CurrentLaw

STATUTE CITATOR 2002-2004

STATUTORY INSTRUMENT CITATOR 2002-2004

THOMSON

™

SWEET & MAXWELL

EUROPE

BELGIUM
Compu-Mark

DENMARK
Forlaget Thomson

FRANCE
Transactive SARL

IRELAND
Round Hall

THE NETHERLANDS
Ellis Publications

SPAIN
Aranzadi

SWEDEN
Fakto Info Direct

ASIA PACIFIC

AUSTRALIA
LBC Information Services

HONG KONG, MALAYSIA AND SINGAPORE
Sweet and Maxwell Asia

JAPAN
Brandy International

NEW ZEALAND
Brooker's

LATIN AMERICA

ARGENTINA
La Ley

BRAZIL
IOB

NORTH AMERICA

CANADA
Carswell

UNITED STATES
West Group, Creative Solutions,
Fast-Tax Trust Services,
Practitioners Publishing Company (PPC), RIA

CurrentLaw

STATUTE CITATOR 2002-2004

STATUTORY INSTRUMENT CITATOR 2002-2004

Sweet & Maxwell Editorial and Production Team
Shahnaila Aziz
Alexandra Carter
Philip Dye
Roger Greenwood
Duncan Wood

London
Sweet & Maxwell
Edinburgh
W. Green

Published in 2005 by
Sweet & Maxwell Limited of
100 Avenue Road, London, NW3 3PF
Typeset by Sweet & Maxwell Limited
Printed in England by Bath Press, CPI Group

**A CIP catalogue record for this book is available
from The British Library**

ISBN This Volume only 0-421-91490-4

ISBN 0-421-91490-4

9 780421 914902

© Sweet & Maxwell 2005

PREFACE

The Sweet & Maxwell Current Law Service

The Current Law Service began in 1947 and provides a comprehensive guide to developments in case law, primary legislation and secondary legislation in the UK and mainland Europe. The Current Law service presently consists of the Monthly Digests, the Year Book, Current Law Statutes, the Statute Citator, the Statutory Instrument Citator, the Case Citator, Current Law Week and European Current Law.

Also available on Current Legal Information which contains an archive of Year Books dating back to 1986 and the present year's cumulated Monthly Digests, as well as a range of other Sweet & Maxwell current awareness products such as the Current Law Case Citator, Current Law Statute Citator, the Legal Journals Index and the Financial Journals Index.

The Statute Citators and the Statutory Instrument Citators

The Current Law Statute Citators comprise six volumes covering the years 1947-1971, 1972-1988, 1989-1995, 1996-1999, 2000-2001 and 2002-2004. The Statutory Instrument Citators cover the years 1993-1995, 1996-1999, 2000-2001 and 2002-2004.

Monthly updates to these Citators are available in Current Law Statutes. The Citators list all amendments, modifications, repeals, etc. to primary and secondary legislation made in the years indicated. This volume contains the Statute Citator 2002-2004 and the Statutory Instrument Citator 2002-2004.

The Statute Citator

The material within the Statute Citator is arranged in chronological order and the following information is provided:

(a) in respect of any Act passed between 1947 and 1959, where the Act is summarised in the Current Law Yearbook, and for any Act thereafter the sate of Royal Assent;

(b) in respect of any Act of any date, whether it has been repealed, amended or otherwise modified since 1947;

(c) in respect of any Act of any date, the cases in which it has been judicially considered since 1947;

(d) in respect of any Act of any date, the Statutory Instruments which have been made under its provisions; and

(e) in respect of any Act of any date, where it has been consolidated by an Act passed between 2002 to 2004.

The Statutory Instrument Citator

The material within the Statutory Instrument Citator is arranged in chronological order and the following information is provided:

(a) in respect of any SI passed of any date, whether it has been repealed, amended or otherwise modified between 2002 and 2004;
(b) in respect of any SI of any date, the cases in which it has been judicially considered between 2002 and 2004;
(c) in respect of any SI of any date, the Statutory Instruments issued between 2002-2004 which have been made under its provisions; and
(d) in respect of any SI of any date, where it has been consolidated by an Act passed between 2002 to 2004.

HOW TO USE THIS BOOK

The following fictional entries to the Statute and Statutory Instrument Citators indicate how to determine developments which hace occurred to the piece of legislation in which you are interested. Entries to the Citators are arranged chronologically.

Statute Citator	
12. Example Act 2001	— Chapter number, name of Act and year
Royal Assent May 5, 2001	— Date of Royal Assent
Commencement Orders: SI 2002/1234; SI 2003/78	— Commencement orders bringing provisions into force
s.1, enabling SI 2002/1234; SI 2003/78	— Statutory Instruments made under the powers of s.1 of the Act
s.2, see *R. v Brown* [2003] Crim.L.R. 43	— Case judicially considering s.2
s.3, amended: 2004 c.3 s.2	— s.3 amended by Act (s.2 of chapter 3 of 2004) and two SI's
s.3, enabling: SI 2001/82; S2004/70	
s.4, repealed: 2004 c.3 Sch. 4	— s.4 repealed by Schedule 4 of chapter 3 of 2004
s.4A added: SI 2002/42	— s.4A added by SI Number 42 of 2002
Sch. 8, C 2002 c.1 s.89	— Schedule 8 considered by s.89 of chapter 1 of 2002
SI Citator	
1234 Example Regulation 2001.	— Number, name and year of SI
Reg. 2, amended: SI 2002/65 Art. 2	— reg. 2 amended by article 2 of SI number 65 of 2002
Reg. 3, revoked: 2002 c.23 Sch. 15	— reg. 3 revoked by Schedule 15 of chapter 23 of 2002
Reg. 4, see *R v. Smith* [2002] C.O.D. 54	— Case judicially considering reg. 4
Reg. 5, C. 2004 c.7 Sch 4	— reg. 5 consolidated by Schedule 4 of chapter 7 of 2004

CONTENTS

TABLE OF ABBREVIATIONS

Publishers name follows reports and journals.

(S&M = Sweet & Maxwell; ICLR = Incorporated Council of Law Reporting for England and Wales; LBC = Law Book Company of Australia; OUP = Oxford University Press; Kluwer = Kluwer Law International; Cass = Frank Cass & Co Ltd; CUP = Cambridge University Press; CLP = Central Law Publishing; TSO = The Stationery Office. LLP = Lloyd's of London Press Ltd.) All other names are in full.

A. & S.L. = Air and Space Law (*Kluwer*)
A.A. & L. = Art Antiquity and Law (*Kluwer*)
A.B. = Advising Business (*EMIS Professional Publishing Ltd*)
A.C. = Appeal Cases (*ICLR*)
A.C.D. = Administrative Court Digest (*S&M*)
A.D.R.L.J. = Arbitration and Dispute Resolution Law Journal (*LLP*)
A.I. & L. = Artificial Intelligence and Law (*Kluwer*)
A.L.Q. = Arab Law Quarterly (*Kluwer*)
Accountancy = Accountancy (*Institute of Chartered Accountants in England and Wales*)
Accountancy Irl. = Accountancy Ireland (*Institute of Chartered Accountants in Ireland*)
Ad. & Fos. = Adoption & Fostering (*British Adoption Agency Institute*)
Admin. L.R. = Administrative Law Reports (*Barry Rose*)
Adviser = Adviser (*NACAB*)
All E.R. = All England Law Reports (*Butterworth Tolley Publishing*)
All E.R. (Comm) = All England Law Reports (Commercial Cases) (*Butterworth Tolley Publishing*)
All E.R. (EC) = All England Law Reports European Cases (*Butterworth Tolley Publishing*)
A.P.L.R. = Asia Pacific Law Review (*Kluwer Law International*)
Arbitration = Arbitration (*Institute of Arbitrators*)
Arbitration Int. = Arbitration International (*Kluwer*)
Arch. News = Archbold News (*S&M*)
Axiom = Axiom (*GT: Specialist Publishers*)

B.C.C. = British Company Cases (*S&M*)
B.C.L.C. = Butterworths Company Law Cases (*Butterworth Tolley Publishing*)
B.H.R.C. = Butterworths Human Rights Cases (*Butterworth Tolley Publishing*)
B.I.F.D. = Bulletin for International Fiscal Documentation (*IBFD Publications BV*)
B.J.I.B. & F.L. = Butterworths Journal of International Banking & Financial Law (*Butterworth Tolley Publishing*)
B.L.E. = Business Law Europe (*S&M*)
B.L.G.R. = Butterworths Local Government Reports (*Butterworth Tolley Publishing*)
B.L.R. = Building Law Reports (*LLB*)
B.M.L.R. = Butterworths Medico-Legal Reports (*Butterworth Tolley Publishing*)
B.P.I.L.S. = Butterworths Personal Injury Litigation Services (*Butterworth Tolley Publishing*)
B.P.I.R. = Bankruptcy and Personal Insolvency Reports (*Jordan*)
B.S.L.R. = BIO-Science Law Review (*Lawtext Publishing Ltd*)
B.T.C. = British Tax Cases (*CCH Editions*)
B.T.R. = British Tax Review (*S&M*)
B.V.C = British Value Added Tax Reporter (*CCH Editions*)

B.Y.B.I.L. = British Year Book of International Law (*OUP*)
Bracton L.J. = Bracton Law Journal (*University of Exeter*)
Brit. J. Criminol. = British Journal of Criminology (*OUP*)
Build. L.M. = Building Law Monthly (*Monitor Press*)
Building = Building (*Tower Publishing*)
Bull. J.S.B. = Bulletin of the Judicial Studies Board
Bus. L.B. = Business Law Bulletin (*W. Green*)
Bus. L.R. = Business Law Review (*Kluwer*)
Buyer = Buyer (*Informa Publishing Group*)

c. = chapter (*of an Act of Parliament*)
C. & E.L. = Construction & Engineering Law (*CLP*)
C. & F.L. = Credit and Finance Law (*Monitor Press*)
C. & F.L.U. = Child & Family Law Update (*SLS Legal Publications*)
C.C.L.R. = Consumer Credit Law Reports (*incorporated within Encyclopedia of Consumer Credit Law - S&M*)
C.C.L. Rep = Community Care Law Reports (*Legal Action Group*)
C.C.R. = Chambers Client Report (*Chambers and Partners Publishing*)
C.D.F.N. = Clinical Disputes Forum Newsletter (*Clinical Disputes Forum*)
C.E.C. = European Community Cases (*S&M*)
C.F.I.L.R. = Company Financial and Insolvency Law Review (*Informa Publishing Group*)
C.F.L.Q. = Child and Family Law Quarterly (*Jordan*)
C.G. = Corporate Governance (*Blackwell Publishers*)
C.I.C.C. = Current Issues in Consumer Credit (*incorporated within Consumer Credit Control - S&M*)
C.I.L. = Contemporary Issues in Law (*Lawtext Publishing Ltd*)
C.I.L.L. = Construction Industry Law Letter (*Monitor Press*)
C.I.P.A.J. = Chartered Institute of Patent Agents Journal (*Chartered Institute of Patent Agents*)
C.J. = Contract Journal (*Reed Business Information*)
C.J.Q. = Civil Justice Quarterly (*S&M*)
C.L. = Current Law Monthly Digest (*S&M*)
C.L. = Commercial Lawyer (*Commercial Lawyer*)
C.L. & P. = Computer Law & Practice (*Butterworth Tolley Publishing*)
C.L. & P.R. = Charity Law and Practice Review (*Key Haven*)
C.L. Pract. = Commercial Law Practitioner (*Round Hall/S&M*)
C.L.B. = Commonwealth Law Bulletin (*Commonwealth Secretariat*)
C.L.C. = Commercial Law Cases (*S&M*)

ix

C.L.C. = Current Law Consolidation (*1947-1951*) (*S&M*)

C.L.J. = Cambridge Law Journal (*CUP*)

C.L.L. Rev. = Commercial Liability Law Review (*Informa Publishing Group*)

C.L.M. = Company Law Monitor (*Monitor Press*)

C.L.P. = Current Legal Problems (*OUP*)

C.L.S.R. = Computer Law & Security Report (*Elsevier Science*)

C.L.W. = Current Law Week (*S&M*)

C.L.W.R. = Common Law World Review (*Vathek Publishing Ltd*)

C.L.Y. = Current Law Yearbook (*S&M*)

C.M. = Compliance Monitor (*CTA Financial Publishing*)

C.M.L. Rev. = Common Market Law Review (*Kluwer*)

C.M.L.R. (AR) = Common Market Law Reports (*S&M*)

C. McK. Env. L.B. = Cameron McKenna Environmental Law Bulletin

C.O.D. = Crown Office Digest (now Administrative Court Digest) (*S&M*)

C.P.L.R. = Civil Practice Law Reports (*CLT Publishing*)

C.P.N. = Civil Procedure News (*S&M*)

C.P. Rep. = Civil Procedure Reports (Online) (*S&M*)

C.P. Rev. = Consumer Policy Review (*Consumer's Association*)

C.Risk. = Clinical Risk (*Royal Society of Medicine Press*)

C.S. = case summaries (*in The Independent*)

C.S.R. = Company Secretary's Review (*Butterworth Tolley Publishing*)

C.S.R. & E.M. = Corporate Social Responsibility and Environmental Management (*John Wiley & Sons Ltd*)

C.T.L.R. = Computer and Telecommunications Law Review (*S&M ESC Publishing*)

C.T.R. = Corporate Tax Review (*Key Haven Publications Ltd*)

C.T.P. = Capital Tax Planning (*S&M*)

C.W. = Copyright World (*Intellectual Property*)

CA = Court of Appeal

Cambrian L.R. = Cambrian Law Review (*University of Wales*)

Can. C.L. = Canadian Current Law (*Carswell*)

CCH. T.C. = CCH Tax Cases (*CCH Editions*)

CEC = Customs and Excise Commissioners

CFI = Court of First Instance

Ch. = Chancery (*Law Reports*) (*ICLR*)

Childright = Childright (*Children's Legal Centre*)

Civ. Lit. = Civil Litigation (*CLT Professional Publishing*)

Civ. P.B. = Civil Practice Bulletin (*W. Green*)

Clarity = Clarity (*Mark Adler*)

CMAC = Courts Martial Appeal Court

Co. Law. = Company Lawyer (*S&M*)

Com. Cas. = Commercial Cases

Com. Jud. J. = Commonwealth Judicial Journal (*Commonwealth Magistrates & Judges Association*)

Comm.Lawyer = The Commonwealth Lawyer (*Commonwealth Lawyers Association(*)

Comm. Leases = Commercial Leases (*Monitor Press*)

Comm. L.J. = Commercial Law Journal (*Legalease Ltd*)

Comms. L. = Communications Law (*Butterworth Tolley Publishing*)

Comp. & Law = Computers & Law (*Society for Computers*)

Comp. L.I. = Competition Law Insight (*Informa Group Ltd*)

Comp. L.J. = Competition Law Journal (*Jordan*)

Comp. L.M. = Competition Law Monitor (*Informa Publishing Group*)

Comp. Law. = Company Lawyer (*S&M*)

Comp. Law E.C. = Competition Law in the European Communities (*Bryan Harris*)

Con. L.R. = Construction Law Reports (*Butterworth Tolley Publishing*)

Cons. L. Today = Consumer Law Today (*Monitor Press*)

Cons. Law = Construction Law (*Eclipse*)

Const. L.J. = Construction Law Journal (*S&M*)

Conv. = Conveyancer and Property Lawyer (*S&M*)

Corp. Brief. = Corporate Briefing (*Monitor Press*)

Corp. C. = Corporate Counsel (*Commercial Lawyer*)

Costs L.R. = Costs Law Reports (*CLT Professional Publishing*)

Counsel = Counsel (*Butterworth Tolley Publishing*)

Cox C.C. = Cox's Criminal Cases

Cr. App. R. = Criminal Appeal Reports (*S&M*)

Cr. App. R. (*S.*) = Criminal Appeal Reports (Sentencing) (*S&M*)

Crim. L.J. = Criminal Law Journal (*LBC*)

Crim. L.B. = Criminal Law Bulletin (*W. Green*)

Crim. L.R. = Criminal Law Review (*S&M*)

Crim. Law. = Criminal Lawyer (*Butterworth Tolley Publishing*)

Criminologist = Criminologist (*Barry Rose*)

D.L.R. = Dominion Law Reports

D.P.L. & P. = Data Protection Law and Policy (*Cecile Publishing Ltd*)

D.P. & P.P. = Data Protection and Privacy Practice (*Masons Solicitors*)

D.U.L.J. = Dublin University Law Journal

Denning L.J. = Denning Law Journal (*University of Buckingham*)

Dir. = Directive

Disc.L.R. = Discrimination Law Reports (*Central Law Training Ltd*)

E. & L. = Education and the Law (*Carfax*)

E. & P. = International Journal of Evidence & Proof (*Blackstone Press*)

E.B.L. = Electronic Business Law (*Eclipse Group*)

E.B. Mag. = Environment Business Magazine (*S&M/GEE*)

E.B.L.R. = European Business Law Review (*Kluwer*)

E.B.O.R. = European Business Organization Law Review (*Kluwer*)

E.C.A. = Elderly Client Adviser (*Ark Publishing*)

E.C.C. = European Commercial Cases (*S&M*)

E.C.D.R. = European Copyright and Design Reports (*S&M*)

E.C.R. = European Court Reports (*TSO*)

E.C.L. & P. = E-Commerce Law & Policy (*Cecile Park Publishing*)

E.C.L.R. = European Competition Law Review (*S&M*)

E.D.D. & R.M. = Environmental Due Diligence & Risk Management (*CLT Professional Publishing*)

E.E.F.N. = Eastern European Forum Newsletter (*International Bar Association*)

E.E.L.R. = European Environmental Law Review (*Kluwer*)

E.F.A. Rev. = European Foreign Affairs Review (*Kluwer Law International*)

E.F.S.L. = European Financial Services Law (*Kluwer*)

E.G. = Estates Gazette (*Estates Gazette Ltd*)

E.G.C.S. = Estates Gazette Case Summaries (*Estates Gazette Ltd*)

E.G.L.R. = Estates Gazette Law Reports (*Estates Gazette Ltd*)

E.H.L.R. = Environmental Health Law Reports (*S&M*)

E.H.R.L.R. = European Human Rights Law Review (*S&M*)

E.H.R.R. = European Human Rights Reports (*S&M*)

E.I.B. = Environment Information Bulletin (*Eclipse*)

E.I.P.R. = European Intellectual Property Review (*S&M*)

E.I.R.R. = European Industrial Relations Review (*Eclipse*)

E.J.C. = European Journal of Criminology (*Sage Publications Ltd*)

E.J.C.L. = Electronic Journal of Comparative Law

E.J.H.L. = European Journal of Health Law (*Kluwer*)

E.J.I.L. = European Journal of International Law (*S&M*)

E.J.S.S. = European Journal of Social Security (*Kluwer*)

E.L. = Equitable Lawyer (*Gostick Hall Publications*)

E.L.A. Briefing = Employment Lawyers Association Briefing (*S&M*)

E.L.B. = Environmental Law Brief (*Monitor Press*)

E.L.J. = European Law Journal (*Blackwell*)

E.L.L.R. = Environmental Liability Law Review (*Kluwer*)

E.L.M. = Environmental Law and Management (*Chancery Law Publishing Ltd*)

E.L.R. = Education Law Reports (*Jordan*)

E.L.Rev. = European Law Review (*S&M*)

E.M.L.R. = Entertainment and Media Law Reports (*S&M*)

E.O.R. = Equal Opportunities Review (*Eclipse*)

E.O.R. Dig. = Equal Opportunities Review and Discrimination Case Law Digest (*Eclipse*)

E.P.L. = European Public Law (*Kluwer*)

E.P.L.I. = Education, Public Law and the Individual (*John Wiley & Sons Ltd*)

E.P.O.R. = European Patent Office Reports (*S&M*)

E.P.S. = EMIS Property Service (*EMIS Professional Publishing*)

E.R.P.L. = European Review of Private Law (*Kluwer*)

E.T.M.R. = European Trade Marks Reports (*S&M*)

E.W.C.B. = European Works Councils Bulletin (*Eclipse*)

EAT = Employment Appeal Tribunal

EC C.P.N. = European Commission Competition Policy Newsletter (*Commission of the European Communities*)

EC T.J. = EC Tax Journal (*Key Haven*)

EC T.R. = EC Tax Review (*Kluwer*)

Ecc. L.J. = Ecclesiastical Law Journal (*Ecclesiastical Law Society*)

Ed. C.R. = Education Case Reports (*S&M*)

EDI L.R. = Electronic Data Interchange Law Review (*Kluwer*)

ECJ = European Court of Justice

Ed. Law. = Education Law Journal (*Jordan*)

Ed. L.M. = Education Law Monitor (*Monitor Press*)

Edin. L.R. = Edinburgh Law Review (*Butterworth Tolley Publishing*)

E-Law Rev. = E-Law Review (*S&M/W. Green*)

Emp. L. = Employers' Law (*Reed Business Information ltd*)

Emp. L. & L. = Employment Law & Litigation (*EMIS Professional Publishing*)

Emp. L. Brief. = Employment Law Briefing (*S&M*)

Emp. L.B. = Employment Law Bulletin (*W. Green*)

Emp L.J. = Employment Law Journal (*Legalease Ltd*)

Emp. Lit. = Employment Litigation (*CLP*)

ENDS = ENDS Report (*Environmental Data Services*)

Ent. L.R. = Entertainment Law Review (*S&M*)

Ent. Law = Entertainment Law (*Frank Cass Publishers*)

Env. L.B. = Environmental Law Bulletin (*W. Green*)

Env. L.M. = Environmental Law Monthly (*Monitor Press*)

Env. L.R. = Environmental Law Reports (*S&M*)

Env. L. Rev. = Environmental Law Review (*Vathek Publishing*)

Env. Law = Environmental Law (*S&M*)

Env. Liability = Environmental Liability (*Lawtext*)

EU Focus = European Union Focus (*S&M*)

Eu. L.R. = European Law Reports (*John Wiley & Sons Ltd*)

Eur. Counsel = European Counsel (*Legal & Commercial Publishing*)

Eur. J. Crime Cr. L. Cr. J. = European Journal of Crime, Criminal Law and Criminal Justice (*Kluwer*)

Euro. Env. = European Environment (*John Wiley & Sons Ltd*)

Euro. Law. = European Lawyer (*H.S. Legal Publishing*)

Euro. L.M. = European Law Monitor (*Monitor Press*)

Euro. Tax. = European Taxation (*IBFD*)

EWCA Civ = Media neutral citation from Court of Appeal (Civil Division)

EWCA Crim = Media neutral citation from Court of Appeal (Criminal Division)

EWHC Admin = Media neutral citation from High Court (Administrative Court)

Expert = Expert (*Academy of Experts S&M*)

F & C.L. = Finance & Credit Law (*Monitor Press*)

F. & D.L.R. = Futures & Derivatives Law Review (*Cavendish*)

F. & D.L.M. = Food & Drink Law Monthly (*Agra Europe Ltd*)

F.C.R. = Family Court Reporter (*Tolleys Ltd*)

F.D. & D.I.B. = Food, Drinks & Drugs Industry Bulletin (*Monitor*)

F.I. = Fraud Intelligence (*Informa Publishing Group*)

F.I.T.A.R. = Financial Instruments Tax & Accounting Review (*CTA Financial Publishing*)

F.L.R. = Family Law Reports (*Jordan*)

F.L.T. = Family Law Today (*Monitor Press*)

F.O.I. = Freedom of Information (*Privacy & Data Protection*)

F.R. = Financial Regulator (*Central Banking Publications Ltd*)

F.S.B. = Financial Services Brief (*S&M*)

F.S. Bulletin = Financial Services Bulletin (*Informa Publishing Group*)

F.S.R. = Fleet Street Reports (*S&M*)

Fairplay = Fairplay (*Fairplay Publication*)

Fam. = Family Division (*Law Reports*) (*ICLR*)

Fam. L.R. = Greens Family Law Reports (*W. Green*)

Fam. Law = Family Law (*Jordan*)

Fam. M. = Family Matters (*S&M*)

Fam. Med. = Family Mediation (*National Association of Family Mediation & Conciliation Services*)

Farm Law = Farm Law (*Informa Publishing Group*)

Farm T.B. = Farm Tax Brief (*Monitor Press*)

Fem. L.S. = Feminist Legal Studies (*Deborah Charles*)

G.C.R. = Global Competition Review (*Law Business Research Ltd*)
G.I.L.S.I. = Gazette Incorporated Law Society of Ireland (*The Law Society*)
G.L. & B. = Global Law & Business (*Global Law & Business*)
G.L.J. = Guernsey Law Journal (*Greffier*)
G.T.B. = Global Telecoms Business (*Euromoney*)
G.W.D. = Green's Weekly Digest (*W. Green*)
Global Counsel = Global Counsel (*Legal & Commercial Publishing*)

H. & S.B. = Health and Safety Bulletin (*Eclipse*)
H. & S.L. = Health and Safety Law (*Emis Professional Publishing*)
H. & S.M. = Health & Safety Monitor (*Monitor Press*)
H. & S.W. = Health & Safety at Work (*Butterworth Tolley Publishing*)
Hert.L.J. = Hertfordshire Law Journal (*University of Hertfordshire*)
H.L.J. = Hibernian Law Journal (*Law Society of Ireland*)
H.L.M. = Housing Law Monitor (*Monitor Press*)
H.L.R. = Housing Law Reports (*S&M*)
H.R.C.D. = Human Rights Case Digest (*S&M*)
H.R.L.R. = Human Rights Law Reports (*S&M*)
H.R. & UK P. = Human Rights & UK Practice (*CLT Professional Publishing*)
H.S. = Hazardous Substances (*Monitor Press*)
HC = House of Commons
Health Law = Health Law (*Monitor Press*)
HL = House of Lords
Hous. L.R. = Greens Housing Law Reports (*W. Green*)
Howard Journal = Howard Journal of Criminal Justice (*Blackwell*)

I. & C.T.L. = Information & Communications Technology Law (*Carfax*)
I. & N.L. & P. = Immigration & Nationality Law & Practice (*Butterworth Tolley Publishing*)
I.B.I.S. Rep. = Information Benefits Service Report (*Charles D. Spencer & Associates Inc.*)
I.B.L. = International Business Lawyer (*Blackwell*)
I.B.R. = Irish Banking Review (*The Irish Banking Review*)
I. Bull. = Interights Bulletin (*Interights*)
I.C.C.L.R. = International Company and Commercial Law Review (*S&M*)
I.C.L.J. = Irish Criminal Law Journal (*Round Hall/S&M*)
I.C.L.Q. = International & Comparative Law Quarterly (*British Institute of International and Comparative Law*)
I.C.L.R. = International Construction Law Review (*LLP*)
I.C.L. Rev. = International Construction Law Review (*Informa Publishing Group*)
I.C.R. = Industrial Cases Reports (*ICLR*)
I.E.L.T.R. = International Energy Law and Taxation Review (*S&M*)
I.E.L.J. = Irish Employment Law Journal (*Round Hall/S&M*)
I.F.L. = International Family Law (*Jordan*)
I.F.L. Rev. = International Financial Law Review (*Euromoney*)
I.H.L. = In-House Lawyer (*Legalease Ltd*)

I.I.E.L. = Immigration and International Employment Law (*Eclipse Group Ltd*)
I.I.L. Rev. = International Internet Law Review (*Euromoney Institutional Investor Plc*)
I.I.R. = International Insolvency Review (*Chancery Law*)
I.J.C.L. = International Journal of Constitutional Law (*OUP*)
I.J.C.L.P. = International Journal of Communications Law and Policy (http://www.digital-Law.Net/WCLP/)
I.J.D.G. = International Journal of Disclosure and Governance (*Henry Stewart Publications*)
I.J.D.L. = International Journal of Discrimination and the Law (*A B Academic*)
I.J.E.L. = Irish Journal of European Law (*Round Hall/S&M*)
I.J.H.R. = International Journal of Human Rights (*Taylor & Francis Group*)
I.J.I.L. = International Journal of Insurance Law (*LLP*)
I.J.L & I.T. = International Journal of Law & Information Technology (*OUP*)
I.J.L.P. = International Journal of the Legal Profession (*Carfax*)
I.J.M.C.L. = International Journal of Marine & Coastal Law (*Kluwer*)
I.J.O.S.L. = International Journal Of Shipping Law (*LLP*)
I.J.R.L. = International Journal of Refugee Law (*OUP*)
I.J.S.L. = International Journal for the Semiotics of Law (*Deborah Charles*)
I.L. & P. = Insolvency Law & Practice (*Butterworth Tolley Publishing*)
I.L.D. = Immigration Law Digest (*Immigration Advisory Service*)
I.L.J. = Industrial Law Journal (*Industrial Law Society*)
I.L.P. = International Legal Practitioner (*International Bar Association*)
I.L.Pr. = International Litigation Procedure (*S&M*)
I.L.T. = Irish Law Times (*Round Hall/S&M*)
I.L.T.R. = Irish Law Times Reports (*Round Hall/S&M*)
I.M.L. = International Media Law (*S&M*)
I.N.L. = Internet Newsletter for Lawyers (*Delia Venables*)
I.N.L.R. = Immigration and Nationality Law Reports (*Jordan*)
I.P. = International Peacekeeping (*Kluwer*)
I.P. & I.T. Law = Intellectual Property and Information Technology Law (*CLP*)
I.P. & I.T.L.U. = Intellectual Property and Information Technology Law Updates (*EMIS Publishing*)
I.P. & T. = Intellectual Property and Technology (*Butterworth Tolley Publishing*)
I.P. News. = Intellectual Property Newsletter (*Monitor Press*)
I.P.D. = Intellectual Property Decisions (*Monitor Press*)
I.P.E.L.J. = Irish Planning and Environmental Law Journal (*Round Hall/S&M*)
I.P.Q. = Intellectual Property Quarterly (*S&M*)
I.P.S.P.I. = Insolvency Practitioner of the Society of Practitioners of Insolvency (*Society of Practitioners of Insolvency*)
I.R.L.A. = Insurance & Reinsurance Law Alert (*LLP Ltd*)
I. & R.L.B. = Insurance & Reinsurance Law Briefing (*S&M*)
I.R.L.B. = Industrial Relations Law Bulletin (*Eclipse*)
I.R.L.C.T. = International Review of Law Computers & Technology (*Carfax*)

I.R.L.R. = Industrial Relations Law Reports (*Eclipse*)

I.R.T.B. = Inland Revenue Tax Bulletin (*Inland Revenue*)

I.R.V. = International Review of Victimology (*A B Academic*)

I.S.L.J. = International Sports Law Journal (*TMC Asser Instituut for International Law*)

I.T. & C.L.J. = Information Technology & Communications Law Journal (*Legalease Ltd*)

IT & C.L.R. = IT &Communications Law Reports (*Legalease Ltd*)

I.T.E.L.R. = International Trust and Estate Law Reports (*Butterworth Tolley Publishing*)

I.T.L.J. = International Travel Law Journal (*Travel Law Centre*)

I.T.L.Q. = Internationnal Trade Law Quarterly (*LLP Ltd*)

I.T.P.J. = International Transfer Pricing Journal (*IBFD Publications BV*)

I.T.R. = Industrial Tribunal Reports

I.T.R. = International Tax Review (*Euromoney*)

I.T. Rep. = International Tax Report (*Monitor*)

I.T. rev. = International Tax Review (*Euromoney*)

I.V.M. = International VAT Monitor (*IBFD*)

IDS Brief = IDS Brief, Employment Law and Practice (*Income Data Services Ltd*)

IDS DW = IDS Diversity of Work (*Incomes Data Services*)

IDS P.L.R. = IDS Pensions Law Reports (*Income Data Services Ltd*)

IH = Inner House of the Court of Session

IIC = International Review of Industrial Property and Copyright Law (*John Wiley & Sons Ltd*)

Imm. A.R. = Immigration Appeals Reports (*TSO*)

In Comp. = In Competition (*S&M*)

Independent = Independent Law Reports

Info. T.L.R. = Information Technology Law Reports (*Lawtext Publishing*)

Ins. L.M. = Insurance Law Monthly (*Monitor Press*)

Insolv. B. = Insolvency Bulletin (*Armstrong Information Ltd*)

Insolv. Int. = Insolvency Intelligence (*S&M*)

Insolvency = Insolvency (*Griffin Multimedia*)

Int. Acc. = International Accountants (*Association of International Accountants*)

Int. A.L.R. = International Arbitration Law Review (*S&M*)

Int. C.L.R. = International Criminal Law Review (*Kluwer*)

Int. J. Comp. L.L.I.R. = International Journal of Comparative Labour Law and Industrial Relations (*Kluwer*)

Int. J.F.L. = International Journal of Franchising Law (*Richmond Law & Tax Ltd*)

Int. J. Law & Fam. = International Journal of Law, Policy and the Family (*OUP*)

Int. J. Soc. L. = International Journal of the Sociology of Law (*Academic Press Ltd*)

Int. Rel. = International Relations (*David Davies Memorial Institute*)

Int. T.L.R. = International Trade Law & Regulation (*S&M ESC Publishing*)

Intertax = Intertax (*Kluwer*)

IP Scan = IP Scan (*Net Searchers*)

Ir. B.L. = Irish Business Law (*Inns Quay Publishing*)

Ir. T.R. = Irish Tax Review (*Institute of Taxation in Ireland*)

IT L.T. = IT Law Today (*Monitor Press*)

J.A.C.L. = Journal of Armed Conflict Law (*Nottingham University Press*)

J.A.L. = Journal of African Law (*CUP*)

J.B.L. = Journal of Business Law (*S&M*)

J.C. = Justiciary Cases

J.C.L.E. = Journal of Clinical Legal Education (*Northumbria Law Press*)

J.C.L.L.E. = Journal of Commonwealth Law and Legal Education (*Cavendish Publishing*)

J.C.L.P. = Journal of Competition Law & Policy (*OECD Publications Service*)

J.C. & S.L. = Journal of Conflict & Security Law (*Oxford University Press*)

J. Civ. Lib. = Journal of Civil Liberties (*Northumbria Law Press*)

J. Com. Mar. St. = Journal of Common Market Studies (*Blackwell*)

J. Crim. L. = Journal of Criminal Law (*Pageant*)

J.E.C.L. & P. = Journal of Electronic Commerce Law and Practice (*Butterworth Tolley Publishing*)

J.E.L.P. = Journal of Employment Law & Practice (*Butterworth Tolley Publishing*)

J.E.L.S. = Journal of Empirical Legal Studies (*Blackwells*)

J. En. & Nat. Res. L. = Journal of Energy & Natural Resources Law (*Kluwer*)

J. Env. L. = Journal of Environmental Law (*OUP*)

J.E.R.L. = Journal of Energy & Natural Resources Law (*Kluwer*)

J.F.C. = Journal of Financial Crime (*Henry Stewart*)

J.F.R. & C. = Journal of Financial Regulation and Compliance (*Henry Stewart*)

J.H.L. = Journal of Housing Law (*S&M*)

J.I.B.L. = Journal of International Banking Law (*S&M*)

J.I.B.R. = Journal of International Banking Regulation (*Euromoney Publications*)

J.I.C.J. = Journal of International Criminal Justice (*OUP*)

J.I.E.L. = Journal of International Economic Law (*OUP*)

J.I.F.D.L. = Journal of International Franchising & Distribution Law (*Butterworth Tolley Publishing*)

J.I.F.M. = Journal of International Financial Markets (*S&M*)

J.I.L.T. = Journal of Information, Law & Technology (*http://elj.warwick.ac.uk/jilt*)

J.I.M.L. = Journal of International Maritime Law (*Lawtext Publishers*)

J. Int. Arb. = Journal of International Arbitration (*Kluwer*)

J. Int. P. = Journal of International Trust and Corporate Planning (*John Wiley*)

J.J. = Justice Journal (*Justice*)

J.L.E. & O. = Journal of Law, Economics & Organization (*Oxford University Press*)

J.L.S. = Journal of Legislative Studies (*Cass*)

J.L.S.S. = Journal of the Law Society of Scotland (*Law Society of Scotland*)

J. Law & Soc. = Journal of Law and Society (*Blackwell*)

J. Leg. Hist. = Journal of Legal History (*Cass*)

J.M.L. & P. = Journal of Media Law & Practice (*Butterworth Tolley Publishing*)

J.M.L.C. = Journal of Money Laundering Control (*Henry Stewart Publications*)

J.N.I. = Journal of Network Industries (*Kluwer*)

J.O. & R. = Journal of Obligations and Remedies (*Northumbria Law Press*)

J.P. = Justice of the Peace (*Justice of the Peace Ltd*)

J.P.I.L. = Journal of Personal Injury Litigation (*S&M*)

J.P.L. = Journal of Planning & Environment Law (*S&M*)

J.P.M. & M. = Journal of Pensions Management and Marketing (*Henry Stewart*)

J.P.N. = Justice of the Peace Reports & Local Government Notes of Cases (*Justice of the Peace Ltd*)

J.P. Rep. = Justice of the Peace and Local Government Law Reports (*Justice of the Peace Ltd*)

J.R. = Judicial Review (*Hart Publishing Ltd*)

J.S.B.J. = Judicial Studies Board Journal (*Blackstone Press*)

J.S.S.L. = Journal of Social Security Law (*S&M*)

J. Soc. Wel. & Fam. L. = Journal of Social Welfare and Family Law (*Routledge*)

J.W.T. = Journal of World Trade (*Kluwer*)

Jersey L.R. = Jersey Law Review (*The Jersey Law Review*)

Jur. Rev. = Juridical Review (*W. Green*)

K.B. = Kings Bench (*Law Reports*) (*ICLR*)

K.C.L.J. = Kings College Law Journal (*King's College London*)

K.I.R. = Knights Industrial Reports

L. & T. Review = Landlord & Tenant Review (*S&M*)

L. Ex. = Legal Executive (*ILEX*)

L.E. = Lawyers' Europe (*Butterworth Tolley Publishing*)

L.F. = Litigation Funding (*Law Society Publishing*)

L.G. Rev. = Local Government Review (*Barry Rose*)

L.G.C. Law & Admin. = Local Government Chronicle Law & Administration (*Local Government Chronicle Ltd*)

L.G.C. = Local Government Chronicle (*Local Government Chronicle Ltd*)

L.G.D. = Law, Social Justice & Global Development (*Electronic Law Journals*)

L.G.L.R. = Local Government Law Reports (*S&M*)

L.I.E.I. = Legal Issues of European Integration (*Kluwer*)

L.I.M. = Legal Information Management (*S&M*)

L.M.C.L.Q. = Lloyd's Maritime & Commercial Law Quarterly (*LLP*)

L.P. or L.V.C. = references to denote Lands Tribunal decision (*transcripts available from the Lands Tribunal*)

L.P. & R. = Law Probability & Risk (*OUP*)

L.P.I.C.T. = Law & Practice of International Courts and Tribunals (*Kluwer*)

L.Q.R. = Law Quarterly Review (*S&M*)

L.R. = Licensing Review (*Benedict Books*)

L.R. App. Cas. = Law Reports Appeal Cases

L.R.L.R. = Lloyd's Reinsurance Law Reports (*LLP*)

L.S. = Legal Studies (*Butterworth Tolley Publishing*)

L.S.G. = Law Society Gazette (*The Law Society*)

L.S. & P = Law, Science & Policy (*A B Academic Publishers*)

L. & T.R. = Landlord and Tenant Reports (*S&M*)

L.W.G. = Legal Week Global (*Butterworth Tolley Publishing*)

Law & Crit. = Law and Critique (*Deborah Charles*)

Law & Just. = Law & Justice (*Plowden*)

Law & Pol. = Law & Policy (*Blackwell*)

Law Lib. = Law Librarian (*S&M*)

Law Teach. = Law Teacher (*S&M*)

Lawyer = Lawyer (*Centaur Communications Group*)

Lawyer 2B = Lawyer 2B (*Centaur Communications*)

Legal Action = Legal Action (*Legal Action Group*)

Legal Bus. = Legal Business (*Legalease Ltd*)

Legal Ethics = Legal Ethics (*Hart Publishing Ltd*)

Legal IT = Legal IT (*Global Professional Publishing*)

Legal Week (*WDIS Ltd*)

Link AWS = Link AWS (*Association of Women Solicitors*)

Lit. = Litigation (*Barry Rose*)

Liverpool L.R. = Liverpool Law Review (*Deborah Charles*)

Lloyd's Rep. = Lloyd's Law Reports (*LLP*)

Lloyd's Rep. Bank. = Lloyd's Law Reports Banking (*LLP*)

Lloyd's Rep. I.R. = Lloyd's Law Reports Insurance & Reinsurance (*LLP*)

Lloyd's Rep. Med. = Lloyd's Law Report Medical (*LLP*)

Lloyd's Rep. P.N. = Lloyd's Law Reports Professional Negligence (*LLP*)

Ll. Rep. = Lloyd's List Reports (*LLP*)

LVAC = Land Valuation Appeal Court

M.A.L.Q.R. = Model Arbitration Law Quarterly Review (*Simmons & Hill Publishing Ltd*)

M. Advocate = Maritime Advocate (*Merlin Legal Publishing*)

M.C.P. = Magistrates' Courts Practice (*CLP*)

M.D.U. Jour. = Medical Defence Union Journal (*Medical Defence Union*)

M.E.C.L.R. = Middle East Commercial Law Review (*S&M*)

M.I.P. = Managing Intellectual Property (*Euromoney*)

M.J. = Maastricht Journal of European and Comparative Law (*Roger Bayliss*)

M. Jour. = Municipal Journal (*Hemming Information Services*)

M.J.L.S. = Mountbatten Journal of Legal Studies (*Southampton Institute*)

M.L.B. = Manx Law Bulletin (*Central Reference*)

M.L.J.I. = Medico-Legal Journal of Ireland (*Round Hall/S&M*)

M.L.N. = Media Lawyer Newsletter (*Tom Welsh*)

M.L.R. = Modern Law Review (*Blackwell*)

M.R.I. = Maritime Risk International (*Informa*)

M.World = Media World (*Informa*)

Magistrate = Magistrate (*Magistrate's Association*)

Masons C.L.R. = Masons Computer Law Reports

Med. L. Int. = Medical Law International (*A B Academic Publishing*)

Med. L. Mon. = Medical Law Monitor (*Monitor Press*)

Med. L. Rev. = Medical Law Review (*OUP*)

Med. L.R. = Medical Law Reports (*OUP*)

Med. Leg. J. = Medico-Legal Journal (*Dramrite Printers*)

Med. Lit. = Medical Litigation (*Medical Litigation Strategies*)

Med. Sci. Law = Medicine, Science & the Law (*Chiltern*)

N.I. = Northern Ireland Law Reports (*Butterworth Tolley Publishing*)

N.I.L.Q. = Northern Ireland Legal Quarterly (*SLS Legal Publications*)

N.L.J. = New Law Journal (*Butterworth Tolley Publishing*)

N.P.C. = New Property Cases (*New Property Cases Ltd*)

N.Q.H.R. = Netherlands Quarterly of Human Rights (*Kluwer*)

N.Z.L.R. = New Zealand Law Reports

Nott. L.J. = Nottingham Law Journal (*Nottingham Trent University*)

O.D. and I.L. = Ocean Development and International Law (*Taylor & Francis Ltd*)

O.H.R. = Occupational Health Review (*Eclipse Group Ltd*)

O.J.L.S. = Oxford Journal of Legal Studies (*OUP*)

O.P.L.R. = Occupational Pensions Law Reports (*Eclipse Group*)

O.S.S. Bull. = Office for the Supervision of Solicitors Bulletin (*The Law Society's Gazette*)

O.T.R. = Offshore Taxation Review (*Key Haven*)

Offshore Red = Offshore Red (*Campden Publishing*)

Occ. Pen. = Occupational Pensions (*Eclipse*)

OJ = Official Journal of the European Communities

OJEPO = European Patent Office Official Journal

O.U.C.L.J. = Oxford University Commonwealth Law Journal (*Hart Publishing*)

P. = Probate, Divorce and Admiralty (*Law Reports*)

P. & C.R. = Property, Planning & Compensation Reports (*S&M*)

P. & D.P. = Privacy & Data Protection

P. & P. = Practice and Procedure (*S&M*)

P. & S. = Punishment & Society (*Sage*)

P. Injury = Personal Injury (*CLP*)

P.A.D. = Planning Appeal Decisions (*S&M*)

P.C.B. = Private Client Business (*S&M*)

P.C.L.B. = Practitioners' Child Law Bulletin (*S&M*)

P.E.B.L. = Perspectives on European Business Law (*European Perspectives Publications*)

P.I. = Personal Injury (*John Wiley & Sons Ltd*)

P.I.C. = Palmer's In Company (*S&M*)

P.I. Comp = Personal Injury Compensation (*Informa Publishing Group*)

P.I.J. = Planning Inspectorate Journal (*The Planning Inspectorate*)

P.I.L.J. = Personal Injury Law Journal (*Legalease Ltd*)

P.I.Q.R. = Personal Injuries and Quantum Reports (*S&M*)

P.L. & B.I.N. = Privacy Laws & Business International Newsletter (*Privacy Law & Business*)

P.L. = Public Law (*S&M*)

P.L. & B.U.K.N. = Privacy Laws & Business United Kingdom Newsletter (*Privacy Laws & Business*)

P.L.B. = Property Law Bulletin (*S&M*)

P.L.C. = Practical Law for Companies (*Legal & Commercial Publishing*)

P.L.C.R. = Planning Law Case Reports (*S&M*)

P.L.J. = Property Law Journal (*Legalease Ltd*)

P.L.R. = Planning Law Reports (*Estates Gazette Ltd*)

P.N. = Professional Negligence (*Butterworth Tolley Publishing*)

P.N.L.R. = Professional Negligence and Liability Reports (*S&M*)

P.P.L. = Practical Planning Law (*CLP*)

P.P.L.R. = Public Procurement Law Review (*S&M*)

P.S.T. = Pension Scheme Trustee (*S&M*)

P.T. = Pensions Today (*Monitor Press*)

P.T.P.R. = Personal Tax Planning Review (*Key Haven*)

P.W. = Patent World (*Intellectual Property*)

P. Week = Property Week (*Property Media Ltd*)

Parl. Aff. = Parliamentary Affairs (*OUP*)

Pay Mag. = Pay Magazine (*S&M/GEE*)

Pen. = Pensions (*Henry Stewart*)

Pen. Law = Pension Lawyer (*Keith Wallace*) (formerly B.P.L. = British Pension Lawyer

Pen. World = Pensions World (*Butterworth Tolley Publishing*)

Pens. L.R. = IDS Pensions Law Reports (*Income Data Services Ltd*)

Pers. Today = Personnel Today (*Reed Business Information*)

Pol. J. = Police Journal (*Barry Rose*)

Policing T. = Policing Today (*Police Review*)

Prison Serv. J. = Prison Service Journal (*HM Prison, Leyhill*)

Probat. J. = Probation Journal (*National Association of Probation Officers*)

Prop. L.B. = Property Law Bulletin (*W. Green*)

Public F. = Public Finance (*Public Finance*)

Q.A. = Quarterly Account (*Money Advice Association*)

Q.B. = Queen's Bench (*Law Reports*) (*ICLR*)

Q.B.D. = Law Reports Queen's Bench Division

Q.R. = Quantum Reports (*S&M*)

R.A. = Rating Appeals (*Rating Publishers*)

R.A.D.I.C. = African Journal of International and Comparative Law (*African Society*)

R.C.I.S.G. = Review of the Convention on Contracts for the International Sale of Goods (*Kluwer*)

R.E.C.I.E.L. = Review of European Community and International Environmental Law (*Blackwell*)

R.L.R. = Restitution Law Review (*Mansfield Press*)

R.P.C. = Reports of Patent, Design and Trade Mark Cases (*The Patent Office*)

R.R.L.R. = Rent Review & Lease Renewal (*MCB University Press*)

R.T.I. = Road Traffic Indicator (*S&M*) (Ceased publication September 2000)

R.T.R. = Road Traffic Reports (*S&M*)

R.V.R. = Rating and Valuation Reporter (*Rating Publishers*)

R.W.L.R. = Rights of Way Law Review (*Rights of Way Law Review*)

Ratio Juris = Ratio Juris (*Blackwell*)

Recovery = Recovery (*Society of Practitioners of Insolvency*)

Rep. B. = Reparation Bulletin (*W. Green*)

Rep. L.R. = Greens Reparation Law Reports (*W. Green*)

Res Publica = Res Publica (*Deborah Charles*)

Rev. C.E.E. Law = Review of Central and East European Law (*Kluwer*)

ROW Bulletin = Rights of Women Bulletin (*Rights of Women*)

RPC = Restrictive Practices Court

S. & C.L. = Sports and Character Licensing (*Informa Publishing Group*)

S. & L.J. = Sport and the Law Journal (*British Association for Sport & Law*)

S. & L.S. = Social & Legal Studies (*Sage*)

S. & T.L.I. = Shipping & Transport Lawyer International (*Guthrum House Ltd*)

S. News = Sentencing News (*S&M*)

S.B.T. & F. = Small Business Tax & Finance (*Cyan Publishing*)

S.C. = Session Cases (*S&M/W. Green*)

S.C. (*HL*) = Session Cases (*House of Lords*)

S.C.C.R. = Scottish Criminal Case Reports (*The Law Society of Scotland*)

S.C.L.R. = Scottish Civil Law Reports (*The Law Society of Scotland*)

S.C.L. Rev. = Scottish Construction Law Review (*W. Green*)

S.C.P. News = Supreme Court Practice News (*S&M*)

S.H.R.J. = Scottish Human Rights Journal (*S&M/W. Green*)

TABLE OF ABBREVIATIONS

S.J. = Solicitors Journal (*S&M*)

S.J.L.B. = Solicitors Journal LawBrief (*S&M*)

S.L.A. & P. = Sports Law Administration & Practice (*Monitor Press*)

S.L.B. = Sports Law Bulletin (*Anglia Sports Law Research Centre*)

S.L.C.R. = Scottish Land Court Reports

S.L.C.R. Apps. = Scottish Land Court Reports (*appendix*)

S.L.G. = Scottish Law Gazette (*Scottish Law Agents Society*)

S.L.L.P. = Scottish Licensing Law & Practice (*Scottish Licensing Services Ltd*)

S.L.Rev. = Student Law Review (*Cavendish*)

S.L.T. = Scots Law Times (*S&M/W. Green*)

S.L.T. (Land Ct) = Scots Law Times Land Court Reports (*S&M/W. Green*)

S.L.T. (Lands Tr) = Scots Law Times Lands Tribunal Reports (*S&M/W. Green*)

S.L.T. (Lyon Ct) = Scots Law Times Lyon Court Reports (*S&M/W. Green*)

S.L.T. News = Scots Law Times News Section (*S&M/W. Green*)

S.L.T. (Notes) = Scots Law Times Notes of Recent Decisions (*1946-1981*) (*S&M/W. Green*)

S.L.T. (Sh Ct) = Scots Law Times Sheriff Court Reports (*S&M/W. Green*)

S.N. = Session Notes

S.P.C.L.R. = Scottish Private Client Law Review (*Sweet & Maxwell*)

S.P.E.L. = Scottish Planning and Environmental Law (*Planning Exchange*)

S.P.T.L. Reporter = Society of Public Teachers of Law Reporter (*Queen Mary*)

S.T.C. = Simons Tax Cases (*Butterworth Tolley Publishing*)

S.T.C. (SCD) = Simons Tax Cases: Special Commissioners Decisions (*Butterworth Tolley Publishing*)

S.T.I. (SCD) = Simons Tax Intelligence (*Butterworth Tolley Publishing*)

S.T.L. = Shipping and Trade Law (*Informa Publishing Group*)

S.W.T.I. = Simon's Weekly Tax Intelligence (*Butterworth Tolley Publishing*)

SCOLAG = SCOLAG (*Scottish Legal Action Group*)

SI = Statutory Instrument

S. & C.L. = Sports and Character Licensing (*Informa Publishing Group*)

Soc. L. = Socialist Lawyer (*Haldane Society*)

Stat. L.R. = Statute Law Review (*OUP*)

Step Journal = The Step Journal (*Barker Brooks Ltd*)

Sudebnik = Sudebnik (*Simmonds & Hill*)

T. & T. = Trusts & Trustees (*Gostick Hall*)

T.A.Q. = The Aviation Quarterly (*LLP*)

T.B. = Technical Bulletin (*Association of Business Recovery Professionals*)

T.B.S.P.I. = Technical Bulletin of the Society of Practitioners of Insolvency (*Society of Practitioners of Insolvency*)

T.C. or Tax.Cas. = Tax Cases (*TSO*)

T.C.L.R. = Technology and Construction Law Reports (*S&M*)

T.E.L.L. = Tolley's Employment Law-Line (*Butterworth Tolley Publishing*)

T.E.L. & T.J. = Trusts and Estates Law & Tax Journal (*Legalease Publications*)

T.L.P. = Transport Law & Policy (*Waterfront Partnership*)

T.M.I.F. = Tax Management International Forum (*BNA International*)

T.N.I.B. = Tolley's National Insurance Brief (*Butterworth Tolley Publishing*)

T.O.C. = Transnational Organized Crime (*Cass*)

T.P.I.A.P.F. = Tax Planning International Asia.Pacific Focus (*BNA International Inc*)

T.P.I.E.U.F. = Tax Planning International European Union Focus (*BNA International Inc*)

T.P.I.I.T = Tax Planning International Indirect Tax (*BNA International Inc*)

T.P.I.R. = Tax Planning International Review (*BNA International Inc*)

T.P.T.N. = Tolley's Practical Tax Newsletter (*Butterworth Tolley Publishing*)

T.P.T.S. = Tolley's Practical Tax Service (*Butterworth Tolley Publishing*)

T.P.V.N. = Tolley's Practical VAT Newsletter (*Butterworth Tolley Publishing*)

T.P.V.S. = Tolley's Practical VAT Service (*Butterworth Tolley Publishing*)

T.Q.R. = Trust Quarterly Review (*Barker Brooks Ltd*)

T.W. = Trademark World (*Intellectual Property*)

Tax A. = Taxation Adviser (*The Manson Group Ltd*)

Tax B. = Tax Briefing (*Office of the Revenue Commissioners*)

Tax Bus. = Tax Business (*Legalease Publication*)

Tax J. = Tax Journal (*Butterworth Tolley Publishing*)

Tax. = Taxation (*Butterworth Tolley Publishing*)

Taxline = Taxline (*Tax Faculty*)

Theo. Crim. = Theoretical Criminology (*Sage Publications*)

Tr. & Est. = Trusts & Estates (*Monitor Press*)

Tr. L.R. = Trading Law Reports (*Barry Rose*)

Trans. ref. = Transcript reference number

Tribunals = Tribunals (*OUP*)

Tru. L.I. = Trust Law International (*Butterworth Tolley Publishing*)

TSO = The Stationery Office

The Times = Times Law Reports

U.L.R. = Utilities Law Review (*Chancery Law Publishing Ltd*)

UCELNET = Universities and Colleges Education Law Network (*University of Stirling*)

U.K.C.L.R. = UK Competition Law Reports (*Jordan*)

UKHL = Media neutral citation from House of Lords

U.K.H.R.R. = United Kingdom Human Rights Reports (*Jordan*)

UKPC = Media neutral citation from Privy Council

V. & D.R. = Value Added Tax and Duties Reports (*TSO*)

V.A.T.T.R. = Value Added Tax Tribunal Reports (*TSO*)

VAT Int. = VAT Intelligence (*Gee Publishing*)

VAT Plan. = VAT Planning (*Butterworth Tolley Publishing*)

W. Comp. = World Competition (*Kluwer*)

W.B. = Welfare Benefits (*CLP*)

W.E.C. & I.P.R. = World E-Commerce & IP Report (*BNA International Inc*)

WL = Westlaw UK (*S&M*)

W.L. = Water Law (*Chancery Law Publishing Ltd*)

W.L.L.R. = World Licensing Law Report (*BNA International Inc*)

W.L.R. = Weekly Law Reports (*ICLR*)

W.M. = Waste Management (*IWM Business Services*)

W.O.G.L.R. = World Online Gambling Law Report (*Cecile Part Publishing*)

TABLE OF ABBREVIATIONS

W.T.L.R. = Wills & Trusts Law Reports (*Legalease Ltd*)

Web J.C.L.I. = Web Journal of Current Legal Issues (*Blackstone*) http://webjcli.ncl.ac.uk

Welf. R. Bull. = Welfare Rights Bulletin (*Child Poverty*)

World I.L.R. = World Internet Law Report (*BNA International Inc*)

W.S.L.R. = World Sport Law Report (*Cecile Park Publishing Ltd*)

World T.R. = World Trade Review (*CUP*)

Worldlaw Bus. = Worldlaw Business (*Euromoney Publications*)

Writ = Writ (*Northern Ireland Law Society*)

Y.J. = Youth Justice (*Russell House Publishing Ltd*)

YSG Mag. = Young Solicitors Group Magazine (*Butterworth Tolley Publishing*)

ALPHABETICAL TABLE OF STATUTES

This table lists all the statutes cited in the Statute Citator

Aberdeen Harbour Order Confirmation Act 1960 (c.i)
Aberdeen Harbour Order Confirmation Act 1987 (c.xxi)
Abolition of Domestic Rates Etc (Scotland) Act 1987 (c.47)
Abolition of Feudal Tenure etc (Scotland) Act 2000 (asp 5)
Abolition of Poindings and Warrant Sales Act 2001 (asp 1)
Abortion Act 1967 (c.87)
Access to Health Records Act 1990 (c.23)
Access to Information Act 1985 (c.)
Access to Justice Act 1999 (c.22)
Access to Neighbouring Land Act 1992 (c.23)
Access to Personal Files Act 1987 (c.37)
Accessories and Abettors Act 1861 (c.94)
Accommodation Agencies Act 1953 (c.23)
Acquisition of Land (Authorisation Procedure) (Scotland) Act 1947 (c.42)
Acquisition of Land (Authorisation Procedure) Act 1946 (c.49)
Acquisition of Land Act 1981 (c.67)
Act of Settlement 1700 (c.2)
Activity Centres (Young Persons Safety) Act 1995 (c.15)
Administration of Estates (Small Payments) (Northern Ireland) Act 1967 (c.5)
Administration of Estates (Small Payments) Act 1965 (c.32)
Administration of Estates Act 1925 (c.23)
Administration of Justice (Appeals) Act 1934 (c.40)
Administration of Justice (Miscellaneous Provisions) Act 1933 (c.36)
Administration of Justice (Northern Ireland) Act 1954 (c.9)
Administration of Justice (Scotland) Act 1972 (c.59)
Administration of Justice Act 1932 (c.)
Administration of Justice Act 1960 (c.65)
Administration of Justice Act 1964 (c.42)
Administration of Justice Act 1965 (c.2)
Administration of Justice Act 1969 (c.58)
Administration of Justice Act 1970 (c.31)
Administration of Justice Act 1973 (c.15)
Administration of Justice Act 1977 (c.38)
Administration of Justice Act 1982 (c.53)
Administration of Justice Act 1985 (c.61)
Administrative and Financial Provisions Act (Northern Ireland) 1962 (c.7)
Admiralty Pensions Act 1921 (c.39)
Adoption (Intercountry Aspects) Act (Northern Ireland) 2001 (c.11)
Adoption (Intercountry Aspects) Act 1999 (c.18)
Adoption (Scotland) Act 1978 (c.28)
Adoption Act 1950 (c.26)
Adoption Act 1958 (c.5)
Adoption Act 1976 (c.36)
Adoption and Children Act 2002 (c.38)
Adoption of Children Act 1926 (c.29)
Adoption of Children Act 1949 (c.98)
Adults with Incapacity (Scotland) Act 2000 (asp 4)
Age of Majority Act (Northern Ireland) 1969 (c.28)
Age-Related Payments Act 2004 (c.10)
Aggravated Vehicle-Taking Act 1992 (c.11)
Agricultural Holdings (Scotland) Act 1991 (c.55)

Agricultural Holdings (Scotland) Act 2003 (asp 11)
Agricultural Holdings Act 1986 (c.5)
Agricultural Land (Removal of Surface Soil) Act 1953 (c.10)
Agricultural Land (Utilisation) Act 1931 (c.41)
Agricultural Marketing Act 1958 (c.47)
Agricultural Marketing Act 1983 (c.3)
Agricultural Produce (Meat Regulations and Pig Industry) Act (Northern Ireland) 1962 (c.13)
Agricultural Returns Act (Northern Ireland) 1939 (c.35)
Agricultural Statistics Act 1979 (c.13)
Agricultural Tenancies Act 1995 (c.8)
Agricultural Training Board Act 1982 (c.9)
Agricultural Training Board Act 1985 (c.36)
Agricultural Training Board Act 1987 (c.29)
Agricultural Wages (Scotland) Act 1949 (c.30)
Agricultural Wages Act 1948 (c.47)
Agriculture (Amendment) Act 1984 (c.20)
Agriculture (Miscellaneous Provisions) (Northern Ireland) Act 1965 (c.3)
Agriculture (Miscellaneous Provisions) Act 1943 (c.16)
Agriculture (Miscellaneous Provisions) Act 1944 (c.28)
Agriculture (Miscellaneous Provisions) Act 1954 (c.39)
Agriculture (Miscellaneous Provisions) Act 1963 (c.11)
Agriculture (Miscellaneous Provisions) Act 1968 (c.34)
Agriculture (Miscellaneous Provisions) Act 1972 (c.62)
Agriculture (Miscellaneous Provisions) Act 1976 (c.55)
Agriculture (Safety, Health and Welfare Provisions) Act 1956 (c.49)
Agriculture (Scotland) Act 1948 (c.45)
Agriculture (Silo Subsidies) Act 1956 (c.5)
Agriculture Act (Northern Ireland) 1949 (c.2)
Agriculture Act 1947 (c.48)
Agriculture Act 1957 (c.57)
Agriculture Act 1958 (c.71)
Agriculture Act 1967 (c.22)
Agriculture Act 1970 (c.40)
Agriculture Act 1986 (c.49)
Agriculture Act 1993 (c.37)
Agriculture and Horticulture Act 1964 (c.28)
AIDS (Control) Act 1987 (c.33)
Air Corporations Act 1966 (c.11)
Air Corporations Act 1969 (c.43)
Air Force (Constitution) Act 1917 (c.51)
Air Force Act 1955 (c.19)
Aircraft and Shipbuilding Industries Act 1977 (c.3)
Airports Act 1986 (c.31)
Alcoholic Liquor Duties Act 1979 (c.4)
Alexandra Park and Palace (Public Purposes) Act 1900 (c.cclix)
Alexandra Park and Palace Act 1913 (c.cxi)
Alexandra Park and Palace Act 1985 (c.xxiii)
Aliens Restriction (Amendment) Act 1919 (c.92)
Allotments Act 1950 (c.31)
Allowances to Members of the Assembly Act (Northern Ireland) 2000 (c.3)
An Act for making a Railway from the Warrington and Newton Railway at Warrington in the County of Lancaster to Birmingham in the County of War-

ALPHABETICAL TABLE OF STATUTES

ALPHABETICAL TABLE OF STATUTORY INSTRUMENTS

This table lists all the Statutory Instruments cited in the Statutory Instruments Citator.

5 Boroughs Partnership National Health Service Trust (Establishment) and the Warrington Community Health Care National Health Service Trust (Dissolution) Order 2001 (S.I. 4120)

A435 Trunk Road (Alcester to Gorcott Hill) De-Trunking Order 1993 (S.I. 80)

A435 Trunk Road (Studley Bypass and Slip Roads) Order 1993 (S.I. 81)

A46 Trunk Road (Ashchurch Station Bridge) Order 2002 (S.I. 1594)

Aberdeen and Grampian Tourist Board Scheme Amendment Order 1995 (S.I. 2211)

Aberdeen and Grampian Tourist Board Scheme Order 1995 (S.I. 1879)

Aberdeen Harbour Revision Order 1972 (S.I. 1704)

Aberdeen Harbour Revision Order 1972 (S.I. 275)

Aberdeen Harbour Revision Order 1976 (S.I. 817)

Aberdeen Harbour Revisions Order 1990 (S.I. 2359)

Abolition of the Intervention Board for Agricultural Produce (Consequential Provisions) (Scotland) Regulations 2001 (S.S.I. 390)

Abolition of the NHS Tribunal (Consequential Provisions) Regulations 2001 (S.I. 3744)

Abolition of the NHS Tribunal (Consequential Provisions) Regulations 2002 (S.I. 1920)

Abortion (Scotland) Regulations 1991 (S.I. 460)

Abortion Regulations 1991 (S.I. 499)

ABRO Trading Fund Order 2002 (S.I. 719)

Abstract of Special Regulations (Highly Flammable Liquids and Liquefied Petroleum Gases) Order 1974 (S.I. 1587)

ACAS (Flexible Working) Arbitration Scheme (England and Wales) Order 2003 (S.I. 694)

ACAS Arbitration Scheme (England and Wales) Order 2001 (S.I. 1185)

Access for Community Air Carriers to Intra-Community Air Routes Regulations 1992 (S.I. 2993)

Access to Health Records (Northern Ireland) Order 1993 (S.I. 1250)

Access to Justice (Northern Ireland) Order 2003 (S.I. 435)

Access to Justice Act 1999 (Destination of Appeals) Order 2000 (S.I. 1071)

Access to the Countryside (Exclusions and Restrictions) (England) Regulations 2003 (S.I. 2713)

Access to the Countryside (Provisional and Conclusive Maps) (England) Regulations 2002 (S.I. 1710)

Accession (Immigration and Worker Registration) Regulations 2004 (S.I. 1219)

Accounts and Audit (Amendment) (England) Regulations 2001 (S.I. 3244)

Accounts and Audit Regulations 1996 (S.I. 590)

Accounts and Audit Regulations 2003 (S.I. 533)

Act of Adjournal (Criminal Procedure Rules) 1996 (S.I. 13946)

Act of Adjournal (Criminal Procedure Rules) 1996 (S.I. 513)

Act of Sederunt (Amendment of Ordinary Cause and Summary Cause Rules) (Written Statements) 1989 (S.I. 436)

Act of Sederunt (Amendment of Ordinary Cause, Summary Cause and Small Claim Rules) 1992 (S.I. 249)

Act of Sederunt (Amendment of Sheriff Court Ordinary Cause, and Summary Cause, Rules) 1988 (S.I. 1978)

Act of Sederunt (Amendment of Sheriff Court Ordinary Cause, Summary Cause, and Small Claim, Rules) (No.2) 1990 (S.I. 2105)

Act of Sederunt (Amendment of Sheriff Court Ordinary Cause, Summary Cause, and Small Claim, Rules) 1990 (S.I. 661)

Act of Sederunt (Amendment of Summary Cause and Small Claim Rules) 1991 (S.I. 821)

Act of Sederunt (Child Care and Maintenance Rules 1997 (S.I. 291)

Act of Sederunt (Child Care and Maintenance Rules) 1997 (S.I. 291)

Act of Sederunt (Child Support Act 1991) (Amendment of Ordinary Cause and Summary Cause Rules) 1993 (S.I. 919)

Act of Sederunt (Civil Jurisdiction of the Sheriff Court) 1986 (S.I. 1946)

Act of Sederunt (Confirmation of Executors) 1964 (S.I. 1143)

Act of Sederunt (Debt Arrangement and Attachment (Scotland) Act 2002) 2002 (S.S.I. 560)

Act of Sederunt (Fees in the Scottish Record Office) 1990 (S.I. 44)

Act of Sederunt (Fees of Messengers-at-Arms) (Amendment) 1998 (S.I. 3256)

Act of Sederunt (Fees of Messengers-at-Arms) (No.2) 1994 (S.I. 3268)

Act of Sederunt (Fees of Messengers-at-Arms) (No.2) 2002 (S.S.I. 566)

Act of Sederunt (Fees of Messengers-at-Arms) 1994 (S.I. 391)

Act of Sederunt (Fees of Messengers-at-Arms) 1995 (S.I. 3094)

Act of Sederunt (Fees of Messengers-at-Arms) 1996 (S.I. 2855)

Act of Sederunt (Fees of Messengers-at-Arms) 1997 (S.I. 2825)

Act of Sederunt (Fees of Messengers-at-Arms) 1998 (S.I. 2668)

Act of Sederunt (Fees of Messengers-at-Arms) 1999 (S.S.I. 151)

Act of Sederunt (Fees of Messengers-At-Arms) 2000 (S.S.I. 421)

Act of Sederunt (Fees of Messengers-At-Arms) 2001 (S.S.I. 440)

Act of Sederunt (Fees of Messengers-At-Arms) 2002 (S.S.I. 513)

Act of Sederunt (Fees of Sheriff Officers) (No.2) 1994 (S.I. 3267)

Act of Sederunt (Fees of Sheriff Officers) (No.2) 2002 (S.S.I. 567)

Act of Sederunt (Fees of Sheriff Officers) 1994 (S.I. 392)

Act of Sederunt (Fees of Sheriff Officers) 1995 (S.I. 3095)

Act of Sederunt (Fees of Sheriff Officers) 1996 (S.I. 2858)

Act of Sederunt (Fees of Sheriff Officers) 1997 (S.I. 2824)

Act of Sederunt (Fees of Sheriff Officers) 1998 (S.I. 2669)

Act of Sederunt (Fees of Sheriff Officers) 1999 (S.S.I. 150)

Act of Sederunt (Fees of Sheriff Officers) 2000 (S.S.I. 419)

Act of Sederunt (Fees of Sheriff Officers) 2001 (S.S.I. 439)

Act of Sederunt (Fees of Sheriff Officers) 2002 (S.S.I. 515)

Act of Sederunt (Fees of Solicitors and Witnesses in the Sheriff Court) (Amendment) 2004 (S.S.I. 152)

Act of Sederunt (Fees of Solicitors in the Sheriff Court) (Amendment and Further Provisions) 1993 (S.I. 3080)

Act of Sederunt (Fees of Solicitors in the Sheriff Court) (Amendment No 2) 2002 (S.S.I. 274)

Act of Sederunt (Fees of Witnesses and Shorthand Writers in the Sheriff Court) 1992 (S.I. 1878)

Act of Sederunt (Form of Charge for Payment) 1988 (S.I. 2059)

Act of Sederunt (Messengers-at-Arms and Sheriff Officers Rules) 1991 (S.I. 1397)

Act of Sederunt (Miscellaneous Amendments) 1986 (S.I. 1966)

Act of Sederunt (Ordinary Cause Rules, Sheriff Court) 1983 (S.I. 747)

Act of Sederunt (Proceedings in the Sheriff Court under the Debtors (Scotland) Act 1987) (Amendment) 1996 (S.I. 2709)

Act of Sederunt (Proceedings in the Sheriff Court under the Debtors (Scotland) Act 1987) 1988 (S.I. 2013)

Act of Sederunt (Rules of Court, consolidation and amendment) 1965 (S.I. 321)

Act of Sederunt (Rules of the Court of Session 1994 (S.I. 1443)

Act of Sederunt (Rules of the Court of Session 1994) 1994 (S.I. 1443)

Act of Sederunt (Rules of the Court of Session Amendment No.2) (Personal Injuries Actions) 2002 (S.I. 570)

Act of Sederunt (Rules of the Court of Session) 1994 (S.I. 1443)

Act of Sederunt (Sheriff Court Bankruptcy Rules) 1996 (S.I. 2507)

Act of Sederunt (Sheriff Court Company Insolvency Rules) 1986 (S.I. 2297)

Act of Sederunt (Sheriff Court Ordinary Cause Rules 1993 (S.I. 1956)

Act of Sederunt (Sheriff Court Ordinary Cause Rules) 1993 (S.I. 1956)

Act of Sederunt (Small Claim Rules) 1988 (S.I. 1976)

Act of Sederunt (Small Claim Rules) 2002 (S.S.I. 133)

Act of Sederunt (Summary Applications, Statutory Applications and Appeals etc Rules) 1999 (S.I. 929)

Act of Sederunt (Summary Cause Rules Sheriff Court) (Amendment) Order 1980 (S.I. 455)

Act of Sederunt (Summary Cause Rules) 1976 (S.I. 476)

Act of Sederunt (Summary Cause Rules) 2002 (S.S.I. 132)

Act of Sederunt (Summary Cause Rules, Sheriff Court) (Amendment No 2) 1978 (S.I. 1805)

Act of Sederunt (Summary Cause Rules, Sheriff Court) (Amendment) 1978 (S.I. 112)

Act of Sederunt (Summary Cause Rules, Sheriff Court) 1976 (S.I. 476)

Act of Sederunt (Summary Suspension) 1993 (S.I. 3128)

Action for Learning Partnership, Bedford Education Action Zone Order 1999 (S.I. 3399)

Action Programme for Nitrate Vulnerable Zones (England and Wales) Regulations 1998 (S.I. 1202)

Action Programme for Nitrate Vulnerable Zones (Scotland) Regulations 1998 (S.I. 2927)

Action Programme for Nitrate Vulnerable Zones (Scotland) Regulations 2003 (S.S.I. 51)

Active Implantable Medical Devices (Amendment and Transitional Provisions) Regulations 1995 (S.I. 1671)

Active Implantable Medical Devices Regulations 1992 (S.I. 3146)

Addenbrooke's National Health Service Trust (Establishment) Order 1992 (S.I. 2567)

Administration of Insolvent Estates of Deceased Persons Order (Northern Ireland) 1991 (365)

Administration of Insolvent Estates of Deceased Persons Order 1986 (S.I. 1999)

Administration of Oaths (Summary Appeal Court) (Air Force) Order 2000 (S.I. 2378)

Administration of Oaths (Summary Appeal Court) (Army) Order 2000 (S.I. 2377)

Administration of Oaths (Summary Appeal Court) (Navy) Order 2000 (S.I. 2376)

Adoption (Designation of Overseas Adoptions) Order 1973 (S.I. 19)

Adoption (Northern Ireland) Order 1987 (S.I. 2203)

Adoption Agencies (Scotland) Regulations 1984 (S.I. 988)

Adoption Agencies (Scotland) Regulations 1996 (S.I. 3266)

Adoption Agencies Regulations (Northern Ireland) 1989 (253)

Adoption Agencies Regulations 1983 (S.I. 1964)

Adoption Allowance Regulations 1991 (S.I. 2030)

Adoption and Children Act 2002 (Commencement No 1) (Wales) Order 2003 (S.I. 181)

Adoption of Children from Overseas (Scotland) Regulations 2001 (S.S.I. 236)

Adoption of Children from Overseas (Wales) Regulations 2001 (S.I. 1272)

Adoption of Children from Overseas Regulations 2001 (S.I. 1251)

Adoption Rules 1984 (S.I. 265)

Adult Placement Schemes (England) Regulations 2004 (S.I. 2071)

Adult Placement Schemes (Wales) Regulations 2004 (S.I. 1756)

Adults with Incapacity (Countersignatories of Applications for Authority to Intromit) (Scotland) Regulations 2001 (S.S.I. 78)

Adults with Incapacity (Ethics Committee) (Scotland) Regulations 2002 (S.S.I. 190)

Adults with Incapacity (Public Guardian's Fees) (Scotland) Regulations 2001 (S.S.I. 75)

Adults with Incapacity (Scotland) Act 2000 (Commencement No 1) Order 2001 (S.S.I. 81)

Adults with Incapacity (Scotland) Act 2000 (Commencement No 3) Order 2003 (S.S.I. 136)

Adults with Incapacity (Specified Medical Treatments) (Scotland) Regulations 2002 (S.S.I. 275)

Advanced Television Services (Amendment) Regulations 1996 (S.I. 3197)

Advanced Television Services Regulations 1996 (S.I. 3151)

Advanced Television Services Regulations 2003 (S.I. 1901)

Adventure Activities (Enforcing Authority and Licensing Amendment) Regulations 1996 (S.I. 1647)

Adventure Activities Licensing Regulations 1996 (S.I. 772)

Adventure Activities Licensing Regulations 2004 (S.I. 1309)

Air Navigation (Dangerous Goods) Regulations 2002 (S.I. 2786)

Air Navigation (General) Regulations 1993 (S.I. 1622)

Air Navigation (Hong Kong) Order 1995 (S.I. 2700)

Air Navigation (Jersey) Order 2000 (S.I. 1346)

Air Navigation (No.2) Order 1995 (S.I. 1970)

Air Navigation (Noise Certification) Order 1990 (S.I. 1514)

Air Navigation (Overseas Territories) Order 2001 (S.I. 2128)

Air Navigation Order 2000 (S.I. 1562)

Air Passenger Duty and Other Indirect Taxes (Interest Rate) Regulations 1998 (S.I. 1461)

Air Quality (England) Regulations 2000 (S.I. 928)

Air Quality (Scotland) Regulations 2000 (S.S.I. 97)

Air Quality (Wales) Regulations 2000 (S.I. 1940)

Air Quality Limit Values (Amendment) Regulations 2002 (S.I. 3117)

Air Quality Limit Values (Scotland) Amendment Regulations 2002 (S.S.I. 556)

Air Quality Limit Values (Scotland) Regulations 2001 (S.S.I. 224)

Air Quality Limit Values (Scotland) Regulations 2003 (S.S.I. 428)

Air Quality Limit Values (Wales) Regulations 2001 (S.I. 2683)

Air Quality Limit Values (Wales) Regulations 2002 (S.I. 3183)

Air Quality Limit Values Regulations (Northern Ireland) 2002 (94)

Air Quality Limit Values Regulations 2001 (S.I. 2315)

Air Quality Limit Values Regulations 2003 (S.I. 2121)

Air Quality Standards Regulations (Northern Ireland) 1990 (145)

Air Quality Standards Regulations 1989 (S.I. 317)

Aircraft (Customs and Excise) Regulations 1981 (S.I. 1259)

Airedale Primary Care Trust (Establishment) Order 2000 (S.I. 1942)

Airports (Groundhandling) Regulations 1997 (S.I. 2389)

Airports (Northern Ireland) Order 1994 (S.I. 426)

Airports Act 1986 (Modifications in Schedule 4 to the Transport Act 1968) Order 1986 (S.I. 1801)

Airports Slot Allocation Regulations 1993 (S.I. 1067)

Alcoholometers and Alcohol Hydrometers (EEC Requirements) Regulations 1977 (S.I. 1753)

Alexandra Health Care National Health Service Trust (Establishment) Order 1994 (S.I. 169)

Alexandra Health Care, the Kidderminster Health Care, the Worcestershire Community Healthcare and the Worcester Royal Infirmary National Health Service Trusts (Dissolution) Order 1999 (S.I. 3471)

Alexandra Park and Palace Order 1966 (S.I. 199)

Allington, the East Suffolk Local Health Services and the Mid Anglia Community Health National Health Service Trusts (Dissolution) Order 1999 (S.I. 850)

Allocation of Housing (England) Regulations 2000 (S.I. 702)

Allocation of Housing (England) Regulations 2002 (S.I. 3264)

Allocation of Housing (Wales) Regulations 2000 (S.I. 1080)

Allocation of Housing and Homelessness (Amendment) (No.2) Regulations 1997 (S.I. 2046)

Al-Qa'ida and Taliban (United Nations Measures) (Channel Islands) Order 2002 (S.I. 258)

Al-Qa'ida and Taliban (United Nations Measures) (Isle of Man) Order 2002 (S.I. 259)

Al-Qa'ida and Taliban (United Nations Measures) (Overseas Territories) Order 2002 (S.I. 112)

Al-Qa'ida and Taliban (United Nations Measures) Order 2002 (S.I. 111)

Alternative Names in Welsh Order 1994 (S.I. 2889)

Alton Station Light Railway Order 1985 (S.I. 810)

Amber Valley Primary Care Trust (Establishment) Order 2001 (S.I. 130)

Ammonium Nitrate Mixtures Exemption Order 1967 (S.I. 1485)

Anatomy (Northern Ireland) Order 1992 (S.I. 1718)

Ancient Monuments (Class Consents) (Scotland) Order 1996 (S.I. 1507)

Andover District Community Health Care National Health Service Trust (Dissolution) Order 2000 (S.I. 847)

Andover District Community Health Care National Health Service Trust (Establishment) Order 1992 (S.I. 2505)

Anglian Harbours National Health Service Trust Dissolution Order 1997 (S.I. 1987)

Anglian Water Parks Byelaws (Extension) Order 2003 (S.I. 757)

Angola (United Nations Prohibition of Flights) (Dependent Territories) Order 1997 (S.I. 2570)

Angola (United Nations Prohibition of Flights) Order 1997 (S.I. 2571)

Angola (United Nations Sanctions) (Amendment) Order 2000 (S.I. 1818)

Angola (United Nations Sanctions) (Channel Islands) (Amendment) Order 2000 (S.I. 1837)

Angola (United Nations Sanctions) (Channel Islands) Order 1993 (S.I. 2357)

Angola (United Nations Sanctions) (Channel Islands) Order 1997 (S.I. 2594)

Angola (United Nations Sanctions) (Channel Islands) Order 1998 (S.I. 1756)

Angola (United Nations Sanctions) (Dependent Territories) Order 1993 (S.I. 2356)

Angola (United Nations Sanctions) (Dependent Territories) Order 1997 (S.I. 2573)

Angola (United Nations Sanctions) (Dependent Territories) Order 1998 (S.I. 1753)

Angola (United Nations Sanctions) (Isle of Man) (Amendment) Order 2000 (S.I. 1836)

Angola (United Nations Sanctions) (Isle of Man) Order 1993 (S.I. 2358)

Angola (United Nations Sanctions) (Isle of Man) Order 1997 (S.I. 2595)

Angola (United Nations Sanctions) (Isle of Man) Order 1998 (S.I. 1757)

Angola (United Nations Sanctions) (Overseas Territories) (Amendment) Order 2000 (S.I. 1819)

Angola (United Nations Sanctions) Order 1993 (S.I. 2355)

Angola (United Nations Sanctions) Order 1997 (S.I. 2572)

Angola (United Nations Sanctions) Order 1998 (S.I. 1752)

Anguilla Constitution Order 1982 (S.I. 334)

Angus and City of Dundee Tourist Board Scheme Amendment Order 1995 (S.I. 2212)

Angus and City of Dundee Tourist Board Scheme Order 1995 (S.I. 1880)

Animal By-Products (Amendment) (England) Order 2001 (S.I. 1704)

Animal By-Products (Amendment) (Wales) Order 2001 (S.I. 1735)

Animal By-Products (Amendment) Regulations (Northern Ireland) 1998 (108)

Animal By-Products (Identification) Regulations (Northern Ireland) 1999 (418)

Ashington Education Action Zone Order 1999 (S.I. 3391)

Ashton, Leigh and Wigan Primary Care Trust (Establishment) Order 2001 (S.I. 3488)

Ashworth, Broadmoor and Rampton Hospital Authorities (Functions and Membership) Regulations 1996 (S.I. 489)

Assured Tenancies and Agricultural Occupancies (Forms) (Amendment) (England) Regulations 2002 (S.I. 337)

Assured Tenancies and Agricultural Occupancies (Forms) Regulations 1997 (S.I. 194)

Asylum (Designated Countries of Destination and Designated Safe Third Countries) Order 1996 (S.I. 2671)

Asylum Appeals (Procedure) Rules 1996 (S.I. 2070)

Asylum Support (Amendment) (No.2) Regulations 2002 (S.I. 2619)

Asylum Support (Amendment) (No.2) Regulations 2003 (S.I. 755)

Asylum Support (Amendment) Regulations 2000 (S.I. 3053)

Asylum Support (Interim Provisions) Regulations 1999 (S.I. 3056)

Asylum Support (Repeal) Order 2002 (S.I. 782)

Asylum Support Appeals (Procedure) Rules 2000 (S.I. 541)

Asylum Support Regulations 2000 (S.I. 704)

Audit (Northern Ireland) Order 1987 (S.I. 460)

Audit and Accountability (Northern Ireland) Order 2003 (S.I. 418)

Avalon, Somerest, National Health Service Trust (Establishment) Order 1992 (S.I. 2588)

Avalon, Somerset, National Health Service Trust (Change of Name) Order 1999 (S.I. 3050)

Aviation Security (Anguilla) Order 1987 (S.I. 451)

Avon (Coroners) Order 1996 (S.I. 656)

Avon (Staff Transfer) Order 1996 (S.I. 400)

Avon (Structural Change) Order 1995 (S.I. 493)

Avon Ambulance Service National Health Service Trust (Establishment) Order 1991 (S.I. 2320)

Avon and Western Wiltshire Mental Health Care National Health Service Trust (Change of Name) Order 2001 (S.I. 271)

Avon Fire Services (Combination Scheme) Order 1995 (S.I. 3127)

Awards For All (England) Joint Scheme (Authorisation) Order 2002 (S.I. 638)

Awards for All (England) Joint Scheme (Authorisation) Order 2003 (S.I. 664)

Aycliffe School Instrument of Management Order 1973 (S.I. 56)

Aylesbury Vale Community Healthcare National Health Service Trust (Dissolution) Order 2001 (S.I. 334)

Aylesbury Vale Community Healthcare National Health Service Trust (Establishment) Amendment Order 1992 (S.I. 1822)

Aylesbury Vale Community Healthcare National Health Service Trust (Establishment) Amendment Order 2000 (S.I. 2663)

Ayrshire and Arran Acute Hospitals National Health Service Trust (Establishment) Amendment (No.2) Order 1999 (S.S.I. 197)

Ayrshire and Arran Acute Hospitals National Health Service Trust (Establishment) Amendment Order 1999 (S.S.I. 100)

Ayrshire and Arran Acute Hospitals National Health Service Trust (Establishment) Amendment Order 2001 (S.S.I. 340)

Ayrshire and Arran Acute Hospitals National Health Service Trust (Establishment) Order 1998 (S.I. 2735)

Ayrshire and Arran Primary Care National Health Service Trust (Establishment) Amendment (No.2) Order 1999 (S.S.I. 165)

Ayrshire and Arran Primary Care National Health Service Trust (Establishment) Amendment Order 2001 (S.S.I. 339)

Ayrshire and Arran Primary Care National Health Service Trust (Establishment) Order 1998 (S.I. 2715)

Ayrshire and Arran Tourist Board Scheme Amendment Order 1995 (S.I. 2232)

Ayrshire and Arran Tourist Board Scheme Order 1995 (S.I. 1882)

Banking Act 1987 (Exempt Transactions) Regulations 1997 (S.I. 817)

Bankruptcy (Scotland) Regulations 1985 (S.I. 1925)

Bankruptcy and Companies (Department of Trade &amp Industry) Fees (Amendment) Order 1990 (S.I. 559)

Bankruptcy and Companies (Department of Trade and Industry) Fees (Amendment) Order 1991 (S.I. 494)

Bankruptcy Fees (Amendment) Order 1985 (S.I. 1783)

Bankruptcy Fees Order 1984 (S.I. 880)

Banks (Administration Proceedings) Order 1989 (S.I. 1276)

Barbados Independence Order 1966 (S.I. 1455)

Barking and Dagenham Primary Care Trust (Establishment) Order 2001 (S.I. 348)

Barking Barrage Order 1995 (S.I. 519)

Barking, Havering and Redbridge Hospitals National Health Service Trust (Establishment) Order 2000 (S.I. 1413)

Barnet and Chase Farm Hospitals National Health Service Trust (Establishment) Order 1999 (S.I. 892)

Barnet Community Healthcare, the Enfield Community Care and the Haringey Health Care National Health Service Trusts (Dissolution) Order 2001 (S.I. 1331)

Barnet Primary Care Trust (Establishment) Order 2001 (S.I. 328)

Barnet, Enfield and Haringey Mental Health National Health Service Trust (Establishment) Order 2001 (S.I. 1330)

Barnsley Community and Priority Services National Health Service Trust (Dissolution) Order 2002 (S.I. 1294)

Barnsley Community and Priority Services National Health Service Trust (Establishment) Order 1991 (S.I. 2323)

Barnsley District General Hospital National Health Service Trust (Establishment) Order 1992 (S.I. 2480)

Barnsley Primary Care Trust (Establishment) Order 2001 (S.I. 4133)

Barts National Health Service Trust Dissolution Order 1993 (S.I. 697)

Basildon and Thurrock General Hospitals National Health Service Trust (Change of Name) Order 2002 (S.I. 2617)

Basildon and Thurrock General Hospitals National Health Service Trust (Establishment) Order 1991 (S.I. 2325)

Basildon Primary Care Trust (Establishment) Order 2001 (S.I. 388)

Bassetlaw Primary Care Trust (Establishment) Order 2001 (S.I. 186)

Bath and North East Somerset District Council (Staff Transfer) Order 1996 (S.I. 377)

Bath and North East Somerset Primary Care Trust (Establishment) Order 2001 (S.I. 473)

Birmingham Northern Relief Road Toll Order 1998 (S.I. 124)

Birmingham Specialist Community Health National Health Service Trust (Establishment) Amendment Order 2000 (S.I. 2044)

Birmingham Specialist Community Health National Health Service Trust (Establishment) Order 1999 (S.I. 3467)

Birmingham Women's Health Care National Health Service Trust (Establishment) Order 1993 (S.I. 2541)

Births and Deaths Registration (Northern Ireland) Order 1976 (S.I. 1041)

Births, Deaths and Marriages (Fees) Order (Northern Ireland) 1998 (330)

Births, Deaths and Marriages Registration (Northern Ireland) Order 1973 (S.I. 600)

Births, Deaths, Marriages and Divorces (Fees) (Scotland) Regulations 1998 (S.I. 643)

Bishop Auckland Hospitals National Health Service Trust (Dissolution) Order 1998. 1998 (S.I. 823)

Bishop Auckland Hospitals National Health Service Trust (Establishment) Amendment Order 1996 (S.I. 989)

Bishop Auckland Hospitals National Health Service Trust (Establishment) Order 1993 (S.I. 2616)

Bitton Light Railway Order 1991 (S.I. 134)

Black Country Mental Health National Health Service Trust (Change of Name) and (Establishment) Amendment Order 2003 (S.I. 844)

Black Country Mental Health National Health Service Trust (Establishment) Amendment Order 1998 (S.I. 1187)

Black Country Mental Health National Health Service Trust (Establishment) Order 1994 (S.I. 3177)

Blackburn with Darwen Primary Care Trust (Establishment) Order 2000 (S.I. 1167)

Blackburn, Hyndburn and Ribble Valley Health Care National Health Service Trust (Establishment) Amendment Order 1999 (S.I. 2308)

Blackburn, Hyndburn and Ribble Valley Health Care National Health Service Trust (Establishment) Order 1993 (S.I. 2592)

Blackpool Primary Care Trust (Establishment) Order 2001 (S.I. 3661)

Blackpool Victoria Hospital National Health Service Trust (Establishment) Order 1993 (S.I. 2598)

Blackpool, Fylde and Wyre Hospitals National Health Service Trust (Establishment) and the Blackpool, Wyre and Fylde Community Health Services National Health Service Trust and the Blackpool Victoria Hospital National Health Service Trust (Dissolu 2002 (S.I. 1243)

Blackpool, Wyre and Fylde Community Health Services National Health Service Trust (Establishment) Amendment Order 2000 (S.I. 993)

Blackpool, Wyre and Fylde Community Health Services National Health Service Trust (Establishment) Order 1993 (S.I. 2597)

Blaenau Gwent and Caerphilly (Tredegar and Rhymney) Order 2002 (S.I. 651)

Blood Tests (Evidence of Paternity) Regulations (Northern Ireland) 1978 (379)

Blood Tests (Evidence of Paternity) Regulations 1971 (S.I. 1861)

Bluebell Extension Light Railway Order 1986 (S.I. 343)

Blyth Harbour Act 1986 (Amendment) Order 1995 (S.I. 2645)

Boarding-out and Fostering of Children (Scotland) Regulations 1985 (S.I. 1799)

Bodmin and Wenford Light Railway Order 1996 (S.I. 2867)

Bodmin Moor Railway Centre Light Railway Order 1989 (S.I. 1625)

Bolton Education Action Zone Order 1999 (S.I. 3393)

Bolton Hospitals National Health Service Trust (Establishment) Order 1993 (S.I. 2604)

Bolton Primary Care Trust (Establishment) Order 2001 (S.I. 3662)

Bolton Sixth Form College (Government) Regulations 1998 (S.I. 1332)

Bolton, Salford and Trafford Mental Health National Health Service Trust (Establishment) and the Mental Health Services of Salford National Health Service Trust (Dissolution) Order 2003 (S.I. 759)

Bo'ness and Kinneil Light Railway Order 1986 (S.I. 174)

Bootle and Litherland Primary Care Trust (Establishment) Order 2001 (S.I. 437)

Borders General Hospital National Health Service Trust (Establishment) Amendment Order 2000 (S.S.I. 353)

Borders General Hospital National Health Service Trust (Establishment) Amendment Order 2001 (S.S.I. 341)

Borders General Hospital National Health Service Trust (Establishment) Order 1994 (S.I. 2998)

Borders Primary Care National Health Service Trust (Establishment) Amendment Order 1999 (S.S.I. 92)

Borders Primary Care National Health Service Trust (Establishment) Amendment Order 2001 (S.S.I. 344)

Borders Primary Care National Health Service Trust (Establishment) Order 1998 (S.I. 2709)

Borehole Sites and Operations (Northern Ireland) 1995 (491)

Borehole Sites and Operations Regulations 1995 (S.I. 2038)

Borough of Allerdale (Electoral Changes) Order 1998 (S.I. 2569)

Borough of Amber Valley (Electoral Changes) Order 1999 (S.I. 2690)

Borough of Ashford (Electoral Changes) Order 2001 (S.I. 3563)

Borough of Barnsley (Electoral Arrangements) Order 1978 (S.I. 1639)

Borough of Barnsley (Electoral Changes) (Amendment) Order 2004 (S.I. 128)

Borough of Barnsley (Electoral Changes) Order 2003 (S.I. 3090)

Borough of Barrow-in-Furness (Electoral Changes) Order 1998 (S.I. 2571)

Borough of Basingstoke and Deane (Electoral Changes) Order 2001 (S.I. 1019)

Borough of Bedford (Electoral Changes) Order 2001 (S.I. 4066)

Borough of Berwick-upon-Tweed (Electoral Changes) Order 1998 (S.I. 2346)

Borough of Blackburn (Parishes and Electoral Changes) Order 1997 (S.I. 782)

Borough of Blackburn with Darwen (Electoral Changes) Order 2002 (S.I. 3223)

Borough of Blackburn with Darwen and the City of Peterborough (Changes to Years of Elections) Order 2002 (S.I. 2876)

Borough of Blackpool (Electoral Changes) Order 1997 (S.I. 783)

Borough of Blackpool (Electoral Changes) Order 2002 (S.I. 2240)

Borough of Blyth Valley (Electoral Changes) Order 1998 (S.I. 2345)

Borough of Bolton (Electoral Arrangements) Order 1979 (S.I. 1321)

Borough of Bolton (Electoral Changes) Order 2004 (S.I. 356)

Borough of Boston (Electoral Changes) Order 1998 (S.I. 2333)

Borough of Bournemouth (Electoral Arrangements) Order 1978 (S.I. 1813)

Borough of Bournemouth (Electoral Changes) Order 2002 (S.I. 1783)

Borough of Bracknell Forest (Electoral Changes) Order 2002 (S.I. 2371)

Borough of Brentwood (Electoral Changes) Order 2001 (S.I. 2441)

Borough of Broxbourne (Electoral Changes) Order 1998 (S.I. 2551)

Borough of Broxtowe (Electoral Changes) Order 2000 (S.I. 3296)

Borough of Burnley (Electoral Changes) (Amendment) Order 2002 (S.I. 2992)

Borough of Burnley (Electoral Changes) Order 2001 (S.I. 2473)

Borough of Bury (Electoral Arrangements) Order 1978 (S.I. 1722)

Borough of Bury (Electoral Changes) Order 2004 (S.I. 357)

Borough of Calderdale (Electoral Arrangements) Order 1979 (S.I. 1320)

Borough of Calderdale (Electoral Changes) Order 2003 (S.I. 3088)

Borough of Castle Morpeth (Electoral Changes) Order 1998 (S.I. 2344)

Borough of Castle Point (Electoral Changes) Order 2001 (S.I. 2440)

Borough of Charnwood (Electoral Arrangements) Order 1980 (S.I. 777)

Borough of Charnwood (Electoral Changes) Order 2002 (S.I. 2886)

Borough of Chelmsford (Electoral Changes) Order 2001 (S.I. 2439)

Borough of Cheltenham (Electoral Changes) Order 2001 (S.I. 3882)

Borough of Chesterfield (Electoral Changes) Order 1999 (S.I. 2692)

Borough of Christchurch (Electoral Arrangements) Order 1978 (S.I. 1841)

Borough of Christchurch (Electoral Changes) Order 2002 (S.I. 2241)

Borough of Colchester (Electoral Changes) Order 2001 (S.I. 2438)

Borough of Congleton (Electoral Changes) Order 1998 (S.I. 2843)

Borough of Copeland (Electoral Changes) Order 1998 (S.I. 2570)

Borough of Corby (Electoral Changes) Order 1998 (S.I. 2506)

Borough of Crawley (Electoral Arrangements) Order 1977 (S.I. 1433)

Borough of Crawley (Electoral Changes) Order 2002 (S.I. 2990)

Borough of Crewe and Nantwich (Electoral Changes) Order 1998 (S.I. 2845)

Borough of Dacorum (Electoral Changes) Order 1998 (S.I. 2552)

Borough of Darlington (Electoral Changes) Order 2001 (S.I. 3357)

Borough of Dartford (Electoral Changes) Order 2001 (S.I. 3560)

Borough of Doncaster (Electoral Arrangements) Order 1979 (S.I. 1027)

Borough of Doncaster (Electoral Changes) Order 2004 (S.I. 121)

Borough of Dudley (Electoral Arrangements) Order 1980 (S.I. 447)

Borough of Dudley (Electoral Changes) Order 2003 (S.I. 2767)

Borough of East Staffordshire (Electoral Changes) Order 2001 (S.I. 1443)

Borough of Eastbourne (Electoral Changes) Order 2001 (S.I. 4057)

Borough of Eastleigh (Parishes and Electoral Changes) Order 2001 (S.I. 1021)

Borough of Ellesmere Port &amp Neston (Electoral Changes) Order 1998 (S.I. 2844)

Borough of Elmbridge (Electoral Changes) Order 1999 (S.I. 2465)

Borough of Epsom and Ewell (Electoral Changes) Order 1999 (S.I. 2474)

Borough of Erewash (Electoral Changes) Order 1999 (S.I. 2694)

Borough of Fareham (Electoral Changes) Order 2001 (S.I. 1020)

Borough of Fylde (Electoral Changes) Order 2001 (S.I. 2475)

Borough of Gateshead (Electoral Changes) Order 2004 (S.I. 361)

Borough of Gedling (Electoral Changes) Order 2000 (S.I. 3297)

Borough of Gosport (Electoral Changes) Order 2001 (S.I. 1022)

Borough of Gravesham (Electoral Changes) Order 2001 (S.I. 3587)

Borough of Great Yarmouth (Electoral Arrangements) Order 1979 (S.I. 710)

Borough of Great Yarmouth (Electoral Changes) Order 2002 (S.I. 3228)

Borough of Guildford (Electoral Changes) Order 1999 (S.I. 2475)

Borough of Halton (Electoral Changes) Order 1997 (S.I. 779)

Borough of Halton (Electoral Changes) Order 2002 (S.I. 2242)

Borough of Harrogate (Electoral Changes) Order 2000 (S.I. 2601)

Borough of Hartlepool (Electoral Arrangements) Order 1975 (S.I. 2103)

Borough of Hartlepool (Electoral Changes) Order 2003 (S.I. 1088)

Borough of Hastings (Electoral Changes) Order 2001 (S.I. 4056)

Borough of Havant (Electoral Changes) Order 2001 (S.I. 1025)

Borough of Hertsmere (Electoral Changes) Order 1998 (S.I. 2554)

Borough of High Peak (Electoral Changes) Order 1999 (S.I. 2695)

Borough of Hinckley and Bosworth (Electoral Arrangements) Order 1980 (S.I. 138)

Borough of Hinckley and Bosworth (Electoral Changes) Order 2002 (S.I. 2888)

Borough of Hyndburn (Electoral Changes) Order 2001 (S.I. 2469)

Borough of Ipswich (Electoral Changes) Order 2001 (S.I. 3890)

Borough of Kettering (Electoral Changes) Order 1998 (S.I. 2508)

Borough of King's Lynn and West Norfolk (Electoral Changes) Order 2002 (S.I. 3227)

Borough of Kirklees (Electoral Arrangements) Order 1980 (S.I. 1463)

Borough of Kirklees (Electoral Changes) Order 2003 (S.I. 3091)

Borough of Knowsley (Electoral Arrangements) Order 1980 (S.I. 1402)

Borough of Knowsley (Electoral Changes) Order 2003 (S.I. 2156)

Borough of Langbaurgh (Electoral Arrangements) Order 1991 (S.I. 720)

Borough of Luton (Electoral Arrangements) Order 1975 (S.I. 1918)

Borough of Luton (Electoral Changes) Order 2002 (S.I. 1787)

Borough of Macclesfield (Electoral Changes) Order 1998 (S.I. 2847)

Borough of Maidstone (Electoral Changes) Order 2001 (S.I. 3586)

Borough of Medway (Electoral Changes) Order 2002 (S.I. 2235)

Borough of Melton (Electoral Arrangements) Order 1977 (S.I. 731)

Borough of Melton (Electoral Changes) Order 2002 (S.I. 2599)

Borough of Middlesbrough (Electoral Arrangements) Order 1976 (S.I. 1131)

Borough of Middlesbrough (Electoral Changes) Order 2003 (S.I. 159)

Borough of Milton Keynes (Electoral Changes) (Amendment) Order 2002 (S.I. 1034)

Borough of Milton Keynes (Electoral Changes) Order 2001 (S.I. 4062)

Borough of Newcastle-under-Lyme (Electoral Changes) Order 2001 (S.I. 1445)

Borough of North East Lincolnshire (Electoral Changes) Order 2001 (S.I. 3361)

Borough of North Lincolnshire (Electoral Changes) Order 2001 (S.I. 3359)

Borough of North Tyneside (Electoral Changes) Order 2004 (S.I. 364)

Borough of North Warwickshire (Electoral Changes) Order 2000 (S.I. 1675)

Borough of Northampton (Electoral Changes) Order 1998 (S.I. 2511)

Borough of Nuneaton and Bedworth (Electoral Changes) Order 2000 (S.I. 2058)

Borough of Oadby and Wigston (Electoral Arrangements) Order 1977 (S.I. 723)

Borough of Oadby and Wigston (Electoral Changes) Order 2002 (S.I. 2889)

Borough of Oldham (Electoral Arrangements) Order 1978 (S.I. 1605)

Borough of Oldham (Electoral Changes) Order 2004 (S.I. 124)

Borough of Oswestry (Electoral Changes) Order 2000 (S.I. 1418)

Borough of Pendle (Electoral Changes) Order 2001 (S.I. 2471)

Borough of Poole (Electoral Arrangements) Order 1979 (S.I. 1347)

Borough of Poole (Electoral Changes) Order 2002 (S.I. 2887)

Borough of Preston (Electoral Changes) Order 2001 (S.I. 2472)

Borough of Reading (Electoral Arrangements) Order 1979 (S.I. 1346)

Borough of Reading (Electoral Changes) Order 2002 (S.I. 2892)

Borough of Redcar and Cleveland (Electoral Changes) Order 2003 (S.I. 162)

Borough of Redditch (Electoral Changes) Order 2002 (S.I. 2986)

Borough of Reigate and Banstead (Electoral Changes) Order 1999 (S.I. 2477)

Borough of Restormel (Electoral Arrangements) Order 1979 (S.I. 1670)

Borough of Restormel (Electoral Changes) Order 2002 (S.I. 2601)

Borough of Ribble Valley (Electoral Changes) Order 2001 (S.I. 2429)

Borough of Rochdale (Electoral Arrangements) Order 1979 (S.I. 1341)

Borough of Rochdale (Electoral Changes) (Amendment) Order 2004 (S.I. 1073)

Borough of Rochdale (Electoral Changes) Order 2004 (S.I. 125)

Borough of Rossendale (Electoral Changes) Order 2001 (S.I. 2430)

Borough of Rotherham (Electoral Arrangements) Order 1979 (S.I. 1323)

Borough of Rotherham (Electoral Changes) Order 2004 (S.I. 123)

Borough of Rugby (Electoral Changes) (No.2) Order 2000 (S.I. 3363)

Borough of Rugby (Electoral Changes) Order 2000 (S.I. 1676)

Borough of Runnymede (Electoral Changes) Order 1999 (S.I. 2478)

Borough of Rushcliffe (Electoral Changes) Order 2000 (S.I. 3301)

Borough of Rushmoor (Electoral Changes) Order 2001 (S.I. 1016)

Borough of Sandwell (Electoral Arrangements) Order 1978 (S.I. 610)

Borough of Sandwell (Electoral Changes) Order 2003 (S.I. 2510)

Borough of Scarborough (Electoral Changes) Order 2000 (S.I. 2604)

Borough of Sedgefield (Electoral Changes) Order 1999 (S.I. 2582)

Borough of Sefton (Electoral Changes) Order 1999 (S.I. 2782)

Borough of Sefton (Electoral Changes) Order 2003 (S.I. 1977)

Borough of Shrewsbury and Atcham (Electoral Changes) Order 2000 (S.I. 1725)

Borough of Slough (Electoral Arrangements) Order 1980 (S.I. 429)

Borough of Slough (Electoral Changes) Order 2002 (S.I. 2600)

Borough of Solihull (Electoral Arrangements) Order 1978 (S.I. 1606)

Borough of Solihull (Electoral Changes) Order 2003 (S.I. 2508)

Borough of South Ribble (Electoral Changes) (Amendment) Order 2002 (S.I. 1031)

Borough of South Ribble (Electoral Changes) Order 2001 (S.I. 2431)

Borough of South Tyneside (Electoral Arrangements) Order 1980 (S.I. 430)

Borough of South Tyneside (Electoral Changes) Order 2004 (S.I. 358)

Borough of Southend-on-Sea (Electoral Changes) Order 2000 (S.I. 1487)

Borough of Spelthorne (Electoral Changes) Order 1999 (S.I. 2479)

Borough of St Edmundsbury (Electoral Changes) Order 2001 (S.I. 3895)

Borough of St Helens (Electoral Arrangements) Order 1979 (S.I. 1348)

Borough of St Helens (Electoral Changes) Order 2003 (S.I. 1979)

Borough of Stafford (Electoral Changes) Order 2001 (S.I. 1447)

Borough of Stevenage (Electoral Changes) Order 1998 (S.I. 2557)

Borough of Stockport (Electoral Arrangements) Order 1979 (S.I. 1324)

Borough of Stockport (Electoral Changes) Order 2004 (S.I. 360)

Borough of Stockton-on-Tees (Electoral Arrangements) Order 1976 (S.I. 1053)

Borough of Stockton-on-Tees (Electoral Changes) Order 2003 (S.I. 2506)

Borough of Sunderland (Electoral Arrangements) Order 1980 (S.I. 756)

Borough of Surrey Heath (Electoral Changes) Order 1999 (S.I. 2481)

Borough of Swale (Electoral Changes) Order 2001 (S.I. 3555)

Common Agricultural Policy (Wine) (Amendment) Regulations 1999 (S.I. 482)

Common Agricultural Policy (Wine) (England and Northern Ireland) Regulations 2001 (S.I. 686)

Common Agricultural Policy (Wine) (Scotland) Regulations 2002 (S.S.I. 325)

Common Agricultural Policy (Wine) (Wales) Regulations 2001 (S.I. 2193)

Common Agricultural Policy (Wine) Regulations 1993 (S.I. 517)

Common Agricultural Policy (Wine) Regulations 1994 (S.I. 674)

Common Agricultural Policy (Wine) Regulations 1995 (S.I. 615)

Common Agricultural Policy (Wine) Regulations 1996 (S.I. 696)

Common Agricultural Policy Support Schemes (Modulation) (Scotland) Regulations 2000 (S.S.I. 429)

Common Agricultural Policy Support Schemes (Modulation) (Wales) Regulations 2000 (S.I. 3294)

Common Agricultural Policy Support Schemes (Modulation) Regulations 2000 (S.I. 3127)

Common Investment (Amendment) Scheme 1999 (S.I. 551)

Common Investment (Closure of High Yield Fund) (Amendment) Scheme 2003 (S.I. 1027)

Common Investment (Closure of High Yield Fund) Scheme 2003 (S.I. 778)

Common Investment Scheme 1991 (S.I. 1209)

Common Services Agency (Membership and Procedure) Regulations 1991 (S.I. 564)

Commons Registration (General) Regulations 1966 (S.I. 1471)

Commons Registration (New Land) Regulations 1969 (S.I. 1843)

Commonwealth Foundation (Immunities and Privileges) Order 1983 (S.I. 143)

Commonwealth Telecommunications Organisation (Immunities and Privileges) Order 1983 (S.I. 144)

CommuniCare National Health Service Trust (Dissolution) Order 2002 (S.I. 1500)

CommuniCare National Health Service Trust (Establishment) Order 1993 (S.I. 2596)

Communications (Bailiwick of Guernsey) Order 2003 (S.I. 3195)

Communications (Bailiwick of Guernsey) Order 2004 (S.I. 307)

Communications (Isle of Man) Order 2003 (S.I. 3198)

Communications (Jersey) Order 2003 (S.I. 3197)

Communications Act 2003 (Commencement No 1) Order 2003 (S.I. 1900)

Community Bus Regulations 1986 (S.I. 1245)

Community Care (Direct Payments) (Scotland) Amendment Regulations 2000 (S.S.I. 183)

Community Care (Direct Payments) (Scotland) Amendment Regulations 2001 (S.S.I. 447)

Community Care (Direct Payments) (Scotland) Regulations 1997 (S.I. 693)

Community Care (Direct Payments) Amendment (Wales) Regulations 2000 (S.I. 1868)

Community Care (Direct Payments) Amendment Regulations 2000 (S.I. 11)

Community Care (Direct Payments) Regulations 1997 (S.I. 734)

Community Care (Disregard of Resources) (Scotland) Order 2002 (S.S.I. 264)

Community Care and Health (Scotland) Act 2002 (Commencement No 2) Order 2003 (S.S.I. 62)

Community Care, Services for Carers and Children's Services (Direct Payments) (England) Regulations 2003 (S.I. 762)

Community Charges (Administration and Enforcement) Regulations 1989 (S.I. 438)

Community Charges (Deductions from Income Support) (No.2) Regulations 1990 (S.I. 545)

Community Charges (Deductions from Income Support) (Scotland) Regulations 1989 (S.I. 507)

Community Drivers Hours and Recording Equipment (Exemptions and Supplementary Provisions) Regulations 1986 (S.I. 1456)

Community Health Care North Durham National Health Service Trust (Dissolution) Order 1998 (S.I. 822)

Community Health Care North Durham National Health Service Trust (Establishment) Amendment Order 1994 (S.I. 194)

Community Health Care North Durham National Health Service Trust (Establishment) Order 1993 (S.I. 2612)

Community Health Care Service (North Derbyshire) National Health Service Trust (Establishment) Order 1993 (S.I. 2606)

Community Health Councils Amendment (Wales) Regulations 2000 (S.I. 479)

Community Health Councils Regulations 1996 (S.I. 640)

Community Health Councils Regulations 2004 (S.I. 905)

Community Health Services, Southern Derbyshire National Health Service Trust (Dissolution) Order 2001 (S.I. 1612)

Community Health Services, Southern Derbyshire National Health Service Trust (Establishment) Order 1992 (S.I. 2481)

Community Health Sheffield National Health Service Trust (Change of Name) and (Establishment) Amendment Order 2003 (S.I. 760)

Community Health Sheffield National Health Service Trust (Establishment) Order 1993 (S.I. 2896)

Community Health South London National Health Service Trust (Establishment) Order 1999 (S.I. 898)

Community Healthcare Bolton National Health Service Trust (Dissolution) Order 2002 (S.I. 1492)

Community Healthcare Bolton National Health Service Trust (Establishment) Order 1993 (S.I. 2595)

Community Learning Partnership Barrow-in-Furness Education Action Zone Order 1999 (S.I. 3384)

Community Legal Service (Cost Protection) Regulations 2000 (S.I. 824)

Community Legal Service (Costs) Regulations 2000 (S.I. 441)

Community Legal Service (Costs) Regulations 2000 (S.I. Reg.12(5)

Community Legal Service (Financial) Regulations 2000 (S.I. 516)

Community Legal Service (Funding) (Counsel in Family Proceedings) Order 2001 (S.I. 1077)

Community Legal Service (Funding) Order 2000 (S.I. 627)

Community Radio Order 2004 (S.I. 1944)

Community Trade Mark Regulations 1996 (S.I. 1908)

Companies (1990 Order) (Eligibility for Appointment as Company Auditor) (Consequential Amendments) Regulations (Northern Ireland) 1993 (67)

Companies (Acquisition of Own Shares) (Treasury Shares) Regulations 2003 (S.I. 1116)

Companies (Department of Trade and Industry) Fees Order 1985 (S.I. 1784)

Companies (Disclosure of Information) (Designated Authorities) (No.2) Order 2002 (S.I. 1889)

Companies (Disclosure of Information) (Designated Authorities) Order 1988 (S.I. 1334)

Council Tax (Chargeable Dwellings, Exempt Dwellings and Discount Disregards) Amendment Order 1997 (S.I. 656)

Council Tax (Deductions from Income Support) Regulations 1993 (S.I. 494)

Council Tax (Demand Notices) (Wales) Regulations 1993 (S.I. 255)

Council Tax (Discount Disregards) Order 1992 (S.I. 548)

Council Tax (Discounts) (Scotland) Amendment Order 1994 (S.I. 626)

Council Tax (Discounts) (Scotland) Amendment Order 1995 (S.I. 599)

Council Tax (Discounts) (Scotland) Amendment Order 1997 (S.I. 586)

Council Tax (Discounts) (Scotland) Amendment Order 1998 (S.I. 341)

Council Tax (Discounts) (Scotland) Consolidation and Amendment Order 2003 (S.S.I. 176)

Council Tax (Discounts) (Scotland) Order 1992 (S.I. 1408)

Council Tax (Dwellings and Part Residential Subjects) (Scotland) Amendment Regulations 2002 (S.I. 102)

Council Tax (Dwellings and Part Residential Subjects) (Scotland) Regulations 1992 (S.I. 2955)

Council Tax (Exempt Dwellings) (Scotland) Order 1997 (S.I. 728)

Council Tax (Exempt Dwellings) Order 1992 (S.I. 558)

Council Tax (Liability for Owners) Regulations 1992 (S.I. 551)

Council Tax (Liability of Owners) (Scotland) Regulations 1992 (S.I. 1331)

Council Tax (Prescribed Classes of Dwellings) (England) Regulations 2003 (S.I. 3011)

Council Tax (Prescribed Classes of Dwellings) (Wales) Regulations 1998 (S.I. 105)

Council Tax (Reductions for Disabilities) Regulations 1992 (S.I. 554)

Council Tax (Valuation of Dwellings) (Scotland) Regulations 1992 (S.I. 1329)

Council Tax and Non-Domestic Rating (Demand Notices) (England) (Amendment) (No.2) Regulations 2000 (S.I. 534)

Council Tax and Non-Domestic Rating (Demand Notices) (England) (Amendment) (Rural Rate Relief) Regulations 1998 (S.I. 47)

Council Tax and Non-Domestic Rating (Demand Notices) (England) (Amendment) Regulations 1997 (S.I. 394)

Council Tax and Non-Domestic Rating (Demand Notices) (England) Amendment Regulations 1995 (S.I. 121)

Council Tax and Non-Domestic Rating (Demand Notices) (England) Regulations 1993 (S.I. 191)

Council Tax and Non-Domestic Rating (Demand Notices) (England) Regulations 2003 (S.I. 2613)

Council Tax and Non-Domestic Rating (Electronic Communications) (England) Order 2003 (S.I. 2604)

Council Tax Benefit (General) Amendment Regulations 1997 (S.I. 1841)

Council Tax Benefit (General) Amendment Regulations 1998 (S.I. 911)

Council Tax Benefit (General) Regulations 1992 (S.I. 1814)

Counter Fraud and Security Management Service (Establishment and Constitution) Order 2002 (S.I. 3039)

Counter Fraud and Security Management Service Regulations 2002 (S.I. 3040)

Countess of Chester Hospital National Health Service Trust (Establishment) Order 1992 (S.I. 2463)

Countryside Access (Appeals Procedures) (Wales) Regulations 2002 (S.I. 1794)

Countryside Access (Draft Maps) (Wales) Regulations 2001 (S.I. 4001)

Countryside Access (Exclusion or Restriction of Access) (Wales) Regulations 2003 (S.I. 142)

Countryside Premium Scheme (Scotland) Regulations 1997 (S.I. 330)

Countryside Stewardship Regulations 2000 (S.I. 3048)

County Borough of Bridgend (Electoral Arrangements) Order 1998 (S.I. 3134)

County Borough of Caerphilly (Electoral Arrangements) Order 1998 (S.I. 3135)

County Borough of Conwy (Electoral Arrangements) Order 1998 (S.I. 3137)

County Borough of Newport (Electoral Changes) Order 2002 (S.I. 3276)

County Borough of Rhondda Cynon Taff (Electoral Arrangements) Order 1998 (S.I. 3138)

County Borough of The Vale of Glamorgan (Electoral Changes) Order 2002 (S.I. 3277)

County Borough of Torfaen (Electoral Changes) Order 2002 (S.I. 3279)

County Borough of Wrexham (Electoral Arrangements) Order 1998 (S.I. 3142)

County Court (Blood Tests) Rules (Northern Ireland) 1978 (378)

County Court Fees (Amendment No 2) Order 2003 (S.I. 718)

County Court Fees (Amendment No 4) Order 2000 (S.I. 2310)

County Court Fees (Amendment) Order 1999 (S.I. 2548)

County Court Fees (Amendment) Order 2000 (S.I. 639)

County Court Fees (Amendment) Order 2003 (S.I. 648)

County Court Fees (Amendment) Order 2004 (S.I. 2098)

County Court Fees Order (Northern Ireland) 1996 (103)

County Court Fees Order 1999 (S.I. 689)

County Court Remedies Regulations 1991 (S.I. 1222)

County Court Rules (Northern Ireland) 1981 (225)

County Court Rules 1981 (S.I. 1687)

County Courts (Interest on Judgment Debts) Order 1991 (S.I. 1184)

County Courts (Northern Ireland) Order 1980 (S.I. 397)

County Durham and Darlington Acute Hospitals National Health Service Trust (Establishment) and the North Durham Health Care National Health Service Trust and South Durham Health Care National Health Service Trust (Dissolution) Order 2002 (S.I. 2420)

County Durham Health Authority (Change of Name) Order 2000 (S.I. 1241)

County Fees (Amendment No 2) Order 2000 (S.I. 939)

County of Carmarthenshire (Electoral Arrangements) Order 1998 (S.I. 3136)

County of Ceredigion (Electoral Changes) Order 2002 (S.I. 3278)

County of Cheshire (Electoral Changes) Order 2000 (S.I. 2486)

County of Cumbria (Electoral Changes) (Amendment) Order 2001 (S.I. 790)

County of Cumbria (Electoral Changes) Order 2000 (S.I. 2485)

County of Denbighshire (Electoral Arrangements) Order 1998 (S.I. 3139)

County of Derbyshire (Electoral Arrangements) Order 1980 (S.I. 1985)

County of Devon (Electoral Arrangements) Order 1981 (S.I. 1748)

County of Essex (Electoral Arrangements) Order 1981 (S.I. 141)

County of Flintshire (Electoral Arrangements) Order 1998 (S.I. 3140)

County of Gloucestershire (Electoral Arrangements) Order 1983 (S.I. 829)

County of Gwynedd (Electoral Changes) Order 2002 (S.I. 3274)

County of Herefordshire District Council (Electoral Changes) Order 2002 (S.I. 187)

County of Hertfordshire (Electoral Changes) Order 2000 (S.I. 2487)

County of Kent (Electoral Arrangements) Order 1981 (S.I. 85)

County of Lincolnshire (Electoral Changes) Order 2000 (S.I. 2488)

County of Monmouthshire (Electoral Changes) Order 2002 (S.I. 3275)

County of Northamptonshire (Electoral Changes) Order 2000 (S.I. 2489)

County of Northumberland (Electoral Changes) Order 2000 (S.I. 2490)

County of Nottinghamshire (Electoral Arrangements) Order 1980 (S.I. 1344)

County of Powys (Electoral Arrangements) Order 1998 (S.I. 3143)

County of Shropshire (Electoral Arrangements) Order 1980 (S.I. 1297)

County of Somerset (Electoral Changes) Order 2000 (S.I. 2491)

County of Staffordshire (Electoral Arrangements) Order 1980 (S.I. 1702)

County of Surrey (Electoral Arrangements) Order (1980) 1980 (S.I. 1830)

County of Warwickshire (Electoral Arrangements) Order 1981 (S.I. 118)

County of Wiltshire (Electoral Arrangements) Order 1993 (S.I. 679)

Court Funds Rules 1987 (S.I. 821)

Court of Protection (Enduring Powers of Attorney) Rules 2001 (S.I. 825)

Court of Protection Rules 1994 (S.I. 3046)

Court of Protection Rules 2001 (S.I. 824)

Court of Session etc Fees Order 1997 (S.I. 688)

Courts Boards Areas Order 2004 (S.I. 1192)

Courts-Martial (Army) Rules 1997 (S.I. 169)

Courts-Martial (Royal Air Force) Rules 1997 (S.I. 171)

Courts-Martial (Royal Navy) Rules 1997 (S.I. 170)

Coventry Healthcare National Health Service Trust (Establishment) Amendment Order 1998 (S.I. 1170)

Coventry Healthcare National Health Service Trust (Establishment) Order 1994 (S.I. 170)

Coventry Millennium Education Action Zone Order 1999 (S.I. 3394)

Coventry Primary Care Trust (Establishment) Order 2002 (S.I. 940)

Craven, Harrogate and Rural District Primary Care Trust (Establishment) Order 2002 (S.I. 149)

Crawley Horsham National Health Service Trust (Establishment) Order 1992 (S.I. 2521)

Credit Cards (Merchant Acquisition) Order 1990 (S.I. 2158)

Credit Cards (Price Discrimination) Order 1990 (S.I. 2159)

Credit Unions (Authorised Investments) Order 1993 (S.I. 3100)

Credit Unions (Increase in Limits of Shareholding, of Deposits by persons too young to be members and of Loans) Order 1989 (S.I. 2423)

Credit Unions (Increase in Limits on Deposits by persons too young to be members and of Periods for the Repayment of Loans) Order 2001 (S.I. 811)

Cremation (Scotland) Regulations 1935 (S.I. 247)

Creosote (Prohibition on Use and Marketing) Regulations 2003 (S.I. 721)

Creosote (Prohibition on Use and Marketing) (No.2) Regulations 2003 (S.I. 1511)

Crime (International Co-operation) Act 2003 (Designation of Prosecuting Authorities) Order 2004 (S.I. 1034)

Crime and Disorder Act 1998 (Service of Prosecution Evidence) Regulations 2000 (S.I. 3305)

Crime and Disorder Strategies (Prescribed Descriptions) (Amendment) Order 1998 (S.I. 2513)

Crime and Disorder Strategies (Prescribed Descriptions) (Amendment) Order 1999 (S.I. 483)

Crime and Disorder Strategies (Prescribed Descriptions) (Amendment) Order 2000 (S.I. 300)

Crime and Disorder Strategies (Prescribed Descriptions) (England) Order 2004 (S.I. 118)

Crime and Disorder Strategies (Prescribed Descriptions) Order 1998 (S.I. 2452)

Crime Prevention (Designated Areas) Order 2003 (S.I. 2208)

Criminal Appeal (Reference of Points of Law) Rules 1973 (S.I. 1114)

Criminal Appeal Rules 1968 (S.I. 1262)

Criminal Attempts and Conspiracy (Northern Ireland) Order 1983 (S.I. 1120)

Criminal Damage (Northern Ireland) Order 1977 (S.I. 426)

Criminal Defence Service (Choice in Very High Cost Cases) Regulations 2001 (S.I. 1169)

Criminal Defence Service (Funding) (Amendment No 3) Order 1989 (S.I. 3341)

Criminal Defence Service (Funding) Order 2001 (S.I. 855)

Criminal Defence Service (General) (No.2) Regulations 2001 (S.I. 1437)

Criminal Defence Service (Recovery of Defence Costs Orders) Regulations 2001 (S.I. 856)

Criminal Defence Service (Representation Order Appeals) Regulations 2001 (S.I. 1168)

Criminal Evidence (Northern Ireland) Order 1988 (S.I. 1987)

Criminal Evidence (Northern Ireland) Order 1999 (S.I. 2789)

Criminal Injuries Compensation (Northern Ireland) Order 2002 (S.I. 796)

Criminal Justice (Children) (Northern Ireland) Order 1998 (S.I. 1504)

Criminal Justice (Children) (Northern Ireland) Order 1998 (S.I. 9)

Criminal Justice (Confiscation) (Northern Ireland) Order 1990 (S.I. 2588)

Criminal Justice (Evidence etc.) (Northern Ireland) Order 1988 (S.I. 1847)

Criminal Justice (Firearms) (Northern Ireland) Order 1988 (S.I. 1845)

Criminal Justice (International Co-operation) Act 1990 (Enforcement of Overseas Forfeiture Orders) (Northern Ireland) Order 1991 (S.I. 1464)

Criminal Justice (International Co-operation) Act 1990 (Enforcement of Overseas Forfeiture Orders) Order 1991 (S.I. 1463)

Criminal Justice (Northern Ireland) Order 1980 (S.I. 704)

Criminal Justice (Northern Ireland) Order 1991 (S.I. 1711)

Dartford and Gravesham National Health Service Trust (Establishment) Amendment Order 1996 (S.I. 994)

Dartford and Gravesham National Health Service Trust (Establishment) Order 1993 (S.I. 2642)

Dartford, Gravesham and Swanley Primary Care Trust (Establishment) Order 2000 (S.I. 2043)

Dartford-Thurrock Crossing (Amendment) Regulations 1999 (S.I. 2208)

Dartford-Thurrock Crossing (Amendment) Regulations 2000 (S.I. 2151)

Dartford-Thurrock Crossing (Amendment) Regulations 2001 (S.I. 2973)

Dartford-Thurrock Crossing Regulations 1998 (S.I. 1908)

Data Protection (Subject Access Modification) (Social Work) Order 2000 (S.I. 415)

Data Protection Tribunal (Enforcement Appeals) Rules 2000 (S.I. 189)

Daventry and South Northamptonshire Primary Care Trust (Establishment) Order 2000 (S.I. 211)

Day Care and Child Minding (National Standards) (England) Regulations 2001 (S.I. 1828)

Debt Arrangement and Attachment (Scotland) Act 2002 (Commencement) Order 2004 (S.S.I. 401)

Debt Arrangement Scheme (Scotland) Regulations 2004 (S.S.I. 468)

Deductions from Income Support (Miscellaneous Amendments) Regulations 1993 (S.I. 495)

Definition of Independent Visitors (Children) Regulations 1991 (S.I. 892)

Delayed Discharges (Mental Health Care) (England) Order 2003 (S.I. 2276)

Democratic Republic of the Congo (Restrictive Measures) (Overseas Territories) Order 2003 (S.I. 2627)

Denbighshire (Rhuddlan, Rhyl, Dyserth and Prestatyn) Order 2003 (S.I. 3134)

Denbighshire and Wrexham (Areas) Order 1996 (S.I. 2914)

Dental Auxiliaries Regulations 1986 (S.I. 887)

Dental Charges (Amendment) Regulations (Northern Ireland) 2001 (124)

Dental Charges (Amendment) Regulations (Northern Ireland) 2002 (84)

Dental Charges Regulations (Northern Ireland) 1989 (111)

Dental Practice Board Regulations 1992 (S.I. 655)

Dental Practice Boards (Personal Dental Services) Regulations 1998 (S.I. 2223)

Dental Vocational Training Authority Regulations 1993 (S.I. 2210)

Dentists Act 1984 (Amendment) Order 2001 (S.I. 3926)

Department for Transport (Driver Licensing and Vehicle Registration Fees) Order 2003 (S.I. 2994)

Department of Trade and Industry (Fees) Order 1988 (S.I. 93)

Department of Transport (Fees) Order 1988 (S.I. 643)

Departments (Northern Ireland) Order 1982 (S.I. 846)

Departments (Northern Ireland) Order 1999 (S.I. 283)

Deposits in the Sea (Exemptions) Order 1985 (S.I. 1699)

Derby City General Hospital National Health Service Trust (Dissolution) Order 1998 (S.I. 850)

Derby City General Hospital National Health Service Trust (Establishment) Order 1992 (S.I. 2476)

Derby North East Education Action Zone Order 2000 (S.I. 864)

Derbyshire (City of Derby) (Structural Change) Order 1995 (S.I. 1773)

Derbyshire (Coroners) Order 1997 (S.I. 496)

Derbyshire Ambulance Service National Health Service Trust (Establishment) Order 1993 (S.I. 2546)

Derbyshire Ambulance Service, the Leicestershire Ambulance and Paramedic Service and the Nottinghamshire Ambulance Service National Health Service Trusts (Dissolution) Order 1999 (S.I. 791)

Derbyshire County Council (City of Derby) (Staff Transfer) Order 1997 (S.I. 459)

Derbyshire Dales and South Derbyshire Primary Care Trust (Establishment) Order 2001 (S.I. 4137)

Derbyshire Fire Services (Combination Scheme) Order 1996 (S.I. 2919)

Derbyshire Royal Infirmary National Health Service Trust (Dissolution) Order 1998 (S.I. 849)

Derbyshire Royal Infirmary National Health Service Trust (Establishment) Order 1993 (S.I. 2547)

Deregulation (Building) (Initial Notices and Final Certificates) Order 1996 (S.I. 1905)

Deregulation (Fair Trading Act 1973) (Amendment) (Merger Reference Time Limits) Order 1996 (S.I. 345)

Deregulation (Salmon Fisheries (Scotland) Act 1868) Order 1996 (S.I. 1211)

Deregulation and Contracting Out (Northern Ireland) Order 1996 (S.I. 1632)

Derwen National Health Service Trust (Dissolution) Order 1997 (S.I. 875)

Derwen National Health Service Trust (Establishment) Order 1993 (S.I. 2835)

Derwent Valley Railway (Transfer) Light Railway Order 1987 (S.I. 75)

Derwentside Primary Care Trust (Establishment) Order 2002 (S.I. 145)

Designation of Schools Having a Religious Character (Wales) Order 1999 (S.I. 1814)

Detention Centre Rules 2001 (S.I. 238)

Devon (City of Plymouth and Borough of Torbay) (Structural Change) Order 1996 (S.I. 1865)

Devon (Coroners) Order 1998 (S.I. 355)

Devon Ambulance Service National Health Service Trust (Establishment) Amendment Order 1992 (S.I. 1327)

Devon Ambulance Service National Health Service Trust Dissolution Order 1993 (S.I. 809)

Devon and Cornwall (Police Area and Authority) Order 1997 (S.I. 1849)

Devon County Council (City of Plymouth and Borough of Torbay) (Staff Transfer) Order 1998 (S.I. 451)

Devon Fire Services (Combination Scheme) Order 1997 (S.I. 2698)

Dewsbury Health Care National Health Service Trust (Establishment) Order 1993 (S.I. 2548)

Dingle Granby Toxteth Education Action Zone Order 1999 (S.I. 3383)

Diplomatic Privileges (British Nationals) Order 1999 (S.I. 670)

Disability Discrimination (Employment) Regulations 1996 (S.I. 1456)

Disability Discrimination (Guidance and Code of Practice) (Appointed Day) Order 1996 (S.I. 1996)

Disability Discrimination (Meaning of Disability) Regulations 1996 (S.I. 1455)

Disability Discrimination (Prescribed Periods for Accessibility Strategies and Plans for Schools) (Wales) Regulations 2003 (S.I. 2531)

Disability Discrimination (Providers of Services) (Adjustment of Premises) Regulations 2001 (S.I. 3253)

Disability Discrimination (Questions and Replies) Order 1996 (S.I. 2793)

District of Adur (Electoral Arrangements) Order 1978 (S.I. 1434)

District of Adur (Electoral Changes) Order 2002 (S.I. 2991)

District of Adur (Scheme for Elections of Specified Council) Order 2003 (S.I. 984)

District of Alnwick (Electoral Changes) Order 1998 (S.I. 2347)

District of Arun (Electoral Arrangements) Order 1980 (S.I. 652)

District of Arun (Electoral Changes) Order 2002 (S.I. 2885)

District of Ashfield (Electoral Changes) Order 2000 (S.I. 3295)

District of Aylesbury Vale (Electoral Arrangements) Order 1975 (S.I. 2083)

District of Aylesbury Vale (Electoral Changes) Order 2002 (S.I. 1788)

District of Babergh (Electoral Changes) (Amendment) Order 2002 (S.I. 1036)

District of Babergh (Electoral Changes) Order 2001 (S.I. 3894)

District of Basildon (Electoral Changes) Order 2001 (S.I. 2443)

District of Bassetlaw (Electoral Changes) Order 2000 (S.I. 3285)

District of Bath and North East Somerset (Electoral Changes) Order 1998 (S.I. 2700)

District of Beaconsfield (Electoral Arrangements) Order 1980 (S.I. 428)

District of Blaby (Electoral Arrangements) Order 1980 (S.I. 1341)

District of Blaby (Electoral Changes) Order 2002 (S.I. 2882)

District of Bolsover (Electoral Changes) Order 1999 (S.I. 2691)

District of Bracknell (Electoral Arrangements) Order 1977 (S.I. 1273)

District of Braintree (Electoral Changes) Order 2001 (S.I. 2442)

District of Breckland (Electoral Arrangements) Order 1978 (S.I. 1612)

District of Breckland (Electoral Changes) Order 2002 (S.I. 3221)

District of Bridgnorth (Electoral Changes) Order 2000 (S.I. 1417)

District of Broadland (Electoral Arrangements) Order 1977 (S.I. 1390)

District of Broadland (Electoral Changes) Order 2003 (S.I. 157)

District of Bromsgrove (Electoral Arrangements) Order 1977 (S.I. 1277)

District of Bromsgrove (Electoral Arrangements) Order 1995 (S.I. 44)

District of Bromsgrove (Electoral Changes) Order 2003 (S.I. 158)

District of Cannock Chase (Electoral Changes) Order 2001 (S.I. 1442)

District of Caradon (Electoral Arrangements) Order 1980 (S.I. 757)

District of Caradon (Electoral Changes) Order 2002 (S.I. 2602)

District of Carrick (Electoral Arrangements) Order 1978 (S.I. 1370)

District of Carrick (Electoral Changes) Order 2002 (S.I. 2594)

District of Cherwell (Electoral Changes) Order 2001 (S.I. 4065)

District of Chester-le-Street (Electoral Changes) Order 1999 (S.I. 2503)

District of Chichester (Electoral Arrangements) Order 1977 (S.I. 865)

District of Chichester (Electoral Changes) Order 2002 (S.I. 2883)

District of Chiltern (Electoral Arrangements) Order 1975 (S.I. 1990)

District of Chiltern (Electoral Changes) Order 2002 (S.I. 1784)

District of Cotswold (Electoral Changes) Order 2001 (S.I. 3885)

District of Craven (Electoral Changes) Order 2000 (S.I. 2599)

District of Craven (Ribble Banks Parish Council) (Electoral Changes) Order 2002 (S.I. 1032)

District of Daventry (Electoral Changes) Order 1998 (S.I. 2507)

District of Derbyshire Dales (Electoral Changes) Order 1999 (S.I. 2693)

District of Derwentside (Electoral Changes) Order 1999 (S.I. 2580)

District of Dover (Electoral Changes) Order 2001 (S.I. 3588)

District of Easington (Electoral Changes) Order 1999 (S.I. 2581)

District of East Cambridgeshire (Electoral Arrangements) Order 1980 (S.I. 1340)

District of East Cambridgeshire (Electoral Changes) Order 2002 (S.I. 2596)

District of East Devon (Electoral Changes) Order 1999 (S.I. 2467)

District of East Dorset (Electoral Changes) Order 2002 (S.I. 2238)

District of East Hampshire (Electoral Changes) Order 2001 (S.I. 1017)

District of East Hertfordshire (Electoral Changes) Order 1998 (S.I. 2553)

District of East Lindsey (Electoral Changes) Order 1998 (S.I. 2335)

District of East Northamptonshire (Electoral Changes) Order 1998 (S.I. 2512)

District of East Riding (Electoral Changes) (Amendment) Order 2002 (S.I. 1033)

District of East Riding (Electoral Changes) Order 2001 (S.I. 3358)

District of Eden (Electoral Changes) Order 1998 (S.I. 2547)

District of Epping Forest (Electoral Changes) (Amendment) Order 2002 (S.I. 2982)

District of Epping Forest (Electoral Changes) Order 2001 (S.I. 2444)

District of Fenland (Electoral Arrangements) Order 1975 (S.I. 2088)

District of Fenland (Electoral Changes) Order 2002 (S.I. 2595)

District of Forest Heath (Electoral Changes) Order 2001 (S.I. 3893)

District of Forest of Dean (Electoral Changes) (Amendment) Order 2002 (S.I. 1035)

District of Forest of Dean (Electoral Changes) Order 2001 (S.I. 3880)

District of Hambleton (Electoral Changes) Order 2000 (S.I. 2600)

District of Harborough (Electoral Arrangements) Order 1979 (S.I. 1112)

District of Harborough (Electoral Changes) Order 2002 (S.I. 2597)

District of Harlow (Electoral Changes) Order 2001 (S.I. 2437)

District of Hart (Parishes and Electoral Changes) Order 2001 (S.I. 1023)

District of Herefordshire (Electoral Changes) Order 1997 (S.I. 1213)

District of Horsham (Electoral Arrangements) Order 1978 (S.I. 1861)

District of Horsham (Electoral Changes) Order 2002 (S.I. 2890)

District of Huntingdon (Electoral Arrangements) Order 1976 (S.I. 401)

District of Huntingdonshire (Electoral Changes) Order 2002 (S.I. 2984)

District of Kennet (Electoral Changes) Order 1999 (S.I. 2922)

District of Kerrier (Electoral Arrangements) Order 1978 (S.I. 1356)

District of Kerrier (Electoral Changes) Order 2002 (S.I. 2604)

District of Leominster (Electoral Arrangements) Order 1978 (S.I. 1843)

District of Lewes (Electoral Changes) Order 2001 (S.I. 4052)

District of Lichfield (Electoral Changes) Order 2001 (S.I. 1444)

District of Maldon (Electoral Changes) Order 2001 (S.I. 2436)

District of Malvern Hills (Electoral Arrangements) Order 1976 (S.I. 1757)

District of Malvern Hills (Electoral Changes) Order 2002 (S.I. 3224)

District of Mansfield (Electoral Changes) Order 2000 (S.I. 3298)

District of Mendip (Electoral Changes) Order 1998 (S.I. 2464)

District of Mid Bedfordshire (Electoral Changes) Order 2001 (S.I. 4067)

District of Mid Devon (Electoral Changes) Order 1999 (S.I. 2470)

District of Mid Suffolk (Electoral Changes) Order 2001 (S.I. 3891)

District of Mid Sussex (Electoral Arrangements) Order 1980 (S.I. 653)

District of Mid Sussex (Electoral Changes) Order 2002 (S.I. 2891)

District of Mole Valley (Electoral Changes) Order 1999 (S.I. 2476)

District of New Forest (Parishes and Electoral Changes) Order 2001 (S.I. 1026)

District of Newark and Sherwood (Electoral Changes) Order 2000 (S.I. 3299)

District of North Cornwall (Electoral Arrangements) Order 1978 (S.I. 1806)

District of North Cornwall (Electoral Changes) Order 2002 (S.I. 2603)

District of North Devon (Electoral Changes) Order 1999 (S.I. 2469)

District of North Dorset (Electoral Arrangements) Order 1980 (S.I. 1487)

District of North Dorset (Electoral Changes) Order 2002 (S.I. 2239)

District of North East Derbyshire (Electoral Changes) Order 1999 (S.I. 2696)

District of North Hertfordshire (Electoral Changes) Order 1998 (S.I. 2555)

District of North Kesteven (Parishes and Electoral Changes) Order 1998 (S.I. 2338)

District of North Norfolk (Electoral Arrangements) Order 1978 (S.I. 1438)

District of North Norfolk (Electoral Changes) Order 2003 (S.I. 160)

District of North Shropshire (Electoral Changes) Order 2000 (S.I. 1419)

District of North Somerset (Electoral Changes) Order 1998 (S.I. 2702)

District of North West Leicestershire (Electoral Arrangements) Order 1980 (S.I. 778)

District of North West Leicestershire (Electoral Changes) Order 2002 (S.I. 2598)

District of North Wiltshire (Electoral Changes) Order 1999 (S.I. 2923)

District of Penwith (Electoral Arrangements) Order 1978 (S.I. 1505)

District of Penwith (Electoral Changes) Order 2002 (S.I. 2593)

District of Purbeck (Electoral Changes) Order 1998 (S.I. 2159)

District of Redditch (Electoral Arrangements) Order 1980 (S.I. 231)

District of Richmondshire (Electoral Changes) Order 2000 (S.I. 2602)

District of Rochford (Electoral Changes) Order 2001 (S.I. 2624)

District of Rother (Electoral Changes) Order 2001 (S.I. 4054)

District of Rutland (Electoral Arrangements) Order 1977 (S.I. 1865)

District of Rutland (Electoral Changes) Order 2003 (S.I. 322)

District of Ryedale (Electoral Changes) Order 2000 (S.I. 2603)

District of Salisbury (Electoral Changes) Order 1999 (S.I. 2924)

District of Sedgemoor (Electoral Changes) Order 1998 (S.I. 2465)

District of Selby (Electoral Changes) Order 2000 (S.I. 2605)

District of Sevenoaks (Electoral Changes) Order 2001 (S.I. 3557)

District of Shepway (Electoral Changes) Order 2001 (S.I. 3558)

District of South Bedfordshire (Electoral Changes) Order 2001 (S.I. 4068)

District of South Bucks (Electoral Changes) Order 2002 (S.I. 1785)

District of South Cambridgeshire (Electoral Arrangements) Order 1975 (S.I. 1991)

District of South Cambridgeshire (Electoral Changes) (Amendment) Order 2003 (S.I. 711)

District of South Cambridgeshire (Electoral Changes) Order 2002 (S.I. 2374)

District of South Derbyshire (Electoral Changes) Order 1999 (S.I. 2697)

District of South Gloucestershire (Electoral Changes) Order 1998 (S.I. 2701)

District of South Hams (Electoral Changes) Order 1998 (S.I. 2487)

District of South Herefordshire (Electoral Arrangements) Order 1977 (S.I. 438)

District of South Herefordshire (Electoral Arrangements) Order 1991 (S.I. 816)

District of South Holland (Electoral Changes) Order 1998 (S.I. 2336)

District of South Kesteven (Electoral Changes) Order 1998 (S.I. 2337)

District of South Lakeland (Electoral Changes) Order 1998 (S.I. 2548)

District of South Norfolk (Electoral Arrangements) Order 1977 (S.I. 237)

District of South Norfolk (Electoral Changes) Order 2002 (S.I. 3218)

District of South Northamptonshire (Electoral Changes) Order 1998 (S.I. 2509)

District of South Oxfordshire (Electoral Arrangements) Order 1980 (S.I. 1343)

District of South Oxfordshire (Electoral Changes) Order 2002 (S.I. 49)

District of South Shropshire (Electoral Changes) (Amendment) Order 2000 (S.I. 3364)

District of South Shropshire (Electoral Changes) Order 2000 (S.I. 1420)

District of South Somerset (Electoral Changes) Order 1998 (S.I. 2462)

District of South Staffordshire (Electoral Changes) Order 2001 (S.I. 1446)

District of Staffordshire Moorlands (Electoral Changes) Order 2001 (S.I. 1448)

District of Stratford on Avon (Electoral Changes) Order 2000 (S.I. 2059)

East Berkshire Community Health National Health Service Trust (Establishment) Order 1992 (S.I. 2582)

East Berkshire National Health Service Trust for People with Learning Disabilities and the West Berkshire Priority Care Service National Health Service Trust (Dissolution) Order 2001 (S.I. 326)

East Birmingham Hospital National Health Service Trust (Change of Name) Order 1993 (S.I. 122)

East Birmingham Hospital National Health Service Trust (Establishment) Amendment Order 1994 (S.I. 2690)

East Cheshire National Health Service Trust (Establishment) Order 1992 (S.I. 2461)

East Devon Primary Care Trust (Establishment) Order 2001 (S.I. 468)

East Durham and Houghall Community College (Government) Regulations 1999 (S.I. 707)

East Elmbridge and Mid Surrey Primary Care Trust (Establishment) Order 2002 (S.I. 982)

East Glamorgan National Health Service Trust (Establishment) Amendment Order 1998 (S.I. 2034)

East Glamorgan National Health Service Trust (Establishment) Order 1994 (S.I. 316)

East Gloucestershire National Health Service Trust (Establishment) Amendment Order 2000 (S.I. 2741)

East Hampshire Primary Care Trust (Establishment) Order 2001 (S.I. 331)

East Hertfordshire and the North Hertfordshire National Health Service Trusts (Dissolution) Order 2000 (S.I. 536)

East Hertfordshire Health National Health Service Trust (Change of Name) Order 1992 (S.I. 2014)

East Kent Coastal Primary Care Trust (Establishment) Order 2002 (S.I. 990)

East Kent Hospitals National Health Service Trust (Establishment) Amendment Order 1999 (S.I. 1858)

East Kent Hospitals National Health Service Trust (Establishment) Order 1999 (S.I. 896)

East Kent Light Railway Order 1993 (S.I. 2154)

East Lancashire (Heywood Extension) Light Railway Order 2002 (S.I. 1384)

East Lancashire Hospitals National Health Service Trust (Establishment) and the Blackburn, Hyndburn and Ribble Valley Health Care National Health Service Trust and Burnley Health Care National Health Service Trust (Dissolution) Order 2002 (S.I. 2073)

East Lancashire Light Railway Order 1986 (S.I. 277)

East Leeds Primary Care Trust (Establishment) Order 2001 (S.I. 3620)

East Lincolnshire Primary Care Trust (Establishment) Order 2001 (S.I. 4135)

East London and The City Mental Health National Health Service Trust (Establishment) Amendment Order 2000 (S.I. 1669)

East London and The City Mental Health National Health Service Trust (Establishment) Order 2000 (S.I. 522)

East Manchester Education Action Zone (Variation) Order 2000 (S.I. 3326)

East Midlands Ambulance Service National Health Service Trust (Establishment) Order 1999 (S.I. 910)

East Riding Health Authority (Change of Name) Order 2000 (S.I. 1240)

East Riding of Yorkshire District Council (Staff Transfer) Order 1996 (S.I. 378)

East Staffordshire Primary Care Trust (Establishment) Order 2002 (S.I. 951)

East Suffolk Local Health Services National Health Service Trust (Establishment) Order 1992 (S.I. 2583)

East Surrey Hospital and Community Healthcare National Health Service Trust (Change of Name) Order 1995 (S.I. 968)

East Surrey Hospital and Community Healthcare National Health Service Trust (Establishment) Order 1992 (S.I. 2522)

East Surrey Learning Disability and Mental Health Service National Health Service Trust (Change of Name) Order 1995 (S.I. 2379)

East Surrey Learning Disability and Mental Health Service National Health Service Trust (Establishment) Order 1994 (S.I. 181)

East Surrey Primary Care Trust (Establishment) Order 2002 (S.I. 988)

East Sussex (Boroughs of Brighton and Hove) (Structural Change) Order 1995 (S.I. 1770)

East Sussex (Coroners) Order 1997 (S.I. 488)

East Sussex County Council (Boroughs of Brighton and Hove) (Staff Transfer) Order 1997 (S.I. 461)

East Sussex Fire Services (Combination Scheme) Order 1996 (S.I. 2922)

East Sussex Hospitals National Health Service Trust (Establishment) and the Eastbourne Hospitals National Health Service Trust and Hastings and Rother National Health Service Trust (Dissolution) Amendment Order 2003 (S.I. 1063)

East Sussex Hospitals National Health Service Trust (Establishment) and the Eastbourne Hospitals National Health Service Trust and Hastings and Rother National Health Service Trust (Dissolution) Order 2003 (S.I. 216)

East Wiltshire Health Care National Health Service Trust (Establishment) Order 1993 (S.I. 2549)

East Yorkshire Community Healthcare and the Hull and Holderness Community Health National Health Service Trusts (Dissolution) Order 1999 (S.I. 2687)

East Yorkshire Community Healthcare National Health Service Trust (Establishment) Amendment Order 1996 (S.I. 1002)

East Yorkshire Community Healthcare National Health Service Trust (Establishment) Order 1993 (S.I. 2550)

East Yorkshire Hospitals and the Royal Hull Hospitals National Health Service Trusts (Dissolution) Order 1999 (S.I. 2674)

East Yorkshire Hospitals National Health Service Trust (Establishment) Amendment Order 1998 (S.I. 2485)

East Yorkshire Hospitals National Health Service Trust (Establishment) Order 1992 (S.I. 2500)

East Yorkshire Primary Care Trust (Establishment) Order 2001 (S.I. 511)

Eastbourne and County Healthcare National Health Service Trust (Establishment) Order 1992 (S.I. 2534)

Eastbourne and County National Health Service Trust Change of Name and (Establishment) Amendment Order (No.2) 2002 (S.I. 2397)

Eastbourne and County National Health Service Trust Change of Name and (Establishment) Amendment Order 2002 (S.I. 1495)

Eastbourne Hospitals National Health Service Trust (Establishment) Order 1991 (S.I. 2344)

Eastern Birmingham Primary Care Trust (Establishment) Order 2002 (S.I. 939)

Eastern Cheshire Primary Care Trust (Establishment) Order 2002 (S.I. 726)

Eastern Hull Primary Care Trust (Establishment) Order 2001 (S.I. 502)

Food Protection (Emergency Prohibitions) (Amnesic Shellfish Poisoning) (West Coast) (No.14) (Scotland) Order 2001 (S.S.I. 451)

Food Protection (Emergency Prohibitions) (Amnesic Shellfish Poisoning) (West Coast) (No.14) (Scotland) Order 2002 (S.S.I. 482)

Food Protection (Emergency Prohibitions) (Amnesic Shellfish Poisoning) (West Coast) (No.14) (Scotland) Partial Revocation Order 2002 (S.S.I. 553)

Food Protection (Emergency Prohibitions) (Amnesic Shellfish Poisoning) (West Coast) (No.15) (Scotland) Order 2002 (S.S.I. 511)

Food Protection (Emergency Prohibitions) (Amnesic Shellfish Poisoning) (West Coast) (No.16) (Scotland) Order 2002 (S.S.I. 544)

Food Protection (Emergency Prohibitions) (Amnesic Shellfish Poisoning) (West Coast) (No.2) (Scotland) Order 2001 (S.S.I. 281)

Food Protection (Emergency Prohibitions) (Amnesic Shellfish Poisoning) (West Coast) (No.2) (Scotland) Order 2002 (S.S.I. 65)

Food Protection (Emergency Prohibitions) (Amnesic Shellfish Poisoning) (West Coast) (No.2) (Scotland) Order 2003 (S.S.I. 245)

Food Protection (Emergency Prohibitions) (Amnesic Shellfish Poisoning) (West Coast) (No.2) (Scotland) Order 2004 (S.S.I. 43)

Food Protection (Emergency Prohibitions) (Amnesic Shellfish Poisoning) (West Coast) (No.2) (Scotland) Partial Revocation Order 2001 (S.S.I. 434)

Food Protection (Emergency Prohibitions) (Amnesic Shellfish Poisoning) (West Coast) (No.2) (Scotland) Partial Revocation Order 2002 (S.S.I. 67)

Food Protection (Emergency Prohibitions) (Amnesic Shellfish Poisoning) (West Coast) (No.3) (Scotland) Order 2000 (S.S.I. 303)

Food Protection (Emergency Prohibitions) (Amnesic Shellfish Poisoning) (West Coast) (No.3) (Scotland) Order 2003 (S.S.I. 365)

Food Protection (Emergency Prohibitions) (Amnesic Shellfish Poisoning) (West Coast) (No.4) (Scotland) Order 2001 (S.S.I. 289)

Food Protection (Emergency Prohibitions) (Amnesic Shellfish Poisoning) (West Coast) (No.4) (Scotland) Order 2002 (S.S.I. 231)

Food Protection (Emergency Prohibitions) (Amnesic Shellfish Poisoning) (West Coast) (No.4) (Scotland) Order 2003 (S.S.I. 374)

Food Protection (Emergency Prohibitions) (Amnesic Shellfish Poisoning) (West Coast) (No.4) (Scotland) Order 2004 (S.S.I. 319)

Food Protection (Emergency Prohibitions) (Amnesic Shellfish Poisoning) (West Coast) (No.4) (Scotland) Partial Revocation (No.2) Order 2002 (S.S.I. 19)

Food Protection (Emergency Prohibitions) (Amnesic Shellfish Poisoning) (West Coast) (No.4) (Scotland) Partial Revocation (No.2) Order 2004 (S.S.I. 65)

Food Protection (Emergency Prohibitions) (Amnesic Shellfish Poisoning) (West Coast) (No.4) (Scotland) Partial Revocation (No.3) Order 2004 (S.S.I. 69)

Food Protection (Emergency Prohibitions) (Amnesic Shellfish Poisoning) (West Coast) (No.4) (Scotland) Partial Revocation Order 2001 (S.S.I. 473)

Food Protection (Emergency Prohibitions) (Amnesic Shellfish Poisoning) (West Coast) (No.4) (Scotland) Partial Revocation Order 2004 (S.S.I. 42)

Food Protection (Emergency Prohibitions) (Amnesic Shellfish Poisoning) (West Coast) (No.5) (Scotland) Order 2001 (S.S.I. 295)

Food Protection (Emergency Prohibitions) (Amnesic Shellfish Poisoning) (West Coast) (No.5) (Scotland) Order 2002 (S.S.I. 306)

Food Protection (Emergency Prohibitions) (Amnesic Shellfish Poisoning) (West Coast) (No.5) (Scotland) Order 2003 (S.S.I. 381)

Food Protection (Emergency Prohibitions) (Amnesic Shellfish Poisoning) (West Coast) (No.5) (Scotland) Order 2003 Partial Revocation Order 2004 (S.S.I. 61)

Food Protection (Emergency Prohibitions) (Amnesic Shellfish Poisoning) (West Coast) (No.5) (Scotland) Partial Revocation (No.2) Order 2002 (S.S.I. 409)

Food Protection (Emergency Prohibitions) (Amnesic Shellfish Poisoning) (West Coast) (No.5) (Scotland) Partial Revocation Order 2002 (S.S.I. 383)

Food Protection (Emergency Prohibitions) (Amnesic Shellfish Poisoning) (West Coast) (No.5) (Scotland) Partial Revocation Order 2003 (S.S.I. 606)

Food Protection (Emergency Prohibitions) (Amnesic Shellfish Poisoning) (West Coast) (No.6) (Scotland) Order 2002 (S.S.I. 307)

Food Protection (Emergency Prohibitions) (Amnesic Shellfish Poisoning) (West Coast) (No.6) (Scotland) Order 2003 (S.S.I. 392)

Food Protection (Emergency Prohibitions) (Amnesic Shellfish Poisoning) (West Coast) (No.6) (Scotland) Order 2003 Partial Revocation Order 2004 (S.S.I. 125)

Food Protection (Emergency Prohibitions) (Amnesic Shellfish Poisoning) (West Coast) (No.6) (Scotland) Partial Revocation Order 2002 (S.S.I. 551)

Food Protection (Emergency Prohibitions) (Amnesic Shellfish Poisoning) (West Coast) (No.7) (Scotland) Order 2001 (S.S.I. 322)

Food Protection (Emergency Prohibitions) (Amnesic Shellfish Poisoning) (West Coast) (No.7) (Scotland) Order 2002 (S.S.I. 332)

Food Protection (Emergency Prohibitions) (Amnesic Shellfish Poisoning) (West Coast) (No.7) (Scotland) Order 2003 (S.S.I. 397)

Food Protection (Emergency Prohibitions) (Amnesic Shellfish Poisoning) (West Coast) (No.8) (Scotland) Order 2001 (S.S.I. 374)

Food Protection (Emergency Prohibitions) (Amnesic Shellfish Poisoning) (West Coast) (No.8) (Scotland) Order 2002 (S.S.I. 333)

Food Protection (Emergency Prohibitions) (Amnesic Shellfish Poisoning) (West Coast) (No.8) (Scotland) Order 2003 (S.S.I. 402)

Food Protection (Emergency Prohibitions) (Amnesic Shellfish Poisoning) (West Coast) (No.9) (Scotland) Order 2001 (S.S.I. 388)

Food Protection (Emergency Prohibitions) (Amnesic Shellfish Poisoning) (West Coast) (No.9) (Scotland) Order 2002 (S.S.I. 350)

Food Protection (Emergency Prohibitions) (Amnesic Shellfish Poisoning) (West Coast) (No.9) (Scotland) Order 2003 (S.S.I. 409)

Food Protection (Emergency Prohibitions) (Amnesic Shellfish Poisoning) (West Coast) (No.9) (Scotland) Partial Revocation Order 2001 (S.S.I. 469)

Food Protection (Emergency Prohibitions) (Amnesic Shellfish Poisoning) (West Coast) (Scotland) Order 2002 (S.S.I. 49)

Forest Reproductive Material Regulations (Northern Ireland) 1977 (194)

Forest Reproductive Material Regulations 1973 (S.I. 944)

Forest Reproductive Material Regulations 1977 (S.I. 891)

Forestry (Felling of Trees) Regulations 1979 (S.I. 791)

Former Yugoslavia (United Nations Sanctions) (Channel Islands) Order 1994 (S.I. 2675)

Former Yugoslavia (United Nations Sanctions) (Dependent Territories) Order 1994 (S.I. 2674)

Former Yugoslavia (United Nations Sanctions) (Isle of Man) Order 1994 (S.I. 2676)

Former Yugoslavia (United Nations Sanctions) Order 1994 (S.I. 2673)

Forth Valley Acute Hospitals National Health Service Trust (Establishment) Amendment Order 1999 (S.S.I. 79)

Forth Valley Acute Hospitals National Health Service Trust (Establishment) Amendment Order 2001 (S.S.I. 348)

Forth Valley Acute Hospitals National Health Service Trust (Establishment) Order 1998 (S.I. 2725)

Forth Valley Primary Care National Health Service Trust (Establishment) Amendment (No.2) Order 1999 (S.S.I. 164)

Forth Valley Primary Care National Health Service Trust (Establishment) Amendment Order 2001 (S.S.I. 347)

Forth Valley Primary Care National Health Service Trust (Establishment) Order 1998 (S.I. 2713)

Fosse Health, Leicestershire Community National Health Service Trust (Establishment) Order 1992 (S.I. 2484)

Fosse Health, Leicestershire Community National Health Service Trust (Establishment) Order 1994 (S.I. 3185)

Fosse Health, Leicestershire Community National Health Service Trust Dissolution Order 1995 (S.I. 478)

Fossil Fuel Levy (Scotland) Regulations 1996 (S.I. 293)

Foster Placement (Children) and Adoption Agencies Amendment (England) Regulations 2001 (S.I. 2992)

Foster Placement (Children) Regulations (Northern Ireland) 1996 (467)

Foster Placement (Children) Regulations 1991 (S.I. 910)

Fostering of Children (Scotland) Regulations 1996 (S.I. 3263)

Fostering Services (Wales) Regulations 2003 (S.I. 237)

Fostering Services Regulations 2002 (S.I. 57)

Foundation Subject (Amendment) (England) Order 2000 (S.I. 1146)

Foundation Subject (Amendment) (Wales) Order 2000 (S.I. 1882)

Foxfield Light Railway Order 1995 (S.I. 1236)

Foyle Area and Carlingford Area (Licensing of Fishing Engines) Regulations 2001 (397)

Freedom of Information (Additional Public Authorities) Order 2002 (S.I. 2623)

Freedom of Information (Additional Public Authorities) Order 2004 (S.I. 938)

Freedom of Information Act 2000 (Commencement No 2) Order 2002 (S.I. 2812)

Freeman Group of Hospitals and the Royal Victoria Infirmary and Associated Hospitals National Health Service Trusts (Dissolution) Order 1998 (S.I. 831)

Freight Containers (Safety Convention) Regulations 1984 (S.I. 1890)

Frenchay Healthcare and the Southmead Health Services National Health Service Trusts (Dissolution) Order 1999 (S.I. 626)

Frenchay Healthcare National Health Service Trust (Establishment) Amendment Order 1998 (S.I. 193)

Fresh Meat (Beef Controls) (No.2) Regulations 1996 (S.I. 2097)

Fresh Meat (Beef Controls) Regulations (Northern Ireland) 1996 (404)

Fresh Meat (Hygiene and Inspection) Regulations (Northern Ireland) 1997 (493)

Fresh Meat (Hygiene and Inspection) Regulations 1995 (S.I. 539)

Fresh Meat (Import Conditions) Regulations (Northern Ireland) 1997 (218)

Fresh Meat (Import Conditions) Regulations 1996 (S.I. 3125)

Friendly Societies (Modification of the Corporation Tax Acts) Regulations 1997 (S.I. 473)

Fruit Juices and Fruit Nectars (Amendment) Regulations 1982 (S.I. 1311)

Fruit Juices and Fruit Nectars (England, Wales and Scotland) (Amendment) Regulations 1991 (S.I. 1284)

Fruit Juices and Fruit Nectars (England, Wales and Scotland) (Amendment) Regulations 1995 (S.I. 236)

Fruit Juices and Fruit Nectars (Scotland) (Amendment) Regulations 1982 (S.I. 1619)

Fruit Juices and Fruit Nectars (Scotland) Amendment Regulations 1977 (S.I. 1883)

Fruit Juices and Fruit Nectars (Scotland) Regulations 1977 (S.I. 1026)

Fruit Juices and Fruit Nectars (Wales) Regulations 2003 (S.I. 3041)

Fruit Juices and Fruit Nectars Regulations 1977 (S.I. 927)

Fugitive Offenders (Anguilla) Order 1987 (S.I. 452)

Fugitive Offenders (Bermuda) Order 1967 (S.I. 1905)

Fugitive Offenders (British Indian Ocean Territory) Order 1968 (S.I. 183)

Fugitive Offenders (Cayman Islands) Order 1968 (S.I. 112)

Fugitive Offenders (Falkland Islands and Dependencies) Order 1968 (S.I. 113)

Fugitive Offenders (Gibraltar) Order 1967 (S.I. 1909)

Fugitive Offenders (Montserrat) Order 1967 (S.I. 1913)

Fugitive Offenders (Overseas Territories) (No.2) Order 1968 (S.I. 1375)

Fugitive Offenders (Overseas Territories) Order 1968 (S.I. 292)

Fugitive Offenders (Pitcairn) Order 1968 (S.I. 884)

Fugitive Offenders (Sovereign Base Areas of Akrotiri and Dhekelia) Order 1967 (S.I. 1916)

Fugitive Offenders (St Helena) Order 1968 (S.I. 184)

Fugitive Offenders (Turks and Caicos Islands) Order 1968 (S.I. 185)

Fugitive Offenders (Virgin Islands) Order 1967 (S.I. 1915)

Functions of Traffic Wardens Order 1970 (S.I. 1958)

Fur Farming (Compensation Scheme) (England) Order 2001 (S.I. 3853)

Fur Farming (Compensation Scheme) (England) Order 2002 (S.I. 221)

Furness Hospitals National Health Service Trust (Dissolution) Order 1998 (S.I. 820)

Furness Hospitals National Health Service Trust (Establishment) Order 1994 (S.I. 179)

General Medical Council (Constitution) Order 1979 (S.I. 112)

General Medical Council (Fitness to Practise Committees) (Amendment) Rules Order of Council 2002 (S.I. 2572)

General Medical Council (Fitness to Practise Committees) Rules Order of Council 2000 (S.I. 2051)

General Medical Council (Fitness to Practise) Rules Order of Council 2004 (S.I. 2608)

General Medical Council (Interim Orders Committee) (Procedure) Rules Order of Council 2000 (S.I. 2053)

General Medical Council (Interim Orders Committee) (Transitional Provisions) Rules Order of Council 2000 (S.I. 2054)

General Medical Council (Legal Assessors) (Amendment) Rules 1997 (S.I. 1861)

General Medical Council (Legal Assessors) (Amendment) Rules 2000 (S.I. 1881)

General Medical Council (Legal Assessors) Amendment (Scotland) Rules 2000 (S.S.I. 308)

General Medical Council (Legal Assessors) Rules 1980 (S.I. 941)

General Medical Council (Professional Performance) Rules Order of Council 1997 (S.I. 1529)

General Medical Council (Registration (Fees) Regulations) Order of Council 1986 (S.I. 149)

General Medical Council (Registration Regulations) Order of Council 1979 (S.I. 844)

General Medical Council (Restoration and Registration Fees Amendment) Regulations Order of Council 2003 (S.I. 1342)

General Medical Council (Suspension and Removal of Members from Office) Rules Order of Council 2004 (S.I. 215)

General Medical Council (Voluntary Erasure and Restoration following Voluntary Erasure) Regulations Order of Council 2003 (S.I. 1341)

General Medical Council (Voluntary Erasure and Restoration) Regulations Order of Council 2000 (S.I. 2033)

General Medical Council Health Committee (Procedure) Rules 1987 (S.I. 2174)

General Medical Council Health Committee (Procedure) Rules Order of Council 1987 (S.I. 2174)

General Medical Council Preliminary Proceedings Committee and Professional Conduct Committee (Procedure) Rules Order of Council 1988 (S.I. 2255)

General Medical Council Professional Conduct Committee (EC Practitioners) (Procedure) Rules Order of Council 1989 (S.I. 1837)

General Medical Services (Transitional and Other Ancillary Provisions) (Scotland) Order 2004 (S.S.I. 142)

General Medical Services and Personal Medical Services Transitional and Consequential Provisions Order 2004 (S.I. 865)

General Medical Services and Section 17C Agreements (Transitional and other Ancillary Provisions) (Scotland) Order 2004 (S.S.I. 163)

General Medical Services Regulations (Northern Ireland) 1997 (380)

General Medical Services Transitional and Consequential Provisions (Wales) Order 2004 (S.I. 477)

General Medical Services Transitional and Consequential Provisions Order 2004 (S.I. 433)

General Optical Council (Disciplinary Committee (Constitution) Rules) Order of Council 1998 (S.I. 1338)

General Optical Council (Registration and Enrolment (Amendment) Rules) Order of Council 2001 (S.I. 1131)

General Optical Council (Registration and Enrolment (Amendment) Rules) Order of Council 2002 (S.I. 775)

General Optical Council (Registration and Enrolment (Amendment) Rules) Order of Council 2003 (S.I. 1080)

General Optical Council (Registration and Enrolment Rules) Order of Council 1977 (S.I. 176)

General Osteopathic Council (Application for Registration and Fees) Rules Order of Council 2000 (S.I. 1038)

General Osteopathic Council (Registration) Rules Order of Council 1998 (S.I. 1328)

General Product Safety Regulations 1994 (S.I. 2328)

General Social Care Council (Appointments and Procedure) Regulations 2001 (S.I. 1744)

General Teaching Council for England (Additional Functions) Order 2001 (S.I. 1214)

General Teaching Council for England (Constitution) Regulations 1999 (S.I. 1726)

General Teaching Council for England (Deduction of Fees) Regulations 2001 (S.I. 3993)

General Teaching Council for England (Disciplinary Functions) Regulations 2001 (S.I. 1268)

General Teaching Council for Wales (Constitution) Regulations 1999 (S.I. 1619)

General Teaching Council for Wales (Disciplinary Functions) Regulations 2001 (S.I. 1424)

General Teaching Council for Wales (Fees) Regulations 2002 (S.I. 326)

General Teaching Council for Wales (Functions) Regulations 2000 (S.I. 1979)

General Teaching Council for Wales Order 1998 (S.I. 2911)

Genetically Modified and Novel Foods (Labelling) (England) Regulations 2000 (S.I. 768)

Genetically Modified and Novel Foods (Labelling) (Scotland) Regulations 2000 (S.S.I. 83)

Genetically Modified and Novel Foods (Labelling) (Wales) Regulations 2000 (S.I. 1925)

Genetically Modified Organisms (Contained Use) Regulations (Northern Ireland) 2001 (295)

Genetically Modified Organisms (Contained Use) Regulations 2000 (S.I. 2831)

Genetically Modified Organisms (Deliberate Release and Risk Assessment) (Amendment) Regulations (Northern Ireland) 1997 (534)

Genetically Modified Organisms (Deliberate Release and Risk Assessment-Amendment) Regulations 1997 (S.I. 1900)

Genetically Modified Organisms (Deliberate Release) (Amendment) Regulations (Northern Ireland) 1995 (413)

Genetically Modified Organisms (Deliberate Release) (Scotland) Regulations 2002 (S.S.I. 541)

Genetically Modified Organisms (Deliberate Release) Regulations (Northern Ireland) 1994 (144)

Genetically Modified Organisms (Deliberate Release) Regulations (Northern Ireland) 2003 (167)

Genetically Modified Organisms (Deliberate Release) Regulations 1992 (S.I. 3280)

Genetically Modified Organisms (Deliberate Release) Regulations 1993 (S.I. 152)

Genetically Modified Organisms (Deliberate Release) Regulations 1995 (S.I. 304)

Genetically Modified Organisms (Deliberate Release) Regulations 2002 (S.I. 2443)

Genetically Modified Organisms (Northern Ireland) Order 1991 (S.I. 1714)

George Eliot Hospital National Health Service Trust (Establishment) Order 1993 (S.I. 2551)

Greater Manchester (Light Rapid Transit System) (Ashton-under-Lyne Extension) Order 1998 (S.I. 1936)

Greater Manchester (Light Rapid Transit System) (Eccles Extension) Order 1996 (S.I. 2714)

Greater Manchester (Light Rapid Transit System) (Trafford Depot) Order 2002 (S.I. 1327)

Greater Manchester Ambulance Service National Health Service Trust (Establishment) Amendment Order 1997 (S.I. 2518)

Greater Manchester Ambulance Service National Health Service Trust (Establishment) Order 1993 (S.I. 2600)

Greater Yardley Primary Care Trust (Establishment) Order 2000 (S.I. 2339)

Greenhouse Gas Emissions Trading Scheme Regulations 2003 (S.I. 3311)

Greenwich Healthcare National Health Service Trust (Establishment) Amendment Order 1998 (S.I. 1417)

Greenwich Healthcare National Health Service Trust (Establishment) Order 1992 (S.I. 2533)

Greenwich Healthcare National Health Service Trust Change of Name and (Establishment) Amendment Order 2001 (S.I. 1435)

Greenwich Park (Vehicle Parking) Regulations 2000 (S.I. 934)

Greenwich Primary Care Trust (Establishment) Order 2001 (S.I. 528)

Grimsby and Louth Light Railway Order 1991 (S.I. 2210)

Grimsby Health National Health Service Trust (Change of Name) Order 1996 (S.I. 2034)

Grimsby Health National Health Service Trust (Establishment) Order 1992 (S.I. 2496)

Groundwater Regulations (Northern Ireland) 1998 (401)

Groundwater Regulations 1998 (S.I. 2746)

Guardian's Allowance (General) Regulations 2003 (S.I. 495)

Guild Community Healthcare National Health Service Trust (Establishment) Order 1993 (S.I. 2623)

Guildford and Waverley Primary Care Trust (Establishment) Order 2002 (S.I. 986)

Guy's and Lewisham National Health Service Trust Dissolution Order 1993 (S.I. 696)

Guy's and St Thomas National Health Service Trust (Establishment) Order 1993 (S.I. 693)

Gwent Community Health National Health Service Trust (Establishment) Amendment Order 1995 (S.I. 2797)

Gwent Community Health National Health Service Trust (Establishment) Order 1992 (S.I. 2730)

Gwent Healthcare National Health Service Trust (Establishment) Order 1998 (S.I. 3321)

Gwynedd Community Health National Health Service Trust (Establishment) Order 1993 (S.I. 2839)

Gwynedd Hospitals National Health Service Trust (Establishment) Order 1993 (S.I. 2841)

Habitat (Broadleaved Woodland) (Wales) Regulations 1994 (S.I. 3099)

Habitat (Coastal Belt) (Wales) Regulations 1994 (S.I. 3101)

Habitat (Salt-Marsh) Regulations 1994 (S.I. 1293)

Habitat (Species-Rich Grassland) (Wales) Regulations 1994 (S.I. 3102)

Habitat (Water Fringe) (Wales) Regulations 1994 (S.I. 3100)

Habitat (Water Fringe) Regulations 1994 (S.I. 1291)

Habitats (Scotland) Regulations 1994 (S.I. 2710)

Haiti (United Nations Sanctions) (Channel Islands) Order 1994 (S.I. 1325)

Haiti (United Nations Sanctions) (Dependent Territories) Order 1994 (S.I. 1324)

Haiti (United Nations Sanctions) (Isle of Man) Order 1994 (S.I. 1326)

Haiti (United Nations Sanctions) Order 1994 (S.I. 1323)

Hallmarking (International Convention) Order 1976 (S.I. 730)

Halton General Hospital and the Warrington Hospital National Health Service Trusts (Dissolution) Order 2001 (S.I. 1665)

Halton General Hospital National Health Service Trust (Establishment) Order 1992 (S.I. 2466)

Halton Primary Care Trust (Establishment) Order 2002 (S.I. 66)

Hambleton and Richmondshire Primary Care Trust (Establishment) Order 2002 (S.I. 357)

Hammersmith and Fulham Primary Care Trust (Establishment) Order 2001 (S.I. 3851)

Hammersmith Hospitals National Health Service Trust (Establishment) Order 1994 (S.I. 853)

Hampshire (Cities of Portsmouth and Southampton) (Structural Change) Order 1995 (S.I. 1775)

Hampshire (Coroners) Order 1997 (S.I. 489)

Hampshire Ambulance Service National Health Service Trust (Establishment) Order 1992 (S.I. 2504)

Hampshire County Council (Cities of Portsmouth and Southampton) (Staff Transfer) Order 1997 (S.I. 468)

Hampshire Fire Services (Combination Scheme) Order 1996 (S.I. 2923)

Harbour Authorities (Constitution) Order 1985 (S.I. 1504)

Harbour Works (Assessment of Environmental Effects) (Amendment) Regulations (Northern Ireland) 1996 (369)

Harbour Works (Assessment of Environmental Effects) Regulations (Northern Ireland) 1990 (181)

Hares (Control of Importation) Order 1965 (S.I. 2040)

Haringey Health Care National Health Service Trust (Establishment) Order 1993 (S.I. 2634)

Haringey Primary Care Trust (Establishment) Order 2001 (S.I. 329)

Harlow Primary Care Trust (Establishment) Order 2000 (S.I. 2820)

Harrow and Hillingdon Healthcare National Health Service Trust (Establishment) Amendment Order 1998 (S.I. 1992)

Harrow and Hillingdon Healthcare National Health Service Trust (Establishment) Order 1994 (S.I. 848)

Harrow College (Government) Regulations 1999 (S.I. 1328)

Harrow Community Health Services National Health Service Trust Dissolution Order 1994 (S.I. 858)

Hartlepool and East Durham National Health Service Trust (Establishment) Order 1996 (S.I. 873)

Hartlepool and East Durham, the North Tees Health and the South Tees Community and Mental Health National Health Service Trusts (Dissolution) Order 1999 (S.I. 800)

Hartlepool and Peterlee Hospitals National Health Service Trust (Establishment) Order 1993 (S.I. 2627)

Hartlepool and Peterlee Hospitals National Health Service Trust Dissolution Order 1996 (S.I. 879)

Hartlepool Community Care National Health Service Trust (Establishment) Order 1993 (S.I. 2591)

Hartlepool Community Care National Health Service Trust Dissolution Order 1996 (S.I. 887)

Hartlepool Primary Care Trust (Establishment) Order 2001 (S.I. 515)

Hastings and Rother National Health Service Trust (Establishment) Order 1991 (S.I. 2356)

Hastings and St Leonards Primary Care Trust (Establishment) Order 2001 (S.I. 282)

Havering Hospitals National Health Service Trust (Establishment) Order 1992 (S.I. 2512)

Havering Primary Care Trust (Establishment) Order 2001 (S.I. 527)

Health Act 1999 (Fund-holding Practices) (Transfer of Assets, Savings, Rights and Liabilities and Transitional Provisions) Order 1999 (S.I. 2541)

Health Act 1999 (Supplementary and Consequential Provisions) Order 1999 (S.I. 2795)

Health and Medicines (Northern Ireland) Order 1988 (S.I. 2249)

Health and Personal Social Service (Assessment of Resources) Regulations (Northern Ireland) 1993 (127)

Health and Personal Social Service (General Ophthalmic Services) Regulations (Northern Ireland) 1986 (163)

Health and Personal Social Services (Fund-holding Practices) Regulations (Northern Ireland) 1993 (142)

Health and Personal Social Services (Northern Ireland) Order 1972 (S.I. 1265)

Health and Personal Social Services (Northern Ireland) Order 1978 (S.I. 1907)

Health and Personal Social Services (Northern Ireland) Order 1991 (S.I. 194)

Health and Personal Social Services (Northern Ireland) Order 1994 (S.I. 429)

Health and Personal Social Services (Optical Charges and Payments) Regulations (Northern Ireland) 1997 (191)

Health and Personal Social Services (Quality, Improvement and Regulation) (Northern Ireland) Order 2003 (S.I. 431)

Health and Personal Social Services (Superannuation) (Additional Voluntary Contributions) Regulations (Northern Ireland) 1999 (294)

Health and Personal Social Services (Superannuation) Regulations (Northern Ireland) 1995 (95)

Health and Personal Social Services General Dental Services Regulations (Northern Ireland) 1993 (326)

Health and Safety (Consultation with Employees) Regulations 1996 (S.I. 1513)

Health and Safety (Display Screen Equipment) Regulations 1992 (S.I. 2792)

Health and Safety (Enforcing Authority) Regulations (Northern Ireland) 1999 (90)

Health and Safety (Enforcing Authority) Regulations 1998 (S.I. 494)

Health and Safety (Fees) Regulations (Northern Ireland) 1998 (125)

Health and Safety (Fees) Regulations 2001 (S.I. 2626)

Health and Safety (Fees) Regulations 2002 (S.I. 655)

Health and Safety (Fees) Regulations 2003 (S.I. 547)

Health and Safety (Fees) Regulations 2004 (S.I. 456)

Health and Safety (First-Aid) Regulations 1981 (S.I. 917)

Health and Safety (Safety Signs and Signals) Regulations (Northern Ireland) 1996 (119)

Health and Safety (Safety Signs and Signals) Regulations 1996 (S.I. 341)

Health and Safety at Work (Amendment) (Northern Ireland) Order 1998 (S.I. 2795)

Health and Safety at Work (Northern Ireland) Order 1978 (S.I. 1039)

Health and Safety at Work etc Act 1974 (Application outside Great Britain) Order 2001 (S.I. 2127)

Health and Safety at Work etc Act 1974 (Application to Environmentally Hazardous Substances) (Amendment) Regulations 1999 (S.I. 40)

Health and Safety at Work etc Act 1974 (Application to Environmentally Hazardous Substances) Regulations 1996 (S.I. 2075)

Health and Safety at Work etc Act 1974 (Application to Environmentally Hazardous Substances) Regulations 2002 (S.I. 282)

Health and Safety at Work Order (Application to Environmentally Hazardous Substances) (Amendment) Regulations 2000 (86)

Health and Safety at Work Order (Application to Environmentally Hazardous Substances) Regulations (Northern Ireland) 1996 (525)

Health and Safety Licensing Appeals (Hearings Procedure) (Scotland) Rules 1974 (S.I. 2068)

Health and Safety Licensing Appeals (Hearings Procedure) Rules 1974 (S.I. 2040)

Health and Social Care (Community Health and Standards) Act 2003 (Commencement No 1) (Wales) Order 2004 (S.I. 480)

Health and Social Care (Community Health and Standards) Act 2003 (Supplementary and Consequential Provision) (NHS Foundation Trusts) Order 2004 (S.I. 696)

Health and Social Care (Community Health and Standards) Act 2003 Commencement (No.2) Order 2004 (S.I. 288)

Health and Social Care (Community Health and Standards) Act 2003 Commencement (No.3) Order 2004 (S.I. 759)

Health and Social Care Act 2001 (Commencement No 3) (Wales) Order 2002 (S.I. 1919)

Health and Social Care Act 2001 (Commencement No 6) (England) Order 2001 (S.I. 3738)

Health and Social Care Act 2001 (Commencement No 8) Order 2002 (S.I. 1095)

Health and Social Services Trusts (Consequential Amendments) Regulations (Northern Ireland) 1994 (65)

Health and Social Services Trusts (Exercise of Functions) Regulations (Northern Ireland) 1994 (64)

Health Authorities (England) Establishment Order 1996 (S.I. 624)

Health Authorities (England) Establishment Order 1996 Amendment and the Cambridgeshire and Norfolk Health Authorities (Establishment etc.) (Amendment) Order 1999 (S.I. 1024)

Health Authorities (England) Establishment Order 1996 Amendment and the Cambridgeshire and Norfolk Health Authorities (Establishment etc.) Order 1999 (S.I. 616)

Health Authorities (Establishment and Abolition) (England) Order 2001 (S.I. 740)

Health Authorities (Establishment and Abolition) (England) Order 2002 (S.I. 553)

Health Authorities (Membership and Procedure) Amendment Regulations 2000 (S.I. 696)

Health Authorities (Membership and Procedure) Regulations 1996 (S.I. 707)

Health Authorities (Transfer of Functions, Staff, Property, Rights and Liabilities and Abolition) (Wales) Order 2003 (S.I. 813)

Health Authorities (Wales) Establishment Order 1996 (S.I. 146)

Health Boards (Membership and Procedure) (Scotland) Regulations 2001 (S.S.I. 302)

Health Development Agency Regulations 1999 (S.I. 3432)

Health Education Board for Scotland Order 1990 (S.I. 2639)

Health Professions (Operating Department Practitioners and Miscellaneous Amendments) Order 2004 (S.I. 2033)

Health Professions (Parts of and Entries in the Register) Order of Council 2003 (S.I. 1571)

Health Professions Council (Registration and Fees) Rules Order of Council 2003 (S.I. 1572)

Health Professions Order 2001 (Consequential Amendments) Order 2003 (S.I. 1590)

Health Professions Order 2002 (S.I. 254)

Health Professions Wales (Establishment, Membership, Constitution and Functions) Order 2004 (S.I. 551)

Health Protection Agency (Yr Asiantaeth Diogelu Iechyd) (Establishment) Order 2003 (S.I. 505)

Health Protection Agency (Yr Asiantaeth Diogelu Iechyd) Regulations 2003 (S.I. 506)

Health Service (Control of Patient Information) Regulations 2002 (S.I. 1438)

Health Service Medicines (Control of Prices of Branded Medicines) Regulations 2000 (S.I. 123)

Health Service Medicines (Control of Prices of Specified Generic Medicines) Regulations 2000 (S.I. 1763)

Health Service Medicines (Information on the Prices of Specified Generic Medicines) Regulations 2001 (S.I. 3798)

Health Services (Primary Care) (Northern Ireland) Order 1997 (S.I. 1177)

Health Technology Board for Scotland Order 2000 (S.S.I. 47)

Healthlands Mental Health National Health Service Trust (Establishment) Order 1994 (S.I. 184)

Heart of Birmingham Teaching Primary Care Trust (Establishment) Order 2002 (S.I. 958)

Heather and Grass etc (Burning) (Amendment) Regulations 1987 (S.I. 1208)

Heather and Grass etc (Burning) Regulations 1986 (S.I. 428)

Heather Moorland (Livestock Extensification) (Scotland) Regulations 1995 (S.I. 891)

Heatherwood and Wexham Park Hospitals National Health Service Trust (Establishment) Order 1991 (S.I. 2357)

Heathrow Express Railway Extension Order 2002 (S.I. 1064)

Hedgerows Regulations 1997 (S.I. 1160)

Hemp (Third Country Imports) Regulations 2002 (S.I. 787)

Hereford and Worcester (Coroners) Order 1998 (S.I. 359)

Hereford and Worcester (Staff Transfer) Order 1998 (S.I. 444)

Hereford and Worcester (Structural, Boundary and Electoral Changes) Order 1996 (S.I. 1867)

Hereford and Worcester Ambulance Service National Health Service Trust (Establishment) Amendment Order 1998 (S.I. 2841)

Hereford and Worcester Ambulance Service National Health Service Trust (Establishment) Order 1993 (S.I. 2553)

Hereford and Worcester Fire Services (Combination Scheme) Order 1997 (S.I. 2700)

Hereford Hospitals National Health Service Trust (Establishment) Amendment Order 1996 (S.I. 990)

Hereford Hospitals National Health Service Trust (Establishment) Order 1993 (S.I. 2552)

Herefordshire Community Health National Health Service Trust (Dissolution) Order 2000 (S.I. 1749)

Herefordshire Community Health National Health Service Trust (Establishment) Amendment Order 1998 (S.I. 2948)

Herefordshire Primary Care Trust (Establishment) Order 2000 (S.I. 1748)

Hertfordshire (Coroners Districts) (Amendment) Order 1998 (S.I. 1799)

Hertfordshire (Coroners Districts) Order 1974 (S.I. 374)

Hertfordshire (Coroners Districts) Order 2002 (S.I. 3084)

Hertfordshire Partnership National Health Service Trust (Establishment) Order 2001 (S.I. 269)

Hertsmere Primary Care Trust (Establishment) Order 2000 (S.I. 1384)

Heywood and Middleton Primary Care Trust (Establishment) Order 2001 (S.I. 438)

High Court and County Courts (Allocation of Arbitration Proceedings) Order 1996 (S.I. 3215)

High Court Enforcement Officers Regulations 2004 (S.I. 400)

High Court of Justiciary (Proceedings in the Netherlands) (United Nations) Order 1998 (S.I. 2251)

High Peak and Dales Primary Care Trust (Establishment) Order 2001 (S.I. 3659)

Highland Acute Hospitals National Health Service Trust (Establishment) Amendment Order 1999 (S.S.I. 80)

Highland Acute Hospitals National Health Service Trust (Establishment) Amendment Order 2001 (S.S.I. 352)

Highland Acute Hospitals National Health Service Trust (Establishment) Order 1998 (S.I. 2722)

Highland Primary Care National Health Service Trust (Establishment) Amendment (No.2) Order 1999 (S.S.I. 93)

Highland Primary Care National Health Service Trust (Establishment) Amendment Order 1999 (S.I. 1069)

Highland Primary Care National Health Service Trust (Establishment) Amendment Order 2001 (S.S.I. 353)

Highland Primary Care National Health Service Trust (Establishment) Order 1998 (S.I. 2721)

Highlands of Scotland Tourist Board Scheme Amendment Order 1995 (S.I. 2236)

Highlands of Scotland Tourist Board Scheme Order 1995 (S.I. 1886)

Highly Flammable Liquids and Liquefied Petroleum Gases Regulations (Northern Ireland) 1975 (256)

Highly Flammable Liquids and Liquefied Petroleum Gases Regulations 1972 (S.I. 917)

Highways (Road Humps) Regulations 1999 (S.I. 1025)

Highways (Traffic Calming) Regulations 1999 (S.I. 1026)

Hill Farm Allowance Regulations 2002 (S.I. 271)

Hill Farm Allowance Regulations 2003 (S.I. 289)

Hill Farm Allowance Regulations 2004 (S.I. 145)

Hill Livestock (Compensatory Allowances) (Scotland) Regulations 1999 (S.S.I. 185)

Hill Livestock (Compensatory Allowances) (Scotland) Regulations 1999 (S.S.I. 187)

Hill Livestock (Compensatory Allowances) Regulations 1996 (S.I. 1500)

Hillingdon Community Health National Health Service Trust Dissolution Order 1994 (S.I. 863)

Hillingdon Hospital National Health Service Trust (Establishment) Amendment Order 1999 (S.I. 1769)

Hillingdon Primary Care Trust (Establishment) Order 2000 (S.I. 209)

Hinchingbrooke Health Care National Health Service Trust (Establishment) Order 1993 (S.I. 823)

Hinchingbrooke Health Care National Health Service Trust Dissolution Order 1993 (S.I. 822)

Housing Benefit (General) Amendment Regulations 1995 (S.I. 1644)

Housing Benefit (General) Regulations (Northern Ireland) 1987 (461)

Housing Benefit (General) Regulations 1987 (S.I. 1971)

Housing Benefit (State Pension Credit) Regulations (Northern Ireland) 2003 (197)

Housing Benefit (Supply of Information) Regulations 1988 (S.I. 662)

Housing Benefit and Council Tax Benefit (Abolition of Benefit Periods) Amendment Regulations 2004 (S.I. 14)

Housing Benefit and Council Tax Benefit (Decisions and Appeals) Regulations 2001 (S.I. 1002)

Housing Benefit and Council Tax Benefit (General) Amendment Regulations 1997 (S.I. 852)

Housing Benefit and Council Tax Benefit (State Pension Credit and Miscellaneous Amendments) Regulations 2003 (S.I. 2275)

Housing Benefit and Council Tax Benefit (State Pension Credit) (Abolition of Benefit Periods) Amendment Regulations 2003 (S.I. 1338)

Housing Benefit and Council Tax Benefit (State Pension Credit) Regulations 2003 (S.I. 325)

Housing Grants (Additional Purposes) (England) Order 2000 (S.I. 1492)

Housing Grants (Additional Purposes) (Wales) Order 2001 (S.I. 2070)

Housing Grants (Assessment of Contributions) (Scotland) Regulations 2003 (S.S.I. 461)

Housing Renewal Grants (Common Parts) Order 1999 (S.I. 68)

Housing Renewal Grants (Prescribed Form and Particulars) (Welsh Form and Particulars) Regulations 1998 (S.I. 1113)

Housing Renewal Grants (Prescribed Form and Particulars) Regulations 1996 (S.I. 2891)

Housing Renewal Grants and Home Repair Assistance (Amendment) Regulations 1996 (S.I. 3119)

Housing Renewal Grants Regulations 1996 (S.I. 2890)

Housing Renovation etc Grants (Reduction of Grant) Regulations (Northern Ireland) 1997 (456)

Housing Support Services (Northern Ireland) Order 2002 (S.I. 3154)

Hovercraft (Fees) Regulations 1997 (S.I. 320)

Hovercraft (General) Order 1972 (S.I. 674)

Huddersfield Central Primary Care Trust (Establishment) Order 2002 (S.I. 358)

Huddersfield Health Care Services National Health Service Trust (Establishment) Order 1992 (S.I. 2487)

Hull and East Riding Community Health National Health Service Trust (Establishment) Order 1999 (S.I. 2688)

Hull and East Yorkshire Hospitals National Health Service Trust (Establishment) Order 1999 (S.I. 2675)

Hull and Holderness Community Health National Health Service Trust (Establishment) Amendment Order 1996 (S.I. 988)

Hull and Holderness Community Health National Health Service Trust (Establishment) Order 1993 (S.I. 2554)

Human Organ Transplants (Northern Ireland) Order 1989 (S.I. 2408)

Human Organ Transplants (Supply of Information) Regulations 1989 (S.I. 2108)

Human Rights Act 1998 (Designated Derogation) Order 2001 (S.I. 3644)

Humber Bridge (Revision of Tolls and Vehicle Classification) Order 1997 (S.I. 1950)

Humber Bridge (Revision of Tolls and Vehicle Classification) Order 2000 (S.I. 264)

Humber Bridge (Revision of Tolls) Order 2002 (S.I. 786)

Humberside (Coroners) (Amendment) Order 1996 (S.I. 787)

Humberside (Coroners) Order 1996 (S.I. 658)

Humberside (Staff Transfer) Order 1996 (S.I. 397)

Humberside (Structural Change) Order 1995 (S.I. 600)

Humberside Ambulance Service National Health Service Trust (Establishment) Amendment Order 1993 (S.I. 318)

Humberside Ambulance Service National Health Service Trust (Establishment) Order 1992 (S.I. 2488)

Humberside Fire Services (Combination Scheme) Order 1995 (S.I. 3132)

Huntingdonshire Primary Care Trust (Establishment) Order 2001 (S.I. 543)

Hyde Park and The Regent's Park (Vehicle Parking) Regulations 1995 (S.I. 993)

Hydrocarbon (Heavy) Oil Regulations 1991 (S.I. 269)

Hydrocarbon Oil (Amendment) (No.2) Regulations 1994 (S.I. 694)

Hydrocarbon Oil (Amendment) Regulations 1985 (S.I. 1033)

Hydrocarbon Oil (Designated Markers) Regulations 1996 (S.I. 1251)

Hydrocarbon Oil (Marking) Regulations 2002 (S.I. 1773)

Hydrocarbon Oil Regulations 1973 (S.I. 1311)

Hyndburn and Ribble Valley Primary Care Trust (Establishment) Order 2001 (S.I. 3489)

Immigration (Control of Entry through Republic of Ireland) Order 1972 (S.I. 1610)

Immigration (Designation of Travel Bans) (Amendment No 2) Order 2002 (S.I. 795)

Immigration (Designation of Travel Bans) (Amendment No 3) Order 2002 (S.I. 3018)

Immigration (Designation of Travel Bans) (Amendment) Order 2001 (S.I. 2377)

Immigration (Designation of Travel Bans) (Amendment) Order 2002 (S.I. 192)

Immigration (Designation of Travel Bans) (Amendment) Order 2003 (S.I. 236)

Immigration (Designation of Travel Bans) Order 2000 (S.I. 2724)

Immigration (European Economic Area) (Amendment) Regulations 2001 (S.I. 865)

Immigration (European Economic Area) Regulations 2000 (S.I. 2326)

Immigration (Guernsey) Order 1993 (S.I. 1796)

Immigration (Jersey) Order 1993 (S.I. 1797)

Immigration (Leave to Enter and Remain) Order 2000 (S.I. 1161)

Immigration (Leave to Remain) (Fees) Regulations 2003 (S.I. 1711)

Immigration (Leave to Remain) (Prescribed Forms and Procedures) Regulations 2003 (S.I. 1712)

Immigration (Passenger Transit Visa) Order 2003 (S.I. 1185)

Immigration (Provision of Physical Data) Regulations 2003 (S.I. 1875)

Immigration (Regularisation Period for Overstayers) Regulations 2000 (S.I. 265)

Immigration (Removal Directions) Regulations 2000 (S.I. 2243)

Immigration (Restrictions on Employment) Order 1996 (S.I. 3225)

Immigration (Transit Visa) (Amendment No 2) Order 1998 (S.I. 1014)

Leeds Community and Mental Health Services Teaching National Health Service Trust (Establishment) Amendment Order 1998 (S.I. 322)

Leeds Community and Mental Health Services Teaching National Health Service Trust (Establishment) Order 1992 (S.I. 2497)

Leeds North East Primary Care Trust (Establishment) Order 2001 (S.I. 3610)

Leeds North West Primary Care Trust (Establishment) Order 2001 (S.I. 3660)

Leeds Supertram (Extension) Order 2001 (S.I. 1347)

Leeds Teaching Hospitals National Health Service Trust (Establishment) Order 1998 (S.I. 837)

Leeds West Primary Care Trust (Establishment) Order 2001 (S.I. 3609)

Legal Advice and Assistance (Amendment No 2) Regulations (Northern Ireland) 2001 (113)

Legal Advice and Assistance (Amendment) Regulations (Northern Ireland) 2002 (62)

Legal Advice and Assistance (Amendment) Regulations 1986 (S.I. 275)

Legal Advice and Assistance (Financial Conditions) Regulations (Northern Ireland) 2001 (112)

Legal Advice and Assistance (Financial Conditions) Regulations (Northern Ireland) 2002 (61)

Legal Advice and Assistance Regulations (Northern Ireland) 1981 (366)

Legal Advice and Assistance Regulations 1989 (S.I. 340)

Legal Aid (Assessment of Resources) Regulations (Northern Ireland) 1981 (189)

Legal Aid (Financial Conditions) Regulations (Northern Ireland) 2001 (111)

Legal Aid (Financial Conditions) Regulations (Northern Ireland) 2002 (60)

Legal Aid (Remuneration of Solicitors and Counsel in County Court Proceedings) (Amendment) Order (Northern Ireland) 1982 (350)

Legal Aid (Remuneration of Solicitors and Counsel in County Court Proceedings) Order (Northern Ireland) 1981 (179)

Legal Aid in Criminal and Care Proceedings (Costs) Regulations 1989 (S.I. 343)

Legal Aid in Criminal and Care Proceedings (General) Regulations 1989 (S.I. 344)

Legal Aid in Criminal and Care Proceedings Regulations 1989 (S.I. 343)

Legal Aid in Criminal Proceedings (Costs) (Amendment) Rules (Northern Ireland) 1992 (314)

Legal Aid in Family Proceedings (Remuneration) Regulations 1991 (S.I. 2038)

Legal Aid, Advice and Assistance (Northern Ireland) Order 1981 (S.I. 228)

Legal Officers (Annual Fees) Order 2001 (S.I. 2665)

Legal Officers (Annual Fees) Order 2002 (S.I. 1893)

Leicester City West Primary Care Trust (Establishment) Order 2001 (S.I. 136)

Leicester College (Government) Regulations 1999 (S.I. 709)

Leicester General Hospital National Health Service Trust (Establishment) Order 1992 (S.I. 2472)

Leicester North Station Light Railway Order 1991 (S.I. 1965)

Leicester Royal Infirmary National Health Service Trust (Establishment) Order 1992 (S.I. 2483)

Leicestershire (City of Leicester and District of Rutland) (Structural Change) Order 1996 (S.I. 507)

Leicestershire (Coroners) Order 1997 (S.I. 490)

Leicestershire Ambulance and Paramedic Service National Health Service Trust (Establishment) Amendment (No.2) Order 1997 (S.I. 1482)

Leicestershire Ambulance and Paramedic Service National Health Service Trust (Establishment) Amendment Order 1997 (S.I. 1325)

Leicestershire Ambulance and Paramedic Service National Health Service Trust (Establishment) Order 1993 (S.I. 2558)

Leicestershire and Rutland Healthcare National Health Service Trust (Establishment) Amendment Order 1999 (S.I. 1825)

Leicestershire and Rutland Healthcare National Health Service Trust (Establishment) Order 1998 (S.I. 3069)

Leicestershire and Rutland Healthcare National Health Service Trust Change of Name and (Establishment) Amendment Order 2002 (S.I. 1437)

Leicestershire County Council (City of Leicester and District of Rutland) (Staff Transfer) Order 1997 (S.I. 476)

Leicestershire Fire Services (Combination Scheme) Order 1996 (S.I. 2912)

Leicestershire Mental Health Service and the Fosse Health, Leicestershire Community National Health Service Trusts (Dissolution) Order 1998 (S.I. 3068)

Leicestershire Mental Health Service National Health Service Trust (Establishment) Order 1993 (S.I. 2559)

Leigh Park Education Action Zone Order 1999 (S.I. 3390)

Lerwick Harbour Revision Order 1999 (S.I. 1170)

Less Favoured Area Support Scheme (Scotland) Regulations 2001 (S.S.I. 50)

Less Favoured Area Support Scheme (Scotland) Regulations 2002 (S.S.I. 139)

Less Favoured Area Support Scheme (Scotland) Regulations 2003 (S.S.I. 129)

Less Favoured Area Support Scheme (Scotland) Regulations 2004 (S.S.I. 70)

Levying Bodies (General) Regulations 1992 (S.I. 2903)

Lewisham Hospital National Health Service Trust (Establishment) Order 1993 (S.I. 694)

Liberia (Freezing of Funds and Economic Resources) (Amendment) Regulations 2004 (S.I. 1710)

Liberia (Freezing of Funds and Economic Resources) Regulations 2004 (S.I. 1264)

Liberia (Restrictive Measures) (Overseas Territories) (Amendment) Order 2004 (S.I. 1112)

Liberia (Restrictive Measures) (Overseas Territories) Order 2004 (S.I. 347)

Liberia (United Nations Sanctions) (Channel Islands) Order 2001 (S.I. 949)

Liberia (United Nations Sanctions) (Isle of Man) Order 2001 (S.I. 948)

Liberia (United Nations Sanctions) (Isle of Man) Order 2004 (S.I. 305)

Liberia (United Nations Sanctions) (Overseas Territories) (No.2) Order 2001 (S.I. 1867)

Liberia (United Nations Sanctions) (Overseas Territories) Order 2001 (S.I. 946)

Liberia (United Nations Sanctions) Order 2001 (S.I. 947)

Liberia (United Nations Sanctions) (Channel Islands) Order 2004 (S.I. 306)

Libya (United Nations Sanctions) (Channel Islands) Order 1992 (S.I. 977)

Libya (United Nations Sanctions) (Channel Islands) Order 1993 (S.I. 2811)

Libya (United Nations Sanctions) (Dependent Territories) Order 1992 (S.I. 976)

Libya (United Nations Sanctions) (Dependent Territories) Order 1993 (S.I. 2808)

Milk Marketing Board (Residuary Functions) Regulations 1994 (S.I. 2759)

Milton Keynes Community Health National Health Service Trust (Dissolution) Order 2000 (S.I. 2662)

Milton Keynes General National Health Service Trust (Establishment) Order 1991 (S.I. 2372)

Milton Keynes Primary Care Trust (Establishment) Order 2000 (S.I. 2015)

Minced Meat and Meat Preparations (Hygiene) Regulations (Northern Ireland) 1997 (495)

Minced Meat and Meat Preparations (Hygiene) Regulations 1995 (S.I. 3205)

Mineral Hydrocarbons in Food Regulations 1966 (S.I. 1073)

Mines (Medical Examinations) Regulations 1964 (S.I. 209)

Mines (Safety of Exit) Regulations 1988 (S.I. 1729)

Mineworkers Pension Scheme (Modification) Regulations 1994 (S.I. 2577)

Minibus and Other Section 19 Permit Buses Regulations 1987 (S.I. 1230)

Ministry of Agriculture, Fisheries and Food (Dissolution) Order 2002 (S.I. 794)

Ministry of Defence Police (Representation at Disciplinary Proceedings) Regulations 1988 (S.I. 1099)

Ministry of Defence Police Appeal Tribunals Regulations 2004 (S.I. 652)

Mink Keeping (England) Order 2000 (S.I. 3402)

Mink Keeping Order 1997 (S.I. 3002)

Miscellaneous Food Additives (Amendment) (England) (No.2) Regulations 2001 (S.I. 3775)

Miscellaneous Food Additives (Amendment) (England) Regulations 2001 (S.I. 60)

Miscellaneous Food Additives (Amendment) (England) Regulations 2003 (S.I. 1008)

Miscellaneous Food Additives (Amendment) (England) Regulations 2004 (S.I. 2601)

Miscellaneous Food Additives (Amendment) (Wales) Regulations 2001 (S.I. 1787)

Miscellaneous Food Additives (Amendment) (Wales) Regulations 2002 (S.I. 329)

Miscellaneous Food Additives (Amendment) (Wales) Regulations 2003 (S.I. 945)

Miscellaneous Food Additives (Amendment) Regulations (Northern Ireland) 1999 (244)

Miscellaneous Food Additives (Amendment) Regulations (Northern Ireland) 2001 (46)

Miscellaneous Food Additives (Amendment) Regulations 1997 (S.I. 1413)

Miscellaneous Food Additives (Amendment) Regulations 1999 (S.I. 1136)

Miscellaneous Food Additives Amendment (Scotland) Regulations 2004 (S.S.I. 413)

Miscellaneous Food Additives Regulations 1995 (S.I. 3187)

Miscellaneous Products of Animal Origin (Import Conditions) Regulations (Northern Ireland) 1999 (189)

Miscellaneous Products of Animal Origin (Import Conditions) Regulations 1999 (S.I. 157)

Misuse of Drugs (Amendment) (No.2) Regulations (Northern Ireland) 1995 (480)

Misuse of Drugs (Amendment) Regulations (Northern Ireland) 1987 (68)

Misuse of Drugs (Amendment) Regulations (Northern Ireland) 1988 (206)

Misuse of Drugs (Amendment) Regulations (Northern Ireland) 1989 (346)

Misuse of Drugs (Amendment) Regulations (Northern Ireland) 1991 (1)

Misuse of Drugs (Amendment) Regulations (Northern Ireland) 1995 (305)

Misuse of Drugs (Amendment) Regulations (Northern Ireland) 1996 (353)

Misuse of Drugs (Amendment) Regulations (Northern Ireland) 1998 (128)

Misuse of Drugs (Amendment) Regulations (Northern Ireland) 1999 (251)

Misuse of Drugs (Licence Fees) (Amendment) Regulations 1987 (S.I. 298)

Misuse of Drugs (Licence Fees) (Amendment) Regulations 1988 (S.I. 311)

Misuse of Drugs (Licence Fees) (Amendment) Regulations 1989 (S.I. 245)

Misuse of Drugs (Licence Fees) (Amendment) Regulations 1991 (S.I. 339)

Misuse of Drugs (Licence Fees) (Amendment) Regulations 1992 (S.I. 315)

Misuse of Drugs (Licence Fees) (Amendment) Regulations 1993 (S.I. 539)

Misuse of Drugs (Licence Fees) (Amendment) Regulations 1994 (S.I. 535)

Misuse of Drugs (Licence Fees) (Amendment) Regulations 1995 (S.I. 506)

Misuse of Drugs (Licence Fees) (Amendment) Regulations 1996 (S.I. 596)

Misuse of Drugs (Licence Fees) (Amendment) Regulations 1999 (S.I. 741)

Misuse of Drugs (Licence Fees) Regulations 1986 (S.I. 416)

Misuse of Drugs (Northern Ireland) Regulations 1986 (52)

Misuse of Drugs Regulations (Northern Ireland) 2002 (1)

Misuse of Drugs Regulations 2001 (S.I. 3998)

Money Laundering Regulations 1993 (S.I. 1933)

Money Laundering Regulations 2001 (S.I. 3641)

Money Laundering Regulations 2003 (S.I. 3075)

Montrose Harbour Revision Order 1991 (S.I. 1745)

Montrose Harbour Revision Order 1999 (S.S.I. 200)

Moorfields Eye Hospital National Health Service Trust (Establishment) Order 1994 (S.I. 403)

Morecambe Bay Hospitals National Health Service Trust (Establishment) Order 1998 (S.I. 816)

Morecambe Bay Primary Care Trust (Establishment) Order 2000 (S.I. 2392)

Morriston Hospital National Health Service Trust (Establishment) Order 1994 (S.I. 317)

Motor Cars (Driving Instruction) Regulations (Northern Ireland) 1991 (373)

Motor Cars (Driving Instruction) Regulations 1989 (S.I. 2057)

Motor Cycles Etc (EC Type Approval) Regulations 1999 (S.I. 2920)

Motor Cycles Etc (Single Vehicle Approval) Regulations 2003 (S.I. 1959)

Motor Fuel (Composition and Content) Regulations 1999 (S.I. 3107)

Motor Vehicle Testing (Amendment) (Fees) Regulations (Northern Ireland) 1999 (78)

Motor Vehicle Testing (Amendment) (Fees) Regulations (Northern Ireland) 2001 (246)

Motor Vehicle Testing (Amendment) (Fees) Regulations (Northern Ireland) 2002 (47)

Motor Vehicle Testing (Amendment) (Fees) Regulations (Northern Ireland) 2003 (101)

Motor Vehicle Testing (Amendment) Regulations (Northern Ireland) 1996 (140)

Motor Vehicle Testing (Amendment) Regulations (Northern Ireland) 1998 (74)

Motor Vehicle Testing (Amendment) Regulations (Northern Ireland) 2000 (151)

Motor Vehicle Testing (Amendment) Regulations (Northern Ireland) 2001 (364)

National Assistance (Sums for Personal Requirements) (England) Regulations 2002 (S.I. 411)

National Assistance (Sums for Personal Requirements) (England) Regulations 2003 (S.I. 628)

National Assistance (Sums for Personal Requirements) (Scotland) Regulations 2001 (S.S.I. 100)

National Assistance (Sums for Personal Requirements) (Scotland) Regulations 2002 (S.S.I. 85)

National Assistance (Sums for Personal Requirements) (Scotland) Regulations 2003 (S.S.I. 86)

National Assistance (Sums for Personal Requirements) (Wales) Regulations 2001 (S.I. 1408)

National Assistance (Sums for Personal Requirements) (Wales) Regulations 2002 (S.I. 815)

National Assistance (Sums for Personal Requirements) (Wales) Regulations 2003 (S.I. 892)

National Assistance (Sums for Personal Requirements) Regulations 2000 (S.I. 798)

National Blood Authority Regulations 1993 (S.I. 586)

National Board for Nursing, Midwifery and Health Visiting for England (Constitution and Administration) Amendment Order 1997 (S.I. 1963)

National Board for Nursing, Midwifery and Health Visiting for England (Constitution and Administration) Amendment Order 1999 (S.I. 766)

National Care Standards Commission (Children's Rights Director) Regulations 2002 (S.I. 1250)

National Care Standards Commission (Director of Private and Voluntary Health Care) Regulations 2002 (S.I. 603)

National Care Standards Commission (Fees and Frequency of Inspections) (Adoption Agencies) Regulations 2003 (S.I. 368)

National Care Standards Commission (Fees and Frequency of Inspections) (Amendment) Regulations 2002 (S.I. 1505)

National Care Standards Commission (Fees and Frequency of Inspections) Amendment (No.2) Regulations 2002 (S.I. 2070)

National Care Standards Commission (Fees and Frequency of Inspections) Amendment (No.3) Regulations 2002 (S.I. 3211)

National Care Standards Commission (Fees and Frequency of Inspections) Regulations 2001 (S.I. 3980)

National Care Standards Commission (Fees and Frequency of Inspections) Regulations 2003 (S.I. 753)

National Care Standards Commission (Inspection of Schools and Colleges) Regulations 2002 (S.I. 552)

National Care Standards Commission (Membership and Procedure) Regulations 2001 (S.I. 1042)

National Care Standards Commission (Registration) (Amendment) Regulations 2003 (S.I. 369)

National Care Standards Commission (Registration) Regulations 2001 (S.I. 3969)

National Clinical Assessment Authority (Establishment and Constitution) Order 2000 (S.I. 2961)

National Clinical Assessment Authority Regulations 2000 (S.I. 2962)

National Crime Squad (Complaints) (Amendment) Regulations 1999 (S.I. 1266)

National Crime Squad (Complaints) Regulations 1998 (S.I. 638)

National Crime Squad (Discipline) (Senior Police Members) Regulations 1998 (S.I. 637)

National Crime Squad (Dispensation from Requirement to Investigate Complaints) Regulations 2003 (S.I. 2601)

National Crime Squad (Secretary of State's Objectives) Order 1999 (S.I. 821)

National Crime Squad (Senior Police Members) (Appeals) Order 1998 (S.I. 639)

National Health Service (Amendments concerning Supplementary and Independent Nurse Prescribing) (Wales) Regulations 2003 (S.I. 2624)

National Health Service (Amendments Relating to Prescribing by Nurses and Pharmacists etc.) (England) Regulations 2003 (S.I. 699)

National Health Service (Appointment of Consultants) (Scotland) Regulations 1993 (S.I. 994)

National Health Service (Appointment of Consultants) (Wales) Regulations 1996 (S.I. 1313)

National Health Service (Appointment of Consultants) Regulations 1996 (S.I. 701)

National Health Service (Association of Community Health Councils) Regulations 1977 (S.I. 874)

National Health Service (Borrowing and Loans from Endowments) (Scotland) Regulations 2004 (S.S.I. 16)

National Health Service (Charges for Appliances) Regulations 1974 (S.I. 284)

National Health Service (Charges for Drugs and Appliances and Travelling Expenses and Remission of Charges) Amendment Regulations 1999 (S.I. 767)

National Health Service (Charges for Drugs and Appliances) (Scotland) Regulations 2001 (S.S.I. 430)

National Health Service (Charges for Drugs and Appliances) (Wales) Regulations 2001 (S.I. 1358)

National Health Service (Charges for Drugs and Appliances) Regulations 2000 (S.I. 620)

National Health Service (Charges to Overseas Visitors) (Scotland) Regulations 1989 (S.I. 364)

National Health Service (Charges to Overseas Visitors) Regulations 1989 (S.I. 306)

National Health Service (Choice of Medical Practitioner) (Scotland) Amendment Regulations 2000 (S.S.I. 191)

National Health Service (Choice of Medical Practitioner) (Scotland) Amendment Regulations 2001 (S.S.I. 85)

National Health Service (Choice of Medical Practitioner) (Scotland) Regulations 1998 (S.I. 659)

National Health Service (Choice of Medical Practitioner) Amendment (Wales) Regulations 2000 (S.I. 1708)

National Health Service (Choice of Medical Practitioner) Amendment Regulations 1999 (S.I. 3179)

National Health Service (Choice of Medical Practitioner) Regulations 1998 (S.I. 668)

National Health Service (Clinical Negligence and Other Risks Indemnity Scheme) (Scotland) Regulations 2000 (S.S.I. 54)

National Health Service (Clinical Negligence Scheme) Regulations 1996 (S.I. 251)

National Health Service (Compensation for Premature Retirement) (Scotland) Amendment Regulations 1985 (S.I. 2036)

National Health Service (Compensation for Premature Retirement) (Scotland) Regulations 1981 (S.I. 1785)

National Health Service (Compensation for Premature Retirement) Amendment Regulations 1985 (S.I. 1659)

National Health Service (Compensation for Premature Retirement) Regulations 1981 (S.I. 1263)

National Health Service (Compensation for Premature Retirement) Regulations 2002 (S.I. 1311)

National Health Service (Constitution of Health Boards) (Scotland) Order 1974 (S.I. 267)

National Health Service (Dental Charges) (Scotland) Amendment (No.2) Regulations 1998 (S.I. 2258)

National Health Service (General Medical Services) (Amendment) (No.3) (Wales) Regulations 2003 (S.I. 1005)

National Health Service (General Medical Services) (Amendment) (Wales) (No.2) Regulations 2002 (S.I. 1896)

National Health Service (General Medical Services) (Amendment) (Wales) Regulations 2002 (S.I. 916)

National Health Service (General Medical Services) (Amendment) (Wales) Regulations 2003 (S.I. 143)

National Health Service (General Medical Services) (Electronic Communications) Order 2001 (S.I. 2890)

National Health Service (General Medical Services) (Scotland) Amendment (No.2) Regulations 1997 (S.I. 1473)

National Health Service (General Medical Services) (Scotland) Amendment (No.2) Regulations 1998 (S.I. 660)

National Health Service (General Medical Services) (Scotland) Amendment (No.2) Regulations 1999 (S.I. 1057)

National Health Service (General Medical Services) (Scotland) Amendment (No.2) Regulations 2000 (S.S.I. 190)

National Health Service (General Medical Services) (Scotland) Amendment (No.2) Regulations 2003 (S.S.I. 310)

National Health Service (General Medical Services) (Scotland) Amendment (No.3) Regulations 1999 (S.I. 1620)

National Health Service (General Medical Services) (Scotland) Amendment (No.3) Regulations 2003 (S.S.I. 443)

National Health Service (General Medical Services) (Scotland) Amendment (No.4) Regulations 1999 (S.S.I. 54)

National Health Service (General Medical Services) (Scotland) Amendment Regulations 1995 (S.I. 3199)

National Health Service (General Medical Services) (Scotland) Amendment Regulations 1996 (S.I. 842)

National Health Service (General Medical Services) (Scotland) Amendment Regulations 1997 (S.I. 943)

National Health Service (General Medical Services) (Scotland) Amendment Regulations 1998 (S.I. 4)

National Health Service (General Medical Services) (Scotland) Amendment Regulations 1999 (S.I. 749)

National Health Service (General Medical Services) (Scotland) Amendment Regulations 2000 (S.S.I. 28)

National Health Service (General Medical Services) (Scotland) Amendment Regulations 2001 (S.S.I. 119)

National Health Service (General Medical Services) (Scotland) Amendment Regulations 2002 (S.S.I. 438)

National Health Service (General Medical Services) (Scotland) Amendment Regulations 2003 (S.S.I. 11)

National Health Service (General Medical Services) (Scotland) Amendment Regulations 2004 (S.S.I. 41)

National Health Service (General Medical Services) (Scotland) Regulations 1995 (S.I. 416)

National Health Service (General Medical Services) Amendment (No.2) (Wales) Regulations 2000 (S.I. 1992)

National Health Service (General Medical Services) Amendment (No.2) (Wales) Regulations 2001 (S.I. 1788)

National Health Service (General Medical Services) Amendment (No.2) Regulations 1993 (S.I. 2421)

National Health Service (General Medical Services) Amendment (No.2) Regulations 1994 (S.I. 2620)

National Health Service (General Medical Services) Amendment (No.2) Regulations 1995 (S.I. 3093)

National Health Service (General Medical Services) Amendment (No.2) Regulations 1997 (S.I. 981)

National Health Service (General Medical Services) Amendment (No.2) Regulations 1998 (S.I. 2838)

National Health Service (General Medical Services) Amendment (No.2) Regulations 1999 (S.I. 1627)

National Health Service (General Medical Services) Amendment (No.2) Regulations 2000 (S.I. 601)

National Health Service (General Medical Services) Amendment (No.2) Regulations 2001 (S.I. 1178)

National Health Service (General Medical Services) Amendment (No.3) (Wales) Regulations 2000 (S.I. 1887)

National Health Service (General Medical Services) Amendment (No.3) Regulations 1997 (S.I. 2468)

National Health Service (General Medical Services) Amendment (No.3) Regulations 2000 (S.I. 1645)

National Health Service (General Medical Services) Amendment (No.3) Regulations 2001 (S.I. 3386)

National Health Service (General Medical Services) Amendment (No.3) Regulations 2002 (S.I. 1768)

National Health Service (General Medical Services) Amendment (No.4) Regulations 2000 (S.I. 2383)

National Health Service (General Medical Services) Amendment (No.4) Regulations 2001 (S.I. 3742)

National Health Service (General Medical Services) Amendment (Wales) Regulations 2000 (S.I. 1707)

National Health Service (General Medical Services) Amendment (Wales) Regulations 2001 (S.I. 1833)

National Health Service (General Medical Services) Amendment Regulations 1992 (S.I. 2412)

National Health Service (General Medical Services) Amendment Regulations 1993 (S.I. 540)

National Health Service (General Medical Services) Amendment Regulations 1994 (S.I. 633)

National Health Service (General Medical Services) Amendment Regulations 1995 (S.I. 80)

National Health Service (General Medical Services) Amendment Regulations 1996 (S.I. 702)

National Health Service (General Medical Services) Amendment Regulations 1997 (S.I. 730)

National Health Service (General Medical Services) Amendment Regulations 1998 (S.I. 682)

National Health Service (General Medical Services) Amendment Regulations 1999 (S.I. 326)

National Health Service (General Medical Services) Amendment Regulations 2000 (S.I. 220)

National Health Service (General Medical Services) Amendment Regulations 2001 (S.I. 706)

National Health Service (General Medical Services) Amendment Regulations 2002 (S.I. 554)

National Health Service (General Medical Services) and (Pharmaceutical Services) (Amendment) (Wales) Regulations 2003 (S.I. 139)

National Health Service (General Medical Services) Regulations 1992 (S.I. 635)

Natural Mineral Water, Spring Water and Bottled Drinking Water Regulations (Northern Ireland) 1999 (301)

Natural Mineral Water, Spring Water and Bottled Drinking Water Regulations 1999 (S.I. 1540)

Nature Conservation and Amenity Lands (Amendment) (Northern Ireland) 1989 (S.I. 492)

Nature Conservation and Amenity Lands (Northern Ireland) Order 1985 (S.I. 170)

Naval Custody Rules 2000 (S.I. 2367)

Naval, Military and Air Forces Etc (Disablement and Death) Service Pensions Order 1983 (S.I. 883)

NCIS (Complaints) (Amendment) Regulations 1999 (S.I. 1273)

NCIS (Complaints) Regulations 1998 (S.I. 641)

NCIS (Secretary of State's Objectives) Order 1999 (S.I. 822)

Neath Port Talbot and Swansea (Trebanos and Clydach) Order 2002 (S.I. 652)

Nelson and West Merton Primary Care Trust (Establishment) Order 2000 (S.I. 254)

Nene Valley Light Railway Order 1986 (S.I. 1000)

Network Rail (West Coast Main Line) Order 2003 (S.I. 1075)

Nevill Hall and District National Health Service Trust (Establishment) Amendment Order 1997 (S.I. 2605)

Nevill Hall and District National Health Service Trust (Establishment) Order 1993 (S.I. 2840)

New Forest (Confirmation of the Byelaws of the Verderers of the New Forest) Order 1999 (S.I. 2134)

New Forest Primary Care Trust (Establishment) Order 2001 (S.I. 601)

New Northern Ireland Assembly Elections (Returning Officer's Charges) Order 1998 (S.I. 1493)

New Possibilities National Health Service Trust (Establishment) Order 1993 (S.I. 2629)

New Possibilities National Health Service Trust Dissolution Order 1993 (S.I. 3141)

New Roads and Street Works Act 1991 (Commencement No.5 and Transitional Provisions and Savings) Order 1992 (S.I. 2984)

New School (Admissions) (England) Regulations 1999 (S.I. 2666)

New Schools (General) (England) Regulations 2003 (S.I. 1558)

Newark and Sherwood Primary Care Trust (Establishment) Order 2000 (S.I. 223)

Newbury and Community Primary Care Trust (Establishment) Order 2001 (S.I. 524)

Newcastle City Health and the Northumberland Mental Health National Health Service Trusts (Dissolution) Order 2001 (S.I. 214)

Newcastle City Health National Health Service Trust (Establishment) Order 1994 (S.I. 851)

Newcastle Mental Health National Health Service Trust Dissolution Order 1994 (S.I. 861)

Newcastle Primary Care Trust (Establishment) Order 2001 (S.I. 513)

Newcastle upon Tyne Hospitals National Health Service Trust (Establishment) Amendment Order 2001 (S.I. 931)

Newcastle upon Tyne Hospitals National Health Service Trust (Establishment) Order 1998 (S.I. 827)

Newcastle, North Tyneside and Northumberland Mental Health National Health Service Trust (Establishment) Order 2001 (S.I. 213)

Newcastle-under-Lyme Primary Care Trust (Establishment) Order 2001 (S.I. 3829)

Newham Community Health Services National Health Service Trust (Establishment) Amendment Order 1999 (S.I. 1773)

Newham Community Health Services National Health Service Trust (Establishment) Order 1995 (S.I. 842)

Newham Education Action Zone (Variation) Order 2000 (S.I. 3337)

Newham Healthcare National Health Service Trust (Establishment) Order 1994 (S.I. 308)

Newham Primary Care Trust (Establishment) Order 2001 (S.I. 350)

Newport (Caerleon and Malpas) Order 2002 (S.I. 3271)

NHS 24 (Scotland) Order 2001 (S.S.I. 137)

NHS Bodies and Local Authorities Partnership Arrangements Regulations 2000 (S.I. 617)

NHS Education for Scotland Order 2002 (S.S.I. 103)

NHS Professionals Special Health Authority (Establishment and Constitution) Amendment Order 2004 (S.I. 648)

NHS Professionals Special Health Authority (Establishment and Constitution) Order 2003 (S.I. 3059)

NHS Professionals Special Health Authority Regulations 2003 (S.I. 3060)

NHS Quality Improvement Scotland Order 2002 (S.S.I. 534)

NHSU Regulations 2003 (S.I. 2773)

Nitrate Sensitive Areas Regulations 1994 (S.I. 1729)

Nitrate Vulnerable Zones (Additional Designations) (England) Regulations 2002 (S.I. 2525)

Nitrate Vulnerable Zones (Grants) (Scotland) Scheme 2003 (S.S.I. 52)

Non Commercial Movement of Pet Animals (England) Regulations 2004 (S.I. 2363)

Non Domestic Rating (Alteration of Lists and Appeals) (Amendment) Regulations 1994 (S.I. 1809)

Non-automatic Weighing Instruments Regulations 2000 (S.I. 3236)

Non-Contentious Probate Fees Order 1999 (S.I. 688)

Non-Contentious Probate Rules 1987 (S.I. 2024)

Non-Domestic Rates (Levying) (Scotland) Regulations 2001 (S.S.I. 71)

Non-Domestic Rates (Levying) (Scotland) Regulations 2002 (S.S.I. 91)

Non-Domestic Rates (Levying) (Scotland) Regulations 2003 (S.S.I. 160)

Non-Domestic Rating (Alteration of Lists and Appeals) (Amendment) (England) Regulations 2003 (S.I. 1999)

Non-Domestic Rating (Alteration of Lists and Appeals) Regulations 1993 (S.I. 291)

Non-Domestic Rating (Alteration of Lists and Appeals) (Amendment) (England) Regulations 2002 (S.I. 498)

Non-Domestic Rating (Caravan Sites) Regulations 1990 (S.I. 673)

Non-Domestic Rating (Chargeable Amounts) (England) Regulations 1999 (S.I. 3379)

Non-Domestic Rating (Chargeable Amounts) Regulations 1994 (S.I. 3279)

Non-Domestic Rating (Collection and Enforcement) (Local Lists) Regulations 1989 (S.I. 1058)

Non-Domestic Rating (Demand Notices) (Wales) Regulations 1993 (S.I. 252)

Non-Domestic Rating (Miscellaneous Provisions) (No.2) Regulations 1989 (S.I. 2303)

Non-Domestic Rating (Railways, Telecommunications and Canals) Regulations 1994 (S.I. 3123)

Non-Domestic Rating (Rural Areas and Rateable Value Limits) (Scotland) Order 1997 (S.I. 2827)

Non-Domestic Rating (Rural Settlements) (Wales) Order 1998 (S.I. 2963)

North Mersey Community National Health Service Trust (Establishment) Amendment Order 1993 (S.I. 155)

North Mersey Community National Health Service Trust (Establishment) Amendment Order 2001 (S.I. 1625)

North Mersey Community National Health Service Trust (Establishment) Order 1991 (S.I. 2376)

North Middlesex Hospital National Health Service Trust (Change of Name) Order 2001 (S.I. 2407)

North Norfolk (Extension and Amendment) Light Railway Order 1987 (S.I. 950)

North Norfolk Primary Care Trust (Establishment) Order 2001 (S.I. 4131)

North Peterborough Primary Care Trust (Establishment) Order 2000 (S.I. 283)

North Sefton & West Lancashire Community National Health Service Trust (Establishment) Amendment Order 2001 (S.I. 1889)

North Sefton & West Lancashire Community National Health Service Trust (Establishment) Order 1999 (S.I. 888)

North Sheffield Primary Care Trust (Establishment) Order 2001 (S.I. 131)

North Staffordshire Combined Healthcare National Health Service Trust (Establishment) Amendment Order 1998 (S.I. 2972)

North Staffordshire Combined Healthcare National Health Service Trust (Establishment) Amendment Order 1999 (S.I. 640)

North Staffordshire Combined Healthcare National Health Service Trust (Establishment) Order 1993 (S.I. 2635)

North Staffordshire Hospital Centre National Health Service Trust (Change of Name) Order 1993 (S.I. 713)

North Staffordshire Hospital Centre National Health Service Trust (Establishment) Order 1992 (S.I. 2559)

North Staffordshire Hospital National Health Service Trust (Change of Name) Order 2003 (S.I. 792)

North Stoke Primary Care Trust (Establishment) Order 2000 (S.I. 2014)

North Tees and Hartlepool National Health Service Trust (Establishment) Order 1999 (S.I. 801)

North Tees Primary Care Trust (Establishment) Order 2001 (S.I. 500)

North Tyneside Health Care National Health Service Trust (Establishment) Order 1993 (S.I. 2624)

North Tyneside Primary Care Trust (Establishment) Order 2001 (S.I. 505)

North Tyneside Steam Railway Light Railway Order 1991 (S.I. 933)

North Wales Ambulance National Health Service Trust (Dissolution) Order 1998 (S.I. 670)

North Wales Ambulance National Health Service Trust (Establishment) Order 1993 (S.I. 2836)

North Warwickshire National Health Service Trust (Establishment) Amendment Order 1998 (S.I. 814)

North Warwickshire National Health Service Trust (Establishment) Order 1992 (S.I. 2552)

North Warwickshire Primary Care Trust (Establishment) Order 2002 (S.I. 634)

North West Anglia Health Care National Health Service Trust (Establishment) Order 1992 (S.I. 2570)

North West London Hospitals National Health Service Trust (Establishment) Order 1999 (S.I. 913)

North West London Mental Health National Health Service Trust (Establishment) Order 1993 (S.I. 34)

North West Wales National Health Service Trust (Establishment) Order 1998 (S.I. 3314)

North Yorkshire (District of York) (Staff Transfer) Order 1996 (S.I. 388)

North Yorkshire (District of York) (Structural and Boundary Changes) Order 1995 (S.I. 610)

North Yorkshire Ambulance Service National Health Service Trust (Establishment) Order 1992 (S.I. 2489)

North Yorkshire Fire Services (Combination Scheme) Order 1995 (S.I. 3133)

Northallerton Health Services National Health Service Trust (Dissolution) Order 2002 (S.I. 1342)

Northallerton Health Services National Health Service Trust (Establishment) Amendment Order 1998 (S.I. 323)

Northallerton Health Services National Health Service Trust (Establishment) Order 1991 (S.I. 2378)

Northampton and Lamport Light Railway Order 1995 (S.I. 1300)

Northampton Community Healthcare and the Rockingham Forest National Health Service Trusts (Dissolution) Order 2001 (S.I. 1291)

Northampton Community Healthcare National Health Service Trust (Establishment) Order 1993 (S.I. 2615)

Northampton General Hospital National Health Service Trust (Establishment) Order 1993 (S.I. 2561)

Northampton Primary Care Trust (Establishment) Order 2002 (S.I. 980)

Northamptonshire Healthcare National Health Service Trust (Establishment) Order 2001 (S.I. 286)

Northamptonshire Heartlands Primary Care Trust (Establishment) Order 2002 (S.I. 997)

Northern Birmingham Community Health and the Southern Birmingham Community Health National Health Service Trusts (Dissolution) Order 1999 (S.I. 3466)

Northern Birmingham Community Health National Health Service Trust (Establishment) Order 1993 (S.I. 2542)

Northern Birmingham Mental Health National Health Service Trust (Establishment) Amendment Order 1999 (S.I. 2955)

Northern Birmingham Mental Health National Health Service Trust (Establishment) Order 1994 (S.I. 173)

Northern Combined Fire Services Area Administration Scheme Order 1995 (S.I. 2633)

Northern Combined Police Area Amalgamation Scheme Order 1995 (S.I. 2641)

Northern Ireland (Date of Next Assembly Poll) Order 2001 (S.I. 3959)

Northern Ireland (Location of Victims Remains) Act 1999 (Immunities and Privileges) Order 1999 (S.I. 1437)

Northern Ireland (Modification of Enactments-;No 1) Order 1973 (S.I. 2163)

Northern Ireland (Modification of Enactments-No 1) Order 1999 (S.I. 663)

Northern Ireland Act 2000 (Restoration of Devolved Government) (No.2) Order 2001 (S.I. 3231)

Northern Ireland Arms Decommissioning Act 1997 (Amnesty Period) Order 2003 (S.I. 426)

Northern Ireland Assembly (Elections) Order 2001 (S.I. 2599)

Northern Ireland Health and Social Care Council (Appointments and Procedure) Regulations (Northern Ireland) 2001 (313)

Northern Lincolnshire and Goole Hospitals National Health Service Trust (Establishment) Order 2000 (S.I. 2885)

Northgate and Prudhoe National Health Service Trust (Establishment) Order 1994 (S.I. 198)

Northgate National Health Service Trust Dissolution Order 1994 (S.I. 829)

Open-ended Investment Companies (Tax) Regulations 1997 (S.I. 1154)

Open-Ended Investment Companies Regulations 2001 (S.I. 1228)

Organic Aid (Scotland) Regulations 1994 (S.I. 1701)

Organic Aid (Scotland) Regulations 2004 (S.S.I. 143)

Organic Farming (Aid) Regulations 1994 (S.I. 1721)

Organic Farming (England Rural Development Programme) Regulations 2001 (S.I. 432)

Organic Farming (England Rural Development Programme) Regulations 2003 (S.I. 1235)

Organic Farming (Northern Ireland) Regulations 2001 (5)

Organic Farming Regulations 1999 (S.I. 590)

Organic Farming Scheme (Wales) Regulations 2001 (S.I. 424)

Organic Products (Amendment) Regulations 1993 (S.I. 405)

Organic Products (Amendment) Regulations 1994 (S.I. 2286)

Organic Products (Amendment) Regulations 1997 (S.I. 166)

Organic Products (Wales) Regulations 2002 (S.I. 3159)

Organic Products Regulations 1992 (S.I. 2111)

Organic Products Regulations 2001 (S.I. 430)

Organisation for Joint Armament Cooperation (Immunities and Privileges) Order 2000 (S.I. 1105)

Organisation for the Prohibition of Chemical Weapons (Immunities and Privileges) Order 2001 (S.I. 3921)

Origin of Goods (Petroleum Products) (Amendment) Regulations 1992 (S.I. 3289)

Origin of Goods (Petroleum Products) Regulations 1988 (S.I. 1)

Orkney Tourist Board Scheme Amendment Order 1995 (S.I. 2238)

Orkney Tourist Board Scheme Order 1995 (S.I. 1888)

OSPAR Commission (Immunities and Privileges) Order 1997 (S.I. 2975)

Oswestry Light Railway Order 1995 (S.I. 2142)

Other Fuel Substitutes (Payment of Excise Duty etc) Regulations 1995 (S.I. 2717)

Other Fuel Substitutes (Rates of Excise Duty etc) Order 1995 (S.I. 2716)

Overhead Lines (Exemption) Regulations 1990 (S.I. 2035)

Overseas Insurers (Tax Representatives) Regulations 1999 (S.I. 881)

Overseas Territories (Zimbabwe) (Restrictive Measures) (Amendment) Order 2004 (S.I. 1111)

Overseas Territories (Zimbabwe) (Restrictive Measures) Order 2002 (S.I. 1077)

Oxford City Primary Care Trust (Establishment) Order 2001 (S.I. 490)

Oxford Radcliffe Hospital National Health Service Trust (Change of Name) Order 1998 (S.I. 1227)

Oxford Radcliffe Hospitals National Health Service Trust (Establishment) Amendment Order 2000 (S.I. 961)

Oxfordshire Ambulance National Health Service Trust (Establishment) Order 1993 (S.I. 2564)

Oxfordshire Community Health National Health Service Trust (Dissolution) Order 2001 (S.I. 771)

Oxfordshire Community Health National Health Service Trust (Establishment) Order 1993 (S.I. 2565)

Oxfordshire Learning Disability National Health Service Trust (Establishment) Order 1992 (S.I. 2574)

Oxfordshire Mental Healthcare National Health Service Trust (Establishment) Amendment Order 1998 (S.I. 1285)

Oxfordshire Mental Healthcare National Health Service Trust (Establishment) Order 1993 (S.I. 2566)

Ozone Monitoring and Information Regulations 1994 (S.I. 440)

Package Holidays and Package Tours Regulations 1992 (S.I. 3288)

Package Travel, Package Holidays and Package Tours Regulations 1992 (S.I. 3288)

Packaging (Essential Requirements) Regulations 1998 (S.I. 1165)

Packaging (Essential Requirements) Regulations 2003 (S.I. 1941)

Packaging of Explosives for Carriage Regulations 1991 (S.I. 2097)

Packaging, Labelling and Carriage of Radioactive Material by Rail Regulations (Northern Ireland) 1998 (132)

Packaging, Labelling and Carriage of Radioactive Material by Rail Regulations 1996 (S.I. 2090)

Packaging, Labelling and Carriage of Radioactive Material by Rail Regulations 2002 (S.I. 2099)

Panels of Persons to Safeguard the Interests of Children (Scotland) Regulations 2001 (S.S.I. 476)

Papworth Hospital National Health Service Trust (Establishment) Order 1992 (S.I. 2568)

Parent Governor Representatives (England) Regulations 2001 (S.I. 478)

Parental Responsibility Agreement Regulations 1991 (S.I. 1478)

Parish Councils (Model Code of Conduct) Order 2001 (S.I. 3576)

Parkside National Health Service Trust (Establishment) Amendment Order 1999 (S.I. 908)

Parkside National Health Service Trust (Establishment) Order 1991 (S.I. 2384)

Parliamentary Constituencies (Wales) Order 1995 (S.I. 1036)

Parliamentary Pensions (Additional Voluntary Contributions Scheme) Regulations 1993 (S.I. 3252)

Parliamentary Pensions (Consolidation and Amendment) Regulations 1993 (S.I. 3253)

Parliamentary Writs Order 1983 (S.I. 605)

Parochial Fees Order 2001 (S.I. 2666)

Parochial Fees Order 2002 (S.I. 1894)

Parochial Fees Order 2003 (S.I. 1932)

Partnerships (Unrestricted Size) No 16 Regulations 2001 (S.I. 1389)

Part-time Workers (Prevention of Less Favourable Treatment) Regulations (Northern Ireland) 2000 (219)

Part-time Workers (Prevention of Less Favourable Treatment) Regulations 2000 (S.I. 1551)

Passenger and Goods Vehicles (Recording Equipment) (Approval of fitters and workshops) (Fees) Regulations 1986 (S.I. 2128)

Passenger and Goods Vehicles (Recording Equipment) Regulations (Northern Ireland) 1996 (145)

Passenger Car (Fuel Consumption and CO2 Emissions Information) Regulations 2001 (S.I. 3523)

Passenger Transport Executives (Capital Finance) Order 1990 (S.I. 720)

Patent Office Trading Fund Order 1991 (S.I. 1796)

Patents (Fees) Rules 1998 (S.I. 1778)

Patents Act 1977 (Isle of Man) (Variation) Order 1990 (S.I. 2295)

Patents Act 1977 (Isle of Man) Order 1978 (S.I. 621)

Patents Rules 1995 (S.I. 2093)

Paternity and Adoption Leave Regulations (Northern Ireland) 2002 (377)

Paternity and Adoption Leave Regulations 2002 (S.I. 2788)

Pathfinder National Health Service Trust (Change of Name) Order 1999 (S.I. 1384)

Pesticides (Maximum Residue Levels in Crops, Food and Feeding Stuffs) (National Limits) (Amendment) Regulations (Northern Ireland) 1995 (460)

Pesticides (Maximum Residue Levels in Crops, Food and Feeding Stuffs) (National Limits) (Amendment) Regulations (Northern Ireland) 1997 (243)

Pesticides (Maximum Residue Levels in Crops, Food and Feeding Stuffs) (National Limits) (Amendment) Regulations (Northern Ireland) 1999 (320)

Pesticides (Maximum Residue Levels in Crops, Food and Feeding Stuffs) (National Limits) Regulations (Northern Ireland) 1995 (32)

Pesticides (Maximum Residue Levels in Crops, Food and Feeding Stuffs) (Scotland) Amendment (No.2) Regulations 2001 (S.S.I. 221)

Pesticides (Maximum Residue Levels in Crops, Food and Feeding Stuffs) (Scotland) Amendment (No.2) Regulations 2002 (S.S.I. 489)

Pesticides (Maximum Residue Levels in Crops, Food and Feeding Stuffs) (Scotland) Amendment (No.2) Regulations 2003 (S.S.I. 445)

Pesticides (Maximum Residue Levels in Crops, Food and Feeding Stuffs) (Scotland) Amendment (No.2) Regulations 2004 (S.S.I. 220)

Pesticides (Maximum Residue Levels in Crops, Food and Feeding Stuffs) (Scotland) Amendment (No.3) Regulations 2001 (S.S.I. 435)

Pesticides (Maximum Residue Levels in Crops, Food and Feeding Stuffs) (Scotland) Amendment Regulations 2001 (S.S.I. 84)

Pesticides (Maximum Residue Levels in Crops, Food and Feeding Stuffs) (Scotland) Amendment Regulations 2002 (S.S.I. 271)

Pesticides (Maximum Residue Levels in Crops, Food and Feeding Stuffs) (Scotland) Amendment Regulations 2003 (S.S.I. 118)

Pesticides (Maximum Residue Levels in Crops, Food and Feeding Stuffs) (Scotland) Amendment Regulations 2004 (S.S.I. 104)

Pesticides (Maximum Residue Levels in Crops, Food and Feeding Stuffs) (Scotland) Regulations 2000 (S.S.I. 22)

Pesticides (Maximum Residue Levels in Crops, Food and Feeding Stuffs) Regulations (Northern Ireland) 2002 (20)

Pesticides (Maximum Residue Levels in Crops, Food, and Feeding Stuffs) (National Limits) (Amendment) Regulations (Northern Ireland) 1996 (526)

Pet Travel Scheme (Pilot Arrangements) (England) (Amendment) (No.2) Order 2002 (S.I. 2850)

Pet Travel Scheme (Pilot Arrangements) (England) (Amendment) (No.3) Order 2000 (S.I. 1641)

Pet Travel Scheme (Pilot Arrangements) (England) (Amendment) Order 2000 (S.I. 1298)

Pet Travel Scheme (Pilot Arrangements) (England) (Amendment) Order 2001 (S.I. 6)

Pet Travel Scheme (Pilot Arrangements) (England) (Amendment) Order 2002 (S.I. 1011)

Pet Travel Scheme (Pilot Arrangements) (England) (Amendment) Order 2004 (S.I. 828)

Pet Travel Scheme (Pilot Arrangements) (England) Order 1999 (S.I. 3443)

Pet Travel Scheme (Scotland) Order 2003 (S.S.I. 229)

Peterborough (Coroners) Order 1998 (S.I. 362)

Peterborough Hospitals National Health Service Trust (Establishment) Order 1992 (S.I. 2572)

Peterhead Bay Harbour Trust and Transfer Order 1983 (S.I. 316)

Peterlee Education Action Zone Order 1999 (S.I. 3381)

Petroleum (Carbide of Calcium) Order (Northern Ireland) 1949 (79)

Petroleum (Carbide of Calcium) Order 1929 (S.I. 992)

Petroleum (Carbide of Calcium) Order 1947 (S.I. 1442)

Petroleum (Carbide of Clacium) Order (Northern Ireland) 1930 (20)

Petroleum (Compressed Gases) Order 1930 (S.I. 34)

Petroleum (Consolidation) Act 1928 (Enforcement) Regulations 1979 (S.I. 427)

Petroleum (Current Model Clauses) Order 1999 (S.I. 160)

Petroleum (Liquid Methane) Order (Northern Ireland) 1973 (528)

Petroleum (Liquid Methane) Order, 1957 (S.I. 859)

Petroleum Revenue Tax (Nomination Scheme for Disposals and Appropriations) Regulations 1987 (S.I. 1338)

Petroleum Spirit (Plastic Containers) Regulations (Northern Ireland) 1983 (43)

Petroleum-spirit (Motor Vehicles etc.) Regulations 1929 (S.I. 952)

Petroleum-spirit (Motor Vehicles, &c.) Regulations 1930 (11)

Petroleum-Spirit (Plastic Containers) Regulations 1982 (S.I. 630)

Pharmaceutical Services Regulations (Northern Ireland) 1997 (381)

Pharmaceutical Society (Statutory Committee) Order of Council 1978 (S.I. 20)

Pharmaceutical Society of Northern Ireland (General) Regulations (Northern Ireland) 1994 (202)

Pharmacy (Northern Ireland) Order 1976 (S.I. 1213)

Phoenix National Health Service Trust (Dissolution) Order 2000 (S.I. 846)

Piccadilly Line (Heathrow T5 Extension) Order 2002 (S.I. 1065)

Pig Carcase (Grading) Amendment (Scotland) Regulations 2003 (S.S.I. 565)

Pig Carcase (Grading) Regulations 1994 (S.I. 2155)

Pig Industry Restructuring Grant (Wales) Scheme 2001 (S.I. 643)

Pigs (Records, Identification and Movement) (Interim Measures) (England) (No.2) (Amendment) Order 2003 (S.I. 28)

Pigs (Records, Identification and Movement) (Interim Measures) (England) (No.2) Order 2002 (S.I. 2154)

Pigs (Records, Identification and Movement) (Interim Measures) (England) Order 2002 (S.I. 241)

Pigs (Records, Identification and Movement) (Interim Measures) (Wales) (No.2) (Amendment) (No.2) Order 2003 (S.I. 2763)

Pigs (Records, Identification and Movement) (Interim Measures) (Wales) (No.2) (Amendment) Order 2003 (S.I. 170)

Pigs (Records, Identification and Movement) (Interim Measures) (Wales) (No.2) Order 2002 (S.I. 2303)

Pigs (Records, Identification and Movement) (Interim Measures) (Wales) Order 2002 (S.I. 281)

Pigs (Records, Identification and Movement) Order 1995 (S.I. 11)

Pilgrim Health National Health Service Trust (Establishment) Order 1993 (S.I. 2567)

Pilotage Act 1987 (Pilotage Commission Transfer of Property, Rights and Liabilities) Order 1990 (S.I. 1338)

Processed Cereal-based Foods and Baby Foods for Infants and Young Children Amendment (Scotland) Regulations 2000 (S.S.I. 214)

Processed Cereal-based Foods and Baby Foods for Infants and Young Children Regulations 1997 (S.I. 2042)

Producer Responsibility Obligations (Northern Ireland) Order 1998 (S.I. 1762)

Producer Responsibility Obligations (Packaging Waste) (Amendment) Regulations (Northern Ireland) 1999 (115)

Producer Responsibility Obligations (Packaging Waste) Regulations 1997 (S.I. 648)

Products of Animal Origin (Import and Export) Amendment (Scotland) Regulations 2001 (S.S.I. 257)

Products of Animal Origin (Import and Export) Regulations (Northern Ireland) 1998 (45)

Products of Animal Origin (Import and Export) Regulations 1996 (S.I. 3124)

Products of Animal Origin (Third Country Imports) (England) (Amendment No 2) Regulations 2004 (S.I. 390)

Products of Animal Origin (Third Country Imports) (England) (Amendment) (No 4) Regulations 2002 (S.I. 3206)

Products of Animal Origin (Third Country Imports) (England) (Amendment) (No.2) Regulations 2002 (S.I. 2570)

Products of Animal Origin (Third Country Imports) (England) (Amendment) (No.3) Regulations 2002 (S.I. 2639)

Products of Animal Origin (Third Country Imports) (England) (Amendment) Regulations 2002 (S.I. 2151)

Products of Animal Origin (Third Country Imports) (England) (Amendment) Regulations 2003 (S.I. 812)

Products of Animal Origin (Third Country Imports) (England) (Amendment) Regulations 2004 (S.I. 82)

Products of Animal Origin (Third Country Imports) (England) (No.2) Regulations 2004 (S.I. 1740)

Products of Animal Origin (Third Country Imports) (England) Regulations 2002 (S.I. 1227)

Products of Animal Origin (Third Country Imports) (England) Regulations 2003 (S.I. 3177)

Products of Animal Origin (Third Country Imports) (England) Regulations 2004 (S.I. 1214)

Products of Animal Origin (Third Country Imports) (Scotland) Regulations 2002 (S.S.I. 445)

Products of Animal Origin (Third Country Imports) (Wales) (Amendment) (No.2) Regulations 2002 (S.I. 3230)

Products of Animal Origin (Third Country Imports) (Wales) (Amendment) Regulations 2003 (S.I. 976)

Products of Animal Origin (Third Country Imports) (Wales) Regulations 2002 (S.I. 1387)

Products of Animal Origin (Third Country Imports) Regulations (Northern Ireland) 2002 (340)

Professions Supplementary to Medicine (Disciplinary Committees) (Procedure) Rules 1964 (S.I. 1203)

Professions Supplementary to Medicine (Disciplinary Committees) (Procedure) Rules Order of Council 1964 (S.I. 1203)

Professions Supplementary to Medicine (Registration (Appeals) Rules) Order of Council 1962 (S.I. 2545)

Prohibition of Fishing with Multiple Trawls (No.2) (Scotland) Order 2000 (S.S.I. 405)

Prohibition of Fishing with Multiple Trawls Order 2001 (S.I. 650)

Prohibition of Keeping or Release of Live Fish (Specified Species) Order 1998 (S.I. 2409)

Property (Northern Ireland) Order 1997 (S.I. 1179)

Property Misdescriptions (Specified Matters) Order 1992 (S.I. 2834)

Prosecution of Offences (Custody Time Limits) Regulations 1987 (S.I. 299)

Prosecution of Offences (Northern Ireland) Order 1972 (S.I. 538)

Prosecution of Offences (Youth Courts Time Limits) Regulations 1999 (S.I. 2743)

Protected Rights (Transfer Payment) Regulations (Northern Ireland) 1996 (509)

Protected Rights (Transfer Payment) Regulations 1996 (S.I. 1461)

Protection from Harassment (Northern Ireland) Order 1997 (S.I. 1180)

Protection of Children (Northern Ireland) Order 1978 (S.I. 1047)

Protection of Children Act Tribunal Regulations 2000 (S.I. 2619)

Protection of Children and Vulnerable Adults (Northern Ireland) Order 2003 (S.I. 417)

Protection of Children and Vulnerable Adults and Care Standards Tribunal Regulations 2002 (S.I. 816)

Protection of Military Remains Act 1986 (Designation of Vessels and Controlled Sites) Order 2002 (S.I. 1761)

Protection of Trading Interests Act 1980 (Hong Kong) Order 1990 (S.I. 2291)

Protection of Water Against Agricultural Nitrate Pollution (England and Wales) Regulations 1996 (S.I. 888)

Protection of Wrecks (Designation No 1 Order 1980) (Amendment) Order 1980 (S.I. 1306)

Protection of Wrecks (Designation No 1) Order 1980 (S.I. 645)

Protection of Wrecks (Designation No 1) Order 1985 (S.I. 699)

Protection of Wrecks (Designation No 1) Order 1989 (S.I. 2089)

Protection of Wrecks (Designation No 1) Order 1994 (S.I. 1842)

Protection of Wrecks (Designation No 2) Order 1998 (S.I. 2708)

Protection of Wrecks (Designation No 3) Order 1989 (S.I. 2295)

Provision and Use of Work Equipment Regulations (Northern Ireland) 1999 (305)

Provision and Use of Work Equipment Regulations 1992 (S.I. 2932)

Provision and Use of Work Equipment Regulations 1998 (S.I. 2306)

Public Airport Companies (Capital Finance) Order 1996 (S.I. 604)

Public Appointments and Public Bodies etc (Scotland) Act 2003 (Commencement No 4) Order 2003 (S.S.I. 602)

Public Finance and Accountability (Scotland) Act 2000 (Access to Documents and Information) (Relevant Persons) Order 2002 (S.S.I. 78)

Public Finance and Accountability (Scotland) Act 2000 (Economy, efficiency and effectiveness examinations) (Specified bodies etc.) Order 2002 (S.S.I. 77)

Public Health (Infectious Diseases) Regulations 1988 (S.I. 1546)

Public Interest Disclosure (Northern Ireland) Order 1998 (S.I. 1763)

Public Interest Disclosure (Prescribed Persons) (Amendment) Order 2003 (S.I. 1993)

Public Interest Disclosure (Prescribed Persons) Order 1999 (S.I. 1549)

Salford Community Health Care National Health Service Trust (Dissolution) Order 2001 (S.I. 1666)

Salford Community Health Care National Health Service Trust (Establishment) Order 1993 (S.I. 2611)

Salford Hospitals National Health Service Trust (Change of Name) Order 1994 (S.I. 1269)

Salford Hospitals National Health Service Trust (Establishment) Order 1994 (S.I. 164)

Salford Primary Care Trust (Establishment) Order 2001 (S.I. 519)

Salford Royal Hospitals National Health Service Trust (Establishment) Amendment Order 1999 (S.I. 2176)

Salisbury Health Care National Health Service Trust (Establishment) Order 1993 (S.I. 2575)

Salmon (Definition of Methods of Net Fishing and Construction of Nets) (Scotland) Regulations 1992 (S.I. 1974)

Salmon (Fish Passes and Screens) (Scotland) Regulations 1994 (S.I. 2524)

Salmon (Weekly Close Time) (Scotland) Regulations 1988 (S.I. 390)

Sandwell and West Birmingham Hospitals National Health Service Trust (Establishment) Amendment Order 2003 (S.I. 2345)

Sandwell and West Birmingham Hospitals National Health Service Trust (Establishment) and the City Hospital National Health Service Trust and Sandwell Healthcare National Health Service Trust (Dissolution) Order 2002 (S.I. 1364)

Sandwell Healthcare National Health Service Trust (Establishment) Amendment Order 1999 (S.I. 62)

Sandwell Healthcare National Health Service Trust (Establishment) Order 1994 (S.I. 172)

Satellite Communications Services Regulations 1995 (S.I. 1947)

Saundersfoot Steam Railway (Light Railway) Order 1991 (S.I. 2682)

Savings Certificates (Yearly Plan) Regulations 1984 (S.I. 779)

Savings Certificates Regulations 1991 (S.I. 1031)

Scarborough, Whitby and Ryedale Primary Care Trust (Establishment) Order 2002 (S.I. 137)

Scheme for Construction Contracts (England and Wales) Regulations 1998 (S.I. 649)

Scheme for Construction Contracts (Scotland) Regulations 1998 (S.I. 687)

School Budget Shares (Prescribed Purposes) (England) Regulations 2002 (S.I. 378)

School Budget Shares (Prescribed Purposes) (England) Regulations 2002 (S.I. 278)

School Companies Regulations 2002 (S.I. 2978)

School Governance (Collaboration) (England) Regulations 2003 (S.I. 1962)

School Governance (Constitution) (England) Regulations 2003 (S.I. 348)

School Governance (Constitution, Procedures and New Schools) (England) (Amendment) Regulations 2004 (S.I. 450)

School Governance (Procedures) (England) Regulations 2003 (S.I. 1377)

School Government (Terms of Reference) (Wales) Regulations 2000 (S.I. 3027)

School Governors Annual Reports (Wales) Regulations 2001 (S.I. 1110)

School Organisation Proposals by the Learning and Skills Council for England Regulations 2001 (S.I. 798)

School Organisation Proposals by the Learning and Skills Council for England Regulations 2003 (S.I. 507)

School Organisation Proposals by the National Council for Education and Training for Wales Regulations 2002 (S.I. 432)

School Premises (General Requirements and Standards) (Scotland) Regulations 1967 (S.I. 1199)

School Pupil Records (Scotland) Regulations 1990 (S.I. 1551)

School Staffing (England) Regulations 2003 (S.I. 1963)

School Standards and Framework Act 1998 (Admissions and Standard Numbers) (Modification) Regulations 1999 (S.I. 1064)

School Standards and Framework Act 1998 (Admissions) (Modifications No 2) Regulations 1998 (S.I. 3130)

School Standards and Framework Act 1998 (Admissions) (Modifications) Regulations 1998 (S.I. 2230)

School Standards and Framework Act 1998 (Education Action Zones) (Modification) Regulations 1998 (S.I. 1878)

School Standards and Framework Act 1998 (Home-School Agreements) (Modification) Regulations 1998 (S.I. 2834)

School Standards and Framework Act 1998 (Infant Class Sizes) (Modification) Regulations 1998 (S.I. 1968)

School Standards and Framework Act 1998 (Intervention in Schools Causing Concern) (Modification) Regulations 1998 (S.I. 2248)

School Standards and Framework Act 1998 (Modification) (No.2) Regulations 1998 (S.I. 3217)

School Standards and Framework Act 1998 (Modification) Regulations 1998 (S.I. 2670)

School Standards and Framework Act 1998 (Proposals under section 211 of the Education Act 1996) (Transitional Provisions) Regulations 1998 (S.I. 3172)

School Standards and Framework Act 1998 (School Attendance Targets) (Modification) Regulations 1999 (S.I. 129)

School Standards and Framework Act 1998 (School Playing Fields) (Modification) (England) Regulations 1999 (S.I. 1)

School Standards and Framework Act 1998 (School Teachers Pay and Conditions) (Transitional Provisions) Regulations 1998 (S.I. 2115)

School Teachers Pay and Conditions Act 1991 (Commencement No 2 and Transitional Provision) Order 1992 (S.I. 532)

School Teachers Pay and Conditions Act 1991 (Commencement No 3) Order 1992 (S.I. 988)

School Teachers Pay and Conditions Act 1991 (Commencement No.1) Order 1991 (S.I. 1874)

School Teachers Pay and Conditions Act 1991 (Commencement No.4) Order 1992 (S.I. 3070)

School Teachers Remuneration Order 2000 (S.I. 2324)

School Teachers Remuneration Order 2002 (S.I. 2103)

School Teachers Remuneration, Professional Duties and Working Time Order 1992 (S.I. 3069)

Schools (Scotland) Code 1956 (S.I. 894)

Schools Forums (England) Regulations 2002 (S.I. 2114)

Schools General (Scotland) Regulations 1975 (S.I. 1135)

Schools Regulations 1959 (S.I. 364)

Scotland Act 1998 (Agency Arrangements) (Specification) (No.2) Order 2002 (S.I. 800)

Scotland Act 1998 (Agency Arrangements) (Specification) Order 2001 (S.I. 3917)

Scotland Act 1998 (Consequential Modifications) (No.1) Order 1999 (S.I. 1042)

Sheep and Goats Spongiform Encephalopathy (Compensation) Amendment (Scotland) Order 2001 (S.S.I. 458)

Sheep and Goats Spongiform Encephalopathy (Compensation) Order 1998. 1998 (S.I. 1647)

Sheep and Goats Spongiform Encephalopathy Order 1998 (S.I. 1645)

Sheep and Goats Spongiform Encephalopathy Regulations 1998 (S.I. 1646)

Sheep Annual Premium and Suckler Cow Premium Quotas Regulations 1997 (S.I. 2844)

Sheep Annual Premium and Suckler Cow Premium Quotas Regulations 2003 (S.I. 2261)

Sheep Annual Premium Regulations (Northern Ireland) 1992 (476)

Sheep Annual Premium Regulations 1992 (S.I. 2677)

Sheffield Children's Hospital National Health Service Trust (Establishment) Order 1991 (S.I. 2399)

Sheffield Children's Hospital National Health Service Trust Change of Name and (Establishment) Amendment Order 2002 (S.I. 1297)

Sheffield South West Primary Care Trust (Establishment) Order 2001 (S.I. 183)

Sheffield Teaching Hospitals National Health Service Trust (Establishment) Order 2000 (S.I. 2909)

Sheffield West Primary Care Trust (Establishment) Order 2001 (S.I. 182)

Shellfish and Specified Fish (Third Country Imports) Order 1992 (S.I. 3301)

Sheriff Court Fees Order 1997 (S.I. 687)

Shetland Islands Regulated Fishery (Scotland) Order 1999 (S.S.I. 194)

Shetland Tourist Board Scheme Amendment Order 1995 (S.I. 2240)

Shetland Tourist Board Scheme Order 1995 (S.I. 1891)

Shipbuilding and Ship-repairing Regulations (Northern Ireland) 1971 (372)

Shipbuliding and Ship-Repairing Regulations 1960 (S.I. 1932)

Ship's Report, Importation and Exportation by Sea Regulations 1981 (S.I. 1260)

Shoreham Port Authority Revision Order 1968 (S.I. 2042)

Shoreham Port Authority Revision Order 1978 (S.I. 647)

Shoreham Port Authority Revision Order 1985 (S.I. 1251)

Shrewsbury and Telford Hospital National Health Service Trust (Establishment) and the Princess Royal Hospital National Health Service Trust and the Royal Shrewsbury Hospitals National Health Service Trust (Dissolution) Order 2003 (S.I. 2346)

Shropshire (Coroners) Order 1998 (S.I. 363)

Shropshire (District of The Wrekin) (Structural Change) Order 1996 (S.I. 1866)

Shropshire County Council (District of The Wrekin) (Staff Transfer) Order 1998 (S.I. 448)

Shropshire County Primary Care Trust (Establishment) Order 2002 (S.I. 941)

Shropshire Fire Services (Combination Scheme) Order 1997 (S.I. 2702)

Shropshire's Community and Mental Health Services National Health Service Trust (Establishment) Order 1998 (S.I. 500)

Shropshire's Community Health Service National Health Service Trust (Dissolution) Order 1998 (S.I. 515)

Shropshire's Community Health Service National Health Service Trust (Establishment) Order 1993 (S.I. 2630)

Shropshire's Mental Health National Health Service Trust (Dissolution) Order 1998 (S.I. 518)

Shropshire's Mental Health National Health Service Trust (Establishment) Amendment Order 1993 (S.I. 156)

Shropshire's Mental Health National Health Service Trust (Establishment) Order 1992 (S.I. 2557)

Sight Testing (Examination and Prescription) (No.2) Regulations 1989 (S.I. 1230)

Simple Pressure Vessels (Safety) Regulations 1991 (S.I. 2749)

Six Pit and Upper Bank Junctions Light Railway Order 1985 (S.I. 747)

Slaughter Premium Regulations (Northern Ireland) 2001 (199)

Slough Primary Care Trust (Establishment) Order 2001 (S.I. 346)

Sludge (Use in Agriculture) Regulations (Northern Ireland) 1990 (245)

Smoke Control Areas (Authorised Fuels) (England) Regulations 2001 (S.I. 3745)

Smoke Control Areas (Authorised Fuels) (Scotland) Regulations 2001 (S.S.I. 433)

Smoke Control Areas (Authorised Fuels) (Wales) Regulations 2001 (S.I. 3762)

Smoke Control Areas (Exempted Fireplaces) (Amendment) Regulations (Northern Ireland) 1999 (289)

Social Fund (Applications) Regulations (Northern Ireland) 1988 (130)

Social Fund (Applications) Regulations 1988 (S.I. 524)

Social Fund (Cold Weather Payments) (General) Regulations (Northern Ireland) 1988 (368)

Social Fund (Maternity and Funeral Expenses) (General) (Amendment) Regulations (Northern Ireland) 2002 (14)

Social Fund (Maternity and Funeral Expenses) (General) Regulations (Northern Ireland) 1987 (150)

Social Fund (Recovery by Deductions from Benefits) Regulations (Northern Ireland) 1988 (21)

Social Fund (Recovery by Deductions from Benefits) Regulations 1988 (S.I. 35)

Social Fund Cold Weather Payments (General) Regulations 1988 (S.I. 1724)

Social Fund Maternity and Funeral Expenses (General) Amendment Regulations 2002 (S.I. 79)

Social Fund Maternity and Funeral Expenses (General) Regulations 1987 (S.I. 481)

Social Fund Winter Fuel Payment Regulations (Northern Ireland) 2000 (91)

Social Fund Winter Fuel Payment Regulations 2000 (S.I. 729)

Social Security (1998 Order) (Commencement No 7 and Savings, Consequential and Transitional Provisions) Order (Northern Ireland) 1999 (310)

Social Security (Abolition of Earnings Rule) (Consequential) Regulations (Northern Ireland) 1989 (373)

Social Security (Abolition of Earnings Rule) (Consequential) Regulations 1989 (S.I. 1642)

Social Security (Adjudication) Regulations 1995 (S.I. 1801)

Social Security (Amendment) (Residential Care and Nursing Homes) Regulations (Northern Ireland) 2002 (132)

Social Security (Attendance Allowance) Regulations (Northern Ireland) 1992 (20)

Social Security (Attendance Allowance) Regulations 1991 (S.I. 2740)

Social Security (Attendence Allowance and Claims and Payments) Amendment Regulations 1990 (S.I. 1871)

Social Security (Australia) Order 2000 (S.I. 3255)

Social Security (Back to Work Bonus and Lone Parent Run-on) (Amendment and Revocation) Regulations 2003 (S.I. 1589)

Social Security (Back to Work Bonus) (No.2) Regulations (Northern Ireland) 1996 (519)

Social Security (Back to Work Bonus) (No.2) Regulations 1996 (S.I. 2570)

Social Security (Benefits for Widows and Widowers) (Consequential Amendments) Regulations (Northern Ireland) 2001 (108)

Social Security (Benefits for Widows and Widowers) (Consequential Amendments) Regulations 2000 (S.I. 1483)

Social Security (Breach of Community Order) Regulations 2001 (S.I. 1395)

Social Security (Categorisation of Earners) Regulations (Northern Ireland) 1978 (401)

Social Security (Categorisation of Earners) Regulations 1978 (S.I. 1689)

Social Security (Child Benefit Consequential) Regulations (Northern Ireland) 1977 (73)

Social Security (Child Benefit Consequential) Regulations 1977 (S.I. 342)

Social Security (Child Maintenance Bonus) Regulations (Northern Ireland) 1996 (622)

Social Security (Child Maintenance Bonus) Regulations 1996 (S.I. 3195)

Social Security (Child Maintenance Premium and Miscellaneous Amendments) Regulations (Northern Ireland) 2001 (25)

Social Security (Child Maintenance Premium and Miscellaneous Amendments) Regulations 2000 (S.I. 3176)

Social Security (Claims and Information) Regulations (Northern Ireland) 2001 (175)

Social Security (Claims and Information) Regulations 1999 (S.I. 3108)

Social Security (Claims and Payments and Adjudication) (Amendment) (Regulations (Northern Ireland) 1997 (416)

Social Security (Claims and Payments and Adjudication) (Amendment) Regulations (Northern Ireland) 1996 (432)

Social Security (Claims and Payments and Adjudication) Amendment No 2 Regulations 1997 (S.I. 2290)

Social Security (Claims and Payments and Adjudication) Amendment Regulations 1996 (S.I. 2306)

Social Security (Claims and Payments and Miscellaneous Amendments No 2) Regulations (Northern Ireland) 2002 (327)

Social Security (Claims and Payments and Miscellaneous Amendments) (No.2) Regulations 2002 (S.I. 2441)

Social Security (Claims and Payments and Miscellaneous Amendments) (No.3) Regulations 2002 (S.I. 2660)

Social Security (Claims and Payments and Miscellaneous Amendments) Regulations (Northern Ireland) 2002 (67)

Social Security (Claims and Payments and Miscellaneous Amendments) Regulations 2002 (S.I. 428)

Social Security (Claims and Payments and Payments on account, Overpayments and Recovery) Amendment Regulations 1989 (S.I. 136)

Social Security (Claims and Payments Etc.) (Amendment) Regulations (Northern Ireland) 1996 (85)

Social Security (Claims and Payments Etc.) Amendment Regulations 1996 (S.I. 672)

Social Security (Claims and Payments) (Amendment No 2) Regulations (Northern Ireland) 1988 (141)

Social Security (Claims and Payments) (Amendment No 2) Regulations (Northern Ireland) 1989 (398)

Social Security (Claims and Payments) (Amendment No 2) Regulations (Northern Ireland) 1992 (271)

Social Security (Claims and Payments) (Amendment No 2) Regulations (Northern Ireland) 1993 (217)

Social Security (Claims and Payments) (Amendment No 2) Regulations (Northern Ireland) 1994 (456)

Social Security (Claims and Payments) (Amendment No 3) Regulations (Northern Ireland) 1993 (375)

Social Security (Claims and Payments) (Amendment No 3) Regulations (Northern Ireland) 2002 (297)

Social Security (Claims and Payments) (Amendment No 4) Regulations (Northern Ireland) 1994 (484)

Social Security (Claims and Payments) (Amendment No.2) Regulations (Northern Ireland) 2002 (254)

Social Security (Claims and Payments) (Amendment) Regulations (Northern Ireland) 1988 (67)

Social Security (Claims and Payments) (Amendment) Regulations (Northern Ireland) 1992 (7)

Social Security (Claims and Payments) (Amendment) Regulations (Northern Ireland) 1994 (345)

Social Security (Claims and Payments) (Amendment) Regulations (Northern Ireland) 1999 (365)

Social Security (Claims and Payments) (Amendment) Regulations (Northern Ireland) 2000 (181)

Social Security (Claims and Payments) (Amendment) Regulations (Northern Ireland) 2001 (22)

Social Security (Claims and Payments) (Amendment) Regulations (Northern Ireland) 2002 (59)

Social Security (Claims and Payments) (Amendment) Regulations 1993 (146)

Social Security (Claims and Payments) (Amendments) Regulations (Northern Ireland) 1989 (40)

Social Security (Claims and Payments) (Jobseeker's Allowance Consequential Amendments) Regulations (Northern Ireland) 1996 (354)

Social Security (Claims and Payments) (Jobseeker's Allowance Consequential Amendments) Regulations 1996 (S.I. 1460)

Social Security (Claims and Payments) Amendment (No.2) Regulations 1993 (S.I. 1113)

Social Security (Claims and Payments) Amendment (No.2) Regulations 1994 (S.I. 2943)

Social Security (Claims and Payments) Amendment (No.2) Regulations 1996 (S.I. 2988)

Social Security (Claims and Payments) Amendment (No.2) Regulations 1998 (S.I. 3039)

Social Security (Claims and Payments) Amendment (No.2) Regulations 2002 (S.I. 1950)

Social Security (Claims and Payments) Amendment (No.3) Regulations 1993 (S.I. 2113)

Social Security (Claims and Payments) Amendment (No.3) Regulations 1994 (S.I. 2944)

Social Security (Claims and Payments) Amendment (No.4) Regulations 1994 (S.I. 3196)

Social Security (Claims and Payments) Amendment Regulations 1988 (S.I. 522)

Social Security (Claims and Payments) Amendment Regulations 1990 (S.I. 725)

Social Security (Claims and Payments) Amendment Regulations 1991 (S.I. 2741)

Social Security (Claims and Payments) Amendment Regulations 1992 (S.I. 1026)

Social Security (Claims and Payments) Amendment Regulations 1993 (S.I. 478)

Social Security (Claims and Payments) Amendment Regulations 1994 (S.I. 2319)

Social Security (Claims and Payments) Amendment Regulations 1995 (S.I. 3055)

Social Security (Claims and Payments) Amendment Regulations 1997 (S.I. 3034)

Social Security (Claims and Payments) Amendment Regulations 1998 (S.I. 1381)

Social Security (Claims and Payments) Amendment Regulations 1999 (S.I. 2358)

Social Security (Claims and Payments) Amendment Regulations 2000 (S.I. 1366)

Social Security (Claims and Payments) Amendment Regulations 2001 (S.I. 18)

Social Security (Claims and Payments) Amendment Regulations 2002 (S.I. 355)

Social Security (Claims and Payments) Regulations (Northern Ireland) 1987 (465)

Social Security (Claims and Payments) Regulations 1987 (S.I. 1968)

Social Security (Common Provisions) (Miscellaneous Amendments) Regulations (Northern Ireland) 1988 (369)

Social Security (Common Provisions) Miscellaneous Amendment Regulations 1988 (S.I. 1725)

Social Security (Contributions) (Amendment No 2) Regulations 2002 (S.I. 307)

Social Security (Contributions) (Amendment No 4) Regulations 2001 (S.I. 2187)

Social Security (Contributions) (Re-rating and National Insurance Fund Payments) Order 1996 (S.I. 597)

Social Security (Contributions) (Re-rating and National Insurance Funds Payments) Order 2000 (S.I. 755)

Social Security (Contributions) (Re-rating and National Insurance Funds Payments) Order 2002 (S.I. 830)

Social Security (Contributions) Regulations 1975 (S.I. 492)

Social Security (Contributions) Regulations 1979 (S.I. 591)

Social Security (Contributions) Regulations 2001 (S.I. 1004)

Social Security (Contributions) (Amendment No 5) Regulations 2002 (S.I. 2929)

Social Security (Crediting and Treatment of Contributions, and National Insurance Numbers) Regulations (Northern Ireland) 2001 (102)

Social Security (Crediting and Treatment of Contributions, and National Insurance Numbers) Regulations 2001 (S.I. 769)

Social Security (Credits) Regulations (Northern Ireland) 1975 (113)

Social Security (Credits) Regulations 1975 (S.I. 1483)

Social Security (Credits) Regulations 1975 (S.I. 556)

Social Security (Disability Living Allowance and Claims and Payments) (Amendment) Regulations 1996 (225)

Social Security (Disability Living Allowance and Claims and Payments) Amendment Regulations 1996 (S.I. 1436)

Social Security (Disability Living Allowance) Regulations (Northern Ireland 1992 (32)

Social Security (Disability Living Allowance) Regulations 1991 (S.I. 2890)

Social Security (Earnings Factor) Regulations (Northern Ireland) 1979 (193)

Social Security (Earnings Factor) Regulations 1979 (S.I. 676)

Social Security (Electronic Communications) (Child Benefit) Order 2002 (S.I. 1789)

Social Security (Employed Earners Employments for Industrial Injuries Purposes) Regulations 1975 (S.I. 467)

Social Security (General Benefit) Regulations (Northern Ireland) 1984 (92)

Social Security (General Benefit) Regulations 1982 (S.I. 1408)

Social Security (Graduated Retirement Benefit) (No.2) Regulations (Northern Ireland) 1978 (105)

Social Security (Graduated Retirement Benefit) (No.2) Regulations 1978 (S.I. 393)

Social Security (Guardian's Allowance) (Amendment) Regulations (Northern Ireland) 1998 (263)

Social Security (Guardian's Allowances) (Amendment) Regulations (Northern Ireland) 1985 (227)

Social Security (Guardian's Allowances) (Amendment) Regulations (Northern Ireland) 2002 (87)

Social Security (Guardian's Allowances) Amendment Regulations 1985 (S.I. 1327)

Social Security (Guardian's Allowances) Amendment Regulations 1998 (S.I. 1811)

Social Security (Guardian's Allowances) Amendment Regulations 2002 (S.I. 492)

Social Security (Guardian's Allowances) Regulations (Northern Ireland) 1975 (98)

Social Security (Guardian's Allowances) Regulations 1975 (S.I. 515)

Social Security (Hospital In-Patients and Miscellaneous Amendments) Regulations (Northern Ireland) 2003 (261)

Social Security (Hospital In-Patients) (Amendment) Regulations (Northern Ireland) 1977 (316)

Social Security (Hospital In-Patients) (Amendment) Regulations (Northern Ireland) 1987 (391)

Social Security (Hospital In-Patients) (Amendment) Regulations (Northern Ireland) 2001 (115)

Social Security (Hospital In-Patients) Regulations (Northern Ireland) 1975 (109)

Social Security (Hospital In-Patients) Regulations 1975 (S.I. 555)

Social Security (Hospital In-Patients, Attendance Allowance and Disability Living Allowance) (Amendment) Regulations 1999 (S.I. 1326)

Social Security (Immigration and Asylum) Consequential Amendments Regulations (Northern Ireland) 2000 (71)

Social Security (Immigration and Asylum) Consequential Amendments Regulations 2000 (S.I. 636)

Social Security (Incapacity Benefit Increases for Dependants) Regulations (Northern Ireland) 1994 (485)

Social Security (Incapacity Benefit Increases for Dependants) Regulations 1994 (S.I. 2945)

Social Security (Incapacity Benefit Work-focused Interviews) Regulations 2003 (S.I. 2439)

Social Security (Incapacity Benefit) (Consequential and Transitional Amendments and Savings) Regulations (Northern Ireland) 1995 (150)

Social Security (Incapacity Benefit) (Consequential and Transitional Amendments and Savings) Regulations 1995 (S.I. 829)

Social Security (Incapacity Benefit) (Miscellaneous Amendments) Regulations (Northern Ireland) 2000 (404)

Social Security (Incapacity Benefit) (Miscellaneous Amendments) Regulations (Northern Ireland) 2001 (316)

Social Security (Incapacity Benefit) (Transitional) Regulations (Northern Ireland) 1995 (35)

Social Security (Incapacity Benefit) (Transitional) Regulations 1995 (S.I. 310)

Social Security (Incapacity Benefit) Miscellaneous Amendments Regulations 2000 (S.I. 3120)

Social Security (Incapacity Benefit) Regulations (Northern Ireland) 1994 (461)

Social Security (Incapacity Benefit) Regulations 1994 (S.I. 2946)

Social Security (Incapacity for Work and Miscellaneous Amendments) Regulations 1996 (S.I. 3207)

Social Security (Incapacity for Work) (General) Regulations (Northern Ireland) 1995 (41)

Social Security (Incapacity for Work) (General) Regulations 1995 (S.I. 311)

Social Security (Incapacity for Work) (Northern Ireland) Order 1994 (S.I. 1898)

Social Security (Income Support and Claims and Payments) (Amendment) Regulations (Northern Ireland) 1995 (301)

Social Security (Income Support and Claims and Payments) Amendment Regulations 1995 (S.I. 1613)

Social Security (Income Support, Claims and Payments and Adjudication) Amendment Regulations 1995 (S.I. 2927)

Social Security (Income Support, Jobseeker's Allowance and Claims and Payments) (Miscellaneous Amendments) Regulations (Northern Ireland) 1997 (165)

Social Security (Industrial Diseases) (Prescribed Diseases) (Amendment) Regulations (Northern Ireland) 1993 (148)

Social Security (Industrial Diseases) (Prescribed Diseases) (Amendment) Regulations (Northern Ireland) 1996 (57)

Social Security (Industrial Injuries and Diseases) (Miscellaneous Amendments) Regulations 1996 (S.I. 425)

Social Security (Industrial Injuries) (Dependency) (Permitted Earnings Limits) Order (Northern Ireland) 2001 (107)

Social Security (Industrial Injuries) (Dependency) (Permitted Earnings Limits) Order (Northern Ireland) 2002 (107)

Social Security (Industrial Injuries) (Prescribed Diseases) (Amendment No 2) Regulations (Northern Ireland) 1987 (454)

Social Security (Industrial Injuries) (Prescribed Diseases) Regulations (Northern Ireland) 1986 (179)

Social Security (Industrial Injuries) (Prescribed Diseases) Regulations 1985 (S.I. 967)

Social Security (Invalid Care Allowance) (Amendment) Regulations (Northern Ireland) 1996 (521)

Social Security (Invalid Care Allowance) Amendment Regulations 1996 (S.I. 2744)

Social Security (Invalid Care Allowance) Regulations (Northern Ireland) 1976 (99)

Social Security (Invalid Care Allowance) Regulations (Northern Ireland) 1976 (S.I. 99)

Social Security (Invalid Care Allowance) Regulations 1976 (S.I. 409)

Social Security (Jobcentre Plus Interviews for Partners) Regulations 2003 (S.I. 1886)

Social Security (Jobcentre Plus Interviews) Regulations 2001 (S.I. 3210)

Social Security (Jobcentre Plus Interviews) Regulations 2002 (S.I. 1703)

Social Security (Jobseeker's Allowance and Payments on Account) (Miscellaneous Amendments) Regulations (Northern Ireland) 1996 (464)

Social Security (Jobseeker's Allowance and Payments on Account) (Miscellaneous Amendments) Regulations 1996 (S.I. 2519)

Social Security (Jobseeker's Allowance Consequential Amendments) (Deductions) Regulations 1996 (S.I. 2344)

Social Security (Joint Claims Consequential Amendments) Regulations (Northern Ireland) 2000 (365)

Social Security (Joint Claims Consequential Amendments) Regulations 2000 (S.I. 1982)

Social Security (Loss of Benefit) Regulations (Northern Ireland) 2002 (79)

Social Security (Loss of Benefit) Regulations 2001 (S.I. 4022)

Social Security (Mariners Benefits) Regulations 1975 (S.I. 529)

Social Security (Maternity Allowance) (Earnings) Regulations (Northern Ireland) 2000 (104)

Social Security (Maternity Allowance) (Earnings) Regulations 2000 (S.I. 688)

Social Security (Maternity Allowance) Regulations (Northern Ireland) 1987 (170)

Social Security (Maternity Allowance) Regulations 1987 (S.I. 416)

Social Security (Medical Evidence) Regulations 1976 (S.I. 615)

Social Security (Medical Evidence, Claims and Payments) Amendment Regulations 1989 (S.I. 1686)

Social Security (Miscellaneous Amendments No 2) Regulations (Northern Ireland) 1997 (156)

Social Security (Miscellaneous Amendments No 2) Regulations (Northern Ireland) 1998 (81)

Social Security (Miscellaneous Amendments No 2) Regulations (Northern Ireland) 1999 (381)

Social Security (Miscellaneous Amendments No 4) Regulations (Northern Ireland) 1997 (435)

Social Security (Miscellaneous Amendments) (No.2) Regulations 1997 (S.I. 793)

Social Security (Miscellaneous Amendments) (No.2) Regulations 1999 (S.I. 2556)

Social Security (Miscellaneous Amendments) (No.2) Regulations 2002 (S.I. 2380)

Social Security (Miscellaneous Amendments) (No.4) Regulations 1997 (S.I. 2305)

Social Security (Miscellaneous Amendments) (No.4) Regulations 1998 (S.I. 1174)

Social Security (Miscellaneous Amendments) Regulations (Northern Ireland) 2001 (78)

Social Security (Miscellaneous Amendments) Regulations 2001 (S.I. 488)

Social Security (Miscellaneous Provisions) (Amendment No 3) Regulations 1992 (453)

Social Security (Miscellaneous Provisions) (Amendment) Regulations (Northern Ireland) 1990 (398)

Social Security (Miscellaneous Provisions) (Amendment) Regulations (Northern Ireland) 1991 (488)

Social Security (Miscellaneous Provisions) (Amendment) Regulations (Northern Ireland) 1992 (83)

Social Security (Miscellaneous Provisions) Amendment (No.2) Regulations 1992 (S.I. 2595)

Social Security (Miscellaneous Provisions) Amendment Regulations 1990 (S.I. 2208)

Social Security (Miscellaneous Provisions) Amendment Regulations 1991 (S.I. 2284)

Social Security (Miscellaneous Provisions) Amendment Regulations 1992 (S.I. 247)

Social Security (Miscellaneous Provisions) Amendment Regulations 1993 (S.I. 846)

Social Security (National Insurance Number Information Exemption) Regulations (Northern Ireland) 2000 (135)

Social Security (National Insurance Number Information Exemption) Regulations 1997 (S.I. 2676)

Social Security (National Insurance Number Information Exemption) Regulations 2000 (S.I. 1082)

Social Security (Northern Ireland) Order 1986 (S.I. 1888)

Social Security (Northern Ireland) Order 1988 (S.I. 594)

Social Security (Northern Ireland) Order 1989 (S.I. 1342)

Social Security (Northern Ireland) Order 1990 (S.I. 1511)

Social Security (Northern Ireland) Order 1993 (S.I. 592)

Social Security (Northern Ireland) Order 1998 (S.I. 1506)

Social Security (Notification of Change of Circumstances) Regulations (Northern Ireland) 2001 (420)

Social Security (Notification of Change of Circumstances) Regulations 2001 (S.I. 3252)

Social Security (Overlapping Benefirs) Regulations (Northern Ireland) 1979 (242)

Social Security (Overlapping Benefits) Regulations 1979 (S.I. 597)

Social Security (Payments on Account, Overpayments and Recovery) (Amendment) Regulations (Northern Ireland) 1993 (175)

Social Security (Payments on Account, Overpayments and Recovery) (Amendment) Regulations (Northern Ireland) 2000 (266)

Social Security (Payments on account, Overpayments and Recovery) Amendment Regulations 1988 (S.I. 688)

Social Security (Payments on account, Overpayments and Recovery) Amendment Regulations 1993 (S.I. 650)

Social Security (Payments on account, Overpayments and Recovery) Amendment Regulations 2000 (S.I. 2336)

Social Security (Payments on account, Overpayments and Recovery) Regulations (Northern Ireland) 1988 (142)

Social Security (Payments on account, Overpayments and Recovery) Regulations 1988 (S.I. 664)

Social Security (Persons from Abroad) (Miscellaneous Amendments) Regulations (Northern Ireland) 1996 (11)

Social Security (Persons From Abroad) Miscellaneous Amendments Regulations 1996 (S.I. 30)

Social Security (Quarterly Work-focused Interviews for Certain Lone Parents) Regulations 2004 (S.I. 2244)

Social Security (Recovery of Benefits) Regulations 1997 (S.I. 2205)

Social Security (Severe Disablement Allowance and Invalid Care Allowance) (Amendment) Regulations (Northern Ireland) 1994 (370)

Social Security (Severe Disablement Allowance) Regulations (Northern Ireland) 1984 (317)

Social Security (Severe Disablement Allowance) Regulations 1984 (S.I. 1303)

Social Security (Social Fund and Claims and Payments) (Miscellaneous Amendments) Regulations (Northern Ireland) 1997 (155)

Social Security (Social Fund and Claims and Payments) (Miscellaneous Amendments) Regulations 1997 (S.I. 792)

Social Security (Students and Income-Related Benefits Amendment) Regulations (Northern Ireland) 2003 (329)

Social Security (Sweden) Order 1988 (S.I. 590)

Social Security (Welfare to Work) Regulations 1998 (S.I. 2231)

Social Security (Widow's Benefit and Retirement Pensions) Regulations (Northern Ireland) 1979 (243)

Social Security (Widow's Benefit and Retirement Pensions) Regulations 1979 (S.I. 642)

Social Security (Work-focused Interviews for Lone Parents Amendment) Regulations (Northern Ireland) 2002 (106)

Social Security (Work-focused Interviews for Lone Parents) and Miscellaneous Amendments Regulations 2000 (S.I. 1926)

Social Security (Work-focused Interviews for Lone Parents) Regulations (Northern Ireland) 2001 (152)

Social Security (Work-focused Interviews) Regulations (Northern Ireland) 2001 (176)

Social Security (Work-focused Interviews) Regulations 2000 (S.I. 897)

Social Security (Working Neighbourhoods) Regulations 2004 (S.I. 959)

Social Security (Working Tax Credit and Child Tax Credit) (Consequential Amendments) Regulations 2003 (S.I. 455)

Social Security Act 1998 (Commencement No 10, and Savings and Consequential and Transitional Provisions) Order (Northern Ireland) 1999 (428)

Social Security Act 1998 (Commencement No 11, and Savings and Consequential and Transitional Provisions) Order 1999 (S.I. 2860)

Social Security Act 1998 (Commencement No 12 and Consequential and Transitional Provisions) Order 1999 (S.I. 3178)

Social Security Act 1998 (Commencement No 6 and Consequential and Transitional Provisions) Order (Northern Ireland) 1999 (246)

Social Security Act 1998 (Commencement No 7 and Consequential and Transitional Provisions) Order 1999 (S.I. 1510)

Social Security Act 1998 (Commencement No 8, and Savings and Consequential and Transitional Provisions) Order 1999 (S.I. 1958)

Social Security Act 1998 (Commencement No 9, and Savings and Consequential and Transitional Provisions) Order 1999 (S.I. 2422)

Social Security Act 1998 (Commencement No 11 and Consequential and Transitional Provisions) Order (Northern Ireland) 1999 (472)

Social Security Administration (Fraud) (Northern Ireland) Order 1997 (S.I. 1182)

Social Security Amendment (Joint Claim Amendments) Regulations (Northern Ireland) 2001 (120)

Social Security Amendment (Joint Claims) Regulations 2001 (S.I. 518)

Social Security Amendment (Residential Care and Nursing Homes) Regulations 2001 (S.I. 3767)

Social Security Amendment (Residential Care and Nursing Homes) Regulations 2002 (S.I. 398)

Social Security Amendment (Students and Income-related Benefits) Regulations 2003 (S.I. 1701)

Social Security and Child Support (Decisions and Appeals) (Amendment) Regulations (Northern Ireland) 2001 (23)

Social Security and Child Support (Decisions and Appeals) and Jobseeker's Allowance (Amendment) Regulations (Northern Ireland) 1999 (408)

South Tyneside Health Care National Health Service Trust (Establishment) Order 1992 (S.I. 2543)

South Tyneside Primary Care Trust (Establishment) Order 2002 (S.I. 166)

South Wales Sea Fisheries Committee (Levies) Regulations 2001 (S.I. 3811)

South Warwickshire Combined Care National Health Service Trust (Establishment) Order 1998 (S.I. 517)

South Warwickshire General Hospitals National Health Service Trust (Establishment) Order 1992 (S.I. 2556)

South Warwickshire Mental Health National Health Service Trust (Establishment) Order 1993 (S.I. 2580)

South Warwickshire Primary Care Trust (Establishment) Order 2002 (S.I. 942)

South West Dorset Primary Care Trust (Establishment) Order 2001 (S.I. 322)

South West Durham Mental Health National Health Service Trust (Establishment) Order 1992 (S.I. 2547)

South West Durham Mental Health National Health Service Trust Dissolution Order 1996 (S.I. 876)

South West Kent Primary Care Trust (Establishment) Order 2001 (S.I. 284)

South West London Community National Health Service Trust (Establishment) Order 1999 (S.I. 794)

South West Oxfordshire Primary Care Trust (Establishment) Order 2001 (S.I. 525)

South West Yorkshire Mental Health National Health Service Trust (Establishment) and the Wakefield and Pontefract Community National Health Service Trust (Dissolution) Order 2002 (S.I. 1313)

South Wiltshire Primary Care Trust (Establishment) Order 2001 (S.I. 335)

South Worcestershire Community National Health Service Trust (Establishment) Order 1992 (S.I. 2555)

South Worcestershire Community National Health Service Trust Dissolution Order 1996 (S.I. 884)

South Worcestershire Primary Care Trust (Establishment) Order 2002 (S.I. 947)

South Yorkshire Metropolitan Ambulance and Paramedic Service National Health Service Trust (Establishment) Amendment Order 1997 (S.I. 2767)

South Yorkshire Metropolitan Ambulance and Paramedic Service National Health Service Trust (Establishment) Order 1991 (S.I. 2404)

Southampton Community Health Services National Health Service Trust (Establishment) Amendment (No.2) Order 2001 (S.I. 3203)

Southampton Community Health Services National Health Service Trust (Establishment) Amendment Order 1998 (S.I. 3098)

Southampton Community Health Services National Health Service Trust (Establishment) Amendment Order 2001 (S.I. 1916)

Southampton Community Health Services National Health Service Trust (Establishment) Order 1992 (S.I. 2584)

Southampton East Healthcare Primary Care Trust (Establishment) Order 2000 (S.I. 257)

Southampton University Hospitals National Health Service Trust (Establishment) Amendment Order 1999 (S.I. 884)

Southampton University Hospitals National Health Service Trust (Establishment) Order 1992 (S.I. 2509)

Southend Community Care Services and the Thameside Community Healthcare National Health Service Trusts (Dissolution) Order 2000 (S.I. 407)

Southend Community Care Services National Health Service Trust (Establishment) Amendment Order 1999 (S.I. 1167)

Southend Health Care Services National Health Service Trust (Change of Name) Order 1997 (S.I. 2938)

Southend on Sea Primary Care Trust (Establishment) Order 2000 (S.I. 307)

Southern Derbyshire Acute Hospitals National Health Service Trust (Establishment) Order 1998 (S.I. 848)

Southern Derbyshire Mental Health National Health Service Trust (Establishment) Order 1992 (S.I. 2473)

Southern Derbyshire Mental Health National Health Service Trust Change of Name and (Establishment) Amendment Order 2001 (S.I. 1606)

Southern Derbyshire Mental Health National Health Service Trust Change of Name and (Establishment) Amendment Order and the Community Health Care Service (North Derbyshire) National Health Service Trust (Dissolution) Order 2002 (S.I. 1296)

Southern Norfolk Primary Care Trust (Establishment) Order 2001 (S.I. 3258)

Southport &amp Ormskirk Hospital National Health Service Trust (Establishment) Order 1999 (S.I. 890)

Southport and Formby Community Health Services National Health Service Trust (Establishment) Order 1992 (S.I. 2465)

Southport and Formby Primary Care Trust (Establishment) Order 2001 (S.I. 520)

Southport and Formby, the Southport and Formby Community Health Services and the West Lancashire National Health Service Trusts (Dissolution) Order 1999 (S.I. 889)

Southwark Primary Care Trust (Establishment) Order 2002 (S.I. 1003)

Special Commissioners (Jurisdiction and Procedure) Regulations 1994 (S.I. 1811)

Special Constables (Amendment) Regulations 1992 (S.I. 1526)

Special Constables Regulations 1965 (S.I. 536)

Special Educational Needs (Provision of Information by Local Education Authorities) (England) Regulations 2001 (S.I. 2218)

Special Educational Needs and Disability Tribunal (General Provisions and Disability Claims Procedure) Regulations 2002 (S.I. 1985)

Special Educational Needs Tribunal Regulations 1995 (S.I. 3113)

Special Educational Needs Tribunal Regulations 2001 (S.I. 600)

Special Health Authorities (Amendment) Regulations 1998 (S.I. 1576)

Special Immigration Appeals Commission (Procedure) (Amendment) Rules 2000 (S.I. 1849)

Special Immigration Appeals Commission (Procedure) Rules 1998 (S.I. 1881)

Special Roads (Notice of Opening) (Scotland) Regulations 1964 (S.I. 1003)

Special Waste Amendment (Scotland) Regulations 2004 (S.S.I. 112)

Special Waste Regulations (Northern Ireland) 1998 (289)

Special Waste Regulations 1996 (S.I. 972)

Specialized Agencies of the United Nations (Immunities and Privileges) (Amendment) (No.2) Order 1985 (S.I. 753)

Specialized Agencies of the United Nations (Immunities and Privileges) Order 1974 (S.I. 1260)

Specified Animal Pathogens Order (Northern Ireland) 1999 (434)

Specified Animal Pathogens Order 1998 (S.I. 463)

Specified Diseases (Notification and Movement Restrictions) Order (Northern Ireland) 1997 (352)

Specified Diseases (Notification and Slaughter) Order 1992 (S.I. 3159)

Specified Diseases (Notification) Order 1996 (S.I. 2628)

Specified Risk Material (Amendment) (England) Order 2000 (S.I. 2726)

Specified Risk Material (Amendment) (England) Order 2001 (S.I. 2650)

Specified Risk Material (Amendment) (Wales) (No.2) Regulations 2001 (S.I. 3546)

Specified Risk Material (Amendment) (Wales) Order 2000 (S.I. 2811)

Specified Risk Material (Amendment) Regulations 1997 (S.I. 3062)

Specified Risk Material (Amendment) Regulations 1998 (S.I. 2405)

Specified Risk Material (Coming into Force Date) (Amendment) Regulations 1998 (S.I. 2431)

Specified Risk Material (Inspection Charges) Regulations 1999 (S.I. 539)

Specified Risk Material Amendment (No.2) (Scotland) Regulations 2001 (S.S.I. 86)

Specified Risk Material Amendment (No.3) (Scotland) Regulations 2001 (S.S.I. 288)

Specified Risk Material Amendment (Scotland) Regulations 2000 (S.S.I. 345)

Specified Risk Material Amendment (Scotland) Regulations 2001 (S.S.I. 3)

Specified Risk Material Order (Northern Ireland) 1997 (551)

Specified Risk Material Order 1997 (S.I. 2964)

Specified Risk Material Order Amendment (Scotland) Regulations 2000 (S.S.I. 344)

Specified Risk Material Regulations (Northern Ireland) 1997 (552)

Specified Risk Material Regulations 1997 (S.I. 2965)

Specified Sugar Products (Amendment) Regulations 1982 (S.I. 255)

Specified Sugar Products (England) Regulations 2003 (S.I. 1563)

Specified Sugar Products (Scotland) Amendment Regulations 1982 (S.I. 410)

Specified Sugar Products (Scotland) Regulations 1976 (S.I. 946)

Specified Sugar Products (Scotland) Regulations 2003 (S.S.I. 527)

Specified Sugar Products (Wales) Regulations 2003 (S.I. 3047)

Specified Sugar Products Regulations (Northern Ireland) 1976 (165)

Specified Sugar Products Regulations (Northern Ireland) 1982 (311)

Specified Sugar Products Regulations 1976 (S.I. 509)

Speke Garston Excellent Education Action Zone Order 1999 (S.I. 3408)

Spongiform Encephalopathy (Miscellaneous Amendments) Order 1994 (S.I. 2627)

Sports Grounds and Sporting Events (Designation) (Scotland) Amendment Order 2001 (S.S.I. 209)

Sports Grounds and Sporting Events (Designation) (Scotland) Amendment Order 2002 (S.S.I. 382)

Sports Grounds and Sporting Events (Designation) (Scotland) Order 1998 (S.I. 2314)

St Albans and Harpenden Primary Care Trust (Establishment) Order 2001 (S.I. 386)

St Albans and Hemel Hempstead National Health Service Trust (Establishment) Order 1994 (S.I. 177)

St Austell College (Government) Regulations 1993 (S.I. 271)

St Christopher and Nevis Constitution Order 1983 (S.I. 881)

St George's Healthcare National Health Service Trust (Establishment) Amendment Order 1999 (S.I. 1168)

St George's Healthcare National Health Service Trust (Establishment) Order 1993 (S.I. 352)

St Helens and Knowsley Community Health National Health Service Trust (Dissolution) Order 2002 (S.I. 1489)

St Helens and Knowsley Community Health National Health Service Trust (Establishment) Order 1991 (S.I. 2394)

St Helens and Knowsley Hospital Services National Health Service Trust (Establishment) Amendment Order 1999 (S.I. 632)

St Helens Primary Care Trust (Establishment) Order 2002 (S.I. 70)

St James and Seacroft University Hospitals National Health Service Trust (Dissolution) Order 1998 (S.I. 839)

St James's and Seacroft University Hospitals National Health Service Trust (Establishment) Amendment Order 1996 (S.I. 996)

St James's and Seacroft University Hospitals National Health Service Trust (Establishment) Order 1994 (S.I. 3183)

St James's University Hospital National Health Service Trust Dissolution Order 1995 (S.I. 480)

St Mary's Hospital National Health Service Trust (Establishment) Order 1992 (S.I. 2507)

St Mary's Hospital National Health Service Trust Dissolution Order 1996 (S.I. 2767)

St Mary's Music School (Aided Places) (Scotland) Regulations 2001 (S.S.I. 223)

St Mary's National Health Service Trust (Establishment) Order 1991 (S.I. 2395)

St Thomas Hospital National Health Service Trust Dissolution Order 1993 (S.I. 695)

Staffing of Grant-maintained and Grant-maintained Special Schools (Transitional Provisions) Regulations 1999 (S.I. 705)

Staffordshire (City of Stoke-on-Trent) (Structural and Boundary Changes) Order 1995 (S.I. 1779)

Staffordshire (Coroners) Order 1997 (S.I. 492)

Staffordshire Ambulance Service National Health Service Trust (Establishment) Amendment Order 1997 (S.I. 2788)

Staffordshire County Council (City of Stoke-on-Trent) (Staff Transfer) Order 1997 (S.I. 469)

Staffordshire Fire Services (Combination Scheme) Order 1996 (S.I. 2917)

Staffordshire Moorlands Primary Care Trust (Establishment) Order 2001 (S.I. 3821)

Stakeholder Pension Schemes (Amendment No 2) Regulations (Northern Ireland) 2001 (119)

Stakeholder Pension Schemes (Amendment) Regulations (Northern Ireland) 2002 (216)

Stakeholder Pension Schemes Regulations (Northern Ireland) 2000 (262)

Stakeholder Pension Schemes Regulations 2000 (S.I. 1403)

Stamp Duty (Collection and Recovery of Penalties) Regulations 1999 (S.I. 2537)

Stamp Duty (Disadvantaged Areas) (Application of Exemptions) Regulations 2003 (S.I. 1056)

Stamp Duty (Disadvantaged Areas) Regulations 2001 (S.I. 3747)

Stamp Duty (Exempt Instruments) (Amendment) Regulations 1999 (S.I. 2539)

Stamp Duty (Exempt Instruments) Regulations 1987 (S.I. 516)

Town and Country Planning (London Borough of Camden) Special Development Order 2004 (S.I. 1231)

Town and Country Planning (Prescription of County Matters) Regulations 1980 (S.I. 2010)

Town and Country Planning (Special Enforcement Notices) (Scotland) Regulations 1992 (S.I. 478)

Town and Country Planning (Structure and Local Plans) (Scotland) Regulations 1983 (S.I. 1590)

Town and Country Planning (Telecommunication Networks) (Railway Operational Land) Special Development Order 1982 (S.I. 817)

Town and Country Planning (Tree Preservation Order) (Amendment) and (Trees in Conservation Areas) (Exempted Cases) Regulations 1975 (S.I. 148)

Town and Country Planning (Tree Preservation Order) Regulations 1969 (S.I. 17)

Town and Country Planning (Trees) Regulations 1999 (S.I. 1892)

Town and Country Planning (Use Classes) (Scotland) Order 1997 (S.I. 3061)

Town and Country Planning (Use Classes) Order 1987 (S.I. 764)

Town and Country Planning Appeals (Determination by Appointed Person) (Inquiries Procedure) (Scotland) Rules 1997 (S.I. 750)

Town and Country Planning Appeals (Determination by Inspectors) (Inquiries Procedure) (England) Rules 2000 (S.I. 1625)

Town and Country Planning Appeals (Determination by Inspectors) (Inquiries Procedure) (Wales) Rules 2003 (S.I. 1267)

Town and Country Planning Appeals (Determination by Inspectors) (Inquiries Procedure) Rules 1992 (S.I. 2039)

Toy (Safety) Regulations 1995 (S.I. 204)

Toys (Safety) Regulations 1995 (S.I. 204)

Trade in Controlled Goods (Embargoed Destinations) Order 2004 (S.I. 318)

Trade Mark Rules 1994 (S.I. 2583)

Trade Marks (EC Measures Relating to Counterfeit Goods) Regulations 1995 (S.I. 1444)

Trade Marks (International Registration) Order 1996 (S.I. 714)

Trade Marks Act 1994 (Isle of Man) Order 1996 (S.I. 729)

Trade Marks Rules 2000 (S.I. 136)

Trade Union and Labour Relations (Northern Ireland) Order 1995 (S.I. 1980)

Trade Union Ballots and Elections (Independent Scrutineer Qualifications) Order 1993 (S.I. 1909)

Trade Union Elections and Ballots (Independent Scrutineer Qualifications) Order (Northern Ireland) 1992 (241)

Traded Securities (Disclosure) Regulations 1994 (S.I. 188)

Traffic Signs (Amendment) Regulations and General Directions 1995 (S.I. 3107)

Traffic Signs General (Amendment) Directions 1995 (S.I. 2769)

Traffic Signs General (Amendment) Directions 1999 (S.I. 1723)

Traffic Signs Regulations (Northern Ireland) 1997 (386)

Traffic Signs Regulations and General Directions 1994 (S.I. 1519)

Traffic Signs Regulations and General Directions 2002 (S.I. 3113)

Trafford Healthcare National Health Service Trust (Establishment) Order 1994 (S.I. 180)

Trafford North Primary Care Trust (Establishment) Order 2001 (S.I. 440)

Trafford South Primary Care Trust (Establishment) Order 2000 (S.I. 1168)

Transfer of Functions (Financial Services) Order 1992 (S.I. 1315)

Transfer of Functions (Legal Aid and Maintenance Orders) (Northern Ireland) Order 1982 (S.I. 159)

Transfer of Functions (Ministry of Food) Order, 1955 (S.I. 554)

Transfer of Functions (Wales) (No.1) Order 1978 (S.I. 272)

Transfer of Functions (Wales) Order 1969 (S.I. 388)

Transfer of Undertakings (Protection of Employment) Regulations 1981 (S.I. 1794)

Transnational Information and Consultation of Employees Regulations 1999 (S.I. 3323)

Transport (Scotland) Act 2001 (Conditions attached to PSV Operator's Licence and Competition Test for Exercise of Bus Functions) Order 2001 (S.I. 2748)

Transport Act 1985 (Modifications in Schedule 4 to the Transport Act 1968) Order 1985 (S.I. 1903)

Transport Act 2000 (Civil Aviation Authority Pension Scheme) Order 2001 (S.I. 853)

Transport Act 2000 (Commencement No 8 and Transitional Provisions) Order 2002 (S.I. 658)

Transport Act 2000 (Consequential Amendments) Order 2001 (S.I. 4050)

Transport and Works (Applications and Objections Procedure) (England and Wales) Rules 2000 (S.I. 2190)

Transport and Works (Applications and Objections Procedure) Rules 1992 (S.I. 2902)

Transport and Works (Descriptions of Works Interfering with Navigation) Order 1992 (S.I. 3230)

Transport and Works (Inquiries Procedure) Rules 1992 (S.I. 2817)

Transport of Animals (Cleansing and Disinfection) (England) (No.2) Order 2000 (S.I. 1618)

Transport of Animals (Cleansing and Disinfection) (England) (No.2) Order 2003 (S.I. 1336)

Transport of Animals (Cleansing and Disinfection) (England) Order 2003 (S.I. 255)

Transport of Animals (Cleansing and Disinfection) (Wales) (No.2) Order 2003 (S.I. 1470)

Transport of Animals (Cleansing and Disinfection) (Wales) (No.3) Order 2003 (S.I. 1968)

Transport of Animals (Cleansing and Disinfection) (Wales) Order 2001 (S.I. 2662)

Transport of Animals (Cleansing and Disinfection) (Wales) Order 2003 (S.I. 482)

Transport of Dangerous Goods (Safety Advisers) Regulations 1999 (S.I. 257)

Transport Tribunal Rules 2000 (S.I. 3226)

Transportable Pressure Vessels Regulations 2001 (S.I. 1426)

Travel Documents (Fees) Regulations 1999 (S.I. 3339)

Travellers Allowances Order 1994 (S.I. 955)

Travelling Expenses and Remission of Charges Regulations (Northern Ireland) 1989 (348)

Treasury Bills Regulations 1968 (S.I. 414)

Treatment of Offenders (Northern Ireland) Order 1976 (S.I. 226)

Treatment of Offenders (Northern Ireland) Order 1989 (S.I. 1344)

Treatment of Spruce Bark (Amendment) Order 1994 (S.I. 3093)

Treatment of Spruce Bark Order 1993 (S.I. 1282)

Trecare National Health Service Trust (Dissolution) Order 1999 (S.I. 634)

Tribunals and Inquiries (Discretionary Inquiries) Order 1975 (S.I. 1379)

Tryptophan in Food (Scotland) Regulations 1990 (S.I. 1792)

Walton Centre for Neurology and Neurosurgery National Health Service Trust (Establishment) Amendment Order 1996 (S.I. 982)

Walton Centre for Neurology and Neurosurgery National Health Service Trust (Establishment) Order 1991 (S.I. 2411)

Wandsworth Community Health National Health Service Trust (Establishment) Order 1993 (S.I. 2578)

Warehousekeepers and Owners of Warehoused Goods Regulations 1999 (S.I. 1278)

Warrenpoint Harbour Authority (Amendment) Order (Northern Ireland) 1994 (399)

Warrenpoint Harbour Authority Order (Northern Ireland) 1971 (136)

Warrenpoint Harbour Authority Order (Northern Ireland) 1973 (4)

Warrenpoint Harbour Authority Order (Northern Ireland) 1974 (215)

Warrington Community Health Care National Health Service Trust (Establishment) Order 1992 (S.I. 2464)

Warrington Hospital National Health Service Trust (Establishment) Amendment Order 1999 (S.I. 58)

Warrington Hospital National Health Service Trust (Establishment) Order 1993 (S.I. 28)

Warrington Primary Care Trust (Establishment) Order 2002 (S.I. 65)

Warwickshire Ambulance Service National Health Service Trust (Establishment) Amendment Order 1998 (S.I. 2949)

Warwickshire Ambulance Service National Health Service Trust-(Establishment) Order 1993 (S.I. 2579)

Waste and Contaminated Land (Northern Ireland) Order 1997 (S.I. 2778)

Waste Collection and Disposal Regulations (Northern Ireland) 1992 (254)

Waste Management Licensing (Amendment) (England) Regulations 2003 (S.I. 595)

Waste Management Licensing (Amendment) (Wales) Regulations 2003 (S.I. 780)

Waste Management Licensing Amendment (Scotland) Regulations 2003 (S.S.I. 171)

Waste Management Licensing Regulations 1994 (S.I. 1056)

Water (Northern Ireland) Order 1999 (S.I. 662)

Water and Sewerage Authorities (Rate of Return) (Scotland) Order 1996 (S.I. 744)

Water and Sewerage Charges (Exemption) (Scotland) Regulations 2002 (S.S.I. 167)

Water and Sewerage Services (Northern Ireland) Order 1973 (S.I. 70)

Water Appointment (Competition Commission) Regulations 1999 (S.I. 3088)

Water Environment (Water Framework Directive) (England and Wales) Regulations 2003 (S.I. 3242)

Water Industry (Charges) (Vulnerable Groups) Regulations 1999 (S.I. 3441)

Water Services Charges (Billing and Collection) (Scotland) Order 1996 (S.I. 325)

Water Services Charges (Billing and Collection) (Scotland) Order 1997 (S.I. 362)

Water Services Charges (Billing and Collection) (Scotland) Order 1998 (S.I. 634)

Water Services Charges (Billing and Collection) (Scotland) Order 2002 (S.S.I. 33)

Water Supply (Water Fittings) Regulations 1999 (S.I. 1148)

Water Supply (Water Quality) (Scotland) Regulations 2001 (S.S.I. 207)

Water Supply (Water Quality) Regulations 1989 (S.I. 1147)

Water Supply (Water Quality) Regulations 2000 (S.I. 3184)

Water Undertakers (Rateable Values) (Wales) Order 2000 (S.I. 299)

Water Undertakings (Rateable Values) (Scotland) Order 2000 (S.S.I. 90)

Water Undertakings (Rateable Values) (Scotland) Variation Order 2002 (S.S.I. 159)

Watford and South of St Albans-Redbourn-Kidney Wood, Luton, Special Road Scheme 1957 (S.I. 448)

Watford and Three Rivers Primary Care Trust (Establishment) Order 2001 (S.I. 364)

Weald of Kent Community National Health Service Trust (Establishment) Order 1994 (S.I. 174)

Weald of Kent Community National Health Service Trust Dissolution Order 1997 (S.I. 417)

Wednesbury and West Bromwich Primary Care Trust (Establishment) Order 2002 (S.I. 957)

Weighing Equipment (Automatic Catchweighing Instruments) Regulations 2003 (S.I. 2761)

Weighing Equipment (Automatic Gravimetric Filling Instruments) Regulations 2000 (S.I. 388)

Weighing Equipment (Automatic Rail-weighbridges) Regulations 2003 (S.I. 2454)

Weighing Equipment (Beltweighers Regulations (Northern Ireland) 1985 (319)

Weighing Equipment (Beltweighers) Regulations 2001 (S.I. 1208)

Weighing Equipment (Filling and Discontinuous Totalising Automatic Weighing Machines) Regulations (Northern Ireland) 1986 (311)

Weighing Equipment (Filling and Discontinuous Totalisting Automatic Weighing Machines) Regulations 1986 (S.I. 1320)

Weighing Equipment (Non-automatic Weighing Machines) Regulations (Northern Ireland) 1991 (266)

Weighing Equipment (Non-automatic Weighing Machines) Regulations 2000 (S.I. 932)

Weights and Measures (Northern Ireland) Order 1981 (S.I. 231)

Weights and Measures (Prescribed Stamp) Regulations (Northern Ireland) 1969 (11)

Weights and Measures (Testing and Adjustment Fees) Regulations (Northern Ireland) 1992 (483)

Weights and Measures Regulations 1963 (S.I. 1710)

Welfare Food (Amendment No 2) Regulations 2003 (S.I. 1864)

Welfare Food (Amendment) Regulations 1997 (S.I. 857)

Welfare Food (Amendment) Regulations 1998 (S.I. 691)

Welfare Food (Amendment) Regulations 1999 (S.I. 2561)

Welfare Food (Amendment) Regulations 2001 (S.I. 758)

Welfare Food (Amendment) Regulations 2002 (S.I. 550)

Welfare Food (Amendment) Regulations 2003 (S.I. 702)

Welfare Food Regulations 1996 (S.I. 1434)

Welfare Foods Regulations (Northern Ireland) 1988 (137)

Welfare of Animals (Slaughter or Killing) Regulations (Northern Ireland) 1996 (558)

Welfare of Animals (Slaughter or Killing) Regulations 1995 (S.I. 731)

Welfare of Animals (Transport) Order 1997 (S.I. 1480)

Welfare of Farmed Animals (England) Regulations 2000 (S.I. 1870)

Welfare of Farmed Animals (England) Regulations 2000 (S.I. Reg.3(2)

Welfare of Farmed Animals (Scotland) Amendment Regulations 2002 (S.S.I. 334)

Welfare of Farmed Animals (Scotland) Regulations 2000 (S.S.I. 442)

Welfare of Farmed Animals (Wales) Regulations 2001 (S.I. 2682)

Welfare of Farmed Animals Regulations (Northern Ireland) 2000 (270)

Welfare Reform and Pensions (1999 Order) (Commencement No 10) Order (Northern Ireland) 2002 (25)

Welfare Reform and Pensions (1999 Order) (Commencement No 9) Order (Northern Ireland) 2001 (438)

Welfare Reform and Pensions (Northern Ireland) Order 1999 (S.I. 3147)

Welfare Reform and Pensions Act 1999 (Commencement No 12) Order 2001 (S.I. 4049)

Wellhouse National Health Service Trust (Establishment) Amendment Order 1996 (S.I. 992)

Welsh Ambulance Services National Health Service Trust (Establishment) Order 1998 (S.I. 678)

Welsh Highland Railway Order 1999 (S.I. 2129)

Welsh Language Schemes (Public Bodies) Order 1996 (S.I. 1898)

Welsh Language Schemes (Public Bodies) Order 2001 (S.I. 2550)

Welwyn Hatfield Primary Care Trust (Establishment) Order 2001 (S.I. 365)

West Berkshire Priority Care Service National Health Service Trust (Establishment) Order 1992 (S.I. 2581)

West Cheshire National Health Service Trust (Establishment) Order 1993 (S.I. 2620)

West Cheshire National Health Service Trust Dissolution Order 1997 (S.I. 832)

West Cumbria Health Care National Health Service Trust (Establishment) Order 1992 (S.I. 2549)

West Cumbria Primary Care Trust (Establishment) Order 2001 (S.I. 512)

West Dorset Community Health National Health Service Trust Dissolution Order 1994 (S.I. 833)

West Dorset Mental Health National Health Service Trust Dissolution Order 1994 (S.I. 831)

West Gloucestershire Primary Care Trust (Establishment) Order 2001 (S.I. 4141)

West Hampshire National Health Service Trust (Establishment) Order 2001 (S.I. 1198)

West Hertfordshire Hospitals National Health Service Trust (Establishment) Order 2000 (S.I. 732)

West Herts Community Health National Health Service Trust (Establishment) Order 1994 (S.I. 854)

West Hull Primary Care Trust (Establishment) Order 2001 (S.I. 509)

West Kent National Health Service and Social Care Trust (Establishment) and the Thames Gateway National Health Service Trust and Invicta Community Care National Health Service Trust (Dissolution) Order 2002 (S.I. 1337)

West Lambeth Community Care National Health Service Trust (Change of Name) Order 1996 (S.I. 1769)

West Lancashire National Health Service Trust (Establishment) Order 1992 (S.I. 2468)

West Lancashire Primary Care Trust (Establishment) Order 2001 (S.I. 522)

West Lincolnshire Primary Care Trust (Establishment) Order 2001 (S.I. 274)

West Lindsey National Health Service Trust (Establishment) Amendment Order 1994 (S.I. 1534)

West Lindsey National Health Service Trust (Establishment) Order 1992 (S.I. 2471)

West London Healthcare National Health Service Trust (Establishment) Order 1992 (S.I. 2539)

West London Mental Health National Health Service Trust (Establishment) Order 2000 (S.I. 2562)

West Lothian Healthcare National Health Service Trust (Establishment) Amendment Order 1999 (S.S.I. 91)

West Lothian Healthcare National Health Service Trust (Establishment) Amendment Order 2001 (S.S.I. 365)

West Lothian Healthcare National Health Service Trust (Establishment) Order 1998 (S.I. 2731)

West Mercia (Police Area and Authority) Order 1997 (S.I. 1844)

West Middlesex University Hospital National Health Service Trust (Establishment) Amendment Order 1996 (S.I. 985)

West Middlesex University Hospital National Health Service Trust (Establishment) Order 1992 (S.I. 2585)

West Midlands (Coroners Districts) Order 1974 (S.I. 583)

West Midlands Ambulance Service National Health Service Trust (Establishment) Amendment Order 2003 (S.I. 2344)

West Midlands Ambulance Service National Health Service Trust (Establishment) Order 1993 (S.I. 29)

West Norfolk Primary Care Trust (Establishment) Order 2000 (S.I. 1718)

West of Cornwall Primary Care Trust (Establishment) Order 2001 (S.I. 1175)

West Suffolk Hospitals National Health Service Trust (Establishment) Amendment Order 2000 (S.I. 2387)

West Suffolk Hospitals National Health Service Trust (Establishment) Order 1992 (S.I. 2565)

West Sussex Health and Social Care National Health Service Trust (Establishment) and the Worthing Priority National Health Service Trust and Sussex Weald and Downs National Health Service Trust (Dissolution) Order 2002 (S.I. 1362)

West Wales Ambulance National Health Service Trust (Dissolution) Order 1998 (S.I. 677)

West Wales Ambulance National Health Service Trust (Establishment) Order 1995 (S.I. 141)

West Wiltshire Primary Care Trust (Establishment) Order 2001 (S.I. 470)

West Yorkshire Metropolitan Ambulance Service National Health Service Trust (Establishment) Amendment Order 1997 (S.I. 1400)

West Yorkshire Metropolitan Ambulance Service National Health Service Trust (Establishment) Order 1992 (S.I. 2493)

Westcountry Ambulance Service National Health Service Trust (Establishment) Order 1993 (S.I. 814)

Western Isles Islands Council (Ardveenish) Harbour Revision Order 1992 (S.I. 1975)

Western Isles Islands Council (Breasclete) Harbour Revision Order 1992 (S.I. 1976)

Western Isles Islands Council (Brevig) Harbour Empowerment Order 1993 (S.I. 2908)

Western Isles Islands Council (Leverburgh) Harbour Revision Order 1995 (S.I. 2971)

Western Isles Islands Council (Various Harbours Jurisdiction and Byelaws) Harbour Revision Order 1995 (S.I. 2007)

Western Isles Tourist Board Scheme Amendment Order 1995 (S.I. 2241)

Western Isles Tourist Board Scheme Order 1995 (S.I. 1892)

Western Sussex Primary Care Trust (Establishment) Order 2002 (S.I. 987)

STATUTE CITATOR 2002 - 2004

The Current Law Statute Citator covers the period 2002 - 2004 and is up to date to **January 1, 2005** (orders and Acts received). It covers both public and local statutes and comprises in a single table:

 (i) Statutes passed during this period;
 (ii) Statutes affected during this period by Statute or Statutory Instrument;
 (iii) Statutes judicially considered during this period;
 (iv) Statutes repealed and amended during this period;
 (v) Statutes under which Statutory Instruments have been made during this period.

The material is arranged in numerical order under the relevant year.

Definitions of legislative effects:

"added"	: new provisions are inserted by subsequent legislation
"amended"	: text of legislation is modified by subsequent legislation
"applied"	: brought to bear, or exercised by subsequent legislation
"consolidated"	: used where previous Acts in the same subject area are brought together in subsequent legislation, with or without amendments
"disapplied"	: an exception made to the application of an earlier enactment
"enabling"	: giving power for the relevant SI to be made
"referred to"	: direction from other legislation without specific effect or application
"repealed"	: rescinded by subsequent legislation
"restored"	: reinstated by subsequent legislation (where previously repealed/ revoked)
"substituted"	: text of provision is completely replaced by subsequent legislation
"varied"	: provisions modified in relation to their application to specified areas or circumstances, however the text itself remains unchanged

ACTS OF THE SCOTTISH PARLIAMENT

CAP.

1999

asp 1. Mental Health (Public Safety and Appeals) (Scotland) Act 1999
repealed: 2003 asp 13 Sch.5 Part 1
s.1, see *Anderson v Scottish Ministers* [2001] UKPC D5, [2003] 2 A.C. 602 (PC (Sc)), Lord Hope of Craighead

2000

asp 1. Public Finance and Accountability (Scotland) Act 2000
applied: 2004 asp 2 s.3
referred to: 2003 asp 6 s.10, 2004 asp 2 s.9
s.4, applied: 2002 asp 7 s.3, s.6, 2003 asp 6 s.3, s.6, 2004 asp 2 s.5, s.6
s.21, applied: 2002 asp 11 Sch.5
s.22, applied: 2002 asp 11 Sch.5
s.23, amended: 2002 asp 3 Sch.7 para.27

CAP.

2000–cont.

asp 1. Public Finance and Accountability (Scotland) Act 2000–*cont.*
s.23, applied: 2002 asp 11 Sch.5, SSI 2004/ 482 Art.2, Sch.1
s.23, referred to: SSI 2002/77 Art.2, SSI 2004/482
s.23, enabling: SSI 2002/77, SSI 2004/482
s.24, applied: SSI 2002/78 Art.2, SSI 2003/ 530 Art.2, Art.3
s.24, referred to: SSI 2002/78 Art.2
s.24, enabling: SSI 2002/78, SSI 2003/530
s.25, applied: 2002 asp 11 Sch.5
s.26, enabling: SSI 2002/176
s.27, applied: SSI 2002/176
Sch.1 para.2, repealed: 2004 asp 7 Sch.2
Sch.1 para.6, repealed: 2002 asp 3 Sch.7 para.27

CAP.

2000–cont.

asp 1. Public Finance and Accountability (Scotland) Act 2000–cont.

Sch.4 para.12, repealed (in part): 2002 asp 3 Sch.7 para.27

asp 4. Adults with Incapacity (Scotland) Act 2000

Commencement Orders: SSI 2002/172 Art.2; SSI 2002/189 Art.2; SSI 2003/136 Art.2; SSI 2003/267 Art.2; SSI 2003/516 Art.2

applied: SSI 2002/494 Reg.14, Reg.36, 2003 asp 13 s.4, s.14, s.15, s.16, 2004 c.30 Sch.4 para.9, Sch.4 para.12, SSI 2004/115 Sch.5 para.15, SSI 2004/116 Sch.1 para.8, Sch.2 para.9

referred to: 2002 asp 11 Sch.4 para.11, SSI 2002/96 Reg.2, SSI 2002/97 Reg.2

Part 4, applied: SSI 2003/231 Sch.4 para.12

s.1, applied: SSI 2002/494 Reg.5

s.3, applied: SSI 2002/494 Reg.14

s.7, enabling: SSI 2002/131

s.9, amended: 2003 asp 13 Sch.5 Part 1

s.9, repealed (in part): 2003 asp 13 Sch.5 Part 1

s.10, referred to: SSI 2002/533 Sch.1

s.10, enabling: SSI 2002/95

s.12, amended: 2003 asp 13 Sch.5 Part 1

s.14, applied: SSI 2002/494 Reg.14

s.19, applied: 2003 asp 13 s.13

s.20, applied: SSI 2002/494 Reg.14

s.26, applied: SSI 2002/494 Reg.14

s.35, amended: 2003 asp 13 Sch.4 para.9, Sch.5 Part 1

s.37, applied: SSI 2003/155 Reg.2, Reg.3, SSI 2003/266 Reg.2, Reg.3

s.37, enabling: SSI 2003/155, SSI 2003/226, SSI 2003/266

s.38, repealed (in part): 2003 asp 13 Sch.5 Part 1

s.39, applied: SSI 2003/155 Reg.4, SSI 2003/266 Reg.4

s.39, enabling: SSI 2003/155, SSI 2003/226, SSI 2003/266

s.41, applied: SSI 2003/155 Reg.5, SSI 2003/266 Reg.5

s.41, enabling: SSI 2003/155, SSI 2003/226, SSI 2003/266

s.47, amended: 2003 asp 13 Sch.4 para.9, Sch.5 Part 1

s.47, applied: SSI 2002/208 Reg.2, SSI 2002/275 Reg.2

s.47, disapplied: SSI 2002/275 Reg.2

s.47, enabling: SSI 2002/208

s.48, applied: SSI 2002/275 Reg.2

s.48, repealed (in part): 2003 asp 13 Sch.5 Part 1

s.48, enabling: SSI 2002/275, SSI 2002/302

s.50, applied: SSI 2002/494 Reg.14

s.51, amended: SI 2004/1031 Sch.10 para.21

s.51, applied: SI 2004/1031 Reg.14, Sch.2 para.2, SSI 2002/190 Reg.6

CAP.

2000–cont.

asp 4. Adults with Incapacity (Scotland) Act 2000–cont.

s.51, referred to: SI 2004/1031 Reg.16, SSI 2002/190 Reg.2

s.51, enabling: SSI 2002/190

s.52, applied: SSI 2002/494 Reg.14

s.53, applied: SSI 2002/494 Reg.14, 2003 asp 13 s.13

s.57, amended: 2003 asp 13 Sch.4 para.9, Sch.5 Part 1

s.57, applied: SI 2003/762 Reg.2, SI 2004/1748 Sch.1, SSI 2002/96 Reg.3, Reg.4, Reg.5, Reg.6, SSI 2002/494 Reg.14

s.57, referred to: SSI 2002/96 Reg.6

s.57, enabling: SSI 2002/96

s.58, applied: 2003 asp 13 s.13

s.70, applied: SSI 2002/98 Reg.2, Reg.3

s.70, enabling: SSI 2002/98

s.71, applied: SSI 2002/494 Reg.14

s.73, applied: 2002 asp 11 Sch.4 para.11, SSI 2002/97 Reg.3-11

s.73, enabling: SSI 2002/97

s.74, applied: SSI 2002/494 Reg.14

s.86, enabling: SSI 2002/95, SSI 2002/96, SSI 2002/97, SSI 2002/131, SSI 2002/190, SSI 2003/155, SSI 2003/226, SSI 2003/266

s.87, amended: 2003 asp 13 Sch.4 para.9, 2004 c.33 Sch.30

s.87, repealed (in part): 2003 asp 13 Sch.5 Part 1, 2004 c.33 Sch.30

s.89, enabling: SSI 2002/172, SSI 2002/189, SSI 2003/136, SSI 2003/227, SSI 2003/267, SSI 2003/516

Sch.1 para.1, repealed (in part): 2003 asp 13 Sch.5 Part 1

Sch.4 para.1, applied: 2003 asp 13 s.13

Sch.5 para.17, repealed (in part): 2003 asp 13 Sch.5 Part 1

asp 5. Abolition of Feudal Tenure etc (Scotland) Act 2000

Commencement Orders: 2003 asp 9 Sch.15; SSI 2003/455 Art.2; SSI 2003/456 Art.2; SSI 2003/620 Art.2

applied: 2003 c.14 Sch.4 para.17, SSI 2004/478 Art.2

referred to: 2003 c.14 s.72, s.117

s.5, enabling: SSI 2004/318

s.17, see *Sheltered Housing Management Ltd v Cairns* 2003 S.L.T. 578 (OH), Lord Nimmo Smith

s.17, amended: 2003 asp 9 Sch.13 para.2, Sch.15

s.17, applied: 2003 asp 9 s.81

s.17, disapplied: 2003 asp 9 s.63

s.18, amended: 2003 asp 9 Sch.13 para.3

s.18, applied: 2003 asp 4 s.14, 2003 asp 9 s.105

s.18A, added: 2003 asp 9 s.114

s.18B, added: 2003 asp 9 s.114

s.18C, added: 2003 asp 9 s.114

2000–cont.

asp 5. Abolition of Feudal Tenure etc (Scotland) Act 2000–cont.

s.18C, amended: 2004 asp 7 Sch.2

s.19, applied: 2003 asp 9 s.105

s.20, amended: 2003 asp 9 Sch.13 para.4, SSI 2003/503 Sch.1 para.4

s.20, applied: 2003 asp 9 s.105, SSI 2003/452 r.4, Sch.1

s.20, repealed (in part): 2003 asp 9 Sch.13 para.4, Sch.15

s.23, repealed: 2003 asp 9 Sch.15

s.24, amended: 2003 asp 9 Sch.15

s.25, amended: 2003 asp 9 Sch.13 para.5

s.26, repealed: 2003 asp 9 Sch.15

s.27, amended: 2003 asp 9 Sch.13 para.6

s.27A, added: 2003 asp 9 s.114

s.28, amended: 2003 asp 9 Sch.15

s.28A, added: 2003 asp 9 s.114

s.29, repealed: 2003 asp 9 Sch.15

s.30, repealed: 2003 asp 9 Sch.15

s.31, repealed: 2003 asp 9 Sch.15

s.32, repealed: 2003 asp 9 Sch.15

s.42, amended: 2003 asp 9 Sch.13 para.7

s.43, amended: 2003 asp 9 Sch.13 para.8

s.44, applied: SSI 2003/452 Sch.1

s.45, applied: SSI 2004/478 Art.2

s.45, enabling: SSI 2004/478

s.46, amended: 2003 asp 9 Sch.13 para.9, Sch.15

s.46, applied: SSI 2004/478 Art.3

s.46, enabling: SSI 2004/478

s.49, amended: 2003 asp 9 Sch.13 para.10

s.49, repealed (in part): 2003 asp 9 Sch.15

s.54, amended: 2003 asp 9 Sch.13 para.11

s.56, amended: 2003 asp 9 Sch.13 para.12

s.60, applied: 2003 asp 9 s.58

s.60, repealed (in part): 2003 asp 9 Sch.15

s.65A, added: 2003 asp 9 s.114

s.71, applied: 2002 asp 17 s.60, 2002 c.23 s.97

s.71, enabling: SSI 2003/456

s.73, amended: 2003 asp 9 Sch.13 para.13

s.75, substituted: 2003 asp 9 Sch.13 para.14

s.76, enabling: SSI 2004/535

s.77, amended: 2003 asp 9 Sch.13 para.15, Sch.15, SSI 2003/503 Sch.1 para.5

s.77, repealed (in part): 2003 asp 9 Sch.15

s.77, enabling: SSI 2003/455, SSI 2003/620

Sch.1, referred to: 2003 asp 9 s.128

Sch.2, referred to: 2003 asp 9 s.128

Sch.3, referred to: 2003 asp 9 s.128

Sch.4, referred to: 2003 asp 9 s.128

Sch.5, referred to: 2003 asp 9 s.128

Sch.5A, added: 2003 asp 9 Sch.13 para.16

Sch.5A, referred to: 2003 asp 9 s.128

Sch.5B, added: 2003 asp 9 Sch.13 para.16

Sch.5B, referred to: 2003 asp 9 s.128

Sch.5C, added: 2003 asp 9 Sch.13 para.16

Sch.5C, referred to: 2003 asp 9 s.128

Sch.6, referred to: 2003 asp 9 s.128

2000–cont.

asp 5. Abolition of Feudal Tenure etc (Scotland) Act 2000–cont.

Sch.7, referred to: 2003 asp 9 s.128

Sch.8, amended: 2003 asp 9 Sch.15

Sch.8, referred to: 2003 asp 9 s.128

Sch.8, substituted: 2003 asp 9 Sch.13 para.17

Sch.8A, added: 2003 asp 9 Sch.13 para.18

Sch.8A, referred to: 2003 asp 9 s.128

Sch.9, referred to: 2003 asp 9 s.128

Sch.10, referred to: 2003 asp 9 s.128

Sch.11, referred to: 2003 asp 9 s.128

Sch.11A, added: 2003 asp 9 Sch.13 para.19

Sch.11A, referred to: 2003 asp 9 s.128

Sch.12 Part 1 para.2, repealed: 2003 asp 9 Sch.15

Sch.12 Part 1 para.7, repealed (in part): 2003 asp 9 Sch.15

Sch.12 Part 1 para.9, amended: 2003 asp 9 Sch.13 para.20, Sch.15

Sch.12 Part 1 para.9, repealed (in part): 2003 asp 9 Sch.15

Sch.12 Part 1 para.15, repealed (in part): 2003 asp 9 Sch.15

Sch.12 Part 1 para.16, repealed (in part): 2003 asp 9 Sch.15

Sch.12 Part 1 para.18, repealed (in part): 2003 asp 9 Sch.15

Sch.12 Part 1 para.30, repealed (in part): 2003 asp 9 Sch.15

Sch.12 Part 1 para.39, repealed (in part): 2003 asp 9 Sch.15

Sch.13 Part 1, amended: 2003 asp 9 Sch.15

asp 6. Standards in Scotland's Schools etc (Scotland) Act 2000

Commencement Orders: SSI 2002/72 Art.2; SSI 2003/84 Art.2; SSI 2004/528 Art.2

s.9, applied: SSI 2003/231 Sch.4 para.19

s.10A, added: 2004 asp 12 s.2

s.10B, added: 2004 asp 12 s.2

s.10C, added: 2004 asp 12 s.2

s.15, referred to: 2004 asp 4 Sch.2 para.3

s.24, repealed (in part): 2004 asp 12 Sch.2

s.35, applied: 2004 asp 4 Sch.2 para.2

s.43, repealed (in part): 2004 asp 4 Sch.3 para.11

s.44, repealed (in part): 2004 asp 4 Sch.3 para.11

s.58, amended: 2003 asp 9 Sch.14 para.12, 2004 asp 12 Sch.1 para.2

s.61, enabling: SSI 2002/72, SSI 2003/84, SSI 2004/528

asp 7. Ethical Standards in Public Life etc (Scotland) Act 2000

Commencement Orders: SSI 2003/74 Art.2

s.3, applied: SSI 2002/55 Art.2, SSI 2003/122 Art.2, SSI 2003/135 Reg.4

s.3, enabling: SSI 2002/55, SSI 2003/122

s.7, enabling: SSI 2003/135, SSI 2003/203

s.8, amended: 2002 asp 11 Sch.6 para.21

s.9, applied: 2002 asp 11 Sch.2 para.21, SI 2003/409 Sch.1 Part I

2000–cont.

asp 7. Ethical Standards in Public Life etc (Scotland) Act 2000–*cont.*

s.19, applied: SI 2003/3190 Reg.4

s.23, applied: 2003 asp 13 Sch.1 para.4, Sch.1 para.5

s.28, enabling: SSI 2003/119, SSI 2003/279, SSI 2004/543

s.30, applied: SSI 2003/199, SSI 2004/473

s.30, enabling: SSI 2003/199, SSI 2004/473

s.37, enabling: SSI 2003/74

Sch.3, amended: 2002 asp 3 Sch.7 para.28, SSI 2002/201 Art.15, 2003 asp 4 Sch.4 para.15, SSI 2003/1 Art.15, SSI 2003/119 Art.2, SSI 2003/279 Art.2

asp 8. Education and Training (Scotland) Act 2000

s.1, enabling: SSI 2004/83, SSI 2004/270, SSI 2004/469

s.2, applied: 2003 c.1 s.255, SSI 2004/83 Reg.2, Reg.9

s.2, enabling: SSI 2004/83, SSI 2004/270, SSI 2004/469

s.3, enabling: SSI 2004/83, SSI 2004/270, SSI 2004/469

asp 10. National Parks (Scotland) Act 2000

applied: 2002 asp 3 s.54, SSI 2002/201 Art.12, SSI 2003/1 Art.12

s.1, applied: SSI 2003/1 Art.7

s.6, applied: SSI 2002/62 Art.5A, SSI 2002/201, SSI 2002/541 Reg.12, SSI 2003/1

s.6, enabling: SSI 2002/201, SSI 2003/1

s.7, enabling: SSI 2002/201, SSI 2003/1

s.8, applied: SSI 2002/201 Sch.1 para.1

s.8, referred to: SSI 2003/1 Sch.1 para.1

s.9, applied: SSI 2002/201 Art.8, Sch.1 para.2

s.9, referred to: SSI 2003/1 Art.8, Sch.1 para.2

s.9, enabling: SSI 2002/201, SSI 2003/1

s.10, enabling: SSI 2002/201, SSI 2003/1

s.11, applied: SSI 2002/201 Sch.1 para.3

s.12, applied: SSI 2002/201 Sch.1 para.3

s.13, applied: SSI 2002/201 Sch.1 para.3

s.14, applied: SSI 2002/201 Sch.1 para.3

s.15, applied: SSI 2002/201 Art.15, Sch.1 para.4, SSI 2003/1 Art.15

s.15, referred to: SSI 2003/1 Sch.1 para.3

s.16, applied: SSI 2002/201 Sch.1 para.5

s.16, referred to: SSI 2003/1 Sch.1 para.4

s.17, applied: SSI 2002/201 Sch.1 para.6

s.17, referred to: SSI 2003/1 Sch.1 para.5

s.18, applied: SSI 2002/201 Sch.1 para.6

s.18, referred to: SSI 2003/1 Sch.1 para.5

s.19, applied: SSI 2002/201 Sch.1 para.7

s.19, referred to: SSI 2003/1 Sch.1 para.6

s.20, applied: SSI 2002/201 Sch.1 para.7

s.20, referred to: SSI 2003/1 Sch.1 para.6

s.21, applied: SSI 2002/201 Sch.1 para.7

s.21, referred to: SSI 2003/1 Sch.1 para.6

s.22, applied: SSI 2002/201 Sch.1 para.7

s.22, referred to: SSI 2003/1 Sch.1 para.6

2000–cont.

asp 10. National Parks (Scotland) Act 2000–*cont.*

s.23, applied: SSI 2002/201 Art.14, Sch.1 para.7

s.23, referred to: SSI 2003/1 Sch.1 para.6

s.23, varied: SSI 2003/1 Art.14

s.24, applied: SSI 2002/201 Art.14, Sch.1 para.7

s.24, referred to: SSI 2003/1 Sch.1 para.6

s.24, varied: SSI 2003/1 Art.14

s.25, applied: SSI 2002/201 Art.14, Sch.1 para.7

s.25, referred to: SSI 2003/1 Sch.1 para.6

s.25, varied: SSI 2003/1 Art.14

s.26, applied: SSI 2002/201 Art.14, Sch.1 para.7

s.26, referred to: SSI 2003/1 Sch.1 para.6

s.26, varied: SSI 2003/1 Art.14

s.27, applied: SSI 2002/201 Sch.1 para.7

s.27, referred to: SSI 2003/1 Sch.1 para.6

s.29, applied: SSI 2002/201 Sch.1 para.8

s.29, referred to: SSI 2003/1 Sch.1 para.7

s.33, enabling: SSI 2002/201, SSI 2003/1

s.34, applied: SSI 2002/202, SSI 2003/2

s.34, enabling: SSI 2002/201, SSI 2003/1

s.36, applied: SSI 2002/201 Sch.1 para.9

s.36, referred to: SSI 2003/1 Sch.1 para.8

Sch.1, applied: 2002 asp 13 Sch.1 para.73

Sch.1 para.3, applied: SSI 2002/201 Art.5, Art.7, Art.10, SSI 2003/1 Art.5, Art.7, Art.10

Sch.1 para.3, enabling: SSI 2002/201, SSI 2003/1

Sch.1 para.4, enabling: SSI 2002/201, SSI 2002/202, SSI 2003/1, SSI 2003/2

Sch.1 para.11, applied: SSI 2002/201 Art.10

Sch.1 para.11, referred to: SSI 2003/1 Art.10

Sch.1 para.16, disapplied: SSI 2002/201 Art.7, SSI 2003/1 Art.7

Sch.1 para.16, enabling: SSI 2002/201, SSI 2003/1

Sch.1 para.18, disapplied: SSI 2004/473 Art.2

Sch.1 para.19, applied: SSI 2002/201 Art.10

Sch.1 para.19, referred to: SSI 2003/1 Art.10

Sch.2 para.3, referred to: SSI 2002/201 Sch.1 para.2, SSI 2003/1 Sch.1 para.2

Sch.2 para.5, referred to: SSI 2002/201 Sch.1 para.2, SSI 2003/1 Sch.1 para.2

Sch.2 para.6, referred to: SSI 2002/201 Sch.1 para.2, SSI 2003/1 Sch.1 para.2

Sch.2 para.8, applied: SSI 2002/201 Art.8

Sch.2 para.8, disapplied: SSI 2003/1 Art.8

Sch.2 para.11, referred to: SSI 2002/201 Sch.1 para.2, SSI 2003/1 Sch.1 para.2

Sch.2 para.12, referred to: SSI 2002/201 Sch.1 para.2, SSI 2003/1 Sch.1 para.2SSI 2002/201 Sch.1 para.2, SSI 2003/1 Sch.1 para.2

Sch.4, applied: SSI 2002/201 Art.12, SSI 2003/1 Art.12

Sch.5 para.2, referred to: SSI 2002/201 Sch.1 para.9, SSI 2003/1 Sch.1 para.8

CAP.

2000–cont.

asp 10. National Parks (Scotland) Act 2000–*cont.*

Sch.5 para.4, referred to: SSI 2002/201 Sch.1 para.9, SSI 2003/1 Sch.1 para.8

Sch.5 para.5, repealed: 2002 asp 11 Sch.6 para.22

Sch.5 para.6, referred to: SSI 2002/201 Sch.1 para.9, SSI 2003/1 Sch.1 para.8

Sch.5 para.7, referred to: SSI 2002/201 Sch.1 para.9, SSI 2003/1 Sch.1 para.8

Sch.5 para.8, referred to: SSI 2002/201 Sch.1 para.9, SSI 2003/1 Sch.1 para.8

Sch.5 para.9, referred to: SSI 2002/201 Sch.1 para.9, SSI 2003/1 Sch.1 para.8

Sch.5 para.10, referred to: SSI 2002/201 Sch.1 para.9, SSI 2003/1 Sch.1 para.8

Sch.5 para.11, referred to: SSI 2002/201 Sch.1 para.9, SSI 2003/1 Sch.1 para.8

Sch.5 para.12, referred to: SSI 2002/201 Sch.1 para.9, SSI 2003/1 Sch.1 para.8

Sch.5 para.14, referred to: SSI 2002/201 Sch.1 para.9, SSI 2003/1 Sch.1 para.8

Sch.5 para.16, referred to: SSI 2002/201 Sch.1 para.9, SSI 2003/1 Sch.1 para.8

Sch.5 para.17, referred to: SSI 2002/201 Sch.1 para.9, SSI 2003/1 Sch.1 para.8

asp 11. Regulation of Investigatory Powers (Scotland) Act 2000

applied: SSI 2003/181, SSI 2003/183 Art.2

s.7, applied: SSI 2002/205 Reg.3

s.7, referred to: SSI 2002/205 Reg.3, SSI 2002/206 Art.4

s.7, enabling: SSI 2002/205, SSI 2002/206

s.8, enabling: SSI 2003/50

s.19, varied: SSI 2002/206 Art.6

s.19, enabling: SSI 2002/206

s.20, applied: SSI 2002/207 Reg.2

s.20, enabling: SSI 2002/207

s.24, applied: SSI 2003/181, SSI 2003/183

s.24, referred to: SSI 2003/181, SSI 2003/183

s.24, enabling: SSI 2003/181, SSI 2003/183

2001

asp 1. Abolition of Poindings and Warrant Sales Act 2001

Commencement Orders: 2002 asp 17 Sch.3 para.27

repealed: 2002 asp 17 Sch.3 para.27

asp 2. Transport (Scotland) Act 2001

Commencement Orders: SSI 2002/291 Art.2; SSI 2003/588 Art.2

s.8, applied: SSI 2002/291 Art.3

s.22, applied: SSI 2002/291 Art.3

s.32, applied: SSI 2002/291 Art.3

s.34, applied: SSI 2002/291 Art.3

s.38, enabling: SSI 2002/289

s.39, applied: SSI 2002/291 Art.3

s.39, disapplied: SSI 2002/291 Art.3

s.41, applied: SSI 2002/199 Reg.3

CAP.

2001–cont.

asp 2. Transport (Scotland) Act 2001–*cont.*

s.41, enabling: SSI 2002/199

s.50, enabling: SSI 2003/292

s.51, applied: SSI 2003/292 Reg.4

s.52, applied: SSI 2003/292 Reg.5

s.54, enabling: SSI 2004/519

s.67, applied: SSI 2003/282 Reg.2

s.67, enabling: SSI 2003/282

s.68, amended: 2003 asp 1 s.44

s.69, enabling: SSI 2002/178

s.72, referred to: SSI 2002/69 Reg.2

s.72, enabling: SSI 2002/69

s.74, applied: SSI 2002/177 Reg.16, SSI 2002/292 Reg.5, Reg.16

s.74, referred to: SSI 2002/177 Reg.5

s.74, enabling: SSI 2002/177, SSI 2002/292

s.81, applied: SSI 2002/178, SSI 2002/199

s.81, enabling: SSI 2002/69, SSI 2002/177, SSI 2002/178, SSI 2002/199, SSI 2002/289, SSI 2002/291, SSI 2002/292, SSI 2003/282, SSI 2003/292, SSI 2004/519

s.84, enabling: SSI 2002/291, SSI 2003/588

asp 3. Salmon Conservation (Scotland) Act 2001

repealed: 2003 asp 15 Sch.4 Part 2

asp 4. Budget (Scotland) Act 2001

s.3, amended: SSI 2002/134 Sch.1, 2003 asp 6 s.8

s.3, referred to:

s.5, amended: SSI 2002/134 Art.2

s.6, repealed: 2002 asp 7 s.8

s.7, applied: SSI 2002/134

s.7, enabling: SSI 2002/134

Sch.1, amended: SSI 2002/134 Art.2, Sch.2 para.2, 2003 asp 6 s.8

Sch.1, referred to:

Sch.2 Part 3, amended: SSI 2002/134 Sch.3

Sch.2 Part 4, amended: SSI 2002/134 Art.2, Sch.3

Sch.2 Part 8, amended: SSI 2002/134 Sch.3

Sch.2 Part 9, amended: SSI 2002/134 Sch.3

Sch.3, amended: SSI 2002/134 Art.2

Sch.4 Part 1, amended: SSI 2002/134 Art.2

asp 6. Education (Graduate Endowment and Student Support) (Scotland) Act 2001

s.1, enabling: SSI 2004/469

7. Convention Rights (Compliance) (Scotland) Act 2001

see *Currie (Dennis) v HM Advocate* 2003 S.C.C.R. 676 (HCJ), Lord Hamilton, Lady Cosgrove, Lord Cullen L.J.G.; see *Flynn (Patrick Anthony) v HM Advocate* 2003 J.C. 153 (HCJ), Lord Cullen L.J.G., Lord Hamilton, Lord Osborne; see *Wright (Gavin Raymond) v HM Advocate* 2003 J.C. 135 (HCJ), Lord Gill L.J.C., Lord Kirkwood, Lord Marnoch, Lord McCluskey, Lord Reed

2001–cont.

asp 7. Convention Rights (Compliance) (Scotland) Act 2001

Sch.para.13, see *McCreaddie (Derek Alexander) v HM Advocate (Appeal against Sentence)* 2002 S.L.T. 1311 (HCJ Appeal), Lord Cullen L.J.G., Lord Hamilton, Lord Marnoch; see *Stewart (William) v HM Advocate (Sentencing)* 2002 S.L.T. 1307 (HCJ Appeal), Lord Cullen L.J.G., Lord Hamilton, Lord Marnoch

Sch.1 Part 1 para.7A, added: 2003 asp 7 s.39

Sch.1 Part 1 para.12, applied: SSI 2003/179 Reg.3, Reg.9

Sch.1 Part 1 para.16, amended: 2003 asp 7 Sch.4 para.5

Sch.1 Part 1 para.19, amended: 2003 asp 7 Sch.4 para.5

Sch.1 Part 4 para.49A, added: 2003 asp 7 s.39

Sch.1 Part 4 para.50, amended: 2003 asp 7 s.39

Sch.1 Part 4 para.53, amended: 2003 asp 7 s.39

Sch.1 Part 4 para.54, amended: 2003 asp 7 s.39

Sch.1 Part 4 para.59, applied: SSI 2003/179 Reg.3, Reg.9

Sch.1 Part 4 para.67, substituted: 2003 asp 7 s.39

Sch.1 para.13., see *Walker (Andrew) v HM Advocate (Sentencing)* 2003 S.L.T. 130 (HCJ), Lord Cullen L.J.G., Lord Clarke, Lord Marnoch

asp 8. Regulation of Care (Scotland) Act 2001

Commencement Orders: SSI 2002/162 Art.2, Art.3; SSI 2003/205 Art.2; SSI 2004/100 Art.3, Art.2; SSI 2003/205 Art.3; SSI 2003/596 Art.3; SSI 2002/162 Art.4

applied: 2002 c.38 s.144, SI 2004/293 Sch.2 para.16, SI 2004/2695 Sch.1 para.28, SSI 2002/162 Art.7

Part 1, applied: SI 2002/635 Reg.2, SI 2002/896 Sch.1 para.9, SI 2002/2005 Reg.14, SSI 2002/112 Art.2, SSI 2002/115 Sch.1 para.12, SSI 2002/162 Art.3, Art.6, 2003 asp 5 Sch.2 para.11, SSI 2003/140 Sch.1 para.1, Sch.1 para.2, SSI 2003/152 Art.2, SSI 2003/587 Art.2, SSI 2004/93 Art.2

Part 1, referred to: SSI 2002/108 Art.2

Part 2, applied: SI 2002/2005 Reg.14, SSI 2002/112 Art.2, SSI 2002/115 Sch.1 para.12, SSI 2002/162 Art.3, SSI 2003/152 Art.2, SSI 2004/93 Art.2

Part 3, applied: SSI 2003/231 Sch.1 para.15

s.2, applied: SI 2002/2005 Reg.14, 2003 asp 7 s.14

s.2, referred to: 2002 asp 5 s.1, SSI 2002/113 Sch.1 para.7, SSI 2002/115 Reg.2, Reg.3, 2004 asp 8 s.81, s.83, SSI 2004/375 Reg.2

2001–cont.

asp 8. Regulation of Care (Scotland) Act 2001–*cont.*

s.2, repealed (in part): 2003 asp 13 Sch.5 Part 1

s.2, varied: SSI 2002/120 Reg.2, Reg.3, Reg.4, Reg.5

s.2, enabling: SSI 2002/120, SSI 2003/571

s.4, applied: SSI 2002/113 Art.6

s.4, enabling: SSI 2002/113

s.7, applied: SI 2004/2695 Sch.1 para.30, SSI 2002/106 Reg.4, SSI 2002/113 Art.2, SSI 2002/162 Art.6, Art.13, SSI 2003/140 Sch.1 para.2, SSI 2003/231 Sch.1 para.9

s.7, enabling: SSI 2002/113, SSI 2003/151, SSI 2003/570, SSI 2004/95

s.8, applied: SSI 2002/113 Art.2, SSI 2003/231 Sch.1 para.9

s.8, enabling: SSI 2003/150

s.9, applied: SSI 2002/162 Art.7

s.9, disapplied: SSI 2002/162 Art.7

s.10, applied: SSI 2002/115 Sch.1 para.9

s.12, applied: SI 2004/2695 Sch.1 para.30

s.13, applied: SSI 2002/162 Art.11, Art.12

s.14, applied: SSI 2002/113 Art.4, Art.5, SSI 2002/162 Art.9, Art.11, Art.12, SSI 2003/231 Sch.1 para.9

s.14, enabling: SSI 2002/113, SSI 2003/151

s.16, referred to: SSI 2002/162 Art.11, Art.12

s.17, applied: SSI 2002/162 Art.8

s.21, applied: SI 2002/635 Sch.1 para.2, SI 2002/896 Sch.1 para.66, SI 2004/2695 Sch.1 para.12

s.22, applied: SI 2002/635 Sch.1 para.2, SI 2002/896 Sch.1 para.66, SI 2004/2695 Sch.1 para.12

s.24, applied: SSI 2002/112, SSI 2002/112 Art.3, SSI 2003/152 Art.3, SSI 2004/93 Art.3

s.24, enabling: SSI 2002/112, SSI 2003/152, SSI 2003/573, SSI 2004/93

s.25, applied: SSI 2004/268 Art.2

s.27, applied: SSI 2004/268 Art.2

s.28, applied: SSI 2002/115, SSI 2003/148, SSI 2004/96

s.28, referred to: SSI 2002/115 Reg.5

s.28, enabling: SI 2003/148, SSI 2002/115, SSI 2003/148, SSI 2004/96

s.29, applied: SI 2002/635 Sch.1 para.2, SI 2002/896 Sch.1 para.66, SI 2004/2695 Sch.1 para.12, SSI 2002/114, SSI 2002/114 Reg.18, SSI 2003/149, SSI 2003/150, SSI 2003/150 Reg.11, SSI 2003/572, SSI 2004/94

s.29, enabling: SSI 2002/114, SSI 2003/149, SSI 2003/150, SSI 2003/572, SSI 2004/94

s.30, applied: SSI 2002/18 Art.2, SSI 2002/108

s.30, enabling: SSI 2002/18, SSI 2002/108

s.33, applied: SSI 2002/113 Art.3, Art.3A, SSI 2002/162 Art.3

2001–cont.

asp 8. Regulation of Care (Scotland) Act 2001–cont.

s.33, enabling: SSI 2002/113, SSI 2004/95

s.36, applied: SSI 2002/113 Art.4

s.36, enabling: SSI 2004/95

s.41, applied: SSI 2002/115 Sch.1 para.10

s.43, applied: SI 2002/797 Art.3

s.44, applied: SSI 2004/268, SSI 2004/268 Art.2

s.44, enabling: SSI 2004/268

s.64, applied: SSI 2002/162 Art.11

s.66, repealed: 2002 asp 11 Sch.6 para.24

s.73, enabling: SSI 2003/608

s.77, amended: 2003 asp 13 Sch.4 para.10, Sch.5 Part 1, 2004 asp 7 Sch.1 para.3

s.77, referred to: SSI 2004/375 Reg.2

s.80, applied: SSI 2004/293, SSI 2004/377

s.80, enabling: SSI 2003/587, SSI 2004/293, SSI 2004/377

s.81, enabling: SSI 2002/162, SSI 2003/205, SSI 2003/596, SSI 2004/100

Sch.1 para.2, applied: SSI 2002/106 Reg.2

Sch.1 para.4, applied: SSI 2002/106 Reg.2

Sch.1 para.7, enabling: SSI 2002/106

Sch.2 para.7, enabling: SSI 2002/60

Sch.3 para.11, repealed (in part): 2003 asp 13 Sch.5 Part 1

asp 10. Housing (Scotland) Act 2001

Commencement Orders: SSI 2002/168 Art.2, Art.3, Sch.1; SSI 2002/321 Art.2, Sch.1; SSI 2002/433 Art.2, Sch.1; SSI 2003/434 Art.2, Art.3, Art.4, Sch.1

applied: 2004 c.33 s.112

Part 1, referred to: SSI 2002/533 Sch.1, Sch.3

Part 3, applied: 2002 c.40 s.255

s.1, applied: 2003 asp 10 s.3

s.5, amended: 2003 asp 10 s.5

s.6, applied: SSI 2002/413 Art.2

s.6, enabling: SSI 2002/413

s.11, amended: SSI 2003/331 Sch.1 para.8

s.11, applied: SSI 2002/318 Art.3

s.11, repealed (in part): SSI 2003/331 Sch.1 para.8

s.11, enabling: SSI 2002/318, SSI 2002/415

s.12, referred to: SSI 2002/318 Art.4

s.14, amended: 2003 asp 10 Sch.1 para.4

s.14, applied: SSI 2002/320 Reg.2

s.14, referred to: 2003 asp 10 s.11

s.14, enabling: SSI 2002/320

s.16, applied: SSI 2002/318 Art.4

s.18, applied: SSI 2002/313 Art.2, Art.8

s.18, enabling: SSI 2002/313

s.22, applied: SSI 2002/318 Art.4, Art.5

s.27, applied: SSI 2002/316 Reg.4, Reg.6

s.27, enabling: SSI 2002/316

s.30, applied: SSI 2002/312 Reg.3, Reg.4, Reg.5

s.30, enabling: SSI 2002/312

s.31, amended: 2004 c.33 Sch.28 para.63

s.34, amended: 2003 asp 10 s.6

2001–cont.

asp 10. Housing (Scotland) Act 2001–cont.

s.34, applied: SSI 2002/315 Reg.2

s.34, enabling: SSI 2002/315

s.35, amended: 2004 asp 8 Sch.4 para.6

s.35, disapplied: SSI 2002/321 Art.5

s.36, amended: 2003 asp 10 Sch.1 para.4

s.36, applied: SSI 2002/319 Reg.2

s.36, referred to: 2003 asp 10 s.11

s.36, enabling: SSI 2002/319

s.37, amended: 2003 asp 10 s.6

s.53, enabling: SSI 2002/416

s.56, amended: SSI 2003/331 Sch.1 para.8

s.57, applied: SSI 2002/78 Sch.1, Sch.2, SSI 2003/461 Reg.31, Reg.33

s.57, referred to: SSI 2002/411 Art.2, 2003 c.14 s.129

s.57, enabling: SSI 2002/411

s.65, applied: SSI 2002/312 Reg.4, 2003 asp 2 s.40, 2003 asp 11 s.27

s.79, amended: 2003 asp 10 s.11

s.85, enabling: SSI 2003/532

s.89, applied: 2003 asp 10 s.3

s.91, applied: SI 2002/1792 Sch.5 para.20, SI 2002/2006 Reg.19, SI 2002/2264 Art.3, Art.4, SSI 2002/444, SSI 2002/444 Reg.3, Reg.4, SSI 2003/140, SSI 2004/108, SSI 2004/348

s.91, enabling: SSI 2002/444, SSI 2003/140, SSI 2004/108, SSI 2004/348

s.92, referred to: 2003 asp 1 s.22

s.93, applied: SSI 2004/117

s.93, enabling: SSI 2004/117

s.94, enabling: SSI 2004/105

s.108, amended: 2004 c.33 Sch.28 para.64

s.108, applied: 2004 asp 8 s.101

s.108, varied: 2004 c.33 Sch.21 para.50

s.109, enabling: SSI 2002/168, SSI 2002/312, SSI 2002/313, SSI 2002/314, SSI 2002/315, SSI 2002/316, SSI 2002/318, SSI 2002/319, SSI 2002/320, SSI 2002/321, SSI 2002/415, SSI 2002/434, SSI 2002/444, SSI 2003/434, SSI 2003/532, SSI 2004/105, SSI 2004/117

s.110, enabling: SSI 2002/318, SSI 2002/413

s.113, enabling: SSI 2002/168, SSI 2002/321, SSI 2002/433, SSI 2003/434

Sch.1 para.3, applied: SSI 2002/314 Reg.2

Sch.1 para.3, enabling: SSI 2002/314, SSI 2002/434

Sch.2 Part 1, referred to: SSI 2002/312 Reg.4

Sch.2 Part 1 para.5, amended: 2004 c.33 Sch.28 para.65

Sch.2 Part 1 para.9, applied: SSI 2002/318 Art.4

Sch.2 Part 1 para.10, applied: SSI 2002/318 Art.4

Sch.2 Part 1 para.11, applied: SSI 2002/318 Art.4

Sch.2 Part 1 para.12, applied: SSI 2002/318 Art.4

CAP.

2001–cont.

asp 10. Housing (Scotland) Act 2001–*cont.*
Sch.2 Part 1 para.13, applied: SSI 2002/318 Art.4

Sch.2 Part 1 para.14, applied: SSI 2002/318 Art.4

Sch.2 Part 1 para.15, amended: 2004 c.33 Sch.28 para.65

Sch.2 Part 1 para.15, applied: SSI 2002/318 Art.4

Sch.3 para.2, amended: 2004 c.33 Sch.28 para.66

Sch.3 para.2, referred to: SSI 2002/318 Art.5

Sch.6 para.2, amended: 2004 asp 8 Sch.4 para.6

Sch.6 para.5A, added: 2003 asp 10 s.5

Sch.7 Part 2 para.4, amended: 2003 asp 13 Sch.4 para.11

asp 11. Mortgage Rights (Scotland) Act 2001
s.1, amended: 2003 asp 9 Sch.14 para.13

s.1, varied: 2004 c.33 Sch.21 para.51

s.2, amended: SSI 2004/468 Sch.3 para.3

s.4, amended: 2003 asp 9 Sch.14 para.13, 2003 asp 10 Sch.1 para.5

s.4, referred to: 2003 asp 10 s.11

asp 13. International Criminal Court (Scotland) Act 2001
s.1, applied: 2003 c.41 s.65, s.137, s.138, s.196, 2003 c.42 Sch.5 para.108, SI 2004/1910 Sch.3

s.1, referred to: 2003 c.41 s.64

s.2, applied: 2003 c.41 s.64, s.65, s.137, s.138, s.196

s.7, applied: 2003 c.41 s.196

s.7, referred to: 2003 c.41 s.64, s.65, s.137, s.138

s.10, repealed: 2002 asp 9 s.9

s.25, repealed: 2003 asp 13 Sch.5 Part 1

s.26, applied: SSI 2004/360 Reg.4

s.26, enabling: SSI 2004/360, SSI 2004/437

s.28, amended: 2002 c.8 s.2

Sch.5 Part 1 para.5, enabling: SSI 2003/27

asp 14. Protection from Abuse (Scotland) Act 2001
applied: 2004 c.33 s.114

s.2, enabling: SSI 2002/128, SSI 2002/514, SSI 2003/26

s.3, enabling: SSI 2002/128, SSI 2002/514

s.5, applied: SSI 2003/179 Reg.3, Reg.9

s.5, enabling: SSI 2002/514

asp 15. Police and Fire Services (Finance) (Scotland) Act 2001
Commencement Orders: SSI 2002/84 Art.2

s.3, enabling: SSI 2002/84

CAP.

2002

asp 1. Scottish Local Government (Elections) Act 2002

asp 2. School Education (Amendment) (Scotland) Act 2002
Commencement Orders: SSI 2002/74 Art.2, Art.3

s.3, enabling: SSI 2002/74

asp 3. Water Industry (Scotland) Act 2002
Commencement Orders: SSI 2002/118 Art.2, Sch.1

applied: 1968 c.47 s.2, s.4, s.10, s.11, 1980 c.45 s.24A, s.76, SI 2002/653 Art.5, Art.7

Part 3, disapplied: SI 2002/653 Art.6

s.2, applied: 1976 c.74 Sch.1A Part III, SSI 2002/62 Sch.3

s.2, enabling: SSI 2002/473

s.20, applied: SI 1998/366 Sch.2 para.3, 2004 c.36 Sch.1 para.32

s.21, applied: SI 2002/653 Art.3

s.22, applied: SI 2002/653 Art.3, Art.4

s.24, enabling: SSI 2002/166, SSI 2002/277

s.26, applied: SSI 2002/166 Art.5

s.27, applied: SSI 2002/166 Art.5

s.31, applied: SSI 2002/166 Art.4

s.32, applied: SSI 2002/166 Art.4

s.37, applied: 1987 c.18 s.1, s.5, SI 1992/1332 Reg.28A, Reg.17, Reg.28, SSI 2002/494 Sch.2 para.10

s.40, enabling: SSI 2002/167, SSI 2003/65, SSI 2004/68

s.41, applied: SSI 2002/165 Art.3

s.41, enabling: SSI 2002/165

s.42, applied: 2003 asp 6 Sch.5, 2004 asp 2 Sch.5

s.42, referred to: 2002 asp 7 Sch.5

s.45, applied: SSI 2002/165 Art.3

s.46, amended: 2003 asp 3 Sch.3 para.24

s.46, referred to: 1968 c.47 s.23, s.48

s.47, applied: 1980 c.45 s.18

s.54, amended: 2004 asp 6 Sch.7 para.13

s.54, repealed (in part): 2004 asp 6 Sch.7 para.13

s.68, applied: SSI 2003/331

s.68, enabling: SSI 2002/118, SSI 2002/166, SSI 2002/473, SSI 2003/331

s.69, enabling: SSI 2002/166, SSI 2003/331

s.70, applied: 1974 c.40 s.62, 1987 c.18 s.1, s.5

s.72, enabling: SSI 2002/118

Sch.1 Part 2 para.5, applied: SI 2003/409 Sch.1 Part I

Sch.3, applied: 2004 c.36 Sch.1 para.32

Sch.4 para.1, referred to: SI 1992/1332 Reg.30

Sch.4 para.2, amended: 2002 asp 17 Sch.3 para.28

Sch.4 para.2, applied: SI 1992/1332 Reg.30

Sch.7 para.23, applied: SSI 2002/118 Art.3

CAP.

2002–cont.

asp 4. Criminal Procedure (Amendment) (Scotland) Act 2002

asp 5. Community Care and Health (Scotland) Act 2002

Commencement Orders: SSI 2002/170 Art.2; SSI 2003/62 Art.2; SSI 2004/33 Art.2, Sch.1; SSI 2004/34 Art.3

Part 2, applied: SSI 2004/386 Sch.1 para.5

s.1, amended: SSI 2002/233 Art.2

s.1, applied: 1968 c.49 s.87, SI 1991/2740 Reg.7, SI 1991/2890 Reg.9, SSI 2002/265 Reg.2, Reg.3, SSI 2002/303 Reg.2, Reg.3

s.1, referred to: SSI 2002/264 Art.2, SSI 2002/265 Reg.2

s.1, enabling: SSI 2002/303, SSI 2002/304

s.2, applied: SSI 2002/303 Reg.2

s.2, enabling: SSI 2002/303

s.4, amended: 2003 asp 13 Sch.4 para.12

s.4, enabling: SSI 2002/265

s.6, amended: 2003 asp 13 Sch.4 para.12

s.6, applied: SSI 2002/265 Reg.2, SSI 2002/266 Reg.2, Reg.4

s.6, referred to: SSI 2002/266 Reg.2, SSI 2002/533 Sch.1, Sch.3

s.6, enabling: SSI 2002/266

s.13, applied: SSI 2002/533 Reg.2, Sch.1, 2004 c.17 s.4

s.13, enabling: SSI 2002/533

s.14, applied: SSI 2002/533 Reg.3, Sch.2, 2004 c.17 s.4

s.14, enabling: SSI 2002/533

s.15, applied: SSI 2002/533 Reg.4, Reg.5, Reg.10, Reg.11, Sch.2, Sch.3, 2004 c.17 s.4

s.15, enabling: SSI 2002/533

s.17, applied: SSI 2002/533 Reg.13, Reg.14, Sch.2, Sch.3, Sch.4

s.17, enabling: SSI 2002/533

s.18, referred to: SSI 2003/63 Art.2

s.18, repealed: 2004 asp 1 Sch.1 para.3

s.19, repealed: SSI 2004/167 Sch.1 para.6

s.20, repealed (in part): 2003 c.43 Sch.14 Part 3

s.22, repealed (in part): 2004 asp 7 Sch.2

s.23, applied: SSI 2002/303, SSI 2002/304

s.23, enabling: SSI 2002/265, SSI 2002/266, SSI 2002/303, SSI 2003/62

s.24, enabling: SSI 2002/233, SSI 2003/63, SSI 2004/34

s.27, enabling: SSI 2002/170, SSI 2003/62, SSI 2004/33

Sch.2 para.2, amended: 2004 asp 1 Sch.1 para.3

Sch.2 para.2, repealed (in part): 2004 asp 1 Sch.1 para.3, SSI 2004/167 Sch.1 para.6

asp 6. Protection of Wild Mammals (Scotland) Act 2002

Commencement Orders: SSI 2002/181 Art.2

s.12, enabling: SSI 2002/181

s.100, see *Adams v Scottish Ministers* 2003 S.C.171 (OH), Lord Nimmo Smith

CAP.

2002–cont.

asp 7. Budget (Scotland) Act 2002

s.3, amended: SSI 2003/157 Art.2

s.5, amended: SSI 2002/542 Art.2, SSI 2003/157 Art.2

s.6, repealed: 2003 asp 6 s.9

s.7, applied: SSI 2002/542, SSI 2003/157

s.7, enabling: SSI 2002/542, SSI 2003/157

Sch.1, amended: SSI 2002/542 Art.2, SSI 2003/157 Art.2

Sch.2 Part 1, amended: SSI 2003/157 Art.2

Sch.2 Part 2, amended: SSI 2002/542 Art.2, SSI 2003/157 Art.2

Sch.2 Part 3, amended: SSI 2002/542 Art.2, SSI 2003/157 Art.2

Sch.2 Part 4, amended: SSI 2002/542 Art.2, SSI 2003/157 Art.2

Sch.2 Part 5, amended: SSI 2002/542 Art.2, SSI 2003/157 Art.2

Sch.2 Part 6, amended: SSI 2002/542 Art.2, SSI 2003/157 Art.2

Sch.2 Part 7, amended: SSI 2002/542 Art.2, SSI 2003/157 Art.2

Sch.2 Part 8, amended: SSI 2002/542 Art.2

Sch.2 Part 9, amended: SSI 2002/542 Art.2

Sch.2 Part 10, amended: SSI 2002/542 Art.2, SSI 2003/157 Art.2

Sch.2 Part 11, amended: SSI 2002/542 Art.2

Sch.3, amended: SSI 2002/542 Art.2, SSI 2003/157 Art.2

Sch.4 Part 1, amended: SSI 2002/542 Art.2

Sch.4 Part 3, amended: SSI 2002/542 Art.2

Sch.4 Part 4, amended: SSI 2002/542 Art.2, SSI 2003/157 Art.2

Sch.5, amended: SSI 2003/157 Art.2

asp 8. Marriage (Scotland) Act 2002

Commencement Orders: SSI 2002/184 Art.2

s.2, enabling: SSI 2002/184

asp 9. Sexual Offences (Procedure and Evidence) (Scotland) Act 2002

Commencement Orders: SSI 2002/443 Art.3

s.8, see *Cumming (Hugh Leishman) v HM Advocate* 2003 S.C.C.R. 261 (HCJ), Lord Cullen L.J.G., Lord McCluskey, Lord Osborne

s.11, enabling: SSI 2002/443

asp 10. Fur Farming (Prohibition) (Scotland) Act 2002

Commencement Orders: SSI 2002/519 Art.2

s.2, applied: SI 1996/513 Sch.2 para.45a

s.6, enabling: SSI 2002/519

asp 11. Scottish Public Services Ombudsman Act 2002

Commencement Orders: SSI 2002/467 Art.2

applied: 1967 c.13 s.11A, 1985 c.42 s.1, 1986 c.47 s.34, 1993 c.46 s.18, SI 1995/574 Sch.1 Part II, 1997 c.8 Sch.4 para.8, 1997 c.9 Sch.3 para.7, 1997 c.10 Sch.1 para.7, 1998 c.38 Sch.9 para.27, SI 1999/686 Sch.1 Part II, SI 2004/1823 Art.3, Art.4, SSI 2001/137, 2002 asp 13 s.63, SSI

2002–cont.

asp 11. Scottish Public Services Ombuds-man Act 2002–*cont.*

applied: 1967 c.13 s.11A–*cont.*
2002/103 Sch.1 Part II, SSI 2002/305 Sch.1 Part II
referred to: 2000 c.36 s.76, SI 2004/1823 Art.4
s.3, enabling: SSI 2002/468
s.7, amended: 2004 c.17 Sch.3 para.18
s.19, amended: 2002 asp 13 Sch.4 para.1
s.19, applied: 1974 c.7 s.33
s.25, enabling: SSI 2003/242
s.26, enabling: SSI 2002/469
s.27, enabling: SSI 2002/467
Sch.2 Part 1 para.4, repealed (in part): 2004 asp 7 Sch.2
Sch.2 Part 1 para.5, amended: 2004 asp 1 Sch.1 para.4
Sch.2 Part 2, added: 2004 c.17 Sch.3 para.18
Sch.2 Part 2 para.21A, added: 2003 asp 4 Sch.4 para.16
Sch.2 Part 2 para.45A, added: 2002 asp 13 s.71
Sch.2 Part 2 para.47, repealed: 2003 asp 4 Sch.4 para.16
Sch.2 Part 2 para.80, repealed: 2004 c.17 Sch.4
Sch.2 Part 2 para.86, repealed: SSI 2002/468 Art.2
Sch.3 para.2, repealed: 2004 asp 12 Sch.2
Sch.3 para.4A, added: 2003 asp 13 Sch.4 para.13
Sch.4 para.14, amended: 2004 asp 1 Sch.1 para.4
Sch.5, amended: 2002 asp 13 Sch.4 para.2
Sch.6 para.6, repealed: 2003 asp 13 Sch.5 Part 1

asp 12. Education (Disability Strategies and Pupils Educational Records) (Scotland) Act 2002

Commencement Orders: SSI 2002/367 Art.2
s.1, enabling: SSI 2002/391
s.2, enabling: SSI 2002/391
s.3, applied: SSI 2002/391 Reg.3
s.3, enabling: SSI 2002/391, SSI 2003/10
s.4, enabling: SSI 2003/581
s.5, applied: SSI 2003/10, SSI 2003/581
s.5, enabling: SSI 2002/391, SSI 2003/10
s.7, enabling: SSI 2002/367

asp 13. Freedom of Information (Scotland) Act 2002

Commencement Orders: SSI 2002/437 Art.2; SSI 2003/477 Art.3; SSI 2004/203 Art.3, Sch.1
applied: SSI 2004/467 Reg.3
referred to: 1937 c.43 s.7
Part 4, applied: 2002 asp 11 Sch.5
s.9, applied: SSI 2004/467, SSI 2004/467 Reg.4
s.9, enabling: SSI 2004/467

2002–cont.

asp 13. Freedom of Information (Scotland) Act 2002–*cont.*

s.12, applied: SSI 2004/467, SSI 2004/467 Reg.5
s.12, enabling: SSI 2004/467
s.13, applied: SSI 2004/376, SSI 2004/376 Reg.4
s.13, enabling: SSI 2004/376
s.42, applied: SI 2003/409 Sch.1 Part I
s.44, applied: 2002 asp 11 Sch.5
s.63, applied: 2002 asp 11 s.19
s.72, applied: SSI 2004/467
s.75, enabling: SSI 2002/437, SSI 2003/477, SSI 2004/203
Sch.1 Part 4 para.30, repealed: 2004 asp 7 Sch.2
Sch.1 Part 4 para.31, repealed: 2004 asp 7 Sch.2
Sch.1 Part 4 para.33, amended: 2004 asp 1 Sch.1 para.5
Sch.1 Part 4 para.34, amended: 2004 asp 1 Sch.1 para.5
Sch.1 Part 4 para.44, repealed: 2003 asp 4 Sch.4 para.17
Sch.1 Part 4 para.46, repealed: 2003 asp 4 Sch.4 para.17
Sch.1 Part 7 para.55, repealed: 2003 asp 4 Sch.4 para.17
Sch.1 Part 7 para.62A, added: 2003 asp 4 Sch.4 para.17
Sch.1 Part 7 para.67A, added: 2003 asp 4 Sch.4 para.17
Sch.1 Part 7 para.68, repealed: 2003 asp 4 Sch.4 para.17
Sch.1 Part 7 para.82, repealed: 2003 asp 4 Sch.4 para.17

asp 14. Scottish Qualifications Authority Act 2002

Commencement Orders: SSI 2002/355 Art.3; SSI 2004/347 Art.2
s.3, applied: SI 2003/409 Sch.1 Part I
s.3, referred to: SSI 2002/293 Reg.4
s.3, enabling: SSI 2002/293
s.6, enabling: SSI 2002/355, SSI 2004/347

asp 15. University of St Andrews (Postgraduate Medical Degrees) Act 2002

asp 16. Scottish Parliamentary Standards Commissioner Act 2002

s.13, applied: SI 2003/2278 Art.2
s.14, applied: SI 2003/2278 Art.2
s.20, applied: SI 2003/2278 Art.2

asp 17. Debt Arrangement and Attachment (Scotland) Act 2002

Commencement Orders: SSI 2004/401 Art.3; SSI 2004/416 Art.2
applied: 1985 c.66 s.7, s.14, s.15, SI 1997/687 Art.9, SSI 2002/560 Art.2, Sch.1 para.4, Sch.1 para.21, Sch.1 Part CHAPTER, SSI 2002/566 Sch.1 para.15, SSI 2002/567 Sch.1 para.17, SSI 2004/468 Reg.16

CAP.

CAP.

2002–cont.

asp 17. Debt Arrangement and Attachment (Scotland) Act 2002–*cont.*

Part 1, applied: 2001 asp 11 s.2, SSI 2004/448 Art.3, SSI 2004/468 Sch.4 para.3

Part 2, applied: SSI 2002/560 Sch.1 para.3, SSI 2004/468 Sch.4 para.5

Part 3, applied: SSI 2002/494 Reg.33, SSI 2002/560 Sch.1 para.3, SSI 2004/468 Sch.4 para.5

s.2, applied: SSI 2004/468 Reg.20

s.2, enabling: SSI 2004/468, SSI 2004/470

s.3, applied: SSI 2004/468 Reg.20, Reg.37

s.4, amended: SSI 2004/468 Reg.35

s.4, enabling: SSI 2004/468, SSI 2004/470

s.5, applied: SSI 2004/468 Reg.37

s.5, enabling: SSI 2004/468, SSI 2004/470

s.6, enabling: SSI 2004/468, SSI 2004/470

s.7, applied: SSI 2004/468 Reg.20

s.7, enabling: SSI 2004/468, SSI 2004/470

s.8, enabling: SSI 2004/448

s.10, applied: 1985 c.66 s.7

s.11, applied: SSI 2002/494 Reg.33, SSI 2004/468 Reg.30

s.12, applied: 1987 c.18 s.70, SSI 2002/560 Sch.1 para.7

s.12, enabling: SSI 2002/560

s.16, applied: SSI 2002/560 Sch.1 para.8, Sch.1 para.16

s.17, applied: SSI 2002/560 Sch.1 para.13

s.17, enabling: SSI 2002/560

s.18, applied: SSI 2002/560 Sch.1 para.8, Sch.1 para.14

s.18, enabling: SSI 2002/560

s.20, applied: SSI 2002/560 Sch.1 para.15

s.21, applied: SSI 2002/560 Sch.1 para.10, Sch.1 para.11, Sch.1 para.12

s.22, applied: SSI 2002/560 Sch.1 para.16

s.23, applied: SSI 2002/560 Sch.1 para.9

s.24, applied: SSI 2002/560 Sch.1 para.17

s.25, referred to: 1987 c.18 s.9

s.26, applied: SSI 2002/560 Sch.1 para.18

s.27, applied: SSI 2002/560 Sch.1 para.19

s.29, applied: SSI 2002/560 Sch.1 para.20

s.30, disapplied: SI 1994/1774 Reg.43

s.30, referred to: SI 1996/1527 Reg.49

s.32, applied: SSI 2002/560 Sch.1 para.21

s.32, enabling: SSI 2002/560

s.33, applied: SSI 2002/560 Sch.1 para.22

s.34, applied: SSI 2002/560 Sch.1 para.23

s.35, applied: SSI 2002/560 Sch.1 para.8, Sch.1 para.23

s.36, applied: SSI 2002/560 Sch.1 para.24

s.39, applied: 1997 c.16 s.52

s.39, referred to: 1970 c.9 s.63A, 1983 c.53 Sch.1 para.3, SI 1986/1711 Sch.1 Part II, 1992 c.5 s.121B, 1992 c.14 Sch.8 para.4, SI 1999/2537 Sch.1 Part II

s.47, amended: SSI 2004/468 Sch.3 para.4

s.47, applied: SSI 2002/560 Sch.1 para.25, Sch.1 para.26, Sch.1 para.29

2002–cont.

asp 17. Debt Arrangement and Attachment (Scotland) Act 2002–*cont.*

s.49, applied: SSI 2002/560 Sch.1 para.30

s.50, applied: SSI 2002/560 Sch.1 para.31, Sch.1 para.32, Sch.1 para.33

s.53, applied: SSI 2002/560 Sch.1 para.19

s.55, applied: SSI 2002/494 Reg.33, SSI 2002/560 Sch.1 para.34

s.56, applied: SSI 2002/560 Sch.1 para.8, Sch.1 para.35

s.56, enabling: SSI 2002/560

s.57, applied: SSI 2002/560 Sch.1 para.36, SSI 2002/566 Art.3, SSI 2002/567 Art.3

s.58, applied: SSI 2002/560 Art.5

s.62, applied: SSI 2004/468

s.62, enabling: SSI 2004/448, SSI 2004/468, SSI 2004/470

s.64, enabling: SSI 2002/560, SSI 2004/401, SSI 2004/416

Sch.2, applied: SSI 2004/468 Reg.30

2003

asp 1. Local Government in Scotland Act 2003

Commencement Orders: SSI 2003/134 Sch.1, Art.2; SSI 2004/28 Art.2

applied: 2003 c.26 s.101

Part 1, applied: 1973 c.65 s.102

Part 2, applied: 1973 c.65 s.102, 1992 c.19 s.1

s.1, applied: 1973 c.65 s.97A, s.99, 1992 c.19 s.1

s.7, amended: 2003 asp 8 Sch.6 para.25

s.13, applied: SSI 2003/286 Reg.2, Reg.3

s.13, enabling: SSI 2003/286

s.15, applied: 1973 c.65 s.99, 1978 c.29 s.4B

s.16, applied: 1973 c.65 s.99

s.17, applied: 1973 c.65 s.99

s.28, referred to: 1997 c.29 Sch.2 para.4

s.29, applied: 1997 c.29 Sch.2 para.3

s.31, referred to: 1963 c.12 s.14

s.35, applied: SSI 2004/29 Reg.2

s.35, enabling: SSI 2004/29

s.39, applied: SSI 2004/29

s.46, applied: 1988 c.53 s.95, SI 2004/953 Art.2

s.50, amended: SSI 2003/607 Art.2

s.50, enabling: SSI 2003/607

s.58, applied: SSI 2003/567

s.58, enabling: SSI 2003/567

s.62, enabling: SSI 2003/134, SSI 2004/28

asp 2. Land Reform (Scotland) Act 2003

Commencement Orders: SSI 2003/427 Art.2; SSI 2004/247 Art.2

referred to: SI 2003/2250

Part 2, applied: 2003 asp 11 s.27, 2004 asp 6 s.48

Part 3, applied: 1993 c.45 s.1, 2003 asp 11 s.27

s.32, amended: SI 2003/2155 Sch.1 para.15, Sch.2

s.33, applied: SSI 2004/296 Art.2

CAP.

CAP.

2003–cont.

asp 2. Land Reform (Scotland) Act 2003– *cont.*

s.33, enabling: SSI 2004/296

s.34, applied: SSI 2004/228 Reg.3

s.35, applied: 1947 c.42 s.1

s.36, enabling: SSI 2004/230, SSI 2004/231

s.37, applied: 1970 c.35 s.25, 1979 c.33 s.4, SSI 2004/229 Reg.3, SSI 2004/233 Reg.2, Reg.3

s.37, referred to: SSI 2004/233 Reg.4

s.37, enabling: SSI 2004/231, SSI 2004/233

s.40, applied: 1970 c.35 s.25, 1979 c.33 s.4

s.43, applied: 1979 c.33 s.4

s.48, applied: SSI 2004/233 Reg.5

s.48, enabling: SSI 2004/233

s.49, applied: SSI 2004/233 Reg.6

s.49, enabling: SSI 2004/233

s.52, referred to: SSI 2004/228 Reg.7

s.52, enabling: SSI 2004/228

s.54, applied: SSI 2004/229 Reg.3

s.56, applied: SSI 2004/229 Reg.3

s.57, applied: SSI 2004/229 Reg.3

s.61, applied: SSI 2004/228 Reg.8

s.62, applied: SSI 2004/228 Reg.8

s.63, applied: SSI 2004/229 Reg.2, Reg.3, Reg.4, Reg.5

s.63, enabling: SSI 2004/229

s.71, applied: SSI 2004/227 Reg.3

s.72, applied: 1947 c.42 s.1

s.73, applied: SSI 2004/224 Reg.2

s.73, enabling: SSI 2004/224

s.75, enabling: SSI 2004/227

s.82, applied: SSI 2004/224 Reg.3, SSI 2004/226 Art.4

s.82, enabling: SSI 2004/224

s.85, applied: SSI 2004/226 Art.3

s.87, applied: SSI 2004/226 Art.3

s.89, applied: SSI 2004/225 Reg.2, Reg.3, Sch.1 para.2, SSI 2004/226 Art.2, Art.4, Art.5, Art.6

s.89, enabling: SSI 2004/226

s.90, applied: SSI 2004/225 Reg.2, Reg.4

s.90, enabling: SSI 2004/225

s.91, applied: SSI 2004/227 Reg.8

s.98, applied: SSI 2004/296

s.100, enabling: SSI 2003/427, SSI 2004/247

Sch.1 para.11, amended: SI 2003/2155 Sch.1 para.15

Sch.1 para.12, amended: SI 2003/2155 Sch.1 para.15

Sch.1 para.13, amended: SI 2003/2155 Sch.1 para.15

asp 3. Water Environment and Water Services (Scotland) Act 2003

Commencement Orders: SSI 2003/562 Art.2

Part 1, applied: SI 2003/3245 Reg.6, SI 2004/99 Reg.5, SSI 2003/610 Art.2

s.4, applied: SSI 2003/610 Art.2

2003–cont.

asp 3. Water Environment and Water Services (Scotland) Act 2003–*cont.*

s.4, varied: SI 2003/3245 Reg.6, SI 2004/99 Sch.4 para.2

s.4, enabling: SSI 2003/610

s.5, varied: SI 2003/3245 Reg.6, SI 2004/99 Sch.4 para.2

s.6, varied: SI 2003/3245 Reg.6, SI 2004/99 Sch.4 para.2

s.7, varied: SI 2003/3245 Reg.6, SI 2004/99 Sch.4 para.2

s.7, enabling: SSI 2004/516

s.8, varied: SI 2003/3245 Reg.6, SI 2004/99 Sch.4 para.2

s.9, varied: SI 2003/3245 Reg.6, SI 2004/99 Sch.4 para.2

s.10, varied: SI 2003/3245 Reg.6, SI 2004/99 Sch.4 para.2

s.11, varied: SI 2003/3245 Reg.6, SI 2004/99 Sch.4 para.2

s.12, varied: SI 2003/3245 Reg.6, SI 2004/99 Sch.4 para.2

s.13, varied: SI 2003/3245 Reg.6, SI 2004/99 Sch.4 para.2

s.14, varied: SI 2003/3245 Reg.6, SI 2004/99 Sch.4 para.2

s.15, varied: SI 2003/3245 Reg.6, SI 2004/99 Sch.4 para.2

s.16, varied: SI 2003/3245 Reg.6, SI 2004/99 Sch.4 para.3

s.17, varied: SI 2003/3245 Reg.6, SI 2004/99 Sch.4 para.2

s.18, varied: SI 2003/3245 Reg.6, SI 2004/99 Sch.4 para.4

s.19, varied: SI 2003/3245 Reg.6, SI 2004/99 Sch.4 para.2

s.20, applied: SI 2004/99 Reg.5

s.20, varied: SI 2003/3245 Reg.6, SI 2004/99 Sch.4 para.5

s.22, applied: SI 2004/99 Reg.5

s.22, varied: SI 2003/3245 Reg.6, SI 2004/99 Sch.4 para.5

s.23, applied: SI 2004/99 Reg.5

s.25, applied: SI 2004/99 Reg.5

s.26, varied: SI 2003/3245 Reg.6, SI 2004/99 Sch.4 para.6

s.27, varied: SI 2003/3245 Reg.6, SI 2004/99 Sch.4 para.7

s.36, applied: SSI 2003/610

s.36, enabling: SSI 2003/610

s.38, enabling: SSI 2003/562

Sch.2 Part 1 para.2, varied: SI 2003/3245 Reg.6, SI 2004/99 Sch.4 para.5

Sch.2 Part 2 para.20, amended: 2004 asp 8 Sch.2 para.6

asp 4. Public Appointments and Public Bodies etc (Scotland) Act 2003

Commencement Orders: SSI 2003/219 Art.2; SSI 2003/348 Art.2; SSI 2003/602 Art.2; SSI 2004/45 Art.2; SSI 2004/198 Art.2;

CAP.

CAP.

2003–cont.

asp 4. Public Appointments and Public Bodies etc (Scotland) Act 2003–*cont.*
  –*cont.*
    SSI 2004/148 Art.2; SSI 2003/384 Art.2; SSI 2004/232 Art.2
    s.5, amended: 2004 asp 7 Sch.2
    s.5, applied: SSI 2004/15 Reg.2, SSI 2004/46, SSI 2004/285 Reg.2
    s.5, repealed (in part): 2004 asp 7 Sch.2
    s.5, enabling: SSI 2004/15, SSI 2004/46, SSI 2004/285
    s.6, applied: 1978 c.29 s.12G
    s.6, repealed: 2004 asp 7 Sch.2
    s.7, amended: 2004 asp 7 Sch.1 para.4
    s.7, applied: SSI 2004/16 Reg.2, Reg.3, SSI 2004/284 Reg.2, Reg.3
    s.7, repealed (in part): 2004 asp 7 Sch.2
    s.7, enabling: SSI 2004/16, SSI 2004/284
    s.8, amended: 2004 asp 7 Sch.2
    s.8, applied: SSI 2004/47
    s.8, repealed (in part): 2004 asp 7 Sch.2
    s.8, enabling: SSI 2004/47
    s.9, amended: 2004 asp 7 Sch.1 para.4, Sch.2
    s.10, repealed (in part): 2004 asp 7 Sch.2
    s.18, applied: SSI 2004/46, SSI 2004/47
    s.18, enabling: SSI 2004/46, SSI 2004/47
    s.21, enabling: SSI 2003/219, SSI 2003/348, SSI 2003/384, SSI 2003/602, SSI 2004/45, SSI 2004/148, SSI 2004/198, SSI 2004/232
    Sch.2, amended: 2004 asp 7 Sch.2
    Sch.4 para.2, referred to: 1953 c.49 s.3
    Sch.4 para.5, repealed (in part): SSI 2004/167 Sch.1 para.7

asp 5. Protection of Children (Scotland) Act 2003
  Commencement Orders: SSI 2004/522 Art.2
    s.5, applied: SI 1999/929 r.3.25.5
    s.6, applied: SI 1999/929 r.3.25.5
    s.7, applied: SI 1999/929 r.3.25.2, r.3.25.3
    s.8, enabling: SSI 2004/523
    s.10, amended: 2004 asp 5 s.24
    s.10, applied: SI 1996/513 Sch.2 para.47a,
    s.14, applied: SI 1999/929 r.3.25.2, r.3.25.4
    s.15, applied: SI 1999/929 r.3.25.2, r.3.25.5, r.3.25.6
    s.21, enabling: SSI 2004/523
    s.22, enabling: SSI 2004/522

asp 6. Budget (Scotland) Act 2003
    s.3, amended: SSI 2003/330 Art.2, SSI 2003/603 Art.2, SSI 2004/147 Art.2
    s.5, amended: SSI 2003/603 Art.2, SSI 2004/147 Art.2
    s.6, repealed: 2004 asp 2 s.8
    s.7, applied: SSI 2003/330, SSI 2004/147
    s.7, enabling: SSI 2003/330, SSI 2003/603, SSI 2004/147
    Sch.1, amended: SSI 2003/330 Art.2, SSI 2003/603 Art.2, SSI 2004/147 Art.2

2003–cont.

asp 6. Budget (Scotland) Act 2003–*cont.*
    Sch.2 Part 1, amended: SSI 2003/603 Art.2, SSI 2004/147 Art.2
    Sch.2 Part 2, amended: SSI 2003/603 Art.2, SSI 2004/147 Art.2
    Sch.2 Part 3, amended: SSI 2003/603 Art.2
    Sch.2 Part 4, amended: SSI 2003/603 Art.2, SSI 2004/147 Art.2
    Sch.2 Part 5, amended: SSI 2004/147 Art.2
    Sch.2 Part 6, amended: SSI 2003/603 Art.2, SSI 2004/147 Art.2
    Sch.2 Part 7, amended: SSI 2004/147 Art.2
    Sch.2 Part 8, amended: SSI 2003/603 Art.2, SSI 2004/147 Art.2
    Sch.2 Part 9, amended: SSI 2003/603 Art.2
    Sch.2 Part 10, amended: SSI 2003/603 Art.2, SSI 2004/147 Art.2
    Sch.2 Part 11, amended: SSI 2003/603 Art.2
    Sch.3, amended: SSI 2003/330 Art.2, SSI 2003/603 Art.2, SSI 2004/147 Art.2
    Sch.5, amended: SSI 2004/147 Art.2

asp 7. Criminal Justice (Scotland) Act 2003
  Commencement Orders: SSI 2003/288 Art.2, Sch.1; SSI 2003/438 Art.2; SSI 2003/475 Art.3, Sch.1, Art.2, 2004 asp 8 Sch.5; SSI 2004/240 Art.2; SSI 2004/451 Art.2
    s.13, applied: SSI 2003/438 Art.2
    s.14, amended: 2004 c.33 Sch.28 para.67
    s.14, applied: 1995 c.46 s.288C, SSI 2003/441 Art.2, SSI 2003/563 Art.3
    s.14, enabling: SSI 2003/441, SSI 2003/519, SSI 2003/563, SSI 2004/287
    s.15A, added: 2004 asp 3 s.3
    s.16, applied: SSI 2004/411 Art.2
    s.16, enabling: SSI 2004/411
    s.18, applied: SSI 2003/440 Art.2
    s.18, enabling: SSI 2003/440
    s.21, amended: 2003 c.42 Sch.6 para.49
    s.21, applied: 1995 c.46 s.201
    s.22, applied: 2002 c.29 Sch.4 para.8A, 2003 c.42 Sch.5 para.109, 2004 c.19 s.14, SI 2004/1910 Sch.3, SSI 2004/411 Sch.1 para.21
    s.27, referred to: SSI 2003/287 Art.2
    s.28, referred to: SSI 2003/287 Art.2
    s.33, referred to: 1997 c.43 Sch.2 para.7
    s.38, referred to: SSI 2003/287 Art.2
    s.42, applied: 1995 c.46 s.234D, s.234H, s.232
    s.42, referred to: 1995 c.46 s.228
    s.42, enabling: SSI 2003/290
    s.44, repealed: 2004 asp 8 Sch.5
    s.45, repealed: 2004 asp 8 Sch.5
    s.53, applied: SSI 2003/424 Art.2, Art.3
    s.53, referred to: SSI 2003/424 Art.3
    s.53, enabling: SSI 2003/424
    s.54, referred to: SSI 2003/287 Art.3
    s.56, applied: SSI 2004/257 Reg.19
    s.62, applied: 1995 c.46 s.107

13

2003–cont.

asp 7. Criminal Justice (Scotland) Act 2003–*cont.*

s.74, applied: 2003 c.42 Sch.5 para.110, SSI 2004/411 Sch.1 para.29

s.83, repealed: 2004 asp 8 Sch.5

s.84, enabling: SSI 2003/287, SSI 2003/438

s.88, applied: SSI 2003/563

s.89, enabling: SSI 2003/288, SSI 2003/ 439, SSI 2003/475, SSI 2004/240, SSI 2004/451

asp 8. Building (Scotland) Act 2003

Commencement Orders: SSI 2004/404 Art.2, Art.4, Sch.1, Sch.2, Sch.3

applied: SSI 2004/428 Reg.32, Reg.54, Reg.59

Part 2, applied: SSI 2004/428 Reg.53

Part 3, applied: SSI 2004/428 Reg.53

Part 4, applied: SSI 2004/428 Reg.53

Part 5, applied: SSI 2004/428 Reg.53

s.1, applied: SSI 2004/406

s.1, enabling: SSI 2004/406

s.3, applied: SSI 2004/406 Reg.16, SSI 2004/428 Reg.21, Reg.25, Reg.28, Reg.29, Reg.60

s.3, enabling: SSI 2004/406

s.7, applied: SSI 2004/428 Reg.30, Reg.31, Reg.35, Reg.37, Reg.38, Reg.40

s.8, applied: SSI 2004/406 Reg.5, SSI 2004/ 428 Reg.6

s.8, enabling: SSI 2004/406

s.9, applied: SSI 2004/428 Reg.3, Reg.4, Reg.5, Reg.9, Reg.12, Reg.17, Reg.18, Reg.20, Reg.23, Reg.33, Reg.34, Reg.56

s.9, enabling: SSI 2004/428

s.10, applied: SSI 2004/428 Sch.2 para.4

s.11, applied: SSI 2004/428 Reg.17, Reg.32, Reg.33, Reg.34, Sch.1 para.9

s.12, applied: SSI 2004/428 Reg.20

s.14, applied: SSI 2004/428 Reg.16

s.15, referred to: SSI 2004/428 Reg.7

s.17, applied: SSI 2004/428 Reg.16, Reg.41, Reg.42, Reg.43, Reg.44, Reg.46, Reg.59, Reg.60

s.17, referred to: SSI 2004/428 Reg.41

s.18, applied: SSI 2004/428 Reg.20, Reg.23, Reg.43, Reg.46

s.19, applied: SSI 2004/428 Reg.32, Reg.41, Reg.46

s.21, applied: SSI 2004/428 Reg.49

s.22, applied: SSI 2004/428 Reg.13, Reg.14, Reg.41, Reg.50, Reg.60

s.23, applied: SSI 2004/428 Reg.14

s.24, enabling: SSI 2004/428

s.25, applied: SSI 2004/428 Reg.51, Reg.57

s.26, applied: SSI 2004/428 Reg.51, Reg.57

s.27, applied: SSI 2004/428 Reg.51, Reg.57

s.28, applied: SSI 2004/428 Reg.51, Reg.57

s.29, applied: SSI 2004/428 Reg.51, Reg.57

s.30, applied: SSI 2004/428 Reg.51, Reg.57

s.31, varied: SSI 2004/404 Art.3

s.31, enabling: SSI 2004/506

2003–cont.

asp 8. Building (Scotland) Act 2003–*cont.*

s.33, enabling: SSI 2004/428

s.36, enabling: SSI 2004/428

s.38, enabling: SSI 2004/428, SSI 2004/508

s.42, applied: SSI 2004/428 Reg.52

s.47, applied: SSI 2004/428 Reg.51, Reg.60

s.47, enabling: SSI 2004/428

s.54, enabling: SSI 2004/404, SSI 2004/ 406, SSI 2004/428, SSI 2004/506, SSI 2004/508

s.56, applied: SSI 2004/406 Reg.4

s.56, enabling: SSI 2004/406

s.59, enabling: SSI 2004/404

Sch.1, enabling: SSI 2004/406

Sch.1 para.3, applied: SSI 2004/406 Reg.6

Sch.2, enabling: SSI 2004/428

Sch.2 para.3, applied: SSI 2004/428 Reg.38

Sch.2 para.9, applied: SSI 2004/428 Reg.39

Sch.3, enabling: SSI 2004/428

asp 9. Title Conditions (Scotland) Act 2003

Commencement Orders: SSI 2003/454 Art.2

applied: 2004 asp 11 Sch.1 para.3.1

referred to: 2004 asp 11 s.25

Part 9, applied: SSI 2003/452 r.28

s.3, amended: 2004 asp 11 Sch.4 para.2

s.4, amended: SSI 2003/503 Sch.1 para.7, 2004 asp 11 Sch.4 para.3

s.4, applied: 1979 c.33 s.6

s.6, applied: 2000 asp 5 s.17

s.10, amended: 2004 asp 11 Sch.4 para.4

s.10, applied: 1979 c.33 s.12

s.10A, added: 2004 asp 11 Sch.4 para.5

s.10A, applied: 1979 c.33 s.12

s.11, amended: 2004 asp 11 Sch.4 para.6

s.21, applied: 1947 c.42 Sch.1 para.3B, 1967 c.10 Sch.5 para.2, SI 1984/467 Reg.6, Sch.4

s.21, referred to: 1967 c.10 Sch.5 para.2

s.23, applied: SSI 2003/452 Sch.1, SSI 2004/479 r.2

s.23, referred to: SSI 2003/452 r.5

s.25, amended: 2004 asp 11 Sch.4 para.7

s.29, amended: 2004 asp 11 Sch.4 para.8

s.29, repealed (in part): 2004 asp 11 Sch.4 para.8

s.31A, added: 2004 asp 11 Sch.4 para.9

s.33, amended: 2004 asp 11 Sch.4 para.10

s.34, applied: SSI 2004/479 r.2

s.35, amended: 2004 asp 11 Sch.4 para.11

s.36, applied: SI 1984/467 Reg.6, Sch.4

s.37, amended: SSI 2003/503 Sch.1 para.8

s.37, applied: SSI 2003/452 Sch.1, SSI 2004/ 479 r.2

s.37, referred to: SSI 2003/452 r.5

s.38, applied: SSI 2003/453 Art.2, Sch.1 Part I, Sch.1 Part II

s.38, enabling: SSI 2003/453, SSI 2003/ 621, SSI 2004/400

s.41, applied: 1979 c.33 s.3

CAP.

2003–cont.

asp 9. Title Conditions (Scotland) Act 2003–*cont.*

s.43, amended: 2004 asp 11 Sch.4 para.12
s.43, applied: SSI 2004/477 Art.2
s.43, enabling: SSI 2004/477
s.45, repealed (in part): 2004 asp 11 Sch.4 para.13
s.46, amended: 2004 asp 7 Sch.2
s.49, applied: 1979 c.33 s.9
s.50, applied: 1979 c.33 s.6, s.9
s.52, applied: 2000 asp 5 s.17
s.53, amended: 2004 asp 11 Sch.4 para.14
s.53, applied: 2000 asp 5 s.17
s.54, applied: 2000 asp 5 s.17
s.55, applied: 2000 asp 5 s.17
s.56, applied: 2000 asp 5 s.17, s.73
s.58, applied: 1979 c.33 s.9
s.63, applied: 2000 asp 5 s.18
s.71, applied: 2004 asp 11 s.4
s.73, applied: SSI 2003/452 Sch.1, SSI 2004/479 r.2
s.73, referred to: SSI 2003/452 r.5
s.75, applied: 1979 c.33 s.6
s.80, applied: 1979 c.33 s.6, s.9
s.86, applied: SSI 2003/452 Sch.1
s.88, referred to: 1973 c.52 Sch.1 para.2
s.90, amended: SSI 2003/503 Sch.1 para.9, 2004 asp 11 Sch.4 para.15
s.90, applied: SSI 2003/452 r.6, r.21, Sch.1
s.91, applied: SSI 2003/452 r.6, r.21, Sch.1
s.93, applied: SSI 2003/452 r.13
s.95, applied: SSI 2003/452 r.21
s.97, applied: SSI 2003/452 r.28
s.98, amended: 2004 asp 11 Sch.4 para.16
s.99, amended: SSI 2003/503 Sch.1 para.10, 2004 asp 11 Sch.4 para.17
s.99, applied: SSI 2003/452 r.28
s.101, enabling: SSI 2003/452
s.102, applied: SSI 2003/452 Sch.1
s.103, applied: SSI 2003/452 r.28
s.104, amended: SSI 2003/503 Sch.1 para.11
s.104, enabling: SSI 2003/452
s.106, amended: SSI 2003/503 Sch.1 para.12
s.106, applied: 1947 c.42 Sch.1 para.4, 1967 c.10 Sch.5 para.6C
s.107, applied: SI 1984/467 Reg.6, Sch.4, SSI 2003/451 r.2
s.107, referred to: SSI 2003/452 r.5
s.109, amended: SSI 2003/503 Sch.1 para.13
s.110, amended: SSI 2003/503 Sch.1 para.14
s.119, repealed (in part): 2004 asp 11 Sch.4 para.18
s.122, amended: SSI 2003/503 Sch.1 para.15, 2004 asp 11 Sch.4 para.19
s.122, applied: 1993 c.44 s.16, 2000 asp 5 s.56
s.122, referred to: 1967 c.10 Sch.5 para.2
s.124, applied: 1947 c.42 Sch.1 para.3A, Sch.1 para.6C, 1967 c.10 Sch.5 para.2
s.126, applied: SSI 2003/451

CAP.

2003–cont.

asp 9. Title Conditions (Scotland) Act 2003–*cont.*

s.126, enabling: SSI 2003/451, SSI 2004/479
s.127, applied: SSI 2003/503
s.128, enabling: SSI 2003/503
s.129, enabling: SSI 2003/454
Sch.1, referred to: 1924 c.27 s.8
Sch.1A, added: 2004 asp 11 Sch.4 para.20

asp 10. Homelessness etc (Scotland) Act 2003

Commencement Orders: SSI 2003/609 Art.2; SSI 2004/288 Art.2
s.14, enabling: SSI 2003/609, SSI 2004/288

asp 11. Agricultural Holdings (Scotland) Act 2003

Commencement Orders: SSI 2003/305 Art.2; SSI 2003/248 Art.2; SSI 2003/548 Art.2, Sch.1 para.2, para.4, para.5, para.7, para.8, para.1, para.3, para.6; SSI 2004/511 Art.2
applied: 1907 c.51 s.37A, 1970 c.35 Sch.1 para.5, 1971 c.58 s.37, 1973 c.56 s.31, s.52, 1974 c.38 s.8, 1986 c.49 Sch.2 para.10, Sch.2 para.11, 1987 c.26 s.256, 1988 c.36 s.33, 1988 c.43 Sch.4 para.6, 1993 c.44 s.29, 1993 c.45 s.1, Sch.1 para.6, 1995 c.36 s.76
disapplied: 1973 c.56 s.55, 1994 c.33 s.106, 1999 c.33 s.149
referred to: 1958 c.69 s.26, 1993 c.44 s.30, 1993 c.45 s.1, SSI 2003/583 Art.2
Part 2, applied: 1991 c.55 s.60
s.2, applied: 1991 c.55 s.21
s.3, applied: 1958 c.69 Sch.6 para.31
s.9, applied: 1958 c.69 s.14A
s.10, applied: 1958 c.69 s.14A, 1987 c.26 Sch.8 para.13
s.17, applied: 1958 c.69 s.14A, 1973 c.56 s.55, SSI 2004/143 Reg.16
s.17, disapplied: 1973 c.56 s.55
s.17, varied: 1973 c.56 s.44
s.21, applied: 1964 c.41 s.16, s.29, SSI 2004/143 Reg.16
s.22, applied: SSI 2004/143 Reg.16
s.25, enabling: SSI 2004/496, SSI 2004/497
s.26, enabling: SSI 2004/497
s.40, applied: 1991 c.55 s.45A, s.85
s.41, applied: 1991 c.55 s.45A, s.85
s.47, applied: 1987 c.26 Sch.8 para.13
s.49, applied: 1987 c.26 Sch.8 para.13
s.53, applied: 1958 c.69 s.24, 1993 c.44 Sch.2 para.11
s.54, applied: 1973 c.56 s.44, s.55
s.71, amended: 2004 c.33 Sch.28 para.68
s.72, applied: SSI 2003/294 Art.2, Art.3
s.72, enabling: SSI 2003/294
s.73, applied: 1991 c.55 s.21
s.84, applied: 1991 c.55
s.84, disapplied: 1991 c.55 s.7
s.91, applied: SSI 2003/583

2003–cont.

asp 11. Agricultural Holdings (Scotland) Act 2003–cont.

s.91, enabling: SSI 2003/248, SSI 2003/294, SSI 2003/305, SSI 2003/548, SSI 2003/583

s.92, enabling: SSI 2003/583

s.95, enabling: SSI 2003/248, SSI 2003/305, SSI 2003/548, SSI 2004/511

asp 13. Mental Health (Care and Treatment) (Scotland) Act 2003

Commencement Orders: SSI 2003/316 Art.2; SSI 2004/153 Sch.2, Art.3, Sch.1, Art.2; SSI 2004/367 Art.2, Sch.1, Sch.2, Art.2, Art.3

applied: SSI 2004/402 Reg.4

s.3, repealed (in part): 2004 asp 7 Sch.2

s.250, applied: SSI 2004/388 Reg.2, SSI 2004/430 Reg.2

s.250, enabling: SSI 2004/388, SSI 2004/430

s.253, applied: SSI 2004/388 Reg.2, SSI 2004/430 Reg.2

s.253, enabling: SSI 2004/388, SSI 2004/430

s.254, amended: 2004 c.33 Sch.28 para.69

s.275, applied: SSI 2004/387 Reg.2, SSI 2004/429 Reg.2

s.275, enabling: SSI 2004/387, SSI 2004/429

s.311, applied: 2003 c.42 Sch.3 para.58, SSI 2004/411 Sch.1 para.18

s.313, amended: 2004 c.33 Sch.28 para.70

s.313, applied: 2003 c.42 Sch.3 para.59

s.315, applied: 2003 c.42 Sch.5 para.111

s.326, applied: SSI 2003/498

s.328, applied: 2004 asp 3 s.11

s.330, enabling: SSI 2003/498, SSI 2004/533

s.333, enabling: SSI 2003/316, SSI 2004/153, SSI 2004/367

Sch.2 Part 1 para.1, referred to: SSI 2004/373 Reg.2, SSI 2004/374 Reg.2, SSI 2004/375 Reg.2

Sch.2 Part 1 para.1, enabling: SSI 2004/154, SSI 2004/374, SSI 2004/375

Sch.2 Part 1 para.2, referred to: SSI 2004/373 Reg.2

Sch.2 Part 1 para.3, enabling: SSI 2004/155, SSI 2004/373

Sch.2 Part 1 para.5, referred to: SSI 2004/402 Reg.3

Sch.2 Part 1 para.5, enabling: SSI 2004/402

Sch.2 Part 2 para.7, referred to: SSI 2004/373 Reg.2

Sch.2 Part 2 para.8, referred to: SSI 2004/373 Reg.2

Sch.2 Part 3, enabling: SSI 2004/286

Sch.2 Part 4 para.15, referred to: SSI 2004/373 Reg.2

Sch.2 Part 4 para.16, referred to: SSI 2004/373 Reg.2

2003–cont.

asp 14. Council of the Law Society of Scotland Act 2003

applied: 1987 c.26 s.24, s.33

asp 18. Education (School Meals) (Scotland) Act 2003

s.1, applied: SSI 2003/350

2004

asp 1. Primary Medical Services (Scotland) Act 2004

Commencement Orders: SSI 2004/58 Sch.1, Art.2

Royal Assent, January 27, 2004

s.7, applied: SSI 2004/114 Reg.3, Reg.16, SSI 2004/115 Reg.3, Reg.27, SSI 2004/116 Reg.3, Reg.23, Reg.27, SSI 2004/167

s.7, enabling: SSI 2004/142, SSI 2004/163, SSI 2004/167, SSI 2004/212, SSI 2004/223, SSI 2004/372

s.9, enabling: SSI 2004/58

Sch.1 para.1, disapplied: SSI 2004/163 Art.97

Sch.1 para.2, applied: SSI 2004/163 Art.49

Sch.1 para.2, disapplied: SSI 2004/163 Art.49

asp 2. Budget (Scotland) Act 2004

Royal Assent, March 23, 2004

s.3, amended: SSI 2004/290 Art.2

s.7, applied: SSI 2004/290

s.7, enabling: SSI 2004/290

Sch.3, amended: SSI 2004/290 Art.2

asp 4. Education (Additional Support for Learning) (Scotland) Act 2004

Royal Assent, May 07, 2004

s.4, applied: 2001 asp 10 s.35, Sch.6 para.2

asp 5. Criminal Procedure (Amendment) (Scotland) Act 2004

Commencement Orders: SSI 2004/405 Art.2, Art.3, Art.5, Sch.1, Sch.2

Royal Assent, June 04, 2004

s.27, enabling: SSI 2004/405

asp 6. Nature Conservation (Scotland) Act 2004

Commencement Orders: SSI 2004/407 Art.2; SSI 2004/495 Art.2

Royal Assent, June 11, 2004

applied: SSI 2004/474 Art.2

Part 2, applied: 1970 c.30 s.10, 1993 c.45 s.1, SI 1994/2716 Reg.3, 1997 c.8 s.54

Part 2 c.2, applied: SI 1994/2716 Reg.19

Part 2 c.3, applied: SI 1994/2716 Reg.19

s.3, applied: SSI 2004/475 Reg.20

s.6, applied: SSI 2004/475 Reg.20

s.6, disapplied: SSI 2004/475 Reg.20

s.13, applied: SI 1994/2716 Reg.53A

s.15, applied: SSI 2004/475 Reg.20

s.15, enabling: SSI 2004/474

s.16, applied: SI 1994/2716 Reg.53A, SSI 2004/475 Reg.20

s.23, applied: SSI 2004/475 Reg.21

s.23, varied: SI 1994/2716 Reg.20

CAP.

2004–cont.

asp 6. Nature Conservation (Scotland) Act 2004–*cont.*

s.24, varied: SI 1994/2716 Reg.20
s.25, varied: SI 1994/2716 Reg.20
s.26, varied: SI 1994/2716 Reg.20
s.27, varied: SI 1994/2716 Reg.20
s.28, varied: SI 1994/2716 Reg.20
s.29, varied: SI 1994/2716 Reg.21
s.30, varied: SI 1994/2716 Reg.21
s.31, varied: SI 1994/2716 Reg.21
s.32, varied: SI 1994/2716 Reg.21
s.33, varied: SI 1994/2716 Reg.21
s.34, varied: SI 1994/2716 Reg.21
s.35, varied: SI 1994/2716 Reg.21
s.36, varied: SI 1994/2716 Reg.21
s.37, varied: SI 1994/2716 Reg.21
s.38, varied: SI 1994/2716 Reg.22
s.39, applied: SI 1994/2716 Reg.19
s.39, varied: SI 1994/2716 Reg.22
s.40, applied: SI 1994/2716 Reg.19
s.40, varied: SI 1994/2716 Reg.22
s.41, applied: SI 1994/2716 Reg.19
s.41, varied: SI 1994/2716 Reg.22
s.42, varied: SI 1994/2716 Reg.22
s.43, applied: SI 1994/2716 Reg.19
s.43, varied: SI 1994/2716 Reg.22
s.44, applied: SI 1994/2716 Reg.19
s.44, varied: SI 1994/2716 Reg.22
s.45, applied: SI 1994/2716 Reg.19
s.45, varied: SI 1994/2716 Reg.22
s.46, applied: SI 1994/2716 Reg.19
s.46, varied: SI 1994/2716 Reg.22
s.47, varied: SI 1994/2716 Reg.22
s.48, varied: SI 1994/2716 Reg.22
s.49, varied: SI 1994/2716 Reg.22
s.53, enabling: SSI 2004/474
s.59, enabling: SSI 2004/407, SSI 2004/495
Sch.1 para.4, applied: SSI 2004/475 Reg.20
Sch.2, applied: SI 1994/2716 Reg.19
Sch.2 para.5, applied: SSI 2004/475 Reg.21
Sch.3, applied: SI 1994/2716 Reg.19
Sch.5 para.2, applied: SSI 2004/475 Reg.20
Sch.5 para.4, varied: SSI 2004/475 Reg.20
Sch.5 para.11, varied: SSI 2004/475 Reg.21

asp 7. National Health Service Reform (Scotland) Act 2004

Commencement Orders: SSI 2004/335 Art.2; SSI 2004/361 Art.2
Royal Assent, June 11, 2004
s.12, enabling: SSI 2004/335, SSI 2004/361

asp 8. Antisocial Behaviour etc (Scotland) Act 2004

Commencement Orders: SSI 2004/420 Art.2, Art.3, Art.4, Sch.1, Sch.2, Sch.3, Sch.4, Sch.5

CAP.

2004–cont.

asp 8. Antisocial Behaviour etc (Scotland) Act 2004–*cont.*

Royal Assent, July 26, 2004
s.4, applied: 1995 c.46 s.234AA
s.5, applied: SI 1999/929 r.3.27.2
s.8, applied: SI 1999/929 r.3.27.4
s.9, applied: 1995 c.46 s.234AA, s.44
s.11, applied: 1995 c.46 s.234AA
s.12, applied: 1995 c.36 s.52, s.73
s.13, applied: SI 1999/929 r.3.27.5
s.27, applied: SI 1999/929 r.3.27.6
s.27, referred to: SI 1999/929 r.3.27.6
s.27, enabling: SSI 2004/455
s.28, applied: SI 1999/929 r.3.27.6, r.3.27.7
s.32, applied: SI 1999/929 r.3.27.8
s.33, applied: SI 1999/929 r.3.27.9
s.34, applied: SI 1999/929 r.3.27.10
s.35, applied: SI 1999/929 r.3.27.11
s.61, applied: SI 1999/929 r.3.27.11
s.63, applied: SI 1999/929 r.3.27.11
s.64, applied: SI 1999/929 r.3.27.11
s.71, applied: SI 1999/929 r.3.27.12
s.73, applied: SI 1999/929 r.3.27.13
s.74, applied: SI 1999/929 r.3.27.12
s.76, applied: SI 1999/929 r.3.27.14
s.94, applied: SI 1999/929 r.3.27.12
s.97, applied: SI 1999/929 r.3.27.12
s.105, applied: SI 1999/929 r.3.27.15
s.123, applied: SSI 2004/419 Reg.2
s.123, enabling: SSI 2004/419
s.141, enabling: SSI 2004/420
s.145, enabling: SSI 2004/420
Sch.1 para.1, varied: 1990 c.43 s.81

asp 9. Local Governance (Scotland) Act 2004

Commencement Orders: SSI 2004/351 Art.2, Art.3
Royal Assent, July 29, 2004
Part 2, applied: 1990 c.43 s.36
s.4, applied: 1973 c.65 s.16
s.16, enabling: SSI 2004/351
s.17, enabling: SSI 2004/351

asp 11. Tenements (Scotland) Act 2004

Commencement Orders: SSI 2004/487 Art.2
Royal Assent, October 22, 2004
s.12, applied: 1973 c.52 Sch.1 para.1, 1979 c.33 s.12
s.12, disapplied: 2003 asp 9 s.10
s.13, applied: 1979 c.33 s.12
s.13, enabling: SSI 2004/490
s.34, enabling: SSI 2004/487
Sch.2, amended: SSI 2004/490 Art.2

ACTS OF THE NORTHERN IRELAND ASSEMBLY

CAP.

12 & 13 Geo. 5 (1922)

20. Uniformity of Laws Act (Northern Ireland) 1922
Sch.5, referred to: SR 2003/152 Sch.7 para.1

14 & 15 Geo. 5 (1924)

5. Explosives Act (Northern Ireland) 1924
applied: SR 2002/147 Reg.3, SR 2002/301 Reg.3

18 & 19 Geo. 5 (1928)

25. Game Preservation Act (Northern Ireland) 1928
s.6, applied: 2002 c.26 Sch.4 para.1
s.7, amended: 2002 c.2 (NI) s.1
s.7A, substituted: 2002 c.2 (NI) s.2
s.7D, amended: 2002 c.2 (NI) s.1
s.7F, amended: 2002 c.2 (NI) s.1, (NI) s.3

19 & 20 Geo. 5 (1929)

13. Petroleum (Consolidation) Act (Northern Ireland) 1929
s.2, amended: SR 2003/152 Sch.7 para.2
s.2, applied: SR 2003/152 Reg.17
s.2, repealed (in part): SR 2003/152 Sch.8 Part I
s.5, applied: SR 2002/301 Reg.8
s.9, applied: SR 2003/152 Reg.17
s.9, repealed: SR 2003/152 Sch.7 para.2, Sch.8 Part I
s.17, repealed: SR 2003/152 Sch.7 para.2, Sch.8 Part I
s.18, amended: SR 2003/152 Sch.7 para.2
s.19, applied: SR 2002/301 Reg.8
s.23, amended: SR 2003/152 Sch.7 para.2
s.24A, amended: SR 2003/152 Sch.7 para.2, Sch.8 Part I
s.24A, substituted: SR 2003/152 Sch.7 para.2

23 & 24 Geo. 5 (1932-33)

6. Stormont Regulation and Government Property Act (Northern Ireland) 1933
s.5, disapplied: SI 2002/3153 Art.41, SI 2003/410 Art.10

1 & 2 Geo. 6 (1937-38)

iv. Belfast Harbour Act 1938
s.17, repealed: SR 2002/40 Sch.2

8 & 9 Geo. 6 (1944-45)

6. Disabled Persons (Employment) Act (Northern Ireland) 1945
s.2, applied: SR 2003/28 Sch.2 para.14
s.3, applied: SR 2003/28 Sch.2 para.14

CAP.

8 & 9 Geo. 6 (1944-45)–cont.

6. Disabled Persons (Employment) Act (Northern Ireland) 1945–cont.
s.4, applied: SI 2003/493 Reg.6, Reg.10

14. Summary Jurisdiction (Separation and Maintenance) Act (Northern Ireland) 1945
applied: SI 2003/435 Sch.2 para.2

15. Criminal Justice Act (Northern Ireland) 1945
s.18, applied: 2002 c.26 Sch.12 para.1, 2004 c.11 s.21, s.22
s.19, repealed: 2002 c.26 Sch.13
s.25, applied: 2003 c.44 Sch.17 para.24
s.35, applied: 2002 c.29 s.186, s.187, s.188
s.35, varied: 2002 c.29 s.185

9 & 10 Geo. 6 (1945-46)

16. Marriage and Matrimonial Causes Act (Northern Ireland) 1946
repealed: SI 2003/413 Sch.1

14 Geo. 6 (1950)

iv. Belfast Harbour Act 1950
s.21, repealed: SR 2002/40 Sch.2

29. Employment and Training Act (Northern Ireland) 1950
applied: SR 2002/79 Reg.11
s.1, applied: 2002 c.21 s.1, SR 2003/28 Sch.2 para.14

1 & 2 Eliz. 2 (1952-53)

2. Forestry Act (Northern Ireland) 1953
s.9, amended: 2002 c.2 (NI) s.2, (NI) Sch.1
s.10, repealed (in part): 2002 c.2 (NI) s.2, (NI) Sch.1

18. Prison Act (Northern Ireland) 1953
applied: SR 2003/28 Reg.5
s.10, applied: 2002 c.26 Sch.4 para.1
s.19, applied: 2002 c.26 Sch.4 para.1

2 & 3 Eliz. 2 (1953-54)

21. Marriages Act (Northern Ireland) 1954
repealed: SI 2003/413 Sch.1

33. Interpretation Act (Northern Ireland) 1954
applied: SI 2003/412 Art.2, SR 2003/240 Reg.1, SR 2003/256 Reg.1, SR 2003/308 Reg.1, SR 2003/312 Reg.1, SR 2003/314 Reg.2, SR 2003/324 Reg.2

CAP.

3 & 4 Eliz. 2 (1954-55)

15. **Lough Neagh and Lower Bann Drainage and Navigation Act (Northern Ireland) 1955**
    s.17, amended: 2003 c.21 Sch.17 para.25
29. **Registration of Births, Deaths, and Marriages (Fees, etc.) Act (Northern Ireland) 1955**
    repealed: SI 2003/413 Sch.1
    s.2, amended: SR 2002/242 Sch.1

4 & 5 Eliz. 2 (1955-56)

iv. **Belfast Harbour Act 1956**
    s.21, repealed: SR 2002/40 Sch.2
4. **Malone and Whiteabbey Training Schools Act (Northern Ireland) 1956**
    applied: SR 2003/137 Art.3
    repealed: 2004 c.4 s.9, Sch.4
5. **Births, Deaths and Marriages Registration Act (Northern Ireland) 1956**
    repealed: SI 2003/413 Sch.1

7 & 8 Eliz. 2 (1958-59)

15. **Coroners Act (Northern Ireland) 1959**
    s.1, amended: 2002 c.26 Sch.3 para.12
    s.2, amended: 2002 c.26 s.18, Sch.3 para.13
    s.2, repealed (in part): 2002 c.26 Sch.13
    s.3, amended: 2002 c.26 Sch.3 para.14
    s.6, amended: 2002 c.26 Sch.3 para.15
    s.34, applied: 2002 c.26 s.80
    s.36, enabling: SR 2002/37
25. **County Courts Act (Northern Ireland) 1959**
    s.102, amended: 2002 c.26 Sch.3 para.3, Sch.5 para.1, Sch.12 para.4
    s.102A, added: 2002 c.26 s.13
    s.103, amended: 2002 c.26 s.18
    s.105, referred to: 2002 c.26 Sch.12 para.5
    s.105, repealed (in part): 2002 c.26 Sch.13
    s.106, amended: 2002 c.26 Sch.12 para.5
    s.107, amended: 2002 c.26 Sch.3 para.4, Sch.13
    s.134, amended: 2002 c.26 Sch.3 para.5
    s.136, repealed (in part): 2002 c.26 Sch.13
    s.136A, added: 2002 c.26 Sch.3 para.6

10 & 11 Eliz. 2 (1961-62)

7. **Administrative and Financial Provisions Act (Northern Ireland) 1962**
    s.18, applied: SR 2003/184
    s.18, referred to: SR 2002/95
    s.18, enabling: SR 2003/227
13. **Agricultural Produce (Meat Regulations and Pig Industry) Act (Northern Ireland) 1962**
    s.8, applied: 2002 c.26 Sch.4 para.1
14. **Electoral Law Act (Northern Ireland) 1962**
    applied: SI 2003/435 Sch.2 para.4
    s.47, applied: 2002 c.26 Sch.4 para.1

CAP.

10 & 11 Eliz. 2 (1961-62)–cont.

14. **Electoral Law Act (Northern Ireland) 1962**–cont.
    s.73, applied: 2002 c.26 Sch.12 para.6
    s.96, applied: 2002 c.26 Sch.12 para.6
    s.97, applied: 2002 c.26 Sch.12 para.6
    s.106, applied: 2002 c.26 Sch.12 para.6
    s.120, applied: 2002 c.26 Sch.12 para.6
    Sch.5, amended: SI 2003/1245 Art.2
    Sch.5, repealed (in part): SI 2003/1245 Art.2
    Sch.8, applied: 2002 c.26 Sch.12 para.6
19. **Human Tissue Act (Northern Ireland) 1962**
    repealed: 2004 c.30 Sch.7 Part 1

1964

21. **Magistrates Court Act (Northern Ireland) 1964**
    s.1, amended: 2002 c.26 Sch.13
    s.7, repealed: 2002 c.26 Sch.13
    s.9, amended: 2002 c.26 s.18, Sch.3 para.8, Sch.5 para.2
    s.9, repealed (in part): 2002 c.26 Sch.13
    s.10, amended: 2002 c.26 Sch.3 para.9, Sch.13
    s.11, repealed: 2002 c.26 Sch.13
    s.12A, amended: 2002 c.26 Sch.4 para.14, Sch.13
    s.168, amended: 2002 c.26 Sch.3 para.10
29. **Lands Tribunal and Compensation Act (Northern Ireland) 1964**
    s.1, amended: 2002 c.26 Sch.3 para.35
    s.2, amended: 2002 c.26 Sch.13
    s.2, applied: SI 2002/2843 Art.4
    s.2, repealed (in part): 2002 c.26 Sch.13
    s.2, enabling: SR 2003/227
    s.3, amended: 2002 c.26 Sch.3 para.36
    s.3, applied: 2002 c.26 Sch.1, Sch.6

1965

3. **Agriculture (Miscellaneous Provisions) (Northern Ireland) Act 1965**
    s.16, repealed: SI 2004/1109 Sch.1
13. **New Towns Act (Northern Ireland) 1965**
    s.25, amended: 2003 c.21 Sch.17 para.31
20. **Factories Act (Northern Ireland) 1965**
    s.32, repealed: SR 2003/152 Sch.8 Part I
22. **Seeds Act (Northern Ireland) 1965**
    s.1, applied: SR 2002/404, SR 2003/42
    s.1, enabling: SR 2002/169, SR 2002/257, SR 2002/404, SR 2002/407, SR 2003/42
    s.2, enabling: SR 2002/257, SR 2002/404, SR 2002/407, SR 2003/42

1966

6. **National Insurance Act (Northern Ireland) 1966**
    applied: SR 2002/352 Sch.3, SR 2002/353 Reg.15

1966–cont.

6. National Insurance Act (Northern Ireland) 1966–cont.
Part III, applied: SR 2002/352 Reg.99
s.35, varied: SR 2002/99 Art.11, SR 2003/155 Art.12
s.36, amended: SR 2003/155 Art.12
s.36, varied: SR 2002/99 Art.11
s.55, disapplied: SR 2002/353 Reg.15
s.56, applied: SR 2002/353 Reg.15

35. Maintenance and Affiliation Orders Act (Northern Ireland) 1966
s.13, applied: SI 2003/435 Sch.2 para.2

1967

7. Diseases of Fish Act (Northern Ireland) 1967
s.1, referred to: SR 2003/87 Art.3
s.1, varied: SR 2003/87 Sch.1, SR 2003/243 Sch.1
s.1, enabling: SR 2003/87, SR 2003/242, SR 2003/243

14. Misrepresentation Act (Northern Ireland) 1967
applied: SI 2003/1593 Sch.1 Part II

21. Livestock Marketing Commission Act (Northern Ireland) 1967
s.4, varied: SR 2003/20 Reg.2
s.4, enabling: SR 2003/20, SR 2003/21, SR 2003/104
s.9, substituted: SI 2003/418 Sch.1 para.11
s.10, repealed (in part): SI 2003/418 Sch.3

28. Plant Health Act (Northern Ireland) 1967
applied: SR 2002/404 Sch.5 para.1
s.2, enabling: SR 2002/7, SR 2002/269, SR 2002/273, SR 2002/285, SR 2003/175, SR 2003/193
s.3, enabling: SR 2002/7, SR 2002/269, SR 2002/273, SR 2002/285, SR 2003/175, SR 2003/193, SR 2003/235
s.3A, enabling: SR 2002/273, SR 2002/285, SR 2003/175
s.3B, enabling: SR 2002/7, SR 2002/273, SR 2002/285, SR 2003/175, SR 2003/193
s.4, enabling: SR 2002/7, SR 2002/269, SR 2002/273, SR 2002/285, SR 2003/175, SR 2003/193

32. Marriage (Registration of Buildings) Act (Northern Ireland) 1967
repealed: SI 2003/413 Sch.1

37. Transport Act (Northern Ireland) 1967
see *R. (on the application of McParland) v Department of the Environment in Northern Ireland* [2002] N.I. 292 (CA (NI)), Carswell, L.C.J.
referred to: SR 2003/217 Reg.2
s.6A, amended: SR 2003/217 Reg.3
s.7A, added: SR 2003/217 Reg.4
s.10B, applied: SR 2003/37 Reg.4
s.28A, amended: SR 2003/217 Reg.5

1967–cont.

37. Transport Act (Northern Ireland) 1967–cont.
s.34, amended: SR 2003/217 Reg.7
s.45, enabling: SR 2003/14
s.46A, substituted: SR 2003/217 Reg.6
s.67F(2), varied: SI 2003/410 Art.20
s.67F(9), varied: SI 2003/410 Art.20

1968

10. Costs in Criminal Cases Act (Northern Ireland) 1968
s.1, amended: SI 2003/1247 Art.35, Sch.2
s.2, amended: 2002 c.26 Sch.11 para.1
s.2, referred to: 2003 c.41 s.62, s.135
s.4, amended: SI 2003/435 Sch.4 para.1, SI 2004/1500 Art.28
s.4, applied: SI 2003/435 Art.21
s.5, referred to: 2003 c.41 s.62, s.135
s.6, amended: SI 2003/435 Sch.4 para.1
s.6, applied: SI 2003/435 Art.21
s.7, applied: 2003 c.41 s.62, s.135
s.10, amended: SI 2003/1247 Art.35

28. Criminal Justice (Miscellaneous Provisions) Act (Northern Ireland) 1968
s.1, applied: 2003 c.21 Sch.6 para.10, SI 2004/1501 Art.31
s.1, varied: 2003 c.21 Sch.6 para.10
s.7, applied: 2003 c.44 Sch.17 para.26, SI 2004/702 Sch.4 para.3

29. Treatment of Offenders Act (Northern Ireland) 1968
s.5, applied: 2002 c.29 s.186, s.187
s.9, amended: 2002 c.26 Sch.11 para.2
s.18, applied: 2002 c.29 s.187
s.19, applied: SI 2003/417 Art.34
s.21, amended: 2002 c.26 Sch.4 para.15
s.21, applied: 2002 c.26 s.10

34. Children and Young Persons Act (Northern Ireland) 1968
applied: SI 2002/635 Reg.2, SI 2002/896 Sch.1 para.2
s.1, applied: SI 2002/896 Sch.1 para.7
s.1, applied: SI 2002/635 Reg.2
s.9, applied: SI 2002/635 Sch.1 para.3, SI 2002/896 Sch.1 para.77
s.11, applied: SI 2002/635 Reg.2, SI 2002/896 Sch.1 para.8
s.14, applied: SI 2002/635 Sch.1 para.3, SI 2002/896 Sch.1 para.76
s.15, applied: SI 2002/635 Reg.2, SI 2002/896 Sch.1 para.8
s.20, applied: 2003 c.44 Sch.17 para.27
s.21, applied: 2002 c.29 Sch.5 para.8, 2003 c.44 Sch.17 para.79
s.22, amended: SI 2003/1247 Art.22
s.22, applied: 2003 c.44 Sch.17 para.80, SI 2003/1184 Sch.2 para.41
s.32, applied: SI 2002/896 Sch.1 para.75
s.97, applied: SI 2003/435 Sch.2 para.2

CAP.

1968–cont.

34. Children and Young Persons Act (Northern Ireland) 1968–cont.

s.127, applied: SI 2002/635 Reg.2, Sch.1 para.3, SI 2002/896 Sch.1 para.5, Sch.1 para.78

s.129, applied: SI 2002/635 Sch.1 para.3, SI 2002/896 Sch.1 para.78

s.137, applied: SI 2002/2006 Reg.19

s.138, applied: SR 2003/61 Sch.3

s.140, applied: SI 2002/896 Sch.1 para.75

s.143, applied: SI 2003/435 Sch.2 para.2

s.144, applied: SI 2002/896 Sch.1 para.75, SI 2003/435 Sch.2 para.2

s.178, amended: 2002 c.26 s.11

s.178, repealed (in part): 2002 c.26 Sch.13

Sch.1, amended: SI 2003/1247 Sch.1 para.6

Sch.1, applied: SI 2002/635 Sch.1 para.3, SI 2002/896 Sch.1 para.68

Sch.1, referred to: SI 2003/237 Sch.4 para.6, SSI 2003/19 Sch.5 para.13

Sch.2, amended: 2002 c.26 s.11

Sch.2, applied: 2002 c.26 Sch.6

Sch.2, repealed (in part): 2002 c.26 Sch.13, Sch.13

1969

9. Livestock Marketing Commission (Amendment) Act (Northern Ireland) 1969

s.1, enabling: SR 2003/21, SR 2003/104

15. Grand Jury (Abolition) Act (Northern Ireland) 1969

s.2, amended: 2002 c.26 Sch.13

s.2, applied: 2002 c.26 s.44, s.89, 2002 c.29 s.233

s.2, repealed (in part): 2002 c.26 Sch.13

16. Theft Act (Northern Ireland) 1969

s.1, applied: 2004 c.19 s.14

s.8, applied: 2003 c.44 Sch.17 para.28

s.8, applied: SI 2004/1500 Sch.2 para.16

s.9, applied: 2003 c.44 Sch.17 para.29, Sch.17 para.81

s.9, amended: SI 2003/1247 Sch.1 para.7

s.10, applied: 2003 c.44 Sch.17 para.30

s.14, repealed (in part): SI 2003/2908 Sch.2

s.15, applied: 2004 c.19 s.14

s.15, referred to: SI 2002/796 Art.17

s.16, applied: 2004 c.19 s.14

s.17, applied: 2004 c.19 s.14

s.20, applied: 2002 c.29 Sch.5 para.9

s.21, applied: 2004 c.19 s.14

s.27, applied: 2002 c.29 s.308

s.32, amended: SI 2003/2908 Sch.1 para.2, Sch.2

24. Industrial and Provident Societies Act (Northern Ireland) 1969

applied: SI 2003/3075 Reg.2

referred to: SI 2004/353 Reg.2

s.6, applied: 2002 c.29 Sch.9 para.2, SI 2003/3075 Reg.2

CAP.

1969–cont.

24. Industrial and Provident Societies Act (Northern Ireland) 1969–cont.

s.7, applied: 2002 c.29 Sch.9 para.2, SI 2003/3075 Reg.2

28. Age of Majority Act (Northern Ireland) 1969

Sch.1, amended: SI 2003/413 Sch.1

1970

1. Harbours Act (Northern Ireland) 1970

s.10, enabling: SR 2003/249, SR 2003/250, SR 2003/251, SR 2003/252

10. Explosives Act (Northern Ireland) 1970

applied: SR 2002/301 Reg.3

s.1, disapplied: SR 2002/147 Reg.12

s.1, enabling: SR 2002/147

s.3, enabling: SR 2002/147

18. Land Registration Act (Northern Ireland) 1970

applied: 2002 c.29 s.195, s.249

s.25, enabling: SR 2002/400, SR 2002/401

s.66, applied: 2002 c.29 s.195, s.249

s.67, applied: 2002 c.29 s.195, s.249

s.81, enabling: SR 2002/229

s.85, enabling: SR 2002/229

Sch.2, applied: SR 2002/400 Art.2, SR 2002/401 Art.2

Sch.11, added: SI 2002/3153 Art.50

Sch.11, amended: SI 2002/3153 Art.50

32. Equal Pay Act (Northern Ireland) 1970

s.2, applied: SI 2003/2902 Sch.2, Sch.3, Sch.4

s.6B, added: SI 2003/2902 Art.30

1971

32. Nursing Homes and Nursing Agencies Act (Northern Ireland) 1971

repealed: SI 2003/431 Sch.5

35. Pensions (Increase) Act (Northern Ireland) 1971

applied: SR 2002/352 Reg.51, Reg.92, Reg.126, Reg.139

s.1, applied: SR 2002/102 Art.3, Art.4, SR 2003/169 Art.3, Art.4

s.8, applied: SR 2002/102 Art.2

1972

4. Fish Industry Act (Northern Ireland) 1972

s.1, applied: SR 2003/163 Art.3

s.1, varied: SR 2003/163 Art.3

s.6, referred to: SR 2003/163 Art.3

s.7, referred to: SR 2003/163 Art.3

7. Welfare of Animals Act (Northern Ireland) 1972

referred to: SR 2003/115 Reg.6

s.2, enabling: SR 2002/259, SR 2003/244

1972–cont.

9. **Local Government Act (Northern Ireland) 1972**
applied: 2002 c.4 (NI) s.4, SR 2003/46 Sch.6 para.3
s.36, applied: SR 2002/352 Sch.6 para.26
s.36, enabling: SR 2003/125
s.51, enabling: SR 2002/231
s.98, disapplied: SI 2002/3153 Art.19, SR 2003/46 Reg.27
s.115, varied: SR 2003/73 Sch.1
s.137, applied: SR 2003/61 Reg.6
Sch.6, applied: 2003 c.21 Sch.4 para.5, SI 2003/410 Sch.2 para.2, Sch.2 para.4, SR 2003/46 Sch.6 para.8
Sch.6, varied: 2003 c.21 Sch.4 para.5, SI 2003/410 Sch.2 para.2, Sch.2 para.4

11. **Miscellaneous Transferred Excise Duties Act (Northern Ireland) 1972**
s.29, amended: 2002 c.2 (NI) s.2
s.35, amended: 2002 c.2 (NI) s.2
s.37, amended: 2002 c.2 (NI) s.2, (NI) Sch.1
s.41, amended: 2002 c.2 (NI) s.2
s.42, amended: 2002 c.2 (NI) s.2, (NI) Sch.1

2000

1. **Financial Assistance for Political Parties Act (Northern Ireland) 2000**
applied: 2003 c.25

2. **Appropriation (Northern Ireland) Act 2000**
repealed: SI 2003/1885 Sch.4

3. **Allowances to Members of the Assembly Act (Northern Ireland) 2000**
s.1, amended: SI 2003/2696 Art.4
s.3, amended: SR 2002/230 Art.2
s.3, enabling: SR 2002/230

4. **Child Support, Pensions and Social Security Act (Northern Ireland) 2000**
Commencement Orders: SR 2003/53 Art.3, Art.5, Art.2, Art.4, Art.6, Art.7, Art.8, Sch.1
referred to: SR 2002/68 Art.1, SR 2002/118 Art.1
s.10, referred to: SR 2002/391 Art.1
s.26, varied: SR 2002/247 Reg.2
s.26, enabling: SR 2002/247
s.28, enabling: SR 2002/164, SR 2003/57, SR 2003/84, SR 2003/91
s.53, applied: SR 2002/79 Reg.3, Reg.5
s.54, applied: SR 2002/79 Reg.3, Reg.5
s.60, enabling: SR 2002/80, SR 2003/154
s.68, enabling: SR 2002/68, SR 2002/118, SR 2003/53
Sch.5, referred to: SR 2002/109 Sch.1
Sch.6, repealed (in part): 2004 c.3 Sch.2 Part 1
Sch.7, enabling: SR 2002/80, SR 2003/189, SR 2003/224, SR 2003/312

2001

3. **Health and Personal Social Services Act (Northern Ireland) 2001**
Commencement Orders: SR 2003/69 Art.2; SR 2002/180 Art.2
Part I, applied: SR 2002/386 Reg.4
s.1, enabling: SR 2002/349
s.3, applied: SR 2003/139 Art.2
s.3, enabling: SR 2003/139
s.10, amended: SI 2003/431 Art.46
s.15, amended: SI 2003/431 Sch.4
s.20, repealed: SI 2003/431 Sch.5
s.21, repealed: SI 2003/431 Sch.5
s.22, substituted: SI 2003/431 Sch.4
s.23, applied: SR 2002/52 Reg.3
s.23, enabling: SR 2002/52
s.25, enabling: SR 2002/52, SR 2002/373
s.32, enabling: SR 2002/52
s.37, enabling: SR 2002/52, SR 2002/373
s.57, enabling: SR 2002/52, SR 2002/349, SR 2002/373
s.58, enabling: SR 2002/66
s.61, enabling: SR 2002/73, SR 2002/180
Sch.1, enabling: SR 2002/349

5. **Ground Rents Act (Northern Ireland) 2001**
Commencement Orders: SR 2002/251 Art.2
s.4, enabling: SR 2002/229
s.5, enabling: SR 2002/228, SR 2002/229
s.6, enabling: SR 2002/229
s.7, enabling: SR 2002/229
s.23, enabling: SR 2002/229
s.26, enabling: SR 2002/229
s.31, enabling: SR 2002/229
s.32, enabling: SR 2002/251
Sch.1, applied: SR 2002/228 Art.2, Art.3
Sch.1, enabling: SR 2002/228

6. **Government Resources and Accounts Act (Northern Ireland) 2001**
s.6, applied: 2002 c.3 (NI) s.2, (NI) s.6, 2002 c.7 (NI) s.3, SI 2003/420 Art.4, Art.8, SI 2004/707 Art.4, Art.8
s.8, applied: 2002 c.3 (NI) s.3, 2002 c.7 (NI) s.4, SI 2003/420 Art.5, SI 2004/707 Art.4, Art.5, Art.8
s.10, applied: SI 2002/3126 Art.2
s.11, applied: SI 2002/3126 Art.2
s.12, repealed: SI 2003/418 Sch.3
s.13, amended: SI 2003/418 Sch.2 para.6
s.14, applied: SR 2003/268
s.15, applied: SR 2003/268 Art.2
s.15, enabling: SR 2003/268
s.16, applied: SI 2002/3126 Art.2
s.21, repealed (in part): SI 2003/418 Sch.3

8. **Street Trading Act (Northern Ireland) 2001**
s.18, applied: 2002 c.26 Sch.4 para.1

9. **Electronic Communications Act (Northern Ireland) 2001**
s.1, enabling: SR 2003/3
s.2, enabling: SR 2003/3

CAP.

2001–cont.

9. Electronic Communications Act (Northern Ireland) 2001–*cont.*
   s.4, amended: 2003 c.21 Sch.17 para.170
11. Adoption (Intercountry Aspects) Act (Northern Ireland) 2001
   s.1, applied: SI 2003/431 Art.15, Art.40
   s.1, enabling: SR 2003/16
   s.2, amended: SI 2003/431 Sch.4
   s.8, repealed: SI 2003/431 Sch.5
   s.12, referred to: SR 2002/22 Art.2
   s.14, referred to: SR 2002/22 Art.2
   s.16, enabling: SR 2002/22, SR 2002/45
12. Family Law Act (Northern Ireland) 2001
   Commencement Orders: SR 2002/138 Art.2, Art.3
   s.4, enabling: SR 2002/138
14. Trustee Act (Northern Ireland) 2001
   Commencement Orders: SR 2002/253 Art.2
   s.45, enabling: SR 2002/253 Art.2
16. Budget (No.2) Act (Northern Ireland) 2001
   Sch.2, disapplied: 2002 c.3 (NI) s.3
17. Social Security Fraud Act (Northern-Ireland) 2001
   Commencement Orders: SR 2002/165 Art.2; SR 2002/392 Art.2; SR 2002/406 Art.2
   s.6, applied: SR 2002/79 Reg.2, Reg.9, SR 2002/80
   s.6, referred to: SR 2002/79 Reg.2, Reg.6, Reg.7, Reg.20
   s.6, repealed (in part): 2002 c.21 Sch.6
   s.6, enabling: SR 2002/79
   s.7, applied: SR 2002/79 Reg.11, Reg.15
   s.7, disapplied: SR 2002/79 Reg.12, Reg.13
   s.7, referred to: SR 2002/79 Reg.4
   s.7, enabling: SR 2002/79
   s.8, applied: SR 2002/79 Reg.9
   s.8, referred to: SR 2002/79 Reg.6, Reg.7, Reg.20
   s.8, enabling: SR 2002/79
   s.9, enabling: SR 2002/79
   s.12, applied: SR 2002/80
   s.17, enabling: SR 2002/75, SR 2002/165, SR 2002/392, SR 2002/406
   s.123, applied: SR 2002/79 Reg.5

2002

1. Industrial Development Act (Northern Ireland) 2002
   Commencement Orders: SR 2002/134 Art.2
   s.6, repealed: SI 2003/419 Sch.5
   s.7, enabling: SR 2002/134
2. Game Preservation (Amendment) Act (Northern Ireland) 2002
   Commencement Orders: SR 2002/130 Art.2
   s.4, enabling: SR 2002/130
3. Budget Act (Northern Ireland) 2002
   s.6, disapplied: SI 2003/420 Art.4

CAP.

2002–cont.

4. Local Government (Best Value) Act (Northern Ireland) 2002
5. Personal Social Services (Preserved Rights) Act (Northern Ireland) 2002
   Commencement Orders: SR 2002/131 Art.2, Art.3
   s.1, applied: SR 2002/136 Reg.3, Reg.4
   s.1, disapplied: SR 2002/136 Reg.2
   s.1, enabling: SR 2002/136
   s.3, enabling: SR 2002/132
   s.6, enabling: SR 2002/131, SR 2002/136
   s.7, enabling: SR 2002/131
6. Carers and Direct Payments Act (Northern Ireland) 2002
   Commencement Orders: SR 2003/201 Art.2
   s.2, applied: SR 2003/226 Reg.2
   s.2, enabling: SR 2003/226
   s.8, applied: SR 2003/253 Art.3
   s.10, enabling: SR 2003/226
   s.11, enabling: SR 2003/201
7. Budget (No.2) Act (Northern Ireland) 2002
   s.3, disapplied: SI 2003/420 Art.4
   s.4, disapplied: SI 2003/420 Art.4
   s.4, substituted: SI 2003/420 Art.5
8. Railway Safety Act (Northern Ireland) 2002
9. Health and Personal Social Services Act (Northern Ireland) 2002
   Commencement Orders: SR 2002/311 Art.2
   s.2, enabling: SR 2002/386
   Sch.1, enabling: SR 2002/386
10. Social Security Act (Northern Ireland) 2002
   Commencement Orders: SR 2002/351 Art.2; SR 2002/358 Art.2; SR 2002/351 Sch.1; SR 2002/358 Art.3, Sch.1
   applied: SR 2002/354
   s.9, enabling: SR 2002/351, SR 2002/358, SR 2003/396
11. Children (Leaving Care) Act (Northern Ireland) 2002
12. Limited Liability Partnerships Act (Northern Ireland) 2002
13. Open-Ended Investment Companies Act (Northern Ireland) 2002
   applied: SI 2002/3150 Sch.1 para.6
   s.1, applied: 2000 c.8 Sch.5 para.1
14. State Pension Credit Act (Northern Ireland) 2002
   Commencement Orders: SR 2002/366 Art.2; SR 2003/29 Art.2; SR 2003/211 Sch.1
   applied: SI 2002/2008 Reg.4, SR 2003/28, SR 2003/28 Reg.4, SR 2003/191
   referred to: SR 2003/191 Reg.34
   s.1, enabling: SR 2003/28, SR 2003/191
   s.2, applied: SR 2003/28 Reg.6, Sch.3 para.2, SR 2003/191 Reg.34
   s.2, varied: SR 2003/28 Reg.6
   s.2, enabling: SR 2003/28, SR 2003/191, SR 2003/261

CAP.

2002–cont.

14. State Pension Credit Act (Northern Ireland) 2002–*cont.*
s.3, applied: SR 2003/28 Reg.9, Sch.3 para.2
s.3, referred to: SR 2003/28 Reg.7
s.3, varied: SR 2003/28 Sch.3 para.1
s.3, enabling: SR 2003/28, SR 2003/191
s.4, varied: SR 2003/28 Sch.3 para.1
s.4, enabling: SR 2003/28
s.5, varied: SR 2003/28 Sch.3 para.1
s.5, enabling: SR 2003/28
s.6, applied: SR 2003/28 Reg.10
s.6, enabling: SR 2003/28
s.7, applied: SR 2003/28 Reg.10
s.7, enabling: SR 2003/28, SR 2003/191
s.9, applied: SR 2003/191 Reg.34
s.9, enabling: SR 2003/28

CAP.

2002–cont.

14. State Pension Credit Act (Northern Ireland) 2002–*cont.*
s.12, applied: SR 2003/28 Sch.3 para.1
s.12, enabling: SR 2003/28, SR 2003/191
s.13, enabling: SR 2003/191, SR 2003/261
s.15, applied: SR 2003/28 Reg.15
s.15, enabling: SR 2003/28, SR 2003/191
s.16, amended: SR 2003/28 Reg.16
s.16, applied: SR 2003/28 Reg.18
s.16, enabling: SR 2003/28
s.17, enabling: SR 2003/28, SR 2003/191
s.19, enabling: SR 2003/191, SR 2003/261
s.21, enabling: SR 2003/29, SR 2003/211, SR 2003/373
Sch.1, enabling: SR 2003/191

ACTS OF THE PARLIAMENT OF ENGLAND, WALES & THE UNITED KINGDOM

CAP.

1449

6. Leases Act 1449
applied: 2003 asp 15 s.66

1469

3. Reversion Act 1469
repealed: 2003 asp 9 s.89

35 Eliz. 1 (1592)

141. Compensation Act 1592
see *Construction Centre Group Ltd v Highland Council* 2003 S.C. 464 (Ex Div), Lord Hamilton, Lord Carloway, Lord Osborne

1607

6. Theft Act 1607
amended: 2003 asp 15 Sch.4 Part 2

1621

18. Bankruptcy Act 1621
applied: 2002 c.29 s.422

13 Cha. 3 (1661)

247. Redemptions Act 1661
repealed: 2003 asp 9 Sch.15

29 Car. 2 (1677)

3. Statute of Frauds 1677
s.4, disapplied: SI 2003/3226 Reg.4

CAP.

33 Car. 2 (1681)

79. Declinature Act 1681 [S] 1681
varied: 2004 c.33 Sch.21 para.1

1700

2. Act of Settlement 1700
s.3, applied: 2002 c.24 s.10
s.3, disapplied: 2003 c.39 s.42, Sch.2 para.14

1702

1. Crown Lands Act 1702
applied: 2002 c.ii
s.5, applied: 2002 c.ii
s.5, disapplied: 2002 c.ii s.3

6 Anne (1706-07)

11. Union with Scotland Act 1706
Art.XXII, see *Lord Gray's Motion, Re* [2002] 1 A.C. 124 (HL), Lord Slynn of Hadley

1707

7. Treaty of Union with England Act 1707
Art.XXII, see *Lord Gray's Motion, Re* [2002] 1 A.C. 124 (HL), Lord Slynn of Hadley

7 Ann. (1708)

14. Parochial Libraries Act 1708
s.2, amended: 2004 c.14 Sch.1 Part 6
s.5, amended: 2004 c.14 Sch.1 Part 6
s.6, repealed: 2004 c.14 Sch.1 Part 6
s.7, repealed: 2004 c.14 Sch.1 Part 6
s.10, amended: 2003 c.39 Sch.8 para.1, Sch.10, 2004 c.14 Sch.1 Part 6

CAP.

4 Geo. 2 (1730)

Landlord Tenant Act 1730
   s.1, see *Peninsular Business Services Ltd v Citation Plc (No.1)* [2004] F.S.R. 17 (Ch D), Judge Maddocks

11 Geo. 2 (1737-38)

19. Distress for Rent Act 1737
   s.4, amended: 2003 c.39 Sch.8 para.2, Sch.10
   s.16, amended: 2003 c.39 Sch.8 para.3, Sch.10

1743

40. Universities (Wine Licences) Act 1743
   repealed: 2003 c.17 Sch.6 para.1, Sch.7

25 Geo. 2 (1751)

36. Disorderly Houses Act 1751
   disapplied: 2003 c.17 Sch.6 para.2

13 Geo. 3 (1772-03)

81. Inclosure Act 1773
   s.4, amended: 2003 c.39 Sch.8 para.4, Sch.10

14 Geo. 3 (1774)

48. Life Assurance Act 1774
   s.1, see *Feasey v Sun Life Assurance Co of Canada* [2002] EWHC 868, [2002] 2 All E.R. (Comm) 492 (QBD (Comm Ct)), Langley, J.; see *Feasey v Sun Life Assurance Co of Canada* [2003] EWCA Civ 885, [2003] 2 All E.R. (Comm) 587 (CA), Waller, L.J.
   s.1, applied: 2004 c.33 s.253
   s.3, see *Feasey v Sun Life Assurance Co of Canada* [2002] EWHC 868, [2002] 2 All E.R. (Comm) 492 (QBD (Comm Ct)), Langley, J.; see *Feasey v Sun Life Assurance Co of Canada* [2003] EWCA Civ 885, [2003] 2 All E.R. (Comm) 587 (CA), Waller, L.J.
   s.3, applied: 2004 c.33 s.253
78. Fires Prevention (Metropolis) Act 1774
   s.86, see *Johnson (t/a Johnson Butchers) v BJW Property Developments Ltd* [2002] EWHC 1131, [2002] 3 All E.R. 574 (QBD (T&CC)), Judge Anthony Thornton Q.C.

1780

49. Sunday Observance Act 1780
   repealed: 2003 c.17 Sch.6 para.3, Sch.7

37 Geo. 3 (1797)

127. Meeting of Parliament Act 1797
   applied: 2004 c.36 s.28

CAP.

1804

xlv. Solway act 1804
   repealed: 2003 asp 15 Sch.4 Part 2
43. Clergy Ordination Act 1804
   Royal Assent, May 03, 2004
   repealed: 2004 c.14 Sch.1 Part 6

48 Geo. 3 (1808)

149. Probate and Legacy Duties Act 1808
   s.42, amended: 2004 c.12 s.294

54 Geo. 3 (1814)

96. Apprentices Act 1814
   repealed: 2004 c.14 Sch.1 Part 8

56 Geo. 3 (1816)

50. Sale of Farming Stock Act 1816
   s.10, amended: 2003 c.39 Sch.8 para.5
141. Burial Act 1816
   s.2, amended: 2003 c.39 Sch.8 para.6, Sch.10

57 Geo. 3 (1817)

97. Duchy of Lancaster Act 1817
   s.25, applied: 2002 c.15 s.108, s.172

59 Geo. 3 (1819)

1. Unlawful Drilling Act 1819
   disapplied: SI 2004/702 Art.49

5 Geo. 4 (1824)

83. Vagrancy Act 1824
   s.3, disapplied: 2003 c.44 Sch.25 para.1
   s.4, amended: 2003 c.42 Sch.7, 2003 c.44 Sch.32 para.146
   s.4, disapplied: 2003 c.44 Sch.25 para.2
   s.4, substituted: 2003 c.44 Sch.32 para.146
   s.5, repealed (in part): 2003 c.44 Sch.37 Part 9
   s.10, repealed (in part): 2003 c.44 Sch.37 Part 9

11 Geo. 4 & 1 Will 4 (1830)

68. Carriers Act 1830
   s.1, amended: 2004 c.14 Sch.2 para.1
   s.3, amended: 2004 c.14 Sch.1 Part 17

1 & 2 Will. 4 (1831)

22. London Hackney Carriage Act 1831
   s.56, amended: 2004 c.14 Sch.1 Part 14
   s.74, amended: 2004 c.14 Sch.1 Part 14
32. Game Act 1831
   s.35, amended: 2004 c.37 Sch.3

CAP.

2 & 3 Will. 4 (1832)

68. Game (Scotland) Act 1832
s.4, repealed: 2002 asp 6 Sch.1 para.1

71. Prescription Act 1832
s.4, see *Smith v Brudenell-Bruce* [2002] 2 P.
& C.R. 4 (Ch D), Pumfrey, J.

3 & 4 Will. 4 (1833)

xxxiv. An Act for making a Railway from the Warrington and Newton Railway at Warrington in the County of Lancaster to Birmingham in the County of Warwick, to be called the Grand Junction Railway 1833
s.180, disapplied: SI 2003/1075 Art.9

27. Real Property Limitation Act 1833
see *Wills v Wills* [2003] UKPC 84, [2004] 1 P.
& C.R. 37 (PC (Jam)), Lord Walker of
Gestingthorpe

35. Inclosure and Drainage (Rates) Act 1833
s.1, amended: 2003 c.39 Sch.8 para.7, Sch.10
s.2, amended: 2003 c.39 Sch.8 para.8,
Sch.10

41. Judicial Committee Act 1833
see *Attorney General for St Christopher and
Nevis v Rodionov* [2004] UKPC 38,
[2004] 1 W.L.R. 2796 (PC (StC)), Lord
Bingham of Cornhill
s.5A, added: 2004 c.14 Sch.2 para.2
s.14, repealed: 2004 c.14 Sch.1 Part 1
s.23, repealed: 2004 c.14 Sch.1 Part 1
s.24, amended: 2004 c.14 Sch.1 Part 1
s.24, enabling: SI 2003/1879

85. Saint Helena Act 1833
s.112, applied: SI 2002/2627
s.112, enabling: SI 2002/1077, SI 2002/1822,
SI 2002/2627, SI 2003/2627, SI 2004/
347, SI 2004/349, SI 2004/1111, SI
2004/1112, SI 2004/1979, SI 2004/1980,
SI 2004/3039

5 & 6 Will. 4 (1835)

50. Highway Act 1835
s.72, applied: 2002 c.30 Sch.4 para.11A,
Sch.4 para.1, Sch.5 para.8A, Sch.5 para.1,
SI 2004/915 Sch.1 para.1, Sch.1 para.9

62. Statutory Declarations Act 1835
s.2, amended: 2004 c.14 Sch.1 Part 5
s.13, varied: 2002 c.26 Sch.4 para.7
s.15, varied: 2002 c.26 Sch.4 para.7
s.16, varied: 2002 c.26 Sch.4 para.7
s.18, varied: 2002 c.26 Sch.4 para.7

6 & 7 Will. 4 (1836)

cxi. Manchester and Leeds Railway Act 1836
referred to: SI 2002/1384 Art.8

CAP.

6 & 7 Will. 4 (1836)–cont.

ixvi. Newport (Monmouthshire) Harbour Act 1836
s.100, repealed: SI 2003/2679 Sch.3

71. Tithe Act 1836
applied: SI 2002/1894 Sch.1 Part I, SI 2004/
1890 Sch.1 Part I

77. Ecclesiastical Commissioners Act 1836
repealed: 2004 c.14 Sch.1 Part 6
s.9, repealed: 2004 c.14 Sch.1 Part 6
s.10, repealed: 2004 c.14 Sch.1 Part 6
s.12, repealed: 2004 c.14 Sch.1 Part 6
s.13, repealed: 2004 c.14 Sch.1 Part 6
s.14, repealed: 2004 c.14 Sch.1 Part 6
s.15, repealed: 2004 c.14 Sch.1 Part 6
s.16, repealed: 2004 c.14 Sch.1 Part 6
s.17, repealed: 2004 c.14 Sch.1 Part 6

7 Will. 4 & 1 Vict. (1837)

cx. Bridlington Harbour Act 1837
s.7, repealed: SI 2004/1426 Sch.3
s.9, repealed: SI 2004/1426 Sch.3
s.16, repealed: SI 2004/1426 Sch.3
s.20, repealed: SI 2004/1426 Sch.3
s.23, repealed: SI 2004/1426 Sch.3
s.26, repealed: SI 2004/1426 Sch.3
s.28, repealed: SI 2004/1426 Sch.3

xxiv. Manchester and Leeds Railway Act 1837
referred to: SI 2002/1384 Art.8

2. Civil List Act 1837
applied: 2002 c.16 s.16

26. Wills Act 1837
s.3, see *Bath and Wells Diocesan Board of
Finance v Jenkinson* [2002] EWHC 218,
[2003] Ch. 89 (Ch D), Etherton, J.
s.9, see *Sherrington v Sherrington* [2004]
EWHC 1613, [2004] W.T.L.R. 895 (Ch D),
Lightman, J.
s.9, applied: 2004 c.30 s.3, s.4
s.15, applied: 2004 c.33 Sch.4 para.3
s.15, referred to: 2004 c.33 Sch.4 para.3
s.16, amended: 2004 c.33 Sch.4 para.4
s.18B, added: 2004 c.33 Sch.4 para.2
s.18C, added: 2004 c.33 Sch.4 para.2
s.33, see *Ling v Ling* [2002] W.T.L.R. 553 (Ch
D), Etherton, J.

45. Parish Notices Act 1837
repealed: 2004 c.14 Sch.1 Part 6

88. Piracy Act 1837
s.3, repealed: 2003 c.44 Sch.32 para.1,
Sch.37 Part 7

1 & 2 Vict. (1837-38)

20. Queen Anne's Bounty Act 1838
repealed: 2004 c.14 Sch.1 Part 6

106. Pluralities Act 1838
s.28, repealed: 2004 c.14 Sch.1 Part 6
s.29, repealed: 2004 c.14 Sch.1 Part 6

CAP.

1 & 2 Vict. (1837-38)–cont.

106. Pluralities Act 1838–cont.
s.30, repealed: 2004 c.14 Sch.1 Part 6
s.31, repealed: 2004 c.14 Sch.1 Part 6

110. Judgments Act 1838
see *Powell v Herefordshire HA* [2002] EWCA
Civ 1786, [2003] 3 All E.R. 253 (CA), Kay,
L.J.; see *Wills v Crown Estate
Commissioners* [2003] EWHC 1718,
[2003] 4 Costs L.R. 581 (Ch D), Peter
Smith, J.
s.12, amended: 2003 c.39 Sch.8 para.9
s.17, referred to: 2002 c.29 s.12, 2002 c.40
s.113

2 & 3 Vict. (1839)

**lv. Manchester and Leeds Railway Act
1839**
referred to: SI 2002/1384 Art.8

45. Highway (Railway Crossing) Act 1839
disapplied: 2004 asp 10 Sch.4 Part 3

47. Metropolitan Police Act 1839
s.41, repealed: 2003 c.17 Sch.7
s.75, substituted: 2003 c.39 Sch.8 para.10

3 & 4 Vict. (1840)

48. Entail Sites Act 1840
applied: 2003 asp 9 s.87

59. Evidence (Scotland) Act 1840
s.3, see *Gerrard v RW Sives Ltd* 2003 S.C. 475
(Ex Div), Lord Johnston, Lord Osborne,
Lord Weir

92. Non-parochial Registers Act 1840
s.1, repealed: 2004 c.14 Sch.1 Part 17
s.4, repealed: 2004 c.14 Sch.1 Part 17
s.17A, added: 2004 c.14 Sch.2 para.3

97. Railway Regulation Act 1840
s.16, see *R. (on the application of Mair) v
Criminal Injuries Compensation Board*
[2001] EWHC Admin 412, [2002] P.I.Q.R.
P4 (QBD (Admin Ct)), Stanley Burnton, J.
s.16, amended: 2003 c.44 Sch.26 para.1

**113. Ecclesiastical Commissioners Act
1840**
s.83, repealed: 2004 c.14 Sch.1 Part 6
s.87, repealed: 2004 c.14 Sch.1 Part 6
s.89, repealed: 2004 c.14 Sch.1 Part 6
s.90, repealed: 2004 c.14 Sch.1 Part 6

4 & 5 Vict. (1841)

14. Trading Partnerships Act 1841
repealed: 2004 c.14 Sch.1 Part 6

30. Ordnance Survey Act 1841
s.2, amended: 2003 c.39 Sch.8 para.11

38. Schools Sites Act 1841
referred to: 2002 c.15 Sch.2 para.3
s.2, see *Bath and Wells Diocesan Board of
Finance v Jenkinson* [2002] EWHC 218,
[2003] Ch. 89 (Ch D), Etherton, J.; see
Fraser v Canterbury Diocesan Board of

CAP.

4 & 5 Vict. (1841)–cont.

38. Schools Sites Act 1841–cont.
s.2–cont.
Finance (No.2) [2003] EWHC 1075,
[2003] W.T.L.R. 1125 (Ch D), Lewison, J.
s.2, applied: 2003 asp 9 s.86
s.2, referred to: 2003 asp 9 s.86

**39. Ecclesiastical Commissioners Act
1841**
s.1, repealed: 2004 c.14 Sch.1 Part 6
s.30, repealed: 2004 c.14 Sch.1 Part 6

5 & 6 Vict. (1842)

55. Railway Regulation Act 1842
s.9, disapplied: 2004 asp 10 Sch.4 Part 3
s.10, referred to: 2002 c.8 (NI) s.1
s.17, amended: 2003 c.39 Sch.8 para.12,
Sch.10, 2003 c.44 Sch.37 Part 9
s.17, disapplied: 2003 c.44 Sch.25 para.3

94. Defence Act 1842
applied: 2002 c.i, s.5
s.24, amended: 2003 c.39 Sch.8 para.13,
Sch.10

**97. Limitations of Actions and Costs Act
1842**
s.2, repealed: 2004 c.14 Sch.1 Part 1

6 & 7 Vict. (1843)

86. London Hackney Carriages Act 1843
s.18, amended: 2004 c.14 Sch.1 Part 14
s.24, amended: 2003 c.39 Sch.8 para.14
s.28, amended: 2003 c.44 Sch.32 para.147,
Sch.37 Part 9
s.28, disapplied: 2003 c.44 Sch.25 para.4
s.47, repealed: 2004 c.14 Sch.1 Part 14

7 & 8 Vict. (1844)

**xvi. Manchester and Leeds Railway Act
1844**
referred to: SI 2002/1384 Art.8

32. Bank Charter Act 1844
s.27, repealed: 2004 c.14 Sch.1 Part 17

69. Judicial Committee Act 1844
s.1, see *Attorney General for St Christopher
and Nevis v Rodionov* [2004] UKPC 38,
[2004] 1 W.L.R. 2796 (PC (StC)), Lord
Bingham of Cornhill
s.1, enabling: SI 2003/1879

81. Marriages (Ireland) Act 1844
repealed: SI 2003/413 Sch.1
s.7, amended: SR 2002/242 Sch.1
s.8, amended: SR 2002/242 Sch.1
s.10, amended: SR 2002/242 Sch.1
s.14, amended: SR 2002/242 Sch.1
s.16, amended: SR 2002/242 Sch.1
s.21, amended: SR 2002/242 Sch.1
s.27, amended: SR 2002/242 Sch.1
s.28, amended: SR 2002/242 Sch.1
s.31, amended: SR 2002/242 Sch.1
s.68, amended: SR 2002/242 Sch.1

CAP.

7 & 8 Vict. (1844)–cont.

81. Marriages (Ireland) Act 1844–cont.
s.69, amended: SR 2002/242 Sch.1
s.70, amended: SR 2002/242 Sch.1

8 & 9 Vict. (1845)

clxxi. Manchester and Leeds Railway Act No 1 1845
referred to: SI 2002/1384 Art.8

liv. Manchester and Leeds Railway Act No 2 1845
referred to: SI 2002/1384 Art.8

cxvi. North Union and Ribble Navigation Branch Railway Act 1845
applied: SI 2002/2398 Sch.1

cxii. Trent Valley Railway Act 1845
referred to: SI 2004/389 Art.9

16. Companies Clauses Consolidation Act 1845
s.3, amended: 2003 c.39 Sch.8 para.15, Sch.10
s.18, amended: 2003 c.39 Sch.8 para.16
s.33, amended: 2003 c.39 Sch.8 para.17, 2004 c.14 Sch.1 Part 17

17. Companies Clauses Consolidation (Scotland) Act 1845
s.114, amended: 2002 asp 17 Sch.3 para.1

18. Lands Clauses Consolidation Act 1845
applied: 2002 c.i, s.5, 2004 asp 10 s.14, s.25, s.30
consolidated: 2004 asp 10 s.37
varied: 2004 asp 10 s.14
Part II, applied: 2003 c.21 Sch.4 para.9
s.1, applied: 2003 c.21 Sch.4 para.9
s.3, amended: 2003 c.39 Sch.8 para.19, Sch.10
s.63, see *Bridgestart Properties Ltd v London Underground Ltd* [2004] R.V.R. 18 (Lands Tr), George Bartlett Q.C. (President)
s.77, see *Rhondda Cynon Taff CBC v Watkins* [2003] EWCA Civ 129, [2003] 1 W.L.R. 1864 (CA), Schiemann, L.J.
s.133, applied: 2003 c.21 Sch.4 para.9
s.134, applied: 2003 c.21 Sch.4 para.9
s.135, applied: 2003 c.21 Sch.4 para.9
s.136, applied: 2003 c.21 Sch.4 para.9
s.137, applied: 2003 c.21 Sch.4 para.9
s.138, applied: 2003 c.21 Sch.4 para.9
s.139, applied: 2003 c.21 Sch.4 para.9
s.140, applied: 2003 c.21 Sch.4 para.9
s.141, applied: 2003 c.21 Sch.4 para.9
s.142, applied: 2003 c.21 Sch.4 para.9
s.143, applied: 2003 c.21 Sch.4 para.9
s.144, applied: 2003 c.21 Sch.4 para.9
s.145, applied: 2003 c.21 Sch.4 para.9
s.146, applied: 2003 c.21 Sch.4 para.9
s.147, applied: 2003 c.21 Sch.4 para.9
s.148, applied: 2003 c.21 Sch.4 para.9
s.149, applied: 2003 c.21 Sch.4 para.9
s.152, applied: 2003 c.21 Sch.4 para.9
s.153, applied: 2003 c.21 Sch.4 para.9

CAP.

8 & 9 Vict. (1845)–cont.

19. Lands Clauses Consolidation (Scotland) Act 1845
applied: 2004 asp 10 s.14, s.25, s.30
disapplied: SSI 2004/171 Art.24
varied: 2004 asp 10 s.14
consolidated: 2004 asp 10 s.37
s.1, consolidated: 2004 asp 10 s.37
s.11, amended: 2002 asp 17 Sch.3 para.2
s.61, varied: 2004 asp 10 s.14
s.83, applied: 2004 asp 10 s.24, SSI 2004/171 Art.16
s.84, applied: 2004 asp 10 s.24, SSI 2004/171 Art.16
s.85, applied: 2004 asp 10 s.24, SSI 2004/171 Art.16
s.86, applied: 2004 asp 10 s.24, SSI 2004/171 Art.16
s.87, applied: 2004 asp 10 s.24, SSI 2004/171 Art.16
s.88, applied: 2004 asp 10 s.24, SSI 2004/171 Art.16
s.89, applied: 2004 asp 10 s.24
s.90, disapplied: 2004 asp 10 s.14, s.21
s.120, disapplied: 2002 asp 3 s.46, SSI 2004/171 Art.4
s.121, disapplied: 2002 asp 3 s.46, SSI 2004/171 Art.4
s.122, disapplied: 2002 asp 3 s.46, SSI 2004/171 Art.4
s.123, disapplied: 2002 asp 3 s.46, SSI 2004/171 Art.4
s.124, disapplied: 2002 asp 3 s.46, SSI 2004/171 Art.4
s.125, consolidated: 2004 asp 10 s.37
s.125, disapplied: 2002 asp 3 s.46, SSI 2004/171 Art.4
s.126, consolidated: 2004 asp 10 s.37
s.128, consolidated: 2004 asp 10 s.37
s.129, consolidated: 2004 asp 10 s.37
s.130, consolidated: 2004 asp 10 s.37
s.131, consolidated: 2004 asp 10 s.37
s.132, consolidated: 2004 asp 10 s.37
s.133, consolidated: 2004 asp 10 s.37
s.134, consolidated: 2004 asp 10 s.37
s.135, consolidated: 2004 asp 10 s.37
s.136, consolidated: 2004 asp 10 s.37
s.137, consolidated: 2004 asp 10 s.37
s.138, consolidated: 2004 asp 10 s.37
s.139, consolidated: 2004 asp 10 s.37
s.140, consolidated: 2004 asp 10 s.37
s.141, consolidated: 2004 asp 10 s.37
s.142, consolidated: 2004 asp 10 s.37
s.143, consolidated: 2004 asp 10 s.37
s.144, consolidated: 2004 asp 10 s.37
Sch.A, amended: SSI 2003/503 Sch.1 para.2
Sch.A, consolidated: 2004 asp 10 s.37
Sch.B, consolidated: 2004 asp 10 s.37

CAP.

8 & 9 Vict. (1845)–cont.

20. Railway Clauses Consolidation Act 1845

s.3, amended: 2003 c.39 Sch.8 para.20, Sch.10

s.7, varied: SI 2002/1384 Art.3

s.8, referred to: SI 2002/1384 Art.3

s.9, varied: SI 2002/1384 Art.3

s.10, varied: SI 2002/1384 Art.3

s.11, referred to: SI 2002/1384 Art.3

s.12, referred to: SI 2002/1384 Art.3

s.13, referred to: SI 2002/1384 Art.3

s.15, referred to: SI 2002/1384 Art.3

s.17, referred to: SI 2002/1384 Art.3

s.18, applied: SI 2002/366 Art.3

s.18, referred to: SI 2002/366 Sch.2 para.10

s.24, applied: SI 2002/366 Art.3, SI 2002/1064 Art.3, SI 2003/1075 Art.3, SI 2003/3364 Art.3, SI 2004/389 Art.3

s.24, varied: SI 2003/1075 Art.3, SI 2004/389 Art.3

s.32, referred to: SI 2002/1384 Art.3

s.33, referred to: SI 2002/1384 Art.3

s.34, referred to: SI 2002/1384 Art.3

s.35, referred to: SI 2002/1384 Art.3

s.36, referred to: SI 2002/1384 Art.3

s.37, referred to: SI 2002/1384 Art.3

s.38, referred to: SI 2002/1384 Art.3

s.39, referred to: SI 2002/1384 Art.3

s.40, referred to: SI 2002/1384 Art.3

s.41, referred to: SI 2002/1384 Art.3

s.42, referred to: SI 2002/1384 Art.3

s.43, referred to: SI 2002/1384 Art.3

s.44, referred to: SI 2002/1384 Art.3

s.46, amended: 2003 c.39 Sch.8 para.22, Sch.10

s.46, applied: SI 2003/3364 Art.3

s.46, varied: SI 2002/1384 Art.3, SI 2003/3364 Art.3

s.47, referred to: 2002 c.8 (NI) s.1, SI 2002/1384 Art.3

s.47, varied: SI 2002/1997 Art.3

s.48, referred to: SI 2002/1384 Art.3

s.49, referred to: SI 2002/1384 Art.3

s.50, referred to: SI 2002/1384 Art.3

s.51, referred to: SI 2002/1384 Art.3

s.52, referred to: SI 2002/1384 Art.3

s.53, referred to: SI 2002/1384 Art.3

s.54, referred to: SI 2002/1384 Art.3

s.55, referred to: SI 2002/1384 Art.3

s.56, referred to: SI 2002/1384 Art.3

s.57, referred to: SI 2002/1384 Art.3

s.58, applied: SI 2002/366 Art.3, SI 2002/1064 Art.3, SI 2003/3364 Art.3, SI 2004/389 Art.3

s.58, varied: SI 2002/1384 Art.3, SI 2003/1075 Art.3

s.59, amended: 2003 c.39 Sch.8 para.23, Sch.10

s.59, referred to: SI 2002/1384 Art.3

s.60, referred to: SI 2002/1384 Art.3

CAP.

8 & 9 Vict. (1845)–cont.

20. Railway Clauses Consolidation Act 1845–*cont.*

s.61, referred to: SI 2002/1384 Art.3

s.62, referred to: SI 2002/1384 Art.3

s.63, referred to: SI 2002/1384 Art.3

s.64, referred to: SI 2002/1384 Art.3

s.65, referred to: SI 2002/1384 Art.3

s.66, referred to: SI 2002/1384 Art.3

s.68, applied: SI 2002/366 Art.3, SI 2002/1064 Art.3, SI 2003/1075 Art.3, SI 2003/3364 Art.3, SI 2004/389 Art.3

s.68, disapplied: SI 2002/1943 Art.3, SI 2004/389 Art.9

s.68, referred to: SI 2002/1384 Art.3

s.71, applied: SI 2002/366 Art.3, SI 2002/1064 Art.3, SI 2003/3364 Art.3, SI 2004/389 Art.3

s.71, referred to: SI 2002/1384 Art.3

s.71, varied: SI 2003/1075 Art.3

s.72, applied: SI 2002/366 Art.3, SI 2002/1064 Art.3, SI 2003/1075 Art.3, SI 2003/3364 Art.3, SI 2004/389 Art.3

s.72, referred to: SI 2002/1384 Art.3

s.73, applied: SI 2002/366 Art.3, SI 2002/1064 Art.3, SI 2003/1075 Art.3, SI 2003/3364 Art.3, SI 2004/389 Art.3

s.73, referred to: SI 2002/1384 Art.3

s.75, applied: SI 2002/366 Art.3, SI 2003/3364 Art.3

s.75, referred to: SI 2002/1384 Art.3

s.77, applied: SI 2002/366 Art.3, SI 2002/1064 Art.3, SI 2003/1075 Art.3, SI 2003/3364 Art.3, Art.8, SI 2004/389 Art.3, Art.11

s.77, referred to: SI 2002/1384 Art.3

s.78, applied: SI 2002/366 Art.3, SI 2002/1064 Art.3, SI 2003/1075 Art.3, SI 2003/3364 Art.3, Art.8, SI 2004/389 Art.3, Art.11

s.78, referred to: SI 2002/1384 Art.3

s.78A, applied: SI 2002/366 Art.3, SI 2002/1064 Art.3, SI 2003/1075 Art.3, SI 2003/3364 Art.3, Art.8, SI 2004/389 Art.3, Art.11

s.78A, referred to: SI 2002/1384 Art.3

s.79, applied: SI 2002/366 Art.3, SI 2002/1064 Art.3, SI 2003/1075 Art.3, SI 2003/3364 Art.3, Art.8, SI 2004/389 Art.3, Art.11

s.79, referred to: SI 2002/1384 Art.3

s.79A, applied: SI 2002/366 Art.3, SI 2002/1064 Art.3, SI 2003/1075 Art.3, SI 2003/3364 Art.3, Art.8, SI 2004/389 Art.3, Art.11

s.79A, referred to: SI 2002/1384 Art.3

s.79B, applied: SI 2002/366 Art.3, SI 2002/1064 Art.3, SI 2003/1075 Art.3, SI 2003/3364 Art.3, Art.8, SI 2004/389 Art.3, Art.11

s.79B, referred to: SI 2002/1384 Art.3

8 & 9 Vict. (1845)–cont.

20. Railway Clauses Consolidation Act 1845–*cont.*

s.80, applied: SI 2002/366 Art.3, SI 2002/1064 Art.3, SI 2003/1075 Art.3, SI 2003/3364 Art.3, Art.8, SI 2004/389 Art.3, Art.11

s.80, referred to: SI 2002/1384 Art.3

s.81, applied: SI 2002/366 Art.3, SI 2002/1064 Art.3, SI 2003/1075 Art.3, SI 2003/3364 Art.3, Art.8, SI 2004/389 Art.3, Art.11

s.81, referred to: SI 2002/1384 Art.3

s.82, applied: SI 2002/366 Art.3, SI 2002/1064 Art.3, SI 2003/1075 Art.3, SI 2003/3364 Art.3, Art.8, SI 2004/389 Art.3, Art.11

s.82, referred to: SI 2002/1384 Art.3

s.83, applied: SI 2002/366 Art.3, SI 2002/1064 Art.3, SI 2003/1075 Art.3, SI 2003/3364 Art.3, Art.8, SI 2004/389 Art.3, Art.11

s.83, referred to: SI 2002/1384 Art.3

s.84, applied: SI 2002/366 Art.3, SI 2002/1064 Art.3, SI 2003/1075 Art.3, SI 2003/3364 Art.3, Art.8, SI 2004/389 Art.3, Art.11

s.84, referred to: SI 2002/1384 Art.3

s.85, applied: SI 2002/366 Art.3, SI 2002/1064 Art.3, SI 2003/1075 Art.3, SI 2003/3364 Art.3, Art.8, SI 2004/389 Art.3, Art.11

s.85, referred to: SI 2002/1384 Art.3

s.85A, applied: SI 2002/366 Art.3, SI 2002/1064 Art.3, SI 2003/1075 Art.3, SI 2003/3364 Art.3, Art.8, SI 2004/389 Art.3, Art.11

s.85A, referred to: SI 2002/1384 Art.3

s.85B, applied: SI 2002/366 Art.3, SI 2002/1064 Art.3, SI 2003/1075 Art.3, SI 2003/3364 Art.3, Art.8, SI 2004/389 Art.3, Art.11

s.85B, referred to: SI 2002/1384 Art.3

s.85C, applied: SI 2002/366 Art.3, SI 2002/1064 Art.3, SI 2003/1075 Art.3, SI 2003/3364 Art.3, Art.8, SI 2004/389 Art.3, Art.11

s.85C, referred to: SI 2002/1384 Art.3

s.85D, applied: SI 2002/366 Art.3, SI 2002/1064 Art.3, SI 2003/1075 Art.3, SI 2003/3364 Art.3, Art.8, SI 2004/389 Art.3, Art.11

s.85D, referred to: SI 2002/1384 Art.3

s.85E, applied: SI 2002/366 Art.3, SI 2002/1064 Art.3, SI 2003/1075 Art.3, SI 2003/3364 Art.3, Art.8, SI 2004/389 Art.3, Art.11

s.85E, referred to: SI 2002/1384 Art.3

s.87, applied: SI 2002/366 Art.3

s.88, referred to: SI 2002/1384 Art.3

s.89, referred to: SI 2002/1384 Art.3

s.90, referred to: SI 2002/1384 Art.3

s.91, referred to: SI 2002/1384 Art.3

8 & 9 Vict. (1845)–cont.

20. Railway Clauses Consolidation Act 1845–*cont.*

s.92, referred to: SI 2002/1384 Art.3

s.93, referred to: SI 2002/1384 Art.3

s.94, referred to: SI 2002/1384 Art.3

s.95, referred to: SI 2002/1384 Art.3

s.97, referred to: SI 2003/1615 Sch.1 para.2

s.103, applied: SI 2002/366 Art.3, SI 2002/1064 Art.3

s.103, referred to: SI 2003/1615 Sch.1 para.2

s.104, applied: SI 2002/366 Art.3, SI 2002/1064 Art.3

s.104, referred to: SI 2003/1615 Sch.1 para.2

s.105, applied: SI 2002/366 Art.3, SI 2002/1064 Art.3, SI 2003/3364 Art.3

s.105, referred to: SI 2003/1615 Sch.1 para.2

s.112, referred to: SI 2002/1384 Art.3

s.113, referred to: SI 2002/1384 Art.3

s.114, referred to: SI 2002/1384 Art.3

s.115, applied: SI 2002/366 Art.3

s.115, referred to: SI 2002/1384 Art.3

s.116, applied: SI 2002/366 Art.3

s.116, referred to: SI 2002/1384 Art.3

s.117, applied: SI 2002/366 Art.3

s.117, referred to: SI 2002/1384 Art.3

s.118, applied: SI 2002/366 Art.3

s.118, referred to: SI 2002/1384 Art.3

s.119, applied: SI 2002/366 Art.3

s.119, referred to: SI 2002/1384 Art.3

s.120, referred to: SI 2002/1384 Art.3

s.121, referred to: SI 2002/1384 Art.3

s.122, referred to: SI 2002/1384 Art.3

s.123, referred to: SI 2002/1384 Art.3

s.124, referred to: SI 2002/1384 Art.3

s.144, referred to: SI 2003/1615 Sch.1 para.2

s.145, applied: SI 2002/366 Art.3, SI 2002/1064 Art.3, SI 2003/1075 Art.3, SI 2003/3364 Art.3, SI 2004/389 Art.3

s.154, applied: SI 2002/366 Art.3, SI 2002/1064 Art.3, SI 2003/1075 Art.3, SI 2004/389 Art.3

s.162, referred to: SI 2002/1384 Art.3

Sch.1, applied: SI 2002/366 Art.3, SI 2002/1064 Art.3, SI 2003/3364 Art.8, SI 2004/389 Art.11

Sch.1, referred to: SI 2002/1384 Art.3

Sch.2, applied: SI 2003/3364 Art.8, SI 2004/389 Art.11

Sch.2, referred to: SI 2002/1384 Art.3

Sch.2 para.1, applied: SI 2002/366 Art.3, SI 2002/1064 Art.3

Sch.2 para.2, applied: SI 2002/366 Art.3, SI 2002/1064 Art.3

Sch.3, applied: SI 2003/3364 Art.8, SI 2004/389 Art.11

Sch.3, referred to: SI 2002/1384 Art.3

33. Railways Clauses Consolidation (Scotland) Act 1845

s.2, consolidated: 2004 asp 10 s.37

s.3, consolidated: 2004 asp 10 s.37

8 & 9 Vict. (1845)–cont.

33. Railways Clauses Consolidation (Scotland) Act 1845–cont.
s.4, consolidated: 2004 asp 10 s.37
s.5, consolidated: 2004 asp 10 s.37
s.6, applied: 2002 asp 3 s.46, 2004 asp 10 s.17
s.6, consolidated: 2004 asp 10 s.37
s.10, consolidated: 2004 asp 10 s.37
s.11, consolidated: 2004 asp 10 s.37
s.12, consolidated: 2004 asp 10 s.37
s.13, consolidated: 2004 asp 10 s.37
s.14, consolidated: 2004 asp 10 s.37
s.15, consolidated: 2004 asp 10 s.37
s.16, consolidated: 2004 asp 10 s.37
s.18, consolidated: 2004 asp 10 s.37
s.21, consolidated: 2004 asp 10 s.37
s.24, consolidated: 2004 asp 10 s.37
s.25, consolidated: 2004 asp 10 s.37
s.26, consolidated: 2004 asp 10 s.37
s.27, consolidated: 2004 asp 10 s.37
s.28, consolidated: 2004 asp 10 s.37
s.29, consolidated: 2004 asp 10 s.37
s.30, consolidated: 2004 asp 10 s.37
s.31, consolidated: 2004 asp 10 s.37
s.32, consolidated: 2004 asp 10 s.37
s.33, consolidated: 2004 asp 10 s.37
s.34, consolidated: 2004 asp 10 s.37
s.35, consolidated: 2004 asp 10 s.37
s.36, applied: 2004 asp 10 s.17
s.36, consolidated: 2004 asp 10 s.37
s.37, consolidated: 2004 asp 10 s.37
s.38, consolidated: 2004 asp 10 s.37
s.39, consolidated: 2004 asp 10 s.37
s.40, consolidated: 2004 asp 10 s.37
s.40, disapplied: 2004 asp 10 Sch.4 Part 3
s.41, consolidated: 2004 asp 10 s.37
s.42, consolidated: 2004 asp 10 s.37
s.43, consolidated: 2004 asp 10 s.37
s.44, consolidated: 2004 asp 10 s.37
s.45, consolidated: 2004 asp 10 s.37
s.46, consolidated: 2004 asp 10 s.37
s.47, consolidated: 2004 asp 10 s.37
s.48, consolidated: 2004 asp 10 s.37
s.49, consolidated: 2004 asp 10 s.37
s.50, consolidated: 2004 asp 10 s.37
s.51, consolidated: 2004 asp 10 s.37
s.52, consolidated: 2004 asp 10 s.37
s.53, consolidated: 2004 asp 10 s.37
s.54, consolidated: 2004 asp 10 s.37
s.55, consolidated: 2004 asp 10 s.37
s.56, consolidated: 2004 asp 10 s.37
s.57, consolidated: 2004 asp 10 s.37
s.58, consolidated: 2004 asp 10 s.37
s.59, consolidated: 2004 asp 10 s.37
s.60, consolidated: 2004 asp 10 s.37
s.60, referred to: 2004 asp 10 s.9
s.61, consolidated: 2004 asp 10 s.37
s.62, consolidated: 2004 asp 10 s.37
s.63, consolidated: 2004 asp 10 s.37
s.64, consolidated: 2004 asp 10 s.37

8 & 9 Vict. (1845)–cont.

33. Railways Clauses Consolidation (Scotland) Act 1845–cont.
s.65, consolidated: 2004 asp 10 s.37
s.66, consolidated: 2004 asp 10 s.37
s.67, consolidated: 2004 asp 10 s.37
s.68, consolidated: 2004 asp 10 s.37
s.69, consolidated: 2004 asp 10 s.37
s.70, applied: 2002 asp 3 s.46, SSI 2004/171 Art.4
s.70, consolidated: 2004 asp 10 s.37
s.71, applied: 2002 asp 3 s.46
s.71, consolidated: 2004 asp 10 s.37
s.71A, applied: 2002 asp 3 s.46
s.71A, consolidated: 2004 asp 10 s.37
s.72, applied: 2002 asp 3 s.46
s.72, consolidated: 2004 asp 10 s.37
s.72A, applied: 2002 asp 3 s.46
s.72A, consolidated: 2004 asp 10 s.37
s.72B, applied: 2002 asp 3 s.46
s.72B, consolidated: 2004 asp 10 s.37
s.73, applied: 2002 asp 3 s.46
s.73, consolidated: 2004 asp 10 s.37
s.74, applied: 2002 asp 3 s.46
s.74, consolidated: 2004 asp 10 s.37
s.75, applied: 2002 asp 3 s.46
s.75, consolidated: 2004 asp 10 s.37
s.76, applied: 2002 asp 3 s.46
s.76, consolidated: 2004 asp 10 s.37
s.77, applied: 2002 asp 3 s.46, SI 2003/1075 Art.12
s.77, consolidated: 2004 asp 10 s.37
s.78, applied: 2002 asp 3 s.46, SI 2003/1075 Art.12
s.78, consolidated: 2004 asp 10 s.37
s.78A, applied: SI 2003/1075 Art.12
s.78A, consolidated: 2004 asp 10 s.37
s.78B, applied: SI 2003/1075 Art.12
s.78B, consolidated: 2004 asp 10 s.37
s.78C, applied: SI 2003/1075 Art.12
s.78C, consolidated: 2004 asp 10 s.37
s.78D, applied: SI 2003/1075 Art.12
s.78D, consolidated: 2004 asp 10 s.37
s.79, applied: SI 2003/1075 Art.12
s.79, consolidated: 2004 asp 10 s.37
s.79A, applied: SI 2003/1075 Art.12
s.79A, consolidated: 2004 asp 10 s.37
s.80, applied: SI 2003/1075 Art.12
s.80, consolidated: 2004 asp 10 s.37
s.81, applied: SI 2003/1075 Art.12
s.81, consolidated: 2004 asp 10 s.37
s.82, applied: SI 2003/1075 Art.12
s.82, consolidated: 2004 asp 10 s.37
s.83, applied: SI 2003/1075 Art.12
s.83, consolidated: 2004 asp 10 s.37
s.84, applied: SI 2003/1075 Art.12
s.84, consolidated: 2004 asp 10 s.37
s.85, applied: SI 2003/1075 Art.12
s.85, consolidated: 2004 asp 10 s.37
s.85E, applied: SI 2003/1075 Art.12
s.85E, consolidated: 2004 asp 10 s.37

8 & 9 Vict. (1845)–cont.

33. Railways Clauses Consolidation (Scotland) Act 1845–cont.
s.86, consolidated: 2004 asp 10 s.37
s.87, consolidated: 2004 asp 10 s.37
s.88, consolidated: 2004 asp 10 s.37
s.89, consolidated: 2004 asp 10 s.37
s.90, consolidated: 2004 asp 10 s.37
s.91, consolidated: 2004 asp 10 s.37
s.92, consolidated: 2004 asp 10 s.37
s.93, consolidated: 2004 asp 10 s.37
s.94, consolidated: 2004 asp 10 s.37
s.95, consolidated: 2004 asp 10 s.37
s.96, consolidated: 2004 asp 10 s.37
s.97, consolidated: 2004 asp 10 s.37
s.98, consolidated: 2004 asp 10 s.37
s.99, consolidated: 2004 asp 10 s.37
s.100, consolidated: 2004 asp 10 s.37
s.101, consolidated: 2004 asp 10 s.37
s.102, consolidated: 2004 asp 10 s.37
s.103, consolidated: 2004 asp 10 s.37
s.104, consolidated: 2004 asp 10 s.37
s.105, consolidated: 2004 asp 10 s.37
s.106, consolidated: 2004 asp 10 s.37
s.107, consolidated: 2004 asp 10 s.37
s.108, consolidated: 2004 asp 10 s.37
s.109, consolidated: 2004 asp 10 s.37
s.110, consolidated: 2004 asp 10 s.37
s.111, consolidated: 2004 asp 10 s.37
s.112, consolidated: 2004 asp 10 s.37
s.113, consolidated: 2004 asp 10 s.37
s.114, consolidated: 2004 asp 10 s.37
s.115, consolidated: 2004 asp 10 s.37
s.116, consolidated: 2004 asp 10 s.37
s.117, consolidated: 2004 asp 10 s.37
s.118, consolidated: 2004 asp 10 s.37
s.119, consolidated: 2004 asp 10 s.37
s.120, consolidated: 2004 asp 10 s.37
s.121, consolidated: 2004 asp 10 s.37
s.122, consolidated: 2004 asp 10 s.37
s.123, consolidated: 2004 asp 10 s.37
s.124, consolidated: 2004 asp 10 s.37
s.125, consolidated: 2004 asp 10 s.37
s.126, consolidated: 2004 asp 10 s.37
s.127, consolidated: 2004 asp 10 s.37
s.128, consolidated: 2004 asp 10 s.37
s.129, consolidated: 2004 asp 10 s.37
s.130, consolidated: 2004 asp 10 s.37
s.131, consolidated: 2004 asp 10 s.37
s.132, amended: 2002 asp 17 Sch.3 para.3
s.132, consolidated: 2004 asp 10 s.37
s.133, consolidated: 2004 asp 10 s.37
s.134, consolidated: 2004 asp 10 s.37
s.135, consolidated: 2004 asp 10 s.37
s.136, consolidated: 2004 asp 10 s.37
s.137, consolidated: 2004 asp 10 s.37
s.138, consolidated: 2004 asp 10 s.37
s.138, repealed: 2002 asp 17 Sch.3 para.3
s.139, consolidated: 2004 asp 10 s.37
s.139, repealed: 2002 asp 17 Sch.3 para.3
s.140, consolidated: 2004 asp 10 s.37

8 & 9 Vict. (1845)–cont.

33. Railways Clauses Consolidation (Scotland) Act 1845–cont.
s.141, consolidated: 2004 asp 10 s.37
s.142, consolidated: 2004 asp 10 s.37
s.143, consolidated: 2004 asp 10 s.37
s.144, consolidated: 2004 asp 10 s.37
s.145, consolidated: 2004 asp 10 s.37
s.146, consolidated: 2004 asp 10 s.37
s.147, consolidated: 2004 asp 10 s.37
s.148, consolidated: 2004 asp 10 s.37
s.149, consolidated: 2004 asp 10 s.37
s.150, consolidated: 2004 asp 10 s.37
s.151, consolidated: 2004 asp 10 s.37
s.152, consolidated: 2004 asp 10 s.37
s.153, consolidated: 2004 asp 10 s.37
s.154, consolidated: 2004 asp 10 s.37
s.155, consolidated: 2004 asp 10 s.37
Sch.1, applied: SI 2003/1075 Art.12
Sch.2, applied: SI 2003/1075 Art.12
Sch.3, applied: SI 2003/1075 Art.12
63. Geological Survey Act 1845
s.1, amended: 2003 c.39 Sch.8 para.25
s.6, amended: 2003 c.39 Sch.8 para.26
118. Inclosure Act 1845
s.163A, added: SI 2003/2867 Sch.1 para.1

9 & 10 Vict. (1846)

48. Art Unions Act 1846
repealed: 2004 c.14 Sch.1 Part 17
72. Marriages (Ireland) Act 1846
repealed: SI 2003/413 Sch.1

10 & 11 Vict. (1847)

lii. Belfast Harbour Act 1847
s.5, amended: SR 2002/40 Art.9
s.55, repealed: SR 2002/40 Sch.2
s.72, repealed: SR 2002/40 Sch.2
s.111, repealed: SR 2002/40 Sch.2
clxiii. Manchester and Leeds Railway Act No 3 1847
referred to: SI 2002/1384 Art.8
14. Markets and Fairs Clauses Act 1847
s.3, amended: 2003 c.39 Sch.8 para.27, Sch.10
s.38, amended: 2002 asp 17 Sch.3 para.4
s.39, amended: 2002 asp 17 Sch.3 para.4
16. Commissioners Clauses Act 1847
varied: SI 2002/2730 Art.2, SI 2003/2679 Art.14
s.9, disapplied: SI 2002/2586 Art.17
s.12, disapplied: SI 2002/2586 Art.17
s.14, disapplied: SI 2002/2586 Art.17
s.15, varied: 2002 c.v s.3
s.37, varied: SR 2002/395 Art.11
s.53, varied: 2002 c.v s.3
s.56, varied: 2002 c.v s.3
s.58, varied: 2002 c.v s.3
s.59, varied: 2002 c.v s.3

10 & 11 Vict. (1847)–cont.

16. Commissioners Clauses Act 1847– cont.

s.60, applied: SI 2003/2724 Art.2, SI 2004/ 1426 Art.2, SSI 2002/294 Art.2, SSI 2002/310 Art.2, SSI 2003/258 Art.2, SSI 2003/435 Art.2

s.60, varied: SI 2003/2574 Art.2, SSI 2003/ 491 Art.2

s.62, varied: 2002 c.v s.3

s.63, varied: 2002 c.v s.3

s.64, varied: 2002 c.v s.3

s.67, varied: 2002 c.v s.3

s.109, varied: 2002 c.v s.3

s.110, varied: 2002 c.v s.3

s.111, varied: 2002 c.v s.3

27. Harbours, Docks, and Piers Clauses Act 1847

applied: SI 2004/2190 Art.15

varied: SI 2004/2190 Art.3

varied: SSI 2002/410 Art.3

s.1, varied: SSI 2002/410 Art.3

s.3, amended: 2003 c.39 Sch.8 para.28, Sch.10

s.5, disapplied: SSI 2002/410 Art.3

s.6, disapplied: SSI 2002/410 Art.3

s.7, disapplied: SSI 2002/410 Art.3

s.8, disapplied: SSI 2002/410 Art.3

s.9, disapplied: SSI 2002/410 Art.3

s.10, disapplied: SSI 2002/410 Art.3

s.11, disapplied: SSI 2002/410 Art.3

s.12, disapplied: SSI 2002/410 Art.3

s.13, disapplied: SSI 2002/410 Art.3

s.14, disapplied: SSI 2002/410 Art.3

s.15, disapplied: SSI 2002/410 Art.3

s.16, disapplied: SSI 2002/410 Art.3

s.17, disapplied: SSI 2002/410 Art.3

s.18, disapplied: SSI 2002/410 Art.3

s.19, disapplied: SSI 2002/410 Art.3

s.20, varied: SSI 2002/410 Art.3

s.21, varied: SSI 2002/410 Art.3

s.22, disapplied: SSI 2002/410 Art.3

s.23, repealed: SR 2002/40 Art.10, SR 2002/ 41 Art.10

s.23, varied: SR 2002/395 Art.11, SSI 2002/ 410 Art.3

s.24, disapplied: SSI 2002/410 Art.3

s.25, disapplied: SSI 2002/410 Art.3

s.26, disapplied: SSI 2002/410 Art.3

s.27, varied: SSI 2002/410 Art.3

s.28, disapplied: SSI 2002/410 Art.3

s.29, varied: SSI 2002/410 Art.3

s.30, disapplied: SSI 2002/410 Art.3

s.31, varied: SSI 2002/410 Art.3

s.32, varied: SSI 2002/410 Art.3

s.33, varied: SSI 2002/410 Art.3

s.34, varied: SSI 2002/410 Art.3

s.35, varied: SSI 2002/410 Art.3

s.36, varied: SSI 2002/410 Art.3

s.37, disapplied: SSI 2002/410 Art.3

s.38, disapplied: SSI 2002/410 Art.3

10 & 11 Vict. (1847)–cont.

27. Harbours, Docks, and Piers Clauses Act 1847–cont.

s.39, disapplied: SSI 2002/410 Art.3

s.40, disapplied: SSI 2002/410 Art.3

s.41, disapplied: SSI 2002/410 Art.3

s.42, disapplied: SSI 2002/410 Art.3

s.43, varied: SSI 2002/410 Art.3

s.44, disapplied: SSI 2002/410 Art.3

s.45, disapplied: SSI 2002/410 Art.3

s.46, amended: 2002 asp 17 Sch.3 para.5

s.46, applied: SSI 2002/410 Art.46

s.46, disapplied: SSI 2002/410 Art.3

s.47, disapplied: SSI 2002/410 Art.3

s.48, disapplied: SSI 2002/410 Art.3

s.49, disapplied: SSI 2002/410 Art.3

s.50, disapplied: SSI 2002/410 Art.3

s.51, disapplied: SSI 2002/410 Art.3

s.52, applied: 2002 c.v s.17, SI 2003/2574 Art.20, SI 2004/148 Art.16, SI 2004/ 2469 Art.15

s.52, varied: 2002 c.v s.3, SSI 2002/410 Art.3

s.53, applied: SI 2004/2469 Art.15

s.53, varied: SSI 2002/410 Art.3

s.54, varied: SSI 2002/410 Art.3

s.55, varied: SSI 2002/410 Art.3

s.56, varied: SSI 2002/410 Art.3

s.57, applied: SSI 2002/410 Art.26

s.57, varied: SSI 2002/410 Art.3

s.58, applied: SI 2004/2469 Art.16, SSI 2002/410 Art.14

s.58, varied: SSI 2002/410 Art.3

s.59, varied: SSI 2002/410 Art.3

s.60, varied: SSI 2002/410 Art.3

s.61, varied: SSI 2002/410 Art.3

s.62, varied: SSI 2002/410 Art.3

s.63, varied: SSI 2002/410 Art.3

s.64, applied: SSI 2002/121 Art.4

s.64, referred to: SSI 2004/207 Art.4

s.64, varied: SSI 2002/410 Art.3

s.65, applied: SSI 2002/121 Art.4

s.65, referred to: SSI 2004/207 Art.4

s.65, varied: SSI 2002/410 Art.3

s.66, varied: SSI 2002/410 Art.3

s.67, disapplied: SSI 2002/410 Art.3

s.68, varied: SSI 2002/410 Art.3

s.69, varied: SSI 2002/410 Art.3

s.70, varied: SSI 2002/410 Art.3

s.71, varied: SSI 2002/410 Art.3

s.72, disapplied: SSI 2002/410 Art.3

s.73, varied: SSI 2002/410 Art.3

s.74, disapplied: SSI 2002/410 Art.3

s.75, disapplied: SSI 2002/410 Art.3

s.76, disapplied: SSI 2002/410 Art.3

s.77, varied: SSI 2002/410 Art.3

s.78, varied: SSI 2002/410 Art.3

s.79, applied: 2002 c.26 Sch.4 para.1, SI 2003/3006 Sch.2

s.79, disapplied: SSI 2002/410 Art.3

s.80, applied: 2002 c.26 Sch.4 para.1

s.80, disapplied: SSI 2002/410 Art.3

10 & 11 Vict. (1847)–cont.

27. Harbours, Docks, and Piers Clauses Act 1847–cont.

s.81, disapplied: SSI 2002/410 Art.3
s.82, disapplied: SSI 2002/410 Art.3
s.83, disapplied: SSI 2002/410 Art.3
s.84, disapplied: SSI 2002/410 Art.3
s.85, disapplied: SSI 2002/410 Art.3
s.86, disapplied: SSI 2002/410 Art.3
s.87, disapplied: SSI 2002/410 Art.3
s.88, disapplied: SSI 2002/410 Art.3
s.89, disapplied: SSI 2002/410 Art.3
s.90, disapplied: SSI 2002/410 Art.3
s.91, disapplied: SSI 2002/410 Art.3
s.92, varied: SSI 2002/410 Art.3
s.93, disapplied: SSI 2002/410 Art.3
s.94, varied: SSI 2002/410 Art.3
s.95, disapplied: SSI 2002/410 Art.3
s.96, disapplied: SSI 2002/410 Art.3
s.97, disapplied: SSI 2002/410 Art.3
s.98, disapplied: SSI 2002/410 Art.3
s.99, disapplied: SSI 2002/410 Art.3
s.100, disapplied: SSI 2002/410 Art.3
s.101, disapplied: SSI 2002/410 Art.3
s.102, disapplied: SSI 2002/410 Art.3
s.103, disapplied: SSI 2002/410 Art.3
s.104, disapplied: SSI 2002/410 Art.3

34. Towns Improvement Clauses Act 1847

s.3, amended: 2003 c.39 Sch.8 para.29, Sch.10

65. Cemeteries Clauses Act 1847

s.3, amended: 2003 c.39 Sch.8 para.30, Sch.10

89. Town Police Clauses Act 1847

s.3, amended: 2003 c.39 Sch.8 para.31, Sch.10
s.26, amended: 2003 c.44 Sch.32 para.148
s.26, disapplied: 2003 c.44 Sch.25 para.5
s.28, amended: 2003 c.42 Sch.7, 2003 c.44 Sch.32 para.149, Sch.37 Part 9
s.28, disapplied: 2003 c.44 Sch.25 para.6
s.29, amended: 2003 c.44 Sch.32 para.150, Sch.37 Part 9
s.29, disapplied: 2003 c.44 Sch.25 para.7
s.35, repealed: 2003 c.17 Sch.6 para.4, Sch.7
s.36, amended: 2003 c.44 Sch.32 para.151, Sch.37 Part 9
s.36, disapplied: 2003 c.44 Sch.25 para.8
s.37, see *R. (on the application of Maud) v Castle Point BC* [2002] EWCA Civ 1526, [2003] R.T.R. 7 (CA), Keene, L.J.; see *R. (on the application of Royden) v Wirral MBC* [2002] EWHC 2484, [2003] B.L.G.R. 290 (QBD (Admin Ct)), Sir Christopher Bellamy, Q.C.

11 & 12 Vict. (1848)

x. Liverpool Docks Act 1848

s.23, disapplied: SI 2002/3127 Art.7

11 & 12 Vict. (1848)–cont.

12. Treason Felony Act 1848

s.3, see *R. (on the application of Rusbridger) v Attorney General* [2003] UKHL 38, [2004] 1 A.C. 357 (HL), Lord Steyn

29. Hares Act 1848

s.2, amended: 2003 c.39 Sch.8 para.32

42. Indictable Offences Act 1848

s.13, amended: 2003 c.39 Sch.8 para.33, Sch.10

13 & 14 Vict. (1850)

7. London Hackney Carriages Act 1850

s.2, repealed: 2004 c.14 Sch.1 Part 14

94. Ecclesiastical Commissioners Act 1850

s.24, repealed: 2004 c.14 Sch.1 Part 6
s.28, repealed: 2004 c.14 Sch.1 Part 6

14 & 15 Vict. (1851)

42. Crown Lands Act 1851

s.22, applied: SI 2003/1908 Art.2

83. Court of Chancery Act 1851

repealed: 2004 c.14 Sch.1 Part 1

90. Fines Act (Ireland) 1851

s.10, applied: SI 2003/1247 Art.24

99. Evidence Act 1851

s.7, see *R. v Mauricia (Richard Audberto)* [2002] EWCA Crim 676, [2002] 2 Cr. App. R. 27 (CA (Crim Div)), Longmore, L.J.
s.13, amended: 2003 c.39 Sch.8 para.34

15 & 16 Vict. (1852)

cxxi. Belfast Port and Harbour Conservancy Act 1852

s.18, repealed: SR 2002/40 Sch.2
s.20, repealed: SR 2002/40 Sch.2
s.23, repealed: SR 2002/40 Sch.2

28. Commissioners of Works Act 1852

s.2, applied: 2003 c.39 s.3

84. Metropolis Water Act 1852

s.1, repealed: 2003 c.37 Sch.7 para.37, Sch.9 Part 3
s.17, see *Thames Water Utilities Ltd v Digginwell Plant & Construction Ltd* [2002] EWHC 1171, [2003] Env. L.R. 21 (QBD (T&CC)), Judge Richard Seymour Q.C.

16 & 17 Vict. (1853)

47. Battersea Park Act 1853

repealed: 2004 c.14 Sch.1 Part 17

94. Entail Amendment Act 1853

s.16, amended: 2002 asp 17 Sch.3 para.6

127. London Hackney Carriage (No.2) Act 1853

repealed: 2004 c.14 Sch.1 Part 14

CAP.

17 & 18 Vict. (1854)

xlv. Belfast Dock Act 1854
s.23, repealed: SR 2002/40 Sch.2
s.24, repealed: SR 2002/40 Sch.2
xxxi. Hereford Improvement Act 1854
s.21, repealed: 2003 c.iv Sch.1
s.28, repealed: 2003 c.iv Sch.1
s.29, repealed: 2003 c.iv Sch.1
s.30, repealed: 2003 c.iv Sch.1
s.31, repealed: 2003 c.iv Sch.1
clxxvii. Londonderry Port and Harbour Act 1854
s.59, repealed: SR 2002/41 Sch.2
s.91, repealed: SR 2002/41 Sch.2
19. Naval Pay and Prize Act 1854
varied: 2004 c.14 Sch.1 Part 17
67. Defence Act 1854
applied: 2002 c.i, s.5
81. Oxford University Act 1854
s.5, repealed: 2004 c.14 Sch.1 Part 7
s.48, amended: 2004 c.14 Sch.1 Part 7
94. Public Revenue and Consolidated Fund Charges Act 1854
s.1, amended: 2004 c.14 Sch.1 Part 9
Sch.A, repealed: 2004 c.14 Sch.1 Part 9
112. Literary and Scientific Institutions Act 1854
referred to: 2002 c.15 Sch.2 para.3

19 & 20 Vict. (1856)

xvii. Cambridge Award Act 1856
s.9, repealed: 2003 c.17 Sch.6 para.5, Sch.7
s.11, repealed: 2003 c.17 Sch.6 para.5, Sch.7
88. Cambridge University Act 1856
s.5, amended: 2004 c.14 Sch.1 Part 7
s.17, amended: 2004 c.14 Sch.1 Part 7
119. Marriage and Registration Act 1856
repealed: 2004 c.14 Sch.1 Part 17

20 & 21 Vict. (1857)

26. Registration of Leases (Scotland) Act 1857
applied: 2003 asp 2 s.83
s.3, amended: 2003 asp 9 Sch.14 para.1
s.3, repealed (in part): 2003 asp 9 Sch.15
31. Inclosure Act 1857
see *R. (on the application of Laing Homes Ltd) v Buckinghamshire CC* [2003] EWHC 1578, [2004] 1 P. & C.R. 36 (QBD (Admin Ct)), Sullivan, J.
s.12, see *Oxfordshire CC v Oxford City Council* [2004] EWHC 12, [2004] Ch. 253 (Ch D), Lightman, J.; see *Rabett v Poole* [2003] 3 E.G.L.R. 143 (CC (Bury St Edmunds)), Judge Langan Q.C.

21 & 22 Vict. (1858)

25. Births and Deaths Registration Act 1858
repealed: 2004 c.14 Sch.1 Part 17

CAP.

21 & 22 Vict. (1858)–cont.

56. Confirmation of Executors (Scotland) Act 1858
s.2, amended: 2003 asp 4 Sch.4 para.1

22 & 23 Vict. (1859)

12. Defence Act 1859
applied: 2002 c.i, s.5
25. Convict Prisons Abroad Act 1859
varied: 2004 c.14 Sch.1 Part 17
43. Inclosure Act 1859
s.4, amended: 2003 c.39 Sch.8 para.35
s.6, amended: 2003 c.39 Sch.8 para.36

23 & 24 Vict. (1860)

18. Marriage (Society of Friends) Act 1860
repealed (in part): SI 2003/413 Sch.1
32. Ecclesiastical Courts Jurisdiction Act 1860
s.2, amended: 2003 c.39 Sch.8 para.37
s.2, disapplied: 2003 c.44 Sch.25 para.9
s.2, repealed (in part): 2003 c.44 Sch.37 Part 9
s.3, amended: 2003 c.39 Sch.8 para.38
90. Game Licences Act 1860
s.5, amended: 2002 asp 6 Sch.1 para.2, 2004 c.37 Sch.3
s.16A, added: 2004 c.14 Sch.2 para.4
112. Defence Act 1860
s.47, amended: 2003 c.39 Sch.8 para.40, Sch.10

24 & 25 Vict. (1861)

3. Bank of England Act 1861
repealed: SI 2004/1662 Sch.1 para.2
70. Locomotive Act 1861
s.7, repealed: 2004 c.14 Sch.1 Part 14
94. Accessories and Abettors Act 1861
s.8, applied: SI 2004/1910 Sch.6
100. Offences against the Person Act 1861
see *R. v Dias (Fernando Augusto)* [2001] EWCA Crim 2986, [2002] 2 Cr. App. R. 5 (CA (Crim Div)), Keene, L.J.
s.4, applied: 2003 c.42 Sch.5 para.5, Sch.5 para.118, 2003 c.44 Sch.4 para.3, Sch.5 para.3, Sch.5 para.32, Sch.5 para.37, Sch.15 para.4, Sch.17 para.6, SI 2004/1500 Sch.2 para.3, SI 2004/1910 Sch.6
s.16, applied: SI 2002/896 Sch.1 para.5, 2003 c.42 Sch.5 para.6, Sch.5 para.119, 2003 c.44 Sch.15 para.5, Sch.17 para.7, SI 2004/1910 Sch.6
s.18, see *Attorney General's Reference (No.132 of 2001), Re* [2002] EWCA Crim 1418, [2003] 1 Cr. App. R. (S.) 41 (CA (Crim Div)), Potter, L.J.; see *Attorney General's Reference (No.18 of 2002), Re* [2002] EWCA Crim 1127, [2003] 1 Cr. App. R. (S.)

24 & 25 Vict. (1861)–cont.

100. Offences against the Person Act 1861–cont.

s.18–cont.

9 (CA (Crim Div)), Rose, L.J.; see *Attorney General's Reference (No.29 of 2001), Re* [2001] EWCA Crim 1491, [2002] 1 Cr. App. R. (S.) 60 (CA (Crim Div)), Potter, L.J.; see *R. v Arnold (Kenneth)* [2004] EWCA Crim 1293, (2004) 148 S.J.L.B. 660 (CA (Crim Div)), Hooper, L.J.; see *R. v Close (Craig)* [2001] EWCA Crim 1066, [2002] 1 Cr. App. R. (S.) 16 (CA (Crim Div)), Leveson, J.; see *R. v LM* [2002] EWCA Crim 3047, [2003] 2 Cr. App. R. (S.) 26 (CA (Crim Div)), Judge Gordon; see *R. v Noorkoiv (Leo Robert)* [2002] EWCA Crim 530, [2002] 2 Cr. App. R. (S.) 91 (CA (Crim Div)), Gibbs, J.

s.18, applied: SI 2002/896 Sch.1 para.6, 2003 c.42 Sch.5 para.7, Sch.5 para.120, 2003 c.44 Sch.4 para.5, Sch.15 para.6, Sch.17 para.8, 2004 c.31 s.58, SI 2004/1500 Sch.2 para.5, SI 2004/1910 Sch.6

s.20, see *R. (on the application of C) v Grimsby and Cleethorpes Magistrates Court* [2004] EWHC 2239, (2004) 168 J.P. 569 (QBD (Admin)), Dyson, L.J.; see *R. v Ashbridge (Dallas)* [2002] EWCA Crim 384, [2002] 2 Cr. App. R. (S.) 89 (CA (Crim Div)), Pitchford, J.; see *R. v Bell (Dean Vernon)* [2002] EWCA Crim 2378, [2003] 1 Cr. App. R. (S.) 105 (CA (Crim Div)), Wright, J.; see *R. v Bridle (Steven Charles)* [2002] EWCA Crim 908, [2003] 1 Cr. App. R. (S.) 3 (CA (Crim Div)), McKinnon, J.; see *R. v Dica (Mohammed)* [2004] EWCA Crim 1103, [2004] Q.B. 1257 (CA (Crim Div)), Lord Woolf of Barnes, L.C.J.; see *R. v LM* [2002] EWCA Crim 3047, [2003] 2 Cr. App. R. (S.) 26 (CA (Crim Div)), Judge Gordon

s.20, applied: SI 2002/896 Sch.1 para.6, 2003 c.42 Sch.5 para.8, Sch.5 para.121, 2003 c.44 Sch.15 para.7, Sch.17 para.9, 2004 c.31 s.58, SI 2004/702 Sch.4 para.2, SI 2004/1910 Sch.6

s.21, applied: 2003 c.42 Sch.5 para.9, Sch.5 para.122, 2003 c.44 Sch.15 para.8, Sch.17 para.10, SI 2004/702 Sch.4 para.2, SI 2004/1910 Sch.6

s.22, applied: 2003 c.42 Sch.5 para.10, Sch.5 para.123, 2003 c.44 Sch.15 para.9, Sch.17 para.11, SI 2004/702 Sch.4 para.2, SI 2004/1910 Sch.6

s.23, see *R. v Rogers (Stephen)* [2003] EWCA Crim 945, [2003] 1 W.L.R. 1374 (CA (Crim Div)), Rose, L.J.

s.23, applied: 2003 c.42 Sch.5 para.11, Sch.5 para.124, 2003 c.44 Sch.15 para.10, Sch.17 para.12, SI 2004/1910 Sch.6

s.27, applied: 2003 c.42 Sch.5 para.12, Sch.5 para.125, 2003 c.44 Sch.15 para.11, Sch.17 para.13, SI 2004/1910 Sch.6

24 & 25 Vict. (1861)–cont.

100. Offences against the Person Act 1861–cont.

s.28, applied: 2003 c.42 Sch.5 para.13, Sch.5 para.126, 2003 c.44 Sch.15 para.12, Sch.17 para.14, SI 2004/1910 Sch.6

s.29, applied: 2003 c.42 Sch.5 para.14, Sch.5 para.127, 2003 c.44 Sch.15 para.13, Sch.17 para.15, SI 2004/1910 Sch.6

s.30, applied: 2003 c.42 Sch.5 para.15, Sch.5 para.128, 2003 c.44 Sch.15 para.14, Sch.17 para.16, SI 2004/702 Sch.4 para.2, SI 2004/1910 Sch.6

s.31, applied: 2003 c.42 Sch.5 para.16, Sch.5 para.129, 2003 c.44 Sch.15 para.15, Sch.17 para.17

s.32, applied: 2003 c.42 Sch.5 para.17, Sch.5 para.130, 2003 c.44 Sch.15 para.16, Sch.17 para.18, SI 2004/702 Sch.4 para.2, SI 2004/1910 Sch.6

s.33, applied: SI 2004/1910 Sch.6

s.35, see *R. v Bridle (Steven Charles)* [2002] EWCA Crim 908, [2003] 1 Cr. App. R. (S.) 3 (CA (Crim Div)), McKinnon, J.

s.35, applied: 2003 c.42 Sch.5 para.18, Sch.5 para.131, 2003 c.44 Sch.15 para.17, Sch.17 para.19

s.37, applied: 2003 c.42 Sch.5 para.19, Sch.5 para.132, 2003 c.44 Sch.15 para.18, Sch.17 para.20

s.38, applied: 2003 c.42 Sch.5 para.20, 2003 c.44 Sch.15 para.19

s.44, amended: 2003 c.39 Sch.8 para.41, Sch.10

s.45, see *Wong v Parkside Health NHS Trust* [2001] EWCA Civ 1721, [2003] 3 All E.R. 932 (CA), Hale, L.J.

s.47, see *T v DPP* [2003] EWHC 266, [2003] Crim. L.R. 622 (QBD (Admin Ct)), Maurice Kay, J.

s.47, applied: SI 2002/896 Sch.1 para.6, 2003 c.42 Sch.5 para.21, Sch.5 para.133, 2003 c.44 Sch.15 para.20, Sch.17 para.21, 2004 c.31 s.58, SI 2004/702 Sch.4 para.2, SI 2004/1910 Sch.6

s.47, disapplied: SSI 2003/19 Sch.5 para.2, Sch.5 para.13

s.48, applied: SI 2003/1184 Sch.2 para.32

s.52, see *Attorney General for Northern Ireland's Reference (No.1 of 2003), Re* [2004] N.I. 30 (CA (Crim Div) (NI)), Lord Carswell L.C.J.

s.52, applied: 2003 c.42 Sch.2 para.2, Sch.3 para.62, 2003 c.44 Sch.17 para.65, SI 2003/1184 Sch.2 para.33, SI 2004/1910 Sch.4

s.53, applied: 2003 c.42 Sch.2 para.2, Sch.3 para.63, 2003 c.44 Sch.17 para.66, SI 2004/702 Sch.4 para.2, SI 2004/1910 Sch.4

s.54, applied: 2003 c.42 Sch.2 para.2, Sch.3 para.63, 2003 c.44 Sch.17 para.67, SI 2004/702 Sch.4 para.2

24 & 25 Vict. (1861)–cont.

100. Offences against the Person Act 1861–cont.

s.55, applied: 2003 c.44 Sch.17 para.68, SI 2004/702 Sch.4 para.2

s.57, applied: 2004 c.19 s.14

s.58, see *R. (on the application of Smeaton) v Secretary of State for Health* [2002] EWHC 610, [2002] 2 F.L.R. 146 (QBD (Admin Ct)), Munby, J.

s.59, see *R. (on the application of Smeaton) v Secretary of State for Health* [2002] EWHC 610, [2002] 2 F.L.R. 146 (QBD (Admin Ct)), Munby, J.

s.61, amended: SI 2003/1247 Sch.1 para.1

s.61, applied: SI 2002/57 Sch.4 para.7, 2003 c.42 Sch.3 para.64, Sch.4 para.1, SI 2003/1184 Sch.2 para.34

s.61, disapplied: SSI 2003/19 Sch.5 para.13

s.61, referred to: SI 2003/237 Sch.4 para.6

s.61, repealed: 2003 c.42 Sch.7

s.62, see *Attorney General of Northern Ireland's Reference (No.2 of 2002), Re* [2003] N.I. 21 (CA (NI)), Carswell, L.C.J.; see *McR's Application for Judicial Review, Re* [2003] N.I. 1 (QBD (NI)), Kerr, J.

s.62, amended: SI 2003/1247 Sch.1 para.2

s.62, applied: 2003 c.42 Sch.3 para.65, Sch.3 para.66, SI 2003/1184 Sch.2 para.35

s.62, repealed: 2003 c.42 Sch.7

s.63, applied: SI 2003/1247 Art.18

s.65, amended: 2003 c.39 Sch.8 para.42, Sch.10

25 & 26 Vict. (1862)

53. Land Registry Act 1862

applied: 2002 c.9 s.122

repealed: 2002 c.9 Sch.13

97. Salmon Fisheries (Scotland) Act 1862

applied: 2003 asp 15 s.37, s.43, SSI 2003/615 Sch.2 para.4

s.6, applied: SSI 2002/138 Sch.2, 2003 asp 15 s.36, s.37, s.40

114. Poaching Prevention Act 1862

s.1, amended: 2003 c.39 Sch.8 para.44, Sch.10

s.2, amended: 2003 c.39 Sch.8 para.45, Sch.10

s.3, amended: 2003 c.39 Sch.8 para.46, Sch.10

26 & 27 Vict. (1863)

13. Town Gardens Protection Act 1863

s.5, amended: 2003 c.44 Sch.37 Part 9

s.5, disapplied: 2003 c.44 Sch.25 para.10

27. Marriage Law (Ireland) Amendment Act 1863

repealed: SI 2003/413 Sch.1

s.12, amended: SR 2002/242 Sch.1

26 & 27 Vict. (1863)–cont.

49. Duchy of Cornwall, Management Act 1863

s.8, applied: 2002 c.15 s.108, s.172

90. Registration of Marriages (Ireland) Act 1863

repealed: SI 2003/413 Sch.1

s.17, amended: SR 2002/242 Sch.1

s.18, amended: SR 2002/242 Sch.1

s.19, amended: SR 2002/242 Sch.1

92. Railways Clauses Act 1863

Part I, consolidated: 2004 asp 10 s.37

s.3, consolidated: 2004 asp 10 s.37

s.6, disapplied: 2004 asp 10 Sch.4 Part 3

s.6, varied: SI 2002/1997 Art.3

s.12, applied: SI 2002/1064 Art.3, SI 2003/3364 Art.3

s.15, consolidated: 2004 asp 10 s.37

s.16, consolidated: 2004 asp 10 s.37

s.17, consolidated: 2004 asp 10 s.37

s.18, consolidated: 2004 asp 10 s.37

27 & 28 Vict. (1864)

118. Salmon Fisheries (Scotland) Act 1864

applied: 2003 asp 15 s.37, s.43, SSI 2003/615 Sch.2 para.4

28 & 29 Vict. (1865)

ccxcii. Chester and West Cheshire Junction Railway Act 1865

s.31, disapplied: SI 2002/412 Art.37

18. Criminal Procedure Act 1865

s.2, applied: 2003 c.44 s.62, SI 2004/1500 Art.21

s.3, applied: 2003 c.44 s.112, s.119, SI 2004/1501 Art.17, Art.23

s.4, applied: 2003 c.44 s.119, SI 2004/1501 Art.23

s.5, applied: 2003 c.44 s.119, SI 2004/1501 Art.23

s.6, amended: 2003 c.39 Sch.8 para.47, 2003 c.44 Sch.36 para.79, Sch.37 Part 5, SI 2004/1501 Sch.1 para.1, Sch.2

56. Trespass (Scotland) Act 1865

s.3, amended: 2003 asp 2 Sch.2 para.1

s.3, substituted: 2003 asp 2 Sch.2 para.1

63. Colonial Laws Validity Act 1865

referred to: 2003 c.7 s.24

69. Parsonages Act 1865

s.4, amended: 2004 c.14 Sch.1 Part 6

73. Naval and Marine Pay and Pensions Act 1865

applied: SI 2002/1792 Sch.4 para.1, SI 2004/291 Sch.4, SI 2004/478 Sch.4, SI 2004/627 Sch.2, SR 2003/28 Sch.4 para.1, SSI 2004/115 Sch.3

s.3, amended: 2004 c.32 s.4

s.3, applied: SI 2002/1792 Sch.4 para.17

s.3, enabling: SI 2002/792, SI 2003/434, SI 2004/708

CAP.

28 & 29 Vict. (1865)–cont.

87. Post Office Extension Act 1865
varied: SI 2003/1542 Art.2

89. Greenwich Hospital Act 1865
s.5, added: 2004 c.33 Sch.26 para.1

94. Carriers Act Amendment Act 1865
repealed: 2004 c.14 Sch.1 Part 17

111. Navy and Marines (Property of Deceased) Act 1865
s.3, applied: 2004 c.32 s.2
s.4, amended: 2004 c.33 Sch.26 para.2
s.5, applied: 2004 c.32 s.2

125. Dockyard Ports Regulation Act 1865
s.2, amended: 2003 c.39 Sch.8 para.48, Sch.10
s.22, amended: 2003 c.39 Sch.8 para.49

29 & 30 Vict. (1866)

Greenock Port and Harbours Act 1866
see *Wilson v Inverclyde Council* 2003 S.C. 366 (Ex Div), Lord Osborne, Lord Coulsfield, Lord Drummond Young

39. Exchequer and Audit Departments Act 1866
s.2, amended: 2004 c.14 Sch.1 Part 9
s.6, applied: SI 2003/418 Art.4
s.10, applied: 2002 c.23 s.137, 2003 c.14 s.129, s.130
s.10, varied: 2002 c.21 s.2, 2002 c.23 Sch.13 para.26, 2004 c.12 s.115

111. Ecclesiastical Commissioners Act 1866
s.1, amended: 2004 c.14 Sch.1 Part 6

122. Metropolitan Commons Act 1866
s.33, added: SI 2003/2867 Sch.1 para.2

30 & 31 Vict. (1867)

133. Consecration of Churchyards Act 1867
applied: SI 2002/1893 para.1, SI 2003/1936 para.1

134. Metropolitan Streets Act 1867
s.19, repealed: 2004 c.14 Sch.1 Part 14
s.20, repealed: 2004 c.14 Sch.1 Part 14

31 & 32 Vict. (1868)

cxiii. Gun Barrel Proof Act 1868
applied: 2002 c.40 Sch.15

37. Documentary Evidence Act 1868
varied: 2002 c.9 Sch.7 para.6, SI 2002/1397 Art.3, Art.4, SI 2002/2626 Art.19, 2003 c.21 s.403, SI 2003/1887 Art.3
Sch.1, varied: 2002 c.9 Sch.7 para.6

45. Sea Fisheries Act 1868
s.64, amended: SI 2002/790 Art.7

64. Land Registers (Scotland) Act 1868
s.25, applied: SSI 2004/318 r.5
s.25, enabling: SSI 2004/507

72. Promissory Oaths Act 1868
applied: 2003 c.39 s.22, s.24

CAP.

31 & 32 Vict. (1868)–cont.

72. Promissory Oaths Act 1868–cont.
s.4, repealed: 2002 c.26 Sch.13
s.6, repealed: 2002 c.26 Sch.13
Sch.1 Part 2, amended: 2002 c.26 Sch.13

101. Titles to Land Consolidation (Scotland) Act 1868
s.138, amended: 2003 asp 9 Sch.14 para.2
s.155, applied: 2002 c.29 s.123, s.258

118. Public Schools Act 1868
s.20, repealed (in part): 2004 c.14 Sch.1 Part 7
s.21, repealed: 2004 c.14 Sch.1 Part 7

119. Regulation of Railways Act 1868
s.22, referred to: 2002 c.8 (NI) s.1

123. Salmon Fisheries (Scotland) Act 1868
applied: 2003 asp 15 s.37, s.43, SSI 2003/615 Sch.2 para.4
repealed: 2003 asp 15 Sch.4 Part 2
s.9, applied: 2003 asp 15 s.37
s.31, applied: SI 2003/336 Sch.1 Part 2

32 & 33 Vict. (1869)

cxviii. Newport (Monmouthshire) Harbour Act 1869
s.3, varied: SI 2003/2679 Art.14
s.17, repealed: SI 2003/2679 Sch.3
s.24, repealed: SI 2003/2679 Sch.3
s.34, repealed: SI 2003/2679 Sch.3
s.40, repealed: SI 2003/2679 Sch.3
s.49, repealed: SI 2003/2679 Sch.3
s.50, repealed: SI 2003/2679 Sch.3

24. Newspapers, Printers, and Reading Rooms Repeal Act 1869
Sch.2 Part 1, amended: 2003 c.39 Sch.8 para.50, Sch.10
Sch.2 Part 4, amended: 2003 c.39 Sch.8 para.50

62. Debtors Act 1869
see *Corbett v Corbett* [2003] EWCA Civ 559, [2003] 2 F.L.R. 385 (CA), Thorpe, L.J.
s.5, amended: SI 2002/439 Art.3, 2004 c.14 Sch.1 Part 17
s.10, substituted: SI 2002/439 Art.4

33 & 34 Vict. (1870)

xcvii. Belfast Harbour Act 1870
repealed: SR 2002/40 Sch.2

2. Owens Extension College, Manchester, Act 1870
applied: 2004 c.iv
repealed: 2004 c.iv Sch.3

35. Apportionment Act 1870
s.2, see *Maconnachie v Leisure Leagues UK Ltd* [2002] I.R.L.R. 600 (EAT), Judge A Wilkie Q.C.

52. Extradition Act 1870
see *R. (on the application of Al-Fawwaz) v Governor of Brixton Prison* [2001] UKHL 69, [2002] 1 A.C. 556 (HL), Lord Slynn of Hadley

CAP.

33 & 34 Vict. (1870)–cont.

52. Extradition Act 1870–*cont.*
applied: 2003 c.41 Sch.3 para.4, Sch.3 para.6, Sch.3 para.8, Sch.3 para.12, Sch.3 para.14
s.2, applied: SI 2002/1831, SI 2002/1831 Art.2, 2003 c.41 Sch.3 para.10, Sch.3 para.11
s.62, applied: SI 2002/1831
s.188, applied: 2002 c.40 s.191

71. National Debt Act 1870
s.3, amended: SI 2002/2521 Sch.2 Part I, SI 2004/1662 Sch.1 para.3, SI 2004/2744 Sch.1 para.1
s.13, amended: SI 2002/2521 Sch.1 para.1
s.13, substituted: SI 2004/1662 Sch.1 para.3
s.14, amended: SI 2002/2521 Sch.1 para.1, SI 2004/1662 Sch.1 para.3
s.14, substituted: SI 2004/2744 Sch.1 para.1
s.15, substituted: SI 2004/1662 Sch.1 para.3, SI 2004/2744 Sch.1 para.1
s.16, amended: SI 2002/2521 Sch.1 para.1, SI 2004/2744 Sch.1 para.1
s.16, substituted: SI 2004/1662 Sch.1 para.3
s.55, amended: SI 2002/2521 Sch.2 Part I, SI 2004/1662 Sch.1 para.3
s.59, amended: SI 2002/2521 Sch.1 para.1
s.59, applied: 2002 c.23 s.138
s.59, substituted: SI 2004/1662 Sch.1 para.3
s.66, amended: SI 2004/1662 Sch.1 para.3
s.66, applied: 2002 c.23 s.138

78. Tramways Act 1870
s.25, see *Roe v Sheffield City Council (No.1)* [2003] EWCA Civ 1, [2004] Q.B. 653 (CA), Pill, L.J.
s.28, see *Roe v Sheffield City Council (No.1)* [2003] EWCA Civ 1, [2004] Q.B. 653 (CA), Pill, L.J.

110. Matrimonial Causes and Marriage Law (Ireland) Amendment Act 1870
s.4, repealed: SI 2003/413 Sch.1
s.32, repealed: SI 2003/413 Sch.1
s.33, repealed: SI 2003/413 Sch.1
s.34, repealed: SI 2003/413 Sch.1
s.35, amended: SR 2002/242 Sch.1
s.35, repealed: SI 2003/413 Sch.1
s.36, repealed: SI 2003/413 Sch.1
s.37, repealed: SI 2003/413 Sch.1
s.38, repealed: SI 2003/413 Sch.1
s.39, repealed: SI 2003/413 Sch.1
s.40, repealed: SI 2003/413 Sch.1
s.41, repealed: SI 2003/413 Sch.1
s.42, repealed: SI 2003/413 Sch.1
Sch.A, repealed: SI 2003/413 Sch.1

34 & 35 Vict. (1871)

cxlvii. Owens College Act 1871
referred to: 2004 c.iv
repealed: 2004 c.iv Sch.3

xvii. Shotts Iron Companys Act 1871
repealed: 2004 c.14 Sch.1 Part 15

CAP.

34 & 35 Vict. (1871)–cont.

cciv. Wimbledon and Putney Commons Act 1871
s.79, repealed: 2004 c.14 Sch.1 Part 17

36. Pensions Commutation Act 1871
s.4, amended: 2004 c.33 Sch.26 para.3

45. Sequestration Act 1871
s.2, amended: 2004 c.14 Sch.1 Part 6

48. Promissory Oaths Act 1871
applied: 2003 c.39 s.22, s.24
s.2, amended: 2003 c.39 Sch.8 para.51

49. Matrimonial Causes and Marriage Law (Ireland) Amendment Act 1871
repealed: SI 2003/413 Sch.1

56. Dogs Act 1871
s.2, see *Shufflebottom v Chief Constable of Greater Manchester* [2003] EWHC 246, (2003) 167 J.P. 153 (QBD (Admin Ct)), Mackay, J.

78. Regulation of Railways Act 1871
referred to: 2002 c.8 (NI) s.1

96. Pedlars Act 1871
s.3, see *Croydon LBC v Burdon* [2002] EWHC 1961, [2003] E.H.L.R.1 (QBD (Admin Ct)), Judge Wilkie

112. Prevention of Crimes Act 1871
s.18, amended: 2003 c.39 Sch.8 para.52

35 & 36 Vict. (1872)

cxix. Hereford Improvement Act 1872
s.24, repealed: 2003 c.iv Sch.1

10. Marriage (Society of Friends) Act 1872
repealed (in part): SI 2003/413 Sch.1

94. Licensing Act 1872
s.12, amended: 2003 c.44 Sch.26 para.2.5 para.1, SI 2002/1837 Sch.1 Part II, SI 2004/915 Sch.1 para.1

36 & 37 Vict. (1873)

xcix. Bank of Scotland Act 1873
s.4, repealed: 2004 c.14 Sch.1 Part 15
s.5, repealed: 2004 c.14 Sch.1 Part 15
s.6, repealed: 2004 c.14 Sch.1 Part 15
s.7, repealed: 2004 c.14 Sch.1 Part 15
s.8, repealed: 2004 c.14 Sch.1 Part 15
s.9, repealed: 2004 c.14 Sch.1 Part 15

16. Marriage Law (Ireland) Amendment Act 1873
repealed: SI 2003/413 Sch.1

37. Fairs Act 1873
s.6, varied: 2003 c.39 Sch.8 para.53

50. Places of Worship Sites Act 1873
referred to: 2002 c.15 Sch.2 para.3
s.3, amended: 2004 c.14 Sch.1 Part 6

57. Consolidated Fund (Permanent Charges Redemption) Act 1873
repealed: 2004 c.14 Sch.1 Part 9

37 & 38 Vict. (1874)

cii. Lancashire and Yorkshire Railway (New Works and Additional Powers) Act 1874
referred to: SI 2002/1384 Art.8

xlix. Londonderry Port and Harbour Act 1874
s.58, repealed: SR 2002/41 Sch.2

81. Great Seal (Offices) Act 1874
s.9, enabling: SI 2003/92

94. Conveyancing (Scotland) Act 1874
s.32, referred to: 2003 asp 9 s.119
s.32, repealed: 2003 asp 9 Sch.15
Sch.H, repealed: 2003 asp 9 Sch.15

38 & 39 Vict. (1875)

17. Explosives Act 1875
applied: SR 2002/147 Reg.3, SR 2002/301 Reg.3, 2003 c.22 s.14, SSI 2004/406 Sch.1 para.1
s.4, applied: SI 2004/1836 Reg.9
s.5, applied: SI 2004/1836 Reg.9, SR 2002/147 Reg.9, Reg.11
s.5, disapplied: SR 2002/147 Reg.11
s.6, applied: SI 2002/655 Sch.9 Part I, SI 2003/547 Sch.9 Part 1, SI 2004/456 Sch.8 Part 1
s.12, applied: SI 2002/655 Sch.9 Part I, SI 2003/547 Sch.9 Part 1, SI 2004/456 Sch.8 Part 1
s.15, applied: SI 2003/547 Sch.9 Part II, SI 2004/456 Sch.8 Part II
s.15, referred to: SI 2002/655 Sch.9 Part II
s.18, applied: SI 2003/547 Sch.9 Part II, SI 2004/456 Sch.8 Part II
s.18, referred to: SI 2002/655 Sch.9 Part II
s.21, applied: SI 2003/547 Sch.9 Part II, SI 2004/456 Sch.8 Part II, SI 2004/1836 Reg.9
s.21, referred to: SI 2002/655 Sch.9 Part II
s.30, repealed: 2003 c.22 Sch.1
s.31, applied: SI 2003/1593 Sch.1 Part I
s.31, repealed: 2003 c.22 Sch.1
s.32, applied: SI 2004/1836 Reg.9
s.32, repealed: 2003 c.22 Sch.1
s.39, applied: SI 2002/655 Sch.9 Part I, SI 2003/1593 Sch.1 Part I
s.39, referred to: SI 2004/456 Sch.8 Part 1
s.40, amended: 2003 c.22 Sch.1
s.40, applied: SI 2002/655 Sch.9 Part I, Sch.9 Part V, Sch.9 Part VI, SI 2003/547 Sch.9 Part 1, Sch.9 Part V, Sch.9 Part VI, SI 2004/456 Sch.8 Part 1, Sch.8 Part V, Sch.8 Part VI
s.40, referred to: SI 2004/456 Sch.8 Part 1
s.43, applied: SSI 2003/231 Sch.1 para.10, Sch.3 para.4, Sch.4 para.4
s.67, amended: 2004 c.21 Sch.1 para.1
s.80, applied: SI 2002/1837 Sch.1 Part I, Sch.1 Part II
s.80, repealed: 2003 c.22 Sch.1

38 & 39 Vict. (1875)–cont.

25. Public Stores Act 1875
s.8, amended: 2003 c.44 Sch.37 Part 9
s.8, disapplied: 2003 c.44 Sch.25 para.11

55. Public Health Act 1875
s.4, see *Bradford MDC v Yorkshire Water Services Ltd* [2001] EWHC Admin 687, [2002] Env. L.R. 16 (QBD (Admin Ct)), Brooke, L.J.
s.164, applied: SI 2004/1777 Art.25, SI 2004/1778 Art.25
s.265, varied: 2002 c.i Sch.3 para.15, SI 2004/1777 Art.19, SI 2004/1778 Art.19

89. Public Works Loans Act 1875
s.33, amended: 2004 c.14 Sch.1 Part 9
s.57, repealed (in part): 2004 c.14 Sch.1 Part 9

39 & 40 Vict. (1876)

Council Directive 92/12 on the general arrangements for products subject to excise duty and on the holding, movement and monitoring of such products Customs Consolidation Act 1876
s.42, see *Masterson v DPP* [2003] Eu. L.R. 25 (HC (Irl)), Roderick H Murphy, J.

iii. Manchester Post Office Act 1876
repealed: SI 2003/1542 Sch.2

lxxv. Western Bank of Scotland (Liquidation) Act 1876
repealed: 2004 c.14 Sch.1 Part 15

36. Customs Consolidation Act 1876
s.42, see *R. v Forbes (Giles)* [2001] UKHL 40, [2002] 2 A.C. 512 (HL), Lord Hutton
s.42, applied: SI 2002/635 Sch.1 para.4, SI 2002/896 Sch.1 para.42, Sch.1 para.59, Sch.1 para.71, 2003 c.42 Sch.3 para.14, Sch.3 para.44, Sch.3 para.78, 2003 c.44 Sch.15 para.100, Sch.16 para.9, Sch.17 para.83, SI 2004/2695 Sch.1 para.18, SSI 2003/19 Sch.5 para.7, Sch.5 para.10, Sch.5 para.17

56. Commons Act 1876
s.20, amended: 2003 c.39 Sch.8 para.54
s.29, see *Oxfordshire CC v Oxford City Council* [2004] EWHC 12, [2004] Ch. 253 (Ch D), Lightman, J.; see *Rabett v Poole* [2003] 3 E.G.L.R. 143 (CC (Bury St Edmunds)), Judge Langan Q.C.

59. Appellate Jurisdiction Act 1876
applied: 2002 c.41 Sch.5 para.3
s.5, applied: 2003 c.41 s.32, s.114, SI 2003/458 Art.12
s.6, amended: 2002 c.26 s.18
s.25, applied: 2002 c.26 s.8, s.24, s.43

40 & 41 Vict. (1877)

cxxi. New Forest Act 1877
see *Verderers of the New Forest v Young (No.2)* [2003] EWHC 3253, [2004] 1 E.G.L.R. 1 (QBD (Admin Ct)), Rose, L.J.

CAP.

40 & 41 Vict. (1877)–cont.

cxxi. New Forest Act 1877–*cont.*
  s.25, see *Verderers of the New Forest v Young (No.2)* [2003] EWHC 3253, [2004] 1 E.G.L.R.1 (QBD (Admin Ct)), Rose, L.J.
  s.25, enabling: SI 2003/3298
  s.29, see *Verderers of the New Forest v Young (No.2)* [2003] EWHC 3253, [2004] 1 E.G.L.R.1 (QBD (Admin Ct)), Rose, L.J.
  Sch.1 para.2, referred to: SI 2003/3298 Sch.1 para.23

xviii. Shotts Iron Companys Act 1877
  repealed: 2004 c.14 Sch.1 Part 15

ccxl. Solway Salmon Fisheries Commissioners (Scotland) Act 1877
  repealed: 2003 asp 15 Sch.4 Part 2

2. Treasury Bills Act 1877
  applied: SI 2003/1633 Reg.14
  s.2, varied: SI 2003/1633 Sch.1 para.2
  s.4, varied: SI 2003/1633 Sch.1 para.3, Sch.1 para.4
  s.8, varied: SI 2003/1633 Sch.1 para.5
  s.9, varied: SI 2003/1633 Sch.1 para.6

40. Writs Execution (Scotland) Act 1877
  s.3, amended: 2002 asp 17 Sch.3 para.7

41. Crown Office Act 1877
  s.3, enabling: SI 2002/3131

48. Universities of Oxford and Cambridge Act 1877
  s.2, amended: 2004 c.14 Sch.1 Part 7
  s.24, repealed: 2004 c.14 Sch.1 Part 7
  s.57, repealed: 2004 c.14 Sch.1 Part 7

41 & 42 Vict. (1878)

cxv. Pier and Harbour Orders Confirmation Act 1878 (No.2) 1878
  repealed: SSI 2002/410 Sch.2 Part I
  s.3, referred to: SSI 2002/410 Sch.2 Part I
  s.4, referred to: SSI 2002/410 Sch.2 Part I
  s.5, referred to: SSI 2002/410 Sch.2 Part I
  s.6, referred to: SSI 2002/410 Sch.2 Part I
  s.31, referred to: SSI 2002/410 Sch.2 Part I
  s.32, referred to: SSI 2002/410 Sch.2 Part I

31. Bills of Sale Act 1878
  applied: SI 2004/3121 Sch.1
  s.15, applied: SI 2004/3121 Sch.1

52. Public Health (Ireland) Act 1878
  s.108, amended: SI 2002/3153 Sch.5 para.1
  s.110, applied: SI 2003/412 Art.142

54. Debtors Act 1878
  s.1, amended: 2004 c.14 Sch.1 Part 17

73. Territorial Waters Jurisdiction Act 1878
  s.3, disapplied: SI 2002/1355 Reg.18, 2004 c.20 s.86, s.98, s.113
  s.4, amended: 2003 c.44 Sch.3 para.29

CAP.

42 & 43 Vict. (1879)

cxcviii. Metropolis Management (Thames River Prevention of Floods) Amendment Act 1879
  s.5, applied: SI 2003/1075 Sch.13 para.39, SI 2004/389 Sch.13 para.39

cxciv. New Forest Act 1879
  s.2, applied: SI 2003/3298 Sch.1 para.4

clxxv. River Bann Navigation Act 1879
  s.3, repealed: SR 2002/395 Sch.2 Part I
  s.8, repealed: SR 2002/395 Sch.2 Part II
  s.9, repealed: SR 2002/395 Sch.2 Part II
  s.10, repealed: SR 2002/395 Sch.2 Part II
  s.12, repealed: SR 2002/395 Sch.2 Part II
  s.15, repealed: SR 2002/395 Sch.2 Part II
  s.16, repealed: SR 2002/395 Sch.2 Part II
  s.17, repealed: SR 2002/395 Sch.2 Part II
  s.18, repealed: SR 2002/395 Sch.2 Part II
  s.19, repealed: SR 2002/395 Sch.2 Part II
  s.20, repealed: SR 2002/395 Sch.2 Part II
  s.21, repealed: SR 2002/395 Sch.2 Part II
  s.22, repealed: SR 2002/395 Sch.2 Part II
  s.23, repealed: SR 2002/395 Sch.2 Part II
  s.24, repealed: SR 2002/395 Sch.2 Part II
  s.25, repealed: SR 2002/395 Sch.2 Part II
  s.26, repealed: SR 2002/395 Sch.2 Part II
  s.27, repealed: SR 2002/395 Sch.2 Part II
  s.28, repealed: SR 2002/395 Sch.2 Part II
  s.29, repealed: SR 2002/395 Sch.2 Part II
  s.30, repealed: SR 2002/395 Sch.2 Part II
  s.31, repealed: SR 2002/395 Sch.2 Part II
  s.32, repealed: SR 2002/395 Sch.2 Part II
  s.33, repealed: SR 2002/395 Sch.2 Part II
  s.34, repealed: SR 2002/395 Sch.2 Part II
  s.35, repealed: SR 2002/395 Sch.2 Part II
  s.36, repealed: SR 2002/395 Sch.2 Part II
  s.37, repealed: SR 2002/395 Sch.2 Part II
  s.38, repealed: SR 2002/395 Sch.2 Part II
  s.39, repealed: SR 2002/395 Sch.2 Part II
  s.40, repealed: SR 2002/395 Sch.2 Part II
  s.55, repealed: SR 2002/395 Sch.2 Part I
  s.95, repealed: SR 2002/395 Sch.2 Part I
  s.96, repealed: SR 2002/395 Sch.2 Part I
  s.97, repealed: SR 2002/395 Sch.2 Part I
  s.98, repealed: SR 2002/395 Sch.2 Part I
  s.99, repealed: SR 2002/395 Sch.2 Part I
  s.100, repealed: SR 2002/395 Sch.2 Part I
  s.101, repealed: SR 2002/395 Sch.2 Part I
  s.104, repealed: SR 2002/395 Sch.2 Part I
  s.105, repealed: SR 2002/395 Sch.2 Part I
  s.106, repealed: SR 2002/395 Sch.2 Part I
  s.107, repealed: SR 2002/395 Sch.2 Part I
  s.108, repealed: SR 2002/395 Sch.2 Part I
  s.109, repealed: SR 2002/395 Sch.2 Part I

11. Bankers Books Evidence Act 1879
  applied: 2002 c.iii s.13, 2002 c.iv s.12, 2003 c.32 Sch.1 para.7
  referred to: 2003 c.44 s.337
  varied: SI 2004/1611 Reg.7
  s.4, amended: 2003 c.44 Sch.37 Part 4, Sch.3 para.30

42 & 43 Vict. (1879)–cont.

11. Bankers Books Evidence Act 1879– cont.
s.4, applied: 2002 c.iii s.13, 2002 c.iv s.12
s.5, amended: 2003 c.44 Sch.37 Part 4, Sch.3 para.30
s.9, applied: 2002 c.iii s.13

42. Valuation of Lands (Scotland) Amendment Act 1879
s.7, enabling: SSI 2002/340

58. Public Offices Fees Act 1879
s.2, applied: SI 2003/1417 r.207
s.2, enabling: SI 2003/165, SI 2003/2092
s.3, applied: SI 2003/1417 r.207
s.3, enabling: SI 2003/165, SI 2003/2092

43 & 44 Vict. (1880)

26. Married Women's Policies of Assurance (Scotland) Act 1880
s.2, applied: 2004 c.33 s.132

47. Ground Game Act 1880
s.1, amended: 2002 c.2 (NI) s.2
s.1, repealed (in part): 2002 c.2 (NI) s.2, (NI) Sch.1
s.10, repealed: 2002 c.2 (NI) s.2, (NI) Sch.1

44 & 45 Vict. (1881)

24. Summary Jurisdiction (Process) Act 1881
disapplied: SI 2003/425 Art.4, Art.6, Art.12, Art.14, Art.16, Art.22
s.4, applied: 2003 c.44 s.302, Sch.11 para.24
s.4, referred to: 2003 asp 7 s.81
s.4, varied: 2003 c.44 Sch.13 para.22

41. Conveyancing Act 1881
s.19, applied: SI 2003/412 Art.117
s.21, applied: SI 2003/412 Art.117
s.22, applied: SI 2003/412 Art.117

64. Central Criminal Court (Prisons) Act 1881
repealed: 2004 c.14 Sch.1 Part 1

45 & 46 Vict. (1882)

clxxi. Belfast Harbour Act 1882
s.3, amended: SR 2002/40 Art.9
s.50, repealed: SR 2002/40 Sch.2
s.52, repealed: SR 2002/40 Sch.2
s.53, repealed: SR 2002/40 Sch.2

cxlii. Londonderry Port and Harbour Act 1882
s.51, repealed: SR 2002/41 Sch.2

15. Commonable Rights Compensation Act 1882
s.2, see *Attorney General v Hyde* [2002] W.T.L.R. 1419 (Ch D), Lawrence Collins, J.
s.4, see *Attorney General v Hyde* [2002] W.T.L.R. 1419 (Ch D), Lawrence Collins, J.

38. Settled Land Act 1882
s.21, referred to: SI 2003/412 Art.86, Art.103
s.63, referred to: SI 2003/412 Art.86, Art.103

45 & 46 Vict. (1882)–cont.

43. Bills of Sale Act (1878) Amendment Act 1882
applied: SI 2004/3121 Sch.1

50. Municipal Corporations Act 1882
s.153, amended: 2003 c.39 Sch.8 para.55, Sch.10

61. Bills of Exchange Act 1882
s.21, see *Dextra Bank & Trust Co Ltd v Bank of Jamaica* [2002] 1 All E.R. (Comm) 193 (PC (Jam)), Lord Bingham of Cornhill
s.29, see *Company (No.2634 of 2002), Re* [2002] EWHC 944, [2002] 2 B.C.L.C. 591 (Ch D (Companies Court)), Rimer, J.
s.92, applied: SI 2004/674 Reg.23, Reg.24, SI 2004/1864 Reg.4, SI 2004/2065 Reg.19
s.92, referred to: SI 2003/2682 Reg.82, Reg.115, Sch.1 para.20

62. Public Works Loans Act 1882
repealed: 2004 c.14 Sch.1 Part 9

72. Revenue, Friendly Societies, and National Debt Act 1882
s.18, substituted: SI 2004/1662 Sch.1 para.4

75. Married Women's Property Act 1882
s.11, varied: 2004 c.33 s.70

77. Citation Amendment (Scotland) Act 1882
s.4, disapplied: SSI 2002/132 Sch.1 para.4.5

46 & 47 Vict. (1883)

1. Consolidated Fund (Permanent Charges Redemption) Act 1883
repealed: 2004 c.14 Sch.1 Part 9

3. Explosive Substances Act 1883
referred to: 2003 c.44 s.337
s.2, applied: 2003 c.42 Sch.5 para.22, Sch.5 para.76, Sch.5 para.134, 2003 c.44 Sch.4 para.26, Sch.5 para.23, Sch.5 para.44, Sch.15 para.21, Sch.17 para.22, SI 2004/1500 Sch.2 para.18, SI 2004/1910 Sch.1
s.3, see *R. v Wildy (Geoffrey Howard)* [2004] 1 Cr. App. R. (S.) 11 (CA (Crim Div)), Cox, J
s.3, applied: 2003 c.42 Sch.5 para.23, Sch.5 para.77, Sch.5 para.135, 2003 c.44 Sch.4 para.27, Sch.5 para.24, Sch.5 para.45, Sch.15 para.22, Sch.17 para.23, SI 2004/1500 Sch.2 para.19, SI 2004/1910 Sch.1
s.4, applied: SI 2004/1910 Sch.1
s.6, amended: 2003 c.39 Sch.8 para.56, Sch.10, 2004 c.33 Sch.27 para.1
s.6, repealed (in part): 2003 c.44 Sch.37 Part 4, Sch.3 para.31
s.9, amended: 2003 c.39 Sch.8 para.57

32. Greenwich Hospital Act 1883
s.2, amended: 2004 c.33 Sch.26 para.4

55. Revenue Act 1883
repealed: 2004 c.14 Sch.1 Part 9

CAP.

47 & 48 Vict. (1884)

31. Colonial Prisoners Removal Act 1884
s.3, applied: SI 2002/313 Sch.1
s.10, amended: 2004 c.28 Sch.10 para.1

55. Pensions and Yeomanry Pay Act 1884
applied: SI 2002/1792 Sch.4 para.1, SR 2003/28 Sch.4 para.1
s.2, enabling: SI 2002/792, SI 2003/434, SI 2004/708
s.4, amended: 2004 c.33 Sch.26 para.5
s.4, applied: 2004 c.32 s.2

62. Revenue Act 1884
s.14, amended: 2004 c.14 Sch.1 Part 9

48 & 49 Vict. (1885)

Thames Preservation Act 1885
s.4, see *Rowland v Environment Agency* [2002] EWHC 2785, [2003] Ch. 581 (Ch D), Lightman, J.

69. Criminal Law Amendment Act 1885
s.2, applied: 2002 c.29 Sch.5 para.8, 2003 c.42 Sch.2 para.2, Sch.3 para.67, 2003 c.44 Sch.17 para.69
s.2, repealed (in part): 2003 c.42 Sch.6 para.5, Sch.7
s.3, applied: 2002 c.29 Sch.5 para.8, 2003 c.42 Sch.2 para.2, Sch.3 para.68, 2003 c.44 Sch.17 para.70
s.4, applied: 2003 c.42 Sch.2 para.2, Sch.3 para.69, 2003 c.44 Sch.17 para.71, SI 2003/1184 Sch.2 para.36, SI 2004/1500 Sch.2 para.9, SI 2004/1910 Sch.4
s.5, applied: SI 2002/57 Sch.4 para.7, 2003 c.42 Sch.2 para.2, Sch.3 para.70, 2003 c.44 Sch.17 para.72, SI 2003/1184 Sch.2 para.37, SI 2004/1910 Sch.4
s.5, disapplied: SSI 2003/19 Sch.5 para.13
s.5, referred to: SI 2003/237 Sch.4 para.6
s.6, applied: 2003 c.44 Sch.17 para.73
s.7, applied: 2003 c.42 Sch.2 para.2, Sch.3 para.71, 2003 c.44 Sch.17 para.74
s.8, applied: 2002 c.29 Sch.5 para.8, 2003 c.44 Sch.17 para.75
s.11, applied: SI 2002/57 Sch.4 para.7, 2003 c.42 Sch.3 para.72, Sch.4 para.1, SI 2003/1184 Sch.2 para.38
s.11, disapplied: SSI 2003/19 Sch.5 para.13
s.11, referred to: SI 2003/237 Sch.4 para.6
s.11, repealed: 2003 c.42 Sch.6 para.5, Sch.7
s.13(3), applied: 2002 c.29 Sch.5 para.8

49 & 50 Vict. (1886)

li. Post Office (Sites) Act 1886
repealed: SI 2003/1542 Sch.2

29. Crofters Holdings (Scotland) Act 1886
s.2, applied: SSI 2004/143 Reg.16
s.33, see *McEntee v MacLennan* 2002 S.L.C.R. 84 (Land Ct (Full Ct)), Lord McGhie, DJ Houston, J Kinloch

CAP.

50 & 51 Vict. (1887)

37. Public Works Loans Act 1887
repealed: 2004 c.14 Sch.1 Part 9

40. Savings Banks Act 1887
s.10, amended: SR 2002/242 Sch.1
s.10, substituted: SSI 2002/389 Sch.1
s.10, varied: SI 2002/3076 Sch.1

54. British Settlements Act 1887
applied: SI 2002/249, SI 2002/2627
enabling: SI 2002/249, SI 2002/1077, SI 2002/1822, SI 2002/2627, SI 2002/2638, SI 2003/2627, SI 2004/347, SI 2004/1112, SI 2004/1979, SI 2004/1980, SI 2004/2669, SI 2004/3039

55. Sheriffs Act 1887
s.7, amended: 2003 c.39 Sch.8 para.58
s.17, amended: 2003 c.39 Sch.8 para.59
s.23, amended: 2003 c.39 Sch.8 para.60
s.26, amended: 2003 c.39 Sch.8 para.61
s.26, substituted: 2003 c.39 Sch.8 para.61
s.29, amended: 2003 c.39 Sch.8 para.62
s.38, amended: 2003 c.39 Sch.8 para.63, Sch.10

70. Appellate Jurisdiction Act 1887
s.5, disapplied: 2002 c.26 s.8, s.24, s.43

51 & 52 Vict. (1888)

21. Law of Distress Amendment Act 1888
s.8, enabling: SI 2003/1858, SI 2003/2141

41. Local Government Act 1888
s.28, amended: 2003 c.39 Sch.8 para.64
s.69, repealed: 2004 c.14 Sch.1 Part 10
s.78, amended: 2004 c.14 Sch.1 Part 10
s.87, repealed: 2004 c.14 Sch.1 Part 10

52 & 53 Vict. (1889)

cxliv. Newport (Monmouthshire) Corporation Act 1889
s.62, repealed: SI 2003/2679 Sch.3
s.67, repealed: SI 2003/2679 Sch.3
s.69, repealed: SI 2003/2679 Sch.3

cvi. Pier and Harbour Orders Confirmation (No 3) Act 1889
varied: SI 2002/3268 Sch.3

ccix. Post Office (Sites) Act 1889
repealed: SI 2003/1542 Sch.2

6. National Debt Act 1889
s.4, amended: SI 2004/1662 Sch.1 para.5
s.4, applied: SI 2004/1662 Sch.1 para.20
s.5, varied: SI 2003/1633 Sch.2 para.1

10. Commissioners for Oaths Act 1889
s.1, applied: SI 2003/1887 Sch.1

30. Board of Agriculture Act 1889
s.5, repealed (in part): SI 2002/794 Sch.2
s.6, applied: SI 2002/794 Art.5
s.6, repealed: SI 2002/794 Sch.2
s.6, varied: SI 2002/794 Art.5
s.7, applied: SI 2002/794 Art.5
s.7, referred to: SI 2002/794 Art.5
s.7, repealed: SI 2002/794 Sch.2

52 & 53 Vict. (1889)–cont.

30. Board of Agriculture Act 1889–*cont.*
s.7, varied: SI 2002/794 Art.5
s.8, repealed: SI 2002/794 Sch.2

39. Judicial Factors (Scotland) Act 1889
s.6, disapplied: 2002 c.29 Sch.3 para.8
s.11A, applied: SI 2002/2822 Reg.43, 2004 c.35 s.121

42. Revenue Act 1889
s.26, repealed (in part): SI 2004/470 Art.3

45. Factors Act 1889
s.2, see *Marcq v Christie Manson & Woods Ltd (t/a Christie's)* [2002] EWHC 2148, [2002] 4 All E.R. 1005 (QBD), Jack, J.

57. Regulation of Railways Act 1889
applied: SI 2002/1384 Art.3
s.1, referred to: 2002 c.8 (NI) s.1
s.4, referred to: 2002 c.8 (NI) s.1
s.5, amended: 2003 c.44 Sch.26 para.3

69. Public Bodies Corrupt Practices Act 1889
applied: SI 2003/284 Art.116
s.1, see *R. v Natji (Naci Vedat)* [2002] EWCA Crim 271, [2002] 1 W.L.R. 2337 (CA (Crim Div)), Bennett, J.
s.1, applied: 2003 asp 7 s.69
s.7, see *R. v Natji (Naci Vedat)* [2002] EWCA Crim 271, [2002] 1 W.L.R. 2337 (CA (Crim Div)), Bennett, J.

53 & 54 Vict. (1890)

cxliv. Newport (Monmouthshire) Harbour Act 1890
s.4, varied: SI 2003/2679 Art.14
s.16, repealed: SI 2003/2679 Sch.3
s.28, repealed: SI 2003/2679 Sch.3
s.30, repealed: SI 2003/2679 Sch.3
s.32, repealed: SI 2003/2679 Sch.3
s.33, repealed: SI 2003/2679 Sch.3
s.36, repealed: SI 2003/2679 Sch.3
s.38, repealed: SI 2003/2679 Sch.3
s.42, amended: SI 2003/2679 Sch.3
s.46, amended: SI 2003/2679 Sch.3
s.47, repealed: SI 2003/2679 Sch.3
s.49, repealed: SI 2003/2679 Sch.3
s.54, amended: SI 2003/2679 Sch.3
s.55, repealed: SI 2003/2679 Sch.3
s.57, repealed: SI 2003/2679 Sch.3
s.69, repealed: SI 2003/2679 Sch.3
s.78, repealed: SI 2003/2679 Sch.3
s.79, repealed: SI 2003/2679 Sch.3
s.82, repealed: SI 2003/2679 Sch.3
s.84, repealed: SI 2003/2679 Sch.3
s.85, amended: SI 2003/2679 Sch.3
s.101, repealed: SI 2003/2679 Sch.3
s.102, repealed: SI 2003/2679 Sch.3
s.104, repealed: SI 2003/2679 Sch.3
s.107, repealed: SI 2003/2679 Sch.3

xcvii. Pier and Harbour Orders Confirmation (No 3) Act 1890
varied: SI 2002/3268 Sch.3

53 & 54 Vict. (1890)–cont.

21. Inland Revenue Regulation Act 1890
applied: 2002 c.21 s.2, s.53
varied: 2002 c.22 s.5
s.1, see *Al-Fayed v Advocate General for Scotland* [2002] S.T.C. 910 (OH), Lord Gill L.J.C.
s.4, applied: 2002 c.21 s.53
s.4, varied: 2002 c.21 s.2, 2002 c.22 s.5
s.4A, applied: 2002 c.23 Sch.29 para.141
s.4A, disapplied: 2003 c.14 Sch.13 para.45
s.13, see *Al-Fayed v Advocate General for Scotland* [2002] S.T.C. 910 (OH), Lord Gill L.J.C.
s.13, applied: 2002 c.21 s.53
s.13, referred to: 2002 c.21 s.40
s.13, varied: 2002 c.21 s.2
s.21, disapplied: 2002 c.22 s.5
s.22, disapplied: 2002 c.22 s.5
s.35, disapplied: 2002 c.22 s.5
s.39, applied: 2002 c.21 s.53
s.39, varied: 2002 c.21 s.2

39. Partnership Act 1890
see *Dave v Robinska* [2003] I.C.R. 1248 (EAT), Judge McMullen Q.C.
s.2, amended: 2004 c.33 Sch.27 para.2
s.5, see *Bank of Scotland v Henry Butcher & Co* [2003] EWCA Civ 67, [2003] 2 All E.R. (Comm) 557 (CA), Munby, J.; see *JJ Coughlan Ltd v Ruparelia* [2003] EWCA Civ 1057, [2004] P.N.L.R. 4 (CA), Dyson, L.J.
s.6, applied: SI 2004/1611 Reg.23
s.10, see *Dubai Aluminium Co Ltd v Salaam* [2002] UKHL 48, [2003] 2 A.C. 366 (HL), Lord Nicholls of Birkenhead; see *JJ Coughlan Ltd v Ruparelia* [2003] EWCA Civ 1057, [2004] P.N.L.R. 4 (CA), Dyson, L.J.
s.19, see *Charlton v Hawking* 570 of 2002 (Ch D), Judge not specified
s.20, see *Fengate Developments v Customs and Excise Commissioners* [2004] EWHC 152, [2004] S.T.C. 772 (Ch D), Evans-Lombe, J.
s.21, see *Charlton v Hawking* 570 of 2002 (Ch D), Judge not specified
s.24, see *Emerson (Emerson's Executrix) v Emerson's Estate* [2004] EWCA Civ 170, [2004] 1 B.C.L.C. 575 (CA), Brooke, L.J.
s.35, see *Mullins v Laughton* [2002] EWHC 2761, [2003] Ch. 250 (Ch D), Neuberger, J.
s.36, see *Hussein (t/a Pressing Dry Cleaners) v Customs and Excise Commissioners* [2003] V. & D.R. 439 (VAT and Duties Tribunal (London)), John Walters Q.C. (Chairman)
s.42, see *Emerson (Emerson's Executrix) v Emerson's Estate* [2004] EWCA Civ 170, [2004] 1 B.C.L.C. 575 (CA), Brooke, L.J.
s.44, see *Hurst v Bryk* [2002] 1 A.C. 185 (HL), Lord Millett

CAP.

53 & 54 Vict. (1890)–cont.

59. Public Health Acts, Amendment Act 1890
s.9, amended: 2004 c.14 Sch.1 Part 13
s.12, repealed (in part): 2004 c.14 Sch.1 Part 13

54 & 55 Vict. (1891)

xcix. Lancashire and Yorkshire Railway Act 1891
referred to: SI 2002/1384 Art.8

24. Public Accounts and Charges Act 1891
s.1, repealed (in part): 2004 c.14 Sch.1 Part 5

39. Stamp Act 1891
applied: 2002 c.23 s.116, Sch.34 para.11, Sch.35 para.12, Sch.36 para.10, 2003 c.14 s.125, s.128, s.129, s.130
s.12, applied: 2003 c.14 s.128, 2003 c.21 Sch.2 para.5, 2003 c.26 Sch.5 para.12, 2003 c.39 Sch.2 para.8, 2004 c.20 Sch.9 para.34
s.14, applied: 2003 c.14 s.130
s.14, disapplied: 2002 c.23 s.115
s.15A, applied: 2002 c.23 s.115, Sch.34 para.5, Sch.35 para.6, 2003 c.14 Sch.19 para.8
s.15B, amended: 2002 c.23 s.114
s.15B, applied: 2002 c.23 s.115, 2003 c.14 Sch.19 para.8
s.17, applied: 2003 c.14 s.130
s.56, see *Keston v Inland Revenue Commissioners* [2004] EWHC 59, [2004] S.T.C. 902 (Ch D), Lightman, J.
s.58, see *Keston v Inland Revenue Commissioners* [2004] EWHC 59, [2004] S.T.C. 902 (Ch D), Lightman, J.
s.58, referred to: 2002 c.23 Sch.36 para.5, 2003 c.14 Sch.20 para.2
s.58, varied: 2002 c.23 Sch.37 para.2
s.122, amended: SI 2002/2521 Sch.2 Part I, SI 2004/1662 Sch.1 para.6

43. Forged Transfers Act 1891
s.1, amended: 2004 c.14 Sch.1 Part 9
s.2, amended: 2004 c.21 Sch.1 para.2
s.3, amended: 2004 c.14 Sch.1 Part 9

55 & 56 Vict. (1892)

6. Colonial Probates Act 1892
s.2, enabling: SI 2003/185

9. Gaming Act 1892
s.1, see *Rio Properties Inc v Al-Midani* [2003] B.P.I.R. 128 (Ch D), Judge Maddocks

17. Sheriff Courts (Scotland) Extracts Act 1892
s.7, amended: 2002 asp 17 Sch.3 para.8

23. Foreign Marriage Act 1892
applied: 2004 c.33 s.244
s.1, amended: 2002 c.8 s.2

36. Forged Transfers Act 1892
s.2, amended: 2004 c.14 Sch.1 Part 9

CAP.

55 & 56 Vict. (1892)–cont.

39. National Debt (Stockholders Relief) Act 1892
s.2, amended: SI 2004/1662 Sch.1 para.7
s.3, amended: SI 2004/1662 Sch.1 para.7
s.8, substituted: SI 2004/1662 Sch.1 para.7
s.9, amended: SI 2002/2521 Sch.2 Part I
s.9, repealed: SI 2004/1662 Sch.1 para.7

48. Bank Act 1892
s.5, repealed: 2004 c.14 Sch.1 Part 17

64. Witnesses (Public Inquiries) Protection Act 1892
s.2, amended: 2003 c.44 Sch.26 para.4

1893

xxxii. Post Office (Sites) Act 1893
repealed: SI 2003/1542 Sch.2

5. Regimental Debts Act 1893
s.10, amended: 2004 c.33 Sch.26 para.6
s.24, amended: 2004 c.33 Sch.26 para.7

7. Customs and Inland Revenue Act 1893
repealed: 2004 c.14 Sch.1 Part 17

17. North Sea Fisheries Act 1893
s.2, amended: 2003 c.44 Sch.37 Part 9
s.2, disapplied: 2003 c.44 Sch.25 para.12
s.3, amended: 2003 c.44 Sch.37 Part 9
s.3, disapplied: 2003 c.44 Sch.25 para.13

44. Sheriff Courts Consignations (Scotland) Act 1893
applied: SSI 2002/132 Sch.1 para.23.5

57 & 58 Vict. (1894)

ccxii. London County Council (General Powers) Act 1894
s.4, repealed: 2004 c.21 Sch.2

2. Behring Sea Award Act 1894
Sch.2, amended: 2003 c.39 Sch.8 para.65

13. Arbitration (Scotland) Act 1894
applied: SSI 2003/359 Art.8
disapplied: SSI 2002/110 Sch.2 para.24

60. Merchant Shipping Act 1894
Part I, applied: SSI 2002/504 Art.6
s.542, applied: 2002 c.26 Sch.4 para.1
s.634, referred to: SSI 2004/171 Art.3
s.735, applied: SI 2004/1284
s.735, enabling: SI 2002/3132, SI 2003/1877, SI 2004/1284

73. Local Government Act 1894
s.8, repealed (in part): 2004 c.14 Sch.1 Part 10
s.26, amended: 2004 c.14 Sch.1 Part 10
s.26, repealed (in part): 2004 c.14 Sch.1 Part 10

58 & 59 Vict. (1895)

14. Courts of Law Fees (Scotland) Act 1895
s.2, enabling: SSI 2002/269, SSI 2002/270, SSI 2003/97

CAP.

58 & 59 Vict. (1895)–cont.

16. Finance Act 1895
s.12, amended: 2003 c.14 Sch.20 para.4
s.12, applied: 2004 c.25 s.4
s.12, disapplied: 2002 c.23 Sch.37 para.4,
2003 c.14 s.125, 2003 c.26 Sch.5 para.12

33. Extradition Act 1895
varied: 2004 c.14 Sch.1 Part 17

44. Judicial Committee Amendment Act 1895
Sch.1, amended: 2004 c.14 Sch.1 Part 1

59 & 60 Vict. (1896)

35. Judicial Trustees Act 1896
s.1, see *Practice Direction (Judicial Trustees: Remuneration)* [2003] 1 W.L.R. 1653 (Ch D), Chief Chancery Master Winegarten

48. Light Railways Act 1896
applied: SSI 2003/359 Art.3
s.7, enabling: SI 2002/1384, SSI 2003/359
s.9, applied: SI 2002/1384
s.9, enabling: SSI 2003/359
s.10, enabling: SI 2002/1384, SSI 2003/359
s.11, enabling: SI 2002/1384, SSI 2003/359
s.12, enabling: SI 2002/1384, SSI 2003/359

60 & 61 Vict. (1897)

cxxx. Lancashire and Yorkshire Railway Act 1897
referred to: SI 2002/1384 Art.8

clxvi. Post Office (Sites) Act 1897
repealed: SI 2003/1542 Sch.2

30. Police (Property) Act 1897
applied: SI 2003/336 Sch.1 Part 2
s.2, amended: 2002 c.30 s.77
s.2, enabling: SI 2002/2313
s.2A, added: 2002 c.30 s.77
s.2A, enabling: SI 2002/2313

30. Police Property Act 1897
s.1, see *Haley v Chief Constable of Northumbria* [2002] EWHC 1942, (2002) 166 J.P. 719 (QBD (Admin Ct)), Silber, J.

38. Public Health (Scotland) Act 1897
s.73, applied: SSI 2004/406 Sch.1 para.12
s.153, amended: 2002 asp 17 Sch.3 para.9
s.154, amended: 2002 asp 17 Sch.3 para.9
s.172, applied: SSI 2004/38 Reg.3

61 & 62 Vict. (1898)

cv. Belfast Harbour Act 1898
s.2, amended: SR 2002/40 Art.9
s.49, repealed: SR 2002/40 Sch.2

35. Vexatious Actions (Scotland) Act 1898
see *HM Advocate v Bell (Jamie)* 2002 S.L.T. 527 (Ex Div), Lord Coulsfield, Lord Cowie, Lord Marnoch

CAP.

61 & 62 Vict. (1898)–cont.

36. Criminal Evidence Act 1898
s.1, see *R. v El-Delbi (Zakaria Ramadan)* [2003] EWCA Crim 1767, (2003) 147 S.J.L.B. 784 (CA (Crim Div)), Hallett, J.
s.1, amended: 2003 c.44 Sch.36 para.80
s.1, repealed (in part): 2003 c.44 Sch.37 Part 5

39. Vagrancy Act 1898
repealed: 2003 c.42 Sch.6 para.6, Sch.7
s.1, applied: 2003 c.44 Sch.17 para.76
s.1 (1), applied: 2002 c.29 Sch.5 para.8

46. Revenue Act 1898
s.9, amended: 2004 c.14 Sch.1 Part 9

60. Inebriates Act 1898
Sch.1, amended: 2003 c.17 Sch.6 para.6, Sch.7

62 & 63 Vict. (1899)

Chc. Inverness Harbour Act 1899
s.39, repealed: SSI 2002/557 Sch.3

clxxv. Owens College Act 1899
referred to: 2004 c.iv
repealed: 2004 c.iv Sch.3

27. Marriages Validity Act 1899
repealed (in part): SI 2003/413 Sch.1

30. Commons Act 1899
applied: 2002 c.i, s.34
s.1, applied: SI 2004/1777 Art.25, SI 2004/1778 Art.25
s.2, applied: SI 2004/1777 Art.25, SI 2004/1778 Art.25
s.3, applied: SI 2004/1777 Art.25, SI 2004/1778 Art.25

38. Telegraph Act 1899
repealed: 2003 c.21 Sch.19

63 & 64 Vict. (1900)

cclix. Alexandra Park and Palace (Public Purposes) Act 1900
referred to: SI 2004/160

ccvi. Post Office (Sites) Act 1900
repealed: SI 2003/1542 Sch.2

27. Railway Employment (Prevention of Accidents) Act 1900
referred to: 2002 c.8 (NI) s.1

1 Edw. 7 (1901)

cxxxiii. Belfast Harbour Act 1901
s.2, amended: SR 2002/40 Art.9

2 Edw. 7 (1902)

cxciv. Post Office (Sites) Act 1902
repealed: SI 2003/1542 Sch.2

8. Cremation Act 1902
s.7, enabling: SSI 2003/301

28. Licensing Act 1902
s.2, amended: 2003 c.44 Sch.26 para.5
s.6, amended: 2003 c.17 Sch.6 para.8

CAP.

2 Edw. 7 (1902)–cont.

28. Licensing Act 1902–cont.
s.8A, added: 2003 c.17 Sch.6 para.9

29. Freshwater Fish (Scotland) Act 1902
repealed: 2003 asp 15 Sch.4 Part 2

3 Edw. 7 (1903)

clvi. Post Office (Sites) Act 1903
repealed: SI 2003/1542 Sch.2

clvii. Scottish American Mortgage Company Limited Act 1903
repealed: 2004 c.14 Sch.1 Part 15

20. Patriotic Fund Reorganisation Act 1903
referred to: SI 2002/1057 Art.2
repealed: 2004 c.32 Sch.3
s.3, repealed (in part): 2004 c.14 Sch.1 Part 5 Sch.1 para.1, amended: SI 2002/1057 Art.3
Sch.1 para.16, added: SI 2002/1057 Art.3

31. Board of Agriculture and Fisheries Act 1903
s.2, repealed (in part): SI 2002/794 Sch.2

44. General Dealers (Ireland) Act 1903
s.5, amended: 2002 c.26 Sch.4 para.8

4 Edw. 7 (1904)

clviii. Post Office (Sites) Act 1904
repealed: SI 2003/1542 Sch.2

xiii. Victoria University of Manchester Act 1904
repealed: 2004 c.iv Sch.3

5 Edw. 7 (1905)

clxxix. Humber Conservancy Act 1905
s.9, applied: SI 2004/2190 Art.8

11. Railway Fires Act 1905
s.2, referred to: SI 2003/1615 Sch.1 para.2

23. Provisional Order (Marriages) Act 1905
applied: SI 2003/1237
enabling: SI 2003/1237

6 Edw. 7 (1906)

xl. Mersey Docks and Harbour Board Act 1906
s.13, disapplied: SI 2002/3127 Art.7

lxii. Newport Harbour Act 1906
s.5, repealed: SI 2003/2679 Sch.3
s.7, repealed: SI 2003/2679 Sch.3

cxviii. Post Office (Sites) Act 1906
repealed: SI 2003/1542 Sch.2

5. Seamen's and Soldiers False Characters Act 1906
s.1, amended: 2003 c.44 Sch.32 para.152
s.1, disapplied: 2003 c.44 Sch.25 para.14

21. Ground Game (Amendment) Act 1906
repealed: 2002 c.2 (NI) Sch.1

25. Open Spaces Act 1906
s.2, amended: 2003 c.14 Sch.20 para.3

CAP.

6 Edw. 7 (1906)–cont.

25. Open Spaces Act 1906–cont.
s.15, applied: SI 2004/1777 Art.25, SI 2004/1778 Art.25

32. Dogs Act 1906
s.9, repealed: 2004 c.14 Sch.1 Part 17

34. Prevention of Corruption Act 1906
applied: SI 2004/653 Reg.24
s.1, see *R. v Natji (Naci Vedat)* [2002] EWCA Crim 271, [2002] 1 W.L.R. 2337 (CA (Crim Div)), Bennett, J.
s.1, applied: 2003 asp 7 s.69

41. Marine Insurance Act 1906
s.17, see *Agapitos v Agnew (The Aegeon) (No.1)* [2002] EWCA Civ 247, [2003] Q.B. 556 (CA), Mance, L.J.; see *Agapitos v Agnew (The Aegeon) (No.1)* [2002] Lloyd's Rep. I.R. 191 (QBD (Comm Ct)), Toulson, J.; see *Manifest Shipping Co Ltd v Uni-Polaris Insurance Co Ltd (The Star Sea)* [2001] UKHL 1, [2003] 1 A.C. 469 (HL), Lord Hobhouse of Woodborough
s.18, see *New Hampshire Insurance Co v Oil Refineries Ltd (Avoidance for Non Disclosure)* [2002] 2 Lloyd's Rep. 462 (QBD (Comm Ct)), Judge Chambers Q.C.; see *WISE Underwriting Agency Ltd v Grupo Nacional Provincial SA* [2004] EWCA Civ 962, [2004] 2 All E.R. (Comm) 613 (CA), Peter Gibson, L.J.
s.39, see *Manifest Shipping Co Ltd v Uni-Polaris Insurance Co Ltd (The Star Sea)* [2001] UKHL 1, [2003] 1 A.C. 469 (HL), Lord Hobhouse of Woodborough; see *Project Asia Line Inc v Shone (The Pride of Donegal)* [2002] EWHC 24, [2002] 1 Lloyd's Rep. 659 (QBD (Comm Ct)), Andrew Smith, J.
s.44, see *Nima SARL v Deves Insurance Public Co Ltd (The Prestrioka)* [2002] EWCA Civ 1132, [2002] 2 All E.R. (Comm) 449 (CA), Potter, L.J.
s.53, see *Heath Lambert Ltd v Sociedad de Corretaje de Seguros* [2003] EWHC 2269, [2004] 1 Lloyd's Rep. 495 (QBD (Comm Ct)), Jonathan Hirst, Q.C.; see *Heath Lambert Ltd v Sociedad de Corretaje de Seguros* [2004] EWCA Civ 792, [2004] 1 W.L.R. 2820 (CA), Lord Phillips of Worth Matravers, M.R.
s.61, see *Kastor Navigation Co Ltd v AGF MAT (The Kastor Too)* [2002] EWHC 2601, [2003] 1 All E.R. (Comm) 277 (QBD (Comm Ct)), Tomlinson, J.; see *Kastor Navigation Co Ltd v AGF MAT (The Kastor Too)* [2004] EWCA Civ 277, [2004] 2 Lloyd's Rep. 119 (CA), Tuckey, L.J.
s.62, see *Kastor Navigation Co Ltd v AGF MAT (The Kastor Too)* [2002] EWHC 2601, [2003] 1 All E.R. (Comm) 277 (QBD (Comm Ct)), Tomlinson, J.; see *Kastor Navigation Co Ltd v AGF MAT (The Kastor*

6 Edw. 7 (1906)–cont.

41. Marine Insurance Act 1906–cont.
s.62–cont.
Too) [2004] EWCA Civ 277, [2004] 2 Lloyd's Rep. 119 (CA), Tuckey, L.J.

55. Public Trustee Act 1906
s.6, amended: 2004 c.33 Sch.4 para.6
s.7, repealed: 2002 c.35 s.1
s.9, amended: 2002 c.35 s.2
s.9, repealed (in part): 2002 c.35 s.2
s.9, enabling: SI 2002/2232, SI 2003/690, SI 2004/799

7 Edw. 7 (1907)

cxxxvi. National Trust Act 1907
varied: 2004 c.14 Sch.1 Part 17
s.10, repealed: 2004 c.14 Sch.1 Part 17
s.38, repealed: 2004 c.14 Sch.1 Part 17
s.39, repealed: 2004 c.14 Sch.1 Part 17

cxxxii. Post Office (Sites) Act 1907
repealed: SI 2003/1542 Sch.2

24. Limited Partnerships Act 1907
disapplied: SI 2002/376 Reg.2
referred to: SI 2003/1660 Reg.14
varied: SI 2002/376 Reg.2
s.3, referred to: SI 2003/1661 Reg.14
s.4, amended: SI 2002/3203 Art.3, SI 2003/2904 Sch.1

51. Sheriff Courts (Scotland) Act 1907
Appendix1., amended: SSI 2002/7 Sch.1, SSI 2002/128 Sch.1, SSI 2003/25 r.2, Sch.1, SSI 2003/26 r.2, SSI 2003/601 Sch.1
s.5, applied: 2003 asp 15 s.40
s.34, applied: SSI 2002/132 Sch.1 para.30.6, Sch.1 para.30.7
s.35, applied: SSI 2002/132 Sch.1 para.30.6, Sch.1 para.30.7
s.36, applied: SSI 2002/132 Sch.1 para.30.3, Sch.1 para.30.6, Sch.1 para.30.7
s.37, applied: SSI 2002/132 Sch.1 para.30.3, Sch.1 para.30.6, Sch.1 para.30.7
s.37A, added: 2003 asp 11 Sch.1 para.1
s.37A, applied: SSI 2002/132 Sch.1 para.30.3, Sch.1 para.30.7
s.38, applied: SSI 2002/132 Sch.1 para.30.1, Sch.1 para.30.3, Sch.1 para.30.7
s.40, enabling: SSI 2002/235, SSI 2002/274, SSI 2002/280, SSI 2002/328, SSI 2002/515, SSI 2002/567, SSI 2002/568, SSI 2003/162, SSI 2003/246, SSI 2003/538, SSI 2004/149, SSI 2004/152, SSI 2004/196, SSI 2004/513
s.50, applied: SSI 2002/410 Art.35
Sch.1 Part 3 para.2, amended: SSI 2002/7 r.2
Sch.1 Part 3 para.3, amended: SSI 2002/7 r.2
Sch.1 Part 5 para.2, amended: SSI 2002/7 r.2
Sch.1 Part 5 para.3, referred to: SSI 2003/601 r.3
Sch.1 Part 5 para.4, amended: SSI 2003/26 r.2

7 Edw. 7 (1907)–cont.

51. Sheriff Courts (Scotland) Act 1907–cont.
Sch.1 Part 5 para.4, referred to: SSI 2003/601 r.3
Sch.1 Part 5 para.5, amended: SSI 2003/26 r.2
Sch.1 Part 5 para.5, referred to: SSI 2003/601 r.3
Sch.1 Part 5 para.6, referred to: SSI 2003/601 r.3
Sch.1 Part 20 para.4, amended: SSI 2003/26 r.2
Sch.1 Part 20 para.5A, added: SSI 2003/26 r.2
Sch.1 Part 23 para.1, amended: SSI 2003/26 r.2
Sch.1 Part 28 para.14, amended: SSI 2003/601 r.4
Sch.1 Part 28 para.14A, added: SSI 2003/601 r.4
Sch.1 Part 33 para.6, amended: SSI 2003/26 r.2
Sch.1 Part 33 para.22A, applied: SSI 2002/494 Reg.18
Sch.1 Part 33 para.51, amended: SSI 2003/26 r.2
Sch.1 Part 33 para.88, amended: SSI 2003/26 r.2
Sch.1 Part 33 para.90, amended: SSI 2003/26 r.2
Sch.1 Part 33 para.91, amended: SSI 2003/26 r.2
Sch.1 Part 34 para.12, added: SSI 2002/7 r.2
Sch.1 Part 41 para.1, added: SSI 2002/128 r.2
Sch.1 Part 41 para.2, added: SSI 2002/128 r.2
Sch.1 Part 41 para.2, amended: SSI 2003/26 r.2
Sch.1 Part 41 para.3, added: SSI 2002/128 r.2
Sch.1 Part 41 para.4, added: SSI 2002/128 r.2
Sch.1 Part 41 para.5, added: SSI 2002/128 r.2
Sch.1 Part 42 para.1, added: SSI 2004/350 r.2
Sch.1 Part 42 para.2, added: SSI 2004/350 r.2

53. Public Health Acts Amendment Act 1907
s.94, amended: 2003 c.39 Sch.8 para.66

8 Edw. 7 (1908)

clxi. Post Office (Sites) Act 1908
repealed: SI 2003/1542 Sch.2

45. Punishment of Incest Act 1908
s.1, applied: 2003 c.42 Sch.2 para.2, Sch.3 para.73, 2003 c.44 Sch.5 para.38, Sch.17 para.77, SI 2003/1184 Sch.2 para.39, SI 2004/1500 Sch.2 para.10
s.2, applied: 2003 c.42 Sch.2 para.2, Sch.3 para.74, 2003 c.44 Sch.17 para.78, SI 2003/1184 Sch.2 para.40

51. Appellate Jurisdiction Act 1908
s.1, repealed: 2004 c.14 Sch.1 Part 1

CAP.

8 Edw. 7 (1908)–cont.

51. Appellate Jurisdiction Act 1908–*cont.*
s.3, repealed: 2004 c.14 Sch.1 Part 1
Sch.1, repealed: 2004 c.14 Sch.1 Part 1

53. Law of Distress Amendment Act 1908
s.4, amended: 2004 c.33 Sch.27 para.3
s.6, applied: 2004 c.34 Sch.3 para.12

9 Edw. 7 (1909)

15. Board of Agriculture and Fisheries Act 1909
s.1, repealed (in part): SI 2002/794 Sch.2

10 Edw. 7 & 1 Geo. 5 (1910)

8. Finance (1909-10) Act 1910
see *Robinson Webster (Holdings) Ltd v Agombar* [2002] 1 P. & C.R. 20 (Ch D), Etherton, J.

1 & 2 Geo. 5 (1911)

cxxi. Inverness Harbour Order Confirmation 1911
s.6, repealed: SSI 2002/557 Sch.3
s.24, repealed: SSI 2002/557 Sch.3
s.34, repealed: SSI 2002/557 Sch.3
s.35, repealed: SSI 2002/557 Sch.3
s.41, repealed: SSI 2002/557 Sch.3
s.91, repealed: SSI 2002/557 Sch.3
s.92, amended: SSI 2002/557 Sch.3
s.94, amended: SSI 2002/557 Sch.3
s.95, amended: SSI 2002/557 Sch.3
s.96, varied: SSI 2002/557 Art.13
s.101, varied: SSI 2002/557 Art.13
s.105, amended: SSI 2002/557 Sch.3

6. Perjury Act 1911
varied: 2004 c.33 s.80
s.1, applied: 2003 c.32 s.30, s.31
s.2, applied: 2002 c.38 s.41
s.3, applied: 2004 c.19 s.14
s.4, applied: 2004 c.19 s.14
s.5, applied: 2002 c.29 s.360, Sch.6 para.2, 2002 c.38 s.41, 2004 c.27 Sch.7 para.3
s.7, applied: 2004 c.19 s.14

27. Protection of Animals Act 1911
s.1, see *Cornwall CC v Baker* [2003] EWHC 374, [2003] 1 W.L.R. 1813 (QBD (Admin Ct)), Toulson, J.; see *RSPCA v Shinton* [2003] EWHC 1696, (2003) 167 J.P. 512 (QBD (Admin Ct)), Leveson, J.
s.1, varied: 2004 c.37 Sch.2 para.3
s.8, applied: SI 2003/3241 Reg.22

28. Official Secrets Act 1911
applied: 2002 asp 11 s.19
varied: 2003 c.21 Sch.17 para.2
s.9, applied: SI 2003/2273 Sch.1 para.4
s.12, amended: 2002 c.26 Sch.7 para.24

CAP.

1 & 2 Geo. 5 (1911)–cont.

46. Copyright Act 1911
s.5, see *Novello & Co Ltd v Keith Prowse Music Publishing Co Ltd* [2004] EWHC 766, [2004] E.M.L.R. 16 (Ch D), Patten, J.
s.15, referred to: 2003 c.28
s.15, repealed: 2003 c.28 Sch.1

49. Small Landholders (Scotland) Act 1911
s.2, applied: SSI 2002/110 Sch.2 para.1
s.21, varied: 2004 c.33 Sch.21 para.2
s.32, applied: SSI 2002/110 Sch.2 para.1

2 & 3 Geo. 5 (1912-13)

14. Protection of Animals (Scotland) Act 1912
s.1, repealed (in part): 2002 asp 6 Sch.1 para.3
s.7, applied: SSI 2003/579 Reg.22

20. Criminal Law Amendment Act 1912
s.7, applied: 2002 c.29 Sch.5 para.8
s.7, repealed: 2003 c.42 Sch.7

3 & 4 Geo. 5 (1913)

cxi. Alexandra Park and Palace Act 1913
referred to: SI 2004/160

cxvi. Post Office (London) Railway Act 1913
varied: SI 2003/1542 Art.2

20. Bankruptcy (Scotland) Act 1913
referred to: 2002 c.29 s.421

4 & 5 Geo. 5 (1914)

18. Injuries in War Compensation Act 1914 (Session 2) 1914
applied: 2003 c.1 s.641

30. Injuries in War (Compensation) Act 1914
applied: 2003 c.1 s.641

47. Deeds of Arrangement Act 1914
applied: 2004 c.35 s.121, SI 2004/400 Reg.5

59. Bankruptcy Act 1914
applied: 2002 c.29 s.418, SI 2003/3363 Sch.1 para.1, SI 2004/593 Art.4
s.14, see *Woodland-Ferrari v UCL Group Retirement Benefits Scheme* [2002] EWHC 1354, [2003] Ch. 115 (Ch D), Ferris, J.
s.27, referred to: 2002 c.29 s.419
s.42, referred to: 2002 c.29 s.419
s.44, referred to: 2002 c.29 s.419
s.133, enabling: SI 2004/593

91. Welsh Church Act 1914
s.3, amended: 2004 c.14 Sch.1 Part 6
s.4, amended: 2004 c.14 Sch.1 Part 6
s.4, repealed (in part): 2004 c.14 Sch.1 Part 6
s.6, repealed (in part): 2004 c.14 Sch.1 Part 6
s.7, repealed: 2004 c.14 Sch.1 Part 6
s.8, repealed (in part): 2004 c.14 Sch.1 Part 6
s.10, repealed: 2004 c.14 Sch.1 Part 6

4 & 5 Geo. 5 (1914)–cont.

91. Welsh Church Act 1914–*cont.*
s.11, repealed: 2004 c.14 Sch.1 Part 6
s.12, repealed: 2004 c.14 Sch.1 Part 6
s.14, repealed: 2004 c.14 Sch.1 Part 6
s.15, repealed: 2004 c.14 Sch.1 Part 6
s.16, repealed: 2004 c.14 Sch.1 Part 6
s.17, repealed: 2004 c.14 Sch.1 Part 6
s.18, repealed: 2004 c.14 Sch.1 Part 6
s.20, repealed: 2004 c.14 Sch.1 Part 6
s.22, repealed (in part): 2004 c.14 Sch.1 Part 6
s.24, repealed (in part): 2004 c.14 Sch.1 Part 6
s.26, repealed: 2004 c.14 Sch.1 Part 6
s.27, amended: 2004 c.14 Sch.1 Part 6
s.27, repealed (in part): 2004 c.14 Sch.1 Part 6
s.29, repealed (in part): 2004 c.14 Sch.1 Part 6
s.30, repealed: 2004 c.14 Sch.1 Part 6
s.31, repealed: 2004 c.14 Sch.1 Part 6
s.32, repealed: 2004 c.14 Sch.1 Part 6
s.33, repealed (in part): 2004 c.14 Sch.1 Part 6
s.34, repealed: 2004 c.14 Sch.1 Part 6
s.35, amended: 2004 c.14 Sch.1 Part 6
s.38, amended: 2004 c.14 Sch.1 Part 6
Sch.3 Part I, repealed: 2004 c.14 Sch.1 Part 6
Sch.3 Part II, repealed: 2004 c.14 Sch.1 Part 6
Sch.3 Part III, repealed: 2004 c.14 Sch.1 Part 6
Sch.3 Part IV, repealed: 2004 c.14 Sch.1 Part 6
Sch.4, repealed: 2004 c.14 Sch.1 Part 6
Sch.5, repealed: 2004 c.14 Sch.1 Part 6

5 & 6 Geo. 5 (1914-15)

28. Naval Medical Compassionate Fund Act 1915
s.1, amended: 2004 c.33 Sch.26 para.8
54. Munitions of War Act 1915
varied: 2004 c.14 Sch.1 Part 17
83. Naval and Military War Pensions &c Act 1915
referred to: SI 2002/1057 Art.2
s.6, repealed: 2004 c.32 Sch.3
89. Finance (No.2) Act 1915
s.48, amended: SI 2002/2521 Sch.1 para.2, SI 2004/1662 Sch.1 para.8
90. Indictments Act 1915
s.2, amended: 2003 c.39 Sch.8 para.67
s.5, see *R. v Palmer (John)* [2002] EWCA Crim 892, Times, April 18, 2002 (CA (Crim Div)), Rose, L.J.
s.5, amended: 2003 c.44 Sch.36 para.40

6 & 7 Geo. 5 (1916)

24. Finance Act 1916
s.65, substituted: SI 2004/1662 Sch.1 para.9
s.66, amended: SI 2002/2521 Sch.1 para.3, SI 2004/1662 Sch.1 para.9
s.67, amended: SI 2002/2521 Sch.2 Part I, SI 2004/1662 Sch.1 para.9
31. Police, Factories, &amp C (Miscellaneous Provisions) Act 1916
varied: 2002 c.i s.21

6 & 7 Geo. 5 (1916)–cont.

38. Small Holding Colonies Act 1916
repealed: 2004 c.14 Sch.1 Part 3
60. Sailors and Soldiers (Gifts for Land Settlement) Act 1916
s.1, repealed (in part): 2004 c.14 Sch.1 Part 3
64. Prevention of Corruption Act 1916
s.2, see *R. v Natji (Naci Vedat)* [2002] EWCA Crim 271, [2002] 1 W.L.R. 2337 (CA (Crim Div)), Bennett, J.
s.4, see *R. v Natji (Naci Vedat)* [2002] EWCA Crim 271, [2002] 1 W.L.R. 2337 (CA (Crim Div)), Bennett, J.

7 & 8 Geo. 5 (1917)

14. Naval and Military War Pensions etc (Administrative Expenses) Act 1917
s.5, amended: 2004 c.33 Sch.26 para.9
s.6, amended: 2004 c.33 Sch.26 para.9
19. Coroners (Emergency Provisions) Act 1917
varied: 2004 c.14 Sch.1 Part 17
51. Air Force (Constitution) Act 1917
applied: SI 2004/291 Sch.4, SI 2004/478 Sch.4, SI 2004/627 Sch.2, SR 2002/56 Reg.4, SSI 2004/115 Sch.3
s.2, applied: SI 2002/1792 Sch.4 para.17
s.2, enabling: SI 2002/792, SI 2003/434, SI 2004/708
55. Chequers Estate Act 1917
s.3A, added: SI 2003/2867 Sch.1 para.3

7 & 8 Geo. 5 (1918)

xviii. Belfast Harbour Act 1918
s.2, amended: SR 2002/40 Art.9
s.24, repealed: SR 2002/40 Sch.2
s.29, repealed: SR 2002/40 Sch.2
7. Increase of Rent etc (Amendment) Act 1918
varied: 2004 c.14 Sch.1 Part 17
57. War Pensions (Administrative Provisions) Act 1918
s.7, repealed: 2004 c.32 Sch.3

9 & 10 Geo. 5 (1919)

lxviii. Londonderry Port and Harbour Act 1919
s.12, repealed: SR 2002/41 Sch.2
lxxxiv. National Trust Charity Scheme Confirmation Act 1919
varied: 2004 c.14 Sch.1 Part 17
7. Increase of Rent and Mortgage Interest (Restrictions) Act 1919
varied: 2004 c.14 Sch.1 Part 17
21. Ministry of Health Act 1919
s.2, referred to: SI 2002/2375 Sch.1 Part 2
53. War Pensions (Administrative Provisions) Act 1919
s.8, amended: 2004 c.33 Sch.26 para.10

CAP.

9 & 10 Geo. 5 (1919)–cont.

59. Land Settlement (Facilities) Act 1919
s.11, repealed: 2004 c.14 Sch.1 Part 3

65. Welsh Church (Temporalities) Act 1919
s.1, repealed: 2004 c.14 Sch.1 Part 6
s.3, repealed: 2004 c.14 Sch.1 Part 6
s.4, repealed: 2004 c.14 Sch.1 Part 6
s.5, repealed: 2004 c.14 Sch.1 Part 6

91. Ministry of Agriculture and Fisheries Act 1919
s.1, amended: SI 2002/794 Sch.2
s.1, applied: SI 2002/794 Art.5
s.1, repealed (in part): SI 2002/794 Sch.2
s.1, varied: SI 2002/794 Art.5

92. Aliens Restriction (Amendment) Act 1919
s.3, amended: 2003 c.44 Sch.32 para.153
s.3, disapplied: 2003 c.44 Sch.25 para.15
s.6, disapplied: 2003 c.39 Sch.2 para.14

10 & 11 Geo. 5 (1920)

lxxxix. London County Council (General Powers) Act 1920
s.18, amended: SI 2002/254 Sch.4 para.1

lxxv. Londonderry Port and Harbour Act 1920
s.24, repealed: SR 2002/41 Sch.2
s.30, repealed: SR 2002/41 Sch.2
s.34, amended: SR 2002/41 Sch.2

23. War Pensions Act 1920
s.7, amended: 2004 c.33 Sch.26 para.11
s.8, amended: 2004 c.33 Sch.26 para.12

33. Maintenance Orders (Facilities for Enforcement) Act 1920
applied: SI 2002/788 Art.4, SI 2002/789
s.2, applied: SI 2002/788 Art.4
s.3, amended: 2003 c.39 Sch.8 para.68, Sch.10
s.3, applied: SI 2002/788 Art.4
s.4, amended: 2003 c.39 Sch.8 para.69
s.4, applied: SI 2002/788 Art.4
s.7, amended: 2003 c.39 Sch.8 para.70

41. Census Act 1920
s.8, amended: 2002 asp 13 s.38
Sch.1 para.5, amended: 2004 c.33 Sch.27 para.4

55. Emergency Powers Act 1920
repealed: 2004 c.36 Sch.3
s.2, amended: 2003 c.44 Sch.26 para.6

72. Roads Act 1920
applied: SI 2002/2742 Reg.46, Sch.2 para.4
repealed: 2004 c.14 Sch.1 Part 14

75. Official Secrets Act 1920
applied: 2002 asp 11 s.19

11 & 12 Geo. 5 (1921)

20. Tithe Annuities Apportionment Act 1921
repealed: 2004 c.14 Sch.1 Part 6

CAP.

11 & 12 Geo. 5 (1921)–cont.

39. Admiralty Pensions Act 1921
s.2, amended: 2004 c.33 Sch.26 para.13

52. Exchequer and Audit Departments Act 1921
s.9, repealed (in part): 2004 c.14 Sch.1 Part 9

58. Trusts (Scotland) Act 1921
applied: 2003 asp 4 s.7
s.4, applied: 2003 asp 4 s.7
s.19, applied: SI 2004/1611 Reg.26
s.20, varied: 2003 c.14 Sch.20 para.3
s.21, applied: SI 2004/1611 Reg.26

12 & 13 Geo. 5 (1922)

16. Law of Property Act 1922
s.188, repealed (in part): SI 2002/794 Sch.2
Sch.15 para.5, substituted: 2002 c.15 Sch.5 para.1
Sch.15 para.6, amended: SI 2002/794 Sch.1 para.1
Sch.15 para.10, amended: SI 2002/794 Sch.1 para.1
Sch.15 para.12, amended: SI 2002/794 Sch.1 para.1
Sch.15 para.16, amended: SI 2002/794 Sch.1 para.1

35. Celluloid and Cinematograph Film Act 1922
s.2, amended: SI 2002/2776 Sch.6 para.1, 2003 c.17 Sch.6 para.10, SR 2003/152 Sch.7 para.1
s.9, amended: 2004 c.21 Sch.1 para.3

13 & 14 Geo. 5 (1923)

8. Industrial Assurance Act 1923
s.5, amended: SI 2002/1555 Art.2

9. Criminal Evidence Act (Northern Ireland) 1923
s.1, amended: SI 2004/1501 Sch.1 para.2
s.1, repealed (in part): SI 2004/1501 Sch.1 para.2, Sch.2

11. Special Constables Act 1923
s.3, applied: SI 2003/527 Reg.42, SSI 2004/257 Reg.42

17. Explosives Act 1923
applied: SSI 2004/406 Sch.1 para.1

20. Mines (Working Facilities and Support) Act 1923
s.15, applied: SI 2002/1064 Art.3
s.15, disapplied: 2002 asp 3 s.46
s.15, referred to: SI 2002/366 Art.3, SI 2003/1075 Art.3

21. Forestry (Transfer of Woods) Act 1923
varied: 2004 c.14 Sch.1 Part 17

33. Universities of Oxford and Cambridge Act 1923
see *Evans v University of Cambridge* [2002] EWHC 1382, [2003] E.L.R. 8 (QBD (Admin Ct)), Scott Baker, J.
s.5, repealed: 2004 c.14 Sch.1 Part 7

14 & 15 Geo. 5 (1924)

lxxxii. Teignmouth Harbour Order 1924
referred to: SI 2003/2574 Art.1
varied: SI 2003/2574 Sch.2 para.21
s.5, repealed (in part): SI 2003/2574 Sch.3
s.7, repealed: SI 2003/2574 Sch.3
s.11, repealed: SI 2003/2574 Sch.3
s.28, repealed: SI 2003/2574 Sch.3
s.31, repealed: SI 2003/2574 Sch.3

20. Marriages Validity (Provisional Orders) Act 1924
applied: SI 2003/1237
enabling: SI 2003/1237

27. Conveyancing (Scotland) Act 1924
s.8, amended: 2003 asp 9 Sch.14 para.3
s.9, repealed: 2003 asp 9 Sch.15
s.40, amended: 2003 asp 9 Sch.14 para.3
s.40, repealed (in part): 2003 asp 9 Sch.15
Sch.B, amended: 2003 asp 9 Sch.15
Sch.E, repealed: 2003 asp 9 Sch.15
Sch.O, amended: 2003 asp 9 Sch.15

15 & 16 Geo. 5 (1925)

xvii. Imperial Institute Act 1925
repealed: 2002 c.39 s.1, Sch.3

cx. Mersey Tunnel Act 1925
applied: 2004 c.ii

1. Interpretation Measure 1925
s.4, repealed: 2004 c.14 Sch.1 Part 6

3. Diocesan Boards of Finance Measure 1925
applied: SI 2002/1892 Sch.1 Part TABLE, SI 2003/1933 Sch.1 Part I, SI 2004/1888 Sch.1 Part TABLE

18. Settled Land Act 1925
applied: 2002 c.9 s.33, s.89, Sch.1 para.2, Sch.3 para.2, SI 2003/1417 r.186
s.15, repealed: 2004 c.14 Sch.1 Part 12
s.19, applied: SI 2003/1417 Sch.7 para.13
s.71, applied: 2002 c.15 s.109
s.73, applied: 2002 c.15 s.109
s.84, amended: SI 2002/794 Sch.1 para.2
s.88, amended: SI 2002/794 Sch.1 para.3
s.115, amended: SI 2002/794 Sch.1 para.4
s.116, amended: SI 2002/794 Sch.1 para.5
s.117, repealed (in part): SI 2002/794 Sch.2
s.118, repealed: 2004 c.14 Sch.1 Part 12
s.119, repealed (in part): 2002 c.9 Sch.13
Sch.1, repealed: 2004 c.14 Sch.1 Part 12
Sch.4 para.1, repealed: 2004 c.14 Sch.1 Part 12
Sch.4 para.2, repealed: 2004 c.14 Sch.1 Part 12
Sch.4 para.3, repealed: 2004 c.14 Sch.1 Part 12
Sch.4 para.4, repealed: 2004 c.14 Sch.1 Part 12
Sch.4 para.5, repealed: 2004 c.14 Sch.1 Part 12
Sch.4 para.6, repealed: 2004 c.14 Sch.1 Part 12

15 & 16 Geo. 5 (1925)–cont.

18. Settled Land Act 1925–cont.
Sch.4 para.7, repealed: 2004 c.14 Sch.1 Part 12
Sch.4 para.8, repealed: 2004 c.14 Sch.1 Part 12
Sch.4 para.9, repealed: 2004 c.14 Sch.1 Part 12
Sch.4 para.10, repealed: 2004 c.14 Sch.1 Part 12
Sch.4 para.11, repealed: 2004 c.14 Sch.1 Part 12
Sch.4 para.12, repealed: 2004 c.14 Sch.1 Part 12
Sch.4 para.13, repealed: 2004 c.14 Sch.1 Part 12
Sch.4 para.14, repealed: 2004 c.14 Sch.1 Part 12
Sch.4 para.15, repealed: 2004 c.14 Sch.1 Part 12
Sch.4 para.16, repealed: 2004 c.14 Sch.1 Part 12

19. Trustee Act 1925
s.15, see *Bradstock Group Pension Scheme Trustees Ltd v Bradstock Group Plc* [2002] EWHC 651, [2002] I.C.R. 1427 (Ch D), Charles Aldous Q.C.
s.31, amended: 2004 c.33 Sch.27 para.5
s.32, see *D (A Child) v O* [2004] EWHC 1036, [2004] 3 All E.R. 780 (Ch D), Lloyd, J.
s.33, amended: 2004 c.33 Sch.27 para.6
s.40, applied: SI 2003/1417 r.161
s.51, amended: SI 2004/1662 Sch.1 para.10
s.60, amended: 2003 c.14 Sch.20 para.3
s.61, see *Segbedzi (Minors) v Segbedzi* [2002] W.T.L.R. 83 (CA), Jonathan Parker, J.
s.66, amended: SI 2004/1662 Sch.1 para.10

20. Law of Property Act 1925
see *Credit & Mercantile Plc v Marks* [2004] EWCA Civ 568, [2004] 3 W.L.R. 489 (CA), Clarke, L.J.; see *Silven Properties Ltd v Royal Bank of Scotland Plc* [2002] EWHC 1976, [2003] B.P.I.R. 171 (Ch D), Patten, J.
applied: 2002 c.15 s.66, s.69, 2003 c.17 s.178, 2004 c.34 s.50, s.74, s.97, s.129, Sch.3 para.13, Sch.7 para.23
referred to: SI 2003/1417 r.67
s.1, applied: 2002 c.9 s.27, s.90, Sch.2 para.6, Sch.2 para.7
s.2, see *Active Estates Ltd v Parness* [2002] EWHC 893, [2002] B.P.I.R. 865 (Ch D), Neuberger, J.
s.39, repealed (in part): 2004 c.14 Sch.1 Part 12
s.44, amended: 2002 c.9 Sch.11 para.2
s.49, see *Omar v El-Wakil* [2001] EWCA Civ 1090, [2002] 2 P. & C.R. 3 (CA), Arden, L.J.
s.53, disapplied: SI 2003/3226 Reg.4

15 & 16 Geo. 5 (1925)–cont.

20. Law of Property Act 1925–cont.

s.62, see *Commission for New Towns v JJ Gallagher Ltd* [2002] EWHC 2668, [2003] 2 P. & C.R. 3 (Ch D), Neuberger, J.; see *Harbour Estates Ltd v HSBC Bank Plc* [2004] EWHC 1714, [2004] 3 All E.R. 1057 (Ch D), Lindsay, J.; see *P&S Platt Ltd v Crouch* [2002] EWHC 2195, [2002] 45 E.G.C.S. 153 (Ch D), Judge Richard Seymour Q.C.; see *P&S Platt Ltd v Crouch* [2003] EWCA Civ 1110, [2004] 1 P. & C.R. 18 (CA), Peter Gibson, L.J.

s.62, applied: 2002 c.9 s.27

s.62, disapplied: SI 2003/1417 r.71

s.63, see *First National Bank Plc v Achampong* [2003] EWCA Civ 487, [2004] 1 F.C.R. 18 (CA), Blackburne, J.; see *Harbour Estates Ltd v HSBC Bank Plc* [2004] EWHC 1714, [2004] 3 All E.R. 1057 (Ch D), Lindsay, J.

s.64, applied: 2004 c.20 Sch.5 para.6, Sch.21 para.7, 2004 c.23 Sch.3 para.1

s.74, see *Bolton MBC v Torkington* [2003] EWCA Civ 1634, [2004] Ch. 66 (CA), Peter Gibson, L.J.

s.75, disapplied: 2002 c.9 s.91

s.76, applied: SI 2003/1417 r.67

s.77, applied: SI 2003/1417 r.67

s.77, referred to: 2002 c.9 Sch.10 para.3, SI 2003/1417 r.69

s.78, see *Crest Nicholson Residential (South) Ltd v McAllister* [2004] EWCA Civ 410, [2004] 1 W.L.R. 2409 (CA), Auld, L.J.

s.84, see *Azfar's Application, Re* [2002] 1 P. & C.R. 17 (Lands Tr), NJ Rose; see *Broomhead's Application, Re* [2003] 2 E.G.L.R. 157 (Lands Tr), Norman Rose FRICS; see *Girls Day School Trust (1872)'s Application, Re* [2002] 2 E.G.L.R. 89 (Lands Tr), PH Clarke FRICS; see *Hotchkin v McDonald* [2004] EWCA Civ 519, [2004] 18 E.G.C.S. 100 (CA), Thorpe, L.J.; see *Luckies v Simons* [2002] EWHC 2504, [2003] 2 P. & C.R. 30 (Ch D), Judge Rich Q.C.; see *MCA East Ltd, Re* [2002] EWHC 1684, [2003] 1 P. & C.R. 9 (Ch D), Blackburne, J.; see *Pennington's Application, Re* [2002] R.V.R. 271 (Lands Tr), NJ Rose, FRICS

s.84, amended: 2002 c.9 Sch.13

s.85, amended: 2002 c.9 Sch.11 para.2

s.86, amended: 2002 c.9 Sch.11 para.2

s.87, amended: 2002 c.9 Sch.11 para.2

s.89, applied: 2002 c.15 s.89

s.94, amended: 2002 c.9 Sch.11 para.2

s.97, amended: 2002 c.9 Sch.11 para.2

s.101, amended: 2002 c.15 Sch.5 para.2

s.104, see *Corbett v Halifax Building Society* [2002] EWCA Civ 1849, [2003] 1 W.L.R. 964 (CA), Pumfrey, J.

s.105, see *Barclays Bank Plc v Burgess* [2002] EWCA Civ 291, [2002] 12 E.G.C.S. 135 (CA), Chadwick, L.J.

15 & 16 Geo. 5 (1925)–cont.

20. Law of Property Act 1925–cont.

s.105, applied: 2002 c.9 s.54

s.112, repealed: 2004 c.14 Sch.1 Part 12

s.115, amended: 2002 c.9 Sch.11 para.2

s.125, amended: 2002 c.9 Sch.11 para.2

s.136, disapplied: SI 2003/3226 Reg.4

s.138, amended: 2002 c.35 s.2

s.139, see *PW & Co v Milton Gate Investments Ltd* [2003] EWHC 1994, [2004] Ch. 142 (Ch D), Neuberger, J.

s.141, see *Muscat v Smith* [2003] EWCA Civ 962, [2003] 1 W.L.R. 2853 (CA), Sedley, L.J.; see *Rother District Investments Ltd v Corke* [2004] EWHC 14, [2004] 2 P. & C.R. 17 (Ch D), Lightman, J.

s.142, see *Cardwell v Walker* [2003] EWHC 3117, [2004] 2 P. & C.R. 9 (Ch D), Neuberger, J.; see *Muscat v Smith* [2003] EWCA Civ 962, [2003] 1 W.L.R. 2853 (CA), Sedley, L.J.

s.146, see *Abidogun v Frolan Health Care Ltd* [2001] EWCA Civ 1821, [2002] L. & T.R. 16 (CA), Arden, L.J.; see *Duarte v Mount Cook Land Ltd* [2002] L. & T.R. 21 (QBD), John Crowley Q.C.; see *Landmaster Properties Ltd v Thackeray Property Services Ltd* [2003] EWHC 959, [2004] L. & T.R. 4 (QBD), Cox, J.; see *Mohammadi v Anston Investments Ltd* [2003] EWCA Civ 981, [2004] H.L.R. 8 (CA), May, L.J.; see *Mount Eden Land Ltd v Towerstone Ltd* [2002] 31 E.G.C.S. 97 (Ch D), Nicholas Strauss Q.C.; see *Smith v Spaul* [2002] EWCA Civ 1830, [2003] Q.B. 983 (CA), Arden, L.J.

s.146, applied: 2002 c.15 s.169, SI 2004/3056 art4(2), SI 2004/3056 art4(3)

s.146, disapplied: 2002 c.15 s.168

s.149, amended: 2002 c.15 Sch.5 para.3, 2004 c.33 Sch.8 para.1

s.149, applied: 2002 c.15 s.76

s.153, repealed (in part): 2004 c.14 Sch.1 Part 12

s.187, see *Bettison v Langton* [2001] UKHL 24, [2002] 1 A.C. 27 (HL), Lord Scott of Foscote

s.193, see *Bakewell Management Ltd v Brandwood* [2002] EWHC 472, Times, April 19, 2002 (Ch D), Park, J.; see *Bakewell Management Ltd v Brandwood* [2003] EWCA Civ 23, [2003] 1 W.L.R. 1429 (CA), Ward, L.J.; see *Bakewell Management Ltd v Brandwood* [2004] UKHL 14, [2004] 2 A.C. 519 (HL), Lord Bingham of Cornhill

s.194, see *Rabett v Poole* [2003] 3 E.G.L.R. 143 (CC (Bury St Edmunds)), Judge Langan Q.C.

s.194, amended: 2003 c.21 Sch.17 para.3

s.194, applied: 2002 c.i s.10, s.35, SI 2004/1777 Art.25, SI 2004/1778 Art.25

15 & 16 Geo. 5 (1925)–cont.

20. Law of Property Act 1925–*cont.*

s.196, see *Blunden v Frogmore Investments Ltd* [2002] EWCA Civ 573, [2003] 2 P. & C.R. 6 (CA), Robert Walker, L.J.; see *WX Investments Ltd v Begg* [2002] EWHC 925, [2002] 1 W.L.R. 2849 (Ch D), Patten, J.

s.198, disapplied: 2003 c.38 s.75

s.205, see *Barclays Bank Plc v Bean* [2004] 41 E.G. 152 (Ch D), Judge Langan; see *Corbett v Halifax Building Society* [2002] EWCA Civ 1849, [2003] 1 W.L.R. 964 (CA), Pumfrey, J.

s.205, amended: 2002 c.9 Sch.11 para.2, Sch.13, 2004 c.33 Sch.27 para.7

s.206, repealed: 2004 c.14 Sch.1 Part 12

Sch.1 Part VI, repealed: 2004 c.14 Sch.1 Part 12

Sch.2 Part VII, varied: SI 2003/1417 r.69

Sch.2 Part VIII, varied: SI 2003/1417 r.69

Sch.5, repealed: 2004 c.14 Sch.1 Part 12

Sch.6 Part SPECIMENNO1, repealed: 2004 c.14 Sch.1 Part 12

Sch.6 Part SPECIMENNO2, repealed: 2004 c.14 Sch.1 Part 12

Sch.6 Part SPECIMENNO3, repealed: 2004 c.14 Sch.1 Part 12

Sch.6 Part SPECIMENNO4, repealed: 2004 c.14 Sch.1 Part 12

Sch.6 Part SPECIMENNO5, repealed: 2004 c.14 Sch.1 Part 12

21. Land Registration Act 1925

see *Credit & Mercantile Plc v Marks* [2004] EWCA Civ 568, [2004] 3 W.L.R. 489 (CA), Clarke, L.J.

applied: 2002 c.9 Sch.12 para.2, 2002 c.29 s.248, 2002 c.i s.4, Sch.1 para.7, SI 2003/1953 Art.4, Art.5

referred to: 2002 c.9 Sch.3 para.2A, Sch.12 para.2, 2002 c.29 s.47

repealed: 2002 c.9 Sch.13

Part V, disapplied: SI 2003/1953 Art.24

s.3, see *Kingsalton Ltd v Thames Water Developments Ltd* [2001] EWCA Civ 20, [2002] 1 P. & C.R. 15 (CA), Peter Gibson, L.J.; see *UCB Group Ltd v Hedworth (No.1)* [2002] EWCA Civ 708, [2002] 3 E.G.L.R. 76 (CA), Jonathan Parker, L.J.

s.5, see *Kingsalton Ltd v Thames Water Developments Ltd* [2001] EWCA Civ 20, [2002] 1 P. & C.R. 15 (CA), Peter Gibson, L.J.

s.20, see *Kingsalton Ltd v Thames Water Developments Ltd* [2001] EWCA Civ 20, [2002] 1 P. & C.R. 15 (CA), Peter Gibson, L.J.

s.24, see *Scottish & Newcastle Plc v Raguz* [2003] EWCA Civ 1070, [2004] L. & T.R. 11 (CA), Sir Andrew Morritt V.C.

s.30, applied: SI 2003/1953 Art.25

s.30, varied: SI 2003/1953 Art.5

15 & 16 Geo. 5 (1925)–cont.

21. Land Registration Act 1925–*cont.*

s.34, see *Bristol & West Plc v Bartlett* [2002] EWCA Civ 1181, [2003] 1 W.L.R. 284 (CA), Longmore, L.J.

s.35, see *Bristol & West Plc v Bartlett* [2002] EWCA Civ 1181, [2003] 1 W.L.R. 284 (CA), Longmore, L.J.

s.37, see *P&O Overseas Holdings Ltd v Rhys Braintree Ltd* [2002] EWCA Civ 296, [2002] 2 P. & C.R. 27 (CA), Sir Andrew Morritt V.C.

s.47, applied: SI 2003/165 Art.4

s.49, amended: 2002 c.15 s.104

s.53, applied: 2002 c.9 Sch.12 para.16

s.54, see *Speciality Shops Ltd v Yorkshire & Metropolitan Estates Ltd* [2002] EWHC 2969, [2003] 2 P. & C.R. 31 (Ch D), Park, J.

s.54, applied: 2002 c.9 Sch.12 para.17, SI 2003/1417 r.198, SI 2003/1953 Art.6

s.54, enabling: SI 2002/2539

s.55, applied: SI 2003/1417 r.219, r.220, r.221

s.56, see *R. (on the application of Kelly) v Hammersmith and Fulham LBC* [2004] EWHC 435, (2004) 7 C.C.L. Rep. 542 (QBD (Admin Ct)), Wilson, J.

s.56, applied: SI 2003/1417 r.219

s.57, applied: 2002 c.29 s.47, s.248

s.58, applied: SI 2003/165 Sch.4

s.64, amended: 2002 c.15 s.104

s.70, see *Johnson v Shaw* [2003] EWCA Civ 894, [2004] 1 P. & C.R. 10 (CA), Peter Gibson, L.J.; see *Lloyd v Dugdale* [2001] EWCA Civ 1754, [2002] 2 P. & C.R. 13 (CA), Sir Christopher Slade; see *Malory Enterprises Ltd v Cheshire Homes (UK) Ltd* [2002] EWCA Civ 151, [2002] Ch. 216 (CA), Arden, L.J.; see *UCB Group Ltd v Hedworth (No.1)* [2002] EWCA Civ 708, [2002] 3 E.G.L.R. 76 (CA), Jonathan Parker, L.J.

s.70, applied: 2002 c.9 Sch.3 para.2A, Sch.12 para.12, Sch.12 para.13

s.73, applied: SI 2003/1953 Art.6

s.75, applied: 2002 c.9 Sch.12 para.18, SI 2003/1417 r.224

s.79, disapplied: SI 2003/1953 Art.5

s.82, see *Buckinghamshire CC v Briar* [2002] EWHC 2821, [2003] Env. L.R. 25 (Ch D), Lawrence Collins, J.; see *Kingsalton Ltd v Thames Water Developments Ltd* [2001] EWCA Civ 20, [2002] 1 P. & C.R. 15 (CA), Peter Gibson, L.J.; see *Malory Enterprises Ltd v Cheshire Homes (UK) Ltd* [2002] EWCA Civ 151, [2002] Ch. 216 (CA), Arden, L.J.

s.83, see *Prestige Properties Ltd v Scottish Provident Institution* [2002] EWHC 330, [2003] Ch. 1 (Ch D), Lightman, J.

s.110, see *P&O Overseas Holdings Ltd v Rhys Braintree Ltd* [2002] EWCA Civ 296, [2002] 2 P. & C.R. 27 (CA), Sir Andrew Morritt V.C.

CAP.

15 & 16 Geo. 5 (1925)–cont.

21. Land Registration Act 1925–cont.
s.111A, added: 2002 c.15 s.104
s.112, enabling: SI 2002/2539
s.113, referred to: SI 2003/1953 Art.29
s.123A, disapplied: SI 2003/165 Art.2
s.123A, referred to: SI 2003/1953 Art.23
s.129, applied: SI 2003/165 Sch.3 Part IV
s.144, amended: SI 2002/794 Sch.1 para.6
s.144, applied: SI 2002/2539, SI 2003/165
s.144, enabling: SI 2002/2539
s.145, applied: SI 2003/165 Sch.4
s.145, referred to: SI 2003/165 Art.4, Art.5
s.145, enabling: SI 2003/165

23. Administration of Estates Act 1925
applied: SI 2003/1417 Sch.7 para.11
s.25, see *CI v NS* [2004] EWHC 659, [2004]
W.T.L.R. 1113 (Fam Div), Baron, J
s.43, amended: 2002 c.9 Sch.11 para.3
s.46, amended: 2004 c.33 Sch.4 para.7
s.47, amended: 2004 c.33 Sch.4 para.8
s.47A, amended: 2004 c.33 Sch.4 para.9
s.48, amended: 2004 c.33 Sch.4 para.10
s.51, amended: 2004 c.33 Sch.4 para.11
s.55, amended: 2004 c.33 Sch.4 para.12

24. Universities and College Estates Act 1925
s.32, repealed (in part): 2004 c.14 Sch.1 Part 7

33. Church of Scotland (Property and Endowments) Act 1925
s.22, applied: 2003 asp 9 s.85
s.22, disapplied: 2003 asp 9 s.85
s.22, repealed (in part): 2003 asp 9 Sch.15

71. Public Health Act 1925
s.10, amended: 2003 c.21 Sch.17 para.4

73. National Library of Scotland Act 1925
s.5, amended: 2003 c.28 s.15

86. Criminal Justice Act 1925
varied: 2004 c.14 Sch.1 Part 17
s.33, amended: 2003 c.39 Sch.10
s.33, applied: 2002 c.38 s.143, 2003 c.17
s.188, 2004 c.11 s.21, s.22, SI 2004/1769
Sch.2 para.11
s.49, repealed (in part): 2003 c.44 Sch.37
Part 4, Sch.3 para.32

16 & 17 Geo. 5 (1926)

lii. Post Office (Sites) Act 1926
repealed: SI 2003/1542 Sch.2

11. Law of Property (Amendment) Act 1926
s.5, repealed: 2002 c.9 Sch.13

16. Execution of Diligence (Scotland) Act 1926
s.6, enabling: SSI 2002/513, SSI 2002/515,
SSI 2002/566, SSI 2002/567, SSI 2003/
536, SSI 2003/538, SSI 2004/513, SSI
2004/515

29. Adoption of Children Act 1926
referred to: 2002 c.38 Sch.4 para.20

CAP.

16 & 17 Geo. 5 (1926)–cont.

29. Adoption of Children Act 1926–cont.
s.5, see *Upton v National Westminster Bank
Plc* [2004] EWHC 1962, [2004] W.T.L.R.
1339 (Ch D), Judge Behrens

36. Parks Regulation (Amendment) Act 1926
s.2, enabling: SI 2004/1307, SI 2004/1308

52. Small Holdings and Allotments Act 1926
s.1, repealed: 2004 c.14 Sch.1 Part 3
s.2, repealed: 2004 c.14 Sch.1 Part 3
s.3, repealed: 2004 c.14 Sch.1 Part 3
s.4, repealed: 2004 c.14 Sch.1 Part 3
s.13, repealed (in part): 2004 c.14 Sch.1 Part 3
s.19, repealed: 2004 c.14 Sch.1 Part 3
Sch.1, amended: 2004 c.14 Sch.1 Part 3

57. Prisons (Scotland) Act 1926
applied: SSI 2002/472 r.2

61. Judicial Proceedings (Regulation of Reports) Act 1926
s.1, amended: 2003 c.44 Sch.26 para.7, 2004
c.33 Sch.27 para.8
s.1, repealed (in part): 2004 c.33 Sch.27
para.8, Sch.30

17 & 18 Geo. 5 (1927)

xxxi. Post Office (Sites) Act 1927
repealed: SI 2003/1542 Sch.2

12. Auctions (Bidding Agreements) Act 1927
s.2, repealed: 2004 c.14 Sch.1 Part 17

36. Landlord and Tenant Act 1927
s.3, see *Norfolk Capital Group Ltd v Cadogan
Estates Ltd* [2004] EWHC 384, [2004] 1
W.L.R. 1458 (Ch D), Etherton, J.
s.18, see *Mason v Totalfinaelf UK Ltd* [2003]
EWHC 1604, [2003] 3 E.G.L.R. 91 (Ch D),
Blackburne, J.
s.19, varied: 2002 c.15 Sch.7 para.1
s.23, see *Beanby Estates Ltd v Egg Stores
(Stamford Hill) Ltd* [2003] EWHC 1252,
[2003] 1 W.L.R. 2064 (Ch D), Neuberger,
J.; see *Blunden v Frogmore Investments Ltd*
[2002] EWCA Civ 573, [2003] 2 P. & C.R.
6 (CA), Robert Walker, L.J.; see *CA Webber
(Transport) Ltd v Railtrack Plc* [2003]
EWCA Civ 1167, [2004] 1 W.L.R. 320
(CA), Peter Gibson, L.J.; see *Norwich
Union Linked Life Assurance Ltd v
Mercantile Credit Co Ltd* [2003] EWHC
3064, [2004] 4 E.G.C.S. 109 (Ch D),
David Richards, J

18 & 19 Geo. 5 (1928)

lxix. Bridlington Harbour Confirmation Act 1928
s.7, repealed: SI 2004/1426 Sch.3
s.8, amended: SI 2004/1426 Sch.3
s.8, repealed (in part): SI 2004/1426 Sch.3
s.9, repealed: SI 2004/1426 Sch.3

18 & 19 Geo. 5 (1928)–cont.

lxix. Bridlington Harbour Confirmation Act 1928–*cont.*
s.11, repealed: SI 2004/1426 Sch.3
s.13, repealed: SI 2004/1426 Sch.3
s.23, repealed: SI 2004/1426 Sch.3
s.31, repealed: SI 2004/1426 Sch.3

32. Petroleum (Consolidation) Act 1928
s.2, amended: SI 2002/2776 Sch.7 Part 1, 2004 c.21 Sch.1 para.4
s.2, applied: SI 2002/2776 Reg.17
s.4, applied: SI 2003/547 Sch.9 Part II, SI 2004/456 Sch.8 Part II
s.4, disapplied: SI 2002/655 Reg.11, SI 2003/547 Reg.11, SI 2004/456 Reg.10
s.4, referred to: SI 2002/655 Sch.9 Part II
s.5, applied: SI 2002/1689 Reg.8
s.9, referred to: SI 2002/2776 Reg.17
s.9, repealed: SI 2002/2776 Sch.7 Part 1
s.17, repealed: SI 2002/2776 Sch.7 Part 1
s.18, amended: SI 2002/2776 Sch.6 para.2, SI 2004/568 Sch.13 para.1
s.19, applied: SI 2002/1689 Reg.8, SI 2003/547 Sch.9 Part II, SI 2004/456 Sch.8 Part II
s.23, amended: SI 2002/2776 Sch.6 para.2
s.25A, amended: SI 2002/2776 Sch.7 Part 1
s.25A, substituted: SI 2002/2776 Sch.6 para.2

19 & 20 Geo. 5 (1929)

17. Local Government Act 1929
s.131, amended: 2004 c.14 Sch.1 Part 10

27. Savings Banks Act 1929
varied: 2004 c.14 Sch.1 Part 17

29. Government Annuities Act 1929
s.23, applied: 2002 c.26 Sch.4 para.1
s.36, repealed (in part): 2004 c.14 Sch.1 Part 9
s.66, amended: 2004 c.14 Sch.1 Part 9

34. Infant Life (Preservation) Act 1929
s.1, applied: 2003 c.42 Sch.5 para.24, 2003 c.44 Sch.15 para.23, SI 2004/1910 Sch.2

20 & 21 Geo. 5 (1930)

cixxix. Bristol Cattle Market Act 1930
s.20, amended: SI 2003/1542 Sch.2

clviii. London Building Act 1930
s.143, amended: 2004 c.21 Sch.1 para.5

Third Party (Rights gainst Insurers) Act 1930
see *T&N Ltd (In Administration) v Royal & Sun Alliance Plc* [2003] EWHC 1016, [2003] 2 All E.R. (Comm.) 939 (Ch D), Lawrence Collins, J.

8. Benefices (Transfer of Rights of Patronage) Measure 1930
s.2, applied: SI 2002/1893 para.1, para.4, SI 2003/1936 para.1, para.4

20 & 21 Geo. 5 (1930)–cont.

25. Third Parties (Rights against Insurers) Act 1930
see *Aitken v Financial Services Compensation Scheme Ltd* 2003 S.L.T. 878 (OH), Lord Drummond Young; see *Cavaliere v Legal Services Commission* [2003] EWHC 323, [2003] 3 Costs L.R. 350 (QBD), Leveson, J.; see *OT Computers Ltd (In Administration), Re* [2004] EWCA Civ 653, [2004] Ch. 317 (CA), Jonathan Parker, L.J.; see *Phillips v Syndicate 992 Gunner* [2003] EWHC 1084, [2003] 2 C.L.C. 152 (QBD), Eady, J.; see *Tarbuck v Avon Insurance Plc* [2002] Q.B. 571 (QBD (Comm Ct)), Toulson, J.
s.1, see *Centre Reinsurance International Co v Curzon Insurance Ltd* [2004] EWHC 200, [2004] 2 All E.R. (Comm) 28 (Ch D), Blackburne, J.; see *OT Computers Ltd (In Administration), Re* [2003] EWHC 2490, [2004] 1 All E.R. (Comm) 320 (Ch D), Sir Robert Andrew Morritt V.C.
s.1, amended: SI 2003/2096 Sch.1 para.2
s.2, see *OT Computers Ltd (In Administration), Re* [2003] EWHC 2490, [2004] 1 All E.R. (Comm) 320 (Ch D), Sir Robert Andrew Morritt V.C.
s.2, amended: SI 2003/2096 Sch.1 para.3

28. Finance Act 1930
s.42, amended: 2003 c.14 Sch.20 para.3
s.42, applied: 2004 c.25 s.4

43. Road Traffic Act 1930
see *Hayling v Harper* [2003] EWCA Civ 1147, [2004] 1 P. & C.R. 35 (CA), Ward, L.J.

21 & 22 Geo. 5 (1931)

Companies Act (Isle of Man) 1931
s.206, see *Impex Services Worldwide Ltd, Re* [2004] B.P.I.R. 564 (HC (IoM)), Deemster Doyle

xxvi. Scottish United Investors Limited Order Confirmation Act 1931
repealed: 2004 c.14 Sch.1 Part 15

4. Channel Islands (Church Legislation) Measure 1931
applied: 2003 c.1 s.4
referred to: 2003 c.2 s.7, 2003 c.3 s.48

4. Statute of Westminster 1931
applied: 2002 c.39 Sch.2 para.2

28. Finance Act 1931
s.28, amended: SI 2003/2867 Sch.1 para.4
Sch.2, applied: 2003 c.14 Sch.10 para.1

41. Agricultural Land (Utilisation) Act 1931
Sch.2, amended: 2004 c.14 Sch.1 Part 3

22 & 23 Geo. 5 (1931-32)

Administration of Justice Act 1932
s.21, see *Pennington v Waine (No.2)* [2003] W.T.L.R. 1011 (Ch D), Judge Hegarty Q.C.

CAP.

22 & 23 Geo. 5 (1931-32)–cont.

xxxvii. Thames Conservancy Act 1932
see *Rowland v Environment Agency* [2003] EWCA Civ 1885, [2004] 3 W.L.R. 249 (CA), Mance, L.J.

12. Destructive Imported Animals Act 1932
s.5, repealed (in part): SI 2004/100 Art.2
s.10, enabling: SI 2004/100, SSI 2003/528

20. Chancel Repairs Act 1932
see *Aston Cantlow and Wilmcote with Billesley Parochial Church Council v Wallbank* [2001] EWCA Civ 713, [2002] Ch. 51 (CA), Sir Andrew Morritt V.C.; see *Aston Cantlow and Wilmcote with Billesley Parochial Church Council v Wallbank* [2003] UKHL 37, [2004] 1 A.C. 546 (HL), Lord Hobhouse of Woodborough

34. British Museum Act 1932
repealed: 2003 c.28 Sch.1

51. Sunday Entertainments Act 1932
repealed: 2003 c.17 Sch.6 para.11, Sch.7

23 & 24 Geo. 5 (1932-33)

xliv. London Overground Wires etc Act 1933
s.11, amended: 2003 c.21 Sch.17 para.5
s.14, amended: 2003 c.21 Sch.17 para.5

6. Visiting Forces (British Commonwealth) Act 1933
s.4, applied: 2002 c.39 Sch.2 para.2

12. Children and Young Persons Act 1933
s.1, see *R. v Laut (Caroline Ann)* [2001] EWCA Crim 2474, [2002] 2 Cr. App. R. (S.) 7 (CA (Crim Div)), Poole, J.
s.1, applied: SI 2002/896 Sch.1 para.7, 2003 c.42 Sch.5 para.25, 2003 c.44 Sch.15 para.24, 2004 c.31 s.58
s.1, repealed (in part): 2004 c.31 Sch.5 Part 5
s.4, amended: 2003 c.44 Sch.37 Part 9
s.4, applied: SI 2003/1593 Sch.1 Part I
s.5, amended: 2003 c.17 Sch.6 para.13
s.7, amended: 2003 c.39 Sch.8 para.72
s.7, applied: 2002 c.30 Sch.4 para.7, Sch.5 para.6, SI 2003/1376 Sch.1, SI 2004/915 Sch.1 para.6
s.12, amended: 2003 c.17 Sch.6 para.14, Sch.7
s.16, amended: 2003 c.44 Sch.37 Part 7
s.18, see *Ashby v Addison (t/a Brayton News)* [2003] I.C.R. 667 (EAT), Judge Burke Q.C.
s.25, amended: 2003 c.39 Sch.8 para.73
s.25, applied: SI 2003/3319 Reg.24, SSI 2003/231 Sch.1 para.6, Sch.3 para.4
s.29, see *T v DPP* [2003] EWHC 2408, (2004) 168 J.P. 194 (QBD (Admin Ct)), Brooke, L.J.
s.30, see *Ashby v Addison (t/a Brayton News)* [2003] I.C.R. 667 (EAT), Judge Burke Q.C.
s.34, applied: SI 2003/2818 Art.5, Art.14

CAP.

23 & 24 Geo. 5 (1932-33)–cont.

12. Children and Young Persons Act 1933–cont.
s.39, see *Briffett v DPP* [2001] EWHC Admin 841, (2002) 166 J.P. 66 (QBD (Admin Ct)), Laws, L.J.; see *S (A Child) (Identification: Restrictions on Publication), Re* [2003] EWCA Civ 963, [2004] Fam. 43 (CA), Hale, L.J.; see *S (A Child) (Identification: Restrictions on Publication), Re* [2004] UKHL 47, [2004] 3 W.L.R. 1129 (HL), Lord Bingham of Cornhill
s.42, amended: 2003 c.44 Sch.3 para.33
s.44, see *R. v Poulton (Sarah Jane)* [2002] EWCA Crim 2487, [2003] 4 All E.R. 869 (CA (Crim Div)), Rose, L.J.
s.45, applied: 2003 c.39 s.66, Sch.9 para.13
s.45, substituted: 2003 c.39 s.50
s.46, amended: 2003 c.39 Sch.8 para.74
s.48, amended: 2003 c.39 Sch.8 para.75
s.49, see *T v DPP* [2003] EWHC 2408, (2004) 168 J.P. 194 (QBD (Admin Ct)), Brooke, L.J.
s.49, amended: 2003 c.44 Sch.32 para.2
s.53, see *R. (on the application of Smith) v Secretary of State for the Home Department* [2003] EWHC 692, [2003] 1 W.L.R. 2176 (QBD (Admin Ct)), Kennedy, L.J.; see *R. v Parchment (Jamal Sky)* [2003] EWCA Crim 2428, (2003) 147 S.J.L.B. 1088 (CA (Crim Div)), Mantell, L.J.
s.96, amended: 2004 c.31 Sch.2 para.1, Sch.5 Part 4
s.101, repealed: 2003 c.39 Sch.8 para.76, Sch.10
s.102, amended: 2003 c.39 Sch.8 para.77
s.107, see *T v DPP* [2003] EWHC 2408, (2004) 168 J.P. 194 (QBD (Admin Ct)), Brooke, L.J.
s.107, amended: 2003 c.17 Sch.6 para.15, Sch.7
Sch.1, see *R. (on the application of J) v West Sussex CC* [2002] EWHC 1143, [2002] 2 F.L.R. 1192 (QBD (Admin Ct)), Sullivan, J.
Sch.1, amended: 2003 c.42 Sch.6 para.7, 2004 c.28 Sch.10 para.2
Sch.1, applied: SI 2004/478 Sch.6 para.111, SSI 2004/116 Sch.1 para.66
Sch.1, referred to: SI 2004/291 Reg.5, Sch.6 para.113, SI 2004/478 Reg.5, SI 2004/627 Reg.5, Sch.5 para.105, SSI 2003/19 Sch.5 para.2, SSI 2004/115 Reg.5, Sch.5 para.101, SSI 2004/116 Reg.3
Sch.2 Part I para.1, repealed: 2003 c.39 s.50, Sch.10
Sch.2 Part I para.2, repealed: 2003 c.39 s.50, Sch.10
Sch.2 Part I para.2A, repealed: 2003 c.39 s.50, Sch.10
Sch.2 Part I para.3, repealed: 2003 c.39 s.50, Sch.10
Sch.2 Part I para.4, repealed: 2003 c.39 s.50, Sch.10

CAP.

23 & 24 Geo. 5 (1932-33)–cont.

12. Children and Young Persons Act 1933–
cont.
Sch.2 Part I para.5, repealed: 2003 c.39 s.50, Sch.10
Sch.2 Part I para.6, repealed: 2003 c.39 s.50, Sch.10
Sch.2 Part I para.7, repealed: 2003 c.39 s.50, Sch.10
Sch.2 Part I para.8, repealed: 2003 c.39 s.50, Sch.10
Sch.2 Part I para.8A, repealed: 2003 c.39 s.50, Sch.10
Sch.2 Part I para.9, repealed: 2003 c.39 s.50, Sch.10
Sch.2 Part I para.10, repealed: 2003 c.39 s.50, Sch.10
Sch.2 Part I para.11, repealed: 2003 c.39 s.50, Sch.10
Sch.2 Part I para.12, repealed: 2003 c.39 s.50, Sch.10
Sch.2 Part II para.13, repealed: 2003 c.39 s.50, Sch.10
Sch.2 Part II para.14, repealed: 2003 c.39 s.50, Sch.10
Sch.2 Part II para.15, repealed: 2003 c.39 s.50, Sch.10
Sch.2 Part II para.15A, repealed: 2003 c.39 s.50, Sch.10
Sch.2 Part II para.16, repealed: 2003 c.39 s.50, Sch.10
Sch.2 Part II para.17, repealed: 2003 c.39 s.50, Sch.10
Sch.2 Part II para.18, repealed: 2003 c.39 s.50, Sch.10
Sch.2 Part II para.19, repealed: 2003 c.39 s.50, Sch.10
Sch.2 Part III para.20, repealed: 2003 c.39 s.50, Sch.10
Sch.2 Part III para.21, repealed: 2003 c.39 s.50, Sch.10

13. Foreign Judgments (Reciprocal Enforcement) Act 1933
Part I, applied: 2003 c.20 Sch.6 para.8
s.1, enabling: SI 2003/2618
s.3, amended: 2003 c.39 Sch.8 para.78
s.4, see *Habib Bank Ltd v Ahmed* [2001] EWCA Civ 1270, [2002] 1 Lloyd's Rep. 444 (CA), Mummery, L.J.

14. London Passenger Transport Act 1933
s.5, repealed (in part): 2004 c.14 Sch.1 Part 14
s.19, amended: 2004 c.14 Sch.1 Part 14
s.19, repealed: SI 2003/1615 Sch.1 para.1
s.23, repealed: SI 2003/1615 Sch.1 para.1
s.81, repealed: 2004 c.14 Sch.1 Part 14
s.89, repealed (in part): 2004 c.14 Sch.1 Part 14
s.93, varied: SI 2003/1615 Sch.2 para.1
s.98, varied: SI 2003/1615 Sch.2 para.1

35. Trout (Scotland) Act 1933
repealed: 2003 asp 15 Sch.4 Part 2

CAP.

23 & 24 Geo. 5 (1932-33)–cont.

36. Administration of Justice (Miscellaneous Provisions) Act 1933
s.2, see *R. v GDM* [2002] EWCA Crim 3067, [2003] Crim. L.R. 471 (CA (Crim Div)), Laws, L.J.
s.2, amended: 2003 c.44 Sch.37 Part 4, Sch.3 para.34, SI 2004/2035 Sch.1 para.1
s.2, applied: 2002 c.29 s.85
s.2, repealed (in part): 2003 c.44 Sch.37 Part 4, Sch.3 para.34

44. Church of Scotland (Property and Endowments) (Amendment) Act 1933
s.9, amended: 2003 asp 9 s.108, Sch.15
s.9, enabling: SSI 2004/538

51. Local Government Act 1933
applied: SI 2003/527 Reg.2

53. Road and Rail Traffic Act 1933
disapplied: 2004 asp 10 Sch.4 Part 3

24 & 25 Geo. 5 (1933-34)

xcvi. London Passenger Transport Act 1934
Part VIII, varied: SI 2003/1615 Sch.2 para.2

xxvii. Post Office (Sites) Act 1934
repealed: SI 2003/1542 Sch.2

21. Protection of Animals Act 1934
s.2, amended: 2003 c.44 Sch.37 Part 9
s.2, disapplied: 2003 c.44 Sch.25 para.17

40. Administration of Justice (Appeals) Act 1934
s.1, see *Practice Note (CA: Civil Division: Handing Down of Reserved Judgments)* [2002] 1 W.L.R. 344 (CA), Lord Phillips of Worth Matravers, M.R.

41. Law Reform (Miscellaneous Provisions) Act 1934
see *Thakerar v Northwich Park Hospital NHS Trust* [2002] EWCA Civ 617, [2002] C.P. Rep. 50 (CA), Sedley, L.J.
s.1, see *Soutar's Executors v James Murray & Co (Cupar) Ltd* [2002] I.R.L.R. 22 (EAT), Lord Johnston
s.3, amended: 2004 c.14 Sch.1 Part 1
s.3, repealed (in part): 2004 c.14 Sch.1 Part 1

58. Betting and Lotteries Act 1934
repealed: 2004 c.14 Sch.1 Part 17

25 & 26 Geo. 5 (1935)

cx. London Passenger Transport Act 1935
Part VII, varied: SI 2003/1615 Sch.2 para.3
s.52, repealed: SI 2003/1615 Sch.1 para.20
s.85, repealed: SI 2003/1615 Sch.1 para.20

26 Geo. 5 & Edw. 8 (1935-36)

cxiii. Hereford Corporation Act 1936
Part IV, repealed: 2003 c.iv Sch.1
s.3, repealed (in part): 2003 c.iv Sch.1

xliii. Post Office (Sites) Act 1936
repealed: SI 2003/1542 Sch.2

CAP.

26 Geo. 5 & Edw. 8 (1935-36)–cont.

5. Ecclesiastical Commissioners (Powers) Measure 1936
s.2, repealed (in part): 2004 c.14 Sch.1 Part 6

6. Public Order Act 1936
s.7, amended: 2003 c.44 Sch.26 para.8

17. Voluntary Hospitals (Paying Patients) Act 1936
referred to: 2003 c.43 Sch.4 para.1
s.1, amended: 2003 c.43 Sch.4 para.2

26. Land Registration Act 1936
applied: 2002 c.i s.4, Sch.1 para.7
repealed: 2002 c.9 Sch.13

27. Petroleum (Transfer of Licences) Act 1936
s.1, applied: SI 2003/547 Sch.9 Part II, SI 2004/456 Sch.8 Part II
s.1, disapplied: SI 2002/655 Reg.11, SI 2003/547 Reg.11, SI 2004/456 Reg.10
s.1, referred to: SI 2002/655 Sch.9 Part II

43. Tithe Act 1936
s.1, repealed: 2004 c.14 Sch.1 Part 6
s.4, repealed: 2004 c.14 Sch.1 Part 6
s.6, repealed: 2004 c.14 Sch.1 Part 6
s.21, repealed: 2004 c.14 Sch.1 Part 6
s.32, repealed: 2004 c.14 Sch.1 Part 6
s.33, repealed: 2004 c.14 Sch.1 Part 6
s.36, repealed (in part): 2004 c.14 Sch.1 Part 6
s.39, repealed: 2004 c.14 Sch.1 Part 6
s.40, repealed: 2004 c.14 Sch.1 Part 6
s.41, repealed: 2004 c.14 Sch.1 Part 6
s.42, repealed: 2004 c.14 Sch.1 Part 6
s.44, repealed: 2004 c.14 Sch.1 Part 6
s.47, amended: 2004 c.14 Sch.1 Part 6
s.47, repealed (in part): 2004 c.14 Sch.1 Part 6
Sch.2 para.1, repealed: 2004 c.14 Sch.1 Part 6
Sch.2 para.2, repealed: 2004 c.14 Sch.1 Part 6
Sch.2 para.3, repealed: 2004 c.14 Sch.1 Part 6
Sch.2 para.4, repealed: 2004 c.14 Sch.1 Part 6
Sch.2 para.5, repealed: 2004 c.14 Sch.1 Part 6
Sch.2 para.6, repealed: 2004 c.14 Sch.1 Part 6
Sch.2 para.7, repealed: 2004 c.14 Sch.1 Part 6
Sch.2 para.8, repealed: 2004 c.14 Sch.1 Part 6
Sch.2 para.9, repealed: 2004 c.14 Sch.1 Part 6
Sch.2 para.10, repealed: 2004 c.14 Sch.1 Part 6
Sch.2 para.11, repealed: 2004 c.14 Sch.1 Part 6
Sch.2 para.12, repealed: 2004 c.14 Sch.1 Part 6

49. Public Health Act 1936
Part II, see *Sefton MBC v United Utilities Water Ltd* [2001] EWCA Civ 1284, [2002] E.H.L.R. 7 (CA), Robert Walker, L.J.
Part XI, see *Sefton MBC v United Utilities Water Ltd* [2001] EWCA Civ 1284, [2002] E.H.L.R. 7 (CA), Robert Walker, L.J.
s.205, amended: 2004 c.14 Sch.1 Part 13
s.226, amended: 2003 c.17 Sch.6 para.16
s.226, repealed (in part): 2003 c.17 Sch.6 para.16, Sch.7

CAP.

26 Geo. 5 & Edw. 8 (1935-36)–cont.

49. Public Health Act 1936–*cont.*
s.263, amended: 2004 c.14 Sch.1 Part 13
s.264, see *Griffiths v Last Cawthra Feather* [2002] P.N.L.R. 27 (QBD (T&CC)), Judge Grenfell
s.264, amended: 2004 c.14 Sch.1 Part 13
s.275, varied: 2004 c.i Sch.1
s.278, varied: 2004 c.i Sch.1
s.283, varied: 2004 c.i Sch.1
s.285, varied: 2004 c.i Sch.1
s.287, amended: 2003 c.44 Sch.37 Part 9
s.287, disapplied: 2003 c.44 Sch.25 para.18
s.287, varied: 2004 c.i Sch.1
s.289, varied: 2003 c.38 s.76, 2004 c.i Sch.1
s.290, varied: 2004 c.i Sch.1
s.291, varied: 2004 c.i Sch.1
s.297, varied: 2004 c.i Sch.1
s.300, applied: 2002 c.i s.27
s.300, varied: 2004 c.i Sch.1
s.301, applied: 2002 c.i s.27
s.302, applied: 2002 c.i s.27
s.309, amended: 2004 c.14 Sch.1 Part 13
s.341, varied: 2004 c.i Sch.1
s.343, amended: 2004 c.21 Sch.2

52. Private Legislation Procedure (Scotland) Act 1936
applied: SI 2003/409 Sch.1 Part I

789. Petroleum (Compressed Gases) Order (Northern Ireland) 1936
repealed: SR 2003/152 Sch.8 Part I

1 Edw. 8 & 1 Geo. 6 (1936-37)

xc. London Passenger Transport Act 1937
Part VII, varied: SI 2003/1615 Sch.2 para.5

lvii. National Trust Act 1937
varied: 2004 c.14 Sch.1 Part 17
s.6, repealed (in part): 2004 c.14 Sch.1 Part 17
s.12, repealed (in part): 2004 c.14 Sch.1 Part 17
s.13, repealed: 2004 c.14 Sch.1 Part 17
s.16, repealed: 2004 c.14 Sch.1 Part 17

28. Harbours, Piers and Ferries (Scotland) Act 1937
s.10, applied: SSI 2002/410 Art.3

32. Civil List Act 1937
applied: 2002 c.16 s.16

33. Diseases of Fish Act 1937
applied: 2004 c.11 s.3
s.1, disapplied: SI 2004/853 Sch.6
s.3, referred to: 2003 asp 15 s.8
s.8, applied: SI 2003/336 Sch.1 Part 2

37. Children and Young Persons (Scotland) Act 1937
varied: 2004 c.14 Sch.1 Part 17
s.12, see *F v General Teaching Council for Scotland* 2002 S.L.T. 1178 (2 Div), Lord Abernethy, Lord Cullen L.J.C., Lord Weir
s.12, amended: 2003 asp 7 s.51

CAP.

1 Edw. 8 & 1 Geo. 6 (1936-37)–cont.

37. Children and Young Persons (Scotland) Act 1937–*cont.*
s.12, applied: 2003 asp 5 Sch.1 para.1, 2003 c.42 Sch.5 para.78, SI 2004/1910 Sch.3, SSI 2003/441 Sch.1 para.6, SSI 2004/411 Sch.1 para.8

s.12, repealed (in part): 2003 asp 7 s.51

s.15, applied: 2003 asp 5 Sch.1 para.1

s.18, applied: SI 2003/1593 Sch.1 Part I

s.22, applied: 2003 asp 5 Sch.1 para.1

s.33, applied: 2003 asp 5 Sch.1 para.1

s.46, applied: 2004 asp 8 s.111

43. Public Records (Scotland) Act 1937
s.7, amended: 2002 asp 13 s.70

s.10, applied: SSI 2003/234 Sch.1 Part I

s.10, enabling: SSI 2003/234

s.12, applied: SSI 2003/522

s.12, enabling: SSI 2003/522

s.12A, added: 2002 asp 13 s.70

46. Physical Training and Recreation Act 1937
see *Bath and North East Somerset Council v Attorney General* [2002] EWHC 1623, [2002] W.T.L.R. 1257 (Ch D), Hart, J.

s.7, repealed: 2004 c.14 Sch.1 Part 13

54. Finance Act 1937
s.5, amended: 2004 c.14 Sch.1 Part 9, Sch.2 para.5

s.28, amended: SI 2002/2521 Sch.2 Part I, SI 2004/1662 Sch.1 para.11

s.28, repealed (in part): SI 2004/1662 Sch.1 para.11

59. Cinematograph Films (Animals) Act 1937
s.1, amended: 2003 c.44 Sch.26 para.9

1 & 2 Geo. 6 (1937-38)

xciii. Green Belt (London and Home Counties) Act 1938
see *R. (on the application of O'Byrne) v Secretary of State for the Environment, Transport and the Regions* [2001] EWCA Civ 499, [2002] H.L.R. 30 (CA), Buxton, L.J.

s.5, see *R. (on the application of O'Byrne) v Secretary of State for the Environment, Transport and the Regions* [2002] UKHL 45, [2002] 1 W.L.R. 3250 (HL), Lord Scott of Foscote

xcii. London Passenger Transport Act 1938
Part VII, varied: SI 2003/1615 Sch.2 para.6

liv. Redcar Corporation Act 1938
s.176, varied: SI 2003/2155 Sch.1 para.16

ii. River Bann Navigation Act (Northern Ireland) 1938
s.4, repealed (in part): SR 2002/395 Sch.2 Part I

3. Parsonages Measure 1938
s.21, repealed: 2004 c.14 Sch.1 Part 6

CAP.

1 & 2 Geo. 6 (1937-38)–cont.

12. Population (Statistics) Act 1938
Sch.1 para.2, amended: 2004 c.33 Sch.27 para.9

13. Superannuation (Various Services) Act 1938
Sch.1 Part I, amended: 2004 c.14 Sch.1 Part 11

22. Trade Marks Act 1938
s.4, see *D Green & Co (Stoke Newington) Ltd v Regalzone Ltd* [2001] EWCA Civ 639, [2002] E.T.M.R. 22 (CA), Chadwick, L.J.

s.9, see *ST Dupont v El du Pont de Nemours & Co (Trade Marks: Distinctiveness)* [2002] EWHC 2455, Times, November 28, 2002 (Ch D), Neuberger, J.; see *ST Dupont v El Du Pont de Nemours & Co (Trade Marks: Distinctiveness)* [2003] EWCA Civ 1368, [2004] F.S.R. 15 (CA), Aldous, L.J.

s.10, see *ST Dupont v El du Pont de Nemours & Co (Trade Marks: Distinctiveness)* [2002] EWHC 2455, Times, November 28, 2002 (Ch D), Neuberger, J.; see *ST Dupont v El Du Pont de Nemours & Co (Trade Marks: Distinctiveness)* [2003] EWCA Civ 1368, [2004] F.S.R. 15 (CA), Aldous, L.J.

s.11, see *ST Dupont v El du Pont de Nemours & Co (Trade Marks: Distinctiveness)* [2002] EWHC 2455, Times, November 28, 2002 (Ch D), Neuberger, J.; see *ST Dupont v El Du Pont de Nemours & Co (Trade Marks: Distinctiveness)* [2003] EWCA Civ 1368, [2004] F.S.R. 15 (CA), Aldous, L.J.

s.12, see *Citicorp v Link Interchange Network Ltd* [2002] E.T.M.R. 94 (Ch D), Jacob, J.

s.18, see *El du Pont de Nemours & Co v ST Dupont (Appeals: Procedure)* Times, November 7, 2002 (Ch D), Neuberger, J.

s.26, see *Ferrero SpA's Trade Marks* [2004] R.P.C. 29 (Appointed Person), David Kitchin Q.C.; see *Gerber Products Co v Gerber Foods International Ltd* [2002] EWCA Civ 1888, [2003] R.P.C. 34 (CA), Auld, L.J.; see *Gerber Products Co v Gerber Foods International Ltd* [2002] EWHC 428, [2002] E.T.M.R. 77 (Ch D), Sir Robert Andrew Morritt V.C.

s.29, see *Ferrero SpA's Trade Marks* [2004] R.P.C. 29 (Appointed Person), David Kitchin Q.C.

s.68, see *Ferrero SpA's Trade Marks* [2004] R.P.C. 29 (Appointed Person), David Kitchin Q.C.

Trade Marks Act 1994 s.13, see *Mars UK Ltd v Societe des Produits Nestle SA* [2003] EWHC 3052, [2004] R.P.C. 27 (Ch D), Lloyd, J.

24. Conveyancing Amendment (Scotland) Act 1938
s.9, repealed: 2003 asp 9 Sch.15

CAP.

1 & 2 Geo. 6 (1937-38)–cont.

34. Leasehold Property (Repairs) Act 1938
s.1, see *Landmaster Properties Ltd v Thackeray Property Services Ltd* [2003] EWHC 959, [2004] L. & T.R. 4 (QBD), Cox, J.; see *Smith v Spaul* [2002] EWCA Civ 1830, [2003] Q.B. 983 (CA), Arden, L.J.

36. Infanticide Act 1938
s.1, applied: SI 2002/896 Sch.1 para.8, 2003 c.42 Sch.5 para.26, 2003 c.44 Sch.15 para.25, SI 2004/1910 Sch.2

51. Essential Commodities Reserves Act 1938
s.4, amended: 2003 c.44 Sch.37 Part 9
s.4, disapplied: 2003 c.44 Sch.25 para.19

70. Holidays with Pay Act 1938
repealed: 2004 c.14 Sch.1 Part 8

73. Nursing Homes Registration (Scotland) Act 1938
applied: SSI 2002/106 Reg.4, SSI 2002/113 Sch.1 para.20, SSI 2002/162 Art.4, Art.9, Art.13
s.1, applied: SSI 2002/162 Art.7, Art.9
s.3, applied: SSI 2002/162 Art.9, Art.13

2 & 3 Geo. 6 (1938-39)

xcvii. London Building Acts (Amendment) Act 1939
s.11, amended: 2003 c.17 Sch.6 para.17
s.13, amended: 2003 c.17 Sch.6 para.17
s.20, amended: 2004 c.21 Sch.1 para.8, Sch.1 para.9
s.34, amended: 2004 c.21 Sch.1 para.9.1 para.9
s.35, repealed (in part): 2004 c.34 s.53, Sch.16
s.36, amended: 2004 c.21 Sch.1 para.9, 2004 c.34 s.53, Sch.16
s.37, amended: 2004 c.21 Sch.1 para.9, 2004 c.34 s.53
s.38, amended: 2004 c.21 Sch.1 para.9
s.39, amended: 2004 c.21 Sch.1 para.9
s.142, amended: 2003 c.44 Sch.37 Part 9, 2004 c.21 Sch.1 para.9
s.142, disapplied: 2003 c.44 Sch.25 para.20

lxxxix. London Passenger Transport Act 1939
Part VII, varied: SI 2003/1615 Sch.2 para.7

lxxxvi. National Trust Act 1939
varied: 2004 c.14 Sch.1 Part 17
s.16, repealed (in part): 2004 c.14 Sch.1 Part 17
s.17, repealed: 2004 c.14 Sch.1 Part 17

lxv. Tiverton Corporation Act 1939
s.89, varied: SI 2003/2155 Sch.1 para.16

5. Infanticide Act (Northern Ireland) 1939
s.1, applied: 2003 c.44 Sch.17 para.25

13. Cancer Act 1939
applied: SI 2003/1376 Sch.1
s.4, amended: 2003 c.44 Sch.37 Part 9
s.4, applied: SI 2003/1593 Sch.1 Part I

CAP.

2 & 3 Geo. 6 (1938-39)–cont.

13. Cancer Act 1939–*cont.*
s.4, disapplied: 2003 c.44 Sch.25 para.21
s.5, applied: SI 2003/1593 Sch.1 Part I
s.7, applied: SI 2003/1593 Sch.1 Part I

20. Reorganisation of Offices (Scotland) Act 1939
s.1, applied: SSI 2002/103 Art.4, SSI 2002/305 Art.4, SSI 2002/534 Art.4

21. Limitation Act 1939
see *McDonnell v Congregation of Christian Brothers Trustees (formerly Irish Christian Brothers)* [2001] EWCA Civ 2095, [2002] C.P. Rep. 31 (CA), Ward, L.J.; see *McDonnell v Congregation of Christian Brothers Trustees (formerly Irish Christian Brothers)* [2003] UKHL 63, [2004] 1 A.C. 1101 (HL), Lord Bingham of Cornhill

31. Civil Defence Act 1939
repealed: 2004 c.36 Sch.2 para.1, Sch.3
s.77, amended: 2003 c.44 Sch.37 Part 9
s.77, disapplied: 2003 c.44 Sch.25 para.22

33. Marriage Act 1939
applied: SI 2004/291 Sch.4

35. Agricultural Returns Act (Northern Ireland) 1939
repealed: SI 2004/1109 Sch.1

44. House to House Collections Act 1939
varied: 2002 c.i s.21
s.8, amended: 2003 c.44 Sch.26 para.10

69. Import, Export and Customs Powers (Defence) Act 1939
applied: SI 2003/2629 Art.3
s.1, amended: 2002 c.28 s.15
s.1, enabling: SI 2002/315, SI 2002/2059, SI 2003/1555, SI 2003/1938
s.3, amended: 2002 c.28 s.15
s.3, repealed (in part): 2002 c.28 s.15
s.7, repealed (in part): 2002 c.28 s.15

82. Personal Injuries (Emergency Provisions) Act 1939
applied: SI 2004/291 Sch.4, SI 2004/478 Sch.4, SI 2004/627 Sch.2, SSI 2004/115 Sch.3
s.1, enabling: SI 2002/672, SI 2003/637, SI 2004/717
s.2, enabling: SI 2002/672, SI 2003/637, SI 2004/717
s.8, amended: 2004 c.14 Sch.1 Part 11

83. Pensions (Navy, Army, Air Force and Mercantile Marine) Act 1939
applied: SI 2004/478 Sch.4, SI 2004/627 Sch.2, SSI 2004/115 Sch.3
s.3, applied: 2003 c.1 s.641
s.4, applied: 2003 c.1 s.641
s.5, applied: 2003 c.1 s.641

121. Official Secrets Act 1939
applied: 2002 asp 11 s.19

CAP.

3 & 4 Geo. 6 (1939-40)
xxx. Christchurch Corporation Act 1940
s.101, varied: SI 2003/2155 Sch.1 para.16
28. Evidence and Powers of Attorney Act 1940
s.4, applied: SI 2003/1417 r.61

5 & 6 Geo. 6 (1941-42)
1. Ecclesiastical Commissioners (Powers) Measure 1942
repealed: 2004 c.14 Sch.1 Part 6
13. Landlord and Tenant (Requisitioned Land) Act 1942
s.13, amended: 2004 c.33 Sch.27 para.10
21. Finance Act 1942
s.47, amended: 2002 c.23 s.140, SI 2002/2521 Sch.1 para.4, SI 2004/1486 Art.2
s.47, applied: 2002 c.23 s.140, SI 2004/1486 Art.1, Art.3, SI 2004/1662 Sch.1 para.20
s.47, referred to: SI 2004/1450 Reg.12
s.47, repealed (in part): SI 2002/2521 Sch.2 Part I
s.47, enabling: SI 2004/1611
s.48, repealed: SI 2004/1662 Sch.1 para.12
23. Minister of Works Act 1942
applied: SI 2002/2626 Art.17
s.5, applied: SI 2002/2626 Art.17
26. Pensions (Mercantile Marine) Act 1942
applied: SI 2004/291 Sch.4, SI 2004/478 Sch.4, SI 2004/627 Sch.2, SSI 2004/115 Sch.3
35. Greenwich Hospital Act 1942
s.1, amended: 2004 c.33 Sch.26 para.14

6 & 7 Geo. 6 (1942-43)
1. New Parishes Measure 1943
s.17, repealed (in part): 2004 c.14 Sch.1 Part 6
2. Episcopal Endowments and Stipends Measure 1943
s.1, amended: 2004 c.14 Sch.1 Part 6
s.8, amended: 2004 c.14 Sch.1 Part 6
16. Agriculture (Miscellaneous Provisions) Act 1943
Sch.3, amended: 2004 c.14 Sch.1 Part 2
39. Pensions Appeal Tribunals Act 1943
referred to: 2004 c.32, s.5
s.1, amended: 2004 c.14 Sch.1 Part 11, 2004 c.33 Sch.26 para.15
s.5A, amended: 2004 c.32 Sch.1 para.2, Sch.3
s.5A, repealed (in part): 2004 c.32 Sch.3
s.6, amended: 2004 c.32 Sch.1 para.3
s.6, repealed (in part): 2004 c.32 Sch.1 para.3, Sch.3
s.6, enabling: SR 2003/316
s.6A, added: 2004 c.32 Sch.1 para.4
s.6D, added: 2004 c.32 Sch.1 para.4
s.8, amended: 2004 c.32 Sch.1 para.5, Sch.3
s.8, repealed (in part): 2004 c.32 Sch.3

CAP.

6 & 7 Geo. 6 (1942-43)–cont.
39. Pensions Appeal Tribunals Act 1943–cont.
s.10, amended: 2004 c.14 Sch.1 Part 11
s.11A, added: 2004 c.32 Sch.1 para.6
s.12, amended: 2004 c.32 Sch.1 para.7
s.13, amended: 2004 c.32 Sch.1 para.8
s.13, repealed (in part): 2004 c.32 Sch.3
s.14, amended: 2004 c.32 Sch.1 para.9
Sch.1 para.5, amended: 2004 c.14 Sch.1 Part 11, 2004 c.32 Sch.1 para.10
Sch.1 para.5, repealed (in part): 2004 c.32 Sch.3
Sch.1 para.5, enabling: SR 2003/316
Sch.1 para.6, amended: 2004 c.32 Sch.1 para.10
Sch.1 para.6, enabling: SR 2003/316
Sch.1 para.6A, amended: 2004 c.32 Sch.1 para.10
Sch.1 para.6B, added: 2004 c.32 Sch.1 para.10

7 & 8 Geo. 6 (1943-44)
28. Agriculture (Miscellaneous Provisions) Act 1944
repealed: 2004 c.14 Sch.1 Part 2

8 & 9 Geo. 6 (1944-45)
Indictments Act (Northern Ireland) 1945
s.5, see *R. v Drake (Anthony Patrick)* [2002] N.I. 144 (CA (Crim Div) (NI)), Carswell, L.C.J.
7. British Settlements Act 1945
applied: SI 2002/249, SI 2002/2627
enabling: SI 2002/249, SI 2002/1077, SI 2002/1822, SI 2002/2627, SI 2002/2638, SI 2003/2627, SI 2004/347, SI 2004/1980, SI 2004/2669, SI 2004/3039
10. Compensation of Displaced Officers (War Service) Act 1945
repealed: 2004 c.14 Sch.1 Part 10
16. Limitation (Enemies and War Prisoners) Act 1945
applied: 2002 c.9 Sch.6 para.8
s.2, amended: 2004 c.33 Sch.27 para.11
18. Statutory Orders (Special Procedure) Act 1945
s.11, amended: 2004 c.21 Sch.1 para.10
28. Law Reform (Contributory Negligence) Act 1945
see *Vellino v Chief Constable of Greater Manchester* [2001] EWCA Civ 1249, [2002] 1 W.L.R. 218 (CA), Schiemann, L.J.
s.1, see *Russell v Smith* [2003] EWHC 2060, (2003) 147 S.J.L.B. 1118 (QBD), Judge Rich Q.C.; see *Standard Chartered Bank v Pakistan National Shipping Corp (No.2)* [2002] UKHL 43, [2003] 1 A.C. 959 (HL), Lord Hoffmann
s.1, applied: 2003 c.43 s.153, s.156

CAP.

8 & 9 Geo. 6 (1944-45)-cont.

43. Requisitioned Land and War Works Act 1945
s.37, amended: 2002 c.9 Sch.11 para.4
s.37, repealed (in part): 2002 c.9 Sch.13

9 & 10 Geo. 6 (1945-46)

27. Bank of England Act 1946
Sch.1 para.4, repealed: 2004 c.14 Sch.1 Part 17

36. Statutory Instruments Act 1946
applied: 2003 c.21 s.403, 2003 c.39 s.72, s.79, SI 2003/284 Art.133, SI 2004/293 Reg.120
varied: SI 2003/1592 Sch.4 para.1, 2004 c.30 Sch.2 para.22
s.1, applied: SI 2002/3135 Art.16, SI 2003/1250 Art.25, SI 2004/293 Reg.15, SI 2004/1267 Reg.16
s.5, applied: 2002 c.26 s.90, 2003 c.6 s.44, 2003 c.39 s.102, SI 2003/435 Art.46, SI 2003/1247 Art.17, 2004 c.4 s.21, 2004 c.23 s.16, 2004 c.33 Sch.15 para.14, Sch.15 para.23, Sch.15 para.31, Sch.15 para.50, Sch.16 para.2, Sch.17 para.14, SI 2004/702 Art.75, Art.80, SI 2004/1500 Art.34, SI 2004/1501 Art.45
s.6, applied: SI 2003/1688, SI 2004/1308, SI 2004/1611, SSI 2003/522
s.6, referred to: SI 2004/160
s.6, enabling: SI 2004/1307, SI 2004/1308

45. United Nations Act 1946
s.1, applied: SI 2002/313 Sch.1, SI 2004/1818 Reg.3
s.1, enabling: SI 2002/111, SI 2002/112, SI 2002/251, SI 2002/258, SI 2002/259, SI 2002/266, SI 2002/2628, SI 2002/2629, SI 2002/2630, SI 2002/2631, SI 2003/1347, SI 2003/1516, SI 2003/1519, SI 2003/1521, SI 2003/1522, SI 2003/1868, SI 2003/1876, SI 2003/2614, SI 2003/2616, SI 2004/305, SI 2004/306, SI 2004/348, SI 2004/1113, SI 2004/1120, SI 2004/1498, SI 2004/1978, SI 2004/1982, SI 2004/1983, SI 2004/2036, SI 2004/2671

46. Police Act 1946
applied: SI 2003/527 Reg.2

49. Acquisition of Land (Authorisation Procedure) Act 1946
Sch.2 para.3, see *Rhondda Cynon Taff CBC v Watkins* [2003] EWCA Civ 129, [2003] 1 W.L.R. 1864 (CA), Schiemann, L.J.

59. Coal Industry Nationalisation Act 1946
s.36, see *Coal Authority v HJ Banks & Co Ltd* [2002] EWCA Civ 841, [2002] 2 C.M.L.R. 54 (CA), Ward, L.J.

73. Hill Farming Act 1946
applied: SSI 2003/129 Sch.2 para.5
referred to: SSI 2004/70 Sch.2 para.5
s.10, repealed: 2004 c.14 Sch.1 Part 2
s.19, amended: 2003 c.44 Sch.37 Part 9

CAP.

9 & 10 Geo. 6 (1945-46)-cont.

73. Hill Farming Act 1946-cont.
s.19, disapplied: 2003 c.44 Sch.25 para.23
s.36, amended: 2004 c.14 Sch.1 Part 2
s.37, repealed (in part): 2004 c.14 Sch.1 Part 2

80. Atomic Energy Act 1946
applied: SI 2002/2533 Art.2
s.18, enabling: SI 2002/2533
s.20, repealed (in part): 2004 c.14 Sch.1 Part 16

10 & 11 Geo. 6 (1946-47)

iv. Forth Road Bridge Order Confirmation Act 1947
repealed (in part): SSI 2002/178 Sch.4
s.67, applied: SSI 2002/178 Art.11
Sch.1, amended: SSI 2002/178 Sch.3 para.1

xlvi. London County Council (General Powers) Act 1947
s.6, amended: 2003 c.17 Sch.6 para.19

xlvii. London Passenger Transport Act 1947
Part VI, varied: SI 2003/1615 Sch.2 para.8

2. Church Commissioners Measure 1947
s.15, repealed (in part): 2004 c.14 Sch.1 Part 6
s.17, amended: 2004 c.14 Sch.1 Part 6

5. Greenwich Hospital Act 1947
s.2, amended: 2004 c.33 Sch.26 para.16

19. Polish Resettlement Act 1947
applied: SI 2004/291 Sch.4, SI 2004/478 Sch.4, SI 2004/627 Sch.2, SSI 2004/115 Sch.3
s.1, amended: 2004 c.33 Sch.26 para.17
s.1, enabling: SI 2002/671
s.2, amended: 2004 c.33 Sch.26 para.18
s.3, applied: SI 2002/1792 Reg.15
s.6, repealed: 2004 c.14 Sch.1 Part 7
s.11, repealed (in part): 2004 c.14 Sch.1 Part 7
Sch.1 Part II, applied: SI 2002/1792 Reg.15
Sch.1 Part II para.7, amended: 2003 c.44 Sch.32 para.154
Sch.1 Part II para.7, disapplied: 2003 c.44 Sch.25 para.24

22. Civic Restaurants Act 1947
s.1, amended: 2003 c.17 Sch.6 para.18

24. Naval Forces (Enforcement of Maintenance Liabilities) Act 1947
s.1, amended: 2004 c.33 Sch.26 para.19

33. Foreign Marriage Act 1947
s.3, applied: 2004 c.33 s.244

39. Statistics of Trade Act 1947
s.10, amended: 2004 c.33 Sch.27 para.12

40. Industrial Organisation and Development Act 1947
applied: SI 2003/409 Sch.1 Part I
s.1, applied: SI 2002/1676, SI 2002/3062, SI 2004/964
s.1, enabling: SI 2002/1676, SI 2002/3062, SI 2003/908, SI 2004/964
s.2, enabling: SI 2003/908

10 & 11 Geo. 6 (1946-47)-cont.

40. Industrial Organisation and Development Act 1947-cont.

s.3, enabling: SI 2002/3062, SI 2003/908, SI 2004/964

s.4, applied: SI 2002/3062, SI 2003/908, SI 2004/964

s.4, referred to: SI 2002/1676

s.4, enabling: SI 2002/1676, SI 2002/3062, SI 2003/908, SI 2004/964

s.6, enabling: SI 2003/908

s.7, amended: SI 2003/1326 Art.4

s.8, applied: SI 2002/1676, SI 2002/3062, SI 2003/908, SI 2004/964

s.8, enabling: SI 2002/1676, SI 2002/3062, SI 2003/908, SI 2003/909, SI 2004/964

s.14, enabling: SI 2002/1676, SI 2003/908

41. Fire Services Act 1947

applied: SI 2002/325 Reg.24, SI 2002/327 Reg.31, SI 2002/1792 Sch.6 para.2, 2003 asp 1 s.16, SI 2003/1021 Reg.3, Reg.34, SI 2003/3171 Sch.1 Part I, SI 2003/3172 Sch.2 Part I, Sch.2 Part II

referred to: 2003 c.26 s.128, s.129, 2003 c.36 s.3

repealed (in part): 2004 c.21 Sch.2

s.3, amended: 2003 c.16 s.2

s.5, applied: 2004 c.21 s.4

s.6, amended: 2003 c.10 Sch.1 para.1, 2003 c.26 Sch.7 para.1

s.6, applied: 2004 c.21 s.4

s.10, amended: 2003 c.10 Sch.1 para.1

s.18, enabling: SI 2004/481, SSI 2004/527

s.19, repealed (in part): 2003 c.26 Sch.8 Part 1

s.24, applied: 2003 asp 1 s.25, 2004 c.21 s.28

s.26, amended: 2004 c.33 Sch.25 para.1

s.26, applied: 2004 c.21 s.36, SI 2004/2306 Art.3, Sch.1

s.26, referred to: SI 2004/2918 Art.3

s.26, varied: SI 2004/2918 Sch.1

s.26, enabling: SI 2004/1912, SSI 2004/385

s.27A, applied: SI 2004/2306 Sch.1

s.27A, varied: SI 2004/2918 Sch.1

s.31, amended: 2003 c.44 Sch.26 para.11

s.31, applied: SI 2002/1837 Sch.1 Part I

s.35, applied: SI 2004/2306 Sch.1

s.35, varied: SI 2004/2918 Sch.1

s.36, amended: 2002 asp 3 Sch.7 para.1, 2003 asp 1 s.11

s.36, applied: 2002 asp 11 Sch.2 para.13, SI 2003/3172 Sch.2 Part I, Sch.2 Part II

s.36, enabling: SSI 2002/141

s.37, amended: 2003 c.16 s.2

s.39, applied: SI 2004/2306 Sch.1

s.39, varied: SI 2004/2918 Sch.1

Sch.3, applied: SI 2004/2306 Sch.1

Sch.3, varied: SI 2004/2918 Sch.1

10 & 11 Geo. 6 (1946-47)-cont.

42. Acquisition of Land (Authorisation Procedure) (Scotland) Act 1947

applied: 2002 asp 3 s.47, 2003 asp 2 s.16, 2003 asp 8 s.45, 2003 c.21 Sch.4 para.4, SSI 2003/168 Sch.1 para.4

referred to: SSI 2004/171 Art.23

varied: 2004 asp 6 s.39

s.1, amended: 2003 asp 2 Sch.2 para.2, SSI 2003/331 Sch.1 para.1

s.1, referred to: 2002 asp 3 s.47

Sch.1, applied: SSI 2003/446 Reg.3

Sch.1 Part I para.2, applied: SSI 2003/446 Reg.3

Sch.1 Part I para.2, enabling: SSI 2003/446

Sch.1 Part I para.3, amended: 2003 asp 9 s.109

Sch.1 Part I para.3, applied: 2003 asp 9 s.106, SSI 2003/446 Reg.3

Sch.1 Part I para.3, referred to: SSI 2003/446 Sch.1

Sch.1 Part I para.3, enabling: SSI 2003/446

Sch.1 Part I para.3A, added: 2003 asp 9 s.109

Sch.1 Part I para.3A, amended: 2003 asp 9 s.109

Sch.1 Part I para.3A, applied: SSI 2003/446 Reg.3

Sch.1 Part I para.3B, added: 2003 asp 9 s.109

Sch.1 Part I para.3B, amended: 2003 asp 9 s.109

Sch.1 Part I para.4, amended: 2003 asp 9 s.109

Sch.1 Part I para.6, applied: SSI 2003/446 Reg.3

Sch.1 Part I para.6, referred to: SSI 2003/446 Sch.1

Sch.1 Part I para.6, enabling: SSI 2003/446

Sch.1 Part I para.6A, added: 2003 asp 9 s.109

Sch.1 Part I para.6B, added: 2003 asp 9 s.109

Sch.1 Part I para.6C, added: 2003 asp 9 s.109

Sch.1 Part I para.6D, added: 2003 asp 9 s.109

Sch.1 Part III, applied: SSI 2003/446 Reg.3, Sch.1

Sch.1 Part III para.13, applied: SSI 2003/446 Reg.3

Sch.1 Part III para.13, referred to: SSI 2003/446 Sch.1

Sch.1 Part III para.13, enabling: SSI 2003/446

Sch.1 Part V para.18, enabling: SSI 2003/446

Sch.1 para.15, see *Prestige Assets Ltd v Renfrewshire Council* 2003 S.C. 88 (OH), Lord Mackay of Drumadoon

43. Local Government (Scotland) Act 1947

s.247, amended: 2002 asp 17 Sch.3 para.10

s.247, enabling: SSI 2002/560

s.247A, amended: 2002 asp 17 Sch.3 para.10

44. Crown Proceedings Act 1947

applied: 2002 c.22 Sch.1 para.5, 2002 c.28 s.16, 2002 c.29 s.350, s.385, SI 2002/2836 Sch.1 para.5, 2003 c.14 Sch.14 para.7, 2004 c.35 s.313

10 & 11 Geo. 6 (1946-47)-cont.

44. Crown Proceedings Act 1947-*cont.*
Part II, applied: 2002 c.22 Sch.1 para.5, SI 2002/2836 Sch.1 para.5, 2003 c.14 Sch.14 para.7, SI 2003/1660 Reg.36, SI 2003/1661 Reg.36
Part III, applied: SI 2003/1660 Reg.36, SI 2003/1661 Reg.36
Part IV, applied: SI 2003/1660 Reg.36, SI 2003/1661 Reg.36
Part V, applied: SI 2003/1660 Reg.36, SI 2003/1661 Reg.36
s.2, see *Matthews v Ministry of Defence* [2003] UKHL 4, [2003] 1 A.C. 1163 (HL), Lord Bingham of Cornhill; see *Quinland v Governor of Swaleside Prison* [2002] EWCA Civ 174, [2003] Q.B. 306 (CA), Kennedy, L.J.
s.10, see *Matthews v Ministry of Defence* [2002] EWCA Civ 773, [2002] 1 W.L.R. 2621 (CA), Lord Phillips of Worth Matravers, M.R.; see *Matthews v Ministry of Defence* [2002] EWHC 13, [2002] C.P. Rep. 26 (QBD), Keith, J.; see *Matthews v Ministry of Defence* [2003] UKHL 4, [2003] 1 A.C. 1163 (HL), Lord Bingham of Cornhill
s.20, disapplied: SI 2003/1660 Reg.36, SI 2003/1661 Reg.36
s.21, see *Davidson v Scottish Ministers (No.1)* 2002 S.C. 205 (Ex Div), Lord Marnoch, Lord Hardie, Lord Weir; see *Davidson v Scottish Ministers (No.1)* 2002 S.C.L.R. 166 (OH), Lord Johnston
s.22, applied: SI 2002/796 Art.16
s.23, applied: SI 2003/1660 Reg.36, SI 2003/1661 Reg.36
s.38, see *Davidson v Scottish Ministers (No.1)* 2002 S.C. 205 (Ex Div), Lord Marnoch, Lord Hardie, Lord Weir
s.38, referred to: SI 2004/2443 Sch.4 para.11
s.40, amended: 2002 c.35 s.1
s.44, see *Davidson v Scottish Ministers (No.1)* 2002 S.C. 205 (Ex Div), Lord Marnoch, Lord Hardie, Lord Weir
s.44, disapplied: SI 2003/1660 Reg.36, SI 2003/1661 Reg.36

45. Public Offices (Site) Act 1947
s.7, repealed: 2003 c.39 Sch.8 para.79, Sch.10

46. Wellington Museum Act 1947
s.2, applied: SI 2002/445 Art.2
s.5, applied: SI 2002/445 Art.2

48. Agriculture Act 1947
applied: 2002 c.15 Sch.2 para.2
s.14, amended: 2003 c.44 Sch.37 Part 9
s.14, disapplied: 2003 c.44 Sch.25 para.25
s.58, repealed: 2004 c.14 Sch.1 Part 3
s.59, repealed: 2004 c.14 Sch.1 Part 3
s.83, repealed: 2004 c.14 Sch.1 Part 2
s.84, repealed: 2004 c.14 Sch.1 Part 2
s.86, repealed: 2004 c.14 Sch.1 Part 2

10 & 11 Geo. 6 (1946-47)-cont.

48. Agriculture Act 1947-*cont.*
s.88, repealed: 2004 c.14 Sch.1 Part 2
s.89, repealed: 2004 c.14 Sch.1 Part 2
s.92, repealed: 2004 c.14 Sch.1 Part 2
s.93, repealed: 2004 c.14 Sch.1 Part 2
s.94, repealed: 2004 c.14 Sch.1 Part 2
s.95, amended: 2003 c.44 Sch.37 Part 9
s.95, applied: 2003 c.44 Sch.25 para.25
s.95, disapplied: 2003 c.44 Sch.25 para.26
s.95, repealed: 2004 c.14 Sch.1 Part 2
s.109, applied: SI 2002/302 Art.4, SI 2002/303 Art.4, SI 2003/285 Art.4, SI 2003/286 Art.4, SI 2004/368 Art.4, SI 2004/369 Art.4
Sch.2 para.1, repealed: 2004 c.14 Sch.1 Part 2
Sch.2 para.2, repealed: 2004 c.14 Sch.1 Part 2
Sch.2 para.3, repealed: 2004 c.14 Sch.1 Part 2
Sch.2 para.4, repealed: 2004 c.14 Sch.1 Part 2
Sch.2 para.5, repealed: 2004 c.14 Sch.1 Part 2
Sch.8 Part II, amended: 2004 c.14 Sch.1 Part 3
Sch.9 para.14, applied: SI 2003/409 Sch.1 Part I
Sch.9 para.15, applied: SI 2003/409 Sch.1 Part I
Sch.11 para.1, repealed: 2004 c.14 Sch.1 Part 2
Sch.11 para.2, repealed: 2004 c.14 Sch.1 Part 2

51. Town and Country Planning Act 1947
s.92, see *Henry Boot Homes Ltd v Bassetlaw DC* [2002] EWHC 546, [2002] J.P.L. 1224 (QBD (Admin Ct)), Sullivan, J.

11 & 12 Geo. 6 (1947-48)

xli. Ipswich Corporation Act 1948
s.173, varied: SI 2003/2155 Sch.1 para.16

4. Judges Pensions (India and Burma) Act 1948
repealed: 2004 c.14 Sch.1 Part 11

5. Civil Defence Act 1948
applied: SI 2002/1040 Sch.4
repealed: 2004 c.36 Sch.2 para.3, Sch.3
s.1, amended: 2004 c.21 Sch.1 para.11
s.3, substituted: 2002 c.5 s.1
s.4, amended: 2003 c.44 Sch.37 Part 9
s.4, disapplied: 2003 c.44 Sch.25 para.27
s.5, amended: 2004 c.21 Sch.1 para.11, Sch.2
s.9, amended: 2004 c.21 Sch.2
s.9, applied: SI 2002/2633 Art.2

23. Law Reform (Miscellaneous Provisions) Act (Northern Ireland) 1948
s.2, applied: 2003 c.43 s.153

29. National Assistance Act 1948
see *R. (on the application of Kelly) v Hammersmith and Fulham LBC* [2004] EWHC 435, (2004) 7 C.C.L. Rep. 542 (QBD (Admin Ct)), Wilson, J.
referred to: 2003 c.43 Sch.4 para.3

CAP.

11 & 12 Geo. 6 (1947-48)–cont.

29. National Assistance Act 1948–*cont.*

see *R. (on the application of Kelly) v Hammersmith and Fulham LBC* [2004] EWHC 435, (2004) 7 C.C.L. Rep. 542 (QBD (Admin Ct)), Wilson, J.

enabling: SI 2002/2531

Part III, applied: 2003 c.5 s.15

s.21, see *Anufrijeva v Southwark LBC* [2003] EWCA Civ 1406, [2004] Q.B. 1124 (CA), Lord Woolf of Barnes, L.C.J.; see *B (A Child) v Todd* [2002] P.I.Q.R. P11 (QBD), Stanley Burnton, J.; see *Crookdake v Drury* [2003] EWHC 1938, (2004) 76 B.M.L.R. 99 (QBD), Owen, J.; see *Murua v Croydon LBC* (2002) 5 C.C.L. Rep. 51 (QBD (Admin Ct)), Rafferty, J.; see *R. (on the application of A) v National Asylum Support Service* [2003] EWCA Civ 1473, [2004] 1 W.L.R. 752 (CA), Waller, L.J.; see *R. (on the application of AA) v Lambeth LBC* [2001] EWHC Admin 741, (2002) 5 C.C.L. Rep. 36 (QBD (Admin Ct)), Forbes, J.; see *R. (on the application of Ali) v Birmingham City Council* [2002] EWHC 1511, [2002] H.L.R. 51 (QBD (Admin Ct)), Moses, J.; see *R. (on the application of Bernard) v Enfield LBC* [2002] EWHC 2282, [2003] H.R.L.R. 4 (QBD (Admin Ct)), Sullivan, J.; see *R. (on the application of H) v Kingston upon Thames RLBC* [2002] EWHC 3158, (2003) 6 C.C.L. Rep. 240 (QBD (Admin Ct)), Elias, J.; see *R. (on the application of Heather) v Leonard Cheshire Foundation* [2002] EWCA Civ 366, [2002] 2 All E.R. 936 (CA), Lord Woolf of Barnes, L.C.J.; see *R. (on the application of J) v Enfield LBC* [2002] EWHC 432, [2002] 2 F.L.R. 1 (QBD (Admin Ct)), Elias, J.; see *R. (on the application of Khan) v Oxfordshire CC* [2002] EWHC 2211, [2003] H.L.R. 23 (QBD (Admin Ct)), Moses, J.; see *R. (on the application of Khan) v Oxfordshire CC* [2004] EWCA Civ 309, [2004] H.L.R. 41 (CA), Ward, L.J.; see *R. (on the application of Khana) v Southwark LBC* [2001] EWCA Civ 999, [2002] H.L.R. 31 (CA), Mance, L.J.; see *R. (on the application of M) v Slough BC* [2004] EWHC 1109, [2004] B.L.G.R. 657 (QBD (Admin Ct)), Collins, J.; see *R. (on the application of Mani) v Lambeth LBC* [2002] EWHC 735, (2002) 5 C.C.L. Rep. 486 (QBD (Admin Ct)), Wilson, J.; see *R. (on the application of Mani) v Lambeth LBC* [2003] EWCA Civ 836, [2004] H.L.R. 5 (CA), Simon Brown, L.J.; see *R. (on the application of O) v Haringey LBC* [2004] EWCA Civ 535, [2004] 2 F.L.R. 476 (CA), Lord Woolf of Barnes, L.C.J.; see *R. (on the application of Wahid) v Tower Hamlets LBC* [2002] EWCA Civ 287, [2003] H.L.R. 2 (CA), Pill, L.J.; see *R. (on the application of*

CAP.

11 & 12 Geo. 6 (1947-48)–cont.

29. National Assistance Act 1948–*cont.*

s.21–*cont.*

Westminster City Council) v National Asylum Support Service [2002] UKHL 38, [2002] 1 W.L.R. 2956 (HL), Lord Hoffmann

s.21, amended: 2002 c.41 s.45

s.21, applied: 2002 c.41 Sch.3 para.1, SI 2002/1792 Reg.15, SI 2003/284 Sch.2 para.2, SI 2003/969 Reg.2, SI 2003/2382 Reg.5, SI 2004/293 Sch.2 para.16, SI 2004/692 Sch.4 para.5

s.21, enabling: SI 2003/969

s.22, see *B (A Child) v Todd* [2002] P.I.Q.R. P11 (QBD), Stanley Burnton, J.; see *Crookdake v Drury* [2003] EWHC 1938, (2004) 76 B.M.L.R. 99 (QBD), Owen, J.

s.22, amended: 2003 c.5 s.17

s.22, applied: 2002 asp 5 s.2, SI 2002/411 Reg.2, SI 2002/815 Reg.2, SI 2002/1792 Reg.15, SI 2003/628 Reg.2, SI 2003/892 Reg.2, SI 2003/2382 Reg.5, SI 2004/1024 Reg.2, SSI 2002/76 Reg.3, SSI 2002/85 Reg.2, SSI 2002/264 Art.2, SSI 2003/86 Reg.2, SSI 2004/106 Reg.2

s.22, referred to: SI 2003/969 Reg.2

s.22, enabling: SI 2002/410, SI 2002/411, SI 2002/814, SI 2002/815, SI 2002/2531, SI 2003/627, SI 2003/628, SI 2003/892, SI 2003/897, SI 2003/931, SI 2003/2343, SI 2003/2530, SI 2004/760, SI 2004/1023, SI 2004/1024, SI 2004/2328, SI 2004/2879, SSI 2002/85, SSI 2003/69, SSI 2003/86, SSI 2003/156, SSI 2003/425, SSI 2003/577, SSI 2004/103, SSI 2004/106, SSI 2004/389

s.23, applied: SI 2002/1792 Reg.15, SI 2003/2382 Reg.5

s.24, amended: 2003 c.43 Sch.4 para.4

s.24, applied: SI 2002/1792 Reg.15, SI 2002/2005 Sch.1 para.9, SI 2003/2382 Reg.5

s.26, see *B (A Child) v Todd* [2002] P.I.Q.R. P11 (QBD), Stanley Burnton, J.; see *R. (on the application of Heather) v Leonard Cheshire Foundation* [2002] EWCA Civ 366, [2002] 2 All E.R. 936 (CA), Lord Woolf of Barnes, L.C.J.

s.26, amended: 2002 c.17 Sch.2 para.38, 2003 c.5 s.17

s.26, applied: 2002 asp 5 s.2, SI 2002/2006 Reg.19, SI 2003/2382 Reg.5, SSI 2002/76 Reg.3

s.29, see *R. (on the application of A) v East Sussex CC (No.1)* [2002] EWHC 2771, [2003] B.L.G.R. 529 (QBD (Admin Ct)), Munby, J.

s.29, applied: 2002 c.41 Sch.3 para.1, SI 2002/1792 Sch.1 para.1, Sch.1 para.2, Sch.2 para.14, Sch.6 para.4, SI 2002/2005 Reg.14, SI 2002/2007 Reg.8, SI 2003/284 Sch.2 para.2, SI 2004/293 Sch.2 para.16, SI 2004/1748 Reg.3

CAP.

11 & 12 Geo. 6 (1947-48)–cont.

29. National Assistance Act 1948–*cont.*
s.30, see *R. (on the application of A) v East Sussex CC (No.1)* [2002] EWHC 2771, [2003] B.L.G.R. 529 (QBD (Admin Ct)), Munby, J.
s.42, applied: 2002 asp 5 s.4
s.43, amended: 2003 c.39 Sch.8 para.80
s.47, amended: 2003 c.39 Sch.8 para.81
s.47, referred to: SSI 2002/533 Sch.1, Sch.3
s.48, referred to: SSI 2002/533 Sch.1, Sch.3
s.51, amended: 2003 c.44 Sch.26 para.12
s.52, amended: 2003 c.44 Sch.26 para.12
s.65, applied: 2002 asp 5 s.2
s.65, repealed (in part): 2003 c.39 Sch.8 para.82, Sch.10

36. House of Commons Members Fund Act 1948
s.4, amended: 2004 c.33 Sch.25 para.2

38. Companies Act 1948
applied: 2002 c.iii, 2002 c.iv
Sch.1 Reg.29, see *Pennington v Waine (No.2)* [2003] W.T.L.R. 1011 (Ch D), Judge Hegarty Q.C.
Sch.1 Reg.30, see *Pennington v Waine (No.2)* [2003] W.T.L.R. 1011 (Ch D), Judge Hegarty Q.C.
Sch.1 Table A Reg.30, see *Pennington v Crampton* [2003] EWHC 2691, [2004] B.C.C. 611 (Ch D), Lloyd, J.
Sch.1 Reg.31, see *Pennington v Waine (No.2)* [2003] W.T.L.R. 1011 (Ch D), Judge Hegarty Q.C.
Sch.1 Table A Reg.31, see *Pennington v Crampton* [2003] EWHC 2691, [2004] B.C.C. 611 (Ch D), Lloyd, J.
Sch.1 Reg.32, see *Pennington v Waine (No.2)* [2003] W.T.L.R. 1011 (Ch D), Judge Hegarty Q.C.

45. Agriculture (Scotland) Act 1948
s.57, applied: 2003 asp 11 s.54
s.64, applied: 2003 asp 11 s.54
Sch.6, referred to: 2003 asp 11 s.7, s.18

47. Agricultural Wages Act 1948
s.3A, amended: 2004 c.24 s.46
s.5, applied: SI 2004/2178 Reg.2
s.5, repealed: SI 2004/2178 Sch.1 Part I
s.11A, added: 2004 c.24 s.47
s.11A, applied: 2004 c.24 s.47
s.12, amended: 2003 c.44 Sch.37 Part 9, 2004 c.24 s.47
s.12, applied: 2004 c.24 s.47
s.12, disapplied: 2003 c.44 Sch.25 para.28
s.12, repealed (in part): 2004 c.24 s.47, Sch.2
s.15A, amended: 2004 c.24 Sch.1 para.1
s.20, repealed (in part): 2004 c.14 Sch.1 Part 2

53. Nurseries and Child-Minders Regulation Act 1948
s.1, applied: SI 2002/635 Reg.2, SI 2002/896 Sch.1 para.8, SI 2004/2695 Sch.1 para.28

CAP.

11 & 12 Geo. 6 (1947-48)–cont.

53. Nurseries and Child-Minders Regulation Act 1948–*cont.*
s.5, applied: SI 2002/635 Reg.2, SI 2002/896 Sch.1 para.8, SI 2004/2695 Sch.1 para.28

56. British Nationality Act 1948
applied: SI 2003/527 Reg.44, SSI 2004/257 Reg.44
s.1, referred to: SI 2003/548 Sch.2 para.15
s.3, applied: SI 2002/798 Art.24
s.5, applied: SI 2003/548 Sch.2 para.11

58. Criminal Justice Act 1948
s.27, amended: 2003 c.44 Sch.3 para.35
s.37, amended: 2003 c.39 Sch.8 para.83
s.41, repealed (in part): 2003 c.44 Sch.37 Part 4, Sch.3 para.35
s.80, amended: 2003 c.44 Sch.37 Part 4, Sch.3 para.35

12, 13 & 14 Geo. 6 (1948-49)

xxix. British Transport Commission Act 1949
s.53, applied: 2003 c.20 s.73
s.53, repealed: 2003 c.20 Sch.8
s.54, referred to: SI 2003/1615 Sch.1 para.2
s.55, see *R. (on the application of Mair) v Criminal Injuries Compensation Board* [2001] EWHC Admin 412, [2002] P.I.Q.R. P4 (QBD (Admin Ct)), Stanley Burnton, J.
s.55, applied: 2002 c.30 s.43, SI 2002/1837 Sch.1 Part II, SI 2004/915 Sch.1 para.11
s.55, referred to: SI 2003/1615 Sch.1 para.2
s.56, applied: 2002 c.30 s.43, SI 2002/1837 Sch.1 Part II, SI 2004/915 Sch.1 para.11
s.56, referred to: SI 2003/1615 Sch.1 para.2
s.57, referred to: SI 2003/1615 Sch.1 para.2
s.57, varied: SI 2002/3269 Art.8
s.59, referred to: SI 2003/1615 Sch.1 para.2

lv. London County Council (General Powers) Act 1949
s.7, amended: 2003 c.21 Sch.17 para.21
s.51, repealed: 2004 c.21 Sch.2

lix. Shoreham Harbour Act 1949
s.13, repealed: SI 2004/1506 Sch.3
s.26, repealed: SI 2004/1506 Sch.3
s.28, repealed: SI 2004/1506 Sch.3
s.49, amended: SI 2004/1506 Sch.3
s.50, amended: SI 2004/1506 Art.12, Sch.3
s.52, amended: SI 2004/1506 Sch.3
s.53, amended: SI 2004/1506 Sch.3

2. Agriculture Act (Northern Ireland) 1949
s.39, repealed: SI 2004/1109 Sch.1

30. Agricultural Wages (Scotland) Act 1949
referred to: 2004 c.24 s.45, s.46
s.3A, amended: SSI 2003/283 Reg.2
s.3A, applied: 2003 c.8 s.2
s.5, applied: SSI 2004/384 Reg.2
s.5, repealed: SSI 2004/384 Reg.2

CAP.

12, 13 & 14 Geo. 6 (1948-49)–cont.

42. Lands Tribunal Act 1949
varied: 2003 asp 2 s.62
s.1, see *BP Oil UK Ltd v Kent CC* [2003] EWCA Civ 798, [2004] 1 P. & C.R. 25 (CA), Carnwath, L.J.; see *Matthews v Walsall MBC* [2003] R.V.R. 163 (Lands Tr), PH Clarke, FRICS
s.1, applied: SSI 2003/452 r.11, r.12
s.3, see *Girls Day School Trust (1872) v Dadak* [2001] EWCA Civ 380, [2002] 1 P. & C.R. 4 (CA), Robert Walker, L.J.; see *Goldstein v Conley* [2001] EWCA Civ 637, [2002] 1 W.L.R. 281 (CA), Clarke, L.J.; see *R. (on the application of Sinclair Gardens Investments (Kensington) Ltd) v Lands Tribunal* [2004] EWHC 1910, [2004] R.V.R. 230 (QBD (Admin Ct)), Sullivan, J.
s.3, applied: 2002 c.15 s.175, SSI 2003/452 r.20, r.26, 2004 c.34 s.231
s.3, enabling: SI 2002/770, SI 2003/2945, SSI 2003/452, SSI 2003/521, SSI 2004/480

45. U.S.A Veterans Pensions (Administration) Act 1949
repealed: 2004 c.14 Sch.1 Part 11

47. Finance Act 1949
s.47, repealed: 2004 c.14 Sch.1 Part 9
s.48, amended: SI 2004/1662 Sch.1 para.13

54. Wireless Telegraphy Act 1949
applied: 2002 c.11 s.6, 2003 c.21 s.14, s.159, s.163, s.164, s.175, s.192, s.364, Sch.1 para.1, Sch.6 para.1
referred to: 2003 c.21 s.393, s.404, SI 2004/692 Reg.7
varied: 2003 c.21 Sch.18 para.55, SI 2003/1903 Reg.3
s.1, amended: 2003 c.21 s.165, Sch.17 para.6, Sch.19
s.1, applied: SI 2002/1700 Reg.4, 2003 c.21 s.160, s.172, s.173, s.174, s.175, s.190, Sch.8 para.27
s.1, disapplied: SI 2003/74 Reg.4
s.1, referred to: 2003 c.21 s.156
s.1, repealed (in part): 2003 c.21 Sch.19
s.1, enabling: SI 2002/1590, SI 2003/74
s.1AA, added: 2003 c.21 s.166
s.1C, amended: 2003 c.21 Sch.17 para.7
s.1D, amended: 2003 c.21 Sch.17 para.8
s.1D, applied: 2003 c.21 Sch.8 para.28
s.1D, repealed (in part): 2003 c.21 Sch.19
s.1D, varied: 2003 c.21 Sch.18 para.20
s.1E, applied: 2003 c.21 s.169
s.1E, substituted: 2003 c.21 s.169
s.1F, applied: SI 2004/2068 r.6
s.1F, repealed: 2003 c.21 Sch.19
s.1F, varied: 2003 c.21 Sch.18 para.23
s.2, repealed: 2003 c.21 Sch.19
s.2, enabling: SI 2002/641, SI 2003/663
s.3, amended: 2003 c.21 Sch.17 para.9, Sch.19
s.3, applied: 2003 c.21 s.190, Sch.8 para.29

CAP.

12, 13 & 14 Geo. 6 (1948-49)–cont.

54. Wireless Telegraphy Act 1949–*cont.*
s.3, enabling: SI 2003/74
s.5, applied: 2003 c.21 s.401, Sch.1 para.1, SI 2003/3104 Reg.3
s.5, enabling: SI 2003/3104
s.6, applied: 2003 c.21 Sch.1 para.1
s.7, applied: 2003 c.21 Sch.1 para.1
s.9, applied: 2003 c.21 Sch.17 para.10
s.9, repealed: 2003 c.21 Sch.19
s.10, amended: 2003 c.21 Sch.17 para.11, Sch.19
s.10, applied: 2003 c.21 Sch.8 para.30
s.11, amended: 2003 c.21 Sch.17 para.12, Sch.19
s.11, disapplied: 2003 c.44 Sch.25 para.29
s.11, repealed (in part): 2003 c.21 Sch.19
s.11, varied: 2003 c.21 s.178
s.12, amended: 2003 c.21 Sch.17 para.13
s.12, varied: 2003 c.21 s.178
s.13A, added: 2003 c.21 s.171
s.13A, applied: 2003 c.21 s.177
s.13B, added: 2003 c.21 s.171
s.13B, applied: 2003 c.21 Sch.8 para.31
s.14, amended: 2003 c.21 s.171, s.179, Sch.17 para.14, 2003 c.44 Sch.37 Part 9
s.14, applied: 2003 c.44 Sch.25 para.29
s.14, repealed (in part): 2003 c.21 Sch.19
s.15, amended: 2003 c.21 Sch.17 para.15
s.15, applied: 2003 c.21 s.182, Sch.7 para.1, Sch.8 para.32
s.15, repealed (in part): 2003 c.21 Sch.19
s.16, amended: 2003 c.21 Sch.17 para.16
s.19, amended: 2003 c.21 s.183, Sch.17 para.17
s.19, referred to: 2003 c.21 s.184
s.19, repealed (in part): 2003 c.21 Sch.19
s.20, applied: SI 2003/3197
s.20, enabling: SI 2003/3195, SI 2003/3196, SI 2003/3197, SI 2003/3198, SI 2004/307, SI 2004/308, SI 2004/309
Sch.1 para.3, substituted: 2003 c.21 Sch.17 para.18
Sch.2 para.1, repealed: 2003 c.21 Sch.19
Sch.2 para.2, repealed: 2003 c.21 Sch.19
Sch.2 para.3, repealed: 2003 c.21 Sch.19
Sch.2 para.4, repealed: 2003 c.21 Sch.19
Sch.2 para.5, repealed: 2003 c.21 Sch.19
Sch.2 para.6, repealed: 2003 c.21 Sch.19
Sch.2 para.7, repealed: 2003 c.21 Sch.19

55. Prevention of Damage by Pests Act 1949
s.3, amended: 2004 c.14 Sch.1 Part 13
s.8, repealed (in part): 2004 c.14 Sch.1 Part 13
s.15, amended: 2003 c.39 Sch.8 para.84, Sch.10
s.18, repealed (in part): 2004 c.14 Sch.1 Part 13
s.19, repealed (in part): 2004 c.14 Sch.1 Part 13
s.22, amended: 2003 c.44 Sch.37 Part 9
s.22, applied: 2003 c.44 Sch.25 para.30

CAP.

12, 13 & 14 Geo. 6 (1948-49)–cont.

55. Prevention of Damage by Pests Act 1949–cont.

s.25, repealed (in part): 2004 c.14 Sch.1 Part 13

s.27, repealed (in part): 2004 c.14 Sch.1 Part 13

s.30, repealed (in part): 2004 c.14 Sch.1 Part 13

67. Civil Aviation Act 1949

s.8, enabling: SI 2003/433, SI 2004/2038

s.41, enabling: SI 2003/433, SI 2004/2038

s.57, enabling: SI 2003/433, SI 2004/2038

s.58, enabling: SI 2003/433, SI 2004/2038

s.59, enabling: SI 2003/433, SI 2004/2038

s.61, enabling: SI 2003/433, SI 2004/2038

69. New Forest Act 1949

applied: SI 2002/794 Art.3, SI 2002/2626 Art.6

s.1, amended: SI 2002/794 Sch.1 para.7

s.9, enabling: SI 2003/3298

s.14, applied: SI 2003/3298 Sch.1 para.18

s.15, applied: SI 2003/3298 Sch.1 para.20

s.16, amended: SI 2002/794 Sch.1 para.8, SI 2002/2626 Sch.2 para.1

s.17, amended: SI 2002/794 Sch.1 para.9, SI 2002/2626 Sch.2 para.1

70. Docking and Nicking of Horses Act 1949

s.1, amended: 2003 c.44 Sch.26 para.13

s.2, amended: 2003 c.44 Sch.26 para.13

s.2, repealed (in part): 2004 c.14 Sch.1 Part 17

s.5, repealed (in part): 2004 c.14 Sch.1 Part 17

74. Coast Protection Act 1949

Part I, applied: SSI 2002/410 Art.57

s.5, applied: SI 2002/1278 Reg.2, Reg.3, Reg.4, SI 2003/1847 Reg.5, Reg.6

s.5, referred to: SI 2003/1847 Reg.4

s.5, enabling: SI 2002/1278, SI 2003/1847

s.25, amended: 2003 c.44 Sch.37 Part 9

s.25, applied: 2003 c.44 Sch.25 para.31

s.34, applied: SSI 2002/410 Art.57, 2003 asp 19 Sch.1 para.5

s.35, amended: 2004 c.20 s.99

s.36, applied: SSI 2002/410 Art.57

s.44, enabling: SI 2002/1278, SI 2003/1847

s.47, amended: 2003 c.21 Sch.17 para.19

Sch.4 para.83, amended: SI 2003/1915 Reg.2

Sch.4 para.113, enabling: SI 2003/1915

76. Marriage Act 1949

see *Gandhi v Patel* [2002] 1 F.L.R. 603 (Ch D), Park, J.

applied: 2002 c.38 s.79, SI 2002/1893 para.1, SI 2003/1936 para.1, 2004 c.19 s.20

Part III, applied: 2004 c.19 s.19, s.20

s.1, amended: 2004 c.7 Sch.4 para.2, 2004 c.33 Sch.27 para.13

s.1, repealed (in part): 2004 c.33 Sch.27 para.13, Sch.30

CAP.

12, 13 & 14 Geo. 6 (1948-49)–cont.

76. Marriage Act 1949–cont.

s.3, amended: 2002 c.38 Sch.3 para.2, Sch.3 para.3, Sch.3 para.4, Sch.3 para.5, 2003 c.39 Sch.8 para.85

s.3, referred to: 2002 c.38 Sch.3 para.1

s.5, applied: SI 2003/1237

s.5B, added: 2004 c.7 Sch.4 para.3

s.27, amended: 2004 c.33 Sch.27 para.14

s.27, applied: 2004 c.19 s.19

s.27A, see *R. (on the application of CPS) v Registrar General of Births, Deaths and Marriages* [2002] EWCA Civ 1661, [2003] Q.B. 1222 (CA), Waller, L.J.

s.28, varied: 2004 c.19 s.20

s.28A, amended: 2004 c.33 Sch.27 para.15

s.31, see *R. (on the application of CPS) v Registrar General of Births, Deaths and Marriages* [2002] EWCA Civ 1661, [2003] Q.B. 1222 (CA), Waller, L.J.

s.39, applied: 2004 c.33 s.244

s.46A, enabling: SI 2003/1961

s.48, varied: 2004 c.19 s.20

s.63, amended: SI 2002/3076 Sch.1

s.64, amended: SI 2002/3076 Sch.1

s.65, amended: SI 2002/3076 Sch.1

s.68, varied: 2004 c.33 Sch.21 para.3

s.78, amended: 2004 c.33 Sch.27 para.16

Sch.1, referred to: 2002 c.38 s.74

Sch.1 Part I, substituted: 2004 c.33 Sch.27 para.17

Sch.1 Part II, substituted: 2004 c.33 Sch.27 para.17

Sch.1 Part III, substituted: 2004 c.33 Sch.27 para.17

87. Patents Act 1949

see *Oystertec Plc v Edward Evans Barker (A Firm)* [2002] EWHC 2324, [2003] R.P.C. 29 (Pat Ct), Jacob, J.

88. Registered Designs Act 1949

see *Apple Computer Inc v Design Registry* [2002] E.C.D.R. 19 (Registered Designs Appeal Tribunal), Jacob, J.

applied: 2002 c.40 s.86

s.1A, amended: SI 2003/550 Reg.2

s.11A, repealed (in part): 2002 c.40 Sch.26

s.11AB, added: 2002 c.40 Sch.25 para.1

s.11AB, varied: SI 2003/1592 Sch.4 para.2

s.11ZB, amended: SI 2003/550 Reg.2

s.13, enabling: SI 2004/3336

s.17, amended: 2003 c.44 Sch.37 Part 6

s.20, amended: SI 2003/550 Reg.2

s.37, enabling: SI 2004/3336

s.44, amended: SI 2003/550 Reg.2

89. Vehicles (Excise) Act 1949

applied: SI 2002/2742 Reg.46, Sch.2 para.4

93. National Health Service (Amendment) Act 1949

repealed (in part): 2003 c.43 Sch.14 Part 4

97. National Parks and Access to the Countryside Act 1949

applied: SI 2003/54 Art.4

CAP.

12, 13 & 14 Geo. 6 (1948-49)–cont.

97. National Parks and Access to the Countryside Act 1949–cont.
s.12, amended: 2003 c.17 Sch.6 para.20
s.12, applied: SI 2004/1777 Art.25, SI 2004/1778 Art.25
s.16, applied: SI 2003/2261 Sch.3 Part I, Sch.4 para.3
s.20, amended: 2003 c.21 Sch.17 para.20
s.20, applied: 2004 asp 6 s.20, s.44
s.21, applied: SI 2004/1777 Art.25, SI 2004/1778 Art.25
s.23, applied: 2004 asp 6 Sch.5 para.8
s.54, amended: 2003 c.17 Sch.6 para.20
s.60, amended: 2003 c.21 Sch.17 para.20
s.60, referred to: 2002 c.i s.42
s.64, applied: SI 2004/1777 Art.25, SI 2004/1778 Art.25
s.68, amended: 2003 c.39 Sch.8 para.86, Sch.10
s.87, applied: SI 2003/54 Art.3
s.89, applied: SI 2004/1777 Art.25, SI 2004/1778 Art.25
s.90, applied: SI 2004/1777 Art.25, SI 2004/1778 Art.25
s.92, applied: 2002 c.i s.15, SI 2004/1777 Art.25, SI 2004/1778 Art.25
s.99, applied: SI 2004/1777 Art.25, SI 2004/1778 Art.25
s.106, applied: 2004 asp 6 s.20
s.107, applied: 2004 asp 6 s.20
Sch.2, referred to: 2002 c.i s.42
98. Adoption of Children Act 1949
s.12, referred to: 2002 c.38 Sch.4 para.20
101. Justices of the Peace Act 1949
Part II, applied: 2003 c.39 Sch.9 para.11
Part III, applied: 2003 c.39 Sch.9 para.11
s.42, applied: 2003 c.39 Sch.9 para.11

14 Geo. 6 (1950)

v. City of London (Various Powers) Act 1950
s.18, amended: SI 2003/1542 Sch.2
Sch.1, amended: SI 2003/1542 Sch.2
European Convention on Human Rights Act 1950
Art.6, see *Kansal v United Kingdom (21413/02)* (2004) 39 E.H.R.R. 31 (ECHR), Judge Pellonpaa (President)
xxiv. Forth Road Bridge Order Confirmation Act 1950
repealed: SSI 2002/178 Sch.4
iii. Gun Barrel Proof Act 1950
applied: 2002 c.40 Sch.15
Inquiries (Evidence) Act 1950
s.1, see *Mount Murray Country Club Ltd v Macleod* [2003] UKPC 53, [2003] S.T.C. 1525 (PC (IoM)), Lord Walker of Gestingthorpe
xlv. Ipswich Dock Act 1950
s.23, repealed: SI 2002/3269 Art.9

CAP.

14 Geo. 6 (1950)–cont.

3. Exchequer and Financial Provisions Act (Northern Ireland) 1950
s.2, applied: SI 2002/3126 Art.2
s.11, varied: SI 2003/1633 Sch.1 para.15
s.40, varied: SI 2003/1633 Sch.1 para.16
Sch.1, varied: SI 2003/1633 Sch.1 para.17
10. Royal Patriotic Fund Corporation Act 1950
s.1, amended: 2004 c.33 Sch.26 para.20
s.2, repealed: 2004 c.32 Sch.3
15. Finance Act 1950
s.39, amended: SI 2004/2310 Sch.1 para.1
26. Adoption Act 1950
referred to: 2002 c.38 Sch.4 para.20
s.18, referred to: 2002 c.38 Sch.4 para.20
27. Arbitration Act 1950
s.19A, see *Aslam v South Bedfordshire DC (Rate of Interest)* [2001] EWCA Civ 515, [2002] R.V.R. 16 (CA), Chadwick, L.J.
s.22, see *Fletamentos Maritimos SA v Effjohn International BV (Wasted Costs)* [2003] Lloyd's Rep. PN 26 (CA), Simon Brown, L.J.
29. Employment and Training (Northern Ireland) Act 1950
applied: SI 2003/418 Art.4
s.1, applied: SI 2002/2006 Reg.19, SI 2003/335 Sch.1, SR 2003/28 Sch.5 para.15, SSI 2003/93 Sch.1
31. Allotments Act 1950
s.6, amended: 2004 c.14 Sch.1 Part 3
37. Maintenance Orders Act 1950
applied: SI 2004/3114 Sch.1, SSI 2002/494 Reg.33
s.16, amended: 2004 c.33 Sch.27 para.18
s.17, amended: 2003 c.39 Sch.8 para.87
s.18, amended: 2003 c.39 Sch.8 para.88
s.22, amended: 2003 c.39 Sch.8 para.89
s.22, applied: SI 2003/435 Sch.2 para.2
s.24, amended: 2003 c.39 Sch.8 para.90
s.25, amended: 2003 c.39 Sch.8 para.91
s.25, repealed (in part): 2003 c.39 Sch.8 para.91, Sch.10
s.28, amended: 2003 c.39 Sch.8 para.92, Sch.10
39. Public Utilities Street Works Act 1950
s.22, see *Road Management Services (A13) Plc v London Power Networks Plc* [2003] B.L.R. 303 (QBD (T&CC)), Forbes, J.
s.31, see *Road Management Services (A13) Plc v London Power Networks Plc* [2003] B.L.R. 303 (QBD (T&CC)), Forbes, J.
Sch.4, see *Road Management Services (A13) Plc v London Power Networks Plc* [2003] B.L.R. 303 (QBD (T&CC)), Forbes, J.

14 & 15 Geo. 6 (1950-51)

xxxix. British Transport Commission Act 1951
s.15, applied: SI 2003/1615 Sch.1 para.21

CAP.

14 & 15 Geo. 6 (1950-51)–cont.

xxv. Pier and Harbour Order (Lymington) Confirmation Act 1951
referred to: SI 2002/2586 Art.1
s.3, repealed (in part): SI 2002/2586 Sch.3
s.7, amended: SI 2002/2586 Sch.3
s.9, repealed: SI 2002/2586 Sch.3
s.17, repealed: SI 2002/2586 Sch.3
s.46, repealed (in part): SI 2002/2586 Sch.3
s.54, repealed: SI 2002/2586 Sch.3
s.55, repealed: SI 2002/2586 Sch.3
s.58, repealed: SI 2002/2586 Sch.3
s.59, repealed: SI 2002/2586 Sch.3

26. Salmon and Freshwater Fisheries (Protection) (Scotland) Act 1951
repealed: 2003 asp 15 Sch.4 Part 2
s.19, applied: SI 2003/336 Sch.1 Part 2
s.20, applied: SI 2003/336 Sch.1 Part 2
s.24, applied: SSI 2002/11 Reg.2, SSI 2003/230 Reg.2, SSI 2004/259 Reg.2, Reg.3

27. Fire Services Act 1951
repealed (in part): 2004 c.21 Sch.2
s.1, applied: SI 2004/2306 Sch.1
s.1, varied: SI 2004/2918 Sch.1

35. Pet Animals Act 1951
applied: 2003 c.44 Sch.25 para.32
s.4, disapplied: 2003 c.44 Sch.25 para.32
s.5, amended: 2003 c.44 Sch.37 Part 9
s.5, repealed (in part): 2003 c.44 Sch.37 Part 9

38. Leasehold Property (Temporary Provisions) Act 1951
applied: 2002 c.15 s.77

39. Common Informers Act 1951
Sch.1, amended: 2003 c.17 Sch.7

55. Nurses (Scotland) Act 1951
applied: SSI 2002/113 Sch.1 para.20, SSI 2002/162 Art.4, Art.13
s.28, applied: SSI 2002/162 Art.7, Art.10

62. Tithe Act 1951
s.8, repealed: 2004 c.14 Sch.1 Part 6
s.10, amended: 2004 c.14 Sch.1 Part 6
s.10, repealed (in part): 2004 c.14 Sch.1 Part 6
s.12, repealed (in part): 2004 c.14 Sch.1 Part 6

65. Reserve and Auxiliary Forces (Protection of Civil Interests) Act 1951
s.14, amended: 2003 c.17 Sch.6 para.22
s.18, amended: 2003 c.17 Sch.6 para.23
s.23, amended: 2004 c.33 Sch.26 para.21
s.25, amended: 2004 c.33 Sch.26 para.22
s.27, amended: 2003 c.17 Sch.6 para.24, 2004 c.33 Sch.26 para.23
s.38, amended: 2004 c.33 Sch.26 para.24
s.46, amended: 2004 c.21 Sch.1 para.12, 2004 c.33 Sch.26 para.25
s.46, applied: SI 2004/2306 Sch.1
s.46, varied: SI 2004/2918 Sch.1
s.52, amended: 2004 c.33 Sch.26 para.26
s.57, amended: SI 2002/1555 Art.3
s.57, varied: SI 2002/1555 Art.4
s.61, amended: 2004 c.21 Sch.1 para.12

CAP.

14 & 15 Geo. 6 (1950-51)–cont.

65. Reserve and Auxiliary Forces (Protection of Civil Interests) Act 1951–cont.
s.61, applied: SI 2004/2306 Sch.1
s.61, varied: SI 2004/2918 Sch.1
Sch.2 Part I, amended: 2002 c.17 Sch.1 para.36, Sch.2 para.39, 2004 c.21 Sch.1 para.12
Sch.2 Part II, repealed: 2003 c.39 Sch.8 para.93, Sch.10
Sch.3 para.1, amended: 2004 c.33 Sch.26 para.27
Sch.3 para.2, amended: 2004 c.33 Sch.26 para.27

66. Rivers (Prevention of Pollution) (Scotland) Act 1951
s.35, amended: 2002 asp 3 Sch.7 para.2

15 & 16 Geo. 6 & 1 Eliz. 2 (1951-52)

xxxviii. City of London (Guild Churches) Act 1952
amended: 2004 c.14 Sch.1 Part 6
s.3, amended: 2004 c.14 Sch.1 Part 6
s.4, amended: 2004 c.14 Sch.1 Part 6
s.22, amended: 2004 c.14 Sch.1 Part 6
s.33, repealed: 2004 c.14 Sch.1 Part 6
s.36, amended: 2004 c.14 Sch.1 Part 6
s.36, repealed (in part): 2004 c.14 Sch.1 Part 6

5. Foyle Fisheries Act (Northern Ireland) 1952
s.13, applied: SR 2003/114
s.13, enabling: SR 2003/114
s.63, applied: 2002 c.26 Sch.4 para.1
s.64, see *Foyle Carlingford and Irish Lights Commission v McGillion* [2002] N.I. 86 (CA (NI)), Carswell, L.C.J.

23. Miners Welfare Act 1952
s.12, applied: 2003 c.17 s.66

37. Civil List Act 1952
applied: 2002 c.16 s.16

39. Motor Vehicles (International Circulation) Act 1952
s.1, applied: SI 2004/1992
s.1, enabling: SI 2004/1992

46. Hypnotism Act 1952
s.1, amended: 2003 c.17 Sch.6 para.26
s.1, repealed (in part): 2003 c.17 Sch.6 para.26, Sch.7
s.2, amended: 2003 c.17 Sch.6 para.27

52. Prison Act 1952
applied: SI 2002/325 Reg.3, SI 2002/1792 Reg.5, SI 2003/527 Sch.2 para.1, SI 2004/645 Reg.16
s.5A, amended: 2002 c.41 s.66
s.7, amended: SI 2002/3135 Sch.1 para.1
s.7, applied: SI 2002/1882 Reg.10, SI 2003/250 Reg.10, SI 2003/2644 Reg.10, SI 2004/585 Reg.10, SI 2004/1020 Reg.10
s.19, amended: 2003 c.39 Sch.8 para.94, Sch.10
s.21, disapplied: 2003 c.44 s.186

CAP.

15 & 16 Geo. 6 & 1 Eliz. 2 (1951-52)– cont.

52. Prison Act 1952–*cont.*
s.37, enabling: SI 2002/77, SI 2002/78
s.43, applied: SI 2002/327 Reg.3
s.43, varied: 2003 c.44 Sch.3 para.36
s.47, applied: 2003 c.44 s.257
s.47, enabling: SI 2002/2116, SI 2002/2117, SI 2003/3005, SI 2003/3301
s.49, amended: 2003 c.44 s.186
s.49, applied: 2003 c.44 s.245, s.261
s.53, amended: 2003 c.44 Sch.32 para.3

55. Magistrates Courts Act 1952
see *R. (on the application of DPP) v Camberwell Green Youth Court* [2003] EWHC 3217, (2004) 168 J.P. 157 (QBD (Admin Ct)), Jackson, J.

59. Cockfighting Act 1952
s.1, amended: 2003 c.44 Sch.37 Part 9
s.1, disapplied: 2003 c.44 Sch.25 para.33

64. Intestates Estates Act 1952
s.5, amended: 2004 c.33 Sch.4 para.13
Sch.2 para.1, amended: 2004 c.33 Sch.4 para.13
Sch.2 para.2, amended: 2004 c.33 Sch.4 para.13
Sch.2 para.3, amended: 2004 c.33 Sch.4 para.13
Sch.2 para.4, amended: 2004 c.33 Sch.4 para.13
Sch.2 para.5, amended: 2004 c.33 Sch.4 para.13
Sch.2 para.6, amended: 2004 c.33 Sch.4 para.13
Sch.2 para.7, amended: 2004 c.33 Sch.4 para.13

67. Visiting Forces Act 1952
applied: SI 2002/1093 Reg.5, 2004 c.18 s.90
varied: 2003 c.1 s.303
Part I, applied: 2003 c.1 s.303, SI 2004/568 Reg.6
s.1, amended: 2002 c.39 Sch.2 para.3
s.1, applied: SI 2002/1093 Reg.5
s.3, applied: 2003 c.20 s.90, s.101
s.8, applied: 2002 c.39 Sch.2 para.3
s.12, applied: 2003 c.20 s.90, s.101
Sch.1 para.1, amended: 2003 c.31 s.7, 2003 c.42 Sch.6 para.8, Sch.7
Sch.1 para.1, repealed (in part): 2003 c.42 Sch.7

1 & 2 Eliz. 2 (1952-53)

xli. Berkshire County Council Act 1953
s.85, varied: SI 2003/2155 Sch.1 para.16

xlii. British Transport Commission Act 1953
s.52, applied: SI 2003/1615 Sch.1 para.22

vii. National Trust Act 1953
s.3, repealed (in part): 2004 c.14 Sch.1 Part 17
s.5, repealed: 2004 c.14 Sch.1 Part 17

CAP.

1 & 2 Eliz. 2 (1952-53)–cont.

2. Diocesan Stipends Funds Measure 1953
s.10, repealed: 2004 c.14 Sch.1 Part 6
s.11, repealed (in part): 2004 c.14 Sch.1 Part 6

10. Agricultural Land (Removal of Surface Soil) Act 1953
see *Staffordshire CC v Riley* [2001] EWCA Civ 257, [2002] P.L.C.R. 5 (CA), Pill, L.J.
disapplied: 2003 c.44 Sch.25 para.34
s.2, amended: 2003 c.44 Sch.37 Part 9
s.2, repealed (in part): 2003 c.44 Sch.37 Part 9

14. Prevention of Crime Act 1953
s.1, see *R. v Poulton (Sarah Jane)* [2002] EWCA Crim 2487, [2003] 4 All E.R. 869 (CA (Crim Div)), Rose, L.J.

18. Prison Act (Northern Ireland) 1953
s.10, amended: SI 2004/704 Art.3
s.15A, added: SI 2004/704 Art.4
s.19A, added: SI 2004/704 Art.5
s.19B, added: SI 2004/704 Art.6
s.26, amended: SI 2003/1247 Sch.1 para.3
s.26, repealed (in part): 2004 c.4 Sch.4
s.40, repealed: SI 2004/704 Art.7

20. Births and Deaths Registration Act 1953
see *KB v National Health Service Pensions Agency (C117/01)* [2004] All E.R. (EC) 1089 (ECJ), Judge Skouris (President)
applied: 2002 c.38 s.78, SI 2002/1419(a), 2004 c.7 Sch.3 para.7, Sch.3 para.10
referred to: 2003 c.24 s.2
s.1, enabling: SI 2003/3048
s.9, amended: 2003 c.24 Sch.1 para.1
s.9, enabling: SI 2003/3048
s.10, amended: 2002 c.38 Sch.3 para.6, Sch.5, 2003 c.24 Sch.1 para.2
s.10A, amended: 2002 c.38 Sch.3 para.7, 2003 c.24 Sch.1 para.4, Sch.1 para.5
s.10A, applied: 2004 c.7 Sch.3 para.7
s.10A, varied: 2004 c.7 Sch.3 para.7
s.10A, enabling: SI 2003/3048
s.10ZA, added: 2003 c.24 Sch.1 para.3
s.10ZA, varied: 2003 c.24 s.3
s.11, applied: SI 2004/291 Sch.4, SI 2004/478 Sch.4, SI 2004/627 Sch.2
s.14, applied: 2002 c.38 Sch.1 para.5
s.14, varied: 2004 c.7 Sch.3 para.7
s.14A, varied: 2004 c.7 Sch.3 para.7
s.15, applied: 2004 c.30 s.1, s.5
s.22, applied: 2004 c.30 s.1, s.5
s.29, amended: SI 2002/1419 Art.2
s.29A, added: SI 2002/1419 Art.2
s.30, amended: SI 2002/3076 Sch.1
s.31, amended: SI 2002/3076 Sch.1
s.33, applied: 2004 c.7 Sch.3 para.6
s.33, varied: SI 2002/3076 Sch.1
s.34, varied: 2004 c.7 Sch.3 para.10
s.39, enabling: SI 2003/3048
s.41, amended: 2004 c.33 Sch.27 para.19

CAP.

1 & 2 Eliz. 2 (1952-53)—cont.

20. Births and Deaths Registration Act 1953—cont.

s.41, enabling: SI 2003/3048

23. Accommodation Agencies Act 1953

applied: SI 2003/1376 Sch.1, SI 2003/1593 Sch.1 Part I

s.1, amended: 2003 c.44 Sch.37 Part 9

s.1, disapplied: 2003 c.44 Sch.25 para.35

26. Local Government (Miscellaneous Provisions) Act 1953

s.6, amended: 2003 c.21 Sch.17 para.22

s.18, repealed (in part): 2004 c.14 Sch.1 Part 13

s.19, repealed (in part): 2004 c.14 Sch.1 Part 13

28. Dogs (Protection of Livestock) Act 1953

s.1, amended: 2002 asp 6 Sch.1 para.4

37. Registration Service Act 1953

applied: 2002 c.38 s.78

s.18, repealed: 2004 c.14 Sch.1 Part 17

s.22, repealed (in part): 2004 c.14 Sch.1 Part 17

Sch.1 para.1, repealed: 2004 c.14 Sch.1 Part 17

Sch.1 para.4, repealed: 2004 c.14 Sch.1 Part 17

Sch.1 para.5, repealed: 2004 c.14 Sch.1 Part 17

Sch.1 para.7, repealed: 2004 c.14 Sch.1 Part 17

Sch.1 para.8, repealed: 2004 c.14 Sch.1 Part 17

Sch.1 para.10, repealed: 2004 c.14 Sch.1 Part 17

Sch.1 para.11, repealed: 2004 c.14 Sch.1 Part 17

Sch.1 para.12, repealed: 2004 c.14 Sch.1 Part 17

Sch.1 para.13, repealed: 2004 c.14 Sch.1 Part 17

Sch.1 para.14, repealed (in part): 2004 c.14 Sch.1 Part 17

Sch.1 para.15, repealed (in part): 2004 c.14 Sch.1 Part 17

37. Registration Services Act 1953

s.6, see *Hopper v Lincolnshire CC* [2002] I.C.R. 1301 (EAT), Wall, J.

49. Historic Buildings and Ancient Monuments Act 1953

s.2, repealed (in part): 2003 asp 4 Sch.4 para.2

s.3, amended: 2003 asp 4 Sch.4 para.2

s.9, amended: 2003 asp 4 Sch.4 para.2

s.9, repealed (in part): 2003 asp 4 Sch.4 para.2

52. Enemy Property Act 1953

s.4, varied: SI 2003/1633 Sch.2 para.2

2 & 3 Eliz. 2 (1953-54)

x. Forth Road Bridge Order Confirmation Act 1954

repealed: SSI 2002/178 Sch.4

CAP.

2 & 3 Eliz. 2 (1953-54)—cont.

Law Reform (Limitation of Actions, &c.) Act 1954

see *McDonnell v Congregation of Christian Brothers Trustees (formerly Irish Christian Brothers)* [2001] EWCA Civ 2095, [2002] C.P. Rep. 31 (CA), Ward, L.J.

lii. Newport Corporation Act 1954

s.61, repealed: SI 2003/2679 Sch.3

xxix. Post Office (Site and Railway) Act 1954

varied: SI 2003/1542 Art.2

1. New Housing Areas (Church Buildings) Measure 1954

s.2, repealed: 2004 c.14 Sch.1 Part 6

9. Administration of Justice (Northern Ireland) Act 1954

s.20, applied: 2002 c.29 s.203

12. Currency and Bank Notes Act 1954

s.4, repealed (in part): 2004 c.14 Sch.1 Part 17

17. Vehicles (Excise) Act (Northern Ireland) 1954

applied: SI 2002/2742 Reg.46

23. Hill Farming Act 1954

repealed: 2004 c.14 Sch.1 Part 2

32. Atomic Energy Authority Act 1954

applied: SI 2003/409 Sch.1 Part I

s.2, repealed (in part): 2004 c.20 Sch.23 Part 1

s.3, applied: 2004 c.20 Sch.8 para.7, Sch.8 para.13, Sch.10 para.7

s.6, amended: 2004 c.14 Sch.1 Part 16

s.9, repealed (in part): 2004 c.14 Sch.1 Part 16, 2004 c.20 Sch.23 Part 1

Sch.1 para.4, repealed: 2004 c.20 Sch.23 Part 1

Sch.1 para.7, applied: 2004 c.17 Sch.1 para.18, 2004 c.20 Sch.10 para.7, Sch.1 para.6

Sch.2 para.3, repealed: 2004 c.14 Sch.1 Part 16

Sch.3, repealed: 2004 c.20 Sch.23 Part 1

33 (N.I.). Interpretation Act (Northern Ireland) 1954

applied: SI 2003/431 Art.2

33. Interpretation Act (Northern Ireland) 1954

applied: 2002 c.1 (NI) Sch.1 para.1, SI 2002/2836 Art.2, SI 2002/3149 Art.2, SI 2002/3150 Art.2, SI 2002/3151 Art.2, SI 2002/3152 Art.2, SI 2002/3153 Art.2, SI 2002/3154 Art.2, SI 2002/3155 Art.2, 2003 c.32 s.73, SI 2003/410 Art.2, SI 2003/413 Art.2, SI 2003/417 Art.2, SI 2003/418 Art.2, SI 2003/419 Art.2, SI 2003/420 Art.2, SI 2003/424 Art.2, SI 2003/430 Art.2, SI 2003/435 Art.2, SI 2003/439 Art.2, SI 2003/1247 Art.2, SI 2003/1885 Art.2, SI 2003/2902 Art.2, SI 2003/2903 Art.2, SI 2003/2904 Art.2, SI 2003/3194 Art.2, SI 2003/3202 Art.2, SI 2004/310 Art.2, SI 2004/311 Art.2, SI 2004/702 Art.2, SI 2004/704 Art.2, SI 2004/707 Art.2, SI

2 & 3 Eliz. 2 (1953-54)–cont.

33. Interpretation Act (Northern Ireland) 1954–cont.

applied: 2002 c.1 (NI) Sch.1 para.1–cont.

2004/1109 Art.2, SI 2004/1272 Art.2, SI 2004/1500 Art.2, SI 2004/1501 Art.2, SI 2004/1987 Art.2, SI 2004/1988 Art.2, SR 2002/1 Reg.2, SR 2002/6 Reg.2, SR 2002/14 Reg.1, SR 2002/16 Reg.1, SR 2002/20 Reg.2, SR 2002/21 Reg.1, SR 2002/27 Reg.1, SR 2002/28 Reg.2, SR 2002/29 Reg.2, SR 2002/30 Reg.2, SR 2002/33 Reg.2, SR 2002/50 Reg.1, SR 2002/58 Reg.1, SR 2002/59 Reg.1, SR 2002/67 Reg.1, SR 2002/70 Reg.2, SR 2002/74 Reg.1, SR 2002/80 Reg.1, SR 2002/86 Reg.1, SR 2002/88 Reg.3, SR 2002/90 Reg.1, SR 2002/93 Reg.2, SR 2002/94 Reg.2, SR 2002/98 Art.1, SR 2002/99 Art.2, SR 2002/105 Reg.1, SR 2002/109 Reg.1, SR 2002/114 Reg.1, SR 2002/116 Reg.1, SR 2002/121 Reg.1, SR 2002/125 Reg.1, SR 2002/128 Reg.1, SR 2002/132 Reg.1, SR 2002/203 Reg.1, SR 2002/222 Reg.1, SR 2002/223 Reg.1, SR 2002/225 Reg.3, SR 2002/226 Reg.2, SR 2002/243 Reg.1, SR 2002/246 Reg.1, SR 2002/249 Reg.2, SR 2002/250 Reg.1, SR 2002/254 Reg.1, SR 2002/263 Reg.1, SR 2002/267 Reg.1, SR 2002/270 Reg.1, SR 2002/275 Reg.1, SR 2002/278 Reg.2, SR 2002/280 Reg.1, SR 2002/284 Reg.1, SR 2002/289 Reg.1, SR 2002/291 Reg.2, SR 2002/292 Art.1, SR 2002/295 Reg.1, SR 2002/296 Reg.2, SR 2002/297 Reg.1, SR 2002/298 Reg.1, SR 2002/299 Reg.1, SR 2002/300 Reg.2, SR 2002/301 Reg.2, SR 2002/304 Reg.1, SR 2002/309 Reg.3, SR 2002/315 Reg.1, SR 2002/322 Reg.1, SR 2002/323 Reg.1, SR 2002/327 Reg.1, SR 2002/332 Reg.1, SR 2002/334 Reg.2, SR 2002/335 Reg.2, SR 2002/339 Art.1, SR 2002/340 Reg.2, SR 2002/354 Reg.1, SR 2002/357 Reg.1, SR 2002/359 Reg.1, SR 2002/363 Reg.1, SR 2002/368 Reg.2, SR 2002/369 Reg.1, SR 2002/370 Art.1, SR 2002/395 Sch.1 para.2, SR 2002/410 Reg.1, SR 2003/1 Reg.1, SR 2003/8 Reg.1, SR 2003/28 Reg.1, SR 2003/36 Reg.2, SR 2003/37 Reg.2, SR 2003/46 Reg.2, SR 2003/52 Reg.2, SR 2003/70 Reg.1, SR 2003/79 Reg.1, SR 2003/80 Reg.1, SR 2003/95 Art.2, SR 2003/105 Reg.2, SR 2003/106 Reg.2, SR 2003/107 Reg.1, SR 2003/108 Reg.1, SR 2003/109 Reg.2, SR 2003/115 Reg.1, SR 2003/117 Reg.1, SR 2003/118 Reg.1, SR 2003/119 Reg.2, SR 2003/123 Reg.1, SR 2003/136 Reg.2, SR 2003/150 Art.1, SR 2003/154 Reg.1, SR 2003/155 Art.2, SR 2003/164 Reg.1, SR 2003/165 Reg.2, SR 2003/167 Reg.2, SR 2003/187 Reg.1, SR 2003/189 Reg.1, SR 2003/192 Reg.2, SR 2003/195 Reg.1, SR 2003/196 Reg.1, SR 2003/

206 Reg.2, SR 2003/208 Reg.2, SR 2003/213 Reg.1, SR 2003/215 Reg.1, SR 2003/219 r.1, SR 2003/244 Reg.1, SR 2003/264 Reg.1, SR 2003/278 Reg.1, SR 2003/287 Reg.1, SR 2003/349 Reg.1, SR 2003/351 Reg.1, SR 2003/353 Reg.2, SR 2003/360 Reg.2

2 & 3 Eliz. 2 (1953-54)–cont.

33. Interpretation Act (Northern Ireland) 1954–cont.

disapplied: SR 2003/122 r.4

s.1, applied: SI 2003/419 Sch.1 para.9

s.7, applied: SI 2004/702 Art.77

s.17, applied: SI 2003/431 Art.48

s.17, referred to: SI 2003/435 Art.46

s.18, applied: SR 2002/352 Sch.6 para.23

s.18, varied: 2004 c.19 s.24

s.19, applied: SI 2003/410 Sch.1 para.1, SI 2003/435 Sch.1 para.1

s.20, applied: 2002 c.26 Sch.12 para.2

s.20, disapplied: SR 2002/6 Reg.2, SR 2002/88 Reg.3

s.20, varied: SI 2002/3153 Art.23, SI 2004/1500 Art.31, SI 2004/1769 Sch.4 para.1, SR 2003/46 Reg.33, SR 2003/115 Reg.24

33 (N.I.). Interpretation Act (Northern Ireland) 1954

s.21, applied: SI 2003/3075 Reg.18

33. Interpretation Act (Northern Ireland) 1954

s.24, applied: SR 2002/12 r.14, SR 2003/17 r.12

s.24, varied: SI 2004/1109 Art.2

s.26, amended: 2002 c.26 Sch.4 para.9

s.26, applied: 2002 c.26 Sch.4 para.2

s.28, applied: SI 2002/3153 Sch.4 para.1

s.28, referred to: SI 2003/435 Art.48, SR 2002/353 Reg.22

s.29, applied: SI 2002/3153 Sch.4 para.1

s.29, referred to: SI 2003/435 Art.48, SR 2002/265 Reg.18, SR 2002/353 Reg.22

s.39, disapplied: SR 2002/74 Reg.1, SR 2002/127 Reg.1

s.41, applied: 2002 c.21 s.66, 2002 c.26 s.90, SI 2002/790 Sch.1 para.4, Sch.2 para.3, Sch.3 para.3, Sch.3 para.4, Sch.3 para.7, 2003 c.33 s.28, 2004 c.7 s.24, 2004 c.17 s.2, s.12

33 (N.I.). Interpretation Act (Northern Ireland) 1954

s.42, applied: SI 2003/3075 Reg.18

33. Interpretation Act (Northern Ireland) 1954

s.42, amended: 2002 c.26 Sch.13

s.44, amended: SI 2003/418 Sch.2 para.1

39. Agriculture (Miscellaneous Provisions) Act 1954

s.3, repealed: 2004 c.14 Sch.1 Part 3

s.6, repealed (in part): 2004 c.14 Sch.1 Part 2

CAP.

2 & 3 Eliz. 2 (1953-54)-cont.

40. Protection of Animals (Amendment) Act 1954
s.2, amended: 2003 c.44 Sch.26 para.14

44. Finance Act 1954
s.34, amended: 2004 c.14 Sch.1 Part 9
s.34, repealed (in part): 2004 c.14 Sch.1 Part 9
s.35, repealed (in part): 2004 c.14 Sch.1 Part 9

46. Protection of Animals (Anaesthetics) Act 1954
s.1, enabling: SI 2002/3215, SI 2003/1328, SI 2003/1844, SSI 2003/476
Sch.1 para.6, amended: SI 2003/1328 Art.2, SI 2003/1844 Art.2
Sch.1 para.6, substituted: SSI 2003/476 Art.2

56. Landlord and Tenant Act 1954
see *Adegbulu v Southwark LBC* [2003] EWHC 1930, [2003] 2 P. & C.R. D20 (Ch D), Bartley Jones Q.C.; see *Brighton and Hove City Council v Collinson* [2004] EWCA Civ 678, [2004] L. & T.R. 24 (CA), Brooke, L.J.; see *Pankhania v Hackney LBC* [2002] N.P.C. 123 (Ch D), Rex Tedd Q.C.
applied: SI 2004/1005 Sch.2
Part I, see *R. (on the application of Morris) v London Rent Assessment Committee* [2002] EWCA Civ 276, [2002] H.L.R. 48 (CA), Mummery, L.J.
Part I, applied: 2002 c.15 s.77
Part I s.17, see *Tiffany Investments Ltd v Bircham & Co Nominees (No.2) Ltd* [2003] EWHC 143, [2003] 2 P. & C.R. 29 (Ch D), Lindsay, J.
Part II, see *Hawkesbrook Leisure Ltd v Reece-Jones Partnership* [2003] EWHC 3333, [2004] L. & T.R. 28 (Ch D), Etherton, J.; see *Hazel v Akhtar* [2001] EWCA Civ 1883, [2002] 2 P. & C.R. 17 (CA), Sir Anthony Evans; see *Pankhania v Hackney LBC (Damages)* [2004] EWHC 323, [2004] 1 E.G.L.R. 135 (Ch D), Geoffrey Vos Q.C.; see *Walji v Mount Cook Land Ltd* [2002] 1 P. & C.R. 13 (CA), Charles, J.
Part II, applied: 2002 c.15 s.75, 2003 c.14 Sch.17A para.9, Sch.5 para.6, SI 2004/1005 Sch.1, Sch.2
Part 2, see *Aran Caterers Ltd v Stepien Lake Gilbert & Paling (A Firm)* [2002] 1 E.G.L.R. 69 (Ch D), Judge Howarth
s., see *Zarvos v Pradhan* [2003] EWCA Civ 208, [2003] 2 P.& C.R. 9 (CA), Ward, L.J.
s.s.30, see *Bentley & Skinner (Bond Street Jewellers) Ltd v Searchmap Ltd* [2003] EWHC 1621, [2003] 2 P. & C.R. D18 (Ch D), Lightman, J.
s.3, see *St Ermins Property Co Ltd v Patel (No.2)* [2001] EWCA Civ 804, [2002] H.L.R. 11 (CA), Sir Martin Nourse
s.4, see *St Ermins Property Co Ltd v Patel (No.2)* [2001] EWCA Civ 804, [2002] H.L.R. 11 (CA), Sir Martin Nourse
s.4, applied: SI 2004/1005 Sch.2
s.14A, added: SI 2003/3096 Sch.5 para.2

CAP.

2 & 3 Eliz. 2 (1953-54)-cont.

56. Landlord and Tenant Act 1954-*cont.*
s.23, see *Hawkesbrook Leisure Ltd v Reece-Jones Partnership* [2003] EWHC 3333, [2004] L. & T.R. 28 (Ch D), Etherton, J.
s.23, amended: SI 2003/3096 Art.13
s.24, see *Bishopsgate Space Management Ltd v London Underground Ltd* [2004] 2 E.G.L.R. 175 (Lands Tr), George Bartlett Q.C. (President); see *Pennycook v Shaws (EAL) Ltd* [2004] EWCA Civ 100, [2004] Ch. 296 (CA), Thorpe, L.J.
s.24, amended: SI 2003/3096 Art.3
s.24, applied: SI 2003/3096 Art.29
s.24, referred to: SI 2004/1005 Sch.2
s.24, repealed (in part): SI 2003/3096 Sch.6
s.24A, referred to: SI 2004/1005 Sch.2
s.24A, substituted: SI 2003/3096 Art.18
s.24B, referred to: SI 2004/1005 Sch.2
s.24C, referred to: SI 2004/1005 Sch.2
s.24D, referred to: SI 2004/1005 Sch.2
s.25, see *Barclays Bank Plc v Bee* [2001] EWCA Civ 1126, [2002] 1 W.L.R. 332 (CA), Aldous, L.J.; see *Beanby Estates Ltd v Egg Stores (Stamford Hill) Ltd* [2003] EWHC 1252, [2003] 1 W.L.R. 2064 (Ch D), Neuberger, J.; see *Bentley & Skinner (Bond Street Jewellers) Ltd v Searchmap Ltd* [2003] EWHC 1621, [2003] 2 P. & C.R. D18 (Ch D), Lightman, J.; see *Blunden v Frogmore Investments Ltd* [2002] EWCA Civ 573, [2003] 2 P. & C.R. 6 (CA), Robert Walker, L.J.; see *CA Webber (Transport) Ltd v Railtrack Plc* [2003] EWCA Civ 1167, [2004] 1 W.L.R. 320 (CA), Peter Gibson, L.J.; see *Pennycook v Shaws (EAL) Ltd* [2004] EWCA Civ 100, [2004] Ch. 296 (CA), Thorpe, L.J.; see *Surrey CC v Single Horse Properties Ltd* [2002] EWCA Civ 367, [2002] 1 W.L.R. 2106 (CA), Arden, L.J.
s.25, amended: SI 2003/3096 Art.4, Art.11
s.25, applied: SI 2003/3096 Art.29, SI 2004/1005 Sch.1, Sch.2
s.25, referred to: SI 2004/1005 Sch.2
s.25, repealed (in part): SI 2003/3096 Sch.6
s.26, amended: SI 2003/3096 Art.12, Sch.5 para.3
s.26, applied: SI 2003/3096 Art.29, SI 2004/1005 Sch.1, Sch.2
s.26, referred to: SI 2004/1005 Sch.2
s.27, amended: SI 2003/3096 Art.25, Sch.6
s.27, applied: SI 2003/3096 Art.29
s.27, referred to: SI 2004/1005 Sch.2
s.28, see *Bishopsgate Space Management Ltd v London Underground Ltd* [2004] 2 E.G.L.R. 175 (Lands Tr), George Bartlett Q.C. (President)
s.28, referred to: SI 2004/1005 Sch.2
s.29, see *Parsons v George* [2004] EWCA Civ 912, [2004] 1 W.L.R. 3264 (CA), Sir Andrew Morritt V.C.; see *Pennycook v*

CAP.

2 & 3 Eliz. 2 (1953-54)–cont.
56. Landlord and Tenant Act 1954–*cont.*
s.29–*cont.*

Shaws (EAL) Ltd [2004] EWCA Civ 100, [2004] Ch. 296 (CA),Thorpe, L.J.

s.29, referred to: SI 2004/1005 Sch.2

s.29, substituted: SI 2003/3096 Art.5

s.29A, added: SI 2003/3096 Art.10

s.29A, applied: SI 2004/1005 Sch.2

s.29A, referred to: SI 2004/1005 Sch.2

s.29B, added: SI 2003/3096 Art.10

s.29B, referred to: SI 2004/1005 Sch.2

s.30, see *Ambrose v Kaye* [2002] EWCA Civ 91, [2002] C.P. Rep. 33 (CA), Chadwick, L.J.; see *Hazel v Akhtar* [2001] EWCA Civ 1883, [2002] 2 P. & C.R. 17 (CA), Sir Anthony Evans; see *Ivorygrove Ltd v Global Grange Ltd* [2003] EWHC 1409, [2003] 1 W.L.R. 2090 (Ch D), Lawrence Collins, J.; see *Marazzi v Global Grange Ltd* [2002] EWHC 3010, [2003] 2 E.G.L.R. 42 (Ch D), Park, J.; see *Pumperninks of Piccadilly Ltd v Land Securities Plc* [2002] EWCA Civ 621, [2002] Ch. 332 (CA), Charles, J.; see *Yoga for Health Foundation v Guest* [2002] EWHC 2658, [2002] N.P.C. 161 (Ch D), Hart, J.

s.30, amended: SI 2003/3096 Art.6, Art.14

s.30, applied: 2002 c.iv s.14

s.30, disapplied: 2002 c.iii s.14

s.30, referred to: SI 2004/1005 Sch.2

s.30, repealed (in part): SI 2003/3096 Sch.6

s.31, amended: SI 2003/3096 Art.7

s.31A, see *Pumperninks of Piccadilly Ltd v Land Securities Plc* [2002] EWCA Civ 621, [2002] Ch. 332 (CA), Charles, J.

s.31A, amended: SI 2003/3096 Art.8

s.31A, referred to: SI 2004/1005 Sch.2

s.33, amended: SI 2003/3096 Art.26

s.34, see *J Murphy & Sons Ltd v Railtrack Plc* [2002] EWCA Civ 679, [2003] 1 P. & C.R. 7 (CA), Peter Gibson, L.J.

s.34, amended: SI 2003/3096 Art.9, Art.15

s.34, referred to: SI 2004/1005 Sch.2

s.35, amended: SI 2003/3096 Art.27

s.35, referred to: SI 2004/1005 Sch.2

s.37, see *Evis v Commission for New Towns* [2002] 2 E.G.L.R. 167 (Lands Tr), George Bartlett Q.C.

s.37, amended: SI 2003/3096 Art.19

s.37, applied: SI 2004/1005 Sch.2

s.37A, added: SI 2003/3096 Art.20

s.38, amended: SI 2003/3096 Art.21, Sch.5 para.4

s.38, applied: SI 2003/3096 Art.29

s.38, repealed (in part): SI 2003/3096 Sch.6

s.38A, added: SI 2003/3096 Art.22

s.38A, applied: SI 2003/3096 Sch.4 para.2, Sch.4 para.3, Sch.4 para.4, Sch.4 para.5

s.38A, referred to: SI 2003/3096 Art.29, Sch.4 para.1, Sch.4 para.2, Sch.4 para.4

CAP.

2 & 3 Eliz. 2 (1953-54)–cont.
56. Landlord and Tenant Act 1954–*cont.*

s.40, applied: SI 2003/3096 Art.29, SI 2004/1005 Sch.1, Sch.2

s.40, referred to: SI 2004/1005 Sch.2

s.40, substituted: SI 2003/3096 Art.23

s.40A, added: SI 2003/3096 Art.24

s.40B, added: SI 2003/3096 Art.24

s.40B, referred to: SI 2004/1005 Sch.2

s.41A, amended: SI 2003/3096 Sch.5 para.5

s.42, amended: SI 2003/3096 Art.16, Sch.6

s.44, amended: SI 2003/3096 Art.27

s.44, applied: SI 2004/1005 Sch.1

s.44, referred to: SI 2004/1005 Sch.2

s.46, amended: SI 2003/3096 Art.17, Sch.5 para.6

s.46, referred to: SI 2004/1005 Sch.2

s.46, substituted: SI 2003/3096 Art.17

s.55, repealed: SI 2003/3096 Sch.6

s.57, amended: SI 2003/3096 Sch.5 para.7

s.57, applied: SI 2004/1005 Sch.1, Sch.2

s.57, referred to: SI 2004/1005 Sch.2

s.58, amended: SI 2003/3096 Sch.5 para.7

s.58, applied: SI 2004/1005 Sch.1, Sch.2

s.59, amended: SI 2003/3096 Sch.5 para.8

s.59, referred to: SI 2004/1005 Sch.2

s.60, applied: SI 2004/1005 Sch.1, Sch.2

s.60A, applied: SI 2004/1005 Sch.1, Sch.2

s.64, see *Surrey CC v Single Horse Properties Ltd* [2002] EWCA Civ 367, [2002] 1 W.L.R. 2106 (CA), Arden, L.J.

s.64, amended: SI 2003/3096 Sch.5 para.9

s.66, enabling: SI 2002/1715, SI 2002/3187, SI 2002/3209, SI 2003/991, SI 2004/1005

s.67, amended: SI 2003/3096 Sch.6

s.67, referred to: SI 2004/1005 Sch.2

Sch.2, referred to: SI 2004/1005 Sch.2

Sch.3 para.1, amended: 2004 c.33 Sch.8 para.2

Sch.6 para.6, applied: SI 2004/1005 Sch.1, Sch.2

58. Charitable Trusts (Validation) Act 1954
s.4, repealed (in part): 2004 c.14 Sch.1 Part 17

61. Pharmacy Act 1954
applied: 2002 c.17 s.26, SI 2002/2376 Reg.4

s.2, amended: SI 2003/3148 Reg.8

s.4, see *R. (on the application of Mahmood) v Royal Pharmaceutical Society of Great Britain* [2001] EWCA Civ 1245, [2002] 1 W.L.R. 879 (CA), Kennedy, L.J.

s.4, amended: SI 2003/3148 Reg.8

s.4A, amended: SI 2003/3148 Reg.8, SI 2004/1947 Reg.13

s.4A, applied: SI 2003/835 Reg.9, SI 2004/2152 Reg.9

s.4A, repealed (in part): SI 2003/3148 Reg.8

s.4B, added: SI 2003/3148 Reg.8

s.8, amended: SI 2003/3148 Reg.8

s.8, applied: 2002 c.17 s.29

s.15, amended: 2003 c.43 Sch.12 para.1

CAP.

2 & 3 Eliz. 2 (1953-54)–cont.

61. Pharmacy Act 1954–*cont.*
s.16, see *R. (on the application of Mahmood) v Royal Pharmaceutical Society of Great Britain* [2001] EWCA Civ 1245, [2002] 1 W.L.R. 879 (CA), Kennedy, L.J.
s.17, amended: 2004 c.33 Sch.27 para.20
s.24, amended: SI 2003/3148 Reg.8, SI 2004/1947 Reg.13
s.24, referred to: SSI 2002/190 Reg.3
Sch.1A, amended: SI 2004/1947 Reg.13
Sch.1A, substituted: SI 2003/3148 Sch.3
Sch.1 para.3A, added: 2003 c.43 Sch.12 para.1
Sch.1A para.1, substituted: SI 2003/3148 Sch.3
Sch.1A para.2, substituted: SI 2003/3148 Sch.3
Sch.1A para.3, substituted: SI 2003/3148 Sch.3
Sch.1A para.4, substituted: SI 2003/3148 Sch.3
Sch.1A para.5, substituted: SI 2003/3148 Sch.3
Sch.1A para.6, substituted: SI 2003/3148 Sch.3
Sch.1A para.7, substituted: SI 2003/3148 Sch.3
Sch.1A para.8, substituted: SI 2003/3148 Sch.3
Sch.1A para.9, substituted: SI 2003/3148 Sch.3
Sch.1A para.10, substituted: SI 2003/3148 Sch.3
Sch.1A para.11, substituted: SI 2003/3148 Sch.3

64. Transport Charges &c (Miscellaneous Provisions) Act 1954
s.11, repealed: 2004 c.14 Sch.1 Part 14
s.13, referred to: SI 2003/1615 Sch.1 para.2

66. Civil Defence (Armed Forces) Act 1954
repealed: 2004 c.36 Sch.3

70. Mines and Quarries Act 1954
applied: SSI 2004/406 Sch.5 para.4.5
s.180, applied: SI 2002/2776 Reg.3

3 & 4 Eliz. 2 (1954-55)

6. Miscellaneous Financial Provisions Act 1955
s.4, repealed (in part): 2004 c.14 Sch.1 Part 14
s.5, amended: SI 2002/2521 Sch.2 Part I, SI 2004/1662 Sch.1 para.14
s.5, repealed (in part): SI 2004/1662 Sch.1 para.14

18. Army Act 1955
applied: 2003 c.41 s.3, s.5, s.71, s.73, 2003 c.44 Sch.7 para.6, SI 2003/2273 Art.12, SSI 2003/176 Art.3, 2004 c.30 s.39, Sch.4 para.5

CAP.

3 & 4 Eliz. 2 (1954-55)–cont.

18. Army Act 1955–*cont.*
referred to: SI 2002/1820 Art.2, 2003 c.44 s.337, SI 2004/1496 Art.2
s.19, amended: 2003 c.44 Sch.37 Part 9
s.19, disapplied: 2003 c.44 Sch.25 para.36
s.34A, amended: 2003 c.20 Sch.7 para.9
s.44B, amended: 2003 c.21 Sch.17 para.23, Sch.19
s.61, amended: 2003 c.44 Sch.32 para.155
s.70, amended: 2003 c.42 Sch.6 para.9, Sch.7
s.70, applied: 2003 c.42 s.137, Sch.3 para.93, Sch.5 para.172, 2003 c.44 s.233, s.329, 2004 c.28 s.8
s.71A, applied: 2003 c.42 s.131
s.71AA, applied: 2003 c.42 s.131
s.76, applied: SI 2004/1937 Art.4
s.76AA, applied: SI 2004/1937 Art.4
s.76B, applied: SI 2004/1937 Art.4
s.83, applied: SI 2004/1937 Art.4
s.83A, applied: SI 2004/1937 Art.3
s.83ZA, amended: SI 2004/1937 Art.5
s.83ZC, enabling: SI 2004/1950
s.83ZD, amended: SI 2004/1937 Art.5
s.83ZJ, enabling: SI 2004/1950
s.83ZK, enabling: SI 2004/1937
s.92, enabling: SI 2002/230
s.99, amended: 2003 c.44 Sch.36 para.81
s.103, enabling: SI 2002/230
s.113C, amended: 2003 c.44 s.272
s.116, substituted: 2004 c.28 Sch.3 para.1
s.116B, applied: SI 2004/293 Sch.4 para.4
s.131, applied: SI 2003/2273 Sch.1 para.10
s.138, applied: SI 2003/336 Sch.1 Part 2
s.143, enabling: SI 2002/230
s.150, amended: 2004 c.33 Sch.26 para.28
s.151, amended: 2004 c.33 Sch.26 para.29
s.161, amended: 2003 c.44 Sch.37 Part 9
s.161, disapplied: 2003 c.44 Sch.25 para.37
s.171, amended: 2003 c.44 Sch.37 Part 9
s.171, disapplied: 2003 c.44 Sch.25 para.38
s.187, amended: 2003 c.44 Sch.3 para.37
s.189, amended: 2002 c.26 Sch.4 para.10, 2003 c.39 Sch.8 para.95
s.191, amended: 2003 c.44 Sch.37 Part 9
s.191, disapplied: 2003 c.44 Sch.25 para.39
s.193, amended: 2003 c.44 Sch.37 Part 9
s.193, disapplied: 2003 c.44 Sch.25 para.40
s.196, amended: 2003 c.44 Sch.37 Part 9
s.196, disapplied: 2003 c.44 Sch.25 para.41
s.197, amended: 2003 c.44 Sch.37 Part 9
s.197, disapplied: 2003 c.44 Sch.25 para.42
s.199, amended: 2003 c.39 Sch.8 para.95
s.225, amended: 2002 c.39 Sch.2 para.1, 2004 c.28 Sch.3 para.2
s.225, applied: 2003 c.20 s.90, s.101
s.225, enabling: SI 2004/1937
Sch.5A para.5, applied: 2003 c.42 s.134
Sch.5A para.10, applied: 2003 c.42 s.131

3 & 4 Eliz. 2 (1954-55)–cont.

19. Air Force Act 1955

applied: 2003 c.41 s.3, s.5, s.71, s.73, 2003 c.44 Sch.7 para.7, SI 2003/2273 Art.12, SSI 2003/176 Art.3, 2004 c.30 s.39, Sch.4 para.5

referred to: SI 2002/1820 Art.2, 2003 c.41 s.216, 2003 c.44 s.337, SI 2004/1496 Art.2

s.19, amended: 2003 c.44 Sch.37 Part 9Sch.25 para.43

s.22, enabling: SI 2003/786

s.23, enabling: SI 2003/786

s.34A, amended: 2003 c.20 Sch.7 para.10

s.44B, amended: 2003 c.21 Sch.17 para.24, Sch.19

s.61, amended: 2003 c.44 Sch.32 para.156

s.70, amended: 2003 c.42 Sch.6 para.10, Sch.7

s.70, applied: 2003 c.42 s.137, Sch.3 para.93, Sch.5 para.172, 2003 c.44 s.233, s.329, 2004 c.28 s.8

s.71A, applied: 2003 c.42 s.131

s.71AA, applied: 2003 c.42 s.131

s.76, applied: SI 2004/1937 Art.4

s.76AA, applied: SI 2004/1937 Art.4

s.76B, applied: SI 2004/1937 Art.4

s.83, applied: SI 2004/1937 Art.4

s.83A, applied: SI 2004/1937 Art.3

s.83ZA, amended: SI 2004/1937 Art.5

s.83ZC, enabling: SI 2004/1951

s.83ZD, amended: SI 2004/1937 Art.5

s.83ZJ, enabling: SI 2004/1951

s.83ZK, enabling: SI 2004/1937

s.92, enabling: SI 2002/229

s.99, amended: 2003 c.44 Sch.36 para.82

s.103, enabling: SI 2002/229

s.113C, amended: 2003 c.44 s.272

s.116, substituted: 2004 c.28 Sch.3 para.1

s.131, applied: SI 2003/2273 Sch.1 para.10

s.138, applied: SI 2003/336 Sch.1 Part 2

s.143, enabling: SI 2002/229

s.150, amended: 2004 c.33 Sch.26 para.30

s.151, amended: 2004 c.33 Sch.26 para.31

s.161, amended: 2003 c.44 Sch.37 Part 9

s.161, disapplied: 2003 c.44 Sch.25 para.44

s.171, amended: 2003 c.44 Sch.37 Part 9

s.171, disapplied: 2003 c.44 Sch.25 para.45

s.187, amended: 2003 c.44 Sch.3 para.38

s.189, amended: 2002 c.26 Sch.4 para.11, 2003 c.39 Sch.8 para.96

s.191, amended: 2003 c.44 Sch.37 Part 9

s.191, disapplied: 2003 c.44 Sch.25 para.46

s.193, amended: 2003 c.44 Sch.37 Part 9

s.193, disapplied: 2003 c.44 Sch.25 para.47

s.196, amended: 2003 c.44 Sch.37 Part 9

s.196, disapplied: 2003 c.44 Sch.25 para.48

s.197, amended: 2003 c.44 Sch.37 Part 9

s.197, disapplied: 2003 c.44 Sch.25 para.49

s.199, amended: 2003 c.39 Sch.8 para.96

3 & 4 Eliz. 2 (1954-55)–cont.

19. Air Force Act 1955–*cont.*

s.223, amended: 2002 c.39 Sch.2 para.1, 2004 c.28 Sch.3 para.2

s.223, enabling: SI 2004/1937

Sch.5A para.5, applied: 2003 c.42 s.134

Sch.5A para.10, applied: 2003 c.42 s.131

22. Pensions (India, Pakistan and Burma) Act 1955

applied: 2003 c.1 s.654

28. Children and Young Persons (Harmful Publications) Act 1955

s.2, amended: 2003 c.44 Sch.26 para.15

4 & 5 Eliz. 2 (1955-56)

xl. Gloucestershire County Council Act 1956

s.97, varied: SI 2003/2155 Sch.1 para.16

xlix. Leicester Corporation Act 1956

s.96, varied: SI 2003/2155 Sch.1 para.16

5. Agriculture (Silo Subsidies) Act 1956

repealed: 2004 c.14 Sch.1 Part 2

49. Agriculture (Safety, Health and Welfare Provisions) Act 1956

s.7, repealed: 2004 c.14 Sch.1 Part 2

60. Valuation and Rating (Scotland) Act 1956

referred to: SSI 2003/187 Art.9

s.6, applied: SSI 2003/160 Reg.15, SSI 2004/92 Reg.3

s.6, varied: SSI 2003/187 Art.7

s.6A, amended: 2003 asp 1 s.32

s.7B, applied: SSI 2003/143 Art.2, SSI 2003/160 Reg.15, SSI 2004/92 Reg.3

s.7B, enabling: SSI 2003/143

s.8C, added: 2003 asp 1 s.30

62. Hotel Proprietors Act 1956

s.2, applied: 2004 c.i s.24

s.2, varied: 2004 c.i s.24

Sch.1, applied: 2004 c.i s.24

Sch.1, varied: 2004 c.i s.24

69. Sexual Offences Act 1956

s.1, see *R. v K (Age of Consent: Reasonable Belief)* [2001] UKHL 41, [2002] 1 A.C. 462 (HL), Lord Bingham of Cornhill

s.1, applied: SI 2002/896 Sch.1 para.9, 2003 c.42 Sch.3 para.1, 2003 c.44 Sch.4 para.7, Sch.4 para.8, Sch.5 para.6, Sch.5 para.7, Sch.15 para.66, SI 2003/1184 Sch.2 para.1, SSI 2003/19 Sch.5 para.1

s.1, repealed: 2003 c.42 Sch.7

s.2, applied: 2002 c.29 Sch.2 para.8, SI 2002/896 Sch.1 para.10, 2003 c.44 Sch.15 para.67

s.2, repealed: 2003 c.42 Sch.7

s.3, applied: 2002 c.29 Sch.2 para.8, SI 2002/896 Sch.1 para.10, 2003 c.44 Sch.15 para.68

s.3, repealed: 2003 c.42 Sch.7

s.4, applied: SI 2002/896 Sch.1 para.11, 2003 c.44 Sch.15 para.69

4 & 5 Eliz. 2 (1955-56)–cont.

69. Sexual Offences Act 1956–cont.

s.4, repealed: 2003 c.42 Sch.7

s.5, applied: SI 2002/896 Sch.1 para.12, 2003 c.42 Sch.3 para.2, 2003 c.44 Sch.4 para.9, Sch.5 para.8, Sch.15 para.70, SI 2003/1184 Sch.2 para.2

s.5, repealed: 2003 c.42 Sch.7

s.6, see *Attorney General's Reference (No.42 of 2003), Re* [2003] EWCA Crim 3068, [2004] 1 Cr.App.R.(S.) 79 (CA (Crim Div)), Kay, L.J.; see *R. v Figg (Joseph Albert)* [2003] EWCA Crim 2751, [2004] 1 Cr. App. R. (S.) 68 (CA (Crim Div)), Leveson, J.; see *R. v J* [2002] EWCA Crim 2983, [2003] 1 W.L.R. 1590 (CA (Crim Div)), Potter, L.J.; see *R. v J* [2004] UKHL 42, [2004] 3 W.L.R. 1019 (HL), Lord Bingham of Cornhill; see *R. v Kirk (Craig)* [2002] EWCA Crim 1580, Times, June 26, 2002 (CA (Crim Div)), Judge, L.J.

s.6, applied: SI 2002/896 Sch.1 para.13, 2003 c.42 Sch.3 para.3, 2003 c.44 Sch.15 para.71, SI 2003/1184 Sch.2 para.3

s.6, disapplied: SSI 2003/19 Sch.5 para.2

s.6, repealed: 2003 c.42 Sch.7

s.7, applied: SI 2002/896 Sch.1 para.14, 2003 c.44 Sch.15 para.72

s.7, repealed: 2003 c.42 Sch.7

s.9, applied: 2002 c.29 Sch.2 para.8, SI 2002/896 Sch.1 para.15, 2003 c.44 Sch.15 para.73

s.9, repealed: 2003 c.42 Sch.7

s.10, applied: SI 2002/896 Sch.1 para.16, 2003 c.42 Sch.3 para.4, 2003 c.44 Sch.4 para.10, Sch.5 para.9, Sch.15 para.74, SI 2003/1184 Sch.2 para.4

s.10, referred to: 2002 c.38 s.74

s.10, repealed: 2003 c.42 Sch.7

s.11, applied: SI 2002/896 Sch.1 para.17, 2003 c.44 Sch.15 para.75, SI 2003/1184 Sch.2 para.5

s.11, referred to: 2002 c.38 s.74

s.11, repealed: 2003 c.42 Sch.7

s.12, applied: SI 2002/896 Sch.1 para.18, 2003 c.42 Sch.3 para.5, Sch.4 para.1, SI 2003/1184 Sch.2 para.6

s.12, disapplied: SSI 2003/19 Sch.5 para.2

s.12, repealed: 2003 c.42 Sch.7

s.13, applied: SI 2002/896 Sch.1 para.19, 2003 c.42 Sch.3 para.6, Sch.4 para.1, SI 2003/1184 Sch.2 para.7

s.13, disapplied: SSI 2003/19 Sch.5 para.2

s.13, repealed: 2003 c.42 Sch.7

s.14, see *R. v Figg (Joseph Albert)* [2003] EWCA Crim 2751, [2004] 1 Cr. App. R. (S.) 68 (CA (Crim Div)), Leveson, J.; see *R. v J* [2002] EWCA Crim 2983, [2003] 1 W.L.R. 1590 (CA (Crim Div)), Potter, L.J.; see *R. v J* [2004] UKHL 42, [2004] 3 W.L.R. 1019 (HL), Lord Bingham of Cornhill; see *R. v K (Age of Consent: Reasonable Belief)* [2001] UKHL 41,

4 & 5 Eliz. 2 (1955-56)–cont.

69. Sexual Offences Act 1956–cont.

s.14–cont.

[2002] 1 A.C. 462 (HL), Lord Bingham of Cornhill

s.14, applied: SI 2002/896 Sch.1 para.20, 2003 c.42 Sch.3 para.7, 2003 c.44 Sch.15 para.76, SI 2003/1184 Sch.2 para.8

s.14, repealed: 2003 c.42 Sch.7

s.15, applied: SI 2002/896 Sch.1 para.20, 2003 c.42 Sch.3 para.8, 2003 c.44 Sch.15 para.77, SI 2003/1184 Sch.2 para.9

s.15, repealed: 2003 c.42 Sch.7

s.16, applied: SI 2002/896 Sch.1 para.21, 2003 c.42 Sch.3 para.9, 2003 c.44 Sch.15 para.78, SI 2003/1184 Sch.2 para.10

s.16, repealed: 2003 c.42 Sch.7

s.17, applied: SI 2002/896 Sch.1 para.22, 2003 c.44 Sch.15 para.79

s.17, repealed: 2003 c.42 Sch.7

s.19, applied: SI 2002/896 Sch.1 para.23, 2003 c.44 Sch.15 para.80

s.19, repealed: 2003 c.42 Sch.7

s.20, applied: SI 2002/896 Sch.1 para.23, 2003 c.44 Sch.15 para.81

s.20, repealed: 2003 c.42 Sch.7

s.21, applied: SI 2002/896 Sch.1 para.24, 2003 c.44 Sch.15 para.82

s.21, repealed: 2003 c.42 Sch.7

s.22, applied: 2002 c.29 Sch.2 para.8, SI 2002/896 Sch.1 para.25, 2003 c.44 Sch.15 para.83

s.22, repealed: 2003 c.42 Sch.7

s.23, applied: SI 2002/896 Sch.1 para.26, 2003 c.44 Sch.15 para.84

s.23, repealed: 2003 c.42 Sch.7

s.24, applied: 2002 c.29 Sch.2 para.8, SI 2002/896 Sch.1 para.27, 2003 c.44 Sch.15 para.85

s.24, repealed: 2003 c.42 Sch.7

s.25, applied: SI 2002/896 Sch.1 para.28, 2003 c.44 Sch.15 para.86

s.25, repealed: 2003 c.42 Sch.7

s.26, applied: SI 2002/896 Sch.1 para.28, 2003 c.44 Sch.15 para.87

s.26, repealed: 2003 c.42 Sch.7

s.27, applied: SI 2002/896 Sch.1 para.29, 2003 c.44 Sch.15 para.88

s.27, repealed: 2003 c.42 Sch.7

s.28, amended: 2002 c.38 Sch.3 para.8, Sch.5

s.28, applied: 2002 c.29 Sch.2 para.8, SI 2002/896 Sch.1 para.30, 2003 c.42 Sch.3 para.10, 2003 c.44 Sch.15 para.89

s.28, repealed: 2003 c.42 Sch.7

s.29, applied: 2002 c.29 Sch.2 para.8, SI 2002/896 Sch.1 para.31, 2003 c.44 Sch.15 para.90

s.29, repealed: 2003 c.42 Sch.7

s.30, applied: 2002 c.29 Sch.2 para.8, SI 2002/896 Sch.1 para.32

4 & 5 Eliz. 2 (1955-56)–cont.

69. Sexual Offences Act 1956–*cont.*
s.30, repealed: 2003 c.42 Sch.7
s.31, applied: 2002 c.29 Sch.2 para.8, SI 2002/896 Sch.1 para.33
s.31, repealed: 2003 c.42 Sch.7
s.32, applied: 2003 c.44 Sch.15 para.91
s.32, repealed: 2003 c.42 Sch.7
s.33, applied: 2002 c.29 Sch.2 para.8, 2003 c.44 Sch.15 para.92
s.33A, added: 2003 c.42 s.55
s.34, applied: 2002 c.29 Sch.2 para.8
s.36, amended: 2003 c.42 Sch.1 para.1
s.37, see *R. v J* [2004] UKHL 42, [2004] 3 W.L.R. 1019 (HL), Lord Bingham of Cornhill
s.41, repealed: 2003 c.42 Sch.7
s.42, repealed: 2003 c.42 Sch.7
s.43, repealed: 2003 c.42 Sch.7
s.44, repealed: 2003 c.42 Sch.7
s.45, repealed: 2003 c.42 Sch.7
s.46, repealed: 2003 c.42 Sch.7
s.46A, repealed: 2003 c.42 Sch.7
s.47, repealed: 2003 c.42 Sch.7
Sch.2 Part I, amended: 2003 c.42 Sch.7
Sch.2 Part II, added: 2003 c.42 s.55
Sch.2 Part II, amended: 2003 c.42 Sch.7
Sch.2 para.10, see *R. v J* [2004] UKHL 42, [2004] 3 W.L.R. 1019 (HL), Lord Bingham of Cornhill

74. Copyright Act 1956
s.4, see *Gabrin v Universal Music Operations Ltd* [2003] EWHC 1335, [2004] E.C.D.R. 4 (Ch D), Patten, J.
s.11, see *Beckingham v Hodgens* [2003] EWCA Civ 143, [2004] E.C.D.R. 6 (CA), Jonathan Parker, L.J.
s.36, see *Novello & Co Ltd v Keith Prowse Music Publishing Co Ltd* [2004] EWHC 766, [2004] E.M.L.R. 16 (Ch D), Patten, J.
Sch.7 Part IV para.28, see *Novello & Co Ltd v Keith Prowse Music Publishing Co Ltd* [2004] EWHC 766, [2004] E.M.L.R. 16 (Ch D), Patten, J.

5 & 6 Eliz. 2 (1957)

xxxiii. British Transport Commission Act 1957
s.66, disapplied: 2004 asp 10 Sch.4 Part 3

x. City of London (Various Powers) Act 1957
Part II, applied: 2002 c.vi, s.2
s.4, amended: 2002 c.vi Sch.1 para.3, Sch.2
s.4, repealed (in part): 2002 c.vi Sch.2
s.6, amended: 2002 c.vi s.3, Sch.1 para.1
s.6, applied: 2002 c.vi s.3, s.4, s.5, s.8
s.6, disapplied: 2002 c.vi s.3
s.6, referred to: 2002 c.vi s.3
s.6, repealed (in part): 2002 c.vi Sch.2
s.7, amended: 2002 c.vi Sch.1 para.2
s.7, applied: 2002 c.vi s.8
s.9, applied: 2002 c.vi s.8

5 & 6 Eliz. 2 (1957)–cont.

xxxvii. East Ham Corporation Act 1957
s.38, repealed (in part): SI 2003/3030 Reg.2

1. Channel Islands (Church Legislation) Measure, 1931 (Amendment) Measure 1957
applied: 2003 c.1 s.4
referred to: 2003 c.2 s.7, 2003 c.3 s.48

11. Homicide Act 1957
s.2, see *R. v Dietschmann (Anthony)* [2001] EWCA Crim 2052, [2002] Crim. L.R. 132 (CA (Crim Div)), Rose, L.J.; see *R. v Dietschmann (Anthony)* [2003] UKHL 10, [2003] 1 A.C. 1209 (HL), Lord Hutton; see *R. v Lambert (Steven)* [2002] Q.B. 1112 (CA (Crim Div)), Lord Woolf of Barnes, L.C.J.
s.2, referred to: 2003 c.44 Sch.21 para.11
s.3, see *Attorney General's Reference (Nos.74, 95 and 118 of 2002), Re* [2002] EWCA Crim 2982, [2003] 2 Cr. App. R. (S.) 42 (CA (Crim Div)), Mantell, L.J.
s.4, see *Attorney General's Reference (No.1 of 2004), Re* [2004] EWCA Crim 1025, [2004] 1 W.L.R. 2111 (CA (Crim Div)), Lord Woolf of Barnes, L.C.J.

12. Public Trustee (Fees) Act 1957
s.1, amended: 2002 c.35 s.2
s.1, applied: SI 2004/799
s.1, referred to: SI 2002/2232, SI 2003/690

16. Nurses Agencies Act 1957
applied: SI 2002/3210 Art.4, SI 2003/753 Reg.5, SI 2003/2527 Sch.5 para.1, Sch.5 para.2, Sch.5 para.5, SI 2004/662 Reg.5
s.2, applied: SI 2002/3210 Art.4, SI 2003/2527 Sch.5 para.2, Sch.5 para.3, Sch.5 para.4

31. Occupiers Liability Act 1957
see *Wattleworth v Goodwood Road Racing Co Ltd* [2004] EWHC 140, [2004] P.I.Q.R. P25 (QBD), Davis, J.
applied: 2002 c.i s.42
s.1, varied: 2002 c.i s.12
s.2, see *Eden v West & Co* [2002] EWCA Civ 991, [2003] P.I.Q.R. Q2 (CA), Pill, L.J.; see *Fairchild v Glenhaven Funeral Services Ltd (t/a GH Dovener & Son)* [2001] EWCA Civ 1881, [2002] 1 W.L.R. 1052 (CA), Brooke, L.J.; see *Gwilliam v West Hertfordshire Hospitals NHS Trust* [2002] EWCA Civ 1041, [2003] Q.B. 443 (CA), Lord Woolf of Barnes, L.C.J.; see *Tomlinson v Congleton BC* [2003] UKHL 47, [2004] 1 A.C. 46 (HL), Lord Hoffmann

38. Housing and Town Development (Scotland) Act 1957
s.10, amended: SSI 2003/331 Sch.1 para.2
s.11, repealed: SSI 2003/331 Sch.1 para.2
s.12, repealed: SSI 2003/331 Sch.1 para.2
s.15, repealed (in part): SSI 2003/331 Sch.1 para.2
s.16, amended: SSI 2003/331 Sch.1 para.2
s.19, amended: SSI 2003/331 Sch.1 para.2

CAP.

5 & 6 Eliz. 2 (1957)–cont.

38. Housing and Town Development (Scotland) Act 1957–cont.
Sch.2 para.1, amended: SSI 2003/331 Sch.1 para.2
Sch.2 para.3, repealed: SSI 2003/331 Sch.1 para.2
Sch.2 para.4, amended: SSI 2003/331 Sch.1 para.2

45. Exchequer and Audit Departments Act 1957
s.1, repealed (in part): 2004 c.14 Sch.1 Part 9
s.2, repealed (in part): 2004 c.14 Sch.1 Part 9

52. Geneva Conventions Act 1957
s.1, applied: 2003 c.41 s.196, 2003 c.44 Sch.4 para.29, Sch.5 para.26, Sch.5 para.47, SI 2004/1500 Sch.2 para.21
s.5, amended: 2003 c.44 Sch.3 para.39
s.8, enabling: SI 2002/1076

53. Naval Discipline Act 1957
applied: 2003 c.41 s.3, s.5, s.71, s.73, s.155, 2003 c.44 Sch.7 para.5, SI 2003/2273 Art.12, SSI 2003/176 Art.3, 2004 c.30 s.39, Sch.4 para.5
referred to: SI 2002/1820 Art.2, 2003 c.44 s.337, SI 2004/66, SI 2004/1496 Art.2
s.12A, amended: 2003 c.20 Sch.7 para.11
s.29B, amended: 2003 c.21 Sch.17 para.26, Sch.19
s.34A, amended: 2003 c.44 Sch.32 para.157
s.42, applied: 2003 c.42 s.137, Sch.3 para.93, Sch.5 para.172, 2003 c.44 s.233, s.329, 2004 c.28 s.8
s.43A, applied: 2003 c.42 s.131
s.43AA, applied: 2003 c.42 s.131
s.47, amended: 2002 c.26 Sch.4 para.12
s.47M, amended: SI 2004/66 Art.2
s.48, amended: 2003 c.42 Sch.6 para.12, Sch.7
s.51, applied: SI 2003/2273 Art.12, Sch.1 para.10
s.52B, applied: SI 2004/1937 Art.4
s.52D, applied: SI 2004/1937 Art.4
s.52F, applied: SI 2004/1937 Art.4
s.52FF, amended: SI 2004/1937 Art.6
s.52FG, amended: SI 2004/66 Art.2
s.52FH, enabling: SI 2004/1949
s.52FJ, amended: SI 2004/66 Art.2, SI 2004/1937 Art.6
s.52FP, enabling: SI 2004/1949
s.52FQ, enabling: SI 2004/1937
s.52H, applied: SI 2004/1937 Art.3
s.53B, amended: SI 2004/66 Art.2
s.53C, amended: SI 2004/66 Art.2
s.56, amended: 2004 c.28 Sch.3 para.4
s.58, enabling: SI 2002/231
s.59, amended: SI 2004/66 Art.2
s.63, substituted: 2004 c.28 Sch.3 para.3
s.64A, amended: 2003 c.44 Sch.36 para.83
s.71AC, amended: 2003 c.44 s.272
s.76, applied: SI 2003/336 Sch.1 Part 2
s.93, disapplied: 2003 c.44 Sch.25 para.50

CAP.

5 & 6 Eliz. 2 (1957)–cont.

53. Naval Discipline Act 1957–cont.
s.96, amended: 2003 c.44 Sch.37 Part 9
s.99, amended: 2003 c.44 Sch.37 Part 9
s.99, disapplied: 2004 c.44 Sch.25 para.51
s.101, amended: 2004 c.33 Sch.26 para.32
s.109, amended: 2003 c.44 Sch.3 para.40
s.110, amended: 2002 c.26 Sch.4 para.12, 2003 c.39 Sch.8 para.97
s.129B, amended: 2003 c.39 Sch.8 para.97
s.135, amended: 2002 c.39 Sch.2 para.1, 2004 c.28 Sch.3 para.5
s.135, enabling: SI 2004/1937
Sch.4A para.5, applied: 2003 c.42 s.134
Sch.4A para.10, applied: 2003 c.42 s.131

56. Housing Act 1957
Part V, see *Gulliksen v Pembrokeshire CC* [2002] EWCA Civ 968, [2003] Q.B. 123 (CA), Sedley, L.J.

57. Agriculture Act 1957
applied: SI 2002/2843 Art.2
s.5, applied: SI 2002/2843 Art.2
s.6, applied: SI 2002/2843 Art.2
s.6, varied: SI 2002/2843 Art.2
s.7, amended: 2003 c.44 Sch.26 para.16
s.9, disapplied: SI 2002/2843 Art.2
s.9, varied: SI 2002/2843 Art.2
s.32, repealed: 2004 c.14 Sch.1 Part 2
s.35, disapplied: SI 2002/2843 Art.2
s.37, amended: 2004 c.14 Sch.1 Part 2
s.37, repealed (in part): 2004 c.14 Sch.1 Part 2

58. Registration of Births, Deaths and Marriages (Special Provisions) Act 1957
applied: SI 2002/1419(a), 2004 c.33 s.211
s.1, amended: 2004 c.33 Sch.27 para.21
s.1, enabling: SI 2002/3122
s.2, enabling: SI 2002/3122
s.3, amended: SI 2002/1419 Art.3
s.3, enabling: SI 2002/3122
s.3A, added: SI 2002/1419 Art.3
s.5, enabling: SI 2002/3122
s.6, enabling: SI 2002/3122
s.7, repealed (in part): 2004 c.14 Sch.1 Part 17

6 & 7 Eliz. 2 (1957-58)

vi. Forth Road Bridge Order Confirmation Act 1958
repealed (in part): SSI 2002/178 Sch.4
Sch.1, added: SSI 2002/178 Sch.3 para.2

5. Adoption Act 1958
referred to: 2002 c.38 Sch.4 para.20
s.21, referred to: 2002 c.38 Sch.4 para.20

7. Manoeuvres Act 1958
applied: SI 2004/568 Reg.6
s.3, amended: 2003 c.39 Sch.10
s.3, amended: 2003 c.39 Sch.8 para.105

14. Overseas Service Act 1958
applied: 2003 c.1 s.652
s.2, applied: 2003 c.1 s.652

CAP.

6 & 7 Eliz. 2 (1957-58)–cont.

14. Overseas Service Act 1958–cont.
s.4, applied: 2003 c.1 s.652

16. Commonwealth Institute Act 1958
repealed: 2002 c.39 Sch.3
s.2, amended: SI 2002/1397 Sch.1 para.1
s.2, applied: SI 2002/1397 Art.5

17. Recreational Charities Act 1958
s.2, applied: 2003 c.17 s.66
s.3, amended: 2004 c.14 Sch.1 Part 17
s.3, repealed (in part): 2004 c.14 Sch.1 Part 17

23. Milford Haven Conservancy Act 1958
referred to: 2002 c.v

23. Trustee Act (Northern Ireland) 1958
s.1, varied: SI 2003/1633 Sch.2 para.13
s.7, varied: SI 2003/1633 Sch.2 para.13,
Sch.2 para.14, Sch.2 para.16

24. Land Drainage (Scotland) Act 1958
s.17, amended: SI 2003/2155 Sch.1 para.2
Sch.2 para.3, amended: SI 2003/2155 Sch.1
para.2

33. Disabled Persons (Employment) Act 1958
s.3, referred to: SSI 2002/533 Sch.1, Sch.3

38. Defence Contracts Act 1958
s.6, repealed (in part): 2004 c.36 Sch.2
para.5, Sch.3

39. Maintenance Orders Act 1958
applied: SI 2004/3114 Sch.1
s.2, amended: 2003 c.39 Sch.8 para.98
s.3, amended: 2003 c.39 Sch.8 para.99
s.4, amended: 2003 c.39 Sch.8 para.100,
2004 c.33 Sch.27 para.22
s.5, amended: 2003 c.39 Sch.8 para.101
s.18, amended: 2003 c.39 Sch.8 para.102
s.19, enabling: SI 2002/789
s.20, amended: 2003 c.39 Sch.8 para.103
s.21, amended: 2003 c.39 Sch.8 para.104,
Sch.10

47. Agricultural Marketing Act 1958
s.1, referred to: SI 2002/2843 Art.3
s.2, referred to: SI 2002/2843 Art.3
s.3, amended: 2004 c.14 Sch.1 Part 2
s.3, referred to: SI 2002/2843 Art.3
s.3, repealed (in part): 2004 c.14 Sch.1 Part 2
s.4, referred to: SI 2002/2843 Art.3
s.5, referred to: SI 2002/2843 Art.3
s.6, referred to: SI 2002/2843 Art.3
s.7, referred to: SI 2002/2843 Art.3
s.8, referred to: SI 2002/2843 Art.3
s.9, referred to: SI 2002/2843 Art.3
s.13, varied: SI 2002/2843 Art.3
s.16, referred to: SI 2002/2843 Art.3
s.19, referred to: SI 2002/2843 Art.3
s.19A, amended: 2002 c.40 Sch.25 para.2,
Sch.26
s.19A, referred to: SI 2002/2843 Art.3
s.20, referred to: SI 2002/2843 Art.3
s.21, referred to: SI 2002/2843 Art.3
s.26, referred to: SI 2002/2843 Art.3
s.28, referred to: SI 2002/2843 Art.3

CAP.

6 & 7 Eliz. 2 (1957-58)–cont.

47. Agricultural Marketing Act 1958–cont.
s.30, referred to: SI 2002/2843 Art.3
s.31, referred to: SI 2002/2843 Art.3
s.32, referred to: SI 2002/2843 Art.3
s.34, repealed: 2004 c.14 Sch.1 Part 2
s.35, repealed: 2004 c.14 Sch.1 Part 2
s.36, repealed: 2004 c.14 Sch.1 Part 2
s.37, repealed: 2004 c.14 Sch.1 Part 2
s.38, repealed: 2004 c.14 Sch.1 Part 2
s.39, repealed: 2004 c.14 Sch.1 Part 2
s.39A, repealed: 2004 c.14 Sch.1 Part 2
s.40, repealed: 2004 c.14 Sch.1 Part 2
s.41, repealed: 2004 c.14 Sch.1 Part 2
s.41A, repealed: 2004 c.14 Sch.1 Part 2
s.42, repealed: 2004 c.14 Sch.1 Part 2
s.43, referred to: SI 2002/2843 Art.3
s.43, repealed: 2004 c.14 Sch.1 Part 2
s.44, referred to: SI 2002/2843 Art.3
s.44, repealed: 2004 c.14 Sch.1 Part 2
s.45, amended: 2003 c.44 Sch.37 Part 9
s.45, disapplied: 2003 c.44 Sch.25 para.52
s.45, referred to: SI 2002/2843 Art.3
s.45, repealed: 2004 c.14 Sch.1 Part 2
s.46, repealed: 2004 c.14 Sch.1 Part 2
s.47, amended: 2002 c.40 Sch.25 para.2,
2004 c.14 Sch.1 Part 2
s.52, applied: SI 2002/2843 Art.3
s.52, repealed (in part): 2004 c.14 Sch.1 Part 2
s.53, repealed (in part): SI 2004/1109 Sch.1
s.54, repealed (in part): 2004 c.14 Sch.1 Part 2
s.55, repealed (in part): 2004 c.14 Sch.1 Part 2
Sch.1 para.6, referred to: 2004 c.14 Sch.2
para.13

49. Trading Representations (Disabled Persons) Act 1958
s.1, amended: SI 2002/1397 Sch.1 para.2
s.1, applied: SI 2002/1397 Art.7

50. Local Government (Omnibus Shelters and Queue Barriers) (Scotland) Act 1958
s.3, amended: SI 2003/2155 Sch.1 para.3

51. Public Records Act 1958
referred to: 2003 c.43 Sch.4 para.5
s.2, enabling: SI 2003/871, SI 2004/750
s.8, applied: 2002 c.38 s.98
Sch.1 Part 1, amended: SI 2002/794 Sch.1
para.10, SI 2002/2469 Sch.1 para.1, 2003
c.43 Sch.4 para.6, SI 2003/1887 Sch.2
para.1
Sch.1 Part 2, amended: 2002 c.11 Sch.1
para.23, 2002 c.17 Sch.6 para.16, Sch.7
para.20, 2002 c.40 Sch.25 para.3,
Sch.26, 2003 c.26 Sch.4 para.21, 2003
c.37 Sch.7 para.16, 2003 c.43 Sch.9
para.1, Sch.14 Part 2, SI 2003/438 Art.2,
2004 c.8 Sch.6 para.1, 2004 c.11 Sch.1
para.1, 2004 c.20 Sch.1 para.14, 2004 c.25
Sch.5 para.16, 2004 c.35 Sch.12 para.1
Sch.1 para.3, amended: 2004 c.20 Sch.14
para.1, 2004 c.30 Sch.2 para.23
Sch.1 para.3A, enabling: SI 2003/438

CAP.

6 & 7 Eliz. 2 (1957-58)–cont.

51. Public Records Act 1958–cont.
Sch.1 para.4, amended: 2004 c.14 Sch.2
para.6

53. Variation of Trusts Act 1958
see *D (A Child) v O* [2004] EWHC 1036,
[2004] 3 All E.R. 780 (Ch D), Lloyd, J.

55. Local Government Act 1958
applied: SI 2003/527 Reg.2
s.63, repealed: 2004 c.14 Sch.1 Part 10

56. Finance Act 1958
s.35, amended: 2003 c.14 Sch.20 para.3

61. Interest on Damages (Scotland) Act 1958
s.1, see *Manson v Skinner* 2002 S.L.T. 448 (2
Div), Lord Gill, Lord Maclean, Lord Weir

65. Children Act 1958
s.4, applied: SI 2002/635 Reg.2, SI 2002/
896 Sch.1 para.6, SI 2004/2695 Sch.1
para.27
s.14, applied: SI 2002/635 Sch.1 para.1, SI
2002/896 Sch.1 para.45, SI 2004/2695
Sch.1 para.3

69. Opencast Coal Act 1958
referred to: SSI 2003/583 Sch.1 para.1
s.7, varied: SI 2004/1822 Sch.1 para.1
s.14A, amended: SSI 2003/583 Sch.1 para.2
s.24, amended: SSI 2003/583 Sch.1 para.3
s.26, amended: SSI 2003/583 Sch.1 para.4
s.45, amended: 2003 c.21 Sch.17 para.27,
Sch.19
s.52, amended: SSI 2003/583 Sch.1 para.5
Sch.6 para.31, amended: SSI 2003/583
Sch.1 para.6
Sch.7 Part VI para.25, amended: SSI 2003/
583 Sch.1 para.7

71. Agriculture Act 1958
s.1, repealed: 2004 c.14 Sch.1 Part 2
s.8, amended: 2004 c.14 Sch.1 Part 2
s.9, amended: 2004 c.14 Sch.1 Part 2
s.10, repealed (in part): 2004 c.14 Sch.1 Part 2
Sch.1 Part I para.2, repealed: 2004 c.14 Sch.1
Part 2
Sch.4 para.1, repealed: 2004 c.14 Sch.1 Part 2
Sch.4 para.2, repealed: 2004 c.14 Sch.1 Part 2
Sch.4 para.10, repealed: 2004 c.14 Sch.1 Part
2
Sch.4 para.13, repealed: 2004 c.14 Sch.1 Part
2
Sch.4 para.14, repealed: 2004 c.14 Sch.1 Part
2

7 & 8 Eliz. 2 (1958-59)

Civil Aviation (Carriers Liability) Act 1959
see *Povey v Civil Aviation Safety Authority*
(2003) 71 B.M.L.R.130 (Sup Ct (Vic)),
Bongiorno, J.

CAP.

7 & 8 Eliz. 2 (1958-59)–cont.

Fisheries (Consolidation) Act (Ireland) 1959
s.223A, see *Browne v Attorney General*
[2004] 1 C.M.L.R. 25 (Sup Ct (Irl)),
Keane, C.J.

xlvi. Humber Bridge Act 1959
see *R. (on the application of Confederation of
Passenger Transport UK) v Humber Bridge
Board* [2002] EWHC 2261, [2002] N.P.C.
136 (QBD (Admin Ct)), Newman, J.

15. Coroners Act (Northern Ireland) 1959
s.34, applied: 2004 c.4 Sch.3 para.3

24. Building (Scotland) Act 1959
applied: 2003 asp 1 s.7
repealed: 2003 asp 8 Sch.6 para.1
s.3, applied: SSI 2002/40
s.3, enabling: SSI 2002/40
s.24, enabling: SSI 2002/40
s.29, enabling: SSI 2002/40
Sch.4, enabling: SSI 2002/40

25. Highways Act 1959
s.7, applied: 2004 c.5 s.32, s.73
s.9, applied: 2004 c.5 s.32, s.73
s.11, applied: 2004 c.5 s.32, s.73
s.13, applied: 2004 c.5 s.32, s.73
s.20, applied: 2004 c.5 s.32, s.73
s.38, see *Gulliksen v Pembrokeshire CC*
[2002] EWCA Civ 968, [2003] Q.B. 123
(CA), Sedley, L.J.

32. Eisteddfod Act 1959
repealed: 2004 c.14 Sch.1 Part 10

43. Post Office Works Act 1959
referred to: SI 2003/2908 Art.2

44. Fire Services Act 1959
referred to: 2003 c.26 s.128
repealed (in part): 2004 c.21 Sch.2
s.7, referred to: 2003 c.26 s.129
s.7, repealed (in part): 2003 c.26 Sch.8 Part 1
s.8, applied: SI 2004/2306 Sch.1
s.8, varied: SI 2004/2918 Sch.1
s.9, applied: SI 2004/2306 Sch.1
s.9, varied: SI 2004/2918 Sch.1
s.10, applied: SI 2004/2306 Sch.1
s.10, varied: SI 2004/2918 Sch.1

49. Chevening Estate Act 1959
s.2A, added: SI 2003/2867 Sch.1 para.5
Sch.1, referred to: 2003 c.1 s.101

53. Town and Country Planning Act 1959
s.23, repealed (in part): 2004 c.14 Sch.1 Part
10
s.57, amended: 2004 c.14 Sch.1 Part 10
Sch.4 Part I para.9., substituted: 2004 c.21
Sch.1 para.13

54. Weeds Act 1959
applied: SSI 2004/70 Sch.3 para.2, SSI
2004/143 Sch.5 para.4
referred to: 2003 c.40 s.2
s.1A, added: 2003 c.40 s.1
s.10, repealed (in part): 2004 c.14 Sch.1 Part 2

57. Street Offences Act 1959
s.1, amended: 2003 c.42 Sch.1 para.2

CAP.

7 & 8 Eliz. 2 (1958-59)–cont.

57. Street Offences Act 1959–cont.
s.2, amended: 2003 c.42 Sch.1 para.3

66. Obscene Publications Act 1959
s.2, amended: 2003 c.17 Sch.6 para.28
s.3, amended: 2003 c.39 Sch.8 para.106, Sch.10
s.3, applied: SI 2003/336 Sch.1 Part 2

70. Town and Country Planning (Scotland) Act 1959
Sch.4 para.2, amended: 2004 c.36 Sch.3
Sch.4 para.3, substituted: SSI 2003/331 Sch.1 para.3

72. Mental Health Act 1959
s.127, repealed: 2003 c.42 Sch.7
s.128, applied: SI 2002/896 Sch.1 para.34, 2003 c.44 Sch.15 para.93
s.128, repealed: 2003 c.42 Sch.7

8 & 9 Eliz. 2 (1959-60)

i. Aberdeen Harbour Order Confirmation Act 1960
s.5, repealed (in part): SSI 2002/310 Sch.3
s.7, repealed (in part): SSI 2002/310 Sch.3
s.9, repealed: SSI 2002/310 Sch.3
s.11, repealed: SSI 2002/310 Sch.3
s.29, repealed: SSI 2002/310 Sch.3
s.31, repealed: SSI 2002/310 Sch.3
Sch.1, repealed: SSI 2002/310 Sch.3

xxx. City of London (Guild Churches) Act 1960
s.5, amended: 2004 c.14 Sch.1 Part 6
s.5, repealed (in part): 2004 c.14 Sch.1 Part 6
s.6, repealed (in part): 2004 c.14 Sch.1 Part 6

iii. Forth Road Bridge Order Confirmation Act 1960
repealed: SSI 2002/178 Sch.4

xlix. Hertfordshire County Council Act 1960
s.41, varied: SI 2003/2155 Sch.1 para.16

xlii. Southampton Corporation Act 1960
s.70, varied: SI 2003/2155 Sch.1 para.16

Trade Marks Act (Sweden) 1960
s.4, see *Mast Jagermeister AG v V&S Vin & Spirit AB* [2004] E.T.M.R. 13 (Hogsta Domstolen (Sweden)), Judge Lars K Beckman

1. Church Property (Miscellaneous Provisions) Measure 1960
s.15, repealed: 2004 c.14 Sch.1 Part 6
s.18, amended: 2004 c.14 Sch.1 Part 6
s.22, repealed: 2004 c.14 Sch.1 Part 6
s.24, amended: 2004 c.14 Sch.1 Part 6

3. Attempted Rape, etc., Act (Northern Ireland) 1960
s.2, amended: SI 2003/1247 Sch.1 para.4
s.2, applied: SI 2004/1500 Sch.2 para.8

16. Road Traffic Act 1960
s.232, amended: 2004 c.14 Sch.1 Part 14
s.232, varied: 2004 c.14 Sch.2 para.7
s.242, varied: 2004 c.14 Sch.2 para.8

CAP.

8 & 9 Eliz. 2 (1959-60)–cont.

16. Road Traffic Act 1960–cont.
s.243, amended: 2003 c.39 Sch.8 para.107
s.248, repealed: 2004 c.14 Sch.1 Part 14
s.249, repealed: 2004 c.14 Sch.1 Part 14
s.266, repealed: 2004 c.14 Sch.1 Part 14
s.270, repealed: 2004 c.14 Sch.1 Part 14
Sch.20 Part I para.1, repealed: 2004 c.14 Sch.1 Part 14
Sch.20 Part II para.2, repealed: 2004 c.14 Sch.1 Part 14
Sch.20 Part II para.3, repealed: 2004 c.14 Sch.1 Part 14
Sch.20 Part II para.4, repealed: 2004 c.14 Sch.1 Part 14
Sch.20 Part II para.5, repealed: 2004 c.14 Sch.1 Part 14

22. Horticulture Act 1960
s.9, repealed: 2004 c.14 Sch.1 Part 2
s.10, repealed: 2004 c.14 Sch.1 Part 2
s.11, repealed: 2004 c.14 Sch.1 Part 2
s.12, repealed: 2004 c.14 Sch.1 Part 2
s.13, repealed: 2004 c.14 Sch.1 Part 2
s.14, repealed: 2004 c.14 Sch.1 Part 2
s.15, repealed: 2004 c.14 Sch.1 Part 2
s.16, repealed: 2004 c.14 Sch.1 Part 2
s.17, repealed: 2004 c.14 Sch.1 Part 2
s.18, repealed: 2004 c.14 Sch.1 Part 2
s.19, repealed: 2004 c.14 Sch.1 Part 2
s.21, repealed: 2004 c.14 Sch.1 Part 2
Sch.1 para.1, repealed: 2004 c.14 Sch.1 Part 2
Sch.1 para.2, repealed: 2004 c.14 Sch.1 Part 2
Sch.1 para.3, repealed: 2004 c.14 Sch.1 Part 2
Sch.1 para.4, repealed: 2004 c.14 Sch.1 Part 2
Sch.1 para.5, repealed: 2004 c.14 Sch.1 Part 2
Sch.1 para.6, repealed: 2004 c.14 Sch.1 Part 2
Sch.1 para.7, repealed: 2004 c.14 Sch.1 Part 2
Sch.1 para.8, repealed: 2004 c.14 Sch.1 Part 2
Sch.1 para.9, repealed: 2004 c.14 Sch.1 Part 2

30. Occupiers Liability (Scotland) Act 1960
s.2, see *Duff v East Dunbartonshire Council* 2002 Rep. L.R. 98 (1 Div), Lord Kirkwood, Lord Cullen, L.P., Lord Marnoch; see *Falconer v Edinburgh City Transport Longstone Social Club* 2003 Rep. L.R. 39 (OH), Temporary Judge TG Coutts Q.C.; see *Graham v East of Scotland Water Authority* 2002 S.C.L.R. 340 (OH), Lord Emslie; see *McCallie v North Ayrshire Council* 2002 S.C.L.R. 178 (Sh Ct (North Strathclyde)), Colin G McKay
s.3, see *McCallie v North Ayrshire Council* 2002 S.C.L.R. 178 (Sh Ct (North Strathclyde)), Colin G McKay
see *Gallagher v Kleinwort Benson (Trustees) Ltd* 2003 S.C.L.R. 384 (OH), Lord Reed; see *Simpson v Transocean Offshore (UK) Inc* 2003 S.L.T. (Sh Ct) 119 (Sh Pr), Sir SST Young, Sheriff Principal
applied: 2003 asp 2 s.22

CAP.

8 & 9 Eliz. 2 (1959-60)–cont.

31. Highlands and Islands Shipping Services Act 1960
s.2, applied: SI 2003/409 Sch.1 Part I

32. Population (Statistics) Act 1960
s.1, repealed (in part): 2004 c.14 Sch.1 Part 17
s.5, repealed (in part): 2004 c.14 Sch.1 Part 17

33. Indecency with Children Act 1960
repealed: 2003 c.42 Sch.7
s.1, applied: SI 2002/896 Sch.1 para.35, 2003 c.42 Sch.3 para.11, 2003 c.44 Sch.15 para.94, SI 2003/1184 Sch.2 para.11, SSI 2003/19 Sch.5 para.3

36. Game Laws (Amendment) Act 1960
s.3, amended: 2003 c.39 Sch.10, 2004 c.14 Sch.1 Part 17
s.5, repealed: 2004 c.14 Sch.1 Part 17
s.6, repealed (in part): 2004 c.14 Sch.1 Part 17

44. Finance Act 1960
s.74A, added: SI 2003/2867 Sch.1 para.6

55. Nigeria Independence Act 1960
Sch.2 para.15, repealed: 2002 c.39 Sch.3

58. Charities Act 1960
s.28, amended: 2004 c.14 Sch.1 Part 17
s.48, repealed (in part): 2004 c.14 Sch.1 Part 17

61. Mental Health (Scotland) Act 1960
see *Hutchison Reid v United Kingdom (50272/99)* (2003) 37 E.H.R.R. 9 (ECHR), G Ress (President)
applied: SI 2004/675 Sch.1 para.64

62. Caravan Sites and Control of Development Act 1960
applied: SSI 2004/406 Sch.1 para.12
Part I, applied: SI 2003/1594 Art.2
s.5, amended: 2004 c.21 Sch.1 para.14
s.7, amended: 2003 c.39 Sch.8 para.108, Sch.10
s.8, amended: 2003 c.39 Sch.8 para.109, Sch.10, 2004 c.21 Sch.1 para.14
s.23, applied: SI 2004/1777 Art.25, SI 2004/1778 Art.25
s.24, see *O'Connor v Secretary of State for Transport, Local Government and the Regions* [2002] EWHC 2649, [2003] J.P.L. 1128 (QBD (Admin Ct)), Field, J.; see *Wrexham CBC v National Assembly for Wales* [2003] EWCA Civ 835, [2003] E.H.L.R. 20 (CA), Auld, L.J.
s.24, amended: 2004 c.21 Sch.1 para.14
s.24, see *O'Connor v Secretary of State for Transport, Local Government and the Regions* [2002] EWHC 2649, [2003] J.P.L. 1128 (QBD (Admin Ct)), Field, J.; see *Wrexham CBC v National Assembly for Wales* [2003] EWCA Civ 835, [2003] E.H.L.R. 20 (CA), Auld, L.J.
s.24, applied: SI 2004/1777 Art.25, SI 2004/1778 Art.25
s.29, see *Howard v Charlton* [2002] EWCA Civ 1086, [2003] 1 P. & C.R. 21 (CA), Carnwath, L.J.; see *Oades v Eke*

CAP.

8 & 9 Eliz. 2 (1959-60)–cont.

62. Caravan Sites and Control of Development Act 1960–cont.
s.29–cont.
(Valuation Officer) [2004] R.A. 161 (Lands Tr), PR Francis FRICS
s.29, amended: 2004 c.21 Sch.1 para.14
s.32, amended: 2003 c.39 Sch.8 para.110, Sch.10

65. Administration of Justice Act 1960
s.1, applied: 2003 c.17 s.130, 2003 c.32 s.60
s.1, disapplied: 2003 c.44 s.274, Sch.22 para.14
s.2, amended: 2003 c.39 s.88, Sch.8 para.111, Sch.10
s.3, repealed: 2003 c.39 Sch.8 para.112, Sch.10
s.12, see *G (A Child) (Contempt: Committal Order), Re* [2003] EWCA Civ 489, [2003] 1 W.L.R. 2051 (CA), Dame Elizabeth Butler-Sloss (President); see *G (A Child) (Litigants In Person), Re* [2003] EWCA Civ 1055, [2003] 2 F.L.R. 963 (CA), Thorpe, L.J.; see *Kent CC v B (A Child)* [2004] EWHC 411, [2004] 2 F.L.R. 142 (Fam Div), Munby, J.; see *M (A Child) (Children and Family Reporter: Disclosure), Re* [2002] EWCA Civ 1199, [2003] Fam. 26 (CA), Thorpe, L.J.; see *R. (on the application of T) v Mental Health Review Tribunal* [2002] EWHC 247, [2002] Lloyd's Rep. Med. 354 (QBD (Admin Ct)), Scott Baker, J.
s.12, amended: 2002 c.38 s.101, 2004 c.31 s.62
s.13, see *Barnet LBC v Hurst* [2002] EWCA Civ 1009, [2003] 1 W.L.R. 722 (CA), Brooke, L.J.; see *R. v Moore (Peter Oliver) (Costs)* [2003] EWCA Crim 1574, [2003] 1 W.L.R. 2170 (CA (Crim Div)), Rose, L.J.; see *Sierra Leone v Davenport (No.2)* [2002] EWCA Civ 230, [2002] C.P.L.R. 236 (CA), Jonathan Parker, L.J.

66. Professions Supplementary to Medicine Act 1960
applied: 2002 c.17 s.25, s.29, SI 2002/254 Art.6, Art.9, Art.13, Sch.1 para.3, Sch.2 para.3, Sch.2 para.13, Sch.2 para.16, Sch.2 para.17, SI 2003/1571 Art.6, SI 2003/1572 Sch.1, SI 2003/1579 Sch.1, SI 2003/1700 Art.12, SR 2002/386 Reg.4, SSI 2002/190 Reg.3, SSI 2002/305 Sch.1 Part III
varied: SI 2002/254 Sch.2 para.17, SI 2003/1700 Art.1
s.2, applied: SI 2002/254 Sch.2 para.11, Sch.2 para.24
s.3, applied: SI 2002/254 Sch.2 para.11, Sch.2 para.18, SI 2003/1700 Art.6
s.8, applied: SI 2003/1700 Art.3, Art.5
s.8, referred to: SI 2002/254 Sch.2 para.17
s.9, see *Collier v Council for Professions Supplementary to Medicine* [2003] UKPC 72, (2004) 78 B.M.L.R. 156 (Privy Council (United Kingdom)), Lord Steyn

CAP.

8 & 9 Eliz. 2 (1959-60)–cont.

66. Professions Supplementary to Medicine Act 1960–*cont.*
s.9, applied: SI 2002/254 Sch.2 para.18, SI 2003/1700 Art.5, Art.6, Art.10, Art.11
Sch.1 Part II para.4, amended: SI 2002/1397 Sch.1 para.3
Sch.1 Part II para.4, applied: SI 2002/1397 Art.5

67. Public Bodies (Admission to Meetings) Act 1960
applied: SI 2003/505 Art.6, SI 2003/2772 Art.6, 2004 c.17 Sch.1 para.15, 2004 c.23 s.26, SI 2004/569 Art.6, SI 2004/667 Art.6, SSI 2002/103 Sch.1 Part II, SSI 2002/305 Sch.1 Part II, SSI 2002/534 Sch.1 Part II
s.1, applied: SI 2003/149 Sch.3 para.8, 2004 c.23 s.24, s.26
Sch.1 para.1, amended: 2002 c.17 Sch.5 para.1, Sch.7 para.21, SI 2002/2469 Sch.1 para.2, 2003 c.43 Sch.9 para.2, 2003 c.4 Sch.3 para.1, 2003 c.37 Sch.7 para.17
Sch.1 para.1, repealed (in part): 2003 c.43 Sch.14 Part 2

9 & 10 Eliz. 2 (1960-61)

xxxvi. British Transport Commission Act 1961
s.26, varied: SI 2002/3269 Art.8

xlv. Devon County Council Act 1961
s.30, varied: SI 2003/2155 Sch.1 para.16

xxi. Forth Road Bridge Order Confirmation Act 1961
repealed: SSI 2002/178 Sch.4

1. Tanganyika Independence Act 1961
Sch.2 para.16, repealed: 2002 c.39 Sch.3

2. Baptismal Registers Measure 1961
s.2, applied: SI 2002/1894 Sch.1 Part I

3. Clergy Pensions Measure 1961
referred to: 2003 c.2, s.7
s.19, applied: 2003 c.2 s.2
s.19, repealed: 2003 c.2 Sch.1
s.20, applied: 2003 c.2 s.2
s.20, repealed: 2003 c.2 Sch.1
s.26, amended: 2003 c.2 s.3
s.26, applied: 2003 c.2 s.1
s.26, repealed (in part): 2003 c.2 Sch.1
s.28, applied: 2003 c.2 s.2

16. Sierra Leone Independence Act 1961
Sch.3 para.16, repealed: 2002 c.39 Sch.3

27. Carriage by Air Act 1961
see *GKN Westland Helicopters Ltd v Korean Air Lines Co Ltd* [2003] EWHC 1120, [2003] 2 All E.R. (Comm.) 578 (QBD (Comm Ct)), Morison, J.
applied: SI 2004/1899 Art.8
disapplied: SI 2004/1899 Art.8
s.2, varied: SI 2004/1899 Art.5, Art.6
s.3, varied: SI 2004/1899 Art.7
s.4, varied: SI 2004/1899 Art.7

CAP.

9 & 10 Eliz. 2 (1960-61)–cont.

27. Carriage by Air Act 1961–*cont.*
s.4A, varied: SI 2004/1899 Art.7
s.5, varied: SI 2004/1899 Art.5, Art.6
s.6, varied: SI 2004/1899 Art.7
s.8, varied: SI 2004/1899 Art.5, Art.6
s.8A, enabling: SI 2002/263
s.10, enabling: SI 2004/1899
s.11, varied: SI 2004/1899 Art.7
s.12, varied: SI 2004/1899 Art.7
s.14, amended: SI 2004/1418 Reg.5
s.14, repealed (in part): 2004 c.14 Sch.1 Part 4
Sch.1B, referred to: SI 2004/1899 Sch.1 Part I
Sch.1 Part I Art.17, see *King v Bristow Helicopters Ltd* [2002] UKHL 7, [2002] 2 A.C. 628 (HL), Lord Hope of Craighead

33. Land Compensation Act 1961
see *Mean Fiddler Holdings Ltd v Islington LBC (No.1)* [2003] EWCA Civ 160, [2003] 2 P. & C.R. 7 (CA), Carnwath, L.J.; see *Roberts v South Gloucestershire Council* [2002] EWCA Civ 1568, [2003] 1 P. & C.R. 26 (CA), Carnwath, L.J.; see *Second Sidcup (St Johns) Scout Group Trustees v Bexley LBC* [2004] R.V.R. 35 (Lands Tr), PR Francis FRICS
applied: SI 2002/1327 Art.26, 2004 c.5 s.38
varied: SI 2002/1064 Art.17
Part I, applied: SI 2002/412 Art.13, Art.19, Art.22, Art.28, SI 2002/1064 Art.7, Art.8, Art.14, Art.19, SI 2002/1065 Art.7, Art.8, Art.19, SI 2002/1066 Art.10, Art.16, Art.18, Art.25, Art.27, Art.28, Art.31, Art.34, SI 2002/1327 Art.10, Art.15, Art.23, SI 2002/1943 Art.8, Art.9, SI 2002/3127 Art.7, SI 2003/1075 Art.8, SI 2003/3364 Art.8, Art.11, Art.16, Art.17, Art.20, SI 2004/389 Art.7, Art.8, Art.9, Art.11, Art.12, Art.20, Art.21, Art.27, Art.28, SI 2004/757 Art.10, Art.19, Art.21, Art.29, Art.30, Art.31, Art.32, Art.35, Art.39
Part III, see *Stevens v Bath and North East Somerset DC* [2004] R.V.R. 189 (Lands Tr), PH Clarke, FRICS
s.4, see *Purfleet Farms Ltd v Secretary of State for Transport, Local Government and the Regions* [2002] EWCA Civ 1430, [2003] 1 P. & C.R. 20 (CA), Potter, L.J.
s.5, see *Prielipp v Secretary of State for the Environment, Transport and the Regions* [2002] 3 E.G.L.R. 143 (Lands Tr), PR Francis FRICS; see *Railtrack Plc (In Railway Administration) v Guinness Ltd* [2003] EWCA Civ 188, [2003] 1 E.G.L.R. 124 (CA), Carnwath, L.J.; see *Ryde International Plc v London Regional Transport* [2003] R.V.R. 49 (Lands Tr), PR Francis FRICS; see *Yorkshire Traction Co Ltd v South Yorkshire Passenger Transport Executive* [2003] R.V.R. 67 (Lands Tr), PH Clarke, FRICS

CAP.

9 & 10 Eliz. 2 (1960-61)–cont.

33. Land Compensation Act 1961–*cont.*
s.5 r, see *Corton Caravans & Chalets Ltd v Anglian Water Services Ltd* [2003] R.V.R. 323 (Lands Tr), George Bartlett Q.C. (President); see *Ryde International Plc v London Regional transport* [2004] EWCA Civ 232, [2004] 2 E.G.L.R. 1 (CA), Sir Andrew Morritt V.C.

s.5A, added: 2004 c.5 s.103

s.5 rule 6, see *Ryde International Plc v London Regional Transport* [2003] R.V.R. 273 (LandsTr), PR Francis FRICS

s.6, see *Waters v Welsh Development Agency* [2004] UKHL 19, [2004] 1 W.L.R. 1304 (HL), Lord Nicholls of Birkenhead

s.9, see *Thomas Executors v Merthyr Tydfil CBC* [2003] R.V.R. 246 (LandsTr), George Bartlett Q.C. (President)

s.14, see *Pentrehobyn Trustees v National Assembly for Wales* [2003] R.V.R. 140 (LandsTr), George Bartlett Q.C. (President)

s.15, see *Pentrehobyn Trustees v National Assembly for Wales* [2003] R.V.R. 140 (LandsTr), George Bartlett Q.C. (President)

s.16, see *Pentrehobyn Trustees v National Assembly for Wales* [2003] R.V.R. 140 (LandsTr), George Bartlett Q.C. (President)

s.17, see *Pentrehobyn Trustees v National Assembly for Wales* [2003] R.V.R. 140 (LandsTr), George Bartlett Q.C. (President)

s.29, amended: 2004 c.21 Sch.1 para.15

34. Factories Act 1961
applied: SI 2002/655 Reg.3, SI 2003/547 Reg.3, SSI 2004/406 Sch.5 para.4.5

s.31, repealed: SI 2002/2776 Sch.7 Part 2

s.178, amended: SI 2002/3076 Sch.1, SSI 2002/389 Sch.1

39. Criminal Justice Act 1961
s.23, amended: 2003 c.44 s.186

s.26, see *R. (on the application of McFetrich) v Secretary of State for the Home Department* [2003] EWHC 1542, [2003] 4 All E.R. 1093 (QBD (Admin Ct)), Scott Baker, L.J.

41. Flood Prevention (Scotland) Act 1961
s.3, amended: SI 2003/2155 Sch.1 para.4

s.4, amended: 2002 asp 3 Sch.7 para.3

s.12, amended: 2002 asp 3 Sch.7 para.3

s.15, amended: 2002 asp 3 Sch.7 para.3

Sch.1 para.2, amended: SI 2003/2155 Sch.1 para.4

Sch.2 para.3, amended: SI 2003/2155 Sch.1 para.4

47. Mock Auctions Act 1961
applied: SI 2003/1376 Sch.1, SI 2003/1593 Sch.1 Part I

50. Rivers (Prevention of Pollution) Act 1961
s.12, amended: 2003 c.44 Sch.37 Part 9

s.12, disapplied: 2003 c.44 Sch.25 para.53

CAP.

9 & 10 Eliz. 2 (1960-61)–cont.

54. Human Tissue Act 1961
see *A v Leeds Teaching Hospital NHS Trust* [2004] EWHC 644, [2004] 2 F.L.R. 365 (QBD), Gage, J.

referred to: 2003 c.43 Sch.4 para.7, 2004 c.30 s.59

repealed (in part): 2004 c.30 Sch.7 Part 1

s.1, amended: 2003 c.43 Sch.4 para.8

s.1, referred to: 2004 c.30 s.59

s.2, amended: SI 2002/3135 Sch.1 para.2

55. Crown Estate Act 1961
s.7, applied: SI 2004/1308

60. Suicide Act 1961
s.2, see *R. (on the application of Pretty) v DPP* [2001] UKHL 61, [2002] 1 A.C. 800 (HL), Lord Bingham of Cornhill

62. Trustee Investments Act 1961
applied: SSI 2002/132 Sch.1 para.26.4, 2003 asp 4 s.7

s.6, applied: 2003 asp 4 s.7

Sch.1 Part I para.1, varied: SI 2003/1633 Sch.2 para.2, Sch.2 para.8

Sch.1 Part I para.2, varied: SI 2003/1633 Sch.2 para.2, Sch.2 para.8

Sch.1 Part II, applied: 2003 asp 4 s.7

Sch.1 Part II para.1, varied: SI 2003/1633 Sch.2 para.2, Sch.2 para.8

Sch.1 Part II para.2, varied: SI 2003/1633 Sch.2 para.2, Sch.2 para.8

Sch.1 Part II para.3, varied: SI 2003/1633 Sch.2 para.2, Sch.2 para.8

Sch.1 Part II para.4, varied: SI 2003/1633 Sch.2 para.2, Sch.2 para.8

Sch.1 Part II para.4A, varied: SI 2003/1633 Sch.2 para.2, Sch.2 para.8

Sch.1 Part II para.5, varied: SI 2003/1633 Sch.2 para.2, Sch.2 para.8

Sch.1 Part II para.5A, varied: SI 2003/1633 Sch.2 para.2, Sch.2 para.8

Sch.1 Part II para.5B, varied: SI 2003/1633 Sch.2 para.2, Sch.2 para.8

Sch.1 Part II para.6, varied: SI 2003/1633 Sch.2 para.2, Sch.2 para.8

Sch.1 Part II para.7, varied: SI 2003/1633 Sch.2 para.2, Sch.2 para.8

Sch.1 Part II para.8, varied: SI 2003/1633 Sch.2 para.2, Sch.2 para.8

Sch.1 Part II para.9, varied: SI 2003/1633 Sch.2 para.2, Sch.2 para.8

Sch.1 Part II para.9A, varied: SI 2003/1633 Sch.2 para.2, Sch.2 para.8

Sch.1 Part II para.10, varied: SI 2003/1633 Sch.2 para.2, Sch.2 para.8

Sch.1 Part II para.10A, varied: SI 2003/1633 Sch.2 para.2, Sch.2 para.8

Sch.1 Part II para.11, varied: SI 2003/1633 Sch.2 para.2, Sch.2 para.8

Sch.1 Part II para.12, varied: SI 2003/1633 Sch.2 para.2, Sch.2 para.8

Sch.1 Part II para.13, varied: SI 2003/1633 Sch.2 para.2, Sch.2 para.8

CAP.

9 & 10 Eliz. 2 (1960-61)–cont.

62. Trustee Investments Act 1961–cont.

Sch.1 Part II para.14, varied: SI 2003/1633 Sch.2 para.2, Sch.2 para.8

Sch.1 Part II para.15, varied: SI 2003/1633 Sch.2 para.2, Sch.2 para.8

Sch.1 Part II para.16, varied: SI 2003/1633 Sch.2 para.2, Sch.2 para.8

Sch.1 Part II para.17, varied: SI 2003/1633 Sch.2 para.2, Sch.2 para.8

Sch.1 Part II para.18, varied: SI 2003/1633 Sch.2 para.2, Sch.2 para.8

Sch.1 Part II para.19, amended: 2002 c.1 Sch.3 para.1

Sch.1 Part II para.19, varied: SI 2003/1633 Sch.2 para.2, Sch.2 para.8

Sch.1 Part II para.20, varied: SI 2003/1633 Sch.2 para.2, Sch.2 para.8

Sch.1 Part II para.21, varied: SI 2003/1633 Sch.2 para.2, Sch.2 para.8

Sch.1 Part II para.22, varied: SI 2003/1633 Sch.2 para.2, Sch.2 para.8

Sch.1 Part II para.23, varied: SI 2003/1633 Sch.2 para.2, Sch.2 para.8

Sch.1 Part II para.24, varied: SI 2003/1633 Sch.2 para.2, Sch.2 para.8

Sch.1 Part III para.1, varied: SI 2003/1633 Sch.2 para.2, Sch.2 para.8

Sch.1 Part III para.2, varied: SI 2003/1633 Sch.2 para.2, Sch.2 para.8

Sch.1 Part III para.2A, varied: SI 2003/1633 Sch.2 para.2, Sch.2 para.8

Sch.1 Part III para.3, varied: SI 2003/1633 Sch.2 para.2, Sch.2 para.8

Sch.1 Part III para.4, varied: SI 2003/1633 Sch.2 para.2, Sch.2 para.8

Sch.1 Part III para.5, varied: SI 2003/1633 Sch.2 para.2, Sch.2 para.8

Sch.1 Part III para.6, varied: SI 2003/1633 Sch.2 para.2, Sch.2 para.8

Sch.1 Part IV para.1, varied: SI 2003/1633 Sch.2 para.2, Sch.2 para.8

Sch.1 Part IV para.2, varied: SI 2003/1633 Sch.2 para.2, Sch.2 para.8

Sch.1 Part IV para.2A, varied: SI 2003/1633 Sch.2 para.2, Sch.2 para.8

Sch.1 Part IV para.3, varied: SI 2003/1633 Sch.2 para.2, Sch.2 para.8

Sch.1 Part IV para.3A, varied: SI 2003/1633 Sch.2 para.2, Sch.2 para.8

Sch.1 Part IV para.4, varied: SI 2003/1633 Sch.2 para.2, Sch.2 para.3, Sch.2 para.8

Sch.1 Part IV para.4A, varied: SI 2003/1633 Sch.2 para.2, Sch.2 para.8

Sch.1 Part IV para.5, varied: SI 2003/1633 Sch.2 para.2, Sch.2 para.8

Sch.1 Part IV para.6, varied: SI 2003/1633 Sch.2 para.2, Sch.2 para.8

Sch.1 Part IV para.6A, varied: SI 2003/1633 Sch.2 para.2, Sch.2 para.8

Sch.1 Part IV para.7, varied: SI 2003/1633 Sch.2 para.2, Sch.2 para.8

CAP.

9 & 10 Eliz. 2 (1960-61)–cont.

63. Highways (Miscellaneous Provisions) Act 1961

applied: SI 2003/1075 Art.12

Part I, applied: SI 2003/1075 Art.9, Art.13, Art.22, Art.23, Art.30, Art.33

s.3, applied: 2004 c.5 s.32, s.73

64. Public Health Act 1961

s.74, see *Wandsworth LBC v Railtrack Plc* [2001] EWCA Civ 1236, [2002] Q.B. 756 (CA), Kennedy, L.J.

s.75, amended: 2004 c.21 Sch.1 para.16

s.86, repealed (in part): 2004 c.14 Sch.1 Part 13

Sch.4, amended: SI 2003/2908 Sch.2

10 & 11 Eliz. 2 (1961-62)

9. Local Government (Financial Provisions etc.) (Scotland) Act 1962

s.4, applied: SSI 2002/91 Reg.16, Reg.18, SSI 2003/160 Reg.17, Reg.19, SSI 2004/92 Reg.3, Reg.5

12. Education Act 1962

applied: SI 2002/3200 Reg.13

s.1, applied: SI 2002/535 Sch.1, SI 2002/1330 Reg.7, Reg.9, SI 2002/3199 Sch.1 para.13, Sch.1 para.14, SI 2003/1994 Reg.7, Reg.9, SI 2003/3118 Sch.1 para.13, Sch.1 para.14, SI 2003/3170 Sch.1 para.13, Sch.1 para.14

s.1, disapplied: SI 2002/1330 Reg.6

s.1, enabling: SI 2002/173, SI 2002/232, SI 2002/1330, SI 2002/2089, SI 2002/3060, SI 2003/1994, SI 2004/1038, SI 2004/1792

s.2, applied: SI 2002/535 Sch.1, SI 2002/1330 Reg.6, SI 2002/3199 Sch.1 para.14, SI 2003/3118 Sch.1 para.14, SI 2003/3170 Sch.1 para.14

s.4, enabling: SI 2002/173, SI 2002/232, SI 2002/1330, SI 2002/2089, SI 2002/3060, SI 2003/1994, SI 2004/1038, SI 2004/1792

Sch.1, applied: SI 2002/1330 Reg.7, SI 2003/1994 Reg.7

Sch.1 para.2, applied: SI 2002/1330 Reg.9, SI 2003/1994 Reg.9

Sch.1 para.2, varied: SI 2002/1330 Reg.8, SI 2003/1994 Reg.8

Sch.1 para.3, enabling: SI 2002/173, SI 2002/232, SI 2002/1330, SI 2002/2089, SI 2002/3060, SI 2003/1994, SI 2004/1038, SI 2004/1792

Sch.1 para.4, enabling: SI 2002/173, SI 2002/232, SI 2002/1330, SI 2002/2089, SI 2002/3060, SI 2003/1994, SI 2004/1038, SI 2004/1792

13. Vehicles (Excise) Act 1962

applied: SI 2002/2742 Reg.46, Sch.2 para.4

14. Electoral Law Act (Northern Ireland) 1962

Appendix 1., amended: SI 2002/2835 Art.9

10 & 11 Eliz. 2 (1961-62)–cont.

14. Electoral Law Act (Northern Ireland) 1962–*cont.*
s.14, applied: SI 2004/1267 Reg.20
s.14A, applied: SI 2004/1267 Reg.20
s.110, amended: 2002 c.26 Sch.4 para.13
Sch.5, amended: SI 2002/2835 Art.4, Art.5, Art.6, Art.7, Art.8
Sch.9, applied: SI 2003/1557 Reg.3
Sch.9, varied: SI 2003/1557 Reg.3

19. West Indies Act 1962
s.5, enabling: SI 2002/2637, SI 2003/1515, SI 2004/2029, SI 2004/2673
s.7, enabling: SI 2002/2637, SI 2003/1515, SI 2004/2029, SI 2004/2673

26. Animals (Cruel Poisons) Act 1962
s.1, amended: 2003 c.44 Sch.26 para.17

31. Sea Fish Industry Act 1962
s.17, applied: SI 2002/790 Sch.3 para.1

40. Jamaica Independence Act 1962
Sch.2 para.15, repealed: 2002 c.39 Sch.3

43. Carriage by Air (Supplementary Provisions) Act 1962
applied: SI 2004/1899 Art.8
s.2, amended: 2004 c.14 Sch.1 Part 4
s.3, amended: 2004 c.14 Sch.1 Part 4
s.3, varied: SI 2004/1899 Art.7
s.4, repealed: 2004 c.14 Sch.1 Part 4
s.4A, enabling: SI 2002/263
s.5, applied: SI 2004/1899
s.5, repealed (in part): 2004 c.14 Sch.1 Part 4
s.6, repealed (in part): 2004 c.14 Sch.1 Part 4
s.7, repealed (in part): 2004 c.14 Sch.1 Part 4

46. Transport Act 1962
s.10, amended: SI 2003/1545 Art.2
s.13, amended: 2003 c.20 Sch.2 para.19
s.24, applied: SSI 2002/263 Art.4
s.27, applied: SSI 2002/263 Art.4
s.52, varied: SI 2003/1615 Sch.1 para.2
s.54, repealed: SI 2003/1615 Sch.1 para.2
s.63, varied: SI 2004/1822 Sch.1 para.2
s.67, applied: SI 2002/1064 Art.23
s.67, repealed (in part): SI 2003/1615 Sch.1 para.2
s.86, amended: SI 2002/2626 Sch.2 para.2
Sch.2 Part I, varied: SI 2003/1615 Sch.1 para.2
Sch.2 Part III, varied: SI 2003/1615 Sch.1 para.2
Sch.2 Part IV, varied: SI 2003/1615 Sch.1 para.2
Sch.6 para.1, varied: SI 2003/1615 Sch.1 para.2
Sch.6 para.2, varied: SI 2003/1615 Sch.1 para.2
Sch.6 para.3, amended: 2003 c.14 Sch.20 para.3
Sch.6 para.3, varied: SI 2003/1615 Sch.1 para.2
Sch.6 para.4, varied: SI 2003/1615 Sch.1 para.2

10 & 11 Eliz. 2 (1961-62)–cont.

46. Transport Act 1962–*cont.*
Sch.6 para.6, varied: SI 2003/1615 Sch.1 para.2

47. Education (Scotland) Act 1962
s.1, disapplied: SI 2003/1994 Reg.6
s.2, applied: SI 2003/1994 Reg.6

54. Trinidad and Tobago Independence Act 1962
Sch.2 para.15, repealed: 2002 c.39 Sch.3

56. Local Government (Records) Act 1962
varied: SI 2004/1777 Art.21, SI 2004/1778 Art.21

57. Uganda Independence Act 1962
Sch.3 para.14, repealed: 2002 c.39 Sch.3

58. Pipe-lines Act 1962
applied: 2004 c.20 s.188
s.9, amended: 2004 c.20 s.151, Sch.23 Part 1
s.9A, amended: 2004 c.20 s.151, Sch.23 Part 1
s.10, amended: 2004 c.20 s.151
s.10B, repealed: 2004 c.20 s.151, Sch.23 Part 1
s.10C, amended: 2004 c.20 s.151, Sch.23 Part 1
s.37, amended: 2004 c.21 Sch.1 para.17
s.37, varied: SI 2004/1822 Sch.1 para.3
s.40, amended: 2003 c.21 Sch.17 para.28
s.44, varied: SI 2004/1822 Sch.1 para.3
s.66, amended: 2004 c.20 s.151, Sch.23 Part 1
s.66, varied: SI 2004/1822 Sch.1 para.3

59. Road Traffic Act 1962
repealed: 2004 c.14 Sch.1 Part 14

1963

xxxvii. Durham County Council Act 1963
s.44, varied: SI 2003/2155 Sch.1 para.16

xvii. London County Council (General Powers) Act 1963
s.9, amended: SI 2003/1615 Sch.1 para.23
s.17, amended: 2003 c.21 Sch.17 para.29, SI 2003/1615 Sch.1 para.23

xxiv. London Transport Act 1963
s.11, see *Bridgestart Properties Ltd v London Underground Ltd* [2004] R.V.R. 18 (Lands Tr), George Bartlett Q.C. (President)

1. Ecclesiastical Jurisdiction Measure 1963
applied: SI 2002/1892 Sch.1 Part TABLEb, SI 2002/1893 para.1, para.4, 2003 c.3 s.7, s.26, s.27, s.29, s.38, s.47, SI 2003/1933 Sch.1 Part III, SI 2003/1936 para.1, SI 2004/1888 Sch.1 Part TABLEb
referred to: 2003 c.3 s.44, s.47, Sch.1 para.1
Part III, applied: 2003 c.3 s.47
Part IV, repealed: 2003 c.3 Sch.2
Part V, repealed: 2003 c.3 Sch.2
Part IX, applied: 2003 c.3 s.47
Part IX, repealed: 2003 c.3 Sch.2
s.1, amended: 2003 c.3 Sch.1 para.2, Sch.2

1963–cont.

1. Ecclesiastical Jurisdiction Measure 1963–*cont.*

s.3, amended: 2003 c.3 Sch.1 para.3

s.3, referred to: 2003 c.3, s.20

s.6, amended: 2003 c.3 Sch.2, 2004 c.14 Sch.1 Part 6

s.6, referred to: SI 2003/1933 Sch.1 Part III, SI 2004/1888 Sch.1 Part TABLEb

s.7, amended: 2003 c.3 Sch.1 para.4, Sch.2

s.9, repealed: 2003 c.3 Sch.2

s.10, referred to: SI 2003/1933 Sch.1 Part III, SI 2004/1888 Sch.1 Part TABLEb

s.11, repealed (in part): 2003 c.3 Sch.2

s.12, amended: 2003 c.3 Sch.1 para.5

s.14, amended: 2003 c.3 Sch.2

s.15, amended: 2003 c.3 Sch.2

s.16, amended: 2003 c.3 Sch.2

s.31, applied: SI 2002/1893 para.4, SI 2003/1936 para.4

s.46, amended: 2003 c.3 Sch.2

s.47, amended: 2003 c.3 Sch.1 para.6

s.47, applied: SI 2002/1892 Sch.1 Part TABLE, Sch.1 Part TABLEa, SI 2003/1933 Sch.1 Part I, Sch.1 Part II, SI 2004/1888 Sch.1 Part TABLE, Sch.1 Part TABLEa

s.49, amended: 2003 c.3 Sch.1 para.7

s.50, amended: 2003 c.3 Sch.1 para.8

s.52, amended: 2003 c.3 Sch.1 para.9

s.54, repealed: 2003 c.3 Sch.2

s.55, referred to: SI 2002/1893 para.4

s.58, varied: 2003 c.3 s.35

s.60, varied: 2003 c.3 s.35

s.61, varied: 2003 c.3 s.35

s.62, applied: SI 2003/1933 Sch.1 Part III, SI 2004/1888 Sch.1 Part TABLEb

s.62, varied: 2003 c.3 s.35

s.63, varied: 2003 c.3 s.35

s.66, amended: 2003 c.3 Sch.1 para.10

s.67, amended: 2003 c.3 Sch.1 para.11

s.68, repealed: 2003 c.3 Sch.2

s.69, amended: 2003 c.3 Sch.1 para.12, Sch.2

s.70, amended: 2003 c.3 Sch.2

s.71, varied: 2003 c.3 s.35

s.72, varied: 2003 c.3 s.35

s.73, varied: 2003 c.3 s.35

s.74, amended: 2003 c.3 Sch.1 para.13

s.74, varied: 2003 c.3 s.35

s.75, varied: 2003 c.3 s.35

s.76, amended: 2003 c.3 Sch.1 para.14

s.76, varied: 2003 c.3 s.35

s.77, repealed: 2003 c.3 Sch.2

s.78, varied: 2003 c.3 s.35

s.79, repealed: 2003 c.3 Sch.2

s.80, varied: 2003 c.3 s.35

s.81, varied: 2003 c.3 s.35

s.82, repealed: 2004 c.14 Sch.1 Part 6

s.83, varied: 2003 c.3 s.35

s.88, repealed: 2004 c.14 Sch.1 Part 6

Sch.2, repealed: 2003 c.3 Sch.2

Sch.4, amended: 2004 c.14 Sch.1 Part 6

1963–cont.

2. Betting, Gaming and Lotteries Act 1963

applied: 2004 c.25 s.9, s.12

referred to: 2004 c.25 s.10

s.1, amended: 2004 c.25 Sch.2 para.2, Sch.6

s.1, disapplied: 2004 c.25 s.9

s.3, amended: 2004 c.25 Sch.2 para.3, Sch.6

s.4, applied: 2004 c.25 s.9

s.4, disapplied: 2004 c.25 s.9

s.4, referred to: 2004 c.25 s.9

s.4, substituted: 2004 c.25 s.10

s.4A, applied: 2004 c.25 s.9

s.4A, disapplied: 2004 c.25 s.9

s.4A, referred to: 2004 c.25 s.9

s.4A, substituted: 2004 c.25 s.10

s.4B, substituted: 2004 c.25 s.10

s.5, amended: 2004 c.25 Sch.2 para.4, Sch.6

s.6, amended: 2004 c.25 Sch.2 para.5, Sch.6

s.8, amended: 2003 c.44 Sch.37 Part 9

s.8, disapplied: 2003 c.44 Sch.25 para.54

s.9, amended: 2004 c.25 Sch.2 para.6, Sch.6

s.9, applied: 2004 c.25 s.9

s.9, referred to: 2004 c.25 s.9

s.9, repealed (in part): 2004 c.25 Sch.2 para.6, Sch.6

s.10, amended: 2003 c.17 Sch.6 para.30

s.10, applied: SI 2002/1930

s.10, enabling: SI 2002/1930

s.10A, amended: 2003 c.39 Sch.8 para.113

s.11, amended: 2003 c.39 Sch.8 para.114, 2004 c.25 Sch.2 para.7

s.12, repealed: 2004 c.25 Sch.2 para.8, Sch.6

s.13, amended: 2004 c.25 Sch.4 para.2

s.13, applied: 2004 c.25 s.17

s.14, repealed: 2004 c.25 Sch.2 para.9, Sch.6

s.15, repealed: 2004 c.25 Sch.2 para.10, Sch.6

s.16, amended: 2004 c.25 Sch.2 para.11

s.24, amended: 2004 c.25 Sch.2 para.12

s.24, referred to: 2004 c.25 s.15

s.24, repealed (in part): 2004 c.25 Sch.2 para.12, Sch.6

s.25, referred to: 2004 c.25 s.15

s.26, referred to: 2004 c.25 s.15

s.26, enabling: SI 2003/1909

s.27, referred to: 2004 c.25 s.15

s.28, referred to: 2004 c.25 s.15

s.29, referred to: 2004 c.25 s.15

s.30, amended: 2004 c.25 Sch.2 para.13

s.30, referred to: 2004 c.25 s.15

s.31, amended: 2004 c.25 Sch.2 para.14, Sch.6

s.52, amended: 2004 c.25 Sch.2 para.15

s.55, amended: 2004 c.25 Sch.2 para.16, Sch.4 para.3, Sch.6

Sch.1A, referred to: 2004 c.25 s.10

Sch.1 para.1, amended: 2003 c.39 Sch.8 para.115

Sch.1 para.2, amended: 2003 c.39 Sch.8 para.115

1963–cont.

2. Betting, Gaming and Lotteries Act 1963–cont.

Sch.1 para.19, see *William Hill (Caledonian) Ltd v Glasgow City Licensing Board* 2003 S.C. 289 (Ex Div), Lord Kirkwood, Lord Johnston, Lady Paton

Sch.1 para.19, amended: 2004 c.25 Sch.2 para.17, Sch.6

Sch.1 para.20A, amended: 2003 c.39 Sch.8 para.115

Sch.1 para.25A, repealed: 2004 c.25 Sch.4 para.4

Sch.1 para.36, repealed: 2004 c.25 Sch.4 para.4

Sch.1A Part I para.1, substituted: 2004 c.25 Sch.1

Sch.1A Part I para.2, substituted: 2004 c.25 Sch.1

Sch.1A Part I para.3, substituted: 2004 c.25 Sch.1

Sch.1A Part II para.4, substituted: 2004 c.25 Sch.1

Sch.1A Part II para.5, substituted: 2004 c.25 Sch.1

Sch.1A Part II para.6, substituted: 2004 c.25 Sch.1

Sch.1A Part II para.7, substituted: 2004 c.25 Sch.1

Sch.1A Part II para.8, substituted: 2004 c.25 Sch.1

Sch.1A Part II para.9, substituted: 2004 c.25 Sch.1

Sch.1A Part III para.10, substituted: 2004 c.25 Sch.1

Sch.1A Part III para.11, substituted: 2004 c.25 Sch.1

Sch.1A Part III para.12, substituted: 2004 c.25 Sch.1

Sch.1A Part III para.13, substituted: 2004 c.25 Sch.1

Sch.1A Part III para.14, substituted: 2004 c.25 Sch.1

Sch.1A Part III para.15, substituted: 2004 c.25 Sch.1

Sch.1A Part III para.16, substituted: 2004 c.25 Sch.1

Sch.1A Part III para.17, substituted: 2004 c.25 Sch.1

Sch.1A Part III para.18, substituted: 2004 c.25 Sch.1

Sch.1A Part III para.19, substituted: 2004 c.25 Sch.1

Sch.1A Part III para.20, substituted: 2004 c.25 Sch.1

Sch.1A Part III para.21, substituted: 2004 c.25 Sch.1

Sch.1A Part III para.22, substituted: 2004 c.25 Sch.1

Sch.1A Part III para.23, substituted: 2004 c.25 Sch.1

1963–cont.

2. Betting, Gaming and Lotteries Act 1963–cont.

Sch.1A Part III para.24, substituted: 2004 c.25 Sch.1

Sch.4 para.10, amended: 2003 c.17 Sch.6 para.31

Sch.4 para.10, substituted: SI 2002/1930 Art.2

Sch.4 para.11, amended: SI 2002/1930 Art.2

11. Agriculture (Miscellaneous Provisions) Act 1963

s.16, repealed: 2004 c.14 Sch.1 Part 6

s.23, repealed (in part): 2004 c.14 Sch.1 Part 2

s.26, repealed: 2004 c.14 Sch.1 Part 2

s.27, repealed (in part): 2004 c.14 Sch.1 Part 2

s.29, amended: 2004 c.14 Sch.1 Part 2, Sch.1 Part 6

12. Local Government (Financial Provisions) (Scotland) Act 1963

s.14, amended: 2003 asp 1 s.31

14. Corn Rents Act 1963

s.3, repealed (in part): 2004 c.14 Sch.1 Part 6

Sch.1, repealed: 2004 c.14 Sch.1 Part 6

15. Fort William Pulp and Paper Mills Act 1963

repealed: 2004 c.14 Sch.1 Part 15

18. Stock Transfer Act 1963

applied: 2002 c.iii s.10, 2002 c.iv s.13, SI 2004/1611 Reg.15

s.1, see *Pennington v Waine (No.1)* [2002] EWCA Civ 227, [2002] 1 W.L.R. 2075 (CA), Arden, L.J.

s.4, amended: 2004 c.21 Sch.1 para.18

22. Sheriff Courts (Civil Jurisdiction and Procedure) (Scotland) Act 1963

s.3, applied: SSI 2002/132 Sch.1 para.32.1, Sch.1 para.32.2

24. British Museum Act 1963

s.10, enabling: SI 2004/1392

Sch.3 Part II para.4, substituted: SI 2004/1392 Art.2

33. London Government Act 1963

applied: SI 2003/527 Reg.2

s.52, repealed (in part): 2003 c.17 Sch.7

Sch.12, applied: 2003 c.17 Sch.4 para.2, Sch.8 para.31

Sch.12 para.1, repealed: 2003 c.17 Sch.7

Sch.12 para.2, repealed: 2003 c.17 Sch.7

Sch.12 para.2A, repealed: 2003 c.17 Sch.7

Sch.12 para.3, repealed: 2003 c.17 Sch.7

Sch.12 para.3A, repealed: 2003 c.17 Sch.7

Sch.12 para.3B, repealed: 2003 c.17 Sch.7

Sch.12 para.3C, repealed: 2003 c.17 Sch.7

Sch.12 para.4, repealed: 2003 c.17 Sch.7

Sch.12 para.5, repealed: 2003 c.17 Sch.7

Sch.12 para.6, repealed: 2003 c.17 Sch.7

Sch.12 para.6A, repealed: 2003 c.17 Sch.7

Sch.12 para.6B, repealed: 2003 c.17 Sch.7

Sch.12 para.6C, repealed: 2003 c.17 Sch.7

Sch.12 para.6D, repealed: 2003 c.17 Sch.7

CAP.

1963–cont.

33. London Government Act 1963–cont.
Sch.12 para.7, repealed: 2003 c.17 Sch.7
Sch.12 para.8, repealed: 2003 c.17 Sch.7
Sch.12 para.9, repealed: 2003 c.17 Sch.7
Sch.12 para.9A, repealed: 2003 c.17 Sch.7
Sch.12 para.10, see *Toye v Southwark LBC* [2002] EWHC 292, (2002) 166 J.P. 389 (QBD (Admin Ct)), Forbes, J.
Sch.12 para.10, repealed: 2003 c.17 Sch.7
Sch.12 para.11, repealed: 2003 c.17 Sch.7
Sch.12 para.11A, added: SI 2002/3205 Art.3
Sch.12 para.11A, repealed: 2003 c.17 Sch.7
Sch.12 para.12, applied: 2004 c.i s.22
Sch.12 para.12, repealed: 2003 c.17 Sch.7
Sch.12 para.12, varied: 2004 c.i s.21
Sch.12 para.12A, repealed: 2003 c.17 Sch.7
Sch.12 para.12B, repealed: 2003 c.17 Sch.7
Sch.12 para.12C, repealed: 2003 c.17 Sch.7
Sch.12 para.13, repealed: 2003 c.17 Sch.7
Sch.12 para.14, repealed: 2003 c.17 Sch.7
Sch.12 para.15, repealed: 2003 c.17 Sch.7
Sch.12 para.16, repealed: 2003 c.17 Sch.7
Sch.12 para.17, repealed: 2003 c.17 Sch.7
Sch.12 para.18, repealed: 2003 c.17 Sch.7
Sch.12 para.18A, repealed: 2003 c.17 Sch.7
Sch.12 para.19, repealed: 2003 c.17 Sch.7
Sch.12 para.19A, repealed: 2003 c.17 Sch.7
Sch.12 para.19AA, repealed: 2003 c.17 Sch.7
Sch.12 para.20, repealed: 2003 c.17 Sch.7

35. Malaysia Act 1963
Sch.2 para.1, repealed (in part): 2002 c.39 Sch.3

37. Children and Young Persons Act 1963
s.16, repealed (in part): 2003 c.44 Sch.37 Part 5
s.17, repealed (in part): 2003 c.39 Sch.10
s.26, amended: SI 2002/3135 Sch.1 para.4
s.29, see *A v DPP* [2002] EWHC 403, [2002] 2 Cr. App. R. (S.) 88 (DC), Goldring, J.; see *T v DPP* [2003] EWHC 2408, (2004) 168 J.P. 194 (QBD (Admin Ct)), Brooke, L.J.
s.37, amended: 2003 c.17 Sch.6 para.32
s.40, amended: 2003 c.44 Sch.37 Part 9
s.40, disapplied: 2003 c.44 Sch.25 para.55
s.42, applied: SI 2003/3319 Reg.24
s.56, amended: 2004 c.31 Sch.5 Part 4
Sch.2 Part II para.14, repealed: 2003 c.39 Sch.10
Sch.2 Part II para.15, repealed: 2003 c.39 Sch.10

41. Offices, Shops and Railway Premises Act 1963
s.2, amended: 2004 c.33 Sch.27 para.23
s.46, amended: 2003 c.39 Sch.8 para.116, Sch.10
s.84, amended: 2002 c.39 Sch.2 para.4
s.90, amended: 2003 c.17 Sch.6 para.33, Sch.7

CAP.

1963–cont.

43. Animal Boarding Establishments Act 1963
disapplied: 2003 c.44 Sch.25 para.56
s.2, applied: 2003 c.44 Sch.25 para.56
s.3, amended: 2003 c.44 Sch.37 Part 9
s.3, repealed (in part): 2003 c.44 Sch.37 Part 9

47. Limitation Act 1963
see *McDonnell v Congregation of Christian Brothers Trustees (formerly Irish Christian Brothers)* [2003] UKHL 63, [2004] 1 A.C. 1101 (HL), Lord Bingham of Cornhill
s.1, see *McDonnell v Congregation of Christian Brothers Trustees (formerly Irish Christian Brothers)* [2001] EWCA Civ 2095, [2002] C.P. Rep. 31 (CA), Ward, L.J.

48. Peerage Act 1963
s.4, see *Lord Gray's Motion, Re* [2002] 1 A.C. 124 (HL), Lord Slynn of Hadley

51. Land Compensation (Scotland) Act 1963
applied: 2004 asp 10 s.8, s.9, s.10, s.16, s.17, s.22, s.23, s.27, SSI 2004/171 Art.14, Art.15
Part II, applied: SSI 2003/452 r.7
s.5, applied: SSI 2003/452 r.8
s.11, applied: SSI 2003/452 r.28

54. Kenya Independence Act 1963
Sch.2 para.13, repealed: 2002 c.39 Sch.3

55. Zanzibar Act 1963
Sch.1 Part I para.13, repealed: 2002 c.39 Sch.3

1964

xxxviii. British Transport Docks Act 1964
s.51, disapplied: SI 2002/3269 Art.8
s.54, varied: SI 2002/3269 Art.8

iv. City of London (Courts) Act 1964
s.7, amended: 2004 c.14 Sch.1 Part 1

5. International Headquarters and Defence Organisations Act 1964
Sch.1 para.1, applied: 2003 c.20 s.101
Sch.1 para.2, applied: 2003 c.20 s.101

6. Clergy (Ordination and Miscellaneous Provisions) Measure 1964
s.1, repealed (in part): 2004 c.14 Sch.1 Part 6
s.11, repealed: 2004 c.14 Sch.1 Part 6
s.12, repealed: 2004 c.14 Sch.1 Part 6

8. Church Commissioners Measure 1964
s.2, repealed (in part): 2004 c.14 Sch.1 Part 6
s.3, repealed: 2004 c.14 Sch.1 Part 6

14. Plant Varieties and Seeds Act 1964
applied: SI 2002/3171 Reg.23
s.16, applied: SI 2002/3172, SI 2002/3174, SI 2002/3175, SI 2002/3176, SI 2002/3176 Reg.8, SI 2003/56, SI 2003/3101, SSI 2002/520, SSI 2002/526, SSI 2002/564, SSI 2003/304, SSI 2004/317
s.16, enabling: SI 2002/1554, SI 2002/1563, SI 2002/1870, SI 2002/3171, SI 2002/3172, SI 2002/3173, SI 2002/3174, SI

CAP.

1964–cont.

14. Plant Varieties and Seeds Act 1964– *cont.*

s.16, enabling:–*cont.*
2002/3175, SI 2002/3176, SI 2003/56, SI 2003/2529, SI 2003/3101, SI 2004/1316, SI 2004/2385, SI 2004/2386, SI 2004/ 2387, SI 2004/2388, SI 2004/2389, SI 2004/2390, SI 2004/2881, SSI 2002/ 520, SSI 2002/526, SSI 2002/564, SSI 2003/304, SSI 2004/250, SSI 2004/317, SSI 2004/380

s.17, applied: SI 2002/3171 Reg.24, SI 2002/ 3172 Reg.27, SI 2002/3173 Reg.27, SI 2002/3174 Reg.27, SI 2002/3175 Reg.27, SI 2004/2881 Reg.27, SSI 2004/317 Reg.23

s.24, applied: SI 2002/3176 Reg.33

s.24, enabling: SI 2002/3176, SI 2004/2390

s.26, applied: SI 2002/3176 Reg.32, Reg.33

s.26, repealed (in part): 2004 c.14 Sch.1 Part 2

s.26, enabling: SI 2002/3176, SI 2004/2390

s.27, amended: 2003 c.44 Sch.26 para.18

s.31, amended: 2004 c.14 Sch.1 Part 2

s.36, enabling: SI 2002/1554, SI 2002/1563, SI 2002/1870, SI 2002/3171, SI 2002/ 3172, SI 2002/3173, SI 2002/3174, SI 2002/3175, SI 2002/3176, SI 2003/56, SI 2003/2529, SI 2003/3101, SI 2004/ 2385, SI 2004/2386, SI 2004/2387, SI 2004/2388, SI 2004/2389, SI 2004/ 2390, SI 2004/2881, SSI 2002/520, SSI 2002/526, SSI 2002/564, SSI 2003/ 304, SSI 2004/317, SSI 2004/380

s.39, amended: SI 2002/2843 Art.5

s.41, repealed (in part): 2004 c.14 Sch.1 Part 2

16. Industrial Training Act 1964

applied: SI 2003/409 Sch.1 Part I

26. Licensing Act 1964

see *Lethem v Secretary of State for Transport, Local Government and the Regions* [2002] EWHC 1549, [2003] 1 P.& C.R. 2 (QBD (Admin Ct)), George Bartlett Q.C.; see *R. (on the application of RBNB) v Warrington Crown Court* [2002] UKHL 24, [2002] 1 W.L.R.1954 (HL), Lord Bingham of Cornhill

applied: SI 2002/493, 2003 c.17 Sch.4 para.2, Sch.8 para.12

repealed: 2003 c.17 Sch.7

Appendix 1., repealed: 2003 c.17 Sch.7

s.6, applied: 2003 c.17 Sch.8 para.12

s.12, see *R. (on the application of Bushell) v Newcastle Upon Tyne Licensing Justices* [2004] EWHC 446, [2004] N.P.C. 44 (QBD (Admin Ct)), Lightman, J.

s.15, see *R. (on the application of Bushell) v Newcastle Upon Tyne Licensing Justices* [2004] EWCA Civ 767, [2004] 3 All E.R. 493 (CA), Jacob, L.J.; see *R. (on the application of Bushell) v Newcastle Upon Tyne Licensing Justices* [2004] EWHC 446, [2004] N.P.C. 44 (QBD (Admin Ct)), Lightman, J.

CAP.

1964–cont.

26. Licensing Act 1964–*cont.*

s.59, referred to: 2003 c.17 Sch.8 para.29

s.66, repealed: 2003 c.17 Sch.7

s.67, repealed: 2003 c.17 Sch.7

s.74, see *Carter-Pascoe v Birmingham Justices* [2002] EWHC 1202, [2002] N.P.C. 83 (QBD (Admin Ct)), Lightman, J.; see *Gough v Avon and Somerset Police Licensing Bureau* [2002] EWHC 658, (2003) 2 J.P. 79 (QBD), Lord Woolf, L.C.J.

s.77, see *R. (on the application of Luminar Leisure Ltd) v Norwich Crown Court* [2003] EWHC 2227, (2003) 167 J.P. 561 (QBD (Admin Ct)), Stanley Burnton, J.; see *R. (on the application of Luminar Leisure Ltd) v Norwich Crown Court* [2004] EWCA Civ 281, [2004] 1 W.L.R. 2512 (CA), Peter Gibson, L.J.

s.77A, see *Westminster City Council v O'Reilly (Leave to Appeal: Jurisdiction)* [2003] EWCA Civ 1007, [2004] 1 W.L.R. 195 (CA), Auld, L.J.; see *Westminster City Council v O'Reilly* [2003] EWHC 485, [2003] 1 W.L.R. 1411 (QBD (Admin Ct)), Mackay, J.

s.86A, referred to: 2003 c.17 s.173

s.87, referred to: 2003 c.17 s.173

s.95, amended: SI 2002/493 Art.2

s.160, see *Haringey LBC v Marks & Spencer Plc* [2004] EWHC 1141, [2004] 3 All E.R. 868 (QBD (Admin Ct)), Maurice Kay, L.J.

s.168E, applied: SI 2002/1837 Sch.1 Part II

s.169A, see *Haringey LBC v Marks & Spencer Plc* [2004] EWHC 1141, [2004] 3 All E.R. 868 (QBD (Admin Ct)), Maurice Kay, L.J.

s.169A, applied: SI 2002/1837 Sch.1 Part I

s.169C, applied: SI 2002/1837 Sch.1 Part I, Sch.1 Part II

s.169F, applied: SI 2002/1837 Sch.1 Part I

s.182, see *Toye v Southwark LBC* [2002] EWHC 292, (2002) 166 J.P. 389 (QBD (Admin Ct)), Forbes, J.

s.182, disapplied: 2003 c.17 Sch.8 para.1

s.199, applied: 2003 c.17 Sch.8 para.1

s.199, referred to: 2003 c.17 s.196

Sch.8 para.1, repealed: 2003 c.17 Sch.7

Sch.8 para.2, repealed: 2003 c.17 Sch.7

Sch.8 para.3, repealed: 2003 c.17 Sch.7

Sch.8 para.4, repealed: 2003 c.17 Sch.7

Sch.8 para.5, repealed: 2003 c.17 Sch.7

Sch.8 para.6, repealed: 2003 c.17 Sch.7

Sch.8 para.7, repealed: 2003 c.17 Sch.7

Sch.8 para.7A, repealed: 2003 c.17 Sch.7

28. Agriculture and Horticulture Act 1964

Part III, applied: SI 2003/1846 Reg.2, SSI 2003/502 Reg.2

Part III, disapplied: 2003 c.44 Sch.25 para.57

s.11, see *Department for Environment, Food and Rural Affairs v ASDA Stores Ltd* [2003] UKHL 71, [2004] 1 W.L.R. 105 (HL), Lord Nicholls of Birkenhead

1964–cont.

28. Agriculture and Horticulture Act 1964–*cont.*

s.11, applied: SI 2003/1846 Reg.2, SSI 2003/502 Reg.2

s.11, enabling: SI 2003/1846, SI 2004/2604, SSI 2003/502, SSI 2004/245

s.12, see *Department for Environment, Food and Rural Affairs v ASDA Stores Ltd* [2003] UKHL 71, [2004] 1 W.L.R. 105 (HL), Lord Nicholls of Birkenhead

s.14, see *Department for Environment, Food and Rural Affairs v ASDA Stores Ltd* [2002] EWHC 1335, [2002] 2 C.M.L.R. 66 (QBD (Admin Ct)), Rose, L.J.; see *Department for Environment, Food and Rural Affairs v ASDA Stores Ltd* [2003] UKHL 71, [2004] 1 W.L.R. 105 (HL), Lord Nicholls of Birkenhead

s.15, applied: 2003 c.44 Sch.25 para.57

s.20, amended: 2003 c.44 Sch.37 Part 9

s.21, repealed: 2004 c.14 Sch.1 Part 2

s.22, applied: SI 2003/1846 Reg.2, SSI 2003/502 Reg.2

s.23, applied: SI 2003/1846, SI 2004/2604, SSI 2004/245

s.24, see *Department for Environment, Food and Rural Affairs v ASDA Stores Ltd* [2002] EWHC 1335, [2002] 2 C.M.L.R. 66 (QBD (Admin Ct)), Rose, L.J.

s.26, amended: 2004 c.14 Sch.1 Part 2

29. Continental Shelf Act 1964

applied: 2002 asp 11 s.9, SI 2002/1861 Reg.3

s.1, applied: SI 2002/1587 Reg.3, 2003 c.1 s.40, s.382, SI 2003/1660 Reg.9, SI 2003/1661 Reg.9, 2004 c.20 s.91, s.188

s.6, repealed: 2003 c.21 Sch.19

s.6, varied: 2003 c.21 Sch.18 para.63

s.8, amended: 2004 c.20 s.103, Sch.23 Part 1

38. Emergency Powers Act 1964

s.1, repealed: 2004 c.36 Sch.3

40. Harbours Act 1964

applied: SI 2002/1998, SI 2003/527 Reg.2, SSI 2004/421 Art.8

referred to: SSI 2002/410 Art.60, SSI 2004/421 Art.7

s.14, applied: SI 2002/311, SI 2002/2476, SI 2002/2586, SI 2002/2618, SI 2002/2730, SI 2002/3127, SI 2002/3268, SI 2002/3269, SI 2003/2556, SI 2003/2574, SI 2003/2679, SI 2003/2724, SI 2003/3006 Sch.2, SI 2004/148, SI 2004/1280, SI 2004/1426, SI 2004/1506, SI 2004/2469, SSI 2002/121, SSI 2002/294, SSI 2002/310, SSI 2002/410, SSI 2002/410 Art.58, SSI 2002/504, SSI 2002/557, SSI 2003/211, SSI 2003/258, SSI 2003/435, SSI 2003/491, SSI 2004/485

s.14, referred to: SI 2002/2476, SI 2002/2618, SI 2002/3127, SI 2002/3269, SI 2003/2556, SI 2004/1280, SI 2004/1426, SSI 2002/410, SSI 2003/258

1964–cont.

40. Harbours Act 1964–*cont.*

s.14, enabling: SI 2002/311, SI 2002/2476, SI 2002/2586, SI 2002/2618, SI 2002/2730, SI 2002/3127, SI 2002/3268, SI 2002/3269, SI 2003/2556, SI 2003/2574, SI 2003/2679, SI 2003/2724, SI 2004/148, SI 2004/1280, SI 2004/1426, SI 2004/1506, SI 2004/2190, SI 2004/2469, SSI 2002/121, SSI 2002/294, SSI 2002/310, SSI 2002/410, SSI 2002/504, SSI 2002/557, SSI 2003/190, SSI 2003/211, SSI 2003/258, SSI 2003/435, SSI 2003/491, SSI 2004/207, SSI 2004/421, SSI 2004/485

s.15, applied: SI 2002/306

s.15, enabling: SI 2002/306

s.16, applied: SSI 2004/171

s.16, enabling: SSI 2004/171

s.27A, applied: SI 2003/1809 Reg.14

s.30, applied: SSI 2002/410 Art.43, Art.45, SSI 2004/421 Art.4

s.31, applied: SI 2003/1809 Reg.14, SSI 2002/410 Art.43, SSI 2004/421 Art.4

s.31, varied: SI 2003/1809 Reg.14

s.32, applied: SSI 2004/421 Art.4

s.40, applied: SSI 2004/421 Art.4

s.53, amended: 2003 c.21 Sch.17 para.30

s.57, applied: SSI 2002/410 Art.4

s.57, referred to: SSI 2002/410 Art.43, SSI 2004/421 Art.4

Sch.2 para.9B, applied: SI 2003/2679 Sch.2 para.13

Sch.2 para.9B, disapplied: SSI 2002/294 Sch.2 para.13, SSI 2002/310 Sch.2 para.15

Sch.2 para.9B, referred to: 2002 c.v Sch.2 para.6, SI 2002/2476 Sch.2 para.15, SI 2002/2586 Sch.2 para.13, SI 2002/2730 Sch.2 para.13, SI 2002/3268 Sch.2 para.10, SI 2003/2574 Sch.2 para.13, SI 2003/2724 Sch.2 para.13, SI 2004/148 Sch.2 para.13, SI 2004/1426 Sch.2 para.13, SI 2004/1506 Sch.2 para.13

Sch.3 Part I para.1, amended: 2004 asp 6 Sch.7 para.1

Sch.3 Part I para.2, applied: SSI 2004/421

Sch.3 Part I para.3, applied: SI 2002/306, SSI 2002/294, SSI 2002/504

Sch.3 Part I para.3, enabling: SSI 2002/294, SSI 2002/504, SSI 2004/421

Sch.3 Part I para.4, enabling: SI 2002/2618, SSI 2004/485

Sch.3 Part 1 para.4, applied: SI 2002/2618

Sch.3 Part I para.4B, applied: SSI 2004/485

Sch.3 Part I para.5, applied: SSI 2004/171

Sch.3 Part I para.5, enabling: SSI 2004/171

Sch.3 Part 1 para.8, applied: SI 2002/2618

Sch.3 Part 1 para.15, applied: SI 2002/2618

Sch.3 Part 1 para.18, applied: SI 2002/2618, SI 2004/1426, SI 2004/2469, SSI 2003/258

Sch.3 Part II para.8, applied: SSI 2004/485

CAP.

1964–cont.

40. Harbours Act 1964–*cont.*

Sch.3 Part III para.10, applied: SI 2002/311, SI 2002/2476, SI 2002/2586, SI 2002/2730, SI 2002/3127, SI 2002/3268, SI 2002/3269, SI 2003/2574, SI 2003/2679, SI 2003/2724, SI 2004/148, SI 2004/1280, SI 2004/1506, SSI 2002/121, SSI 2003/491, SSI 2004/207

Sch.3 Part III para.10, enabling: SI 2002/311, SI 2002/2476, SI 2002/2586, SI 2002/3127, SI 2002/3268, SI 2002/3269, SI 2003/2574, SI 2003/2679, SI 2003/2724, SI 2004/148, SI 2004/1280, SI 2004/1506, SSI 2002/121, SSI 2003/435, SSI 2003/491, SSI 2004/207

Sch.3 Part VIII para.15, applied: SSI 2004/485

41. Succession (Scotland) Act 1964

applied: 2003 asp 11 s.21, s.77

Part I, applied: 2003 asp 11 s.21

s.1, amended: 2004 c.33 Sch.28 para.1

s.2, amended: 2004 c.33 Sch.28 para.2

s.5, amended: 2004 c.33 Sch.28 para.3

s.8, amended: 2004 c.33 Sch.28 para.4

s.9, amended: 2004 c.33 Sch.28 para.5

s.10, amended: 2004 c.33 Sch.28 para.6

s.15, amended: 2004 c.33 Sch.28 para.7

s.16, amended: 2003 asp 11 s.20, Sch.1 para.2, 2004 c.33 Sch.28 para.8

s.16, applied: 2003 asp 11 s.21, s.22, s.23

s.29, amended: 2003 asp 11 Sch.1 para.2

s.31, amended: 2004 c.33 Sch.28 para.9

s.36, amended: 2004 c.33 s.131, Sch.28 para.10

42. Administration of Justice Act 1964

s.19, amended: 2003 c.39 Sch.8 para.117

s.26, amended: 2003 c.39 Sch.8 para.118, Sch.10

Sch.3 Part II para.10, repealed: 2004 c.14 Sch.1 Part 1

Sch.3 Part II para.31, repealed: 2003 c.17 Sch.7

46. Malawi Independence Act 1964

Sch.2 para.14, repealed: 2002 c.39 Sch.3

48. Police Act 1964

applied: SI 2002/412 Art.31, SI 2003/527 Reg.2, Reg.21

s.21, applied: SI 2003/527 Reg.21

s.21A, applied: SI 2003/527 Reg.21

s.53C, varied: SI 2003/527 Reg.40

49. Finance Act 1964

s.24, repealed: SI 2002/2521 Sch.2 Part I

Sch.8 para.1, repealed: SI 2002/2521 Sch.2 Part I

Sch.8 para.3, repealed: SI 2002/2521 Sch.2 Part I

Sch.8 para.9, repealed: SI 2002/2521 Sch.2 Part I

53. Hire Purchase Act 1964

s.27, see *Shogun Finance Ltd v Hudson* [2001] EWCA Civ 1000, [2002] Q.B. 834 (CA), Sedley, L.J.; see *Shogun Finance Ltd*

CAP.

1964–cont.

53. Hire Purchase Act 1964–*cont.*

s.27–*cont.*

v Hudson [2003] UKHL 62, [2004] 1 A.C. 919 (HL), Lord Nicholls of Birkenhead

55. Perpetuities and Accumulations Act 1964

s.9, see *Wilson v Truelove* [2003] EWHC 750, [2003] 2 E.G.L.R. 63 (Ch D), Simon Berry Q.C.

60. Emergency Laws (Re-enactments and Repeals) Act 1964

Sch.1 para.1, amended: 2003 c.44 Sch.37 Part 9

Sch.1 para.1, disapplied: 2003 c.44 Sch.25 para.58

Sch.1 para.2, amended: 2003 c.44 Sch.37 Part 9

Sch.1 para.2, disapplied: 2003 c.44 Sch.25 para.58

63. Law of Property (Joint Tenants) Act 1964

s.3, amended: 2002 c.9 Sch.11 para.5

65. Zambia Independence Act 1964

Sch.1 Part I para.10, repealed: 2002 c.39 Sch.3

69. Scrap Metal Dealers Act 1964

applied: 2003 c.ii s.7

s.8, repealed: 2004 c.14 Sch.1 Part 16

s.10, amended: 2004 c.14 Sch.1 Part 16

s.10, repealed (in part): 2004 c.14 Sch.1 Part 16

s.11, repealed (in part): 2004 c.14 Sch.1 Part 16

70. Riding Establishments Act 1964

disapplied: 2003 c.44 Sch.25 para.59

s.2, applied: 2003 c.44 Sch.25 para.59

s.4, amended: 2003 c.44 Sch.37 Part 9

71. Trading Stamps Act 1964

s.2, amended: 2004 c.14 Sch.1 Part 16

s.3, repealed (in part): 2004 c.14 Sch.1 Part 16

s.9, repealed: 2004 c.14 Sch.1 Part 16

s.11, repealed (in part): 2004 c.14 Sch.1 Part 16

75. Public Libraries and Museums Act 1964

applied: SI 2004/803

s.2, amended: SI 2004/803 Art.3

s.2, applied: SI 2004/803

81. Diplomatic Privileges Act 1964

see *B (A Child) (Care Proceedings: Diplomatic Immunity), Re* [2002] EWHC 1751, [2003] Fam. 16 (Fam Div), Dame Elizabeth Butler-Sloss (President)

applied: SI 2003/2621 Art.2, Art.3

Sch.1, applied: SI 2002/1826 Art.8, Art.14, Art.15, Art.16, Art.17, Art.18, Art.19

83. New Forest Act 1964

applied: SI 2002/794 Art.3, SI 2002/2626 Art.6

s.3, amended: SI 2002/794 Sch.1 para.11

s.4, amended: SI 2002/794 Sch.1 para.12, SI 2002/2626 Sch.2 para.3

1964–cont.

84. Criminal Procedure (Insanity) Act 1964

s.3, see *R. (on the application of South West Yorkshire Mental Health NHS Trust) v Bradford Crown Court* [2003] EWCA Civ 1857, [2004] 1 W.L.R. 1664 (CA), Pill, L.J.

s.4, see *R. v H (Fitness to Plead)* [2001] EWCA Crim 2024, [2002] 1 W.L.R. 824 (CA (Crim Div)), Rose, L.J.

s.4, amended: 2004 c.28 s.22

s.4, applied: 2003 c.44 s.48, 2004 c.28 s.36

s.4, referred to: 2003 c.44 s.75

s.4A, see *R. (on the application of Young) v Central Criminal Court* [2002] EWHC 548, [2002] 2 Cr. App. R. 12 (QBD (Admin Ct)), Rose, L.J.; see *R. v Grant (Heather)* [2001] EWCA Crim 2611, [2002] Q.B. 1030 (CA (Crim Div)), Richards, J.; see *R. v H (Fitness to Plead)* [2001] EWCA Crim 2024, [2002] 1 W.L.R. 824 (CA (Crim Div)), Rose, L.J.; see *R. v H (Fitness to Plead)* [2003] UKHL 1, [2003] 1 W.L.R. 411 (HL), Lord Bingham of Cornhill; see *R. v M (Witness Statement)* [2003] EWCA Crim 357, [2003] 2 Cr. App. R. 21 (CA (Crim Div)), Potter, L.J.

s.4A, amended: 2004 c.28 s.22

s.4A, applied: 2003 c.44 s.48, s.107, s.125, 2004 c.28 s.19, s.36

s.5, see *R. (on the application of South West Yorkshire Mental Health NHS Trust) v Bradford Crown Court* [2003] EWCA Civ 1857, [2004] 1 W.L.R. 1664 (CA), Pill, L.J.; see *R. (on the application of South West Yorkshire Mental Health NHS Trust) v Bradford Crown Court* [2003] EWHC 640, [2003] A.C.D. 68 (QBD (Admin Ct)), Newman, J.

s.5, applied: SI 2002/896 Sch.1 para.10, SI 2003/495 Reg.7

s.5, substituted: 2004 c.28 s.24

s.7, repealed: 2004 c.28 Sch.11

s.8, amended: SI 2002/3135 Sch.1 para.5, 2004 c.28 Sch.10 para.3, Sch.11

s.8, repealed (in part): 2004 c.28 Sch.11

Sch.1A Part I para.1, added: 2004 c.28 Sch.2

Sch.1A Part I para.1, varied: 2004 c.28 Sch.12 para.9

Sch.1A Part II para.2, added: 2004 c.28 Sch.2

Sch.1A Part II para.2, varied: 2004 c.28 Sch.12 para.9

Sch.1A Part II para.3, added: 2004 c.28 Sch.2

Sch.1A Part II para.3, varied: 2004 c.28 Sch.12 para.9

Sch.1A Part II para.4, added: 2004 c.28 Sch.2

Sch.1A Part II para.4, varied: 2004 c.28 Sch.12 para.9

Sch.1A Part II para.5, added: 2004 c.28 Sch.2

Sch.1A Part II para.5, varied: 2004 c.28 Sch.12 para.9

Sch.1A Part II para.6, added: 2004 c.28 Sch.2

1964–cont.

84. Criminal Procedure (Insanity) Act 1964–*cont.*

Sch.1A Part II para.6, varied: 2004 c.28 Sch.12 para.9

Sch.1A Part II para.7, added: 2004 c.28 Sch.2

Sch.1A Part II para.7, varied: 2004 c.28 Sch.12 para.9

Sch.1A Part II para.8, added: 2004 c.28 Sch.2

Sch.1A Part II para.8, varied: 2004 c.28 Sch.12 para.9

Sch.1A Part III para.9, added: 2004 c.28 Sch.2

Sch.1A Part III para.9, varied: 2004 c.28 Sch.12 para.9

Sch.1A Part III para.10, added: 2004 c.28 Sch.2

Sch.1A Part III para.10, varied: 2004 c.28 Sch.12 para.9

Sch.1A Part III para.11, added: 2004 c.28 Sch.2

Sch.1A Part III para.11, varied: 2004 c.28 Sch.12 para.9

Sch.1A Part III para.12, added: 2004 c.28 Sch.2

Sch.1A Part III para.12, varied: 2004 c.28 Sch.12 para.9

Sch.1A Part III para.13, added: 2004 c.28 Sch.2

Sch.1A Part III para.13, varied: 2004 c.28 Sch.12 para.9

Sch.1A Part III para.14, added: 2004 c.28 Sch.2

Sch.1A Part III para.14, varied: 2004 c.28 Sch.12 para.9

86. Malta Independence Act 1964

Sch.2 para.14, repealed: 2002 c.39 Sch.3

88. Refreshment Houses Act 1964

repealed: 2003 c.17 Sch.7

89. Hairdressers (Registration) Act 1964

s.2, amended: 2004 c.14 Sch.1 Part 16

s.3, amended: 2004 c.14 Sch.1 Part 16

s.3, repealed (in part): 2004 c.14 Sch.1 Part 16

s.7, amended: 2004 c.14 Sch.1 Part 16

s.15, amended: 2004 c.14 Sch.1 Part 16

Sch.1 Part I para.1, amended: 2004 c.14 Sch.1 Part 16

Sch.1 Part I para.2, repealed: 2004 c.14 Sch.1 Part 16

Sch.1 Part II para.5, repealed: 2004 c.14 Sch.1 Part 16

Sch.1 Part II para.6, repealed (in part): 2004 c.14 Sch.1 Part 16

93. Gambia Independence Act 1964

Sch.2 para.13, repealed: 2002 c.39 Sch.3

1965

xxxix. City of London (Various Powers) Act 1965

s.6, amended: SI 2003/1615 Sch.1 para.24

1965–cont.

Trade Union Act 1965
s.6, see *Stevedoring Services Ltd v Burgess* [2002] UKPC 39, [2002] 1 W.L.R. 2838 (PC (Ber)), Lord Hoffmann

2. Administration of Justice Act 1965
Sch.1, amended: 2004 c.14 Sch.1 Part 1, Sch.1 Part 9

4. Science and Technology Act 1965
s.1, applied: SSI 2003/176 Sch.3 para.11
Sch.2, amended: 2003 c.39 Sch.10

12. Industrial and Provident Societies Act 1965
see *Boyle v Collins* [2004] EWHC 271, [2004] 2 B.C.L.C. 471 (Ch D), Lewison, J.
applied: 2002 c.20, 2002 c.40 s.255, SI 2003/1102 Reg.2, SI 2004/2030 Art.2, SSI 2004/468 Reg.10
referred to: SI 2004/353 Reg.2
s.1, disapplied: 2002 c.20 s.2
s.3, amended: 2003 c.15 Sch.1
s.5, amended: 2003 c.15 s.5, Sch.1
s.5, repealed (in part): 2003 c.15 Sch.1
s.5A, added: 2003 c.15 s.2
s.6, applied: 2002 c.29 Sch.9 para.2, Sch.9 para.3, SI 2003/3075 Reg.2
s.7, applied: 2002 c.29 Sch.9 para.2, Sch.9 para.3, SI 2003/3075 Reg.2
s.7A, added: 2003 c.15 s.3
s.7B, added: 2003 c.15 s.3
s.7C, added: 2003 c.15 s.3
s.7D, added: 2003 c.15 s.3
s.7E, added: 2003 c.15 s.3
s.7F, added: 2003 c.15 s.3
s.10, disapplied: 2002 c.20 s.2
s.16, amended: 2003 c.44 Sch.37 Part 9
s.16, disapplied: 2002 c.20 s.2, 2003 c.44 Sch.25 para.60
s.17, disapplied: 2002 c.20 s.2
s.18, disapplied: 2002 c.20 s.2
s.20, applied: SI 2002/704 Art.2
s.23, amended: 2004 c.33 Sch.27 para.24
s.23, disapplied: 2002 c.20 s.2
s.24, disapplied: 2002 c.20 s.2
s.25, amended: 2004 c.33 Sch.27 para.25
s.25, disapplied: 2002 c.20 s.2
s.26, disapplied: 2002 c.20 s.2
s.27, disapplied: 2002 c.20 s.2
s.29A, added: 2003 c.15 s.4
s.29B, added: 2003 c.15 s.5
s.29C, added: 2003 c.15 s.5
s.29C, varied: 2002 c.9 s.91
s.29D, added: 2003 c.15 s.5
s.29E, added: 2003 c.15 s.5
s.29F, added: 2003 c.15 s.5
s.29G, added: 2003 c.15 s.5
s.31, amended: 2004 c.21 Sch.1 para.19
s.31, varied: SI 2003/1633 Sch.2 para.14
s.36, repealed: 2003 c.15 Sch.1
s.39, referred to: SI 2002/1501 Art.7
s.48, amended: 2003 c.44 Sch.37 Part 9

1965–cont.

12. Industrial and Provident Societies Act 1965–*cont.*
s.48, disapplied: 2003 c.44 Sch.25 para.61
s.49, applied: SI 2003/3075 Reg.26
s.50, disapplied: 2002 c.20 s.2
s.51, disapplied: 2002 c.20 s.2
s.52, amended: 2002 c.20 s.1
s.52, disapplied: 2002 c.20 s.2
s.53, applied: 2004 c.27 s.56
s.53, disapplied: 2002 c.20 s.2
s.54, disapplied: 2002 c.20 s.2
s.55, disapplied: 2002 c.20 s.2
s.56, disapplied: 2002 c.20 s.2
s.58, disapplied: 2002 c.20 s.2
s.59, disapplied: 2002 c.20 s.2
s.74, applied: 2003 c.17 s.65
s.76, amended: 2003 c.15 s.4, s.5
Sch.1 para.13, substituted: 2003 c.15 s.5

13. Rivers (Prevention of Pollution) (Scotland) Act 1965
s.13, repealed (in part): 2003 asp 15 Sch.4 Part 2

14. Cereals Marketing Act 1965
applied: SI 2002/2843 Art.6
Part I, applied: SI 2002/1461, SI 2003/1512, SI 2004/1445
s.7, applied: SI 2002/2843 Art.6
s.13, applied: SI 2002/1461, SI 2002/2843 Art.6, SI 2003/1512, SI 2004/1445
s.13, enabling: SI 2002/1461, SI 2003/1512, SI 2004/1445
s.16, applied: SI 2002/2843 Art.6
s.17, amended: 2003 c.44 Sch.37 Part 9
s.17, disapplied: 2003 c.44 Sch.25 para.62
s.17, varied: SI 2002/2843 Art.6
s.21, amended: SI 2003/1326 Art.5
s.21, referred to: SI 2002/2843 Art.6
s.21, varied: SI 2002/2843 Art.6
s.23, enabling: SI 2002/1461, SI 2003/1512, SI 2004/1445
s.24, enabling: SI 2002/1461, SI 2003/1512, SI 2004/1445
Sch.3, applied: SI 2002/2843 Art.6

16. Teaching Council (Scotland) Act 1965
s.11, see *Peace v General Teaching Council for Scotland* 2003 S.C. 299 (Ex Div), Lord Marnoch, Lord MacLean, Lord McCluskey

17. Museum of London Act 1965
s.4, amended: SI 2004/1939 Art.2

19. Teaching Council (Scotland) Act 1965
s.2, applied: SSI 2004/390
s.6, amended: 2003 asp 5 s.13
s.6, applied: SSI 2004/390
s.6, enabling: SSI 2004/390
s.7, applied: SSI 2004/390
s.7, enabling: SSI 2004/390
s.14, enabling: SSI 2004/542
Sch.1 Part I para.1, amended: 2004 asp 4 Sch.3 para.1
Sch.1 Part I para.1, enabling: SSI 2004/542

1965–cont.

20NI. Factories Act (Northern Ireland) 1965
applied: SI 2003/431 Art.11

22. Law Commissions Act 1965
s.1, amended: 2002 c.26 Sch.12 para.8
s.1, repealed (in part): 2002 c.26 Sch.13
s.3, amended: 2002 c.26 Sch.12 para.9

23. Land Development Values (Compensation) Act (Northern Ireland) 1965
Part 3, applied: 2003 c.21 Sch.4 para.8
s.31, applied: 2003 c.21 Sch.4 para.8
s.40, applied: 2003 c.21 Sch.4 para.8
s.40, varied: 2003 c.21 Sch.4 para.8
Sch.2, amended: SI 2002/3153 Sch.5 para.2

25. Finance Act 1965
s.47, see *Strand Options & Futures Ltd v Vojak (Inspector of Taxes)* [2002] S.T.C. (S.C.D.) 398 (Sp Comm), John F Avery Jones; see *Strand Options & Futures Ltd v Vojak (Inspector of Taxes)* [2003] EWHC 67, [2003] S.T.C. 331 (Ch D), Etherton, J.
s.90, amended: 2003 c.14 Sch.20 para.3
s.92, applied: SI 2002/2023 Art.3

32. Administration of Estates (Small Payments) Act 1965
Sch.1 Part I, amended: 2004 c.14 Sch.1 Part 11

36. Gas Act 1965
s.12, amended: 2002 c.9 Sch.11 para.6, SI 2004/2043 Sch.1 para.1
s.13, amended: 2002 c.9 Sch.11 para.6
s.15, varied: SI 2004/1822 Sch.1 para.4
s.17, amended: 2004 c.21 Sch.1 para.20
s.17, varied: SI 2004/1822 Sch.1 para.4
s.28, amended: 2004 c.21 Sch.1 para.20
s.28, varied: SI 2004/1822 Sch.1 para.4
Sch.2 Part IV para.17, varied: SI 2004/1822 Sch.1 para.4
Sch.3 para.7, amended: 2004 c.5 Sch.7 para.1
Sch.4 Part II para.5, varied: SI 2004/1822 Sch.1 para.4
Sch.4 Part II para.9, varied: SI 2004/1822 Sch.1 para.4
Sch.6 para.2, varied: SI 2004/1822 Sch.1 para.4
Sch.6 para.9, amended: 2003 c.44 Sch.37 Part 9
Sch.6 para.9, disapplied: 2003 c.44 Sch.25 para.63
Sch.6 para.11, varied: SI 2004/1822 Sch.1 para.4

37. Carriage of Goods by Road Act 1965
see *Quantum Corp Inc v Plane Trucking Ltd* [2002] EWCA Civ 350, [2002] 1 W.L.R. 2678 (CA), Mance, L.J.

45. Backing of Warrants (Republic of Ireland) Act 1965
repealed: 2003 c.41 s.218
s.1, amended: 2003 c.39 Sch.8 para.119
s.2, applied: SI 2002/313 Sch.1, SI 2003/435 Art.25
s.4, amended: 2003 c.39 Sch.8 para.120

1965–cont.

45. Backing of Warrants (Republic of Ireland) Act 1965–*cont.*
s.5, amended: SI 2003/1247 Sch.1 para.5, Sch.2
s.6, amended: 2003 c.39 Sch.8 para.121
s.8, amended: 2003 c.39 Sch.8 para.122
Sch.1 para.2, substituted: 2003 c.39 Sch.8 para.123
Sch.1 para.2A, substituted: 2003 c.39 Sch.8 para.123
Sch.1 para.3, amended: 2003 c.39 Sch.8 para.123
Sch.1 para.4, amended: 2003 c.44 Sch.37 Part 4, Sch.3 para.41

49. Registration of Births, Deaths and Marriages (Scotland) Act 1965
s.5, referred to: 2004 c.33 s.126
s.18, amended: 2003 c.24 Sch.1 para.6
s.18A, varied: 2004 c.7 Sch.3 para.18
s.18ZA, added: 2003 c.24 Sch.1 para.7
s.18ZA, varied: 2003 c.24 s.3
s.20, varied: 2004 c.7 Sch.3 para.18
s.21, applied: SSI 2004/115 Sch.3
s.28A, enabling: SSI 2002/390, SSI 2003/89
s.34, applied: 2004 c.33 s.98, s.99
s.37, applied: 2004 c.33 s.98
s.37, enabling: SSI 2002/390, SSI 2003/89
s.38, applied: 2004 c.7 Sch.3 para.15, 2004 c.33 s.98
s.38, enabling: SSI 2002/390, SSI 2003/89
s.40, applied: 2004 c.7 Sch.3 para.17
s.40, enabling: SSI 2002/390, SSI 2003/89
s.41, applied: 2004 c.7 Sch.3 para.20
s.42, varied: 2004 c.7 Sch.3 para.18
s.43, varied: 2004 c.7 Sch.3 para.18
s.43, enabling: SSI 2002/390, SSI 2003/89
s.44, applied: 2004 c.33 s.98
s.47, enabling: SSI 2002/390, SSI 2003/89
s.53, applied: 2004 c.19 s.14
s.54, enabling: SSI 2002/390, SSI 2003/89
s.56, amended: 2004 c.33 s.136
s.56, enabling: SSI 2002/390, SSI 2003/89

51. National Insurance Act 1965
applied: 2004 c.12 Sch.28 para.2, Sch.28 para.16
s.36, amended: SI 2002/668 Art.11, SI 2003/526 Art.12
s.36, referred to: SI 2004/552 Art.12
s.36, varied: SI 2004/552 Art.12
s.37, varied: SI 2002/668 Art.11, SI 2003/526 Art.12, SI 2004/552 Art.12

56. Compulsory Purchase Act 1965
see *BP Oil UK Ltd v Kent CC* [2003] EWCA Civ 798, [2004] 1 P. & C.R. 25 (CA), Carnwath, L.J.
applied: SI 2002/1064 Art.18, SI 2002/1066 Art.23, SI 2003/1075 Art.26, SI 2003/3364 Art.14, Art.19, Sch.4 para.3, SI 2004/389 Art.30, Sch.9 para.3, SI 2004/757 Art.34

1965–cont.

56. Compulsory Purchase Act 1965–cont.
disapplied: SI 2003/1075 Art.32
referred to: SI 2004/389 Art.24, SI 2004/757 Art.26
varied: SI 2002/412 Sch.4 para.3, SI 2002/1065 Sch.3 para.3, SI 2002/1066 Art.22, SI 2002/1327 Sch.4 para.3, SI 2002/1943 Art.4, SI 2003/1075 Sch.9 para.3, SI 2004/757 Sch.8 para.3
Part I, applied: SI 2002/1064 Sch.2 para.3, SI 2002/1066 Art.32, SI 2002/1327 Art.27, SI 2002/1943 Art.4, Art.10, 2003 c.21 Sch.4 para.9, SI 2003/1075 Art.25, Art.34, SI 2004/389 Art.23, Art.31, Art.32, Sch.9 para.3, SI 2004/757 Art.37, Sch.8 para.3
Part I, disapplied: SI 2002/412 Art.23
s.1, repealed (in part): 2003 c.39 Sch.8 para.124, Sch.10
s.1, varied: SI 2002/412 Art.17, SI 2002/1064 Art.10, SI 2002/1066 Art.21, Sch.7 para.3, SI 2002/1327 Art.19, SI 2003/1075 Art.25, Sch.9 para.3, SI 2004/389 Art.23, SI 2004/757 Art.24
s.2, varied: SI 2002/412 Art.17, SI 2002/1064 Art.10, SI 2002/1066 Art.21, Sch.7 para.3, SI 2002/1327 Art.19, SI 2003/1075 Art.25, Sch.9 para.3, SI 2004/389 Art.23, SI 2004/757 Art.24
s.3, varied: SI 2002/412 Art.17, SI 2002/1064 Art.10, SI 2002/1066 Art.21, Sch.7 para.3, SI 2002/1327 Art.19, SI 2003/1075 Art.25, Sch.9 para.3, SI 2004/389 Art.23, SI 2004/757 Art.24
s.4, applied: SI 2002/1066 Art.30
s.4, disapplied: 2003 c.21 Sch.4 para.9
s.4, referred to: SI 2002/1066 Art.21
s.4, varied: SI 2002/412 Art.17, SI 2002/1064 Art.10, SI 2002/1065 Art.10, SI 2002/1066 Art.21, Sch.7 para.3, SI 2002/1327 Art.19, SI 2002/1943 Art.4, SI 2003/1075 Art.25, Sch.9 para.3, SI 2003/3364 Art.14, SI 2004/389 Art.23, SI 2004/757 Art.24
s.5, disapplied: 2003 c.21 Sch.4 para.9
s.5, varied: SI 2002/412 Art.17, SI 2002/1064 Art.10, SI 2002/1066 Art.21, Sch.7 para.3, SI 2002/1327 Art.19, SI 2003/1075 Art.25, Sch.9 para.3, SI 2004/389 Art.23, SI 2004/757 Art.24
s.6, disapplied: 2003 c.21 Sch.4 para.9
s.6, varied: SI 2002/412 Art.17, SI 2002/1064 Art.10, SI 2002/1066 Art.21, Sch.7 para.3, SI 2002/1327 Art.19, SI 2003/1075 Art.25, Sch.9 para.3, SI 2004/389 Art.23, SI 2004/757 Art.24
s.7, applied: SI 2002/1065 Sch.3 para.2, SI 2002/1066 Sch.7 para.2, SI 2003/1075 Sch.9 para.2, SI 2004/389 Sch.9 para.2, SI 2004/757 Sch.8 para.2
s.7, disapplied: 2003 c.21 Sch.4 para.9

1965–cont.

56. Compulsory Purchase Act 1965–cont.
s.7, varied: SI 2002/412 Art.17, Sch.4 para.4, SI 2002/1064 Art.10, Sch.2 para.4, SI 2002/1065 Sch.3 para.4, SI 2002/1066 Art.21, Sch.7 para.3, SI 2002/1327 Art.19, Sch.4 para.4, SI 2003/1075 Art.25, Sch.9 para.3, Sch.9 para.4, SI 2003/3364 Sch.4 para.4, SI 2004/389 Art.23, Sch.9 para.4, SI 2004/757 Art.24, Sch.8 para.4
s.8, applied: SI 2002/412 Art.18, SI 2002/1064 Art.11, Art.12, Art.13, SI 2002/1065 Sch.3 para.2, SI 2002/1066 Art.23, Sch.7 para.2, SI 2002/1327 Art.21, SI 2003/1075 Art.26, Sch.9 para.2, SI 2003/3364 Art.15, SI 2004/389 Art.24, Sch.9 para.2, SI 2004/757 Art.26, Sch.8 para.2
s.8, disapplied: SI 2002/412 Art.21, SI 2002/1064 Art.18, SI 2002/1066 Art.30, SI 2002/1327 Art.25, 2003 c.21 Sch.4 para.9, SI 2003/1075 Art.32, SI 2003/3364 Art.19, SI 2004/389 Art.30, SI 2004/757 Art.34
s.8, referred to: SI 2002/1065 Art.18
s.8, varied: SI 2002/412 Art.17, Sch.4 para.5, SI 2002/1064 Art.10, Sch.2 para.5, SI 2002/1065 Sch.3 para.5, SI 2002/1066 Art.21, Sch.7 para.3, SI 2002/1327 Art.19, Sch.4 para.5, SI 2003/1075 Art.25, Sch.9 para.3, Sch.9 para.5, SI 2003/3364 Sch.4 para.5, SI 2004/389 Art.23, Sch.9 para.5, SI 2004/757 Art.24, Sch.8 para.5
s.9, varied: SI 2002/412 Art.17, Sch.4 para.6, SI 2002/1064 Art.10, Sch.2 para.6, SI 2002/1065 Sch.3 para.6, SI 2002/1066 Art.21, Sch.7 para.3, Sch.7 para.6, SI 2002/1327 Art.19, Sch.4 para.6, SI 2003/1075 Art.25, Sch.9 para.3, Sch.9 para.6, SI 2003/3364 Sch.4 para.6, SI 2004/389 Art.23, Sch.9 para.6, SI 2004/757 Art.24, Sch.8 para.6
s.10, see *Ocean Leisure Ltd v Westminster City Council* [2004] EWCA Civ 970, [2004] B.L.R. 393 (CA), Potter, L.J.; see *Puttock v Bexley LBC* [2004] R.V.R. 216 (Lands Tr), PR Francis FRICS
s.10, applied: SI 2002/1064 Art.7, Art.14, Art.15, SI 2002/1065 Art.7, Art.14, Art.15, SI 2002/1066 Art.16, Art.27, Art.28, SI 2002/1943 Art.9, SI 2003/1075 Art.22, Art.30, SI 2003/3364 Art.16, Art.17, SI 2004/389 Art.20, Art.28, SI 2004/757 Art.19, Art.30, Art.31
s.10, varied: SI 2002/412 Art.17, SI 2002/1064 Art.10, Sch.2 para.6, SI 2002/1065 Sch.3 para.6, SI 2002/1066 Art.21, Sch.7 para.3, SI 2002/1327 Art.19, SI 2002/1943 Art.5, SI 2003/1075 Art.25, Sch.9 para.3, SI 2004/389 Art.23, SI 2004/757 Art.24
s.11, applied: SI 2002/412 Art.22, SI 2002/1064 Art.19, SI 2002/1065 Art.19, SI 2002/1066 Art.27, Art.31, SI 2002/1327 Art.26, SI 2002/1943 Art.4, Art.8, SI

1965–cont.

56. Compulsory Purchase Act 1965–cont.

s.11, applied:–cont.

2003/1075 Art.33, Sch.13 para.42, SI 2003/3364 Art.20, Sch.7 para.2, SI 2004/389 Art.31, Sch.13 para.42, SI 2004/757 Art.30, Art.35, Sch.13 para.4, Sch.16 para.42

s.11, disapplied: SI 2002/1066 Sch.11 para.2, Sch.11 para.17

s.11, referred to: SI 2002/412 Sch.6 para.2, SI 2002/1066 Sch.14 para.42

s.11, varied: SI 2002/412 Art.17, Sch.4 para.7, SI 2002/1064 Art.10, Sch.2 para.7, SI 2002/1065 Art.10, Sch.3 para.7, SI 2002/1066 Art.21, Sch.7 para.3, Sch.7 para.7, SI 2002/1327 Art.19, Sch.4 para.7, SI 2003/1075 Art.25, Sch.9 para.3, Sch.9 para.7, SI 2003/3364 Art.14, Sch.4 para.7, SI 2004/389 Art.23, Sch.9 para.7, SI 2004/757 Art.24, Sch.8 para.7

s.12, varied: SI 2002/412 Art.17, Sch.4 para.7, SI 2002/1064 Art.10, SI 2002/1066 Art.21, Sch.7 para.3, Sch.7 para.7, SI 2002/1327 Art.19, SI 2003/1075 Art.25, Sch.9 para.3, Sch.9 para.7, SI 2004/389 Art.23, Sch.9 para.7, SI 2004/757 Art.24, Sch.8 para.7

s.13, varied: SI 2002/412 Art.17, Sch.4 para.7, SI 2002/1064 Art.10, SI 2002/1066 Art.21, Sch.7 para.3, Sch.7 para.7, SI 2002/1327 Art.19, SI 2003/1075 Art.25, Sch.9 para.3, Sch.9 para.7, SI 2004/389 Art.23, Sch.9 para.7, SI 2004/757 Art.24, Art.30, Art.31, Sch.8 para.7

s.14, varied: SI 2002/412 Art.17, SI 2002/1064 Art.10, SI 2002/1066 Art.21, Sch.7 para.3, SI 2002/1327 Art.19, SI 2003/1075 Art.25, Sch.9 para.3, SI 2004/389 Art.23, SI 2004/757 Art.24

s.15, varied: SI 2002/412 Art.17, SI 2002/1064 Art.10, SI 2002/1066 Art.21, Sch.7 para.3, SI 2002/1327 Art.19, SI 2003/1075 Art.25, Sch.9 para.3, SI 2004/389 Art.23, SI 2004/757 Art.24

s.16, varied: SI 2002/412 Art.17, SI 2002/1064 Art.10, SI 2002/1066 Art.21, Sch.7 para.3, SI 2002/1327 Art.19, SI 2003/1075 Art.25, Sch.9 para.3, SI 2004/389 Art.23, SI 2004/757 Art.24

s.17, varied: SI 2002/412 Art.17, SI 2002/1064 Art.10, SI 2002/1066 Art.21, Sch.7 para.3, SI 2002/1327 Art.19, SI 2003/1075 Art.25, Sch.9 para.3, SI 2004/389 Art.23, SI 2004/757 Art.24

s.18, varied: SI 2002/412 Art.17, SI 2002/1064 Art.10, SI 2002/1066 Art.21, Sch.7 para.3, SI 2002/1327 Art.19, SI 2003/1075 Art.25, Sch.9 para.3, SI 2004/389 Art.23, SI 2004/757 Art.24

s.19, varied: SI 2002/412 Art.17, SI 2002/1064 Art.10, SI 2002/1066 Art.21, Sch.7 para.3, SI 2002/1327 Art.19, SI 2003/

1965–cont.

56. Compulsory Purchase Act 1965–cont.

s.19, varied:–cont.

1075 Art.25, Sch.9 para.3, SI 2004/389 Art.23, SI 2004/757 Art.24

s.20, see *Bishopsgate Space Management Ltd v London Underground Ltd* [2004] 2 E.G.L.R. 175 (Lands Tr), George Bartlett Q.C. (President)

s.20, varied: SI 2002/412 Art.17, Sch.4 para.8, SI 2002/1064 Art.10, Sch.2 para.8, SI 2002/1065 Sch.3 para.8, SI 2002/1066 Art.21, Sch.7 para.3, Sch.7 para.8, SI 2002/1327 Art.19, Sch.4 para.8, SI 2003/1075 Art.25, Sch.9 para.3, Sch.9 para.8, SI 2003/3364 Sch.4 para.8, SI 2004/389 Art.23, Sch.9 para.8, SI 2004/757 Art.24, Sch.8 para.8

s.21, varied: SI 2002/412 Art.17, SI 2002/1064 Art.10, SI 2002/1066 Art.21, Sch.7 para.3, SI 2002/1327 Art.19, SI 2003/1075 Art.25, Sch.9 para.3, SI 2004/389 Art.23, SI 2004/757 Art.24

s.22, varied: SI 2002/412 Art.17, Sch.4 para.9, SI 2002/1064 Art.10, Sch.2 para.9, SI 2002/1065 Sch.3 para.9, SI 2002/1066 Art.21, Sch.7 para.3, Sch.7 para.9, SI 2002/1327 Art.19, Sch.4 para.9, SI 2003/1075 Art.25, Sch.9 para.3, Sch.9 para.9, SI 2003/3364 Sch.4 para.9, SI 2004/389 Art.23, Sch.9 para.9, SI 2004/757 Art.24, Sch.8 para.9

s.23, varied: SI 2002/412 Art.17, SI 2002/1064 Art.10, SI 2002/1066 Art.21, Sch.7 para.3, SI 2002/1327 Art.19, SI 2003/1075 Art.25, Sch.9 para.3, SI 2004/389 Art.23, SI 2004/757 Art.24

s.24, varied: SI 2002/412 Art.17, SI 2002/1064 Art.10, SI 2002/1066 Art.21, Sch.7 para.3, SI 2002/1327 Art.19, SI 2003/1075 Art.25, Sch.9 para.3, SI 2004/389 Art.23, SI 2004/757 Art.24

s.25, varied: SI 2002/412 Art.17, SI 2002/1064 Art.10, SI 2002/1066 Art.21, Sch.7 para.3, SI 2002/1327 Art.19, SI 2003/1075 Art.25, Sch.9 para.3, SI 2004/389 Art.23, SI 2004/757 Art.24

s.26, varied: SI 2002/412 Art.17, SI 2002/1064 Art.10, SI 2002/1066 Art.21, Sch.7 para.3, SI 2002/1327 Art.19, SI 2003/1075 Art.25, Sch.9 para.3, SI 2004/389 Art.23, SI 2004/757 Art.24

s.27, varied: SI 2002/412 Art.17, SI 2002/1064 Art.10, SI 2002/1066 Art.21, Sch.7 para.3, SI 2002/1327 Art.19, SI 2003/1075 Art.25, Sch.9 para.3, SI 2004/389 Art.23, SI 2004/757 Art.24

s.28, varied: SI 2002/412 Art.17, SI 2002/1064 Art.10, SI 2002/1066 Art.21, Sch.7 para.3, SI 2002/1327 Art.19, SI 2003/1075 Art.25, Sch.9 para.3, SI 2004/389 Art.23, SI 2004/757 Art.24

CAP.

1965–cont.

56. Compulsory Purchase Act 1965–*cont.*
s.29, varied: SI 2002/412 Art.17, SI 2002/
1064 Art.10, SI 2002/1066 Art.21, Sch.7
para.3, SI 2002/1327 Art.19, SI 2003/
1075 Art.25, Sch.9 para.3, SI 2004/389
Art.23, SI 2004/757 Art.24

s.30, varied: SI 2002/412 Art.17, SI 2002/
1064 Art.10, SI 2002/1066 Art.21, Sch.7
para.3, SI 2002/1327 Art.19, SI 2003/
1075 Art.25, Sch.9 para.3, SI 2004/389
Art.23, SI 2004/757 Art.24

s.31, applied: 2003 c.21 Sch.4 para.9

s.31, varied: SI 2002/412 Art.17, SI 2002/
1064 Art.10, SI 2002/1066 Art.21, Sch.7
para.3, SI 2002/1327 Art.19, SI 2003/
1075 Art.25, Sch.9 para.3, SI 2004/389
Art.23, SI 2004/757 Art.24

s.32, varied: SI 2002/412 Art.17, SI 2002/
1064 Art.10, SI 2002/1066 Art.21, Sch.7
para.3, SI 2002/1327 Art.19, SI 2003/
1075 Art.25, Sch.9 para.3, SI 2004/389
Art.23, SI 2004/757 Art.24

Sch.1 para.10, varied: SI 2002/412 Sch.4
para.6, SI 2002/1066 Sch.7 para.6, SI
2002/1327 Sch.4 para.6, SI 2003/1075
Sch.9 para.6, SI 2003/3364 Sch.4 para.6,
SI 2004/389 Sch.9 para.6, SI 2004/757
Sch.8 para.6

Sch.2 para.2, varied: SI 2002/412 Sch.4
para.6, SI 2002/1064 Sch.2 para.6, SI
2002/1065 Sch.3 para.6, SI 2002/1066
Sch.7 para.6, SI 2002/1327 Sch.4 para.6,
SI 2003/1075 Sch.9 para.6, SI 2003/
3364 Sch.4 para.6, SI 2004/389 Sch.9
para.6, SI 2004/757 Sch.8 para.6

Sch.3 para.3, referred to: SI 2002/1066
Art.21

Sch.3 para.3, varied: SI 2002/1065 Art.10, SI
2002/1066 Art.21, SI 2002/1943 Art.4, SI
2003/1075 Art.25, SI 2004/757 Art.24

Sch.4 para.2, varied: SI 2002/412 Sch.4
para.6, SI 2002/1064 Sch.2 para.6, SI
2002/1065 Sch.3 para.6, SI 2002/1066
Sch.7 para.6, SI 2002/1327 Sch.4 para.6,
SI 2003/1075 Sch.9 para.6, SI 2003/
3364 Sch.4 para.6, SI 2004/389 Sch.9
para.6, SI 2004/757 Sch.8 para.6

Sch.4 para.7, varied: SI 2002/412 Sch.4
para.6, SI 2002/1064 Sch.2 para.6, SI
2002/1065 Sch.3 para.6, SI 2002/1066
Sch.7 para.6, SI 2002/1327 Sch.4 para.6,
SI 2003/1075 Sch.9 para.6, SI 2003/
3364 Sch.4 para.6, SI 2004/389 Sch.9
para.6, SI 2004/757 Sch.8 para.6

57. Nuclear Installations Act 1965
applied: SSI 2004/406 Sch.1 para.2

referred to: 2004 c.20 s.76

s.3, varied: SI 2004/1822 Sch.1 para.5

s.27, amended: 2004 c.20 s.78

s.27, repealed (in part): 2004 c.20 Sch.23
Part 1

CAP.

1965–cont.

57. Nuclear Installations Act 1965–*cont.*
Sch.1 para.4, repealed (in part): 2004 c.20
Sch.23 Part 1

Sch.1 para.7, repealed (in part): 2004 c.20
Sch.23 Part 1

63. Public Works Loans Act 1965
s.2, amended: 2003 c.26 Sch.7 para.2, 2003
c.39 Sch.8 para.125, 2004 c.21 Sch.1
para.21, SI 2004/533 Art.7

s.2, applied: SI 2004/533 Art.7

s.2, repealed (in part): 2003 c.39 Sch.8
para.125, Sch.10

64. Commons Registration Act 1965
see *R. (on the application of Laing Homes Ltd)
v Buckinghamshire CC* [2003] EWHC
1578, [2004] 1 P. & C.R. 36 (QBD (Admin
Ct)), Sullivan, J.

applied: 2002 c.9 s.27, s.33, Sch.3 para.3,
2002 c.i, s.4, s.23, Sch.1 para.7, SI 2003/
2713 Reg.8

s.1, amended: 2002 c.9 Sch.11 para.7

s.3, applied: SI 2002/1710 Reg.12

s.4, amended: 2002 c.9 Sch.11 para.7

s.5, see *R. (on the application of Whitmey) v
Commons Commissioners* [2004] EWCA
Civ 951, [2004] 3 W.L.R. 1343 (CA (Civ
Div)), Waller, L.J.

s.8, amended: 2002 c.9 Sch.11 para.7

s.9, amended: 2002 c.9 Sch.11 para.7

s.9, applied: SI 2004/1777 Art.25, SI 2004/
1778 Art.25

s.12, amended: 2002 c.9 Sch.11 para.7

s.13, see *R. (on the application of Beresford) v
Sunderland City Council* [2001] EWCA Civ
1218, [2002] Q.B. 874 (CA), Dyson, L.J.;
see *R. (on the application of Whitmey) v
Commons Commissioners* [2004] EWCA
Civ 951, [2004] 3 W.L.R. 1343 (CA (Civ
Div)), Waller, L.J.

s.14, see *R. (on the application of Cheltenham
Builders Ltd) v South Gloucestershire DC*
[2003] EWHC 2803, [2004] 1 E.G.L.R.
85 (QBD (Admin Ct)), Sullivan, J.; see *R.
(on the application of Whitmey) v Commons
Commissioners* [2004] EWCA Civ 951,
[2004] 3 W.L.R. 1343 (CA (Civ Div)),
Waller, L.J.

s.15, see *Bettison v Langton* [2001] UKHL 24,
[2002] 1 A.C. 27 (HL), Lord Scott of
Foscote

s.19, enabling: SI 2003/994, SI 2003/2260

s.22, see *Oxfordshire CC v Oxford City
Council* [2004] EWHC 12, [2004] Ch.
253 (Ch D), Lightman, J.; see *R. (on the
application of Beresford) v Sunderland
City Council* [2001] EWCA Civ 1218,
[2002] Q.B. 874 (CA), Dyson, L.J.; see *R.
(on the application of Beresford) v
Sunderland City Council* [2003] UKHL
60, [2004] 1 A.C. 889 (HL), Lord
Bingham of Cornhill; see *R. (on the
application of Cheltenham Builders Ltd) v*

CAP.

1965–cont.

64. Commons Registration Act 1965–*cont.*
s.22–*cont.*
South Gloucestershire DC [2003] EWHC 2803, [2004] 1 E.G.L.R. 85 (QBD (Admin Ct)), Sullivan, J.
s.22, amended: 2002 c.9 Sch.11 para.7

69. Criminal Procedure (Attendance of Witnesses) Act 1965
s.2, applied: SI 2003/421 r.38
s.2, amended: 2003 c.39 Sch.8 para.126, 2003 c.44 Sch.3 para.42
s.2, repealed (in part): 2003 c.44 Sch.37 Part 4, Sch.3 para.42
s.2B, amended: 2003 c.39 Sch.8 para.126
s.2C, amended: 2003 c.39 Sch.8 para.126
s.2E, amended: 2003 c.39 Sch.8 para.126

70. Hon Lady Hylton-Foster's Annuity Act 1965
repealed: 2004 c.14 Sch.1 Part 11

71. Murder (Abolition of Death Penalty) Act 1965
s.1, see R. v Lichniak (Daniella Helen) [2001] EWHC Admin 294, [2002] Q.B. 296 (QBD (Admin Ct)), Kennedy, L.J.; see R. v Lichniak (Daniella Helen) [2002] UKHL 47, [2003] 1 A.C. 903 (HL), Lord Bingham of Cornhill; see R. v Mason (Kenneth) [2002] EWCA Crim 699, [2002] 2 Cr. App. R. 32 (CA (Crim Div)), Clarke, L.J.
s.1, repealed (in part): 2003 c.44 Sch.37 Part 8

1966

xxviii. Greater London (General Powers) Act 1966
s.21, amended: 2003 c.17 Sch.6 para.35
s.21, applied: 2003 c.17 Sch.8 para.31
s.21, referred to: 2003 c.17 Sch.2 para.4
s.22, amended: 2003 c.17 Sch.6 para.36

xli. Lee Valley Regional Park Act 1966
s.13, amended: SI 2003/1615 Sch.1 para.25

2. Church of England Convocations Act 1966
s.1, amended: 2004 c.14 Sch.1 Part 6

4. Mines (Working Facilities and Support) Act 1966
applied: 2003 asp 9 Sch.11 para.1

6 (N.I). National Insurance Act (Northern Ireland) 1966
applied: SR 2002/352 Reg.39

11. Air Corporations Act 1966
repealed: 2004 c.14 Sch.1 Part 4

13. Universities (Scotland) Act 1966
Sch.6 para.17, disapplied: 2002 asp 15 s.1

14. Guyana Independence Act 1966
Sch.2 para.12, repealed: 2002 c.39 Sch.3

17. Fisheries Act (Northern Ireland) 1966
s.11, applied: SR 2003/136 Reg.3, SR 2003/163 Art.3

CAP.

1966–cont.

17. Fisheries Act (Northern Ireland) 1966–*cont.*
s.11, varied: SR 2003/163 Art.3
s.11A, varied: SR 2003/163 Art.3
s.11B, varied: SR 2003/163 Art.3
s.11C, varied: SR 2003/163 Art.3
s.16, amended: SI 2002/790 Art.6
s.26, enabling: SR 2002/11, SR 2002/274, SR 2002/371, SR 2002/372, SR 2003/271
s.30, substituted: SI 2003/418 Sch.1 para.4
s.31, repealed: SI 2003/418 Sch.1 para.4
s.32, amended: SI 2003/418 Sch.3
s.37, enabling: SR 2002/274, SR 2002/371, SR 2002/372, SR 2003/271
s.70, enabling: SR 2002/274
s.114, applied: 2002 c.26 Sch.4 para.1
s.124, amended: SI 2002/790 Art.6
s.181, applied: 2002 c.26 Sch.4 para.1
s.185B, varied: SR 2003/163 Art.3
s.206, amended: SI 2002/790 Art.6, Sch.4 Sch.1, varied: SR 2003/163 Art.3

18. Finance Act 1966
s.2, repealed: 2004 c.12 Sch.42 Part 5
s.2, varied: 2004 c.12 s.323

19. Law Reform (Miscellaneous Provisions) (Scotland) Act 1966
s.8, applied: 2004 c.33 s.227

23. Botswana Independence Act 1966
Sch.1 Part I para.9, repealed: 2002 c.39 Sch.3

24. Lesotho Independence Act 1966
Sch.1 Part I para.10, repealed: 2002 c.39 Sch.3

25. Post Office Subway Act 1966
referred to: SI 2003/2908 Art.2

26. Office and Shop Premises Act (Northern Ireland) 1966
applied: SI 2003/431 Art.11

28. Docks and Harbours Act 1966
s.37, applied: 2002 c.v s.22

29. Singapore Act 1966
Sch.1 para.12, repealed: 2002 c.39 Sch.3

34. Industrial Development Act 1966
Sch.2, amended: SSI 2002/263 Sch.1

35. Family Provision Act 1966
s.1, amended: 2004 c.33 Sch.4 para.14

36. Veterinary Surgeons Act 1966
applied: SI 2003/2919 Art.10
referred to: SI 2003/2919 Art.11
s.2, amended: SI 2003/2919 Sch.1 para.1
s.2, applied: SI 2003/2919 Art.10
s.5A, applied: SI 2004/2143 Sch.1
s.5A, disapplied: SI 2003/2919 Art.3
s.5A, referred to: SI 2003/2919 Art.6
s.5A, substituted: SI 2003/2919 Sch.1 para.2
s.5B, added: SI 2003/2919 Sch.1 para.3
s.5B, applied: SI 2004/2143 Sch.1
s.5B, disapplied: SI 2003/2919 Art.4
s.5B, referred to: SI 2003/2919 Art.6
s.5C, added: SI 2003/2919 Sch.1 para.4

CAP.

1966–cont.

36. Veterinary Surgeons Act 1966–*cont.*
s.5C, applied: SI 2004/2143 Sch.1
s.5C, referred to: SI 2004/2143 Sch.1
s.5D, added: SI 2003/2919 Sch.1 para.5
s.5D, applied: SI 2004/2143
s.6, amended: SI 2003/2919 Sch.1 para.6
s.7, applied: SI 2003/3342 Sch.1
s.8, applied: SI 2003/3342 Sch.1
s.10, disapplied: SI 2003/2919 Art.10
s.11, applied: SI 2003/219, SI 2003/219 Sch.1, SI 2003/3342, SI 2003/3342 Sch.1
s.11, disapplied: SI 2003/2919 Art.10
s.11, enabling: SI 2003/3342, SI 2004/3317
s.13, applied: SI 2003/3342 Sch.1
s.16, see *Kirk v Royal College of Veterinary Surgeons* 51 of 2002 (PC (UK)), Lord Hoffmann
s.16, applied: SI 2003/2919 Art.8, SI 2003/3342 Sch.1, SI 2004/1680 Sch.1
s.17, applied: SI 2003/2919 Art.9, SI 2003/3342 Sch.1
s.18, applied: SI 2004/1680 Sch.1
s.19, applied: SI 2002/794 Art.3, SI 2002/1479, SI 2002/2584, SI 2002/2584 Art.4, Art.5, SI 2003/2919 Art.10, SI 2004/1504 Art.3, SI 2004/2780 Art.2
s.19, referred to: SI 2002/2584 Art.4
s.19, enabling: SI 2002/1479, SI 2002/2584, SI 2004/1504, SI 2004/2780
s.20, applied: SI 2003/2919 Art.10
s.25, applied: SI 2003/219, SI 2004/2143
s.25, enabling: SI 2003/219, SI 2003/3342, SI 2004/3317
s.26, applied: SI 2004/1680 Sch.1Sch.1 para.7
s.28, repealed (in part): 2004 c.14 Sch.1 Part 17
s.29, repealed (in part): 2004 c.14 Sch.1 Part 17
Sch.1A, substituted: SI 2003/2919 Sch.1 para.8
Sch.1 para.12, repealed: 2004 c.14 Sch.1 Part 17
Sch.1 para.13, repealed: 2004 c.14 Sch.1 Part 17
Sch.1A para.1, substituted: SI 2003/2919 Sch.1 para.8
Sch.1A para.2, substituted: SI 2003/2919 Sch.1 para.8
Sch.1A para.3, substituted: SI 2003/2919 Sch.1 para.8
Sch.2 Part II para.5, applied: SI 2004/1680
Sch.2 Part II para.5, enabling: SI 2004/1680
Sch.3 Part 1 para.6, substituted: SI 2002/1479 Art.2
Sch.3 Part 1 para.7, added: SI 2002/1479 Art.2

37. Barbados Independence Act 1966
Sch.2 para.13, repealed: 2002 c.39 Sch.3

CAP.

1966–cont.

38. Sea Fisheries Regulation Act 1966
see *R. (on the application of South Wales Sea Fisheries Committee) v National Assembly for Wales* [2001] EWHC Admin 1162, [2002] R.V.R. 134 (QBD (Admin Ct)), Richards, J.
s.1, enabling: SI 2003/3036
s.2, enabling: SI 2003/3036

42. Local Government Act 1966
s.43, repealed: 2004 c.14 Sch.1 Part 10
Sch.5 para.1, repealed: 2004 c.14 Sch.1 Part 10
Sch.5 para.2, repealed: 2004 c.14 Sch.1 Part 10
Sch.5 para.3, repealed: 2004 c.14 Sch.1 Part 10
Sch.5 para.4, repealed: 2004 c.14 Sch.1 Part 10
Sch.5 para.5, repealed: 2004 c.14 Sch.1 Part 10
Sch.5 para.6, repealed: 2004 c.14 Sch.1 Part 10
Sch.5 para.7, repealed: 2004 c.14 Sch.1 Part 10
Sch.5 para.8, repealed: 2004 c.14 Sch.1 Part 10

45. Armed Forces Act 1966
s.2, applied: SR 2003/28 Sch.6 para.2
s.2, enabling: SI 2002/201, SI 2003/2305
s.8, amended: 2003 c.44 Sch.37 Part 9
s.8, disapplied: 2003 c.44 Sch.25 para.64

49. Housing (Scotland) Act 1966
s.8, see *MacKenzie v Aberdeen City Council* 2002 Hous. L.R. 88 (Sh Ct (Grampian, Highland and Islands)), DJ Cusine

51. Local Government (Scotland) Act 1966
s.24, applied: SSI 2002/91 Reg.16, SSI 2003/160 Reg.17, SSI 2004/92 Reg.3
s.24A, applied: SSI 2002/91 Reg.17, SSI 2003/160 Reg.18, SSI 2004/92 Reg.3
s.24A, referred to: SSI 2003/160 Reg.18
s.25A, applied: SSI 2002/91 Reg.18, SSI 2003/160 Reg.19, SSI 2004/92 Reg.5
s.46, amended: 2002 asp 3 Sch.7 para.4

1967

xlii. City of London (Various Powers) Act 1967
s.10, amended: SI 2003/1615 Sch.1 para.26
s.11, amended: SI 2003/1615 Sch.1 para.26
s.19, amended: SI 2003/1615 Sch.1 para.26

1. Clergy Pensions (Amendment) Measure 1967
s.4, amended: 2003 c.2 s.2

3. Education Act 1967
repealed (in part): 2002 c.32 Sch.22 Part 3
s.4, repealed (in part): 2002 c.32 s.18

1967–cont.

3. **Overseas and Other Clergy (Ministry and Ordination) Measure 1967**
   applied: SI 2002/1892 Sch.1 Part TABLEd, SI 2003/1933 Sch.1 Part II, Sch.1 Part IV, SI 2004/1888 Sch.1 Part TABLEd

5. **Administration of Estates (Small Payments) (Northern Ireland) Act 1967**
   s.6, applied: SR 2002/352 Reg.96

7. **Misrepresentation Act 1967**
   see *Procter & Gamble (Health and Beauty Care) Ltd v Carrier Holdings Ltd* [2003] EWHC 83, [2003] B.L.R. 255 (QBD (T&CC)), Forbes, J.
   applied: SI 2003/1593 Sch.1 Part I
   s.2, see *Inntrepreneur Pub Co (CPC) Ltd v Sweeney* [2002] EWHC 1060, [2003] E.C.C. 17 (Ch D), Park, J.; see *MCI WorldCom International Inc v Primus Telecommunications Inc* [2003] EWHC 2182, [2004] 1 All E.R. (Comm) 138 (QBD (Comm Ct)), Colman, J.; see *Pankhania v Hackney LBC (Damages)* [2004] EWHC 323, [2004] 1 E.G.L.R. 135 (Ch D), Geoffrey Vos Q.C.; see *Rushton v Worcester City Council* [2001] EWCA Civ 367, [2002] H.L.R. 9 (CA), Potter, L.J.; see *Spice Girls Ltd v Aprilia World Service BV* [2002] EWCA Civ 15, [2002] E.M.L.R. 27 (CA), Sir Andrew Morritt V.C.; see *Thomson v Christie Manson & Woods Ltd* [2004] EWHC 1101, [2004] P.N.L.R. 42 (QBD), Jack, J.

8. **Plant Health Act 1967**
   applied: SI 2002/3026 Sch.5 para.1
   s.2, enabling: SI 2002/295, SI 2002/927, SI 2002/1067, SI 2002/1299, SI 2002/1350, SI 2002/1478, SI 2002/1805, SI 2002/2573, SI 2002/2589, SI 2002/2762, SI 2003/1157, SI 2003/1851, SI 2004/1452, SI 2004/2365, SI 2004/2590, SI 2004/2697, SI 2004/3213, SSI 2002/223, SSI 2002/483, SSI 2003/224, SSI 2004/255, SSI 2004/440, SSI 2004/488
   s.3, amended: 2003 c.44 Sch.27 para.1
   s.3, enabling: SI 2002/295, SI 2002/296, SI 2002/927, SI 2002/1067, SI 2002/1299, SI 2002/1350, SI 2002/1478, SI 2002/1805, SI 2002/2573, SI 2002/2589, SI 2002/2762, SI 2003/1157, SI 2003/1851, SI 2004/1404, SI 2004/1452, SI 2004/1684, SI 2004/2365, SI 2004/2590, SI 2004/2697, SI 2004/3213, SI 2004/3367, SSI 2002/223, SSI 2002/483, SSI 2003/224, SSI 2004/248, SSI 2004/255, SSI 2004/440, SSI 2004/488
   s.4, enabling: SI 2002/1067, SI 2002/1299, SI 2002/1350, SI 2002/1805, SI 2002/2573, SI 2002/2762, SI 2003/1851, SI 2004/1452, SI 2004/2590, SI 2004/2697, SI 2004/3367, SSI 2002/223, SSI 2002/483, SSI 2004/255, SSI 2004/488

1967–cont.

8. **Plant Health Act 1967**–*cont.*
   s.4A, enabling: SI 2004/1404, SI 2004/1684, SSI 2004/248

9. **General Rate Act 1967**
   see *R. (on the application of Corus UK Ltd) v Valuation Office Agency* [2001] EWHC Admin 1108, [2002] R.A. 1 (QBD (Admin Ct)), Sullivan, J.
   s.48, applied: SI 2002/1792 Sch.2 para.6

10. **Forestry Act 1967**
    applied: SSI 2003/129 Sch.2 para.13
    referred to: SSI 2004/70 Sch.2 para.13
    Part II, applied: SSI 2003/209 Art.5
    s.1, applied: SSI 2004/474 Sch.1
    s.9, see *R. (on the application of Grundy & Co Excavations Ltd) v Halton Division Magistrates Court* [2003] EWHC 272, (2003) 167 J.P. 387 (QBD (Admin Ct)), Clarke, L.J.
    s.9, applied: SSI 2003/209 Art.5
    s.10, amended: 2004 asp 6 Sch.7 para.2
    s.10, applied: SSI 2003/209 Art.5
    s.10, enabling: SI 2002/226
    s.12, amended: 2004 asp 6 Sch.7 para.2
    s.15, repealed (in part): SI 2002/794 Sch.2
    s.17, see *R. (on the application of Grundy & Co Excavations Ltd) v Halton Division Magistrates Court* [2003] EWHC 272, (2003) 167 J.P. 387 (QBD (Admin Ct)), Clarke, L.J.
    s.17A, applied: SSI 2003/209 Art.5
    s.19, repealed (in part): SI 2002/794 Sch.2
    s.24, applied: SSI 2003/209 Art.5
    s.32, enabling: SI 2002/226
    s.49, amended: SI 2002/794 Sch.1 para.13, Sch.2
    Sch.1, applied: SI 2002/794 Art.3
    Sch.3 para.4, repealed: SI 2002/794 Sch.2
    Sch.5 Part I para.2, amended: 2003 asp 9 s.110
    Sch.5 Part I para.2, applied: 2003 asp 9 s.106
    Sch.5 Part I para.3, amended: 2003 asp 9 s.110
    Sch.5 Part I para.4, amended: 2003 asp 9 s.110
    Sch.5 Part I para.6, amended: 2003 asp 9 s.110
    Sch.5 Part I para.6A, added: 2003 asp 9 s.110
    Sch.5 Part I para.6B, added: 2003 asp 9 s.110
    Sch.5 Part I para.6C, added: 2003 asp 9 s.110
    Sch.5 Part I para.6D, added: 2003 asp 9 s.110

13. **Parliamentary Commissioner Act 1967**
    applied: 2002 asp 11 s.21
    s.3, amended: SI 2004/1823 Art.5
    s.4, enabling: SI 2003/2921, SI 2004/2670
    s.5, amended: 2004 c.28 Sch.7 para.2
    s.5, enabling: SI 2003/2921
    s.7, amended: 2004 c.28 Sch.7 para.3
    s.8, amended: 2004 c.28 Sch.7 para.4
    s.10, amended: 2004 c.28 Sch.7 para.5

CAP.

13. **Parliamentary Commissioner Act 1967**–*cont.*

s.11A, amended: 2004 c.34 Sch.15 para.1, SI 2004/1823 Art.5

s.11AA, referred to: 2002 asp 13 s.63

s.12, amended: 2004 c.28 Sch.7 para.6

Sch.2, amended: 2002 c.17 Sch.6 para.17, 2002 c.29 Sch.11 para.2, 2002 c.39 Sch.3, 2002 c.40 Sch.1 para.14, Sch.26, SI 2002/253 Sch.5 para.1, SI 2002/794 Sch.1 para.14, Sch.2, SI 2002/1397 Sch.1 para.4, SI 2002/2626 Sch.2 para.4, 2003 c.20 Sch.2 para.19, 2003 c.21 Sch.19, 2003 c.26 Sch.4 para.22, 2003 c.37 Sch.7 para.18, Sch.9 Part 3, 2003 c.43 Sch.2 para.17, Sch.9 para.3, Sch.14 Part 2, SI 2003/2921 Art.3, 2004 c.8 Sch.6 para.2, 2004 c.11 Sch.1 para.2, 2004 c.14 Sch.1 Part 5, 2004 c.17 Sch.3 para.1, Sch.4, 2004 c.20 Sch.1 para.15, 2004 c.25 Sch.4 para.5, Sch.5 para.10, 2004 c.27 Sch.3 para.8, Sch.4 para.5, 2004 c.30 Sch.2 para.24, 2004 c.35 Sch.1 para.33, Sch.13 Part 1, SI 2004/2670 Art.2

Sch.2, applied: SI 2004/1957 Art.2

Sch.2, referred to: SI 2003/55 Art.2

Sch.2, varied: SI 2004/664 Art.11, Art.12, Art.13, Art.14

Sch.2 paraA.1, added: 2002 c.29 Sch.11 para.2

Sch.2 paraA.1, amended: 2003 c.20 Sch.2 para.19

Sch.2 para.1, amended: 2003 c.20 Sch.2 para.19

Sch.2 para.1A, amended: 2003 c.20 Sch.2 para.19

Sch.2 para.1B, amended: 2003 c.20 Sch.2 para.19

Sch.2 para.2, amended: 2003 c.20 Sch.2 para.19

Sch.2 para.2A, added: SI 2003/2921 Art.3

Sch.2 para.2A, amended: 2003 c.20 Sch.2 para.19

Sch.2 para.3, amended: 2003 c.20 Sch.2 para.19

Sch.2 para.4, amended: 2003 c.20 Sch.2 para.19, SI 2003/2921 Art.3

Sch.2 para.5, amended: 2003 c.20 Sch.2 para.19

Sch.2 para.6, amended: 2003 c.20 Sch.2 para.19

Sch.2 para.7, amended: 2003 c.20 Sch.2 para.19

Sch.2 para.8, amended: 2003 c.20 Sch.2 para.19

Sch.2 para.8A, amended: 2003 c.20 Sch.2 para.19, SI 2003/2921 Art.3

Sch.2 para.9, amended: 2003 c.20 Sch.2 para.19

Sch.2 para.10, amended: 2003 c.20 Sch.2 para.19

CAP.

13. **Parliamentary Commissioner Act 1967**–*cont.*

Sch.2 para.11, amended: 2003 c.20 Sch.2 para.19

Sch.2 para.12, added: 2004 c.17 Sch.3 para.1

Sch.2 para.12, amended: 2003 c.20 Sch.2 para.19

Sch.2 para.13, added: SI 2004/2670 Art.2

Sch.2 para.13, amended: 2003 c.20 Sch.2 para.19

Sch.3 para.4, substituted: 2003 c.41 Sch.3 para.2

Sch.3 para.8, amended: SI 2002/2469 Sch.1 para.3, 2003 c.43 Sch.13 para.1, Sch.14 Part 4, Sch.14 Part 7

Sch.3 para.10, amended: 2002 c.1 Sch.3 para.2

Sch.4, amended: SI 2003/1398 Sch.1 para.1, SI 2003/2921 Art.4, 2004 c.35 s.211, Sch.4 para.16

18. **Criminal Law Act (Northern Ireland) 1967**

s.6, amended: 2003 c.44 Sch.36 para.43

19. **Private Places of Entertainment (Licensing) Act 1967**

applied: 2003 c.17 Sch.4 para.2

repealed: 2003 c.17 Sch.7

22. **Agriculture Act 1967**

s.3, amended: 2004 c.14 Sch.1 Part 2

s.6, amended: 2003 c.44 Sch.26 para.19, Sch.37 Part 9

s.6, disapplied: 2003 c.44 Sch.25 para.65

s.9, amended: 2003 c.44 Sch.27 para.2

s.14, amended: 2003 c.44 Sch.37 Part 9

s.14, disapplied: 2003 c.44 Sch.25 para.66

s.16, repealed: 2004 c.14 Sch.1 Part 2

s.19, amended: SI 2003/1326 Art.6

s.21, amended: 2003 c.44 Sch.26 para.19

s.22, repealed: 2004 c.14 Sch.1 Part 2

s.33, repealed: 2004 c.14 Sch.1 Part 2

s.34, repealed: 2004 c.14 Sch.1 Part 2

s.58, amended: 2004 c.14 Sch.1 Part 2

s.61, repealed: 2004 c.14 Sch.1 Part 2

s.62, amended: 2004 c.14 Sch.1 Part 2

s.62, repealed (in part): 2004 c.14 Sch.1 Part 2

s.64, amended: 2004 c.14 Sch.1 Part 2

s.64, repealed (in part): 2004 c.14 Sch.1 Part 2

s.65, repealed: 2004 c.14 Sch.1 Part 2

s.69, amended: 2003 c.44 Sch.37 Part 9

s.69, disapplied: 2003 c.44 Sch.25 para.67

s.75, amended: 2004 c.14 Sch.1 Part 2

s.75, repealed (in part): 2004 c.14 Sch.1 Part 2

Sch.1 Part I para.10A, amended: SI 2004/1317 Reg.15

Sch.1 Part I para.10A, substituted: SSI 2004/280 Reg.15

28. **Superannuation (Miscellaneous Provisions) Act 1967**

s.15, applied: SI 2002/1043 Art.2, SI 2002/2143 Art.2

1967–cont.

41. Marine, &c., Broadcasting (Offences) Act 1967
applied: 2002 c.11 s.6
referred to: 2003 c.21 s.393, s.404
s.3, amended: 2002 c.8 s.2
s.4, amended: 2003 c.21 Sch.17 para.32
s.5, amended: 2003 c.21 Sch.17 para.32, Sch.17 para.33
s.6, amended: 2002 c.26 Sch.7 para.25, 2003 c.21 Sch.17 para.34
s.6, repealed (in part): 2003 c.21 Sch.19
s.7A, amended: 2003 c.21 Sch.17 para.35
s.7A, applied: 2003 c.21 Sch.1 para.2
s.9, amended: 2003 c.21 Sch.17 para.36

48. Industrial and Provident Societies Act 1967
s.4, disapplied: SI 2003/3226 Reg.4

49. Llangollen International Musical Eisteddfod Act 1967
repealed: 2004 c.14 Sch.1 Part 10

50. Farm and Garden Chemicals Act 1967
s.1, repealed (in part): 2004 c.14 Sch.1 Part 2

51. Licensing (Amendment) Act 1967
repealed: 2003 c.17 Sch.7

54. Finance Act 1967
s.5, amended: 2003 c.17 Sch.6 para.37, Sch.7
s.5, repealed (in part): 2003 c.17 Sch.6 para.37, Sch.7
s.27, applied: 2004 c.25 s.4
s.45, repealed (in part): 2003 c.17 Sch.7, 2004 c.14 Sch.1 Part 17
Sch.7 para.1, repealed: 2003 c.17 Sch.7
Sch.7 para.2, repealed: 2003 c.17 Sch.7
Sch.7 para.3, repealed: 2003 c.17 Sch.7
Sch.7 para.4, repealed: 2003 c.17 Sch.7
Sch.7 para.5, repealed: 2003 c.17 Sch.7
Sch.7 para.6, repealed: 2003 c.17 Sch.7
Sch.7 para.7, repealed: 2003 c.17 Sch.7
Sch.7 para.8, repealed: 2003 c.17 Sch.7
Sch.7 para.9, repealed: 2003 c.17 Sch.7
Sch.7 para.10, repealed: 2003 c.17 Sch.7
Sch.7 para.11, repealed: 2003 c.17 Sch.7
Sch.7 para.12, repealed: 2003 c.17 Sch.7
Sch.7 para.13, repealed: 2003 c.17 Sch.7
Sch.7 para.14, repealed: 2003 c.17 Sch.7
Sch.7 para.15, repealed: 2003 c.17 Sch.7
Sch.7 para.16, repealed: 2003 c.17 Sch.7
Sch.7 para.17, repealed: 2003 c.17 Sch.7
Sch.7 para.18, repealed: 2003 c.17 Sch.7
Sch.7 para.19, repealed: 2003 c.17 Sch.7
Sch.7 para.20, repealed: 2003 c.17 Sch.7
Sch.7 para.21, repealed: 2003 c.17 Sch.7
Sch.7 para.22, repealed: 2003 c.17 Sch.7
Sch.7 para.23, repealed: 2003 c.17 Sch.7
Sch.7 para.24, repealed: 2003 c.17 Sch.7

58. Criminal Law Act 1967
s.3, see *R. v Jones (Margaret)* [2004] EWCA Crim 1981, [2004] 3 W.L.R. 1362 (CA (Crim Div)), Latham, L.J.
s.5, applied: SI 2002/1837 Sch.1 Part I

1967–cont.

58. Criminal Law Act 1967–*cont.*
s.6, see *R. v Fitzgerald (John Cornelius)* [2003] EWCA Crim 576, [2003] 2 Cr. App. R. 17 (CA (Crim Div)), Pill, L.J.; see *R. v Morrison (Richard)* [2003] EWCA Crim 1722, [2003] 1 W.L.R. 1859 (CA (Crim Div)), Lord Woolf of Barnes, L.C.J.36 para.41
s.6, repealed (in part): 2004 c.28 s.11

60. Sexual Offences Act 1967
s.1, repealed: 2003 c.42 Sch.6 para.15, Sch.7
s.4, applied: SI 2002/896 Sch.1 para.36, 2003 c.44 Sch.15 para.95
s.4, repealed: 2003 c.42 Sch.6 para.15, Sch.7
s.5, applied: 2002 c.29 Sch.2 para.8, SI 2002/896 Sch.1 para.37, 2003 c.44 Sch.15 para.96
s.5, repealed: 2003 c.42 Sch.6 para.15, Sch.7
s.7, repealed: 2003 c.42 Sch.6 para.15, Sch.7
s.8, repealed: 2003 c.42 Sch.6 para.15, Sch.7
s.10, repealed: 2003 c.42 Sch.6 para.15, Sch.7

61. Public Works Loans Act 1967
s.2, amended: 2003 c.26 Sch.7 para.3, SI 2004/533 Art.7

63. Bermuda Constitution Act 1967
s.1, enabling: SI 2003/456

68. Fugitive Offenders Act 1967
applied: SI 2002/1823 Sch.2 para.19

72. Wireless Telegraphy Act 1967
applied: 2002 c.11 s.6
referred to: 2003 c.21 s.393, s.404
varied: SI 2003/1903 Reg.3
s.4, repealed: 2003 c.21 Sch.19
s.6, amended: 2003 c.21 s.367
s.6, referred to: 2003 c.21 s.367
s.6, enabling: SI 2004/692
s.7, amended: 2003 c.21 Sch.17 para.37
s.7, applied: 2003 c.21 s.182, Sch.1 para.1, Sch.7 para.1, Sch.7 para.9
s.7, disapplied: 2003 c.21 s.182
s.7, repealed (in part): 2003 c.21 Sch.19
s.8, amended: 2003 c.21 Sch.17 para.38
s.13, amended: 2003 c.21 Sch.17 para.39

75. Matrimonial Homes Act 1967
s.2, applied: SI 2003/1953 Art.20

76. Road Traffic Regulation Act 1967
repealed: 2004 c.14 Sch.1 Part 14

77. Police (Scotland) Act 1967
applied: 2002 asp 11 Sch.2 para.14, Sch.4 para.1, 2002 asp 13 Sch.1 para.51, 2002 c.29 s.139, 2003 asp 1 s.16, SI 2003/527 Reg.3, 2004 c.20 s.66, 2004 c.36 Sch.1 para.14, SSI 2004/257 Reg.2
referred to: 2002 c.30 s.108
s.1, applied: SI 2003/2617 Sch.1 para.1, SI 2003/3171 Sch.1 Part I, SI 2003/3172 Sch.1, SSI 2002/62 Sch.1
s.2, applied: SSI 2002/62 Sch.1, 2003 c.14 Sch.9 para.1, SSI 2004/257 Reg.11
s.3AA, applied: SSI 2004/257 Reg.44

CAP.

1967–cont.

77. Police (Scotland) Act 1967–*cont.*
s.4, applied: SSI 2004/257 Reg.11
s.5, substituted: 2003 asp 7 s.75
s.7, amended: 2003 asp 7 s.75
s.7, enabling: SSI 2004/257
s.9, amended: 2003 asp 7 s.76
s.9, applied: SSI 2003/231 Sch.4 para.8, SSI 2004/257 Reg.24
s.9A, added: 2003 asp 7 s.76
s.9B, added: 2003 asp 7 s.76
s.11, amended: SI 2004/1573 Art.12
s.11, varied: 2003 c.20 Sch.5 para.4
s.12, amended: 2004 c.20 Sch.14 para.2, SI 2004/1573 Art.12
s.12, varied: 2003 c.20 Sch.5 para.4
s.16, applied: SSI 2004/257 Reg.10
s.16, varied: 2003 c.20 s.24, s.25
s.16, enabling: SSI 2004/257
s.17, varied: 2003 c.20 Sch.5 para.4
s.19, applied: 2003 c.14 Sch.9 para.1
s.20, applied: SSI 2002/458
s.20, referred to: SSI 2002/140
s.20, enabling: SSI 2002/140, SSI 2002/458
s.21, applied: SSI 2002/458
s.21, referred to: SSI 2002/140
s.21, enabling: SSI 2002/140, SSI 2002/458
s.21B, applied: SSI 2002/458
s.21B, enabling: SSI 2002/458
s.26, amended: 2003 asp 7 s.75
s.26, applied: 2002 c.30 s.82, SSI 2003/21
s.26, enabling: SSI 2003/21, SSI 2003/220, SSI 2004/121, SSI 2004/257
s.27, enabling: SSI 2004/257
s.31, amended: 2003 asp 7 s.75
s.32, enabling: SSI 2002/116, SSI 2003/172, SSI 2004/120
s.33, applied: 2003 asp 1 s.25, 2003 c.20 s.63, s.64, s.67, SI 2003/409 Sch.1 Part I
s.38, amended: 2002 c.29 Sch.11 para.3
s.38, applied: SSI 2004/257 Reg.21, Reg.24
s.38A, amended: 2002 c.1 Sch.3 para.3, Sch.4, 2002 c.29 Sch.11 para.3, 2002 c.30 Sch.7 para.1
s.38A, applied: SSI 2004/257 Reg.21, Reg.24, Reg.40, Reg.44
s.39, amended: 2002 c.30 s.102, s.103, 2003 asp 7 s.76
s.39, applied: SI 2004/1127 Art.2
s.39, enabling: SI 2004/1127
s.41, see *Walsh v McFadyen* 2002 J.C. 93 (HCJ Appeal), Lord McCluskey, Lord Cameron of Lochbroom, Lord Marnoch
s.41, amended: 2002 c.30 s.104, 2003 asp 7 s.76
s.41, applied: SI 2004/1127 Art.2, SSI 2003/441 Sch.1 para.7
s.41, varied: 2003 c.32 s.84, 2004 c.20 s.68
s.41, enabling: SI 2004/1127
s.42, amended: 2004 c.20 s.68
s.42, applied: SSI 2004/257 Reg.24

CAP.

1967–cont.

77. Police (Scotland) Act 1967–*cont.*
s.42, varied: 2003 c.20 Sch.5 para.4
s.43, amended: 2003 asp 7 s.76, 2004 c.20 s.68
s.43, applied: SSI 2004/257 Reg.24
s.43, referred to: 2003 c.20 Sch.5 para.3
s.44, amended: 2003 asp 7 s.76
s.44, applied: SSI 2004/257 Reg.24
s.45, amended: 2003 asp 7 s.76
s.48, enabling: SSI 2004/257
s.50, applied: 2003 c.20 Sch.4 para.7
s.51, amended: 2003 asp 7 s.76, 2003 c.20 Sch.5 para.4
s.51, varied: 2003 c.20 Sch.5 para.4

80. Criminal Justice Act 1967
referred to: 2003 c.44 s.189
s.9, see *R. (on the application of Islington LBC) v Jordan* [2002] EWHC 2645, (2003) 167 J.P. 1 (QBD (Admin Ct)), McCombe, J.
s.9, amended: 2003 c.39 Sch.4 para.1, 2003 c.44 Sch.37 Part 4, Sch.3 para.43
s.9, applied: 2003 c.21 Sch.6 para.10, 2003 c.41 s.205, 2003 c.44 s.127
s.9, varied: 2003 c.21 Sch.6 para.10
s.10, applied: 2003 c.41 s.205
s.10, varied: 2003 c.41 s.205
s.17, amended: 2003 c.44 Sch.36 para.42
s.20, repealed: 2003 c.44 Sch.37 Part 9
s.22, amended: 2003 c.44 s.17, Sch.37 Part 2
s.32, amended: 2003 c.44 Sch.32 para.5
s.34, repealed: 2003 c.41 Sch.4
s.36, amended: 2003 c.44 Sch.37 Part 4, Sch.3 para.43
s.67, see *R. v Armstrong (Christopher Andrew)* [2002] EWCA Crim 441, [2002] 2 Cr. App. R. (S.) 87 (CA (Crim Div)), Rose, L.J.; see *R. v Broomfield (Neil Robert)* [2004] EWCA Crim 363, [2004] 2 Cr. App. R. (S.) 70 (CA (Crim Div)), Keene, L.J.
s.67, applied: 2003 c.44 s.241
s.72, applied: 2003 c.41 s.142
s.91, applied: 2002 c.30 Sch.5 para.1, SI 2002/1837 Sch.1 Part I, Sch.1 Part II, SI 2004/915 Sch.1 para.1
s.104, amended: 2003 c.44 Sch.32 para.6, Sch.37 Part 7
s.104, repealed (in part): 2003 c.44 Sch.32 para.6, Sch.37 Part 7

81. Companies Act 1967
applied: 2002 c.iv

83. Sea Fisheries (Shellfish) Act 1967
s.1, applied: SI 2002/1885 Reg.2, SSI 2002/185, SSI 2002/186, SSI 2002/272, SSI 2004/1, SSI 2004/5
s.1, enabling: SI 2002/1885, SSI 2002/185, SSI 2002/186, SSI 2002/272, SSI 2004/1, SSI 2004/5
s.7, applied: SSI 2002/186 Art.5, SSI 2002/272 Art.5, SSI 2004/5 Art.5

1967–cont.

83. Sea Fisheries (Shellfish) Act 1967– cont.

s.7, enabling: SSI 2002/185, SSI 2002/186, SSI 2002/272, SSI 2004/5

s.14, amended: 2003 c.44 Sch.37 Part 9

s.14, disapplied: 2003 c.44 Sch.25 para.68

Sch.1, applied: SSI 2002/185, SSI 2002/186, SSI 2004/1

Sch.1, enabling: SSI 2002/185, SSI 2002/186, SSI 2004/1, SSI 2004/5

Sch.1 para.1, applied: SSI 2002/185, SSI 2002/186, SSI 2002/272, SSI 2004/1, SSI 2004/5

Sch.1 para.2, applied: SSI 2002/185, SSI 2002/186, SSI 2002/272, SSI 2004/1, SSI 2004/5

Sch.1 para.3, applied: SSI 2002/185, SSI 2002/186, SSI 2002/272, SSI 2004/1, SSI 2004/5

84. Sea Fish (Conservation) Act 1967

applied: SI 2002/790 Sch.1 para.1, SI 2004/12 Art.8

referred to: SI 2004/12 Art.8

s.1, applied: SI 2002/790 Sch.1 para.2, Sch.1 para.3, SI 2004/12 Art.6

s.1, enabling: SI 2002/1897, SI 2004/12

s.3, see *Urquhart v Sinclair* 2003 S.L.T. 824 (HCJ), Lord Cullen L.J.G., Lord Caplan, Lord Marnoch

s.3, applied: SI 2002/790 Sch.1 para.2, Sch.1 para.3, SI 2002/2870 Art.4, SI 2003/2513 Art.5, SI 2003/3035 Art.4, SI 2004/2567 Art.5, SI 2004/2696 Art.5, SSI 2004/261 Art.4

s.3, enabling: SI 2002/2870, SI 2003/1560, SI 2003/2513, SI 2004/12, SI 2004/2567, SI 2004/2696, SI 2004/3397, SSI 2003/167, SSI 2004/261

s.4, applied: SI 2002/790 Sch.1 para.2, Sch.1 para.3, Sch.1 para.4, SI 2003/229 Art.6, SI 2003/1535 Art.6, SI 2003/2669 Art.9, SR 2003/59 Art.6

s.4, varied: SI 2002/790 Sch.1 para.4

s.4A, applied: SI 2002/790 Sch.1 para.2, Sch.1 para.3, Sch.1 para.4

s.4A, varied: SI 2002/790 Sch.1 para.4

s.4B, applied: SI 2002/790 Sch.1 para.3, Sch.1 para.4

s.4B, disapplied: SI 2002/790 Sch.1 para.4

s.5, applied: SI 2002/676 Art.5, SI 2002/790 Sch.1 para.3, SI 2003/607 Art.4, SI 2003/1855 Art.4, SSI 2002/58 Art.4, SSI 2003/79 Art.4, SSI 2004/55 Art.4

s.5, referred to: SI 2003/1559 Art.4

s.5, varied: SI 2002/676 Art.5

s.5, enabling: SI 2002/676, SI 2003/607, SI 2003/1559, SI 2003/1855, SI 2003/3035, SI 2004/3397, SSI 2002/58, SSI 2003/79, SSI 2003/100, SSI 2003/166, SSI 2003/371, SSI 2004/55

s.5A, enabling: SI 2003/607, SI 2004/3397

1967–cont.

84. Sea Fish (Conservation) Act 1967– cont.

s.6, applied: SI 2002/676 Art.5, SI 2002/790 Sch.1 para.2, Sch.1 para.3

s.6, varied: SI 2002/676 Art.5, SI 2002/790 Sch.1 para.4

s.6, enabling: SI 2002/676

s.8, applied: SI 2002/790 Sch.1 para.3, Sch.1 para.4

s.8, varied: SI 2002/790 Sch.1 para.4

s.9, applied: SI 2002/790 Sch.1 para.3

s.10, applied: SI 2002/790 Sch.1 para.3

s.11, applied: SI 2003/336 Sch.1 Part 2

s.14, applied: SI 2003/2513 Art.1, SI 2004/2567 Art.1

s.14, referred to: SI 2003/1559 Art.1, SI 2004/12 Art.1, SI 2004/2696 Art.1

s.15, applied: SI 2002/790 Sch.1 para.3

s.15, enabling: SI 2002/676, SI 2002/1897, SI 2002/2870, SI 2003/607, SI 2003/1559, SI 2003/1560, SI 2003/1855, SI 2003/2513, SI 2003/3035, SI 2004/12, SI 2004/2567, SI 2004/2696, SI 2004/3397, SSI 2002/58, SSI 2003/79, SSI 2003/100, SSI 2003/371, SSI 2004/55, SSI 2004/261

s.18, amended: 2003 asp 15 Sch.4 para.1

s.20, disapplied: SI 2002/790 Sch.1 para.4

s.20, enabling: SI 2003/1559, SI 2003/1560, SI 2004/12

s.22, enabling: SSI 2002/58, SSI 2003/79, SSI 2003/100, SSI 2003/166, SSI 2003/167, SSI 2004/55

s.22A, applied: SI 2002/790 Sch.1 para.1

86. Countryside (Scotland) Act 1967

referred to: 2003 asp 2 Sch.2 para.3

s.10, repealed: 2003 asp 2 Sch.2 para.4

s.11, amended: SI 2003/2155 Sch.1 para.5

s.11, repealed: 2003 asp 2 Sch.2 para.4

s.12, repealed: 2003 asp 2 Sch.2 para.4

s.13, repealed: 2003 asp 2 Sch.2 para.4

s.14, repealed: 2003 asp 2 Sch.2 para.4

s.15, repealed: 2003 asp 2 Sch.2 para.4

s.16, repealed: 2003 asp 2 Sch.2 para.4

s.17, repealed: 2003 asp 2 Sch.2 para.4

s.18, repealed: 2003 asp 2 Sch.2 para.4

s.19, repealed: 2003 asp 2 Sch.2 para.4

s.20, repealed: 2003 asp 2 Sch.2 para.4

s.21, applied: 2003 asp 2 Sch.2 para.6

s.21, referred to: 2003 asp 2 Sch.2 para.6

s.21, repealed: 2003 asp 2 Sch.2 para.4

s.22, referred to: 2003 asp 2 Sch.2 para.6

s.22, repealed: 2003 asp 2 Sch.2 para.4

s.23, referred to: 2003 asp 2 Sch.2 para.6

s.23, repealed: 2003 asp 2 Sch.2 para.4

s.24, repealed: 2003 asp 2 Sch.2 para.4

s.25, repealed: 2003 asp 2 Sch.2 para.4

s.26, repealed: 2003 asp 2 Sch.2 para.4

s.27, referred to: 2003 asp 2 Sch.2 para.6

s.27, repealed: 2003 asp 2 Sch.2 para.4

s.28, repealed: 2003 asp 2 Sch.2 para.4

CAP.

1967–cont.

86. Countryside (Scotland) Act 1967– cont.
s.29, repealed: 2003 asp 2 Sch.2 para.4
s.30, applied: 2003 asp 2 s.22
s.30, repealed: 2003 asp 2 Sch.2 para.4
s.31, applied: 2003 asp 2 s.22
s.31, repealed: 2003 asp 2 Sch.2 para.4
s.32, applied: 2003 asp 2 s.22
s.32, repealed: 2003 asp 2 Sch.2 para.4
s.33, applied: 2003 asp 2 s.22
s.33, repealed: 2003 asp 2 Sch.2 para.4
s.34, applied: 2003 asp 2 s.22
s.34, repealed: 2003 asp 2 Sch.2 para.4
s.35, applied: 2003 asp 2 s.22
s.35, repealed: 2003 asp 2 Sch.2 para.4
s.36, applied: 2003 asp 2 s.22
s.36, repealed: 2003 asp 2 Sch.2 para.4
s.37, repealed: 2003 asp 2 Sch.2 para.4
s.38, amended: SI 2003/2155 Sch.1 para.5
s.38, repealed: 2003 asp 2 Sch.2 para.4
s.43, repealed: 2003 asp 2 Sch.2 para.4
s.47, amended: 2003 asp 2 Sch.2 para.5
s.49A, applied: SI 2003/2261 Sch.3 Part I, Sch.4 para.3, 2004 asp 10 s.35
s.54, amended: 2003 asp 2 Sch.2 para.4, SI 2003/2155 Sch.1 para.5
s.55, repealed: 2003 asp 2 Sch.2 para.4
s.61, amended: 2002 asp 3 Sch.7 para.5
s.63, amended: 2002 asp 3 Sch.7 para.5
s.65, applied: SSI 2002/201 Art.8
s.78, amended: 2002 asp 3 Sch.7 para.5
Sch.3 Part I para.1, amended: 2003 asp 2 Sch.2 para.4
Sch.3 Part I para.2, amended: 2003 asp 2 Sch.2 para.4

87. Abortion Act 1967
referred to: 2003 c.43 Sch.4 para.9
s.1, see *An NHS Trust v D* [2003] EWHC 2793, [2004] 1 F.L.R. 1110 (Fam Div), Coleridge, J.; see *SS (Medical Treatment: Late Termination), Re* [2002] 1 F.L.R. 445 (Fam Div), Wall, J.
s.1, amended: 2003 c.43 Sch.4 para.10
s.1, applied: SSI 2003/231 Sch.1 para.8, Sch.4 para.3
s.2, applied: SI 2002/325 Reg.40
s.2, enabling: SI 2002/887, SI 2002/2879

88. Leasehold Reform Act 1967
applied: 2002 c.15 s.159, SI 2004/1005 Sch.1
referred to: 2003 c.43 Sch.4 para.11
Part I, applied: SI 2002/1715 Reg.3, SI 2002/3187 Reg.3, SI 2003/1989 Reg.2, SI 2004/699 Reg.2, SI 2004/1005 Sch.2
Part II, applied: SI 2004/1005 Sch.2
s.1, see *Collins v Howard de Walden Estates Ltd* [2003] EWCA Civ 545, [2003] H.L.R. 70 (CA), Aldous, L.J.; see *Earl Cadogan v Search Guarantees Plc* [2004] EWCA Civ 969, [2004] 1 W.L.R. 2768 (CA), Jonathan Parker, L.J.; see *Malekshad v Howard de Walden Estates*

CAP.

1967–cont.

88. Leasehold Reform Act 1967– cont.
s.1–cont.
Ltd (No.1) [2002] UKHL 49, [2003] 1 A.C. 1013 (HL), Lord Scott of Foscote
s.1, amended: 2002 c.15 s.138, s.139, s.140, Sch.14, 2004 c.33 Sch.8 para.3, Sch.8 para.4
s.1, repealed (in part): 2002 c.15 Sch.14
s.1AA, amended: 2002 c.15 s.141, Sch.14
s.1AA, repealed (in part): 2002 c.15 Sch.14
s.2, see *Collins v Howard de Walden Estates Ltd* [2003] EWCA Civ 545, [2003] H.L.R. 70 (CA), Aldous, L.J.; see *Malekshad v Howard de Walden Estates Ltd (No.1)* [2001] EWCA Civ 761, [2002] Q.B. 364 (CA), Robert Walker, L.J.; see *Malekshad v Howard de Walden Estates Ltd (No.1)* [2002] UKHL 49, [2003] 1 A.C. 1013 (HL), Lord Scott of Foscote; see *Rosen v Campden Charities Trustees* [2002] Ch. 69 (CA), Evans-Lombe, J.
s.2, amended: 2002 c.15 s.138, Sch.14
s.2, referred to: SI 2004/1005 Sch.2
s.3, see *Skinns v Greenwood* [2002] EWCA Civ 424, [2002] H.L.R. 50 (CA), Kennedy, L.J.
s.3, amended: 2002 c.15 Sch.14, 2004 c.33 Sch.8 para.5
s.5, see *South v Chamberlayne* [2002] L. & T.R. 26 (Ch D), Lightman, J.
s.5, amended: 2002 c.9 Sch.11 para.8
s.6, amended: 2002 c.15 s.138, Sch.14
s.6, repealed (in part): 2002 c.15 Sch.14
s.6A, added: 2002 c.15 s.142
s.7, amended: 2002 c.15 s.138, Sch.14, 2004 c.33 Sch.8 para.6
s.7, repealed (in part): 2002 c.15 Sch.14
s.7, varied: 2004 c.33 Sch.21 para.4
s.8, applied: SI 2002/3012 Sch.2 para.5
s.9, see *Rosen v Campden Charities Trustees* [2002] Ch. 69 (CA), Evans-Lombe, J.; see *Shalson v John Lyon Free Grammar School Governors* [2003] UKHL 32, [2004] 1 A.C. 802 (HL), Lord Bingham of Cornhill; see *Speedwell Estates Ltd v Dalziel* [2001] EWCA Civ 1277, [2002] H.L.R. 43 (CA), Rimer, J.
s.9, amended: 2002 c.15 s.139, s.143, s.145, s.146, s.147, Sch.13 para.2, Sch.14
s.9, repealed (in part): 2002 c.15 Sch.14
s.9A, amended: 2002 c.15 s.147
s.14, amended: 2002 c.15 Sch.13 para.3
s.14, applied: SI 2002/3012 Sch.2 para.5
s.16, amended: 2002 c.15 s.143, Sch.14
s.16, repealed (in part): 2002 c.15 Sch.14
s.17, applied: SI 2004/1005 Sch.2
s.18, amended: 2004 c.33 Sch.8 para.7
s.18, applied: SI 2004/1005 Sch.2
s.18, varied: 2004 c.33 Sch.21 para.5
s.19, applied: 2002 c.15 s.159
s.20, amended: 2002 c.15 Sch.13 para.4

CAP.

1967–cont.

88. Leasehold Reform Act 1967–*cont.*

s.21, amended: 2002 c.15 s.149, Sch.13 para.5

s.21, applied: SI 2003/2099 Sch.1 para.1, Sch.2 para.1, SI 2004/681 Sch.1 para.1, Sch.2 para.1

s.21, repealed (in part): 2002 c.15 Sch.14

s.22, see *Collins v Howard de Walden Estates Ltd* [2002] 2 E.G.L.R. 61 (CC (Central London)), Judge Hallgarten Q.C.

s.22, applied: SI 2003/991

s.22, referred to: SI 2004/1005

s.22, enabling: SI 2003/1989, SI 2004/699

s.23, amended: 2002 c.15 s.139

s.27, amended: 2002 c.15 s.148, s.149

s.27, applied: SI 2002/3012 Sch.2 para.5

s.28, amended: SI 2002/2469 Sch.1 para.4, 2003 c.43 Sch.4 para.12, 2004 c.5 Sch.7 para.3

s.28, applied: SI 2004/1005 Sch.2

s.37, amended: 2002 c.15 Sch.14

Sch.2 para.8, amended: 2002 c.15 Sch.13 para.6

Sch.3 Part I para.2, amended: SI 2003/3096 Sch.5 para.11

Sch.3 Part I para.2, repealed (in part): SI 2003/3096 Sch.6

Sch.3 Part I para.2A, added: SI 2003/3096 Sch.5 para.12

Sch.3 Part II para.6, see *Speedwell Estates Ltd v Dalziel* [2001] EWCA Civ 1277, [2002] H.L.R. 43 (CA), Rimer, J.

Sch.3 Part II para.6, amended: 2002 c.15 s.142, Sch.14

Sch.3 Part II para.6, repealed (in part): 2002 c.15 Sch.14

Sch.3 Part II para.7, applied: SI 2002/3209 Reg.3, SI 2003/991 Reg.3

Sch.3 Part II para.10, amended: SI 2003/3096 Sch.5 para.13

Sch.3 Part II para.10, applied: SI 2004/1005 Sch.1, Sch.2

Sch.3 para.3, see *Malekshad v Howard de Walden Estates Ltd (No.2)* [2003] EWHC 3106, [2004] 1 W.L.R. 862 (Ch D), Neuberger, J.

Sch.3 para.6, see *Earl Cadogan v Strauss* [2004] EWCA Civ 211, [2004] H.L.R. 33 (CA), Brooke, L.J.; see *Malekshad v Howard de Walden Estates Ltd (No.2)* [2003] EWHC 3106, [2004] 1 W.L.R. 862 (Ch D), Neuberger, J.

Sch.4 Part I para.1, amended: 2002 c.9 Sch.11 para.8

Sch.4A para.2, amended: 2002 c.15 s.144

Sch.4A para.3, amended: 2002 c.15 Sch.14

1968

xxxvii. City of London (Various Powers) Act 1968

s.5, amended: 2003 c.17 Sch.6 para.53

CAP.

1968–cont.

xxxix. Greater London Council (General Powers) Act 1968

s.16, amended: 2004 c.21 Sch.1 para.23

s.17, amended: 2004 c.21 Sch.1 para.23

s.19, amended: 2004 c.21 Sch.1 para.23

s.20, amended: 2004 c.21 Sch.1 para.23

s.21, amended: 2004 c.21 Sch.1 para.23

s.24, amended: 2004 c.21 Sch.1 para.23

s.47, repealed: 2003 c.17 Sch.7

s.48, repealed: 2003 c.17 Sch.7

s.49, repealed: 2003 c.17 Sch.7

s.50, repealed: 2003 c.17 Sch.7

s.51, repealed: 2003 c.17 Sch.7

s.52, repealed: 2003 c.17 Sch.7

s.53, repealed: 2003 c.17 Sch.7

s.54, repealed: 2003 c.17 Sch.7

s.55, repealed: 2003 c.17 Sch.7

xxxii. Port of London Act 1968

Part X, applied: SI 2003/3006 Sch.2

s.2, amended: SI 2003/2556 Art.7

s.34, repealed: SI 2003/2556 Art.6

s.70, disapplied: SI 2004/757 Art.4

s.73, disapplied: SI 2004/757 Art.4

s.111, amended: SI 2003/2556 Art.3

s.120, amended: SI 2003/2556 Art.7

s.124, substituted: SI 2003/2556 Art.4

s.132, substituted: SI 2003/2556 Art.4

s.154, applied: SI 2003/527 Reg.42

s.154, referred to: SSI 2004/257 Reg.42

s.162, amended: SI 2003/2556 Art.5

s.164, substituted: SI 2003/2556 Art.5

s.165, repealed: SI 2003/2556 Art.7

Sch.10, amended: SI 2003/2556 Art.7

Sch.12, referred to: SI 2004/757 Sch.17 para.13

2. Provisional Collection of Taxes Act 1968

s.1, amended: 2003 c.14 Sch.18 para.1

4. Erskine Bridge Tolls Act 1968

s.17, amended: SSI 2002/176 Art.2

7. London Cab Act 1968

s.3, amended: SI 2003/1615 Sch.1 para.3

s.3, repealed (in part): 2004 c.14 Sch.1 Part 14

s.5, repealed (in part): 2004 c.14 Sch.1 Part 14

8. Mauritius Independence Act 1968

Sch.2 para.12, repealed: 2002 c.39 Sch.3

13. National Loans Act 1968

applied: 2002 c.29 Sch.9 para.1, SI 2003/3075 Reg.2, SI 2004/1450 Reg.12

varied: SI 2003/1633 Sch.2 para.2

s.12, applied: 2004 c.12 s.324

s.13, applied: 2004 c.12 s.324

s.14, amended: SI 2002/2521 Sch.2 Part I, SI 2004/1662 Sch.1 para.15

s.14, applied: 2004 c.12 s.324

s.14A, applied: 2004 c.12 s.324

s.15, amended: 2003 c.14 s.210

s.15, applied: 2004 c.12 s.324

s.15, repealed (in part): 2003 c.14 Sch.43 Part 5

1968–cont.

13. National Loans Act 1968–*cont.*

s.16, amended: SI 2002/2521 Sch.1 para.5, SI 2004/1662 Sch.1 para.15

s.16, applied: 2004 c.12 s.324

s.17, applied: 2004 c.12 s.324

s.17, repealed (in part): 2004 c.14 Sch.1 Part 9

s.18, applied: 2004 c.12 s.324

s.18, repealed (in part): 2004 c.14 Sch.1 Part 9

s.19, amended: 2003 c.14 s.211

s.19, applied: 2004 c.12 s.324

s.19, repealed (in part): 2003 c.14 Sch.43 Part 5

s.20, applied: 2004 c.12 s.324

s.20A, applied: 2004 c.12 s.324

s.21, amended: 2003 c.14 s.212

s.21, repealed (in part): 2003 c.14 s.212, Sch.43 Part 5

Sch.1, amended: 2004 c.14 Sch.1 Part 9

Sch.4 para.1, amended: 2003 c.39 Sch.8 para.127, 2004 c.21 Sch.1 para.22

Sch.4 para.1, repealed (in part): 2003 c.39 Sch.8 para.127, Sch.10

Sch.5A, applied: 2004 c.12 s.324

Sch.5A para.8, repealed: 2003 c.14 Sch.43 Part 5

Sch.5A para.11, amended: 2003 c.14 s.214

Sch.5A para.13, repealed (in part): 2003 c.14 Sch.43 Part 5

14. Public Expenditure and Receipts Act 1968

s.4, repealed: 2004 c.36 Sch.2 para.6, Sch.3

s.5, enabling: SI 2002/3076, SSI 2002/389

Sch.3, amended: 2004 c.14 Sch.1 Part 9, Sch.1 Part 14, Sch.1 Part 17

Sch.3 para.1, enabling: SI 2002/3076, SSI 2002/389

Sch.3 para.2, enabling: SI 2002/3076

16. New Towns (Scotland) Act 1968

applied: 2003 c.14 Sch.9 para.1

s.7, applied: 2003 asp 11 s.54

s.14, amended: SI 2003/2155 Sch.1 para.6

s.19, amended: SI 2003/2155 Sch.1 para.6

s.24, amended: SI 2003/2155 Sch.1 para.6

s.26, amended: SI 2003/2155 Sch.1 para.6

s.36A, amended: SI 2003/2155 Sch.1 para.6

18. Consular Relations Act 1968

s.1, amended: 2002 c.8 s.2

19. Criminal Appeal Act 1968

see *R. (on the application of Christofides) v Secretary of State for the Home Department* [2002] EWHC 1083, [2002] 1 W.L.R. 2769 (QBD (Admin Ct)), Sedley, L.J.

applied: 2002 c.29 s.89, 2003 c.44 s.274

referred to: 2002 c.29 s.90, 2003 c.44 s.47, s.97, Sch.22 para.14

Part I, applied: 2003 c.39 s.87, SI 2003/428 r.14, r.15, r.16, r.21

Part I, added: 2004 c.28 s.25

Part II, applied: 2003 c.44 s.71

s.1, amended: 2003 c.44 Sch.3 para.44

1968–cont.

19. Criminal Appeal Act 1968–*cont.*

s.2, see *R. v Pendleton (Donald)* [2001] UKHL 66, [2002] 1 W.L.R. 72 (HL), Lord Bingham of Cornhill

s.3, see *R. v Briggs (Linda Joan)* [2003] EWCA Crim 3662, [2004] 1 Cr. App. R. 34 (CA (Crim Div)), Judge, L.J.; see *R. v Duggan (John William Patrick)* [2002] EWCA Crim 2627, [2003] 1 Cr. App. R. 26 (CA (Crim Div)), Rose, L.J.

s.3, amended: 2003 c.44 s.316

s.3A, added: 2003 c.44 s.316

s.6, amended: 2004 c.28 s.24

s.6, applied: SI 2002/896 Sch.1 para.10, SI 2003/495 Reg.7

s.7, amended: 2003 c.44 Sch.36 para.44

s.8, see *R. v Jones (Paul Garfield)* [2002] EWCA Crim 2284, [2003] 1 Cr. App. R. 20 (CA (Crim Div)), Kay, L.J.

s.9, amended: 2003 c.44 s.271, Sch.37 Part 4, Sch.3 para.44

s.10, amended: 2003 c.17 Sch.6 para.39, 2003 c.44 s.319, Sch.32 para.8

s.10, repealed (in part): 2003 c.44 Sch.32 para.8, Sch.37 Part 7, Sch.37 Part 12

s.11, see *R. v Gosling (John)* [2002] EWCA Crim 1682, [2003] 1 Cr. App. R. (S.) 62 (CA (Crim Div)), Wright, J.; see *R. v Matthews (Jonathan Edward)* [2002] EWCA Crim 677, [2002] 1 W.L.R. 2578 (CA (Crim Div)), Johnson, J.; see *R. v Ruddick (David)* [2003] EWCA Crim 1061, [2004] 1 Cr. App. R. (S.) 7 (CA (Crim Div)), Morison, J.

s.11, amended: 2003 c.44 s.319, Sch.37 Part 12

s.11, repealed (in part): 2003 c.44 Sch.32 para.9, Sch.37 Part 7

s.14, amended: 2004 c.28 s.24

s.14, applied: SI 2002/896 Sch.1 para.10, SI 2003/495 Reg.7

s.14A, applied: SI 2002/896 Sch.1 para.10

s.14A, repealed: 2004 c.28 s.24, Sch.11

s.15, amended: 2004 c.28 Sch.10 para.4

s.18, applied: 2002 c.29 s.15, 2004 c.28 s.19

s.18, disapplied: 2003 c.44 s.231

s.18, varied: 2003 c.44 s.48, 2004 c.28 s.19

s.23, see *R. v Clark (Sally) (Appeal against Conviction) (No.2)* [2003] EWCA Crim 1020, [2003] 2 F.C.R. 447 (CA (Crim Div)), Kay, L.J.; see *R. v Jones (Wayne Daniel)* [2003] EWCA Crim 1966, [2004] 1 Cr. App. R. 5 (CA (Crim Div)), Auld, L.J.; see *R. v Pinfold (Terence Joseph)* [2003] EWCA Crim 3643, [2004] 2 Cr. App. R. 5 (CA (Crim Div)), Lord Woolf of Barnes, L.C.J.; see *R. v Steel (Anthony)* [2003] EWCA Crim 1640, (2003) 147 S.J.L.B. 751 (CA (Crim Div)), Rix, L.J.

s.23A, see *R. v Shillibier (Marc James)* [2003] EWCA Crim 2757, [2004] 1 Cr. App. R. 31 (CA (Crim Div)), David Clarke, J.

CAP.

1968–cont.

19. Criminal Appeal Act 1968–*cont.*

s.23A, amended: 2003 c.44 s.313

s.23A, disapplied: SI 2004/1629 Art.3

s.31, see *R. v Oates (Emma Louise)* [2002] EWCA Crim 1071, [2002] 1 W.L.R. 2833 (CA (Crim Div)), Rose, L.J.

s.31, amended: 2003 c.17 Sch.6 para.40, 2003 c.39 s.87, 2003 c.44 Sch.36 para.87

s.31, referred to: SI 2003/428 r.16, r.18, r.19, r.22

s.31A, amended: 2003 c.39 s.87, Sch.10, 2003 c.44 Sch.36 para.88

s.31B, added: 2003 c.39 s.87

s.31C, added: 2003 c.39 s.87

s.33, amended: 2002 c.29 Sch.11 para.4, 2003 c.44 s.47, s.68, s.81

s.33, applied: 2003 c.17 s.130

s.33, disapplied: 2003 c.44 s.274, Sch.22 para.14

s.33, referred to: 2002 c.29 s.90

s.34, amended: 2003 c.39 s.88, 2003 c.44 s.81

s.36, amended: 2003 c.44 s.47, s.68

s.37, amended: 2004 c.28 Sch.10 para.5

s.38, amended: 2003 c.44 s.81

s.44, amended: 2003 c.17 Sch.6 para.41

s.44A, amended: 2004 c.33 Sch.27 para.26

s.45, amended: 2003 c.39 Sch.8 para.128, 2003 c.44 Sch.36 para.89

s.48, repealed: 2003 c.39 Sch.8 para.129, Sch.10

s.50, see *Attorney General's Reference (Nos.114, 115 and 116 of 2002), Re* [2003] EWCA Crim 3374, (2003) 147 S.J.L.B. 1400 (CA (Crim Div)), Rose, L.J. (Vice President)

s.50, amended: 2002 c.29 Sch.11 para.4, 2003 c.17 Sch.6 para.42

s.51, amended: SI 2002/3135 Sch.1 para.6, 2003 c.44 Sch.36 para.90, Sch.37 Part 12, 2004 c.28 Sch.10 para.6

Sch.2, substituted: 2003 c.44 s.131

Sch.2 para.2, see *Attorney General's Reference (No.82a of 2000), Re* [2002] EWCA Crim 215, [2002] 2 Cr. App. R. 24 (CA (Crim Div)), Lord Woolf of Barnes, L.C.J.

Sch.2 para.2, amended: 2003 c.44 Sch.32 para.10

Sch.4 para.1, repealed: 2003 c.39 Sch.8 para.130, Sch.10

Sch.4 para.2, repealed: 2003 c.39 Sch.8 para.130, Sch.10

Sch.4 para.3, repealed: 2003 c.39 Sch.8 para.130, Sch.10

Sch.4 para.4, repealed: 2003 c.39 Sch.8 para.130, Sch.10

20. Courts-Martial (Appeals) Act 1968

referred to: 2003 c.44 s.337

Part II, added: 2004 c.28 Sch.3 para.13

s.8, amended: 2003 c.44 s.271

1968–cont.

20. Courts-Martial (Appeals) Act 1968–*cont.*

s.14, amended: 2003 c.44 s.318

s.14A, added: 2003 c.44 s.318

s.16, substituted: 2004 c.28 Sch.3 para.7

s.21, amended: 2004 c.28 Sch.3 para.8

s.22, amended: 2004 c.28 Sch.3 para.9

s.23, substituted: 2004 c.28 Sch.3 para.10

s.24, amended: 2004 c.28 Sch.3 para.11

s.25, substituted: 2004 c.28 Sch.3 para.12

s.36, amended: 2003 c.39 s.90, Sch.10

s.36A, amended: 2003 c.39 s.90, Sch.10

s.36B, added: 2003 c.39 s.90

s.36B, applied: 2003 c.39 s.90

s.36C, added: 2003 c.39 s.90

s.36C, applied: 2003 c.39 s.90

s.40, amended: 2003 c.39 s.91

s.46, applied: SI 2003/336 Sch.1 Part 2

s.48A, amended: 2004 c.33 Sch.26 para.33

s.55, repealed: 2003 c.39 Sch.8 para.131, Sch.10

s.57, amended: 2004 c.28 Sch.3 para.14

Sch.1 Part I para.1, substituted: 2003 c.44 Sch.7 para.5

Sch.1 Part II para.3, substituted: 2003 c.44 Sch.7 para.6

Sch.1 Part III para.5, substituted: 2003 c.44 Sch.7 para.7

Sch.2 para.1, repealed: 2003 c.39 Sch.8 para.131, Sch.10

Sch.2 para.2, repealed: 2003 c.39 Sch.8 para.131, Sch.10

Sch.2 para.3, repealed: 2003 c.39 Sch.8 para.131, Sch.10

Sch.2 para.4, repealed: 2003 c.39 Sch.8 para.131, Sch.10

Sch.2 para.5, repealed: 2003 c.39 Sch.8 para.131, Sch.10

Sch.2 para.6, repealed: 2003 c.39 Sch.8 para.131, Sch.10

Sch.2 para.7, repealed: 2003 c.39 Sch.8 para.131, Sch.10

Sch.3 para.3, amended: 2004 c.28 Sch.3 para.15

Sch.3 para.3, repealed (in part): 2004 c.28 Sch.3 para.15, Sch.11

Sch.3 para.3A, added: 2004 c.28 Sch.3 para.15

27. Firearms Act 1968

see *McIntyre v Council of the Law Society of Scotland* 2002 S.C.L.R. 169 (Ex Div), Lord Prosser, Lord Coulsfield, Lord Hamilton

applied: 2003 c.17 Sch.4 para.3, 2003 c.44 s.203, SI 2003/2764 Art.11, SSI 2003/231 Sch.1 para.5, Sch.3 para.4

Part II, applied: 2003 c.38 s.39

s.1, see *R. v Morgan (Norman David)* [2003] EWCA Crim 1607, [2004] 1 Cr. App. R. (S.) 20 (CA (Crim Div)), Treacy, J.

s.1, amended: 2003 c.38 s.39

1968–cont.

27. Firearms Act 1968–*cont.*

s.1, applied: 2003 c.38 s.39, SI 2004/702 Art.18

s.1, disapplied: SI 2003/3300 Art.5

s.3, applied: 2002 c.29 Sch.2 para.5, Sch.4 para.5

s.5, see *R. v Morgan (Norman David)* [2003] EWCA Crim 1607, [2004] 1 Cr. App. R. (S.) 20 (CA (Crim Div)), Treacy, J.

s.5, amended: 2003 c.38 s.39

s.5, applied: SI 2003/2764 Art.21, SI 2004/1910 Sch.5

s.5, disapplied: 2003 c.38 s.39

s.5, referred to: 2003 c.38 s.39

s.6, applied: SI 2004/702 Art.56

s.6, enabling: SI 2003/3228

s.7, applied: SSI 2003/231 Sch.1 para.5, Sch.3 para.4

s.8, referred to: 2003 c.38 s.39

s.9, applied: SSI 2003/231 Sch.1 para.5, Sch.3 para.4

s.13, applied: SSI 2003/231 Sch.1 para.5, Sch.3 para.4

s.16, applied: 2003 c.42 Sch.5 para.27, Sch.5 para.79, 2003 c.44 Sch.15 para.26, SI 2004/1910 Sch.5, SSI 2004/411 Sch.1 para.24

s.16A, see *Attorney General's Reference (No.36 of 2001), Re* [2001] EWCA Crim 1489, [2002] 1 Cr. App. R. (S.) 57 (CA (Crim Div)), Potter, L.J.; see *Attorney General's Reference (No.75 of 2001), Re* [2001] EWCA Crim 1928, [2002] 1 Cr. App. R. (S.) 103 (CA (Crim Div)), Rose, L.J.; see *R. v Brown (Sean Lloyd)* [2003] EWCA Crim 2197, [2004] 1 Cr. App. R. (S.) 28 (CA (Crim Div)), Mance, L.J.

s.16A, applied: 2003 c.42 Sch.5 para.28, Sch.5 para.80, 2003 c.44 Sch.15 para.27, SI 2004/1910 Sch.5, SSI 2004/411 Sch.1 para.24

s.17, see *R. v Bentham (Peter)* [2003] EWCA Crim 3751, [2004] 2 All E.R. 549 (CA (Crim Div)), Kennedy, L.J.

s.17, applied: 2003 c.42 Sch.5 para.29, Sch.5 para.30, Sch.5 para.81, Sch.5 para.82, 2003 c.44 Sch.15 para.28, Sch.15 para.29, SI 2004/1910 Sch.5, SSI 2004/411 Sch.1 para.24

s.18, see *R. v Townsend (Tony)* [2003] EWCA Crim 2210, [2004] 1 Cr. App. R. (S.) 47 (CA (Crim Div)), Buxton, L.J.

s.18, applied: 2003 c.42 Sch.5 para.31, Sch.5 para.83, 2003 c.44 Sch.15 para.30, SI 2004/1910 Sch.5, SSI 2004/411 Sch.1 para.24

s.18; Crime, see *R. v Flamson (Lee Andrew)* [2001] EWCA Crim 3030, [2002] 2 Cr. App. R. (S.) 48 (CA (Crim Div)), Mance, L.J.

s.19, amended: 2003 c.38 s.37

1968–cont.

27. Firearms Act 1968–*cont.*

s.19, applied: SI 2004/1910 Sch.5, SSI 2004/411 Sch.1 para.24

s.20, applied: SSI 2004/411 Sch.1 para.24

s.21, amended: 2003 c.44 Sch.32 para.12

s.21, applied: SI 2004/702 Art.63

s.22, amended: 2003 c.38 s.38

s.22, repealed (in part): 2003 c.38 Sch.3

s.23, amended: 2003 c.38 s.38, Sch.3

s.24, amended: 2003 c.38 s.38

s.30C, see *Evans v Chief Constable of Central Scotland* 2002 S.L.T. (Sh Ct) 152 (Sh Pr), CGB Nicholson Q.C., Sheriff Principal

s.32A, applied: SI 2003/2764 Art.11

s.45, applied: SI 2004/702 Art.26

s.51A, added: 2003 c.44 s.287

s.51A, applied: 2003 c.44 s.142, s.150, s.152, s.153, s.174, s.291, s.305

s.52, amended: 2003 c.44 Sch.32 para.13

s.52, applied: SI 2003/336 Sch.1 Part 2

s.54, amended: 2004 c.20 Sch.14 para.3, SI 2004/1573 Art.12

s.54, varied: 2003 c.20 Sch.5 para.4, SI 2003/2818 Art.9

s.57, amended: 2003 c.20 Sch.5 para.4

s.57, referred to: 2003 c.44 Sch.4 para.24

s.57, varied: 2003 c.20 Sch.5 para.4

Sch.1, referred to: 2003 c.44 Sch.15 para.29

Sch.1 para.6, substituted: 2003 c.42 Sch.6 para.16

Sch.6 Part I, amended: 2003 c.38 s.37, s.38, Sch.3, 2003 c.44 s.288

Sch.6 Part II para.3, repealed: 2003 c.44 Sch.37 Part 4

Sch.6 Part II para.7, amended: 2003 c.38 s.38

Sch.6 Part II para.8, amended: 2003 c.38 s.38

28. Wills Act 1968

s.1, applied: 2004 c.33 Sch.4 para.3

29. Trade Descriptions Act 1968

see *R. (on the application of North Yorkshire Trading Standards Service) v Coleman* [2001] EWHC Admin 818, (2002) 166 J.P. 76 (QBD (Admin Ct)), Burton, J.; see *R. v Richards (Robert)* [2004] EWCA Crim 192, [2004] 2 Cr. App. R. (S.) 51 (CA (Crim Div)), Scott Baker, L.J.

applied: 2002 c.40 Sch.14, Sch.15, SI 2003/419 Art.63, SI 2003/1376 Sch.1, SI 2003/1593 Sch.1 Part I

referred to: 2003 c.21 s.393, SI 2003/750 Sch.5 para.12, SI 2003/751 Sch.6 para.12, SI 2004/1468 Sch.6 para.12

s.1, see *R. (on the application of Newham LBC) v Stratford Magistrates Court* [2004] EWHC 2506, (2004) 168 J.P. 658 (QBD (Admin)), Davis, J.

s.1, applied: 2003 c.17 Sch.4 para.4

s.14, see *R. v Killian (John)* [2002] EWCA Crim 404, (2002) 166 J.P. 169 (CA (Crim Div)), Rose, L.J.

1968–cont.

29. Trade Descriptions Act 1968–*cont.*
s.28, repealed (in part): 2002 c.40 Sch.26

34. Agriculture (Miscellaneous Provisions) Act 1968
s.2, applied: SI 2002/794 Art.3, SI 2002/1898, SI 2003/299, SSI 2002/334, SSI 2003/488
s.2, enabling: SI 2002/1646, SI 2002/1898, SI 2003/299, SI 2003/1726, SSI 2002/334, SSI 2003/488
s.3, applied: SI 2002/794 Art.3
s.5, applied: SI 2002/794 Art.3
s.6, amended: 2004 c.14 Sch.1 Part 17
s.7, amended: 2003 c.44 Sch.26 para.21
s.12, amended: 2004 c.5 Sch.7 para.4
s.54, repealed (in part): 2004 c.14 Sch.1 Part 17

41. Countryside Act 1968
s.4, applied: SI 2003/2261 Sch.3 Part I, Sch.4 para.3, SI 2004/1777 Art.25, SI 2004/1778 Art.25
s.7, applied: SI 2004/1777 Art.25, SI 2004/1778 Art.25
s.9, applied: SI 2004/1777 Art.25, SI 2004/1778 Art.25
s.10, applied: SI 2004/1777 Art.25, SI 2004/1778 Art.25
s.15, applied: SI 2003/2261 Sch.3 Part I, Sch.4 para.3
s.27, applied: SI 2004/1777 Art.25, SI 2004/1778 Art.25
s.41, amended: 2003 c.21 Sch.17 para.40
s.41, applied: SI 2004/1777 Art.25, SI 2004/1778 Art.25
s.43, applied: SI 2004/1777 Art.25, SI 2004/1778 Art.25
s.45, applied: SI 2004/1777 Art.25, SI 2004/1778 Art.25
Sch.2 para.3, amended: 2004 c.5 Sch.7 para.5
Sch.2 para.6, amended: 2003 c.21 Sch.17 para.40

44. Finance Act 1968
s.54, amended: SI 2004/2353 Reg.2
s.54, applied: 2004 c.12 s.325
s.54, repealed (in part): SI 2004/2353 Reg.2
Sch.18, applied: 2004 c.12 s.325
Sch.18 para.3, repealed: SI 2004/2353 Reg.2
Sch.18 para.6, repealed: SI 2004/2353 Reg.2
Sch.18 para.10, repealed: SI 2004/2353 Reg.2
Sch.18 para.11, amended: SI 2004/2353 Reg.2
Sch.18 para.14, repealed: SI 2004/2353 Reg.2
Sch.18 para.15, amended: SI 2004/2353 Reg.2
Sch.18 para.15, repealed (in part): SI 2004/2353 Reg.2
Sch.18 para.16, repealed: SI 2004/2353 Reg.2

1968–cont.

46. Health Services and Public Health Act 1968
referred to: 2002 c.38 Sch.3 para.9, 2003 c.43 Sch.4 para.13, Sch.11 para.2
s.45, amended: 2002 c.41 s.45
s.45, applied: 2002 c.41 Sch.3 para.1
s.59, amended: 2003 c.43 Sch.11 para.3, Sch.14 Part 4, SI 2004/957 Sch.1 para.1
s.59, varied: SI 2004/288 Art.7, SI 2004/480 Art.6
s.63, amended: 2002 c.17 Sch.2 para.40, Sch.5 para.2, Sch.9 Part 1, SI 2002/2202 Art.4, SI 2002/2469 Sch.1 para.5, 2003 c.43 Sch.4 para.14, Sch.11 para.4, Sch.14 Part 1, Sch.14 Part 4, 2004 c.31 s.55, SI 2004/957 Sch.1 para.1
s.63, applied: SI 2002/195 Reg.4, Reg.10, Reg.12, Reg.28, SI 2002/1330 Reg.12, Reg.23, SI 2002/2375 Reg.9, Reg.10, SI 2002/3200 Reg.4, Reg.10, Reg.12, Reg.27, Sch.3 para.1, Sch.3 para.9, SI 2003/1994 Reg.12, Reg.23, Sch.3 para.4, SI 2004/551 Art.3, SI 2004/667 Art.3, SR 2002/224 Reg.4, Reg.10, Reg.12, Reg.29, Sch.3 para.1
s.63, disapplied: SI 2002/195 Sch.3 para.1
s.63, referred to: SI 2002/2375 Sch.1 Part1, SI 2002/3200 Sch.3 para.4
s.63, varied: SI 2004/288 Art.7, SI 2004/480 Art.6
s.63, enabling: SI 2002/2375
s.64, amended: 2002 c.38 Sch.3 para.10, 2003 c.43 Sch.11 para.5, SI 2004/957 Sch.1 para.1
s.64, referred to: SI 2002/2375 Sch.1 Part 2
s.65, amended: 2002 c.38 Sch.3 para.11

47. Sewerage (Scotland) Act 1968
applied: 2002 asp 3 s.46, s.49, s.52, s.53, s.60, s.70
referred to: 2002 asp 3 s.71,
s.1, amended: 2002 asp 3 Sch.5 para.2, Sch.5 para.3, Sch.5 para.4, Sch.5 para.5, 2003 asp 3 s.29, Sch.3 para.2
s.2, amended: 2002 asp 3 Sch.5 para.6, 2003 asp 3 Sch.3 para.3
s.3, amended: 2002 asp 3 Sch.5 para.2, Sch.5 para.3, Sch.5 para.7, 2003 asp 3 Sch.3 para.4
s.3, repealed (in part): 2002 asp 3 Sch.5 para.7
s.3A, amended: 2002 asp 3 Sch.5 para.2, Sch.5 para.3, Sch.5 para.4, Sch.5 para.8, 2003 asp 3 s.30, Sch.3 para.5
s.4, amended: 2002 asp 3 Sch.5 para.2, Sch.5 para.4, Sch.5 para.9, 2003 asp 3 Sch.3 para.6
s.6, repealed: 2002 asp 3 Sch.5 para.10
s.7, amended: 2002 asp 3 Sch.5 para.2, Sch.5 para.11, 2003 asp 3 Sch.3 para.7
s.7, repealed (in part): 2002 asp 3 Sch.5 para.11

1968–cont.

47. Sewerage (Scotland) Act 1968–cont.

s.8, amended: 2002 asp 3 Sch.5 para.4, Sch.5 para.12, 2003 asp 3 s.30, Sch.3 para.8

s.8, repealed (in part): 2003 asp 3 s.30

s.9, amended: 2002 asp 3 Sch.5 para.13

s.10, amended: 2002 asp 3 Sch.5 para.2, Sch.5 para.4, Sch.5 para.14

s.11, amended: 2002 asp 3 Sch.5 para.2, Sch.5 para.3, Sch.5 para.4, Sch.5 para.15, 2003 asp 3 Sch.3 para.9

s.12, amended: 2002 asp 3 Sch.5 para.2, Sch.5 para.3, Sch.5 para.4, Sch.5 para.16, 2003 asp 3 s.30, Sch.3 para.10, 2004 asp 8 Sch.2 para.1

s.12, applied: 2002 asp 3 s.39

s.13, repealed: 2002 asp 3 Sch.5 para.17

s.14, amended: 2002 asp 3 Sch.5 para.2, Sch.5 para.4, Sch.5 para.18, 2003 asp 3 Sch.3 para.11

s.14A, added: 2003 asp 3 s.30

s.14B, added: 2003 asp 3 s.30

s.14C, added: 2003 asp 3 s.30

s.15, amended: 2002 asp 3 Sch.5 para.2, Sch.5 para.3, Sch.5 para.19, 2003 asp 3 Sch.3 para.12

s.16, amended: 2002 asp 3 Sch.5 para.2, Sch.5 para.3, Sch.5 para.4, Sch.5 para.20, 2003 asp 3 Sch.3 para.13

s.16A, amended: 2002 asp 3 Sch.5 para.2, Sch.5 para.3, Sch.5 para.21, 2003 asp 3 s.30, Sch.3 para.14

s.17, amended: 2002 asp 3 Sch.5 para.2, Sch.5 para.3, Sch.5 para.22, 2003 asp 3 Sch.3 para.15

s.20, amended: 2002 asp 3 Sch.5 para.2, Sch.5 para.3, Sch.5 para.4, Sch.5 para.23

s.21, amended: 2002 asp 3 Sch.5 para.3, Sch.5 para.4, Sch.5 para.24, 2003 asp 3 Sch.3 para.16, 2003 asp 8 Sch.6 para.2

s.22, amended: 2002 asp 3 Sch.5 para.2, SI 2003/2155 Sch.1 para.7

s.23, amended: 2002 asp 3 Sch.5 para.2, Sch.5 para.3, Sch.5 para.25, 2003 asp 3 Sch.3 para.17

s.24, amended: 2002 asp 3 Sch.5 para.2, Sch.5 para.4, 2004 asp 8 Sch.2 para.1

s.25, amended: 2002 asp 3 Sch.5 para.2

s.26, amended: 2002 asp 3 Sch.5 para.2, Sch.5 para.4

s.27, amended: 2002 asp 3 Sch.5 para.2, Sch.5 para.4, Sch.5 para.26

s.27, repealed (in part): 2002 asp 3 Sch.5 para.26

s.28, amended: 2002 asp 3 Sch.5 para.2, Sch.5 para.4, Sch.5 para.27

s.29, amended: 2002 asp 3 Sch.5 para.2, Sch.5 para.4, Sch.5 para.28

s.29, applied: 2002 asp 3 s.31

s.30, amended: 2002 asp 3 Sch.5 para.2, Sch.5 para.29

1968–cont.

47. Sewerage (Scotland) Act 1968–cont.

s.31, amended: 2002 asp 3 Sch.5 para.3, Sch.5 para.4

s.32, amended: 2002 asp 3 Sch.5 para.2, Sch.5 para.3, Sch.5 para.4, Sch.5 para.30

s.33, amended: 2002 asp 3 Sch.5 para.3

s.34, amended: 2002 asp 3 Sch.5 para.3

s.35, amended: 2002 asp 3 Sch.5 para.3, Sch.5 para.4

s.36, amended: 2002 asp 3 Sch.5 para.2, Sch.5 para.3, Sch.5 para.4, Sch.5 para.31

s.37, amended: 2002 asp 3 Sch.5 para.2, Sch.5 para.3, Sch.5 para.4, Sch.5 para.32

s.37A, amended: 2002 asp 3 Sch.5 para.2, Sch.5 para.4, Sch.5 para.33

s.37B, varied: SI 2004/1822 Sch.1 para.6

s.37C, added: 2002 asp 3 s.63

s.38, amended: 2002 asp 3 Sch.5 para.2, Sch.5 para.4, Sch.5 para.34

s.39, amended: 2002 asp 3 Sch.5 para.2, Sch.5 para.35, 2003 asp 3 Sch.3 para.18

s.41, amended: 2002 asp 3 Sch.5 para.36, 2003 asp 3 Sch.3 para.19

s.42, amended: 2002 asp 3 Sch.5 para.3, Sch.5 para.37

s.44, amended: 2002 asp 3 Sch.5 para.2, Sch.5 para.38

s.45, amended: 2002 asp 3 Sch.5 para.2, Sch.5 para.4, 2003 asp 3 Sch.3 para.20

s.46, amended: 2003 asp 3 Sch.3 para.21, 2004 asp 8 Sch.2 para.1

s.48, amended: 2002 asp 3 Sch.5 para.2, Sch.5 para.3, Sch.5 para.4, Sch.5 para.39, 2003 asp 3 Sch.3 para.22

s.51, amended: 2002 asp 3 Sch.5 para.3, Sch.5 para.4

s.53, amended: 2002 asp 3 Sch.5 para.2

s.55, amended: 2002 asp 3 Sch.5 para.40

s.59, amended: 2002 asp 3 Sch.5 para.41, 2003 asp 3 s.33, Sch.3 para.23

48. International Organisations Act 1968

referred to: 2002 c.1 s.12

s.1, enabling: SI 2002/1826, SI 2002/1827, SI 2002/1828, SI 2004/1282, SI 2004/3334

s.2, enabling: SI 2002/1826

s.10, applied: SI 2002/1826, SI 2002/1827, SI 2002/1828, SI 2004/1282

s.10, enabling: SI 2002/1826, SI 2002/1827, SI 2002/1828

Sch.1 Part I, applied: 2003 c.25 s.1

Sch.1 Part II, applied: 2003 c.25 s.1

Sch.1 Part III, applied: 2003 c.25 s.1

Sch.1 Part IV, disapplied: SI 2002/1826 Art.14, Art.15, Art.19, SI 2004/1282 Art.14, Art.15

Sch.1 Part V, applied: 2003 c.25 s.1

49. Social Work (Scotland) Act 1968

applied: 2002 asp 5 s.2, s.4, s.5, s.6, SSI 2002/106 Reg.4, SSI 2002/113 Sch.1 para.20, SSI 2002/162 Art.4, Art.13, SSI

1968–cont.

49. Social Work (Scotland) Act 1968–cont.
applied: 2002 asp 5 s.2–cont.
2002/303 Reg.2, Reg.3, SSI 2003/376 Reg.4, Sch.2, SSI 2003/460 Reg.4
Part II, applied: 2003 asp 13 s.259
s.4, amended: 2003 asp 13 Sch.4 para.1
s.4, referred to: SSI 2002/533 Sch.1, Sch.3
s.5, amended: 2003 asp 13 Sch.4 para.1
s.5, applied: 2003 asp 13 s.259, 2003 c.14 Sch.36 para.4
s.5, referred to: 2002 asp 5 s.26
s.5A, amended: 2003 asp 13 Sch.4 para.1
s.5A, referred to: SSI 2002/533 Sch.1, Sch.3
s.5B, applied: SSI 2003/608 Reg.16, Reg.20
s.5B, referred to: SSI 2002/533 Sch.1, Sch.3
s.6, amended: 2003 asp 13 Sch.4 para.1
s.6, applied: 2002 asp 13 Sch.1 para.19
s.12, see *Robertson v Fife Council* [2002] UKHL 35, 2002 S.C. (H.L.) 145 (HL), Lord Hope of Craighead
s.12, amended: 2002 asp 5 s.3, 2002 c.41 s.46
s.12, applied: 2002 asp 5 s.5, 2002 c.41 Sch.3 para.1, SSI 2002/264 Art.2
s.12, referred to: SSI 2002/264 Art.2, SSI 2002/533 Sch.1, Sch.3
s.12, enabling: SSI 2002/264
s.12A, see *Robertson v Fife Council* [2002] UKHL 35, 2002 S.C. (H.L.) 145 (HL), Lord Hope of Craighead
s.12A, amended: 2002 asp 5 s.8
s.12A, applied: SSI 2002/304 Reg.2, 2003 asp 13 s.62, s.227, s.228
s.12A, referred to: SSI 2002/533 Sch.1, Sch.3
s.12A, repealed (in part): 2002 asp 5 s.9
s.12A, varied: 2002 asp 5 s.1
s.12AA, added: 2002 asp 5 s.9
s.12AA, applied: 2002 asp 5 s.12
s.12AA, referred to: SSI 2002/533 Sch.3
s.12AB, added: 2002 asp 5 s.9
s.12AB, referred to: SSI 2002/533 Sch.3
s.12B, amended: 2002 asp 5 s.7, Sch.2 para.1
s.12B, applied: SI 2002/2006 Reg.19, SSI 2002/494 Reg.33, Sch.2 para.5, Sch.3 para.8, SSI 2003/243 Reg.2, Reg.3, Reg.4, Reg.5, Reg.6
s.12B, referred to: SSI 2002/533 Sch.1, Sch.3
s.12B, enabling: SSI 2003/243
s.12C, amended: 2002 asp 5 Sch.2 para.1
s.12C, referred to: SSI 2002/533 Sch.1, Sch.3
s.13, referred to: SSI 2002/533 Sch.1, Sch.3
s.13A, see *Robertson v Fife Council* [2002] UKHL 35, 2002 S.C. (H.L.) 145 (HL), Lord Hope of Craighead
s.13A, amended: 2002 asp 5 Sch.2 para.1, 2002 c.41 s.46
s.13A, applied: 2002 asp 5 s.5, 2002 c.41 Sch.3 para.1
s.13A, disapplied: 2002 asp 5 s.5
s.13A, referred to: SSI 2002/533 Sch.1, Sch.3
s.13B, amended: 2002 c.41 s.46

1968–cont.

49. Social Work (Scotland) Act 1968–cont.
s.13B, applied: SI 2002/1792 Reg.15
s.13B, referred to: SSI 2002/533 Sch.1, Sch.3
s.14, referred to: SSI 2002/533 Sch.1, Sch.3
s.16, applied: SI 2002/635 Reg.2, SI 2002/896 Sch.1 para.4, SI 2004/2695 Sch.1 para.24
s.17, applied: SI 2002/635 Sch.1 para.2, SI 2002/896 Sch.1 para.64, SI 2004/2695 Sch.1 para.10
s.21, applied: SI 2002/2006 Reg.19
s.27, amended: 2003 asp 7 s.71, 2004 asp 8 Sch.4 para.1, Sch.5
s.27, referred to: 2003 asp 7 s.71
s.27A, amended: 2003 asp 7 s.71, s.72
s.27B, applied: SSI 2002/444 Reg.4
s.27ZA, added: 2003 asp 7 s.71
s.44, applied: SI 2002/635 Reg.2, SI 2002/896 Sch.1 para.3, SI 2004/2695 Sch.1 para.23
s.59, amended: 2003 asp 13 Sch.4 para.1
s.59, applied: SI 2002/1792 Reg.15, SI 2002/2779 Sch.3 para.2, 2003 asp 5 Sch.2 para.2, SI 2004/293 Sch.2 para.16
s.59, referred to: SSI 2002/533 Sch.1, Sch.3
s.60, applied: SI 2002/635 Sch.1 para.2, SI 2002/896 Sch.1 para.55, SI 2004/2695 Sch.1 para.11
s.61, applied: SI 2002/635 Sch.1 para.2, SI 2002/896 Sch.1 para.55, SI 2002/2779 Sch.3 para.2, SI 2004/2695 Sch.1 para.11
s.62, applied: SI 2002/635 Reg.2, Sch.1 para.2, SI 2002/896 Sch.1 para.9, Sch.1 para.55, SI 2004/2695 Sch.1 para.11, Sch.1 para.29, SSI 2002/162 Art.7, Art.11
s.63A, applied: SSI 2002/162 Art.11
s.64, applied: SSI 2002/162 Art.13
s.71, applied: SI 2002/635 Sch.1 para.2, SI 2002/896 Sch.1 para.64, SI 2004/2695 Sch.1 para.10
s.86, amended: 2003 asp 13 Sch.4 para.1
s.87, amended: 2002 asp 5 s.1
s.87, applied: 2002 asp 5 s.2, s.6, SSI 2002/76 Reg.3, SSI 2002/85, SSI 2003/69, SSI 2003/86, SSI 2003/86 Reg.2, SSI 2003/156, SSI 2003/425, SSI 2003/577, SSI 2004/103, SSI 2004/106, SSI 2004/106 Reg.2, SSI 2004/389
s.94, see *S v N* 2002 S.L.T. 589 (Ex Div), Lord Emslie, Lord Cameron of Lochbroom, Lord Reed
s.94, amended: 2002 asp 5 Sch.2 para.1, 2003 asp 13 Sch.4 para.1, 2003 c.44 Sch.32 para.14, Sch.37 Part 7
s.94, referred to: SSI 2003/243 Reg.2
s.94, enabling: SSI 2002/264

50. Hearing Aid Council Act 1968
s.12, amended: SI 2004/1715 Art.2
s.12, repealed (in part): SI 2004/1715 Art.2

CAP.

CAP.

1968–cont.

52. Caravan Sites Act 1968

Part I, see *R. (on the application of Smith) v Barking and Dagenham LBC* [2002] EWHC 2400, [2002] 48 E.G.C.S. 141 (QBD (Admin Ct)), Burton, J.

s.1, amended: 2004 c.34 s.209

s.2, referred to: 2004 c.34 s.209

s.3, amended: 2004 c.33 Sch.8 para.8, 2004 c.34 s.210

s.3, referred to: 2004 c.34 s.209

s.4, see *Somerset CC v Isaacs* [2002] EWHC 1014, [2002] E.H.L.R. 18 (QBD (Admin Ct)), Stanley Burnton, J.

s.4, amended: 2004 c.34 s.211

s.4, referred to: 2004 c.34 s.209

54. Theatres Act 1968

applied: 2003 c.17 Sch.8 para.1

s.1, repealed (in part): 2003 c.17 Sch.6 para.44

s.12, repealed (in part): 2003 c.17 Sch.6 para.44

s.13, amended: 2003 c.44 Sch.37 Part 9

s.13, applied: 2003 c.17 Sch.4 para.2

s.13, disapplied: 2003 c.44 Sch.25 para.69

s.13, repealed (in part): 2003 c.17 Sch.6 para.44

s.14, repealed (in part): 2003 c.17 Sch.6 para.44

s.15, amended: 2003 c.17 Sch.6 para.45

s.15, repealed (in part): 2003 c.17 Sch.6 para.45, Sch.7

s.17, repealed: 2003 c.17 Sch.6 para.46, Sch.7

s.18, repealed (in part): 2003 c.17 Sch.6 para.47, Sch.7

Sch.1 para.1, repealed (in part): 2003 c.17 Sch.6 para.44

Sch.1 para.2, repealed (in part): 2003 c.17 Sch.6 para.44

Sch.1 para.3, repealed (in part): 2003 c.17 Sch.6 para.44

Sch.1 para.4, repealed (in part): 2003 c.17 Sch.6 para.44

Sch.1 para.5, repealed (in part): 2003 c.17 Sch.6 para.44

Sch.1 para.6, repealed (in part): 2003 c.17 Sch.6 para.44

Sch.1 para.7, repealed (in part): 2003 c.17 Sch.6 para.44

Sch.1 para.7A, repealed (in part): 2003 c.17 Sch.6 para.44

Sch.1 para.7B, repealed (in part): 2003 c.17 Sch.6 para.44

Sch.1 para.7C, repealed (in part): 2003 c.17 Sch.6 para.44

Sch.2, amended: 2003 c.17 Sch.7

55. Friendly and Industrial and Provident Societies Act 1968

s.4A, repealed (in part): 2004 c.34 Sch.16

56. Swaziland Independence Act 1968

Sch.1 Part I para.10, repealed: 2002 c.39 Sch.3

1968–cont.

59. Hovercraft Act 1968

applied: SR 2002/40 Art.8, SR 2002/41 Art.8, SR 2002/395 Art.9

referred to: SR 2002/42 Art.8

60. Theft Act 1968

applied: 2003 c.ii

s.1, see *R. v Sookoo (Neil Dexter)* [2002] EWCA Crim 800, Times, April 10, 2002 (CA (Crim Div)), Douglas Brown, J.

s.1, applied: SI 2002/1837 Sch.1 Part I, SI 2002/1917 Art.2, 2003 c.17 Sch.4 para.5, 2004 c.19 s.14, SI 2004/1910 Sch.2

s.3, see *R. v Briggs (Linda Joan)* [2003] EWCA Crim 3662, [2004] 1 Cr. App. R. 34 (CA (Crim Div)), Judge, L.J.

s.8, see *Attorney General's Reference (No.83 of 2001), Re* [2001] EWCA Crim 2443, [2002] 1 Cr. App. R. (S.) 139 (CA (Crim Div)), Judge, L.J.; see *R. v Benfield (Anthony John)* [2003] EWCA Crim 2223, [2004] 1 Cr. App. R. 8 (CA (Crim Div)), Lord Woolf of Barnes, L.C.J.

s.8, applied: 2003 c.17 Sch.4 para.5, 2003 c.42 Sch.5 para.32, 2003 c.44 Sch.4 para.24, Sch.15 para.31, SI 2004/1910 Sch.2

s.9, amended: 2003 c.42 Sch.7

s.9, applied: SI 2002/896 Sch.1 para.38, 2003 c.17 Sch.4 para.5, 2003 c.42 Sch.5 para.33, 2003 c.44 Sch.15 para.32, Sch.15 para.97, SI 2004/1910 Sch.2

s.10, applied: 2003 c.17 Sch.4 para.5, 2003 c.42 Sch.5 para.34, 2003 c.44 Sch.15 para.33, SI 2004/1910 Sch.2

s.11, applied: 2003 c.17 Sch.4 para.5

s.12, applied: SI 2002/1917 Art.2

s.12A, amended: 2003 c.44 s.285

s.12A, applied: SI 2002/1917 Art.2, 2003 c.17 Sch.4 para.5, 2003 c.42 Sch.5 para.35, 2003 c.44 Sch.15 para.34, SI 2004/1910 Sch.2

s.13, applied: 2003 c.17 Sch.4 para.5

s.14, repealed (in part): SI 2003/2908 Sch.2

s.15, see *R. (on the application of Newham LBC) v Stratford Magistrates Court* [2004] EWHC 2506, (2004) 168 J.P. 658 (QBD (Admin)), Davis, J.; see *R. v Smith (Wallace Duncan) (No.4)* [2004] EWCA Crim 631, [2004] Q.B. 1418 (CA (Crim Div)), Lord Woolf of Barnes, L.C.J.

s.15, applied: 2003 c.17 Sch.4 para.5, 2004 c.19 s.14

s.15A, applied: 2003 c.17 Sch.4 para.5

s.16, see *Hewison v Meridian Shipping Services Pte Ltd* [2002] EWCA Civ 1821, [2003] I.C.R. 766 (CA), Clarke, L.J.

s.16, applied: 2003 c.17 Sch.4 para.5, 2004 c.19 s.14

s.17, see *Attorney General's Reference (No.1 of 2001), Re* [2002] EWCA Crim 1768, [2003] 1 W.L.R. 395 (CA (Crim Div)), Kennedy, L.J.; see *R. v Atkinson (Layean)*

CAP.

1968–cont.

60. Theft Act 1968–*cont.*

s.17–*cont.*

[2003] EWCA Crim 3031, [2004] Crim. L.R. 226 (CA (Crim Div)), May, L.J.

s.17, applied: 2003 c.17 Sch.4 para.5, 2004 c.19 s.14

s.19, applied: 2003 c.17 Sch.4 para.5

s.20, see *R. v Pope (Alan) (No.1)* [2002] UKHL 26, [2002] 1 W.L.R. 1966 (HL), Lord Hobhouse of Woodborough; see *R. v Stewart (Christopher) (Costs)* [2004] 3 Costs L.R. 501 (Crown Ct (Middlesex Guildhall)), Senior Costs Judge Hurst

s.20, applied: 2003 c.17 Sch.4 para.5

s.21, applied: 2002 c.29 Sch.2 para.9, 2003 c.17 Sch.4 para.5

s.22, applied: SI 2002/1917 Art.2, 2003 c.17 Sch.4 para.5, 2004 c.19 s.14

s.23, applied: SI 2002/1917 Art.2

s.24A, applied: 2003 c.17 Sch.4 para.5

s.25, applied: 2003 c.17 Sch.4 para.5

s.26, applied: SI 2003/2273 Sch.1 para.4

s.27, repealed (in part): 2003 c.44 Sch.37 Part 4, Sch.3 para.46

s.30, amended: 2004 c.33 Sch.27 para.27, Sch.30

s.30, substituted: 2004 c.33 Sch.27 para.27

s.31, amended: 2004 c.33 Sch.27 para.28

s.34, amended: SI 2003/2908 Sch.1 para.1

Sch.1 para.2, amended: 2003 c.44 Sch.37 Part 9

Sch.1 para.2, disapplied: 2003 c.44 Sch.25 para.70

63. Domestic and Appellate Proceedings (Restriction of Publicity) Act 1968

s.2, amended: 2004 c.33 Sch.27 para.29

64. Civil Evidence Act 1968

s.11, applied: 2002 c.40 s.228

s.14, amended: 2004 c.33 Sch.27 para.30

65. Gaming Act 1968

applied: SI 2003/335 Sch.1, SSI 2003/93 Sch.1, 2004 c.35 Sch.3, Sch.8

referred to: SI 2002/460(a)

s.6, amended: 2003 c.17 Sch.6 para.49

s.7, amended: 2003 c.17 Sch.6 para.50

s.7, applied: 2003 c.17 Sch.4 para.6

s.8, amended: 2003 c.17 Sch.6 para.51

s.13, enabling: SI 2002/1130, SI 2002/1407

s.14, repealed (in part): SI 2002/460 Art.2

s.14, enabling: SI 2002/1902

s.15, enabling: SI 2002/1130

s.19, see *Kingsley v United Kingdom (35605/97)* (2002) 35 E.H.R.R.10 (European Court of Human Rights (Grand Chamber)), L Wildhaber (President)

s.20, amended: SI 2002/1904 Art.2

s.20, enabling: SI 2002/1904

s.21, amended: SI 2002/1904 Art.3

s.21, enabling: SI 2002/1904

s.22, enabling: SI 2002/1910, SI 2003/1513

s.26, amended: SI 2003/3275 Art.2

CAP.

1968–cont.

65. Gaming Act 1968–*cont.*

s.31, amended: SI 2003/3275 Art.2

s.32, amended: SI 2002/460 Art.3

s.34, amended: SI 2002/460 Art.3, SI 2003/3275 Art.2

s.37, amended: SI 2003/3275 Art.2

s.38, amended: SI 2003/3275 Art.2

s.43, amended: 2004 c.21 Sch.1 para.24

s.44, repealed (in part): 2004 c.14 Sch.1 Part 17

s.48, amended: SI 2002/642 Sch.1, SI 2003/509 Sch.1, SI 2004/531 Sch.1, SSI 2003/403 Sch.1

s.48, referred to: SI 2003/508 Art.2, SI 2003/509 Art.2, SI 2004/531 Art.2, SSI 2002/281 Art.2, SSI 2003/403 Art.2

s.48, enabling: SI 2002/637, SI 2002/642, SI 2003/508, SI 2003/509, SI 2004/531, SSI 2002/281, SSI 2003/403

s.51, amended: 2004 c.14 Sch.1 Part 17

s.51, enabling: SI 2002/637, SI 2002/642, SI 2002/1130, SI 2002/1407, SI 2002/1904, SI 2002/1910, SI 2003/508, SI 2003/509, SI 2003/1513, SI 2004/531, SSI 2002/281, SSI 2003/403

s.54, repealed (in part): 2004 c.14 Sch.1 Part 17

Sch.1 para.6, amended: 2004 c.25 Sch.2 para.18

Sch.2 para.1, amended: 2003 c.39 Sch.8 para.132

Sch.2 para.2, amended: 2003 c.39 Sch.8 para.132, 2004 c.21 Sch.1 para.24

Sch.2 para.5, amended: 2004 c.21 Sch.1 para.24

Sch.2 para.13, amended: 2004 c.21 Sch.1 para.24

Sch.2 para.14, amended: 2004 c.21 Sch.1 para.24

Sch.2 para.20, amended: 2004 c.21 Sch.1 para.24

Sch.2 para.35A, amended: 2004 c.33 Sch.27 para.31

Sch.2 para.48, amended: 2003 c.39 Sch.8 para.132

Sch.3 para.3, amended: 2004 c.21 Sch.1 para.24

Sch.3 para.4, amended: 2004 c.21 Sch.1 para.24

Sch.3 para.6, amended: 2004 c.21 Sch.1 para.24

Sch.3 para.12, amended: 2003 c.39 Sch.8 para.133

Sch.3 para.13, amended: 2003 c.39 Sch.8 para.133, 2004 c.14 Sch.1 Part 17

Sch.3 para.15, amended: 2003 c.39 Sch.8 para.133

Sch.3 para.16, amended: 2003 c.39 Sch.8 para.133

Sch.3 para.17, amended: 2003 c.39 Sch.8 para.133

CAP.

1968–cont.

65. Gaming Act 1968–*cont.*

Sch.3 para.23, amended: 2003 c.39 Sch.8 para.133

Sch.3 para.24, amended: 2003 c.39 Sch.8 para.133

Sch.4 para.8, amended: 2004 c.21 Sch.1 para.24

Sch.7 para.3, amended: 2003 c.39 Sch.8 para.134

Sch.7 para.4, amended: 2003 c.39 Sch.8 para.134

Sch.7 para.11, amended: 2003 c.39 Sch.8 para.134

Sch.7 para.13, amended: 2003 c.39 Sch.8 para.134

Sch.7 para.14, amended: 2003 c.39 Sch.8 para.134

Sch.7 para.20, amended: 2003 c.39 Sch.8 para.134

Sch.7 para.24, amended: 2003 c.39 Sch.8 para.134

Sch.7 para.25, amended: 2003 c.39 Sch.8 para.134

Sch.9 para.1, amended: 2003 c.17 Sch.6 para.52

Sch.9 para.1A, added: 2003 c.17 Sch.6 para.52

Sch.9 para.10A, amended: 2003 c.17 Sch.6 para.52

Sch.9 para.11, amended: 2003 c.17 Sch.6 para.52

Sch.9 para.11, repealed (in part): 2003 c.17 Sch.6 para.52, Sch.7

Sch.9 para.14, repealed: 2003 c.17 Sch.6 para.52, Sch.7

Sch.9 para.21, amended: 2003 c.17 Sch.6 para.52

Sch.9 para.23, substituted: 2003 c.17 Sch.6 para.52

Sch.9 para.24, repealed: 2003 c.17 Sch.6 para.52, Sch.7

67. Medicines Act 1968

applied: SI 2002/794 Art.3, SI 2002/1689 Reg.3, SI 2003/1076 Art.1, Sch.1 para.1, SI 2004/291 Sch.6 para.43, SI 2004/478 Sch.6 para.43, Sch.6 para.51, SI 2004/627 Sch.5 para.42, SI 2004/1031 Reg.49, Sch.7 para.5, Sch.7 para.6, Sch.7 para.8, Sch.7 para.9, Sch.7 para.13, SR 2002/1 Reg.11, Reg.17, SR 2002/301 Reg.3, SSI 2004/115 Sch.5 para.41, SSI 2004/116 Sch.1 para.13

referred to: SI 2004/1031 Reg.4, Sch.9 para.1

Part III, applied: SI 2004/291 Sch.6 para.52, SI 2004/627 Sch.5 para.52, SSI 2004/115 Sch.5 para.45, SSI 2004/116 Sch.1 para.16

s.1, amended: SI 2002/794 Sch.1 para.15, Sch.2

s.1, referred to: SI 2004/1031 Sch.5 para.3, Sch.8 para.5

s.1, enabling: SI 2002/542

s.3, amended: SI 2004/1031 Sch.10 para.1

CAP.

1968–cont.

67. Medicines Act 1968–*cont.*

s.4, amended: SI 2004/1031 Sch.10 para.2

s.4, applied: SI 2003/409 Sch.1 Part I

s.5, amended: SI 2002/794 Sch.1 para.16, Sch.2

s.5, applied: SI 2002/794 Art.3

s.7, amended: SI 2004/1031 Sch.10 para.3

s.8, amended: SI 2002/236 Reg.2, SI 2004/1031 Sch.10 para.4

s.11, amended: SI 2004/1771 Sch.1 para.10

s.14, amended: SI 2002/236 Reg.2

s.18, amended: SI 2002/236 Reg.2

s.21, applied: SI 2004/2750 Reg.13

s.23, amended: SI 2004/1031 Sch.10 para.5

s.24, amended: SI 2002/236 Reg.2

s.24, repealed (in part): SI 2002/236 Reg.2

s.25, repealed (in part): 2004 c.14 Sch.1 Part 17

s.26, repealed: 2004 c.14 Sch.1 Part 17

s.28, amended: SI 2002/236 Reg.2

s.28, applied: SI 2004/2750 Reg.6

s.31, repealed: SI 2004/1031 Sch.10 para.6

s.35, amended: SI 2004/1031 Sch.10 para.7

s.35, repealed (in part): SI 2004/1031 Sch.10 para.7

s.36, amended: SI 2004/1031 Sch.10 para.8

s.36, enabling: SI 2003/3309

s.37, amended: SI 2004/1031 Sch.10 para.9

s.37, repealed (in part): 2004 c.14 Sch.1 Part 17, SI 2004/1031 Sch.10 para.9

s.38, amended: SI 2004/1031 Sch.10 para.10

s.38, applied: SI 2004/2750 Reg.13

s.38, enabling: SI 2003/3309

s.39, amended: SI 2004/1031 Sch.10 para.11

s.44, amended: SI 2004/1031 Sch.10 para.12

s.45, amended: SI 2004/1031 Sch.10 para.13

s.46, amended: SI 2004/1031 Sch.10 para.14

s.47, amended: SI 2004/1031 Sch.10 para.15

s.47, enabling: SI 2003/3309, SI 2004/1678

s.49A, amended: SI 2002/236 Reg.2

s.50, amended: SI 2004/1031 Sch.10 para.16

s.51, enabling: SI 2002/933

s.52, disapplied: SI 2004/2779 Art.3

s.52, referred to: SI 2004/2779 Art.3

s.55, amended: SI 2004/1771 Sch.1 para.10

s.57, enabling: SI 2003/696, SI 2003/697, SI 2004/1, SI 2004/1190, SI 2004/2779

s.58, see *Department for the Environment, Food and Rural Affairs v Atkinson* [2002] EWHC 2028, [2002] 3 C.M.L.R. 38 (QBD (Admin Ct)), Brooke, L.J.; see *Hughes (Robert John) v HM Advocate (Sentencing)* 2002 S.C.C.R. 937 (HCJ), Lord Coulsfield, Lord Hamilton; see *R. v Andrews (Christopher Kenneth)* [2002] EWCA Crim 3021, [2003] Crim. L.R. 477 (CA (Crim Div)), Laws, L.J.; see *R. v Groombridge (Mark)* [2003] EWCA Crim 1371, [2004] 1 Cr. App. R. (S.) 9 (CA (Crim Div)), Treacy, J.

1968–cont.

67. Medicines Act 1968–cont.

s.58, amended: SI 2002/253 Sch.5 para.2, SI 2003/1590 Sch.1 para.6

s.58, applied: SI 2002/327 Reg.21, SI 2002/549, SI 2002/2677 Reg.5, SI 2003/696, SI 2003/2915, SI 2004/2, SI 2004/291 Sch.6 para.44, SI 2004/478 Sch.6 para.44, SI 2004/627 Sch.5 para.43, SI 2004/1189, SI 2004/2693

s.58, disapplied: SI 2004/2779 Art.3

s.58, referred to: SI 2003/1571 Art.6, SI 2004/2779 Art.3

s.58, enabling: SI 2002/549, SI 2003/696, SI 2003/2915, SI 2004/2, SI 2004/1189, SI 2004/2693, SI 2004/2779

s.58A, amended: SI 2002/236 Reg.2

s.59, enabling: SI 2002/549

s.61, enabling: SI 2003/698

s.62, applied: SI 2002/3170

s.62, enabling: SI 2002/3170

s.66, enabling: SI 2003/698

s.67, see *R. v Andrews (Christopher Kenneth)* [2002] EWCA Crim 3021, [2003] Crim. L.R. 477 (CA (Crim Div)), Laws, L.J.; see *R. v Groombridge (Mark)* [2003] EWCA Crim 1371, [2004] 1 Cr. App. R. (S.) 9 (CA (Crim Div)), Treacy, J.

s.75, applied: SI 2002/1689 Reg.14, SR 2002/301 Reg.14

s.75, enabling: SI 2002/3024, SI 2003/3141, SI 2004/3197

s.76, enabling: SI 2002/3024, SI 2003/3141, SI 2004/3197

s.80, applied: 2002 c.17 s.29

s.85, enabling: SI 2003/3309

s.86, amended: SI 2002/236 Reg.2

s.86, enabling: SI 2003/3309

s.87, referred to: SI 2003/2317 Reg.5

s.87, enabling: SI 2003/2317

s.88, enabling: SI 2003/2317

s.91, enabling: SI 2003/2317, SI 2003/3309

s.92, amended: SI 2003/2498 Sch.1 para.19, Sch.2

s.95, enabling: SI 2004/1480

s.99, repealed (in part): 2004 c.14 Sch.1 Part 17

s.103, enabling: SI 2002/549

s.104, amended: SI 2004/1031 Sch.10 para.17

s.104, applied: SI 2002/1689 Reg.3, SR 2002/301 Reg.3

s.104, referred to: SI 2002/2677 Sch.2d (medicinal.product)

s.105, amended: SI 2004/1031 Sch.10 para.18

s.105, applied: SI 2002/1689 Reg.3, SR 2002/301 Reg.3

s.105, referred to: SI 2002/2677 Sch.2d (medicinal.product)

s.107, varied: SI 2004/1031 Sch.9 para.2

s.108, applied: SI 2002/794 Art.3

s.108, varied: SI 2004/1031 Sch.9 para.3

s.109, varied: SI 2004/1031 Sch.9 para.4

1968–cont.

67. Medicines Act 1968–cont.

s.110, applied: SR 2002/1 Reg.8, Reg.9

s.110, varied: SI 2004/1031 Sch.9 para.5

s.111, applied: SI 2002/3170 Art.3

s.111, varied: SI 2004/1031 Sch.9 para.6

s.112, applied: SI 2002/3170 Art.3

s.112, varied: SI 2004/1031 Sch.9 para.7

s.114, amended: 2004 c.33 Sch.27 para.32

s.115, varied: SI 2004/1031 Sch.9 para.8

s.116, varied: SI 2004/1031 Sch.9 para.9

s.118, varied: SI 2004/1031 Sch.9 para.10

s.119, varied: SI 2004/1031 Sch.9 para.11

s.120, repealed: 2004 c.14 Sch.1 Part 17

s.121, varied: SI 2004/1031 Sch.9 para.12

s.122, varied: SI 2004/1031 Sch.9 para.13

s.124, varied: SI 2004/1031 Sch.9 para.14

s.125, varied: SI 2004/1031 Sch.9 para.15

s.127, varied: SI 2004/1031 Sch.9 para.16

s.129, applied: SI 2002/542, SI 2002/549, SI 2002/933, SI 2002/2569, SI 2002/3024, SI 2002/3170, SI 2003/625, SI 2003/696, SI 2003/697, SI 2003/698, SI 2003/2317, SI 2003/2321, SI 2003/2915, SI 2003/2957, SI 2003/3141, SI 2003/3309, SI 2004/1, SI 2004/2, SI 2004/666, SI 2004/1189, SI 2004/1190, SI 2004/1480, SI 2004/1678, SI 2004/2693, SI 2004/2750

s.129, varied: SI 2004/1031 Sch.9 para.17

s.129, enabling: SI 2002/549, SI 2002/933, SI 2002/3024, SI 2002/3170, SI 2003/696, SI 2003/697, SI 2003/698, SI 2003/2317, SI 2003/2915, SI 2003/3141, SI 2003/3309, SI 2004/1, SI 2004/2, SI 2004/1189, SI 2004/1190, SI 2004/1480, SI 2004/1678, SI 2004/2693, SI 2004/3197

s.130, applied: SI 2002/1689 Reg.3, SR 2002/301 Reg.3

s.130, referred to: SI 2002/2677 Sch.2d (medicinal.product)

s.131, varied: SI 2004/1031 Sch.9 para.18

s.132, amended: SI 2002/236 Reg.2, SI 2003/2321 Reg.2, SI 2004/1031 Sch.10 para.19

s.132, varied: SI 2004/1031 Sch.9 para.19

s.135, amended: 2004 c.14 Sch.1 Part 17

Sch.3, applied: SI 2002/3170 Art.3, SR 2002/1 Reg.8

Sch.3, referred to: SR 2002/1 Reg.9

Sch.3 para.1, varied: SI 2004/1031 Sch.9 para.20

Sch.3 para.16, varied: SI 2004/1031 Sch.9 para.20

Sch.3 para.17, varied: SI 2004/1031 Sch.9 para.20

Sch.3 para.19, varied: SI 2004/1031 Sch.9 para.20

Sch.3 para.20, varied: SI 2004/1031 Sch.9 para.20

1968–cont.

67. Medicines Act 1968–cont.

Sch.3 para.21, varied: SI 2004/1031 Sch.9 para.20

Sch.3 para.22, varied: SI 2004/1031 Sch.9 para.20

Sch.3 para.24, varied: SI 2004/1031 Sch.9 para.20

Sch.3 para.27, varied: SI 2004/1031 Sch.9 para.20

Sch.5 para.1, repealed: 2004 c.14 Sch.1 Part 17

69. Justices of the Peace Act 1968

s.1, applied: 2003 c.39 Sch.9 para.11

Sch.3 Part III para.16, applied: 2003 c.39 Sch.9 para.11

70. Law Reform (Miscellaneous Provisions) (Scotland) Act 1968

s.10, applied: 2002 c.40 s.228

73. Transport Act 1968

Commencement Orders: SI 2003/1985 Art.2

Part II, applied: SSI 2002/62 Sch.1

s.9, applied: 2004 c.ii, SI 2004/118 Art.3

s.9A, amended: 2003 asp 1 s.60

s.10, see *Smith v Strathclyde Passenger Transport Executive* 2003 S.L.T. (Sh Ct) 97 (Sh Ct (Glasgow and Strathkelvin)), EF Bowen Q.C., Sheriff Principal

s.15, disapplied: SI 2002/412 Art.32

s.24, repealed: SSI 2002/263 Sch.1

s.26, repealed: SSI 2002/263 Sch.1

s.27, repealed: SSI 2002/263 Sch.1

s.28, repealed: SSI 2002/263 Sch.1

s.29, repealed: SSI 2002/263 Sch.1

s.32, repealed: 2004 c.14 Sch.1 Part 14

s.44, repealed (in part): SSI 2002/263 Sch.1

s.48, amended: SSI 2002/263 Sch.1

s.50, amended: SI 2003/1545 Art.3, SSI 2002/263 Sch.1l 2002/263 Sch.1

s.52, amended: SSI 2002/263 Sch.1

s.63, see *Smith v Strathclyde Passenger Transport Executive* 2003 S.L.T. (Sh Ct) 97 (Sh Ct (Glasgow and Strathkelvin)), EF Bowen Q.C., Sheriff Principal

s.97, see *Pritchard v Crown Prosecution Service* [2003] EWHC 1851, [2004] R.T.R. 22 (QBD (Admin Ct)), McCombe, J.; see *Vehicle & Operators Services Agency v North Leicester Vehicle Movements Ltd* [2003] EWHC 2638, (2004) 168 J.P. 285 (QBD (Admin Ct)), Mitting, J.; see *Vehicle Inspectorate v Sam Anderson (Newhouse) Ltd* [2001] EWHC Admin 893, [2002] R.T.R. 13 (QBD (Admin Ct)), Poole, J.

s.99, see *John Mann International Ltd v Vehicle Inspectorate* [2004] EWHC 1236, [2004] 1 W.L.R. 2731 (QBD (Admin Ct)), Owen, J.

s.102, amended: 2004 c.21 Sch.1 para.25

s.105, applied: SI 2003/1075 Sch.13 para.49, SI 2004/389 Sch.13 para.49

s.109, varied: SI 2004/1822 Sch.1 para.7

1968–cont.

73. Transport Act 1968–cont.

s.112, varied: SI 2004/1822 Sch.1 para.7

s.113, varied: SI 2004/1822 Sch.1 para.7

s.116, amended: SI 2003/1615 Sch.1 para.4

s.116, varied: SI 2002/1384 Art.3, SI 2002/1997 Art.9, SI 2003/1615 Sch.1 para.4, SI 2004/1817 Art.3

s.117, amended: SI 2003/1615 Sch.1 para.4

s.117, varied: SI 2002/1384 Art.3, SI 2002/1997 Art.9, SI 2003/1615 Sch.1 para.4, SI 2004/1817 Art.3

s.118, amended: SI 2003/1615 Sch.1 para.4

s.118, varied: SI 2002/1384 Art.3, SI 2002/1997 Art.9, SI 2003/1615 Sch.1 para.4, SI 2004/1817 Art.3

s.119, amended: SI 2003/1615 Sch.1 para.4

s.119, varied: SI 2002/1384 Art.3, SI 2003/1615 Sch.1 para.4

s.121, amended: SI 2003/1615 Sch.1 para.4

s.121, varied: SI 2003/1615 Sch.1 para.4

s.121, enabling: SI 2002/1384

s.137, amended: SI 2002/2626 Sch.2 para.5

s.139, repealed: 2004 c.14 Sch.1 Part 14

s.145, repealed: 2004 c.14 Sch.1 Part 14

s.157, amended: 2004 c.14 Sch.1 Part 14

s.159, amended: SSI 2002/263 Sch.1

s.161, repealed: 2004 c.14 Sch.1 Part 14

s.166, enabling: SI 2003/1985

Sch.1 para.6, amended: SSI 2002/263 Sch.1

Sch.2 para.5, repealed: SSI 2002/263 Sch.1

Sch.4 para.5, amended: SSI 2002/263 Sch.1

Sch.4 para.13, amended: 2003 c.14 Sch.20 para.3

Sch.8 para.1, repealed: 2004 c.14 Sch.1 Part 14

Sch.8 para.2, repealed: 2004 c.14 Sch.1 Part 14

Sch.8 para.3, repealed: 2004 c.14 Sch.1 Part 14

Sch.8 para.4, repealed: 2004 c.14 Sch.1 Part 14

Sch.8 para.5, repealed: 2004 c.14 Sch.1 Part 14

Sch.8 para.6, repealed: 2004 c.14 Sch.1 Part 14

Sch.8 para.7, repealed: 2004 c.14 Sch.1 Part 14

Sch.8 para.8, repealed: 2004 c.14 Sch.1 Part 14

Sch.8 para.9, repealed: 2004 c.14 Sch.1 Part 14

Sch.8 para.10, repealed: 2004 c.14 Sch.1 Part 14

Sch.8 para.11, repealed: 2004 c.14 Sch.1 Part 14

Sch.13 para.5, varied: SI 2004/1822 Sch.1 para.7

Sch.16 para.4, amended: SI 2003/1615 Sch.1 para.4, SSI 2002/263 Sch.1

Sch.16 para.4, repealed (in part): SSI 2002/263 Sch.1

1968–cont.

77. Sea Fisheries Act 1968
s.5, applied: SI 2002/790 Sch.3 para.2, Sch.3 para.3
s.18, disapplied: SI 2002/790 Sch.3 para.3

1969

lii. Greater London Council (General Powers) Act 1969
s.7, amended: 2003 c.21 Sch.17 para.41, SI 2003/1615 Sch.1 para.28
s.9, amended: SI 2003/1615 Sch.1 para.28
s.13, amended: 2004 c.5 Sch.7 para.6
s.16, amended: SI 2003/1615 Sch.1 para.28
s.17, amended: SI 2003/1615 Sch.1 para.28
s.18A, amended: SI 2003/1615 Sch.1 para.28
s.24, amended: SI 2003/1615 Sch.1 para.28
s.30, amended: 2004 c.21 Sch.1 para.26

2. Synodical Government Measure 1969
Appendix 1., added: 2003 c.1 s.1
Appendix 1., amended: 2003 c.1 s.1
Appendix 1., added: 2003 c.1 s.1
Appendix 2., added: 2003 c.1 s.1
Appendix 2., amended: 2003 c.1 s.1, Sch.1 para.9
r.1, added: 2003 c.1 s.1
r.1, amended: 2003 c.1 s.1
r.2, amended: 2003 c.1 s.1
r.4, added: 2003 c.1 s.1
r.5, amended: 2003 c.1 s.1
r.6, amended: 2003 c.1 s.1
r.9, amended: 2003 c.1 s.1
r.12, added: 2003 c.1 s.1
r.12, amended: 2003 c.1 s.1
r.16, amended: 2003 c.1 s.1
r.18, amended: 2003 c.1 s.1
r.40(1), amended: 2003 c.1 s.1
r.44, amended: 2003 c.1 s.1
r.45, amended: 2003 c.1 s.1
r.46, amended: 2003 c.1 s.1
r.46A, added: 2003 c.1 s.1
r.48, amended: 2003 c.1 s.1
s.3, repealed (in part): 2004 c.14 Sch.1 Part 6
s.4, amended: 2003 c.1 s.1
s.7, repealed (in part): 2004 c.14 Sch.1 Part 6
s.7, enabling: SI 2004/1889
s.9, amended: 2004 c.14 Sch.1 Part 6
Sch.3, added: SI 2004/1889 r.17
Sch.3, amended: 2003 c.1 Sch.1 para.2, Sch.1 para.3, Sch.1 para.4, Sch.1 para.6, Sch.1 para.7, SI 2004/1889 r.1, r.2, r.3, r.4, r.5, r.6, r.7, r.8, r.9, r.11, r.12, r.13, r.14, r.15, r.16, r.17, r.18
Sch.3, applied: 2003 c.1 s.1, 2003 c.3 s.21, SI 2004/1889
Sch.3, repealed (in part): 2003 c.1 Sch.1 para.6, Sch.1 para.8, SI 2004/1889 r.12
Sch.3, substituted: 2003 c.1 Sch.1 para.5
Sch.4, repealed (in part): 2004 c.14 Sch.1 Part 6, Sch.1 Part 6

6. Mines Act (Northern Ireland) 1969
s.156, applied: SR 2003/152 Reg.3

1969–cont.

10. Mines and Quarries (Tips) Act 1969
s.34, amended: 2003 asp 8 Sch.6 para.3

12. Genocide Act 1969
s.1, amended: 2002 c.26 Sch.7 para.26

14. Horserace Betting Levy Act 1969
referred to: 2004 c.25 s.15
s.5, amended: 2004 c.25 Sch.2 para.19

22. Redundant Churches and Other Religious Buildings Act 1969
s.1, applied: SI 2003/829 Art.2, Art.3
s.1, enabling: SI 2003/829
s.3, repealed: 2004 c.14 Sch.1 Part 6
s.7, repealed (in part): 2004 c.14 Sch.1 Part 6

24NI. Industrial and Provident Societies Act (Northern Ireland) 1969
applied: SI 2003/1102 Reg.2
s.6, applied: 2002 c.29 Sch.9 para.3
s.7, applied: 2002 c.29 Sch.9 para.3

32. Finance Act 1969
s.58, amended: 2003 c.1 Sch.6 para.122, 2004 c.5 Sch.7 para.2
s.59, repealed: 2004 c.25 Sch.4 para.6

35. Transport (London) Act 1969
varied: SI 2003/1615 Sch.2 para.1
s.25, amended: SI 2003/1615 Sch.1 para.27

43. Air Corporations Act 1969
repealed: 2004 c.14 Sch.1 Part 4

46. Family Law Reform Act 1969
Part II, referred to: 2002 c.38 Sch.4 para.19
s.22, enabling: SI 2004/596
Sch.1 Part II, amended: SI 2004/1662 Sch.1 para.18

48. Post Office Act 1969
varied: 2004 c.14 Sch.1 Part 17
s.24, applied: SI 2002/799
s.24, enabling: SI 2002/799
s.86, amended: SI 2003/2908 Sch.2
s.87, enabling: SI 2002/799
s.108, repealed (in part): 2004 c.14 Sch.1 Part 9
s.137, repealed (in part): SI 2003/2908 Sch.2
s.139, amended: SI 2003/2908 Sch.1 para.3
s.141, repealed: SI 2003/2908 Sch.2
Sch.4 Part II para.14, repealed: SI 2003/2908 Sch.2
Sch.4 Part II para.27, repealed: 2002 c.9 Sch.13
Sch.4 Part II para.30, repealed: SI 2003/2908 Sch.2
Sch.4 Part II para.70, repealed: SI 2003/2908 Sch.2
Sch.9 para.14, repealed: SI 2003/2908 Sch.2

51. Development of Tourism Act 1969
s.6, amended: SSI 2002/176 Art.3

53. Late Night Refreshment Houses Act 1969
applied: 2003 c.17 Sch.4 para.2
repealed: 2003 c.17 Sch.7

54. Children and Young Persons Act 1969
s.1, applied: SI 2002/896 Sch.1 para.2

CAP.

1969–cont.

54. Children and Young Persons Act 1969–
cont.
s.7, applied: SI 2002/896 Sch.1 para.2
s.12AA, applied: SI 2002/635 Reg.2, SI
2002/896 Sch.1 para.2, SI 2004/2695
Sch.1 para.22
s.23, see *H v DPP* [2003] EWHC 878, (2003)
167 J.P. 486 (QBD (Admin Ct)), Gage, J.;
see *R. (on the application of SR) v
Nottingham Magistrates Court* [2001]
EWHC Admin 802, (2002) 166 J.P. 132
(QBD (Admin Ct)), Brooke, L.J.
s.23, amended: 2003 c.41 s.201, 2003 c.44
Sch.32 para.15
s.23, applied: 2003 c.44 s.242
s.23, referred to: 2003 c.41 s.201
s.23A, amended: 2003 c.39 Sch.8 para.136,
Sch.10
s.23AA, amended: 2003 c.39 Sch.8 para.135
s.23AA, enabling: SI 2002/845
s.23B, added: 2003 c.38 s.90
s.32, applied: SI 2002/635 Sch.1 para.4, SI
2002/896 Sch.1 para.43, Sch.1 para.56,
Sch.1 para.69, SI 2004/2695 Sch.1 para.20
**56. Auctions (Bidding Agreements) Act
1969**
s.3, repealed (in part): 2004 c.14 Sch.1 Part 17
s.5, repealed (in part): 2004 c.14 Sch.1 Part 17
**57. Employers Liability (Compulsory Insur-
ance) Act 1969**
see *T&N Ltd (In Administration) v Royal & Sun
Alliance Plc* [2003] EWHC 1016, [2003] 2
All E.R. (Comm.) 939 (Ch D), Lawrence
Collins, J.
applied: 2002 c.30 Sch.2 para.7
referred to: 2003 c.43 Sch.4 para.15, 2003
c.44 Sch.19 para.5, Sch.19 para.6
s.1, see *R. (on the application of Geologistics
Ltd) v Financial Services Compensation
Scheme* [2003] EWHC 629, [2003] 1
W.L.R. 1696 (QBD (Admin Ct)), Davis, J.
s.2, amended: 2004 c.33 Sch.27 para.33
s.2, varied: 2004 c.33 Sch.21 para.6
s.3, amended: 2002 c.17 Sch.5 para.3, 2003
c.43 Sch.4 para.16
s.3, enabling: SI 2004/2882
s.6, enabling: SI 2004/2882
58. Administration of Justice Act 1969
s.36, repealed (in part): 2004 c.14 Sch.1 Part 1
Sch.1, amended: 2004 c.14 Sch.1 Part 1
59. Law of Property Act 1969
s.6, repealed: SI 2003/3096 Sch.6
s.16, repealed: 2004 c.14 Sch.1 Part 12
s.17, repealed (in part): 2004 c.14 Sch.1 Part 12
s.24, amended: 2002 c.9 Sch.11 para.9
s.28, repealed (in part): 2002 c.9 Sch.13,
2004 c.14 Sch.1 Part 12
61. Expiring Laws Act 1969
varied: 2004 c.14 Sch.1 Part 17
63. Police Act 1969
s.2, applied: SSI 2004/257 Reg.40

CAP.

1969–cont.

63. Police Act 1969–*cont.*
s.2, varied: SI 2003/527 Reg.40

1970

**lxxvi. Greater London Council (General
Powers) Act 1970**
s.15, amended: SI 2003/1615 Sch.1 para.29
**xxiv. Huntingdon and Peterborough
County Council Act 1970**
s.14, varied: SI 2003/2155 Sch.1 para.16
Income Tax Act 1970
s.106, see *Mount Murray Country Club Ltd v
Macleod* [2003] UKPC 53, [2003] S.T.C.
1525 (PC (IoM)), Lord Walker of
Gestingthorpe
Social Services Act 1970
s.7, see *R. (on the application of Heffernan) v
Sheffield City Council* [2004] EWHC 1377,
(2004) 7 C.C.L. Rep. 350 (QBD (Admin
Ct)), Collins, J.
1. Harbours Act (Northern Ireland) 1970
s.1, applied: SR 2002/40, SR 2002/41, SR
2002/42, SR 2002/394, SR 2002/395
s.1, enabling: SR 2002/40, SR 2002/41, SR
2002/42, SR 2002/394, SR 2002/395
s.37, amended: 2003 c.21 Sch.17 para.42
Sch.1, enabling: SR 2002/40, SR 2002/41,
SR 2002/42, SR 2002/394, SR 2002/395
Sch.2, enabling: SR 2002/40, SR 2002/41,
SR 2002/42, SR 2002/394, SR 2002/395
9. Taxes Management Act 1970
see *Al-Fayed v Advocate General for Scotland*
[2002] S.T.C. 910 (OH), Lord Gill L.J.C.; see
*Lee-Phipps v Inland Revenue
Commissioners* [2003] B.P.I.R. 803 (Ch
D), Launcelot Henderson Q.C.; see *R. (on
the application of Carvill) v Inland Revenue
Commissioners* [2003] EWHC 1852,
[2003] S.T.C. 1539 (QBD (Admin Ct)),
McCombe, J.; see *Two Settlors v Inland
Revenue Commissioners* [2004] S.T.C.
(S.C.D.) 45 (Sp Comm), John F Avery
Jones
applied: SI 2003/2718 Reg.5, 2004 c.6 s.23,
2004 c.12 Sch.11 para.4, Sch.11 para.8,
Sch.11 para.12, SI 2004/674 Reg.23
referred to: 2002 c.23 Sch.18 para.13, 2003
c.14 s.199, 2003 c.1 Sch.6 para.123, SI
2003/415 Art.2, SI 2004/1450 Reg.37
varied: SI 2002/2836 Sch.1 para.3
Part IV, applied: SI 2002/2172 Reg.14, SI
2003/2682 Reg.80, Reg.110, Reg.204
Part V, applied: 2002 c.21 s.39, SI 2002/2172
Reg.8, Reg.14, SI 2003/2682 Reg.110,
Reg.204, 2004 c.6 s.23, 2004 c.12 s.114,
SI 2004/1450 Reg.28
Part VA, applied: SI 2003/2682 Reg.204
Part VI, applied: 2002 c.21 s.29, Sch.2 para.7,
SI 2002/2172 Reg.14, SI 2002/2820
Reg.8, SI 2003/2682 Reg.80, Reg.110,

1970–cont.

9. Taxes Management Act 1970–*cont.*
Part VI, applied:–*cont.*
Reg.204, SI 2004/1450 Reg.22, SR 2002/
379 Reg.8, 2004 c.6 s.21
s.1, see *R. (on the application of Wilkinson) v
Inland Revenue Commissioners* [2002]
EWHC 182, [2002] S.T.C. 347 (QBD
(Admin Ct)), Moses, J.; see *R. (on the
application of Wilkinson) v Inland Revenue
Commissioners* [2003] EWCA Civ 814,
[2003] 1 W.L.R. 2683 (CA), Lord Phillips
of Worth Matravers
s.1, varied: 2003 c.14 Sch.17 para.1
s.2, referred to: 2003 c.1 Sch.5 para.59
s.2, varied: 2003 c.14 Sch.17 para.1
s.2A, applied: SI 2003/233
s.2A, disapplied: SI 2003/207 Art.3
s.2A, referred to: SI 2003/415 Art.1
s.2A, varied: 2003 c.14 Sch.17 para.1, SI
2003/415 Sch.1
s.2A, enabling: SSI 2003/233
s.3, varied: 2003 c.14 Sch.17 para.1
s.3A, referred to: SI 2003/415 Art.1
s.3A, varied: 2003 c.14 Sch.17 para.1, SI
2003/415 Sch.1
s.4, amended: 2003 c.39 Sch.8 para.137
s.4, applied: 2003 c.39 Sch.9 para.2
s.4, referred to: 2003 c.1 Sch.2 para.100,
Sch.3 para.49, Sch.4 para.37, Sch.5
para.59
s.4, varied: 2003 c.14 Sch.17 para.1
s.4A, varied: 2003 c.14 Sch.17 para.1
s.5, varied: 2003 c.14 Sch.17 para.1
s.6, applied: 2002 c.21 s.53
s.6, varied: 2002 c.21 s.2, 2002 c.22 s.5,
2003 c.14 Sch.17 para.1
s.7, amended: 2003 c.1 Sch.6 para.124
s.7, applied: 2004 c.12 s.108
s.7, varied: 2004 c.12 s.109
s.8, see *Osborne (Deceased) v Dickinson
(Inspector of Taxes)* [2004] S.T.C. (S.C.D.)
104 (Sp Comm), John Clark
s.8, applied: 2002 c.23 s.98, SI 2003/282
Reg.2, SI 2003/2682 Reg.146, Reg.185,
2004 c.12 s.108, SI 2004/1864 Reg.8
s.8, referred to: 2002 c.21 s.19
s.8, varied: 2004 c.12 s.109
s.8A, applied: SI 2003/282 Reg.2, SI 2003/
2682 Reg.185, 2004 c.12 s.108, SI 2004/
1864 Reg.8
s.8A, varied: 2004 c.12 s.109
s.9, amended: 2003 c.1 Sch.6 para.125, 2004
c.12 Sch.35 para.1
s.9, applied: SI 2003/282 Reg.2, SI 2003/
2682 Sch.1 para.25, 2004 c.12 s.108
s.9, varied: 2004 c.12 s.109
s.9A, see *Hall v Couch (Inspector of Taxes)*
[2004] S.T.C. (S.C.D.) 353 (Sp Comm),
John F Avery Jones; see *Langham
(Inspector of Taxes) v Veltema* [2002]
EWHC 2689, [2002] S.T.C. 1557 (Ch D),

1970–cont.

9. Taxes Management Act 1970–*cont.*
s.9A–*cont.*
Park, J.; see *Langham (Inspector of Taxes) v
Veltema* [2004] EWCA Civ 193, [2004]
S.T.C. 544 (CA), Auld, L.J.; see *Siwek v Inland Revenue Commissioners* [2002] S.T.C.
(S.C.D.) 247 (Sp Comm), J Gordon Reid
Q.C.
s.9A, amended: 2004 c.12 Sch.5 para.1
s.9A, applied: 2002 c.21 s.19, SI 2003/282
Reg.2
s.9A, see *Murat v Ornoch (Inspector of Taxes)*
[2004] S.T.C. (S.C.D.) 115 (Sp Comm),
Theodore Wallace
s.9B, applied: SI 2003/282 Reg.2
s.9C, applied: 2002 c.21 s.20, SI 2003/282
Reg.2
s.9D, applied: SI 2003/282 Reg.2
s.9ZA, applied: 2002 c.21 s.20, 2002 c.23
Sch.22 para.17
s.9ZB, applied: 2002 c.21 s.20
s.12AA, applied: SI 2003/282 Reg.2, SI
2004/1864 Reg.8
s.12AB, amended: 2002 c.23 Sch.40 Part 3
s.12AB, applied: SI 2003/282 Reg.2
s.12ABA, applied: 2002 c.21 s.20, 2002 c.23
Sch.22 para.17
s.12ABB, applied: 2002 c.21 s.20
s.12AC, applied: SI 2003/282 Reg.2
s.12AD, applied: SI 2003/282 Reg.2
s.12AE, applied: SI 2003/282 Reg.2
s.12B, amended: 2004 c.12 Sch.12 para.1
s.12B, disapplied: 2004 c.12 s.33
s.15, amended: 2003 c.1 Sch.6 para.126
s.16A, substituted: 2003 c.1 Sch.6 para.127
s.17, applied: 2003 c.14 s.199, SI 2003/3297
Reg.15, Reg.16
s.18, applied: 2003 c.14 s.199, SI 2003/3297
Reg.15, Reg.16
s.19A, see *Parto v Bratherton (Inspector of
Taxes)* [2004] S.T.C. (S.C.D.) 339 (Sp
Comm), JD Demack (Chairman)
s.20, see *Fox v Uxbridge General
Commissioners* [2002] S.T.C. 455 (Ch D),
Jacob, J.; see *Morris v Roberts (Inspector of
Taxes)* [2004] S.T.C. (S.C.D.) 245 (Sp
Comm), John F Avery Jones; see *R. (on
the application of Morgan Grenfell & Co
Ltd) v Special Commissioner of Income Tax*
[2001] EWCA Civ 329, [2002] 2 W.L.R.
255 (CA), Blackburne, J.; see *R. (on the
application of Morgan Grenfell & Co Ltd) v
Special Commissioner of Income Tax*
[2002] UKHL 21, [2003] 1 A.C. 563 (HL),
Lord Hoffmann; see *R. (on the application
of Werner) v Inland Revenue Commissioners*
[2002] EWCA Civ 979, [2002] S.T.C. 1213
(CA), Hart, J.; see *R. v Allen (Brian Roger)*
[2001] UKHL 45, [2002] 1 A.C. 509 (HL),
Lord Hutton
s.20, varied: 2002 c.21 s.25
s.20B, referred to: 2002 c.21 s.25

1970–cont.

9. Taxes Management Act 1970–*cont.*

s.20BA, applied: 2002 c.21 s.36, 2002 c.29 s.323

s.20BB, referred to: 2002 c.21 s.25, s.36

s.20C, see *R. (on the application of H) v Inland Revenue Commissioners* [2002] EWHC 2164, [2002] S.T.C. 1354 (QBD (Admin Ct)), Stanley Burnton, J.

s.20C, applied: 2002 c.21 s.36, 2002 c.29 s.323

s.20CC, see *R. (on the application of H) v Inland Revenue Commissioners* [2002] EWHC 2164, [2002] S.T.C. 1354 (QBD (Admin Ct)), Stanley Burnton, J.

s.20CC, referred to: 2002 c.21 s.36

s.20D, amended: 2003 c.39 Sch.4 para.2

s.28A, applied: 2002 c.21 s.20

s.28A, referred to: 2002 c.21 s.19

s.28B, applied: 2002 c.21 s.20

s.29, see *Hall v Couch (Inspector of Taxes)* [2004] S.T.C. (S.C.D.) 353 (Sp Comm), John F Avery Jones; see *Langham (Inspector of Taxes) v Veltema* [2002] EWHC 2689, [2002] S.T.C. 1557 (Ch D), Park, J.; see *Langham (Inspector of Taxes) v Veltema* [2004] EWCA Civ 193, [2004] S.T.C. 544 (CA), Auld, L.J.; see *Osborne (Deceased) v Dickinson (Inspector of Taxes)* [2004] S.T.C. (S.C.D.) 104 (Sp Comm), John Clark; see *Parto v Bratherton (Inspector of Taxes)* [2004] S.T.C. (S.C.D.) 339 (Sp Comm), JD Demack (Chairman)

s.29, applied: 2002 c.21 s.20, 2002 c.29 s.319, 2003 c.1 s.312

s.30, see *Guthrie (Inspector of Taxes) v Twickenham Film Studios Ltd* [2002] EWHC 1936, [2002] S.T.C. 1374 (Ch D), Lloyd, J.

s.30, applied: SI 2003/2682 Reg.14, Reg.188

s.30, varied: SI 2003/2495 Reg.4

s.30A, varied: SI 2003/2495 Reg.4

s.31, applied: SI 2003/2682 Reg.217

s.31A, applied: SI 2003/2495 Reg.6, SI 2003/2682 Reg.217

s.31B, applied: SI 2003/2495 Reg.6, SI 2003/2682 Reg.217

s.31D, applied: 2002 c.21 s.39, SI 2003/2495 Reg.6, SI 2003/2682 Reg.217, 2004 c.6 s.23

s.32, applied: 2002 c.21 s.20

s.33, see *Howard v Inland Revenue Commissioners* [2002] S.T.C. (S.C.D.) 408 (Sp Comm), Theodore Wallace; see *McClymont v Jarman (Inspector of Taxes)* [2003] S.T.I. 2277 (Sp Comm), Colin Bishopp; see *Wall v Inland Revenue Commissioners* [2002] S.T.C. (S.C.D.) 122 (Sp Comm), Nuala Brice

s.33, applied: 2002 c.21 s.20

s.35, substituted: 2004 c.12 Sch.17 para.3

1970–cont.

9. Taxes Management Act 1970–*cont.*

s.36, see *Lord Hanson v Mansworth (Inspector of Taxes)* [2004] S.T.C. (S.C.D.) 288 (Sp Comm), Nuala Brice

s.36, amended: 2002 c.21 Sch.6

s.37A, amended: 2002 c.21 Sch.6

s.42, see *Howard v Inland Revenue Commissioners* [2002] S.T.C. (S.C.D.) 408 (Sp Comm), Theodore Wallace

s.42, amended: 2003 c.1 Sch.6 para.128

s.42, disapplied: SI 2004/1450 Reg.28

s.43A, amended: 2002 c.21 Sch.6, 2003 c.14 s.207

s.43C, added: 2003 c.14 s.207

s.44, applied: SI 2003/2682 Reg.80

s.44, varied: 2002 c.22 Sch.1 para.2, Sch.1 para.4, SI 2003/1382 Reg.4

s.45, applied: SI 2003/2682 Reg.80

s.45, varied: 2002 c.22 Sch.1 para.2, Sch.1 para.4

s.46, applied: 2002 c.21 s.39, 2003 c.1 Sch.5 para.48, Sch.5 para.50, Sch.5 para.56, Sch.5 para.57, SI 2003/2682 Reg.80, 2004 c.6 s.23, 2004 c.12 s.156, s.159, s.170, s.253, s.269, s.271, Sch.33 para.6

s.46, varied: 2002 c.22 Sch.1 para.2, Sch.1 para.4, SI 2003/1382 Reg.5

s.46A, applied: SI 2003/2682 Reg.80

s.46A, varied: 2002 c.22 Sch.1 para.2, Sch.1 para.4, SI 2003/1382 Reg.6

s.46A, enabling: SI 2002/2976

s.46B, amended: 2003 c.1 Sch.6 para.129

s.46B, applied: SI 2003/2682 Reg.80

s.46B, varied: 2002 c.22 Sch.1 para.2, Sch.1 para.4

s.46C, applied: SI 2003/2682 Reg.80

s.46C, varied: 2002 c.22 Sch.1 para.2, Sch.1 para.4

s.46D, applied: SI 2003/2682 Reg.80

s.46D, varied: 2002 c.22 Sch.1 para.2, Sch.1 para.4

s.47, applied: SI 2003/2682 Reg.80

s.47, varied: 2002 c.22 Sch.1 para.2, Sch.1 para.4

s.47A, applied: SI 2003/2682 Reg.80

s.47A, varied: 2002 c.22 Sch.1 para.2, Sch.1 para.4

s.47B, applied: SI 2003/2682 Reg.80

s.47B, varied: 2002 c.22 Sch.1 para.2, Sch.1 para.4

s.48, applied: SI 2003/2682 Reg.80

s.48, varied: 2002 c.22 Sch.1 para.2, Sch.1 para.4, SI 2003/1382 Reg.7

s.49, see *Consultants Ltd v Inspector of Taxes* [2002] S.T.C. (S.C.D.) 162 (Sp Comm), John F Avery Jones

s.49, applied: SI 2003/2682 Reg.80

s.49, varied: 2002 c.22 Sch.1 para.2, Sch.1 para.4, SI 2003/1382 Reg.8

s.50, applied: SI 2003/2682 Reg.80

s.50, disapplied: SI 2003/2682 Reg.204

CAP.

1970–cont.

9. Taxes Management Act 1970–*cont.*

s.50, varied: 2002 c.22 Sch.1 para.2, Sch.1 para.4

s.51, applied: SI 2003/2682 Reg.80

s.51, varied: 2002 c.22 Sch.1 para.2, Sch.1 para.4

s.52, applied: SI 2003/2682 Reg.80

s.52, varied: 2002 c.22 Sch.1 para.2, Sch.1 para.4

s.53, applied: SI 2003/2682 Reg.80

s.53, varied: 2002 c.22 Sch.1 para.2, Sch.1 para.4, SI 2003/1382 Reg.10

s.54, see *Ahajot (Count Artsrunik) v Waller (Inspector of Taxes)* [2004] S.T.C. (S.C.D.) 151 (Sp Comm), Nuala Brice; see *Sun Chemical Ltd v Smith (Inspector of Taxes)* [2002] S.T.C. (S.C.D.) 510 (Sp Comm), John F Avery Jones

s.54, applied: 2002 c.21 s.63, SI 2003/2682 Reg.80, 2004 c.6 s.24

s.54, varied: 2002 c.22 Sch.1 para.2, Sch.1 para.4, SI 2002/2926 Reg.3, SI 2003/1382 Reg.9

s.55, see *Pumahaven Ltd v Williams (Inspector of Taxes)* [2002] EWHC 2237, [2002] S.T.C. 1423 (Ch D), Park, J.

s.55, applied: 2002 c.23 Sch.16 para.45

s.55, disapplied: SI 2002/2172 Reg.14

s.55, varied: 2002 c.22 Sch.1 para.2, Sch.1 para.4

s.56, see *Hudson (Inspector of Taxes) v JDC Services Ltd* [2004] EWHC 602, [2004] S.T.C. 834 (Ch D), Lightman, J.

s.56, applied: SI 2003/2682 Reg.80

s.56, referred to: 2003 c.14 Sch.17 para.9

s.56, varied: 2002 c.22 Sch.1 para.2, Sch.1 para.4, SI 2003/1382 Reg.10

s.56A, see *Pumahaven Ltd v Williams (Inspector of Taxes)* [2003] EWCA Civ 700, [2003] S.T.C. 890 (CA), Peter Gibson, L.J.

s.56A, applied: SI 2003/2682 Reg.80

s.56A, referred to: 2003 c.14 Sch.17 para.9

s.56A, varied: 2002 c.22 Sch.1 para.2, Sch.1 para.4, SI 2003/1382 Reg.10

s.56B, applied: 2002 c.21 s.39, 2002 c.29 s.320, SI 2003/2682 Reg.80, 2004 c.6 s.23

s.56B, varied: 2002 c.22 Sch.1 para.2, Sch.1 para.4

s.56B, enabling: SI 2003/968, SI 2004/1363

s.56C, applied: SI 2003/2682 Reg.80

s.56C, varied: 2002 c.22 Sch.1 para.2, Sch.1 para.4

s.56D, applied: SI 2003/2682 Reg.80

s.56D, varied: 2002 c.22 Sch.1 para.2, Sch.1 para.4

s.57, applied: SI 2003/2682 Reg.80

s.57, varied: 2002 c.22 Sch.1 para.2, Sch.1 para.4

s.57A, applied: SI 2003/2682 Reg.80

CAP.

1970–cont.

9. Taxes Management Act 1970–*cont.*

s.57A, varied: 2002 c.22 Sch.1 para.2, Sch.1 para.4

s.57B, applied: SI 2003/2682 Reg.80

s.57B, varied: 2002 c.22 Sch.1 para.2, Sch.1 para.4

s.58, amended: 2002 c.21 Sch.6

s.58, applied: SI 2003/2682 Reg.80

s.58, referred to: 2003 c.14 Sch.17 para.9

s.58, varied: 2002 c.22 Sch.1 para.2, Sch.1 para.4, SI 2003/1382 Reg.10

s.59, applied: SI 2003/2682 Reg.80

s.59, varied: 2002 c.22 Sch.1 para.2, Sch.1 para.4

s.59A, applied: 2004 c.12 s.108

s.59A, referred to: SI 2003/2682 Reg.185

s.59A, amended: 2003 c.1 Sch.6 para.130, 2003 c.14 s.145, 2004 c.12 Sch.17 para.10

s.59B, applied: SI 2003/2682 Reg.185, 2004 c.12 s.108

s.59B, referred to: SI 2003/2682 Reg.185, Reg.186, Reg.187

s.59B, varied: 2004 c.12 s.109

s.59B, amended: 2003 c.14 s.145, 2003 c.1 Sch.6 para.131

s.59C, see *Bancroft v Crutchfield (Inspector of Taxes)* [2002] S.T.C. (S.C.D.) 347 (Sp Comm), Dr JF Avery Jones CBE (Chairman); see *Gladders v Prior (Inspector of Taxes)* [2003] S.T.C. (S.C.D.) 245 (Sp Comm), John F Avery Jones; see *Thompson (Inspector of Taxes) v Minzly* [2002] S.T.C. 450 (Ch D), Ferris, J.

s.59D, amended: 2002 c.23 s.40, 2004 c.12 Sch.12 para.2

s.59DA, amended: 2004 c.12 Sch.12 para.3

s.59DA, applied: SI 2003/282 Reg.2

s.59E, amended: 2002 c.23 s.92

s.59E, applied: SI 2003/282 Reg.2

s.60, varied: SI 2002/2836 Sch.1 para.2, Sch.1 para.4, SI 2003/2682 Reg.84, Reg.109

s.61, varied: SI 2002/2836 Sch.1 para.2, Sch.1 para.4, SI 2003/2682 Reg.84, Reg.109

s.62, amended: 2003 c.1 Sch.6 para.132, 2004 c.12 Sch.12 para.4

s.62, varied: SI 2002/2836 Sch.1 para.2, Sch.1 para.4, SI 2003/2682 Reg.84, Reg.109

s.63, amended: 2002 asp 17 Sch.3 para.11, 2003 c.1 Sch.6 para.133, 2004 c.12 Sch.12 para.5

s.63, varied: SI 2002/2836 Sch.1 para.2, Sch.1 para.4, SI 2003/2682 Reg.84, Reg.109

s.63, enabling: SSI 2002/560

s.63A, amended: 2002 asp 17 Sch.3 para.11

s.63A, varied: SI 2002/2836 Sch.1 para.2, Sch.1 para.4, SI 2003/2682 Reg.84, Reg.109

1970–cont.

9. Taxes Management Act 1970–*cont.*

s.64, amended: 2003 c.1 Sch.6 para.134, 2004 c.12 Sch.12 para.6

s.64, varied: SI 2002/2836 Sch.1 para.2, Sch.1 para.4, SI 2003/2682 Reg.84, Reg.109

s.65, applied: SI 2002/2172 Reg.14, SI 2002/2820 Reg.8, SI 2003/2682 Reg.84, Reg.109, SR 2002/379 Reg.8

s.65, varied: SI 2002/2836 Sch.1 para.2, Sch.1 para.4, SI 2003/2682 Reg.84, Reg.109

s.66, applied: SI 2002/2172 Reg.14, SI 2002/2820 Reg.8, SI 2003/2682 Reg.84, Reg.109, SR 2002/379 Reg.8

s.66, varied: SI 2002/2836 Sch.1 para.2, Sch.1 para.4, SI 2003/2682 Reg.84, Reg.109

s.67, applied: SI 2002/2172 Reg.14, SI 2002/2820 Reg.8, SI 2003/2682 Reg.84, Reg.109, SR 2002/379 Reg.8

s.67, varied: SI 2002/2836 Sch.1 para.2, Sch.1 para.4, SI 2003/2682 Reg.84, Reg.109

s.68, varied: SI 2002/2836 Sch.1 para.2, Sch.1 para.4, SI 2003/2682 Reg.84, Reg.109

s.69, varied: SI 2002/2836 Sch.1 para.2, Sch.1 para.4, SI 2003/2682 Reg.84, Reg.109

s.70, see *McCullough (Inspector of Taxes) v Ahluwalia* [2004] EWCA Civ 889, [2004] S.T.C. 1295 (CA), Waller, L.J.

s.70, amended: 2003 c.1 Sch.6 para.135

s.70, varied: SI 2002/2836 Sch.1 para.2, Sch.1 para.4, SI 2003/2682 Reg.84, Reg.109

s.70A, varied: SI 2002/2836 Sch.1 para.2, Sch.1 para.4, SI 2003/2682 Reg.84, Reg.109

s.72, varied: SI 2004/1450 Reg.29

s.73, varied: SI 2004/1450 Reg.29

s.75, disapplied: 2002 c.29 Sch.10, Sch.10 para.1

s.77, disapplied: 2002 c.29 Sch.10, Sch.10 para.1

s.86, applied: SI 2003/2682 Reg.72, Reg.81

s.87, see *Mellham Ltd v Burton (Inspector of Taxes)* [2003] EWCA Civ 173, [2003] S.T.C. 441 (CA), Buxton, L.J.

s.87A, amended: 2002 c.23 Sch.29 para.69

s.91, amended: 2003 c.1 Sch.6 para.136

s.93, see *Gladders v Prior (Inspector of Taxes)* [2003] S.T.C. (S.C.D.) 245 (Sp Comm), John F Avery Jones

s.94, see *Lessex Ltd v Spence (Inspector of Taxes)* [2004] S.T.C. (S.C.D.) 79 (Sp Comm), David Williams

s.95, applied: 2003 c.1 s.164, 2004 c.12 s.33, s.313

s.95A, applied: 2004 c.12 s.33

1970–cont.

9. Taxes Management Act 1970–*cont.*

s.98, see *Fox v Uxbridge General Commissioners* [2002] S.T.C. 455 (Ch D), Jacob, J.

s.98, amended: 2002 c.23 s.94, s.96, Sch.17 para.1, Sch.21 para.7, Sch.33 para.15, Sch.34 para.6, Sch.34 para.10, Sch.35 para.7, Sch.35 para.11, 2003 c.14 s.199, s.203, Sch.22 para.47, Sch.28 para.6, Sch.30 para.6, 2003 c.1 Sch.6 para.137, Sch.8 Part 1, 2004 c.12 s.55, s.105, s.258, Sch.12 para.7, Sch.21 para.1, Sch.42 Part 2, Sch.42 Part 3

s.98A, amended: 2003 c.1 Sch.6 para.138, 2004 c.3 Sch.2 Part 1, 2004 c.12 Sch.12 para.8

s.98A, applied: SI 2003/2682 Reg.73, Reg.146

s.98A, referred to: SI 2004/1864 Reg.9

s.98C, added: 2004 c.12 s.315

s.98C, referred to: 2004 c.12 s.313

s.99, applied: 2004 c.12 s.33

s.100, amended: 2004 c.12 s.260, s.315, Sch.42 Part 3

s.100, applied: SI 2003/2682 Reg.210, SI 2003/3297 Reg.14

s.100A, applied: SI 2003/3297 Reg.14

s.100B, applied: SI 2003/3297 Reg.14

s.100C, amended: 2004 c.12 s.315

s.102, applied: SI 2003/2682 Reg.203, SI 2003/3297 Reg.14

s.103, applied: SI 2003/3297 Reg.14

s.103A, applied: SI 2003/2682 Reg.210

s.105, amended: 2003 c.14 s.206

s.108, amended: 2003 c.14 Sch.41 para.2

s.115, see *Spring Salmon & Seafood Ltd v Advocate General for Scotland* [2004] S.T.C. 444 (OH), Lady Smith

s.118, see *Howard v Inland Revenue Commissioners* [2002] S.T.C. (S.C.D.) 408 (Sp Comm), Theodore Wallace

s.118, amended: 2003 c.1 Sch.6 para.139, 2003 c.14 Sch.43 Part 3

s.118, applied: 2002 c.22 s.11, 2002 c.29 s.326, SI 2002/2836 Art.12, SI 2003/1417 r.140, SI 2003/3297 Reg.14

s.119, amended: 2003 c.1 Sch.6 para.140

Sch.1A, applied: SI 2003/282 Reg.2

Sch.1AA, applied: 2002 c.21 s.36

Sch.1AA, referred to: 2002 c.21 s.36

Sch.1AA para.9, amended: 2003 c.39 Sch.4 para.2

Sch.1A para.4, amended: 2003 c.1 Sch.6 para.141

Sch.1A para.5, see *Forthright (Wales) Ltd v Davies (Inspector of Taxes)* [2004] EWHC 524, [2004] S.T.C. 875 (Ch D), Lightman, J.

Sch.1A para.7, see *Forthright (Wales) Ltd v Davies (Inspector of Taxes)* [2004] EWHC 524, [2004] S.T.C. 875 (Ch D), Lightman, J.

1970–cont.

9. Taxes Management Act 1970–*cont.*

Sch.1B para.2, see *Blackburn (Inspector of Taxes) v Keeling* [2003] EWCA Civ 1221, [2003] S.T.C. 1162 (CA), Carnwath, L.J.; see *Blackburn (Inspector of Taxes) v Keeling* [2003] EWHC 754, [2003] S.T.C. 639 (Ch D), Peter Smith, J.

Sch.3 para.1, applied: 2004 c.12 s.156, s.159, s.170, s.269, s.271, Sch.33 para.6

Sch.3 para.1, varied: 2004 c.12 s.253

Sch.3 para.2, applied: 2004 c.12 s.156, s.159, s.170, s.269, s.271, Sch.33 para.6

Sch.3 para.2, varied: 2004 c.12 s.253

Sch.3 para.3, amended: 2003 c.1 Sch.6 para.142

Sch.3 para.3, applied: SI 2003/2495 Reg.6, SI 2003/2682 Reg.18, Reg.80, Reg.110, Reg.127, Reg.217

Sch.3 para.8, applied: SI 2003/2495 Reg.6, 2004 c.12 s.156, s.159, s.170, s.269, s.271, Sch.33 para.6

Sch.3 para.8, varied: 2004 c.12 s.253

Sch.3 para.9, applied: 2004 c.12 s.156, s.159, s.170, s.269, s.271, Sch.33 para.6

Sch.3 para.9, varied: 2004 c.12 s.253

Sch.3A Part I para.2, amended: 2003 c.1 Sch.6 para.143

10. Income and Corporation Taxes Act 1970

s.26, see *Venables v Hornby (Inspector of Taxes)* [2002] EWCA Civ 1277, [2002] S.T.C. 1248 (CA), Chadwick, L.J.

s.280, see *Whitehall Electric Investments Ltd v Owen (Inspector of Taxes)* [2002] S.T.C. (S.C.D.) 229 (Sp Comm), Nuala Brice

s.306, see *Howard v Inland Revenue Commissioners* [2002] S.T.C. (S.C.D.) 408 (Sp Comm), Theodore Wallace

11. Sea Fish Industry Act 1970

s.14, disapplied: SI 2002/790 Art.7

s.42, disapplied: SI 2002/790 Art.7

21. New Forest Act 1970

applied: SI 2002/794 Art.3

s.2, amended: SI 2002/794 Sch.1 para.17

22. Tonga Act 1970

Sch.1 Part I para.8, repealed: 2002 c.39 Sch.3

24. Finance Act 1970

Part II c.II, applied: 2003 c.1 s.594

s.6, amended: 2003 c.17 Sch.6 para.54, Sch.7

30. Conservation of Seals Act 1970

s.3, enabling: SSI 2002/404, SSI 2004/283

s.10, amended: 2004 asp 6 Sch.7 para.3

31. Administration of Justice Act 1970

s.36, see *Royal Bank of Scotland Plc v Miller* [2001] EWCA Civ 344, [2002] Q.B. 255 (CA), Dyson, L.J.

s.36, repealed (in part): 2004 c.14 Sch.1 Part 12

s.40, applied: SI 2003/1376 Sch.1, SI 2003/1593 Sch.1 Part I

s.41, amended: 2003 c.39 Sch.8 para.138

1970–cont.

31. Administration of Justice Act 1970–*cont.*

s.41, applied: SI 2002/1998 Art.17

s.41, repealed (in part): 2004 c.14 Sch.1 Part 1

s.44, applied: SI 2003/1372 r.56

s.54, amended: 2004 c.14 Sch.1 Part 1

s.54, repealed (in part): 2004 c.14 Sch.1 Part 1

Sch.2 para.26, repealed: 2004 c.14 Sch.1 Part 12

Sch.2 para.28, repealed: 2004 c.14 Sch.1 Part 12

Sch.8 para.15, added: 2004 c.33 Sch.27 para.34

Sch.9 Part I, applied: SI 2002/1998 Art.17

Sch.9 Part I para.13, added: 2004 c.28 s.14

33. Law Reform (Miscellaneous Provisions) Act 1970

s.3, see *Cox v Jones* [2004] EWHC 1486, [2004] 2 F.L.R. 1010 (Ch D), Mann, J.

35. Conveyancing and Feudal Reform Act 1970

s.25, see *Davidson v Clydesdale Bank Plc* 2002 S.L.T. 1088 (OH), Judge TG Coutts Q.C.

35. Conveyancing and Feudal Reform (Scotland) Act 1970

see *Gardiner v Jacques Vert Plc* 2002 S.L.T. 928 (Ex Div), Lord Cameron of Lochbroom, Lord Dawson, Lord Marnoch

applied: SI 2004/1484 Reg.1

s.1, see *Strathclyde Joint Police Board v Elderslie Estates Ltd* 2002 S.L.T. (Lands Tr) 2 (Lands Tr (Scot)), Lord McGhie

s.1, repealed: 2003 asp 9 Sch.15

s.2, repealed: 2003 asp 9 Sch.15

s.7, repealed: 2003 asp 9 Sch.15

s.9, amended: 2003 asp 9 Sch.14 para.4

s.9, applied: SSI 2002/494 Sch.2 para.11, SSI 2003/168 Sch.1 para.5

s.10, see *J Sykes & Sons (Fish Merchants) Ltd v Grieve* 2002 S.L.T. (Sh Ct) 15 (Sh Pr), JC McInnes Q.C., Sheriff Principal

s.13, amended: 2003 asp 9 s.111

s.13, referred to: 2003 asp 9 s.111

s.19, amended: 2003 asp 9 Sch.14 para.4

s.19, applied: 2003 asp 2 s.37, s.73

s.19A, amended: 2003 asp 9 Sch.14 para.4

s.19B, added: 2003 asp 10 Sch.1 para.1

s.19B, referred to: 2003 asp 10 s.11

s.20, applied: 2003 asp 2 s.67, 2003 asp 11 s.30

s.21, amended: 2003 asp 10 Sch.1 para.1

s.21, applied: 2003 asp 2 s.37, s.73

s.22, applied: 2003 asp 2 s.73

s.23, applied: 2003 asp 2 s.67, 2003 asp 11 s.30

s.24, see *GMAC-RFA Ltd v Murray* 2003 Hous. L.R. 50 (Sh Pr), Sheriff Principal EF Bowen Q.C.

s.24, amended: 2003 asp 9 Sch.14 para.4, 2003 asp 10 Sch.1 para.1

CAP.

CAP.

1970–cont.

35. Conveyancing and Feudal Reform (Scotland) Act 1970–*cont.*

s.24, applied: 2003 asp 2 s.37, s.67, s.73, 2003 asp 11 s.27, s.30

s.24, disapplied: 2003 asp 2 s.40

s.24, referred to: 2003 asp 10 s.11

s.25, amended: 2003 asp 2 s.40

s.27, referred to: SSI 2004/171 Art.18

s.53, amended: 2003 asp 9 Sch.15

Sch.1 para.5, amended: 2003 asp 11 Sch.1 para.3

38. Building (Scotland) Act 1970

repealed: 2003 asp 8 Sch.6 para.4

39. Local Authorities (Goods and Services) Act 1970

applied: SI 2002/522 Art.2, SI 2002/1729 Art.2, SI 2002/2244 Art.2, SI 2002/2624 Art.2, 2003 asp 1 s.22, SI 2003/354 Art.2, SI 2003/1018 Art.2, SI 2003/2069 Art.2, SI 2004/485 Art.2, SI 2004/2878 Art.2

varied: 2002 asp 3 s.61, SI 2004/1777 Art.30, SI 2004/1778 Art.30

s.1, amended: 2003 asp 1 s.8

s.1, repealed (in part): 2003 asp 1 s.8

s.1, enabling: SI 2002/522, SI 2002/1729, SI 2002/2244, SI 2002/2624, SI 2003/354, SI 2003/1018, SI 2003/2069, SI 2003/2558, SI 2004/485, SI 2004/2475, SI 2004/2878

s.2, amended: 2003 asp 1 s.8

s.2, repealed (in part): 2003 asp 1 s.8

40. Agriculture Act 1970

applied: SI 2002/892, SI 2003/1296, SI 2003/2912, SI 2004/1301, SI 2004/1749, SI 2004/2688, SSI 2003/277

referred to: SI 2002/1797, SI 2003/1677 Reg.9, SI 2003/2912 Reg.8, SI 2003/3119, SI 2004/2734, SR 2002/263, SSI 2004/458

Part IV, referred to: SI 2003/1677 Reg.10

s.2, applied: SI 2004/2734

s.28, enabling: SI 2003/2726

s.29, applied: SSI 2002/44 Art.3

s.29, referred to: SSI 2002/43 Art.3, SSI 2003/52 Art.7

s.29, enabling: SI 2003/562, SI 2003/2726, SI 2004/1606, SSI 2002/43, SSI 2003/52, SSI 2003/518, SSI 2004/236

s.34, repealed: 2004 c.14 Sch.1 Part 2

s.52, amended: 2004 c.14 Sch.1 Part 3

s.52, repealed (in part): 2004 c.14 Sch.1 Part 3

s.66, applied: SI 2002/1689 Reg.3, SR 2002/301 Reg.3

s.66, referred to: SI 2003/1677

s.66, enabling: SI 2002/892, SI 2002/1797, SI 2003/1296, SI 2003/1503, SI 2003/1677, SI 2003/1850, SI 2003/2912, SI 2003/3119, SI 2004/1301, SI 2004/1749, SI 2004/2146, SI 2004/2688, SI 2004/2734, SI 2004/3091, SR 2002/263, SR 2003/287, SSI 2002/285, SSI 2003/277,

1970–cont.

40. Agriculture Act 1970–*cont.*

s.66, enabling:–*cont.*

SSI 2003/312, SSI 2003/474, SSI 2004/208, SSI 2004/414, SSI 2004/458

s.67, applied: SI 2002/843 Sch.9 para.2, SI 2003/1082 Reg.9, SI 2004/2412 Reg.4, SSI 2002/255 Sch.9 para.2, SSI 2004/433 Reg.4, SSI 2004/438 Reg.3

s.67, referred to: SI 2003/2912 Reg.10, SI 2003/3119 Reg.10

s.67, varied: SI 2002/1416 Sch.9 para.2

s.68, amended: 2003 c.44 Sch.26 para.22

s.68, enabling: SI 2002/892, SI 2002/1797, SI 2003/1503, SI 2003/1850, SR 2002/263, SSI 2002/285, SSI 2003/312

s.69, amended: 2003 c.44 Sch.26 para.22

s.69, enabling: SI 2002/892, SI 2002/1797, SI 2003/1503, SI 2003/1850, SR 2002/263, SSI 2002/285, SSI 2003/312

s.70, amended: 2003 c.44 Sch.26 para.22

s.71, amended: 2003 c.44 Sch.26 para.22

s.73, amended: 2003 c.44 Sch.26 para.22

s.73A, amended: 2003 c.44 Sch.26 para.22

s.74A, amended: 2003 c.44 Sch.26 para.22

s.74A, applied: SI 2003/2912 Reg.3

s.74A, referred to: SI 2003/3119 Reg.3

s.74A, enabling: SI 2002/892, SI 2002/1797, SI 2003/1503, SI 2003/1850, SI 2003/2912, SI 2003/3119, SI 2004/1301, SI 2004/1749, SI 2004/2688, SI 2004/3091, SR 2002/263, SSI 2002/285, SSI 2003/277, SSI 2003/312, SSI 2003/474, SSI 2004/208, SSI 2004/458

s.75, referred to: SI 2003/1677

s.75, enabling: SI 2002/892, SI 2002/1797, SI 2003/1296, SI 2003/1503, SI 2003/1677, SI 2003/1850, SR 2002/263, SR 2003/287, SSI 2002/285, SSI 2003/277, SSI 2003/312, SSI 2004/414

s.76, referred to: SI 2003/1677, SI 2003/1677 Reg.11, SI 2003/2912 Reg.11, SI 2003/3119 Reg.11

s.76, varied: SI 2004/2334 Reg.6, SSI 2004/433 Reg.6

s.76, enabling: SI 2002/892, SI 2002/1797, SI 2003/1296, SI 2003/1503, SI 2003/1677, SI 2003/1850, SR 2002/263, SR 2003/287, SSI 2002/285, SSI 2003/277, SSI 2003/312, SSI 2004/414

s.77, referred to: SI 2003/1677, SI 2003/1677 Reg.12

s.77, varied: SI 2004/2334 Reg.6, SSI 2004/433 Reg.6

s.77, enabling: SI 2002/892, SI 2002/1797, SI 2003/1296, SI 2003/1677, SI 2004/1749, SI 2004/2146, SI 2004/2734, SI 2004/3091, SR 2002/263, SR 2003/287, SSI 2002/285, SSI 2003/277, SSI 2004/414

s.78, referred to: SI 2003/1677, SI 2003/1677 Reg.12

1970–cont.

40. Agriculture Act 1970–*cont.*

s.78, varied: SI 2004/2334 Reg.6, SSI 2004/433 Reg.6

s.78, enabling: SI 2002/892, SI 2002/1797, SI 2003/1296, SI 2003/1677, SI 2004/2146, SI 2004/2734, SR 2002/263, SR 2003/287, SSI 2002/285, SSI 2003/277, SSI 2004/414

s.79, amended: 2003 c.44 Sch.26 para.22

s.79, referred to: SI 2003/1677

s.79, varied: SI 2004/2334 Reg.6, SSI 2004/433 Reg.6

s.79, enabling: SI 2002/892, SI 2002/1797, SI 2003/1296, SI 2003/1677, SI 2004/3091, SR 2002/263, SR 2003/287, SSI 2002/285, SSI 2003/277, SSI 2004/414

s.80, varied: SI 2004/2334 Reg.6, SSI 2004/433 Reg.6

s.81, varied: SI 2004/2334 Reg.6, SSI 2004/433 Reg.6

s.82, varied: SI 2004/2334 Reg.6, SSI 2004/433 Reg.6

s.83, amended: 2003 c.44 Sch.26 para.22

s.83, referred to: SI 2003/1677 Reg.13

s.83, varied: SI 2004/2334 Reg.6, SSI 2004/433 Reg.6

s.84, applied: SI 2002/892, SI 2002/1797, SI 2003/1503, SI 2003/1677, SI 2003/1850, SI 2003/2912, SI 2003/3119, SI 2004/1301, SI 2004/1749, SI 2004/2688, SI 2004/2734, SR 2002/263, SR 2003/287, SSI 2002/285, SSI 2003/474, SSI 2004/208, SSI 2004/458

s.84, referred to: SI 2003/1677, SI 2004/2146, SSI 2003/312

s.84, enabling: SI 2002/892, SI 2002/1797, SI 2003/1296, SI 2003/1503, SI 2003/1677, SI 2003/1850, SI 2003/2912, SI 2003/3119, SI 2004/1301, SI 2004/1749, SI 2004/2146, SI 2004/2688, SI 2004/2734, SI 2004/3091, SR 2002/263, SR 2003/287, SSI 2002/285, SSI 2003/277, SSI 2003/312, SSI 2003/474, SSI 2004/208, SSI 2004/414, SSI 2004/458

s.86, enabling: SR 2003/287

s.87, repealed (in part): 2004 c.14 Sch.1 Part 2

s.102, repealed: 2004 c.14 Sch.1 Part 2

s.106, amended: 2003 c.44 Sch.26 para.22, Sch.37 Part 9

s.106, disapplied: 2003 c.44 Sch.25 para.71

s.110, varied: SI 2004/2334 Reg.6, SSI 2004/433 Reg.6

s.111, amended: 2004 c.14 Sch.1 Part 2

Sch.3 para.8, repealed: 2004 c.14 Sch.1 Part 3

41. Equal Pay Act 1970

see *Alabaster v Woolwich Plc* [2002] EWCA Civ 211, [2002] 1 C.M.L.R. 56 (CA), Mummery, L.J.; see *Lawrence v Regent Office Care Ltd (C320/00)* [2002] 3 C.M.L.R. 27 (ECJ), GC Rodriguez Iglesias (President); see *Preston v Wolverhampton Healthcare NHS Trust (No.3)* [2002]

1970–cont.

41. Equal Pay Act 1970–*cont.*

see–*cont.*

O.P.L.R. 323 (ET), JK Macmillan; see *South Ayrshire Council v Morton* 2002 S.L.T. 656 (2 Div), Lord Gill L.J.C., Lord Caplan, Lord MacLean

applied: SI 2004/1861 Sch.1 para.61

s.1, see *Cadman v Health and Safety Executive* [2004] I.C.R. 378 (EAT), Judge Burke Q.C.; see *Department for Environment Food and Rural Affairs v Robertson* [2004] I.C.R. 1289 (EAT), Burton, J.; see *Milligan v South Ayrshire Council* 2003 S.C. 274 (2 Div), Lord Gill L.J.C., Lord Caplan, Lord MacLean; see *Ministry of Defence v Armstrong* [2004] I.R.L.R. 672 (EAT), Cox, J.; see *Nelson v Carillion Services Ltd* [2003] EWCA Civ 544, [2003] I.C.R. 1256 (CA), Simon Brown, L.J.; see *Parliamentary Commissioner for Administration v Fernandez* [2004] 2 C.M.L.R. 4 (EAT), Judge Peter Clark

s.1, amended: SI 2003/1656 Reg.10

s.2, see *Powerhouse Retail Ltd v Burroughs* [2004] EWCA Civ 1281, [2004] I.R.L.R. 979 (CA (Civ Div)), Pill, L.J.; see *Preston v Wolverhampton Healthcare NHS Trust (No.3)* [2004] I.C.R. 993 (EAT), Judge J McMullen Q.C.

s.2, amended: SI 2003/1656 Reg.3

s.2, applied: 2002 c.22 Sch.3, Sch.4, Sch.5, SI 2004/1861 Sch.1 para.22

s.2A, amended: SI 2004/2352 Reg.2

s.2A, applied: SI 2004/1861 Reg.20, SI 2004/2352 Reg.1

s.2ZA, added: SI 2003/1656 Reg.4

s.2ZB, added: SI 2003/1656 Reg.5

s.2ZC, added: SI 2003/1656 Reg.5

s.7A, amended: SI 2003/1656 Reg.6

s.7AA, added: SI 2003/1656 Reg.7

s.7AB, added: SI 2003/1656 Reg.8

s.7AC, added: SI 2003/1656 Reg.8

s.7B, added: 2002 c.22 s.42

s.7B, applied: SI 2003/722 Art.3, Art.4

s.7B, referred to: SI 2003/722 Art.2, SI 2004/752 Reg.14

s.7B, enabling: SI 2003/722

s.11, amended: SI 2003/1656 Reg.9

42. Local Authority Social Services Act 1970

applied: 2002 c.38 s.3, 2004 c.31 s.18

referred to: 2002 c.38 Sch.3 para.12

s.2, repealed (in part): 2004 c.14 Sch.1 Part 10, 2004 c.31 s.55, Sch.5 Part 4

s.3, repealed: 2004 c.31 s.55, Sch.5 Part 4

s.3A, repealed: 2004 c.31 s.55, Sch.5 Part 4

s.4, repealed: 2004 c.31 s.55, Sch.5 Part 4

s.5, repealed: 2004 c.31 s.55, Sch.5 Part 4

s.6, amended: 2004 c.31 Sch.2 para.2

s.6, repealed (in part): 2004 c.14 Sch.1 Part 10

CAP.

1970–cont.

42. Local Authority Social Services Act 1970–*cont.*

s.7, see *A Local Authority (Inquiry: Restraint on Publication), Re* [2003] EWHC 2746, [2004] Fam. 96 (Fam Div), Dame Elizabeth Butler-Sloss (President); see *C (Adoption: Religious Observance), Re* [2002] 1 F.L.R. 1119 (QBD (Admin Ct)), Wilson, J.; see *F v Lambeth LBC* [2002] 1 F.L.R. 217 (Fam Div), Munby, J.

s.7, applied: 2003 c.43 s.79, s.80

s.7B, repealed: 2003 c.43 Sch.14 Part 2

s.7D, amended: 2002 c.38 Sch.3 para.13

s.14, repealed (in part): 2004 c.14 Sch.1 Part 10

s.15, repealed (in part): 2004 c.14 Sch.1 Part 10

Sch.1, amended: 2002 c.38 Sch.3 para.14, Sch.5, SI 2002/2469 Sch.1 para.6, 2003 c.5 s.13, 2003 c.43 Sch.9 para.4, 2004 c.14 Sch.1 Part 10, 2004 c.15 s.4, 2004 c.31 s.56, Sch.2 para.2

Sch.1, disapplied: SI 2003/1716 Art.2

Sch.1, referred to: 2004 c.31 s.45

Sch.1, substituted: 2004 c.31 s.55

44. Chronically Sick and Disabled Persons Act 1970

s.1, referred to: SSI 2002/533 Sch.1, Sch.3

s.2, see *R. (on the application of Spink) v Wandsworth LBC* [2004] EWHC 2314, [2004] 3 F.C.R. 471 (QBD (Admin)), Richards, J.

s.2, referred to: SSI 2002/533 Sch.1, Sch.3

s.6, amended: 2003 asp 8 Sch.6 para.5

s.17, referred to: SI 2002/2375 Sch.1 Part 2

s.21, amended: 2004 c.18 s.94

s.21, applied: 2004 c.18 s.79

s.21, referred to: SSI 2002/450

s.21, enabling: SSI 2002/451, SSI 2002/547

s.23, repealed (in part): 2004 c.32 Sch.3

46. Radiological Protection Act 1970

repealed: 2004 c.17 Sch.3 para.2, Sch.4

s.1, applied: SI 2002/1093 Reg.68, SI 2004/905 Reg.9

50. Fiji Independence Act 1970

Sch.2 para.10, repealed: 2002 c.39 Sch.3

69. New Forest Act 1970

applied: SI 2002/2626 Art.6

s.2, amended: SI 2002/2626 Sch.2 para.6

999. Land Registration Act (Northern Ireland) 1970

Sch.11, added: SI 2003/412 Sch.4 para.1

Sch.11, substituted: SI 2003/412 Sch.4 para.1

1971

xlvii. Humber Bridge Act 1971

see *R. (on the application of Confederation of Passenger Transport UK) v Humber Bridge Board* [2002] EWHC 2261, [2002] N.P.C. 136 (QBD (Admin Ct)), Newman, J.

CAP.

1971–cont.

xiv. Ipswich Dock Act 1971

s.78, applied: SI 2002/3269 Art.8

s.80, repealed: SI 2002/3269 Art.9

s.81, repealed: SI 2002/3269 Art.9

xl. London Transport Act 1971

varied: SI 2003/1615 Sch.2 para.2

s.26, amended: SI 2003/1615 Sch.1 para.30

s.27, amended: SI 2003/1615 Sch.1 para.30

lxii. London Transport (No.2) Act 1971

varied: SI 2003/1615 Sch.2 para.3

vi. National Trust Act 1971

s.7, repealed (in part): 2004 c.14 Sch.1 Part 17

s.8, repealed (in part): 2004 c.14 Sch.1 Part 17

s.12, repealed (in part): 2004 c.14 Sch.1 Part 17

s.28, repealed: 2004 c.14 Sch.1 Part 17

s.32, repealed: 2004 c.14 Sch.1 Part 17

s.34, repealed: 2004 c.14 Sch.1 Part 17

lx. Torbay Corporation (No.2) Act 1971

s.61, varied: SI 2003/2155 Sch.1 para.16

7. Leasehold (Enlargement and Extension) Act (Northern Ireland) 1971

s.33, varied: SR 2003/73 Sch.1

10. Vehicles (Excise) Act 1971

applied: SI 2002/2742 Reg.46, Sch.2 para.4

11. Atomic Energy Authority Act 1971

s.4, amended: 2004 c.20 Sch.23 Part 1

s.4, repealed (in part): 2004 c.20 Sch.23 Part 1

s.5, amended: 2004 c.14 Sch.1 Part 16

s.5, repealed (in part): 2004 c.14 Sch.1 Part 16

s.6, amended: 2004 c.14 Sch.1 Part 16

s.7, repealed: 2004 c.14 Sch.1 Part 16

s.8, amended: 2004 c.14 Sch.1 Part 16

s.8, repealed (in part): 2004 c.14 Sch.1 Part 16

s.9, repealed (in part): 2004 c.14 Sch.1 Part 16

s.11, amended: 2004 c.20 s.197

s.11, repealed (in part): 2004 c.14 Sch.1 Part 16, 2004 c.20 Sch.23 Part 1

s.12, amended: 2004 c.20 s.197

s.17, repealed (in part): 2004 c.14 Sch.1 Part 16

s.19, applied: SI 2003/403 Reg.22, SI 2003/2310 Art.2, SI 2003/2311 Art.2, SI 2003/2312 Art.2

s.19, repealed: 2004 c.20 Sch.23 Part 1

s.19, enabling: SI 2003/2310, SI 2003/2311, SI 2003/2312

s.20, repealed (in part): 2004 c.20 Sch.23 Part 1

s.24, amended: 2004 c.14 Sch.1 Part 16

19. Carriage of Goods by Sea Act 1971

see *JI MacWilliam Co Inc v Mediterranean Shipping Co SA (The Rafaela S)* [2003] EWCA Civ 556, [2004] Q.B. 702 (CA), Rix, L.J.

s.4, enabling: SI 2002/3147

22. Animals Act 1971

s.2, see *Mirvahedy v Henley* [2001] EWCA Civ 1749, [2002] Q.B. 769 (CA), Hale, L.J.; see *Mirvahedy v Henley* [2003]

1971–cont.

22. Animals Act 1971–*cont.*

s.2–*cont.*

UKHL 16, [2003] 2 A.C. 491 (HL), Lord Nicholls of Birkenhead

23. Courts Act 1971

Part IV, applied: SI 2003/1887 Sch.1

s.20, repealed (in part): 2004 c.14 Sch.1 Part 1

s.27, amended: SI 2003/1887 Sch.2 para.2

s.27, applied: 2003 c.39 Sch.9 para.2

s.27, repealed: 2003 c.39 Sch.8 para.139, Sch.10

s.28, amended: SI 2002/2626 Sch.2 para.7, SI 2003/1887 Sch.2 para.2

s.28, applied: SI 2003/1887 Art.7

s.28, repealed: 2003 c.39 Sch.8 para.139, Sch.10

s.29, amended: SI 2003/1887 Sch.2 para.2

s.30, amended: SI 2003/1887 Sch.2 para.2

s.41, repealed: 2004 c.14 Sch.1 Part 1

s.42, repealed (in part): 2004 c.14 Sch.1 Part 1

s.43, repealed: 2004 c.14 Sch.1 Part 1

s.52, amended: 2003 c.39 Sch.8 para.140

s.53, repealed: 2004 c.14 Sch.1 Part 1

s.55, repealed (in part): 2004 c.14 Sch.1 Part 1

s.59, amended: 2004 c.14 Sch.1 Part 1

s.59, repealed (in part): 2004 c.14 Sch.1 Part 1

Sch.2 Part I para.1, repealed: 2004 c.14 Sch.1 Part 1

Sch.2 Part I para.3, amended: 2004 c.14 Sch.1 Part 1

Sch.2 Part II para.8, repealed: 2004 c.14 Sch.1 Part 1

Sch.3 para.1, repealed: 2003 c.39 Sch.8 para.139, Sch.10

Sch.3 para.2, amended: SI 2003/1887 Sch.2 para.2

Sch.3 para.2, repealed: 2003 c.39 Sch.8 para.139, Sch.10

Sch.3 para.3, repealed: 2003 c.39 Sch.8 para.139, Sch.10

Sch.3 para.4, repealed: 2003 c.39 Sch.8 para.139, Sch.10

Sch.3 para.5, amended: SI 2003/1887 Sch.2 para.2

Sch.3 para.5, repealed: 2003 c.39 Sch.8 para.139, Sch.10

Sch.3 para.6, repealed: 2003 c.39 Sch.8 para.139, Sch.10

Sch.3 para.7, repealed: 2003 c.39 Sch.8 para.139, Sch.10

Sch.3 para.8, repealed: 2003 c.39 Sch.8 para.139, Sch.10

Sch.3 para.9, repealed: 2003 c.39 Sch.8 para.139, Sch.10

Sch.3 para.10, repealed: 2003 c.39 Sch.8 para.139, Sch.10

Sch.3 para.11, repealed: 2003 c.39 Sch.8 para.139, Sch.10

Sch.3 para.12, repealed: 2003 c.39 Sch.8 para.139, Sch.10

1971–cont.

23. Courts Act 1971–*cont.*

Sch.5 Part I para.1, repealed: 2004 c.14 Sch.1 Part 1

Sch.5 Part I para.2, repealed: 2004 c.14 Sch.1 Part 1

Sch.5 Part I para.3, repealed: 2004 c.14 Sch.1 Part 1

Sch.5 Part I para.4, repealed: 2004 c.14 Sch.1 Part 1

Sch.5 Part I para.5, repealed: 2004 c.14 Sch.1 Part 1

Sch.5 Part II para.6, repealed: 2004 c.14 Sch.1 Part 1

Sch.5 Part II para.7, repealed: 2004 c.14 Sch.1 Part 1

Sch.5 Part II para.8, repealed: 2004 c.14 Sch.1 Part 1

Sch.5 Part II para.9, repealed: 2004 c.14 Sch.1 Part 1

Sch.5 Part III para.10, repealed: 2004 c.14 Sch.1 Part 1

Sch.5 Part III para.11, repealed: 2004 c.14 Sch.1 Part 1

Sch.5 Part III para.12, repealed: 2004 c.14 Sch.1 Part 1

Sch.5 Part III para.13, repealed: 2004 c.14 Sch.1 Part 1

Sch.5 Part III para.14, repealed: 2004 c.14 Sch.1 Part 1

Sch.6 para.7, repealed: 2003 c.17 Sch.7

Sch.6 para.13, repealed: 2003 c.17 Sch.7

Sch.7 para.4, repealed: 2004 c.14 Sch.1 Part 1

Sch.7 para.5, repealed: 2004 c.14 Sch.1 Part 1

Sch.8 Part II para.14, repealed: 2004 c.14 Sch.1 Part 1

Sch.8 Part II para.17, repealed: 2003 c.39 Sch.10

Sch.8 Part II para.42, repealed: 2003 c.17 Sch.7

Sch.8 Part II para.48, amended: 2003 c.44 Sch.37 Part 2

Sch.8 Part II para.49, repealed: 2003 c.39 Sch.10

Sch.8 Part II para.55, repealed: 2004 c.14 Sch.1 Part 1

Sch.8 Part II para.59, repealed: 2004 c.14 Sch.1 Part 1

Sch.8 Part II para.60, repealed (in part): 2004 c.14 Sch.1 Part 1

Sch.9 Part I, amended: 2003 c.17 Sch.7, 2004 c.14 Sch.1 Part 1

Sch.10 Part I para.1, repealed (in part): 2004 c.14 Sch.1 Part 1

Sch.10 Part I para.2, repealed: 2004 c.14 Sch.1 Part 1

Sch.10 Part I para.3, repealed: 2004 c.14 Sch.1 Part 1

Sch.10 Part I para.4, repealed: 2004 c.14 Sch.1 Part 1

Sch.10 Part II para.5, repealed: 2004 c.14 Sch.1 Part 1

CAP.

1971—cont.

23. Courts Act 1971—*cont.*
Sch.10 Part II para.6, repealed: 2004 c.14
Sch.1 Part 1
Sch.10 Part IV para.10, repealed: 2004 c.14
Sch.1 Part 1
Sch.10 Part IV para.17, repealed: 2004 c.14
Sch.1 Part 1

27. Powers of Attorney Act 1971
s.3, applied: SI 2003/1417 r.61
s.8, repealed: 2004 c.14 Sch.1 Part 17
s.11, repealed (in part): 2004 c.14 Sch.1 Part 17

29. National Savings Bank Act 1971
s.2, enabling: SI 2003/2895
s.3, amended: 2003 c.14 s.208
s.3, applied: SI 2003/2895
s.4, applied: SI 2003/2895
s.6, amended: 2003 c.14 s.208
s.6, applied: SI 2003/2895
s.7, applied: SI 2003/2895
s.8, amended: 2003 c.14 s.208
s.8, applied: SI 2003/2895
s.9, applied: SI 2003/2895
s.9A, added: 2003 c.14 s.208

30. Unsolicited Goods and Services Act 1971
applied: 2002 c.40 Sch.15
s.3, see *Supporting Link Alliance Ltd, Re* [2004] EWHC 523, [2004] 1 W.L.R. 1549 (Ch D), Sir Andrew Morritt V.C.
s.3A, applied: SI 2004/2095 Reg.15

32. Attachment of Earnings Act 1971
applied: SI 2004/176 Reg.4
referred to: SI 2004/176 Reg.12
s.1, varied: SI 2004/176 Reg.4
s.3, amended: 2003 c.39 Sch.8 para.141
s.3, repealed (in part): SI 2004/176 Reg.4
s.4, applied: 2004 c.14 Sch.2 para.9
s.4, varied: 2004 c.14 Sch.2 para.10
s.6, amended: 2003 c.39 Sch.8 para.142
s.6, varied: SI 2004/176 Reg.4
s.6, enabling: SI 2003/1236
s.7, varied: SI 2004/176 Reg.4
s.8, varied: SI 2004/176 Reg.4
s.9, disapplied: SI 2004/176 Reg.4
s.9, varied: SI 2004/176 Reg.4
s.12, varied: SI 2004/176 Reg.4
s.12, enabling: SI 2003/1236
s.14, varied: SI 2004/176 Reg.4
s.15, varied: SI 2004/176 Reg.4
s.17, varied: SI 2004/176 Reg.4
s.18, amended: 2003 c.39 Sch.8 para.143
s.21, amended: 2003 c.39 Sch.8 para.144
s.23, applied: SI 2004/3114 Sch.1
s.24, amended: 2002 c.21 Sch.3 para.1
s.25, amended: 2003 c.39 Sch.10
s.25, varied: SI 2004/176 Reg.4
Sch.1 para.15, added: 2004 c.33 Sch.27 para.35
Sch.1 para.16, added: 2004 c.33 Sch.27 para.35

CAP.

1971—cont.

32. Attachment of Earnings Act 1971—*cont.*
Sch.3 Part I para.1, varied: SI 2004/176 Reg.4
Sch.3 Part I para.2, varied: SI 2004/176 Reg.4
Sch.3 Part I para.3, varied: SI 2004/176 Reg.4
Sch.3 Part I para.4, varied: SI 2004/176 Reg.4
Sch.3 Part I para.5, varied: SI 2004/176 Reg.4
Sch.3 Part I para.6, varied: SI 2004/176 Reg.4

33. Armed Forces Act 1971
Sch.2 para.1, repealed (in part): 2003 c.39 Sch.10

36. Civil Evidence Act (Northern Ireland) 1971
s.7, applied: 2002 c.40 s.228

37. Welsh National Opera Company Act 1971
repealed: 2004 c.14 Sch.1 Part 10

38. Misuse of Drugs Act 1971
see *Attorney General's Reference (No.90 of 2001), Re* [2002] EWCA Crim 3173, [2003] 2 Cr. App. R. (S.) 33 (CA (Crim Div)), Kennedy, L.J.; see *Haney v HM Advocate (No.1)* 2003 J.C. 43 (HCJ), Lord Gill L.J.C., Lord Maclean, Lord McCluskey; see *Haney v HM Advocate (No.2)* 2003 J.C. 46 (HCJ), Lord Gill L.J.C., Lord MacLean, Lord McCluskey; see *McFarlane v Gilchrist* 2002 S.L.T. 521 (HCJ Appeal), Lord Coulsfield, Lord Carloway, Lord Wheatley; see *R. v Dias (Fernando Augusto)* [2001] EWCA Crim 2986, [2002] 2 Cr. App. R. 5 (CA (Crim Div)), Keene, L.J.; see *R. v Taylor (Paul Simon)* [2001] EWCA Crim 2263, [2002] 1 Cr. App. R. 37 (CA (Crim Div)), Rose, L.J.; see *Rimmer (Roy William) v HM Advocate* 2002 S.C.C.R. 22 (HCJ Appeal), Lord Roger L.J.G., Lord Clarke, Lord Sutherland
applied: SI 2002/1689 Reg.3, SI 2004/291 Sch.6 para.39, Sch.6 para.42, Sch.6 para.43, SI 2004/478 Sch.6 para.39, Sch.6 para.42, Sch.6 para.43, SI 2004/627 Sch.5 para.38, Sch.5 para.41, Sch.5 para.42, SR 2002/1 Reg.22, SR 2002/301 Reg.3, 2003 c.38 s.11, SSI 2003/64 Sch.1 para.9, SSI 2004/115 Sch.5 para.39, Sch.5 para.41, SSI 2004/116 Sch.1 para.11, Sch.1 para.13
referred to: SSI 2004/116 Sch.1 para.13
s.1, applied: 2003 c.38 s.11
s.2, applied: 2003 c.38 s.11
s.2, referred to: 2003 c.44 Sch.4 para.19, Sch.4 para.20, Sch.4 para.21, Sch.4 para.22, Sch.4 para.23, Sch.5 para.18, Sch.5 para.19, Sch.5 para.20, Sch.5 para.21, Sch.5 para.39, Sch.5 para.40, Sch.5 para.41, Sch.5 para.42, SI 2004/1500 Sch.2 para.11, Sch.2 para.12, Sch.2 para.13, Sch.2 para.14, Sch.2 para.15
s.2, enabling: SI 2003/1243, SI 2003/3201
s.3, applied: 2002 c.29 Sch.2 para.1, Sch.4 para.2, Sch.5 para.1, SR 2002/1 Reg.4

1971–cont.

38. Misuse of Drugs Act 1971–*cont.*

s.3, disapplied: SR 2002/1 Reg.4

s.4, see *Clark (James Michael) v HM Advocate* 2002 S.C.C.R. 675 (HCJ Appeal), Lord Coulsfield, Lord Hamilton, Lord McCluskey; see *HM Advocate v McIntosh (Robert) (No.2)* 2002 S.C.C.R. 287 (HCJ), Lord Eassie; see *HM Advocate v Urquhart (Robert David)* 2002 S.L.T. 1143 (HCJ), Lord Mackay of Drumadoon; see *Lennox (John Adam) v HM Advocate* 2002 S.C.C.R. 954 (HCJ), Lord Cullen L.J.G., Lord Marnoch, Lord Weir; see *Smith (Stephen) v HM Advocate* 2002 S.C.C.R. 1059 (HCJ), Lord Cullen L.J.G., Lord Cameron of Lochbroom, Lord Marnoch

s.4, applied: 2002 c.29 Sch.2 para.1, Sch.4 para.2, Sch.5 para.1, SI 2002/896 Sch.1 para.39, 2003 c.17 s.97, 2003 c.44 Sch.4 para.23, SI 2004/1500 Sch.2 para.14, Sch.2 para.15, SI 2004/1910 Sch.1, SR 2002/1 Reg.5, Reg.6, 2003 c.17 Sch.4 para.7, 2003 c.44 Sch.4 para.22, Sch.5 para.21, Sch.5 para.42

s.4, disapplied: SI 2002/1689 Reg.3, SR 2002/1 Reg.4, Reg.6, Reg.8, Reg.9, Reg.11

s.4, referred to: SR 2002/301 Reg.3

s.5, see *Attorney General for Northern Ireland's Reference (No.11 of 2003), Re* [2004] N.I. 144 (CA (Crim Div) (NI)), Lord Carswell L.C.J.; see *Lochridge v Miller (Procurator Fiscal)* 2002 S.L.T. 906 (HCJ Appeal), Lord Coulsfield, Lord MacLean, Lord Sutherland; see *R. v Lambert (Steven)* [2001] UKHL 37, [2002] 2 A.C. 545 (HL), Lord Slynn of Hadley; see *R. v Lambert (Steven)* [2002] Q.B. 1112 (CA (Crim Div)), Lord Woolf of Barnes, L.C.J.; see *R. v Murphy (Andrew)* [2002] EWCA Crim 1587, [2003] 1 W.L.R. 422 (CA (Crim Div)), Longmore, L.J.

s.5, applied: 2002 c.29 Sch.2 para.1, Sch.4 para.2, Sch.5 para.1, SI 2004/1910 Sch.1, SR 2002/1 Reg.5, Reg.6, 2003 c.17 Sch.4 para.7, 2003 c.38 s.11

s.5, disapplied: SR 2002/1 Reg.4, Reg.6, Reg.10, Reg.11

s.6, applied: 2003 c.38 s.11

s.6, disapplied: SR 2002/1 Reg.12

s.7, applied: SI 2002/1689 Reg.3, SI 2003/2429, SR 2002/301 Reg.3

s.7, enabling: SI 2003/2429, SR 2002/1, SR 2003/314, SR 2003/324

s.8, see *R. v Auguste (Paul David)* [2003] EWCA Crim 3929, [2004] 1 W.L.R. 917 (CA (Crim Div)), Kay, L.J.

s.8, applied: 2002 c.29 Sch.2 para.1, Sch.4 para.2, Sch.5 para.1, 2003 c.17 Sch.4 para.7, SI 2004/1910 Sch.1

s.8, disapplied: SR 2002/1 Reg.13

s.9, applied: SI 2004/1910 Sch.1

s.10, applied: SI 2003/1653, SI 2003/2429

1971–cont.

38. Misuse of Drugs Act 1971–*cont.*

s.10, enabling: SI 2003/1432, SI 2003/1653, SI 2003/2429, SR 2002/1, SR 2003/314, SR 2003/324

s.20, see *R. v P (Telephone Intercepts: Admissibility of Evidence)* [2002] 1 A.C. 146 (HL), Lord Hobhouse of Woodborough

s.20, applied: 2002 c.29 Sch.2 para.1, Sch.4 para.2, Sch.5 para.1, SI 2004/1910 Sch.1

s.21, amended: 2002 c.29 Sch.12

s.22, applied: SI 2003/1653, SI 2003/2429

s.22, enabling: SI 2003/1653, SI 2003/2429, SR 2002/1, SR 2003/324

s.23, see *Graham v Higson* 2002 S.L.T. 1382 (HCJ), Lord Cameron of Lochbroom, Lord Caplan, Lord Marnoch; see *Hepburn v Chief Constable of Thames Valley* [2002] EWCA Civ 1841, Times, December 19, 2002 (CA), Sedley, L.J.; see *Jeffrey v Higson* 2003 S.L.T. 1053 (HCJ), Temporary Judge CGB Nicholson Q.C., Lord Osborne, Lady Paton; see *Knaup v Hutchison* 2003 S.L.T. 1264 (HCJ), Lord Kirkwood, Lord Abernethy, Temporary Judge EF Bowen Q.C.; see *R. (on the application of Cronin) v Sheffield Justices* [2002] EWHC 2568, [2003] 1 W.L.R. 752 (QBD (Admin Ct)), Lord Woolf of Barnes, L.C.J.

s.23, amended: 2002 c.29 Sch.12

s.27, amended: 2002 c.29 Sch.11 para.5

s.27, applied: 2002 c.29 s.13, s.82, s.97, s.148, s.163, s.230, SI 2003/336 Sch.1 Part 2

s.28, see *R. v Lambert (Steven)* [2001] UKHL 37, [2002] 2 A.C. 545 (HL), Lord Slynn of Hadley; see *R. v Lambert (Steven)* [2002] Q.B. 1112 (CA (Crim Div)), Lord Woolf of Barnes, L.C.J.

s.30, enabling: SI 2003/611

s.31, applied: SI 2003/611, SI 2003/1653, SI 2003/2429, SR 2002/1, SR 2003/314, SR 2003/324

s.31, enabling: SI 2003/611, SI 2003/1432, SI 2003/1653, SI 2003/2429, SR 2002/1, SR 2003/314, SR 2003/324

s.37, amended: 2004 c.14 Sch.1 Part 17

s.37, repealed (in part): 2004 c.14 Sch.1 Part 17

s.37, enabling: SI 2003/611

s.38, applied: SR 2003/314, SR 2003/324

s.38, referred to: SR 2002/1

s.40, repealed (in part): 2004 c.14 Sch.1 Part 17

Sch.2 Part I para.1, amended: SI 2003/1243 Art.2, SI 2003/3201 Art.2

Sch.2 Part II para.1, amended: SI 2003/3201 Art.2

Sch.2 Part III para.1, amended: SI 2003/1243 Art.2, SI 2003/3201 Art.2

Sch.4, amended: 2003 c.44 Sch.28 para.1

40. Fire Precautions Act 1971

s.1, amended: 2004 c.21 Sch.1 para.28

1971–cont.

40. Fire Precautions Act 1971–cont.

s.3, amended: 2004 c.21 Sch.1 para.28

s.4, amended: 2004 c.21 Sch.1 para.28

s.5, see *City Logistics Ltd v Northamptonshire County Fire Officer* [2001] EWCA Civ 1216, [2002] 1 W.L.R. 1124 (CA), Kennedy, L.J.

s.5, amended: 2004 c.21 Sch.1 para.28

s.5A, amended: 2004 c.21 Sch.1 para.28

s.5B, amended: 2004 c.21 Sch.1 para.28

s.6, amended: 2004 c.21 Sch.1 para.28

s.8, amended: 2004 c.21 Sch.1 para.28

s.8A, amended: 2004 c.21 Sch.1 para.28

s.8B, amended: 2004 c.21 Sch.1 para.28

s.9, amended: 2004 c.21 Sch.1 para.28

s.9A, amended: 2004 c.21 Sch.1 para.28

s.9D, amended: 2004 c.21 Sch.1 para.28

s.10, amended: 2004 c.21 Sch.1 para.28

s.12, amended: 2004 c.21 Sch.1 para.28

s.13, see *City Logistics Ltd v Northamptonshire County Fire Officer* [2001] EWCA Civ 1216, [2002] 1 W.L.R. 1124 (CA), Kennedy, L.J.

s.13, amended: 2004 c.21 Sch.1 para.28

s.16, amended: 2004 c.21 Sch.1 para.28

s.17, amended: 2003 asp 8 Sch.6 para.6, 2004 c.21 Sch.1 para.28

s.18, amended: 2004 c.21 Sch.1 para.28

s.20, amended: 2004 c.21 Sch.1 para.29

s.27, amended: 2004 c.21 Sch.1 para.28

s.27A, amended: 2004 c.21 Sch.1 para.28

s.29, repealed (in part): 2004 c.21 Sch.2

s.33, repealed: 2004 c.14 Sch.1 Part 13

s.34, repealed: 2004 c.14 Sch.1 Part 13

s.40, amended: 2004 c.21 Sch.1 para.31

s.41, amended: 2004 c.21 Sch.1 para.32

s.43, amended: 2003 c.39 Sch.8 para.146, Sch.10, 2004 c.21 Sch.1 para.33

Sch.1 Part III para.1, repealed: 2004 c.14 Sch.1 Part 13

Sch.1 Part III para.2, repealed: 2004 c.14 Sch.1 Part 13

Sch.1 Part III para.3, repealed: 2004 c.14 Sch.1 Part 13

Sch.1 Part III para.4, repealed: 2004 c.14 Sch.1 Part 13

Sch.1 Part III para.5, repealed: 2004 c.14 Sch.1 Part 13

Sch.1 Part IV para.1, repealed: 2004 c.14 Sch.1 Part 13

Sch.1 Part IV para.2, repealed: 2004 c.14 Sch.1 Part 13

Sch.1 Part IV para.3, repealed: 2004 c.14 Sch.1 Part 13

Sch.1 Part IV para.4, repealed: 2004 c.14 Sch.1 Part 13

Sch.1 Part IV para.5, repealed: 2004 c.14 Sch.1 Part 13

Sch.1 Part IV para.6, repealed: 2004 c.14 Sch.1 Part 13

Sch.2 Part II para.3, amended: 2004 c.21 Sch.1 para.28

1971–cont.

41. Highways Act 1971

s.1, applied: 2004 c.5 s.32, s.73

s.10, applied: 2004 c.5 s.32, s.73

48. Criminal Damage Act 1971

s.1, see *R. v Cakmak (Kenan)* [2002] EWCA Crim 500, [2002] 2 Cr. App. R. 10 (CA (Crim Div)), Aikens, J.; see *R. v G* [2002] EWCA Crim 1992, [2003] 3 All E.R. 206 (CA (Crim Div)), Dyson, L.J.; see *R. v G* [2003] UKHL 50, [2004] 1 A.C. 1034 (HL), Lord Bingham of Cornhill

s.1, applied: SI 2002/1837 Sch.1 Part I, 2003 c.42 Sch.5 para.36, Sch.5 para.37, 2003 c.44 Sch.4 para.25, Sch.5 para.22, Sch.15 para.35, Sch.15 para.36, SI 2004/1910 Sch.2

s.2, see *R. v Cakmak (Kenan)* [2002] EWCA Crim 500, [2002] 2 Cr. App. R. 10 (CA (Crim Div)), Aikens, J.

s.2, applied: SI 2004/1910 Sch.2

s.3, applied: SI 2004/1910 Sch.2

s.5, see *R. v Jones (Margaret)* [2004] EWCA Crim 1981, [2004] 3 W.L.R. 1362 (CA (Crim Div)), Latham, L.J.; see *R. v Kelleher (Paul)* [2003] EWCA Crim 3525, (2003) 147 S.J.L.B. 1395 (CA (Crim Div)), Mantell, L.J.; see *R. v Mitchell (Carl)* [2003] EWCA Crim 2188, [2004] R.T.R. 14 (CA (Crim Div)), Tuckey, L.J.

s.9, amended: 2004 c.33 Sch.27 para.36

54. Land Registration and Land Charges Act 1971

repealed: 2002 c.9 Sch.13

s.4, enabling: SI 2002/2539

56. Pensions (Increase) Act 1971

applied: 2003 c.1 s.629, s.643, SI 2003/973 Art.9, SI 2004/558 Reg.3, SI 2004/1711 Reg.3

varied: SI 2003/2623 Reg.3

s.1, applied: SI 2003/681 Art.3, Art.4, SI 2004/758 Art.3, Art.4

s.5, enabling: SI 2003/2623, SI 2004/558, SI 2004/1711

s.8, referred to: SI 2002/699 Art.2

s.15, repealed (in part): 2004 c.21 Sch.2

Sch.2 Part I, referred to: SI 2003/2623 Reg.3

Sch.2 Part I para.3, amended: 2004 c.14 Sch.1 Part 11

Sch.2 Part I para.15, amended: 2002 c.1 Sch.3 para.4

Sch.2 Part I para.16, applied: SI 2004/2306 Sch.1

Sch.2 Part I para.16, substituted: 2004 c.21 Sch.1 para.35

Sch.2 Part I para.16, varied: SI 2004/2918 Sch.1

Sch.2 Part I para.16A, applied: SI 2004/2306 Sch.1

Sch.2 Part I para.16A, substituted: 2004 c.21 Sch.1 para.35

CAP.

1971-cont.

56. Pensions (Increase) Act 1971-*cont.*
Sch.2 Part I para.16A, varied: SI 2004/2918 Sch.1

Sch.2 Part I para.28, repealed: 2004 c.14 Sch.1 Part 11

Sch.2 Part II, referred to: SI 2004/558 Reg.3

Sch.2 Part II para.44, applied: SI 2004/2306 Sch.1

Sch.2 Part II para.44, substituted: 2004 c.21 Sch.1 para.35

Sch.2 Part II para.44, varied: SI 2004/2918 Sch.1

Sch.2 Part II para.45, repealed (in part): 2004 c.21 Sch.2

Sch.3 para.6, amended: 2004 c.21 Sch.1 para.36

58. Sheriff Courts (Scotland) Act 1971
applied: SSI 2002/132 Sch.1 para.32.1

s.32, amended: 2002 asp 17 s.43, 2004 asp 3 s.14

s.32, applied: 2002 c.29 s.155, s.386, s.403, s.408, SSI 2002/516, SSI 2002/563, SSI 2003/25, SSI 2003/26, SSI 2003/27, SSI 2003/319, SSI 2003/388

s.32, enabling: SSI 2002/7, SSI 2002/128, SSI 2002/129, SSI 2002/130, SSI 2002/132, SSI 2002/133, SSI 2002/146, SSI 2002/516, SSI 2002/560, SSI 2002/563, SSI 2003/25, SSI 2003/26, SSI 2003/27, SSI 2003/44, SSI 2003/98, SSI 2003/261, SSI 2003/319, SSI 2003/346, SSI 2003/388, SSI 2003/556, SSI 2003/601, SSI 2004/197, SSI 2004/222, SSI 2004/334, SSI 2004/350, SSI 2004/455, SSI 2004/505, SSI 2004/534

s.34, applied: SSI 2002/7, SSI 2002/128, SSI 2002/129, SSI 2002/130, SSI 2002/132, SSI 2002/133, SSI 2002/146, SSI 2002/560, SSI 2002/563, SSI 2003/25, SSI 2003/26, SSI 2003/27, SSI 2003/44, SSI 2003/98, SSI 2003/261, SSI 2003/319, SSI 2003/346, SSI 2003/388, SSI 2003/601, SSI 2004/197, SSI 2004/222, SSI 2004/334, SSI 2004/350, SSI 2004/455, SSI 2004/505

s.34, referred to: SSI 2003/556

s.35, see *Hoy Trust v Thomson* 2003 S.L.T. (Sh Ct) 20 (Sh Pr), Sir SST Young Q.C., Sheriff Principal

s.36B, applied: SSI 2002/133 Sch.1 para.19.1

s.37, see *Donnelly v Safeway Stores Plc* 2003 S.C. 236 (1 Div), Lord Marnoch, Lord Caplan, Lord Cullen L.P.; see *Gallagher v Birse* 2003 S.C.L.R. 623 (Sh Ct (Tayside, Central and Fife)), Sheriff Richard Davidson

s.37, amended: 2003 asp 11 s.86

60. Prevention of Oil Pollution Act 1971
applied: SSI 2002/410 Art.57, 2004 c.20 s.188

61. Mineral Workings (Offshore Installations) Act 1971
applied: SR 2002/1 Reg.8

CAP.

1971-cont.

61. Mineral Workings (Offshore Installations) Act 1971-*cont.*
s.12, varied: SI 2002/2175 Reg.3

68. Finance Act 1971
Sch.3 Part I para.8, referred to: 2003 c.1 s.583, s.623

69. Medicines Act 1971
applied: SI 2002/794 Art.3, SI 2003/1076 Sch.1 para.1

s.1, amended: SI 2004/1031 Sch.10 para.20

s.1, applied: SI 2002/542

s.1, enabling: SI 2002/542, SI 2002/2569, SI 2003/625, SI 2003/2321, SI 2003/2957, SI 2004/666, SI 2004/2750, SI 2004/3081

72. Industrial Relations Act 1971
s.116, see *Dunnachie v Kingston upon Hull City Council* [2004] UKHL 36, [2004] 3 W.L.R. 310 (HL), Lord Nicholls of Birkenhead

77. Immigration Act 1971
see *A (Children) (Care Proceedings: Asylum Seekers), Re* [2003] EWHC 1086, [2003] 2 F.L.R. 921 (Fam Div), Munby, J.; see *R. (on the application of Saadi) v Secretary of State for the Home Department* [2002] UKHL 41, [2002] 1 W.L.R. 3131 (HL), Lord Slynn of Hadley; see *R. (on the application of Tum) v Secretary of State for the Home Department* [2004] EWCA Civ 788, [2004] 2 C.M.L.R. 48 (CA), Lord Woolf of Barnes, L.C.J.

applied: 2002 c.41 s.67, s.77, s.78, SI 2002/195 Reg.2, Sch.1 para.1, SI 2002/1330 Reg.13, Sch.3 para.1, SI 2002/1792 Reg.2, SI 2002/3200 Reg.2, Sch.1 para.1, 2003 c.31 s.6, 2003 c.32 s.48, SI 2003/612 Art.3, SI 2003/1185 Art.2, SI 2003/1994 Reg.13, Sch.3 para.1, SI 2003/2818 Art.11, Art.13, 2004 c.19 s.19, s.23, 2004 c.33 Sch.23 para.1, SI 2004/1219 Reg.2, Reg.6, Reg.7, SR 2002/224 Reg.2, Sch.1 para.1, SR 2002/265 Sch.1 para.2, Sch.7 para.1, SR 2003/28 Reg.2, SSI 2004/273 Sch.1 para.1

disapplied: 2003 c.32 s.48

referred to: 2002 c.38 s.74, SI 2003/754 Sch.2 para.2, SI 2003/1252 Art.1, SI 2003/2900 Art.1, Sch.1

Part II, applied: SI 2003/754 Sch.2 para.2, Sch.2 para.4

Part III, applied: 2004 c.19 s.2, s.35, SI 2004/1219 Reg.9

s.1, applied: 2002 c.41 s.130

s.2, applied: 2002 c.41 s.11, SI 2003/548 Sch.2 para.11, SI 2003/1875 Reg.8, 2004 c.6 s.2

s.3, see *Khalil v Secretary of State for the Home Department* 2002 S.L.T. 1039 (OH), Lord Carloway; see *M v Secretary of State for the Home Department* [2003] EWCA

1971–cont.

77. Immigration Act 1971 *–cont.*

s.3*–cont.*

Civ 146, [2003] 1 W.L.R. 1980 (CA), Laws, L.J.

s.3, amended: 2002 c.8 s.2, 2002 c.41 s.10, Sch.9

s.3, applied: 2002 c.41 s.10, s.130, 2003 c.44 s.259, SI 2003/754 Sch.2 para.2

s.3, referred to: SI 2003/2900 Sch.1

s.3A, applied: 2002 c.41 s.62

s.3A, referred to: SI 2003/1252 Sch.1, SI 2003/2900 Sch.1

s.3A, enabling: SI 2004/475

s.3B, referred to: SI 2003/1252 Sch.1, SI 2003/2900 Sch.1

s.3C, applied: SI 2003/754 Sch.2 para.2

s.3C, referred to: SI 2003/2900 Sch.1

s.3C, substituted: 2002 c.41 s.118

s.4, see *R. (on the application of Hashmi) v Secretary of State for the Home Department* [2001] EWHC Admin 908, [2002] Imm. A.R. 257 (QBD (Admin Ct)), Cresswell, J.; see *R. (on the application of Hashmi) v Secretary of State for the Home Department* [2002] EWCA Civ 728, [2002] I.N.L.R. 377 (CA), Sir Swinton Thomas

s.4, applied: SI 2003/658 Reg.6

s.4, varied: SI 2003/2818 Sch.2 para.1

s.5, see *AC v Immigration Appeal Tribunal* [2003] EWHC 389, [2003] I.N.L.R. 507 (QBD (Admin Ct)), Jack, J.

s.5, amended: 2004 c.33 Sch.27 para.37

s.5, applied: SI 2002/313 Sch.1, SI 2003/754 Sch.2 para.2, SI 2004/1219 Reg.6

s.7, amended: 2002 c.41 s.75, 2003 c.44 Sch.32 para.16

s.7, repealed (in part): 2002 c.41 Sch.9

s.8, applied: 2002 c.41 s.11

s.8, enabling: SI 2004/3171

s.8A, referred to: SI 2003/2900 Sch.1

s.8B, referred to: SI 2003/2900 Sch.1

s.8B, enabling: SI 2002/192, SI 2002/795, SI 2002/3018, SI 2003/236, SI 2003/3285, SI 2004/3316

s.9, applied: SI 2002/1832 Art.2

s.10, applied: SI 2002/1832

s.10, enabling: SI 2002/1832

s.11, see *Kaya v Haringey LBC* [2001] EWCA Civ 677, [2002] H.L.R. 1 (CA), Buxton, L.J.; see *R. (on the application of Tum) v Secretary of State for the Home Department* [2003] EWHC 2745, [2004] 1 C.M.L.R. 33 (QBD (Admin Ct)), Davis, J.

s.11, amended: 2002 c.41 s.62, SI 2003/1016 Sch.1 para.1

s.11, applied: 2002 c.41 s.11, 2004 c.19 s.2

s.13, applied: SI 2003/754 Sch.2 para.2

s.14, applied: SI 2003/754 Sch.2 para.2

s.15, applied: SI 2003/658 Reg.3, SI 2003/754 Sch.2 para.2

1971–cont.

77. Immigration Act 1971 *–cont.*

s.16, applied: SI 2003/754 Sch.2 para.2

s.17, applied: SI 2003/754 Sch.2 para.2

s.19, see *R. (on the application of Boafo) v Secretary of State for the Home Department* [2002] EWCA Civ 44, [2002] 1 W.L.R. 1919 (CA), Auld, L.J.

s.20, referred to: SI 2003/754 Sch.2 para.4

s.21, applied: SI 2003/754 Sch.2 para.2

s.24, see *Addey and Stanhope School Governing Body v Vakante* [2003] I.C.R. 290 (EAT), Judge Serota Q.C.; see *Vakante v Addey and Stanhope School* [2004] EWCA Civ 1065, [2004] 4 All E.R. 1056 (CA), Brooke, L.J.

s.24, amended: 2002 c.41 s.62

s.24, applied: 2002 c.41 s.129, s.134

s.24A, see *R. v Ali (Nasir)* [2001] EWCA Crim 2874, [2002] 2 Cr. App. R. (S.) 32 (CA (Crim Div)), May, L.J.

s.24A, applied: 2002 c.41 s.129, s.134

s.24A, referred to: SI 2003/2900 Sch.1

s.24A, repealed (in part): 2002 c.41 Sch.9

s.24A, varied: SI 2003/2818 Art.12

s.25, see *R. v Woop (Michael Thomas)* [2002] EWCA Crim 58, [2002] 2 Cr. App. R. (S.) 65 (CA (Crim Div)), Mitchell, J.

s.25, amended: 2002 c.8 s.2, 2004 c.19 s.1

s.25, applied: 2002 c.29 Sch.2 para.4, Sch.4 para.4, Sch.5 para.4, 2002 c.41 s.146, SI 2004/1910 Sch.1, SI 2004/2877 Art.2

s.25, referred to: SI 2003/2900 Sch.1

s.25, substituted: 2002 c.41 s.143

s.25, enabling: SI 2004/2877

s.25A, applied: 2002 c.29 Sch.2 para.4, Sch.5 para.4, SI 2004/1910 Sch.1

s.25A, referred to: SI 2003/2900 Sch.1

s.25A, substituted: 2002 c.41 s.144

s.25A, varied: SI 2003/2818 Art.12

s.25B, applied: 2002 c.29 Sch.2 para.4, Sch.5 para.4, SI 2004/1910 Sch.1

s.25B, varied: SI 2003/2818 Art.12

s.25C, amended: 2004 c.19 s.1, s.5

s.25C, applied: 2002 c.41 s.146

s.25C, substituted: 2004 c.19 s.5

s.25C, varied: 2004 c.19 s.5

s.25D, amended: 2002 c.41 s.144, 2003 c.39 Sch.8 para.147

s.25D, applied: 2002 c.41 s.146

s.25D, repealed (in part): 2002 c.41 Sch.9

s.25D, varied: 2004 c.19 s.5

s.26, amended: 2002 c.41 s.151, Sch.9

s.26, applied: 2002 c.41 s.129, s.134, SI 2003/2818 Art.3

s.26, referred to: SI 2003/2900 Sch.1

s.26, varied: SI 2003/2818 Art.12

s.26A, added: 2002 c.41 s.148

s.26B, added: 2002 c.41 s.149

s.27, varied: SI 2003/2818 Art.12

s.28, amended: 2002 c.41 Sch.9

CAP.

1971–cont.

77. Immigration Act 1971–*cont.*

s.28, applied: 2004 c.19 s.2, s.35, SI 2004/1219 Reg.9

s.28A, amended: 2002 c.41 s.144, s.150, Sch.9

s.28A, applied: SI 2003/2818 Art.13

s.28A, referred to: SI 2003/2900 Sch.1

s.28A, repealed (in part): 2002 c.41 Sch.9

s.28AA, added: 2002 c.41 s.152

s.28B, amended: 2002 c.41 s.144, s.150

s.28B, applied: 2004 c.19 s.2, s.35, SI 2004/1219 Reg.9

s.28B, referred to: SI 2003/2900 Sch.1

s.28C, amended: 2002 c.41 s.144

s.28C, referred to: SI 2003/2900 Sch.1

s.28C, varied: 2004 c.19 s.14

s.28CA, added: 2002 c.41 s.153

s.28D, amended: 2002 c.41 s.144, s.150

s.28D, applied: 2004 c.19 s.2, s.35, SI 2004/1219 Reg.9

s.28D, referred to: SI 2003/2900 Sch.1

s.28E, applied: 2004 c.19 s.2, s.35, SI 2004/1219 Reg.9

s.28E, referred to: SI 2003/2900 Sch.1

s.28E, varied: 2004 c.19 s.14

s.28F, amended: 2002 c.41 s.144

s.28F, referred to: SI 2003/2900 Sch.1

s.28F, varied: 2004 c.19 s.14

s.28FA, added: 2002 c.41 s.154

s.28FB, added: 2002 c.41 s.154

s.28FB, varied: SI 2002/2811 Art.6

s.28G, applied: 2004 c.19 s.2, s.35, SI 2004/1219 Reg.9

s.28G, referred to: SI 2003/2900 Sch.1

s.28G, varied: 2004 c.19 s.14

s.28H, applied: 2004 c.19 s.2, s.35, SI 2004/1219 Reg.9

s.28H, referred to: SI 2003/2900 Sch.1

s.28H, varied: 2004 c.19 s.14

s.28I, referred to: SI 2003/2900 Sch.1

s.28I, varied: 2004 c.19 s.14

s.28J, referred to: SI 2003/2900 Sch.1

s.28K, amended: 2003 c.39 Sch.8 para.148

s.28K, referred to: SI 2003/2900 Sch.1

s.28L, amended: 2002 c.29 Sch.11 para.6, 2002 c.41 s.155

s.28L, referred to: SI 2003/2900 Sch.1

s.28L, substituted: 2002 c.41 s.155

s.29, repealed: 2002 c.41 s.58, Sch.9

s.31, repealed (in part): 2002 c.41 s.58, Sch.9

s.31A, amended: 2002 c.41 s.121

s.31A, enabling: SI 2003/1712, SI 2004/581, SI 2004/2576

s.32, amended: 2002 c.41 s.158, 2004 c.19 s.44

s.33, amended: 2002 c.8 s.1, 2002 c.38 Sch.3 para.15, 2002 c.41 s.10, s.144, Sch.7 para.1

s.33, applied: 2002 c.41 s.10, s.130, 2003 c.44 s.259, SI 2003/918 Reg.4, 2004 c.6 s.2, 2004 c.19 s.13, SSI 2004/83 Reg.3

CAP.

1971–cont.

77. Immigration Act 1971–*cont.*

s.33, varied: SI 2003/2818 Sch.2 para.1

s.36, enabling: SI 2003/1252

Sch.2, see *R. (on the application of Nadarajah) v Secretary of State for the Home Department* [2003] EWCA Civ 1768, [2004] I.N.L.R. 139 (CA), Lord Phillips of Worth Matravers, M.R.

Sch.2, applied: 2002 c.41 s.62, s.133, 2003 c.32 s.48, 2003 c.44 s.260

Sch.2 Part I para.1, amended: 2004 c.17 Sch.3 para.3

Sch.2 Part I para.1, applied: 2002 c.41 s.133

Sch.2 Part I para.1, varied: SI 2003/2818 Sch.2 para.1

Sch.2 Part I para.2, varied: SI 2003/2818 Sch.2 para.1

Sch.2 Part I para.2A, amended: 2002 c.41 Sch.7 para.2, 2004 c.19 s.18

Sch.2 Part I para.2A, applied: 2002 c.41 s.92

Sch.2 Part I para.2A, referred to: SI 2003/2900 Sch.1

Sch.2 Part I para.4, amended: 2002 c.41 Sch.7 para.3

Sch.2 Part I para.6, amended: 2002 c.41 s.119

Sch.2 Part I para.6, applied: SI 2003/658 Reg.6

Sch.2 Part I para.7, referred to: SI 2003/2900 Sch.1

Sch.2 Part I para.8, amended: 2002 c.41 Sch.7 para.4

Sch.2 Part I para.8, applied: 2002 c.41 s.62, SI 2002/313 Sch.1, SI 2004/1219 Reg.6

Sch.2 Part I para.8, varied: SI 2002/1832 Art.2, SI 2003/2818 Sch.2 para.1

Sch.2 Part I para.9, applied: 2002 c.41 s.62, SI 2002/313 Sch.1, SI 2004/1219 Reg.6

Sch.2 Part I para.9, varied: SI 2002/1832 Art.2, SI 2003/2818 Sch.2 para.1

Sch.2 Part I para.10, applied: 2002 c.41 s.62, SI 2002/313 Sch.1, SI 2004/1219 Reg.6

Sch.2 Part I para.10, referred to: 2002 c.41 s.62

Sch.2 Part I para.10A, added: 2002 c.41 s.73

Sch.2 Part I para.10A, applied: 2002 c.41 s.62, SI 2004/1219 Reg.6

Sch.2 Part I para.11, varied: SI 2002/1832 Art.2

Sch.2 Part I para.12, applied: 2002 c.41 s.82, SI 2002/313 Sch.1

Sch.2 Part I para.13, applied: SI 2002/313 Sch.1

Sch.2 Part I para.14, applied: 2002 c.41 s.62, SI 2002/313 Sch.1

Sch.2 Part I para.16, see *R. (on the application of Saadi) v Secretary of State for the Home Department* [2001] EWCA Civ 1512, [2002] 1 W.L.R. 356 (CA), Lord Phillips of Worth Matravers, M.R.

Sch.2 Part I para.16, amended: 2002 c.41 s.73

Sch.2 Part I para.16, applied: 2002 c.41 s.71

CAP.

1971–cont.

77. Immigration Act 1971–*cont.*

Sch.2 Part I para.16, referred to: 2002 c.41 s.62

Sch.2 Part I para.16, varied: SI 2003/2818 Sch.2 para.1

Sch.2 Part I para.17, amended: 2002 c.41 s.63, s.64

Sch.2 Part I para.17, applied: SI 2003/2818 Art.13

Sch.2 Part I para.20, disapplied: 2003 c.32 s.48

Sch.2 Part I para.21, applied: 2002 c.41 s.30, s.62, s.69, s.70, s.71, s.130

Sch.2 Part I para.21, referred to: 2002 c.41 s.62, SI 2003/2900 Sch.1

Sch.2 Part I para.22, amended: 2004 c.19 Sch.2 para.1

Sch.2 Part I para.23, amended: 2003 c.39 Sch.8 para.149, 2004 c.19 Sch.2 para.1

Sch.2 Part I para.24, amended: 2003 c.39 Sch.8 para.149, 2004 c.19 Sch.2 para.1

Sch.2 Part I para.25, amended: 2002 c.41 Sch.7 para.5, 2004 c.19 Sch.2 para.1

Sch.2 Part I para.25A, referred to: SI 2003/2900 Sch.1

Sch.2 Part I para.25B, referred to: SI 2003/2900 Sch.1

Sch.2 Part I para.25C, referred to: SI 2003/2900 Sch.1

Sch.2 Part I para.25D, referred to: SI 2003/2900 Sch.1

Sch.2 Part I para.25E, referred to: SI 2003/2900 Sch.1

Sch.2 Part I para.26, referred to: SI 2003/2900 Sch.1

Sch.2 Part I para.26, varied: SI 2003/2818 Sch.2 para.1

Sch.2 Part I para.27B, amended: 2004 c.19 s.16

Sch.2 Part I para.27B, referred to: SI 2003/2900 Sch.1

Sch.2 Part I para.27C, referred to: SI 2003/2900 Sch.1

Sch.2 Part II para.28, applied: SI 2003/754 Sch.2 para.2

Sch.2 Part II para.29, amended: 2002 c.41 Sch.7 para.6, 2004 c.19 Sch.2 para.1, Sch.4

Sch.2 Part II para.29, applied: 2002 c.41 s.69, SI 2003/754 Sch.2 para.2

Sch.2 Part II para.29, repealed (in part): 2004 c.19 Sch.2 para.1, Sch.4

Sch.2 Part II para.30, amended: 2004 c.19 Sch.2 para.1

Sch.2 Part II para.31, amended: 2003 c.39 Sch.8 para.149, 2004 c.19 Sch.2 para.1

Sch.2 Part II para.32, amended: 2004 c.19 Sch.2 para.1

Sch.2 Part II para.33, amended: 2003 c.39 Sch.8 para.149, 2004 c.19 Sch.2 para.1

CAP.

1971–cont.

77. Immigration Act 1971–*cont.*

Sch.2 para.8, see *R. (on the application of Tu) v Secretary of State for the Home Department* [2002] EWHC 2678, [2003] Imm. A.R. 288 (QBD (Admin Ct)), Cooke, J.; see *Zeqaj v Secretary of State for the Home Department* [2002] EWCA Civ 1919, [2003] Imm. A.R. 298 (CA), Latham, L.J.

Sch.2 para.16, see *R. (on the application of Khadir) v Secretary of State for the Home Department* [2003] EWCA Civ 475, [2003] I.N.L.R. 426 (CA), Kennedy, L.J.

Sch.3, see *R. (on the application of Sezek) v Secretary of State for the Home Department (Bail Application)* [2001] EWCA Civ 795, [2002] 1 W.L.R. 348 (CA), Peter Gibson, L.J.

Sch.3, applied: 2003 c.44 s.260

Sch.3 para.1, applied: SI 2002/313 Sch.1

Sch.3 para.2, see *R. (on the application of Sezek) v Secretary of State for the Home Department (Bail Application)* [2001] EWCA Civ 795, [2002] 1 W.L.R. 348 (CA), Peter Gibson, L.J.

Sch.3 para.2, amended: 2002 c.41 Sch.7 para.7, 2004 c.19 s.34

Sch.3 para.2, applied: 2002 c.41 s.30, s.69, s.70, s.130

Sch.3 para.3, applied: SI 2003/754 Sch.2 para.2

Sch.3 para.3, substituted: 2002 c.41 Sch.7 para.8

Sch.3 para.5, applied: 2002 c.41 s.69

Sch.3 para.6, amended: 2003 c.39 Sch.8 para.150, Sch.10

Sch.3 para.8, amended: 2003 c.39 Sch.8 para.150

78. Town and Country Planning Act 1971

s.43, see *Ceredigion CC v National Assembly for Wales* [2001] EWHC Admin 694, [2002] 2 P. & C.R. 6 (QBD (Admin Ct)), Richards, J.; see *Field v First Secretary of State* [2004] EWHC 147, [2004] J.P.L. 1286 (QBD (Admin Ct)), Sullivan, J.

s.51, see *Aslam v South Bedfordshire DC (Rate of Interest)* [2001] EWCA Civ 515, [2002] R.V.R. 16 (CA), Chadwick, L.J.

s.170, see *Aslam v South Bedfordshire DC (Rate of Interest)* [2001] EWCA Civ 515, [2002] R.V.R. 16 (CA), Chadwick, L.J.

Sch.24 para.21, see *Field v First Secretary of State* [2004] EWHC 147, [2004] J.P.L. 1286 (QBD (Admin Ct)), Sullivan, J.

80. Banking and Financial Dealings Act 1971

applied: 2002 asp 3 s.35, 2002 c.29 s.335, s.336, SI 2002/1891 Sch.2 para.9, SI 2002/2779 Art.80, Sch.2 para.3, Sch.3 para.6, 2003 c.44 s.88, s.89, s.91, SI 2003/284 Art.84, Sch.2 para.6, Sch.5 para.2, SI 2003/1375 Art.7, SI 2004/870

1971–cont.

80. Banking and Financial Dealings Act 1971–*cont.*
applied: 2002 asp 3 s.35–*cont.*
Reg.18, SI 2004/1962 Art.11, Sch.1, SI 2004/2682 Reg.9, SSI 2003/2 Art.16
referred to: SI 2002/2742 Sch.2 para.13, SI 2004/753 Sch.1 para.225S
s.1, applied: SI 2003/1417 r.216

1972

European Communities Act (Ireland) 1972
s.3, see *Sam McCauley Chemists (Blackpool) Ltd v Pharmaceutical Society of Ireland* [2003] Eu. L.R. 37 (HC (Irl)), McCracken, J.

xl. Greater London Council (General Powers) Act 1972
s.17, amended: SI 2004/2035 Sch.1 para.3

xlii. London Transport Act 1972
varied: SI 2003/1615 Sch.2 para.4

xlv. Thames Barrier and Flood Prevention Act 1972
s.20, amended: 2003 c.21 Sch.17 para.43

xiv. Thames Barrier and Flood Prevention Act 1972
s.56, amended: 2003 c.44 Sch.32 para.17

2. Repair of Benefice Buildings Measure 1972
s.32, repealed: 2004 c.14 Sch.1 Part 6
Sch.1, repealed (in part): 2004 c.14 Sch.1 Part 6, Sch.1 Part 6

5. Local Employment Act 1972
s.2, applied: SI 2004/1005 Sch.1, Sch.2

6. Summer Time Act 1972
s.1, amended: SI 2002/262 Art.2
s.2, repealed: SI 2002/262 Art.2
s.3, amended: SI 2002/262 Art.2

7. Civil List Act 1972
applied: 2002 c.16 s.16

9 (N.I.). Local Government Act (Northern Ireland) 1972
applied: SI 2003/3172 Sch.2 Part III
s.23, varied: 2002 c.17 Sch.7 para.19
s.27, varied: 2002 c.17 Sch.7 para.19
s.74, applied: SI 2003/418 Art.1, Art.8
s.74, substituted: SI 2003/418 Art.7
s.75, substituted: SI 2003/418 Art.7
s.97, applied: SI 2002/3153 Art.41
Sch.6, applied: SI 2002/3153 Art.41

10. Vehicles (Excise) Act (Northern Ireland) 1972
applied: SI 2002/2742 Reg.46

11. Superannuation Act 1972
see *Bain, Petitioner* 2002 S.L.T. 1112 (Court of Session (Inner House, Extra Division)), Lord Cameron of Lochbroom, Lord Johnston, Lord Wheatley
applied: 2002 c.26 Sch.8 para.3, Sch.9 para.3, Sch.9 para.4, 2002 c.40 Sch.3 para.6, 2003 c.26 s.17, 2003 c.43 Sch.2

1972–cont.

11. Superannuation Act 1972–*cont.*
applied: 2002 c.26 Sch.8 para.3–*cont.*
para.5, Sch.9 para.6, 2004 c.28 Sch.8 para.5, 2004 c.31 Sch.1 para.6, 2004 c.35 s.211, s.274, Sch.1 para.34
referred to: 2004 c.8 s.52
s.1, applied: 2002 c.26 Sch.8 para.2, Sch.8 para.3, Sch.9 para.3, Sch.9 para.4, 2002 c.30 Sch.2 para.7, 2002 c.40 Sch.3 para.6, SI 2002/1311 Reg.6, SI 2002/1913 Art.2, Art.3, SI 2002/2143 Art.2, 2003 c.20 Sch.1 para.12, 2003 c.39 Sch.9 para.11, 2003 c.43 Sch.2 para.5, SI 2003/973 Art.6, Art.9, SI 2003/1073 Art.2, Art.3, SI 2003/2623 Reg.3, 2004 c.27 Sch.3 para.3, 2004 c.35 s.211, s.274, Sch.1 para.34, Sch.5 para.28, SI 2004/1711 Reg.3, SSI 2003/344 Reg.5, 2004 c.8 s.5
s.1, enabling: SI 2002/1913, SI 2003/1073, SI 2004/1927
s.2, applied: 2003 c.39 Sch.9 para.11, SI 2004/1711 Reg.3
s.7, see *Nicholls v Greenwich LBC* [2003] EWCA Civ 416, [2003] I.C.R. 1020 (CA), Mummery, L.J.
s.7, applied: 2002 asp 11 Sch.2 para.16, SI 2002/769, SI 2003/973 Art.9, SI 2003/1021 Reg.11, Reg.21, SI 2004/558 Reg.3, SSI 2002/311, SSI 2003/138, SSI 2004/134
s.7, enabling: SI 2002/206, SI 2002/819, SI 2002/1852, SI 2003/1022, SI 2003/2249, SI 2003/2437, SI 2003/2719, SI 2003/3004, SI 2004/573, SI 2004/928, SI 2004/3372, SSI 2002/311, SSI 2003/138, SSI 2004/134
s.9, applied: 2002 asp 11 Sch.2 para.16, SI 2002/3058, SI 2004/587, SSI 2002/288, SSI 2003/423, SSI 2004/89
s.9, enabling: SI 2002/3058, SI 2004/587, SSI 2002/288, SSI 2003/423, SSI 2004/89
s.10, applied: SSI 2003/55, SSI 2003/270, SSI 2003/517, SSI 2004/62
s.10, enabling: SI 2002/561, SI 2002/610, SI 2003/631, SI 2003/2322, SI 2004/665, SSI 2003/55, SSI 2003/270, SSI 2003/517, SSI 2004/62
s.11, enabling: SI 2002/819
s.12, see *Nicholls v Greenwich LBC* [2003] EWCA Civ 416, [2003] I.C.R. 1020 (CA), Mummery, L.J.
s.12, enabling: SI 2002/206, SI 2002/561, SI 2002/3058, SI 2003/631, SI 2003/2249, SI 2003/2322, SI 2003/3004, SI 2004/573, SI 2004/587, SI 2004/665, SI 2004/1912, SI 2004/3372, SSI 2002/288, SSI 2002/311, SSI 2003/55, SSI 2003/270, SSI 2003/423, SSI 2003/517, SSI 2004/62, SSI 2004/89, SSI 2004/385

CAP.

1972–cont.

11. Superannuation Act 1972–*cont.*
s.16, applied: SI 2004/1912, SI 2004/2306 Sch.1
s.16, repealed (in part): 2004 c.21 Sch.2
s.16, varied: SI 2004/2918 Sch.1
s.16, enabling: SSI 2004/385
s.22, repealed (in part): SI 2002/254 Sch.4 para.2
s.24, amended: 2004 c.21 Sch.1 para.37
s.24, applied: SI 2002/1311 Reg.6, SI 2003/973 Art.9, SI 2004/2306 Sch.1, SSI 2003/344 Reg.5
s.24, varied: SI 2004/2918 Sch.1
s.24, enabling: SI 2002/768, SI 2002/769, SI 2002/1311, SI 2003/631, SI 2003/1022, SI 2004/587, SI 2004/928, SSI 2003/344
s.27, repealed: 2004 c.14 Sch.1 Part 5
s.30, amended: 2004 c.14 Sch.1 Part 5
Sch.1, amended: 2002 c.26 Sch.8 para.3, Sch.9 para.4, 2002 c.30 Sch.7 para.2, Sch.8, 2002 c.39 Sch.3, 2002 c.40 Sch.25 para.4, SI 2002/1913 Art.2, Art.3, Art.4, SI 2002/2143 Art.2, 2003 c.37 Sch.7 para.19, 2003 c.43 Sch.2 para.5, Sch.9 para.5, 2003 c.44 Sch.19 para.6, SI 2003/1073 Art.2, Art.3, 2004 c.8 s.5, Sch.6 para.3, Sch.7, 2004 c.11 Sch.1 para.3, 2004 c.25 Sch.5 para.20, 2004 c.28 Sch.8 para.5, 2004 c.31 Sch.1 para.6, 2004 c.35 Sch.12 para.2, SI 2004/1927 Art.2, Art.3, Art.4
Sch.1, applied: 2002 c.30 s.28
Sch.2 Part I, referred to: SI 2004/1711 Reg.3
Sch.3, enabling: SI 2002/561, SI 2002/610, SI 2002/3058, SI 2004/587, SI 2004/665, SSI 2002/288, SSI 2003/55, SSI 2003/270, SSI 2003/423, SSI 2003/517, SSI 2004/62, SSI 2004/89
Sch.3 para.1, enabling: SI 2003/631
Sch.3 para.2, enabling: SI 2003/631
Sch.3 para.4, enabling: SI 2003/631, SI 2003/2322
Sch.3 para.8, enabling: SI 2002/1311, SI 2003/2322, SSI 2003/344
Sch.3 para.9, enabling: SI 2002/1311, SSI 2003/344
Sch.3 para.13, enabling: SI 2002/1311, SI 2003/631, SI 2003/2322, SSI 2003/344
Sch.4, amended: SI 2002/254 Sch.4 para.2
Sch.6 para.16, repealed: 2002 c.9 Sch.13

18. Maintenance Orders (Reciprocal Enforcement) Act 1972
applied: SI 2002/788 Art.4, SI 2002/789, SI 2004/3114 Sch.1, SSI 2002/494 Reg.33
referred to: SI 2002/788 Art.4
Part I, applied: SI 2002/788 Art.3, SI 2003/435 Sch.2 para.2
Part II, applied: SI 2002/2839 Art.2, SI 2003/435 Sch.2 para.2
s.1, enabling: SI 2002/788
s.2, applied: SI 2002/788 Art.4

CAP.

1972–cont.

18. Maintenance Orders (Reciprocal Enforcement) Act 1972–*cont.*
s.3, applied: SI 2002/788 Art.4
s.4, applied: SI 2002/788 Art.4
s.5, varied: SI 2002/788 Art.4
s.7, amended: 2003 c.39 Sch.8 para.151
s.7, applied: SI 2002/788 Art.4
s.7, varied: SI 2002/788 Art.4
s.8, amended: 2003 c.39 Sch.8 para.152
s.8, varied: SI 2002/788 Art.4
s.9, amended: 2003 c.39 Sch.8 para.153
s.9, varied: SI 2002/788 Art.4
s.10, varied: SI 2002/788 Art.4
s.11, varied: SI 2002/788 Art.4
s.12, varied: SI 2002/788 Art.4
s.13, varied: SI 2002/788 Art.4
s.14, varied: SI 2002/788 Art.4
s.15, varied: SI 2002/788 Art.4
s.16, varied: SI 2002/788 Art.4
s.17, amended: 2003 c.39 Sch.8 para.154
s.17, varied: SI 2002/788 Art.4
s.18, amended: 2003 c.39 Sch.8 para.155
s.18, referred to: SI 2002/1734
s.18, varied: SI 2002/788 Art.4
s.18, enabling: SI 2002/1734
s.19, varied: SI 2002/788 Art.4
s.20, varied: SI 2002/788 Art.4
s.21, see *Cartwright v Cartwright* [2002] EWCA Civ 931, [2002] 2 F.L.R. 610 (CA), Arden, L.J.
s.21, amended: 2003 c.39 Sch.8 para.156, Sch.10
s.21, varied: SI 2002/788 Art.4
s.23, amended: 2003 c.39 Sch.8 para.157
s.24, enabling: SI 2002/788
s.25, enabling: SI 2002/2839
s.26, amended: 2003 c.39 Sch.8 para.158
s.27B, amended: 2003 c.39 Sch.8 para.159
s.27C, amended: 2003 c.39 Sch.8 para.160
s.32, amended: 2003 c.39 Sch.8 para.161
s.34, amended: 2003 c.39 Sch.8 para.162
s.34A, amended: 2003 c.39 Sch.8 para.163, Sch.10
s.38A, amended: SI 2004/2035 Sch.1 para.2
s.38A, repealed (in part): SI 2004/2035 Sch.1 para.2
s.40, enabling: SI 2002/2838, SI 2003/776
s.45, enabling: SI 2002/2838, SI 2002/2839, SI 2003/776
s.47, amended: 2003 c.39 Sch.8 para.164

26. Sunday Theatre Act 1972
repealed: 2003 c.17 Sch.6 para.55, Sch.7

27. Road Traffic (Foreign Vehicles) Act 1972
s.1, applied: SI 2002/2426 Reg.2
Sch.1, amended: SI 2002/1415 Reg.2
Sch.2, amended: SI 2002/1415 Reg.2

30. Civil Evidence Act 1972
s.2, repealed (in part): 2003 c.39 Sch.8 para.165, Sch.10

CAP.

1972–cont.

30. Civil Evidence Act 1972–*cont.*
s.3, see *Malmstedt v EMI Records Ltd* [2004] EWHC 3228, [2003] E.C.D.R.15 (Ch D), N Strauss Q.C.

35. Defective Premises Act 1972
s.4, see *Ratcliffe v Sandwell MBC* [2002] EWCA Civ 6, [2002] 1 W.L.R. 1488 (CA), Chadwick, L.J.
s.4, varied: 2002 c.15 Sch.7 para.2

41. Finance Act 1972
Sch.9 Part I para.1, see *Cheltenham & Gloucester Plc v Ashford* [2001] EWCA Civ 1713, [2002] B.T.C. 81 (CA), Chadwick, L.J.

45. Trading Representations (Disabled Persons) Amendment Act 1972
s.1, repealed (in part): 2004 c.14 Sch.1 Part 16
s.2, repealed: 2004 c.14 Sch.1 Part 16
s.3, repealed (in part): 2004 c.14 Sch.1 Part 16
Sch.1, amended: 2004 c.14 Sch.1 Part 16

48. Parliamentary and other Pensions Act 1972
s.27, amended: 2004 c.33 Sch.25 para.3
s.27, varied: 2004 c.33 Sch.21 para.7
s.32, repealed: 2004 c.14 Sch.1 Part 11

52. Town and Country Planning (Scotland) Act 1972
applied: SI 2004/352 Sch.6 para.12
s.109, applied: 2003 c.21 Sch.4 para.9

54. British Library Act 1972
s.4, repealed (in part): 2003 c.28 Sch.1

58. National Health Service (Scotland) Act 1972
s.32, amended: SI 2003/1590 Sch.1 para.5

59. Administration of Justice (Scotland) Act 1972
s.1, see *Harwood v Jackson* 2003 S.L.T. 1026 (OH), Temporary Judge J Gordon Reid Q.C.
s.1, applied: SSI 2002/132 Sch.1 para.8.5, Sch.1 para.18.3, Sch.1 para.34.4
s.3, applied: 2004 asp 10 s.30
s.3, disapplied: SI 2004/753 Sch.1 para.211S, SI 2004/2333 Sch.1 para.162S

61. Land Charges Act 1972
applied: 2002 c.9 s.86, s.87, 2002 c.29 s.248
referred to: 2002 c.29 s.47
s.4, see *Fisher v Merer* [2003] EWCA Civ 747, (2003) 147 S.J.L.B. 596 (CA), Arden, L.J.
s.6, referred to: 2002 c.9 s.87
s.14, amended: 2002 c.9 Sch.11 para.10
s.17, amended: 2002 c.9 Sch.11 para.10
s.18, repealed (in part): 2004 c.14 Sch.1 Part 12
Sch.2 para.1, repealed (in part): 2004 c.36 Sch.3

62. Agriculture (Miscellaneous Provisions) Act 1972
s.4, repealed: 2004 c.14 Sch.1 Part 2
s.8, repealed (in part): 2004 c.14 Sch.1 Part 2
s.11, repealed: 2004 c.14 Sch.1 Part 2
s.12, repealed (in part): 2004 c.14 Sch.1 Part 2

CAP.

1972–cont.

62. Agriculture (Miscellaneous Provisions) Act 1972–*cont.*
s.14, repealed: 2004 c.14 Sch.1 Part 2
s.17, repealed (in part): 2004 c.14 Sch.1 Part 2
s.20, applied: SI 2002/295, SI 2002/296, SI 2002/927, SI 2002/1805, SI 2004/1452, SI 2004/2590, SI 2004/2697, SSI 2004/255
s.20, referred to: SI 2003/1851, SSI 2004/488
s.21, repealed: 2004 c.14 Sch.1 Part 2
s.27, amended: 2004 c.14 Sch.1 Part 2
s.27, repealed (in part): 2004 c.14 Sch.1 Part 2
Sch.5, amended: SSI 2004/384 Sch.1

65. National Debt Act 1972
s.11, applied: 2004 c.12 s.325, SI 2004/1450 Reg.12
s.11, enabling: SI 2003/1085, SI 2004/2353

66. Poisons Act 1972
Sch.1 para.3, amended: SI 2002/794 Sch.1 para.18
Sch.1 para.3, applied: SI 2002/794 Art.3

68. European Communities Act 1972
applied: 2002 c.18 Sch.2 Part 2, Sch.2 Part 22, SI 2002/2315, SI 2002/2325, SI 2002/3026 Reg.2, 2003 c.13 Sch.2 Part 2, Sch.2 Part 26, SR 2003/8, 2004 c.9 Sch.2 Part 2, Sch.2 Part 25
s.1, amended: 2002 c.3 s.1, 2003 c.35 s.1
s.1, applied: SI 2002/3139, SI 2003/1891, SI 2003/1891 Art.2, SI 2004/304, SI 2004/345, SI 2004/1499 Art.2
s.1, referred to: SI 2002/2841 Art.2, SI 2002/3139 Art.2, 2003 c.7 s.2, SI 2003/1554 Art.2, SI 2003/1556 Art.2, SI 2004/304 Art.2, SI 2004/345 Art.2, SI 2004/2037 Art.2
s.1, varied: SI 2004/346 Sch.1
s.1, enabling: SI 2002/2841, SI 2002/3139, SI 2003/1554, SI 2003/1556, SI 2003/1891, SI 2004/304, SI 2004/345, SI 2004/346, SI 2004/1499, SI 2004/2037, SI 2004/3331
s.2, see *Thoburn v Sunderland City Council* [2002] EWHC 195, [2003] Q.B. 151 (QBD (Admin Ct)), Laws, L.J.
s.2, applied: SI 2002/2, SI 2002/76, SI 2002/119, SI 2002/120, SI 2002/203, SI 2002/247, SI 2002/248 Art.2, SI 2002/269, SI 2002/271, SI 2002/318, SI 2002/430, SI 2002/431, SI 2002/467, SI 2002/468, SI 2002/501, SI 2002/526, SI 2002/528, SI 2002/542, SI 2002/618, SI 2002/655, SI 2002/677, SI 2002/744, SI 2002/765, SI 2002/787, SI 2002/794 Art.3, SI 2002/811, SI 2002/820, SI 2002/821, SI 2002/826, SI 2002/843, SI 2002/868, SI 2002/897, SI 2002/956, SI 2002/1037, SI 2002/1080 Art.2, SI 2002/1144, SI 2002/1166, SI 2002/1227, SI 2002/1240, SI 2002/1241, SI 2002/1253, SI 2002/1267, SI 2002/1354, SI 2002/

CAP.

1972–cont.

68. European Communities Act 1972–*cont.*
s.2, applied:–*cont.*

1415, SI 2002/1476, SI 2002/1597, SI
2002/1674, SI 2002/1767, SI 2002/1773,
SI 2002/1775, SI 2002/1797, SI 2002/
1806, SI 2002/1819 Art.2, Art.3, SI
2002/1835, SI 2002/1890, SI 2002/
1924, SI 2002/2013, SI 2002/2015, SI
2002/2036, SI 2002/2125, SI 2002/
2127, SI 2002/2151, SI 2002/2201, SI
2002/2295, SI 2002/2296, SI 2002/
2350, SI 2002/2351, SI 2002/2357, SI
2002/2426, SI 2002/2569, SI 2002/
2677, SI 2002/2706, SI 2002/2723, SI
2002/2759, SI 2002/2761, SI 2002/
2840 Art.2, Art.3, SI 2002/2932, SI
2002/3011, SI 2002/3045, SI 2002/
3050, SI 2002/3051, SI 2002/3061, SI
2002/3080, SI 2002/3082, SI 2002/
3153 Sch.1 para.20, SI 2002/3226, SI
2002/3230, 2003 c.20 Sch.6 para.6,
2003 c.44 s.307, SI 2003/3078(b), SI
2003/46, SI 2003/114, SI 2003/151, SI
2003/289, SI 2003/330, SI 2003/419
Art.53, SI 2003/432 Art.2, SI 2003/467,
SI 2003/488, SI 2003/545, SI 2003/547,
SI 2003/549, SI 2003/602, SI 2003/625,
SI 2003/721, SI 2003/750, SI 2003/751,
SI 2003/835, SI 2003/976, SI 2003/
992, SI 2003/1019, SI 2003/1099, SI
2003/1102, SI 2003/1230, SI 2003/1246
Art.2, SI 2003/1296, SI 2003/1297, SI
2003/1482, SI 2003/1511, SI 2003/1557,
SI 2003/1618, SI 2003/1636, SI 2003/
1677, SI 2003/1684, SI 2003/1697, SI
2003/1742, SI 2003/1810, SI 2003/
1846, SI 2003/1850, SI 2003/1852, SI
2003/1888 Art.2, SI 2003/1901, SI
2003/1922, SI 2003/1958, SI 2003/
2066, SI 2003/2109, SI 2003/2209, SI
2003/2288, SI 2003/2292, SI 2003/
2299, SI 2003/2321, SI 2003/2428, SI
2003/2430, SI 2003/2455, SI 2003/
2457, SI 2003/2562, SI 2003/2577, SI
2003/2617 Art.6, SI 2003/2650, SI
2003/2750, SI 2003/2780, SI 2003/
2821, SI 2003/2901 Art.2, Art.3, Art.4, SI
2003/2912, SI 2003/2957, SI 2003/3031,
SI 2003/3049, SI 2003/3073, SI 2003/
3100, SI 2003/3102, SI 2003/3119, SI
2003/3131, SI 2003/3148, SI 2003/
3183, SI 2003/3188, SI 2003/3274,
2004 c.33 s.260, SI 2004/291 Sch.6
para.43, SI 2004/303, SI 2004/312, SI
2004/353, SI 2004/392, SI 2004/478
Sch.6 para.43, SI 2004/590, SI 2004/
627 Sch.5 para.42, SI 2004/676, SI
2004/685, SI 2004/694, SI 2004/706
Art.2, Art.3, Art.4, SI 2004/756, SI 2004/
800, SI 2004/1110 Art.2, SI 2004/1236, SI
2004/1257, SI 2004/1264, SI 2004/1283
Art.2, SI 2004/1301, SI 2004/1468, SI
2004/1633, SI 2004/1749, SI 2004/1769

CAP.

Reg.14, SI 2004/1818, SI 2004/1984
Art.2, Art.3, SI 2004/2146, SI 2004/
2326, SI 2004/2599, SI 2004/2642
Art.2, SI 2004/2688, SI 2004/2689, SI
2004/2731, SR 2002/27, SR 2002/28,
SR 2002/30, SR 2002/50, SR 2002/70,
SR 2002/72, SR 2002/88, SR 2002/93,
SR 2002/94, SR 2002/116, SR 2002/
125, SR 2002/140, SR 2002/141, SR
2002/161, SR 2002/162, SR 2002/210,
SR 2002/217, SR 2002/223, SR 2002/
225, SR 2002/226, SR 2002/246, SR
2002/249, SR 2002/250, SR 2002/259,
SR 2002/263, SR 2002/278, SR 2002/
289, SR 2002/291, SR 2002/293, SR
2002/296, SR 2002/300, SR 2002/301,
SR 2002/302, SR 2002/304, SR 2002/
307, SR 2002/331, SR 2002/334, SR
2002/335, SR 2002/340, SR 2002/357,
SR 2002/368, SR 2002/374, SR 2002/
374 Reg.2, SR 2002/404, SR 2002/404
Reg.2, SR 2003/36, SR 2003/70, SR
2003/79, SR 2003/97, SR 2003/105, SR
2003/106, SR 2003/115, SR 2003/119, SR
2003/123, SR 2003/136, SR 2003/162,
SR 2003/165, SR 2003/167, SR 2003/
192, SR 2003/206, SR 2003/208, SR
2003/210, SR 2003/259 Reg.6, SR
2003/278, SSI 2002/87, SSI 2002/234,
2003 c.20 s.103, Sch.6 para.10, 2003 c.21
s.409, SI 2004/2152, SSI 2004/115 Sch.5
para.41, SSI 2004/116 Sch.1 para.13, SSI
2004/245

1972–cont.

68. European Communities Act 1972–*cont.*
s.2, referred to: SI 2002/458, SI 2003/415
Art.5, SI 2004/2030 Art.7

s.2, enabling: SI 2002/2, SI 2002/8, SI 2002/
42, SI 2002/47, SI 2002/50, SI 2002/63,
SI 2002/85, SI 2002/94, SI 2002/95, SI
2002/118, SI 2002/119, SI 2002/120, SI
2002/129, SI 2002/130, SI 2002/183, SI
2002/203, SI 2002/236, SI 2002/247, SI
2002/248, SI 2002/262, SI 2002/269, SI
2002/271, SI 2002/273, SI 2002/274, SI
2002/282, SI 2002/284, SI 2002/304, SI
2002/316, SI 2002/318, SI 2002/430, SI
2002/431, SI 2002/457, SI 2002/458, SI
2002/467, SI 2002/468, SI 2002/526, SI
2002/528, SI 2002/542, SI 2002/618, SI
2002/646, SI 2002/655, SI 2002/675, SI
2002/677, SI 2002/696, SI 2002/697, SI
2002/744, SI 2002/765, SI 2002/773, SI
2002/774, SI 2002/787, SI 2002/811, SI
2002/820, SI 2002/821, SI 2002/826, SI
2002/843, SI 2002/849, SI 2002/868, SI
2002/889, SI 2002/892, SI 2002/897, SI
2002/931, SI 2002/956, SI 2002/1037, SI
2002/1039, SI 2002/1080, SI 2002/1090,
SI 2002/1144, SI 2002/1166, SI 2002/
1174, SI 2002/1227, SI 2002/1240, SI
2002/1241, SI 2002/1253, SI 2002/1267,
SI 2002/1354, SI 2002/1387, SI 2002/
1415, SI 2002/1416, SI 2002/1460, SI

CAP.

CAP.

1972–cont.

68. European Communities Act 1972–*cont.*
s.2, enabling:–*cont.*

2002/1476, SI 2002/1597, SI 2002/1614, SI 2002/1649, SI 2002/1674, SI 2002/1689, SI 2002/1726, SI 2002/1728, SI 2002/1767, SI 2002/1770, SI 2002/1773, SI 2002/1775, SI 2002/1797, SI 2002/1798, SI 2002/1806, SI 2002/1819, SI 2002/1835, SI 2002/1890, SI 2002/1891, SI 2002/1924, SI 2002/1951, SI 2002/2013, SI 2002/2015, SI 2002/2033, SI 2002/2036, SI 2002/2125, SI 2002/2127, SI 2002/2151, SI 2002/2176, SI 2002/2201, SI 2002/2295, SI 2002/2296, SI 2002/2297, SI 2002/2315, SI 2002/2325, SI 2002/2350, SI 2002/2351, SI 2002/2357, SI 2002/2426, SI 2002/2443, SI 2002/2498, SI 2002/2530, SI 2002/2569, SI 2002/2570, SI 2002/2614, SI 2002/2639, SI 2002/2677, SI 2002/2706, SI 2002/2723, SI 2002/2733, SI 2002/2743, SI 2002/2759, SI 2002/2761, SI 2002/2840, SI 2002/2842, SI 2002/2860, SI 2002/2874, SI 2002/2902, SI 2002/2932, SI 2002/2934, SI 2002/2980, SI 2002/3011, SI 2002/3026, SI 2002/3041, SI 2002/3045, SI 2002/3050, SI 2002/3051, SI 2002/3061, SI 2002/3080, SI 2002/3082, SI 2002/3117, SI 2002/3118, SI 2002/3128, SI 2002/3159, SI 2002/3183, SI 2002/3188, SI 2002/3206, SI 2002/3226, SI 2002/3230, SI 2003/33, SI 2003/37, SI 2003/46, SI 2003/114, SI 2003/115, SI 2003/151, SI 2003/164, SI 2003/171, SI 2003/289, SI 2003/330, SI 2003/411, SI 2003/429, SI 2003/432, SI 2003/467, SI 2003/488, SI 2003/504, SI 2003/529, SI 2003/545, SI 2003/547, SI 2003/549, SI 2003/550, SI 2003/595, SI 2003/602, SI 2003/625, SI 2003/660, SI 2003/661, SI 2003/721, SI 2003/750, SI 2003/751, SI 2003/752, SI 2003/812, SI 2003/835, SI 2003/976, SI 2003/978, SI 2003/989, SI 2003/992, SI 2003/1019, SI 2003/1026, SI 2003/1052, SI 2003/1099, SI 2003/1102, SI 2003/1116, SI 2003/1118, SI 2003/1119, SI 2003/1230, SI 2003/1235, SI 2003/1246, SI 2003/1296, SI 2003/1297, SI 2003/1473, SI 2003/1482, SI 2003/1503, SI 2003/1557, SI 2003/1618, SI 2003/1626, SI 2003/1636, SI 2003/1656, SI 2003/1657, SI 2003/1660, SI 2003/1661, SI 2003/1673, SI 2003/1677, SI 2003/1684, SI 2003/1697, SI 2003/1722, SI 2003/1736, SI 2003/1742, SI 2003/1776, SI 2003/1787, SI 2003/1788, SI 2003/1809, SI 2003/1810, SI 2003/1846, SI 2003/1848, SI 2003/1850, SI 2003/1852, SI 2003/1888, SI 2003/1901, SI 2003/1903, SI 2003/1922, SI 2003/1940, SI 2003/1941, SI 2003/1956, SI 2003/1957,

SI 2003/1958, SI 2003/2002, SI 2003/2037, SI 2003/2066, SI 2003/2074, SI 2003/2109, SI 2003/2121, SI 2003/2209, SI 2003/2254, SI 2003/2261, SI 2003/2264, SI 2003/2288, SI 2003/2292, SI 2003/2299, SI 2003/2316, SI 2003/2321, SI 2003/2426, SI 2003/2428, SI 2003/2430, SI 2003/2455, SI 2003/2457, SI 2003/2498, SI 2003/2500, SI 2003/2501, SI 2003/2562, SI 2003/2577, SI 2003/2591, SI 2003/2635, SI 2003/2650, SI 2003/2742, SI 2003/2750, SI 2003/2756, SI 2003/2770, SI 2003/2780, SI 2003/2821, SI 2003/2827, SI 2003/2828, SI 2003/2901, SI 2003/2910, SI 2003/2912, SI 2003/2919, SI 2003/2949, SI 2003/2988, SI 2003/3003, SI 2003/3031, SI 2003/3049, SI 2003/3075, SI 2003/3078, SI 2003/3100, SI 2003/3102, SI 2003/3119, SI 2003/3131, SI 2003/3144, SI 2003/3148, SI 2003/3177, SI 2003/3183, SI 2003/3188, SI 2003/3204, SI 2003/3226, SI 2003/3229, SI 2003/3241, SI 2003/3242, SI 2003/3245, SI 2003/3272, SI 2003/3274, SI 2003/3310, SI 2003/3311, SI 2004/73, SI 2004/77, SI 2004/82, SI 2004/99, SI 2004/105, SI 2004/106, SI 2004/129, SI 2004/142, SI 2004/145, SI 2004/147, SI 2004/189, SI 2004/221, SI 2004/245, SI 2004/293, SI 2004/302, SI 2004/303, SI 2004/312, SI 2004/353, SI 2004/371, SI 2004/373, SI 2004/390, SI 2004/392, SI 2004/432, SI 2004/437, SI 2004/456, SI 2004/463, SI 2004/546, SI 2004/559, SI 2004/590, SI 2004/666, SI 2004/676, SI 2004/685, SI 2004/694, SI 2004/695, SI 2004/706, SI 2004/756, SI 2004/800, SI 2004/816, SI 2004/850, SI 2004/853, SI 2004/911, SI 2004/946, SI 2004/994, SI 2004/1031, SI 2004/1036, SI 2004/1039, SI 2004/1045, SI 2004/1046, SI 2004/1079, SI 2004/1110, SI 2004/1117, SI 2004/1151, SI 2004/1157, SI 2004/1159, SI 2004/1165, SI 2004/1178, SI 2004/1188, SI 2004/1214, SI 2004/1219, SI 2004/1230, SI 2004/1236, SI 2004/1256, SI 2004/1257, SI 2004/1261, SI 2004/1262, SI 2004/1264, SI 2004/1265, SI 2004/1266, SI 2004/1267, SI 2004/1283, SI 2004/1315, SI 2004/1317, SI 2004/1374, SI 2004/1393, SI 2004/1397, SI 2004/1418, SI 2004/1430, SI 2004/1432, SI 2004/1464, SI 2004/1468, SI 2004/1473, SI 2004/1480, SI 2004/1487, SI 2004/1495, SI 2004/1505, SI 2004/1518, SI 2004/1604, SI 2004/1628, SI 2004/1633 Reg.2, SI 2004/1656, SI 2004/1660, SI 2004/1661, SI 2004/1710, SI 2004/1713, SI 2004/1727, SI 2004/1733, SI 2004/1740, SI 2004/1749, SI 2004/1769, SI 2004/1779, SI 2004/1804, SI 2004/1810, SI 2004/1816, SI 2004/1862, SI 2004/

CAP.

1972–cont.

68. European Communities Act 1972–*cont.*
s.2, enabling:–*cont.*

1882, SI 2004/1947, SI 2004/1948, SI 2004/1958, SI 2004/1974, SI 2004/1977, SI 2004/1984, SI 2004/2034, SI 2004/2043, SI 2004/2095, SI 2004/2110, SI 2004/2145, SI 2004/2152, SI 2004/2178, SI 2004/2186, SI 2004/2245, SI 2004/2309, SI 2004/2326, SI 2004/2330, SI 2004/2332, SI 2004/2334, SI 2004/2352, SI 2004/2361, SI 2004/2363, SI 2004/2411, SI 2004/2412, SI 2004/2516, SI 2004/2518, SI 2004/2519, SI 2004/2520, SI 2004/2539, SI 2004/2559, SI 2004/2574, SI 2004/2599, SI 2004/2603, SI 2004/2604, SI 2004/2640, SI 2004/2642, SI 2004/2661, SI 2004/2662, SI 2004/2688, SI 2004/2689, SI 2004/2690, SI 2004/2692, SI 2004/2731, SI 2004/2734, SI 2004/2735, SI 2004/2750, SI 2004/2885, SI 2004/2886, SI 2004/2888, SI 2004/2919, SI 2004/2949, SI 2004/2990, SI 2004/3037, SI 2004/3081, SI 2004/3091, SI 2004/3099, SI 2004/3100, SI 2004/3193, SI 2004/3196, SI 2004/3201, SI 2004/3219, SI 2004/3221, SI 2004/3222, SI 2004/3223, SI 2004/3224, SI 2004/3227, SI 2004/3254, SI 2004/3278, SI 2004/3279, SI 2004/3280, SI 2004/3284, SI 2004/3298, SI 2004/3330, SI 2004/3349, SI 2004/3378, SI 2004/3385, SI 2004/3390, SI 2004/3391, SR 2002/6, SR 2002/20, SR 2002/21, SR 2002/27, SR 2002/28, SR 2002/29, SR 2002/30, SR 2002/33, SR 2002/53, SR 2002/70, SR 2002/72, SR 2002/88, SR 2002/93, SR 2002/94, SR 2002/125, SR 2002/140, SR 2002/141, SR 2002/161, SR 2002/162, SR 2002/210, SR 2002/217, SR 2002/223, SR 2002/225, SR 2002/226, SR 2002/249, SR 2002/250, SR 2002/259, SR 2002/263, SR 2002/278, SR 2002/289, SR 2002/291, SR 2002/293, SR 2002/296, SR 2002/300, SR 2002/301, SR 2002/302, SR 2002/304, SR 2002/307, SR 2002/334, SR 2002/335, SR 2002/340, SR 2002/357, SR 2002/368, SR 2002/374, SR 2002/404, SR 2003/8, SR 2003/36, SR 2003/52, SR 2003/70, SR 2003/79, SR 2003/97, SR 2003/105, SR 2003/106, SR 2003/115, SR 2003/119, SR 2003/123, SR 2003/136, SR 2003/162, SR 2003/165, SR 2003/167, SR 2003/192, SR 2003/206, SR 2003/208, SR 2003/210, SR 2003/215, SR 2003/219, SR 2003/240, SR 2003/244, SR 2003/259, SR 2003/287, SR 2003/353, SR 2003/360, SR 2003/361, SSI 2002/1, SSI 2002/6, SSI 2002/21, SSI 2002/22, SSI 2002/35, SSI 2002/36, SSI 2002/39, SSI 2002/76,

CAP.

SSI 2002/109, SSI 2002/110, SSI 2002/117, SSI 2002/125, SSI 2002/139, SSI 2002/148, SSI 2002/149, SSI 2002/164, SSI 2002/169, SSI 2002/179, SSI 2002/196, SSI 2002/228, SSI 2002/238, SSI 2002/255, SSI 2002/271, SSI 2002/276, SSI 2002/278, SSI 2002/279, SSI 2002/285, SSI 2002/300, SSI 2002/324, SSI 2002/325, SSI 2002/335, SSI 2002/356, SSI 2002/424, SSI 2002/425, SSI 2002/445, SSI 2002/449, SSI 2002/489, SSI 2002/518, SSI 2002/531, SSI 2002/537, SSI 2002/541, SSI 2002/546, SSI 2002/556, SSI 2002/565, SSI 2003/51, SSI 2003/85, SSI 2003/101, SSI 2003/118, SSI 2003/129, SSI 2003/164, SSI 2003/165, SSI 2003/169, SSI 2003/174, SSI 2003/198, SSI 2003/225, SSI 2003/273, SSI 2003/277, SSI 2003/299, SSI 2003/302, SSI 2003/328, SSI 2003/333, SSI 2003/341, SSI 2003/382, SSI 2003/396, SSI 2003/405, SSI 2003/411, SSI 2003/413, SSI 2003/414, SSI 2003/418, SSI 2003/428, SSI 2003/445, SSI 2003/466, SSI 2003/474, SSI 2003/493, SSI 2003/502, SSI 2003/547, SSI 2003/558, SSI 2003/565, SSI 2003/568, SSI 2003/576, SSI 2003/579, SSI 2003/593, SSI 2004/13, SSI 2004/27, SSI 2004/56, SSI 2004/70, SSI 2004/104, SSI 2004/111, SSI 2004/112, SSI 2004/118, SSI 2004/128, SSI 2004/143, SSI 2004/174, SSI 2004/186, SSI 2004/187, SSI 2004/204, SSI 2004/208, SSI 2004/210, SSI 2004/220, SSI 2004/249, SSI 2004/258, SSI 2004/267, SSI 2004/272, SSI 2004/275, SSI 2004/277, SSI 2004/278, SSI 2004/279, SSI 2004/280, SSI 2004/302, SSI 2004/368, SSI 2004/381, SSI 2004/383, SSI 2004/384, SSI 2004/391, SSI 2004/394, SSI 2004/395, SSI 2004/398, SSI 2004/399, SSI 2004/433, SSI 2004/438, SSI 2004/439, SSI 2004/453, SSI 2004/458, SSI 2004/471, SSI 2004/475, SSI 2004/491, SSI 2004/493, SSI 2004/498, SSI 2004/512, SSI 2004/518, SSI 2004/520, SSI 2004/536

1972–cont.

68. European Communities Act 1972–*cont.*
s.3, see *Browne v Attorney General* [2002] Eu. L.R. 635 (HC (Irl)), Kearns, J.

Sch.1 Part II, amended: 2002 c.3 s.2

Sch.2 para.1, amended: 2003 c.44 Sch.27 para.3

Sch.2 para.1, disapplied: 2002 c.40 s.209, 2003 c.44 s.307

Sch.2 para.1, referred to: 2003 c.44 s.307

Sch.2 para.2, applied: SI 2003/1626, SI 2003/1660, SI 2003/1661, SSI 2002/541, 2004 c.33 s.260, SI 2004/1818

Sch.2 para.2, enabling: SI 2004/3391

Sch.2 para.3, applied: 2004 c.33 s.260

CAP.

1972–cont.

69. Horserace Totalisator and Betting Levy Boards Act 1972

repealed: 2004 c.25 Sch.6

70. Local Government Act 1972

applied: 2003 c.10 s.4, 2003 c.ii s.3, 2003 c.iv, SI 2003/284 Art.23, Art.110, Art.123, SI 2003/527 Reg.2, 2004 c.23 s.26, 2004 c.iii, SI 2004/870 Reg.15

referred to: SI 2002/803 Art.2, SI 2002/808 Art.2, SI 2002/1057 Art.2, 2003 c.43 Sch.4 para.17

Part IV, applied: 2004 c.21 s.2, s.4

Part V, applied: 2004 c.21 s.2

Part VA, applied: 2002 c.17 s.19, SI 2002/802 Reg.11, SI 2002/3038 Sch.2 para.1

Part VA, referred to: 2002 c.17 Sch.6 para.5

Part VII, applied: SI 2004/533 Art.7

Part XI, applied: 2004 c.5 s.29

s.2, applied: 2003 c.14 s.61, s.66

s.7, repealed (in part): SI 2002/1723 Sch.1

s.21, applied: 2003 c.14 s.61, s.66

s.28, applied: SI 2004/218 Art.2

s.54, applied: SI 2002/652, SI 2002/654, SI 2002/1129, SI 2002/3270, SI 2002/3271, SI 2002/3272, SI 2002/3273, SI 2003/3132, SI 2003/3134, SI 2003/3137, SI 2004/2746, SI 2004/2747

s.54, enabling: SI 2002/1129

s.55, applied: SI 2002/1129

s.55, enabling: SI 2002/1129

s.57, applied: SI 2004/218 Art.2

s.58, applied: SI 2002/652, SI 2002/654, SI 2002/1129, SI 2002/3270, SI 2002/3271, SI 2002/3272, SI 2002/3273, SI 2002/3274, SI 2002/3275, SI 2002/3276, SI 2002/3277, SI 2002/3278, SI 2002/3279, SI 2003/3132, SI 2003/3134, SI 2003/3137, SI 2004/218 Art.2, SI 2004/2746, SI 2004/2747

s.58, enabling: SI 2002/651, SI 2002/652, SI 2002/654, SI 2002/1129, SI 2002/1432, SI 2002/3270, SI 2002/3271, SI 2002/3272, SI 2002/3273, SI 2002/3274, SI 2002/3275, SI 2002/3276, SI 2002/3277, SI 2002/3278, SI 2002/3279, SI 2003/974, SI 2003/3132, SI 2003/3134, SI 2003/3137, SI 2004/2746, SI 2004/2747

s.64, applied: SI 2002/3274, SI 2002/3275, SI 2002/3276, SI 2002/3277, SI 2002/3278, SI 2002/3279

s.64, repealed: 2004 c.14 Sch.1 Part 10

s.64, enabling: SI 2002/3274, SI 2002/3275, SI 2002/3276, SI 2002/3278, SI 2002/3279

s.67, enabling: SI 2002/1129, SI 2002/1432, SI 2002/3274, SI 2002/3275, SI 2002/3276, SI 2002/3277, SI 2002/3278, SI 2002/3279

s.70, amended: SI 2002/808 Art.3

s.74, repealed (in part): 2004 c.14 Sch.1 Part 10

CAP.

1972–cont.

70. Local Government Act 1972–*cont.*

s.78, amended: 2003 c.17 Sch.6 para.57, Sch.7, 2004 c.14 Sch.1 Part 10

s.79, amended: SI 2002/808 Art.4

s.80, see *Islington LBC v Camp* [2004] B.L.G.R. 58 (QBD), Richards, J.

s.80, amended: 2002 c.40 s.267

s.80, disapplied: SI 2002/808 Art.41

s.81, repealed (in part): 2002 c.40 Sch.26

s.82, amended: SI 2002/808 Art.6

s.83, applied: SI 2002/1895 Reg.4, SI 2003/895 Reg.4

s.83, enabling: SI 2004/1508

s.85, applied: SI 2003/3190 Reg.4

s.85, varied: SI 2004/1777 Art.13, SI 2004/1778 Art.13

s.86, see *Islington LBC v Camp* [2004] B.L.G.R. 58 (QBD), Richards, J.

s.87, applied: SI 2004/218 Art.2

s.89, applied: 2003 c.26 s.103, 2004 c.2 Sch.1 para.2

s.89, referred to: 2003 c.26 s.104

s.89, varied: SI 2004/218 Art.3

s.90, amended: 2004 c.14 Sch.1 Part 10

s.92, varied: SI 2004/1777 Art.12, SI 2004/1778 Art.12

s.94, varied: SI 2004/1777 Art.14

s.95, amended: 2004 c.33 Sch.27 para.38

s.95, varied: SI 2004/1777 Art.14

s.96, amended: 2004 c.33 Sch.27 para.39

s.96, varied: SI 2004/1777 Art.14

s.97, varied: SI 2004/1777 Art.14

s.98, amended: SI 2002/1555 Art.5

s.98, varied: SI 2003/1633 Sch.2 para.8, SI 2004/1777 Art.14

s.99, varied: SI 2004/1777 Sch.3 para.7, SI 2004/1778 Sch.3 para.7

s.100, varied: SI 2004/1777 Sch.3 para.7, SI 2004/1778 Sch.3 para.7

s.100A, amended: SI 2002/715 Art.2

s.100A, applied: SI 2002/3038 Sch.2 para.1, 2004 c.23 s.26

s.100A, varied: SI 2002/3038 Sch.2 para.1, 2004 c.23 s.24, SI 2004/1777 Art.21, SI 2004/1778 Art.21

s.100B, applied: SI 2002/3038 Sch.2 para.1, 2004 c.23 s.24

s.100B, varied: SI 2002/3038 Sch.2 para.1, 2004 c.23 s.24, SI 2004/1777 Art.21, SI 2004/1778 Art.21

s.100C, applied: SI 2002/3038 Sch.2 para.1, 2004 c.23 s.26

s.100C, varied: SI 2002/3038 Sch.2 para.1, 2004 c.23 s.24, SI 2004/1777 Art.21, SI 2004/1778 Art.21

s.100D, applied: SI 2002/3038 Sch.2 para.1, 2004 c.23 s.26

s.100D, varied: SI 2002/3038 Sch.2 para.1, 2004 c.23 s.24, SI 2004/1777 Art.21, SI 2004/1778 Art.21

1972–cont.

70. Local Government Act 1972–cont.

s.100E, varied: 2004 c.23 s.24, SI 2004/1777 Art.21, SI 2004/1778 Art.21

s.100F, varied: 2004 c.23 s.24, SI 2004/1777 Art.21, SI 2004/1778 Art.21

s.100G, varied: 2004 c.23 s.24, SI 2004/1777 Art.21, SI 2004/1778 Art.21

s.100H, see *Lillie v Newcastle City Council* [2002] EWHC 1600, (2002) 146 S.J.L.B. 225 (QBD), Eady, J.

s.100H, varied: SI 2002/3038 Sch.2 para.1, 2004 c.23 s.24, SI 2004/1777 Art.21, SI 2004/1778 Art.21

s.100I, varied: 2004 c.23 s.24, SI 2004/1777 Art.21, SI 2004/1778 Art.21

s.100J, amended: 2004 c.21 Sch.1 para.39

s.100J, repealed (in part): 2004 c.21 Sch.2

s.100J, varied: 2004 c.23 s.24, SI 2004/1777 Art.21, SI 2004/1778 Art.21

s.100K, varied: 2004 c.23 s.24, SI 2004/1777 Art.21, SI 2004/1778 Art.21

s.100K, enabling: SI 2002/715

s.101, amended: 2003 c.17 Sch.6 para.58

s.101, applied: 2002 c.32 s.183, SI 2002/802 Reg.3, Reg.4, Reg.5, Reg.11, 2003 c.iii s.10, 2004 c.5 s.4, 2004 c.18 s.81, Sch.9 para.6

s.101, disapplied: SI 2002/803 Art.7, 2004 c.23 s.25

s.101, referred to: 2002 c.i s.20

s.101, repealed (in part): 2004 c.31 Sch.5 Part 4

s.101, varied: SI 2004/1777 Art.17, SI 2004/1778 Art.17

s.102, applied: SI 2004/1778 Art.17

s.102, disapplied: SI 2004/1777 Art.17

s.102, varied: SI 2004/1777 Art.17, SI 2004/1778 Art.17

s.103, varied: SI 2004/1777 Art.17, SI 2004/1778 Art.17

s.104, varied: SI 2004/1777 Art.17, SI 2004/1778 Art.17

s.105, varied: SI 2004/1777 Art.14

s.106, varied: SI 2004/1777 Art.17, SI 2004/1778 Art.17

s.111, see *R. (on the application of A) v East Sussex CC (No.1)* [2002] EWHC 2771, [2003] B.L.G.R. 529 (QBD (Admin Ct)), Munby, J.; see *R. (on the application of Comninos) v Bedford BC* [2003] EWHC 121, [2003] B.L.G.R. 271 (QBD (Admin Ct)), Sullivan, J.; see *Tower Hamlets LBC v Sherwood* [2002] EWCA Civ 229, [2002] E.H.L.R. 13 (CA), Chadwick, L.J.

s.111, disapplied: 2003 c.26 s.93

s.111, referred to: SI 2004/1777 Art.26, SI 2004/1778 Art.26

s.112, repealed (in part): 2004 c.21 Sch.2

s.112, varied: SI 2004/1777 Art.17, SI 2004/1778 Art.17

1972–cont.

70. Local Government Act 1972–cont.

s.113, amended: SI 2002/2469 Sch.1 para.7, 2003 c.43 Sch.4 para.18, 2004 c.17 Sch.3 para.4

s.113, varied: SI 2004/1777 Art.17, SI 2004/1778 Art.17

s.114, varied: SI 2004/1777 Art.17, SI 2004/1778 Art.17

s.115, varied: SI 2004/1777 Art.17, SI 2004/1778 Art.17

s.116, varied: SI 2004/1777 Art.17, SI 2004/1778 Art.17

s.117, varied: SI 2004/1777 Art.17, SI 2004/1778 Art.17

s.118, varied: SI 2004/1777 Art.17, SI 2004/1778 Art.17

s.119, varied: SI 2004/1777 Art.17, SI 2004/1778 Art.17

s.121, applied: SI 2004/2595 Reg.3, SI 2004/2732 Reg.3

s.122, see *R. (on the application of Beresford) v Sunderland City Council* [2003] UKHL 60, [2004] 1 A.C. 889 (HL), Lord Bingham of Cornhill

s.123, see *R. (on the application of Beresford) v Sunderland City Council* [2003] UKHL 60, [2004] 1 A.C. 889 (HL), Lord Bingham of Cornhill; see *R. (on the application of Molinaro) v Kensington and Chelsea RLBC* [2001] EWHC Admin 896, [2002] B.L.G.R. 336 (QBD (Admin Ct)), Elias, J.

s.123, disapplied: 2002 c.i s.18

s.125, applied: SI 2004/2595 Reg.3, SI 2004/2732 Reg.3

s.127, applied: SI 2004/533 Art.7

s.132, varied: SI 2004/1777 Art.29, SI 2004/1778 Art.29

s.135, applied: SI 2002/803 Art.7, SI 2003/1021 Reg.7, Reg.8, Reg.26

s.135, varied: SI 2004/1777 Art.29, SI 2004/1778 Art.29

s.136, varied: SI 2004/1777 Art.29, SI 2004/1778 Art.29

s.137, amended: 2003 c.26 s.118, Sch.7 para.4, 2004 c.23 Sch.2 para.1, Sch.4

s.137, applied: SI 2002/2878 Art.2

s.137, referred to: 2003 c.26 s.128

s.137, repealed (in part): 2003 c.26 Sch.8 Part 1

s.137, enabling: SI 2002/2878

s.138, repealed (in part): 2004 c.36 Sch.2 para.7, Sch.3

s.139, varied: SI 2004/1777 Art.29, SI 2004/1778 Art.29

s.140, varied: SI 2004/1777 Art.29, SI 2004/1778 Art.29

s.140A, varied: SI 2004/1777 Art.29, SI 2004/1778 Art.29

s.140C, varied: SI 2004/1777 Art.29, SI 2004/1778 Art.29

CAP.

1972–cont.

70. Local Government Act 1972–*cont.*

s.141, varied: SI 2004/1777 Art.29, SI 2004/1778 Art.29

s.142, amended: 2003 c.21 s.349

s.142, varied: SI 2004/1777 Art.29, SI 2004/1778 Art.29

s.144, varied: SI 2004/1777 Art.29, SI 2004/1778 Art.29

s.145, amended: 2003 c.17 Sch.6 para.59

s.151, applied: SI 2002/377 Sch.1 para.27, SI 2002/3199 Sch.1 para.21, 2003 c.26 s.25, SI 2003/3118 Sch.1 para.19, SI 2003/3170 Sch.1 para.21

s.151, varied: SI 2004/1777 Art.23, SI 2004/1778 Art.23

s.153, applied: SI 2004/533 Art.7

s.168, amended: 2004 c.21 Sch.1 para.41

s.168, varied: SI 2004/1777 Art.23, SI 2004/1778 Art.23

s.169, repealed: 2004 c.14 Sch.1 Part 10

s.173, applied: SI 2002/2899 Reg.7, SI 2002/3178 Sch.1 para.3, SI 2003/895 Reg.5, Reg.6, Reg.9, Reg.12, SI 2003/3227 Sch.1 para.3

s.173, disapplied: SI 2003/1021 Reg.34

s.173, referred to: 2002 c.32 s.52

s.173, enabling: SI 2003/895

s.173A, disapplied: SI 2003/1021 Reg.34

s.173A, referred to: 2002 c.32 s.52

s.174, applied: SI 2002/3178 Sch.1 para.3, SI 2003/3227 Sch.1 para.3, SI 2004/1777 Art.15, SI 2004/1778 Art.15

s.174, disapplied: SI 2002/1895 Reg.20, SI 2003/895 Reg.15, SI 2003/1021 Reg.34, SI 2004/2555 Reg.20

s.174, referred to: 2002 c.32 s.52

s.174, varied: SI 2002/2899 Reg.7

s.175, applied: SI 2003/895 Reg.9, Reg.10, SI 2004/1777 Art.15, SI 2004/1778 Art.15

s.175, disapplied: SI 2002/1895 Reg.20, SI 2003/1021 Reg.34, SI 2004/2555 Reg.20

s.175, enabling: SI 2003/895

s.176, applied: SI 2002/1895 Reg.16, SI 2003/895 Reg.9, Reg.12, SI 2004/1777 Art.15, SI 2004/1778 Art.15

s.176, disapplied: SI 2003/1021 Reg.34

s.176, varied: SI 2002/1895 Reg.20

s.177, amended: 2002 c.32 Sch.21 para.1

s.177, disapplied: SI 2002/1895 Reg.20

s.177, enabling: SI 2003/895

s.178, enabling: SI 2003/895

s.180, applied: SI 2004/1777 Art.25, SI 2004/1778 Art.25

s.190, repealed: 2004 c.14 Sch.1 Part 10

s.191, amended: 2004 c.14 Sch.1 Part 10

s.195, see *R. (on the application of Heather) v Leonard Cheshire Foundation* [2002] EWCA Civ 366, [2002] 2 All E.R. 936 (CA), Lord Woolf of Barnes, L.C.J.

s.197, repealed (in part): 2004 c.14 Sch.1 Part 10

CAP.

1972–cont.

70. Local Government Act 1972–*cont.*

s.204, repealed: 2003 c.17 Sch.6 para.60, Sch.7

s.213, repealed (in part): 2004 c.14 Sch.1 Part 10

s.219, amended: 2004 c.14 Sch.1 Part 10

s.221, repealed: 2004 c.14 Sch.1 Part 10

s.222, see *Brighton and Hove City Council v Woolworths Plc* [2002] EWHC 2565, (2003) 167 J.P. 21 (QBD (Admin Ct)), Field, J.; see *Monks v East Northamptonshire DC* [2002] EWHC 473, (2002) 166 J.P. 592 (QBD (Admin Ct)), Silber, J.; see *Nottingham City Council v Zain* [2001] EWCA Civ 1248, [2002] 1 W.L.R. 607 (CA), Schiemann, L.J.; see *Worcestershire CC v Tongue* [2004] EWCA Civ 140, [2004] Ch. 236 (CA), Peter Gibson, L.J.

s.222, applied: 2003 c.38 s.91

s.222, referred to: 2003 c.38 s.91

s.222, varied: SI 2004/1777 Art.29, SI 2004/1778 Art.29

s.223, varied: SI 2004/1777 Art.29, SI 2004/1778 Art.29

s.224, varied: SI 2004/1777 Art.21, SI 2004/1778 Art.21

s.225, applied: SI 2002/1710 Reg.10, Reg.11, Reg.12

s.225, varied: SI 2004/1777 Art.21, SI 2004/1778 Art.21

s.228, applied: SI 2002/1710 Reg.10, Reg.11, Reg.12

s.228, varied: SI 2004/1777 Art.21, SI 2004/1778 Art.21

s.229, varied: SI 2004/1777 Art.21, SI 2004/1778 Art.21

s.230, applied: SI 2004/1777 Art.22, SI 2004/1778 Art.22

s.230, varied: SI 2004/1777 Art.21, SI 2004/1778 Art.21

s.231, disapplied: 2003 c.17 s.184

s.231, varied: SI 2004/1777 Art.21, SI 2004/1778 Art.21

s.232, varied: SI 2004/1777 Art.21, SI 2004/1778 Art.21

s.233, applied: 2003 c.iii s.19, SI 2004/2443 Sch.4 para.1

s.233, disapplied: 2003 c.17 s.184

s.233, referred to: SI 2004/2443 Sch.4 para.1, Sch.4 para.12

s.233, varied: 2004 c.34 s.246, SI 2004/1777 Art.21, SI 2004/1778 Art.21

s.234, varied: SI 2004/1777 Art.21, SI 2004/1778 Art.21

s.235, applied: SI 2004/1777 Art.25, SI 2004/1778 Art.25

s.236, applied: 2002 c.i s.24

s.236, referred to: 2002 c.i s.15

s.236, varied: 2002 c.i s.24, SI 2004/1777 Art.21, SI 2004/1778 Art.21

1972–cont.

70. Local Government Act 1972–*cont.*
s.237, varied: SI 2004/1777 Art.21, SI 2004/1778 Art.21
s.238, referred to: 2002 c.i s.15
s.238, varied: 2002 c.i s.24, SI 2004/1777 Art.21, SI 2004/1778 Art.21
s.239, applied: 2003 c.ii, 2003 c.iii, 2004 c.iii
s.239, referred to: 2002 c.i
s.239, varied: SI 2004/1777 Art.32, SI 2004/1778 Art.32
s.245, amended: SI 2002/1057 Art.5
s.246, applied: SI 2003/533 Reg.9
s.250, applied: 2002 c.38 s.17, 2002 c.i s.36, SI 2002/2780 Reg.2, 2003 c.43 s.134, s.135, 2004 c.20 Sch.16 para.6, 2004 c.21 s.56, 2004 c.31 s.4, SI 2004/652 Reg.11
s.250, varied: SI 2002/2127 Reg.15, SI 2003/164 Reg.11, SI 2003/3311 Sch.3 para.5, 2004 c.31 s.3, SI 2004/1769 Reg.17
s.254, repealed (in part): 2004 c.14 Sch.1 Part 10
s.257, repealed: 2004 c.14 Sch.1 Part 10
s.258, repealed: 2004 c.14 Sch.1 Part 10
s.261, repealed: 2004 c.14 Sch.1 Part 10
s.262, enabling: SI 2004/80, SI 2004/1281
s.265, enabling: SI 2004/1412
s.270, see *R. (on the application of Beresford) v Sunderland City Council* [2003] UKHL 60, [2004] 1 A.C. 889 (HL), Lord Bingham of Cornhill
s.270, amended: SI 2002/808 Art.9, 2004 c.14 Sch.1 Part 10
s.270, applied: SI 2002/1895 Reg.18, SI 2003/895 Reg.13, SI 2003/1021 Reg.7, Reg.8, SI 2004/1962 Sch.1, SI 2004/2555 Reg.18
s.270, enabling: SI 2003/895
s.271, repealed (in part): 2004 c.14 Sch.1 Part 10
s.273, repealed (in part): 2004 c.14 Sch.1 Part 10
s.274, amended: 2004 c.14 Sch.1 Part 10
Sch.1 Part III para.6, varied: SI 2003/1633 Sch.2 para.17
Sch.3 para.2, repealed: 2004 c.14 Sch.1 Part 10
Sch.3 para.4, repealed: 2004 c.14 Sch.1 Part 10
Sch.3 para.5, repealed: 2004 c.14 Sch.1 Part 10
Sch.3 para.6, repealed: 2004 c.14 Sch.1 Part 10
Sch.3 para.7, repealed: 2004 c.14 Sch.1 Part 10
Sch.3 para.8, repealed: 2004 c.14 Sch.1 Part 10
Sch.3 para.9, repealed: 2004 c.14 Sch.1 Part 10
Sch.3 para.11, repealed: 2004 c.14 Sch.1 Part 10

1972–cont.

70. Local Government Act 1972–*cont.*
Sch.3 para.12, amended: 2004 c.14 Sch.1 Part 10
Sch.3 para.12, repealed (in part): 2004 c.14 Sch.1 Part 10
Sch.3 para.13, repealed (in part): 2004 c.14 Sch.1 Part 10
Sch.3 para.15, repealed: 2004 c.14 Sch.1 Part 10
Sch.3 para.16, repealed: 2004 c.14 Sch.1 Part 10
Sch.3 para.17, repealed: 2004 c.14 Sch.1 Part 10
Sch.5 para.3, repealed: 2004 c.14 Sch.1 Part 10
Sch.5 para.4, repealed: 2004 c.14 Sch.1 Part 10
Sch.5 para.5, repealed: 2004 c.14 Sch.1 Part 10
Sch.5 para.6, repealed: 2004 c.14 Sch.1 Part 10
Sch.5 para.7, repealed: 2004 c.14 Sch.1 Part 10
Sch.5 para.8, repealed: 2004 c.14 Sch.1 Part 10
Sch.5 para.9, repealed: 2004 c.14 Sch.1 Part 10
Sch.5 para.10, repealed: 2004 c.14 Sch.1 Part 10
Sch.12A, applied: SI 2002/3038 Sch.2 para.1
Sch.12 Part I para.1, amended: SI 2002/1057 Art.6
Sch.12 Part II para.10, amended: 2003 c.17 Sch.6 para.61
Sch.12 Part III para.14, amended: 2003 c.17 Sch.6 para.61
Sch.12 Part IV para.26, amended: 2003 c.17 Sch.6 para.61
Sch.12 Part V para.32, amended: 2003 c.17 Sch.6 para.61
Sch.12 Part VI para.39, varied: SI 2004/1777 Sch.3 para.7, SI 2004/1778 Sch.3 para.7
Sch.12 Part VI para.40, varied: SI 2004/1777 Sch.3 para.7, SI 2004/1778 Sch.3 para.7
Sch.12 Part VI para.41, varied: SI 2004/1777 Sch.3 para.7, SI 2004/1778 Sch.3 para.7
Sch.12 Part VI para.42, varied: SI 2004/1777 Sch.3 para.7, SI 2004/1778 Sch.3 para.7
Sch.12 Part VI para.43, varied: SI 2004/1777 Sch.3 para.7, SI 2004/1778 Sch.3 para.7
Sch.12 Part VI para.44, varied: SI 2004/1777 Sch.3 para.7, SI 2004/1778 Sch.3 para.7
Sch.12 Part VI para.45, applied: SI 2004/1777 Sch.3 para.7, SI 2004/1778 Sch.3 para.7
Sch.12 Part VI para.45, varied: SI 2004/1777 Sch.3 para.7, SI 2004/1778 Sch.3 para.7
Sch.12 Part VI para.46, varied: SI 2004/1777 Sch.3 para.7, SI 2004/1778 Sch.3 para.7
Sch.12A Part I, applied: SI 2002/3038 Sch.2 para.1

1972–cont.

70. Local Government Act 1972–*cont.*

Sch.12A Part I para.1, varied: SI 2002/3038 Sch.2 para.1

Sch.12A Part I para.2A, varied: SI 2002/3038 Sch.2 para.1

Sch.12A Part I para.3, varied: SI 2002/3038 Sch.2 para.1

Sch.12A Part I para.5, varied: SI 2002/3038 Sch.2 para.1

Sch.12A Part I para.6, varied: SI 2002/3038 Sch.2 para.1

Sch.12A Part I para.6A, varied: SI 2002/3038 Sch.2 para.1

Sch.12A Part I para.6B, varied: SI 2002/3038 Sch.2 para.1, SI 2004/1016 Art.85

Sch.12A Part I para.13, varied: SI 2002/3038 Sch.2 para.1

Sch.12A Part II, applied: SI 2002/3038 Sch.2 para.1

Sch.12A Part II para.1, varied: SI 2002/3038 Sch.2 para.1

Sch.12A Part II para.7, varied: SI 2002/3038 Sch.2 para.1

Sch.12A Part III para.1, applied: SI 2002/3038 Sch.2 para.1

Sch.12B para.1, added: 2003 c.26 s.118

Sch.12B para.2, added: 2003 c.26 s.118

Sch.12B para.3, added: 2003 c.26 s.118

Sch.12B para.4, added: 2003 c.26 s.118

Sch.12B para.5, added: 2003 c.26 s.118

Sch.12B para.6, added: 2003 c.26 s.118

Sch.12B para.7, added: 2003 c.26 s.118

Sch.13 Part I para.1, applied: SI 2004/533 Art.7

Sch.14 Part I para.3, repealed: 2004 c.14 Sch.1 Part 13

Sch.14 Part I para.19, repealed: 2004 c.14 Sch.1 Part 13

Sch.14 Part I para.21, repealed: 2004 c.14 Sch.1 Part 13

Sch.14 Part II para.24, amended: 2004 c.14 Sch.1 Part 13

Sch.14 Part II para.25, amended: 2004 c.14 Sch.1 Part 13

Sch.14 Part II para.33, repealed: 2004 c.14 Sch.1 Part 13

Sch.14 Part II para.35, repealed: 2004 c.14 Sch.1 Part 13

Sch.14 Part II para.36, repealed: 2004 c.14 Sch.1 Part 13

Sch.14 Part II para.44, repealed: 2004 c.14 Sch.1 Part 13

Sch.15 para.1, repealed: 2004 c.14 Sch.1 Part 13

Sch.15 para.2, repealed: 2004 c.14 Sch.1 Part 13

Sch.15 para.3, repealed: 2004 c.14 Sch.1 Part 13

Sch.15 para.4, repealed: 2004 c.14 Sch.1 Part 13

1972–cont.

70. Local Government Act 1972–*cont.*

Sch.23, see *R. (on the application of Heather) v Leonard Cheshire Foundation* [2002] EWCA Civ 366, [2002] 2 All E.R. 936 (CA), Lord Woolf of Barnes, L.C.J.

Sch.23 para.11, repealed: 2004 c.14 Sch.1 Part 10

Sch.24 Part I para.1, repealed: 2004 c.14 Sch.1 Part 10

Sch.24 Part I para.3, repealed: 2004 c.14 Sch.1 Part 10

Sch.25 Part I para.1, repealed: 2003 c.17 Sch.7

Sch.25 Part I para.2, repealed: 2003 c.17 Sch.7

Sch.25 Part I para.3, repealed: 2003 c.17 Sch.7

Sch.25 Part I para.4, repealed: 2003 c.17 Sch.7

Sch.25 Part I para.5, repealed: 2003 c.17 Sch.7

Sch.25 Part I para.6, repealed: 2003 c.17 Sch.7

Sch.25 Part I para.7, repealed: 2003 c.17 Sch.7

Sch.25 Part I para.8, repealed: 2003 c.17 Sch.7

Sch.25 Part I para.9, repealed: 2003 c.17 Sch.7

Sch.28, repealed: 2004 c.14 Sch.1 Part 10

Sch.29 Part II para.9, repealed (in part): 2004 c.14 Sch.1 Part 10

Sch.29 Part II para.10, repealed (in part): 2004 c.14 Sch.1 Part 10

Sch.29 Part II para.11, repealed: 2004 c.14 Sch.1 Part 3

Sch.29 Part II para.12, repealed: 2004 c.14 Sch.1 Part 10

Sch.29 Part II para.16, repealed: 2004 c.14 Sch.1 Part 10

Sch.29 Part II para.17, repealed (in part): 2004 c.14 Sch.1 Part 10

Sch.29 Part II para.26, repealed: 2002 c.9 Sch.13, 2004 c.14 Sch.1 Part 10

Sch.29 Part II para.35, repealed: 2004 c.14 Sch.1 Part 10

Sch.29 Part II para.41, amended: 2004 c.14 Sch.1 Part 17

Sch.29 Part II para.45, repealed: 2004 c.14 Sch.1 Part 10

71. Criminal Justice Act 1972

s.36, see *Attorney General's Reference (No.2 of 2001), Re* [2003] UKHL 68, [2004] 2 A.C. 72 (HL), Lord Bingham of Cornhill

s.46, repealed (in part): 2003 c.44 Sch.37 Part 4, Sch.3 para.47

s.48, repealed: 2003 c.42 Sch.7

s.51, amended: 2003 c.39 Sch.8 para.166

CAP.

1973

xiv. Cromarty Firth Port Authority Order 1973
applied: SSI 2003/491 Art.1

xvi. Cromarty Firth Port Authority Order 1973
s.3, amended: SSI 2003/491 Sch.3
s.6, repealed: SSI 2003/491 Sch.3
s.8, amended: SSI 2003/491 Sch.3
s.60, repealed: SSI 2003/491 Sch.3
s.61, repealed: SSI 2003/491 Sch.3

xxx. Greater London Council (General Powers) Act 1973
s.24, amended: 2004 c.5 Sch.7 para.8, Sch.9

xi. London Transport Act 1973
varied: SI 2003/1615 Sch.2 para.5

4. Atomic Energy Authority (Weapons Group) Act 1973
s.3, amended: 2004 c.14 Sch.1 Part 16
s.3, repealed (in part): 2004 c.14 Sch.1 Part 16
s.4, amended: 2004 c.14 Sch.1 Part 16

13. Supply of Goods (Implied Terms) Act 1973
applied: SI 2003/1593 Sch.1 Part I
s.9, referred to: SI 2003/1374 Sch.1
s.10, amended: SI 2002/3045 Reg.13
s.10, referred to: SI 2003/1374 Sch.1
s.11, referred to: SI 2003/1374 Sch.1
s.15, amended: SI 2002/3045 Reg.13

15. Administration of Justice Act 1973
applied: 2003 c.39 s.22
referred to: SI 2002/1057 Art.2
s.5, amended: 2003 c.39 Sch.8 para.167, Sch.10
s.6, repealed: 2004 c.14 Sch.1 Part 1
s.8, see *Rees Investments Ltd v Groves* [2002] 1 P. & C.R. D9 (Ch D), Neuberger, J.; see *Royal Bank of Scotland Plc v Miller* [2001] EWCA Civ 344, [2002] Q.B. 255 (CA), Dyson, L.J.
s.8, repealed (in part): 2004 c.14 Sch.1 Part 12
s.9, amended: 2002 c.26 Sch.12 para.11
s.12, amended: 2002 c.26 Sch.12 para.12
Sch.1 Part II para.7, repealed: 2003 c.39 Sch.8 para.168, Sch.10
Sch.1 Part II para.7A, added: SI 2002/1057 Art.7
Sch.1 Part II para.7A, repealed: 2003 c.39 Sch.8 para.168, Sch.10
Sch.1 Part II para.7B, added: SI 2002/1057 Art.7
Sch.1 Part II para.7B, repealed: 2003 c.39 Sch.8 para.168, Sch.10
Sch.1 Part IV para.10, repealed (in part): 2003 c.39 Sch.8 para.168, Sch.10
Sch.2 Part I, repealed: 2004 c.14 Sch.1 Part 1

16. Education Act 1973
s.3, enabling: SI 2002/173, SI 2002/232, SI 2002/1330, SI 2002/2089, SI 2002/3060, SI 2003/1994, SI 2004/1038, SI 2004/1792

CAP.

1973–cont.

18. Matrimonial Causes Act 1973
see *Kimber v Brookman Solicitors* [2004] 2 F.L.R. 221 (Fam Div), Coleridge, J.
Part II, applied: 2004 c.33 s.72
Part II, referred to: 2004 c.33 s.72
s.1, see *Bhaiji v Chauhan* [2003] 2 F.L.R. 485 (Fam Div), Wilson, J.
s.10A, added: 2002 c.27 s.1
s.11, see *Bellinger v Bellinger* [2001] EWCA Civ 1140, [2002] Fam. 150 (CA), Dame Elizabeth Butler-Sloss (President); see *Bellinger v Bellinger* [2003] UKHL 21, [2003] 2 A.C. 467 (HL), Lord Nicholls of Birkenhead; see *KB v National Health Service Pensions Agency (C117/01)* [2004] All E.R. (EC) 1089 (ECJ), Judge Skouris (President)
s.11, amended: 2004 c.33 Sch.27 para.40
s.12, see *P v R (Forced Marriage: Annulment: Procedure)* [2003] 1 F.L.R. 661 (Fam Div), Coleridge, J.
s.12, amended: 2004 c.7 Sch.2 para.2, Sch.4 para.5
s.13, amended: 2004 c.7 Sch.2 para.3, Sch.4 para.6
s.14, amended: 2004 c.33 Sch.27 para.41
s.22, see *G v G (Maintenance Pending Suit: Legal Costs)* [2002] EWHC 306, [2003] 2 F.L.R. 71 (Fam Div), Charles, J.
s.22A, applied: 2003 c.14 Sch.3 para.3
s.23, see *Nunn (Bankruptcy: Divorce: Pension Rights), Re* [2004] 1 F.L.R. 1123 (Ch D), Nicholas Strauss Q.C.
s.23A, applied: 2003 c.14 Sch.3 para.3
s.24, see *C v C (Financial Provision: Post Nuptial Settlements)* [2004] EWCA Civ 1030, [2004] 2 F.L.R. 1093 (CA), Thorpe, L.J.; see *C v C (Financial Provision: Post Nuptial Settlements)* [2004] EWHC 742, [2004] Fam. 141 (Fam Div), Wilson, J.; see *Customs and Excise Commissioners v A* [2002] EWCA Civ 1039, [2003] Fam. 55 (CA), Schiemann, L.J.; see *Customs and Excise Commissioners v A* [2002] EWHC 611, [2002] 2 F.L.R. 274 (QBD (Admin Ct)), Munby, J.; see *Mountney v Treharne* [2002] 2 F.L.R. 406 (Ch D), Stanley Burnton, J.; see *Mountney v Treharne* [2002] EWCA Civ 1174, [2003] Ch. 135 (CA), Jonathan Parker, L.J.
s.24A, amended: 2004 c.33 Sch.27 para.42
s.24A, applied: 2003 c.14 Sch.3 para.3
s.25, see *Akintola v Akintola (Transfer of Tenancy)* [2001] EWCA Civ 1989, [2002] 1 F.L.R. 701 (CA), Thorpe, L.J.; see *CO v CO (Ancillary Relief: Pre Marriage Cohabitation)* [2004] EWHC 287, [2004] 1 F.L.R. 1095 (Fam Div), Coleridge, J.; see *Cowan v Cowan* [2001] EWCA Civ 679, [2002] Fam. 97 (CA), Thorpe, L.J.; see *G (Financial Provision: Liberty to Restore Application for Lump Sum), Re* [2004]

1973–cont.

18. Matrimonial Causes Act 1973–*cont.*

s.25–*cont.*

EWHC 88, [2004] 1 F.L.R. 997 (Fam Div), Singer, J.; see *H v H* [2002] 1 F.C.R. 55 (Fam Div), Coleridge, J.; see *J v J (Ancillary Relief: Periodical Payments)* [2004] EWHC 53, [2004] 1 F.C.R. 709 (Fam Div), Bennett, J.; see *K v K (Ancillary Relief: Prenuptial Agreement)* [2003] 1 F.L.R. 120 (Fam Div), Rodger Hayward-Smith Q.C.; see *Lambert v Lambert* [2002] 1 F.L.R. 642 (Fam Div), Connell, J.; see *Lambert v Lambert* [2002] EWCA Civ 1685, [2003] Fam. 103 (CA), Thorpe, L.J.; see *M v L (Financial Relief after Overseas Divorce)* [2003] EWHC 328, [2003] 2 F.L.R. 425 (Fam Div), Coleridge, J.; see *McFarlane v McFarlane* [2004] EWCA Civ 872, [2004] 3 W.L.R. 1480 (CA), Thorpe, L.J.; see *McMinn v McMinn (Ancillary Relief: Death of Party to Proceedings)* [2002] EWHC 1194, [2003] 2 F.L.R. 823 (Fam Div), Black, J.; see *McMinn v McMinn (Ancillary Relief: Death of Party to Proceedings: Costs)* [2003] 2 F.L.R. 839 (Fam Div), Black, J.; see *Norris v Norris* [2002] EWHC 2996, [2003] 1 F.L.R. 1142 (Fam Div), Bennett, J.; see *R v R (Lump Sum Repayments)* [2003] EWHC 3197, [2004] 1 F.L.R. 928 (Fam Div), Wilson, J.; see *X v X* [2002] 1 F.L.R. 508 (Fam Div), Munby, J.

s.25A, see *F v F (Clean Break: Balance of Fairness)* [2003] 1 F.L.R. 847 (Fam Div), Singer, J.; see *McFarlane v McFarlane* [2004] EWCA Civ 872, [2004] 3 W.L.R. 1480 (CA), Thorpe, L.J.; see *P v P (Divorce: Financial Provision: Clean Break)* [2002] EWCA Civ 1886, [2003] 1 F.L.R. 942 (CA), Thorpe, L.J.

s.25E, added: 2004 c.35 Sch.12 para.3

s.28, amended: 2004 c.33 Sch.27 para.43

s.31, see *Fleming v Fleming* [2003] EWCA Civ 1841, [2004] 1 F.L.R. 667 (CA), Thorpe, L.J.; see *W v W (Ancillary Relief: Non-Disclosure)* [2003] EWHC 2254, [2004] 1 F.L.R. 494 (Fam Div), Nicholas Mostyn Q.C.; see *Westbury v Sampson* [2001] EWCA Civ 407, [2002] 1 F.L.R. 166 (CA), Bodey, J.

s.34, see *H v H* [2002] 1 F.C.R. 55 (Fam Div), Coleridge, J.

s.35, amended: 2003 c.39 Sch.8 para.169, 2004 c.33 Sch.27 para.44

s.37, see *F v F (Financial Provision: Bankruptcy: Reviewable Disposition)* [2002] EWHC 2814, [2003] 1 F.L.R. 911 (Fam Div), Coleridge, J.; see *Field v Field* [2003] 1 F.L.R. 376 (Fam Div), Wilson, J.

s.38, amended: 2003 c.39 Sch.8 para.170, 2004 c.33 Sch.27 para.45

s.41, see *Practice Direction (Fam Div: Conciliation)* [2004] 1 W.L.R. 1287 (Fam Div), Senior District Judge Waller

1973–cont.

18. Matrimonial Causes Act 1973–*cont.*

s.52, amended: 2004 c.33 Sch.27 para.46

Sch.1 Part II para.11, amended: 2004 c.7 Sch.2 para.4

21. Overseas Pensions Act 1973

applied: 2002 c.18 Sch.2 Part 2, Sch.2 Part 22, 2003 c.13 Sch.2 Part 2, Sch.2 Part 26, 2003 c.1 s.566, 2004 c.9 Sch.2 Part 2, Sch.2 Part 25

s.1, applied: 2003 c.1 s.629, s.643, s.651

s.1, disapplied: 2003 c.1 s.643

s.2, amended: 2002 c.1 Sch.3 para.5

s.2, applied: 2003 c.1 s.650, s.652, s.654

s.2, referred to: 2003 c.1 s.650, s.652

26. Land Compensation Act 1973

applied: SI 2003/3364 Sch.4 para.2, SI 2004/757 Sch.8 para.2

varied: SI 2002/1066 Sch.7 para.2, Sch.7 para.3

Part I, see *Nesbitt v National Assembly for Wales* [2003] R.V.R. 302 (Lands Tr), NJ Rose, FRICS

Part III, applied: SI 2004/1005 Sch.2

Part III, added: 2004 c.5 s.106

s.7, varied: SI 2002/1066 Sch.7 para.4

s.8, varied: SI 2002/1066 Sch.7 para.5

s.9, see *Brunt v Southampton International Airport Ltd* [2004] R.V.R. 81 (Lands Tr), George Bartlett Q.C. (President)

s.12A, amended: 2002 c.15 Sch.8 para.1, Sch.14

s.29, see *Ingle v Scarborough BC* [2002] EWCA Civ 290, [2002] H.L.R. 36 (CA), May, L.J.

s.29, amended: 2004 c.5 Sch.7 para.7, 2004 c.34 Sch.15 para.3

s.29A, amended: 2004 c.33 Sch.9 para.17

s.30, applied: SI 2003/1706 Reg.3, SI 2004/1631 Reg.2, SI 2004/1758 Reg.2

s.30, varied: SI 2003/1856 Reg.2

s.30, enabling: SI 2003/1706, SI 2003/1856, SI 2004/1631, SI 2004/1758

s.33A, disapplied: 2004 c.5 s.106

s.33B, added: 2004 c.5 s.107

s.33B, disapplied: 2004 c.5 s.107

s.33C, added: 2004 c.5 s.107

s.33C, disapplied: 2004 c.5 s.107

s.33D, added: 2004 c.5 s.108

s.33D, amended: 2004 c.34 Sch.15 para.4

s.33D, disapplied: 2004 c.5 s.108

s.33E, added: 2004 c.5 s.109

s.33F, added: 2004 c.5 s.109

s.33G, added: 2004 c.5 s.109

s.33H, added: 2004 c.5 s.109

s.33I, added: 2004 c.5 s.109

s.33J, added: 2004 c.5 s.109

s.33K, added: 2004 c.5 s.109

s.34, repealed: 2004 c.5 Sch.9

s.35, repealed: 2004 c.5 Sch.9

s.36, repealed: 2004 c.5 Sch.9

1973–cont.

26. Land Compensation Act 1973–*cont.*
s.37, see *Evis v Commission for New Towns* [2002] 2 E.G.L.R. 167 (Lands Tr), George Bartlett Q.C.
s.37, amended: 2004 c.34 Sch.15 para.5, Sch.16
s.39, amended: 2004 c.34 Sch.15 para.6, Sch.16
s.39, applied: SI 2002/3264 Reg.3, SI 2003/239 Reg.3
s.44, varied: SI 2002/412 Sch.4 para.2, SI 2002/1064 Sch.2 para.2, SI 2002/1065 Sch.3 para.2, SI 2002/1066 Sch.7 para.2, SI 2002/1327 Sch.4 para.2, SI 2003/1075 Sch.9 para.2, SI 2003/3364 Sch.4 para.2, SI 2004/389 Sch.9 para.2, SI 2004/757 Sch.8 para.2
s.52, see *Wiberg v Swansea City and County Council* [2002] R.V.R. 143 (Lands Tr), George Bartlett Q.C.
s.52, amended: 2004 c.5 s.104
s.52A, amended: 2004 c.5 s.104
s.52ZA, added: 2004 c.5 s.104
s.52ZB, added: 2004 c.5 s.104
s.52ZC, added: 2004 c.5 s.104
s.58, varied: SI 2002/412 Sch.4 para.2, SI 2002/1064 Sch.2 para.2, SI 2002/1065 Sch.3 para.2, SI 2002/1066 Sch.7 para.2, SI 2002/1327 Sch.4 para.2, SI 2003/1075 Sch.9 para.2, SI 2003/3364 Sch.4 para.2, SI 2004/389 Sch.9 para.2, SI 2004/757 Sch.8 para.2
s.87, amended: 2004 c.5 Sch.9

27. Bahamas Independence Act 1973
Sch.2 para.10, repealed: 2002 c.39 Sch.3

32. National Health Service Reorganisation Act 1973
Sch.4 para.92, repealed: 2003 c.42 Sch.7

33. Protection of Wrecks Act 1973
applied: SI 2002/1858 Art.2, SI 2004/2395 Art.2
s.1, enabling: SI 2002/1858, SI 2004/2395, SI 2004/3243, SI 2004/3249
s.3, enabling: SI 2004/2395

35. Employment Agencies Act 1973
applied: SI 2003/335 Sch.1, 2004 c.11 s.27
disapplied: 2004 c.11 s.27
referred to: SI 2003/3319 Reg.29, Reg.30
s.3C, applied: SI 2004/1861 Sch.1 para.53
s.5, enabling: SI 2003/3319, SI 2004/14
s.6, disapplied: SI 2003/3319 Reg.26
s.6, enabling: SI 2003/3319, SI 2004/14
s.9, applied: SI 2003/3319 Reg.29
s.12, applied: SI 2003/3319
s.12, enabling: SI 2003/3319, SI 2004/14

36. Northern Ireland Constitution Act 1973
s.10, repealed (in part): 2002 c.26 Sch.13
s.34, repealed: 2002 c.26 Sch.13
s.35, amended: 2002 c.26 s.18, s.20, Sch.7 para.14

1973–cont.

39. Statute Law (Repeals) Act 1973
Sch.2, repealed: 2004 c.14 Sch.1 Part 2

41. Fair Trading Act 1973
applied: 2002 c.40 Sch.15, Sch.24 para.16, Sch.24 para.17, SI 2003/419 Art.63
referred to: 2003 c.21 s.393
Part I, applied: 2002 c.40 Sch.14
Part II, applied: 2002 c.40 Sch.14
Part II, referred to: 2002 c.40 s.10, SI 2003/750 Sch.5 para.12, SI 2003/751 Sch.6 para.12
Part II, repealed: 2002 c.40 Sch.26
Part III, applied: 2002 c.40 Sch.14, SI 2003/1397 Art.7
Part III, referred to: SI 2003/750 Sch.5 para.12, SI 2003/751 Sch.6 para.12
Part IV, applied: 2002 c.40 s.243, Sch.14
Part V, applied: 2002 c.40 s.121, s.243, Sch.14, Sch.24 para.13
Part VI, applied: 2002 c.40 s.243, Sch.14
Part VII, applied: 2002 c.40 Sch.14
Part VIII, applied: 2002 c.40 Sch.14
Part XI, see *Alpha Club (UK) Ltd, Re* [2002] EWHC 884, [2002] 2 B.C.L.C. 612 (Ch D), John Jarvis Q.C.
Part XI, applied: 2002 c.40 Sch.14
s.1, repealed: 2002 c.40 Sch.26
s.2, repealed: 2002 c.40 Sch.26
s.3, repealed: 2002 c.40 s.10, Sch.26
s.5, amended: 2002 c.40 Sch.25 para.5
s.5, repealed (in part): 2002 c.40 Sch.26, SI 2003/3180 Sch.1 para.1
s.6, repealed: 2002 c.40 Sch.26
s.7, repealed: 2002 c.40 Sch.26
s.8, repealed: 2002 c.40 Sch.26
s.9, repealed: 2002 c.40 Sch.26
s.10, repealed: 2002 c.40 Sch.26
s.11, repealed: 2002 c.40 Sch.26
s.12, repealed: 2002 c.40 Sch.26
s.23, applied: SI 2003/1376 Sch.1
s.30, amended: 2002 c.40 Sch.26, 2004 c.33 Sch.27 para.47
s.30, repealed (in part): 2002 c.40 Sch.26
s.34, repealed: 2002 c.40 Sch.26
s.35, repealed: 2002 c.40 Sch.26
s.36, repealed: 2002 c.40 Sch.26
s.37, repealed: 2002 c.40 Sch.26
s.38, repealed: 2002 c.40 Sch.26
s.39, repealed: 2002 c.40 Sch.26
s.40, repealed: 2002 c.40 Sch.26
s.41, repealed: 2002 c.40 Sch.26
s.41A, repealed: 2002 c.40 Sch.26
s.42, repealed: 2002 c.40 Sch.26
s.44, applied: 2002 c.40 Sch.24 para.14
s.44, repealed: 2002 c.40 Sch.26
s.45, repealed: 2002 c.40 Sch.26
s.46, repealed: 2002 c.40 Sch.26
s.47, repealed: 2002 c.40 Sch.26
s.48, repealed: 2002 c.40 Sch.26
s.49, repealed: 2002 c.40 Sch.26

1973–cont.

41. Fair Trading Act 1973–*cont.*
s.50, applied: 2002 c.40 Sch.24 para.14
s.50, repealed: 2002 c.40 Sch.26
s.51, amended: SI 2002/2626 Sch.2 para.8
s.51, applied: 2002 c.40 Sch.24 para.14, SI 2002/794 Art.3
s.51, repealed: 2002 c.40 Sch.26
s.52, repealed: 2002 c.40 Sch.26
s.53, repealed: 2002 c.40 Sch.26
s.54, repealed: 2002 c.40 Sch.26
s.55, repealed: 2002 c.40 Sch.26
s.56, applied: 2002 c.40 Sch.24 para.15, Sch.24 para.17, SI 2002/3204, SI 2003/52, SI 2004/2181 Sch.2
s.56, repealed: 2002 c.40 Sch.26
s.56, enabling: SI 2002/3204, SI 2003/52
s.56A, applied: 2002 c.40 Sch.24 para.15, Sch.24 para.16
s.56A, repealed: 2002 c.40 Sch.26
s.56B, repealed: 2002 c.40 Sch.26
s.56C, repealed: 2002 c.40 Sch.26
s.56D, repealed: 2002 c.40 Sch.26
s.56E, repealed: 2002 c.40 Sch.26
s.56F, applied: 2002 c.40 Sch.24 para.15, Sch.24 para.16
s.56F, repealed: 2002 c.40 Sch.26
s.56G, repealed: 2002 c.40 Sch.26
s.57, applied: 2002 c.40 s.121, SI 2003/3180 Art.3
s.57, repealed: 2003 c.21 Sch.19
s.58, applied: 2002 c.40 s.69, s.121, 2003 c.21 Sch.18 para.62, SI 2003/3180 Art.3
s.58, referred to: SI 2003/3180 Art.3
s.58, repealed: 2003 c.21 Sch.19
s.59, applied: 2002 c.40 s.69, s.121
s.59, repealed: 2003 c.21 Sch.19
s.60, applied: 2002 c.40 s.121
s.60, repealed: 2003 c.21 Sch.19
s.61, applied: 2002 c.40 s.121
s.61, repealed: 2003 c.21 Sch.19
s.62, repealed: 2003 c.21 Sch.19
s.63, repealed: 2002 c.40 Sch.26
s.64, applied: 2002 c.40 Sch.24 para.13
s.64, repealed: 2002 c.40 Sch.26
s.65, repealed: 2002 c.40 Sch.26
s.66, repealed: 2002 c.40 Sch.26
s.66A, repealed: 2002 c.40 Sch.26
s.67, repealed: 2002 c.40 Sch.26
s.68, repealed: 2002 c.40 Sch.26
s.69, repealed: 2002 c.40 Sch.26
s.70, repealed: 2002 c.40 Sch.26
s.71, repealed: 2002 c.40 Sch.26
s.72, repealed: 2002 c.40 Sch.26
s.73, applied: 2002 c.40 Sch.24 para.15, Sch.24 para.17
s.73, repealed: 2002 c.40 Sch.26
s.74, applied: 2002 c.40 Sch.24 para.15, Sch.24 para.17
s.74, repealed: 2002 c.40 Sch.26
s.75, amended: 2002 c.8 s.2

1973–cont.

41. Fair Trading Act 1973–*cont.*
s.75, applied: 2002 c.40 Sch.24 para.13
s.75, repealed: 2002 c.40 Sch.26
s.75A, repealed: 2002 c.40 Sch.26
s.75B, applied: 2002 c.40 Sch.24 para.13
s.75B, repealed: 2002 c.40 Sch.26
s.75C, applied: 2002 c.40 Sch.24 para.13
s.75C, repealed: 2002 c.40 Sch.26
s.75D, repealed: 2002 c.40 Sch.26
s.75E, repealed: 2002 c.40 Sch.26
s.75F, repealed: 2002 c.40 Sch.26
s.75G, applied: 2002 c.40 Sch.24 para.13, Sch.24 para.15, Sch.24 para.16, SI 2003/1397 Art.4
s.75G, repealed: 2002 c.40 Sch.26
s.75H, repealed: 2002 c.40 Sch.26
s.75J, applied: 2002 c.40 Sch.24 para.16
s.75J, repealed: 2002 c.40 Sch.26
s.75K, applied: 2002 c.40 Sch.24 para.15, Sch.24 para.17
s.75K, repealed: 2002 c.40 Sch.26
s.76, repealed: 2002 c.40 Sch.26
s.77, repealed (in part): 2002 c.40 Sch.26, SI 2003/3180 Sch.1 para.1
s.78, repealed: 2002 c.40 Sch.26
s.79, repealed: 2002 c.40 Sch.26
s.80, repealed: 2002 c.40 Sch.26
s.81, repealed: 2002 c.40 Sch.26
s.82, amended: 2002 c.40 Sch.26
s.82, repealed (in part): 2002 c.40 Sch.26, SI 2003/3180 Sch.1 para.1
s.83, amended: 2002 c.40 Sch.26
s.83, repealed: SI 2003/3180 Sch.1 para.1
s.84, repealed: 2002 c.40 Sch.26
s.85, repealed: SI 2003/3180 Sch.1 para.1
s.86, repealed: 2002 c.40 Sch.26
s.87, repealed: SI 2003/3180 Sch.1 para.1
s.88, applied: 2002 c.40 Sch.24 para.15, Sch.24 para.16, SI 2003/1397 Art.4, SI 2004/2181 Sch.1, SI 2004/3233 Art.4
s.88, repealed: 2002 c.40 Sch.26
s.89, applied: 2002 c.40 Sch.24 para.15, Sch.24 para.17
s.89, repealed: 2002 c.40 Sch.26
s.89, enabling: SI 2002/108
s.90, repealed: 2002 c.40 Sch.26
s.90, enabling: SI 2002/108, SI 2002/3204, SI 2003/52
s.91, applied: SI 2002/3204, SI 2003/52
s.91, repealed: 2002 c.40 Sch.26
s.92, repealed: 2002 c.40 Sch.26
s.93, disapplied: 2002 c.40 Sch.24 para.15
s.93, repealed: 2002 c.40 Sch.26
s.93A, disapplied: 2002 c.40 Sch.24 para.15
s.93A, repealed: 2002 c.40 Sch.26
s.93B, amended: 2002 c.40 Sch.25 para.5, Sch.26, 2003 c.21 Sch.19
s.93B, repealed (in part): SI 2003/3180 Sch.1 para.1
s.94, amended: 2004 c.14 Sch.1 Part 16

1973–cont.

41. Fair Trading Act 1973–cont.

s.120, see *Alpha Club (UK) Ltd, Re* [2002] EWHC 884, [2002] 2 B.C.L.C. 612 (Ch D), John Jarvis Q.C.

s.124, repealed: 2002 c.40 Sch.26

s.125, referred to: SI 2003/750 Sch.5 para.12, SI 2003/751 Sch.6 para.12

s.125, repealed: 2002 c.40 Sch.26

s.129, amended: 2002 c.40 Sch.26

s.130, repealed: 2002 c.40 Sch.26

s.131, repealed: 2002 c.40 Sch.26

s.132, amended: 2002 c.40 Sch.26, SI 2003/ 3180 Sch.1 para.1

s.133, amended: 2003 c.20 Sch.2 para.19

s.133, referred to: 2003 c.20 s.115

s.133, repealed: 2002 c.40 Sch.26

s.134, disapplied: 2002 c.40 Sch.24 para.17

s.134, enabling: SI 2002/108, SI 2002/3204, SI 2003/52

s.137, amended: 2002 c.40 Sch.26, 2003 c.21 Sch.17 para.44, SI 2003/3180 Sch.1 para.1

s.137, repealed (in part): SI 2003/3180 Sch.1 para.1

s.138, amended: 2002 c.40 Sch.26

s.140, repealed (in part): 2004 c.14 Sch.1 Part 16

Sch.1 para.1, repealed: 2002 c.40 Sch.26

Sch.1 para.2, repealed: 2002 c.40 Sch.26

Sch.1 para.3, repealed: 2002 c.40 Sch.26

Sch.1 para.4, repealed: 2002 c.40 Sch.26

Sch.1 para.5, repealed: 2002 c.40 Sch.26

Sch.1 para.6, repealed: 2002 c.40 Sch.26

Sch.1 para.7, repealed: 2002 c.40 Sch.26

Sch.2 para.1, repealed: 2002 c.40 Sch.26

Sch.2 para.2, repealed: 2002 c.40 Sch.26

Sch.2 para.3, repealed: 2002 c.40 Sch.26

Sch.2 para.4, repealed: 2002 c.40 Sch.26

Sch.2 para.5, repealed: 2002 c.40 Sch.26

Sch.2 para.6, repealed: 2002 c.40 Sch.26

Sch.2 para.7, repealed: 2002 c.40 Sch.26

Sch.2 para.8, repealed: 2002 c.40 Sch.26

Sch.2 para.9, repealed: 2002 c.40 Sch.26

Sch.3 Part I para.2, applied: SI 2003/1376 Art.4

Sch.4 para.1, repealed: 2002 c.40 Sch.26

Sch.4 para.2, repealed: 2002 c.40 Sch.26

Sch.4 para.3, repealed: 2002 c.40 Sch.26

Sch.4 para.4, repealed: 2002 c.40 Sch.26

Sch.4 para.5, repealed: 2002 c.40 Sch.26

Sch.4 para.6, repealed: 2002 c.40 Sch.26

Sch.4 para.6, substituted: SI 2002/253 Sch.5 para.3

Sch.4 para.7, amended: SI 2002/253 Sch.5 para.3

Sch.4 para.7, repealed: 2002 c.40 Sch.26

Sch.4 para.8, repealed: 2002 c.40 Sch.26

Sch.4 para.9, repealed: 2002 c.40 Sch.26

Sch.4 para.10, repealed: 2002 c.40 Sch.26

Sch.4 para.10A, repealed: 2002 c.40 Sch.26

1973–cont.

41. Fair Trading Act 1973–cont.

Sch.4 para.11, repealed: 2002 c.40 Sch.26

Sch.4 para.12, repealed: 2002 c.40 Sch.26

Sch.4 para.13, repealed: 2002 c.40 Sch.26

Sch.4 para.14, repealed: 2002 c.40 Sch.26

Sch.4 para.15, repealed: 2002 c.40 Sch.26

Sch.5 Part I para.1, repealed: 2002 c.40 Sch.26

Sch.5 Part I para.3, repealed: 2002 c.40 Sch.26

Sch.5 Part I para.4, repealed: 2002 c.40 Sch.26

Sch.5 Part I para.5, repealed: 2002 c.40 Sch.26

Sch.5 Part I para.6, repealed: 2002 c.40 Sch.26

Sch.5 Part I para.7, repealed: 2002 c.40 Sch.26

Sch.6 para.1, repealed: 2002 c.40 Sch.26

Sch.6 para.2, repealed: 2002 c.40 Sch.26

Sch.6 para.3, repealed: 2002 c.40 Sch.26

Sch.6 para.4, repealed: 2002 c.40 Sch.26

Sch.6 para.5, repealed: 2002 c.40 Sch.26

Sch.6 para.6, repealed: 2002 c.40 Sch.26

Sch.7 Part I para.1, repealed: 2002 c.40 Sch.26

Sch.7 Part I para.2, repealed: 2002 c.40 Sch.26

Sch.7 Part I para.3, repealed: 2002 c.40 Sch.26

Sch.7 Part I para.4, repealed: 2002 c.40 Sch.26

Sch.7 Part I para.5, repealed: 2002 c.40 Sch.26

Sch.7 Part I para.6, repealed: 2002 c.40 Sch.26

Sch.7 Part I para.7, repealed: 2002 c.40 Sch.26

Sch.7 Part I para.8, repealed: 2002 c.40 Sch.26

Sch.7 Part I para.9, repealed: 2002 c.40 Sch.26

Sch.7 Part II, repealed: 2002 c.40 Sch.26

Sch.7 Part III, repealed: 2002 c.40 Sch.26

Sch.8 Part I para.1, repealed: 2002 c.40 Sch.26

Sch.8 Part I para.1, enabling: SI 2002/3204, SI 2003/52

Sch.8 Part I para.2, repealed: 2002 c.40 Sch.26

Sch.8 Part I para.2, enabling: SI 2002/3204, SI 2003/52

Sch.8 Part I para.3, repealed: 2002 c.40 Sch.26

Sch.8 Part I para.4, repealed: 2002 c.40 Sch.26

Sch.8 Part I para.4, enabling: SI 2003/52

Sch.8 Part I para.5, repealed: 2002 c.40 Sch.26

Sch.8 Part I para.6, repealed: 2002 c.40 Sch.26

1973–cont.

41. Fair Trading Act 1973–*cont.*

Sch.8 Part I para.7, repealed: 2002 c.40 Sch.26

Sch.8 Part I para.8, repealed: 2002 c.40 Sch.26

Sch.8 Part I para.8, enabling: SI 2003/52

Sch.8 Part I para.9, repealed: 2002 c.40 Sch.26

Sch.8 Part I para.9, enabling: SI 2003/52

Sch.8 Part I para.9A, repealed: 2002 c.40 Sch.26

Sch.8 Part I para.10, repealed: 2002 c.40 Sch.26

Sch.8 Part I para.11, repealed: 2002 c.40 Sch.26

Sch.8 Part I para.12, repealed: 2002 c.40 Sch.26

Sch.8 Part I para.12A, repealed: 2002 c.40 Sch.26

Sch.8 Part I para.12B, repealed: 2002 c.40 Sch.26

Sch.8 Part I para.12C, repealed: 2002 c.40 Sch.26

Sch.8 Part I para.13, repealed: 2002 c.40 Sch.26

Sch.8 Part II para.14, repealed: 2002 c.40 Sch.26

Sch.8 Part II para.14, enabling: SI 2002/3204

Sch.8 Part II para.15, repealed: 2002 c.40 Sch.26

Sch.9, applied: SI 2002/3204

Sch.9 para.1, repealed: 2002 c.40 Sch.26

Sch.9 para.2, repealed: 2002 c.40 Sch.26

Sch.9 para.3, repealed: 2002 c.40 Sch.26

Sch.9 para.4, repealed: 2002 c.40 Sch.26

Sch.11 para.1, applied: SI 2003/1397 Art.6

Sch.11 para.9, applied: SI 2003/1397 Art.6

43. Hallmarking Act 1973

applied: 2002 c.40 Sch.14, Sch.15, SI 2002/506 Art.4, Art.5, SI 2003/1376 Sch.1, SI 2003/1593 Sch.1 Part I

s.2, applied: SI 2002/506 Art.3, Art.6

s.2, enabling: SI 2002/506

s.4, applied: SI 2002/506 Art.5

s.4, varied: SI 2002/506 Art.5

s.21, enabling: SI 2002/506

Sch.2 Part I para.1, referred to: SI 2002/506 Art.6

Sch.4 para.19, amended: SI 2003/1326 Art.8

45. Domicile and Matrimonial Proceedings Act 1973

s.5, see *Armstrong v Armstrong* [2003] EWHC 777, [2003] 2 F.L.R. 375 (Fam Div), Dame Elizabeth Butler-Sloss (President); see *Ikimi v Ikimi (Divorce: Habitual Residence)* [2001] EWCA Civ 873, [2002] Fam. 72 (CA), Thorpe, L.J.; see *O v O (Appeal against Stay: Divorce Petition)* [2002] EWCA Civ 949, [2003] 1 F.L.R. 192 (CA), Thorpe, L.J.

Sch.1, applied: 2004 c.33 s.223

1973–cont.

45. Domicile and Matrimonial Proceedings Act 1973–*cont.*

Sch.1 para.9, see *Armstrong v Armstrong* [2003] EWHC 777, [2003] 2 F.L.R. 375 (Fam Div), Dame Elizabeth Butler-Sloss (President)

Sch.3, applied: 2004 c.33 s.226

49. Bangladesh Act 1973

Sch.1 para.11, repealed: 2002 c.39 Sch.3

50. Employment and Training Act 1973

applied: SI 2003/1325 Art.2, SI 2003/1660 Reg.19, SI 2003/1661 Reg.19, SSI 2003/93 Sch.1

s.2, applied: 2002 c.21 s.1, SI 2002/1792 Sch.2 para.14, SI 2002/2005 Reg.9, Reg.18, SI 2002/2006 Reg.16, Reg.19, SI 2002/3200 Reg.29, SI 2003/335 Sch.1, SI 2003/673 Art.3, SI 2003/1660 Reg.19, SI 2003/1661 Reg.19, SI 2003/2041 Reg.2, SI 2003/3237 Reg.4, SI 2004/118 Art.3, SI 2004/959 Reg.4, SSI 2003/93 Sch.1, SSI 2003/176 Art.8

s.8, applied: 2003 c.42 s.21, SI 2003/3237 Reg.4

s.9, applied: 2003 c.42 s.21, SI 2003/335 Sch.1, SI 2003/3237 Reg.4, SSI 2003/93 Sch.1

s.10, applied: SI 2002/2897 Reg.14, 2003 c.42 s.21, SI 2003/3237 Reg.4

s.12, repealed (in part): 2004 c.14 Sch.1 Part 8

s.15, amended: 2004 c.14 Sch.1 Part 8

s.15, repealed (in part): 2004 c.14 Sch.1 Part 8

Sch.3 para.1, repealed: 2004 c.14 Sch.1 Part 8

Sch.3 para.2, repealed: 2004 c.14 Sch.1 Part 8

Sch.3 para.8, repealed: 2004 c.14 Sch.1 Part 8

Sch.3 para.11, repealed (in part): 2004 c.14 Sch.1 Part 8

51. Finance Act 1973

s.56, applied: SI 2002/1144 Reg.15, SI 2004/1882, SI 2004/2689

s.56, enabling: SI 2002/401, SI 2002/511, SI 2002/537, SI 2002/538, SI 2002/539, SI 2002/542, SI 2002/618, SI 2002/1415, SI 2002/2928, SI 2002/2942, SI 2003/551, SI 2003/625, SI 2003/1118, SI 2003/1811, SI 2003/1812, SI 2003/1813, SI 2003/2258, SI 2003/2321, SI 2003/2327, SI 2004/579, SI 2004/666, SI 2004/686, SI 2004/1157, SI 2004/1300, SI 2004/1604, SI 2004/1882, SI 2004/1883, SI 2004/1884, SI 2004/1885, SI 2004/1911, SI 2004/1977, SI 2004/2106, SI 2004/2407, SI 2004/2640, SI 2004/2643, SI 2004/2689, SI 2004/2750, SI 2004/2886, SI 2004/3081, SR 2002/50, SR 2002/309

Sch.8 para.7, applied: 2003 c.1 Sch.7 para.56

Sch.15, referred to: 2003 c.1 Sch.6 para.144

Sch.15 para.2, amended: 2003 c.1 Sch.6 para.145

Sch.15 para.5, amended: 2003 c.1 Sch.6 para.146

CAP.

1973–cont.

52. Prescription and Limitation (Scotland) Act 1973

Part I, applied: 2003 asp 9 s.18

s.1, see *Mason's Executors v Smith* 2002 S.L.T. 1169 (OH), Lord Mackay of Drumadoon

s.1, amended: 2003 asp 9 Sch.14 para.5

s.3, applied: 2003 asp 9 s.75

s.6, see *Adams v Thorntons WS* 2002 S.C.L.R. 787 (OH), Lord Macfadyen; see *BP Exploration Operating Co Ltd v Chevron Shipping Co* [2001] UKHL 50, [2003] 1 A.C. 197 (HL), Lord Hope of Craighead; see *Ghani v Peter T McCann & Co* 2002 S.L.T. (Sh Ct) 135 (Sh Pr), EF Bowen Q.C., Sheriff Principal; see *Glasgow City Council v Morrison Developments Ltd* 2003 S.L.T. 263 (OH), Lord Eassie; see *Orkney Islands Council v Charles Brand Ltd* 2002 S.L.T. 100 (OH), Lord Johnston

s.6, applied: 2003 asp 9 s.18

s.6, disapplied: 2004 c.12 s.321

s.7, see *K v Gilmartin's Executrix* 2002 S.C. 602 (OH), Lady Paton

s.7, applied: 2003 asp 9 s.18

s.8A, applied: 2003 asp 9 s.18

s.9, see *Orkney Islands Council v Charles Brand Ltd* 2002 S.L.T. 100 (OH), Lord Johnston; see *RM Supplies (Inverkeithing) Ltd v EMS Trans Schiffahrisges mbH & Co* 2003 S.L.T. 133 (OH), Lord Dawson

s.9, varied: 2003 asp 9 s.18

s.10, see *Wilkie v Direct Line Insurance Plc (No.2)* 2002 S.L.T. 530 (OH), Lord Kingarth

s.10, varied: 2003 asp 9 s.18

s.11, see *Adams v Thorntons WS* 2002 S.C.L.R. 787 (OH), Lord Macfadyen; see *Ghani v Peter T McCann & Co* 2002 S.L.T. (Sh Ct) 135 (Sh Pr), EF Bowen Q.C., Sheriff Principal; see *K v Gilmartin's Executrix* 2002 S.C. 602 (OH), Lady Paton

s.14, disapplied: 2003 asp 9 s.18

s.14, varied: 2003 asp 9 s.18

s.17, see *Agnew v Scott Lithgow Ltd (No.2)* 2003 S.C. 448 (Court of Session (Inner House, Extra Division)), Lady Cosgrove, Lord Abernethy, Lord Marnoch; see *Lambie v Toffolo Jackson Ltd (In Liquidation)* 2003 S.L.T. 1415 (1 Div), Lord Cullen L.P., Lord Kirkwood, Lord Macfadyen; see *Murray v National Association of Round Tables of Great Britain and Ireland* 2002 S.L.T. 204 (Ex Div), Lord McCluskey, Lady Cosgrove, Lord Coulsfield; see *Tudhope v Finlay Park (t/a Park Hutchison Solicitors)* 2003 S.L.T. 1305 (OH), Lady Paton

s.19A, see *Agnew v Scott Lithgow Ltd (No.2)* 2003 S.C. 448 (Court of Session (Inner House, Extra Division)), Lady Cosgrove, Lord Abernethy, Lord Marnoch; see *Campbell (or Pearson) v Imray* [2004]

CAP.

1973–cont.

52. Prescription and Limitation (Scotland) Act 1973–*cont.*

s.19A–*cont.*

P.N.L.R. 1 (OH), Lord Emslie; see *Gorrie v Marist Brothers* 2002 S.C.L.R. 436 (Sh Pr), JC McInnes Q.C., Sheriff Principal; see *Morrice v Martin Retail Group Ltd* 2003 S.C.L.R. 289 (OH), Lord Clarke

s.19B, added: 2002 c.29 s.288

s.23A, see *Kleinwort Benson Ltd v Glasgow City Council (No.3)* 2002 S.L.T. 1190 (OH), Lord Macfadyen

Sch.1 para.1, amended: 2003 asp 9 s.88, Sch.14 para.5, 2004 asp 11 s.15

Sch.1 para.2, see *Glasgow City Council v Morrison Developments Ltd* 2003 S.L.T. 263 (OH), Lord Eassie

Sch.1 para.2, amended: 2003 asp 9 s.88, 2004 asp 11 s.15

Sch.1 para.4, substituted: 2003 asp 9 Sch.14 para.5

Sch.3, amended: 2003 asp 9 Sch.14 para.5

Sch.3 s.8 para., see *Mason's Executors v Smith* 2002 S.L.T. 1169 (OH), Lord Mackay of Drumadoon

56. Land Compensation (Scotland) Act 1973

s.27, amended: 2003 asp 8 Sch.6 para.7

s.31, amended: SSI 2003/583 Sch.1 para.8

s.34, amended: 2003 asp 8 Sch.6 para.7

s.36, amended: 2003 asp 8 Sch.6 para.7

s.44, amended: SSI 2003/583 Sch.1 para.8

s.52, amended: SSI 2003/583 Sch.1 para.8

s.55, amended: SSI 2003/583 Sch.1 para.8

s.80, amended: SSI 2003/583 Sch.1 para.8

60. Breeding of Dogs Act 1973

disapplied: 2003 c.44 Sch.25 para.72

s.2, disapplied: 2003 c.44 Sch.25 para.72

s.3, amended: 2003 c.39 Sch.8 para.171, 2003 c.44 Sch.37 Part 9

s.3, repealed (in part): 2003 c.44 Sch.37 Part 9

62. Powers of Criminal Courts Act 1973

s.42, see *R. v Pope (Alan) (No.1)* [2002] UKHL 26, [2002] 1 W.L.R. 1966 (HL), Lord Hobhouse of Woodborough

63. Government Trading Funds Act 1973

applied: SI 2002/719(a), SI 2002/1951, SI 2003/1076(a), SI 2003/942, SI 2003/2094, SI 2004/1037

applied: SI 2002/831

s.1, applied: SI 2003/942, SI 2003/1076, SI 2004/1037

s.1, enabling: SI 2002/719, SI 2002/831, SI 2002/1951, SI 2003/105, SI 2003/942, SI 2003/1076, SI 2003/2094, SI 2004/1037, SI 2004/3277

s.2, applied: SI 2002/719, SI 2002/1951, SI 2003/1076, SI 2003/2094, SI 2004/1037

1973–cont.

63. Government Trading Funds Act 1973– *cont.*

s.2, enabling: SI 2002/719, SI 2002/831, SI 2003/942, SI 2003/1076, SI 2003/2094, SI 2004/1037, SI 2004/3277

s.2A, applied: SI 2002/719 Art.5, SI 2003/1076 Art.5, SI 2004/1037 Art.6

s.2A, enabling: SI 2002/719, SI 2003/105, SI 2003/942, SI 2003/1076, SI 2004/1037

s.2AA, enabling: SI 2002/719, SI 2003/105, SI 2003/1076, SI 2004/1037

s.2B, applied: SI 2002/719 Art.5, SI 2003/1076 Art.5, SI 2004/1037 Art.6

s.2C, enabling: SI 2002/719, SI 2003/1076, SI 2004/1037

s.4, varied: SI 2003/1633 Sch.2 para.2

s.6, applied: SI 2002/719, SI 2002/1951, SI 2003/942, SI 2003/1076, SI 2003/2094, SI 2004/1037

s.6, enabling: SI 2002/719, SI 2002/831, SI 2002/1951, SI 2003/105, SI 2003/942, SI 2003/1076, SI 2003/2094, SI 2004/3277

65. Local Government (Scotland) Act 1973

referred to: SI 2002/2779 Art.81, SSI 2004/257 Reg.2

Part II, applied: SI 2003/409 Sch.1 Part I

Part IIIA, applied: SSI 2002/201 Art.11, SSI 2003/1 Art.11

Part IV, applied: 2004 asp 6 s.48

Part VII, applied: 2002 asp 11 Sch.5, 2003 asp 1 s.14, s.39

s.12, varied: 2004 asp 9 s.4

s.13, varied: 2004 asp 9 s.4

s.14, applied: SSI 2002/154, SSI 2002/155, SSI 2002/156, SSI 2002/157

s.14, varied: 2004 asp 9 s.4

s.15, varied: 2004 asp 9 s.4

s.16, amended: 2004 asp 9 s.4

s.16, varied: 2004 asp 9 s.4

s.17, applied: SSI 2002/154, SSI 2002/155, SSI 2002/156, SSI 2002/157, 2004 asp 9 s.1

s.17, varied: 2004 asp 9 s.4

s.17, enabling: SSI 2002/154, SSI 2002/155, SSI 2002/156, SSI 2002/157

s.18, amended: 2004 asp 9 s.4

s.18, applied: 2004 asp 9 s.4

s.18, varied: 2004 asp 9 s.4

s.19, varied: 2004 asp 9 s.4

s.20, repealed: 2004 asp 9 s.4

s.20, varied: 2004 asp 9 s.4

s.21, varied: 2004 asp 9 s.4

s.22, varied: 2004 asp 9 s.4

s.23, varied: 2004 asp 9 s.4

s.24, varied: 2004 asp 9 s.4

s.25, varied: 2004 asp 9 s.4

s.26, varied: 2004 asp 9 s.4

s.27, varied: 2004 asp 9 s.4

s.28, amended: 2004 asp 9 s.4

1973–cont.

65. Local Government (Scotland) Act 1973–*cont.*

s.28, varied: 2004 asp 9 s.4

s.29, amended: 2004 asp 9 s.8, s.12

s.31, repealed (in part): 2004 asp 9 s.7

s.31A, added: 2004 asp 9 s.7

s.35, applied: SI 2003/3190 Reg.4

s.36, amended: 2002 asp 1 s.4

s.37, amended: 2002 asp 1 s.3, s.4

s.37, disapplied: 2002 asp 1 s.3

s.45, enabling: SSI 2002/15, SSI 2004/146

s.47, enabling: SSI 2002/15, SSI 2004/146

s.50A, amended: SI 2003/2155 Sch.1 para.8

s.51, applied: SSI 2002/62 Sch.3

s.56, applied: 2002 asp 11 Sch.2 para.9

s.64, amended: 2003 asp 13 Sch.4 para.2

s.67, substituted: 2004 asp 9 s.10

s.74, amended: 2003 asp 1 s.11

s.83, amended: 2003 asp 1 s.60

s.83, repealed (in part): 2003 asp 1 s.60

s.92, varied: SI 2003/1633 Sch.2 para.8

s.93, amended: 2003 asp 1 s.41

s.93, applied: SSI 2003/580 Reg.2

s.93, enabling: SSI 2003/580

s.94, applied: 2002 asp 7 s.5, 2003 asp 6 s.5

s.94, repealed: 2003 asp 1 s.60

s.96, referred to: SSI 2002/33 Art.13

s.97, amended: 2003 asp 1 s.53

s.97, applied: 2002 asp 11 Sch.5, 2003 asp 1 s.53, SI 2003/409 Sch.1 Part I

s.97A, amended: 2003 asp 1 s.6

s.97A, applied: 2002 asp 11 Sch.5

s.97B, amended: 2003 asp 1 s.54

s.99, amended: 2003 asp 1 s.55

s.99, referred to: 2003 asp 1 s.12

s.100, amended: 2003 asp 1 s.54

s.102, amended: 2003 asp 1 s.56

s.102, applied: 2002 asp 11 Sch.5, 2003 asp 1 s.3

s.103, applied: 2002 asp 11 Sch.5

s.103, repealed (in part): 2003 asp 1 s.4

s.103B, applied: 2003 asp 1 s.4

s.103C, applied: 2003 asp 1 s.4

s.103C, disapplied: 2003 asp 1 s.4

s.103D, applied: 2003 asp 1 s.3, s.4, s.5, s.23

s.103D, varied: 2003 asp 1 s.4

s.103E, applied: 2003 asp 1 s.5

s.105A, applied: 2002 asp 11 Sch.5

s.106, applied: 2003 asp 1 s.14, s.39

s.122A, repealed: 2003 asp 1 s.60

s.147, applied: 2002 asp 11 Sch.2 para.13, SI 2003/3172 Sch.2 Part I, Sch.2 Part II

s.170A, amended: 2002 asp 3 Sch.7 para.6

s.170B, amended: 2002 asp 3 Sch.7 para.6

s.171A, repealed: 2003 asp 1 s.60

s.171B, repealed: 2003 asp 1 s.60

s.171C, repealed: 2003 asp 1 s.60

s.192, applied: 2003 asp 8 s.37

s.192, varied: 2003 asp 8 s.37

CAP.

1973–cont.

65. Local Government (Scotland) Act 1973–*cont.*

s.202, applied: SSI 2002/410 Art.30, 2003 asp 2 s.12

s.202, referred to: SSI 2002/178 Art.8

s.202, varied: 2003 asp 2 s.12

s.202A, applied: 2003 asp 2 s.12

s.202B, applied: 2003 asp 2 s.12

s.202C, applied: 2003 asp 2 s.12

s.203, applied: 2003 asp 2 s.12

s.204, applied: 2003 asp 2 s.12

s.210, applied: SSI 2002/6 Reg.15, 2003 asp 8 s.52, 2004 asp 6 Sch.2 para.11, 2004 c.20 Sch.16 para.6

s.210, varied: SI 2003/3311 Sch.3 para.6, 2004 asp 6 Sch.2 para.11, 2004 c.31 s.6, SI 2004/652 Reg.11, SI 2004/1769 Reg.17

s.235, applied: 2002 asp 13 Sch.1 para.22, SSI 2002/62 Sch.1

s.235, enabling: SSI 2002/15, SSI 2004/146

Sch.5 para.1, repealed: 2004 asp 9 s.4

Sch.5 para.2, repealed: 2004 asp 9 s.4

Sch.6, applied: 2004 asp 9 s.4

Sch.6 para.1, amended: 2004 asp 9 s.4

Sch.7, applied: SSI 2002/201 Art.11, SSI 2003/1 Art.11

Sch.7 para.1, varied: SSI 2002/201 Art.10, 2003 asp 1 s.43, SSI 2003/1 Art.10

Sch.7 para.2, amended: 2003 asp 1 s.43

Sch.7 para.2, varied: SSI 2002/201 Art.10, 2003 asp 1 s.43, SSI 2003/1 Art.10

Sch.7 para.3, varied: SSI 2002/201 Art.10, 2003 asp 1 s.43, SSI 2003/1 Art.10

Sch.7 para.4, varied: SSI 2002/201 Art.10, 2003 asp 1 s.43, SSI 2003/1 Art.10

Sch.7 para.5, varied: SSI 2002/201 Art.10, 2003 asp 1 s.43, SSI 2003/1 Art.10

Sch.7 para.6, varied: SSI 2002/201 Art.10, 2003 asp 1 s.43, SSI 2003/1 Art.10

Sch.7 para.7, varied: SSI 2002/201 Art.10, 2003 asp 1 s.43, SSI 2003/1 Art.10

Sch.7 para.8, varied: SSI 2002/201 Art.10, 2003 asp 1 s.43, SSI 2003/1 Art.10

Sch.7 para.9, varied: SSI 2002/201 Art.10, 2003 asp 1 s.43, SSI 2003/1 Art.10

Sch.7 para.10, varied: SSI 2002/201 Art.10, 2003 asp 1 s.43, SSI 2003/1 Art.10

Sch.15 Part I para.1, repealed: 2003 asp 8 Sch.6 para.8

Sch.15 Part I para.2, repealed: 2003 asp 8 Sch.6 para.8

Sch.15 Part I para.3, repealed: 2003 asp 8 Sch.6 para.8

Sch.15 Part I para.4, repealed: 2003 asp 8 Sch.6 para.8

Sch.15 Part I para.5, repealed: 2003 asp 8 Sch.6 para.8

Sch.15 Part I para.6, repealed: 2003 asp 8 Sch.6 para.8

Sch.15 Part I para.7, repealed: 2003 asp 8 Sch.6 para.8

CAP.

1973–cont.

65. Local Government (Scotland) Act 1973–*cont.*

Sch.15 Part I para.8, repealed: 2003 asp 8 Sch.6 para.8

Sch.15 Part I para.9, repealed: 2003 asp 8 Sch.6 para.8

Sch.15 Part I para.10, repealed: 2003 asp 8 Sch.6 para.8

Sch.15 Part I para.11, repealed: 2003 asp 8 Sch.6 para.8

Sch.15 Part I para.12, repealed: 2003 asp 8 Sch.6 para.8

Sch.15 Part I para.13, repealed: 2003 asp 8 Sch.6 para.8

Sch.15 Part I para.14, repealed: 2003 asp 8 Sch.6 para.8

Sch.15 Part I para.15, repealed: 2003 asp 8 Sch.6 para.8

Sch.15 Part I para.16, repealed: 2003 asp 8 Sch.6 para.8

Sch.15 Part I para.17, repealed: 2003 asp 8 Sch.6 para.8

Sch.15 Part I para.18, repealed: 2003 asp 8 Sch.6 para.8

Sch.15 Part I para.19, repealed: 2003 asp 8 Sch.6 para.8

Sch.15 Part I para.20, repealed: 2003 asp 8 Sch.6 para.8

Sch.15 Part I para.21, repealed: 2003 asp 8 Sch.6 para.8

Sch.15 Part I para.22, repealed: 2003 asp 8 Sch.6 para.8

Sch.15 Part I para.23, repealed: 2003 asp 8 Sch.6 para.8

Sch.15 Part I para.24, repealed: 2003 asp 8 Sch.6 para.8

Sch.27 Part II para.205, repealed: 2004 c.14 Sch.1 Part 2

1974

xxiv. Greater London Council (General Powers) Act 1974

s.14, amended: SI 2003/1615 Sch.1 para.31

s.15, amended: SI 2003/1615 Sch.1 para.31, 2004 c.21 Sch.1 para.43

s.15, applied: 2004 c.18 Sch.7 para.3

s.21, amended: SI 2003/1615 Sch.1 para.31

i. Harwich Harbour Act 1974

s.28, amended: SI 2002/2618 Art.16

Health and Safety at Work Act 1974

s.3, see *R. (on the application of Junttan Oy) v Bristol Magistrates Court* [2002] EWHC 566, [2002] 4 All E.R. 965 (QBD (Admin Ct)), Lord Woolf of Barnes, L.C.J.

s.6, see *R. (on the application of Junttan Oy) v Bristol Magistrates Court* [2002] EWHC 566, [2002] 4 All E.R. 965 (QBD (Admin Ct)), Lord Woolf of Barnes, L.C.J.

xx. Lerwick Harbour Order Confirmation Act 1974

s.10, applied: SSI 2003/211 Art.17

CAP.

1974–cont.

viii. Zetland County Council Act 1974
Part II, amended: SSI 2003/190 Art.2

3. Slaughterhouses Act 1974
s.4, amended: 2003 c.44 Sch.32 para.158
s.4, disapplied: 2003 c.44 Sch.25 para.73
s.10, amended: 2004 c.33 Sch.27 para.48
s.20, amended: 2003 c.44 Sch.26 para.23
s.21, amended: 2003 c.44 Sch.26 para.23
s.23, amended: 2003 c.44 Sch.26 para.23
s.38, amended: 2003 c.44 Sch.27 para.4, Sch.37 Part 9

4. Legal Aid Act 1974
see *R. v Conroy (Costs)* [2004] 1 Costs L.R. 182 (Crown Ct (Bristol)), Judge Crowther Q.C.

5. Horticulture (Special Payments) Act 1974
repealed: 2004 c.14 Sch.1 Part 2

6. Biological Weapons Act 1974
s.1, applied: SI 2004/1910 Sch.1
s.2, amended: 2002 c.26 Sch.7 para.27
s.4, applied: SI 2003/2273 Sch.1 para.4

7. Local Government Act 1974
referred to: SI 2002/808 Art.2, SI 2002/1057 Art.2
Part III, applied: 2002 asp 11 s.21, SI 2002/152 Reg.24, 2003 c.43 s.114, SI 2004/344 Art.2, SI 2004/1777 Art.24, SI 2004/1778 Art.24
s.1, repealed: 2004 c.14 Sch.1 Part 10
s.2, repealed: 2004 c.14 Sch.1 Part 10
s.3, repealed: 2004 c.14 Sch.1 Part 10
s.4, repealed: 2004 c.14 Sch.1 Part 10
s.5, repealed: 2004 c.14 Sch.1 Part 10
s.10, amended: 2004 c.14 Sch.1 Part 10
s.10, repealed (in part): 2004 c.14 Sch.1 Part 10
s.23, amended: SI 2004/2359 Art.2
s.23, repealed (in part): SI 2004/2359 Art.2
s.25, amended: 2002 c.32 Sch.21 para.2, 2004 c.21 Sch.1 para.42
s.25, repealed (in part): 2002 c.32 Sch.22 Part 3
s.25, enabling: SI 2004/344
s.26, see *R. (on the application of Maxhuni) v Commissioner for Local Administration* [2002] EWCA Civ 973, [2003] B.L.G.R. 113 (CA), Simon Brown, L.J.; see *R. (on the application of Umo) v Commissioner for Local Adminstration in England* [2003] EWHC 3202, [2004] E.L.R. 265 (QBD (Admin Ct)), Beatson, J.
s.26, applied: 2003 c.43 s.114
s.30, see *R. (on the application of Maxhuni) v Commissioner for Local Administration* [2002] EWCA Civ 973, [2003] B.L.G.R. 113 (CA), Simon Brown, L.J.
s.30, amended: SI 2002/1057 Art.8
s.32A, added: SI 2004/2359 Art.2
s.33, amended: 2004 c.34 Sch.15 para.7, Sch.16, SI 2004/1823 Art.6

CAP.

1974–cont.

7. Local Government Act 1974–*cont.*
s.34, amended: SI 2002/1057 Art.8
s.35, amended: SI 2003/1615 Sch.1 para.5
Sch.2 Part I para.1, repealed: 2004 c.14 Sch.1 Part 10
Sch.2 Part I para.2, repealed: 2004 c.14 Sch.1 Part 10
Sch.2 Part I para.3, repealed: 2004 c.14 Sch.1 Part 10
Sch.2 Part I para.3A, repealed: 2004 c.14 Sch.1 Part 10
Sch.2 Part I para.4, repealed: 2004 c.14 Sch.1 Part 10
Sch.2 Part II para.5, repealed: 2004 c.14 Sch.1 Part 10
Sch.2 Part II para.6, repealed: 2004 c.14 Sch.1 Part 10
Sch.2 Part III para.7, repealed: 2004 c.14 Sch.1 Part 10
Sch.2 Part III para.8, repealed: 2004 c.14 Sch.1 Part 10
Sch.2 Part III para.9, repealed: 2004 c.14 Sch.1 Part 10
Sch.2 Part III para.10, repealed: 2004 c.14 Sch.1 Part 10
Sch.2 Part III para.11, repealed: 2004 c.14 Sch.1 Part 10
Sch.4 para.1, amended: 2004 c.34 s.228
Sch.4 para.6, amended: 2003 c.26 Sch.7 para.5
Sch.4 para.8, amended: 2003 c.26 Sch.7 para.5
Sch.4 para.8A, added: 2003 c.26 Sch.7 para.5
Sch.6 para.24, repealed: 2003 c.17 Sch.7

8. Statutory Corporations (Financial Provisions) Act 1974
Sch.2 para.3, repealed: 2004 c.14 Sch.1 Part 9

11. Charlwood and Horley Act 1974
s.2, repealed (in part): 2004 c.14 Sch.1 Part 10

23. Juries Act 1974
applied: SI 2004/291 Sch.4, SI 2004/478 Sch.4, SI 2004/627 Sch.2
referred to: 2003 c.44 Sch.33 para.1
s.1, see *R. v Smith (Lance Percival)* [2003] EWCA Crim 283, [2003] 1 W.L.R. 2229 (CA (Crim Div)), Pill, L.J.
s.1, referred to: SI 2004/921 r.1
s.1, substituted: 2003 c.44 Sch.33 para.2
s.2, amended: 2003 c.44 Sch.37 Part 10
s.9, amended: 2003 c.39 Sch.8 para.172, 2003 c.44 Sch.33 para.4, Sch.33 para.5, Sch.33 para.6, Sch.37 Part 10
s.9, repealed (in part): 2003 c.44 Sch.37 Part 10
s.9A, amended: 2003 c.39 Sch.8 para.172, 2003 c.44 Sch.33 para.7, Sch.33 para.8, Sch.33 para.9, Sch.33 para.10, Sch.33 para.11
s.9AA, added: 2003 c.44 Sch.33 para.12
s.9B, amended: 2003 c.39 Sch.4 para.3

CAP.

1974–cont.

23. Juries Act 1974–cont.

s.10, amended: 2003 c.39 Sch.4 para.4, Sch.10

s.11, amended: 2004 c.28 Sch.10 para.8, Sch.11

s.11, repealed (in part): 2004 c.28 Sch.10 para.8, Sch.11

s.14, amended: 2003 c.39 Sch.8 para.173

s.19, amended: 2003 c.44 Sch.33 para.13

s.20, see *R. v Dodds (Raymond)* [2002] EWCA Crim 1328, [2003] 1 Cr. App. R. 3 (CA (Crim Div)), Hedley, J.

s.20, amended: 2003 c.44 Sch.33 para.14

Sch.1, referred to: SI 2004/921 r.1

Sch.1 Part I, amended: 2002 c.30 Sch.7 para.3, 2003 c.39 Sch.8 para.174, Sch.10

Sch.1 Part I, substituted: 2003 c.44 Sch.33 para.15

Sch.1 Part I para.1, substituted: 2003 c.44 Sch.33 para.15

Sch.1 Part I para.2, substituted: 2003 c.44 Sch.33 para.15

Sch.1 Part I para.3, substituted: 2003 c.44 Sch.33 para.15

Sch.1 Part I para.4, repealed (in part): 2004 c.28 Sch.11

Sch.1 Part I para.4, substituted: 2003 c.44 Sch.33 para.15

Sch.1 Part II, substituted: 2003 c.44 Sch.33 para.15

Sch.1 Part II para.5, substituted: 2003 c.44 Sch.33 para.15

Sch.1 Part II para.6, substituted: 2003 c.44 Sch.33 para.15

Sch.1 Part II para.7, substituted: 2003 c.44 Sch.33 para.15

Sch.1 Part II para.8, substituted: 2003 c.44 Sch.33 para.15

Sch.1 Part III, amended: 2002 c.24 Sch.3 para.2

Sch.1 Part III, substituted: 2003 c.44 Sch.33 para.15

24. Prices Act 1974

applied: 2002 c.40 Sch.14, Sch.15

s.2, applied: SI 2003/2253, SI 2004/102

s.2, repealed: 2004 c.14 Sch.1 Part 16

s.4, amended: 2004 c.14 Sch.2 para.11

s.4, applied: SI 2003/1593 Sch.1 Part I, SI 2004/102

s.4, referred to: SI 2003/1376 Sch.1

s.4, enabling: SI 2003/2253, SI 2004/102

s.5, repealed: 2004 c.14 Sch.1 Part 16

s.7, amended: 2004 c.14 Sch.1 Part 16

s.9, repealed (in part): 2004 c.14 Sch.1 Part 16

Sch.1, applied: SI 2003/1376 Sch.1

Sch.1 para.5, amended: 2004 c.14 Sch.1 Part 16

Sch.1 para.5, repealed (in part): 2004 c.14 Sch.1 Part 16

Sch.1 para.11, repealed: 2004 c.14 Sch.1 Part 16

CAP.

1974–cont.

24. Prices Act 1974–cont.

Sch.1 para.12, repealed (in part): 2002 c.40 Sch.26, 2004 c.14 Sch.1 Part 16

Sch.1 para.14, amended: 2004 c.14 Sch.1 Part 16

30. Finance Act 1974

s.24, amended: 2003 c.1 Sch.6 para.147

s.55, repealed: 2004 c.14 Sch.1 Part 14

35. Carriage of Passengers by Road Act 1974

repealed: 2004 c.14 Sch.1 Part 14

37. Health and Safety at Work etc Act 1974

applied: SI 2002/377 Sch.1 para.27, Sch.4 para.22, SI 2002/655 Reg.20, Reg.21, SI 2002/1093 Reg.7, SI 2002/1689 Reg.14, SI 2002/3199 Sch.1 para.21, SI 2003/403 Reg.27, SI 2003/453 Sch.3 para.22, SI 2003/547 Reg.19, Reg.20, Reg.21, Reg.22, SI 2003/1082 Reg.12, SI 2003/3118 Sch.1 para.19, SI 2003/3170 Sch.1 para.21, SI 2003/3247 Sch.3 para.22, 2004 c.20 s.86, SI 2004/456 Reg.18, Reg.19, Reg.20, Reg.21, SI 2004/1836 Reg.9, SI 2004/2507 Sch.1 para.22

see *Thames Trains Ltd v Health and Safety Executive* [2002] EWHC 1415, [2003] P.I.Q.R. P14 (QBD), Morland, J.

Part I, applied: 2002 c.40 Sch.15, SI 2003/750 Sch.5 para.12, SI 2003/751 Sch.6 para.12

Part I, referred to: SI 2004/1468 Sch.6 para.12

s.1, applied: SI 2002/1689 Reg.17, SI 2002/2675 Reg.26, SI 2002/2676 Reg.14, SI 2002/2677 Reg.17, SI 2002/2776 Reg.12

s.1, varied: SI 2002/282 Reg.3, SI 2002/2677 Reg.19

s.2, see *R. v Fresha Bakeries Ltd* [2002] EWCA Crim 1451, [2003] 1 Cr. App. R. (S.) 44 (CA (Crim Div)), Field, J.

s.2, applied: SI 2002/1689 Reg.17, SI 2002/2675 Reg.26, SI 2002/2676 Reg.14, SI 2002/2677 Reg.17, SI 2002/2776 Reg.12

s.2, varied: SI 2002/2677 Reg.19

s.2, enabling: SI 2002/655

s.2, see *Duthie v Bath and North East Somerset Council* [2003] I.C.R. 1405 (EAT), Judge Ansell; see *R. v Avon Lippiatt Hobbs (Contractors) Ltd* [2003] EWCA Crim 627, [2003] 2 Cr. App. R. (S.) 71 (CA (Crim Div)), Sachs, J.; see *R. v Colthrop Board Mills Ltd* [2002] EWCA Crim 520, [2002] 2 Cr. App. R. (S.) 80 (CA (Crim Div)), Gibbs, J.

s.3, see *R. v Fresha Bakeries Ltd* [2002] EWCA Crim 1451, [2003] 1 Cr. App. R. (S.) 44 (CA (Crim Div)), Field, J.

s.3, applied: SI 2002/1689 Reg.17, SI 2002/2675 Reg.26, SI 2002/2676 Reg.14, SI 2002/2677 Reg.17, SI 2002/2776 Reg.12

s.3, varied: SI 2002/2677 Reg.19, Reg.20

1974—cont.

37. Health and Safety at Work etc Act 1974—*cont.*

s.3, see *Davies v Health and Safety Executive* [2002] EWCA Crim 2949, [2003] I.C.R. 586 (CA (Crim Div)),Tuckey, L.J.; see *R. v Avon Lippiatt Hobbs (Contractors) Ltd* [2003] EWCA Crim 627, [2003] 2 Cr. App. R. (S.) 71 (CA (Crim Div)), Sachs, J.; see *R. v Yorkshire Sheeting & Insulation Ltd* [2003] EWCA Crim 458, [2003] 2 Cr. App. R. (S.) 93 (CA (Crim Div)), Davis, J.

s.4, applied: SI 2002/1689 Reg.17, SI 2002/2675 Reg.26, SI 2002/2676 Reg.14, SI 2002/2677 Reg.17, SI 2002/2776 Reg.12

s.4, varied: SI 2002/2677 Reg.19

s.5, applied: SI 2002/1689 Reg.17, SI 2002/2675 Reg.26, SI 2002/2676 Reg.14, SI 2002/2677 Reg.17, SI 2002/2776 Reg.12

s.5, varied: SI 2002/2677 Reg.19

s.6, applied: SI 2002/1689 Reg.17, SI 2002/2675 Reg.26, SI 2002/2676 Reg.14, SI 2002/2677 Reg.17, SI 2002/2776 Reg.12

s.6, varied: SI 2002/2677 Reg.19

s.6, see *R. (on the application of Junttan Oy) v Bristol Magistrates Court* [2003] UKHL 55, [2004] 2 All E.R. 555 (HL), Lord Hobhouse of Woodborough

s.7, applied: SI 2002/1689 Reg.17, SI 2002/2099 Reg.20, SI 2002/2675 Reg.26, SI 2002/2676 Reg.14, SI 2002/2677 Reg.17, SI 2002/2776 Reg.12

s.7, varied: SI 2002/2677 Reg.19

s.8, applied: SI 2002/1689 Reg.17, SI 2002/2099 Reg.20, SI 2002/2675 Reg.26, SI 2002/2676 Reg.14, SI 2002/2677 Reg.17, SI 2002/2776 Reg.12

s.8, varied: SI 2002/2677 Reg.19

s.9, applied: SI 2002/1689 Reg.17, SI 2002/2675 Reg.26, SI 2002/2676 Reg.14, SI 2002/2677 Reg.17, SI 2002/2776 Reg.12

s.9, varied: SI 2002/2677 Reg.19

s.10, applied: SI 2002/1689 Reg.17, SI 2002/2675 Reg.26, SI 2002/2676 Reg.14, SI 2002/2677 Reg.17, SI 2002/2776 Reg.12, SI 2004/1818 Reg.3

s.10, varied: SI 2002/2677 Reg.19

s.11, applied: SI 2002/63, SI 2002/655, SI 2002/1689, SI 2002/1689 Reg.17, SI 2002/2099, SI 2002/2174, SI 2002/2675, SI 2002/2675 Reg.26, SI 2002/2676, SI 2002/2676 Reg.14, SI 2002/2677, SI 2002/2677 Reg.17, SI 2002/2776, SI 2002/2776 Reg.12, SI 2002/2979, SI 2003/547, SI 2003/579, SI 2003/978, SI 2003/1431, SI 2003/1889, SI 2003/2457, SI 2003/2563, SI 2004/456, SI 2004/568

s.11, varied: SI 2002/2677 Reg.19

s.12, applied: SI 2002/1689 Reg.17, SI 2002/2675 Reg.26, SI 2002/2676 Reg.14, SI 2002/2677 Reg.17, SI 2002/2776 Reg.12

s.12, varied: SI 2002/2677 Reg.19

1974—cont.

37. Health and Safety at Work etc Act 1974—*cont.*

s.13, applied: SI 2002/1689 Reg.17, SI 2002/2675 Reg.26, SI 2002/2676 Reg.14, SI 2002/2677 Reg.17, SI 2002/2776 Reg.12, SI 2003/547 Sch.17, SI 2004/456 Sch.16, SI 2004/756 Sch.2 para.8

s.13, varied: SI 2002/2677 Reg.19

s.14, applied: SI 2002/1689 Reg.17, SI 2002/2675 Reg.26, SI 2002/2676 Reg.14, SI 2002/2677 Reg.17, SI 2002/2776 Reg.12

s.14, varied: SI 2002/2677 Reg.19

s.15, amended: SI 2002/794 Sch.2

s.15, applied: SI 2002/282 Reg.3, SI 2002/1689 Reg.17, SI 2002/2675 Reg.26, SI 2002/2676 Reg.14, SI 2002/2677 Reg.17, SI 2002/2776 Reg.12

s.15, varied: SI 2002/2677 Reg.19

s.15, enabling: SI 2002/63, SI 2002/1689, SI 2002/2099, SI 2002/2174, SI 2002/2175, SI 2002/2176, SI 2002/2675, SI 2002/2676, SI 2002/2677, SI 2002/2776, SI 2002/2979, SI 2003/403, SI 2003/579, SI 2003/978, SI 2003/1082, SI 2003/1431, SI 2003/1889, SI 2003/2457, SI 2003/2563, SI 2004/568, SI 2004/3386

s.16, amended: 2004 c.17 Sch.3 para.5

s.16, applied: SI 2002/1689 Reg.14, Reg.17, SI 2002/2675 Reg.26, SI 2002/2676 Reg.14, SI 2002/2677 Reg.17, SI 2002/2776 Reg.12

s.16, varied: SI 2002/2677 Reg.19

s.17, applied: SI 2002/1689 Reg.14, Reg.17, SI 2002/2675 Reg.26, SI 2002/2676 Reg.14, SI 2002/2677 Reg.17, SI 2002/2776 Reg.12

s.17, varied: SI 2002/2677 Reg.19

s.18, applied: SI 2002/528 Reg.10, SI 2002/1689 Reg.14, Reg.17, SI 2002/2675 Reg.26, SI 2002/2676 Reg.14, SI 2002/2677 Reg.17, SI 2002/2776 Reg.12

s.18, varied: SI 2002/2677 Reg.19, SI 2004/1309 Reg.17

s.18, enabling: SI 2002/2675, SI 2003/1082, SI 2004/1359

s.18, see *Lane Group Plc v Farmiloe* [2004] P.I.Q.R. P22 (EAT), Judge Peter Clark

s.19, applied: SI 2002/528 Reg.10, SI 2002/1689 Reg.14, Reg.17, SI 2002/2675 Reg.26, SI 2002/2676 Reg.14, SI 2002/2677 Reg.17, Sch.9 para.1, Sch.9 para.2, SI 2002/2776 Reg.12, SI 2003/403 Reg.23

s.19, varied: SI 2002/1166 Reg.31, SI 2002/2677 Reg.19, SI 2003/403 Reg.23, SI 2004/129 Reg.23, SI 2004/1309 Reg.17

s.20, amended: 2004 c.33 S ...'7 para.49

s.20, applied: SI 2002/528 Reg.10, Reg.11, SI 2002/1689 Reg.14, Reg.17, SI 2002/2675 Reg.26, SI 2002/2676 Reg.14, SI 2002/2677 Reg.17, SI 2002/2776 Reg.12, SI 2003/403 Reg.23

1974–cont.

37. Health and Safety at Work etc Act 1974–*cont.*

s.20, varied: SI 2002/1166 Reg.31, SI 2002/2677 Reg.19, SI 2003/403 Reg.23, SI 2004/129 Reg.23, SI 2004/1309 Reg.17

s.20, enabling: SI 2003/1082

s.20, see *HM Advocate v Shell UK Ltd* 2003 S.L.T. 1296 (HCJ), Lady Smith, Lady Cosgrove, Lord Cullen L.J.G.; see *R. (on the application of Wandsworth LBC) v South Western Magistrates Court* [2003] EWHC 1158, [2003] I.C.R. 1287 (QBD (Admin Ct)), Scott Baker, L.J.

s.21, applied: SI 2002/528 Reg.10, Reg.11, SI 2002/1689 Reg.14, Reg.17, SI 2002/2675 Reg.26, SI 2002/2676 Reg.14, SI 2002/2677 Reg.17, SI 2002/2776 Reg.12, SI 2004/129 Reg.25, Reg.27

s.21, varied: SI 2002/1166 Reg.31, SI 2002/2677 Reg.19, SI 2004/129 Reg.23, SI 2004/1309 Reg.17

s.22, applied: SI 2002/528 Reg.10, SI 2002/1689 Reg.14, Reg.17, SI 2002/2675 Reg.26, SI 2002/2676 Reg.14, SI 2002/2677 Reg.17, SI 2002/2776 Reg.12, SI 2004/129 Reg.25, Reg.27

s.22, varied: SI 2002/1166 Reg.31, SI 2002/2677 Reg.19, SI 2004/129 Reg.23, SI 2004/1309 Reg.17

s.23, amended: 2004 c.21 Sch.1 para.44

s.23, applied: SI 2002/528 Reg.10, SI 2002/1689 Reg.14, Reg.17, SI 2002/2675 Reg.26, SI 2002/2676 Reg.14, SI 2002/2677 Reg.17, SI 2002/2776 Reg.12

s.23, varied: SI 2002/1166 Reg.31, SI 2002/2677 Reg.19, SI 2004/129 Reg.23, SI 2004/1309 Reg.17

s.24, applied: SI 2002/528 Reg.10, SI 2002/655 Reg.22, SI 2002/1689 Reg.14, Reg.17, SI 2002/2675 Reg.26, SI 2002/2676 Reg.14, SI 2002/2677 Reg.17, SI 2002/2776 Reg.12, SI 2004/456 Reg.21, SI 2004/1861 Reg.16, Sch.4 para.6, Sch.4 para.8

s.24, disapplied: SI 2003/547 Reg.22

s.24, varied: SI 2002/1166 Reg.31, SI 2002/2677 Reg.19, SI 2004/129 Reg.23, SI 2004/1309 Reg.17

s.24, enabling: SI 2004/1861

s.25, applied: SI 2002/528 Reg.10, SI 2002/1689 Reg.14, Reg.17, SI 2002/2675 Reg.26, SI 2002/2676 Reg.14, SI 2002/2677 Reg.17, SI 2002/2776 Reg.12

s.25, varied: SI 2002/2677 Reg.19, SI 2004/1309 Reg.17

s.25A, applied: SI 2002/528 Reg.10, SI 2002/1689 Reg.14, Reg.17, SI 2002/2675 Reg.26, SI 2002/2676 Reg.14, SI 2002/2677 Reg.17, SI 2002/2776 Reg.12

s.25A, varied: SI 2002/2677 Reg.19, SI 2004/129 Reg.23

1974–cont.

37. Health and Safety at Work etc Act 1974–*cont.*

s.26, applied: SI 2002/528 Reg.10, SI 2002/1689 Reg.14, Reg.17, SI 2002/2675 Reg.26, SI 2002/2676 Reg.14, SI 2002/2677 Reg.17, SI 2002/2776 Reg.12, SI 2003/403 Reg.23

s.26, varied: SI 2002/1166 Reg.31, SI 2002/2677 Reg.19, SI 2004/129 Reg.23, SI 2004/1309 Reg.17

s.27, applied: SI 2002/1689 Reg.17, SI 2002/2675 Reg.26, SI 2002/2676 Reg.14, SI 2002/2677 Reg.17, SI 2002/2776 Reg.12, SI 2003/403 Reg.23

s.27, varied: SI 2002/2677 Reg.19, SI 2003/403 Reg.23, SI 2004/129 Reg.23, SI 2004/1309 Reg.17

s.27A, applied: SI 2002/1689 Reg.17, SI 2002/2675 Reg.26, SI 2002/2676 Reg.14, SI 2002/2677 Reg.17, SI 2002/2776 Reg.12

s.27A, varied: SI 2002/2677 Reg.19, SI 2004/129 Reg.23

s.28, amended: 2003 c.20 s.105

s.28, applied: SI 2002/1689 Reg.17, SI 2002/2675 Reg.26, SI 2002/2676 Reg.14, SI 2002/2677 Reg.17, SI 2002/2776 Reg.12, SI 2003/403 Reg.23

s.28, varied: SI 2002/2677 Reg.19, SI 2003/403 Reg.23, SI 2004/1822 Sch.1 para.8

s.29, applied: SI 2002/1689 Reg.17, SI 2002/2675 Reg.26, SI 2002/2676 Reg.14, SI 2002/2677 Reg.17, SI 2002/2776 Reg.12

s.29, varied: SI 2002/2677 Reg.19

s.30, applied: SI 2002/1689 Reg.17, SI 2002/2675 Reg.26, SI 2002/2676 Reg.14, SI 2002/2677 Reg.17, SI 2002/2776 Reg.12

s.30, varied: SI 2002/2677 Reg.19

s.31, applied: SI 2002/1689 Reg.17, SI 2002/2675 Reg.26, SI 2002/2676 Reg.14, SI 2002/2677 Reg.17, SI 2002/2776 Reg.12

s.31, varied: SI 2002/2677 Reg.19

s.32, applied: SI 2002/1689 Reg.17, SI 2002/2675 Reg.26, SI 2002/2676 Reg.14, SI 2002/2677 Reg.17, SI 2002/2776 Reg.12

s.32, varied: SI 2002/2677 Reg.19

s.33, applied: SI 2002/1166 Reg.31, SI 2002/1689 Reg.14, Reg.17, SI 2002/2675 Reg.26, SI 2002/2676 Reg.14, SI 2002/2677 Reg.17, SI 2002/2776 Reg.12, SI 2003/403 Reg.23, Reg.25

s.33, referred to: SI 2003/403 Reg.28

s.33, varied: SI 2002/1166 Reg.31, SI 2002/2677 Reg.19, SI 2003/403 Reg.23, SI 2004/129 Reg.23, SI 2004/1309 Reg.17

s.33, see *Davies v Health and Safety Executive* [2002] EWCA Crim 2949, [2003] I.C.R. 586 (CA (Crim Div)), Tuckey, L.J.

s.34, applied: SI 2002/1689 Reg.14, Reg.17, SI 2002/2675 Reg.26, SI 2002/2676 Reg.14, SI 2002/2677 Reg.17, SI 2002/2776 Reg.12

1974–cont.

37. Health and Safety at Work etc Act 1974–*cont.*

s.34, varied: SI 2002/1166 Reg.31, SI 2002/2677 Reg.19, SI 2004/129 Reg.23, SI 2004/1309 Reg.17

s.35, applied: SI 2002/1689 Reg.14, Reg.17, SI 2002/2675 Reg.26, SI 2002/2676 Reg.14, SI 2002/2677 Reg.17, SI 2002/2776 Reg.12, SI 2003/403 Reg.23

s.35, varied: SI 2002/1166 Reg.31, SI 2002/2677 Reg.19, SI 2003/403 Reg.23, SI 2004/129 Reg.23

s.36, applied: SI 2002/1689 Reg.14, Reg.17, SI 2002/2675 Reg.26, SI 2002/2676 Reg.14, SI 2002/2677 Reg.17, SI 2002/2776 Reg.12, SI 2003/403 Reg.23

s.36, varied: SI 2002/1166 Reg.31, SI 2002/2677 Reg.19, SI 2003/403 Reg.23, SI 2004/129 Reg.23, SI 2004/1309 Reg.17

s.37, applied: SI 2002/1689 Reg.14, Reg.17, SI 2002/2675 Reg.26, SI 2002/2676 Reg.14, SI 2002/2677 Reg.17, SI 2002/2776 Reg.12, SI 2003/403 Reg.23

s.37, varied: SI 2002/1166 Reg.31, SI 2002/2677 Reg.19, SI 2003/403 Reg.23, SI 2004/129 Reg.23, SI 2004/1309 Reg.17

s.38, applied: SI 2002/1689 Reg.14, Reg.17, SI 2002/2675 Reg.26, SI 2002/2676 Reg.14, SI 2002/2677 Reg.17, SI 2002/2776 Reg.12, SI 2003/403 Reg.23

s.38, varied: SI 2002/1166 Reg.31, SI 2002/2677 Reg.19, SI 2003/403 Reg.23, SI 2004/129 Reg.23, SI 2004/1309 Reg.17

s.39, applied: SI 2002/1689 Reg.14, Reg.17, SI 2002/2675 Reg.26, SI 2002/2676 Reg.14, SI 2002/2677 Reg.17, SI 2002/2776 Reg.12

s.39, varied: SI 2002/1166 Reg.31, SI 2002/2677 Reg.19, SI 2004/129 Reg.23, SI 2004/1309 Reg.17

s.40, applied: SI 2002/1689 Reg.14, Reg.17, SI 2002/2675 Reg.26, SI 2002/2676 Reg.14, SI 2002/2677 Reg.17, SI 2002/2776 Reg.12

s.40, varied: SI 2002/1166 Reg.31, SI 2002/2677 Reg.19, SI 2004/129 Reg.23, SI 2004/1309 Reg.17

s.41, applied: SI 2002/1689 Reg.14, Reg.17, SI 2002/2675 Reg.26, SI 2002/2676 Reg.14, SI 2002/2677 Reg.17, SI 2002/2776 Reg.12

s.41, varied: SI 2002/1166 Reg.31, SI 2002/2677 Reg.19, SI 2004/129 Reg.23, SI 2004/1309 Reg.17

s.42, applied: SI 2002/1689 Reg.14, Reg.17, SI 2002/2675 Reg.26, SI 2002/2676 Reg.14, SI 2002/2677 Reg.17, SI 2002/2776 Reg.12, SI 2003/403 Reg.23

s.42, varied: SI 2002/1166 Reg.31, SI 2002/2677 Reg.19, SI 2003/403 Reg.23, SI 2004/129 Reg.23, SI 2004/1309 Reg.17

s.43, amended: SI 2002/794 Sch.2

1974–cont.

37. Health and Safety at Work etc Act 1974–*cont.*

s.43, applied: SI 2002/655 Reg.15, SI 2002/1689 Reg.17, SI 2002/2675 Reg.26, SI 2002/2676 Reg.14, SI 2002/2677 Reg.17, SI 2002/2776 Reg.12

s.43, referred to: SI 2002/655 Reg.13, SI 2003/547 Reg.13, Reg.15, SI 2004/456 Reg.12, Reg.14

s.43, varied: SI 2002/2677 Reg.19

s.43, enabling: SI 2002/655, SI 2003/547, SI 2004/456, SI 2004/568

s.43A, added: 2003 c.20 s.105

s.43A, applied: SI 2002/1689 Reg.17, SI 2002/2675 Reg.26, SI 2002/2676 Reg.14, SI 2002/2677 Reg.17, SI 2002/2776 Reg.12

s.43A, varied: SI 2002/2677 Reg.19

s.44, applied: SI 2002/1689 Reg.17, SI 2002/2675 Reg.26, SI 2002/2676 Reg.14, SI 2002/2677 Reg.17, SI 2002/2776 Reg.12, SI 2004/1309 Reg.15

s.44, varied: SI 2002/2677 Reg.19

s.45, applied: SI 2002/1689 Reg.17, SI 2002/2675 Reg.26, SI 2002/2676 Reg.14, SI 2002/2677 Reg.17, SI 2002/2776 Reg.12

s.45, varied: SI 2002/2677 Reg.19

s.46, applied: SI 2002/1689 Reg.17, SI 2002/2675 Reg.26, SI 2002/2676 Reg.14, SI 2002/2677 Reg.17, SI 2002/2776 Reg.12, SI 2003/403 Reg.23

s.46, varied: SI 2002/2677 Reg.19, SI 2003/403 Reg.23, SI 2004/1309 Reg.17

s.47, applied: SI 2002/1689 Reg.14, Reg.17, SI 2002/2675 Reg.26, SI 2002/2676 Reg.14, SI 2002/2677 Reg.17, SI 2002/2776 Reg.12

s.47, varied: SI 2002/2677 Reg.19

s.47, enabling: SI 2003/2457

s.48, applied: SI 2002/1689 Reg.17, SI 2002/2675 Reg.26, SI 2002/2676 Reg.14, SI 2002/2677 Reg.17, SI 2002/2776 Reg.12

s.48, varied: SI 2002/2677 Reg.19, SI 2004/129 Reg.23

s.49, amended: SI 2002/794 Sch.2

s.49, applied: SI 2002/1689 Reg.17, SI 2002/2675 Reg.26, SI 2002/2676 Reg.14, SI 2002/2677 Reg.17, SI 2002/2776 Reg.12

s.49, varied: SI 2002/2677 Reg.19

s.50, amended: 2004 c.17 Sch.3 para.5

s.50, applied: SI 2002/63, SI 2002/1689, SI 2002/1689 Reg.17, SI 2002/2099, SI 2002/2174, SI 2002/2175, SI 2002/2675, SI 2002/2675 Reg.26, SI 2002/2676, SI 2002/2676 Reg.14, SI 2002/2677, SI 2002/2677 Reg.17, SI 2002/2776, SI 2002/2776 Reg.12, SI 2002/2979, SI 2003/403, SI 2003/579, SI 2003/978, SI 2003/1082, SI 2003/1431, SI 2003/1889, SI 2003/2457, SI 2003/2563, SI 2004/568, SI 2004/1359

s.50, varied: SI 2002/2677 Reg.19

1974–cont.

37. Health and Safety at Work etc Act 1974–*cont.*

s.50, enabling: SI 2003/403

s.51, applied: SI 2002/1689 Reg.17, SI 2002/2675 Reg.26, SI 2002/2676 Reg.14, SI 2002/2677 Reg.17, SI 2002/2776 Reg.12

s.51, varied: SI 2002/2677 Reg.19

s.51A, amended: 2002 c.30 s.95

s.51A, applied: SI 2002/1689 Reg.17, SI 2002/2675 Reg.26, SI 2002/2676 Reg.14, SI 2002/2677 Reg.17, SI 2002/2776 Reg.12

s.51A, varied: SI 2002/2677 Reg.19

s.52, amended: SI 2002/794 Sch.2

s.52, applied: SI 2002/1689 Reg.17, SI 2002/2675 Reg.26, SI 2002/2676 Reg.14, SI 2002/2677 Reg.17, SI 2002/2776 Reg.12

s.52, varied: SI 2002/2677 Reg.19

s.52, enabling: SI 2002/2677, SI 2004/3386

s.53, applied: SI 2002/1689 Reg.17, SI 2002/2675 Reg.26, SI 2002/2676 Reg.14, SI 2002/2677 Reg.17, SI 2002/2776 Reg.12, SSI 2002/410 Art.57

s.53, referred to: SI 2002/3199 Sch.1 para.21, SI 2003/3118 Sch.1 para.19, SI 2003/3170 Sch.1 para.21

s.53, varied: SI 2002/2677 Reg.19

s.54, applied: SI 2002/1689 Reg.17, SI 2002/2675 Reg.26, SI 2002/2676 Reg.14, SI 2002/2677 Reg.17, SI 2002/2776 Reg.12

s.54, varied: SI 2002/2677 Reg.19

s.56, amended: SI 2002/3135 Sch.1 para.7

s.60, amended: 2002 c.17 Sch.2 para.41, SI 2002/3135 Sch.1 para.7

s.75, repealed: 2003 asp 8 Sch.6 para.9

s.77, repealed: 2004 c.17 Sch.4

s.80, amended: SI 2002/794 Sch.2

s.80, applied: SI 2002/1689 Reg.17, SI 2002/2675 Reg.26, SI 2002/2676 Reg.14, SI 2002/2677 Reg.17, SI 2002/2776 Reg.12, SSI 2002/410 Art.57

s.80, enabling: SI 2002/2776, SI 2004/568

s.81, applied: SI 2002/1689 Reg.17, SI 2002/2675 Reg.26, SI 2002/2676 Reg.14, SI 2002/2677 Reg.17, SI 2002/2776 Reg.12

s.82, amended: 2003 c.20 s.105

s.82, applied: SI 2002/1689 Reg.17, SI 2002/2675 Reg.26, SI 2002/2676 Reg.14, SI 2002/2677 Reg.17, SI 2002/2776 Reg.12

s.82, enabling: SI 2002/63, SI 2002/655, SI 2002/1689, SI 2002/2099, SI 2002/2174, SI 2002/2175, SI 2002/2176, SI 2002/2675, SI 2002/2676, SI 2002/2677, SI 2002/2776, SI 2002/2979, SI 2003/403, SI 2003/547, SI 2003/579, SI 2003/978, SI 2003/1082, SI 2003/1889, SI 2003/2563, SI 2004/456, SI 2004/568, SI 2004/3386

Sch.1, amended: 2003 c.22 Sch.1

Sch.3 para.1, enabling: SI 2002/1689, SI 2002/2099, SI 2002/2174, SI 2002/2176, SI 2002/2675, SI 2002/2676, SI

1974–cont.

37. Health and Safety at Work etc Act 1974–*cont.*

Sch.3 para.1, enabling:–*cont.* 2002/2677, SI 2002/2776, SI 2002/2979, SI 2003/403, SI 2003/978, SI 2003/1082, SI 2003/1431, SI 2003/1889, SI 2004/568, SI 2004/3386

Sch.3 para.2, enabling: SI 2002/1689, SI 2002/2677, SI 2003/1082, SI 2003/1431, SI 2003/1889, SI 2004/568

Sch.3 para.3, enabling: SI 2002/1689, SI 2002/2099, SI 2002/2675, SI 2003/403, SI 2003/1431, SI 2004/568

Sch.3 para.4, enabling: SI 2002/2099, SI 2003/403, SI 2003/1431, SI 2004/568

Sch.3 para.5, varied: SI 2002/2677 Reg.19

Sch.3 para.6, varied: SI 2002/2677 Reg.19

Sch.3 para.6, enabling: SI 2002/2675, SI 2002/2676, SI 2002/2677, SI 2002/2776, SI 2003/1431, SI 2004/568

Sch.3 para.7, enabling: SI 2002/2676

Sch.3 para.8, enabling: SI 2002/2174, SI 2002/2675, SI 2002/2676, SI 2002/2677, SI 2003/579, SI 2004/3386

Sch.3 para.9, enabling: SI 2002/2174, SI 2002/2675, SI 2002/2676, SI 2002/2677, SI 2002/2776, SI 2004/3386

Sch.3 para.10, enabling: SI 2002/2174, SI 2002/2675

Sch.3 para.11, enabling: SI 2002/2174, SI 2002/2675, SI 2002/2676, SI 2002/2677, SI 2002/2776, SI 2004/3386

Sch.3 para.14, enabling: SI 2002/2099, SI 2002/2174, SI 2002/2675, SI 2002/2676, SI 2002/2677, SI 2002/2776, SI 2004/568, SI 2004/3386

Sch.3 para.15, enabling: SI 2002/63, SI 2002/1689, SI 2002/2099, SI 2002/2675, SI 2002/2676, SI 2002/2677, SI 2002/2979, SI 2003/403, SI 2003/579, SI 2003/1082, SI 2004/568, SI 2004/3386

Sch.3 para.16, enabling: SI 2002/63, SI 2002/1689, SI 2002/2099, SI 2002/2675, SI 2002/2676, SI 2002/2677, SI 2002/2776, SI 2003/403, SI 2003/1082, SI 2003/1431, SI 2004/568, SI 2004/3386

Sch.3 para.18, enabling: SI 2002/2776

Sch.3 para.20, enabling: SI 2002/2675, SI 2002/2677, SI 2002/2776, SI 2004/568, SI 2004/3386

Sch.3 para.21, enabling: SI 2003/403

Sch.7 para.1, repealed: 2003 asp 8 Sch.6 para.9

Sch.7 para.2, repealed: 2003 asp 8 Sch.6 para.9

Sch.7 para.3, repealed: 2003 asp 8 Sch.6 para.9

Sch.7 para.4, repealed: 2003 asp 8 Sch.6 para.9

CAP.

1974–cont.

37. Health and Safety at Work etc Act 1974*–cont.*
Sch.7 para.5, repealed: 2003 asp 8 Sch.6 para.9

Sch.7 para.6, repealed: 2003 asp 8 Sch.6 para.9

Sch.7 para.7, repealed: 2003 asp 8 Sch.6 para.9

Sch.7 para.8, repealed: 2003 asp 8 Sch.6 para.9

Sch.7 para.9, repealed: 2003 asp 8 Sch.6 para.9

38. Land Tenure Reform (Scotland) Act 1974
s.2, amended: 2003 asp 9 Sch.14 para.6

s.8, amended: 2003 asp 11 Sch.1 para.4

s.19, amended: 2003 asp 9 Sch.15

39. Consumer Credit Act 1974
see *Thew v Cole* [2003] EWCA Civ 1828, [2004] R.T.R. 25 (CA), Tuckey, L.J.

applied: 2002 c.40 Sch.14, Sch.15, SI 2003/ 419 Art.63, SI 2003/1376 Sch.1, SI 2003/ 1593 Sch.1 Part I, SI 2004/400 Reg.5, SI 2004/2095 Reg.11, Reg.12, Reg.29, SSI 2002/132 Sch.1 para.4.3, SSI 2004/468 Sch.5 para.1

referred to: 2003 c.21 s.393

Part I, referred to: SI 2003/1374 Sch.1

Part II, applied: SI 2002/2742 Sch.4 para.1

Part III, referred to: SI 2003/1374 Sch.1

Part IV, referred to: SI 2003/1374 Sch.1

Part V, referred to: SI 2003/1374 Sch.1

Part VII, referred to: SI 2003/1374 Sch.1

Part VIII, referred to: SI 2003/1374 Sch.1

Part IX, referred to: SI 2003/1374 Sch.1

s.1, amended: 2002 c.40 Sch.25 para.6

s.1, referred to: SI 2003/1374 Sch.1

s.2, amended: 2002 c.40 Sch.25 para.6

s.2, referred to: SI 2003/1374 Sch.1

s.3, amended: 2002 c.40 Sch.25 para.6

s.3, referred to: SI 2003/1374 Sch.1

s.4, amended: 2002 c.40 Sch.25 para.6

s.4, referred to: SI 2003/1374 Sch.1

s.5, amended: 2002 c.40 Sch.25 para.6

s.5, referred to: SI 2003/1374 Sch.1

s.5, repealed: 2002 c.40 Sch.26

s.6, amended: 2002 c.40 Sch.25 para.6

s.7, amended: 2002 c.40 Sch.25 para.6

s.8, see *McMillan Williams (A Firm) v Range* [2004] EWCA Civ 294, [2004] 1 W.L.R. 1858 (CA), Ward, L.J.

s.8, referred to: SI 2003/1374 Sch.1

s.9, see *McGinn v Grangewood Securities Ltd* [2002] EWCA Civ 522, Times, May 30, 2002 (CA), Clarke, L.J.; see *McMillan Williams (A Firm) v Range* [2004] EWCA Civ 294, [2004] 1 W.L.R. 1858 (CA), Ward, L.J.; see *Wilson v First County Trust Ltd (No.2)* [2001] EWCA Civ 633, [2002] Q.B. 74 (CA), Sir Andrew Morritt V.C.

s.9, referred to: SI 2003/1374 Sch.1

CAP.

1974–cont.

39. Consumer Credit Act 1974*–cont.*
s.10, referred to: SI 2003/1374 Sch.1

s.11, referred to: SI 2003/1374 Sch.1

s.12, referred to: SI 2003/1374 Sch.1

s.13, referred to: SI 2003/1374 Sch.1

s.14, referred to: SI 2003/1374 Sch.1

s.15, see *Lagden v O'Connor* [2002] EWCA Civ 510, [2003] Q.B. 36 (CA), Aldous, L.J.

s.15, referred to: SI 2003/1374 Sch.1

s.16, amended: 2003 c.21 Sch.17 para.47

s.16, applied: SI 2002/195 Reg.39, SI 2002/ 3200 Reg.38, SR 2002/224 Reg.40

s.16, referred to: SI 2003/1374 Sch.1

s.17, referred to: SI 2003/1374 Sch.1

s.18, referred to: SI 2003/1374 Sch.1

s.19, referred to: SI 2003/1374 Sch.1

s.20, referred to: SI 2003/1374 Sch.1

s.22, amended: 2002 c.40 Sch.25 para.6

s.25, amended: 2002 c.40 Sch.25 para.6

s.27, amended: 2002 c.40 Sch.25 para.6

s.28, amended: 2002 c.40 Sch.25 para.6

s.29, amended: 2002 c.40 Sch.25 para.6

s.30, amended: 2002 c.40 Sch.25 para.6

s.31, amended: 2002 c.40 Sch.25 para.6

s.32, amended: 2002 c.40 Sch.25 para.6

s.33, amended: 2002 c.40 Sch.25 para.6

s.34, amended: 2002 c.40 Sch.25 para.6

s.35, amended: 2002 c.40 Sch.25 para.6

s.36, amended: 2002 c.40 Sch.25 para.6

s.39, amended: 2002 c.40 Sch.25 para.6

s.40, amended: 2002 c.40 Sch.25 para.6

s.41, amended: 2002 c.40 Sch.25 para.6

s.44, enabling: SI 2004/1484, SI 2004/2619

s.47, applied: SI 2004/1484 Reg.12

s.49, amended: 2002 c.40 Sch.25 para.6

s.55, enabling: SI 2004/1481

s.58, referred to: SI 2004/1481 Reg.2

s.60, amended: 2002 c.40 Sch.25 para.6

s.60, enabling: SI 2004/1482, SI 2004/2619

s.61, see *Broadwick Financial Services Ltd v Spencer* [2002] EWCA Civ 35, [2002] 1 All E.R. (Comm) 446 (CA), Dyson, L.J.; see *Dimond v Lovell* [2002] 1 A.C. 384 (HL), Lord Hoffmann

s.61, enabling: SI 2004/1482, SI 2004/2619

s.64, amended: 2002 c.40 Sch.25 para.6

s.64, enabling: SI 2004/2619

s.65, see *Wilson v First County Trust Ltd (No.2)* [2001] EWCA Civ 633, [2002] Q.B. 74 (CA), Sir Andrew Morritt V.C.

s.74, amended: 2002 c.40 Sch.25 para.6

s.75, see *OT Computers Ltd (In Administration), Re* [2003] EWHC 2490, [2004] 1 All E.R. (Comm) 320 (Ch D), Sir Robert Andrew Morritt V.C.

s.75, referred to: SI 2003/1374 Sch.1

s.76, applied: SI 2004/1483 Reg.5

s.76, referred to: SI 2003/1374 Sch.1

s.76, enabling: SI 2004/3237

s.77, referred to: SI 2003/1374 Sch.1

1974–cont.

39. Consumer Credit Act 1974–*cont.*
s.78, referred to: SI 2003/1374 Sch.1
s.79, referred to: SI 2003/1374 Sch.1
s.80, referred to: SI 2003/1374 Sch.1
s.81, referred to: SI 2003/1374 Sch.1
s.82, referred to: SI 2003/1374 Sch.1
s.83, applied: SI 2004/2095 Reg.14
s.83, referred to: SI 2003/1374 Sch.1
s.84, amended: SI 2004/2095 Reg.14
s.84, referred to: SI 2003/1374 Sch.1
s.85, referred to: SI 2003/1374 Sch.1
s.86, referred to: SI 2003/1374 Sch.1
s.88, enabling: SI 2004/3237
s.94, applied: SI 2004/1483 Reg.2, Reg.5
s.95, enabling: SI 2004/1483, SI 2004/2619
s.96, applied: SI 2004/1483 Reg.3
s.97, enabling: SI 2004/1483
s.98, applied: SI 2004/1483 Reg.5
s.98, enabling: SI 2004/3237
s.99, applied: SI 2004/1483 Reg.2
s.101, amended: 2002 c.40 Sch.25 para.6
s.105, enabling: SI 2004/1482, SI 2004/2619
s.113, amended: 2002 c.40 Sch.25 para.6
s.114, enabling: SI 2004/1482, SI 2004/2619
s.127, see *McGinn v Grangewood Securities Ltd* [2002] EWCA Civ 522, Times, May 30, 2002 (CA), Clarke, L.J.; see *Wilson v First County Trust Ltd (No.2)* [2001] EWCA Civ 633, [2002] Q.B. 74 (CA), Sir Andrew Morritt V.C.; see *Wilson v First County Trust Ltd (No.2)* [2003] UKHL 40, [2004] 1 A.C. 816 (HL), Lord Nicholls of Birkenhead
s.129, see *Director General of Fair Trading v First National Bank Plc* [2001] UKHL 52, [2002] 1 A.C. 481 (HL), Lord Bingham of Cornhill
s.129, applied: SSI 2004/468 Reg.26
s.136, see *Director General of Fair Trading v First National Bank Plc* [2001] UKHL 52, [2002] 1 A.C. 481 (HL), Lord Bingham of Cornhill
s.137, see *Batooneh v Asombang* [2003] EWHC 2111, [2004] B.P.I.R. 1 (QBD), Buckley, J.; see *Broadwick Financial Services Ltd v Spencer* [2002] EWCA Civ 35, [2002] 1 All E.R. (Comm) 446 (CA), Dyson, L.J.
s.138, see *Batooneh v Asombang* [2003] EWHC 2111, [2004] B.P.I.R. 1 (QBD), Buckley, J.; see *Broadwick Financial Services Ltd v Spencer* [2002] EWCA Civ 35, [2002] 1 All E.R. (Comm) 446 (CA), Dyson, L.J.; see *Paragon Finance Plc (formerly National Home Loans Corp) v Nash* [2001] EWCA Civ 1466, [2002] 1 W.L.R. 685 (CA), Dyson, L.J.
s.139, see *Batooneh v Asombang* [2003] EWHC 2111, [2004] B.P.I.R. 1 (QBD), Buckley, J.; see *Paragon Finance Plc (formerly National Home Loans Corp) v*

1974–cont.

39. Consumer Credit Act 1974–*cont.*
s.139–*cont.*
 Nash [2001] EWCA Civ 1466, [2002] 1 W.L.R. 685 (CA), Dyson, L.J.
s.140, see *Batooneh v Asombang* [2003] EWHC 2111, [2004] B.P.I.R. 1 (QBD), Buckley, J.
s.141, referred to: SI 2003/1374 Sch.1
s.142, referred to: SI 2003/1374 Sch.1
s.143, referred to: SI 2003/1374 Sch.1
s.144, referred to: SI 2003/1374 Sch.1
s.145, amended: SI 2003/1475 Art.21
s.145, referred to: SI 2003/1374 Sch.1
s.146, amended: SI 2003/1475 Art.21
s.146, referred to: SI 2003/1374 Sch.1
s.147, referred to: SI 2003/1374 Sch.1
s.148, amended: 2002 c.40 Sch.25 para.6
s.148, referred to: SI 2003/1374 Sch.1
s.149, amended: 2002 c.40 Sch.25 para.6
s.149, referred to: SI 2003/1374 Sch.1
s.150, referred to: SI 2003/1374 Sch.1
s.151, referred to: SI 2003/1374 Sch.1
s.151, enabling: SI 2004/1484, SI 2004/2619
s.152, referred to: SI 2003/1374 Sch.1
s.153, referred to: SI 2003/1374 Sch.1
s.154, referred to: SI 2003/1374 Sch.1
s.155, amended: SI 2003/1475 Art.22
s.155, referred to: SI 2003/1374 Sch.1
s.156, referred to: SI 2003/1374 Sch.1
s.157, referred to: SI 2003/1374 Sch.1
s.158, referred to: SI 2003/1374 Sch.1
s.159, amended: 2002 c.40 Sch.25 para.6
s.159, referred to: SI 2003/1374 Sch.1
s.160, amended: 2002 c.40 Sch.25 para.6
s.160, referred to: SI 2003/1374 Sch.1
s.161, amended: 2002 c.40 Sch.25 para.6
s.161, applied: SI 2003/1376 Art.4
s.161, repealed (in part): 2002 c.40 Sch.25 para.6, Sch.26
s.162, amended: 2002 c.40 Sch.25 para.6
s.165, amended: 2004 c.33 Sch.27 para.50
s.166, amended: 2002 c.40 Sch.25 para.6
s.167, applied: SI 2004/1484 Reg.12
s.170, amended: 2002 c.40 Sch.25 para.6
s.173, amended: 2002 c.40 Sch.25 para.6
s.174, amended: 2003 c.20 Sch.2 para.19
s.174, applied: 2002 c.40 s.231
s.174, referred to: 2003 c.20 s.115
s.174, repealed: 2002 c.40 Sch.26
s.177, amended: 2002 c.9 Sch.11 para.11
s.179, referred to: SI 2003/1374 Sch.1
s.180, referred to: SI 2003/1374 Sch.1
s.180, enabling: SI 2004/2619
s.181, referred to: SI 2003/1374 Sch.1
s.182, referred to: SI 2003/1374 Sch.1
s.182, enabling: SI 2004/1481, SI 2004/1482, SI 2004/1483, SI 2004/1484, SI 2004/2619
s.183, amended: 2002 c.40 Sch.25 para.6
s.183, referred to: SI 2003/1374 Sch.1

1974–cont.

39. Consumer Credit Act 1974–*cont.*

s.184, amended: 2004 c.33 Sch.27 para.51, Sch.30

s.184, referred to: SI 2003/1374 Sch.1

s.184, varied: 2004 c.33 Sch.21 para.8

s.185, referred to: SI 2003/1374 Sch.1

s.186, referred to: SI 2003/1374 Sch.1

s.187, referred to: SI 2003/1374 Sch.1

s.188, referred to: SI 2003/1374 Sch.1

s.189, amended: 2002 c.40 Sch.25 para.6, Sch.26

s.189, applied: 2003 c.ii s.7

s.189, referred to: SI 2003/1374 Sch.1

s.189, enabling: SI 2004/1481, SI 2004/1482, SI 2004/1483, SI 2004/1484, SI 2004/2619, SI 2004/3237

s.189A, referred to: SI 2003/1374 Sch.1

s.190, referred to: SI 2003/1374 Sch.1

s.191, amended: 2002 c.40 Sch.25 para.6

s.191, referred to: SI 2003/1374 Sch.1

s.192, referred to: SI 2003/1374 Sch.1

s.193, referred to: SI 2003/1374 Sch.1

Sch.1, amended: 2002 c.40 Sch.25 para.6

Sch.2 Part I, referred to: SI 2003/1374 Sch.1

Sch.2 Part II, referred to: SI 2003/1374 Sch.1

Sch.3 Part II, referred to: SI 2003/1374 Sch.1

Sch.3 Part III, referred to: SI 2003/1374 Sch.1

Sch.3 Part IV, referred to: SI 2003/1374 Sch.1

Sch.3 Part V, referred to: SI 2003/1374 Sch.1

Sch.3 Part VI, referred to: SI 2003/1374 Sch.1

Sch.3 Part VII, referred to: SI 2003/1374 Sch.1

Sch.3 Part VIII, referred to: SI 2003/1374 Sch.1

Sch.3 Part IX para.42, referred to: SI 2003/1374 Sch.1

Sch.3 Part IX para.43, referred to: SI 2003/1374 Sch.1

Sch.3 Part X, referred to: SI 2003/1374 Sch.1

Sch.3 Part XII, referred to: SI 2003/1374 Sch.1

Sch.4 Part I para.1, referred to: SI 2003/1374 Sch.1

Sch.4 Part I para.2, referred to: SI 2003/1374 Sch.1

Sch.4 Part I para.3, referred to: SI 2003/1374 Sch.1

Sch.4 Part I para.4, referred to: SI 2003/1374 Sch.1

Sch.4 Part I para.5, referred to: SI 2003/1374 Sch.1

Sch.4 Part I para.6, referred to: SI 2003/1374 Sch.1

Sch.4 Part I para.7, referred to: SI 2003/1374 Sch.1

Sch.4 Part I para.8, referred to: SI 2003/1374 Sch.1

Sch.4 Part I para.9, referred to: SI 2003/1374 Sch.1

Sch.4 Part I para.10, referred to: SI 2003/1374 Sch.1

1974–cont.

39. Consumer Credit Act 1974–*cont.*

Sch.4 Part I para.11, referred to: SI 2003/1374 Sch.1

Sch.4 Part I para.12, referred to: SI 2003/1374 Sch.1

Sch.4 Part I para.13, referred to: SI 2003/1374 Sch.1

Sch.4 Part I para.14, referred to: SI 2003/1374 Sch.1

Sch.4 Part I para.15, referred to: SI 2003/1374 Sch.1

Sch.4 Part I para.16, referred to: SI 2003/1374 Sch.1

Sch.4 Part I para.17, referred to: SI 2003/1374 Sch.1

Sch.4 Part I para.18, referred to: SI 2003/1374 Sch.1

Sch.4 Part I para.19, referred to: SI 2003/1374 Sch.1

Sch.4 Part I para.20, referred to: SI 2003/1374 Sch.1

Sch.4 Part I para.21, referred to: SI 2003/1374 Sch.1

Sch.4 Part I para.22, referred to: SI 2003/1374 Sch.1

Sch.4 Part I para.23, referred to: SI 2003/1374 Sch.1

Sch.4 Part I para.24, referred to: SI 2003/1374 Sch.1

Sch.4 Part I para.25, referred to: SI 2003/1374 Sch.1

Sch.4 Part I para.26, referred to: SI 2003/1374 Sch.1

Sch.4 Part I para.27, referred to: SI 2003/1374 Sch.1

Sch.4 Part I para.28, referred to: SI 2003/1374 Sch.1

Sch.4 Part I para.28, repealed: 2002 c.40 Sch.26

Sch.4 Part I para.29, referred to: SI 2003/1374 Sch.1

Sch.4 Part I para.30, referred to: SI 2003/1374 Sch.1

Sch.4 Part I para.31, referred to: SI 2003/1374 Sch.1

Sch.4 Part I para.32, referred to: SI 2003/1374 Sch.1

Sch.4 Part I para.33, referred to: SI 2003/1374 Sch.1

Sch.4 Part I para.34, referred to: SI 2003/1374 Sch.1

Sch.4 Part I para.35, referred to: SI 2003/1374 Sch.1

Sch.4 Part I para.36, referred to: SI 2003/1374 Sch.1

Sch.4 Part I para.37, referred to: SI 2003/1374 Sch.1

Sch.4 Part I para.37, repealed: SI 2003/3180 Sch.1 para.2

Sch.4 Part II para.38, referred to: SI 2003/1374 Sch.1

1974–cont.

39. Consumer Credit Act 1974–*cont.*

Sch.4 Part II para.39, referred to: SI 2003/1374 Sch.1

Sch.4 Part II para.40, referred to: SI 2003/1374 Sch.1

Sch.4 Part II para.41, referred to: SI 2003/1374 Sch.1

Sch.4 Part II para.42, referred to: SI 2003/1374 Sch.1

Sch.4 Part II para.43, referred to: SI 2003/1374 Sch.1

Sch.4 Part II para.44, referred to: SI 2003/1374 Sch.1

Sch.4 Part II para.45, referred to: SI 2003/1374 Sch.1

Sch.4 Part II para.46, referred to: SI 2003/1374 Sch.1

Sch.4 Part II para.47, referred to: SI 2003/1374 Sch.1

Sch.4 Part II para.48, referred to: SI 2003/1374 Sch.1

Sch.4 Part II para.49, referred to: SI 2003/1374 Sch.1

Sch.4 Part II para.50, referred to: SI 2003/1374 Sch.1

Sch.4 Part II para.51, referred to: SI 2003/1374 Sch.1

40. Control of Pollution Act 1974

applied: SSI 2002/410 Art.57, SSI 2003/129 Sch.2 para.1

referred to: SSI 2004/70 Sch.2 para.1

s.9, varied: SSI 2003/168 Sch.1 para.6

s.11, varied: SSI 2003/168 Sch.1 para.6

s.12, applied: SSI 2003/168 Sch.1 para.5

s.30B, enabling: SSI 2003/85

s.30F, amended: 2004 asp 8 Sch.2 para.2

s.30F, applied: 2003 asp 15 s.28, 2004 asp 10 s.12

s.30H, amended: SSI 2003/331 Sch.1 para.4

s.30I, applied: 2004 asp 10 s.12

s.31A, enabling: SSI 2003/531

s.31B, applied: SI 2003/2261 Sch.3 Part I

s.36, amended: SSI 2003/331 Sch.1 para.4

s.41, enabling: SSI 2003/168

s.46, referred to: SSI 2003/168 Reg.3

s.46A, applied: SSI 2003/168 Reg.4

s.46A, enabling: SSI 2003/168

s.46B, applied: SSI 2003/168 Reg.8

s.46B, enabling: SSI 2003/168

s.46C, applied: SSI 2003/168 Reg.3, Reg.4

s.46C, enabling: SSI 2003/168

s.46D, amended: 2004 asp 8 Sch.2 para.2

s.46D, referred to: SSI 2003/168 Reg.3

s.49A, amended: 2004 asp 8 Sch.2 para.2

s.51, applied: SSI 2003/531 Reg.8

s.56, amended: SSI 2003/331 Sch.1 para.4

s.60, applied: SI 2002/461 Art.2, SI 2002/1066 Art.43, SI 2002/1795 Art.2, SI 2003/1075 Art.35, SI 2004/757 Art.50

s.60, referred to: SSI 2002/104 Art.2

s.61, amended: 2003 asp 8 Sch.6 para.10

1974–cont.

40. Control of Pollution Act 1974–*cont.*

s.61, applied: SI 2002/1066 Art.43, SI 2003/1075 Art.35, SI 2004/389 Art.33, SI 2004/757 Art.50

s.61, disapplied: SI 2002/1066 Art.43, SI 2003/1075 Art.35, SI 2004/389 Art.33, SI 2004/757 Art.50

s.62, amended: SSI 2003/331 Sch.1 para.4, 2004 c.21 Sch.1 para.45

s.65, applied: SI 2002/1066 Art.43, SI 2003/1075 Art.35, SI 2004/389 Art.33, SI 2004/757 Art.50

s.65, disapplied: SI 2002/1066 Art.43, SI 2003/1075 Art.35, SI 2004/389 Art.33, SI 2004/757 Art.50

s.71, enabling: SI 2002/461, SI 2002/1795, SSI 2002/104

s.104, enabling: SI 2002/461, SI 2002/1795, SSI 2002/104, SSI 2003/85, SSI 2003/168, SSI 2003/531

s.105, enabling: SSI 2003/168, SSI 2003/531

s.109, amended: 2004 c.14 Sch.1 Part 13

Sch.2 para.4, repealed: 2004 c.14 Sch.1 Part 13

Sch.2 para.5, repealed: 2004 c.14 Sch.1 Part 13

Sch.2 para.20, repealed: 2004 c.14 Sch.1 Part 13

Sch.3 para.1, repealed: 2004 c.14 Sch.1 Part 13

Sch.3 para.2, repealed: 2004 c.14 Sch.1 Part 13

Sch.3 para.3, repealed: 2004 c.14 Sch.1 Part 13

Sch.3 para.4, repealed: 2004 c.14 Sch.1 Part 13

Sch.3 para.11, repealed (in part): 2003 asp 15 Sch.4 Part 2

46. Friendly Societies Act 1974

s.7, applied: 2002 c.40 s.255

s.66, amended: 2004 c.33 Sch.27 para.52

s.102, substituted: 2003 c.39 Sch.8 para.175

s.105A, added: SI 2003/2867 Sch.1 para.7

s.111, applied: 2003 c.17 s.65

Sch.9 para.21, repealed: 2004 c.14 Sch.1 Part 9

47. Solicitors Act 1974

see *Arumugam v Law Society (No.2)* [2002] EWHC 2722, (2003) 147 S.J.L.B. 27 (QBD), Rose, L.J.; see *Miller v Law Society* [2002] EWHC 1453, [2002] 4 All E.R. 312 (Ch D), Geoffrey Vos Q.C.

applied: SI 2003/1887 Sch.1

Part III, applied: SI 2004/3114 Sch.1, SI 2004/3121 Sch.1

s.2, amended: SI 2003/1887 Sch.2 para.3

s.11, amended: SI 2002/3235 Art.2, SI 2003/1887 Sch.2 para.3

s.12A, amended: SI 2003/1887 Sch.2 para.3

s.14, amended: SI 2003/1887 Sch.2 para.3

s.22, amended: 2002 c.9 Sch.11 para.12

1974–cont.

47. Solicitors Act 1974–*cont.*

s.23, applied: SI 2004/2951 Reg.4

s.28, amended: SI 2003/1887 Sch.2 para.3

s.31, amended: SI 2003/1887 Sch.2 para.3

s.34, see *Law Society v Sephton & Co* [2004] EWHC 544, [2004] P.N.L.R. 27 (Ch D), Michael Briggs Q.C.

s.36, see *Law Society v Sephton & Co* [2004] EWHC 544, [2004] P.N.L.R. 27 (Ch D), Michael Briggs Q.C.

s.37A, see *R. (on the application of White) v Office for the Supervision of Solicitors* [2001] EWHC Admin 1149, (2002) 152 N.L.J. 21 (QBD (Admin Ct)), Lightman, J.

s.38, amended: 2003 c.39 Sch.8 para.176

s.38, repealed (in part): 2003 c.39 Sch.8 para.176, Sch.10

s.46, amended: SI 2003/1887 Sch.2 para.3

s.47, see *Camacho v Law Society (No.2)* [2004] EWHC 1675, [2004] 1 W.L.R. 3037 (QBD (Admin Ct)), Thomas, L.J.

s.47, amended: SI 2003/1887 Sch.2 para.3

s.49, see *Lucas v Millman* [2002] EWHC 2470, [2003] 1 W.L.R. 271 (QBD (Admin Ct)), Kennedy, L.J.

s.56, amended: 2002 c.9 Sch.11 para.12, SI 2003/1887 Sch.2 para.3

s.69, see *Ralph Hume Garry (A Firm) v Gwillim* [2002] EWCA Civ 1500, [2003] 1 W.L.R. 510 (CA), Ward, L.J.

s.70, see *Joseph v Boyd & Hutchinson* [2003] EWHC 413, [2003] 3 Costs L.R. 358 (Ch D), Patten, J.; see *MacPherson v Bevan Ashford (A Firm)* [2003] EWHC 636, [2003] 3 Costs L.R. 389 (Ch D), Patten, J.; see *McIlwraith v McIlwraith* [2002] EWHC 1757, [2003] W.T.L.R. 413 (Ch D), Judge Rich Q.C.; see *Pine v Law Society (No.2)* [2002] EWCA Civ 175, [2002] 1 W.L.R. 2189 (CA), Sir Andrew Morritt V.C.

s.71, see *MacPherson v Bevan Ashford (A Firm)* [2003] EWHC 636, [2003] 3 Costs L.R. 389 (Ch D), Patten, J.; see *Marsden v Guide Dogs for the Blind Association* [2004] EWHC 593, [2004] 3 All E.R. 222 (Ch D), Lloyd, J.; see *McIlwraith v McIlwraith* [2002] EWHC 1757, [2003] W.T.L.R. 413 (Ch D), Judge Rich Q.C.; see *Pine v Law Society (No.2)* [2002] EWCA Civ 175, [2002] 1 W.L.R. 2189 (CA), Sir Andrew Morritt V.C.

s.73, see *Clifford Harris & Co v Solland International Ltd* [2004] EWHC 2488, (2004) 148 S.J.L.B. 1400 (Ch D), David Richards, J.; see *Rohm & Haas Co v Collag Ltd (No.2)* [2002] B.P.I.R. 837 (Ch D), Pumfrey, J.

s.74, see *Lynch v Paul Davidson Taylor (A Firm)* [2004] EWHC 89, [2004] 1 W.L.R. 1753 (QBD), Hughes, J.

s.75, repealed (in part): 2002 c.9 Sch.13

s.81A, amended: SI 2003/1887 Sch.2 para.3

1974–cont.

47. Solicitors Act 1974–*cont.*

Sch.1 Part I para.1, see *Holder v Law Society* [2003] EWCA Civ 39, [2003] 1 W.L.R. 1059 (CA), Carnwath, L.J.

Sch.1 Part II, see *Dooley v Law Society* Times, January 16, 2002 (Ch D), Lightman, J.

Sch.1 Part II para.6, see *Dooley v Law Society* Times, January 16, 2002 (Ch D), Lightman, J.; see *Halley v Law Society* [2003] EWCA Civ 97, [2003] W.T.L.R. 845 (CA), Carnwath, L.J.; see *Holder v Law Society* [2002] EWHC 1559, Times, September 9, 2002 (Ch D), Peter Smith, J.

Sch.1 Part II para.9, see *Holder v Law Society* [2002] EWHC 1559, Times, September 9, 2002 (Ch D), Peter Smith, J.

Sch.1 Part II para.13, see *Pine v Law Society (No.2)* [2002] EWCA Civ 175, [2002] 1 W.L.R. 2189 (CA), Sir Andrew Morritt V.C.

Sch.1A para.1, amended: SI 2003/1887 Sch.2 para.3

Sch.1A para.2, amended: SI 2003/1887 Sch.2 para.3

Sch.1A para.3, amended: SI 2003/1887 Sch.2 para.3

Sch.1A para.4, amended: SI 2003/1887 Sch.2 para.3

Sch.1A para.5, see *R. (on the application of White) v Office for the Supervision of Solicitors* [2001] EWHC Admin 1149, (2002) 152 N.L.J. 21 (QBD (Admin Ct)), Lightman, J.

Sch.1A para.5, amended: SI 2003/1887 Sch.2 para.3

Sch.1A para.6, amended: SI 2003/1887 Sch.2 para.3

Sch.1A para.7, amended: SI 2003/1887 Sch.2 para.3

Sch.1A para.8, amended: SI 2003/1887 Sch.2 para.3

Sch.1A para.9, amended: SI 2003/1887 Sch.2 para.3

50. Road Traffic Act 1974

s.18, repealed: 2003 c.22 Sch.1

s.23, repealed (in part): 2004 c.14 Sch.1 Part 14

53. Rehabilitation of Offenders Act 1974

applied: SI 2002/233 Reg.5, SI 2002/324 Sch.2 para.7, SI 2002/325 Sch.2 para.8, SI 2002/327 Sch.2 para.7, SI 2002/812 Sch.2 para.7, SI 2002/919 Sch.2 para.9A, Sch.3 para.13A, Sch.8 para.9, Sch.8 para.9A, 2003 c.17 s.114, SI 2003/781 Sch.2 para.7, SI 2003/2527 Sch.2 para.9, SI 2004/2541 Sch.1, SI 2004/2542 Sch.1, SI 2004/2695 Sch.1 para.2, SSI 2002/143 Reg.6, SSI 2002/504 Sch.1, SSI 2002/541 Reg.35, SSI 2004/421 Sch.2

s.1, see *Munro v Highland Council* 2003 S.C. 239 (1 Div), Lord Cullen L.P., Lord Caplan, Lord Marnoch

CAP.

1974–cont.

53. Rehabilitation of Offenders Act 1974– cont.

s.1, amended: 2002 c.29 Sch.11 para.7, 2004 c.28 Sch.10 para.9

s.1, applied: SI 2002/57 Sch.1 para.7, Sch.3 para.13, SI 2002/324 Reg.19, SI 2002/325 Reg.18, SI 2002/327 Reg.26, Sch.2 para.7, SI 2002/812 Reg.16, Sch.2 para.7, SI 2002/919 Reg.5, Sch.1 para.1, Sch.1 para.16, Sch.3 para.8, Sch.7 para.1, Sch.7 para.13, SI 2002/3212 Sch.3 para.4, SI 2002/3214 Sch.3 para.4

s.4, see *R. (on the application of Pearson) v Driver and Vehicle Licensing Agency* [2002] EWHC 2482, [2003] R.T.R. 20 (QBD (Admin Ct)), Maurice Kay, J.

s.4, disapplied: SSI 2003/231 Art.3, Art.4, Art.5

s.4, varied: SI 2003/415 Sch.1

s.4, enabling: SI 2002/441, SI 2003/965, SSI 2003/231

s.5, see *Munro v Highland Council* 2003 S.C. 239 (1 Div), Lord Cullen L.P., Lord Caplan, Lord Marnoch

s.5, amended: 2003 c.44 Sch.32 para.18

s.6, see *Munro v Highland Council* 2003 S.C. 239 (1 Div), Lord Cullen L.P., Lord Caplan, Lord Marnoch

s.7, amended: 2002 c.30 Sch.7 para.4, 2003 c.42 Sch.6 para.19, 2004 c.33 Sch.27 para.53

s.7, varied: SI 2003/415 Sch.1

s.7, enabling: SI 2002/441, SI 2003/965, SSI 2003/231

s.10, applied: SSI 2003/231

s.10, enabling: SI 2002/441, SI 2003/965, SSI 2003/231

1975

xxii. Dart Harbour and Navigation Author-ity Act 1975

referred to: SI 2002/2730 Art.1

s.2, amended: SI 2002/2730 Art.18, Sch.3

s.5, repealed: SI 2002/2730 Sch.3

s.19, repealed: SI 2002/2730 Sch.3

s.30, see *R. (on the application of Dart Harbour and Navigation Authority) v Secretary of State for Transport, Local Government and the Regions* [2003] EWHC 1494, [2003] 2 Lloyd's Rep. 607 (QBD (Admin Ct)), Lightman, J.

s.33, see *R. (on the application of Dart Harbour and Navigation Authority) v Secretary of State for Transport, Local Government and the Regions* [2003] EWHC 1494, [2003] 2 Lloyd's Rep. 607 (QBD (Admin Ct)), Lightman, J.

s.41, amended: SI 2002/2730 Art.18

s.65, amended: SI 2002/2730 Art.15

s.65, referred to: SI 2002/2730 Art.17

s.66, amended: SI 2002/2730 Art.16

CAP.

1975–cont.

xxii. Dart Harbour and Navigation Author-ity Act 1975–cont.

s.66, referred to: SI 2002/2730 Art.17

Sch.1, repealed: SI 2002/2730 Sch.3

Sch.2, repealed: SI 2002/2730 Sch.3

xxx. Greater London Council (General Powers) Act 1975

s.3, amended: SI 2002/1397 Sch.1 para.5, 2004 c.21 Sch.1 para.46

s.3, applied: SI 2002/1397 Art.11

Inheritance (Provision for Family and Dependents) Act 1975

see *Churchill v Roach* [2002] EWHC 3230, [2004] 2 F.L.R. 989 (Ch D), Judge Norris Q.C.; see *Wade v Varney* [2003] EWCA Civ 1279, [2003] W.T.L.R. 1535 (CA), Tuckey, L.J.

s.1, see *Robinson v Bird* [2003] EWCA Civ 1820, [2004] W.T.L.R. 257 (CA), Mance, L.J.

s.3, see *Parnall v Hurst* [2003] W.T.L.R. 997 (Ch D), Peter Langan Q.C.

Labour Relations Act 1975

s.9, see *Stevedoring Services Ltd v Burgess* [2002] UKPC 39, [2002] 1 W.L.R. 2838 (PC (Ber)), Lord Hoffmann

xxxi. London Transport Act 1975

varied: SI 2003/1615 Sch.2 para.6

s.24, amended: SI 2003/1615 Sch.1 para.32

xxviii. Milford Haven Conservancy Act 1975

referred to: 2002 c.v

xx. Plymouth City Council Act 1975

applied: SI 2003/655 Reg.8

1. Church Commissioners (Miscellaneous Provisions) Measure 1975

s.1, repealed (in part): 2004 c.14 Sch.1 Part 6

4. Biological Standards Act 1975

s.6, repealed: 2004 c.14 Sch.1 Part 17

s.8, amended: 2004 c.14 Sch.1 Part 17

s.9, repealed (in part): 2004 c.14 Sch.1 Part 17

7. Finance Act 1975

Sch.12 para.5, repealed: 2002 c.9 Sch.13

8. Offshore Petroleum Development (Scotland) Act 1975

applied: SSI 2002/410 Art.57

13. Unsolicited Goods and Services (Amendment) Act 1975

s.2, repealed (in part): 2004 c.14 Sch.1 Part 16

s.3, repealed (in part): 2004 c.14 Sch.1 Part 16

s.4, repealed (in part): 2004 c.14 Sch.1 Part 16

14. Social Security Act 1975

applied: SI 2004/865 Art.101, SI 2004/1016 Art.77

s.126A, applied: SI 2002/668 Art.4, SI 2003/526 Art.4

s.126A, varied: SI 2004/552 Art.4

15. Social Security (Northern Ireland) Act 1975

s.120, varied: SR 2002/99 Art.4, SR 2003/155 Art.4

1975–cont.

21. Criminal Procedure (Scotland) Act 1975
applied: 2004 c.33 s.115

s.338, amended: 2002 asp 4 s.1

22. OIL TAXATION ACT 1975
applied: SI 2003/2718 Reg.5, SI 2004/352 Sch.2 para.11, Sch.4 para.10, Sch.6 para.10

referred to: SI 2004/352 Sch.3 para.12

Sch.2 para.2, applied: SI 2003/2718 Sch.1 para.1

Sch.2 para.5, applied: SI 2003/2718 Sch.1 para.2

Sch.2 para.8, applied: 2004 c.12 s.313

Sch.4 para.2, amended: 2004 c.12 s.287

Sch.5 para.1, applied: SI 2003/2718 Sch.1 para.3

Sch.5 para.2, applied: SI 2003/2718 Sch.1 para.4

Sch.6 para.1, applied: SI 2003/2718 Sch.1 para.5

Sch.7 para.1, applied: SI 2003/2718 Sch.1 para.6

Sch.8 para.1, applied: SI 2003/2718 Sch.1 para.7

Sch.8 para.4, applied: SI 2003/2718 Sch.1 para.8

23. Reservoirs Act 1975
applied: 2003 asp 8 s.55, 2003 c.37 s.74

s.1, amended: 2002 asp 3 Sch.7 para.7, 2003 c.37 s.74

s.2, amended: 2003 c.37 s.74, s.78

s.2, applied: 2003 c.37 s.74

s.3, amended: 2003 c.37 s.74

s.8, amended: 2003 c.37 s.75

s.12A, added: 2003 c.37 s.77

s.12B, added: 2003 c.37 s.78

s.13, amended: 2003 c.37 s.74

s.15, amended: 2003 c.37 s.75, s.76

s.17, amended: 2003 c.37 s.75

s.20, amended: 2003 c.37 s.74

s.21, amended: 2003 c.37 s.74

s.22, amended: 2003 c.37 s.74, s.79, Sch.9 Part 3

s.22A, added: 2003 c.37 s.76

s.24, amended: 2003 c.37 s.74

s.25, amended: 2003 c.37 s.74

s.27, amended: 2003 c.37 s.74

s.27A, added: 2003 c.37 s.80

Sch.1, amended: 2003 c.37 s.74, Sch.7 para.38, Sch.9 Part 3

Sch.1, repealed (in part): 2003 c.37 Sch.9 Part 3

24. House of Commons Disqualification Act 1975
referred to: 2003 c.43 Sch.4 para.19

s.1, applied: 2002 c.24 s.10

s.4, referred to: 2002 c.24 s.10

Sch.1 Part I, amended: 2002 c.9 Sch.9 para.9

Sch.1 Part II, amended: 2002 asp 3 Sch.7 para.8, 2002 c.11 Sch.1 para.21, 2002 c.17 Sch.6 para.18, Sch.7 para.22, 2002 c.26

1975–cont.

24. House of Commons Disqualification Act 1975–*cont.*
Sch.1 Part II, amended:–*cont.*

Sch.2 para.18, Sch.9 para.13, 2002 c.30 Sch.7 para.5, Sch.8, 2002 c.40 Sch.1 para.15, Sch.2 para.10, Sch.3 para.17, SI 2002/1723 Sch.1, 2003 c.26 Sch.4 para.23, 2003 c.37 Sch.7 para.20, 2003 c.43 Sch.9 para.7, Sch.14 Part 2, SI 2003/2246 Art.3, SSI 2002/263 Sch.1, 2003 asp 4 Sch.4 para.3, 2003 c.4 Sch.3 para.2, 2003 c.20 Sch.2 para.21, 2003 c.21 Sch.17 para.48, Sch.19, 2004 c.11 Sch.1 para.4, 2004 c.17 Sch.4, 2004 c.19 Sch.2 para.2, 2004 c.20 Sch.10 para.17, Sch.1 para.16, 2004 c.30 Sch.2 para.25, 2004 c.35 Sch.1 para.31, Sch.5 para.26, Sch.13 Part 1

Sch.1 Part II, referred to: 2002 c.24 s.10

Sch.1 Part II, varied: SI 2004/1822 Sch.1 para.9

Sch.1 Part III, amended: 2002 c.8 s.1, 2002 c.9 Sch.7 para.7, 2002 c.26 s.23, Sch.8 para.14, 2002 c.32 Sch.11 para.5, Sch.18 para.14, 2002 c.39 Sch.3, 2002 c.40 Sch.26, 2002 c.41 Sch.7 para.9, SI 2002/253 Sch.5 para.4, SI 2002/2469 Sch.1 para.8, 2003 c.20 Sch.8, 2003 c.21 Sch.19, 2003 c.37 Sch.7 para.20, Sch.9 Part 3, 2003 c.43 Sch.2 para.18, Sch.4 para.20, Sch.13 para.2, Sch.14 Part 4, Sch.14 Part 7, 2004 c.7 Sch.1 para.10, 2004 c.8 Sch.6 para.4, 2004 c.17 Sch.3 para.6, 2004 c.19 Sch.2 para.2, Sch.4, 2004 c.20 s.45, 2004 c.25 Sch.4 para.7, Sch.5 para.11, 2004 c.27 Sch.3 para.9, Sch.4 para.6, 2004 c.28 Sch.8 para.10, 2004 c.31 Sch.1 para.12, 2004 c.35 s.211, s.274, Sch.1 para.31, Sch.4 para.14, SI 2004/1823 Art.7

Sch.1 Part III, referred to: 2002 c.24 s.10

Sch.2, amended: SI 2002/794 Sch.2

25. Northern Ireland Assembly Disqualification Act 1975
Sch.1 Part I, amended: 2002 c.9 Sch.9 para.9, 2002 c.26 Sch.13

Sch.1 Part II, amended: 2002 c.9 (NI) Sch.1 para.16, 2002 c.11 Sch.1 para.21, 2002 c.17 Sch.7 para.23, 2002 c.1 (NI) Sch.1 para.20, (NI) Sch.4, 2002 c.26 Sch.2 para.19, Sch.9 para.14, SI 2002/1723 Sch.1, 2003 c.21 Sch.17 para.49, Sch.19, 2003 c.43 Sch.14 Part 2, SI 2003/410 Sch.1 para.22, SI 2003/419 Sch.1 para.12, SI 2003/431 Sch.4, 2004 c.11 Sch.1 para.5, 2004 c.19 Sch.2 para.3, 2004 c.20 Sch.1 para.16, 2004 c.35 Sch.5 para.27, Sch.13 Part 1

Sch.1 Part II, varied: SI 2004/664 Art.11, Art.12, Art.13, Art.14

Sch.1 Part III, added: 2004 c.31 Sch.1 para.13

Sch.1 Part III, amended: 2002 c.1 (NI) Sch.4, 2002 c.9 Sch.7 para.7, 2002 c.26 s.23, Sch.8 para.15, 2002 c.40 Sch.26, SI

CAP.

1975–cont.

25. Northern Ireland Assembly Disqualification Act 1975–cont.
Sch.1 Part III, amended:–cont.
2002/253 Sch.5 para.5, 2003 c.21 Sch.19, SI 2003/419 Sch.5, SI 2003/439 Sch.2 para.13, 2004 c.7 Sch.1 para.11, 2004 c.17 Sch.3 para.7, 2004 c.19 Sch.2 para.3, Sch.4, 2004 c.20 s.45, 2004 c.25 Sch.5 para.12, 2004 c.35 s.211, Sch.4 para.15, SI 2004/1823 Art.8

26. Ministers of the Crown Act 1975
s.1, applied: SI 2002/794, SI 2002/2626, SI 2002/2633
s.1, enabling: SI 2002/794, SI 2002/1397, SI 2002/2633, SI 2003/1887, SI 2003/2922, SI 2003/3191
s.2, applied: SI 2002/2626
s.2, enabling: SI 2002/1397, SI 2003/1887
s.5, applied: SI 2002/794
s.5, enabling: SI 2002/794

27. Ministerial and other Salaries Act 1975
applied: 2003 c.1 s.295
Sch.1 Part I, amended: SI 2002/794 Sch.2

30. Local Government (Scotland) Act 1975
referred to: SSI 2003/187 Art.9
Part II, applied: SSI 2002/201 Art.12, SSI 2003/1 Art.12
Part II, referred to: 2002 asp 11 Sch.7 para.1
s.1, applied: SSI 2002/504 Art.6
s.2, amended: SSI 2002/158 Art.18
s.2, varied: SSI 2003/187 Art.8
s.3, varied: SSI 2003/187 Art.8
s.6, applied: SSI 2002/91 Reg.15, SSI 2002/158, SSI 2002/158 Art.19, SSI 2002/159, SSI 2003/160 Reg.15, Reg.16, SSI 2003/187, SSI 2003/187 Art.3, Art.4, Art.5
s.6, enabling: SSI 2002/158, SSI 2002/159, SSI 2003/187
s.7, applied: SSI 2002/504 Art.6
s.7B, applied: SSI 2002/89 Art.2, SSI 2003/123 Art.2, SSI 2004/59 Art.2
s.7B, enabling: SSI 2002/89, SSI 2003/123, SSI 2004/59
s.21, applied: 2002 asp 11 Sch.7 para.1
s.21, repealed: 2002 asp 11 Sch.6 para.1
s.22, repealed: 2002 asp 11 Sch.6 para.1
s.23, repealed: 2002 asp 11 Sch.6 para.1
s.24, repealed: 2002 asp 11 Sch.6 para.1
s.25, repealed: 2002 asp 11 Sch.6 para.1
s.26, repealed: 2002 asp 11 Sch.6 para.1
s.27, repealed: 2002 asp 11 Sch.6 para.1
s.28, repealed: 2002 asp 11 Sch.6 para.1
s.29, repealed: 2002 asp 11 Sch.6 para.1
s.29A, repealed: 2002 asp 11 Sch.6 para.1
s.30, repealed: 2002 asp 11 Sch.6 para.1
s.31, repealed: 2002 asp 11 Sch.6 para.1
s.32, repealed: 2002 asp 11 Sch.6 para.1
s.35, enabling: SSI 2002/158, SSI 2002/159, SSI 2003/187

CAP.

1975–cont.

30. Local Government (Scotland) Act 1975–cont.
s.37, applied: 2002 asp 3 s.62, SSI 2002/91 Reg.9, Reg.10, SSI 2003/160 Reg.9, Reg.10
s.37, enabling: SSI 2002/89, SSI 2002/158, SSI 2002/159, SSI 2003/123, SSI 2003/187, SSI 2004/59
Sch.4 para.1, repealed: 2002 asp 11 Sch.6 para.1
Sch.4 para.2, repealed: 2002 asp 11 Sch.6 para.1
Sch.4 para.3, repealed: 2002 asp 11 Sch.6 para.1
Sch.4 para.4, repealed: 2002 asp 11 Sch.6 para.1
Sch.4 para.5, repealed: 2002 asp 11 Sch.6 para.1
Sch.4 para.6, repealed: 2002 asp 11 Sch.6 para.1
Sch.5 para.1, repealed: 2002 asp 11 Sch.6 para.1
Sch.5 para.2, repealed: 2002 asp 11 Sch.6 para.1
Sch.5 para.3, repealed: 2002 asp 11 Sch.6 para.1
Sch.5 para.4, repealed: 2002 asp 11 Sch.6 para.1
Sch.5 para.5, repealed: 2002 asp 11 Sch.6 para.1

32. Prices Act 1975
repealed: 2004 c.14 Sch.1 Part 16

34. Evidence (Proceedings in Other Jurisdictions) Act 1975
see *Commerce & Industry Insurance Co (Canada) v Lloyd's Underwriters* [2002] 1 W.L.R. 1323 (QBD (Comm Ct)), Moore-Bick, J.; see *Refco Capital Markets Ltd v Credit Suisse First Boston Ltd* [2001] EWCA Civ 1733, [2002] C.P. Rep. 15 (CA), Waller, L.J.
s.7, amended: 2003 c.39 Sch.8 para.177

35. Farriers (Registration) Act 1975
s.7, amended: SI 2002/1597 Sch.2 para.1, Sch.2 para.2, Sch.2 para.3
s.7A, added: SI 2002/1597 Sch.2 para.4
s.7B, added: SI 2002/1597 Sch.2 para.5
s.9, substituted: SI 2002/1597 Sch.2 para.6

45. Finance (No.2) Act 1975
s.73, amended: SI 2002/2521 Sch.2 Part I, SI 2004/1662 Sch.1 para.19

47. Litigants in Person (Costs and Expenses) Act 1975
applied: SSI 2002/132 Sch.1 para.23.3
s.2, repealed (in part): 2004 c.14 Sch.1 Part 1

51. Salmon and Freshwater Fisheries Act 1975
applied: SI 2004/933 Art.19
referred to: SI 2003/2830 Sch.2 para.13, SI 2003/2831 Art.19

1975–cont.

51. Salmon and Freshwater Fisheries Act 1975–cont.

Sch.4 Part II para.14, amended: 2003 c.39 Sch.8 para.178

52. Safety of Sports Grounds Act 1975

applied: SI 2002/1754 Art.2, SI 2002/2893 Art.2, SI 2003/1256 Art.2, SI 2003/1637 Art.2, SI 2004/1907 Art.2

s.1, enabling: SI 2002/1754, SI 2002/2893, SI 2003/1256, SI 2003/1637, SI 2004/1907

s.3, amended: 2004 c.21 Sch.1 para.47

s.4, amended: 2004 c.21 Sch.1 para.47

s.5, amended: 2004 c.21 Sch.1 para.47

s.10, amended: 2004 c.21 Sch.1 para.47

s.10A, amended: 2004 c.21 Sch.1 para.47

s.11, amended: 2004 c.21 Sch.1 para.47

s.17, amended: 2003 asp 8 Sch.6 para.11, 2003 c.39 Sch.8 para.179, Sch.10

s.18, referred to: SI 2002/2893, SI 2003/1256, SI 2003/1637

s.18, enabling: SI 2002/1754, SI 2002/2893

54. Limitation Act 1975

see *McDonnell v Congregation of Christian Brothers Trustees (formerly Irish Christian Brothers)* [2003] UKHL 63, [2004] 1 A.C. 1101 (HL), Lord Bingham of Cornhill

55. Statutory Corporations (Financial Provisions) Act 1975

Sch.4 para.4, repealed: 2004 c.14 Sch.1 Part 9

59. Criminal Jurisdiction Act 1975

s.11, amended: 2002 c.26 Sch.7 para.28

Sch.1 Part I para.9, substituted: SI 2004/702 Sch.7 para.1

Sch.3 para.1, repealed: 2003 c.41 Sch.4

60. Social Security Pensions Act 1975

applied: SSI 2002/494 Sch.2 para.8

s.59, applied: SI 2002/699 Art.6, SI 2002/1311 Sch.1 para.3, SI 2003/681 Art.6, SI 2004/758 Art.6, SSI 2003/344 Sch.1 para.3

s.59, enabling: SI 2002/699, SI 2003/681, SI 2004/758

s.59A, applied: SI 2002/699 Art.5, SI 2003/681 Art.5, SI 2004/758 Art.5

s.61, repealed: 2004 c.14 Sch.1 Part 11

s.67, repealed: 2004 c.14 Sch.1 Part 11

s.68, repealed (in part): 2004 c.14 Sch.1 Part 11

Sch.4 para.4, repealed: 2004 c.14 Sch.1 Part 11

Sch.4 para.21, repealed: 2004 c.14 Sch.1 Part 11

Sch.4 para.34, repealed: 2004 c.14 Sch.1 Part 11

Sch.4 para.65, repealed: 2004 c.14 Sch.1 Part 11

1975–cont.

63. Inheritance (Provision for Family and Dependants) Act 1975

see *Marsh v Sofaer* [2003] EWHC 3334, [2004] P.N.L.R. 24 (Ch D), Sir Robert Andrew Morritt V.C.; see *Nathan v Leonard* [2002] EWHC 1701, [2003] 1 W.L.R. 827 (Ch D), John Martin Q.C.; see *Robinson v Bird* [2003] EWHC 30, [2003] W.T.L.R. 529 (Ch D), Blackburne, J.

s.1, see *G (Decree Absolute: Prejudice), Re* [2002] EWHC 2834, [2003] 1 F.L.R. 870 (Fam Div), Bennett, J.; see *Gully v Dix* [2004] EWCA Civ 139, [2004] 1 W.L.R. 1399 (CA), Ward, L.J.; see *Murphy v Murphy* [2003] EWCA Civ 1862, [2004] 1 F.C.R. 1 (CA), Thomas, L.J.

s.1, amended: 2004 c.33 Sch.4 para.15

s.2, see *Murphy v Murphy* [2003] EWCA Civ 1862, [2004] 1 F.C.R. 1 (CA), Thomas, L.J.

s.2, amended: 2004 c.33 Sch.4 para.16

s.3, see *Stephanides v Cohen* [2002] EWHC 1869, [2002] W.T.L.R. 1373 (Fam Div), District Judge Kenworthy-Browne

s.3, amended: 2004 c.33 Sch.4 para.17, Sch.4 para.18, Sch.30

s.4, see *McNulty v McNulty* [2002] EWHC 123, [2002] W.T.L.R. 737 (Ch D), Launcelot Henderson Q.C.

s.6, amended: 2004 c.33 Sch.4 para.19

s.9, see *Murphy v Murphy* [2003] EWCA Civ 1862, [2004] 1 F.C.R. 1 (CA), Thomas, L.J.

s.14A, added: 2004 c.33 Sch.4 para.20

s.15B, added: 2004 c.33 Sch.4 para.22

s.15ZA, added: 2004 c.33 Sch.4 para.21

s.16, amended: 2004 c.33 Sch.4 para.23

s.17, amended: 2004 c.33 Sch.4 para.24

s.18A, added: 2004 c.33 Sch.4 para.25

s.19, amended: 2004 c.33 Sch.4 para.26

s.25, see *Gandhi v Patel* [2002] 1 F.L.R. 603 (Ch D), Park, J.

s.25, amended: 2004 c.33 Sch.4 para.27

65. Sex Discrimination Act 1975

see *1 Pump Court Chambers v Horton* [2004] EWCA Civ 941, [2004] 3 All E.R. 852 (CA), Peter Gibson, L.J.; see *Advocate General for Scotland v MacDonald* 2002 S.C.1 (Court of Session (Inner House, Extra Division)), Lord Prosser, Lord Caplan, Lord Kirkwood; see *Chief Constable of West Yorkshire v A* [2002] I.C.R. 552 (EAT), Lindsay, J. (President); see *Department for Work and Pensions v Thompson* [2004] I.R.L.R. 348 (EAT), Keith, J.; see *X v Stevens (Commissioner of Police of the Metropolis)* [2003] I.C.R. 1031 (EAT), Burton, J.

applied: SI 2004/753 Sch.1 para.168, SI 2004/1861 Sch.1 para.61

Part II, applied: SI 2004/1861 Sch.1 para.22

s.1, see *Advocate General for Scotland v MacDonald* [2003] UKHL 34, [2004] 1 All E.R. 339 (HL), Lord Nicholls of

CAP.

1975–cont.

65. Sex Discrimination Act 1975–*cont.*

s.1–*cont.*

Birkenhead; see *Chief Constable of Avon and Somerset v Chew* [2002] Emp. L.R. 370 (EAT), Charles, J.; see *Chief Constable of West Yorkshire v A* [2004] UKHL 21, [2004] 2 W.L.R. 1209 (HL), Lord Bingham of Cornhill; see *Coker v Lord Chancellor* [2001] EWCA Civ 1756, [2002] I.C.R. 321 (CA), Lord Phillips of Worth Matravers, M.R.; see *Hardman v Mallon (t/a Orchard Lodge Nursing Home)* [2002] 2 C.M.L.R. 59 (EAT), J McMullen Q.C.; see *Hayes v Charman Underwriting Agencies Ltd* [2002] Emp. L.R. 130 (EAT), Judge Peter Clark; see *University of Huddersfield v Wolff* [2004] I.C.R. 828 (EAT), Burton, J.

s.1, repealed (in part): 2004 c.33 Sch.30

s.2, see *Chief Constable of West Yorkshire v A* [2004] UKHL 21, [2004] 2 W.L.R. 1209 (HL), Lord Bingham of Cornhill

s.3, substituted: 2004 c.33 s.251

s.4, see *McGlennon v Chief Constable of Cumbria* [2002] I.C.R. 1156 (EAT), Commissioner Howell Q.C.; see *Royal National Orthopaedic Hospital Trust v Howard* [2002] I.R.L.R. 849 (EAT), Judge JR Reid Q.C.; see *St Helens MBC v Derbyshire* [2004] I.R.L.R. 851 (EAT), Cox, J.

s.5, see *Advocate General for Scotland v MacDonald* [2003] UKHL 34, [2004] 1 All E.R. 339 (HL), Lord Nicholls of Birkenhead; see *Hardman v Mallon (t/a Orchard Lodge Nursing Home)* [2002] 2 C.M.L.R. 59 (EAT), J McMullen Q.C.

s.5, amended: 2004 c.33 s.251

s.6, see *Chief Constable of West Yorkshire v A* [2004] UKHL 21, [2004] 2 W.L.R. 1209 (HL), Lord Bingham of Cornhill; see *Hayes v Charman Underwriting Agencies Ltd* [2002] Emp. L.R. 130 (EAT), Judge Peter Clark; see *Pearce v Mayfield Secondary School Governing Body* [2001] EWCA Civ 1347, [2002] I.C.R. 198 (CA), Hale, L.J.; see *Rhys-Harper v Relaxion Group Plc* [2003] UKHL 33, [2003] 4 All E.R. 1113 (HL), Lord Nicholls of Birkenhead; see *Royal National Orthopaedic Hospital Trust v Howard* [2002] I.R.L.R. 849 (EAT), Judge JR Reid Q.C.

s.6, varied: SI 2003/1964 Sch.1

s.7, see *Chief Constable of West Yorkshire v A* [2002] EWCA Civ 1584, [2003] 1 All E.R. 255 (CA), Kennedy, L.J.; see *Chief Constable of West Yorkshire v A* [2002] I.C.R. 552 (EAT), Lindsay, J. (President); see *Chief Constable of West Yorkshire v A* [2004] UKHL 21, [2004] 2 W.L.R. 1209 (HL), Lord Bingham of Cornhill

s.7, amended: 2004 c.33 s.251

s.7, varied: SI 2003/1964 Sch.1

CAP.

1975–cont.

65. Sex Discrimination Act 1975–*cont.*

s.7A, amended: 2004 c.7 Sch.6 para.2

s.7B, see *Chief Constable of West Yorkshire v A* [2002] I.C.R. 552 (EAT), Lindsay, J. (President)

s.7B, amended: 2004 c.7 Sch.6 para.3

s.9, amended: 2004 c.7 Sch.6 para.4

s.9, varied: SI 2003/1964 Sch.1

s.11, see *Dave v Robinska* [2003] I.C.R. 1248 (EAT), Judge McMullen Q.C.

s.11, amended: 2004 c.7 Sch.6 para.5

s.17, see *Chief Constable of Kent v Baskerville* [2003] EWCA Civ 1354, [2003] I.C.R. 1463 (CA), Peter Gibson, L.J.; see *McGlennon v Chief Constable of Cumbria* [2002] I.C.R. 1156 (EAT), Commissioner Howell Q.C.

s.17, amended: SI 2003/1657 Reg.2

s.20A, added: SI 2003/1657 Reg.3

s.26, applied: 2004 asp 4 Sch.2 para.3

s.35C, added: SI 2003/1657 Reg.4

s.41, see *Chief Constable of Kent v Baskerville* [2003] EWCA Civ 1354, [2003] I.C.R. 1463 (CA), Peter Gibson, L.J.

s.41, varied: SI 2003/1964 Sch.1

s.42, see *Sinclair Roche & Temperley v Heard* [2004] I.R.L.R. 763 (EAT), Burton, J.

s.42A, added: 2002 c.2 s.1

s.44, referred to: 2004 c.7 s.19

s.56A, applied: SI 2003/2865, SI 2003/2865 Art.2

s.56A, enabling: SI 2003/2865

s.63, applied: 2002 c.22 Sch.3, Sch.4, Sch.5, SI 2004/1861 Sch.1 para.22

s.63A, see *Barton v Investec Henderson Crosthwaite Securities Ltd* [2003] I.C.R. 1205 (EAT), Judge Ansell; see *Chamberlin Solicitors v Emokpae* [2004] I.C.R. 1476 (EAT), Judge McMullen Q.C.; see *Nelson v Carillion Services Ltd* [2003] EWCA Civ 544, [2003] I.C.R. 1256 (CA), Simon Brown, L.J.; see *University of Huddersfield v Wolff* [2004] I.C.R. 828 (EAT), Burton, J.

s.65, see *Vince-Cain v Orthet Ltd* [2004] I.R.L.R. 857 (EAT), Judge McMullen Q.C.

s.65, amended: 2004 c.33 s.251

s.68, applied: SI 2004/1861 Reg.16

s.74, referred to: SI 2004/752 Reg.14

s.76, see *Commissioner of Police of the Metropolis v Hendricks* [2002] Emp. L.R. 32 (EAT), Judge Serota Q.C.; see *Kells v Pilkington Plc* [2002] 2 C.M.L.R. 63 (EAT), Lindsay, J. (President); see *Stott v Prison Service* [2003] EWCA Civ 1513, (2003) 147 S.J.L.B. 1206 (CA), Simon Brown, L.J.

s.76, amended: 2004 c.8 s.19

s.77, applied: SI 2004/754 Art.2, Art.3

s.77, enabling: SI 2004/754, SI 2004/2515

1975–cont.

65. Sex Discrimination Act 1975–cont.
s.82, see *Croft v Royal Mail Group Plc* [2003] EWCA Civ 1045, [2003] I.C.R. 1425 (CA), Pill, L.J.
s.82, amended: 2004 c.33 Sch.27 para.54
s.82, varied: SI 2003/1964 Sch.1
Sch.2 para.4, repealed: 2002 c.32 Sch.21 para.3, Sch.22 Part 3
Sch.2 para.4A, added: 2002 c.32 Sch.21 para.3

68. Industry Act 1975
Sch.3, applied: SI 2003/409 Sch.1 Part I

70. Welsh Development Agency Act 1975
s.7, applied: SI 2004/1005 Sch.2
s.8, applied: SI 2004/1005 Sch.2
s.16, applied: SI 2004/907 Art.2
s.16, enabling: SI 2004/907
s.18, applied: SI 2004/1826 Art.2
s.18, enabling: SI 2004/1826
s.19, amended: 2003 c.21 Sch.17 para.50, Sch.19
s.27, amended: 2004 c.14 Sch.1 Part 16
s.29, repealed (in part): 2004 c.14 Sch.1 Part 16
Sch.1 para.20A, added: SI 2003/2867 Sch.1 para.8
Sch.1 para.21, substituted: SI 2002/1555 Art.6
Sch.4 Part I para.2, repealed: 2004 c.5 Sch.9
Sch.4 Part I para.3, amended: 2004 c.5 Sch.7 para.9

71. Employment Protection Act 1975
s.111, repealed (in part): 2004 c.14 Sch.1 Part 8
s.124, amended: 2004 c.14 Sch.1 Part 8
Sch.9 Part II para.2, repealed (in part): SI 2004/2178 Sch.1 Part I
Sch.10 Part II para.2, repealed (in part): SSI 2004/384 Sch.1
Sch.13 para.5, repealed: 2004 c.14 Sch.1 Part 8
Sch.13 para.7, repealed: 2004 c.14 Sch.1 Part 8
Sch.14 para.6, repealed: 2004 c.14 Sch.1 Part 8
Sch.15 para.1, repealed: 2004 c.14 Sch.1 Part 8
Sch.15 para.4, repealed: 2004 c.14 Sch.1 Part 8
Sch.15 para.5, repealed: 2004 c.14 Sch.1 Part 8
Sch.15 para.7, repealed: 2004 c.14 Sch.1 Part 8
Sch.15 para.8, repealed: 2004 c.14 Sch.1 Part 8
Sch.15 para.10, repealed: 2004 c.14 Sch.1 Part 8
Sch.15 para.11, repealed: 2004 c.14 Sch.1 Part 8
Sch.15 para.14, repealed: 2004 c.14 Sch.1 Part 8
Sch.15 para.16, repealed (in part): 2004 c.14 Sch.1 Part 8

1975–cont.

71. Employment Protection Act 1975–cont.
Sch.15 para.18, repealed: 2004 c.14 Sch.1 Part 8
Sch.15 para.20, repealed: 2004 c.14 Sch.1 Part 8
Sch.15 para.21, repealed: 2004 c.14 Sch.1 Part 8

72. Children Act 1975
s.34, applied: SI 2002/1330 Sch.3 para.1, SI 2002/3200 Reg.15, Sch.3 para.1, SI 2003/1994 Sch.3 para.1
s.34, disapplied: SI 2002/195 Reg.15, Sch.3 para.1

75. Policyholders Protection Act 1975
s.6, see *Aitken v Financial Services Compensation Scheme Ltd* 2003 S.L.T. 878 (OH), Lord Drummond Young; see *R. (on the application of Geologistics Ltd) v Financial Services Compensation Scheme* [2003] EWCA Civ 1905, [2004] 1 W.L.R. 1719 (CA), Waller, L.J.; see *R. (on the application of Geologistics Ltd) v Financial Services Compensation Scheme* [2003] EWHC 629, [2003] 1 W.L.R. 1696 (QBD (Admin Ct)), Davis, J.

76. Local Land Charges Act 1975
s.10, see *Pound v Ashford BC* [2003] EWHC 1088, [2004] 1 P. & C.R. 2 (Ch D), Laddie, J.; see *Smith v South Gloucestershire DC* [2002] EWCA Civ 1131, [2002] 3 E.G.L.R. 1 (CA), Sir Martin Nourse
s.10, amended: 2002 c.9 Sch.11 para.13
s.14, enabling: SI 2003/2502
s.19, referred to: 2002 c.9 Sch.12 para.13
s.19, repealed (in part): 2002 c.9 Sch.13
s.20, repealed (in part): 2004 c.14 Sch.1 Part 12
Sch.1, amended: 2004 c.14 Sch.1 Part 2, Sch.1 Part 12
Sch.1, repealed: 2002 c.9 Sch.13

82. Civil List Act 1975
applied: 2002 c.16 s.16

1976

Constitution of the Republic of Trinidad and Tobago Act 1976
s.5, see *Matthew v Trinidad and Tobago* [2004] UKPC 33, [2004] 3 W.L.R. 812 (PC (Trin)), Lord Hoffmann

xxvi. Greater London Council (General Powers) Act 1976
s.5, repealed: 2003 c.17 Sch.7
s.6, repealed: 2003 c.17 Sch.7
s.7, repealed: 2003 c.17 Sch.7
s.8, repealed: 2003 c.17 Sch.7

xxxvii. London Transport Act 1976
s.13, see *Thames Water Utilities Ltd v London Underground Ltd* [2004] EWCA Civ 615, (2004) 148 S.J.L.B. 633 (CA), Brooke, L.J.

1976–cont.

xxi. Stornoway Harbour Order Confirmation Act 1976
referred to: SSI 2003/435 Art.1
s.2, amended: SSI 2003/435 Sch.3
s.4, repealed (in part): SSI 2003/435 Sch.3
s.5, repealed: SSI 2003/435 Sch.3
s.6, repealed: SSI 2003/435 Sch.3
s.7, repealed: SSI 2003/435 Sch.3
s.8, amended: SSI 2003/435 Art.17
Sch.1, repealed: SSI 2003/435 Sch.3

2. Ecclesiastical Judges and Legal Officers Measure 1976
s.5, amended: 2003 c.3 s.44
s.5, applied: 2003 c.3 s.5
s.5, referred to: 2003 c.3

3. Church of England (Miscellaneous Provisions) Measure 1976
s.1, repealed (in part): 2004 c.14 Sch.1 Part 6
s.2, repealed (in part): 2004 c.14 Sch.1 Part 6
s.7, repealed: 2004 c.14 Sch.1 Part 6
s.8, repealed (in part): 2004 c.14 Sch.1 Part 6

3. Road Traffic (Drivers Ages and Hours of Work) Act 1976
s.2, repealed (in part): 2004 c.14 Sch.1 Part 14
s.4, repealed (in part): 2004 c.14 Sch.1 Part 14

4. Endowments and Glebe Measure 1976
s.6, repealed (in part): 2004 c.14 Sch.1 Part 6
s.10, repealed (in part): 2004 c.14 Sch.1 Part 6
s.13, repealed: 2004 c.14 Sch.1 Part 6
s.38, repealed (in part): 2004 c.14 Sch.1 Part 6
s.49, repealed (in part): 2004 c.14 Sch.1 Part 6
Sch.5, repealed: 2002 c.9 Sch.13
Sch.6, repealed (in part): 2004 c.14 Sch.1 Part 6, Sch.1 Part 6

13. Damages (Scotland) Act 1976
s.1, see *Gillies v Lynch (No.1)* 2002 S.L.T.1420 (OH), Lord Macfadyen
s.1, applied: 2003 c.43 Sch.10 para.7
Sch.1 para.1, amended: 2004 c.33 Sch.28 para.42, Sch.30

14. Fatal Accidents and Sudden Deaths Inquiry (Scotland) Act 1976
applied: 2002 asp 13 s.34, s.37
s.6, see *Leighton v Lord Advocate* 2003 S.L.T. 800 (OH), Lord Mackay of Drumadoon

18. Licensing (Amendment) Act 1976
repealed: 2003 c.17 Sch.7

19. Seychelles Act 1976
Sch.1 para.8, repealed: 2002 c.39 Sch.3

22. Freshwater and Salmon Fisheries (Scotland) Act 1976
repealed: 2003 asp 15 Sch.4 Part 2
s.1, enabling: SSI 2004/260
Sch.1, applied: SSI 2004/260

23. Atomic Energy Authority (Special Constables) Act 1976
s.1, repealed: 2004 c.20 Sch.23 Part 1
s.2, repealed: 2004 c.20 Sch.23 Part 1
s.4, repealed: 2004 c.20 Sch.23 Part 1

1976–cont.

25. Fair Employment (Northern Ireland) Act 1976
s.16, see *Gill v Northern Ireland Council for Ethnic Minorities* [2002] I.R.L.R. 74 (CA (NI)), Sir Robert Carswell, L.C.J.
s.17, see *Gill v Northern Ireland Council for Ethnic Minorities* [2002] I.R.L.R. 74 (CA (NI)), Sir Robert Carswell, L.C.J.
s.42, see *Devenney v United Kingdom (24265/94)* (2002) 35 E.H.R.R. 24 (ECHR), J-P Costa (President); see *Devlin v United Kingdom (29545/95)* [2002] I.R.L.R. 155 (ECHR), J-P Costa (President)

26. Explosives (Age of Purchase &c.) Act 1976
repealed: 2003 c.22 Sch.1

27. Theatres Trust Act 1976 25 para.4

30. Fatal Accidents Act 1976
see *Edwards v United Kingdom (46477/99)* (2002) 35 E.H.R.R. 19 (ECHR), Judge Cabral Barreto (President); see *R. (on the application of Wright) v Secretary of State for the Home Department* [2001] EWHC Admin 520, [2002] H.R.L.R. 1 (QBD (Admin Ct)), Jackson, J.; see *Thakerar v Northwich Park Hospital NHS Trust* [2002] EWCA Civ 617, [2002] C.P. Rep. 50 (CA), Sedley, L.J.; see *Toth v Ledger* [2002] P.I.Q.R. P1 (CA), Laws, L.J.; see *White v ESAB Group (UK) Ltd* [2002] P.I.Q.R. Q6 (QBD), Nelson, J.
applied: 2003 c.43 Sch.10 para.6
s.1, amended: 2004 c.33 s.83
s.1, varied: 2004 c.33 Sch.21 para.9
s.1A, amended: SI 2002/644 Art.2, 2004 c.33 s.83
s.1A, enabling: SI 2002/644
s.3, amended: 2004 c.33 s.83
s.4, see *H (A Child) v S (Damages)* [2002] EWCA Civ 792, [2003] Q.B 965 (CA), Kennedy, L.J.; see *L (A Child) v Barry May Haulage* [2002] P.I.Q.R. Q3 (QBD), Stuart Brown Q.C.; see *Roerig v Valiant Trawlers Ltd* [2002] EWCA Civ 21, [2002] 1 W.L.R. 2304 (CA), Waller, L.J.

31. Legitimacy Act 1976
referred to: 2002 c.38 Sch.3 para.16
s.4, amended: 2002 c.38 Sch.3 para.17
s.6, amended: 2002 c.38 Sch.3 para.18

32. Lotteries and Amusements Act 1976
applied: SI 2003/335 Sch.1, SSI 2003/93 Sch.1, 2004 c.35 Sch.3, Sch.8
Part I, applied: SI 2003/1376 Sch.1, SI 2003/1593 Sch.1 Part I
s.1, see *Alpha Club (UK) Ltd, Re* [2002] EWHC 884, [2002] 2 B.C.L.C. 612 (Ch D), John Jarvis Q.C.
s.11, amended: SI 2002/1410 Art.2, Art.3, Art.4
s.14, applied: SI 2003/1376 Sch.1, SI 2003/1593 Sch.1 Part I

CAP.

1976–cont.

32. Lotteries and Amusements Act 1976– *cont.*

s.18, enabling: SI 2002/639, SI 2002/1410, SI 2004/532

s.22, applied: 2003 c.17 Sch.1 para.10

s.24, enabling: SI 2002/639, SI 2002/1410, SI 2004/532

s.25, repealed (in part): 2004 c.14 Sch.1 Part 17

Sch.1A, applied: SI 2002/639 Art.5

Sch.1A Part I para.2, applied: SI 2002/639 Art.3, SI 2004/532 Art.3

Sch.1A Part I para.6, applied: SI 2002/639 Art.5, Art.6, SI 2004/532 Art.5, Art.6

Sch.1A Part I para.6, enabling: SI 2002/639, SI 2004/532

Sch.1A Part II para.10, applied: SI 2002/639 Art.7, SI 2004/532 Art.7

Sch.2, applied: SI 2002/639 Art.5, SI 2004/532 Art.5

Sch.2 para.6A, applied: SI 2002/639 Art.7, SI 2004/532 Art.7

Sch.2 para.7, applied: SI 2002/639 Art.4, Art.5, Art.6, SI 2004/532 Art.4, Art.5, Art.6

Sch.2 para.7, enabling: SI 2002/639, SI 2004/532

Sch.2A Part I para.1, applied: SI 2002/639 Art.8, SI 2004/532 Art.8

Sch.3 para.1, amended: 2003 c.17 Sch.6 para.63, Sch.7

Sch.3 para.8, amended: 2003 c.17 Sch.6 para.64

Sch.3 para.8, repealed (in part): 2003 c.17 Sch.6 para.64, Sch.7

Sch.3 para.11, repealed: 2003 c.17 Sch.6 para.65, Sch.7

Sch.3 para.18, amended: 2003 c.17 Sch.6 para.66

Sch.4 para.7, repealed: 2004 c.14 Sch.1 Part 17

Sch.4 para.9, repealed: 2004 c.14 Sch.1 Part 10

33. Restrictive Practices Court Act 1976

s.9, amended: 2002 c.40 Sch.25 para.7

35. Police Pensions Act 1976

s.1, enabling: SI 2002/2529, SI 2002/3202, SI 2003/27, SI 2003/535, SI 2003/2716, SI 2003/2717, SI 2004/1491, SI 2004/1760, SI 2004/2354, SSI 2003/406, SSI 2004/486

s.2, enabling: SI 2002/3202, SI 2003/27, SI 2003/2716, SI 2003/2717, SI 2004/1491, SSI 2003/406, SSI 2004/486

s.3, enabling: SI 2002/3202, SI 2003/27, SI 2003/2716, SI 2003/2717, SI 2004/1491, SSI 2003/406, SSI 2004/486

s.4, enabling: SI 2002/3202, SI 2003/27, SI 2003/2716, SI 2003/2717, SI 2004/1491, SI 2004/1760, SSI 2003/406, SSI 2004/486

CAP.

1976–cont.

35. Police Pensions Act 1976–*cont.*

s.5, enabling: SI 2002/3202, SI 2003/27, SI 2003/2716, SI 2003/2717, SI 2004/1491, SSI 2003/406, SSI 2004/486

s.6, enabling: SI 2002/3202, SI 2003/27, SI 2003/535, SI 2003/2716, SI 2003/2717, SI 2004/1491, SSI 2003/406, SSI 2004/486

s.7, amended: 2002 c.1 Sch.3 para.6

s.7, enabling: SI 2002/3202, SI 2003/27, SI 2003/2716, SI 2003/2717, SI 2004/1491, SSI 2003/406, SSI 2004/486

s.11, amended: 2002 c.1 Sch.3 para.6, 2002 c.30 Sch.7 para.7

36. Adoption Act 1976

see *L Teaching Hospitals NHS Trust v A* [2003] EWHC 259, [2003] 1 F.L.R. 1091 (QBD), Dame Elizabeth Butler-Sloss (President)

applied: 2002 c.38 s.87, SI 2002/816 Reg.3, SI 2004/3114 Sch.1

referred to: 2002 c.38 s.145, Sch.4 para.20, Sch.4 para.22

repealed: 2002 c.38 Sch.5

Part I, applied: SI 2003/365 Sch.1 para.3

Part IV, applied: 2002 c.38 s.66

s.1, applied: 2002 c.38 Sch.4 para.3

s.1, repealed: 2002 c.38 Sch.5

s.2, repealed: 2002 c.38 Sch.5

s.3, applied: SI 2003/152 Art.3, SI 2003/365 Sch.1 para.6

s.3, repealed: 2002 c.38 Sch.5

s.4, applied: SI 2003/365 Sch.1 para.2, Sch.1 para.3, Sch.1 para.4

s.4, repealed: 2002 c.38 Sch.5

s.5, applied: SI 2003/365 Sch.1 para.3, Sch.1 para.5, Sch.1 para.6

s.5, repealed: 2002 c.38 Sch.5

s.6, see *R. (on the application of W) v Leicestershire CC* [2003] EWHC 704, [2003] 2 F.L.R. 185 (QBD (Admin Ct)), Wilson, J.

s.6, applied: SI 2003/118 Reg.26, Reg.29

s.6, repealed: 2002 c.38 Sch.5

s.7, applied: SI 2003/118 Reg.26, Reg.29

s.7, repealed: 2002 c.38 Sch.5

s.8, applied: SI 2003/365 Sch.1 para.3

s.8, repealed: 2002 c.38 Sch.5

s.9, amended: 2002 c.38 Sch.4 para.4

s.9, referred to: 2002 c.38 Sch.4 para.4

s.9, repealed: 2002 c.38 Sch.5

s.9, varied: 2002 c.38 s.145

s.9, enabling: SI 2003/118, SI 2003/367, SI 2003/370, SI 2003/710, SI 2003/1173, SI 2003/1348, SI 2003/1634, SI 2003/2555, SI 2003/3223, SI 2004/190, SI 2004/1011, SI 2004/1081, SI 2004/1868

s.9A, added: 2002 c.38 Sch.4 para.5

s.9A, applied: SI 2004/190 Reg.2

s.9A, repealed: 2002 c.38 Sch.5

s.9A, varied: 2002 c.38 s.145

1976–cont.

36. Adoption Act 1976–cont.

s.9A, enabling: SI 2004/190, SI 2004/1081, SI 2004/1868

s.10, repealed: 2002 c.38 Sch.5

s.11, see *M (Adoption: International Adoption Trade), Re* [2003] EWHC 219, [2003] 1 F.L.R. 1111 (Fam Div), Munby, J.

s.11, repealed: 2002 c.38 Sch.5

s.12, applied: 2002 c.38 Sch.4 para.8, Sch.4 para.21

s.12, repealed: 2002 c.38 Sch.5

s.12, varied: SI 2003/118 Sch.3

s.13, amended: 2002 c.38 Sch.4 para.10

s.13, applied: SI 2003/1173 Reg.6

s.13, disapplied: SI 2003/1173 Reg.6

s.13, repealed (in part): 2002 c.38 Sch.4 para.10, Sch.5

s.13, varied: SI 2003/1173 Reg.6

s.14, applied: SI 2003/118 Reg.28

s.14, repealed: 2002 c.38 Sch.5

s.15, see *B v P (Adoption by Unmarried Father)* [2001] UKHL 70, [2002] 1 W.L.R. 258 (HL), Lord Nicholls of Birkenhead

s.15, applied: SI 2003/118 Reg.28

s.15, repealed: 2002 c.38 Sch.5

s.15, varied: 2003 c.24 s.3

s.16, see *J (A Child) (Adoption: Consent of Foreign Public Authority), Re* [2002] EWHC 766, [2002] 2 F.L.R. 618 (Fam Div), Charles, J.

s.16, repealed: 2002 c.38 Sch.5

s.16, varied: SI 2003/118 Sch.3

s.17, applied: SI 2003/118 Reg.21, Reg.32, Reg.37

s.17, repealed: 2002 c.38 Sch.5

s.17, enabling: SI 2003/118

s.18, see *Family Proceedings (Allocation to Judiciary) (Amendment) Directions 2003* [2003] 2 F.L.R. 373 (Fam Div), Lord Irvine of Lairg, L.C.; see *S (A Child) (Freeing for Adoption), Re* [2002] EWCA Civ 798, [2002] 2 F.L.R. 681 (CA), Thorpe, L.J.

s.18, applied: 2002 c.38 Sch.4 para.6, Sch.4 para.7, Sch.4 para.21, SI 2003/118 Reg.25, Reg.27, Reg.32, SR 2003/16 Reg.23, Reg.25, Reg.30, SSI 2003/19 Reg.22, Reg.24, Reg.30

s.18, referred to: 2002 c.38 Sch.4 para.23

s.18, repealed: 2002 c.38 Sch.5

s.19, applied: 2002 c.38 Sch.4 para.7

s.19, repealed: 2002 c.38 Sch.5

s.20, see *A (Adoption: Placement Outside Jurisdiction), Re* [2004] EWCA Civ 515, [2004] 3 W.L.R. 1207 (CA), Thorpe, L.J.

s.20, applied: 2002 c.38 Sch.4 para.7

s.20, repealed: 2002 c.38 Sch.5

s.20, varied: 2002 c.38 Sch.4 para.7

s.21, applied: 2002 c.38 Sch.4 para.7

s.21, disapplied: SI 2004/3114 Sch.1

s.21, repealed: 2002 c.38 Sch.5

1976–cont.

36. Adoption Act 1976–cont.

s.22, applied: 2002 c.38 Sch.4 para.9, SI 2003/118 Reg.15, SI 2003/1173 Reg.5

s.22, repealed: 2002 c.38 Sch.5

s.22, varied: SI 2003/118 Sch.3

s.23, repealed: 2002 c.38 Sch.5

s.24, repealed: 2002 c.38 Sch.5

s.25, repealed: 2002 c.38 Sch.5

s.26, repealed: 2002 c.38 Sch.5

s.27, repealed: 2002 c.38 Sch.5

s.27, varied: SI 2003/118 Sch.3

s.28, repealed: 2002 c.38 Sch.5

s.29, repealed: 2002 c.38 Sch.5

s.30, see *R. (on the application of W) v Leicestershire CC* [2003] EWHC 704, [2003] 2 F.L.R. 185 (QBD (Admin Ct)), Wilson, J.

s.30, applied: SI 2002/2788 Reg.22, SI 2002/2822 Reg.22, SR 2002/377 Reg.22, SR 2002/378 Reg.22

s.30, repealed: 2002 c.38 Sch.5

s.30, varied: SI 2003/118 Sch.3

s.31, see *R. (on the application of W) v Leicestershire CC* [2003] EWHC 704, [2003] 2 F.L.R. 185 (QBD (Admin Ct)), Wilson, J.

s.31, repealed: 2002 c.38 Sch.5

s.31, varied: SI 2003/118 Sch.3

s.32, repealed: 2002 c.38 Sch.5

s.33, repealed: 2002 c.38 Sch.5

s.34, repealed: 2002 c.38 Sch.5

s.35, repealed: 2002 c.38 Sch.5

s.36, repealed: 2002 c.38 Sch.5

s.36A, repealed: 2002 c.38 Sch.5

s.37, repealed: 2002 c.38 Sch.5

s.38, amended: 2002 c.38 Sch.3 para.19

s.39, see *Upton v National Westminster Bank Plc* [2004] EWHC 1962, [2004] W.T.L.R. 1339 (Ch D), Judge Behrens

s.47, amended: 2002 c.8 s.2

s.50, repealed: 2002 c.38 Sch.5

s.51, applied: SI 2003/365 Sch.1 para.3

s.51, repealed: 2002 c.38 Sch.5

s.51A, repealed: 2002 c.38 Sch.5

s.52, amended: 2002 c.38 Sch.4 para.15

s.52, repealed: 2002 c.38 Sch.5

s.53, applied: SI 2003/118 Reg.19, Reg.24

s.53, repealed: 2002 c.38 Sch.5

s.54, repealed: 2002 c.38 Sch.5

s.55, see *A (Adoption: Placement Outside Jurisdiction), Re* [2004] EWCA Civ 515, [2004] 3 W.L.R. 1207 (CA), Thorpe, L.J.; see *G (Adoption: Ordinary Residence), Re* [2002] EWHC 2447, [2003] 2 F.L.R. 944 (Fam Div), Wall, J.; see *S (A Child) (Freeing for Adoption), Re* [2002] EWCA Civ 798, [2002] 2 F.L.R. 681 (CA), Thorpe, L.J.

s.55, referred to: 2002 c.38 Sch.4 para.23

s.55, repealed: 2002 c.38 Sch.5

1976–cont.

36. Adoption Act 1976–*cont.*

s.56, see *A (Adoption: Placement Outside Jurisdiction), Re* [2004] EWCA Civ 515, [2004] 3 W.L.R. 1207 (CA),Thorpe, L.J.

s.56, amended: 2002 c.38 Sch.4 para.11

s.56, repealed: 2002 c.38 Sch.5

s.56A, amended: 2002 c.38 Sch.4 para.12

s.56A, applied: SI 2003/1173 Reg.3, Reg.5, Reg.6

s.56A, repealed: 2002 c.38 Sch.5

s.56A, enabling: SI 2003/1173

s.57, see *M (Adoption: International Adoption Trade), Re* [2003] EWHC 219, [2003] 1 F.L.R. 1111 (Fam Div), Munby, J.

s.57, disapplied: 2002 c.38 Sch.4 para.3

s.57, repealed: 2002 c.38 Sch.5

s.57A, applied: SI 2002/1330 Sch.3 para.1, SI 2002/2006 Reg.19, SI 2002/3200 Reg.15, Sch.3 para.1, SI 2003/1994 Sch.3 para.1

s.57A, disapplied: SI 2002/195 Reg.15, Sch.3 para.1

s.57A, repealed: 2002 c.38 Sch.5

s.57A, enabling: SI 2004/1011

s.58, amended: 2002 c.38 Sch.4 para.14

s.58, referred to: 2002 c.38 Sch.4 para.16

s.58, repealed: 2002 c.38 Sch.5

s.58A, repealed: 2002 c.38 Sch.5

s.59, repealed: 2002 c.38 Sch.5

s.60, repealed: 2002 c.38 Sch.5

s.61, amended: SI 2004/2035 Sch.1 para.5

s.61, repealed: 2002 c.38 Sch.5

s.62, amended: SI 2004/2035 Sch.1 para.6

s.62, repealed: 2002 c.38 Sch.5

s.63, repealed: 2002 c.38 Sch.5

s.64, repealed: 2002 c.38 Sch.5

s.65, amended: SI 2004/2035 Sch.1 para.7

s.65, repealed: 2002 c.38 Sch.5

s.65, enabling: SI 2003/183

s.65A, repealed: 2002 c.38 Sch.5

s.66, amended: 2004 c.31 s.62, SI 2004/2035 Sch.1 para.8

s.66, repealed (in part): 2002 c.38 Sch.5, SI 2004/2035 Sch.1 para.8

s.66, enabling: SI 2003/183

s.67, repealed: 2002 c.38 Sch.5

s.67, enabling: SI 2003/118, SI 2003/183, SI 2003/367, SI 2003/370, SI 2003/710, SI 2003/1173, SI 2003/1255, SI 2003/1348, SI 2004/190, SI 2004/1011, SI 2004/1868

s.68, repealed: 2002 c.38 Sch.5

s.69, repealed: 2002 c.38 Sch.5

s.70, repealed: 2002 c.38 Sch.5

s.71, repealed: 2002 c.38 Sch.5

s.72, see *S (A Child) (Freeing for Adoption), Re* [2002] EWCA Civ 798, [2002] 2 F.L.R. 681 (CA),Thorpe, L.J.

s.72, amended: SI 2004/2035 Sch.1 para.9

s.72, repealed (in part): 2002 c.38 Sch.4 para.13, Sch.5

s.73, repealed: 2002 c.38 Sch.5

s.74, repealed: 2002 c.38 Sch.5

1976–cont.

36. Adoption Act 1976–*cont.*

Sch.1, repealed: 2002 c.38 Sch.5

Sch.1 para.3, applied: SI 2003/1255 Reg.2, Reg.3, Reg.4, Reg.5, Reg.6

Sch.1 para.3, enabling: SI 2003/1255

Sch.2, repealed: 2002 c.38 Sch.5

Sch.2 para.7, repealed: 2002 c.38 Sch.5

Sch.2 para.8, repealed: 2002 c.38 Sch.5

Sch.3 Part I para.1, repealed: 2002 c.38 Sch.5

Sch.3 Part I para.2, repealed: 2002 c.38 Sch.5

Sch.3 Part I para.3, repealed: 2002 c.38 Sch.5

Sch.3 Part I para.4, repealed: 2002 c.38 Sch.5

Sch.3 Part I para.5, repealed: 2002 c.38 Sch.5

Sch.3 Part I para.6, repealed: 2002 c.38 Sch.5

Sch.3 Part I para.7, repealed: 2002 c.38 Sch.5

Sch.3 Part I para.8, repealed: 2002 c.38 Sch.5

Sch.3 Part I para.9, repealed: 2002 c.38 Sch.5

Sch.3 Part I para.10, repealed: 2002 c.38 Sch.5

Sch.3 Part I para.11, repealed: 2002 c.38 Sch.5

Sch.3 Part I para.12, repealed: 2002 c.38 Sch.5

Sch.3 Part I para.13, repealed: 2002 c.38 Sch.5

Sch.3 Part I para.14, repealed: 2002 c.38 Sch.5

Sch.3 Part I para.15, repealed: 2002 c.38 Sch.5

Sch.3 Part I para.16, repealed: 2002 c.38 Sch.5

Sch.3 Part I para.17, repealed: 2002 c.38 Sch.5

Sch.3 Part I para.18, repealed: 2002 c.38 Sch.5

Sch.3 Part I para.19, repealed: 2002 c.38 Sch.5

Sch.3 Part I para.20, repealed: 2002 c.38 Sch.5

Sch.3 Part I para.21, repealed: 2002 c.38 Sch.5

Sch.3 Part I para.22, repealed: 2002 c.38 Sch.5

Sch.3 Part I para.23, repealed: 2002 c.38 Sch.5

Sch.3 Part I para.24, repealed: 2002 c.38 Sch.5

Sch.3 Part II para.25, repealed: 2002 c.38 Sch.5

Sch.3 Part II para.26, repealed: 2002 c.38 Sch.5

Sch.3 Part II para.27, repealed: 2002 c.38 Sch.5

CAP.

1976–cont.

36. Adoption Act 1976–*cont.*

Sch.3 Part II para.28, repealed: 2002 c.38 Sch.5

Sch.3 Part II para.29, repealed: 2002 c.38 Sch.5

Sch.3 Part II para.30, repealed: 2002 c.38 Sch.5

Sch.3 Part II para.31, repealed: 2002 c.38 Sch.5

Sch.3 Part II para.32, repealed: 2002 c.38 Sch.5

Sch.3 Part II para.33, repealed: 2002 c.38 Sch.5

Sch.3 Part II para.34, repealed: 2002 c.38 Sch.5

Sch.3 Part II para.35, repealed: 2002 c.38 Sch.5

Sch.3 Part II para.36, repealed: 2002 c.38 Sch.5

Sch.3 Part II para.37, repealed: 2002 c.38 Sch.5

Sch.3 Part II para.38, repealed: 2002 c.38 Sch.5

Sch.3 Part II para.39, repealed: 2002 c.38 Sch.5

Sch.3 Part II para.40, repealed: 2002 c.38 Sch.5

Sch.3 Part II para.41, repealed: 2002 c.38 Sch.5

Sch.3 Part II para.42, repealed: 2002 c.38 Sch.5

Sch.3 Part II para.43, repealed: 2002 c.38 Sch.5

Sch.3 Part II para.44, repealed: 2002 c.38 Sch.5

39. Divorce (Scotland) Act 1976

s.1, substituted: 2004 c.7 Sch.2 para.6

s.2, amended: 2004 c.7 Sch.2 para.7

s.5, applied: SSI 2002/494 Reg.33

52. Armed Forces Act 1976

referred to: 2003 c.44 s.337

s.8, amended: 2003 c.44 Sch.32 para.19

Sch.3 para.11, amended: 2003 c.44 Sch.36 para.84

Sch.3 para.17, applied: SI 2003/336 Sch.1 Part 2

55. Agriculture (Miscellaneous Provisions) Act 1976

s.1, repealed: 2004 c.14 Sch.1 Part 2

s.3, amended: 2004 c.14 Sch.1 Part 2

s.26, amended: 2004 c.14 Sch.1 Part 2

s.27, amended: 2004 c.14 Sch.1 Part 2

s.27, repealed (in part): 2004 c.14 Sch.1 Part 2

57. Local Government (Miscellaneous Provisions) Act 1976

referred to: SI 2002/808 Art.2

s.16, applied: 2003 c.i s.2

s.16, varied: 2003 c.i s.2

s.27, repealed (in part): 2004 c.14 Sch.1 Part 13

s.30, varied: SI 2004/1778 Art.17

CAP.

1976–cont.

57. Local Government (Miscellaneous Provisions) Act 1976–*cont.*

s.38, varied: SI 2004/1777 Art.29, SI 2004/1778 Art.29

s.41, amended: SI 2002/808 Art.11

s.41, varied: SI 2004/1777 Art.21, SI 2004/1778 Art.21, Art.29

s.42, applied: 2004 c.i s.9

s.44, amended: SI 2002/808 Art.11

s.45, varied: SI 2004/1778 Art.29

s.47, see *R. (on the application of Maud) v Castle Point BC* [2002] EWCA Civ 1526, [2003] R.T.R. 7 (CA), Keene, L.J.

s.60, see *Leeds City Council v Hussain* [2002] EWHC 1145, [2003] R.T.R. 13 (QBD (Admin Ct)), Silber, J.

s.61, see *Leeds City Council v Hussain* [2002] EWHC 1145, [2003] R.T.R. 13 (QBD (Admin Ct)), Silber, J.

s.64, applied: 2004 c.18 Sch.7 para.4

s.70, see *Kelly v Liverpool City Council* [2003] EWCA Civ 197, [2003] 2 All E.R. 772 (CA), Schiemann, L.J.

s.83, repealed (in part): 2004 c.14 Sch.1 Part 13

58. International Carriage of Perishable Foodstuffs Act 1976

s.3, enabling: SI 2003/1693

s.4, enabling: SI 2003/1693

60. Insolvency Act 1976

repealed: 2004 c.14 Sch.1 Part 17

s.12, referred to: 2004 c.14 Sch.2 para.9

s.216, see *Archer Structures Ltd v Griffiths* [2003] EWHC 957, [2004] B.C.C. 156 (Ch D), Judge Kirkham

s.217, see *Archer Structures Ltd v Griffiths* [2003] EWHC 957, [2004] B.C.C. 156 (Ch D), Judge Kirkham

63. Bail Act 1976

see *R. (on the application of Sezek) v Secretary of State for the Home Department (Bail Application)* [2001] EWCA Civ 795, [2002] 1 W.L.R. 348 (CA), Peter Gibson, L.J.; see *R. v Ashley (Phillip Martin)* [2003] EWCA Crim 2571, [2004] 1 W.L.R. 2057 (CA (Crim Div)), Rose, L.J.

s.1, amended: 2003 c.41 s.198

s.2, amended: 2003 c.39 Sch.8 para.180, Sch.10, 2003 c.41 s.198, Sch.4, 2003 c.44 Sch.32 para.21, Sch.37 Part 7

s.3, see *R. (on the application of Crown Prosecution Service) v Chorley Justices* [2002] EWHC 2162, (2002) 166 J.P. 764 (QBD (Admin Ct)), Latham, L.J.

s.3, amended: 2003 c.44 s.13, s.19, Sch.3 para.48, Sch.37 Part 2

s.3, applied: 2003 c.44 s.13, s.16, s.17

s.3, repealed (in part): 2003 c.44 Sch.37 Part 4, Sch.3 para.48

1976–cont.

63. Bail Act 1976–cont.

s.3A, amended: 2003 c.44 s.13, s.19, Sch.37 Part 2

s.3AA, amended: 2003 c.39 Sch.8 para.181

s.3AA, enabling: SI 2002/844

s.4, amended: 2003 c.41 s.198, Sch.4, 2003 c.44 Sch.32 para.22

s.4, applied: 2003 c.44 s.90

s.5, see *R. (on the application of Stevens) v Truro Magistrates Court* [2001] EWHC Admin 558, [2002] 1 W.L.R. 144 (QBD (Admin)), Brooke, L.J.

s.5, amended: 2003 c.39 Sch.8 para.182, 2003 c.44 Sch.36 para.2, Sch.3 para.48, Sch.37 Part 2, Sch.37 Part 12

s.5, repealed (in part): 2003 c.44 Sch.37 Part 4, Sch.3 para.48, Sch.37 Part 2

s.5A, amended: 2003 c.44 Sch.37 Part 2

s.5B, amended: 2003 c.39 Sch.8 para.183, Sch.10, 2003 c.41 s.198

s.5B, applied: 2003 c.44 s.16

s.6, see *Practice Direction (CA (Crim Div): Bail: Failure to Surrender and Trials in Absence)* [2004] 1 W.L.R. 589 (CA (Crim Div)), Lord Woolf of Barnes, L.C.J.; see *R. v Hourigan (Rudolph)* [2003] EWCA Crim 2306, (2003) 147 S.J.L.B. 901 (CA (Crim Div)), Scott Baker, L.J.

s.6, amended: 2003 c.39 Sch.8 para.184, 2003 c.44 s.15, Sch.3 para.48

s.7, see *R. (on the application of Vickers) v West London Magistrates Court* [2003] EWHC 1809, (2003) 167 J.P. 473 (QBD (Admin Ct)), Gage, J.

s.7, amended: 2003 c.39 Sch.8 para.185, Sch.10, 2003 c.41 s.198, Sch.4

s.7, applied: 2003 c.41 s.142, 2003 c.44 s.15

s.8, amended: 2003 c.39 Sch.8 para.186, Sch.10

s.9, amended: 2003 c.44 Sch.3 para.48

Sch.1 Part I, added: 2003 c.44 s.19

Sch.1 Part I para.1, substituted: 2003 c.41 s.198

Sch.1 Part I para.2, applied: 2003 c.44 s.20

Sch.1 Part I para.2, substituted: 2003 c.44 s.20

Sch.1 Part I para.2A, applied: 2003 c.44 s.20

Sch.1 Part I para.2A, substituted: 2003 c.44 s.14

Sch.1 Part I para.2B, added: 2003 c.41 s.198

Sch.1 Part I para.6, amended: 2003 c.41 s.198

Sch.1 Part I para.6, substituted: 2003 c.44 s.15

Sch.1 Part I para.8, amended: 2003 c.44 s.13, s.19

Sch.1 Part I para.9, amended: 2003 c.44 s.20

Sch.1 Part I para.9AA, added: 2003 c.44 s.14

Sch.1 Part I para.9AB, added: 2003 c.44 s.15

Sch.1 Part II para.5, substituted: 2003 c.44 s.13

1976–cont.

63. Bail Act 1976–cont.

Sch.1 Part III para.2, substituted: 2003 c.44 Sch.36 para.3

Sch.1 Part III para.4, amended: 2003 c.44 Sch.32 para.23

Sch.2 para.33, repealed: 2003 c.41 Sch.4

64. Valuation and Rating (Exempted Classes) (Scotland) Act 1976

s.1, applied: SSI 2002/262

s.1, enabling: SSI 2002/262

66. Licensing (Scotland) Act 1976

see *Coakley v Secretary of State for Transport (Locus of Commissioner to Appear)* 2003 S.C. 455 (Court of Session (Inner House, Extra Division)), Lord Kirkwood, Lady Cosgrove, Lord Marnoch

applied: 2002 asp 11 Sch.2 para.10, SSI 2004/157 Art.2

s.1, applied: 2002 asp 13 Sch.1 para.23, SSI 2002/62 Sch.1

s.8, enabling: SSI 2004/157

s.9, referred to: SSI 2004/157 Sch.1 Part I

s.20, applied: SI 2004/293 Reg.4

s.21, referred to: SSI 2004/157 Sch.1 Part I

s.23, amended: 2003 asp 8 Sch.6 para.12

s.25, referred to: SSI 2004/157 Sch.1 Part I

s.26, referred to: SSI 2004/157 Sch.1 Part I

s.27, referred to: SSI 2004/157 Sch.1 Part I

s.32, referred to: SSI 2004/157 Sch.1 Part I

s.33, referred to: SSI 2004/157 Sch.1 Part I

s.34, applied: SSI 2002/167 Reg.6

s.34, referred to: SSI 2004/157 Sch.1 Part I

s.35, referred to: SSI 2004/157 Sch.1 Part I

s.36, referred to: SSI 2004/157 Sch.1 Part I

s.40, referred to: SSI 2004/157 Sch.1 Part I

s.41, referred to: SSI 2004/157 Sch.1 Part I

s.42, referred to: SSI 2004/157 Sch.1 Part I

s.43, referred to: SSI 2004/157 Sch.1 Part I

s.57, referred to: SSI 2004/157 Sch.1 Part I

s.58, referred to: SSI 2004/157 Sch.1 Part I

s.59, referred to: SSI 2004/157 Sch.1 Part I

s.64, see *Catscratch Ltd v Glasgow City Licensing Board (No.2)* 2002 S.L.T. 503 (OH), Lord Johnston; see *WGR Trading Ltd v Highland Licensing Board* 2003 S.L.T. 1019 (OH), Lord Nimmo Smith

s.64, referred to: SSI 2004/157 Sch.1 Part I

s.65, referred to: SSI 2004/157 Sch.1 Part I

s.135, enabling: SSI 2004/157

Sch.7 para.9, repealed (in part): 2003 c.17 Sch.7

Sch.7 para.10, repealed: 2003 c.17 Sch.7

Sch.7 para.11, repealed: 2003 c.17 Sch.7

Sch.7 para.12, repealed: 2003 c.17 Sch.7

67. Sexual Offences (Scotland) Act 1976

s.2A, applied: SI 2003/1184 Sch.2 para.23

s.2B, applied: SI 2003/1184 Sch.2 para.24

s.2C, applied: SI 2003/1184 Sch.2 para.25

s.3, applied: SI 2003/1184 Sch.2 para.21

s.4, applied: SI 2003/1184 Sch.2 para.22

CAP.

1976-cont.

67. Sexual Offences (Scotland) Act 1976– cont.

s.5, see *A v HM Advocate* 2003 S.L.T. 497 (HCJ), Lord Gill L.J.C., Lord Kirkwood, Lord MacLean

70. Land Drainage Act 1976

s.34, see *R. (on the application of the Environment Agency) v Davis* [2002] EWHC 2804, [2003] E.H.L.R. 12 (QBD (Admin Ct)), Goldring, J.

Sch.5 para.1, amended: SI 2002/794 Sch.1 para.19

72. Endangered Species (Import and Export) Act 1976

referred to: SR 2003/115 Reg.6

74. Race Relations Act 1976

see *1 Pump Court Chambers v Horton* [2004] EWCA Civ 941, [2004] 3 All E.R. 852 (CA), Peter Gibson, L.J.; see *Chief Constable of Bedfordshire v Liversidge* [2002] EWCA Civ 894, [2002] I.C.R. 1135 (CA), Peter Gibson, L.J.

applied: SI 2004/753 Sch.1 para.168, SI 2004/1861 Sch.1 para.61

referred to: 2003 c.43 Sch.4 para.21

Part II, applied: SI 2004/1861 Sch.1 para.22

Part X, added: SI 2003/1626 Reg.49

s.1, see *Coker v Lord Chancellor* [2001] EWCA Civ 1756, [2002] I.C.R. 321 (CA), Lord Phillips of Worth Matravers, M.R.; see *Hussain v Midland Cosmetic Sales Plc* [2002] Emp. L.R. 713 (EAT), Recorder Burke Q.C.; see *R. (on the application of European Roma Rights Centre) v Immigration Officer, Prague Airport* [2003] EWCA Civ 666, [2004] Q.B. 811 (CA), Simon Brown, L.J.

s.1, amended: SI 2003/1626 Reg.3

s.2, see *Jiad v Byford* [2003] EWCA Civ 135, [2003] I.R.L.R. 232 (CA), May, L.J.

s.3, amended: SI 2003/1626 Reg.4

s.3, applied: SI 2004/118 Art.3

s.3A, added: SI 2003/1626 Reg.5

s.4, see *Hussain v HM Prison Service* [2002] Emp. L.R. 874 (EAT), Lindsay, J.; see *Hussain v King's College Hospital NHS Trust* [2002] EWCA Civ 1269, [2002] I.C.R. 1433 (CA), Pill, L.J.; see *Patterson v Legal Services Commission* [2003] EWCA Civ 1558, [2004] I.C.R. 312 (CA), Clarke, L.J.; see *Patterson v Legal Services Commission* [2003] I.R.L.R. 742 (EAT), Judge McMullen Q.C.; see *Rhys-Harper v Relaxion Group Plc* [2003] UKHL 33, [2003] 4 All E.R. 1113 (HL), Lord Nicholls of Birkenhead

s.4, amended: SI 2003/1626 Reg.6

s.4, varied: SI 2003/1964 Sch.1

s.4A, added: SI 2003/1626 Reg.7

s.5, amended: SI 2003/1626 Reg.8

s.5, varied: SI 2003/1964 Sch.1

s.6, amended: SI 2003/1626 Reg.9

CAP.

1976-cont.

74. Race Relations Act 1976–*cont.*

s.7, amended: SI 2003/1626 Reg.10

s.7, varied: SI 2003/1964 Sch.1

s.8, amended: SI 2003/1626 Reg.11

s.9, amended: SI 2003/1651 Art.2

s.10, amended: SI 2003/1626 Reg.12

s.11, see *Sadek v Medical Protection Society* [2004] EWCA Civ 865, [2004] 4 All E.R. 118 (CA), Dame Elizabeth Butler-Sloss (President)

s.11, amended: SI 2003/1626 Reg.13

s.12, see *Carter v Ahsan (No.1)* [2004] I.C.R. 938 (EAT), Burton, J.; see *Pathak v Secretary of State for Health* (2004) 80 B.M.L.R. 151 (EAT), Judge Pugsley; see *Patterson v Legal Services Commission* [2003] EWCA Civ 1558, [2004] I.C.R. 312 (CA), Clarke, L.J.; see *Patterson v Legal Services Commission* [2003] I.R.L.R. 742 (EAT), Judge McMullen Q.C.; see *Triesman v Ali* [2002] EWCA Civ 93, [2002] I.C.R. 1026 (CA), Peter Gibson, L.J.

s.12, amended: SI 2003/1626 Reg.14

s.13, see *Hussain v King's College Hospital NHS Trust* [2002] EWCA Civ 1269, [2002] I.C.R. 1433 (CA), Pill, L.J.

s.13, amended: SI 2003/1626 Reg.15

s.14, amended: SI 2003/1626 Reg.16

s.15, amended: SI 2003/1626 Reg.17

s.16, see *Chief Constable of Bedfordshire v Liversidge* [2002] I.R.L.R. 15 (EAT), Lindsay, J. (President)

s.17, amended: SI 2003/1626 Reg.18

s.17, substituted: SI 2003/1626 Reg.18

s.18, amended: SI 2003/1626 Reg.19

s.18A, amended: SI 2003/1626 Reg.19

s.18B, amended: SI 2003/1626 Reg.19

s.18D, amended: SI 2003/1626 Reg.19

s.19B, see *R. (on the application of European Roma Rights Centre) v Immigration Officer, Prague Airport* [2002] EWHC 1989, [2003] A.C.D. 15 (QBD (Admin Ct)), Burton, J.

s.19B, amended: SI 2003/1626 Reg.20

s.19B, applied: 2002 c.41 s.84, SI 2003/658 Reg.5

s.19B, varied: SI 2003/2818 Art.11

s.19C, amended: SI 2003/1016 Sch.1 para.2, SI 2003/1626 Reg.21

s.19D, see *R. (on the application of the Tamil Information Centre) v Secretary of State for the Home Department* [2002] EWHC 2155, Times, October 30, 2002 (QBD (Admin Ct)), Forbes, J.

s.19D, amended: 2002 c.41 s.6, 2004 c.19 s.14

s.19D, varied: SI 2003/2818 Art.11

s.19E, amended: 2002 c.41 s.6

s.19E, applied: SI 2003/409 Sch.1 Part I

s.19E, repealed (in part): 2002 c.41 s.6, Sch.9

1976–cont.

74. Race Relations Act 1976–*cont.*

s.19D 3, see *R. (on the application of the Tamil Information Centre) v Secretary of State for the Home Department* [2002] EWHC 2155, Times, October 30, 2002 (QBD (Admin Ct)), Forbes, J.

s.20, amended: SI 2003/1626 Reg.22

s.21, amended: SI 2003/1626 Reg.23

s.22, amended: SI 2003/1626 Reg.24

s.23, amended: SI 2003/1626 Reg.25

s.24, amended: SI 2003/1626 Reg.26

s.26A, amended: SI 2003/1626 Reg.27

s.26B, amended: SI 2003/1626 Reg.28

s.27A, added: SI 2003/1626 Reg.29

s.28, amended: SI 2003/1626 Reg.30

s.30, amended: SI 2003/1626 Reg.31

s.31, amended: SI 2003/1626 Reg.32

s.32, see *Chief Constable of Bedfordshire v Liversidge* [2002] I.R.L.R. 15 (EAT), Lindsay, J. (President)

s.32, varied: SI 2003/1964 Sch.1

s.33, see *Chief Constable of Bedfordshire v Liversidge* [2002] I.R.L.R. 15 (EAT), Lindsay, J. (President)

s.34, amended: SI 2003/1626 Reg.33

s.36, amended: SI 2003/1626 Reg.34

s.41, amended: SI 2003/1626 Reg.35

s.43, amended: SI 2003/1626 Reg.36

s.43, repealed (in part): 2004 c.14 Sch.1 Part 5

s.47, amended: SI 2003/1626 Reg.37

s.50, amended: SI 2003/1626 Reg.38

s.53, amended: 2002 c.41 Sch.7 para.11, SI 2003/1626 Reg.39

s.54, see *British Medical Association v Chaudhary (No.1)* [2003] EWCA Civ 645, [2003] Lloyd's Rep. Med. 409 (CA), Mummery, L.J.; see *Essa v Laing Ltd* [2003] I.C.R. 1110 (EAT), Judge Serota Q.C.; see *Pathak v Secretary of State for Health* (2004) 80 B.M.L.R. 151 (EAT), Judge Pugsley

s.54, amended: SI 2003/1626 Reg.40

s.54, applied: 2002 c.22 Sch.3, Sch.4, Sch.5, SI 2004/1861 Sch.1 para.22

s.54A, added: SI 2003/1626 Reg.41

s.56, see *Essa v Laing Ltd* [2004] EWCA Civ 2, [2004] I.C.R. 746 (CA), Pill, L.J.; see *Khan v Trident Safeguards Ltd* [2004] EWCA Civ 624, [2004] I.R.L.R. 961 (CA), Buxton, L.J.

s.57, see *Essa v Laing Ltd* [2004] EWCA Civ 2, [2004] I.C.R. 746 (CA), Pill, L.J.; see *Khan v Trident Safeguards Ltd* [2004] EWCA Civ 624, [2004] I.R.L.R. 961 (CA), Buxton, L.J.

s.57, amended: SI 2003/1626 Reg.42

s.57A, amended: 2002 c.41 Sch.7 para.12

s.57ZA, added: SI 2003/1626 Reg.43

s.58, amended: SI 2003/1626 Reg.44

s.59, applied: SI 2004/1861 Reg.16

s.62, amended: 2002 c.41 Sch.7 para.13, SI 2003/1626 Reg.45

1976–cont.

74. Race Relations Act 1976–*cont.*

s.64, amended: SI 2003/1626 Reg.46

s.65, amended: 2002 c.41 Sch.7 para.14, SI 2003/1626 Reg.47

s.65, applied: SI 2003/1626 Reg.2

s.65, referred to: SI 2003/1626 Reg.2, SI 2004/752 Reg.14

s.66, amended: 2002 c.41 Sch.7 para.15

s.67, see *Ahmed v University of Oxford* [2002] EWCA Civ 1907, [2003] 1 W.L.R. 995 (CA), Waller, L.J.

s.68, see *Afolabi v Southwark LBC* [2003] EWCA Civ 15, [2003] I.C.R. 800 (CA), Peter Gibson, L.J.; see *British Medical Association v Chaudhary (No.1)* [2003] EWCA Civ 645, [2003] Lloyd's Rep. Med. 409 (CA), Mummery, L.J.; see *Commissioner of Police of the Metropolis v Hendricks* [2002] Emp. L.R. 32 (EAT), Judge Serota Q.C.; see *Robertson v Bexley Community Centre (t/a Leisure Link)* [2003] EWCA Civ 576, [2003] I.R.L.R. 434 (CA), Auld, L.J.

s.68, amended: 2004 c.8 s.19

s.71, applied: SI 2002/1435, SI 2002/3111, SI 2003/3006 Art.2, SSI 2002/62, SSI 2002/62 Art.2, SSI 2003/566

s.71, enabling: SI 2002/1435, SI 2002/3111, SI 2003/3006, SI 2003/3007, SI 2004/3125, SI 2004/3127, SSI 2002/62, SSI 2003/566, SSI 2004/521

s.71A, amended: 2002 c.41 s.6, Sch.9

s.71C, applied: SI 2002/1435, SI 2002/3111

s.71C, referred to: SI 2002/3111

s.72, amended: SI 2003/1626 Reg.48

s.72, applied: SI 2004/754 Art.2, Art.3

s.72, enabling: SI 2004/754, SI 2004/2515

s.73, enabling: SI 2003/1651

s.74, enabling: SSI 2003/566, SSI 2004/521

s.76, amended: SI 2003/1626 Reg.50

s.76ZA, added: SI 2003/1626 Reg.51

s.78, see *Essex Strategic HA (formerly North Essex HA) v David-John* [2004] I.C.R. 112 (EAT), Judge DM Levy Q.C.; see *Mingeley v Pennock (t/a Amber Cars)* [2004] EWCA Civ 328, [2004] I.C.R. 727 (CA), Buxton, L.J.; see *Patterson v Legal Services Commission* [2003] EWCA Civ 1558, [2004] I.C.R. 312 (CA), Clarke, L.J.

s.78, amended: SI 2003/1626 Reg.52, 2004 c.33 Sch.27 para.55

Sch.1A, referred to: SSI 2002/62 Art.5

Sch.1A Part I para.5, amended: SI 2002/2469 Sch.1 para.9, SI 2003/3007 Art.2

Sch.1A Part I para.8A, added: 2003 c.43 Sch.4 para.22

Sch.1A Part I para.21, substituted: 2004 c.21 Sch.1 para.48

Sch.1A Part I para.23, repealed: 2002 asp 3 Sch.7 para.9

Sch.1A Part I para.29, amended: 2004 c.36 Sch.2 para.10

CAP.

1976–cont.

74. Race Relations Act 1976–*cont.*
Sch.1A Part I para.45, repealed: 2003 c.39 Sch.8 para.187, Sch.10

Sch.1A Part II, amended: 2003 asp 4 Sch.4 para.4, 2003 c.37 Sch.7 para.22, 2003 c.39 Sch.8 para.187, Sch.10, 2003 c.43 Sch.13 para.3, Sch.14 Part 4, Sch.14 Part 7, SI 2003/1250 Sch.9 para.1, SI 2003/1590 Sch.1 para.4, SI 2003/3007 Art.2, 2004 c.17 Sch.3 para.8, Sch.4, 2004 c.20 Sch.14 para.4, 2004 c.25 Sch.2 para.20, Sch.4 para.8, Sch.6, SI 2004/803 Art.3, SI 2004/1771 Sch.1 para.9

Sch.1A Part III, added: SI 2003/3007 Sch.1

Sch.1A Part III, referred to: SI 2003/3006 Art.4

Sch.2 para.2, repealed: 2004 c.14 Sch.1 Part 5

Sch.2 para.3, repealed: 2004 c.14 Sch.1 Part 5

Sch.2 para.4, repealed: 2004 c.14 Sch.1 Part 5

Sch.2 para.5, repealed: 2004 c.14 Sch.1 Part 5

Sch.2 para.6, repealed: 2004 c.14 Sch.1 Part 5

Sch.2 para.7, repealed: 2004 c.14 Sch.1 Part 5

Sch.2 para.8, repealed: 2004 c.14 Sch.1 Part 5

Sch.2 para.9, repealed: 2004 c.14 Sch.1 Part 5

Sch.2 para.10, repealed: 2004 c.14 Sch.1 Part 5

76. Energy Act 1976
applied: 2004 c.20 s.188
s.5, added: 2004 c.36 Sch.2 para.14
Sch.2 para.6, amended: 2002 c.26 Sch.13

78. Industrial Common Ownership Act 1976
s.1, repealed: 2004 c.14 Sch.1 Part 16

80. Rent (Agriculture) Act 1976
applied: 2004 c.34 s.124, Sch.7 para.18, SI 2004/1005 Sch.2
referred to: 2004 c.34 s.33
s.3, amended: 2004 c.33 Sch.8 para.9
s.4, amended: 2004 c.33 Sch.8 para.10
s.5, disapplied: 2004 c.34 s.124, Sch.7 para.4, Sch.7 para.12, Sch.7 para.18
s.31, amended: 2004 c.33 Sch.8 para.11
Sch.2, disapplied: 2004 c.34 s.124, Sch.7 para.4, Sch.7 para.12, Sch.7 para.18
Sch.4 Part I para.1, amended: 2004 c.33 Sch.8 para.12

82. Sexual Offences (Amendment) Act 1976
s.1, repealed (in part): 2003 c.42 Sch.7
s.7, amended: 2003 c.42 Sch.6 para.20
s.7, repealed (in part): 2003 c.42 Sch.7

86. Fishery Limits Act 1976
s.2, applied: SI 2002/790 Sch.3 para.4
s.2, disapplied: SI 2002/790 Sch.3 para.4
s.6, disapplied: SI 2002/790 Sch.3 para.4
s.8, referred to: SI 2004/2696 Art.2
Sch.2 para.12, repealed (in part): 2003 asp 15 Sch.4 Part 2

CAP.

1977

xii. London Transport Act 1977
varied: SI 2003/1615 Sch.2 para.7

Protection of Eviction Act 1977
s.5, see *Lewisham LBC v Lasisi-Agiri* [2003] EWHC 2392, [2003] 45 E.G.C.S. 175 (Ch D), Hart, J.

1. Incumbents (Vacation of Benefices) Measure 1977
applied: SI 2002/1893 para.4, SI 2003/1936 para.4
s.1A, applied: SI 2002/1893 para.4, SI 2003/1936 para.4

3. Aircraft and Shipbuilding Industries Act 1977
Part 1, repealed: 2004 c.14 Sch.1 Part 16
s.1, repealed (in part): 2004 c.14 Sch.1 Part 16
s.10, repealed (in part): 2004 c.14 Sch.1 Part 16
s.12, amended: 2004 c.14 Sch.1 Part 16
s.18, repealed (in part): 2004 c.14 Sch.1 Part 16
s.21, repealed: 2004 c.14 Sch.1 Part 16
s.22, repealed: 2004 c.14 Sch.1 Part 16
s.23, repealed: 2004 c.14 Sch.1 Part 16
s.24, repealed: 2004 c.14 Sch.1 Part 16
s.25, repealed: 2004 c.14 Sch.1 Part 16
s.26, repealed: 2004 c.14 Sch.1 Part 16
s.27, repealed: 2004 c.14 Sch.1 Part 16
s.28, repealed: 2004 c.14 Sch.1 Part 16
s.29, repealed: 2004 c.14 Sch.1 Part 16
s.30, repealed: 2004 c.14 Sch.1 Part 16
s.31, repealed: 2004 c.14 Sch.1 Part 16
s.32, repealed: 2004 c.14 Sch.1 Part 16
s.33, repealed: 2004 c.14 Sch.1 Part 16
s.34, repealed: 2004 c.14 Sch.1 Part 16
s.35, repealed: 2004 c.14 Sch.1 Part 16
s.36, repealed: 2004 c.14 Sch.1 Part 16
s.37, repealed: 2004 c.14 Sch.1 Part 16
s.38, repealed: 2004 c.14 Sch.1 Part 16
s.39, repealed: 2004 c.14 Sch.1 Part 16
s.41, repealed: 2004 c.14 Sch.1 Part 16
s.50, repealed: 2004 c.14 Sch.1 Part 16
s.51, repealed: 2004 c.14 Sch.1 Part 16
s.54, amended: 2004 c.14 Sch.1 Part 16
s.54, repealed (in part): 2004 c.14 Sch.1 Part 16
s.56, amended: 2004 c.14 Sch.1 Part 16
Sch.4 para.1, repealed: 2004 c.14 Sch.1 Part 16
Sch.4 para.2, repealed: 2004 c.14 Sch.1 Part 16
Sch.4 para.3, repealed: 2004 c.14 Sch.1 Part 16
Sch.4 para.4, repealed: 2004 c.14 Sch.1 Part 16
Sch.4 para.5, repealed: 2004 c.14 Sch.1 Part 16
Sch.4 para.6, repealed: 2004 c.14 Sch.1 Part 16
Sch.4 para.7, repealed: 2004 c.14 Sch.1 Part 16

1977–cont.

3. Aircraft and Shipbuilding Industries Act 1977–*cont.*

Sch.5 para.1, repealed: 2004 c.14 Sch.1 Part 16

Sch.5 para.2, repealed: 2004 c.14 Sch.1 Part 16

Sch.5 para.3, repealed: 2004 c.14 Sch.1 Part 16

Sch.5 para.4, repealed: 2004 c.14 Sch.1 Part 16

Sch.5 para.5, repealed: 2004 c.14 Sch.1 Part 16

Sch.5 para.6, repealed: 2004 c.14 Sch.1 Part 16

Sch.5 para.7, repealed: 2004 c.14 Sch.1 Part 16

Sch.5 para.8, repealed: 2004 c.14 Sch.1 Part 16

Sch.5 para.9, repealed: 2004 c.14 Sch.1 Part 16

Sch.6 para.1, repealed: 2004 c.14 Sch.1 Part 16

Sch.6 para.2, repealed: 2004 c.14 Sch.1 Part 16

Sch.6 para.3, repealed: 2004 c.14 Sch.1 Part 16

Sch.6 para.4, repealed: 2004 c.14 Sch.1 Part 16

Sch.6 para.5, repealed: 2004 c.14 Sch.1 Part 16

Sch.6 para.6, repealed: 2004 c.14 Sch.1 Part 16

Sch.6 para.7, repealed: 2004 c.14 Sch.1 Part 16

Sch.6 para.8, repealed: 2004 c.14 Sch.1 Part 16

Sch.6 para.9, repealed: 2004 c.14 Sch.1 Part 16

Sch.6 para.10, repealed: 2004 c.14 Sch.1 Part 16

Sch.6 para.11, repealed: 2004 c.14 Sch.1 Part 16

Sch.6 para.12, repealed: 2004 c.14 Sch.1 Part 16

Sch.6 para.13, repealed: 2004 c.14 Sch.1 Part 16

Sch.6 para.14, repealed: 2004 c.14 Sch.1 Part 16

Sch.6 para.14, varied: SI 2003/1633 Sch.2 para.13

Sch.6 para.15, repealed: 2004 c.14 Sch.1 Part 16

Sch.6 para.16, repealed: 2004 c.14 Sch.1 Part 16

Sch.6 para.17, repealed: 2004 c.14 Sch.1 Part 16

5. Social Security (Miscellaneous Provisions) Act 1977

s.12, applied: SI 2002/792, SI 2002/1792 Sch.4 para.1, SI 2003/434, SI 2004/708, SR 2003/28 Sch.4 para.1

1977–cont.

5. Social Security (Miscellaneous Provisions) Act 1977–*cont.*

s.12, enabling: SI 2002/792, SI 2003/434, SI 2004/708

s.24, enabling: SI 2002/792, SI 2003/434, SI 2004/708

7. Nuclear Industry (Finance) Act 1977

s.1, amended: 2004 c.20 Sch.23 Part 1

s.1, applied: 2004 c.20 Sch.7 para.3, Sch.7 para.5

s.2, amended: 2004 c.20 s.197

s.2, applied: 2004 c.20 Sch.7 para.5

s.2, referred to: 2004 c.20 Sch.7 para.5

s.2, repealed (in part): 2004 c.20 Sch.23 Part 1

8. Job Release Act 1977

repealed: 2004 c.14 Sch.1 Part 8

15. Marriage (Scotland) Act 1977

applied: 2004 c.19 s.22

s.2, amended: 2004 c.7 Sch.4 para.7

s.3, see *Sohrab v Khan* 2002 S.C. 382 (OH), Lord McEwan

s.3, amended: 2004 c.33 Sch.28 para.43

s.3, applied: 2004 c.19 s.21

s.3, enabling: SSI 2002/390, SSI 2003/89

s.4, applied: 2004 c.19 s.21

s.5, see *Sohrab v Khan* 2002 S.C. 382 (OH), Lord McEwan

s.5, amended: 2004 c.33 Sch.28 para.44

s.6, applied: 2004 c.19 s.21

s.13, see *Sohrab v Khan* 2002 S.C. 382 (OH), Lord McEwan

s.18, amended: 2002 asp 8 s.1

s.18A, added: 2002 asp 8 s.1

s.18A, applied: SSI 2002/260, SSI 2002/260 Reg.9, Reg.15, Reg.16

s.18A, enabling: SSI 2002/260

s.19, enabling: SSI 2003/89

s.23A, see *Sohrab v Khan* 2002 S.C. 382 (OH), Lord McEwan

s.24, amended: 2002 asp 8 s.1

s.25, enabling: SSI 2002/390, SSI 2003/89

s.26, enabling: SSI 2002/390, SSI 2003/89

26. Licensing (Amendment) Act 1977

repealed: 2003 c.17 Sch.7

27. Presumption of Death (Scotland) Act 1977

s.1, amended: 2004 c.33 Sch.28 para.45

s.1, applied: 2004 c.33 s.210, s.211

s.3, amended: 2004 c.33 Sch.28 para.46

30. Rentcharges Act 1977

s.1, applied: SI 2002/1792 Sch.2 para.13

s.17, repealed (in part): 2004 c.14 Sch.1 Part 12

s.18, repealed (in part): 2004 c.14 Sch.1 Part 12

31. Farriers (Registration) (Amendment) Act 1977

s.1, repealed (in part): 2004 c.14 Sch.1 Part 17

s.2, repealed (in part): 2004 c.14 Sch.1 Part 17

1977–cont.

32. Torts (Interference with Goods) Act 1977

s.12, applied: SI 2003/1593 Sch.1 Part I

36. Finance Act 1977

s.11, repealed: 2002 c.23 Sch.40 Part 5

s.56, repealed: 2004 c.14 Sch.1 Part 6

Sch.9 Part V, repealed: 2004 c.14 Sch.1 Part 6

37. Patents Act 1977

see *Dranez Anstalt v Hayek* [2002] EWCA Civ 1729, [2003] 1 B.C.L.C. 278 (CA), Chadwick, L.J.

applied: 2002 c.40 s.86, SI 2002/247 Reg.20, Reg.26, SI 2002/3052 Sch.1 para.1, Sch.2 para.1, SI 2004/1818 Reg.3, SI 2004/2357 Art.21

varied: SI 2002/247 Reg.26, Reg.27, SI 2003/1249 Art.3

Part I, added: 2004 c.16 s.13

s.1, see *Hutchins' Application* [2002] R.P.C. 8 (PO), Stephen Probert; see *Practice Notice (PO: Patents Act 1977: Interpreting Section 1(2))* [2002] R.P.C. 40 (PO), A Brimelow

s.1, amended: 2004 c.16 Sch.2 para.2

s.1, varied: SI 2003/1249 Sch.1 para.1

s.2, see *Dendron GmbH v University of California (Amendment of Claim)* [2003] EWHC 2771, [2004] F.S.R. 23 (Pat Ct), Patten, J.; see *ITP SA v Coflexip Stena Offshore Ltd* 2003 S.L.T. 1197 (OH), Lord Nimmo Smith; see *Memcor Australia Pty Ltd v Norit Membraan Technologie BV* [2003] F.S.R. 43 (PCC), Judge Fysh Q.C.; see *Synthon BV v Smithkline Beecham Plc (No.2)* [2003] EWCA Civ 861, [2003] R.P.C. 43 (CA), Aldous, L.J.; see *Woolard v Comptroller General of Patents* [2002] EWHC 535, [2002] R.P.C. 39 (Pat Ct), Laddie, J.; see *Zbinden's Patent Application* [2002] R.P.C. 13 (PO), HJ Edwards

s.2, repealed (in part): 2004 c.16 Sch.2 para.3, Sch.3

s.3, see *Memcor Australia Pty Ltd v Norit Membraan Technologie BV* [2003] F.S.R. 43 (PCC), Judge Fysh Q.C.; see *Sabaf SpA v MFI Furniture Centres Ltd* [2002] EWCA Civ 976, [2003] R.P.C. 14 (CA), Peter Gibson, L.J.

s.4, see *Teva Pharmaceutical Industries Ltd v Istituto Gentili SpA* [2003] EWHC 5, [2003] F.S.R. 29 (Pat Ct), Jacob, J.

s.4, amended: 2004 c.16 Sch.3

s.4, repealed (in part): 2004 c.16 Sch.3

s.4A, added: 2004 c.16 s.1

s.5, amended: SI 2004/2357 Art.3

s.5, applied: SI 2004/2357 Art.20, Art.21

s.5, varied: SI 2003/1249 Sch.1 para.2

s.7, see *Markem Corp v Zipher Ltd (No.1)* [2004] R.P.C. 10 (Pat Ct), Judge Fysh Q.C.; see *Xtralite (Rooflights) Ltd v Hartington Conway Ltd* [2003] EWHC 1872, [2004] R.P.C. 7 (Pat Ct), Pumfrey, J.

1977–cont.

37. Patents Act 1977–*cont.*

s.8, see *Markem Corp v Zipher Ltd (No.1)* [2004] R.P.C. 10 (Pat Ct), Judge Fysh Q.C.; see *Xtralite (Rooflights) Ltd v Hartington Conway Ltd* [2003] EWHC 1872, [2004] R.P.C. 7 (Pat Ct), Pumfrey, J.

s.8, amended: 2004 c.16 s.6

s.11, amended: 2004 c.16 s.6

s.12, see *Markem Corp v Zipher Ltd (No.1)* [2004] R.P.C. 10 (Pat Ct), Judge Fysh Q.C.; see *Minnesota Mining & Manufacturing Co's International Patent Application* [2003] R.P.C. 28 (PO), Peter Hayward

s.12, amended: 2004 c.16 Sch.2 para.5

s.13, see *Minnesota Mining & Manufacturing Co's International Patent Application* [2003] R.P.C. 28 (PO), Peter Hayward

s.14, amended: SI 2004/2357 Art.4

s.14, applied: SI 2002/3052 Sch.1 para.1, SI 2004/2357 Art.20, Art.21

s.14, disapplied: SI 2004/2357 Art.20, Art.21

s.14, repealed (in part): SI 2004/2357 Art.4

s.14, enabling: SI 2003/513

s.15, applied: SI 2004/2357 Art.20, Art.21, Art.22

s.15, referred to: SI 2004/2357 Art.20

s.15, substituted: SI 2004/2357 Art.5

s.15A, disapplied: SI 2004/2357 Art.20, Art.21, Art.22

s.15A, substituted: SI 2004/2357 Art.5

s.16, see *Smart Card Solutions Ltd's Patent Application* [2004] R.P.C. 12 (PO), Stephen Probert

s.17, amended: SI 2004/2357 Art.6

s.17, applied: SI 2002/3052 Sch.2 para.1, SI 2004/2357 Art.20, Art.21, Art.22

s.17, repealed (in part): SI 2004/2357 Art.6

s.17, enabling: SI 2003/513

s.18, see *Smart Card Solutions Ltd's Patent Application* [2004] R.P.C. 12 (PO), Stephen Probert

s.18, amended: SI 2004/2357 Art.7

s.18, applied: SI 2002/3052 Sch.2 para.1, SI 2004/2357 Art.20, Art.21, Art.22

s.19, applied: SI 2002/3052 Sch.1 para.1

s.20A, added: SI 2004/2357 Art.8

s.20B, added: SI 2004/2357 Art.8

s.20B, amended: 2004 c.16 Sch.2 para.7

s.21, applied: SI 2002/3052 Sch.1 para.1

s.22, amended: 2004 c.16 Sch.2 para.8

s.22, applied: SI 2004/1818 Reg.3

s.22, varied: SI 2003/1249 Sch.1 para.3

s.23, amended: 2004 c.16 s.7

s.23, applied: SI 2004/1818 Reg.3

s.23, varied: SI 2003/1249 Sch.1 para.3

s.24, amended: 2004 c.16 Sch.2 para.9

s.25, amended: 2004 c.16 s.8

s.25, applied: SI 2004/2357 Art.23

s.27, amended: 2004 c.16 s.2

1977–cont.

37. Patents Act 1977–*cont.*

s.28, amended: 2004 c.16 s.8, SI 2004/2357 Art.9

s.30, see *Xtralite (Rooflights) Ltd v Hartington Conway Ltd* [2004] R.P.C. 6 (PO), Peter Hayward

s.30, amended: SI 2004/2357 Art.10

s.31, see *Roadvert Ltd v Pitt* 2002 S.C.L.R. 323 (OH), Lord Clarke

s.32, amended: 2003 c.44 Sch.37 Part 6, 2004 c.16 s.13

s.36, amended: 2004 c.16 s.9

s.37, see *Markem Corp v Zipher Ltd (No.1)* [2004] R.P.C. 10 (Pat Ct), Judge Fysh Q.C.

s.38, amended: 2004 c.16 Sch.2 para.10

s.40, see *Entertainment UK Ltd's Patent* [2002] R.P.C. 11 (PO), P Hayward

s.40, amended: 2004 c.16 s.10

s.41, amended: 2004 c.8 Sch.6 para.5, 2004 c.16 s.10, Sch.2 para.11

s.41, repealed (in part): 2004 c.16 Sch.3

s.41, varied: SI 2003/1249 Sch.1 para.4

s.43, amended: 2004 c.16 s.10

s.44, varied: SI 2003/1249 Sch.1 para.5

s.45, varied: SI 2003/1249 Sch.1 para.5

s.46, amended: 2004 c.16 s.8

s.48, applied: SI 2002/247 Reg.22, Reg.24, Reg.26

s.48, varied: SI 2003/1249 Sch.1 para.6

s.48A, disapplied: SI 2002/247 Reg.26

s.48B, disapplied: SI 2002/247 Reg.26

s.49, disapplied: SI 2002/247 Reg.26

s.50, disapplied: SI 2002/247 Reg.26

s.50, varied: SI 2003/1249 Sch.1 para.7

s.50A, added: 2002 c.40 Sch.25 para.8

s.50A, varied: SI 2003/1592 Sch.4 para.3

s.51, repealed (in part): 2002 c.40 Sch.26

s.51, varied: SI 2003/1249 Sch.1 para.8

s.52, disapplied: SI 2002/247 Reg.26

s.52, varied: SI 2003/1249 Sch.1 para.9

s.53, amended: 2002 c.40 Sch.25 para.8

s.53, repealed (in part): 2004 c.16 Sch.3

s.53, varied: SI 2003/1249 Sch.1 para.8, SI 2003/1592 Sch.4 para.3

s.54, varied: SI 2003/1249 Sch.1 para.10

s.56, amended: 2003 c.43 Sch.11 para.6, SI 2004/957 Sch.1 para.2

s.56, varied: SI 2004/288 Art.7, SI 2004/480 Art.6

s.58, amended: 2004 c.16 s.2, s.3

s.58, varied: SI 2003/1249 Sch.1 para.11

s.60, see *Menashe Business Mercantile Ltd v William Hill Organisation Ltd* [2002] EWCA Civ 1702, [2003] 1 W.L.R. 1462 (CA), Aldous, L.J.; see *Menashe Business Mercantile Ltd v William Hill Organisation Ltd* [2002] EWHC 397, [2002] 3 All E.R. 597 (Pat Ct), Jacob, J.; see *Sabaf SpA v MFI Furniture Centres Ltd* [2002] EWCA Civ 976, [2003] R.P.C. 14 (CA), Peter Gibson, L.J.; see *Spring Form Inc v Toy*

1977–cont.

37. Patents Act 1977–*cont.*

s.60–*cont.*

Brokers Ltd [2002] F.S.R. 17 (Pat Ct), Pumfrey, J.; see *Stena Rederi AB v Irish Ferries Ltd* [2002] EWHC 737, [2002] R.P.C. 50 (Pat Ct), Laddie, J.; see *Stena Rederi AB v Irish Ferries Ltd* [2003] EWCA Civ 66, [2003] R.P.C. 36 (CA), Aldous, L.J.

s.60, amended: SI 2004/2357 Art.11

s.60, repealed (in part): 2004 c.16 Sch.3

s.60, varied: SI 2003/1249 Sch.1 para.12

s.61, see *Spring Form Inc v Toy Brokers Ltd* [2002] F.S.R. 17 (Pat Ct), Pumfrey, J.; see *Xtralite (Rooflights) Ltd v Hartington Conway Ltd* [2003] EWHC 1872, [2004] R.P.C. 7 (Pat Ct), Pumfrey, J.

s.61, amended: 2004 c.16 s.11, Sch.2 para.14

s.62, see *Smithkline Beecham Plc v Apotex Europe Ltd* [2002] EWHC 2556, [2003] F.S.R. 30 (Pat Ct), Jacob, J.; see *Spring Form Inc v Toy Brokers Ltd* [2002] F.S.R. 17 (Pat Ct), Pumfrey, J.

s.62, amended: 2004 c.16 s.2, Sch.2 para.15

s.63, see *Smithkline Beecham Plc v Apotex Europe Ltd* [2002] EWHC 2556, [2003] F.S.R. 30 (Pat Ct), Jacob, J.

s.63, amended: 2004 c.16 s.2, s.3, Sch.2 para.16

s.68, see *LG Electronics Inc v NCR Financial Solutions Group Ltd* [2003] F.S.R. 24 (Pat Ct), Jacob, J.

s.69, see *Spring Form Inc v Toy Brokers Ltd* [2002] F.S.R. 17 (Pat Ct), Pumfrey, J.

s.70, see *Kenburn Waste Management Ltd v Bergmann* [2002] EWCA Civ 98, [2002] C.L.C 644 (CA), Robert Walker, L.J.

s.70, amended: 2004 c.16 s.12, Sch.2 para.17

s.71, see *Memcor Australia Pty Ltd v Norit Membraan Technologie BV* [2003] F.S.R. 43 (PCC), Judge Fysh Q.C.

s.72, see *American Home Products Corp v Novartis Pharmaceuticals UK Ltd* [2002] E.N.P.R. 13 (CA), Aldous, L.J.; see *Cairnstores Ltd v Aktiebolaget Hassle* [2002] F.S.R. 35 (Pat Ct), Pumfrey, J.; see *Kirin-Amgen Inc v Transkaryotic Therapies Inc (No.1)* [2002] R.P.C. 1 (Pat Ct), Neuberger, J.; see *Oystertec Plc v Edward Evans Barker (A Firm)* [2002] EWHC 2324, [2003] R.P.C. 29 (Pat Ct), Jacob, J.; see *R. (on the application of Ash & Lacy Building Products Ltd) v Comptroller General of Patents, Designs and Trade Marks* [2002] EWHC 541, [2002] R.P.C. 46 (QBD (Admin Ct)), Laddie, J.

s.72, amended: 2004 c.16 s.4, Sch.2 para.18, Sch.3, SI 2004/2357 Art.12

s.72, applied: SI 2004/2357 Art.20, Art.21

s.73, see *Thibierge & Comar SA v Rexam CFP Ltd* [2002] R.P.C. 18 (Pat Ct), Jacob, J.

s.74, amended: 2004 c.16 s.13

s.75, amended: 2004 c.16 s.2, Sch.2 para.19

1977–cont.

37. Patents Act 1977–cont.

s.76, see *Baker Hughes Inc v Halliburton Energy Services Inc* [2002] EWHC 2524, (2003) 26(1) I.P.D. 26003 (Pat Ct), Jacob, J.

s.76, amended: SI 2004/2357 Art.13

s.76, applied: SI 2004/2357 Art.20, Art.21

s.76A, varied: SI 2003/1249 Sch.1 para.13

s.77, amended: 2004 c.16 Sch.1 para.2

s.78, amended: 2004 c.16 Sch.1 para.3, SI 2004/2357 Art.14

s.78, applied: SI 2004/2357 Art.20, Art.21.1 para.4

s.81, amended: 2004 c.16 Sch.1 para.5, SI 2004/2357 Art.15

s.81, applied: SI 2004/2357 Art.21

s.81, repealed (in part): 2004 c.16 Sch.3

s.86, repealed: 2004 c.16 Sch.3

s.87, repealed: 2004 c.16 Sch.3

s.89, repealed (in part): 2004 c.16 Sch.3

s.89A, applied: SI 2002/529 r.1, SI 2004/2357 Art.22

s.89B, amended: 2004 c.16 Sch.1 para.8, SI 2004/2357 Art.16

s.89B, applied: SI 2004/2357 Art.22

s.91, amended: 2004 c.16 Sch.2 para.20

s.93, varied: SI 2003/1249 Sch.1 para.14

s.95, amended: 2004 c.16 Sch.2 para.21, Sch.3

s.96, varied: SI 2003/1249 Sch.1 para.15

s.97, varied: SI 2003/1249 Sch.1 para.16

s.103, amended: 2004 c.16 Sch.3

s.105, amended: 2004 c.16 Sch.3

s.106, amended: 2004 c.16 s.14, Sch.3

s.107, amended: 2004 c.16 s.15

s.107, varied: SI 2003/1249 Sch.1 para.17

s.109, varied: SI 2003/1249 Sch.1 para.18

s.117, amended: SI 2004/2357 Art.17

s.117, applied: SI 2002/3052 Sch.1 para.1

s.117A, added: SI 2004/2357 Art.18

s.117A, amended: 2004 c.16 Sch.2 para.23

s.117B, added: SI 2004/2357 Art.18

s.118, see *Buralls of Wisbech Ltd's Patent Application* [2004] R.P.C. 14 (PO), Peter Hayward; see *Haberman v Comptroller General of Patents* [2003] EWHC 430, [2004] R.P.C. 21 (Pat Ct), Peter Prescott Q.C.

s.120, amended: 2004 c.16 Sch.2 para.24

s.121, amended: 2004 c.16 Sch.2 para.25, Sch.3

s.123, amended: 2004 c.16 Sch.2 para.26

s.123, applied: SI 2002/247 Reg.20, Reg.22, Reg.24

s.123, repealed (in part): 2004 c.16 Sch.2 para.26, Sch.3

s.123, enabling: SI 2002/529, SI 2003/513, SI 2004/2358

s.124, applied: SI 2002/247 Reg.20

s.124, enabling: SI 2003/1249

s.124A, added: SI 2003/512 Art.2

1977–cont.

37. Patents Act 1977–cont.

s.124A, varied: SI 2003/1249 Sch.1 para.19

s.125, see *Pharmacia Corp v Merck & Co Inc* [2002] E.N.P.R. 7 (Pat Ct), Pumfrey, J.

s.125A, varied: SI 2003/1249 Sch.1 para.20

s.130, see *Coflexip SA v Stolt Offshore MS Ltd* [2004] EWCA Civ 213, [2004] F.S.R. 34 (CA), Sir Martin Nourse; see *Dendron GmbH v University of California (Preliminary Issue: Exclusive Licensee)* [2004] EWHC 1163, [2004] F.S.R. 43 (Pat Ct), Pumfrey, J.; see *Xtralite (Rooflights) Ltd v Hartington Conway Ltd* [2004] R.P.C. 6 (PO), Peter Hayward

s.130, amended: SI 2003/512 Art.3, 2004 c.16 Sch.1 para.9, Sch.2 para.27, Sch.3, SI 2004/2357 Art.19

s.130, applied: SI 2004/2357 Art.20, Art.21

s.130, repealed (in part): 2004 c.16 Sch.1 para.9

s.130, varied: SI 2003/1249 Sch.1 para.21

s.131, amended: 2004 c.16 Sch.2 para.28

s.132, enabling: SI 2003/1249

Sch.A1 para.1, varied: SI 2003/1249 Sch.1 para.22

Sch.A1 para.2, varied: SI 2003/1249 Sch.1 para.22

Sch.A1 para.3, varied: SI 2003/1249 Sch.1 para.22

Sch.A1 para.4, varied: SI 2003/1249 Sch.1 para.22

Sch.A1 para.5, varied: SI 2003/1249 Sch.1 para.22

Sch.A1 para.6, varied: SI 2003/1249 Sch.1 para.22

Sch.A1 para.7, varied: SI 2003/1249 Sch.1 para.22

Sch.A1 para.8, varied: SI 2003/1249 Sch.1 para.22

Sch.A1 para.9, varied: SI 2003/1249 Sch.1 para.22

Sch.A1 para.10, varied: SI 2003/1249 Sch.1 para.22

Sch.A1 para.11, varied: SI 2003/1249 Sch.1 para.22

Sch.A1 para.12, varied: SI 2003/1249 Sch.1 para.22

Sch.A2 para.1, varied: SI 2003/1249 Sch.1 para.22

Sch.A2 para.2, varied: SI 2003/1249 Sch.1 para.22

Sch.A2 para.3, varied: SI 2003/1249 Sch.1 para.22

Sch.A2 para.4, varied: SI 2003/1249 Sch.1 para.22

Sch.A2 para.5, varied: SI 2003/1249 Sch.1 para.22

Sch.A2 para.6, varied: SI 2003/1249 Sch.1 para.22

Sch.A2 para.7, varied: SI 2003/1249 Sch.1 para.22

1977–cont.

37. Patents Act 1977–*cont.*

Sch.A2 para.8, varied: SI 2003/1249 Sch.1 para.22

Sch.A2 para.9, varied: SI 2003/1249 Sch.1 para.22

Sch.A2 para.10, varied: SI 2003/1249 Sch.1 para.22

Sch.A2 para.11, varied: SI 2003/1249 Sch.1 para.22

Sch.5 para.7, repealed: 2002 c.40 Sch.26

38. Administration of Justice Act 1977

s.1, repealed: 2004 c.14 Sch.1 Part 1

s.2, repealed (in part): 2004 c.14 Sch.1 Part 1

s.5, repealed (in part): 2004 c.14 Sch.1 Part 1

s.11, repealed: 2004 c.14 Sch.1 Part 1

s.12, repealed: 2004 c.14 Sch.1 Part 1

s.19, repealed (in part): 2004 c.14 Sch.1 Part 1

s.22, repealed: 2003 c.39 Sch.8 para.188, Sch.10

s.24, repealed: 2002 c.9 Sch.13

s.26, repealed: 2002 c.9 Sch.13

s.32, repealed (in part): 2004 c.14 Sch.1 Part 1

Sch.2 Part I para.3, repealed: 2004 c.14 Sch.1 Part 1

Sch.2 Part I para.4, repealed: 2004 c.14 Sch.1 Part 1

Sch.2 Part I para.6, repealed: 2004 c.14 Sch.1 Part 1

42. Rent Act 1977

see *Rajah v Arogol Co Ltd* [2001] EWCA Civ 454, [2002] H.L.R. 21 (CA), Hale, L.J.; see *Wandsworth LBC v Michalak* [2002] EWCA Civ 271, [2003] 1 W.L.R. 617 (CA), Brooke, L.J.

applied: 2004 c.34 s.124, Sch.7 para.18, SI 2004/1005 Sch.2

referred to: 2004 c.34 s.33

Part IV, applied: 2002 c.15 Sch.11 para.1

s.2, see *Moreland Properties (UK) Ltd v Dhokia* [2003] EWCA Civ 1639, [2004] L. & T.R. 20 (CA), Brooke, L.J.

s.11, amended: 2003 c.17 Sch.6 para.67

s.14, disapplied: 2004 c.34 s.124, Sch.7 para.4, Sch.7 para.12, Sch.7 para.18

s.15, disapplied: 2004 c.34 s.124, Sch.7 para.4, Sch.7 para.12, Sch.7 para.18

s.16, disapplied: 2004 c.34 s.124, Sch.7 para.4, Sch.7 para.12, Sch.7 para.18

s.62, amended: SI 2003/973 Art.10

s.63, amended: SI 2003/973 Art.11

s.63, applied: SI 2003/437 Sch.1 Part 2, SI 2003/973 Art.2

s.64B, enabling: SI 2003/973

s.66, amended: SI 2003/973 Art.12

s.70, see *R. (on the application of Wolters (London) Ltd) v London Rent Assessment Committee* [2003] EWHC 1465, [2003] 3 E.G.L.R. 17 (QBD (Admin Ct)), Harrison, J.

s.71, applied: 2002 c.15 Sch.11 para.1

1977–cont.

42. Rent Act 1977–*cont.*

s.98, see *Akram v Adam (No.1)* [2002] EWCA Civ 1679, [2003] H.L.R. 28 (CA), Chadwick, L.J.

s.102, see *Clements v Simmonds* [2002] EWHC 1652, [2002] 3 E.G.L.R. 22 (QBD), Burton, J.

s.116, see *Akram v Adam (No.1)* [2002] EWCA Civ 1679, [2003] H.L.R. 28 (CA), Chadwick, L.J.

s.116, amended: SI 2002/1860 Sch.1 para.1, Sch.6

s.116(2), see *Akram v Adam (No.1)* [2002] EWCA Civ 1679, [2003] H.L.R. 28 (CA), Chadwick, L.J.

s.136, amended: 2002 c.9 Sch.11 para.14

s.137, see *Moreland Properties (UK) Ltd v Dhokia* [2003] EWCA Civ 1639, [2004] L. & T.R. 20 (CA), Brooke, L.J.

Sch.1 Part I para.2, amended: 2004 c.33 Sch.8 para.13

Sch.1 para.2, see *Ghaidan v Godin-Mendoza* [2002] EWCA Civ 1533, [2003] Ch. 380 (CA), Buxton, L.J.; see *Ghaidan v Godin-Mendoza* [2004] UKHL 30, [2004] 2 A.C. 557 (HL), Lord Nicholls of Birkenhead

Sch.1 para.3, see *Ghaidan v Godin-Mendoza* [2002] EWCA Civ 1533, [2003] Ch. 380 (CA), Buxton, L.J.

Sch.10, applied: 2002 c.15 s.173, Sch.12 para.5, Sch.12 para.8, SI 2003/409 Sch.1 Part I, SI 2003/437 Sch.1 Part 1, SI 2003/2099 Reg.12, Reg.13, 2004 c.34 s.229, SI 2004/681 Reg.12, Reg.13

Sch.15 Part I para.9, amended: 2004 c.33 Sch.8 para.14

Sch.15 Case 9, see *Clements v Simmonds* [2002] EWHC 1652, [2002] 3 E.G.L.R. 22 (QBD), Burton, J.

43. Protection from Eviction Act 1977

applied: 2002 c.41 s.32

s.1, see *Attorney General's Reference (No.1 of 2004), Re* [2004] EWCA Crim 1025, [2004] 1 W.L.R. 2111 (CA (Crim Div)), Lord Woolf of Barnes, L.C.J.; see *Cowan v Chief Constable of Avon and Somerset* [2002] H.L.R. 44 (CA), Keene, L.J.; see *R. (on the application of McGowan) v Brent Justices* [2001] EWHC Admin 814, (2002) 166 J.P. 29 (QBD (Admin Ct)), Tuckey, L.J.

s.2, see *Belgravia Property Investment & Development Co Ltd v Webb* [2001] EWCA Civ 2075, [2002] L. & T.R. 29 (CA), Robert Walker, L.J.

s.3A, see *Sumeghova v McMahon* [2002] EWCA Civ 1581, [2003] H.L.R. 26 (CA), Longmore, L.J.

s.3A, amended: 2002 c.41 s.32

s.3A, applied: SI 2003/2436 Art.2

s.3A, enabling: SI 2003/2436

s.4, amended: 2004 c.33 Sch.8 para.15

1977–cont.

45. Criminal Law Act 1977

s.1, see *R. v Gleeson (John Vincent)* [2003] EWCA Crim 3357, [2004] 1 Cr. App. R. 29 (CA (Crim Div)), Auld, L.J.; see *R. v Hobbs (Stephen Paul)* [2002] EWCA Crim 387, [2002] 2 Cr. App. R. 22 (CA (Crim Div)), Pill, L.J.; see *R. v Hussain (Akhtar)* [2002] EWCA Crim 6, [2002] 2 Cr. App. R. 26 (CA (Crim Div)), May, L.J.; see *R. v Taylor (Robert John)* [2001] EWCA Crim 1044, [2002] Crim. L.R. 205 (CA (Crim Div)), Rougier, J.

s.1, applied: 2003 c.44 Sch.4 para.39, Sch.5 para.29, SI 2004/1910 Sch.2

s.2, amended: 2004 c.33 Sch.27 para.56

s.3, see *R. v Mason (Kenneth)* [2002] EWCA Crim 699, [2002] 2 Cr. App. R. 32 (CA (Crim Div)), Clarke, L.J.; see *R. v Taylor (Robert John)* [2001] EWCA Crim 1044, [2002] Crim. L.R. 205 (CA (Crim Div)), Rougier, J.

s.3, amended: 2003 c.44 Sch.32 para.24

s.8, amended: 2003 c.44 Sch.26 para.24

s.10, amended: 2003 c.39 Sch.8 para.189

s.39, amended: 2003 c.44 Sch.36 para.6

s.47, applied: 2002 c.29 s.38

s.48, amended: 2003 c.39 Sch.8 para.190

s.51, see *R. v Mason (Auburn)* [2001] EWCA Crim 1138, [2002] 1 Cr. App. R. (S.) 29 (CA (Crim Div)), Butterfield, J.

s.51, applied: SI 2004/1910 Sch.2

s.54, applied: SI 2002/896 Sch.1 para.40, 2003 c.42 Sch.3 para.12, 2003 c.44 Sch.15 para.98, SI 2003/1184 Sch.2 para.12, SSI 2003/19 Sch.5 para.4

s.54, referred to: 2002 c.38 s.74

s.54, repealed: 2003 c.42 Sch.7

Sch.12 para.1, amended: 2002 c.38 Sch.5, 2003 c.44 Sch.37 Part 4, Sch.37 Part 10

Sch.12 para.2, amended: 2002 c.38 Sch.5, 2003 c.44 Sch.37 Part 4, Sch.37 Part 10

Sch.12 para.3, amended: 2002 c.38 Sch.5, 2003 c.44 Sch.37 Part 4, Sch.37 Part 10

Sch.12 para.4, amended: 2002 c.38 Sch.5, 2003 c.41 Sch.4, 2003 c.44 Sch.37 Part 4, Sch.37 Part 10

Sch.12 para.6, amended: 2002 c.38 Sch.5, 2003 c.44 Sch.37 Part 4, Sch.37 Part 10

Sch.12 para.7, amended: 2002 c.38 Sch.5, 2003 c.44 Sch.37 Part 4, Sch.37 Part 10

Sch.12 para.8, amended: 2002 c.38 Sch.5, 2003 c.44 Sch.37 Part 4, Sch.37 Part 10

Sch.12 para.9, amended: 2002 c.38 Sch.5, 2003 c.44 Sch.37 Part 4, Sch.37 Part 10

Sch.12 para.10, amended: 2002 c.38 Sch.5, 2003 c.44 Sch.37 Part 4, Sch.37 Part 10

Sch.12 para.11, amended: 2002 c.38 Sch.5, 2003 c.44 Sch.37 Part 4, Sch.37 Part 10

Sch.12 para.12, amended: 2002 c.38 Sch.5, 2003 c.44 Sch.37 Part 4, Sch.37 Part 10

1977–cont.

49. National Health Service Act 1977

applied: SI 2002/324 Reg.3, SI 2002/325 Reg.4, SI 2002/2375 Reg.3, Reg.9, Reg.11, SI 2003/993 Reg.17, SI 2003/1587 Reg.18, SI 2003/1617 Reg.2, SI 2003/2123 Reg.2, SI 2004/291 Reg.15, Sch.4, Sch.5 para.1, Sch.6 para.2, Sch.6 para.79, Sch.6 para.104, SI 2004/478 Reg.15, Sch.4, Sch.5 para.1, Sch.6 para.2, Sch.6 para.77, Sch.6 para.102, SI 2004/627 Reg.19, Sch.2, Sch.3, Sch.5 para.3, Sch.5 para.75, SI 2004/629 Sch.2, SI 2004/865 Art.108, SI 2004/905 Reg.14, Reg.15, Reg.25, SI 2004/1016 Art.84, SI 2004/1022 Sch.2, SI 2004/1031 Reg.28

referred to: SI 2002/3038 Reg.5, 2003 c.43 s.40, s.187, Sch.4 para.23, Sch.11 para.7, SI 2003/250 Reg.2, SI 2003/2123 Reg.4

varied: 2002 c.17 Sch.6 para.6, Sch.7 para.5, 2003 c.43 s.187, Sch.6 para.3, Sch.7 para.3, SI 2003/1250 Sch.2 para.4

enabling: SI 2002/544

Part I, applied: 2002 c.17 s.17, SI 2002/2375 Reg.3, Reg.4, SI 2003/2124 Reg.3, 2004 c.31 s.12, s.29, SI 2004/118 Art.3, SI 2004/905 Reg.20, SSI 2004/386 Reg.7

Part I, added: 2003 c.43 s.175

Part II, applied: 2002 c.17 s.17, SI 2002/325 Reg.3, Reg.4, SI 2002/545 Reg.2, SI 2002/2469 Sch.12 para.2, SI 2003/2124 Reg.3, SI 2003/2382 Reg.6, SI 2004/865 Art.60, Art.61, SI 2004/905 Reg.20, SSI 2004/386 Reg.7

Part II, enabling: SI 2002/2802

s.1, applied: 2003 c.43 s.3

s.1, referred to: SI 2002/2375 Sch.2

s.2, applied: SI 2002/2375 Reg.6

s.2, referred to: SI 2002/2375 Sch.1 Part 1

s.3, amended: SI 2002/2759 Reg.3, 2003 c.43 Sch.11 para.8, Sch.14 Part 4

s.3, applied: SI 2002/1792 Reg.4, 2003 c.43 s.3

s.3, referred to: SI 2002/2375 Sch.1 Part 2

s.3, varied: SI 2004/865 Art.109, SI 2004/1016 Art.85

s.4, applied: SI 2002/1792 Reg.5, SI 2002/2375 Reg.8

s.4, referred to: SI 2002/2375 Sch.1 Part 2

s.5, applied: SI 2002/2005 Reg.9, Reg.13, SI 2002/2375 Reg.3, Reg.8, SI 2003/505 Art.10, Sch.1 para.2

s.5, referred to: SI 2002/2375 Sch.1 Part 1, Sch.1 Part 2

s.5, repealed (in part): SI 2002/2759 Reg.3, 2003 c.43 s.171, Sch.13 para.4, Sch.14 Part 4, Sch.14 Part 7

s.7, applied: SI 2003/409 Sch.1 Part I

s.8, applied: SI 2002/195 Reg.12, SI 2002/253 Sch.2 para.18, SI 2002/2375 Reg.6, SI 2002/3200 Reg.12, SI 2003/1617 Reg.2, SR 2002/224 Reg.12, 2003 c.14 s.61, s.66, 2004 c.28 s.9

1977–cont.

49. National Health Service Act 1977– *cont.*

s.8, substituted: 2002 c.17 s.1

s.8, enabling: SI 2002/553, SI 2003/250, SI 2003/1617, SI 2004/37

s.11, applied: SI 2002/195 Reg.12, SI 2002/3200 Reg.12, SI 2003/2644 Reg.3, SI 2003/3171 Sch.1 Part II, SR 2002/224 Reg.12, 2003 c.14 s.61, s.66, 2004 c.36 Sch.1 para.9

s.11, referred to: SI 2002/559, 2003 c.43 s.187

s.11, enabling: SI 2002/34, SI 2002/559, SI 2002/1760, SI 2002/2621, SI 2002/3039, SI 2003/505, SI 2003/1077, SI 2003/1827, SI 2003/2772, SI 2003/3059, SI 2004/569, SI 2004/648, SI 2004/667, SI 2004/951, SI 2004/2147

s.12, amended: 2002 c.17 Sch.1 para.2

s.15, amended: 2002 c.17 Sch.2 para.2, Sch.3 para.11, SI 2002/2861 Reg.16, 2003 c.43 Sch.11 para.9

s.15, applied: SI 2002/545 Reg.2, SI 2003/2824 Reg.2, Reg.3

s.15, varied: SI 2004/288 Art.7, SI 2004/480 Art.6

s.15, enabling: SI 2002/545, SI 2002/558, SI 2002/918, SI 2002/1881, SI 2002/2548, SI 2003/26, SI 2003/138, SI 2003/1976, SI 2003/2824

s.16, amended: 2002 c.17 Sch.1 para.3, Sch.5 para.5

s.16, enabling: SI 2002/1759, SI 2002/2375, SI 2002/3040, SI 2003/1497, SI 2003/2773, SI 2003/3060, SI 2004/570, SI 2004/668

s.16A, amended: 2002 c.17 s.2

s.16A, applied: SI 2002/64, SI 2002/65, SI 2002/66, SI 2002/67, SI 2002/68, SI 2002/69, SI 2002/70, SI 2002/71, SI 2002/137, SI 2002/138, SI 2002/139, SI 2002/140, SI 2002/141, SI 2002/142, SI 2002/143, SI 2002/144, SI 2002/145, SI 2002/146, SI 2002/147, SI 2002/148, SI 2002/149, SI 2002/150, SI 2002/166, SI 2002/356, SI 2002/357, SI 2002/358, SI 2002/616, SI 2002/617, SI 2002/634, SI 2002/722, SI 2002/723, SI 2002/724, SI 2002/725, SI 2002/726, SI 2002/727, SI 2002/728, SI 2002/729, SI 2002/730, SI 2002/893, SI 2002/894, SI 2002/895, SI 2002/938, SI 2002/939, SI 2002/940, SI 2002/941, SI 2002/942, SI 2002/943, SI 2002/944, SI 2002/945, SI 2002/946, SI 2002/947, SI 2002/948, SI 2002/950, SI 2002/951, SI 2002/957, SI 2002/958, SI 2002/959, SI 2002/960, SI 2002/980, SI 2002/981, SI 2002/982, SI 2002/983, SI 2002/984, SI 2002/985, SI 2002/986, SI 2002/987, SI 2002/988, SI 2002/989, SI 2002/990, SI 2002/991, SI 2002/992, SI 2002/994, SI 2002/995, SI 2002/996, SI

1977–cont.

49. National Health Service Act 1977– *cont.*

s.16A, applied:–*cont.*

2002/997, SI 2002/998, SI 2002/999, SI 2002/1000, SI 2002/1001, SI 2002/1002, SI 2002/1003, SI 2002/1004, SI 2002/1005, SI 2002/1007, SI 2002/1008, SI 2002/1009, SI 2002/1010, SI 2002/1112, SI 2002/1113, SI 2002/1114, SI 2002/1115, SI 2002/1116, SI 2002/1117, SI 2002/1118, SI 2002/1119, SI 2002/1120, SI 2002/1121, SI 2002/1122, SI 2002/1123, SI 2002/1133, SI 2002/1235, SI 2002/1325, SI 2002/1392, SI 2002/1393, SI 2002/1405, SI 2002/2006 Reg.19, SI 2002/2233, 2003 c.14 s.61, s.66, SI 2003/1064, SI 2003/1067, SI 2003/1740, 2004 c.28 s.9, 2004 c.36 Sch.1 para.7, SI 2004/904, SI 2004/1630, SI 2004/1643

s.16A, enabling: SI 2002/64, SI 2002/65, SI 2002/66, SI 2002/67, SI 2002/68, SI 2002/69, SI 2002/70, SI 2002/71, SI 2002/137, SI 2002/138, SI 2002/139, SI 2002/140, SI 2002/141, SI 2002/142, SI 2002/143, SI 2002/144, SI 2002/145, SI 2002/146, SI 2002/147, SI 2002/148, SI 2002/149, SI 2002/150, SI 2002/166, SI 2002/356, SI 2002/357, SI 2002/358, SI 2002/616, SI 2002/617, SI 2002/634, SI 2002/722, SI 2002/723, SI 2002/724, SI 2002/725, SI 2002/726, SI 2002/727, SI 2002/728, SI 2002/729, SI 2002/730, SI 2002/893, SI 2002/894, SI 2002/895, SI 2002/938, SI 2002/939, SI 2002/940, SI 2002/941, SI 2002/942, SI 2002/943, SI 2002/944, SI 2002/945, SI 2002/946, SI 2002/947, SI 2002/948, SI 2002/949, SI 2002/950, SI 2002/951, SI 2002/957, SI 2002/958, SI 2002/959, SI 2002/960, SI 2002/980, SI 2002/981, SI 2002/982, SI 2002/983, SI 2002/984, SI 2002/985, SI 2002/986, SI 2002/987, SI 2002/988, SI 2002/989, SI 2002/990, SI 2002/991, SI 2002/992, SI 2002/993, SI 2002/994, SI 2002/995, SI 2002/996, SI 2002/997, SI 2002/998, SI 2002/999, SI 2002/1000, SI 2002/1001, SI 2002/1002, SI 2002/1003, SI 2002/1004, SI 2002/1005, SI 2002/1006, SI 2002/1007, SI 2002/1008, SI 2002/1009, SI 2002/1010, SI 2002/1112, SI 2002/1113, SI 2002/1114, SI 2002/1115, SI 2002/1116, SI 2002/1117, SI 2002/1118, SI 2002/1119, SI 2002/1120, SI 2002/1121, SI 2002/1122, SI 2002/1123, SI 2002/1133, SI 2002/1235, SI 2002/1325, SI 2002/1392, SI 2002/1393, SI 2002/1405, SI 2002/2233, SI 2003/1064, SI 2003/1066, SI 2003/1067, SI 2003/1501, SI 2003/1740, SI 2003/1983, SI 2003/2168, SI 2003/2649, SI 2003/2662, SI 2003/2663, SI 2003/2664, SI 2003/2766, SI 2003/

CAP.

1977–cont.

49. National Health Service Act 1977– cont.

s.16A, enabling:–cont.
2944, SI 2004/543, SI 2004/904, SI 2004/1413, SI 2004/1630, SI 2004/1643, SI 2004/2248

s.16B, amended: 2002 c.17 Sch.1 para.4, Sch.5 para.6, 2003 c.43 s.182

s.16B, applied: 2004 c.36 Sch.1 para.8

s.16B, enabling: SI 2002/2375, SI 2003/1497

s.16BA, added: 2002 c.17 s.6

s.16BA, applied: 2003 c.14 s.61, s.66, SI 2003/148 Art.4, 2004 c.28 s.9

s.16BA, enabling: SI 2003/148, SI 2003/1740

s.16BB, added: 2002 c.17 s.6

s.16BB, amended: 2003 c.43 Sch.11 para.10

s.16BB, applied: SI 2004/478 Reg.23, Sch.6 para.63, Sch.6 para.76, SI 2004/1016 Art.22

s.16BB, enabling: SI 2003/150, SI 2003/815, SI 2003/816, SI 2004/905

s.16BC, added: 2002 c.17 s.6

s.16BC, amended: 2003 c.43 s.182, Sch.11 para.11

s.16BC, enabling: SI 2003/149

s.16C, amended: 2002 c.17 Sch.1 para.5, Sch.5 para.7

s.16CA, added: 2003 c.43 s.170

s.16CA, varied: 2003 c.43 s.150

s.16CB, added: 2003 c.43 s.171

s.16CC, added: 2003 c.43 s.174

s.16CC, applied: SI 2004/291 Sch.6 para.83, SI 2004/478 Sch.6 para.81, SI 2004/627 Sch.5 para.79, SI 2004/1768 Reg.6, Reg.20

s.16CC, varied: 2003 c.43 s.150

s.16D, amended: 2002 c.17 s.3, Sch.1 para.6

s.16D, applied: 2002 c.17 Sch.6 para.6, Sch.7 para.5, 2003 c.43 s.187, Sch.6 para.3, Sch.7 para.3, SI 2003/1250 Sch.2 para.4

s.16D, disapplied: SI 2002/2375 Reg.6

s.16D, referred to: 2003 c.43 s.187

s.16D, varied: 2004 c.17 Sch.1 para.2

s.16D, enabling: SI 2002/2375, SI 2003/1497

s.17, enabling: SI 2004/905

s.17, applied: SI 2004/627 Reg.13, Reg.14, Sch.5 para.86

s.17, amended: 2002 c.17 Sch.1 para.7

s.17, applied: SI 2002/2375 Reg.6, Reg.7, SI 2004/291 Reg.23, Sch.6 para.64, SI 2004/627 Reg.13, Sch.5 para.63, Sch.5 para.73, Sch.5 para.91, SI 2004/865 Art.23

s.17, referred to: SI 2002/2375 Sch.2, Sch.3

s.17, enabling: SI 2002/555, SI 2002/2375, SI 2002/3048, SI 2003/993, SI 2003/1497, SI 2003/1587, SI 2003/2824, SI 2004/1427

s.17A, substituted: 2002 c.17 s.3

CAP.

1977–cont.

49. National Health Service Act 1977– cont.

s.17B, amended: 2002 c.17 s.3, Sch.1 para.8, Sch.9 Part 1

s.18, amended: 2002 c.17 s.3, Sch.1 para.9, 2003 c.4 Sch.4

s.18, repealed (in part): 2002 c.17 s.3, Sch.9 Part 1, 2003 c.4 Sch.4

s.18, enabling: SI 2002/555, SI 2002/2375, SI 2004/1768

s.18A, amended: 2003 c.43 Sch.4 para.24, Sch.11 para.12, Sch.14 Part 4

s.18A, varied: SI 2004/288 Art.7, SI 2004/480 Art.6

s.19A, amended: 2003 c.43 Sch.9 para.9

s.19A, applied: 2002 c.17 s.19, SI 2004/291 Sch.6 para.92, SI 2004/478 Sch.6 para.90, SI 2004/627 Sch.5 para.86, SI 2004/905 Reg.22, SI 2004/1768 Reg.11

s.19A, referred to: SI 2003/2124 Reg.5

s.20, applied: 2002 c.17 s.22

s.20, repealed (in part): 2003 c.4 Sch.4

s.20A, added: 2003 c.4 s.1

s.20A, applied: SI 2004/905 Reg.3, Sch.1 para.1

s.21, applied: 2002 c.41 Sch.3 para.1

s.22, amended: 2002 c.17 Sch.1 para.10, Sch.5 para.8, Sch.9 Part 1, 2003 c.43 Sch.4 para.25, Sch.14 Part 1

s.22, repealed (in part): 2003 c.43 Sch.14 Part 1

s.23, amended: 2002 c.17 Sch.1 para.11, Sch.5 para.9

s.23, applied: SI 2002/1792 Reg.4, SI 2003/2382 Reg.10, SI 2004/1768 Reg.20

s.23, referred to: SI 2002/2375 Sch.1 Part 1

s.26, amended: 2002 c.17 Sch.1 para.12, Sch.5 para.10, SI 2002/2861 Reg.17, 2003 c.43 Sch.11 para.13, Sch.14 Part 4

s.26, applied: SI 2002/2202 Art.2

s.26, referred to: SI 2002/2375 Sch.1 Part 1

s.26, varied: SI 2004/288 Art.7, SI 2004/480 Art.6, SI 2004/865 Art.109, SI 2004/1016 Art.85

s.27, amended: 2002 c.17 Sch.1 para.13, Sch.5 para.11

s.27, applied: SI 2002/2202 Art.2

s.27, referred to: SI 2002/2375 Sch.1 Part 1

s.28, amended: 2002 c.17 Sch.1 para.14, Sch.5 para.12, 2003 c.43 Sch.4 para.26

s.28A, amended: 2002 c.17 Sch.1 para.15, Sch.5 para.13, Sch.9 Part 1, 2003 c.43 Sch.4 para.27

s.28A, applied: 2004 c.17 s.4

s.28BB, amended: 2002 c.17 Sch.1 para.16, Sch.5 para.14

s.28BB, applied: 2004 c.17 s.4

s.28C, amended: 2003 c.43 Sch.11 para.14

s.28C, applied: 2002 c.17 s.17, SI 2003/1250 Art.10, Sch.8 para.22, SI 2003/2124 Reg.3, SI 2004/118 Art.3, SI 2004/433 Art.43, SI

1977–cont.

49. National Health Service Act 1977– *cont.*

s.28C, applied:–*cont.*

2004/477 Art.43, SI 2004/478 Sch.6 para.34, Sch.6 para.35, Sch.6 para.69, SI 2004/627 Sch.5 para.86, Sch.5 para.105, SI 2004/865 Art.58, SI 2004/905 Reg.20, SI 2004/1768 Reg.2, Reg.7

s.28C, repealed (in part): 2003 c.43 Sch.14 Part 4

s.28D, amended: 2003 c.43 s.177, Sch.11 para.15, Sch.14 Part 4, SI 2004/957 Sch.1 para.3

s.28D, applied: SI 2004/291 Reg.8, SI 2004/478 Reg.8, SI 2004/627 Reg.5, Sch.5 para.80

s.28D, referred to: SI 2004/627 Reg.4, SI 2004/865 Art.60, SI 2004/1772 Art.4, SI 2004/1825 Art.3

s.28D, repealed (in part): 2003 c.43 Sch.14 Part 4

s.28D, varied: SI 2004/288 Art.7, SI 2004/480 Art.6, SI 2004/865 Art.109, SI 2004/1016 Art.85

s.28D, enabling: SI 2004/291, SI 2004/478, SI 2004/627, SI 2004/2694

s.28DA, applied: SI 2003/1250 Art.10, Sch.8 para.22

s.28DA, repealed (in part): 2003 c.43 Sch.14 Part 4

s.28E, amended: 2003 c.43 s.177

s.28E, applied: SI 2004/627 Reg.13, Reg.14

s.28E, repealed (in part): 2003 c.43 Sch.14 Part 4

s.28E, enabling: SI 2004/627, SI 2004/906, SI 2004/2694

s.28EE, amended: 2003 c.43 Sch.11 para.16

s.28F, repealed (in part): 2003 c.43 s.177, Sch.14 Part 4

s.28G, repealed (in part): 2003 c.43 s.177, Sch.14 Part 4

s.28H, repealed (in part): 2003 c.43 s.177, Sch.14 Part 4

s.28I, amended: SI 2002/2861 Reg.18, 2003 c.43 Sch.11 para.17

s.28I, varied: SI 2004/288 Art.8, SI 2004/480 Art.7

s.28K, added: 2003 c.43 s.172

s.28K, varied: 2003 c.43 s.150

s.28L, added: 2003 c.43 s.172

s.28M, added: 2003 c.43 s.172

s.28N, added: 2003 c.43 s.172

s.28O, added: 2003 c.43 s.172

s.28P, added: 2003 c.43 s.172

s.28Q, added: 2003 c.43 s.175

s.28Q, applied: SI 2004/865 Art.109, Art.115

s.28Q, varied: 2003 c.43 s.150

s.28R, added: 2003 c.43 s.175

s.28R, applied: SI 2004/291 Reg.15, SI 2004/478 Reg.15

s.28R, enabling: SI 2004/291, SI 2004/478

1977–cont.

49. National Health Service Act 1977– *cont.*

s.28S, added: 2003 c.43 s.175

s.28S, applied: SI 2004/1772 Art.3, Art.4, SI 2004/1825 Art.3

s.28S, referred to: SI 2004/291 Sch.6 para.85, Sch.6 para.86, Sch.6 para.105, Sch.6 para.113, SI 2004/478 Sch.6 para.83, Sch.6 para.84, Sch.6 para.103, Sch.6 para.111, SI 2004/627 Reg.19

s.28S, enabling: SI 2004/291, SI 2004/478, SI 2004/2694

s.28T, added: 2003 c.43 s.175

s.28T, applied: SI 2004/291 Reg.22, Reg.23, SI 2004/478 Reg.22, Reg.23

s.28U, added: 2003 c.43 s.175

s.28U, applied: SI 2004/291 Sch.6 para.42, Sch.6 para.43, Sch.6 para.50, SI 2004/478 Sch.6 para.42, Sch.6 para.43, Sch.6 para.49, SI 2004/627 Sch.5 para.41, Sch.5 para.42, Sch.5 para.50

s.28U, enabling: SI 2004/629, SI 2004/1022, SI 2004/3215

s.28V, added: 2003 c.43 s.175

s.28V, enabling: SI 2004/291, SI 2004/478, SI 2004/906, SI 2004/1017, SI 2004/2694

s.28W, added: 2003 c.43 s.175

s.28W, applied: SI 2004/291 Sch.6 para.102, SI 2004/478 Sch.6 para.100

s.28W, enabling: SI 2004/291, SI 2004/478, SI 2004/2694

s.28X, added: 2003 c.43 s.179

s.28X, amended: 2003 c.43 s.179

s.28X, applied: SI 2003/3190 Reg.4, SI 2003/3279 Reg.4, SI 2004/585 Reg.8, SI 2004/1020 Reg.8

s.28X, enabling: SI 2004/585, SI 2004/1020, SI 2004/2694

s.28Y, added: 2003 c.43 s.180

s.29, amended: 2002 c.17 Sch.2 para.3, Sch.8 para.2, SI 2002/3135 Sch.1 para.8

s.29, applied: SI 2002/2202 Art.2, SI 2002/2469 Sch.12 para.2, Sch.12 para.4, SI 2002/2548 Reg.3, 2003 c.43 s.176, SI 2003/1250 Art.10, Sch.8 para.22, SI 2004/118 Art.3, SI 2004/291 Reg.29, SI 2004/433 Art.2, Art.5, Art.24, Art.26, Art.27, Art.28, Art.32, SI 2004/477 Art.2, Art.5, Art.24, Art.26, Art.28, Art.32, SI 2004/478 Reg.29, SI 2004/865 Art.2, Art.60, SI 2004/1016 Art.2, SI 2004/1772 Art.2, SI 2004/1825 Art.2

s.29, referred to: SI 2002/1882 Reg.10

s.29, repealed (in part): 2003 c.43 Sch.14 Part 4

s.29, enabling: SI 2002/551, SI 2002/554, SI 2002/916, SI 2002/1768, SI 2002/1804, SI 2002/1882, SI 2002/1896, SI 2002/2548, SI 2002/2802, SI 2002/3189, SI 2003/26, SI 2003/139, SI 2003/143, SI 2003/699, SI 2003/784, SI 2003/1005,

1977–cont.

49. National Health Service Act 1977– *cont.*

s.29, enabling:–*cont.*

SI 2003/1084, SI 2003/2624, SI 2003/ 2644, SI 2003/2863, SI 2004/1018

s.29A, amended: 2002 c.17 Sch.2 para.4

s.29A, applied: SI 2002/2469 Sch.12 para.2, Sch.12 para.4

s.29A, repealed (in part): 2003 c.43 Sch.14 Part 4

s.29A, enabling: SI 2002/554, SI 2002/916, SI 2002/1896, SI 2002/2802, SI 2003/ 2644

s.29B, amended: 2002 c.17 Sch.2 para.5, Sch.9 Part 1

s.29B, applied: SI 2002/1095 Art.4, SI 2002/ 2469 Sch.12 para.4, SI 2002/3038 Reg.5, SI 2002/3040 Reg.3, SI 2003/506 Reg.3, SI 2003/1250 Art.10, Sch.8 para.22, SI 2003/2123 Reg.4, SI 2003/2773 Reg.3, SI 2003/3060 Reg.3, SI 2003/3190 Reg.4, SI 2003/3279 Reg.4, SI 2004/570 Reg.3, SI 2004/668 Reg.3

s.29B, repealed (in part): 2003 c.43 Sch.14 Part 4

s.29B, enabling: SI 2002/554, SI 2002/916, SI 2002/1896, SI 2002/2802, SI 2003/ 2644

s.30, repealed (in part): 2003 c.43 Sch.14 Part 4

s.31, amended: 2002 c.17 Sch.2 para.6

s.31, applied: SI 2003/1250 Sch.6 para.1, SI 2003/2644 Reg.4, SI 2004/865 Art.110, SI 2004/1016 Art.86

s.31, disapplied: SI 2004/1016 Art.86

s.31, referred to: SI 2004/865 Art.110

s.31, repealed (in part): 2003 c.43 Sch.14 Part 4, SI 2003/1250 Sch.9 para.2

s.31, varied: SI 2004/865 Art.110

s.32, amended: 2002 c.17 Sch.2 para.7

s.32, disapplied: SI 2004/1016 Art.86

s.32, referred to: SI 2004/865 Art.110

s.32, repealed (in part): 2003 c.43 Sch.14 Part 4, SI 2003/1250 Sch.9 para.2

s.33, amended: 2002 c.17 Sch.2 para.8, Sch.9 Part 1

s.33, repealed (in part): 2003 c.43 Sch.14 Part 4

s.34, repealed (in part): 2003 c.43 Sch.14 Part 4

s.34A, repealed (in part): 2003 c.43 Sch.14 Part 4

s.35, amended: 2002 c.17 Sch.2 para.9

s.35, applied: 2003 c.43 s.173, SI 2004/1768 Reg.2

s.35, repealed: 2003 c.43 s.172, Sch.14 Part 4

s.35, enabling: SI 2002/558, SI 2002/918, SI 2002/1881, SI 2003/138, SI 2003/250, SI 2003/782, SI 2003/1702, SI 2003/1976, SI 2003/2863

s.36, amended: 2002 c.17 Sch.2 para.10

1977–cont.

49. National Health Service Act 1977– *cont.*

s.36, applied: SI 2002/2469 Sch.12 para.4

s.36, repealed: 2003 c.43 s.172, Sch.14 Part 4

s.36, enabling: SI 2002/558, SI 2002/918, SI 2002/1881, SI 2003/138, SI 2003/250, SI 2003/782, SI 2003/1702, SI 2003/1976, SI 2003/2863

s.37, amended: 2002 c.17 Sch.1 para.17

s.37, applied: SI 2003/2382 Reg.12

s.37, repealed: 2003 c.43 Sch.14 Part 4

s.37, enabling: SI 2002/1881, SI 2002/2353, SI 2003/250, SI 2003/1702, SI 2003/ 2382

s.38, amended: 2002 c.17 Sch.2 para.11

s.38, applied: SI 2002/2469 Sch.12 para.4, SI 2004/291 Sch.5 para.1, SI 2004/478 Sch.5 para.1, SI 2004/627 Sch.3, SI 2004/1768 Reg.2

s.38, enabling: SI 2002/547, SI 2002/601, SI 2002/917, SI 2002/1883, SI 2002/2802, SI 2003/301, SI 2003/657, SI 2003/837, SI 2003/955, SI 2003/2381, SI 2003/ 2863, SI 2004/642, SI 2004/936, SI 2004/1014, SI 2004/1042, SI 2004/1138

s.39, amended: 2002 c.17 Sch.2 para.12

s.39, applied: SI 2002/2469 Sch.12 para.4

s.39, enabling: SI 2002/601, SI 2002/917, SI 2002/1883, SI 2002/2802, SI 2003/301, SI 2003/657, SI 2003/837, SI 2003/955

s.41, amended: 2002 c.17 Sch.2 para.13, SI 2002/253 Sch.5 para.6, 2003 c.43 Sch.11 para.18, SI 2003/1590 Sch.1 para.3, SI 2004/1771 Sch.1 para.8

s.41, applied: SI 2002/327 Reg.21, SI 2004/ 1768 Reg.2

s.41, enabling: SI 2002/551, SI 2002/888, SI 2002/2016, SI 2002/2861, SI 2002/3189, SI 2003/139, SI 2003/699, SI 2003/783, SI 2003/1084, SI 2003/2624, SI 2003/ 2863, SI 2003/3236, SI 2004/922, SI 2004/1018, SI 2004/1021

s.41A, amended: 2002 c.17 Sch.2 para.14

s.41B, amended: 2002 c.17 Sch.2 para.15

s.42, amended: 2002 c.17 Sch.2 para.16

s.42, applied: SI 2002/2469 Sch.12 para.4

s.42, enabling: SI 2002/551, SI 2002/888, SI 2002/2016, SI 2002/2861, SI 2002/3189, SI 2003/139, SI 2003/699, SI 2003/783, SI 2003/1084, SI 2003/2624, SI 2003/ 2863, SI 2003/3236, SI 2004/922, SI 2004/1018, SI 2004/1021

s.43, amended: 2002 c.17 Sch.2 para.17, 2003 c.43 Sch.11 para.19

s.43, applied: SI 2002/2469 Sch.12 para.4

s.43, varied: SI 2004/288 Art.7, SI 2004/480 Art.6

s.43, enabling: SI 2002/551, SI 2002/2016, SI 2002/2861, SI 2002/3189, SI 2003/ 139, SI 2003/699, SI 2003/1084, SI 2003/2624, SI 2003/3236, SI 2004/ 922, SI 2004/1018, SI 2004/1021

1977–cont.

49. National Health Service Act 1977– *cont.*

s.43C, amended: 2002 c.17 Sch.2 para.19, Sch.8 para.3, 2003 c.43 Sch.14 Part 4

s.43C, varied: SI 2004/288 Art.7, SI 2004/480 Art.6

s.43D, amended: 2002 c.17 Sch.2 para.20, 2003 c.43 Sch.11 para.20

s.43D, applied: SI 2002/2469 Sch.12 para.2, Sch.12 para.3, Sch.12 para.4, SI 2003/250 Reg.8, SI 2003/1250 Art.10, Sch.8 para.22, SI 2003/3190 Reg.4, SI 2003/3279 Reg.4

s.43D, repealed (in part): 2003 c.43 Sch.11 para.20, Sch.14 Part 4

s.43D, varied: SI 2004/288 Art.7, SI 2004/480 Art.6

s.43D, enabling: SI 2002/848, SI 2002/1882, SI 2002/2802, SI 2003/250, SI 2003/1702, SI 2003/2644

s.43ZA, amended: 2002 c.17 Sch.2 para.18

s.43ZA, applied: SI 2002/2469 Sch.12 para.4, SI 2002/3038 Reg.5, SI 2002/3040 Reg.3, SI 2003/506 Reg.3

s.43ZA, repealed (in part): 2003 c.43 Sch.14 Part 4

s.43ZA, enabling: SI 2002/554, SI 2002/558, SI 2002/601, SI 2002/1881, SI 2002/1883, SI 2002/1896, SI 2002/2802, SI 2003/2644

s.44, amended: 2002 c.17 s.5, Sch.9 Part 1, SI 2002/2861 Reg.19, 2003 c.43 Sch.11 para.21

s.44, applied: SI 2002/553 Art.9, SI 2002/2469 Sch.12 para.5

s.44, referred to: SI 2002/2548 Reg.11

s.44, repealed (in part): 2003 c.43 Sch.11 para.21, Sch.14 Part 4

s.44, varied: SI 2004/288 Art.7, SI 2004/480 Art.6

s.45, amended: 2002 c.17 s.5, SI 2002/2861 Reg.20, 2003 c.43 Sch.11 para.22, Sch.14 Part 4

s.45, repealed (in part): 2003 c.43 Sch.11 para.22, Sch.14 Part 4

s.45, varied: SI 2004/288 Art.7, SI 2004/480 Art.6

s.45, enabling: SI 2002/2861

s.45A, added: 2003 c.43 Sch.11 para.23

s.45A, applied: SI 2004/291 Reg.27, SI 2004/478 Reg.27, SI 2004/865 Art.60, Art.104, SI 2004/1016 Art.80

s.45A, varied: SI 2004/865 Art.109, SI 2004/1016 Art.85

s.45A, enabling: SI 2004/291, SI 2004/478

s.45B, added: 2003 c.43 Sch.11 para.23

s.45B, varied: SI 2004/480 Art.6

s.46, applied: SI 2002/1920 Reg.6, SI 2002/2469 Sch.12 para.44, Sch.12 para.45, SSI 2004/386 Reg.7

s.46, varied: SI 2002/2469 Reg.16

s.49A, varied: SI 2002/2469 Reg.16

1977–cont.

49. National Health Service Act 1977– *cont.*

s.49F, amended: 2002 c.17 Sch.2 para.21

s.49F, applied: SI 2002/1920 Reg.6, SI 2002/2469 Sch.12 para.4, Sch.12 para.42, SI 2002/3038 Reg.5, SI 2002/3040 Reg.3, SI 2003/250 Reg.10, SI 2003/506 Reg.3, SI 2003/2773 Reg.3, SI 2003/3279 Reg.4, SI 2004/291 Reg.5, Sch.6 para.113, SI 2004/478 Reg.5, Sch.6 para.111, SI 2004/585 Reg.10, SI 2004/627 Reg.5, Sch.5 para.105

s.49F, referred to: SI 2002/1882 Reg.10, SI 2002/3038 Reg.5, SI 2002/3040 Reg.3, SI 2003/2123 Reg.4, SI 2003/3060 Reg.3, SI 2003/3190 Reg.4, SI 2004/570 Reg.3, SI 2004/668 Reg.3, SI 2004/1020 Reg.10

s.49F, repealed (in part): 2003 c.43 Sch.14 Part 4

s.49F, enabling: SI 2002/1881, SI 2002/1883, SI 2002/1896, SI 2002/2802

s.49G, amended: 2002 c.17 Sch.2 para.21

s.49G, applied: SI 2002/3038 Reg.5, SI 2002/3040 Reg.3, SI 2003/506 Reg.3, SI 2003/3190 Reg.4, SI 2003/3279 Reg.4

s.49H, amended: 2003 c.43 Sch.14 Part 4

s.49I, amended: 2002 c.17 Sch.2 para.21

s.49I, applied: SI 2002/1920 Reg.6, SI 2002/2469 Sch.12 para.4, Sch.12 para.43, SI 2002/3038 Reg.5, SI 2002/3040 Reg.3, SI 2003/506 Reg.3, SI 2003/3190 Reg.4, SI 2003/3279 Reg.4

s.49I, enabling: SI 2002/1881, SI 2002/1883, SI 2002/1896, SI 2002/2802

s.49J, amended: 2002 c.17 Sch.2 para.22

s.49L, amended: 2002 c.17 Sch.2 para.23

s.49L, applied: SI 2002/2469 Sch.12 para.4

s.49L, enabling: SI 2002/1881, SI 2002/1883, SI 2002/1896, SI 2002/2802

s.49M, amended: 2002 c.17 Sch.2 para.24, 2003 c.43 s.179

s.49M, applied: SI 2002/1920 Reg.3, SI 2002/2469 Sch.12 para.4, Sch.12 para.39

s.49M, enabling: SI 2002/1881, SI 2002/1883, SI 2002/1896, SI 2002/2802

s.49N, see *Kataria v Essex Strategic Health Authority* [2004] EWHC 641, [2004] 3 All E.R. 572 (QBD (Admin Ct)), Stanley Burnton, J.

s.49N, amended: 2002 c.17 Sch.2 para.25, 2003 c.43 Sch.11 para.24

s.49N, applied: SI 2002/1920 Reg.4, Reg.5, Reg.6, SI 2002/2469 Sch.12 para.4, Sch.12 para.40, SI 2002/3038 Reg.5, SI 2002/3040 Reg.3, SI 2003/506 Reg.3, SI 2003/2773 Reg.3, SI 2003/3060 Reg.3

s.49N, referred to: SI 2002/1882 Reg.20, SI 2003/250 Reg.19, SI 2004/585 Reg.19, SI 2004/1020 Reg.19

CAP.

1977–cont.

49. National Health Service Act 1977– cont.

s.49N, varied: SI 2003/250 Reg.19, SI 2003/2644 Reg.19, SI 2004/288 Art.7, SI 2004/480 Art.6, SI 2004/585 Reg.19, SI 2004/1020 Reg.19

s.49N, enabling: SI 2002/1881, SI 2002/1883, SI 2002/1896, SI 2002/2802, SI 2003/250, SI 2003/2644

s.49O, amended: 2002 c.17 Sch.2 para.26

s.49O, applied: SI 2002/2469 Sch.12 para.4

s.49O, enabling: SI 2002/554, SI 2002/558, SI 2002/601, SI 2002/1881, SI 2002/1883, SI 2002/1896, SI 2003/2644

s.49P, amended: 2002 c.17 Sch.2 para.27

s.49P, applied: SI 2002/2469 Sch.12 para.4

s.49P, enabling: SI 2002/1881, SI 2002/1883, SI 2002/1896, SI 2002/2802, SI 2003/2644

s.49Q, amended: 2002 c.17 Sch.2 para.28

s.49Q, applied: SI 2002/2469 Sch.12 para.4

s.49Q, enabling: SI 2002/554, SI 2002/558, SI 2002/601, SI 2002/1883, SI 2002/1896, SI 2002/2802, SI 2003/2644

s.49R, enabling: SI 2002/554, SI 2002/558, SI 2002/601, SI 2002/1881, SI 2002/1883, SI 2002/1896, SI 2002/2802, SI 2003/2644

s.49S, amended: 2002 c.17 Sch.1 para.18

s.49S, applied: SI 2002/3038 Reg.5, SI 2002/3040 Reg.3, SI 2003/506 Reg.3, SI 2003/2123 Reg.4, SI 2003/2773 Reg.3, SI 2003/3060 Reg.3

s.51, amended: 2002 c.17 Sch.1 para.19, Sch.5 para.15, Sch.9 Part 1

s.51, applied: SI 2002/2375 Reg.6, Reg.9, Reg.10, 2003 c.43 s.3

s.51, referred to: SI 2002/2375 Sch.1 Part 1

s.51, enabling: SI 2002/2375

s.52, amended: 2003 c.43 Sch.14 Part 4

s.52, referred to: SI 2002/2375 Sch.1 Part 2

s.52, varied: SI 2004/288 Art.7, SI 2004/480 Art.6

s.53, repealed (in part): 2003 c.43 Sch.14 Part 4

s.54, amended: 2002 c.17 Sch.2 para.29, 2003 c.43 Sch.11 para.26

s.54, applied: SI 2004/291 Sch.6 para.69, SI 2004/478 Sch.6 para.68

s.54, referred to: SI 2004/627 Sch.5 para.69

s.54, varied: SI 2004/865 Art.109, SI 2004/1016 Art.85

s.54, enabling: SI 2004/906, SI 2004/1017

s.56, amended: 2002 c.17 Sch.2 para.30

s.56, repealed (in part): 2003 c.43 Sch.14 Part 4

s.63, amended: 2003 c.43 Sch.4 para.28

s.63, referred to: SI 2002/2375 Sch.1 Part 2

s.65, amended: 2002 c.17 Sch.1 para.20, 2003 c.43 Sch.4 para.29

CAP.

1977–cont.

49. National Health Service Act 1977– cont.

s.65, applied: SI 2004/291 Sch.5 para.1, SI 2004/478 Sch.5 para.1, SI 2004/627 Sch.3

s.65, enabling: SI 2002/1896

s.72, amended: 2003 c.43 Sch.11 para.27, Sch.14 Part 4

s.72, applied: SI 2004/865 Art.40, SI 2004/1016 Art.37

s.72, referred to: SI 2002/2375 Sch.1 Part 2

s.72, substituted: 2003 c.43 Sch.11 para.27

s.72, varied: SI 2004/288 Art.7, SI 2004/480 Art.6, SI 2004/865 Art.109, SI 2004/1016 Art.85

s.77, amended: 2003 c.43 Sch.11 para.28

s.77, enabling: SI 2002/548, SI 2002/1386, SI 2002/2352, SI 2003/585, SI 2003/699, SI 2003/1084, SI 2003/2624, SI 2004/663, SI 2004/1018, SI 2004/1605

s.78, amended: 2003 c.43 Sch.11 para.29, Sch.14 Part 4

s.78, repealed (in part): 2003 c.43 Sch.14 Part 4

s.78, enabling: SI 2002/35, SI 2002/547, SI 2002/917, SI 2002/2353, SI 2003/301, SI 2003/657, SI 2003/955, SI 2003/2381, SI 2004/642, SI 2004/936, SI 2004/1042

s.78A, substituted: 2003 c.43 s.183

s.78A, enabling: SI 2004/1091

s.79, substituted: 2003 c.43 s.183

s.79, varied: 2003 c.43 s.183

s.79, enabling: SI 2002/2353, SI 2003/138

s.79A, substituted: 2003 c.43 s.183

s.79A, enabling: SI 2002/544, SI 2002/2353, SI 2003/138, SI 2003/586, SI 2004/1091

s.81, amended: 2003 c.43 Sch.4 para.30

s.81, repealed (in part): 2003 c.43 Sch.14 Part 4

s.82, amended: 2003 c.43 Sch.4 para.31

s.82, repealed (in part): 2003 c.43 Sch.14 Part 4

s.82, enabling: SI 2002/2353

s.83, amended: 2002 c.17 Sch.2 para.31, 2003 c.43 Sch.11 para.30

s.83, repealed (in part): 2003 c.43 Sch.14 Part 4

s.83, enabling: SI 2002/2352

s.83A, amended: 2002 c.17 Sch.2 para.32, 2003 c.43 Sch.4 para.32, Sch.11 para.31

s.83A, enabling: SI 2002/548, SI 2002/580, SI 2002/2352, SI 2002/2353, SI 2003/671, SI 2003/975, SI 2003/1084, SI 2003/2382, SI 2003/2561, SI 2004/663, SI 2004/871, SI 2004/936, SI 2004/1018, SI 2004/1042

s.84, see *R. (on the application of Howard) v Secretary of State for Health* [2002] EWHC 396, [2003] Q.B. 830 (QBD (Admin Ct)), Scott Baker, J.

197

1977–cont.

49. National Health Service Act 1977– *cont.*

s.84, amended: 2003 c.43 Sch.4 para.33

s.84A, amended: 2002 c.17 Sch.1 para.21, Sch.5 para.16

s.84B, amended: 2002 c.17 Sch.1 para.22, Sch.5 para.17

s.85, amended: 2002 c.17 Sch.1 para.23, Sch.5 para.18, 2003 c.43 Sch.11 para.32

s.85, repealed (in part): 2003 c.43 Sch.11 para.32, Sch.14 Part 4

s.85, varied: SI 2002/2861 Reg.21

s.86, varied: SI 2002/2861 Reg.22

s.87, referred to: SI 2002/2375 Sch.2

s.90, amended: 2002 c.17 Sch.1 para.24

s.91, amended: 2002 c.17 Sch.1 para.25, 2003 c.43 Sch.4 para.34

s.92, amended: 2002 c.17 Sch.1 para.26, Sch.2 para.33, Sch.5 para.19, 2003 c.43 Sch.4 para.35

s.92, applied: SI 2002/553 Art.4, SI 2002/560, SI 2002/562, SI 2002/563, SI 2002/564, SI 2002/565, SI 2002/566, SI 2002/567, SI 2002/568, SI 2002/569, SI 2002/570, SI 2002/571, SI 2002/572, SI 2002/573, SI 2002/574, SI 2002/575, SI 2002/576, SI 2002/577, SI 2002/578, SI 2002/581, SI 2002/582, SI 2002/583, SI 2002/584, SI 2002/585, SI 2002/586, SI 2002/587, SI 2002/588, SI 2002/589, SI 2002/590, SI 2002/591, SI 2002/592, SI 2002/594, SI 2002/595, SI 2002/596, SI 2002/597, SI 2002/598, SI 2002/599, SI 2002/600, SI 2002/604, SI 2002/605, SI 2002/606, SI 2002/607, SI 2002/608, SI 2002/609, SI 2002/619, SI 2002/620, SI 2002/621, SI 2002/622, SI 2002/623, SI 2002/624, SI 2002/625, SI 2002/626, SI 2002/627, SI 2002/628, SI 2002/630, SI 2002/631, SI 2002/847, SI 2002/850, SI 2002/851, SI 2002/852, SI 2002/853, SI 2002/854, SI 2002/855, SI 2002/856, SI 2002/858, SI 2002/861, SI 2002/862, SI 2002/863, SI 2002/864, SI 2002/866, SI 2002/867, SI 2002/869, SI 2002/870, SI 2002/871, SI 2002/872, SI 2002/873, SI 2002/874, SI 2002/875, SI 2002/876, SI 2002/877, SI 2002/878, SI 2002/879, SI 2002/1692, SI 2002/2269, SI 2002/2270, SI 2002/2271, SI 2002/2272, SI 2002/2273, SI 2002/2274, SI 2002/2275, SI 2002/2276, SI 2002/2277, SI 2002/2278, SI 2002/2279, SI 2002/2280, SI 2002/2281, SI 2002/2282, SI 2002/2283, SI 2003/613, SI 2003/614, SI 2003/615, SI 2003/616, SI 2003/618, SI 2003/619, SI 2003/620, SI 2003/621, SI 2003/623, SI 2003/624, SI 2003/632, SI 2003/633, SI 2003/3189, SI 2004/436, SI 2004/465, SI 2004/466, SI 2004/467, SI 2004/468, SI 2004/471, SI 2004/541, SI 2004/542, SI 2004/563, SI 2004/2605, SI 2004/2606

1977–cont.

49. National Health Service Act 1977– *cont.*

s.92, enabling: SI 2002/560, SI 2002/562, SI 2002/563, SI 2002/564, SI 2002/565, SI 2002/566, SI 2002/567, SI 2002/568, SI 2002/569, SI 2002/570, SI 2002/571, SI 2002/572, SI 2002/573, SI 2002/574, SI 2002/575, SI 2002/576, SI 2002/577, SI 2002/578, SI 2002/579, SI 2002/581, SI 2002/582, SI 2002/583, SI 2002/584, SI 2002/585, SI 2002/586, SI 2002/587, SI 2002/588, SI 2002/589, SI 2002/590, SI 2002/591, SI 2002/592, SI 2002/593, SI 2002/594, SI 2002/595, SI 2002/596, SI 2002/597, SI 2002/598, SI 2002/599, SI 2002/600, SI 2002/604, SI 2002/605, SI 2002/606, SI 2002/607, SI 2002/608, SI 2002/609, SI 2002/619, SI 2002/620, SI 2002/621, SI 2002/622, SI 2002/623, SI 2002/624, SI 2002/625, SI 2002/626, SI 2002/627, SI 2002/628, SI 2002/630, SI 2002/631, SI 2002/632, SI 2002/633, SI 2002/636, SI 2002/847, SI 2002/850, SI 2002/851, SI 2002/852, SI 2002/853, SI 2002/854, SI 2002/855, SI 2002/856, SI 2002/857, SI 2002/858, SI 2002/859, SI 2002/861, SI 2002/862, SI 2002/863, SI 2002/864, SI 2002/866, SI 2002/867, SI 2002/869, SI 2002/870, SI 2002/871, SI 2002/872, SI 2002/873, SI 2002/874, SI 2002/875, SI 2002/876, SI 2002/877, SI 2002/878, SI 2002/879, SI 2002/1692, SI 2002/2269, SI 2002/2270, SI 2002/2271, SI 2002/2272, SI 2002/2273, SI 2002/2274, SI 2002/2275, SI 2002/2276, SI 2002/2277, SI 2002/2278, SI 2002/2279, SI 2002/2280, SI 2002/2281, SI 2002/2282, SI 2002/2283, SI 2003/613, SI 2003/614, SI 2003/615, SI 2003/616, SI 2003/618, SI 2003/619, SI 2003/620, SI 2003/621, SI 2003/623, SI 2003/624, SI 2003/632, SI 2003/633, SI 2003/3189, SI 2004/436, SI 2004/465, SI 2004/466, SI 2004/467, SI 2004/468, SI 2004/471, SI 2004/541, SI 2004/542, SI 2004/563, SI 2004/1607, SI 2004/2605, SI 2004/2606

s.96, amended: 2002 c.17 Sch.1 para.27

s.96, varied: 2003 c.43 Sch.4 para.36

s.96, enabling: SI 2004/465, SI 2004/466, SI 2004/467, SI 2004/468, SI 2004/471, SI 2004/541, SI 2004/542, SI 2004/563, SI 2004/2605, SI 2004/2606

s.96A, amended: 2002 c.17 Sch.1 para.28, Sch.2 para.34, Sch.5 para.20, 2003 c.43 Sch.4 para.37

s.96C, applied: SI 2002/2375 Reg.8

s.96C, referred to: SI 2002/2375 Sch.1 Part 2

s.97, amended: 2002 c.17 s.7, s.10

s.97, repealed (in part): 2002 c.17 Sch.9 Part 1

s.97, varied: SI 2002/2478 Art.4

s.97A, amended: 2002 c.17 Sch.8 para.4

s.97AA, amended: 2002 c.17 Sch.8 para.5

1977–cont.

49. National Health Service Act 1977–
cont.

s.97C, substituted: 2002 c.17 s.8

s.97C, varied: SI 2002/2478 Art.4

s.97D, amended: 2002 c.17 Sch.9 Part 3

s.97E, amended: 2002 c.17 Sch.8 para.7

s.97F, added: 2002 c.17 s.9

s.97G, added: 2002 c.17 s.9

s.97H, added: 2002 c.17 s.9

s.98, amended: 2002 c.17 Sch.1 para.29, Sch.5 para.21, 2003 c.43 Sch.11 para.33, Sch.14 Part 4, SI 2003/1324 Sch.2 para.1, 2004 c.23 Sch.2 para.2, SI 2004/1714 Sch.2 para.1

s.98, applied: SI 2002/553 Art.5, 2004 c.23 s.61

s.98, disapplied: SI 2003/983 Art.2, SI 2004/1416 Art.2

s.98, repealed (in part): 2003 c.4 Sch.4, 2003 c.43 Sch.11 para.33, Sch.14 Part 4

s.99, amended: 2002 c.17 Sch.1 para.30, Sch.5 para.22, 2003 c.43 Sch.11 para.34

s.99, repealed (in part): 2003 c.43 Sch.11 para.34, Sch.14 Part 4

s.100, amended: 2003 c.43 Sch.11 para.35

s.100, repealed (in part): 2003 c.43 Sch.11 para.35, Sch.14 Part 4

s.102, repealed (in part): 2003 c.43 Sch.14 Part 4, SI 2003/1250 Sch.9 para.2

s.103, amended: 2002 c.17 Sch.2 para.35, Sch.9 Part 1, SI 2002/2861 Reg.23, 2003 c.43 Sch.4 para.38, Sch.11 para.36, Sch.14 Part 4

s.103, repealed (in part): 2002 c.17 Sch.9 Part 1

s.103, varied: SI 2004/288 Art.7, SI 2004/480 Art.6

s.104, amended: 2002 c.17 Sch.8 para.8

s.105, amended: 2002 c.17 Sch.8 para.9, 2003 c.43 Sch.4 para.39, Sch.11 para.37

s.121, referred to: SI 2002/2375 Sch.1 Part 2

s.121, enabling: SI 2004/614, SI 2004/1433

s.122, amended: 2003 c.43 Sch.4 para.40

s.124, amended: 2002 c.17 Sch.2 para.36

s.124A, amended: 2002 c.38 Sch.3 para.20, Sch.5

s.125, amended: 2002 c.17 Sch.1 para.31, Sch.5 para.23, Sch.9 Part 1, 2003 c.43 Sch.4 para.41, Sch.14 Part 1

s.125, repealed (in part): 2003 c.43 Sch.14 Part 1

s.126, amended: 2002 c.17 s.6, Sch.1 para.32, Sch.8 para.10, Sch.9 Part 1, 2003 c.4 s.1, 2003 c.43 s.183, Sch.11 para.38, Sch.14 Part 4

s.126, repealed (in part): 2002 c.17 s.6, SI 2003/1250 Sch.9 para.2

s.126, enabling: SI 2002/34, SI 2002/35, SI 2002/38, SI 2002/64, SI 2002/65, SI 2002/66, SI 2002/67, SI 2002/68, SI 2002/69, SI 2002/70, SI 2002/71, SI

1977–cont.

49. National Health Service Act 1977–
cont.

s.126, enabling:–*cont.*

2002/137, SI 2002/138, SI 2002/139, SI 2002/140, SI 2002/141, SI 2002/142, SI 2002/143, SI 2002/144, SI 2002/145, SI 2002/146, SI 2002/147, SI 2002/148, SI 2002/149, SI 2002/150, SI 2002/166, SI 2002/186, SI 2002/308, SI 2002/356, SI 2002/357, SI 2002/358, SI 2002/442, SI 2002/545, SI 2002/547, SI 2002/548, SI 2002/553, SI 2002/554, SI 2002/555, SI 2002/556, SI 2002/557, SI 2002/558, SI 2002/559, SI 2002/560, SI 2002/562, SI 2002/563, SI 2002/564, SI 2002/565, SI 2002/566, SI 2002/567, SI 2002/568, SI 2002/569, SI 2002/570, SI 2002/571, SI 2002/572, SI 2002/573, SI 2002/574, SI 2002/575, SI 2002/576, SI 2002/577, SI 2002/578, SI 2002/579, SI 2002/580, SI 2002/581, SI 2002/582, SI 2002/583, SI 2002/584, SI 2002/585, SI 2002/586, SI 2002/587, SI 2002/588, SI 2002/589, SI 2002/590, SI 2002/591, SI 2002/592, SI 2002/593, SI 2002/594, SI 2002/595, SI 2002/596, SI 2002/597, SI 2002/598, SI 2002/599, SI 2002/600, SI 2002/601, SI 2002/604, SI 2002/605, SI 2002/606, SI 2002/607, SI 2002/608, SI 2002/609, SI 2002/616, SI 2002/617, SI 2002/619, SI 2002/620, SI 2002/621, SI 2002/622, SI 2002/623, SI 2002/624, SI 2002/625, SI 2002/626, SI 2002/627, SI 2002/628, SI 2002/630, SI 2002/631, SI 2002/632, SI 2002/633, SI 2002/634, SI 2002/636, SI 2002/647, SI 2002/722, SI 2002/723, SI 2002/724, SI 2002/725, SI 2002/726, SI 2002/727, SI 2002/728, SI 2002/729, SI 2002/730, SI 2002/731, SI 2002/847, SI 2002/850, SI 2002/851, SI 2002/852, SI 2002/853, SI 2002/854, SI 2002/855, SI 2002/856, SI 2002/857, SI 2002/858, SI 2002/859, SI 2002/861, SI 2002/862, SI 2002/863, SI 2002/864, SI 2002/866, SI 2002/867, SI 2002/869, SI 2002/870, SI 2002/871, SI 2002/872, SI 2002/873, SI 2002/874, SI 2002/875, SI 2002/876, SI 2002/877, SI 2002/878, SI 2002/879, SI 2002/888, SI 2002/891, SI 2002/893, SI 2002/894, SI 2002/895, SI 2002/916, SI 2002/917, SI 2002/918, SI 2002/938, SI 2002/939, SI 2002/940, SI 2002/941, SI 2002/942, SI 2002/943, SI 2002/944, SI 2002/945, SI 2002/946, SI 2002/947, SI 2002/948, SI 2002/949, SI 2002/950, SI 2002/951, SI 2002/957, SI 2002/958, SI 2002/959, SI 2002/960, SI 2002/980, SI 2002/981, SI 2002/982, SI 2002/983, SI 2002/984, SI 2002/985, SI 2002/986, SI 2002/987, SI 2002/988, SI 2002/989, SI 2002/990, SI 2002/991, SI 2002/992, SI 2002/993, SI 2002/994, SI 2002/995, SI 2002/996, SI 2002/997, SI 2002/998, SI

CAP.

2002/999, SI 2002/1000, SI 2002/1001, SI 2002/1002, SI 2002/1003, SI 2002/1004, SI 2002/1005, SI 2002/1006, SI 2002/1007, SI 2002/1008, SI 2002/1009, SI 2002/1010, SI 2002/1073, SI 2002/1112, SI 2002/1113, SI 2002/1114, SI 2002/1115, SI 2002/1116, SI 2002/1117, SI 2002/1118, SI 2002/1119, SI 2002/1120, SI 2002/1121, SI 2002/1122, SI 2002/1123, SI 2002/1133, SI 2002/1234, SI 2002/1235, SI 2002/1243, SI 2002/1244, SI 2002/1293, SI 2002/1294, SI 2002/1295, SI 2002/1296, SI 2002/1297, SI 2002/1313, SI 2002/1322, SI 2002/1323, SI 2002/1324, SI 2002/1325, SI 2002/1335, SI 2002/1337, SI 2002/1338, SI 2002/1341, SI 2002/1342, SI 2002/1360, SI 2002/1361, SI 2002/1362, SI 2002/1363, SI 2002/1364, SI 2002/1386, SI 2002/1392, SI 2002/1393, SI 2002/1405, SI 2002/1437, SI 2002/1489, SI 2002/1490, SI 2002/1491, SI 2002/1492, SI 2002/1494, SI 2002/1495, SI 2002/1496, SI 2002/1497, SI 2002/1498, SI 2002/1499, SI 2002/1500, SI 2002/1506, SI 2002/1615, SI 2002/1690, SI 2002/1692, SI 2002/1759, SI 2002/1760, SI 2002/1768, SI 2002/1791, SI 2002/1804, SI 2002/1881, SI 2002/1882, SI 2002/1883, SI 2002/1896, SI 2002/1921, SI 2002/2016, SI 2002/2025, SI 2002/2073, SI 2002/2106, SI 2002/2199, SI 2002/2233, SI 2002/2269, SI 2002/2270, SI 2002/2271, SI 2002/2272, SI 2002/2273, SI 2002/2274, SI 2002/2275, SI 2002/2276, SI 2002/2277, SI 2002/2278, SI 2002/2279, SI 2002/2280, SI 2002/2281, SI 2002/2282, SI 2002/2283, SI 2002/2352, SI 2002/2353, SI 2002/2375, SI 2002/2397, SI 2002/2419, SI 2002/2420, SI 2002/2548, SI 2002/2616, SI 2002/2617, SI 2002/2621, SI 2002/2802, SI 2002/2861, SI 2002/3040, SI 2002/3048, SI 2002/3189, SI 2003/26, SI 2003/138, SI 2003/139, SI 2003/143, SI 2003/148, SI 2003/150, SI 2003/216, SI 2003/250, SI 2003/301, SI 2003/506, SI 2003/585, SI 2003/613, SI 2003/614, SI 2003/615, SI 2003/616, SI 2003/617, SI 2003/618, SI 2003/619, SI 2003/620, SI 2003/621, SI 2003/622, SI 2003/623, SI 2003/624, SI 2003/629, SI 2003/632, SI 2003/633, SI 2003/657, SI 2003/671, SI 2003/699, SI 2003/759, SI 2003/760, SI 2003/782, SI 2003/783, SI 2003/784, SI 2003/791, SI 2003/792, SI 2003/815, SI 2003/816, SI 2003/817, SI 2003/818, SI 2003/834, SI 2003/837, SI 2003/844, SI 2003/866, SI 2003/868, SI 2003/955, SI 2003/975, SI 2003/993, SI 2003/1005, SI 2003/1063, SI 2003/1064, SI 2003/1066, SI 2003/1067, SI 2003/1077, SI 2003/1084, SI 2003/1096, SI 2003/1276, SI 2003/1496, SI 2003/

CAP.

1977–cont.

49. National Health Service Act 1977–*cont.*

s.126, enabling:–*cont.*

1497, SI 2003/1499, SI 2003/1500, SI 2003/1501, SI 2003/1587, SI 2003/1616, SI 2003/1617, SI 2003/1702, SI 2003/1740, SI 2003/1827, SI 2003/1976, SI 2003/1983, SI 2003/2149, SI 2003/2150, SI 2003/2168, SI 2003/2344, SI 2003/2345, SI 2003/2346, SI 2003/2381, SI 2003/2382, SI 2003/2427, SI 2003/2434, SI 2003/2561, SI 2003/2624, SI 2003/2644, SI 2003/2649, SI 2003/2662, SI 2003/2663, SI 2003/2664, SI 2003/2766, SI 2003/2773, SI 2003/2863, SI 2003/2944, SI 2003/3060, SI 2003/3189, SI 2003/3236, SI 2004/17, SI 2004/18, SI 2004/19, SI 2004/20, SI 2004/21, SI 2004/37, SI 2004/75, SI 2004/291, SI 2004/465, SI 2004/466, SI 2004/467, SI 2004/468, SI 2004/469, SI 2004/471, SI 2004/478, SI 2004/487, SI 2004/541, SI 2004/542, SI 2004/543, SI 2004/563, SI 2004/570, SI 2004/585, SI 2004/614, SI 2004/627, SI 2004/629, SI 2004/642, SI 2004/648, SI 2004/663, SI 2004/668, SI 2004/766, SI 2004/864, SI 2004/871, SI 2004/904, SI 2004/905, SI 2004/906, SI 2004/922, SI 2004/936, SI 2004/951, SI 2004/1014, SI 2004/1017, SI 2004/1018, SI 2004/1020, SI 2004/1021, SI 2004/1022, SI 2004/1042, SI 2004/1091, SI 2004/1138, SI 2004/1390, SI 2004/1413, SI 2004/1427, SI 2004/1433, SI 2004/1605, SI 2004/1607, SI 2004/1624, SI 2004/1625, SI 2004/1626, SI 2004/1630, SI 2004/1643, SI 2004/1659, SI 2004/2147, SI 2004/2248, SI 2004/2391, SI 2004/2394, SI 2004/2397, SI 2004/2605, SI 2004/2606, SI 2004/2694, SI 2004/2893, SI 2004/2894, SI 2004/2895, SI 2004/2896, SI 2004/2897, SI 2004/2898, SI 2004/3215, SI 2004/3365

s.127, amended: 2003 c.43 Sch.13 para.4, Sch.14 Part 7

s.127, enabling: SI 2002/917, SI 2003/301, SI 2003/955

s.128, amended: 2002 c.17 Sch.1 para.33, SI 2002/2861 Reg.24, 2003 c.43 Sch.4 para.42, Sch.11 para.39, Sch.14 Part 4

s.128, varied: SI 2004/288 Art.7, SI 2004/480 Art.6

s.128, enabling: SI 2002/556, SI 2002/580, SI 2003/301, SI 2003/975, SI 2003/2561, SI 2004/871, SI 2004/1042

Sch.1, applied: SI 2002/2375 Reg.3

Sch.1 para.1, amended: 2003 c.43 Sch.14 Part 4

Sch.1 para.1, referred to: SI 2002/2375 Sch.1 Part 2

Sch.1 para.2, amended: 2003 c.43 Sch.14 Part 4

1977–cont.

49. National Health Service Act 1977– cont.

Sch.1 para.3, amended: 2003 c.43 Sch.14 Part 4

Sch.1 para.4, amended: 2003 c.43 Sch.14 Part 4

Sch.1 para.25, amended: 2003 c.43 Sch.14 Part 4

Sch.1 para.60, amended: 2003 c.43 Sch.14 Part 4

Sch.2, applied: SI 2002/2005 Reg.9, Reg.13

Sch.2 para.1, referred to: SI 2002/2375 Sch.1 Part 2

Sch.2 para.2, referred to: SI 2002/2375 Sch.1 Part 2

Sch.3 Part I para.1, repealed: 2003 c.43 Sch.13 para.4, Sch.14 Part 7

Sch.3 Part I para.2, repealed: 2003 c.43 Sch.13 para.4, Sch.14 Part 7

Sch.3 Part I para.3, repealed: 2003 c.43 Sch.13 para.4, Sch.14 Part 7

Sch.3 Part I para.4, repealed: 2003 c.43 Sch.13 para.4, Sch.14 Part 7

Sch.3 Part I para.5, repealed: 2003 c.43 Sch.13 para.4, Sch.14 Part 7

Sch.3 Part I para.6, repealed: 2003 c.43 Sch.13 para.4, Sch.14 Part 7

Sch.3 Part I para.7, repealed: 2003 c.43 Sch.13 para.4, Sch.14 Part 7

Sch.3 Part I para.8, repealed: 2003 c.43 Sch.13 para.4, Sch.14 Part 7

Sch.3 Part I para.9, repealed: 2003 c.43 Sch.13 para.4, Sch.14 Part 7

Sch.3 Part I para.10, repealed: 2003 c.43 Sch.13 para.4, Sch.14 Part 7

Sch.3 Part II para.11, repealed: 2003 c.43 Sch.13 para.4, Sch.14 Part 7

Sch.3 Part II para.12, repealed: 2003 c.43 Sch.13 para.4, Sch.14 Part 7

Sch.3 Part II para.13, repealed: 2003 c.43 Sch.13 para.4, Sch.14 Part 7

Sch.3 Part II para.14, repealed: 2003 c.43 Sch.13 para.4, Sch.14 Part 7

Sch.3 Part II para.15, repealed: 2003 c.43 Sch.13 para.4, Sch.14 Part 7

Sch.3 Part II para.16, repealed: 2003 c.43 Sch.13 para.4, Sch.14 Part 7

Sch.3 Part II para.17, repealed: 2003 c.43 Sch.13 para.4, Sch.14 Part 7

Sch.3 Part II para.18, repealed: 2003 c.43 Sch.13 para.4, Sch.14 Part 7

Sch.5, referred to: 2003 c.43 s.187

Sch.5 Part I para.1, amended: 2002 c.17 Sch.1 para.34

Sch.5 Part I para.2, amended: 2002 c.17 Sch.1 para.34

Sch.5 Part I para.2, enabling: SI 2002/556

Sch.5 Part I para.2, amended: 2002 c.17 Sch.1 para.34

Sch.5 Part I para.3, amended: 2002 c.17 Sch.1 para.34

1977–cont.

49. National Health Service Act 1977– cont.

Sch.5 Part I para.3, enabling: SI 2002/556

Sch.5 Part I para.3, amended: 2002 c.17 Sch.1 para.34

Sch.5 Part I para.4, amended: 2002 c.17 Sch.1 para.34

Sch.5 Part I para.4A, added: 2002 c.17 Sch.1 para.34

Sch.5 Part I para.4A, amended: 2002 c.17 Sch.1 para.34

Sch.5 Part I para.5, amended: 2002 c.17 Sch.1 para.34

Sch.5 Part III para.8, amended: 2002 c.17 Sch.1 para.34

Sch.5 Part III para.9, amended: 2002 c.17 Sch.1 para.34

Sch.5 Part III para.9, applied: SI 2002/3039 Art.5, SI 2002/3040 Reg.10, SI 2003/505 Art.5, SI 2003/506 Reg.10, SI 2003/2772 Art.5, SI 2003/3059 Art.5, SI 2004/569 Art.5, SI 2004/570 Reg.10, SI 2004/667 Art.5

Sch.5 Part III para.9, referred to: SI 2002/2375 Sch.2, Sch.3

Sch.5 Part III para.9, enabling: SI 2002/3039, SI 2003/505, SI 2003/2772, SI 2003/3059, SI 2004/569, SI 2004/667

Sch.5 Part III para.10, enabling: SI 2003/2773, SI 2003/3060, SI 2004/17, SI 2004/20, SI 2004/21, SI 2004/570, SI 2004/668, SI 2004/3365

Sch.5 Part III para.12, enabling: SI 2002/34, SI 2002/556, SI 2002/1759, SI 2002/3040, SI 2003/506, SI 2003/2773, SI 2003/3060, SI 2004/17, SI 2004/20, SI 2004/21, SI 2004/570, SI 2004/668, SI 2004/3365

Sch.5 Part III para.16, enabling: SI 2002/3040, SI 2003/506, SI 2003/2773, SI 2003/3060, SI 2004/570, SI 2004/668

Sch.5A Part I para.1, applied: SI 2002/2233 Art.1

Sch.5A Part I para.1, enabling: SI 2002/64, SI 2002/65, SI 2002/66, SI 2002/67, SI 2002/68, SI 2002/69, SI 2002/70, SI 2002/71, SI 2002/137, SI 2002/138, SI 2002/139, SI 2002/140, SI 2002/141, SI 2002/142, SI 2002/143, SI 2002/144, SI 2002/145, SI 2002/146, SI 2002/147, SI 2002/148, SI 2002/149, SI 2002/150, SI 2002/166, SI 2002/356, SI 2002/357, SI 2002/358, SI 2002/616, SI 2002/617, SI 2002/634, SI 2002/722, SI 2002/723, SI 2002/724, SI 2002/725, SI 2002/726, SI 2002/727, SI 2002/728, SI 2002/893, SI 2002/894, SI 2002/895, SI 2002/938, SI 2002/939, SI 2002/940, SI 2002/941, SI 2002/942, SI 2002/943, SI 2002/944, SI 2002/945, SI 2002/946, SI 2002/947, SI 2002/948, SI 2002/949, SI 2002/950, SI 2002/951, SI 2002/957, SI 2002/958, SI

CAP.

1977–cont.

49. National Health Service Act 1977– cont.

Sch.5A Part I para.1, enabling:–*cont.*

2002/959, SI 2002/960, SI 2002/980, SI 2002/981, SI 2002/982, SI 2002/983, SI 2002/984, SI 2002/985, SI 2002/986, SI 2002/987, SI 2002/988, SI 2002/989, SI 2002/990, SI 2002/991, SI 2002/992, SI 2002/993, SI 2002/994, SI 2002/995, SI 2002/996, SI 2002/997, SI 2002/998, SI 2002/999, SI 2002/1000, SI 2002/1001, SI 2002/1002, SI 2002/1003, SI 2002/1004, SI 2002/1005, SI 2002/1006, SI 2002/1007, SI 2002/1010, SI 2002/1116, SI 2002/1117, SI 2002/1119, SI 2002/1121, SI 2002/1122, SI 2002/1123, SI 2002/1133, SI 2002/2233, SI 2003/1064, SI 2003/1067, SI 2003/1983, SI 2003/2168, SI 2003/2649, SI 2003/2662, SI 2003/2663, SI 2003/2664, SI 2003/2766, SI 2003/2944

Sch.5A Part I para.2, amended: 2002 c.17 s.2

Sch.5A Part I para.2, applied: SI 2002/2233 Art.1

Sch.5A Part I para.2, enabling: SI 2002/64, SI 2002/65, SI 2002/66, SI 2002/67, SI 2002/68, SI 2002/69, SI 2002/70, SI 2002/71, SI 2002/137, SI 2002/138, SI 2002/139, SI 2002/140, SI 2002/141, SI 2002/142, SI 2002/143, SI 2002/144, SI 2002/145, SI 2002/146, SI 2002/147, SI 2002/148, SI 2002/149, SI 2002/150, SI 2002/166, SI 2002/356, SI 2002/357, SI 2002/358, SI 2002/616, SI 2002/617, SI 2002/634, SI 2002/722, SI 2002/723, SI 2002/724, SI 2002/725, SI 2002/726, SI 2002/727, SI 2002/728, SI 2002/894, SI 2002/895, SI 2002/938, SI 2002/939, SI 2002/940, SI 2002/941, SI 2002/942, SI 2002/943, SI 2002/944, SI 2002/945, SI 2002/946, SI 2002/947, SI 2002/949, SI 2002/951, SI 2002/957, SI 2002/958, SI 2002/959, SI 2002/980, SI 2002/997, SI 2002/1116, SI 2002/2233

Sch.5A Part II para.5, enabling: SI 2002/38, SI 2002/557, SI 2003/1616, SI 2004/18, SI 2004/3365

Sch.5A Part II para.8, enabling: SI 2004/3365

Sch.5A Part II para.10, amended: 2002 c.17 Sch.1 para.35

Sch.5A Part II para.10A, added: 2002 c.17 Sch.2 para.37

Sch.5A Part III para.13, amended: SI 2003/1937 Sch.1 para.1

Sch.5A Part III para.16, amended: 2002 c.17 s.2

Sch.5A Part III para.20, amended: 2002 c.17 Sch.1 para.35, 2003 c.43 Sch.4 para.43

Sch.5A Part IV para.21, amended: 2002 c.17 Sch.1 para.35

CAP.

1977–cont.

49. National Health Service Act 1977– cont.

Sch.5A Part V para.23, amended: 2002 c.17 Sch.1 para.35

Sch.5A Part V para.23, applied: SI 2002/2819 Reg.2, Reg.5

Sch.5B Part I para.1, added: 2002 c.17 Sch.4

Sch.5B Part I para.1, enabling: SI 2003/148

Sch.5B Part I para.2, added: 2002 c.17 Sch.4

Sch.5B Part I para.2, enabling: SI 2003/148

Sch.5B Part II para.3, added: 2002 c.17 Sch.4

Sch.5B Part II para.4, added: 2002 c.17 Sch.4

Sch.5B Part II para.5, added: 2002 c.17 Sch.4

Sch.5B Part II para.6, added: 2002 c.17 Sch.4

Sch.5B Part II para.6, enabling: SI 2003/149

Sch.5B Part II para.7, added: 2002 c.17 Sch.4

Sch.5B Part II para.8, added: 2002 c.17 Sch.4

Sch.5B Part II para.9, added: 2002 c.17 Sch.4

Sch.5B Part II para.10, added: 2002 c.17 Sch.4

Sch.5B Part II para.11, added: 2002 c.17 Sch.4

Sch.5B Part II para.12, added: 2002 c.17 Sch.4

Sch.5B Part II para.12, applied: SI 2003/149 Reg.15

Sch.5B Part III para.13, added: 2002 c.17 Sch.4

Sch.5B Part III para.14, added: 2002 c.17 Sch.4

Sch.5B Part III para.15, added: 2002 c.17 Sch.4

Sch.5B Part III para.16, added: 2002 c.17 Sch.4

Sch.5B Part III para.17, added: 2002 c.17 Sch.4

Sch.5B Part III para.18, added: 2002 c.17 Sch.4

Sch.5B Part III para.19, added: 2002 c.17 Sch.4

Sch.5B Part III para.20, added: 2002 c.17 Sch.4

Sch.5B Part III para.20, applied: SI 2003/473

Sch.5B Part III para.20, enabling: SI 2003/473

Sch.5B Part III para.21, added: 2002 c.17 Sch.4

Sch.5B Part III para.21, enabling: SI 2003/473

Sch.5B Part III para.22, added: 2002 c.17 Sch.4

Sch.5B Part III para.22, enabling: SI 2003/818

Sch.5B Part III para.23, added: 2002 c.17 Sch.4

Sch.5B Part III para.24, added: 2002 c.17 Sch.4

Sch.5B Part III para.25, added: 2002 c.17 Sch.4

Sch.5B Part III para.26, added: 2002 c.17 Sch.4

Sch.7, applied: SI 2002/2202 Art.2

Sch.7, referred to: SI 2003/2660 Art.2

1977–cont.

49. National Health Service Act 1977– *cont.*

Sch.7 para.1, repealed (in part): 2003 c.4 Sch.4

Sch.7 para.2, amended: 2002 c.17 Sch.5 para.24

Sch.7 para.2, repealed (in part): 2003 c.4 Sch.4

Sch.7 para.2, enabling: SI 2002/2106

Sch.7 para.3, repealed (in part): 2003 c.4 Sch.4

Sch.7 para.4, repealed (in part): 2003 c.4 Sch.4

Sch.7 para.5, applied: 2002 c.17 s.22

Sch.7 para.5, repealed (in part): 2003 c.4 Sch.4

Sch.7 para.6, repealed (in part): 2003 c.4 Sch.4

Sch.7 para.7, amended: 2002 c.17 Sch.8 para.11

Sch.7 para.7, repealed (in part): 2003 c.4 Sch.4

Sch.7 para.8, repealed (in part): 2003 c.4 Sch.4

Sch.7A para.1, added: 2003 c.4 Sch.1

Sch.7A para.2, added: 2003 c.4 Sch.1

Sch.7A para.2, enabling: SI 2004/905

Sch.7A para.3, added: 2003 c.4 Sch.1

Sch.7A para.3, amended: 2003 c.43 Sch.11 para.40, Sch.14 Part 4

Sch.7A para.3, enabling: SI 2004/905

Sch.7A para.4, added: 2003 c.4 Sch.1

Sch.7A para.4, enabling: SI 2004/905

Sch.7A para.5, added: 2003 c.4 Sch.1

Sch.8A, applied: 2002 c.17 s.17, SI 2003/2124 Reg.3, SI 2004/905 Reg.20

Sch.8 para.2, amended: 2002 c.41 s.45

Sch.8A para.1, amended: 2003 c.43 Sch.4 para.44, Sch.11 para.41

Sch.8A para.1, varied: SI 2004/288 Art.7, SI 2004/480 Art.6

Sch.9A, enabling: SI 2002/1921

Sch.9 para.3, varied: SI 2002/2469 Reg.16

Sch.9A para.6, amended: 2003 c.43 Sch.11 para.42

Sch.9A para.6, varied: SI 2004/288 Art.7, SI 2004/480 Art.6

Sch.9A para.10, amended: 2003 c.43 Sch.11 para.42

Sch.9A para.10, substituted: 2003 c.43 Sch.11 para.42

Sch.9A para.10, varied: SI 2004/288 Art.7, SI 2004/480 Art.6

Sch.9A para.17, amended: 2003 c.43 Sch.11 para.42

Sch.10 para.1, applied: SI 2004/906 Reg.7

Sch.10 para.1, varied: SI 2002/1095 Art.3

Sch.10 para.1, enabling: SI 2004/906

Sch.10 para.3, amended: 2003 c.43 Sch.11 para.43

1977–cont.

49. National Health Service Act 1977– *cont.*

Sch.11 para.8, amended: 2003 c.44 Sch.37 Part 9

Sch.11 para.8, disapplied: 2003 c.44 Sch.25 para.74

Sch.11 para.9, amended: 2003 c.44 Sch.37 Part 9

Sch.11 para.9, disapplied: 2003 c.44 Sch.25 para.74

Sch.12 para.1, amended: SI 2002/2861 Reg.25, 2003 c.43 Sch.11 para.44

Sch.12 para.2, amended: 2003 c.43 Sch.14 Part 4

Sch.12 para.2, repealed (in part): 2003 c.43 Sch.14 Part 4

Sch.12 para.2, enabling: SI 2002/547, SI 2002/917, SI 2002/2353, SI 2003/301, SI 2003/657, SI 2003/955, SI 2003/2381, SI 2004/642, SI 2004/1014

Sch.12 para.2A, enabling: SI 2002/35, SI 2002/186, SI 2002/547, SI 2002/917, SI 2002/1326, SI 2002/1506, SI 2003/301, SI 2003/657, SI 2003/955, SI 2003/2381, SI 2004/642, SI 2004/936, SI 2004/1014, SI 2004/1042, SI 2004/1138, SI 2004/1659

Sch.12 para.3, repealed: 2003 c.43 Sch.14 Part 4

Sch.12 para.3, enabling: SI 2002/544, SI 2003/586, SI 2004/1091

Sch.12 para.6, repealed: 2003 c.43 Sch.14 Part 4

Sch.12A para.1, amended: 2003 c.43 Sch.11 para.45

Sch.12A para.1, repealed (in part): 2003 c.43 Sch.14 Part 4

Sch.12A para.1, varied: SI 2002/2478 Art.4

Sch.12A para.2, amended: 2003 c.43 Sch.11 para.45

Sch.12A para.2, repealed (in part): 2003 c.43 Sch.14 Part 4

Sch.12A para.2, varied: SI 2002/2478 Art.4

Sch.12A para.3, amended: 2002 c.17 s.10

Sch.12A para.3, varied: SI 2002/2478 Art.4

Sch.12A para.4, amended: 2002 c.17 s.10, Sch.8 para.12, Sch.9 Part 1, 2003 c.43 Sch.11 para.45

Sch.12A para.4, repealed (in part): 2003 c.43 Sch.14 Part 4

Sch.12A para.4, varied: SI 2002/2478 Art.4

Sch.12A para.5, amended: 2002 c.17 s.10, Sch.8 para.12, Sch.9 Part 1, 2003 c.43 Sch.11 para.45

Sch.12A para.5, repealed (in part): 2003 c.43 Sch.14 Part 4

Sch.12A para.5, varied: SI 2002/2478 Art.4

Sch.12A para.6, substituted: 2002 c.17 s.10

Sch.12A para.6, varied: SI 2002/2478 Art.4

Sch.12A para.6A, added: 2002 c.17 s.10

CAP.

1977–cont.

49. National Health Service Act 1977– cont.

Sch.12A para.6A, amended: 2003 c.43 Sch.11 para.45

Sch.12A para.6A, repealed (in part): 2003 c.43 Sch.14 Part 4

Sch.12A para.6A, varied: SI 2002/2478 Art.4

Sch.12A para.6B, added: 2002 c.17 s.10

Sch.12A para.6B, amended: 2003 c.43 Sch.11 para.45

Sch.12A para.6B, repealed (in part): 2003 c.43 Sch.14 Part 4

Sch.12A para.6B, varied: SI 2002/2478 Art.4

Sch.12A para.6C, added: 2002 c.17 s.10

Sch.12A para.6C, varied: SI 2002/2478 Art.4

Sch.12A para.7, amended: 2002 c.17 s.10, Sch.9 Part 1, 2003 c.43 Sch.4 para.45

Sch.12A para.7, varied: SI 2002/2478 Art.4

Sch.12ZA para.1, added: 2003 c.43 s.183

Sch.12ZA para.2, added: 2003 c.43 s.183

Sch.12ZA para.3, added: 2003 c.43 s.183

Sch.12ZA para.4, added: 2003 c.43 s.183

Sch.12ZA para.5, added: 2003 c.43 s.183

Sch.12ZA para.6, added: 2003 c.43 s.183

Sch.12ZA para.7, added: 2003 c.43 s.183

Sch.15 para.29, repealed: 2003 c.42 Sch.7

50. Unfair Contract Terms Act 1977

see *Bacardi Martini Beverages Ltd v Thomas Hardy Packaging Ltd* [2002] 1 Lloyd's Rep. 62 (QBD (Comm Ct)), Tomlinson, J; see *Bank of Scotland v Fuller Peiser* 2002 S.L.T. 574 (OH), Lord Eassie; see *Britvic Soft Drinks Ltd v Messer UK Ltd* [2002] EWCA Civ 548, [2002] 2 All E.R. (Comm) 321 (CA), Mance, L.J.; see *Feldarol Foundry Plc v Hermes Leasing (London) Ltd* [2004] EWCA Civ 747, (2004) 101(24) L.S.G. 32 (CA), Kennedy, L.J.; see *SAM Business Systems Ltd v Hedley & Co* [2002] EWHC 2733, [2003] 1 All E.R. (Comm) 465 (QBD (T&CC)), Judge Bowsher Q.C.

applied: SI 2003/1593 Sch.1 Part I

s.3, see *Hadley Design Associates Ltd v Westminster City Council* [2003] EWHC 1617, [2004] T.C.L.R. 1 (QBD (T&CC)), Judge Richard Seymour Q.C.; see *Paragon Finance Plc (formerly National Home Loans Corp) v Nash* [2001] EWCA Civ 1466, [2002] 1 W.L.R. 685 (CA), Dyson, L.J.; see *Sweeney v Peninsula Business Services Ltd* [2004] I.R.L.R. 49 (EAT), Rimer, J.

s.6, see *Bacardi Martini Beverages Ltd v Thomas Hardy Packaging Ltd* [2002] EWCA Civ 549, [2002] 2 All E.R. (Comm) 335 (CA), Mance, L.J.

s.6, referred to: SI 2003/1374 Sch.1

s.7, referred to: SI 2003/1374 Sch.1

s.12, amended: SI 2002/3045 Reg.14

s.20, referred to: SI 2003/1374 Sch.1

CAP.

1977–cont.

50. Unfair Contract Terms Act 1977–cont.

s.21, referred to: SI 2003/1374 Sch.1

s.25, amended: SI 2002/3045 Reg.14

s.26, see *Amiri Flight Authority v BAE Systems Plc* [2002] EWHC 2481, [2003] 1 All E.R. (Comm) 1 (QBD (Comm Ct)), Tomlinson, J.; see *Amiri Flight Authority v BAE Systems Plc* [2003] EWCA Civ 1447, [2004] 1 All E.R. (Comm) 385 (CA), Mance, L.J.

s.27, referred to: SI 2003/1374 Sch.1

Sch.2, see *Granville Oil & Chemicals Ltd v Davies Turner & Co Ltd* [2003] EWCA Civ 570, [2003] 1 All E.R. (Comm) 819 (CA), Tuckey, L.J.

1978

xiii. Greater London Council (General Powers) Act 1978

s.3, repealed: 2003 c.17 Sch.7

s.3, repealed: 2003 c.17 Sch.6 para.69

s.4, repealed: 2003 c.17 Sch.7

s.5, applied: 2003 c.17 Sch.8 para.31

s.5, repealed (in part): 2003 c.17 Sch.7

s.5, amended: 2003 c.17 Sch.6 para.70

s.5, repealed (in part): 2003 c.17 Sch.6 para.70

xii. King's College London Act 1978

Part III, amended: SI 2004/1194 Art.4

s.10, amended: SI 2004/1194 Art.5

s.11, repealed: SI 2004/1194 Art.6

s.12, amended: SI 2004/1194 Art.7

s.12, repealed (in part): SI 2004/1194 Art.7

s.13, substituted: SI 2004/1194 Art.8

s.15, amended: SI 2004/1194 Art.9

s.15, repealed (in part): SI 2004/1194 Art.9

s.16, amended: SI 2004/1194 Art.10

xv. London Transport Act 1978

varied: SI 2003/1615 Sch.2 para.8

New Zealand Securities Act 1978

s.37, see *Christchurch Pavilion Partnership No.1 v Deloitte & Touche Tohmatsu Trustee Co Ltd* [2002] UKPC 4, [2002] B.C.C. 636 (PC (NZ)), Lord Scott of Foscote

1. Dioceses Measure 1978

applied: SI 2002/1893 para.1, SI 2003/1936 para.1

s.9, repealed (in part): 2004 c.14 Sch.1 Part 6

s.15, repealed (in part): 2004 c.14 Sch.1 Part 6

s.25, repealed (in part): 2004 c.14 Sch.1 Part 6

2. Parochial Registers and Records Measure 1978

s.23, repealed: 2004 c.14 Sch.1 Part 6

s.27, repealed (in part): 2004 c.14 Sch.1 Part 6

3. Church of England (Miscellaneous Provisions) Measure 1978

s.3, repealed (in part): 2004 c.14 Sch.1 Part 6

s.12, repealed: 2004 c.14 Sch.1 Part 6

s.13, repealed (in part): 2004 c.14 Sch.1 Part 6

1978–cont.

3. Refuse Disposal (Amenity) Act 1978
referred to: 2003 c.iii s.20
s.2, amended: 2003 c.44 Sch.26 para.25
s.2, applied: SSI 2002/410 Art.28
s.3, applied: 2004 c.i s.6, s.8
s.3, enabling: SI 2002/746, SSI 2002/538
s.4, applied: 2004 c.i s.3, s.6, s.7
s.4, varied: 2004 c.i s.3
s.4, enabling: SI 2002/746, SSI 2002/538
s.5, varied: 2004 c.i s.4
s.6, applied: SI 2004/1777 Art.25, SI 2004/1778 Art.25
s.8, applied: SI 2004/1777 Art.25, SI 2004/1778 Art.25
s.11, varied: 2004 c.i s.5

4. Local Government (Scotland) Act 1978
s.4, repealed: 2002 asp 11 Sch.6 para.2

6. Employment Subsidies Act 1978
repealed: 2004 c.14 Sch.1 Part 8

9. Gun Barrel Proof Act 1978
applied: 2002 c.40 Sch.15

10. European Parliamentary Elections Act 1978
repealed: 2002 c.24 Sch.4
s.1, consolidated: 2002 c.24 s.1
s.2, consolidated: 2002 c.24 s.1
s.3, consolidated: 2002 c.24 s.2
s.3A, consolidated: 2002 c.24 s.3
s.3C, consolidated: 2002 c.24 s.8
s.3D, consolidated: 2002 c.24 s.4, s.13
s.4, consolidated: 2002 c.24 s.9
s.5, consolidated: 2002 c.24 Sch.3 para.2, Sch.3 para.3
s.6, applied: 2002 c.3 s.3
s.6, consolidated: 2002 c.24 s.12
s.7, consolidated: 2002 c.24 s.6
s.8, consolidated: 2002 c.24, s.9, s.10, Sch.1 para.4
s.9, consolidated: 2002 c.24 s.13
Sch.1 para.2, consolidated: 2002 c.24 s.2, s.7, s.13
Sch.1 para.3, consolidated: 2002 c.24 s.5, s.13
Sch.1 para.4, consolidated: 2002 c.24 s.6
Sch.1 para.5, consolidated: 2002 c.24, s.10, s.13
Sch.1 para.6, consolidated: 2002 c.24 s.6, s.11, s.13
Sch.2 Part I para.1, consolidated: 2002 c.24 Sch.1 para.1, Sch.1 para.2, Sch.1 para.3
Sch.2 Part I para.2, consolidated: 2002 c.24 Sch.1 para.1, Sch.1 para.2, Sch.1 para.3
Sch.2 Part I para.3, consolidated: 2002 c.24 Sch.1 para.1, Sch.1 para.2, Sch.1 para.3
Sch.2 Part I para.4, consolidated: 2002 c.24 Sch.1 para.4
Sch.2 Part I para.8, consolidated: 2002 c.24 s.5
Sch.2 para.4, consolidated: 2002 c.24 s.13, Sch.1 para.4

1978–cont.

15. Solomon Islands Act 1978
Sch.1 para.8, repealed: 2002 c.39 Sch.3

17. Internationally Protected Persons Act 1978
referred to: 2003 c.32 Sch.5 para.1
s.1, amended: 2003 c.42 Sch.6 para.22, Sch.7
s.2, amended: 2002 c.26 Sch.7 para.29, Sch.13, 2003 c.32 Sch.5 para.2

19. Oaths Act 1978
s.5, applied: SI 2004/1048 r.7

20. Tuvalu Act 1978
Sch.2 para.8, repealed: 2002 c.39 Sch.3

22. Domestic Proceedings and Magistrates Courts Act 1978
applied: 2004 c.33 s.72
Part I, applied: 2004 c.33 Sch.6 para.43, Sch.6 para.46
s.4, amended: 2004 c.33 Sch.27 para.57
s.6, amended: 2003 c.39 Sch.8 para.191
s.20ZA, amended: 2003 c.39 Sch.8 para.192
s.26, amended: 2004 c.31 Sch.3 para.1
s.27, amended: 2003 c.39 Sch.8 para.193
s.28, applied: 2004 c.33 Sch.6 para.46
s.29, applied: 2004 c.33 Sch.6 para.46
s.30, amended: 2003 c.39 Sch.8 para.194
s.31, applied: 2004 c.33 Sch.6 para.46
s.32, amended: 2003 c.39 Sch.8 para.195
s.32, applied: 2004 c.33 Sch.6 para.43
s.35, amended: 2003 c.39 Sch.8 para.196, 2004 c.33 Sch.27 para.58
s.73, repealed (in part): 2002 c.38 Sch.5
s.74, repealed (in part): 2002 c.38 Sch.5
s.88, amended: 2003 c.39 Sch.8 para.197, Sch.10
Sch.2 para.2, repealed: 2003 c.39 Sch.10
Sch.2 para.6, repealed: 2003 c.39 Sch.10
Sch.2 para.9, repealed: 2003 c.39 Sch.10

23. Judicature (Northern Ireland) Act 1978
Art.47, applied: 2002 c.26 Sch.5 para.6
s.2, amended: 2002 c.26 Sch.13, SI 2004/1985 Art.2
s.2, enabling: SI 2004/1985
s.3, amended: 2002 c.26 Sch.13
s.4, amended: 2002 c.26 Sch.13
s.7, amended: 2002 c.26 s.18, Sch.3 para.1, Sch.5 para.4
s.7, applied: 2002 c.26 Sch.1, Sch.6
s.9, substituted: 2002 c.26 s.18
s.12, amended: 2004 c.4 s.4
s.12, substituted: 2002 c.26 s.4
s.12B, added: 2002 c.26 s.6
s.12B, referred to: 2002 c.26 s.7
s.13, repealed: 2002 c.26 Sch.13
s.14, amended: 2002 c.26 Sch.12 para.13
s.41, applied: 2003 c.32 s.62
s.47, amended: 2002 c.26 Sch.5 para.5
s.48, amended: 2002 c.26 Sch.5 para.6, 2003 c.44 Sch.36 para.45

1978–cont.

23. Judicature (Northern Ireland) Act 1978–*cont.*
s.51, amended: 2002 c.26 Sch.13
s.51, applied: 2002 c.26 s.10
s.51A, amended: 2002 c.26 Sch.13
s.52, enabling: SR 2003/71
s.53, amended: 2002 c.26 s.17, Sch.5 para.7
s.54, amended: 2002 c.26 s.17, s.73
s.55, applied: SR 2003/54
s.55, enabling: SR 2002/15, SR 2002/202, SR 2003/54, SR 2003/263
s.58, amended: 2002 c.26 Sch.5 para.8
s.60, amended: 2002 c.26 Sch.5 para.9
s.68, amended: 2002 c.26 Sch.5 para.10
s.69, applied: 2002 c.26 s.79, 2004 c.4 Sch.3 para.1
s.70, amended: 2002 c.26 s.18, Sch.3 para.17
s.70, applied: 2002 c.26 Sch.1, Sch.6
s.71, repealed (in part): 2002 c.26 Sch.13
s.74, amended: 2002 c.26 Sch.3 para.18
s.74, applied: 2002 c.26 Sch.1, Sch.6
s.75, amended: 2002 c.26 Sch.5 para.11
s.75, repealed (in part): 2002 c.26 Sch.13
s.99, repealed (in part): 2002 c.26 Sch.13
s.103, amended: 2002 c.26 s.18, Sch.4 para.17
s.103A, added: 2002 c.26 Sch.4 para.18
s.107, amended: 2002 c.26 s.18
s.116, enabling: SR 2002/341, SR 2002/342, SR 2002/343
s.119, amended: 2002 c.26 Sch.13
s.201, applied: 2002 c.29 s.239
Sch.2, amended: 2002 c.26 Sch.13
Sch.3, amended: 2002 c.26 s.17, s.18, Sch.13
Sch.5, amended: 2002 c.26 Sch.13

25. Nuclear Safeguards and Electricity (Finance) Act 1978
referred to: SI 2004/1289 Art.2
s.1, varied: SI 2004/1288 Sch.1 para.1, SI 2004/1289 Sch.1 para.1, SI 2004/1290 Sch.1 para.1
s.2, referred to: SI 2004/1288 Art.2, SI 2004/1290 Art.2
s.2, varied: SI 2004/1288 Sch.1 para.2, SI 2004/1289 Sch.1 para.2, SI 2004/1290 Sch.1 para.2
s.3, varied: SI 2004/1288 Sch.1 para.3, SI 2004/1289 Sch.1 para.3, SI 2004/1290 Sch.1 para.3
s.4, varied: SI 2004/1288 Sch.1 para.4, SI 2004/1290 Sch.1 para.4
s.5, varied: SI 2004/1288 Sch.1 para.5, SI 2004/1289 Sch.1 para.4, SI 2004/1290 Sch.1 para.5
s.6, varied: SI 2004/1288 Sch.1 para.6, SI 2004/1289 Sch.1 para.5, SI 2004/1290 Sch.1 para.6

26. Suppression of Terrorism Act 1978
applied: SI 2002/1823 Sch.2 para.24
referred to: 2003 c.32 Sch.5 para.3
s.1, applied: SI 2002/1823 Sch.2 para.24

1978–cont.

26. Suppression of Terrorism Act 1978–*cont.*
s.1, repealed: 2003 c.41 Sch.4
s.2, repealed: 2003 c.41 Sch.4
s.4, amended: 2002 c.26 Sch.13, 2003 c.32 Sch.5 para.4, 2003 c.42 Sch.7
s.5, applied: SI 2002/1823 Sch.2 para.24
s.5, substituted: 2003 c.41 Sch.3 para.5
s.8, amended: 2003 c.41 Sch.4
s.8, repealed (in part): 2003 c.41 Sch.4
s.8, enabling: SI 2003/6, SI 2003/1863
Sch.1 para.3, amended: 2003 c.42 Sch.6 para.23
Sch.1 para.9, substituted: 2003 c.42 Sch.6 para.23
Sch.1 para.11, repealed: 2003 c.42 Sch.7
Sch.1 para.15, substituted: SI 2004/702 Sch.7 para.2

28. Adoption (Scotland) Act 1978
applied: 2002 c.38 s.96
referred to: 2002 c.38 Sch.3 para.21, Sch.4 para.16
s.3, applied: SSI 2002/113 Sch.1 para.20
s.6, see *Edinburgh City Council v W* 2002 Fam. L.R. 67 (Sh Pr), CGB Nicholson Q.C., Sheriff Principal; see *X, Petitioner* 2003 Fam L.R. 6 (Sh Ct (South Strathclyde, Dumfries and Galloway)), IC Simpson
s.6, applied: SSI 2003/19 Reg.23, Reg.26
s.6A, applied: SSI 2003/19 Reg.23, Reg.26
s.7, applied: SSI 2003/19 Reg.23, Reg.26
s.9, enabling: SSI 2003/19
s.11, amended: 2002 c.38 Sch.3 para.22
s.11, applied: 2002 c.38 s.123
s.12, varied: SSI 2003/19 Sch.3
s.13, varied: SSI 2003/19 Sch.3
s.15, amended: 2003 c.24 Sch.1 para.11
s.16, see *East Lothian Council v A* 2002 S.C. 106 (Ex Div), Lord Coulsfield, Lord Cameron of Lochbroom, Lord McCluskey
s.16, amended: 2002 c.38 Sch.3 para.23
s.16, varied: SSI 2003/19 Sch.3
s.17, applied: SSI 2003/19 Reg.30, Reg.35
s.18, see *G v Edinburgh City Council (Adoption: Paternal Rights)* 2002 S.C. 440 (Ex Div), Lord Coulsfield, Lord Caplan, Lady Cosgrove; see *G v Edinburgh City Council (Adoption: Paternal Rights)* 2002 S.L.T. (Sh Ct) 58 (Sh Pr), CGB Nicholson Q.C., Sheriff Principal
s.18, applied: 2002 c.38 s.47, SI 2003/118 Reg.25, Reg.27, Reg.32, SR 2003/16 Reg.23, Reg.25, Reg.30, SSI 2003/19 Reg.22, Reg.24, Reg.26, Reg.30
s.18, varied: 2002 c.38 s.105
s.19, applied: SSI 2003/19 Reg.24, Reg.26
s.20, varied: 2002 c.38 s.105
s.21, varied: 2002 c.38 s.105
s.22, applied: SSI 2003/19 Reg.13
s.22, varied: SSI 2003/19 Sch.3

CAP.

1978–cont.

28. Adoption (Scotland) Act 1978–*cont.*
s.25, varied: 2002 c.38 s.105
s.27, applied: 2002 c.38 s.105
s.27, varied: SSI 2003/19 Sch.3
s.28, applied: 2002 c.38 s.105
s.29, amended: 2002 c.38 Sch.3 para.24
s.29, varied: 2002 c.38 s.105
s.29A, added: 2002 c.38 s.132
s.30, applied: SI 2002/2788 Reg.22, SI 2002/2822 Reg.22, SR 2002/377 Reg.22, SR 2002/378 Reg.22
s.30, varied: SSI 2003/19 Sch.3
s.31, varied: SSI 2003/19 Sch.3
s.41, amended: 2002 c.8 s.2, 2004 c.33 s.86
s.45, amended: 2002 c.38 Sch.3 para.25
s.45, applied: 2002 c.38 s.107, Sch.2 para.3
s.47, amended: 2002 c.38 Sch.3 para.26
s.49, applied: 2002 c.38 s.85
s.50, amended: 2002 c.38 s.133, Sch.3 para.27, Sch.5
s.50, applied: 2002 c.38 s.123
s.50A, substituted: 2002 c.38 s.133
s.50A, enabling: SSI 2003/19
s.51, applied: SI 2002/2006 Reg.19
s.52, referred to: 2002 c.38 Sch.4 para.16
s.52, repealed: 2002 c.38 Sch.3 para.28, Sch.5
s.53, amended: 2002 c.38 Sch.3 para.29, Sch.5
s.53, applied: SSI 2003/19 Reg.17, Reg.21
s.53A, added: 2002 c.38 Sch.3 para.30
s.53B, added: 2002 c.38 Sch.3 para.30
s.53C, added: 2002 c.38 Sch.3 para.30
s.54, amended: 2002 c.38 Sch.3 para.31
s.56, amended: 2002 c.38 Sch.3 para.32
s.59, amended: 2002 c.38 Sch.3 para.33
s.59, enabling: SSI 2003/44, SSI 2004/52
s.60, amended: 2002 c.38 Sch.3 para.34
s.60, enabling: SSI 2003/67
s.65, see *G v Edinburgh City Council (Adoption: Paternal Rights)* 2002 S.L.T. (Sh Ct) 58 (Sh Pr), CGB Nicholson Q.C., Sheriff Principal
s.65, amended: 2002 c.38 s.133, s.134, Sch.3 para.35
s.65, repealed (in part): 2002 c.38 Sch.5
Sch.1 para.1, enabling: SSI 2003/67
Sch.1 para.3, enabling: SSI 2003/67

29. National Health Service (Scotland) Act 1978
applied: 2002 asp 13 Sch.1 para.33, 2003 asp 4 s.8, 2003 asp 13 s.259, s.288, SI 2003/409 Sch.1 Part I, SI 2004/629 Sch.2, SI 2004/1022 Sch.2, SI 2004/1031 Reg.28, SSI 2002/103 Art.4, SSI 2002/120 Reg.4, SSI 2002/534 Art.4, SSI 2003/64 Sch.1 para.4, SSI 2003/376 Reg.3, Reg.7, SSI 2003/460 Reg.7, SSI 2004/47 Sch.1, SSI 2004/115 Sch.3, Sch.4 para.1, Sch.5 para.2, Sch.5 para.71, Sch.5 para.94, SSI

CAP.

1978–cont.

29. National Health Service (Scotland) Act 1978–*cont.*
applied: 2002 asp 13 Sch.1 para.33–*cont.*
2004/116 Reg.24, Sch.1 para.59, SSI 2004/163 Art.95, SSI 2004/386 Reg.3
referred to: 2004 asp 1 s.7
Part I, applied: SSI 2002/190 Reg.3, SSI 2004/386 Reg.7
Part I, added: 2004 asp 1 s.4
Part I, added: 2004 asp 1 s.5
Part II, applied: 2002 asp 11 Sch.2 para.5, 2002 asp 13 Sch.1 para.33, SSI 2003/376 Reg.5, SSI 2003/460 Reg.5, SSI 2004/163 Art.51, Art.52, SSI 2004/386 Reg.7
Part II, disapplied: SSI 2003/376 Reg.5
Part II, referred to: SSI 2003/460 Reg.5
s.1, referred to: SSI 2002/534 Art.4
s.1A, added: 2004 asp 7 s.9
s.2, amended: 2004 asp 7 Sch.1 para.1
s.2, applied: 2002 asp 13 Sch.1 para.27, SI 2002/195 Reg.12, SI 2002/3200 Reg.12, SR 2002/224 Reg.12, SSI 2002/103 Sch.1 Part I, SSI 2002/305 Sch.1 Part I, SSI 2002/534 Sch.1 Part I, 2003 c.14 s.61, s.66, 2004 c.36 Sch.1 para.17, SSI 2004/115 Sch.5 para.70, SSI 2004/116 Reg.21, Sch.1 para.36, SSI 2004/163 Art.21
s.2, referred to: 2002 asp 5 s.26, 2003 asp 4 s.9
s.2, enabling: SSI 2002/99, SSI 2002/103, SSI 2002/111, SSI 2002/153, SSI 2002/192, SSI 2002/239, SSI 2002/268, SSI 2002/305, SSI 2002/534, SSI 2003/131, SSI 2003/154, SSI 2003/217, SSI 2003/422, SSI 2003/443, SSI 2004/292, SSI 2004/386
s.2A, added: 2004 asp 7 s.9
s.2B, added: 2004 asp 7 s.7
s.2C, added: 2004 asp 1 s.1
s.2C, amended: 2004 asp 7 Sch.1 para.1
s.2C, applied: SSI 2004/114 Reg.3, Reg.4, Reg.10, SSI 2004/115 Sch.5 para.75, SSI 2004/116 Sch.1 para.41, SSI 2004/163 Art.88
s.2D, added: 2004 asp 7 s.4
s.3, applied: SI 2003/409 Sch.1 Part I
s.3, repealed: 2003 asp 4 Sch.4 para.5
s.4, enabling: SSI 2003/158
s.4A, added: 2004 asp 7 s.2
s.4B, added: 2004 asp 7 s.2
s.4B, applied: SSI 2004/386 Reg.10
s.4B, enabling: SSI 2004/386
s.5, amended: SSI 2002/176 Art.4
s.7, applied: 2002 asp 13 Sch.1 para.30, 2004 asp 7 s.8
s.7, repealed: 2004 asp 7 Sch.2
s.8, amended: 2004 asp 7 Sch.2
s.9, amended: 2004 asp 7 Sch.2
s.9, applied: SSI 2004/115 Reg.27, SSI 2004/116 Reg.23
s.9, enabling: SSI 2004/115, SSI 2004/116

1978–cont.

29. National Health Service (Scotland) Act 1978–cont.

s.10, amended: 2004 asp 7 Sch.2

s.10, applied: SSI 2002/103 Sch.1 Part I, SSI 2002/305 Sch.1 Part I, SSI 2002/534 Sch.1 Part I, 2003 c.14 s.61, s.66, SSI 2003/306, 2004 c.36 Sch.1 para.38

s.10, referred to: 2002 asp 5 s.26

s.10, enabling: SSI 2003/159, SSI 2003/306

s.11, amended: SSI 2002/176 Art.4

s.11, applied: 2003 asp 4 s.5, SSI 2004/46 Reg.7

s.11, repealed: 2003 asp 4 Sch.4 para.5

s.12A, applied: SI 2002/2819 Reg.2, SSI 2002/62 Sch.1, 2003 c.14 s.61, s.66

s.12A, referred to: 2002 asp 5 s.26, SSI 2002/533 Sch.2 para.2

s.12A, repealed: 2004 asp 7 s.1

s.12A, enabling: SSI 2003/189, SSI 2003/259, SSI 2003/325, SSI 2003/448, SSI 2003/597, SSI 2004/107

s.12AA, referred to: SSI 2002/533 Sch.2 para.2

s.12AA, repealed: 2004 asp 7 Sch.2

s.12B, applied: SI 2002/2819 Reg.2, Reg.5

s.12B, repealed: 2004 asp 7 Sch.2

s.12C, repealed: 2004 asp 7 Sch.2

s.12D, referred to: 2003 asp 4 s.6

s.12D, repealed: 2004 asp 7 Sch.2

s.12DA, added: SI 2003/2867 Sch.1 para.9

s.12DA, repealed: 2004 asp 7 Sch.2

s.12E, repealed: 2004 asp 7 Sch.2

s.12F, repealed: 2004 asp 7 Sch.2

s.12G, amended: 2003 asp 4 s.10

s.12G, repealed: 2004 asp 7 Sch.2

s.12H, amended: 2004 asp 7 Sch.1 para.1

s.12I, added: 2004 asp 7 s.3

s.12J, added: 2004 asp 7 s.5

s.13, amended: 2004 asp 7 Sch.2

s.13, applied: SSI 2002/103 Sch.1 Part I, SSI 2002/305 Sch.1 Part I, SSI 2002/534 Sch.1 Part I

s.13A, applied: SSI 2002/103 Sch.1 Part I, SSI 2002/305 Sch.1 Part I, SSI 2002/534 Sch.1 Part I

s.15, amended: 2004 asp 1 Sch.1 para.1

s.15, applied: SSI 2002/534 Sch.1 Part I

s.15, varied: SSI 2002/534 Sch.1 Part I, SSI 2004/163 Art.96

s.16, applied: SSI 2002/103 Art.4, SSI 2002/305 Art.4, SSI 2002/534 Art.4

s.16A, amended: 2002 asp 5 Sch.2 para.2, 2004 asp 4 Sch.3 para.2

s.16A, referred to: 2002 asp 5 s.13

s.16A, repealed (in part): 2004 asp 4 Sch.3 para.2

s.16B, applied: SSI 2002/103 Art.4, SSI 2002/305 Art.4, SSI 2002/534 Art.4

s.17A, amended: 2004 c.17 Sch.3 para.9

1978–cont.

29. National Health Service (Scotland) Act 1978–cont.

s.17A, applied: SSI 2002/103 Sch.1 Part I, SSI 2002/305 Sch.1 Part I, SSI 2002/534 Sch.1 Part I, SSI 2004/115 Reg.10, Sch.5 para.91, Sch.5 para.92, SSI 2004/116 Reg.7, Reg.8, Sch.1 para.56, Sch.1 para.57, SSI 2004/163 Art.59

s.17A, referred to: 2002 asp 11 Sch.4 para.7

s.17A, repealed (in part): 2003 c.43 Sch.14 Part 4, 2004 asp 7 Sch.2

s.17A, varied: SSI 2004/115 Reg.10

s.17A, enabling: SSI 2004/115

s.17C, amended: 2002 c.17 Sch.3 para.12, 2004 asp 1 s.2

s.17C, applied: 2002 asp 11 Sch.2 para.5, 2002 asp 13 Sch.1 para.34, SI 2003/1250 Art.10, Sch.8 para.22, SSI 2002/190 Reg.3, 2004 asp 1 s.2, SSI 2004/115 Sch.5 para.34, Sch.5 para.35, Sch.5 para.63, Sch.6 para.1, Sch.6 para.5, SSI 2004/116 Reg.26, SSI 2004/163 Art.49

s.17C, referred to: 2004 asp 1 Sch.1 para.1

s.17C, repealed (in part): 2004 asp 1 s.2

s.17D, amended: 2003 c.43 Sch.11 para.46, 2004 asp 1 s.2, Sch.1 para.1

s.17D, applied: SSI 2004/116 Reg.3, Reg.6, Sch.1 para.42

s.17D, repealed (in part): 2004 asp 7 Sch.2

s.17D, enabling: SSI 2004/116

s.17E, amended: 2004 asp 1 s.2

s.17E, applied: SSI 2004/116 Reg.20, Reg.21, Sch.1 para.27

s.17E, repealed (in part): SI 2003/1250 Sch.9 para.3, 2004 asp 1 s.2

s.17E, enabling: SSI 2004/116, SSI 2004/162, SSI 2004/217

s.17EA, amended: 2002 asp 5 s.18

s.17EA, applied: SI 2003/1250 Art.10, Sch.8 para.22

s.17EA, repealed: 2004 asp 1 Sch.1 para.1

s.17EB, added: 2002 asp 5 s.18

s.17EB, amended: SI 2003/1250 Sch.9 para.3

s.17EB, repealed (in part): SI 2003/1250 Sch.9 para.3, 2004 asp 1 Sch.1 para.1

s.17F, repealed (in part): 2004 asp 1 Sch.1 para.1

s.17H, repealed: 2004 asp 1 s.2

s.17I, amended: 2004 asp 1 Sch.1 para.1

s.17J, applied: SSI 2004/163 Art.96

s.17K, applied: SSI 2004/115 Reg.15

s.17K, enabling: SSI 2004/115, SSI 2004/215

s.17L, applied: SSI 2004/115 Reg.8, SSI 2004/116 Reg.24

s.17L, referred to: SSI 2004/115 Sch.5 para.77, Sch.5 para.78, Sch.5 para.101, SSI 2004/116 Reg.24

s.17L, enabling: SSI 2004/115

s.17M, applied: SSI 2004/115 Reg.22, Reg.23, Sch.5 para.57

1978–cont.

29. National Health Service (Scotland) Act 1978–*cont.*

s.17N, applied: SSI 2004/115 Sch.5 para.40, Sch.5 para.41, SSI 2004/116 Sch.1 para.12, Sch.1 para.13

s.17N, enabling: SSI 2004/115, SSI 2004/162, SSI 2004/215

s.17O, enabling: SSI 2004/115, SSI 2004/215

s.17P, applied: SSI 2004/386 Reg.3

s.17P, enabling: SSI 2004/114, SSI 2004/216, SSI 2004/271

s.17Q, added:

s.18, amended: 2004 asp 1 s.1

s.19, amended: SI 2002/3135 Sch.1 para.9

s.19, applied: 2002 asp 11 Sch.4 para.14, SI 2003/1250 Art.10, Sch.8 para.22, SSI 2002/190 Reg.3, SSI 2003/64 Reg.4, Reg.6, 2004 asp 1 s.7, SSI 2004/115 Reg.29, SSI 2004/142 Art.2, Art.24, Art.27, Art.28, Art.32, SSI 2004/163 Art.2, Art.77, Art.78, Art.81, Art.82, Art.83, Art.84, Art.97

s.19, referred to: SSI 2002/533 Sch.2 para.1

s.19, repealed: 2004 asp 1 Sch.1 para.1

s.19, enabling: SSI 2002/100, SSI 2002/111, SSI 2002/153, SSI 2002/438, SSI 2003/11, SSI 2003/64, SSI 2003/130, SSI 2003/298, SSI 2003/310, SSI 2003/443, SSI 2004/38, SSI 2004/40, SSI 2004/41, SSI 2004/66

s.19A, amended: 2003 asp 4 Sch.4 para.5

s.19A, repealed: 2004 asp 1 Sch.1 para.1

s.19B, amended: 2003 asp 4 Sch.4 para.5

s.19B, applied: SI 2003/1250 Art.10, Sch.8 para.22

s.19B, repealed: 2004 asp 1 Sch.1 para.1

s.20, amended: 2002 asp 5 Sch.2 para.2, 2003 asp 4 Sch.4 para.5

s.20, repealed: 2004 asp 1 Sch.1 para.1

s.20, varied: SSI 2004/38 Reg.26

s.21, amended: 2003 asp 4 Sch.4 para.5

s.21, applied: SI 2003/1250 Sch.6 para.1, SSI 2003/64 Reg.9, SSI 2004/163 Art.97

s.21, repealed: SI 2003/1250 Sch.9 para.3, 2004 asp 1 Sch.1 para.1

s.22, amended: 2003 asp 4 Sch.4 para.5

s.22, applied: SSI 2004/163 Art.97

s.22, repealed: SI 2003/1250 Sch.9 para.3, 2004 asp 1 Sch.1 para.1

s.23, amended: 2003 asp 4 Sch.4 para.5, SI 2003/1250 Sch.9 para.3

s.23, applied: SI 2003/1250 Art.10, Sch.8 para.22, SSI 2004/142 Art.9

s.23, repealed: 2004 asp 1 Sch.1 para.1

s.23, varied: SSI 2004/142 Art.9

s.24, applied: SI 2003/1250 Art.10, Sch.8 para.22

s.24, repealed: 2003 asp 4 Sch.4 para.5

s.24A, repealed: 2004 asp 1 Sch.1 para.1

s.24B, amended: 2002 asp 5 s.18

1978–cont.

29. National Health Service (Scotland) Act 1978–*cont.*

s.24B, applied: SI 2003/1250 Art.10, Sch.8 para.22

s.24B, referred to: SSI 2003/63 Art.2

s.24B, repealed: 2004 asp 1 Sch.1 para.1

s.24B, enabling: SSI 2003/64, SSI 2003/298, SSI 2004/38, SSI 2004/40

s.24C, added: 2002 asp 5 s.18

s.24C, amended: SI 2003/1250 Sch.9 para.3

s.24C, repealed (in part): SI 2003/1250 Sch.9 para.3, 2004 asp 1 Sch.1 para.1

s.24C, enabling: SSI 2003/64, SSI 2003/298

s.25, applied: 2002 asp 11 Sch.4 para.14

s.25, referred to: SSI 2002/533 Sch.2 para.1

s.25, varied: SSI 2004/38 Reg.26

s.25, enabling: SSI 2002/99, SSI 2002/100, SSI 2002/192, SSI 2002/268, SSI 2003/131, SSI 2003/158, SSI 2003/422, SSI 2004/37, SSI 2004/38, SSI 2004/292

s.26, applied: 2002 asp 11 Sch.4 para.14, SSI 2003/64 Sch.1 para.11

s.26, disapplied: SSI 2004/115 Sch.4 para.1

s.26, referred to: SSI 2002/533 Sch.2 para.1, SSI 2003/64 Sch.1 para.11

s.26, varied: SSI 2004/38 Reg.26

s.26, enabling: SSI 2002/17, SSI 2002/86, SSI 2002/224, SSI 2003/201, SSI 2003/218, SSI 2003/431, SSI 2003/432, SSI 2004/36, SSI 2004/38, SSI 2004/97, SSI 2004/98, SSI 2004/168, SSI 2004/169

s.27, see *Lloyds Pharmacy Ltd v National Appeal Panel for Entry to the Pharmaceutical Lists* 2003 S.L.T. 830 (OH), Lady Smith

s.27, amended: SI 2003/1590 Sch.1 para.2, 2004 asp 7 Sch.2, SI 2004/1771 Sch.1 para.6

s.27, applied: 2002 asp 11 Sch.4 para.14

s.27, referred to: SSI 2002/533 Sch.2 para.1

s.27, varied: SSI 2004/38 Reg.26

s.27, enabling: SSI 2002/100, SSI 2002/111, SSI 2002/153, SSI 2003/130, SSI 2003/295, SSI 2003/296, SSI 2004/38, SSI 2004/39, SSI 2004/66

s.28, amended: 2004 asp 1 Sch.1 para.1

s.28, enabling: SSI 2002/111, SSI 2002/153, SSI 2003/296, SSI 2003/443, SSI 2004/115, SSI 2004/116

s.28A, amended: 2004 asp 1 Sch.1 para.1

s.28A, enabling: SSI 2002/111, SSI 2002/153

s.28B, amended: 2004 asp 1 Sch.1 para.1

s.28C, amended: 2004 asp 1 Sch.1 para.1

s.29, amended: 2002 asp 5 Sch.2 para.2, 2004 asp 1 s.5, SSI 2004/167 Sch.1 para.1

s.29, applied: SSI 2003/64 Reg.5, SSI 2004/31 Art.3, SSI 2004/38 Reg.3, Reg.3A, SSI 2004/114 Reg.7, Reg.12, SSI 2004/163

1978–cont.

29. National Health Service (Scotland) Act 1978–*cont.*

s.29, applied:–*cont.*
Art.79, Art.80, Art.81, Art.89, Art.91, Art.93, SSI 2004/386 Reg.7

s.29, referred to: SSI 2004/34 Art.3

s.29, varied: SSI 2004/31 Art.3

s.29, enabling: SSI 2004/38, SSI 2004/122, SSI 2004/271

s.29A, amended: 2002 asp 5 Sch.2 para.2

s.29A, repealed (in part): 2004 asp 1 Sch.1 para.1

s.29A, enabling: SSI 2004/38, SSI 2004/122

s.29B, amended: 2002 asp 5 Sch.2 para.2, 2004 asp 1 Sch.1 para.1

s.29B, applied: SSI 2004/38 Reg.21, Reg.28, SSI 2004/114 Reg.7, Reg.9

s.29B, repealed (in part): 2004 asp 1 Sch.1 para.1

s.29C, amended: SSI 2004/167 Sch.1 para.1

s.29C, applied: SSI 2004/38 Reg.21

s.30, amended: 2002 asp 5 Sch.2 para.2

s.30, applied: SSI 2003/64 Reg.5, SSI 2004/38 Reg.24, Reg.25, Reg.28, Reg.29, SSI 2004/114 Reg.7, Reg.9, Reg.12, SSI 2004/163 Art.79, Art.80, Art.81, Art.93

s.31, amended: 2002 asp 5 Sch.2 para.2, SSI 2004/167 Sch.1 para.1

s.31, applied: SSI 2004/38 Reg.28, SSI 2004/114 Reg.7, Reg.9

s.31, referred to: SSI 2004/38 Reg.28

s.32, enabling: SSI 2004/38, SSI 2004/122

s.32A, amended: 2002 asp 5 Sch.2 para.2, SSI 2004/167 Sch.1 para.1

s.32A, applied: SSI 2004/38 Reg.15, Reg.22, Reg.23, Reg.27, SSI 2004/114 Reg.7, Reg.9, SSI 2004/163 Art.79, Art.80, Art.81

s.32A, referred to: SSI 2004/34 Art.3

s.32A, varied: SSI 2004/31 Art.3

s.32B, amended: 2002 asp 5 Sch.2 para.2

s.32B, applied: SSI 2004/38 Reg.20, Reg.21, Reg.27, SSI 2004/114 Reg.7, Reg.9

s.32B, referred to: SSI 2004/34 Art.3

s.32B, varied: SSI 2004/31 Art.3

s.32C, enabling: SSI 2004/38, SSI 2004/122

s.32D, amended: 2002 asp 5 Sch.2 para.2, SSI 2004/167 Sch.1 para.1

s.32D, applied: SSI 2004/114 Reg.7, Reg.9

s.32E, enabling: SSI 2004/40, SSI 2004/114

s.35, amended: 2004 asp 1 Sch.1 para.1

s.35, applied: SSI 2004/116 Sch.1 para.32

s.35, referred to: SSI 2004/115 Sch.5 para.62

s.35, varied: SSI 2004/163 Art.96

s.35, enabling: SSI 2004/162

s.35A, repealed: 2004 asp 7 Sch.2

s.36, applied: SSI 2002/305 Art.4, SSI 2002/533 Reg.5

s.36, referred to: SSI 2002/533 Sch.2 para.1

s.37, applied: SSI 2002/305 Art.4

s.37, referred to: SSI 2002/533 Sch.2 para.1

s.39, applied: SSI 2004/386 Reg.3

1978–cont.

29. National Health Service (Scotland) Act 1978–*cont.*

s.40, repealed (in part): 2004 asp 1 Sch.1 para.1

s.41, applied: SSI 2002/305 Art.4

s.42, applied: SSI 2002/305 Art.4, SSI 2002/534 Art.4

s.45, referred to: SSI 2002/533 Sch.2 para.1

s.46, applied: SI 2002/2005 Reg.9, Reg.13

s.47, applied: SSI 2002/305 Art.4, SSI 2002/534 Art.4

s.47, referred to: SSI 2002/103 Art.4, 2003 asp 4 s.8

s.48, applied: SSI 2002/305 Art.4

s.57, applied: SSI 2003/64 Sch.1 para.11, SSI 2004/115 Sch.4 para.1

s.64, applied: SSI 2004/163 Art.32

s.69, applied: SSI 2003/376 Reg.3, Reg.5, SSI 2003/460 Reg.3, Reg.5

s.69, enabling: SSI 2002/100, SSI 2003/130, SSI 2003/295, SSI 2004/66

s.70, applied: SSI 2003/376 Reg.3, Reg.5, SSI 2003/460 Reg.3, Reg.5

s.70, enabling: SSI 2002/17, SSI 2002/86, SSI 2002/99, SSI 2002/224, SSI 2003/158, SSI 2003/218, SSI 2003/431, SSI 2004/97, SSI 2004/101, SSI 2004/168

s.71, applied: SSI 2003/158 Reg.3, SSI 2003/376 Reg.3, Reg.5, SSI 2003/460 Reg.3, Reg.5

s.71, enabling: SSI 2002/99, SSI 2003/158, SSI 2004/101

s.71A, enabling: SSI 2002/99, SSI 2003/158, SSI 2004/101

s.73, repealed (in part): 2004 asp 7 Sch.2

s.73, enabling: SSI 2002/86, SSI 2003/158, SSI 2003/218, SSI 2004/97

s.74, repealed (in part): 2004 asp 7 Sch.2

s.74, enabling: SSI 2002/86, SSI 2003/158, SSI 2003/218, SSI 2004/97, SSI 2004/101, SSI 2004/168

s.75, enabling: SSI 2003/158

s.75A, amended: 2004 asp 7 Sch.1 para.1

s.75A, applied: SSI 2003/158 Reg.7

s.75A, repealed (in part): 2004 asp 7 Sch.2

s.75A, enabling: SSI 2003/376, SSI 2003/460, SSI 2004/102, SSI 2004/166

s.76, applied: 2002 asp 11 Sch.4 para.12

s.77, applied: SSI 2002/103 Sch.1 Part I, SSI 2002/305 Sch.1 Part I, SSI 2002/534 Sch.1 Part I

s.77, repealed (in part): 2003 asp 4 Sch.4 para.5, 2004 asp 7 Sch.2

s.78A, added: 2004 asp 7 s.6

s.78B, added: 2004 asp 7 s.6

s.79, amended: 2004 asp 7 Sch.1 para.1

s.79, applied: SSI 2002/103 Art.4, Sch.1 Part I, SSI 2002/305 Art.4, Sch.1 Part I, SSI 2002/534 Art.4, Sch.1 Part I

s.82, amended: 2003 asp 4 s.10, 2004 asp 7 s.1, Sch.2

CAP.

1978–cont.

29. National Health Service (Scotland) Act 1978–*cont.*

s.83, amended: 2003 asp 4 s.10

s.83, applied: SSI 2002/103 Sch.1 Part I, SSI 2002/305 Sch.1 Part I, SSI 2002/534 Sch.1 Part I

s.83, repealed (in part): 2004 asp 7 Sch.2

s.84, amended: 2004 asp 7 Sch.2

s.84, applied: SSI 2002/103 Sch.1 Part I, SSI 2002/305 Sch.1 Part I, SSI 2002/534 Sch.1 Part I

s.84A, amended: 2004 asp 7 Sch.2

s.84A, applied: SSI 2002/103 Sch.1 Part I, SSI 2002/305 Sch.1 Part I, SSI 2002/534 Sch.1 Part I

s.84A, repealed (in part): 2004 asp 7 Sch.2

s.85, applied: SSI 2002/103 Sch.1 Part I, SSI 2002/305 Sch.1 Part I, SSI 2002/534 Sch.1 Part I, 2003 asp 13 Sch.1 para.9

s.85, repealed (in part): 2003 asp 4 Sch.4 para.5, 2004 asp 7 Sch.2

s.85A, amended: 2004 asp 7 Sch.2

s.85A, applied: SSI 2002/103 Sch.1 Part I, SSI 2002/305 Sch.1 Part I, 2003 asp 13 Sch.1 para.9

s.85AA, amended: 2004 asp 1 Sch.1 para.1

s.85AA, applied: SSI 2002/103 Sch.1 Part I, SSI 2002/305 Sch.1 Part I, SSI 2002/534 Sch.1 Part I

s.85AA, repealed (in part): 2004 asp 1 Sch.1 para.1, 2004 asp 7 Sch.2

s.85B, amended: 2002 asp 5 s.21, 2004 asp 7 Sch.2

s.85B, applied: SSI 2002/103 Sch.1 Part I, SSI 2002/305 Sch.1 Part I, SSI 2002/534 Sch.1 Part I

s.85B, repealed (in part): 2004 asp 7 Sch.2

s.85B, enabling: SSI 2002/239

s.86, amended: 2004 asp 7 Sch.1 para.1

s.86, applied: SSI 2002/103 Sch.1 Part I, SSI 2002/305 Sch.1 Part I, SSI 2002/534 Sch.1 Part I, 2003 asp 13 Sch.1 para.9

s.86, repealed (in part): 2004 asp 7 Sch.2

s.87, applied: SSI 2002/103 Sch.1 Part I, SSI 2002/305 Sch.1 Part I, SSI 2002/534 Sch.1 Part I

s.88, repealed (in part): 2003 asp 4 Sch.4 para.5

s.98, enabling: SSI 2004/369

s.101, amended: 2004 asp 7 Sch.2

s.101, applied: SSI 2002/103 Sch.1 Part I, SSI 2002/305 Sch.1 Part I, SSI 2002/534 Sch.1 Part I

s.102, amended: 2003 asp 13 Sch.4 para.3, Sch.5 Part 1, 2004 asp 7 Sch.1 para.1

s.102, disapplied: 2003 asp 13 s.193, s.210, s.212, s.215

s.102, repealed (in part): 2003 asp 13 s.280

s.104A, added: SI 2003/2867 Sch.1 para.9

s.105, amended: 2004 asp 7 Sch.1 para.1

s.105, repealed (in part): 2004 asp 7 Sch.2

CAP.

1978–cont.

29. National Health Service (Scotland) Act 1978–*cont.*

s.105, enabling: SSI 2002/17, SSI 2002/86, SSI 2002/99, SSI 2002/100, SSI 2002/103, SSI 2002/105, SSI 2002/111, SSI 2002/153, SSI 2002/192, SSI 2002/224, SSI 2002/239, SSI 2002/268, SSI 2002/305, SSI 2002/438, SSI 2002/534, SSI 2002/535, SSI 2003/11, SSI 2003/64, SSI 2003/130, SSI 2003/131, SSI 2003/153, SSI 2003/154, SSI 2003/158, SSI 2003/189, SSI 2003/201, SSI 2003/218, SSI 2003/259, SSI 2003/295, SSI 2003/296, SSI 2003/298, SSI 2003/306, SSI 2003/310, SSI 2003/325, SSI 2003/376, SSI 2003/422, SSI 2003/431, SSI 2003/432, SSI 2003/443, SSI 2003/448, SSI 2003/460, SSI 2003/597, SSI 2004/36, SSI 2004/37, SSI 2004/38, SSI 2004/39, SSI 2004/40, SSI 2004/41, SSI 2004/66, SSI 2004/97, SSI 2004/98, SSI 2004/101, SSI 2004/102, SSI 2004/107, SSI 2004/114, SSI 2004/115, SSI 2004/116, SSI 2004/122, SSI 2004/162, SSI 2004/166, SSI 2004/168, SSI 2004/169, SSI 2004/215, SSI 2004/216, SSI 2004/217, SSI 2004/271, SSI 2004/292, SSI 2004/369, SSI 2004/386

s.106, enabling: SSI 2002/111, SSI 2002/153, SSI 2004/38, SSI 2004/115, SSI 2004/116, SSI 2004/122, SSI 2004/217

s.108, amended: 2002 asp 5 Sch.2 para.2, 2003 asp 4 Sch.4 para.5, 2004 asp 1 Sch.1 para.1, 2004 asp 7 Sch.2

s.108, referred to: 2003 asp 13 s.13

s.108, enabling: SSI 2002/17, SSI 2002/86, SSI 2002/99, SSI 2002/100, SSI 2002/105, SSI 2002/111, SSI 2002/153, SSI 2002/192, SSI 2002/224, SSI 2002/239, SSI 2002/268, SSI 2002/438, SSI 2002/535, SSI 2003/11, SSI 2003/130, SSI 2003/131, SSI 2003/153, SSI 2003/158, SSI 2003/201, SSI 2003/218, SSI 2003/295, SSI 2003/296, SSI 2003/298, SSI 2003/310, SSI 2003/376, SSI 2003/422, SSI 2003/431, SSI 2003/432, SSI 2003/443, SSI 2003/460, SSI 2004/36, SSI 2004/37, SSI 2004/38, SSI 2004/39, SSI 2004/40, SSI 2004/41, SSI 2004/66, SSI 2004/97, SSI 2004/98, SSI 2004/101, SSI 2004/102, SSI 2004/114, SSI 2004/115, SSI 2004/116, SSI 2004/122, SSI 2004/162, SSI 2004/166, SSI 2004/168, SSI 2004/169, SSI 2004/215, SSI 2004/216, SSI 2004/217, SSI 2004/271, SSI 2004/292, SSI 2004/369

Sch.1 Part I para.1, applied: SSI 2002/103 Sch.1 Part I, SSI 2002/305 Sch.1 Part I, SSI 2002/534 Sch.1 Part I

Sch.1 Part I para.2, applied: SSI 2002/103 Sch.1 Part I, SSI 2002/305 Sch.1 Part I, SSI 2002/534 Sch.1 Part I

1978–cont.

29. **National Health Service (Scotland) Act 1978**–*cont.*

Sch.1 Part I para.4, applied: SSI 2002/103 Art.4, Sch.1 Part I, SSI 2002/305 Art.4, Sch.1 Part I, SSI 2002/534 Art.4, Sch.1 Part I

Sch.1 Part I para.5, applied: SSI 2002/103 Sch.1 Part I, SSI 2002/305 Sch.1 Part I, SSI 2002/534 Sch.1 Part I

Sch.1 Part I para.5A, applied: SSI 2002/103 Sch.1 Part I, SSI 2002/305 Sch.1 Part I, SSI 2002/534 Sch.1 Part I

Sch.1 Part I para.6, applied: SSI 2002/103 Sch.1 Part I, SSI 2002/305 Sch.1 Part I, SSI 2002/534 Sch.1 Part I

Sch.1 Part I para.6, enabling: SSI 2004/386

Sch.1 Part I para.7, applied: SSI 2002/103 Sch.1 Part I, SSI 2002/305 Sch.1 Part I, SSI 2002/534 Sch.1 Part I

Sch.1 Part I para.7A, applied: SSI 2002/103 Sch.1 Part I, SSI 2002/305 Sch.1 Part I, SSI 2002/534 Sch.1 Part I

Sch.1 Part I para.7A, enabling: SSI 2002/105, SSI 2002/535

Sch.1 Part I para.7B, applied: SSI 2002/103 Sch.1 Part I, SSI 2002/305 Sch.1 Part I, SSI 2002/534 Sch.1 Part I

Sch.1 Part I para.7C, applied: SSI 2002/105, SSI 2002/535

Sch.1 Part I para.8A, amended: 2004 asp 7 Sch.1 para.1

Sch.1 Part II para.11, applied: SSI 2002/103 Sch.1 Part I, SSI 2002/305 Sch.1 Part I, SSI 2002/534 Sch.1 Part I

Sch.1 Part II para.11, enabling: SSI 2002/111, SSI 2002/153, SSI 2003/296, SSI 2004/386

Sch.1 Part II para.11A, applied: SSI 2002/103 Sch.1 Part I, SSI 2002/305 Sch.1 Part I, SSI 2002/534 Sch.1 Part I

Sch.1 Part II para.12, applied: SSI 2002/103 Sch.1 Part I, SSI 2002/305 Sch.1 Part I, SSI 2002/534 Sch.1 Part I

Sch.1 Part II para.13, applied: SSI 2002/103 Art.4, Sch.1 Part I, SSI 2002/305 Art.4, SSI 2002/534 Art.4, Sch.1 Part I

Sch.1 Part II para.13, varied: SSI 2002/305 Sch.1 Part I

Sch.1 Part II para.14, applied: SSI 2002/103 Sch.1 Part I, SSI 2002/305 Sch.1 Part I, SSI 2002/534 Sch.1 Part I

Sch.1 Part II para.15, applied: SSI 2002/103 Sch.1 Part I, SSI 2002/305 Sch.1 Part I, SSI 2002/534 Sch.1 Part I

Sch.1 Part II para.16, repealed: 2003 asp 4 Sch.4 para.5

Sch.1 Part II para.17, repealed: 2003 asp 4 Sch.4 para.5

Sch.2 para.1, repealed: 2003 asp 4 Sch.4 para.5

Sch.2 para.2, repealed: 2003 asp 4 Sch.4 para.5

1978–cont.

29. **National Health Service (Scotland) Act 1978**–*cont.*

Sch.2 para.2A, repealed: 2003 asp 4 Sch.4 para.5

Sch.2 para.3, repealed: 2003 asp 4 Sch.4 para.5

Sch.2 para.4, repealed: 2003 asp 4 Sch.4 para.5

Sch.2 para.5, repealed: 2003 asp 4 Sch.4 para.5

Sch.2 para.15, repealed: 2003 asp 4 Sch.4 para.5

Sch.5 para.7B, applied: SSI 2002/103 Sch.1 Part I, SSI 2002/305 Sch.1 Part I, SSI 2002/534 Sch.1 Part I

Sch.5 para.7B, enabling: SSI 2002/535, SSI 2003/153

Sch.5 para.7C, applied: SSI 2002/103 Sch.1 Part I, SSI 2002/305 Sch.1 Part I, SSI 2002/534 Sch.1 Part I

Sch.5 para.8A, amended: 2004 asp 7 Sch.1 para.1

Sch.5 para.8B, applied: SSI 2002/535, SSI 2003/153

Sch.6, referred to: 2003 asp 4 Sch.4 para.8

Sch.6 Part I para.1, repealed: 2003 asp 4 Sch.4 para.5

Sch.6 Part I para.2, repealed: 2003 asp 4 Sch.4 para.5

Sch.6 Part I para.3, repealed: 2003 asp 4 Sch.4 para.5

Sch.6 Part II para.4, applied: 2003 asp 4 s.5, SSI 2004/46 Reg.2, Reg.4

Sch.6 Part II para.4, repealed: 2003 asp 4 Sch.4 para.5

Sch.6 Part II para.5, repealed: 2003 asp 4 Sch.4 para.5

Sch.6 Part II para.6, repealed: 2003 asp 4 Sch.4 para.5

Sch.6 Part II para.7, repealed: 2003 asp 4 Sch.4 para.5

Sch.6 Part II para.8, repealed: 2003 asp 4 Sch.4 para.5

Sch.6 Part II para.9, repealed: 2003 asp 4 Sch.4 para.5

Sch.6 Part II para.10, applied: SSI 2004/46 Reg.7

Sch.6 Part II para.10, repealed: 2003 asp 4 Sch.4 para.5

Sch.7A Part I para.1, repealed: 2004 asp 7 s.1

Sch.7A Part I para.1, enabling: SSI 2003/259

Sch.7A Part I para.2, repealed: 2004 asp 7 s.1

Sch.7A Part I para.3, repealed: 2004 asp 7 s.1

Sch.7A Part I para.3, enabling: SSI 2003/259

Sch.7A Part I para.4, repealed: 2004 asp 7 s.1

Sch.7A Part I para.5, repealed: 2004 asp 7 s.1

Sch.7A Part II para.6, referred to: 2002 asp 5 s.26, 2003 asp 4 s.9

Sch.7A Part II para.6, repealed: 2004 asp 7 s.1

Sch.7A Part II para.7, repealed: 2004 asp 7 s.1

Sch.7A Part II para.8, repealed: 2004 asp 7 s.1

1978–cont.

29. National Health Service (Scotland) Act 1978–cont.

Sch.7A Part II para.9, repealed: 2004 asp 7 s.1

Sch.7A Part II para.10, repealed: 2004 asp 7 s.1

Sch.7A Part II para.11, repealed: 2004 asp 7 s.1

Sch.7A Part II para.12, repealed: 2004 asp 7 s.1

Sch.7A Part II para.13, repealed: 2004 asp 7 s.1

Sch.7A Part II para.14, repealed: 2004 asp 7 s.1

Sch.7A Part II para.15, repealed: 2004 asp 7 s.1

Sch.7A Part II para.16, repealed: 2004 asp 7 s.1

Sch.7A Part II para.17, amended: 2002 asp 5 Sch.2 para.2

Sch.7A Part II para.17, repealed: 2004 asp 7 s.1

Sch.7A Part II para.18, repealed: 2004 asp 7 s.1

Sch.7A Part II para.19, repealed: 2004 asp 7 s.1

Sch.7A Part II para.20, applied: SSI 2003/ 344 Reg.5

Sch.7A Part II para.20, repealed: 2004 asp 7 s.1

Sch.7A Part II para.21, repealed: 2004 asp 7 s.1

Sch.7A Part III para.22, repealed: 2004 asp 7 s.1

Sch.7A Part III para.23, repealed: 2004 asp 7 s.1

Sch.7A Part III para.24, repealed: 2004 asp 7 s.1

Sch.7A Part IV para.25, applied: SSI 2003/ 189, SSI 2003/325, SSI 2003/448, SSI 2003/597, SSI 2004/107

Sch.7A Part IV para.25, repealed: 2004 asp 7 s.1

Sch.7A Part IV para.25, enabling: SSI 2003/ 189, SSI 2003/325, SSI 2003/448, SSI 2003/597, SSI 2004/107

Sch.7A Part IV para.26, amended: 2004 asp 7 s.1

Sch.7A Part IV para.26, repealed: 2004 asp 7 s.1

Sch.7A Part IV para.27, repealed: 2004 asp 7 s.1

Sch.7A Part IV para.28, repealed: 2004 asp 7 s.1

Sch.7B para.1, repealed: 2004 asp 7 Sch.2

Sch.7B para.2, repealed: 2004 asp 7 Sch.2

Sch.7B para.2A, applied: 2003 asp 6 Sch.5

Sch.7B para.2A, referred to: 2002 asp 7 Sch.5

Sch.7B para.2A, repealed: 2004 asp 7 Sch.2

Sch.7B para.2B, repealed: 2004 asp 7 Sch.2

Sch.7B para.3, repealed: 2004 asp 7 Sch.2

1978–cont.

29. National Health Service (Scotland) Act 1978–cont.

Sch.7B para.4, repealed: 2004 asp 7 Sch.2

Sch.7B para.5, repealed: 2004 asp 7 Sch.2

Sch.7B para.6, repealed: 2004 asp 7 Sch.2

Sch.7B para.7, repealed: 2004 asp 7 Sch.2

Sch.7B para.8, repealed: 2004 asp 7 Sch.2

Sch.8 para.7, enabling: SSI 2004/38

Sch.8 para.8, varied: SSI 2004/31 Art.3

Sch.9 para.1, amended: 2003 asp 4 Sch.4 para.5

Sch.9 para.1, applied: SSI 2004/162 Reg.7

Sch.9 para.1, enabling: SSI 2004/162

Sch.11 para.2, applied: SSI 2003/158 Reg.2, Reg.5

Sch.11 para.2, enabling: SSI 2002/17, SSI 2002/86, SSI 2002/224, SSI 2003/158, SSI 2003/218, SSI 2003/431, SSI 2004/ 97, SSI 2004/168

Sch.11 para.2A, enabling: SSI 2002/17, SSI 2002/86, SSI 2002/224, SSI 2003/218, SSI 2003/431, SSI 2004/97, SSI 2004/ 168

Sch.11 para.3, applied: SSI 2003/158 Reg.3, Reg.4, Reg.5

Sch.11 para.3, enabling: SSI 2003/158, SSI 2004/101

Sch.11 para.7, applied: SSI 2003/158 Sch.2

30. Interpretation Act 1978

see *Spring Salmon & Seafood Ltd v Advocate General for Scotland* [2004] S.T.C. 444 (OH), Lady Smith

applied: 2002 c.40 s.211, 2003 c.17 s.198, 2003 c.26 s.21, s.93, 2004 c.30 s.35, SI 2004/1662 Art.3, SI 2004/1680 Sch.1

referred to: SI 2004/1611 Reg.35, SI 2004/ 1771 Art.1, SI 2004/2744 Art.3

s.5, see *Haringey LBC v Marks & Spencer Plc* [2004] EWHC 1141, [2004] 3 All E.R. 868 (QBD (Admin Ct)), Maurice Kay, J.; see *Rosser v Inland Revenue Commissioners* [2003] S.T.C. (S.C.D.) 311 (Sp Comm), Michael Tildesley; see *Verderers of the New Forest v Young (No.2)* [2003] EWHC 3253, [2004] 1 E.G.L.R. 1 (QBD (Admin Ct)), Rose, L.J.

s.6, see *Caurti v DPP* [2001] EWHC Admin 867, [2002] Crim. L.R. 131 (QBD (Admin Ct)), Cresswell, J.

s.7, see *Beanby Estates Ltd v Egg Stores (Stamford Hill) Ltd* [2003] EWHC 1252, [2003] 1 W.L.R. 2064 (Ch D), Neuberger, J.; see *CA Webber (Transport) Ltd v Railtrack Plc* [2003] EWCA Civ 1167, [2004] 1 W.L.R. 320 (CA), Peter Gibson, L.J.; see *Chelminski v Gdynia America Shipping Lines (London) Ltd* [2004] EWCA Civ 871, [2004] 3 All E.R. 666 (CA), Pill, L.J.; see *R. (on the application of Durham CC) v North Durham Justices* [2004] EWHC 1073, (2004) 168 J.P. 269 (QBD (Admin Ct)), Moses, J.; see *Scotford*

1978–cont.

30. Interpretation Act 1978–cont.

s.7–cont.

v *Smithkline Beecham* [2002] I.C.R. 264 (EAT), Recorder Langstaff Q.C.; see *Zietsman (t/a Berkshire Orthodontics) v Stubbington* [2002] I.C.R. 249 (EAT), Judge Peter Clark

s.7, applied: 2002 c.40 s.126, 2002 c.i s.37, SI 2002/412 Art.41, SI 2002/1064 Art.31, SI 2002/1065 Art.27, SI 2002/1066 Art.46, SI 2002/1327 Art.33, SI 2002/1891 Sch.2 para.14, SI 2002/3171 Reg.27, SI 2002/3172 Reg.30, SI 2002/3173 Reg.30, SI 2002/3174 Reg.30, SI 2002/3175 Reg.30, SI 2002/3176 Reg.41, 2003 c.14 s.84, 2003 c.17 s.184, 2003 c.21 s.364, s.394, 2003 c.32 s.71, 2003 c.38 s.79, SI 2003/750 Sch.5 para.15, SI 2003/751 Sch.6 para.15, SI 2003/1075 Art.44, SI 2003/1996 Reg.9, SI 2003/2496 Art.9, SI 2003/3241 Reg.25, SI 2003/3311 Reg.4, SI 2003/3364 Art.27, 2004 c.20 s.193, 2004 c.21 s.47, 2004 c.35 s.303, SI 2004/389 Art.42, SI 2004/757 Art.53, SI 2004/1495 Reg.20, SI 2004/1818 Reg.6, SI 2004/2881 Reg.30, SSI 2002/400 Reg.16, SSI 2003/71 Reg.16, SSI 2003/579 Reg.25, SSI 2004/86 Reg.16, SSI 2004/171 Art.27, SSI 2004/317 Reg.24

s.7, disapplied: SI 2003/1369 Reg.5, Reg.8, Reg.11, Reg.12, Reg.13

s.7, referred to: SI 2004/1468 Sch.6 para.15

s.14, applied: 2002 c.32 Sch.15 para.8, SI 2002/1501 Art.13

s.16, see *Road Management Services (A13) Plc v London Power Networks Plc* [2003] B.L.R. 303 (QBD (T&CC)), Forbes, J.

s.16, applied: SI 2002/920 Sch.1 para.2, Sch.1 para.4, SI 2002/2439 Sch.1 para.7, SI 2002/3185 Art.7, SI 2003/3311 Reg.4

s.16, referred to: 2002 c.23 s.81, SI 2002/920 Sch.1 para.2, SI 2003/895 Reg.15, 2004 c.12 s.283

s.17, applied: 2002 c.23 s.20, 2004 c.24 s.47

s.17, disapplied: 2002 c.1 Sch.5 para.1, 2002 c.24 Sch.2 para.5, SI 2002/3171 Reg.29, SI 2002/3172 Reg.32, SI 2002/3173 Reg.32, SI 2002/3174 Reg.32, SI 2002/3175 Reg.32, 2003 c.1 Sch.7 para.6, SI 2003/2682 Sch.1 para.12, SI 2004/2881 Reg.32, SSI 2004/317 Reg.27

s.17, referred to: 2002 c.23 s.81, SI 2002/1330 Reg.6, SI 2003/1994 Reg.6, 2004 c.12 s.283

s.18, see *R. (on the application of Junttan Oy) v Bristol Magistrates Court* [2003] UKHL 55, [2004] 2 All E.R. 555 (HL), Lord Hobhouse of Woodborough

s.20, disapplied: 2003 c.8 s.2

s.21, applied: 2002 c.29 s.323, 2002 c.40 s.230, s.246

1978–cont.

30. Interpretation Act 1978–cont.

s.23, applied: SI 2002/920 Sch.1 para.2, Sch.1 para.4

s.23, referred to: SI 2002/920 Sch.1 para.2, Sch.1 para.4

Sch.1, see *Verderers of the New Forest v Young (No.2)* [2003] EWHC 3253, [2004] 1 E.G.L.R. 1 (QBD (Admin Ct)), Rose, L.J.

Sch.1, amended: 2002 c.8 s.1, 2002 c.26 Sch.13, SI 2002/253 Sch.5 para.7, SI 2002/3135 Sch.1 para.10, 2003 c.1 Sch.6 para.148, 2003 c.44 Sch.3 para.49, 2004 c.33 Sch.27 para.59, SI 2004/1771 Sch.1 para.7

Sch.1, referred to: 2003 c.1 s.721

Sch.1, repealed (in part): 2003 c.44 Sch.37 Part 4, Sch.3 para.49

31. Theft Act 1978

s.1, see *R. v Smith (Wallace Duncan) (No.4)* [2004] EWCA Crim 631, [2004] Q.B. 1418 (CA (Crim Div)), Lord Woolf of Barnes, L.C.J.; see *R. v Sofroniou (Leon Florenzous)* [2003] EWCA Crim 3681, [2004] Q.B. 1218 (CA (Crim Div)), May, L.J.

s.1, applied: 2003 c.17 Sch.4 para.8, 2004 c.19 s.14

s.2, applied: 2003 c.17 Sch.4 para.8, 2004 c.19 s.14

s.14, see *R. v Smith (Wallace Duncan) (No.4)* [2004] EWCA Crim 631, [2004] Q.B. 1418 (CA (Crim Div)), Lord Woolf of Barnes, L.C.J.

33. State Immunity Act 1978

see *Al-Adsani v United Kingdom (35763/97)* (2002) 34 E.H.R.R. 11 (ECHR), L Wildhaber (President); see *Fogarty v United Kingdom (37112/97)* [2002] I.R.L.R. 148 (ECHR), L Wildhaber (President)

s.4, amended: 2002 c.8 s.2

35. Import of Live Fish (Scotland) Act 1978

s.1, applied: SSI 2003/560

s.1, enabling: SSI 2003/560

36. House of Commons (Administration) Act 1978

s.3, applied: 2004 c.9 Sch.2 Part 55

37. Protection of Children Act 1978

see *R. v Grosvenor (Michael James)* [2003] EWCA Crim 1627, [2004] 1 Cr. App. R. (S.) 17 (CA (Crim Div)), Cox, J.

s.1, see *R. v Pardue (Graeme John)* [2003] EWCA Crim 1562, [2004] 1 Cr. App. R. (S.) 13 (CA (Crim Div)), Mitting, J.; see *R. v Smethurst (John Russell)* [2001] EWCA Crim 772, [2002] 1 Cr. App. R. 6 (CA (Crim Div)), Lord Woolf of Barnes, L.C.J.; see *R. v Smith (Graham Westgarth)* [2002] EWCA Crim 683, [2003] 1 Cr. App. R. 13 (CA (Crim Div)), Dyson, L.J.; see *R. v Turpin (Nicholas Victor)* [2001] EWCA Crim

CAP.

1978–cont.

37. Protection of Children Act 1978–*cont.*
s.1–*cont.*
1600, [2002] 1 Cr. App. R. (S.) 77 (CA (Crim Div)), Grigson, J.
s.1, amended: 2003 c.42 Sch.6 para.24
s.1, applied: SI 2002/896 Sch.1 para.41, 2003 c.42 Sch.2 para.1, Sch.3 para.13, 2003 c.44 Sch.15 para.99, SI 2003/1184 Reg.8, Sch.2 para.13, SSI 2003/19 Sch.5 para.5
s.1A, added: 2003 c.42 s.45
s.1A, amended: 2004 c.33 Sch.27 para.60
s.1B, added: 2003 c.42 s.46
s.2, amended: 2003 c.42 s.45
s.4, amended: 2003 c.39 Sch.8 para.199, Sch.10
s.5, amended: 2003 c.39 Sch.8 para.200
s.7, amended: 2003 c.42 s.45
s.7, applied: 2003 c.42 Sch.3 para.97

39. Local Government Act 1978
s.1, amended: 2002 asp 11 Sch.6 para.3

40. Rating (Disabled Persons) Act 1978
applied: SSI 2002/91 Reg.16, SSI 2003/160 Reg.17, SSI 2004/92 Reg.3

42. Finance Act 1978
s.77, repealed: 2003 c.14 Sch.43 Part 5

47. Civil Liability (Contribution) Act 1978
see *Bellefield Computer Services Ltd v E Turner & Sons Ltd* [2002] EWCA Civ 1823, [2003] T.C.L.R. 10 (CA), Potter, L.J.; see *Cape & Dalgleish v Fitzgerald* [2002] UKHL 16, [2002] C.P. Rep. 51 (HL), Lord Mackay of Clashfern; see *Dingles Building (NI) Ltd v Brooks* [2003] P.N.L.R. 8 (CA (NI)), Lord Carswell, L.C.J.; see *Knight v Rochdale Healthcare NHS Trust* [2003] EWHC 1831, [2004] 1 W.L.R. 371 (QBD), Crane, J.; see *Luke v Kingsley Smith & Co* [2003] EWHC 1559, [2004] P.N.L.R. 12 (QBD), Davis, J.; see *Parkman Consulting Engineers v Cumbrian Industrials Ltd* [2001] EWCA Civ 1621, [2002] B.L.R. 64 (CA), Henry, L.J.; see *Rolls Royce Power Engineering Plc v Ricardo Consulting Engineers Ltd* [2003] EWHC 2871, [2004] 2 All E.R. (Comm) 129 (QBD (T&CC)), Judge Richard Seymour Q.C.; see *Webb v Barclays Bank Plc* [2001] EWCA Civ 1141, [2002] P.I.Q.R. P8 (CA), Henry, L.J.
s.1, see *Abbey National Bank Plc v Matthews & Son* [2003] EWHC 925, [2003] 1 W.L.R. 2042 (Ch D), Simon Berry Q.C.; see *Cooperative Retail Services Ltd v Taylor Young Partnership Ltd* [2002] UKHL 17, [2002] 1 W.L.R. 1419 (HL), Lord Hope of Craighead; see *Dubai Aluminium Co Ltd v Salaam* [2002] UKHL 48, [2003] 2 A.C. 366 (HL), Lord Nicholls of Birkenhead; see *Eastgate Group Ltd v Lindsey Morden Group Inc* [2001] EWCA Civ 1446, [2002] 1 W.L.R. 642 (CA), Longmore, L.J.; see *Hampton v Minns* [2002] 1 W.L.R. 1 (Ch

CAP.

1978–cont.

47. Civil Liability (Contribution) Act 1978–*cont.*
s.1–*cont.*
D), Kevin Garnett Q.C.; see *Hurstwood Developments Ltd v Motor & General & Andersley & Co Insurance Services Ltd* [2001] EWCA Civ 1785, [2002] Lloyd's Rep. I.R. 185 (CA), Keene, L.J.; see *Linklaters v HSBC Bank Plc* [2003] EWHC 1113, [2003] 2 Lloyd's Rep. 545 (QBD (Comm Ct)), Gross, J.; see *Niru Battery Manufacturing Co v Milestone Trading Ltd (No.2)* [2003] EWHC 1032, [2003] 2 All E.R. (Comm) 365 (QBD (Comm Ct)), Moore-Bick, J.; see *Royal Brompton Hospital NHS Trust v Hammond (No.3)* [2002] UKHL 14, [2002] 1 W.L.R. 1397 (HL), Lord Steyn; see *Skrine & Co v Euromoney Publications Plc* [2002] I.L.Pr. 22 (QBD), Morland, J.; see *Thames Water Utilities Ltd v Digginwell Plant & Construction Ltd* [2002] EWHC 1171, [2003] Env. L.R. 21 (QBD (T&CC)), Judge Richard Seymour Q.C.
s.2, see *Abbey National Bank Plc v Matthews & Son* [2003] EWHC 925, [2003] 1 W.L.R. 2042 (Ch D), Simon Berry Q.C.
s.6, see *Hurstwood Developments Ltd v Motor & General & Andersley & Co Insurance Services Ltd* [2001] EWCA Civ 1785, [2002] Lloyd's Rep. I.R. 185 (CA), Keene, L.J.; see *Niru Battery Manufacturing Co v Milestone Trading Ltd (No.2)* [2003] EWHC 1032, [2003] 2 All E.R. (Comm) 365 (QBD (Comm Ct)), Moore-Bick, J.; see *Niru Battery Manufacturing Co v Milestone Trading Ltd (No.2)* [2004] EWCA Civ 487, [2004] 2 All E.R. (Comm) 289 (CA), Dame Elizabeth Butler-Sloss (President)

1979

xxiii. Greater London Council (General Powers) Act 1979
s.3, repealed: 2003 c.17 Sch.7

2. Customs and Excise Management Act 1979
applied: 2002 c.29 s.289, s.451, 2002 c.40 Sch.14, SI 2002/1227 Reg.16, Reg.28, SI 2002/1387 Reg.16, Reg.28, SI 2002/1478 Art.3, SI 2002/2573 Art.4, SI 2002/2677 Reg.4, 2003 c.27 s.4, SI 2003/2759 Art.7, SI 2003/3075 Reg.23, SI 2003/3177 Reg.16, Reg.28, 2004 c.20 s.86, SI 2004/1214 Reg.16, Reg.28, SI 2004/1430 Reg.16, Reg.28, SI 2004/1740 Reg.16, SI 2004/2640 Reg.16, Reg.28, SR 2003/97 Reg.5, SR 2003/193 Art.4, SR 2003/303 Reg.6, SSI 2002/445 Reg.28
referred to: 2003 c.44 s.337, SI 2004/1473 Reg.8, SI 2004/1740 Reg.28

1979–cont.

2. **Customs and Excise Management Act 1979**–*cont.*

s.1, applied: 2002 c.28 s.11, SI 2002/111 Art.19, SI 2002/2628 Art.15, SI 2003/1519 Art.19, SI 2004/348 Art.14

s.1, referred to: SI 2003/336 Sch.1 Part 1

s.5, applied: SI 2002/1227 Reg.16, SI 2002/1387 Reg.16, SI 2003/3177 Reg.16, SI 2004/1430 Reg.16, SI 2004/1740 Reg.16, SI 2004/2640 Reg.16, SSI 2002/445 Reg.16

s.6, applied: 2002 c.29 s.454

s.17, applied: 2002 c.23 s.137

s.21, amended: 2003 c.44 Sch.26 para.26

s.33, amended: 2003 c.44 Sch.26 para.26

s.34, amended: 2003 c.44 Sch.26 para.26

s.35, applied: SI 2003/3113 Sch.1

s.50, amended: 2003 c.44 s.293, SI 2004/702 Sch.7 para.3

s.50, applied: 2002 c.29 Sch.2 para.1, Sch.4 para.2, Sch.5 para.1, SI 2002/528 Reg.5, 2003 c.44 Sch.4 para.19, Sch.5 para.18, Sch.5 para.39, SI 2004/1500 Sch.2 para.11, SI 2004/1910 Sch.1

s.50, disapplied: SR 2002/1 Reg.4

s.68, amended: 2003 c.44 s.293, SI 2004/702 Sch.7 para.4

s.68, applied: 2002 c.29 Sch.2 para.1, Sch.2 para.5, Sch.4 para.2, Sch.4 para.5, Sch.5 para.1, Sch.5 para.5, 2003 c.44 Sch.4 para.20, Sch.5 para.19, Sch.5 para.40, SI 2004/1500 Sch.2 para.12, SI 2004/1910 Sch.1

s.68, disapplied: SR 2002/1 Reg.4

s.68, varied: SI 2003/2764 Art.21

s.80, applied: SI 2003/3113 Sch.1

s.92, see *TDG (UK) Ltd v Customs and Excise Commissioners* [2002] V. & D.R. 323 (V&DTr), Nuala Brice (Chairman)

s.92, applied: SI 2004/2065 Reg.6

s.93, enabling: SI 2002/501, SI 2002/1265, SI 2004/1003, SI 2004/2064, SI 2004/2065

s.100A, enabling: SI 2002/1418, SI 2004/2742

s.100G, applied: SI 2002/3057 Reg.4, Reg.5

s.100G, enabling: SI 2002/501, SI 2002/3057, SI 2004/1003, SI 2004/2064, SI 2004/2065

s.100H, amended: 2002 c.23 Sch.3 para.2

s.100H, enabling: SI 2002/501, SI 2002/3057, SI 2004/1003, SI 2004/2064, SI 2004/2065

s.100J, applied: SI 2002/501 Reg.25, SI 2003/2758 Art.4

s.108, applied: SI 2002/1928 Reg.4, SI 2004/2065 Reg.8

s.116, applied: SI 2002/1928 Reg.6, SI 2004/2065 Reg.19

s.118A, enabling: SI 2002/501, SI 2002/1265, SI 2002/1928, SI 2004/2065

1979–cont.

2. **Customs and Excise Management Act 1979**–*cont.*

s.120, enabling: SI 2002/2266

s.127A, enabling: SI 2004/2065

s.133, amended: 2002 c.23 s.21

s.133, repealed (in part): 2002 c.23 Sch.40 Part 1

s.138, applied: SI 2002/868 Reg.4, SI 2004/221 Reg.4, SI 2004/373 Reg.4, SI 2004/432 Reg.4, SI 2004/559 Reg.4, SI 2004/1315 Reg.4

s.139, see *Customs and Excise Commissioners v Everwine Ltd* [2003] EWCA Civ 953, (2003) 147 S.J.L.B. 870 (CA), Keene, L.J.; see *Customs and Excise Commissioners v Venn, Mather & Marquis Publications* [2001] EWHC Admin 1055, (2002) 166 J.P. 53 (QBD (Admin Ct)), Harrison, J.; see *Gora v Customs and Excise Commissioners* [2003] EWCA Civ 525, [2004] Q.B. 93 (CA), Pill, L.J.

s.139, applied: SI 2004/1473 Reg.7

s.140, see *Customs and Excise Commissioners v Everwine Ltd* [2003] EWCA Civ 953, (2003) 147 S.J.L.B. 870 (CA), Keene, L.J.

s.141, see *Customs and Excise Commissioners v Helman* [2002] EWHC 2254, (2002) 166 J.P. 725 (QBD (Admin Ct)), Davis, J.; see *Fox v Customs and Excise Commissioners* [2002] EWHC 1244, [2003] 1 W.L.R. 1331 (QBD (Admin Ct)), Lightman, J.

s.144, applied: SI 2004/1473 Reg.7

s.145, applied: SI 2002/868 Reg.4, SI 2003/2764 Art.21, SI 2003/2765 Art.12, SI 2004/221 Reg.4, SI 2004/318 Art.11, SI 2004/373 Reg.4, SI 2004/432 Reg.4, SI 2004/559 Reg.4, SI 2004/1315 Reg.4, SI 2004/1473 Reg.7

s.145, disapplied: SI 2004/221 Reg.4, SI 2004/373 Reg.4, SI 2004/559 Reg.4, SI 2004/1315 Reg.4

s.145, referred to: SI 2002/868 Reg.4

s.145, varied: SI 2004/318 Art.11

s.146, applied: SI 2002/868 Reg.4, SI 2003/2764 Art.21, SI 2003/2765 Art.12, SI 2004/221 Reg.4, SI 2004/373 Reg.4, SI 2004/432 Reg.4, SI 2004/559 Reg.4, SI 2004/1315 Reg.4, SI 2004/1473 Reg.7

s.146, varied: SI 2004/318 Art.11

s.146A, applied: SI 2002/868 Reg.4, SI 2003/2764 Art.21, SI 2003/2765 Art.12, SI 2004/221 Reg.4, SI 2004/373 Reg.4, SI 2004/432 Reg.4, SI 2004/559 Reg.4, SI 2004/1315 Reg.4

s.146A, varied: SI 2004/318 Art.11

s.147, applied: SI 2002/868 Reg.4, SI 2003/2764 Art.21, SI 2003/2765 Art.12, SI 2004/221 Reg.4, SI 2004/373 Reg.4, SI 2004/432 Reg.4, SI 2004/559 Reg.4, SI 2004/1315 Reg.4

CAP.

1979–cont.

2. Customs and Excise Management Act 1979–*cont.*

s.147, repealed (in part): 2003 c.44 Sch.37 Part 4, Sch.3 para.50

s.147, varied: SI 2004/318 Art.11

s.148, applied: SI 2002/868 Reg.4, SI 2003/ 2764 Art.21, SI 2003/2765 Art.12, SI 2004/221 Reg.4, SI 2004/373 Reg.4, SI 2004/432 Reg.4, SI 2004/559 Reg.4, SI 2004/1315 Reg.4

s.148, varied: SI 2004/318 Art.11

s.150, applied: SI 2002/868 Reg.4, SI 2003/ 2764 Art.21, SI 2003/2765 Art.12, SI 2004/221 Reg.4, SI 2004/373 Reg.4, SI 2004/432 Reg.4, SI 2004/559 Reg.4, SI 2004/1315 Reg.4

s.150, varied: SI 2004/318 Art.11

s.151, applied: SI 2002/868 Reg.4, SI 2003/ 2764 Art.21, SI 2003/2765 Art.12, SI 2004/221 Reg.4, SI 2004/373 Reg.4, SI 2004/432 Reg.4, SI 2004/559 Reg.4, SI 2004/1315 Reg.4

s.151, varied: SI 2004/318 Art.11

s.152, see *Customs and Excise Commissioners v Helman* [2002] EWHC 2254, (2002) 166 J.P. 725 (QBD (Admin Ct)), Davis, J.; see *Gascoyne v Customs and Excise Commissioners* [2003] EWHC 257, [2003] Ch. 292 (Ch D), Neuberger, J.; see *Gora v Customs and Excise Commissioners* [2003] EWCA Civ 525, [2004] Q.B. 93 (CA), Pill, L.J.

s.152, applied: SI 2002/868 Reg.4, SI 2003/ 2764 Art.21, SI 2003/2765 Art.12, SI 2004/221 Reg.4, SI 2004/373 Reg.4, SI 2004/432 Reg.4, SI 2004/559 Reg.4, SI 2004/1315 Reg.4, SI 2004/1473 Reg.7

s.152, varied: SI 2004/318 Art.11

s.153, applied: SI 2002/868 Reg.4, SI 2003/ 2764 Art.21, SI 2003/2765 Art.12, SI 2004/221 Reg.4, SI 2004/373 Reg.4, SI 2004/432 Reg.4, SI 2004/559 Reg.4, SI 2004/1315 Reg.4, SI 2004/1473 Reg.7

s.153, varied: SI 2004/318 Art.11

s.154, applied: SI 2002/868 Reg.4, SI 2003/ 2764 Art.21, SI 2003/2765 Art.12, SI 2004/221 Reg.4, SI 2004/373 Reg.4, SI 2004/432 Reg.4, SI 2004/559 Reg.4, SI 2004/1315 Reg.4, SI 2004/1473 Reg.7

s.154, varied: SI 2004/318 Art.11

s.155, applied: SI 2002/868 Reg.4, SI 2003/ 2764 Art.21, SI 2003/2765 Art.12, SI 2004/221 Reg.4, SI 2004/373 Reg.4, SI 2004/432 Reg.4, SI 2004/559 Reg.4, SI 2004/1315 Reg.4, SI 2004/1473 Reg.7

s.155, varied: SI 2004/318 Art.11

s.163, see *R. (on the application of Hoverspeed Ltd) v Customs and Excise Commissioners* [2002] EWCA Civ 1804, [2003] Q.B.1041 (CA), Mance, L.J.

CAP.

1979–cont.

2. Customs and Excise Management Act 1979–*cont.*

s.163A, see *R. (on the application of Hoverspeed Ltd) v Customs and Excise Commissioners* [2002] EWCA Civ 1804, [2003] Q.B.1041 (CA), Mance, L.J.

s.164, applied: 2002 c.29 s.289

s.167, see *Customs and Excise Commissioners v Everwine Ltd* [2003] EWCA Civ 953, (2003) 147 S.J.L.B. 870 (CA), Keene, L.J.

s.167, applied: SI 2003/3102 Sch.1, SI 2003/ 3113 Sch.1

s.168, applied: SI 2003/3102 Sch.1

s.170, see *Beacom (Michael) v HM Advocate* 2002 S.L.T. 349 (HCJ Appeal), Lord Clarke; see *R. v Chuni (Narinder Nath)* [2002] EWCA Crim 453, [2002] 2 Cr. App. R. (S.) 82 (CA (Crim Div)), Gibbs, J.; see *R. v Forbes (Giles)* [2001] UKHL 40, [2002] 2 A.C. 512 (HL), Lord Hutton; see *R. v Matudi (Misawki Kurawku)* [2003] EWCA Crim 697, [2003] E.H.L.R. 13 (CA (Crim Div)), Scott Baker, L.J.; see *R. v Smith (David Cadman)* [2001] UKHL 68, [2002] 1 W.L.R. 54 (HL), Lord Rodger of Earlsferry; see *R. v Taylor (Robert John)* [2001] EWCA Crim 1044, [2002] Crim. L.R. 205 (CA (Crim Div)), Rougier, J.; see *R. v Unlu (Ali)* [2002] EWCA Crim 2220, [2003] 1 Cr. App. R. (S.) 101 (CA (Crim Div)), Clarke, L.J.

s.170, amended: 2003 c.44 s.293, SI 2004/ 702 Sch.7 para.5

s.170, applied: 2002 c.29 Sch.2 para.1, Sch.2 para.5, Sch.4 para.2, Sch.4 para.5, Sch.5 para.1, Sch.5 para.5, SI 2002/528 Sch.1 para.33, SI 2002/635 Sch.1 para.4, SI 2002/896 Sch.1 para.42, Sch.1 para.59, Sch.1 para.71, 2003 c.17 Sch.4 para.9, 2003 c.42 Sch.3 para.14, Sch.3 para.44, Sch.3 para.78, 2003 c.44 Sch.4 para.21, Sch.5 para.20, Sch.5 para.41, Sch.15 para.100, Sch.16 para.9, Sch.17 para.83, SI 2004/1500 Sch.2 para.13, SI 2004/1910 Sch.1, SI 2004/2695 Sch.1 para.18, SSI 2003/19 Sch.5 para.7, Sch.5 para.10, Sch.5 para.17

s.170, disapplied: SR 2002/1 Reg.4

s.170, varied: SI 2003/2764 Art.21

s.170A, varied: SI 2003/2758 Sch.1 para.13

s.170B, see *Customs and Excise Commissioners v Everwine Ltd* [2003] EWCA Civ 953, (2003) 147 S.J.L.B. 870 (CA), Keene, L.J.

s.170B, applied: 2003 c.17 Sch.4 para.9

Sch.1 para.2, amended: 2003 c.44 Sch.28 para.2

Sch.3, see *Gascoyne v Customs and Excise Commissioners* [2003] EWHC 257, [2003] Ch. 292 (Ch D), Neuberger, J.; see *Gora v Customs and Excise Commissioners*

1979–cont.

2. **Customs and Excise Management Act 1979**–*cont.*
Sch.3–*cont.*
[2003] EWCA Civ 525, [2004] Q.B. 93 (CA), Pill, L.J.
Sch.3, applied: SI 2004/1473 Reg.7
Sch.3 para.3, see *Customs and Excise Commissioners v Dickinson* [2003] EWHC 2358, [2004] 1 W.L.R. 1160 (Ch D), Peter Smith, J.
Sch.3 para.6, see *Customs and Excise Commissioners v Helman* [2002] EWHC 2254, (2002) 166 J.P. 725 (QBD (Admin Ct)), Davis, J.; see *Customs and Excise Commissioners v Newbury* [2003] EWHC 702, [2003] 1 W.L.R. 2131 (QBD (Admin Ct)), Hale, L.J.; see *R. (on the application of Mudie) v Dover Magistrates Court* [2003] EWCA Civ 237, [2003] Q.B. 1238 (CA), Laws, L.J.
Sch.3 para.8, see *R. (on the application of Mudie) v Dover Magistrates Court* [2003] EWCA Civ 237, [2003] Q.B. 1238 (CA), Laws, L.J.
Sch.4 para.12, amended: 2003 c.17 Sch.7

3. **Customs and Excise Duties (General Reliefs) Act 1979**
applied: 2004 c.20 s.86
s.7, enabling: SI 2004/1002
s.12, applied: SI 2002/501 Reg.3
s.13, enabling: SI 2002/2691, SI 2004/1002
s.13A, applied: SI 2002/501 Reg.3
s.13B, amended: 2002 c.1 Sch.3 para.7

4. **Alcoholic Liquor Duties Act 1979**
applied: SI 2004/674 Sch.1 Part 1
s.1, repealed (in part): 2002 c.23 Sch.40 Part 1
s.4, amended: 2003 c.17 Sch.6 para.72, Sch.7
s.4, repealed (in part): 2003 c.17 Sch.6 para.72, Sch.7
s.36, amended: 2002 c.23 Sch.1 para.1, 2003 c.14 s.2, 2004 c.12 s.2
s.36A, added: 2002 c.23 Sch.1 para.2
s.36B, added: 2002 c.23 Sch.1 para.2
s.36C, added: 2002 c.23 Sch.1 para.2
s.36C, amended: SI 2004/1296 Art.3
s.36D, added: 2002 c.23 Sch.1 para.2
s.36D, amended: SI 2004/1296 Art.3
s.36E, added: 2002 c.23 Sch.1 para.2
s.36E, amended: SI 2004/1296 Art.3
s.36F, added: 2002 c.23 Sch.1 para.2
s.36F, amended: SI 2004/1296 Art.3
s.36G, added: 2002 c.23 Sch.1 para.2
s.36H, added: 2002 c.23 Sch.1 para.2
s.36H, enabling: SI 2004/1296
s.41A, applied: SI 2002/501 Reg.3
s.47, applied: SI 2002/501 Reg.3
s.49, amended: 2002 c.23 Sch.1 para.3
s.49, applied: SI 2003/2758 Art.4
s.49, enabling: SI 2002/1265
s.54, applied: SI 2002/501 Reg.3

1979–cont.

4. **Alcoholic Liquor Duties Act 1979**–*cont.*
s.55, applied: SI 2002/501 Reg.3
s.62, amended: 2002 c.23 s.2
s.62, applied: SI 2002/501 Reg.3
s.64A, added: 2004 c.12 s.4
s.71, amended: 2003 c.17 Sch.6 para.73, Sch.7
s.71, repealed (in part): 2003 c.17 Sch.6 para.73, Sch.7
Sch.1, amended: 2003 c.14 s.3, 2004 c.12 s.3
Sch.2A para.1, added: 2004 c.12 Sch.1
Sch.2A para.2, added: 2004 c.12 Sch.1
Sch.2A para.3, added: 2004 c.12 Sch.1
Sch.2A para.4, added: 2004 c.12 Sch.1
Sch.2A para.5, added: 2004 c.12 Sch.1
Sch.2A para.6, added: 2004 c.12 Sch.1
Sch.2A para.7, added: 2004 c.12 Sch.1
Sch.2A para.8, added: 2004 c.12 Sch.1
Sch.2A para.9, added: 2004 c.12 Sch.1
Sch.2A para.10, added: 2004 c.12 Sch.1
Sch.2A para.11, added: 2004 c.12 Sch.1
Sch.2A para.12, added: 2004 c.12 Sch.1
Sch.2A para.13, added: 2004 c.12 Sch.1
Sch.2A para.14, added: 2004 c.12 Sch.1
Sch.2A para.15, added: 2004 c.12 Sch.1
Sch.3 para.5, repealed: 2003 c.17 Sch.7

5. **Hydrocarbon Oil Duties Act 1979**
applied: SI 2002/1826 Art.11, Art.15, Art.16, SI 2004/674 Sch.1 Part 1, SI 2004/1282 Art.13, Art.15, SI 2004/2063 Art.1, Art.5, SI 2004/2064 Reg.4, Reg.5
referred to: SI 2004/2063 Art.5
s.1, amended: 2004 c.12 s.7
s.2A, amended: 2002 c.23 s.5, 2004 c.12 s.7, s.8, s.10
s.2AA, added: 2002 c.23 s.5
s.2AB, added: 2004 c.12 s.10
s.3, varied: SI 2002/1928 Reg.3, SI 2004/2065 Reg.3
s.5, substituted: 2004 c.12 s.6
s.6, amended: 2003 c.14 s.4, 2004 c.12 s.5, s.7
s.6, varied: SI 2004/2063 Art.3
s.6A, amended: 2002 c.23 s.7, Sch.2 para.2, 2004 c.12 s.10, s.12
s.6A, applied: 2004 c.12 s.10, SI 2004/2064 Reg.5
s.6A, enabling: SI 2002/3042, SI 2004/2062
s.6AA, added: 2002 c.23 s.5
s.6AA, amended: 2003 c.14 s.4, 2004 c.12 s.5, s.11, Sch.42 Part 1
s.6AA, applied: SI 2002/1928 Reg.3, SI 2004/2064 Reg.5
s.6AA, varied: SI 2004/2063 Art.3
s.6AB, added: 2002 c.23 s.5
s.6AB, amended: 2002 c.23 Sch.2 para.7, Sch.40 Part 1
s.6AB, applied: SI 2002/1928 Reg.3, SI 2004/2065 Reg.3

1979–cont.

5. Hydrocarbon Oil Duties Act 1979–cont.

s.6AC, added: 2002 c.23 s.5

s.6AC, enabling: SI 2002/1928, SI 2004/2065

s.6AD, added: 2004 c.12 s.10

s.6AE, added: 2004 c.12 s.10

s.6AE, applied: SI 2004/2065 Reg.3

s.6AF, added: 2004 c.12 s.10

s.6AF, enabling: SI 2004/2065

s.8, amended: 2004 c.12 s.6

s.8, applied: SI 2004/2064 Reg.5

s.9, applied: SI 2002/1471 Reg.8, Reg.10, SI 2002/1773 Reg.5

s.11, amended: 2002 c.23 Sch.2 para.3, 2003 c.14 s.5, 2004 c.12 s.5, s.10

s.11, applied: SI 2002/1773 Reg.4

s.11, varied: SI 2004/2063 Art.4

s.12, see *Tyler v Customs and Excise Commissioners* [2003] V. & D.R. 358 (VAT and Duties Tribunal (London)), John Walters Q.C. (Chairman)

s.12, amended: 2002 c.23 Sch.3 para.6, Sch.3 para.7

s.13A, amended: 2003 c.14 s.4, 2004 c.12 s.5, s.7

s.13AA, amended: 2004 c.12 s.7, s.10

s.13AA, applied: SI 2002/1773 Reg.4

s.13AA, varied: SI 2004/2063 Art.4

s.14, amended: 2003 c.14 s.5, 2004 c.12 s.5, s.10

s.14, applied: SI 2002/1471 Reg.7, SI 2002/1773 Reg.4

s.14, varied: SI 2004/2063 Art.4

s.15, varied: SI 2002/1928 Reg.3, SI 2004/2065 Reg.3

s.17A, added: 2002 c.23 Sch.2 para.4

s.17A, applied: SI 2002/1928 Reg.8, SI 2004/2065 Reg.28

s.19, varied: SI 2002/1928 Reg.3, SI 2004/2065 Reg.3

s.20, varied: SI 2002/1928 Reg.3, SI 2004/2065 Reg.3

s.20AA, varied: SI 2004/2065 Reg.3

s.20AA, enabling: SI 2004/2065, SI 2004/2069

s.20AAA, amended: 2002 c.23 Sch.2 para.5

s.20AAA, applied: 2004 c.12 s.9

s.20AAA, substituted: 2004 c.12 s.9

s.20AAB, amended: 2002 c.23 Sch.2 para.5, 2004 c.12 s.9, Sch.42 Part 1

s.20AB, enabling: SI 2003/1597

s.21, amended: 2004 c.12 s.6

s.21, varied: SI 2002/1928 Reg.3, SI 2004/2065 Reg.3

s.21, enabling: SI 2002/1928, SI 2004/2064, SI 2004/2065

s.22, amended: 2002 c.23 Sch.2 para.5, 2004 c.12 s.10

s.23A, added: 2002 c.23 Sch.3 para.1

s.23A, applied: SI 2002/3057 Reg.8

1979–cont.

5. Hydrocarbon Oil Duties Act 1979–cont.

s.23A, disapplied: SI 2002/3057 Reg.3, Reg.6

s.23B, added: 2002 c.23 Sch.3 para.1

s.23B, enabling: SI 2002/3057

s.23C, added: 2004 c.12 s.13

s.23C, enabling: SI 2004/2064

s.24, amended: 2002 c.23 Sch.3 para.8

s.24, enabling: SI 2002/1471, SI 2002/1773, SI 2002/1928, SI 2004/2065

s.24A, enabling: SI 2002/1773

s.24AA, added: 2002 c.23 Sch.3 para.3

s.24AA, enabling: SI 2002/3057

s.27, amended: 2002 c.23 Sch.2 para.6, Sch.3 para.4, Sch.3 para.9, 2004 c.12 s.7, s.10

Sch.2A Part I para.1, repealed: 2004 c.12 Sch.42 Part 1

Sch.2A Part I para.2, repealed: 2004 c.12 Sch.42 Part 1

Sch.2A Part I para.2A, repealed: 2004 c.12 Sch.42 Part 1

Sch.2A Part I para.3, repealed: 2004 c.12 Sch.42 Part 1

Sch.2A Part II para.4, repealed: 2004 c.12 Sch.42 Part 1

Sch.2A Part II para.5, repealed: 2004 c.12 Sch.42 Part 1

Sch.2A Part II para.6, repealed: 2004 c.12 Sch.42 Part 1

Sch.2A Part II para.6A, repealed: 2004 c.12 Sch.42 Part 1

Sch.2A Part II para.7, repealed: 2004 c.12 Sch.42 Part 1

Sch.2A Part IIA para.7A, repealed: 2004 c.12 Sch.42 Part 1

Sch.2A Part IIB para.7B, added: 2002 c.23 Sch.2 para.5

Sch.2A Part IIB para.7B, repealed: 2004 c.12 Sch.42 Part 1

Sch.2A Part III para.8, repealed: 2004 c.12 Sch.42 Part 1

Sch.2A Part III para.9, amended: 2002 c.23 Sch.2 para.5

Sch.2A Part III para.9, repealed: 2004 c.12 Sch.42 Part 1

Sch.2A Part III para.10, amended: 2002 c.23 Sch.2 para.5

Sch.2A Part III para.10, repealed: 2004 c.12 Sch.42 Part 1

Sch.2A Part III para.11, repealed: 2004 c.12 Sch.42 Part 1

Sch.3 Part I para.3, varied: SI 2004/2065 Reg.3

Sch.3 Part I para.3, enabling: SI 2004/2064, SI 2004/2065

Sch.3 Part I para.11, varied: SI 2002/1928 Reg.3, SI 2004/2065 Reg.3

Sch.3 Part I para.11, enabling: SI 2002/1928, SI 2004/2064, SI 2004/2065

Sch.3 Part III para.19, enabling: SI 2004/2064

1979–cont.

5. Hydrocarbon Oil Duties Act 1979–*cont.*
Sch.3 Part III para.25, enabling: SI 2004/2064
Sch.4, enabling: SI 2002/1471, SI 2002/1773
Sch.4 para.3, amended: 2002 c.23 Sch.2 para.4
Sch.4 para.3, enabling: SI 2002/1928, SI 2004/2065
Sch.4 para.17, varied: SI 2004/2065 Reg.3
Sch.4 para.17, enabling: SI 2004/2065
Sch.4 para.21, varied: SI 2004/2065 Reg.3
Sch.4 para.21, enabling: SI 2004/2065

7. Tobacco Products Duty Act 1979
applied: SI 2004/674 Sch.1 Part 1
s.1, repealed (in part): SI 2003/1471 Art.3
s.1, enabling: SI 2003/1471
s.7, applied: SI 2002/501 Reg.3, SI 2003/2758 Art.4
s.7, enabling: SI 2003/1523, SI 2004/1003
s.8G, applied: 2003 c.17 Sch.4 para.10
s.8H, applied: 2003 c.17 Sch.4 para.10
Sch.1, amended: 2002 c.23 s.1, 2003 c.14 s.1
Sch.1, substituted: 2004 c.12 s.1

8. Excise Duties (Surcharges or Rebates) Act 1979
s.1, amended: 2002 c.23 Sch.40 Part 1
s.1, enabling: SI 2004/2063, SI 2004/3160, SI 2004/3162
s.2, enabling: SI 2004/2063, SI 2004/3160, SI 2004/3162

10. Public Lending Right Act 1979
s.2, amended: SI 2003/839 Art.2
s.2, applied: SI 2003/839, SI 2003/839 Art.2
s.2, enabling: SI 2003/839
s.3, enabling: SI 2002/3123, SI 2003/3045, SI 2004/1258, SI 2004/3128
Sch.1 para.2, applied: SI 2003/839 Art.2

13. Agricultural Statistics Act 1979
s.2, repealed: 2004 c.14 Sch.1 Part 2
s.3, amended: 2004 c.14 Sch.1 Part 2
s.3, repealed (in part): 2004 c.14 Sch.1 Part 2
s.4, amended: 2004 c.14 Sch.1 Part 2
s.6, amended: SI 2002/794 Sch.1 para.20
s.8, repealed (in part): 2004 c.14 Sch.1 Part 2

14. Capital Gains Tax Act 1979
s.1, see *Smith v Inland Revenue Commissioners* [2004] S.T.C. (S.C.D.) 60 (Sp Comm), J Gordon Reid Q.C.
s.27, see *Jerome v Kelly (Inspector of Taxes)* [2002] EWCA Civ 1879, [2003] S.T.C. 206 (CA), Jonathan Parker, L.J.; see *Jerome v Kelly (Inspector of Taxes)* [2002] EWHC 604, [2002] S.T.C. 609 (Ch D), Park, J.; see *Jerome v Kelly (Inspector of Taxes)* [2004] UKHL 25, [2004] 1 W.L.R. 1409 (HL), Lord Nicholls of Birkenhead; see *Smith v Inland Revenue Commissioners* [2004] S.T.C. (S.C.D.) 60 (Sp Comm), J Gordon Reid Q.C.

1979–cont.

14. Capital Gains Tax Act 1979–*cont.*
s.29A, see *Mansworth (Inspector of Taxes) v Jelley* [2002] EWHC 442, [2002] S.T.C. 1013 (Ch D), Lightman, J.
s.46, see *Jerome v Kelly (Inspector of Taxes)* [2002] EWCA Civ 1879, [2003] S.T.C. 206 (CA), Jonathan Parker, L.J.
s.137, see *Mansworth (Inspector of Taxes) v Jelley* [2002] EWCA Civ 1829, [2003] S.T.C. 53 (CA), Chadwick, L.J.
s.150, see *Ellis (Inspector of Taxes) v Norbury Hill Ltd* [2004] R.V.R. 86 (Lands Tr), PH Clarke, FRICS

16. Criminal Evidence Act 1979
repealed (in part): SI 2004/1501 Sch.2
s.1, amended: 2003 c.44 Sch.37 Part 5

17. Vaccine Damage Payments Act 1979
s.1, amended: SI 2002/1592 Art.2
s.1, applied: SI 2002/1592 Art.1, Sch.1 para.3, Sch.1 para.5
s.1, referred to: SI 2002/1592 Sch.1 para.3
s.3, amended: SI 2002/1592 Art.3
s.3, referred to: SI 2002/1592 Sch.1 para.3, Sch.1 para.6
s.4, enabling: SI 2002/1379, SI 2004/3368
s.7B, amended: SI 2002/1592 Art.5

23. Public Health Laboratory Service Act 1979
s.1, repealed (in part): 2003 c.43 Sch.14 Part 7
s.2, repealed: 2003 c.43 Sch.14 Part 7

27. Kiribati Act 1979
Sch.1 para.9, repealed: 2002 c.39 Sch.3

28. Carriage by Air and Road Act 1979
Commencement Orders: 2004 c.14 Sch.1 Part 4
s.3, repealed (in part): 2004 c.14 Sch.1 Part 14
s.4, amended: 2004 c.14 Sch.1 Part 14
s.4, repealed (in part): 2004 c.14 Sch.1 Part 14
s.5, amended: 2004 c.14 Sch.1 Part 14
s.6, repealed (in part): 2004 c.14 Sch.1 Part 14
Sch.2 para.5, repealed: 2004 c.14 Sch.1 Part 4

33. Land Registration (Scotland) Act 1979
Commencement Orders: SSI 2002/432 Art.2
s.2, amended: 2003 asp 9 Sch.14 para.7
s.3, amended: 2003 asp 9 Sch.14 para.7
s.3, disapplied: 2003 asp 9 s.4, s.71, s.73, s.75
s.3, referred to: 2003 asp 9 s.119
s.4, amended: 2003 asp 2 s.66
s.6, amended: 2003 asp 9 s.112, Sch.14 para.7
s.6, applied: 2003 asp 9 s.51
s.9, see *Mutch v Mavisbank Properties Ltd* 2002 S.L.T. (Sh Ct) 91 (Sh Pr), EF Bowen Q.C., Sheriff Principal
s.9, amended: 2003 asp 9 s.112
s.9, applied: 2003 asp 9 s.51
s.12, amended: 2003 asp 9 Sch.14 para.7, 2004 asp 11 s.13
s.15, amended: 2003 asp 9 Sch.14 para.7, Sch.15
s.15, applied: 2003 asp 9 s.41, s.60
s.15, disapplied: 2003 asp 9 s.60

CAP.

1979–cont.

33. Land Registration (Scotland) Act 1979–*cont.*
s.16, applied: 2004 c.20 Sch.5 para.6
s.16, varied: 2004 c.20 Sch.21 para.7
s.17, repealed: 2003 asp 9 Sch.15
s.18, repealed: 2003 asp 9 Sch.15
s.27, enabling: SSI 2004/476
s.28, amended: 2003 asp 2 s.22, 2003 asp 9 Sch.14 para.7
s.28, applied: 2004 asp 10 s.16
s.30, enabling: SSI 2002/432

34. Credit Unions Act 1979
Commencement Orders: SI 2003/306 Art.2
referred to: SI 2003/256 Art.2
s.1, amended: SI 2002/1501 Art.2, SI 2003/256 Art.3
s.1, applied: SSI 2004/468 Reg.10
s.2, amended: SI 2002/1501 Art.2
s.3, amended: SI 2003/256 Art.4
s.4, repealed (in part): SI 2002/1555 Art.7
s.5, repealed (in part): SI 2002/1501 Art.2
s.8, repealed (in part): SI 2002/1501 Art.2
s.9, amended: SI 2002/1501 Art.2
s.9, repealed (in part): SI 2002/1501 Art.2
s.9A, added: SI 2003/256 Art.5
s.10, amended: SI 2002/1501 Art.2
s.10, repealed (in part): SI 2002/1501 Art.2
s.11, amended: SI 2002/1501 Art.2
s.11, repealed (in part): SI 2002/1501 Art.2
s.11C, applied: SI 2002/704 Art.5
s.13, repealed: SI 2002/1501 Art.2
s.14, repealed (in part): SI 2002/1501 Art.2
s.15, repealed: SI 2002/1501 Art.2
s.17, repealed (in part): SI 2002/1501 Art.2
s.18, amended: SI 2002/1501 Art.2
s.18, applied: SI 2003/3075 Reg.26
s.19, applied: SI 2002/704 Art.5, SI 2002/1501 Art.6
s.19, repealed: SI 2002/1501 Art.2
s.20, amended: SI 2002/1501 Art.2
s.21, amended: SI 2002/1501 Art.2
s.23, amended: SI 2002/1501 Art.2
s.23, repealed (in part): SI 2002/1501 Art.2
s.24, amended: SI 2002/1501 Art.2
s.27, applied: SI 2002/704 Art.6
s.27, repealed: SI 2002/1501 Art.2
s.31, amended: SI 2002/1501 Art.2, SI 2002/1555 Art.7, 2004 c.33 Sch.27 para.61
s.31, varied: 2004 c.33 Sch.21 para.10
s.32, amended: SI 2002/1555 Art.7
s.33, enabling: SI 2003/306
Sch.1 para.7, amended: SI 2002/1501 Art.2
Sch.1 para.11, amended: SI 2002/1501 Art.2
Sch.1 para.13, repealed (in part): SI 2002/1501 Art.2
Sch.2, applied: SI 2002/1501 Art.6
Sch.2 para.1, disapplied: SI 2002/1501 Art.6
Sch.2 para.1, repealed: SI 2002/1501 Art.2
Sch.2 para.2, repealed: SI 2002/1501 Art.2
Sch.2 para.2, varied: SI 2002/1501 Art.6

CAP.

1979–cont.

34. Credit Unions Act 1979–*cont.*
Sch.2 para.3, repealed: SI 2002/1501 Art.2
Sch.2 para.4, repealed: SI 2002/1501 Art.2
Sch.2 para.5, repealed: SI 2002/1501 Art.2
Sch.2 para.6, repealed: SI 2002/1501 Art.2

36. Nurses, Midwives and Health Visitors Act 1979
Sch.7 para.19, repealed: SI 2003/431 Sch.5
Sch.7 para.20, repealed: SI 2003/431 Sch.5
Sch.7 para.21, repealed: SI 2003/431 Sch.5
Sch.7 para.22, repealed: SI 2003/431 Sch.5

37. Banking Act 1979
s.51, repealed (in part): 2004 c.14 Sch.1 Part 17
s.52, repealed (in part): 2004 c.14 Sch.1 Part 17

38. Estate Agents Act 1979
applied: 2002 c.40 s.231, Sch.14, Sch.15, SI 2003/419 Art.63, SI 2003/1376 Sch.1, SI 2003/1593 Sch.1 Part I, 2004 c.34 s.175
amended: 2002 c.40 Sch.25 para.9
s.3, amended: 2002 c.40 Sch.25 para.9
s.3, referred to: 2004 c.34 s.175
s.4, amended: 2002 c.40 Sch.25 para.9
s.5, amended: 2002 c.40 Sch.25 para.9
s.6, amended: 2002 c.40 Sch.25 para.9
s.7, amended: 2002 c.40 Sch.25 para.9
s.8, amended: 2002 c.40 Sch.25 para.9
s.9, amended: 2002 c.40 Sch.25 para.9
s.9, repealed (in part): 2002 c.40 Sch.26
s.10, amended: 2003 c.20 Sch.2 para.19
s.10, referred to: 2003 c.20 s.115
s.10, repealed: 2002 c.40 Sch.26
s.11, amended: 2002 c.40 Sch.25 para.9
s.13, amended: 2002 c.40 Sch.25 para.9
s.15, amended: 2002 c.40 Sch.25 para.9
s.17, amended: 2002 c.40 Sch.25 para.9
s.19, amended: 2002 c.40 Sch.25 para.9
s.20, amended: 2002 c.40 Sch.25 para.9
s.21, amended: 2002 c.40 Sch.25 para.9
s.25, amended: 2002 c.40 Sch.25 para.9
s.26, amended: 2002 c.40 Sch.25 para.9
s.26, applied: SI 2003/1376 Art.4
s.26, repealed (in part): 2002 c.40 Sch.25 para.9, Sch.26
s.27, amended: 2004 c.33 Sch.27 para.62
s.29, amended: 2002 c.40 Sch.25 para.9
s.30, amended: 2002 c.40 Sch.25 para.9
s.32, amended: 2004 c.33 Sch.27 para.63, Sch.30
s.32, varied: 2004 c.33 Sch.21 para.11
s.33, amended: 2002 c.40 Sch.25 para.9, Sch.26
Sch.2 Part I para.1, amended: 2002 c.40 Sch.25 para.9
Sch.2 Part I para.2, amended: 2002 c.40 Sch.25 para.9
Sch.2 Part I para.3, amended: 2002 c.40 Sch.25 para.9

1979–cont.

38. Estate Agents Act 1979–*cont.*

Sch.2 Part I para.4, amended: 2002 c.40 Sch.25 para.9

Sch.2 Part I para.5, amended: 2002 c.40 Sch.25 para.9

Sch.2 Part I para.6, amended: 2002 c.40 Sch.25 para.9

Sch.2 Part I para.7, amended: 2002 c.40 Sch.25 para.9

Sch.2 Part I para.8, amended: 2002 c.40 Sch.25 para.9

Sch.2 Part I para.9, amended: 2002 c.40 Sch.25 para.9

Sch.2 Part I para.10, amended: 2002 c.40 Sch.25 para.9

Sch.2 Part II para.11, amended: 2002 c.40 Sch.25 para.9

Sch.2 Part II para.12, amended: 2002 c.40 Sch.25 para.9

Sch.2 Part II para.13, amended: 2002 c.40 Sch.25 para.9

Sch.2 Part II para.14, amended: 2002 c.40 Sch.25 para.9

39. Merchant Shipping Act 1979

s.21, see *Ziemniak v ETPM Deep Sea Ltd* [2003] EWCA Civ 636, [2003] 2 All E.R. (Comm) 283 (CA), Kay, L.J.

41. Pneumoconiosis etc (Workers Compensation) Act 1979

applied: SI 2002/1792 Reg.15, 2004 c.33 s.254, SI 2004/726 Reg.1

s.1, enabling: SI 2004/726

s.7, enabling: SI 2004/726

42. Arbitration Act 1979

see *North Range Shipping Ltd v Seatrans Shipping Corp (The Western Triumph)* [2002] EWCA Civ 405, [2002] 1 W.L.R. 2397 (CA), Tuckey, L.J.

s.1, see *Nagusina Naviera v Allied Maritime Inc* [2002] C.L.C. 385 (QBD (Comm Ct)), Andrew Smith, J.

46. Ancient Monuments and Archaeological Areas Act 1979

applied: SI 2003/1075 Art.23, SI 2004/389 Art.21, SSI 2003/129 Sch.2 para.9

referred to: SSI 2004/70 Sch.2 para.9

s.1, applied: 2003 asp 8 s.35, SSI 2004/406 Sch.1 para.3

s.11, applied: SI 2004/1777 Art.25, SI 2004/1778 Art.25

s.12, applied: SI 2004/1777 Art.25, SI 2004/1778 Art.25

s.13, applied: SI 2004/1777 Art.25, SI 2004/1778 Art.25

s.14, applied: SI 2004/1777 Art.25, SI 2004/1778 Art.25

s.15, applied: SI 2004/1777 Art.25, SI 2004/1778 Art.25

s.16, applied: SI 2004/1777 Art.25, SI 2004/1778 Art.25

1979–cont.

46. Ancient Monuments and Archaeological Areas Act 1979–*cont.*

s.17, amended: 2002 c.14 s.2, 2003 asp 9 Sch.14 para.8

s.17, applied: SI 2004/1777 Art.25, SI 2004/1778 Art.25

s.19, applied: SI 2004/1777 Art.25, SI 2004/1778 Art.25

s.20, applied: SI 2004/1777 Art.25, SI 2004/1778 Art.25

s.21, applied: SI 2004/1777 Art.25, SI 2004/1778 Art.25

s.22, repealed (in part): 2003 asp 4 Sch.4 para.6

s.23, amended: 2003 asp 4 Sch.4 para.6

s.24, amended: 2002 c.14 s.2

Sch.4 para.6, repealed: 2003 asp 8 Sch.6 para.13

50. European Assembly (Pay and Pensions) Act 1979

applied: SI 2003/2922 Art.2

s.2, amended: SI 2003/2922 Art.2

s.3, amended: 2002 c.24 Sch.3 para.4

s.3, applied: 2003 c.1 s.291

s.4, amended: SI 2003/2922 Art.2

s.4, enabling: SI 2003/1416, SI 2004/2418

s.6, amended: SI 2003/2922 Art.2

s.7, amended: 2002 c.24 Sch.3 para.4, SI 2003/2922 Art.2

s.8, amended: 2002 c.24 Sch.3 para.4, SI 2003/2922 Art.2

53. Charging Orders Act 1979

s.1, see *Field v Field* [2003] 1 F.L.R. 376 (Fam Div), Wilson, J.

s.1, applied: 2002 c.15 s.39

s.2, see *Beckenham MC Ltd v Centralex Ltd* [2004] EWHC 1287, [2004] B.P.I.R. 1112 (Ch D), Hart, J.

s.3, amended: 2002 c.9 Sch.11 para.15

s.3, repealed (in part): 2002 c.9 Sch.13

s.5, amended: SI 2002/439 Art.5

s.5, repealed (in part): SI 2002/439 Art.5

s.7, repealed (in part): 2002 c.9 Sch.13

54. Sale of Goods Act 1979

see *Feldarol Foundry Plc v Hermes Leasing (London) Ltd* [2004] EWCA Civ 747, (2004) 101 (24) L.S.G. 32 (CA), Kennedy, L.J.

applied: SI 2003/1593 Sch.1 Part I

s.12, see *HiTech Autoparts Ltd v Towergate Two Ltd (No.1)* [2002] F.S.R. 15 (PCC), Christopher Floyd Q.C.; see *Louis Dreyfus Trading Ltd v Reliance Trading Ltd* [2004] EWHC 525, [2004] 2 Lloyd's Rep. 243 (QBD (Comm Ct)), Andrew Smith, J.

s.13, see *Clegg v Andersson (t/a Nordic Marine)* [2003] EWCA Civ 320, [2003] 1 All E.R. (Comm) 721 (CA), Sir Robert Andrew Morritt V.C.

s.13, referred to: SI 2003/1374 Sch.1

CAP.

1979–cont.

54. Sale of Goods Act 1979–*cont.*

s.14, see *Bramhill v Edwards* [2004] EWCA Civ 403, [2004] 2 Lloyd's Rep. 653 (CA), Auld, L.J.; see *Britvic Soft Drinks Ltd v Messer UK Ltd* [2002] EWCA Civ 548, [2002] 2 All E.R. (Comm) 321 (CA), Mance, L.J.; see *Clegg v Andersson (t/a Nordic Marine)* [2003] EWCA Civ 320, [2003] 1 All E.R. (Comm) 721 (CA), Sir Robert Andrew Morritt V.C.; see *Jewson Ltd v Boyhan* [2003] EWCA Civ 1030, [2004] 1 Lloyd's Rep. 505 (CA), Clarke, L.J.; see *Jewson Ltd v Kelly (Preliminary Issues)* Times, October 3, 2002 (QBD), David Foskett Q.C.

s.14, amended: SI 2002/3045 Reg.3

s.14, referred to: SI 2003/1374 Sch.1

s.15, see *Munns v Perkins* [2002] B.P.I.R. 120 (Ch D), Evans-Lombe, J.

s.15, referred to: SI 2003/1374 Sch.1

s.15B, referred to: SI 2003/1374 Sch.1

s.16, see *Customs and Excise Commissioners v Everwine Ltd* [2003] EWCA Civ 953, (2003) 147 S.J.L.B. 870 (CA), Keene, L.J.

s.17, see *Customs and Excise Commissioners v Everwine Ltd* [2003] EWCA Civ 953, (2003) 147 S.J.L.B. 870 (CA), Keene, L.J.

s.19, see *Transpacific Eternity SA v Kanematsu Corp (The Antares III)* [2002] 1 Lloyd's Rep. 233 (QBD (Comm Ct)), David Steel, J.

s.20, amended: SI 2002/3045 Reg.4

s.20, referred to: SI 2003/1374 Sch.1

s.24, see *Marcq v Christie Manson & Woods Ltd (t/a Christie's)* [2002] EWHC 2148, [2002] 4 All E.R. 1005 (QBD), Jack, J.

s.25, see *Marcq v Christie Manson & Woods Ltd (t/a Christie's)* [2002] EWHC 2148, [2002] 4 All E.R. 1005 (QBD), Jack, J.

s.32, amended: SI 2002/3045 Reg.4

s.32, referred to: SI 2003/1374 Sch.1

s.35, see *Clegg v Andersson (t/a Nordic Marine)* [2003] EWCA Civ 320, [2003] 1 All E.R. (Comm) 721 (CA), Sir Robert Andrew Morritt V.C.

s.48A, added: SI 2002/3045 Reg.5

s.48A, referred to: SI 2003/1374 Sch.1

s.48B, added: SI 2002/3045 Reg.5

s.48B, referred to: SI 2003/1374 Sch.1

s.48C, added: SI 2002/3045 Reg.5

s.48C, referred to: SI 2003/1374 Sch.1

s.48D, added: SI 2002/3045 Reg.5

s.48D, referred to: SI 2003/1374 Sch.1

s.48E, added: SI 2002/3045 Reg.5

s.48E, referred to: SI 2003/1374 Sch.1

s.48F, added: SI 2002/3045 Reg.5

s.48F, referred to: SI 2003/1374 Sch.1

s.53, see *Louis Dreyfus Trading Ltd v Reliance Trading Ltd* [2004] EWHC 525, [2004] 2 Lloyd's Rep. 243 (QBD (Comm Ct)), Andrew Smith, J.

s.61, amended: SI 2002/3045 Reg.6

CAP.

1979–cont.

55. Justices of the Peace Act 1979

referred to: 2003 c.39 Sch.9 para.11

58. Isle of Man Act 1979

s.1, repealed (in part): 2004 c.14 Sch.1 Part 9

s.7, repealed: 2004 c.14 Sch.1 Part 9

1980

i. Ardveenish Harbour Order Confirmation Act 1980

repealed: SSI 2002/410 Sch.2 Part I

s.1, referred to: SSI 2002/410 Sch.2 Part I

s.2, referred to: SSI 2002/410 Sch.2 Part I

s.4, referred to: SSI 2002/410 Sch.2 Part I

s.5, referred to: SSI 2002/410 Sch.2 Part I

s.6, referred to: SSI 2002/410 Sch.2 Part I

s.9, referred to: SSI 2002/410 Sch.2 Part I

s.10, referred to: SSI 2002/410 Sch.2 Part I

s.11, referred to: SSI 2002/410 Sch.2 Part I

s.12, referred to: SSI 2002/410 Sch.2 Part I

s.13, referred to: SSI 2002/410 Sch.2 Part I

s.14, referred to: SSI 2002/410 Sch.2 Part I

s.15, referred to: SSI 2002/410 Sch.2 Part I

xxvii. Breasclete Harbour Confirmation Act 1980

repealed: SSI 2002/410 Sch.2 Part I

s.1, referred to: SSI 2002/410 Sch.2 Part I

s.2, referred to: SSI 2002/410 Sch.2 Part I

s.6, referred to: SSI 2002/410 Sch.2 Part I

s.7, referred to: SSI 2002/410 Sch.2 Part I

s.8, referred to: SSI 2002/410 Sch.2 Part I

s.9, referred to: SSI 2002/410 Sch.2 Part I

s.10, referred to: SSI 2002/410 Sch.2 Part I

s.15, referred to: SSI 2002/410 Sch.2 Part I

x. County of Merseyside Act 1980

applied: 2004 c.ii

Part XIII, applied: 2004 c.ii

s.48, repealed: 2004 c.34 s.53, Sch.16

s.49, repealed (in part): 2004 c.34 s.53, Sch.16

s.91, substituted: 2004 c.ii Sch.1 para.1

s.96, substituted: 2004 c.ii Sch.1 para.2

s.99, repealed: 2004 c.ii Sch.3

s.101, repealed: 2004 c.ii Sch.3

s.102, amended: 2004 c.ii Sch.1 para.3

s.103, amended: 2004 c.ii Sch.1 para.4

s.109A, added: 2004 c.ii Sch.2

s.132, amended: 2004 c.34 Sch.16

s.139, repealed (in part): 2004 c.34 Sch.16

Court Funds Investment Act (Laws of Trinidad and Tobago) 1980

see *Kirvek Management & Consulting Services Ltd v Attorney General of Trinidad and Tobago* [2002] UKPC 43, [2002] 1 W.L.R. 2792 (PC (Trin)), Lord Scott of Foscote

xxxii. London Transport Act 1980

varied: SI 2003/1615 Sch.2 para.9

1980–cont.

Magistrates Court Act 1980
s.122, see *Hayes v Chelmsford Crown Court* [2003] EWHC 73, (2003) 167 J.P. 65 (QBD (Admin Ct)), Henriques, J.

xxxvii. South Yorkshire Act 1980
s.39, repealed: SI 2003/3030 Reg.2

xiv. West Yorkshire Act 1980
see *Leeds City Council v Watkins* [2003] EWHC 598, [2003] U.K.C.L.R. 467 (Ch D), Peter Smith, J.
s.50, repealed: SI 2003/3030 Reg.2

1. Petroleum Revenue Tax Act 1980
s.1, applied: SI 2003/2718 Sch.1 para.9

2. Papua New Guinea, Western Samoa and Nauru (Miscellaneous Provisions) Act 1980
Sch.1 para.6, repealed: 2002 c.39 Sch.3

6. Foster Children Act 1980
s.10, applied: SI 2002/635 Reg.2, SI 2002/896 Sch.1 para.6, SI 2004/2695 Sch.1 para.27
s.16, applied: SI 2002/635 Sch.1 para.1, SI 2002/896 Sch.1 para.45, SI 2004/2695 Sch.1 para.3

9. Reserve Forces Act 1980
s.140, applied: SI 2002/1792 Sch.4 para.17
s.151, applied: SI 2002/1792 Sch.4 para.17

11. Protection of Trading Interests Act 1980
s.5, see *Lewis v Eliades* [2003] EWCA Civ 1758, [2004] 1 W.L.R. 692 (CA), Potter, L.J.; see *Lewis v Eliades* [2003] EWHC 368, [2003] 1 All E.R. (Comm) 850 (QBD), Nelson, J.

16. New Hebrides Act 1980
Sch.1 para.7, repealed: 2002 c.39 Sch.3

17. National Heritage Act 1980
s.11, amended: 2003 c.14 Sch.20 para.3
s.11A, added: SI 2003/2867 Sch.1 para.10
s.15, repealed: 2004 c.14 Sch.1 Part 5

20. Education Act 1980
s.313, see *R. (on the application of Independent Panel for Special Educational Advice Ltd) v Secretary of State for Education and Skills* [2003] EWCA Civ 7, [2003] E.L.R. 393 (CA), Hale, L.J.
s.324, see *R. (on the application of Independent Panel for Special Educational Advice Ltd) v Secretary of State for Education and Skills* [2003] EWCA Civ 7, [2003] E.L.R. 393 (CA), Hale, L.J.

21. Competition Act 1980
applied: 2002 c.40 Sch.14, Sch.15, SI 2003/419 Art.63
referred to: 2003 c.21 s.393
s.11, amended: 2002 c.40 Sch.25 para.10, SI 2003/1615 Sch.1 para.6
s.11, applied: 2002 c.40 s.243, SI 2003/1397 Art.8
s.11, repealed (in part): 2002 asp 3 Sch.7 para.10, 2002 c.40 Sch.26

1980–cont.

21. Competition Act 1980–*cont.*
s.11, varied: SI 2004/1822 Sch.1 para.10
s.11A, added: 2002 c.40 Sch.25 para.10
s.11B, added: 2002 c.40 Sch.25 para.10
s.11B, referred to: SI 2003/1371
s.11B, enabling: SI 2003/1371
s.11C, added: 2002 c.40 Sch.25 para.10
s.11C, amended: 2003 c.21 Sch.16 para.1
s.11D, added: 2002 c.40 Sch.25 para.10
s.12, amended: 2002 c.40 Sch.25 para.10
s.13, repealed: 2002 c.40 Sch.26
s.15, repealed (in part): SI 2003/3180 Sch.1 para.3
s.16, amended: 2002 c.40 Sch.26
s.16, repealed (in part): 2002 c.40 Sch.26
s.17, amended: 2002 c.40 Sch.25 para.10, Sch.26
s.18, repealed: 2002 c.40 Sch.26
s.19, amended: SI 2002/1555 Art.8, 2003 c.20 Sch.2 para.19
s.19, referred to: 2003 c.20 s.115
s.19, repealed (in part): 2002 c.40 s.247, Sch.26
s.20, repealed: 2002 c.40 Sch.26
s.21, repealed: 2002 c.40 Sch.26
s.24, repealed: 2002 c.40 Sch.26
s.31, amended: 2002 c.40 Sch.25 para.10, Sch.26
s.31, repealed (in part): 2002 c.40 Sch.25 para.10, Sch.26
s.33, amended: 2002 c.40 Sch.25 para.10

23. Consular Fees Act 1980
s.1, applied: SI 2002/1618, SI 2002/1618 Art.2, 2004 c.19 s.42
s.1, enabling: SI 2002/1627, SI 2002/2634, SI 2003/1871, SI 2003/2920

26. British Aerospace Act 1980
s.1, repealed (in part): 2004 c.14 Sch.1 Part 16
s.2, repealed: 2004 c.14 Sch.1 Part 16
s.3, repealed: 2004 c.14 Sch.1 Part 16
s.5, repealed: 2004 c.14 Sch.1 Part 16
s.6, repealed: 2004 c.14 Sch.1 Part 16
s.7, repealed: 2004 c.14 Sch.1 Part 16
s.8, repealed: 2004 c.14 Sch.1 Part 16
s.9, repealed (in part): 2004 c.14 Sch.1 Part 16
s.10, repealed (in part): 2004 c.14 Sch.1 Part 16
s.11, repealed: 2004 c.14 Sch.1 Part 16
s.14, repealed (in part): 2004 c.14 Sch.1 Part 16
s.15, amended: 2004 c.14 Sch.1 Part 16
Sch.2 para.1, repealed: 2004 c.14 Sch.1 Part 16
Sch.2 para.2, repealed: 2004 c.14 Sch.1 Part 16
Sch.2 para.3, repealed: 2004 c.14 Sch.1 Part 16
Sch.2 para.4, repealed: 2004 c.14 Sch.1 Part 16

CAP.

1980–cont.

26. British Aerospace Act 1980–*cont.*
Sch.2 para.5, repealed: 2004 c.14 Sch.1 Part 16
Sch.2 para.6, repealed: 2004 c.14 Sch.1 Part 16

27. Import of Live Fish (England and Wales) Act 1980
s.1, applied: SI 2003/25, SI 2003/416
s.1, enabling: SI 2003/25, SI 2003/416

30. Social Security Act 1980
s.16, repealed (in part): 2004 c.32 Sch.3
Sch.4 para.1, amended: 2004 c.14 Sch.1 Part 7

32. Licensed Premises (Exclusion of Certain Persons) Act 1980
s.2, amended: 2003 c.44 Sch.26 para.27
s.4, amended: 2003 c.17 Sch.6 para.74, 2003 c.39 Sch.8

33. Industry Act 1980
s.2A, added: SI 2003/2867 Sch.1 para.11
s.6, repealed (in part): 2004 c.14 Sch.1 Part 16
s.8, repealed (in part): 2004 c.14 Sch.1 Part 16
s.9, repealed: 2004 c.14 Sch.1 Part 16
s.19, repealed: 2004 c.14 Sch.1 Part 16
s.20, repealed: 2004 c.14 Sch.1 Part 16
s.22, amended: 2004 c.14 Sch.1 Part 16

34. Transport Act 1980
s.45, repealed (in part): 2004 c.14 Sch.1 Part 5
s.46, repealed (in part): 2004 c.14 Sch.1 Part 5
s.47, repealed: 2004 c.14 Sch.1 Part 5
s.48, repealed: 2004 c.14 Sch.1 Part 5
s.62, repealed (in part): 2004 c.14 Sch.1 Part 14
s.66, repealed: 2004 c.14 Sch.1 Part 5
s.67, repealed: 2004 c.14 Sch.1 Part 5
Sch.6 para.1, amended: 2004 c.14 Sch.1 Part 5
Sch.6 para.1, repealed (in part): 2004 c.14 Sch.1 Part 5
Sch.6 para.4, repealed (in part): 2004 c.14 Sch.1 Part 5

40. Licensing (Amendment) Act 1980
repealed: 2003 c.17 Sch.7

43. Magistrates Courts Act 1980
applied: 2002 c.29 s.67, SI 2002/1227 Reg.21, SI 2002/1998 Art.16, SI 2002/2127 Reg.24, SI 2002/2295 Reg.6, SI 2002/2296 Reg.6, SI 2002/2350 Reg.6, SI 2002/2351 Reg.6, 2003 c.17 s.165, 2003 c.39 s.98, 2003 c.44 s.302, SI 2003/284 Art.127, SI 2003/1119 Reg.6, SI 2003/1478 Reg.8, SI 2003/1721 Reg.8, SI 2003/1722 Reg.6, SI 2003/1940 Reg.6, SI 2003/1956 Reg.6, SI 2003/2074 Reg.6, SI 2003/2254 Reg.6, SI 2003/2288 Reg.6, SI 2003/2455 Reg.6, SI 2003/2910 Reg.6, SI 2003/3177 Reg.21, 2004 c.33 Sch.6 para.41, SI 2004/1214 Reg.21, SI 2004/1430 Reg.21, SI 2004/2640 Reg.21
disapplied: 2003 c.39 s.26
referred to: 2002 c.38 Sch.3 para.36, SI 2004/176 Reg.6, Reg.9, Reg.12
Part I, added: 2003 c.39 Sch.3

CAP.

1980–cont.

43. Magistrates Courts Act 1980–*cont.*
Part II, added: 2003 c.39 s.48
Part III, applied: 2003 c.39 Sch.5 para.1, Sch.6 para.1, 2003 c.44 s.300, s.301, SI 2003/229 Art.13, SI 2003/772 Art.5, SI 2003/1535 Art.13, SI 2004/398 Art.15, SI 2004/1237 Art.6
Part III, referred to: SI 2002/272 Art.5
s.1, amended: 2003 c.39 s.43, 2003 c.44 s.31, Sch.36 para.8, Sch.37 Part 12
s.1, applied: 2002 c.29 s.85, 2003 c.41 s.142, 2003 c.44 s.29, s.30
s.1, referred to: 2003 c.44 s.30
s.1, repealed (in part): 2003 c.39 s.43, Sch.10
s.2, see *Verderers of the New Forest v Young (No.2)* [2003] EWHC 3253, [2004] 1 E.G.L.R. 1 (QBD (Admin Ct)), Rose, L.J.
s.2, amended: 2003 c.44 Sch.3 para.51
s.2, substituted: 2003 c.39 s.44
s.3, repealed: 2003 c.39 Sch.8 para.201, Sch.10
s.3B, repealed: 2003 c.39 s.46, Sch.10
s.4, repealed: 2003 c.44 Sch.37 Part 4, Sch.3 para.51
s.5, repealed: 2003 c.44 Sch.37 Part 4, Sch.3 para.51
s.5A, repealed: 2003 c.44 Sch.37 Part 4, Sch.3 para.51
s.5B, repealed: 2003 c.44 Sch.37 Part 4, Sch.3 para.51
s.5C, repealed: 2003 c.44 Sch.37 Part 4, Sch.3 para.51
s.5D, repealed: 2003 c.44 Sch.37 Part 4, Sch.3 para.51
s.5E, repealed: 2003 c.44 Sch.37 Part 4, Sch.3 para.51
s.5F, repealed: 2003 c.44 Sch.37 Part 4, Sch.3 para.51
s.6, amended: 2003 c.39 Sch.8 para.202
s.6, applied: 2004 c.28 Sch.12 para.3
s.6, referred to: 2004 c.28 Sch.12 para.3
s.6, repealed: 2003 c.44 Sch.37 Part 4, Sch.3 para.51
s.7, repealed: 2003 c.44 Sch.37 Part 4, Sch.3 para.51
s.8, repealed: 2003 c.44 Sch.37 Part 4, Sch.3 para.51
s.8B, amended: 2003 c.44 Sch.37 Part 4, Sch.3 para.51
s.9, see *R. (on the application of Crown Prosecution Service) v Blaydon Youth Court* [2004] EWHC 2296, (2004) 168 J.P. 638 (QBD (Admin Ct)), Keene, L.J.
s.10, see *DPP v Shuttleworth* [2002] EWHC 621, (2002) 166 J.P. 417 (QBD (Admin Ct)), Roderick Evans, J.; see *R. (on the application of Crown Prosecution Service) v Blaydon Youth Court* [2004] EWHC 2296, (2004) 168 J.P. 638 (QBD (Admin Ct)), Keene, L.J.
s.10, applied: 2003 c.44 s.16

1980–cont.

43. Magistrates Courts Act 1980–*cont.*

s.11, see *R. (on the application of Durham CC) v North Durham Justices* [2004] EWHC 1073, (2004) 168 J.P. 269 (QBD (Admin Ct)), Moses, J.

s.11, amended: 2003 c.44 Sch.32 para.26

s.11, applied: 2003 c.44 s.164

s.12, amended: 2003 c.39 Sch.8 para.203

s.12, applied: 2003 c.44 s.162, s.164

s.12, repealed (in part): 2003 c.44 s.308, Sch.37 Part 12

s.12A, amended: 2003 c.39 Sch.8 para.204

s.13, amended: 2003 c.44 s.31, Sch.37 Part 12

s.14, amended: 2003 c.39 Sch.8 para.205

s.15, see *DPP v Shuttleworth* [2002] EWHC 621, (2002) 166 J.P. 417 (QBD (Admin Ct)), Roderick Evans, J.

s.17A, amended: 2003 c.44 Sch.3 para.2

s.17C, applied: 2003 c.44 s.16

s.17D, added: 2003 c.44 Sch.3 para.3

s.17E, added: 2003 c.44 Sch.3 para.3

s.18, amended: 2003 c.44 Sch.3 para.4

s.18, applied: 2003 c.44 s.16

s.19, applied: 2003 c.44 s.170

s.19, substituted: 2003 c.44 Sch.3 para.5

s.20, substituted: 2003 c.44 Sch.3 para.6

s.21, substituted: 2003 c.44 Sch.3 para.7

s.22, see *R. v Alden (Paul Stuart)* [2002] EWCA Crim 421, [2002] 2 Cr. App. R. (S.) 74 (CA (Crim Div)), Rose, L.J.

s.23, amended: 2003 c.44 Sch.3 para.8

s.24, see *R. (on the application of D) v Manchester City Youth Court* [2001] EWHC Admin 860, [2002] 1 Cr. App. R. (S.) 135 (QBD (Admin Ct)), Gage, J.; see *R. (on the application of D) v Sheffield Youth Court* [2003] EWHC 35, (2003) 167 J.P. 159 (QBD (Admin Ct)), Stanley Burnton, J.; see *R. (on the application of H) v Balham Youth Court* [2003] EWHC 3267, (2004) 168 J.P. 177 (QBD (Admin Ct)), Rose, L.J.; see *R. (on the application of W) v Southampton Youth Court* [2002] EWHC 1640, [2003] 1 Cr. App. R. (S.) 87 (QBD (Admin Ct)), Lord Woolf of Barnes, L.C.J.; see *R. (on the application of W) v Thetford Youth Court* [2002] EWHC 1252, (2002) 166 J.P. 453 (QBD (Admin Ct)), Gage, J.; see *R. v H (Anthony)* [2002] EWCA Crim 2938, (2003) 167 J.P. 30 (CA (Crim Div)), Mance, L.J.

s.24, amended: 2003 c.44 s.42, Sch.3 para.9

s.24, applied: 2004 c.28 s.6

s.24, repealed (in part): 2003 c.44 Sch.37 Part 4, Sch.3 para.9

s.24A, added: 2003 c.44 Sch.3 para.10

s.24A, applied: 2004 c.28 s.6

s.24B, added: 2003 c.44 Sch.3 para.10

s.24B, applied: 2004 c.28 s.6

s.24C, added: 2003 c.44 Sch.3 para.10

s.24C, applied: 2003 c.44 s.16, 2004 c.28 s.6

1980–cont.

43. Magistrates Courts Act 1980–*cont.*

s.24D, added: 2003 c.44 Sch.3 para.10

s.24D, applied: 2004 c.28 s.6

s.25, see *R. (on the application of C) v Grimsby and Cleethorpes Magistrates Court* [2004] EWHC 2239, (2004) 168 J.P. 569 (QBD (Admin)), Dyson, L.J.; see *R. (on the application of DPP) v Camberwell Green Youth Court* [2003] EWHC 3217, (2004) 168 J.P. 157 (QBD (Admin Ct)), Jackson, J.; see *R. (on the application of H) v Balham Youth Court* [2003] EWHC 3267, (2004) 168 J.P. 177 (QBD (Admin Ct)), Rose, L.J.

s.25, amended: 2003 c.44 s.42, Sch.3 para.11

s.25, applied: 2004 c.28 s.6

s.25, repealed (in part): 2003 c.44 Sch.37 Part 4, Sch.3 para.11

s.26, amended: 2003 c.44 Sch.3 para.12

s.29, amended: 2003 c.44 Sch.3 para.51

s.32, amended: 2003 c.44 s.282

s.33, amended: 2003 c.44 Sch.32 para.27

s.33, repealed (in part): 2003 c.44 Sch.37 Part 4, Sch.3 para.13

s.42, repealed: 2003 c.44 Sch.37 Part 4, Sch.3 para.14

s.43, amended: 2003 c.39 Sch.8 para.206

s.43B, disapplied: 2003 c.44 s.88

s.44, applied: SI 2004/1910 Sch.2

s.47, amended: 2003 c.39 Sch.8 para.207

s.51, substituted: 2003 c.39 s.47

s.52, see *Shufflebottom v Chief Constable of Greater Manchester* [2003] EWHC 246, (2003) 167 J.P. 153 (QBD (Admin Ct)), Mackay, J.

s.52, applied: SI 2002/2998 r.12

s.52, substituted: 2003 c.39 s.47

s.59, amended: 2003 c.39 Sch.8 para.208, 2004 c.33 Sch.27 para.64

s.59, applied: 2004 c.33 Sch.6 para.35, Sch.6 para.36, Sch.6 para.37, Sch.6 para.38

s.59, referred to: 2004 c.33 Sch.6 para.38

s.59A, amended: 2003 c.39 Sch.8 para.209

s.59B, amended: 2003 c.39 Sch.8 para.210

s.60, amended: 2003 c.39 Sch.8 para.211, Sch.10

s.60, applied: 2004 c.33 Sch.6 para.42

s.61, amended: 2003 c.39 Sch.8 para.212

s.62, amended: 2003 c.39 Sch.8 para.213

s.63, applied: 2004 c.33 Sch.6 para.42

s.65, amended: 2002 c.38 Sch.3 para.37, 2003 c.39 Sch.8 para.214, 2004 c.33 Sch.27 para.65

s.65, referred to: 2003 c.39 s.26, s.66

s.66, see *Tameside MBC v Grant* [2002] Fam. 194 (Fam Div), Wall, J.

s.66, amended: 2003 c.39 Sch.8 para.215

s.66, applied: SI 2003/2960 r.8

CAP.

CAP.

1980–cont.

43. Magistrates Courts Act 1980–*cont.*

s.67, see *Tameside MBC v Grant* [2002] Fam. 194 (Fam Div), Wall, J.

s.67, applied: 2003 c.39 s.66, Sch.9 para.12

s.67, substituted: 2003 c.39 s.49

s.67, enabling: SI 2003/2960

s.68, repealed: 2003 c.39 s.49, Sch.10

s.69, amended: 2002 c.38 Sch.3 para.38

s.70, amended: 2003 c.39 Sch.8 para.216

s.70, applied: 2004 c.33 Sch.6 para.47

s.71, amended: 2002 c.38 Sch.3 para.39, Sch.5

s.74, amended: 2003 c.39 Sch.8 para.217

s.75, varied: 2002 c.29 s.35

s.76, applied: 2003 c.39 Sch.6 para.2

s.76, varied: 2002 c.29 s.35

s.77, amended: 2003 c.39 Sch.8 para.218

s.77, applied: SI 2002/272 Art.5, SI 2003/229 Art.13, SI 2004/1237 Art.6

s.77, varied: 2002 c.29 s.35, SI 2003/772 Art.5, SI 2003/1535 Art.13, SI 2004/398 Art.15

s.78, amended: 2003 c.39 Sch.8 para.219

s.78, applied: SI 2002/272 Art.5, SI 2003/229 Art.13, SI 2004/176 Reg.10, SI 2004/1237 Art.6

s.78, varied: 2002 c.29 s.35, SI 2003/772 Art.5, SI 2003/1535 Art.13, SI 2004/398 Art.15

s.79, amended: 2003 c.39 Sch.8 para.219

s.79, varied: 2002 c.29 s.35

s.80, varied: 2002 c.29 s.35

s.81, applied: 2003 c.44 s.300, s.301

s.81, varied: 2002 c.29 s.35

s.82, amended: 2003 c.39 Sch.8 para.220

s.82, applied: 2003 c.44 s.165

s.82, repealed (in part): 2003 c.44 Sch.37 Part 7

s.82, varied: 2002 c.29 s.35

s.83, varied: 2002 c.29 s.35, SI 2004/176 Reg.12

s.84, amended: 2003 c.39 Sch.8 para.221, 2003 c.44 Sch.37 Part 9

s.84, applied: 2003 c.39 Sch.6 para.2

s.84, disapplied: 2003 c.44 Sch.25 para.75

s.84, varied: 2002 c.29 s.35

s.85, amended: 2003 c.39 Sch.8 para.222, 2003 c.44 Sch.32 para.28

s.85, varied: 2002 c.29 s.35

s.85A, varied: 2002 c.29 s.35

s.86, varied: 2002 c.29 s.35

s.87, amended: 2003 c.39 Sch.8 para.223

s.87, applied: 2003 c.39 Sch.6 para.2

s.87, referred to: SI 2004/176 Reg.9

s.87, repealed (in part): 2003 c.39 Sch.8 para.223, Sch.10

s.87, varied: 2002 c.29 s.35, SI 2004/176 Reg.9

s.87A, amended: 2002 c.40 Sch.17 para.2, 2003 c.39 Sch.8 para.224

43. Magistrates Courts Act 1980–*cont.*

s.87A, repealed (in part): 2003 c.39 Sch.8 para.224, Sch.10

s.87A, varied: 2002 c.29 s.35, SI 2004/176 Reg.12

s.88, applied: 2003 c.39 Sch.6 para.2

s.88, varied: 2002 c.29 s.35

s.89, amended: 2003 c.39 Sch.8 para.225

s.89, varied: 2002 c.29 s.35, SI 2004/176 Reg.6

s.90, amended: 2003 c.39 Sch.8 para.226

s.90, applied: SI 2002/272 Art.5, SI 2003/229 Art.13, SI 2003/1535 Art.13, SI 2004/398 Art.15, SSI 2002/51 Art.6, SSI 2003/56 Art.13, SSI 2003/88 Art.6, SSI 2004/44 Art.16, SSI 2004/209 Art.7, SSI 2004/392 Art.11

s.90, varied: 2002 c.29 s.35, SI 2004/176 Reg.6

s.91, amended: 2003 c.39 Sch.8 para.227

s.91, varied: 2002 c.29 s.35, SI 2004/176 Reg.6

s.92, varied: 2002 c.29 s.35

s.93, amended: 2003 c.39 Sch.8 para.228

s.93, varied: 2002 c.29 s.35

s.94, varied: 2002 c.29 s.35

s.94A, varied: 2002 c.29 s.35

s.95, amended: 2003 c.39 Sch.8 para.229

s.95, varied: 2002 c.29 s.35

s.96, varied: 2002 c.29 s.35

s.96A, varied: 2002 c.29 s.35

s.97, see *R. (on the application of Howe) v South Durham Magistrates Court* [2004] EWHC 362, (2004) 168 J.P. 424 (QBD (Admin Ct)), Rose, L.J.

s.97, amended: 2003 c.39 Sch.8 para.230, Sch.10

s.97A, amended: 2003 c.39 Sch.8 para.231, Sch.10

s.97A, repealed (in part): 2003 c.39 Sch.8 para.231, Sch.10, 2003 c.44 Sch.37 Part 4, Sch.3 para.51

s.99, amended: 2003 c.39 Sch.8 para.232

s.101, see *DPP v Barker* [2004] EWHC 2502, (2004) 168 J.P. 617 (QBD (Admin)), Collins, J.; see *R. (on the application of Grundy & Co Excavations Ltd) v Halton Division Magistrates Court* [2003] EWHC 272, (2003) 167 J.P. 387 (QBD (Admin Ct)), Clarke, L.J.

s.103, amended: 2003 c.42 Sch.6 para.26, Sch.7

s.103, repealed: 2003 c.44 Sch.37 Part 4, Sch.3 para.51

s.106, repealed: 2003 c.44 Sch.37 Part 4, Sch.3 para.51

s.107, amended: 2003 c.39 Sch.8 para.233

s.108, amended: 2004 c.28 Sch.10 para.10

s.109, amended: 2003 c.39 Sch.8 para.234

1980–cont.
43. Magistrates Courts Act 1980–*cont.*

s.111, see *R. (on the application of Food Standards Agency) v Brent Justices* [2004] EWHC 459, (2004) 168 J.P. 241 (QBD (Admin Ct)), Stanley Burnton, J.

s.111, applied: 2002 c.29 s.14, SI 2002/1891 Sch.2 para.6, Sch.2 para.10, 2003 c.17 s.130, 2003 c.32 s.60, SI 2003/750 Sch.5 para.9, SI 2003/751 Sch.6 para.9, SI 2003/1901 Sch.1 para.7, SI 2004/1468 Sch.6 para.9

s.114, amended: 2003 c.39 Sch.8 para.235

s.114, substituted: 2003 c.39 Sch.8 para.235

s.116, amended: 2003 c.39 Sch.8 para.236, Sch.10

s.116, repealed (in part): 2003 c.39 Sch.8 para.236, Sch.10

s.120, see *R. (on the application of Hart) v Bow Street Magistrates Court* [2001] EWHC Admin 1141, [2002] 1 W.L.R. 1242 (QBD (Admin Ct)), Ouseley, J.

s.121, amended: 2003 c.39 Sch.8 para.237, Sch.10

s.121, repealed (in part): 2003 c.39 Sch.8 para.237, Sch.10

s.123, see *DPP v Short* [2001] EWHC Admin 885, (2002) 166 J.P. 474 (QBD (Admin Ct)), Owen, J.

s.125, amended: 2003 c.39 Sch.8 para.238

s.125, applied: SI 2004/176 Reg.10

s.125A, applied: SI 2004/176 Reg.10

s.125A, enabling: SI 2004/1835

s.125B, amended: 2003 c.39 Sch.8 para.239

s.125B, applied: SI 2004/176 Reg.10

s.125B, repealed (in part): 2003 c.39 Sch.8 para.239, Sch.10

s.125BA, added: 2004 c.28 s.27

s.125BA, applied: SI 2004/176 Reg.10

s.125C, amended: 2003 c.39 Sch.8 para.240, Sch.10

s.125C, applied: SI 2004/176 Reg.10

s.125CA, added: 2004 c.28 s.28

s.125CA, applied: SI 2004/176 Reg.10

s.125CB, added: 2004 c.28 s.28

s.125CB, applied: SI 2004/176 Reg.10

s.125D, applied: SI 2004/176 Reg.10

s.126, amended: 2003 c.39 Sch.8 para.241

s.126, applied: SI 2004/176 Reg.10

s.127, see *Customs and Excise Commissioners v Venn, Mather & Marquis Publications* [2001] EWHC Admin 1055, (2002) 166 J.P. 53 (QBD (Admin Ct)), Harrison, J.; see *John Mann International Ltd v Vehicle Inspectorate* [2004] EWHC 1236, [2004] 1 W.L.R. 2731 (QBD (Admin Ct)), Owen, J.

s.127, applied: 2003 c.17 s.186

s.127, disapplied: SI 2002/111 Art.20, SI 2002/2628 Art.16, 2003 c.21 s.174, 2003 c.44 s.162, SI 2003/1519 Art.20, SI 2004/348 Art.15

1980–cont.
43. Magistrates Courts Act 1980–*cont.*

s.128, amended: 2003 c.44 Sch.37 Part 4, Sch.3 para.51

s.129, amended: 2003 c.44 Sch.3 para.51

s.130, amended: 2003 c.44 Sch.37 Part 4, Sch.3 para.51

s.131, amended: 2003 c.44 Sch.32 para.29

s.132, see *R. v Hourigan (Rudolph)* [2003] EWCA Crim 2306, (2003) 147 S.J.L.B. 901 (CA (Crim Div)), Scott Baker, L.J.

s.132, applied: 2003 c.44 s.154

s.133, amended: 2003 c.44 s.155, Sch.32 para.30

s.133, applied: 2003 c.44 s.154

s.133, repealed (in part): 2003 c.44 s.155, Sch.37 Part 7

s.137, repealed: 2003 c.39 Sch.8 para.242, Sch.10

s.138, repealed: 2003 c.39 Sch.8 para.242, Sch.10

s.139, amended: 2003 c.39 Sch.8 para.243, 2004 c.28 Sch.10 para.11

s.139, applied: 2003 c.39 s.39

s.140, disapplied: SI 2003/1901 Sch.1 para.8

s.141, applied: 2003 c.17 s.131

s.141, repealed: 2003 c.39 Sch.8 para.244, Sch.10

s.142, see *R. (on the application of Denny) v Acton Youth Court* [2004] EWHC 948, [2004] 1 W.L.R. 3051 (QBD (Admin Ct)), Maurice Kay, L.J.

s.143, amended: 2003 c.44 s.323

s.144, amended: 2003 c.39 Sch.8 para.245, Sch.10

s.144, applied: 2002 c.38 s.141, SI 2002/193, SI 2002/194, SI 2002/1687, SI 2002/1734, SI 2002/2782, 2003 c.44 s.30, s.127, SI 2003/423, SI 2003/1236, SI 2004/1514

s.144, referred to: 2003 c.44 s.30

s.144, repealed (in part): 2003 c.39 Sch.8 para.245, Sch.10

s.144, enabling: SI 2002/194, SI 2002/1135, SI 2002/1687, SI 2002/1734, SI 2002/2782, SI 2002/2784, SI 2002/2998, SI 2003/423, SI 2003/638, SI 2003/1236, SI 2003/1645, SI 2003/2840, SI 2003/2960, SI 2003/3367, SI 2004/184, SI 2004/247, SI 2004/1048, SI 2004/1051, SI 2004/1052, SI 2004/1053, SI 2004/1054, SI 2004/2419, SI 2004/2993

s.145, amended: 2004 c.31 s.62

s.145, applied: SI 2003/1236

s.145, repealed (in part): 2003 c.39 Sch.10, 2003 c.44 Sch.37 Part 4, Sch.3 para.51

s.145, enabling: SI 2002/2998, SI 2003/1645

s.146, repealed: 2003 c.39 s.50, Sch.10

s.147, repealed: 2003 c.39 Sch.8 para.247, Sch.10

s.148, amended: 2003 c.39 Sch.8 para.248

CAP.

1980–cont.

43. Magistrates Courts Act 1980–cont.
s.149, repealed: 2003 c.39 Sch.8 para.249, Sch.10
s.150, amended: 2003 c.39 Sch.8 para.250, Sch.10, 2003 c.44 Sch.36 para.9, Sch.37 Part 4, Sch.3 para.51
s.150, applied: SI 2004/1048 r.11
s.150, varied: SI 2004/176 Reg.6
s.152, amended: 2003 c.39 Sch.8 para.251
s.153, repealed: 2003 c.39 Sch.8 para.252, Sch.10
s.155, amended: 2003 c.39 Sch.8 para.253, 2003 c.44 Sch.37 Part 4, Sch.3 para.51
Sch.1, referred to: 2003 c.44 s.282
Sch.1 para.1A, added: 2003 c.44 s.320
Sch.1 para.23, repealed: 2003 c.42 Sch.7
Sch.1 para.27, repealed: 2003 c.42 Sch.7
Sch.1 para.28, see *R. v McGrath (Henry Paul)* [2003] EWCA Crim 2062, [2004] 1 Cr. App. R. 15 (CA (Crim Div)), Laws, L.J.
Sch.1 para.32, repealed: 2003 c.42 Sch.7
Sch.3, applied: 2002 c.38 s.143, 2003 c.17 s.188, 2004 c.11 s.21, s.22, SI 2004/1769 Sch.2 para.11
Sch.3 para.2, repealed (in part): 2003 c.44 Sch.37 Part 4, Sch.3 para.51
Sch.3 para.6, amended: 2003 c.44 Sch.3 para.51
Sch.4A para.1, added: 2004 c.28 Sch.4
Sch.4A para.2, added: 2004 c.28 Sch.4
Sch.4A para.3, added: 2004 c.28 Sch.4
Sch.4A para.4, added: 2004 c.28 Sch.4
Sch.4A para.5, added: 2004 c.28 Sch.4
Sch.5 para.2, repealed: 2003 c.44 Sch.37 Part 4, Sch.3 para.51
Sch.5 para.5, amended: 2003 c.44 Sch.3 para.51
Sch.6A, amended: 2003 c.44 Sch.37 Part 7
Sch.6 Part I, amended: 2002 c.16 Sch.2 para.25, 2002 c.21 Sch.3 para.2, 2002 c.38 Sch.3 para.40
Sch.6 Part I, applied: 2002 c.38 Sch.4 para.7
Sch.6 Part I, referred to: SI 2003/3184 Reg.7
Sch.6 Part I, repealed: 2003 c.39 Sch.8 para.254, Sch.10
Sch.6 Part II para.1, repealed: 2003 c.39 Sch.8 para.254, Sch.10
Sch.6 Part II para.2, repealed: 2003 c.39 Sch.8 para.254, Sch.10
Sch.6 Part III para.1, repealed: 2003 c.39 Sch.8 para.254, Sch.10
Sch.6 Part III para.2, repealed: 2003 c.39 Sch.8 para.254, Sch.10
Sch.6 Part III para.3, repealed: 2003 c.17 Sch.6 para.75, Sch.7, 2003 c.39 Sch.8 para.254, Sch.10
Sch.6 Part III para.4, repealed: 2003 c.39 Sch.8 para.254, Sch.10
Sch.6 Part III para.5, repealed: 2003 c.17 Sch.6 para.75, Sch.7, 2003 c.39 Sch.8 para.254, Sch.10

CAP.

1980–cont.

43. Magistrates Courts Act 1980–cont.
Sch.7 para.5, repealed: 2003 c.39 Sch.10
Sch.7 para.8, repealed: 2003 c.39 Sch.10
Sch.7 para.18, repealed: 2003 c.42 Sch.6 para.26, Sch.7
Sch.7 para.45, repealed: 2003 c.17 Sch.7
Sch.7 para.46, repealed: 2003 c.17 Sch.7
Sch.7 para.47, repealed: 2003 c.17 Sch.7
Sch.7 para.48, repealed: 2003 c.17 Sch.7
Sch.7 para.50, repealed: 2003 c.17 Sch.7
Sch.7 para.73, repealed: 2003 c.44 Sch.37 Part 4
Sch.7 para.101, repealed (in part): 2003 c.39 Sch.10
Sch.7 para.106, repealed: 2003 c.39 Sch.10
Sch.7 para.107, repealed: 2003 c.39 Sch.10
Sch.7 para.113, repealed: 2003 c.39 Sch.10
Sch.7 para.131, repealed: 2003 c.39 Sch.10
Sch.7 para.141, repealed: 2002 c.38 Sch.5, SI 2004/2035 Sch.1 para.10
Sch.7 para.142, repealed: 2002 c.38 Sch.5, SI 2004/2035 Sch.1 para.10
Sch.7 para.151, repealed: 2003 c.39 Sch.10

44. Education (Scotland) Act 1980
see *South Ayrshire Council v Morton* 2002 S.L.T. 656 (2 Div), Lord Gill L.J.C., Lord Caplan, Lord MacLean
applied: 2002 asp 13 Sch.1 para.10, Sch.1 para.48, SI 2002/195 Reg.4, Reg.28, SI 2002/2779 Art.63, Art.64, Sch.2 para.32, 2004 asp 4 s.30, SI 2004/293 Reg.67, Sch.1 para.24, SSI 2002/113 Sch.1 para.33, SSI 2002/120 Reg.3
s.1, applied: SI 2003/1660 Reg.20, SI 2003/1661 Reg.20, SSI 2002/62 Sch.2 Part II, SSI 2002/90 Art.2, Art.3
s.1, repealed (in part): 2004 asp 4 Sch.3 para.3
s.1, enabling: SSI 2002/90
s.2, referred to: 2004 asp 4 s.24
s.2, enabling: SSI 2003/75
s.4, amended: 2004 asp 4 Sch.3 para.3
s.14, see *Proudfoot v Glasgow City Council* 2003 S.L.T. (Sh Ct) 23 (Sh Ct (Glasgow and Strathkelvin)), JK Mitchell
s.14, amended: 2003 asp 13 s.277
s.21, referred to: SI 2003/1660 Reg.39
s.23, amended: 2004 asp 4 Sch.3 para.3
s.23, applied: 2004 asp 4 s.29
s.28A, see *Wokoma v Aberdeen City Council* 2002 S.C. 352 (OH), Lord Drummond Young
s.28A, amended: 2002 asp 2 s.1, 2004 asp 4 Sch.3 para.3
s.28A, disapplied: 2004 asp 4 Sch.2 para.1
s.28B, amended: 2004 asp 4 Sch.3 para.3
s.28C, see *Wokoma v Aberdeen City Council* 2002 S.C. 352 (OH), Lord Drummond Young
s.28C, disapplied: 2004 asp 4 Sch.2 para.1
s.28D, amended: 2004 asp 4 Sch.3 para.3

1980–cont.

44. Education (Scotland) Act 1980–*cont.*

s.28D, applied: 2004 asp 4 s.19, Sch.2 para.5

s.28E, see *Wokoma v Aberdeen City Council* 2002 S.C. 352 (OH), Lord Drummond Young

s.28E, disapplied: 2004 asp 4 Sch.2 para.1

s.28E, repealed (in part): 2004 asp 4 Sch.3 para.3

s.28F, see *Wokoma v Aberdeen City Council* 2002 S.C. 352 (OH), Lord Drummond Young

s.28F, disapplied: 2004 asp 4 Sch.2 para.1

s.28G, amended: 2002 asp 2 s.1

s.28G, disapplied: 2004 asp 4 Sch.2 para.1

s.28H, see *Proudfoot v Glasgow City Council* 2003 S.L.T. (Sh Ct) 23 (Sh Ct (Glasgow and Strathkelvin)), JK Mitchell

s.31, applied: SSI 2003/19 Reg.11

s.32, applied: SSI 2002/90 Art.2

s.33, applied: SSI 2004/273 Reg.3

s.38, amended: 2004 asp 4 Sch.3 para.3

s.38, applied: SSI 2002/289 Reg.3

s.40, repealed (in part): 2004 asp 4 Sch.3 para.3

s.49, enabling: SSI 2004/469

s.51, amended: 2003 asp 1 s.45

s.51, applied: SSI 2002/289 Reg.3, SSI 2002/290 Art.3

s.53, amended: 2003 asp 18 s.1

s.53, applied: SSI 2003/350 Reg.3

s.53, enabling: SSI 2003/350

s.54, amended: 2004 asp 4 Sch.3 para.3

s.60, see *D, Petitioners* 2003 S.L.T.1323 (OH), Lord Philip

s.60, repealed: 2004 asp 4 Sch.3 para.3

s.61, see *D, Petitioners* 2003 S.L.T.1323 (OH), Lord Philip

s.61, repealed: 2004 asp 4 Sch.3 para.3

s.62, see *D, Petitioners* 2003 S.L.T.1323 (OH), Lord Philip; see *G (A Child) v Edinburgh City Council (Educational Needs: Judicial Review)* 2002 S.C.L.R. 92 (OH), Lord Emslie

s.62, applied: 2004 asp 4 s.30

s.62, repealed: 2004 asp 4 Sch.3 para.3

s.63, repealed: 2004 asp 4 Sch.3 para.3

s.64, see *D, Petitioners* 2003 S.L.T.1323 (OH), Lord Philip

s.64, repealed: 2004 asp 4 Sch.3 para.3

s.65, repealed: 2004 asp 4 Sch.3 para.3

s.65A, repealed: 2004 asp 4 Sch.3 para.3

s.65B, repealed: 2004 asp 4 Sch.3 para.3

s.65C, repealed: 2004 asp 4 Sch.3 para.3

s.65D, repealed: 2004 asp 4 Sch.3 para.3

s.65E, repealed: 2004 asp 4 Sch.3 para.3

s.65F, repealed: 2004 asp 4 Sch.3 para.3

s.65G, repealed: 2004 asp 4 Sch.3 para.3

s.66, applied: SSI 2002/162 Art.4, SSI 2003/231 Sch.4 para.19

s.66B, added: 2004 asp 12 s.1

s.66C, added: 2004 asp 12 s.1

1980–cont.

44. Education (Scotland) Act 1980–*cont.*

s.66D, added: 2004 asp 12 s.1

s.73, applied: SI 2002/195 Reg.10, Reg.12, Reg.28, SI 2002/1330 Sch.3 para.1, SI 2002/2086 Reg.3, Reg.7, SI 2002/3200 Reg.10, Reg.12, Reg.27, Sch.3 para.1, SI 2003/1917 Reg.3, Reg.7, SI 2003/1994 Sch.3 para.1, SR 2002/224 Reg.10, Reg.12, Reg.29, Sch.3 para.1, SSI 2004/273 Reg.3

s.73, disapplied: SI 2002/195 Sch.3 para.1

s.73, enabling: SI 2002/2859, SI 2004/1175, SI 2004/2752, SSI 2002/248, SSI 2002/423, SSI 2003/280, SSI 2003/401, SSI 2004/238, SSI 2004/273, SSI 2004/301, SSI 2004/469

s.73A, applied: SI 2002/3200 Sch.3 para.1

s.73B, amended: 2003 c.1 Sch.6 para.149

s.73B, applied: SI 2002/2820 Reg.4, SI 2002/3200 Sch.3 para.1, SR 2002/379 Reg.4

s.73B, enabling: SI 2002/2859, SI 2004/1175, SI 2004/2752, SSI 2004/469

s.73C, applied: SI 2002/3200 Sch.3 para.1

s.73D, applied: SI 2002/3200 Sch.3 para.1

s.73E, applied: SI 2002/3200 Sch.3 para.1

s.74, applied: SI 2002/195 Reg.10, Reg.12, Reg.28, SI 2002/1330 Sch.3 para.1, SI 2002/3200 Reg.10, Reg.12, Reg.27, Sch.3 para.1, SI 2003/1994 Sch.3 para.1, SR 2002/224 Reg.10, Reg.12, Reg.29, Sch.3 para.1

s.74, disapplied: SI 2002/195 Sch.3 para.1

s.74, enabling: SSI 2002/248, SSI 2002/423, SSI 2003/280, SSI 2003/401, SSI 2004/238, SSI 2004/469

s.75A, see *Mackay-Ludgate v Lord Advocate* 2002 S.C.L.R. 109 (OH), Lord Philip

s.75A, applied: SSI 2002/249, SSI 2003/281, SSI 2004/239

s.75A, enabling: SSI 2002/249, SSI 2003/281, SSI 2004/239

s.75B, enabling: SSI 2002/249, SSI 2003/281, SSI 2004/239

s.84, amended: SSI 2002/389 Sch.1

s.87A, applied: 2003 asp 1 s.50

s.98, amended: 2004 asp 12 s.4, Sch.1 para.1, Sch.2

s.98, applied: SSI 2002/113 Sch.1 para.33

s.98, repealed (in part): 2004 asp 12 Sch.2

s.98A, substituted: 2004 asp 12 s.4

s.98E, added: 2004 asp 12 s.5

s.99, amended: 2004 asp 12 s.5, Sch.1 para.1, Sch.2

s.100, amended: 2004 asp 12 s.5, Sch.1 para.1

s.101, amended: 2004 asp 12 s.5, Sch.1 para.1, Sch.2

s.102, amended: 2004 asp 12 s.6, Sch.1 para.1, Sch.2

s.102, applied: SSI 2003/231 Sch.1 para.7

s.103, substituted: 2004 asp 12 s.6

CAP.

1980–cont.

44. Education (Scotland) Act 1980–cont.
s.103A, added: 2004 asp 12 s.7

s.103B, added: 2004 asp 12 s.7

s.131, amended: 2003 asp 13 s.277

s.133, amended: 2004 asp 12 Sch.1 para.1

s.135, see *D, Petitioners* 2003 S.L.T. 1323 (OH), Lord Philip

s.135, amended: 2004 asp 4 Sch.3 para.3, 2004 asp 12 s.3, Sch.1 para.1, Sch.2

s.135, applied: SI 2003/1660 Reg.20, SI 2003/1661 Reg.20, SSI 2002/62 Sch.2 Part I, Sch.2 Part II, SSI 2002/314 Reg.2, SSI 2003/231 Sch.1 para.7

Sch.A2 para.1, repealed: 2004 asp 4 Sch.3 para.3

Sch.A2 para.2, repealed: 2004 asp 4 Sch.3 para.3

Sch.A2 para.3, disapplied: 2002 asp 2 s.1

Sch.A2 para.3, repealed: 2004 asp 4 Sch.3 para.3

Sch.A2 para.4, repealed: 2004 asp 4 Sch.3 para.3

Sch.A2 para.5, repealed: 2004 asp 4 Sch.3 para.3

Sch.A2 para.6, repealed: 2004 asp 4 Sch.3 para.3

Sch.2, applied: 2002 asp 11 Sch.3 para.2

Sch.2 para.1, repealed: 2004 asp 12 Sch.2

Sch.2 para.2, repealed: 2004 asp 12 Sch.2

Sch.2 para.3, repealed: 2004 asp 12 Sch.2

Sch.2 para.4, repealed: 2004 asp 12 Sch.2

Sch.2 para.5, repealed: 2004 asp 12 Sch.2

45. Water (Scotland) Act 1980
applied: 2002 asp 3 s.35, s.49, s.52, s.53, s.60, s.70

referred to: 2002 asp 3 s.71,

s.1, amended: 2002 asp 3 Sch.6 para.2

s.6, amended: 2002 asp 3 Sch.6 para.3, 2003 asp 3 s.29

s.6, applied: 2002 asp 3 s.39

s.8, amended: 2002 asp 3 Sch.6 para.4

s.9, amended: 2002 asp 3 Sch.6 para.5

s.9A, amended: 2002 asp 3 Sch.6 para.6

s.9A, applied: 2002 asp 3 s.29

s.10, amended: 2002 asp 3 Sch.6 para.7

s.11, amended: 2002 asp 3 Sch.6 para.8

s.11, repealed (in part): 2002 asp 3 Sch.6 para.8

s.12, repealed: 2002 asp 3 Sch.6 para.9

s.13, amended: 2002 asp 3 Sch.6 para.10

s.13, repealed (in part): 2002 asp 3 Sch.6 para.10

s.13A, amended: 2002 asp 3 Sch.6 para.11

s.14, amended: 2002 asp 3 Sch.6 para.12

s.16, amended: 2002 asp 3 Sch.6 para.13

s.17, amended: 2002 asp 3 Sch.6 para.14

s.17, applied: 2002 asp 3 s.47

s.18, amended: 2002 asp 3 Sch.6 para.15

s.18, applied: 2002 asp 3 s.47

s.21, amended: 2002 asp 3 Sch.6 para.16, 2003 asp 3 s.32

CAP.

1980–cont.

45. Water (Scotland) Act 1980–cont.
s.21, substituted: 2003 asp 3 s.32

s.22, amended: 2002 asp 3 Sch.6 para.17, 2003 asp 3 Sch.4 para.1

s.22, substituted: 2003 asp 3 Sch.4 para.1

s.23, amended: 2002 asp 3 Sch.6 para.18, 2003 asp 3 s.32, Sch.4 para.2

s.23A, added: 2003 asp 3 s.31

s.23B, added: 2003 asp 3 s.31

s.23C, added: 2003 asp 3 s.31

s.24, amended: 2003 asp 3 Sch.4 para.3

s.24A, amended: 2002 asp 3 Sch.6 para.19

s.24B, added: 2002 asp 3 s.64

s.25, amended: 2002 asp 3 Sch.6 para.20

s.26, amended: 2002 asp 3 Sch.6 para.21

s.28, amended: 2002 asp 3 Sch.6 para.22

s.29, amended: 2002 asp 3 Sch.6 para.23

s.31, amended: 2002 asp 3 Sch.6 para.24

s.32, amended: 2002 asp 3 Sch.6 para.25

s.33, amended: 2002 asp 3 Sch.6 para.26

s.34, amended: 2002 asp 3 Sch.6 para.27

s.35, amended: 2002 asp 3 Sch.6 para.28, 2002 asp 17 Sch.3 para.12

s.36, amended: 2002 asp 3 Sch.6 para.29

s.38, amended: 2002 asp 3 Sch.6 para.30

s.41A, amended: 2002 asp 3 Sch.6 para.31

s.45, applied: SI 2002/1792 Sch.2 para.6

s.47, applied: 2002 asp 3 s.29

s.50, amended: 2002 asp 3 Sch.6 para.32

s.51, amended: 2002 asp 3 Sch.6 para.33

s.52, amended: 2002 asp 3 Sch.6 para.34

s.53, amended: 2002 asp 3 Sch.6 para.35

s.54, amended: 2002 asp 3 Sch.6 para.36

s.55, amended: 2002 asp 3 Sch.6 para.37

s.55, repealed (in part): 2002 asp 3 Sch.6 para.37

s.56, amended: 2002 asp 3 Sch.6 para.38

s.58, amended: 2002 asp 3 Sch.6 para.39

s.58, repealed (in part): 2002 asp 3 Sch.6 para.39

s.59, amended: 2002 asp 3 Sch.6 para.40

s.63, amended: 2002 asp 3 Sch.6 para.41

s.68, amended: 2002 asp 3 Sch.6 para.42

s.69, amended: 2002 asp 3 Sch.6 para.43

s.70, amended: 2002 asp 3 Sch.6 para.44

s.71, amended: 2002 asp 3 Sch.6 para.45

s.71, repealed (in part): 2002 asp 3 Sch.6 para.45

s.72, amended: 2002 asp 3 s.65, Sch.6 para.46

s.72, enabling: SSI 2003/433, SSI 2003/489, SSI 2004/449, SSI 2004/450

s.73, amended: 2002 asp 3 Sch.6 para.47

s.75, amended: 2004 asp 8 Sch.2 para.3

s.75, repealed (in part): 2004 asp 8 Sch.2 para.3

s.76, amended: 2002 asp 3 Sch.6 para.48

s.76A, amended: 2002 asp 3 Sch.6 para.49

s.76B, amended: 2002 asp 3 Sch.6 para.50

s.76C, amended: 2002 asp 3 Sch.6 para.51

1980–cont.

45. Water (Scotland) Act 1980–*cont.*

s.76D, amended: 2002 asp 3 Sch.6 para.52
s.76E, amended: 2002 asp 3 Sch.6 para.53
s.76F, amended: 2002 asp 3 Sch.6 para.54
s.76G, amended: 2002 asp 3 Sch.6 para.55
s.76H, amended: 2002 asp 3 Sch.6 para.56
s.76I, amended: 2002 asp 3 Sch.6 para.57
s.76L, amended: 2002 asp 3 Sch.6 para.58
s.100, amended: 2002 asp 3 Sch.6 para.59
s.103, amended: 2002 asp 3 Sch.6 para.60
s.107, amended: 2002 asp 3 Sch.6 para.61
s.107, repealed (in part): 2002 asp 3 Sch.6 para.61
s.109, amended: 2002 asp 3 Sch.6 para.62
s.110, amended: 2002 asp 3 Sch.6 para.63
Sch.1 Part I para.1, amended: 2002 asp 3 Sch.6 para.64
Sch.1 Part I para.2, amended: 2002 asp 3 Sch.6 para.64
Sch.1 Part I para.3, amended: 2002 asp 3 Sch.6 para.64
Sch.1 Part I para.4, amended: 2002 asp 3 Sch.6 para.64
Sch.1 Part I para.5, amended: 2002 asp 3 Sch.6 para.64
Sch.1 Part I para.8, amended: 2002 asp 3 Sch.6 para.64
Sch.1 Part II para.11, amended: 2002 asp 3 Sch.6 para.64
Sch.1 Part II para.12, amended: 2002 asp 3 Sch.6 para.64
Sch.1 Part II para.14, amended: 2002 asp 3 Sch.6 para.64
Sch.1 Part II para.15, amended: 2002 asp 3 Sch.6 para.64
Sch.1 Part II para.17, amended: 2002 asp 3 Sch.6 para.64
Sch.1 Part III para.19, amended: 2002 asp 3 Sch.6 para.64
Sch.1 Part III para.20, amended: 2002 asp 3 Sch.6 para.64
Sch.1 Part III para.23, amended: 2002 asp 3 Sch.6 para.64
Sch.1 Part IV para.24, amended: 2002 asp 3 Sch.6 para.64
Sch.1 Part IV para.26, amended: 2002 asp 3 Sch.6 para.64
Sch.1 Part IV para.27, amended: 2002 asp 3 Sch.6 para.64
Sch.1 Part IV para.30, amended: 2002 asp 3 Sch.6 para.64
Sch.1 Part IV para.31, amended: 2002 asp 3 Sch.6 para.64
Sch.2 para.4, amended: 2002 asp 3 Sch.6 para.65
Sch.2 para.6, amended: 2002 asp 3 Sch.6 para.65
Sch.3 Part I para.1, amended: 2002 asp 3 Sch.6 para.66
Sch.3 Part I para.2, amended: 2002 asp 3 Sch.6 para.66

1980–cont.

45. Water (Scotland) Act 1980–*cont.*

Sch.3 Part II para.4, amended: 2002 asp 3 Sch.6 para.66, 2003 asp 3 Sch.4 para.4
Sch.3 Part II para.5, amended: 2002 asp 3 Sch.6 para.66
Sch.3 Part II para.6, amended: 2002 asp 3 Sch.6 para.66, 2003 asp 3 Sch.4 para.4
Sch.3 Part II para.7, amended: 2002 asp 3 Sch.6 para.66
Sch.3 Part II para.9, amended: 2002 asp 3 Sch.6 para.66
Sch.4 Part II para.4, amended: SI 2003/2155 Sch.1 para.9
Sch.4 Part IV, applied: 2002 asp 3 s.46
Sch.4 Part VII para.34, amended: 2003 asp 3 Sch.4 para.5
Sch.4 Part VII para.36, amended: SI 2003/2155 Sch.1 para.9, 2004 c.20 Sch.19 para.1
Sch.10 Part I, repealed: 2002 asp 3 Sch.6 para.67

46. Solicitors (Scotland) Act 1980

applied: SI 2002/427 Reg.13, Reg.15
referred to: SSI 2004/383 Reg.1, Reg.2
s.1, amended: 2003 asp 4 s.12
s.3, amended: 2003 asp 4 s.12
s.3A, added: 2003 asp 14 s.1
s.9, see *Danskin v Council of the Law Society of Scotland* 2002 S.L.T. 900 (OH), Lady Cosgrove
s.23B, added: SSI 2004/383 Reg.3
s.26, amended: SSI 2004/383 Reg.4
s.28, amended: SSI 2004/383 Reg.5
s.30, varied: SSI 2004/383 Reg.13
s.31, see *Ross & Liddell Ltd v Haggerty* 2003 S.C.L.R. 491 (Sh Ct (Glasgow and Strathkelvin)), Sheriff Brian Kearney
s.31, amended: SSI 2004/383 Reg.6
s.32, see *Bank of Scotland v Mitchell* 2002 S.L.T. (Sh Ct) 55 (Sh Ct (Tayside, Central and Fife)), RA Davidson; see *Ross & Liddell Ltd v Haggerty* 2003 S.C.L.R. 491 (Sh Ct (Glasgow and Strathkelvin)), Sheriff Brian Kearney
s.32, amended: 2003 asp 4 Sch.4 para.7, SSI 2004/383 Reg.7
s.33B, added: SSI 2004/383 Reg.8
s.34, amended: SSI 2004/383 Reg.9
s.34, applied: SSI 2004/383 Reg.14
s.35, applied: SSI 2004/383 Reg.14
s.36, applied: SSI 2004/383 Reg.14
s.37, applied: SSI 2004/383 Reg.14
s.37, varied: SSI 2004/383 Reg.13
s.38, varied: SSI 2004/383 Reg.13
s.39, varied: SSI 2004/383 Reg.13
s.39A, varied: SSI 2004/383 Reg.13
s.40, varied: SSI 2004/383 Reg.13
s.41, applied: SI 2002/1792 Reg.24, SR 2003/28 Reg.24
s.41, referred to: 2002 c.21 s.45
s.41, varied: SSI 2004/383 Reg.13
s.42, varied: SSI 2004/383 Reg.13

CAP.

1980–cont.

46. Solicitors (Scotland) Act 1980–*cont.*
s.42A, varied: SSI 2004/383 Reg.13
s.42B, varied: SSI 2004/383 Reg.13
s.42C, varied: SSI 2004/383 Reg.13
s.43, amended: SSI 2004/383 Reg.10
s.43, varied: SSI 2004/383 Reg.13
s.44, applied: SSI 2004/383 Reg.14
s.44, varied: SSI 2004/383 Reg.13
s.45, varied: SSI 2004/383 Reg.13
s.50, amended: 2003 asp 4 s.13
s.51, amended: 2003 asp 4 s.13
s.52, amended: 2003 asp 4 s.13
s.52, applied: SSI 2004/383 Reg.14
s.53, varied: SSI 2004/383 Reg.13
s.53A, varied: SSI 2004/383 Reg.13
s.53B, varied: SSI 2004/383 Reg.13
s.53C, varied: SSI 2004/383 Reg.13
s.54, varied: SSI 2004/383 Reg.13
s.55, varied: SSI 2004/383 Reg.13
s.56, varied: SSI 2004/383 Reg.13
s.56A, varied: SSI 2004/383 Reg.13
s.60A, amended: SSI 2004/383 Reg.11
s.60A, repealed (in part): SSI 2004/383
Reg.11
s.61, varied: SSI 2004/383 Reg.13
s.61A, varied: SSI 2004/383 Reg.13
s.62A, varied: SSI 2004/383 Reg.13
s.63, varied: SSI 2004/383 Reg.13
s.64, varied: SSI 2004/383 Reg.13
s.64C, repealed (in part): SI 2003/1398 Sch.1
para.2
s.64CA, added: SI 2003/1398 Sch.1 para.2
s.64CB, added: SI 2003/1398 Sch.1 para.2
s.65, amended: 2003 asp 4 s.12
Sch.1 para.2, amended: 2003 asp 14 s.2
Sch.1 para.3, amended: 2003 asp 14 s.2
Sch.3 Part I para.1B, added: SSI 2004/383
Reg.12
Sch.3 Part I para.4, applied: SSI 2004/383
Reg.14
Sch.3 Part II para.5, varied: SSI 2004/383
Reg.13
Sch.4 Part I para.1, varied: SSI 2004/383
Reg.13
Sch.4 Part I para.2, varied: SSI 2004/383
Reg.13
Sch.4 Part I para.3, varied: SSI 2004/383
Reg.13
Sch.4 Part I para.4, varied: SSI 2004/383
Reg.13
Sch.4 Part I para.5, varied: SSI 2004/383
Reg.13
Sch.4 Part I para.6, varied: SSI 2004/383
Reg.13
Sch.4 Part II para.7, varied: SSI 2004/383
Reg.13
Sch.4 Part II para.8, varied: SSI 2004/383
Reg.13
Sch.4 Part II para.8A, varied: SSI 2004/383
Reg.13

CAP.

1980–cont.

46. Solicitors (Scotland) Act 1980–*cont.*
Sch.4 Part II para.9, varied: SSI 2004/383
Reg.13
Sch.4 Part II para.10, varied: SSI 2004/383
Reg.13
Sch.4 Part II para.11, varied: SSI 2004/383
Reg.13
Sch.4 Part II para.12, varied: SSI 2004/383
Reg.13
Sch.4 Part II para.13, varied: SSI 2004/383
Reg.13
Sch.4 Part II para.14, varied: SSI 2004/383
Reg.13
Sch.4 Part II para.14A, varied: SSI 2004/383
Reg.13
Sch.4 Part II para.15, varied: SSI 2004/383
Reg.13
Sch.4 Part II para.16, varied: SSI 2004/383
Reg.13
Sch.4 Part II para.17, varied: SSI 2004/383
Reg.13
Sch.4 Part II para.18, varied: SSI 2004/383
Reg.13
Sch.4 Part II para.18A, varied: SSI 2004/383
Reg.13
Sch.4 Part II para.19, varied: SSI 2004/383
Reg.13
Sch.4 Part II para.20, varied: SSI 2004/383
Reg.13
Sch.4 Part II para.21, varied: SSI 2004/383
Reg.13
Sch.4 Part II para.22, varied: SSI 2004/383
Reg.13
Sch.4 Part II para.23, varied: SSI 2004/383
Reg.13
Sch.4 Part II para.24, varied: SSI 2004/383
Reg.13
Sch.4 Part II para.25, varied: SSI 2004/383
Reg.13

47. Criminal Appeal (Northern Ireland) Act 1980
Part II, amended: SI 2004/1500 Art.27
Part II, applied: SI 2004/1500 Art.30
s.6, amended: 2003 c.44 Sch.36 para.46
s.7, amended: SI 2003/435 Sch.5
s.9, amended: 2002 c.26 Sch.12 para.15
s.11, applied: SI 2003/495 Reg.7
s.13, applied: SI 2003/495 Reg.7
s.15, amended: 2002 c.26 s.41
s.16, applied: 2002 c.29 s.165
s.19, amended: 2003 c.44 Sch.36 para.92
s.19, repealed: SI 2003/435 Sch.4 para.5,
Sch.5
s.25A, disapplied: SI 2004/1629 Art.3
s.28, amended: 2003 c.44 Sch.36 para.93, SI
2003/435 Sch.5
s.28, repealed (in part): SI 2003/435 Sch.5
s.30, amended: 2002 c.29 Sch.11 para.9,
Sch.12, SI 2003/435 Sch.4 para.5

1980–cont.

47. Criminal Appeal (Northern Ireland) Act 1980–*cont.*

s.31, amended: 2002 c.29 Sch.11 para.9, 2003 c.44 Sch.36 para.94, SI 2004/1500 Art.27

s.35, amended: SI 2004/1500 Art.27

s.37, repealed: SI 2003/435 Sch.4 para.5, Sch.5

s.45, amended: 2003 c.44 Sch.36 para.95

s.45, repealed (in part): SI 2003/435 Sch.5

s.47A, applied: SI 2003/435 Art.25

Sch.1, repealed: SI 2003/435 Sch.4 para.5, Sch.5

Sch.1, substituted: SI 2004/1501 Art.34

48. Finance Act 1980

s.17, amended: 2002 c.23 Sch.40 Part 5

s.17, repealed (in part): 2002 c.23 Sch.40 Part 5, 2003 c.14 Sch.43 Part 5

s.97, amended: 2003 c.14 Sch.20 para.3

s.97, applied: 2003 c.14 Sch.19 para.7

s.97, referred to: 2003 c.14 Sch.19 para.7

s.120, amended: 2003 c.14 Sch.43 Part 5

s.120, repealed (in part): 2003 c.14 Sch.43 Part 5

Sch.17 Part I para.3, applied: SI 2003/2718 Sch.1 para.10

Sch.17 Part III, substituted: 2004 c.12 s.288

51. Housing Act 1980

Part I c.I, applied: SI 2003/3239 Reg.9

s.54, amended: 2004 c.33 Sch.8 para.16, Sch.30

s.76, amended: 2004 c.33 Sch.8 para.17

s.89, see *Hackney LBC v Side by Side (Kids) Ltd* [2003] EWHC 1813, [2004] 1 W.L.R. 363 (QBD), Stanley Burnton, J.

s.142, amended: 2002 c.15 Sch.13 para.7, Sch.14

s.142, repealed (in part): 2002 c.15 Sch.14

s.142, substituted: 2002 c.15 Sch.13 para.7

Sch.21 para.1, repealed (in part): 2002 c.15 Sch.14, Sch.14

Sch.22 Part I para.1, repealed (in part): 2002 c.15 Sch.14

Sch.22 Part I para.2, repealed (in part): 2002 c.15 Sch.14

Sch.22 Part I para.3, repealed (in part): 2002 c.15 Sch.14

Sch.22 Part I para.4, repealed (in part): 2002 c.15 Sch.14

Sch.22 Part I para.5, repealed (in part): 2002 c.15 Sch.14

Sch.22 Part I para.6, repealed (in part): 2002 c.15 Sch.14

Sch.22 Part I para.7, repealed (in part): 2002 c.15 Sch.14

Sch.22 Part II para.8, repealed (in part): 2002 c.15 Sch.14

52. Tenants Rights etc (Scotland) Act 1980

s.7, see *Fox v Argyll and Bute DC* 2002 Hous. L.R. 52 (Lands Tr (Scot)), WDC Andrews

1980–cont.

52. Tenants Rights etc (Scotland) Act 1980–*cont.*

s.10, see *Fox v Argyll and Bute DC* 2002 Hous. L.R. 52 (Lands Tr (Scot)), WDC Andrews

s.19, see *Fox v Argyll and Bute DC* 2002 Hous. L.R. 52 (Lands Tr (Scot)), WDC Andrews

s.82, see *Fox v Argyll and Bute DC* 2002 Hous. L.R. 52 (Lands Tr (Scot)), WDC Andrews

53. Health Services Act 1980

s.8, amended: 2004 c.14 Sch.1 Part 5

s.8, repealed (in part): 2004 c.14 Sch.1 Part 5

s.9, repealed (in part): 2004 c.14 Sch.1 Part 5

Sch.2 para.1, repealed: 2004 c.14 Sch.1 Part 5

Sch.2 para.2, repealed: 2004 c.14 Sch.1 Part 5

Sch.2 para.3, repealed: 2004 c.14 Sch.1 Part 5

Sch.2 para.4, repealed: 2004 c.14 Sch.1 Part 5

Sch.2 para.5, repealed: 2004 c.14 Sch.1 Part 5

Sch.2 para.6, repealed: 2004 c.14 Sch.1 Part 5

Sch.2 para.7, repealed: 2004 c.14 Sch.1 Part 5

Sch.2 para.8, repealed: 2004 c.14 Sch.1 Part 5

Sch.2 para.9, repealed: 2004 c.14 Sch.1 Part 5

Sch.2 para.10, repealed: 2004 c.14 Sch.1 Part 5

Sch.2 para.11, repealed: 2004 c.14 Sch.1 Part 5

Sch.2 para.16, repealed: 2004 c.14 Sch.1 Part 5

Sch.5 Part I para.2, repealed (in part): 2003 c.43 Sch.14 Part 4

Sch.5 Part I para.4, repealed (in part): 2003 c.43 Sch.14 Part 4

Sch.6 para.1, repealed: 2004 asp 7 Sch.2

55. Law Reform (Miscellaneous Provisions) (Scotland) Act 1980

Sch.1 Part II, amended: 2003 asp 7 s.78, 2003 c.44 Sch.32 para.31

58. Limitation Act 1980

see *Anglo Manx Group Ltd v Aitken* [2002] B.P.I.R. 215 (Ch D), John Jarvis Q.C.; see *Norfolk v My Travel Group Plc* [2004] 1 Lloyd's Rep. 106 (CC (Plymouth)), Judge Overend; see *R. (on the application of Daejan Properties Ltd) v London Leasehold Valuation Tribunal* [2001] EWCA Civ 1095, [2002] H.L.R. 25 (CA), Simon Brown, L.J.; see *Salford City Council v Garner* [2004] EWCA Civ 364, [2004] H.L.R. 35 (CA), Chadwick, L.J.; see *Secretary of State for the Environment, Food and Rural Affairs v Maltco 3 Ltd* [2003] EWHC 469, [2003] 2 C.M.L.R. 5 (QBD), Davis, J.

applied: 2002 c.9 s.11, s.12, Sch.1 para.15, Sch.8 para.8

s.2, see *Deutsche Morgan Grenfell Group Plc v Inland Revenue Commissioners* [2003] EWHC 1779, [2003] 4 All E.R. 645 (Ch D), Park, J.; see *Hatton v Chafes (A Firm)* [2003] EWCA Civ 341, [2003] P.N.L.R. 24 (CA), Clarke, L.J.; see *Khan v RM Falvey & Co* [2002] EWCA Civ 400, [2002] Lloyd's Rep. P.N. 369 (CA), Sir

1980–cont.

58. Limitation Act 1980–*cont.*

s.2–*cont.*

Murray Stuart-Smith; see *McCarroll v Statham Gill Davies (A Firm)* [2002] EWHC 2558, [2003] Lloyd's Rep. P.N. 115 (QBD), Gray, J.; see *McCarroll v Statham Gill Davies (A Firm)* [2003] EWCA Civ 425, [2003] Lloyd's Rep. P.N.167 (CA), Pill, L.J.

s.5, see *Bristol & West Plc v Bartlett* [2002] EWCA Civ 1181, [2003] 1 W.L.R. 284 (CA), Longmore, L.J.; see *Heath Lambert Ltd v Sociedad de Corretaje de Seguros* [2003] EWHC 2269, [2004] 1 Lloyd's Rep. 495 (QBD (Comm Ct)), Jonathan Hirst, Q.C.; see *Kleinwort Benson Ltd v Glasgow City Council (No.3)* 2002 S.L.T. 1190 (OH), Lord Macfadyen; see *Scottish Equitable Plc v Thompson* [2003] EWCA Civ 225, [2003] H.L.R. 48 (CA), Mummery, L.J.

s.8, see *Scottish Equitable Plc v Thompson* [2003] EWCA Civ 225, [2003] H.L.R. 48 (CA), Mummery, L.J.

s.9, see *Bridgestart Properties Ltd v London Underground Ltd* [2004] R.V.R. 18 (Lands Tr), George Bartlett Q.C. (President); see *Wiberg v Swansea City and County Council* [2002] R.V.R. 143 (Lands Tr), George Bartlett Q.C.

s.10, see *Hampton v Minns* [2002] 1 W.L.R. 1 (Ch D), Kevin Garnett Q.C.; see *Knight v Rochdale Healthcare NHS Trust* [2003] EWHC 1831, [2004] 1 W.L.R. 371 (QBD), Crane, J.

s.11, see *Adams v Bracknell Forest BC* [2004] UKHL 29, [2004] 3 W.L.R. 89 (HL), Lord Hoffmann; see *Godfrey v Gloucestershire Royal Infirmary NHS Trust* [2003] EWHC 549, [2003] Lloyd's Rep. Med. 398 (QBD), Leveson, J.; see *H v Northampton CC* [2004] EWCA Civ 526, (2004) 148 S.J.L.B. 540 (CA), Pill, L.J.; see *KR v Bryn Alyn Community (Holdings) Ltd (In Liquidation)* [2003] EWCA Civ 85, [2003] 3 W.L.R. 107 (CA), Auld, L.J.; see *Meherali v Hampshire CC* [2002] EWHC 2655, [2003] E.L.R. 338 (QBD), Judge Zucker Q.C.; see *Rowbottom v Royal Masonic Hospital* [2002] EWCA Civ 87, [2003] P.I.Q.R. P1 (CA), Mantell, L.J.; see *Rowe v Kingston upon Hull City Council* [2003] EWCA Civ 1281, [2003] E.L.R. 771 (CA), Keene, L.J.; see *Young (Deceased) v Western Power Distribution (South West) Plc* [2003] EWCA Civ 1034, [2003] 1 W.L.R. 2868 (CA), Simon Brown, L.J.

s.12, see *Young (Deceased) v Western Power Distribution (South West) Plc* [2003] EWCA Civ 1034, [2003] 1 W.L.R. 2868 (CA), Simon Brown, L.J.

1980–cont.

58. Limitation Act 1980–*cont.*

s.14, see *Adams v Bracknell Forest BC* [2003] EWCA Civ 706, [2003] E.L.R. 409 (CA), Tuckey, L.J.; see *Adams v Bracknell Forest BC* [2004] UKHL 29, [2004] 3 W.L.R. 89 (HL), Lord Hoffmann; see *C v Cairns* [2003] Lloyd's Rep. Med. 90 (QBD), Cox, J.; see *Godfrey v Gloucestershire Royal Infirmary NHS Trust* [2003] EWHC 549, [2003] Lloyd's Rep. Med. 398 (QBD), Leveson, J.; see *H v Northampton CC* [2004] EWCA Civ 526, (2004) 148 S.J.L.B. 540 (CA), Pill, L.J.; see *KR v Bryn Alyn Community (Holdings) Ltd (In Liquidation)* [2003] EWCA Civ 85, [2003] 3 W.L.R. 107 (CA), Auld, L.J.; see *McDonnell v Congregation of Christian Brothers Trustees (formerly Irish Christian Brothers)* [2003] UKHL 63, [2004] 1 A.C. 1101 (HL), Lord Bingham of Cornhill; see *Rowbottom v Royal Masonic Hospital* [2002] EWCA Civ 87, [2003] P.I.Q.R. P1 (CA), Mantell, L.J.; see *Rowe v Kingston upon Hull City Council* [2003] EWCA Civ 1281, [2003] E.L.R. 771 (CA), Keene, L.J.

s.14A, see *Babicki v Rowlands* [2001] EWCA Civ 1720, [2002] Lloyd's Rep. P.N. 121 (CA), Lord Woolf of Barnes, L.C.J.; see *Daniels v Thompson* [2004] EWCA Civ 307, [2004] P.N.L.R. 33 (CA), Dyson, L.J.; see *Graham v Entec Europe Ltd (t/a Exploration Associates)* [2003] EWCA Civ 1177, [2003] 4 All E.R. 1345 (CA), Potter, L.J.; see *Hatton v Chafes (A Firm)* [2003] EWCA Civ 341, [2003] P.N.L.R. 24 (CA), Clarke, L.J.; see *Haward v Fawcetts (A Firm)* [2003] P.N.L.R. 36 (QBD), Judge Playford Q.C.; see *Haward v Fawcetts (A Firm)* [2004] EWCA Civ 240, [2004] P.N.L.R. 34 (CA), Potter, L.J.; see *McCarroll v Statham Gill Davies (A Firm)* [2002] EWHC 2558, [2003] Lloyd's Rep. P.N. 115 (QBD), Gray, J.; see *McCarroll v Statham Gill Davies (A Firm)* [2003] EWCA Civ 425, [2003] Lloyd's Rep. P.N. 167 (CA), Pill, L.J.; see *Swansea Building Society v Bradford & Bingley (t/a BBG Surveyors)* [2003] P.N.L.R. 38 (QBD), Judge David Tyzack Q.C.

s.15, see *Inglewood Investment Co Ltd v Baker* [2002] EWCA Civ 1733, [2003] 2 P. & C.R. 23 (CA), Aldous, L.J.; see *Rhondda Cynon Taff CBC v Watkins* [2003] EWCA Civ 129, [2003] 1 W.L.R. 1864 (CA), Schiemann, L.J.

s.15, applied: 2002 c.9 Sch.6 para.11

s.15, disapplied: 2002 c.9 s.96

s.16, disapplied: 2002 c.9 s.96

s.17, disapplied: 2002 c.9 s.96

s.17, repealed (in part): 2002 c.9 Sch.13

s.19A, added: 2002 c.15 Sch.5 para.4

CAP.

1980–cont.

58. Limitation Act 1980–*cont.*

s.20, see *Bristol & West Plc v Bartlett* [2002] EWCA Civ 1181, [2003] 1 W.L.R. 284 (CA), Longmore, L.J.; see *Scottish Equitable Plc v Thompson* [2003] EWCA Civ 225, [2003] H.L.R. 48 (CA), Mummery, L.J.

s.21, see *DEG-Deutsche Investitions- und Entwicklungsgesellschaft mbH v Koshy (Account of Profits: Limitations)* [2002] 1 B.C.L.C. 478 (Ch D), Rimer, J.; see *DEG-Deutsche Investitions- und Entwicklungsgesellschaft mbH v Koshy (Account of Profits: Limitations)* [2003] EWCA Civ 1048, [2004] 1 B.C.L.C. 131 (CA), Mummery, L.J.; see *JJ Harrison (Properties) Ltd v Harrison* [2001] EWCA Civ 1467, [2002] B.C.C. 729 (CA), Chadwick, L.J.; see *Miller v Bain (Director's Breach of Duty)* [2002] 1 B.C.L.C. 266 (Ch D (Companies Court)), Judge Richard Field Q.C.

s.24, see *Bennett v Bank of Scotland* [2004] EWCA Civ 988, [2004] B.P.I.R. 1122 (CA), Mummery, L.J.; see *Hill v Bailey* [2003] EWHC 2835, [2004] 1 All E.R. 1210 (Ch D), Lightman, J.

s.27A, added: 2002 c.29 s.288

s.28, see *H v Northampton CC* [2004] EWCA Civ 526, (2004) 148 S.J.L.B. 540 (CA), Pill, L.J.; see *Masterman-Lister v Jewell* [2002] EWCA Civ 1889, [2003] 1 W.L.R. 1511 (CA), Kennedy, L.J.

s.29, see *Cadle Co v Hearley* [2002] 1 Lloyd's Rep. 143 (QBD (Merc Ct)), Judge Havelock-Allan, Q.C.; see *Good Challenger Navegante SA v Metalexportimport SA* [2003] EWCA Civ 1668, [2004] 1 Lloyd's Rep. 67 (CA), Mantell, L.J.; see *Good Challenger Navegante SA v Metalexportimport SA* [2003] EWHC 10, [2003] 1 Lloyd's Rep. 471 (QBD (Comm Ct)), Michael Crane Q.C.; see *UCB Corporate Services Ltd v Kohli* [2004] EWHC 1126, [2004] 2 All E.R. (Comm) 422 (Ch D), Richard Sheldon Q.C.

s.30, see *Cadle Co v Hearley* [2002] 1 Lloyd's Rep. 143 (QBD (Merc Ct)), Judge Havelock-Allan, Q.C.; see *Good Challenger Navegante SA v Metalexportimport SA* [2003] EWCA Civ 1668, [2004] 1 Lloyd's Rep. 67 (CA), Mantell, L.J.; see *Good Challenger Navegante SA v Metalexportimport SA* [2003] EWHC 10, [2003] 1 Lloyd's Rep. 471 (QBD (Comm Ct)), Michael Crane Q.C.; see *UCB Corporate Services Ltd v Kohli* [2004] EWHC 1126, [2004] 2 All E.R. (Comm) 422 (Ch D), Richard Sheldon Q.C.

s.31, see *UCB Corporate Services Ltd v Kohli* [2004] EWHC 1126, [2004] 2 All E.R. (Comm) 422 (Ch D), Richard Sheldon Q.C.

CAP.

1980–cont.

58. Limitation Act 1980–*cont.*

s.32, see *Biggs v Sotnicks (A Firm)* [2002] EWCA Civ 272, [2002] Lloyd's Rep. P.N. 331 (CA), Arden, L.J.; see *Brocklesby v Armitage & Guest* [2002] 1 W.L.R. 598 (CA), Morritt, L.J.; see *Cave v Robinson Jarvis & Rolf* [2001] EWCA Civ 245, [2002] 1 W.L.R. 581 (CA), Potter, L.J.; see *Cave v Robinson Jarvis & Rolf* [2002] UKHL 18, [2003] 1 A.C. 384 (HL), Lord Scott of Foscote; see *Deutsche Morgan Grenfell Group Plc v Inland Revenue Commissioners* [2003] EWHC 1779, [2003] 4 All E.R. 645 (Ch D), Park, J.; see *Ezekiel v Lehrer* [2002] EWCA Civ 16, [2002] Lloyd's Rep. P.N. 260 (CA), Ward, L.J.; see *Law Society v Sephton & Co* [2004] EWHC 544, [2004] P.N.L.R. 27 (Ch D), Michael Briggs Q.C.; see *McCarroll v Statham Gill Davies (A Firm)* [2002] EWHC 2558, [2003] Lloyd's Rep. P.N. 115 (QBD), Gray, J.; see *McCarroll v Statham Gill Davies (A Firm)* [2003] EWCA Civ 425, [2003] Lloyd's Rep. P.N. 167 (CA), Pill, L.J.; see *Prettys v Carter* [2002] P.N.L.R. 11 (QBD), Judge Playford Q.C.; see *Procter & Gamble (Health and Beauty Care) Ltd v Carrier Holdings Ltd* [2003] EWHC 83, [2003] B.L.R. 255 (QBD (T&CC)), Forbes, J.; see *Skerratt v Linfax Ltd (t/a Go Karting for Fun)* [2003] EWCA Civ 695, [2004] P.I.Q.R. P10 (CA), Waller, L.J.; see *Swansea Building Society v Bradford & Bingley (t/a BBG Surveyors)* [2003] P.N.L.R. 38 (QBD), Judge David Tyzack Q.C.; see *Williams v Fanshaw Porter & Hazelhurst* [2004] EWCA Civ 157, [2004] 1 W.L.R. 3185 (CA), Brooke, L.J.

s.32, disapplied: 2004 c.12 s.320

s.32A, see *Steedman v BBC* [2001] EWCA Civ 1534, [2002] E.M.L.R. 17 (CA), David Steel, J.

s.33, see *Adams v Bracknell Forest BC* [2004] UKHL 29, [2004] 3 W.L.R. 89 (HL), Lord Hoffmann; see *Burke v Ashe Construction Ltd* [2003] EWCA Civ 717, [2004] P.I.Q.R. P11 (CA), Potter, L.J.; see *C v Cairns* [2003] Lloyd's Rep. Med. 90 (QBD), Cox, J.; see *Godfrey v Gloucestershire Royal Infirmary NHS Trust* [2003] EWHC 549, [2003] Lloyd's Rep. Med. 398 (QBD), Leveson, J.; see *H v Northampton CC* [2004] EWCA Civ 526, (2004) 148 S.J.L.B. 540 (CA), Pill, L.J.; see *KR v Bryn Alyn Community (Holdings) Ltd (In Liquidation)* [2003] EWCA Civ 85, [2003] 3 W.L.R. 107 (CA), Auld, L.J.; see *Meherali v Hampshire CC* [2002] EWHC 2655, [2003] E.L.R. 338 (QBD), Judge Zucker Q.C.; see *Piggott v Aulton (Deceased)* [2003] EWCA Civ 24, [2003] C.P. Rep. 35 (CA), Arden, L.J.; see *Rowe v*

CAP.

1980–cont.
58. Limitation Act 1980–*cont.*
s.33–*cont.*

Kingston upon Hull City Council [2003] EWCA Civ 1281, [2003] E.L.R. 771 (CA), Keene, L.J.; see *Skerratt v Linfax Ltd (t/a Go Karting for Fun)* [2003] EWCA Civ 695, [2004] P.I.Q.R. P10 (CA), Waller, L.J.; see *Smith v White Knight Laundry Ltd* [2001] EWCA Civ 660, [2002] 1 W.L.R. 616 (CA), Jonathan Parker, L.J.; see *Young (Deceased) v Western Power Distribution (South West) Plc* [2003] EWCA Civ 1034, [2003] 1 W.L.R. 2868 (CA), Simon Brown, L.J.

s.35, see *Hemmingway v Smith Roddam (A Firm)* [2003] EWCA Civ 1342, (2003) 147 S.J.L.B. 1089 (CA), Clarke, L.J.; see *Horne-Roberts v Smithkline Beecham Plc* [2001] EWCA Civ 2006, [2002] 1 W.L.R. 1662 (CA), Keene, L.J.; see *Kleinwort Benson Ltd v Glasgow City Council (No.3)* 2002 S.L.T. 1190 (OH), Lord Macfadyen

s.35, applied: 2004 c.12 s.320

s35., see *Bajwa v Furini* [2004] EWCA Civ 412, [2004] 1 W.L.R. 1971 (CA), Mummery, L.J.

Sch.1 Part I para.6, disapplied: 2002 c.9 Sch.6 para.11

Sch.1 para.5, see *Williams v Jones* [2002] EWCA Civ 1097, [2002] 3 E.G.L.R. 69 (CA), Buxton, L.J.

Sch.1 para.8, see *Rhondda Cynon Taff CBC v Watkins* [2003] EWCA Civ 129, [2003] 1 W.L.R. 1864 (CA), Schiemann, L.J.

60. Civil Aviation Act 1980
s.2, repealed: 2004 c.14 Sch.1 Part 4
s.3, repealed (in part): 2004 c.14 Sch.1 Part 4
s.8, repealed (in part): 2004 c.14 Sch.1 Part 4
s.9, repealed: 2004 c.14 Sch.1 Part 4
s.10, repealed (in part): 2004 c.14 Sch.1 Part 4
s.27, repealed: 2004 c.14 Sch.1 Part 4
s.28, repealed: 2004 c.14 Sch.1 Part 4
Sch.3 Part II, repealed: 2004 c.14 Sch.1 Part 4

62. Criminal Justice (Scotland) Act 1980
s.80, applied: SI 2003/1184 Sch.2 para.26

63. Overseas Development and Co-operation Act 1980
applied: 2002 c.18 Sch.2 Part 2
disapplied: 2002 c.18 Sch.2 Part 22
repealed: 2002 c.1 Sch.4
s.2, applied: SSI 2002/103 Sch.1 Part II
s.3, repealed: 2002 c.1 s.15
s.6, applied: 2002 c.1 Sch.5 para.1
s.7, repealed: 2002 c.1 s.15
s.8, repealed: 2002 c.1 s.15
s.10, applied: 2002 c.1 Sch.5 para.3
s.12, applied: SI 2003/527 Reg.44, SSI 2004/257 Reg.44
s.12, referred to: 2002 c.1 Sch.5 para.4
Sch.1, applied: SSI 2002/103 Sch.1 Part II

CAP.

1980–cont.
65. Local Government, Planning and Land Act 1980
applied: 2004 c.5 s.26
s.1, repealed (in part): 2004 c.14 Sch.1 Part 10
s.2, amended: 2004 c.21 Sch.1 para.49, 2004 c.23 Sch.2 para.3
s.2, repealed (in part): 2004 c.14 Sch.1 Part 10
s.4, amended: SI 2002/2626 Sch.2 para.9
s.4, applied: SI 2002/2626 Art.4
s.4, repealed (in part): SI 2002/2626 Sch.2 para.9
s.5, repealed (in part): 2003 asp 1 s.60
s.6, repealed (in part): 2003 asp 1 s.60
s.7, repealed (in part): 2003 asp 1 s.60
s.8, repealed (in part): 2003 asp 1 s.60
s.9, repealed (in part): 2003 asp 1 s.60
s.10, repealed (in part): 2003 asp 1 s.60
s.11, repealed (in part): 2003 asp 1 s.60
s.12, repealed (in part): 2003 asp 1 s.60
s.13, repealed (in part): 2003 asp 1 s.60
s.14, repealed (in part): 2003 asp 1 s.60
s.14A, repealed (in part): 2003 asp 1 s.60
s.14B, repealed (in part): 2003 asp 1 s.60
s.15, repealed (in part): 2003 asp 1 s.60
s.16, repealed (in part): 2003 asp 1 s.60
s.17, repealed (in part): 2003 asp 1 s.60
s.18, repealed (in part): 2003 asp 1 s.60
s.19, repealed (in part): 2003 asp 1 s.60
s.19A, repealed (in part): 2003 asp 1 s.60
s.19B, repealed (in part): 2003 asp 1 s.60
s.20, repealed (in part): 2003 asp 1 s.60
s.21, repealed (in part): 2003 asp 1 s.60
s.22, repealed (in part): 2003 asp 1 s.60
s.23, repealed (in part): 2003 asp 1 s.60
s.32, applied: SI 2003/1269 r.13
s.48, repealed: 2004 c.14 Sch.1 Part 10
s.49, repealed: 2004 c.14 Sch.1 Part 10
s.50, repealed: 2004 c.14 Sch.1 Part 10
s.51, repealed: 2004 c.14 Sch.1 Part 10
s.52, repealed: 2004 c.14 Sch.1 Part 10
s.53, repealed: 2004 c.14 Sch.1 Part 10
s.54, repealed: 2004 c.14 Sch.1 Part 10
s.55, repealed: 2004 c.14 Sch.1 Part 10
s.56, repealed: 2004 c.14 Sch.1 Part 10
s.57, repealed: 2004 c.14 Sch.1 Part 10
s.58, repealed: 2004 c.14 Sch.1 Part 10
s.59, repealed: 2004 c.14 Sch.1 Part 10
s.60, repealed: 2004 c.14 Sch.1 Part 10
s.61, repealed: 2004 c.14 Sch.1 Part 10
s.62, repealed: 2004 c.14 Sch.1 Part 10
s.63, repealed: 2004 c.14 Sch.1 Part 10
s.63A, repealed: 2004 c.14 Sch.1 Part 10
s.64, repealed: 2004 c.14 Sch.1 Part 10
s.65, repealed: 2004 c.14 Sch.1 Part 10
s.66, repealed: 2004 c.14 Sch.1 Part 10
s.67, repealed: 2004 c.14 Sch.1 Part 10
s.68, repealed: 2004 c.14 Sch.1 Part 10
s.69, repealed (in part): 2004 c.14 Sch.1 Part 10
s.120, applied: 2002 asp 3 s.47

1980–*cont.*

65. Local Government, Planning and Land Act 1980–*cont.*

s.131, repealed: 2003 c.17 Sch.6 para.77, Sch.7

s.132, repealed: 2003 c.17 Sch.6 para.77, Sch.7

s.133, amended: 2003 c.17 Sch.6 para.78

s.133, repealed (in part): 2003 c.17 Sch.7

s.134, enabling: SI 2003/2896, SI 2004/1642, SI 2004/3370

s.135, applied: 2003 c.14 Sch.9 para.1

s.135, enabling: SI 2003/2896, SI 2004/1642, SI 2004/3370

s.142, amended: 2004 c.5 Sch.9

s.143, amended: 2004 c.5 Sch.9

s.144, amended: 2004 c.5 Sch.9

s.146, amended: 2003 c.17 Sch.6 para.79

s.152, amended: 2004 c.21 Sch.1 para.49

s.184, repealed (in part): 2002 asp 11 Sch.6 para.4

Sch.4 para.1, repealed: 2004 c.14 Sch.1 Part 10

Sch.4 para.2, repealed: 2004 c.14 Sch.1 Part 10

Sch.4 para.3, repealed: 2004 c.14 Sch.1 Part 10

Sch.4 para.4, repealed: 2004 c.14 Sch.1 Part 10

Sch.4 para.5, repealed: 2004 c.14 Sch.1 Part 10

Sch.4 para.6, repealed: 2004 c.14 Sch.1 Part 10

Sch.4 para.7, repealed: 2004 c.14 Sch.1 Part 10

Sch.4 para.8, repealed: 2004 c.14 Sch.1 Part 10

Sch.4 para.9, repealed: 2004 c.14 Sch.1 Part 10

Sch.4 para.10, repealed: 2004 c.14 Sch.1 Part 10

Sch.4 para.11, repealed: 2004 c.14 Sch.1 Part 10

Sch.4 para.12, repealed: 2004 c.14 Sch.1 Part 10

Sch.5 para.1, repealed: 2004 c.14 Sch.1 Part 10

Sch.5 para.2, repealed: 2004 c.14 Sch.1 Part 10

Sch.5 para.3, repealed: 2004 c.14 Sch.1 Part 10

Sch.5 para.4, repealed: 2004 c.14 Sch.1 Part 10

Sch.5 para.5, repealed: 2004 c.14 Sch.1 Part 10

Sch.8, repealed: 2004 c.14 Sch.1 Part 10

Sch.9 para.1, repealed: 2004 c.14 Sch.1 Part 10

Sch.9 para.2, repealed: 2004 c.14 Sch.1 Part 10

Sch.9 para.3, repealed: 2004 c.14 Sch.1 Part 10

1980–*cont.*

65. Local Government, Planning and Land Act 1980–*cont.*

Sch.10 Part I para.1, repealed: 2004 c.14 Sch.1 Part 10

Sch.10 Part I para.2, repealed: 2004 c.14 Sch.1 Part 10

Sch.10 Part I para.3, repealed: 2004 c.14 Sch.1 Part 10

Sch.10 Part II para.4, repealed: 2004 c.14 Sch.1 Part 10

Sch.10 Part II para.5, repealed: 2004 c.14 Sch.1 Part 10

Sch.10 Part II para.6, repealed: 2004 c.14 Sch.1 Part 10

Sch.10 Part III para.7, repealed: 2004 c.14 Sch.1 Part 10

Sch.10 Part III para.8, repealed: 2004 c.14 Sch.1 Part 10

Sch.10 Part III para.9, repealed: 2004 c.14 Sch.1 Part 10

Sch.10 Part III para.10, repealed: 2004 c.14 Sch.1 Part 10

Sch.26, added: 2004 c.5 Sch.7 para.10

Sch.26 para.1, enabling: SI 2003/2896, SI 2004/1642, SI 2004/3370

Sch.28 Part I para.1, amended: 2004 c.5 Sch.9

Sch.28 Part III para.5, amended: 2003 c.21 Sch.17 para.52

Sch.28 Part III para.6, amended: 2003 c.21 Sch.17 para.52

Sch.28 Part III para.13, amended: 2003 c.21 Sch.17 para.52

Sch.28 Part III para.14, amended: 2003 c.21 Sch.17 para.52

Sch.28 Part III para.16, amended: 2003 c.21 Sch.17 para.52

Sch.32, applied: SI 2002/1223 r.13, SI 2002/2685 r.11, SI 2003/1266 r.11, SI 2003/1267 r.11, SI 2003/1270 r.11

Sch.32, referred to: SI 2002/2686 r.13

Sch.32 Part I para.5, applied: 2004 c.5 s.26

Sch.32 Part IV para.31, repealed: 2004 c.14 Sch.1 Part 10

Sch.33 para.3, applied: SSI 2003/452 r.26

66. Highways Act 1980

see *R. (on the application of Brown) v Secretary of State for Transport* [2003] EWHC 819, [2004] Env. L.R. 2 (QBD (Admin Ct)), Collins, J.

applied: SI 2002/1998 Art.28, Art.29, 2003 c.iii Sch.2 para.7, SI 2003/1075 Sch.12 para.3, SI 2003/3364 Sch.6 para.3, 2004 c.5 s.38, SI 2004/389 Sch.12 para.3

s.1, applied: 2004 c.36 Sch.1 para.28

s.8, applied: SI 2004/2595 Reg.3, SI 2004/2732 Reg.3

s.10, applied: SI 2003/2990, SI 2003/2991, 2004 c.5 s.32, s.73

1980–cont.

66. Highways Act 1980–*cont.*

s.10, enabling: SI 2002/75, SI 2002/207, SI 2002/215, SI 2002/216, SI 2002/217, SI 2002/309, SI 2002/340, SI 2002/341, SI 2002/342, SI 2002/343, SI 2002/434, SI 2002/780, SI 2002/781, SI 2002/898, SI 2002/1029, SI 2002/1030, SI 2002/1058, SI 2002/1168, SI 2002/1178, SI 2002/1179, SI 2002/1180, SI 2002/1181, SI 2002/1182, SI 2002/1183, SI 2002/1184, SI 2002/1185, SI 2002/1186, SI 2002/1205, SI 2002/1206, SI 2002/1207, SI 2002/1208, SI 2002/1209, SI 2002/1210, SI 2002/1211, SI 2002/1212, SI 2002/1213, SI 2002/1214, SI 2002/1215, SI 2002/1315, SI 2002/1395, SI 2002/1594, SI 2002/1595, SI 2002/1678, SI 2002/1679, SI 2002/2107, SI 2002/2108, SI 2002/2422, SI 2002/2423, SI 2002/2424, SI 2002/2425, SI 2002/2757, SI 2003/89, SI 2003/90, SI 2003/91, SI 2003/93, SI 2003/94, SI 2003/111, SI 2003/125, SI 2003/126, SI 2003/127, SI 2003/128, SI 2003/724, SI 2003/725, SI 2003/726, SI 2003/727, SI 2003/728, SI 2003/809, SI 2003/1007, SI 2003/1061, SI 2003/1120, SI 2003/1122, SI 2003/1123, SI 2003/1124, SI 2003/1139, SI 2003/1140, SI 2003/1141, SI 2003/1142, SI 2003/1143, SI 2003/1144, SI 2003/1145, SI 2003/1158, SI 2003/1159, SI 2003/1160, SI 2003/1199, SI 2003/1204, SI 2003/1313, SI 2003/1388, SI 2003/1389, SI 2003/1423, SI 2003/1424, SI 2003/1425, SI 2003/1426, SI 2003/1599, SI 2003/1600, SI 2003/1601, SI 2003/1743, SI 2003/1978, SI 2003/1991, SI 2003/2206, SI 2003/2207, SI 2003/2423, SI 2003/2424, SI 2003/2425, SI 2003/2460, SI 2003/2720, SI 2003/2721, SI 2003/2722, SI 2003/2774, SI 2003/2776, SI 2003/2777, SI 2003/2778, SI 2003/2801, SI 2003/2825, SI 2003/2990, SI 2003/2991, SI 2003/2995, SI 2003/3147, SI 2003/3149, SI 2003/3151, SI 2003/3152, SI 2003/3153, SI 2003/3154, SI 2003/3155, SI 2003/3162, SI 2003/3163, SI 2003/3260, SI 2004/79, SI 2004/449, SI 2004/1801, SI 2004/1893, SI 2004/1894, SI 2004/2027, SI 2004/2088, SI 2004/2155, SI 2004/2563, SI 2004/2623, SI 2004/2666, SI 2004/2675, SI 2004/2679, SI 2004/2691, SI 2004/2754, SI 2004/2890, SI 2004/2901, SI 2004/3133, SI 2004/3173, SI 2004/3174, SI 2004/3209

s.12, applied: SI 2003/2990, SI 2003/2991

s.12, enabling: SI 2002/75, SI 2002/207, SI 2002/215, SI 2002/216, SI 2002/217, SI 2002/309, SI 2002/340, SI 2002/341, SI 2002/342, SI 2002/343, SI 2002/434, SI 2002/1058, SI 2002/1168, SI 2002/1179,

1980–cont.

66. Highways Act 1980–*cont.*

s.12, enabling:–*cont.*

SI 2002/1180, SI 2002/1181, SI 2002/1182, SI 2002/1183, SI 2002/1184, SI 2002/1185, SI 2002/1186, SI 2002/1205, SI 2002/1206, SI 2002/1207, SI 2002/1208, SI 2002/1209, SI 2002/1210, SI 2002/1211, SI 2002/1212, SI 2002/1213, SI 2002/1214, SI 2002/1215, SI 2002/1395, SI 2002/1595, SI 2002/1678, SI 2002/1679, SI 2002/2107, SI 2002/2108, SI 2002/2423, SI 2002/2424, SI 2002/2425, SI 2003/89, SI 2003/90, SI 2003/91, SI 2003/93, SI 2003/94, SI 2003/125, SI 2003/126, SI 2003/127, SI 2003/128, SI 2003/724, SI 2003/725, SI 2003/726, SI 2003/727, SI 2003/728, SI 2003/809, SI 2003/1007, SI 2003/1120, SI 2003/1122, SI 2003/1123, SI 2003/1124, SI 2003/1139, SI 2003/1140, SI 2003/1141, SI 2003/1142, SI 2003/1143, SI 2003/1144, SI 2003/1145, SI 2003/1158, SI 2003/1159, SI 2003/1160, SI 2003/1199, SI 2003/1204, SI 2003/1313, SI 2003/1388, SI 2003/1389, SI 2003/1423, SI 2003/1424, SI 2003/1425, SI 2003/1426, SI 2003/1743, SI 2003/2206, SI 2003/2207, SI 2003/2423, SI 2003/2722, SI 2003/2774, SI 2003/2801, SI 2003/2990, SI 2003/2991, SI 2003/2995, SI 2003/3147, SI 2003/3149, SI 2003/3151, SI 2003/3152, SI 2003/3153, SI 2003/3154, SI 2003/3155, SI 2003/3162, SI 2003/3163, SI 2004/79, SI 2004/1801, SI 2004/1893, SI 2004/1894, SI 2004/2088, SI 2004/2155, SI 2004/2623, SI 2004/2666, SI 2004/2675, SI 2004/2691, SI 2004/2890, SI 2004/2901, SI 2004/3174, SI 2004/3209

s.14, applied: 2004 c.5 s.32, s.73

s.16, applied: 2004 c.5 s.32, s.73

s.16, enabling: SI 2002/343, SI 2003/406, SI 2003/913, SI 2003/3261, SI 2003/3339, SI 2004/445, SI 2004/446, SI 2004/448, SI 2004/2562, SI 2004/3058, SI 2004/3107

s.17, enabling: SI 2002/343, SI 2003/406, SI 2003/913, SI 2003/3261, SI 2004/445, SI 2004/446, SI 2004/448, SI 2004/2562, SI 2004/3058

s.18, applied: 2004 c.5 s.32, s.73

s.19, enabling: SI 2002/343, SI 2003/913, SI 2003/3261, SI 2004/445, SI 2004/446, SI 2004/448, SI 2004/2562, SI 2004/3058

s.25, applied: SI 2004/1777 Art.25, SI 2004/1778 Art.25

s.28, applied: SI 2003/1479 Reg.6

s.28, varied: SI 2003/1075 Art.8

s.28, enabling: SI 2003/1479

s.31, see *Applegarth v Secretary of State for the Environment, Transport and the Regions* [2001] EWHC Admin 487,

1980–cont.

66. Highways Act 1980–*cont.*

s.31–*cont.*

[2002] 1 P. & C.R. 9 (QBD (Admin Ct)), Munby, J.; see *Burrows v Secretary of State for Environment, Food and Rural Affairs* [2004] EWHC 132, (2004) 101(5) L.S.G. 30 (QBD (Admin Ct)), Andrew Nicol Q.C.; see *R. (on the application of Godmanchester Town Council) v Secretary of State for the Environment, Food and Rural Affairs* [2004] EWHC 1217, [2004] 4 All E.R. 342 (QBD (Admin Ct)), Maurice Kay, L.J.; see *Robinson Webster (Holdings) Ltd v Agombar* [2002] 1 P. & C.R. 20 (Ch D), Etherton, J.

s.32, see *Robinson Webster (Holdings) Ltd v Agombar* [2002] 1 P. & C.R. 20 (Ch D), Etherton, J.

s.35, amended: 2003 c.21 Sch.17 para.53

s.36, see *Gulliksen v Pembrokeshire CC* [2002] EWCA Civ 968, [2003] Q.B. 123 (CA), Sedley, L.J.; see *Gulliksen v Pembrokeshire CC* [2002] Q.B. 825 (QBD), Neuberger, J.

s.41, see *Gorringe v Calderdale MBC* [2002] EWCA Civ 595, [2002] R.T.R. 27 (CA), Potter, L.J.; see *Gorringe v Calderdale MBC* [2004] UKHL 15, [2004] 1 W.L.R. 1057 (HL), Lord Steyn; see *Roe v Sheffield City Council (No.1)* [2003] EWCA Civ 1, [2004] Q.B. 653 (CA), Pill, L.J.

s.41, amended: 2003 c.20 s.111

s.41, enabling: SI 2002/781, SI 2002/898, SI 2002/1030, SI 2002/1594, SI 2002/2757, SI 2003/1601, SI 2003/2206, SI 2003/2720, SI 2003/2721, SI 2003/2776, SI 2003/2777, SI 2003/2778, SI 2003/2825, SI 2003/3163, SI 2003/3260, SI 2004/449, SI 2004/2563, SI 2004/2679, SI 2004/2754, SI 2004/3173

s.47, amended: 2003 c.39 Sch.8 para.256

s.58, see *Gulliksen v Pembrokeshire CC* [2002] EWCA Civ 968, [2003] Q.B. 123 (CA), Sedley, L.J.

s.62, see *Sandhar v Department of Transport, Environment and the Regions* [2004] EWHC 28, (2004) 101(5) L.S.G. 30 (QBD), Newman, J.

s.64, applied: SI 2002/412 Art.3, SI 2002/1066 Art.3, SI 2004/757 Art.3

s.68, applied: SI 2002/3113 Reg.16

s.75, applied: SI 2002/3113 Reg.16

s.90A, applied: SI 2002/3113 Reg.16, Reg.34

s.90G, applied: SI 2002/3113 Reg.16

s.90H, amended: 2004 c.36 Sch.2 para.15

s.106, applied: SI 2002/1134 Sch.1, SI 2002/1809 Sch.1, SI 2002/1810 Sch.1, SI 2002/3238 Sch.1, SI 2002/3239 Sch.1, SI 2003/2917 Sch.1, SI 2003/3056 Sch.1, 2004 c.5 s.32, s.73, SI 2004/2447 Sch.1

1980–cont.

66. Highways Act 1980–*cont.*

s.106, enabling: SI 2002/1134, SI 2002/1809, SI 2002/1810, SI 2002/1868, SI 2002/3238, SI 2002/3239, SI 2003/2917, SI 2003/3056, SI 2004/2447, SI 2004/2754

s.108, applied: 2004 c.5 s.32, s.73

s.108, enabling: SI 2002/1868

s.115, see *Tower Hamlets LBC v Sherwood* [2002] E.H.L.R. 3 (Ch D), S Proudman Q.C.

s.115A, amended: SI 2003/1615 Sch.1 para.7

s.115D, amended: 2003 c.21 Sch.17 para.54

s.115H, amended: SI 2003/1615 Sch.1 para.7

s.115J, amended: SI 2003/1615 Sch.1 para.7

s.116, amended: 2003 c.39 Sch.8 para.257

s.118B, applied: SI 2003/1479 Reg.3, SI 2003/2208 Art.3, SI 2004/1239 Art.3

s.118B, referred to: SI 2003/1479 Reg.3

s.118B, enabling: SI 2003/1479, SI 2003/2208, SI 2004/1239, SI 2004/2674

s.119, see *R. (on the application of Hargrave) v Stroud DC* [2002] EWCA Civ 1281, [2003] 1 P.& C.R. 1 (CA), Schiemann, L.J.

s.119B, referred to: SI 2003/1479 Reg.3

s.119B, enabling: SI 2003/1479

s.121, applied: SI 2003/1479, SI 2003/1479 Reg.6

s.130, see *Nottingham City Council v Zain* [2001] EWCA Civ 1248, [2002] 1 W.L.R. 607 (CA), Schiemann, L.J.

s.130A, applied: SI 2004/317 Reg.3, SI 2004/370 Reg.2

s.130A, enabling: SI 2004/317, SI 2004/370

s.130B, applied: SI 2004/317 Reg.3, SI 2004/370 Reg.2, Reg.3

s.130B, enabling: SI 2004/317, SI 2004/370

s.130C, applied: SI 2004/317 Reg.3, SI 2004/370 Reg.2

s.130C, enabling: SI 2004/317, SI 2004/370

s.137, see *Westminster City Council v Haw* [2002] EWHC 2073, (2002) 146 S.J.L.B. 221 (QBD), Gray, J.

s.137, applied: 2004 c.29

s.137ZA, see *R. (on the application of Ashbrook) v East Sussex CC* [2002] EWCA Civ 1701, [2003] 1 P. & C.R. 13 (CA), Schiemann, L.J.

s.137ZA, applied: 2004 c.29, s.1

s.139, amended: 2004 c.18 s.70

s.140A, substituted: 2004 c.18 s.66

s.140B, added: 2004 c.18 s.67

s.140C, added: 2004 c.18 s.70

s.142, amended: 2003 c.21 Sch.17 para.55

s.143, see *R. (on the application of Ashbrook) v East Sussex CC* [2002] EWCA Civ 1701, [2003] 1 P. & C.R. 13 (CA), Schiemann, L.J.

s.144, amended: 2003 c.21 Sch.17 para.56

s.149, applied: 2003 c.iii s.17

CAP.

1980–cont.

66. Highways Act 1980–cont.

s.150, see *Devon CC v Webber* [2002] EWCA Civ 602,Times, May 27, 2002 (CA), Keene, L.J.

s.151, see *Devon CC v Webber* [2002] EWCA Civ 602,Times, May 27, 2002 (CA), Keene, L.J.

s.169, amended: 2003 c.21 Sch.17 para.56, SI 2003/1615 Sch.1 para.7

s.170, amended: 2003 c.21 Sch.17 para.56

s.171A, substituted: 2004 c.18 s.68

s.171B, added: 2004 c.18 s.69

s.171C, added: 2004 c.18 s.70

s.174, amended: 2004 c.18 s.71

s.177, amended: 2003 c.21 Sch.17 para.56

s.178, amended: 2003 c.21 Sch.17 para.56

s.184, applied: 2003 c.iii s.16

s.219, amended: SI 2003/1615 Sch.1 para.7

s.232, amended: 2004 c.5 Sch.7 para.11

s.245A, added: 2004 c.18 s.13

s.245A, amended: 2004 c.18 s.13

s.251, repealed (in part): 2002 c.9 Sch.13

s.258, applied: SI 2002/2626 Art.5

s.259, repealed: 2004 c.5 Sch.9

s.281A, added: SI 2003/2867 Sch.1 para.12

s.300, applied: SI 2002/2626 Art.5

s.301A, amended: 2004 c.18 s.62

s.301A, applied: 2004 c.18 s.29, s.60

s.301A, varied: 2004 c.18 s.29

s.307, applied: SI 2003/1075 Art.8

s.307, varied: SI 2003/1075 Art.8

s.314, amended: 2004 c.29 s.1

s.314, applied: 2004 c.29, s.1

s.314A, added: 2004 c.18 s.64

s.322, amended: 2004 c.18 s.64

s.325, amended: 2004 c.18 s.70

s.326, enabling: SI 2003/406, SI 2003/913, SI 2003/3339, SI 2004/445, SI 2004/446

s.329, amended: 2003 c.21 Sch.17 para.56, SI 2003/1615 Sch.1 para.7, 2004 c.36 Sch.2 para.15

s.334, amended: 2003 c.21 Sch.17 para.56

Sch.1 Part I para.7, applied: SI 2002/2626 Art.5

Sch.1 Part I para.8, applied: SI 2002/2626 Art.5

Sch.1 Part II para.14, applied: SI 2002/2626 Art.5

Sch.1 Part II para.15, applied: SI 2002/2626 Art.5

Sch.1 Part III para.18, applied: SI 2002/2626 Art.5

Sch.1 Part III para.19, applied: SI 2002/2626 Art.5

Sch.1 Part III para.21, applied: SI 2002/2626 Art.5

Sch.2 para.1, applied: SI 2002/1134 Art.1, SI 2002/1809 Art.1, SI 2002/1810 Art.1, SI 2003/2917 Art.1, SI 2003/3056 Art.1, SI 2004/2447 Art.1

Sch.4, applied: SI 2004/2562 Art.3

CAP.

1980–cont.

66. Highways Act 1980–cont.

Sch.4, referred to: SI 2002/343 Art.3, SI 2003/406, SI 2003/3261 Art.3, SI 2004/448 Art.3

Sch.6 Part I para.1, applied: SI 2003/1479 Reg.4, Reg.5

Sch.6 Part I para.1, enabling: SI 2003/1479

Sch.6 Part I para.3, amended: 2004 c.21 Sch.1 para.50

Sch.6 Part I para.3, enabling: SI 2003/1479

Sch.6 Part II para.4, applied: SI 2003/1479 Reg.4, Reg.5

Sch.6 Part II para.4, enabling: SI 2003/1479

Sch.6 Part II para.6, enabling: SI 2003/1479

Sch.22A, added: 2004 c.18 Sch.5

Sch.22B para.1, added: 2004 c.18 Sch.6

Sch.22B para.2, added: 2004 c.18 Sch.6

Sch.22B para.3, added: 2004 c.18 Sch.6

Sch.22B para.4, added: 2004 c.18 Sch.6

Sch.22B para.5, added: 2004 c.18 Sch.6

Sch.22B para.6, added: 2004 c.18 Sch.6

Sch.22B para.7, added: 2004 c.18 Sch.6

Sch.22B para.8, added: 2004 c.18 Sch.6

Sch.22B para.9, added: 2004 c.18 Sch.6

Sch.24 para.12, repealed: 2003 c.17 Sch.7

1981

Book Prices Act (France) 1981

s.4, see *Le Grand Livre du Mois v Syndicat National de la Librairie* [2002] E.C.C. 27 (Cass (F)), M Canivet (President)

s.6, see *Le Grand Livre du Mois v Syndicat National de la Librairie* [2002] E.C.C. 27 (Cass (F)), M Canivet (President)

xvii. Greater London Council (General Powers) Act 1981

s.9, amended: 2004 c.34 Sch.15 para.8

xxxii. London Transport Act 1981

varied: SI 2003/1615 Sch.2 para.10

6. Industry Act 1981

s.2, repealed (in part): 2004 c.14 Sch.1 Part 16

s.3, amended: 2004 c.14 Sch.2 para.12

s.3, repealed (in part): 2004 c.14 Sch.1 Part 16

s.7, amended: 2004 c.14 Sch.1 Part 16

s.7, repealed (in part): 2004 c.14 Sch.1 Part 16

14. Public Passenger Vehicles Act 1981

applied: SI 2003/409 Sch.1 Part I, SI 2003/1594 Art.2

Part II, applied: SI 2002/2977 Sch.1 para.4

s.1, see *Vehicle & Operator Services Agency v Johnson* [2003] EWHC 2104, (2003) 167 J.P. 497 (QBD (Admin Ct)), Pitchford, J.

s.1, varied: SI 2002/412 Art.2

s.5, amended: SI 2003/1615 Sch.1 para.8

s.5, enabling: SI 2004/2682

s.6, applied: SI 2002/2742 Sch.2 para.13

s.6, enabling: SI 2002/335

s.10, enabling: SI 2002/335, SI 2002/489, SI 2003/1817, SI 2004/1880

1981–cont.

14. Public Passenger Vehicles Act 1981– cont.

s.12, see *Vehicle & Operator Services Agency v Johnson* [2003] EWHC 2104, (2003) 167 J.P. 497 (QBD (Admin Ct)), Pitchford, J.

s.14, applied: SI 2002/2535 Reg.3, SI 2004/1876 Reg.3

s.19, amended: SI 2003/2096 Sch.1 para.4

s.24, enabling: SI 2002/1724

s.25, enabling: SI 2002/1724

s.46, amended: 2002 c.32 Sch.21 para.4

s.52, enabling: SI 2002/489, SI 2002/2534, SI 2002/2535, SI 2002/2536, SI 2002/2537, SI 2003/1817, SI 2004/1876, SI 2004/1880, SI 2004/2250, SI 2004/2251, SI 2004/2252, SSI 2004/415

s.54, applied: SI 2002/1014 Art.3, SSI 2002/291 Art.3

s.60, enabling: SI 2002/335, SI 2002/489, SI 2002/1724, SI 2002/2534, SI 2002/2535, SI 2002/2536, SI 2002/2537, SI 2003/1817, SI 2004/10, SI 2004/1876, SI 2004/1880, SI 2004/2250, SI 2004/2251, SI 2004/2252, SI 2004/2682, SSI 2002/548, SSI 2004/415

s.61, applied: SI 2002/182, SI 2002/335, SI 2002/489, SI 2002/1724, SI 2002/2534, SI 2002/2535, SI 2002/2536, SI 2002/2537, SI 2003/1817, SI 2004/10, SI 2004/1876, SI 2004/1880, SI 2004/2250, SI 2004/2252, SI 2004/2682, SSI 2002/548, SSI 2004/415

s.69, repealed (in part): 2004 c.14 Sch.1 Part 14

s.89, repealed (in part): 2004 c.14 Sch.1 Part 14

Sch.3 para.1, amended: 2003 c.44 Sch.32 para.32

17. Energy Conservation Act 1981

repealed: 2004 c.14 Sch.1 Part 16

18. Disused Burial Grounds (Amendment) Act 1981

s.9, amended: 2004 c.33 Sch.27 para.66

20. Judicial Pensions Act 1981

referred to: SI 2003/2916 Reg.2

s.14A, varied: SI 2003/2916 Reg.3

22. Animal Health Act 1981

applied: SI 2002/280 Art.12, SI 2002/2304 Art.10, SI 2002/3113 Reg.29, SI 2002/3159 Reg.10, SI 2003/255 Art.1, SI 2003/326 Art.9, SI 2003/1078 Art.13, SI 2003/1079 Art.12, SI 2003/1470 Art.1, SI 2003/1724 Art.1, SI 2004/1604 Reg.13, SSI 2002/139 Reg.6, Reg.9, SSI 2002/255 Reg.3, SSI 2003/129 Reg.10, Reg.11, SSI 2003/353 Art.2, SSI 2003/354 Art.14, SSI 2003/411 Reg.2, SSI 2004/70 Reg.10, Reg.11

referred to: SI 2003/326 Art.14

varied: SSI 2002/255 Reg.3

1981–cont.

22. Animal Health Act 1981–*cont.*

s.1, enabling: SI 2002/202, SI 2002/240, SI 2002/241, SI 2002/242, SI 2002/280, SI 2002/281, SI 2002/283, SI 2002/764, SI 2002/882, SI 2002/907, SI 2002/1038, SI 2002/1328, SI 2002/1348, SI 2002/1349, SI 2002/1356, SI 2002/1357, SI 2002/1358, SI 2002/1764, SI 2002/1765, SI 2002/2060, SI 2002/2061, SI 2002/2152, SI 2002/2153, SI 2002/2154, SI 2002/2300, SI 2002/2302, SI 2002/2303, SI 2002/2304, SI 2002/2480, SI 2002/3229, SI 2003/28, SI 2003/29, SI 2003/30, SI 2003/31, SI 2003/130, SI 2003/167, SI 2003/168, SI 2003/169, SI 2003/170, SI 2003/253, SI 2003/254, SI 2003/255, SI 2003/326, SI 2003/399, SI 2003/481, SI 2003/482, SI 2003/483, SI 2003/502, SI 2003/946, SI 2003/1078, SI 2003/1079, SI 2003/1279, SI 2003/1336, SI 2003/1414, SI 2003/1428, SI 2003/1470, SI 2003/1723, SI 2003/1724, SI 2003/1728, SI 2003/1729, SI 2003/1966, SI 2003/1967, SI 2003/1968, SI 2003/2329, SI 2003/2456, SI 2003/2632, SI 2003/2763, SI 2003/2913, SI 2003/3273, SI 2004/996, SI 2004/1202, SI 2004/1803, SI 2004/2364, SI 2004/2891, SSI 2002/34, SSI 2002/38, SSI 2002/221, SSI 2002/369, SSI 2002/530, SSI 2002/540, SSI 2003/91, SSI 2003/202, SSI 2003/228, SSI 2003/334, SSI 2003/353, SSI 2003/354, SSI 2003/426, SSI 2003/586, SSI 2004/537

s.2, enabling: SSI 2003/202

s.6A, added: 2002 c.42 s.16

s.6A, applied: SI 2003/2035 Art.2

s.6A, enabling: SI 2003/2035

s.6B, added: 2002 c.42 s.16

s.7, enabling: SI 2002/202, SI 2002/241, SI 2002/242, SI 2002/280, SI 2002/281, SI 2002/283, SI 2002/1328, SI 2002/1358, SI 2002/1764, SI 2002/1765, SI 2002/2060, SI 2002/2061, SI 2002/2152, SI 2002/2304, SI 2003/31, SI 2003/130, SI 2003/169, SI 2003/253, SI 2003/254, SI 2003/255, SI 2003/326, SI 2003/481, SI 2003/482, SI 2003/483, SI 2003/1078, SI 2003/1079, SI 2003/1279, SI 2003/1336, SI 2003/1414, SI 2003/1428, SI 2003/1470, SI 2003/1723, SI 2003/1724, SI 2003/1729, SI 2003/1966, SI 2003/1967, SI 2003/1968, SI 2003/2329, SI 2003/2456, SI 2003/2913, SI 2003/3273, SI 2004/1202, SI 2004/1803, SI 2004/2891, SSI 2002/34, SSI 2002/221, SSI 2002/369, SSI 2002/530, SSI 2003/91, SSI 2003/228, SSI 2003/334, SSI 2003/354, SSI 2003/426, SSI 2003/586, SSI 2004/537

s.8, applied: SI 2002/242 Art.3, SI 2002/280 Art.3, SI 2002/2152 Art.3, SI 2002/2304 Art.3, SSI 2002/34 Art.3

CAP.

1981–cont.

22. Animal Health Act 1981–*cont.*

s.8, enabling: SI 2002/202, SI 2002/240, SI 2002/241, SI 2002/242, SI 2002/280, SI 2002/281, SI 2002/283, SI 2002/764, SI 2002/907, SI 2002/1038, SI 2002/1328, SI 2002/1348, SI 2002/1349, SI 2002/1356, SI 2002/1357, SI 2002/1358, SI 2002/1764, SI 2002/1765, SI 2002/2060, SI 2002/2061, SI 2002/2152, SI 2002/2153, SI 2002/2154, SI 2002/2300, SI 2002/2302, SI 2002/2303, SI 2002/2304, SI 2002/2480, SI 2002/3229, SI 2003/28, SI 2003/29, SI 2003/30, SI 2003/31, SI 2003/130, SI 2003/167, SI 2003/168, SI 2003/169, SI 2003/170, SI 2003/253, SI 2003/254, SI 2003/326, SI 2003/399, SI 2003/481, SI 2003/483, SI 2003/502, SI 2003/946, SI 2003/1078, SI 2003/1079, SI 2003/1279, SI 2003/1414, SI 2003/1723, SI 2003/1728, SI 2003/1729, SI 2003/1966, SI 2003/1967, SI 2003/2329, SI 2003/2456, SI 2003/2632, SI 2003/2763, SI 2003/2913, SI 2003/3273, SI 2004/996, SI 2004/1202, SI 2004/1803, SSI 2002/34, SSI 2002/38, SSI 2002/221, SSI 2002/369, SSI 2002/530, SSI 2002/540, SSI 2003/91, SSI 2003/202, SSI 2003/228, SSI 2003/353, SSI 2003/354, SSI 2003/426, SSI 2003/586

s.10, enabling: SI 2002/882, SI 2002/1011, SI 2002/2850, SI 2004/828, SI 2004/2364, SSI 2003/229

s.10A, added: 2002 c.42 s.17

s.14, enabling: SSI 2003/202

s.14A, added: 2002 c.42 s.18

s.14A, applied: SI 2003/2036 Art.2

s.14A, enabling: SI 2003/2036

s.14B, added: 2002 c.42 s.15

s.15, enabling: SI 2003/130, SI 2003/326, SI 2003/1078, SI 2003/1079, SI 2003/2329, SI 2003/2456, SI 2003/2913, SI 2003/3273, SSI 2003/91, SSI 2003/354, SSI 2003/426, SSI 2003/586

s.16, amended: 2002 c.42 s.7

s.16A, added: 2002 c.42 s.5

s.16A, applied: SI 2003/1734 Art.2

s.16A, enabling: SI 2003/1734

s.17, applied: SI 2002/457 Reg.12, Reg.15, SI 2002/843 Sch.7 para.5, SI 2002/897 Reg.12, Reg.15, SI 2002/1416 Sch.7 para.4, SSI 2002/110 Reg.12, Reg.14, SSI 2002/255 Sch.7 para.4

s.17, enabling: SI 2002/3229, SI 2003/130, SI 2003/326, SI 2003/399, SI 2003/1078, SI 2003/1079, SI 2003/2329, SI 2003/2456, SI 2003/2913, SI 2003/3273, SSI 2003/91, SSI 2003/353, SSI 2003/354, SSI 2003/426, SSI 2003/586

s.23, enabling: SI 2002/3229, SI 2003/130, SI 2003/326, SI 2003/399, SI 2003/1078, SI 2003/1079, SI 2003/1428, SI 2003/

CAP.

1981–cont.

22. Animal Health Act 1981–*cont.*

s.23, enabling:–*cont.*
2329, SI 2003/2456, SI 2003/2913, SI 2003/3273, SI 2004/2891, SSI 2003/91, SSI 2003/334, SSI 2003/353, SSI 2003/354, SSI 2003/426, SSI 2003/586, SSI 2004/537

s.24, enabling: SI 2002/882, SI 2004/2364

s.25, enabling: SI 2003/130, SI 2003/326, SI 2003/1078, SI 2003/1079, SI 2003/2329, SI 2003/2456, SI 2003/2913, SI 2003/3273, SSI 2003/91, SSI 2003/354, SSI 2003/426, SSI 2003/586

s.28, enabling: SI 2003/1078, SI 2003/1079, SI 2003/2329, SI 2003/2456, SI 2003/2913, SI 2003/3273, SSI 2003/353, SSI 2003/354, SSI 2003/426, SSI 2003/586

s.28A, added: 2002 c.42 s.12

s.28B, added: 2002 c.42 s.12

s.32, applied: SI 2002/843 Sch.7 para.5, SI 2002/1416 Sch.7 para.4, SI 2003/130 Art.13, SI 2003/326 Art.13, SSI 2002/255 Sch.7 para.4, Sch.9 para.6, Sch.9 para.11, SSI 2003/91 Art.13

s.32, varied: SSI 2003/586 Art.2

s.32, enabling: SI 2003/130, SI 2003/326, SSI 2003/91

s.32A, added: 2002 c.42 s.2

s.32A, enabling: SI 2003/1734

s.32B, added: 2002 c.42 s.3

s.32B, applied: SI 2003/2035 Art.3

s.32B, enabling: SI 2003/2035

s.32C, added: 2002 c.42 s.3

s.32D, added: 2002 c.42 s.4

s.34, see *R. (on the application of Dixon) v Secretary of State for the Environment, Food and Rural Affairs* [2002] EWHC 831, Times, April 22, 2002 (QBD (Admin Ct)), Jack Beatson, Q.C.

s.34, enabling: SI 2003/130, SI 2003/326, SSI 2003/91

s.35, amended: 2002 c.42 s.2

s.35, enabling: SI 2003/130, SI 2003/326, SI 2003/1078, SI 2003/1079, SI 2003/2329, SI 2003/2456, SI 2003/2913, SI 2003/3273, SSI 2003/91, SSI 2003/354, SSI 2003/426, SSI 2003/586

s.36, enabling: SI 2003/130, SI 2003/326, SSI 2003/91

s.37, enabling: SI 2003/255, SI 2003/482, SI 2003/1336, SI 2003/1470, SI 2003/1724, SI 2003/1968

s.38, amended: SI 2003/1615 Sch.1 para.9

s.38, enabling: SI 2003/2329, SI 2003/2456, SI 2003/2913, SI 2003/3273

s.60, amended: 2002 c.42 s.11

s.62A, added: 2002 c.42 s.8

s.62B, added: 2002 c.42 s.8

s.62C, added: 2002 c.42 s.8

s.62D, added: 2002 c.42 s.9

s.62D, applied: SI 2003/1734 Art.3

CAP.

1981–cont.

22. Animal Health Act 1981–*cont.*
s.62D, enabling: SI 2003/1734
s.62E, added: 2002 c.42 s.9
s.62F, added: 2002 c.42 s.9
s.65A, added: 2002 c.42 s.10
s.66A, added: 2002 c.42 s.8
s.71A, added: 2002 c.42 s.14
s.75, substituted: 2002 c.42 s.13
s.77, amended: 2004 c.14 Sch.1 Part 17
s.83, enabling: SI 2002/202, SI 2002/242, SI 2002/280, SI 2002/283, SI 2002/2152, SI 2002/2154, SI 2002/2303, SI 2002/2304, SI 2002/3229, SI 2003/30, SI 2003/31, SI 2003/130, SI 2003/168, SI 2003/169, SI 2003/253, SI 2003/254, SI 2003/326, SI 2003/399, SI 2003/481, SI 2003/483, SI 2003/1078, SI 2003/1079, SI 2003/1279, SI 2003/1414, SI 2003/1723, SI 2003/1729, SI 2003/1966, SI 2003/1967, SI 2003/2329, SI 2003/2456, SI 2003/2763, SI 2003/2913, SI 2003/3273, SI 2004/1202, SI 2004/1803, SSI 2002/34, SSI 2002/540, SSI 2003/91, SSI 2003/426, SSI 2003/586
s.84, applied: SI 2002/2875
s.84, enabling: SI 2002/2875, SSI 2002/529
s.86, amended: SI 2002/794 Sch.2
s.87, applied: SI 2002/280 Art.14
s.87, varied: SI 2002/242 Art.14, SI 2002/3229 Art.2, SI 2003/255 Art.1, SI 2003/399 Art.2, SI 2003/482 Art.1, SI 2003/1078 Art.2, SI 2003/1079 Art.2, SI 2003/1470 Art.1, SI 2003/1724 Art.1, SSI 2003/353 Art.2, SSI 2003/354 Art.2
s.87, enabling: SI 2002/241, SI 2002/242, SI 2002/280, SI 2002/281, SI 2002/1764, SI 2002/2061, SI 2002/2152, SI 2002/2304, SI 2002/3229, SI 2003/255, SI 2003/399, SI 2003/482, SI 2003/1078, SI 2003/1079, SI 2003/1336, SI 2003/1470, SI 2003/1724, SI 2003/1968, SSI 2003/353, SSI 2003/354
s.88, varied: SI 2002/3229 Art.2, SI 2003/130 Art.3, SI 2003/255 Art.1, SI 2003/326 Art.3, SI 2003/399 Art.2, SI 2003/482 Art.1, SI 2003/1078 Art.2, SI 2003/1079 Art.2, SI 2003/1470 Art.1, SI 2003/1724 Art.1, SSI 2003/91 Art.3, SSI 2003/353 Art.2, SSI 2003/354 Art.2, SSI 2003/586 Art.2
s.88, enabling: SI 2002/3229, SI 2003/130, SI 2003/255, SI 2003/326, SI 2003/399, SI 2003/482, SI 2003/1078, SI 2003/1079, SI 2003/1336, SI 2003/1470, SI 2003/1724, SI 2003/1968, SSI 2003/91, SSI 2003/353, SSI 2003/354, SSI 2003/586
s.94, repealed (in part): 2004 c.14 Sch.1 Part 17
s.95, enabling: SI 2004/2364
Sch.1 para.6, amended: 2003 c.44 Sch.37 Part 9

CAP.

1981–cont.

22. Animal Health Act 1981–*cont.*
Sch.1 para.6, disapplied: 2003 c.44 Sch.25 para.76
Sch.2A, added: 2002 c.42 s.12
Sch.3 para.3, amended: 2002 c.42 s.1
Sch.3 para.5, amended: SI 2003/1734 Art.4
Sch.3 para.5, applied: SI 2003/2035 Art.3
Sch.5 para.4, repealed: 2004 c.14 Sch.1 Part 17

23. Local Government (Miscellaneous Provisions) (Scotland) Act 1981
Sch.1 para.1, repealed: 2002 asp 11 Sch.6 para.5

24. Matrimonial Homes and Property Act 1981
s.4, repealed: 2002 c.9 Sch.13

27. Criminal Justice (Amendment) Act 1981
repealed: 2003 c.44 Sch.37 Part 4

28. Licensing (Alcohol Education and Research) Act 1981
s.3, amended: SI 2002/1555 Art.9
s.3, varied: SI 2003/1633 Sch.2 para.8
s.10, amended: SI 2003/1326 Art.9

29. Fisheries Act 1981
s.1, applied: SI 2002/675 Reg.11, SR 2002/6 Reg.11
s.2, applied: SI 2002/675 Reg.11, SR 2002/6 Reg.11
s.3, repealed (in part): 2002 c.1 Sch.4
s.5, amended: 2003 c.44 Sch.37 Part 9
s.5, disapplied: 2003 c.44 Sch.25 para.77
s.11, amended: SI 2003/1326 Art.10, SI 2004/1715 Art.3
s.11, repealed (in part): SI 2004/1715 Art.3
s.12, amended: SI 2002/790 Art.7
s.13, amended: 2004 c.14 Sch.1 Part 5
s.13, repealed (in part): 2004 c.14 Sch.1 Part 5
s.15, applied: SI 2002/790 Sch.2 para.2
s.15, disapplied: SI 2002/790 Sch.2 para.2
s.15, varied: SI 2002/790 Sch.2 para.2
s.15, enabling: SI 2003/2669, SI 2004/2467, SSI 2003/87, SSI 2003/116, SSI 2004/379
s.16, amended: SI 2003/1326 Art.10, SI 2004/1715 Art.3
s.16, applied: SI 2002/790 Sch.2 para.2
s.16, disapplied: SI 2002/790 Sch.2 para.2
s.16, repealed (in part): SI 2004/1715 Art.3
s.16, varied: SI 2002/790 Sch.2 para.2
s.17, applied: SI 2003/2669 Art.14, SI 2004/2467 Art.8, SSI 2003/116 Art.10, SSI 2004/379 Art.10
s.30, applied: SI 2002/272 Art.4, SI 2002/790 Sch.2 para.3, SI 2003/229 Art.1, SI 2003/772 Art.1, Art.4, SI 2004/1237 Art.1, SSI 2002/51 Art.5, Art.13, SSI 2003/88 Art.5, Art.13, SSI 2004/209 Art.6, Art.14
s.30, disapplied: SI 2002/790 Sch.2 para.3

CAP.

CAP.

1981–cont.

29. Fisheries Act 1981–cont.

s.30, referred to: SI 2002/272 Art.1, SI 2002/ 677 Reg.2, SI 2003/1535 Art.1, SI 2004/ 398 Art.1, SR 2003/59 Art.1, SSI 2003/ 56 Art.1, SSI 2004/44 Art.1, SSI 2004/ 392 Art.1

s.30, enabling: SI 2002/272, SI 2002/426, SI 2003/229, SI 2003/559, SI 2003/772, SI 2003/1535, SI 2004/38, SI 2004/398, SI 2004/1237, SI 2004/3226, SR 2003/59, SSI 2002/51, SSI 2002/56, SSI 2002/81, SSI 2003/56, SSI 2003/66, SSI 2003/88, SSI 2003/300, SSI 2003/623, SSI 2004/ 44, SSI 2004/81, SSI 2004/209, SSI 2004/392

s.33, applied: 2003 asp 15 s.19

s.40, amended: SI 2002/790 Art.6

s.43, amended: SI 2002/790 Art.7

Sch.3 para.4, repealed: 2004 c.14 Sch.1 Part 5

Sch.3 para.5, repealed: 2004 c.14 Sch.1 Part 5

Sch.3 para.6, repealed: 2004 c.14 Sch.1 Part 5

Sch.3 para.7, repealed: 2004 c.14 Sch.1 Part 5

Sch.4 Part II para.18, repealed (in part): 2003 asp 15 Sch.4 Part 2

Sch.4 Part II para.19, repealed (in part): 2003 asp 15 Sch.4 Part 2

Sch.4 Part II para.20, repealed (in part): 2003 asp 15 Sch.4 Part 2

Sch.4 Part II para.21, repealed (in part): 2003 asp 15 Sch.4 Part 2

Sch.4 Part II para.22, repealed (in part): 2003 asp 15 Sch.4 Part 2

Sch.4 Part II para.23, repealed (in part): 2003 asp 15 Sch.4 Part 2

Sch.4 Part II para.24, repealed (in part): 2003 asp 15 Sch.4 Part 2

Sch.4 Part II para.25, repealed (in part): 2003 asp 15 Sch.4 Part 2

30. Horserace Betting Levy Act 1981

referred to: 2004 c.25 s.15

31. Insurance Companies Act 1981

repealed: SI 2002/1555 Art.10

34. Representation of the People Act 1981

applied: SI 2002/2779 Sch.2 para.15, Sch.2 para.16, Sch.2 para.17, Sch.2 para.21, Sch.2 para.22, SI 2003/284 Sch.5 para.18, SI 2004/293 Sch.1 para.13, Sch.1 para.17, SI 2004/1267 Sch.1 para.15

referred to: SI 2003/284 Sch.5 para.13, Sch.5 para.14, Sch.5 para.18, SI 2004/293 Sch.1 para.17, SI 2004/1267 Sch.1 para.12, Sch.1 para.15

35. Finance Act 1981

s.107, amended: 2003 c.14 Sch.20 para.3

s.108, referred to: 2003 c.14 Sch.19 para.7

Sch.8 Part III para.24, repealed: 2003 c.17 Sch.7

Sch.8 Part III para.25, repealed: 2003 c.17 Sch.7

1981–cont.

36. Town and Country Planning (Minerals) Act 1981

s.7, see *Earthline Ltd v Secretary of State for Transport, Local Government and the Regions* [2002] EWCA Civ 1599, [2003] 1 P. & C.R. 24 (CA), Brooke, L.J.

37. Zoo Licensing Act 1981

applied: SI 2002/242 Art.3, SI 2002/280 Art.3, SI 2002/2152 Art.3, SI 2002/2304 Art.3, SI 2002/3080 Reg.28, SI 2003/254 Art.3, SI 2003/992 Reg.3, Reg.4, SI 2003/ 1279 Art.3, SI 2003/1414 Art.3, SI 2003/ 1729 Art.3, SSI 2003/174 Reg.28

disapplied: SI 2003/483 Art.3, SI 2003/ 1966 Art.3

referred to: SI 2002/3080 Reg.3, SSI 2003/ 174 Reg.3

s.1, amended: SI 2002/3080 Reg.4, SI 2003/ 992 Sch.1 para.1, SSI 2003/174 Reg.4

s.1, repealed (in part): 2004 c.14 Sch.1 Part 17

s.1A, added: SI 2002/3080 Reg.5, SI 2003/ 992 Sch.1 para.2, SSI 2003/174 Reg.5

s.1A, referred to: SI 2002/3080 Reg.27, SI 2003/992 Reg.3, SSI 2003/174 Reg.27

s.2, amended: SI 2002/3080 Reg.6, SI 2003/992 Sch.1 para.3, SSI 2003/174 Reg.6

s.3, amended: 2004 c.21 Sch.1 para.51

s.4, amended: SI 2002/3080 Reg.7, SI 2003/ 992 Sch.1 para.4, SSI 2003/174 Reg.7

s.4, repealed (in part): SI 2002/3080 Reg.7, SI 2003/992 Sch.1 para.4, SSI 2003/174 Reg.7

s.4, substituted: SSI 2003/174 Reg.7

s.5, amended: SI 2002/3080 Reg.8, SI 2003/992 Sch.1 para.5, SSI 2003/174 Reg.8

s.5, repealed (in part): SI 2002/3080 Reg.8, SI 2003/992 Sch.1 para.5, SSI 2003/174 Reg.8

s.6, amended: SI 2002/3080 Reg.9, SI 2003/992 Sch.1 para.6, SSI 2003/174 Reg.9

s.7, amended: SI 2002/3080 Reg.10, SI 2003/992 Sch.1 para.7, SSI 2003/174 Reg.10

s.8, amended: SI 2002/3080 Reg.11, SI 2003/992 Sch.1 para.8, SSI 2003/174 Reg.11

s.8, substituted: SSI 2003/174 Reg.11

s.9, applied: SI 2002/3080 Reg.27, SI 2003/ 992 Reg.3, SSI 2003/174 Reg.27

s.9A, added: SI 2002/3080 Reg.12, SI 2003/ 992 Sch.1 para.9, SSI 2003/174 Reg.12

s.10, amended: SI 2002/3080 Reg.13, SI 2003/992 Sch.1 para.10, SSI 2003/174 Reg.13

s.11, amended: SI 2002/3080 Reg.14, SI 2003/992 Sch.1 para.11, SSI 2003/174 Reg.14

1981–cont.

37. Zoo Licensing Act 1981–*cont.*

s.11A, added: SI 2002/3080 Reg.15, SI 2003/992 Sch.1 para.12, SSI 2003/174 Reg.15

s.12, amended: SI 2002/3080 Reg.16, SI 2003/992 Sch.1 para.13, SSI 2003/174 Reg.16

s.13, amended: SI 2002/3080 Reg.17, SI 2003/992 Sch.1 para.14, SSI 2003/174 Reg.17

s.14, amended: SI 2002/3080 Reg.18, SI 2003/992 Sch.1 para.15, SSI 2003/174 Reg.18

s.15, amended: SI 2002/3080 Reg.19, SI 2003/992 Sch.1 para.16, SSI 2003/174 Reg.19

s.16, amended: SI 2002/3080 Reg.20, SI 2003/992 Sch.1 para.17, SSI 2003/174 Reg.20

s.16, applied: SI 2002/3080 Reg.27, SI 2003/992 Reg.3, SSI 2003/174 Reg.27

s.16, varied: SI 2002/3080 Reg.27, SI 2003/992 Reg.3, SSI 2003/174 Reg.27

s.16A, added: SI 2002/3080 Reg.21, SI 2003/992 Sch.1 para.18, SSI 2003/174 Reg.21

s.16B, added: SI 2002/3080 Reg.21, SI 2003/992 Sch.1 para.18, SSI 2003/174 Reg.21

s.16C, added: SI 2002/3080 Reg.21, SI 2003/992 Sch.1 para.18, SSI 2003/174 Reg.21

s.16C, disapplied: SI 2002/3080 Reg.28, SI 2003/992 Reg.4, SSI 2003/174 Reg.28

s.16D, added: SI 2002/3080 Reg.21, SI 2003/992 Sch.1 para.18, SSI 2003/174 Reg.21

s.16E, added: SI 2002/3080 Reg.21, SI 2003/992 Sch.1 para.18, SSI 2003/174 Reg.21

s.16F, added: SI 2002/3080 Reg.21, SI 2003/992 Sch.1 para.18, SSI 2003/174 Reg.21

s.16G, added: SI 2002/3080 Reg.21, SI 2003/992 Sch.1 para.18, SSI 2003/174 Reg.21

s.17, repealed (in part): SI 2002/3080 Reg.22, SI 2003/992 Sch.1 para.19, SSI 2003/174 Reg.22

s.18, amended: SI 2002/3080 Reg.23, 2003 c.39 Sch.8 para.258, Sch.10, SI 2003/992 Sch.1 para.20, SSI 2003/174 Reg.23

s.18, applied: SI 2002/3080 Reg.27, SI 2003/992 Reg.3, SSI 2003/174 Reg.27

s.19, amended: SI 2002/3080 Reg.24, SI 2003/992 Sch.1 para.21, SSI 2003/174 Reg.24

s.19A, added: SI 2002/3080 Reg.25, SI 2003/992 Sch.1 para.22, SSI 2003/174 Reg.25

s.20, repealed: 2004 c.14 Sch.1 Part 17

1981–cont.

37. Zoo Licensing Act 1981–*cont.*

s.21, amended: SI 2002/3080 Reg.26, SI 2003/992 Sch.1 para.23, SSI 2003/174 Reg.26

s.22, repealed (in part): 2004 c.14 Sch.1 Part 17

s.22A, added: SI 2002/3080 Reg.2

s.22A, repealed (in part): SI 2003/992 Reg.2

s.23, repealed (in part): 2004 c.14 Sch.1 Part 17

38. British Telecommunications Act 1981

varied: 2004 c.14 Sch.1 Part 17

s.66, see *Consignia Plc v Hays Plc* Times, January 24, 2002 (Ch D), Jacob, J.

s.88, amended: 2003 c.21 Sch.19

Sch.2 para.12, amended: 2003 c.14 Sch.20 para.3

Sch.3 Part II para.51, repealed (in part): SI 2003/2908 Sch.2

Sch.4 para.2, repealed: 2003 c.21 Sch.19

Sch.4 para.3, repealed: 2003 c.21 Sch.19

Sch.4 para.4, repealed: 2003 c.21 Sch.19

Sch.4 para.5, repealed: 2003 c.21 Sch.19

Sch.4 para.6, repealed: 2003 c.21 Sch.19

Sch.4 para.7, repealed: 2003 c.21 Sch.19

Sch.4 para.8, repealed: 2003 c.21 Sch.19

Sch.4 para.9, repealed: 2003 c.21 Sch.19

Sch.4 para.10, repealed: 2003 c.21 Sch.19

Sch.4 para.11, repealed: 2003 c.21 Sch.19

Sch.4 para.12, repealed: 2003 c.21 Sch.19

Sch.4 para.13, repealed: 2003 c.21 Sch.19

Sch.4 para.14, repealed: 2003 c.21 Sch.19

Sch.4 para.15, repealed: 2003 c.21 Sch.19

Sch.4 para.16, repealed: 2003 c.21 Sch.19

Sch.4 para.17, repealed: 2003 c.21 Sch.19

Sch.4 para.18, repealed: 2003 c.21 Sch.19

Sch.4 para.21, repealed: 2003 c.21 Sch.19

Sch.4 para.22, repealed: 2003 c.21 Sch.19

Sch.5 Part II para.3, repealed: 2003 c.21 Sch.19

Sch.5 Part II para.4, repealed: 2003 c.21 Sch.19

Sch.5 Part II para.5, repealed: 2003 c.21 Sch.19

Sch.5 Part II para.6, repealed: 2003 c.21 Sch.19

Sch.5 Part II para.7, repealed: 2003 c.21 Sch.19

Sch.5 Part II para.8, repealed: 2003 c.21 Sch.19

Sch.5 Part II para.9, repealed: 2003 c.21 Sch.19

Sch.5 Part II para.10, repealed: 2003 c.21 Sch.19

Sch.5 Part II para.11, repealed: 2003 c.21 Sch.19

Sch.5 Part II para.12, repealed: 2003 c.21 Sch.19

Sch.5 Part III para.13, repealed: 2003 c.21 Sch.19

1981–cont.

38. British Telecommunications Act 1981– cont.

Sch.5 Part III para.14, repealed: 2003 c.21 Sch.19

Sch.5 Part III para.15, repealed: 2003 c.21 Sch.19

Sch.5 Part III para.16, repealed: 2003 c.21 Sch.19

Sch.5 Part III para.17, repealed: 2003 c.21 Sch.19

Sch.5 Part III para.18, repealed: 2003 c.21 Sch.19

Sch.5 Part III para.19, repealed: 2003 c.21 Sch.19

Sch.5 Part III para.20, repealed: 2003 c.21 Sch.19

Sch.5 Part III para.21, repealed: 2003 c.21 Sch.19

Sch.5 Part III para.22, repealed: 2003 c.21 Sch.19

40. Licensing (Amendment) Act 1981
repealed: 2003 c.17 Sch.7

42. Indecent Displays (Control) Act 1981
s.1, amended: 2003 c.17 Sch.6 para.80

43. Disabled Persons Act 1981
Commencement Orders: 2004 c.14 Sch.1 Part 13

s.6, repealed: 2004 c.14 Sch.1 Part 13

s.9, repealed (in part): 2004 c.14 Sch.1 Part 13

45. Forgery and Counterfeiting Act 1981
Part I, applied: 2004 c.11 s.12

s.1, applied: 2003 c.17 Sch.4 para.11, 2004 c.19 s.14

s.2, applied: 2003 c.17 Sch.4 para.11, 2004 c.19 s.14

s.3, see *Attorney General's Reference (No.1 of 2001), Re* [2002] EWCA Crim 1768, [2003] 1 W.L.R. 395 (CA (Crim Div)), Kennedy, L.J.; see *R. v Balasubramaniam (Ravindran)* [2001] EWCA Crim 2680, [2002] 2 Cr. App. R. (S.) 17 (CA (Crim Div)), Sullivan, J.

s.3, applied: 2003 c.17 Sch.4 para.11, 2004 c.19 s.14

s.4, applied: 2003 c.17 Sch.4 para.11, 2004 c.19 s.14

s.5, see *R. v Cheema (Gurmit Singh)* [2002] EWCA Crim 325, [2002] 2 Cr. App. R. (S.) 79 (CA (Crim Div)), Pill, L.J.; see *R. v Fitzgerald (John Cornelius)* [2003] EWCA Crim 576, [2003] 2 Cr. App. R. 17 (CA (Crim Div)), Pill, L.J.

s.5, amended: 2003 c.32 s.88, 2004 c.19 s.3, 2004 c.33 Sch.27 para.67

s.5, applied: 2003 c.17 Sch.4 para.11, 2004 c.19 s.14

s.5, referred to: 2003 c.32

s.6, applied: 2003 c.17 Sch.4 para.11

s.7, applied: 2003 c.17 Sch.4 para.11, SI 2003/336 Sch.1 Part 2

s.8, applied: 2003 c.17 Sch.4 para.11

1981–cont.

45. Forgery and Counterfeiting Act 1981– cont.

s.9, applied: 2003 c.17 Sch.4 para.11

s.9, referred to: 2004 c.11 s.12

s.10, applied: 2003 c.17 Sch.4 para.11

s.11, applied: 2003 c.17 Sch.4 para.11

s.12, applied: 2003 c.17 Sch.4 para.11

s.13, applied: 2003 c.17 Sch.4 para.11

s.14, applied: 2002 c.29 Sch.2 para.6, Sch.4 para.6, Sch.5 para.6, 2003 c.17 Sch.4 para.11

s.15, applied: 2002 c.29 Sch.2 para.6, Sch.4 para.6, Sch.5 para.6, 2003 c.17 Sch.4 para.11

s.16, applied: 2002 c.29 Sch.2 para.6, Sch.4 para.6, Sch.5 para.6, 2003 c.17 Sch.4 para.11

s.17, applied: 2002 c.29 Sch.2 para.6, Sch.4 para.6, Sch.5 para.6, 2003 c.17 Sch.4 para.11

s.20, applied: 2003 c.17 Sch.4 para.11

s.21, applied: 2003 c.17 Sch.4 para.11

s.22, applied: 2003 c.17 Sch.4 para.11

s.23, applied: 2003 c.17 Sch.4 para.11

s.23, repealed (in part): 2003 c.44 Sch.37 Part 7

s.24, applied: 2003 c.17 Sch.4 para.11, SI 2003/336 Sch.1 Part 2

s.25, applied: 2003 c.17 Sch.4 para.11

s.26, applied: 2003 c.17 Sch.4 para.11

s.27, applied: 2003 c.17 Sch.4 para.11

s.28, applied: 2003 c.17 Sch.4 para.11

s.31, applied: 2003 c.17 Sch.4 para.11

s.32, applied: 2003 c.17 Sch.4 para.11

s.33, applied: 2003 c.17 Sch.4 para.11

s.34, applied: 2003 c.17 Sch.4 para.11

47. Criminal Attempts Act 1981
s.1, applied: 2003 c.44 Sch.4 para.2, Sch.4 para.8, Sch.4 para.14, Sch.5 para.2, Sch.5 para.7, Sch.5 para.13, SI 2004/1910 Sch.2

s.2, amended: 2003 c.44 Sch.37 Part 4, Sch.3 para.52

s.4, amended: 2003 c.44 Sch.32 para.33

s.4, repealed (in part): 2003 c.42 Sch.7

s.9, amended: 2003 c.44 Sch.26 para.28

s.9, applied: SI 2002/1917 Art.2

48. Atomic Energy (Miscellaneous Provisions) Act 1981
s.1, disapplied: 2004 c.20 s.48

s.1, referred to: 2004 c.20 s.48

s.1, repealed (in part): 2004 c.20 Sch.23 Part 1

49. Contempt of Court Act 1981
referred to: 2003 c.44 s.337

s.2, see *HM Advocate v Beggs (No.1)* 2002 S.L.T. 135 (HCJ), Lord Osborne; see *HM Advocate v Beggs (No.2)* 2002 S.L.T. 139 (HCJ), Lord Osborne; see *HTV Cymru (Wales) Ltd, Ex p.* [2002] E.M.L.R. 11 (Crown Ct (Cardiff)), Aikens, J.

s.3, repealed (in part): 2004 c.14 Sch.1 Part 1

1981–cont.

49. Contempt of Court Act 1981–*cont.*

s.4, see *BBC, Petitioners (No.3)* 2002 J.C. 27 (HCJ Appeal), Lord Rodger L.J.G., Lord Abernethy, Lord Kirkwood; see *HM Advocate v Beggs (No.1)* 2002 S.L.T. 135 (HCJ), Lord Osborne; see *Practice Direction (Criminal Proceedings: Consolidation)* [2002] 1 W.L.R. 2870 (CA (Crim Div)), Lord Woolf of Barnes, L.C.J.; see *R. v News Group Newspapers Ltd* [2002] E.M.L.R. 9 (CA (Crim Div)), Lord Bingham of Cornhill, L.C.J.

s.4, amended: 2003 c.44 Sch.3 para.53

s.4, repealed (in part): 2003 c.44 Sch.37 Part 4, 2004 c.14 Sch.1 Part 1

s.8, see *Attorney General v Scotcher* [2003] EWHC 1380, [2004] A.C.D. 2 (QBD (Admin Ct)), Scott Baker, L.J.; see *R. v Mirza (Shabbir Ali)* [2002] EWCA Crim 1235, [2002] Crim. L.R. 921 (CA (Crim Div)), Rose, L.J.; see *R. v Mirza (Shabbir Ali)* [2004] UKHL 2, [2004] 1 A.C. 1118 (HL), Lord Steyn

s.10, see *Ashworth Hospital Authority v MGN Ltd* [2002] UKHL 29, [2002] 1 W.L.R. 2033 (HL), Lord Woolf of Barnes, L.C.J.; see *Interbrew SA v Financial Times Ltd* [2002] EWCA Civ 274, [2002] 2 Lloyd's Rep. 229 (CA), Sedley, L.J.

s.13, repealed (in part): SI 2003/435 Sch.5

Sch.2 Part III para.1, repealed: 2004 c.14 Sch.1 Part 1

52. Belize Act 1981

Sch.2 para.8, repealed: 2002 c.39 Sch.3

53. Deep Sea Mining (Temporary Provisions) Act 1981

s.1, amended: 2002 c.8 s.2

54. Supreme Court Act 1981

s.s.28A, see *Kilhey Court Hotels Ltd v Wigan MBC* [2004] EWCA 2890 (QBD (Admin)), Forbes, J.

s.2, amended: SI 2002/2837 Art.2, 2003 c.39 s.63

s.2, applied: SI 2002/2837

s.2, enabling: SI 2002/2837

s.4, amended: SI 2003/775 Art.2

s.4, applied: SI 2003/775

s.4, enabling: SI 2003/775

s.8, amended: 2003 c.39 s.65, Sch.8 para.259

s.9, see *Coppard v Customs and Excise Commissioners* [2003] EWCA Civ 511, [2003] Q.B. 1428 (CA), Sedley, L.J.; see *Fawdry & Co v Murfitt* [2002] EWCA Civ 643, [2003] Q.B. 104 (CA), Hale, L.J.

s.9, amended: 2003 c.39 Sch.8 para.260

s.15, see *R. (on the application of Sezek) v Secretary of State for the Home Department (Bail Application)* [2001] EWCA Civ 795, [2002] 1 W.L.R. 348 (CA), Peter Gibson, L.J.

1981–cont.

54. Supreme Court Act 1981–*cont.*

s.16, see *Aoun v Bahri (No.1)* [2002] EWCA Civ 1141, [2003] C.P. Rep. 6 (CA), Brooke, L.J.

s.18, see *R. (on the application of Aru) v Chief Constable of Merseyside* [2004] EWCA Civ 199, [2004] 1 W.L.R. 1697 (CA), Waller, L.J.; see *R. (on the application of South West Yorkshire Mental Health NHS Trust) v Bradford Crown Court* [2003] EWCA Civ 1857, [2004] 1 W.L.R. 1664 (CA), Pill, L.J.; see *Westminster City Council v O'Reilly (Leave to Appeal: Jurisdiction)* [2003] EWCA Civ 1007, [2004] 1 W.L.R. 195 (CA), Auld, L.J.

s.18, amended: 2004 c.33 Sch.27 para.68

s.18, disapplied: 2003 c.44 s.274, Sch.22 para.14

s.28, amended: 2003 c.17 Sch.7

s.28, applied: 2003 c.17 s.130

s.28A, see *Westminster City Council v O'Reilly (Leave to Appeal: Jurisdiction)* [2003] EWCA Civ 1007, [2004] 1 W.L.R. 195 (CA), Auld, L.J.

s.29, see *R. (on the application of Kenneally) v Snaresbrook Crown Court* [2001] EWHC Admin 968, [2002] Q.B. 1169 (QBD (Admin Ct)), Pill, L.J.; see *R. (on the application of Rogerson) v Stafford Crown Court* [2001] EWHC Admin 961, [2002] Crim.L.R. 318 (QBD (Admin Ct)), Crane, J.; see *R. (on the application of Salubi) v Bow Street Magistrates Court* [2002] EWHC 919, [2002] 1 W.L.R. 3073 (QBD (Admin Ct)), Auld, L.J.

s.29, amended: SI 2004/1033 Art.3

s.31, see *R. (on the application of Comninos) v Bedford BC* [2003] EWHC 121, [2003] B.L.G.R. 271 (QBD (Admin Ct)), Sullivan, J.; see *R. (on the application of Gavin) v Haringey LBC* [2003] EWHC 2591, [2004] 2 P. & C.R. 13 (QBD (Admin Ct)), Richards, J.

s.31, amended: SI 2004/1033 Art.4

s.31, applied: 2004 c.23 s.36

s.32A, see *A v National Blood Authority (No. 2)* [2002] Lloyd's Rep. Med. 487 (QBD), Burton, J.

s.32A, applied: 2003 c.43 s.157

s.33, see *Black v Sumitomo Corp* [2001] EWCA Civ 1819, [2002] 1 W.L.R. 1562 (CA), Rix, L.J.

s.34, see *Individual Homes Ltd v Macbream Investments Ltd* Times, November 14, 2002 (Ch D), AG Steinfeld Q.C.

s.35A, see *Sempra Metals Ltd (formerly Metallgesellschaft Ltd) v Inland Revenue Commissioners* [2004] EWHC 2387, [2004] S.T.C. 1178 (Ch D), Park, J.

s.37, see *Donohue v Armco Inc* [2001] UKHL 64, [2002] 1 All E.R. 749 (HL), Lord Bingham of Cornhill; see *Field v Field*

CAP.

1981–cont.
54. Supreme Court Act 1981–*cont.*
s.37–*cont.*

[2003] 1 F.L.R. 376 (Fam Div), Wilson, J.; see *Moore v Moore* [2004] EWCA Civ 1243, [2004] 3 F.C.R. 461 (CA), Thorpe, L.J.; see *Rio Properties Inc v Gibson Dunn & Crutcher* [2004] EWCA Civ 1043, [2004] 1 W.L.R. 2702 (CA (Civ Div)), Jonathan Parker, L.J.

s.37, applied: 2004 c.33 Sch.7 para.18

s.40A, amended: SI 2002/439 Art.6

s.42, see *Attorney General v Ebert* [2001] EWHC Admin 695, [2002] 2 All E.R. 789 (QBD (Admin Ct)), Brooke, L.J.; see *Attorney General v Oakes* [2002] B.P.I.R. 231 (QBD), Klevan, J.; see *Bhamjee v Forsdick* [2003] EWCA Civ 1113, [2004] 1 W.L.R. 88 (CA), Lord Phillips of Worth Matravers, M.R.; see *Ebert v Official Receiver (No.2)* [2001] EWCA Civ 340, [2002] 1 W.L.R. 320 (CA), Buxton, L.J.

s.43, amended: SI 2004/1033 Art.5

s.45, see *HTV Cymru (Wales) Ltd, Ex p.* [2002] E.M.L.R. 11 (Crown Ct (Cardiff)), Aikens, J.; see *R. v G* [2004] EWCA Crim 1368, [2004] 1 W.L.R. 2932 (CA (Crim Div)), Rose, L.J.

s.49, see *A v National Blood Authority (No. 2)* [2002] Lloyd's Rep. Med. 487 (QBD), Burton, J.

s.51, see *AB v Leeds Teaching Hospitals NHS Trust* [2003] EWHC 1034, [2003] 3 Costs L.R. 405 (QBD), Gage, J.; see *Associated Newspapers Ltd v Impac Ltd* [2002] F.S.R. 18 (QBD), Master Turner; see *Brown v Bennett (Wasted Costs) (No.1)* [2002] 1 W.L.R. 713 (Ch D), Neuberger, J.; see *Byrne v Sefton HA* [2001] EWCA Civ 1904, [2002] 1 W.L.R. 775 (CA), Chadwick, L.J.; see *CIBC Mellon Trust Co v Mora Hotel Corp NV* [2002] EWCA Civ 1688, [2003] 1 All E.R. 564 (CA), Peter Gibson, L.J.; see *Contract Facilities Ltd v Rees Estate (Application to Strike Out)* [2003] EWCA Civ 1105, (2003) 147 S.J.L.B. 933 (CA), Waller, L.J.; see *Daly v Hubner (Wasted Costs)* [2002] Lloyd's Rep. P.N. 461 (Ch D), Etherton, J.; see *Dempsey v Johnstone* [2003] EWCA Civ 1134, [2004] 1 Costs L.R. 41 (CA), Aldous, L.J.; see *Floods of Queensferry Ltd v Shand Construction Ltd (Costs)* [2002] EWCA Civ 918, [2003] Lloyd's Rep. I.R. 181 (CA), Buxton, L.J.; see *Hamilton v Al-Fayed (Costs)* [2002] EWCA Civ 665, [2003] Q.B. 1175 (CA), Simon Brown, L.J.; see *Individual Homes Ltd v Macbream Investments Ltd* Times, November 14, 2002 (Ch D), AG Steinfeld Q.C.; see *Isaacs Partnership (A Firm) v Umm Al-Jawaby Oil Service Co Ltd* [2003] EWHC 2539, [2004] P.N.L.R. 9 (QBD), Gross, J.; see *J v Oyston* [2002]

CAP.

1981–cont.
54. Supreme Court Act 1981–*cont.*
s.51–*cont.*

EWHC 819, [2002] C.P.L.R. 563 (QBD), McKinnon, J.; see *John v Pricewaterhouse-Coopers (formerly Price Waterhouse) (Costs)* [2002] 1 W.L.R. 953 (Ch D), Ferris, J.; see *Medcalf v Mardell (Wasted Costs Order)* [2002] UKHL 27, [2003] 1 A.C. 120 (HL), Lord Bingham of Cornhill; see *Melchior v Vettivel* [2002] C.P. Rep. 24 (Ch D), Patten, J.; see *North West Holdings Plc (In Liquidation) (Costs), Re* [2001] EWCA Civ 67, [2002] B.C.C. 441 (CA), Aldous, L.J.; see *Radford & Co v Charles* [2003] EWHC 3180, [2004] P.N.L.R. 25 (Ch D), Neuberger, J.; see *Ross (A Bankrupt) (Costs), Re* [2002] B.P.I.R. 185 (CA), Nourse, L.J.; see *Ryan Developments Ltd, Re* [2002] EWHC 1121, [2002] 2 B.C.L.C. 792 (Ch D), Neuberger, J.; see *Wagstaff v Colls* [2003] EWCA Civ 469, [2003] C.P. Rep. 50 (CA), Ward, L.J.

s.52, amended: SI 2004/2035 Sch.1 para.12

s.52, enabling: SI 2003/421

s.53, applied: 2002 c.29 s.89, 2003 c.44 s.47, s.74

s.54, see *Noueiri v Paragon Finance Plc (No.1)* [2001] EWCA Civ 1114, [2002] C.P. Rep. 2 (CA), Robert Walker, L.J.

s.55, see *R. v Coates (Victor Henry)* [2004] EWCA Crim 2253, [2004] 1 W.L.R. 3043 (CA (Crim Div)), Judge, L.J.

s.55, amended: 2004 c.28 Sch.10 para.14, Sch.11

s.56A, repealed: 2003 c.39 Sch.10

s.68, see *Coppard v Customs and Excise Commissioners* [2003] EWCA Civ 511, [2003] Q.B. 1428 (CA), Sedley, L.J.

s.68, applied: SI 2004/293 Reg.49

s.69, see *Phillips v Commissioner of Police of the Metropolis* [2003] EWCA Civ 382, [2003] C.P. Rep. 48 (CA), Scott Baker, L.J.; see *Spencer v Sillitoe* [2002] EWCA Civ 1579, [2003] E.M.L.R. 10 (CA), Buxton, L.J.

s.70, see *Independent Insurance Co Ltd (In Provisional Liquidation), Re (No.1)* [2002] EWHC 1577, [2002] 2 B.C.L.C. 709 (Ch D (Companies Court)), Ferris, J.

s.72, amended: 2004 c.33 Sch.27 para.69

s.73, amended: SI 2004/2035 Sch.1 para.12

s.74, amended: SI 2004/2035 Sch.1 para.12

s.75, amended: 2003 c.39 Sch.8 para.261

s.76, amended: 2003 c.44 Sch.36 para.47, Sch.3 para.54

s.76, applied: 2003 c.39 s.86

s.76, repealed (in part): 2003 c.39 Sch.10, 2003 c.44 Sch.37 Part 4, Sch.3 para.54

s.77, amended: 2003 c.44 Sch.3 para.54, SI 2004/2035 Sch.1 para.13

s.77, repealed (in part): 2003 c.44 Sch.37 Part 4, Sch.3 para.54

1981–cont.

54. Supreme Court Act 1981–*cont.*
s.79, see *Hayes v Chelmsford Crown Court* [2003] EWHC 73, (2003) 167 J.P. 65 (QBD (Admin Ct)), Henriques, J.

s.80, amended: 2003 c.44 Sch.3 para.54

s.81, amended: 2003 c.44 Sch.36 para.4, Sch.37 Part 2, Sch.37 Part 4, Sch.3 para.54, 2004 c.28 Sch.10 para.15, SI 2004/1033 Art.6, SI 2004/2035 Sch.1 para.14

s.81, applied: 2003 c.44 s.17

s.81, disapplied: 2003 c.44 s.89

s.81, repealed (in part): 2003 c.44 Sch.36 para.4, Sch.37 Part 4, Sch.3 para.54

s.84, amended: SI 2004/2035 Sch.1 para.15

s.84, applied: SI 2003/428

s.84, enabling: SI 2002/1688, SI 2002/2783, SI 2002/2997, SI 2003/421, SI 2003/422, SI 2003/428, SI 2003/639, SI 2003/1646, SI 2003/1664, SI 2004/185, SI 2004/1047, SI 2004/1292, SI 2004/1293, SI 2004/2420, SI 2004/2991, SI 2004/2992

s.86, amended: SI 2004/2035 Sch.1 para.16

s.86, repealed (in part): SI 2004/2035 Sch.1 para.16

s.86, enabling: SI 2002/1688, SI 2002/2783, SI 2002/2997, SI 2003/421, SI 2003/422, SI 2003/428, SI 2003/639, SI 2003/1646, SI 2003/1664, SI 2004/185, SI 2004/1047, SI 2004/1292, SI 2004/1293, SI 2004/2420, SI 2004/2991, SI 2004/2992

s.87, amended: SI 2004/2035 Sch.1 para.17

s.87, enabling: SI 2003/428, SI 2004/2992

s.91, applied: 2003 c.39 s.64

s.92, amended: 2003 c.39 s.89, Sch.10

s.92, repealed (in part): 2003 c.39 s.89, Sch.10

s.109, amended: 2004 c.12 s.294

s.109, repealed (in part): 2004 c.12 s.294, Sch.42 Part 4

s.125, amended: 2003 c.39 Sch.8 para.262

s.126, amended: 2003 c.39 Sch.8 para.262

s.127, applied: 2003 c.39 s.76

s.127, enabling: SI 2003/185, SI 2004/2985

s.130, applied: SI 2002/222, SI 2003/646, SI 2003/647, SI 2003/717, SI 2003/1239, SI 2004/2100

s.130, repealed: 2003 c.39 Sch.8 para.263, Sch.10

s.130, enabling: SI 2002/222, SI 2003/646, SI 2003/647, SI 2003/717, SI 2003/1239, SI 2004/2100

s.134, amended: 2003 c.39 Sch.8 para.262

s.138, repealed: 2003 c.39 Sch.10

s.138A, repealed: 2003 c.39 Sch.10

s.138B, repealed: 2003 c.39 Sch.10

s.141, repealed: 2004 c.14 Sch.1 Part 1

s.151, amended: SI 2004/2035 Sch.1 para.18

s.151, repealed (in part): 2003 c.39 Sch.8 para.265, Sch.10

1981–cont.

54. Supreme Court Act 1981–*cont.*
s.152, repealed (in part): 2004 c.14 Sch.1 Part 1

Sch.1 para.3, amended: 2004 c.33 Sch.27 para.70

Sch.2, applied: SI 2003/409 Sch.1 Part I

Sch.5 Part 1, amended: 2004 c.14 Sch.1 Part 1

Sch.5 Part 2, amended: 2003 c.39 Sch.10

55. Armed Forces Act 1981
s.13, applied: SI 2002/325 Reg.3

s.24, repealed (in part): 2004 c.14 Sch.1 Part 5

Sch.3 Part II para.9, repealed: SI 2003/413 Sch.1

56. Transport Act 1981
s.8, varied: SI 2002/3269 Art.8

s.9, disapplied: SI 2002/3269 Art.8

s.9, varied: SI 2002/3269 Art.8

s.15, amended: 2004 c.14 Sch.1 Part 5

s.15, repealed (in part): 2004 c.14 Sch.1 Part 5

s.16, amended: 2004 c.14 Sch.1 Part 5

s.16, repealed (in part): 2004 c.14 Sch.1 Part 5

Sch.3 para.1, varied: SI 2002/3269 Art.8

Sch.3 para.2, varied: SI 2002/3269 Art.8

Sch.3 para.3, varied: SI 2002/3269 Art.8

Sch.3 para.4, varied: SI 2002/3269 Art.8

Sch.3 para.5, varied: SI 2002/3269 Art.8

Sch.3 para.6, varied: SI 2002/3269 Art.8

Sch.3 para.7, varied: SI 2002/3269 Art.8

Sch.3 para.8, varied: SI 2002/3269 Art.8

Sch.3 para.9, varied: SI 2002/3269 Art.8

Sch.3 para.10, varied: SI 2002/3269 Art.8

Sch.3 para.11, varied: SI 2002/3269 Art.8

Sch.3 para.12, varied: SI 2002/3269 Art.8

Sch.3 para.13, varied: SI 2002/3269 Art.8

Sch.3 para.14, varied: SI 2002/3269 Art.8

Sch.3 para.15, varied: SI 2002/3269 Art.8

Sch.3 para.16, varied: SI 2002/3269 Art.8

Sch.3 para.17, varied: SI 2002/3269 Art.8

Sch.3 para.18, varied: SI 2002/3269 Art.8

Sch.3 para.19, varied: SI 2002/3269 Art.8

Sch.3 para.20, varied: SI 2002/3269 Art.8

Sch.3 para.21, varied: SI 2002/3269 Art.8

Sch.3 para.22, varied: SI 2002/3269 Art.8

Sch.3 para.23, varied: SI 2002/3269 Art.8

Sch.3 para.24, varied: SI 2002/3269 Art.8

Sch.3 para.25, varied: SI 2002/3269 Art.8

Sch.3 para.26, varied: SI 2002/3269 Art.8

Sch.3 para.27, varied: SI 2002/3269 Art.8

Sch.3 para.28, varied: SI 2002/3269 Art.8

Sch.3 para.29, varied: SI 2002/3269 Art.8

Sch.3 para.30, varied: SI 2002/3269 Art.8

Sch.3 para.31, amended: SI 2003/1615 Sch.1 para.10, SSI 2002/263 Art.5, Sch.1

Sch.3 para.31, varied: SI 2002/3269 Art.8

Sch.3 para.32, varied: SI 2002/3269 Art.8

Sch.5 Part I para.1, repealed: 2004 c.14 Sch.1 Part 5

Sch.5 Part I para.2, repealed: 2004 c.14 Sch.1 Part 5

CAP.

1981–cont.

56. Transport Act 1981–*cont.*

Sch.5 Part I para.3, repealed: 2004 c.14 Sch.1 Part 5

Sch.5 Part I para.4, repealed: 2004 c.14 Sch.1 Part 5

Sch.5 Part I para.6, repealed (in part): 2004 c.14 Sch.1 Part 5

Sch.5 Part I para.7, repealed: 2004 c.14 Sch.1 Part 5

Sch.5 Part I para.12, repealed: 2004 c.14 Sch.1 Part 5

57. Employment and Training Act 1981

s.9, repealed (in part): 2004 c.14 Sch.1 Part 8

s.11, amended: 2004 c.14 Sch.1 Part 8

Sch.2 Part II para.5, repealed: 2004 c.14 Sch.1 Part 8

Sch.2 Part II para.10, repealed: 2004 c.14 Sch.1 Part 8

Sch.2 Part II para.11, repealed: 2004 c.14 Sch.1 Part 8

Sch.2 Part II para.13, repealed: 2004 c.14 Sch.1 Part 8

Sch.2 Part II para.16, repealed: 2004 c.14 Sch.1 Part 8

58. Education (Scotland) Act 1981

s.3, repealed (in part): 2004 asp 4 Sch.3 para.4

s.4, repealed (in part): 2004 asp 4 Sch.3 para.4

Sch.2 para.4, repealed (in part): 2004 asp 4 Sch.3 para.4

Sch.2 para.6, repealed: 2004 asp 4 Sch.3 para.4

Sch.2 para.7, repealed: 2004 asp 4 Sch.3 para.4

Sch.2 para.8, repealed: 2004 asp 4 Sch.3 para.4

59. Matrimonial Homes (Family Protection) (Scotland) Act 1981

s.1, see *Stevenson v Roy* 2002 S.L.T. 445 (OH), Lord Drummond Young

s.1, applied: 2003 asp 4 s.14

s.6, see *Stevenson v Roy* 2002 S.L.T. 445 (OH), Lord Drummond Young

s.6, applied: 2003 asp 4 s.14

s.8, applied: 2003 asp 4 s.14

s.11, amended: 2002 asp 17 Sch.3 para.13

s.13, amended: 2003 asp 11 Sch.1 para.5

s.17, applied: SSI 2003/179 Reg.3, Reg.9

60. Education Act 1981

see *Carty v Croydon LBC* [2004] EWHC 228, [2004] E.L.R. 226 (QBD), Gibbs, J.

s.5, see *Keating v Bromley LBC* [2003] EWHC 1070, [2003] E.L.R. 590 (QBD), Stanley Burnton, J.

61. British Nationality Act 1981

amended: 2002 c.8 s.1, s.2

applied: 2002 c.1 s.14, 2002 c.8 s.3, s.6, 2002 c.41 s.14, s.130, s.131, s.146, 2003 asp 7 s.22, 2003 c.31 s.6, 2003 c.42 s.60, SI 2003/118 Reg.21, SI 2003/527 Reg.44,

CAP.

1981–cont.

61. British Nationality Act 1981–*cont.*

applied: 2002 c.1 s.14–*cont.*

SI 2003/3157 Reg.6, Sch.1, SR 2003/16 Reg.19, 2004 c.19 s.5, SSI 2004/257 Reg.44

referred to: 2002 c.38 s.74, 2002 c.41 s.92

s.1, amended: 2002 c.8 Sch.1 para.1, 2002 c.38 s.137, Sch.5

s.1, applied: SI 2003/548 Sch.2 para.1, Sch.2 para.2, Sch.2 para.3, SSI 2003/19 Reg.30

s.1, referred to: SI 2003/118 Reg.12, SSI 2003/19 Reg.10

s.2, amended: 2002 c.8 Sch.1 para.2

s.3, see *R. (on the application of Ullah (Azad))* v *Secretary of State for the Home Department* [2001] EWCA Civ 659, [2002] Q.B. 525 (CA), Latham, L.J.

s.3, amended: 2002 c.8 Sch.1 para.3, 2002 c.41 s.9, 2004 c.33 Sch.27 para.71

s.3, applied: SI 2003/548 Reg.14, Sch.2 para.4, Sch.2 para.5, Sch.2 para.6

s.3, repealed (in part): 2002 c.41 s.9, Sch.9

s.4, applied: 2002 c.41 s.11, SI 2003/548 Reg.4, Sch.2 para.7, Sch.2 para.8

s.4A, added: 2002 c.8 s.4

s.4A, applied: SI 2003/548 Sch.2 para.9

s.4B, added: 2002 c.41 s.12

s.4B, applied: SI 2003/548 Sch.2 para.10

s.4C, added: 2002 c.41 s.13

s.4C, applied: SI 2003/548 Sch.2 para.11

s.5, applied: SI 2003/548 Reg.4, Sch.2 para.12, SI 2003/3157 Sch.1

s.6, see *R. (on the application of Ullah (Azad))* v *Secretary of State for the Home Department* [2001] EWCA Civ 659, [2002] Q.B. 525 (CA), Latham, L.J.

s.6, amended: 2004 c.33 Sch.27 para.72

s.6, applied: SI 2003/548 Reg.5A, Sch.2 para.13, Sch.2 para.14, SI 2003/3157 Sch.1

s.7, repealed: 2002 c.41 Sch.2 para.1, Sch.9

s.8, repealed: 2002 c.41 Sch.2 para.1, Sch.9

s.9, repealed: 2002 c.41 Sch.2 para.1, Sch.9

s.10, amended: 2002 c.41 s.5, Sch.9, 2004 c.33 Sch.27 para.73

s.10, applied: SI 2003/548 Sch.2 para.15, Sch.2 para.16

s.12, amended: 2004 c.33 Sch.27 para.74

s.12, applied: SI 2003/3157 Sch.1

s.13, applied: SI 2003/548 Sch.2 para.17, Sch.2 para.18

s.14, amended: 2002 c.41 s.12, s.13

s.15, amended: 2002 c.38 s.137

s.17, amended: 2002 c.41 s.9, 2004 c.33 Sch.27 para.75

s.17, repealed (in part): 2002 c.41 s.9, Sch.9

s.18, amended: 2004 c.33 Sch.27 para.76

s.18, applied: SI 2003/3157 Sch.1

s.19, repealed: 2002 c.41 Sch.2 para.1, Sch.9

s.20, repealed: 2002 c.41 Sch.2 para.1, Sch.9

s.21, repealed: 2002 c.41 Sch.2 para.1, Sch.9

1981–cont.

61. British Nationality Act 1981–*cont.*

s.22, amended: 2002 c.41 s.5, Sch.9, 2004 c.33 Sch.27 para.77

s.24, applied: SI 2003/3157 Sch.1

s.27, repealed (in part): 2002 c.41 Sch.2 para.1, Sch.9

s.28, repealed: 2002 c.41 Sch.2 para.1, Sch.9

s.29, applied: SI 2003/3157 Sch.1

s.33, repealed: 2002 c.41 Sch.2 para.1, Sch.9

s.34, applied: SI 2003/3157 Sch.1

s.37, amended: 2002 c.8 Sch.1 para.4

s.40, applied: 2002 c.41 s.4, SI 2003/548 Reg.10

s.40, substituted: 2002 c.41 s.4

s.40A, amended: 2004 c.19 Sch.2 para.4

s.40A, repealed (in part): 2004 c.19 Sch.2 para.4, Sch.4

s.40A, enabling: SI 2003/652

s.41, amended: 2002 c.41 s.1, Sch.1 para.4, Sch.1 para.5, Sch.1 para.6, Sch.1 para.7

s.41, applied: 2002 c.41 Sch.1 para.8, SI 2003/548 Reg.6A, Sch.3 para.3, 2004 c.19 s.42

s.41, enabling: SI 2003/539, SI 2003/540, SI 2003/548, SI 2003/3157, SI 2003/3158, SI 2003/3159, SI 2004/1726, SI 2004/2109

s.42, applied: SI 2003/548 Reg.6A, Reg.6, Sch.3 para.3, SI 2003/3157 Reg.4

s.42, substituted: 2002 c.41 Sch.1 para.1

s.43, amended: 2002 c.8 Sch.2

s.43, applied: SI 2003/548 Reg.2, SI 2003/1034 r.2

s.44, repealed (in part): 2002 c.41 s.7, Sch.9

s.45, applied: SI 2003/548 Reg.13

s.46, amended: 2003 c.44 Sch.26 para.29

s.47, repealed: 2002 c.41 s.9, Sch.9

s.50, amended: 2002 c.8 s.1, Sch.1 para.5, Sch.2, 2002 c.38 s.137, 2002 c.41 s.9

s.50, applied: 2002 c.41 s.11, 2003 c.42 s.60, SI 2003/409 Sch.1 Part I, SI 2003/3156 Art.4

s.51, amended: 2002 c.8 Sch.1 para.6

Sch.1, applied: 2002 c.41 s.11

Sch.1 para.1, amended: 2002 c.41 s.1

Sch.1 para.2, amended: 2002 c.41 s.1

Sch.1 para.2, applied: SI 2003/548 Sch.2 para.13

Sch.1 para.3, amended: 2002 c.41 s.2

Sch.1 para.4, amended: 2002 c.41 s.2, Sch.9, 2004 c.33 Sch.27 para.78

Sch.1 para.4, applied: SI 2003/548 Sch.2 para.14

Sch.1 para.7, amended: 2002 c.41 s.2

Sch.1 para.8, amended: 2002 c.41 s.2, Sch.9, 2004 c.33 Sch.27 para.78

Sch.2, amended: 2002 c.8 s.1

Sch.2 para.1, amended: 2002 c.41 s.9, Sch.9

Sch.2 para.2, amended: 2002 c.41 s.9, Sch.9

Sch.2 para.3, amended: 2002 c.41 Sch.9

1981–cont.

61. British Nationality Act 1981–*cont.*

Sch.2 para.3, applied: SI 2003/548 Sch.2 para.19

Sch.2 para.4, amended: 2002 c.8 s.2

Sch.2 para.4, applied: SI 2003/548 Sch.2 para.20

Sch.2 para.5, applied: SI 2003/548 Sch.2 para.21

Sch.2 para.6, applied: SI 2003/548 Sch.2 para.19, Sch.2 para.20

Sch.3, applied: SI 2003/548 Sch.3 para.1

Sch.3, referred to: 2003 c.1 s.615, s.649, SI 2003/548 Reg.4, Reg.9, 2004 c.33 s.240

Sch.4 para.2, amended: 2002 c.41 Sch.9

Sch.4 para.6, repealed: 2002 c.41 Sch.9

Sch.5, substituted: 2002 c.41 Sch.1 para.2

Sch.5 para.1, substituted: 2002 c.41 Sch.1 para.2

Sch.5 para.2, substituted: 2002 c.41 Sch.1 para.2

Sch.5 para.3, substituted: 2002 c.41 Sch.1 para.2

Sch.5 para.4, substituted: 2002 c.41 Sch.1 para.2

Sch.6, amended: 2002 c.8 s.1

Sch.6, referred to: 2002 c.1 s.2, 2002 c.8 s.1

63. Betting and Gaming Duties Act 1981

s.2, amended: 2002 c.23 Sch.4 para.3

s.2, repealed (in part): 2002 c.23 Sch.40 Part 1

s.3, amended: 2002 c.23 s.13

s.4, amended: 2002 c.23 Sch.4 para.4

s.4, substituted: 2004 c.12 s.15

s.5, amended: 2003 c.14 s.6, 2004 c.12 s.15

s.5A, repealed: 2003 c.14 Sch.43 Part 1

s.5AA, added: 2003 c.14 s.6

s.5AB, added: 2003 c.14 s.7

s.5B, amended: 2003 c.14 s.7, 2004 c.12 s.15

s.5C, amended: 2003 c.14 s.7, Sch.43 Part 1

s.5C, repealed (in part): 2003 c.14 Sch.43 Part 1

s.5D, enabling: SI 2003/2631, SI 2004/768

s.6, substituted: 2002 c.23 Sch.4 para.2

s.7, substituted: 2002 c.23 Sch.4 para.2

s.7A, applied: 2002 c.23 Sch.4 para.13

s.7A, substituted: 2002 c.23 Sch.4 para.2

s.7B, amended: 2004 c.12 s.15, Sch.42 Part 1

s.7B, substituted: 2002 c.23 Sch.4 para.2

s.7C, substituted: 2002 c.23 Sch.4 para.2

s.7D, substituted: 2002 c.23 Sch.4 para.2

s.7E, substituted: 2002 c.23 Sch.4 para.2

s.7F, substituted: 2002 c.23 Sch.4 para.2

s.7ZA, added: 2003 c.14 s.6

s.7ZA, substituted: 2002 c.23 Sch.4 para.2

s.8, substituted: 2002 c.23 Sch.4 para.2

s.9, amended: 2002 c.23 Sch.4 para.6, Sch.4 para.7, Sch.40 Part 1, 2004 c.12 s.15

s.9, repealed (in part): 2002 c.23 Sch.40 Part 1

s.9A, added: 2002 c.23 s.14

1981–cont.

63. Betting and Gaming Duties Act 1981– *cont.*

s.9B, added: 2002 c.23 s.14

s.10, amended: 2004 c.12 s.15

s.11, repealed: 2002 c.23 Sch.4 para.8, Sch.40 Part 1

s.12, amended: 2002 c.23 Sch.4 para.9, Sch.40 Part 1, 2003 c.14 s.8, 2004 c.12 s.15, Sch.42 Part 1

s.17, substituted: 2003 c.14 s.9

s.18, substituted: 2003 c.14 s.9

s.19, substituted: 2003 c.14 s.9

s.20, substituted: 2003 c.14 s.9

s.21, amended: 2002 c.23 s.8, 2003 c.14 s.10

s.23, amended: 2002 c.23 s.9, 2004 c.12 s.17

s.24, amended: 2003 c.14 s.12

s.25, amended: 2002 c.23 s.8, 2003 c.14 s.10

s.26, amended: 2002 c.23 Sch.40 Part 1, 2003 c.14 s.10, Sch.43 Part 1

s.26, repealed (in part): 2003 c.14 Sch.43 Part 1

s.26A, added: 2003 c.14 s.11

Sch.1 para.1, amended: 2002 c.23 Sch.4 para.10

Sch.1 para.2, enabling: SI 2003/2631, SI 2004/768

Sch.1 para.2A, added: 2002 c.23 Sch.4 para.10

Sch.1 para.3, amended: 2002 c.23 Sch.40 Part 1

Sch.1 para.4, amended: 2002 c.23 Sch.4 para.10

Sch.1 para.4, applied: 2002 c.23 Sch.4 para.14

Sch.1 para.4, repealed (in part): 2002 c.23 Sch.40 Part 1

Sch.1 para.5, amended: 2002 c.23 Sch.4 para.10

Sch.1 para.6, repealed (in part): 2002 c.23 Sch.40 Part 1

Sch.1 para.8, repealed: 2002 c.23 Sch.40 Part 1

Sch.1 para.10, amended: 2004 c.12 Sch.42 Part 1

Sch.1 para.12, repealed: 2002 c.23 Sch.40 Part 1

Sch.1 para.13, amended: 2002 c.23 Sch.4 para.10

Sch.1 para.14, amended: 2002 c.23 Sch.40 Part 1

Sch.1 para.15, amended: 2002 c.23 Sch.4 para.10, 2003 c.39 Sch.8 para.266

Sch.3 Part I para.1, amended: 2003 c.14 s.9

Sch.3 Part I para.2, substituted: 2003 c.14 s.9

Sch.3 Part I para.2B, added: 2003 c.14 s.9

Sch.3 Part I para.5, amended: 2003 c.14 s.9, SI 2004/155 Art.2

Sch.3 Part I para.6, amended: 2003 c.14 s.9

Sch.3 Part I para.7, enabling: SI 2004/155

Sch.3 Part II para.9, enabling: SI 2003/2503

Sch.3 Part II para.10, amended: 2003 c.14 s.9

1981–cont.

63. Betting and Gaming Duties Act 1981– *cont.*

Sch.3 Part II para.10, applied: SI 2003/2503 Reg.4

Sch.3 Part II para.11, repealed: 2003 c.14 Sch.43 Part 1

Sch.3 Part II para.12, repealed: 2003 c.14 Sch.43 Part 1

Sch.3 Part II para.15, repealed: 2003 c.14 Sch.43 Part 1

Sch.3 Part II para.16, amended: 2003 c.14 s.9

Sch.3 Part II para.16, repealed (in part): 2003 c.14 Sch.43 Part 1

Sch.4 Part II para.15, amended: 2003 c.39 Sch.8 para.267

Sch.4A para.7, amended: 2003 c.14 s.12

Sch.6 para.5, amended: 2002 c.23 s.14

64. New Towns Act 1981

applied: 2003 c.14 Sch.9 para.1, SI 2004/692 Sch.4 para.6

s.1, applied: 2004 c.5 s.32, s.73

s.16, amended: 2003 c.21 Sch.17 para.57

s.18, amended: 2003 c.17 Sch.6 para.81

s.19, amended: 2003 c.21 Sch.17 para.57

s.24, amended: 2003 c.21 Sch.17 para.57

s.26, amended: 2003 c.21 Sch.17 para.57

s.36, referred to: SI 2002/86 Art.4, SI 2004/586 Art.4, Art.5

s.37, varied: SI 2002/86 Art.5, SI 2004/586 Art.5

s.39, amended: 2003 c.21 Sch.17 para.57

s.67, amended: SI 2003/1326 Art.11

s.68, amended: SI 2003/1326 Art.11

s.70, amended: SI 2003/1326 Art.11

s.80, amended: 2004 c.21 Sch.1 para.52

Sch.2 para.2, repealed: 2003 c.17 Sch.7

Sch.12 para.1, repealed: 2003 c.17 Sch.7

Sch.12 para.29, repealed (in part): 2003 c.17 Sch.7

66. Compulsory Purchase (Vesting Declarations) Act 1981

applied: SI 2004/757 Art.25

varied: SI 2002/412 Art.16, SI 2002/1066 Art.22, SI 2002/1327 Art.20, SI 2002/1943 Art.4, SI 2004/757 Art.25

s.3, varied: SI 2002/1066 Art.22, SI 2002/1327 Art.20, SI 2002/1943 Art.4, SI 2004/757 Art.25

s.4, applied: SI 2002/1066 Art.27, Art.32, SI 2004/757 Art.30, Art.37

s.4, disapplied: SI 2002/412 Art.23, SI 2002/1943 Art.10

s.5, varied: SI 2002/1066 Art.22, SI 2002/1327 Art.20, SI 2002/1943 Art.4, SI 2004/757 Art.25

s.7, varied: SI 2002/1066 Art.22, SI 2002/1327 Art.20, SI 2002/1943 Art.4, SI 2004/757 Art.25

s.10, see *Bhattacharjee v Blackburn with Darwen BC* [2002] R.V.R. 55 (Lands Tr), George Bartlett Q.C. (President)

1981–cont.

67. Acquisition of Land Act 1981

applied: SI 2002/1064 Art.10, SI 2002/1065 Art.10, SI 2002/1066 Art.21, 2003 c.21 Sch.4 para.3, 2003 c.43 Sch.4 para.46, SI 2003/1075 Art.25, SI 2004/389 Art.23, SI 2004/757 Art.24

referred to: SI 2002/412 Art.17, 2003 c.43 Sch.4 para.47

Part II, applied: 2003 c.43 Sch.4 para.46, SI 2004/2595 Reg.1, SI 2004/2732 Reg.1

s.1, amended: 2004 c.14 Sch.1 Part 3

s.4, varied: SI 2002/1943 Art.7

s.5A, added: 2004 c.5 s.105

s.5B, added: 2004 c.5 s.105

s.6, amended: 2004 c.5 s.100

s.7, amended: 2004 c.5 s.100, 2004 c.21 Sch.1 para.53

s.7, enabling: SI 2004/2594, SI 2004/2595, SI 2004/2730, SI 2004/2732

s.10, applied: SI 2004/2595 Reg.3, SI 2004/2732 Reg.3

s.10, enabling: SI 2004/2595, SI 2004/2732

s.11, amended: 2004 c.5 s.100

s.11, applied: 2004 c.5 s.100, s.102, Sch.6 para.7, Sch.7 para.5, Sch.7 para.9, Sch.7 para.10, Sch.7 para.11, Sch.7 para.13, Sch.7 para.14, Sch.7 para.15, Sch.7 para.18, Sch.7 para.21, SI 2004/2595 Reg.3, SI 2004/2730 Reg.1, SI 2004/2732 Reg.1, Reg.3

s.11, enabling: SI 2004/2595, SI 2004/2732

s.12, amended: 2004 c.5 s.100

s.12, applied: SI 2004/2594 Reg.5, SI 2004/2595 Reg.3, SI 2004/2730 Reg.5, SI 2004/2732 Reg.3

s.12, enabling: SI 2004/2595, SI 2004/2732

s.13, substituted: 2004 c.5 s.100

s.13A, applied: SI 2004/2594 Reg.3, SI 2004/2730 Sch.1

s.13A, enabling: SI 2004/2594, SI 2004/2730

s.13B, enabling: SI 2004/2594, SI 2004/2730

s.14A, added: 2004 c.5 s.102

s.14A, applied: SI 2004/2595 Reg.3, SI 2004/2732 Reg.3

s.15, applied: SI 2004/2594 Reg.10, SI 2004/2595 Reg.3, SI 2004/2732 Reg.3

s.15, substituted: 2004 c.5 s.100

s.15, enabling: SI 2004/2595, SI 2004/2732

s.16, amended: 2002 c.17 Sch.5 para.25, Sch.9 Part 1, 2003 c.43 Sch.4 para.48

s.16, applied: SI 2004/2595 Reg.3, SI 2004/2732 Reg.3

s.17, amended: 2003 c.43 Sch.4 para.49

s.19, applied: SI 2004/2595 Reg.3, SI 2004/2732 Reg.3

s.22, applied: SI 2004/2595 Reg.3, SI 2004/2732 Reg.3

s.22, enabling: SI 2004/2595, SI 2004/2732

1981–cont.

67. Acquisition of Land Act 1981–*cont.*

s.23, see *Ainsdale Investments Ltd v First Secretary of State* [2004] EWHC 1010, [2004] H.L.R. 50 (QBD (Admin Ct)), Owen, J.; see *R. (on the application of Baker) v First Secretary of State* [2003] EWHC 2511, [2004] R.V.R. 13 (QBD (Admin Ct)), Nicholas Blake Q.C.; see *R. (on the application of Lock) v Secretary of State for the Environment, Transport and the Regions* [2002] EWHC 1654, [2002] 3 E.G.L.R. 5 (QBD (Admin Ct)), Harrison, J.

s.24, see *Ainsdale Investments Ltd v First Secretary of State* [2004] EWHC 1010, [2004] H.L.R. 50 (QBD (Admin Ct)), Owen, J.

s.28, amended: 2003 c.21 Sch.17 para.58

s.28, repealed (in part): 2003 c.21 Sch.19

s.29, amended: 2004 c.5 Sch.7 para.12

s.32, amended: 2003 c.21 Sch.17 para.58

Sch.1, applied: SI 2002/1943 Art.4

Sch.1 para.1, applied: SI 2004/2595 Reg.1, SI 2004/2732 Reg.1

Sch.1 para.2, amended: 2004 c.5 s.101

Sch.1 para.2, applied: 2004 c.5 s.101, Sch.6 para.7, Sch.7 para.10, Sch.7 para.11, Sch.7 para.15, Sch.7 para.18, Sch.7 para.21, SI 2004/2595 Reg.3, SI 2004/2730 Reg.1, SI 2004/2732 Reg.1, Reg.3

Sch.1 para.2, enabling: SI 2004/2595, SI 2004/2732

Sch.1 para.3, amended: 2004 c.5 s.101

Sch.1 para.3, applied: SI 2004/2594 Reg.5, SI 2004/2595 Reg.3, SI 2004/2730 Reg.5, SI 2004/2732 Reg.3

Sch.1 para.3, enabling: SI 2004/2595, SI 2004/2732

Sch.1 para.4, substituted: 2004 c.5 s.101

Sch.1 para.4A, applied: SI 2004/2594 Reg.3, SI 2004/2730 Sch.1

Sch.1 para.4A, enabling: SI 2004/2594, SI 2004/2730

Sch.1 para.6, applied: SI 2004/2594 Reg.10, SI 2004/2595 Reg.3, SI 2004/2732 Reg.3

Sch.1 para.6, substituted: 2004 c.5 s.101

Sch.1 para.6, enabling: SI 2004/2595, SI 2004/2732

Sch.2 Part II para.2, varied: SI 2002/412 Art.39, SI 2002/1943 Art.6

Sch.2 Part III para.3, varied: SI 2002/412 Art.39

Sch.2 Part III para.4, varied: SI 2002/412 Art.39

Sch.2 Part III para.5, varied: SI 2002/412 Art.39

Sch.2 Part III para.6, varied: SI 2002/412 Art.39

Sch.2 Part III para.7, varied: SI 2002/412 Art.39

Sch.2 Part III para.8, varied: SI 2002/412 Art.39

1981–cont.

67. Acquisition of Land Act 1981–cont.

Sch.2 Part III para.9, varied: SI 2002/412 Art.39

Sch.3 Part II para.3, applied: SI 2004/2595 Reg.3, SI 2004/2732 Reg.3

Sch.3 Part II para.6, applied: SI 2004/2595 Reg.3, SI 2004/2732 Reg.3

Sch.3 Part II para.9, applied: SI 2004/2595 Reg.3, SI 2004/2732 Reg.3

Sch.3 Part II para.9, enabling: SI 2004/2595, SI 2004/2732

Sch.4 para.1, amended: 2003 c.39 Sch.10, 2004 c.14 Sch.1 Part 2

Sch.4 para.3, repealed: 2004 c.14 Sch.1 Part 2

Sch.4 para.19, repealed: 2003 c.39 Sch.10

69. Wildlife and Countryside Act 1981

see *R. (on the application of Newsum) v Welsh Assembly* [2004] EWHC 50, [2004] Env. L.R. 39 (QBD (Admin Ct)), Pitchford, J.; see *R. (on the application of Trailer & Marina (Leven) Ltd) v Secretary of State for the Environment, Food and Rural Affairs* [2004] EWHC 153, [2004] Env. L.R. 40 (QBD (Admin Ct)), Ouseley, J.

applied: SI 2002/1772 Reg.3, Reg.12, SSI 2003/129 Sch.2 para.10, 2004 c.i s.9

referred to: SI 2002/2127 Reg.13, 2003 asp 7 s.77, s.89, Sch.3 para.1, SSI 2004/70 Sch.2 para.10

Part I, applied: 2003 asp 7 s.77, Sch.3 para.2

Part I, referred to: SI 2004/1733 Reg.3

Part 2, see *R. (on the application of Brown) v Secretary of State for Transport* [2003] EWHC 819, [2004] Env. L.R. 2 (QBD (Admin Ct)), Collins, J.

s.1, amended: 2003 asp 7 Sch.5, 2004 asp 6 Sch.6 para.2, SI 2004/1487 Reg.3

s.1, repealed (in part): 2003 asp 7 Sch.5, SI 2004/1487 Reg.3

s.2, amended: 2004 asp 6 Sch.6 para.3

s.2, repealed (in part): 2004 asp 6 Sch.6 para.3

s.3, amended: 2004 asp 6 Sch.6 para.4

s.3, repealed (in part): 2003 asp 7 Sch.5, 2004 asp 6 Sch.6 para.4

s.4, amended: 2004 asp 6 Sch.6 para.5.5, 2004 asp 6 Sch.6 para.6

s.5, repealed (in part): 2004 asp 6 Sch.6 para.6

s.6, amended: 2003 asp 7 Sch.3 para.2

s.6, repealed (in part): 2003 asp 7 Sch.5

s.7, amended: 2003 asp 7 Sch.3 para.2, Sch.3 para.3, Sch.5, 2004 asp 6 Sch.6 para.7

s.7, enabling: SI 2003/3235, SI 2004/640

s.8, see *RSPCA v Shinton* [2003] EWHC 1696, (2003) 167 J.P. 512 (QBD (Admin Ct)), Leveson, J.

s.8, amended: 2003 asp 7 Sch.5

s.9, amended: 2004 asp 6 Sch.6 para.8

s.10, amended: 2004 asp 6 Sch.6 para.9

s.11, amended: 2004 asp 6 Sch.6 para.10

1981–cont.

69. Wildlife and Countryside Act 1981–cont.

s.13, amended: 2004 asp 6 Sch.6 para.11

s.14, amended: 2004 asp 6 Sch.6 para.12

s.14A, added: 2004 asp 6 Sch.6 para.13

s.14B, added: 2004 asp 6 Sch.6 para.13

s.15A, added: 2004 asp 6 Sch.6 para.14

s.16, see *RSPCA v Cundey* [2001] EWHC Admin 906, (2002) 166 J.P. 125 (QBD (Admin Ct)), Silber, J.

s.16, amended: 2004 asp 6 Sch.6 para.15

s.18, see *RSPCA v Cundey* [2001] EWHC Admin 906, (2002) 166 J.P. 125 (QBD (Admin Ct)), Silber, J.

s.19, see *Hughes v DPP* [2003] EWHC 2470, (2003) 167 J.P. 589 (QBD (Admin Ct)), Stanley Burnton, J.

s.19, amended: 2003 asp 7 Sch.3 para.4, 2004 asp 6 Sch.6 para.16

s.19ZC, added: 2004 asp 6 Sch.6 para.17

s.19ZD, added: 2004 asp 6 Sch.6 para.17

s.20, amended: 2003 asp 7 Sch.3 para.5, 2004 asp 6 Sch.6 para.18

s.20, repealed (in part): 2003 asp 7 Sch.3 para.5

s.21, amended: 2003 asp 7 Sch.3 para.6, 2004 asp 6 Sch.6 para.19

s.21, repealed (in part): 2003 asp 7 Sch.3 para.6

s.22, amended: 2004 asp 6 Sch.6 para.20

s.22, repealed (in part): 2004 asp 6 Sch.6 para.20

s.26, amended: 2004 asp 6 Sch.6 para.21

s.26A, added: 2004 asp 6 Sch.6 para.22

s.26A, enabling: SSI 2004/475

s.27, see *Hughes v DPP* [2003] EWHC 2470, (2003) 167 J.P. 589 (QBD (Admin Ct)), Stanley Burnton, J.

s.27, amended: 2002 asp 3 Sch.7 para.11, 2004 asp 6 Sch.6 para.23, SI 2004/1487 Reg.4

s.27, applied: 2004 c.37 Sch.1 para.1, Sch.1 para.2

s.27ZA, added: SI 2004/1487 Reg.5

s.27ZA, repealed: SI 2004/1733 Reg.3

s.28, see *R. (on the application of Fisher) v English Nature* [2003] EWHC 1599, [2004] 1 W.L.R. 503 (QBD (Admin Ct)), Lightman, J.; see *R. (on the application of Fisher) v English Nature* [2004] EWCA Civ 663, [2004] 4 All E.R. 861 (CA), Auld, L.J.; see *William Sinclair Holdings Ltd v English Nature* [2001] EWHC Admin 408, [2002] Env. L.R. 4 (QBD (Admin Ct)), Turner, J.

s.28, applied: 2002 asp 3 s.54, 2002 c.i s.39, SI 2002/1730 Sch.1, SSI 2003/129 Sch.2 para.5, 2004 asp 6 Sch.6 para.2, Sch.5 para.3, Sch.5 para.7, Sch.5 para.9, Sch.5 para.13, SSI 2004/70 Sch.2 para.5

s.28, repealed (in part): 2004 asp 6 Sch.7 para.4

1981–cont.

69. Wildlife and Countryside Act 1981– cont.

s.28A, applied: 2002 c.i s.39

s.28A, repealed (in part): 2004 asp 6 Sch.7 para.4

s.28B, applied: 2002 c.i s.39

s.28B, repealed (in part): 2004 asp 6 Sch.7 para.4

s.28C, applied: 2002 c.i s.39

s.28C, repealed (in part): 2004 asp 6 Sch.7 para.4

s.28D, applied: 2002 c.i s.39

s.28D, repealed (in part): 2004 asp 6 Sch.7 para.4

s.28E, applied: 2002 c.i s.39, SI 2002/1772 Reg.8

s.28E, repealed (in part): 2004 asp 6 Sch.7 para.4

s.28F, applied: 2002 c.i s.39

s.28F, repealed (in part): 2004 asp 6 Sch.7 para.4

s.28F, enabling: SI 2002/1772

s.28G, applied: 2002 c.i s.39

s.28G, repealed (in part): 2004 asp 6 Sch.7 para.4

s.28H, applied: 2002 c.i s.39

s.28H, repealed (in part): 2004 asp 6 Sch.7 para.4

s.28I, applied: 2002 c.i s.39

s.28I, repealed (in part): 2004 asp 6 Sch.7 para.4

s.28J, applied: 2002 c.i s.39

s.28J, repealed (in part): 2004 asp 6 Sch.7 para.4

s.28K, applied: 2002 c.i s.39

s.28K, repealed (in part): 2004 asp 6 Sch.7 para.4

s.28L, applied: 2002 c.i s.39

s.28L, repealed (in part): 2004 asp 6 Sch.7 para.4

s.28L, enabling: SI 2002/1772

s.28M, applied: 2002 c.i s.39

s.28M, repealed (in part): 2004 asp 6 Sch.7 para.4

s.28N, applied: 2002 c.i s.39

s.28N, repealed (in part): 2004 asp 6 Sch.7 para.4

s.28O, applied: 2002 c.i s.39

s.28O, repealed (in part): 2004 asp 6 Sch.7 para.4

s.28P, applied: 2002 c.i s.39

s.28P, repealed (in part): 2004 asp 6 Sch.7 para.4

s.28Q, applied: 2002 c.i s.39

s.28Q, repealed (in part): 2004 asp 6 Sch.7 para.4

s.28R, applied: 2002 c.i s.39

s.28R, repealed (in part): 2004 asp 6 Sch.7 para.4

1981–cont.

69. Wildlife and Countryside Act 1981– cont.

s.29, see *R. (on the application of Aggregate Industries UK Ltd) v English Nature* [2002] EWHC 908, [2003] Env. L.R. 3 (QBD (Admin Ct)), Forbes, J.

s.29, applied: 2002 c.i s.39, 2004 asp 6 Sch.5 para.11

s.29, repealed (in part): 2004 asp 6 Sch.7 para.4

s.30, applied: 2002 c.i s.39

s.30, repealed (in part): 2004 asp 6 Sch.7 para.4

s.31, applied: 2002 c.i s.39

s.31, repealed (in part): 2004 asp 6 Sch.7 para.4

s.32, applied: 2002 c.i s.39

s.32, repealed (in part): 2004 asp 6 Sch.7 para.4

s.33, applied: 2002 c.i s.39

s.33, repealed (in part): 2004 asp 6 Sch.7 para.4

s.34, repealed (in part): 2004 asp 6 Sch.7 para.4

s.36, amended: 2002 asp 3 Sch.7 para.11

s.39, applied: SI 2003/2261 Sch.3 Part I, Sch.4 para.3

s.41, repealed (in part): 2004 asp 6 Sch.7 para.4

s.42, applied: SI 2002/80, SI 2002/80 Art.2, Art.3

s.42, enabling: SI 2002/80

s.50, repealed (in part): 2004 asp 6 Sch.7 para.4

s.51, applied: 2004 asp 6 Sch.5 para.7

s.51, repealed (in part): 2004 asp 6 Sch.7 para.4

s.52, repealed (in part): SI 2002/794 Sch.2

s.52, enabling: SI 2002/80

s.53, see *Applegarth v Secretary of State for the Environment, Transport and the Regions* [2001] EWHC Admin 487, [2002] 1 P. & C.R. 9 (QBD (Admin Ct)), Munby, J.; see *Burrows v Secretary of State for Environment, Food and Rural Affairs* [2004] EWHC 132, (2004) 101 (5) L.S.G. 30 (QBD (Admin Ct)), Andrew Nicol Q.C.; see *Todd v Secretary of State for the Environment, Food and Rural Affairs* [2004] EWHC 1450, [2004] 1 W.L.R. 2471 (QBD (Admin Ct)), Evans-Lombe, J.

s.62, applied: SI 2004/1777 Art.25, SI 2004/1778 Art.25

s.74, repealed (in part): 2004 asp 6 Sch.7 para.4

Sch.A1, added: 2004 asp 6 Sch.6 para.24

Sch.1A, added: 2004 asp 6 Sch.6 para.25

Sch.11, applied: 2004 asp 6 Sch.5 para.11

Sch.11, referred to: 2004 asp 6 Sch.5 para.11

Sch.11 para.6, applied: 2004 asp 6 Sch.5 para.11

CAP.

1981–cont.

69. Wildlife and Countryside Act 1981– cont.

Sch.13, applied: SI 2003/409 Sch.1 Part I

Sch.15 para.6, see *Todd v Secretary of State for the Environment, Food and Rural Affairs* [2004] EWHC 1450, [2004] 1 W.L.R. 2471 (QBD (Admin Ct)), Evans-Lombe, J.

Sch.15 para.7, see *Todd v Secretary of State for the Environment, Food and Rural Affairs* [2004] EWHC 1450, [2004] 1 W.L.R. 2471 (QBD (Admin Ct)), Evans-Lombe, J.

Sch.15 para.12, see *Applegarth v Secretary of State for the Environment, Transport and the Regions* [2001] EWHC Admin 487, [2002] 1 P. & C.R. 9 (QBD (Admin Ct)), Munby, J.; see *Burrows v Secretary of State for Environment, Food and Rural Affairs* [2004] EWHC 132, (2004) 101 (5) L.S.G. 30 (QBD (Admin Ct)), Andrew Nicol Q.C.

1982

i. Greater London Council (General Powers) Act 1982

s.5, amended: 2004 c.i s.11

s.5, repealed (in part): 2004 c.i s.11

s.7, repealed: 2003 c.17 Sch.7

xiv. Lloyd's Act 1982

s.2, applied: SSI 2003/231 Sch.2 para.6, Sch.2 Part 2

v. London Transport Act 1982

varied: SI 2003/1615 Sch.2 para.11

s.19, amended: SI 2003/1615 Sch.1 para.33

Sch.2, amended: SI 2003/1615 Sch.1 para.33

xxi. London Transport (General Powers) Act 1982

varied: SI 2003/1615 Sch.2 para.12

ii. Western Isles Islands Council (Loch Roag) Order Confirmation Act 1982

repealed: SSI 2002/410 Sch.2 Part I

s.1, referred to: SSI 2002/410 Sch.2 Part I

s.2, referred to: SSI 2002/410 Sch.2 Part I

s.31, referred to: SSI 2002/410 Sch.2 Part I

s.32, referred to: SSI 2002/410 Sch.2 Part I

s.33, referred to: SSI 2002/410 Sch.2 Part I

s.34, referred to: SSI 2002/410 Sch.2 Part I

s.35, referred to: SSI 2002/410 Sch.2 Part I

s.36, referred to: SSI 2002/410 Sch.2 Part I

s.37, referred to: SSI 2002/410 Sch.2 Part I

1. Civil Aviation (Amendment) Act 1982

repealed: 2004 c.14 Sch.1 Part 4

2. Clergy Pensions (Amendment) Measure 1982

s.2, repealed (in part): 2003 c.2 Sch.1

s.12, repealed (in part): 2003 c.2 Sch.1

s.28, repealed: 2003 c.2 Sch.1

5. Hops Marketing Act 1982

repealed: 2004 c.14 Sch.1 Part 2

9. Agricultural Training Board Act 1982

repealed: 2004 c.14 Sch.1 Part 2

1982–cont.

10. Industrial Training Act 1982

applied: 2002 asp 11 s.3, SI 2003/409 Sch.1 Part I

s.1, applied: SI 2004/369

s.8, amended: SI 2003/1326 Art.12

s.11, applied: SI 2002/302, SI 2002/303, SI 2003/285, SI 2003/286, SI 2004/368, SI 2004/369

s.11, referred to: SI 2002/302, SI 2002/303, SI 2003/285, SI 2003/286, SI 2004/368, SI 2004/369

s.11, enabling: SI 2002/302, SI 2002/303, SI 2003/285, SI 2003/286, SI 2004/368, SI 2004/369

s.12, applied: SI 2002/302, SI 2002/303, SI 2003/285, SI 2004/368, SI 2004/369, SI 2004/1861 Reg.16

s.12, enabling: SI 2002/302, SI 2002/303, SI 2003/285, SI 2003/286, SI 2004/368, SI 2004/369

s.20, repealed (in part): 2004 c.14 Sch.1 Part 8

Sch.2 para.1, repealed: 2004 c.14 Sch.1 Part 8

Sch.2 para.2, repealed: 2004 c.14 Sch.1 Part 8

Sch.2 para.3, repealed: 2004 c.14 Sch.1 Part 8

Sch.2 para.4, repealed: 2004 c.14 Sch.1 Part 8

Sch.2 para.5, repealed: 2004 c.14 Sch.1 Part 8

16. Civil Aviation Act 1982

applied: SI 2003/335 Sch.1, SSI 2003/93 Sch.1, 2004 c.20 s.86

s.4, amended: 2002 c.40 Sch.25 para.11

s.4, disapplied: SI 2004/1958 Reg.3

s.7, applied: SI 2002/2786 Reg.18

s.21, repealed (in part): SI 2004/77 Reg.2

s.23, amended: SI 2004/77 Reg.2

s.23, applied: SI 2004/77 Reg.2

s.23, repealed (in part): SI 2004/77 Reg.2

s.35, enabling: SI 2002/2421

s.44, amended: 2003 c.44 Sch.26 para.30, SI 2004/1755 Art.2

s.48, amended: 2003 c.21 Sch.17 para.60

s.57, applied: 2002 c.26 Sch.4 para.1

s.60, see *R. v Tagg (Heather Susan)* [2001] EWCA Crim 1230, [2002] 1 Cr. App. R. 2 (CA (Crim Div)), Rose, L.J.

s.60, disapplied: SI 2003/777

s.60, referred to: SI 2002/264

s.60, enabling: SI 2002/264, SI 2002/798, SI 2002/1078, SI 2002/1628, SI 2003/777, SI 2003/2905, SI 2004/705

s.61, see *R. v Tagg (Heather Susan)* [2001] EWCA Crim 1230, [2002] 1 Cr. App. R. 2 (CA (Crim Div)), Rose, L.J.

s.61, amended: 2003 c.19 s.2

s.61, enabling: SI 2002/264, SI 2002/798, SI 2002/1628, SI 2003/777, SI 2003/2905, SI 2004/705, SI 2004/2038

s.69A, amended: SI 2004/1256 Reg.2

s.71, applied: SI 2003/1741

s.71, enabling: SI 2003/1741

s.73, applied: SI 2002/2817 Reg.13

s.75, amended: 2003 c.44 Sch.26 para.30

CAP.

CAP.

1982–cont.

16. Civil Aviation Act 1982–*cont.*

s.76, see *Glen v Korean Airlines Co Ltd* [2003] EWHC 643, [2003] Q.B. 1386 (QBD), Simon, J.; see *Hatton v United Kingdom (36022/97)* (2003) 37 E.H.R.R. 28 (European Court of Human Rights (Grand Chamber)), Judge Wildhaber (President)

s.77, enabling: SI 2003/2905, SI 2004/705

s.78, see *Hatton v United Kingdom (36022/97)* (2003) 37 E.H.R.R. 28 (European Court of Human Rights (Grand Chamber)), Judge Wildhaber (President)

s.78, applied: SI 2003/1742 Reg.4

s.82, amended: 2003 c.44 Sch.37 Part 9

s.82, disapplied: 2003 c.44 Sch.25 para.78

s.85, applied: SI 2004/77 Reg.2

s.85, repealed: SI 2004/77 Reg.2

s.92, amended: 2002 c.26 Sch.13

s.92, repealed (in part): 2002 c.26 Sch.13

s.101, enabling: SI 2002/798, SI 2003/2905, SI 2004/705

s.102, applied: SI 2002/798

s.102, enabling: SI 2002/264, SI 2002/798, SI 2002/1078, SI 2002/1628, SI 2003/777, SI 2003/2905, SI 2004/705

s.105, see *Glen v Korean Airlines Co Ltd* [2003] EWHC 643, [2003] Q.B. 1386 (QBD), Simon, J.

s.105, amended: 2002 c.8 s.2

Sch.2 para.2, repealed: 2004 c.36 Sch.3

Sch.2 para.3, varied: SI 2004/1822 Sch.1 para.11

Sch.2 para.4, amended: 2004 c.34 Sch.16

Sch.11 para.1, repealed: SI 2004/77 Reg.2

Sch.11 para.2, repealed: SI 2004/77 Reg.2

Sch.11 para.3, repealed: SI 2004/77 Reg.2

Sch.11 para.4, repealed: SI 2004/77 Reg.2

Sch.11 para.5, repealed: SI 2004/77 Reg.2

Sch.13, enabling: SI 2002/264, SI 2002/1078, SI 2002/1628, SI 2003/777, SI 2003/2905, SI 2004/705

Sch.13 Part II, amended: 2004 c.20 s.101, SI 2004/77 Reg.2

Sch.13 Part III para.1, enabling: SI 2003/1741

Sch.13 Part III para.2, enabling: SI 2003/1741

Sch.13 Part III para.6, amended: 2004 c.20 s.101

Sch.13 Part III para.7, added: 2004 c.20 s.101

Sch.14 para.12, repealed: 2004 c.14 Sch.1 Part 4

Sch.15 para.6, repealed: 2004 c.14 Sch.1 Part 4

Sch.15 para.16, repealed: 2004 c.14 Sch.1 Part 4

22. Gaming (Amendment) Act 1982

Sch.1 para.2, repealed: 2004 c.14 Sch.1 Part 17

Sch.1 para.6, repealed (in part): 2004 c.14 Sch.1 Part 17

Sch.1 para.14, repealed: 2004 c.14 Sch.1 Part 17

1982–cont.

24. Social Security and Housing Benefits Act 1982

see *Taylor Gordon & Co Ltd (t/a Plan Personnel) v Timmons* [2004] I.R.L.R. 180 (EAT), Recorder Luba Q.C.

27. Civil Jurisdiction and Judgments Act 1982

see *C v C (Financial Provision: Post Nuptial Settlements)* [2004] EWHC 742, [2004] Fam. 141 (Fam Div), Wilson, J.; see *Marie Brizzard et Roger International SA v William Grant & Sons Ltd (No.1)* 2002 S.L.T. 1359 (OH), Lord Mackay of Drumadoon; see *Marie Brizzard et Roger International SA v William Grant & Sons Ltd (No.2)* 2002 S.L.T. 1365 (OH), Lord Mackay of Drumadoon; see *Phillips v Symes (Stay of Proceedings)* [2002] 1 W.L.R. 853 (Ch D), Hart, J.

applied: SSI 2002/494 Reg.33

Part I, applied: 2004 c.33 Sch.11 para.2

s.1, referred to: SI 2003/1372 r.45

s.2, see *Turner v Grovit* [2001] UKHL 65, [2002] 1 W.L.R. 107 (HL), Lord Hobhouse of Woodborough

s.4, applied: SSI 2002/494 Reg.46

s.4, enabling: SSI 2004/52

s.5, amended: 2003 c.39 Sch.8 para.268

s.5, applied: SSI 2002/494 Reg.46

s.12, referred to: SI 2002/2972

s.12, enabling: SSI 2004/52

s.15, amended: 2003 c.39 Sch.8 para.269

s.18, amended: 2002 c.29 Sch.11 para.11, SI 2003/425 Art.34

s.18, enabling: SI 2002/2972

s.25, see *Lewis v Eliades* [2002] EWHC 335, [2002] C.P. Rep. 28 (QBD), McCombe, J.; see *Motorola Credit Corp v Uzan (No.6)* [2003] EWCA Civ 752, [2004] 1 W.L.R. 113 (CA), Potter, L.J.

s.31, amended: 2004 c.14 Sch.1 Part 14

s.32, amended: 2004 c.14 Sch.1 Part 14

s.33, see *Starlight International Inc v Bruce* [2002] EWHC 374, [2002] I.L.Pr. 35 (Ch D), Lawrence Collins, J.

s.40, repealed (in part): SI 2003/435 Sch.5

s.41, applied: SSI 2002/132 Sch.1 para.7.3

s.42, applied: SSI 2002/132 Sch.1 para.7.3

s.46, see *Tehrani v Secretary of State for the Home Department* 2003 S.L.T. 808 (OH), Lord Philip

s.48, referred to: SI 2002/2972

s.48, enabling: SI 2002/194, SR 2002/159, SSI 2004/52

s.49, see *Marodi Service de D Mialich v Mikkal Myklebusthaug Rederi A/S* 2002 S.L.T. 1013 (OH), Judge TG Coutts Q.C.

Sch.1, see *Kenburn Waste Management Ltd v Bergmann* [2002] F.S.R. 44 (Ch D), Pumfrey, J.

Sch.1, applied: SSI 2002/132 Sch.1 para.7.3

CAP.

1982–cont.

27. Civil Jurisdiction and Judgments Act 1982–cont.

Sch.1, referred to: SSI 2002/132 Sch.1 para.5.7

Sch.3, see *Tradigrain SA v SIAT SpA* [2002] EWHC 106, [2002] 2 Lloyd's Rep. 553 (QBD (Comm Ct)), Colman, J.

Sch.3C, applied: SSI 2002/132 Sch.1 para.7.3

Sch.3C, referred to: SSI 2002/132 Sch.1 para.5.7

Sch.4 Art.5, see *Ennstone Building Products Ltd v Stanger Ltd (No.1)* [2002] B.L.R. 82 (QBD (T&CC)), Judge Kirkham

Sch.4 Art.13, see *ICS Computing Ltd v Capital One Services Inc* [2002] N.I. 76 (QBD (NI)), Weatherup, J.

Sch.4 Art.17, see *McGowan v Summit at Lloyds* 2002 S.C. 638 (Ex Div), Lord Reed, Lady Cosgrove, Lord Marnoch

Sch.6, applied: SI 2002/2972 Reg.5

Sch.6 para.2, enabling: SI 2002/2972

Sch.6 para.4, enabling: SI 2002/2972

Sch.8 r.3, see *Prostar Management Ltd v Twaddle* 2003 S.L.T. (Sh Ct) 11 (Sh Pr), EF Bowen Q.C., Sheriff Principal; see *Semple Fraser WS v Quayle* 2002 S.L.T. (Sh Ct) 33 (Sh Ct (Glasgow and Strathkelvin)), JA Taylor

28. Taking of Hostages Act 1982

s.1, applied: SI 2002/1823 Sch.2 para.25, 2003 c.41 s.16, s.83, 2003 c.42 Sch.5 para.38, Sch.5 para.84, Sch.5 para.150, 2003 c.44 Sch.4 para.31, Sch.5 para.28, Sch.5 para.49, Sch.15 para.37, Sch.17 para.38, SI 2004/1500 Sch.2 para.23, SI 2004/1910 Sch.1

29. Supply of Goods and Services Act 1982

applied: SI 2003/1593 Sch.1 Part I

s.3, referred to: SI 2003/1374 Sch.1

s.4, amended: SI 2002/3045 Reg.7

s.4, referred to: SI 2003/1374 Sch.1

s.5, referred to: SI 2003/1374 Sch.1

s.9, amended: SI 2002/3045 Reg.10

s.11C, referred to: SI 2003/1374 Sch.1

s.11D, amended: SI 2002/3045 Reg.8

s.11D, referred to: SI 2003/1374 Sch.1

s.11E, referred to: SI 2003/1374 Sch.1

s.11J, amended: SI 2002/3045 Reg.11

s.11M, added: SI 2002/3045 Reg.9

s.11M, referred to: SI 2003/1374 Sch.1

s.11N, added: SI 2002/3045 Reg.9

s.11N, referred to: SI 2003/1374 Sch.1

s.11P, added: SI 2002/3045 Reg.9

s.11P, referred to: SI 2003/1374 Sch.1

s.11Q, added: SI 2002/3045 Reg.9

s.11Q, referred to: SI 2003/1374 Sch.1

s.11R, added: SI 2002/3045 Reg.9

s.11R, referred to: SI 2003/1374 Sch.1

s.11S, added: SI 2002/3045 Reg.9

s.11S, referred to: SI 2003/1374 Sch.1

CAP.

1982–cont.

29. Supply of Goods and Services Act 1982–cont.

s.13, referred to: SI 2003/1374 Sch.1

s.18, amended: SI 2002/3045 Reg.12

30. Local Government (Miscellaneous Provisions) Act 1982

s.1, repealed: 2003 c.17 Sch.6 para.83, Sch.7

s.3, applied: 2003 c.17 Sch.8 para.32

s.4, repealed: 2003 c.17 Sch.6 para.83, Sch.7

s.5, repealed: 2003 c.17 Sch.6 para.83, Sch.7

s.6, applied: 2003 c.17 Sch.4 para.2

s.6, repealed: 2003 c.17 Sch.6 para.83, Sch.7

s.7, repealed: 2003 c.17 Sch.7

s.9, amended: 2004 c.21 Sch.1 para.54

s.10, amended: 2003 c.17 Sch.6 para.84, 2004 c.21 Sch.1 para.54

s.11, repealed: 2004 c.14 Sch.1 Part 10

s.15, amended: 2003 c.26 s.120

s.16, amended: SI 2004/2035 Sch.1 para.19

s.18, referred to: 2003 c.17 Sch.8 para.32

s.27, repealed (in part): 2004 c.14 Sch.1 Part 10

s.33, varied: SI 2004/1777 Art.26, SI 2004/1778 Art.26

s.39, repealed (in part): 2004 c.14 Sch.1 Part 10

s.40, repealed (in part): 2002 c.32 Sch.22 Part 3

s.41, amended: SI 2003/1615 Sch.1 para.11

s.41, varied: SI 2004/1777 Art.29

s.45, varied: SI 2004/1777 Art.29

s.46, repealed: 2004 c.14 Sch.1 Part 10

s.49, amended: 2004 c.14 Sch.1 Part 10

Sch.1, applied: 2003 c.17 Sch.4 para.2

Sch.1 para.1, repealed: 2003 c.17 Sch.6 para.83, Sch.7

Sch.1 para.2, repealed: 2003 c.17 Sch.6 para.83, Sch.7

Sch.1 para.3, repealed: 2003 c.17 Sch.6 para.83, Sch.7

Sch.1 para.4, repealed: 2003 c.17 Sch.6 para.83, Sch.7

Sch.1 para.5, repealed: 2003 c.17 Sch.6 para.83, Sch.7

Sch.1 para.6, repealed: 2003 c.17 Sch.6 para.83, Sch.7

Sch.1 para.6A, repealed: 2003 c.17 Sch.6 para.83, Sch.7

Sch.1 para.7, repealed: 2003 c.17 Sch.6 para.83, Sch.7

Sch.1 para.8, repealed: 2003 c.17 Sch.6 para.83, Sch.7

Sch.1 para.9, repealed: 2003 c.17 Sch.6 para.83, Sch.7

Sch.1 para.10, repealed: 2003 c.17 Sch.6 para.83, Sch.7

Sch.1 para.11, repealed: 2003 c.17 Sch.6 para.83, Sch.7

Sch.1 para.11A, repealed: 2003 c.17 Sch.6 para.83, Sch.7

Sch.1 para.12, amended: SI 2004/916 Art.4

1982–cont.

30. Local Government (Miscellaneous Provisions) Act 1982–cont.

Sch.1 para.12, repealed: 2003 c.17 Sch.6 para.83, Sch.7

Sch.1 para.13, repealed: 2003 c.17 Sch.6 para.83, Sch.7

Sch.1 para.13A, added: SI 2002/3205 Art.4

Sch.1 para.13A, repealed: 2003 c.17 Sch.6 para.83, Sch.7

Sch.1 para.14, repealed: 2003 c.17 Sch.6 para.83, Sch.7

Sch.1 para.15, repealed: 2003 c.17 Sch.6 para.83, Sch.7

Sch.1 para.16, repealed: 2003 c.17 Sch.6 para.83, Sch.7

Sch.1 para.16A, repealed: 2003 c.17 Sch.6 para.83, Sch.7

Sch.1 para.17, repealed: 2003 c.17 Sch.6 para.83, Sch.7

Sch.1 para.18, repealed: 2003 c.17 Sch.6 para.83, Sch.7

Sch.1 para.19, repealed: 2003 c.17 Sch.6 para.83, Sch.7

Sch.1 para.20, repealed: 2003 c.17 Sch.6 para.83, Sch.7

Sch.1 para.21, repealed: 2003 c.17 Sch.6 para.83, Sch.7

Sch.1 para.22, repealed: 2003 c.17 Sch.6 para.83, Sch.7

Sch.2 para.1, repealed: 2003 c.17 Sch.7

Sch.2 para.2, repealed: 2003 c.17 Sch.7

Sch.2 para.3, repealed: 2003 c.17 Sch.7

Sch.2 para.4, repealed: 2003 c.17 Sch.7

Sch.2 para.5, repealed: 2003 c.17 Sch.7

Sch.2 para.6, repealed: 2003 c.17 Sch.7

Sch.3 para.3, amended: 2003 c.17 Sch.6 para.85

Sch.3 para.3, applied: 2003 c.17 Sch.8 para.33

Sch.3 para.3A, amended: 2003 c.17 Sch.6 para.85

Sch.3 para.3A, disapplied: 2003 c.17 Sch.8 para.32

Sch.3 para.3A, referred to: 2003 c.17 Sch.8 para.32

32. Local Government Finance Act 1982

s.8, repealed: 2004 c.14 Sch.1 Part 10

s.9, repealed: 2004 c.14 Sch.1 Part 10

s.10, repealed: 2004 c.14 Sch.1 Part 10

s.20, see *Porter v Magill* [2001] UKHL 67, [2002] 2 A.C. 357 (HL), Lord Bingham of Cornhill

Sch.2 para.1, repealed: 2004 c.14 Sch.1 Part 10

Sch.2 para.2, repealed: 2004 c.14 Sch.1 Part 10

Sch.2 para.3, repealed: 2004 c.14 Sch.1 Part 10

Sch.2 para.4, repealed: 2004 c.14 Sch.1 Part 10

1982–cont.

32. Local Government Finance Act 1982–cont.

Sch.2 para.5, repealed: 2004 c.14 Sch.1 Part 10

Sch.2 para.6, repealed: 2004 c.14 Sch.1 Part 10

Sch.2 para.7, repealed: 2004 c.14 Sch.1 Part 10

Sch.2 para.8, repealed: 2004 c.14 Sch.1 Part 10

Sch.2 para.9, repealed: 2004 c.14 Sch.1 Part 10

Sch.2 para.10, repealed: 2004 c.14 Sch.1 Part 10

34. Forfeiture Act 1982

s.1, see *Dalton v Latham* [2003] EWHC 796, [2003] W.T.L.R. 687 (Ch D), Patten, J

s.3, amended: 2004 c.33 Sch.27 para.79

s.4, amended: 2004 c.32 s.7

36. Aviation Security Act 1982

applied: SI 2003/527 Reg.3

s.1, applied: 2003 c.42 Sch.5 para.39, Sch.5 para.85, Sch.5 para.151, 2003 c.44 Sch.4 para.32, Sch.15 para.38, Sch.17 para.39, SI 2004/1500 Sch.2 para.24, SI 2004/1910 Sch.1

s.2, applied: 2003 c.42 Sch.5 para.40, Sch.5 para.86, Sch.5 para.152, 2003 c.44 Sch.4 para.33, Sch.15 para.39, Sch.17 para.40, SI 2004/1500 Sch.2 para.25, SI 2004/1910 Sch.1

s.3, applied: 2003 c.42 Sch.5 para.41, Sch.5 para.87, Sch.5 para.153, 2003 c.44 Sch.15 para.40, Sch.17 para.41, SI 2004/1910 Sch.1

s.4, see *R. v Burrows (David John)* [2004] EWCA Crim 677, [2004] 2 Cr. App. R. (S.) 89 (CA (Crim Div)), Forbes, J.

s.4, applied: 2003 c.42 Sch.5 para.42, Sch.5 para.88, Sch.5 para.154, 2003 c.44 Sch.15 para.41, Sch.17 para.42, SI 2004/1910 Sch.1

s.30, applied: SSI 2004/257 Reg.43

s.30, varied: SI 2003/527 Reg.43

s.36, repealed (in part): 2004 c.14 Sch.1 Part 4

s.38, amended: 2002 c.8 s.2

Sch.1 para.5, amended: 2003 asp 9 Sch.15

Sch.2 para.8, repealed: 2004 c.14 Sch.1 Part 4

39. Finance Act 1982

s.152, repealed (in part): 2003 c.14 Sch.43 Part 5

s.156, repealed: 2004 c.14 Sch.1 Part 5

41. Stock Transfer Act 1982

s.1, amended: 2003 c.26 Sch.8 Part 1

Sch.1 para.4, amended: 2002 c.1 Sch.3 para.8

Sch.2 para.1, repealed (in part): 2004 c.14 Sch.1 Part 9

42. Derelict Land Act 1982

s.1, applied: SI 2002/2053 Art.2

s.1, enabling: SI 2002/2053

1982–cont.

43. Local Government and Planning (Scotland) Act 1982

s.14, amended: 2002 asp 3 Sch.7 para.12

s.14, repealed (in part): 2002 asp 3 Sch.7 para.12

45. Civic Government (Scotland) Act 1982

referred to: 2003 asp 15 s.65

s.10, see *Falconer v South Ayrshire Council* 2002 S.L.T. 1033 (OH), Lord Hamilton

s.20, amended: 2002 c.37 s.2, 2003 asp 1 s.49

s.20, applied: SSI 2003/73 Reg.2

s.20, enabling: SSI 2002/500, SSI 2002/521, SSI 2003/73, SSI 2004/88

s.24, see *Stewart v Perth and Kinross Council* 2003 S.C. 551 (Ex Div), Lord Coulsfield, Lord Johnston, Lord McCluskey

s.44, applied: SSI 2003/463

s.44, enabling: SSI 2002/161, SSI 2003/463

s.48, repealed: 2003 asp 12 s.17

s.52, see *Lord Advocate's Reference (No.1 of 2002)* 2002 S.L.T. 1017 (HCJ), Lord Kirkwood, Lord Cameron of Lochbroom, Lord Caplan; see *Ogilvie (Alan Joseph) v HM Advocate (Sentencing)* 2002 J.C. 74 (HCJ Appeal), Lord Sutherland, Lord Abernethy, Lord Rodger L.J.G.

s.52, amended: 2003 asp 7 s.19

s.52, applied: SI 2002/635 Sch.1 para.2, SI 2002/896 Sch.1 para.60, 2003 c.42 Sch.3 para.45, Sch.3 para.97, 2003 c.44 Sch.16 para.10, SI 2003/1184 Reg.8, Sch.2 para.27, SI 2004/1910 Sch.3, SI 2004/2695 Sch.1 para.8, SSI 2003/19 Sch.5 para.11, SSI 2004/411 Sch.1 para.22

s.52, referred to: SI 2002/57 Sch.4 para.4, SI 2003/237 Sch.4 para.4

s.52A, see *Arnott (Neil Paterson) v McFadyen* 2002 S.C.C.R. 96 (HCJ Appeal), Lord Marnoch, Lord Bonomy, Lord Dawson; see *Lord Advocate's Reference (No.1 of 2002)* 2002 S.L.T. 1017 (HCJ), Lord Kirkwood, Lord Cameron of Lochbroom, Lord Caplan; see *Ogilvie (Alan Joseph) v HM Advocate (Sentencing)* 2002 J.C. 74 (HCJ Appeal), Lord Sutherland, Lord Abernethy, Lord Rodger L.J.G.

s.52A, amended: 2003 asp 7 s.19

s.52A, applied: SI 2002/635 Sch.1 para.2, SI 2002/896 Sch.1 para.60, 2003 c.42 Sch.3 para.46, 2003 c.44 Sch.16 para.11, SI 2004/1910 Sch.3, SI 2004/2695 Sch.1 para.8, SSI 2003/19 Sch.5 para.11, SSI 2004/411 Sch.1 para.22

s.52A, referred to: SI 2002/57 Sch.4 para.4, SI 2003/237 Sch.4 para.4

s.53, applied: 2003 asp 2 s.5

s.54, amended: 2002 asp 3 Sch.7 para.13

s.58, see *Stevens (Andrew) v HM Advocate* 2002 S.L.T. 1249 (HCJ), Lady Paton

s.62, applied: 2004 asp 8 s.21

1982–cont.

45. Civic Government (Scotland) Act 1982–cont.

s.63, see *Aberdeen Bon Accord Loyal Orange Lodge 701 v Aberdeen City Council* 2002 S.L.T. (Sh Ct) 52 (Sh Ct (Grampian, Highland and Islands)), AM Cowan; see *Wishart Arch Defenders Loyal Orange Lodge 404 v Angus Council* 2002 S.L.T. (Sh Ct) 43 (Sh Ct (Tayside, Central and Fife)), ID Dunbar

s.68, see *Debidin v Chief Constable of the Northern Constabulary* 2002 S.L.T. (Sh Ct) 125 (Sh Pr), JC McInnes Q.C., Sheriff Principal

s.76, see *Debidin v Chief Constable of the Northern Constabulary* 2002 S.L.T. (Sh Ct) 125 (Sh Pr), JC McInnes Q.C., Sheriff Principal

s.86A, amended: 2002 c.29 Sch.11 para.12

s.86A, referred to: SSI 2003/210 Art.7

s.87, amended: 2003 asp 8 Sch.6 para.14

s.87, repealed (in part): 2003 asp 8 Sch.6 para.14

s.89, amended: 2003 asp 8 Sch.6 para.14

s.120, amended: 2003 asp 2 Sch.2 para.8

s.121, amended: 2003 asp 2 Sch.2 para.8

s.121, applied: SSI 2002/201 Art.8, SSI 2003/1 Art.8

s.121, repealed (in part): 2003 asp 2 Sch.2 para.8

s.123, amended: 2003 asp 2 Sch.2 para.8

Sch.1 para.5, see *Falconer v South Ayrshire Council* 2002 S.L.T. 1033 (OH), Lord Hamilton; see *Stewart v Perth and Kinross Council* 2003 S.C. 551 (Ex Div), Lord Coulsfield, Lord Johnston, Lord McCluskey

Sch.1 para.15, applied: 2003 asp 15 s.65

Sch.1 para.18, see *Falconer v South Ayrshire Council* 2002 S.L.T. 1033 (OH), Lord Hamilton

Sch.2A para.8, amended: 2002 c.29 Sch.11 para.12

46. Employment Act 1982

repealed: 2004 c.14 Sch.1 Part 8

48. Criminal Justice Act 1982

s.32, amended: 2003 c.44 Sch.32 para.35

s.41, repealed: 2004 c.36 Sch.3

s.61, repealed: 2003 c.44 Sch.37 Part 4

s.70, repealed: 2003 c.44 Sch.37 Part 9

Sch.1 Part I para.2, repealed: 2003 c.42 Sch.7

Sch.1 Part II, repealed: 2003 c.42 Sch.7

Sch.1 Part II, added: 2002 c.29 Sch.11 para.13, 2003 c.42 Sch.6 para.27, 2004 c.28 Sch.10 para.16

Sch.9 para.1, repealed (in part): 2003 c.44 Sch.37 Part 4

Sch.13 Part III para.7, amended: 2003 c.44 Sch.32 para.36

Sch.13 Part III para.9, amended: 2003 c.44 Sch.32 para.36

1982–cont.

48. Criminal Justice Act 1982–*cont.*
Sch.14 para.35, repealed: 2003 c.44 Sch.37 Part 10

49. Transport Act 1982
s.70, amended: 2002 c.16 Sch.2 para.26, 2002 c.21 Sch.3 para.9
Sch.5 para.5, repealed (in part): SSI 2002/263 Sch.1

50. Insurance Companies Act 1982
Sch.2, see *Scottish Provident Institution v Shore* 2003 S.L.T. 73 (OH), Lord Carloway
Sch.3A para.2, see *American Motorists Insurance Co (AMICO) v Cellstar Corp* [2003] EWCA Civ 206, [2003] 2 C.L.C. 599 (CA), Mance, L.J.

51. Mental Health (Amendment) Act 1982
s.34, amended: 2004 c.14 Sch.1 Part 17
Sch.3 Part I para.29, repealed: 2003 c.42 Sch.7
Sch.3 Part I para.33, repealed: 2004 c.14 Sch.1 Part 17
Sch.3 Part I para.34, repealed: 2003 c.42 Sch.7
Sch.3 Part I para.44, repealed: 2004 c.14 Sch.1 Part 17
Sch.3 Part I para.47, repealed: 2004 c.14 Sch.1 Part 17
Sch.3 Part I para.48, repealed: 2003 c.44 Sch.37 Part 10
Sch.3 Part I para.50, repealed: 2004 c.14 Sch.1 Part 17
Sch.3 Part I para.51, repealed: 2004 c.14 Sch.1 Part 17

52. Industrial Development Act 1982
Part II, applied: 2002 c.23 Sch.29 para.103
s.1, amended: 2004 c.14 Sch.1 Part 16
s.1, applied: SI 2004/1005 Sch.2
s.1, repealed (in part): 2004 c.14 Sch.1 Part 16
s.2, repealed: 2004 c.14 Sch.1 Part 16
s.3, repealed: 2004 c.14 Sch.1 Part 16
s.4, repealed: 2004 c.14 Sch.1 Part 16
s.5, repealed: 2004 c.14 Sch.1 Part 16
s.6, repealed: 2004 c.14 Sch.1 Part 16
s.7, varied: SI 2002/1630 Sch.1
s.8, amended: SI 2002/151 Art.2, 2003 c.11 s.1, SI 2003/849 Art.2
s.8, applied: SI 2002/151, SI 2003/849
s.8, varied: SI 2002/1630 Sch.1
s.8, enabling: SI 2002/151, SI 2003/849
s.11, repealed (in part): 2004 c.14 Sch.1 Part 16
s.15, amended: 2004 c.14 Sch.1 Part 16, Sch.2 para.14
s.15, repealed (in part): 2004 c.14 Sch.1 Part 16
s.16, repealed (in part): 2004 c.14 Sch.1 Part 16
s.18, amended: 2004 c.14 Sch.1 Part 16
Sch.1 para.1, repealed: 2004 c.14 Sch.1 Part 16
Sch.1 para.2, repealed: 2004 c.14 Sch.1 Part 16
Sch.1 para.3, repealed: 2004 c.14 Sch.1 Part 16

1982–cont.

52. Industrial Development Act 1982–*cont.*
Sch.1 para.4, repealed: 2004 c.14 Sch.1 Part 16
Sch.1 para.5, repealed: 2004 c.14 Sch.1 Part 16
Sch.1 para.6, repealed: 2004 c.14 Sch.1 Part 16
Sch.2 Part I para.1, repealed: 2004 c.14 Sch.1 Part 16
Sch.2 Part I para.2, repealed: 2004 c.14 Sch.1 Part 16
Sch.2 Part II para.6, repealed: 2004 c.14 Sch.1 Part 16
Sch.2 Part II para.9, repealed: 2004 c.14 Sch.1 Part 16

53. Administration of Justice Act 1982
s.3, repealed (in part): 2004 c.14 Sch.1 Part 1
s.6, repealed (in part): 2004 c.14 Sch.1 Part 1
s.8, see *Cusick v Campbell* 2002 S.C.L.R. 581 (1 Div), Lord Cullen L.P., Lord MacLean, Lady Paton; see *Graham v Dryden* 2002 Rep. L.R. 104 (OH), Lady Paton; see *Moohan v Glasgow City Council* 2003 S.L.T. 745 (OH), Lord Brodie; see *Sturgeon v Gallagher* 2003 S.L.T. 67 (OH), Lord Emslie
s.9, see *Graham v Dryden* 2002 Rep. L.R. 104 (OH), Lady Paton; see *Moohan v Glasgow City Council* 2003 S.L.T. 745 (OH), Lord Brodie; see *Murray v Weldex International Offshore Ltd* 2002 S.C.L.R. 591 (OH), Lord Eassie
s.10, see *Cantwell v Criminal Injuries Compensation Board* [2001] UKHL 36, 2002 S.C. (H.L.) 1 (HL), Lord Hope of Craighead
s.12, see *Young v Scottish Coal (Deep Mining) Co Ltd* 2002 S.L.T. 1215 (OH), Lord Mackay of Drumadoon
s.12, applied: SSI 2002/132 Sch.1 para.34.3, Sch.1 para.34.7, 2003 c.43 s.157
s.13, amended: 2004 c.33 Sch.28 para.47
s.13, varied: 2004 c.33 Sch.21 para.12
s.20, see *Bell v Georgiou* [2002] EWHC 1080, [2002] W.T.L.R. 1105 (Ch D), Blackburne, J.
s.21, see *Hodgson v Clare* [2002] W.T.L.R. 619 (Ch D), Stanley Burnton Q.C.
s.23, amended: 2003 c.39 Sch.8 para.270
s.34, repealed (in part): 2004 c.14 Sch.1 Part 1
s.35, repealed: 2004 c.14 Sch.1 Part 1
s.38, enabling: SI 2003/375, SI 2003/720
s.42, applied: SI 2004/266 Art.3, Sch.1 para.2
s.42, enabling: SI 2003/778, SI 2003/1027, SI 2004/266
s.46, repealed (in part): 2004 c.14 Sch.1 Part 1
s.49, repealed: 2004 c.14 Sch.1 Part 1
s.50, repealed: 2004 c.14 Sch.1 Part 1
s.59, repealed (in part): 2004 c.14 Sch.1 Part 1
s.66, repealed: 2002 c.9 Sch.13
s.67, repealed: 2002 c.9 Sch.13
s.72, repealed (in part): 2002 c.26 Sch.13
s.73, repealed (in part): 2004 c.14 Sch.1 Part 1

CAP.

1982–cont.

53. Administration of Justice Act 1982– cont.

s.77, repealed (in part): 2004 c.14 Sch.1 Part 1
Sch.3 Part II para.4, repealed (in part): 2004 c.14 Sch.1 Part 1
Sch.3 Part III para.7, repealed: 2004 c.14 Sch.1 Part 1
Sch.5, repealed: 2002 c.9 Sch.13
Sch.6 para.10, applied: 2003 c.43 s.157
Sch.8 para.2, repealed: 2002 c.26 Sch.13
Sch.8 para.3, repealed: 2004 c.14 Sch.1 Part 1

1983

Companies Act 1983

s.320, see *Conegrade Ltd, Re* [2002] EWHC 2411, [2003] B.P.I.R. 358 (Ch D (Companies Court)), Lloyd, J.

Health and Social Services and Social Security Adjudicators Act 1983

s.17, see *R. (on the application of Spink) v Wandsworth LBC* [2004] EWHC 2314, [2004] 3 F.C.R. 471 (QBD (Admin)), Richards, J.

xix. Milford Haven Conservancy Act 1983

referred to: 2002 c.v
Part I, repealed: 2002 c.v s.24
s.9, applied: 2002 c.v s.22
s.15, applied: 2002 c.v s.15
Sch.1, repealed: 2002 c.v s.24

xviii. Staffordshire Act 1983

s.18, repealed: SI 2003/3030 Reg.2

1. Pastoral Measure 1983

applied: SI 2002/1893 para.1
referred to: SI 2003/1936 para.1
Part II, applied: SI 2002/1893 para.1, SI 2003/1936 para.1
Part III, applied: SI 2003/472 Art.1
s.2A, added: 2003 c.1 s.2
s.3, amended: 2003 c.1 s.2
s.25, applied: 2003 c.3 s.41
s.44, applied: SI 2003/472 Art.3
s.52, applied: SI 2003/472 Art.2
s.53, applied: SI 2003/472 Art.3
s.53, enabling: SI 2003/472
Sch.1, amended: 2003 c.1 s.2
Sch.1, repealed: 2003 c.1 s.2
Sch.3, varied: 2004 c.14 Sch.2 para.15
Sch.4, applied: 2003 c.3 s.41
Sch.8, repealed: 2004 c.14 Sch.1 Part 6

2. Church of England (Miscellaneous Provisions) Measure 1983

applied: SI 2002/1893 para.1, SI 2003/1936 para.1
s.8, repealed (in part): 2004 c.14 Sch.1 Part 6
s.12, repealed: 2004 c.14 Sch.1 Part 6
s.13, repealed (in part): 2004 c.14 Sch.1 Part 6

2. Representation of the People Act 1983

see *Ahmed v Kennedy* [2002] EWHC 2061, [2002] EWHC 2060, [2002] 4 All E.R. 764 (QBD), Hooper, J.

CAP.

1983–cont.

2. Representation of the People Act 1983– cont.

applied: 2002 c.24 s.9, SI 2002/185 Sch.3 para.21, SI 2002/2779 Art.81, 2003 c.12 s.1, SI 2003/284 Art.111, Art.116, Art.123, Art.124, Sch.6 para.4, SI 2003/435 Sch.2 para.4, SI 2003/1557 Reg.2, SI 2003/1887 Sch.1, SI 2004/291 Sch.4, SI 2004/293 Sch.2 para.2, Sch.2 para.7, SI 2004/478 Sch.4, SI 2004/627 Sch.2, SI 2004/870 Reg.10, Reg.15, SSI 2004/115 Sch.3
referred to: SI 2002/1057 Art.2, 2003 c.3 s.1, SI 2003/284 Art.111, Art.124, SI 2003/1557 Reg.4
varied: SI 2004/870 Reg.8
Part II, applied: SI 2002/185 Sch.4 para.9, SI 2003/1907 Art.11, SI 2004/293 Sch.6 para.1
Part III, applied: SSI 2002/202 Art.7, SSI 2003/2 Art.7, 2004 asp 9 s.3
s.1, applied: SI 2002/2626 Sch.1, SI 2004/870 Reg.10
s.2, applied: SI 2002/2626 Sch.1, SI 2004/870 Reg.10
s.3, see *Hirst v United Kingdom (74025/01)* (2004) 38 E.H.R.R. 40 (ECHR), Judge Pellonpaa (President)
s.3, applied: SI 2002/2626 Sch.1, SI 2004/870 Reg.10
s.3, referred to: 2003 c.7 s.17
s.3A, amended: 2004 c.28 Sch.10 para.17
s.3A, applied: SI 2002/2626 Sch.1, SI 2004/870 Reg.10
s.3A, referred to: 2003 c.7 s.17
s.4, applied: SI 2002/2626 Sch.1, SI 2004/870 Reg.10
s.4, applied: SI 2002/2626 Sch.1, SI 2002/2779 Art.22, SI 2004/870 Reg.10
s.4, varied: SI 2003/1557 Reg.2
s.5, applied: SI 2002/2626 Sch.1, SI 2004/870 Reg.10
s.5, referred to: 2003 c.7 s.17
s.6, applied: SI 2002/2626 Sch.1, SI 2004/870 Reg.10
s.6, referred to: 2003 c.7 s.17
s.7, applied: SI 2002/2626 Sch.1, SI 2003/284 Sch.2 para.1, SI 2004/870 Reg.10
s.7, disapplied: SI 2004/293 Sch.2 para.2
s.7, applied: SI 2002/2626 Sch.1, SI 2003/284 Art.7, SI 2004/870 Reg.10, SI 2004/1267 Reg.7
s.7, disapplied: SI 2002/2779 Art.8
s.7, referred to: 2003 c.7 s.17
s.7A, applied: SI 2002/2626 Sch.1, SI 2003/284 Art.7, Sch.2 para.1, SI 2004/870 Reg.10
s.7A, disapplied: SI 2002/2779 Art.8, SI 2004/293 Sch.2 para.2
s.7A, referred to: 2003 c.7 s.17

1983–cont.

2. Representation of the People Act 1983–*cont.*

s.7B, applied: SI 2002/2626 Sch.1, SI 2002/2779 Sch.3 para.1, SI 2003/284 Sch.2 para.1, SI 2004/870 Reg.10, SI 2004/1962 Sch.1

s.7B, varied: SI 2003/1557 Reg.2

s.7C, applied: SI 2002/2626 Sch.1, SI 2004/870 Reg.10, SI 2004/1267 Reg.7

s.8, applied: SI 2002/2626 Sch.1, SI 2003/409 Sch.1 Part I, SI 2004/870 Reg.8, Reg.10, SI 2004/1962 Art.6

s.9, applied: SI 2002/2626 Sch.1, SI 2004/870 Reg.10

s.10, amended: 2002 c.13 s.1

s.10, applied: SI 2002/1871 Reg.4, SI 2002/1872 Reg.4, Sch.1 Part I, SI 2002/1873 Reg.4, SI 2002/2626 Sch.1, SI 2003/1899 Reg.3, SI 2003/1942 Reg.3, SI 2003/2696 Art.2, SI 2004/870 Reg.10, SI 2004/1267 Reg.8, Reg.9, Sch.1 para.37, Sch.1 para.46, SI 2004/1848 Reg.3, SI 2004/1960 Reg.3

s.10, referred to: SI 2003/1892 Reg.3

s.10, enabling: SI 2002/1871, SI 2002/1872, SI 2002/1873, SI 2003/1892, SI 2003/1899, SI 2003/1942, SI 2004/1848, SI 2004/1960

s.10A, amended: 2002 c.13 s.1

s.10A, applied: SI 2002/2626 Sch.1, SI 2004/870 Reg.10, SI 2004/1267 Reg.8, Reg.9, Sch.1 para.37, Sch.1 para.46

s.10A, enabling: SI 2002/1871, SI 2002/1872, SI 2002/1873

s.11, applied: SI 2002/2626 Sch.1, SI 2004/870 Reg.10

s.12, applied: SI 2002/2626 Sch.1, SI 2004/870 Reg.10

s.13, applied: SI 2002/1872 Reg.2, SI 2002/1873 Reg.2, SI 2002/2626 Sch.1, SI 2002/2779 Art.22, Sch.1 para.1, Sch.1 para.2, SI 2004/870 Reg.10

s.13, varied: SI 2003/2696 Art.2, Art.3

s.13A, amended: 2002 c.13 s.1

s.13A, applied: SI 2002/2626 Sch.1, SI 2002/2779 Sch.1 para.1, Sch.1 para.2, SI 2003/284 Art.4, SI 2004/870 Reg.10, SI 2004/1267 Reg.8, Reg.9, Reg.22, Sch.1 para.37, Sch.1 para.46

s.13A, disapplied: SI 2002/2779 Art.4

s.13A, varied: SI 2003/2696 Art.3

s.13A, enabling: SI 2002/1871, SI 2002/1872, SI 2002/1873

s.13B, applied: SI 2002/2626 Sch.1, SI 2002/2779 Art.4, Art.5, Sch.1 para.1, Sch.1 para.2, SI 2004/870 Reg.10, SI 2004/1267 Reg.22

s.13B, varied: SI 2004/870 Sch.3

s.13B, enabling: SI 2002/1871, SI 2002/1872, SI 2002/1873

s.13C, added: 2002 c.13 s.4

1983–cont.

2. Representation of the People Act 1983–*cont.*

s.13C, applied: SI 2002/2626 Sch.1, SI 2004/870 Reg.10, SI 2004/1267 Sch.1 para.37

s.13C, enabling: SI 2002/1873

s.13D, added: 2002 c.13 s.7

s.13D, applied: SI 2002/2626 Sch.1, SI 2004/870 Reg.10

s.14, amended: 2004 c.33 Sch.27 para.80

s.14, applied: SI 2002/2626 Sch.1, SI 2002/2779 Art.13, SI 2003/284 Art.14, SI 2004/870 Reg.10

s.15, applied: SI 2002/2626 Sch.1, SI 2004/870 Reg.10

s.15, referred to: SI 2002/834 Art.4

s.15, varied: SI 2003/1557 Reg.2

s.16, amended: 2004 c.33 Sch.27 para.81

s.16, applied: SI 2002/2626 Sch.1, SI 2002/2779 Sch.3 para.1, SI 2003/284 Sch.2 para.1, SI 2004/870 Reg.10

s.16, varied: SI 2002/834 Art.23, SI 2003/1557 Reg.2

s.17, applied: SI 2002/2626 Sch.1, SI 2004/870 Reg.10

s.17, varied: SI 2003/1557 Reg.2

s.18, applied: SI 2002/2626 Sch.1, SI 2002/2779 Art.6, SI 2003/284 Art.6, SI 2004/870 Reg.10

s.19, applied: SI 2002/2626 Sch.1, SI 2004/870 Reg.10

s.20, applied: SI 2002/2626 Sch.1, SI 2004/870 Reg.10

s.21, applied: SI 2002/2626 Sch.1, SI 2004/870 Reg.10

s.22, applied: SI 2002/2626 Sch.1, SI 2004/870 Reg.10

s.23, applied: SI 2002/2626 Sch.1, SI 2004/870 Reg.10

s.24, amended: SI 2002/1057 Art.9

s.24, applied: SI 2002/2626 Sch.1, SI 2004/870 Reg.10

s.24, enabling: SI 2004/1204

s.25, applied: 2002 c.24 s.6, SI 2002/2626 Sch.1, SI 2002/2779 Art.15, SI 2003/409 Sch.1 Part I, SI 2004/870 Reg.10

s.26, applied: SI 2002/2626 Sch.1, SI 2004/870 Reg.10

s.27, applied: SI 2002/2626 Sch.1, SI 2004/870 Reg.10

s.28, amended: SI 2002/1057 Art.10

s.28, applied: 2002 c.24 s.6, SI 2002/2626 Sch.1, SI 2004/870 Reg.10

s.29, applied: SI 2002/2626 Sch.1, SI 2002/2779 Sch.5 para.3, SI 2003/122 Art.3, Art.4, SI 2004/294 Reg.6, SI 2004/870 Reg.10

s.29, varied: SI 2002/2779 Art.19, Sch.5 para.3, SI 2004/294 Reg.6

s.29, enabling: SI 2003/122, SI 2003/3029

s.30, applied: SI 2002/2626 Sch.1, SI 2004/870 Reg.10

1983–cont.

2. Representation of the People Act 1983–cont.

s.30, varied: SI 2004/294 Reg.6

s.31, applied: SI 2002/2626 Sch.1

s.31, varied: SI 2002/185 Sch.2, SI 2004/870 Sch.3

s.32, applied: SI 2002/2626 Sch.1, SI 2004/870 Reg.10

s.32, referred to: SI 2003/284 Sch.2 para.10

s.33, applied: SI 2002/2626 Sch.1, SI 2004/870 Reg.10

s.34, applied: SI 2002/2626 Sch.1, SI 2004/870 Reg.10

s.35, applied: SI 2002/2626 Sch.1, SI 2003/284 Art.17, SI 2004/870 Reg.10, Reg.11, SI 2004/2443 Reg.6

s.35, varied: SI 2002/185 Sch.2, SI 2004/870 Sch.3, SI 2004/1962 Sch.2 Part 2

s.36, applied: SI 2002/2626 Sch.1, 2003 c.26 s.103, s.104, SI 2003/284 Sch.4 para.2, Sch.4 para.3, SI 2004/294 Reg.5, Reg.6, SI 2004/870 Reg.10

s.36, varied: SI 2002/185 Sch.2, SI 2003/284 Sch.4 para.3, SI 2004/294 Reg.6, SI 2004/870 Sch.3

s.36, enabling: SI 2004/223, SI 2004/224, SI 2004/227, SI 2004/294, SI 2004/1040, SI 2004/1041

s.37, applied: SI 2002/2626 Sch.1, SI 2004/218 Art.2, SI 2004/870 Reg.10

s.37, disapplied: SI 2004/222 Art.2

s.38, applied: SI 2002/2626 Sch.1, SI 2004/870 Reg.10

s.39, applied: SI 2002/185 Sch.3 para.54, SI 2002/2626 Sch.1, SI 2004/870 Reg.10

s.39, varied: SI 2002/185 Sch.2

s.40, applied: SI 2002/2626 Sch.1, SI 2004/870 Reg.10

s.40, varied: SI 2002/185 Sch.2

s.41, applied: SI 2002/2626 Sch.1, SI 2002/2779 Art.15, SI 2004/870 Reg.10, SSI 2002/202 Art.3, SSI 2003/2 Art.3

s.42, applied: 2002 asp 1 s.6, SI 2002/2626 Sch.1, SI 2002/2779 Sch.5 para.2, SI 2004/870 Reg.10

s.42, repealed (in part): 2004 asp 9 s.5

s.42, varied: SI 2002/2779 Sch.5 para.3

s.42, enabling: SSI 2002/457, SSI 2002/522

s.43, amended: 2002 asp 1 s.2, s.4

s.43, applied: SI 2002/2626 Sch.1, SI 2004/870 Reg.10

s.44, applied: SI 2002/2626 Sch.1, SI 2004/870 Reg.10

s.45, applied: SI 2002/2626 Sch.1, SI 2004/870 Reg.10

s.46, applied: SI 2002/2626 Sch.1, SI 2004/870 Reg.10

s.46, varied: SI 2002/185 Sch.2

s.47, applied: SI 2002/2626 Sch.1, SI 2004/870 Reg.10

1983–cont.

2. Representation of the People Act 1983–cont.

s.47, varied: SI 2002/185 Sch.2, SI 2004/870 Sch.3, Sch.4, SI 2004/1962 Sch.2 Part 2

s.48, see *Knight v Nicholls* [2004] EWCA Civ 68, [2004] 1 W.L.R. 1653 (CA), Tuckey, L.J.

s.48, applied: SI 2002/2626 Sch.1, SI 2004/870 Reg.10

s.48, varied: SI 2002/185 Sch.2

s.49, applied: SI 2002/2626 Sch.1, SI 2004/870 Reg.10

s.49, varied: SI 2003/1557 Reg.2, SI 2004/870 Sch.3, SI 2004/1962 Sch.2 Part 2

s.50, applied: SI 2002/2626 Sch.1, SI 2004/870 Reg.10

s.50, varied: SI 2002/185 Sch.2, SI 2004/1962 Sch.2 Part 2

s.51, applied: SI 2002/2626 Sch.1, SI 2004/870 Reg.10

s.52, applied: SI 2002/2626 Sch.1, SI 2004/870 Reg.10

s.52, varied: SI 2002/185 Sch.2, SI 2004/1962 Sch.2 Part 2

s.53, applied: SI 2002/2626 Sch.1, 2003 c.7 s.17, SI 2004/870 Reg.10

s.53, enabling: SI 2002/1871, SI 2002/1872, SI 2002/1873, SI 2003/1892, SI 2003/1899, SI 2003/1942, SI 2004/1848, SI 2004/1960, SSI 2002/561

s.54, applied: SI 2004/293 Sch.6 para.1, SI 2004/870 Reg.10

s.54, varied: SI 2002/185 Sch.2, SI 2004/1962 Sch.2 Part 2

s.55, applied: SI 2002/2626 Sch.1, SI 2004/870 Reg.10

s.56, applied: SI 2002/2626 Sch.1, SI 2002/2779 Art.5, SI 2003/284 Art.4, Art.5, SI 2004/870 Reg.10

s.56, disapplied: SI 2002/2779 Art.4

s.56, varied: SI 2004/1962 Sch.2 Part 2

s.57, applied: SI 2002/2626 Sch.1, SI 2002/2779 Art.5, SI 2004/870 Reg.10

s.58, applied: SI 2002/2626 Sch.1, SI 2004/870 Reg.10

s.59, amended: 2004 c.33 Sch.27 para.82

s.59, applied: SI 2002/2626 Sch.1, SI 2002/2779 Art.13, SI 2004/870 Reg.10

s.59, referred to: SI 2002/2779 Art.88, SI 2003/284 Sch.2 para.14

s.59, varied: SI 2002/2779 Art.13, SI 2003/284 Art.14

s.60, applied: SI 2002/2626 Sch.1, SI 2004/870 Reg.10

s.60, disapplied: SI 2002/2779 Art.81

s.60, varied: 2004 c.2 s.6, SI 2004/870 Sch.3, Sch.4, SI 2004/1962 Sch.2 Part 2

s.61, amended: 2004 c.33 Sch.27 para.83

s.61, applied: 2002 c.24 s.9, SI 2002/2626 Sch.1, SI 2004/870 Reg.10

1983–cont.

2. **Representation of the People Act 1983**–*cont.*

s.61, varied: SI 2002/185 Sch.2, SI 2003/ 1557 Reg.2, SI 2004/870 Sch.3, Sch.4, SI 2004/1962 Sch.2 Part 2

s.62, applied: SI 2002/2626 Sch.1, SI 2004/ 870 Reg.10

s.62, varied: SI 2003/1557 Reg.2

s.63, applied: SI 2002/2626 Sch.1, SI 2004/ 870 Reg.10

s.63, varied: SI 2004/1962 Sch.2 Part 2

s.64, applied: SI 2002/2626 Sch.1, SI 2004/ 870 Reg.10

s.65, applied: SI 2002/2626 Sch.1, SI 2004/ 870 Reg.10

s.65, varied: SI 2004/870 Sch.3, SI 2004/ 1962 Sch.2 Part 2

s.65A, applied: SI 2002/2626 Sch.1, SI 2004/870 Reg.10

s.66, applied: SI 2002/185 Sch.3 para.27, SI 2002/2626 Sch.1, SI 2004/870 Reg.10

s.66, referred to: SI 2004/1962 Sch.1, SSI 2002/561 Reg.7

s.66, varied: SI 2004/870 Sch.3, Sch.4, SI 2004/1962 Sch.2 Part 2

s.66A, applied: SI 2002/2626 Sch.1, SI 2004/870 Reg.10

s.66A, varied: SI 2004/870 Sch.3, Sch.4, SI 2004/1962 Sch.2 Part 2

s.67, applied: SI 2002/185 Sch.3 para.9, SI 2002/2626 Sch.1, SI 2003/284 Sch.6 para.8, SI 2004/870 Reg.10

s.67, varied: SI 2002/185 Sch.2

s.68, applied: SI 2002/2626 Sch.1, SI 2004/ 870 Reg.10

s.69, applied: SI 2002/2626 Sch.1, SI 2004/ 870 Reg.10

s.70, applied: SI 2002/2626 Sch.1, SI 2004/ 870 Reg.10

s.70A, applied: SI 2002/2626 Sch.1, SI 2004/870 Reg.10

s.71, applied: SI 2002/2626 Sch.1, SI 2004/ 870 Reg.10

s.71A, applied: SI 2002/2626 Sch.1, SI 2004/ 870 Reg.10

s.72, applied: SI 2002/2626 Sch.1, SI 2004/ 870 Reg.10

s.73, applied: SI 2002/2626 Sch.1, SI 2004/ 870 Reg.10

s.74, applied: SI 2002/2626 Sch.1, SI 2004/ 870 Reg.10

s.74A, applied: SI 2002/2626 Sch.1, SI 2004/870 Reg.10

s.75, applied: SI 2002/2626 Sch.1, SI 2004/ 870 Reg.10

s.75, disapplied: 2002 asp 1 s.5, SI 2003/ 1907 Art.11

s.75, varied: SI 2002/185 Sch.2

s.76, amended: SSI 2003/76 Art.2

s.76, applied: SI 2002/2626 Sch.1, SI 2004/ 870 Reg.10

1983–cont.

2. **Representation of the People Act 1983**–*cont.*

s.76, varied: SI 2002/185 Sch.2

s.76A, applied: SI 2002/2626 Sch.1, SI 2004/870 Reg.10

s.76A, enabling: SSI 2003/76

s.77, applied: SI 2002/2626 Sch.1, SI 2004/ 870 Reg.10

s.78, applied: SI 2002/2626 Sch.1, SI 2004/ 870 Reg.10

s.79, applied: SI 2002/2626 Sch.1, SI 2004/ 870 Reg.10

s.80, applied: SI 2002/2626 Sch.1, SI 2004/ 870 Reg.10

s.81, applied: SI 2002/2626 Sch.1, SI 2003/ 284 Sch.6 para.10, SI 2004/870 Reg.10

s.82, applied: SI 2002/2626 Sch.1, SI 2004/ 870 Reg.10

s.83, applied: SI 2002/2626 Sch.1, SI 2004/ 870 Reg.10

s.84, applied: SI 2002/2626 Sch.1, SI 2004/ 870 Reg.10

s.85, applied: SI 2002/2626 Sch.1, SI 2004/ 870 Reg.10

s.85, varied: SI 2002/185 Sch.2

s.85A, applied: SI 2002/2626 Sch.1, SI 2004/870 Reg.10

s.85A, varied: SI 2002/185 Sch.2

s.86, applied: SI 2002/2626 Sch.1, SI 2004/ 870 Reg.10

s.87, applied: SI 2002/2626 Sch.1, SI 2004/ 870 Reg.10

s.87A, applied: SI 2002/2626 Sch.1, SI 2004/870 Reg.10

s.88, applied: SI 2002/2626 Sch.1, SI 2004/ 870 Reg.10

s.89, applied: SI 2002/2626 Sch.1, SI 2004/ 870 Reg.10

s.90, applied: SI 2002/2626 Sch.1, SI 2004/ 870 Reg.10

s.90A, applied: SI 2002/2626 Sch.1, SI 2004/870 Reg.10

s.90B, applied: SI 2002/2626 Sch.1, SI 2004/870 Reg.10

s.90C, applied: SI 2002/2626 Sch.1, SI 2004/870 Reg.10

s.90D, applied: SI 2002/2626 Sch.1, SI 2004/870 Reg.10

s.90D, varied: SI 2002/185 Sch.2

s.91, applied: SI 2002/2626 Sch.1, SI 2004/ 870 Reg.10

s.92, amended: 2003 c.21 Sch.17 para.61

s.92, applied: SI 2002/2626 Sch.1, SI 2004/ 870 Reg.10

s.92, varied: SI 2004/870 Sch.3, SI 2004/ 1962 Sch.2 Part 2

s.93, amended: 2003 c.21 Sch.17 para.62

s.93, applied: SI 2002/2626 Sch.1, SI 2004/ 870 Reg.10

s.93, varied: SI 2002/185 Sch.2

1983–cont.

2. **Representation of the People Act 1983**–cont.

s.94, applied: SI 2002/2626 Sch.1, SI 2004/ 870 Reg.10

s.94, varied: SI 2002/185 Sch.2, SI 2004/ 870 Sch.3

s.95, applied: SI 2002/2626 Sch.1, SI 2004/ 870 Reg.10

s.96, applied: SI 2002/2626 Sch.1, SI 2004/ 870 Reg.10

s.96, varied: SI 2002/185 Sch.2, SI 2004/ 870 Sch.3

s.97, applied: SI 2002/2626 Sch.1, SI 2004/ 870 Reg.10

s.97, varied: SI 2002/185 Sch.2, SI 2004/ 870 Sch.3, SI 2004/1962 Sch.2 Part 2

s.98, applied: SI 2002/2626 Sch.1, SI 2004/ 870 Reg.10

s.99, applied: SI 2002/2626 Sch.1, SI 2004/ 870 Reg.10

s.99, varied: SI 2002/185 Sch.2, SI 2004/ 1962 Sch.2 Part 2

s.100, applied: SI 2002/2626 Sch.1, SI 2004/ 870 Reg.10

s.100, varied: SI 2004/870 Sch.3, SI 2004/ 1962 Sch.2 Part 2

s.101, applied: SI 2002/2626 Sch.1, SI 2004/ 870 Reg.10

s.102, applied: SI 2002/2626 Sch.1, SI 2004/ 870 Reg.10

s.103, applied: SI 2002/2626 Sch.1, SI 2004/ 870 Reg.10

s.104, applied: SI 2002/2626 Sch.1, SI 2004/ 870 Reg.10

s.105, applied: SI 2002/2626 Sch.1, SI 2004/ 870 Reg.10

s.106, applied: SI 2002/2626 Sch.1, SI 2004/ 870 Reg.10

s.107, applied: SI 2002/2626 Sch.1, SI 2004/ 870 Reg.10

s.108, applied: SI 2002/2626 Sch.1, SI 2004/ 870 Reg.10

s.109, applied: SI 2002/2626 Sch.1, SI 2004/ 870 Reg.10

s.109, varied: SI 2004/870 Sch.3, SI 2004/ 1962 Sch.2 Part 2

s.110, applied: SI 2002/2626 Sch.1, SI 2004/ 870 Reg.10

s.110, varied: SI 2004/293 Reg.74, SI 2004/ 870 Sch.3

s.111, applied: SI 2002/2626 Sch.1, SI 2004/ 870 Reg.10

s.111, varied: SI 2004/870 Sch.3, SI 2004/ 1962 Sch.2 Part 2

s.112, applied: SI 2002/2626 Sch.1, SI 2004/ 870 Reg.10

s.112, varied: SI 2004/870 Sch.3, SI 2004/ 1962 Sch.2 Part 2

s.113, applied: SI 2002/2626 Sch.1, SI 2004/ 870 Reg.10

1983–cont.

2. **Representation of the People Act 1983**–cont.

s.113, varied: SI 2004/870 Sch.3, SI 2004/ 1962 Sch.2 Part 2

s.114, applied: SI 2002/2626 Sch.1, SI 2004/ 870 Reg.10

s.114, varied: SI 2004/870 Sch.3, SI 2004/ 1962 Sch.2 Part 2

s.115, applied: SI 2002/2626 Sch.1, SI 2004/ 870 Reg.10

s.115, varied: SI 2004/870 Sch.3, SI 2004/ 1962 Sch.2 Part 2

s.116, applied: SI 2002/2626 Sch.1, SI 2004/ 870 Reg.10

s.116, varied: SI 2004/870 Sch.3, SI 2004/ 1962 Sch.2 Part 2

s.117, applied: SI 2002/2626 Sch.1, SI 2004/ 870 Reg.10

s.117, varied: SI 2004/1962 Sch.2 Part 2

s.118, applied: SI 2002/2626 Sch.1, SI 2004/ 870 Reg.10

s.118, varied: SI 2004/870 Sch.3, SI 2004/ 1962 Sch.2 Part 2

s.118A, applied: SI 2002/2626 Sch.1, SI 2004/870 Reg.10

s.118A, varied: SI 2002/185 Sch.2

s.119, applied: SI 2002/2626 Sch.1, SI 2004/ 870 Reg.10

s.119, varied: SI 2004/870 Sch.3, SI 2004/ 1962 Sch.2 Part 2

s.120, applied: SI 2002/2626 Sch.1, SI 2004/ 870 Reg.10

s.120, varied: SI 2002/185 Reg.6, SI 2002/ 2779 Sch.6 Part I, Sch.6 Part II

s.121, applied: SI 2002/2626 Sch.1, SI 2004/ 870 Reg.10

s.121, varied: SI 2002/185 Reg.6, SI 2002/ 2779 Sch.6 Part I, Sch.6 Part II

s.122, applied: SI 2002/2626 Sch.1, SI 2004/ 870 Reg.10

s.122, varied: SI 2002/185 Reg.6, SI 2002/ 2779 Sch.6 Part I, Sch.6 Part II

s.123, applied: SI 2002/2626 Sch.1, 2003 c.7 s.23, SI 2004/870 Reg.10

s.123, varied: SI 2002/185 Reg.6, SI 2002/ 2779 Sch.6 Part I, Sch.6 Part II

s.124, applied: SI 2002/2626 Sch.1, SI 2004/ 870 Reg.10

s.124, varied: SI 2002/185 Reg.6

s.125, applied: SI 2002/2626 Sch.1, SI 2004/ 870 Reg.10

s.125, varied: SI 2002/185 Reg.6, SI 2002/ 2779 Sch.6 Part I, Sch.6 Part II

s.126, applied: SI 2002/2626 Sch.1, SI 2004/ 870 Reg.10

s.126, varied: SI 2002/185 Reg.6, SI 2002/ 2779 Sch.6 Part I, Sch.6 Part II

s.127, applied: SI 2002/2626 Sch.1, SI 2004/ 870 Reg.10

s.127, varied: SI 2002/185 Reg.6

1983–cont.

2. **Representation of the People Act 1983**–*cont.*

s.128, applied: SI 2002/2626 Sch.1, SI 2004/870 Reg.10

s.128, varied: SI 2002/185 Reg.6, SI 2004/870 Reg.15, Sch.5

s.129, applied: SI 2002/2626 Sch.1, SI 2004/870 Reg.10

s.129, varied: SI 2002/185 Reg.6, SI 2004/870 Reg.15, Sch.5

s.130, applied: SI 2002/2626 Sch.1, SI 2004/870 Reg.10, Reg.15

s.130, varied: SI 2002/185 Reg.6, SI 2004/870 Reg.15, Sch.5

s.131, applied: SI 2002/2626 Sch.1, SI 2004/870 Reg.10

s.131, varied: SI 2002/185 Reg.6, SI 2004/870 Reg.15, Sch.5

s.132, applied: SI 2002/2626 Sch.1, SI 2004/870 Reg.10

s.132, varied: SI 2002/185 Reg.6, SI 2004/870 Reg.15

s.133, applied: SI 2002/2626 Sch.1, SI 2004/870 Reg.10

s.133, varied: SI 2002/185 Reg.6, SI 2004/870 Reg.15, Sch.5

s.134, applied: SI 2002/2626 Sch.1, SI 2004/870 Reg.10

s.134, varied: SI 2002/185 Reg.6

s.135, applied: SI 2002/2626 Sch.1, SI 2004/870 Reg.10

s.135, varied: SI 2002/185 Reg.6

s.135A, applied: SI 2002/2626 Sch.1, SI 2004/870 Reg.10

s.135A, varied: SI 2002/185 Reg.6

s.136, see *Ahmed v Kennedy* [2002] EWCA Civ 1793, [2003] 1 W.L.R. 1820 (CA), Simon Brown, L.J.

s.136, applied: SI 2002/2626 Sch.1, SI 2004/870 Reg.10

s.136, varied: SI 2002/185 Reg.6, SI 2002/2779 Sch.6 Part I, Sch.6 Part II, SI 2004/870 Reg.15, Sch.5

s.136, enabling: SI 2003/971, SI 2003/972

s.137, applied: SI 2002/2626 Sch.1, SI 2004/870 Reg.10

s.137, varied: SI 2002/185 Reg.6, SI 2002/2779 Sch.6 Part I, Sch.6 Part II, SI 2004/870 Reg.15, Sch.5

s.138, applied: SI 2002/2626 Sch.1, SI 2004/870 Reg.10

s.138, varied: SI 2002/185 Reg.6, SI 2002/2779 Sch.6 Part I, SI 2004/870 Reg.15, Sch.5

s.139, applied: SI 2002/2626 Sch.1, SI 2004/870 Reg.10

s.139, varied: SI 2002/185 Reg.6, SI 2002/2779 Sch.6 Part I, Sch.6 Part II, SI 2004/870 Reg.15, Sch.5

s.140, applied: SI 2002/2626 Sch.1, SI 2004/870 Reg.10

1983–cont.

2. **Representation of the People Act 1983**–*cont.*

s.140, varied: SI 2002/185 Reg.6, SI 2002/2779 Sch.6 Part I, Sch.6 Part II, SI 2004/870 Reg.15, Sch.5

s.141, amended: 2004 c.33 Sch.27 para.84

s.141, applied: SI 2002/2626 Sch.1, SI 2004/870 Reg.10

s.141, varied: SI 2002/185 Reg.6, SI 2002/2779 Sch.6 Part I, Sch.6 Part II, SI 2004/870 Reg.15, Sch.5

s.142, applied: SI 2002/2626 Sch.1, SI 2004/870 Reg.10

s.142, varied: SI 2002/185 Reg.6, SI 2004/870 Reg.15

s.143, applied: SI 2002/2626 Sch.1, SI 2004/870 Reg.10

s.143, varied: SI 2002/185 Reg.6, SI 2002/2779 Sch.6 Part I, Sch.6 Part II, SI 2004/870 Reg.15, Sch.5

s.144, applied: SI 2002/2626 Sch.1, SI 2004/870 Reg.10

s.144, varied: SI 2002/185 Reg.6, SI 2002/2779 Sch.6 Part I, Sch.6 Part II

s.145, applied: SI 2002/2626 Sch.1, SI 2004/870 Reg.10

s.145, varied: SI 2002/185 Reg.6, SI 2004/870 Reg.15, Sch.5

s.145A, applied: SI 2002/2626 Sch.1, SI 2004/870 Reg.10

s.145A, varied: SI 2002/185 Reg.6

s.146, applied: SI 2002/2626 Sch.1, SI 2004/870 Reg.10

s.146, varied: SI 2002/185 Reg.6, SI 2002/2779 Sch.6 Part I, SI 2004/870 Reg.15, Sch.5

s.147, applied: SI 2002/2626 Sch.1, SI 2004/870 Reg.10

s.147, varied: SI 2002/185 Reg.6, SI 2002/2779 Sch.6 Part I, SI 2004/870 Reg.15, Sch.5

s.148, applied: SI 2002/2626 Sch.1, SI 2004/870 Reg.10

s.148, varied: SI 2002/185 Reg.6

s.149, applied: SI 2002/2626 Sch.1, SI 2004/870 Reg.10

s.149, varied: SI 2002/185 Reg.6

s.150, applied: SI 2002/2626 Sch.1, SI 2004/870 Reg.10

s.150, varied: SI 2002/185 Reg.6

s.151, applied: SI 2002/2626 Sch.1, SI 2004/870 Reg.10

s.151, varied: SI 2002/185 Reg.6

s.152, applied: SI 2002/2626 Sch.1, SI 2004/870 Reg.10

s.152, varied: SI 2002/185 Reg.6

s.153, applied: SI 2002/2626 Sch.1, SI 2004/870 Reg.10

s.153, varied: SI 2002/185 Reg.6

s.154, applied: SI 2002/2626 Sch.1, SI 2004/870 Reg.10

1983–cont.

2. **Representation of the People Act 1983**–*cont.*

s.154, varied: SI 2002/185 Reg.6, SI 2002/2779 Sch.6 Part I, Sch.6 Part II, SI 2004/870 Reg.15, Sch.5

s.155, applied: SI 2002/2626 Sch.1, SI 2004/870 Reg.10

s.155, varied: SI 2002/185 Reg.6, SI 2002/2779 Sch.6 Part I, Sch.6 Part II, SI 2004/870 Reg.15, Sch.5

s.156, applied: SI 2002/2626 Sch.1, SI 2004/870 Reg.10

s.156, varied: SI 2002/185 Reg.6, SI 2002/2779 Sch.6 Part I, SI 2004/870 Reg.15, Sch.5

s.157, applied: SI 2002/2626 Sch.1, SI 2004/870 Reg.10

s.157, varied: SI 2002/185 Reg.6, SI 2002/2779 Sch.6 Part I, Sch.6 Part II, SI 2004/870 Reg.15, Sch.5

s.158, applied: SI 2002/2626 Sch.1, SI 2004/870 Reg.10

s.158, varied: SI 2002/185 Reg.6, SI 2002/2779 Sch.6 Part I

s.159, applied: SI 2002/2626 Sch.1, SI 2004/870 Reg.10

s.159, varied: SI 2002/185 Reg.6, SI 2002/2779 Sch.6 Part I

s.160, applied: SI 2002/2626 Sch.1, SI 2004/870 Reg.10

s.160, disapplied: SI 2002/2779 Art.81

s.160, referred to: SI 2003/284 Art.110, Art.111

s.160, varied: SI 2002/185 Reg.6, SI 2002/2779 Sch.6 Part I, Sch.6 Part II, SI 2004/870 Reg.15, Sch.5

s.161, applied: SI 2004/870 Reg.10

s.161, disapplied: SI 2003/1887 Sch.1

s.161, varied: SI 2002/185 Reg.6, SI 2002/2779 Sch.6 Part I, SI 2004/870 Reg.15, Sch.5

s.162, applied: SI 2002/2626 Sch.1, SI 2004/870 Reg.10

s.162, varied: SI 2002/185 Reg.6, SI 2002/2779 Sch.6 Part I, SI 2004/870 Reg.15, Sch.5

s.163, applied: SI 2002/2626 Sch.1, SI 2004/870 Reg.10

s.163, varied: SI 2002/185 Reg.6, SI 2002/2779 Sch.6 Part I, SI 2004/870 Reg.15, Sch.5

s.164, applied: SI 2002/2626 Sch.1, SI 2004/870 Reg.10, Reg.15

s.164, varied: SI 2002/185 Reg.6, SI 2002/2779 Sch.6 Part I, SI 2004/870 Reg.15, Sch.5

s.165, applied: SI 2002/2626 Sch.1, SI 2004/870 Reg.10

s.165, varied: SI 2002/185 Reg.6, SI 2002/2779 Sch.6 Part I

s.166, amended: 2004 asp 9 s.5

1983–cont.

2. **Representation of the People Act 1983**–*cont.*

s.166, applied: SI 2002/2626 Sch.1, SI 2004/870 Reg.10

s.166, varied: SI 2002/185 Reg.6, SI 2002/2779 Sch.6 Part I

s.167, applied: SI 2002/2626 Sch.1, SI 2002/2779 Art.73, SI 2004/870 Reg.10

s.167, varied: SI 2002/185 Reg.6, SI 2002/2779 Sch.6 Part I, Sch.6 Part II, SI 2004/870 Reg.15, Sch.3, Sch.5, SI 2004/1962 Sch.2 Part 2

s.168, applied: SI 2002/2626 Sch.1, SI 2004/870 Reg.10

s.168, varied: SI 2002/185 Reg.6, SI 2002/2779 Sch.6 Part I, Sch.6 Part II, SI 2004/870 Sch.3, SI 2004/1962 Sch.2 Part 2

s.169, applied: SI 2002/2626 Sch.1, SI 2004/870 Reg.10

s.169, varied: SI 2002/185 Reg.6, SI 2002/2779 Sch.6 Part I, Sch.6 Part II, SI 2004/870 Sch.3, SI 2004/1962 Sch.2 Part 2

s.170, applied: SI 2002/2626 Sch.1, SI 2004/870 Reg.10

s.170, varied: SI 2002/185 Reg.6, SI 2002/2779 Sch.6 Part I, Sch.6 Part II, SI 2004/870 Sch.3, SI 2004/1962 Sch.2 Part 2

s.171, applied: SI 2002/2626 Sch.1, SI 2004/870 Reg.10

s.171, varied: SI 2002/185 Reg.6

s.172, applied: SI 2002/2626 Sch.1, SI 2004/870 Reg.10

s.172, varied: SI 2002/185 Reg.6

s.173, applied: SI 2002/2626 Sch.1, SI 2002/2779 Art.27, Art.39, Art.60, SI 2004/870 Reg.10

s.173, varied: SI 2002/185 Reg.6, SI 2002/2779 Sch.6 Part I, SI 2004/870 Sch.3

s.173A, applied: SI 2002/2626 Sch.1, SI 2004/870 Reg.10

s.173A, varied: SI 2002/185 Reg.6, SI 2002/2779 Sch.6 Part I, Sch.6 Part II

s.174, applied: SI 2002/2626 Sch.1, SI 2003/284 Art.110, Art.111, Art.122, Art.123, Art.124, SI 2004/870 Reg.10

s.174, varied: SI 2002/185 Reg.6, SI 2002/2779 Sch.6 Part I, Sch.6 Part II, SI 2003/284 Art.110, Art.111, Art.123, Art.124, SI 2004/870 Sch.3

s.175, applied: SI 2002/2626 Sch.1, SI 2004/870 Reg.10

s.175, varied: SI 2002/185 Reg.6, SI 2002/2779 Sch.6 Part I, Sch.6 Part II, SI 2004/870 Sch.3, SI 2004/1962 Sch.2 Part 2

s.176, applied: SI 2002/2626 Sch.1, 2004 c.2 s.7, SI 2004/870 Reg.10

s.176, varied: SI 2002/185 Reg.6, SI 2002/2779 Sch.6 Part I, Sch.6 Part II, SI 2004/870 Sch.3, SI 2004/1962 Sch.2 Part 2

s.177, applied: SI 2002/2626 Sch.1, SI 2004/870 Reg.10

1983–cont.

2. Representation of the People Act 1983–cont.

s.177, varied: SI 2002/185 Reg.6, SI 2004/870 Sch.3, SI 2004/1962 Sch.2 Part 2

s.178, applied: 2002 c.24 s.9, SI 2002/2626 Sch.1, SI 2004/870 Reg.10

s.178, varied: SI 2002/185 Reg.6, SI 2002/2779 Sch.6 Part I, Sch.6 Part II, SI 2004/870 Sch.3, SI 2004/1962 Sch.2 Part 2

s.179, applied: SI 2002/2626 Sch.1, SI 2004/870 Reg.10

s.179, varied: SI 2002/185 Reg.6, SI 2002/2779 Sch.6 Part I, Sch.6 Part II, SI 2004/870 Sch.3, SI 2004/1962 Sch.2 Part 2

s.180, applied: SI 2002/2626 Sch.1, SI 2004/870 Reg.10

s.180, varied: SI 2002/185 Reg.6, SI 2002/2779 Sch.6 Part I, Sch.6 Part II, SI 2004/870 Reg.15, Sch.5

s.180A, applied: SI 2002/2626 Sch.1, SI 2004/870 Reg.10

s.180A, varied: SI 2002/185 Reg.6, SI 2002/2779 Sch.6 Part I, Sch.6 Part II, SI 2004/1962 Sch.2 Part 2

s.181, applied: SI 2002/2626 Sch.1, SI 2004/870 Reg.10

s.181, varied: SI 2002/185 Reg.6, SI 2002/2779 Sch.6 Part I, Sch.6 Part II, SI 2004/870 Sch.3, SI 2004/1962 Sch.2 Part 2

s.182, see *Ahmed v Kennedy* [2002] EWCA Civ 1793, [2003] 1 W.L.R. 1820 (CA), Simon Brown, L.J.

s.182, applied: SI 2002/2626 Sch.1, SI 2004/870 Reg.10

s.182, varied: SI 2002/185 Reg.6

s.182, enabling: SI 2003/971, SI 2003/972

s.183, applied: SI 2002/2626 Sch.1, SI 2004/870 Reg.10

s.183, varied: SI 2002/185 Reg.6, SI 2002/2779 Sch.6 Part I, Sch.6 Part II, SI 2004/870 Reg.15, Sch.5

s.184, applied: SI 2002/2626 Sch.1, SI 2004/870 Reg.10

s.184, varied: SI 2002/185 Reg.6, SI 2002/2779 Sch.6 Part I, Sch.6 Part II, SI 2004/870 Reg.15, Sch.5, SI 2004/1962 Sch.2 Part 2

s.185, amended: 2003 c.17 Sch.6 para.87

s.185, applied: SI 2002/2626 Sch.1, SI 2004/870 Reg.10

s.185, varied: SI 2002/185 Reg.6, SI 2002/2779 Sch.6 Part I, Sch.6 Part II, SI 2004/870 Reg.15, Sch.3, Sch.5, SI 2004/1962 Sch.2 Part 2

s.185, enabling: SI 2003/971, SI 2003/972

s.186, applied: SI 2002/2626 Sch.1, SI 2004/870 Reg.10

s.186, varied: SI 2002/185 Reg.6, SI 2002/2779 Sch.6 Part I, Sch.6 Part II, SI 2004/1962 Sch.2 Part 2

s.187, amended: 2004 asp 9 s.5

1983–cont.

2. Representation of the People Act 1983–cont.

s.187, applied: SI 2002/2626 Sch.1, SI 2004/870 Reg.10

s.188, applied: SI 2002/2626 Sch.1, SI 2004/870 Reg.10

s.188, repealed: 2004 asp 9 s.5

s.189, applied: SI 2002/2626 Sch.1, SI 2004/870 Reg.10

s.189A, applied: SI 2002/2626 Sch.1, SI 2004/870 Reg.10

s.190, applied: SI 2002/2626 Sch.1, SI 2004/870 Reg.10

s.191, amended: 2002 c.vi Sch.1 para.4

s.191, applied: SI 2002/2626 Sch.1, SI 2004/870 Reg.10

s.192, applied: SI 2002/2626 Sch.1, SI 2004/870 Reg.10

s.193, applied: SI 2002/2626 Sch.1, SI 2004/870 Reg.10

s.194, applied: SI 2002/2626 Sch.1, SI 2004/870 Reg.10

s.195, applied: SI 2002/2626 Sch.1, SI 2004/870 Reg.10

s.196, applied: SI 2002/2626 Sch.1, SI 2004/870 Reg.10

s.197, applied: SI 2002/2626 Sch.1, SI 2004/870 Reg.10

s.198, applied: SI 2002/2626 Sch.1, SI 2004/870 Reg.10

s.199, applied: SI 2002/2626 Sch.1, SI 2004/870 Reg.10

s.199A, added: SI 2002/2626 Sch.2 para.10

s.199A, applied: SI 2002/2626 Sch.1, SI 2004/870 Reg.10

s.199A, repealed: SI 2003/1887 Sch.2 para.4

s.200, applied: SI 2002/2626 Sch.1, SI 2004/870 Reg.10

s.200, varied: SI 2004/870 Sch.3, SI 2004/1962 Sch.2 Part 2

s.200A, applied: SI 2002/2626 Sch.1, SI 2004/870 Reg.10

s.201, applied: SI 2002/2626 Sch.1, SI 2004/870 Reg.10, SSI 2002/561

s.201, enabling: SI 2002/1871, SI 2002/1872, SI 2002/1873, SI 2003/1156, SI 2003/1892, SI 2003/1899, SI 2003/1942, SI 2004/1848, SI 2004/1960

s.202, applied: SI 2002/1871 (b), SI 2002/1872 (b), SI 2002/2626 Sch.1, SI 2003/1899, SI 2004/870 Reg.10

s.202, consolidated: 2002 c.24 Sch.1 para.4

s.202, varied: SI 2003/1557 Reg.2, SI 2004/870 Sch.3, SI 2004/1962 Sch.2 Part 2

s.202, enabling: SI 2002/1873

s.203, applied: SI 2002/2626 Sch.1, 2004 c.2 s.9, SI 2004/870 Reg.10, SI 2004/1962 Art.6

s.203, varied: SI 2002/185 Sch.2, SI 2004/870 Sch.3, SI 2004/1962 Sch.2 Part 2

s.204, amended: 2004 asp 9 s.5

1983–cont.

2. Representation of the People Act 1983–*cont.*

s.204, applied: SI 2002/2626 Sch.1, SI 2004/870 Reg.10

s.205, applied: SI 2002/2626 Sch.1, SI 2004/870 Reg.10

s.206, applied: SI 2002/2626 Sch.1, SI 2004/870 Reg.10

s.207, applied: SI 2002/2626 Sch.1, SI 2004/870 Reg.10

s.210, applied: SI 2002/2626 Sch.1, SI 2004/870 Reg.10

Sch.1, applied: 2003 c.12 s.2, SI 2004/294 Sch.2 para.1

Sch.1, referred to: SI 2004/294 Reg.5

Sch.1 Part I, applied: SI 2002/2626 Sch.1, SI 2004/870 Reg.10

Sch.1 Part 1, applied: SI 2004/870 Reg.10

Sch.1 Part 1, varied: SI 2004/294 Reg.8

Sch.1 Part 1, applied: SI 2004/870 Reg.10

Sch.1 Part 1, varied: SI 2004/294 Reg.8, Sch.2 para.29

Sch.1 Part I para.1, varied: 2004 c.2 Sch.1 para.1, SI 2004/294 Reg.8

Sch.1 Part 1 para.1, varied: SI 2004/294 Reg.8

Sch.1 Part 1 para.1, varied: SI 2004/294 Reg.8, Sch.2 para.28

Sch.1 Part I para.1A, varied: SI 2004/294 Reg.8

Sch.1 Part I para.2, varied: SI 2004/294 Reg.8

Sch.1 Part 1 para.2, varied: SI 2004/294 Reg.8

Sch.1 Part 1 para.2, varied: SI 2004/294 Reg.8, Sch.2 para.28

Sch.1 Part 1 para.2A, varied: SI 2004/294 Reg.8

Sch.1 Part 1 para.3, varied: SI 2004/294 Reg.8

Sch.1 Part 1 para.3, varied: SI 2004/294 Reg.8, Sch.2 para.28

Sch.1 Part 1 para.3A, varied: SI 2004/294 Reg.8

Sch.1 Part 1 para.4, varied: SI 2004/294 Reg.8

Sch.1 Part 1 para.4, varied: SI 2004/294 Reg.8, Sch.2 para.28

Sch.1 Part 1 para.5, varied: SI 2004/294 Reg.8, Sch.2 para.28

Sch.1 Part II, applied: SI 2002/2626 Sch.1, SI 2004/870 Reg.10

Sch.1 Part II, applied: SI 2004/870 Reg.10

Sch.1 Part II para.3, applied: SI 2002/2626 Sch.1

Sch.1 Part II para.3, varied: SI 2004/294 Reg.8

Sch.1 Part II para.4, applied: SI 2002/2626 Sch.1

Sch.1 Part II para.4, varied: SI 2004/294 Reg.8

Sch.1 Part II para.5, applied: SI 2002/2626 Sch.1

Sch.1 Part II para.5, varied: SI 2004/294 Reg.8

1983–cont.

2. Representation of the People Act 1983–*cont.*

Sch.1 Part II para.6, applied: SI 2002/2626 Sch.1

Sch.1 Part II para.6, varied: SI 2004/294 Reg.8

Sch.1 Part II para.6A, applied: SI 2002/2626 Sch.1

Sch.1 Part II para.6A, varied: SI 2004/294 Reg.8

Sch.1 Part II para.6B, applied: SI 2002/2626 Sch.1

Sch.1 Part II para.6B, varied: SI 2004/294 Reg.8

Sch.1 Part II para.6C, applied: SI 2002/2626 Sch.1

Sch.1 Part II para.6C, varied: SI 2004/294 Reg.8

Sch.1 Part II para.7, applied: SI 2002/2626 Sch.1

Sch.1 Part II para.7, varied: SI 2004/294 Reg.8

Sch.1 Part II para.8, applied: SI 2002/2626 Sch.1

Sch.1 Part II para.8, varied: SI 2004/294 Reg.8

Sch.1 Part II para.8A, applied: SI 2002/2626 Sch.1

Sch.1 Part II para.8A, varied: SI 2004/294 Reg.8

Sch.1 Part II para.9, applied: SI 2002/2626 Sch.1

Sch.1 Part II para.9, varied: SI 2004/294 Reg.8

Sch.1 Part II para.10, applied: SI 2002/2626 Sch.1

Sch.1 Part II para.10, varied: SI 2004/294 Reg.8

Sch.1 Part II para.10A, varied: SI 2004/294 Reg.8

Sch.1 Part II para.10B, varied: SI 2004/294 Reg.8

Sch.1 Part II para.11, amended: 2004 c.33 Sch.27 para.85

Sch.1 Part II para.11, applied: SI 2002/2626 Sch.1

Sch.1 Part II para.11, varied: SI 2004/294 Reg.8

Sch.1 Part II para.11A, varied: SI 2004/294 Reg.8

Sch.1 Part II para.12, applied: SI 2002/2626 Sch.1

Sch.1 Part II para.12, varied: SI 2004/294 Reg.8

Sch.1 Part II para.13, applied: SI 2002/2626 Sch.1

Sch.1 Part II para.13, varied: SI 2004/294 Reg.8

Sch.1 Part II para.14, applied: SI 2002/2626 Sch.1

Sch.1 Part II para.14, varied: SI 2004/294 Reg.8

CAP.

1983–*cont.*

2. Representation of the People Act 1983–*cont.*

Sch.1 Part II para.15, applied: SI 2002/2626 Sch.1

Sch.1 Part II para.15, varied: SI 2004/294 Reg.8

Sch.1 Part II para.16, applied: SI 2002/2626 Sch.1

Sch.1 Part II para.16, varied: SI 2004/294 Reg.8

Sch.1 Part II para.17, applied: SI 2002/2626 Sch.1

Sch.1 Part II para.17, varied: SI 2004/294 Reg.8

Sch.1 Part III, applied: SI 2004/870 Reg.10

Sch.1 Part III para.18, varied: SI 2004/294 Reg.8

Sch.1 Part III para.19, applied: SI 2002/2626 Sch.1

Sch.1 Part III para.19, varied: SI 2004/294 Reg.8, Sch.2 para.4

Sch.1 Part III para.20, applied: SI 2002/2626 Sch.1

Sch.1 Part III para.20, varied: SI 2004/294 Reg.8

Sch.1 Part III para.21, applied: SI 2002/2626 Sch.1

Sch.1 Part III para.21, varied: SI 2004/294 Reg.8

Sch.1 Part III para.22, applied: SI 2002/2626 Sch.1

Sch.1 Part III para.22, varied: SI 2004/294 Reg.8

Sch.1 Part III para.23, applied: SI 2002/2626 Sch.1

Sch.1 Part III para.23, referred to: SI 2004/294 Reg.5

Sch.1 Part III para.23, varied: SI 2004/294 Reg.8, Sch.2 para.5

Sch.1 Part III para.24, amended: 2002 c.13 s.3

Sch.1 Part III para.24, applied: SI 2002/2626 Sch.1

Sch.1 Part III para.24, referred to: SI 2004/294 Reg.5

Sch.1 Part III para.24, substituted: 2002 c.13 s.3

Sch.1 Part III para.24, varied: SI 2004/294 Reg.8

Sch.1 Part III para.24, enabling: SI 2002/1871, SI 2002/1872, SI 2002/1873

Sch.1 Part III para.25, applied: SI 2002/2626 Sch.1

Sch.1 Part III para.25, referred to: SI 2004/294 Reg.5

Sch.1 Part III para.25, varied: SI 2004/294 Reg.8

Sch.1 Part III para.26, applied: SI 2002/2626 Sch.1

Sch.1 Part III para.26, referred to: SI 2004/294 Reg.5

CAP.

1983–*cont.*

2. Representation of the People Act 1983–*cont.*

Sch.1 Part III para.26, varied: SI 2004/294 Reg.8

Sch.1 Part III para.26A, varied: SI 2004/294 Reg.8

Sch.1 Part III para.27, varied: SI 2004/294 Reg.8

Sch.1 Part III para.28, applied: SI 2002/2626 Sch.1

Sch.1 Part III para.28, varied: SI 2004/294 Reg.8, Sch.2 para.6

Sch.1 Part III para.29, applied: SI 2002/2626 Sch.1

Sch.1 Part III para.29, referred to: SI 2004/294 Reg.5

Sch.1 Part III para.29, varied: SI 2004/294 Reg.8, Sch.2 para.7, Sch.2 para.8, Sch.2 para.9

Sch.1 Part III para.29A, varied: SI 2004/294 Reg.8

Sch.1 Part III para.30, applied: SI 2002/2626 Sch.1

Sch.1 Part III para.30, varied: SI 2004/294 Reg.8, Sch.2 para.10

Sch.1 Part III para.31, applied: SI 2002/2626 Sch.1

Sch.1 Part III para.31, referred to: SI 2004/294 Reg.5

Sch.1 Part III para.31, varied: SI 2004/294 Reg.8

Sch.1 Part III para.32, applied: SI 2002/2626 Sch.1

Sch.1 Part III para.32, referred to: SI 2004/294 Reg.5

Sch.1 Part III para.32, varied: SI 2004/294 Reg.8, Sch.2 para.11

Sch.1 Part III para.33, applied: SI 2002/2626 Sch.1

Sch.1 Part III para.33, referred to: SI 2004/294 Reg.5

Sch.1 Part III para.33, varied: SI 2004/294 Reg.8

Sch.1 Part III para.34, applied: SI 2002/2626 Sch.1

Sch.1 Part III para.34, varied: SI 2004/294 Reg.8

Sch.1 Part III para.35, amended: 2002 c.13 s.2, 2004 c.33 Sch.27 para.85

Sch.1 Part III para.35, applied: SI 2002/2626 Sch.1

Sch.1 Part III para.35, varied: SI 2004/294 Reg.8, Sch.2 para.12

Sch.1 Part III para.36, applied: SI 2002/2626 Sch.1, 2004 c.2 s.6

Sch.1 Part III para.36, varied: SI 2004/294 Reg.8

Sch.1 Part III para.37, amended: 2002 c.13 s.2, s.4, SI 2003/1156 Reg.3

Sch.1 Part III para.37, applied: SI 2002/2626 Sch.1

1983–cont.

2. Representation of the People Act 1983–*cont.*

Sch.1 Part III para.37, repealed (in part): SI 2003/1156 Reg.3

Sch.1 Part III para.37, varied: SI 2004/294 Reg.8, Sch.2 para.13

Sch.1 Part III para.37, enabling: SI 2002/1873, SI 2003/1156

Sch.1 Part III para.38, applied: SI 2002/2626 Sch.1

Sch.1 Part III para.38, varied: SI 2004/294 Reg.8, Sch.2 para.14

Sch.1 Part III para.39, amended: 2002 c.13 s.5, 2004 c.33 Sch.27 para.85

Sch.1 Part III para.39, applied: SI 2002/2626 Sch.1

Sch.1 Part III para.39, varied: SI 2004/294 Reg.8, Sch.2 para.15

Sch.1 Part III para.40, amended: 2002 c.13 s.2

Sch.1 Part III para.40, applied: SI 2002/2626 Sch.1

Sch.1 Part III para.40, varied: SI 2004/294 Reg.8, Sch.2 para.16

Sch.1 Part III para.40A, varied: SI 2004/294 Reg.8

Sch.1 Part III para.41, applied: SI 2002/2626 Sch.1

Sch.1 Part III para.41, varied: SI 2004/294 Reg.8

Sch.1 Part III para.42, applied: SI 2002/2626 Sch.1

Sch.1 Part III para.42, varied: SI 2004/294 Reg.8, Sch.2 para.17

Sch.1 Part III para.43, applied: SI 2002/2626 Sch.1

Sch.1 Part III para.43, varied: SI 2004/294 Reg.8, Sch.2 para.18, Sch.2 para.19

Sch.1 Part III para.43A, applied: SI 2002/2626 Sch.1

Sch.1 Part III para.43A, varied: SI 2004/294 Reg.8

Sch.1 Part III para.43B, applied: SI 2002/2626 Sch.1

Sch.1 Part III para.43B, varied: SI 2004/294 Reg.8

Sch.1 Part III para.44, amended: 2004 c.33 Sch.27 para.85

Sch.1 Part III para.44, applied: SI 2002/2626 Sch.1

Sch.1 Part III para.44, varied: SI 2004/294 Reg.8, Sch.2 para.20, Sch.2 para.21

Sch.1 Part III para.44A, applied: SI 2002/2626 Sch.1

Sch.1 Part III para.44A, varied: SI 2004/294 Reg.8

Sch.1 Part III para.44B, applied: SI 2002/2626 Sch.1

Sch.1 Part III para.44B, varied: SI 2004/294 Reg.8

Sch.1 Part III para.44B, applied: SI 2002/2626 Sch.1

1983–cont.

2. Representation of the People Act 1983–*cont.*

Sch.1 Part III para.44B, varied: SI 2004/294 Reg.8

Sch.1 Part III para.44C, applied: SI 2002/2626 Sch.1

Sch.1 Part III para.44C, varied: SI 2004/294 Reg.8

Sch.1 Part III para.44D, applied: SI 2002/2626 Sch.1

Sch.1 Part III para.44D, varied: SI 2004/294 Reg.8

Sch.1 Part III para.44E, applied: SI 2002/2626 Sch.1

Sch.1 Part III para.44E, varied: SI 2004/294 Reg.8

Sch.1 Part III para.44F, applied: SI 2002/2626 Sch.1

Sch.1 Part III para.44F, varied: SI 2004/294 Reg.8

Sch.1 Part III para.44G, applied: SI 2002/2626 Sch.1

Sch.1 Part III para.44G, varied: SI 2004/294 Reg.8

Sch.1 Part III para.44H, applied: SI 2002/2626 Sch.1

Sch.1 Part III para.44H, varied: SI 2004/294 Reg.8

Sch.1 Part III para.44J, applied: SI 2002/2626 Sch.1

Sch.1 Part III para.44J, varied: SI 2004/294 Reg.8

Sch.1 Part III para.44K, applied: SI 2002/2626 Sch.1

Sch.1 Part III para.44K, varied: SI 2004/294 Reg.8

Sch.1 Part III para.44L, applied: SI 2002/2626 Sch.1

Sch.1 Part III para.44L, varied: SI 2004/294 Reg.8

Sch.1 Part III para.44M, varied: SI 2004/294 Reg.8

Sch.1 Part III para.45, amended: 2002 c.13 s.3

Sch.1 Part III para.45, applied: SI 2002/2626 Sch.1

Sch.1 Part III para.45, referred to: SI 2004/294 Reg.5

Sch.1 Part III para.45, varied: SI 2004/294 Reg.8, Sch.2 para.22, Sch.2 para.23, Sch.2 para.24

Sch.1 Part III para.46, applied: SI 2002/2626 Sch.1

Sch.1 Part III para.46, varied: SI 2004/294 Reg.8

Sch.1 Part III para.46A, varied: SI 2004/294 Reg.8

Sch.1 Part III para.47, applied: SI 2002/2626 Sch.1

Sch.1 Part III para.47, varied: SI 2004/294 Reg.8

1983–cont.

2. **Representation of the People Act 1983**–*cont.*

Sch.1 Part III para.48, varied: SI 2004/294 Reg.8

Sch.1 Part III para.48A, applied: SI 2002/2626 Sch.1

Sch.1 Part III para.48A, varied: SI 2004/294 Reg.8

Sch.1 Part III para.48B, applied: SI 2002/2626 Sch.1

Sch.1 Part III para.48B, varied: SI 2004/294 Reg.8

Sch.1 Part III para.48C, applied: SI 2002/2626 Sch.1

Sch.1 Part III para.48C, varied: SI 2004/294 Reg.8

Sch.1 Part III para.49, varied: SI 2004/294 Reg.8

Sch.1 Part IV, applied: SI 2004/870 Reg.10

Sch.1 Part IV para.50, applied: SI 2002/2626 Sch.1

Sch.1 Part IV para.50, varied: SI 2004/294 Reg.8

Sch.1 Part IV para.51, varied: SI 2004/294 Reg.8

Sch.1 Part IV para.52, varied: SI 2004/294 Reg.8

Sch.1 Part IV para.53, varied: SI 2004/294 Reg.8

Sch.1 Part V, applied: SI 2004/870 Reg.10

Sch.1 Part V para.54, varied: SI 2004/294 Reg.8, Sch.2 para.25

Sch.1 Part V para.55, varied: SI 2004/294 Reg.8, Sch.2 para.26

Sch.1 Part V para.56, varied: SI 2004/294 Reg.8

Sch.1 Part V para.57, varied: SI 2004/294 Reg.8

Sch.1 Part V para.58, varied: SI 2004/294 Reg.8

Sch.1 Part V para.59, varied: SI 2004/294 Reg.8

Sch.1 Part VI, applied: SI 2004/870 Reg.10

Sch.1 Part VI para.60, varied: SI 2004/294 Reg.8, Sch.2 para.27

Sch.1 Part VI para.61, varied: SI 2004/294 Reg.8

Sch.2, enabling: SSI 2002/561

Sch.2 para.1, amended: 2002 c.13 s.6

Sch.2 para.1, enabling: SI 2002/1873

Sch.2 para.10, applied: SI 2003/1942 Reg.3

Sch.2 para.10, enabling: SI 2002/1871, SI 2002/1872, SI 2002/1873, SI 2003/1892, SI 2003/1899, SI 2003/1942, SI 2004/1848, SI 2004/1960

Sch.2 para.10A, enabling: SI 2002/1871, SI 2002/1872, SI 2002/1873

Sch.2 para.10B, enabling: SI 2002/1871, SI 2002/1872, SI 2002/1873

Sch.2 para.11, enabling: SI 2002/1871, SI 2002/1872, SI 2002/1873

1983–cont.

2. **Representation of the People Act 1983**–*cont.*

Sch.2 para.11A, enabling: SI 2002/1871, SI 2002/1872, SI 2002/1873

Sch.2 para.12, enabling: SI 2002/1871, SI 2002/1872, SI 2002/1873

Sch.2 para.13, enabling: SI 2002/1871, SI 2002/1872, SI 2002/1873

Sch.2A Part I para.1, applied: SI 2004/293 Sch.6 para.1, SI 2004/870 Reg.10

Sch.2A Part I para.2, applied: SI 2002/2779 Art.57, SI 2004/870 Reg.10

Sch.2A Part I para.3, applied: SI 2004/870 Reg.10

Sch.2A Part I para.4, applied: SI 2004/870 Reg.10

Sch.2A Part I para.5, applied: SI 2004/870 Reg.10

Sch.2A Part II para.6, applied: SI 2004/870 Reg.10

Sch.2A Part II para.7, applied: SI 2003/1645 r.1, SI 2004/870 Reg.10

Sch.2A Part II para.8, applied: SI 2004/870 Reg.10

Sch.2A Part II para.9, applied: SI 2004/870 Reg.10

Sch.2A Part III para.10, applied: SI 2004/870 Reg.10

Sch.2A Part III para.11, applied: SI 2004/870 Reg.10

Sch.2A Part III para.12, applied: SI 2004/870 Reg.10

Sch.5, applied: SI 2004/293 Sch.8 para.3

Sch.6 para.1, amended: 2002 c.vi Sch.1 para.5

Sch.6 para.5, amended: 2002 c.vi Sch.1 para.6

Sch.6 para.6, amended: 2002 c.vi Sch.2

Sch.7 Part I, applied: SI 2004/870 Reg.10

Sch.7 Part I para.4, repealed: 2003 c.17 Sch.6 para.88, Sch.7

Sch.7 Part II, applied: SI 2004/870 Reg.10

Sch.8 Part 1, applied: SI 2004/870 Reg.10

Sch.8 Part 1 para.7, repealed: 2003 c.17 Sch.7

Sch.8 Part 1 para.8, repealed: 2003 c.17 Sch.7

Sch.8 Part 1 para.9, repealed: 2003 c.17 Sch.7

Sch.8 Part 1 para.10, repealed: 2003 c.17 Sch.7

Sch.8 Part 1 para.21, consolidated: 2002 c.24 s.9

Sch.8 Part 1 para.21, repealed: 2002 c.24 Sch.4

Sch.8 Part 1 para.22, repealed: 2002 c.24 Sch.4

Sch.8 Part 1 para.23, repealed: 2002 c.24 Sch.4

Sch.8 Part 2, applied: SI 2004/870 Reg.10

Sch.8 Part 2 para.28, repealed: SI 2003/435 Sch.5

Sch.9 Part I, applied: SI 2004/870 Reg.10

Sch.9 Part II, applied: SI 2004/870 Reg.10

Sch.9 Part III, applied: SI 2002/2626 Sch.1

CAP.

1983–cont.

3. **Agricultural Marketing Act 1983**
applied: SI 2002/2843 Art.7
s.4, repealed (in part): 2004 c.14 Sch.1 Part 2
s.5, amended: SI 2003/1326 Art.13
s.5, referred to: SI 2002/2843 Art.7
s.5, varied: SI 2002/2843 Art.7
s.7, applied: SI 2002/794 Art.3
s.9, amended: 2004 c.14 Sch.1 Part 2
s.9, repealed (in part): 2004 c.14 Sch.1 Part 2
Sch.2 para.3, repealed: 2004 c.14 Sch.1 Part 2

6. **British Nationality (Falkland Islands) Act 1983**
s.1, amended: 2002 c.8 s.2
s.1, repealed (in part): 2002 c.8 Sch.2
s.2, repealed: 2002 c.8 Sch.2
s.4, amended: SI 2003/1016 Sch.1 para.3
s.4, repealed (in part): 2002 c.41 Sch.9
s.5, amended: 2002 c.8 s.2

8. **British Fishing Boats Act 1983**
referred to: SI 2002/790 Sch.3 para.5
s.1, applied: SI 2002/790 Sch.3 para.6, Sch.3 para.7
s.1, disapplied: SI 2002/790 Sch.3 para.7
s.1, varied: SI 2002/790 Sch.3 para.7

9. **Currency Act 1983**
s.2, repealed (in part): 2004 c.14 Sch.1 Part 17
s.3, repealed (in part): 2004 c.14 Sch.1 Part 17

10. **Transport Act 1983**
s.10, repealed: 2004 c.14 Sch.1 Part 14

14. **International Transport Conventions Act 1983**
Sch.2 para.3, repealed: 2004 c.14 Sch.1 Part 14

15. **British Shipbuilders Act 1983**
s.1, repealed (in part): 2004 c.14 Sch.1 Part 16
s.2, repealed (in part): 2004 c.14 Sch.1 Part 16
s.3, repealed (in part): 2004 c.14 Sch.1 Part 16

16. **Level Crossings Act 1983**
applied: SI 2003/547 Sch.17, SI 2004/456 Sch.16
s.1, applied: SI 2002/3113 Reg.56
s.1, disapplied: 2004 asp 10 Sch.4 Part 3

18. **Nuclear Material (Offences) Act 1983**
referred to: 2003 c.32 Sch.5 para.7
s.2, applied: SI 2004/1910 Sch.1
s.3, amended: 2002 c.26 Sch.7 para.30, 2003 c.32 Sch.5 para.8

19. **Matrimonial Homes Act 1983**
applied: 2004 c.33 Sch.9 para.25
s.2, applied: SI 2003/1953 Art.20

20. **Mental Health Act 1983**
see *AD v East Kent Community NHS Trust* [2002] EWHC 2256, [2002] 3 F.C.R. 658 (QBD), Cooke, J.; see *B (A Child) v Todd* [2002] P.I.Q.R. P11 (QBD), Stanley Burnton, J.; see *Masterman-Lister v Jewell* [2002] EWHC 417, [2002] Lloyd's Rep. Med. 239 (QBD), Wright, J.; see *Mersey Care NHS Trust v Ackroyd* [2003] EWCA Civ 663, [2003] E.M.L.R. 36 (CA), May,

CAP.

1983–cont.

20. **Mental Health Act 1983**–*cont.*
see–*cont.*
L.J.; see *R (Execution of Statutory Will), Re* [2003] W.T.L.R. 1051 (Ch D), Ferris, J.; see *R. (on the application of G) v Ealing LBC (No.2)* [2002] EWHC 250, Times, March 18, 2002 (QBD (Admin Ct)), Munby, J.; see *R. (on the application of KB) v Mental Health Review Tribunal (Damages)* [2003] EWHC 193, [2004] Q.B. 936 (QBD (Admin Ct)), Stanley Burnton, J.; see *R. (on the application of KB) v Mental Health Review Tribunal* [2002] EWHC 639, (2002) 5 C.C.L. Rep. 458 (QBD (Admin Ct)), Stanley Burnton, J.; see *R. (on the application of N) v M* [2002] EWHC 1911, [2003] A.C.D. 17 (QBD (Admin Ct)), Silber, J.; see *R. (on the application of S) v Airedale NHS Trust* [2002] EWHC 1780, [2003] Lloyd's Rep. Med. 21 (QBD (Admin Ct)), Stanley Burnton, J.; see *R. v Drew (Anthony James)* [2001] EWCA Crim 2861, [2002] 2 Cr. App. R. (S.) 45 (CA (Crim Div)), Kennedy, L.J.
applied: SI 2002/325 Reg.42, Sch.3 para.1, SI 2002/1792 Reg.5, SI 2002/2978 Sch.1 para.13, SI 2002/3177 Sch.1 para.13, 2003 c.44 s.166, s.207, s.327, SI 2003/348 Sch.6 para.4, SI 2003/409 Sch.1 Part I, SI 2003/1558 Sch.2 para.4, SI 2004/675 Sch.1 para.64, SI 2004/2608 Sch.1
referred to: 2003 c.43 Sch.4 para.50
Part III, applied: 2003 c.44 s.142
Part VIII, applied: 2004 c.33 Sch.5 para.78
s.2, see *R. (on the application of von Brandenburg) v East London and the City Mental Health NHS Trust* [2001] EWCA Civ 239, [2002] Q.B. 235 (CA), Lord Phillips of Worth Matravers, M.R.; see *R. (on the application of von Brandenburg) v East London and the City Mental Health NHS Trust* [2003] UKHL 58, [2004] 2 A.C. 280 (HL), Lord Bingham of Cornhill
s.3, see *AD v East Kent Community NHS Trust* [2002] EWCA Civ 1872, [2003] 3 All E.R. 1167 (CA), Judge, L.J.; see *D v South Tyneside Health Care NHS Trust* [2003] EWCA Civ 878, [2004] P.I.Q.R. P12 (CA), Lord Phillips of Worth Matravers, M.R.; see *R. (on the application of A) v Partnerships in Care Ltd* [2002] EWHC 529, [2002] 1 W.L.R. 2610 (QBD (Admin Ct)), Keith, J.; see *R. (on the application of B) v Ashworth Hospital Authority* [2003] EWCA Civ 547, [2003] 1 W.L.R. 1886 (CA), Dyson, L.J.; see *R. (on the application of C) v Mental Health Review Tribunal* [2001] EWCA Civ 1110, [2002] 1 W.L.R. 176 (CA), Lord Phillips of Worth Matravers, M.R.; see *R. (on the application of DR) v Mersey Care NHS Trust* Times, October 11, 2002 (QBD (Admin Ct)), Wilson, J.; see *R. (on the*

1983–cont.

20. Mental Health Act 1983–cont.

s.3–cont.

application of H) v Ashworth Hospital Authority [2001] EWHC Admin 901, (2002) 5 C.C.L. Rep. 78 (QBD (Admin Ct)), Stanley Burnton, J.; see *R. (on the application of H) vAshworth Hospital Authority* [2002] EWCA Civ 923, [2003] 1 W.L.R. 127 (CA), Dyson, L.J.; see *R. (on the application of PD) v West Midlands and North West Mental Health Review Tribunal* [2004] EWCA Civ 311, (2004) 148 S.J.L.B. 384 (CA), Lord Phillips of Worth Matravers, M.R.; see *R. (on the application of S) v Secretary of State for the Home Department* [2002] EWHC 2424, Times, November 13, 2002 (QBD (Admin Ct)), Maurice Kay, J.; see *R. (on the application of Stennett) v Manchester City Council* [2002] UKHL 34, [2002] 2 A.C. 1127 (HL), Lord Steyn; see *R. (on the application of von Brandenburg) v East London and the City Mental Health NHS Trust* [2001] EWCA Civ 239, [2002] Q.B. 235 (CA), Lord Phillips of Worth Matravers, M.R.; see *R. (on the application of von Brandenburg) v East London and the City Mental Health NHS Trust* [2003] UKHL 58, [2004] 2 A.C. 280 (HL), Lord Bingham of Cornhill; see *SS (Medical Treatment: Late Termination), Re* [2002] 1 F.L.R. 445 (Fam Div), Wall, J.

s.7, applied: SI 2003/762 Reg.2, SI 2004/1748 Sch.1

s.12, amended: 2003 c.43 Sch.4 para.51, 2004 c.33 Sch.27 para.86

s.12, applied: SI 2002/2375 Reg.3, Reg.7, 2003 c.44 s.207

s.12, referred to: SI 2002/2375 Sch.2, Sch.3

s.12, varied: 2004 c.33 Sch.21 para.13

s.13, see *R. (on the application of H) v Ashworth Hospital Authority* [2002] EWCA Civ 923, [2003] 1 W.L.R. 127 (CA), Dyson, L.J.; see *R. (on the application of von Brandenburg) v East London and the City Mental Health NHS Trust* [2001] EWCA Civ 239, [2002] Q.B. 235 (CA), Lord Phillips of Worth Matravers, M.R.

s.14, amended: 2004 c.31 Sch.5 Part 4

s.17, see *R. (on the application of A) v Secretary of State for the Home Department* [2002] EWHC 1618, [2003] 1 W.L.R. 330 (QBD (Admin Ct)), Crane, J.

s.17, applied: SI 2003/762 Reg.2, SI 2004/1748 Sch.1, SSI 2003/243 Reg.2

s.19, amended: 2003 c.43 Sch.4 para.52

s.20, see *R. (on the application of DR) v Mersey Care NHS Trust* Times, October 11, 2002 (QBD (Admin Ct)), Wilson, J.

s.23, see *R. (on the application of T) v Central and North West London Mental Health NHS Trust* [2002] EWHC 2803, Times,

1983–cont.

20. Mental Health Act 1983–cont.

s.23–cont.

December 13, 2002 (QBD (Admin Ct)), Forbes, J.

s.23, amended: 2003 c.43 Sch.4 para.53

s.24, amended: 2003 c.43 Sch.4 para.54

s.25A, amended: 2002 c.17 Sch.2 para.43

s.25A, applied: SI 2003/762 Reg.2, SI 2004/1748 Sch.1, SSI 2003/243 Reg.2

s.25C, amended: 2002 c.17 Sch.2 para.44, 2004 c.33 Sch.27 para.86

s.25C, varied: 2004 c.33 Sch.21 para.14

s.25F, amended: 2002 c.17 Sch.2 para.45

s.26, see *R. (on the application of M) v Secretary of State for Health* [2003] EWHC 1094, [2003] U.K.H.R.R. 746 (QBD (Admin Ct)), Maurice Kay, J.

s.28, amended: 2002 c.38 Sch.3 para.41

s.29, see *R. (on the application of M) v Secretary of State for Health* [2003] EWHC 1094, [2003] U.K.H.R.R. 746 (QBD (Admin Ct)), Maurice Kay, J.; see *R. (on the application of S) v Plymouth City Council* [2002] EWCA Civ 388, [2002] 1 W.L.R 2583 (CA), Hale, L.J.

s.32, amended: 2003 c.43 Sch.4 para.55

s.35, applied: 2003 c.44 s.242

s.36, applied: 2003 c.44 s.242

s.37, see *R. (on the application of B) v Ashworth Hospital Authority* [2003] EWCA Civ 547, [2003] 1 W.L.R. 1886 (CA), Dyson, L.J.; see *R. (on the application of H) v Secretary of State for the Home Department* [2001] EWHC Admin 1037, (2002) 5 C.C.L. Rep. 62 (QBD (Admin Ct)), Bell, J.; see *R. (on the application of H) v Secretary of State for the Home Department* [2003] UKHL 59, [2004] 2 A.C. 253 (HL), Lord Bingham of Cornhill; see *R. (on the application of K) v Camden and Islington HA* [2001] EWCA Civ 240, [2002] Q.B. 198 (CA), Lord Phillips of Worth Matravers, M.R.; see *R. (on the application of S) v Mental Health Review Tribunal* [2002] EWHC 2522, Times, December 6, 2002 (QBD (Admin Ct)), Stanley Burnton, J.; see *R. (on the application of South West Yorkshire Mental Health NHS Trust) v Bradford Crown Court* [2003] EWHC 640, [2003] A.C.D. 68 (QBD (Admin Ct)), Newman, J.; see *R. (on the application of W) v Doncaster MBC* [2004] EWCA Civ 378, [2004] B.L.G.R. 743 (CA), Judge, L.J.; see *R. v Drew (Anthony James)* [2003] UKHL 25, [2003] 1 W.L.R. 1213 (HL), Lord Bingham of Cornhill; see *R. v Kearney (Mark Michael)* [2002] EWCA Crim 2772, [2003] 2 Cr. App. R. (S.) 17 (CA (Crim Div)), Holman, J.; see *R. v Walton (Peter Howard)* [2003] EWCA Crim 2254, [2004] 1 Cr. App. R. (S.) 35 (CA (Crim Div)), Rix, L.J.; see *Wallis Ltd*

1983–cont.

20. Mental Health Act 1983–*cont.*

s.37–*cont.*

v *Customs and Excise Commissioners* [2003] V. & D.R.151 (VATand DutiesTribunal (London)), Theodore Wallace (Chairman)

s.37, amended: 2003 c.44 Sch.32 para.38, Sch.37 Part 7

s.37, applied: 2003 c.42 s.135, 2003 c.44 s.207, s.246, s.260, SI 2003/495 Reg.7, SI 2003/762 Reg.2, SI 2004/1748 Sch.1

s.38, applied: 2003 c.44 s.242, SI 2003/495 Reg.7

s.39, amended: 2002 c.17 Sch.2 para.46

s.41, see *R. (on the application of A) v Secretary of State for the Home Department* [2002] EWHC 1618, [2003] 1 W.L.R. 330 (QBD (Admin Ct)), Crane, J.; see *R. (on the application of H) v Secretary of State for the Home Department* [2001] EWHC Admin 1037, (2002) 5 C.C.L. Rep. 62 (QBD (Admin Ct)), Bell, J.; see *R. (on the application of K) v Camden and Islington HA* [2001] EWCA Civ 240, [2002] Q.B. 198 (CA), Lord Phillips of Worth Matravers, M.R.; see *R. (on the application of S) v Mental Health Review Tribunal* [2002] EWHC 2522, Times, December 6, 2002 (QBD (Admin Ct)), Stanley Burnton, J.; see *R. (on the application of South West Yorkshire Mental Health NHS Trust) v Bradford Crown Court* [2003] EWHC 640, [2003] A.C.D. 68 (QBD (Admin Ct)), Newman, J.; see *R. (on the application of W) v Doncaster MBC* [2004] EWCA Civ 378, [2004] B.L.G.R. 743 (CA), Judge, L.J.; see *R. v Drew (Anthony James)* [2003] UKHL 25, [2003] 1 W.L.R. 1213 (HL), Lord Bingham of Cornhill; see *R. v Kearney (Mark Michael)* [2002] EWCA Crim 2772, [2003] 2 Cr. App. R. (S.) 17 (CA (Crim Div)), Holman, J.; see *R. v Walton (Peter Howard)* [2003] EWCA Crim 2254, [2004] 1 Cr. App. R. (S.) 35 (CA (Crim Div)), Rix, L.J.

s.42, see *R. (on the application of A) v Secretary of State for the Home Department* [2002] EWHC 1618, [2003] 1 W.L.R. 330 (QBD (Admin Ct)), Crane, J.

s.42, applied: SI 2003/762 Reg.2, 2004 c.28 s.38, s.41, s.44, SI 2004/1748 Sch.1, SSI 2003/243 Reg.2, 2004 c.28 s.37, s.40, s.43

s.43, amended: 2003 c.44 Sch.3 para.55

s.43, repealed (in part): 2003 c.44 Sch.37 Part 9

s.45A, amended: 2003 c.44 Sch.32 para.39, Sch.37 Part 7

s.45A, applied: 2003 c.44 s.246, s.260, SI 2003/495 Reg.7

s.47, see *R. (on the application of D) v Secretary of State for the Home Department* [2002] EWHC 2805, [2003]

1983–cont.

20. Mental Health Act 1983–*cont.*

s.47–*cont.*

1 W.L.R. 1315 (QBD (Admin Ct)), Stanley Burnton, J.; see *R. (on the application of M) v Nottinghamshire Healthcare NHS Trust* [2002] EWCA Civ 1728, [2003] 1 All E.R. 784 (CA), Pill, L.J.; see *R. v Drew (Anthony James)* [2003] UKHL 25, [2003] 1 W.L.R. 1213 (HL), Lord Bingham of Cornhill

s.47, amended: 2004 c.28 Sch.10 para.18

s.47, applied: SI 2002/2375 Reg.3, 2003 c.44 s.246, s.260

s.48, amended: 2002 c.41 s.62, 2004 c.14 Sch.1 Part 17

s.48, applied: SI 2002/2375 Reg.3, 2003 c.44 s.242

s.49, see *R. (on the application of D) v Secretary of State for the Home Department* [2002] EWHC 2805, [2003] 1 W.L.R. 1315 (QBD (Admin Ct)), Stanley Burnton, J.; see *R. v Drew (Anthony James)* [2003] UKHL 25, [2003] 1 W.L.R. 1213 (HL), Lord Bingham of Cornhill

s.50, see *R. (on the application of M) v Nottinghamshire Healthcare NHS Trust* [2002] EWCA Civ 1728, [2003] 1 All E.R. 784 (CA), Pill, L.J.

s.50, amended: 2003 c.44 s.294

s.51, see *R. (on the application of Kenneally) v Snaresbrook Crown Court* [2001] EWHC Admin 968, [2002] Q.B. 1169 (QBD (Admin Ct)), Pill, L.J.

s.52, amended: 2003 c.44 Sch.37 Part 4, Sch.3 para.55

s.53, varied: 2002 c.41 s.62

s.54, applied: 2003 c.44 s.207

s.58, see *R. (on the application of N) v M* [2002] EWCA Civ 1789, [2003] 1 W.L.R. 562 (CA), Dyson, L.J.; see *R. (on the application of Wooder) v Feggetter* [2002] EWCA Civ 554, [2003] Q.B. 219 (CA), Brooke, L.J.

s.58, applied: 2003 c.42 s.135

s.63, see *R. (on the application of B) v Ashworth Hospital Authority* [2003] EWCA Civ 547, [2003] 1 W.L.R. 1886 (CA), Dyson, L.J.

s.65, applied: SI 2003/2251 Art.2, Sch.1

s.65, enabling: SI 2003/2251

s.69, amended: 2004 c.28 Sch.10 para.19, Sch.11

s.69, applied: 2004 c.28 s.37, s.38, s.40, s.41, s.43, s.44

s.70, see *R. (on the application of C) v Secretary of State for the Home Department* [2002] EWCA Civ 647, Times, May 24, 2002 (CA), Lord Phillips of Worth Matravers, M.R.

s.70, applied: 2004 c.28 s.37, s.38, s.40, s.41, s.43, s.44

1983–cont.
20. Mental Health Act 1983–cont.
s.71, see *R. (on the application of C) v Secretary of State for the Home Department* [2002] EWCA Civ 647, Times, May 24, 2002 (CA), Lord Phillips of Worth Matravers, M.R.

s.71, applied: 2004 c.28 s.37, s.38, s.40, s.41, s.43, s.44

s.71, repealed (in part): 2004 c.28 Sch.10 para.20, Sch.11

s.72, see *MP v Nottinghamshire Healthcare NHS Trust* [2003] EWHC 1782, [2003] A.C.D. 99 (QBD (Admin Ct)), Silber, J.; see *R. (on the application of B) v Ashworth Hospital Authority* [2003] EWCA Civ 547, [2003] 1 W.L.R. 1886 (CA), Dyson, L.J.; see *R. (on the application of H) v Ashworth Hospital Authority* [2001] EWHC Admin 901, (2002) 5 C.C.L. Rep. 78 (QBD (Admin Ct)), Stanley Burnton, J.; see *R. (on the application of H) v Mental Health Review Tribunal for North and East London Region* [2001] EWCA Civ 415, [2002] Q.B.1 (CA), Lord Phillips of Worth Matravers, M.R.; see *R. (on the application of Secretary of State for the Home Department) v Mental Health Review Tribunal* (2002) 63 B.M.L.R. 181 (QBD (Admin Ct)), Collins, J.

s.73, see *MP v Nottinghamshire Healthcare NHS Trust* [2003] EWHC 1782, [2003] A.C.D. 99 (QBD (Admin Ct)), Silber, J.; see *R. (on the application of A) v Secretary of State for the Home Department* [2002] EWHC 1618, [2003] 1 W.L.R. 330 (QBD (Admin Ct)), Crane, J.; see *R. (on the application of C) v Secretary of State for the Home Department* [2002] EWCA Civ 647, Times, May 24, 2002 (CA), Lord Phillips of Worth Matravers, M.R.; see *R. (on the application of H) v Mental Health Review Tribunal for North and East London Region* [2001] EWCA Civ 415, [2002] Q.B.1 (CA), Lord Phillips of Worth Matravers, M.R.; see *R. (on the application of H) v Secretary of State for the Home Department* [2001] EWHC Admin 1037, (2002) 5 C.C.L. Rep. 62 (QBD (Admin Ct)), Bell, J.; see *R. (on the application of H) v Secretary of State for the Home Department* [2002] EWCA Civ 646, [2003] Q.B. 320 (CA), Lord Phillips of Worth Matravers, M.R.; see *R. (on the application of W) v Doncaster MBC* [2004] EWCA Civ 378, [2004] B.L.G.R. 743 (CA), Judge, L.J.

s.73, applied: SI 2003/762 Reg.2, SI 2004/1748 Sch.1, SSI 2003/243 Reg.2

s.74, amended: 2003 c.44 s.295

s.75, applied: SI 2003/762 Reg.2, SI 2004/1748 Sch.1, SSI 2003/243 Reg.2, 2004 c.28 s.37, s.38, s.40, s.41, s.43, s.44

1983–cont.
20. Mental Health Act 1983–cont.
s.78, see *R. (on the application of Secretary of State for the Home Department) v Mental Health Review Tribunal* (2002) 63 B.M.L.R. 181 (QBD (Admin Ct)), Collins, J.; see *R. (on the application of T) v Mental Health Review Tribunal* [2002] EWHC 247, [2002] Lloyd's Rep. Med. 354 (QBD (Admin Ct)), Scott Baker, J.

s.79, amended: 2004 c.28 Sch.10 para.21

s.79, repealed (in part): 2004 c.28 Sch.10 para.21, Sch.11

s.84, amended: 2004 c.28 Sch.10 para.22

s.86, applied: SI 2002/313 Sch.1

s.94, see *Masterman-Lister v Jewell* [2002] EWCA Civ 1889, [2003] 1 W.L.R. 1511 (CA), Kennedy, L.J.; see *Tait v Wedgwood* [2002] EWHC 2594, [2003] W.T.L.R. 121 (Ch D), Rimer, J.

s.103, amended: 2003 c.44 Sch.37 Part 9

s.103, disapplied: 2003 c.44 Sch.25 para.79

s.106, applied: SI 2004/1291

s.106, referred to: SI 2002/833

s.106, enabling: SI 2002/832, SI 2002/833, SI 2002/1944, SI 2003/1733, SI 2004/1291

s.107, enabling: SI 2002/832, SI 2002/833

s.108, enabling: SI 2002/832, SI 2002/833, SI 2002/1944, SI 2003/1733, SI 2004/1291

s.117, see *R. (on the application of H) v Ashworth Hospital Authority* [2001] EWHC Admin 901, (2002) 5 C.C.L. Rep. 78 (QBD (Admin Ct)), Stanley Burnton, J.; see *R. (on the application of K) v Camden and Islington HA* [2001] EWCA Civ 240, [2002] Q.B. 198 (CA), Lord Phillips of Worth Matravers, M.R.; see *R. (on the application of Stennett) v Manchester City Council* [2002] UKHL 34, [2002] 2 A.C. 1127 (HL), Lord Steyn; see *R. (on the application of W) v Doncaster MBC* [2003] EWHC 192, (2003) 6 C.C.L. Rep. 301 (QBD (Admin Ct)), Stanley Burnton, J.; see *R. (on the application of W) v Doncaster MBC* [2004] EWCA Civ 378, [2004] B.L.G.R. 743 (CA), Judge, L.J.; see *R. (on the application of Wahid) v Tower Hamlets LBC* [2002] EWCA Civ 287, [2003] H.L.R. 2 (CA), Pill, L.J.

s.117, amended: 2002 c.17 Sch.2 para.47

s.117, applied: SI 2003/762 Reg.5, SI 2004/1748 Reg.6

s.118, see *R. (on the application of Munjaz) v Mersey Care NHS Trust* [2003] EWCA Civ 1036, [2004] Q.B. 395 (CA), Lord Phillips of Worth Matravers, M.R.

s.127, see *R. v Spedding (Steffan Anthony)* [2001] EWCA Crim 2190, [2002] 1 Cr. App. R. (S.) 119 (CA (Crim Div)), Tomlinson, J

1983–cont.

20. Mental Health Act 1983–cont.

s.127, applied: 2003 c.42 Sch.5 para.43, 2003 c.44 Sch.15 para.42

s.129, amended: 2003 c.44 Sch.37 Part 9

s.129, disapplied: 2003 c.44 Sch.25 para.80

s.134, amended: 2002 c.17 s.19, SI 2002/2469 Sch.1 para.10, SI 2004/1823 Art.9

s.134, applied: SI 2003/2042 Reg.2

s.134, referred to: SI 2003/2042 Reg.2

s.135, see *Ward v Commissioner of Police of the Metropolis* [2003] EWCA Civ 1152, [2003] 1 W.L.R. 2413 (CA), Latham, L.J.

s.139, amended: SI 2002/2469 Sch.1 para.10, 2003 c.43 Sch.4 para.56

s.140, amended: 2002 c.17 Sch.2 para.48

s.142, applied: SI 2004/291 Sch.4, SI 2004/478 Sch.4, SI 2004/627 Sch.2, SSI 2004/115 Sch.3

s.145, amended: 2002 c.17 Sch.2 para.49, SI 2002/2469 Sch.1 para.10, 2003 c.43 Sch.4 para.57

s.149, repealed (in part): 2004 c.14 Sch.1 Part 17

Sch.3, amended: 2004 c.14 Sch.1 Part 17

Sch.4 para.6, repealed: 2002 c.9 Sch.13

Sch.4 para.9, repealed: 2004 c.14 Sch.1 Part 11

Sch.4 para.15, repealed: 2003 c.42 Sch.7

Sch.4 para.19, repealed: 2004 c.14 Sch.1 Part 17

Sch.4 para.30, repealed: 2004 c.14 Sch.1 Part 17

Sch.4 para.33, repealed: 2004 c.14 Sch.1 Part 17

Sch.4 para.36, repealed: 2004 c.14 Sch.1 Part 17

Sch.4 para.37, repealed: 2003 c.44 Sch.37 Part 10

Sch.4 para.45, repealed: 2002 c.38 Sch.5

Sch.4 para.52, repealed: 2004 c.14 Sch.1 Part 17

Sch.4 para.53, repealed: 2004 c.14 Sch.1 Part 17

Sch.4 para.54, repealed: 2004 c.14 Sch.1 Part 17

Sch.5 para.4, repealed: 2004 c.14 Sch.1 Part 17

Sch.5 para.5, repealed: 2004 c.14 Sch.1 Part 17

Sch.5 para.7, repealed: 2004 c.14 Sch.1 Part 17

Sch.5 para.8, repealed: 2004 c.14 Sch.1 Part 17

Sch.5 para.9, repealed (in part): 2004 c.14 Sch.1 Part 17

Sch.5 para.10, repealed: 2004 c.14 Sch.1 Part 17

Sch.5 para.11, repealed: 2004 c.14 Sch.1 Part 17

Sch.5 para.12, repealed: 2004 c.14 Sch.1 Part 17

1983–cont.

20. Mental Health Act 1983–cont.

Sch.5 para.13, repealed: 2004 c.14 Sch.1 Part 17

Sch.5 para.14, repealed: 2004 c.14 Sch.1 Part 17

Sch.5 para.18, repealed: 2004 c.14 Sch.1 Part 17

Sch.5 para.19, repealed: 2004 c.14 Sch.1 Part 17

Sch.5 para.21, substituted: 2004 c.28 Sch.10 para.23

Sch.5 para.22, repealed: 2004 c.14 Sch.1 Part 17

Sch.5 para.26, repealed: 2004 c.14 Sch.1 Part 17

Sch.5 para.37, amended: 2004 c.28 Sch.10 para.23

24. Licensing (Occasional Permissions) Act 1983

applied: 2003 c.17 Sch.4 para.2

repealed: 2003 c.17 Sch.7

29. Miscellaneous Financial Provisions Act 1983

s.4, repealed (in part): 2002 c.1 Sch.4

Sch.2, amended: SSI 2002/263 Sch.1

30. Diseases of Fish Act 1983

s.7, amended: SI 2002/794 Sch.1 para.21

s.7, enabling: SSI 2002/193, SSI 2002/220

32. Marriage Act 1983

applied: SR 2002/242 Art.3

s.3, amended: SR 2002/242 Sch.1

s.3, applied: SR 2002/242 Art.3

s.3, repealed: SI 2003/413 Sch.1

s.4, amended: SR 2002/242 Sch.1

s.4, repealed: SI 2003/413 Sch.1

s.5, repealed: SI 2003/413 Sch.1

s.5, substituted: SR 2002/242 Sch.1

s.6, repealed: SI 2003/413 Sch.1

s.7, repealed: SI 2003/413 Sch.1

s.8, repealed: SI 2003/413 Sch.1

s.9, applied: SR 2002/242

s.9, repealed: SI 2003/413 Sch.1

s.10, repealed: SI 2003/413 Sch.1

s.11, repealed: SI 2003/413 Sch.1

s.12, repealed (in part): SI 2003/413 Sch.1

34. Mobile Homes Act 1983

see *Howard v Charlton* [2002] EWCA Civ 1086, [2003] 1 P. & C.R. 21 (CA), Carnwath, L.J.; see *R. (on the application of Smith) v Barking and Dagenham LBC* [2002] EWHC 2400, [2002] 48 E.G.C.S. 141 (QBD (Admin Ct)), Burton, J.

disapplied: 2004 c.34 s.270

s.1, substituted: 2004 c.34 s.206

s.2, amended: 2004 c.34 s.206, Sch.15 para.9

s.2A, added: 2004 c.34 s.208

s.2A, applied: 2004 c.34 s.208

s.3, amended: 2004 c.33 Sch.27 para.87

1983–cont.

34. Mobile Homes Act 1983–*cont.*
s.5, see *Somerset CC v Isaacs* [2002] EWHC
1014, [2002] E.H.L.R. 18 (QBD (Admin
Ct)), Stanley Burnton, J.
s.5, amended: 2004 c.33 Sch.27 para.88,
2004 c.34 s.206
s.5, varied: 2004 c.33 Sch.21 para.15
Sch.1 Part I para.6, amended: 2004 c.34
s.207, Sch.16
Sch.1 Part I para.8, amended: 2004 c.34
s.207
Sch.1 Part I para.9, substituted: 2004 c.34
s.207
Sch.1 Part III para.1, added: 2004 c.34 s.207
Sch.1 Part III para.2, added: 2004 c.34 s.207

35. Litter Act 1983
s.5, applied: SI 2004/1777 Art.25, SI 2004/
1778 Art.25

**40. Education (Fees and Awards) Act
1983**
s.1, applied: 2004 c.8 s.29
s.1, repealed (in part): 2002 c.32 Sch.21
para.5, Sch.22 Part 3
s.1, enabling: SI 2003/3280, SSI 2004/469
s.2, enabling: SI 2003/3280, SSI 2004/469

**41. Health and Social Services and Social
Security Adjudications Act 1983**
s.10, repealed: SI 2002/797 Art.2
s.14, repealed (in part): 2003 c.43 Sch.14 Part
4
s.15, repealed (in part): 2003 c.43 Sch.14 Part
4
s.17, amended: 2003 c.5 s.17
s.23, amended: 2003 asp 9 Sch.14 para.9
s.27, repealed: 2004 c.14 Sch.1 Part 5
s.33, repealed (in part): 2004 c.14 Sch.1 Part 5
Sch.2 para.29, repealed: 2002 c.38 Sch.5
Sch.2 para.30, repealed: 2002 c.38 Sch.5
Sch.2 para.31, repealed: 2002 c.38 Sch.5
Sch.2 para.32, repealed: 2002 c.38 Sch.5
Sch.2 para.33, repealed: 2002 c.38 Sch.5
Sch.2 para.35, repealed: 2002 c.38 Sch.5
Sch.2 para.36, repealed: 2002 c.38 Sch.5
Sch.3 Part I para.1, repealed: SI 2002/797
Art.2
Sch.3 Part I para.2, repealed: SI 2002/797
Art.2
Sch.3 Part I para.3, repealed: SI 2002/797
Art.2
Sch.3 Part I para.4, repealed: SI 2002/797
Art.2
Sch.3 Part I para.5, repealed: SI 2002/797
Art.2
Sch.3 Part I para.6, repealed: SI 2002/797
Art.2
Sch.3 Part I para.7, repealed: SI 2002/797
Art.2
Sch.3 Part I para.8, repealed: SI 2002/797
Art.2
Sch.3 Part I para.9, repealed: SI 2002/797
Art.2

1983–cont.

**41. Health and Social Services and Social
Security Adjudications Act 1983**–*cont.*
Sch.3 Part II para.10, repealed: SI 2002/797
Art.2
Sch.3 Part II para.11, repealed: SI 2002/797
Art.2
Sch.3 Part II para.12, repealed: SI 2002/797
Art.2
Sch.3 Part II para.13, repealed: SI 2002/797
Art.2
Sch.3 Part II para.14, repealed: SI 2002/797
Art.2
Sch.3 Part II para.15, repealed: SI 2002/797
Art.2
Sch.3 Part II para.16, repealed: SI 2002/797
Art.2
Sch.3 Part II para.17, repealed: SI 2002/797
Art.2
Sch.3 Part II para.18, repealed: SI 2002/797
Art.2
Sch.3 Part II para.19, repealed: SI 2002/797
Art.2
Sch.3 Part II para.20, repealed: SI 2002/797
Art.2
Sch.3 Part II para.21, repealed: SI 2002/797
Art.2
Sch.3 Part II para.22, repealed: SI 2002/797
Art.2
Sch.3 Part II para.23, repealed: SI 2002/797
Art.2
Sch.3 Part II para.24, repealed: SI 2002/797
Art.2
Sch.3 Part II para.25, repealed: SI 2002/797
Art.2
Sch.3 Part II para.26, repealed: SI 2002/797
Art.2
Sch.3 Part II para.27, repealed: SI 2002/797
Art.2
Sch.3 Part II para.28, repealed: SI 2002/797
Art.2
Sch.6 para.2, repealed (in part): 2003 c.43
Sch.14 Part 4
Sch.9 Part I para.19, repealed: 2002 c.38
Sch.5

44. National Audit Act 1983
applied: 2002 c.40 Sch.15
referred to: 2003 c.43 Sch.4 para.58
Part II, applied: SI 2002/1889 Art.2
s.6, amended: 2003 c.43 Sch.4 para.59
s.7, applied: 2003 c.4 Sch.2 para.25, Sch.2
para.26
s.10, substituted: 2004 c.14 Sch.1 Part 9
s.11, substituted: 2004 c.14 Sch.1 Part 9
s.15, amended: 2004 c.14 Sch.1 Part 9
s.15, repealed (in part): 2004 c.14 Sch.1 Part 9
Sch.4 Part I, amended: SSI 2002/263 Sch.1

**45. County Courts (Penalties for
Contempt) Act 1983**
s.2, repealed (in part): 2004 c.14 Sch.1 Part 1

47. National Heritage Act 1983
s.24, amended: SI 2002/794 Sch.1 para.22

1983–cont.

47. National Heritage Act 1983–*cont.*

s.25, amended: SI 2002/794 Sch.1 para.23

s.29, amended: SI 2002/794 Sch.1 para.24

s.32, referred to: 2002 c.14 s.3

s.33, amended: 2002 c.14 s.1, s.4, s.7

s.33, applied: SI 2002/2427, SI 2002/2427 Art.3, Art.4

s.33, enabling: SI 2002/2427

s.33A, added: 2002 c.14 s.4

s.33B, added: 2002 c.14 s.4

s.33C, added: 2002 c.14 s.6

s.34, amended: 2002 c.14 s.2

s.34, applied: 2002 c.14 s.3

s.35, amended: 2002 c.14 s.5

s.39, repealed: 2004 c.14 Sch.1 Part 5

Sch.1 Part IV para.33, amended: SI 2002/794 Sch.1 para.25

Sch.1 Part IV para.34, amended: SI 2002/794 Sch.1 para.25

Sch.1 Part IV para.37, amended: SI 2002/794 Sch.1 para.25

Sch.1 Part IV para.39, amended: SI 2002/794 Sch.1 para.25

Sch.1 Part IV para.40, amended: SI 2002/794 Sch.1 para.25

Sch.3 para.2, varied: 2002 c.14 s.3

Sch.3 para.12, amended: SI 2003/1326 Art.14

Sch.3 para.13, amended: SI 2003/1326 Art.14

49. Finance (No.2) Act 1983

s.15, amended: 2003 c.14 Sch.20 para.3

53. Car Tax Act 1983

repealed: 2004 c.14 Sch.1 Part 9

Sch.1 para.3, amended: 2002 asp 17 Sch.3 para.14

Sch.1 para.3, enabling: SSI 2002/560

54. Medical Act 1983

applied: SI 2002/2376 Reg.4, SI 2003/1250 Art.7, Art.21, Sch.2 para.1, SI 2004/2610 Art.1, SSI 2003/64 Reg.4

referred to: 2003 c.43 Sch.11 para.47, SSI 2004/114 Reg.4

Part V, applied: SI 2004/215 Sch.1

s.1, amended: SI 2002/3135 Art.3, Art.5

s.1, applied: SI 2003/2644 Reg.6

s.1, referred to: SI 2004/585 Reg.24, SI 2004/1020 Reg.24

s.1, enabling: SI 2002/3136

s.2, amended: SI 2002/3135 Art.9

s.2, applied: SI 2003/1250 Art.8, Sch.2 para.1, Sch.8 para.23

s.2, repealed (in part): SI 2002/3135 Art.9

s.3, amended: SI 2003/3148 Reg.9, SI 2004/1947 Reg.3

s.3, applied: 2002 asp 15 s.1, SI 2003/835 Reg.9, SI 2003/1250 Sch.6 para.1, SI 2004/2152 Reg.9, SI 2004/2607 Sch.1

s.4, repealed (in part): SI 2004/1947 Reg.3

s.5, amended: SI 2003/3148 Reg.9, SI 2004/1947 Reg.3

1983–cont.

54. Medical Act 1983–*cont.*

s.10, amended: SI 2002/3135 Art.15

s.11, amended: 2003 c.43 Sch.11 para.48, Sch.14 Part 4, SI 2004/957 Sch.1 para.4

s.11, applied: SI 2003/1250 Art.10, SI 2004/585 Reg.22, SI 2004/1020 Reg.22

s.11, referred to: SI 2004/865 Art.111

s.11, varied: SI 2004/865 Art.111, SI 2004/1016 Art.87, SSI 2004/163 Art.98

s.12, amended: 2003 c.43 Sch.11 para.49, SI 2004/957 Sch.1 para.4

s.12, referred to: SI 2004/865 Art.111

s.12, varied: SI 2004/865 Art.111, SI 2004/1016 Art.87, SSI 2004/163 Art.98

s.15, applied: SI 2003/1250 Art.10, Sch.8 para.22, SI 2004/2644 Reg.3, SI 2004/291 Sch.6 para.53, SI 2004/478 Sch.6 para.52, SI 2004/585 Reg.22, SI 2004/627 Sch.5 para.53, Sch.5 para.64, SI 2004/1020 Reg.22, SSI 2004/114 Reg.3, SSI 2004/116 Sch.1 para.17

s.15A, applied: SI 2003/1250 Art.10, Sch.8 para.22, SI 2004/291 Sch.6 para.53, SI 2004/478 Sch.6 para.52, SI 2004/585 Reg.22, SI 2004/627 Sch.5 para.53, Sch.5 para.64, SI 2004/1020 Reg.22, SSI 2004/114 Reg.3, SSI 2004/115 Sch.5 para.46, SSI 2004/116 Sch.1 para.17

s.16, amended: SI 2002/3135 Art.9

s.16, applied: SI 2003/1341 Sch.1, SI 2003/1342 Sch.1

s.17, amended: SI 2003/3148 Reg.9, SI 2004/1947 Reg.3

s.18, applied: SI 2004/2607 Sch.1

s.19, applied: 2002 asp 15 s.1, SI 2002/3135 Sch.2 para.2, Sch.2 para.3, Sch.2 para.5, Sch.2 para.16, Sch.2 para.17, Sch.2 para.18

s.19, substituted: SI 2002/3135 Art.6

s.20, applied: SI 2002/3135 Sch.2 para.2

s.20, repealed: SI 2002/3135 Art.6

s.21, amended: SI 2002/3135 Art.6

s.21, applied: SI 2002/3135 Sch.2 para.2, Sch.2 para.3, Sch.2 para.5, Sch.2 para.16, Sch.2 para.17, Sch.2 para.18, SI 2003/1250 Art.10, Sch.8 para.22, SI 2003/2644 Reg.3, SI 2004/291 Sch.6 para.53, SI 2004/478 Sch.6 para.52, SI 2004/585 Reg.22, SI 2004/627 Sch.5 para.53, Sch.5 para.64, SI 2004/1020 Reg.22, SSI 2004/114 Reg.3, SSI 2004/115 Sch.5 para.46, SSI 2004/116 Sch.1 para.17

s.21A, added: SI 2002/3135 Art.6

s.21A, amended: SI 2003/1250 Sch.9 para.5

s.22, amended: SI 2002/3135 Art.6

s.22, applied: 2002 asp 15 s.1, SI 2002/3135 Sch.2 para.16, Sch.2 para.17, Sch.2 para.18

s.24, amended: SI 2002/3135 Art.6

s.25, amended: SI 2002/3135 Art.6

s.26, amended: SI 2002/3135 Art.6

s.26, applied: SI 2003/1341 Sch.1, SI 2003/1342 Sch.1

1983–cont.

54. Medical Act 1983–*cont.*

s.26, repealed (in part): SI 2002/3135 Art.6

s.27, amended: SI 2002/3135 Art.6

s.28, amended: SI 2002/3135 Sch.2 para.3

s.28, applied: SI 2003/1343, SI 2003/1343 Sch.1

s.28, repealed: SI 2002/3135 Art.6

s.28, enabling: SI 2003/1343

s.29, amended: SI 2002/3135 Sch.2 para.3

s.29, applied: SI 2002/3135 Sch.2 para.3

s.29, repealed (in part): SI 2002/3135 Art.6, Sch.2 para.3

s.29A, added: SI 2002/3135 Art.10

s.29A, applied: SI 2002/3135 Sch.2 para.38

s.29B, added: SI 2002/3135 Art.10

s.29C, added: SI 2002/3135 Art.10

s.29D, added: SI 2002/3135 Art.10

s.29E, added: SI 2002/3135 Art.10

s.29F, added: SI 2002/3135 Art.10

s.29G, added: SI 2002/3135 Art.10

s.29H, added: SI 2002/3135 Art.10

s.29J, added: SI 2002/3135 Art.10

s.30, amended: SI 2002/3135 Art.7, Art.12

s.30, applied: SI 2003/1342 Sch.1, SI 2004/ 2612 Sch.1

s.30, repealed (in part): SI 2002/3135 Art.7

s.30, varied: SI 2002/3135 Sch.2 para.3

s.31, amended: SI 2002/3135 Art.7, Art.12

s.31, applied: SI 2003/1342, SI 2003/1342 Sch.1, SI 2004/2612, SI 2004/2612 Sch.1

s.31, repealed (in part): SI 2002/3135 Art.7

s.31, enabling: SI 2003/1342, SI 2004/2612

s.31A, amended: SI 2002/3135 Art.12

s.31A, applied: SI 2003/1341, SI 2003/1341 Sch.1, SI 2004/2609

s.31A, enabling: SI 2003/1341, SI 2004/ 2609

s.32, applied: SI 2003/1074, SI 2003/1074 Sch.1, SI 2003/1342, SI 2003/1342 Sch.1, SI 2004/2612 Sch.1

s.32, enabling: SI 2003/1074, SI 2003/1342

s.34, amended: SI 2002/3135 Art.7

s.34, substituted: SI 2002/3135 Art.7

s.34A, added: SI 2002/3135 Art.7

s.34A, amended: SI 2002/3135 Art.7

s.34B, added: SI 2002/3135 Art.8

s.35, substituted: SI 2002/3135 Art.13

s.35A, applied: SI 2004/2608 Sch.1

s.35A, substituted: SI 2002/3135 Art.13

s.35B, applied: SI 2004/2608 Sch.1

s.35B, substituted: SI 2002/3135 Art.13

s.35C, applied: SI 2002/3135 Sch.2 para.6, Sch.2 para.8, Sch.2 para.9, SI 2004/2608 Sch.1

s.35C, referred to: SI 2002/3135 Sch.2 para.6, Sch.2 para.7, Sch.2 para.8, SI 2004/1731 Art.2, SI 2004/2608 Sch.1

s.35C, substituted: SI 2002/3135 Art.13

s.35CC, amended: SI 2002/3135 Art.13

s.35CC, substituted: SI 2002/3135 Art.13

1983–cont.

54. Medical Act 1983–*cont.*

s.35CC, enabling: SI 2004/2608

s.35D, applied: SI 2002/3135 Sch.2 para.15, SI 2004/215 Sch.1, SI 2004/433 Art.3, SI 2004/477 Art.3, SI 2004/585 Reg.24, Reg.26, SI 2004/1020 Reg.24, Reg.26, SI 2004/2608 Sch.1, SSI 2004/114 Reg.7, Reg.9, SSI 2004/142 Art.3, Art.4

s.35D, referred to: SI 2002/3135 Sch.2 para.10

s.35D, substituted: SI 2002/3135 Art.13

s.35E, substituted: SI 2002/3135 Art.13

s.36, see *Bhadra v General Medical Council* [2002] UKPC 55, [2003] 1 W.L.R. 162 (PC (UK)), Lord Hope of Craighead; see *Otote v General Medical Council* [2003] UKPC 71, (2004) 78 B.M.L.R. 162 (PC (UK)), Lord Walker of Gestingthorpe

s.36, applied: 2002 c.17 s.29, SI 2002/1882 Reg.6, Reg.10, SI 2002/3135 Sch.2 para.10, Sch.2 para.11, Sch.2 para.12, Sch.2 para.13, Sch.2 para.36, SI 2003/ 2644 Reg.6, Reg.10, SI 2004/215 Sch.1, SI 2004/585 Reg.24, Reg.26, SI 2004/ 1020 Reg.24, Reg.26, SSI 2003/64 Reg.7, SSI 2004/114 Reg.7, Reg.9

s.36, substituted: SI 2002/3135 Art.13

s.36A, see *Chaudhury v General Medical Council* [2002] UKPC 41, [2004] Lloyd's Rep. Med. 251 (PC (UK)), Lord Hutton

s.36A, applied: SI 2002/1882 Reg.6, SI 2002/3135 Sch.2 para.10, Sch.2 para.11, Sch.2 para.12, Sch.2 para.13, Sch.2 para.36, SI 2003/2644 Reg.6, SI 2004/ 215 Sch.1, SI 2004/433 Art.3, SI 2004/ 477 Art.3, SI 2004/585 Reg.24, SI 2004/ 1020 Reg.24, SSI 2004/142 Art.3, Art.4

s.36A, substituted: SI 2002/3135 Art.13

s.37, see *Brocklebank v General Medical Council* [2003] UKPC 57, (2004) 79 B.M.L.R. 122 (PC (UK)), Lord Hoffmann; see *Crabbie v General Medical Council* [2002] UKPC 45, [2002] 1 W.L.R. 3104 (PC (UK)), Lord Scott of Foscote

s.37, applied: SI 2002/1882 Reg.6, SI 2002/ 3135 Sch.2 para.10, Sch.2 para.11, Sch.2 para.12, Sch.2 para.13, Sch.2 para.36, SI 2003/2644 Reg.6, Reg.10, SI 2004/215 Sch.1, SI 2004/433 Art.3, SI 2004/477 Art.3, SI 2004/585 Reg.24, Reg.26, SI 2004/1020 Reg.24, Reg.26, SSI 2004/ 114 Reg.10, SSI 2004/142 Art.3, Art.4

s.37, substituted: SI 2002/3135 Art.13

s.38, applied: SI 2002/1882 Reg.10, SI 2002/ 3135 Sch.2 para.10, Sch.2 para.11, Sch.2 para.13, Sch.2 para.14, Sch.2 para.33, Sch.2 para.36, SI 2003/2644 Reg.10, SI 2004/215 Sch.1, SI 2004/433 Art.3, SI 2004/477 Art.3, SI 2004/585 Reg.26, SI 2004/1020 Reg.26, SI 2004/2608 Sch.1, SSI 2003/64 Reg.7, SSI 2004/114 Reg.7, Reg.9, SSI 2004/142 Art.3, Art.4

CAP.

1983–cont.

54. Medical Act 1983–*cont.*

s.38, disapplied: SI 2004/215 Sch.1

s.38, substituted: SI 2002/3135 Art.13

s.39, applied: SI 2002/3135 Sch.2 para.12, Sch.2 para.36

s.39, substituted: SI 2002/3135 Art.13

s.40, see *Bhadra v General Medical Council* [2002] UKPC 55, [2003] 1 W.L.R. 162 (PC (UK)), Lord Hope of Craighead; see *Chaudhury v General Medical Council* [2002] UKPC 41, [2004] Lloyd's Rep. Med. 251 (PC (UK)), Lord Hutton; see *Hall v General Medical Council (No.1)* [2001] UKPC 46, (2002) 65 B.M.L.R. 53 (PC (UK)), Sir Anthony Evans; see *Seyedi v General Medical Council* [2003] UKPC 67, (2004) 78 B.M.L.R. 173 (Privy Council (United Kingdom)), Lord Hope of Craighead; see *Stefan v General Medical Council (No.3)* [2002] UKPC 10, Times, March 29, 2002 (PC (UK)), Lord Steyn

s.40, amended: 2002 c.17 s.30, Sch.8 para.14, SI 2003/1250 Art.30

s.40, applied: SI 2002/3135 Sch.2 para.12, Sch.2 para.13, SI 2003/833 Art.4

s.40, repealed (in part): 2002 c.17 Sch.9 Part 2

s.40, substituted: SI 2002/3135 Art.13

s.41, see *Gosai v General Medical Council* [2003] UKPC 31, (2004) 75 B.M.L.R. 52 (PC (UK)), Sir Philip Otton

s.41, applied: SI 2002/3135 Sch.2 para.12, Sch.2 para.16, Sch.2 para.17, Sch.2 para.18, Sch.2 para.19, Sch.2 para.36, SI 2004/2608 Sch.1

s.41, referred to: SI 2002/3135 Sch.2 para.17, Sch.2 para.19

s.41, substituted: SI 2002/3135 Art.13

s.41A, see *General Medical Council v Pembrey* [2002] EWHC 1602, [2002] Lloyd's Rep. Med. 434 (QBD (Admin Ct)), Crane, J.; see *R. (on the application of George) v General Medical Council* [2003] EWHC 1124, [2004] Lloyd's Rep. Med. 33 (QBD (Admin Ct)), Collins, J.

s.41A, amended: SI 2002/3135 Art.13

s.41A, applied: SI 2002/1882 Reg.10, SI 2002/3135 Sch.2 para.20, Sch.2 para.21, Sch.2 para.22, Sch.2 para.23, Sch.2 para.24, SI 2003/2644 Reg.6, Reg.10, SI 2004/215 Sch.1, SI 2004/291 Sch.6 para.53, SI 2004/433 Art.3, SI 2004/477 Art.3, SI 2004/478 Sch.6 para.52, SI 2004/585 Reg.24, Reg.26, SI 2004/627 Sch.5 para.53, SI 2004/1020 Reg.24, Reg.26, SI 2004/2608 Sch.1, SSI 2004/114 Reg.10, SSI 2004/115 Sch.5 para.46, SSI 2004/116 Sch.1 para.17, SSI 2004/142 Art.3, Art.4

s.41A, disapplied: SI 2004/215 Sch.1

CAP.

1983–cont.

54. Medical Act 1983–*cont.*

s.41A, referred to: SI 2002/3135 Sch.2 para.20, Sch.2 para.21, Sch.2 para.22, Sch.2 para.23

s.41A, substituted: SI 2002/3135 Art.13

s.41B, applied: SI 2002/3135 Sch.2 para.23, Sch.2 para.24, SI 2004/215 Sch.1

s.41B, disapplied: SI 2004/215 Sch.1

s.41B, referred to: SI 2002/3135 Sch.2 para.23

s.41B, substituted: SI 2002/3135 Art.13

s.41C, substituted: SI 2002/3135 Art.13

s.42, applied: SI 2002/1882 Reg.6, SI 2002/3135 Sch.2 para.7, Sch.2 para.9

s.42, substituted: SI 2002/3135 Art.13

s.43, referred to: SI 2004/1731 Art.2

s.43, substituted: SI 2002/3135 Art.13

s.43, enabling: SI 2004/2625

s.44, applied: SI 2002/3135 Sch.2 para.12, Sch.2 para.25, Sch.2 para.36, SI 2004/2607 Sch.1, SI 2004/2610 Art.2, Art.3

s.44, referred to: SI 2002/3135 Sch.2 para.25

s.44, substituted: SI 2002/3135 Art.13

s.44A, applied: SI 2004/2607 Sch.1

s.44A, referred to: SI 2002/3135 Sch.2 para.37

s.44A, substituted: SI 2002/3135 Art.13

s.45, applied: SI 2002/3135 Sch.2 para.12, Sch.2 para.26, Sch.2 para.28, Sch.2 para.29, Sch.2 para.30, Sch.2 para.36

s.45, referred to: SI 2002/3135 Sch.2 para.26, Sch.2 para.27

s.45, substituted: SI 2002/3135 Art.13

s.45, varied: SI 2002/3135 Sch.2 para.28

s.46, amended: SI 2002/3135 Art.12

s.46, applied: SI 2002/3135 Sch.2 para.31

s.46, varied: SI 2002/3135 Sch.2 para.31

s.47, see *R. (on the application of George) v General Medical Council* [2003] EWHC 1124, [2004] Lloyd's Rep. Med. 33 (QBD (Admin Ct)), Collins, J.

s.47, amended: SI 2002/3135 Art.12, Art.15

s.48, amended: SI 2002/3135 Art.12

s.48, disapplied: SI 2002/3135 Sch.2 para.32

s.49A, added: SI 2002/3135 Art.12

s.50, amended: SI 2002/3135 Art.15

s.52A, added: SI 2002/3135 Art.15

s.53, amended: SI 2002/3135 Art.15

s.53, applied: SI 2002/3135 Sch.2 para.33

s.55, amended: SI 2002/3135 Art.15

Sch.1 Part I para.1, amended: SI 2002/3135 Art.4

Sch.1 Part I para.2, amended: SI 2002/3135 Art.4

Sch.1 Part I para.3, amended: SI 2002/3135 Art.4

Sch.1 Part I para.3, enabling: SI 2002/3136

Sch.1 Part I para.4, amended: SI 2002/3135 Art.4, 2003 c.43 Sch.12 para.2

Sch.1 Part I para.4A, added: SI 2002/3135 Art.4

1983–cont.

54. Medical Act 1983–*cont.*

Sch.1 Part I para.4A, amended: SI 2002/3135 Art.4

Sch.1 Part I para.4A, applied: SI 2004/215, SI 2004/215 Sch.1, SI 2004/2608

Sch.1 Part I para.4A, enabling: SI 2004/215, SI 2004/2608

Sch.1 Part I para.4B, added: SI 2002/3135 Art.4

Sch.1 Part I para.4ZA, added: 2003 c.43 Sch.12 para.2

Sch.1 Part I para.5, enabling: SI 2002/3136

Sch.1 Part I para.7, substituted: SI 2002/3135 Art.4

Sch.1 Part I para.7, enabling: SI 2002/3136

Sch.1 Part II para.9A, added: SI 2002/3135 Art.15

Sch.1 Part II para.9B, added: SI 2002/3135 Art.15

Sch.1 Part II para.11, amended: SI 2002/3135 Art.9

Sch.1 Part II para.13, substituted: SI 2002/3135 Art.4

Sch.1 Part II para.13, enabling: SI 2002/3136

Sch.1 Part II para.16, amended: SI 2002/3135 Art.15

Sch.1 Part II para.17, substituted: SI 2002/3135 Art.15

Sch.1 Part III, applied: SI 2004/433 Art.3, SI 2004/477 Art.3, SSI 2004/142 Art.3, Art.4

Sch.1 Part III para.19, substituted: SI 2002/3135 Art.5

Sch.1 Part III para.19A, applied: SI 2002/2572, SI 2003/1344 Sch.1

Sch.1 Part III para.19A, substituted: SI 2002/3135 Art.5

Sch.1 Part III para.19A, enabling: SI 2002/2572, SI 2003/1344, SI 2004/2611

Sch.1 Part III para.19B, applied: SI 2002/2572, SI 2003/1344 Sch.1

Sch.1 Part III para.19B, substituted: SI 2002/3135 Art.5

Sch.1 Part III para.19B, enabling: SI 2004/2611

Sch.1 Part III para.19C, applied: SI 2002/2572, SI 2003/1344 Sch.1

Sch.1 Part III para.19C, substituted: SI 2002/3135 Art.5

Sch.1 Part III para.19C, enabling: SI 2004/2611

Sch.1 Part III para.19D, applied: SI 2002/2572, SI 2003/1344 Sch.1

Sch.1 Part III para.19D, substituted: SI 2002/3135 Art.5

Sch.1 Part III para.19D, enabling: SI 2004/2611

Sch.1 Part III para.19E, applied: SI 2002/2572, SI 2003/1344 Sch.1

Sch.1 Part III para.19E, substituted: SI 2002/3135 Art.5

Sch.1 Part III para.19E, enabling: SI 2004/2611

1983–cont.

54. Medical Act 1983–*cont.*

Sch.1 Part III para.20, applied: SI 2002/2572, SI 2003/1344 Sch.1

Sch.1 Part III para.20, substituted: SI 2002/3135 Art.5

Sch.1 Part III para.20, enabling: SI 2002/2572, SI 2003/1344

Sch.1 Part III para.21, applied: SI 2002/2572, SI 2003/1344 Sch.1

Sch.1 Part III para.21, substituted: SI 2002/3135 Art.5

Sch.1 Part III para.21, enabling: SI 2002/2572, SI 2003/1344

Sch.1 Part III para.21A, applied: SI 2002/2572, SI 2003/1344 Sch.1

Sch.1 Part III para.21A, substituted: SI 2002/3135 Art.5

Sch.1 Part III para.21A, enabling: SI 2002/2572, SI 2003/1344

Sch.1 Part III para.21B, applied: SI 2002/2572, SI 2003/1344 Sch.1

Sch.1 Part III para.21B, substituted: SI 2002/3135 Art.5

Sch.1 Part III para.21B, enabling: SI 2002/2572, SI 2003/1344

Sch.1 Part III para.22, applied: SI 2002/2572, SI 2003/1344 Sch.1

Sch.1 Part III para.22, substituted: SI 2002/3135 Art.5

Sch.1 Part III para.22, enabling: SI 2002/2572, SI 2003/1344

Sch.1 Part III para.23, substituted: SI 2002/3135 Art.5

Sch.1 Part III para.23, enabling: SI 2004/2611

Sch.1 Part III para.23A, substituted: SI 2002/3135 Art.5

Sch.1 Part III para.23B, substituted: SI 2002/3135 Art.5

Sch.1 Part III para.23B, enabling: SI 2004/2611

Sch.1 Part III para.24, applied: SI 2002/2572, SI 2003/1344, SI 2004/2611

Sch.1 Part III para.24, substituted: SI 2002/3135 Art.5

Sch.1 Part III para.25, amended: SI 2002/3135 Art.5

Sch.1 Part IV para.26, amended: SI 2002/3135 Art.15

Sch.1 Part IV para.29, substituted: SI 2002/3135 Art.15

Sch.2, substituted: SI 2003/3148 Sch.4 Part I

Sch.2, amended: SI 2004/1947 Reg.3

Sch.2, substituted: SI 2003/3148 Sch.4 Part I

Sch.2 para.1, substituted: SI 2003/3148 Sch.4 Part I

Sch.2 para.2, substituted: SI 2003/3148 Sch.4 Part I

Sch.2 para.3, substituted: SI 2003/3148 Sch.4 Part I

Sch.3A, applied: SI 2002/3135 Sch.2 para.3, SI 2003/1250 Art.18, Art.23

1983–cont.

54. Medical Act 1983–*cont.*

Sch.3 para.2, amended: SI 2002/3135 Art.9

Sch.3 para.2, repealed (in part): SI 2002/3135 Art.9

Sch.3 para.5, amended: SI 2002/3135 Art.9

Sch.3A para.1, added: SI 2002/3135 Art.8

Sch.3A para.2, added: SI 2002/3135 Art.8

Sch.3A para.3, added: SI 2002/3135 Art.8

Sch.3A para.4, added: SI 2002/3135 Art.8

Sch.3A para.4, applied: SI 2003/1250 Art.23

Sch.3A para.5, added: SI 2002/3135 Art.8

Sch.3A para.6, added: SI 2002/3135 Art.8

Sch.3A para.6, applied: SI 2003/1250 Art.18

Sch.3A para.7, added: SI 2002/3135 Art.8

Sch.3B para.1, added: SI 2002/3135 Art.11

Sch.3B para.2, added: SI 2002/3135 Art.11

Sch.3B para.3, added: SI 2002/3135 Art.11

Sch.3B para.4, added: SI 2002/3135 Art.11

Sch.3B para.5, added: SI 2002/3135 Art.11

Sch.3B para.6, added: SI 2002/3135 Art.11

Sch.3B para.7, added: SI 2002/3135 Art.11

Sch.3B para.8, added: SI 2002/3135 Art.11

Sch.4, applied: SI 2002/3135 Sch.2 para.7, Sch.2 para.10, Sch.2 para.11, Sch.2 para.13, Sch.2 para.17, Sch.2 para.20, Sch.2 para.21, Sch.2 para.22, Sch.2 para.23

Sch.4, referred to: SI 2004/2608 Sch.1

Sch.4 para.1, applied: SI 2002/2572, SI 2003/1343, SI 2003/1343 Sch.1, SI 2004/1731 Art.2, SI 2004/2607, SI 2004/2608

Sch.4 para.1, referred to: SI 2004/1731 Art.2

Sch.4 para.1, substituted: SI 2002/3135 Art.14

Sch.4 para.1, enabling: SI 2002/2572, SI 2003/1343, SI 2004/2607, SI 2004/2608

Sch.4 para.2, applied: SI 2004/2608 Sch.1

Sch.4 para.2, substituted: SI 2002/3135 Art.14

Sch.4 para.3, amended: 2002 c.17 s.30, Sch.9 Part 2

Sch.4 para.3, substituted: SI 2002/3135 Art.14

Sch.4 para.3A, substituted: SI 2002/3135 Art.14

Sch.4 para.4, substituted: SI 2002/3135 Art.14

Sch.4 para.5, applied: SI 2003/1343, SI 2003/1343 Sch.1

Sch.4 para.5, substituted: SI 2002/3135 Art.14

Sch.4 para.5, enabling: SI 2002/2572, SI 2003/1343

Sch.4 para.5A, applied: SI 2002/2572, SI 2002/3135 Sch.2 para.8, Sch.2 para.10, Sch.2 para.11, Sch.2 para.13, Sch.2 para.14, Sch.2 para.15, Sch.2 para.35, SI 2003/2644 Reg.6, SI 2004/215 Sch.1, SI 2004/433 Art.3, SI 2004/477 Art.3, SI 2004/585 Reg.24, Reg.26, SI 2004/1020

1983–cont.

54. Medical Act 1983–*cont.*

Sch.4 para.5A, applied:–*cont.*

Reg.24, Reg.26, SI 2004/1731 Art.2, SI 2004/2608, SI 2004/2608 Sch.1, SSI 2004/114 Reg.7, Reg.9, SSI 2004/142 Art.3, Art.4

Sch.4 para.5A, disapplied: SI 2004/215 Sch.1

Sch.4 para.5A, referred to: SI 2004/1731 Art.2

Sch.4 para.5A, substituted: SI 2002/3135 Art.14

Sch.4 para.5A, enabling: SI 2002/2572, SI 2004/2608

Sch.4 para.5B, substituted: SI 2002/3135 Art.14

Sch.4 para.6, applied: SI 2004/1731 Art.2

Sch.4 para.6, referred to: SI 2004/1731 Art.2

Sch.4 para.6, substituted: SI 2002/3135 Art.14

Sch.4 para.7, applied: SI 2004/1731 Art.2, SI 2004/2625 r.3

Sch.4 para.7, referred to: SI 2004/1731 Art.2

Sch.4 para.7, substituted: SI 2002/3135 Art.14

Sch.4 para.7, enabling: SI 2004/2625

Sch.4 para.8, applied: SI 2002/3135 Sch.2 para.37, SI 2003/1250 Sch.8 para.18, SI 2004/2608 Sch.1, SI 2004/2610 Art.2

Sch.4 para.8, substituted: SI 2002/3135 Art.14

Sch.4 para.9, substituted: SI 2002/3135 Art.14

Sch.4 para.10, see *Bhadra v General Medical Council* [2002] UKPC 55, [2003] 1 W.L.R. 162 (PC (UK)), Lord Hope of Craighead

Sch.4 para.10, amended: 2002 c.17 s.30, Sch.9 Part 2

Sch.4 para.10, repealed (in part): 2002 c.17 Sch.9 Part 2

Sch.4 para.10, substituted: SI 2002/3135 Art.14

Sch.4 para.11, substituted: SI 2002/3135 Art.14

Sch.4 para.12, substituted: SI 2002/3135 Art.14

Sch.4 para.13, substituted: SI 2002/3135 Art.14

Sch.4 para.14, substituted: SI 2002/3135 Art.14

Sch.5 para.16, repealed (in part): 2003 c.43 Sch.14 Part 4

Sch.6 para.11, amended: SI 2002/3135 Art.12, SI 2003/1250 Art.30

Sch.6 para.18, amended: 2002 c.17 Sch.9 Part 2

55. Value Added Tax Act 1983

applied: SSI 2002/301 Sch.2 para.6, SSI 2002/566 Sch.1 para.14, SSI 2002/567 Sch.1 para.16

CAP.

1983–cont.

55. Value Added Tax Act 1983–*cont.*

Sch.6 Group 2, see *Card Protection Plan Ltd v Customs and Excise Commissioners* [2001] UKHL 4, [2002] 1 A.C. 202 (HL), Lord Slynn of Hadley

56. OIL TAXATION ACT 1983

referred to: 2004 c.12 s.285

s.3, amended: 2004 c.12 Sch.37 para.2

s.3A, added: 2004 c.12 Sch.37 para.3

s.4, amended: 2004 c.12 Sch.37 para.4

s.6, amended: 2004 c.12 s.285

s.6A, added: 2004 c.12 s.285

s.6A, referred to: 2004 c.12 Sch.37 para.9

s.6B, added: 2004 c.12 s.285

s.7, amended: 2004 c.12 Sch.37 para.5

s.7A, added: 2004 c.12 Sch.37 para.5

Sch.1 Part I para.3, amended: 2004 c.12 Sch.37 para.6

Sch.1 Part II para.7, amended: 2004 c.12 Sch.37 para.7

Sch.1 Part II para.8, amended: 2004 c.12 Sch.37 para.8

Sch.2 para.12, amended: 2004 c.12 s.285

58. British Shipbuilders (Borrowing Powers) Act 1983

s.1, repealed (in part): 2004 c.14 Sch.1 Part 16

1984

xxi. County of Lancashire Act 1984

s.20, repealed: SI 2003/3030 Reg.2

xxvii. Greater London Council (General Powers) Act 1984

s.4, repealed (in part): 2003 c.17 Sch.7

s.15, amended: 2003 c.17 Sch.6 para.94

s.19, repealed: 2003 c.17 Sch.7

s.20, repealed: 2003 c.17 Sch.7

s.21, repealed: 2003 c.17 Sch.7

s.22, repealed: 2003 c.17 Sch.7

Sch.2, amended: SI 2002/254 Sch.4 para.3

Inheritance Act 1984

Part VI Chap.III, see *Lee v Inland Revenue Commissioners* [2003] S.T.C. (S.C.D.) 41 (Sp Comm), John F Avery Jones

xxx. Lochmaddy and East Loch Tarbert (Improvement of Piers &c.) Order Confirmation Act 1984

repealed: SSI 2002/410 Sch.2 Part I

s.4, referred to: SSI 2002/410 Sch.2 Part I

s.7, referred to: SSI 2002/410 Sch.2 Part I

s.8, referred to: SSI 2002/410 Sch.2 Part I

s.13, referred to: SSI 2002/410 Sch.2 Part I

s.14, referred to: SSI 2002/410 Sch.2 Part I

s.15, referred to: SSI 2002/410 Sch.2 Part I

s.16, referred to: SSI 2002/410 Sch.2 Part I

s.17, referred to: SSI 2002/410 Sch.2 Part I

s.20, referred to: SSI 2002/410 Sch.2 Part I

s.28, referred to: SSI 2002/410 Sch.2 Part I

s.29, referred to: SSI 2002/410 Sch.2 Part I

s.30, referred to: SSI 2002/410 Sch.2 Part I

s.33, referred to: SSI 2002/410 Sch.2 Part I

CAP.

1984–cont.

xxx. Lochmaddy and East Loch Tarbert (Improvement of Piers &c.) Order Confirmation Act 1984–*cont.*

s.34, referred to: SSI 2002/410 Sch.2 Part I

xxv. London Transport Act 1984

varied: SI 2003/1615 Sch.2 para.13

ii. Western Isles Islands Council (Kallin Pier, Harbour Jurisdiction) Order Confirmation Act 1984

repealed: SSI 2002/410 Sch.2 Part I

s.1, referred to: SSI 2002/410 Sch.2 Part I

s.2, referred to: SSI 2002/410 Sch.2 Part I

s.14, referred to: SSI 2002/410 Sch.2 Part I

3. Occupiers Liability Act 1984

s.1, see *Donoghue v Folkestone Properties Ltd* [2003] EWCA Civ 231, [2003] Q.B. 1008 (CA), Lord Phillips of Worth Matravers, M.R.; see *Tomlinson v Congleton BC* [2002] EWCA Civ 309, [2003] 2 W.L.R. 1120 (CA), Ward, L.J.; see *Tomlinson v Congleton BC* [2003] UKHL 47, [2004] 1 A.C. 46 (HL), Lord Hoffmann

7. Pensions Commutation Act 1984

s.1, repealed (in part): 2004 c.14 Sch.1 Part 5

8. Prevention of Terrorism (Temporary Provisions) Act 1984

see *Brennan v United Kingdom (39846/98)* (2002) 34 E.H.R.R. 18 (ECHR), J-P Costa (President)

12. Telecommunications Act 1984

applied: 2002 c.40 s.126, Sch.15, 2003 c.21 s.406, SI 2003/419 Art.63, SI 2003/1075 Sch.13 para.14, SSI 2002/410 Art.31

referred to: 2003 c.21 s.393, s.404, SI 2003/3196 Sch.1 para.1

Part II, repealed: 2003 c.21 Sch.19

Part VI, applied: 2002 c.11 s.6, 2003 c.21 Sch.1 para.1

s.1, repealed: 2003 c.21 Sch.19

s.2, repealed: 2003 c.21 Sch.19

s.3, see *R. (on the application of T-Mobile (UK) Ltd) v Competition Commission* [2003] EWHC 1566, [2003] Eu. L.R. 769 (QBD (Admin Ct)), Moses, J.

s.3, amended: 2002 c.40 Sch.25 para.13

s.3, referred to: SI 2003/33 Reg.3, SI 2003/330 Reg.4

s.3, repealed: 2003 c.21 Sch.19

s.3A, repealed: 2003 c.21 Sch.19

s.4, repealed: 2003 c.21 Sch.19

s.7, applied: SI 2002/399, SI 2002/400, SI 2002/1070, SI 2002/1071, SI 2002/1376, SI 2002/1560, SI 2002/1561, SI 2002/1562, SI 2002/1947, SI 2002/1948, SI 2002/1949, SI 2002/2657, SI 2002/2658, SI 2003/1900 Art.3

s.7, varied: 2003 c.21 Sch.18 para.3, Sch.18 para.4, Sch.18 para.9, Sch.18 para.11, Sch.18 para.12, Sch.18 para.14, Sch.18 para.16, Sch.18 para.17, Sch.18 para.18, Sch.18 para.22

1984–cont.

12. Telecommunications Act 1984–cont.

s.7A, applied: SI 2002/399, SI 2002/1070, SI 2002/1071

s.8, applied: SI 2002/399, SI 2002/1070, SI 2002/1071, SI 2002/1376, SI 2002/1560, SI 2002/1561, SI 2002/1562, SI 2002/1947, SI 2002/1948, SI 2002/1949, SI 2002/2657, SI 2002/2658

s.9, enabling: SI 2002/399, SI 2002/400, SI 2002/1070, SI 2002/1071, SI 2002/1376, SI 2002/1560, SI 2002/1561, SI 2002/1562, SI 2002/1947, SI 2002/1948, SI 2002/1949, SI 2002/2657, SI 2002/2658

s.13, applied: SI 2003/1397 Art.8

s.13, repealed (in part): 2002 c.40 Sch.26

s.13A, added: 2002 c.40 Sch.25 para.13

s.13B, added: 2002 c.40 Sch.25 para.13

s.13B, referred to: SI 2003/1371

s.13B, enabling: SI 2003/1371

s.14, amended: 2002 c.40 Sch.25 para.13

s.34, repealed: 2003 c.21 Sch.19

s.34, varied: 2003 c.21 Sch.18 para.19

s.35, repealed: 2003 c.21 Sch.19

s.35, varied: 2003 c.21 Sch.18 para.19

s.36, repealed: 2003 c.21 Sch.19

s.36, varied: 2003 c.21 Sch.18 para.19

s.37, repealed: 2003 c.21 Sch.19

s.37, varied: 2003 c.21 Sch.18 para.19

s.38, repealed: 2003 c.21 Sch.19

s.38, varied: 2003 c.21 Sch.18 para.19

s.39, repealed: 2003 c.21 Sch.19

s.39, varied: 2003 c.21 Sch.18 para.19

s.40, repealed: 2003 c.21 Sch.19

s.41, repealed: 2003 c.21 Sch.19

s.42, repealed: 2003 c.21 Sch.19

s.42A, see *R. v Stephens (Brian Andrew)* [2002] EWCA Crim 136, [2002] 2 Cr. App. R. (S.) 67 (CA (Crim Div)), Judge Fawcus

s.42A, repealed: 2003 c.21 Sch.19

s.43, see *Ford v Ritchie* 2002 S.C.C.R. 395 (HCJ Appeal), Lord Cameron of Lochbroom, Lord Hamilton, Lord MacLean

s.43, applied: SI 2002/1837 Sch.1 Part I

s.43, repealed: 2003 c.21 Sch.19

s.44, repealed: 2003 c.21 Sch.19

s.45, repealed: 2003 c.21 Sch.19

s.46, repealed: 2003 c.21 Sch.19

s.46A, repealed: 2003 c.21 Sch.19

s.46B, applied: SI 2003/330 Reg.11, SI 2004/2068 r.6

s.46B, repealed: 2003 c.21 Sch.19

s.46B, varied: 2003 c.21 Sch.18 para.23, SI 2003/33 Reg.6

s.47, amended: 2002 c.40 Sch.25 para.13

s.48, amended: 2002 c.40 Sch.25 para.13

s.50, amended: 2002 c.40 Sch.9 para.16, Sch.25 para.13, Sch.26

s.50, repealed (in part): 2002 c.40 Sch.26, 2003 c.21 Sch.19

s.51, repealed: 2003 c.21 Sch.19

1984–cont.

12. Telecommunications Act 1984–cont.

s.52, amended: SI 2003/435 Sch.4 para.7

s.52, repealed: 2003 c.21 Sch.19

s.53, applied: SI 2003/330 Reg.10

s.53, repealed: 2003 c.21 Sch.19

s.54, applied: 2003 c.21 s.31

s.54, repealed: 2003 c.21 Sch.19

s.55, repealed: 2003 c.21 Sch.19

s.56, varied: SI 2003/3196 Art.3

s.57, varied: SI 2003/3196 Art.3

s.58, varied: SI 2003/3196 Art.3

s.59, varied: SI 2003/3196 Art.3

s.60, repealed: 2003 c.21 Sch.19

s.61, repealed (in part): 2003 c.21 Sch.19

s.62, repealed: 2003 c.21 Sch.19

s.63, repealed (in part): 2003 c.21 Sch.19

s.64, repealed: 2003 c.21 Sch.19

s.65, repealed: 2003 c.21 Sch.19

s.66, repealed: 2003 c.21 Sch.19

s.67, repealed: 2003 c.21 Sch.19

s.68, amended: 2003 c.21 s.398

s.69, repealed: 2003 c.21 Sch.19

s.70, repealed: 2003 c.21 Sch.19

s.71, repealed: 2003 c.21 Sch.19

s.72, amended: 2003 c.21 Sch.19

s.72, repealed (in part): 2003 c.21 Sch.19

s.73, repealed: 2003 c.21 Sch.19

s.74, varied: SI 2003/3196 Sch.1 para.3

s.75, varied: SI 2003/3196 Sch.1 para.4

s.76, varied: SI 2003/3196 Sch.1 para.5

s.77, varied: SI 2003/3196 Sch.1 para.5

s.79, amended: 2003 c.21 s.179, Sch.17 para.64, Sch.17 para.65

s.79, applied: 2003 c.21 s.182, Sch.7 para.1

s.79, varied: SI 2003/3196 Sch.1 para.6

s.80, disapplied: 2003 c.21 s.182

s.80, repealed: 2003 c.21 Sch.19

s.80, varied: SI 2003/3196 Sch.1 para.7

s.81, disapplied: 2003 c.21 s.182

s.81, repealed: 2003 c.21 Sch.19

s.81, varied: SI 2003/3196 Sch.1 para.7

s.82, varied: SI 2003/3196 Sch.1 para.8

s.83, amended: 2003 c.21 Sch.17 para.64, Sch.17 para.66

s.83, varied: SI 2003/3196 Sch.1 para.9

s.84, amended: 2003 c.21 Sch.17 para.67

s.84, applied: 2003 c.21 Sch.1 para.1, SI 2003/74 Sch.3 para.2, Sch.4 para.2, Sch.5 para.2, Sch.6 para.2, Sch.7 para.2, Sch.8 para.2, Sch.9 para.2

s.84, referred to: SI 2003/74 Sch.4 para.2

s.84, varied: SI 2003/3196 Sch.1 para.10

s.84, enabling: SI 2003/74

s.85, amended: 2003 c.21 Sch.17 para.64

s.85, varied: SI 2003/3196 Sch.1 para.10

s.86, amended: 2003 c.21 Sch.17 para.64

s.86, varied: SI 2003/3196 Sch.1 para.10

s.87, varied: SI 2003/3196 Sch.1 para.10

s.88, repealed: 2003 c.21 Sch.19

s.88, varied: SI 2003/3196 Sch.1 para.10

1984–cont.

12. Telecommunications Act 1984–*cont.*

s.89, repealed: 2004 c.14 Sch.1 Part 5

s.90, repealed: 2003 c.21 Sch.19

s.90, varied: SI 2003/3196 Sch.1 para.10

s.91, amended: 2003 c.21 Sch.17 para.69, Sch.19

s.91, varied: SI 2003/3196 Sch.1 para.11

s.92, repealed (in part): 2003 c.21 Sch.19

s.92, varied: SI 2003/3196 Sch.1 para.12

s.93, repealed: 2003 c.21 Sch.19

s.94, amended: 2003 c.21 Sch.17 para.70

s.94, varied: 2003 c.21 Sch.18 para.24

s.95, amended: 2002 c.40 Sch.9 para.1

s.95, repealed: 2003 c.21 Sch.19

s.95, varied: SI 2003/1592 Sch.4 para.4

s.96, repealed: 2003 c.21 Sch.19

s.97, repealed: 2003 c.21 Sch.19

s.98, amended: 2003 c.21 Sch.17 para.71, Sch.19, 2004 c.20 Sch.19 para.2

s.98, varied: SI 2004/1822 Sch.1 para.12

s.101, amended: 2002 c.40 Sch.25 para.13, 2003 c.20 Sch.2 para.19, 2003 c.21 Sch.17 para.72, Sch.19, 2003 c.37 Sch.7 para.23

s.101, referred to: 2003 c.20 s.115

s.101, repealed (in part): 2003 c.21 Sch.17 para.72

s.102, repealed: 2003 c.21 Sch.19

s.102, varied: SI 2003/3196 Art.3

s.103, amended: 2002 c.40 Sch.25 para.13

s.103, substituted: 2002 c.40 Sch.25 para.13

s.104, amended: 2003 c.21 Sch.17 para.73, Sch.19

s.104, repealed (in part): 2003 c.21 Sch.19

s.106, amended: 2003 c.21 Sch.17 para.74, Sch.19

s.106, varied: SI 2003/3196 Art.3, Sch.1 para.13

s.107, repealed (in part): 2003 c.21 Sch.19

s.108, enabling: SI 2003/3196, SI 2004/308

s.109, amended: 2003 c.21 Sch.19

s.109, repealed (in part): 2003 c.21 Sch.19

s.109, varied: SI 2003/3196 Art.3, Sch.1 para.14

s.110, varied: SI 2003/3196 Art.3

Sch.2, see *Orange PCS Ltd v Bradford (Valuation Officer)* [2004] EWCA Civ 155, [2004] 2 All E.R. 651 (CA), Auld, L.J.

Sch.2, applied: 2003 c.21 s.394, SI 2003/2553 Reg.2

Sch.2, referred to: SI 2002/1384 Art.7, SI 2002/2398 Art.5, SI 2003/1900 Art.3

Sch.2 para.1, amended: 2003 c.21 Sch.3 para.2, Sch.3 para.3, Sch.3 para.4, Sch.19

Sch.2 para.1, varied: 2003 c.21 Sch.18 para.17

Sch.2 para.2, amended: 2003 c.21 Sch.3 para.5

Sch.2 para.2, varied: 2003 c.21 Sch.18 para.17

Sch.2 para.3, amended: 2003 c.21 Sch.3 para.5

1984–cont.

12. Telecommunications Act 1984–*cont.*

Sch.2 para.3, varied: 2003 c.21 Sch.18 para.17

Sch.2 para.4, amended: 2003 c.21 Sch.3 para.5

Sch.2 para.4, varied: 2003 c.21 Sch.18 para.17

Sch.2 para.5, see *St Leger Davey v First Secretary of State* [2004] EWHC 512, [2004] J.P.L. 1581 (QBD (Admin Ct)), Sullivan, J.

Sch.2 para.5, amended: 2003 c.21 Sch.3 para.5

Sch.2 para.5, varied: 2003 c.21 Sch.18 para.17

Sch.2 para.6, amended: 2003 c.21 Sch.3 para.5

Sch.2 para.6, varied: 2003 c.21 Sch.18 para.17

Sch.2 para.7, amended: 2003 c.21 Sch.3 para.5

Sch.2 para.7, varied: 2003 c.21 Sch.18 para.17

Sch.2 para.8, amended: 2003 c.21 Sch.3 para.5

Sch.2 para.8, varied: 2003 c.21 Sch.18 para.17

Sch.2 para.9, amended: 2003 c.21 Sch.3 para.5, Sch.19

Sch.2 para.9, applied: SI 2002/1066 Sch.10 para.2, SI 2003/2553 Reg.16

Sch.2 para.9, varied: 2003 c.21 Sch.18 para.17

Sch.2 para.10, amended: 2003 c.21 Sch.3 para.5, Sch.3 para.6, Sch.19

Sch.2 para.10, varied: 2003 c.21 Sch.18 para.17

Sch.2 para.11, amended: 2003 c.21 Sch.3 para.5

Sch.2 para.11, varied: 2003 c.21 Sch.18 para.17

Sch.2 para.12, amended: 2003 c.21 Sch.3 para.5

Sch.2 para.12, varied: 2003 c.21 Sch.18 para.17

Sch.2 para.13, amended: 2003 c.21 Sch.3 para.5

Sch.2 para.13, varied: 2003 c.21 Sch.18 para.17

Sch.2 para.14, amended: 2003 c.21 Sch.3 para.5

Sch.2 para.14, varied: 2003 c.21 Sch.18 para.17

Sch.2 para.15, amended: 2003 c.21 Sch.3 para.5

Sch.2 para.15, varied: 2003 c.21 Sch.18 para.17

Sch.2 para.16, amended: 2003 c.21 Sch.3 para.5

Sch.2 para.16, varied: 2003 c.21 Sch.18 para.17

Sch.2 para.17, see *Jones v T Mobile (UK) Ltd* [2003] EWCA Civ 1162, [2004] C.P. Rep. 10 (CA), Kennedy, L.J.

Sch.2 para.17, amended: 2003 c.21 Sch.3 para.5

Sch.2 para.17, varied: 2003 c.21 Sch.18 para.17

CAP.

1984–cont.

12. Telecommunications Act 1984–*cont.*

Sch.2 para.18, see *Jones v T Mobile (UK) Ltd* [2003] EWCA Civ 1162, [2004] C.P. Rep. 10 (CA), Kennedy, L.J.

Sch.2 para.18, amended: 2003 c.21 Sch.3 para.5, Sch.17 para.75

Sch.2 para.18, varied: 2003 c.21 Sch.18 para.17

Sch.2 para.19, amended: 2003 c.21 Sch.3 para.5

Sch.2 para.19, varied: 2003 c.21 Sch.18 para.17

Sch.2 para.20, amended: 2003 c.21 Sch.3 para.5, Sch.3 para.7

Sch.2 para.20, varied: 2003 c.21 Sch.18 para.17

Sch.2 para.21, amended: 2003 c.21 Sch.3 para.5

Sch.2 para.21, varied: 2003 c.21 Sch.18 para.17

Sch.2 para.22, amended: 2003 c.21 Sch.3 para.5

Sch.2 para.22, varied: 2003 c.21 Sch.18 para.17

Sch.2 para.23, amended: 2003 c.21 Sch.3 para.5, Sch.3 para.8

Sch.2 para.23, varied: 2003 c.21 Sch.18 para.17

Sch.2 para.24, amended: 2003 c.21 Sch.3 para.5, Sch.3 para.9

Sch.2 para.24, varied: 2003 c.21 Sch.18 para.17

Sch.2 para.25, amended: 2003 c.21 Sch.3 para.5

Sch.2 para.25, varied: 2003 c.21 Sch.18 para.17

Sch.2 para.26, amended: 2003 c.21 Sch.3 para.5, Sch.3 para.10

Sch.2 para.26, varied: 2003 c.21 Sch.18 para.17

Sch.2 para.27, amended: 2003 c.21 Sch.3 para.5, Sch.19

Sch.2 para.27, varied: 2003 c.21 Sch.18 para.17

Sch.2 para.28, amended: 2003 c.21 Sch.3 para.5

Sch.2 para.28, varied: 2003 c.21 Sch.18 para.17

Sch.2 para.29, added: 2003 c.21 Sch.3 para.11

Sch.2 para.29, applied: 2002 c.40 s.128, s.234

Sch.2 para.29, varied: 2003 c.21 Sch.18 para.17

Sch.3 para.1, varied: SI 2003/3196 Art.3, Sch.1 para.15

Sch.3 para.2, varied: SI 2003/3196 Art.3

Sch.3 para.3, varied: SI 2003/3196 Art.3

Sch.4 para.2, repealed: 2003 c.21 Sch.19

Sch.4 para.3, repealed: 2003 c.21 Sch.19

Sch.4 para.12, repealed: 2003 c.21 Sch.19

CAP.

1984–cont.

12. Telecommunications Act 1984–*cont.*

Sch.4 para.16, repealed: 2003 c.21 Sch.19

Sch.4 para.28, repealed (in part): 2003 c.21 Sch.19

Sch.4 para.40, repealed: 2003 c.21 Sch.19

Sch.4 para.55, repealed (in part): 2003 c.21 Sch.19

Sch.4 para.57, repealed: 2002 c.40 Sch.26

Sch.4 para.60, repealed (in part): 2002 c.40 Sch.26

Sch.4 para.65, repealed: 2003 c.21 Sch.19

Sch.4 para.72, repealed: 2002 c.40 Sch.26

Sch.4 para.73, repealed: 2002 c.40 Sch.26

Sch.4 para.80, repealed (in part): 2003 c.21 Sch.19

Sch.4 para.86, repealed (in part): 2003 c.21 Sch.19

Sch.4 para.88, amended: SI 2003/2155 Sch.1 para.1

Sch.4 para.89, repealed (in part): 2003 c.21 Sch.19

Sch.4 para.90, repealed: 2003 c.21 Sch.19

Sch.5 Part I para.1, repealed: 2003 c.21 Sch.19

Sch.5 Part I para.2, repealed: 2003 c.21 Sch.19

Sch.5 Part I para.3, repealed: 2003 c.21 Sch.19

Sch.5 Part I para.4, repealed: 2003 c.21 Sch.19

Sch.5 Part I para.5, repealed: 2003 c.21 Sch.19

Sch.5 Part I para.6, repealed: 2003 c.21 Sch.19

Sch.5 Part I para.7, repealed: 2003 c.21 Sch.19

Sch.5 Part I para.8, repealed (in part): 2003 c.21 Sch.19

Sch.5 Part I para.9, repealed: 2003 c.21 Sch.19

Sch.5 Part I para.10, repealed: 2003 c.21 Sch.19

Sch.5 Part I para.11, repealed: 2003 c.21 Sch.19

Sch.5 Part I para.12, repealed: 2003 c.21 Sch.19

Sch.5 Part I para.13, repealed: 2003 c.21 Sch.19

Sch.5 Part I para.14, repealed: 2003 c.21 Sch.19

Sch.5 Part I para.16, repealed: 2003 c.21 Sch.19

Sch.5 Part I para.17, repealed: 2003 c.21 Sch.19

Sch.5 Part I para.18, repealed: 2003 c.21 Sch.19

Sch.5 Part I para.19, repealed: 2003 c.21 Sch.19

Sch.5 Part II para.20, repealed: 2003 c.21 Sch.19

1984–cont.

12. Telecommunications Act 1984–cont.

Sch.5 Part II para.21, repealed: 2003 c.21 Sch.19

Sch.5 Part II para.22, repealed: 2003 c.21 Sch.19

Sch.5 Part II para.23, repealed: 2003 c.21 Sch.19

Sch.5 Part II para.24, repealed: 2003 c.21 Sch.19

Sch.5 Part II para.25, repealed: 2003 c.21 Sch.19

Sch.5 Part II para.26, repealed: 2003 c.21 Sch.19

Sch.5 Part II para.27, repealed: 2003 c.21 Sch.19

Sch.5 Part II para.28, repealed: 2003 c.21 Sch.19

Sch.5 Part II para.29, repealed: 2003 c.21 Sch.19

Sch.5 Part II para.31, repealed: 2003 c.21 Sch.19

Sch.5 Part II para.32, repealed: 2003 c.21 Sch.19

Sch.5 Part II para.33, repealed: 2003 c.21 Sch.19

Sch.5 Part II para.35, repealed: 2003 c.21 Sch.19

Sch.5 Part II para.38, repealed: 2003 c.21 Sch.19

Sch.5 Part II para.39, repealed: 2003 c.21 Sch.19

Sch.5 Part II para.40, repealed: 2003 c.21 Sch.19

Sch.5 Part II para.41, repealed: 2003 c.21 Sch.19

Sch.5 Part II para.42, repealed: 2003 c.21 Sch.19

Sch.5 Part II para.47, repealed: 2003 c.21 Sch.19

Sch.5 Part II para.48, amended: 2003 c.21 Sch.19

Sch.5 Part II para.49, repealed: 2003 c.21 Sch.19

Sch.5 Part II para.50, repealed: 2003 c.21 Sch.19

Sch.5 Part II para.51, repealed: 2003 c.21 Sch.19

Sch.6 para.1, repealed: 2003 c.21 Sch.19

Sch.6 para.2, repealed: 2003 c.21 Sch.19

Sch.6 para.3, repealed: 2003 c.21 Sch.19

Sch.6 para.4, repealed: 2003 c.21 Sch.19

Sch.6 para.5, repealed: 2003 c.21 Sch.19

Sch.6 para.6, repealed: 2003 c.21 Sch.19

Sch.6 para.7, repealed: 2003 c.21 Sch.19

Sch.6 para.8, repealed: 2003 c.21 Sch.19

Sch.6 para.9, repealed: 2003 c.21 Sch.19

Sch.6 para.10, repealed: 2003 c.21 Sch.19

Sch.6 para.11, repealed: 2003 c.21 Sch.19

Sch.6 para.12, repealed: 2003 c.21 Sch.19

Sch.6 para.13, repealed: 2003 c.21 Sch.19

Sch.6 para.14, repealed: 2003 c.21 Sch.19

1984–cont.

12. Telecommunications Act 1984–cont.

Sch.7 Part IV, varied: SI 2003/3196 Art.3, Sch.1 para.16

14. Anatomy Act 1984

applied: 2004 c.30 s.10

referred to: 2004 c.30 s.59

repealed (in part): 2004 c.30 Sch.7 Part 1

s.4, amended: 2004 c.30 Sch.6 para.2

s.4, applied: 2004 c.30 s.10

s.4, referred to: 2004 c.30 s.59

s.6, applied: 2004 c.30 s.10

s.11, amended: 2003 c.44 Sch.26 para.31, Sch.27 para.5

20. Agriculture (Amendment) Act 1984

s.2, repealed (in part): 2004 c.14 Sch.1 Part 2

s.3, repealed (in part): 2004 c.14 Sch.1 Part 2

22. Public Health (Control of Disease) Act 1984

applied: SI 2002/1882 Reg.10, SI 2003/250 Reg.10, SI 2003/2644 Reg.10, SI 2004/585 Reg.10, SI 2004/1020 Reg.10

referred to: 2003 c.43 Sch.4 para.60

s.1, amended: SI 2002/2469 Sch.1 para.11

s.2, applied: 2004 c.36 Sch.1 para.10

s.2, enabling: SI 2002/2000

s.4, enabling: SI 2002/2000

s.5, amended: 2004 c.14 Sch.1 Part 13

s.11, amended: 2002 c.17 Sch.2 para.50

s.12, amended: 2002 c.17 Sch.2 para.50

s.13, amended: SI 2002/2469 Sch.1 para.11, 2003 c.43 Sch.4 para.61

s.29, amended: 2003 c.44 Sch.26 para.32

s.30, amended: 2003 c.44 Sch.26 para.32

s.37, amended: SI 2002/2469 Sch.1 para.11, 2003 c.43 Sch.4 para.62

s.39, amended: 2002 c.17 Sch.2 para.50

s.41, amended: SI 2002/2469 Sch.1 para.11, 2003 c.43 Sch.4 para.63

s.62, amended: 2003 c.44 Sch.26 para.32

s.79, repealed (in part): 2004 c.14 Sch.1 Part 13

Sch.1 para.4, repealed: 2004 c.14 Sch.1 Part 13

23. Registered Homes Act 1984

see *Bogdal v Kingston upon Hull City Council* [2002] R.A. 145 (CA), Stuart-Smith, L.J.; see *Douce v Staffordshire CC* [2002] EWCA Civ 506, (2002) 5 C.C.L. Rep. 347 (CA), Sir Denis Henry; see *John Grooms (Registered Charity) v Bond (Listing Officer)* [2003] R.V.R. 218 (Valuation Tribunal); see *Kingscrest Associates Ltd (t/a Kingscrest Residential Care Homes) v Customs and Excise Commissioners* [2003] B.V.C. 2592 (V&DTr), Adrian Shipwright (Chairman)

applied: SI 2002/816 Reg.3, SI 2002/921 Reg.5, Reg.6, Reg.7, Reg.8, SI 2003/284 Sch.2 para.2, SI 2003/753 Reg.5, SI 2004/661 Reg.5, SI 2004/662 Reg.5

referred to: SI 2002/920 Sch.1 para.2

CAP.

1984–cont.

23. Registered Homes Act 1984–*cont.*

Part I, applied: SI 2002/920 Sch.1 para.2, Sch.1 para.5, Sch.1 para.6, Sch.1 para.7, Sch.1 para.8, Sch.1 para.9, Sch.1 para.10, SI 2002/921 Reg.3, SI 2003/284 Sch.2 para.2

Part II, see *R. (on the application of A) v Partnerships in Care Ltd* [2002] EWHC 529, [2002] 1 W.L.R. 2610 (QBD (Admin Ct)), Keith, J.

Part II, applied: SI 2002/920 Sch.1 para.2, Sch.1 para.5, Sch.1 para.6, Sch.1 para.7, Sch.1 para.8, Sch.1 para.9, Sch.1 para.10

s.1, applied: SI 2003/284 Sch.2 para.2

s.1, varied: SI 2002/920 Sch.1 para.2

s.2, varied: SI 2002/920 Sch.1 para.2

s.3, applied: SI 2002/920 Sch.1 para.5, Sch.1 para.6

s.3, varied: SI 2002/920 Sch.1 para.2

s.4, varied: SI 2002/920 Sch.1 para.2

s.5, varied: SI 2002/920 Sch.1 para.2

s.6, varied: SI 2002/920 Sch.1 para.2

s.7, varied: SI 2002/920 Sch.1 para.2

s.8, varied: SI 2002/920 Sch.1 para.2

s.8A, varied: SI 2002/920 Sch.1 para.2

s.9, varied: SI 2002/920 Sch.1 para.2

s.10, varied: SI 2002/920 Sch.1 para.2

s.11, applied: SI 2002/920 Sch.1 para.2

s.11, varied: SI 2002/920 Sch.1 para.2

s.12, applied: SI 2002/920 Sch.1 para.2, Sch.1 para.7, Sch.1 para.8

s.12, varied: SI 2002/920 Sch.1 para.2

s.13, referred to: SI 2002/920 Sch.1 para.2

s.13, varied: SI 2002/920 Sch.1 para.2

s.14, applied: SI 2002/920 Sch.1 para.2, Sch.1 para.8, Sch.1 para.9

s.14, varied: SI 2002/920 Sch.1 para.2

s.15, varied: SI 2002/920 Sch.1 para.2

s.16, varied: SI 2002/920 Sch.1 para.2

s.17, varied: SI 2002/920 Sch.1 para.2

s.18, varied: SI 2002/920 Sch.1 para.2

s.19, varied: SI 2002/920 Sch.1 para.2

s.20, varied: SI 2002/920 Sch.1 para.2

s.21, varied: SI 2002/920 Sch.1 para.2

s.22, varied: SI 2002/920 Sch.1 para.2

s.23, varied: SI 2002/920 Sch.1 para.2

s.24, varied: SI 2002/920 Sch.1 para.2

s.25, varied: SI 2002/920 Sch.1 para.2

s.26, varied: SI 2002/920 Sch.1 para.2

s.27, varied: SI 2002/920 Sch.1 para.2

s.28, varied: SI 2002/920 Sch.1 para.2

s.29, varied: SI 2002/920 Sch.1 para.2

s.30, varied: SI 2002/920 Sch.1 para.2

s.31, applied: SI 2002/920 Sch.1 para.7, Sch.1 para.8

s.31, varied: SI 2002/920 Sch.1 para.2

s.32, varied: SI 2002/920 Sch.1 para.2

s.33, applied: SI 2002/920 Sch.1 para.8, Sch.1 para.9

s.33, varied: SI 2002/920 Sch.1 para.2

CAP.

1984–cont.

23. Registered Homes Act 1984–*cont.*

s.34, varied: SI 2002/920 Sch.1 para.2

s.35, varied: SI 2002/920 Sch.1 para.2

s.36, varied: SI 2002/920 Sch.1 para.2

s.37, varied: SI 2002/920 Sch.1 para.2

s.38, varied: SI 2002/920 Sch.1 para.2

s.42, amended: SI 2002/253 Sch.5 para.8

24. Dentists Act 1984

applied: 2002 c.17 s.31, SI 2002/1625 Art.2, SI 2002/2376 Reg.4, 2003 c.43 Sch.1 para.16, SI 2003/1250 Art.18, SI 2004/1031 Sch.4 para.3

referred to: SI 2002/1625 Art.4

s.2, enabling: SI 2003/1081, SI 2004/67

s.14, applied: SI 2003/1250 Art.18

s.15, amended: SI 2003/3148 Reg.6, SI 2004/1947 Reg.11

s.15, applied: SSI 2004/292 Reg.2

s.16, amended: SI 2003/3148 Reg.6

s.17, amended: SI 2003/3148 Reg.6

s.21A, amended: SI 2003/3148 Reg.6

s.27, applied: 2002 c.17 s.29, SI 2003/250 Reg.10

s.28, applied: SI 2003/250 Reg.6, Reg.10

s.28, referred to: SI 2003/250 Reg.10

s.29, amended: 2002 c.17 s.31, Sch.8 para.16

s.29, applied: SI 2003/833 Art.4

s.29, repealed (in part): 2002 c.17 Sch.9 Part 2

s.30, applied: SI 2003/250 Reg.10

s.32, applied: SI 2003/250 Reg.10

s.34A, amended: 2002 c.17 s.31

s.34A, applied: SI 2004/68 Sch.1

s.34A, enabling: SI 2004/68

s.34B, applied: SI 2004/68 Sch.1

s.37, amended: SI 2002/3135 Sch.1 para.11

s.40, amended: 2003 c.43 Sch.11 para.50, Sch.14 Part 4

s.41, amended: 2004 c.33 Sch.27 para.89

s.44, amended: 2002 c.17 s.31

s.44, applied: SI 2003/833 Art.4

s.45, applied: SI 2002/1671, SI 2003/3105

s.45, enabling: SI 2002/1671, SI 2003/3105

s.46, applied: SI 2002/1399

s.46, disapplied: SI 2002/1399 Art.2

s.46, enabling: SI 2002/1399

s.51, amended: 2002 c.17 Sch.9 Part 2

Sch.1 Part I para.1, amended: 2003 c.43 Sch.12 para.3

Sch.1 Part I para.1, applied: SI 2002/1625 Art.2

Sch.1 Part I para.1, referred to: SI 2002/1625 Art.4

Sch.1 Part I para.2, amended: 2003 c.43 Sch.12 para.3

Sch.1 Part I para.2, applied: SI 2002/2464 Sch.1 para.2

Sch.1 Part I para.2A, added: 2003 c.43 Sch.12 para.3

1984-cont.

24. Dentists Act 1984—*cont.*

Sch.1 Part I para.3, applied: SI 2002/1625 Art.4

Sch.1 Part I para.3, enabling: SI 2002/2463

Sch.1 Part I para.3, applied: SI 2002/2463, SI 2002/2464 Sch.1 para.2

Sch.1 Part I para.4, applied: SI 2002/1625 Art.4

Sch.1 Part I para.4, enabling: SI 2002/2464

Sch.1 Part I para.4, applied: SI 2002/2464

Sch.2 Part I para.1, amended: SI 2003/3148 Reg.6, SI 2004/1947 Reg.11

Sch.2 Part I para.6A, added: SI 2003/3148 Reg.6

Sch.2 Part I para.8, added: SI 2004/1947 Reg.11

Sch.2 Part I para.9, added: SI 2004/1947 Reg.11

Sch.2 Part I para.10, added: SI 2004/1947 Reg.11

Sch.2 Part II, amended: SI 2004/1947 Reg.11

Sch.2 Part II, substituted: SI 2003/3148 Sch.2 Part I

Sch.3, applied: SI 2004/68 Sch.1

Sch.3A, applied: SI 2004/68 Sch.1

Sch.3A para.2, enabling: SI 2004/68

Sch.5 para.6, repealed: 2002 c.40 Sch.26

Sch.5 para.8, repealed: 2003 c.43 Sch.14 Part 4

26. Inshore Fishing (Scotland) Act 1984

s.1, enabling: SSI 2003/404, SSI 2003/514, SSI 2004/276h.1 Part 2

s.7, amended: 2003 asp 15 Sch.4 para.2

27. Road Traffic Regulation Act 1984

see *DPP v Broomfield* [2002] EWHC 1962, (2002) 166 J.P. 736 (QBD (Admin Ct)), Judge Wilkie Q.C.

applied: SI 2003/1075 Art.10, SI 2003/2334 Art.6, SI 2003/2336 Art.6, SI 2003/2677 Art.6, SI 2003/2711 Art.6, 2004 c.18 s.97, SI 2004/389 Art.13, SI 2004/757 Art.47, SI 2004/1402 Art.6

referred to: SI 2002/1485 Art.6, SI 2003/634 Art.6, SI 2003/635 Art.6, SI 2003/898 Art.6, SI 2003/1261 Art.6, SI 2003/1984 Art.6, SI 2004/1608 Art.6, SI 2004/2028 Art.6, SI 2004/2111 Art.6, SI 2004/2188 Art.6, SI 2004/2193 Art.6, SI 2004/2194 Art.6, SI 2004/2212 Art.6, SI 2004/2260 Art.6

varied: SI 2004/13 Art.6

Part III, applied: SI 2004/389 Art.15

s.1, applied: SSI 2002/178 Art.9, SSI 2002/450 Reg.4, Reg.6, Reg.7, 2004 c.18 s.85, s.86

s.1, enabling: SI 2003/2723

s.2, applied: SSI 2002/178 Art.9

s.2, enabling: SI 2003/2723

s.4, applied: SSI 2002/178 Art.9

s.5, applied: 2004 c.18 Sch.7 para.4

1984-cont.

27. Road Traffic Regulation Act 1984—*cont.*

s.6, applied: 2003 c.iii s.14, SI 2003/1615 Art.5, SSI 2002/450 Reg.6, Reg.7, 2004 c.18 s.85, s.86, Sch.7 para.7

s.6, enabling: SI 2002/1672

s.7, applied: SI 2002/1672

s.8, applied: 2004 c.18 Sch.7 para.3

s.8, repealed (in part): 2004 c.18 Sch.12 Part 1

s.8, varied: 2003 c.iii s.7

s.9, applied: 2003 c.iii s.14, SI 2003/1615 Art.5, SSI 2002/178 Art.9, SSI 2002/450 Reg.4, Reg.6, Reg.7

s.11, applied: 2004 c.18 Sch.7 para.3, Sch.7 para.4

s.11, repealed (in part): 2004 c.18 Sch.12 Part 1

s.11, varied: 2003 c.iii s.7

s.14, applied: SI 2002/3113 Reg.10, SSI 2002/178 Art.9, 2003 asp 1 s.46

s.16, applied: 2003 asp 1 s.46, 2004 c.18 Sch.7 para.3, Sch.7 para.4

s.16C, applied: 2004 c.18 Sch.7 para.3, Sch.7 para.4

s.17, applied: 2003 asp 1 s.46

s.17, enabling: SI 2002/1651, SI 2002/2403, SI 2002/2936, SI 2003/2186, SI 2003/2187, SI 2003/2188, SI 2003/2615, SI 2004/180, SI 2004/3258, SI 2004/3261, SSI 2004/53, SSI 2004/54

s.22, referred to: SSI 2002/450

s.22, repealed (in part): 2004 asp 6 Sch.7 para.5

s.22B, added: 2003 c.20 s.108

s.22C, added: 2004 c.36 Sch.2 para.16

s.22D, added: 2004 c.36 Sch.2 para.16

s.23, see *R. (on the application of Wainwright) v Richmond upon Thames LBC* [2001] EWCA Civ 2062, Times, January 16, 2002 (CA), Clarke, L.J.

s.25, applied: SI 2002/3113 Reg.49, 2004 c.18 Sch.7 para.3, Sch.7 para.4

s.25, referred to: SI 2002/3113 Reg.18

s.26, applied: SI 2002/377 Reg.4, SI 2002/3199 Reg.4, SI 2003/3118 Reg.2, SI 2003/3170 Reg.4

s.28, enabling: SI 2002/3020, SSI 2002/549

s.32, see *Isle of Wight Council v Customs and Excise Commissioners* [2004] B.V.C. 2181 (V&DTr), Stephen Oliver Q.C. (Chairman)

s.32, applied: 2004 c.18 Sch.8 para.8

s.35, applied: SSI 2002/450 Reg.4, Reg.6, Reg.7

s.35A, applied: 2004 c.18 Sch.7 para.3, Sch.7 para.4

s.36, varied: 2003 c.iii s.7

s.45, applied: SSI 2002/450 Reg.4, Reg.6, Reg.7, Reg.8, 2003 c.iii s.14, 2004 c.18 Sch.8 para.8

s.46, amended: 2004 c.18 Sch.11 para.1

s.46, applied: SSI 2002/450 Reg.4, Reg.6, Reg.7, Reg.8

1984–cont.

27. Road Traffic Regulation Act 1984–*cont.*

s.46, varied: SI 2002/37 Sch.2 para.1, SI 2002/126 Sch.2 para.1, SI 2002/276 Sch.2 para.1, SI 2002/421 Sch.2 para.1, SI 2002/422 Sch.2 para.1, SI 2002/1351 Sch.2 para.1, SI 2002/1352 Sch.2 para.1, SI 2002/1353 Sch.2 para.1, SI 2002/1485 Sch.2 para.1, SI 2002/1486 Sch.2 para.1, SI 2002/1504 Sch.2 para.1, SI 2002/1621 Sch.2 para.1, SI 2002/2012 Sch.2 para.1, SI 2002/2183 Sch.2 para.1, SI 2002/2184 Sch.2 para.1, SI 2002/2185 Sch.2 para.1, SI 2002/2186 Sch.2 para.1, SI 2002/2187 Sch.2 para.1, SI 2002/2188 Sch.2 para.1, SI 2002/2520 Sch.2 para.1, SI 2002/2705 Sch.2 para.1, SI 2002/3265 Sch.2 para.1, SI 2002/3266 Sch.2 para.1, SI 2003/95 Sch.2 para.1, SI 2003/251 Sch.2 para.1, SI 2003/634 Sch.2 para.1, SI 2003/635 Sch.2 para.1, SI 2003/898 Sch.2 para.1, SI 2003/1261 Sch.2 para.1, SI 2003/1262 Sch.2 para.1, SI 2003/1924 Sch.2 para.1, SI 2003/1984 Sch.2 para.1, SI 2003/2152 Sch.2 para.1, SI 2003/2153 Sch.2 para.1, SI 2003/2326 Sch.2 para.1, SI 2003/2334 Sch.2 para.1, SI 2003/2336 Sch.2 para.1, SI 2003/2440 Sch.2 para.1, SI 2003/2677 Sch.2 para.1, SI 2003/2711 Sch.2 para.1, SI 2004/13 Sch.2 para.1, SI 2004/104 Sch.2 para.1, SI 2004/914 Sch.2 para.1, SI 2004/1278 Sch.2 para.1, SI 2004/1285 Sch.2 para.9, SI 2004/1305 Sch.2 para.1, SI 2004/1402 Sch.2 para.1, SI 2004/1608 Sch.2 para.1, SI 2004/2028 Sch.3 para.1, SI 2004/2111 Sch.2 para.1, SI 2004/2188 Sch.2 para.1, SI 2004/2193 Sch.2 para.1, SI 2004/2194 Sch.2 para.1, SI 2004/2212 Sch.2 para.1, SI 2004/2260 Sch.2 para.1, SI 2004/2424 Sch.3 para.1, SI 2004/2616 Sch.2 para.1, SSI 2002/398 Sch.3 para.1, SSI 2003/70 Sch.3 para.1, SSI 2004/87 Sch.3 para.1

s.47, amended: 2004 c.18 Sch.12 Part 1

s.47, applied: 2004 c.18 Sch.7 para.4

s.53, applied: 2004 c.18 Sch.7 para.4

s.55, amended: SI 2003/1924 Sch.2 para.2, 2004 c.18 s.95

s.55, applied: 2003 c.26 s.100, 2004 c.18 s.88

s.55, referred to: 2004 c.18 s.88

s.55, varied: SI 2002/37 Sch.2 para.2, SI 2002/126 Sch.2 para.2, SI 2002/276 Sch.2 para.2, SI 2002/421 Sch.2 para.2, SI 2002/422 Sch.2 para.2, SI 2002/1351 Sch.2 para.2, SI 2002/1352 Sch.2 para.2, SI 2002/1353 Sch.2 para.2, SI 2002/1484 Sch.2 para.2, SI 2002/1485 Sch.2 para.2, SI 2002/1486 Sch.2 para.2, SI 2002/1504 Sch.2 para.2, SI 2002/1621 Sch.2 para.2, SI 2002/2012 Sch.2 para.2, SI 2002/2183 Sch.2 para.2, SI 2002/2184 Sch.2 para.2, SI 2002/2185 Sch.2 para.2, SI 2002/2186 Sch.2 para.2, SI 2002/2187

1984–cont.

27. Road Traffic Regulation Act 1984–*cont.*

s.55, varied:–*cont.*

Sch.2 para.2, SI 2002/2188 Sch.2 para.2, SI 2002/2520 Sch.2 para.2, SI 2002/2705 Sch.2 para.2, SI 2002/3265 Sch.2 para.2, SI 2002/3266 Sch.2 para.2, 2003 c.iii s.12, SI 2003/95 Sch.2 para.2, SI 2003/251 Sch.2 para.2, SI 2003/634 Sch.2 para.2, SI 2003/635 Sch.2 para.2, SI 2003/898 Sch.2 para.2, SI 2003/1261 Sch.2 para.2, SI 2003/1262 Sch.2 para.2, SI 2003/1924 Sch.2 para.2, SI 2003/1984 Sch.2 para.2, SI 2003/2152 Sch.2 para.2, SI 2003/2153 Sch.2 para.2, SI 2003/2326 Sch.2 para.2, SI 2003/2334 Sch.2 para.2, SI 2003/2336 Sch.2 para.2, SI 2003/2440 Sch.2 para.2, SI 2003/2677 Sch.2 para.2, SI 2003/2711 Sch.2 para.2, SI 2004/13 Sch.2 para.2, SI 2004/104 Sch.2 para.2, SI 2004/914 Sch.2 para.2, SI 2004/1278 Sch.2 para.2, SI 2004/1285 Sch.2 para.10, SI 2004/1305 Sch.2 para.2, SI 2004/1402 Sch.2 para.2, SI 2004/1608 Sch.2 para.2, SI 2004/2028 Sch.3 para.2, SI 2004/2111 Sch.2 para.2, SI 2004/2188 Sch.2 para.2, SI 2004/2193 Sch.2 para.2, SI 2004/2194 Sch.2 para.2, SI 2004/2212 Sch.2 para.2, SI 2004/2260 Sch.2 para.2, SI 2004/2424 Sch.3 para.2, SI 2004/2616 Sch.2 para.2, SI 2004/2684 Art.4, SSI 2002/398 Sch.3 para.2, SSI 2003/70 Sch.3 para.2, SSI 2004/87 Sch.3 para.2

s.61, applied: 2004 c.18 Sch.7 para.3, Sch.7 para.4

s.63A, amended: SI 2003/251 Sch.2 para.3, 2004 c.18 Sch.11 para.2

s.63A, applied: SI 2002/3113 Reg.4, SSI 2002/399 Reg.2, 2003 c.iii s.15, SSI 2003/72 Reg.2, 2004 c.18 s.76, SSI 2004/85 Reg.2

s.63A, varied: SI 2002/37 Sch.2 para.3, SI 2002/126 Sch.2 para.3, SI 2002/276 Sch.2 para.3, SI 2002/421 Sch.2 para.3, SI 2002/422 Sch.2 para.3, SI 2002/1351 Sch.2 para.3, SI 2002/1352 Sch.2 para.3, SI 2002/1353 Sch.2 para.3, SI 2002/1484 Sch.2 para.3, SI 2002/1485 Sch.2 para.3, SI 2002/1486 Sch.2 para.3, SI 2002/1504 Sch.2 para.3, SI 2002/1621 Sch.2 para.3, SI 2002/2012 Sch.2 para.3, SI 2002/2183 Sch.2 para.3, SI 2002/2184 Sch.2 para.3, SI 2002/2185 Sch.2 para.3, SI 2002/2186 Sch.2 para.3, SI 2002/2187 Sch.2 para.3, SI 2002/2188 Sch.2 para.3, SI 2002/2520 Sch.2 para.3, SI 2002/2705 Sch.2 para.3, SI 2002/3265 Sch.2 para.3, SI 2002/3266 Sch.2 para.3, SI 2003/95 Sch.2 para.3, SI 2003/634 Sch.2 para.3, SI 2003/635 Sch.2 para.3, SI 2003/898 Sch.2 para.3, SI 2003/1261 Sch.2 para.3, SI 2003/1262 Sch.2 para.3, SI 2003/1924 Sch.2 para.3, SI 2003/

1984–cont.

27. **Road Traffic Regulation Act 1984**–*cont.*
s.63A, varied:–*cont.*
1984 Sch.2 para.3, SI 2003/2152 Sch.2
para.3, SI 2003/2153 Sch.2 para.3, SI
2003/2326 Sch.2 para.3, SI 2003/2334
Sch.2 para.3, SI 2003/2336 Sch.2 para.3,
SI 2003/2440 Sch.2 para.3, SI 2003/2677
Sch.2 para.3, SI 2003/2711 Sch.2 para.3, SI
2004/13 Sch.2 para.3, SI 2004/104 Sch.2
para.3, SI 2004/914 Sch.2 para.3, SI 2004/
1278 Sch.2 para.3, SI 2004/1285 Sch.2
para.11, SI 2004/1305 Sch.2 para.3, SI
2004/1402 Sch.2 para.3, SI 2004/1608
Sch.2 para.3, SI 2004/2028 Sch.3 para.3,
SI 2004/2111 Sch.2 para.3, SI 2004/2188
Sch.2 para.3, SI 2004/2193 Sch.2 para.3,
SI 2004/2194 Sch.2 para.3, SI 2004/
2212 Sch.2 para.3, SI 2004/2260 Sch.2
para.3, SI 2004/2424 Sch.3 para.3, SI
2004/2616 Sch.2 para.3, SSI 2002/398
Sch.3 para.3, SSI 2003/70 Sch.3 para.3,
SSI 2004/87 Sch.3 para.3
s.63A, enabling: SSI 2002/399, SSI 2003/
72, SSI 2004/85
s.64, applied: SI 2002/412 Art.27, SI 2002/
3113 Reg.8, Reg.49, SI 2003/1075 Art.10
s.64, enabling: SI 2002/3113
s.65, applied: SI 2002/412 Art.27, SI 2002/
3113 Reg.49, Reg.53, SI 2003/1075 Art.10
s.65, enabling: SI 2002/3113, SI 2003/393,
SI 2004/1275
s.67, amended: 2004 c.36 Sch.2 para.16
s.67, applied: SI 2002/3113 Reg.53, 2004
c.18 s.7
s.74, amended: SI 2002/2626 Sch.2 para.11
s.74, applied: SI 2002/2626 Art.4
s.82, applied: SSI 2002/178 Art.9
s.84, applied: SSI 2002/178 Art.9
s.85, enabling: SI 2002/3113
s.87, amended: 2004 c.21 Sch.1 para.55
s.87, referred to: SI 2004/389 Art.15
s.88, applied: 2003 asp 1 s.46
s.88, enabling: SSI 2002/371
s.89, applied: 2003 asp 1 s.46, 2003 c.32
Sch.3 para.2
s.95, applied: SSI 2003/231 Sch.4 para.8
s.95, enabling: SI 2002/2975
s.96, amended: 2002 c.30 s.44, Sch.8
s.96, referred to: 2002 c.30 s.108
s.96, repealed (in part): 2002 c.30 s.44,
Sch.8
s.96, enabling: SI 2002/2975
s.99, see *Clarke v Chief Constable of West
Midlands* [2001] EWCA Civ 1169, [2002]
R.T.R. 5 (CA), Longmore, L.J.
s.99, applied: 2002 c.30 Sch.4 para.10, Sch.5
para.7, 2004 c.18 s.9, SI 2004/915 Sch.1
para.7, SSI 2003/72 Reg.2
s.99, referred to: SSI 2002/399 Reg.2, SSI
2004/85 Reg.2

1984–cont.

27. **Road Traffic Regulation Act 1984**–*cont.*
s.99, enabling: SI 2002/746, SI 2002/2777,
SI 2003/2186, SSI 2002/538
s.100, applied: 2004 c.18 s.9
s.101, amended: SI 2003/251 Sch.2 para.4,
2004 c.18 Sch.11 para.3
s.101, applied: 2004 c.18 s.9
s.101, repealed (in part): 2004 c.18 Sch.11
para.3, Sch.12 Part 1
s.101, varied: SI 2002/37 Sch.2 para.4, SI
2002/126 Sch.2 para.4, SI 2002/276
Sch.2 para.4, SI 2002/421 Sch.2 para.4,
SI 2002/422 Sch.2 para.4, SI 2002/1351
Sch.2 para.4, SI 2002/1352 Sch.2 para.4,
SI 2002/1353 Sch.2 para.4, SI 2002/
1484 Sch.2 para.4, SI 2002/1485 Sch.2
para.4, SI 2002/1486 Sch.2 para.4, SI
2002/1504 Sch.2 para.4, SI 2002/1621
Sch.2 para.4, SI 2002/2012 Sch.2 para.4,
SI 2002/2183 Sch.2 para.4, SI 2002/
2184 Sch.2 para.4, SI 2002/2185 Sch.2
para.4, SI 2002/2186 Sch.2 para.4, SI
2002/2187 Sch.2 para.4, SI 2002/2188
Sch.2 para.4, Sch.2 para.5, SI 2002/2520
Sch.2 para.4, SI 2002/2705 Sch.2 para.4,
SI 2002/3265 Sch.2 para.4, SI 2002/3266
Sch.2 para.4, SI 2003/95 Sch.2 para.4, SI
2003/251 Sch.2 para.4, SI 2003/634
Sch.2 para.4, SI 2003/635 Sch.2 para.4,
SI 2003/898 Sch.2 para.4, SI 2003/1261
Sch.2 para.4, SI 2003/1262 Sch.2 para.4,
SI 2003/1924 Sch.2 para.4, SI 2003/
1984 Sch.2 para.4, SI 2003/2152 Sch.2
para.4, SI 2003/2153 Sch.2 para.4, SI
2003/2326 Sch.2 para.4, SI 2003/2334
Sch.2 para.4, SI 2003/2336 Sch.2 para.4,
SI 2003/2440 Sch.2 para.4, SI 2003/2677
Sch.2 para.4, SI 2003/2711 Sch.2 para.4, SI
2004/13 Sch.2 para.4, SI 2004/104 Sch.2
para.4, SI 2004/914 Sch.2 para.4, SI 2004/
1278 Sch.2 para.4, SI 2004/1285 Sch.2
para.12, SI 2004/1305 Sch.2 para.4, SI
2004/1402 Sch.2 para.4, SI 2004/1608
Sch.2 para.4, SI 2004/2028 Sch.3 para.4,
SI 2004/2111 Sch.2 para.4, SI 2004/2188
Sch.2 para.4, SI 2004/2193 Sch.2 para.4,
SI 2004/2194 Sch.2 para.4, SI 2004/
2212 Sch.2 para.4, SI 2004/2260 Sch.2
para.4, SI 2004/2424 Sch.3 para.4, SSI
2004/2616 Sch.2 para.4, SSI 2002/398
Sch.3 para.4, SSI 2003/70 Sch.3 para.4,
SSI 2004/87 Sch.3 para.4
s.101, enabling: SI 2002/746, SSI 2002/538
s.101A, added: 2004 c.18 Sch.11 para.3
s.101A, applied: 2004 c.18 s.9
s.101B, added: 2004 c.18 Sch.11 para.3
s.101B, applied: 2004 c.18 s.9
s.102, amended: SI 2003/251 Sch.2 para.5,
2004 c.18 Sch.11 para.4, Sch.12 Part 1
s.102, applied: 2004 c.18 s.9, Sch.9 para.1

CAP.

1984–cont.

27. Road Traffic Regulation Act 1984–*cont.*

s.102, varied: SI 2002/37 Sch.2 para.5, SI 2002/126 Sch.2 para.5, SI 2002/276 Sch.2 para.5, SI 2002/421 Sch.2 para.5, SI 2002/422 Sch.2 para.5, SI 2002/1351 Sch.2 para.5, SI 2002/1352 Sch.2 para.5, SI 2002/1353 Sch.2 para.5, SI 2002/1485 Sch.2 para.5, SI 2002/1486 Sch.2 para.5, SI 2002/1504 Sch.2 para.5, SI 2002/1621 Sch.2 para.5, SI 2002/2012 Sch.2 para.5, SI 2002/2183 Sch.2 para.5, SI 2002/2184 Sch.2 para.5, SI 2002/2185 Sch.2 para.5, SI 2002/2186 Sch.2 para.5, SI 2002/2187 Sch.2 para.5, SI 2002/2520 Sch.2 para.5, SI 2002/2705 Sch.2 para.5, SI 2002/3265 Sch.2 para.5, SI 2002/3266 Sch.2 para.5, SI 2003/95 Sch.2 para.5, SI 2003/251 Sch.2 para.5, SI 2003/634 Sch.2 para.5, SI 2003/635 Sch.2 para.5, SI 2003/898 Sch.2 para.5, SI 2003/1261 Sch.2 para.5, SI 2003/1262 Sch.2 para.5, SI 2003/1924 Sch.2 para.5, SI 2003/1984 Sch.2 para.5, SI 2003/2152 Sch.2 para.5, SI 2003/2153 Sch.2 para.5, SI 2003/2326 Sch.2 para.5, SI 2003/2334 Sch.2 para.5, SI 2003/2336 Sch.2 para.5, SI 2003/2440 Sch.2 para.5, SI 2003/2677 Sch.2 para.5, SI 2003/2711 Sch.2 para.5, SI 2004/13 Sch.2 para.5, SI 2004/104 Sch.2 para.5, SI 2004/914 Sch.2 para.5, SI 2004/1278 Sch.2 para.5, SI 2004/1285 Sch.2 para.13, SI 2004/1305 Sch.2 para.5, SI 2004/1402 Sch.2 para.5, SI 2004/1608 Sch.2 para.5, SI 2004/2028 Sch.3 para.5, SI 2004/2111 Sch.2 para.5, SI 2004/2188 Sch.2 para.5, SI 2004/2193 Sch.2 para.5, SI 2004/2194 Sch.2 para.5, SI 2004/2212 Sch.2 para.5, SI 2004/2260 Sch.2 para.5, SI 2004/2424 Sch.3 para.5, SI 2004/2616 Sch.2 para.5, SI 2004/2684 Art.4, SSI 2002/398 Sch.3 para.5, SSI 2003/70 Sch.3 para.5, SSI 2004/87 Sch.3 para.5

s.103, enabling: SI 2002/2777

s.115, applied: 2003 c.iii s.13

s.115, referred to: 2003 c.iii s.13

s.117, amended: 2004 c.18 s.94

s.117, applied: 2004 c.18 s.79

s.121A, applied: SSI 2003/70 Sch.1

s.121B, amended: 2004 c.18 s.63

s.121B, applied: 2004 c.18 s.29, s.60

s.121B, varied: 2004 c.18 s.29

s.122, see *R. (on the application of LPC Group Plc) v Leicester City Council* [2002] EWHC 2485, [2003] R.T.R. 11 (QBD (Admin Ct)), Sir Christopher Bellamy, Q.C.; see *R. (on the application of Westminster City Council) v Mayor of London* [2002] EWHC 2440, [2003] B.L.G.R. 611 (QBD (Admin Ct)), Maurice Kay, J.

s.124, enabling: SSI 2002/31, SSI 2002/450, SSI 2002/547

s.124C, varied: 2004 c.18 s.61

CAP.

1984–cont.

27. Road Traffic Regulation Act 1984–*cont.*

s.129, applied: SI 2002/2780 Reg.2

s.131, applied: 2004 c.18 s.90

s.134, applied: SI 2002/3113(a), SI 2002/746, SI 2002/1651, SI 2002/2777, SI 2002/2936, SI 2002/3020, SI 2003/2187, SI 2003/2188, SI 2003/2615, SI 2004/180, SSI 2002/31, SSI 2002/399, SSI 2002/450, SSI 2002/538, SSI 2002/547, SSI 2002/549, SSI 2003/72, SSI 2004/53, SSI 2004/54, SSI 2004/85

s.134, varied: SSI 2002/398 Sch.3 para.6, SSI 2003/70 Sch.3 para.6, SSI 2004/87 Sch.3 para.6

s.142, amended: SI 2003/251 Sch.2 para.6

s.142, varied: SI 2002/37 Sch.2 para.6, SI 2002/126 Sch.2 para.6, SI 2002/276 Sch.2 para.6, SI 2002/421 Sch.2 para.6, SI 2002/422 Sch.2 para.6, SI 2002/1351 Sch.2 para.6, SI 2002/1352 Sch.2 para.6, SI 2002/1353 Sch.2 para.6, SI 2002/1484 Sch.2 para.6, SI 2002/1485 Sch.2 para.6, SI 2002/1486 Sch.2 para.6, SI 2002/1504 Sch.2 para.6, SI 2002/1621 Sch.2 para.6, SI 2002/2012 Sch.2 para.6, SI 2002/2183 Sch.2 para.6, SI 2002/2184 Sch.2 para.6, SI 2002/2185 Sch.2 para.6, SI 2002/2186 Sch.2 para.6, SI 2002/2187 Sch.2 para.6, SI 2002/2188 Sch.2 para.6, SI 2002/2520 Sch.2 para.6, SI 2002/2705 Sch.2 para.6, SI 2002/3265 Sch.2 para.6, SI 2002/3266 Sch.2 para.6, SI 2003/95 Sch.2 para.6, SI 2003/634 Sch.2 para.6, SI 2003/635 Sch.2 para.6, SI 2003/898 Sch.2 para.6, SI 2003/1261 Sch.2 para.6, SI 2003/1262 Sch.2 para.6, SI 2003/1924 Sch.2 para.6, SI 2003/1984 Sch.2 para.6, SI 2003/2152 Sch.2 para.6, SI 2003/2153 Sch.2 para.6, SI 2003/2326 Sch.2 para.6, SI 2003/2334 Sch.2 para.6, SI 2003/2336 Sch.2 para.6, SI 2003/2440 Sch.2 para.6, SI 2003/2677 Sch.2 para.6, SI 2003/2711 Sch.2 para.6, SI 2004/13 Sch.2 para.6, SI 2004/104 Sch.2 para.6, SI 2004/914 Sch.2 para.6, SI 2004/1278 Sch.2 para.6, SI 2004/1285 Sch.2 para.14, SI 2004/1305 Sch.2 para.6, SI 2004/1402 Sch.2 para.6, SI 2004/1608 Sch.2 para.6, SI 2004/2028 Sch.3 para.6, SI 2004/2111 Sch.2 para.6, SI 2004/2188 Sch.2 para.6, SI 2004/2193 Sch.2 para.6, SI 2004/2194 Sch.2 para.6, SI 2004/2212 Sch.2 para.6, SI 2004/2260 Sch.2 para.6, SI 2004/2424 Sch.3 para.6, SI 2004/2616 Sch.2 para.6, SSI 2002/398 Sch.3 para.7, SSI 2003/70 Sch.3 para.7, SSI 2004/87 Sch.3 para.7

s.145, repealed: 2004 c.14 Sch.1 Part 14

Sch.1 para.7, referred to: 2004 c.18 Sch.7 para.3

Sch.1 para.8, referred to: 2004 c.18 Sch.7 para.3

CAP.

CAP.

1984–cont.

27. Road Traffic Regulation Act 1984–*cont.*

Sch.2 para.1, repealed: 2004 c.14 Sch.1 Part 14

Sch.2 para.2, repealed: 2004 c.14 Sch.1 Part 14

Sch.2 para.3, repealed: 2004 c.14 Sch.1 Part 14

Sch.2 para.4, repealed: 2004 c.14 Sch.1 Part 14

Sch.2 para.5, repealed: 2004 c.14 Sch.1 Part 14

Sch.2 para.6, repealed: 2004 c.14 Sch.1 Part 14

Sch.2 para.7, repealed: 2004 c.14 Sch.1 Part 14

Sch.2 para.8, repealed: 2004 c.14 Sch.1 Part 14

Sch.2 para.9, repealed: 2004 c.14 Sch.1 Part 14

Sch.2 para.10, repealed: 2004 c.14 Sch.1 Part 14

Sch.5, amended: SI 2002/2626 Sch.2 para.11

Sch.8 Part II para.3, substituted: 2004 c.14 Sch.2 para.16

Sch.9 Part I para.1, amended: 2004 c.36 Sch.2 para.16

Sch.9 Part I para.12A, added: 2004 c.36 Sch.2 para.16

Sch.9 Part I para.12B, added: 2004 c.36 Sch.2 para.16

Sch.9 Part III, enabling: SSI 2002/31

Sch.9 Part III para.21, enabling: SSI 2002/450, SSI 2002/547

Sch.9 Part III para.22, enabling: SSI 2002/450, SSI 2002/547

Sch.9 Part III para.25, enabling: SSI 2002/450, SSI 2002/547

Sch.9 Part IV, enabling: SI 2002/1672

Sch.9 Part VI, see *R. (on the application of Deutsch) v Hackney LBC* [2003] EWHC 2692, [2004] A.C.D. 11 (QBD (Admin Ct)), Hooper, J.

Sch.9 para.35, see *R. (on the application of LPC Group Plc) v Leicester City Council* [2002] EWHC 2485, [2003] R.T.R. 11 (QBD (Admin Ct)), Sir Christopher Bellamy, Q.C.

Sch.10 para.18, repealed: 2004 c.14 Sch.1 Part 14

Sch.10 para.20, repealed: 2004 c.14 Sch.1 Part 14

Sch.13 para.2, repealed: 2004 c.14 Sch.1 Part 14

Sch.13 para.5, repealed: 2004 c.14 Sch.1 Part 14

Sch.13 para.39, repealed: 2004 c.14 Sch.1 Part 14

28. County Courts Act 1984

applied: 2003 c.20 Sch.4 para.7

referred to: 2003 c.39 s.76

1984–cont.

28. County Courts Act 1984–*cont.*

Part VI, applied: 2004 c.14 Sch.2 para.17

s.6, applied: 2003 c.39 s.77, SI 2003/409 Sch.1 Part I

s.14, amended: 2003 c.44 Sch.26 para.33

s.24, amended: 2004 c.14 Sch.1 Part 1

s.51, applied: 2003 c.43 s.157

s.55, applied: SI 2002/457 Sch.1 para.18, SI 2002/897 Sch.1 para.18

s.66, amended: 2003 c.39 Sch.8 para.271

s.69, see *Sempra Metals Ltd (formerly Metallgesellschaft Ltd) v Inland Revenue Commissioners* [2004] EWHC 2387, [2004] S.T.C. 1178 (Ch D), Park, J.

s.73, applied: 2003 c.39 Sch.9 para.16

s.73, repealed: 2003 c.39 Sch.8 para.272, Sch.10

s.73A, repealed: 2003 c.39 Sch.8 para.272, Sch.10

s.80, amended: 2003 c.39 Sch.8 para.271

s.86, see *Ropaigealach v Allied Irish Bank Plc* [2001] EWCA Civ 1790, [2002] 1 E.G.L.R. 83 (CA), Hale, L.J.

s.92, amended: 2003 c.44 Sch.26 para.33

s.95, amended: 2003 c.39 Sch.8 para.271

s.97, applied: SI 2004/3114 Sch.1, SI 2004/3121 Sch.1

s.98, amended: 2003 c.39 Sch.8 para.273

s.99, amended: 2003 c.39 Sch.8 para.274

s.99, repealed (in part): 2003 c.39 Sch.10

s.104, substituted: 2003 c.39 Sch.8 para.275

s.109, amended: SI 2002/439 Art.7

s.110, amended: SI 2002/439 Art.8

s.110, repealed (in part): SI 2002/439 Art.8

s.112, applied: 2003 c.39 s.98, SI 2004/400 Reg.5

s.112A, applied: 2003 c.39 s.98

s.128, applied: SI 2002/223, SI 2003/648, SI 2003/718, SI 2004/2098

s.128, repealed: 2003 c.39 Sch.8 para.276, Sch.10

s.128, enabling: SI 2002/223, SI 2003/648, SI 2003/718, SI 2004/2098

s.138, see *Mohammadi v Anston Investments Ltd* [2003] EWCA Civ 981, [2004] H.L.R. 8 (CA), May, L.J.

s.147, amended: SI 2002/439 Art.9, 2003 c.39 Sch.8 para.277, Sch.10

Sch.2 Part V para.22, repealed: 2004 c.14 Sch.1 Part 1

Sch.2 Part V para.24, repealed: 2004 c.14 Sch.1 Part 1

Sch.2 Part V para.30, repealed: 2004 c.14 Sch.1 Part 1

Sch.2 Part V para.35, repealed: 2004 c.14 Sch.1 Part 1

Sch.2 Part V para.36, repealed: 2004 c.14 Sch.1 Part 1

Sch.2 Part V para.38, repealed: 2004 c.14 Sch.1 Part 1

1984–cont.

28. County Courts Act 1984–*cont.*

Sch.2 Part V para.39, repealed: 2004 c.14 Sch.1 Part 1

Sch.2 Part V para.43, repealed: 2003 c.39 Sch.10

Sch.2 Part V para.44, repealed: 2004 c.14 Sch.1 Part 1

Sch.2 Part V para.45, repealed: 2004 c.14 Sch.1 Part 1

Sch.2 Part V para.46, repealed: 2004 c.14 Sch.1 Part 1

Sch.2 Part V para.48, repealed: 2004 c.14 Sch.1 Part 1

Sch.2 Part V para.50, repealed: 2004 c.14 Sch.1 Part 1

Sch.2 Part V para.57, repealed: 2004 c.14 Sch.1 Part 1

Sch.2 Part V para.58, repealed: 2002 c.38 Sch.5

Sch.2 Part V para.59, repealed: 2004 c.14 Sch.1 Part 17

Sch.2 Part V para.60, repealed: 2004 c.14 Sch.1 Part 17

Sch.2 Part V para.63, repealed: 2004 c.14 Sch.1 Part 1

Sch.2 Part V para.73, repealed: 2004 c.14 Sch.1 Part 1

Sch.2 Part V para.74, repealed: 2004 c.14 Sch.1 Part 1

Sch.2 Part V para.76, repealed: 2004 c.14 Sch.1 Part 1

Sch.2 Part V para.77, repealed: 2004 c.14 Sch.1 Part 1

30. Food Act 1984

applied: 2003 c.iv s.3

s.50, referred to: 2004 c.iii s.6

s.50, varied: 2003 c.iv s.3, 2004 c.iii s.6

s.51, varied: 2003 c.iv s.3, 2004 c.iii s.6

s.52, varied: 2003 c.iv s.3, 2004 c.iii s.6

s.53, varied: 2003 c.iv s.3, 2004 c.iii s.6

s.54, varied: 2003 c.iv s.3, 2004 c.iii s.6

s.55, varied: 2003 c.iv s.3, 2004 c.iii s.6

s.56, varied: 2003 c.iv s.3, 2004 c.iii s.6

s.57, varied: 2003 c.iv s.3, 2004 c.iii s.6

s.57A, varied: 2003 c.iv s.3, 2004 c.iii s.6

s.58, varied: 2003 c.iv s.3, 2004 c.iii s.6

s.59, varied: 2003 c.iv s.3, 2004 c.iii s.6

s.60, amended: 2004 c.21 Sch.1 para.56

s.60, varied: 2003 c.iv s.3, 2004 c.iii s.6

s.61, amended: 2004 c.21 Sch.1 para.56

s.61, varied: 2003 c.iv s.3, 2004 c.iii s.6

s.68, repealed (in part): SI 2003/1281 Art.3

s.69, amended: SI 2003/1281 Art.4

32. London Regional Transport Act 1984

s.41A, amended: 2003 c.20 Sch.2 para.19

34. Juries (Disqualification) Act 1984

repealed: 2003 c.44 Sch.37 Part 10

35. Data Protection Act 1984

s.5, see *Information Commissioner v Islington LBC* [2002] EWHC 1036, [2003] B.L.G.R. 38 (QBD), Hallett, J.

1984–cont.

36. Mental Health (Scotland) Act 1984

see *Anderson v Scottish Ministers* [2001] UKPC D5, [2003] 2 A.C. 602 (PC (Sc)), Lord Hope of Craighead; see *Smith v Angiolini* 2002 S.L.T. 934 (HCJ), Lord Kirkwood, Lord Abernethy, Judge EF Bowen Q.C.

applied: SI 2002/1792 Reg.5, SSI 2002/303 Reg.2, SSI 2003/231 Sch.1 para.4

repealed: 2003 asp 13 Sch.5 Part 1

Part V, applied: 2003 asp 7 s.7, SSI 2003/179 Reg.3, Reg.9

s.1, see *Hampson (Stewart) v HM Advocate* 2003 S.L.T. 94 (HCJ), Lord Cullen L.J.G., Lord Cameron of Lochbroom, Lord Marnoch

s.1, applied: SSI 2002/494 Reg.5

s.2, amended: 2003 asp 13 Sch.1 para.10

s.2, applied: SSI 2002/113 Art.6

s.6, amended: 2003 asp 13 Sch.1 para.10

s.7, amended: 2002 c.41 s.46

s.7, applied: 2002 asp 5 s.2, s.4, s.6, SI 2002/1792 Reg.15, SSI 2002/76 Reg.2, SSI 2002/303 Reg.3, 2003 asp 5 Sch.2 para.2

s.7, referred to: SSI 2002/533 Sch.1, Sch.3

s.8, amended: 2002 c.41 s.46

s.8, applied: SSI 2002/303 Reg.3

s.8, referred to: SSI 2002/533 Sch.1, Sch.3

s.9, referred to: SSI 2002/533 Sch.1

s.11, referred to: SSI 2002/533 Sch.1, Sch.3

s.17, see *Hutchison Reid v United Kingdom (50272/99)* (2003) 37 E.H.R.R. 9 (ECHR), G Ress (President)

s.20, applied: SSI 2003/155 Reg.3, SSI 2003/266 Reg.3

s.25, applied: 2003 asp 13 s.299

s.26, see *M, Petitioner* 2003 S.C. 52 (OH), Lord Eassie

s.27, applied: SI 2003/762 Reg.2, SI 2004/1748 Sch.1, SSI 2003/243 Reg.2

s.33, amended: 2003 asp 13 Sch.6 para.2

s.33, applied: 2002 asp 11 Sch.4 para.11

s.35A, applied: SI 2003/762 Reg.2, SI 2004/1748 Sch.1, SSI 2003/243 Reg.2

s.35I, applied: 2002 asp 11 Sch.4 para.11

s.50, applied: 2002 asp 11 Sch.4 para.11

s.53, amended: 2004 c.33 Sch.28 para.50

s.54, amended: 2004 c.33 Sch.28 para.51

s.63, applied: SI 2003/762 Reg.2, SI 2004/1748 Sch.1

s.64, amended: 2003 asp 13 Sch.6 para.3, SSI 2003/498 Art.2

s.64, applied: SI 2003/762 Reg.2, SI 2004/1748 Sch.1, SSI 2003/243 Reg.2

s.64, repealed (in part): 2003 asp 13 Sch.6 para.3

s.66, amended: 2003 asp 13 Sch.6 para.4

s.68, applied: SI 2003/762 Reg.2, SI 2004/1748 Sch.1, SSI 2003/243 Reg.2

s.71, amended: 2002 c.41 s.62

s.71, applied: 2003 asp 7 s.7

1984–cont.

36. Mental Health (Scotland) Act 1984–
cont.
s.74, amended: 2002 c.41 s.62
s.90, applied: SI 2002/1792 Reg.5
s.91, applied: SI 2003/409 Sch.1 Part I
s.105, applied: 2003 c.42 Sch.5 para.89
s.106, applied: 2003 c.42 Sch.3 para.47, SSI
    2003/441 Sch.1 para.14, SSI 2004/411
    Sch.1 para.17
s.107, applied: 2003 c.42 Sch.3 para.48, SSI
    2003/441 Sch.1 para.14, SSI 2004/411
    Sch.1 para.17
s.115, amended: 2002 asp 11 Sch.6 para.6
s.125, applied: 2003 asp 7 s.7

37. Child Abduction Act 1984
applied: 2002 c.38 Sch.4 para.21
referred to: 2003 c.32 Sch.5 para.9
s.1, amended: 2002 c.38 Sch.3 para.42,
    Sch.5
s.1, applied: SI 2002/896 Sch.1 para.43
s.2, see *R. v JA* [2001] EWCA Crim 1974,
    [2002] 1 Cr. App. R. (S.) 108 (CA (Crim
    Div)), Kay, L.J.
s.6, applied: SI 2002/635 Sch.1 para.2, SI
    2002/896 Sch.1 para.61, SI 2004/2695
    Sch.1 para.10
s.11, amended: 2003 c.32 Sch.5 para.10
Sch.1 para.3, amended: 2002 c.38 Sch.3
    para.43
Sch.1 para.5, amended: 2002 c.38 Sch.3
    para.43

39. Video Recordings Act 1984
applied: 2002 c.40 Sch.14, Sch.15
s.3, amended: SI 2002/253 Sch.5 para.9, SI
    2002/254 Sch.4 para.4, 2003 c.17 Sch.6
    para.89
s.3, applied: 2003 c.17 Sch.8 para.33
s.10, see *R. v Passley (Allen Martin)* [2003]
    EWCA Crim 2727, [2004] 1 Cr.App.R.(S.)
    70 (CA (Crim Div)), Henriques, J.

40. Animal Health and Welfare Act 1984
s.4, repealed: 2004 c.14 Sch.1 Part 17
s.10, amended: 2003 c.44 Sch.26 para.34
s.10, enabling: SI 2002/824, SI 2002/1131, SI
    2004/3231, SSI 2002/191
s.12, repealed: 2004 c.14 Sch.1 Part 17
s.17, repealed (in part): 2004 c.14 Sch.1 Part 17

**42. Matrimonial and Family Proceedings
Act 1984**
s.12, amended: 2004 c.33 Sch.27 para.90
s.13, see *Emin v Yeldag* [2002] 1 F.L.R. 956
    (Fam Div), Sumner, J.
s.16, see *M v L (Financial Relief after Overseas
    Divorce)* [2003] EWHC 328, [2003] 2
    F.L.R. 425 (Fam Div), Coleridge, J.
s.17, see *M v L (Financial Relief after Overseas
    Divorce)* [2003] EWHC 328, [2003] 2
    F.L.R. 425 (Fam Div), Coleridge, J.
s.18, see *M v L (Financial Relief after Overseas
    Divorce)* [2003] EWHC 328, [2003] 2
    F.L.R. 425 (Fam Div), Coleridge, J.

1984–cont.

**42. Matrimonial and Family Proceedings
Act 1984–**cont.
s.18, amended: 2004 c.35 Sch.12 para.4
s.21, amended: 2004 c.35 Sch.12 para.4
s.32, amended: 2004 c.33 Sch.27 para.91
s.36A, added: 2004 c.33 Sch.27 para.92
s.36B, added: 2004 c.33 Sch.27 para.92
s.36C, added: 2004 c.33 Sch.27 para.92
s.36D, added: 2004 c.33 Sch.27 para.92
s.38, amended: 2004 c.33 Sch.27 para.93
s.39, amended: 2004 c.33 Sch.27 para.94
s.40, amended: 2002 c.38 Sch.3 para.44,
    Sch.5, 2004 c.31 s.62, 2004 c.33 Sch.27
    para.95
s.40, applied: SI 2003/2839
s.40, repealed: 2003 c.39 Sch.8 para.278,
    Sch.10
s.40, enabling: SI 2003/184, SI 2003/2839
s.41, applied: SI 2003/645, SI 2003/719
s.41, repealed: 2003 c.39 Sch.8 para.278,
    Sch.10
s.41, enabling: SI 2003/645, SI 2003/719, SI
    2004/2103.27 para.96
Sch.1 para.13, repealed (in part): 2003 c.39
    Sch.10
Sch.1 para.20, repealed (in part): 2002 c.38
    Sch.5, SI 2004/2035 Sch.1 para.20

43. Finance Act 1984
s.15, see *TDG (UK) Ltd v Customs and Excise
    Commissioners* [2002] V. & D.R. 323
    (V&DTr), Nuala Brice (Chairman)
s.16, repealed (in part): 2004 c.14 Sch.1 Part 9
s.110, amended: 2003 c.14 Sch.20 para.3

47. Repatriation of Prisoners Act 1984
applied: 2003 c.32 s.48
s.1, applied: SI 2002/313 Sch.1
s.2, amended: 2003 c.44 Sch.32 para.41,
    Sch.37 Part 8
s.2, applied: SI 2002/313 Sch.1
s.3, amended: 2003 asp 7 s.33
s.3, repealed (in part): 2003 c.44 Sch.37 Part
    8
s.4, applied: SI 2002/313 Sch.1
Sch.1, amended: SI 2004/702 Sch.7 para.7
Sch.1 para.2, amended: 2003 c.44 Sch.32
    para.43
Sch.1 para.2, substituted: 2003 asp 7 s.33
Sch.1 para.3, repealed (in part): 2003 asp 7
    s.33, 2003 c.44 Sch.37 Part 8
Sch.1 para.8, amended: SI 2004/702 Sch.7
    para.7

48. Health and Social Security Act 1984
s.6, repealed (in part): 2003 c.4 Sch.4
Sch.3 para.5, repealed: 2003 c.43 Sch.14
    Part 4
Sch.3 para.15, repealed (in part): 2003 c.4
    Sch.4

51. Inheritance Tax Act 1984
applied: 2002 c.29 s.321, 2003 c.14 s.195,
    2004 c.12 Sch.15 para.10, Sch.15 para.11,
    Sch.15 para.12, SI 2004/2543 Reg.7

CAP.

1984–cont.

51. Inheritance Tax Act 1984–*cont.*
referred to: 2003 c.1 Sch.6 para.150
Part III c.III, applied: 2002 c.29 s.322, 2004 c.12 Sch.36 para.56, Sch.36 para.57
s.3, see *Melville v Inland Revenue Commissioners* [2001] EWCA Civ 1247, [2002] 1 W.L.R. 407 (CA), Peter Gibson, L.J.
s.5, see *Curnock v Inland Revenue Commissioners* [2003] S.T.C (S.C.D.) 283 (Sp Comm), John F Avery Jones; see *Daffodil v Inland Revenue Commissioners* [2002] S.T.C. (S.C.D.) 224 (Sp Comm), AN Brice (Chairman); see *Kempe v Inland Revenue Commissioners* [2004] S.T.C. (S.C.D.) 467 (Sp Comm), Nuala Brice; see *Melville v Inland Revenue Commissioners* [2001] EWCA Civ 1247, [2002] 1 W.L.R. 407 (CA), Peter Gibson, L.J.; see *Sillars v Inland Revenue Commissioners* [2004] S.T.C. (S.C.D.) 180 (Sp Comm), John F Avery Jones
s.6, amended: 2003 c.14 s.186
s.8, applied: SI 2003/841 Art.2, SI 2004/771 Art.2
s.8, disapplied: 2002 c.23 s.118
s.8, enabling: SI 2002/701, SI 2003/841, SI 2004/771
s.11, applied: 2004 c.12 Sch.15 para.10
s.12, amended: 2004 c.12 s.203
s.12, repealed (in part): 2004 c.12 Sch.42 Part 3
s.13, amended: 2003 c.1 Sch.6 para.151
s.14, amended: 2003 c.1 Sch.6 para.152
s.17, applied: 2004 c.12 Sch.15 para.16
s.18, see *Inland Revenue Commissioners v Eversden* [2002] EWHC 1360, [2002] S.T.C. 1109 (Ch D), Lightman, J.; see *Inland Revenue Commissioners v Eversden* [2002] S.T.C. (S.C.D.) 39 (Sp Comm), Nuala Brice; see *Inland Revenue Commissioners v Eversden* [2003] EWCA Civ 668, [2003] S.T.C. 822 (CA), Carnwath, L.J.
s.18, applied: SI 2004/2543 Reg.5
s.19, applied: 2004 c.12 Sch.15 para.10
s.20, applied: 2004 c.12 Sch.15 para.10
s.21, see *McDowall's Executors v Inland Revenue Commissioners* [2004] S.T.C. (S.C.D.) 22 (Sp Comm), J Gordon Reid Q.C. (Chairman)
s.23, applied: SI 2004/2543 Reg.5
s.23, varied: 2002 c.23 Sch.18 para.9
s.25, applied: SI 2004/2543 Reg.5
s.43, see *Rysaffe Trustee Co (CI) Ltd v Inland Revenue Commissioners* [2002] EWHC 1114, [2002] S.T.C. 872 (Ch D), Park, J.; see *Rysaffe Trustee Co (CI) Ltd v Inland Revenue Commissioners* [2003] EWCA Civ 356, [2003] S.T.C. 536 (CA), Mummery, L.J.
s.47A, added: 2002 c.23 s.119

CAP.

1984–cont.

51. Inheritance Tax Act 1984–*cont.*
s.48, amended: 2003 c.14 s.186
s.48, applied: 2004 c.12 Sch.15 para.12
s.49, amended: 2002 c.23 s.119
s.50, amended: 2002 c.23 s.119
s.51, amended: 2002 c.23 s.119
s.52, amended: 2002 c.23 s.119
s.53, amended: 2002 c.23 s.119
s.54, amended: 2002 c.23 s.119
s.54A, amended: 2002 c.23 s.119
s.54B, amended: 2002 c.23 s.119
s.55, amended: 2002 c.23 s.119
s.55A, added: 2002 c.23 s.119
s.55A, amended: 2002 c.23 s.119
s.56, amended: 2002 c.23 s.119
s.57, amended: 2002 c.23 s.119
s.57, applied: SI 2002/1731d (an.excepted.transfer)
s.57A, amended: 2002 c.23 s.119
s.58, amended: 2004 c.12 s.203, Sch.42 Part 3
s.58, referred to: 2004 c.12 Sch.36 para.58
s.64, see *Rysaffe Trustee Co (CI) Ltd v Inland Revenue Commissioners* [2002] EWHC 1114, [2002] S.T.C. 872 (Ch D), Park, J.
s.72, amended: 2003 c.1 Sch.6 para.151
s.86, amended: 2003 c.1 Sch.6 para.151
s.97, amended: 2002 c.23 s.42
s.104, disapplied: SI 2004/2543 Reg.4
s.105, see *Inland Revenue Commissioners v George* [2002] S.T.C. (S.C.D.) 358 (Sp Comm), John F Avery Jones; see *Inland Revenue Commissioners v George* [2003] EWCA Civ 1763, [2004] S.T.C. 147 (CA), Carnwath, L.J.; see *Inland Revenue Commissioners v George* [2003] EWHC 318, [2003] S.T.C. 468 (Ch D), Laddie, J.
s.115, see *Dixon v Inland Revenue Commissioners* [2002] S.T.C. (S.C.D.) 53 (Sp Comm), Nuala Brice; see *Higginson's Executors v Inland Revenue Commissioners* [2002] S.T.C. (S.C.D.) 483 (Sp Comm), BMF O'Brien; see *Lloyds TSB (Personal Representative of Antrobus (Deceased)) v Inland Revenue Commissioners* [2002] S.T.C. (S.C.D.) 468 (Sp Comm), Nuala Brice; see *Rosser v Inland Revenue Commissioners* [2003] S.T.C. (S.C.D.) 311 (Sp Comm), Michael Tildesley
s.116, see *Dixon v Inland Revenue Commissioners* [2002] S.T.C. (S.C.D.) 53 (Sp Comm), Nuala Brice; see *Rosser v Inland Revenue Commissioners* [2003] S.T.C. (S.C.D.) 311 (Sp Comm), Michael Tildesley
s.116, disapplied: SI 2004/2543 Reg.4
s.117, see *Rosser v Inland Revenue Commissioners* [2003] S.T.C. (S.C.D.) 311 (Sp Comm), Michael Tildesley

1984–cont.

51. InheritanceTax Act 1984–*cont.*

s.142, see *Soutter's Executry v Inland Revenue Commissioners* [2002] S.T.C. (S.C.D.) 385 (Sp Comm),T Gordon Coutts Q.C.

s.142, amended: 2002 c.23 s.120

s.142, applied: SI 2004/2543 Reg.3

s.151, amended: 2004 c.12 s.203

s.151, applied: 2004 c.12 Sch.36 para.56, Sch.36 para.58

s.151, repealed (in part): 2004 c.12 Sch.42 Part 3

s.152, amended: 2004 c.12 s.203

s.154, applied: SI 2003/1239 Art.3

s.155, amended: 2002 c.8 s.2

s.158, amended: 2003 c.14 s.198

s.161, see *Arkwright (Williams Personal Representative) v Inland Revenue Commissioners* [2004] EWHC 1720, [2004] S.T.C.1323 (Ch D), Gloster, J.

s.178, amended: 2003 c.14 s.186, Sch.43 Part 4

s.190, amended: 2003 c.14 Sch.18 para.2

s.216, see *Robertson v Inland Revenue Commissioners (No.1)* [2002] S.T.C. (S.C.D.) 182 (Sp Comm), J Gordon Reid Q.C.

s.216, applied: SI 2002/1731 Reg.3, 2004 c.12 s.295, SI 2004/2543 Reg.3, Reg.6, Reg.8

s.216, disapplied: SI 2002/1732 Reg.4, SI 2002/1733 Reg.4

s.217, applied: 2004 c.12 s.295

s.218A, added: 2002 c.23 s.120

s.218A, referred to: 2004 c.12 s.295

s.220A, amended: 2003 c.14 s.198

s.221, see *McDowall's Executors v Inland Revenue Commissioners* [2004] S.T.C. (S.C.D.) 22 (Sp Comm), J Gordon Reid Q.C. (Chairman); see *Two Settlors v Inland Revenue Commissioners* [2004] S.T.C. (S.C.D.) 45 (Sp Comm), John F Avery Jones

s.222, see *Arkwright (Williams Personal Representative) v Inland Revenue Commissioners* [2004] S.T.C. (S.C.D.) 89 (Sp Comm), Nuala Brice

s.224, see *Rosser v Inland Revenue Commissioners* [2003] S.T.C. (S.C.D.) 311 (Sp Comm), Michael Tildesley; see *Smith (Lesley Ann) v Inland Revenue Commissioners* [2002] S.T.C. (S.C.D.) 411 (Sp Comm), JF Avery Jones

s.231, amended: 2003 c.14 Sch.20 para.3

s.233, see *Prosser (Jempson's Personal Representative) v Inland Revenue Commissioners* [2003] S.T.C. (S.C.D.) 250 (Sp Comm), John F Avery Jones

s.237, applied: 2002 c.9 s.31

s.238, amended: 2002 c.9 Sch.11 para.17

s.238, applied: 2002 c.9 s.31

s.245, amended: 2004 c.12 s.295

1984–cont.

51. InheritanceTax Act 1984–*cont.*

s.245, varied: 2004 c.12 s.295

s.245A, amended: 2002 c.23 s.120, 2004 c.12 s.295

s.245A, varied: 2004 c.12 s.295

s.247, see *Robertson v Inland Revenue Commissioners (No.1)* [2002] S.T.C. (S.C.D.) 182 (Sp Comm), J Gordon Reid Q.C.

s.247, amended: 2004 c.12 s.295

s.247, applied: 2004 c.12 s.313

s.256, amended: 2004 c.12 s.293

s.256, repealed (in part): 2004 c.12 Sch.42 Part 4

s.256, enabling: SI 2002/1731, SI 2002/1732, SI 2002/1733, SI 2003/1658, SI 2004/2543

s.264, applied: SI 2002/1731 Reg.7, SI 2002/1732 Reg.8, SI 2002/1733 Reg.8, SI 2004/2543 Reg.10

s.267, applied: SI 2004/2543 Reg.4

s.267, referred to: SI 2002/1733 Reg.3

s.268, see *RysaffeTrustee Co (CI) Ltd v Inland Revenue Commissioners* [2002] EWHC 1114, [2002] S.T.C. 872 (Ch D), Park, J.; see *Rysaffe Trustee Co (CI) Ltd v Inland Revenue Commissioners* [2003] EWCA Civ 356, [2003] S.T.C. 536 (CA), Mummery, L.J.

s.268, referred to: 2004 c.12 Sch.15 para.11

s.272, see *Daffodil v Inland Revenue Commissioners* [2002] S.T.C. (S.C.D.) 224 (Sp Comm), AN Brice (Chairman); see *Rysaffe Trustee Co (CI) Ltd v Inland Revenue Commissioners* [2003] EWCA Civ 356, [2003] S.T.C. 536 (CA), Mummery, L.J.

s.272, amended: 2002 c.23 s.119, 2003 c.14 s.186, 2004 c.12 s.203

Sch.1, amended: SI 2002/701 Art.2, SI 2003/841 Art.2, SI 2004/771 Art.2

Sch.1, substituted: 2002 c.23 s.118

Sch.4 Part I para.3, applied: 2004 c.12 Sch.15 para.11

Sch.8 para.1, repealed: 2002 c.9 Sch.13

53. Local Government (Interim Provisions) Act 1984

repealed: 2004 c.14 Sch.1 Part 10

54. Roads (Scotland) Act 1984

applied: 2003 asp 15 s.55, SI 2003/1594 Art.2

s.1, applied: SI 2002/3113 Reg.16

s.2, applied: SI 2002/3113 Reg.16

s.7, amended: 2002 asp 3 Sch.7 para.14

s.27, applied: SI 2002/3113 Reg.16

s.34, see *Syme v Scottish Borders Council* 2003 S.L.T. 601 (OH), 7 Lord Clarke

s.36, applied: SI 2002/3113 Reg.16, Reg.34

s.38, applied: SSI 2002/419

s.38, enabling: SSI 2002/419

s.39A, applied: SI 2002/3113 Reg.16

CAP.

1984–cont.

54. Roads (Scotland) Act 1984–*cont.*
s.39B, enabling: SSI 2002/419
s.39BA, added: 2004 c.36 Sch.2 para.17
s.40, amended: 2004 c.36 Sch.2 para.17
s.50, amended: SI 2003/2155 Sch.1 para.10
s.75, amended: SI 2003/2155 Sch.1 para.10
s.76, amended: 2002 asp 3 Sch.7 para.14
s.78, amended: SI 2003/2155 Sch.1 para.10
s.87, see *David Runciman & Sons v Scottish Borders Council* 2003 S.L.T. 1405 (OH), Lord Drummond Young
s.132, amended: SI 2003/2155 Sch.1 para.10
s.135, amended: 2002 asp 3 Sch.7 para.14
s.143, enabling: SSI 2002/419
s.151, see *David Runciman & Sons v Scottish Borders Council* 2003 S.L.T. 1405 (OH), Lord Drummond Young
s.151, amended: 2002 asp 3 Sch.7 para.14, SI 2003/2155 Sch.1 para.10, Sch.2
s.151, applied: 2003 asp 2 s.5
s.151, referred to: SSI 2002/178 Art.9
Sch.1 Part I para.3, amended: 2002 asp 3 Sch.7 para.14
Sch.1 Part II para.10, amended: 2002 asp 3 Sch.7 para.14
Sch.9 para.7, repealed (in part): 2003 c.22 Sch.1
Sch.9 para.24, repealed: 2004 c.14 Sch.1 Part 14
Sch.9 para.51, repealed: 2003 asp 8 Sch.6 para.15

55. Building Act 1984
see *R. (on the application of Bello) v Lewisham LBC* [2003] EWCA Civ 353, (2004) 20 Const. L.J. 89 (CA), Schiemann, L.J.
s.1, amended: 2004 c.22 s.1
s.1, referred to: 2004 c.22 s.6
s.1, enabling: SI 2002/440, SI 2002/2871, SI 2002/2872, SI 2003/2692, SI 2003/3030, SI 2003/3133, SI 2004/1465, SI 2004/1466, SI 2004/1808, SI 2004/3210
s.1A, added: 2004 c.22 s.2
s.2, enabling: SI 2002/440
s.2A, added: 2004 c.22 s.4
s.3, enabling: SI 2004/1808, SI 2004/3210
s.4, see *Manchester City Council v Railtrack Plc* [2002] EWHC 2719, [2003] E.H.L.R. 8 (QBD (Admin Ct)), Silber, J.
s.4, amended: 2002 c.32 Sch.21 para.6
s.4, repealed: 2004 c.22 s.5, Sch.1
s.4, enabling: SI 2002/440
s.11, repealed (in part): 2004 c.14 Sch.1 Part 13
s.11, enabling: SI 2002/440
s.12, repealed (in part): 2004 c.14 Sch.1 Part 13
s.14, applied: SI 2002/440, SI 2002/2871, SI 2002/2872, SI 2003/2692, SI 2003/3030, SI 2004/1465, SI 2004/1466, SI 2004/1808
s.15, amended: 2004 c.21 Sch.1 para.57

CAP.

1984–cont.

55. Building Act 1984–*cont.*
s.16, applied: SI 2002/2871 Reg.3, SI 2003/2692 Reg.3, SI 2003/3030 Reg.3, SI 2004/1808 Reg.3
s.24, amended: 2003 c.17 Sch.6 para.91, 2004 c.21 Sch.1 para.57
s.33, amended: 2004 c.22 s.4
s.35, see *Manchester City Council v Railtrack Plc* [2002] EWHC 2719, [2003] E.H.L.R. 8 (QBD (Admin Ct)), Silber, J.
s.35, enabling: SI 2002/2872, SI 2003/3133
s.36, see *R. (on the application of Bello) v Lewisham LBC* [2002] EWHC 1332, [2002] E.H.L.R. 19 (QBD (Admin Ct)), Silber, J.
s.38, amended: 2004 c.22 s.4
s.40, amended: 2003 c.39 Sch.8 para.279, Sch.10
s.44, amended: 2004 c.22 s.3, s.4
s.45, amended: 2004 c.22 s.3
s.47, amended: 2004 c.22 s.8
s.47, applied: SI 2002/2871 Reg.3, SI 2002/2872 Reg.3, Reg.4, SI 2003/2692 Reg.3, SI 2004/1808 Reg.3
s.47, enabling: SI 2002/2871, SI 2002/2872, SI 2003/3133, SI 2004/1466
s.48, amended: 2004 c.21 Sch.1 para.57
s.50, applied: SI 2002/2871 Reg.3, SI 2002/2872 Reg.3, SI 2003/2692 Reg.3, SI 2004/1808 Reg.3
s.51A, applied: SI 2002/2871 Reg.3, SI 2002/2872 Reg.3, Reg.4, SI 2003/2692 Reg.3, SI 2004/1808 Reg.3
s.51B, amended: 2004 c.21 Sch.1 para.57
s.52, amended: 2004 c.22 s.8
s.55, amended: 2003 c.39 Sch.8 para.280, Sch.10
s.56, repealed (in part): 2004 c.22 Sch.1
s.57, amended: 2004 c.22 s.8
s.59, amended: SI 2002/440 Reg.4
s.59, repealed (in part): 2004 c.22 s.5, Sch.1
s.71, amended: 2004 c.21 Sch.1 para.57
s.72, amended: 2004 c.21 Sch.1 para.57
s.72, repealed (in part): 2004 c.34 s.53, Sch.16
s.74, repealed (in part): 2003 c.17 Sch.6 para.92, Sch.7
s.81, amended: 2004 c.21 Sch.1 para.57
s.81, applied: 2004 c.i s.10
s.81, varied: 2004 c.i s.10
s.82, amended: 2004 c.21 Sch.1 para.57
s.91A, added: 2004 c.22 s.7
s.96, amended: 2003 c.44 Sch.37 Part 9
s.96, disapplied: 2003 c.44 Sch.25 para.81
s.99, applied: 2004 c.i s.10
s.107, referred to: 2004 c.i s.10
s.107, varied: 2004 c.i s.10
s.108, varied: 2004 c.i s.10
s.109, varied: 2004 c.i s.10
s.110, varied: 2004 c.i s.10

1984–cont.

55. Building Act 1984–_cont._

s.126, amended: 2004 c.21 Sch.1 para.57, 2004 c.22 s.1, s.4

Sch.1 para.1, enabling: SI 2002/2871, SI 2002/2872, SI 2003/3133, SI 2004/1465, SI 2004/1466

Sch.1 para.2, enabling: SI 2002/440, SI 2002/2871, SI 2002/2872, SI 2003/2692, SI 2003/3133, SI 2004/1465, SI 2004/1466, SI 2004/1808, SI 2004/3210

Sch.1 para.4, enabling: SI 2002/440, SI 2004/1808, SI 2004/3210

Sch.1 para.4A, added: 2004 c.22 s.8

Sch.1 para.4B, added: 2004 c.22 s.9

Sch.1 para.7, amended: 2004 c.22 s.3

Sch.1 para.7, enabling: SI 2002/2871, SI 2003/2692, SI 2003/3133, SI 2004/1465, SI 2004/1466, SI 2004/1808, SI 2004/3210

Sch.1 para.8, amended: 2004 c.22 s.3

Sch.1 para.8, enabling: SI 2002/2871, SI 2003/2692, SI 2003/3133, SI 2004/1465, SI 2004/1466, SI 2004/1808, SI 2004/3210

Sch.1 para.10, enabling: SI 2002/440, SI 2002/2871, SI 2002/2872, SI 2003/2692, SI 2003/3030, SI 2003/3133, SI 2004/1465, SI 2004/1466, SI 2004/1808, SI 2004/3210

Sch.1 para.11, enabling: SI 2002/440, SI 2003/3030

Sch.5 para.1, repealed: 2004 c.14 Sch.1 Part 13

Sch.5 para.4, repealed: 2004 c.14 Sch.1 Part 13

Sch.6 para.9, repealed: 2004 c.14 Sch.1 Part 13

Sch.6 para.12, repealed: 2004 c.14 Sch.1 Part 13

56. Foster Children (Scotland) Act 1984

s.10, applied: SI 2002/635 Reg.2, SI 2002/896 Sch.1 para.6

s.15, applied: SI 2002/635 Sch.1 para.2, SI 2002/896 Sch.1 para.62, SI 2004/2695 Sch.1 para.10

57. Co-operative Development Agency and Industrial Development Act 1984

s.3, repealed: 2004 c.14 Sch.1 Part 16

s.5, repealed (in part): 2004 c.14 Sch.1 Part 16 1 Part 16

s.7, repealed: 2004 c.14 Sch.1 Part 16

s.8, amended: 2004 c.14 Sch.1 Part 16

Sch.1 Part I, repealed: 2004 c.14 Sch.1 Part 16

Sch.1 Part II para.1, repealed: 2004 c.14 Sch.1 Part 16

Sch.1 Part II para.4, repealed: 2004 c.14 Sch.1 Part 16

Sch.1 Part II para.5, repealed: 2004 c.14 Sch.1 Part 16

Sch.1 Part II para.6, repealed: 2004 c.14 Sch.1 Part 16

1984–cont.

57. Co-operative Development Agency and Industrial Development Act 1984–_cont._

Sch.2 Part I, amended: 2004 c.14 Sch.1 Part 16

Sch.2 Part II, amended: 2004 c.14 Sch.1 Part 16

Sch.2 Part III, amended: 2004 c.14 Sch.1 Part 16

58. Rent (Scotland) Act 1984

s.5, amended: SSI 2003/331 Sch.1 para.5

s.6, amended: 2003 c.14 Sch.20 para.3

s.12A, added: 2003 asp 10 Sch.1 para.2

s.12A, referred to: 2003 asp 10 s.11

s.23A, amended: 2002 c.41 s.32

s.25, amended: 2003 asp 11 Sch.1 para.6

s.43, applied: 2002 asp 13 Sch.1 para.18

s.44, applied: 2002 asp 11 Sch.3 para.5

s.55, applied: SSI 2002/318 Art.5

s.56, applied: SSI 2002/318 Art.5

s.57, applied: SSI 2002/318 Art.5

s.58, applied: SSI 2002/318 Art.5

s.59, applied: SSI 2002/318 Art.5

s.63, amended: SSI 2003/331 Sch.1 para.5

s.115, amended: SSI 2003/331 Sch.1 para.5

Sch.1 para.2, amended: 2004 c.33 Sch.28 para.48

Sch.1 para.6, amended: 2004 c.33 Sch.28 para.48

Sch.1A para.2, amended: 2004 c.33 Sch.28 para.49

Sch.4 para.4, applied: SI 2003/409 Sch.1 Part I

60. Police and Criminal Evidence Act 1984

see *Addison v Chief Constable of the West Midlands* [2004] 1 W.L.R. 29 (CA), Ward, L.J.; see *DPP v Wilson* [2001] EWHC Admin 198, [2002] R.T.R. 6 (QBD (Admin Ct)), Sullivan, J.; see *Perry v United Kingdom (63737/00)* (2004) 39 E.H.R.R. 3 (ECHR), Judge Ress (President); see *R. v Dervish (Mulayim)* [2001] EWCA Crim 2789, [2002] 2 Cr. App. R. 6 (CA (Crim Div)), Kay, L.J.; see *R. v Marrin (Keith Ian)* [2002] EWCA Crim 251, Times, March 5, 2002 (CA (Crim Div)), Keene, L.J.; see *Whitley v DPP* [2003] EWHC 2512, (2004) 168 J.P. 350 (QBD (Admin Ct)), Brooke, L.J.

applied: SI 2002/868 Reg.4, SI 2003/1519 Art.20, SI 2003/2818 Art.13, SI 2004/221 Reg.4, SI 2004/373 Reg.4, SI 2004/432 Reg.4, SI 2004/559 Reg.4, SI 2004/1315 Reg.4

referred to: SI 2004/653 Reg.24

Part IV, applied: 2003 c.20 s.85, s.97, 2003 c.44 s.87, SI 2003/2818 Art.7

s.1, amended: 2003 c.44 s.1, Sch.37 Part 1

s.2, see *DPP v Avery* [2001] EWHC Admin 748, [2002] 1 Cr. App. R. 31 (QBD (Admin Ct)), Newman, J.

1984–cont.

60. Police and Criminal Evidence Act 1984–cont.

s.4, applied: 2002 c.30 Sch.4 para.13

s.6, amended: SI 2004/1573 Art.12

s.6, repealed (in part): 2004 c.20 Sch.23 Part 1

s.8, applied: 2002 c.30 Sch.4 para.16, 2003 c.32 s.16

s.8, varied: 2003 c.32 s.16

s.9, see *R. (on the application of NTL Group Ltd) v Ipswich Crown Court* [2002] EWHC 1585, [2003] Q.B. 131 (QBD (Admin Ct)), Lord Woolf of Barnes, L.C.J.

s.9, amended: 2003 c.39 Sch.4 para.5

s.9, applied: 2002 c.30 Sch.4 para.17, SI 2003/2273 Sch.1 para.3

s.9, varied: SI 2002/2326 Art.4, 2003 c.32 s.16

s.10, see *R. v Davies (Keith)* [2002] EWCA Crim 85, (2002) 166 J.P. 243 (CA (Crim Div)), May, L.J.

s.10, varied: 2003 c.32 s.16

s.11, referred to: SI 2003/2273 Sch.1 para.14

s.11, varied: 2003 c.32 s.16

s.12, varied: 2003 c.32 s.16

s.13, varied: 2003 c.32 s.16

s.14, varied: 2003 c.32 s.16

s.15, amended: SI 2003/174 Art.2

s.15, applied: 2002 c.29 s.355, SI 2003/1901 Sch.1 para.12

s.15, referred to: SI 2003/174 Art.10, Sch.1

s.15, repealed (in part): SI 2003/174 Art.2

s.15, varied: 2002 c.30 Sch.4 para.16, Sch.4 para.17, SI 2002/2326 Art.4, 2003 c.32 s.16

s.16, amended: 2003 c.39 Sch.8 para.281, 2003 c.44 s.2, SI 2003/174 Art.3

s.16, applied: 2002 c.29 s.355, 2002 c.30 Sch.4 para.24A, Sch.4 para.20, SI 2003/1901 Sch.1 para.12

s.16, referred to: SI 2003/174 Art.10, Sch.1

s.16, repealed (in part): SI 2003/174 Art.3

s.16, varied: 2002 c.30 Sch.4 para.16, Sch.4 para.17, 2003 c.14 Sch.13 para.52, 2003 c.32 s.16

s.17, see *Hobson v Chief Constable of Cheshire* [2003] EWHC 3011, (2004) 168 J.P. 111 (QBD (Admin Ct)), Maurice Kay, J.

s.17, amended: 2002 c.30 s.49

s.17, applied: 2002 c.30 Sch.4 para.8, SI 2003/1901 Sch.1 para.13

s.17, varied: 2003 c.32 s.16

s.18, see *R. (on the application of) v Commissioner of Police of the Metropolis* [2002] UKHL 20, [2002] 2 A.C. 692 (HL), Lord Hutton

s.18, amended: 2002 c.30 Sch.7 para.9, 2003 c.44 Sch.1 para.2

s.18, applied: 2002 c.30 Sch.4 para.18, SI 2003/1901 Sch.1 para.13

1984–cont.

60. Police and Criminal Evidence Act 1984–cont.

s.18, varied: 2002 c.30 Sch.4 para.18, 2003 c.32 s.16

s.19, see *R. (on the application of) v Commissioner of Police of the Metropolis* [2002] UKHL 20, [2002] 2 A.C. 692 (HL), Lord Hutton

s.19, applied: 2002 c.29 s.67, 2002 c.30 Sch.4 para.19

s.19, varied: 2002 c.30 Sch.4 para.16, Sch.4 para.17, Sch.4 para.18, Sch.4 para.19, 2003 c.32 s.16

s.20, applied: SI 2003/425 Art.6, SI 2003/1901 Sch.1 para.12

s.20, disapplied: SI 2003/425 Art.15, Art.25

s.20, varied: 2002 c.30 Sch.4 para.16, Sch.4 para.17, Sch.4 para.18, SI 2002/2326 Art.4, 2003 c.32 s.16, SI 2003/425 Art.5

s.21, amended: 2003 c.44 Sch.1 para.3, SI 2003/174 Art.4

s.21, applied: 2002 c.29 s.355, SI 2003/1901 Sch.1 para.12

s.21, referred to: 2002 c.30 Sch.4 para.24A, SI 2003/174 Art.10, Sch.1

s.21, varied: 2002 c.30 Sch.4 para.16, Sch.4 para.17, Sch.4 para.18, Sch.4 para.19, Sch.4 para.20, SI 2002/2326 Art.4, 2003 c.32 s.16, s.22

s.22, amended: 2003 c.44 Sch.1 para.4, SI 2003/174 Art.5

s.22, applied: 2002 c.29 s.355, SI 2003/1901 Sch.1 para.13

s.22, referred to: SI 2003/174 Art.10, Sch.1

s.22, repealed (in part): SI 2003/174 Art.5

s.22, varied: 2002 c.30 Sch.4 para.16, Sch.4 para.18, Sch.4 para.19, SI 2002/2326 Art.4, 2003 c.32 s.16

s.23, amended: 2004 c.20 s.103, Sch.23 Part 1

s.23, applied: SI 2003/1901 Sch.1 para.13

s.23, varied: 2003 c.32 s.16

s.24, amended: 2002 c.30 s.48

s.24, applied: SI 2002/868 Reg.4, SI 2002/2628 Art.16, SI 2003/1519 Art.20, 2004 c.2 s.6, 2004 c.11 s.14, SI 2004/432 Reg.4, SI 2004/559 Reg.4

s.24, varied: SI 2002/111 Art.20, SI 2004/221 Reg.4, SI 2004/348 Art.15, SI 2004/373 Reg.4, SI 2004/1315 Reg.4

s.27, applied: 2002 c.30 Sch.4 para.25

s.27, enabling: SI 2003/2823

s.28, see *Taylor v Chief Constable of Thames Valley* [2004] EWCA Civ 858, [2004] 1 W.L.R. 3155 (CA), Sir Andrew Morritt V.C.

s.30, amended: 2003 c.44 s.4

s.30, applied: 2002 c.30 Sch.4 para.34

s.30, varied: 2002 c.30 Sch.4 para.34

s.30A, added: 2003 c.44 s.4

s.30B, added: 2003 c.44 s.4

s.30C, added: 2003 c.44 s.4

1984–cont.

60. Police and Criminal Evidence Act 1984–*cont.*

s.30D, added: 2003 c.44 s.4

s.31, applied: 2002 c.30 Sch.4 para.21

s.31, varied: 2002 c.30 Sch.4 para.21

s.34, see *Williamson v Chief Constable of the West Midlands* [2003] EWCA Civ 337, [2004] 1 W.L.R. 14 (CA), Dyson, L.J.

s.34, amended: 2002 c.30 s.53, 2003 c.20 Sch.7 para.12, 2003 c.44 Sch.1 para.5

s.34, applied: 2003 c.44 s.87

s.34, varied: SI 2003/2818 Art.15, Art.16

s.35, amended: 2003 c.44 Sch.1 para.6

s.35, applied: SI 2003/2818 Art.7, Art.14, Art.16

s.35, varied: 2003 c.20 Sch.5 para.4, SI 2003/2818 Art.15, Art.16

s.36, amended: 2003 c.44 Sch.1 para.7

s.36, applied: SI 2003/2818 Art.5, Art.14

s.36, varied: 2002 c.30 Sch.4 para.23, 2003 c.20 Sch.5 para.4, SI 2003/2818 Art.16

s.37, amended: 2003 c.44 Sch.2 para.2

s.37, applied: SI 2003/2818 Art.7

s.37, varied: 2002 c.30 Sch.4 para.23, 2003 c.44 s.87, SI 2003/2818 Art.15, Art.16

s.37A, added: 2003 c.44 Sch.2 para.3

s.37A, varied: SI 2003/2818 Art.15, Art.16

s.37B, added: 2003 c.44 Sch.2 para.3

s.37B, amended: 2003 c.44 Sch.2 para.3

s.37B, varied: SI 2003/2818 Art.15, Art.16

s.37C, added: 2003 c.44 Sch.2 para.3

s.37C, varied: SI 2003/2818 Art.15, Art.16

s.37D, added: 2003 c.44 Sch.2 para.3

s.37D, varied: SI 2003/2818 Art.15, Art.16

s.38, amended: 2003 c.44 s.5, Sch.32 para.44, Sch.36 para.5

s.38, applied: 2003 c.44 s.88

s.38, referred to: 2003 c.44 s.88

s.38, varied: 2003 c.44 s.88, SI 2003/2818 Art.15, Art.16

s.39, varied: 2002 c.30 Sch.4 para.22, Sch.4 para.35, SI 2003/2818 Art.15, Art.16

s.40, amended: 2002 c.30 s.52, 2003 c.44 Sch.2 para.4

s.40, applied: SI 2003/2397 Reg.3, SI 2003/2818 Art.7

s.40, varied: 2003 c.44 s.87, SI 2003/2818 Art.15, Art.16

s.40A, amended: 2003 c.44 s.6

s.40A, applied: SI 2003/2818 Art.7

s.40A, varied: SI 2003/2818 Art.15, Art.16

s.41, amended: 2003 c.44 Sch.1 para.8

s.41, applied: SI 2003/2818 Art.7

s.41, referred to: SI 2003/2818 Art.7

s.41, varied: SI 2003/2818 Art.15, Art.16

s.42, amended: 2003 c.44 s.7

s.42, applied: SI 2003/2818 Art.7

s.42, varied: 2003 c.44 s.87, SI 2003/2818 Art.15, Art.16

s.43, applied: SI 2003/2818 Art.7

1984–cont.

60. Police and Criminal Evidence Act 1984–*cont.*

s.43, varied: SI 2003/2818 Art.15, Art.16

s.44, varied: SI 2003/2818 Art.15, Art.16

s.45, varied: SI 2003/2818 Art.15, Art.16

s.45A, amended: 2003 c.44 Sch.1 para.9

s.45A, varied: SI 2003/2818 Art.15, Art.16

s.45A, enabling: SI 2003/2397, SI 2004/1503

s.46, amended: 2003 c.39 Sch.8 para.282

s.46, disapplied: 2003 c.44 s.88

s.46, varied: SI 2003/2818 Art.15, Art.16

s.46A, amended: 2003 c.44 Sch.2 para.5

s.46A, varied: SI 2003/2818 Art.15, Art.16

s.47, amended: 2003 c.39 Sch.8 para.283, 2003 c.44 Sch.1 para.10, Sch.2 para.6

s.47, disapplied: 2003 c.44 s.88

s.47, varied: SI 2003/2818 Art.15, Art.16

s.47A, amended: 2003 c.39 Sch.8 para.284

s.47A, varied: SI 2003/2818 Art.15, Art.16

s.48, varied: SI 2003/2818 Art.15, Art.16

s.49, varied: SI 2003/2818 Art.15, Art.16

s.50, varied: SI 2003/2818 Art.15, Art.16

s.51, varied: SI 2003/2818 Art.15, Art.16

s.52, varied: SI 2003/2818 Art.15, Art.16

s.54, see *Chief Constable of West Yorkshire v A* [2002] EWCA Civ 1584, [2003] 1 All E.R. 255 (CA), Kennedy, L.J.; see *Chief Constable of West Yorkshire v A* [2004] UKHL 21, [2004] 2 W.L.R. 1209 (HL), Lord Bingham of Cornhill

s.54, amended: 2003 c.44 s.8, Sch.37 Part 1

s.54, applied: 2002 c.30 Sch.4 para.34, Sch.4 para.35, SI 2003/2273 Art.17, SI 2003/2818 Art.5, Art.14

s.54, referred to: 2003 c.41 s.171

s.54, varied: 2002 c.30 Sch.4 para.26, SI 2003/3106 Art.2

s.54A, amended: 2002 c.30 Sch.7 para.9, 2003 c.41 s.169

s.54A, applied: 2002 c.30 Sch.4 para.27

s.55, see *Chief Constable of West Yorkshire v A* [2002] I.C.R. 552 (EAT), Lindsay, J. (President)

s.55, applied: SI 2003/2818 Art.5, Art.14

s.55, referred to: 2003 c.41 s.171

s.55, varied: 2002 c.30 Sch.4 para.28, SI 2003/3106 Art.2

s.56, amended: 2002 c.29 Sch.11 para.14

s.56, applied: SI 2003/2818 Art.5, Art.14

s.56, referred to: 2003 c.41 s.171

s.56, varied: SI 2003/3106 Art.2

s.58, see *Campbell v DPP* [2002] EWHC 1314, (2002) 166 J.P. 742 (QBD (Admin Ct)), Goldring, J.; see *Kennedy v CPS* [2002] EWHC 2297, (2003) 167 J.P. 267 (QBD (Admin Ct)), Kennedy, L.J.; see *Kirkup v DPP* [2003] EWHC 2354, (2004) 168 J.P. 255 (QBD (Admin Ct)), Jackson, J.; see *Myles v DPP* [2004]

CAP.

1984–cont.

60. Police and Criminal Evidence Act 1984–cont.

s.58–*cont.*

EWHC 594, [2004] 2 All E.R. 902 (QBD (Admin Ct)), Kennedy, L.J.

s.58, amended: 2002 c.29 Sch.11 para.14

s.58, applied: SI 2003/2818 Art.5, Art.14

s.58, referred to: 2003 c.41 s.171

s.58, varied: SI 2003/3106 Art.2

s.60, applied: SI 2003/703, SI 2003/705, SI 2004/1887

s.60, referred to: SI 2003/703 Art.2, SI 2004/1887 Art.2

s.60, enabling: SI 2003/703, SI 2003/705

s.60A, applied: SI 2002/1069, SI 2002/1266, SI 2002/2527, SI 2004/1887, SI 2004/1887 Art.2

s.60A, enabling: SI 2002/1069, SI 2002/1266, SI 2002/2527, SI 2003/2463

s.61, amended: 2002 c.30 Sch.7 para.9, 2003 c.41 s.169, 2003 c.44 s.9

s.61, applied: 2002 c.30 Sch.4 para.29, SI 2003/2818 Art.14

s.62, amended: 2002 c.30 s.53, s.54, 2003 c.44 Sch.3 para.56

s.62, applied: 2002 c.30 Sch.4 para.30, SI 2003/2818 Art.14

s.62, repealed (in part): 2003 c.44 Sch.37 Part 4, Sch.3 para.56

s.63, amended: 2002 c.30 Sch.7 para.9, 2003 c.41 s.169, 2003 c.44 s.10, Sch.37 Part 1

s.63, applied: SI 2003/527 Reg.19, SI 2003/2818 Art.14

s.63, varied: 2002 c.30 Sch.4 para.31

s.63A, applied: 2002 c.30 Sch.4 para.32

s.63A, varied: 2003 c.20 Sch.5 para.4

s.63B, amended: 2003 c.44 s.5, 2004 c.31 Sch.5 Part 4

s.63C, amended: 2003 c.44 Sch.26 para.35

s.64, see *R. (on the application of S) v Chief Constable of South Yorkshire* [2002] EWCA Civ 1275, [2002] 1 W.L.R. 3223 (CA), Lord Woolf of Barnes, L.C.J.; see *R. (on the application of S) v Chief Constable of South Yorkshire* [2002] EWHC 478, Times, April 4, 2002 (QBD (Admin Ct)), Leveson, J.; see *R. (on the application of S) v Chief Constable of South Yorkshire* [2004] UKHL 39, [2004] 1 W.L.R. 2196 (HL), Lord Steyn

s.64A, amended: 2002 c.30 Sch.7 para.9, 2003 c.41 s.169

s.64A, applied: 2002 c.30 Sch.4 para.33

s.65, amended: 2002 c.29 Sch.12, 2002 c.30 s.54, 2003 c.41 s.169

s.65, applied: 2003 c.41 s.174, SI 2003/2461 Art.2

s.65, enabling: SI 2003/2461

s.66, see *R. v Williams (Hugh)* [2003] EWCA Crim 3200, (2003) 147 S.J.L.B. 1305 (CA (Crim Div)), Latham, L.J.

CAP.

1984–cont.

60. Police and Criminal Evidence Act 1984–cont.

s.66, applied: SI 2002/615 Art.2, SI 2002/3075, SI 2003/703, SI 2004/1887, SI 2004/1887 Art.2

s.66, referred to: SI 2002/3075 Art.2, SI 2003/703 Art.2

s.66, varied: SI 2002/615 Sch.1

s.66, enabling: SI 2002/3075, SI 2003/703

s.67, see *R. v Gill (Sewa Singh)* [2003] EWCA Crim 2256, [2004] 1 W.L.R. 469 (CA (Crim Div)), Clarke, L.J.

s.67, amended: 2002 c.30 Sch.7 para.9, Sch.8, 2003 c.44 s.11, Sch.37 Part 1

s.67, applied: SI 2002/1069, SI 2002/1266, SI 2002/2527, SI 2002/3075, SI 2003/703, SI 2003/705, SI 2004/1887

s.67, disapplied: 2002 c.29 s.377

s.67, enabling: SI 2002/615, SI 2002/1069, SI 2002/1150, SI 2002/1266, SI 2002/1863, SI 2002/3075, SI 2003/703, SI 2003/704, SI 2003/705, SI 2003/712, SI 2004/78, SI 2004/1887

s.71, amended: 2003 c.44 Sch.37 Part 4, Sch.3 para.56

s.73, amended: 2003 c.39 Sch.8 para.285

s.74, see *R. v Hayter (Paul Ali)* [2003] EWCA Crim 1048, [2003] 1 W.L.R. 1910 (CA (Crim Div)), Mantell, L.J.

s.74, amended: 2003 c.44 Sch.36 para.85, Sch.37 Part 5

s.76, see *R. v De Silva (Marc Anthony)* [2002] EWCA Crim 2673, [2003] 2 Cr. App. R. 5 (CA (Crim Div)), Hughes, J.; see *R. v Wahab (Azizul) (Appeal against Conviction)* [2002] EWCA Crim 1570, [2003] 1 Cr. App. R. 15 (CA (Crim Div)), Judge, L.J.

s.76, applied: 2003 c.44 s.128

s.76, repealed (in part): 2003 c.44 Sch.37 Part 4, Sch.3 para.56

s.76A, added: 2003 c.44 s.128

s.77, amended: 2003 c.44 Sch.36 para.48

s.78, see *Armstrong v United Kingdom (48521/99)* (2003) 36 E.H.R.R. 30 (ECHR), Judge Pellonpaa (President); see *Attorney General's Reference (No.5 of 2002), Re* [2003] EWCA Crim 1632, [2003] 1 W.L.R. 2902 (CA (Crim Div)), Clarke, L.J.; see *Campbell v DPP* [2002] EWHC 1314, (2002) 166 J.P. 742 (QBD (Admin Ct)), Goldring, J.; see *DPP v Kennedy* [2003] EWHC 2583, (2004) 168 J.P. 185 (QBD (Admin Ct)), Kennedy, L.J.; see *DPP v Robertson* [2002] EWHC 542, (2002) 166 J.P. 649 (QBD (Admin Ct)), Newman, J.; see *Kirkup v DPP* [2003] EWHC 2354, (2004) 168 J.P. 255 (QBD (Admin Ct)), Jackson, J.; see *R. (on the application of Bozkurt) v Thames Magistrates Court* [2001] EWHC Admin 400, [2002] R.T.R. 15 (QBD (Admin Ct)), Lord Woolf of Barnes, L.C.J.; see *R. (on*

1984–cont.

60. Police and Criminal Evidence Act 1984–*cont.*

s.78–*cont.*

the application of DPP) v BE [2002] EWHC 2976, (2003) 167 J.P. 144 (QBD (Admin Ct)), Maurice Kay, J.; see *R. v Claydon (Colette Dawn)* [2001] EWCA Crim 1359, [2004] 1 W.L.R. 1575 (CA (Crim Div)), Henry, L.J.; see *R. v De Silva (Marc Anthony)* [2002] EWCA Crim 2673, [2003] 2 Cr. App. R. 5 (CA (Crim Div)), Hughes, J.; see *R. v Elleray (Colin Woods)* [2003] EWCA Crim 553, [2003] 2 Cr. App. R. 11 (CA (Crim Div)), Lord Woolf of Barnes, L.C.J.; see *R. v Gill (Sewa Singh)* [2003] EWCA Crim 2256, [2004] 1 W.L.R. 469 (CA (Crim Div)), Clarke, L.J.; see *R. v Hardy (Brian)* [2002] EWCA Crim 3012, [2003] 1 Cr. App. R. 30 (CA (Crim Div)), Hughes, J.; see *R. v Hartnett (Kevin Patrick)* [2003] EWCA Crim 345, [2003] Crim. L.R. 719 (CA (Crim Div)), Lord Woolf of Barnes; see *R. v Jenkins (Nigel)* [2002] EWCA Crim 2475, [2003] Crim. L.R. 107 (CA (Crim Div)), Potter, L.J.; see *R. v Lyons (Isidore Jack) (No.3)* [2001] EWCA Crim 2860, [2002] 2 Cr. App. R. 15 (CA (Crim Div)), Rose, L.J.; see *R. v P (Telephone Intercepts: Admissibility of Evidence)* [2002] 1 A.C. 146 (HL), Lord Hobhouse of Woodborough; see *R. v Sed (Ali Dahir)* [2004] EWCA Crim 1294, [2004] 1 W.L.R. 3218 (CA (Crim Div)), Auld, L.J.; see *R. v Senior (Dianne)* [2004] EWCA Crim 454, [2004] 3 All E.R. 9 (CA (Crim Div)), Potter, L.J.; see *R. v Wahab (Azizul) (Appeal against Conviction)* [2002] EWCA Crim 1570, [2003] 1 Cr. App. R. 15 (CA (Crim Div)), Judge, L.J.; see *R. v Williams (Hugh)* [2003] EWCA Crim 3200, (2003) 147 S.J.L.B. 1305 (CA (Crim Div)), Latham, L.J.; see *Taylor-Sabori v United Kingdom (47114/99)* (2003) 36 E.H.R.R. 17 (ECHR), J-P Costa (President); see *Watson v DPP* [2003] EWHC 1466, (2004) 168 J.P. 116 (QBD (Admin Ct)), Goldring, J.

s.78, applied: 2003 c.44 s.126

s.78, repealed (in part): 2003 c.44 Sch.37 Part 4, Sch.3 para.56

s.80, see *R. (on the application of CPS) v Registrar General of Births, Deaths and Marriages* [2002] EWCA Civ 1661, [2003] Q.B. 1222 (CA), Waller, L.J.; see *R. v Pearce (Gary James)* [2001] EWCA Crim 2834, [2002] 1 W.L.R. 1553 (CA (Crim Div)), Kennedy, L.J.

s.80, amended: 2003 c.42 Sch.6 para.28, Sch.7, 2004 c.33 Sch.27 para.97

s.80A, amended: 2004 c.33 Sch.27 para.98

s.81, amended: 2003 c.39 Sch.8 para.286

s.81, applied: 2003 c.44 s.127

1984–cont.

60. Police and Criminal Evidence Act 1984–*cont.*

s.82, see *Mawdesley v Chief Constable of Cheshire* [2003] EWHC 1586, [2004] 1 W.L.R. 1035 (QBD (Admin Ct)), Owen, J.

s.96, applied: 2002 c.30 s.9

s.113, amended: 2003 c.44 s.11, Sch.37 Part 1

s.113, applied: SI 2003/2272 Art.4, SI 2003/2315, SI 2003/2315 Art.2

s.113, referred to: 2003 c.44 s.337

s.113, enabling: SI 2003/2315

s.114, applied: 2002 c.29 s.67

s.114A, referred to: SI 2002/2326 Art.3

s.114A, enabling: SI 2002/2326

s.116, amended: 2002 c.29 Sch.11 para.14

s.116, applied: SI 2004/643 Reg.2, Reg.5

s.118, amended: 2002 c.30 Sch.7 para.9, 2003 c.20 Sch.5 para.4

s.118, varied: 2003 c.20 Sch.5 para.4

Sch.1, see *Gordon v Summers* [2003] F.S.R. 40 (Ch D), Neuberger, J.; see *R. (on the application of NTL Group Ltd) v Ipswich Crown Court* [2002] EWHC 1585, [2003] Q.B.131 (QBD (Admin Ct)), Lord Woolf of Barnes, L.C.J.

Sch.1, applied: 2002 c.30 Sch.4 para.17, SI 2002/2326 Art.3, 2003 c.32 s.16

Sch.1, see *Gordon v Summers* [2003] F.S.R. 40 (Ch D), Neuberger, J.; see *R. (on the application of NTL Group Ltd) v Ipswich Crown Court* [2002] EWHC 1585, [2003] Q.B.131 (QBD (Admin Ct)), Lord Woolf of Barnes, L.C.J.

Sch.1, added: 2003 c.39 Sch.4 para.6

Sch.1A, added: 2003 c.44 s.3

Sch.1A, added: 2003 c.21 s.181

Sch.1A, added: 2003 c.44 s.3

Sch.1A, added: 2003 c.17 Sch.6 para.93

Sch.1 para.1, amended: 2003 c.39 Sch.4 para.6

Sch.1 para.1, varied: 2002 c.30 Sch.4 para.17, SI 2002/2326 Art.4

Sch.1 para.2, amended: 2003 c.39 Sch.4 para.6

Sch.1 para.2, varied: 2002 c.30 Sch.4 para.17, SI 2002/2326 Art.4

Sch.1 para.3, amended: 2003 c.39 Sch.4 para.6

Sch.1 para.3, varied: 2002 c.30 Sch.4 para.17, SI 2002/2326 Art.4

Sch.1 para.4, amended: 2003 c.39 Sch.4 para.6

Sch.1 para.4, varied: 2002 c.30 Sch.4 para.17, SI 2002/2326 Art.4

Sch.1 para.5, amended: 2003 c.39 Sch.4 para.6

Sch.1 para.5, varied: 2002 c.30 Sch.4 para.17, SI 2002/2326 Art.4

Sch.1 para.6, amended: 2003 c.39 Sch.4 para.6

CAP.

1984–cont.

60. Police and Criminal Evidence Act 1984–*cont.*

Sch.1 para.6, varied: 2002 c.30 Sch.4 para.17, SI 2002/2326 Art.4

Sch.1 para.7, amended: 2003 c.39 Sch.4 para.6

Sch.1 para.7, varied: 2002 c.30 Sch.4 para.17, SI 2002/2326 Art.4

Sch.1 para.8, amended: 2003 c.39 Sch.4 para.6

Sch.1 para.8, varied: 2002 c.30 Sch.4 para.17, SI 2002/2326 Art.4

Sch.1 para.9, amended: 2003 c.39 Sch.4 para.6

Sch.1 para.9, varied: 2002 c.30 Sch.4 para.17, SI 2002/2326 Art.4

Sch.1 para.10, amended: 2003 c.39 Sch.4 para.6

Sch.1 para.10, varied: 2002 c.30 Sch.4 para.17, SI 2002/2326 Art.4

Sch.1 para.11, amended: 2003 c.39 Sch.4 para.6

Sch.1 para.11, varied: 2002 c.30 Sch.4 para.17, SI 2002/2326 Art.4

Sch.1 para.12, amended: 2003 c.39 Sch.4 para.6

Sch.1 para.12, varied: 2002 c.30 Sch.4 para.17, SI 2002/2326 Art.4

Sch.1 para.13, amended: 2003 c.39 Sch.4 para.6

Sch.1 para.13, varied: 2002 c.30 Sch.4 para.17, SI 2002/2326 Art.4

Sch.1 para.14, amended: 2003 c.39 Sch.4 para.6

Sch.1 para.14, varied: 2002 c.30 Sch.4 para.17, SI 2002/2326 Art.4

Sch.1 para.15, amended: 2003 c.39 Sch.4 para.6

Sch.1 para.15, varied: 2002 c.30 Sch.4 para.17, SI 2002/2326 Art.4

Sch.1 para.16, amended: 2003 c.39 Sch.4 para.6

Sch.1 para.16, varied: 2002 c.30 Sch.4 para.17, SI 2002/2326 Art.4

Sch.1 para.17, amended: 2003 c.39 Sch.4 para.6

Sch.1 para.17, varied: 2002 c.30 Sch.4 para.17, SI 2002/2326 Art.4

Sch.1A para.1, added: 2002 c.30 Sch.6

Sch.1A para.2, added: 2002 c.30 Sch.6

Sch.1A para.2A, added: 2002 c.30 Sch.6

Sch.1A para.2ZA, added: 2002 c.30 Sch.6

Sch.1A para.3, added: 2002 c.30 Sch.6

Sch.1A para.4, added: 2002 c.30 Sch.6

Sch.1A para.4, repealed: 2003 c.42 Sch.7

Sch.1A para.5, added: 2002 c.30 Sch.6

Sch.1A para.5A, added: 2002 c.30 Sch.6, 2003 c.38 s.37

Sch.1A para.6, added: 2002 c.30 Sch.6

Sch.1A para.6A, added: 2002 c.30 Sch.6

Sch.1A para.7, added: 2002 c.30 Sch.6

CAP.

1984–cont.

60. Police and Criminal Evidence Act 1984–*cont.*

Sch.1A para.8, added: 2002 c.30 Sch.6

Sch.1A para.9, added: 2002 c.30 Sch.6

Sch.1A para.10, added: 2002 c.30 Sch.6

Sch.1A para.11, added: 2002 c.30 Sch.6

Sch.1A para.11A, added: 2002 c.30 Sch.6, 2003 c.19 s.1

Sch.1A para.12, added: 2002 c.30 Sch.6

Sch.1A para.13, added: 2002 c.30 Sch.6

Sch.1A para.14, added: 2002 c.30 Sch.6

Sch.1A para.14A, added: 2002 c.30 Sch.6, 2004 c.28 s.10

Sch.1A para.15, added: 2002 c.30 Sch.6

Sch.1A para.16, added: 2002 c.30 Sch.6

Sch.1A para.17, added: 2002 c.30 Sch.6

Sch.1A para.17A, added: 2002 c.30 Sch.6, 2003 c.44 s.3

Sch.1A para.18, added: 2002 c.30 Sch.6

Sch.1A para.19, added: 2002 c.30 Sch.6

Sch.1A para.20, added: 2002 c.30 Sch.6

Sch.1A para.21, added: 2002 c.30 Sch.6

Sch.1A para.22, added: 2002 c.30 Sch.6

Sch.1A para.23, added: 2002 c.30 Sch.6

Sch.1A para.24, added: 2002 c.30 Sch.6

Sch.1A para.25, added: 2002 c.30 Sch.6

Sch.1A para.26, added: 2002 c.30 Sch.6

Sch.1A para.27, added: 2002 c.30 Sch.6, 2003 c.42 Sch.6 para.28

Sch.2, amended: 2004 c.36 Sch.3

Sch.5 Part I para.4, repealed: 2003 c.42 Sch.7

Sch.5 Part I para.6, repealed: 2003 c.42 Sch.7

Sch.5 Part I para.7, repealed: 2003 c.42 Sch.7

Sch.5 Part I para.8, repealed: 2003 c.42 Sch.7

Sch.5 Part II, added: 2004 c.28 Sch.10 para.24

Sch.5 Part II para.2, repealed: 2003 c.42 Sch.7

Sch.5 Part II para.18, added: 2003 c.42 Sch.6 para.28

Sch.5 Part II para.19, added: 2003 c.42 Sch.6 para.28

Sch.5 Part II para.20, added: 2003 c.42 Sch.6 para.28

Sch.5 Part II para.21, added: 2003 c.42 Sch.6 para.28

Sch.5 Part II para.22, added: 2003 c.42 Sch.6 para.28

Sch.5 Part II para.23, added: 2003 c.42 Sch.6 para.28

Sch.5 Part II para.24, added: 2003 c.42 Sch.6 para.28

Sch.5 Part II para.25, added: 2003 c.42 Sch.6 para.28

Sch.6 Part I para.9, repealed: 2003 c.42 Sch.7

Sch.6 Part II para.40, repealed: 2004 c.14 Sch.1 Part 9

1985

Access to Information Act 1985
para.13, see *Sherman v Minister of National Revenue* 2003 FCA 202 (CA (Can)), Desjardins, J.A.

xxiii. Alexandra Park and Palace Act 1985
referred to: SI 2004/160
s.6, repealed (in part): SI 2004/160

xlii. Hereford City Council Act 1985
s.20, repealed: SI 2002/1998 Sch.2

xvii. Leicestershire Act 1985
s.30, repealed: SI 2003/3030 Reg.2
s.54, repealed (in part): 2004 c.34 s.53, Sch.16

i. London Transport (Tower Hill) Act 1985
varied: SI 2003/1615 Sch.2 para.14

3. Brunei and Maldives Act 1985
Sch.1 para.3, repealed: 2002 c.39 Sch.3

4. Milk (Cessation of Production) Act 1985
s.7, repealed (in part): 2004 c.14 Sch.1 Part 2

6. Companies Act 1985
see *OTV Birwelco Ltd v Technical & General Guarantee Co Ltd* [2002] EWHC 2240, [2002] 4 All E.R. 668 (QBD (T&CC)), Judge Thornton Q.C.
applied: 2002 asp 3 s.25, 2002 asp 11 Sch.2 para.27, 2002 c.9 s.121, 2002 c.15 s.66, s.69, Sch.3 para.16, 2002 c.23 Sch.29 para.46, 2002 c.29 s.364, s.398, 2002 c.40 Sch.15, Sch.17 para.3, 2002 c.iii, 2002 c.iv s.3, SI 2002/915 Reg.11, Reg.14, 2003 c.v, s.5, SI 2003/1660 Reg.9, SI 2003/1661 Reg.9, SI 2003/3319 Sch.2 para.11, SI 2003/3363 Sch.1 para.1, 2004 c.12 s.50, s.51, s.52, s.54, 2004 c.20 Sch.6 para.2, Sch.7 para.9, 2004 c.25 s.5, s.7, s.12, 2004 c.27 s.16, s.37, s.54, SI 2004/593 Art.4, SI 2004/675 Sch.1 para.2, Sch.1 para.15, Sch.1 para.29, Sch.1 para.52, Sch.1 para.65, Sch.1 para.70, Sch.1 para.71, Sch.1 para.80, Sch.1 para.83, Sch.1 para.86, Sch.1 para.93, SI 2004/1829 Reg.12, SI 2004/1863 Sch.1 para.7, SI 2004/2326 Reg.13, Reg.85, Reg.87, Reg.88, Reg.89, SI 2004/3121 Sch.1, SSI 2002/121, SSI 2004/207, SSI 2004/396 Sch.1 para.9, SSI 2004/397 Sch.1 para.9
disapplied: 2003 c.v s.6
referred to: 2002 c.32 s.13, SI 2003/61 Reg.1, SI 2003/62 Reg.1, 2004 c.27 s.34, s.63, SI 2004/2326 Reg.14
varied: SI 2004/2326 Sch.4 para.3
Part I c.I, applied: SI 2004/2621 Sch.4
Part II, applied: SI 2004/2621 Sch.4
Part VII c.I, added: SI 2002/1986 Reg.3
Part XI c.V, applied: 2004 c.27 s.43
Part XII, see *Arthur D Little Ltd (In Administration) v Ableco Finance LLC* [2002] EWHC 701, [2003] 5 Ch. 217 (Ch D), Roger Kaye Q.C.
Part XII, applied: 2002 c.9 s.121, SI 2004/2620 Sch.3, SI 2004/2621 Sch.4

1985–cont.

6. Companies Act 1985–*cont.*
Part XIIIA, see *Winpar Holdings Ltd v Joseph Holt Group Plc* [2001] EWCA Civ 770, [2002] B.C.C. 174 (CA), Peter Gibson, L.J.
Part XIV, applied: SI 2002/912 Sch.1, SI 2002/915 Sch.1, SI 2003/335 Sch.1, SI 2004/3322 Art.13, SSI 2003/93 Sch.1, 2004 c.35 Sch.3, Sch.8
Part XXII c.II, applied: SI 2004/2621 Sch.4
Part XXIII c.II, applied: 2004 c.12 Sch.11 para.12
Part XXIII c.III, applied: 2002 c.9 s.121
Part XXIV, referred to: 2004 c.27 s.58
Part XXV, referred to: 2004 c.27 s.58
s.2, applied: 2002 c.15 s.34
s.2, disapplied: 2002 c.15 s.74, Sch.3 para.4, SI 2004/2326 Sch.4 para.1
s.3, disapplied: 2002 c.15 s.74, Sch.3 para.4
s.4, applied: 2002 c.15 Sch.3 para.4, 2004 c.27 s.37, s.54
s.5, amended: SI 2003/1116 Sch.1 para.1
s.5, applied: 2002 c.15 Sch.3 para.4, 2004 c.27 s.37, s.54
s.7, applied: 2004 c.27 s.32
s.7, disapplied: SI 2004/2326 Sch.4 para.1
s.8, disapplied: 2002 c.15 s.74, Sch.3 para.4
s.10, amended: SI 2002/912 Sch.2 para.1
s.10, applied: SI 2002/691 Reg.2, SI 2002/912 Reg.8, Reg.11, SI 2003/62 Reg.2, 2004 c.27 s.36, SI 2004/2326 Reg.87
s.10, disapplied: SI 2004/2326 Sch.4 para.1
s.10, enabling: SI 2002/691, SI 2003/62
s.12, applied: 2002 c.15 Sch.3 para.17, 2004 c.27 s.36, SI 2004/2326 Reg.87
s.12, varied: SI 2004/2326 Reg.87
s.13, applied: 2002 c.15 Sch.1 para.2, 2004 c.27 s.36, SI 2004/1829 Reg.19
s.13, disapplied: SI 2004/2326 Sch.4 para.6
s.17, applied: 2004 c.27 s.37, s.54
s.22, applied: 2002 c.15 Sch.3 para.15
s.22, disapplied: SI 2004/2326 Sch.4 para.7
s.23, applied: 2002 c.15 Sch.3 para.15
s.24, added: SI 2003/1116 Sch.1 para.2
s.25, disapplied: 2004 c.27 s.33
s.26, amended: 2004 c.27 Sch.6 para.2
s.27, amended: 2004 c.27 Sch.6 para.3, Sch.8
s.28, see *Halifax Plc v Halifax Repossessions Ltd* [2004] EWCA Civ 331, [2004] B.C.C. 281 (CA), Latham, L.J.
s.28, applied: 2002 c.15 Sch.1 para.3, 2004 c.27 s.38, s.39, s.40, s.55, SI 2004/1829 Reg.19, SI 2004/2326 Reg.88, SI 2004/2621 Sch.4
s.30, amended: 2004 c.27 Sch.6 para.4
s.33, amended: 2004 c.27 Sch.6 para.5
s.34, varied: SI 2004/2326 Sch.4 para.8
s.34A, added: 2004 c.27 Sch.6 para.6
s.35, see *Bayoumi v Women's Total Abstinence Educational Union Ltd* [2003] EWCA Civ 1548, [2004] Ch. 46 (CA), Chadwick, L.J.

CAP.

1985–cont.

6. Companies Act 1985–*cont.*

s.35A, see *Bayoumi v Women's Total Abstinence Educational Union Ltd* [2003] EWCA Civ 1548, [2004] Ch. 46 (CA), Chadwick, L.J.; see *Cottrell v King* [2004] EWHC 397, [2004] B.C.C. 307 (Ch D), Kevin Garnett Q.C.; see *Criterion Properties Plc v Stratford UK Properties LLC* [2004] UKHL 28, [2004] 1 W.L.R. 1846 (HL), Lord Nicholls of Birkenhead; see *EIC Services Ltd v Phipps* [2003] EWHC 1507, [2003] 1 W.L.R. 2360 (Ch D), Neuberger, J.; see *Smith v Henniker-Major & Co* [2002] B.C.C. 544 (Ch D), Rimer, J.; see *Smith v Henniker-Major & Co* [2002] EWCA Civ 762, [2003] Ch. 182 (CA), Robert Walker, L.J.

s.35B, see *Criterion Properties Plc v Stratford UK Properties LLC* [2004] UKHL 28, [2004] 1 W.L.R. 1846 (HL), Lord Nicholls of Birkenhead

s.36A, varied: 2002 c.9 s.91

s.36C, see *Braymist Ltd v Wise Finance Co Ltd* [2002] EWCA Civ 127, [2002] Ch. 273 (CA), Arden, L.J.

s.43, amended: 2004 c.27 Sch.6 para.7

s.43, applied: 2004 c.27 s.52

s.44, amended: 2004 c.14 Sch.1 Part 17

s.47, applied: 2004 c.27 s.52

s.49, applied: 2004 c.27 s.52

s.53, applied: 2004 c.27 s.52

s.54, amended: SI 2003/1116 Sch.1 para.3

s.55, applied: 2004 c.27 s.52

s.81, amended: SI 2004/355 Art.2

s.88, amended: SI 2003/2868 Reg.2

s.88, referred to: SI 2003/2868 Reg.2

s.88, repealed (in part): SI 2003/2868 Reg.2

s.89, amended: SI 2003/1116 Sch.1 para.4, SI 2003/3031 Reg.2

s.89, applied: SI 2003/3031 Reg.2

s.94, amended: SI 2003/1116 Sch.1 para.5

s.95, see *CAS (Nominees) Ltd v Nottingham Forest FC Plc* [2002] B.C.C. 145 (Ch D), Hart, J.

s.95, amended: SI 2003/1116 Sch.1 para.6

s.103, amended: SI 2003/1116 Sch.1 para.7, 2004 c.14 Sch.1 Part 17

s.117, applied: SI 2004/2199 Reg.9

s.117, disapplied: SI 2004/2326 Sch.4 para.9

s.117, referred to: SI 2004/2326 Sch.4 para.9

s.122, disapplied: SI 2004/2326 Sch.4 para.9

s.125, see *Smiths of Smithfield Ltd, Re* [2003] EWHC 568, [2003] B.C.C. 769 (Ch D), Leslie Kosmin Q.C.

s.125, amended: SI 2003/1116 Sch.1 para.8

s.127, amended: SI 2003/1116 Sch.1 para.9

s.131, amended: SI 2003/1116 Sch.1 para.10

s.143, amended: SI 2003/1116 Sch.1 para.11

s.151, see *Chaston v SWP Group Plc* [2002] EWCA Civ 1999, [2003] B.C.C. 140 (CA), Arden, L.J.; see *Dyment v Boyden* [2004]

CAP.

1985–cont.

6. Companies Act 1985–*cont.*

s.151–*cont.*

EWHC 350, [2004] 2 B.C.L.C. 423 (Ch D), Hart, J.; see *MacPherson v European Strategic Bureau Ltd* [2002] B.C.C. 39 (CA), Chadwick, L.J.; see *MT Realisations Ltd (In Liquidation) v Digital Equipment Co Ltd* [2002] EWHC 1628, [2002] 2 B.C.L.C. 688 (Ch D), Laddie, J.; see *MT Realisations Ltd (In Liquidation) v Digital Equipment Co Ltd* [2003] EWCA Civ 494, [2003] B.C.C. 415 (CA), Mummery, L.J.

s.152, see *MT Realisations Ltd (In Liquidation) v Digital Equipment Co Ltd* [2003] EWCA Civ 494, [2003] B.C.C. 415 (CA), Mummery, L.J.

s.153, varied: 2004 c.33 Sch.21 para.16

s.155, see *In a Flap Envelope Co Ltd, Re* [2003] EWHC 3047, [2003] B.C.C. 487 (Ch D (Companies Court)), Jonathan Crow

s.156, see *In a Flap Envelope Co Ltd, Re* [2003] EWHC 3047, [2003] B.C.C. 487 (Ch D (Companies Court)), Jonathan Crow

s.160, see *Strand Options & Futures Ltd v Vojak (Inspector of Taxes)* [2003] EWHC 67, [2003] S.T.C. 331 (Ch D), Etherton, J.

s.162, see *Strand Options & Futures Ltd v Vojak (Inspector of Taxes)* [2003] EWHC 67, [2003] S.T.C. 331 (Ch D), Etherton, J.

s.162, amended: SI 2003/1116 Reg.2

s.162A, added: SI 2003/1116 Reg.3

s.162B, added: SI 2003/1116 Reg.3

s.162C, added: SI 2003/1116 Reg.3

s.162D, added: SI 2003/1116 Reg.3

s.162E, added: SI 2003/1116 Reg.3

s.162F, added: SI 2003/1116 Reg.3

s.162G, added: SI 2003/1116 Reg.3

s.169, amended: SI 2003/1116 Sch.1 para.12, SI 2003/3031 Reg.3

s.169, applied: SI 2003/2982 Reg.2

s.169, enabling: SI 2003/2982

s.169A, added: SI 2003/1116 Sch.1 para.13

s.169A, applied: SI 2003/2982 Reg.2

s.169A, enabling: SI 2003/2982

s.170, amended: SI 2003/1116 Sch.1 para.14

s.196, disapplied: SI 2003/3226 Reg.10

s.198, amended: SI 2003/1116 Sch.1 para.15

s.199, amended: SI 2003/2066 Reg.13

s.203, amended: 2004 c.33 Sch.27 para.99

s.203, varied: 2004 c.33 Sch.21 para.17

s.209, amended: SI 2002/765 Reg.2

s.214, amended: SI 2003/1116 Sch.1 para.16

s.223, applied: SI 2004/2326 Reg.83

s.224, applied: SI 2004/2326 Reg.83, Sch.4 para.11

s.225, amended: 2002 c.40 Sch.17 para.4

s.225, applied: SI 2004/16 Reg.7

s.226, applied: 2004 c.12 Sch.11 para.12, 2004 c.35 s.44

1985–cont.

6. Companies Act 1985–*cont.*

s.228, varied: SI 2003/1633 Sch.2 para.8
s.232, amended: SI 2002/1986 Reg.2
s.234, amended: 2004 c.27 s.9
s.234ZA, added: 2004 c.27 s.9
s.235, amended: SI 2002/1986 Reg.4
s.237, amended: SI 2002/1986 Reg.5, Reg.6, Reg.10
s.238, amended: SI 2002/1986 Reg.10
s.239, amended: SI 2002/1986 Reg.10
s.241, amended: SI 2002/1986 Reg.10
s.241, applied: 2004 c.12 Sch.11 para.12
s.241A, added: SI 2002/1986 Reg.7
s.242, see *R. (on the application of POW Trust) v Chief Executive and Registrar of Companies* [2002] EWHC 2783, [2004] B.C.C. 268 (QBD (Admin Ct)), Lightman, J.
s.242, amended: SI 2002/1986 Reg.10
s.242, applied: 2004 c.12 Sch.11 para.12
s.242, varied: 2004 c.27 s.34
s.242A, see *R. (on the application of POW Trust) v Chief Executive and Registrar of Companies* [2002] EWHC 2783, [2004] B.C.C. 268 (QBD (Admin Ct)), Lightman, J.; see *Registrar of Companies v Radio-Tech Engineering Ltd* [2004] B.C.C. 277 (Ch D), Judge Moseley Q.C.
s.244, see *Registrar of Companies v Radio-Tech Engineering Ltd* [2004] B.C.C. 277 (Ch D), Judge Moseley Q.C.
s.245, see *Company (No.7466 of 2003), Re* [2004] EWHC 60, [2004] 1 W.L.R. 1357 (Ch D (Companies Ct)), Peter Leaver Q.C.
s.245, amended: SI 2002/1986 Reg.10
s.245B, amended: SI 2002/1986 Reg.10
s.245C, amended: 2004 c.27 s.10
s.245C, applied: 2004 c.27 s.15
s.245C, repealed (in part): 2004 c.27 Sch.8
s.245D, added: 2004 c.27 s.11
s.245D, applied: 2004 c.27 s.15
s.245D, referred to: 2004 c.27 s.15
s.245E, added: 2004 c.27 s.11
s.245E, applied: 2004 c.27 s.15
s.245E, referred to: 2004 c.27 s.15
s.245E, varied: 2004 c.27 s.15
s.245F, added: 2004 c.27 s.12
s.245F, applied: 2004 c.27 s.15
s.245F, referred to: 2004 c.27 s.15
s.245F, varied: 2004 c.27 s.15
s.245G, added: 2004 c.27 s.12
s.245G, applied: 2004 c.27 s.15
s.245G, referred to: 2004 c.27 s.15
s.247, amended: SI 2004/16 Reg.2
s.247, applied: SI 2004/16 Reg.7
s.247, referred to: SI 2003/1370 Art.7
s.248, see *Slater Ltd v Beacontree General Commissioners (No.1)* [2002] S.T.C. 246 (Ch D), Lightman, J.
s.249, amended: SI 2004/16 Reg.3
s.249, applied: SI 2004/16 Reg.7
s.249, referred to: SI 2003/1370 Art.7

1985–cont.

6. Companies Act 1985–*cont.*

s.249A, amended: SI 2004/16 Reg.4
s.249AA, applied: SI 2004/2326 Reg.80
s.249B, amended: SI 2004/16 Reg.5
s.249D, amended: SI 2004/16 Reg.6
s.249D, referred to: SI 2003/3319 Sch.2 para.10
s.249E, amended: 2004 c.27 Sch.2 para.6
s.251, amended: SI 2002/1986 Reg.8
s.251, enabling: SI 2002/1780
s.256, repealed (in part): 2004 c.27 Sch.8
s.257, amended: 2004 c.27 s.13
s.257, applied: SI 2002/1986, SI 2004/2947
s.257, enabling: SI 2002/1986, SI 2004/16, SI 2004/2947
s.258, applied: SI 2004/2541 Sch.1, SI 2004/2542 Sch.1
s.262, amended: SI 2002/765 Reg.2, SI 2002/1986 Reg.10
s.262, referred to: SI 2003/1370 Art.7
s.262A, amended: SI 2002/1986 Reg.10
s.263, see *Clydebank Football Club Ltd v Steedman* 2002 S.L.T. 109 (OH), Lord Hamilton; see *Inland Revenue Commissioners v Richmond* [2003] EWHC 999, [2003] S.T.C. 1394 (Ch D (Companies Court)), Etherton, J.; see *Liquidator of Marini Ltd v Dickenson* [2003] EWHC 334, [2004] B.C.C. 172 (Ch D (Companies Ct)), Judge Richard Seymour Q.C.; see *MacPherson v European Strategic Bureau Ltd* [2002] B.C.C. 39 (CA), Chadwick, L.J.
s.263, applied: 2004 c.20 Sch.6 para.6
s.264, applied: 2004 c.20 Sch.6 para.6
s.270, see *Bairstow v Queens Moat Houses Plc* [2001] EWCA Civ 712, [2002] B.C.C. 91 (CA), Robert Walker, L.J.; see *Inland Revenue Commissioners v Richmond* [2003] EWHC 999, [2003] S.T.C. 1394 (Ch D (Companies Court)), Etherton, J.
s.270, applied: 2004 c.25 s.6
s.270, varied: 2004 c.20 Sch.6 para.7
s.271, applied: 2004 c.25 s.6
s.271, varied: 2004 c.20 Sch.6 para.7
s.272, applied: 2004 c.25 s.6
s.272, varied: 2004 c.20 Sch.6 para.7
s.273, applied: 2004 c.25 s.6
s.273, varied: 2004 c.20 Sch.6 para.7
s.274, applied: 2004 c.25 s.6
s.274, varied: 2004 c.20 Sch.6 para.7
s.275, applied: 2004 c.25 s.6
s.275, varied: 2004 c.20 Sch.6 para.7
s.276, applied: 2004 c.25 s.6
s.276, varied: 2004 c.20 Sch.6 para.7
s.288, amended: SI 2002/912 Sch.2 para.2
s.288, applied: SI 2002/691 Reg.2, SI 2002/912 Reg.11, Reg.14, SI 2002/915 Reg.11, SI 2003/62 Reg.2, 2004 c.12 Sch.11 para.12, 2004 c.27 s.45, SI 2004/2326 Reg.79
s.288, disapplied: 2004 c.27 s.46

CAP.

1985–cont.

6. Companies Act 1985–cont.

s.288, repealed (in part): SI 2002/912 Sch.2 para.2

s.288, varied: 2004 c.27 s.45

s.288, enabling: SI 2002/691, SI 2003/62

s.288A, added: SI 2002/915 Sch.2 para.2

s.288A, applied: SI 2002/915 Reg.11, SI 2003/61 Reg.2

s.288A, referred to: SI 2002/690 Reg.2

s.288A, enabling: SI 2002/690, SI 2003/61

s.289, amended: SI 2002/912 Sch.2 para.3

s.289, applied: SI 2002/912 Reg.14

s.290, amended: SI 2002/912 Sch.2 para.4

s.290, applied: SI 2002/912 Reg.14

s.309A, added: 2004 c.27 s.19

s.309B, added: 2004 c.27 s.19

s.309C, added: 2004 c.27 s.19

s.310, amended: 2004 c.27 s.19, Sch.8

s.310, applied: SI 2004/675 Sch.1 para.93

s.310, referred to: SI 2004/675 Sch.1 para.94

s.320, see *Clydebank Football Club Ltd v Steedman* 2002 S.L.T. 109 (OH), Lord Hamilton; see *Walker v WA Personnel Ltd* [2002] B.P.I.R. 621 (Ch D), Judge Havelock-Allan Q.C.

s.322, see *Clydebank Football Club Ltd v Steedman* 2002 S.L.T. 109 (OH), Lord Hamilton

s.322A, see *Rubin v Gunner* [2004] EWHC 316, [2004] 2 B.C.L.C. 110 (Ch D (Companies Ct)), Etherton, J.

s.323, amended: SI 2003/3031 Reg.4

s.327, amended: 2004 c.33 Sch.27 para.100

s.327, varied: 2004 c.33 Sch.21 para.18

s.328, amended: 2004 c.33 Sch.27 para.101

s.328, varied: 2004 c.33 Sch.21 para.19

s.330, see *Ciro Citterio Menswear Plc v Thakrar* [2002] EWHC 662, [2002] 1 W.L.R. 2217 (Ch D (Companies Court)), Anthony Mann Q.C.; see *Company (No.1641 of 2003), Re* [2003] EWHC 2652, [2004] 1 B.C.L.C. 210 (Ch D), Judge Norris Q.C.; see *Currencies Direct Ltd v Ellis* [2002] 1 B.C.L.C. 193 (QBD), Gage, J.

s.337A, added: 2004 c.27 s.20

s.341, see *Ciro Citterio Menswear Plc v Thakrar* [2002] EWHC 662, [2002] 1 W.L.R. 2217 (Ch D (Companies Court)), Anthony Mann Q.C.; see *Currencies Direct Ltd v Ellis* [2002] 1 B.C.L.C. 193 (QBD), Gage, J.

s.346, see *Clydebank Football Club Ltd v Steedman* 2002 S.L.T. 109 (OH), Lord Hamilton

s.346, amended: SI 2003/1116 Sch.1 para.17, 2004 c.33 Sch.27 para.102

s.346, varied: 2004 c.33 Sch.21 para.20

s.348, applied: SI 2003/1376 Sch.1, SI 2003/1593 Sch.1 Part I

s.349, applied: SI 2003/1376 Sch.1, SI 2003/1593 Sch.1 Part I

CAP.

1985–cont.

6. Companies Act 1985–cont.

s.351, amended: 2004 c.27 Sch.6 para.8

s.351, applied: SI 2003/1376 Sch.1, SI 2003/1593 Sch.1 Part I

s.352, amended: SI 2003/1116 Sch.1 para.18

s.352, applied: 2002 c.15 Sch.3 para.11, Sch.3 para.14

s.356, see *Pelling v Families Need Fathers Ltd* [2001] EWCA Civ 1280, [2002] 2 All E.R. 440 (CA), Mummery, L.J.

s.359, see *Greenwich Millennium Exhibition Ltd v New Millennium Experience Co Ltd* [2003] EWHC 1823, [2004] 1 All E.R. 687 (Ch D (Companies Ct)), Lawrence Collins, J.

s.363, applied: SI 2002/691 Reg.2, SI 2003/61 Reg.2, SI 2003/62 Reg.2, 2004 c.12 Sch.11 para.12, SI 2004/2620 Sch.3, SI 2004/2621 Sch.4

s.363, referred to: SI 2002/690 Reg.3

s.363, enabling: SI 2002/690, SI 2002/691, SI 2003/61, SI 2003/62

s.364, applied: 2004 c.12 Sch.11 para.12

s.364, enabling: SI 2002/3081

s.364A, applied: 2004 c.12 Sch.11 para.12

s.365, applied: 2004 c.12 Sch.11 para.12

s.368, see *PNC Telecom Plc v Thomas* [2002] EWHC 2848, [2003] B.C.C. 202 (Ch D), Sir Andrew Morritt V.C.; see *Woven Rugs Ltd, Re* [2002] 1 B.C.L.C. 324 (Ch D), A Mann Q.C.

s.368, amended: SI 2003/1116 Sch.1 para.19

s.369, amended: SI 2003/1116 Sch.1 para.20

s.369, applied: SI 2004/675 Sch.1 para.92

s.369, referred to: SI 2004/675 Sch.1 para.89

s.370, amended: SI 2003/1116 Sch.1 para.21

s.371, see *Might SA v Redbus Interhouse Plc* [2003] EWHC 3514, [2004] 2 B.C.L.C. 449 (Ch D), Lindsay, J.; see *Union Music Ltd v Watson* [2003] EWCA Civ 180, [2004] B.C.C. 37 (CA), Peter Gibson, L.J.; see *Vectone Entertainment Holding Ltd v South Entertainment Ltd* [2004] EWHC 744, [2004] 2 B.C.L.C. 224 (Ch D), Richard Sheldon Q.C.; see *Woven Rugs Ltd, Re* [2002] 1 B.C.L.C. 324 (Ch D), A Mann Q.C.

s.373, amended: SI 2003/1116 Sch.1 para.22

s.376, amended: SI 2003/1116 Sch.1 para.23

s.378, amended: SI 2003/1116 Sch.1 para.24

s.380, amended: SI 2003/1116 Sch.1 para.25

s.380, applied: 2004 c.27 s.37, s.54

s.380, varied: 2004 c.27 s.37

s.389A, applied: 2004 c.27 s.43

s.389A, substituted: 2004 c.27 s.8

s.389B, applied: 2004 c.27 s.43

s.390A, amended: 2004 c.27 s.7

s.390A, repealed (in part): 2004 c.27 s.7, Sch.8

s.390B, substituted: 2004 c.27 s.7

1985–cont.

6. Companies Act 1985–*cont.*

s.394, see *P&P Design Plc v PricewaterhouseCoopers* [2002] EWHC 446, [2002] 2 B.C.L.C. 648 (Ch D), Ferris, J.

s.395, see *Igroup Ltd v Ocwen* [2003] EWHC 2431, [2004] 1 W.L.R. 451 (Ch D (Companies Court)), Lightman, J.; see *Namco UK Ltd, Re* [2003] EWHC 989, [2003] 2 B.C.L.C. 78 (Ch D), Blackburne, J.; see *Smith (Administrator of Cosslett (Contractors) Ltd) v Bridgend CBC* [2001] UKHL 58, [2002] 1 A.C. 336 (HL), Lord Hoffmann; see *TXU Europe Group Plc (In Administration), Re* [2003] EWHC 3105, [2004] 1 B.C.L.C. 519 (Ch D), Blackburne, J.

s.395, disapplied: SI 2003/3226 Reg.4

s.396, see *Namco UK Ltd, Re* [2003] EWHC 989, [2003] 2 B.C.L.C. 78 (Ch D), Blackburne, J.; see *Obaray v Gateway (London) Ltd* [2004] 1 B.C.L.C. 555 (Ch D (Companies Court)), Hazel Williamson Q.C.

s.404, see *Igroup Ltd v Ocwen* [2003] EWHC 2431, [2004] 1 W.L.R. 451 (Ch D (Companies Court)), Lightman, J.

s.410, see *Arthur D Little Ltd (In Administration) v Ableco Finance LLC* [2002] EWHC 701, [2003] 5 Ch. 217 (Ch D), Roger Kaye Q.C.

s.410, disapplied: SI 2003/3226 Reg.5

s.425, see *Drax Holdings Ltd, Re* [2003] EWHC 2743, [2004] 1 W.L.R. 1049 (Ch D (Companies Ct)), Lawrence Collins, J.; see *Equitable Life Assurance Society (No.1), Re* [2002] B.C.C. 319 (Ch D (Companies Court)), Lloyd, J.; see *Equitable Life Assurance Society (No.2), Re* [2002] EWHC 140, [2002] B.C.C. 319 (Ch D (Companies Ct)), Lloyd, J.; see *Hawk Insurance Co Ltd, Re* [2001] EWCA Civ 241, [2002] B.C.C. 300 (CA), Chadwick, L.J.; see *HIH Casualty & General Insurance Ltd, Re* [2002] EWCA Civ 300, [2002] 2 B.C.L.C. 228 (CA), Jonathan Parker, L.J.; see *Practice Statement (Ch D: Schemes of Arrangements with Creditors)* [2002] 1 W.L.R. 1345 (Ch D), Sir Robert Andrew Morritt V.C.; see *Telewest Communications Plc (No.1), Re* [2004] EWHC 924, [2004] B.C.C. 342 (Ch D (Companies Ct)), David Richards, J.; see *Waste Recycling Group Plc, Re* [2003] EWHC 2065, [2004] B.C.C. 328 (Ch D), Lloyd, J.

s.425, amended: 2002 c.40 Sch.17 para.5

s.425, applied: 2002 c.40 s.255, 2003 c.1 Sch.3 para.37, Sch.3 para.38, Sch.4 para.26, SI 2003/1102 Reg.5, SI 2004/353 Reg.5, SI 2004/1045 Reg.4

s.427A, amended: 2002 c.40 Sch.17 para.6

1985–cont.

6. Companies Act 1985–*cont.*

s.428, see *Winpar Holdings Ltd v Joseph Holt Group Plc* [2001] EWCA Civ 770, [2002] B.C.C. 174 (CA), Peter Gibson, L.J.

s.428, amended: SI 2003/3031 Reg.5

s.428, applied: 2003 c.1 Sch.3 para.37, Sch.3 para.38, Sch.4 para.26

s.429, see *Diamix Plc, Re* [2002] EWHC 770, [2002] B.C.C. 707 (Ch D), Peter Leaver Q.C.; see *Winpar Holdings Ltd v Joseph Holt Group Plc* [2001] EWCA Civ 770, [2002] B.C.C. 174 (CA), Peter Gibson, L.J.

s.429, amended: SI 2003/1116 Sch.1 para.26, SI 2003/3031 Reg.6

s.429, applied: 2003 c.1 Sch.3 para.37, Sch.3 para.38, Sch.4 para.26

s.430, applied: 2003 c.1 Sch.3 para.37, Sch.3 para.38, Sch.4 para.26

s.430A, amended: SI 2003/1116 Sch.1 para.27, SI 2003/3031 Reg.7

s.430C, see *Diamix Plc, Re* [2002] EWHC 770, [2002] B.C.C. 707 (Ch D), Peter Leaver Q.C.; see *Greythorn Ltd, Re* [2002] B.C.C. 559 (Ch D), Robert Hildyard Q.C.

s.430E, amended: 2004 c.33 Sch.27 para.103

s.430E, varied: 2004 c.33 Sch.21 para.21

s.431, amended: SI 2003/1116 Sch.1 para.28

s.431, applied: SI 2003/3075 Reg.26

s.432, applied: SI 2003/3075 Reg.26

s.434, see *R. v Lyons (Isidore Jack) (No.3)* [2002] UKHL 44, [2003] 1 A.C. 976 (HL), Lord Bingham of Cornhill

s.442, applied: SI 2003/3075 Reg.26

s.446, applied: SI 2003/3075 Reg.26

s.447, see *Forcesun Ltd, Re* [2002] EWHC 443, [2002] 2 B.C.L.C. 302 (Ch D), Neuberger, J.

s.447, applied: SI 2002/912 Sch.1, SI 2002/915 Sch.1, SI 2003/3075 Reg.26, 2004 c.35 Sch.3, Sch.8, SI 2004/3322 Art.12, Art.13

s.447, substituted: 2004 c.27 s.21

s.447A, added: 2004 c.27 Sch.2 para.17

s.447A, applied: SI 2004/3322 Art.12, Art.13

s.448, applied: SI 2004/3322 Art.12, Art.13

s.448A, added: 2004 c.27 s.22

s.449, amended: 2004 c.35 Sch.4 para.18, Sch.12 para.5

s.449, applied: SI 2002/1889 Art.2

s.449, substituted: 2004 c.27 Sch.2 para.18

s.449, enabling: SI 2002/1889

s.451, substituted: 2004 c.27 Sch.2 para.19

s.451A, amended: 2004 c.27 Sch.2 para.20

s.452, amended: 2004 c.27 Sch.2 para.21

s.453A, added: 2004 c.27 s.23

s.453B, added: 2004 c.27 s.23

s.453C, added: 2004 c.27 s.24

s.458, see *V v C* [2001] EWCA Civ 1509, [2002] C.P. Rep. 8 (CA), Waller, L.J.

1985–cont.

6. Companies Act 1985–*cont.*

s.459, see *Anderson v Hogg* 2002 S.C. 190 (Court of Session (Inner House, Extra Division)), Lord Coulsfield, Lord Hamilton, Lord Prosser; see *Atlasview Ltd v Brightview Ltd* [2004] EWHC 1056, [2004] 2 B.C.L.C. 191 (Ch D (Companies Ct)), Jonathan Crow; see *Bhullar v Bhullar* [2003] EWCA Civ 424, [2003] B.C.C. 711 (CA), Jonathan Parker, L.J.; see *Brown v Scottish Border Springs Ltd* 2002 S.L.T. 1213 (OH), Lord McEwan; see *CAS (Nominees) Ltd v Nottingham Forest FC Plc* [2002] B.C.C. 145 (Ch D), Hart, J.; see *Ciro Citterio Menswear Plc, Re* [2002] EWHC 897, [2002] B.P.I.R. 903 (Ch D), Pumfrey, J.; see *Clark v Cutland* [2003] EWCA Civ 810, [2004] 1 W.L.R. 783 (CA), Arden, L.J.; see *Colen v Cebrian (UK) Ltd* [2003] EWCA Civ 1676, [2004] I.C.R. 568 (CA), Peter Gibson, L.J.; see *Exeter City AFC Ltd v Football Conference Ltd* [2004] EWHC 831, [2004] 1 W.L.R. 2910 (Ch D), Judge Weeks Q.C.; see *Gross v Rackind* [2004] EWCA Civ 815, [2004] 4 All E.R. 735 (CA), Keene, L.J.; see *Hateley v Morris* [2004] EWHC 252, [2004] 1 B.C.L.C. 582 (Ch D), Mann, J.; see *Incasep Ltd v Jones* [2002] EWCA Civ 961, [2003] B.C.C. 226 (CA), Arden, L.J.; see *Larvin v Phoenix Office Supplies Ltd* [2002] EWCA Civ 1740, [2003] B.C.C. 11 (CA), Auld, L.J.; see *Larvin v Phoenix Office Supplies Ltd* [2002] EWHC 591, [2002] 2 B.C.L.C. 556 (Ch D), Blackburne, J.; see *Lloyd v Casey* [2002] 1 B.C.L.C. 454 (Ch D), Ferris, J.; see *McKee v O'Reilly* [2003] EWHC 2008, [2004] 2 B.C.L.C. 145 (Ch D), Sir Donald Rattee; see *Nugent v Benfield Greig Group Plc* [2001] EWCA Civ 397, [2002] B.C.C. 256 (CA), Aldous, L.J.; see *Phoneer Ltd, Re* [2002] 2 B.C.L.C. 241 (Ch D), Roger Kaye Q.C.; see *Premier Electronics (GB) Ltd, Re* [2002] B.C.C. 911 (Ch D), Pumfrey, J.; see *Profinance Trust SA v Gladstone* [2001] EWCA Civ 1031, [2002] 1 W.L.R. 1024 (CA), Robert Walker, L.J.; see *Reid (Nicholas Landon) v Reid (Michael John)* [2003] EWHC 2329, [2003] 2 B.C.L.C. 319 (Ch D (Companies Court)), Kevin Garnett Q.C.; see *Rock Nominees Ltd v RCO (Holdings) Plc (In Members Voluntary Liquidation)* [2003] EWHC 936, [2003] 2 B.C.L.C. 493 (Ch D (Companies Ct)), Peter Smith, J.; see *Smiths of Smithfield Ltd, Re* [2003] EWHC 568, [2003] B.C.C. 769 (Ch D), Leslie Kosmin Q.C.; see *Wilson v Inverness Retail & Business Park Ltd* 2003 S.L.T. 301 (OH), Lord Eassie

1985–cont.

6. Companies Act 1985–*cont.*

s.461, see *Atlasview Ltd v Brightview Ltd* [2004] EWHC 1056, [2004] 2 B.C.L.C. 191 (Ch D (Companies Ct)), Jonathan Crow; see *Brown v Scottish Border Springs Ltd* 2002 S.L.T. 1213 (OH), Lord McEwan; see *McKee v O'Reilly* [2003] EWHC 2008, [2004] 2 B.C.L.C. 145 (Ch D), Sir Donald Rattee; see *Profinance Trust SA v Gladstone* [2001] EWCA Civ 1031, [2002] 1 W.L.R. 1024 (CA), Robert Walker, L.J.

s.462, referred to: 2002 c.29 s.430

s.484, applied: 2002 c.32 s.18

s.615, referred to: 2002 c.29 s.427

s.615A, referred to: 2002 c.29 s.427

s.615B, referred to: 2002 c.29 s.427

s.651, see *Smith v White Knight Laundry Ltd* [2001] EWCA Civ 660, [2002] 1 W.L.R. 616 (CA), Jonathan Parker, L.J.

s.651, applied: 2004 c.27 s.51

s.652, see *Walji v Mount Cook Land Ltd* [2002] 1 P. & C.R. 13 (CA), Charles, J.

s.652, applied: 2002 c.15 s.87, s.105, 2004 c.27 s.51

s.652A, applied: 2002 c.15 s.87, s.105, 2004 c.27 s.51, SI 2004/2620 Sch.3, SI 2004/2621 Sch.4

s.652B, amended: 2002 c.40 Sch.17 para.7

s.652B, applied: 2004 c.27 s.51

s.652C, amended: 2002 c.40 Sch.17 para.8

s.653, see *Regent Leisuretime Ltd v NatWest Finance Ltd (formerly County NatWest Ltd)* [2003] EWCA Civ 391, [2003] B.C.C. 587 (CA), Jonathan Parker, L.J.

s.653, applied: 2004 c.27 s.51

s.654, see *Scarr v Boyden* [2004] B.P.I.R. 318 (Ch D), Registrar Baister

s.654, disapplied: 2002 c.iii s.11, 2002 c.iv s.15

s.663, enabling: SI 2004/593

s.664, enabling: SI 2004/593

s.690A, applied: SI 2004/2621 Sch.4

s.691, amended: SI 2002/912 Sch.2 para.5

s.691, applied: SI 2002/691 Reg.2, SI 2002/912 Reg.8, Reg.11, Reg.14, 2004 c.12 Sch.11 para.12, 2004 c.20 Sch.20 para.35, SI 2004/2621 Sch.4

s.691, enabling: SI 2002/691

s.692, amended: SI 2002/912 Sch.2 para.6

s.692, applied: SI 2002/691 Reg.2, SI 2002/912 Reg.11, Reg.14, 2004 c.12 Sch.11 para.12, SI 2004/2621 Sch.4

s.692, enabling: SI 2002/691

s.693, applied: 2004 c.12 Sch.11 para.12

s.695, see *Rakusens Ltd v Baser Ambalaj Plastik Sanayi Ticaret AS* [2001] EWCA Civ 1820, [2002] 1 B.C.L.C. 104 (CA), Buxton L.J.

s.695, applied: SI 2002/1861 Reg.6

s.699, applied: 2004 c.12 Sch.11 para.12

1985–cont.

6. Companies Act 1985–*cont.*

s.699A, amended: SI 2002/765 Reg.2

s.704, applied: SI 2004/2326 Sch.2 para.1

s.705, varied: SI 2004/2326 Sch.2 para.2

s.706, applied: SI 2004/2326 Sch.2 para.3

s.706, enabling: SI 2002/690

s.707A, applied: SI 2004/2326 Sch.2 para.3

s.707B, applied: SI 2004/2326 Sch.2 para.3

s.708, varied: SI 2004/2326 Sch.4 para.10

s.708, enabling: SI 2002/317, SI 2002/502, SI 2002/503, SI 2002/2894, SI 2002/2895, SI 2004/2620, SI 2004/2621

s.709, applied: SI 2002/912 Reg.14, Reg.15, SI 2002/915 Reg.14, Reg.15, SI 2004/2620 Sch.3, SI 2004/2621 Sch.4

s.710, applied: SI 2004/2620 Sch.3, SI 2004/2621 Sch.4

s.713, applied: SI 2004/2326 Sch.2 para.4

s.716, amended: SI 2002/1555 Art.11

s.716, repealed: SI 2002/3203 Art.2

s.717, repealed: SI 2002/3203 Art.2

s.717, enabling: SI 2002/376

s.718, applied: 2004 c.20 Sch.20 para.35

s.718, repealed (in part): 2004 c.14 Sch.1 Part 17

s.723, applied: SI 2002/690 Reg.2

s.723B, applied: SI 2002/689 Reg.3, SI 2002/690 Reg.4, SI 2002/691 Reg.3, SI 2002/912 Reg.3, Reg.4, Reg.10, Reg.11, Reg.17, SI 2002/915 Reg.3, Reg.4, Reg.10, Reg.17, SI 2003/62 Reg.3, SI 2004/2326 Reg.79, Reg.80

s.723B, varied: SI 2002/913 Sch.1

s.723B, enabling: SI 2002/912, SI 2002/915

s.723C, applied: SI 2004/2326 Reg.80

s.723C, varied: SI 2002/913 Sch.1

s.723C, enabling: SI 2002/912, SI 2002/915

s.723D, applied: SI 2002/912 Reg.12, SI 2002/915 Reg.12, SI 2004/2326 Reg.80

s.723D, varied: SI 2002/913 Sch.1

s.723D, enabling: SI 2002/912, SI 2002/915

s.723E, applied: SI 2004/2326 Reg.80

s.723E, enabling: SI 2002/912, SI 2002/915

s.723F, applied: SI 2002/912, SI 2002/915, SI 2004/2326 Reg.80

s.723F, varied: SI 2002/913 Sch.1

s.723F, enabling: SI 2002/915

s.725, see *Spring Salmon & Seafood Ltd v Advocate General for Scotland* [2004] S.T.C. 444 (OH), Lady Smith

s.725, applied: SI 2002/1861 Reg.6

s.727, see *Bairstow v Queens Moat Houses Plc* [2001] EWCA Civ 712, [2002] B.C.C. 91 (CA), Robert Walker, L.J.; see *Extrasure Travel Insurances Ltd v Scattergood* [2003] 1 B.C.L.C. 598 (Ch D), Jonathan Crow; see *Globalink Telecommunications Ltd v Wilmbury Ltd* [2002] EWHC 1988, [2002] B.C.C. 958 (QBD), Stanley Burnton, J.; see *Inland Revenue Commissioners v Richmond*

1985–cont.

6. Companies Act 1985–*cont.*

s.727–*cont.*

[2003] EWHC 999, [2003] S.T.C. 1394 (Ch D (Companies Court)), Etherton, J.; see *Inn Spirit Ltd v Burns* [2002] EWHC 1731, [2002] 2 B.C.L.C. 780 (Ch D), Rimer, J.; see *Liquidator of Marini Ltd v Dickenson* [2003] EWHC 334, [2004] B.C.C. 172 (Ch D (Companies Ct)), Judge Richard Seymour Q.C.

s.732, amended: 2004 c.27 Sch.2 para.7, Sch.2 para.22

s.733, amended: 2004 c.27 Sch.2 para.8, Sch.2 para.23

s.734, amended: 2004 c.27 Sch.2 para.9, Sch.2 para.24, Sch.8

s.735, applied: 2004 c.35 s.44

s.735, referred to: SI 2004/2326 Reg.80

s.735, varied: SI 2004/2326 Sch.4 para.5

s.736, applied: 2002 asp 3 s.43, 2002 c.40 s.223, 2002 c.iv s.14, SI 2002/1065 Art.21, SI 2003/3311 Reg.8, SSI 2003/231 Sch.3 para.7, 2004 c.20 s.37, 2004 c.35 s.45, s.57, 2004 c.i s.9, SI 2004/1931 Art.3, SI 2004/2541 Sch.1, SI 2004/2542 Sch.1

s.736, referred to: SI 2003/403 Reg.22

s.736, varied: 2002 c.40 s.79

s.736A, applied: 2002 c.iv s.14, 2004 c.20 s.37, SI 2004/2541 Sch.1, SI 2004/2542 Sch.1

s.736A, varied: 2002 c.40 s.79

s.736B, applied: SI 2004/2541 Sch.1, SI 2004/2542 Sch.1

s.741, applied: SI 2004/2326 Reg.79, 2004/2541 Sch.1, SI 2004/2542 Sch.1

s.742A, amended: 2004 c.33 Sch.27 para.104, SI 2004/355 Art.2

s.742A, varied: 2004 c.33 Sch.21 para.22

s.744, enabling: SI 2002/376, SI 2002/691, SI 2002/3081, SI 2003/62, SI 2003/2982

s.744A, amended: SI 2003/1116 Sch.1 para.29

s.744A, applied: SI 2004/2326 Reg.3

Sch.1, applied: SI 2002/912 Reg.8

Sch.1 para.5, added: SI 2002/912 Sch.2 para.7

Sch.4 Part III para.38, amended: SI 2003/1116 Sch.1 para.30

Sch.4A para.1, amended: 2004 c.27 s.7, Sch.8

Sch.4A para.10, amended: SI 2003/1116 Sch.1 para.31

Sch.6 Part I para.1, added: SI 2002/1986 Reg.10

Sch.6 Part I para.1, amended: SI 2002/1986 Reg.10

Sch.6 Part I para.2, added: SI 2002/1986 Reg.10

Sch.6 Part I para.3, added: SI 2002/1986 Reg.10

1985–cont.

6. Companies Act 1985–*cont.*

Sch.6 Part I para.4, added: SI 2002/1986 Reg.10

Sch.6 Part I para.5, added: SI 2002/1986 Reg.10

Sch.6 Part I para.6, added: SI 2002/1986 Reg.10

Sch.6 Part I para.7, added: SI 2002/1986 Reg.10

Sch.6 Part I para.8, added: SI 2002/1986 Reg.10

Sch.6 Part I para.9, added: SI 2002/1986 Reg.10

Sch.6 Part I para.10, added: SI 2002/1986 Reg.10

Sch.6 Part I para.11, added: SI 2002/1986 Reg.10

Sch.6 Part I para.12, added: SI 2002/1986 Reg.10

Sch.6 Part I para.13, added: SI 2002/1986 Reg.10

Sch.6 Part I para.14, added: SI 2002/1986 Reg.10

Sch.7B, applied: 2004 c.27 s.15

Sch.7 Part I para.2B, amended: 2004 c.33 Sch.27 para.105

Sch.7A Part I para.1, added: SI 2002/1986 Sch.1

Sch.7A Part II para.2, added: SI 2002/1986 Sch.1

Sch.7A Part II para.3, added: SI 2002/1986 Sch.1

Sch.7A Part II para.4, added: SI 2002/1986 Sch.1

Sch.7A Part II para.5, added: SI 2002/1986 Sch.1

Sch.7A Part III para.6, added: SI 2002/1986 Sch.1

Sch.7A Part III para.7, added: SI 2002/1986 Sch.1

Sch.7A Part III para.8, added: SI 2002/1986 Sch.1

Sch.7A Part III para.9, added: SI 2002/1986 Sch.1

Sch.7A Part III para.10, added: SI 2002/1986 Sch.1

Sch.7A Part III para.11, added: SI 2002/1986 Sch.1

Sch.7A Part III para.12, added: SI 2002/1986 Sch.1

Sch.7A Part III para.13, added: SI 2002/1986 Sch.1

Sch.7A Part III para.14, added: SI 2002/1986 Sch.1

Sch.7A Part III para.15, added: SI 2002/1986 Sch.1

Sch.7A Part IV para.16, added: SI 2002/1986 Sch.1

Sch.7A Part IV para.17, added: SI 2002/1986 Sch.1

1985–cont.

6. Companies Act 1985–*cont.*

Sch.7A Part IV para.18, added: SI 2002/1986 Sch.1

Sch.7A Part IV para.19, added: SI 2002/1986 Sch.1

Sch.7A Part IV para.20, added: SI 2002/1986 Sch.1

Sch.7A Part IV para.21, added: SI 2002/1986 Sch.1

Sch.7B Part I para.1, added: 2004 c.27 Sch.1

Sch.7B Part I para.2, added: 2004 c.27 Sch.1

Sch.7B Part I para.3, added: 2004 c.27 Sch.1

Sch.7B Part I para.4, added: 2004 c.27 Sch.1

Sch.7B Part I para.5, added: 2004 c.27 Sch.1

Sch.7B Part I para.6, added: 2004 c.27 Sch.1

Sch.7B Part II para.7, added: 2004 c.27 Sch.1

Sch.7B Part II para.8, added: 2004 c.27 Sch.1

Sch.7B Part II para.9, added: 2004 c.27 Sch.1

Sch.7B Part II para.10, added: 2004 c.27 Sch.1

Sch.7B Part II para.11, added: 2004 c.27 Sch.1

Sch.7B Part II para.12, added: 2004 c.27 Sch.1

Sch.7B Part II para.13, added: 2004 c.27 Sch.1

Sch.7B Part II para.14, added: 2004 c.27 Sch.1

Sch.7B Part III para.15, added: 2004 c.27 Sch.1

Sch.7B Part III para.16, added: 2004 c.27 Sch.1

Sch.7B Part III para.16, referred to: 2004 c.27 s.15

Sch.7B Part III para.17, added: 2004 c.27 Sch.1

Sch.9A, applied: SI 2003/2714 Reg.3

Sch.9 Part 1 para.1, varied: SI 2003/1633 Sch.2 para.2

Sch.9 Part IV para.3, amended: SI 2002/1555 Art.12

Sch.15B para.10, amended: SI 2003/1116 Sch.1 para.32

Sch.15B para.12, amended: SI 2003/1116 Sch.1 para.32

Sch.15C para.1, added: 2004 c.27 Sch.2 para.25

Sch.15C para.2, added: 2004 c.27 Sch.2 para.25

Sch.15C para.3, added: 2004 c.27 Sch.2 para.25

Sch.15C para.4, added: 2004 c.27 Sch.2 para.25

Sch.15C para.5, added: 2004 c.27 Sch.2 para.25

Sch.15C para.6, added: 2004 c.27 Sch.2 para.25

Sch.15C para.7, added: 2004 c.27 Sch.2 para.25

Sch.15C para.8, added: 2004 c.27 Sch.2 para.25

1985–cont.

6. Companies Act 1985–*cont.*

Sch.15C para.9, added: 2004 c.27 Sch.2 para.25

Sch.15C para.10, added: 2004 c.27 Sch.2 para.25

Sch.15D para.1, added: 2004 c.27 Sch.2 para.25

Sch.15D para.2, added: 2004 c.27 Sch.2 para.25

Sch.15D para.3, added: 2004 c.27 Sch.2 para.25

Sch.15D para.4, added: 2004 c.27 Sch.2 para.25

Sch.15D para.5, added: 2004 c.27 Sch.2 para.25

Sch.15D para.6, added: 2004 c.27 Sch.2 para.25

Sch.15D para.7, added: 2004 c.27 Sch.2 para.25

Sch.15D para.8, added: 2004 c.27 Sch.2 para.25

Sch.15D para.9, added: 2004 c.27 Sch.2 para.25

Sch.15D para.10, added: 2004 c.27 Sch.2 para.25

Sch.15D para.11, added: 2004 c.27 Sch.2 para.25

Sch.15D para.12, added: 2004 c.27 Sch.2 para.25

Sch.15D para.13, added: 2004 c.27 Sch.2 para.25

Sch.15D para.13, substituted: 2004 c.35 Sch.12 para.5

Sch.15D para.13A, added: 2004 c.27 Sch.2 para.25, 2004 c.35 Sch.12 para.5

Sch.15D para.14, added: 2004 c.27 Sch.2 para.25

Sch.15D para.15, added: 2004 c.27 Sch.2 para.25

Sch.15D para.16, added: 2004 c.27 Sch.2 para.25

Sch.15D para.17, added: 2004 c.27 Sch.2 para.25

Sch.15D para.18, added: 2004 c.27 Sch.2 para.25

Sch.15D para.19, added: 2004 c.27 Sch.2 para.25

Sch.15D para.20, added: 2004 c.27 Sch.2 para.25

Sch.15D para.21, added: 2004 c.27 Sch.2 para.25

Sch.15D para.22, added: 2004 c.27 Sch.2 para.25

Sch.15D para.23, added: 2004 c.27 Sch.2 para.25

Sch.15D para.24, added: 2004 c.27 Sch.2 para.25

Sch.15D para.25, added: 2004 c.27 Sch.2 para.25

Sch.15D para.26, added: 2004 c.27 Sch.2 para.25

1985–cont.

6. Companies Act 1985–*cont.*

Sch.15D para.27, added: 2004 c.27 Sch.2 para.25

Sch.15D para.28, added: 2004 c.27 Sch.2 para.25

Sch.15D para.29, added: 2004 c.27 Sch.2 para.25

Sch.15D para.30, added: 2004 c.27 Sch.2 para.25

Sch.15D para.31, added: 2004 c.27 Sch.2 para.25

Sch.15D para.32, added: 2004 c.27 Sch.2 para.25

Sch.15D para.33, added: 2004 c.27 Sch.2 para.25

Sch.15D para.34, added: 2004 c.27 Sch.2 para.25

Sch.15D para.35, added: 2004 c.27 Sch.2 para.25

Sch.15D para.36, added: 2004 c.27 Sch.2 para.25

Sch.15D para.37, added: 2004 c.27 Sch.2 para.25

Sch.15D para.38, added: 2004 c.27 Sch.2 para.25

Sch.15D para.39, added: 2004 c.27 Sch.2 para.25

Sch.15D para.40, added: 2004 c.27 Sch.2 para.25

Sch.15D para.41, added: 2004 c.27 Sch.2 para.25

Sch.15D para.42, added: 2004 c.27 Sch.2 para.25

Sch.15D para.43, added: 2004 c.27 Sch.2 para.25

Sch.15D para.44, added: 2004 c.27 Sch.2 para.254 c.27 Sch.2 para.25, 2004 c.35 Sch.4 para.19

Sch.15D para.45, added: 2004 c.27 Sch.2 para.25

Sch.15D para.46, added: 2004 c.27 Sch.2 para.25

Sch.15D para.47, added: 2004 c.27 Sch.2 para.25

Sch.15D para.48, added: 2004 c.27 Sch.2 para.25

Sch.15D para.49, added: 2004 c.27 Sch.2 para.25

Sch.21A, applied: SI 2002/912 Reg.8, Reg.11, Reg.14

Sch.21C, applied: 2002 c.23 Sch.26 para.19

Sch.21D, applied: 2002 c.23 Sch.26 para.19

Sch.21A para.1, applied: SI 2002/691 Reg.2, SI 2004/2621 Sch.4

Sch.21A para.1, enabling: SI 2002/691

Sch.21A para.2, amended: SI 2002/912 Sch.2 para.8

Sch.21A para.3, amended: SI 2002/912 Sch.2 para.8

Sch.21A para.4A, added: SI 2002/912 Sch.2 para.8

CAP.

1985–cont.

6. Companies Act 1985–*cont.*

Sch.21A para.4A, applied: SI 2002/691 Reg.2

Sch.21A para.4A, enabling: SI 2002/691

Sch.21A para.7, applied: SI 2002/691 Reg.2, SI 2004/2621 Sch.4

Sch.21A para.7, enabling: SI 2002/691

Sch.21A para.9, added: SI 2002/912 Sch.2 para.8

Sch.21A para.9, applied: SI 2002/691 Reg.2

Sch.21A para.9, enabling: SI 2002/691

Sch.24, amended: SI 2002/1986 Reg.10, SI 2003/1116 Sch.1 para.33, 2004 c.27 Sch.2 para.10, Sch.2 para.26, Sch.6 para.9, Sch.8

7. Business Names Act 1985

applied: SI 2003/1376 Sch.1, SI 2003/1593 Sch.1 Part I

9. Companies Consolidation (Consequential Provisions) Act 1985

s.21, repealed: 2004 c.14 Sch.1 Part 17

s.27, repealed: 2004 c.14 Sch.1 Part 17

s.28, repealed: 2004 c.14 Sch.1 Part 17

Sch.2, amended: 2002 c.40 Sch.26, 2003 c.21 Sch.19, 2004 c.14 Sch.1 Part 5, Sch.1 Part 9, Sch.1 Part 16, Sch.1 Part 17

13. Cinemas Act 1985

applied: 2003 c.17 Sch.4 para.2

repealed (in part): 2003 c.17 Sch.6 para.95

s.3, repealed (in part): 2003 c.17 Sch.7

s.4, enabling: SI 2002/1903, SSI 2003/144

s.5, applied: 2003 c.17 Sch.8 para.33

s.6, applied: 2003 c.17 Sch.8 para.33

s.9, repealed: 2003 c.17 Sch.7

s.17, repealed: 2003 c.17 Sch.7

s.18, repealed: 2003 c.17 Sch.7

s.19, repealed (in part): 2003 c.17 Sch.7

s.20, applied: 2003 c.17 Sch.8 para.33

s.21, amended: 2003 c.21 Sch.17 para.76

s.21, applied: 2003 c.17 Sch.8 para.33

Sch.2 para.2, repealed: 2003 c.17 Sch.7

Sch.2 para.3, repealed: 2003 c.17 Sch.7

Sch.2 para.6, repealed: 2003 c.17 Sch.7

Sch.2 para.7, repealed: 2003 c.17 Sch.7

Sch.2 para.8, repealed: 2003 c.17 Sch.7

Sch.2 para.12, repealed: 2003 c.39 Sch.10

Sch.2 para.14, repealed: 2003 c.17 Sch.7

Sch.2 para.15, repealed: 2003 c.17 Sch.7

Sch.2 para.16, repealed (in part): 2003 c.17 Sch.7

15. Hong Kong Act 1985

Sch.1 para.2, amended: 2002 c.8 s.2

Sch.1 para.3, enabling: SI 2002/1824

17. Reserve Forces (Safeguard of Employment) Act 1985

applied: SI 2002/2822 Reg.37, SI 2004/291 Sch.4, SI 2004/478 Sch.4, SI 2004/627 Sch.2, SR 2002/378 Reg.37, SSI 2004/115 Sch.3

s.1, referred to: SI 2002/2822 Reg.37, SR 2002/378 Reg.37

CAP.

1985–cont.

21. Films Act 1985

s.1, repealed (in part): 2004 c.14 Sch.1 Part 5

s.3, repealed (in part): 2004 c.14 Sch.1 Part 5

Sch.1 para.4, enabling: SI 2002/1398, SI 2002/2635, SI 2003/828, SI 2003/2630, SI 2004/724, SI 2004/2031, SI 2004/3043

22. Dangerous Vessels Act 1985

s.6A, added: 2003 c.16 Sch.2 para.1

23. Prosecution of Offences Act 1985

Part II, applied: 2003 c.41 s.135

Part II, referred to: 2003 c.41 s.62

s.1, disapplied: 2003 c.44 s.92

s.3, amended: 2002 c.30 Sch.7 para.10, 2003 c.38 s.86, Sch.3, 2003 c.41 s.190, 2004 c.19 s.7

s.5, amended: 2003 c.41 s.190

s.7, amended: 2003 c.39 Sch.8 para.287

s.7A, amended: 2003 c.44 Sch.36 para.50, Sch.3 para.57

s.14, amended: 2003 c.41 s.190

s.15, amended: 2003 c.41 s.190, 2003 c.44 Sch.36 para.10

s.16, see *R. (on the application of Hale) v North Sefton Justices* [2002] EWHC 257, Times, January 29, 2002 (QBD (Admin Ct)), Auld, L.J.; see *R. v Martin (Costs)* [2004] 1 Costs L.R. 167 (Supreme Court Costs Office), Costs Judge Rogers

s.16, amended: 2003 c.44 s.69, s.312, Sch.3 para.57, 2004 c.28 Sch.10 para.25, Sch.11

s.16, repealed (in part): 2003 c.44 Sch.37 Part 4, Sch.3 para.57

s.18, amended: 2003 c.44 s.69, s.312

s.19, enabling: SI 2004/2408

s.19A, enabling: SI 2004/2408

s.19B, added: 2003 c.39 s.93

s.19B, enabling: SI 2004/2408

s.20, amended: 2003 c.39 Sch.8 para.288

s.20, applied: 2003 c.41 s.62, s.135

s.20, repealed (in part): 2003 c.39 Sch.8 para.288, Sch.10

s.20, enabling: SI 2004/2408

s.21, amended: 2003 c.39 Sch.8 para.289, 2003 c.44 Sch.3 para.57

s.22, see *R. (on the application of Gibson) v Winchester Crown Court* [2004] EWHC 361, [2004] 1 W.L.R. 1623 (QBD (Admin Ct)), Lord Woolf of Barnes, L.C.J.; see *R. (on the application of O) v Harrow Crown Court* [2003] EWHC 868, [2003] 1 W.L.R. 2756 (QBD (Admin Ct)), Kennedy, L.J.; see *R. (on the application of Rippe) v Chelmsford Crown Court* [2001] EWHC Admin 1115, [2002] Crim L.R. 485 (QBD (Admin Ct)), Keene, L.J.

s.22, amended: 2003 c.44 s.70, Sch.36 para.51, Sch.3 para.57

s.22, enabling: SI 2003/917

s.22A, enabling: SI 2003/917

s.22B, amended: 2003 c.44 Sch.36 para.17

1985–cont.

23. Prosecution of Offences Act 1985–
cont.
s.23, amended: 2003 c.39 Sch.8 para.290,
2003 c.44 Sch.3 para.57
s.23A, amended: 2003 c.44 Sch.37 Part 4,
Sch.3 para.57
Sch.1 Part I para.2, repealed: 2003 c.44
Sch.37 Part 4
Sch.1 Part I para.3, repealed: 2003 c.44
Sch.37 Part 4
**26. Intoxicating Substances (Supply) Act
1985**
applied: SI 2003/1593 Sch.1 Part I
s.1, applied: SI 2003/1376 Sch.1
**29. Enduring Powers of Attorney Act
1985**
see *Gregory v Turner* [2003] EWCA Civ 183,
[2003] 1 W.L.R. 1149 (CA), Brooke, L.J.
s.3, amended: 2004 c.33 Sch.27 para.106
s.6, see *F (Enduring Power of Attorney), Re*
[2004] EWHC 725, [2004] 3 All E.R. 277
(Ch D), Patten, J.
s.7, applied: SI 2003/1417 r.61
s.8, applied: SI 2003/1417 r.61
s.13, applied: 2003 c.17 s.27
Sch.1 Part I para.2, amended: 2004 c.33
Sch.27 para.107
**31. Wildlife and Countryside (Amendment)
Act 1985**
referred to: 2004 asp 6 Sch.5 para.2
35. Gaming (Bingo) Act 1985
referred to: SI 2002/460(a)
s.1, amended: SI 2002/460 Art.4
s.2, applied: SI 2002/1909 Art.2
s.2, enabling: SI 2002/1909
s.3, enabling: SI 2002/1901
Sch.1 para.5, enabling: SI 2002/640
36. Agricultural Training Board Act 1985
repealed: 2004 c.14 Sch.1 Part 2
37. Family Law (Scotland) Act 1985
see *Sweeney v Sweeney* 2003 S.L.T. 892
(OH), Lord Kingarth
applied: SSI 2002/494 Reg.33
s.1, amended: 2004 c.33 Sch.28 para.11
s.2, amended: 2004 c.33 Sch.28 para.12
s.5, see *Paterson v Paterson* 2002 S.L.T. (Sh
Ct) 65 (Sh Ct (Grampian, Highland and
Islands)), DJ Cusine
s.6, see *Christie v Christie* 2003 S.L.T. (Sh Ct)
115 (Sh Ct (South Strathclyde, Dumfries
and Galloway)), Sheriff HK Small
s.6, amended: 2004 c.33 Sch.28 para.13
s.8, see *Cameron v Cameron* 2002 S.L.T. (Sh
Ct) 23 (Sh Pr), CGB Nicholson Q.C., Sheriff
Principal
s.8, amended: 2004 c.33 Sch.28 para.14
s.8, applied: SSI 2002/494 Reg.33, 2003
c.14 Sch.3 para.3
s.9, see *Haugan v Haugan (No.1)* 2002 S.C.
631 (Ex Div), Lord Hamilton, Lord
McCluskey, Lord Menzies; see *Quinn v*

1985–cont.

37. Family Law (Scotland) Act 1985–*cont.*
s.9–*cont.*
Quinn 2003 S.L.T. (Sh Ct) 5 (Sh Ct
(Lothian and Border)), AM Bell
s.9, amended: 2004 c.33 Sch.28 para.15
s.10, see *Bremner v Bremner* 2002 Fam. L.R.
140 (Sh Ct), DJ Cusine; see *Cordiner v
Cordiner* 2003 Fam. L.R. 39 (Sh Pr), Sir
SST Young Q.C., Sheriff Principal
s.10, amended: 2004 c.33 Sch.28 para.16,
Sch.30
s.11, amended: 2004 c.33 Sch.28 para.17
s.12, see *Christie v Christie* 2003 S.L.T. (Sh Ct)
115 (Sh Ct (South Strathclyde, Dumfries
and Galloway)), Sheriff HK Small
s.12, amended: 2004 c.33 Sch.28 para.18
s.12A, amended: 2004 c.33 Sch.28 para.19
s.13, see *Haugan v Haugan (No.1)* 2002 S.C.
631 (Ex Div), Lord Hamilton, Lord
McCluskey, Lord Menzies
s.13, amended: 2004 c.33 Sch.28 para.20
s.14, see *Robertson (James Gregor) v
Robertson (Mary)* 2003 S.L.T. 208 (OH),
Judge TG Coutts Q.C.
s.14, amended: 2004 c.33 Sch.28 para.21
s.14, applied: 2003 c.14 Sch.3 para.3
s.16, amended: 2004 c.33 Sch.28 para.22
s.17, amended: 2004 c.33 Sch.28 para.23
s.18, amended: 2004 c.33 Sch.28 para.24
s.21, amended: 2004 c.33 Sch.28 para.25
s.22, amended: 2004 c.33 Sch.28 para.26
s.24, amended: 2004 c.33 Sch.28 para.27
s.25, amended: 2004 c.33 Sch.28 para.28
s.26, amended: 2004 c.33 Sch.28 para.29
s.27, amended: 2004 c.33 Sch.28 para.30
**38. Prohibition of Female Circumcision
Act 1985**
see *Ahmed v General Medical Council* [2001]
UKPC 49, (2002) 66 B.M.L.R. 52 (Privy
Council (United Kingdom)), Lord Rodger
of Earlsferry
repealed (in part): 2003 c.31 s.7
s.1, applied: 2003 c.42 Sch.5 para.44, Sch.5
para.90, Sch.5 para.155, 2003 c.44 Sch.15
para.43, Sch.17 para.43, SI 2004/1910
Sch.3
39. Controlled Drugs (Penalties) Act 1985
s.2, repealed: 2004 c.14 Sch.1 Part 17
40. Licensing (Amendment) Act 1985
repealed: 2003 c.17 Sch.7
**42. Hospital Complaints Procedure Act
1985**
s.1, amended: 2002 asp 11 Sch.6 para.7, 2002
c.17 Sch.1 para.37, Sch.5 para.26, 2003
c.43 Sch.14 Part 2
s.1, repealed (in part): 2003 c.43 Sch.14 Part 2
44. Sexual Offences Act 1985
amended: 2003 c.42 Sch.1 para.4
s.1, amended: 2003 c.42 Sch.1 para.4
s.2, amended: 2003 c.42 Sch.1 para.4

1985–cont.

44. Sexual Offences Act 1985–*cont.*
 s.3, see *R. v Figg (Joseph Albert)* [2003] EWCA Crim 2751, [2004] 1 Cr. App. R. (S.) 68 (CA (Crim Div)), Leveson, J.
 s.3, repealed: 2003 c.42 Sch.7
 s.4, amended: 2003 c.42 Sch.1 para.4
 s.4, repealed (in part): 2003 c.42 Sch.7
 s.5, repealed (in part): 2003 c.42 Sch.7

46. Insurance (Fees) Act 1985
 repealed: SI 2002/1555 Art.13

47. Further Education Act 1985
 s.2, amended: 2004 c.8 Sch.6 para.6
 s.3, amended: 2004 c.23 Sch.2 para.4

48. Food and Environment Protection Act 1985
 see *R. v Searby (Alan Edward)* [2003] EWCA Crim 1910, [2003] 3 C.M.L.R.15 (CA (Crim Div)), Buxton, L.J.
 applied: 2002 asp 7 Sch.2 Part 1, 2004 asp 2 Sch.2 Part 1, SI 2004/2040 Art.3
 Part I, applied: SR 2002/339 Art.3, SSI 2002/49 Art.3, SSI 2002/65 Art.3, SSI 2002/80 Art.3, SSI 2002/231 Art.3, SSI 2002/306 Art.3, SSI 2002/307 Art.3, SSI 2002/332 Art.3, SSI 2002/333 Art.3, SSI 2002/345 Art.3, SSI 2002/350 Art.3, SSI 2002/353 Art.3, SSI 2002/357 Art.3, SSI 2002/408 Art.3, SSI 2002/430 Art.3, SSI 2002/465 Art.3, SSI 2002/482 Art.3, SSI 2002/511 Art.3, SSI 2002/544 Art.3, SSI 2003/244 Art.3, SSI 2003/245 Art.3, SSI 2003/260 Art.3, SSI 2003/321 Art.3, SSI 2003/365 Art.3, SSI 2003/366 Art.3, SSI 2003/369 Art.3, SSI 2003/374 Art.3, SSI 2003/392 Art.3, SSI 2003/393 Art.3, SSI 2003/397 Art.3, SSI 2003/402 Art.3, SSI 2003/409 Art.3, SSI 2003/410 Art.3, SSI 2003/429 Art.3, SSI 2004/21 Art.3, SSI 2004/43 Art.3, SSI 2004/221 Art.3, SSI 2004/237 Art.3, SSI 2004/298 Art.3, SSI 2004/319 Art.3, SSI 2004/322 Art.3, SSI 2004/323 Art.3, SSI 2004/330 Art.3, SSI 2004/340 Art.3, SSI 2004/341 Art.3, SSI 2004/344 Art.3, SSI 2004/352 Art.3, SSI 2004/359 Art.3, SSI 2004/378 Art.3, SSI 2004/412 Art.3, SSI 2004/417 Art.3, SSI 2004/418 Art.3, SSI 2004/435 Art.3, SSI 2004/436 Art.3, SSI 2004/447 Art.3, SSI 2004/484 Art.3
 Part II, applied: SSI 2002/410 Art.57, 2004 c.20 s.188
 Part III, applied: SSI 2003/129 Sch.2 para.7
 Part III, referred to: SSI 2004/70 Sch.2 para.7
 s.1, applied: SI 2002/457 Reg.12, Reg.15, SI 2002/897 Reg.12, Reg.15, SI 2004/2040 Art.2, SR 2002/88 Reg.12, Reg.15, SR 2002/339, SSI 2002/110 Reg.12, Reg.14
 s.1, varied: SSI 2003/365 Sch.1, SSI 2003/366 Sch.1, SSI 2003/380 Sch.1, SSI 2003/381 Sch.1, SSI 2003/394 Sch.1, SSI 2003/501 Sch.1, SSI 2003/561 Sch.1, SSI 2004/221 Sch.1

1985–cont.

48. Food and Environment Protection Act 1985–*cont.*
 s.1, enabling: SI 2003/2185, SI 2004/2040, SI 2004/2123, SI 2004/2686, SR 2002/339, SR 2002/369, SSI 2002/9, SSI 2002/19, SSI 2002/20, SSI 2002/48, SSI 2002/49, SSI 2002/57, SSI 2002/65, SSI 2002/66, SSI 2002/67, SSI 2002/80, SSI 2002/82, SSI 2002/126, SSI 2002/127, SSI 2002/152, SSI 2002/160, SSI 2002/182, SSI 2002/183, SSI 2002/197, SSI 2002/198, SSI 2002/218, SSI 2002/231, SSI 2002/306, SSI 2002/307, SSI 2002/332, SSI 2002/333, SSI 2002/345, SSI 2002/350, SSI 2002/353, SSI 2002/357, SSI 2002/383, SSI 2002/384, SSI 2002/388, SSI 2002/401, SSI 2002/402, SSI 2002/403, SSI 2002/408, SSI 2002/409, SSI 2002/421, SSI 2002/422, SSI 2002/430, SSI 2002/431, SSI 2002/465, SSI 2002/482, SSI 2002/510, SSI 2002/511, SSI 2002/544, SSI 2002/545, SSI 2002/550, SSI 2002/551, SSI 2002/552, SSI 2002/553, SSI 2002/558, SSI 2003/17, SSI 2003/18, SSI 2003/22, SSI 2003/23, SSI 2003/24, SSI 2003/81, SSI 2003/90, SSI 2003/115, SSI 2003/195, SSI 2003/197, SSI 2003/244, SSI 2003/245, SSI 2003/260, SSI 2003/315, SSI 2003/321, SSI 2003/365, SSI 2003/366, SSI 2003/369, SSI 2003/374, SSI 2003/375, SSI 2003/380, SSI 2003/381, SSI 2003/392, SSI 2003/393, SSI 2003/394, SSI 2003/397, SSI 2003/402, SSI 2003/409, SSI 2003/410, SSI 2003/429, SSI 2003/494, SSI 2003/495, SSI 2003/501, SSI 2003/557, SSI 2003/561, SSI 2003/589, SSI 2003/590, SSI 2003/591, SSI 2003/592, SSI 2003/598, SSI 2003/605, SSI 2003/606, SSI 2004/19, SSI 2004/21, SSI 2004/22, SSI 2004/42, SSI 2004/43, SSI 2004/48, SSI 2004/61, SSI 2004/65, SSI 2004/69, SSI 2004/79, SSI 2004/124, SSI 2004/125, SSI 2004/129, SSI 2004/130, SSI 2004/131, SSI 2004/135, SSI 2004/139, SSI 2004/159, SSI 2004/177, SSI 2004/178, SSI 2004/179, SSI 2004/181, SSI 2004/192, SSI 2004/221, SSI 2004/237, SSI 2004/298, SSI 2004/315, SSI 2004/319, SSI 2004/322, SSI 2004/323, SSI 2004/330, SSI 2004/340, SSI 2004/341, SSI 2004/344, SSI 2004/345, SSI 2004/349, SSI 2004/352, SSI 2004/359, SSI 2004/378, SSI 2004/412, SSI 2004/417, SSI 2004/418, SSI 2004/435, SSI 2004/436, SSI 2004/446, SSI 2004/447, SSI 2004/463, SSI 2004/484, SSI 2004/500, SSI 2004/501, SSI 2004/502, SSI 2004/510, SSI 2004/547
 s.2, varied: SSI 2003/365 Sch.1, SSI 2003/366 Sch.1, SSI 2003/380 Sch.1, SSI 2003/381 Sch.1, SSI 2003/394 Sch.1, SSI 2003/

1985–cont.

48. Food and Environment Protection Act 1985–*cont.*

s.2, varied:–*cont.*

501 Sch.1, SSI 2003/561 Sch.1, SSI 2004/221 Sch.1

s.3, varied: SSI 2003/365 Sch.1, SSI 2003/366 Sch.1, SSI 2003/380 Sch.1, SSI 2003/381 Sch.1, SSI 2003/394 Sch.1, SSI 2003/501 Sch.1, SSI 2003/561 Sch.1, SSI 2004/221 Sch.1

s.4, varied: SSI 2003/365 Sch.1, SSI 2003/366 Sch.1, SSI 2003/380 Sch.1, SSI 2003/381 Sch.1, SSI 2003/394 Sch.1, SSI 2003/501 Sch.1, SSI 2003/561 Sch.1, SSI 2004/221 Sch.1

s.16, applied: SI 2003/3241 Reg.24, SR 2002/20

s.16, enabling: SR 2002/20, SR 2002/27, SR 2002/250

s.19, varied: SI 2003/3241 Reg.24, SR 2002/20 Reg.4, SSI 2003/579 Reg.24

s.22, varied: SR 2002/20 Reg.4

s.24, enabling: SI 2003/2185, SI 2004/2040, SI 2004/2123, SI 2004/2686, SR 2002/339, SR 2002/369, SSI 2002/19, SSI 2002/49, SSI 2002/65, SSI 2002/66, SSI 2002/67, SSI 2002/80, SSI 2002/231, SSI 2002/306, SSI 2002/307, SSI 2002/332, SSI 2002/333, SSI 2002/345, SSI 2002/350, SSI 2002/353, SSI 2002/357, SSI 2002/383, SSI 2002/388, SSI 2002/408, SSI 2002/409, SSI 2002/421, SSI 2002/430, SSI 2002/465, SSI 2002/482, SSI 2002/510, SSI 2002/511, SSI 2002/544, SSI 2002/545, SSI 2002/551, SSI 2002/552, SSI 2002/553, SSI 2002/558, SSI 2003/22, SSI 2003/90, SSI 2003/244, SSI 2003/245, SSI 2003/260, SSI 2003/315, SSI 2003/321, SSI 2003/365, SSI 2003/366, SSI 2003/369, SSI 2003/374, SSI 2003/375, SSI 2003/380, SSI 2003/381, SSI 2003/392, SSI 2003/393, SSI 2003/394, SSI 2003/397, SSI 2003/402, SSI 2003/409, SSI 2003/410, SSI 2003/429, SSI 2003/501, SSI 2003/557, SSI 2003/561, SSI 2003/592, SSI 2003/606, SSI 2004/21, SSI 2004/42, SSI 2004/43, SSI 2004/48, SSI 2004/61, SSI 2004/65, SSI 2004/69, SSI 2004/125, SSI 2004/139, SSI 2004/221, SSI 2004/237, SSI 2004/298, SSI 2004/319, SSI 2004/322, SSI 2004/323, SSI 2004/330, SSI 2004/340, SSI 2004/341, SSI 2004/344, SSI 2004/352, SSI 2004/359, SSI 2004/378, SSI 2004/412, SSI 2004/417, SSI 2004/418, SSI 2004/435, SSI 2004/436, SSI 2004/447, SSI 2004/484, SSI 2004/500

s.27, repealed: 2004 c.14 Sch.1 Part 2

Sch.2 para.1, varied: SI 2003/3241 Reg.24, SR 2002/20 Reg.4, SSI 2003/579 Reg.24

1985–cont.

48. Food and Environment Protection Act 1985–*cont.*

Sch.2 para.2, varied: SI 2003/3241 Reg.24, SR 2002/20 Reg.4, SSI 2003/579 Reg.24

Sch.2 para.2A, amended: 2004 c.33 Sch.27 para.109

Sch.2 para.2A, varied: SR 2002/20 Reg.4

Sch.2 para.3, varied: SR 2002/20 Reg.4

Sch.2 para.4, varied: SI 2003/3241 Reg.24, SR 2002/20 Reg.4, SSI 2003/579 Reg.24

Sch.2 para.5, varied: SI 2003/3241 Reg.24, SR 2002/20 Reg.4, SSI 2003/579 Reg.24

Sch.2 para.6, varied: SI 2003/3241 Reg.24, SR 2002/20 Reg.4, SSI 2003/579 Reg.24

Sch.2 para.7, varied: SI 2003/3241 Reg.24, SR 2002/20 Reg.4, SSI 2003/579 Reg.24

Sch.2 para.8, varied: SI 2003/3241 Reg.24, SR 2002/20 Reg.4, SSI 2003/579 Reg.24

Sch.2 para.9, varied: SI 2003/3241 Reg.24, SR 2002/20 Reg.4, SSI 2003/579 Reg.24

Sch.2 para.10, varied: SR 2002/20 Reg.4

49. Surrogacy Arrangements Act 1985

s.2, disapplied: 2003 c.44 Sch.25 para.82

s.3, amended: 2003 c.21 Sch.17 para.77

s.3, repealed (in part): 2003 c.21 Sch.19

s.4, amended: 2003 c.44 Sch.37 Part 9

s.4, repealed (in part): 2003 c.44 Sch.37 Part 9

50. Representation of the People Act 1985

applied: SI 2003/1887 Sch.1, SI 2004/870 Reg.10

s.1, applied: SI 2002/2626 Sch.1, SI 2004/1267 Reg.11

s.1, referred to: 2003 c.7 s.17

s.2, applied: SI 2002/2626 Sch.1

s.2, referred to: 2003 c.7 s.17

s.3, applied: 2002 c.24 s.8, Sch.1 para.4, SI 2002/2626 Sch.1

s.4, applied: SI 2002/2626 Sch.1

s.5, applied: SI 2002/2626 Sch.1

s.6, amended: 2002 c.13 s.3

s.6, applied: SI 2003/284 Sch.2 para.10

s.6, referred to: SI 2003/284 Sch.2 para.10

s.7, amended: 2002 c.13 s.3

s.11, applied: SI 2002/2626 Sch.1

s.12, applied: SI 2002/2626 Sch.1

s.13, applied: SI 2002/2626 Sch.1

s.14, applied: SI 2002/2626 Sch.1

s.15, applied: SI 2002/2626 Sch.1, SI 2004/293 Reg.11, Sch.2 para.27, SI 2004/294 Reg.4, Reg.6, Reg.8, SI 2004/1267 Reg.115, SSI 2002/457 r.4, SSI 2002/561 Reg.3, Reg.9, Reg.11

s.15, varied: SI 2002/185 Sch.2, 2003 c.26 Sch.7 para.7

s.15, enabling: SI 2004/294

s.16, applied: SI 2002/2626 Sch.1, 2003 c.26 s.104

s.16, disapplied: 2003 c.26 s.103, SI 2004/218 Art.2, SI 2004/222 Art.2

1985–cont.

50. Representation of the People Act 1985–*cont.*

s.17, applied: SI 2002/2626 Sch.1

s.18, applied: SI 2002/2626 Sch.1

s.19, applied: SI 2002/2626 Sch.1

s.20, applied: SI 2002/2626 Sch.1

s.21, applied: SI 2002/2626 Sch.1

s.22, applied: SI 2002/2626 Sch.1, SI 2004/1233, SI 2004/1234

s.23, applied: SI 2002/2626 Sch.1

s.24, applied: SI 2002/2626 Sch.1

s.25, applied: SI 2002/2626 Sch.1

s.26, applied: SI 2002/2626 Sch.1

s.27, amended: SI 2002/2626 Sch.2 para.12

s.27, applied: SI 2002/2626 Sch.1

s.27, repealed (in part): SI 2003/1887 Sch.2 para.5

s.28, applied: SI 2002/2626 Sch.1

s.29, applied: SI 2002/2626 Sch.1

s.31, applied: SI 2002/2626 Sch.1

s.37, applied: SI 2002/2626 Sch.1

Sch.1 Part I, applied: SI 2002/2626 Sch.1

Sch.1 Part II, applied: SI 2002/2626 Sch.1

Sch.1 Part III, applied: SI 2002/2626 Sch.1

Sch.1 Part IV, applied: SI 2002/2626 Sch.1

Sch.2 Part I, applied: SI 2002/2626 Sch.1

Sch.2 Part II, applied: SI 2002/2626 Sch.1

Sch.2 Part II para.9, applied: SI 2003/284 Sch.2 para.10

Sch.2 Part III, applied: SI 2002/2626 Sch.1

Sch.3 para.1, applied: SI 2002/2626 Sch.1

Sch.3 para.2, applied: SI 2002/2626 Sch.1

Sch.3 para.3, applied: SI 2002/2626 Sch.1

Sch.3 para.4, applied: SI 2002/2626 Sch.1

Sch.3 para.5, applied: SI 2002/2626 Sch.1

Sch.3 para.6, applied: SI 2002/2626 Sch.1

Sch.3 para.7, applied: SI 2002/2626 Sch.1

Sch.3 para.8, applied: SI 2002/2626 Sch.1

Sch.3 para.9, applied: SI 2002/2626 Sch.1

Sch.3 para.10, applied: SI 2002/2626 Sch.1

Sch.3 para.11, applied: SI 2002/2626 Sch.1

Sch.4, applied: SI 2002/2626 Sch.1

Sch.5, applied: SI 2002/2626 Sch.1

51. Local Government Act 1985

applied: 2004 c.ii

referred to: SI 2002/1057 Art.2

Part IV, applied: 2003 c.26 s.23, s.33, s.103, SI 2003/1021 Reg.3, Reg.34

s.7, repealed (in part): 2004 c.14 Sch.1 Part 10

s.10, applied: 2003 c.26 s.23, s.33, SI 2003/530 Art.3, SI 2003/1021 Reg.8

s.11, repealed (in part): 2004 c.14 Sch.1 Part 10

s.14, repealed: 2004 c.14 Sch.1 Part 10

s.26, applied: 2004 c.36 Sch.2 para.10

s.28, applied: 2004 c.ii

s.30, repealed: 2004 c.14 Sch.1 Part 10

s.35, disapplied: SI 2002/808 Art.41

s.38, repealed: 2004 c.14 Sch.1 Part 10

s.42, repealed (in part): 2004 c.21 Sch.2

1985–cont.

51. Local Government Act 1985–*cont.*

s.48, repealed (in part): 2004 c.14 Sch.1 Part 10

s.49, repealed: 2004 c.14 Sch.1 Part 10

s.50, repealed: 2004 c.14 Sch.1 Part 10

s.51, repealed: 2004 c.14 Sch.1 Part 10

s.55, repealed: 2004 c.14 Sch.1 Part 10

s.56, repealed: 2004 c.14 Sch.1 Part 10

s.57, repealed (in part): 2004 c.14 Sch.1 Part 10

s.59, repealed: 2004 c.14 Sch.1 Part 10

s.60, amended: 2004 c.21 Sch.1 para.60

s.63, repealed: 2004 c.14 Sch.1 Part 10

s.64, repealed: 2004 c.14 Sch.1 Part 10

s.65, repealed: 2004 c.14 Sch.1 Part 10

s.69, repealed: 2004 c.14 Sch.1 Part 10

s.73, applied: 2003 c.26 s.25

s.78, repealed: 2004 c.14 Sch.1 Part 10

s.79, repealed: 2004 c.14 Sch.1 Part 10

s.80, repealed: 2004 c.14 Sch.1 Part 10

s.81, repealed: 2004 c.14 Sch.1 Part 10

s.82, repealed: 2004 c.14 Sch.1 Part 10

s.83, repealed: 2004 c.14 Sch.1 Part 10

s.85, repealed: 2004 c.14 Sch.1 Part 10

s.86, repealed: 2004 c.14 Sch.1 Part 10

s.87, applied: 2003 c.iii

s.87, repealed (in part): 2004 c.14 Sch.1 Part 10

s.91, repealed: 2004 c.14 Sch.1 Part 10

s.92, repealed: 2004 c.14 Sch.1 Part 10

s.93, repealed: 2004 c.14 Sch.1 Part 10

s.95, repealed: 2004 c.14 Sch.1 Part 10

s.96, repealed: 2004 c.14 Sch.1 Part 10

s.97, repealed: 2004 c.14 Sch.1 Part 10

s.99, repealed: 2003 c.39 Sch.8 para.291, Sch.10

Sch.7 para.1, repealed: 2004 c.14 Sch.1 Part 10

Sch.7 para.2, repealed: 2004 c.14 Sch.1 Part 10

Sch.7 para.3, repealed: 2004 c.14 Sch.1 Part 10

Sch.7 para.4, repealed: 2004 c.14 Sch.1 Part 10

Sch.7 para.5, repealed: 2004 c.14 Sch.1 Part 10

Sch.7 para.6, repealed: 2004 c.14 Sch.1 Part 10

Sch.7 para.7, repealed: 2004 c.14 Sch.1 Part 10

Sch.7 para.8, repealed: 2004 c.14 Sch.1 Part 10

Sch.7 para.9, repealed: 2004 c.14 Sch.1 Part 10

Sch.8 para.1, amended: 2003 c.17 Sch.7

Sch.8 para.1, repealed (in part): 2003 c.17 Sch.7

Sch.8 para.2, repealed: 2003 c.17 Sch.7

Sch.8 para.3, repealed: 2003 c.17 Sch.7

Sch.8 para.4, repealed: 2003 c.17 Sch.7

Sch.8 para.5, repealed: 2003 c.17 Sch.7

CAP.

CAP.

1985–cont.

51. Local Government Act 1985–*cont.*

Sch.11 para.2, applied: SI 2003/3171 Sch.1 Part I

Sch.11 para.2, referred to: SI 2003/3172 Sch.2 Part I, Sch.2 Part II

Sch.11 para.2, repealed (in part): 2004 c.21 Sch.2

Sch.11 para.5, amended: 2004 c.21 Sch.1 para.61

Sch.13 para.13, repealed (in part): 2003 c.39 Sch.8 para.292, Sch.10

Sch.15 Part I para.1, repealed: 2004 c.14 Sch.1 Part 10

Sch.15 Part II para.2, repealed: 2004 c.14 Sch.1 Part 10

Sch.15 Part II para.3, repealed: 2004 c.14 Sch.1 Part 10

Sch.15 Part II para.4, repealed: 2004 c.14 Sch.1 Part 10

Sch.15 Part II para.5, repealed: 2004 c.14 Sch.1 Part 10

Sch.15 Part II para.6, repealed: 2004 c.14 Sch.1 Part 10

Sch.15 Part III para.7, repealed: 2004 c.14 Sch.1 Part 10

Sch.16 para.9, repealed: 2004 c.14 Sch.1 Part 10

54. Finance Act 1985

s.10, repealed (in part): 2004 c.14 Sch.1 Part 9

s.82, amended: 2003 c.14 Sch.20 para.3

s.83, amended: 2003 c.14 Sch.20 para.3

s.84, amended: 2003 c.14 Sch.20 para.3

56. Interception of Communications Act 1985

see *Attorney General's Reference (No.5 of 2002), Re* [2003] EWCA Crim 1632, [2003] 1 W.L.R. 2902 (CA (Crim Div)), Clarke, L.J.; see *R. v Allan (John Paul)* [2001] EWCA Crim 1027, [2002] 1 Cr. App. R. (S.) 9 (CA (Crim Div)), Keene, L.J.; see *R. v P (Telephone Intercepts: Admissibility of Evidence)* [2002] 1 A.C. 146 (HL), Lord Hobhouse of Woodborough

s.1, see *R. v Sargent (Ian Michael)* [2001] UKHL 54, [2003] 1 A.C. 347 (HL), Lord Hobhouse of Woodborough

s.2, see *Taylor-Sabori v United Kingdom (47114/99)* (2003) 36 E.H.R.R. 17 (ECHR), J-P Costa (President)

s.9, see *Attorney General's Reference (No.5 of 2002), Re* [2004] UKHL 40, [2004] 3 W.L.R. 957 (HL), Lord Bingham of Cornhill; see *R. v Sargent (Ian Michael)* [2001] UKHL 54, [2003] 1 A.C. 347 (HL), Lord Hobhouse of Woodborough

Sch.2, repealed: 2003 c.21 Sch.19

57. Sporting Events (Control of Alcohol etc.) Act 1985

s.1, amended: 2003 c.17 Sch.6 para.97

s.1A, amended: 2003 c.17 Sch.6 para.97

s.2, amended: 2003 c.17 Sch.6 para.97

1985–cont.

57. Sporting Events (Control of Alcohol etc.) Act 1985–*cont.*

s.2, repealed (in part): 2003 c.17 Sch.6 para.98, Sch.7

s.3, repealed: 2003 c.17 Sch.6 para.99, Sch.7

s.4, repealed: 2003 c.17 Sch.6 para.99, Sch.7

s.5, repealed: 2003 c.17 Sch.6 para.99, Sch.7

s.5A, repealed: 2003 c.17 Sch.6 para.99, Sch.7

s.5B, repealed: 2003 c.17 Sch.6 para.99, Sch.7

s.5C, repealed: 2003 c.17 Sch.6 para.99, Sch.7

s.5D, repealed: 2003 c.17 Sch.6 para.99, Sch.7

s.6, repealed: 2003 c.17 Sch.6 para.99, Sch.7

s.8, amended: 2003 c.17 Sch.6 para.100, 2003 c.44 Sch.26 para.36

s.8, repealed (in part): 2003 c.17 Sch.6 para.100, Sch.7

s.9, amended: 2003 c.17 Sch.6 para.101

s.9, repealed (in part): 2003 c.17 Sch.6 para.101, Sch.7

Sch.1 para.1, repealed: 2003 c.17 Sch.6 para.99, Sch.7

Sch.1 para.2, repealed: 2003 c.17 Sch.6 para.99, Sch.7

Sch.1 para.3, repealed: 2003 c.17 Sch.6 para.99, Sch.7

Sch.1 para.4, repealed: 2003 c.17 Sch.6 para.99, Sch.7

Sch.1 para.5, repealed: 2003 c.17 Sch.6 para.99, Sch.7

Sch.1 para.6, repealed: 2003 c.17 Sch.6 para.99, Sch.7

58. Trustee Savings Banks Act 1985

s.2, repealed: 2004 c.14 Sch.1 Part 5

s.4, amended: 2004 c.14 Sch.1 Part 5

s.4, repealed (in part): 2004 c.14 Sch.1 Part 5

Sch.1 Part III para.11, amended: SI 2002/1501 Art.18

60. Child Abduction and Custody Act 1985

see *H (Children) (Child Abduction: Grave Risk), Re* [2003] EWCA Civ 355, [2003] 2 F.L.R. 141 (CA), Dame Elizabeth Butler-Sloss (President); see *J (Children) (Abduction: Child's Objections to Return), Re* [2004] EWCA Civ 428, [2004] 2 F.L.R. 64 (CA), Wall, L.J.; see *J v K (Child Abduction: Acquiescence)* 2002 S.C. 450 (OH), Lady Paton; see *O v O (Children) (International Abduction: Custody Rights)* 2002 S.C. 430 (OH), Lord Wheatley; see *S (A Child) (Abduction: Residence Order), Re* [2002] EWCA Civ 1941, [2003] 1 F.L.R. 1008 (CA), Thorpe, L.J.; see *W (A Child) (Abduction: Conditions for Return), Re* [2004] EWHC 1247, [2004] 2 F.L.R. 499 (Fam Div), Baron, J.; see *W v W* 2003 S.C.L.R. 478 (OH), Lord Drummond Young

s.2, enabling: SI 2003/1518, SI 2004/3040

CAP.

1985–cont.

60. Child Abduction and Custody Act 1985–*cont.*

s.5, see *C (Abduction: Interim Directions: Accommodation by Local Authority), Re* [2003] EWHC 3065, [2004] 1 F.L.R. 653 (Fam Div), Singer, J.; see *P v S (Child Abduction: Wrongful Removal)* 2002 Fam. L.R. 2 (Ex Div), Lord Prosser, Lord Caplan, Lord Milligan

s.6, amended: 2004 c.31 Sch.3 para.3

s.8, see *G (Abduction: Rights of Custody), Re* [2002] 2 F.L.R. 703 (Fam Div), Sumner, J.; see *H (Child Abduction) (Unmarried Father: Rights of Custody), Re* [2003] EWHC 492, [2003] 2 F.L.R. 153 (Fam Div), Holman, J.

s.11, amended: SI 2003/435 Sch.4 para.8, Sch.5

s.13, enabling: SI 2003/1518, SI 2004/3040

s.21, amended: 2004 c.31 Sch.3 para.3

s.24A, amended: 2004 c.33 Sch.27 para.110

s.27, amended: 2004 c.31 Sch.3 para.4

Sch.1, see *S (Children) (Child Abduction: Asylum Appeal), Re* [2002] EWHC 816, [2002] 2 F.L.R. 437 (Fam Div), Bennett, J.

Sch.1 Art.3, see *S v S (Child Abduction: Custody Rights: Acquiescence)* 2003 S.L.T. 344 (OH), Lord Clarke

Sch.1 Art.7, see *S v S (Child Abduction: Custody Rights: Acquiescence)* 2003 S.L.T. 344 (OH), Lord Clarke

Sch.1 Art.12, see *S v S (Child Abduction: Custody Rights: Acquiescence)* 2003 S.L.T. 344 (OH), Lord Clarke

Sch.1 Art.13, see *S v S (Child Abduction: Custody Rights: Acquiescence)* 2003 S.L.T. 344 (OH), Lord Clarke

Sch.2, see *S (Children) (Child Abduction: Asylum Appeal), Re* [2002] EWHC 816, [2002] 2 F.L.R. 437 (Fam Div), Bennett, J.

Sch.3 Part I para.1, amended: 2002 c.38 Sch.3 para.45, Sch.5

Sch.3 Part I para.1, repealed (in part): 2002 c.38 Sch.3 para.45, Sch.5

61. Administration of Justice Act 1985

applied: SI 2003/1887 Sch.1

s.9, amended: SI 2003/1887 Sch.2 para.6

s.26, see *Colley v Council for Licensed Conveyancers (Right of Appeal)* [2001] EWCA Civ 1137, [2002] 1 W.L.R. 160 (CA), Sir Andrew Morritt V.C.

s.26, amended: SI 2003/1887 Sch.2 para.6

s.34, repealed (in part): 2002 c.9 Sch.13

s.38, amended: SI 2003/1887 Sch.2 para.6

s.51, repealed (in part): 2004 c.14 Sch.1 Part 1

s.53, amended: SI 2003/1887 Sch.2 para.6

s.54, repealed: 2003 c.39 Sch.10

s.60, amended: 2002 c.40 Sch.26

s.69, amended: SI 2003/1887 Sch.2 para.6

Sch.2 para.30, amended: SI 2003/2096 Sch.1 para.6

CAP.

1985–cont.

61. Administration of Justice Act 1985–*cont.*

Sch.2 para.32, amended: SI 2003/2096 Sch.1 para.6

Sch.2 para.37, repealed (in part): 2002 c.9 Sch.13

Sch.3 para.1, amended: SI 2003/1887 Sch.2 para.6

Sch.3 para.2, amended: SI 2003/1887 Sch.2 para.6

Sch.3 para.3, amended: SI 2003/1887 Sch.2 para.6

Sch.3 para.4, amended: SI 2003/1887 Sch.2 para.6

Sch.3 para.5, amended: SI 2003/1887 Sch.2 para.6

Sch.3 para.6, amended: SI 2003/1887 Sch.2 para.6

Sch.3 para.7, amended: SI 2003/1887 Sch.2 para.6

Sch.3 para.8, amended: SI 2003/1887 Sch.2 para.6

Sch.3 para.9, amended: SI 2003/1887 Sch.2 para.6

Sch.3 para.10, amended: SI 2003/1887 Sch.2 para.6

Sch.3 para.11, amended: SI 2003/1887 Sch.2 para.6

Sch.4 para.1, amended: SI 2003/1887 Sch.2 para.6

Sch.4 para.2, amended: SI 2003/1887 Sch.2 para.6

Sch.4 para.3, amended: SI 2003/1887 Sch.2 para.6

Sch.4 para.4, amended: SI 2003/1887 Sch.2 para.6

Sch.6 para.10, amended: SI 2003/2096 Sch.1 para.7

62. Oil and Pipelines Act 1985

Sch.3 para.9, amended: SI 2003/1326 Art.15

63. Water (Fluoridation) Act 1985

s.1, amended: 2003 c.37 s.58

s.5, amended: 2002 asp 3 Sch.7 para.15

65. Insolvency Act 1985

s.219, repealed: 2004 c.14 Sch.1 Part 17

s.236, repealed (in part): 2004 c.14 Sch.1 Part 17

Sch.6 para.4, repealed: 2004 c.27 Sch.8

Sch.6 para.8, repealed: 2004 c.14 Sch.1 Part 17

Sch.8 para.5, repealed: 2002 c.9 Sch.13

Sch.8 para.10, repealed: 2004 c.14 Sch.1 Part 17

Sch.8 para.12, repealed: 2003 c.17 Sch.7

Sch.8 para.14, repealed: 2004 c.14 Sch.1 Part 17

Sch.8 para.17, repealed: 2004 c.14 Sch.1 Part 17

Sch.8 para.20, repealed: 2004 c.14 Sch.1 Part 17

Sch.8 para.22, repealed: 2002 c.40 Sch.26

CAP.

1985–cont.

65. Insolvency Act 1985–*cont.*

Sch.8 para.32, repealed: 2004 c.14 Sch.1 Part 17

Sch.8 para.35, repealed: 2004 c.14 Sch.1 Part 17

Sch.8 para.37, repealed (in part): 2004 c.14 Sch.1 Part 17

Sch.8 para.38, repealed (in part): 2004 c.14 Sch.1 Part 17

66. Bankruptcy (Scotland) Act 1985

see *Sutherland v Campbell* 2003 S.L.T. 1138 (OH), Lord Mackay of Drumadoon

applied: 2002 asp 17 s.40, 2002 c.29 s.150, s.311, SI 2002/427 Reg.13, Reg.14, Reg.15, SI 2003/2093 Art.1, SSI 2002/202 Art.7, SSI 2003/2 Art.7

referred to: 2002 c.29 s.84, s.421, s.432, SI 2003/2109 Reg.3

varied: 2002 c.29 s.420

s.2, applied: 2002 c.29 s.311, s.420

s.5, see *Toni, Petitioner* 2002 S.L.T. (Sh Ct) 159 (Sh Ct (South Strathclyde, Dumfries and Galloway)), KA Ross

s.5, amended: 2002 c.29 Sch.11 para.15, SI 2003/2109 Reg.5

s.5, applied: SSI 2003/179 Reg.3

s.5, referred to: SSI 2003/210 Art.7

s.6, amended: SI 2003/2109 Reg.6

s.6A, added: SI 2003/2109 Reg.7

s.7, amended: 2002 asp 17 Sch.3 para.15, 2002 c.29 Sch.11 para.15, SI 2003/2109 Reg.8, SSI 2004/468 Reg.46

s.7, applied: SI 2003/2553 Reg.16

s.7, referred to: SSI 2003/210 Art.7

s.7, varied: SI 2003/2553 Reg.16

s.8, amended: SI 2003/2109 Reg.9

s.9, amended: SI 2003/2109 Reg.10

s.12, applied: 2002 c.29 s.434, 2004 c.35 s.121

s.14, amended: SSI 2004/468 Sch.3 para.1

s.15, amended: SSI 2004/468 Sch.3 para.2

s.16, amended: 2004 c.33 Sch.28 para.31

s.17, see *Crawford's Trustee v Crawford* 2002 S.C. 464 (Ex Div (Extra Division)), Lord Cameron of Lochbroom, Lord Marnoch, Lord Nimmo Smith

s.17, amended: 2004 c.33 Sch.28 para.32

s.20, amended: 2004 c.33 Sch.28 para.33

s.31, see *Burnett's Trustee v Grainger* 2002 S.C. 580 (Court of Session (Inner House, Extra Division)), Lord Coulsfield, Lord Hamilton, Lord Maclean

s.31, amended: SI 2003/2109 Reg.11

s.31, applied: 2002 c.29 s.421

s.31A, added: 2002 c.29 Sch.11 para.15

s.31A, amended: 2002 c.29 Sch.11 para.15

s.31AA, added: 2002 c.29 Sch.11 para.15

s.31AA, amended: SI 2003/2109 Reg.12

s.31B, added: 2002 c.29 Sch.11 para.15

s.31B, amended: 2002 c.29 Sch.11 para.15

s.31B, referred to: SI 2003/421 r.24

CAP.

1985–cont.

66. Bankruptcy (Scotland) Act 1985–*cont.*

s.31C, added: 2002 c.29 Sch.11 para.15

s.31C, amended: 2002 c.29 Sch.11 para.15

s.32, amended: 2004 c.33 Sch.28 para.34

s.32, applied: 2002 c.29 s.421, SSI 2003/344 Reg.13

s.33, amended: 2002 asp 17 Sch.3 para.15

s.34, amended: 2004 c.33 Sch.28 para.35

s.34, applied: 2002 c.29 s.422, SI 2002/427 Reg.19, SI 2002/836 Reg.19

s.35, applied: SI 2002/427 Reg.19, SI 2002/836 Reg.19

s.36, applied: 2002 c.29 s.422, SI 2002/427 Reg.19, SI 2002/836 Reg.19

s.36B, applied: SI 2002/427 Reg.16, SI 2002/836 Reg.16

s.36C, applied: SI 2002/427 Reg.19, SI 2002/836 Reg.19

s.36C, enabling: SI 2002/427, SI 2002/836

s.36E, applied: SI 2002/427 Reg.18, SI 2002/836 Reg.18

s.36F, applied: SI 2002/427 Reg.19, SI 2002/836 Reg.19

s.36F, enabling: SI 2002/427, SI 2002/836

s.37, amended: 2002 asp 17 Sch.3 para.15

s.37, applied: 2002 asp 17 s.31

s.40, amended: 2004 c.33 Sch.28 para.36

s.41A, added: 2004 c.33 Sch.28 para.37

s.44, amended: 2004 c.33 Sch.28 para.38

s.48, referred to: 2002 c.29 s.420

s.49, disapplied: SI 2003/3226 Reg.15

s.50, substituted: SI 2003/2109 Reg.13

s.51, amended: SI 2003/2109 Reg.14, 2004 c.33 Sch.28 para.39

s.52, amended: SI 2003/2109 Reg.15

s.53, see *Rankin, Noter* 2003 S.L.T. 107 (OH), Lord Nimmo Smith

s.54, see *Thomas's Trustee, Noter* 2003 S.L.T. (Sh Ct) 99 (Sh Ct (Lothian and Border)), Sheriff MM Stephen

s.54, applied: SSI 2004/468 Reg.10, Reg.21

s.55, amended: 2002 c.29 Sch.11 para.15

s.59A, added: SI 2003/2109 Reg.16

s.59B, added: SI 2003/2109 Reg.16

s.59C, added: SI 2003/2109 Reg.16

s.60A, added: SI 2003/2109 Reg.17

s.60B, added: SI 2003/2109 Reg.17

s.63, see *Thomas's Trustee, Noter* 2003 S.L.T. (Sh Ct) 99 (Sh Ct (Lothian and Border)), Sheriff MM Stephen

s.70, amended: 2002 asp 3 Sch.7 para.16, 2003 c.21 Sch.17 para.78

s.71A, added: 2004 c.27 s.59

s.72ZA, added: SI 2003/2109 Reg.18

s.73, amended: SI 2003/2109 Reg.19

s.74, amended: 2004 c.33 Sch.28 para.40

s.74, applied: 2002 c.29 Sch.3 para.3, 2004 c.35 s.38, s.51, s.53, s.57

s.74, varied: 2004 c.33 Sch.21 para.23

s.75, applied: SSI 2004/468 Reg.10, Reg.21

1985–cont.

66. Bankruptcy (Scotland) Act 1985–*cont.*

Sch.1 para.2, amended: 2004 c.33 Sch.28 para.41

Sch.3 Part I para.1, amended: 2003 c.1 Sch.6 para.153

Sch.3 Part I para.1, repealed: 2002 c.40 Sch.26

Sch.3 Part I para.2, repealed: 2002 c.40 Sch.26

Sch.3 Part I para.3, repealed: 2002 c.40 Sch.26

Sch.3 Part II para.8, repealed: 2002 c.40 Sch.26

Sch.3 Part II para.8A, repealed: 2002 c.40 Sch.26

Sch.3 Part II para.8B, repealed: 2002 c.40 Sch.26

Sch.3 Part II para.8C, repealed: 2002 c.40 Sch.26

Sch.7 Part II para.24, amended: 2002 asp 17 Sch.3 para.15

67. Transport Act 1985

referred to: SI 2002/808 Art.2

s.2, applied: SI 2002/1040 Sch.4

s.6, applied: SI 2002/1014 Art.3, SI 2004/10 Reg.13, SSI 2002/291 Art.3

s.6, enabling: SI 2002/182, SI 2004/10

s.7, applied: SI 2004/2682 Reg.4, Reg.6, Reg.7

s.7, enabling: SI 2004/2682

s.9, applied: SI 2004/2682 Reg.7

s.9, enabling: SI 2004/2682

s.16, see *R. (on the application of Maud) v Castle Point BC* [2002] EWCA Civ 1526, [2003] R.T.R. 7 (CA), Keene, L.J.

s.17, amended: 2003 c.39 Sch.8 para.293, Sch.10

s.19, applied: SI 2002/1015 Reg.3, SI 2002/2022 Reg.3

s.22, applied: SI 2002/2090 Sch.1 para.1

s.32, repealed: 2004 c.14 Sch.1 Part 14

s.49, applied: SI 2002/785 Reg.2

s.54, repealed (in part): 2004 c.14 Sch.1 Part 5

s.55, repealed: 2004 c.14 Sch.1 Part 5

s.63, amended: 2003 asp 1 s.60

s.65, amended: SI 2003/1615 Sch.1 para.12

s.65, repealed (in part): SI 2003/1615 Sch.1 para.12

s.88, amended: 2003 asp 1 s.60, SI 2003/1615 Sch.1 para.12

s.89, applied: SI 2002/2090 Reg.3A, Reg.3, Reg.4

s.89, disapplied: SI 2002/2090 Reg.3

s.89, repealed (in part): 2003 asp 1 s.60

s.90, referred to: SI 2002/2090 Reg.5

s.90, repealed (in part): 2003 asp 1 s.60

s.90, enabling: SI 2002/2090

s.91, referred to: SI 2002/2090 Reg.5

s.91, repealed (in part): 2003 asp 1 s.60

s.91, enabling: SI 2002/520, SI 2002/2090, SI 2004/609

1985–cont.

67. Transport Act 1985–*cont.*

s.93, amended: 2002 c.4 s.1, 2003 asp 1 s.44

s.94, applied: SI 2002/1016 Art.3, SI 2002/2023 Art.3, SSI 2002/290 Art.3

s.94, enabling: SI 2002/1016, SI 2002/2023, SSI 2002/290

s.111, applied: SI 2002/1014 Art.3, SSI 2002/291 Art.3

s.111, varied: SI 2002/1014 Art.3, SSI 2002/291 Art.3

s.114, repealed (in part): SI 2003/1398 Sch.1 para.4, 2004 c.14 Sch.1 Part 14

s.117, repealed (in part): 2004 c.14 Sch.1 Part 14

s.134, enabling: SI 2002/2090, SI 2004/609

s.135, amended: 2004 c.14 Sch.1 Part 14

s.139, repealed (in part): 2004 c.14 Sch.1 Part 14

Sch.1, applied: SI 2002/1040 Sch.4

Sch.1 para.6, repealed: 2004 c.14 Sch.1 Part 14

Sch.1 para.7, repealed: 2004 c.14 Sch.1 Part 14

Sch.1 para.9, repealed: 2004 c.14 Sch.1 Part 14

Sch.1 para.10, repealed: 2004 c.14 Sch.1 Part 14

Sch.1 para.12, repealed: 2004 c.14 Sch.1 Part 14

Sch.1 para.14, repealed: 2004 c.14 Sch.1 Part 14

Sch.3 para.1, repealed: 2004 c.14 Sch.1 Part 14

Sch.3 para.5, repealed: 2004 c.14 Sch.1 Part 14

Sch.3 para.9, repealed: 2004 c.14 Sch.1 Part 14

Sch.3 para.10, repealed: 2004 c.14 Sch.1 Part 14

Sch.3 para.11, repealed: 2004 c.14 Sch.1 Part 14

Sch.3 para.14, repealed: 2004 c.14 Sch.1 Part 14

Sch.3 para.24, repealed: 2004 c.14 Sch.1 Part 14

Sch.3 para.25, repealed: 2004 c.14 Sch.1 Part 14

Sch.3 para.26, repealed: 2004 c.14 Sch.1 Part 14

Sch.3 para.27, repealed: 2004 c.14 Sch.1 Part 14

Sch.3 para.28, repealed: 2004 c.14 Sch.1 Part 14

Sch.3 para.32, repealed: 2004 c.14 Sch.1 Part 14

Sch.4 para.11, enabling: SI 2002/643

Sch.4, para.12, see *Coakley v Secretary of State for Transport (Locus of Commissioner to Appear)* 2003 S.C. 455 (Court of Session (Inner House, Extra Division)), Lord Kirkwood, Lady Cosgrove, Lord Marnoch

Sch.6 para.1, repealed: 2004 c.14 Sch.1 Part 14

1985–cont.

67. Transport Act 1985–*cont.*

Sch.6 para.2, repealed: 2004 c.14 Sch.1 Part 14

Sch.6 para.3, repealed: 2004 c.14 Sch.1 Part 14

Sch.6 para.4, repealed: 2004 c.14 Sch.1 Part 14

Sch.6 para.5, repealed: 2004 c.14 Sch.1 Part 14

Sch.6 para.6, amended: 2004 c.14 Sch.1 Part 14

Sch.6 para.8, repealed: 2004 c.14 Sch.1 Part 14

Sch.6 para.9, repealed: 2004 c.14 Sch.1 Part 14

Sch.6 para.10, repealed: 2004 c.14 Sch.1 Part 14

Sch.6 para.11, repealed: 2004 c.14 Sch.1 Part 14

Sch.6 para.12, repealed: 2004 c.14 Sch.1 Part 14

Sch.6 para.14, repealed: 2004 c.14 Sch.1 Part 14

Sch.6 para.16, repealed: 2004 c.14 Sch.1 Part 14

Sch.6 para.17, repealed: 2004 c.14 Sch.1 Part 14

Sch.6 para.18, repealed: 2004 c.14 Sch.1 Part 14

Sch.6 para.20, repealed: 2004 c.14 Sch.1 Part 14

Sch.6 para.22, repealed: 2004 c.14 Sch.1 Part 14

Sch.6 para.24, repealed: 2004 c.14 Sch.1 Part 14

Sch.7 para.4, repealed: 2004 c.14 Sch.1 Part 14

Sch.7 para.5, repealed: 2004 c.14 Sch.1 Part 14

Sch.7 para.11, repealed: 2004 c.14 Sch.1 Part 14

Sch.7 para.16, repealed: 2004 c.14 Sch.1 Part 14

Sch.7 para.26, repealed: 2004 c.14 Sch.1 Part 14

68. Housing Act 1985

see *Oxley v Hiscock* [2004] EWCA Civ 546, [2004] 3 W.L.R. 715 (CA), Chadwick, L.J.; see *R. (on the application of Smith) v Barking and Dagenham LBC* [2002] EWHC 2400, [2002] 48 E.G.C.S. 141 (QBD (Admin Ct)), Burton, J.; see *Tomkins v Basildon DC* [2002] EWCA Civ 876, [2003] L. & T.R. 7 (CA), Hart, J.

applied: SI 2002/1860(a), 2003 c.14 Sch.9 para.1

referred to: 2002 c.30 s.108, SI 2003/940 Art.3, 2004 c.34 s.267

Part II, applied: SI 2003/3239 Reg.9, Reg.18, SI 2004/692 Sch.4 para.6

Part III, applied: SI 2002/3264 Reg.4, SI 2003/239 Reg.4

1985–cont.

68. Housing Act 1985–*cont.*

Part IV, see *Sheffield City Council v Hopkins* [2001] EWCA Civ 1023, [2002] H.L.R. 12 (CA), Lord Woolf of Barnes, L.C.J.

Part V, see *R. (on the application of O'Byrne) v Secretary of State for the Environment, Transport and the Regions* [2002] UKHL 45, [2002] 1 W.L.R. 3250 (HL), Lord Scott of Foscote

Part V, applied: 2002 c.9 s.4, s.27, 2002 c.15 s.76, 2003 c.14 Sch.9 para.1, SI 2003/3146 Reg.14, Reg.19, SI 2003/3239 Reg.9, Reg.10, Reg.17, Reg.18

Part V, referred to: 2002 c.30 s.100

Part VII, applied: SI 2003/239 Reg.4

Part IX, applied: 2004 c.34 s.3, s.9

Part X, applied: 2004 c.34 s.216

Part X, referred to: 2004 c.34 s.216

Part XIV, applied: SI 2002/1860 Art.3

s.4, amended: 2002 c.30 Sch.8

s.8, amended: 2004 c.34 Sch.15 para.11

s.8, applied: 2004 c.34 s.225

s.11, amended: 2003 c.17 Sch.6 para.103

s.17, see *Ainsdale Investments Ltd v First Secretary of State* [2004] EWHC 1010, [2004] H.L.R. 50 (QBD (Admin Ct)), Owen, J.

s.21, see *Akumah v Hackney LBC* [2002] EWCA Civ 582, [2003] H.L.R. 5 (CA), 5employmentMoses, J.

s.23, see *Akumah v Hackney LBC* [2002] EWCA Civ 582, [2003] H.L.R. 5 (CA), 5employmentMoses, J.

s.24, amended: 2003 c.26 s.92

s.24, referred to: 2003 c.26 s.92

s.27, see *R. (on the application of Beale) v Camden LBC* [2004] EWHC 6, [2004] H.L.R. 48 (QBD (Admin Ct)), Munby, J.

s.27, applied: SI 2002/522 Art.2

s.27, substituted: SI 2003/940 Art.2

s.27AB, amended: 2003 c.26 Sch.8 Part 1

s.33, amended: 2004 c.34 s.197

s.35, amended: 2004 c.34 s.195

s.35A, added: 2004 c.34 s.196

s.36, repealed (in part): 2002 c.9 Sch.13

s.36A, added: 2004 c.34 s.197

s.36B, added: 2004 c.34 s.197

s.37, amended: 2002 c.9 Sch.11 para.18, 2004 c.34 s.197

s.37, applied: SI 2003/1417 r.95

s.39, amended: 2004 c.33 Sch.8 para.18, Sch.8 para.19, Sch.30

s.39A, added: 2004 c.34 s.198

s.41, amended: 2004 c.34 s.197

s.44, applied: SI 2003/3239 Reg.9

s.65, see *R. (on the application of Ibrahim) v Redbridge LBC* [2002] EWHC 2756, Times, December 27, 2002 (QBD (Admin Ct)), Lightman, J.

1985–cont.

68. Housing Act 1985–cont.

s.69, see *R. (on the application of Ibrahim) v Redbridge LBC* [2002] EWHC 2756,Times, December 27, 2002 (QBD (Admin Ct)), Lightman, J.

s.79, see *Kay v Lambeth LBC* [2004] EWCA Civ 926, [2004] 3 W.L.R.1396 (CA), Auld, L.J.

s.80, see *Kay v Lambeth LBC* [2004] EWCA Civ 926, [2004] 3 W.L.R.1396 (CA), Auld, L.J.

s.80, applied: 2004 c.34 s.124, Sch.7 para.4, Sch.7 para.12

s.81, see *Kay v Lambeth LBC* [2004] EWCA Civ 926, [2004] 3 W.L.R.1396 (CA), Auld, L.J.

s.82, see *Marshall v Bradford MDC* [2001] EWCA Civ 594, [2002] H.L.R. 22 (CA), Chadwick, L.J.; see *St Brice v Southwark LBC* [2001] EWCA Civ 1138, [2002] 1 W.L.R.1537 (CA), Kennedy, L.J.

s.82, amended: 2003 c.38 s.14

s.82A, added: 2003 c.38 s.14

s.83, see *Kensington and Chelsea RLBC v Hislop* [2003] EWHC 2944, [2004] 1 All E.R. 1036 (Ch D), Waller, L.J.; see *Knowsley Housing Trust v Revell* [2003] EWCA Civ 496, [2003] H.L.R. 63 (CA), Waller, L.J.; see *Swindon BC (formerly Thamesdown BC) v Aston* [2002] EWCA Civ 1850, [2003] H.L.R. 42 (CA), Pumfrey, J.

s.83, amended: 2003 c.38 s.14

s.83, enabling: SI 2004/1627

s.84, see *Kensington and Chelsea RLBC v Hislop* [2003] EWHC 2944, [2004] 1 All E.R. 1036 (Ch D), Lindsay, J.; see *Swindon BC (formerly Thamesdown BC) v Aston* [2002] EWCA Civ 1850, [2003] H.L.R. 42 (CA), Pumfrey, J.

s.85, see *Dunn v Bradford MDC* [2002] EWCA Civ 1137, [2003] H.L.R. 15 (CA), Chadwick, L.J.; see *Manchester City Council v Finn* [2002] EWCA Civ 1998, [2003] H.L.R. 41 (CA), Arden, L.J.; see *Marshall v Bradford MDC* [2001] EWCA Civ 594, [2002] H.L.R. 22 (CA), Chadwick, L.J.; see *Sheffield City Council v Hopkins* [2001] EWCA Civ 1023, [2002] H.L.R. 12 (CA), Lord Woolf of Barnes, L.C.J.; see *St Brice v Southwark LBC* [2001] EWCA Civ 1138, [2002] 1 W.L.R. 1537 (CA), Kennedy, L.J.; see *Swindon BC (formerly Thamesdown BC) v Aston* [2002] EWCA Civ 1850, [2003] H.L.R. 42 (CA), Pumfrey, J.

s.85, amended: 2004 c.33 Sch.9 para.18

s.85A, added: 2003 c.38 s.16

s.87, see *R. (on the application of Gangera) v Hounslow LBC* [2003] EWHC 794, [2003] H.L.R. 68 (QBD (Admin Ct)), Moses, J.

1985–cont.

68. Housing Act 1985–cont.

s.87, amended: 2004 c.33 Sch.8 para.20

s.88, see *R. (on the application of Gangera) v Hounslow LBC* [2003] EWHC 794, [2003] H.L.R. 68 (QBD (Admin Ct)), Moses, J.

s.88, amended: 2004 c.33 Sch.8 para.21

s.89, amended: 2004 c.33 Sch.8 para.22, Sch.30

s.90, amended: 2004 c.33 Sch.8 para.23, Sch.30

s.91, amended: 2004 c.33 Sch.8 para.24, Sch.30

s.92, applied: 2002 c.15 s.77

s.99B, amended: 2004 c.33 Sch.8 para.25, Sch.9 para.19, Sch.30

s.100, repealed (in part): SI 2002/1860 Sch.6

s.101, amended: 2004 c.33 Sch.8 para.26, Sch.9 para.20, Sch.30

s.104, amended: 2004 c.34 s.189, Sch.16

s.105, see *R. (on the application of Beale) v Camden LBC* [2004] EWHC 6, [2004] H.L.R. 48 (QBD (Admin Ct)), Munby, J.

s.105, amended: 2003 c.38 Sch.1 para.2

s.106, amended: 2002 c.7 Sch.1 para.1, Sch.2

s.113, see *Wandsworth LBC v Michalak* [2002] EWCA Civ 271, [2003] 1 W.L.R. 617 (CA), Brooke, L.J.

s.113, amended: 2004 c.33 Sch.8 para.27

s.113, varied: 2004 c.33 Sch.21 para.24

s.118, see *R. (on the application of O'Byrne) v Secretary of State for the Environment, Transport and the Regions* [2002] UKHL 45, [2002] 1 W.L.R. 3250 (HL), Lord Scott of Foscote

s.118, amended: 2002 c.15 Sch.5 para.5

s.119, amended: 2004 c.34 s.180

s.121, amended: 2004 c.34 s.192

s.121A, added: 2004 c.34 s.192

s.121AA, added: 2004 c.34 s.189

s.121B, added: 2004 c.34 s.189

s.122, see *Kensington and Chelsea RLBC v Hislop* [2003] EWHC 2944, [2004] 1 All E.R.1036 (Ch D), Lindsay, J.

s.122, applied: 2002 c.30 s.100, SI 2003/498 Art.4, 2004 c.34 s.180, s.182

s.123, amended: 2004 c.33 Sch.8 para.28

s.125, see *Kensington and Chelsea RLBC v Hislop* [2003] EWHC 2944, [2004] 1 All E.R. 1036 (Ch D), Lindsay, J.; see *Rushton v Worcester City Council* [2001] EWCA Civ 367, [2002] H.L.R. 9 (CA), Potter, L.J.

s.126, applied: 2003 c.14 Sch.9 para.6

s.127, applied: SI 2002/1091 Art.2

s.129, amended: 2004 c.34 s.180

s.130, amended: 2004 c.33 Sch.8 para.29

s.131, see *Rushton v Worcester City Council* [2001] EWCA Civ 367, [2002] H.L.R. 9 (CA), Potter, L.J.

s.131, enabling: SI 2003/498, SI 2003/803

1985–cont.
68. Housing Act 1985–*cont.*

s.138, see *R. (on the application of O'Byrne) v Secretary of State for the Environment, Transport and the Regions* [2001] EWCA Civ 499, [2002] H.L.R. 30 (CA), Buxton, L.J.

s.138, amended: 2004 c.34 s.183, s.193

s.138, applied: 2004 c.34 s.194

s.138, referred to: 2004 c.34 s.194

s.138A, added: 2004 c.34 s.183

s.138B, added: 2004 c.34 s.183

s.138C, added: 2004 c.34 s.183

s.140, amended: 2004 c.34 s.184

s.142A, added: 2004 c.34 s.190

s.143, amended: 2004 c.34 s.190

s.144, amended: 2004 c.34 s.190

s.154, amended: 2002 c.9 Sch.11 para.18

s.154, repealed (in part): 2002 c.9 Sch.13

s.155, amended: 2004 c.34 s.185

s.155, varied: 2004 c.34 s.185

s.155A, added: 2004 c.34 s.185

s.155B, added: 2004 c.34 s.185

s.155C, added: 2004 c.34 s.186

s.156, applied: SI 2002/763 Art.2, SI 2003/1083 Art.2, SI 2003/1853 Art.2, SI 2004/1071 Art.2, SI 2004/1806 Art.2

s.156, repealed (in part): 2002 c.9 Sch.13

s.156, enabling: SI 2002/763, SI 2003/1083, SI 2003/1853, SI 2004/1071, SI 2004/1806

s.156A, added: 2004 c.34 s.188

s.157, amended: 2002 c.9 Sch.11 para.18, 2004 c.34 s.188, Sch.16

s.157, applied: SI 2002/1769 Art.2, Art.3, SI 2003/54 Art.2, Art.3, Art.4, SI 2003/1105 Art.2, Art.3, SI 2003/1417 r.95, 2004 c.34 s.188, SI 2004/418 Art.2, Art.3, SI 2004/2681 Art.2, Art.3

s.157, referred to: 2004 c.34 s.188

s.157, repealed (in part): 2004 c.34 s.188, Sch.16

s.157, enabling: SI 2002/1769, SI 2003/54, SI 2003/1105, SI 2003/1147, SI 2004/418, SI 2004/2681

s.158, amended: 2004 c.34 s.188

s.158, referred to: 2004 c.34 s.188

s.160, amended: 2004 c.33 Sch.8 para.18, Sch.8 para.30, Sch.30

s.162, amended: 2004 c.34 s.188

s.163A, added: 2004 c.34 s.187

s.165, amended: 2002 c.9 Sch.11 para.18

s.167, enabling: SI 2003/1147

s.168, repealed (in part): 2002 c.9 Sch.13

s.171A, applied: 2002 c.9 s.4, s.27, 2003 c.14 Sch.9 para.1

s.171B, amended: 2003 c.38 Sch.1 para.2, 2004 c.33 Sch.8 para.31

s.171C, applied: 2004 c.34 s.192, s.194

s.181, amended: 2004 c.34 s.186

s.186, amended: 2004 c.33 Sch.8 para.27

s.186, varied: 2004 c.33 Sch.21 para.25

1985–cont.
68. Housing Act 1985–*cont.*

s.189, see *R. (on the application of Erskine) v Lambeth LBC* [2003] EWHC 2479, [2003] N.P.C. 118 (QBD (Admin Ct)), Mitting, J.; see *Watson v Rhondda Cynon Taff CBC* [2001] EWHC Admin 913, [2002] R.V.R. 132 (QBD (Admin Ct)), Gibbs, J.

s.189, repealed: 2004 c.34 Sch.16

s.190, repealed: 2004 c.34 Sch.16

s.190A, repealed: 2004 c.34 Sch.16

s.191, repealed: 2004 c.34 Sch.16

s.191A, repealed: 2004 c.34 Sch.16

s.192, repealed: 2004 c.34 Sch.16

s.193, repealed: 2004 c.34 Sch.16

s.194, repealed: 2004 c.34 Sch.16

s.195, repealed: 2004 c.34 Sch.16

s.196, repealed: 2004 c.34 Sch.16

s.197, repealed: 2004 c.34 Sch.16

s.198, repealed: 2004 c.34 Sch.16

s.198A, repealed: 2004 c.34 Sch.16

s.199, repealed: 2004 c.34 Sch.16

s.200, repealed: 2004 c.34 Sch.16

s.201, repealed: 2004 c.34 Sch.16

s.202, repealed: 2004 c.34 Sch.16

s.203, repealed: 2004 c.34 Sch.16

s.204, repealed: 2004 c.34 Sch.16

s.205, repealed: 2004 c.34 Sch.16

s.206, repealed: 2004 c.34 Sch.16

s.207, repealed: 2004 c.34 Sch.16

s.208, repealed: 2004 c.34 Sch.16

s.244, repealed (in part): SI 2002/1860 Sch.6

s.252, amended: 2004 c.34 Sch.15 para.12

s.255, repealed (in part): SI 2002/1860 Sch.6

s.264, repealed: 2004 c.34 Sch.16

s.265, applied: 2004 c.34 s.7, s.49, s.50, Sch.1 para.12, Sch.2 para.8

s.265, substituted: 2004 c.34 s.46

s.267, amended: 2004 c.34 Sch.16

s.267, repealed (in part): 2004 c.34 Sch.16

s.268, applied: 2004 c.34 s.8

s.268, substituted: 2004 c.34 Sch.15 para.13

s.269, amended: 2004 c.34 s.48, Sch.15 para.14

s.269, repealed (in part): 2004 c.34 Sch.16

s.269A, added: 2004 c.34 Sch.15 para.15

s.272, amended: 2004 c.34 s.48

s.274, amended: 2004 c.34 Sch.15 para.16

s.274A, added: 2004 c.34 Sch.15 para.17

s.275, substituted: 2004 c.34 Sch.15 para.18

s.276, repealed: 2004 c.34 Sch.16

s.277, repealed: 2004 c.34 Sch.16

s.278, repealed: 2004 c.34 Sch.16

s.279, repealed: 2004 c.34 Sch.16

s.283, repealed: 2004 c.34 s.52, Sch.16

s.284, repealed: 2004 c.34 s.52, Sch.16

s.285, repealed: 2004 c.34 s.52, Sch.16

s.286, repealed: 2004 c.34 s.52, Sch.16

s.287, repealed: 2004 c.34 s.52, Sch.16

s.288, repealed: 2004 c.34 s.52, Sch.16

1985–cont.

68. Housing Act 1985–*cont.*

s.289, see *R. (on the application of Baker) v First Secretary of State* [2003] EWHC 2511, [2004] R.V.R. 13 (QBD (Admin Ct)), Nicholas Blake Q.C.

s.289, amended: 2004 c.34 s.47, Sch.15 para.19

s.289, applied: 2004 c.34 s.5, s.6, s.7, s.8

s.289, repealed (in part): 2004 c.34 Sch.16

s.295, amended: 2003 c.21 Sch.17 para.79

s.298, amended: 2003 c.21 Sch.17 para.79

s.298, repealed (in part): 2003 c.21 Sch.19

s.300, applied: 2004 c.34 s.6

s.300, substituted: 2004 c.34 Sch.15 para.20

s.304, substituted: 2004 c.34 Sch.15 para.21

s.305, amended: 2004 c.34 Sch.16

s.305, repealed (in part): 2004 c.34 Sch.16

s.307, amended: 2004 c.34 Sch.15 para.22

s.308, amended: 2004 c.34 Sch.15 para.23

s.308, applied: 2004 c.34 s.39

s.310, repealed: 2004 c.34 Sch.15 para.24, Sch.16

s.311, amended: 2004 c.34 Sch.16

s.316, amended: 2004 c.34 Sch.16

s.317, amended: 2004 c.34 s.48, Sch.16

s.318, amended: 2004 c.34 s.48, Sch.15 para.25

s.318, repealed (in part): 2004 c.34 s.48, Sch.16

s.319, amended: 2004 c.34 Sch.16

s.322, substituted: 2004 c.34 Sch.15 para.26

s.323, amended: 2004 c.34 Sch.15 para.27, Sch.16

s.345, see *R. (on the application of Hossack) v Kettering BC* [2002] EWCA Civ 886, [2003] 2 P. & C.R. 34 (CA), Simon Brown, L.J.; see *Stanley v Ealing LBC (No.2)* [2003] EWCA Civ 679, [2003] H.L.R. 71 (CA), Buxton, L.J.

s.345, repealed: 2004 c.34 Sch.16

s.346, repealed: 2004 c.34 Sch.16

s.346A, repealed: 2004 c.34 Sch.16

s.346B, see *Brent LBC v Reynolds* [2001] EWCA Civ 1843, [2002] H.L.R. 15 (CA), Buxton, L.J.

s.346B, repealed: 2004 c.34 Sch.16

s.347, applied: 2004 c.34 s.76

s.347, repealed: 2004 c.34 Sch.16

s.348, see *Brent LBC v Reynolds* [2001] EWCA Civ 1843, [2002] H.L.R. 15 (CA), Buxton, L.J.

s.348, repealed: 2004 c.34 Sch.16

s.348A, repealed: 2004 c.34 Sch.16

s.348B, applied: 2004 c.34 s.76

s.348B, repealed: 2004 c.34 Sch.16

s.348C, repealed: 2004 c.34 Sch.16

s.348D, repealed: 2004 c.34 Sch.16

s.348E, repealed: 2004 c.34 Sch.16

s.348F, repealed: 2004 c.34 Sch.16

s.348G, repealed: 2004 c.34 Sch.16

s.349, repealed: 2004 c.34 Sch.16

1985–cont.

68. Housing Act 1985–*cont.*

s.350, repealed: 2004 c.34 Sch.16

s.351, repealed: 2004 c.34 Sch.16

s.352, see *Stanley v Ealing LBC (No.2)* [2003] EWCA Civ 679, [2003] H.L.R. 71 (CA), Buxton, L.J.; see *Watson v Rhondda Cynon Taff CBC* [2001] EWHC Admin 913, [2002] R.V.R. 132 (QBD (Admin Ct)), Gibbs, J.

s.352, repealed: 2004 c.34 Sch.16

s.352A, repealed: 2004 c.34 Sch.16

s.353, repealed: 2004 c.34 Sch.16

s.353A, repealed: 2004 c.34 Sch.16

s.354, repealed: 2004 c.34 Sch.16

s.355, repealed: 2004 c.34 Sch.16

s.356, repealed: 2004 c.34 Sch.16

s.357, repealed: 2004 c.34 Sch.16

s.358, repealed: 2004 c.34 Sch.16

s.359, repealed: 2004 c.34 Sch.16

s.360, repealed: 2004 c.34 Sch.16

s.361, repealed: 2004 c.34 Sch.16

s.362, repealed: 2004 c.34 Sch.16

s.363, repealed: 2004 c.34 Sch.16

s.364, repealed: 2004 c.34 Sch.16

s.365, amended: 2004 c.21 Sch.1 para.62

s.365, repealed: 2004 c.34 Sch.16

s.366, repealed: 2004 c.34 Sch.16

s.367, repealed: 2004 c.34 Sch.16

s.368, repealed: 2004 c.34 Sch.16

s.369, repealed: 2004 c.34 Sch.16

s.370, repealed: 2004 c.34 Sch.16

s.371, repealed: 2004 c.34 Sch.16

s.372, see *Stanley v Ealing LBC (No.2)* [2003] EWCA Civ 679, [2003] H.L.R. 71 (CA), Buxton, L.J.

s.372, repealed: 2004 c.34 Sch.16

s.373, repealed: 2004 c.34 Sch.16

s.374, repealed: 2004 c.34 Sch.16

s.375, repealed: 2004 c.34 Sch.16

s.376, repealed: 2004 c.34 Sch.16

s.377, repealed: 2004 c.34 Sch.16

s.377A, repealed: 2004 c.34 Sch.16

s.378, repealed: 2004 c.34 Sch.16

s.379, repealed: 2004 c.34 Sch.16

s.380, repealed: 2004 c.34 Sch.16

s.381, repealed: 2004 c.34 Sch.16

s.382, repealed: 2004 c.34 Sch.16

s.383, repealed: 2004 c.34 Sch.16

s.384, repealed: 2004 c.34 Sch.16

s.385, repealed: 2004 c.34 Sch.16

s.386, repealed: 2004 c.34 Sch.16

s.387, repealed: 2004 c.34 Sch.16

s.388, repealed: 2004 c.34 Sch.16

s.389, repealed: 2004 c.34 Sch.16

s.390, repealed: 2004 c.34 Sch.16

s.391, repealed: 2004 c.34 Sch.16

s.392, repealed: 2004 c.34 Sch.16

s.393, repealed: 2004 c.34 Sch.16

s.394, repealed: 2004 c.34 Sch.16

s.395, applied: SI 2003/1417 r.111

1985–cont.

68. Housing Act 1985–*cont.*

s.395, repealed: 2004 c.34 Sch.16

s.395A, repealed: 2004 c.34 Sch.16

s.396, repealed: 2004 c.34 Sch.16

s.397, repealed: 2004 c.34 Sch.16

s.398, repealed: 2004 c.34 Sch.16

s.399, repealed: 2004 c.34 Sch.16

s.400, repealed: 2004 c.34 Sch.16

s.401, applied: SI 2003/1417 r.111

s.410, applied: SI 2003/1417 r.111

s.418, applied: SI 2003/1417 r.111

s.435, amended: SI 2002/1860 Sch.2 para.3

s.435, repealed (in part): SI 2002/1860 Sch.6

s.436, amended: SI 2002/1860 Sch.2 para.4

s.439, amended: SI 2002/1860 Sch.2 para.4

s.439, repealed (in part): 2004 c.34 Sch.15 para.28, Sch.16

s.442, amended: SI 2002/1860 Sch.2 para.4

s.450A, amended: 2002 c.15 Sch.9 para.2

s.450B, amended: 2002 c.15 Sch.9 para.3

s.458, amended: 2002 c.15 Sch.9 para.4

s.459, amended: 2002 c.15 Sch.9 para.5

s.554, amended: 2004 c.33 Sch.8 para.32

s.554, applied: SI 2002/3264 Reg.3, SI 2003/239 Reg.3

s.555, applied: SI 2002/3264 Reg.3, SI 2003/239 Reg.3

s.578A, amended: 2004 c.5 Sch.7 para.13

s.582, amended: 2004 c.34 Sch.15 para.29

s.584A, applied: 2004 c.34 s.24, s.43

s.584A, substituted: 2004 c.34 Sch.15 para.30

s.584B, applied: 2004 c.34 s.24, s.43

s.584B, substituted: 2004 c.34 Sch.15 para.31

s.604, see *R. (on the application of Erskine) v Lambeth LBC* [2003] EWHC 2479, [2003] N.P.C. 118 (QBD (Admin Ct)), Mitting, J.

s.604, applied: 2004 c.34 s.1

s.604, repealed: 2004 c.34 Sch.16

s.604A, repealed: 2004 c.34 Sch.16

s.605, repealed: 2004 c.34 Sch.16

s.606, repealed: 2004 c.34 Sch.16

s.618, applied: 2004 c.34 s.261

s.621A, amended: 2002 c.15 Sch.9 para.6

s.622, applied: SI 2003/3239 Reg.9

s.623, amended: 2004 c.34 Sch.16

s.624, amended: 2004 c.34 Sch.16

Sch.1 para.1B, added: 2003 c.38 Sch.1 para.2

Sch.1 para.2, amended: 2004 c.21 Sch.1 para.62

Sch.1 para.9, amended: 2003 c.17 Sch.6 para.104

Sch.2 Part I, amended: 2004 c.33 Sch.8 para.33

Sch.2 Ground 2, see *Manchester City Council v Romano* [2004] EWCA Civ 834, [2004] 4 All E.R. 21 (CA), Brooke, L.J.

1985–cont.

68. Housing Act 1985–*cont.*

Sch.2 Part III Ground 16, see *Kensington and Chelsea RLBC v Hislop* [2003] EWHC 2944, [2004] 1 All E.R. 1036 (Ch D), Lindsay, J.

Sch.3 Part 2A, added: 2004 c.34 s.191

Sch.3 Part 2A, applied: 2004 c.34 s.194

Sch.4, applied: 2002 c.30 s.100

Sch.4 para.2, amended: 2004 c.33 Sch.8 para.34

Sch.4 para.5, amended: 2004 c.33 Sch.8 para.34

Sch.4 para.5A, amended: 2004 c.33 Sch.8 para.34

Sch.4 para.9A, added: 2003 c.38 Sch.1 para.2

Sch.5 para.11, amended: 2004 c.34 s.181

Sch.5 para.11, applied: 2004 c.34 s.181

Sch.5 para.13, added: 2004 c.34 s.182

Sch.5 para.14, added: 2004 c.34 s.182

Sch.5 para.15, added: 2004 c.34 s.182

Sch.5 para.16, added: 2004 c.34 s.182

Sch.5A para.1, added: 2004 c.34 Sch.9

Sch.5A para.2, added: 2004 c.34 Sch.9

Sch.5A para.3, added: 2004 c.34 Sch.9

Sch.5A para.4, added: 2004 c.34 Sch.9

Sch.5A para.5, added: 2004 c.34 Sch.9

Sch.5A para.6, added: 2004 c.34 Sch.9

Sch.6A, applied: SI 2003/3146 Reg.9, SI 2003/3239 Reg.8

Sch.6A para.1, amended: 2004 c.33 Sch.8 para.35, Sch.30

Sch.6A para.4, amended: 2004 c.33 Sch.8 para.35

Sch.6A para.12, amended: 2004 c.33 Sch.8 para.35

Sch.9A para.2, amended: 2002 c.9 Sch.11 para.18

Sch.9A para.2, repealed (in part): 2002 c.9 Sch.13

Sch.9A para.3, repealed: 2002 c.9 Sch.13

Sch.9A para.4, applied: SI 2003/1417 r.95

Sch.9A para.4, substituted: 2002 c.9 Sch.11 para.18

Sch.9A para.5, amended: 2002 c.9 Sch.11 para.18

Sch.9A para.5, repealed (in part): 2002 c.9 Sch.13

Sch.9A para.6, amended: 2002 c.9 Sch.11 para.18

Sch.9A para.9, amended: 2002 c.9 Sch.11 para.18

Sch.10 para.1, repealed: 2004 c.34 Sch.16

Sch.10 para.2, repealed: 2004 c.34 Sch.16

Sch.10 para.3, repealed: 2004 c.34 Sch.16

Sch.10 para.4, repealed: 2004 c.34 Sch.16

Sch.10 para.5, repealed: 2004 c.34 Sch.16

Sch.10 para.6, repealed: 2004 c.34 Sch.16

Sch.10 para.6A, repealed: 2004 c.34 Sch.16

Sch.10 para.7, repealed: 2004 c.34 Sch.16

Sch.10 para.8, repealed: 2004 c.34 Sch.16

1985–cont.

68. Housing Act 1985–cont.

Sch.13 Part I para.1, repealed: 2004 c.34 Sch.16

Sch.13 Part I para.2, repealed: 2004 c.34 Sch.16

Sch.13 Part I para.3, repealed: 2004 c.34 Sch.16

Sch.13 Part I para.4, repealed: 2004 c.34 Sch.16

Sch.13 Part I para.5, repealed: 2004 c.34 Sch.16

Sch.13 Part I para.6, repealed: 2004 c.34 Sch.16

Sch.13 Part II para.7, repealed: 2004 c.34 Sch.16

Sch.13 Part II para.8, repealed: 2004 c.34 Sch.16

Sch.13 Part II para.9, repealed: 2004 c.34 Sch.16

Sch.13 Part II para.10, repealed: 2004 c.34 Sch.16

Sch.13 Part II para.11, repealed: 2004 c.34 Sch.16

Sch.13 Part II para.12, repealed: 2004 c.34 Sch.16

Sch.13 Part II para.13, repealed: 2004 c.34 Sch.16

Sch.13 Part II para.13A, repealed: 2004 c.34 Sch.16

Sch.13 Part II para.14, repealed: 2004 c.34 Sch.16

Sch.13 Part III para.15, repealed: 2004 c.34 Sch.16

Sch.13 Part III para.16, repealed: 2004 c.34 Sch.16

Sch.13 Part III para.17, repealed: 2004 c.34 Sch.16

Sch.13 Part III para.18, repealed: 2004 c.34 Sch.16

Sch.13 Part III para.19, repealed: 2004 c.34 Sch.16

Sch.13 Part III para.20, repealed: 2004 c.34 Sch.16

Sch.13 Part III para.21, repealed: 2004 c.34 Sch.16

Sch.13 Part IV para.22, repealed: 2004 c.34 Sch.16

Sch.13 Part IV para.23, repealed: 2004 c.34 Sch.16

Sch.13 Part IV para.24, repealed: 2004 c.34 Sch.16

Sch.13 Part IV para.25, repealed: 2004 c.34 Sch.16

Sch.13 Part IV para.26, repealed: 2004 c.34 Sch.16

Sch.17 para.2, amended: 2002 c.9 Sch.11 para.18

Sch.20 Part III para.17, amended: 2002 c.9 Sch.11 para.18

1985–cont.

68. Housing Act 1985–cont.

Sch.24 Part I para.2, see *Farrell v Sandwell MBC* [2001] EWCA Civ 1107, [2002] R.V.R. 11 (CA), Robert Walker, L.J.

69. Housing Associations Act 1985

applied: SI 2003/1417 r.181, r.182, r.183, SI 2004/692 Sch.4 para.6

s.3, applied: SSI 2002/411 Art.2, 2003 c.14 s.129

s.75, amended: 2004 c.23 Sch.2 para.5

s.75, repealed (in part): 2004 c.23 Sch.2 para.5, Sch.4

s.87, amended: 2004 c.34 Sch.11 para.1, Sch.16

s.87, repealed (in part): 2004 c.34 Sch.11 para.1, Sch.16

s.89, applied: 2004 c.12 s.59

s.97, amended: SI 2003/1326 Art.16

s.105, amended: 2004 c.33 Sch.28 para.52

s.105, varied: 2004 c.33 Sch.21 para.26

Sch.1, referred to: SI 2003/1417 r.181, r.182, r.183

70. Landlord and Tenant Act 1985

applied: 2002 c.15 Sch.12 para.9

s.1, see *B Osborn & Co Ltd v Dior* [2003] EWCA Civ 281, [2003] H.L.R. 45 (CA), Arden, L.J.

s.8, see *Ratcliffe v Sandwell MBC* [2002] EWCA Civ 6, [2002] 1 W.L.R. 1488 (CA), Chadwick, L.J.

s.11, see *Niazi Services Ltd v Van der Loo* [2004] EWCA Civ 53, [2004] 1 W.L.R. 1254 (CA), Tuckey, L.J.; see *O'Connor v Old Etonian Housing Association Ltd* [2002] EWCA Civ 150, [2002] Ch. 295 (CA), Lord Phillips of Worth Matravers, M.R.; see *Southwark LBC v McIntosh* [2002] 1 E.G.L.R. 25 (Ch D), Lightman, J.; see *Tomkins v Basildon DC* [2002] EWCA Civ 876, [2003] L. & T.R. 7 (CA), Hart, J.

s.11, applied: 2002 c.15 Sch.7 para.3

s.11, varied: 2002 c.15 Sch.7 para.3

s.18, see *Cinnamon Ltd v Morgan* [2001] EWCA Civ 1616, [2002] 2 P. & C.R. 10 (CA), Chadwick, L.J.; see *Heron Maple House Ltd v Central Estates Ltd* [2004] L. & T.R. 17 (CC (Central London)), Judge Roger Cooke

s.18, amended: 2002 c.15 Sch.9 para.7

s.18, applied: 2002 c.15 s.169, s.172

s.18, varied: 2002 c.15 Sch.7 para.4

s.19, see *Cinnamon Ltd v Morgan* [2001] EWCA Civ 1616, [2002] 2 P. & C.R. 10 (CA), Chadwick, L.J.; see *R. (on the application of Daejan Properties Ltd) v London Leasehold Valuation Tribunal* [2001] EWCA Civ 1095, [2002] H.L.R. 25 (CA), Simon Brown, L.J.

s.19, applied: 2002 c.15 s.172

s.19, repealed (in part): 2002 c.15 Sch.14

s.19, varied: 2002 c.15 Sch.7 para.4

1985–cont.

70. Landlord and Tenant Act 1985–*cont.*

s.20, see *Heron Maple House Ltd v Central Estates Ltd* [2004] L. & T.R. 17 (CC (Central London)), Judge Roger Cooke

s.20, applied: 2002 c.15 s.172, SI 2003/1987 Reg.1, Reg.4, Reg.5, Reg.6, Reg.7, SI 2004/669 Art.2, SI 2004/684 Reg.1, Reg.4, Reg.5, Reg.6, Reg.7

s.20, disapplied: SI 2003/1987 Reg.7

s.20, referred to: SI 2003/1986 Art.3

s.20, substituted: 2002 c.15 s.151

s.20, varied: 2002 c.15 Sch.7 para.4

s.20, enabling: SI 2003/1987, SI 2004/684, SI 2004/2665, SI 2004/2939

s.20A, amended: SI 2002/1860 Sch.1 para.2

s.20A, applied: 2002 c.15 s.172

s.20A, varied: 2002 c.15 Sch.7 para.4

s.20B, see *Gilje v Charlegrove Securities Ltd* [2003] EWHC 1284, [2004] 1 All E.R. 91 (Ch D), Etherton, J.

s.20B, applied: 2002 c.15 s.172

s.20B, varied: 2002 c.15 Sch.7 para.4

s.20C, amended: 2004 c.34 Sch.15 para.32

s.20C, applied: 2002 c.15 s.172, SI 2003/2099 Sch.1 para.7, SI 2004/681 Sch.1 para.7

s.20C, varied: 2002 c.15 Sch.7 para.4

s.20ZA, applied: 2002 c.15 s.172, SI 2003/1987 Reg.5, Reg.7, SI 2003/2098 Reg.2, Reg.3, SI 2003/2099 Sch.1 para.2, SI 2004/681 Sch.1 para.2, SI 2004/683 Reg.3, SI 2004/684 Reg.5, Reg.7

s.20ZA, varied: 2002 c.15 Sch.7 para.4

s.20ZA, enabling: SI 2003/1987, SI 2004/684, SI 2004/2665, SI 2004/2939

s.21, applied: 2002 c.15 s.172

s.21, substituted: 2002 c.15 s.152

s.21, varied: 2002 c.15 Sch.7 para.4

s.21A, applied: 2002 c.15 s.172

s.21A, varied: 2002 c.15 Sch.7 para.4

s.21B, added: 2002 c.15 s.153

s.21B, applied: 2002 c.15 s.172

s.21B, varied: 2002 c.15 Sch.7 para.4

s.22, applied: 2002 c.15 s.172

s.22, substituted: 2002 c.15 s.154

s.22, varied: 2002 c.15 Sch.7 para.4

s.23, applied: 2002 c.15 s.172

s.23, substituted: 2002 c.15 Sch.10 para.1

s.23, varied: 2002 c.15 Sch.7 para.4

s.23A, added: 2002 c.15 Sch.10 para.2

s.23A, applied: 2002 c.15 s.172

s.23A, varied: 2002 c.15 Sch.7 para.4

s.24, applied: 2002 c.15 s.172

s.24, substituted: 2002 c.15 Sch.10 para.3

s.24, varied: 2002 c.15 Sch.7 para.4

s.25, amended: 2002 c.15 Sch.10 para.4

s.25, applied: 2002 c.15 s.172

s.25, varied: 2002 c.15 Sch.7 para.4

s.26, amended: 2002 c.15 Sch.10 para.5

s.26, applied: 2002 c.15 s.172

1985–cont.

70. Landlord and Tenant Act 1985–*cont.*

s.26, varied: 2002 c.15 Sch.7 para.4

s.27, amended: 2002 c.15 Sch.10 para.5

s.27, applied: 2002 c.15 s.172

s.27, varied: 2002 c.15 Sch.7 para.4

s.27A, added: 2002 c.15 s.155

s.27A, applied: 2002 c.15 s.172, SI 2003/2098 Reg.3, SI 2003/2099 Sch.1 para.2, Sch.2 para.2, SI 2004/681 Sch.1 para.2, Sch.2 para.2, SI 2004/683 Reg.3

s.27A, referred to: 2002 c.15 Sch.9 para.13

s.27A, varied: 2002 c.15 Sch.7 para.4

s.28, amended: 2002 c.15 Sch.10 para.6

s.28, applied: 2002 c.15 s.172

s.28, varied: 2002 c.15 Sch.7 para.4

s.29, applied: 2002 c.15 s.172

s.29, varied: 2002 c.15 Sch.7 para.4

s.30, see *Cinnamon Ltd v Morgan* [2001] EWCA Civ 1616, [2002] 2 P. & C.R. 10 (CA), Chadwick, L.J.

s.30, applied: 2002 c.15 s.172

s.30, varied: 2002 c.15 Sch.7 para.4

s.30A, applied: 2002 c.15 s.172

s.30A, varied: 2002 c.15 Sch.7 para.5

s.30B, applied: 2002 c.15 s.172, SI 2003/1988 Reg.3

s.30B, varied: 2002 c.15 Sch.7 para.6

s.31A, repealed (in part): 2002 c.15 Sch.14

s.31B, repealed (in part): 2002 c.15 Sch.14

s.31B, enabling: SI 2003/2269, SI 2003/2270, SI 2004/677, SI 2004/680

s.31C, repealed (in part): 2002 c.15 Sch.14

s.38, amended: 2002 c.15 s.155

s.39, amended: 2002 c.15 s.155, Sch.10 para.7, Sch.14

Sch.1, applied: 2002 c.15 s.172

Sch.1, amended: 2002 c.15 Sch.14

Sch.1, amended: 2002 c.15 Sch.10 para.13

Sch.1 para.1, varied: 2002 c.15 Sch.7 para.5

Sch.1 para.2, amended: 2002 c.15 Sch.10 para.8

Sch.1 para.2, applied: 2002 c.15 s.172

Sch.1 para.2, varied: 2002 c.15 Sch.7 para.5

Sch.1 para.3, applied: 2002 c.15 s.172

Sch.1 para.3, substituted: 2002 c.15 Sch.10 para.9

Sch.1 para.3, varied: 2002 c.15 Sch.7 para.5

Sch.1 para.4, amended: 2002 c.15 Sch.10 para.10

Sch.1 para.4, applied: 2002 c.15 s.172

Sch.1 para.4, varied: 2002 c.15 Sch.7 para.5

Sch.1 para.4A, added: 2002 c.15 Sch.10 para.11

Sch.1 para.4A, applied: 2002 c.15 s.172

Sch.1 para.4A, varied: 2002 c.15 Sch.7 para.5

Sch.1 para.5, amended: 2002 c.15 Sch.10 para.12

Sch.1 para.5, varied: 2002 c.15 Sch.7 para.5

Sch.1 para.6, amended: 2002 c.15 Sch.10 para.13

1985–cont.

70. Landlord and Tenant Act 1985–*cont.*
Sch.1 para.6, varied: 2002 c.15 Sch.7 para.5
Sch.1 para.7, varied: 2002 c.15 Sch.7 para.5
Sch.1 para.8, amended: 2002 c.15 s.165
Sch.1 para.8, applied: SI 2003/2098 Reg.3,
SI 2003/2099 Sch.1 para.2, SI 2004/681
Sch.1 para.2, SI 2004/683 Reg.3
Sch.1 para.8, repealed (in part): 2002 c.15
Sch.14
Sch.1 para.8, varied: 2002 c.15 Sch.7 para.5
Sch.1 para.9, varied: 2002 c.15 Sch.7 para.5
71. Housing (Consequential Provisions) Act 1985
Sch.2 para.24, repealed (in part): 2004 c.34
Sch.16
72. Weights and Measures Act 1985
see *Thoburn v Sunderland City Council*
[2002] EWHC 195, [2003] Q.B. 151
(QBD (Admin Ct)), Laws, L.J.
applied: 2002 c.40 Sch.15, SI 2003/2454
Reg.7, SI 2003/2761 Reg.8, SI 2004/102
Art.5, Art.14
referred to: SI 2002/808 Art.2, SI 2003/750
Sch.5 para.12, SI 2003/751 Sch.6 para.12,
SI 2004/1468 Sch.6 para.12
Part IV, applied: SI 2004/102 Art.5
Part V, applied: SI 2004/102 Art.5
s.5, amended: SI 2002/808 Art.13
s.8, applied: SI 2004/102 Art.7
s.11, applied: SI 2003/2454 Reg.3, SI 2003/
2761 Reg.3, Reg.16
s.15, enabling: SI 2003/214, SI 2003/2110, SI
2003/2454, SI 2003/2761
s.21, applied: SI 2003/1593 Sch.1 Part I
s.22, applied: SI 2003/1376 Sch.1, SI 2003/
1593 Sch.1 Part I
s.23, applied: SI 2003/1376 Sch.1, SI 2003/
1593 Sch.1 Part I
s.25, applied: SI 2003/1376 Sch.1, SI 2003/
1593 Sch.1 Part I
s.28, applied: SI 2003/1376 Sch.1, SI 2003/
1593 Sch.1 Part I
s.29, applied: SI 2003/1376 Sch.1
s.30, applied: SI 2003/1376 Sch.1, SI 2003/
1593 Sch.1 Part I
s.31, applied: SI 2003/1376 Sch.1, SI 2003/
1593 Sch.1 Part I
s.32, applied: SI 2003/1376 Sch.1, SI 2003/
1593 Sch.1 Part I
s.50, applied: SI 2003/1376 Sch.1, SI 2003/
1593 Sch.1 Part I
s.55, repealed: 2004 c.14 Sch.1 Part 5
s.62, repealed (in part): 2004 c.14 Sch.1 Part 5
s.69, applied: 2003 c.17 s.186
s.86, enabling: SI 2003/214, SI 2003/2110,
SI 2003/2454, SI 2003/2761
s.94, enabling: SI 2003/2110
Sch.12 para.6, repealed: 2002 c.40 Sch.26
73. Law Reform (Miscellaneous Provisions) (Scotland) Act 1985
s.7, amended: 2003 asp 11 Sch.1 para.7

1985–cont.

73. Law Reform (Miscellaneous Provisions) (Scotland) Act 1985–*cont.*
s.9, see *Cooperative Wholesale Society Ltd v Ravenseft Properties Ltd (No.2)* 2002
S.C.L.R. 644 (OH), Lord Macfadyen; see
Sheltered Housing Management Ltd v Cairns 2003 S.L.T. 578 (OH), Lord Nimmo
Smith
s.13, referred to: 2004 c.33 s.108
s.14, applied: SSI 2002/132 Sch.1 para.16.3
s.51, repealed (in part): 2003 asp 13 Sch.5
Part 1
s.54, amended: 2003 asp 4 Sch.4 para.8
s.54, repealed (in part): 2003 asp 4 Sch.4
para.8
s.55, repealed: 2002 asp 11 Sch.6 para.8

1986

xxi. Blyth Harbour Act 1986
s.2, amended: SI 2004/148 Sch.3
s.3, repealed: SI 2004/148 Sch.3
s.9, repealed: SI 2004/148 Sch.3
Sch.1, repealed: SI 2004/148 Sch.3
Companies Act 1986
s.429, see *Rock Nominees Ltd v RCO (Holdings) Plc (In Members Voluntary Liquidation)* [2004] EWCA Civ 118,
[2004] 1 B.C.L.C. 439 (CA), Potter, L.J.
s.459, see *Rock Nominees Ltd v RCO (Holdings) Plc (In Members Voluntary Liquidation)* [2004] EWCA Civ 118,
[2004] 1 B.C.L.C. 439 (CA), Potter, L.J.
iv. Greater London Council (General Powers) Act 1986
s.3, repealed: 2003 c.17 Sch.7
xx. Milford Haven Port Authority Act 1986
referred to: 2002 c.v
xix. Western Isles Islands Council (Berneray Harbour) Order Confirmation Act 1986
repealed: SSI 2002/410 Sch.2 Part I
s.1, referred to: SSI 2002/410 Sch.2 Part I
s.2, referred to: SSI 2002/410 Sch.2 Part I
s.4, referred to: SSI 2002/410 Sch.2 Part I
s.21, referred to: SSI 2002/410 Sch.2 Part I
s.22, referred to: SSI 2002/410 Sch.2 Part I
s.23, referred to: SSI 2002/410 Sch.2 Part I
s.24, referred to: SSI 2002/410 Sch.2 Part I
s.25, referred to: SSI 2002/410 Sch.2 Part I
s.26, referred to: SSI 2002/410 Sch.2 Part I
s.27, referred to: SSI 2002/410 Sch.2 Part I
s.28, referred to: SSI 2002/410 Sch.2 Part I
s.29, referred to: SSI 2002/410 Sch.2 Part I
s.30, referred to: SSI 2002/410 Sch.2 Part I
s.31, referred to: SSI 2002/410 Sch.2 Part I
2. Ecclesiastical Fees Measure 1986
applied: SI 2002/1892 Art.3, SI 2002/1893
para.1, SI 2003/1933 Art.3, SI 2003/1936
para.1, SI 2004/1888 Art.3

CAP.

2. **Ecclesiastical Fees Measure 1986**–*cont.*
s.1, applied: SI 2003/1936 para.1
s.1, enabling: SI 2002/1894, SI 2003/1932, SI 2004/1890
s.2, applied: SI 2002/1894, SI 2003/1932
s.2, enabling: SI 2002/1894, SI 2003/1932, SI 2004/1890
s.3, applied: SI 2002/1894 Art.1, SI 2003/1932 Art.1, SI 2003/1936 para.1, SI 2004/1890 Art.1
s.4, applied: SI 2002/1892, SI 2002/1893, SI 2003/1933, SI 2003/1936, SI 2004/1888
s.5, applied: SI 2002/1892 Sch.1 Part TABLEe, SI 2003/1933 Sch.1 Part V, SI 2004/1888 Sch.1 Part TABLEe
s.5, enabling: SI 2002/1893, SI 2003/1936
s.6, applied: SI 2002/1893 para.4, SI 2003/1936 para.4
s.6, enabling: SI 2002/1892, SI 2003/1933, SI 2004/1888
s.7, applied: SI 2003/1936 para.1
s.8, applied: SI 2002/1892 Sch.1 Part TABLEd, SI 2002/1893 Art.2, SI 2003/1933 Sch.1 Part IV, SI 2003/1936 Art.2, SI 2004/1888 Sch.1 Part TABLEd
s.10, amended: 2003 c.3 s.44

3. **Patronage (Benefices) Measure 1986**
Part I, applied: SI 2002/1892 Sch.1 Part TABLEe, SI 2002/1893 para.1, para.4, SI 2003/1933 Sch.1 Part II, Sch.1 Part V, SI 2003/1936 para.1, para.4, SI 2004/1888 Sch.1 Part TABLEe
s.1, applied: SI 2002/1893 para.1
s.3, applied: SI 2002/1893 para.1
s.6, repealed: 2002 c.9 Sch.13
s.7, applied: SI 2002/1893 para.1

5. **Agricultural Holdings Act 1986**
see *Vooght v Hoath* [2002] EWHC 1408, [2002] B.P.I.R. 1047 (Ch D), Neuberger, J.
applied: 2002 c.15 Sch.2 para.2
s.2, see *JS Bloor (Measham) Ltd v Calcott (No.2)* [2002] 1 E.G.L.R. 1 (Ch D), Hart, J.
s.12, see *Secretary of State for Defence v Spencer* [2002] EWHC 2116, [2003] 1 W.L.R. 75 (Ch D), Neuberger, J.
s.25, see *JS Bloor (Measham) Ltd v Calcott (No.2)* [2002] 1 E.G.L.R. 1 (Ch D), Hart, J.
s.26, applied: SI 2002/457 Reg.12, SI 2002/897 Reg.12
s.35, amended: 2004 c.33 Sch.8 para.36
s.36, amended: 2004 c.33 Sch.8 para.37
s.49, amended: 2004 c.33 Sch.8 para.36
s.50, amended: 2004 c.33 Sch.8 para.38
s.96, amended: SI 2002/794 Sch.1 para.27
Sch.2 para.4, see *Secretary of State for Defence v Spencer* [2002] EWHC 2116, [2003] 1 W.L.R. 75 (Ch D), Neuberger, J.; see *Secretary of State for Defence v Spencer* [2003] EWCA Civ 784, [2003] 1 W.L.R. 2701 (CA), Peter Gibson, L.J.

CAP.

5. **Agricultural Holdings Act 1986**–*cont.*
Sch.2 para.6, see *Secretary of State for Defence v Spencer* [2002] EWHC 2116, [2003] 1 W.L.R. 75 (Ch D), Neuberger, J.; see *Secretary of State for Defence v Spencer* [2003] EWCA Civ 784, [2003] 1 W.L.R. 2701 (CA), Peter Gibson, L.J.
Sch.3, applied: SI 2002/457 Reg.12, SI 2002/897 Reg.12
Sch.6 Part I, amended: 2004 c.33 Sch.8 para.39
Sch.6 Part I para.1, amended: 2004 c.33 Sch.8 para.39
Sch.6 Part I para.3, applied: SI 2002/1925 Art.2, SI 2003/4 Art.2, SI 2003/2151 Art.2, SI 2004/1218 Art.2, SI 2004/1811 Art.2
Sch.6 Part I para.4, enabling: SI 2002/1925, SI 2003/4, SI 2003/2151, SI 2004/1218, SI 2004/1811
Sch.6 Part I para.6, amended: 2004 c.33 Sch.8 para.39
Sch.6 Part I para.9, amended: 2004 c.33 Sch.8 para.39
Sch.6 Part I para.10, amended: 2004 c.33 Sch.8 para.39
Sch.11 para.1, applied: SI 2002/457 Sch.1 para.4, Sch.1 para.7, SI 2002/897 Sch.1 para.7
Sch.12 para.4, amended: SI 2003/1615 Sch.1 para.13
Sch.14 para.7, repealed: 2004 c.14 Sch.1 Part 3
Sch.14 para.19, repealed: 2004 c.14 Sch.1 Part 2

9. **Law Reform (Parent and Child) (Scotland) Act 1986**
applied: SI 2004/1309 Reg.3
s.1, applied: 2004 c.33 s.86
s.1, referred to: 2003 c.1 s.721
s.8, amended: SSI 2003/96 Art.7

10. **Local Government Act 1986**
referred to: SI 2002/808 Art.2
s.2, amended: 2003 c.21 s.349
s.2, varied: SI 2004/1777 Art.33, SI 2004/1778 Art.33
s.2A, referred to: 2003 c.26 s.128
s.2A, repealed: 2003 c.26 Sch.8 Part 1
s.2A, varied: SI 2004/1777 Art.33, SI 2004/1778 Art.33
s.3, varied: SI 2004/1777 Art.33, SI 2004/1778 Art.33
s.4, varied: SI 2004/1777 Art.33, SI 2004/1778 Art.33
s.5, amended: 2004 c.23 Sch.2 para.6
s.5, varied: SI 2004/1777 Art.33, SI 2004/1778 Art.33
s.6, amended: SI 2002/808 Art.14
s.6, varied: SI 2004/1777 Art.33, SI 2004/1778 Art.33

CAP.

1986–cont.

14. Animals (Scientific Procedures) Act 1986
applied: 2002 c.18 Sch.2 Part 2, Sch.2 Part 24, 2003 c.13 Sch.2 Part 2, Sch.2 Part 28, 2004 c.9 Sch.2 Part 27

s.8, enabling: SI 2002/473

s.22, amended: 2003 c.44 Sch.37 Part 9

s.22, disapplied: 2003 c.44 Sch.25 para.83

s.23, amended: 2003 c.44 Sch.37 Part 9

s.23, disapplied: 2003 c.44 Sch.25 para.83

s.25, amended: 2003 c.44 Sch.37 Part 9

s.25, disapplied: 2003 c.44 Sch.25 para.83

18. Corneal Tissue Act 1986
referred to: 2004 c.30 s.59

repealed (in part): 2004 c.30 Sch.7 Part 1

20. Horticultural Produce Act 1986
s.7, repealed (in part): 2004 c.14 Sch.1 Part 2

22. Civil Protection in Peacetime Act 1986
repealed: 2004 c.36 Sch.2 para.8, Sch.3

s.2, amended: 2002 c.5 s.1

26. Land Registration Act 1986
s.1, repealed: 2002 c.9 Sch.13

s.2, repealed: 2002 c.9 Sch.13

s.3, repealed: 2002 c.9 Sch.13

s.4, repealed: 2002 c.9 Sch.13

31. Airports Act 1986
see *Commission of the European Communities v United Kingdom (C98/01)* [2003] All E.R. (EC) 878 (ECJ), Judge Rodriguez Iglesias (President)

applied: 2002 c.40 Sch.15, SI 2003/419 Art.63

referred to: SI 2002/808 Art.2

Part IV, applied: SI 2003/335 Sch.1, SSI 2003/93 Sch.1

Part V, applied: SI 2002/2626 Art.6

s.1, repealed: 2004 c.14 Sch.1 Part 4

s.2, repealed: 2004 c.14 Sch.1 Part 4

s.3, repealed: 2004 c.14 Sch.1 Part 4

s.4, repealed (in part): 2004 c.14 Sch.1 Part 4

s.5, repealed: 2004 c.14 Sch.1 Part 4

s.9, repealed: 2004 c.14 Sch.1 Part 4

s.11, repealed: 2004 c.14 Sch.1 Part 4

s.20, amended: 2004 c.33 Sch.27 para.111

s.20, varied: 2004 c.33 Sch.21 para.27

s.22, amended: 2004 c.23 Sch.2 para.7

s.24, amended: 2004 c.23 Sch.2 para.7, Sch.4

s.32, enabling: SI 2004/1946

s.36, amended: SI 2003/1398 Sch.1 para.5

s.43, applied: SI 2003/1397 Art.8

s.44, repealed (in part): 2002 c.40 Sch.26

s.44A, added: 2002 c.40 Sch.25 para.14

s.44B, added: 2002 c.40 Sch.25 para.14

s.44B, referred to: SI 2003/1371

s.44B, enabling: SI 2003/1371

s.45, amended: 2002 c.40 Sch.25 para.14

s.53, repealed (in part): 2004 c.14 Sch.1 Part 4

s.54, amended: 2002 c.40 Sch.9 para.2

s.54, repealed (in part): 2002 c.40 Sch.26

CAP.

1986–cont.

31. Airports Act 1986–*cont.*
s.54, varied: SI 2003/1592 Sch.4 para.5

s.56, amended: 2002 c.40 Sch.25 para.14

s.57, repealed (in part): 2004 c.14 Sch.1 Part 4

s.62, amended: 2003 c.21 Sch.17 para.80

s.62, repealed (in part): 2003 c.21 Sch.19

s.69, applied: SI 2003/335 Sch.1, SSI 2003/93 Sch.1

s.73, applied: SI 2003/335 Sch.1, SSI 2003/93 Sch.1

s.74, amended: 2002 c.40 Sch.25 para.14, 2003 c.20 Sch.2 para.19, 2003 c.37 Sch.7 para.24

s.74, referred to: 2003 c.20 s.115

s.75, amended: 2004 c.14 Sch.1 Part 4

s.76, amended: 2004 c.14 Sch.1 Part 4

s.76A, added: SI 2003/2867 Sch.1 para.13

s.79, amended: 2004 c.14 Sch.1 Part 4

s.79, applied: SI 2004/1946

s.82, applied: 2004 c.36 Sch.1 para.26, Sch.1 para.36

s.85, repealed (in part): 2004 c.14 Sch.1 Part 4

Sch.1 para.13, amended: 2002 c.40 Sch.9 para.3

Sch.2 para.1, amended: SI 2002/2626 Sch.2 para.13, 2004 c.34 Sch.16

Sch.2 para.3, varied: SI 2004/1822 Sch.1 para.13

Sch.4 para.3, repealed: 2002 c.40 Sch.26

Sch.4 para.4, repealed: 2002 c.40 Sch.26

Sch.4 para.6, repealed: 2002 c.40 Sch.26

Sch.4 para.7, repealed: 2002 c.40 Sch.26

Sch.5 para.7, repealed: 2004 c.14 Sch.1 Part 4

Sch.5 para.8, repealed: 2004 c.14 Sch.1 Part 4

Sch.5 para.9, repealed: 2004 c.14 Sch.1 Part 4

32. Drug Trafficking Offences Act 1986
applied: 2002 c.29 s.8, s.94, s.158

s.9, applied: 2002 c.29 s.41, s.49, s.51, s.53, s.79, s.120, s.125, s.128, s.145, s.190, s.197, s.199, s.201, s.227

33. Disabled Persons (Services, Consultation and Representation) Act 1986
see *D, Petitioners* 2003 S.L.T. 1323 (OH), Lord Philip

referred to: 2003 c.43 Sch.4 para.64

s.2, amended: SI 2002/2469 Sch.1 para.12, 2003 asp 13 Sch.4 para.4, 2003 c.43 Sch.4 para.65

s.5, applied: SI 2002/152 Reg.24

s.7, amended: 2002 c.17 Sch.1 para.38, Sch.2 para.51, 2003 asp 13 Sch.5 Part 1, 2003 c.43 Sch.4 para.66

s.8, referred to: SSI 2002/533 Sch.1, Sch.3

s.10, disapplied: 2002 c.32 Sch.18 para.13

s.13, repealed (in part): 2004 asp 4 Sch.3 para.5

s.14, repealed (in part): 2004 asp 4 Sch.3 para.5

s.16, amended: 2002 c.17 Sch.1 para.38, 2003 asp 13 Sch.4 para.4

1986–cont.

35. Protection of Military Remains Act 1986
applied: SI 2002/1761 Art.2
s.1, enabling: SI 2002/1761, SI 2003/405
s.3, amended: 2002 c.8 s.2

38. Outer Space Act 1986
s.2, amended: 2002 c.8 s.2
s.15, repealed (in part): 2004 c.14 Sch.1 Part 4

40. Education Act 1986
s.1, amended: 2002 c.32 Sch.21 para.7
s.1, repealed (in part): 2002 c.32 s.18, Sch.22 Part 3
s.2, repealed (in part): 2002 c.32 Sch.22 Part 3
s.3, repealed (in part): 2002 c.32 Sch.22 Part 3
s.4, repealed (in part): 2002 c.32 Sch.22 Part 3

41. Finance Act 1986
Part V, applied: 2004 c.12 Sch.15 para.11, Sch.15 para.21, Sch.15 para.22
s.66, amended: 2003 c.14 Sch.40 para.2
s.67, amended: 2003 c.14 Sch.20 para.3
s.70, amended: 2003 c.14 Sch.20 para.3
s.75, amended: 2003 c.14 Sch.20 para.3
s.75, applied: 2003 c.14 Sch.7 para.2, Sch.7 para.4
s.76, amended: 2002 c.23 s.112, 2003 c.14 Sch.20 para.3
s.76, applied: 2002 c.23 s.113
s.76, referred to: 2002 c.23 Sch.35 para.3
s.77, amended: 2003 c.14 Sch.20 para.3
s.79, amended: 2003 c.14 Sch.20 para.3
s.80A, referred to: 2002 c.23 s.117
s.80C, referred to: 2002 c.23 s.117
s.88, amended: 2003 c.14 Sch.20 para.3
s.88A, referred to: 2002 c.23 s.117
s.89AA, referred to: 2002 c.23 s.117
s.90, amended: 2003 c.14 Sch.40 para.3
s.92, amended: 2003 c.14 Sch.40 para.4, SI 2003/2868 Reg.4
s.98, applied: 2004 c.12 s.313
s.99, amended: SI 2003/2868 Reg.5
s.102, see *Inland Revenue Commissioners v Eversden* [2002] EWHC 1360, [2002] S.T.C. 1109 (Ch D), Lightman, J.; see *Inland Revenue Commissioners v Eversden* [2002] S.T.C. (S.C.D.) 39 (Sp Comm), Nuala Brice; see *Inland Revenue Commissioners v Eversden* [2003] EWCA Civ 668, [2003] S.T.C. 822 (CA), Carnwath, L.J.
s.102, amended: 2003 c.14 s.185
s.102, applied: 2004 c.12 Sch.15 para.11, Sch.15 para.21, Sch.15 para.22
s.102, disapplied: 2004 c.12 Sch.15 para.11
s.102B, disapplied: 2004 c.12 Sch.15 para.11
s.102C, disapplied: 2004 c.12 Sch.15 para.11
Sch.4 Part I para.2, repealed (in part): 2002 c.23 Sch.40 Part 1

1986–cont.

41. Finance Act 1986–*cont.*
Sch.5, see *Inland Revenue Commissioners v Eversden* [2002] S.T.C. (S.C.D.) 39 (Sp Comm), Nuala Brice
Sch.11, see *Agassi v Robinson (Inspector of Taxes)* [2003] S.T.C. (S.C.D.) 382 (Sp Comm), John Avery-Jones
Sch.20 para.2, disapplied: 2004 c.12 Sch.15 para.11
Sch.20 para.6, disapplied: 2004 c.12 Sch.15 para.11

44. Gas Act 1986
applied: 2002 c.40 Sch.15, SI 2003/419 Art.63, 2004 c.20 s.188, SI 2004/2541 Sch.1, SI 2004/2542 Sch.1
Part I, applied: SI 2002/366 Sch.2 para.8, SI 2002/1384 Art.11, SI 2002/2398 Art.6, SI 2004/2542 Reg.3, SSI 2003/359 Art.7, 2004 c.20 s.150, s.168, s.190
s.4A, applied: 2004 c.20 s.175, s.190
s.4AA, amended: 2003 c.21 Sch.17 para.81, 2004 c.20 s.83, s.149, s.178, s.179
s.4AA, applied: 2002 c.40 s.168, 2004 c.20 s.175, s.190
s.4AB, applied: 2004 c.20 s.175, s.190
s.4B, amended: 2002 c.40 Sch.25 para.15
s.4B, applied: 2004 c.20 s.190
s.5, amended: 2004 c.20 s.149
s.6A, amended: 2004 c.20 s.149
s.6A, applied: SI 2004/2542 Sch.2 para.2
s.6A, enabling: SI 2004/2542
s.7, amended: 2004 c.20 s.149
s.7, applied: 2004 c.36 Sch.1 para.20, Sch.1 para.31, SI 2004/2542 Reg.3
s.7, referred to: 2002 c.40 s.168
s.7, repealed (in part): 2004 c.20 Sch.23 Part 1
s.7A, amended: 2004 c.20 s.149
s.7A, applied: SI 2004/2542 Reg.3, Sch.2 para.4
s.7A, referred to: 2002 c.40 s.168, SI 2004/2542 Sch.2 para.1
s.7B, applied: 2004 c.20 s.191, SI 2004/2542 Reg.8
s.7B, varied: 2004 c.20 s.152
s.7B, enabling: SI 2003/847, SI 2004/2983
s.7ZA, added: 2004 c.20 s.149
s.7ZA, applied: 2004 c.20 s.150, s.152, 2004 c.36 Sch.1 para.20, Sch.1 para.31
s.7ZA, referred to: 2002 c.40 s.168
s.8, amended: 2004 c.20 s.150
s.8, applied: SI 2004/2542 Sch.1
s.8, referred to: SI 2004/2542 Reg.6
s.8, varied: 2004 c.20 s.152
s.10, enabling: SI 2002/1488
s.13, enabling: SI 2002/3130
s.19A, amended: SI 2004/2043 Sch.2 para.1
s.19A, applied: SI 2004/2043 Reg.3
s.19B, amended: SI 2004/2043 Sch.2 para.2
s.19C, amended: SI 2004/2043 Sch.2 para.3
s.19C, applied: SI 2004/2043 Reg.3

CAP.

1986–cont.

44. Gas Act 1986–*cont.*

s.19D, amended: SI 2004/2043 Sch.2 para.4

s.19D, repealed (in part): SI 2004/2043 Sch.2 para.4

s.19DA, added: SI 2004/2043 Sch.2 para.5

s.19E, amended: SI 2004/2043 Sch.2 para.6

s.19E, repealed (in part): SI 2004/2043 Sch.2 para.6

s.23, amended: 2004 c.20 s.150

s.23, applied: SI 2003/1746, SI 2003/1746 Art.4

s.23, enabling: SI 2003/1746

s.24, amended: 2002 c.40 Sch.25 para.15, 2004 c.20 s.149

s.24, applied: SI 2003/1397 Art.8, 2004 c.20 s.177

s.24, repealed (in part): 2002 c.40 Sch.26

s.24A, added: 2002 c.40 Sch.25 para.15

s.24B, added: 2002 c.40 Sch.25 para.15

s.24B, referred to: SI 2003/1371

s.24B, enabling: SI 2003/1371

s.25, amended: 2002 c.40 Sch.25 para.15

s.26, amended: 2004 c.20 s.150

s.26A, amended: 2002 c.40 Sch.25 para.15, 2004 c.20 s.150

s.26A, referred to: SI 2003/1371

s.26A, repealed (in part): 2002 c.40 Sch.26

s.26A, enabling: SI 2003/1371

s.27, amended: 2002 c.40 Sch.9 para.4, 2004 c.20 s.150

s.27, repealed (in part): 2002 c.40 Sch.26

s.27, varied: SI 2003/1592 Sch.4 para.6

s.30A, applied: SI 2002/1111, SI 2002/1111 Art.3

s.30A, enabling: SI 2002/1111

s.33, amended: 2002 c.40 Sch.25 para.15

s.33A, applied: SI 2002/475

s.33A, referred to: SI 2002/475 Reg.10

s.33A, enabling: SI 2002/475, SI 2002/741

s.33AA, applied: SI 2002/741

s.33AA, referred to: SI 2002/475 Reg.10

s.33AA, enabling: SI 2002/741

s.33AB, applied: SI 2002/475 Reg.6

s.33AB, enabling: SI 2002/475, SI 2002/741

s.33B, applied: SI 2002/475 Reg.11

s.33BA, applied: SI 2002/475 Reg.11

s.33BAA, applied: SI 2002/741

s.33BC, enabling: SI 2003/1180, SI 2004/3392

s.33D, enabling: SI 2002/475, SI 2002/741

s.34, amended: 2002 c.40 Sch.25 para.15

s.35, amended: 2002 c.40 Sch.25 para.15

s.36, amended: 2004 c.20 s.149, s.183

s.36A, amended: 2002 c.40 Sch.9 para.17, Sch.25 para.15, SI 2004/1261 Sch.2 para.1

s.36A, repealed (in part): 2002 c.40 Sch.26

s.41C, amended: 2004 c.20 s.149

s.41E, applied: SI 2003/1397 Art.8

s.41E, repealed (in part): 2002 c.40 Sch.26

s.41EA, added: 2002 c.40 Sch.25 para.15

CAP.

1986–cont.

44. Gas Act 1986–*cont.*

s.41EB, added: 2002 c.40 Sch.25 para.15

s.41EB, amended: 2003 c.21 Sch.16 para.2

s.41EB, referred to: SI 2003/1371

s.41EB, enabling: SI 2003/1371

s.41F, amended: 2002 c.40 Sch.25 para.15

s.46, applied: SI 2002/475 Reg.10, Reg.11

s.47, enabling: SI 2002/475, SI 2002/741, SI 2002/1488, SI 2002/3130, SI 2003/847, SI 2004/2983

s.48, amended: 2004 c.20 s.149

s.48, enabling: SI 2003/847

s.49, amended: 2004 c.20 s.183

s.50, repealed (in part): 2004 c.14 Sch.1 Part 5

s.57, repealed: 2004 c.14 Sch.1 Part 5

s.60, enabling: SI 2004/2542

s.62, amended: 2002 c.40 Sch.25 para.15

s.64A, added: 2004 c.20 s.153

Sch.2B para.6A, substituted: 2004 c.20 s.181

Sch.2B para.7, applied: SI 2002/475 Reg.5, Reg.8

Sch.2B para.10, applied: SI 2002/475 Reg.8

Sch.2B para.29, amended: 2002 asp 17 Sch.3 para.16

Sch.5 Part II para.19, amended: 2002 asp 17 Sch.3 para.16

Sch.7 para.15, repealed: 2002 c.40 Sch.26

Sch.7 para.19, repealed: 2002 c.40 Sch.26

Sch.7 para.27, repealed: 2002 c.40 Sch.26

Sch.7 para.28, repealed: 2002 c.40 Sch.26

45. Insolvency Act 1986

see *Darrell v Miller* [2003] EWHC 2811, [2004] B.P.I.R. 470 (Ch D), Lewison, J.; see *Kudos Glass Ltd (In Liquidation), Re* [2002] B.C.C. 416 (Ch D), Richard McCombe Q.C.; see *Kyrris v Oldham* [2003] EWCA Civ 1506, [2004] B.C.C. 111 (CA), Jonathan Parker, L.J.; see *Malcolm v Mackenzie* [2004] EWHC 339, [2004] 1 W.L.R. 1803 (Ch D), Lloyd, J.; see *T&N Ltd, Re* [2004] EWHC 1680, [2004] Pens. L.R. 351 (Ch D (Companies Ct)), David Richards, J.

applied: 2002 c.29 s.311, 2002 c.40 s.249, s.254, Sch.15, Sch.17 para.9, SI 2002/3038 Reg.5, 2003 c.17 s.27, 2003 c.39 s.101, 2003 c.43 s.26, SI 2003/1102 Reg.2, Reg.5, SI 2003/1417 r.184, SI 2003/2093 Art.1, 2004 c.20 Sch.20 para.46, 2004 c.35 s.87, s.121, s.201, Sch.3, Sch.8, SI 2004/353 Reg.2, Reg.5, SI 2004/400 Reg.5, SI 2004/1045 Reg.4, SI 2004/3121 Sch.1

disapplied: 2002 c.29 s.430

referred to: 2002 c.9 s.86, 2002 c.29 s.432, 2002 c.40 Sch.23 para.1, 2003 c.43 s.26, 2004 c.20 Sch.20 para.46, SI 2004/1941 Sch.1 para.1

varied: 2004 c.20 Sch.20 para.41

1986–cont.

45. Insolvency Act 1986–*cont.*

Part I, see *Television Trade Rentals Ltd, Re* [2002] EWHC 211, [2002] B.C.C. 807 (Ch D (Companies Court)), Lawrence Collins, J.

Part I, applied: 2002 c.15 s.87, s.105, 2002 c.29 s.311, 2002 c.40 s.255, SI 2002/2708 Art.11, SI 2002/2709 r.4, r.6, SI 2002/2822 Reg.43, SI 2003/2093 Art.4, 2004 c.20 s.159, 2004 c.35 s.121, SI 2004/353 Reg.4, SI 2004/593 Art.4, Sch.2 para.2, SI 2004/1450 Reg.20

Part I, disapplied: SI 2003/1102 Reg.4

Part I, referred to: SI 2004/1045 Reg.3

Part II, applied: 2002 asp 17 s.40, 2002 c.40 s.255, SI 2003/1730 r.5, SI 2003/2093 Art.3, Art.4, 2004 c.20 s.159, 2004 c.35 s.121, SI 2004/353 Reg.4, SI 2004/593 Art.4, Sch.2 para.2

Part II, disapplied: SI 2003/1102 Reg.4

Part II, referred to: SI 2004/1045 Reg.3

Part III, applied: 2004 c.20 s.159, SI 2004/593 Art.4, Sch.2 para.2

Part IV, applied: 2002 asp 17 s.40, 2002 c.29 s.426, SI 2003/1102 Reg.11, 2004 c.20 s.159, 2004 c.35 s.121, SI 2004/291 Sch.6 para.113, SI 2004/353 Reg.11, SI 2004/478 Sch.6 para.111, SI 2004/593 Art.4, Sch.2 para.2, SI 2004/627 Sch.5 para.105, SI 2004/1045 Reg.12, SSI 2004/115 Sch.5 para.101, SSI 2004/116 Sch.1 para.66

Part IV c.IV, referred to: SI 2004/1045 Reg.3

Part IV c.VI, applied: SI 2004/353 Reg.4

Part IV c.VI, disapplied: SI 2003/1102 Reg.4

Part IV c.VI, referred to: SI 2004/1045 Reg.3

Part V, see *Lancefield v Lancefield* [2002] B.P.I.R. 1108 (Ch D), Neuberger, J.

Part V, applied: 2002 asp 17 s.40, 2002 c.29 s.426, 2004 c.20 s.159, 2004 c.35 s.121, SI 2004/593 Art.4, Sch.2 para.2

Part VI, applied: 2004 c.20 s.159, SI 2004/593 Art.4, Sch.2 para.2

Part VII, applied: 2004 c.20 s.159, SI 2004/593 Art.4, Sch.2 para.2

Part VIII, see *Household Mortgage Corp Plc v Whitehead* [2002] EWCA Civ 1657, [2003] 1 W.L.R. 1173 (CA), Chadwick, L.J.; see *Inland Revenue Commissioners v Bland* [2003] EWHC 1068, [2003] B.P.I.R. 1274 (Ch D), Lloyd, J.; see *Lloyds Bank Plc v Ellicott* [2002] EWCA Civ 1333, [2003] B.P.I.R. 632 (CA), Ward, L.J.

Part VIII, applied: 2002 c.29 s.311, SI 2002/427 Reg.4, Reg.6, SI 2002/836 Reg.4, Reg.6, SI 2002/2712 r.5, r.8, SI 2003/2093 Art.4, 2004 c.35 s.121, SI 2004/400 Reg.5, SI 2004/593 Art.4, Sch.2 para.2

Part VIII, see *Household Mortgage Corp Plc v Whitehead* [2002] EWCA Civ 1657, [2003] 1 W.L.R. 1173 (CA), Chadwick, L.J.; see *Inland Revenue Commissioners v Bland* [2003] EWHC 1068, [2003] B.P.I.R. 1274

1986–cont.

45. Insolvency Act 1986–*cont.*

Part VIII –*cont.*

(Ch D), Lloyd, J.; see *Lloyds Bank Plc v Ellicott* [2002] EWCA Civ 1333, [2003] B.P.I.R. 632 (CA), Ward, L.J.

Part VIII, added: 2002 c.40 Sch.22 para.2

Part IX, applied: 2002 c.29 s.418, SI 2002/427 Reg.4, Reg.6, SI 2002/836 Reg.4, Reg.6, SI 2004/593 Art.4, Sch.2 para.2

Part X, applied: SI 2002/427 Reg.4, Reg.6, SI 2002/836 Reg.4, Reg.6, SI 2004/593 Art.4, Sch.2 para.2

Part XI, applied: SI 2002/427 Reg.4, Reg.6, SI 2002/836 Reg.4, Reg.6, SI 2004/593 Art.4, Sch.2 para.2

Part XIII, applied: 2004 c.20 s.171

s.1, see *Inland Revenue Commissioners v Adam & Partners Ltd* [2002] B.C.C. 247 (CA), Mummery, L.J.; see *Salvage Association, Re* [2003] EWHC 1028, [2004] 1 W.L.R. 174 (Ch D), Blackburne, J.

s.1, amended: 2002 c.40 Sch.17 para.10, SI 2002/1240 Reg.4

s.1, applied: SI 2002/2711 Art.5, SI 2003/1102 Reg.33, SI 2004/353 Reg.33

s.1, varied: 2003 c.43 s.24

s.1A, varied: 2003 c.43 s.24

s.2, applied: 2004 c.35 s.121, SI 2004/3121 Sch.1

s.2, varied: 2003 c.43 s.24

s.3, applied: SI 2002/2708 Art.11, SI 2002/2709 r.4, SI 2002/2710 Reg.2, SI 2002/2711 Art.3, SI 2002/2712 r.3

s.3, varied: 2003 c.43 s.24

s.4, see *Inland Revenue Commissioners v Wimbledon Football Club Ltd* [2004] EWCA Civ 655, [2004] B.C.C. 638 (CA), Lord Woolf of Barnes, L.C.J.

s.4, applied: SI 2003/1102 Reg.4, SI 2004/353 Reg.4, SI 2004/1045 Reg.3

s.4, varied: 2003 c.43 s.24, SI 2003/1102 Reg.33, SI 2004/353 Reg.33

s.4A, applied: SI 2003/1102 Reg.11, Reg.34, Reg.36, SI 2004/353 Reg.11, Reg.34, Reg.36, SI 2004/1045 Reg.12, Reg.19, Reg.21

s.4A, varied: 2003 c.43 s.24

s.4B, varied: 2003 c.43 s.24

s.5, see *McGruther v James Scott Ltd* 2003 S.C. 495 (OH), Lady Smith

s.5, amended: 2002 c.40 Sch.17 para.11

s.5, referred to: SI 2002/2711 Art.3

s.5, varied: 2003 c.43 s.24, 2004 c.20 Sch.20 para.43

s.6, see *Pearson v Albany Marketing Ltd* [2003] EWHC 1437, [2003] B.P.I.R. 1132 (Ch D (Companies Court)), Rimer, J.; see *Swindon Town Properties Ltd v Swindon Town Football Co Ltd* [2003] B.P.I.R. 253 (Ch D), Hart, J.; see *Trident Fashions Plc (In Administration), Re (No.1)* [2004] EWHC 351, [2004] 2 B.C.L.C. 28 (Ch D

CAP.

CAP.

1986–cont.

45. Insolvency Act 1986–*cont.*

s.6–*cont.*

(Companies Ct)), Lindsay, J.; see *Trident Fashions Plc (In Administration), Re (No.2)* [2004] EWHC 293, [2004] 2 B.C.L.C. 35 (Ch D), Lewison, J.

s.6, amended: 2002 c.40 Sch.17 para.12

s.6, applied: SI 2003/1102 Reg.11, SI 2004/ 353 Reg.11, SI 2004/1045 Reg.12

s.6, varied: 2003 c.43 s.24, 2004 c.20 Sch.20 para.44

s.6A, varied: 2003 c.43 s.24

s.7, see *Alman v Approach Housing Ltd* [2002] B.C.C. 723 (Ch D), Rimer, J.; see *County Bookshops Ltd v Grove* [2002] EWHC 1160, [2003] 1 B.C.L.C. 479 (Ch D), Neuberger, J.; see *Pearson v Albany Marketing Ltd* [2003] EWHC 1437, [2003] B.P.I.R. 1132 (Ch D (Companies Court)), Rimer, J.

s.7, varied: 2003 c.43 s.24

s.7A, varied: 2003 c.43 s.24

s.7B, varied: 2003 c.43 s.24

s.8, see *Bee v T&N Shelf Twenty Six Ltd* 2002 S.L.T. 1129 (OH), Lord Macfadyen; see *BRAC Rent-A-Car International Inc, Re* [2003] EWHC 128, [2003] 1 W.L.R. 1421 (Ch D (Companies Court)), Lloyd, J.; see *Designer Room Ltd, Re* [2004] EWHC 720, [2004] 3 All E.R. 679 (Ch D), Rimer, J.; see *Digginwell Plant & Construction Ltd, Re* [2002] B.P.I.R. 299 (Ch D), Neuberger, J.; see *Highberry Ltd v Colt Telecom Group Plc (No.2)* [2002] EWHC 2815, [2003] B.P.I.R. 324 (Ch D (Companies Court)), Jacob, J.; see *Salvage Association, Re* [2003] EWHC 1028, [2004] 1 W.L.R. 174 (Ch D), Blackburne, J.; see *Willmont v AY Bank Ltd* [2002] B.P.I.R. 1231 (Ch D), Pumfrey, J.

s.8, amended: SI 2002/1240 Reg.5, SI 2002/ 1555 Art.14

s.8, applied: SI 2002/1242 Art.3, SI 2003/ 1102 Reg.9, Reg.11, Reg.34, Reg.36, SI 2004/353 Reg.34, SI 2004/1045 Reg.21

s.8, substituted: 2002 c.40 s.248

s.8, varied: 2002 c.40 s.249

s.8, see *Bee v T&N Shelf Twenty Six Ltd* 2002 S.L.T. 1129 (OH), Lord Macfadyen; see *BRAC Rent-A-Car International Inc, Re* [2003] EWHC 128, [2003] 1 W.L.R. 1421 (Ch D (Companies Court)), Lloyd, J.; see *Designer Room Ltd, Re* [2004] EWHC 720, [2004] 3 All E.R. 679 (Ch D), Rimer, J.; see *Digginwell Plant & Construction Ltd, Re* [2002] B.P.I.R. 299 (Ch D), Neuberger, J.; see *Highberry Ltd v Colt Telecom Group Plc (No.2)* [2002] EWHC 2815, [2003] B.P.I.R. 324 (Ch D (Companies Court)), Jacob, J.; see *Salvage Association, Re* [2003] EWHC 1028, [2004] 1 W.L.R. 174 (Ch D), Blackburne, J.; see *Willmont v AY*

1986–cont.

45. Insolvency Act 1986–*cont.*

s.8–*cont.*

Bank Ltd [2002] B.P.I.R. 1231 (Ch D), Pumfrey, J.

s.8, applied: SI 2004/1045 Reg.12, Reg.19

s.8, substituted: 2002 c.40 s.248

s.8, varied: 2002 c.40 s.249

s.9, see *Far East Abrasives Ltd, Re* [2003] B.P.I.R. 375 (Ch D), Judge Norris Q.C.

s.9, applied: SI 2002/1242 Art.5, SI 2003/ 1102 Reg.9

s.9, substituted: 2002 c.40 s.248

s.9, varied: 2002 c.40 s.249

s.10, disapplied: SI 2003/3226 Reg.8

s.10, substituted: 2002 c.40 s.248

s.10, varied: 2002 c.40 s.249

s.11, see *Bee v T&N Shelf Twenty Six Ltd* 2002 S.L.T. 1129 (OH), Lord Macfadyen; see *Canary Riverside Development (Private) Ltd v Timtec International Ltd* (2003) 19 Const. L.J. 283 (QBD), DKR Oliver Q.C.; see *Divine Solutions (UK) Ltd, Re* [2003] EWHC 1931, [2004] B.C.C. 325 (Ch D), Hart, J.; see *London Flight Centre (Stansted) Ltd v Osprey Aviation Ltd* [2002] B.P.I.R. 1115 (Ch D), Hart, J.; see *Railtrack Plc (In Administration) (No.2), Re* [2002] EWCA Civ 955, [2002] 1 W.L.R. 3002 (CA), Lord Woolf of Barnes, L.C.J.

s.11, disapplied: SI 2003/3226 Reg.8

s.11, substituted: 2002 c.40 s.248

s.11, varied: 2002 c.40 s.249

s.12, substituted: 2002 c.40 s.248

s.12, varied: 2002 c.40 s.249

s.13, substituted: 2002 c.40 s.248

s.13, varied: 2002 c.40 s.249, SI 2002/1242 Sch.1 para.1

s.14, see *Designer Room Ltd, Re* [2004] EWHC 720, [2004] 3 All E.R. 679 (Ch D), Rimer, J.

s.14, substituted: 2002 c.40 s.248

s.14, varied: 2002 c.40 s.249

s.15, disapplied: SI 2003/3226 Reg.8

s.15, substituted: 2002 c.40 s.248

s.15, varied: 2002 c.40 s.249

s.16, substituted: 2002 c.40 s.248

s.16, varied: 2002 c.40 s.249

s.17, substituted: 2002 c.40 s.248

s.17, varied: 2002 c.40 s.249

s.18, substituted: 2002 c.40 s.248

s.18, varied: 2002 c.40 s.249, SI 2002/1242 Sch.1 para.2

s.19, see *Antal International Ltd, Re* [2003] EWHC 1339, [2003] 2 B.C.L.C. 406 (Ch D (Companies Court)), Laddie, J.; see *Ciro Citterio Menswear Plc, Re* [2002] EWHC 897, [2002] B.P.I.R. 903 (Ch D), Pumfrey, J.

s.19, substituted: 2002 c.40 s.248

s.19, varied: 2002 c.40 s.249

1986–cont.

45. Insolvency Act 1986–*cont.*

s.20, see *Oakhouse Property Holdings Ltd, Re* [2003] B.P.I.R. 469 (Ch D), Rimer, J.

s.20, substituted: 2002 c.40 s.248

s.20, varied: 2002 c.40 s.249

s.21, substituted: 2002 c.40 s.248

s.21, varied: 2002 c.40 s.249

s.22, substituted: 2002 c.40 s.248

s.22, varied: 2002 c.40 s.249

s.23, substituted: 2002 c.40 s.248

s.23, varied: 2002 c.40 s.249, SI 2002/1242 Sch.1 para.3

s.24, substituted: 2002 c.40 s.248

s.24, varied: 2002 c.40 s.249, SI 2002/1242 Sch.1 para.4

s.25, substituted: 2002 c.40 s.248

s.25, varied: 2002 c.40 s.249, SI 2002/1242 Sch.1 para.5

s.26, substituted: 2002 c.40 s.248

s.26, varied: 2002 c.40 s.249

s.27, applied: SI 2003/1102 Reg.11, SI 2004/1045 Reg.12

s.27, substituted: 2002 c.40 s.248

s.27, varied: 2002 c.40 s.249

s.31, substituted: 2002 c.40 Sch.21 para.1

s.35, see *Munns v Perkins* [2002] B.P.I.R. 120 (Ch D), Evans-Lombe, J.

s.44, see *Rees v Boston BC* [2001] EWCA Civ 1934, [2002] 1 W.L.R. 1304 (CA), Jonathan Parker, L.J.

s.51, amended: 2002 c.40 Sch.17 para.13

s.51, applied: 2004 c.27 s.47

s.53, applied: 2002 asp 17 s.40

s.54, applied: 2002 asp 17 s.40

s.62, amended: SI 2003/2096 Sch.1 para.9

s.72A, added: 2002 c.40 s.250

s.72A, amended: SI 2003/1832 Art.2

s.72A, applied: SI 2003/2095 Art.2

s.72A, referred to: SI 2003/1832 Art.1

s.72B, added: 2002 c.40 s.250

s.72B, referred to: SI 2003/1832 Art.1

s.72C, added: 2002 c.40 s.250

s.72C, referred to: SI 2003/1832 Art.1

s.72D, added: 2002 c.40 s.250

s.72D, referred to: SI 2003/1832 Art.1

s.72DA, added: 2002 c.40 s.250, SI 2003/1832 Art.2

s.72DA, referred to: SI 2003/1832 Art.1

s.72E, added: 2002 c.40 s.250

s.72E, referred to: SI 2003/1832 Art.1

s.72F, added: 2002 c.40 s.250

s.72F, referred to: SI 2003/1832 Art.1

s.72G, added: 2002 c.40 s.250

s.72G, referred to: SI 2003/1832 Art.1

s.72GA, added: 2002 c.40 s.250, SI 2003/1832 Art.2

s.72H, added: 2002 c.40 s.250

s.72H, enabling: SI 2003/1468, SI 2003/1832

s.73, varied: 2003 c.43 s.25

1986–cont.

45. Insolvency Act 1986–*cont.*

s.74, varied: 2003 c.43 s.25

s.75, varied: 2003 c.43 s.25

s.76, varied: 2003 c.43 s.25

s.77, varied: 2003 c.43 s.25

s.78, varied: 2003 c.43 s.25

s.79, varied: 2003 c.43 s.25

s.80, varied: 2003 c.43 s.25

s.81, varied: 2003 c.43 s.25

s.82, varied: 2003 c.43 s.25

s.83, varied: 2003 c.43 s.25

s.84, amended: 2002 c.15 Sch.5 para.6, SI 2003/2096 Sch.1 para.10

s.84, applied: SI 2004/1045 Reg.8

s.84, varied: 2003 c.43 s.25

s.85, varied: 2003 c.43 s.25

s.86, varied: 2003 c.43 s.25

s.87, varied: 2003 c.43 s.25

s.88, disapplied: SI 2003/3226 Reg.10

s.88, varied: 2003 c.43 s.25

s.89, see *Greenwich Millennium Exhibition Ltd v New Millennium Experience Co Ltd* [2003] EWHC 1823, [2004] 1 All E.R. 687 (Ch D (Companies Ct)), Lawrence Collins, J.

s.89, applied: 2004 c.35 s.121, SI 2004/3121 Sch.1

s.89, varied: 2003 c.43 s.25

s.90, varied: 2003 c.43 s.25

s.91, applied: 2002 c.15 s.44, s.45, s.48

s.91, varied: 2003 c.43 s.25

s.92, varied: 2003 c.43 s.25

s.93, varied: 2003 c.43 s.25

s.94, varied: 2003 c.43 s.25

s.95, applied: 2002 c.15 s.48, SI 2003/1102 Reg.9, 2004 c.35 s.121, SI 2004/353 Reg.9, SI 2004/1045 Reg.9

s.95, varied: 2003 c.43 s.25

s.96, applied: 2002 c.15 s.48

s.96, varied: 2003 c.43 s.25

s.97, varied: 2003 c.43 s.25

s.98, applied: SI 2003/3226 Reg.12

s.98, varied: 2003 c.43 s.25

s.99, varied: 2003 c.43 s.25

s.100, amended: 2002 c.40 Sch.17 para.14

s.100, applied: 2002 c.15 s.48, SI 2003/1102 Reg.14, Reg.34, Reg.36, SI 2004/353 Reg.14, Reg.34, Reg.36, SI 2004/1045 Reg.9, Reg.11, Reg.12, Reg.16, Reg.19, Reg.21

s.100, referred to: SI 2003/1102 Reg.9, Reg.11, Reg.18, SI 2004/353 Reg.9, Reg.11, Reg.18

s.100, varied: 2003 c.43 s.25

s.101, varied: 2003 c.43 s.25

s.102, varied: 2003 c.43 s.25

s.103, varied: 2003 c.43 s.25

s.104, varied: 2003 c.43 s.25

s.105, varied: 2003 c.43 s.25

s.106, varied: 2003 c.43 s.25

1986–cont.

45. Insolvency Act 1986–*cont.*

s.107, varied: 2003 c.43 s.25

s.108, see *AMP Enterprises Ltd v Hoffman* [2002] EWHC 1899, [2002] B.C.C. 996 (Ch D (Companies Court)), Neuberger, J.; see *Fielding v Seery* [2004] B.C.C. 315 (Ch D), Judge Maddocks; see *Quicksons (South & West) Ltd v Katz (No.1)* [2003] EWHC 1981, [2003] 4 All E.R. 864 (Ch D (Companies Ct)), Evans-Lombe, J.

s.108, varied: 2003 c.43 s.25

s.109, varied: 2003 c.43 s.25

s.110, varied: 2003 c.43 s.25

s.111, varied: 2003 c.43 s.25

s.112, see *Environment Agency v Hillridge Ltd* [2003] EWHC 3023, [2004] 2 B.C.L.C. 358 (Ch D (Companies Court)), Blackburne, J.

s.112, applied: 2002 c.15 s.48, s.49, SI 2004/353 Reg.11, SI 2004/1045 Reg.12

s.112, varied: 2003 c.43 s.25

s.113, varied: 2003 c.43 s.25

s.114, varied: 2003 c.43 s.25

s.115, see *Buchler v Talbot* [2002] EWCA Civ 228, [2003] B.C.C. 159 (CA), Chadwick, L.J.

s.115, varied: 2003 c.43 s.25

s.116, varied: 2003 c.43 s.25

s.117, amended: SI 2002/1240 Reg.6

s.117, varied: 2003 c.43 s.25

s.118, varied: 2003 c.43 s.25

s.119, varied: 2003 c.43 s.25

s.120, amended: SI 2002/1240 Reg.7

s.120, varied: 2003 c.43 s.25

s.121, varied: 2003 c.43 s.25

s.122, see *Millennium Advanced Technology Ltd, Re* [2004] EWHC 711, [2004] 1 W.L.R. 2177 (Ch D (Companies Ct)), Michael Briggs Q.C.; see *Phoneer Ltd, Re* [2002] 2 B.C.L.C. 241 (Ch D), Roger Kaye Q.C.

s.122, applied: SI 2004/2199 Reg.3, SI 2004/2326 Reg.72

s.122, varied: 2003 c.43 s.25

s.123, applied: SI 2003/187 Sch.1 para.6, SI 2003/2553 Reg.16, 2004 c.20 s.157, SI 2004/291 Sch.6 para.85, SI 2004/478 Sch.6 para.83, SI 2004/627 Sch.5 para.80, SSI 2004/115 Sch.5 para.77, SSI 2004/116 Sch.1 para.42

s.123, varied: 2003 c.43 s.25, SI 2003/2553 Reg.16

s.124, see *TFB Mortgages Ltd v Pimlico Capital Ltd* [2002] EWHC 878, [2002] 2 B.C.L.C. 544 (Ch D (Companies Ct)), Lawrence Collins, J.

s.124, amended: SI 2002/1240 Reg.8, 2003 c.39 Sch.8 para.294, 2004 c.27 s.50, SI 2004/2326 Reg.73

s.124, applied: 2002 c.15 s.50

s.124, varied: 2003 c.43 s.25

1986–cont.

45. Insolvency Act 1986–*cont.*

s.124A, see *Allso v Secretary of State for Trade and Industry* [2004] EWHC 862, [2004] 1 W.L.R. 1566 (Ch D (Companies Court)), Evans-Lombe, J.; see *Alpha Club (UK) Ltd, Re* [2002] EWHC 884, [2002] 2 B.C.L.C. 612 (Ch D), John Jarvis Q.C.; see *Equity & Provident Ltd, Re* [2002] EWHC 186, [2002] 2 B.C.L.C. 78 (Ch D), Patten, J.; see *Marann Brooks CSV Ltd, Re* [2003] B.C.C. 239 (Ch D), Patten, J.

s.124A, amended: 2004 c.27 Sch.2 para.27

s.124A, applied: 2004 c.20 s.157

s.124A, referred to: SI 2004/3322 Art.13

s.124A, varied: 2003 c.43 s.25

s.124B, added: SI 2004/2326 Reg.73

s.124B, varied: 2003 c.43 s.25

s.125, applied: SI 2003/1102 Reg.9, 2004 c.20 s.157, s.160, SI 2004/353 Reg.9, SI 2004/1045 Reg.9, Reg.11

s.125, varied: 2003 c.43 s.25

s.126, varied: 2003 c.43 s.25

s.127, see *Jackson v Royal Bank of Scotland Plc* 2002 S.L.T. 1123 (OH), Lord Drummond Young; see *Rescupine Ltd, Re* [2003] EWHC 216, [2003] 1 B.C.L.C. 661 (Ch D), Hart, J.; see *Rose v AIB Group (UK) Plc* [2003] EWHC 1737, [2003] 1 W.L.R. 2791 (Ch D (Companies Court)), Nicholas Warren Q.C.; see *Royal Bank of Scotland Plc v Bhardwaj* [2002] B.C.C. 57 (Ch D (Companies Ct)), Neuberger, J.

s.127, amended: 2002 c.40 Sch.17 para.15

s.127, disapplied: SI 2003/3226 Reg.10

s.127, substituted: 2002 c.40 Sch.17 para.15

s.127, varied: 2003 c.43 s.25

s.128, varied: 2003 c.43 s.25

s.129, amended: 2002 c.40 Sch.17 para.16

s.129, varied: 2003 c.43 s.25, 2004 c.20 Sch.20 para.45

s.130, see *Flightline Ltd v Edwards* [2002] EWHC 1648, [2002] 1 W.L.R. 2535 (Ch D (Companies Court)), Neuberger, J.; see *Flightline Ltd v Edwards* [2003] EWCA Civ 63, [2003] 1 W.L.R. 1200 (CA), Jonathan Parker, L.J.; see *HIH Casualty & General Insurance Ltd, Re* [2002] EWCA Civ 300, [2002] 2 B.C.L.C. 228 (CA), Jonathan Parker, L.J.; see *Mazur Media Ltd v Mazur Media GmbH* [2004] EWHC 1566, [2004] 1 W.L.R. 2966 (Ch D), Lawrence Collins, J.; see *Namco UK Ltd, Re* [2003] EWHC 989, [2003] 2 B.C.L.C. 78 (Ch D), Blackburne, J.

s.130, varied: 2003 c.43 s.25

s.131, varied: 2003 c.43 s.25

s.132, see *R. v Brady (Paul Clement)* [2004] EWCA Crim 1763, [2004] 1 W.L.R. 3240 (CA (Crim Div)), Tuckey, L.J.

s.132, varied: 2003 c.43 s.25

1986–cont.

45. Insolvency Act 1986–*cont.*

s.133, see *Casterbridge Properties Ltd (No.2), Re* [2003] EWCA Civ 1246, [2004] 1 W.L.R. 602 (CA), Chadwick, L.J.

s.133, varied: 2003 c.43 s.25

s.134, varied: 2003 c.43 s.25

s.135, see *Namco UK Ltd, Re* [2003] EWHC 989, [2003] 2 B.C.L.C. 78 (Ch D), Blackburne, J.

s.135, applied: 2002 c.15 s.51, SI 2003/1102 Reg.9, Reg.11, 2004 c.20 s.160, SI 2004/353 Reg.9, Reg.11, SI 2004/1045 Reg.9, Reg.11, Reg.12

s.135, varied: 2003 c.43 s.25

s.136, varied: 2003 c.43 s.25

s.137, varied: 2003 c.43 s.25

s.138, varied: 2003 c.43 s.25

s.139, varied: 2003 c.43 s.25

s.140, amended: 2002 c.40 Sch.17 para.17

s.140, varied: 2003 c.43 s.25

s.141, varied: 2003 c.43 s.25

s.142, varied: 2003 c.43 s.25

s.143, see *Barings Plc (In Liquidation), Re (No.2)* [2002] 1 B.C.L.C. 401 (Ch D (Companies Ct)), Sir Robert Andrew Morritt V.C.

s.143, varied: 2003 c.43 s.25

s.144, varied: 2003 c.43 s.25

s.145, varied: 2003 c.43 s.25

s.146, varied: 2003 c.43 s.25

s.147, see *McGruther v James Scott Ltd* 2003 S.C. 495 (OH), Lady Smith

s.147, varied: 2003 c.43 s.25

s.148, varied: 2003 c.43 s.25

s.149, varied: 2003 c.43 s.25

s.150, varied: 2003 c.43 s.25

s.151, varied: 2003 c.43 s.25

s.152, varied: 2003 c.43 s.25

s.153, varied: 2003 c.43 s.25

s.154, varied: 2003 c.43 s.25

s.155, varied: 2003 c.43 s.25

s.156, applied: 2004 c.20 s.161

s.156, varied: 2003 c.43 s.25

s.157, applied: 2004 c.20 s.161

s.157, varied: 2003 c.43 s.25

s.158, varied: 2003 c.43 s.25

s.159, varied: 2003 c.43 s.25

s.160, varied: 2003 c.43 s.25

s.161, varied: 2003 c.43 s.25

s.162, varied: 2003 c.43 s.25

s.163, varied: 2003 c.43 s.25

s.164, varied: 2003 c.43 s.25

s.165, varied: 2003 c.43 s.25

s.166, varied: 2003 c.43 s.25

s.167, see *Barings Plc (In Liquidation), Re (No.2)* [2002] 1 B.C.L.C. 401 (Ch D (Companies Ct)), Sir Robert Andrew Morritt V.C.

s.167, varied: 2003 c.43 s.25

1986–cont.

45. Insolvency Act 1986–*cont.*

s.168, see *Barings Plc (In Liquidation), Re (No.2)* [2002] 1 B.C.L.C. 401 (Ch D (Companies Ct)), Sir Robert Andrew Morritt V.C.

s.168, amended: SI 2002/1555 Art.15

s.168, applied: 2002 c.15 s.54, SI 2003/1102 Reg.29

s.168, referred to: SI 2003/1102 Reg.29, SI 2004/353 Reg.29

s.168, varied: 2003 c.43 s.25

s.169, varied: 2003 c.43 s.25

s.170, varied: 2003 c.43 s.25

s.171, varied: 2003 c.43 s.25

s.172, applied: 2002 c.15 s.54

s.172, varied: 2003 c.43 s.25

s.173, varied: 2003 c.43 s.25

s.174, applied: 2002 c.15 s.54

s.174, varied: 2003 c.43 s.25

s.175, see *Buchler v Talbot* [2002] EWCA Civ 228, [2003] B.C.C. 159 (CA), Chadwick, L.J.; see *Buchler v Talbot* [2004] UKHL 9, [2004] 2 A.C. 298 (HL), Lord Nicholls of Birkenhead

s.175, applied: SI 2003/1102 Reg.27, Reg.31, SI 2004/353 Reg.27, Reg.31

s.175, disapplied: SI 2003/1102 Reg.20, SI 2004/353 Reg.20

s.175, varied: 2003 c.43 s.25

s.176, varied: 2003 c.43 s.25

s.176A, added: 2002 c.40 s.252

s.176A, applied: SI 2003/2097 Art.2, Art.3, SI 2004/353 Reg.21

s.176A, disapplied: SI 2003/3226 Reg.10

s.176A, varied: 2003 c.43 s.25

s.176A, enabling: SI 2003/2097

s.177, varied: 2003 c.43 s.25

s.178, see *Environment Agency v Hillridge Ltd* [2003] EWHC 3023, [2004] 2 B.C.L.C. 358 (Ch D (Companies Court)), Blackburne, J.; see *Manning v AIG Europe UK Ltd* [2004] EWHC 1760, [2004] B.P.I.R. 1334 (Ch D (Companies Ct)), Lloyd, J.; see *Scottish Widows Plc v Tripipatkul* [2003] EWHC 1874, [2004] B.C.C. 200 (Ch D), Pumfrey, J.

s.178, disapplied: SI 2003/3226 Reg.10

s.178, varied: 2003 c.43 s.25

s.179, varied: 2003 c.43 s.25

s.180, varied: 2003 c.43 s.25

s.181, varied: 2003 c.43 s.25

s.182, varied: 2003 c.43 s.25

s.183, amended: 2003 c.39 Sch.8 para.295

s.183, applied: 2003 c.39 Sch.7 para.11

s.183, varied: 2003 c.43 s.25

s.184, amended: 2003 c.39 Sch.8 para.296

s.184, applied: 2003 c.39 Sch.7 para.11

s.184, varied: 2003 c.43 s.25

s.185, varied: 2003 c.43 s.25

s.186, varied: 2003 c.43 s.25

s.187, varied: 2003 c.43 s.25

CAP.

1986–cont.

45. Insolvency Act 1986–*cont.*
s.188, varied: 2003 c.43 s.25
s.189, varied: 2003 c.43 s.25
s.190, varied: 2003 c.43 s.25
s.191, varied: 2003 c.43 s.25
s.192, varied: 2003 c.43 s.25
s.193, varied: 2003 c.43 s.25
s.194, varied: 2003 c.43 s.25
s.195, varied: 2003 c.43 s.25
s.196, varied: 2003 c.43 s.25
s.197, varied: 2003 c.43 s.25
s.198, varied: 2003 c.43 s.25
s.199, varied: 2003 c.43 s.25
s.200, varied: 2003 c.43 s.25
s.201, varied: 2003 c.43 s.25
s.202, applied: 2002 c.15 s.54
s.202, varied: 2003 c.43 s.25
s.203, varied: 2003 c.43 s.25
s.204, varied: 2003 c.43 s.25
s.205, applied: 2002 c.15 s.54
s.205, varied: 2003 c.43 s.25
s.206, see *R. v Carass (Clive Louden)* [2001] EWCA Crim 2845, [2002] 1 W.L.R. 1714 (CA (Crim Div)), Waller, L.J.
s.206, varied: 2003 c.43 s.25
s.207, varied: 2003 c.43 s.25
s.208, varied: 2003 c.43 s.25
s.209, varied: 2003 c.43 s.25
s.210, varied: 2003 c.43 s.25
s.211, varied: 2003 c.43 s.25
s.212, see *Cohen v Selby* [2002] B.C.C. 82 (CA), Chadwick, L.J.; see *Inland Revenue Commissioners v Richmond* [2003] EWHC 999, [2003] S.T.C.1394 (Ch D (Companies Court)), Etherton, J.; see *Kyrris v Oldham* [2003] 2 B.C.L.C. 35 (Ch D), Behrens, J.; see *Liquidator of Marini Ltd v Dickenson* [2003] EWHC 334, [2004] B.C.C. 172 (Ch D (Companies Ct)), Judge Richard Seymour Q.C.; see *Rubin v Gunner* [2004] EWHC 316, [2004] 2 B.C.L.C. 110 (Ch D (Companies Ct)), Etherton, J.; see *Whalley v Doney* [2003] EWHC 2277, [2004] 1 B.C.L.C. 217 (Ch D), Park, J.
s.212, amended: 2002 c.40 Sch.17 para.18, Sch.26
s.212, applied: SI 2003/1102 Reg.31, SI 2004/353 Reg.31
s.212, varied: 2003 c.43 s.25
s.213, see *Morphitis v Bernasconi* [2003] EWCA Civ 289, [2003] Ch. 552 (CA), Chadwick, L.J.; see *Morris v Bank of America National Trust and Savings Association (Amendment of claim)* [2002] EWCA Civ 425, [2003] C.P.L.R. 251 (CA), Chadwick, L.J.; see *Morris v Bank of India* [2004] EWHC 528, [2004] 2 B.C.L.C. 279 (Ch D (Companies Court)), Patten, J.; see *Morris v Banque Arabe Internationale d'Investissement SA (No.2)* [2002] B.C.C. 407 (Ch D), Neuberger, J.; see *Morris v*

CAP.

1986–cont.

45. Insolvency Act 1986–*cont.*
s.213–*cont.*
  State Bank of India [2003] EWHC 1868, [2003] B.C.C. 735 (Ch D (Companies Ct)), Patten, J.
s.213, varied: 2003 c.43 s.25
s.214, see *Liquidator of Marini Ltd v Dickenson* [2003] EWHC 334, [2004] B.C.C. 172 (Ch D (Companies Ct)), Judge Richard Seymour Q.C.; see *Rubin v Gunner* [2004] EWHC 316, [2004] 2 B.C.L.C. 110 (Ch D (Companies Ct)), Etherton, J.
s.214, varied: 2003 c.43 s.25
s.214A, varied: 2003 c.43 s.25
s.215, amended: 2004 c.33 Sch.27 para.112
s.215, varied: 2003 c.43 s.25
s.216, see *Inland Revenue Commissioners v Nash* [2003] EWHC 686, [2004] B.C.C. 150 (Ch D), Peter Smith, J.; see *Morphitis v Bernasconi* [2003] EWCA Civ 289, [2003] Ch. 552 (CA), Chadwick, L.J.; see *R. v Doring (Petra)* [2002] EWCA Crim 1695, [2002] B.C.C. 838 (CA (Crim Div)), Buxton, L.J.; see *Ricketts v Ad Valorem Factors Ltd* [2003] EWCA Civ 1706, [2004] 1 All E.R. 894 (CA), Simon Brown, L.J.
s.216, varied: 2003 c.43 s.25
s.217, see *Inland Revenue Commissioners v Nash* [2003] EWHC 686, [2004] B.C.C. 150 (Ch D), Peter Smith, J.; see *Ricketts v Ad Valorem Factors Ltd* [2003] EWCA Civ 1706, [2004] 1 All E.R. 894 (CA), Simon Brown, L.J.
s.217, varied: 2003 c.43 s.25
s.218, varied: 2003 c.43 s.25
s.219, varied: 2003 c.43 s.25
s.221, see *Drax Holdings Ltd, Re* [2003] EWHC 2743, [2004] 1 W.L.R. 1049 (Ch D (Companies Ct)), Lawrence Collins, J.
s.221, amended: SI 2002/1240 Reg.9
s.221, applied: SI 2003/1102 Reg.4, 2004 c.20 s.157, SI 2004/353 Reg.4, SI 2004/1045 Reg.3
s.221, referred to: SI 2004/2443 Sch.4 para.14
s.222, applied: SI 2003/2553 Reg.16, 2004 c.20 s.157
s.222, varied: SI 2003/2553 Reg.16
s.223, applied: SI 2003/2553 Reg.16, 2004 c.20 s.157
s.224, applied: SI 2003/2553 Reg.16, 2004 c.20 s.157
s.225, amended: SI 2002/1240 Reg.10
s.230, repealed (in part): 2002 c.40 Sch.26
s.231, amended: 2002 c.40 Sch.26
s.232, amended: 2002 c.40 Sch.26
s.233, amended: 2002 c.40 Sch.17 para.22, 2003 c.21 Sch.17 para.82
s.233, varied: SI 2004/1822 Sch.1 para.14

CAP.

CAP.

1986–cont.

45. Insolvency Act 1986–*cont.*

s.234, see *Smith (Administrator of Cosslett (Contractors) Ltd) v Bridgend CBC* [2001] UKHL 58, [2002] 1 A.C. 336 (HL), Lord Hoffmann

s.234, amended: 2002 c.40 Sch.17 para.23

s.235, see *Pantmaenog Timber Co Ltd, Re* [2001] EWCA Civ 1227, [2002] Ch. 239 (CA), Chadwick, L.J.; see *R. v Brady (Paul Clement)* [2004] EWCA Crim 1763, [2004] 1 W.L.R. 3240 (CA (Crim Div)), Tuckey, L.J.; see *Shierson v Rastogi* [2002] EWCA Civ 1624, [2003] 1 W.L.R. 586 (CA), Peter Gibson, L.J.

s.235, amended: 2002 c.40 Sch.17 para.24

s.236, see *Akers v Lomas* [2002] 1 B.C.L.C. 655 (Ch D), Patten, J.; see *Miller v Bain* [2002] B.C.C. 899 (Ch D (Companies Ct)), Sir Andrew Morritt V.C.; see *New China Hong Kong Capital Ltd, Re* [2003] EWHC 1573, [2003] B.P.I.R. 1176 (Ch D), Peter Smith, J.; see *Pantmaenog Timber Co Ltd, Re* [2001] EWCA Civ 1227, [2002] Ch. 239 (CA), Chadwick, L.J.; see *Pantmaenog Timber Co Ltd, Re* [2003] UKHL 49, [2004] 1 A.C. 158 (HL), Lord Millett; see *PNC Telecom Plc (In Administration), Re* [2003] EWHC 2220, [2004] B.P.I.R. 314 (Ch D), Evans-Lombe, J.; see *Quicksons (South & West) Ltd v Katz (No.1)* [2003] EWHC 1981, [2003] 4 All E.R. 864 (Ch D (Companies Ct)), Evans-Lombe, J.; see *Shierson v Rastogi* [2002] EWCA Civ 1624, [2003] 1 W.L.R. 586 (CA), Peter Gibson, L.J.; see *Westmead Consultants Ltd (In Liquidation), Re* [2002] 1 B.C.L.C. 384 (Ch D), Judge Weeks Q.C.

s.238, see *Demaglass Ltd (In Liquidation), Re* [2002] EWHC 3138, [2003] 1 B.C.L.C. 412 (Ch D), Anthony Mann Q.C.; see *Imperial Consolidated Financiers Ltd (In Administration) v Schofield* 1628 of 2002 (Ch D), John Behrens Q.C.; see *Lord (Liquidator of Rosshill Properties Ltd) v Sinai Securities Ltd* [2004] EWHC 1764, [2004] B.P.I.R. 1244 (Ch D), Hart, J.; see *Sinai Securities Ltd v Hooper* [2003] EWHC 910, [2004] 2 B.C.L.C. 575 (Ch D), Neuberger, J.; see *Walker v WA Personnel Ltd* [2002] B.P.I.R. 621 (Ch D), Judge Havelock-Allan Q.C.; see *Whalley v Doney* [2003] EWHC 2277, [2004] 1 B.C.L.C. 217 (Ch D), Park, J.

s.238, amended: 2002 c.40 Sch.17 para.25

s.238, applied: 2002 c.29 s.427

s.239, see *Conegrade Ltd, Re* [2002] EWHC 2411, [2003] B.P.I.R. 358 (Ch D (Companies Court)), Lloyd, J.; see *Lord (Liquidator of Rosshill Properties Ltd) v Sinai Securities Ltd* [2004] EWHC 1764, [2004] B.P.I.R. 1244 (Ch D), Hart, J.; see

1986–cont.

45. Insolvency Act 1986–*cont.*

s.239–*cont.*

Whalley v Doney [2003] EWHC 2277, [2004] 1 B.C.L.C. 217 (Ch D), Park, J.

s.239, applied: 2002 c.29 s.427

s.239, referred to: 2002 c.29 s.427

s.240, amended: 2002 c.40 Sch.17 para.26, Sch.26, SI 2002/1240 Reg.11

s.241, amended: 2002 c.40 Sch.17 para.27

s.242, see *Jackson v Royal Bank of Scotland Plc* 2002 S.L.T. 1123 (OH), Lord Drummond Young

s.242, amended: 2002 c.40 Sch.17 para.28

s.242, applied: 2002 c.29 s.427

s.242, referred to: 2002 c.29 s.427

s.243, see *Baillie Marshall Ltd (In Liquidation) v Avian Communications Ltd* 2002 S.L.T. 189 (OH), Lord Kingarth

s.243, amended: 2002 c.40 Sch.17 para.29

s.243, applied: 2002 c.29 s.427

s.243, referred to: 2002 c.29 s.427

s.244, amended: 2002 c.40 Sch.17 para.30

s.245, amended: 2002 c.40 Sch.17 para.31, Sch.26

s.245, disapplied: SI 2003/3226 Reg.10

s.246, amended: 2002 c.40 Sch.17 para.32

s.247, amended: 2002 c.40 Sch.17 para.33, SI 2002/1240 Reg.12

s.247, applied: 2004 c.20 s.157

s.249, applied: 2004 c.35 s.38, s.51, s.53, s.57

s.251, applied: 2004 c.35 s.121

s.252, see *Clarke v Coutts & Co* [2002] B.P.I.R. 762 (QBD), Judge Zucker Q.C.; see *Clarke v Coutts & Co* [2002] EWCA Civ 943, [2002] B.P.I.R. 916 (CA), Peter Gibson, L.J.; see *Hurst v Kroll Buchler Phillips Ltd* [2002] EWHC 2885, [2003] B.P.I.R. 872 (Ch D), Etherton, J.

s.253, see *Welburn v Dibb Lupton Broomhead* [2002] EWCA Civ 1601, [2003] B.P.I.R. 768 (CA), Dyson, L.J.

s.253, applied: SI 2002/2711 Art.5

s.255, see *Hurst v Bennett (No.2)* [2001] EWCA Civ 1398, [2002] B.P.I.R. 102 (CA), Mummery, L.J.

s.255, referred to: SI 2002/2711 Art.4

s.256, see *Inland Revenue Commissioners v Bland* [2003] EWHC 1068, [2003] B.P.I.R. 1274 (Ch D), Lloyd, J.

s.256, applied: 2004 c.35 s.121

s.256A, applied: 2004 c.35 s.121

s.257, see *N (A Debtor), Re* [2002] B.P.I.R. 1024 (Ch D (Bankruptcy Ct)), Registrar Baister; see *Vlieland-Boddy v Dexter Ltd* [2003] EWHC 2592, [2004] B.P.I.R. 235 (Ch D), Roger Kaye Q.C.

s.261, substituted: 2002 c.40 Sch.22 para.1

s.262, see *Fender v Inland Revenue Commissioners* [2003] B.P.I.R. 1304 (Ch D), Judge Norris Q.C.; see *Inland*

1986–cont.

45. Insolvency Act 1986–cont.

s.262–cont.

Revenue Commissioners v Bland [2003] EWHC 1068, [2003] B.P.I.R. 1274 (Ch D), Lloyd, J.; see Plummer, Re [2004] B.P.I.R. 767 (Chancery Division (Bankruptcy Court)), Registrar Baister; see Vlieland-Boddy v Dexter Ltd [2003] EWHC 2592, [2004] B.P.I.R. 235 (Ch D), Roger Kaye Q.C.; see Warley Continental Services Ltd (In Compulsory Liquidation) v Johal [2004] B.P.I.R. 353 (Ch D), Judge Norris Q.C.

s.263B, varied: 2002 c.40 s.264

s.263C, varied: 2002 c.40 s.264

s.263D, varied: 2002 c.40 s.264

s.263E, varied: 2002 c.40 s.264

s.263F, varied: 2002 c.40 s.264

s.263G, varied: 2002 c.40 s.264

s.264, amended: SI 2002/1240 Reg.13

s.264, applied: 2002 c.40 Sch.19 para.6

s.264, varied: 2002 c.29 s.417

s.265, see North v Skipton Building Society Daily Telegraph, June 20, 2002 (Ch D), Kim Lewison Q.C.; see Skjevesland v Geveran Trading (No.4) [2002] EWHC 2898, [2003] B.C.C. 391 (Ch D), Judge Howarth

s.265, amended: SI 2002/1240 Reg.14

s.265, varied: 2002 c.29 s.417

s.266, see John Lewis Plc v Pearson Burton [2004] B.P.I.R. 70 (Ch D), Pumfrey, J.; see Lloyd's v Micklethwait [2002] EWHC 1123, [2003] B.P.I.R. 101 (Ch D), Peter Smith, J.

s.266, varied: 2002 c.29 s.417

s.267, varied: 2002 c.29 s.417

s.268, applied: SI 2003/2553 Reg.16

s.268, varied: 2002 c.29 s.417

s.269, see Barclays Bank Plc v Mogg [2003] EWHC 2645, [2004] B.P.I.R. 259 (Ch D), David Richards, J.

s.269, varied: 2002 c.29 s.417

s.270, varied: 2002 c.29 s.417

s.271, varied: 2002 c.29 s.417

s.272, varied: 2002 c.29 s.417

s.273, applied: SI 2004/593 Art.5

s.273, varied: 2002 c.29 s.417

s.274, applied: SI 2004/593 Art.5

s.274, varied: 2002 c.29 s.417

s.275, applied: SI 2003/1730 r.9, SI 2003/2093 Art.8

s.275, repealed: 2002 c.40 Sch.26

s.275, varied: 2002 c.29 s.417

s.276, varied: 2002 c.29 s.417

s.277, varied: 2002 c.29 s.417

s.278, varied: 2002 c.29 s.417

s.279, see Bagnall v Official Receiver [2003] EWCA Civ 1925, [2004] 1 W.L.R. 2832 (CA), Latham, L.J.; see Bagnall v Official Receiver [2003] EWHC 1398, [2003] 3 All E.R. 613 (Ch D), Evans-Lombe, J.; see

1986–cont.

45. Insolvency Act 1986–cont.

s.279–cont.

Ravichandran, Re [2004] B.P.I.R. 814 (Chancery Division (Bankruptcy Court)), Registrar Nicholls; see Thorogood v Official Receiver [2003] EWHC 1971, [2003] B.P.I.R. 1476 (Ch D), Blackburne, J.

s.279, applied: 2002 c.40 Sch.19 para.4, Sch.19 para.5, SI 2003/2093 Art.8, SSI 2004/468 Reg.10, Reg.21

s.279, disapplied: 2002 c.40 Sch.19 para.3

s.279, substituted: 2002 c.40 s.256

s.279, varied: 2002 c.29 s.417

s.280, amended: 2002 c.40 Sch.23 para.3

s.280, applied: 2002 c.29 s.418, 2002 c.40 Sch.19 para.5, Sch.19 para.6, SSI 2004/468 Reg.10, Reg.21

s.280, varied: 2002 c.29 s.417

s.281, see Anglo Manx Group Ltd v Aitken [2002] B.P.I.R. 215 (Ch D), John Jarvis Q.C.; see Ravichandran, Re [2004] B.P.I.R. 814 (Chancery Division (Bankruptcy Court)), Registrar Nicholls; see Woodland-Ferrari v UCL Group Retirement Benefits Scheme [2002] EWHC 1354, [2003] Ch. 115 (Ch D), Ferris, J.

s.281, amended: 2002 c.29 Sch.11 para.16

s.281, varied: 2002 c.29 s.417

s.281A, added: 2002 c.40 s.257

s.281A, varied: 2002 c.29 s.417

s.282, see Balendran v Law Society (No.2) [2004] EWHC 495, [2004] B.P.I.R. 859 (Ch D), Judge Weeks Q.C.; see Leicester v Plumtree Farms Ltd [2003] EWHC 206, [2004] B.P.I.R. 296 (Ch D), Lloyd, J.; see McKay v Rogers [2002] EWHC 2825, [2004] B.P.I.R. 1272 (Ch D), Hart, J.; see Owo-Samson v Barclays Bank Plc (Annulment of Bankruptcy Order) [2003] B.P.I.R. 1393 (Ch D), Registrar Jaques; see Simmons v Mole Valley DC [2004] EWHC 475, [2004] B.P.I.R. 1022 (Ch D), Lightman, J.

s.282, amended: 2002 c.40 Sch.23 para.4

s.282, applied: 2002 c.40 Sch.19 para.5

s.282, repealed (in part): 2002 c.40 Sch.26

s.282, varied: 2002 c.29 s.417

s.283, see Mountney v Treharne [2002] 2 F.L.R. 406 (Ch D), Stanley Burnton, J.; see Mountney v Treharne [2002] EWCA Civ 1174, [2003] Ch. 135 (CA), Jonathan Parker, L.J.; see Nunn (Bankruptcy: Divorce: Pension Rights), Re [2004] 1 F.L.R. 1123 (Ch D), Nicholas Strauss Q.C.

s.283, varied: 2002 c.29 s.417

s.283A, added: 2002 c.40 s.261

s.283A, amended: 2004 c.33 Sch.27 para.113

s.283A, applied: 2002 c.40 s.261

s.283A, varied: 2002 c.29 s.417, 2002 c.40 s.261

1986–cont.

45. Insolvency Act 1986–cont.

s.284, see *Rio Properties Inc v Al-Midani* [2003] B.P.I.R. 128 (Ch D), Judge Maddocks; see *Treharne v Forrester* [2003] EWHC 2784, [2004] 1 F.L.R. 1173 (Ch D), Lindsay, J.

s.284, varied: 2002 c.29 s.417

s.285, varied: 2002 c.29 s.417

s.286, see *Rio Properties Inc v Gibson Dunn & Crutcher* [2004] EWCA Civ 1043, [2004] 1 W.L.R. 2702 (CA (Civ Div)), Jonathan Parker, L.J.

s.286, applied: 2002 c.29 s.311, s.417

s.286, varied: 2002 c.29 s.417

s.287, see *Inland Revenue Commissioners v Hamilton* [2003] EWHC 3198, [2004] B.P.I.R. 264 (Ch D), Lewison, J.; see *Rio Properties Inc v Gibson Dunn & Crutcher* [2004] EWCA Civ 1043, [2004] 1 W.L.R. 2702 (CA (Civ Div)), Jonathan Parker, L.J.

s.287, varied: 2002 c.29 s.417

s.288, varied: 2002 c.29 s.417

s.289, substituted: 2002 c.40 s.258

s.289, varied: 2002 c.29 s.417

s.290, varied: 2002 c.29 s.417

s.291, see *R. v Kansal (Yash Pal) (Change of Law)* [2001] UKHL 62, [2002] 2 A.C. 69 (HL), Lord Hope of Craighead

s.291, amended: 2002 c.40 Sch.23 para.5

s.291, varied: 2002 c.29 s.417

s.292, amended: 2002 c.40 Sch.26

s.292, varied: 2002 c.29 s.417

s.293, amended: 2002 c.40 Sch.26

s.293, varied: 2002 c.29 s.417

s.294, repealed (in part): 2002 c.40 Sch.26

s.294, varied: 2002 c.29 s.417

s.295, varied: 2002 c.29 s.417

s.296, varied: 2002 c.29 s.417

s.297, amended: 2002 c.40 Sch.26

s.297, repealed (in part): 2002 c.40 Sch.26

s.297, varied: 2002 c.29 s.417

s.298, repealed (in part): 2002 c.40 Sch.26

s.298, varied: 2002 c.29 s.417

s.299, varied: 2002 c.29 s.417

s.300, amended: 2002 c.40 Sch.26

s.300, repealed (in part): 2002 c.40 Sch.26

s.300, varied: 2002 c.29 s.417

s.301, varied: 2002 c.29 s.417

s.302, varied: 2002 c.29 s.417

s.303, see *Engel v Peri* [2002] EWHC 799, [2002] B.P.I.R. 961 (Ch D), Ferris, J.; see *Mulkerrins v PricewaterhouseCoopers* [2003] UKHL 41, [2003] 1 W.L.R. 1937 (HL), Lord Walker of Gestingthorpe; see *Woodbridge v Smith* [2004] B.P.I.R. 247 (Ch D), Registrar Baister

s.303, varied: 2002 c.29 s.417

s.304, see *Brown v Beat* [2002] B.P.I.R. 421 (Ch D), Hart, J.

s.304, varied: 2002 c.29 s.417

s.305, varied: 2002 c.29 s.417

1986–cont.

45. Insolvency Act 1986–cont.

s.306, see *Kaberry v Freethcartwright (A Firm) (formerly Freeth Cartwright Hunt Dickens) (No.2)* [2003] EWCA Civ 1077, [2003] B.P.I.R. 1144 (CA), Chadwick, L.J.; see *Mountney v Treharne* [2002] 2 F.L.R. 406 (Ch D), Stanley Burnton, J.

s.306, applied: SI 2002/427 Reg.5, Reg.6, SI 2002/836 Reg.5, Reg.6

s.306, varied: 2002 c.29 s.417

s.306A, added: 2002 c.29 Sch.11 para.16

s.306A, amended: 2002 c.29 Sch.11 para.16

s.306A, varied: 2002 c.29 s.417

s.306B, added: 2002 c.29 Sch.11 para.16

s.306B, amended: 2002 c.29 Sch.11 para.16

s.306B, referred to: SI 2003/421 r.24

s.306B, varied: 2002 c.29 s.417

s.306C, added: 2002 c.29 Sch.11 para.16

s.306C, amended: 2002 c.29 Sch.11 para.16

s.306C, varied: 2002 c.29 s.417

s.307, amended: 2002 c.40 s.261

s.307, applied: 2002 c.29 s.418, SI 2002/195 Reg.40, SI 2002/3200 Reg.39, SR 2002/224 Reg.41

s.307, varied: 2002 c.29 s.417

s.308, applied: 2002 c.29 s.418

s.308, varied: 2002 c.29 s.417

s.308A, applied: 2002 c.29 s.418

s.308A, varied: 2002 c.29 s.417

s.309, varied: 2002 c.29 s.417

s.310, see *Rowe v Sanders* [2002] EWCA Civ 242, [2002] 2 All E.R. 800 (Note) (CA), Jonathan Parker, L.J.

s.310, amended: 2002 c.40 s.259, Sch.26

s.310, applied: SI 2002/195 Reg.40, SI 2002/1311 Reg.13, SI 2002/3200 Reg.39, SR 2002/224 Reg.41, SSI 2003/344 Reg.13

s.310, varied: 2002 c.29 s.417

s.310A, added: 2002 c.40 s.260

s.310A, varied: 2002 c.29 s.417

s.310, see *Scott v Davis* [2003] B.P.I.R. 1009 (Ch D (Bankruptcy Ct)), Anthony Mann Q.C.

s.311, varied: 2002 c.29 s.417

s.312, varied: 2002 c.29 s.417

s.313, amended: 2002 c.40 s.261, 2004 c.33 Sch.27 para.114

s.313, varied: 2002 c.29 s.417

s.313A, added: 2002 c.40 s.261

s.313A, amended: 2004 c.33 Sch.27 para.115

s.313A, varied: 2002 c.29 s.417

s.314, varied: 2002 c.29 s.417

s.315, varied: 2002 c.29 s.417

s.316, varied: 2002 c.29 s.417

s.317, varied: 2002 c.29 s.417

s.318, varied: 2002 c.29 s.417

s.319, varied: 2002 c.29 s.417

s.320, varied: 2002 c.29 s.417

s.321, varied: 2002 c.29 s.417

s.322, varied: 2002 c.29 s.417

CAP.

1986-cont.

45. Insolvency Act 1986-*cont.*
s.323, varied: 2002 c.29 s.417
s.324, varied: 2002 c.29 s.417
s.325, varied: 2002 c.29 s.417
s.326, varied: 2002 c.29 s.417
s.327, varied: 2002 c.29 s.417
s.328, varied: 2002 c.29 s.417
s.329, amended: 2004 c.33 Sch.27 para.116
s.329, varied: 2002 c.29 s.417
s.330, amended: SI 2002/1240 Reg.15
s.330, varied: 2002 c.29 s.417
s.331, varied: 2002 c.29 s.417
s.332, amended: 2004 c.33 Sch.27 para.117
s.332, varied: 2002 c.29 s.417
s.333, varied: 2002 c.29 s.417
s.334, varied: 2002 c.29 s.417
s.335, varied: 2002 c.29 s.417
s.335A, amended: 2004 c.33 Sch.27 para.118
s.335A, varied: 2002 c.29 s.417
s.336, amended: 2004 c.33 Sch.9 para.21
s.336, varied: 2002 c.29 s.417
s.337, amended: 2004 c.33 Sch.9 para.22
s.337, varied: 2002 c.29 s.417
s.338, varied: 2002 c.29 s.417
s.339, see *Fender v Inland Revenue Commissioners* [2003] B.P.I.R. 1304 (Ch D), Judge Norris Q.C.; see *Pozzuto v Iacovides* [2003] EWHC 431, [2003] B.P.I.R. 999 (Chancery Division (Bankruptcy Court)), Lawrence Collins, J.; see *Reid v Ramlort Ltd* [2003] EWHC 1999, [2003] B.P.I.R. 1444 (Ch D), Judge Norris Q.C.; see *Reid v Ramlort Ltd* [2004] EWCA Civ 800, [2004] B.P.I.R. 985 (CA), Judge, L.J.; see *Simms v Oakes* [2002] EWCA Civ 08, [2002] B.P.I.R. 1244 (CA), Buxton, L.J.
s.339, amended: 2004 c.33 Sch.27 para.119
s.339, applied: SI 2002/427 Reg.10, SI 2002/836 Reg.10, 2004 c.33 Sch.5 para.77
s.339, referred to: 2002 c.29 s.419
s.339, varied: 2002 c.29 s.417
s.340, applied: SI 2002/427 Reg.10, SI 2002/836 Reg.10, 2004 c.33 Sch.5 para.77
s.340, referred to: 2002 c.29 s.419
s.340, varied: 2002 c.29 s.417
s.341, varied: 2002 c.29 s.417
s.342, varied: 2002 c.29 s.417
s.342A, varied: 2002 c.29 s.417
s.342B, applied: SI 2002/427 Reg.7, SI 2002/836 Reg.7
s.342B, varied: 2002 c.29 s.417
s.342C, applied: SI 2002/427 Reg.10, SI 2002/836 Reg.10
s.342C, varied: 2002 c.29 s.417
s.342C, enabling: SI 2002/427, SI 2002/836
s.342D, varied: 2002 c.29 s.417
s.342E, applied: SI 2002/427 Reg.9
s.342E, referred to: SI 2002/836 Reg.9

CAP.

1986-cont.

45. Insolvency Act 1986-*cont.*
s.342E, varied: 2002 c.29 s.417
s.342F, applied: SI 2002/427 Reg.10, SI 2002/836 Reg.10
s.342F, varied: 2002 c.29 s.417
s.342F, enabling: SI 2002/427, SI 2002/836
s.343, varied: 2002 c.29 s.417
s.344, varied: 2002 c.29 s.417
s.345, varied: 2002 c.29 s.417
s.346, amended: 2003 c.39 Sch.8 para.297
s.346, applied: 2003 c.39 Sch.7 para.11
s.346, varied: 2002 c.29 s.417
s.347, amended: 2003 c.39 Sch.8 para.298
s.347, varied: 2002 c.29 s.417
s.348, varied: 2002 c.29 s.417
s.349, varied: 2002 c.29 s.417
s.349A, varied: 2002 c.29 s.417
s.350, amended: 2002 c.40 Sch.21 para.2
s.350, varied: 2002 c.29 s.417
s.351, varied: 2002 c.29 s.417
s.352, see *Attorney General's Reference (No.1 of 2004), Re* [2004] EWCA Crim 1025, [2004] 1 W.L.R. 2111 (CA (Crim Div)), Lord Woolf of Barnes, L.C.J.; see *R. v Daniel (Anthony Lala)* [2002] EWCA Crim 959, [2003] 1 Cr. App. R. 6 (CA (Crim Div)), Auld, L.J.
s.352, varied: 2002 c.29 s.417
s.353, see *Attorney General's Reference (No.1 of 2004), Re* [2004] EWCA Crim 1025, [2004] 1 W.L.R. 2111 (CA (Crim Div)), Lord Woolf of Barnes, L.C.J.
s.353, varied: 2002 c.29 s.417
s.354, see *R. v Kearns (Nicholas Gary)* [2002] EWCA Crim 748, [2002] 1 W.L.R. 2815 (CA (Crim Div)), Aikens, J.
s.354, amended: 2002 c.40 Sch.23 para.12
s.354, varied: 2002 c.29 s.417
s.355, amended: 2002 c.40 Sch.23 para.13
s.355, varied: 2002 c.29 s.417
s.356, varied: 2002 c.29 s.417
s.357, see *Attorney General's Reference (No.1 of 2004), Re* [2004] EWCA Crim 1025, [2004] 1 W.L.R. 2111 (CA (Crim Div)), Lord Woolf of Barnes, L.C.J.
s.357, varied: 2002 c.29 s.417
s.358, varied: 2002 c.29 s.417
s.359, varied: 2002 c.29 s.417
s.360, amended: 2002 c.40 Sch.21 para.3
s.360, varied: 2002 c.29 s.417
s.361, repealed: 2002 c.40 Sch.26
s.361, varied: 2002 c.29 s.417
s.362, see *R. v Muhamad (Mithum)* [2002] EWCA Crim 1856, [2003] Q.B. 1031 (CA (Crim Div)), Dyson, L.J.
s.362, repealed: 2002 c.40 Sch.26
s.362, varied: 2002 c.29 s.417
s.363, varied: 2002 c.29 s.417
s.364, varied: 2002 c.29 s.417
s.365, varied: 2002 c.29 s.417
s.366, amended: 2004 c.33 Sch.27 para.120

1986–cont.

45. Insolvency Act 1986–*cont.*

s.366, varied: 2002 c.29 s.417

s.367, varied: 2002 c.29 s.417

s.368, varied: 2002 c.29 s.417

s.369, varied: 2002 c.29 s.417

s.370, varied: 2002 c.29 s.417

s.371, varied: 2002 c.29 s.417

s.372, amended: 2003 c.21 Sch.17 para.82

s.375, see *Boorer v Boorer's Trustee in Bankruptcy* [2002] B.P.I.R. 21 (Ch D), Jacob, J.; see *Egleton v Inland Revenue Commissioners* [2003] EWHC 3226, [2004] B.P.I.R. 476 (Ch D), Lawrence Collins, J.; see *Hurst v Bennett (No.2)* [2001] EWCA Civ 1398, [2002] B.P.I.R. 102 (CA), Mummery, L.J.; see *Hurst v Bennett (Variation of Civil Restraint Order)* [2004] EWCA Civ 230, [2004] B.P.I.R. 732 (CA), Chadwick, L.J.; see *Shepherd v Legal Services Commission* [2003] B.C.C. 728 (Ch D), Gabriel Moss Q.C.; see *Thorogood, Re (No.1)* [2003] EWHC 997, [2003] B.P.I.R.1468 (Ch D), Neuberger, J.

s.376, see *Warley Continental Services Ltd (In Compulsory Liquidation) v Johal* [2004] B.P.I.R. 353 (Ch D), Judge Norris Q.C.

s.382, see *Harper v Buchler* [2004] B.P.I.R. 724 (Ch D), Deputy Registrar Barnett

s.384, amended: 2002 c.40 s.261

s.386, amended: 2002 c.40 s.251

s.387, amended: 2002 c.40 Sch.17 para.34, SI 2002/1240 Reg.16

s.388, amended: SI 2002/1240 Reg.17, SI 2002/2708 Art.3

s.388, applied: 2002 c.29 s.433, Sch.9 para.1, SI 2002/459 Reg.8, SI 2002/912 Sch.1, SI 2002/915 Sch.1, SI 2003/3075 Reg.2

s.388, referred to: SI 2002/2711 Art.5

s.388, varied: 2002 c.29 s.433, 2004 c.35 s.121

s.389, applied: SI 2002/459 Reg.8

s.389A, amended: SI 2004/1941 Sch.1 para.2

s.389B, added: 2002 c.40 Sch.22 para.3

s.390, amended: 2002 c.40 Sch.21 para.4, SI 2004/1941 Sch.1 para.3

s.390, enabling: SI 2002/2710, SI 2002/2748

s.391, applied: SI 2003/3363 Art.2, 2004 c.35 Sch.3, Sch.8

s.392, amended: 2002 c.40 s.270

s.392, applied: SI 2003/3363 Art.4

s.393, applied: SI 2003/3363 Art.3, Art.4

s.399, amended: 2002 c.40 Sch.23 para.14

s.399, applied: SI 2002/912 Sch.1, SI 2002/915 Sch.1

s.405, repealed: 2002 c.40 Sch.26

s.408, substituted: 2002 c.40 s.272

s.411, amended: SI 2002/1037 Reg.3

s.411, applied: 2004 c.20 s.159

1986–cont.

45. Insolvency Act 1986–*cont.*

s.411, enabling: SI 2002/1307, SI 2002/2709, SI 2002/2712, SI 2003/1367, SI 2003/1730, SI 2003/2111, SI 2004/472, SI 2004/584, SI 2004/1070

s.412, amended: SI 2002/1037 Reg.3

s.412, enabling: SI 2002/1307, SI 2002/2712, SI 2003/1730, SI 2004/472, SI 2004/584, SI 2004/1070

s.413, applied: SI 2002/1307, SI 2002/2712, SI 2003/1367, SI 2004/584, SI 2004/1070

s.414, applied: SI 2003/646, SI 2003/648, SI 2003/717, SI 2003/718, SI 2004/2098, SI 2004/2100, SI 2004/3114 Art.7, SI 2004/3121, SI 2004/3121 Art.8

s.414, enabling: SI 2003/646, SI 2003/648, SI 2003/717, SI 2003/718, SI 2004/593, SI 2004/2098, SI 2004/2100, SI 2004/3121

s.415, applied: SI 2003/645, SI 2003/646, SI 2003/648, SI 2003/717, SI 2003/718, SI 2003/719, SI 2004/2098, SI 2004/2100, SI 2004/3114 Art.7, SI 2004/3121, SI 2004/3121 Art.8

s.415, enabling: SI 2003/645, SI 2003/646, SI 2003/648, SI 2003/717, SI 2003/718, SI 2003/719, SI 2004/593, SI 2004/2098, SI 2004/2100, SI 2004/3121

s.415A, added: 2002 c.40 s.270

s.415A, enabling: SI 2003/3363, SI 2004/476

s.416, applied: SI 2003/2553 Reg.16

s.417, applied: SI 2003/2553 Reg.16

s.418, amended: 2002 c.40 s.261

s.418, enabling: SI 2004/547

s.419, enabling: SI 2002/2710, SI 2002/2748, SI 2004/473

s.420, amended: SI 2002/1037 Reg.3

s.420, applied: 2004 c.35 s.121

s.420, referred to: 2002 c.29 s.311

s.420, enabling: SI 2002/1308, SI 2002/2708

s.421, amended: SI 2002/1037 Reg.3

s.421, applied: SI 2002/2822 Reg.43, 2004 c.35 s.121

s.421, referred to: 2002 c.29 s.311

s.421, enabling: SI 2002/1309

s.422, amended: 2002 c.40 Sch.17 para.35, SI 2002/1555 Art.16

s.422, repealed (in part): SI 2003/2096 Sch.1 para.11

s.422, substituted: SI 2002/1555 Art.16

s.423, see *Anglo Eastern Trust Ltd v Kermanshahchi* [2003] EWHC 1939, [2003] B.P.I.R. 1229 (Ch D), Hart, J.; see *Barclays Bank Plc v Bean* [2004] 41 E.G. 152 (Ch D), Judge Langan; see *Beckenham MC Ltd v Centralex Ltd* [2004] EWHC 1287, [2004] B.P.I.R. 1112 (Ch D), Hart, J.; see *Habib Bank Ltd v Ahmed (Permission to Appeal)* [2004] EWCA Civ 805, [2004] B.P.I.R. 864 (CA),

CAP.

1986–cont.

45. Insolvency Act 1986–*cont.*
s.423–*cont.*

Auld, L.J.; see *Habib Bank Ltd v Ahmed* [2003] EWHC 1697, [2004] B.P.I.R. 35 (QBD), Simon, J.; see *Inland Revenue Commissioners v Hashmi* [2002] B.P.I.R. 271 (Ch D), Hart, J.; see *Inland Revenue Commissioners v Hashmi* [2002] EWCA Civ 981, [2002] B.C.C. 943 (CA), Arden, L.J.; see *Kubiangha v Ekpenyong* [2002] EWHC 1567, [2002] 2 B.C.L.C. 597 (Ch D), L Henderson Q.C.; see *Law Society v Southall* [2001] EWCA Civ 2001, [2002] B.P.I.R. 336 (CA), Peter Gibson, L.J.; see *National Westminster Bank Plc v Jones* [2001] EWCA Civ 1541, [2002] 1 B.C.L.C. 55 (CA), Mummery, L.J.; see *Pagemanor Ltd v Ryan (No.2)* [2002] B.P.I.R. 593 (Ch D), Sonia Proudman Q.C.; see *Ram v Ram (No.1)* [2004] EWCA Civ 1452, [2004] 3 F.C.R. 425 (CA (Civ Div)), Potter, L.J.; see *Secretary of State for the Environment, Food and Rural Affairs v Feakins (No.1)* [2002] B.P.I.R. 281 (QBD), Penry-Davey, J.; see *Trowbridge v Trowbridge* [2002] EWHC 3114, [2003] 2 F.L.R. 231 (Ch D), David Richards Q.C.

s.423, amended: 2004 c.33 Sch.27 para.121
s.423, applied: 2002 c.29 s.427, 2004 c.35 s.58
s.423, referred to: 2002 c.29 s.419, 2004 c.35 s.58
s.424, amended: 2002 c.40 Sch.17 para.36
s.425, see *Kubiangha v Ekpenyong* [2002] EWHC 1567, [2002] 2 B.C.L.C. 597 (Ch D), L Henderson Q.C.
s.426, see *Television Trade Rentals Ltd, Re* [2002] EWHC 211, [2002] B.C.C. 807 (Ch D (Companies Court)), Lawrence Collins, J.
s.426, amended: SI 2002/3150 Sch.3 para.2
s.426A, added: 2002 c.40 s.266
s.426A, varied: 2002 c.40 s.266
s.426B, added: 2002 c.40 s.266
s.426B, varied: 2002 c.40 s.266
s.426C, added: 2002 c.40 s.266
s.427, amended: 2002 c.40 Sch.26
s.427, repealed (in part): 2002 c.40 Sch.26
s.429, amended: 2002 c.40 Sch.23 para.15
s.429, applied: 2002 c.30 Sch.2 para.1, Sch.2 para.2, SI 2002/2376 Reg.2, SI 2002/3040 Reg.3, 2003 c.20 Sch.4 para.7, SI 2003/348 Sch.6 para.7, SI 2003/506 Reg.3, SI 2003/1558 Sch.2 para.6, SI 2003/2773 Reg.3, SI 2003/3060 Reg.3, SI 2003/3190 Reg.4, SI 2003/3279 Reg.4, SI 2004/291 Reg.5, Sch.6 para.113, SI 2004/478 Reg.5, Sch.6 para.111, SI 2004/570 Reg.3, SI 2004/627 Reg.5, Sch.5 para.105, SI 2004/668 Reg.3, SSI 2004/115 Sch.5 para.101, SSI 2004/116 Reg.3, Sch.1 para.66

CAP.

1986–cont.

45. Insolvency Act 1986–*cont.*

s.435, amended: 2004 c.33 Sch.27 para.122
s.435, applied: 2004 c.35 s.38, s.43, s.47, s.51, s.53, s.57
s.435, varied: 2004 c.33 Sch.21 para.28
s.436, see *Dear v Reeves* [2001] EWCA Civ 277, [2002] Ch.1 (CA), Mummery, L.J.
s.436, amended: SI 2002/1037 Reg.4
s.436A, added: SI 2002/1240 Reg.18
s.440, amended: 2002 c.40 s.270
Sch.A1 Part I para.1, varied: SI 2003/1633 Sch.2 para.7
Sch.A1 Part I para.2, varied: SI 2003/1633 Sch.2 para.7
Sch.A1 Part I para.3, amended: SI 2002/1990 Reg.3
Sch.A1 Part I para.3, varied: SI 2003/1633 Sch.2 para.7
Sch.A1 Part I para.4, amended: 2002 c.40 Sch.17 para.37
Sch.A1 Part I para.4, varied: SI 2003/1633 Sch.2 para.7
Sch.A1 Part I para.4A, added: SI 2002/1990 Reg.3
Sch.A1 Part I para.4A, varied: SI 2003/1633 Sch.2 para.7
Sch.A1 Part I para.4B, added: SI 2002/1990 Reg.3
Sch.A1 Part I para.4B, varied: SI 2003/1633 Sch.2 para.7
Sch.A1 Part I para.4C, added: SI 2002/1990 Reg.3
Sch.A1 Part I para.4C, varied: SI 2003/1633 Sch.2 para.7
Sch.A1 Part I para.4D, added: SI 2002/1990 Reg.3
Sch.A1 Part I para.4D, varied: SI 2003/1633 Sch.2 para.7
Sch.A1 Part I para.4E, added: SI 2002/1990 Reg.3
Sch.A1 Part I para.4E, varied: SI 2003/1633 Sch.2 para.7
Sch.A1 Part I para.4F, added: SI 2002/1990 Reg.3
Sch.A1 Part I para.4F, varied: SI 2003/1633 Sch.2 para.7
Sch.A1 Part I para.4G, added: SI 2002/1990 Reg.3
Sch.A1 Part I para.4G, varied: SI 2003/1633 Sch.2 para.7
Sch.A1 Part I para.4H, added: SI 2002/1990 Reg.3
Sch.A1 Part I para.4H, varied: SI 2003/1633 Sch.2 para.7
Sch.A1 Part I para.4I, added: SI 2002/1990 Reg.3
Sch.A1 Part I para.4I, varied: SI 2003/1633 Sch.2 para.7
Sch.A1 Part I para.4J, added: SI 2002/1990 Reg.3

1986–cont.

45. Insolvency Act 1986–*cont.*

Sch.A1 Part I para.4J, varied: SI 2003/1633
Sch.2 para.7

Sch.A1 Part I para.4K, added: SI 2002/1990
Reg.3

Sch.A1 Part I para.4K, varied: SI 2003/1633
Sch.2 para.7

Sch.A1 Part I para.5, varied: SI 2003/1633
Sch.2 para.7

Sch.A1 Part I para.5, enabling: SI 2002/1990

Sch.A1 Part I para.5, varied: SI 2003/1633
Sch.2 para.7

Sch.A1 Part II para.6, varied: SI 2003/1633
Sch.2 para.7

Sch.A1 Part II para.7, applied: 2004 c.35 s.121,
SI 2004/3121 Sch.1

Sch.A1 Part II para.7, varied: SI 2003/1633
Sch.2 para.7

Sch.A1 Part II para.8, varied: SI 2003/1633
Sch.2 para.7

Sch.A1 Part II para.9, varied: SI 2003/1633
Sch.2 para.7

Sch.A1 Part II para.10, varied: SI 2003/1633
Sch.2 para.7

Sch.A1 Part II para.11, varied: SI 2003/1633
Sch.2 para.7

Sch.A1 Part III para.12, amended: 2002 c.40
Sch.17 para.37, SI 2004/2326 Reg.73

Sch.A1 Part III para.12, disapplied: SI 2003/
3226 Reg.8

Sch.A1 Part III para.12, varied: SI 2003/1633
Sch.2 para.7

Sch.A1 Part III para.13, varied: SI 2003/1633
Sch.2 para.7

Sch.A1 Part III para.14, varied: SI 2003/1633
Sch.2 para.7

Sch.A1 Part III para.15, varied: SI 2003/1633
Sch.2 para.7

Sch.A1 Part III para.16, varied: SI 2003/1633
Sch.2 para.7

Sch.A1 Part III para.17, varied: SI 2003/1633
Sch.2 para.7

Sch.A1 Part III para.18, varied: SI 2003/1633
Sch.2 para.7

Sch.A1 Part III para.19, varied: SI 2003/1633
Sch.2 para.7

Sch.A1 Part III para.20, disapplied: SI 2003/
3226 Reg.8

Sch.A1 Part III para.20, varied: SI 2003/1633
Sch.2 para.7

Sch.A1 Part III para.21, varied: SI 2003/1633
Sch.2 para.7

Sch.A1 Part III para.22, varied: SI 2003/1633
Sch.2 para.7

Sch.A1 Part III para.23, varied: SI 2003/1633
Sch.2 para.7

Sch.A1 Part IV para.24, varied: SI 2003/1633
Sch.2 para.7

Sch.A1 Part IV para.25, varied: SI 2003/1633
Sch.2 para.7

1986–cont.

45. Insolvency Act 1986–*cont.*

Sch.A1 Part IV para.26, varied: SI 2003/1633
Sch.2 para.7

Sch.A1 Part IV para.27, varied: SI 2003/1633
Sch.2 para.7

Sch.A1 Part IV para.28, varied: SI 2003/1633
Sch.2 para.7

Sch.A1 Part V para.29, varied: SI 2003/1633
Sch.2 para.7

Sch.A1 Part V para.30, varied: SI 2003/1633
Sch.2 para.7

Sch.A1 Part V para.31, varied: SI 2003/1633
Sch.2 para.7

Sch.A1 Part V para.32, varied: SI 2003/1633
Sch.2 para.7

Sch.A1 Part V para.33, varied: SI 2003/1633
Sch.2 para.7

Sch.A1 Part V para.34, varied: SI 2003/1633
Sch.2 para.7

Sch.A1 Part V para.35, varied: SI 2003/1633
Sch.2 para.7

Sch.A1 Part V para.36, varied: SI 2003/1633
Sch.2 para.7

Sch.A1 Part V para.37, varied: SI 2003/1633
Sch.2 para.7

Sch.A1 Part V para.38, varied: SI 2003/1633
Sch.2 para.7

Sch.A1 Part V para.39, varied: SI 2003/1633
Sch.2 para.7

Sch.A1 Part VI para.40, amended: 2002 c.40
Sch.17 para.37, SI 2004/2312 Art.2

Sch.A1 Part VI para.40, varied: SI 2003/1633
Sch.2 para.7

Sch.A1 Part VI para.41, varied: SI 2003/1633
Sch.2 para.7

Sch.A1 Part VI para.42, varied: SI 2003/1633
Sch.2 para.7

Sch.A1 Part VI para.43, varied: SI 2003/1633
Sch.2 para.7

Sch.A1 Part VI para.44, varied: SI 2003/1633
Sch.2 para.7

Sch.A1 Part VI para.45, applied: SI 2002/1990

Sch.A1 Part VI para.45, varied: SI 2003/1633
Sch.2 para.7

Sch.A1 Part VI para.45, enabling: SI 2002/
1990

Sch.B1, see *Transbus International Ltd (In
Liquidation), Re* [2004] EWHC 932,
[2004] 1 W.L.R. 2654 (Ch D), Lawrence
Collins, J.

Sch.B1, applied: 2004 c.20 s.157, SI 2004/
291 Sch.6 para.113, SI 2004/478 Sch.6
para.111, SI 2004/627 Sch.5 para.105, SSI
2004/115 Sch.5 para.101, SSI 2004/116
Sch.1 para.66

Sch.B1, referred to: 2004 c.20 s.159, s.171

Sch.B1 Part 1 para.1, added: 2002 c.40 Sch.16

Sch.B1 Part 1 para.1, applied: 2004 c.20
Sch.20 para.2, 2004 c.35 s.121

Sch.B1 Part 1 para.1, varied: 2004 c.20 Sch.20
para.1, Sch.20 para.5, Sch.20 para.33

1986–cont.

45. Insolvency Act 1986–cont.

Sch.B1 Part1 para.2, added: 2002 c.40 Sch.16

Sch.B1 Part 1 para.2, varied: 2004 c.20 Sch.20 para.1, Sch.20 para.33

Sch.B1 Part1 para.3, added: 2002 c.40 Sch.16

Sch.B1 Part 1 para.3, applied: SI 2004/353 Reg.12, SI 2004/1045 Reg.11

Sch.B1 Part 1 para.3, referred to: SI 2004/1045 Reg.14

Sch.B1 Part 1 para.3, varied: 2004 c.20 Sch.20 para.1, Sch.20 para.33

Sch.B1 Part1 para.4, added: 2002 c.40 Sch.16

Sch.B1 Part 1 para.4, varied: 2004 c.20 Sch.20 para.1, Sch.20 para.33

Sch.B1 Part1 para.5, added: 2002 c.40 Sch.16

Sch.B1 Part 1 para.5, varied: 2004 c.20 Sch.20 para.1, Sch.20 para.33

Sch.B1 Part1 para.6, added: 2002 c.40 Sch.16

Sch.B1 Part 1 para.6, varied: 2004 c.20 Sch.20 para.1, Sch.20 para.33

Sch.B1 Part1 para.7, added: 2002 c.40 Sch.16

Sch.B1 Part1 para.7, varied: 2004 c.20 Sch.20 para.1, Sch.20 para.33

Sch.B1 Part1 para.8, added: 2002 c.40 Sch.16

Sch.B1 Part 1 para.8, varied: 2004 c.20 Sch.20 para.1, Sch.20 para.33

Sch.B1 Part1 para.9, added: 2002 c.40 Sch.16

Sch.B1 Part 1 para.9, applied: SI 2002/1242 Art.3

Sch.B1 Part 1 para.9, varied: 2004 c.20 Sch.20 para.1, Sch.20 para.33

Sch.B1 Part 2 para.10, added: 2002 c.40 Sch.16

Sch.B1 Part 2 para.10, varied: 2004 c.20 Sch.20 para.1, Sch.20 para.33

Sch.B1 Part 2 para.11, added: 2002 c.40 Sch.16

Sch.B1 Part 2 para.11, varied: 2004 c.20 Sch.20 para.1, Sch.20 para.33

Sch.B1 Part 2 para.12, added: 2002 c.40 Sch.16

Sch.B1 Part 2 para.12, amended: 2002 c.40 Sch.16, 2003 c.39 Sch.8 para.299

Sch.B1 Part 2 para.12, applied: SI 2002/1242 Art.5

Sch.B1 Part 2 para.12, varied: 2004 c.20 Sch.20 para.1, Sch.20 para.33

Sch.B1 Part 2 para.13, added: 2002 c.40 Sch.16

Sch.B1 Part 2 para.13, applied: 2004 c.20 s.162, SI 2004/353 Reg.9, Reg.11, Reg.14, Reg.34, Reg.36, SI 2004/1045 Reg.9, Reg.11, Reg.12, Reg.19, Reg.21

Sch.B1 Part 2 para.13, varied: 2004 c.20 Sch.20 para.1, Sch.20 para.33

Sch.B1 Part 3 para.14, added: 2002 c.40 Sch.16

Sch.B1 Part 3 para.14, applied: 2002 c.40 Sch.17 para.1, SI 2002/1242 Art.5, 2004 c.20 s.156, s.163, SI 2004/353 Reg.4,

1986–cont.

45. Insolvency Act 1986–cont.

Sch.B1 Part 3 para.14, applied:–cont. Reg.36, SI 2004/1045 Reg.3, SI 2004/3121 Sch.1

Sch.B1 Part 3 para.14, disapplied: SI 2002/1242 Art.3, 2004 c.20 s.163

Sch.B1 Part 3 para.14, varied: 2004 c.20 Sch.20 para.1, Sch.20 para.33

Sch.B1 Part 3 para.15, added: 2002 c.40 Sch.16

Sch.B1 Part 3 para.15, applied: 2002 c.40 Sch.17 para.1

Sch.B1 Part 3 para.15, varied: 2004 c.20 Sch.20 para.1, Sch.20 para.33

Sch.B1 Part 3 para.16, added: 2002 c.40 Sch.16

Sch.B1 Part 3 para.16, varied: 2004 c.20 Sch.20 para.1, Sch.20 para.33

Sch.B1 Part 3 para.17, added: 2002 c.40 Sch.16

Sch.B1 Part 3 para.17, varied: 2004 c.20 Sch.20 para.1, Sch.20 para.33

Sch.B1 Part 3 para.18, added: 2002 c.40 Sch.16

Sch.B1 Part 3 para.18, applied: SI 2002/1242 Art.5, 2004 c.20 s.163, SI 2004/3121 Sch.1

Sch.B1 Part 3 para.18, varied: 2004 c.20 Sch.20 para.1, Sch.20 para.33

Sch.B1 Part 3 para.19, added: 2002 c.40 Sch.16

Sch.B1 Part 3 para.19, varied: 2004 c.20 Sch.20 para.1, Sch.20 para.33

Sch.B1 Part 3 para.20, added: 2002 c.40 Sch.16

Sch.B1 Part 3 para.20, varied: 2004 c.20 Sch.20 para.1, Sch.20 para.33

Sch.B1 Part 3 para.21, added: 2002 c.40 Sch.16

Sch.B1 Part 3 para.21, varied: 2004 c.20 Sch.20 para.1, Sch.20 para.33

Sch.B1 Part 4 para.22, added: 2002 c.40 Sch.16

Sch.B1 Part 4 para.22, applied: 2002 c.40 Sch.17 para.1, SI 2002/1242 Art.5, 2004 c.20 s.163, SI 2004/353 Reg.4, Reg.36, SI 2004/1045 Reg.3

Sch.B1 Part 4 para.22, disapplied: SI 2002/1242 Art.3, 2004 c.20 s.163

Sch.B1 Part 4 para.22, varied: 2004 c.20 Sch.20 para.1, Sch.20 para.33

Sch.B1 Part 4 para.23, added: 2002 c.40 Sch.16

Sch.B1 Part 4 para.23, varied: 2004 c.20 Sch.20 para.1, Sch.20 para.33

Sch.B1 Part 4 para.24, added: 2002 c.40 Sch.16

Sch.B1 Part 4 para.24, varied: 2004 c.20 Sch.20 para.1, Sch.20 para.33

Sch.B1 Part 4 para.25, added: 2002 c.40 Sch.16

1986–cont.

45. Insolvency Act 1986–*cont.*

Sch.B1 Part 4 para.25, varied: 2004 c.20
Sch.20 para.1, Sch.20 para.33

Sch.B1 Part 4 para.26, added: 2002 c.40
Sch.16

Sch.B1 Part 4 para.26, applied: 2002 c.40
Sch.17 para.1

Sch.B1 Part 4 para.26, varied: 2004 c.20
Sch.20 para.1, Sch.20 para.33

Sch.B1 Part 4 para.27, added: 2002 c.40
Sch.16

Sch.B1 Part 4 para.27, applied: SI 2002/1242
Art.5, SI 2004/3121 Sch.1

Sch.B1 Part 4 para.27, varied: 2004 c.20
Sch.20 para.1, Sch.20 para.33

Sch.B1 Part 4 para.28, added: 2002 c.40
Sch.16

Sch.B1 Part 4 para.28, varied: 2004 c.20
Sch.20 para.1, Sch.20 para.33

Sch.B1 Part 4 para.29, added: 2002 c.40
Sch.16

Sch.B1 Part 4 para.29, applied: 2004 c.20
s.163, SI 2004/3121 Sch.1

Sch.B1 Part 4 para.29, varied: 2004 c.20
Sch.20 para.1, Sch.20 para.33

Sch.B1 Part 4 para.30, added: 2002 c.40
Sch.16

Sch.B1 Part 4 para.30, varied: 2004 c.20
Sch.20 para.1, Sch.20 para.33

Sch.B1 Part 4 para.31, added: 2002 c.40
Sch.16

Sch.B1 Part 4 para.31, varied: 2004 c.20
Sch.20 para.1, Sch.20 para.33

Sch.B1 Part 4 para.32, added: 2002 c.40
Sch.16

Sch.B1 Part 4 para.32, varied: 2004 c.20
Sch.20 para.1, Sch.20 para.33

Sch.B1 Part 4 para.33, added: 2002 c.40
Sch.16

Sch.B1 Part 4 para.33, varied: 2004 c.20
Sch.20 para.1, Sch.20 para.33

Sch.B1 Part 4 para.34, added: 2002 c.40
Sch.16

Sch.B1 Part 4 para.34, varied: 2004 c.20
Sch.20 para.1, Sch.20 para.33

Sch.B1 Part 5 para.35, added: 2002 c.40
Sch.16

Sch.B1 Part 5 para.35, varied: 2004 c.20
Sch.20 para.1, Sch.20 para.33

Sch.B1 Part 5 para.36, added: 2002 c.40
Sch.16

Sch.B1 Part 5 para.36, varied: 2004 c.20
Sch.20 para.1, Sch.20 para.33

Sch.B1 Part 5 para.37, added: 2002 c.40
Sch.16

Sch.B1 Part 5 para.37, varied: 2004 c.20
Sch.20 para.1, Sch.20 para.33

Sch.B1 Part 5 para.38, added: 2002 c.40
Sch.16

Sch.B1 Part 5 para.38, varied: 2004 c.20
Sch.20 para.1, Sch.20 para.33

1986–cont.

45. Insolvency Act 1986–*cont.*

Sch.B1 Part 5 para.39, added: 2002 c.40
Sch.16

Sch.B1 Part 5 para.39, varied: 2004 c.20
Sch.20 para.1, Sch.20 para.33

Sch.B1 Part 6 para.40, added: 2002 c.40
Sch.16

Sch.B1 Part 6 para.40, amended: SI 2004/
2326 Reg.73

Sch.B1 Part 6 para.40, applied: 2004 c.20
Sch.20 para.2

Sch.B1 Part 6 para.40, varied: 2004 c.20
Sch.20 para.1, Sch.20 para.6, Sch.20
para.33

Sch.B1 Part 6 para.41, added: 2002 c.40
Sch.16

Sch.B1 Part 6 para.41, applied: 2004 c.20
Sch.20 para.2

Sch.B1 Part 6 para.41, disapplied: SI 2003/
3226 Reg.8

Sch.B1 Part 6 para.41, varied: 2004 c.20
Sch.20 para.1, Sch.20 para.33, Sch.20
para.37

Sch.B1 Part 6 para.42, added: 2002 c.40
Sch.16

Sch.B1 Part 6 para.42, amended: SI 2004/
2326 Reg.73

Sch.B1 Part 6 para.42, applied: 2004 c.20
Sch.20 para.2

Sch.B1 Part 6 para.42, disapplied: 2004 c.20
Sch.20 para.35

Sch.B1 Part 6 para.42, varied: 2004 c.20
Sch.20 para.1, Sch.20 para.7, Sch.20
para.33

Sch.B1 Part 6 para.43, added: 2002 c.40
Sch.16

Sch.B1 Part 6 para.43, amended: SI 2003/
2096 Art.2

Sch.B1 Part 6 para.43, applied: 2004 c.20
Sch.20 para.2

Sch.B1 Part 6 para.43, disapplied: SI 2003/
3226 Reg.8

Sch.B1 Part 6 para.43, varied: 2004 c.20
Sch.20 para.1, Sch.20 para.33, Sch.20
para.38

Sch.B1 Part 6 para.44, added: 2002 c.40
Sch.16

Sch.B1 Part 6 para.44, applied: 2004 c.20
Sch.20 para.2

Sch.B1 Part 6 para.44, disapplied: 2004 c.20
s.162, s.163

Sch.B1 Part 6 para.44, referred to: SI 2003/
3226 Reg.8

Sch.B1 Part 6 para.44, varied: 2004 c.20
Sch.20 para.1, Sch.20 para.8, Sch.20
para.33, Sch.20 para.39

Sch.B1 Part 6 para.45, added: 2002 c.40
Sch.16

Sch.B1 Part 6 para.45, applied: 2004 c.20
Sch.20 para.2

Sch.B1 Part 6 para.45, varied: 2004 c.20
Sch.20 para.1, Sch.20 para.33

1986–cont.

45. Insolvency Act 1986–*cont.*

Sch.B1 Part 7 para.46, added: 2002 c.40 Sch.16

Sch.B1 Part 7 para.46, applied: 2004 c.20 Sch.20 para.2, Sch.20 para.35

Sch.B1 Part 7 para.46, varied: 2004 c.20 Sch.20 para.1, Sch.20 para.9, Sch.20 para.33

Sch.B1 Part 7 para.47, added: 2002 c.40 Sch.16

Sch.B1 Part 7 para.47, applied: 2004 c.20 Sch.20 para.2

Sch.B1 Part 7 para.47, varied: 2004 c.20 Sch.20 para.1, Sch.20 para.33

Sch.B1 Part 7 para.48, added: 2002 c.40 Sch.16

Sch.B1 Part 7 para.48, applied: 2004 c.20 Sch.20 para.2

Sch.B1 Part 7 para.48, varied: 2004 c.20 Sch.20 para.1, Sch.20 para.33

Sch.B1 Part 7 para.49, added: 2002 c.40 Sch.16

Sch.B1 Part 7 para.49, amended: SI 2002/ 1242 Sch.1 para.1

Sch.B1 Part 7 para.49, applied: 2004 c.20 Sch.20 para.2, Sch.20 para.35

Sch.B1 Part 7 para.49, varied: 2004 c.20 Sch.20 para.1, Sch.20 para.10, Sch.20 para.33

Sch.B1 Part 7 para.50, added: 2002 c.40 Sch.16

Sch.B1 Part 7 para.50, applied: 2004 c.20 Sch.20 para.2

Sch.B1 Part 7 para.50, varied: 2004 c.20 Sch.20 para.1, Sch.20 para.33

Sch.B1 Part 7 para.51, added: 2002 c.40 Sch.16

Sch.B1 Part 7 para.51, varied: 2004 c.20 Sch.20 para.1, Sch.20 para.33

Sch.B1 Part 7 para.52, added: 2002 c.40 Sch.16

Sch.B1 Part 7 para.52, varied: 2004 c.20 Sch.20 para.1, Sch.20 para.33

Sch.B1 Part 7 para.53, added: 2002 c.40 Sch.16

Sch.B1 Part 7 para.53, amended: SI 2002/ 1242 Sch.1 para.2

Sch.B1 Part 7 para.53, varied: 2004 c.20 Sch.20 para.1, Sch.20 para.33

Sch.B1 Part 7 para.54, added: 2002 c.40 Sch.16

Sch.B1 Part 7 para.54, amended: SI 2002/ 1242 Sch.1 para.3

Sch.B1 Part 7 para.54, applied: 2004 c.20 Sch.20 para.2, Sch.20 para.35

Sch.B1 Part 7 para.54, varied: 2004 c.20 Sch.20 para.1, Sch.20 para.11, Sch.20 para.33

Sch.B1 Part 7 para.55, added: 2002 c.40 Sch.16

1986–cont.

45. Insolvency Act 1986–*cont.*

Sch.B1 Part 7 para.55, varied: 2004 c.20 Sch.20 para.1, Sch.20 para.33

Sch.B1 Part 7 para.56, added: 2002 c.40 Sch.16

Sch.B1 Part 7 para.56, varied: 2004 c.20 Sch.20 para.1, Sch.20 para.33

Sch.B1 Part 7 para.57, added: 2002 c.40 Sch.16

Sch.B1 Part 7 para.57, varied: 2004 c.20 Sch.20 para.1, Sch.20 para.33

Sch.B1 Part 7 para.58, added: 2002 c.40 Sch.16

Sch.B1 Part 7 para.58, varied: 2004 c.20 Sch.20 para.1, Sch.20 para.33

Sch.B1 Part 8 para.59, added: 2002 c.40 Sch.16

Sch.B1 Part 8 para.59, applied: 2004 c.20 Sch.20 para.2

Sch.B1 Part 8 para.59, varied: 2004 c.20 Sch.20 para.1, Sch.20 para.33

Sch.B1 Part 8 para.60, added: 2002 c.40 Sch.16

Sch.B1 Part 8 para.60, applied: 2004 c.20 Sch.20 para.2

Sch.B1 Part 8 para.60, varied: 2004 c.20 Sch.20 para.1, Sch.20 para.12, Sch.20 para.33

Sch.B1 Part 8 para.61, added: 2002 c.40 Sch.16

Sch.B1 Part 8 para.61, applied: 2004 c.20 Sch.20 para.2

Sch.B1 Part 8 para.61, disapplied: 2004 c.20 Sch.20 para.35

Sch.B1 Part 8 para.61, varied: 2004 c.20 Sch.20 para.1, Sch.20 para.33

Sch.B1 Part 8 para.62, added: 2002 c.40 Sch.16

Sch.B1 Part 8 para.62, applied: 2004 c.20 Sch.20 para.2

Sch.B1 Part 8 para.62, varied: 2004 c.20 Sch.20 para.1, Sch.20 para.33

Sch.B1 Part 8 para.63, added: 2002 c.40 Sch.16

Sch.B1 Part 8 para.63, applied: 2004 c.20 Sch.20 para.2

Sch.B1 Part 8 para.63, varied: 2004 c.20 Sch.20 para.1, Sch.20 para.33

Sch.B1 Part 8 para.64, added: 2002 c.40 Sch.16

Sch.B1 Part 8 para.64, applied: 2004 c.20 Sch.20 para.2

Sch.B1 Part 8 para.64, varied: 2004 c.20 Sch.20 para.1, Sch.20 para.33, Sch.20 para.40

Sch.B1 Part 8 para.65, added: 2002 c.40 Sch.16

Sch.B1 Part 8 para.65, applied: 2004 c.20 Sch.20 para.2

Sch.B1 Part 8 para.65, varied: 2004 c.20 Sch.20 para.1, Sch.20 para.33

1986–cont.

45. Insolvency Act 1986–*cont.*

Sch.B1 Part 8 para.66, added: 2002 c.40 Sch.16

Sch.B1 Part 8 para.66, applied: 2004 c.20 Sch.20 para.2

Sch.B1 Part 8 para.66, varied: 2004 c.20 Sch.20 para.1, Sch.20 para.33

Sch.B1 Part 8 para.67, added: 2002 c.40 Sch.16

Sch.B1 Part 8 para.67, applied: 2004 c.20 Sch.20 para.2

Sch.B1 Part 8 para.67, varied: 2004 c.20 Sch.20 para.1, Sch.20 para.33

Sch.B1 Part 8 para.68, added: 2002 c.40 Sch.16

Sch.B1 Part 8 para.68, applied: 2004 c.20 Sch.20 para.2

Sch.B1 Part 8 para.68, varied: 2004 c.20 Sch.20 para.1, Sch.20 para.13, Sch.20 para.33

Sch.B1 Part 8 para.69, added: 2002 c.40 Sch.16

Sch.B1 Part 8 para.69, varied: 2004 c.20 Sch.20 para.1, Sch.20 para.33

Sch.B1 Part 8 para.70, added: 2002 c.40 Sch.16

Sch.B1 Part 8 para.70, applied: 2004 c.20 Sch.20 para.2

Sch.B1 Part 8 para.70, disapplied: SI 2003/ 3226 Reg.8

Sch.B1 Part 8 para.70, varied: 2004 c.20 Sch.20 para.1, Sch.20 para.33

Sch.B1 Part 8 para.71, added: 2002 c.40 Sch.16

Sch.B1 Part 8 para.71, applied: 2004 c.20 Sch.20 para.2, Sch.20 para.35

Sch.B1 Part 8 para.71, disapplied: SI 2003/ 3226 Reg.8

Sch.B1 Part 8 para.71, varied: 2004 c.20 Sch.20 para.1, Sch.20 para.14, Sch.20 para.33

Sch.B1 Part 8 para.72, added: 2002 c.40 Sch.16

Sch.B1 Part 8 para.72, applied: 2004 c.20 Sch.20 para.2, Sch.20 para.35

Sch.B1 Part 8 para.72, varied: 2004 c.20 Sch.20 para.1, Sch.20 para.14, Sch.20 para.33

Sch.B1 Part 8 para.73, added: 2002 c.40 Sch.16

Sch.B1 Part 8 para.73, applied: 2004 c.20 Sch.20 para.2

Sch.B1 Part 8 para.73, varied: 2004 c.20 Sch.20 para.1, Sch.20 para.15, Sch.20 para.33

Sch.B1 Part 8 para.74, added: 2002 c.40 Sch.16

Sch.B1 Part 8 para.74, applied: 2004 c.20 Sch.20 para.2

Sch.B1 Part 8 para.74, varied: 2004 c.20 Sch.20 para.1, Sch.20 para.16, Sch.20 para.33

1986–cont.

45. Insolvency Act 1986–*cont.*

Sch.B1 Part 8 para.75, added: 2002 c.40 Sch.16

Sch.B1 Part 8 para.75, applied: 2004 c.20 Sch.20 para.2

Sch.B1 Part 8 para.75, varied: 2004 c.20 Sch.20 para.1, Sch.20 para.17, Sch.20 para.33

Sch.B1 Part 9 para.76, added: 2002 c.40 Sch.16

Sch.B1 Part 9 para.76, amended: SI 2002/ 1242 Sch.1 para.4, Sch.1 para.5

Sch.B1 Part 9 para.76, varied: 2004 c.20 Sch.20 para.1, Sch.20 para.33

Sch.B1 Part 9 para.77, added: 2002 c.40 Sch.16

Sch.B1 Part 9 para.77, varied: 2004 c.20 Sch.20 para.1, Sch.20 para.33

Sch.B1 Part 9 para.78, added: 2002 c.40 Sch.16

Sch.B1 Part 9 para.78, varied: 2004 c.20 Sch.20 para.1, Sch.20 para.33

Sch.B1 Part 9 para.79, added: 2002 c.40 Sch.16

Sch.B1 Part 9 para.79, amended: SI 2002/ 1242 Sch.1 para.6

Sch.B1 Part 9 para.79, applied: 2004 c.20 Sch.20 para.2

Sch.B1 Part 9 para.79, varied: 2004 c.20 Sch.20 para.1, Sch.20 para.18, Sch.20 para.33

Sch.B1 Part 9 para.80, added: 2002 c.40 Sch.16

Sch.B1 Part 9 para.80, varied: 2004 c.20 Sch.20 para.1, Sch.20 para.33

Sch.B1 Part 9 para.81, added: 2002 c.40 Sch.16

Sch.B1 Part 9 para.81, varied: 2004 c.20 Sch.20 para.1, Sch.20 para.33

Sch.B1 Part 9 para.82, added: 2002 c.40 Sch.16

Sch.B1 Part 9 para.82, amended: SI 2004/ 2326 Reg.73

Sch.B1 Part 9 para.82, varied: 2004 c.20 Sch.20 para.1, Sch.20 para.33

Sch.B1 Part 9 para.83, added: 2002 c.40 Sch.16

Sch.B1 Part 9 para.83, applied: 2004 c.20 Sch.20 para.2, SI 2004/353 Reg.14, Reg.34, SI 2004/1045 Reg.9, Reg.11, Reg.16, Reg.19, Reg.21

Sch.B1 Part 9 para.83, disapplied: 2004 c.20 Sch.20 para.35

Sch.B1 Part 9 para.83, referred to: SI 2004/ 353 Reg.9, Reg.18

Sch.B1 Part 9 para.83, varied: 2004 c.20 Sch.20 para.1, Sch.20 para.19, Sch.20 para.33

Sch.B1 Part 9 para.84, added: 2002 c.40 Sch.16

Sch.B1 Part 9 para.84, applied: 2004 c.20 Sch.20 para.2

1986–cont.

45. Insolvency Act 1986–*cont.*

Sch.B1 Part 9 para.84, disapplied: 2004 c.20
Sch.20 para.35

Sch.B1 Part 9 para.84, varied: 2004 c.20
Sch.20 para.1, Sch.20 para.20, Sch.20
para.33

Sch.B1 Part 9 para.85, added: 2002 c.40
Sch.16

Sch.B1 Part 9 para.85, applied: 2004 c.20
Sch.20 para.2

Sch.B1 Part 9 para.85, varied: 2004 c.20
Sch.20 para.1, Sch.20 para.33

Sch.B1 Part 9 para.86, added: 2002 c.40
Sch.16

Sch.B1 Part 9 para.86, applied: 2004 c.20
Sch.20 para.2, Sch.20 para.35, SI 2004/
353 Reg.36

Sch.B1 Part 9 para.86, varied: 2004 c.20
Sch.20 para.1, Sch.20 para.33

Sch.B1 Part 10 para.87, added: 2002 c.40
Sch.16

Sch.B1 Part 10 para.87, amended: 2002 c.40
Sch.16

Sch.B1 Part 10 para.87, applied: 2004 c.20
Sch.20 para.2

Sch.B1 Part 10 para.87, varied: 2004 c.20
Sch.20 para.1, Sch.20 para.21, Sch.20
para.33

Sch.B1 Part 10 para.88, added: 2002 c.40
Sch.16

Sch.B1 Part 10 para.88, applied: 2004 c.20
Sch.20 para.2

Sch.B1 Part 10 para.88, varied: 2004 c.20
Sch.20 para.1, Sch.20 para.33

Sch.B1 Part 10 para.89, added: 2002 c.40
Sch.16

Sch.B1 Part 10 para.89, amended: 2002 c.40
Sch.16

Sch.B1 Part 10 para.89, applied: 2004 c.20
Sch.20 para.2

Sch.B1 Part 10 para.89, varied: 2004 c.20
Sch.20 para.1, Sch.20 para.22, Sch.20
para.33

Sch.B1 Part 10 para.90, added: 2002 c.40
Sch.16

Sch.B1 Part 10 para.90, applied: 2004 c.20
Sch.20 para.2

Sch.B1 Part 10 para.90, varied: 2004 c.20
Sch.20 para.1, Sch.20 para.23, Sch.20
para.33

Sch.B1 Part 10 para.91, added: 2002 c.40
Sch.16

Sch.B1 Part 10 para.91, amended: SI 2002/
1242 Sch.1 para.7

Sch.B1 Part 10 para.91, applied: 2004 c.20
s.171, Sch.20 para.2

Sch.B1 Part 10 para.91, varied: 2004 c.20
Sch.20 para.1, Sch.20 para.24, Sch.20
para.33

Sch.B1 Part 10 para.92, added: 2002 c.40
Sch.16

1986–cont.

45. Insolvency Act 1986–*cont.*

Sch.B1 Part 10 para.92, varied: 2004 c.20
Sch.20 para.1, Sch.20 para.33

Sch.B1 Part 10 para.93, added: 2002 c.40
Sch.16

Sch.B1 Part 10 para.93, varied: 2004 c.20
Sch.20 para.1, Sch.20 para.33

Sch.B1 Part 10 para.94, added: 2002 c.40
Sch.16

Sch.B1 Part 10 para.94, varied: 2004 c.20
Sch.20 para.1, Sch.20 para.33

Sch.B1 Part 10 para.95, added: 2002 c.40
Sch.16

Sch.B1 Part 10 para.95, varied: 2004 c.20
Sch.20 para.1, Sch.20 para.33

Sch.B1 Part 10 para.96, added: 2002 c.40
Sch.16

Sch.B1 Part 10 para.96, varied: 2004 c.20
Sch.20 para.1, Sch.20 para.33

Sch.B1 Part 10 para.97, added: 2002 c.40
Sch.16

Sch.B1 Part 10 para.97, varied: 2004 c.20
Sch.20 para.1, Sch.20 para.33

Sch.B1 Part 10 para.98, added: 2002 c.40
Sch.16

Sch.B1 Part 10 para.98, applied: 2004 c.20
Sch.20 para.2

Sch.B1 Part 10 para.98, varied: 2004 c.20
Sch.20 para.1, Sch.20 para.25, Sch.20
para.33

Sch.B1 Part 10 para.99, added: 2002 c.40
Sch.16

Sch.B1 Part 10 para.99, applied: 2004 c.20
Sch.20 para.2

Sch.B1 Part 10 para.99, varied: 2004 c.20
Sch.20 para.1, Sch.20 para.26, Sch.20
para.33

Sch.B1 Part 11 para.100, added: 2002 c.40
Sch.16

Sch.B1 Part 11 para.100, applied: 2004 c.20
Sch.20 para.2

Sch.B1 Part 11 para.100, varied: 2004 c.20
Sch.20 para.1, Sch.20 para.27, Sch.20
para.33

Sch.B1 Part 11 para.101, added: 2002 c.40
Sch.16

Sch.B1 Part 11 para.101, applied: 2004 c.20
Sch.20 para.2

Sch.B1 Part 11 para.101, varied: 2004 c.20
Sch.20 para.1, Sch.20 para.28, Sch.20
para.33

Sch.B1 Part 11 para.102, added: 2002 c.40
Sch.16

Sch.B1 Part 11 para.102, applied: 2004 c.20
Sch.20 para.2

Sch.B1 Part 11 para.102, varied: 2004 c.20
Sch.20 para.1, Sch.20 para.33

Sch.B1 Part 11 para.103, added: 2002 c.40
Sch.16

Sch.B1 Part 11 para.103, applied: 2004 c.20
s.171, Sch.20 para.2

1986–cont.

45. Insolvency Act 1986–cont.
Sch.B1 Part 11 para.103, varied: 2004 c.20 Sch.20 para.1, Sch.20 para.29, Sch.20 para.33

Sch.B1 Part 11 para.104, added: 2002 c.40 Sch.16

Sch.B1 Part 11 para.104, applied: 2004 c.20 Sch.20 para.2

Sch.B1 Part 11 para.104, varied: 2004 c.20 Sch.20 para.1, Sch.20 para.33

Sch.B1 Part 11 para.105, added: 2002 c.40 Sch.16

Sch.B1 Part 11 para.105, applied: 2004 c.20 Sch.20 para.2

Sch.B1 Part 11 para.105, varied: 2004 c.20 Sch.20 para.1, Sch.20 para.33

Sch.B1 Part 11 para.106, added: 2002 c.40 Sch.16

Sch.B1 Part 11 para.106, applied: 2004 c.20 Sch.20 para.2

Sch.B1 Part 11 para.106, varied: 2004 c.20 Sch.20 para.1, Sch.20 para.30, Sch.20 para.33

Sch.B1 Part 11 para.107, added: 2002 c.40 Sch.16

Sch.B1 Part 11 para.107, applied: 2004 c.20 Sch.20 para.2

Sch.B1 Part 11 para.107, varied: 2004 c.20 Sch.20 para.1, Sch.20 para.33

Sch.B1 Part 11 para.108, added: 2002 c.40 Sch.16

Sch.B1 Part 11 para.108, varied: 2004 c.20 Sch.20 para.1, Sch.20 para.33

Sch.B1 Part 11 para.109, added: 2002 c.40 Sch.16

Sch.B1 Part 11 para.109, applied: 2004 c.20 Sch.20 para.2

Sch.B1 Part 11 para.109, varied: 2004 c.20 Sch.20 para.1, Sch.20 para.31, Sch.20 para.33

Sch.B1 Part 11 para.110, added: 2002 c.40 Sch.16

Sch.B1 Part 11 para.110, applied: 2004 c.20 Sch.20 para.2

Sch.B1 Part 11 para.110, varied: 2004 c.20 Sch.20 para.1, Sch.20 para.33

Sch.B1 Part 11 para.111, added: 2002 c.40 Sch.16

Sch.B1 Part 11 para.111, applied: 2004 c.20 Sch.20 para.2

Sch.B1 Part 11 para.111, varied: 2004 c.20 Sch.20 para.1, Sch.20 para.32, Sch.20 para.33

Sch.B1 Part 11 para.112, added: 2002 c.40 Sch.16

Sch.B1 Part 11 para.112, applied: 2004 c.20 Sch.20 para.2

Sch.B1 Part 11 para.112, varied: 2004 c.20 Sch.20 para.1, Sch.20 para.33

Sch.B1 Part 11 para.113, added: 2002 c.40 Sch.16

1986–cont.

45. Insolvency Act 1986–cont.
Sch.B1 Part 11 para.113, applied: 2004 c.20 Sch.20 para.2

Sch.B1 Part 11 para.113, varied: 2004 c.20 Sch.20 para.1, Sch.20 para.33

Sch.B1 Part 11 para.114, added: 2002 c.40 Sch.16

Sch.B1 Part 11 para.114, applied: 2004 c.20 Sch.20 para.2

Sch.B1 Part 11 para.114, varied: 2004 c.20 Sch.20 para.1, Sch.20 para.33

Sch.B1 Part 11 para.115, added: 2002 c.40 Sch.16

Sch.B1 Part 11 para.115, applied: 2004 c.20 Sch.20 para.2

Sch.B1 Part 11 para.115, varied: 2004 c.20 Sch.20 para.1, Sch.20 para.33

Sch.B1 Part 11 para.116, added: 2002 c.40 Sch.16

Sch.B1 Part 11 para.116, applied: 2004 c.20 Sch.20 para.2

Sch.B1 Part 11 para.116, varied: 2004 c.20 Sch.20 para.1, Sch.20 para.33

Sch.B1 Part 11 para.119, added: 2002 c.40 Sch.16

Sch.B1 Part 11 para.119, varied: 2004 c.20 Sch.20 para.1, Sch.20 para.33

Sch.1, applied: SI 2002/1242 Sch.1 para.8, 2004 c.20 Sch.20 para.36

Sch.1 para.1, varied: 2004 c.20 Sch.20 para.36

Sch.1 para.2, varied: 2004 c.20 Sch.20 para.36

Sch.1 para.3, varied: 2004 c.20 Sch.20 para.36

Sch.1 para.4, varied: 2004 c.20 Sch.20 para.36

Sch.1 para.5, varied: 2004 c.20 Sch.20 para.36

Sch.1 para.6, varied: 2004 c.20 Sch.20 para.36

Sch.1 para.7, varied: 2004 c.20 Sch.20 para.36

Sch.1 para.8, varied: 2004 c.20 Sch.20 para.36

Sch.1 para.9, varied: 2004 c.20 Sch.20 para.36

Sch.1 para.10, varied: 2004 c.20 Sch.20 para.36

Sch.1 para.11, varied: 2004 c.20 Sch.20 para.36

Sch.1 para.12, varied: 2004 c.20 Sch.20 para.36

Sch.1 para.13, see *Designer Room Ltd, Re* [2004] EWHC 720, [2004] 3 All E.R. 679 (Ch D), Rimer, J.

Sch.1 para.13, varied: 2004 c.20 Sch.20 para.36

Sch.1 para.14, varied: 2004 c.20 Sch.20 para.36

1986–cont.

45. Insolvency Act 1986–*cont.*

Sch.1 para.15, varied: 2004 c.20 Sch.20 para.36

Sch.1 para.16, varied: 2004 c.20 Sch.20 para.36

Sch.1 para.17, varied: 2004 c.20 Sch.20 para.36

Sch.1 para.18, see *TXU UK Ltd (In Administration), Re* [2002] EWHC 2784, [2003] 2 B.C.L.C. 341 (Ch D (Companies Ct)), Peter Smith, J.

Sch.1 para.18, varied: 2004 c.20 Sch.20 para.36

Sch.1 para.19, varied: 2004 c.20 Sch.20 para.36

Sch.1 para.20, varied: 2004 c.20 Sch.20 para.36

Sch.1 para.21, varied: 2004 c.20 Sch.20 para.36

Sch.1 para.22, varied: 2004 c.20 Sch.20 para.36

Sch.1 para.23, varied: 2004 c.20 Sch.20 para.36

Sch.2A, referred to: SI 2003/1832 Art.1

Sch.2A para.1, added: 2002 c.40 Sch.18

Sch.2A para.1, amended: SI 2003/1468 Art.2, Art.3

Sch.2A para.1, varied: SI 2003/1633 Sch.2 para.7

Sch.2A para.2, added: 2002 c.40 Sch.18

Sch.2A para.2, varied: SI 2003/1633 Sch.2 para.7

Sch.2A para.3, added: 2002 c.40 Sch.18

Sch.2A para.3, varied: SI 2003/1633 Sch.2 para.7

Sch.2A para.4, added: 2002 c.40 Sch.18

Sch.2A para.4, varied: SI 2003/1633 Sch.2 para.7

Sch.2A para.5, added: 2002 c.40 Sch.18

Sch.2A para.5, varied: SI 2003/1633 Sch.2 para.7

Sch.2A para.6, added: 2002 c.40 Sch.18

Sch.2A para.6, varied: SI 2003/1633 Sch.2 para.7

Sch.2A para.7, added: 2002 c.40 Sch.18

Sch.2A para.7, varied: SI 2003/1633 Sch.2 para.7

Sch.2A para.8, added: 2002 c.40 Sch.18

Sch.2A para.8, varied: SI 2003/1633 Sch.2 para.7

Sch.2A para.9, added: 2002 c.40 Sch.18

Sch.2A para.9, varied: SI 2003/1633 Sch.2 para.7

Sch.2A para.10, added: 2002 c.40 Sch.18

Sch.2A para.10, amended: 2003 c.21 Sch.17 para.82

Sch.2A para.10, repealed (in part): 2003 c.21 Sch.19

Sch.2A para.10, varied: SI 2003/1633 Sch.2 para.7

Sch.2A para.11, added: 2002 c.40 Sch.18

1986–cont.

45. Insolvency Act 1986–*cont.*

Sch.2A para.11, varied: SI 2003/1633 Sch.2 para.7

Sch.4A, applied: 2002 c.40 s.268, SI 2004/ 291 Reg.5, Sch.6 para.113, SI 2004/478 Reg.5, SI 2004/627 Reg.5, Sch.5 para.105, SSI 2004/115 Reg.5, Sch.5 para.101, SSI 2004/116 Reg.3, Sch.1 para.66, SSI 2004/468 Reg.10, Reg.21

Sch.4 Part I para.3A, added: 2002 c.40 s.253

Sch.4A para.1, added: 2002 c.40 Sch.20

Sch.4A para.2, added: 2002 c.40 Sch.20

Sch.4A para.3, added: 2002 c.40 Sch.20

Sch.4A para.4, added: 2002 c.40 Sch.20

Sch.4A para.5, added: 2002 c.40 Sch.20

Sch.4A para.6, added: 2002 c.40 Sch.20

Sch.4A para.7, added: 2002 c.40 Sch.20

Sch.4A para.8, added: 2002 c.40 Sch.20

Sch.4A para.9, added: 2002 c.40 Sch.20

Sch.4A para.10, added: 2002 c.40 Sch.20

Sch.4A para.11, added: 2002 c.40 Sch.20

Sch.4A para.12, added: 2002 c.40 Sch.20

Sch.5, applied: 2002 asp 17 s.40

Sch.5 Part I para.2A, added: 2002 c.40 s.262

Sch.6 para.1, amended: 2003 c.1 Sch.6 para.154

Sch.6 para.1, repealed: 2002 c.40 Sch.26

Sch.6 para.2, repealed: 2002 c.40 Sch.26

Sch.6 para.3, repealed: 2002 c.40 Sch.26

Sch.6 para.3A, repealed: 2002 c.40 Sch.26

Sch.6 para.3B, repealed: 2002 c.40 Sch.26

Sch.6 para.3C, repealed: 2002 c.40 Sch.26

Sch.6 para.3D, repealed: 2002 c.40 Sch.26

Sch.6 para.4, repealed: 2002 c.40 Sch.26

Sch.6 para.5, repealed: 2002 c.40 Sch.26

Sch.6 para.5A, repealed: 2002 c.40 Sch.26

Sch.6 para.5B, repealed: 2002 c.40 Sch.26

Sch.6 para.5C, repealed: 2002 c.40 Sch.26

Sch.6 para.6, repealed: 2002 c.40 Sch.26

Sch.6 para.7, repealed: 2002 c.40 Sch.26

Sch.8 para.2, amended: 2002 c.40 Sch.17 para.38

Sch.8 para.2, substituted: 2002 c.40 Sch.17 para.38

Sch.8 para.10, amended: 2002 c.40 Sch.17 para.38

Sch.8 para.14A, added: 2002 c.40 Sch.17 para.38

Sch.8 para.14B, added: 2002 c.40 Sch.17 para.38

Sch.8 para.16A, added: 2002 c.40 s.271

Sch.8 para.27, enabling: SI 2004/472

Sch.8 para.29, amended: 2002 c.40 Sch.17 para.38

Sch.9 para.8A, added: 2002 c.40 Sch.23 para.16

Sch.9 para.21A, added: 2002 c.40 s.271

Sch.9 para.29A, added: 2002 c.40 Sch.23 para.16

Sch.9 para.30, enabling: SI 2004/472

1986–cont.

45. Insolvency Act 1986–*cont.*

Sch.10, amended: 2002 c.40 Sch.17 para.39, Sch.26

Sch.13 Part I, amended: 2004 c.27 Sch.8

Sch.14, amended: 2002 c.9 Sch.13, 2003 c.17 Sch.7

46. Company Directors Disqualification Act 1986

see *Frewen v Secretary of State for Trade and Industry* [2002] EWHC 2688, [2003] 2 B.C.L.C. 305 (Ch D), Park, J.; see *Official Receiver v Zwirn* [2002] B.C.C. 760 (Ch D), Gabriel Moss Q.C.; see *Secretary of State for Trade and Industry v Blackwood* 2003 S.L.T. 120 (1 Div), Lord Cullen L.P., Lord Kirkwood, Lord Marnoch; see *Secretary of State for Trade and Industry v Lewis* [2003] B.C.C. 567 (Ch D), Neuberger, J.; see *Westminster Property Management Ltd (No.2), Re* [2001] EWCA Civ 111, [2002] B.C.C. 937 (CA), Chadwick, L.J.

applied: 2002 c.30 Sch.2 para.1, Sch.2 para.2, 2002 c.40 Sch.15, Sch.17 para.40, SI 2002/2376 Reg.2, SI 2002/2978 Sch.1 para.3, SI 2002/3038 Reg.5, SI 2002/3040 Reg.3, SI 2002/3150 Art.17, Art.19, Art.22, SI 2002/3177 Sch.1 para.3, 2003 c.20 Sch.4 para.7, SI 2003/348 Sch.6 para.7, SI 2003/506 Reg.3, SI 2003/1558 Sch.2 para.6, SI 2003/2773 Reg.3, SI 2003/3060 Reg.3, SI 2003/3190 Reg.4, SI 2003/3279 Reg.4, SI 2004/291 Reg.5, Sch.6 para.113, SI 2004/400 Reg.5, SI 2004/478 Reg.5, Sch.6 para.111, SI 2004/570 Reg.3, SI 2004/627 Reg.5, Sch.5 para.105, SI 2004/668 Reg.3, SR 2003/346 Art.5, Art.6, SSI 2004/115 Sch.5 para.101, SSI 2004/116 Reg.3, Sch.1 para.66, SSI 2004/386 Reg.7

referred to: 2003 c.43 Sch.4 para.67

see *Frewen v Secretary of State for Trade and Industry* [2002] EWHC 2688, [2003] 2 B.C.L.C. 305 (Ch D), Park, J.; see *Official Receiver v Zwirn* [2002] B.C.C. 760 (Ch D), Gabriel Moss Q.C.; see *Secretary of State for Trade and Industry v Blackwood* 2003 S.L.T. 120 (1 Div), Lord Cullen L.P., Lord Kirkwood, Lord Marnoch; see *Secretary of State for Trade and Industry v Lewis* [2003] B.C.C. 567 (Ch D), Neuberger, J.; see *Westminster Property Management Ltd (No.2), Re* [2001] EWCA Civ 111, [2002] B.C.C. 937 (CA), Chadwick, L.J.

added: 2002 c.40 s.204

s.1, see *R. v Ward (Michael Grainger)* [2001] EWCA Crim 1648, [2002] B.C.C. 953 (CA (Crim Div)), Rose, L.J.

s.1, amended: 2002 c.40 s.204

s.1, applied: SSI 2004/468 Reg.10

s.2, see *Cedarwood Productions Ltd, Re* [2001] EWCA Civ 1083, [2004] B.C.C. 65 (CA), Chadwick, L.J.

1986–cont.

46. Company Directors Disqualification Act 1986–*cont.*

s.2, amended: 2003 c.39 Sch.8 para.300

s.2, applied: SSI 2004/468 Reg.10

s.4, see *Adbury Estates Ltd, Re* [2003] B.C.C. 696 (Ch D), Jacob, J.; see *Denis Hilton Ltd, Re* [2002] 1 B.C.L.C. 302 (Ch D), Ferris, J.

s.5, amended: 2003 c.39 Sch.8 para.300

s.6, see *Cedarwood Productions Ltd, Re* [2001] EWCA Civ 1083, [2004] B.C.C. 65 (CA), Chadwick, L.J.; see *Official Receiver v Ireland* [2002] B.C.C. 428 (Ch D (Companies Court)), Lawrence Collins, J.; see *Pantmaenog Timber Co Ltd, Re* [2003] UKHL 49, [2004] 1 A.C. 158 (HL), Lord Millett; see *Secretary of State for Trade and Industry v Becker* [2002] EWHC 2200, [2003] 1 B.C.L.C. 555 (Ch D), Sir Donald Rattee; see *Secretary of State for Trade and Industry v Creegan* [2001] EWCA Civ 1742, [2002] 1 B.C.L.C. 99 (CA), Sir Martin Nourse; see *Secretary of State for Trade and Industry v Goldberg (No.2)* [2003] EWHC 2843, [2004] 1 B.C.L.C. 597 (Ch D), Lewison, J.; see *Secretary of State for Trade and Industry v Reynard* [2002] EWCA Civ 497, [2002] B.C.C. 813 (CA), Mummery, L.J.

s.6, amended: 2002 c.40 Sch.17 para.41

s.7, see *Blackspur Group Plc (No.3), Re* [2001] EWCA Civ 1595, [2002] 2 B.C.L.C. 263 (CA), Chadwick, L.J.; see *Official Receiver v Broad (Rights of Audience)* [2003] EWCA Civ 404, [2003] C.P. Rep. 59 (CA), Jonathan Parker, L.J.; see *Pantmaenog Timber Co Ltd, Re* [2003] UKHL 49, [2004] 1 A.C. 158 (HL), Lord Millett

s.7, amended: 2002 c.40 Sch.17 para.42

s.7, applied: 2004 c.35 s.87, s.201

s.8, see *Equity & Provident Ltd, Re* [2002] EWHC 186, [2002] 2 B.C.L.C. 78 (Ch D), Patten, J.; see *Secretary of State for Trade and Industry v Amiss* [2003] EWHC 532, [2003] 2 B.C.L.C. 206 (Ch D (Companies Ct)), Peter Smith, J.; see *Secretary of State for Trade and Industry v Bairstow (No.1)* [2003] EWCA Civ 321, [2004] Ch. 1 (CA), Sir Andrew Morritt V.C.

s.8, amended: 2004 c.27 Sch.2 para.28

s.8, applied: 2004 c.35 s.87, s.201

s.8, referred to: SI 2004/3322 Art.12

s.8A, see *Blackspur Group Plc (No.3), Re* [2001] EWCA Civ 1595, [2002] 2 B.C.L.C. 263 (CA), Chadwick, L.J.

s.8A, amended: 2002 c.40 s.204

s.9E, amended: 2003 c.20 Sch.2 para.19, 2003 c.21 Sch.17 para.83, 2003 c.37 Sch.7 para.25

s.11, see *R. v Doring (Petra)* [2002] EWCA Crim 1695, [2002] B.C.C. 838 (CA (Crim Div)), Buxton, L.J.

1986–cont.

46. Company Directors Disqualification Act 1986–*cont.*

s.11, amended: 2002 c.40 Sch.21 para.5

s.12B, added: SI 2004/1941 Art.2

s.13, amended: SI 2004/1941 Art.2

s.14, amended: SI 2004/1941 Art.2

s.15, amended: SI 2004/1941 Art.2

s.16, amended: 2002 c.40 s.204

s.17, see *Blackspur Group Plc (No.3), Re* [2001] EWCA Civ 1595, [2002] 2 B.C.L.C. 263 (CA), Chadwick, L.J.

s.17, amended: 2002 c.40 s.204

s.18, amended: 2002 c.40 s.204, SI 2004/1941 Art.2, Art.3

s.18, enabling: SI 2002/689, SI 2002/1834, SI 2004/1940

s.21, enabling: SI 2003/1367

s.22, see *Secretary of State for Trade and Industry v Becker* [2002] EWHC 2200, [2003] 1 B.C.L.C. 555 (Ch D), Sir Donald Rattee

s.22C, added: 2003 c.43 Sch.4 para.68

Sch.1 Part II para.10, amended: SI 2003/2096 Sch.1 para.12

47. Legal Aid (Scotland) Act 1986

applied: SSI 2002/494 Reg.24, 2003 c.21 s.119, 2003 c.41 s.183

Part II, applied: SSI 2003/179 Reg.3, Reg.4, Reg.5, Reg.6, Reg.7, Reg.8, Reg.10, Reg.11, Reg.12

s.4, amended: SSI 2004/493 Reg.2

s.4, varied: SSI 2002/494 Reg.18

s.6, see *Sutherland-Fisher v Law Society of Scotland* 2003 S.C. 562 (Ex Div), Lord Kirkwood, Lord Emslie, Lord Marnoch

s.8, see *Sutherland-Fisher v Law Society of Scotland* 2003 S.C. 562 (Ex Div), Lord Kirkwood, Lord Emslie, Lord Marnoch

s.8, amended: 2002 c.21 Sch.3 para.11, SSI 2002/144 Reg.3, SSI 2002/329 Reg.3, SSI 2003/180 Reg.3, Reg.4, SSI 2004/140 Reg.3, Reg.4

s.9, applied: SSI 2003/179 Reg.9

s.9, enabling: SSI 2002/37, SSI 2003/179, SSI 2003/500, SSI 2004/307, SSI 2004/308

s.11, amended: 2002 c.21 Sch.3 para.12, SSI 2002/144 Reg.4, SSI 2003/180 Reg.5, SSI 2004/140 Reg.5

s.11, applied: SSI 2002/144 Reg.5, SSI 2003/180 Reg.6, SSI 2004/140 Reg.6

s.11, disapplied: SSI 2003/179 Reg.9

s.11, enabling: SSI 2002/144, SSI 2003/180

s.12, enabling: SSI 2002/495, SSI 2003/163, SSI 2003/421, SSI 2004/49

s.13, enabling: SSI 2002/532

s.14, applied: SSI 2002/494 Reg.5, Reg.18, Reg.19, Reg.20, Reg.27, Reg.29, Reg.31

s.14, varied: SSI 2002/494 Reg.45

1986–cont.

47. Legal Aid (Scotland) Act 1986–*cont.*

s.15, amended: SSI 2002/145 Reg.3, SSI 2002/330 Reg.3, SSI 2003/182 Reg.3, Reg.4, SSI 2004/141 Reg.3, Reg.4, SSI 2004/493 Reg.3

s.15, applied: SSI 2002/494 Reg.18

s.15, varied: SSI 2002/494 Reg.45, Reg.46

s.17, amended: SSI 2002/145 Reg.4, SSI 2002/330 Reg.4, SSI 2003/182 Reg.5, Reg.6, SSI 2004/141 Reg.5, Reg.6

s.17, applied: SSI 2002/494 Reg.14, Reg.17, Reg.39, Reg.40, Reg.46, Sch.3 para.7, SSI 2004/468 Reg.3

s.17, disapplied: SSI 2002/494 Reg.33

s.17, referred to: SSI 2002/494 Sch.3 para.15

s.17, varied: SSI 2002/494 Reg.18, Reg.45, Reg.46

s.17, enabling: SSI 2002/494

s.18, see *Masson v Masson (Assessment of Liability) (No.2)* 2002 S.C.L.R. 382 (Sh Ct (Grampian, Highland and Islands)), DJ Cusine

s.18, applied: SSI 2002/494 Reg.32, Reg.34, Reg.36, Reg.38

s.19, applied: SSI 2002/494 Reg.32, Reg.37

s.19, enabling: SSI 2002/494

s.20, enabling: SSI 2002/494

s.22, amended: 2002 asp 9 s.2, 2004 asp 5 s.10

s.24, applied: SSI 2003/179 Reg.6

s.28A, amended: 2003 asp 7 s.73

s.28A, repealed (in part): 2003 asp 7 s.73

s.28A, enabling: SSI 2003/511

s.29, see *Glasgow City Council v H* 2003 S.L.T. (Sh Ct) 61 (Sh Pr), EF Bowen Q.C., Sheriff Principal

s.31, amended: 2002 asp 9 s.2, 2004 asp 5 s.10

s.31, enabling: SSI 2004/282

s.33, enabling: SSI 2002/246, SSI 2002/247, SSI 2002/440, SSI 2002/442, SSI 2002/496, SSI 2003/178, SSI 2003/249, SSI 2004/51, SSI 2004/126, SSI 2004/262, SSI 2004/263, SSI 2004/264, SSI 2004/281, SSI 2004/305, SSI 2004/316

s.34, amended: 2002 asp 11 Sch.6 para.9

s.36, enabling: SSI 2002/88, SSI 2002/144, SSI 2002/145, SSI 2002/247, SSI 2002/254, SSI 2002/329, SSI 2002/330, SSI 2002/441, SSI 2002/494, SSI 2003/49, SSI 2003/178, SSI 2003/180, SSI 2003/182, SSI 2003/249, SSI 2003/421, SSI 2003/486, SSI 2004/50, SSI 2004/140, SSI 2004/141, SSI 2004/281, SSI 2004/282, SSI 2004/308, SSI 2004/491, SSI 2004/492, SSI 2004/493

s.37, applied: SSI 2002/37, SSI 2002/144, SSI 2002/145, SSI 2002/329, SSI 2002/330, SSI 2002/532, SSI 2003/179, SSI 2003/180, SSI 2003/182, SSI 2003/500, SSI 2004/140, SSI 2004/141, SSI 2004/307, SSI 2004/308

1986–cont.

47. Legal Aid (Scotland) Act 1986–*cont.*
s.37, enabling: SSI 2002/37, SSI 2002/144, SSI 2002/494, SSI 2002/495, SSI 2002/532, SSI 2003/163, SSI 2003/179, SSI 2003/180, SSI 2003/500
s.41A, enabling: SSI 2002/442, SSI 2003/249, SSI 2004/51, SSI 2004/126, SSI 2004/263
s.42, applied: SSI 2002/494 Reg.11
s.42, enabling: SSI 2002/494, SSI 2003/49, SSI 2003/163, SSI 2003/421, SSI 2004/491
s.43A, amended: 2003 asp 4 Sch.4 para.9
Sch.2 Part I para.1, amended: SSI 2002/532 Reg.2
Sch.2 Part II para.4, amended: 2002 asp 17 s.44
Sch.2 Part II para.5, amended: 2002 asp 17 s.44

49. Agriculture Act 1986
s.4, repealed (in part): 2004 c.14 Sch.1 Part 2
s.5, repealed (in part): 2004 c.14 Sch.1 Part 2
s.6, applied: SI 2002/2843 Art.6
s.8, repealed (in part): 2004 c.14 Sch.1 Part 2
s.9, repealed: 2004 c.14 Sch.1 Part 2
s.10, repealed: 2004 c.14 Sch.1 Part 2
s.12, repealed: 2004 c.14 Sch.1 Part 2
s.16, amended: 2003 asp 11 Sch.1 para.9
s.17, amended: SI 2002/794 Sch.1 para.28
s.18, amended: SI 2002/794 Sch.1 para.29, Sch.2
s.18, applied: SI 2003/2261 Sch.3 Part I
s.18, enabling: SI 2004/115
s.24, amended: 2004 c.14 Sch.1 Part 2
Sch.1 Part III para.18, amended: SI 2002/794 Sch.1 para.30
Sch.2 para.2, amended: SSI 2003/583 Sch.1 para.9
Sch.2 para.7, amended: 2003 asp 11 Sch.1 para.10
Sch.2 para.10, amended: 2003 asp 11 Sch.1 para.10
Sch.2 para.11, amended: 2003 asp 11 Sch.1 para.10

50. Social Security Act 1986
s.30, repealed: 2004 c.14 Sch.1 Part 10
s.63, applied: SI 2002/668 Art.4, SI 2003/526 Art.4
s.63, varied: SI 2004/552 Art.4
Sch.10 Part I para.52, repealed: 2004 c.14 Sch.1 Part 10
Sch.10 Part I para.61, repealed: 2002 c.21 Sch.6

51. British Council and Commonwealth Institute Superannuation Act 1986
s.1, amended: 2002 c.39 Sch.1 para.4
s.1, repealed (in part): 2002 c.39 Sch.3
s.2, amended: 2002 c.39 Sch.3

53. Building Societies Act 1986
Commencement Orders: 2004 c.14 Sch.1 Part 17

1986–cont.

53. Building Societies Act 1986–*cont.*
applied: SI 2002/3150 Sch.1 para.7, 2004 c.35 Sch.3, Sch.8
referred to: SI 2002/3152 Art.4
s.6, enabling: SI 2004/3200
s.7, varied: SI 2003/1633 Sch.2 para.11
s.7, enabling: SI 2004/3200
s.8, varied: SI 2003/1633 Sch.2 para.11
s.55, applied: SI 2002/3152 Sch.2 para.13, SI 2003/3075 Reg.26
s.55, varied: SI 2002/3152 Sch.2 para.13
s.56, applied: SI 2003/3075 Reg.26
s.57, varied: SI 2002/3152 Sch.2 para.13
s.60, amended: SI 2003/404 Art.2, Art.29, Art.30
s.61, amended: SI 2003/404 Art.3, Art.30
s.66A, amended: SI 2003/404 Art.30
s.68, amended: SI 2003/404 Art.4
s.69, amended: SI 2003/404 Art.5, 2004 c.14 Sch.2 para.18
s.70, amended: 2004 c.33 Sch.27 para.123
s.70, varied: 2004 c.33 Sch.21 para.29
s.73, enabling: SI 2004/3199
s.75, enabling: SI 2004/3199
s.76, amended: SI 2003/404 Art.6, SI 2004/355 Art.3
s.81, amended: SI 2003/404 Art.7
s.92A, amended: SI 2003/404 Art.30
s.97, applied: 2002 c.23 Sch.29 para.90, 2003 c.14 s.64
s.109A, added: SI 2003/2867 Sch.1 para.14
s.115, amended: SI 2003/404 Art.8
s.119, amended: SI 2003/404 Art.9, SI 2004/1862 Reg.14
s.119, applied: 2002 c.40 s.249
s.119, repealed (in part): 2004 c.14 Sch.1 Part 17
s.122, amended: 2004 c.14 Sch.1 Part 17
s.124, repealed: 2004 c.14 Sch.1 Part 17
s.126, amended: 2004 c.14 Sch.1 Part 17
s.126, repealed (in part): 2004 c.14 Sch.1 Part 17
Sch.2 Part I para.3, amended: SI 2003/404 Art.10
Sch.2 Part I para.9, amended: SI 2003/404 Art.11
Sch.2 Part I para.13, amended: SI 2003/404 Art.12
Sch.2 Part II para.17, amended: SI 2003/404 Art.30
Sch.2 Part III para.20A, amended: SI 2003/404 Art.13, Art.30
Sch.2 Part III para.21, amended: SI 2003/404 Art.29
Sch.2 Part III para.22, amended: SI 2003/404 Art.29
Sch.2 Part III para.22A, added: SI 2003/404 Art.14
Sch.2 Part III para.22B, added: SI 2003/404 Art.14

CAP.

1986–cont.

53. Building Societies Act 1986–*cont.*

Sch.2 Part III para.23, amended: SI 2003/404 Art.29, Art.30

Sch.2 Part III para.24, amended: SI 2003/404 Art.15, Art.29

Sch.2 Part III para.25, amended: SI 2003/404 Art.29

Sch.2 Part III para.27, amended: SI 2003/404 Art.30

Sch.2 Part III para.31, amended: SI 2003/404 Art.30

Sch.2 Part III para.32, amended: SI 2003/404 Art.16

Sch.2 Part III para.33, amended: SI 2003/404 Art.17, Art.30

Sch.2 Part III para.33A, added: SI 2003/404 Art.18

Sch.2 Part III para.34, amended: SI 2003/404 Art.19, Art.29, Art.30

Sch.2 Part III para.35, amended: SI 2003/404 Art.30

Sch.2A para.1, amended: 2002 c.9 Sch.11 para.19, Sch.13

Sch.2A para.1, repealed (in part): 2002 c.9 Sch.13

Sch.8A Part I para.3, amended: SI 2003/404 Art.20

Sch.8A Part II para.9, amended: SI 2003/404 Art.21

Sch.11 para.4, amended: SI 2003/404 Art.22

Sch.11 para.7, amended: SI 2003/404 Art.23

Sch.11 para.8, amended: SI 2003/404 Art.24

Sch.15A Part I para.1, amended: SI 2002/3152 Sch.2 para.14

Sch.15A Part III para.30, amended: SI 2002/3152 Sch.2 para.14

Sch.15A Part III para.30A, added: SI 2002/3152 Sch.2 para.14

Sch.15A Part III para.31A, added: SI 2002/3152 Sch.2 para.14

Sch.16 Part I para.1, amended: SI 2003/404 Art.25

Sch.16 Part II para.4, amended: SI 2003/404 Art.26

Sch.16 Part II para.6, substituted: SI 2003/404 Art.26

Sch.17 Part I para.4, amended: SI 2003/404 Art.27

Sch.17 Part IA para.5C, substituted: SI 2003/404 Art.28

Sch.17 Part IA para.5E, substituted: SI 2003/404 Art.28

Sch.18 Part I para.2, repealed: 2002 c.9 Sch.13

Sch.18 Part I para.3, repealed: 2004 c.14 Sch.1 Part 17

Sch.18 Part I para.19, repealed (in part): 2004 c.14 Sch.1 Part 17

Sch.21 para.1, repealed: 2004 c.14 Sch.1 Part 17

CAP.

1986–cont.

53. Building Societies Act 1986–*cont.*

Sch.21 para.2, repealed: 2004 c.14 Sch.1 Part 17

Sch.21 para.3, repealed: 2004 c.14 Sch.1 Part 17

Sch.21 para.4, repealed: 2004 c.14 Sch.1 Part 17

Sch.21 para.5, repealed: 2004 c.14 Sch.1 Part 17

Sch.21 para.6, repealed: 2004 c.14 Sch.1 Part 17

Sch.21 para.7, repealed: 2004 c.14 Sch.1 Part 17

Sch.21 para.8, repealed: 2004 c.14 Sch.1 Part 17

Sch.21 para.9, repealed (in part): 2002 c.9 Sch.13, 2004 c.14 Sch.1 Part 17

Sch.21 para.10, repealed: 2004 c.14 Sch.1 Part 17

Sch.21 para.11, repealed: 2004 c.14 Sch.1 Part 17

Sch.21 para.12, repealed: 2004 c.14 Sch.1 Part 17

Sch.21 para.13, repealed: 2004 c.14 Sch.1 Part 17

Sch.21 para.14, repealed: 2004 c.14 Sch.1 Part 17

54. Rate Support Grants Act 1986

repealed: 2004 c.14 Sch.1 Part 10

55. Family Law Act 1986

referred to: 2002 c.38 Sch.3 para.46

s.1, amended: 2002 c.8 s.1, 2002 c.38 Sch.3 para.47

s.2, amended: 2002 c.38 Sch.3 para.48

s.2, applied: 2004 c.33 Sch.6 para.47

s.2A, see *B (A Child) (Court's Jurisdiction), Re* [2004] EWCA Civ 681, [2004] 2 F.L.R. 741 (CA), Arden, L.J.

s.3, amended: 2002 c.8 s.1

s.6, amended: 2002 c.8 s.1

s.10, amended: 2002 c.8 s.1

s.11, amended: 2002 c.8 s.1

s.13, see *B (A Child) (Court's Jurisdiction), Re* [2004] EWCA Civ 681, [2004] 2 F.L.R. 741 (CA), Arden, L.J.

s.13, amended: 2002 c.8 s.1

s.14, see *M v M* 2002 S.C. 103 (Ex Div), Lord Prosser, Lord Coulsfield, Lady Paton

s.15, see *M v M* 2002 S.C. 103 (Ex Div), Lord Prosser, Lord Coulsfield, Lady Paton

s.15, amended: 2002 c.8 s.1

s.20, amended: 2002 c.8 s.1

s.23, amended: 2002 c.8 s.1

s.25, amended: 2002 c.8 s.1

s.26, amended: 2002 c.8 s.1

s.27, amended: 2002 c.8 s.1

s.28, amended: 2002 c.8 s.1

s.31, amended: 2002 c.8 s.1

s.32, amended: 2002 c.8 s.1

s.33, amended: 2002 c.8 s.1, 2004 c.33 Sch.27 para.124

1986–cont.

55. Family Law Act 1986–*cont.*

s.35, amended: 2002 c.8 s.1

s.36, amended: 2002 c.8 s.1

s.37, amended: 2002 c.8 s.1

s.41, see *A (Abduction: Declaration of Wrongful Removal), Re* [2002] N.I. 114 (Fam Div (NI)), Gillen, J.; see *B (A Child) (Court's Jurisdiction), Re* [2004] EWCA Civ 681, [2004] 2 F.L.R. 741 (CA), Arden, L.J.; see *S (A Child) (Abduction: Residence Order), Re* [2002] EWCA Civ 1941, [2003] 1 F.L.R. 1008 (CA), Thorpe, L.J.

s.44, see *Sulaiman v Juffali* [2002] 1 F.L.R. 479 (Fam Div), Munby, J.

s.45, see *Sulaiman v Juffali* [2002] 1 F.L.R. 479 (Fam Div), Munby, J.

s.46, see *Baig v Entry Clearance Officer, Islamabad* [2002] UKIAT 4229, [2003] I.N.L.R. 117 (IAT), CMG Ockelton; see *Emin v Yeldag* [2002] 1 F.L.R. 956 (Fam Div), Sumner, J.

s.49, see *Emin v Yeldag* [2002] 1 F.L.R. 956 (Fam Div), Sumner, J.

s.50, amended: 2004 c.33 Sch.27 para.125

s.55A, see *L Teaching Hospitals NHS Trust v A* [2003] EWHC 259, [2003] 1 F.L.R. 1091 (QBD), Dame Elizabeth Butler-Sloss (President)

s.57, amended: 2002 c.38 Sch.3 para.49

s.59, applied: 2002 c.38 s.88

s.60, applied: 2002 c.38 s.88

56. Parliamentary Constituencies Act 1986

applied: SI 2002/2626 Sch.1, 2003 c.14 s.67, SI 2003/1887 Sch.1, SI 2004/1204 Art.1

s.3, applied: 2004 c.13 Sch.3 para.1

s.6A, added: SI 2002/2626 Sch.2 para.14

s.6A, repealed: SI 2003/1887 Sch.2 para.7

Sch.1, applied: SI 2003/409 Sch.1 Part I

Sch.1 para.3, disapplied: SI 2003/1887 Sch.1

57. Public Trustee and Administration of Funds Act 1986

s.3, repealed (in part): 2002 c.35 s.1

s.4, repealed: 2004 c.14 Sch.1 Part 1, Sch.1 Part 17

s.6, repealed (in part): 2004 c.14 Sch.1 Part 17, Sch.1 Part 1

59. Sex Discrimination Act 1986

applied: SI 2004/1861 Sch.1 para.61

s.5, repealed: 2003 c.17 Sch.6 para.105, Sch.7

s.6, applied: SI 2004/1861 Sch.1 para.52

60. Financial Services Act 1986

see *Public Trustee (Gordon's Executor) v Williams* [2002] W.T.L.R. 45 (Ch D), Neuberger, J.; see *R. (on the application of Davies) v Financial Services Authority* [2003] EWCA Civ 1128, [2004] 1 W.L.R. 185 (CA), Mummery, L.J.

applied: 2002 c.40 Sch.15, SI 2002/2848 Sch.1 Part I

1986–cont.

60. Financial Services Act 1986–*cont.*

s.1, see *CR Sugar Trading Ltd (In Administration) v China National Sugar Corp & Alcohol Group* [2003] EWHC 79, [2003] 1 Lloyd's Rep. 279 (QBD (Comm Ct)), David Steel, J.

s.5, see *CR Sugar Trading Ltd (In Administration) v China National Sugar Corp & Alcohol Group* [2003] EWHC 79, [2003] 1 Lloyd's Rep. 279 (QBD (Comm Ct)), David Steel, J.

s.45, applied: SI 2003/3075 Reg.2

s.47, see *R. (on the application of Young) v Central Criminal Court* [2002] EWHC 548, [2002] 2 Cr. App. R. 12 (QBD (Admin Ct)), Rose, L.J.

s.75, see *Russell-Cooke Trust Co v Prentis (No.1)* [2002] EWHC 2227, [2003] 2 All E.R. 478 (Ch D), Lindsay, J.

s.87, applied: SI 2003/1181 Art.4

s.172, see *Winpar Holdings Ltd v Joseph Holt Group Plc* [2001] EWCA Civ 770, [2002] B.C.C. 174 (CA), Peter Gibson, L.J.

Sch.1 Part I para.8 note 4, see *CR Sugar Trading Ltd (In Administration) v China National Sugar Corp & Alcohol Group* [2003] EWHC 79, [2003] 1 Lloyd's Rep. 279 (QBD (Comm Ct)), David Steel, J.

61. Education (No.2) Act 1986

s.49, applied: SI 2002/1394

s.49, repealed (in part): 2002 c.32 Sch.22 Part 3

s.49, enabling: SI 2002/1394

s.50, amended: 2002 c.32 Sch.22 Part 3

s.50, applied: SI 2002/509 Reg.3, SI 2002/1330 Sch.3 para.1, SI 2002/3200 Sch.3 para.1, SI 2003/1994 Sch.3 para.1, SR 2002/224 Sch.3 para.1, SR 2002/265 Sch.7 para.1

s.50, disapplied: SI 2002/195 Sch.3 para.1

s.50, repealed (in part): 2002 c.32 s.18, Sch.22 Part 3

s.50, enabling: SI 2002/508, SI 2002/509, SI 2002/756, SI 2002/1137, SI 2002/3005, SI 2003/3094

s.63, enabling: SI 2002/508, SI 2002/509, SI 2002/756, SI 2002/1137, SI 2002/1394, SI 2002/3005, SI 2003/3094

62. Salmon Act 1986

s.1, repealed (in part): 2003 asp 15 Sch.4 Part 2

s.1, enabling: SSI 2002/138, SSI 2003/615

s.2, applied: SSI 2002/138 Sch.2

s.2, repealed (in part): 2003 asp 15 Sch.4 Part 2

s.2, enabling: SSI 2002/138, SSI 2003/615

s.3, applied: SSI 2002/138 Sch.2

s.3, repealed (in part): 2003 asp 15 Sch.4 Part 2

s.5, repealed (in part): 2003 asp 15 Sch.4 Part 2

1986–cont.

62. Salmon Act 1986–*cont.*

s.6, repealed (in part): 2003 asp 15 Sch.4 Part 2

s.7, repealed (in part): 2003 asp 15 Sch.4 Part 2

s.8, applied: SSI 2002/11, SSI 2003/230, SSI 2003/614, SSI 2004/259

s.8, repealed (in part): 2003 asp 15 Sch.4 Part 2

s.8, enabling: SSI 2002/11, SSI 2003/230, SSI 2003/614, SSI 2004/259

s.9, repealed (in part): 2003 asp 15 Sch.4 Part 2

s.10, repealed (in part): 2003 asp 15 Sch.4 Part 2

s.10A, referred to: SSI 2002/418

s.10A, repealed (in part): 2003 asp 15 Sch.4 Part 2

s.10A, enabling: SSI 2002/418

s.10B, repealed (in part): 2003 asp 15 Sch.4 Part 2

s.10C, repealed (in part): 2003 asp 15 Sch.4 Part 2

s.10D, applied: SSI 2002/418

s.10D, repealed (in part): 2003 asp 15 Sch.4 Part 2

s.10E, repealed (in part): 2003 asp 15 Sch.4 Part 2

s.11, repealed (in part): 2003 asp 15 Sch.4 Part 2

s.12, repealed (in part): 2003 asp 15 Sch.4 Part 2

s.13, repealed (in part): 2003 asp 15 Sch.4 Part 2

s.14, repealed (in part): 2003 asp 15 Sch.4 Part 2

s.15, repealed (in part): 2003 asp 15 Sch.4 Part 2

s.16, repealed (in part): 2003 asp 15 Sch.4 Part 2

s.17, repealed (in part): 2003 asp 15 Sch.4 Part 2

s.18, repealed (in part): 2003 asp 15 Sch.4 Part 2

s.19, repealed (in part): 2003 asp 15 Sch.4 Part 2

s.40, applied: SSI 2004/474 Sch.1

Sch.1, applied: SSI 2002/418, SSI 2003/615

Sch.1, enabling: SSI 2003/615

Sch.1 para.1, repealed (in part): 2003 asp 15 Sch.4 Part 2

Sch.1 para.2, repealed (in part): 2003 asp 15 Sch.4 Part 2

Sch.1 para.3, applied: SSI 2002/11, SSI 2002/138, SSI 2003/230, SSI 2003/614, SSI 2004/259

Sch.1 para.3, repealed (in part): 2003 asp 15 Sch.4 Part 2

Sch.1 para.3, enabling: SSI 2002/11

1986–cont.

62. Salmon Act 1986–*cont.*

Sch.1 para.4, applied: SSI 2002/11, SSI 2002/138, SSI 2003/230, SSI 2003/614, SSI 2004/259

Sch.1 para.4, repealed (in part): 2003 asp 15 Sch.4 Part 2

Sch.1 para.4, enabling: SSI 2002/11

Sch.1 para.5, repealed (in part): 2003 asp 15 Sch.4 Part 2

Sch.1 para.6, repealed (in part): 2003 asp 15 Sch.4 Part 2

Sch.1 para.7, repealed (in part): 2003 asp 15 Sch.4 Part 2

Sch.1 para.8, repealed (in part): 2003 asp 15 Sch.4 Part 2

Sch.1 para.9, repealed (in part): 2003 asp 15 Sch.4 Part 2

Sch.2 Part I para.1, repealed (in part): 2003 asp 15 Sch.4 Part 2

Sch.2 Part I para.2, repealed (in part): 2003 asp 15 Sch.4 Part 2

Sch.2 Part I para.3, repealed (in part): 2003 asp 15 Sch.4 Part 2

Sch.2 Part I para.4, repealed (in part): 2003 asp 15 Sch.4 Part 2

Sch.2 Part I para.5, repealed (in part): 2003 asp 15 Sch.4 Part 2

Sch.2 Part II para.6, repealed (in part): 2003 asp 15 Sch.4 Part 2

Sch.3 para.1, repealed (in part): 2003 asp 15 Sch.4 Part 2

Sch.3 para.2, repealed (in part): 2003 asp 15 Sch.4 Part 2

Sch.3 para.3, repealed (in part): 2003 asp 15 Sch.4 Part 2

Sch.3 para.4, repealed (in part): 2003 asp 15 Sch.4 Part 2

Sch.3 para.5, repealed (in part): 2003 asp 15 Sch.4 Part 2

Sch.3 para.6, repealed (in part): 2003 asp 15 Sch.4 Part 2

Sch.3 para.7, repealed (in part): 2003 asp 15 Sch.4 Part 2

Sch.3 para.8, repealed (in part): 2003 asp 15 Sch.4 Part 2

Sch.3 para.9, repealed (in part): 2003 asp 15 Sch.4 Part 2

Sch.4 para.1, repealed (in part): 2003 asp 15 Sch.4 Part 2

Sch.4 para.2, repealed (in part): 2003 asp 15 Sch.4 Part 2

Sch.4 para.3, repealed (in part): 2003 asp 15 Sch.4 Part 2

Sch.4 para.4, repealed (in part): 2003 asp 15 Sch.4 Part 2

Sch.4 para.5, repealed (in part): 2003 asp 15 Sch.4 Part 2

Sch.4 para.7, repealed (in part): 2003 asp 15 Sch.4 Part 2

Sch.4 para.8, repealed (in part): 2003 asp 15 Sch.4 Part 2

CAP.

1986–cont.

62. Salmon Act 1986–*cont.*

Sch.4 para.9, repealed (in part): 2003 asp 15 Sch.4 Part 2

Sch.4 para.10, repealed (in part): 2003 asp 15 Sch.4 Part 2

Sch.4 para.12, repealed (in part): 2003 asp 15 Sch.4 Part 2

Sch.4 para.15, repealed (in part): 2003 asp 15 Sch.4 Part 2

63. Housing and Planning Act 1986

s.42, applied: SI 2002/2780, SI 2002/2780 Reg.3

s.42, enabling: SI 2002/2780

Sch.5 Part I para.9, repealed (in part): 2002 c.15 Sch.14

Sch.5 Part II para.18, amended: 2003 c.14 Sch.20 para.3

64. Public Order Act 1986

s.1, see *R. v Ghafoor (Imran Hussain)* [2002] EWCA Crim 1857, [2003] 1 Cr. App. R. (S.) 84 (CA (Crim Div)), Dyson, L.J.

s.1, applied: 2003 c.42 Sch.5 para.45, 2003 c.44 Sch.15 para.44, SI 2004/1910 Sch.2

s.2, see *Taylor v Chief Constable of Thames Valley* [2004] EWCA Civ 858, [2004] 1 W.L.R. 3155 (CA), Sir Andrew Morritt V.C.

s.2, applied: 2003 c.42 Sch.5 para.46, 2003 c.44 Sch.15 para.45, SI 2004/1910 Sch.2

s.3, see *I v DPP* [2001] UKHL 10, [2002] 1 A.C. 285 (HL), Lord Hutton

s.3, applied: 2003 c.42 Sch.5 para.47, 2003 c.44 Sch.15 para.46, SI 2004/1910 Sch.2

s.4, see *R. v Clark (Raymond John)* [2003] EWCA Crim 3143, [2004] 2 Cr. App. R. (S.) 1 (CA (Crim Div)), May, L.J.; see *R. v O'Keefe (Matthew)* [2003] EWCA Crim 2629, [2004] 1 Cr. App. R. (S.) 67 (CA (Crim Div)), Jackson, J.

s.4, applied: 2003 c.42 Sch.5 para.59, 2003 c.44 Sch.15 para.59

s.4A, applied: 2003 c.42 Sch.5 para.59, 2003 c.44 Sch.15 para.59

s.5, see *Hammond v DPP* [2004] EWHC 69, (2004) 168 J.P. 601 (QBD (Admin Ct)), May, L.J.; see *Percy v DPP* [2001] EWHC Admin 1125, (2002) 166 J.P. 93 (QBD (Admin Ct)), Hallett, J.; see *R. (on the application of Aru) v Chief Constable of Merseyside* [2004] EWCA Civ 199, [2004] 1 W.L.R. 1697 (CA), Waller, L.J.

s.5, applied: SI 2002/1837 Sch.1 Part I

s.11, applied: 2003 c.38 s.30

s.11, referred to: 2003 c.38 s.30

s.12, amended: 2003 c.44 Sch.26 para.37

s.13, amended: 2003 c.44 Sch.26 para.37

s.14, amended: 2003 c.44 Sch.26 para.37

s.14A, amended: 2003 asp 2 Sch.2 para.9

s.14B, amended: 2003 c.44 Sch.26 para.37

s.16, amended: 2003 c.38 s.57

s.25, applied: SI 2003/336 Sch.1 Part 2

Sch.1 Part I para.4, repealed: 2003 c.17 Sch.7

CAP.

1986–cont.

64. Public Order Act 1986–*cont.*

Sch.1 Part I para.5, repealed: 2003 c.17 Sch.7

Sch.1 Part I para.7, repealed (in part): 2003 c.17 Sch.7

Sch.1 Part I para.8, repealed: 2003 c.17 Sch.7

ss.5, see *R. (on the application of Aru) v Chief Constable of Merseyside* [2004] EWCA Civ 199, [2004] 1 W.L.R. 1697 (CA), Waller, L.J.

65. Housing (Scotland) Act 1986

s.19, repealed: 2003 asp 8 Sch.6 para.16

Sch.2 para.1, repealed: 2003 asp 8 Sch.6 para.16

1987

xxi. Aberdeen Harbour Order Confirmation Act 1987

s.3, repealed: SSI 2002/310 Sch.3

s.6, repealed: SSI 2002/310 Sch.3

s.9, repealed (in part): SSI 2002/310 Sch.3

xx. Essex Act 1987

applied: SI 2003/1688

s.6, applied: 2004 c.18 Sch.7 para.4

s.86, applied: SI 2003/1688

3. Coal Industry Act 1987

s.7, repealed (in part): 2004 c.14 Sch.1 Part 5

Sch.1 para.37, repealed: 2002 c.1 Sch.4

4. Ministry of Defence Police Act 1987

s.1, amended: 2002 c.30 s.79

s.1, applied: 2002 c.26 Sch.4 para.1, SI 2004/672 Art.2

s.1, referred to: SI 2003/527 Reg.42, SSI 2004/257 Reg.42

s.1, enabling: SI 2004/652, SI 2004/653, SI 2004/654

s.2, amended: 2003 c.20 Sch.5 para.4, 2004 c.20 Sch.14 para.5, Sch.23 Part 1

s.2, applied: SI 2004/118 Art.3

s.2, varied: 2003 c.20 Sch.5 para.4

s.2A, amended: 2003 c.20 Sch.5 para.4, 2004 c.20 Sch.14 para.5, Sch.23 Part 1

s.2A, varied: 2003 c.20 Sch.5 para.4

s.2B, added: 2002 c.30 s.78

s.2B, amended: 2003 c.20 Sch.5 para.4, 2004 c.20 Sch.14 para.5, Sch.23 Part 1

s.2B, varied: 2003 c.20 Sch.5 para.4

s.3, referred to: 2004 c.20 s.64, s.65

s.3A, added: 2002 c.30 s.79

s.3A, enabling: SI 2004/653, SI 2004/654

s.4, applied: SI 2004/653 Reg.29

s.4, referred to: SI 2004/653 Reg.12

s.4, enabling: SI 2004/653

s.4A, added: 2002 c.30 s.79

s.4A, enabling: SI 2004/652

s.4B, added: 2002 c.30 s.80

s.4C, added: 2002 c.30 s.80

s.6A, added: 2002 c.30 s.79

s.6A, enabling: SI 2004/652, SI 2004/653, SI 2004/654

s.7, repealed (in part): 2004 c.20 Sch.23 Part 1

1987–cont.

5. Rate Support Grants Act 1987
repealed: 2004 c.14 Sch.1 Part 10

6. Local Government Finance Act 1987
repealed: 2004 c.14 Sch.1 Part 10

11. Gaming (Amendment) Act 1987
s.1, repealed (in part): 2004 c.14 Sch.1 Part 17
s.2, repealed (in part): 2004 c.14 Sch.1 Part 17

12. Petroleum Act 1987
s.21, applied: SI 2002/1063 Art.2, SI 2002/2467 Art.2, SI 2003/845 Art.2, SI 2003/2743 Art.2, SI 2004/343 Art.2, SI 2004/1409 Art.2, SI 2004/1746 Art.2, SI 2004/2641 Art.2
s.22, enabling: SI 2002/1063, SI 2002/2467, SI 2003/845, SI 2003/1710, SI 2003/2743, SI 2004/343, SI 2004/1409, SI 2004/1746, SI 2004/2641
s.23, applied: 2004 c.20 s.86
s.24, applied: SI 2002/1063, SI 2002/2467, SI 2003/845, SI 2003/1710, SI 2003/2743, SI 2004/343, SI 2004/1409, SI 2004/1746, SI 2004/2641

14. Recognition of Trusts Act 1987
s.1, see *C v C (Financial Provision: Post Nuptial Settlements)* [2004] EWHC 742, [2004] Fam. 141 (Fam Div), Wilson, J.

15. Reverter of Sites Act 1987
see *Bath and Wells Diocesan Board of Finance v Jenkinson* [2002] EWHC 218, [2003] Ch. 89 (Ch D), Etherton, J.; see *Fraser v Canterbury Diocesan Board of Finance (No.2)* [2003] EWHC 1075, [2003] W.T.L.R. 1125 (Ch D), Lewison, J.

16. Finance Act 1987
s.50, amended: 2003 c.14 Sch.20 para.3
s.62, applied: SI 2003/2718 Sch.1 para.11
s.65, applied: SI 2003/2718 Sch.1 para.12

18. Debtors (Scotland) Act 1987
applied: SSI 2002/132 Sch.1 para.2.1, Sch.1 para.4.3, Sch.1 para.23.10, SSI 2002/133 Sch.1 para.5.1, SSI 2002/566 Sch.1 para.15, SSI 2002/567 Sch.1 para.17, SSI 2004/468 Sch.4 para.5
s.1, see *Capital Bank Plc v Paterson* 2002 S.L.T. (Sh Ct) 100 (Sh Ct (Glasgow and Strathkelvin)), Sheriff WH Holligan
s.1, amended: 2002 asp 3 Sch.7 para.17
s.1, applied: 2002 asp 17 s.47, SSI 2004/468 Reg.26
s.2, amended: 2002 asp 17 Sch.3 para.17
s.4, applied: 2002 asp 17 s.47
s.5, amended: 2002 asp 3 Sch.7 para.17
s.5, applied: 2002 asp 17 s.47, SSI 2004/468 Reg.26
s.8, amended: 2002 asp 17 Sch.3 para.17
s.9, amended: 2002 asp 17 Sch.3 para.17
s.9, applied: 2002 asp 17 s.25, s.40
s.10, amended: 2002 asp 17 Sch.3 para.17
s.11, applied: 2002 asp 17 s.47
s.13, amended: 2002 asp 17 Sch.3 para.17
s.15, amended: 2002 asp 17 Sch.3 para.17

1987–cont.

18. Debtors (Scotland) Act 1987–*cont.*
s.16, referred to: SSI 2002/494 Reg.33
s.16, repealed: 2002 asp 17 s.58
s.17, repealed: 2002 asp 17 s.58
s.18, repealed: 2002 asp 17 s.58
s.19, repealed: 2002 asp 17 s.58
s.20, repealed: 2002 asp 17 s.58
s.21, repealed: 2002 asp 17 s.58
s.22, repealed: 2002 asp 17 s.58
s.23, applied: SSI 2002/494 Reg.33
s.23, repealed: 2002 asp 17 s.58
s.24, repealed: 2002 asp 17 s.58
s.25, repealed: 2002 asp 17 s.58
s.26, repealed: 2002 asp 17 s.58
s.27, repealed: 2002 asp 17 s.58
s.28, repealed: 2002 asp 17 s.58
s.29, repealed: 2002 asp 17 s.58
s.30, repealed: 2002 asp 17 s.58
s.31, repealed: 2002 asp 17 s.58
s.32, repealed: 2002 asp 17 s.58
s.33, repealed: 2002 asp 17 s.58
s.34, repealed: 2002 asp 17 s.58
s.35, repealed: 2002 asp 17 s.58
s.36, repealed: 2002 asp 17 s.58
s.37, repealed: 2002 asp 17 s.58
s.38, repealed: 2002 asp 17 s.58
s.39, repealed: 2002 asp 17 s.58
s.40, repealed: 2002 asp 17 s.58
s.41, repealed: 2002 asp 17 s.58
s.42, repealed: 2002 asp 17 s.58
s.43, repealed: 2002 asp 17 s.58
s.44, repealed: 2002 asp 17 s.58
s.45, repealed: 2002 asp 17 s.58
s.70, amended: 2002 asp 17 Sch.3 para.17
s.71, applied: SSI 2004/468 Reg.33
s.73, amended: 2002 c.21 Sch.3 para.13
s.74, repealed (in part): 2002 asp 17 s.58
s.79, applied: 2002 asp 17 s.32
s.87, amended: 2002 asp 17 Sch.3 para.17
s.90, amended: 2002 asp 17 Sch.3 para.17
s.90, applied:
s.93, amended: SI 2003/2096 Sch.1 para.13
s.93, applied: 2002 asp 17 s.41
s.93, repealed (in part): 2002 asp 17 Sch.3 para.17
s.94, amended: 2002 asp 17 Sch.3 para.17
s.94, repealed (in part): 2002 asp 17 Sch.3 para.17
s.95, repealed (in part): 2002 asp 17 Sch.3 para.17
s.99, repealed: 2002 asp 17 Sch.3 para.17
s.103, amended: 2002 asp 17 Sch.3 para.17
s.103, repealed (in part): 2002 asp 17 Sch.3 para.17
s.104, amended: 2002 asp 17 Sch.3 para.17
s.104, repealed (in part): 2002 asp 17 Sch.3 para.17
s.106, amended: 2002 asp 3 Sch.7 para.17, 2002 asp 17 Sch.3 para.17, 2004 c.33 Sch.28 para.53

1987–cont.

18. Debtors (Scotland) Act 1987–*cont.*
Sch.1 para.1, repealed: 2002 asp 17 s.58
Sch.1 para.2, repealed: 2002 asp 17 s.58
Sch.1 para.3, repealed: 2002 asp 17 s.58
Sch.1 para.4, repealed: 2002 asp 17 s.58
Sch.1 para.5, repealed: 2002 asp 17 s.58
Sch.1 para.6, repealed: 2002 asp 17 s.58
Sch.1 para.7, repealed: 2002 asp 17 s.58
Sch.1 para.8, repealed: 2002 asp 17 s.58
Sch.1 para.9, repealed: 2002 asp 17 s.58
Sch.1 para.10, repealed: 2002 asp 17 s.58
Sch.1 para.11, repealed: 2002 asp 17 s.58
Sch.1 para.12, repealed: 2002 asp 17 s.58
Sch.4 para.3, repealed: 2004 c.14 Sch.1 Part 9
Sch.5, applied: 2002 asp 17 s.59
Sch.5 para.1, repealed: 2002 asp 17 s.58
Sch.5 para.2, repealed: 2002 asp 17 s.58
Sch.5 para.3, repealed: 2002 asp 17 s.58
Sch.5 para.4, repealed: 2002 asp 17 s.58
Sch.5 para.5, repealed: 2002 asp 17 s.58
Sch.5 para.6, repealed: 2002 asp 17 s.58
Sch.5 para.7, repealed: 2002 asp 17 s.58
Sch.5 para.8, repealed: 2002 asp 17 s.58
Sch.5 para.9, repealed: 2002 asp 17 s.58
Sch.5 para.10, repealed: 2002 asp 17 s.58
Sch.5 para.11, repealed: 2002 asp 17 s.58
Sch.5 para.12, repealed: 2002 asp 17 s.58
Sch.5 para.13, repealed: 2002 asp 17 s.58
Sch.5 para.14, repealed: 2002 asp 17 s.58
Sch.5 para.15, repealed: 2002 asp 17 s.58
Sch.5 para.16, repealed: 2002 asp 17 s.58
Sch.5 para.17, repealed: 2002 asp 17 s.58
Sch.5 para.18, repealed: 2002 asp 17 s.58
Sch.5 para.19, repealed: 2002 asp 17 s.58
Sch.5 para.20, repealed: 2002 asp 17 s.58
Sch.5 para.21, repealed: 2002 asp 17 s.58
Sch.5 para.22, repealed: 2002 asp 17 s.58
Sch.5 para.23, repealed: 2002 asp 17 s.58
Sch.5 para.24, repealed: 2002 asp 17 s.58
Sch.5 para.25, repealed: 2002 asp 17 s.58
Sch.5 para.26, repealed: 2002 asp 17 s.58
Sch.5 para.27, repealed: 2002 asp 17 s.58
Sch.5 para.28, repealed: 2002 asp 17 s.58
Sch.5 para.29, repealed: 2002 asp 17 s.58
Sch.5 para.30, repealed: 2002 asp 17 s.58
Sch.5 para.31, repealed: 2002 asp 17 s.58
Sch.5 para.32, repealed: 2002 asp 17 s.58
Sch.5 para.33, repealed: 2002 asp 17 s.58
Sch.5 para.34, repealed: 2002 asp 17 s.58
Sch.5 para.35, repealed: 2002 asp 17 s.58
Sch.7 para.4, repealed: 2002 asp 17 Sch.3 para.17
Sch.7 para.7, repealed (in part): 2002 asp 17 Sch.3 para.17
Sch.7 para.9, repealed (in part): 2002 asp 17 Sch.3 para.17

21. Pilotage Act 1987
applied: SI 2002/3037, SI 2002/3037 Art.2, 2004 c.20 s.86
referred to: SI 2002/808 Art.2

1987–cont.

21. Pilotage Act 1987–*cont.*
Part I, applied: SR 2002/394 Art.2
s.1, applied: SI 2002/3037
s.1, enabling: SI 2002/3037
s.3, amended: SI 2003/1230 Reg.2
s.7, applied: SR 2002/394
s.24, repealed (in part): 2004 c.14 Sch.1 Part 5
s.25, repealed (in part): 2004 c.14 Sch.1 Part 5
s.26, repealed: 2004 c.14 Sch.1 Part 5
s.28, repealed: 2004 c.14 Sch.1 Part 5
s.29, repealed (in part): 2004 c.14 Sch.1 Part 5
Sch.A1 para.1, added: SI 2003/1230 Reg.2
Sch.A1 para.2, added: SI 2003/1230 Reg.2
Sch.A1 para.3, added: SI 2003/1230 Reg.2
Sch.A1 para.4, added: SI 2003/1230 Reg.2
Sch.A1 para.5, added: SI 2003/1230 Reg.2
Sch.A1 para.6, added: SI 2003/1230 Reg.2
Sch.A1 para.7, added: SI 2003/1230 Reg.2
Sch.A1 para.8, added: SI 2003/1230 Reg.2
Sch.A1 para.9, added: SI 2003/1230 Reg.2
Sch.A1 para.10, added: SI 2003/1230 Reg.2
Sch.A1 para.11, added: SI 2003/1230 Reg.2

22. Banking Act 1987
applied: 2002 c.40 Sch.15
s.3, see *Financial Services Authority (FSA) v Rourke (t/a JE Rourke & Co)* [2002] C.P. Rep. 14 (Ch D), Neuberger, J.
s.35, see *Financial Services Authority (FSA) v Rourke (t/a JE Rourke & Co)* [2002] C.P. Rep. 14 (Ch D), Neuberger, J.

24. Immigration (Carriers Liability) Act 1987
referred to: SI 2003/2900 Sch.1
s.1A, enabling: SI 2002/825, SI 2002/2758

25. Crown Proceedings (Armed Forces) Act 1987
s.1, see *Matthews v Ministry of Defence* [2002] EWHC 13, [2002] C.P. Rep. 26 (QBD), Keith, J.

26. Housing (Scotland) Act 1987
see *McAuley v Highland Council* 2003 S.L.T. 986 (OH), Lady Smith
applied: SSI 2002/321 Art.3
Part II, applied: SSI 2002/312 Reg.4
Part II, referred to: SSI 2002/533 Sch.1, Sch.3, 2003 asp 10 s.2, s.13
Part III, applied: 2003 asp 2 s.40, s.65, s.84, 2003 asp 11 s.27, 2004 c.33 s.112
Part XIII, applied: SSI 2002/312 Reg.5, SSI 2003/434 Art.4
Part XIII, referred to: SSI 2002/533 Sch.1, Sch.3
s.1, referred to: SSI 2002/533 Sch.1, Sch.3
s.2, referred to: SSI 2002/533 Sch.1, Sch.3
s.3, referred to: SSI 2002/533 Sch.1, Sch.3
s.4, referred to: SSI 2002/533 Sch.1, Sch.3
s.5, referred to: SSI 2002/533 Sch.1, Sch.3
s.5A, referred to: SSI 2002/533 Sch.1, Sch.3
s.5B, referred to: SSI 2002/533 Sch.1, Sch.3
s.6, referred to: SSI 2002/533 Sch.1, Sch.3

CAP.

1987–cont.

26. Housing (Scotland) Act 1987–*cont.*
s.7, referred to: SSI 2002/533 Sch.1, Sch.3
s.8, referred to: SSI 2002/533 Sch.1, Sch.3
s.12, applied: 2003 asp 2 s.40, 2003 asp 11 s.27
s.14, applied: SSI 2002/312 Reg.4, 2003 asp 11 s.27
s.14, referred to: 2003 asp 2 s.40
s.20, amended: 2003 asp 10 s.10
s.24, amended: 2003 asp 10 s.5, s.10
s.25, amended: 2003 asp 10 s.1
s.25, applied: 2003 asp 10 s.3
s.27, amended: 2003 asp 10 s.7
s.27, applied: 2004 c.19 s.11
s.28, amended: 2003 asp 10 s.4
s.29, amended: 2003 asp 10 s.9
s.29, applied: 2002 c.41 s.55, Sch.3 para.1
s.29, varied: SSI 2004/489 Art.2
s.29, enabling: SSI 2004/489
s.30, amended: 2003 asp 10 s.4
s.31, amended: 2003 asp 10 s.5, 2004 asp 8 Sch.4 para.2
s.31, applied: SSI 2002/412 Reg.3, SSI 2002/414 Reg.3, Reg.5, 2003 asp 10 s.2, s.3
s.31, disapplied: SSI 2002/412 Reg.3
s.31, enabling: SSI 2002/414
s.32, amended: 2003 asp 10 s.9
s.32, applied: SSI 2002/414, SSI 2002/414 Reg.3, Reg.5, 2003 asp 10 s.2, s.3
s.32, enabling: SSI 2002/414
s.32A, enabling: SSI 2002/412
s.33, amended: 2003 asp 10 s.10
s.33, repealed (in part): 2003 asp 10 s.10
s.33A, added: 2003 asp 10 s.8
s.33B, added: 2003 asp 10 s.8
s.36, amended: 2003 asp 10 s.5
s.44, see *Knowes Housing Association Ltd v Millar* 2002 S.C. 58 (Ex Div), Lord Johnston, Lord Cameron of Lochbroom, Lord Prosser
s.50, see *Smith v Dundee City Council* 2003 Hous. L.R. 55 (Sh Ct (Tayside, Central and Fife)), Sheriff FR Crowe
s.58A, applied: SSI 2002/321 Art.4
s.61, see *Davidson v Dundee City Council* 2002 Hous. L.R. 104 (Lands Tr (Scot)), JN Wright Q.C.; see *McAllister v Queens Cross Housing Association Ltd* 2002 S.L.T. (Lands Tr) 13 (Lands Tr (Scot)), JN Wright Q.C.
s.61, amended: 2002 asp 3 Sch.7 para.18
s.61, applied: SSI 2002/318 Art.4, 2003 asp 9 s.43, s.63, 2003 c.14 Sch.9 para.1
s.61, disapplied: SSI 2002/318 Art.2
s.61, referred to: 2003 asp 9 s.63
s.61A, disapplied: SSI 2002/318 Art.4
s.61A, enabling: SSI 2002/318
s.61B, disapplied: SSI 2002/318 Art.4
s.62, applied: SSI 2002/318 Art.4, 2003 c.14 Sch.9 para.6
s.63, applied: SSI 2002/322 Art.2

CAP.

1987–cont.

26. Housing (Scotland) Act 1987–*cont.*
s.63, enabling: SSI 2002/322
s.70A, applied: SSI 2002/317 Art.2
s.70A, enabling: SSI 2002/317
s.72, repealed (in part): 2003 asp 9 Sch.15
s.81A, applied: 2003 c.14 Sch.9 para.1
s.83, amended: 2004 c.33 Sch.28 para.54
s.83, varied: 2004 c.33 Sch.21 para.30
s.86, applied: SSI 2003/461 Reg.33
s.88, applied: SSI 2003/336 Reg.2, SSI 2003/434 Art.4
s.90, applied: SSI 2003/434 Art.4
s.91, applied: SSI 2003/434 Art.4
s.108, applied: SSI 2003/335 Reg.2, SSI 2003/434 Art.4, SSI 2003/461 Reg.29
s.123, applied: 2004 asp 11 s.21
s.162, applied: SSI 2003/434 Art.4
s.178, applied: 2004 asp 8 s.81, s.83
s.191, applied: SSI 2002/171, SSI 2003/161, SSI 2004/173
s.191, varied: SSI 2004/105 Art.3
s.191, enabling: SSI 2002/171, SSI 2003/161, SSI 2004/173
s.192, varied: SSI 2004/105 Art.3
s.192, enabling: SSI 2002/171, SSI 2003/161, SSI 2004/173
s.193, varied: SSI 2004/105 Art.3
s.203, varied: SSI 2004/105 Art.3
s.204, enabling: SSI 2002/45, SSI 2003/54, SSI 2004/60
s.212, amended: 2002 asp 3 Sch.7 para.18
s.233, amended: 2002 asp 3 Sch.7 para.18
s.236, applied: SSI 2003/461 Reg.3
s.236, referred to: SSI 2003/420 Reg.2, Reg.3
s.237, applied: SSI 2003/420 Reg.2, Reg.3
s.237, enabling: SSI 2003/420
s.240, applied: SSI 2003/314 Art.2
s.240, enabling: SSI 2003/314
s.240A, applied: SSI 2003/461, SSI 2004/456
s.240A, enabling: SSI 2003/461, SSI 2004/456
s.242, applied: SSI 2003/462, SSI 2003/462 Reg.2
s.242, enabling: SSI 2003/462
s.246, applied: SSI 2003/338 Reg.2
s.248, applied: SSI 2003/338 Reg.2, SSI 2003/420 Reg.4, SSI 2003/434 Art.4
s.249, applied: SSI 2003/338 Reg.2, SSI 2003/420 Reg.5, SSI 2003/434 Art.4
s.250, applied: SSI 2003/434 Art.4
s.256, amended: SSI 2003/583 Sch.1 para.10
s.300, amended: 2002 asp 3 Sch.7 para.18
s.330, enabling: SSI 2003/335, SSI 2003/336, SSI 2003/337, SSI 2003/338, SSI 2003/420
s.338, amended: 2002 asp 3 Sch.7 para.18, SSI 2003/583 Sch.1 para.10

1987–cont.

26. Housing (Scotland) Act 1987–*cont.*

Sch.3 Part I para.2, see *Perth and Kinross Council v Gillies* 2002 S.C.L.R. 1104 (Sh Ct (Tayside, Central and Fife)), LDR Foulis

Sch.3 para.7, see *Edinburgh City Council v Watson* 2002 Hous. L.R. 2 (Sh Ct (Lothian and Border)), AM Bell

Sch.8 Part II para.11, amended: SI 2003/2155 Sch.1 para.11

Sch.8 Part IV para.13, amended: SSI 2003/583 Sch.1 para.10

Sch.15 Part I para.1, referred to: SSI 2002/171 Art.3, SSI 2003/161 Art.3

Sch.15 Part II para.3, applied: SSI 2002/171 Sch.2 para.2, SSI 2003/161 Sch.2 para.2, SSI 2004/173 Sch.2 para.2

Sch.19 para.6, applied: SSI 2003/337 Reg.2

Sch.23 para.8, repealed: 2003 asp 8 Sch.6 para.17

27. Fire Safety and Safety of Places of Sport Act 1987

see *City Logistics Ltd v Northamptonshire County Fire Officer* [2001] EWCA Civ 1216, [2002] 1 W.L.R. 1124 (CA), Kennedy, L.J.

s.12, repealed (in part): 2004 c.14 Sch.1 Part 13

s.15, repealed: 2004 c.14 Sch.1 Part 13

s.16, repealed (in part): 2004 c.14 Sch.1 Part 13

s.22, repealed (in part): 2004 c.14 Sch.1 Part 13

s.28, amended: 2004 c.21 Sch.1 para.63

s.29, amended: 2004 c.21 Sch.1 para.63

s.30, amended: 2004 c.21 Sch.1 para.63

s.33, amended: 2003 c.17 Sch.6 para.106

s.35, amended: 2004 c.21 Sch.1 para.63

s.41, amended: 2003 asp 8 Sch.6 para.18, 2003 c.39 Sch.8 para.301, Sch.10

s.42, repealed: 2003 c.17 Sch.7

s.43, repealed: 2003 c.17 Sch.7

s.45, repealed: 2003 c.17 Sch.7

s.46, repealed: 2003 c.17 Sch.7

Sch.3 Part 1 para.1, repealed: 2003 c.17 Sch.7

Sch.3 Part 2 para.2, repealed: 2003 c.17 Sch.7

Sch.3 Part 2 para.3, repealed: 2003 c.17 Sch.7

Sch.3 Part 2 para.4, repealed: 2003 c.17 Sch.7

Sch.3 Part 2 para.5, repealed: 2003 c.17 Sch.7

Sch.3 Part 2 para.6, repealed: 2003 c.17 Sch.7

Sch.3 Part 2 para.7, repealed: 2003 c.17 Sch.7

Sch.3 Part 2 para.8, repealed: 2003 c.17 Sch.7

Sch.3 Part 2 para.9, repealed: 2003 c.17 Sch.7

Sch.3 Part 2 para.10, repealed: 2003 c.17 Sch.7

1987–cont.

27. Fire Safety and Safety of Places of Sport Act 1987–*cont.*

Sch.3 Part 2 para.11, repealed: 2003 c.17 Sch.7

Sch.3 Part 2 para.12, repealed: 2003 c.17 Sch.7

Sch.3 Part 2 para.13, repealed: 2003 c.17 Sch.7

Sch.5 para.1, amended: 2003 c.17 Sch.7

Sch.5 para.1, repealed (in part): 2003 c.17 Sch.7

Sch.5 para.8, repealed: 2003 c.17 Sch.7

Sch.5 para.9, repealed: 2003 c.17 Sch.7

Sch.5 para.10, repealed: 2003 c.17 Sch.7

29. Agricultural Training Board Act 1987

repealed: 2004 c.14 Sch.1 Part 2

30. Northern Ireland (Emergency Provisions) Act 1987

s.15, see *Cullen v Chief Constable of the Royal Ulster Constabulary* [2003] UKHL 39, [2003] 1 W.L.R. 1736 (HL (NI)), Lord Bingham of Cornhill

31. Landlord and Tenant Act 1987

applied: 2002 c.iv s.14, SI 2004/675 Sch.1 para.4

referred to: SI 2002/3012 Sch.2 para.6, Sch.2 para.7

Part II, applied: 2002 c.15 s.79, s.83, s.86, s.88, s.91, s.93, s.94, s.97, s.105, s.172, Sch.12 para.9, SI 2002/3012 Sch.2 para.6

Part III, disapplied: 2002 c.15 Sch.7 para.9

Part IV, applied: 2002 c.15 s.172, Sch.12 para.9, SI 2003/2098 Reg.3, SI 2003/2099 Reg.4, Reg.5, Sch.1 para.6, SI 2004/675 Sch.1 para.4, SI 2004/681 Reg.4, Reg.5, Sch.1 para.6, SI 2004/683 Reg.3

s.4, see *Long Acre Securities Ltd v Karet* [2004] EWHC 442, [2004] 3 W.L.R. 866 (Ch D), Geoffrey Vos Q.C.

s.4, amended: 2004 c.33 Sch.8 para.40, Sch.30

s.4, applied: 2002 c.iv s.14

s.4, disapplied: 2002 c.iii s.14

s.4, varied: 2004 c.33 Sch.21 para.31

s.5, see *Long Acre Securities Ltd v Karet* [2004] EWHC 442, [2004] 3 W.L.R. 866 (Ch D), Geoffrey Vos Q.C.

s.5, varied: 2002 c.15 Sch.7 para.7

s.5B, see *Long Acre Securities Ltd v Karet* [2004] EWHC 442, [2004] 3 W.L.R. 866 (Ch D), Geoffrey Vos Q.C.

s.13, applied: SI 2003/2099 Sch.1 para.1, Sch.2 para.1, SI 2004/681 Sch.1 para.1, Sch.2 para.1

s.19, see *Wandsworth LBC v Manuel* [2002] 2 E.G.L.R. 128 (Ch D), Tomlinson, J.

s.21, amended: 2002 c.15 s.161

s.21, varied: 2002 c.15 Sch.7 para.8

s.22, amended: 2002 c.15 s.160

CAP.

CAP.

1987–cont.

31. Landlord and Tenant Act 1987–*cont.*

s.22, applied: SI 2003/2099 Sch.1 para.5, Sch.2 para.5, SI 2004/681 Sch.1 para.5, Sch.2 para.5

s.22, varied: 2002 c.15 Sch.7 para.8

s.23, amended: 2002 c.15 s.160

s.23, repealed (in part): 2002 c.15 Sch.14

s.23, varied: 2002 c.15 Sch.7 para.8

s.24, see *Maunder Taylor v Blaquiere* [2002] EWCA Civ 1633, [2003] 1 W.L.R. 379 (CA), Aldous, L.J.; see *Orchard Court Residents Association v St Anthony's Homes Ltd* [2003] EWCA Civ 1049, [2003] 2 E.G.L.R. 28 (CA), Keene, L.J.

s.24, amended: 2002 c.9 Sch.11 para.20, 2002 c.15 s.160, Sch.9 para.8, Sch.10 para.14, Sch.11 para.8, Sch.13 para.9

s.24, applied: SI 2003/2098 Reg.3, SI 2003/2099 Sch.1 para.5, Sch.2 para.5, SI 2004/681 Sch.1 para.5, Sch.2 para.5, SI 2004/683 Reg.3

s.24, referred to: 2002 c.15 Sch.7 para.8

s.24, varied: 2002 c.15 Sch.7 para.8

s.24A, repealed (in part): 2002 c.15 Sch.14

s.24A, varied: 2002 c.15 Sch.7 para.8

s.24B, repealed (in part): 2002 c.15 Sch.14

s.24B, varied: 2002 c.15 Sch.7 para.8

s.24B, enabling: SI 2003/2269, SI 2003/2270, SI 2004/677, SI 2004/680

s.28, amended: 2002 c.9 Sch.11 para.20

s.28, applied: SI 2003/1417 r.93

s.28, repealed (in part): 2002 c.9 Sch.13

s.29, amended: 2002 c.15 s.160, Sch.9 para.9, Sch.14

s.30, amended: 2002 c.9 Sch.11 para.20

s.31, applied: SI 2003/2099 Sch.1 para.1, SI 2004/681 Sch.1 para.1

s.34, amended: 2002 c.9 Sch.11 para.20

s.35, amended: 2002 c.15 s.162, s.163

s.35, applied: SI 2002/3012 Sch.2 para.7

s.35, varied: 2002 c.15 Sch.7 para.10

s.35, enabling: SI 2003/2099, SI 2004/681, SI 2004/3098

s.36, amended: 2002 c.15 s.163

s.36, varied: 2002 c.15 Sch.7 para.10

s.37, amended: 2002 c.15 s.163

s.38, amended: 2002 c.15 s.163, Sch.14

s.38, applied: SI 2004/669 Sch.2 para.12

s.38, varied: 2002 c.15 Sch.7 para.10

s.39, amended: 2002 c.15 s.163

s.39, applied: SI 2004/669 Sch.2 para.12

s.39, varied: 2002 c.15 Sch.7 para.10

s.40, amended: 2002 c.15 s.163

s.42, amended: 2002 c.15 Sch.10 para.15, Sch.14

s.42, repealed (in part): 2002 c.15 Sch.14

s.42, varied: 2002 c.15 Sch.7 para.11

s.42A, added: 2002 c.15 s.156

s.42A, varied: 2002 c.15 Sch.7 para.11

s.42B, added: 2002 c.15 s.156

s.42B, varied: 2002 c.15 Sch.7 para.11

1987–cont.

31. Landlord and Tenant Act 1987–*cont.*

s.46, amended: 2002 c.15 Sch.11 para.9

s.46, applied: 2002 c.15 s.172

s.46, varied: 2002 c.15 Sch.7 para.12

s.47, amended: 2002 c.15 Sch.11 para.10, Sch.13 para.10

s.47, applied: 2002 c.15 s.111, s.164, s.172

s.47, varied: 2002 c.15 Sch.7 para.12

s.48, amended: 2002 c.15 Sch.11 para.11, Sch.13 para.11

s.48, applied: 2002 c.15 s.111, s.164, s.172

s.48, varied: 2002 c.15 Sch.7 para.12

s.49, applied: 2002 c.15 s.172

s.52, amended: 2002 c.15 s.163

s.52A, repealed (in part): 2002 c.15 Sch.14

s.53, amended: 2002 c.15 s.156, s.162, Sch.14

s.56, amended: 2002 c.15 s.172

s.56, repealed (in part): 2002 c.15 Sch.14

Sch.2 para.3, repealed (in part): 2002 c.15 Sch.14

Sch.2 para.5, repealed: 2002 c.15 Sch.14

Sch.2 para.6, repealed: 2002 c.15 Sch.14

Sch.2 para.7, repealed (in part): 2002 c.15 Sch.14

Sch.4 para.1, repealed: 2002 c.9 Sch.13

Sch.4 para.2, repealed: 2002 c.9 Sch.13

33. AIDS (Control) Act 1987

referred to: 2003 c.43 Sch.4 para.69

s.1, amended: SI 2002/2469 Sch.1 para.13, 2003 c.43 Sch.4 para.70

34. Motor Cycle Noise Act 1987

Sch.1 para.1, amended: 2003 c.44 Sch.37 Part 9

Sch.1 para.1, disapplied: 2003 c.44 Sch.25 para.84

35. Protection of Animals (Penalties) Act 1987

s.1, repealed (in part): 2004 c.14 Sch.1 Part 17

s.2, repealed (in part): 2004 c.14 Sch.1 Part 17

37. Access to Personal Files Act 1987

see *MG v United Kingdom (39393/98)* [2002] 3 F.C.R. 289 (ECHR), Judge Costa (President)

38. Criminal Justice Act 1987

see *Marlwood Commercial Inc v Kozeny* [2004] EWCA Civ 798, [2004] 3 All E.R. 648 (CA), Peter Gibson, L.J.

applied: 2003 c.44 s.45

referred to: 2003 c.32 Sch.5 para.11

s.1, applied: SI 2003/3335 Art.2, SI 2004/1034 Art.2

s.2, see *R. (on the application of Evans) v Director of the Serious Fraud Office* [2002] EWHC 2304, [2003] 1 W.L.R. 299 (QBD (Admin Ct)), Kennedy, L.J.

s.2, amended: 2003 c.32 Sch.5 para.12, Sch.6, 2003 c.44 Sch.1 para.11, Sch.1 para.12, Sch.1 para.13

s.2, repealed (in part): 2003 c.32 Sch.6

s.3, amended: 2003 c.32 s.80, Sch.6

1987–cont.

38. Criminal Justice Act 1987–cont.

s.4, repealed: 2003 c.44 Sch.37 Part 4, Sch.3 para.58

s.5, repealed: 2003 c.44 Sch.37 Part 4, Sch.3 para.58

s.6, amended: SI 2004/2035 Sch.1 para.22

s.6, repealed: 2003 c.44 Sch.37 Part 4, Sch.3 para.58

s.7, see *R. v Carass (Clive Louden)* [2001] EWCA Crim 2845, [2002] 1 W.L.R. 1714 (CA (Crim Div)), Waller, L.J.; see *R. v G (Interlocutory Appeal: Jurisdiction)* [2001] EWCA Crim 442, [2002] 1 W.L.R. 200 (CA (Crim Div)), Henry, L.J.; see *R. v G* [2004] EWCA Crim 1368, [2004] 1 W.L.R. 2932 (CA (Crim Div)), Rose, L.J.

s.7, amended: 2003 c.44 s.45, s.310, Sch.36 para.53

s.7, varied: 2004 c.28 s.18

s.9, see *R. v Carass (Clive Louden)* [2001] EWCA Crim 2845, [2002] 1 W.L.R. 1714 (CA (Crim Div)), Waller, L.J.; see *R. v G (Interlocutory Appeal: Jurisdiction)* [2001] EWCA Crim 442, [2002] 1 W.L.R. 200 (CA (Crim Div)), Henry, L.J.; see *R. v G* [2004] EWCA Crim 1368, [2004] 1 W.L.R. 2932 (CA (Crim Div)), Rose, L.J.

s.9, amended: 2003 c.44 s.45, s.310, Sch.36 para.54, SI 2004/2035 Sch.1 para.23

s.9, applied: 2003 c.44 s.310, s.312

s.9, repealed (in part): 2003 c.44 Sch.36 para.18, Sch.37 Part 3

s.9, varied: 2004 c.28 s.18

s.10, amended: 2003 c.44 Sch.36 para.55

s.11, amended: 2003 c.44 s.311, Sch.37 Part 4, Sch.3 para.58

s.11, repealed (in part): 2003 c.44 Sch.37 Part 4, Sch.3 para.58

s.11A, amended: 2003 c.44 s.311

s.17, amended: 2003 c.44 s.311

s.40, see *R. v G (Interlocutory Appeal: Jurisdiction)* [2001] EWCA Crim 442, [2002] 1 W.L.R. 200 (CA (Crim Div)), Henry, L.J.

Sch.1 para.5, repealed (in part): 2002 c.26 Sch.13

Sch.2 para.1, repealed: 2003 c.44 Sch.37 Part 4

Sch.2 para.6, repealed: 2002 c.26 Sch.13

Sch.2 para.9, repealed: 2003 c.44 Sch.37 Part 4

Sch.2 para.14, repealed: 2003 c.44 Sch.37 Part 4

41. Criminal Justice (Scotland) Act 1987

Part I, applied: 2002 c.29 s.8, s.94, s.158

42. Family Law Reform Act 1987

see *H and A (Children) (Paternity: Blood Tests), Re* [2002] EWCA Civ 383, [2002] 1 F.L.R. 1145 (CA), Thorpe, L.J.

referred to: 2002 c.38 Sch.3 para.50

Part III, applied: 2002 c.38 s.70

1987–cont.

42. Family Law Reform Act 1987–cont.

Part III, referred to: 2002 c.38 Sch.4 para.19

s.1, see *Upton v National Westminster Bank Plc* [2004] EWHC 1962, [2004] W.T.L.R. 1339 (Ch D), Judge Behrens

s.1, amended: 2002 c.38 Sch.3 para.51

s.1, referred to: 2003 c.1 s.721

s.19, see *Upton v National Westminster Bank Plc* [2004] EWHC 1962, [2004] W.T.L.R. 1339 (Ch D), Judge Behrens

s.19, amended: 2002 c.38 Sch.3 para.52

Sch.3 para.2, repealed: 2002 c.38 Sch.5

Sch.3 para.3, repealed: 2002 c.38 Sch.5

Sch.3 para.4, repealed: 2002 c.38 Sch.5

Sch.3 para.5, repealed: 2002 c.38 Sch.5

43. Consumer Protection Act 1987

see *R. (on the application of North Yorkshire Trading Standards Service) v Coleman* [2001] EWHC Admin 818, (2002) 166 J.P. 76 (QBD (Admin Ct)), Burton, J.

applied: 2002 c.40 Sch.14, Sch.15, SI 2002/618 Reg.62, Reg.64, 2003 c.22 s.11, SI 2003/419 Art.63, SI 2003/721 Reg.8, SI 2003/1511 Reg.8

referred to: SI 2002/618 Reg.61, SI 2002/3041 Reg.15, 2003 c.21 s.393, SI 2003/750 Sch.5 para.12, SI 2003/751 Sch.6 para.12, SI 2004/1468 Sch.6 para.12

Part I, see *Horne-Roberts v Smithkline Beecham Plc* [2001] EWCA Civ 2006, [2002] 1 W.L.R. 1662 (CA), Keene, L.J.

Part II, applied: SI 2002/618 Reg.61, SI 2004/1464 Sch.17 para.1

Part III, applied: SI 2003/1376 Sch.1, SI 2003/1593 Sch.1 Part I

Part IV, applied: SI 2002/3041 Reg.15, SI 2004/1464 Sch.17 para.1

s.11, applied: SI 2002/618, SI 2002/1689 Reg.14, SI 2002/2479, SI 2002/3041, SI 2002/3041 Reg.15, 2003 c.22 s.2, s.12, SI 2003/721, SI 2003/835, SI 2003/835 Reg.13, SI 2003/1101, SI 2003/1316, SI 2003/1511, SI 2003/1697, SI 2003/2762, SI 2003/3310 Reg.7, SI 2003/3314, SI 2004/1417, SI 2004/2030 Sch.1, SI 2004/2152, SI 2004/2152 Reg.13, Reg.15, SI 2004/2988, SR 2002/301 Reg.14

s.11, disapplied: SI 2002/618 Reg.61, SI 2002/1770 Reg.1

s.11, varied: 2003 c.22 s.11

s.11, enabling: SI 2002/618, SI 2002/1415, SI 2002/2479, SI 2002/3010, SI 2002/3041, SI 2003/721, SI 2003/835, SI 2003/1101, SI 2003/1316, SI 2003/1511, SI 2003/1680, SI 2003/1697, SI 2003/2762, SI 2003/3310, SI 2003/3314, SI 2004/1372, SI 2004/1417, SI 2004/1836, SI 2004/2152, SI 2004/2913, SI 2004/2988, SSI 2004/393

CAP.

CAP.

1987–cont.

43. Consumer Protection Act 1987–*cont.*

s.12, see *Brighton and Hove City Council v Woolworths Plc* [2002] EWHC 2565, (2003) 167 J.P. 21 (QBD (Admin Ct)), Field, J.

s.12, applied: SI 2002/618 Reg.61, SI 2002/3041 Reg.15, SI 2003/1101 Reg.9, SI 2003/1376 Sch.1, SI 2003/1680 Reg.7, SI 2004/1464 Reg.21, SI 2004/1836 Reg.9, SI 2004/2152 Reg.6, SR 2002/301 Reg.14

s.12, disapplied: SI 2004/2152 Reg.15

s.13, applied: SI 2002/618 Reg.61, SI 2004/1464 Sch.17 para.1

s.13, varied: SI 2002/1144 Sch.10 para.1, SI 2004/1464 Sch.17 para.1

s.14, see *Brighton and Hove City Council v Woolworths Plc* [2002] EWHC 2565, (2003) 167 J.P. 21 (QBD (Admin Ct)), Field, J.

s.14, applied: SI 2002/618 Reg.61, Reg.63, SI 2003/1680 Reg.3, SI 2004/1464 Sch.17 para.1

s.14, varied: SI 2002/1144 Sch.10 para.1, SI 2003/1941 Sch.4 para.2, SI 2004/1464 Sch.17 para.1

s.15, applied: SI 2002/618 Reg.61, Reg.63, SI 2004/1464 Sch.17 para.1

s.15, varied: SI 2002/1144 Sch.10 para.1, SI 2003/1941 Sch.4 para.2

s.16, applied: SI 2002/618 Reg.61, Reg.63, SI 2004/1464 Sch.17 para.1

s.16, disapplied: SI 2002/618 Reg.62

s.16, varied: SI 2002/1144 Sch.10 para.1

s.17, applied: SI 2002/618 Reg.61, Reg.63, SI 2004/1464 Sch.17 para.1

s.17, disapplied: SI 2002/618 Reg.62

s.17, varied: SI 2002/1144 Sch.10 para.1

s.18, applied: 2003 c.22 s.2, SI 2004/1464 Sch.17 para.1, SI 2004/2030 Sch.1

s.18, varied: SI 2002/1144 Sch.10 para.1

s.25, amended: 2002 c.40 Sch.25 para.16

s.26, amended: 2002 c.40 Sch.25 para.16

s.27, applied: SI 2002/618 Reg.61, 2003 c.22 s.12, SI 2003/1680 Reg.7, SI 2003/3085, SI 2003/3085 Reg.6, SI 2004/1836, SI 2004/2030 Sch.1, SSI 2004/393

s.27, enabling: SI 2002/618, SI 2002/1415, SI 2003/1680, SI 2004/1836, SI 2004/3262, SSI 2004/393

s.28, applied: 2003 c.22 s.12, SI 2003/835 Reg.15, SI 2004/2152 Reg.17

s.28, varied: SI 2002/1144 Sch.10 para.1, SI 2003/1941 Sch.4 para.2

s.28, enabling: SI 2003/835, SI 2004/2152

s.29, applied: SI 2002/1144 Reg.16, 2003 c.22 s.12, SI 2003/835 Reg.15, SI 2004/2152 Reg.17

s.29, varied: SI 2002/1144 Sch.10 para.1, SI 2003/1941 Sch.4 para.2

s.30, applied: 2003 c.22 s.12

1987–cont.

43. Consumer Protection Act 1987–*cont.*

s.30, varied: SI 2002/1144 Sch.10 para.1, SI 2003/1941 Sch.4 para.2

s.30, enabling: SI 2003/835, SI 2004/2152

s.31, varied: SI 2002/1144 Sch.10 para.1, SI 2003/1941 Sch.4 para.2

s.32, applied: 2003 c.22 s.12, SI 2003/1941 Sch.4 para.2

s.32, varied: SI 2002/1144 Sch.10 para.1, SI 2003/1941 Sch.4 para.2

s.33, applied: 2003 c.22 s.12

s.33, varied: SI 2002/1144 Sch.10 para.1, SI 2003/1941 Sch.4 para.2

s.34, applied: 2003 c.22 s.12

s.34, varied: SI 2002/1144 Sch.10 para.1, SI 2003/1941 Sch.4 para.2

s.35, applied: 2003 c.22 s.12

s.35, varied: SI 2002/1144 Sch.10 para.1, SI 2003/1941 Sch.4 para.2

s.37, applied: 2003 c.22 s.12, SI 2004/1464 Sch.17 para.1

s.37, varied: SI 2002/1144 Sch.10 para.1, SI 2003/1941 Sch.4 para.2

s.38, amended: 2003 c.20 Sch.2 para.19

s.38, applied: SI 2002/618 Reg.61, SI 2004/1464 Sch.17 para.1

s.38, referred to: 2003 c.20 s.115

s.38, repealed: 2002 c.40 Sch.26

s.38, varied: SI 2002/1144 Sch.10 para.1, SI 2003/1941 Sch.4 para.2

s.39, applied: SI 2003/1941 Sch.4 para.2

s.40, applied: 2003 c.22 s.11, SI 2003/1941 Sch.4 para.2

s.41, applied: 2003 c.22 s.12

s.42, applied: SI 2004/1464 Sch.17 para.1

s.44, applied: 2003 c.22 s.12

s.44, varied: SI 2002/1144 Sch.10 para.1, SI 2003/1941 Sch.4 para.2

s.47, amended: 2004 c.33 Sch.27 para.126

s.47, applied: 2003 c.22 s.13

s.47, varied: SI 2002/1144 Sch.10 para.1, SI 2003/1941 Sch.4 para.2

Sch.2, applied: SI 2002/618 Reg.61

Sch.4 para.1, repealed: 2003 c.22 Sch.1

Sch.4 para.2, repealed (in part): 2002 c.40 Sch.26

Sch.4 para.3, repealed: 2002 c.40 Sch.26

Sch.4 para.4, repealed: 2002 c.40 Sch.26

Sch.4 para.7, repealed: 2002 c.40 Sch.26

Sch.4 para.9, amended: 2003 c.21 Sch.19

43. Housing (Scotland) Act 1987

s.43, see *McAllister v Queens Cross Housing Association Ltd* 2003 S.C. 514 (2 Div), Lord Gill L.J.C., Lord Kirkwood, Lord Weir

s.45, see *McAllister v Queens Cross Housing Association Ltd* 2003 S.C. 514 (2 Div), Lord Gill L.J.C., Lord Kirkwood, Lord Weir

s.47, see *West Lothian Council v Reape* 2002 Hous. L.R. 58 (Sh Ct (Lothian and Border)), P Gillam

1987–cont.

43. Housing (Scotland) Act 1987–*cont.*
s.48, see *Stirling Council v Magar* 2002 Hous. L.R. 64 (Sh Pr), RA Dunlop Q.C., Sheriff Principal
Sch.3 para.6, see *West Lothian Council v Reape* 2002 Hous. L.R. 58 (Sh Ct (Lothian and Border)), P Gillam
44. Local Government Act 1987
repealed: 2004 c.14 Sch.1 Part 10
45. Parliamentary and other Pensions Act 1987
s.2, enabling: SI 2002/1807, SI 2002/1887, SI 2004/2416, SI 2004/2417
46. Diplomatic and Consular Premises Act 1987
s.5, amended: 2002 c.9 Sch.11 para.21
Sch.1 Part I para.1, amended: 2002 c.9 Sch.11 para.21, Sch.13
47. Abolition of Domestic Rates Etc (Scotland) Act 1987
s.26, referred to: SSI 2002/504 Art.6
Sch.2 para.7, amended: 2002 asp 17 Sch.3 para.18
Sch.2 para.7, enabling: SSI 2002/560
Sch.2 para.7A, varied: 2002 c.16 Sch.2 para.27
Sch.2 para.8, amended: 2002 asp 17 Sch.3 para.18
49. Territorial Sea Act 1987
s.1, applied: SI 2002/676 Art.2
s.4, enabling: SI 2002/250
Sch.4, varied: SI 2002/250 Art.2
51. Finance (No.2) Act 1987
s.98, repealed: 2004 c.12 Sch.42 Part 3
s.102, applied: SI 2002/1618, SI 2002/1618 Art.2, Art.3, SI 2003/2994 Art.2, Art.3, 2004 c.19 s.42, SI 2004/1007 Art.2
s.102, enabling: SI 2002/1618, SI 2003/1094, SI 2003/2994, SI 2004/1007
52. British Shipbuilders (Borrowing Powers) Act 1987
s.1, repealed (in part): 2004 c.14 Sch.1 Part 16
53. Channel Tunnel Act 1987
applied: SI 2003/1594 Art.2
s.1, applied: SI 2002/655 Reg.20, SI 2004/456 Reg.19, SI 2004/2363 Reg.11
s.1, referred to: SI 2003/547 Reg.20
s.9, repealed (in part): 2004 asp 6 Sch.7 para.6
s.11, enabling: SI 2002/2693, SI 2003/2758, SI 2003/2799, SI 2004/1004, SI 2004/2589
s.13, enabling: SI 2002/2693, SI 2003/2758, SI 2004/1004
s.14, amended: SI 2004/1573 Art.12
s.32, substituted: 2003 c.21 Sch.17 para.84
s.33, amended: SI 2003/1398 Sch.1 para.6
s.33, repealed (in part): SI 2003/1398 Sch.1 para.6
s.34, amended: SI 2003/1398 Sch.1 para.6
s.34, enabling: SI 2003/2758, SI 2004/1004

1987–cont.

53. Channel Tunnel Act 1987–*cont.*
Sch.2 Part II para.3, amended: 2003 c.21 Sch.17 para.85
Sch.7 Part X para.1, amended: 2003 c.21 Sch.17 para.86
Sch.7 Part X para.1, repealed (in part): 2003 c.21 Sch.19
Sch.7 Part X para.2, amended: 2003 c.21 Sch.17 para.86
Sch.7 Part X para.3, amended: 2003 c.21 Sch.17 para.86
Sch.7 Part X para.4, amended: 2003 c.21 Sch.17 para.86
Sch.7 Part X para.5, amended: 2003 c.21 Sch.17 para.86
Sch.7 Part X para.6, amended: 2003 c.21 Sch.17 para.86
Sch.7 Part X para.7, amended: 2003 c.21 Sch.17 para.86

1988

xiv. Felixstowe Dock and Railway Act 1988
s.3, repealed (in part): SI 2002/2618 Art.3
Sch.1, repealed: SI 2002/2618 Art.3

Human Rights Act 1988
s.12, see *Roddy (A Child) (Identification: Restriction on Publication), Re* [2003] EWHC 2927, [2004] E.M.L.R. 8 (Fam Div), Munby, J.
Sch.1 Part I Art.8, see *Roddy (A Child) (Identification: Restriction on Publication), Re* [2003] EWHC 2927, [2004] E.M.L.R. 8 (Fam Div), Munby, J.
Sch.1 Part I Art.10, see *Roddy (A Child) (Identification: Restriction on Publication), Re* [2003] EWHC 2927, [2004] E.M.L.R. 8 (Fam Div), Munby, J.

Income and Corporation Tax Act 1988
s.249, see *Howell v Trippier* [2004] S.T.C. (S.C.D.) 132 (Sp Comm), John F Avery Jones
s.686, see *Howell v Trippier* [2004] S.T.C. (S.C.D.) 132 (Sp Comm), John F Avery Jones

Local Government and Finance Act 1988
s.41, see *National Car Parks Ltd v Baird (Valuation Officer)* [2003] R.A. 289 (LandsTr), George Bartlett Q.C. (President)
s.55, see *National Car Parks Ltd v Baird (Valuation Officer)* [2003] R.A. 289 (LandsTr), George Bartlett Q.C. (President)
Sch.5 para.7, see *Pyrke (Valuation Officer), Re* [2003] R.A. 318 (LandsTr), George Bartlett Q.C. (President)
Sch.7A, see *National Car Parks Ltd v Baird (Valuation Officer)* [2003] R.A. 289 (LandsTr), George Bartlett Q.C. (President)

CAP.

1988–cont.

xxvii. South Yorkshire Light Rail Transit Act 1988

s.15, see *Roe v Sheffield City Council (No.1)* [2003] EWCA Civ 1, [2004] Q.B. 653 (CA), Pill, L.J.

1. Income and Corporation Taxes Act 1988

see *Cadbury Schweppes Plc v Inland Revenue Commissioners* [2004] 3 C.M.L.R. 15 (Sp Comm), John F Avery Jones

applied: SR 2002/352 Sch.4 para.10, 2004 c.12 s.285, 2004 c.35 Sch.3, Sch.8

referred to: SI 2002/2661 Reg.2, 2003 c.1 s.515, 2004 c.12 s.285, s.318, SI 2004/2199 Reg.2, SSI 2004/83 Reg.7

Part II, referred to: 2002 c.29 Sch.10 para.12

Part IV, applied: SI 2002/2848 Sch.1 Part III

Part IV c.VII, added: 2004 c.12 s.124

Part IV c.VII, added: 2004 c.12 s.125

Part V c.IV, repealed: 2003 c.1 Sch.8 Part 1

Part VI, applied: 2003 c.14 s.195

Part VI c.VI, added: 2003 c.1 Sch.6 para.34

Part VII c.I, applied: 2002 c.23 Sch.16 para.19, SI 2002/195 Sch.3 para.6, SI 2002/1330 Sch.3 para.6, SI 2002/3200 Sch.3 para.4, Sch.3 para.6, SI 2003/1994 Sch.3 para.6, SR 2002/224 Sch.3 para.6

Part VII c.I, referred to: SR 2002/265 Sch.7 para.6

Part VII c.III, applied: 2002 c.23 s.50, 2003 c.1 Sch.5 para.11

Part VII c.III, referred to: 2002 c.23 s.50, 2004 c.12 Sch.27 para.4, SI 2004/712 Reg.1

Part VII Chapter II, see *Forthright (Wales) Ltd v Davies (Inspector of Taxes)* [2004] EWHC 524, [2004] S.T.C. 875 (Ch D), Lightman, J.

Part X c.I, applied: 2002 c.23 Sch.22 para.4

Part X c.II, applied: 2002 c.23 Sch.22 para.4

Part X c.IV, applied: 2002 c.23 Sch.12 para.14, SI 2004/2502 Reg.2

Part XII c.I, applied: 2002 c.23 Sch.12 para.12, Sch.13 para.22

Part XII c.IV, applied: SI 2003/3297 Reg.16

Part XIII c.II, applied: 2003 c.14 Sch.34 para.3, Sch.34 para.4, Sch.34 para.15, SI 2004/1450 Reg.37, Reg.38

Part XIV, applied: SI 2002/2848 Sch.1 Part III, SR 2002/352 Reg.15, 2004 c.12 Sch.36 para.3

Part XIV c.I, applied: SI 2002/427 Reg.3, Reg.12, SI 2002/836 Reg.3, Reg.12, SI 2002/2006 Reg.3, SI 2002/2848 Sch.1 Part III, SI 2004/1863 Sch.1 para.4, SR 2002/127 Reg.3, 2003 c.14 Sch.24 para.8, 2003 c.1 s.54, s.400, s.492, s.594, 2003 c.20 Sch.4 para.24, 2004 c.12 Sch.36 para.1, Sch.36 para.6

Part XIV c.I, referred to: SR 2002/127 Reg.3

Part XIV c.III, applied: SI 2002/2006 Reg.3, 2003 c.1 s.492

Part XIV c.IV, applied: SI 2002/427 Reg.2, Reg.3, Reg.12, SI 2002/836 Reg.2, Reg.3, Reg.12, SI 2002/2006 Reg.3, SI

CAP.

1988–cont.

1. Income and Corporation Taxes Act 1988–*cont.*

Part XIV c.IV, applied:–*cont.*

2002/2848 Sch.1 Part III, SI 2004/1863 Sch.1 para.4, SR 2002/127 Reg.3, 2003 c.14 Sch.24 para.8, 2003 c.1 s.54, s.492, 2004 c.12 Sch.36 para.1, Sch.36 para.6, Sch.36 para.37

Part XIV c.IV, referred to: 2003 c.1 s.604

Part XV, applied: 2004 c.12 Sch.15 para.8

Part XVII c.I, applied: 2002 c.23 Sch.26 para.24

Part XVII c.IV, applied: 2002 c.23 Sch.29 para.116

Part XVII c.V, applied: 2004 c.12 Sch.26 para.17

Part XVII c.V, disapplied: 2004 c.12 Sch.26 para.17

Part XVII Ch.III, see *R. v Dimsey (Dermot Jeremy)* [2001] UKHL 46, [2002] 1 A.C. 509 (HL), Lord Scott of Foscote

Part XVIII, applied: 2004 c.12 s.107

Part XVIII, disapplied: 2002 c.23 Sch.29 para.66

Part XVIII c.I, applied: 2004 c.12 s.107, s.110, s.111

Part XVIII c.II, applied: 2004 c.12 s.107, s.110, s.111

s.1, amended: SI 2002/707 Art.2, 2003 c.14 s.132, 2003 c.1 Sch.6 para.2, SI 2003/840 Art.2

s.1, applied: SI 2002/707 Art.2, 2003 c.1 s.1, SI 2003/840 Art.2, SI 2003/2682 Reg.7, SI 2004/772 Art.2

s.1, referred to: SI 2004/772 Art.2

s.1, varied: 2002 c.23 s.27

s.1, enabling: SI 2002/707, SI 2003/840, SI 2004/772

s.1A, amended: 2003 c.14 Sch.35 para.1, Sch.43 Part 3

s.4, amended: 2003 c.1 Sch.6 para.3

s.9, amended: 2003 c.1 Sch.6 para.4

s.11, amended: 2003 c.14 s.149

s.11, referred to: 2003 c.14 s.150

s.11AA, added: 2003 c.14 s.149

s.11AA, applied: 2003 c.14 s.149

s.11AA, varied: SI 2003/2714 Reg.3

s.11AA, enabling: SI 2003/2714

s.12, amended: 2003 c.14 Sch.41 para.1

s.12, applied: SI 2004/2502 Reg.2

s.13, see *Gascoines Group Ltd v Inspector of Taxes* [2004] EWHC 640, [2004] S.T.C. 844 (Ch D), Lightman, J.; see *Gascoines Group Ltd v Inspector of Taxes* [2004] S.T.C. (S.C.D.) 11 (Sp Comm), AN Brice; see *Jansen Nielsen Pilkes Ltd v Tomlinson (Inspector of Taxes)* [2004] S.T.C. (S.C.D.) 226 (Sp Comm), John F Avery Jones; see *Land Management Ltd v Fox (Inspector of Taxes)* [2002] S.T.C. (S.C.D.) 152 (Sp Comm), Nuala Brice; see *Strand Options*

1988–cont.

1. Income and Corporation Taxes Act 1988–*cont.*

s.13–*cont.*

& *Futures Ltd v Vojak (Inspector of Taxes)* [2003] EWHC 67, [2003] S.T.C. 331 (Ch D), Etherton, J.

s.13, referred to: 2002 c.23 s.31, 2003 c.14 s.134

s.13, varied: 2004 c.12 s.26

s.13AA, see *Hallamshire Estates Ltd v Walford (Inspector of Taxes)* [2004] S.T.C. (S.C.D.) 330 (Sp Comm), John F Avery Jones

s.13AA, referred to: 2002 c.23 s.32, 2003 c.14 s.135

s.13AA, varied: 2004 c.12 s.27

s.13AB, added: 2004 c.12 s.28

s.14, see *Hoechst UK Ltd v Inland Revenue Commissioners* [2003] EWHC 1002, [2004] S.T.C. 1486 (Ch D), Park, J.; see *Pirelli Cable Holding NV v Inland Revenue Commissioners* [2003] EWHC 32, [2003] S.T.C. 250 (Ch D), Park, J.

s.15, amended: 2002 c.23 Sch.27 para.2, Sch.40 Part 3

s.15, applied: 2003 c.1 s.178

s.15, referred to: SI 2002/2006 Reg.3, Reg.11

s.18, see *Agassi v Robinson (Inspector of Taxes)* [2004] EWHC 487, [2004] S.T.C. 610 (Ch D), Lightman, J.; see *Anise Ltd v Hammond (Inspector of Taxes)* [2003] S.T.C. (S.C.D.) 258 (Sp Comm), Stephen Oliver Q.C.

s.18, amended: 2003 c.1 Sch.6 para.5, 2004 c.12 s.105

s.18, applied: 2002 c.23 Sch.12 para.4, Sch.12 para.5, Sch.12 para.8, Sch.12 para.13, Sch.12 para.15, Sch.13 para.23, Sch.13 para.25, Sch.16 para.27, Sch.22 para.4, Sch.22 para.11, Sch.29 para.30, Sch.29 para.33, Sch.29 para.34, Sch.29 para.36, SI 2002/2006 Reg.12, 2003 c.14 s.151, 2003 c.1 s.6, s.178, s.394, s.397, s.399, s.477, s.515, 2003 c.14 s.195, Sch.36 para.3, 2004 c.12 s.119, s.127, s.131, 2004 c.20 s.28, s.44

s.18, referred to: 2004 c.20 s.28

s.19, see *Ainslie v Buckley (Inspector of Taxes)* [2002] S.T.C. (S.C.D.) 132 (Sp Comm), Theodore Wallace; see *Grimm v Newman* [2002] EWCA Civ 1621, [2003] 1 All E.R. 67 (CA), Sir Andrew Morritt V.C.; see *McBride v Blackburn (Inspector of Taxes)* [2003] S.T.C. (S.C.D.) 139 (Sp Comm), Nuala Brice; see *Wilson (Inspector of Taxes) v Clayton* [2004] EWHC 898, [2004] S.T.C. 1022 (Ch D), Patten, J.

s.19, applied: SI 2002/1792 Reg.17A, 2003 c.1 s.413

s.19, repealed: 2003 c.1 Sch.8 Part 1

s.20, applied: 2003 c.14 s.151, 2003 c.1 s.515

1988–cont.

1. Income and Corporation Taxes Act 1988–*cont.*

s.21, see *Kings v King (Inspector of Taxes)* [2004] S.T.C. (S.C.D.) 186 (Sp Comm), Michael Tildesley

s.21A, amended: 2003 c.1 Sch.6 para.7, 2004 c.12 Sch.35 para.3, Sch.42 Part 3

s.31A, added: 2004 c.12 s.143

s.31A, applied: SI 2004/2664 Reg.2, Reg.3, Reg.4

s.31A, enabling: SI 2004/2664

s.31B, added: 2004 c.12 s.143

s.31B, enabling: SI 2004/2664

s.34, referred to: SI 2002/2006 Reg.14

s.42, applied: SI 2004/2664 Reg.4

s.43A, amended: 2002 c.23 s.103

s.43A, referred to: SI 2004/1863 Sch.1 para.7

s.43A, repealed (in part): 2002 c.23 Sch.40 Part 3

s.46, applied: SI 2002/2006 Reg.10

s.49, amended: SI 2004/2744 Sch.1 para.2

s.50, amended: SI 2002/2521 Sch.2 Part I, SI 2004/2744 Sch.1 para.2

s.51, amended: SI 2004/2744 Sch.1 para.2

s.55, applied: 2002 c.23 Sch.29 para.33

s.56, amended: 2004 c.12 Sch.35 para.4

s.56, applied: 2003 c.14 s.151

s.56, referred to: SI 2002/2006 Reg.14

s.56, repealed (in part): 2002 c.23 Sch.40 Part 3

s.56, varied: SI 2003/1633 Sch.2 para.6

s.56A, referred to: 2002 c.29 Sch.10 para.6, SI 2002/2006 Reg.14

s.56A, varied: SI 2003/1633 Sch.2 para.6

s.58, applied: 2002 c.23 s.50

s.58, repealed: 2003 c.1 Sch.8 Part 1

s.60, applied: 2003 c.14 Sch.36 para.3

s.61, applied: 2002 c.29 Sch.10 para.12, 2003 c.14 Sch.36 para.3, 2004 c.12 s.130

s.62, applied: 2003 c.14 Sch.36 para.3

s.62A, applied: 2003 c.14 Sch.36 para.3

s.63, applied: 2003 c.14 Sch.36 para.3

s.63A, applied: 2003 c.14 Sch.36 para.10, Sch.36 para.15

s.65, amended: 2003 c.1 Sch.8 Part 1

s.65, applied: SI 2002/2006 Reg.12, 2003 c.1 s.613, s.679

s.65, referred to: 2003 c.1 s.575, s.613, s.631, s.635

s.68, applied: 2003 c.1 s.679

s.68, referred to: 2003 c.1 s.575, s.613, s.631, s.635

s.68A, added: 2003 c.1 Sch.6 para.10

s.68A, applied: 2003 c.1 Sch.2 para.87

s.68A, referred to: 2003 c.1 s.515

s.68B, added: 2003 c.1 Sch.6 para.10

s.68B, applied: 2003 c.1 s.493, s.496, s.497, Sch.2 para.79, Sch.2 para.87

s.68B, referred to: 2003 c.1 s.515

s.68C, added: 2003 c.1 Sch.6 para.10

1988–cont.

1. Income and Corporation Taxes Act 1988–cont.

s.68C, applied: 2003 c.1 Sch.2 para.87

s.68C, referred to: 2003 c.1 s.515

s.70, disapplied: 2002 c.23 s.65

s.72, see *Lyons v Kelly (Inspector of Taxes)* [2002] S.T.C. (S.C.D.) 455 (Sp Comm), Nuala Brice

s.74, see *Beauty Consultants Ltd v Inspector of Taxes* [2002] S.T.C. (S.C.D.) 352 (Sp Comm), John F Avery Jones; see *Mars UK Ltd v Small (Inspector of Taxes)* [2004] S.T.C. (S.C.D.) 253 (Sp Comm), Dr Nuala Brice; see *Powell v Jackman (Inspector of Taxes)* [2002] S.T.C. (S.C.D.) 488 (Sp Comm), Nuala Brice; see *Powell v Jackman (Inspector of Taxes)* [2004] EWHC 550, [2004] S.T.C. 645 (Ch D), Lewison, J.

s.74, applied: 2002 c.23 Sch.26 para.22

s.74, disapplied: 2002 c.23 Sch.29 para.8

s.74, referred to: 2002 c.23 Sch.26 para.14

s.74, repealed (in part): 2004 c.12 Sch.42 Part 2

s.75, see *Cadbury Schweppes Plc v Williams (Inspector of Taxes)* [2002] S.T.C. (S.C.D.) 115 (Sp Comm), John F Avery Jones; see *Camas Plc v Atkinson (Inspector of Taxes)* [2003] EWHC 1600, [2003] S.T.C. 968 (Ch D), Patten, J.; see *Camas Plc v Atkinson (Inspector of Taxes)* [2003] S.T.C. (S.C.D.) 1 (Sp Comm), Stephen Oliver Q.C.; see *Camas Plc v Atkinson (Inspector of Taxes)* [2004] EWCA Civ 541, [2004] 1 W.L.R. 2392 (CA), Sir Andrew Morritt V.C.

s.75, applied: 2003 c.14 Sch.23 para.9, Sch.23 para.16, 2004 c.12 s.43, s.44, s.196, s.200, s.246, Sch.36 para.41, 2004 c.20 s.44, SI 2004/2310 Sch.1 para.12

s.75, disapplied: 2004 c.12 s.43

s.75, referred to: SI 2004/2310 Sch.1 para.13, Sch.1 para.14

s.75, substituted: 2004 c.12 s.389

s.75A, added: 2004 c.12 s.39

s.75A, applied: 2004 c.12 s.246

s.75B, added: 2004 c.12 s.45

s.75B, applied: 2004 c.12 s.246

s.76, amended: 2003 c.14 Sch.33 para.6, Sch.33 para.8, Sch.33 para.12

s.76, applied: 2002 c.23 Sch.12 para.13, Sch.13 para.23, Sch.29 para.36, 2003 c.14 Sch.24 para.7, 2003 c.1 s.357, 2003 c.14 Sch.23 para.9, Sch.23 para.16, 2004 c.12 s.44, s.196, s.199, s.200, s.246, Sch.36 para.41

s.76, referred to: 2004 c.12 s.246

s.76, substituted: 2004 c.12 s.40

s.76, varied: 2003 c.14 Sch.33 para.7, 2004 c.12 s.199, SI 2004/2200 Reg.3

s.76B, amended: 2004 c.12 Sch.6 para.1

1988–cont.

1. Income and Corporation Taxes Act 1988–cont.

s.77, see *Cadbury Schweppes Plc v Williams (Inspector of Taxes)* [2002] S.T.C. (S.C.D.) 115 (Sp Comm), John F Avery Jones

s.77, amended: 2004 c.12 Sch.42 Part 2

s.77, repealed (in part): 2002 c.23 Sch.40 Part 3

s.79, amended: SI 2004/2310 Sch.1 para.3

s.79A, amended: SI 2004/2310 Sch.1 para.3

s.79B, added: 2003 c.14 s.180

s.79B, amended: SI 2004/2310 Sch.1 para.3

s.79B, applied: SI 2004/439, SI 2004/439 Art.2, Art.3, Art.4, Art.5

s.79B, enabling: SI 2004/439

s.82A, applied: 2004 c.12 s.53

s.83A, varied: 2002 c.23 Sch.18 para.9

s.84A, amended: 2003 c.1 Sch.6 para.11, SI 2004/2310 Sch.1 para.4

s.85, amended: SI 2004/2310 Sch.1 para.5

s.85A, amended: SI 2004/2310 Sch.1 para.6

s.85B, added: 2003 c.1 Sch.6 para.12

s.86, amended: SI 2004/2310 Sch.1 para.7

s.86, applied: 2004 c.12 s.44

s.86A, amended: 2003 c.1 Sch.6 para.13, SI 2004/2310 Sch.1 para.8

s.88, amended: SI 2004/2310 Sch.1 para.9

s.90, amended: SI 2004/2310 Sch.1 para.10

s.91A, amended: SR 2003/46 Sch.11 para.3

s.91A, repealed (in part): 2002 c.23 Sch.40 Part 3

s.91B, repealed (in part): 2002 c.23 Sch.40 Part 3

s.93, amended: SI 2004/2310 Sch.1 para.11

s.94, see *Wildin & Co v Jowett (Inspector of Taxes)* [2002] S.T.C. (S.C.D.) 390 (Sp Comm), John F Avery Jones

s.95, amended: 2004 c.12 s.137

s.95, repealed (in part): 2003 c.14 Sch.43 Part 3

s.100, amended: 2002 c.23 s.106, 2004 c.12 Sch.5 para.2

s.100, applied: 2002 c.23 Sch.22 para.8

s.100, referred to: 2002 c.29 Sch.10 para.11

s.100, repealed (in part): 2002 c.23 Sch.40 Part 3

s.113, referred to: 2002 c.23 Sch.22 para.3

s.114, applied: 2002 c.23 Sch.26 para.49

s.115, amended: 2003 c.14 s.153

s.117, amended: 2004 c.12 s.124

s.118ZB, substituted: 2004 c.12 s.124

s.118ZD, amended: 2004 c.12 s.124

s.122, applied: 2002 c.23 Sch.18 para.4

s.127, amended: 2004 c.12 Sch.35 para.5

s.128, substituted: 2002 c.23 Sch.27 para.3

s.129B, amended: 2004 c.12 Sch.35 para.6

s.130, see *Cadbury Schweppes Plc v Williams (Inspector of Taxes)* [2002] S.T.C. (S.C.D.) 115 (Sp Comm), John F Avery Jones

s.130, amended: 2004 c.12 s.38

s.131, repealed: 2003 c.1 Sch.8 Part 1

1988–cont.

1. **Income and Corporation Taxes Act 1988**–*cont.*

s.132, applied: 2003 c.1 Sch.7 para.9, Sch.7 para.11

s.132, repealed: 2003 c.1 Sch.8 Part 1

s.133, applied: SI 2002/2006 Reg.5

s.133, repealed: 2003 c.1 Sch.8 Part 1

s.134, repealed: 2003 c.1 Sch.8 Part 1

s.135, see *Bluck v Salton (Inspector of Taxes) (No.1)* [2003] S.T.C. (S.C.D.) 439 (Sp Comm), Malcolm Gammie Q.C.

s.135, amended: 2002 c.23 Sch.6 para.1

s.135, applied: 2003 c.1 Sch.7 para.67

s.135, referred to: 2002 c.29 Sch.10 para.30

s.135, repealed: 2003 c.1 Sch.8 Part 1

s.136, applied: 2003 c.1 Sch.7 para.60, Sch.7 para.67

s.136, repealed: 2003 c.1 Sch.8 Part 1

s.137, repealed: 2003 c.1 Sch.8 Part 1

s.138, amended: 2003 c.1 Sch.6 para.16

s.138, applied: 2003 c.1 s.418

s.139, applied: 2003 c.1 s.418

s.140, see *Bluck v Salton (Inspector of Taxes) (No.1)* [2003] S.T.C. (S.C.D.) 439 (Sp Comm), Malcolm Gammie Q.C.

s.140, applied: 2003 c.1 s.418

s.140, repealed: 2003 c.1 Sch.8 Part 1

s.140A, applied: 2003 c.1 Sch.7 para.47, Sch.7 para.48, Sch.7 para.59

s.140A, referred to: 2002 c.29 Sch.10 para.31

s.140A, repealed: 2003 c.1 Sch.8 Part 1

s.140B, repealed: 2003 c.1 Sch.8 Part 1

s.140C, repealed: 2003 c.1 Sch.8 Part 1

s.140D, applied: 2003 c.1 Sch.7 para.53, Sch.7 para.59

s.140D, repealed: 2003 c.1 Sch.8 Part 1

s.140E, repealed: 2003 c.1 Sch.8 Part 1

s.140F, repealed: 2003 c.1 Sch.8 Part 1

s.140G, applied: 2003 c.1 Sch.7 para.47, Sch.7 para.48, Sch.7 para.53, Sch.7 para.60

s.140G, repealed: 2003 c.1 Sch.8 Part 1

s.140H, repealed: 2003 c.1 Sch.8 Part 1

s.141, repealed: 2003 c.1 Sch.8 Part 1

s.142, see *Allcock v King (Inspector of Taxes)* [2004] S.T.C. (S.C.D.) 122 (Sp Comm), Graham Aaronson Q.C.

s.142, repealed: 2003 c.1 Sch.8 Part 1

s.143, repealed: 2003 c.1 Sch.8 Part 1

s.144, amended: 2002 c.23 Sch.6 para.2

s.144, applied: 2003 c.1 Sch.7 para.19

s.144, disapplied: 2003 c.1 Sch.7 para.20

s.144, repealed: 2003 c.1 Sch.8 Part 1

s.144A, amended: 2002 c.23 Sch.6 para.4

s.144A, repealed: 2003 c.1 Sch.8 Part 1

s.145, repealed: 2003 c.1 Sch.8 Part 1

s.146, repealed: 2003 c.1 Sch.8 Part 1

s.146A, repealed: 2003 c.1 Sch.8 Part 1

s.147, repealed: 2003 c.1 Sch.8 Part 1

1988–cont.

1. **Income and Corporation Taxes Act 1988**–*cont.*

s.148, see *Bluck v Salton (Inspector of Taxes) (No.1)* [2003] S.T.C. (S.C.D.) 439 (Sp Comm), Malcolm Gammie Q.C.; see *Walker v Adams (Inspector of Taxes)* [2003] S.T.C. (S.C.D.) 269 (Sp Comm), BMF O'Brien; see *Wilson (Inspector of Taxes) v Clayton* [2004] EWHC 898, [2004] S.T.C. 1022 (Ch D), Patten, J.

s.148, amended: 2002 c.23 Sch.6 para.5

s.148, applied: SR 2002/352 Sch.4 para.1, 2003 c.1 Sch.7 para.43

s.148, repealed: 2003 c.1 Sch.8 Part 1

s.149, see *McBride v Blackburn (Inspector of Taxes)* [2003] S.T.C. (S.C.D.) 139 (Sp Comm), Nuala Brice

s.149, repealed: 2003 c.1 Sch.8 Part 1

s.150, amended: 2002 c.23 s.35

s.150, repealed: 2003 c.1 Sch.8 Part 1

s.151, repealed: 2003 c.1 Sch.8 Part 1

s.151A, repealed: 2003 c.1 Sch.8 Part 1

s.152, amended: SI 2002/1397 Sch.1 para.6, 2003 c.1 Sch.6 para.23

s.153, repealed: 2003 c.1 Sch.8 Part 1

s.154, see *Dextra Accessories Ltd v Macdonald (Inspector of Taxes)* [2002] S.T.C. (S.C.D.) 413 (Sp Comm), JF Avery Jones; see *Kerr v Brown (Inspector of Taxes) (No.1)* [2002] S.T.C. (S.C.D.) 434 (Sp Comm), Colin Bishopp; see *Lord Hanson v Mansworth (Inspector of Taxes)* [2004] S.T.C. (S.C.D.) 288 (Sp Comm), Nuala Brice; see *McBride v Blackburn (Inspector of Taxes)* [2003] S.T.C. (S.C.D.) 139 (Sp Comm), Nuala Brice; see *Vasili v Christensen (Inspector of Taxes)* [2004] EWHC 476, [2004] S.T.C. 935 (Ch D), Pumfrey, J.; see *Wilson (Inspector of Taxes) v Clayton* [2004] EWHC 898, [2004] S.T.C. 1022 (Ch D), Patten, J.

s.154, applied: SI 2002/2006 Reg.4

s.154, disapplied: SI 2002/205 Reg.3, Reg.4, SI 2002/1596 Reg.3

s.154, repealed: 2003 c.1 Sch.8 Part 1

s.155, repealed: 2003 c.1 Sch.8 Part 1

s.155A, repealed: 2003 c.1 Sch.8 Part 1

s.155AA, repealed: 2003 c.1 Sch.8 Part 1

s.155ZA, applied: SI 2002/1596 Reg.3

s.155ZA, repealed: 2003 c.1 Sch.8 Part 1

s.155ZB, amended: 2002 c.23 s.36

s.155ZB, repealed: 2003 c.1 Sch.8 Part 1

s.155ZB, enabling: SI 2002/205, SI 2002/1596

s.156, see *Kerr v Brown (Inspector of Taxes) (No.1)* [2002] S.T.C. (S.C.D.) 434 (Sp Comm), Colin Bishopp; see *Kerr v Brown (Inspector of Taxes) (No.2)* [2003] S.T.C (S.C.D.) 266 (Sp Comm), Colin Bishopp

s.156, applied: SI 2002/2006 Reg.4

s.156, repealed: 2003 c.1 Sch.8 Part 1

s.156A, repealed: 2003 c.1 Sch.8 Part 1

1988–cont.

1. Income and Corporation Taxes Act 1988–*cont.*

s.157, see *Allcock v King (Inspector of Taxes)* [2004] S.T.C. (S.C.D.) 122 (Sp Comm), Graham Aaronson Q.C.; see *Vasili v Christensen (Inspector of Taxes)* [2004] EWHC 476, [2004] S.T.C. 935 (Ch D), Pumfrey, J.

s.157, amended: 2002 c.23 Sch.6 para.3

s.157, repealed: 2003 c.1 Sch.8 Part 1

s.157A, repealed: 2003 c.1 Sch.8 Part 1

s.158, see *Allcock v King (Inspector of Taxes)* [2004] S.T.C. (S.C.D.) 122 (Sp Comm), Graham Aaronson Q.C.

s.158, amended: 2002 c.23 s.34, SI 2002/706 Art.2

s.158, repealed: 2003 c.1 Sch.8 Part 1

s.158, enabling: SI 2002/706

s.159, repealed: 2003 c.1 Sch.8 Part 1

s.159AA, amended: 2002 c.23 Sch.6 para.3

s.159AA, repealed: 2003 c.1 Sch.8 Part 1

s.159AB, repealed: 2003 c.1 Sch.8 Part 1

s.159AC, amended: 2002 c.23 Sch.6 para.3

s.159AC, repealed: 2003 c.1 Sch.8 Part 1

s.160, repealed: 2003 c.1 Sch.8 Part 1

s.161, repealed: 2003 c.1 Sch.8 Part 1

s.161A, repealed: 2003 c.1 Sch.8 Part 1

s.161B, repealed: 2003 c.1 Sch.8 Part 1

s.162, applied: 2003 c.1 Sch.7 para.29

s.162, referred to: 2002 c.29 Sch.10 para.32

s.162, repealed: 2003 c.1 Sch.8 Part 1

s.163, repealed: 2003 c.1 Sch.8 Part 1

s.164, repealed: 2003 c.1 Sch.8 Part 1

s.165, repealed: 2003 c.1 Sch.8 Part 1

s.166, disapplied: 2003 c.1 Sch.7 para.16

s.166, repealed: 2003 c.1 Sch.8 Part 1

s.167, see *Allcock v King (Inspector of Taxes)* [2004] S.T.C. (S.C.D.) 122 (Sp Comm), Graham Aaronson Q.C.

s.167, repealed: 2003 c.1 Sch.8 Part 1

s.168, see *R. v Allen (Brian Roger)* [2001] UKHL 45, [2002] 1 A.C. 509 (HL), Lord Hutton

s.168, repealed: 2003 c.1 Sch.8 Part 1

s.168A, repealed: 2003 c.1 Sch.8 Part 1

s.168AA, repealed: 2003 c.1 Sch.8 Part 1

s.168AB, repealed: 2003 c.1 Sch.8 Part 1

s.168B, repealed: 2003 c.1 Sch.8 Part 1

s.168C, repealed: 2003 c.1 Sch.8 Part 1

s.168D, repealed: 2003 c.1 Sch.8 Part 1

s.168E, repealed: 2003 c.1 Sch.8 Part 1

s.168F, repealed: 2003 c.1 Sch.8 Part 1

s.168G, repealed: 2003 c.1 Sch.8 Part 1

s.185, applied: 2003 c.1 Sch.7 para.65, Sch.7 para.66, Sch.7 para.76

s.185, repealed: 2003 c.1 Sch.8 Part 1

s.186, amended: 2003 c.1 Sch.6 para.26, Sch.8 Part 1

s.186, applied: 2003 c.1 s.418, Sch.7 para.76

s.186, varied: 2003 c.1 s.418

1988–cont.

1. Income and Corporation Taxes Act 1988–*cont.*

s.187, applied: 2003 c.1 s.418, Sch.7 para.76

s.187, repealed (in part): 2003 c.1 Sch.8 Part 1

s.187, varied: 2003 c.1 s.418

s.187A, repealed: 2003 c.1 Sch.8 Part 1

s.188, see *Bluck v Salton (Inspector of Taxes) (No.1)* [2003] S.T.C. (S.C.D.) 439 (Sp Comm), Malcolm Gammie Q.C.

s.189, repealed: 2003 c.1 Sch.8 Part 1

s.190, repealed: 2003 c.1 Sch.8 Part 1

s.191, repealed: 2003 c.1 Sch.8 Part 1

s.191A, repealed: 2003 c.1 Sch.8 Part 1

s.191B, repealed: 2003 c.1 Sch.8 Part 1

s.192, applied: SI 2002/427 Reg.2, SI 2002/836 Reg.2, SR 2002/127 Reg.2

s.192, repealed: 2003 c.1 Sch.8 Part 1

s.192A, repealed: 2003 c.1 Sch.8 Part 1

s.193, repealed: 2003 c.1 Sch.8 Part 1

s.194, repealed: 2003 c.1 Sch.8 Part 1

s.195, repealed: 2003 c.1 Sch.8 Part 1

s.196, applied: SI 2002/2006 Reg.12

s.196, repealed: 2003 c.1 Sch.8 Part 1

s.197, repealed: 2003 c.1 Sch.8 Part 1

s.197A, repealed: 2003 c.1 Sch.8 Part 1

s.197AA, repealed: 2003 c.1 Sch.8 Part 1

s.197AB, amended: 2002 c.23 s.33

s.197AB, repealed: 2003 c.1 Sch.8 Part 1

s.197AC, repealed: 2003 c.1 Sch.8 Part 1

s.197AD, repealed: 2003 c.1 Sch.8 Part 1

s.197AE, repealed: 2003 c.1 Sch.8 Part 1

s.197AF, repealed: 2003 c.1 Sch.8 Part 1

s.197AH, repealed: 2003 c.1 Sch.8 Part 1

s.197B, repealed: 2003 c.1 Sch.8 Part 1

s.197C, repealed: 2003 c.1 Sch.8 Part 1

s.197D, repealed: 2003 c.1 Sch.8 Part 1

s.197E, repealed: 2003 c.1 Sch.8 Part 1

s.197F, repealed: 2003 c.1 Sch.8 Part 1

s.197G, repealed: 2003 c.1 Sch.8 Part 1

s.198, see *Kirkwood (Inspector of Taxes) v Evans* [2002] EWHC 30, [2002] 1 W.L.R. 1794 (Ch D), Patten, J.; see *Phillips v Hamilton (Inspector of Taxes)* [2003] S.T.C (S.C.D.) 286 (Sp Comm), Nuala Brice

s.198, repealed: 2003 c.1 Sch.8 Part 1

s.199, repealed: 2003 c.1 Sch.8 Part 1

s.200, amended: 2002 c.23 s.41

s.200, repealed: 2003 c.1 Sch.8 Part 1

s.200A, repealed: 2003 c.1 Sch.8 Part 1

s.200A, varied: 2003 c.1 Sch.7 para.34

s.200AA, repealed: 2003 c.1 Sch.8 Part 1

s.200B, see *Silva v Charnock (Inspector of Taxes)* [2002] S.T.C. (S.C.D.) 426 (Sp Comm), JF Avery Jones

s.200B, repealed: 2003 c.1 Sch.8 Part 1

s.200C, see *Silva v Charnock (Inspector of Taxes)* [2002] S.T.C. (S.C.D.) 426 (Sp Comm), JF Avery Jones

s.200C, repealed: 2003 c.1 Sch.8 Part 1

s.200D, repealed: 2003 c.1 Sch.8 Part 1

1988–cont.

1. Income and Corporation Taxes Act 1988–*cont.*

s.200E, repealed: 2003 c.1 Sch.8 Part 1

s.200F, repealed: 2003 c.1 Sch.8 Part 1

s.200G, repealed: 2003 c.1 Sch.8 Part 1

s.200H, repealed: 2003 c.1 Sch.8 Part 1

s.200J, repealed: 2003 c.1 Sch.8 Part 1

s.200ZA, amended: 2002 c.23 s.41

s.200ZA, repealed: 2003 c.1 Sch.8 Part 1

s.201, repealed: 2003 c.1 Sch.8 Part 1

s.201A, repealed: 2003 c.1 Sch.8 Part 1

s.201AA, repealed: 2003 c.1 Sch.8 Part 1

s.202, repealed: 2003 c.1 Sch.8 Part 1

s.202, enabling: SI 2003/1745

s.202A, applied: 2002 c.23 Sch.29 para.113

s.202B, see *White v Inland Revenue Commissioners* [2003] S.T.C. (S.C.D.) 161 (Sp Comm), BMF O'Brien

s.202B, applied: 2002 c.23 Sch.29 para.113

s.203, see *Blackburn (Inspector of Taxes) v Keeling* [2003] EWHC 754, [2003] S.T.C. 639 (Ch D), Peter Smith, J.

s.203, applied: 2002 c.21 s.29, Sch.2 para.7

s.203, enabling: SI 2002/680, SI 2003/536

s.207, applied: 2003 c.1 Sch.7 para.12

s.208, see *Strand Options & Futures Ltd v Vojak (Inspector of Taxes)* [2002] S.T.C. (S.C.D.) 398 (Sp Comm), John F Avery Jones; see *Strand Options & Futures Ltd v Vojak (Inspector of Taxes)* [2003] EWCA Civ 1457, [2004] S.T.C. 64 (CA), Carnwath, L.J.; see *Strand Options & Futures Ltd v Vojak (Inspector of Taxes)* [2003] EWHC 67, [2003] S.T.C. 331 (Ch D), Etherton, J.

s.208, applied: 2004 c.12 Sch.36 para.1

s.209, amended: 2002 c.23 s.102, 2004 c.12 Sch.42 Part 2

s.209, repealed (in part): 2004 c.12 Sch.42 Part 2

s.209A, added: 2002 c.23 s.102

s.209A, referred to: 2004 c.12 s.307

s.209B, added: 2002 c.23 s.102

s.209B, amended: 2003 c.14 Sch.18 para.3

s.212, amended: 2004 c.12 Sch.42 Part 2

s.212, repealed (in part): 2004 c.12 Sch.42 Part 2

s.213, amended: 2003 c.14 Sch.18 para.3

s.214, amended: 2002 c.23 Sch.30 para.1, 2003 c.14 Sch.18 para.3

s.215, amended: 2003 c.14 Sch.18 para.3

s.215, applied: SI 2004/1864 Reg.5

s.219, see *Strand Options & Futures Ltd v Vojak (Inspector of Taxes)* [2002] S.T.C. (S.C.D.) 398 (Sp Comm), John F Avery Jones

s.225, applied: SI 2004/1864 Reg.5

s.227, amended: 2004 c.12 Sch.35 para.7

s.231AA, amended: 2004 c.12 Sch.24 para.1

s.231AB, amended: 2004 c.12 Sch.24 para.1

s.233, amended: 2004 c.12 Sch.24 para.1

s.234, applied: SI 2003/3143 Reg.2

1988–cont.

1. Income and Corporation Taxes Act 1988–*cont.*

s.234A, applied: 2003 c.1 Sch.2 para.80, SI 2003/3143 Reg.2

s.234A, disapplied: 2003 c.1 s.493

s.246N, see *Mellham Ltd v Burton (Inspector of Taxes)* [2003] EWCA Civ 173, [2003] S.T.C. 441 (CA), Buxton, L.J.

s.247, see *Deutsche Morgan Grenfell Group Plc v Inland Revenue Commissioners* [2003] EWHC 1779, [2003] 4 All E.R. 645 (Ch D), Park, J.; see *NEC Semi Conductors Ltd v Inland Revenue Commissioners* [2003] EWHC 2813, [2004] S.T.C. 489 (Ch D), Park, J.; see *Pirelli Cable Holding NV v Inland Revenue Commissioners* [2003] EWCA Civ 1849, [2004] S.T.C. (Ch D), Peter Gibson, L.J.; see *Pirelli Cable Holding NV v Inland Revenue Commissioners* [2003] EWHC 32, [2003] S.T.C. 250 (Ch D), Park, J.

s.249, see *Howell v Trippier* [2004] EWCA Civ 885, [2004] S.T.C. 1245 (CA), Dame Elizabeth Butler-Sloss (President)

s.249, referred to: SI 2002/2006 Reg.14

s.251A, applied: 2003 c.1 Sch.2 para.87

s.251A, referred to: 2003 c.1 s.515

s.251B, applied: 2003 c.1 s.496, Sch.2 para.87

s.251B, referred to: 2003 c.1 s.515

s.251C, applied: 2003 c.1 s.493, s.496, s.497, Sch.2 para.79, Sch.2 para.87

s.251C, referred to: 2003 c.1 s.515

s.251D, applied: 2003 c.1 Sch.2 para.87

s.251D, referred to: 2003 c.1 s.515

s.254, applied: 2003 c.14 s.195

s.257, amended: 2002 c.23 s.28, s.29, SI 2002/2930 Art.2, SI 2003/3215 Art.2, 2004 c.12 s.24, SI 2004/3161 Art.2

s.257, applied: SI 2003/2682 Reg.17, Reg.19, Reg.20, 2004 c.12 s.192, SI 2004/3161 Art.2, SSI 2003/461 Reg.14

s.257, disapplied: 2004 c.12 s.24

s.257, referred to: 2002 c.23 s.28, s.29, SI 2003/2682 Reg.7, Reg.179, SI 2003/3215 Art.2

s.257, varied: 2002 c.23 s.29

s.257A, amended: SI 2002/2930 Art.2, SI 2003/3215 Art.2, SI 2004/3161 Art.2

s.257A, applied: SI 2003/2682 Reg.17, Reg.19, Reg.20, 2004 c.12 s.192, SI 2004/3161 Art.2

s.257A, referred to: SI 2003/2682 Reg.179, SI 2003/3215 Art.2

s.257A, repealed (in part): 2002 c.21 Sch.6

s.257AA, amended: SI 2002/707 Art.2

s.257AA, applied: 2002 c.21 s.1, 2002 c.23 s.27

s.257AA, repealed: 2002 c.21 Sch.6

s.257C, amended: 2002 c.21 Sch.6, 2003 c.1 Sch.6 para.35

1988–cont.

1. **Income and Corporation Taxes Act 1988**–*cont.*

s.257C, applied: SI 2002/707 Art.2, SI 2003/3215 Art.2, SI 2004/3161 Art.2

s.257C, disapplied: 2002 c.23 s.28, s.29

s.257C, varied: 2002 c.23 s.27

s.257C, enabling: SI 2002/707, SI 2002/2930, SI 2003/3215, SI 2004/3161

s.259, applied: SSI 2003/461 Reg.14

s.262, see *R. (on the application of Wilkinson) v Inland Revenue Commissioners* [2002] EWHC 182, [2002] S.T.C. 347 (QBD (Admin Ct)), Moses, J.; see *R. (on the application of Wilkinson) v Inland Revenue Commissioners* [2003] EWCA Civ 814, [2003] 1 W.L.R. 2683 (CA), Lord Phillips of Worth Matravers

s.265, amended: SI 2002/707 Art.2, SI 2002/2930 Art.2, SI 2003/3215 Art.2, 2004 c.12 Sch.35 para.8, SI 2004/3161 Art.2

s.265, applied: 2002 c.23 s.27, SI 2002/707 Art.2, SI 2003/3215 Art.2, SI 2004/3161 Art.2

s.265, referred to: SI 2003/2682 Reg.7, Reg.179, SI 2003/3215 Art.2

s.266, amended: 2004 c.12 Sch.35 para.9

s.266, applied: SI 2002/195 Sch.3 para.6, SI 2002/1330 Sch.3 para.6, SI 2002/3200 Sch.3 para.6, SI 2003/1994 Sch.3 para.6, SR 2002/224 Sch.3 para.6, SR 2002/265 Sch.7 para.6

s.266A, added: 2003 c.1 Sch.6 para.36

s.266A, amended: 2004 c.12 Sch.35 para.10

s.266A, applied: 2003 c.1 s.386

s.268, amended: 2004 c.12 Sch.35 para.11

s.273, amended: 2004 c.12 Sch.35 para.12

s.273, applied: SI 2002/195 Sch.3 para.6, SI 2002/1330 Sch.3 para.6, SI 2002/3200 Sch.3 para.3, Sch.3 para.4, Sch.3 para.6, SI 2003/1994 Sch.3 para.6, SR 2002/224 Sch.3 para.6, SR 2002/265 Sch.7 para.6, 2003 c.1 s.609

s.282A, amended: 2004 c.12 s.91

s.289, see *Forthright (Wales) Ltd v Davies (Inspector of Taxes)* [2004] EWHC 524, [2004] S.T.C. 875 (Ch D), Lightman, J.

s.289, amended: 2004 c.12 Sch.18 para.1, Sch.42 Part 2

s.289A, amended: 2002 c.23 Sch.17 para.2, SI 2003/2096 Sch.1 para.16, 2004 c.12 Sch.18 para.2, Sch.42 Part 2

s.289B, amended: 2004 c.12 Sch.18 para.3

s.290, amended: 2004 c.12 Sch.18 para.4

s.293, amended: SI 2003/2096 Sch.1 para.17, 2004 c.12 Sch.18 para.5, Sch.27 para.4, Sch.42 Part 2

s.297, amended: 2002 c.23 s.103, Sch.40 Part 3, 2004 c.12 Sch.27 para.4

s.298, amended: 2004 c.12 Sch.42 Part 2

s.299, amended: 2002 c.23 Sch.9 para.4

1988–cont.

1. **Income and Corporation Taxes Act 1988**–*cont.*

s.300, see *Fletcher (Inspector of Taxes) v Thompson* [2002] EWHC 1447, [2002] EWHC 1448, [2002] S.T.C. 1149 (Ch D), Lawrence Collins, J.

s.300, amended: 2004 c.12 Sch.18 para.6

s.303, amended: 2004 c.12 Sch.18 para.7

s.303, applied: 2004 c.12 Sch.18 para.8

s.303A, applied: 2004 c.12 Sch.18 para.7, Sch.18 para.8

s.303A, repealed (in part): 2004 c.12 Sch.42 Part 2

s.304, applied: 2002 c.23 s.50

s.304, referred to: 2002 c.23 s.50

s.306, see *Forthright (Wales) Ltd v Davies (Inspector of Taxes)* [2004] EWHC 524, [2004] S.T.C. 875 (Ch D), Lightman, J.

s.306, amended: 2003 c.1 Sch.6 para.37

s.306, applied: SI 2004/1863 Sch.1 para.3

s.307, amended: 2003 c.1 Sch.6 para.38

s.308, amended: 2004 c.12 Sch.18 para.9, Sch.42 Part 2

s.308, repealed (in part): 2004 c.12 Sch.42 Part 2

s.310, amended: 2004 c.12 Sch.18 para.10

s.312, amended: 2002 c.23 Sch.9 para.4, SI 2003/2096 Sch.1 para.18, 2004 c.12 Sch.18 para.11

s.312, applied: 2003 c.1 Sch.5 para.11

s.313, see *RCI (Europe) Ltd v Woods (Inspector of Taxes)* [2003] EWHC 3129, [2004] S.T.C. 315 (Ch D), Lightman, J.; see *RCI (Europe) Ltd v Woods (Inspector of Taxes)* [2003] S.T.C. (S.C.D.) 128 (Sp Comm), John F Avery Jones

s.313, repealed: 2003 c.1 Sch.8 Part 1

s.314, amended: 2003 c.1 Sch.6 para.40

s.314, applied: 2003 c.1 s.6

s.315, repealed: 2003 c.1 Sch.8 Part 1

s.316, repealed: 2003 c.1 Sch.8 Part 1

s.317, repealed: 2003 c.1 Sch.8 Part 1

s.318, repealed: 2003 c.1 Sch.8 Part 1

s.319, repealed: 2003 c.1 Sch.8 Part 1

s.321, repealed: 2003 c.1 Sch.8 Part 1

s.322, amended: 2002 c.8 s.2, 2003 c.1 Sch.6 para.44

s.322, referred to: 2003 c.1 Sch.6 para.167

s.322, repealed (in part): 2003 c.1 Sch.8 Part 1

s.323, amended: 2002 c.8 s.2, 2003 c.1 Sch.6 para.45

s.323, referred to: 2003 c.1 Sch.6 para.167

s.323, repealed (in part): 2003 c.1 Sch.8 Part 1

s.325, applied: SI 2002/2006 Reg.10

s.327A, added: 2003 c.14 s.175

s.327A, applied: SI 2002/2006 Reg.19

s.329AA, amended: 2003 c.39 s.100

s.329AA, applied: SI 2004/1863 Sch.1 para.4

s.329AA, referred to: 2003 c.39 s.101

1988–cont.

1. Income and Corporation Taxes Act 1988–*cont.*

s.329AA, repealed (in part): 2003 c.39 s.100, Sch.10

s.329AA, varied: SI 2004/1819 Art.2

s.329AB, amended: 2003 c.39 s.100

s.329AB, enabling: SI 2004/1819

s.330, repealed: 2003 c.1 Sch.8 Part 1

s.331, applied: SI 2002/2006 Reg.9, 2003 c.1 s.211

s.331, varied: 2003 c.1 s.215

s.331A, applied: SI 2002/2006 Reg.9

s.332, amended: 2003 c.1 Sch.6 para.47

s.332, repealed (in part): 2003 c.1 Sch.8 Part 1

s.333, enabling: SI 2002/453, SI 2002/1974, SI 2002/3158, SI 2003/2747, SI 2003/2748, SI 2004/1676, SI 2004/1677, SI 2004/2996

s.333A, applied: SI 2004/1450 Reg.15

s.333A, enabling: SI 2002/453

s.333B, applied: 2004 c.6 s.14

s.333B, varied: 2004 c.6 s.14

s.333B, enabling: SI 2002/453, SI 2004/2680

s.336, amended: 2003 c.1 Sch.6 para.48, 2004 c.12 Sch.17 para.10, Sch.35 para.13

s.336, repealed (in part): 2004 c.12 Sch.35 para.13, Sch.42 Part 3

s.337, referred to: 2002 c.23 Sch.22 para.3

s.337, substituted: 2002 c.23 Sch.30 para.1

s.337A, substituted: 2002 c.23 Sch.30 para.1

s.338, see *MacNiven (Inspector of Taxes) v Westmoreland Investments Ltd* [2001] UKHL 6, [2003] 1 A.C. 311 (HL), Lord Hoffmann

s.338, applied: 2004 c.20 Sch.4 para.3

s.338, substituted: 2002 c.23 Sch.30 para.1

s.338B, amended: 2003 c.14 s.153

s.342A, added: 2003 c.14 Sch.41 para.3

s.343, applied: 2003 c.1 Sch.5 para.23, 2004 c.12 s.59

s.343, disapplied: 2004 c.20 Sch.9 para.21

s.343, referred to: 2004 c.20 Sch.9 para.17

s.343, varied: 2004 c.20 Sch.9 para.2, Sch.9 para.17

s.344, applied: 2003 c.1 Sch.5 para.23

s.347A, amended: 2003 c.1 Sch.6 para.49

s.347A, applied: SI 2002/2006 Reg.10

s.347B, applied: 2002 c.23 Sch.16 para.19

s.348, amended: 2003 c.1 Sch.6 para.50, 2004 c.12 Sch.35 para.14

s.349, see *Mistletoe Ltd v Flood (Inspector of Taxes)* [2003] S.T.C. (S.C.D.) 66 (Sp Comm), BMF O'Brien

s.349, amended: 2002 c.23 s.95, 2003 c.14 s.202, 2003 c.1 Sch.6 para.51, 2004 c.12 s.105, Sch.35 para.15

s.349, applied: 2004 c.12 s.101, s.102, SI 2004/2622 Reg.8

1988–cont.

1. Income and Corporation Taxes Act 1988–*cont.*

s.349, referred to: 2002 c.23 Sch.26 para.51

s.349, varied: SI 2003/1633 Sch.2 para.6

s.349A, amended: 2002 c.23 s.94

s.349B, amended: 2002 c.23 s.94, SI 2002/2931 Art.2, 2003 c.14 s.153, 2004 c.12 Sch.35 para.16

s.349B, repealed (in part): 2002 c.23 Sch.40 Part 3, 2004 c.12 Sch.35 para.16, Sch.42 Part 3

s.349B, varied: SI 2004/1450 Reg.24

s.349B, enabling: SI 2002/2931

s.349C, amended: 2002 c.23 s.94

s.349D, amended: 2002 c.23 s.94

s.349E, added: 2002 c.23 s.96

s.350, amended: 2002 c.23 s.96

s.350, varied: 2004 c.12 s.101

s.352, applied: SI 2003/3143 Reg.3

s.353, applied: 2002 c.23 Sch.16 para.19, 2003 c.1 s.178

s.360A, amended: 2004 c.12 Sch.35 para.17

s.369, applied: SI 2002/1792 Sch.4 para.10, 2003 c.1 s.178, s.184, s.399, s.416, SR 2003/28 Sch.4 para.10

s.376, amended: 2003 c.1 Sch.6 para.52

s.379A, applied: SI 2002/2006 Reg.3, Reg.11, Reg.12

s.379B, applied: SI 2002/2006 Reg.12

s.380, see *Blackburn (Inspector of Taxes) v Keeling* [2003] EWCA Civ 1221, [2003] S.T.C. 1162 (CA), Carnwath, L.J.; see *Blackburn (Inspector of Taxes) v Keeling* [2003] EWHC 754, [2003] S.T.C. 639 (Ch D), Peter Smith, J.; see *Norton v Thompson (Inspector of Taxes)* [2004] S.T.C. (S.C.D.) 163 (Sp Comm), Adrian Shipwright

s.380, applied: 2003 c.1 s.11, s.329, 2004 c.12 s.119, s.121, s.126, s.128

s.381, see *Walsh v Taylor (Inspector of Taxes)* [2004] S.T.C. (S.C.D.) 48 (Sp Comm), John F Avery Jones

s.381, applied: 2004 c.12 s.119, s.121, s.126, s.128

s.391, amended: 2003 c.1 Sch.6 para.53

s.392, amended: 2003 c.1 Sch.6 para.54

s.392A, amended: SI 2004/2310 Sch.1 para.12

s.392A, applied: 2004 c.20 s.44, SI 2004/2310 Sch.1 para.12

s.392A, referred to: SI 2004/2310 Sch.1 para.13, Sch.1 para.14

s.392B, applied: 2004 c.20 s.44

s.393, applied: 2002 c.23 Sch.13 para.15, Sch.13 para.16, Sch.13 para.19, SI 2002/653 Art.4, 2003 c.14 Sch.33 para.7, 2004 c.20 s.27

s.393A, applied: 2002 c.23 Sch.13 para.15, Sch.13 para.16, 2004 c.20 s.27

s.399, amended: 2002 c.23 Sch.27 para.4

1988–cont.

1. Income and Corporation Taxes Act 1988–cont.

s.400, amended: SI 2004/2310 Sch.1 para.13

s.400, applied: SI 2002/653 Art.4, 2004 c.20 s.44

s.400, varied: SI 2002/653 Art.4, SI 2004/2310 Sch.1 para.13

s.401, applied: 2002 c.23 Sch.12 para.1, Sch.12 para.7, Sch.13 para.2

s.401, disapplied: 2002 c.23 Sch.12 para.20, Sch.13 para.2, Sch.13 para.15, Sch.13 para.28, Sch.15 para.2

s.402, amended: 2003 c.14 s.153

s.403, see *Taylor (Inspector of Taxes) v MEPC Holdings Ltd* [2002] EWCA Civ 883, [2002] S.T.C. 997 (CA), Chadwick, L.J.; see *Taylor (Inspector of Taxes) v MEPC Holdings Ltd* [2002] S.T.C. 430 (Ch D), Sir Donald Rattee; see *Taylor (Inspector of Taxes) v MEPC Holdings Ltd* [2003] UKHL 70, [2004] 1 W.L.R. 82 (HL), Lord Hoffmann

s.403, amended: 2002 c.23 Sch.30 para.2

s.403, applied: 2002 c.23 Sch.13 para.15, Sch.13 para.16, Sch.25 para.61A, Sch.29 para.35, 2004 c.20 s.27

s.403E, amended: 2003 c.14 s.153

s.403ZC, repealed (in part): 2002 c.23 Sch.40 Part 3

s.403ZD, amended: 2002 c.23 Sch.30 para.2, SI 2004/2310 Sch.1 para.14

s.403ZD, repealed (in part): SI 2004/2310 Sch.1 para.14

s.403ZD, varied: SI 2004/2310 Sch.1 para.14

s.403ZE, amended: SI 2004/2310 Sch.1 para.15

s.403ZE, repealed (in part): SI 2004/2310 Sch.1 para.15

s.403ZE, varied: SI 2004/2310 Sch.1 para.15

s.404, amended: SI 2004/2310 Sch.1 para.16

s.404, applied: 2002 c.23 Sch.29 para.55, Sch.29 para.84

s.404, referred to: SI 2004/2310 Sch.1 para.16

s.410, applied: SI 2002/653 Art.5

s.413, see *Marks & Spencer Plc v Halsey (Inspector of Taxes)* [2003] Eu.L.R. 46 (Sp Comm), John F Avery Jones

s.413, applied: SI 2004/2502 Reg.2

s.414, amended: 2004 c.12 Sch.35 para.18

s.415, amended: 2004 c.12 Sch.35 para.19

s.416, see *Gascoines Group Ltd v Inspector of Taxes* [2004] EWHC 640, [2004] S.T.C. 844 (Ch D), Lightman, J.; see *Gascoines Group Ltd v Inspector of Taxes* [2004] S.T.C. (S.C.D.) 11 (Sp Comm), AN Brice

s.416, applied: 2003 c.1 Sch.2 para.94, Sch.3 para.47, Sch.4 para.35, Sch.5 para.10, Sch.5 para.23, 2003 c.14 Sch.7 para.8, SI 2003/412 Art.85, 2004 c.12 Sch.11 para.4, SI 2004/352 Sch.2 para.37, Sch.2 para.38, Sch.3 para.38, Sch.3 para.39, Sch.4

1988–cont.

1. Income and Corporation Taxes Act 1988–cont.

s.416, applied:–cont.

para.36, Sch.6 para.35, Sch.6 para.36, SR 2002/352 Sch.4 para.9, 2003 c.1 s.230

s.416, referred to: SI 2004/352 Sch.4 para.37, SR 2002/352 Sch.4 para.9

s.416, varied: 2002 c.23 Sch.29 para.59, SI 2004/352 Sch.2 para.37, Sch.3 para.38, Sch.4 para.36, Sch.6 para.35

s.417, see *Gascoines Group Ltd v Inspector of Taxes* [2004] EWHC 640, [2004] S.T.C. 844 (Ch D), Lightman, J.

s.418, amended: 2003 c.1 Sch.6 para.55

s.421, referred to: SI 2002/2006 Reg.14

s.431, see *Royal London Mutual Insurance Society Ltd v Barrett (Inspector of Taxes)* [2003] EWCA Civ 789, [2003] S.T.C. 1129 (CA), Arden, L.J.

s.431, amended: 2003 c.14 Sch.33 para.20, Sch.33 para.22, Sch.33 para.25, Sch.33 para.29, 2004 c.12 s.147

s.431, applied: SI 2004/1450 Reg.14

s.431, varied: SI 2004/2200 Reg.3, SI 2004/2680 Reg.5

s.431A, enabling: SI 2004/3266

s.431B, applied: SI 2004/1450 Reg.12

s.431B, substituted: 2004 c.12 Sch.35 para.20

s.431B, varied: 2004 c.12 Sch.36 para.2

s.431C, see *Royal London Mutual Insurance Society Ltd v Barrett (Inspector of Taxes)* [2002] S.T.C. (S.C.D.) 61 (Sp Comm), Nuala Brice

s.431C, varied: SI 2004/2680 Reg.6

s.431C, enabling: SI 2003/1828, SI 2003/2573

s.431D, see *Royal London Mutual Insurance Society Ltd v Barrett (Inspector of Taxes)* [2002] EWHC 1416, [2002] S.T.C. 1020 (Ch D), Peter Smith, J.; see *Royal London Mutual Insurance Society Ltd v Barrett (Inspector of Taxes)* [2002] S.T.C. (S.C.D.) 61 (Sp Comm), Nuala Brice; see *Royal London Mutual Insurance Society Ltd v Barrett (Inspector of Taxes)* [2003] EWCA Civ 789, [2003] S.T.C. 1129 (CA), Arden, L.J.

s.431D, varied: SI 2004/2680 Reg.6

s.431D, enabling: SI 2004/3274

s.431E, enabling: SI 2004/3273

s.431F, varied: SI 2004/2680 Reg.7

s.432A, amended: 2002 c.23 Sch.25 para.46, Sch.40 Part 3, 2003 c.14 Sch.33 para.26, 2004 c.12 Sch.7 para.8

s.432A, applied: 2002 c.23 Sch.29 para.138

s.432A, repealed (in part): 2003 c.14 Sch.43 Part 3

s.432A, varied: SI 2004/2680 Reg.8

s.432AA, varied: SI 2004/2680 Reg.9

1988–cont.

1. Income and Corporation Taxes Act 1988–cont.

s.432AB, amended: SI 2004/2310 Sch.1 para.17

s.432C, varied: SI 2004/2680 Reg.10

s.432D, amended: 2003 c.14 Sch.33 para.9

s.432D, varied: SI 2004/2680 Reg.10

s.432E, applied: SI 2003/1860 Art.2

s.432E, referred to: SI 2003/1860 Art.2

s.432E, enabling: SI 2003/1860

s.432E, amended: 2003 c.14 Sch.33 para.10, Sch.43 Part 3, SI 2004/3266 Art.3

s.432E, repealed (in part): 2003 c.14 Sch.43 Part 3

s.432G, added: SI 2004/3266 Art.4

s.434, amended: 2003 c.14 Sch.33 para.6, Sch.33 para.12

s.434A, amended: 2003 c.14 Sch.33 para.6

s.436, amended: 2003 c.14 Sch.33 para.1, Sch.43 Part 3

s.436, applied: 2002 c.23 Sch.12 para.13, Sch.13 para.23

s.436, varied: SI 2004/2680 Reg.11

s.437, amended: 2003 c.14 Sch.33 para.6, SI 2004/2310 Sch.1 para.18

s.438, amended: 2004 c.12 Sch.7 para.9

s.438, repealed (in part): 2004 c.12 Sch.42 Part 3

s.438, varied: SI 2004/2680 Reg.12

s.438B, amended: 2003 c.14 Sch.33 para.13

s.438B, repealed (in part): 2003 c.14 Sch.43 Part 3

s.439A, enabling: SI 2003/1828

s.439B, amended: 2003 c.14 Sch.33 para.1, Sch.43 Part 3, 2004 c.12 Sch.7 para.9

s.439B, applied: 2002 c.23 Sch.12 para.13, Sch.13 para.23

s.440, amended: 2002 c.23 Sch.27 para.5, 2004 c.12 Sch.10 para.43, Sch.10 para.70

s.440, disapplied: SI 2004/822 Reg.20, SI 2004/2200 Reg.4

s.440, referred to: 2002 c.23 Sch.26 para.29, SI 2004/2200 Reg.4

s.440, varied: SI 2004/2680 Reg.13

s.440A, varied: SI 2004/2680 Reg.14

s.440B, referred to: SI 2004/2200 Reg.4

s.441, amended: 2003 c.14 Sch.33 para.1, Sch.43 Part 3

s.441, applied: 2002 c.23 Sch.12 para.13, Sch.13 para.23

s.442, amended: 2003 c.14 s.153

s.442A, amended: 2003 c.14 Sch.33 para.23, Sch.43 Part 3

s.442A, enabling: SI 2003/1828, SI 2003/2573, SI 2003/2642, SI 2004/2189, SI 2004/2257

s.444A, amended: 2003 c.14 Sch.33 para.24, 2004 c.12 Sch.7 para.1, SI 2004/2310 Sch.1 para.19

s.444A, applied: SI 2004/1864 Reg.5

s.444AA, added: 2003 c.14 Sch.33 para.18

1988–cont.

1. Income and Corporation Taxes Act 1988–cont.

s.444AA, applied: 2003 c.14 Sch.33 para.18

s.444AB, added: 2003 c.14 Sch.33 para.19

s.444AB, amended: 2004 c.12 Sch.7 para.2

s.444AB, applied: 2003 c.14 Sch.33 para.19

s.444AB, referred to: 2004 c.12 Sch.7 para.2, Sch.7 para.3

s.444ABA, added: 2004 c.12 Sch.7 para.3

s.444AC, added: 2003 c.14 Sch.33 para.20

s.444AC, amended: SI 2004/3266 Art.5

s.444AD, added: 2003 c.14 Sch.33 para.20

s.444AD, amended: 2004 c.12 Sch.7 para.4, SI 2004/3266 Art.6

s.444AD, applied: 2003 c.14 Sch.33 para.20

s.444AE, added: 2003 c.14 Sch.33 para.20

s.444BA, enabling: SI 2004/3260

s.444BB, amended: 2003 c.14 s.153

s.444BB, enabling: SI 2004/3260

s.444BC, enabling: SI 2004/3260

s.444BD, enabling: SI 2004/3260

s.458, applied: 2002 c.23 Sch.26 para.12, SI 2003/2172 Reg.2, SI 2003/2173 Reg.2

s.460, amended: 2003 c.14 s.172

s.461A, applied: 2002 c.23 Sch.29 para.55, Sch.29 para.66, Sch.29 para.84

s.463, enabling: SI 2003/23, SI 2004/822

s.464, amended: 2004 c.12 Sch.35 para.21

s.466, amended: 2004 c.12 Sch.35 para.22, Sch.42 Part 3

s.466, varied: 2004 c.12 Sch.36 para.2, SI 2004/2680 Reg.15

s.467, amended: 2004 c.12 Sch.35 para.23

s.468, amended: 2004 c.12 s.28

s.468, repealed (in part): SI 2004/2310 Sch.1 para.20

s.468AA, repealed: 2002 c.23 Sch.40 Part 3

s.468L, amended: 2002 c.23 Sch.27 para.7, 2003 c.14 s.203, SI 2004/2310 Sch.1 para.21

s.468M, applied: SI 2003/1830 Reg.3, Reg.8

s.468M, substituted: 2003 c.14 s.203

s.468M, varied: SI 2003/1830 Reg.4, Reg.7

s.468N, substituted: 2003 c.14 s.203

s.468O, amended: 2003 c.14 s.203

s.468O, applied: SI 2003/1830 Reg.3, Reg.8

s.468O, repealed (in part): 2003 c.14 Sch.43 Part 5

s.468O, varied: SI 2003/1830 Reg.5, Reg.7

s.468P, amended: 2003 c.14 s.203, Sch.43 Part 5

s.468P, applied: SI 2003/1830 Reg.3, Reg.8

s.468P, repealed (in part): 2003 c.14 Sch.43 Part 5

s.468P, varied: SI 2003/1830 Reg.6, Reg.7

s.468PA, added: 2003 c.14 s.203

s.468PB, added: 2003 c.14 s.203

s.468PB, enabling: SI 2003/1830

s.469A, amended: 2003 c.14 s.183, Sch.43 Part 3

1988–cont.

1. **Income and Corporation Taxes Act 1988**–*cont.*

s.469A, repealed (in part): 2003 c.14 Sch.43 Part 3

s.469A, varied: 2003 c.14 s.101

s.472A, added: 2004 c.12 s.54

s.473, amended: 2002 c.23 s.67, Sch.9 para.4, Sch.40 Part 3

s.473, applied: 2002 c.23 Sch.9 para.8

s.477A, amended: 2002 c.23 Sch.25 para.47

s.477A, varied: SI 2003/1633 Sch.2 para.6

s.477B, amended: 2002 c.23 Sch.25 para.48

s.481, applied: SI 2002/1968 Art.2

s.481, varied: SI 2003/1633 Sch.2 para.6

s.481, enabling: SI 2002/1968

s.482, varied: SI 2003/1633 Sch.2 para.6

s.482, enabling: SI 2002/1968

s.486, amended: SI 2002/794 Sch.1 para.31

s.486, applied: 2002 c.23 Sch.29 para.46, Sch.29 para.91

s.487, amended: SI 2004/2310 Sch.1 para.22

s.488, amended: SI 2004/2030 Art.5

s.488, applied: SI 2004/2030 Art.2, Art.3

s.494, amended: 2002 c.23 Sch.23 para.17, 2004 c.12 Sch.5 para.3, Sch.42 Part 2

s.494, repealed (in part): 2004 c.12 Sch.42 Part 2

s.494AA, amended: 2002 c.23 s.103

s.494AA, repealed (in part): 2002 c.23 Sch.40 Part 3

s.496, amended: 2004 c.12 Sch.37 para.11

s.496A, added: 2004 c.12 s.286

s.501A, added: 2002 c.23 s.91

s.501A, amended: 2002 c.23 Sch.23 para.18, Sch.27 para.8

s.501A, applied: 2002 c.23 s.63

s.501B, added: 2002 c.23 s.92

s.503, see *Patel v Maidment (Inspector of Taxes)* [2004] S.T.C. (S.C.D.) 41 (Sp Comm), John F Avery Jones

s.503, amended: 2004 c.12 Sch.35 para.24

s.503, applied: 2002 c.23 Sch.29 para.32

s.504, see *Patel v Maidment (Inspector of Taxes)* [2004] S.T.C. (S.C.D.) 41 (Sp Comm), John F Avery Jones

s.505, amended: 2002 c.23 Sch.30 para.3

s.505, applied: 2003 c.1 s.357, 2004 c.12 s.83, 2004 c.27 s.54

s.506, applied: 2002 c.23 Sch.13 para.6, Sch.13 para.12, SI 2002/302 Art.5, SI 2002/303 Art.5, SI 2003/285 Art.5, SI 2003/286 Art.5, SI 2004/368 Art.5, SI 2004/369 Art.5

s.508, referred to: 2002 c.23 Sch.13 para.6, Sch.13 para.12

s.510A, amended: 2002 c.23 Sch.25 para.49

s.512, repealed (in part): 2004 c.12 Sch.42 Part 3

s.519A, amended: 2002 c.17 Sch.5 para.27, SI 2002/2469 Sch.1 para.14, 2003 c.43 s.33, 2004 c.12 s.148

1988–cont.

1. **Income and Corporation Taxes Act 1988**–*cont.*

s.519A, repealed (in part): 2003 c.43 Sch.13 para.5, Sch.14 Part 4, Sch.14 Part 7

s.539, amended: 2003 c.14 Sch.34 para.1, Sch.34 para.6, Sch.34 para.13, 2004 c.12 Sch.35 para.25

s.539, referred to: 2003 c.14 Sch.34 para.12

s.539A, added: 2003 c.14 Sch.34 para.2

s.539A, applied: 2003 c.14 Sch.34 para.4

s.540, applied: SI 2004/1450 Reg.38

s.540, referred to: 2003 c.14 s.171

s.540, repealed (in part): 2003 c.14 Sch.43 Part 3

s.541, amended: 2002 c.23 s.87

s.541, applied: SI 2004/1450 Reg.24

s.543, amended: 2002 c.23 s.87

s.545, amended: 2003 c.1 Sch.6 para.56

s.546, applied: SI 2004/1450 Reg.12

s.546B, amended: 2002 c.23 s.87

s.547, amended: 2003 c.14 s.153, Sch.34 para.7, Sch.35 para.2

s.547, applied: SI 2002/2006 Reg.10, 2004 c.12 s.147, Sch.15 para.9

s.547, disapplied: 2003 c.14 Sch.34 para.12

s.547, varied: SI 2004/1450 Reg.38

s.547A, amended: 2003 c.14 Sch.34 para.8

s.548, amended: 2003 c.14 Sch.34 para.9

s.549, amended: 2004 c.12 s.140

s.549, applied: SI 2004/1450 Reg.24

s.550, amended: 2003 c.1 Sch.6 para.57, 2003 c.14 Sch.35 para.3

s.550, varied: SI 2004/1450 Reg.38

s.551, amended: 2003 c.14 Sch.34 para.10

s.551A, amended: 2003 c.14 Sch.34 para.11

s.552, referred to: SI 2002/3158 Reg.8, SI 2004/1450 Reg.37

s.552, varied: 2003 c.14 Sch.34 para.5, SI 2004/1450 Reg.38

s.552A, enabling: SI 2002/443, SI 2004/3272

s.552ZA, varied: SI 2004/1450 Reg.38

s.552ZA, enabling: SI 2002/444

s.553C, enabling: SI 2002/455

s.555, see *Agassi v Robinson (Inspector of Taxes)* [2004] EWHC 487, [2004] S.T.C. 610 (Ch D), Lightman, J.

s.555, applied: 2003 c.1 s.48nson (Inspector of Taxes) [2003] S.T.C. (S.C.D.) 382 (Sp Comm), John Avery-Jones; see *Agassi v Robinson (Inspector of Taxes)* [2004] EWHC 487, [2004] S.T.C. 610 (Ch D), Lightman, J.

s.559, amended: 2002 c.23 Sch.40 Part 3, 2003 c.1 Sch.6 para.58

s.559, applied: SI 2002/2820 Reg.4, SI 2003/2682 Reg.70, SR 2002/379 Reg.4, 2003 c.1 s.54

s.559, repealed (in part): 2002 c.23 Sch.40 Part 3, 2004 c.12 Sch.42 Part 2

s.559A, added: 2002 c.23 s.40

1988–cont.

1. **Income and Corporation Taxes Act 1988**–*cont.*

s.559A, applied: 2002 c.23 s.40, SI 2003/2682 Reg.70

s.559A, repealed: 2004 c.12 Sch.42 Part 2

s.559A, enabling: SI 2003/536

s.560, amended: 2002 c.23 Sch.40 Part 3

s.560, applied: 2003 c.1 Sch.7 para.14

s.560, repealed: 2004 c.12 Sch.42 Part 2

s.561, see *Shaw (Inspector of Taxes) v Vicky Construction Ltd* [2002] EWHC 2659, [2002] S.T.C.1544 (Ch D), Ferris, J.

s.561, amended: 2003 c.1 Sch.6 para.59

s.561, applied: 2004 c.12 s.77

s.561, repealed: 2004 c.12 Sch.42 Part 2

s.562, repealed: 2004 c.12 Sch.42 Part 2

s.563, repealed: 2004 c.12 Sch.42 Part 2

s.564, repealed: 2004 c.12 Sch.42 Part 2

s.565, see *Hudson (Inspector of Taxes) v JDC Services Ltd* [2004] EWHC 602, [2004] S.T.C. 834 (Ch D), Lightman, J.; see *Shaw (Inspector of Taxes) v Vicky Construction Ltd* [2002] EWHC 2659, [2002] S.T.C. 1544 (Ch D), Ferris, J.

s.565, amended: 2003 c.1 Sch.6 para.60

s.565, repealed: 2004 c.12 Sch.42 Part 2

s.566, amended: 2003 c.14 s.147, 2003 c.1 Sch.6 para.61

s.566, applied: 2004 c.12 s.77

s.566, repealed: 2004 c.12 Sch.42 Part 2

s.566, enabling: SI 2002/2225, SI 2003/536, SI 2004/1075

s.567, amended: 2003 c.21 Sch.17 para.88

s.567, repealed: 2004 c.12 Sch.42 Part 2

s.573, referred to: 2004 c.12 Sch.27 para.4, SI 2004/712 Reg.1

s.574, referred to: 2004 c.12 Sch.27 para.4, SI 2004/712 Reg.1

s.577, amended: 2003 c.1 Sch.8 Part 1, SI 2004/2310 Sch.1 para.23

s.577, applied: 2002 c.23 Sch.29 para.112, 2003 c.1 s.3572682 Reg.86, Reg.87

s.577, repealed (in part): 2003 c.1 Sch.8 Part 1

s.577A, amended: 2002 c.23 s.68, SI 2004/2310 Sch.1 para.24

s.577A, applied: 2002 c.23 Sch.29 para.112

s.578A, amended: 2002 c.23 s.60, SI 2004/2310 Sch.1 para.25

s.578A, applied: 2002 c.23 Sch.29 para.112

s.578B, amended: 2004 c.12 s.139

s.579, amended: SI 2004/2310 Sch.1 para.26

s.579, repealed (in part): 2003 c.1 Sch.8 Part 1

s.580, repealed (in part): 2003 c.1 Sch.8 Part 1

s.580A, amended: 2003 c.1 Sch.6 para.65

s.580C, added: 2004 c.12 s.147

s.582, amended: 2002 c.23 Sch.25 para.50

s.582A, amended: 2004 c.12 Sch.12 para.10

s.584, applied: SI 2002/2006 Reg.3, 2003 c.1 s.679

1988–cont.

1. **Income and Corporation Taxes Act 1988**–*cont.*

s.584, referred to: 2003 c.1 s.575, s.613, s.635

s.585, amended: 2003 c.1 Sch.8 Part 1

s.585, applied: 2003 c.1 s.613, s.679, Sch.7 para.11

s.585, referred to: 2003 c.1 s.575, s.613, s.635

s.585, repealed (in part): 2003 c.1 Sch.8 Part 1

s.587B, amended: 2002 c.23 s.97, Sch.40 Part 3, 2004 c.12 s.139, Sch.26 para.10, SI 2004/2310 Sch.1 para.27

s.587B, varied: 2002 c.23 s.97

s.587C, added: 2002 c.23 s.97

s.588, amended: 2003 c.1 Sch.6 para.67, SI 2004/2310 Sch.1 para.28

s.588, repealed (in part): 2003 c.1 Sch.8 Part 1

s.588, varied: 2003 c.1 Sch.7 para.37

s.589, repealed: 2003 c.1 Sch.8 Part 1

s.589A, amended: 2003 c.1 Sch.6 para.69, SI 2004/2310 Sch.1 para.29

s.589A, repealed (in part): 2003 c.1 Sch.8 Part 1

s.589B, amended: 2003 c.1 Sch.8 Part 1

s.589B, repealed (in part): 2003 c.1 Sch.8 Part 1

s.590, applied: SI 2002/427 Reg.2, SI 2002/836 Reg.2, SR 2002/127 Reg.2, SR 2002/352 Sch.4 para.1

s.590, repealed: 2004 c.12 Sch.42 Part 3

s.590A, repealed: 2004 c.12 Sch.42 Part 3

s.590B, repealed: 2004 c.12 Sch.42 Part 3

s.590C, applied: SI 2002/427 Reg.2, SI 2002/836 Reg.2, SI 2003/843 Art.2, SR 2002/127 Reg.2, 2004 c.12 Sch.36 para.16, SI 2004/773 Art.2

s.590C, referred to: SI 2002/427 Reg.2, SR 2002/127 Reg.2

s.590C, repealed: 2004 c.12 Sch.42 Part 3

s.590C, varied: SI 2002/700 Art.2

s.590C, enabling: SI 2002/700, SI 2003/843, SI 2004/773

s.591, applied: SI 2002/427 Reg.2, SI 2002/836 Reg.2, SR 2002/127 Reg.2

s.591, repealed: 2004 c.12 Sch.42 Part 3

s.591A, repealed: 2004 c.12 Sch.42 Part 3

s.591B, see *R. (on the application of Mander) v Inland Revenue Commissioners* [2002] S.T.C. 631 (QBD (Admin Ct)), Sullivan, J.

s.591B, referred to: 2004 c.12 Sch.36 para.5

s.591B, repealed: 2004 c.12 Sch.42 Part 3

s.591C, applied: 2003 c.1 s.397

s.591C, repealed: 2004 c.12 Sch.42 Part 3

s.591C, varied: 2004 c.12 Sch.36 para.5

s.591D, repealed (in part): 2003 c.1 Sch.8 Part 1, 2004 c.12 Sch.42 Part 3

s.591D, varied: 2004 c.12 Sch.36 para.5

CAP.

1988–cont.

1. Income and Corporation Taxes Act 1988–*cont.*

s.592, see *Trustees of the Sema Group Pension Scheme v Inland Revenue Commissioners* [2002] EWHC 94, [2002] S.T.C. 276 (Ch D), Lightman, J.

s.592, amended: 2003 c.1 Sch.6 para.72, SI 2004/2310 Sch.1 para.30

s.592, applied: SI 2002/427 Reg.2, SI 2002/836 Reg.2, SI 2003/2682 Reg.15, SR 2002/127 Reg.2, SR 2002/352 Sch.2 para.8, 2003 c.1 s.23, s.315, s.327, s.381, 2004 c.12 Sch.36 para.42

s.592, repealed: 2004 c.12 Sch.42 Part 3

s.593, repealed: 2004 c.12 Sch.42 Part 3

s.594, amended: 2003 c.1 Sch.6 para.73

s.594, applied: 2003 c.1 s.23, s.315, s.327, s.381, SI 2003/2682 Reg.15

s.594, repealed: 2004 c.12 Sch.42 Part 3

s.595, amended: 2002 c.23 Sch.6 para.6

s.595, applied: 2003 c.1 s.395, 2004 c.12 Sch.36 para.52, Sch.36 para.53

s.595, disapplied: SI 2002/427 Reg.2, SI 2002/836 Reg.2, SR 2002/127 Reg.2

s.595, referred to: SR 2002/127 Reg.2

s.595, repealed: 2003 c.1 Sch.8 Part 1

s.596, applied: SI 2002/427 Reg.2, SI 2002/836 Reg.2, SR 2002/127 Reg.2

s.596, referred to: SR 2002/352 Sch.4 para.1

s.596, repealed: 2003 c.1 Sch.8 Part 1

s.596A, repealed: 2003 c.1 Sch.8 Part 1

s.596B, repealed: 2003 c.1 Sch.8 Part 1

s.596C, repealed: 2003 c.1 Sch.8 Part 1

s.597, applied: SI 2002/2006 Reg.5

s.597, repealed: 2003 c.1 Sch.8 Part 1

s.598, applied: SR 2002/352 Reg.88, 2003 c.1 s.583, s.623

s.598, repealed: 2004 c.12 Sch.42 Part 3

s.599, applied: SR 2002/352 Reg.51, Reg.52, Reg.142, Reg.143, 2003 c.1 s.583, s.623

s.599, repealed: 2004 c.12 Sch.42 Part 3

s.599A, repealed (in part): 2003 c.1 Sch.8 Part 1, 2004 c.12 Sch.42 Part 3

s.600, see *Venables v Hornby (Inspector of Taxes)* [2002] EWCA Civ 1277, [2002] S.T.C. 1248 (CA), Chadwick, L.J.

s.600, applied: SI 2002/2006 Reg.5

s.600, repealed: 2003 c.1 Sch.8 Part 1

s.601, repealed: 2004 c.12 Sch.42 Part 3

s.602, repealed: 2004 c.12 Sch.42 Part 3

s.603, repealed: 2004 c.12 Sch.42 Part 3

s.604, repealed: 2004 c.12 Sch.42 Part 3

s.605, applied: SR 2002/352 Reg.4

s.605, referred to: 2004 c.12 Sch.36 para.50

s.605, repealed: 2004 c.12 Sch.42 Part 3

s.605, enabling: SI 2002/3006

s.605A, repealed: 2004 c.12 Sch.42 Part 3

s.606, amended: 2003 c.14 Sch.27 para.1, 2003 c.1 Sch.6 para.79

s.606, repealed: 2004 c.12 Sch.42 Part 3

CAP.

1988–cont.

1. Income and Corporation Taxes Act 1988–*cont.*

s.606, varied: 2003 c.14 s.153

s.606A, repealed: 2004 c.12 Sch.42 Part 3

s.607, amended: 2003 c.1 Sch.6 para.80

s.607, applied: SI 2002/2006 Reg.3

s.607, repealed (in part): 2003 c.1 Sch.8 Part 1, 2004 c.12 Sch.42 Part 3

s.608, applied: SI 2002/427 Reg.2, SI 2002/836 Reg.2, SI 2002/2006 Reg.5, SR 2002/127 Reg.2

s.608, referred to: SR 2002/352 Sch.4 para.1

s.608, repealed (in part): 2003 c.1 Sch.8 Part 1, 2004 c.12 Sch.42 Part 3

s.609, repealed: 2004 c.12 Sch.42 Part 3

s.610, repealed: 2004 c.12 Sch.42 Part 3

s.611, applied: 2004 c.12 Sch.36 para.1

s.611, referred to: SR 2002/352 Sch.4 para.1

s.611, repealed: 2004 c.12 Sch.42 Part 3

s.611A, applied: SI 2002/2006 Reg.3, 2004 c.12 Sch.36 para.4, SI 2004/1863 Sch.1 para.4

s.611A, referred to: SR 2002/352 Sch.4 para.1, 2004 c.12 Sch.36 para.1

s.611A, repealed: 2004 c.12 Sch.42 Part 3

s.611AA, repealed: 2004 c.12 Sch.42 Part 3

s.612, amended: 2003 c.1 Sch.6 para.82

s.612, applied: 2003 c.1 s.400

s.612, repealed: 2004 c.12 Sch.42 Part 3

s.613, amended: 2004 c.12 Sch.35 para.26, Sch.42 Part 3

s.613, applied: SI 2002/2006 Reg.5

s.613, referred to: 2004 c.12 Sch.36 para.1

s.613, repealed (in part): 2003 c.1 Sch.8 Part 1, 2004 c.12 Sch.35 para.26, Sch.42 Part 3

s.614, amended: 2003 c.1 Sch.6 para.84

s.614, applied: SI 2002/427 Reg.2, SI 2002/836 Reg.2, SR 2002/127 Reg.2

s.615, amended: 2002 c.1 Sch.3 para.9

s.615, applied: SI 2002/427 Reg.2, SI 2002/836 Reg.2, 2004 c.12 Sch.36 para.56, SI 2004/1863 Sch.1 para.4, SR 2002/127 Reg.2

s.615, referred to: 2003 c.1 s.412

s.615, repealed (in part): 2002 c.1 Sch.4, 2003 c.1 Sch.8 Part 1

s.616, applied: SI 2002/427 Reg.2, SI 2002/836 Reg.2, SR 2002/127 Reg.2

s.616, repealed: 2003 c.1 Sch.8 Part 1

s.617, amended: 2002 c.16 Sch.2 para.28, 2002 c.21 Sch.6, 2003 c.1 Sch.6 para.87, SI 2004/2310 Sch.1 para.31

s.617, repealed (in part): 2002 c.21 Sch.6, 2003 c.1 Sch.8 Part 1

s.617A, added: 2002 c.21 Sch.3 para.14

s.617A, repealed: 2003 c.1 Sch.8 Part 1

s.618, repealed: 2004 c.12 Sch.42 Part 3

s.619, see *Lonsdale v Braisby (Inspector of Taxes)* [2004] EWHC 1811, [2004] S.T.C. 1606 (Ch D), Lewison, J.

1988–cont.

1. Income and Corporation Taxes Act 1988–*cont.*

s.619, applied: SI 2002/195 Sch.3 para.6, SI 2002/1330 Sch.3 para.6, SI 2002/3200 Sch.3 para.3, Sch.3 para.4, Sch.3 para.6, 2003 c.1 s.315, SI 2003/1994 Sch.3 para.6, SR 2002/224 Sch.3 para.6, SR 2002/265 Sch.7 para.6, 2003 c.1 s.327

s.619, repealed: 2004 c.12 Sch.42 Part 3

s.620, applied: SR 2002/352 Reg.124, Sch.4 para.1, 2004 c.12 Sch.36 para.1, Sch.36 para.37

s.620, referred to: 2003 c.1 s.637, 2004 c.12 Sch.36 para.5

s.620, repealed: 2004 c.12 Sch.42 Part 3

s.621, applied: SR 2002/352 Reg.124, 2004 c.12 Sch.36 para.1, Sch.36 para.37

s.621, repealed: 2004 c.12 Sch.42 Part 3

s.622, applied: 2004 c.12 Sch.36 para.1, Sch.36 para.37

s.622, repealed: 2004 c.12 Sch.42 Part 3

s.623, applied: 2002 c.23 Sch.22 para.4

s.623, repealed: 2004 c.12 Sch.42 Part 3

s.624, amended: 2003 c.1 Sch.6 para.89

s.624, repealed: 2004 c.12 Sch.42 Part 3

s.625, see *Lonsdale v Braisby (Inspector of Taxes)* [2004] EWHC 1811, [2004] S.T.C. 1606 (Ch D), Lewison, J.

s.625, repealed: 2004 c.12 Sch.42 Part 3

s.626, repealed: 2004 c.12 Sch.42 Part 3

s.628, repealed: 2004 c.12 Sch.42 Part 3

s.630, applied: 2003 c.1 s.604

s.630, referred to: SI 2002/427 Reg.2, SI 2002/836 Reg.2, SR 2002/127 Reg.2, 2003 c.14 Sch.24 para.8

s.630, repealed: 2004 c.12 Sch.42 Part 3

s.631, applied: SR 2002/352 Sch.4 para.1

s.631, repealed: 2004 c.12 Sch.42 Part 3

s.631A, repealed: 2004 c.12 Sch.42 Part 3

s.632, repealed: 2004 c.12 Sch.42 Part 3

s.632A, repealed: 2004 c.12 Sch.42 Part 3

s.632B, repealed: 2004 c.12 Sch.42 Part 3

s.633, repealed: 2004 c.12 Sch.42 Part 3

s.634, repealed: 2004 c.12 Sch.42 Part 3

s.634A, applied: 2004 c.12 Sch.36 para.8

s.634A, referred to: 2004 c.12 Sch.36 para.10

s.634A, repealed: 2004 c.12 Sch.42 Part 3

s.635, repealed: 2004 c.12 Sch.42 Part 3

s.636, repealed: 2004 c.12 Sch.42 Part 3

s.636A, repealed: 2004 c.12 Sch.42 Part 3

s.637, repealed: 2004 c.12 Sch.42 Part 3

s.637A, repealed: 2004 c.12 Sch.42 Part 3

s.638, amended: 2003 c.1 Sch.6 para.90, Sch.8 Part 1

s.638, applied: 2003 c.14 s.174

s.638, referred to: 2004 c.12 Sch.36 para.4

s.638, repealed: 2004 c.12 Sch.42 Part 3

s.638A, repealed: 2004 c.12 Sch.42 Part 3

s.638ZA, repealed: 2004 c.12 Sch.42 Part 3

1988–cont.

1. Income and Corporation Taxes Act 1988–*cont.*

s.639, applied: SI 2002/195 Sch.3 para.6, SI 2002/1330 Sch.3 para.6, SI 2002/3200 Sch.3 para.3, Sch.3 para.4, Sch.3 para.6, SI 2003/1994 Sch.3 para.6, SR 2002/224 Sch.3 para.6, SR 2002/265 Sch.7 para.6

s.639, repealed: 2004 c.12 Sch.42 Part 3

s.640, repealed: 2004 c.12 Sch.42 Part 3

s.640A, amended: 2003 c.14 s.174

s.640A, applied: 2003 c.14 s.174

s.640A, repealed: 2004 c.12 Sch.42 Part 3

s.641A, amended: 2003 c.14 s.174

s.641A, repealed: 2004 c.12 Sch.42 Part 3

s.643, amended: 2003 c.1 Sch.8 Part 1

s.643, repealed (in part): 2003 c.1 Sch.8 Part 1, 2004 c.12 Sch.42 Part 3

s.644, amended: 2003 c.1 Sch.6 para.92

s.644, applied: 2002 c.23 Sch.22 para.4, 2003 c.1 s.56

s.644, repealed: 2004 c.12 Sch.42 Part 3

s.645, amended: 2003 c.1 Sch.6 para.93

s.645, applied: 2003 c.1 Sch.7 para.12

s.645, repealed: 2004 c.12 Sch.42 Part 3

s.646, amended: 2003 c.1 Sch.6 para.94

s.646, repealed: 2004 c.12 Sch.42 Part 3

s.646A, amended: 2003 c.1 Sch.6 para.95

s.646A, repealed: 2004 c.12 Sch.42 Part 3

s.646B, repealed: 2004 c.12 Sch.42 Part 3

s.646C, repealed: 2004 c.12 Sch.42 Part 3

s.646D, repealed: 2004 c.12 Sch.42 Part 3

s.647, applied: SI 2002/2006 Reg.5

s.647, repealed: 2003 c.1 Sch.8 Part 1

s.648, repealed: 2003 c.1 Sch.8 Part 1

s.648A, applied: SI 2002/2006 Reg.5

s.648A, repealed: 2003 c.1 Sch.8 Part 1

s.648A, repealed: 2004 c.12 Sch.42 Part 3

s.648B, repealed: 2004 c.12 Sch.42 Part 3

s.649, repealed: 2004 c.12 Sch.42 Part 3

s.650, referred to: 2004 c.12 Sch.36 para.5

s.650, repealed: 2004 c.12 Sch.42 Part 3

s.650A, repealed: 2004 c.12 Sch.42 Part 3

s.650A, varied: 2004 c.12 Sch.36 para.5

s.651, referred to: 2004 c.12 Sch.36 para.50

s.651, repealed: 2004 c.12 Sch.42 Part 3

s.651, varied: 2004 c.12 Sch.36 para.5

s.651A, repealed: 2004 c.12 Sch.42 Part 3

s.653, repealed: 2004 c.12 Sch.42 Part 3

s.653A, repealed: 2004 c.12 Sch.42 Part 3

s.654, repealed: 2004 c.12 Sch.42 Part 3

s.655, see *Lonsdale v Braisby (Inspector of Taxes)* [2004] EWHC 1811, [2004] S.T.C. 1606 (Ch D), Lewison, J.

s.655, repealed: 2004 c.12 Sch.42 Part 3

s.657, amended: 2003 c.1 Sch.6 para.97, 2004 c.12 Sch.35 para.27

s.658A, amended: 2003 c.1 Sch.6 para.98

s.658A, repealed: 2004 c.12 Sch.42 Part 3

s.659A, amended: 2004 c.12 Sch.42 Part 3

1988–cont.

1. **Income and Corporation Taxes Act 1988**–*cont.*

s.659B, amended: 2003 c.1 Sch.6 para.99

s.659B, repealed: 2004 c.12 Sch.42 Part 3

s.659C, repealed: 2004 c.12 Sch.42 Part 3

s.659D, repealed: 2004 c.12 Sch.42 Part 3

s.659E, repealed (in part): 2004 c.12 Sch.42 Part 3

s.660A, see *Jones v Garnett (Inspector of Taxes)* [2004] W.T.L.R. 1209 (Sp Comm), Nuala Brice

s.660A, amended: 2004 c.12 Sch.35 para.28

s.660A, applied: SI 2002/2848 Sch.1 Part III, 2004 c.12 Sch.15 para.8, Sch.15 para.9, Sch.15 para.22

s.660A, referred to: SI 2002/2006 Reg.14

s.660B, applied: SI 2004/1450 Reg.24

s.660B, referred to: SI 2002/2006 Reg.14

s.660G, see *Jones v Garnett (Inspector of Taxes)* [2004] W.T.L.R. 1209 (Sp Comm), Nuala Brice

s.677, amended: 2004 c.12 Sch.4 para.1

s.677, applied: 2003 c.1 s.189, 2004 c.12 Sch.4 para.3

s.677, referred to: SI 2002/2006 Reg.14

s.678, referred to: SI 2002/2006 Reg.14

s.686, see *Howell v Trippier* [2004] EWCA Civ 885, [2004] S.T.C. 1245 (CA), Dame Elizabeth Butler-Sloss (President)

s.686, amended: 2004 c.12 s.29, Sch.35 para.29

s.686B, added: 2003 c.1 Sch.6 para.100

s.686B, applied: 2003 c.1 Sch.2 para.87

s.686B, referred to: 2003 c.1 s.515

s.686C, added: 2003 c.1 Sch.6 para.100

s.686C, applied: 2003 c.1 Sch.2 para.87

s.686C, referred to: 2003 c.1 s.515

s.694, amended: 2004 c.12 Sch.4 para.2

s.695, referred to: SI 2002/2006 Reg.14

s.696, referred to: SI 2002/2006 Reg.14

s.699A, amended: 2003 c.14 Sch.35 para.4

s.703, see *Inland Revenue Commissioners v Laird Group Plc* [2003] UKHL 54, [2003] 1 W.L.R. 2476 (HL), Lord Millett

s.704A, see *Trustees of the Sema Group Pension Scheme v Inland Revenue Commissioners* [2002] EWCA Civ 1857, [2003] S.T.C. 95 (CA), Jonathan Parker, L.J.

s.706, applied: SI 2003/409 Sch.1 Part I

s.707, applied: SI 2004/1864 Reg.5

s.709, see *Inland Revenue Commissioners v Laird Group Plc* [2002] EWCA Civ 576, [2002] S.T.C. 722 (CA), Sir Andrew Morritt V.C.; see *Trustees of the Sema Group Pension Scheme v Inland Revenue Commissioners* [2002] EWCA Civ 1857, [2003] S.T.C. 95 (CA), Jonathan Parker, L.J.; see *Trustees of the Sema Group Pension Scheme v Inland Revenue*

1988–cont.

1. **Income and Corporation Taxes Act 1988**–*cont.*

s.709–*cont.*

Commissioners [2002] EWHC 94, [2002] S.T.C. 276 (Ch D), Lightman, J.

s.710, amended: 2003 c.14 Sch.39 para.5

s.710, repealed (in part): 2004 c.12 Sch.42 Part 2

s.710, varied: SI 2003/1633 Sch.2 para.6

s.711, applied: 2002 c.29 Sch.10 para.4

s.712, applied: 2002 c.29 Sch.10 para.4

s.713, applied: 2002 c.29 Sch.10 para.4

s.713, disapplied: 2002 c.29 Sch.10 para.4

s.714, applied: 2002 c.29 Sch.10 para.4, SI 2004/1450 Reg.24

s.714, referred to: SI 2002/2006 Reg.14

s.715, amended: 2004 c.12 Sch.35 para.30

s.715, applied: 2002 c.29 Sch.10 para.4

s.716, applied: 2002 c.29 Sch.10 para.4

s.716, disapplied: 2002 c.29 Sch.10 para.4

s.716, referred to: SI 2002/2006 Reg.14

s.717, applied: 2002 c.29 Sch.10 para.4

s.718, applied: 2002 c.29 Sch.10 para.4

s.719, applied: 2002 c.29 Sch.10 para.4

s.720, applied: 2002 c.29 Sch.10 para.4

s.721, applied: 2002 c.29 Sch.10 para.4

s.722, applied: 2002 c.29 Sch.10 para.4

s.722A, applied: 2002 c.29 Sch.10 para.4

s.723, applied: 2002 c.29 Sch.10 para.4

s.724, applied: 2002 c.29 Sch.10 para.4

s.725, applied: 2002 c.29 Sch.10 para.4

s.726, applied: 2002 c.29 Sch.10 para.4

s.726A, applied: 2002 c.29 Sch.10 para.4

s.727, applied: 2002 c.29 Sch.10 para.4

s.727A, amended: 2003 c.14 Sch.38 para.4, Sch.38 para.15

s.727A, applied: 2002 c.29 Sch.10 para.4

s.728, applied: 2002 c.29 Sch.10 para.4

s.730, amended: 2002 c.23 Sch.25 para.51

s.730, referred to: SI 2002/2006 Reg.14

s.730A, amended: 2002 c.23 Sch.25 para.52, 2003 c.14 Sch.38 para.5, Sch.38 para.10, Sch.38 para.11, Sch.38 para.16, Sch.38 para.20, 2004 c.12 Sch.10 para.44, Sch.35 para.31, Sch.42 Part 2

s.730A, referred to: SI 2002/2006 Reg.14, SI 2004/1863 Sch.1 para.7

s.730A, repealed (in part): 2004 c.12 Sch.42 Part 2

s.730BB, added: 2003 c.14 Sch.38 para.12

s.730BB, amended: 2004 c.12 Sch.10 para.78

s.730BB, repealed (in part): 2004 c.12 Sch.42 Part 2

s.731, amended: 2003 c.14 Sch.38 para.6

s.737A, amended: 2003 c.14 Sch.38 para.2, Sch.38 para.7

s.737C, amended: 2003 c.14 Sch.38 para.3, Sch.38 para.17, Sch.43 Part 3

s.737C, repealed (in part): 2003 c.14 Sch.43 Part 3

s.737D, amended: 2004 c.12 Sch.35 para.32

CAP.

CAP.

1988–cont.

1. Income and Corporation Taxes Act 1988–*cont.*

s.737E, amended: 2003 c.14 Sch.38 para.8, Sch.38 para.13, 2004 c.12 Sch.24 para.3

s.739, see *Carvill v Inland Revenue Commissioners* [2002] EWHC 1488, [2002] S.T.C. 1167 (Ch D), Hart, J.; see *R. (on the application of Carvill) v Inland Revenue Commissioners* [2003] EWHC 1852, [2003] S.T.C. 1539 (QBD (Admin Ct)), McCombe, J.; see *R. v Dimsey (Dermot Jeremy)* [2001] UKHL 46, [2002] 1 A.C. 509 (HL), Lord Scott of Foscote

s.739, applied: SI 2002/2848 Sch.1 Part III, 2004 c.12 Sch.15 para.9

s.739, referred to: SI 2002/2006 Reg.14

s.740, referred to: SI 2002/2006 Reg.14

s.741, see *Carvill v Inland Revenue Commissioners* [2002] EWHC 1488, [2002] S.T.C. 1167 (Ch D), Hart, J.

s.747, see *Association of British Travel Agents Ltd v Inland Revenue Commissioners* [2003] S.T.C. (S.C.D.) 194 (Sp Comm), John F Avery Jones

s.747, amended: 2002 c.23 s.90

s.747, applied: 2002 c.23 Sch.29 para.116

s.747, referred to: 2002 c.23 Sch.29 para.116

s.747A, amended: 2002 c.23 Sch.23 para.19

s.748, see *Association of British Travel Agents Ltd v Inland Revenue Commissioners* [2003] S.T.C. (S.C.D.) 194 (Sp Comm), John F Avery Jones

s.748, amended: 2002 c.23 s.89

s.748, enabling: SI 2002/1963, SI 2002/2406

s.748A, added: 2002 c.23 s.89

s.748A, amended: 2003 c.14 s.153

s.755A, amended: 2003 c.14 Sch.33 para.13

s.755A, varied: SI 2004/2680 Reg.16

s.756A, added: 2004 c.12 Sch.26 para.3

s.756B, added: 2004 c.12 Sch.26 para.3

s.756B, applied: 2004 c.12 Sch.26 para.17, SI 2004/2572 Reg.2, Reg.3, Reg.4, Reg.5, Reg.6

s.756C, added: 2004 c.12 Sch.26 para.3

s.756C, applied: 2004 c.12 Sch.26 para.17, SI 2004/2572 Reg.3, Reg.4, Reg.5, Reg.7

s.757, amended: 2002 c.23 Sch.9 para.4, 2004 c.12 Sch.26 para.4

s.757, referred to: 2002 c.29 Sch.10 para.7

s.758, amended: 2002 c.23 Sch.9 para.4, 2004 c.12 Sch.26 para.5

s.758, varied: SI 2004/2572 Reg.3

s.758, enabling: SI 2004/2572

s.759, amended: 2004 c.12 Sch.26 para.6

s.759, repealed (in part): 2004 c.12 Sch.42 Part 2

s.760, amended: 2004 c.12 Sch.26 para.7

s.760, disapplied: 2004 c.12 Sch.26 para.17

1988–cont.

1. Income and Corporation Taxes Act 1988–*cont.*

s.760, repealed (in part): 2004 c.12 Sch.42 Part 2

s.760, varied: 2004 c.12 Sch.26 para.17

s.761, applied: SI 2004/1450 Reg.24

s.761, referred to: SI 2002/2006 Reg.14

s.762A, added: 2004 c.12 Sch.26 para.15

s.763, amended: 2004 c.12 Sch.26 para.15, Sch.26 para.16

s.767A, see *Inland Revenue Commissioners v Richmond* [2003] EWHC 999, [2003] S.T.C. 1394 (Ch D (Companies Court)), Etherton, J.

s.768B, amended: 2002 c.23 Sch.27 para.9, 2004 c.12 Sch.6 para.3

s.768B, applied: 2004 c.12 s.43

s.768C, amended: 2002 c.23 Sch.27 para.10, Sch.30 para.4, 2004 c.12 Sch.6 para.4

s.768C, applied: 2004 c.12 s.43

s.768D, amended: 2004 c.12 Sch.6 para.5

s.768E, added: 2002 c.23 Sch.30 para.4

s.768E, amended: 2004 c.12 Sch.6 para.6

s.770, see *Waterloo Plc v Inland Revenue Commissioners* [2002] S.T.C. (S.C.D.) 95 (Sp Comm), Nuala Brice

s.773, see *Waterloo Plc v Inland Revenue Commissioners* [2002] S.T.C. (S.C.D.) 95 (Sp Comm), Nuala Brice

s.776, referred to: SI 2002/2006 Reg.14

s.779, amended: 2003 c.1 Sch.6 para.101, SI 2004/2310 Sch.1 para.32

s.781, amended: 2003 c.1 Sch.6 para.102, SI 2004/2310 Sch.1 para.33

s.785A, added: 2004 c.12 s.135

s.787, amended: 2002 c.23 Sch.25 para.53

s.788, see *NEC Semi Conductors Ltd v Inland Revenue Commissioners* [2003] EWHC 2813, [2004] S.T.C. 489 (Ch D), Park, J.; see *Pirelli Cable Holding NV v Inland Revenue Commissioners* [2003] EWCA Civ 1849, [2004] S.T.C. 130 (CA), Peter Gibson, L.J.

s.788, amended: 2002 c.23 s.88, 2003 c.14 s.198

s.788, applied: 2002 c.23 Sch.16 para.19, Sch.29 para.87, SI 2002/2006 Reg.3, SI 2002/2847, SI 2002/2848, SI 2002/3137, SI 2002/3138, 2003 c.14 s.151, SI 2003/2620, SI 2003/3199, SI 2003/3200, 2004 c.12 s.103, s.189, SI 2004/1274, SI 2004/1863 Sch.1 para.4

s.788, referred to: SI 2003/2619

s.788, varied: 2002 c.23 Sch.29 para.87

s.788, enabling: SI 2002/2847, SI 2002/2848, SI 2002/3137, SI 2002/3138, SI 2003/2619, SI 2003/2620, SI 2003/3199, SI 2003/3200, SI 2004/1274

s.789, varied: 2002 c.23 Sch.29 para.87

s.790, amended: 2002 c.23 s.88, 2003 c.14 s.153

1988–cont.

1. Income and Corporation Taxes Act 1988–cont.

s.790, applied: 2002 c.23 Sch.16 para.19
s.790, varied: 2002 c.23 Sch.29 para.87
s.791, varied: 2002 c.23 Sch.29 para.87
s.791, enabling: SI 2003/2581
s.792, amended: 2002 c.23 s.88, 2004 c.12 s.115
s.792, varied: 2002 c.23 Sch.29 para.87
s.793, varied: 2002 c.23 Sch.29 para.87
s.793A, amended: 2002 c.23 s.88
s.793A, varied: 2002 c.23 Sch.29 para.87
s.794, amended: 2003 c.1 Sch.6 para.103
s.794, varied: 2002 c.23 Sch.29 para.87, 2003 c.14 s.153
s.795, amended: 2002 c.23 Sch.30 para.5, 2004 c.12 s.112
s.795, disapplied: 2004 c.12 s.111
s.795, varied: 2002 c.23 Sch.29 para.87
s.795A, amended: 2002 c.23 s.88
s.795A, varied: 2002 c.23 Sch.29 para.87
s.796, varied: 2002 c.23 Sch.29 para.87
s.797, amended: 2002 c.23 Sch.25 para.54, 2003 c.14 s.154, SI 2004/2310 Sch.1 para.34
s.797, varied: 2002 c.23 Sch.29 para.87
s.797A, amended: 2002 c.23 Sch.25 para.55, Sch.30 para.5, Sch.40 Part 3
s.797A, repealed (in part): 2002 c.23 Sch.40 Part 3
s.797A, varied: 2002 c.23 Sch.29 para.87
s.797B, added: 2002 c.23 Sch.30 para.5
s.797B, varied: 2002 c.23 Sch.29 para.87
s.798, varied: 2002 c.23 Sch.29 para.87
s.798A, varied: 2002 c.23 Sch.29 para.87
s.798B, amended: 2002 c.23 s.103, Sch.23 para.20, Sch.27 para.11
s.798B, varied: 2002 c.23 Sch.29 para.87
s.799, varied: 2002 c.23 Sch.29 para.87
s.800, varied: 2002 c.23 Sch.29 para.87
s.801, amended: 2003 c.14 s.153
s.801, varied: 2002 c.23 Sch.29 para.87
s.801A, varied: 2002 c.23 Sch.29 para.87
s.801B, varied: 2002 c.23 Sch.29 para.87
s.801C, varied: 2002 c.23 Sch.29 para.87
s.802, varied: 2002 c.23 Sch.29 para.87
s.803, varied: 2002 c.23 Sch.29 para.87
s.803A, varied: 2002 c.23 Sch.29 para.87
s.804, varied: 2002 c.23 Sch.29 para.87
s.804A, amended: 2003 c.14 s.153
s.804A, varied: 2002 c.23 Sch.29 para.87
s.804B, amended: 2003 c.14 Sch.33 para.11, 2004 c.12 Sch.7 para.7
s.804B, varied: 2002 c.23 Sch.29 para.87
s.804C, amended: 2003 c.14 Sch.33 para.11
s.804C, varied: 2002 c.23 Sch.29 para.87
s.804D, varied: 2002 c.23 Sch.29 para.87
s.804E, varied: 2002 c.23 Sch.29 para.87
s.804F, varied: 2002 c.23 Sch.29 para.87
s.805, varied: 2002 c.23 Sch.29 para.87

1988–cont.

1. Income and Corporation Taxes Act 1988–cont.

s.806, varied: 2002 c.23 Sch.29 para.87
s.806A, varied: 2002 c.23 Sch.29 para.87
s.806B, varied: 2002 c.23 Sch.29 para.87
s.806C, varied: 2002 c.23 Sch.29 para.87
s.806D, varied: 2002 c.23 Sch.29 para.87
s.806E, varied: 2002 c.23 Sch.29 para.87
s.806F, varied: 2002 c.23 Sch.29 para.87
s.806G, varied: 2002 c.23 Sch.29 para.87
s.806H, varied: 2002 c.23 Sch.29 para.87
s.806H, enabling: SI 2003/1829
s.806J, varied: 2002 c.23 Sch.29 para.87
s.806K, varied: 2002 c.23 Sch.29 para.87, 2003 c.14 s.153
s.806L, amended: 2003 c.14 s.153, Sch.27 para.1
s.806L, varied: 2002 c.23 Sch.29 para.87
s.806M, amended: 2003 c.14 s.153
s.806M, varied: 2002 c.23 Sch.29 para.87
s.807, varied: 2002 c.23 Sch.29 para.87
s.807A, amended: 2002 c.23 Sch.27 para.12, Sch.40 Part 3
s.807A, varied: 2002 c.23 Sch.29 para.87
s.808, varied: 2002 c.23 Sch.29 para.87
s.808A, varied: 2002 c.23 Sch.29 para.87, 2004 c.12 s.103
s.808B, varied: 2002 c.23 Sch.29 para.87, 2004 c.12 s.103
s.809, varied: 2002 c.23 Sch.29 para.87
s.810, varied: 2002 c.23 Sch.29 para.87
s.811, amended: 2002 c.23 Sch.30 para.5, 2004 c.12 s.115
s.811, varied: 2002 c.23 Sch.29 para.87
s.812, amended: 2002 c.23 s.88
s.812, varied: 2002 c.23 Sch.29 para.87
s.813, varied: 2002 c.23 Sch.29 para.87
s.814, varied: 2002 c.23 Sch.29 para.87, 2003 c.14 s.153
s.815, varied: 2002 c.23 Sch.29 para.87
s.815A, amended: 2003 c.14 s.153
s.815A, varied: 2002 c.23 Sch.29 para.87
s.815AA, amended: 2002 c.23 s.88
s.815AA, varied: 2002 c.23 Sch.29 para.87
s.815B, varied: 2002 c.23 Sch.29 para.87
s.815C, amended: 2002 c.23 s.88, 2003 c.14 s.198
s.815C, varied: 2002 c.23 Sch.29 para.87
s.816, amended: 2002 c.23 s.88
s.816, varied: 2002 c.23 Sch.29 para.87
s.817, disapplied: 2002 c.23 Sch.29 para.8
s.824, amended: 2003 c.1 Sch.6 para.104, 2004 c.12 Sch.35 para.33
s.824, applied: SI 2002/2172 Reg.8, SI 2003/2682 Sch.1 para.26, 2004 c.12 s.108
s.826, amended: 2002 c.23 Sch.14 para.1
s.826, applied: 2002 c.23 Sch.13 para.18, SI 2002/2172 Reg.8
s.827, amended: 2003 c.14 s.40, Sch.18 para.3

CAP.

1. Income and Corporation Taxes Act 1988–*cont.*

s.828, amended: 2003 c.14 s.180, 2003 c.1 Sch.6 para.105, 2004 c.12 Sch.35 para.34

s.829, amended: 2002 c.23 s.40, 2004 c.12 Sch.12 para.11

s.830, referred to: 2003 c.1 Sch.3 para.49, Sch.4 para.37, Sch.5 para.59

s.830, repealed (in part): 2003 c.1 Sch.8 Part 1

s.830, varied: 2003 c.14 s.153

s.831, amended: 2003 c.1 Sch.6 para.107

s.831, referred to: 2004 c.12 s.318

s.832, see *Spring Salmon & Seafood Ltd v Advocate General for Scotland* [2004] S.T.C. 444 (OH), Lady Smith

s.832, amended: 2002 c.23 s.103, 2003 c.14 s.148, 2004 c.12 s.50, Sch.27 para.2, Sch.35 para.35

s.832, applied: 2004 c.12 s.280, SI 2004/ 1450 Reg.38

s.832, referred to: 2003 c.1 Sch.2 para.100, Sch.3 para.49, Sch.4 para.37, Sch.5 para.59

s.833, amended: 2003 c.14 Sch.35 para.5, 2003 c.1 Sch.6 para.108

s.833, applied: 2002 c.23 Sch.22 para.4

s.834, amended: 2002 c.23 Sch.27 para.13, Sch.30 para.1, Sch.40 Part 3, 2003 c.14 s.149

s.834, applied: 2004 c.12 s.280

s.835, applied: 2003 c.1 s.331, 2004 c.12 s.280

s.836A, added: 2002 c.23 s.103

s.836A, referred to: 2003 c.1 Sch.5 para.59

s.837A, amended: 2002 c.23 s.103

s.837A, applied: SI 2004/712 Reg.2

s.837A, repealed (in part): 2002 c.23 Sch.40 Part 3

s.837A, enabling: SI 2004/712

s.837C, added: 2004 c.12 Sch.27 para.1

s.838, applied: 2002 c.23 Sch.29 para.54, 2003 c.14 Sch.7 para.1

s.838, referred to: 2003 c.1 Sch.5 para.59

s.838, varied: 2002 c.23 s.73, Sch.29 para.50

s.839, applied: 2002 c.23 s.55, Sch.12 para.19, Sch.13 para.27, Sch.16 para.51, Sch.37 para.2, SI 2002/761 Reg.12, 2003 c.14 s.44, s.45, s.53, s.58, s.59, s.108, Sch.6A para.10, Sch.4 para.1, Sch.4 para.10, Sch.4 para.12, Sch.20 para.2, 2003 c.1 s.718, 2004 c.12 s.161, s.273, s.278, SI 2004/1863 Reg.1, SI 2004/ 1865 Reg.1

s.839, referred to: 2003 c.14 s.54

s.839, varied: 2003 c.14 Sch.15 para.39, 2004 c.12 Sch.15 para.2

s.840, applied: 2002 c.23 Sch.16 para.14, SR 2002/352 Sch.4 para.9, 2003 c.1 s.719, 2004 c.12 s.65

s.840, varied: 2003 c.1 s.69

CAP.

1. Income and Corporation Taxes Act 1988–*cont.*

s.840A, amended: SI 2002/1409 Art.2, 2004 c.12 Sch.35 para.36

s.840A, applied: 2003 c.1 Sch.2 para.49, SI 2004/1450 Reg.12, Reg.14, Reg.20

s.840A, referred to: 2004 c.12 s.307

s.841, referred to: 2003 c.1 Sch.2 para.100, Sch.3 para.49, Sch.4 para.37

s.842, amended: 2002 c.23 Sch.9 para.4, Sch.25 para.56, Sch.40 Part 3, 2004 c.12 s.45

s.842, applied: 2002 c.23 Sch.9 para.8, Sch.26 para.39

s.842A, amended: 2004 c.21 Sch.1 para.64

s.842AA, amended: 2002 c.23 Sch.25 para.57, Sch.33 para.13

s.842AA, applied: 2002 c.23 Sch.26 para.40, Sch.33 para.3, Sch.33 para.5, Sch.33 para.7, Sch.33 para.11, Sch.33 para.12, SI 2002/2661 Reg.7, Reg.8, Reg.9, Reg.11, 2004 c.12 Sch.19 para.16, SI 2004/712 Reg.1, SI 2004/2199 Reg.6, Reg.12, Reg.13, Reg.14

s.842AA, referred to: 2002 c.23 Sch.33 para.9, SI 2004/2199 Reg.3, Reg.14

s.842AA, varied: SI 2004/2199 Reg.13

s.842AA, enabling: SI 2002/2661

s.842B, amended: 2002 c.23 Sch.40 Part 3

s.842B, applied: 2004 c.12 s.280

Sch.A1 Part I para.1, added: 2003 c.14 Sch.25

Sch.A1 Part II para.2, added: 2003 c.14 Sch.25

Sch.A1 Part II para.3, added: 2003 c.14 Sch.25

Sch.A1 Part II para.4, added: 2003 c.14 Sch.25

Sch.A1 Part II para.5, added: 2003 c.14 Sch.25

Sch.A1 Part II para.6, added: 2003 c.14 Sch.25

Sch.A1 Part III para.7, added: 2003 c.14 Sch.25

Sch.A1 Part III para.8, added: 2003 c.14 Sch.25

Sch.A1 Part III para.9, added: 2003 c.14 Sch.25

Sch.A1 Part III para.10, added: 2003 c.14 Sch.25

Sch.A2 Part 1 para.1, added: 2004 c.12 Sch.3

Sch.A2 Part 1 para.2, added: 2004 c.12 Sch.3

Sch.A2 Part 1 para.3, added: 2004 c.12 Sch.3

Sch.A2 Part 1 para.4, added: 2004 c.12 Sch.3

Sch.A2 Part 1 para.5, added: 2004 c.12 Sch.3

Sch.A2 Part 2 para.6, added: 2004 c.12 Sch.3

Sch.A2 Part 2 para.7, added: 2004 c.12 Sch.3

Sch.A2 Part 2 para.8, added: 2004 c.12 Sch.3

Sch.A2 Part 2 para.9, added: 2004 c.12 Sch.3

Sch.A2 Part 2 para.10, added: 2004 c.12 Sch.3

1988–cont.

1. Income and Corporation Taxes Act 1988–*cont.*

Sch.A2 Part 2 para.11, added: 2004 c.12 Sch.3

Sch.A2 Part 2 para.12, added: 2004 c.12 Sch.3

Sch.A2 Part 3 para.13, added: 2004 c.12 Sch.3

Sch.A2 Part 3 para.14, added: 2004 c.12 Sch.3

Sch.A2 Part 3 para.15, added: 2004 c.12 Sch.3

Sch.A2 Part 3 para.16, added: 2004 c.12 Sch.3

Sch.A2 Part 3 para.17, added: 2004 c.12 Sch.3

Sch.A2 Part 3 para.18, added: 2004 c.12 Sch.3

Sch.1, applied: 2003 c.1 Sch.7 para.71

Sch.3, applied: 2003 c.1 s.697, s.701

Sch.4, applied: 2003 c.1 s.697, s.701

Sch.4AA, applied: 2003 c.14 Sch.24 para.8

Sch.4AA, referred to: 2003 c.1 s.515

Sch.4AA para.1, added: 2003 c.1 Sch.6 para.109

Sch.4AA para.1, amended: SI 2004/2310 Sch.1 para.35

Sch.4AA para.2, added: 2003 c.1 Sch.6 para.109

Sch.4AA para.2, applied: 2003 c.14 Sch.23 para.24

Sch.4AA para.3, added: 2003 c.1 Sch.6 para.109

Sch.4AA para.3, applied: 2003 c.14 Sch.23 para.24

Sch.4AA para.4, added: 2003 c.1 Sch.6 para.109

Sch.4AA para.5, added: 2003 c.1 Sch.6 para.109

Sch.4AA para.6, added: 2003 c.1 Sch.6 para.109

Sch.4AA para.7, added: 2003 c.1 Sch.6 para.109

Sch.4AA para.7, amended: SI 2004/2310 Sch.1 para.35

Sch.4AA para.8, added: 2003 c.1 Sch.6 para.109

Sch.4AA para.9, added: 2003 c.1 Sch.6 para.109

Sch.4AA para.9, applied: 2003 c.14 Sch.23 para.24

Sch.4AA para.10, added: 2003 c.1 Sch.6 para.109

Sch.4AA para.10, applied: 2003 c.14 Sch.23 para.24

Sch.4AA para.11, added: 2003 c.1 Sch.6 para.109

Sch.4AA para.11, applied: 2003 c.1 Sch.2 para.85

Sch.4AA para.12, added: 2003 c.1 Sch.6 para.109

1988–cont.

1. Income and Corporation Taxes Act 1988–*cont.*

Sch.4AA para.13, added: 2003 c.1 Sch.6 para.109

Sch.4AA para.13, amended: SI 2004/2310 Sch.1 para.35

Sch.5AA, applied: 2002 c.23 Sch.28 para.6

Sch.5 para.2, amended: 2002 c.23 Sch.40 Part 3

Sch.5 para.6, amended: 2002 c.23 Sch.40 Part 3

Sch.5AA para.1, amended: 2002 c.23 Sch.40 Part 3

Sch.5AA para.1, repealed (in part): 2002 c.23 Sch.40 Part 3

Sch.5AA para.2, amended: 2002 c.23 s.78

Sch.5AA para.2, repealed (in part): 2002 c.23 Sch.40 Part 3

Sch.5AA para.4, amended: 2002 c.23 s.78

Sch.5AA para.4, applied: 2002 c.29 Sch.10 para.8

Sch.5AA para.4, repealed (in part): 2002 c.23 Sch.40 Part 3

Sch.5AA para.4A, amended: 2002 c.23 s.78, Sch.40 Part 3

Sch.5AA para.4A, repealed (in part): 2002 c.23 Sch.40 Part 3

Sch.5AA para.6, amended: 2002 c.23 s.78

Sch.5AA para.6, repealed (in part): 2002 c.23 Sch.40 Part 3

Sch.5AA para.9, repealed: 2002 c.23 Sch.40 Part 3

Sch.6 Part I, repealed: 2003 c.1 Sch.8 Part 1

Sch.6 para.1, repealed: 2003 c.1 Sch.8 Part 1

Sch.6 para.2, repealed: 2003 c.1 Sch.8 Part 1

Sch.6 Part II para.1, repealed: 2003 c.1 Sch.8 Part 1

Sch.6 Part II para.2, repealed: 2003 c.1 Sch.8 Part 1

Sch.6 Part II para.3, repealed: 2003 c.1 Sch.8 Part 1

Sch.6 Part II para.4, repealed: 2003 c.1 Sch.8 Part 1

Sch.6 Part II para.5, repealed: 2003 c.1 Sch.8 Part 1

Sch.6 para.3, repealed: 2003 c.1 Sch.8 Part 1

Sch.6 para.4, repealed: 2003 c.1 Sch.8 Part 1

Sch.6 para.5, repealed: 2003 c.1 Sch.8 Part 1

Sch.6 para.5A, repealed: 2003 c.1 Sch.8 Part 1

Sch.6 para.5B, repealed: 2003 c.1 Sch.8 Part 1

Sch.6 para.5C, repealed: 2003 c.1 Sch.8 Part 1

Sch.6 para.5D, repealed: 2003 c.1 Sch.8 Part 1

Sch.6 para.5E, repealed: 2003 c.1 Sch.8 Part 1

Sch.6 para.5F, repealed: 2003 c.1 Sch.8 Part 1

Sch.6 para.5G, repealed: 2003 c.1 Sch.8 Part 1

1988–cont.

1. **Income and Corporation Taxes Act 1988**–*cont.*

Sch.6 para.6, repealed: 2003 c.1 Sch.8 Part 1

Sch.6 para.7, repealed: 2003 c.1 Sch.8 Part 1

Sch.6 para.8, repealed: 2003 c.1 Sch.8 Part 1

Sch.6 para.9, repealed: 2003 c.1 Sch.8 Part 1

Sch.6 para.10, repealed: 2003 c.1 Sch.8 Part 1

Sch.6A Part I para.1, repealed: 2003 c.1 Sch.8 Part 1

Sch.6A Part I para.2, repealed: 2003 c.1 Sch.8 Part 1

Sch.6A Part I para.3, repealed: 2003 c.1 Sch.8 Part 1

Sch.6A Part II para.4, repealed: 2003 c.1 Sch.8 Part 1

Sch.6A Part II para.5, repealed: 2003 c.1 Sch.8 Part 1

Sch.6A Part II para.6, repealed: 2003 c.1 Sch.8 Part 1

Sch.6A Part II para.7, repealed: 2003 c.1 Sch.8 Part 1

Sch.6A Part II para.8, repealed: 2003 c.1 Sch.8 Part 1

Sch.6A Part II para.9, repealed: 2003 c.1 Sch.8 Part 1

Sch.6A Part III para.10, repealed: 2003 c.1 Sch.8 Part 1

Sch.6A Part III para.11, repealed: 2003 c.1 Sch.8 Part 1

Sch.6A Part III para.12, repealed: 2003 c.1 Sch.8 Part 1

Sch.7 Part I para.1, repealed: 2003 c.1 Sch.8 Part 1

Sch.7 Part I para.2, repealed: 2003 c.1 Sch.8 Part 1

Sch.7 Part II para.3, repealed: 2003 c.1 Sch.8 Part 1

Sch.7 Part II para.4, repealed: 2003 c.1 Sch.8 Part 1

Sch.7 Part II para.5, repealed: 2003 c.1 Sch.8 Part 1

Sch.7 Part II para.5A, repealed: 2003 c.1 Sch.8 Part 1

Sch.7 Part III para.6, repealed: 2003 c.1 Sch.8 Part 1

Sch.7 Part III para.7, repealed: 2003 c.1 Sch.8 Part 1

Sch.7 Part III para.8, repealed: 2003 c.1 Sch.8 Part 1

Sch.7 Part III para.9, repealed: 2003 c.1 Sch.8 Part 1

Sch.7 Part III para.10, repealed: 2003 c.1 Sch.8 Part 1

Sch.7 Part III para.11, repealed: 2003 c.1 Sch.8 Part 1

Sch.7 Part III para.12, repealed: 2003 c.1 Sch.8 Part 1

Sch.7 Part III para.13, repealed: 2003 c.1 Sch.8 Part 1

Sch.7 Part IV para.14, repealed: 2003 c.1 Sch.8 Part 1

1988–cont.

1. **Income and Corporation Taxes Act 1988**–*cont.*

Sch.7 Part IV para.15, repealed: 2003 c.1 Sch.8 Part 1

Sch.7 Part IV para.16, repealed: 2003 c.1 Sch.8 Part 1

Sch.7 Part IV para.17, repealed: 2003 c.1 Sch.8 Part 1

Sch.7 Part IV para.18, repealed: 2003 c.1 Sch.8 Part 1

Sch.7 Part V para.19, repealed: 2003 c.1 Sch.8 Part 1

Sch.7A para.1, repealed: 2003 c.1 Sch.8 Part 1

Sch.7A para.2, repealed: 2003 c.1 Sch.8 Part 1

Sch.7A para.3, repealed: 2003 c.1 Sch.8 Part 1

Sch.7A para.4, repealed: 2003 c.1 Sch.8 Part 1

Sch.7A para.5, repealed: 2003 c.1 Sch.8 Part 1

Sch.7A para.6, repealed: 2003 c.1 Sch.8 Part 1

Sch.8 para.6, see *University of Keele v Price Waterhouse* [2003] EWHC 1595, [2004] P.N.L.R. 8 (Ch D), Hart, J.

Sch.8 para.7, see *University of Keele v Price Waterhouse* [2003] EWHC 1595, [2004] P.N.L.R. 8 (Ch D), Hart, J.

Sch.8 para.8, see *University of Keele v Price Waterhouse* [2003] EWHC 1595, [2004] P.N.L.R. 8 (Ch D), Hart, J.

Sch.9, applied: 2003 c.1 s.418, s.551, s.697, s.701, Sch.7 para.73, Sch.7 para.75, Sch.7 para.76, Sch.7 para.87

Sch.9 Part I para.1, repealed (in part): 2003 c.1 Sch.8 Part 1

Sch.9 Part I para.2, repealed (in part): 2003 c.1 Sch.8 Part 1

Sch.9 Part I para.3, repealed (in part): 2003 c.1 Sch.8 Part 1

Sch.9 Part I para.4, repealed (in part): 2003 c.1 Sch.8 Part 1

Sch.9 Part I para.5, repealed (in part): 2003 c.1 Sch.8 Part 1

Sch.9 Part I para.6, repealed (in part): 2003 c.1 Sch.8 Part 1

Sch.9 Part II para.7, repealed (in part): 2003 c.1 Sch.8 Part 1

Sch.9 Part II para.8, repealed (in part): 2003 c.1 Sch.8 Part 1

Sch.9 Part II para.8A, repealed (in part): 2003 c.1 Sch.8 Part 1

Sch.9 Part II para.9, repealed (in part): 2003 c.1 Sch.8 Part 1

Sch.9 Part II para.10, repealed (in part): 2003 c.1 Sch.8 Part 1

Sch.9 Part II para.11, repealed (in part): 2003 c.1 Sch.8 Part 1

Sch.9 Part II para.11A, repealed (in part): 2003 c.1 Sch.8 Part 1

1988–cont.

1. Income and Corporation Taxes Act 1988–*cont.*

Sch.9 Part II para.12, repealed (in part): 2003 c.1 Sch.8 Part 1

Sch.9 Part II para.13, repealed (in part): 2003 c.1 Sch.8 Part 1

Sch.9 Part II para.14, repealed (in part): 2003 c.1 Sch.8 Part 1

Sch.9 Part II para.15, repealed (in part): 2003 c.1 Sch.8 Part 1

Sch.9 Part III para.16, repealed: 2003 c.1 Sch.8 Part 1

Sch.9 Part III para.17, repealed: 2003 c.1 Sch.8 Part 1

Sch.9 Part III para.18, repealed: 2003 c.1 Sch.8 Part 1

Sch.9 Part III para.19, repealed: 2003 c.1 Sch.8 Part 1

Sch.9 Part III para.20, repealed: 2003 c.1 Sch.8 Part 1

Sch.9 Part III para.21, repealed: 2003 c.1 Sch.8 Part 1

Sch.9 Part III para.22, repealed: 2003 c.1 Sch.8 Part 1

Sch.9 Part III para.23, repealed: 2003 c.1 Sch.8 Part 1

Sch.9 Part III para.24, repealed: 2003 c.1 Sch.8 Part 1

Sch.9 Part III para.25, repealed: 2003 c.1 Sch.8 Part 1

Sch.9 Part III para.26, repealed: 2003 c.1 Sch.8 Part 1

Sch.9 Part IV para.27, repealed: 2003 c.1 Sch.8 Part 1

Sch.9 Part IV para.28, repealed: 2003 c.1 Sch.8 Part 1

Sch.9 Part IV para.29, repealed: 2003 c.1 Sch.8 Part 1

Sch.9 Part V para.34, varied: 2003 c.1 Sch.7 para.85

Sch.9 Part VI para.37, repealed (in part): 2003 c.1 Sch.8 Part 1

Sch.9 Part VI para.38, repealed (in part): 2003 c.1 Sch.8 Part 1

Sch.9 Part VI para.39, repealed (in part): 2003 c.1 Sch.8 Part 1

Sch.9 Part VI para.40, repealed (in part): 2003 c.1 Sch.8 Part 1

Sch.10, applied: 2003 c.1 s.418

Sch.10 para.3, amended: 2003 c.1 Sch.6 para.113

Sch.10 para.6, amended: 2003 c.1 Sch.6 para.113

Sch.10 para.7, amended: 2003 c.1 Sch.6 para.113, Sch.8 Part 1

Sch.11 para.1, repealed: 2003 c.1 Sch.8 Part 1

Sch.11 Part I para.1, repealed: 2003 c.1 Sch.8 Part 1

Sch.11 Part I para.2, repealed: 2003 c.1 Sch.8 Part 1

1988–cont.

1. Income and Corporation Taxes Act 1988–*cont.*

Sch.11 Part I para.3, repealed: 2003 c.1 Sch.8 Part 1

Sch.11 Part I para.4, repealed: 2003 c.1 Sch.8 Part 1

Sch.11 Part I para.5, repealed: 2003 c.1 Sch.8 Part 1

Sch.11 Part I para.6, repealed: 2003 c.1 Sch.8 Part 1

Sch.11 Part I para.7, repealed: 2003 c.1 Sch.8 Part 1

Sch.11 Part I para.8, repealed: 2003 c.1 Sch.8 Part 1

Sch.11 Part I para.9, repealed: 2003 c.1 Sch.8 Part 1

Sch.11 Part I para.10, repealed: 2003 c.1 Sch.8 Part 1

Sch.11 Part I para.11, repealed: 2003 c.1 Sch.8 Part 1

Sch.11 para.2, repealed: 2003 c.1 Sch.8 Part 1

Sch.11 Part II para.12, repealed: 2003 c.1 Sch.8 Part 1

Sch.11 Part II para.13, repealed: 2003 c.1 Sch.8 Part 1

Sch.11 Part II para.14, repealed: 2003 c.1 Sch.8 Part 1

Sch.11 Part II para.15, repealed: 2003 c.1 Sch.8 Part 1

Sch.11 Part II para.16, repealed: 2003 c.1 Sch.8 Part 1

Sch.11 Part II para.17, repealed: 2003 c.1 Sch.8 Part 1

Sch.11 Part II para.18, repealed: 2003 c.1 Sch.8 Part 1

Sch.11 Part II para.19, repealed: 2003 c.1 Sch.8 Part 1

Sch.11 para.3, repealed: 2003 c.1 Sch.8 Part 1

Sch.11 para.4, repealed: 2003 c.1 Sch.8 Part 1

Sch.11 para.5, repealed: 2003 c.1 Sch.8 Part 1

Sch.11 para.6, amended: 2002 c.1 Sch.3 para.10

Sch.11 para.6, repealed: 2003 c.1 Sch.8 Part 1

Sch.11 para.7, repealed: 2003 c.1 Sch.8 Part 1

Sch.11 para.8, repealed: 2003 c.1 Sch.8 Part 1

Sch.11 para.9, repealed: 2003 c.1 Sch.8 Part 1

Sch.11 para.10, repealed: 2003 c.1 Sch.8 Part 1

Sch.11 para.11, repealed: 2003 c.1 Sch.8 Part 1

Sch.11 para.12, repealed: 2003 c.1 Sch.8 Part 1

Sch.11 para.13, repealed: 2003 c.1 Sch.8 Part 1

Sch.11 para.14, repealed: 2003 c.1 Sch.8 Part 1

Sch.11 para.15, repealed: 2003 c.1 Sch.8 Part 1

Sch.11 para.16, repealed: 2003 c.1 Sch.8 Part 1

Sch.11A Part I para.1, repealed: 2003 c.1 Sch.8 Part 1

Sch.11A Part I para.2, repealed: 2003 c.1 Sch.8 Part 1

Sch.11A Part II para.3, repealed: 2003 c.1 Sch.8 Part 1

Sch.11A Part II para.4, repealed: 2003 c.1 Sch.8 Part 1

1988–cont.

1. Income and Corporation Taxes Act 1988–*cont.*

Sch.11A Part II para.5, repealed: 2003 c.1 Sch.8 Part 1

Sch.11A Part II para.6, repealed: 2003 c.1 Sch.8 Part 1

Sch.11A Part III para.7, repealed: 2003 c.1 Sch.8 Part 1

Sch.11A Part III para.8, repealed: 2003 c.1 Sch.8 Part 1

Sch.11A Part III para.9, repealed: 2003 c.1 Sch.8 Part 1

Sch.11A Part III para.10, repealed: 2003 c.1 Sch.8 Part 1

Sch.11A Part III para.11, repealed: 2003 c.1 Sch.8 Part 1

Sch.11A Part III para.12, repealed: 2003 c.1 Sch.8 Part 1

Sch.11A Part III para.13, repealed: 2003 c.1 Sch.8 Part 1

Sch.11A Part III para.14, repealed: 2003 c.1 Sch.8 Part 1

Sch.11A Part III para.15, repealed: 2003 c.1 Sch.8 Part 1

Sch.11A Part IV para.16, repealed: 2003 c.1 Sch.8 Part 1

Sch.11A Part IV para.17, repealed: 2003 c.1 Sch.8 Part 1

Sch.11A Part IV para.18, repealed: 2003 c.1 Sch.8 Part 1

Sch.11A Part IV para.19, repealed: 2003 c.1 Sch.8 Part 1

Sch.11A Part IV para.20, repealed: 2003 c.1 Sch.8 Part 1

Sch.11A Part IV para.21, repealed: 2003 c.1 Sch.8 Part 1

Sch.11A Part IV para.22, repealed: 2003 c.1 Sch.8 Part 1

Sch.11A Part IV para.23, repealed: 2003 c.1 Sch.8 Part 1

Sch.11A Part V para.24, repealed: 2003 c.1 Sch.8 Part 1

Sch.11A Part VI para.25, repealed: 2003 c.1 Sch.8 Part 1

Sch.11A Part VI para.26, repealed: 2003 c.1 Sch.8 Part 1

Sch.11A Part VI para.27, repealed: 2003 c.1 Sch.8 Part 1

Sch.11A Part VI para.28, repealed: 2003 c.1 Sch.8 Part 1

Sch.11A Part VI para.29, repealed: 2003 c.1 Sch.8 Part 1

Sch.12A, see *Kirkwood (Inspector of Taxes) v Evans* [2002] EWHC 30, [2002] 1 W.L.R. 1794 (Ch D), Patten, J.; see *Phillips v Hamilton (Inspector of Taxes)* [2003] S.T.C (S.C.D.) 286 (Sp Comm), Nuala Brice

Sch.12 para.1, repealed: 2003 c.1 Sch.8 Part 1

Sch.12 para.1A, repealed: 2003 c.1 Sch.8 Part 1

Sch.12 para.2, repealed: 2003 c.1 Sch.8 Part 1

1988–cont.

1. Income and Corporation Taxes Act 1988–*cont.*

Sch.12 para.3, repealed: 2003 c.1 Sch.8 Part 1

Sch.12 para.4, repealed: 2003 c.1 Sch.8 Part 1

Sch.12 para.5, repealed: 2003 c.1 Sch.8 Part 1

Sch.12 para.6, repealed: 2003 c.1 Sch.8 Part 1

Sch.12 para.7, repealed: 2003 c.1 Sch.8 Part 1

Sch.12AA para.1, repealed: 2003 c.1 Sch.8 Part 1

Sch.12AA para.2, repealed: 2003 c.1 Sch.8 Part 1

Sch.12AA para.3, repealed: 2003 c.1 Sch.8 Part 1

Sch.12AA para.4, repealed: 2003 c.1 Sch.8 Part 1

Sch.12AA para.5, repealed: 2003 c.1 Sch.8 Part 1

Sch.12AA para.6, repealed: 2003 c.1 Sch.8 Part 1

Sch.12AA para.7, repealed: 2003 c.1 Sch.8 Part 1

Sch.12AA para.8, repealed: 2003 c.1 Sch.8 Part 1

Sch.12A para.1, repealed: 2003 c.1 Sch.8 Part 1

Sch.12A para.2, repealed: 2003 c.1 Sch.8 Part 1

Sch.12A para.3, repealed: 2003 c.1 Sch.8 Part 1

Sch.12A para.4, repealed: 2003 c.1 Sch.8 Part 1

Sch.12A para.5, repealed: 2003 c.1 Sch.8 Part 1

Sch.12A para.6, repealed: 2003 c.1 Sch.8 Part 1

Sch.12A para.7, repealed: 2003 c.1 Sch.8 Part 1

Sch.13B para.1, repealed: 2002 c.21 Sch.6

Sch.13B para.2, repealed: 2002 c.21 Sch.6

Sch.13B para.3, repealed: 2002 c.21 Sch.6

Sch.13B para.4, repealed: 2002 c.21 Sch.6

Sch.13B para.5, repealed: 2002 c.21 Sch.6

Sch.13B para.6, repealed: 2002 c.21 Sch.6

Sch.13B para.7, repealed: 2002 c.21 Sch.6

Sch.13B para.8, repealed: 2002 c.21 Sch.6

Sch.14 Part II para.5, amended: 2003 c.1 Sch.6 para.119

Sch.15B, applied: SI 2004/2199 Reg.13

Sch.15 Part I, amended: 2003 c.14 s.172

Sch.15 Part I para.3, repealed (in part): 2003 c.14 Sch.43 Part 3

Sch.15 Part I para.12, amended: 2003 c.14 s.172

Sch.15 Part I para.17, amended: 2003 c.14 s.153

Sch.15 Part I para.18, amended: 2003 c.14 s.172

Sch.15 Part III para.24, amended: 2003 c.14 Sch.27 para.1

Sch.15 Part III para.25, amended: 2003 c.14 s.153

1988–cont.

1. **Income and Corporation Taxes Act 1988**–*cont.*

Sch.15A para.2, amended: 2003 c.1 Sch.6 para.120

Sch.15B Part I, applied: 2004 c.12 Sch.19 para.7, SI 2004/2199 Reg.11, Reg.13

Sch.15B Part I para.1, amended: 2002 c.23 Sch.17 para.3, 2003 c.14 Sch.40 para.1, 2004 c.12 Sch.19 para.1

Sch.15B Part I para.1, varied: 2004 c.12 s.94

Sch.15B Part I para.3, applied: SI 2004/2199 Reg.4

Sch.15B Part I para.3, referred to: 2002 c.23 Sch.33 para.9

Sch.15B Part I para.3, varied: 2004 c.12 s.94

Sch.15B Part II para.8, amended: 2004 c.12 Sch.19 para.2

Sch.16 para.1, varied: 2004 c.12 s.101

Sch.16 para.2, varied: 2004 c.12 s.101

Sch.16 para.3, varied: 2004 c.12 s.101

Sch.16 para.4, varied: 2004 c.12 s.101

Sch.16 para.5, varied: 2004 c.12 s.101

Sch.16 para.6, amended: 2002 asp 17 Sch.3 para.19

Sch.16 para.6, varied: 2004 c.12 s.101

Sch.16 para.7, varied: 2004 c.12 s.101

Sch.16 para.7A, varied: 2004 c.12 s.101

Sch.16 para.8, varied: 2004 c.12 s.101

Sch.16 para.9, varied: 2004 c.12 s.101

Sch.16 para.10, varied: 2004 c.12 s.101

Sch.16 para.11, varied: 2004 c.12 s.101

Sch.18 para.1, see *Businessman v Inspector of Taxes* [2003] S.T.C. (S.C.D.) 403 (Sp Comm), John F Avery Jones

Sch.18 para.1, varied: 2002 c.23 Sch.29 para.53, 2003 c.14 Sch.7 para.1

Sch.18 para.2, varied: 2002 c.23 Sch.29 para.53, 2003 c.14 Sch.7 para.1

Sch.18 para.3, varied: 2002 c.23 Sch.29 para.53, 2003 c.14 Sch.7 para.1

Sch.18 para.4, varied: 2002 c.23 Sch.29 para.53, 2003 c.14 Sch.7 para.1

Sch.18 para.5, varied: 2002 c.23 Sch.29 para.53, 2003 c.14 Sch.7 para.1

Sch.18 para.5A, varied: 2002 c.23 Sch.29 para.53, 2003 c.14 Sch.7 para.1

Sch.18 para.5B, amended: 2003 c.1 Sch.6 para.121

Sch.18 para.5B, varied: 2002 c.23 Sch.29 para.53, 2003 c.14 Sch.7 para.1

Sch.18 para.5C, varied: 2002 c.23 Sch.29 para.53, 2003 c.14 Sch.7 para.1

Sch.18 para.5D, varied: 2002 c.23 Sch.29 para.53, 2003 c.14 Sch.7 para.1

Sch.18 para.5E, varied: 2002 c.23 Sch.29 para.53, 2003 c.14 Sch.7 para.1

Sch.18 para.5F, varied: 2002 c.23 Sch.29 para.53, 2003 c.14 Sch.7 para.1

Sch.18 para.6, varied: 2002 c.23 Sch.29 para.53, 2003 c.14 Sch.7 para.1

1988–cont.

1. **Income and Corporation Taxes Act 1988**–*cont.*

Sch.18 para.7, varied: 2002 c.23 Sch.29 para.53, 2003 c.14 Sch.7 para.1

Sch.19AA para.1, enabling: SI 2004/3275

Sch.19AA para.4, amended: 2003 c.14 Sch.33 para.27

Sch.19AA para.5, amended: 2003 c.14 s.153

Sch.19AA para.5, varied: SI 2004/2680 Reg.17

Sch.19AB para.1, amended: SI 2002/1409 Art.2

Sch.19AC para.3, varied: SI 2004/2200 Reg.3

Sch.19AC para.4, varied: SI 2004/2200 Reg.3

Sch.19AC para.4A, applied: 2002 c.23 Sch.26 para.28, Sch.29 para.89

Sch.19AC para.4A, varied: SI 2004/2200 Reg.3

Sch.19AC para.5, substituted: SI 2004/2310 Sch.1 para.36

Sch.19AC para.5, varied: SI 2004/2200 Reg.3

Sch.19AC para.5A, varied: SI 2004/2200 Reg.3

Sch.19AC para.5B, varied: SI 2004/2200 Reg.3

Sch.19AC para.5C, varied: SI 2004/2200 Reg.3

Sch.19AC para.6, varied: SI 2004/2200 Reg.3

Sch.19AC para.6A, varied: SI 2004/2200 Reg.3

Sch.19AC para.7, varied: SI 2004/2200 Reg.3

Sch.19AC para.8, varied: SI 2004/2200 Reg.3

Sch.19AC para.9, varied: SI 2004/2200 Reg.3

Sch.19AC para.10AA, varied: SI 2004/2200 Reg.3

Sch.19AC para.10B, varied: SI 2004/2200 Reg.3

Sch.19AC para.10C, varied: SI 2004/2200 Reg.3

Sch.19AC para.11, varied: SI 2004/2200 Reg.3

Sch.19AC para.11C, varied: SI 2004/2200 Reg.3

Sch.19AC para.13, varied: SI 2004/2200 Reg.3

Sch.19AC para.14, varied: SI 2004/2200 Reg.3

Sch.19AC para.14A, varied: SI 2004/2200 Reg.3

Sch.19B Part I para.1, added: 2004 c.12 Sch.38

Sch.19B Part II para.2, added: 2004 c.12 Sch.38

1988–cont.

1. Income and Corporation Taxes Act 1988–*cont.*

Sch.19B Part II para.3, added: 2004 c.12 Sch.38

Sch.19B Part II para.4, added: 2004 c.12 Sch.38

Sch.19B Part II para.5, added: 2004 c.12 Sch.38

Sch.19B Part II para.6, added: 2004 c.12 Sch.38

Sch.19B Part II para.7, added: 2004 c.12 Sch.38

Sch.19B Part II para.8, added: 2004 c.12 Sch.38

Sch.19B Part III para.9, added: 2004 c.12 Sch.38

Sch.19B Part III para.10, added: 2004 c.12 Sch.38

Sch.19B Part III para.11, added: 2004 c.12 Sch.38

Sch.19B Part III para.12, added: 2004 c.12 Sch.38

Sch.19B Part III para.13, added: 2004 c.12 Sch.38

Sch.19B Part III para.14, added: 2004 c.12 Sch.38

Sch.19B Part IV para.15, added: 2004 c.12 Sch.38

Sch.19B Part IV para.16, added: 2004 c.12 Sch.38

Sch.19B Part IV para.17, added: 2004 c.12 Sch.38

Sch.19B Part IV para.18, added: 2004 c.12 Sch.38

Sch.19B Part IV para.19, added: 2004 c.12 Sch.38

Sch.19B Part IV para.20, added: 2004 c.12 Sch.38

Sch.19B Part IV para.21, added: 2004 c.12 Sch.38

Sch.19B Part IV para.22, added: 2004 c.12 Sch.38

Sch.19B Part IV para.23, added: 2004 c.12 Sch.38

Sch.19B Part IV para.24, added: 2004 c.12 Sch.38

Sch.20 Part I para.8, varied: SI 2003/1633 Sch.2 para.6

Sch.22 para.1, repealed: 2004 c.12 Sch.42 Part 3

Sch.22 para.2, repealed: 2004 c.12 Sch.42 Part 3

Sch.22 para.3, repealed: 2004 c.12 Sch.42 Part 3

Sch.22 para.4, repealed: 2004 c.12 Sch.42 Part 3

Sch.22 para.5, repealed: 2004 c.12 Sch.42 Part 3

Sch.22 para.6, referred to: 2004 c.35 s.251

Sch.22 para.6, repealed: 2004 c.12 Sch.42 Part 3

1988–cont.

1. Income and Corporation Taxes Act 1988–*cont.*

Sch.22 para.7, repealed: 2004 c.12 Sch.42 Part 3

Sch.22 para.8, repealed: 2004 c.12 Sch.42 Part 3

Sch.23 para.1, repealed: 2004 c.12 Sch.42 Part 3

Sch.23 para.2, repealed: 2004 c.12 Sch.42 Part 3

Sch.23 para.3, repealed: 2004 c.12 Sch.42 Part 3

Sch.23 para.4, repealed: 2004 c.12 Sch.42 Part 3

Sch.23 para.5, referred to: SR 2002/352 Sch.4 para.9

Sch.23 para.5, repealed: 2004 c.12 Sch.42 Part 3

Sch.23 para.6, repealed: 2004 c.12 Sch.42 Part 3

Sch.23 para.7, repealed: 2004 c.12 Sch.42 Part 3

Sch.23 para.8, repealed: 2004 c.12 Sch.42 Part 3

Sch.23 para.9, repealed: 2004 c.12 Sch.42 Part 3

Sch.23A para.1, enabling: SI 2003/2582

Sch.23A para.2, referred to: SI 2003/3143 Reg.4

Sch.23A para.2A, amended: 2002 c.23 s.108, 2004 c.12 Sch.24 para.2, Sch.42 Part 2

Sch.23A para.2A, referred to: 2004 c.12 Sch.24 para.2

Sch.23A para.2A, repealed (in part): 2004 c.12 Sch.42 Part 2

Sch.23A para.2A, varied: 2004 c.12 Sch.24 para.2

Sch.23A para.3, amended: 2002 c.23 s.108

Sch.23A para.3, applied: SI 2004/1450 Reg.25

Sch.23A para.3, referred to: SI 2003/3143 Reg.4

Sch.23A para.3, varied: 2003 c.14 s.153

Sch.23A para.4, amended: 2002 c.23 Sch.30 para.1, SI 2004/2310 Sch.1 para.37

Sch.23A para.4, applied: SI 2004/1450 Reg.25

Sch.23A para.4, varied: 2003 c.14 s.153

Sch.23A para.4, enabling: SI 2003/2582

Sch.23A para.7, amended: SI 2004/2310 Sch.1 para.37

Sch.23A para.7A, added: 2004 c.12 s.137

Sch.23A para.8, enabling: SI 2003/2582, SI 2004/2310

Sch.23ZA para.1, repealed: 2004 c.12 Sch.42 Part 3

Sch.23ZA para.2, repealed: 2004 c.12 Sch.42 Part 3

Sch.23ZA para.3, repealed: 2004 c.12 Sch.42 Part 3

1988–cont.

1. Income and Corporation Taxes Act 1988–*cont.*

Sch.23ZA para.4, repealed: 2004 c.12 Sch.42 Part 3

Sch.23ZA para.5, repealed: 2004 c.12 Sch.42 Part 3

Sch.23ZA para.6, repealed: 2004 c.12 Sch.42 Part 3

Sch.24 para.1, amended: 2003 c.14 s.153

Sch.24 para.4, applied: 2002 c.23 Sch.29 para.116

Sch.24 para.4, disapplied: 2002 c.23 Sch.29 para.116

Sch.24 para.8, amended: 2003 c.14 s.153

Sch.24 para.13, repealed: 2002 c.23 Sch.40 Part 3

Sch.24 para.14, repealed: 2002 c.23 Sch.40 Part 3

Sch.24 para.15, repealed: 2002 c.23 Sch.40 Part 3

Sch.24 para.16, repealed: 2002 c.23 Sch.40 Part 3

Sch.24 para.17, repealed: 2002 c.23 Sch.40 Part 3

Sch.24 para.18, repealed: 2002 c.23 Sch.40 Part 3

Sch.24 para.19, repealed: 2002 c.23 Sch.40 Part 3

Sch.24 para.20, repealed: 2004 c.12 Sch.42 Part 2

Sch.25 Part II para.5, amended: 2003 c.14 s.201

Sch.25 Part II para.6, amended: 2003 c.14 s.153, Sch.42 para.2, Sch.43 Part 5

Sch.25 Part II para.8, amended: 2003 c.14 s.153

Sch.25 Part II para.11, amended: 2003 c.14 s.153, Sch.42 para.3

Sch.25 Part II para.11A, added: 2003 c.14 Sch.42 para.4

Sch.25 Part II para.11B, added: 2003 c.14 Sch.42 para.4

Sch.26 para.1, amended: SI 2004/2310 Sch.1 para.38

Sch.27, applied: SI 2004/2572 Reg.7

Sch.27, referred to: SI 2004/2572 Reg.6

Sch.27 Part I para.1, varied: SI 2004/2572 Reg.4

Sch.27 Part I para.2, varied: SI 2004/2572 Reg.4

Sch.27 Part I para.3, amended: 2004 c.12 Sch.26 para.8

Sch.27 Part I para.4, varied: SI 2004/2572 Reg.4

Sch.27 Part I para.5, amended: 2004 c.12 Sch.26 para.1, Sch.26 para.2

Sch.27 Part I para.5, applied: 2002 c.23 Sch.26 para.35

Sch.27 Part I para.5, repealed (in part): 2002 c.23 Sch.40 Part 3

1988–cont.

1. Income and Corporation Taxes Act 1988–*cont.*

Sch.27 Part I para.5, varied: SI 2004/2572 Reg.4

Sch.27 Part II para.6, amended: 2004 c.12 Sch.26 para.14

Sch.27 Part II para.7, amended: 2004 c.12 Sch.26 para.14

Sch.27 Part II para.10, repealed: 2004 c.12 Sch.42 Part 2

Sch.27 Part II para.11, amended: 2004 c.12 Sch.26 para.8, Sch.26 para.14, Sch.42 Part 2

Sch.27 Part II para.11, varied: SI 2004/2572 Reg.4

Sch.27 Part II para.12, repealed: 2004 c.12 Sch.42 Part 2

Sch.27 Part II para.13, repealed: 2004 c.12 Sch.42 Part 2

Sch.27 Part II para.14, amended: 2004 c.12 Sch.26 para.14

Sch.27 Part III para.15, varied: SI 2004/2572 Reg.4

Sch.27 Part III para.16, amended: 2004 c.12 Sch.42 Part 2

Sch.27 Part IV, added: 2004 c.12 Sch.26 para.8

Sch.27 Part IV para.21, enabling: SI 2004/2572

Sch.28A, applied: 2004 c.12 s.43

Sch.28AA, see *Meditor Capital Management Ltd v Feighan (Inspector of Taxes)* [2004] S.T.C. (S.C.D.) 273 (Sp Comm), Julian Ghosh

Sch.28AA, applied: 2002 c.23 Sch.26 para.31A, Sch.26 para.27, Sch.29 para.92, 2004 c.12 s.33, s.37

Sch.28AA, disapplied: 2002 c.23 Sch.26 para.28, Sch.29 para.55

Sch.28AA, see *Meditor Capital Management Ltd v Feighan (Inspector of Taxes)* [2004] S.T.C. (S.C.D.) 273 (Sp Comm), Julian Ghosh

Sch.28AA, added: 2004 c.12 s.34

Sch.28AA, see *Meditor Capital Management Ltd v Feighan (Inspector of Taxes)* [2004] S.T.C. (S.C.D.) 273 (Sp Comm), Julian Ghosh

Sch.28AA, see *Meditor Capital Management Ltd v Feighan (Inspector of Taxes)* [2004] S.T.C. (S.C.D.) 273 (Sp Comm), Julian Ghosh

Sch.28AA, added: 2004 c.12 s.31

Sch.28B, applied: 2002 c.23 Sch.33 para.5, SI 2002/2661 Reg.8, Reg.9, SI 2004/2199 Reg.12, Reg.13

Sch.28B, referred to: 2002 c.23 Sch.33 para.9, SI 2002/2661 Reg.8, Reg.9, SI 2004/712 Reg.1

Sch.28B, added: 2004 c.12 Sch.19 para.10

Sch.28B, added: 2004 c.12 Sch.19 para.13

1988–cont.

1. Income and Corporation Taxes Act 1988–*cont.*

Sch.28 Part II para.6, varied: SI 2004/2572 Reg.5

Sch.28 Part III para.9, added: 2004 c.12 Sch.26 para.9

Sch.28 Part III para.9, enabling: SI 2004/2572

Sch.28AA para.1, amended: 2004 c.12 s.31

Sch.28AA para.1, applied: 2002 c.23 Sch.29 para.92

Sch.28AA para.5, amended: 2003 c.14 Sch.43 Part 3, 2004 c.12 s.30, Sch.42 Part 2

Sch.28AA para.5, disapplied: 2002 c.23 Sch.29 para.92

Sch.28AA para.5, referred to: 2002 c.23 Sch.29 para.92

Sch.28AA para.5, repealed (in part): 2004 c.12 Sch.42 Part 2

Sch.28AA para.5B, added: 2004 c.12 s.31

Sch.28AA para.5C, added: 2004 c.12 s.31

Sch.28AA para.5D, added: 2004 c.12 s.31

Sch.28AA para.5E, added: 2004 c.12 s.31

Sch.28AA para.6, amended: 2004 c.12 s.30, s.35

Sch.28AA para.6A, added: 2004 c.12 s.32

Sch.28AA para.6B, added: 2004 c.12 s.32

Sch.28AA para.6C, added: 2004 c.12 s.35

Sch.28AA para.6D, added: 2004 c.12 s.35

Sch.28AA para.6E, added: 2004 c.12 s.35

Sch.28AA para.7A, added: 2004 c.12 s.30

Sch.28AA para.7B, added: 2004 c.12 s.36

Sch.28AA para.7C, added: 2004 c.12 s.36

Sch.28AA para.7D, added: 2004 c.12 s.36

Sch.28AA para.8, amended: 2002 c.23 Sch.23 para.21, Sch.27 para.15

Sch.28AA para.11, amended: 2004 c.12 s.30, Sch.42 Part 2

Sch.28AA para.11, repealed (in part): 2004 c.12 Sch.42 Part 2

Sch.28AA para.12, amended: 2004 c.12 s.30

Sch.28AA para.13, amended: 2004 c.12 s.32

Sch.28AA para.14, amended: 2004 c.12 s.31, s.35, SI 2004/2310 Sch.1 para.40

Sch.28A Part I para.1, amended: SI 2004/2310 Sch.1 para.39

Sch.28A Part I para.2, amended: SI 2004/2310 Sch.1 para.39

Sch.28A Part I para.3, amended: SI 2004/2310 Sch.1 para.39

Sch.28A Part I para.4, amended: SI 2004/2310 Sch.1 para.39

Sch.28A Part I para.5, amended: SI 2004/2310 Sch.1 para.39

Sch.28A Part II para.6, amended: 2002 c.23 Sch.25 para.58, Sch.30 para.4, SI 2004/2310 Sch.1 para.39

Sch.28A Part II para.6A, amended: SI 2004/2310 Sch.1 para.39

1988–cont.

1. Income and Corporation Taxes Act 1988–*cont.*

Sch.28A Part III para.7, amended: 2002 c.23 Sch.25 para.58, Sch.30 para.4, Sch.40 Part 3, 2004 c.12 Sch.10 para.45, SI 2004/2310 Sch.1 para.39

Sch.28A Part III para.7, repealed (in part): 2002 c.23 Sch.40 Part 3

Sch.28A Part III para.8, amended: SI 2004/2310 Sch.1 para.39

Sch.28A Part IV para.9, amended: SI 2004/2310 Sch.1 para.39

Sch.28A Part IV para.10, amended: SI 2004/2310 Sch.1 para.39

Sch.28A Part IV para.11, amended: SI 2004/2310 Sch.1 para.39

Sch.28A Part IV para.11, amended: 2002 c.23 Sch.25 para.58, 2004 c.12 Sch.10 para.45, SI 2004/2310 Sch.1 para.39

Sch.28A Part IV para.12, amended: SI 2004/2310 Sch.1 para.39

Sch.28A Part IVi para.11, amended: SI 2004/2310 Sch.1 para.39

Sch.28A Part V para.13, amended: 2002 c.23 Sch.25 para.58, Sch.30 para.4, SI 2004/2310 Sch.1 para.39

Sch.28A Part V para.13A, amended: SI 2004/2310 Sch.1 para.39

Sch.28A Part VI para.14, amended: SI 2004/2310 Sch.1 para.39

Sch.28A Part VI para.15, amended: SI 2004/2310 Sch.1 para.39

Sch.28A Part VI para.16, amended: 2002 c.23 Sch.25 para.58, Sch.30 para.4, Sch.40 Part 3, 2004 c.12 Sch.10 para.45, SI 2004/2310 Sch.1 para.39

Sch.28A Part VI para.16, repealed (in part): 2002 c.23 Sch.40 Part 3

Sch.28A Part VI para.17, amended: SI 2004/2310 Sch.1 para.39

Sch.28B para.1, applied: SI 2004/2199 Reg.8

Sch.28B para.2, applied: SI 2002/2661 Reg.7, Reg.8, Reg.9

Sch.28B para.2, referred to: SI 2002/2661 Reg.8, Reg.9

Sch.28B para.3, amended: 2004 c.12 Sch.19 para.9, Sch.27 para.5, Sch.42 Part 2

Sch.28B para.4, amended: 2002 c.23 s.103, Sch.40 Part 3, 2004 c.12 Sch.27 para.5

Sch.28B para.5, amended: 2004 c.12 Sch.42 Part 2

Sch.28B para.6, amended: 2004 c.12 Sch.19 para.11

Sch.28B para.6, applied: SI 2002/2661 Reg.7, Reg.8, Reg.9, SI 2004/2199 Reg.8

Sch.28B para.6, repealed (in part): 2004 c.12 Sch.42 Part 2

Sch.28B para.7, applied: SI 2002/2661 Reg.7, Reg.8, Reg.9, SI 2004/2199 Reg.8

Sch.28B para.8, applied: SI 2002/2661 Reg.7, SI 2004/2199 Reg.8

1988–cont.

1. **Income and Corporation Taxes Act 1988**–cont.
   Sch.28B para.9, applied: SI 2002/2661 Reg.7, SI 2004/2199 Reg.13
   Sch.28B para.9, disapplied: SI 2002/2661 Reg.8
   Sch.28B para.9, referred to: SI 2002/2661 Reg.9, SI 2004/2199 Reg.13
   Sch.28B para.10, amended: 2004 c.12 Sch.19 para.12, Sch.42 Part 2
   Sch.28B para.10, repealed (in part): 2004 c.12 Sch.42 Part 2
   Sch.28B para.10B, applied: SI 2002/2661 Reg.7, Reg.8, Reg.9, Reg.11, SI 2004/2199 Reg.13
   Sch.28B para.10C, applied: SI 2002/2661 Reg.5
   Sch.28B para.10D, applied: SI 2002/2661 Reg.4
   Sch.28B para.11, amended: 2004 c.12 Sch.19 para.14, Sch.42 Part 2
   Sch.28B para.11A, amended: SI 2003/2096 Sch.1 para.19, 2004 c.12 Sch.19 para.15
   Sch.28B para.11B, applied: SI 2002/2661 Reg.2, Reg.3
   Sch.28B para.11B, enabling: SI 2002/2661
   Sch.29 para.6, repealed: 2003 c.1 Sch.8 Part 1
   Sch.29 para.32, amended: 2002 c.40 Sch.26, 2003 c.14 Sch.43 Part 4, 2003 c.21 Sch.19, 2004 c.12 Sch.42 Part 3

2. **Arms Control and Disarmament (Privileges and Immunities) Act 1988**
   s.1, applied: SI 2003/2621
   s.1, enabling: SI 2003/2621

3. **Land Registration Act 1988**
   repealed: 2002 c.9 Sch.13

4. **Church of England (Pensions) Measure 1988**
   Sch.12, repealed: 2003 c.2 Sch.1

4. **Norfolk and Suffolk Broads Act 1988**
   applied: SI 2002/1223 r.13, SI 2002/2685 r.11, SI 2002/2686 r.13
   s.25, amended: 2003 c.21 Sch.17 para.89
   Sch.3 Part II para.40, amended: 2003 c.17 Sch.6 para.107

7. **Social Security Act 1988**
   applied: SI 2002/2006 Reg.7
   s.13, applied: SI 2004/291 Sch.4, SI 2004/478 Sch.4, SI 2004/627 Sch.2, SSI 2004/115 Sch.3
   s.13, substituted: 2003 c.43 s.185
   s.13, enabling: SI 2002/550, SI 2003/702, SI 2003/1864, SI 2004/723, SI 2004/2311
   s.15A, amended: 2003 c.43 s.185
   s.15A, repealed (in part): 2003 c.43 s.185, Sch.14 Part 5
   Sch.4 para.1, repealed: 2003 c.1 Sch.8 Part 1

9. **Local Government Act 1988**
   referred to: SI 2002/808 Art.2
   s.1, repealed (in part): 2003 asp 1 s.60

1988–cont.

9. **Local Government Act 1988**–cont.
   s.2, repealed (in part): 2003 asp 1 s.60
   s.3, repealed (in part): 2003 asp 1 s.60
   s.4, repealed (in part): 2003 asp 1 s.60
   s.5, repealed (in part): 2003 asp 1 s.60
   s.6, repealed (in part): 2003 asp 1 s.60
   s.7, repealed (in part): 2003 asp 1 s.60
   s.8, repealed (in part): 2003 asp 1 s.60
   s.9, repealed (in part): 2003 asp 1 s.60
   s.10, repealed (in part): 2003 asp 1 s.60
   s.11, repealed (in part): 2003 asp 1 s.60
   s.12, repealed (in part): 2003 asp 1 s.60
   s.13, repealed (in part): 2003 asp 1 s.60
   s.14, repealed (in part): 2003 asp 1 s.60
   s.15, repealed (in part): 2003 asp 1 s.60
   s.16, repealed (in part): 2003 asp 1 s.60
   s.17, amended: 2003 asp 8 Sch.6 para.19
   s.17, applied: 2003 asp 8 Sch.6 para.19
   s.17, disapplied: 2003 asp 1 s.7
   s.17, varied: SI 2002/678 Art.2
   s.19, amended: SI 2002/808 Art.17
   s.25, amended: SI 2002/1860 Sch.1 para.3, Sch.6
   s.28, referred to: 2003 c.26 s.128
   s.28, repealed: 2003 c.26 Sch.8 Part 1
   s.32, repealed (in part): 2003 asp 1 s.60
   s.33, referred to: 2003 c.26 s.129
   s.33, repealed (in part): 2003 asp 1 s.60, 2003 c.26 Sch.8 Part 1
   s.38, repealed: 2004 c.14 Sch.1 Part 17
   Sch.2 Part 1, amended: SI 2002/808 Art.17, 2004 c.21 Sch.1 para.65
   Sch.3 para.11, repealed: 2002 asp 11 Sch.6 para.10
   Sch.3 para.12, repealed: 2002 asp 11 Sch.6 para.10
   Sch.3 para.13, repealed: 2002 asp 11 Sch.6 para.10
   Sch.3 para.14, repealed: 2002 asp 11 Sch.6 para.10
   Sch.3 para.15, repealed: 2002 asp 11 Sch.6 para.10
   Sch.3 para.16, repealed: 2002 asp 11 Sch.6 para.10
   Sch.3 para.17, repealed: 2002 asp 11 Sch.6 para.10
   Sch.6 para.1, repealed (in part): 2003 asp 1 s.60
   Sch.6 para.2, repealed (in part): 2003 asp 1 s.60
   Sch.6 para.3, repealed (in part): 2003 asp 1 s.60
   Sch.6 para.4, repealed (in part): 2003 asp 1 s.60
   Sch.6 para.5, repealed (in part): 2003 asp 1 s.60
   Sch.6 para.6, repealed (in part): 2003 asp 1 s.60
   Sch.6 para.7, repealed (in part): 2003 asp 1 s.60

1988–cont.

9. Local Government Act 1988–*cont.*

Sch.6 para.8, repealed (in part): 2003 asp 1 s.60

Sch.6 para.9, repealed (in part): 2003 asp 1 s.60

Sch.6 para.10, repealed (in part): 2003 asp 1 s.60

Sch.6 para.11, repealed (in part): 2003 asp 1 s.60

11. Regional Development Grants (Termination) Act 1988

repealed: 2004 c.14 Sch.1 Part 16

12. Merchant Shipping Act 1988

see *Factortame Ltd v Secretary of State for the Environment, Transport and the Regions (Costs) (No.1)* [2002] EWCA Civ 22, [2002] 1 W.L.R. 2438 (CA), Waller, L.J.

13. Coroners Act 1988

s.1, amended: 2003 c.10 Sch.1 para.2

s.1, applied: SI 2004/536 Art.3, SI 2004/1799 Art.5

s.1, enabling: SI 2004/536, SI 2004/1799

s.2, applied: SI 2002/975 Reg.2

s.4, applied: SI 2002/1588, SI 2002/2257, SI 2002/3084, SI 2004/1799

s.4, enabling: SI 2002/1588, SI 2002/2257, SI 2002/3084, SI 2003/2753, SI 2003/3224, SI 2004/535, SI 2004/536, SI 2004/1799, SI 2004/2192

s.7, see *Commissioner of Police of the Metropolis v HM Coroner for Inner South London* [2002] EWHC 2392, [2003] 1 W.L.R. 371 (QBD (Admin Ct)), Pitchers, J.

s.8, applied: SI 2004/921 r.1

s.9, repealed (in part): 2003 c.44 Sch.37 Part 10

s.11, see *R. (on the application of Sacker) v HM Coroner for West Yorkshire* [2004] UKHL 11, [2004] 1 W.L.R. 796 (HL), Lord Bingham of Cornhill

s.13, see *Commissioner of Police of the Metropolis v HM Coroner for Inner South London* [2002] EWHC 2392, [2003] 1 W.L.R. 371 (QBD (Admin Ct)), Pitchers, J.; see *HM Coroner for Wiltshire and Swindon v Ministry of Defence* [2002] EWHC 2567, Times, November 28, 2002 (QBD (Admin Ct)), Lord Woolf of Barnes, L.C.J.; see *R. (on the application of Mulholland) v HM Coroner for St Pancras* [2003] EWHC 2612, (2004) 78 B.M.L.R. 75 (QBD (Admin Ct)), Kennedy, L.J.; see *Terry v East Sussex Coroner* [2001] EWCA Civ 1094, [2002] Q.B. 312 (CA), Simon Brown, L.J.

s.16, see *R. (on the application of Hurst) v HM Coroner for Northern District London* [2003] EWHC 1721, [2004] U.K.H.R.R. 139 (QBD (Admin Ct)), Henriques, J.

s.16, amended: 2003 c.39 Sch.8 para.302, 2003 c.44 Sch.3 para.59, 2004 c.28 Sch.10 para.26, Sch.11

1988–cont.

13. Coroners Act 1988–*cont.*

s.17, amended: 2003 c.39 Sch.8 para.302, 2003 c.44 Sch.3 para.59, 2004 c.28 Sch.10 para.27, Sch.11

s.19, see *Terry v East Sussex Coroner* [2001] EWCA Civ 1094, [2002] Q.B. 312 (CA), Simon Brown, L.J.

s.19, amended: 2004 c.30 Sch.6 para.3

s.21, amended: 2004 c.30 Sch.6 para.3

s.24, enabling: SI 2002/2401

s.32, enabling: SI 2004/921

s.36, enabling: SI 2004/1799

14. Immigration Act 1988

applied: 2002 c.41 s.67, s.77, s.78

s.5, see *Khalil v Secretary of State for the Home Department* 2002 S.L.T. 1039 (OH), Lord Carloway

s.5, applied: SI 2003/754 Sch.2 para.3

s.8, referred to: SI 2003/2900 Sch.1

s.9, referred to: SI 2003/2900 Sch.1

s.10, applied: SI 2002/3019 Reg.36

16. Farm Land and Rural Development Act 1988

s.1, amended: SI 2002/794 Sch.1 para.32

s.1, enabling: SI 2003/2726, SSI 2002/44

s.2, applied: SSI 2003/209

s.2, enabling: SSI 2003/209

17. Licensing Act 1988

repealed: 2003 c.17 Sch.7

19. Employment Act 1988

s.29, amended: 2004 c.14 Sch.1 Part 2

Sch.3 Part II para.13, repealed: 2004 c.14 Sch.1 Part 2

20. Dartford-Thurrock Crossing Act 1988

s.11, applied: SI 2002/1040 Art.2

s.16, applied: SI 2002/1040 Art.2

s.19, amended: SI 2002/2469 Sch.1 para.15, 2004 c.21 Sch.1 para.66

s.25, enabling: SI 2003/496, SI 2004/1441

s.26, enabling: SI 2003/496

s.44, enabling: SI 2003/496

s.46, enabling: SI 2003/496, SI 2004/1441

22. Scotch Whisky Act 1988

s.3, amended: SI 2002/794 Sch.2

s.3, varied: SI 2002/794 Sch.1 para.33

24. Community Health Councils (Access to Information) Act 1988

s.1, amended: 2003 c.4 Sch.3 para.5, 2003 c.43 Sch.11 para.51

s.1, varied: SI 2002/2469 Reg.17, SI 2004/288 Art.7, SI 2004/480 Art.6, SI 2004/865 Art.109, SI 2004/1016 Art.85

25. Licensing (Retail Sales) Act 1988

repealed: 2003 c.17 Sch.7

26. Landlord and Tenant Act 1988

s.1, see *Clinton Cards (Essex) Ltd v Sun Alliance & London Assurance Co Ltd* [2002] EWHC 1576, [2003] L. & T.R. 2 (Ch D), David Oliver Q.C.; see *Design Progression Ltd v Thurloe Properties Ltd* [2004] EWHC 324, [2004] 2 P. & C.R. 31

CAP.

1988–cont.

26. Landlord and Tenant Act 1988–*cont.*
s.1–*cont.*

(Ch D), Peter Smith, J.; see *Go West Ltd v Spigarolo* [2003] EWCA Civ 17, [2003] Q.B.1140 (CA), Munby, J.; see *Mount Eden Land Ltd v Folia Ltd* [2003] EWHC 1815, [2003] N.P.C. 95 (Ch D), Peter Smith, J.; see *Norwich Union Linked Life Assurance Ltd v Mercantile Credit Co Ltd* [2003] EWHC 3064, [2004] 4 E.G.C.S. 109 (Ch D), David Richards, J

s.1, varied: 2002 c.15 Sch.7 para.13

s.3, varied: 2002 c.15 Sch.7 para.13

s.5, see *Norwich Union Linked Life Assurance Ltd v Mercantile Credit Co Ltd* [2003] EWHC 3064, [2004] 4 E.G.C.S. 109 (Ch D), David Richards, J

27. Malicious Communications Act 1988
applied: SI 2003/1593 Sch.1 Part I

s.1, amended: 2003 c.21 Sch.17 para.90

s.1, applied: SI 2003/1376 Sch.1

30. Environment and Safety Information Act 1988
Sch.1, amended: 2004 c.21 Sch.1 para.67

32. Civil Evidence (Scotland) Act 1988
see *Ellison v Inspirations East Ltd* 2003 S.L.T. 291 (OH), Lord Hardie

s.2, applied: SSI 2002/132 Sch.1 para.17.1, SSI 2002/133 Sch.1 para.16.1

s.8, amended: 2004 c.33 Sch.28 para.55

33. Criminal Justice Act 1988
Commencement Orders: SI 2004/2167 Art.2, Art.3

see *Hughes v Customs and Excise Commissioners* [2002] EWCA Civ 734, [2003] 1 W.L.R. 177 (CA), Simon Brown, L.J.; see *Katchis v UPS (London) Ltd* [2003] EWHC 3222, [2004] B.P.I.R. 472 (Ch D), Judge Weeks Q.C.; see *R. v Blee (Julian)* [2003] EWCA Crim 2126, [2004] 1 Cr. App. R. (S.) 33 (CA (Crim Div)), Mance, L.J.

referred to: 2003 c.32 Sch.5 para.13

Part IV, see *R. v Rezvi (Syed)* [2002] UKHL 1, [2003] 1 A.C. 1099 (HL), Lord Steyn

Part IV, applied: SI 2003/2267 Art.2

Part VI, see *R. v Threapleton (Michael) (Costs: Confiscation Order)* [2001] EWCA Crim 2892, [2003] 3 All E.R. 458 (CA (Crim Div)), Stanley Burnton, J.

Part VI, applied: 2002 c.29 s.8, s.94, s.120, s.158

Part VI, see *R. v Threapleton (Michael) (Costs: Confiscation Order)* [2001] EWCA Crim 2892, [2003] 3 All E.R. 458 (CA (Crim Div)), Stanley Burnton, J.

Part VI, repealed: 2002 c.29 Sch.12

Part VI, see *R. v Threapleton (Michael) (Costs: Confiscation Order)* [2001] EWCA Crim 2892, [2003] 3 All E.R. 458 (CA (Crim Div)), Stanley Burnton, J.

CAP.

1988–cont.

33. Criminal Justice Act 1988–*cont.*
Part 6, see *R. v Levin (David)* [2004] EWCA Crim 408, [2004] 2 Cr. App. R. (S.) 61 (CA (Crim Div)), Rose, L.J.

s.23, see *R. v Arnold (Kenneth)* [2004] EWCA Crim 1293, (2004) 148 S.J.L.B. 660 (CA (Crim Div)), Hooper, L.J.; see *R. v M (Witness Statement)* [2003] EWCA Crim 357, [2003] 2 Cr. App. R. 21 (CA (Crim Div)), Potter, L.J.; see *R. v Sed (Ali Dahir)* [2004] EWCA Crim 1294, [2004] 1 W.L.R. 3218 (CA (Crim Div)), Auld, L.J.

s.23, repealed (in part): 2003 c.44 s.136, Sch.37 Part 4, Sch.3 para.60, Sch.37 Part 6

s.23A, repealed: 2003 c.44 s.136, Sch.37 Part 6

s.23B, repealed: 2003 c.44 s.136, Sch.37 Part 6

s.24, see *Department for the Environment, Food and Rural Affairs v Atkinson* [2002] EWHC 2028, [2002] 3 C.M.L.R. 38 (QBD (Admin Ct)), Brooke, L.J.; see *R. v Jenkins (Nigel)* [2002] EWCA Crim 2475, [2003] Crim. L.R. 107 (CA (Crim Div)), Potter, L.J.

s.24, amended: 2003 c.32 Sch.5 para.14

s.24, repealed (in part): 2003 c.44 s.136, Sch.37 Part 4, Sch.3 para.60, Sch.37 Part 6

s.25, applied: 2003 c.32 s.9

s.25, repealed: 2003 c.44 s.136, Sch.37 Part 6

s.26, see *R. v Arnold (Kenneth)* [2004] EWCA Crim 1293, (2004) 148 S.J.L.B. 660 (CA (Crim Div)), Hooper, L.J.; see *R. v M (Witness Statement)* [2003] EWCA Crim 357, [2003] 2 Cr. App. R. 21 (CA (Crim Div)), Potter, L.J.; see *R. v Sed (Ali Dahir)* [2004] EWCA Crim 1294, [2004] 1 W.L.R. 3218 (CA (Crim Div)), Auld, L.J.

s.26, amended: 2003 c.32 Sch.5 para.15, 2003 c.44 Sch.37 Part 4, Sch.3 para.60

s.26, repealed: 2003 c.44 s.136, Sch.37 Part 6

s.27, amended: 2003 c.44 Sch.37 Part 4, Sch.3 para.60

s.27, repealed: 2003 c.44 s.136, Sch.37 Part 6

s.28, repealed: 2003 c.44 s.136, Sch.37 Part 6

s.30, repealed (in part): 2003 c.44 Sch.37 Part 4, Sch.3 para.60

s.31, amended: SI 2004/2035 Sch.1 para.25

s.32, see *R. (on the application of H) v Thames Youth Court* [2002] EWHC 2046, (2002) 166 J.P. 711 (QBD (Admin Ct)), Sullivan, J.

s.32, amended: 2003 c.42 Sch.6 para.29, Sch.7, SI 2004/2035 Sch.1 para.26

s.32, applied: SI 2004/2167 Art.2

s.32, referred to: 2003 c.32 s.29

s.32, repealed (in part): SI 2004/2035 Sch.1 para.26

CAP.

1988–cont.

33. Criminal Justice Act 1988–*cont.*
s.32A, see *R. (on the application of H) v Thames Youth Court* [2002] EWHC 2046, (2002) 166 J.P. 711 (QBD (Admin Ct)), Sullivan, J.

s.33, repealed: 2003 c.44 Sch.37 Part 4

s.35, enabling: SI 2003/2267

s.36, see *Attorney General's Reference (No.14 of 2001), Re* [2001] EWCA Crim 1235, [2002] 1 Cr. App. R. (S.) 25 (CA (Crim Div)), Kennedy, L.J.; see *Attorney General's Reference (No.2 of 1997), Re* [2002] 241 B.C.C. 121 (CA (Crim Div)), Lord Bingham of Cornhill, L.C.J.; see *Attorney General's Reference (No.22 of 2001), Re* [2001] EWCA Crim 1174, [2002] 1 Cr. App. R. (S.) 13 (CA (Crim Div)), Kay, L.J.; see *Attorney General's Reference (No.25 of 2001), Re* [2001] EWCA Crim 1770, [2002] 1 W.L.R. 253 (CA (Crim Div)), Mantell, L.J.; see *Attorney General's Reference (No.28 of 2001), Re* [2001] EWCA Crim 1373, [2002] 1 Cr. App. R. (S.) 59 (CA (Crim Div)), Judge, L.J.; see *Attorney General's Reference (No.30 of 2001), Re* [2001] EWCA Crim 1319, [2002] 1 Cr. App. R. (S.) 39 (CA (Crim Div)), Kennedy, L.J.; see *Attorney General's Reference (No.35 of 2001), Re* [2001] EWCA Crim 1271, [2002] 1 Cr. App. R. (S.) 44 (CA (Crim Div)), Mantell, L.J.; see *Attorney General's Reference (No.36 of 2001), Re* [2001] EWCA Crim 1489, [2002] 1 Cr. App. R. (S.) 57 (CA (Crim Div)), Potter, L.J.; see *Attorney General's Reference (No.43 of 2001), Re* [2001] EWCA Crim 1275, [2002] 1 Cr. App. R. (S.) 30 (CA (Crim Div)), Rose, L.J.; see *Attorney General's Reference (No.50 of 2001), Re* [2001] EWCA Crim 1475, [2002] 1 Cr. App. R. (S.) 58 (CA (Crim Div)), Potter, L.J.; see *Attorney General's Reference (No.51 of 2001), Re* [2001] EWCA Crim 1635, [2002] 1 Cr. App. R. (S.) 80 (CA (Crim Div)), Mantell, L.J.; see *Attorney General's Reference (No.60 of 2001), Re* [2001] EWCA Crim 2026, [2002] 1 Cr. App. R. (S.) 91 (CA (Crim Div)), Kennedy, L.J.; see *Attorney General's Reference (No.63 of 2001), Re* [2001] EWCA Crim 1652, [2002] 1 Cr. App. R. (S.) 78 (CA (Crim Div)), Rose, L.J.; see *Attorney General's Reference (No.64 of 2001), Re* [2001] EWCA Crim 2028, [2002] 1 Cr. App. R. (S.) 94 (CA (Crim Div)), Kennedy, L.J.; see *Attorney General's Reference (No.68 of 2001), Re* [2001] EWCA Crim 1803, [2002] 1 Cr. App. R. (S.) 93 (CA (Crim Div)), Rose, L.J.; see *Attorney General's Reference (No.71 of 2001), Re* [2001] EWCA Crim 2838, [2002] 2 Cr. App. R. (S.) 23 (CA (Crim Div)), Mantell, L.J.; see

CAP.

1988–cont.

33. Criminal Justice Act 1988–*cont.*
s.36–*cont.*
Attorney General's Reference (No.79 of 2001), Re [2001] EWCA Crim 1925, [2002] 1 Cr. App. R. (S.) 104 (CA (Crim Div)), Rose, L.J.; see *Attorney General's Reference (No.82a of 2000), Re* [2002] EWCA Crim 215, [2002] 2 Cr. App. R. 24 (CA (Crim Div)), Lord Woolf of Barnes, L.C.J.; see *Attorney General's Reference (No.91 of 2001), Re* [2001] EWCA Crim 2135, [2002] 1 Cr. App. R. (S.) 106 (CA (Crim Div)), Kay, L.J.; see *Attorney General's Reference (Nos.114, 115 and 116 of 2002), Re* [2003] EWCA Crim 3374, (2003) 147 S.J.L.B. 1400 (CA (Crim Div)), Rose, L.J. (Vice President); see *Attorney General's Reference (Nos.120, 91 and 119 of 2002), Re* [2003] EWCA Crim 5, [2003] 2 All E.R. 955 (CA (Crim Div)), Mantell, L.J.; see *Attorney General's Reference (Nos.19, 20 and 21 of 2001), Re* [2001] EWCA Crim 1432, [2002] 1 Cr. App. R. (S.) 33 (CA (Crim Div)), Kay, L.J.; see *Attorney General's Reference (Nos.33 and 34 of 2001), Re* [2001] EWCA Crim 1908, [2002] 1 Cr. App. R. (S.) 92 (CA (Crim Div)), Kennedy, L.J.; see *Attorney General's Reference (Nos.44 and 45 of 2001), Re* [2001] EWCA Crim 1483, [2002] 1 Cr. App. R. (S.) 67 (CA (Crim Div)), Tomlinson, J; see *Attorney General's Reference (Nos.73 and 74 of 2001), Re* [2001] EWCA Crim 1923, [2002] 1 Cr. App. R. (S.) 102 (CA (Crim Div)), Rose, L.J.

s.36, amended: 2002 c.26 s.41, 2003 c.44 s.272, Sch.32 para.46, Sch.36 para.96

s.36, applied: 2002 c.29 s.15, 2003 c.17 s.131, s.132, 2003 c.44 Sch.22 para.15

s.40, amended: 2003 c.44 Sch.37 Part 4, Sch.3 para.60

s.41, amended: 2003 c.39 Sch.8 para.303, 2004 c.28 Sch.10 para.28

s.41, repealed (in part): 2003 c.39 Sch.8 para.303, Sch.10, 2003 c.44 Sch.37 Part 4, Sch.3 para.60

s.50, amended: 2003 c.44 Sch.32 para.47

s.62, applied: SI 2003/2093 Art.3

s.62, repealed (in part): 2002 c.40 Sch.26

s.67, amended: 2003 c.39 Sch.8 para.304

s.71, see *R. v Alagbala (Michael)* [2004] EWCA Crim 89, [2004] 2 Cr. App. R. (S.) 48 (CA (Crim Div)), Latham, L.J.; see *R. v Davies (Derrick)* [2003] EWCA Crim 3110, [2004] 2 All E.R. 706 (CA (Crim Div)), Waller, L.J.; see *R. v Davy (Michael Alan)* [2003] EWCA Crim 781, [2003] 2 Cr. App. R. (S.) 101 (CA (Crim Div)), Cox, J.; see *R. v Foggon (John James)* [2003] EWCA Crim 270, [2003] S.T.C. 461 (CA (Crim Div)), Jack, J.; see *R. v Jannaway (Terrance Stuart)* [2003] EWCA Crim 459, [2003] 2 Cr. App. R. (S.) 98 (CA (Crim

CAP.

1988–cont.

33. Criminal Justice Act 1988–*cont.*
s.71–*cont.*

Div)), Mance, L.J.; see *R. v McKechnie (Ian Alexander)* [2002] EWCA Crim 3161, [2003] 2 Cr. App. R. (S.) 34 (CA (Crim Div)), Hallett, J.; see *R. v McKinnon (Ross Andrew)* [2004] EWCA Crim 395, [2004] 2 Cr. App. R. (S.) 46 (CA (Crim Div)), Scott Baker, L.J.; see *R. v Olubitan (Ayodele Olusegun)* [2003] EWCA Crim 2940, [2004] 2 Cr. App. R. (S.) 14 (CA (Crim Div)), farMay, L.J.; see *R. v Palmer (John)* [2002] EWCA Crim 2202, [2003] 1 Cr. App. R. (S.) 112 (CA (Crim Div)), Rix, L.J.; see *R. v Pope (Alan) (No.1)* [2001] EWCA Crim 972, [2002] 1 Cr. App. R. (S.) 8 (CA (Crim Div)), Buxton, L.J.; see *R. v Pope (Alan) (No.1)* [2002] UKHL 26, [2002] 1 W.L.R. 1966 (HL), Lord Hobhouse of Woodborough; see *R. v Raphael (Saad Towpheek)* [2003] EWCA Crim 698, (2003) 147 S.J.L.B. 353 (CA (Crim Div)), Holland, J.; see *R. v Rezvi (Syed)* [2002] UKHL 1, [2003] 1 A.C. 1099 (HL), Lord Steyn; see *R. v Sekhon (Daljit Singh)* [2002] EWCA Crim 2954, [2003] 1 W.L.R. 1655 (CA (Crim Div)), Lord Woolf of Barnes, L.C.J.; see *R. v Simpson (Ian McDonald)* [2003] EWCA Crim 1499, [2004] Q.B. 118 (CA (Crim Div)), Lord Woolf of Barnes, L.C.J.; see *R. v Smith (David Cadman)* [2001] UKHL 68, [2002] 1 W.L.R. 54 (HL), Lord Rodger of Earlsferry; see *R. v Threapleton (Michael) (Costs: Confiscation Order)* [2001] EWCA Crim 2892, [2003] 3 All E.R. 458 (CA (Crim Div)), Stanley Burnton, J.; see *R. v Wilkes (Gary John)* [2003] EWCA Crim 848, [2003] 2 Cr. App. R. (S.) 105 (CA (Crim Div)), Gross, J.

s.71, repealed: 2002 c.29 Sch.12

s.72, see *R. v Palmer (John)* [2002] EWCA Crim 2202, [2003] 1 Cr. App. R. (S.) 112 (CA (Crim Div)), Rix, L.J.; see *R. v Rogers (Simon)* [2001] EWCA Crim 1680, [2002] 1 Cr. App. R. (S.) 81 (CA (Crim Div)), Judge Beaumont Q.C.; see *R. v Sekhon (Daljit Singh)* [2002] EWCA Crim 2954, [2003] 1 W.L.R. 1655 (CA (Crim Div)), Lord Woolf of Barnes, L.C.J.; see *R. v Simpson (Ian McDonald)* [2003] EWCA Crim 1499, [2004] Q.B. 118 (CA (Crim Div)), Lord Woolf of Barnes, L.C.J.; see *R. v Smart (David Edwin)* [2003] EWCA Crim 258, [2003] 2 Cr. App. R. (S.) 65 (CA (Crim Div)), Gray, J.; see *R. v Threapleton (Michael) (Costs: Confiscation Order)* [2001] EWCA Crim 2892, [2003] 3 All E.R. 458 (CA (Crim Div)), Stanley Burnton, J.

s.72, repealed: 2002 c.29 Sch.12

s.72A, see *R. v Groombridge (Mark)* [2003] EWCA Crim 1371, [2004] 1 Cr. App. R. (S.) 9 (CA (Crim Div)),Treacy, J.; see *R. v Haisman*

CAP.

1988–cont.

33. Criminal Justice Act 1988–*cont.*
s.72A–*cont.*

(Sharon) [2003] EWCA Crim 2246, [2004] 1 Cr. App. R. (S.) 63 (CA (Crim Div)), Potter, L.J.; see *R. v Jones (Timothy Dale)* [2003] EWCA Crim 1631, [2004] 1 Cr. App. R. (S.) 23 (CA (Crim Div)), Judge Hyam; see *R. v Ruddick (David)* [2003] EWCA Crim 1061, [2004] 1 Cr. App. R. (S.) 7 (CA (Crim Div)), Morison, J.; see *R. v Soneji (Kamlesh Kumar)* [2003] EWCA Crim 1765, [2004] 1 Cr. App. R. (S.) 34 (CA (Crim Div)), Pill, J.; see *R. v Young (Trevor Alan)* [2003] EWCA Crim 3481, [2004] 1 W.L.R. 1587 (CA (Crim Div)), May, L.J.

s.72A, repealed: 2002 c.29 Sch.12

s.72AA, see *R. v Davies (Derrick)* [2003] EWCA Crim 3110, [2004] 2 All E.R. 706 (CA (Crim Div)), Waller, L.J.; see *R. v Smith (John)* [2002] EWCA Crim 2561, [2003] 2 Cr. App. R. (S.) 4 (CA (Crim Div)), Longmore, L.J.; see *R. v Wilkes (Gary John)* [2003] EWCA Crim 848, [2003] 2 Cr. App. R. (S.) 105 (CA (Crim Div)), Gross, J.

s.72AA, repealed: 2002 c.29 Sch.12

s.73, repealed: 2002 c.29 Sch.12

s.73A, repealed: 2002 c.29 Sch.12

s.74, see *R. v Smith (David Cadman)* [2001] UKHL 68, [2002] 1 W.L.R. 54 (HL), Lord Rodger of Earlsferry

s.74, repealed: 2002 c.29 Sch.12

s.77, see *G (Restraint Order), Re* [2001] EWHC Admin 606, [2002] S.T.C. 391 (QBD (Admin Ct)), Stanley Burnton, J.; see *Inland Revenue Commissioners v Piacentini* [2003] EWHC 113, [2003] Q.B. 1497 (QBD (Admin Ct)), Lightman, J.; see *X (Restraint Order: Variation), Re* [2004] EWHC 861, [2004] 3 W.L.R. 906 (QBD (Admin Ct)), Davis, J.

s.77, amended: 2002 c.9 Sch.11 para.22

s.77, repealed (in part): 2002 c.9 Sch.13

s.78, applied: 2002 c.29 s.41, s.49, s.51, s.53, s.79, s.125, s.128, s.145, s.190, s.197, s.199, s.201, s.227

s.79, amended: 2002 c.9 Sch.11 para.22

s.81, see *Inland Revenue Commissioners v Piacentini* [2003] EWHC 113, [2003] Q.B. 1497 (QBD (Admin Ct)), Lightman, J.

s.82, see *Inland Revenue Commissioners v Piacentini* [2003] EWHC 113, [2003] Q.B. 1497 (QBD (Admin Ct)), Lightman, J.; see *X (Restraint Order: Variation), Re* [2004] EWHC 861, [2004] 3 W.L.R. 906 (QBD (Admin Ct)), Davis, J.

s.90, repealed: 2002 c.29 Sch.12

s.91, repealed: 2002 c.29 Sch.12

s.92, repealed: 2002 c.29 Sch.12

s.93, repealed: 2002 c.29 Sch.12

1988–cont.

33. Criminal Justice Act 1988–*cont.*

s.93A, see *Amalgamated Metal Trading Ltd v City of London Police Financial Investigation Unit* [2003] EWHC 703, [2003] 1 W.L.R. 2711 (QBD (Comm Ct)), Tomlinson, J.; see *R. v Alagbala (Michael)* [2004] EWCA Crim 89, [2004] 2 Cr. App. R. (S.) 48 (CA (Crim Div)), Latham, L.J.

s.93A, repealed: 2002 c.29 Sch.12

s.93B, repealed: 2002 c.29 Sch.12

s.93C, see *R. v Hagan (Geoff)* [2003] EWCA Crim 1878, [2004] 1 Cr. App. R. (S.) 31 (CA (Crim Div)), Richards, J.; see *R. v Hussain (Akhtar)* [2002] EWCA Crim 6, [2002] 2 Cr. App. R. 26 (CA (Crim Div)), May, L.J.; see *R. v Montila (Steven William)* [2003] EWCA Crim 3082, [2004] 1 W.L.R. 624 (CA (Crim Div)), Scott Baker, L.J.; see *R. v Montila (Steven William)* [2004] UKHL 50, [2004] 1 W.L.R. 3141 (HL), Lord Bingham of Cornhill

s.93C, repealed: 2002 c.29 Sch.12

s.93D, applied: SI 2003/120 Art.5

s.93D, referred to: SI 2003/120 Art.5

s.93D, repealed: 2002 c.29 Sch.12

s.93E, repealed: 2002 c.29 Sch.12

s.93F, applied: SI 2003/120 Art.6

s.93F, repealed: 2002 c.29 Sch.12

s.93G, applied: SI 2003/120 Art.6

s.93G, repealed: 2002 c.29 Sch.12

s.93H, applied: SI 2003/120 Art.6

s.93H, repealed: 2002 c.29 Sch.12

s.93I, applied: SI 2003/120 Art.6

s.93I, repealed: 2002 c.29 Sch.12

s.93J, applied: SI 2003/120 Art.6

s.93J, repealed: 2002 c.29 Sch.12

s.94, repealed: 2002 c.29 Sch.12

s.95, repealed: 2002 c.29 Sch.12

s.96, repealed: 2002 c.29 Sch.12

s.96, enabling: SI 2002/256, SI 2002/2844, SI 2004/1981

s.97, see *United States v Montgomery (No.2)* [2003] EWCA Civ 392, [2003] 1 W.L.R. 1916 (CA), Lord Woolf of Barnes, L.C.J.; see *United States v Montgomery (No.2)* [2004] UKHL 37, [2004] 1 W.L.R. 2241 (HL), Lord Steyn

s.97, repealed: 2002 c.29 Sch.12

s.98, repealed: 2002 c.29 Sch.12

s.99, repealed: 2002 c.29 Sch.12

s.100, repealed: 2002 c.29 Sch.12

s.101, repealed: 2002 c.29 Sch.12

s.102, repealed: 2002 c.29 Sch.12

s.119, repealed: 2003 c.44 Sch.37 Part 10

s.133, see *McFarland's Application for Judicial Review, Re* [2004] UKHL 17, [2004] 1 W.L.R. 1289 (HL (NI)), Lord Bingham of Cornhill; see *R. (on the application of Christofides) v Secretary of State for the Home Department* [2002] EWHC 1083, [2002] 1 W.L.R. 2769 (QBD (Admin Ct)),

1988–cont.

33. Criminal Justice Act 1988–*cont.*

s.133–*cont.*

Sedley, L.J.; see *R. (on the application of Mullen) v Secretary of State for the Home Department* [2002] EWCA Civ 1882, [2003] Q.B. 993 (CA), Schiemann, L.J.; see *R. (on the application of Mullen) v Secretary of State for the Home Department* [2002] EWHC 230, [2002] 1 W.L.R. 1857 (QBD (Admin Ct)), Simon Brown, L.J.; see *R. (on the application of Mullen) v Secretary of State for the Home Department* [2004] UKHL 18, [2004] 2 W.L.R. 1140 (HL), Lord Bingham of Cornhill

s.133, applied: SI 2003/409 Sch.1 Part I

s.134, applied: 2003 c.42 Sch.5 para.48, Sch.5 para.91, Sch.5 para.157, 2003 c.44 Sch.15 para.47, Sch.17 para.45, SI 2004/1910 Sch.1

s.135, amended: 2002 c.26 Sch.7 para.31

s.139, see *R. (on the application of Bayliss) v DPP* [2003] EWHC 245, [2003] A.C.D. 56 (QBD (Admin Ct)), Pitchford, J.; see *R. v Bown (Mark)* [2003] EWCA Crim 1989, [2004] 1 Cr. App. R. 13 (CA (Crim Div)), Keene, L.J.; see *R. v Jolie (Leroy)* [2003] EWCA Crim 1543, [2004] 1 Cr. App. R. 3 (CA (Crim Div)), Kennedy, L.J.; see *R. v Matthews (Mark Anthony)* [2003] EWCA Crim 813, [2004] Q.B. 690 (CA (Crim Div)), Field, J.; see *R. v Poulton (Sarah Jane)* [2002] EWCA Crim 2487, [2003] 4 All E.R. 869 (CA (Crim Div)), Rose, L.J.; see *R. v Roberts (Leroy Lloyd)* [2003] EWCA Crim 2753, [2004] 1 W.L.R. 181 (CA (Crim Div)), Mantell, L.J.; see *R. v Wang (Cheong)* [2003] EWCA Crim 3228, (2004) 168 J.P. 224 (CA (Crim Div)), Laws, L.J.; see *SL (A Juvenile) v DPP* [2001] EWHC Admin 882, [2003] Q.B. 137 (QBD (Admin Ct)), Pill, L.J.

s.141, amended: SI 2004/702 Sch.7 para.11

s.141, applied: SSI 2002/323

s.141, enabling: SI 2002/1668, SI 2004/1271, SSI 2002/323

s.144, repealed: 2003 c.44 Sch.37 Part 4

s.151, amended: 2002 c.29 Sch.11 para.17, Sch.12

s.152, amended: 2002 c.29 Sch.11 para.17

s.159, amended: SI 2004/2035 Sch.1 para.27

s.160, see *R. v Thompson (Richard)* [2004] EWCA Crim 669, [2004] 2 Cr. App. R. 16 (CA (Crim Div)), Thomas, L.J.

s.160, amended: 2003 c.42 Sch.6 para.29

s.160, applied: SI 2002/896 Sch.1 para.44, 2003 c.42 Sch.2 para.1, Sch.3 para.15, 2003 c.44 Sch.15 para.101, SI 2003/1184 Sch.2 para.14A, SSI 2003/19 Sch.5 para.6

s.160A, added: 2003 c.42 s.45

s.160A, amended: 2004 c.33 Sch.27 para.127

s.171, enabling: SI 2004/2167

CAP.

1988–cont.

33. Criminal Justice Act 1988–*cont.*

s.172, amended: 2002 c.29 Sch.12

Sch.2 para.1, repealed: 2003 c.44 s.136, Sch.37 Part 6

Sch.2 para.2, repealed: 2003 c.44 s.136, Sch.37 Part 6

Sch.2 para.3, repealed: 2003 c.44 s.136, Sch.37 Part 6

Sch.2 para.4, amended: SI 2004/2035 Sch.1 para.28

Sch.2 para.4, repealed: 2003 c.44 s.136, Sch.37 Part 6

Sch.2 para.5, repealed: 2003 c.44 s.136, Sch.37 Part 6

Sch.2 para.6, repealed: 2003 c.44 s.136, Sch.37 Part 6

Sch.3 para.1, applied: 2002 c.29 s.15, s.165

Sch.3 para.12, amended: 2002 c.26 Sch.12 para.41

Sch.4 Part I, repealed: 2002 c.29 Sch.12

Sch.4 Part II para.1, repealed: 2002 c.29 Sch.12

Sch.4 Part II para.2, repealed: 2002 c.29 Sch.12

Sch.4 Part II para.6, repealed (in part): 2002 c.29 Sch.12, 2003 c.44 Sch.37 Part 6

Sch.8 Part I para.8, repealed: 2003 c.44 Sch.37 Part 10

Sch.13 para.2, repealed: 2003 c.44 s.136, Sch.37 Part 6

Sch.13 para.3, repealed: 2003 c.44 s.136, Sch.37 Part 6

Sch.13 para.4, repealed: 2003 c.44 s.136, Sch.37 Part 6

Sch.13 para.5, repealed: 2003 c.44 s.136, Sch.37 Part 6

Sch.13 para.6, amended: 2003 c.32 Sch.5 para.16

Sch.13 para.6, applied: 2003 c.44 s.117, SI 2004/1501 Art.21

Sch.15 para.6, repealed: 2002 c.9 Sch.13

Sch.15 para.7, repealed: 2002 c.9 Sch.13

Sch.15 para.10, repealed: 2003 c.44 Sch.37 Part 4

Sch.15 para.32, repealed: 2003 c.44 Sch.37 Part 6

Sch.15 para.66, repealed: 2003 c.44 Sch.37 Part 4

Sch.15 para.104, repealed: 2003 c.44 Sch.37 Part 4

34. Legal Aid Act 1988

see *R. v Conroy (Costs)* [2004] 1 Costs L.R. 182 (Crown Ct (Bristol)), Judge Crowther Q.C.

applied: SI 2003/1887 Sch.1

Part II, applied: SI 2004/3114 Art.3

Part III, applied: SI 2004/3114 Art.3

Part IV, applied: SI 2004/3114 Art.3, SI 2004/3121 Art.4

CAP.

1988–cont.

34. Legal Aid Act 1988–*cont.*

s.4, see *R. (on the application of Machi) v Legal Services Commission* [2001] EWCA Civ 2010, [2002] 1 W.L.R. 983 (CA), Sedley, L.J.; see *R. (on the application of Machi) v Legal Services Commission* [2001] EWHC Admin 580, [2002] A.C.D. 8 (QBD (Admin Ct)), Ouseley, J.

s.16, see *Cavaliere v Legal Services Commission* [2003] EWHC 323, [2003] 3 Costs L.R. 350 (QBD), Leveson, J.; see *Patel v Legal Services Commission* [2004] EWHC 743, (2004) 148 S.J.L.B. 474 (Ch D), R Sheldon Q.C.

s.16, enabling: SI 2002/3033

s.17, see *Hill v Bailey* [2003] EWHC 2835, [2004] 1 All E.R. 1210 (Ch D), Lightman, J.

s.31, see *Brawley v Marczynski (No.2)* [2002] EWCA Civ 1453, [2003] 1 W.L.R. 813 (CA), Longmore, L.J.

s.34, see *R. (on the application of Machi) v Legal Services Commission* [2001] EWHC Admin 580, [2002] A.C.D. 8 (QBD (Admin Ct)), Ouseley, J.

s.34, referred to: SI 2002/710, SI 2002/3033, SI 2003/1312

s.34, enabling: SI 2002/710, SI 2002/711, SI 2002/3033, SI 2003/1312

s.43, enabling: SI 2002/710, SI 2002/711, SI 2002/3033, SI 2003/1312

Sch.5 para.11, repealed: 2003 c.21 Sch.19

35. British Steel Act 1988

s.1, repealed (in part): 2004 c.14 Sch.1 Part 16

s.2, repealed: 2004 c.14 Sch.1 Part 16

s.3, repealed (in part): 2004 c.14 Sch.1 Part 16

s.12, repealed: 2004 c.14 Sch.1 Part 16

Sch.1 para.4, repealed: 2004 c.14 Sch.1 Part 16

36. Court of Session Act 1988

applied: SSI 2004/115 Sch.3

s.1, enabling: SSI 2004/499

s.5, amended: 2004 asp 3 s.14

s.5, applied: 2002 c.29 s.155, s.396

s.5, enabling: SSI 2002/301, SSI 2002/513, SSI 2002/514, SSI 2002/560, SSI 2002/566, SSI 2002/570, SSI 2003/194, SSI 2003/222, SSI 2003/223, SSI 2003/247, SSI 2003/385, SSI 2003/536, SSI 2003/537, SSI 2004/52, SSI 2004/150, SSI 2004/151, SSI 2004/291, SSI 2004/331, SSI 2004/514, SSI 2004/515

s.9, see *Heasman v JM Taylor & Partners* 2002 S.C. 326 (Ex Div), Lord Coulsfield, Lord Hamilton, Lord Johnston; see *Murray v Lanarkshire Acute Hospitals NHS Trust* 2003 Rep. L.R. 32 (OH), Lord Wheatley

s.11, see *Heasman v JM Taylor & Partners* 2002 S.C. 326 (Ex Div), Lord Coulsfield, Lord Hamilton, Lord Johnston; see *Murray v Lanarkshire Acute Hospitals NHS Trust* 2003 Rep. L.R. 32 (OH), Lord Wheatley

s.12, applied: 2003 asp 7 s.78

1988–cont.

36. Court of Session Act 1988–*cont.*

s.29, see *Tait v Campbell* 2003 Rep. L.R. 35 (Ex Div), Lord Marnoch, Lord Bonomy, Lord Johnston

s.32, see *MacDonald v MacDonald* 2002 S.L.T. (Sh Ct) 144 (Sh Pr), RA Dunlop Q.C., Sheriff Principal

s.33, amended: 2003 asp 11 s.87

s.45, see *Davidson v Scottish Ministers (No.1)* 2002 S.C. 205 (Ex Div), Lord Marnoch, Lord Hardie, Lord Weir

s.45, applied: 2003 asp 13 s.272, 2003 c.21 s.36, s.59, s.95, s.111, s.129, s.331, Sch.9 para.7, 2004 c.20 s.20, s.49, Sch.5 para.4, 2004 c.35 s.71, SI 2004/2326 Reg.73, Reg.76

s.47, see *Britel Fund Trustees Ltd v Scottish and Southern Energy Plc* 2002 S.L.T. 223 (OH), Lord Macfadyen; see *Scottish Power Generation Ltd v British Energy Generation (UK) Ltd* 2002 S.C. 517 (Ex Div), Lord Reed, Lord Cameron of Lochbroom, Lord Emslie; see *Va Tech Wabag UK Ltd v Morgan Est (Scotland) Ltd* 2002 S.L.T. 1290 (OH), Lord Drummond Young

39. Finance Act 1988

s.12, repealed (in part): 2004 c.14 Sch.1 Part 9

s.38, amended: 2004 c.12 Sch.17 para.10

s.46, repealed: 2003 c.1 Sch.8 Part 1

s.47, repealed (in part): 2003 c.1 Sch.8 Part 1

s.48, repealed (in part): 2003 c.1 Sch.8 Part 1

s.49, repealed (in part): 2003 c.1 Sch.8 Part 1

s.54, repealed: 2004 c.12 Sch.42 Part 3

s.55, repealed: 2004 c.12 Sch.42 Part 3

s.56, repealed: 2004 c.12 Sch.42 Part 3

s.57, repealed: 2003 c.1 Sch.8 Part 1

s.68, repealed: 2003 c.1 Sch.8 Part 1

s.69, repealed: 2003 c.1 Sch.8 Part 1

s.73, amended: 2003 c.1 Sch.6 para.155, SI 2004/2310 Sch.1 para.41

s.73, repealed (in part): 2003 c.1 Sch.8 Part 1

s.77, repealed: 2003 c.1 Sch.8 Part 1

s.78, repealed: 2003 c.1 Sch.8 Part 1

s.79, referred to: 2002 c.29 Sch.10 para.33

s.79, repealed: 2003 c.1 Sch.8 Part 1

s.80, repealed: 2003 c.1 Sch.8 Part 1

s.81, repealed: 2003 c.1 Sch.8 Part 1

s.82, repealed: 2003 c.1 Sch.8 Part 1

s.83, repealed: 2003 c.1 Sch.8 Part 1

s.84, repealed: 2003 c.1 Sch.8 Part 1

s.85, applied: 2003 c.1 Sch.7 para.60, Sch.7 para.61

s.85, repealed: 2003 c.1 Sch.8 Part 1

s.86, amended: 2002 c.23 Sch.40 Part 3

s.86, repealed: 2003 c.1 Sch.8 Part 1

s.87, repealed: 2003 c.1 Sch.8 Part 1

s.88, repealed: 2003 c.1 Sch.8 Part 1

s.89, amended: 2003 c.1 Sch.8 Part 1

s.89, repealed (in part): 2003 c.1 Sch.8 Part 1

s.128, repealed: 2003 c.1 Sch.8 Part 1

1988–cont.

39. Finance Act 1988–*cont.*

s.130, amended: 2004 c.12 Sch.12 para.12

s.130, varied: 2003 c.v s.7

s.131, varied: 2003 c.v s.7

s.132, varied: 2003 c.v s.7

Sch.3 Part I para.4, repealed: 2003 c.1 Sch.8 Part 1

Sch.3 Part I para.18, repealed: 2004 c.12 Sch.42 Part 3

Sch.6 para.3, amended: 2002 c.23 Sch.40 Part 3

Sch.6 para.3, repealed (in part): 2002 c.23 Sch.40 Part 3

Sch.10, see *Unmarried Settlor v Inland Revenue Commissioners* [2003] S.T.C (S.C.D.) 274 (Sp Comm), John F Avery Jones

Sch.12 para.1, amended: 2002 c.23 s.105

Sch.12 para.2, repealed: 2002 c.23 Sch.40 Part 3

Sch.13 Part I para.3, repealed: 2003 c.1 Sch.8 Part 1

Sch.13 Part I para.6, repealed: 2004 c.12 Sch.42 Part 3

40. Education Reform Act 1988

applied: 2002 c.40 Sch.15

s.70, applied: SR 2002/265 Reg.7

s.120, applied: SI 2002/1330 Reg.4, SI 2003/1994 Reg.4

s.120, disapplied: 2004 c.31 s.18

s.121, repealed (in part): 2004 c.14 Sch.1 Part 7

s.122A, enabling: SI 2002/1136

s.124, amended: 2002 c.32 Sch.21 para.8

s.124B, amended: 2004 c.23 Sch.2 para.9

s.136, repealed: 2004 c.14 Sch.1 Part 5

s.137, repealed: 2004 c.14 Sch.1 Part 7

s.138, repealed (in part): 2004 c.14 Sch.1 Part 7

s.160, repealed (in part): 2002 c.32 Sch.22 Part 3

s.162, repealed: 2004 c.14 Sch.1 Part 5

s.164, repealed: 2004 c.14 Sch.1 Part 5

s.165, repealed: 2004 c.14 Sch.1 Part 5

s.169, repealed: 2004 c.14 Sch.1 Part 5

s.171, repealed: 2004 c.14 Sch.1 Part 5

s.175, repealed: 2004 c.14 Sch.1 Part 5

s.176, repealed: 2004 c.14 Sch.1 Part 5

s.177, repealed: 2004 c.14 Sch.1 Part 5

s.178, repealed: 2004 c.14 Sch.1 Part 5

s.182, repealed: 2004 c.14 Sch.1 Part 5

s.183, repealed: 2004 c.14 Sch.1 Part 5

s.184, repealed: 2004 c.14 Sch.1 Part 5

s.186, repealed: 2004 c.14 Sch.1 Part 5

s.187, enabling: SI 2002/2003, SI 2002/2760

s.188, repealed: 2004 c.14 Sch.1 Part 5

s.189, repealed: 2004 c.14 Sch.1 Part 5

s.190, amended: 2004 c.5 Sch.7 para.14

s.190, repealed: 2004 c.14 Sch.1 Part 5

1988–cont.

40. Education Reform Act 1988–cont.
s.191, repealed: 2004 c.14 Sch.1 Part 5
s.193, repealed: 2004 c.14 Sch.1 Part 5
s.194, repealed: 2004 c.14 Sch.1 Part 5
s.198, applied: SI 2003/1965 Reg.12, Reg.35, Reg.40, SI 2004/2042 Reg.12
s.198, varied: SI 2004/2042 Reg.40, Reg.45
s.201, amended: 2004 c.5 Sch.7 para.14
s.201, repealed: 2004 c.14 Sch.1 Part 7
s.206, repealed (in part): 2004 c.8 s.46, Sch.7
s.207, repealed (in part): 2004 c.8 Sch.7
s.210, repealed (in part): 2002 c.32 s.18, Sch.22 Part 3
s.211, repealed (in part): 2002 c.32 s.18, Sch.22 Part 3
s.216, applied: SI 2002/1377 Art.2, SI 2002/1667 Art.2, SI 2004/2753 Art.2, SSI 2002/406 Art.2
s.216, enabling: SI 2002/1377, SI 2002/1661, SI 2002/1667, SI 2003/1865, SI 2003/3124, SI 2004/2753, SI 2004/3095, SSI 2002/406, SSI 2004/539
s.218, applied: SI 2002/195 Reg.10, SI 2002/233 Reg.7, SI 2002/324 Reg.7, Reg.9, SI 2002/325 Reg.9, Reg.11, SI 2002/326 Reg.3, Reg.4, SI 2002/327 Reg.6, Reg.8, SI 2002/438 Sch.1 para.10, SI 2002/812 Reg.4B, Reg.4, SI 2002/896 Sch.1 para.2, SI 2002/919 Sch.2 para.9A, Sch.3 para.13A, Sch.8 para.9, Sch.8 para.9A, SI 2002/1330 Reg.12, SI 2002/1434, SI 2002/2978 Sch.1 para.6, SI 2002/3177 Sch.1 para.6, SI 2002/3200 Reg.10, SI 2003/107, SI 2003/543 Sch.1 para.5, SI 2003/781 Reg.5, Reg.7, SI 2003/1662 Sch.2 para.3, SI 2003/2458, SI 2004/2695 Sch.1 para.33, SR 2002/224 Reg.10, SR 2002/265 Reg.7
s.218, referred to: SI 2002/896 Sch.1 para.2, SI 2004/2695 Sch.1 para.33
s.218, repealed (in part): 2002 c.32 Sch.22 Part 3
s.218, enabling: SI 2002/1434, SI 2002/1663, SI 2002/2938, SI 2003/107, SI 2003/140, SI 2003/2458, SI 2004/571
s.218A, repealed (in part): 2002 c.32 Sch.22 Part 3
s.230, amended: 2004 c.14 Sch.1 Part 5, Sch.1 Part 7
s.231, enabling: SI 2002/2003, SI 2002/2760
s.232, enabling: SI 2002/1434, SI 2002/1663, SI 2002/2003, SI 2002/2760, SI 2002/2938, SI 2003/107, SI 2003/140, SI 2003/2458, SI 2004/571, SI 2004/2753
s.236, repealed (in part): 2004 c.14 Sch.1 Part 7

Sch.3 para.8, see R. (on the application of McNally) v Secretary of State for Education and Employment [2001] EWCA

1988–cont.

40. Education Reform Act 1988–cont.
Sch.3 para.8–cont.
Civ 332, [2002] I.C.R. 15 (CA), Kennedy, L.J.
Sch.10, referred to: 2002 c.32 s.24, SI 2003/1965 Reg.12, Reg.35, Reg.40
Sch.10 para.1, varied: SI 2004/2042 Reg.40, Reg.45
Sch.10 para.2, varied: SI 2004/2042 Reg.40, Reg.45
Sch.10 para.3, varied: SI 2004/2042 Reg.40, Reg.45
Sch.10 para.4, varied: SI 2004/2042 Reg.40, Reg.45
Sch.10 para.5, varied: SI 2004/2042 Reg.40, Reg.45
Sch.10 para.6, varied: SI 2004/2042 Reg.40, Reg.45
Sch.10 para.7, varied: SI 2004/2042 Reg.40, Reg.45
Sch.10 para.8, varied: SI 2004/2042 Reg.40, Reg.45
Sch.10 para.9, varied: SI 2004/2042 Reg.40, Reg.45
Sch.10 para.10, varied: SI 2004/2042 Reg.40, Reg.45
Sch.12 Part II para.52, repealed: 2004 c.14 Sch.1 Part 7
Sch.12 Part III para.65, repealed: 2004 c.14 Sch.1 Part 7
Sch.12 Part III para.86, repealed: 2004 c.14 Sch.1 Part 2
Sch.12 Part III para.90, repealed: 2004 c.14 Sch.1 Part 7

41. Local Government Finance Act 1988
see R. (on the application of Corus UK Ltd) v Valuation Office Agency [2001] EWHC Admin 1108, [2002] R.A. 1 (QBD (Admin Ct)), Sullivan, J.; see R. (on the application of HTV Ltd) v Bristol City Council [2004] EWHC 1219, [2004] 1 W.L.R. 2717 (QBD (Admin Ct)), Elias, J.
referred to: SI 2002/808 Art.2
Part III, applied: 2003 c.26 s.59
s.41, see National Car Parks Ltd v Baird (Valuation Officer) [2004] EWCA Civ 967, [2004] R.A. 245 (CA), Sir Andrew Morritt V.C.
s.41, amended: 2003 c.26 s.60
s.42, applied: SI 2004/2443 Sch.2 para.4
s.42A, amended: 2003 c.26 s.63
s.43, see Rees v Boston BC [2001] EWCA Civ 1934, [2002] 1 W.L.R. 1304 (CA), Jonathan Parker, L.J.
s.43, amended: 2003 c.26 s.61, s.63, s.64
s.43, applied: SI 2002/331 Art.3, Art.4, SI 2003/2613 Sch.2 para.5
s.43, referred to: SI 2003/2613 Sch.2 para.5
s.43, enabling: SI 2002/331, SI 2004/3152, SI 2004/3153, SI 2004/3315
s.44, amended: 2003 c.26 s.61

1988–cont.

41. Local Government Finance Act 1988– *cont.*

s.44, applied: SI 2003/2613 Sch.2 para.5

s.44, referred to: SI 2003/2613 Sch.2 para.5

s.44, enabling: SI 2004/3315

s.44A, applied: SI 2003/2613 Sch.2 para.5

s.45, amended: 2003 c.26 s.64

s.45, applied: SI 2003/2613 Sch.2 para.5

s.45, referred to: SI 2003/2613 Sch.2 para.4, Sch.2 para.5

s.45, enabling: SI 2004/3146

s.47, amended: 2003 c.26 s.61, s.63, s.64, Sch.7 para.10

s.47, applied: SI 2002/331 Art.3, SI 2003/2613 Sch.2 para.5

s.47, enabling: SI 2002/331, SI 2004/3153

s.48, amended: 2003 c.26 s.64

s.49, amended: 2003 c.26 Sch.7 para.11

s.50, applied: 2003 c.26 s.48

s.52, amended: 2003 c.26 s.60

s.53, repealed (in part): 2003 c.26 Sch.8 Part 1

s.53, enabling: SI 2003/3225

s.55, see *National Car Parks Ltd v Baird (Valuation Officer)* [2004] EWCA Civ 967, [2004] R.A. 245 (CA), Sir Andrew Morritt V.C.

s.55, enabling: SI 2002/498, SI 2002/1735, SI 2003/1999, SI 2004/3057

s.57A, added: 2003 c.26 s.65

s.57A, enabling: SI 2004/3387

s.58, amended: 2003 c.26 s.65

s.58, applied: SI 2003/2613 Sch.2 para.5

s.58, enabling: SI 2004/1297

s.62, enabling: SI 2003/1714

s.63, applied: 2003 c.26 s.48

s.64, amended: 2003 c.26 s.66

s.65, varied: SI 2002/2779 Art.90, SI 2003/284 Art.146, SI 2004/293 Reg.125, SI 2004/870 Reg.20, SI 2004/1962 Art.13

s.66, see *R. (on the application of Curzon Berkeley Ltd) v Bliss (Valuation Officer)* [2001] EWHC Admin 1130, [2002] R.A. 45 (QBD (Admin Ct)), James Goudie Q.C.; see *Tully v Jorgensen (Valuation Officer)* [2003] R.A. 233 (Lands Tr), George Bartlett Q.C. (President)

s.66, applied: SI 2002/1792 Sch.2 para.6, SI 2004/400 Sch.3

s.67, amended: 2003 c.26 s.64

s.74, amended: 2003 c.10 Sch.1 para.3, 2003 c.39 Sch.8 para.305, 2004 c.21 Sch.1 para.68

s.74, applied: 2003 c.26 s.23, SI 2003/3146 Reg.32

s.74, enabling: SI 2003/3072

s.75, applied: 2003 c.26 s.23

s.76, substituted: 2003 c.26 Sch.7 para.12

s.76, enabling: SI 2003/5, SI 2003/706

s.77A, added: 2003 c.26 Sch.7 para.14

1988–cont.

41. Local Government Finance Act 1988– *cont.*

s.78, applied: 2002 c.18 Sch.2 Part 9, 2003 c.13 Sch.2 Part 2, Sch.2 Part 11

s.78, substituted: 2003 c.26 Sch.7 para.13

s.78, amended: 2003 c.26 Sch.7 para.15

s.78, applied: 2004 c.9 Sch.2 Part 2, Sch.2 Part 10

s.78A, applied: SI 2002/535 Sch.1

s.78A, substituted: 2003 c.26 Sch.7 para.13

s.78A, amended: 2003 c.26 Sch.7 para.15

s.79, substituted: 2003 c.26 Sch.7 para.13

s.80, substituted: 2003 c.26 Sch.7 para.13

s.81, substituted: 2003 c.26 Sch.7 para.13

s.82, substituted: 2003 c.26 Sch.7 para.13

s.83, substituted: 2003 c.26 Sch.7 para.13

s.84, substituted: 2003 c.26 Sch.7 para.13

s.84A, substituted: 2003 c.26 Sch.7 para.13

s.84B, substituted: 2003 c.26 Sch.7 para.13

s.84C, substituted: 2003 c.26 Sch.7 para.13

s.84D, added: 2003 c.26 Sch.2 para.1

s.84E, added: 2003 c.26 Sch.2 para.1

s.84F, added: 2003 c.26 Sch.2 para.1

s.84G, added: 2003 c.26 Sch.2 para.1

s.84H, added: 2003 c.26 Sch.2 para.1

s.84J, added: 2003 c.26 Sch.2 para.1

s.84K, added: 2003 c.26 Sch.2 para.1

s.84L, added: 2003 c.26 Sch.2 para.1

s.84M, added: 2003 c.26 Sch.2 para.1

s.84N, added: 2003 c.26 Sch.2 para.1

s.84P, added: 2003 c.26 Sch.2 para.1

s.85, substituted: 2003 c.26 Sch.7 para.16

s.85, amended: 2003 c.26 Sch.7 para.17

s.86, substituted: 2003 c.26 Sch.7 para.16

s.87, substituted: 2003 c.26 Sch.7 para.16

s.88, substituted: 2003 c.26 Sch.7 para.16

s.88A, substituted: 2003 c.26 Sch.7 para.16

s.88A, applied: SI 2004/2506 Sch.1 para.36

s.88B, applied: 2002 c.18 Sch.2 Part 2, Sch.2 Part 9, SI 2002/377 Sch.1 para.1, SI 2002/535 Sch.1, SI 2002/3199 Reg.1, Sch.2 para.3, 2003 c.13 Sch.2 Part 2, Sch.2 Part 11

s.88B, substituted: 2003 c.26 Sch.7 para.16

s.88B, applied: 2004 c.9 Sch.2 Part 2, Sch.2 Part 10

s.89, amended: 2003 c.10 Sch.1 para.3

s.90, amended: 2003 c.26 Sch.7 para.19

s.91, amended: 2003 c.10 Sch.1 para.3

s.97, amended: 2003 c.26 s.70

s.99, amended: 2003 c.26 s.70

s.111, amended: SI 2002/808 Art.18, 2004 c.21 Sch.1 para.68

s.112, amended: 2004 c.21 Sch.1 para.68

s.112, applied: 2003 c.26 s.25

s.114, amended: SI 2002/808 Art.19

s.114, applied: 2004 c.23 s.25

s.114, referred to: 2003 c.26 s.30

s.114A, applied: 2004 c.23 s.25

s.115, amended: 2003 c.26 s.30

1988–cont.

41. Local Government Finance Act 1988– *cont.*

s.115, applied: 2004 c.23 s.25

s.115A, applied: 2004 c.23 s.25

s.115B, added: SI 2002/808 Art.20

s.115B, applied: 2004 c.23 s.25

s.116, amended: SI 2002/808 Art.20

s.116, applied: 2004 c.23 s.25

s.117, amended: 2003 c.39 Sch.8 para.305, 2004 c.21 Sch.1 para.68

s.118, applied: 2003 c.26 s.23

s.126, repealed: 2004 c.14 Sch.1 Part 10

s.138, amended: 2003 c.26 Sch.7 para.20

s.139, amended: 2003 c.26 Sch.7 para.21

s.140, amended: 2003 c.26 Sch.7 para.22, Sch.8 Part 1

s.140, repealed (in part): 2003 c.26 Sch.7 para.22, Sch.8 Part 1

s.140, enabling: SI 2002/3054, SI 2003/706, SI 2003/944, SI 2003/3211, SI 2003/3225, SI 2004/3232, SI 2004/3387

s.141, amended: 2003 c.26 s.90, Sch.7 para.23

s.143, amended: 2003 c.26 Sch.7 para.24

s.143, repealed (in part): 2003 c.26 Sch.8 Part 1

s.143, enabling: SI 2002/180, SI 2002/498, SI 2002/1735, SI 2002/3021, SI 2002/3054, SI 2003/329, SI 2003/944, SI 2003/1714, SI 2003/1999, SI 2003/2000, SI 2003/2210, SI 2003/2613, SI 2003/3072, SI 2003/3081, SI 2003/3130, SI 2003/3211, SI 2003/3225, SI 2004/1000, SI 2004/1013, SI 2004/1297, SI 2004/1312, SI 2004/1494, SI 2004/3057, SI 2004/3151, SI 2004/3152, SI 2004/3232, SI 2004/3234, SI 2004/3315, SI 2004/3387, SI 2004/3389

s.144, amended: 2004 c.21 Sch.1 para.68

s.146, enabling: SI 2003/1714, SI 2003/2613, SI 2003/3081

Sch.4A, applied: 2003 c.26 Sch.7 para.43

Sch.4 Part II para.6, varied: 2002 c.16 Sch.2 para.29

Sch.5, see *Cartwright v Cherry Valley Farms Ltd* [2003] R.A. 21 (Lands Tr), George Bartlett Q.C. (President)

Sch.5 para.1, see *Withers v Dalling (Valuation Officer)* [2004] R.A. 182 (Lands Tr), NJ Rose, FRICS

Sch.5 para.3, amended: 2003 c.26 s.67

Sch.5 para.7, amended: 2003 c.26 s.67

Sch.5 para.11, amended: 2003 c.26 s.68

Sch.6, see *Holmes v Wills (Valuation Officer)* [2003] R.V.R. 9 (Valuation Tribunal), Judge not specified; see *O'Brien v Harwood (Valuation Officer) (Preliminary Issues)* [2003] R.V.R. 116 (Lands Tr), PH Clarke, FRICS

1988–cont.

41. Local Government Finance Act 1988– *cont.*

Sch.6 para.2, see *Archer Ltd v Robinson (Valuation Officer) (Application for Permission to Appeal)* [2003 EWCA Civ 642, [2003] R.V.R. 447 (CA (Court of Appeal)), Pill, L.J.; see *Orange PCS Ltd v Bradford (Valuation Officer)* [2004] EWCA Civ 155, [2004] 2 All E.R. 651 (CA), Auld, L.J.

Sch.6 para.2, applied: SI 2002/3186 Art.2, SI 2003/329 Art.2

Sch.6 para.2, enabling: SI 2002/3186, SI 2003/329, SI 2004/1000, SI 2004/1494

Sch.6 para.2A, enabling: SI 2004/3151

Sch.6 para.3, see *R. (on the application of Edison First Power Ltd) v Secretary of State for the Environment, Transport and the Regions* [2003] UKHL 20, [2003] 4 All E.R. 209 (HL), Lord Hoffmann

Sch.6 para.3, repealed (in part): 2003 c.26 s.69, Sch.8 Part 1

Sch.6 para.3, enabling: SI 2003/944

Sch.7 Part I para.1, amended: 2003 c.26 s.62

Sch.7 Part I para.3, substituted: 2003 c.26 s.62

Sch.7 Part I para.4, applied: SI 2003/2613 Sch.2 para.3

Sch.7 Part I para.4, substituted: 2003 c.26 s.62

Sch.7 Part I para.5, amended: 2003 c.26 s.62, Sch.7 para.25

Sch.7 Part I para.6, amended: 2003 c.26 s.62, Sch.7 para.25

Sch.7 Part II, applied: SI 2003/2613 Sch.2 para.2

Sch.7 Part II para.9, amended: 2003 c.26 Sch.7 para.25

Sch.7 Part II para.9A, added: 2003 c.26 s.62

Sch.7 Part II para.10, amended: 2003 c.26 Sch.7 para.25

Sch.7 Part II para.11, amended: 2003 c.26 Sch.7 para.25

Sch.7A para.10, enabling: SI 2002/498, SI 2002/1735, SI 2003/2000

Sch.7A para.11, enabling: SI 2002/498, SI 2002/1735, SI 2003/2000

Sch.7A para.12, enabling: SI 2002/498, SI 2002/1735, SI 2003/2000

Sch.8 Part I para.2, amended: 2003 c.26 Sch.7 para.26

Sch.8 Part II para.4, amended: 2003 c.26 s.70, s.71, Sch.7 para.26

Sch.8 Part II para.4, enabling: SI 2002/3021, SI 2002/3054, SI 2003/3130, SI 2003/3211, SI 2004/3232, SI 2004/3234

Sch.8 Part II para.5, amended: 2003 c.26 s.70, 2004 c.23 Sch.2 para.8

Sch.8 Part II para.5, enabling: SI 2002/3054

Sch.8 Part II para.6, amended: 2003 c.26 s.71

1988–cont.

41. Local Government Finance Act 1988–cont.

Sch.8 Part II para.6, enabling: SI 2002/3021, SI 2002/3054, SI 2003/3130, SI 2003/3211, SI 2004/3232, SI 2004/3234

Sch.8 Part III, added: 2003 c.26 Sch.2 para.2

Sch.8 Part III para.8, amended: 2003 c.26 Sch.2 para.2

Sch.8 Part III para.9, amended: 2003 c.26 Sch.2 para.2

Sch.8 Part III para.11, amended: 2003 c.26 Sch.2 para.2

Sch.8 Part III para.11A, added: 2003 c.26 Sch.2 para.2

Sch.8 Part III para.11B, added: 2003 c.26 Sch.2 para.2

Sch.8 Part III para.11C, added: 2003 c.26 Sch.2 para.2

Sch.8 Part III para.12, amended: 2003 c.26 Sch.2 para.2

Sch.8 Part III para.14A, added: 2003 c.26 Sch.2 para.2

Sch.8 Part III para.15, amended: 2003 c.26 Sch.2 para.2

Sch.9, applied: 2003 c.26 s.48

Sch.9, referred to: 2003 c.26 s.128

Sch.9 para.1, enabling: SI 2002/180, SI 2003/414, SI 2003/1714, SI 2003/2210, SI 2003/2613, SI 2003/3081, SI 2004/1013, SI 2004/3389

Sch.9 para.2, enabling: SI 2002/180, SI 2003/414, SI 2003/2613, SI 2003/3081, SI 2004/3389

Sch.9 para.3, enabling: SI 2003/1714, SI 2003/2210, SI 2004/1013

Sch.9 para.5, amended: 2003 c.26 Sch.8 Part 1

Sch.9 para.5, repealed (in part): 2003 c.26 Sch.8 Part 1

Sch.9 para.5A, added: 2003 c.26 s.72

Sch.9 para.5B, added: 2003 c.26 s.72

Sch.9 para.5C, added: 2003 c.26 s.72

Sch.9 para.5D, added: 2003 c.26 s.72

Sch.9 para.5E, added: 2003 c.26 s.72

Sch.9 para.5F, added: 2003 c.26 s.72

Sch.9 para.5G, added: 2003 c.26 s.72

Sch.9 para.5H, added: 2003 c.26 s.72

Sch.9 para.6A, enabling: SI 2003/2613

Sch.11 para.1, amended: 2003 c.26 Sch.7 para.27

Sch.11 para.1, enabling: SI 2004/1312

Sch.11 para.2, amended: 2003 c.26 s.72

Sch.11 para.5, enabling: SI 2004/1312

Sch.11 para.6, amended: 2003 c.26 Sch.7 para.27

Sch.11 para.7, amended: 2003 c.26 Sch.7 para.27

43. Housing (Scotland) Act 1988

see *Bain, Petitioner* 2002 S.L.T. 1112 (Court of Session (Inner House, Extra Division)), Lord Cameron of Lochbroom, Lord

1988–cont.

43. Housing (Scotland) Act 1988–cont.

see–cont.

Johnston, Lord Wheatley; see *Wishaw and District Housing Association Ltd v Neary* 2003 Hous. L.R. 63 (Sh Pr), Sheriff Principal JJ Maguire Q.C.

s.1, applied: SSI 2003/532 Sch.1 para.1

s.2, applied: SI 2004/953 Art.2, SSI 2002/444 Reg.4, SSI 2003/140 Sch.1 para.4

s.7, applied: 2003 asp 6 Sch.5, 2004 asp 2 Sch.5

s.7, referred to: 2002 asp 7 Sch.5

s.16, see *Johnstone v Finneran* 2003 S.C.L.R. 157 (Sh Pr), EF Bowen Q.C., Sheriff Principal

s.18, amended: 2003 asp 10 s.12, 2004 asp 8 s.100

s.19A, added: 2003 asp 10 Sch.1 para.3

s.19A, referred to: 2003 asp 10 s.11

s.20, amended: 2003 asp 10 s.12

s.24, applied: SSI 2002/318 Art.5

s.30, applied: SSI 2002/318 Art.5

s.31, amended: 2004 c.33 Sch.28 para.56

s.32, see *Cavriani v Robinson* 2002 Hous. L.R. 67 (Sh Ct (Lothian and Border)), JA Farrell

s.33, see *Cavriani v Robinson* 2002 Hous. L.R. 67 (Sh Ct (Lothian and Border)), JA Farrell

s.36, see *Scott v Thomson* 2003 S.L.T. 99 (Ex Div), Lord Osborne, Lord Hamilton, Lord McCluskey

s.37, see *Scott v Thomson* 2003 S.L.T. 99 (Ex Div), Lord Osborne, Lord Hamilton, Lord McCluskey

s.43, see *Knowes Housing Association Ltd v Millar* 2002 S.C. 58 (Ex Div), Lord Johnston, Lord Cameron of Lochbroom, Lord Prosser; see *McAllister v Queens Cross Housing Association Ltd* 2002 S.L.T. (Lands Tr) 13 (Lands Tr (Scot)), JN Wright Q.C.

s.43, amended: SSI 2003/331 Sch.1 para.6

s.45, see *Knowes Housing Association Ltd v Millar* 2002 S.C. 58 (Ex Div), Lord Johnston, Lord Cameron of Lochbroom, Lord Prosser

s.45, amended: SSI 2003/331 Sch.1 para.6

s.55, amended: SSI 2003/331 Sch.1 para.6

Sch.2 para.4, repealed: 2002 asp 11 Sch.6 para.11

Sch.4 para.6, amended: SSI 2003/583 Sch.1 para.11

Sch.4 para.9, amended: 2003 c.14 Sch.20 para.3

Sch.4 para.11, amended: SSI 2003/331 Sch.1 para.6

Sch.5 Part I, amended: 2004 c.33 Sch.28 para.57

1988–cont.

44. Foreign Marriage (Amendment) Act 1988
s.1, amended: 2002 c.8 s.2

45. Firearms (Amendment) Act 1988
applied: 2003 c.17 Sch.4 para.12
s.1, amended: 2003 c.38 s.39, Sch.3, 2003 c.44 Sch.32 para.49
s.8, applied: SI 2004/702 Art.2
s.16B, added: 2002 c.30 s.81
s.17, applied: SI 2003/2764 Art.11
s.22, enabling: SI 2002/127
s.27, amended: 2003 c.44 Sch.32 para.50

47. School Boards (Scotland) Act 1988
s.11, amended: 2002 asp 2 s.2
s.15, amended: 2002 asp 2 s.2
Sch.2 para.1, amended: 2002 asp 2 s.2
Sch.2 para.1, disapplied: 2002 asp 2 s.2
Sch.2 para.10, amended: 2002 asp 2 s.2
Sch.2 para.19, amended: 2002 asp 2 s.2

48. Copyright, Designs and Patents Act 1988
see *Apple Computer Inc v Design Registry* [2002] E.C.D.R. 19 (Registered Designs Appeal Tribunal), Jacob, J.; see *Item Software (UK) Ltd v Fassihi* [2003] EWHC 3116, [2003] B.C.C. 858 (Ch D), Nicholas Strauss Q.C.; see *Novello & Co Ltd v Keith Prowse Music Publishing Co Ltd* [2004] EWHC 766, [2004] E.M.L.R. 16 (Ch D), Patten, J.; see *R Griggs Group Ltd v Evans (No.2)* [2004] EWHC 1088, [2004] F.S.R. 48 (Ch D), Peter Prescott Q.C.
applied: 2002 c.40 Sch.14, Sch.15
referred to: 2003 c.43 Sch.4 para.71, SI 2003/2500 Sch.1 Part 1
Part I, applied: SI 2003/2498 Reg.30, Reg.37
Part I c.III, applied: SI 2003/2498 Reg.33
Part I c.III, amended: SI 2003/2498 Sch.2
Part I c.VII, amended: SI 2003/2498 Sch.2
Part II, see *Bamgboye v Reed* [2002] EWHC 2922, [2004] E.M.L.R. 5 (QBD), Hazel Williamson Q.C.
Part II, applied: SI 2003/2498 Reg.30, Reg.35
s.1, amended: SI 2003/2498 Reg.5
s.1, varied: SI 2003/1517 Sch.1 Part I
s.2, varied: SI 2003/1517 Sch.1 Part I
s.3, varied: SI 2003/1517 Sch.1 Part I
s.3A, varied: SI 2003/1517 Sch.1 Part I
s.4, see *HiTech Autoparts Ltd v Towergate Two Ltd (No.1)* [2002] F.S.R. 15 (PCC), Christopher Floyd Q.C.
s.4, varied: SI 2003/1517 Sch.1 Part I
s.5, varied: SI 2003/1517 Sch.1 Part I
s.5A, varied: SI 2003/1517 Sch.1 Part I
s.5B, varied: SI 2003/1517 Sch.1 Part I
s.6, amended: SI 2003/2498 Reg.4, Sch.2
s.6, varied: SI 2003/1517 Sch.1 Part I
s.6A, amended: SI 2003/2498 Reg.5

1988–cont.

48. Copyright, Designs and Patents Act 1988–*cont.*
s.6A, varied: SI 2003/1517 Sch.1 Part I, Sch.1 Part II
s.7, repealed: SI 2003/2498 Sch.2
s.7, varied: SI 2003/1517 Sch.1 Part I, Sch.1 Part II
s.8, varied: SI 2003/1517 Sch.1 Part I
s.9, repealed (in part): SI 2003/2498 Sch.2
s.9, varied: SI 2003/1517 Sch.1 Part I
s.10, see *Bamgboye v Reed* [2002] EWHC 2922, [2004] E.M.L.R. 5 (QBD), Hazel Williamson Q.C.; see *Brighton v Jones* [2004] EWHC 1157, [2004] E.M.L.R. 26 (Ch D), Park, J.
s.10, varied: SI 2003/1517 Sch.1 Part I
s.11, see *Bamgboye v Reed* [2002] EWHC 2922, [2004] E.M.L.R. 5 (QBD), Hazel Williamson Q.C.
s.11, varied: SI 2003/1517 Sch.1 Part I
s.11A, varied: SI 2003/1517 Sch.1 Part I
s.12, amended: SI 2003/2498 Sch.1 para.4
s.12, varied: SI 2003/1517 Sch.1 Part I, Sch.1 Part II
s.13, varied: SI 2003/1517 Sch.1 Part I
s.13A, amended: SI 2003/2498 Reg.29
s.13A, applied: SI 2003/2498 Reg.39
s.13A, repealed (in part): SI 2003/2498 Sch.2
s.13A, varied: SI 2003/1517 Sch.1 Part I, Sch.1 Part II
s.13B, amended: SI 2003/2498 Sch.1 para.4
s.13B, varied: SI 2003/1517 Sch.1 Part I, Sch.1 Part II
s.14, amended: SI 2003/2498 Sch.2
s.14, varied: SI 2003/1517 Sch.1 Part I, Sch.1 Part II
s.15, varied: SI 2003/1517 Sch.1 Part I
s.15A, varied: SI 2003/1517 Sch.1 Part I, Sch.1 Part II
s.16, see *Newspaper Licensing Agency Ltd v Marks & Spencer Plc* [2001] UKHL 38, [2003] 1 A.C. 551 (HL), Lord Hoffmann
s.16, amended: SI 2003/2498 Reg.6
s.16, varied: SI 2003/1517 Sch.1 Part I, Sch.1 Part II
s.17, see *Kabushiki Kaisha Sony Computer Entertainment Inc v Ball (Application for Summary Judgment)* [2004] EWHC 1738, [2004] E.C.D.R. 33 (Ch D), Laddie, J.; see *Sony Music Entertainment (UK) Ltd v Easyinternetcafe Ltd* [2003] EWHC 62, [2003] E.C.D.R. 27 (Ch D), Peter Smith, J.
s.17, amended: SI 2003/2498 Reg.5
s.17, varied: SI 2003/1517 Sch.1 Part I
s.18, see *Sony Music Entertainment (UK) Ltd v Easyinternetcafe Ltd* [2003] EWHC 62, [2003] E.C.D.R. 27 (Ch D), Peter Smith, J.; see *Vermaat (t/a Cotton Productions) v Boncrest Ltd (No.2)* [2002] F.S.R. 21 (Ch D), Alan Steinfeld Q.C.

1988–cont.

48. Copyright, Designs and Patents Act 1988–*cont.*

s.18, varied: SI 2003/1517 Sch.1 Part I, Sch.1 Part II

s.18A, amended: SI 2003/2498 Sch.1 para.6

s.18A, varied: SI 2003/1517 Sch.1 Part I

s.19, amended: SI 2003/2498 Sch.1 para.3

s.19, varied: SI 2003/1517 Sch.1 Part I

s.20, substituted: SI 2003/2498 Reg.6

s.20, varied: SI 2003/1517 Sch.1 Part I

s.21, varied: SI 2003/1517 Sch.1 Part I

s.22, varied: SI 2003/1517 Sch.1 Part I, Sch.1 Part II

s.23, see *Vermaat (t/a Cotton Productions) v Boncrest Ltd (No.2)* [2002] F.S.R. 21 (Ch D), Alan Steinfeld Q.C.

s.23, varied: SI 2003/1517 Sch.1 Part I

s.24, amended: SI 2003/2498 Sch.1 para.5

s.24, varied: SI 2003/1517 Sch.1 Part I, Sch.1 Part II

s.25, varied: SI 2003/1517 Sch.1 Part I

s.26, varied: SI 2003/1517 Sch.1 Part I

s.27, amended: 2002 c.33 s.7, SI 2003/2498 Reg.20, Sch.2

s.27, varied: SI 2003/1517 Sch.1 Part I, Sch.1 Part II

s.28, varied: SI 2003/1517 Sch.1 Part I

s.28A, added: SI 2003/2498 Reg.8

s.28A, varied: SI 2003/1517 Sch.1 Part I

s.29, amended: SI 2003/2498 Reg.9

s.29, repealed (in part): SI 2003/2498 Sch.2

s.29, varied: SI 2003/1517 Sch.1 Part I

s.30, see *Ashdown v Telegraph Group Ltd* [2001] EWCA Civ 1142, [2002] Ch. 149 (CA), Lord Phillips of Worth Matravers, M.R.

s.30, amended: SI 2003/2498 Reg.10

s.30, varied: SI 2003/1517 Sch.1 Part I

s.31, see *Football Association Premier League Ltd v Panini UK Ltd* [2002] EWHC 2779, [2003] E.C.D.R. 21 (Ch D), Peter Smith, J.; see *Football Association Premier League Ltd v Panini UK Ltd* [2003] EWCA Civ 995, [2004] 1 W.L.R. 1147 (CA), Chadwick, L.J.

s.31, amended: SI 2003/2498 Sch.1 para.3, Sch.1 para.6

s.31, varied: SI 2003/1517 Sch.1 Part I

s.31A, added: 2002 c.33 s.1

s.31A, amended: 2002 c.33 s.1

s.31A, varied: SI 2003/1517 Sch.1 Part I

s.31B, added: 2002 c.33 s.2

s.31B, amended: 2002 c.33 s.2

s.31B, varied: SI 2003/1517 Sch.1 Part I

s.31C, added: 2002 c.33 s.3

s.31C, varied: SI 2003/1517 Sch.1 Part I, Sch.1 Part II

s.31D, added: 2002 c.33 s.4

s.31D, varied: SI 2003/1517 Sch.1 Part I, Sch.1 Part II

s.31E, added: 2002 c.33 s.5

1988–cont.

48. Copyright, Designs and Patents Act 1988–*cont.*

s.31E, varied: SI 2003/1517 Sch.1 Part I, Sch.1 Part II

s.31F, added: 2002 c.33 s.6

s.31F, varied: SI 2003/1517 Sch.1 Part I, Sch.1 Part II

s.32, amended: SI 2003/2498 Reg.11

s.32, varied: SI 2003/1517 Sch.1 Part I

s.33, varied: SI 2003/1517 Sch.1 Part I

s.34, amended: SI 2003/2498 Sch.1 para.3

s.34, varied: SI 2003/1517 Sch.1 Part I

s.35, amended: SI 2003/2498 Reg.12, Sch.2

s.35, applied: SI 2003/187, SI 2003/187 Art.2, Art.3, Sch.1, SI 2003/188

s.35, varied: SI 2003/1517 Sch.1 Part I

s.36, amended: SI 2003/2498 Reg.13, Sch.2

s.36, varied: SI 2003/1517 Sch.1 Part I

s.36A, varied: SI 2003/1517 Sch.1 Part I

s.37, varied: SI 2003/1517 Sch.1 Part I, Sch.1 Part II

s.38, amended: SI 2003/2498 Reg.14

s.38, varied: SI 2003/1517 Sch.1 Part I

s.39, amended: SI 2003/2498 Reg.14

s.39, varied: SI 2003/1517 Sch.1 Part I

s.40, varied: SI 2003/1517 Sch.1 Part I

s.40A, varied: SI 2003/1517 Sch.1 Part I, Sch.1 Part II

s.41, varied: SI 2003/1517 Sch.1 Part I

s.42, varied: SI 2003/1517 Sch.1 Part I

s.43, amended: SI 2003/2498 Reg.14

s.43, varied: SI 2003/1517 Sch.1 Part I

s.44, varied: SI 2003/1517 Sch.1 Part I, Sch.1 Part II

s.44A, added: 2003 c.28 s.8

s.44A, varied: SI 2003/1517 Sch.1 Part I

s.45, varied: SI 2003/1517 Sch.1 Part I

s.46, varied: SI 2003/1517 Sch.1 Part I, Sch.1 Part II

s.47, varied: SI 2003/1517 Sch.1 Part I, Sch.1 Part II

s.48, amended: 2003 c.43 Sch.4 para.72

s.48, varied: SI 2003/1517 Sch.1 Part I, Sch.1 Part II

s.49, varied: SI 2003/1517 Sch.1 Part I, Sch.1 Part II

s.50, see *Sony Computer Entertainment v Owen* [2002] EWHC 45, [2002] E.C.D.R. 27 (Ch D), Jacob, J.

s.50, varied: SI 2003/1517 Sch.1 Part I, Sch.1 Part II

s.50A, amended: SI 2003/2498 Reg.15

s.50A, varied: SI 2003/1517 Sch.1 Part I, Sch.1 Part II

s.50B, varied: SI 2003/1517 Sch.1 Part I, Sch.1 Part II

s.50BA, added: SI 2003/2498 Reg.15

s.50BA, varied: SI 2003/1517 Sch.1 Part I

s.50C, amended: SI 2003/2498 Reg.15

s.50C, varied: SI 2003/1517 Sch.1 Part I

1988–cont.

48. Copyright, Designs and Patents Act 1988–cont.

s.50D, varied: SI 2003/1517 Sch.1 Part I, Sch.1 Part II

s.51, see *Hi Tech Autoparts Ltd v Towergate Two Ltd (No.2)* [2002] F.S.R. 16 (PCC), Christopher Floyd Q.C.; see *Lambretta Clothing Co Ltd v Teddy Smith (UK) Ltd* [2003] EWHC 1204, [2003] R.P.C. 41 (Ch D), Etherton, J.

s.51, amended: SI 2003/2498 Sch.1 para.8

s.51, varied: SI 2003/1517 Sch.1 Part I

s.52, varied: SI 2003/1517 Sch.1 Part I, Sch.1 Part II

s.53, varied: SI 2003/1517 Sch.1 Part I, Sch.1 Part II

s.54, varied: SI 2003/1517 Sch.1 Part I

s.55, varied: SI 2003/1517 Sch.1 Part I, Sch.1 Part II

s.56, varied: SI 2003/1517 Sch.1 Part I

s.57, varied: SI 2003/1517 Sch.1 Part I

s.58, amended: SI 2003/2498 Sch.1 para.12, Sch.2

s.58, varied: SI 2003/1517 Sch.1 Part I

s.59, amended: SI 2003/2498 Sch.1 para.5, Sch.1 para.9

s.59, varied: SI 2003/1517 Sch.1 Part I

s.60, varied: SI 2003/1517 Sch.1 Part I

s.61, amended: SI 2003/2498 Reg.16

s.61, varied: SI 2003/1517 Sch.1 Part I, Sch.1 Part II

s.62, amended: SI 2003/2498 Sch.1 para.5, Sch.1 para.14

s.62, varied: SI 2003/1517 Sch.1 Part I

s.63, amended: SI 2003/2498 Reg.17

s.63, varied: SI 2003/1517 Sch.1 Part I

s.64, varied: SI 2003/1517 Sch.1 Part I

s.65, varied: SI 2003/1517 Sch.1 Part I

s.66, varied: SI 2003/1517 Sch.1 Part I, Sch.1 Part II

s.66A, varied: SI 2003/1517 Sch.1 Part I

s.67, see *Phonographic Performance Ltd v Department of Trade and Industry* [2004] EWHC 1795, [2004] 1 W.L.R. 2893 (Ch D), Sir Andrew Morritt V.C.

s.67, varied: SI 2003/1517 Sch.1 Part I

s.67, see *Phonographic Performance Ltd v Department of Trade and Industry* [2004] EWHC 1795, [2004] 1 W.L.R. 2893 (Ch D), Sir Andrew Morritt V.C.

s.67, amended: SI 2003/2498 Reg.18

s.67, varied: SI 2003/1517 Sch.1 Part I

s.68, amended: SI 2003/2498 Sch.2

s.68, varied: SI 2003/1517 Sch.1 Part I

s.69, amended: 2003 c.21 Sch.17 para.91, Sch.19, SI 2003/2498 Sch.1 para.2

s.69, varied: SI 2003/1517 Sch.1 Part I, Sch.1 Part II, SI 2004/1975 Art.9

s.70, see *Sony Music Entertainment (UK) Ltd v Easyinternetcafe Ltd* [2003] EWHC 62, [2003] E.C.D.R. 27 (Ch D), Peter Smith, J.

1988–cont.

48. Copyright, Designs and Patents Act 1988–cont.

s.70, amended: SI 2003/2498 Reg.19, Sch.2

s.70, varied: SI 2003/1517 Sch.1 Part I

s.71, substituted: SI 2003/2498 Reg.20

s.71, varied: SI 2003/1517 Sch.1 Part I

s.72, see *Phonographic Performance Ltd v Department of Trade and Industry* [2004] EWHC 1795, [2004] 1 W.L.R. 2893 (Ch D), Sir Andrew Morritt V.C.

s.72, amended: SI 2003/2498 Reg.21, Sch.2

s.72, varied: SI 2003/1517 Sch.1 Part I

s.73, amended: 2003 c.21 Sch.17 para.92, SI 2003/2498 Reg.22

s.73, varied: SI 2003/1517 Sch.1 Part I, Sch.1 Part II

s.73A, amended: SI 2003/2498 Reg.22

s.73A, referred to: SI 2003/1517 Sch.1 Part I

s.73A, varied: SI 2003/1517 Sch.1 Part I

s.74, amended: SI 2003/2498 Reg.23, Sch.2

s.74, varied: SI 2003/1517 Sch.1 Part I, Sch.1 Part II

s.75, amended: SI 2003/2498 Sch.2

s.75, varied: SI 2003/1517 Sch.1 Part I, Sch.1 Part II

s.76, varied: SI 2003/1517 Sch.1 Part I

s.77, amended: SI 2003/2498 Sch.1 para.8, Sch.1 para.9

s.77, varied: SI 2003/1517 Sch.1 Part I

s.78, varied: SI 2003/1517 Sch.1 Part I

s.79, amended: SI 2003/2498 Sch.1 para.3, Sch.1 para.18

s.79, varied: SI 2003/1517 Sch.1 Part I, Sch.1 Part II

s.80, see *Confetti Records v Warner Music UK Ltd (t/a East West Records)* [2003] EWHC 1274, [2003] E.C.D.R. 31 (Ch D), Lewison, J

s.80, amended: SI 2003/2498 Sch.1 para.10, Sch.1 para.13

s.80, varied: SI 2003/1517 Sch.1 Part I

s.81, varied: SI 2003/1517 Sch.1 Part I, Sch.1 Part II

s.82, amended: SI 2003/2498 Sch.1 para.18, Sch.2

s.82, varied: SI 2003/1517 Sch.1 Part I, Sch.1 Part II

s.83, varied: SI 2003/1517 Sch.1 Part I

s.84, amended: SI 2003/2498 Sch.1 para.10

s.84, varied: SI 2003/1517 Sch.1 Part I

s.85, amended: SI 2003/2498 Sch.1 para.3, Sch.1 para.8

s.85, varied: SI 2003/1517 Sch.1 Part I, Sch.1 Part II

s.86, varied: SI 2003/1517 Sch.1 Part I

s.87, varied: SI 2003/1517 Sch.1 Part I

s.88, varied: SI 2003/1517 Sch.1 Part I

s.89, varied: SI 2003/1517 Sch.1 Part I

s.90, varied: SI 2003/1517 Sch.1 Part I

s.91, varied: SI 2003/1517 Sch.1 Part I

s.92, varied: SI 2003/1517 Sch.1 Part I

1988–cont.

48. **Copyright, Designs and Patents Act 1988**–*cont.*

s.93, varied: SI 2003/1517 Sch.1 Part I

s.93A, varied: SI 2003/1517 Sch.1 Part I

s.93B, varied: SI 2003/1517 Sch.1 Part I

s.93C, varied: SI 2003/1517 Sch.1 Part I

s.94, varied: SI 2003/1517 Sch.1 Part I

s.95, varied: SI 2003/1517 Sch.1 Part I

s.96, varied: SI 2003/1517 Sch.1 Part I

s.97, see *Nottinghamshire Healthcare NHS Trust v News Group Newspapers Ltd* [2002] EWHC 409, [2002] E.M.L.R. 33 (Ch D), Pumfrey, J.; see *Peninsular Business Services Ltd v Citation Plc (No.1)* [2004] F.S.R.17 (Ch D), Judge Maddocks; see *Peninsular Business Services Ltd v Citation Plc (No.2)* [2004] F.S.R 18 (Ch D), Judge Maddocks; see *Sony Computer Entertainment v Owen* [2002] EWHC 45, [2002] E.C.D.R. 27 (Ch D), Jacob, J.

s.97, varied: SI 2003/1517 Sch.1 Part I

s.97A, added: SI 2003/2498 Reg.27

s.97A, varied: SI 2003/1517 Sch.1 Part I

s.98, referred to: SI 2003/1517 Sch.1 Part I

s.98, varied: SI 2003/1517 Sch.1 Part I

s.99, varied: SI 2003/1517 Sch.1 Part I

s.100, varied: SI 2003/1517 Sch.1 Part I, Sch.1 Part II

s.101, varied: SI 2003/1517 Sch.1 Part I

s.101A, added: SI 2003/2498 Reg.28

s.101A, varied: SI 2003/1517 Sch.1 Part I

s.102, varied: SI 2003/1517 Sch.1 Part I

s.103, varied: SI 2003/1517 Sch.1 Part I

s.104, varied: SI 2003/1517 Sch.1 Part I

s.105, amended: SI 2003/2498 Sch.1 para.8

s.105, varied: SI 2003/1517 Sch.1 Part I

s.106, varied: SI 2003/1517 Sch.1 Part I

s.107, amended: 2002 c.25 s.1, SI 2003/2498 Reg.26, Sch.1 para.9

s.107, applied: 2002 c.29 Sch.2 para.7, Sch.4 para.7, Sch.5 para.7, 2003 c.17 Sch.4 para.13, SI 2003/1376 Sch.1, SI 2003/1593 Sch.1 Part I

s.107, disapplied: SI 2003/2498 Reg.40

s.107, varied: SI 2003/1517 Sch.1 Part I, Sch.1 Part II

s.107A, varied: SI 2003/1517 Sch.1 Part I, Sch.1 Part II

s.108, varied: SI 2003/1517 Sch.1 Part I, Sch.1 Part II

s.109, amended: 2002 c.25 s.2, SI 2003/2498 Reg.26

s.109, varied: SI 2003/1517 Sch.1 Part I, Sch.1 Part II

s.110, varied: SI 2003/1517 Sch.1 Part I

s.111, amended: SI 2004/1473 Reg.12

s.111, varied: SI 2003/1517 Sch.1 Part I, Sch.1 Part II

s.112, varied: SI 2003/1517 Sch.1 Part I, Sch.1 Part II

1988–cont.

48. **Copyright, Designs and Patents Act 1988**–*cont.*

s.113, varied: SI 2003/1517 Sch.1 Part I, Sch.1 Part II

s.114, varied: SI 2003/1517 Sch.1 Part I, Sch.1 Part II

s.114A, added: 2002 c.25 s.3

s.114A, amended: SI 2003/2498 Reg.26

s.114A, varied: SI 2003/1517 Sch.1 Part I, Sch.1 Part II

s.114B, added: 2002 c.25 s.3

s.114B, amended: SI 2003/2498 Reg.26

s.114B, referred to: SI 2003/1517 Sch.1 Part I

s.114B, varied: SI 2003/1517 Sch.1 Part I

s.115, varied: SI 2003/1517 Sch.1 Part I, Sch.1 Part II

s.116, see *Universities UK Ltd v Copyright Licensing Agency Ltd* [2002] E.M.L.R. 35 (Copyright Tribunal), Christopher Floyd Q.C. (Chairman)

s.116, varied: SI 2003/1517 Sch.1 Part I, Sch.1 Part II

s.117, amended: SI 2003/2498 Sch.1 para.4

s.117, varied: SI 2003/1517 Sch.1 Part I

s.118, varied: SI 2003/1517 Sch.1 Part I

s.119, varied: SI 2003/1517 Sch.1 Part I

s.120, amended: SI 2003/2498 Reg.21

s.120, varied: SI 2003/1517 Sch.1 Part I

s.121, varied: SI 2003/1517 Sch.1 Part I

s.122, varied: SI 2003/1517 Sch.1 Part I

s.123, varied: SI 2003/1517 Sch.1 Part I

s.124, amended: SI 2003/2498 Sch.1 para.4

s.124, varied: SI 2003/1517 Sch.1 Part I

s.125, varied: SI 2003/1517 Sch.1 Part I

s.126, varied: SI 2003/1517 Sch.1 Part I

s.127, amended: SI 2003/2498 Reg.21

s.127, varied: SI 2003/1517 Sch.1 Part I

s.128, varied: SI 2003/1517 Sch.1 Part I

s.128A, added: SI 2003/2498 Reg.21

s.128A, varied: SI 2003/1517 Sch.1 Part I

s.128B, added: SI 2003/2498 Reg.21

s.128B, varied: SI 2003/1517 Sch.1 Part I

s.129, varied: SI 2003/1517 Sch.1 Part I

s.130, varied: SI 2003/1517 Sch.1 Part I

s.131, amended: SI 2003/2498 Sch.2

s.131, varied: SI 2003/1517 Sch.1 Part I

s.132, amended: SI 2003/2498 Sch.1 para.3

s.132, varied: SI 2003/1517 Sch.1 Part I

s.133, amended: SI 2003/2498 Sch.1 para.3

s.133, varied: SI 2003/1517 Sch.1 Part I

s.134, amended: SI 2003/2498 Sch.2

s.134, varied: SI 2003/1517 Sch.1 Part I, Sch.1 Part II

s.135, varied: SI 2003/1517 Sch.1 Part I

s.135A, amended: SI 2003/2498 Sch.1 para.15, Sch.2

s.135A, varied: SI 2003/1517 Sch.1 Part I

s.135B, amended: SI 2003/2498 Sch.2

s.135B, varied: SI 2003/1517 Sch.1 Part I

s.135C, amended: SI 2003/2498 Sch.2

1988–cont.

48. Copyright, Designs and Patents Act 1988–cont.

s.135C, varied: SI 2003/1517 Sch.1 Part I
s.135D, varied: SI 2003/1517 Sch.1 Part I
s.135E, amended: SI 2003/2498 Sch.2
s.135E, varied: SI 2003/1517 Sch.1 Part I
s.135F, varied: SI 2003/1517 Sch.1 Part I
s.135G, varied: SI 2003/1517 Sch.1 Part I
s.135H, amended: SI 2003/2498 Sch.2
s.135H, varied: SI 2003/1517 Sch.1 Part I, Sch.1 Part II
s.136, varied: SI 2003/1517 Sch.1 Part I
s.137, varied: SI 2003/1517 Sch.1 Part I, Sch.1 Part II
s.138, varied: SI 2003/1517 Sch.1 Part I, Sch.1 Part II
s.139, varied: SI 2003/1517 Sch.1 Part I, Sch.1 Part II
s.140, varied: SI 2003/1517 Sch.1 Part I, Sch.1 Part II
s.141, varied: SI 2003/1517 Sch.1 Part I, Sch.1 Part II
s.142, varied: SI 2003/1517 Sch.1 Part I
s.143, amended: SI 2003/2498 Sch.2
s.143, varied: SI 2003/1517 Sch.1 Part I, Sch.1 Part II
s.143, enabling: SI 2003/187, SI 2003/188
s.144, amended: 2002 c.40 Sch.25 para.18
s.144, referred to: SI 2003/1517 Sch.1 Part I
s.144, varied: SI 2003/1517 Sch.1 Part I, SI 2003/1592 Sch.4 para.7
s.144A, amended: SI 2003/2498 Reg.5, Sch.1 para.15
s.144A, referred to: SI 2003/1517 Sch.1 Part I
s.144A, varied: SI 2003/1517 Sch.1 Part I
s.145, varied: SI 2003/1517 Sch.1 Part I, Sch.1 Part II
s.146, varied: SI 2003/1517 Sch.1 Part I, Sch.1 Part II
s.147, varied: SI 2003/1517 Sch.1 Part I, Sch.1 Part II
s.148, varied: SI 2003/1517 Sch.1 Part I, Sch.1 Part II
s.149, amended: SI 2003/2498 Reg.21, Sch.2
s.149, varied: SI 2003/1517 Sch.1 Part I, Sch.1 Part II
s.150, varied: SI 2003/1517 Sch.1 Part I, Sch.1 Part II
s.151, varied: SI 2003/1517 Sch.1 Part I, Sch.1 Part II
s.151A, amended: SI 2003/2498 Sch.1 para.7
s.151A, varied: SI 2003/1517 Sch.1 Part I
s.152, varied: SI 2003/1517 Sch.1 Part I, Sch.1 Part II
s.153, amended: SI 2003/2498 Sch.2
s.153, varied: SI 2003/1517 Sch.1 Part I
s.154, amended: 2002 c.8 s.2
s.154, repealed (in part): SI 2003/2498 Sch.2
s.154, varied: SI 2003/1517 Sch.1 Part I, Sch.1 Part II

1988–cont.

48. Copyright, Designs and Patents Act 1988–cont.

s.155, varied: SI 2003/1517 Sch.1 Part I, Sch.1 Part II
s.156, amended: SI 2003/2498 Sch.2
s.156, varied: SI 2003/1517 Sch.1 Part I, Sch.1 Part II
s.157, amended: 2002 c.8 s.1
s.157, referred to: SI 2003/1517 Sch.1 Part I
s.157, varied: SI 2003/1517 Sch.1 Part I
s.157, enabling: SI 2003/1517
s.158, referred to: SI 2003/1517 Sch.1 Part I
s.158, varied: SI 2003/1517 Sch.1 Part I
s.159, amended: SI 2003/2498 Sch.2
s.159, varied: SI 2003/1517 Sch.1 Part I, Sch.1 Part II
s.159, enabling: SI 2003/774
s.160, varied: SI 2003/1517 Sch.1 Part I, Sch.1 Part II
s.161, varied: SI 2003/1517 Sch.1 Part I, Sch.1 Part II
s.162, varied: SI 2003/1517 Sch.1 Part I, Sch.1 Part II
s.163, amended: SI 2003/2498 Sch.1 para.11
s.163, varied: SI 2003/1517 Sch.1 Part I, Sch.1 Part II
s.164, varied: SI 2003/1517 Sch.1 Part I, Sch.1 Part II
s.165, amended: SI 2003/2498 Sch.1 para.11
s.165, varied: SI 2003/1517 Sch.1 Part I, Sch.1 Part II
s.166, varied: SI 2003/1517 Sch.1 Part I, Sch.1 Part II
s.166A, referred to: SI 2003/1517 Sch.1 Part I
s.166A, varied: SI 2003/1517 Sch.1 Part I
s.166B, referred to: SI 2003/1517 Sch.1 Part I
s.166B, varied: SI 2003/1517 Sch.1 Part I
s.167, varied: SI 2003/1517 Sch.1 Part I, Sch.1 Part II
s.168, varied: SI 2003/1517 Sch.1 Part I, Sch.1 Part II
s.169, varied: SI 2003/1517 Sch.1 Part I, Sch.1 Part II
s.170, varied: SI 2003/1517 Sch.1 Part I
s.171, see *Ashdown v Telegraph Group Ltd* [2001] EWCA Civ 1142, [2002] Ch. 149 (CA), Lord Phillips of Worth Matravers, M.R.
s.171, varied: SI 2003/1517 Sch.1 Part I, Sch.1 Part II
s.172, varied: SI 2003/1517 Sch.1 Part I, Sch.1 Part II
s.172A, referred to: SI 2003/1517 Sch.1 Part I
s.172A, varied: SI 2003/1517 Sch.1 Part I
s.173, varied: SI 2003/1517 Sch.1 Part I
s.174, varied: SI 2003/1517 Sch.1 Part I, Sch.1 Part II
s.175, amended: SI 2003/2498 Sch.1 para.6
s.175, varied: SI 2003/1517 Sch.1 Part I
s.176, varied: SI 2003/1517 Sch.1 Part I
s.177, varied: SI 2003/1517 Sch.1 Part I

1988–cont.

48. Copyright, Designs and Patents Act 1988–*cont.*

s.178, see *Bamgboye v Reed* [2002] EWHC 2922, [2004] E.M.L.R. 5 (QBD), Hazel Williamson Q.C.

s.178, amended: SI 2003/2498 Sch.1 para.15

s.178, varied: SI 2003/1517 Sch.1 Part I, Sch.1 Part II

s.179, amended: 2002 c.33 s.7, SI 2003/2498 Reg.21, Sch.1 para.15, Sch.2

s.179, varied: SI 2003/1517 Sch.1 Part I, Sch.1 Part II

s.180, amended: SI 2003/2498 Sch.2

s.180, varied: SI 2003/773 Art.3

s.181, varied: SI 2003/773 Art.3

s.182, amended: SI 2003/2498 Sch.2

s.182, repealed (in part): SI 2003/2498 Sch.2

s.182, varied: SI 2003/773 Art.3

s.182A, amended: SI 2003/2498 Reg.8, Sch.2

s.182A, varied: SI 2003/773 Art.3

s.182B, varied: SI 2003/773 Art.3

s.182C, amended: SI 2003/2498 Sch.1 para.6

s.182C, varied: SI 2003/773 Art.3

s.182CA, added: SI 2003/2498 Reg.7

s.182CA, applied: SI 2003/2498 Reg.34, Reg.35

s.182CA, referred to: SI 2003/2498 Reg.34

s.182CA, varied: SI 2003/773 Art.3

s.182D, amended: SI 2003/2498 Reg.7

s.182D, disapplied: SI 2003/2498 Reg.34

s.182D, varied: SI 2003/773 Art.3

s.183, amended: SI 2003/2498 Sch.1 para.13

s.183, varied: SI 2003/773 Art.3

s.184, varied: SI 2003/773 Art.3

s.185, varied: SI 2003/773 Art.3

s.186, amended: SI 2003/2498 Sch.2

s.186, varied: SI 2003/773 Art.3

s.187, amended: SI 2003/2498 Sch.1 para.13

s.187, varied: SI 2003/773 Art.3

s.188, varied: SI 2003/773 Art.3

s.189, varied: SI 2003/773 Art.3

s.190, varied: SI 2003/773 Art.3

s.191, amended: SI 2003/2498 Sch.1 para.8

s.191, varied: SI 2003/773 Art.3

s.191A, amended: SI 2003/2498 Reg.7

s.191A, varied: SI 2003/773 Art.3

s.191B, varied: SI 2003/773 Art.3

s.191C, varied: SI 2003/773 Art.3

s.191D, varied: SI 2003/773 Art.3

s.191E, varied: SI 2003/773 Art.3

s.191F, varied: SI 2003/773 Art.3

s.191G, varied: SI 2003/773 Art.3

s.191H, varied: SI 2003/773 Art.3

s.191I, varied: SI 2003/773 Art.3

s.191J, varied: SI 2003/773 Art.3

s.191JA, added: SI 2003/2498 Reg.27

s.191JA, varied: SI 2003/773 Art.3

s.191K, varied: SI 2003/773 Art.3

s.191L, varied: SI 2003/773 Art.3

1988–cont.

48. Copyright, Designs and Patents Act 1988–*cont.*

s.191M, varied: SI 2003/773 Art.3

s.192, varied: SI 2003/773 Art.3

s.192A, applied: SI 2003/2498 Reg.35

s.192A, varied: SI 2003/773 Art.3

s.192B, varied: SI 2003/773 Art.3

s.193, varied: SI 2003/773 Art.3

s.194, varied: SI 2003/773 Art.3

s.195, varied: SI 2003/773 Art.3

s.196, varied: SI 2003/773 Art.3

s.197, varied: SI 2003/773 Art.3

s.197, amended: SI 2003/2498 Reg.20, Sch.2

s.197, varied: SI 2003/773 Art.3

s.198, amended: 2002 c.25 s.1, SI 2003/2498 Reg.26, Sch.1 para.4

s.198, applied: 2002 c.29 Sch.2 para.7, Sch.4 para.7, Sch.5 para.7, 2003 c.17 Sch.4 para.13, SI 2003/1376 Sch.1, SI 2003/1593 Sch.1 Part I

s.198, disapplied: SI 2003/2498 Reg.40

s.198, varied: SI 2003/773 Art.3

s.198A, varied: SI 2003/773 Art.3

s.199, varied: SI 2003/773 Art.3

s.200, amended: 2002 c.25 s.2, SI 2003/2498 Reg.26

s.200, varied: SI 2003/773 Art.3

s.201, varied: SI 2003/773 Art.3

s.202, varied: SI 2003/773 Art.3

s.203, varied: SI 2003/773 Art.3

s.204, varied: SI 2003/773 Art.3

s.204A, added: 2002 c.25 s.4

s.204A, amended: SI 2003/2498 Reg.26

s.204A, varied: SI 2003/773 Art.3

s.204B, added: 2002 c.25 s.4

s.204B, amended: SI 2003/2498 Reg.26

s.204B, varied: SI 2003/773 Art.3

s.205, varied: SI 2003/773 Art.3

s.205A, varied: SI 2003/773 Art.3

s.205B, varied: SI 2003/773 Art.3

s.206, varied: 2002 c.8 s.2, SI 2003/773 Art.3

s.207, varied: SI 2003/773 Art.3

s.208, varied: SI 2003/773 Art.3

s.208, enabling: SI 2003/773

s.209, varied: SI 2003/773 Art.3

s.210, varied: SI 2003/773 Art.3

s.211, amended: SI 2003/2498 Sch.1 para.15, Sch.2

s.211, varied: SI 2003/773 Art.3

s.212, amended: SI 2003/2498 Sch.1 para.15, Sch.2

s.212, varied: SI 2003/773 Art.3

s.213, see *A Fulton Co Ltd v Totes Isotoner (UK) Ltd* [2003] EWCA Civ 1514, [2004] R.P.C. 16 (CA), Lord Phillips of Worth Matravers, M.R.; see *Lambretta Clothing Co Ltd v Teddy Smith (UK) Ltd* [2003] EWHC 1204, [2003] R.P.C. 41 (Ch D), Etherton, J.; see *Scholes Windows Ltd v*

1988–cont.
48. Copyright, Designs and Patents Act 1988–*cont.*

s.213–*cont.*

Magnet Ltd (No.1) [2001] EWCA Civ 532, [2002] E.C.D.R. 20 (CA), Mummery, L.J.; see *Ultraframe UK Ltd v Clayton (No.2)* [2002] EWHC 1964, [2003] R.P.C. 23 (Ch D), Laddie, J.

s.215, see *Intercase UK Ltd v Time Computers Ltd* [2003] EWHC 2988, [2004] E.C.D.R. 8 (Ch D), Patten, J.; see *Ultraframe UK Ltd v Clayton (No.2)* [2002] EWHC 1964, [2003] R.P.C. 23 (Ch D), Laddie, J.

s.217, varied: 2002 c.8 s.2

s.226, see *A Fulton Co Ltd v Totes Isotoner (UK) Ltd* [2003] EWCA Civ 1514, [2004] R.P.C. 16 (CA), Lord Phillips of Worth Matravers, M.R.

s.238, amended: 2002 c.40 Sch.25 para.18

s.238, varied: SI 2003/1592 Sch.4 para.7

s.240, amended: 2003 c.43 Sch.11 para.52, SI 2004/957 Sch.1 para.5

s.240, repealed (in part): 2003 c.43 Sch.11 para.52, Sch.14 Part 4

s.240, varied: SI 2004/288 Art.7, Art.8, SI 2004/480 Art.6, Art.7

s.287, applied: SI 2004/1473 Reg.9

s.296, see *Kabushiki Kaisha Sony Computer Entertainment Inc v Ball (Application for Summary Judgment)* [2004] EWHC 1738, [2004] E.C.D.R. 33 (Ch D), Laddie, J.; see *Sony Computer Entertainment v Owen* [2002] EWHC 45, [2002] E.C.D.R. 27 (Ch D), Jacob, J.

s.296, applied: SI 2003/2498 Reg.40

s.296, substituted: SI 2003/2498 Reg.24

s.296A, amended: SI 2003/2498 Reg.15

s.296ZA, see *Kabushiki Kaisha Sony Computer Entertainment Inc v Ball (Application for Summary Judgment)* [2004] EWHC 1738, [2004] E.C.D.R. 33 (Ch D), Laddie, J.

s.296ZA, applied: SI 2003/2498 Reg.40

s.296ZB, disapplied: SI 2003/2498 Reg.40

s.296ZD, see *Kabushiki Kaisha Sony Computer Entertainment Inc v Ball (Application for Summary Judgment)* [2004] EWHC 1738, [2004] E.C.D.R. 33 (Ch D), Laddie, J.

s.296ZD, applied: SI 2003/2498 Reg.40

s.296ZE, applied: 2002 c.33 s.7

s.296ZF, see *Kabushiki Kaisha Sony Computer Entertainment Inc v Ball (Application for Summary Judgment)* [2004] EWHC 1738, [2004] E.C.D.R. 33 (Ch D), Laddie, J.

s.296ZG, added: SI 2003/2498 Reg.25

s.297, amended: SI 2003/2498 Sch.2

s.297, applied: 2003 c.17 Sch.4 para.13

s.297, referred to: 2003 c.21 s.125, s.126

1988–cont.
48. Copyright, Designs and Patents Act 1988–*cont.*

s.297A, see *R. v Mainwaring (David Charles)* [2002] F.S.R. 20 (Crown Ct (Oxford)), Judge Peter Crawford Q.C.

s.297A, amended: 2002 c.25 s.1, SI 2003/2498 Sch.2

s.297A, applied: 2002 c.29 Sch.2 para.7, Sch.4 para.7, Sch.5 para.7, 2003 c.17 Sch.4 para.13, SI 2003/1376 Sch.1, SI 2003/1593 Sch.1 Part I

s.297B, added: 2002 c.25 s.2

s.297C, added: 2002 c.25 s.5

s.297D, added: 2002 c.25 s.5

s.298, amended: SI 2003/2498 Sch.2

s.299, amended: SI 2003/2498 Sch.1 para.3, Sch.2

s.301, amended: SI 2003/2498 Sch.1 para.6

Sch.1 para.1, varied: SI 2003/1517 Sch.1 Part III

Sch.1 para.5, varied: SI 2003/1517 Sch.1 Part III

Sch.1 para.6, varied: SI 2003/1517 Sch.1 Part III

Sch.1 para.9, substituted: SI 2003/2498 Sch.1 para.16

Sch.1 para.12, amended: SI 2003/2498 Sch.1 para.18

Sch.1 para.12, varied: SI 2003/1517 Sch.1 Part III

Sch.1 para.13, referred to: SI 2003/1517 Sch.1 Part I

Sch.1 para.14, varied: SI 2003/1517 Sch.1 Part III

Sch.1 para.15, repealed (in part): SI 2003/2498 Sch.2

Sch.1 para.15, varied: SI 2003/1517 Sch.1 Part III

Sch.1 para.17, amended: SI 2003/2498 Sch.1 para.4

Sch.1 para.19, varied: SI 2003/1517 Sch.1 Part III

Sch.1 para.21, referred to: SI 2003/1517 Sch.1 Part I

Sch.1 para.23, varied: SI 2003/1517 Sch.1 Part III

Sch.1 para.28, varied: SI 2003/1517 Sch.1 Part III

Sch.1 para.34, referred to: SI 2003/1517 Sch.1 Part I

Sch.1 para.36, amended: 2002 c.8 s.1

Sch.1 para.36, referred to: SI 2003/1517 Sch.1 Part I

Sch.1 para.37, amended: 2002 c.8 s.1

Sch.1 para.37, referred to: SI 2003/1517 Sch.1 Part I

Sch.1 para.38, varied: SI 2003/1517 Sch.1 Part III

Sch.1 para.39, varied: SI 2003/1517 Sch.1 Part III

Sch.1 para.40, varied: SI 2003/1517 Sch.1 Part III

1988–cont.

48. Copyright, Designs and Patents Act 1988–*cont.*

Sch.1 para.42, varied: SI 2003/1517 Sch.1 Part III

Sch.1 para.43, varied: SI 2003/1517 Sch.1 Part III

Sch.2, applied: SI 2003/2498 Reg.33

Sch.2, amended: SI 2003/2498 Sch.1 para.2

Sch.2, amended: SI 2003/2498 Sch.2

Sch.2, amended: SI 2003/2498 Sch.1 para.2

Sch.2, amended: SI 2003/2498 Sch.2

Sch.2, amended: SI 2003/2498 Reg.22

Sch.2, amended: SI 2003/2498 Sch.2

Sch.2 para.1A, added: SI 2003/2498 Reg.8

Sch.2 para.2, amended: SI 2003/2498 Reg.10

Sch.2 para.3, amended: SI 2003/2498 Sch.1 para.3, Sch.1 para.6

Sch.2 para.4, amended: SI 2003/2498 Reg.11

Sch.2 para.5, amended: SI 2003/2498 Sch.1 para.3

Sch.2 para.6, amended: SI 2003/2498 Reg.12, Sch.2

Sch.2 para.13, amended: SI 2003/2498 Sch.1 para.12, Sch.2

Sch.2 para.15, amended: SI 2003/2498 Reg.18

Sch.2 para.16, amended: SI 2003/2498 Sch.2

Sch.2 para.17, amended: 2003 c.21 Sch.17 para.93, Sch.19

Sch.2 para.17, varied: SI 2004/1975 Art.9

Sch.2 para.17A, added: SI 2003/2498 Reg.19

Sch.2 para.17B, added: SI 2003/2498 Reg.20

Sch.2 para.18, amended: SI 2003/2498 Reg.21, Sch.2

Sch.2 para.19, amended: SI 2003/2498 Reg.22

Sch.2 para.20, amended: SI 2003/2498 Reg.23, Sch.2

Sch.2 para.21, amended: SI 2003/2498 Sch.2

Sch.2A para.1, amended: SI 2003/2498 Reg.7

Sch.2A para.2, amended: SI 2003/2498 Reg.7, Sch.2

Sch.2A para.9, amended: SI 2003/2498 Reg.7, Sch.2

Sch.2A para.16, amended: SI 2003/2498 Sch.1 para.17

Sch.2A para.17, amended: 2002 c.40 Sch.25 para.18

Sch.2A para.17, varied: SI 2003/1592 Sch.4 para.7

Sch.5A Part I, added: SI 2003/2498 Sch.3

Sch.5A Part I, amended: 2002 c.33 s.7

Sch.5A Part II, added: SI 2003/2498 Sch.3

Sch.5A Part III, added: SI 2003/2498 Sch.3

1988–cont.

48. Copyright, Designs and Patents Act 1988–*cont.*

Sch.6 para.2, amended: SI 2003/2498 Sch.1 para.6

Sch.7 para.10, repealed (in part): SI 2003/2498 Sch.2

Sch.7 para.15, repealed: 2002 c.40 Sch.26

Sch.7 para.27, repealed: 2003 c.21 Sch.19

49. Health and Medicines Act 1988

referred to: 2003 c.43 Sch.11 para.53

s.1, repealed (in part): 2004 c.14 Sch.1 Part 5

s.2, amended: 2003 c.43 Sch.14 Part 4

s.2, repealed (in part): SI 2004/957 Sch.1 para.6

s.3, repealed: 2004 c.14 Sch.1 Part 5

s.7, applied: SSI 2002/103 Sch.1 Part II, SSI 2002/305 Sch.1 Part II, SSI 2002/534 Sch.1 Part II

s.8, amended: 2003 c.43 Sch.14 Part 4

s.8, repealed (in part): SI 2004/957 Sch.1 para.6

s.12, amended: 2003 c.43 Sch.11 para.54, Sch.14 Part 4

s.12, repealed (in part): 2003 c.43 Sch.14 Part 4

s.17, amended: 2003 c.43 Sch.11 para.55, Sch.14 Part 4, SSI 2004/167 Sch.1 para.2

s.17, applied: 2002 asp 11 Sch.4 para.14

s.17, varied: SI 2004/288 Art.7, SI 2004/480 Art.6

Sch.2 para.4, repealed: 2003 c.43 Sch.14 Part 4

Sch.2 para.5, repealed: 2003 c.43 Sch.14 Part 4

Sch.2 para.6, repealed: 2003 c.43 Sch.14 Part 4

Sch.2 para.7, repealed (in part): 2003 c.43 Sch.14 Part 4

Sch.2 para.8, repealed (in part): 2003 c.43 Sch.14 Part 4

50. Housing Act 1988

Commencement Orders: 2004 c.14 Sch.1 Part 10

see *Baygreen Properties Ltd v Gil* [2002] EWCA Civ 1340, [2003] H.L.R. 12 (CA), Clarke, L.J.

referred to: 2002 c.30 s.108, 2004 c.34 s.267

Part I, applied: 2004 c.34 s.124, Sch.7 para.18

Part I, referred to: 2004 c.34 s.33, s.124, Sch.7 para.4, Sch.7 para.12, Sch.7 para.18

Part III, applied: 2003 c.14 Sch.9 para.1

s.1, see *Uratemp Ventures Ltd v Collins* [2001] UKHL 43, [2002] 1 A.C. 301 (HL), Lord Millett

s.1, disapplied: 2004 c.34 s.124, Sch.7 para.4, Sch.7 para.12, Sch.7 para.18

s.5, amended: 2004 c.34 s.222

s.7, see *North Devon Homes Ltd v Brazier* [2003] EWHC 574, [2003] H.L.R. 59 (QBD), David Steel, J.

1988–cont.

50. Housing Act 1988–cont.

s.8, see *Knowsley Housing Trust v Revell* [2003] EWCA Civ 496, [2003] H.L.R. 63 (CA), Waller, L.J.; see *North Devon Homes Ltd v Brazier* [2003] EWHC 574, [2003] H.L.R. 59 (QBD), David Steel, J.

s.9, amended: 2004 c.33 Sch.9 para.23

s.9A, added: 2003 c.38 s.16

s.13, see *R. (on the application of Lester) v London Rent Assessment Committee* [2002] EWHC 2790, [2003] H.L.R. 29 (QBD (Admin Ct)), Sir Richard Tucker; see *R. (on the application of Lester) v London Rent Assessment Committee* [2003] EWCA Civ 319, [2003] 1 W.L.R. 1449 (CA), Waller, L.J.

s.13, amended: SI 2003/259 Art.2

s.13, applied: SI 2002/337 Reg.4, SI 2003/259 Art.1, SI 2003/260 Reg.3, SI 2003/307 Reg.3

s.13, enabling: SI 2002/337, SI 2003/260, SI 2003/307

s.17, amended: 2004 c.33 Sch.8 para.41

s.20, see *B Osborn & Co Ltd v Dior* [2003] EWCA Civ 281, [2003] H.L.R. 45 (CA), Arden, L.J.; see *Ravenseft Properties Ltd v Hall* [2001] EWCA Civ 2034, [2002] H.L.R. 33 (CA), Mummery, L.J.; see *Yenula Properties Ltd v Naidu* [2002] EWCA Civ 719, [2003] H.L.R. 18 (CA), Robert Walker, L.J.

s.20B, added: 2003 c.38 s.15

s.21, see *McDonald v Fernandez* [2003] EWCA Civ 1219, [2004] 1 W.L.R. 1027 (CA), Hale, L.J.; see *Poplar Housing & Regeneration Community Association Ltd v Donoghue* [2001] EWCA Civ 595, [2002] Q.B. 48 (CA), Lord Woolf of Barnes, L.C.J.

s.21, amended: 2003 c.38 s.15

s.34, see *Rajah v Arogol Co Ltd* [2001] EWCA Civ 454, [2002] H.L.R. 21 (CA), Hale, L.J.

s.45, see *Goodman v Evely* [2001] EWCA Civ 104, [2002] H.L.R. 53 (CA), Sir Robert Andrew Morritt V.C.

s.45, enabling: SI 2002/337, SI 2003/260, SI 2003/307

s.50, amended: 2004 c.34 Sch.11 para.3, Sch.16

s.52, amended: 2004 c.34 Sch.11 para.4, Sch.16

s.55, repealed: 2004 c.34 Sch.11 para.5, Sch.16

s.57, amended: 2004 c.34 Sch.16

s.59, amended: 2004 c.34 Sch.11 para.6

s.67, applied: SI 2002/1223 r.13, SI 2002/2685 r.11, SI 2002/2686 r.13, SI 2003/1266 r.11, SI 2003/1267 r.11, SI 2003/1269 r.13, SI 2003/1270 r.11

s.79, applied: 2004 c.34 s.204

s.81, amended: 2002 c.9 Sch.11 para.23

s.81, applied: SI 2003/1417 r.95

1988–cont.

50. Housing Act 1988–cont.

s.82, amended: 2004 c.33 Sch.8 para.42

s.88, enabling: SI 2002/86, SI 2004/586

s.90, amended: 2002 c.9 Sch.11 para.23

s.129, amended: SI 2003/986 Art.2

s.130, repealed: 2004 c.34 Sch.16

s.133, amended: 2002 c.9 Sch.11 para.23

s.133, applied: SI 2003/1417 r.95

Sch.1 Part I para.5, amended: 2003 c.17 Sch.6 para.108

Sch.1 Part I para.12, amended: 2002 c.30 Sch.8

Sch.1 Part I para.12, disapplied: 2004 c.34 s.124, Sch.7 para.4, Sch.7 para.12, Sch.7 para.18

Sch.2 Part I, amended: 2004 c.33 Sch.8 para.43

Sch.2 Part II, amended: 2002 c.17 Sch.5 para.28, 2004 c.33 Sch.8 para.43

Sch.2 Part II Ground 14, see *Pollards Hill Housing Association v Marsh* [2002] EWCA Civ 199, [2002] H.L.R. 35 (CA), Kay, L.J.

Sch.2 Ground 8, see *Coltrane v Day* [2003] EWCA Civ 342, [2003] 1 W.L.R. 1379 (CA), Tuckey, L.J.

Sch.2 Ground 14, see *New Charter Housing (North) Ltd v Ashcroft* [2004] EWCA Civ 310, [2004] H.L.R. 36 (CA), Potter, L.J.

Sch.2A para.1, applied: 2002 c.30 s.100

Sch.2A para.2, applied: 2002 c.30 s.100

Sch.2A para.3, applied: 2002 c.30 s.100

Sch.2A para.5A, added: 2003 c.38 s.15

Sch.3 para.3, amended: 2004 c.33 Sch.8 para.44

Sch.10 Part I para.2, repealed: 2004 c.5 Sch.9

Sch.10 Part II para.4, amended: 2003 c.21 Sch.17 para.94

Sch.10 Part II para.5, amended: 2003 c.21 Sch.17 para.94

Sch.10 Part II para.11, amended: 2003 c.21 Sch.17 para.94

Sch.10 Part II para.12, amended: 2003 c.21 Sch.17 para.94

Sch.10 Part II para.14, amended: 2003 c.21 Sch.17 para.94

Sch.10 Part II para.19, repealed: 2003 c.21 Sch.19

Sch.11 para.1, amended: 2004 c.34 s.203

Sch.11 para.1, varied: 2004 c.34 s.203

Sch.11 para.1A, added: 2004 c.34 s.203

Sch.11 para.2, repealed (in part): 2002 c.9 Sch.13

Sch.11 para.2A, added: 2004 c.34 s.204

Sch.11 para.2B, added: 2004 c.34 s.204

Sch.11 para.4, amended: 2004 c.33 Sch.8 para.45, Sch.30

Sch.11 para.6, amended: 2004 c.34 s.204

Sch.11 para.8, added: 2004 c.34 s.205

Sch.15 para.1, repealed: 2004 c.34 Sch.16

Sch.15 para.2, repealed: 2004 c.34 Sch.16

1988–cont.

50. Housing Act 1988–*cont.*

Sch.15 para.3, repealed: 2004 c.34 Sch.16

Sch.15 para.4, repealed: 2004 c.34 Sch.16

Sch.15 para.5, repealed: 2004 c.34 Sch.16

Sch.15 para.6, repealed: 2004 c.34 Sch.16

Sch.15 para.7, repealed: 2004 c.34 Sch.16

Sch.15 para.8, repealed: 2004 c.34 Sch.16

Sch.15 para.9, repealed: 2004 c.34 Sch.16

Sch.15 para.10, repealed: 2004 c.34 Sch.16

Sch.15 para.11, repealed: 2004 c.34 Sch.16

Sch.15 para.12, repealed: 2004 c.34 Sch.16

Sch.15 para.13, repealed: 2004 c.34 Sch.16

Sch.17 Part I para.47, amended: 2004 c.34 Sch.15 para.33

Sch.17 Part I para.79, repealed: 2004 c.14 Sch.1 Part 10

Sch.17 Part I para.83, repealed: 2002 c.29 Sch.12

Sch.17 Part I para.84, repealed: 2002 c.29 Sch.12

51. Rate Support Grants Act 1988

repealed: 2004 c.14 Sch.1 Part 10

52. Road Traffic Act 1988

see *McPhee v Maguire* 2002 J.C. 45 (HCJ Appeal), Lord Coulsfield, Lord Caplan, Lord Osborne

applied: SI 2002/2742 Sch.2 para.4, SI 2003/1594 Art.2

referred to: 2003 c.32 Sch.5 para.17, 2003 c.43 Sch.4 para.73

Part III, applied: 2003 c.32 s.68, s.82, 2003 c.44 s.301, SI 2003/2994 Art.2, SI 2004/1267 Sch.1 para.37

Part III, referred to: SI 2002/2590 Art.2

Part IV, applied: SI 2003/2994 Art.2

Part V, applied: SI 2002/2934 Sch.2 Part 1

Part VI, applied: SI 2004/242 Reg.3

s.1, see *Hughes (Brian Andrew) v HM Advocate* 2002 J.C. 23 (HCJ Appeal), Lord Rodger L.J.G, Lord Cameron of Lochbroom, Lady Paton; see *R. v Davies (John Watkin)* [2001] EWCA Crim 2319, [2002] 1 Cr. App. R. (S.) 136 (CA (Crim Div)), Davis, J.; see *R. v Marchant (Thomas John)* [2003] EWCA Crim 2099, [2004] 1 W.L.R. 442 (CA (Crim Div)), Rose, L.J.

s.1, applied: 2003 c.32 Sch.3 para.3, 2003 c.42 Sch.5 para.49, Sch.5 para.92, 2003 c.44 Sch.15 para.48, SI 2004/1910 Sch.5, SSI 2003/441 Sch.1 para.21, SSI 2004/411 Sch.1 para.30

s.2, see *McLean v McLeod* 2002 S.C.C.R.127 (HCJ Appeal), Lord Coulsfield, Lord Caplan, Lord Philip; see *Young (Steven James) v Barbour* 2002 S.C.C.R. 84 (HCJ Appeal), Lord Cullen L.J.C., Lord Caplan, Lord Philip

s.2, applied: 2003 c.32 Sch.3 para.3

1988–cont.

52. Road Traffic Act 1988–*cont.*

s.2A, see *R. v Conteh (Kondeh)* [2003] EWCA Crim 962, [2004] R.T.R. 1 (CA (Crim Div)), Auld, L.J.; see *R. v Marchant (Thomas John)* [2003] EWCA Crim 2099, [2004] 1 W.L.R. 442 (CA (Crim Div)), Rose, L.J.

s.3, applied: 2002 c.30 s.59, 2003 c.32 Sch.3 para.3, 2004 asp 8 s.126

s.3A, see *Kennedy v CPS* [2002] EWHC 2297, (2003) 167 J.P. 267 (QBD (Admin Ct)), Kennedy, L.J.; see *R. v Drummond (Andrew)* [2002] EWCA Crim 527, [2002] 2 Cr. App. R. 25 (CA (Crim Div)), Longmore, L.J.; see *Ross (Hugh) v HM Advocate (Sentencing)* 2003 S.C.C.R. 1 (HCJ), Lord Cameron of Lochbroom, Lord Sutherland

s.3A, applied: 2003 c.17 Sch.4 para.14, 2003 c.32 Sch.3 para.3, 2003 c.42 Sch.5 para.50, Sch.5 para.93, 2003 c.44 Sch.15 para.49, SI 2004/1910 Sch.5, SSI 2003/441 Sch.1 para.22, SSI 2004/411 Sch.1 para.30

s.4, see *DPP v Robertson* [2002] EWHC 542, (2002) 166 J.P. 649 (QBD (Admin Ct)), Newman, J.

s.4, applied: 2003 c.17 Sch.4 para.14, 2003 c.32 Sch.3 para.3

s.5, see *Brown (Gary John) v Gallacher* 2002 S.L.T. 756 (HCJ Appeal), Lord Cameron of Lochbroom, Lord Hamilton, Lord Morison; see *DPP v Alderton* [2003] EWHC 2917, [2004] R.T.R. 23 (QBD (Admin Ct)), Harrison, J.; see *DPP v Janman* [2004] EWHC 101, [2004] R.T.R. 31 (QBD (Admin Ct)), May, L.J.; see *Goodson v Higson* 2002 S.L.T. 202 (HCJ Appeal), Lord Philip, Lord Caplan, Lord Cullen L.J.C.; see *Grant v DPP* [2003] EWHC 130, (2003) 167 J.P. 459 (QBD (Admin Ct)), Clarke, L.J.; see *Griffiths v DPP* [2002] EWHC 792, (2002) 166 J.P. 629 (QBD (Admin Ct)), Turner, J.; see *Jubb v DPP* [2002] EWHC 2317, (2003) 167 J.P. 50 (QBD (Admin Ct)), McCombe, J.; see *Kennedy v CPS* [2002] EWHC 2297, (2003) 167 J.P. 267 (QBD (Admin Ct)), Kennedy, L.J.; see *Mercer v DPP* [2003] EWHC 225, (2003) 167 J.P. 441 (QBD (Admin Ct)), Pitchford, J.; see *R. (on the application of DPP) v BE* [2002] EWHC 2976, (2003) 167 J.P. 144 (QBD (Admin Ct)), Maurice Kay, J.; see *R. (on the application of McCormack) v DPP* [2002] EWHC 173, [2002] R.T.R. 20 (QBD (Admin Ct)), Maurice Kay, J.; see *R. (on the application of Planton) v DPP* [2001] EWHC Admin 450, (2002) 166 J.P. 324 (QBD (Admin Ct)), Pill, L.J.; see *Sheldrake v DPP* [2003] EWHC 273, [2004] Q.B. 487 (QBD (Admin Ct)), Clarke, L.J.; see *Sheldrake v DPP* [2004]

1988–cont.

52. Road Traffic Act 1988–*cont.*

s.5–*cont.*

UKHL 43, [2004] 3 W.L.R. 976 (HL), Lord Bingham of Cornhill; see *Steadman v DPP* [2002] EWHC 810, [2003] R.T.R. 2 (QBD (Admin Ct)), Keith, J.; see *Stewart v DPP* [2003] EWHC 1323, (2004) 168 J.P. 82 (QBD (Admin Ct)), Goldring, J.

s.5, applied: 2003 c.17 Sch.4 para.14, 2003 c.32 Sch.3 para.3

s.6, see *DPP v Robertson* [2002] EWHC 542, (2002) 166 J.P. 649 (QBD (Admin Ct)), Newman, J.; see *Grant v DPP* [2003] EWHC 130, (2003) 167 J.P. 459 (QBD (Admin Ct)), Clarke, L.J.

s.6, applied: 2003 c.20 s.83, s.96, 2003 c.32 Sch.3 para.3

s.6, substituted: 2003 c.20 Sch.7 para.1

s.6, varied: 2003 c.20 s.83, s.96

s.6A, amended: 2003 c.20 Sch.7 para.1

s.6A, applied: 2003 c.20 s.83, s.96

s.6A, varied: 2003 c.20 s.83, s.96

s.6B, applied: 2003 c.20 s.83, s.96

s.6B, varied: 2003 c.20 s.83, s.96

s.6C, applied: 2003 c.20 s.83, s.96

s.6C, varied: 2003 c.20 s.83, s.96

s.6D, applied: 2003 c.20 s.83, s.96

s.6E, applied: 2003 c.20 s.83, s.96

s.7, see *Brown (Gary John) v Gallacher* 2002 S.L.T. 756 (HCJ Appeal), Lord Cameron of Lochbroom, Lord Hamilton, Lord Morison; see *Brown (Scott) v Gallacher* 2002 S.L.T. 1135 (HCJ), Lord Cameron of Lochbroom, Lord Gill L.J.C., Lord MacLean; see *DPP v Brown (Andrew Earle)* [2001] EWHC Admin 931, (2002) 166 J.P. 1 (QBD (Admin Ct)), Cresswell, J.; see *DPP v Memery* [2002] EWHC 1720, (2003) 167 J.P. 238 (QBD (Admin Ct)), Gibbs, J.; see *Joseph v DPP* [2003] EWHC 3078, (2004) 168 J.P. 575 (QBD (Admin Ct)), Lord Woolf of Barnes, L.C.J.; see *Jubb v DPP* [2002] EWHC 2317, (2003) 167 J.P. 50 (QBD (Admin Ct)), McCombe, J.; see *Kirkup v DPP* [2003] EWHC 2354, (2004) 168 J.P. 255 (QBD (Admin Ct)), Jackson, J.; see *Myles v DPP* [2004] EWHC 594, [2004] 2 All E.R. 902 (QBD (Admin Ct)), Kennedy, L.J.; see *Steadman v DPP* [2002] EWHC 810, [2003] R.T.R. 2 (QBD (Admin Ct)), Keith, J.; see *Stewart v DPP* [2003] EWHC 1323, (2004) 168 J.P. 82 (QBD (Admin Ct)), Goldring, J.; see *Whitley v DPP* [2003] EWHC 2512, (2004) 168 J.P. 350 (QBD (Admin Ct)), Brooke, L.J.

s.7, amended: 2002 c.30 s.55, 2003 c.20 Sch.7 para.2

s.7, applied: 2003 c.20 s.83, s.96, 2003 c.32 Sch.3 para.3

s.7, varied: 2003 c.20 s.83, s.96

s.7A, added: 2002 c.30 s.56

s.7A, applied: 2003 c.20 s.83, s.96

1988–cont.

52. Road Traffic Act 1988–*cont.*

s.8, see *Joseph v DPP* [2003] EWHC 3078, (2004) 168 J.P. 575 (QBD (Admin Ct)), Lord Woolf of Barnes, L.C.J.; see *R. (on the application of DPP) v BE* [2002] EWHC 2976, (2003) 167 J.P. 144 (QBD (Admin Ct)), Maurice Kay, J.

s.8, applied: 2003 c.20 s.83, s.96

s.8, varied: 2003 c.20 s.96

s.9, amended: 2002 c.30 s.56, 2003 c.20 Sch.7 para.3

s.9, applied: 2003 c.20 s.83, s.96

s.10, amended: 2003 c.20 Sch.7 para.4

s.10, applied: 2003 c.20 s.83, s.96

s.10, varied: 2003 c.20 s.83, s.96

s.11, see *Stewart v DPP* [2003] EWHC 1323, (2004) 168 J.P. 82 (QBD (Admin Ct)), Goldring, J.

s.11, amended: 2002 c.30 s.55, 2003 c.20 Sch.7 para.5, Sch.8

s.11, applied: 2003 c.20 s.83, s.96, SI 2003/ 2462 Art.2

s.11, varied: 2003 c.20 s.83, s.96

s.11, enabling: SI 2003/2462

s.12, applied: 2003 c.32 Sch.3 para.4

s.13, enabling: SSI 2002/14

s.14, amended: 2003 c.20 s.110

s.18, applied: SI 2004/2922 Art.2

s.19, applied: 2004 c.18 Sch.7 para.3, Sch.7 para.4

s.21, amended: 2003 c.21 Sch.17 para.95

s.21, applied: 2004 c.18 Sch.7 para.3, Sch.7 para.4

s.25, applied: SI 2002/1917 Art.2

s.34, see *Massey v Boulden* [2002] EWCA Civ 1634, [2003] 1 W.L.R. 1792 (CA), Simon Brown, L.J.

s.34, applied: 2002 c.30 s.59, 2004 asp 8 s.126

s.35, amended: 2004 c.18 s.6

s.35, applied: 2004 c.18 s.6

s.35, varied: 2002 c.30 Sch.4 para.12, Sch.5 para.9, SI 2004/915 Sch.1 para.10

s.36, applied: SI 2002/3113 Reg.10, 2003 asp 1 s.46, 2004 c.18 Sch.7 para.3, Sch.7 para.4, Sch.7 para.8, Sch.7 para.10

s.36, repealed (in part): 2004 c.18 Sch.12 Part 1

s.36, enabling: SI 2002/3113

s.37, amended: 2004 c.18 s.6

s.37, varied: 2002 c.30 Sch.4 para.12, Sch.5 para.9, SI 2004/915 Sch.1 para.10

s.38, see *Gilfillan v Barbour* 2003 S.L.T. 1127 (OH), Lord Reed

s.39, see *Gorringe v Calderdale MBC* [2002] EWCA Civ 595, [2002] R.T.R. 27 (CA), Potter, L.J.; see *Gorringe v Calderdale MBC* [2004] UKHL 15, [2004] 1 W.L.R. 1057 (HL), Lord Steyn

1988–cont.

52. Road Traffic Act 1988–*cont.*

s.40A, see *R. v Marchant (Thomas John)* [2003] EWCA Crim 2099, [2004] 1 W.L.R. 442 (CA (Crim Div)), Rose, L.J.

s.41, applied: SI 2003/1998 Art.53

s.41, enabling: SI 2002/227, SI 2002/335, SI 2002/1474, SI 2002/2126, SI 2003/182, SI 2003/1690, SI 2003/1946, SI 2003/2695, SI 2003/3145, SI 2004/1706, SI 2004/2102

s.41B, see *Kelly Communications Ltd v DPP* [2002] EWHC 2752, (2003) 167 J.P. 73 (QBD (Admin Ct)), Hallett, J.

s.42, applied: SI 2002/1808 Reg.7, SI 2003/300 Reg.7, SSI 2003/212 Reg.7

s.44, see *R. v Marchant (Thomas John)* [2003] EWCA Crim 2099, [2004] 1 W.L.R. 442 (CA (Crim Div)), Rose, L.J.

s.44, enabling: SI 2003/1998

s.45, applied: SI 2002/1808 Reg.9, Reg.19, SI 2002/2742 Sch.2 para.13, SI 2003/300 Reg.9, Reg.19, SI 2003/1113 Reg.25, SI 2004/1896 Reg.3, SR 2003/303 Reg.5, Reg.6, SSI 2003/212 Reg.9, Reg.20

s.45, enabling: SI 2002/488, SI 2002/1698, SI 2003/1113, SI 2003/1698, SI 2003/1815, SI 2004/1632, SI 2004/1879

s.46, applied: SI 2003/1113 Reg.25

s.46, enabling: SI 2002/488, SI 2002/1698, SI 2003/1113, SI 2003/1698, SI 2003/1815, SI 2004/1632, SI 2004/1879

s.47, applied: SI 2004/242 Reg.3, SI 2004/1896 Reg.3

s.47, referred to: SI 2003/1253 Art.2

s.49, referred to: SI 2002/2742 Sch.2 para.13

s.49, enabling: SI 2002/487, SI 2003/1816, SI 2004/1873

s.51, enabling: SI 2002/487, SI 2003/1816, SI 2004/1873

s.52, applied: SI 2002/2742 Sch.2 para.13

s.53, applied: SI 2004/2577 Reg.3

s.53, enabling: SI 2002/487, SI 2003/1816

s.54, applied: SI 2002/2742 Sch.2 para.4, SI 2003/1959 Reg.7, Reg.14, SI 2003/1998 Sch.2 para.2, Sch.2 para.15, Sch.3 para.2, Sch.3 para.8

s.54, enabling: SI 2003/582, SI 2003/1866, SI 2003/1959, SI 2004/623

s.55, applied: SI 2003/1959 Reg.14

s.56, applied: SI 2003/1959 Reg.14

s.57, applied: SI 2002/2742 Sch.2 para.4, SI 2003/1959 Reg.14

s.58, applied: SI 2003/1959 Reg.5, Reg.7, Reg.10, Reg.14

s.60, enabling: SI 2003/1959

s.61, applied: SI 2003/1959 Reg.2

s.61, enabling: SI 2003/582, SI 2003/1866, SI 2003/1959, SI 2003/1960, SI 2003/2258, SI 2004/623, SI 2004/2106

s.63, applied: SI 2003/1959 Reg.13, Reg.14

s.63, disapplied: SR 2003/303 Reg.6

1988–cont.

52. Road Traffic Act 1988–*cont.*

s.63, enabling: SI 2003/1959, SI 2004/623

s.65A, repealed (in part): 2004 c.36 Sch.2 para.9, Sch.3

s.66, referred to: SI 2003/2994 Art.2

s.66, enabling: SI 2003/1959, SI 2004/623, SI 2004/1896, SI 2004/2577

s.67, applied: 2002 c.30 Sch.4 para.11, Sch.5 para.8, SI 2002/2426 Reg.2, SI 2004/915 Sch.1 para.8

s.67A, repealed: 2004 c.14 Sch.1 Part 14

s.67B, repealed: 2004 c.14 Sch.1 Part 14

s.68, applied: SI 2002/2426 Reg.2

s.75, see *Devon CC v DB Cars Ltd* [2001] EWHC Admin 521, (2002) 166 J.P. 38 (QBD (Admin Ct)), Forbes, J.

s.75, applied: SI 2003/1376 Sch.1, SI 2003/1593 Sch.1 Part I

s.76, applied: SI 2003/1376 Sch.1, SI 2003/1593 Sch.1 Part I

s.85, amended: SI 2003/1099 Reg.3, 2004 c.21 Sch.1 para.69

s.87, see *Momoh v Gallacher* 2003 S.L.T. 1155 (HCJ), Lord Hamilton, Lord Clarke, Lord Marnoch

s.88, amended: 2003 c.32 Sch.5 para.18

s.88, enabling: SI 2003/166

s.89, enabling: SI 2002/2590, SI 2002/2641, SI 2003/166, SI 2003/636, SI 2003/2003, SI 2003/3313, SI 2004/3028

s.90, amended: 2003 c.39 Sch.8 para.306, Sch.10

s.92, amended: 2003 c.32 Sch.5 para.19

s.92, enabling: SI 2003/166

s.93, amended: 2003 c.32 s.79

s.94A, amended: 2003 c.32 Sch.5 para.20

s.95, applied: SI 2002/335

s.97, amended: 2003 c.32 s.78, Sch.5 para.21

s.97, applied: 2003 c.32 s.68

s.97, referred to: SI 2003/2994 Art.2

s.97, enabling: SI 2003/166, SI 2003/222, SI 2004/265

s.99, amended: 2003 c.32 s.78

s.99A, applied: 2003 c.32 s.65

s.100, amended: 2003 c.32 Sch.5 para.22, 2003 c.39 Sch.8 para.307, Sch.10

s.101, enabling: SI 2003/166, SI 2004/1519

s.102, substituted: 2003 c.32 s.78

s.102A, added: 2003 c.32 s.76

s.103, amended: 2002 c.30 Sch.7 para.11

s.103, applied: 2003 c.32 Sch.3 para.5

s.103, referred to: 2002 c.30 s.108

s.103, repealed (in part): 2002 c.30 Sch.7 para.11

s.105, amended: 2003 c.32 Sch.5 para.23

s.105, enabling: SI 2002/2641, SI 2003/166, SI 2003/222, SI 2003/636, SI 2003/2003, SI 2003/3313, SI 2004/265, SI 2004/1519, SI 2004/3028

s.107, amended: 2003 c.32 Sch.5 para.24

1988–cont.

52. Road Traffic Act 1988–cont.

s.108, amended: 2003 c.32 Sch.5 para.25, Sch.6

s.108, applied: SI 2002/1593, SI 2002/2379, SI 2002/2379 Art.3, Art.4, SI 2004/301, SI 2004/301 Art.3

s.108, disapplied: SI 2002/1593 Art.2

s.108, enabling: SI 2002/1593, SI 2002/2379, SI 2004/301

s.109, amended: 2003 c.32 Sch.5 para.26

s.109, repealed (in part): 2003 c.32 Sch.6

s.109A, added: 2003 c.32 s.77

s.109B, added: 2003 c.32 s.79

s.109C, added: 2003 c.32 s.79

s.112, see *Secretary of State for Transport, Local Government and the Regions v Snowdon* [2002] EWHC 2394, [2003] R.T.R. 15 (QBD (Admin Ct)), Nigel Pleming Q.C.

s.114, enabling: SI 2003/636, SI 2004/1519

s.119, amended: 2003 c.39 Sch.8 para.308, Sch.10

s.120, enabling: SI 2003/166, SI 2003/636, SI 2004/265, SI 2004/1519

s.121, see *Secretary of State for Transport, Local Government and the Regions v Snowdon* [2002] EWHC 2394, [2003] R.T.R. 15 (QBD (Admin Ct)), Nigel Pleming Q.C.

s.125, enabling: SI 2002/2640, SI 2003/3027, SI 2004/3159

s.132, enabling: SI 2002/2640, SI 2003/3027, SI 2004/2871, SI 2004/3159

s.133, amended: 2003 c.39 Sch.8 para.309

s.134, enabling: SI 2004/3159

s.141, enabling: SI 2004/2871

s.143, see *DPP v Heritage* [2002] EWHC 2139, (2002) 166 J.P. 772 (QBD (Admin Ct)), Jackson, J.; see *Lloyd-Wolper v Moore* [2004] EWCA Civ 766, [2004] 1 W.L.R. 2350 (CA), Pill, L.J.; see *Winter v DPP* [2002] EWHC 1524, [2003] R.T.R. 14 (QBD (Admin Ct)), Michael Supperstone Q.C.

s.143, referred to: SI 2003/1253 Art.2

s.144, amended: 2002 c.17 Sch.5 para.29, 2003 c.43 Sch.4 para.74

s.145, amended: 2003 c.43 Sch.14 Part 3

s.145, applied: SI 2002/3061 Reg.2

s.151, see *Charlton v Fisher* [2001] EWCA Civ 112, [2002] Q.B. 578 (CA), Kennedy, L.J.; see *Lloyd-Wolper v Moore* [2004] EWCA Civ 766, [2004] 1 W.L.R. 2350 (CA), Pill, L.J.; see *Nawaz v Crowe Insurance Group* [2003] EWCA Civ 316, [2003] C.P. Rep. 41 (CA), Lord Woolf of Barnes, L.C.J.

s.152, see *Nawaz v Crowe Insurance Group* [2003] EWCA Civ 316, [2003] C.P. Rep. 41 (CA), Lord Woolf of Barnes, L.C.J.

s.153, amended: SI 2003/2096 Sch.1 para.14

s.157, amended: 2002 asp 5 s.20

s.157, disapplied: 2003 c.43 s.165

s.158, amended: 2002 asp 5 s.20

1988–cont.

52. Road Traffic Act 1988–cont.

s.158, applied: SI 2004/291 Sch.5 para.1, SI 2004/478 Sch.5 para.1, SI 2004/627 Sch.3, SSI 2003/64 Sch.1 para.11, SSI 2004/115 Sch.4 para.1

s.158, disapplied: 2003 c.43 s.165

s.159, disapplied: 2003 c.43 s.165

s.161, repealed (in part): 2003 c.43 s.169, Sch.14 Part 3

s.163, amended: 2002 c.30 s.49, 2004 c.18 s.6

s.163, applied: 2002 c.30 Sch.4 para.11A, Sch.4 para.13, Sch.5 para.8A, SI 2004/915 Sch.1 para.9

s.164, amended: 2003 c.32 Sch.5 para.27, 2003 c.44 Sch.32 para.51

s.167, amended: 2003 c.32 Sch.5 para.28

s.170, applied: 2003 c.32 Sch.3 para.6

s.172, see *Brown v Stott* [2003] 1 A.C. 681 (Privy Council (Scotland)), Lord Bingham of Cornhill, Lord Clyde, Lord Hope, Lord Kirkwood, Lord Steyn; see *DPP v Broomfield* [2002] EWHC 1962, (2002) 166 J.P. 736 (QBD (Admin Ct)), Judge Wilkie Q.C.; see *DPP v Wilson* [2001] EWHC Admin 198, [2002] R.T.R. 6 (QBD (Admin Ct)), Sullivan, J.; see *Francis v DPP* [2004] EWHC 591, (2004) 168 J.P. 492 (QBD (Admin Ct)), Kennedy, L.J.; see *Jones v DPP* [2004] EWHC 236, [2004] R.T.R. 20 (QBD (Admin Ct)), May, L.J.; see *Mawdesley v Chief Constable of Cheshire* [2003] EWHC 1586, [2004] 1 W.L.R. 1035 (QBD (Admin Ct)), Owen, J.; see *Mohindra v DPP* [2004] EWHC 490, (2004) 168 J.P. 448 (QBD (Admin Ct)), Moses, J.

s.172, amended: 2004 c.14 Sch.1 Part 14

s.172, referred to: SI 2003/1253 Art.2

s.173, amended: 2003 c.32 Sch.5 para.29

s.176, amended: 2003 c.32 Sch.5 para.30

s.178, see *Currie v Clamp* 2002 S.L.T. 196 (OH), Lord Clarke

s.183, amended: 2002 c.30 Sch.8

s.183, referred to: 2002 c.30 s.108

s.184, amended: 2003 c.20 Sch.7 para.6

s.192, referred to: SI 2002/3113 Reg.22

s.193A, amended: 2003 c.32 Sch.5 para.31

s.195, applied: SI 2002/3113(a), SI 2002/227, SI 2002/487, SI 2002/488, SI 2002/1698, SI 2002/2126, SI 2002/2641, SI 2003/166, SI 2003/182, SI 2003/222, SI 2003/582, SI 2003/636, SI 2003/1113, SI 2003/1690, SI 2003/1698, SI 2003/1815, SI 2003/1816, SI 2003/1866, SI 2003/1946, SI 2003/1959, SI 2003/1960, SI 2003/2003, SI 2003/2258, SI 2003/2695, SI 2003/3145, SI 2003/3313, SI 2004/265, SI 2004/623, SI 2004/1519, SI 2004/1632, SI 2004/1706, SI 2004/1873, SI 2004/1879, SI 2004/1896, SI

1988–cont.

52. Road Traffic Act 1988–*cont.*

s.195, applied:–*cont.*

2004/2102, SI 2004/2106, SI 2004/2577, SI 2004/2871, SSI 2002/14

s.195, enabling: SSI 2002/14

53. Road Traffic Offenders Act 1988

Commencement Orders: 2004 c.14 Sch.1 Part 14

applied: SI 2004/2541 Sch.1, SI 2004/2542 Sch.1

referred to: 2003 c.32 Sch.5 para.32

Part III, applied: SI 2003/1253 Art.2, SI 2004/2922 Art.2

Part III, referred to: 2002 c.30 s.108

s.1, applied: 2003 c.32 Sch.5 para.36

s.3, amended: 2003 c.32 Sch.5 para.33

s.6, applied: 2003 c.32 Sch.5 para.36

s.7, see *Jubb v DPP* [2002] EWHC 2317, (2003) 167 J.P. 50 (QBD (Admin Ct)), McCombe, J.

s.7, amended: 2003 c.39 Sch.8 para.310

s.8, amended: 2003 c.39 Sch.8 para.311

s.11, applied: 2003 c.32 Sch.5 para.36

s.11, repealed (in part): 2003 c.44 Sch.37 Part 4, Sch.3 para.61

s.12, see *Francis v DPP* [2004] EWHC 591, (2004) 168 J.P. 492 (QBD (Admin Ct)), Kennedy, L.J.; see *Mawdesley v Chief Constable of Cheshire* [2003] EWHC 1586, [2004] 1 W.L.R. 1035 (QBD (Admin Ct)), Owen, J.

s.12, amended: SI 2004/2035 Sch.1 para.30

s.12, applied: 2003 c.32 Sch.5 para.36

s.13, amended: SI 2004/2035 Sch.1 para.31

s.13, repealed (in part): 2003 c.44 Sch.37 Part 4, Sch.3 para.61

s.15, see *DPP v Chambers* [2003] EWHC 2142, (2004) 168 J.P. 231 (QBD (Admin Ct)), Maurice Kay, J.; see *Griffiths v DPP* [2002] EWHC 792, (2002) 166 J.P. 629 (QBD (Admin Ct)), Turner, J.; see *Jones v Crown Prosecution Service* [2003] EWHC 1729, (2003) 167 J.P. 481 (QBD (Admin Ct)), Douglas Brown, J.; see *Jubb v DPP* [2002] EWHC 2317, (2003) 167 J.P. 50 (QBD (Admin Ct)), McCombe, J.; see *Lonergan v DPP* [2002] EWHC 1263, [2003] R.T.R. 12 (QBD (Admin Ct)), Elias, J.; see *R. v Drummond (Andrew)* [2002] EWCA Crim 527, [2002] 2 Cr. App. R. 25 (CA (Crim Div)), Longmore, L.J.

s.15, amended: 2002 c.30 s.57

s.15, applied: 2003 c.20 s.83, s.96

s.15, varied: 2003 c.20 s.83, s.96

s.16, see *Jubb v DPP* [2002] EWHC 2317, (2003) 167 J.P. 50 (QBD (Admin Ct)), McCombe, J.; see *R. (on the application of McCormack) v DPP* [2002] EWHC 173, [2002] R.T.R. 20 (QBD (Admin Ct)), Maurice Kay, J.

s.16, amended: 2002 c.30 s.57

1988–cont.

53. Road Traffic Offenders Act 1988–*cont.*

s.16, applied: 2003 c.20 s.83, s.96

s.16, repealed (in part): 2003 c.44 Sch.37 Part 4, Sch.3 para.61

s.20, repealed (in part): 2003 c.44 Sch.37 Part 4, Sch.3 para.61

s.25, amended: 2003 c.39 Sch.8 para.311

s.26, amended: 2003 c.32 Sch.5 para.34, 2003 c.39 Sch.8 para.312

s.27, amended: 2003 c.39 Sch.8 para.313, 2003 c.44 Sch.32 para.53

s.27, repealed (in part): 2004 c.14 Sch.1 Part 14

s.30, repealed (in part): 2004 c.14 Sch.1 Part 14

s.34, see *DPP v Barker* [2004] EWHC 2502, (2004) 168 J.P. 617 (QBD (Admin)), Collins, J.

s.34, amended: 2002 c.30 s.56, Sch.8

s.34A, applied: 2003 c.32 s.55

s.36, see *DPP v Barker* [2004] EWHC 2502, (2004) 168 J.P. 617 (QBD (Admin)), Collins, J.

s.37, see *DPP v Barker* [2004] EWHC 2502, (2004) 168 J.P. 617 (QBD (Admin)), Collins, J.

s.42, applied: 2003 c.32 s.55, SSI 2003/179 Reg.3

s.46, repealed (in part): 2003 c.44 Sch.32 para.54, Sch.37 Part 7

s.51, enabling: SI 2003/1253, SI 2004/2922

s.52, amended: 2003 c.39 Sch.8 para.314

s.52, repealed (in part): 2004 c.14 Sch.1 Part 14

s.53, amended: 2004 c.28 s.16

s.53, enabling: SI 2003/1254

s.54, amended: 2002 c.30 s.76

s.54, applied: 2002 c.30 Sch.4 para.1, Sch.5 para.1, SI 2004/915 Sch.1 para.1

s.54, varied: 2003 c.20 Sch.5 para.4

s.59, repealed: 2004 c.14 Sch.1 Part 14

s.69, amended: 2003 c.39 Sch.8 para.315

s.70, amended: 2003 c.39 Sch.8 para.316

s.71, amended: 2003 c.39 Sch.8 para.317

s.71, applied: 2003 c.39 Sch.5 para.3

s.74, amended: 2003 c.39 Sch.8 para.318

s.75, amended: 2002 c.30 s.76, 2003 c.20 s.69, 2003 c.39 Sch.8 para.319

s.75, applied: SI 2004/953 Art.2

s.75, varied: 2003 c.20 Sch.5 para.4

s.76, amended: 2002 c.30 s.76, 2003 c.20 s.69, Sch.8

s.82, amended: 2003 c.39 Sch.8 para.320

s.82, repealed (in part): 2003 c.39 Sch.8 para.320, Sch.10

s.83, amended: 2003 c.39 Sch.8 para.321

s.84, amended: 2003 c.39 Sch.8 para.322, 2004 c.28 s.16

s.87, amended: 2002 c.30 s.76

s.87, varied: 2003 c.20 Sch.5 para.4

1988–cont.

53. Road Traffic Offenders Act 1988–*cont.*

s.88, applied: SI 2003/1253, SI 2003/1254, SI 2004/2922

s.89, amended: 2002 c.30 s.76, 2003 c.20 Sch.5 para.4

s.89, varied: 2003 c.20 Sch.5 para.4

s.91A, applied: 2003 c.32 s.55

s.91ZA, added: 2003 c.32 s.77

s.91ZB, added: 2003 c.32 s.77

s.95, substituted: SI 2004/956 Art.2

s.98, amended: 2003 c.32 Sch.5 para.35

s.99, repealed (in part): 2004 c.14 Sch.1 Part 14

Sch.1 para.2, repealed (in part): 2004 c.14 Sch.1 Part 14

Sch.1 para.3, repealed (in part): 2004 c.14 Sch.1 Part 14

Sch.1 para.4, amended: 2002 c.30 s.56, 2003 c.20 Sch.7 para.7, 2003 c.32 Sch.5 para.36, 2004 c.14 Sch.1 Part 14, 2004 c.18 Sch.12 Part 2

Sch.1 para.4, repealed (in part): 2004 c.14 Sch.1 Part 14

Sch.2, see *Mercer v DPP* [2003] EWHC 225, (2003) 167 J.P. 441 (QBD (Admin Ct)), Pitchford, J.; see *R. (on the application of Planton) v DPP* [2001] EWHC Admin 450, (2002) 166 J.P. 324 (QBD (Admin Ct)), Pill, L.J.

Sch.2 Part I, amended: 2002 c.30 s.56, 2003 c.20 Sch.7 para.8, 2003 c.32 Sch.5 para.37, Sch.6, 2003 c.44 s.285, s.286, 2004 c.14 Sch.1 Part 14, 2004 c.18 s.6, Sch.12 Part 2

Sch.2 Part I, applied: SI 2002/3113 Reg.10

Sch.2 Part I, referred to: 2003 c.32 Sch.3 para.7

Sch.2 Part I, substituted: 2003 c.44 Sch.26 para.38

Sch.3, amended: SI 2003/1253 Art.2, 2004 c.18 Sch.12 Part 2, SI 2004/2922 Art.2

Sch.5, amended: 2004 c.14 Sch.1 Part 14

1989

Children's Act 1989

s.31, see *A Local Authority v S* [2004] EWHC 1270, [2004] 2 F.L.R. 129 (Fam Div), Hedley, J.

ii. London Regional Transport Act 1989

varied: SI 2003/1615 Sch.2 para.15

xi. London Regional Transport (No.2) Act 1989

varied: SI 2003/1615 Sch.2 para.16

Superannuation Schemes Act 1989

s.9, see *Bank of New Zealand v Bank of New Zealand Officers Provident Association Management Board* [2003] UKPC 58, [2003] O.P.L.R. 281 (PC (NZ)), Lord Hoffmann

1989–cont.

3. Elected Authorities (Northern Ireland) Act 1989

s.1, enabling: SI 2002/1873

s.2, applied: SI 2003/1557 Reg.4

Sch.1, applied: SI 2003/1557 Reg.4

Sch.1, enabling: SI 2002/1873

Sch.1 Part I, amended: 2002 c.13 s.7

4. Prevention of Terrorism (Temporary Provisions) Act 1989

s.14, see *Cullen v Chief Constable of the Royal Ulster Constabulary* [2003] UKHL 39, [2003] 1 W.L.R. 1736 (HL (NI)), Lord Bingham of Cornhill

6. Official Secrets Act 1989

see *R. v Shayler (David Michael) (Application for Permission to Appeal)* [2003] EWCA Crim 2218, [2003] A.C.D. 79 (CA (Crim Div)), Kennedy, L.J.

applied: 2002 asp 11 s.19

s.1, see *R. v Shayler (David Michael)* [2002] UKHL 11, [2003] 1 A.C. 247 (HL), Lord Bingham of Cornhill

s.4, see *R. v Shayler (David Michael)* [2002] UKHL 11, [2003] 1 A.C. 247 (HL), Lord Bingham of Cornhill

s.7, enabling: SI 2003/1918

s.8, enabling: SI 2003/1918

s.9, amended: 2002 c.26 Sch.7 para.32

s.10, amended: 2003 c.44 Sch.26 para.39

s.11, repealed (in part): 2002 c.30 Sch.8

s.12, amended: 2004 c.20 Sch.14 para.6

s.12, enabling: SI 2003/1918

s.13, referred to: SI 2003/1918

Sch.1 para.1, repealed (in part): 2002 asp 11 Sch.6 para.12

7. Atomic Energy Act 1989

s.5, amended: 2002 c.8 s.2

10. Disabled Persons (Northern Ireland) Act 1989

s.2, amended: SI 2003/431 Sch.4

s.8, disapplied: 2002 c.6 (NI) s.1

13. Dock Work Act 1989

s.1, repealed: 2004 c.14 Sch.1 Part 8

s.2, repealed: 2004 c.14 Sch.1 Part 8

s.3, repealed: 2004 c.14 Sch.1 Part 8

s.4, repealed: 2004 c.14 Sch.1 Part 8

s.5, repealed: 2004 c.14 Sch.1 Part 8

s.7, repealed (in part): 2004 c.14 Sch.1 Part 8

Sch.2 para.1, repealed: 2004 c.14 Sch.1 Part 8

Sch.2 para.3, repealed: 2004 c.14 Sch.1 Part 8

Sch.2 para.4, repealed (in part): 2004 c.14 Sch.1 Part 8

Sch.2 para.8, repealed: 2004 c.14 Sch.1 Part 8

Sch.2 para.9, repealed: 2004 c.14 Sch.1 Part 8

14. Control of Pollution (Amendment) Act 1989

s.7, amended: 2003 c.38 s.55

s.9, amended: 2003 c.38 s.55

s.11, repealed (in part): 2004 c.14 Sch.1 Part 13

CAP.

1989–cont.

15. Water Act 1989

applied: 2002 c.40 Sch.15, SI 2003/419 Art.63

s.112, applied: SI 2003/2261 Sch.3 Part I

s.165, see *Thames Water Utilities Ltd v Digginwell Plant & Construction Ltd* [2002] EWHC 1171, [2003] Env. L.R. 21 (QBD (T&CC)), Judge Richard Seymour Q.C.

s.174, amended: 2002 c.40 Sch.25 para.19, 2003 c.21 Sch.17 para.96, 2003 c.37 Sch.7 para.26, Sch.8 para.1

s.185, repealed (in part): 2003 c.37 Sch.7 para.26, Sch.9 Part 3

Sch.3 para.6, repealed: 2003 c.37 Sch.7 para.26, Sch.9 Part 3

Sch.3 para.7, repealed: 2003 c.37 Sch.7 para.26, Sch.9 Part 3

Sch.4 para.6, repealed: 2003 c.37 Sch.7 para.26, Sch.9 Part 3

Sch.17 para.4, amended: 2003 asp 15 Sch.4 para.3

Sch.17 para.4, substituted: 2003 asp 15 Sch.4 para.3

Sch.25 para.1, repealed (in part): 2004 c.36 Sch.3

Sch.25 para.9, repealed (in part): 2004 c.21 Sch.2

Sch.25 para.45, amended: SI 2003/1398 Sch.1 para.8

Sch.25 para.45, repealed (in part): 2002 c.40 Sch.26

Sch.25 para.47, repealed: 2002 c.40 Sch.26

Sch.25 para.57, repealed: 2002 c.40 Sch.26

Sch.25 para.59, repealed (in part): 2002 c.40 Sch.26

Sch.25 para.68, repealed (in part): 2003 c.37 Sch.7 para.26, Sch.9 Part 3

Sch.25 para.76, repealed (in part): 2003 c.37 Sch.7 para.26, Sch.9 Part 3

20. Licensing (Amendment) Act 1989

repealed: 2003 c.17 Sch.7

22. Road Traffic (Driver Licensing and Information Systems) Act 1989

s.1, amended: 2004 c.14 Sch.1 Part 14

s.1, repealed (in part): 2004 c.14 Sch.1 Part 14

s.9, amended: 2003 c.21 Sch.17 para.97

Sch.1, applied: SI 2003/2994 Art.2

Sch.1 Part I para.1, repealed: 2004 c.14 Sch.1 Part 14

Sch.1 Part I para.2, repealed: 2004 c.14 Sch.1 Part 14

Sch.1 Part I para.3, repealed: 2004 c.14 Sch.1 Part 14

Sch.1 Part I para.4, repealed: 2004 c.14 Sch.1 Part 14

Sch.1 Part I para.5, repealed: 2004 c.14 Sch.1 Part 14

Sch.1 Part I para.6, repealed: 2004 c.14 Sch.1 Part 14

CAP.

1989–cont.

22. Road Traffic (Driver Licensing and Information Systems) Act 1989–*cont.*

Sch.1 Part I para.7, repealed: 2004 c.14 Sch.1 Part 14

Sch.1 Part I para.8, repealed: 2004 c.14 Sch.1 Part 14

Sch.1 Part I para.9, repealed: 2004 c.14 Sch.1 Part 14

Sch.1 Part II para.10, repealed: 2004 c.14 Sch.1 Part 14

Sch.1 Part II para.11, repealed: 2004 c.14 Sch.1 Part 14

Sch.1 Part II para.12, repealed: 2004 c.14 Sch.1 Part 14

Sch.3 para.1, repealed: 2004 c.14 Sch.1 Part 14

Sch.3 para.7, repealed: 2004 c.14 Sch.1 Part 14

Sch.3 para.10, repealed: 2004 c.14 Sch.1 Part 14

Sch.3 para.13, repealed: 2004 c.14 Sch.1 Part 14

Sch.3 para.17, repealed: 2004 c.14 Sch.1 Part 14

Sch.3 para.25, repealed: 2004 c.14 Sch.1 Part 14

Sch.3 para.27, repealed (in part): 2004 c.14 Sch.1 Part 14

Sch.3 para.29, repealed: 2004 c.14 Sch.1 Part 14

Sch.3 para.30, repealed (in part): 2004 c.14 Sch.1 Part 14

Sch.4 para.4, amended: 2003 c.21 Sch.17 para.97

Sch.5 para.8, amended: 2003 c.21 Sch.17 para.97

23. Transport (Scotland) Act 1989

applied: SSI 2002/263

s.14, enabling: SSI 2002/263

24. Social Security Act 1989

Sch.5 Part I para.3, applied: 2004 c.35 s.318

Sch.5 Part I para.5, applied: SI 2002/2788 Reg.14, Reg.27

Sch.5 Part I para.5A, added: 2004 c.35 s.265

Sch.5 Part I para.5A, applied: SI 2002/2788 Reg.14, Reg.27

Sch.5 Part I para.5A, referred to: 2004 c.35 s.265

Sch.5 Part I para.5B, added: 2004 c.35 s.265

Sch.5 Part I para.5B, applied: SI 2002/2788 Reg.14, Reg.27

Sch.5 Part I para.5B, referred to: 2004 c.35 s.265

Sch.5 Part I para.6, applied: SI 2002/2788 Reg.14, Reg.27

26. Finance Act 1989

referred to: 2003 c.1 Sch.6 para.156

s.27, repealed: 2004 c.14 Sch.1 Part 9

s.36, repealed: 2003 c.1 Sch.8 Part 1

s.37, repealed: 2003 c.1 Sch.8 Part 1

s.38, repealed: 2003 c.1 Sch.8 Part 1

1989–cont.

26. Finance Act 1989–*cont.*

s.39, repealed: 2003 c.1 Sch.8 Part 1

s.40, repealed: 2003 c.1 Sch.8 Part 1

s.41, repealed: 2003 c.1 Sch.8 Part 1

s.42, repealed: 2003 c.1 Sch.8 Part 1

s.43, see *Dextra Accessories Ltd v Macdonald (Inspector of Taxes)* [2002] S.T.C. (S.C.D.) 413 (Sp Comm), JF Avery Jones; see *Dextra Accessories Ltd v Macdonald (Inspector of Taxes)* [2004] EWCA Civ 22, [2004] S.T.C. 339 (CA), Potter, L.J.

s.43, amended: 2002 c.23 Sch.40 Part 3, 2003 c.14 Sch.24 para.10, 2004 c.12 Sch.17 para.4

s.43, substituted: 2003 c.1 Sch.6 para.157

s.43, varied: 2003 c.14 Sch.24 para.11

s.44, amended: 2003 c.14 Sch.24 para.10, SI 2004/2310 Sch.1 para.42

s.44, substituted: 2003 c.1 Sch.6 para.158

s.44, varied: 2003 c.14 Sch.24 para.11

s.45, repealed: 2003 c.1 Sch.8 Part 1

s.50, see *Lord Hanson v Mansworth (Inspector of Taxes)* [2004] S.T.C. (S.C.D.) 288 (Sp Comm), Nuala Brice

s.50, repealed: 2003 c.1 Sch.8 Part 1

s.51, repealed: 2003 c.1 Sch.8 Part 1

s.52, repealed: 2003 c.1 Sch.8 Part 1

s.53, amended: 2003 c.1 Sch.8 Part 1

s.53, repealed (in part): 2003 c.1 Sch.8 Part 1, Sch.8 Part 1

s.62, repealed: 2003 c.1 Sch.8 Part 1

s.64, repealed: 2003 c.1 Sch.8 Part 1

s.66, repealed: 2003 c.1 Sch.8 Part 1

s.67, applied: 2003 c.14 Sch.24 para.8

s.67, disapplied: 2003 c.14 s.142

s.69, amended: 2003 c.1 Sch.6 para.160

s.69, applied: 2003 c.1 Sch.2 para.78, 2003 c.14 s.142

s.69, referred to: 2003 c.1 Sch.2 para.78

s.69, varied: 2003 c.14 s.142

s.75, repealed: 2004 c.12 Sch.42 Part 3

s.76, amended: 2003 c.1 Sch.6 para.161, 2004 c.12 Sch.17 para.10, SI 2004/2310 Sch.1 para.43

s.76, applied: 2002 c.23 Sch.29 para.112, 2003 c.1 Sch.7 para.12

s.76, repealed: 2004 c.12 Sch.42 Part 3

s.77, repealed: 2004 c.12 Sch.42 Part 3

s.82, amended: 2004 c.12 Sch.7 para.5

s.82, applied: 2003 c.14 Sch.33 para.1

s.82, substituted: 2003 c.14 Sch.33 para.1

s.82A, enabling: SI 2003/2082

s.82B, varied: 2003 c.14 Sch.33 para.1

s.82C, added: 2004 c.12 Sch.7 para.5

s.83, amended: 2003 c.14 Sch.33 para.2, Sch.43 Part 3, SI 2004/3266 Art.8

s.83, applied: SI 2003/1860 Art.2, SI 2003/2082 Reg.5

s.83, repealed (in part): 2003 c.14 Sch.43 Part 3

1989–cont.

26. Finance Act 1989–*cont.*

s.83A, amended: SI 2002/1409 Art.3, 2003 c.14 Sch.33 para.1, Sch.43 Part 3

s.83AA, amended: 2003 c.14 Sch.43 Part 3

s.83AA, repealed (in part): 2003 c.14 Sch.43 Part 3

s.83AB, amended: 2003 c.14 Sch.33 para.5

s.83AB, repealed (in part): 2003 c.14 Sch.43 Part 3

s.83ZA, added: 2003 c.14 Sch.33 para.3

s.83ZA, amended: SI 2004/3266 Art.9

s.84, amended: 2003 c.14 Sch.33 para.30

s.84, repealed (in part): 2003 c.14 Sch.43 Part 3

s.85, amended: 2004 c.12 Sch.6 para.7

s.85, repealed (in part): 2004 c.12 Sch.42 Part 2

s.86, amended: 2004 c.12 Sch.6 para.8

s.86, disapplied: 2003 c.14 Sch.24 para.7

s.86, repealed (in part): 2004 c.12 Sch.42 Part 2

s.87, amended: 2003 c.14 Sch.43 Part 3, SI 2004/2310 Sch.1 para.44

s.87, applied: 2004 c.12 s.44

s.88, amended: 2003 c.14 Sch.33 para.6, Sch.33 para.13, Sch.43 Part 3, 2004 c.12 Sch.7 para.9, SI 2004/2310 Sch.1 para.45

s.88A, repealed: 2003 c.14 Sch.43 Part 3

s.89, amended: 2003 c.14 Sch.33 para.6, Sch.33 para.7, Sch.33 para.12, Sch.33 para.13, Sch.43 Part 3, 2004 c.12 Sch.7 para.9, SI 2004/2310 Sch.1 para.46

s.89, applied: 2003 c.14 Sch.33 para.6

s.89A, amended: SI 2004/2200 Reg.5

s.90A, added: 2003 c.14 Sch.33 para.31

s.170, repealed (in part): 2004 c.12 Sch.42 Part 3

s.178, amended: 2002 c.22 Sch.1 para.8, SI 2002/2836 Sch.1 para.8, 2003 c.14 Sch.18 para.4, 2003 c.1 Sch.6 para.162, Sch.8 Part 1

s.178, applied: 2002 c.22 Sch.1 para.8, SI 2002/2172 Reg.8, SI 2002/2836 Sch.1 para.8, 2003 c.1 s.181, 2003 c.14 s.87, s.88, s.89, SI 2004/674 Reg.23

s.178, referred to: 2003 c.14 s.114, Sch.5 para.8

s.178, repealed (in part): 2002 c.9 Sch.13

s.178, varied: 2003 c.14 Sch.5 para.8

s.179, repealed (in part): 2002 c.9 Sch.13, 2003 c.1 Sch.8 Part 1

s.182, amended: 2002 c.21 Sch.5 para.11, 2002 c.22 Sch.7 para.1, 2004 c.6 s.18, SI 2004/1823 Art.10

s.182, applied: SI 2003/1830 Reg.10, SI 2003/3297 Reg.16, 2004 c.35 s.88, s.202

s.182, referred to: 2004 c.6 s.24

s.182, repealed (in part): 2004 c.14 Sch.1 Part 5, SI 2004/1823 Art.10

s.182, varied: 2004 c.6 s.24

s.185, repealed: 2004 c.14 Sch.1 Part 6

CAP.

1989–cont.

26. Finance Act 1989–*cont.*

Sch.5, applied: 2003 c.1 s.551

Sch.5 para.4, amended: 2003 c.1 Sch.6 para.163

Sch.5 para.9, amended: 2003 c.1 Sch.6 para.163

Sch.5 para.10, amended: 2003 c.1 Sch.6 para.163

Sch.5 para.18, added: 2003 c.1 Sch.6 para.163

Sch.6 Part I para.1, repealed: 2004 c.12 Sch.42 Part 3

Sch.6 Part I para.2, repealed: 2004 c.12 Sch.42 Part 3

Sch.6 Part I para.3, repealed: 2004 c.12 Sch.42 Part 3

Sch.6 Part I para.4, repealed: 2004 c.12 Sch.42 Part 3

Sch.6 Part I para.5, repealed: 2004 c.12 Sch.42 Part 3

Sch.6 Part I para.6, repealed: 2004 c.12 Sch.42 Part 3

Sch.6 Part I para.7, repealed: 2003 c.1 Sch.8 Part 1, 2004 c.12 Sch.42 Part 3

Sch.6 Part I para.8, repealed: 2003 c.1 Sch.8 Part 1, 2004 c.12 Sch.42 Part 3

Sch.6 Part I para.9, repealed: 2003 c.1 Sch.8 Part 1, 2004 c.12 Sch.42 Part 3

Sch.6 Part I para.10, repealed: 2004 c.12 Sch.42 Part 3

Sch.6 Part I para.11, repealed: 2004 c.12 Sch.42 Part 3

Sch.6 Part I para.12, repealed: 2004 c.12 Sch.42 Part 3

Sch.6 Part I para.13, repealed: 2003 c.1 Sch.8 Part 1, 2004 c.12 Sch.42 Part 3

Sch.6 Part I para.14, repealed: 2004 c.12 Sch.42 Part 3

Sch.6 Part I para.15, repealed: 2004 c.12 Sch.42 Part 3

Sch.6 Part I para.16, repealed: 2004 c.12 Sch.42 Part 3

Sch.6 Part I para.17, repealed: 2004 c.12 Sch.42 Part 3

Sch.6 Part I para.18, amended: 2003 c.1 Sch.8 Part 1

Sch.6 Part I para.18, repealed (in part): 2003 c.1 Sch.8 Part 1, 2004 c.12 Sch.42 Part 3

Sch.6 Part II para.19, repealed: 2004 c.12 Sch.42 Part 3

Sch.6 Part II para.20, repealed: 2004 c.12 Sch.42 Part 3

Sch.6 Part II para.21, repealed: 2004 c.12 Sch.42 Part 3

Sch.6 Part II para.22, repealed: 2004 c.12 Sch.42 Part 3

Sch.6 Part II para.23, repealed: 2004 c.12 Sch.42 Part 3

Sch.6 Part II para.24, repealed: 2004 c.12 Sch.42 Part 3

CAP.

1989–cont.

26. Finance Act 1989–*cont.*

Sch.6 Part II para.25, repealed: 2004 c.12 Sch.42 Part 3

Sch.6 Part II para.26, repealed: 2004 c.12 Sch.42 Part 3

Sch.6 Part II para.27, repealed: 2004 c.12 Sch.42 Part 3

Sch.6 Part II para.28, repealed: 2004 c.12 Sch.42 Part 3

Sch.6 Part II para.29, repealed: 2004 c.12 Sch.42 Part 3

Sch.6 Part II para.30, repealed: 2004 c.12 Sch.42 Part 3

Sch.6 Part III para.31, repealed: 2004 c.12 Sch.42 Part 3

Sch.6 Part III para.32, repealed: 2004 c.12 Sch.42 Part 3

Sch.6 Part III para.33, applied: 2003 c.1 s.583, s.593

Sch.6 Part III para.33, repealed: 2004 c.12 Sch.42 Part 3

Sch.6 Part III para.34, repealed: 2004 c.12 Sch.42 Part 3

Sch.6 Part III para.35, repealed: 2004 c.12 Sch.42 Part 3

Sch.7 Part I para.1, repealed: 2004 c.12 Sch.42 Part 3

Sch.7 Part I para.2, repealed: 2004 c.12 Sch.42 Part 3

Sch.7 Part I para.3, repealed: 2004 c.12 Sch.42 Part 3

Sch.7 Part I para.4, repealed: 2004 c.12 Sch.42 Part 3

Sch.7 Part I para.5, repealed: 2004 c.12 Sch.42 Part 3

Sch.7 Part I para.6, repealed: 2004 c.12 Sch.42 Part 3

Sch.7 Part I para.7, repealed: 2004 c.12 Sch.42 Part 3

Sch.7 Part I para.8, repealed: 2004 c.12 Sch.42 Part 3

Sch.7 Part I para.9, repealed: 2004 c.12 Sch.42 Part 3

Sch.7 Part II para.10, repealed: 2004 c.12 Sch.42 Part 3

Sch.7 Part II para.11, repealed: 2004 c.12 Sch.42 Part 3

Sch.7 Part II para.12, repealed: 2004 c.12 Sch.42 Part 3

Sch.8A para.1, amended: SI 2004/2200 Reg.6

Sch.8A para.1, varied: SI 2004/2200 Reg.6

Sch.8A para.1A, amended: SI 2004/2200 Reg.6

Sch.8A para.1A, varied: SI 2004/2200 Reg.6

Sch.8A para.1AA, amended: SI 2004/2200 Reg.6

Sch.8A para.1AA, varied: SI 2004/2200 Reg.6

Sch.8A para.1B, amended: SI 2004/2200 Reg.6

1989–cont.

26. Finance Act 1989–*cont.*
Sch.8A para.1B, varied: SI 2004/2200 Reg.6
Sch.8A para.1C, amended: SI 2004/2200 Reg.6
Sch.8A para.1C, varied: SI 2004/2200 Reg.6
Sch.8A para.1D, amended: SI 2004/2200 Reg.6
Sch.8A para.1D, varied: SI 2004/2200 Reg.6
Sch.8A para.2, amended: SI 2004/2200 Reg.6
Sch.8A para.2, varied: SI 2004/2200 Reg.6
Sch.12 Part I para.4, varied: SI 2003/1633 Sch.2 para.13
Sch.12 Part II para.8, repealed: 2003 c.1 Sch.8 Part 1
Sch.12 Part II para.15, repealed: 2004 c.12 Sch.42 Part 3
Sch.12 Part II para.16, repealed: 2004 c.12 Sch.42 Part 3

29. Electricity Act 1989
applied: 2002 c.40 Sch.15, SI 2003/419 Art.63, 2004 c.20 s.188, 2004 c.36 Sch.1 para.19, Sch.1 para.30, SI 2004/2541 Sch.1, SI 2004/2542 Sch.1, SSI 2004/406 Sch.5 para.4.5
referred to: 2003 c.9 s.2
Part I, applied: 2004 c.20 s.90, s.91, s.133, s.134, s.137, s.146, s.168, s.190, Sch.17 para.3, SI 2004/2541 Reg.3
Part II, referred to: 2003 c.9 s.2
s.1, varied: 2004 c.20 s.184, s.185
s.2, varied: 2004 c.20 s.184, s.185
s.3, varied: 2004 c.20 s.184, s.185
s.3A, amended: 2003 c.21 Sch.17 para.98, 2004 c.20 s.83, s.147, s.178, s.179, s.190, Sch.19 para.4
s.3A, applied: 2002 c.40 s.168, 2004 c.20 s.175, s.190
s.3A, varied: 2004 c.20 s.184, s.185
s.3B, applied: 2004 c.20 s.175, s.190
s.3B, varied: 2004 c.20 s.184, s.185
s.3C, applied: 2004 c.20 s.175, s.190
s.3C, varied: 2004 c.20 s.184, s.185
s.3D, amended: 2002 c.40 Sch.25 para.20, 2004 c.20 s.99
s.3D, applied: 2004 c.20 s.190
s.3D, varied: 2004 c.20 s.184, s.185
s.4, amended: 2004 c.20 s.89, s.135, s.145, s.179, Sch.23 Part 1
s.4, applied: 2004 c.20 s.86, s.134
s.4, disapplied: SI 2002/823 Art.3, SI 2003/3318 Art.3, Art.4, SI 2004/1179 Art.3
s.4, referred to: SI 2003/2380 Art.3, SI 2004/1776 Art.3
s.4, varied: 2004 c.20 s.184, s.185
s.5, amended: 2004 c.20 s.145
s.5, applied: SI 2002/823, SI 2003/2380, SI 2003/3318, SI 2004/1179, SI 2004/2541 Sch.2 para.3
s.5, varied: 2004 c.20 s.184, s.185

1989–cont.

29. Electricity Act 1989–*cont.*
s.5, enabling: SI 2002/823, SI 2003/2380, SI 2003/3318, SI 2004/1179, SI 2004/1776, SI 2004/3225
s.6, amended: 2004 c.20 s.89, s.136, s.145, Sch.19 para.5, Sch.23 Part 1
s.6, applied: SI 2002/476, SI 2003/1746 Art.3, 2004 c.20 s.134, s.140, s.148, Sch.17 para.1, 2004 c.36 Sch.1 para.19, SI 2004/2541 Reg.3, Sch.2 para.3
s.6, referred to: 2002 c.40 s.168, SI 2004/2541 Sch.2 para.1
s.6, varied: 2004 c.20 s.184, s.185
s.6A, amended: 2004 c.20 Sch.19 para.6
s.6A, applied: SI 2004/2541 Reg.8
s.6A, varied: 2004 c.20 s.148, s.184, s.185
s.6A, enabling: SI 2003/848, SI 2004/2541, SI 2004/2952
s.6B, amended: 2004 c.20 Sch.19 para.7
s.6B, varied: 2004 c.20 s.184, s.185
s.6C, added: 2004 c.20 s.92
s.6C, varied: 2004 c.20 s.184, s.185
s.7, amended: 2004 c.20 s.136
s.7, applied: 2004 c.20 s.191
s.7, varied: 2004 c.20 s.148, s.184, s.185
s.7A, varied: 2004 c.20 s.184, s.185
s.7B, varied: 2004 c.20 s.184, s.185
s.8, varied: 2004 c.20 s.184, s.185
s.8A, amended: 2004 c.20 s.137, s.146
s.8A, applied: SI 2004/2541 Sch.1
s.8A, varied: 2004 c.20 s.148, s.184, s.185
s.9, amended: 2004 c.20 Sch.19 para.8
s.9, varied: 2004 c.20 s.184, s.185
s.10, amended: 2004 c.20 Sch.19 para.9
s.10, varied: 2004 c.20 s.184, s.185
s.11, varied: 2004 c.20 s.184, s.185
s.11A, amended: 2004 c.20 Sch.23 Part 1
s.11A, applied: SI 2003/1746, SI 2003/1746 Art.3
s.11A, varied: 2004 c.20 s.184, s.185
s.11A, enabling: SI 2003/1746
s.12, amended: 2002 c.40 Sch.25 para.20
s.12, applied: SI 2003/1397 Art.8, 2004 c.20 s.177
s.12, repealed (in part): 2002 c.40 Sch.26
s.12, varied: 2004 c.20 s.184, s.185
s.12A, added: 2002 c.40 Sch.25 para.20
s.12A, varied: 2004 c.20 s.184, s.185
s.12B, added: 2002 c.40 Sch.25 para.20
s.12B, referred to: SI 2003/1371
s.12B, varied: 2004 c.20 s.184, s.185
s.12B, enabling: SI 2003/1371
s.13, amended: 2002 c.40 Sch.25 para.20
s.13, varied: 2004 c.20 s.184, s.185
s.14, varied: 2004 c.20 s.184, s.185
s.14A, amended: 2002 c.40 Sch.25 para.20
s.14A, referred to: SI 2003/1371
s.14A, repealed (in part): 2002 c.40 Sch.26
s.14A, varied: 2004 c.20 s.184, s.185
s.14A, enabling: SI 2003/1371

1989–cont.

29. Electricity Act 1989–*cont.*

s.15, amended: 2002 c.40 Sch.9 para.5

s.15, varied: SI 2003/1592 Sch.4 para.8, 2004 c.20 s.184, s.185

s.15A, varied: 2004 c.20 s.184, s.185

s.16, applied: SI 2002/93 Reg.5, SI 2004/2541 Sch.2 para.4

s.16, varied: 2004 c.20 s.184, s.185

s.16A, varied: 2004 c.20 s.184, s.185

s.17, varied: 2004 c.20 s.184, s.185

s.18, varied: 2004 c.20 s.184, s.185

s.18A, varied: 2004 c.20 s.184, s.185

s.19, varied: 2004 c.20 s.184, s.185

s.19, enabling: SI 2002/93, SI 2002/3232

s.20, varied: 2004 c.20 s.184, s.185

s.21, varied: 2004 c.20 s.184, s.185

s.22, varied: 2004 c.20 s.184, s.185

s.23, varied: 2004 c.20 s.184, s.185

s.24, varied: 2004 c.20 s.184, s.185

s.25, referred to: 2004 c.20 s.184, s.185

s.25, varied: 2004 c.20 s.184, s.185

s.26, varied: 2004 c.20 s.184, s.185

s.27, varied: 2004 c.20 s.184, s.185

s.27A, applied: SI 2002/1111, SI 2002/1111 Art.3

s.27A, varied: 2004 c.20 s.184, s.185

s.27A, enabling: SI 2002/1111

s.27B, varied: 2004 c.20 s.184, s.185

s.27C, varied: 2004 c.20 s.184, s.185

s.27D, varied: 2004 c.20 s.184, s.185

s.27E, varied: 2004 c.20 s.184, s.185

s.27F, varied: 2004 c.20 s.184, s.185

s.28, varied: 2004 c.20 s.184, s.185

s.29, amended: 2004 c.20 s.94, s.147, Sch.19 para.10

s.29, applied: 2004 c.20 s.86

s.29, varied: 2004 c.20 s.184, s.185

s.29, enabling: SI 2002/2665

s.30, amended: 2004 c.20 s.94, s.147, Sch.19 para.11

s.30, applied: SI 2002/2665 Reg.30

s.30, varied: 2004 c.20 s.184, s.185

s.30, enabling: SI 2002/2665

s.31, varied: 2004 c.20 s.184, s.185

s.31, enabling: SI 2002/3129

s.32, amended: 2004 c.20 s.115, s.119

s.32, applied: SI 2002/914, SI 2004/924, SSI 2002/163, 2004 c.20 s.115, s.116, s.117, s.118, s.119, SSI 2004/170

s.32, varied: 2004 c.20 s.184, s.185

s.32, enabling: SI 2002/914, SI 2004/924, SSI 2002/163, SSI 2004/170

s.32A, amended: 2004 c.20 s.119

s.32A, varied: 2004 c.20 s.184, s.185

s.32A, enabling: SI 2002/914, SI 2004/924, SSI 2002/163, SSI 2004/170

s.32B, amended: 2004 c.20 s.116

s.32B, applied: SI 2002/914 Art.3, SSI 2002/163 Art.3, Art.4, SSI 2004/170 Art.3, Art.4

s.32B, varied: 2004 c.20 s.184, s.185

1989–cont.

29. Electricity Act 1989–*cont.*

s.32B, enabling: SI 2002/914, SI 2004/924, SSI 2002/163, SSI 2004/170

s.32BA, added: 2004 c.20 s.117

s.32BA, varied: 2004 c.20 s.184, s.185

s.32C, amended: 2004 c.20 s.115, s.118

s.32C, varied: 2004 c.20 s.184, s.185

s.32C, enabling: SI 2002/914, SI 2004/924, SSI 2002/163, SSI 2004/170

s.33, amended: SSI 2002/92 Art.2

s.33, applied: 2003 c.30 s.7, 2004 c.20 s.187

s.33, referred to: 2004 c.20 s.187

s.33, varied: 2004 c.20 s.184, s.185

s.33, enabling: SSI 2002/94

s.34, varied: 2004 c.20 s.184, s.185

s.35, amended: 2004 c.20 Sch.19 para.12

s.35, applied: 2004 c.20 s.86

s.35, varied: 2004 c.20 s.184, s.185

s.36, amended: 2004 c.20 s.93

s.36, applied: 2004 c.20 s.86, s.100

s.36, disapplied: SI 2003/2829 Art.14, SI 2003/2830 Art.16, SI 2003/2831 Art.16, SI 2004/933 Art.16

s.36, varied: SSI 2002/407 Art.3, 2004 c.20 s.184, s.185

s.36, enabling: SSI 2002/407

s.36A, added: 2004 c.20 s.99

s.36A, varied: 2004 c.20 s.100, s.184, s.185

s.36B, added: 2004 c.20 s.99

s.36B, varied: 2004 c.20 s.184, s.185

s.37, applied: 2004 c.20 s.86

s.37, varied: 2004 c.20 s.184, s.185

s.38, varied: 2004 c.20 s.184, s.185

s.39, applied: SI 2002/476, SI 2002/742

s.39, varied: 2004 c.20 s.184, s.185

s.39, enabling: SI 2002/476, SI 2002/742

s.39A, applied: SI 2002/476, SI 2002/742

s.39A, varied: 2004 c.20 s.184, s.185

s.39A, enabling: SI 2002/476, SI 2002/742

s.39B, varied: 2004 c.20 s.184, s.185

s.39B, enabling: SI 2002/476, SI 2002/742

s.40, varied: 2004 c.20 s.184, s.185

s.40A, varied: 2004 c.20 s.184, s.185

s.40B, varied: 2004 c.20 s.184, s.185

s.40B, enabling: SI 2002/476, SI 2002/742

s.41, varied: 2004 c.20 s.184, s.185

s.41A, varied: 2004 c.20 s.184, s.185

s.41A, enabling: SI 2003/1180, SI 2004/3392

s.42, varied: 2004 c.20 s.184, s.185

s.42A, varied: 2004 c.20 s.184, s.185

s.42A, enabling: SI 2002/476, SI 2002/742

s.42AA, varied: 2004 c.20 s.184, s.185

s.42B, varied: 2004 c.20 s.184, s.185

s.42C, varied: 2004 c.20 s.184, s.185

s.43, amended: 2002 c.40 Sch.9 para.18, Sch.25 para.20, Sch.26, 2004 c.20 s.147, SI 2004/1261 Sch.2 para.3

s.43, repealed (in part): 2002 c.40 Sch.26

s.43, varied: 2004 c.20 s.184, s.185

1989–cont.

29. Electricity Act 1989–*cont.*

s.43A, varied: 2004 c.20 s.184, s.185

s.43B, amended: 2004 c.20 Sch.19 para.13

s.43B, varied: 2004 c.20 s.184, s.185

s.44, varied: 2004 c.20 s.184, s.185

s.44A, varied: 2004 c.20 s.184, s.185

s.45, varied: 2004 c.20 s.184, s.185

s.46, varied: 2004 c.20 s.184, s.185

s.46A, amended: 2002 c.40 Sch.25 para.20, 2004 c.20 s.179

s.46A, varied: 2004 c.20 s.184, s.185

s.47, amended: 2002 c.40 Sch.25 para.20

s.47, varied: 2004 c.20 s.184, s.185

s.48, amended: 2002 c.40 Sch.25 para.20, 2004 c.20 s.179

s.48, varied: 2004 c.20 s.184, s.185

s.49, varied: 2004 c.20 s.184, s.185

s.49A, varied: 2004 c.20 s.184, s.185

s.50, varied: 2004 c.20 s.184, s.185

s.51, varied: 2004 c.20 s.184, s.185

s.52, varied: 2004 c.20 s.184, s.185

s.53, varied: 2004 c.20 s.184, s.185

s.54, varied: 2004 c.20 s.184, s.185

s.55, varied: 2004 c.20 s.184, s.185

s.56, varied: 2004 c.20 s.184, s.185

s.56A, varied: 2004 c.20 s.184, s.185

s.56B, varied: 2004 c.20 s.184, s.185

s.56C, applied: SI 2003/1397 Art.8

s.56C, repealed (in part): 2002 c.40 Sch.26

s.56C, varied: 2004 c.20 s.184, s.185

s.56CA, added: 2002 c.40 Sch.25 para.20

s.56CA, varied: 2004 c.20 s.184, s.185

s.56CB, added: 2002 c.40 Sch.25 para.20

s.56CB, amended: 2003 c.21 Sch.16 para.3

s.56CB, referred to: SI 2003/1371

s.56CB, varied: 2004 c.20 s.184, s.185

s.56CB, enabling: SI 2003/1371

s.56D, amended: 2002 c.40 Sch.25 para.20

s.56D, varied: 2004 c.20 s.184, s.185

s.56E, varied: 2004 c.20 s.184, s.185

s.56F, varied: 2004 c.20 s.184, s.185

s.56G, varied: 2004 c.20 s.184, s.185

s.57, varied: 2004 c.20 s.184, s.185

s.58, amended: 2004 c.20 s.147, Sch.19 para.14

s.58, varied: 2004 c.20 s.184, s.185

s.59, applied: 2004 c.20 s.86

s.59, varied: 2004 c.20 s.184, s.185

s.60, varied: 2004 c.20 s.184, s.185

s.60, enabling: SI 2002/93, SI 2002/476, SI 2002/742, SI 2002/2665, SI 2002/3129, SI 2002/3232, SI 2003/848, SI 2004/2541, SI 2004/2952, SSI 2002/94

s.61, amended: 2004 c.20 s.102

s.61, varied: 2004 c.20 s.184, s.185

s.62, amended: 2004 c.20 s.102

s.62, applied: 2004 c.20 Sch.16 para.7

s.62, varied: 2004 c.20 s.184, s.185

s.63, varied: 2004 c.20 s.184, s.185

1989–cont.

29. Electricity Act 1989–*cont.*

s.64, amended: 2004 c.20 s.89, s.102, s.147, s.180, Sch.19 para.15, Sch.23 Part 1

s.64, applied: SI 2004/2542 Reg.8

s.64, referred to: SSI 2002/410 Art.32, Art.33

s.64, varied: 2004 c.20 s.184, s.185

s.64, enabling: SI 2002/93, SI 2002/3232, SI 2003/848

s.72, referred to: 2003 c.9 s.2

s.72, repealed: 2003 c.9 s.2

s.74, repealed: 2003 c.9 s.2

s.84, repealed: 2004 c.14 Sch.1 Part 5

s.85, repealed: 2004 c.14 Sch.1 Part 5

s.86, repealed: 2004 c.14 Sch.1 Part 5

s.87, repealed: 2004 c.14 Sch.1 Part 5

s.88, repealed: 2004 c.14 Sch.1 Part 5

s.89, repealed: 2004 c.14 Sch.1 Part 5

s.91, repealed (in part): 2004 c.14 Sch.1 Part 5

s.92, repealed: 2004 c.14 Sch.1 Part 5

s.98, amended: 2004 c.20 s.147

s.100, amended: SI 2003/1398 Sch.1 para.9

s.108A, added: 2004 c.20 s.102

s.111, enabling: SSI 2002/407

s.113, amended: SI 2003/1398 Sch.1 para.9

Sch.3, applied: SI 2004/2541 Sch.2 para.2

Sch.4, applied: SI 2004/2541 Sch.2 para.2

Sch.4 para.1, varied: 2004 c.20 s.143

Sch.4 para.2, varied: 2004 c.20 s.143

Sch.4 para.3, amended: 2003 c.21 Sch.17 para.99

Sch.4 para.3, varied: 2004 c.20 s.143

Sch.4 para.4, amended: 2003 c.21 Sch.17 para.99

Sch.4 para.4, varied: 2004 c.20 s.143

Sch.4 para.5, amended: 2003 c.21 Sch.17 para.99

Sch.4 para.5, varied: 2004 c.20 s.143

Sch.4 para.6, see *British Waterways Board v London Power Networks Plc* [2002] EWHC 2417, [2003] 1 All E.R. 187 (Ch D), Sir Andrew Morritt V.C.

Sch.4 para.6, varied: 2004 c.20 s.143

Sch.4 para.7, varied: 2004 c.20 s.143

Sch.4 para.8, varied: 2004 c.20 s.143

Sch.4 para.9, varied: 2004 c.20 s.143

Sch.4 para.10, varied: 2004 c.20 s.143

Sch.4 para.11, varied: 2004 c.20 s.143

Sch.4 para.12, amended: 2003 c.21 Sch.19

Sch.4 para.12, varied: 2004 c.20 s.143

Sch.5 para.8, varied: SI 2004/1822 Sch.1 para.15

Sch.5 para.9, varied: SI 2004/1822 Sch.1 para.15

Sch.5 para.12, varied: SI 2004/1822 Sch.1 para.15

Sch.5 para.14, varied: SI 2004/1822 Sch.1 para.15

Sch.6 para.3, applied: SI 2004/2541 Sch.2 para.4

Sch.7 para.2, enabling: SI 2002/3129

1989–cont.

29. Electricity Act 1989–*cont.*

Sch.7 para.3, applied: 2004 c.20 s.86

Sch.7 para.12, amended: 2004 c.20 s.181

Sch.7 para.13, applied: SI 2002/3129

Sch.7 para.13, enabling: SI 2002/3129

Sch.8, applied: 2004 c.20 Sch.16 para.8

Sch.8 para.5A, added: 2004 c.20 s.182

Sch.8 para.7A, added: 2004 c.20 s.93

Sch.8 para.8, amended: 2004 c.20 s.99

Sch.9 para.1, amended: 2004 c.20 Sch.19 para.16

Sch.9 para.3, amended: 2004 c.20 Sch.19 para.16

Sch.9 para.4, amended: 2003 asp 4 Sch.4 para.10

Sch.9 para.5, applied: 2002 asp 13 Sch.1 para.65

Sch.12 para.1, amended: 2003 c.9 s.3, 2004 c.20 s.34

Sch.12 para.1, applied: 2003 c.9 s.4

Sch.12 para.2, amended: 2003 c.9 s.3

Sch.12 para.3, amended: 2003 c.9 s.3

Sch.12 para.3A, added: 2004 c.20 s.34

Sch.12 para.4, repealed: 2003 c.9 s.3

Sch.16 para.1, repealed (in part): 2004 c.34 Sch.16, 2004 c.36 Sch.3

Sch.16 para.4, repealed: 2004 c.36 Sch.3

Sch.16 para.16, repealed: 2002 c.40 Sch.26

Sch.16 para.17, repealed (in part): 2002 c.40 Sch.26

Sch.16 para.24, repealed: 2002 c.40 Sch.26

Sch.16 para.25, repealed: 2002 c.40 Sch.26

Sch.16 para.36, repealed: 2002 c.40 Sch.26

Sch.17 Part II para.29, repealed: 2004 c.14 Sch.1 Part 5

Sch.17 Part II para.30, repealed: 2004 c.14 Sch.1 Part 5

Sch.17 Part II para.31, repealed: 2004 c.14 Sch.1 Part 5

30. Dangerous Dogs Act 1989

s.1, amended: 2003 c.39 Sch.8 para.323

31. Human Organ Transplants Act 1989

applied: 2004 c.19 s.4

referred to: 2004 c.30 s.59

repealed (in part): 2004 c.30 Sch.7 Part 1

s.1, amended: 2003 c.44 Sch.26 para.40, 2004 c.30 Sch.6 para.4

s.1, referred to: 2004 c.30 s.59

s.2, amended: 2003 c.44 Sch.37 Part 9

s.2, disapplied: 2003 c.44 Sch.25 para.85

s.2, referred to: 2004 c.30 s.59

s.3, referred to: 2004 c.30 s.59

s.5, referred to: 2004 c.30 s.59

s.6, referred to: 2004 c.30 s.59

33. Extradition Act 1989

see *R. (on the application of St John) v Governor of Brixton Prison* [2001] EWHC Admin 543, [2002] Q.B. 613 (QBD (Admin Ct)), Harrison, J.

1989–cont.

33. Extradition Act 1989–*cont.*

applied: SI 2002/1825 Art.2, SI 2002/1831, SI 2002/1831 Sch.3 para.1, 2003 c.32 s.86, s.87

referred to: 2003 c.32 s.86

repealed (in part): 2003 c.41 Sch.4

Part III, applied: SI 2002/1823 Sch.2 para.6, Sch.2 para.24, SI 2002/1831 Art.3

Part V, applied: SI 2002/1823 Art.2

s.1, applied: SI 2002/1823 Art.2, SI 2003/1870 Art.2

s.2, applied: SI 2002/1823 Art.2

s.4, applied: SI 2002/1831

s.4, enabling: SI 2002/1829, SI 2002/1830, SI 2002/1831, SI 2003/408, SI 2003/436, SI 2003/1244, SI 2003/1251, SI 2003/1873, SI 2003/1878

s.5, applied: SI 2002/1823 Art.2, Sch.2 para.5

s.5, enabling: SI 2003/1870

s.6, see *Lodhi v Governor of Brixton Prison (No.2)* [2002] EWHC 2029, (2002) 146 S.J.L.B. 230 (QBD (Admin Ct)), Brooke, L.J.; see *R. (on the application of Oncel) v Governor of Brixton Prison* [2001] EWHC Admin 1142, Times, January 17, 2002 (QBD (Admin Ct)), Lord Woolf of Barnes, L.C.J.

s.7, amended: 2003 c.39 Sch.8 para.324

s.7, applied: 2002 c.41 s.94, SI 2002/1823 Art.2

s.8, see *Wright v Scottish Ministers (No.1)* 2003 S.L.T. 840 (OH), Lord Sutherland

s.8, amended: 2003 c.39 Sch.8 para.325

s.8, applied: 2002 c.41 s.94, SI 2002/1823 Art.2, SI 2002/1831 Sch.3 para.2

s.8, disapplied: SI 2002/1831 Sch.3 para.2

s.8, varied: SI 2002/1823 Sch.3 para.2, Sch.4 para.2

s.9, see *R. (on the application of Hart) v Bow Street Magistrates Court* [2001] EWHC Admin 1141, [2002] 1 W.L.R. 1242 (QBD (Admin Ct)), Ouseley, J.

s.9, amended: 2003 c.39 Sch.8 para.326

s.9, applied: SI 2002/1823 Art.2, SI 2003/435 Art.25

s.9, varied: SI 2002/1823 Sch.3 para.3, Sch.3 para.4, Sch.4 para.3

s.10, applied: SI 2002/1823 Art.2

s.11, see *Lodhi v Governor of Brixton Prison (No.2)* [2002] EWHC 2029, (2002) 146 S.J.L.B. 230 (QBD (Admin Ct)), Brooke, L.J.; see *R. (on the application of Kashamu) v Governor of Brixton Prison (No.2)* [2001] EWHC Admin 980, [2002] Q.B. 887 (QBD (Admin Ct)), Rose, L.J.; see *R. (on the application of Oncel) v Governor of Brixton Prison* [2001] EWHC Admin 1142, Times, January 17, 2002 (QBD (Admin Ct)), Lord Woolf of Barnes, L.C.J.

s.11, applied: SI 2002/1823 Art.2

1989–cont.

33. Extradition Act 1989–*cont.*

s.12, see *Brown v Scottish Ministers* 2003 S.L.T. 1002 (OH), Lord Mackay of Drumadoon

s.12, applied: SI 2002/313 Sch.1, SI 2002/1823 Art.2

s.13, amended: 2003 c.39 Sch.8 para.327

s.14, amended: 2003 c.39 Sch.8 para.328

s.14, applied: SI 2002/1823 Art.2

s.14, varied: SI 2002/1823 Sch.3 para.5, Sch.4 para.4

s.14A, enabling: SSI 2002/517

s.16, applied: SI 2002/1823 Art.2

s.17, applied: SI 2002/1823 Art.2

s.17, varied: SI 2002/1823 Sch.3 para.6, Sch.3 para.7, Sch.3 para.8, Sch.4 para.5

s.18, see *R. (on the application of Rogerson) v Stafford Crown Court* [2001] EWHC Admin 961, [2002] Crim.L.R. 318 (QBD (Admin Ct)), Crane, J.

s.19, applied: SI 2002/1823 Art.2

s.19, varied: SI 2002/1823 Sch.3 para.9

s.20, applied: SI 2002/1823 Art.2

s.20, varied: SI 2002/1823 Sch.3 para.10

s.22, amended: 2002 c.29 Sch.11 para.18, Sch.12

s.22, applied: SI 2002/1831

s.22, referred to: SI 2002/1831 Sch.3 para.1

s.22, varied: SI 2003/120 Art.7

s.22, enabling: SI 2002/1831

s.23, applied: SI 2002/1823 Art.2

s.24, amended: SI 2002/419 Sch.9 para.2

s.24, applied: SI 2002/1823 Art.2

s.25, applied: SI 2002/1823 Art.2

s.27, applied: SI 2002/1823 Art.2

s.28, applied: SI 2002/1823 Art.2

s.28, varied: SI 2002/1823 Sch.3 para.11, Sch.4 para.6

s.32, amended: SI 2002/1824 Art.2

s.32, enabling: SI 2002/1823, SI 2002/1825, SI 2004/2036

s.34, enabling: SI 2002/1823

s.34A, added: SI 2002/419 Sch.9 para.3

s.35, amended: SI 2002/419 Sch.9 para.4

s.35, applied: SI 2002/1823 Art.2

s.35, referred to: SI 2002/1823 Sch.2 para.12

s.35, varied: SI 2002/1823 Sch.3 para.12, Sch.3 para.13, Sch.3 para.14, Sch.4 para.7, Sch.4 para.8, Sch.4 para.9

s.36, applied: SI 2002/1823 Art.2

s.37, enabling: SI 2002/1831, SI 2003/1244, SI 2003/1251

Sch.1, applied: SI 2002/1831 Art.2, 2003 c.41 Sch.3 para.7

Sch.1A, referred to: 2003 c.32 s.87

Sch.1 para.4, see *Guisto v Governor of Brixton Prison* [2003] UKHL 19, [2004] 1 A.C. 101 (HL), Lord Hope of Craighead

Sch.1 para.4, amended: 2003 c.39 Sch.8 para.329

Sch.1 para.4, applied: 2002 c.41 s.94

1989–cont.

33. Extradition Act 1989–*cont.*

Sch.1 para.5, amended: 2003 c.39 Sch.8 para.329

Sch.1 para.5, applied: 2002 c.41 s.94

Sch.1 para.6, see *R. (on the application of Kashamu) v Governor of Brixton Prison (No.2)* [2001] EWHC Admin 980, [2002] Q.B. 887 (QBD (Admin Ct)), Rose, L.J.

Sch.1 para.6, applied: SI 2003/435 Art.25

Sch.1. para.7, see *Guisto v Governor of Brixton Prison* [2002] EWHC 1441, [2003] 2 W.L.R. 157 (QBD (Admin Ct)), Gibbs, J.

Sch.1 para.7, see *Guisto v Governor of Brixton Prison* [2003] UKHL 19, [2004] 1 A.C. 101 (HL), Lord Hope of Craighead; see *Warda v Governor of Brixton Prison* [2002] EWHC 194, Times, March 18, 2002 (QBD (Admin Ct)), Keene, L.J.

Sch.1 para.8, applied: SI 2002/313 Sch.1

Sch.1 para.9, amended: 2003 c.39 Sch.8 para.329

Sch.1 para.12, see *Warda v Governor of Brixton Prison* [2002] EWHC 194, Times, March 18, 2002 (QBD (Admin Ct)), Keene, L.J.

Sch.1 para.13, amended: 2003 c.39 Sch.8 para.329

Sch.1 para.15, amended: 2002 c.29 Sch.11 para.18

Sch.1 para.15, varied: SI 2003/120 Art.7

Sch.1 para.20, see *Guisto v Governor of Brixton Prison* [2003] UKHL 19, [2004] 1 A.C. 101 (HL), Lord Hope of Craighead; see *R. (on the application of Al-Fawwaz) v Governor of Brixton Prison* [2001] UKHL 69, [2002] 1 A.C. 556 (HL), Lord Slynn of Hadley

Sch.1A Part 1 para.1, added: SI 2002/419 Sch.9 para.5

Sch.1A Part 1 para.2, added: SI 2002/419 Sch.9 para.5

Sch.1A Part 1 para.3, added: SI 2002/419 Sch.9 para.5

Sch.1A Part 1 para.4, added: SI 2002/419 Sch.9 para.5

Sch.1A Part 1 para.5, added: SI 2002/419 Sch.9 para.5

Sch.1A Part 1 para.5, amended: SI 2002/1662 Reg.2, 2003 c.39 Sch.8 para.330

Sch.1A Part 1 para.6, added: SI 2002/419 Sch.9 para.5

Sch.1A Part 2 para.7, added: SI 2002/419 Sch.9 para.5

Sch.1A Part 2 para.8, added: SI 2002/419 Sch.9 para.5

Sch.1A Part 2 para.9, added: SI 2002/419 Sch.9 para.5

Sch.1A Part 2 para.10, added: SI 2002/419 Sch.9 para.5

Sch.1A Part 2 para.10, repealed (in part): SI 2002/1662 Reg.2

Sch.1A Part 2 para.11, added: SI 2002/419 Sch.9 para.5

CAP.

1989–cont.

33. Extradition Act 1989–*cont.*

Sch.1A Part 2 para.11, amended: SI 2002/1662 Reg.2

Sch.1A Part 2 para.12, added: SI 2002/419 Sch.9 para.5

Sch.2, referred to: SI 2002/1825 Art.2

34. Law of Property (Miscellaneous Provisions) Act 1989

s.1, see *Shah v Shah* [2001] EWCA Civ 527, [2002] Q.B. 35 (CA), Pill, L.J.

s.2, see *Boorer v Boorer's Trustee in Bankruptcy* [2002] B.P.I.R. 21 (Ch D), Jacob, J.; see *Braymist Ltd v Wise Finance Co Ltd* [2002] EWCA Civ 127, [2002] Ch. 273 (CA), Arden, L.J.; see *Butts Park Ventures (Coventry) Ltd v Bryant Homes Central Ltd* [2003] EWHC 2487, [2004] B.C.C. 207 (Ch D), Sir Andrew Morritt V.C.; see *Healey v Brown* [2002] W.T.L.R. 849 (Ch D), David Donaldson Q.C.; see *Nweze v Nwoko* [2004] EWCA Civ 379, [2004] 2 P. & C.R. 33 (CA), Waller, L.J.; see *RG Kensington Management Co Ltd v Hutchinson IDH Ltd* [2002] EWHC 1180, [2003] 2 P. & C.R. 13 (Ch D), Neuberger, J.

37. Football Spectators Act 1989

Part II, applied: SI 2002/1143 Art.3, SI 2004/1029 Art.2, SI 2004/2409 Art.3, Art.4, Art.5

s.2, amended: 2003 c.44 Sch.26 para.41

s.7, see *R. v Smith (Paul Roger)* [2003] EWCA Crim 2480, [2004] 1 Cr. App. R. (S.) 58 (CA (Crim Div)), Penry-Davey, J.

s.7, amended: 2003 c.39 Sch.8 para.331, 2003 c.44 Sch.37 Part 7

s.7, repealed (in part): 2003 c.39 Sch.8 para.331, Sch.10, 2003 c.44 Sch.32 para.56, Sch.37 Part 7

s.11, applied: SI 2003/1280, SI 2004/1737

s.11, enabling: SI 2002/1755, SI 2003/1280, SI 2003/1541, SI 2004/1737

s.13, amended: 2004 c.21 Sch.1 para.70

s.14, enabling: SI 2002/1143, SI 2004/1029, SI 2004/2409

s.14A, see *Gough v Chief Constable of Derbyshire* [2001] EWHC Admin 554, [2002] Q.B. 459 (QBD (Admin Ct)), Laws, L.J.; see *R. v Smith (Paul Roger)* [2003] EWCA Crim 2480, [2004] 1 Cr. App. R. (S.) 58 (CA (Crim Div)), Penry-Davey, J.

s.14A, amended: 2003 c.38 s.86

s.14B, see *Gough v Chief Constable of Derbyshire* [2001] EWHC Admin 554, [2002] Q.B. 459 (QBD (Admin Ct)), Laws, L.J.; see *Gough v Chief Constable of Derbyshire* [2002] EWCA Civ 351, [2002] Q.B. 1213 (CA), Lord Phillips of Worth Matravers, M.R.

s.14E, amended: 2003 c.44 Sch.32 para.57

s.14G, amended: 2003 c.39 Sch.8 para.332

s.14H, amended: 2003 c.39 Sch.8 para.332

CAP.

1989–cont.

37. Football Spectators Act 1989–*cont.*

s.18, amended: 2003 c.39 Sch.8 para.333, 2003 c.44 Sch.32 para.58

s.18, applied: SI 2004/2409 Art.6

s.18, repealed (in part): 2003 c.39 Sch.8 para.333, Sch.10

s.18, enabling: SI 2004/2409

s.20, amended: 2003 c.39 Sch.8 para.334, Sch.10

s.22, amended: 2003 c.39 Sch.8 para.335, Sch.10

s.22A, applied: SI 2004/2409

Sch.1, see *R. v O'Keefe (Matthew)* [2003] EWCA Crim 2629, [2004] 1 Cr. App. R. (S.) 67 (CA (Crim Div)), Jackson, J.

Sch.1 para.1, see *R. v Smith (Paul Roger)* [2003] EWCA Crim 2480, [2004] 1 Cr. App. R. (S.) 58 (CA (Crim Div)), Penry-Davey, J.

Sch.2 para.24, amended: SI 2003/1326 Art.17

Sch.2 para.26A, added: SI 2003/1326 Art.17

Sch.2 para.26B, added: SI 2003/1326 Art.17

38. Employment Act 1989

s.3, repealed (in part): 2004 c.14 Sch.1 Part 8

s.8, repealed (in part): 2004 c.14 Sch.1 Part 8

s.9, repealed (in part): 2004 c.14 Sch.1 Part 8

s.11, applied: SI 2003/1660 Reg.26

s.21, repealed: 2004 c.14 Sch.1 Part 8

s.30, repealed (in part): 2004 c.14 Sch.1 Part 8

Sch.2 Part I, repealed: 2004 c.14 Sch.1 Part 8

Sch.2 Part II para.1, repealed: 2004 c.14 Sch.1 Part 8

Sch.2 Part II para.2, repealed: 2004 c.14 Sch.1 Part 8

Sch.3 Part I, repealed: 2004 c.14 Sch.1 Part 8

Sch.3 Part II, repealed: 2004 c.14 Sch.1 Part 8

Sch.4 para.1, repealed (in part): 2004 c.14 Sch.1 Part 8

Sch.4 para.5, repealed: 2004 c.14 Sch.1 Part 8

Sch.4 para.6, repealed (in part): 2004 c.14 Sch.1 Part 8

Sch.4 para.8, repealed: 2004 c.14 Sch.1 Part 8

Sch.4 para.9, repealed: 2004 c.14 Sch.1 Part 8

Sch.4 para.10, repealed (in part): 2004 c.14 Sch.1 Part 8

Sch.4 para.12, repealed (in part): 2004 c.14 Sch.1 Part 8

Sch.4 para.13, repealed (in part): 2004 c.14 Sch.1 Part 8

Sch.4 para.14, repealed: 2004 c.14 Sch.1 Part 8

Sch.4 para.16, repealed (in part): 2004 c.14 Sch.1 Part 8

Sch.5 para.4, repealed (in part): 2004 c.14 Sch.1 Part 8

Sch.5 para.6, repealed: 2004 c.14 Sch.1 Part 8

Sch.5 para.10, repealed: 2004 c.14 Sch.1 Part 8

Sch.6 para.27, repealed: 2004 c.14 Sch.1 Part 8

1989–cont.

38. Employment Act 1989–*cont.*

Sch.6 para.28, repealed: 2004 c.14 Sch.1 Part 2

Sch.6 para.30, repealed: 2003 c.17 Sch.7

39. Self Governing Schools etc (Scotland) Act 1989

see *Dove v Scottish Ministers* 2002 S.C. 257 (OH), Lord Eassie; see *Dove v Scottish Ministers* 2002 S.L.T. 1296 (Ex Div), Lord Cameron of Lochbroom, Lord Macfadyen, Lord Sutherland

39. Self-Governing Schools etc (Scotland) Act 1989

applied: SSI 2002/62 Sch.2 Part I

s.71, repealed: 2004 asp 4 Sch.3 para.6

s.72, repealed: 2004 asp 4 Sch.3 para.6

Sch.10 para.8, repealed (in part): 2004 asp 4 Sch.3 para.6

40. Companies Act 1989

Commencement Orders: SI 2004/3322 Art.2

applied: 2002 c.40 Sch.15, Sch.17 para.43

Part II, applied: 2002 c.i s.29, 2003 c.21 s.67, 2004 c.27 s.16

Part III, applied: SI 2003/335 Sch.1, SSI 2003/93 Sch.1, 2004 c.35 Sch.3, Sch.8

Part VII, applied: 2002 c.29 s.282

Part VIII, applied: 2002 c.40 s.249

s.25, applied: 2002 c.29 Sch.9 para.1, SI 2002/253 Art.52, SI 2002/254 Art.46, SI 2002/435 Reg.8, SI 2003/1250 Art.29, SI 2003/3075 Reg.2, 2004 c.23 s.14, 2004 c.27 s.43

s.30, amended: 2004 c.27 Sch.2 para.2

s.33, amended: 2004 c.27 s.6

s.40, amended: 2004 c.27 Sch.2 para.3

s.46, amended: 2004 c.27 Sch.2 para.3

s.46, repealed (in part): SI 2004/1261 Sch.2 para.2

s.46A, added: 2004 c.27 s.4

s.47, amended: 2002 c.40 Sch.25 para.21, 2004 c.27 Sch.2 para.3

s.47, repealed: SI 2004/1261 Sch.2 para.2

s.48, repealed (in part): 2004 c.27 Sch.8

s.52, amended: 2004 c.33 Sch.27 para.128

s.52, varied: 2004 c.33 Sch.21 para.32

s.54, repealed: SI 2004/1261 Sch.2 para.2

s.63, repealed: 2004 c.27 Sch.8

s.65, repealed: 2004 c.27 Sch.8

s.67, repealed: 2004 c.27 Sch.8

s.69, repealed (in part): 2004 c.27 Sch.8

s.82, applied: SI 2002/912 Sch.1, SI 2002/915 Sch.1, SI 2003/3075 Reg.5

s.84, applied: SI 2002/912 Sch.1, SI 2002/915 Sch.1, SI 2003/3075 Reg.26, 2004 c.35 Sch.3, Sch.8

s.87, amended: 2002 c.40 Sch.25 para.21, SI 2002/1889 Art.3, 2004 c.27 Sch.2 para.3, Sch.2 para.29, 2004 c.35 Sch.4 para.20, Sch.12 para.6

s.87, applied: SI 2002/1889 Art.3

s.87, enabling: SI 2002/1889

1989–cont.

40. Companies Act 1989–*cont.*

s.120, repealed (in part): 2004 c.14 Sch.1 Part 17, 2004 c.27 Sch.8

s.127, repealed (in part): 2004 c.14 Sch.1 Part 17

s.133, repealed (in part): SI 2003/1116 Sch.1 para.34

s.137, repealed (in part): 2004 c.14 Sch.1 Part 17

s.139, repealed (in part): 2004 c.12 Sch.42 Part 2

s.146, repealed: 2002 c.40 Sch.26

s.147, repealed: 2002 c.40 Sch.26

s.148, repealed: 2002 c.40 Sch.26

s.149, amended: 2002 c.8 s.2

s.149, repealed: 2002 c.40 Sch.26

s.150, repealed: 2002 c.40 Sch.26

s.152, repealed: 2002 c.40 Sch.26

s.158, amended: 2002 c.40 Sch.17 para.44

s.161, amended: 2002 c.40 Sch.17 para.45

s.167, amended: 2002 c.40 Sch.17 para.46

s.175, amended: 2002 c.40 Sch.17 para.47

s.207, enabling: SI 2003/1633

s.215, enabling: SI 2004/3322

Sch.4 para.4, repealed (in part): 2004 c.14 Sch.1 Part 17

Sch.4 para.7, repealed: 2004 c.14 Sch.1 Part 17

Sch.5 para.2, repealed (in part): 2004 c.14 Sch.1 Part 17

Sch.10 Part II para.38, repealed (in part): 2004 c.12 Sch.42 Part 2

Sch.11 Part II, added: 2004 c.27 s.1

Sch.11 Part II para.7, amended: 2004 c.27 s.1

Sch.11 Part II para.8, substituted: 2004 c.27 s.1

Sch.11 Part III para.17, added: 2004 c.27 s.2

Sch.11 Part III para.17, applied: 2004 c.27 s.16

Sch.11 Part III para.18, added: 2004 c.27 s.2

Sch.11 Part III para.18, applied: 2004 c.27 s.16

Sch.11 Part III para.19, added: 2004 c.27 s.2

Sch.11 Part III para.19, applied: 2004 c.27 s.16

Sch.11 Part III para.20, added: 2004 c.27 s.2

Sch.11 Part III para.20, applied: 2004 c.27 s.16

Sch.11 Part III para.21, added: 2004 c.27 s.2

Sch.11 Part III para.22, added: 2004 c.27 s.2

Sch.13, substituted: 2004 c.27 s.5

Sch.13 para.10, amended: 2004 c.27 s.5

Sch.13 para.11, amended: 2004 c.27 s.5

Sch.13 para.13, added: 2004 c.27 s.5

Sch.14 Part I, amended: 2002 c.40 Sch.25 para.21

Sch.14 Part I para.1, amended: 2002 c.40 Sch.25 para.21

Sch.14 Part I para.1, repealed: SI 2004/1261 Sch.2 para.2

Sch.14 Part I para.2, repealed: SI 2004/1261 Sch.2 para.2

Sch.14 Part I para.3, amended: 2002 c.40 Sch.25 para.21

1989–cont.

40. Companies Act 1989–*cont.*

Sch.14 Part I para.3, repealed: SI 2004/1261 Sch.2 para.2

Sch.14 Part I para.4, amended: 2002 c.40 Sch.25 para.21

Sch.14 Part I para.4, repealed (in part): 2002 c.40 Sch.25 para.21, Sch.26, SI 2004/1261 Sch.2 para.2

Sch.14 Part I para.4A, added: 2002 c.40 Sch.25 para.21

Sch.14 Part I para.4A, amended: SI 2003/1398 Sch.1 para.10

Sch.14 Part I para.4A, repealed: SI 2004/1261 Sch.2 para.2

Sch.14 Part I para.4B, added: 2002 c.40 Sch.25 para.21

Sch.14 Part I para.4B, repealed: SI 2004/1261 Sch.2 para.2

Sch.14 Part I para.5, amended: 2002 c.40 Sch.25 para.21

Sch.14 Part I para.5, repealed: SI 2004/1261 Sch.2 para.2

Sch.14 Part I para.6, amended: 2002 c.40 Sch.25 para.21

Sch.14 Part I para.6, repealed: SI 2004/1261 Sch.2 para.2

Sch.14 Part I para.7, amended: 2002 c.40 Sch.25 para.21

Sch.14 Part I para.7, repealed: SI 2004/1261 Sch.2 para.2

Sch.14 Part II para.8, repealed: 2002 c.40 Sch.26, SI 2004/1261 Sch.2 para.2

Sch.14 Part II para.9, repealed: SI 2004/1261 Sch.2 para.2

Sch.14 Part II para.10, repealed: SI 2004/1261 Sch.2 para.2

Sch.18 para.2, repealed: 2004 c.14 Sch.1 Part 17

Sch.18 para.3, repealed: SI 2003/3096 Sch.6

Sch.18 para.11, repealed: 2004 c.14 Sch.1 Part 17

Sch.18 para.19, repealed: 2004 c.14 Sch.1 Part 17

Sch.18 para.26, repealed: 2004 c.14 Sch.1 Part 17

Sch.18 para.28, repealed: 2003 c.21 Sch.19

Sch.18 para.46, repealed: 2003 c.1 Sch.8 Part 1

Sch.20 para.1, repealed: 2004 c.14 Sch.1 Part 17

Sch.20 para.2, repealed (in part): 2003 c.21 Sch.19, 2004 c.14 Sch.1 Part 17

Sch.20 para.3, repealed: 2002 c.40 Sch.26

Sch.20 para.4, repealed: 2002 c.40 Sch.26

Sch.20 para.5, repealed: 2002 c.40 Sch.26

Sch.20 para.6, repealed: 2002 c.40 Sch.26

Sch.20 para.7, repealed: 2002 c.40 Sch.26

Sch.20 para.8, repealed: 2002 c.40 Sch.26

Sch.20 para.9, repealed: 2002 c.40 Sch.26

Sch.20 para.10, repealed: 2002 c.40 Sch.26

Sch.20 para.11, repealed: 2002 c.40 Sch.26

1989–cont.

40. Companies Act 1989–*cont.*

Sch.20 para.12, repealed: SI 2003/3180 Sch.1 para.4

Sch.20 para.13, repealed (in part): SI 2003/3180 Sch.1 para.4, 2004 c.14 Sch.1 Part 17

Sch.20 para.14, repealed: 2002 c.40 Sch.26

Sch.20 para.15, repealed: 2002 c.40 Sch.26

Sch.20 para.16, repealed: 2002 c.40 Sch.26

Sch.20 para.19, repealed: 2002 c.40 Sch.26

Sch.20 para.20, repealed: 2004 c.14 Sch.1 Part 17

41. Children Act 1989

see *A (Children) (Care Proceedings: Asylum Seekers), Re* [2003] EWHC 1086, [2003] 2 F.L.R. 921 (Fam Div), Munby, J.; see *A Health Authority v X (No.1)* [2001] EWCA Civ 2014, [2002] 2 All E.R. 780 (CA), Thorpe, L.J.; see *B (Children) (Removal from Jurisdiction), Re* [2003] EWCA Civ 1149, [2003] 2 F.L.R. 1043 (CA), Thorpe, L.J.; see *Kingscrest Associates Ltd (t/a Kingscrest Residential Care Homes) v Customs and Excise Commissioners* [2003] B.V.C. 2592 (V&DTr), Adrian Shipwright (Chairman); see *R (Litigant in Person: Judicial Intervention), Re* [2001] EWCA Civ 1880, [2002] Fam. Law 268, [2002] 1 F.L.R. 432 (CA), Keene, L.J.; see *S (Children) (Care Order: Implementation of Care Plan), Re* [2002] UKHL 10, [2002] 2 A.C. 291 (HL), Lord Nicholls of Birkenhead; see *U (A Child) (Serious Injury: Standard of Proof), Re* [2004] EWCA Civ 567, [2004] 3 W.L.R. 753 (CA), Dame Elizabeth Butler-Sloss (President)

applied: 2002 c.38 s.1, s.46, SI 2002/377 Sch.1 para.14, SI 2002/438 Sch.1 para.5, SI 2002/816 Reg.3, SI 2002/920 Sch.1 para.4, SI 2002/921 Reg.5, Reg.6, Reg.7, SI 2002/1250 Reg.3, SI 2002/1493 Art.4, SI 2002/3199 Sch.1 para.7, SI 2002/3213 Reg.4, 2003 c.43 s.133, SI 2003/367 Reg.10, SI 2003/753 Reg.5, SI 2003/781 Reg.4, SI 2003/3118 Sch.1 para.7, SI 2003/3170 Sch.1 para.7, 2004 c.33 s.63, Sch.6 para.45, SI 2004/291 Sch.6 para.15, Sch.6 para.93, SI 2004/478 Sch.6 para.15, Sch.6 para.91, SI 2004/615 Reg.3, SI 2004/627 Sch.5 para.14, Sch.5 para.87, SI 2004/662 Reg.5, SI 2004/1309 Reg.3, SSI 2002/162 Art.13

referred to: 2002 c.38 s.145, Sch.3 para.54, SI 2002/920 Sch.1 para.4, 2003 c.43 Sch.4 para.75, SI 2003/1348 Reg.1

Part II, see *R v R (Private Law Proceedings: Residental Assessment)* [2002] 2 F.L.R. 953 (Fam Div), Holman, J.

Part II Sch.2 para.19B, see *R. (on the application of Berhe) v Hillingdon LBC* [2003] EWHC 2075, [2004] 1 F.L.R. 439 (QBD (Admin Ct)), Sullivan, J.

CAP.

1989–cont.

41. Children Act 1989–cont.

Part III, see *R. (on the application of B) v Merton LBC* [2003] EWHC 1689, [2003] 4 All E.R. 280 (QBD (Admin Ct)), Stanley Burnton, J.

Part III, applied: SI 2002/2007 Reg.3, SI 2003/493 Reg.18, SI 2003/2077 Reg.3

Part IV, see *J (A Child) (Care Proceedings: Disclosure), Re* [2003] EWHC 976, [2003] 2 F.L.R. 522 (Fam Div), Wall, J.; see *L (Care Proceedings: Human Rights Claims), Re* [2003] EWHC 665, [2003] 2 F.L.R. 160 (Fam Div), Munby, J.; see *Practice Direction (Fam Div: Care Cases: Judicial Case Management)* [2003] 1 W.L.R. 2209 (Fam Div), Dame Elizabeth Butler-Sloss (President); see *V (A Child) (Care Proceedings: Human Rights Claims), Re* [2004] EWCA Civ 54, [2004] 1 W.L.R. 1433 (CA), Tuckey, L.J.

Part IV, applied: SI 2002/635 Reg.2

Part IV, referred to: SI 2004/2695 Sch.1 para.22

Part V, applied: 2002 c.21 Sch.5 para.10A

Part VII, applied: SI 2002/920 Sch.1 para.9

Part VIII, applied: SI 2002/920 Sch.1 para.5, Sch.1 para.7, Sch.1 para.8, Sch.1 para.9

Part X, applied: SI 2002/635 Reg.2, SI 2002/896 Sch.1 para.8, SI 2002/920 Sch.2 para.2, SI 2004/2695 Sch.1 para.28, SSI 2002/162 Art.4

Part XA, applied: SI 2002/635 Reg.2, SI 2002/812 Reg.3, Reg.9, Reg.17, Reg.23, Sch.2 para.2, SI 2002/896 Reg.3, Sch.1 para.8, SI 2002/920 Sch.2 para.2, Sch.2 para.3, SI 2002/921 Reg.3, Reg.9, SI 2002/2005 Reg.14, SI 2003/1992 Reg.4, SI 2003/1996 Reg.4, 2004 c.31 s.12, s.29, SI 2004/2695 Reg.3, Sch.1 para.28

Part XA, referred to: SI 2002/919 Reg.16

s.1, see *Akintola v Akintola (Transfer of Tenancy)* [2001] EWCA Civ 1989, [2002] 1 F.L.R. 701 (CA), Thorpe, L.J.; see *C (A Child) (Immunisation: Parental Rights), Re* [2003] EWCA Civ 1148, [2003] 2 F.L.R. 1095 (CA), Thorpe, L.J.; see *C (A Child) (Immunisation: Parental Rights), Re* [2003] EWHC 1376, [2003] 2 F.L.R. 1054 (Fam Div), Sumner, J.; see *D (Stay of Children Act Proceedings), Re* [2003] EWHC 565, [2003] 2 F.L.R. 1159 (Fam Div), Bracewell, J.; see *H (A Child) (Residence), Re* [2002] 3 F.C.R. 277 (CA), Thorpe, L.J.; see *Medway Council v BBC* [2002] 1 F.L.R. 104 (Fam Div), Wilson, J.; see *O and N (Children) (Non Accidental Injury: Burden of Proof), Re* [2002] EWCA Civ 1271, [2002] 2 F.L.R. 1167 (CA), Ward, L.J.; see *R. (on the application of R) v Children and Family Court Advisory and Support Service* [2003] EWHC 235, [2003] 1 F.L.R. 953 (QBD (Admin Ct)), Charles, J.; see *S (A Child) (Identification:*

CAP.

1989–cont.

41. Children Act 1989–cont.

s.1–cont.

Restrictions on Publication), Re [2003] EWCA Civ 963, [2004] Fam. 43 (CA), Hale, L.J.; see *W (Wardship: Relatives Rejected as Foster Carers), Re* [2003] EWHC 2206, [2004] 1 F.L.R. 415 (Fam Div), Hedley, J.; see *Y (Leave to Remove from Jurisdiction), Re* [2004] 2 F.L.R. 330 (Fam Div), Hedley, J.

s.1, amended: 2002 c.38 s.115

s.2, amended: 2002 c.38 s.111

s.3, applied: SI 2003/1255 Reg.4, 2004 c.31 s.12, s.29

s.3, referred to: 2002 c.38 Sch.6

s.4, amended: 2002 c.38 s.111, SI 2003/3191 Sch.1 para.1

s.4, applied: SI 2004/3114 Sch.1

s.4, referred to: 2002 c.38 s.111

s.4, varied: SI 2003/3191 Art.3

s.4A, added: 2002 c.38 s.112

s.4A, amended: 2004 c.33 s.75

s.5, amended: 2002 c.38 s.115

s.5, applied: SI 2004/3114 Sch.1

s.6, amended: 2004 c.33 s.76

s.6, applied: SI 2004/3114 Sch.1

s.7, amended: 2004 c.31 Sch.3 para.6

s.7, applied: 2003 c.42 s.21

s.8, see *A (Children) (Shared Residence), Re* [2001] EWCA Civ 1795, [2002] 1 F.C.R. 177 (CA), Hale, L.J.; see *A v Times Newspapers Ltd* [2002] EWHC 2444, [2003] 1 All E.R. 587 (Fam Div), Sumner, J.; see *C (A Child) (Immunisation: Parental Rights), Re* [2003] EWCA Civ 1148, [2003] 2 F.L.R. 1095 (CA), Thorpe, L.J.; see *C (A Child) (Immunisation: Parental Rights), Re* [2003] EWHC 1376, [2003] 2 F.L.R. 1054 (Fam Div), Sumner, J.; see *C v FC (Brussels II: Freestanding Application for Parental Responsibility)* [2004] 1 F.L.R. 317 (Fam Div (Family Division)), Rex Tedd Q.C.; see *F (Abduction: Unmarried Father: Sole Carer), Re* [2002] EWHC 2896, [2003] 1 F.L.R. 839 (Fam Div), Dame Elizabeth Butler-Sloss (President); see *G (Adoption: Ordinary Residence), Re* [2002] EWHC 2447, [2003] 2 F.L.R. 944 (Fam Div), Wall, J.; see *L Teaching Hospitals NHS Trust v A* [2003] EWHC 259, [2003] 1 F.L.R. 1091 (QBD), Dame Elizabeth Butler-Sloss (President); see *Practice Direction (Fam Div: Conciliation)* [2004] 1 W.L.R. 1287 (Fam Div), Senior District Judge Waller; see *W (Wardship: Relatives Rejected as Foster Carers), Re* [2003] EWHC 2206, [2004] 1 F.L.R. 415 (Fam Div), Hedley, J.; see *White v White* [2003] EWCA Civ 924, [2004] 2 F.L.R. 321 (CA), Thorpe, L.J.

s.8, amended: 2002 c.38 Sch.3 para.55, 2004 c.33 Sch.27 para.129

CAP.

1989–cont.

41. Children Act 1989–*cont.*

s.8, applied: 2002 c.38 s.26

s.8, referred to: 2002 c.38 s.29, Sch.6

s.9, amended: 2002 c.38 s.113, s.114

s.9, repealed (in part): 2002 c.38 s.113, Sch.5

s.10, see *J (A Child) (Leave to Issue Application for Residence Order), Re* [2002] EWCA Civ 1346, [2003] 1 F.L.R. 114 (CA), Thorpe, L.J.

s.10, amended: 2002 c.38 Sch.3 para.56, 2004 c.33 s.77

s.10, applied: SI 2004/3114 Sch.1

s.12, amended: 2002 c.38 s.114, Sch.3 para.57

s.12, repealed (in part): 2002 c.38 Sch.3 para.57, Sch.5

s.13, see *Practice Direction (Fam Div: Conciliation)* [2004] 1 W.L.R. 1287 (Fam Div), Senior District Judge Waller

s.13, applied: SI 2004/3114 Sch.1

s.14A, added: 2002 c.38 s.115

s.14A, varied: 2002 c.38 s.29

s.14B, added: 2002 c.38 s.115

s.14C, added: 2002 c.38 s.115

s.14C, disapplied: 2002 c.38 s.29

s.14D, added: 2002 c.38 s.115

s.14E, added: 2002 c.38 s.115

s.14F, added: 2002 c.38 s.115

s.14F, applied: SI 2002/2006 Reg.19

s.14G, added: 2002 c.38 s.115

s.14G, repealed: 2003 c.43 s.117, Sch.14 Part 2

s.15, see *P (A Child) (Financial Provision), Re* [2003] EWCA Civ 837, [2003] 2 F.L.R. 865 (CA), Thorpe, L.J.

s.15, applied: SI 2002/1330 Sch.3 para.1, SI 2002/3200 Reg.15, Sch.3 para.1, SI 2003/1994 Sch.3 para.1

s.15, disapplied: SI 2002/195 Reg.15, Sch.3 para.1

s.16, amended: 2002 c.38 Sch.3 para.58, 2004 c.31 Sch.3 para.7

s.17, see *R. (on the application of A) v Lambeth LBC* [2001] EWCA Civ 1624, [2002] 1 F.L.R. 353 (CA), Laws, L.J.; see *R. (on the application of Ali) v Birmingham City Council* [2002] EWHC 1511, [2002] H.L.R. 51 (QBD (Admin Ct)), Moses, J.; see *R. (on the application of B) v Merton LBC* [2003] EWHC 1689, [2003] 4 All E.R. 280 (QBD (Admin Ct)), Stanley Burnton, J.; see *R. (on the application of Berhe) v Hillingdon LBC* [2003] EWHC 2075, [2004] 1 F.L.R. 439 (QBD (Admin Ct)), Sullivan, J.; see *R. (on the application of CD) v Isle of Anglesey CC* [2004] EWHC 1635, [2004] 3 F.C.R. 171 (QBD (Admin Ct)), Wilson, J.; see *R. (on the application of G) v Barnet LBC* [2003] UKHL 57, [2004] 2 A.C. 208 (HL), Lord Nicholls of Birkenhead; see *R. (on the application of J) v Enfield LBC* [2002]

CAP.

1989–cont.

41. Children Act 1989–*cont.*

s.17–*cont.*

EWHC 432, [2002] 2 F.L.R. 1 (QBD (Admin Ct)), Elias, J.; see *R. (on the application of M) v Barking and Dagenham LBC* [2002] EWHC 2663, (2003) C.C.L. Rep. 87 (QBD (Admin Ct)), Crane, J.; see *R. (on the application of M) v Islington LBC* [2003] EWHC 1388, [2003] 2 F.L.R. 903 (QBD (Admin Ct)), Wilson, J.; see *R. (on the application of O) v Haringey LBC* [2004] EWCA Civ 535, [2004] 2 F.L.R. 476 (CA), Lord Woolf of Barnes, L.C.J.; see *R. (on the application of S) v Wandsworth LBC* [2001] EWHC Admin 709, [2002] 1 F.L.R. 469 (QBD (Admin Ct)), Jack Beatson Q.C.; see *R. (on the application of the Howard League for Penal Reform) v Secretary of State for the Home Department (No.2)* [2002] EWHC 2497, [2003] 1 F.L.R. 484 (QBD (Admin Ct)), Munby, J.; see *R. (on the application of W) v Lambeth LBC* [2002] EWCA Civ 613, [2002] 2 All E.R. 901 (CA), Brooke, L.J.; see *T (Judicial Review: Local Authority Decisions Concerning Child in Need), Re* [2004] 1 F.L.R. 601 (QBD (Admin Ct)), Wall, J.

s.17, amended: 2002 c.21 Sch.3 para.16, 2002 c.38 s.116, 2004 c.31 s.53

s.17, applied: 2002 c.41 Sch.3 para.1, SI 2003/762 Reg.4, SI 2003/2077 Reg.3

s.17, enabling: SI 2003/2077

s.17A, see *R. (on the application of W) v Lambeth LBC* [2002] EWCA Civ 613, [2002] 2 All E.R. 901 (CA), Brooke, L.J.

s.17A, amended: 2002 c.21 Sch.3 para.17, Sch.6

s.17A, applied: SI 2003/762 Reg.3, Reg.4, Reg.5, SI 2003/2077 Reg.3, SI 2004/1748 Reg.4, Reg.6

s.17A, referred to: SI 2003/762 Reg.6, SI 2004/1748 Reg.7

s.17A, enabling: SI 2003/762, SI 2004/1748

s.17B, applied: SI 2003/2077 Reg.3

s.17B, enabling: SI 2003/1216

s.19, amended: 2002 c.32 Sch.22 Part 3

s.20, see *R. (on the application of Ali) v Birmingham City Council* [2002] EWHC 1511, [2002] H.L.R. 51 (QBD (Admin Ct)), Moses, J.; see *R. (on the application of Berhe) v Hillingdon LBC* [2003] EWHC 2075, [2004] 1 F.L.R. 439 (QBD (Admin Ct)), Sullivan, J.; see *R. (on the application of CD) v Isle of Anglesey CC* [2004] EWHC 1635, [2004] 3 F.C.R. 171 (QBD (Admin Ct)), Wilson, J.; see *R. (on the application of Grant) v Lambeth LBC* [2004] EWHC 1524, [2004] 3 F.C.R. 494 (QBD (Admin Ct)), Mitting, J.; see *R. (on the application of O) v Haringey LBC* [2004] EWCA Civ 535, [2004] 2 F.L.R. 476 (CA), Lord Woolf of Barnes, L.C.J.

1989–cont.

41. Children Act 1989–cont.

s.20, amended: 2002 c.38 Sch.3 para.59, Sch.5, 2004 c.31 s.53

s.20, applied: 2002 c.38 s.38, SI 2002/2051 Art.3, 2003 c.42 s.21

s.20, referred to: 2002 c.38 s.30, s.34, s.37, s.38, s.39, s.40

s.21, amended: 2003 c.38 Sch.2 para.5

s.21, applied: 2003 c.42 s.21

s.22, see *F v Lambeth LBC* [2002] 1 F.L.R. 217 (Fam Div), Munby, J.; see *R. (on the application of Berhe) v Hillingdon LBC* [2003] EWHC 2075, [2004] 1 F.L.R. 439 (QBD (Admin Ct)), Sullivan, J.; see *R. (on the application of CD) v Isle of Anglesey CC* [2004] EWHC 1635, [2004] 3 F.C.R. 171 (QBD (Admin Ct)), Wilson, J.; see *R. (on the application of L (A Child)) v Manchester City Council* [2001] EWHC Admin 707, [2002] 1 F.L.R. 43 (QBD (Admin Ct)), Munby, J.; see *R. (on the application of M (A Child)) v Sheffield Magistrates Court* [2004] EWHC 1830, [2004] 3 F.C.R. 281 (QBD (Admin Ct)), Newman, J.

s.22, amended: 2002 c.38 s.116, 2004 c.31 s.52

s.22, applied: SI 2002/57 Reg.33, Reg.36, SI 2002/152 Reg.24, SI 2003/237 Reg.33, Reg.36, SI 2003/2962 Reg.3

s.22, referred to: 2002 c.38 s.53, Sch.6

s.23, see *H (A Child) (Care Order: Appropriate Local Authority), Re* [2003] EWCA Civ 1629, [2004] Fam. 89 (CA), Thorpe, L.J.; see *Kirklees MBC v Brent LBC* [2004] 2 F.L.R. 800 (Fam Div), Bodey, J.; see *R. (on the application of CD) v Isle of Anglesey CC* [2004] EWHC 1635, [2004] 3 F.C.R. 171 (QBD (Admin Ct)), Wilson, J.; see *W (Wardship: Relatives Rejected as Foster Carers), Re* [2003] EWHC 2206, [2004] 1 F.L.R. 415 (Fam Div), Hedley, J.

s.23, amended: 2004 c.31 s.49

s.23, applied: SI 2002/1330 Sch.3 para.1, SI 2002/2006 Reg.19, SI 2002/2007 Reg.3, SI 2002/3200 Reg.15, Sch.3 para.1, 2003 c.14 Sch.36 para.4, 2003 c.42 s.21, s.27, SI 2003/493 Reg.16, SI 2003/1994 Sch.3 para.1, 2004 c.31 s.49, SI 2004/692 Sch.4 para.3

s.23, disapplied: SI 2002/195 Reg.15, Sch.3 para.1

s.23, referred to: 2002 c.38 Sch.6

s.23, enabling: SI 2002/57, SI 2002/546, SI 2002/865, SI 2002/2935, SI 2002/3013, SI 2003/237, SI 2003/896

s.23A, applied: SI 2002/2051 Art.3, SI 2003/2382 Reg.5, SSI 2003/376 Sch.2

s.23A, enabling: SI 2002/546, SI 2002/1855, SI 2002/2935, SI 2004/1732

s.23B, applied: 2003 c.42 s.21, SI 2003/2382 Reg.5, SSI 2003/376 Sch.2

1989–cont.

41. Children Act 1989–cont.

s.23C, see *R. (on the application of Berhe) v Hillingdon LBC* [2003] EWHC 2075, [2004] 1 F.L.R. 439 (QBD (Admin Ct)), Sullivan, J.

s.23C, applied: 2002 c.41 Sch.3 para.1, 2004 c.31 s.10, s.18, s.25, s.50

s.24, amended: 2002 c.38 Sch.3 para.60, 2003 c.43 Sch.4 para.76

s.24, applied: SI 2002/1330 Sch.3 para.1, SI 2002/3200 Reg.15, Sch.3 para.1, SI 2003/1994 Sch.3 para.1, 2004 c.31 s.10, s.18, s.25, s.50

s.24, disapplied: SI 2002/195 Reg.15, Sch.3 para.1

s.24A, amended: 2002 c.38 s.116, Sch.3 para.61

s.24A, applied: 2002 c.41 Sch.3 para.1, 2004 c.31 s.10, s.18, s.25, s.50

s.24B, amended: 2002 c.38 Sch.3 para.62

s.24B, applied: 2002 c.41 Sch.3 para.1, 2004 c.31 s.10, s.18, s.25, s.50

s.24C, amended: 2003 c.43 Sch.4 para.77

s.24C, applied: 2004 c.31 s.10, s.18, s.25, s.50

s.24D, amended: 2002 c.38 s.117

s.24D, applied: 2003 c.43 s.114, 2004 c.31 s.10, s.18, s.25, s.50, SI 2004/719 Reg.3, Reg.4, SI 2004/1448 Reg.3, Reg.4

s.24D, enabling: SI 2004/719, SI 2004/1448

s.25, see *S (A Child) v Knowsley BC* [2004] EWHC 491, [2004] 2 F.L.R. 716 (Fam Div), Charles, J.

s.25, applied: SI 2004/3114 Sch.1

s.25, enabling: SI 2002/546, SI 2002/2935

s.26, amended: 2002 c.38 s.117, s.118, Sch.5, 2003 c.43 s.117, 2004 c.31 Sch.3 para.8

s.26, applied: SI 2002/57 Reg.3, 2003 c.43 s.114, SI 2003/237 Reg.3, SI 2003/370 Sch.1 para.8, Sch.2 para.3, SI 2003/710 Sch.1 para.8, Sch.2 para.3, SI 2004/719 Reg.3, Reg.4, SI 2004/1448 Reg.3, Reg.4

s.26, enabling: SI 2002/546, SI 2002/2935, SI 2002/3013, SI 2004/719, SI 2004/1419, SI 2004/1448, SI 2004/1449, SI 2004/2187, SI 2004/2253

s.26A, added: 2002 c.38 s.119

s.26A, amended: 2003 c.43 s.116

s.26A, applied: SI 2004/719 Reg.3, Reg.5, SI 2004/1448 Reg.3

s.26A, enabling: SI 2004/719, SI 2004/1448

s.26ZA, added: 2003 c.43 s.116

s.26ZB, added: 2003 c.43 s.116

s.27, see *R. (on the application of S) v Wandsworth LBC* [2001] EWHC Admin 709, [2002] 1 F.L.R. 469 (QBD (Admin Ct)), Jack Beatson Q.C.

s.27, amended: 2003 c.43 Sch.4 para.78

s.27, referred to: 2004 c.15 s.3.2 para.30, 2002 c.21 Sch.3 para.18, SI 2002/2469 Sch.1 para.16

CAP.

1989–cont.

41. Children Act 1989–cont.

s.31, see *A and D (Non Accidental Injury: Subdural Haematomas), Re* [2002] 1 F.L.R. 337 (Fam Div), Dame Elizabeth Butler-Sloss (President); see *B (Children) (Care: Interference with Family Life), Re* [2003] EWCA Civ 786, [2003] 2 F.L.R. 813 (CA), Thorpe, L.J.; see *H (A Child) (Care Order: Appropriate Local Authority), Re* [2003] EWCA Civ 1629, [2004] Fam. 89 (CA), Thorpe, L.J.; see *K (Children) (Adoption: Freeing Order), Re* [2004] EWCA Civ 1181, [2004] 3 F.C.R. 123 (CA), Wall, L.J.; see *Kirklees MBC v Brent LBC* [2004] 2 F.L.R. 800 (Fam Div), Bodey, J.; see *M (A Child) (Care Order: Freeing Application), Re* [2003] EWCA Civ 1874, [2004] 1 F.L.R. 826 (CA), Ward, L.J.; see *M (Intractable Contact Dispute: Interim Care Order), Re* [2003] EWHC 1024, [2003] 2 F.L.R. 636 (Fam Div), Wall, J.; see *MH (A Child) (Care Proceedings: Children's Guardian), Re* [2002] 1 W.L.R. 189 (Fam Div), Wall, J.; see *North Yorkshire CC v SA* [2003] EWCA Civ 839, [2003] 2 F.L.R. 849 (CA), Dame Elizabeth Butler-Sloss (President); see *O and N (Children) (Non Accidental Injury: Burden of Proof), Re* [2002] EWCA Civ 1271, [2002] 2 F.L.R. 1167 (CA), Ward, L.J.; see *O and N (Children) (Non-Accidental Injury: Burden of Proof), Re* [2003] UKHL 18, [2004] 1 A.C. 523 (HL), Lord Nicholls of Birkenhead; see *Oxfordshire CC v S* [2003] EWHC 2174, [2004] 1 F.L.R. 426 (Fam Div), Munby, J.; see *R (A Child) (Care: Disclosure: Nature of Proceedings), Re* [2002] 1 F.L.R. 755 (Fam Div), Charles, J.; see *Redbridge LBC v Newport City Council* [2003] EWHC 2967, [2004] 2 F.L.R. 226 (Fam Div), David Hershman Q.C.; see *T (Children) (Abuse: Standard of Proof), Re* [2004] EWCA Civ 558, [2004] 2 F.L.R. 838 (CA), Dame Elizabeth Butler-Sloss (President)

s.31, amended: 2002 c.38 s.120, s.121

s.31, applied: 2002 c.38 s.21, s.22, SI 2002/635 Reg.2, SI 2002/896 Sch.1 para.1, Sch.1 para.2, SI 2002/3213 Sch.4 para.2, 2003 asp 13 s.252, SI 2004/2695 Sch.1 para.21, Sch.1 para.22, SI 2004/3114 Sch.1

s.31, referred to: 2002 c.38 Sch.6

s.31A, added: 2002 c.38 s.121

s.31A, applied: 2002 c.38 s.121

s.33, amended: 2002 c.38 Sch.3 para.63

s.33, applied: 2004 c.33 Sch.2 para.1, SI 2004/3114 Sch.1

s.33, repealed (in part): 2002 c.38 Sch.3 para.63, Sch.5

s.34, see *F v Lambeth LBC* [2002] 1 F.L.R. 217 (Fam Div), Munby, J.; see *G (Adoption: Ordinary Residence), Re* [2002] EWHC 2447, [2003] 2 F.L.R. 944 (Fam Div),

CAP.

1989–cont.

41. Children Act 1989–cont.

s.34–cont.

Wall, J.; see *G (Children) (Permission to Terminate Paternal Contact), Re* [2002] EWCA Civ 761, [2003] 1 F.L.R. 270 (CA), Ward, L.J.

s.34, amended: 2002 c.38 Sch.3 para.64

s.34, applied: 2002 c.38 s.26, SI 2004/3114 Sch.1

s.36, see *Graves v Islington LBC* [2003] EWHC 2817, [2004] E.L.R. 1 (QBD (Admin Ct)), Beatson, J.

s.36, applied: SI 2004/3114 Sch.1

s.37, see *M (Intractable Contact Dispute: Interim Care Order), Re* [2003] EWHC 1024, [2003] 2 F.L.R. 636 (Fam Div), Wall, J.

s.38, see *B (A Child) (Interim Care Order: Directions), Re* [2002] EWCA Civ 25, [2002] 1 F.L.R. 545 (CA), Thorpe, L.J.; see *G (A Child) (Interim Care Order: Residential Assessment), Re* [2004] EWCA Civ 24, [2004] 1 F.L.R. 876 (CA), Dame Elizabeth Butler-Sloss (President); see *Oxfordshire CC v S* [2003] EWHC 2174, [2004] 1 F.L.R. 426 (Fam Div), Munby, J.; see *V (A Child) (Care Proceedings: Human Rights Claims), Re* [2004] EWCA Civ 54, [2004] 1 W.L.R. 1433 (CA), Tuckey, L.J.

s.38, applied: SI 2004/3114 Sch.1

s.38, referred to: 2002 c.38 Sch.6

s.39, see *G (Care: Challenge to Local Authority's Decision), Re* [2003] EWHC 551, [2003] 2 F.L.R. 42 (Fam Div), Munby, J.

s.39, applied: SI 2004/3114 Sch.1

s.41, see *Practice Direction (Family Proceedings: Representation of Children)* [2004] 1 W.L.R. 1180 (Fam Div), Dame Elizabeth Butler-Sloss (President)

s.41, amended: 2002 c.38 s.122, 2004 c.31 Sch.3 para.9

s.41, applied: 2003 c.42 s.21

s.42, see *J (A Child) (Care Proceedings: Disclosure), Re* [2003] EWHC 976, [2003] 2 F.L.R. 522 (Fam Div), Wall, J.

s.42, amended: 2004 c.31 Sch.3 para.10

s.43, applied: SI 2004/3114 Sch.1

s.43, referred to: 2002 c.38 Sch.6

s.44, applied: SI 2002/896 Sch.1 para.46, SI 2004/2695 Sch.1 para.21, SI 2004/3114 Sch.1

s.44A, applied: SI 2004/3114 Sch.1

s.44B, applied: SI 2004/3114 Sch.1

s.45, amended: SI 2002/253 Sch.5 para.10, SI 2004/1771 Sch.1 para.4

s.45, applied: SI 2004/3114 Sch.1

s.46, applied: SI 2004/3114 Sch.1

s.47, see *M (A Child) (Children and Family Reporter: Disclosure), Re* [2002] EWCA Civ 1199, [2003] Fam. 26 (CA), Thorpe,

CAP.

1989–cont.

41. Children Act 1989–*cont.*

s.47–*cont.*

L.J.; see *R. (on the application of the Howard League for Penal Reform) v Secretary of State for the Home Department (No.2)* [2002] EWHC 2497, [2003] 1 F.L.R. 484 (QBD (Admin Ct)), Munby, J.

s.47, amended: 2003 c.43 Sch.4 para.79, 2004 c.31 s.53

s.48, amended: SI 2002/253 Sch.5 para.10, 2004 c.33 Sch.27 para.130, SI 2004/1771 Sch.1 para.4

s.48, applied: SI 2004/3114 Sch.1

s.49, see *R. v JA* [2001] EWCA Crim 1974, [2002] 1 Cr. App. R. (S.) 108 (CA (Crim Div)), Kay, L.J.

s.49, applied: SI 2002/635 Sch.1 para.1, SI 2002/896 Sch.1 para.46, SI 2004/2695 Sch.1 para.3

s.50, amended: 2004 c.33 Sch.27 para.131

s.50, applied: SI 2002/635 Sch.1 para.1, SI 2002/896 Sch.1 para.46, SI 2004/2695 Sch.1 para.3, SI 2004/3114 Sch.1

s.51, applied: SI 2002/327 Reg.15

s.51, enabling: SI 2002/546, SI 2002/2935

s.59, amended: 2004 c.31 s.49

s.59, applied: SI 2002/57 Reg.3, Reg.50, 2003 c.14 Sch.36 para.4, 2003 c.42 s.21, s.27, SI 2003/237 Reg.3, Reg.52, 2004 c.31 s.49, SI 2004/692 Sch.4 para.3

s.59, enabling: SI 2002/57, SI 2002/546, SI 2002/865, SI 2002/2935, SI 2003/237, SI 2003/896, SI 2004/1419, SI 2004/1449, SI 2004/2253

s.60, applied: SI 2002/920 Sch.1 para.5, Sch.1 para.7, Sch.1 para.8, Sch.1 para.9

s.60, referred to: SI 2002/920 Sch.1 para.4, Sch.1 para.9

s.61, applied: SI 2002/57 Reg.33, Reg.36, Reg.41, SI 2003/237 Reg.33, Reg.36, Reg.41

s.61, referred to: 2002 c.38 s.53

s.62, enabling: SI 2002/57, SI 2003/237, SI 2003/896

s.63, applied: SI 2002/635 Sch.1 para.1, SI 2002/896 Sch.1 para.47, SI 2004/2695 Sch.1 para.3

s.63, referred to: SI 2002/920 Sch.1 para.4, Sch.1 para.9

s.65, amended: 2003 c.43 Sch.9 para.10

s.65, applied: SI 2002/816 Sch.3 para.1, SI 2002/920 Sch.3 para.2, Sch.3 para.3, SI 2002/1493 Art.4

s.65, varied: SI 2002/920 Sch.3 para.2, SI 2004/664 Art.11, Art.12, Art.13, Art.14

s.65A, applied: SI 2002/816 Reg.4, Sch.3 para.1, SI 2002/920 Sch.3 para.3, Sch.3 para.4, SI 2002/1493 Art.4

s.65A, varied: SI 2002/920 Sch.3 para.3, Sch.3 para.4

s.66, applied: 2003 c.42 s.27

s.66, referred to: SI 2004/692 Sch.4 para.3

CAP.

1989–cont.

41. Children Act 1989–*cont.*

s.67, amended: 2004 c.31 s.44

s.67, referred to: 2004 c.31 s.45

s.68, amended: 2003 c.44 Sch.32 para.60, Sch.37 Part 7

s.68, applied: SI 2002/635 Reg.2, SI 2002/896 Reg.2, SI 2004/2695 Reg.4

s.68, referred to: 2004 c.31 s.45

s.68, enabling: SI 2002/635, SI 2002/896, SI 2004/2695

s.69, applied: SI 2002/635 Reg.2, SI 2002/896 Sch.1 para.6, SI 2004/2695 Sch.1 para.27

s.69, referred to: 2004 c.31 s.45

s.70, applied: SI 2002/635 Sch.1 para.1, SI 2002/896 Sch.1 para.45, SI 2004/2695 Sch.1 para.3

s.70, referred to: 2004 c.31 s.45

s.71, applied: SI 2002/920 Sch.2 para.3, Sch.2 para.4, Sch.2 para.6, SSI 2002/113 Sch.1 para.20

s.72, applied: SI 2002/920 Sch.2 para.2, Sch.2 para.3, SSI 2002/162 Art.12

s.73, applied: SI 2002/920 Sch.2 para.2, Sch.2 para.3, SSI 2002/162 Art.12

s.75, applied: SSI 2002/162 Art.12

s.77, see *Tameside MBC v Grant* [2002] Fam. 194 (Fam Div), Wall, J.

s.77, applied: SSI 2002/162 Art.12, Art.13

s.78, applied: SI 2002/635 Sch.1 para.1, Sch.1 para.2, SI 2002/896 Sch.1 para.48, Sch.1 para.63, SI 2004/2695 Sch.1 para.10

s.78C, applied: SI 2004/2695 Sch.1 para.3

s.79A, applied: SI 2002/327 Reg.3

s.79A, varied: SI 2003/1992 Reg.3

s.79B, amended: 2002 c.32 Sch.13 para.1, 2004 c.31 Sch.4 para.2, Sch.4 para.6

s.79B, applied: SI 2002/920 Sch.2 para.2

s.79B, varied: SI 2003/1992 Reg.3

s.79C, varied: SI 2003/1992 Reg.3

s.79C, enabling: SI 2002/812, SI 2002/2171, SI 2002/2622, SI 2003/1996, SI 2003/2708, SI 2004/2414, SI 2004/2695

s.79D, applied: SI 2002/635 Sch.1 para.1, SI 2002/896 Sch.1 para.48, SI 2003/1992 Reg.4, SI 2004/2695 Reg.7, Sch.1 para.3, Sch.1 para.10

s.79D, varied: SI 2003/1992 Reg.3

s.79E, amended: 2004 c.31 Sch.4 para.3

s.79E, applied: SI 2002/920 Sch.2 para.6, SI 2004/2695 Sch.1 para.3, Sch.1 para.10

s.79E, varied: SI 2003/1992 Reg.3

s.79E, enabling: SI 2002/919, SI 2002/2171, SI 2002/2622, SI 2003/1995, SI 2003/2709

s.79F, amended: 2004 c.31 Sch.4 para.3

s.79F, applied: SI 2002/635 Sch.1 para.1, SI 2002/896 Sch.1 para.48, SI 2002/920 Sch.2 para.2, Sch.2 para.6, SI 2002/921 Reg.9, SI 2003/463 Art.5, SI 2004/2695 Sch.1 para.3, Sch.1 para.10

1989–cont.

41. Children Act 1989–*cont.*

s.79F, repealed (in part): 2004 c.31 Sch.4 para.3, Sch.5 Part 2

s.79F, varied: SI 2003/1992 Reg.3

s.79F, enabling: SI 2002/921

s.79G, amended: 2004 c.31 Sch.4 para.2, Sch.4 para.4, Sch.5 Part 2

s.79G, varied: SI 2003/1992 Reg.3

s.79H, amended: 2002 c.32 Sch.13 para.2

s.79H, varied: SI 2003/1992 Reg.3

s.79H, enabling: SI 2003/332, SI 2004/3282

s.79J, varied: SI 2003/1992 Reg.3

s.79K, applied: SI 2002/816 Reg.23, Sch.2 para.1, Sch.2 para.3, SI 2002/920 Sch.2 para.2, SI 2003/332 Reg.4

s.79K, referred to: SI 2003/463 Art.15

s.79K, varied: SI 2003/1992 Reg.3

s.79L, applied: SI 2002/816 Sch.2 para.1, Sch.2 para.3, SI 2003/463 Art.11

s.79L, referred to: SI 2002/920 Sch.2 para.2, SI 2003/463 Art.15

s.79L, varied: SI 2003/463 Art.12, SI 2003/1992 Reg.3

s.79M, amended: 2002 c.32 Sch.13 para.3, Sch.22 Part 3

s.79M, applied: SI 2002/816 Reg.4, Sch.2 para.1, SI 2002/920 Sch.2 para.2, SI 2003/463 Art.15, SI 2004/2695 Reg.8

s.79M, referred to: SI 2003/463 Art.12, Art.15

s.79M, varied: SI 2003/1992 Reg.3

s.79M, enabling: SI 2004/2695

s.79N, varied: SI 2003/1992 Reg.3

s.79N, enabling: SI 2004/3136

s.79P, amended: 2002 c.32 Sch.14 para.4

s.79P, repealed (in part): 2002 c.32 Sch.22 Part 3

s.79P, varied: SI 2003/1992 Reg.3

s.79Q, amended: 2002 c.32 Sch.13 para.4

s.79Q, varied: SI 2003/1992 Reg.3

s.79R, varied: SI 2003/1992 Reg.3

s.79S, varied: SI 2003/1992 Reg.3

s.79T, varied: SI 2003/1992 Reg.3

s.79U, amended: 2002 c.32 Sch.13 para.5

s.79U, repealed (in part): 2002 c.32 Sch.13 para.5

s.79U, varied: SI 2003/1992 Reg.3

s.79V, varied: SI 2003/1992 Reg.3

s.79W, varied: SI 2003/1992 Reg.3

s.79X, varied: SI 2003/1992 Reg.3

s.80, amended: 2003 c.43 Sch.4 para.80

s.80, applied: SI 2002/327 Reg.15, 2003 c.43 s.143

s.80, repealed (in part): 2002 c.38 Sch.3 para.65, Sch.5

s.81, repealed (in part): 2002 c.38 Sch.3 para.66, Sch.5

s.82, applied: 2003 c.42 s.21

s.83, amended: 2003 c.39 Sch.8 para.336, 2004 c.31 s.54

s.85, amended: 2003 c.43 Sch.4 para.81

s.85, applied: SI 2002/152 Reg.24

1989–cont.

41. Children Act 1989–*cont.*

s.86, applied: SI 2002/152 Reg.24

s.87, amended: 2003 c.43 s.111, Sch.9 para.10

s.87, applied: SI 2002/152 Reg.24, SI 2002/552 Reg.4, Reg.5, SI 2002/1250 Reg.3, SI 2002/3161 Reg.3, Reg.4, 2003 c.43 s.110, s.144

s.87, referred to: SI 2004/615 Reg.2

s.87, varied: SI 2004/664 Art.11, Art.12, Art.13, Art.14

s.87, enabling: SI 2002/552, SI 2002/3161

s.87D, enabling: SI 2002/3161, SI 2003/753, SI 2004/662

s.88, repealed (in part): 2002 c.38 Sch.3 para.67, Sch.5

s.91, see *C (Children) (Prohibition on Further Applications), Re* [2002] EWCA Civ 292, [2002] 1 F.L.R. 1136 (CA), Dame Elizabeth Butler-Sloss (President); see *G (A Child) (Contempt: Committal Order), Re* [2003] EWCA Civ 489, [2003] 1 W.L.R. 2051 (CA), Dame Elizabeth Butler-Sloss (President)

s.91, amended: 2002 c.38 s.114, Sch.3 para.68

s.93, amended: 2002 c.38 s.122

s.94, amended: 2002 c.38 s.100

s.94, applied: SI 2004/3114 Sch.1

s.97, see *G (A Child) (Litigants In Person), Re* [2003] EWCA Civ 1055, [2003] 2 F.L.R. 963 (CA), Thorpe, L.J.; see *M (A Child) (Children and Family Reporter: Disclosure), Re* [2002] EWCA Civ 1199, [2003] Fam. 26 (CA), Thorpe, L.J.; see *Pelling v Bruce-Williams* [2003] EWHC 1541, [2004] Fam. 22 (Fam Div), Bennett, J.; see *Pelling v Bruce-Williams* [2004] EWCA Civ 845, [2004] Fam. 155 (CA), Thorpe, L.J.

s.97, amended: 2002 c.38 s.101, 2003 c.39 Sch.8 para.337, 2004 c.31 s.62

s.97, repealed (in part): 2003 c.39 Sch.8 para.337, Sch.10

s.98, see *AB (A Child) (Care Proceedings: Disclosure of Medical Evidence to Police), Re* [2002] EWHC 2198, [2003] 1 F.L.R. 579 (Fam Div), Wall, J.; see *D and M (Disclosure: Private Law), Re* [2002] EWHC 2820, [2003] 1 F.L.R. 647 (Fam Div), Hedley, J.

s.98, amended: 2004 c.33 Sch.27 para.132

s.100, see *W (Wardship: Relatives Rejected as Foster Carers), Re* [2003] EWHC 2206, [2004] 1 F.L.R. 415 (Fam Div), Hedley, J.

s.102, amended: SI 2002/253 Sch.5 para.10, SI 2004/1771 Sch.1 para.4

s.102, applied: SI 2004/3114 Sch.1

s.102, repealed (in part): 2002 c.38 Sch.3 para.69, Sch.5

s.104, amended: 2002 c.21 Sch.3 para.19, 2002 c.38 s.111

1989–cont.

41. Children Act 1989–*cont.*

s.104, enabling: SI 2002/546, SI 2002/552, SI 2002/812, SI 2002/896, SI 2002/919, SI 2002/921, SI 2002/1855, SI 2002/2171, SI 2002/2622, SI 2002/2935, SI 2002/3013, SI 2002/3161, SI 2003/332, SI 2003/762, SI 2003/1992, SI 2003/1995, SI 2003/1996, SI 2003/2077, SI 2003/2708, SI 2003/2709, SI 2004/719, SI 2004/1419, SI 2004/1448, SI 2004/1449, SI 2004/1732, SI 2004/1748, SI 2004/2187, SI 2004/2253, SI 2004/2414, SI 2004/2695, SI 2004/3282

s.105, see *G (Adoption: Ordinary Residence), Re* [2002] EWHC 2447, [2003] 2 F.L.R. 944 (Fam Div), Wall, J.; see *H (A Child) (Care Order: Appropriate Local Authority), Re* [2003] EWCA Civ 1629, [2004] Fam. 89 (CA), Thorpe, L.J.; see *Redbridge LBC v Newport City Council* [2003] EWHC 2967, [2004] 2 F.L.R. 226 (Fam Div), David Hershman Q.C.

s.105, amended: 2002 c.38 Sch.3 para.70, SI 2002/2469 Sch.1 para.16, 2004 c.31 Sch.3 para.11, 2004 c.33 s.75

s.105, referred to: 2002 c.38 Sch.6, SI 2002/920 Sch.1 para.4, Sch.1 para.9

s.105, repealed (in part): 2002 c.38 Sch.5

s.105, varied: 2004 c.33 Sch.21 para.33

Sch.1, see *P (A Child) (Financial Provision), Re* [2003] EWCA Civ 837, [2003] 2 F.L.R. 865 (CA), Thorpe, L.J.; see *P (A Child) (Financial Provision), Re* Independent, December 11, 2002 (Fam Div), Judge Brunning; see *White v White* [2003] EWCA Civ 924, [2004] 2 F.L.R. 321 (CA), Thorpe, L.J.

Sch.1, applied: SI 2002/1330 Sch.3 para.1, SI 2002/3200 Reg.15, Sch.3 para.1, SI 2003/1994 Sch.3 para.1

Sch.1, disapplied: SI 2002/195 Reg.15, Sch.3 para.1

Sch.1 para.1, amended: 2002 c.38 Sch.3 para.71

Sch.1 para.1, applied: SI 2004/3114 Sch.1

Sch.1 para.2, amended: 2004 c.33 s.78

Sch.1 para.2, applied: SI 2004/3114 Art.3, Sch.1

Sch.1 para.5, applied: SI 2004/3114 Sch.1

Sch.1 para.6, amended: 2002 c.38 Sch.3 para.71

Sch.1 para.6, applied: SI 2004/3114 Sch.1

Sch.1 para.6A, amended: 2003 c.39 Sch.8 para.338

Sch.1 para.8, amended: 2002 c.38 Sch.3 para.71

Sch.1 para.8, applied: SI 2004/3114 Sch.1

Sch.1 para.10, amended: 2003 c.39 Sch.8 para.339

Sch.1 para.10, applied: SI 2004/3114 Sch.1

Sch.1 para.11, applied: SI 2004/3114 Sch.1

1989–cont.

41. Children Act 1989–*cont.*

Sch.1 para.14, amended: 2002 c.38 Sch.3 para.71

Sch.1 para.14, applied: SI 2004/3114 Sch.1

Sch.1 para.15, amended: 2004 c.33 s.78

Sch.1 para.15, applied: SI 2002/2006 Reg.19

Sch.1 para.16, amended: 2004 c.33 s.78

Sch.2 Part I para.1, see *R. (on the application of M) v Barking and Dagenham LBC* [2002] EWHC 2663, (2003) C.C.L. Rep. 87 (QBD (Admin Ct)), Crane, J.

Sch.2 Part I para.1A, amended: 2002 c.17 Sch.2 para.52, 2003 c.43 Sch.4 para.82, SI 2003/154 Sch.1 para.2

Sch.2 Part I para.1A, applied: SI 2003/154 Reg.7

Sch.2 Part I para.1A, referred to: SI 2003/154 Sch.1 para.1

Sch.2 Part I para.1A, repealed: 2004 c.31 Sch.5 Part 1

Sch.2 Part II para.12, applied: SI 2002/57 Reg.40, SI 2003/237 Reg.40

Sch.2 Part II para.12, enabling: SI 2002/57, SI 2002/546, SI 2002/865, SI 2003/237, SI 2003/896

Sch.2 Part II para.13, enabling: SI 2002/546, SI 2002/2935

Sch.2 Part II para.14, enabling: SI 2002/546, SI 2002/2935

Sch.2 Part II para.15, referred to: 2002 c.38 s.53

Sch.2 Part II para.17, applied: SI 2002/327 Reg.15

Sch.2 Part II para.19, amended: 2002 c.38 Sch.3 para.72

Sch.2 Part II para.19, applied: SI 2002/57 Reg.39, SI 2004/3114 Sch.1

Sch.2 Part II para.19B, enabling: SI 2002/1855

Sch.2 Part II para.19C, applied: 2003 c.42 s.21

Sch.2 Part II para.20, amended: 2003 c.43 Sch.9 para.10

Sch.2 Part III, applied: 2002 c.38 s.53

Sch.2 Part III para.21, amended: 2002 c.21 Sch.3 para.20

Sch.2 Part III para.21, referred to: 2002 c.38 s.53

Sch.2 Part III para.23, applied: SI 2004/3114 Sch.1

Sch.2 Part III para.24, amended: 2003 c.39 Sch.8 para.340

Sch.2 para.6, see *R. (on the application of CD) v Isle of Anglesey CC* [2004] EWHC 1635, [2004] 3 F.C.R. 171 (QBD (Admin Ct)), Wilson, J.

Sch.2 para.19, see *S (A Child) (Freeing for Adoption), Re* [2002] EWCA Civ 798, [2002] 2 F.L.R. 681 (CA), Thorpe, L.J.

Sch.3 Part II para.6, applied: SI 2004/3114 Sch.1

1989–cont.

41. Children Act 1989–*cont.*

Sch.3 Part III para.15, applied: SI 2004/3114 Sch.1

Sch.3 Part III para.17, applied: SI 2004/3114 Sch.1

Sch.3 para.13, see *Graves v Islington LBC* [2003] EWHC 2817, [2004] E.L.R. 1 (QBD (Admin Ct)), Beatson, J.

Sch.4 Part I para.2, enabling: SI 2003/1649

Sch.4 Part III para.4, enabling: SI 2002/546, SI 2002/2935

Sch.5, applied: SI 2002/920 Sch.1 para.9, SI 2002/1493 Art.4

Sch.5, referred to: SI 2002/920 Sch.1 para.4, Sch.1 para.9

Sch.5 Part I para.1, applied: SI 2002/635 Reg.2, Sch.1 para.1, SI 2002/896 Sch.1 para.5, Sch.1 para.47, SI 2004/2695 Sch.1 para.3, Sch.1 para.26

Sch.5 Part I para.2, applied: SI 2002/920 Sch.1 para.7, Sch.1 para.8

Sch.5 Part I para.4, applied: SI 2002/920 Sch.1 para.8, Sch.1 para.9

Sch.5 Part I para.5, applied: SI 2002/920 Sch.3 para.4, SI 2002/1493 Art.4

Sch.5 Part II para.7, enabling: SI 2002/546, SI 2002/2935

Sch.6, applied: SI 2002/920 Sch.1 para.9, Sch.1 para.10, SI 2002/1493 Art.4

Sch.6, referred to: SI 2002/920 Sch.1 para.4, Sch.1 para.9

Sch.6 Part I para.1, applied: SI 2002/635 Reg.2, SI 2002/896 Sch.1 para.5, SI 2004/2695 Sch.1 para.26

Sch.6 Part I para.2, applied: SI 2002/635 Sch.1 para.1, SI 2002/896 Sch.1 para.47, SI 2002/920 Sch.1 para.7, SI 2004/2695 Sch.1 para.3

Sch.6 Part I para.3, referred to: SI 2002/920 Sch.1 para.4

Sch.6 Part I para.4, applied: SI 2002/635 Reg.2, SI 2002/896 Sch.1 para.5, SI 2004/2695 Sch.1 para.26

Sch.6 Part I para.5, applied: SI 2002/920 Sch.1 para.4, Sch.1 para.7, Sch.1 para.8

Sch.6 Part I para.6, referred to: SI 2002/920 Sch.1 para.4

Sch.6 Part I para.7, applied: SI 2002/920 Sch.1 para.8, Sch.1 para.9

Sch.6 Part I para.7, referred to: SI 2002/920 Sch.1 para.4

Sch.6 Part I para.8, applied: SI 2002/920 Sch.3 para.3, SI 2002/1493 Art.4

Sch.6 Part II para.10, enabling: SI 2002/546, SI 2002/2935, SI 2004/1419, SI 2004/2253

Sch.8 para.5, amended: 2002 c.38 Sch.3 para.73

Sch.8 para.6, referred to: 2004 c.31 s.45

Sch.8 para.7, referred to: 2004 c.31 s.45

Sch.8 para.7A, added: 2004 c.31 s.44

1989–cont.

41. Children Act 1989–*cont.*

Sch.8 para.7A, referred to: 2004 c.31 s.45

Sch.8 para.8, referred to: 2004 c.31 s.45

Sch.8 para.9, referred to: 2004 c.31 s.45

Sch.9, applied: SI 2002/920 Sch.2 para.2

Sch.9A, applied: SI 2004/2695 Reg.8

Sch.9A, amended: 2004 c.31 Sch.4 para.4, Sch.5 Part 2

Sch.9 para.1, applied: SI 2002/920 Sch.2 para.6

Sch.9 para.2, applied: SI 2002/896 Reg.4, SI 2002/920 Sch.2 para.2, SI 2004/2695 Reg.6

Sch.9 para.6, applied: SSI 2002/162 Art.7

Sch.9A para.1, applied: SI 2002/2005 Reg.14, SI 2003/3230 Sch.1 para.3

Sch.9A para.1, enabling: SI 2003/1992

Sch.9A para.2, applied: SI 2002/2005 Reg.14

Sch.9A para.2A, added: 2004 c.31 Sch.4 para.7

Sch.9A para.4, amended: 2002 c.32 Sch.13 para.6, Sch.21 para.9, 2003 c.44 Sch.32 para.61, Sch.37 Part 7, 2004 c.31 Sch.4 para.5, Sch.4 para.8, Sch.5 Part 2

Sch.9A para.4, applied: SI 2002/816 Sch.2 para.1, SI 2002/896 Reg.3, SI 2004/2695 Reg.5

Sch.9A para.4, enabling: SI 2002/896, SI 2004/2695

Sch.9A para.5A, added: 2004 c.31 Sch.4 para.9

Sch.9A para.6, applied: SI 2002/919 Reg.18, SI 2002/920 Sch.2 para.4

Sch.9A para.6, disapplied: SI 2002/920 Sch.2 para.4

Sch.9A para.6, enabling: SI 2002/919, SI 2003/2709

Sch.9A para.7, amended: 2004 c.31 Sch.4 para.4

Sch.9A para.7, enabling: SI 2002/921

Sch.10 Part I para.1, repealed: 2002 c.38 Sch.3 para.74, Sch.5

Sch.10 Part I para.2, repealed: 2002 c.38 Sch.3 para.74, Sch.5

Sch.10 Part I para.3, repealed: 2002 c.38 Sch.3 para.74, Sch.5

Sch.10 Part I para.4, repealed: 2002 c.38 Sch.3 para.74, Sch.5

Sch.10 Part I para.5, repealed: 2002 c.38 Sch.3 para.74, Sch.5

Sch.10 Part I para.6, repealed: 2002 c.38 Sch.3 para.74, Sch.5

Sch.10 Part I para.7, repealed: 2002 c.38 Sch.3 para.74, Sch.5

Sch.10 Part I para.8, repealed: 2002 c.38 Sch.3 para.74, Sch.5

Sch.10 Part I para.9, repealed: 2002 c.38 Sch.3 para.74, Sch.5

Sch.10 Part I para.10, repealed: 2002 c.38 Sch.3 para.74, Sch.5

1989–cont.

41. Children Act 1989–*cont.*

Sch.10 Part I para.11, repealed: 2002 c.38 Sch.3 para.74, Sch.5

Sch.10 Part I para.12, repealed: 2002 c.38 Sch.3 para.74, Sch.5

Sch.10 Part I para.13, repealed: 2002 c.38 Sch.3 para.74, Sch.5

Sch.10 Part I para.14, repealed: 2002 c.38 Sch.3 para.74, Sch.5

Sch.10 Part I para.15, repealed: 2002 c.38 Sch.3 para.74, Sch.5

Sch.10 Part I para.16, repealed: 2002 c.38 Sch.3 para.74, Sch.5

Sch.10 Part I para.17, repealed: 2002 c.38 Sch.3 para.74, Sch.5

Sch.10 Part I para.18, repealed: 2002 c.38 Sch.3 para.74, Sch.5

Sch.10 Part I para.19, repealed: 2002 c.38 Sch.3 para.74, Sch.5

Sch.10 Part I para.20, repealed: 2002 c.38 Sch.3 para.74, Sch.5

Sch.10 Part I para.21, repealed: 2002 c.38 Sch.3 para.74, Sch.5

Sch.10 Part I para.22, repealed: 2002 c.38 Sch.3 para.74, Sch.5

Sch.10 Part I para.23, repealed: 2002 c.38 Sch.3 para.74, Sch.5

Sch.10 Part I para.24, repealed: 2002 c.38 Sch.3 para.74, Sch.5

Sch.10 Part I para.25, repealed: 2002 c.38 Sch.3 para.74, Sch.5

Sch.10 Part I para.26, repealed: 2002 c.38 Sch.3 para.74, Sch.5

Sch.10 Part I para.27, repealed: 2002 c.38 Sch.3 para.74, Sch.5

Sch.10 Part I para.28, repealed: 2002 c.38 Sch.3 para.74, Sch.5

Sch.10 Part I para.29, repealed: 2002 c.38 Sch.3 para.74, Sch.5

Sch.10 Part I para.30, repealed: 2002 c.38 Sch.3 para.74, Sch.5

Sch.10 Part I para.31, repealed: 2002 c.38 Sch.3 para.74, Sch.5

Sch.11 Part I, enabling: SI 2003/331

Sch.11 Part I para.1, amended: 2002 c.38 Sch.3 para.75

Sch.11 Part I para.2, amended: 2002 c.38 Sch.3 para.75

Sch.11 Part II para.8, repealed (in part): 2003 c.39 Sch.10

Sch.12 para.11, repealed: 2003 c.42 Sch.7

Sch.12 para.12, repealed: 2003 c.42 Sch.7

Sch.12 para.13, repealed: 2003 c.42 Sch.7

Sch.12 para.14, repealed: 2003 c.42 Sch.7

Sch.12 para.16, repealed: 2003 c.42 Sch.7

Sch.13 para.50, repealed: 2003 asp 13 Sch.5 Part 1

Sch.14 Part 1 para.1, applied: SI 2003/2960 r.3

Sch.14 Part 3 para.11, applied: SI 2004/3114 Sch.1

1989–cont.

41. Children Act 1989–*cont.*

Sch.14 Part 5 para.15, applied: SI 2002/635 Reg.2, SI 2002/896 Sch.1 para.2, SI 2004/2695 Sch.1 para.22

42. Local Government and Housing Act 1989

Commencement Orders: 2004 c.14 Sch.1 Part 10

applied: SI 2002/1860(a), 2003 c.26 s.21, s.22

referred to: SI 2002/803 Art.2, SI 2002/808 Art.2, 2003 c.26 Sch.3 para.1

Part I, applied: SI 2003/409 Sch.1 Part I, SI 2003/437 Sch.1 Part 2, SI 2004/1777 Art.12

Part IV, applied: SI 2003/3146 Reg.33, SI 2004/533 Art.11

Part IV, referred to: SI 2004/533 Art.3, Art.7, Art.8, Art.9

Part V, applied: 2003 c.26 s.18, s.95, 2004 c.23 s.48

Part VII, applied: 2004 c.34 s.3

s.1, varied: SI 2004/1777 Art.12, SI 2004/1778 Art.12

s.2, amended: SI 2002/808 Art.21, 2004 asp 9 s.9, 2004 c.31 Sch.2 para.3

s.2, repealed (in part): 2004 asp 9 s.9, 2004 c.21 Sch.2

s.2, varied: SI 2004/1777 Art.12, SI 2004/1778 Art.12

s.3, applied: 2002 asp 13 Sch.1 para.75, SI 2003/409 Sch.1 Part I

s.3, varied: SI 2004/1777 Art.12, SI 2004/1778 Art.12

s.4, applied: 2003 c.20 Sch.4 para.11

s.4, varied: SI 2004/1777 Art.17, SI 2004/1778 Art.17

s.5, added: SI 2002/808 Art.22

s.5, amended: SI 2002/808 Art.22, 2003 c.26 s.113

s.5, applied: SI 2003/1483 Reg.2, SSI 2002/201 Art.11, SSI 2003/1 Art.11, 2004 c.23 s.25

s.5, varied: SI 2004/1777 Art.17, SI 2004/1778 Art.17

s.5A, added: SI 2002/808 Art.22

s.6, applied: 2003 c.26 s.25

s.7, see *Archibald v Fife Council* [2004] UKHL 32, [2004] 4 All E.R. 303 (HL), Lord Nicholls of Birkenhead

s.7, amended: SI 2003/1673 Reg.31

s.7, repealed (in part): 2004 c.21 Sch.2

s.7, varied: SI 2004/1777 Art.17, SI 2004/1778 Art.17

s.8, amended: SI 2002/803 Art.5

s.8, varied: SI 2004/1777 Art.17, SI 2004/1778 Art.17

s.9, applied: SI 2002/975 Reg.3

s.9, varied: SI 2002/975 Reg.3

s.10, varied: SI 2004/1777 Art.15, SI 2004/1778 Art.15

1989–cont.

42. Local Government and Housing Act 1989–*cont.*

s.12, varied: SI 2004/1777 Art.17, SI 2004/1778 Art.17

s.13, repealed (in part): 2004 c.31 Sch.5 Part 4

s.13, varied: SI 2004/1777 Art.17, SI 2004/1778 Art.17

s.15, applied: SI 2002/339 Reg.3, SI 2002/1895 Reg.4

s.18, applied: SI 2002/975 Reg.2, SI 2003/1021 Reg.3, Reg.6, SI 2003/2437 Reg.2

s.18, disapplied: SI 2003/1021 Reg.34

s.18, enabling: SI 2002/1895, SI 2003/1021, SI 2003/1692, SI 2003/2676, SI 2003/2963, SI 2004/2555, SSI 2002/15, SSI 2004/146

s.19, amended: 2004 c.33 Sch.27 para.133

s.19, varied: SI 2004/1777 Art.14, SI 2004/1778 Art.14

s.20, varied: SI 2004/1777 Sch.3 para.7, SI 2004/1778 Sch.3 para.7

s.21, amended: 2004 c.21 Sch.1 para.71, 2004 c.36 Sch.2 para.10

s.23, repealed (in part): 2002 asp 11 Sch.6 para.13

s.27, repealed: 2002 asp 11 Sch.6 para.13

s.29, repealed: 2002 asp 11 Sch.6 para.13

s.31, repealed (in part): 2003 asp 1 s.60

s.31, varied: SI 2004/1777 Art.14, SI 2004/1778 Art.14

s.39, amended: 2003 c.10 Sch.1 para.4, 2004 c.36 Sch.2 para.10

s.39, applied: SI 2004/533 Art.8, Art.9

s.39, referred to: SI 2004/533 Art.3, Art.10

s.39, repealed (in part): 2003 c.26 Sch.8 Part 1, 2003 c.39 Sch.8 para.341, Sch.10

s.39, enabling: SI 2002/2118, SI 2002/2298, SI 2003/1035

s.40, repealed (in part): 2003 c.26 Sch.8 Part 1

s.41, applied: SI 2002/535 Sch.1

s.41, referred to: SI 2002/3199 Reg.1, SI 2003/533 Reg.7, SI 2003/3118 Reg.2

s.41, repealed (in part): 2003 c.26 Sch.8 Part 1

s.42, repealed (in part): 2003 c.26 Sch.8 Part 1

s.42, enabling: SI 2003/515, SI 2003/915, SI 2004/459

s.43, repealed (in part): 2003 c.26 Sch.8 Part 1

s.43, varied: SI 2003/1633 Sch.1 para.19, Sch.1 para.20, Sch.1 para.21

s.44, repealed (in part): 2003 c.26 Sch.8 Part 1

s.44A, repealed (in part): 2003 c.26 Sch.8 Part 1

s.45, applied: SI 2002/510 Reg.2

s.45, repealed (in part): 2003 c.26 Sch.8 Part 1

1989–cont.

42. Local Government and Housing Act 1989–*cont.*

s.46, repealed (in part): 2003 c.26 Sch.8 Part 1

s.46, varied: SI 2003/1633 Sch.1 para.22

s.47, repealed (in part): 2003 c.26 Sch.8 Part 1

s.48, applied: SI 2003/2938 Sch.1 para.17, SI 2003/3034 Sch.2 para.3, SI 2003/3239 Reg.3

s.48, referred to: SI 2004/533 Art.3

s.48, repealed (in part): 2003 c.26 Sch.8 Part 1

s.48, enabling: SI 2003/515

s.49, applied: SI 2002/110 Reg.2, SI 2003/248 Reg.2, SI 2003/894 Reg.2

s.49, referred to: SI 2004/533 Art.3

s.49, repealed (in part): 2003 c.26 Sch.8 Part 1

s.49, enabling: SI 2002/110, SI 2002/785, SI 2003/248, SI 2003/894

s.50, applied: SI 2003/3239 Reg.3

s.50, repealed (in part): 2003 c.26 Sch.8 Part 1

s.51, repealed (in part): 2003 c.26 Sch.8 Part 1

s.52, referred to: SI 2004/533 Art.3

s.52, repealed (in part): 2003 c.26 Sch.8 Part 1

s.53, repealed (in part): 2003 c.26 Sch.8 Part 1

s.54, applied: SI 2002/906 Art.15

s.54, repealed (in part): 2003 c.26 Sch.8 Part 1

s.55, repealed (in part): 2003 c.26 Sch.8 Part 1

s.56, repealed (in part): 2003 c.26 Sch.8 Part 1

s.57, repealed (in part): 2003 c.26 Sch.8 Part 1

s.58, repealed (in part): 2003 c.26 Sch.8 Part 1

s.58, enabling: SI 2002/451, SI 2002/885

s.59, applied: SI 2003/3146 Reg.16

s.59, referred to: SI 2003/3146 Reg.16

s.59, repealed (in part): 2003 c.26 Sch.8 Part 1

s.59, enabling: SI 2003/43

s.60, applied: SI 2003/2938 Sch.1 para.18, SI 2003/3034 Sch.2 para.3

s.60, repealed (in part): 2003 c.26 Sch.8 Part 1

s.61, repealed (in part): 2003 c.26 Sch.8 Part 1

s.61, enabling: SI 2002/2299

s.62, repealed (in part): 2003 c.26 Sch.8 Part 1

s.63, repealed (in part): 2003 c.26 Sch.8 Part 1

s.64, repealed (in part): 2003 c.26 Sch.8 Part 1

1989–cont.

42. Local Government and Housing Act 1989–*cont.*

s.65, amended: 2004 c.23 Sch.2 para.11

s.65, repealed (in part): 2003 c.26 Sch.8 Part 1

s.66, referred to: SI 2004/533 Art.3

s.66, repealed (in part): 2003 c.26 Sch.8 Part 1

s.66, varied: SI 2003/1633 Sch.1 para.23

s.66, enabling: SI 2002/451, SI 2002/885, SI 2002/1884

s.67, amended: 2003 c.26 Sch.3 para.2, 2004 c.21 Sch.1 para.71, 2004 c.36 Sch.2 para.10

s.67, applied: SI 2004/1777 Art.12, SI 2004/1778 Art.12

s.67, repealed (in part): 2003 c.39 Sch.8 para.342, Sch.10

s.68, applied: 2004 c.23 s.48, SI 2004/1777 Art.12, SI 2004/1778 Art.12

s.69, amended: 2004 c.33 Sch.27 para.134

s.69, applied: 2003 c.26 s.18, SI 2004/1777 Art.12, SI 2004/1778 Art.12

s.70, amended: 2003 c.26 Sch.3 para.3, Sch.7 para.30, 2004 c.23 Sch.2 para.12

s.70, applied: 2003 c.26 s.100, SI 2004/1777 Art.12, SI 2004/1778 Art.12

s.70, varied: 2003 c.26 s.95

s.71, amended: SI 2002/808 Art.25

s.71, applied: SI 2004/1777 Art.12, SI 2004/1778 Art.12

s.72, applied: 2003 c.26 s.18, SI 2004/1777 Art.12, SI 2004/1778 Art.12

s.73, amended: SI 2002/808 Art.25

s.74, applied: SI 2003/533 Reg.7, SI 2003/3239 Reg.18

s.74, referred to: 2003 c.26 s.11

s.79, amended: 2003 c.26 s.89

s.80, amended: 2003 c.26 s.89, Sch.8 Part 1

s.80, repealed (in part): 2003 c.26 Sch.8 Part 1

s.80A, amended: 2003 c.26 Sch.7 para.31

s.80ZA, added: 2003 c.26 s.90

s.87A, added: 2003 c.26 s.91

s.88, amended: 2003 c.21 Sch.17 para.100, 2003 c.26 s.89, Sch.7 para.32

s.89, amended: SI 2002/1860 Sch.5 para.2

s.89, repealed (in part): SI 2002/1860 Sch.6

s.90, repealed: SI 2002/1860 Sch.6

s.91, substituted: SI 2002/1860 Sch.5 para.4

s.92, repealed (in part): SI 2002/1860 Sch.6

s.93, amended: SI 2002/1860 Sch.6

s.93, repealed (in part): SI 2002/1860 Sch.6

s.94, varied: SI 2004/1778 Art.14

s.95, amended: SI 2002/1860 Sch.5 para.6, Sch.6

s.95, repealed (in part): SI 2002/1860 Sch.6

s.95, varied: SI 2004/1778 Art.14

s.96, varied: SI 2004/1778 Art.14

s.97, varied: SI 2004/1778 Art.14

s.98, varied: SI 2004/1778 Art.14

1989–cont.

42. Local Government and Housing Act 1989–*cont.*

s.99, amended: SI 2002/1860 Sch.6

s.100, amended: 2004 c.34 Sch.15 para.34

s.105, varied: SI 2004/1778 Art.14

s.147, repealed: 2004 c.14 Sch.1 Part 10

s.148, repealed: 2004 c.14 Sch.1 Part 10

s.150, enabling: SI 2003/907, SI 2004/2443

s.152, amended: 2004 c.21 Sch.1 para.71, 2004 c.36 Sch.2 para.10

s.152, enabling: SI 2003/907

s.155, amended: 2003 c.26 s.37, Sch.8 Part 1, 2004 c.21 Sch.1 para.71

s.157, applied: SI 2003/3239 Reg.23

s.165, repealed (in part): 2004 c.34 Sch.16

s.167, repealed: 2004 c.34 s.227, Sch.16

s.168, applied: SI 2003/407 Art.2

s.169, repealed (in part): SI 2002/1860 Sch.6

s.173, amended: 2002 c.9 Sch.11 para.24

s.173, applied: SI 2003/1417 r.95

s.190, enabling: SI 2002/451, SI 2002/2299, SI 2003/43, SI 2003/515, SI 2003/1021, SI 2003/1692, SI 2004/459, SSI 2002/15, SSI 2004/146

s.195, amended: 2004 c.34 Sch.15 para.35

Sch.1 para.4, amended: 2004 c.31 s.55, Sch.5 Part 4

Sch.3 Part I para.1, repealed (in part): 2003 c.26 Sch.8 Part 1

Sch.3 Part I para.2, repealed (in part): 2003 c.26 Sch.8 Part 1

Sch.3 Part I para.3, repealed (in part): 2003 c.26 Sch.8 Part 1

Sch.3 Part I para.4, repealed (in part): 2003 c.26 Sch.8 Part 1

Sch.3 Part I para.5, repealed (in part): 2003 c.26 Sch.8 Part 1

Sch.3 Part II para.6, repealed (in part): 2003 c.26 Sch.8 Part 1

Sch.3 Part II para.7, repealed (in part): 2003 c.26 Sch.8 Part 1

Sch.3 Part III, applied: SI 2002/510 Reg.2, SI 2003/3146 Reg.33

Sch.3 Part III para.8, repealed (in part): 2003 c.26 Sch.8 Part 1

Sch.3 Part III para.9, repealed (in part): 2003 c.26 Sch.8 Part 1

Sch.3 Part III para.10, repealed (in part): 2003 c.26 Sch.8 Part 1

Sch.3 Part III para.10A, repealed (in part): 2003 c.26 Sch.8 Part 1

Sch.3 Part III para.10B, repealed (in part): 2003 c.26 Sch.8 Part 1

Sch.3 Part III para.10C, repealed (in part): 2003 c.26 Sch.8 Part 1

Sch.3 Part III para.10D, repealed (in part): 2003 c.26 Sch.8 Part 1

Sch.3 Part III para.10E, repealed (in part): 2003 c.26 Sch.8 Part 1

Sch.3 Part III para.10F, repealed (in part): 2003 c.26 Sch.8 Part 1

1989–cont.
42. Local Government and Housing Act 1989–*cont.*

Sch.3 Part III para.10G, repealed (in part): 2003 c.26 Sch.8 Part 1

Sch.3 Part III para.10H, repealed (in part): 2003 c.26 Sch.8 Part 1

Sch.3 Part III para.10I, repealed (in part): 2003 c.26 Sch.8 Part 1

Sch.3 Part III para.10J, repealed (in part): 2003 c.26 Sch.8 Part 1

Sch.3 Part III para.11, repealed (in part): 2003 c.26 Sch.8 Part 1

Sch.3 Part III para.11, enabling: SI 2002/2299

Sch.3 Part III para.12, repealed (in part): 2003 c.26 Sch.8 Part 1

Sch.3 Part III para.13, repealed (in part): 2003 c.26 Sch.8 Part 1

Sch.3 Part III para.14, repealed (in part): 2003 c.26 Sch.8 Part 1

Sch.3 Part IV para.15, repealed (in part): 2003 c.26 Sch.8 Part 1

Sch.3 Part IV para.15, enabling: SI 2002/2299

Sch.3 Part IV para.16, repealed (in part): 2003 c.26 Sch.8 Part 1

Sch.3 Part IV para.17, repealed (in part): 2003 c.26 Sch.8 Part 1

Sch.3 Part IV para.18, repealed (in part): 2003 c.26 Sch.8 Part 1

Sch.3 Part IV para.19, repealed (in part): 2003 c.26 Sch.8 Part 1

Sch.3 Part IV para.20, repealed (in part): 2003 c.26 Sch.8 Part 1

Sch.4 Part I para.5, repealed: 2003 c.26 Sch.8 Part 1

Sch.4 Part I para.9, substituted: 2003 c.26 Sch.7 para.33

Sch.4 Part II para.2, applied: SI 2003/533 Reg.7

Sch.4 Part II para.2, substituted: SI 2004/533 Art.4

Sch.4 Part II para.4, repealed: 2003 c.26 Sch.8 Part 1

Sch.4 Part II para.5, substituted: 2003 c.26 s.90

Sch.4 Part II para.8, applied: SI 2003/533 Reg.7

Sch.4 Part II para.10, added: 2003 c.26 Sch.7 para.33

Sch.4 Part IV, referred to: 2003 c.26 s.128

Sch.4 Part IV para.3, repealed: 2003 c.26 Sch.8 Part 1

Sch.5 para.37, amended: 2003 c.26 Sch.8 Part 1

Sch.5 para.38, repealed (in part): 2003 c.26 Sch.8 Part 1

Sch.5 para.60, repealed (in part): 2003 c.26 Sch.8 Part 1

Sch.9 Part I para.1, repealed: 2004 c.34 Sch.16

1989–cont.
42. Local Government and Housing Act 1989–*cont.*

Sch.9 Part I para.2, repealed: 2004 c.34 Sch.16

Sch.9 Part I para.3, repealed: 2004 c.34 Sch.16

Sch.9 Part I para.4, repealed: 2004 c.34 Sch.16

Sch.9 Part I para.5, repealed: 2004 c.34 Sch.16

Sch.9 Part I para.6, repealed: 2004 c.34 Sch.16

Sch.9 Part I para.7, repealed: 2004 c.34 Sch.16

Sch.9 Part I para.8, repealed: 2004 c.34 Sch.16

Sch.9 Part I para.9, repealed: 2004 c.34 Sch.16

Sch.9 Part I para.10, repealed: 2004 c.34 Sch.16

Sch.9 Part I para.11, repealed: 2004 c.34 Sch.16

Sch.9 Part I para.12, repealed: 2004 c.34 Sch.16

Sch.9 Part I para.13, repealed: 2004 c.34 Sch.16

Sch.9 Part II para.14, repealed: 2004 c.34 Sch.16

Sch.9 Part II para.16, repealed: 2004 c.34 Sch.16

Sch.9 Part II para.17, repealed (in part): 2004 c.34 Sch.16

Sch.9 Part II para.20, repealed (in part): 2004 c.34 Sch.16

Sch.9 Part II para.21, repealed: 2004 c.34 Sch.16

Sch.9 Part II para.22, repealed: 2004 c.34 Sch.16

Sch.9 Part II para.23, repealed: 2004 c.34 Sch.16

Sch.9 Part II para.25, repealed (in part): 2004 c.34 Sch.16

Sch.9 Part II para.29, repealed: 2004 c.34 Sch.16

Sch.9 Part II para.32, repealed: 2004 c.34 Sch.16

Sch.9 Part II para.33, repealed (in part): 2004 c.34 Sch.16

Sch.9 Part II para.36, repealed: 2004 c.34 Sch.16

Sch.9 Part II para.42, repealed: 2004 c.34 Sch.16

Sch.9 Part II para.43, repealed (in part): 2004 c.34 Sch.16

Sch.9 Part III, see *Stanley v Ealing LBC (No.2)* [2003] EWCA Civ 679, [2003] H.L.R. 71 (CA), Buxton, L.J.

Sch.9 Part III para.44, repealed: 2004 c.34 Sch.16

Sch.9 Part III para.45, repealed: 2004 c.34 Sch.16

CAP.

1989–cont.

42. Local Government and Housing Act 1989–*cont.*

Sch.9 Part III para.46, repealed: 2004 c.34 Sch.16

Sch.9 Part III para.47, repealed: 2004 c.34 Sch.16

Sch.9 Part III para.48, repealed: 2004 c.34 Sch.16

Sch.9 Part III para.49, repealed: 2004 c.34 Sch.16

Sch.9 Part III para.50, repealed: 2004 c.34 Sch.16

Sch.9 Part III para.51, repealed: 2004 c.34 Sch.16

Sch.9 Part III para.52, repealed: 2004 c.34 Sch.16

Sch.9 Part III para.53, repealed: 2004 c.34 Sch.16

Sch.9 Part III para.54, repealed: 2004 c.34 Sch.16

Sch.9 Part III para.55, repealed: 2004 c.34 Sch.16

Sch.9 Part III para.56, repealed: 2004 c.34 Sch.16

Sch.9 Part III para.57, repealed: 2004 c.34 Sch.16

Sch.9 Part III para.58, repealed: 2004 c.34 Sch.16

Sch.9 Part III para.59, repealed: 2004 c.34 Sch.16

Sch.9 Part III para.60, repealed: 2004 c.34 Sch.16

Sch.9 Part III para.61, repealed: 2004 c.34 Sch.16

Sch.9 Part III para.62, repealed: 2004 c.34 Sch.16

Sch.9 Part III para.63, repealed: 2004 c.34 Sch.16

Sch.9 Part III para.64, repealed: 2004 c.34 Sch.16

Sch.9 Part III para.65, repealed: 2004 c.34 Sch.16

Sch.9 Part III para.66, repealed: 2004 c.34 Sch.16

Sch.9 Part III para.67, repealed: 2004 c.34 Sch.16

Sch.9 Part III para.68, repealed: 2004 c.34 Sch.16

Sch.9 Part III para.69, repealed: 2004 c.34 Sch.16

Sch.9 Part III para.70, repealed: 2004 c.34 Sch.16

Sch.9 Part III para.71, repealed: 2004 c.34 Sch.16

Sch.9 Part IV para.75, repealed: 2004 c.34 Sch.16

Sch.9 Part V para.83, repealed: 2004 c.34 Sch.16

Sch.9 Part V para.84, repealed: 2004 c.34 Sch.16

CAP.

1989–cont.

42. Local Government and Housing Act 1989–*cont.*

Sch.9 Part V para.86, repealed: 2004 c.34 Sch.16

Sch.10, applied: 2002 c.15 s.77

Sch.10 para.4, applied: SI 2004/1005 Sch.2

Sch.10 para.4, enabling: SI 2002/2227, SI 2003/233

Sch.10 para.5, amended: 2004 c.33 Sch.8 para.46

Sch.11 para.6, repealed (in part): 2003 c.26 Sch.8 Part 1

Sch.11 para.7, repealed (in part): 2003 c.26 Sch.8 Part 1

Sch.11 para.10, repealed (in part): 2002 c.15 Sch.14

Sch.11 para.44, repealed: 2002 asp 11 Sch.6 para.13

Sch.11 para.45, repealed: 2002 asp 11 Sch.6 para.13

Sch.11 para.46, repealed: 2002 asp 11 Sch.6 para.13

Sch.11 para.59, repealed (in part): 2003 c.26 Sch.8 Part 1

Sch.11 para.91, repealed: 2002 c.15 Sch.14

Sch.11 para.92, repealed: 2004 c.14 Sch.1 Part 10

Sch.11 para.97, repealed (in part): 2003 c.26 Sch.8 Part 1

43. Statute Law (Repeals) Act 1989

Sch.2 Part I para.4, repealed: 2003 c.39 Sch.10

44. Opticians Act 1989

applied: SI 2002/2376 Reg.4, SI 2004/905 Reg.9

s.5, applied: SI 2004/259 Sch.1

s.5, enabling: SI 2004/259

s.9, applied: SR 2002/386 Reg.4

s.10, applied: SI 2004/258

s.10, referred to: SI 2004/258 Sch.1

s.10, enabling: SI 2002/775, SI 2003/1080, SI 2004/258

s.17, applied: 2002 c.17 s.29

s.23, amended: 2002 c.17 s.32, Sch.8 para.17

s.23, applied: SI 2003/833 Art.4

s.29, amended: 2004 c.33 Sch.27 para.135

s.34, applied: SI 2003/1080

s.34, referred to: SI 2004/258

Sch.1 para.2A, added: 2003 c.43 Sch.12 para.4

45. Prisons (Scotland) Act 1989

applied: SI 2002/1792 Reg.5, 2003 asp 7 s.16, SSI 2004/257 Sch.2 para.1

referred to: 2003 asp 7 s.27

s.3A, applied: SSI 2004/38 Reg.3

s.13, amended: 2003 asp 7 s.24

s.14, enabling: SSI 2002/472

s.19, amended: 2003 asp 7 s.23

s.19, applied: SSI 2003/231 Sch.4 para.7

s.22, amended: 2003 asp 7 s.27, s.34

1989–cont.

45. Prisons (Scotland) Act 1989–*cont.*
s.22, applied: 2003 asp 7 s.27, s.40, SI 2003/
762 Reg.2, SI 2004/1748 Sch.1, SSI 2003/
243 Reg.2, SSI 2003/287 Art.2
s.22, referred to: SSI 2003/287 Art.2
s.22, repealed (in part): 2003 asp 7 s.27
s.22A, added: 2003 asp 7 s.34
s.23, repealed: 2003 asp 7 Sch.5
s.26, applied: SI 2003/762 Reg.2, SI 2004/
1748 Sch.1
s.28, amended: 2003 asp 7 s.34
s.28, repealed (in part): 2003 asp 7 s.34
s.39, see *Dudley (Fiona Jacqueline) v HM
Advocate* 2003 J.C. 53 (HCJ), Lord
Cameron of Lochbroom, Lord Gill L.J.C.,
Lord Kirkwood
s.39, applied: SSI 2003/231 Sch.4 para.7
s.39, enabling: SSI 2002/107, SSI 2002/472
s.40, amended: 2003 asp 7 s.23
s.40B, added: 2003 asp 7 s.25
s.42, amended: 2003 asp 7 Sch.4 para.1

1990

vii. London Local Authorities Act 1990
applied: 2003 c.17 Sch.4 para.2
Part III, see *Tower Hamlets LBC v Sherwood*
[2002] EWCA Civ 229, [2002] E.H.L.R.
13 (CA), Chadwick, L.J.
s.2, amended: 2004 c.i Sch.5
s.2, applied: 2003 c.17 Sch.8 para.32
s.4, amended: SI 2003/1615 Sch.1 para.34
s.4, repealed: 2003 c.17 Sch.7
s.4, substituted: 2004 c.i s.19
s.5, repealed: 2003 c.17 Sch.7
s.6, repealed: 2003 c.17 Sch.7
s.7, repealed: 2003 c.17 Sch.7
s.8, repealed: 2003 c.17 Sch.7
s.9, repealed: 2003 c.17 Sch.7
s.10, repealed: 2003 c.17 Sch.7
s.11, repealed: 2003 c.17 Sch.7
s.12, repealed: 2003 c.17 Sch.7
s.13, repealed: 2003 c.17 Sch.7
s.14, repealed: 2003 c.17 Sch.7
s.15, repealed: 2003 c.17 Sch.7
s.16, repealed: 2003 c.17 Sch.7
s.17, repealed: 2003 c.17 Sch.7
s.17, varied: 2004 c.i s.19
s.19, repealed: 2003 c.17 Sch.7
s.20, repealed: 2003 c.17 Sch.7
s.21, see *Croydon LBC v Burdon* [2002]
EWHC 1961, [2003] E.H.L.R. 1 (QBD
(Admin Ct)), Judge Wilkie; see *Tower
Hamlets LBC v Sherwood* [2002] E.H.L.R.
3 (Ch D), S Proudman Q.C.
s.21, amended: 2004 c.i Sch.4 para.1, Sch.4
para.2
s.24, amended: SI 2003/1615 Sch.1 para.34
s.24, amended: 2004 c.i Sch.4 para.3
s.24, repealed (in part): 2004 c.i Sch.4 para.3
s.25, amended: 2004 c.i Sch.4 para.4

1990–cont.

vii. London Local Authorities Act 1990–
cont.
s.34, applied: 2004 c.i Sch.2
s.38, see *R. (on the application of Islington
LBC) v Jordan* [2002] EWHC 2645,
(2003) 167 J.P. 1 (QBD (Admin Ct)),
McCombe, J.
s.38, amended: 2004 c.i Sch.4 para.5
s.38, applied: 2004 c.i Sch.2
s.39, amended: SI 2003/1615 Sch.1 para.34

**xxx. London Local Authorities (No.2) Act
1990**
s.5, amended: 2003 c.21 Sch.17 para.107
s.6, repealed: 2003 c.17 Sch.7

xiv. Nottingham Park Estate Act 1990
s.14, amended: SI 2003/1542 Sch.1 para.1

1. Capital Allowances Act 1990
see *Lonergan v W&P Food Service Ltd* 2002
S.L.T. 908 (OH), Lord Clarke
s.22, see *MF Freeman (Plant) Ltd v Jowett
(Inspector of Taxes)* [2003] S.T.C. (S.C.D.)
423 (Sp Comm), AN Brice
s.24, see *Barclays Mercantile Business
Finance Ltd v Mawson (Inspector of Taxes)*
[2002] EWCA Civ 1853, [2003] S.T.C. 66
(CA), Peter Gibson, L.J.; see *Barclays
Mercantile Business Finance Ltd v
Mawson (Inspector of Taxes)* [2002]
EWHC 1527, [2002] S.T.C. 1068 (Ch D),
Park, J.; see *Barclays Mercantile Business
Finance Ltd v Mawson (Inspector of Taxes)*
[2004] UKHL 51, [2004] 3 W.L.R. 1383
(HL), Lord Nicholls of Birkenhead; see
*BMBF (No.24) Ltd v Inland Revenue
Commissioners* [2002] EWHC 2466,
[2002] S.T.C. 1450 (Ch D), Etherton, J.;
see *BMBF (No.24) Ltd v Inland Revenue
Commissioners* [2002] S.T.C. (S.C.D.) 274
(Sp Comm), Theodore Wallace; see *Shove
(Inspector of Taxes) v Lingfield Park 1991 Ltd*
[2003] EWHC 1684, [2003] S.T.C. 1003
(Ch D), Hart, J.; see *Shove (Inspector of
Taxes) v Lingfield Park 1991 Ltd* [2004]
EWCA Civ 391, [2004] S.T.C. 805 (CA),
Potter, L.J.
s.35, see *Lloyds UDT Finance Ltd v Chartered
Finance Trust Holdings Plc* [2002] EWCA
Civ 806, [2002] S.T.C. 956 (CA),
Jonathan Parker, L.J.
s.36, see *Lloyds UDT Finance Ltd v Chartered
Finance Trust Holdings Plc* [2002] EWCA
Civ 806, [2002] S.T.C. 956 (CA),
Jonathan Parker, L.J.
s.42, see *BMBF (No.24) Ltd v Inland Revenue
Commissioners* [2002] EWHC 2466,
[2002] S.T.C. 1450 (Ch D), Etherton, J.;
see *BMBF (No.24) Ltd v Inland Revenue
Commissioners* [2002] S.T.C. (S.C.D.) 274
(Sp Comm), Theodore Wallace; see *BMBF
(No.24) Ltd v Inland Revenue
Commissioners* [2003] EWCA Civ 1560,
[2004] S.T.C. 97 (CA), Chadwick, L.J.

CAP.

1990–cont.

1. Capital Allowances Act 1990–*cont.*

s.50, see *MF Freeman (Plant) Ltd v Jowett (Inspector of Taxes)* [2003] S.T.C. (S.C.D.) 423 (Sp Comm), AN Brice

s.75, see *Barclays Mercantile Business Finance Ltd v Mawson (Inspector of Taxes)* [2002] EWCA Civ 1853, [2003] S.T.C. 66 (CA), Peter Gibson, L.J.

Sch.AA1 para.2, see *Anchor International Ltd v Inland Revenue Commissioners* [2003] S.T.C. (S.C.D.) 115 (Sp Comm), John F Avery Jones

5. Criminal Justice (International Co-operation) Act 1990

see *Marlwood Commercial Inc v Kozeny* [2004] EWCA Civ 798, [2004] 3 All E.R. 648 (CA), Peter Gibson, L.J.

referred to: 2003 c.32 Sch.5 para.41

s.1, repealed: 2003 c.32 Sch.6

s.2, repealed: 2003 c.32 Sch.6

s.3, see *BOC Ltd v Instrument Technology Ltd* [2001] EWCA Civ 854, [2002] Q.B. 537 (CA), Mummery, L.J.

s.3, repealed: 2003 c.32 Sch.6

s.4, see *R. (on the application of Evans) v Director of the Serious Fraud Office* [2002] EWHC 2304, [2003] 1 W.L.R. 299 (QBD (Admin Ct)), Kennedy, L.J.

s.4, repealed: 2003 c.32 Sch.6

s.5, amended: 2003 c.32 Sch.5 para.43

s.5, applied: SI 2002/313 Sch.1, 2003 c.32 s.47, s.48

s.5, enabling: SI 2002/731

s.7, repealed: 2003 c.32 Sch.6

s.8, repealed: 2003 c.32 Sch.6

s.9, enabling: SI 2002/255, SI 2002/2845

s.10, enabling: SI 2004/1047

s.11, repealed: 2003 c.32 Sch.6

s.12, applied: 2002 c.29 Sch.2 para.1, Sch.4 para.2, Sch.5 para.1, SI 2004/1910 Sch.1

s.13, amended: 2002 c.29 Sch.11 para.21, Sch.12

s.13, referred to: SSI 2003/210 Art.7

s.13, varied: SI 2003/333 Art.10

s.14, repealed: 2002 c.29 Sch.12

s.19, amended: 2003 c.44 Sch.28 para.3

s.19, applied: 2002 c.29 Sch.2 para.1, Sch.4 para.2, Sch.5 para.1

s.22, repealed: 2003 c.41 Sch.4

Sch.1 para.1, repealed: 2003 c.32 Sch.6

Sch.1 para.2, repealed: 2003 c.32 Sch.6

Sch.1 para.3, repealed: 2003 c.32 Sch.6

Sch.1 para.4, repealed: 2003 c.32 Sch.6

Sch.1 para.5, repealed: 2003 c.32 Sch.6

Sch.1 para.6, repealed: 2003 c.32 Sch.6

Sch.1 para.7, repealed: 2003 c.32 Sch.6

Sch.2, referred to: 2002 c.29 Sch.2 para.1, Sch.4 para.2, Sch.5 para.1

Sch.4 para.1, repealed: 2002 c.29 Sch.12

Sch.4 para.6, repealed (in part): 2003 c.32 Sch.6

CAP.

1990–cont.

5. Criminal Justice (International Co-operation) Act 1990–*cont.*

Sch.4 para.8, repealed: 2003 c.32 Sch.6

6. Education (Student Loans) Act 1990

applied: SI 2002/195 Reg.4, Reg.28, SI 2002/3200 Reg.4, SR 2002/224 Reg.4

referred to: 2004 c.8 s.42

s.1, applied: 2002 c.32 s.186, SI 2002/2086 Reg.7, Reg.12, SI 2003/1917 Reg.7, Reg.12

s.1, enabling: SI 2002/1329, SI 2002/1433, SI 2003/1647, SI 2004/1030, SSI 2002/282, SSI 2003/285, SSI 2004/256

Sch.2 para.1, enabling: SI 2002/1329, SI 2002/1433, SI 2003/1647, SI 2004/1030, SSI 2002/282, SSI 2003/285, SSI 2004/256

Sch.2 para.5, varied: 2004 c.8 s.42

8. Town and Country Planning Act 1990

see *Duncan v Epping Forest DC (Preliminary Issues)* [2004] R.V.R. 213 (Lands Tr), George Bartlett Q.C. (President); see *Henriques v Stephens (Valuation Officer)* [2003] R.V.R. 266 (Lands Tr), PR Francis FRICS; see *R. (on the application of Prokopp) v London Underground Ltd* [2003] EWCA Civ 961, [2004] Env. L.R. 8 (CA), Schiemann, L.J.

applied: SI 2002/1066 Art.17, SI 2002/1559 Reg.5, 2003 c.14 s.61, s.66, 2003 c.21 Sch.4 para.3, SI 2003/164 Reg.3, SI 2003/390 Reg.5, SI 2003/2553 Reg.5, 2004 c.5 s.29, s.43, s.51, s.59, SI 2004/352 Sch.6 para.12, SI 2004/757 Art.20, SI 2004/932 Art.5

varied: SI 2002/412 Sch.5, SI 2002/1066 Sch.10 para.1, SI 2002/1327 Sch.5 para.1, SI 2004/757 Sch.12 para.1

Part II c.I, applied: 2004 c.5 Sch.8 para.4, SI 2004/2205 Reg.4

Part II c.I, referred to: 2004 c.5 Sch.8 para.5

Part II c.II, applied: 2004 c.5 Sch.8 para.9, SI 2004/2205 Reg.5

Part III, applied: SI 2002/412 Art.14, SI 2002/432 Reg.8, SI 2002/1066 Art.17, SI 2002/1327 Art.14, SI 2003/507 Reg.19, 2004 c.5 s.18, Sch.4 para.3, Sch.4 para.6, SI 2004/757 Art.20, SI 2004/932 Art.4, SI 2004/1576 Reg.16

Part III, added: 2004 c.5 s.43

Part IV, applied: 2003 c.21 Sch.4 para.6, SI 2004/932 Art.7

Part VI c.II, applied: 2004 c.5 Sch.8 para.16

Part VII, applied: 2004 c.5 s.59

Part VII, added: 2004 c.5 s.52

Part XIII, applied: 2004 c.5 s.87

s.1, referred to: SI 2002/221 Sch.4 para.2, SI 2004/1964 Sch.3 para.2

s.2, amended: 2004 c.23 Sch.2 para.13

s.2, applied: 2003 c.26 s.23, s.33

s.10, repealed (in part): 2004 c.5 Sch.9

s.10A, repealed (in part): 2004 c.5 Sch.9

s.11, repealed (in part): 2004 c.5 Sch.9

1990–cont.

8. Town and Country Planning Act 1990– *cont.*

s.12, applied: 2004 c.5 Sch.8 para.7

s.12, repealed (in part): 2004 c.5 Sch.9

s.12A, repealed (in part): 2004 c.5 Sch.9

s.13, applied: 2004 c.5 Sch.8 para.3, Sch.8 para.5

s.13, repealed (in part): 2004 c.5 Sch.9

s.14, repealed (in part): 2004 c.5 Sch.9

s.15, repealed (in part): SI 2002/794 Sch.2, 2004 c.5 Sch.9

s.16, applied: 2004 c.5 Sch.8 para.4

s.16, repealed (in part): 2004 c.5 Sch.9

s.17, repealed (in part): 2004 c.5 Sch.9

s.18, repealed (in part): SI 2002/794 Sch.2, 2004 c.5 Sch.9

s.19, repealed (in part): 2004 c.5 Sch.9

s.20, amended: 2004 c.5 s.43

s.20, repealed (in part): 2004 c.5 Sch.9

s.21, repealed (in part): 2004 c.5 Sch.9

s.21A, repealed (in part): 2004 c.5 Sch.9

s.22, repealed (in part): 2004 c.5 Sch.9

s.23, repealed (in part): 2004 c.5 Sch.9

s.23A, repealed (in part): 2004 c.5 Sch.9

s.23B, repealed (in part): 2004 c.5 Sch.9

s.23C, repealed (in part): 2004 c.5 Sch.9

s.24, repealed (in part): 2004 c.5 Sch.9

s.25, repealed (in part): 2004 c.5 Sch.9

s.26, applied: 2004 c.5 Sch.8 para.4, Sch.8 para.5

s.26, repealed (in part): 2004 c.5 Sch.9

s.27, applied: 2004 c.5 Sch.8 para.1, Sch.8 para.6, Sch.8 para.16

s.27, repealed (in part): 2004 c.5 Sch.9

s.27A, repealed (in part): 2004 c.5 Sch.9

s.28, applied: 2004 c.5 Sch.8 para.19

s.28, repealed (in part): 2004 c.5 Sch.9

s.28A, repealed (in part): 2004 c.5 Sch.9

s.29, repealed (in part): 2004 c.5 Sch.9

s.29, varied: 2004 c.5 Sch.8 para.10

s.30, repealed (in part): 2004 c.5 Sch.9

s.30, varied: 2004 c.5 Sch.8 para.10

s.31, see *JS Bloor Ltd v Swindon BC* [2001] EWHC Admin 966, [2002] P.L.C.R. 22 (QBD (Admin Ct)), Ouseley, J.

s.31, repealed (in part): 2004 c.5 Sch.9

s.31, varied: 2004 c.5 Sch.8 para.10

s.32, repealed (in part): 2004 c.5 Sch.9

s.32, varied: 2004 c.5 Sch.8 para.10

s.33, applied: 2004 c.5 Sch.8 para.2

s.33, repealed (in part): 2004 c.5 Sch.9

s.33, varied: 2004 c.5 Sch.8 para.10

s.34, repealed (in part): 2004 c.5 Sch.9

s.34, varied: 2004 c.5 Sch.8 para.10

s.35, repealed (in part): 2004 c.5 Sch.9

s.35, varied: 2004 c.5 Sch.8 para.10

s.35A, repealed (in part): 2004 c.5 Sch.9

s.35A, varied: 2004 c.5 Sch.8 para.10

1990–cont.

8. Town and Country Planning Act 1990– *cont.*

s.35B, applied: SI 2002/452 Reg.2, SI 2003/464 Reg.2, SI 2003/1179 Reg.2, SI 2003/2948 Reg.2, SI 2004/1716 Reg.2

s.35B, disapplied: SI 2004/421 Reg.2

s.35B, repealed (in part): 2004 c.5 Sch.9

s.35B, varied: 2004 c.5 Sch.8 para.10

s.35B, enabling: SI 2003/1179, SI 2003/2948, SI 2004/1716

s.35C, repealed (in part): 2004 c.5 Sch.9

s.35C, varied: 2004 c.5 Sch.8 para.10

s.36, see *JS Bloor Ltd v Swindon BC* [2001] EWHC Admin 966, [2002] P.L.C.R. 22 (QBD (Admin Ct)), Ouseley, J.

s.36, applied: 2004 c.5 Sch.8 para.11, Sch.8 para.13

s.36, repealed (in part): 2004 c.5 Sch.9

s.36, varied: 2004 c.5 Sch.8 para.10

s.37, repealed (in part): 2004 c.5 Sch.9

s.37, varied: 2004 c.5 Sch.8 para.10

s.38, repealed (in part): 2004 c.5 Sch.9

s.38, varied: 2004 c.5 Sch.8 para.10

s.39, repealed (in part): 2004 c.5 Sch.9

s.39, varied: 2004 c.5 Sch.8 para.10

s.40, applied: 2004 c.5 Sch.8 para.10

s.40, referred to: 2004 c.5 Sch.8 para.8

s.40, repealed (in part): 2004 c.5 Sch.9

s.40, varied: 2004 c.5 Sch.8 para.10

s.41, repealed (in part): 2004 c.5 Sch.9

s.41, varied: 2004 c.5 Sch.8 para.10

s.42, see *Bersted Parish Council v Arun DC* [2003] EWHC 3149, [2004] 2 P. & C.R. 12 (QBD (Admin Ct)), Richards, J.

s.42, applied: 2004 c.5 Sch.8 para.9, Sch.8 para.10

s.42, repealed (in part): 2004 c.5 Sch.9

s.42, varied: 2004 c.5 Sch.8 para.10

s.43, applied: 2004 c.5 Sch.8 para.11

s.43, repealed (in part): SI 2002/794 Sch.2, 2004 c.5 Sch.9

s.43, varied: 2004 c.5 Sch.8 para.10

s.44, repealed (in part): SI 2002/794 Sch.2, 2004 c.5 Sch.9

s.44, varied: 2004 c.5 Sch.8 para.10

s.45, repealed (in part): 2004 c.5 Sch.9

s.45, varied: 2004 c.5 Sch.8 para.10

s.46, repealed (in part): 2004 c.5 Sch.9

s.46, varied: 2004 c.5 Sch.8 para.10

s.47, repealed (in part): 2004 c.5 Sch.9

s.47, varied: 2004 c.5 Sch.8 para.10

s.48, repealed (in part): 2004 c.5 Sch.9

s.48, varied: 2004 c.5 Sch.8 para.10

s.49, repealed (in part): 2004 c.5 Sch.9

s.49, varied: 2004 c.5 Sch.8 para.10

s.50, repealed (in part): 2004 c.5 Sch.9

s.50, varied: 2004 c.5 Sch.8 para.10

s.51, repealed (in part): 2004 c.5 Sch.9

s.51, varied: 2004 c.5 Sch.8 para.10

s.51A, repealed (in part): 2004 c.5 Sch.9

1990–cont.

8. Town and Country Planning Act 1990– *cont.*

s.51A, varied: 2004 c.5 Sch.8 para.10

s.52, repealed (in part): 2004 c.5 Sch.9

s.52, varied: 2004 c.5 Sch.8 para.10

s.53, applied: 2004 c.5 Sch.8 para.9, Sch.8 para.10

s.53, repealed (in part): 2004 c.5 Sch.9

s.53, varied: 2004 c.5 Sch.8 para.10

s.54, applied: 2004 c.5 Sch.8 para.1, Sch.8 para.2, Sch.8 para.12, Sch.8 para.16

s.54, repealed (in part): 2004 c.5 Sch.9

s.54, varied: 2004 c.5 Sch.8 para.10

s.54A, see *Butler v Secretary of State for the Environment, Transport and the Regions* [2001] EWHC Admin 590, [2002] J.P.L. 428 (QBD (Admin Ct)), Ouseley, J.; see *Guildford BC v Secretary of State for the Environment, Transport and the Regions* [2001] EWHC Admin 819, [2002] J.P.L. 733 (QBD (Admin Ct)), Sullivan, J.; see *R. (on the application of JA Pye (Oxford) Ltd) v Oxford City Council* [2001] EWHC Admin 870, [2002] 2 P. & C.R. 35 (QBD (Admin Ct)), Ouseley, J.; see *R. (on the application of Mount Cook Land Ltd) v Westminster City Council* [2003] EWCA Civ 1346, [2004] C.P. Rep. 12 (CA), Auld, L.J.; see *R. (on the application of Waveney DC) v Secretary of State for Transport, Local Government and the Regions* [2002] EWHC 2397, [2003] J.P.L. 1058 (QBD (Admin Ct)), Sullivan, J.; see *Sefton MBC v Secretary of State for the Environment, Transport and the Regions* [2002] EWHC 119, [2002] P.L.C.R. 23 (QBD (Admin Ct)), Ouseley, J.

s.54A, repealed (in part): 2004 c.5 Sch.9

s.55, see *Belmont Riding Centre v First Secretary of State* [2003] EWHC 1895, [2004] J.P.L. 593 (QBD (Admin Ct)), Richards, J.; see *Eastleigh BC v First Secretary of State* [2004] EWHC 1408, [2004] 24 E.G.C.S. 149 (QBD (Admin Ct)), Collins, J.; see *R. (on the application of Westminster City Council) v Secretary of State for the Environment, Transport and the Regions* [2001] EWHC Admin 270, [2002] 1 P. & C.R. 8 (QBD (Admin Ct)), Jackson, J.; see *Sage v Secretary of State for the Environment, Transport and the Regions* [2001] EWCA Civ 1100, [2002] 1 P. & C.R. 38 (CA), Keene, L.J.; see *Sage v Secretary of State for the Environment, Transport and the Regions* [2003] UKHL 22, [2003] 1 W.L.R. 983 (HL), Lord Hobhouse of Woodborough

s.55, amended: 2004 c.5 s.49, Sch.6 para.2, Sch.9

s.55, applied: 2004 c.5 s.49

s.55, enabling: SI 2002/1875

1990–cont.

8. Town and Country Planning Act 1990– *cont.*

s.56, see *Commercial Land Ltd v Secretary of State for Transport, Local Government and the Regions* [2002] EWHC 1264, [2003] J.P.L. 358 (QBD (Admin Ct)), Ouseley, J.; see *R. (on the application of Hammerton) v London Underground Ltd* [2002] EWHC 2307, [2003] J.P.L. 984 (QBD (Admin Ct)), Ouseley, J.

s.56, amended: 2004 c.5 s.40

s.57, amended: 2004 c.5 s.40

s.58, amended: 2004 c.5 s.40

s.59, applied: 2002 c.i s.40

s.59, enabling: SI 2002/828, SI 2002/1877, SI 2002/1878, SI 2003/2047, SI 2004/1231, SI 2004/1434, SI 2004/2355, SI 2004/3340

s.60, enabling: SI 2002/1878

s.61, enabling: SI 2002/1877, SI 2002/1878

s.61A, added: 2004 c.5 s.40

s.61A, applied: SI 2004/2204 Reg.48

s.61B, added: 2004 c.5 s.40

s.61C, added: 2004 c.5 s.40

s.61D, added: 2004 c.5 s.41

s.62, substituted: 2004 c.5 s.42

s.64, see *R. (on the application of Reprotech (Pebsham) Ltd) v East Sussex CC* [2002] UKHL 8, [2003] 1 W.L.R. 348 (HL), Lord Hoffmann

s.65, see *R. (on the application of Pridmore) v Salisbury DC* [2004] EWHC 2511, [2004] 47 E.G.C.S. 165 (QBD (Admin)), Newman, J.

s.65, enabling: SI 2002/1877

s.69, applied: 2004 c.5 Sch.4 para.4

s.69, substituted: 2004 c.5 Sch.6 para.3

s.69, enabling: SI 2002/828, SI 2002/1877, SI 2004/1434, SI 2004/3340

s.70, see *Guildford BC v Secretary of State for the Environment, Transport and the Regions* [2001] EWHC Admin 819, [2002] J.P.L. 733 (QBD (Admin Ct)), Sullivan, J.; see *R. (on the application of Kides) v South Cambridgeshire DC* [2002] EWCA Civ 1370, [2003] 1 P. & C.R. 19 (CA), Jonathan Parker, L.J.; see *R. (on the application of Mount Cook Land Ltd) v Westminster City Council* [2003] EWCA Civ 1346, [2004] C.P. Rep. 12 (CA), Auld, L.J.; see *R. (on the application of Redditch BC) v First Secretary of State* [2003] EWHC 650, [2003] 2 P. & C.R. 25 (QBD (Admin Ct)), Wilson, J.

s.70A, added: 2004 c.5 s.43

s.71, enabling: SI 2002/1877, SI 2003/2047

s.73, see *Kebbell Development Ltd v First Secretary of State* [2003] EWCA Civ 1855, [2004] J.P.L. 1710 (CA), Keene, L.J.; see *Kebbell Development Ltd v First Secretary of State* [2003] EWHC 902, [2004] J.P.L. 353 (QBD (Admin Ct)), Sir

1990–cont.

8. Town and Country Planning Act 1990– *cont.*

s.73–*cont.*

RichardTucker; see *R. (on the application of Barker) v Waverley BC* [2001] EWCA Civ 566, [2002] 1 P. & C.R. 6 (CA), Pill, L.J.; see *R. (on the application of Reid) v Secretary of State forTransport, Local Government and the Regions* [2002] EWHC 2174, [2002] 42 E.G.C.S. 158 (QBD (Admin Ct)), Sullivan, J.

s.73, amended: 2004 c.5 s.51

s.73, applied: SI 2004/932 Art.4

s.73, repealed (in part): 2004 c.5 s.42, Sch.9

s.73, enabling: SI 2002/1877

s.73A, see *R. (on the application of Gosbee) v First Secretary of State* [2003] EWHC 770, [2004] 1 P. & C.R. 22 (QBD (Admin Ct)), Elias, J.

s.74, enabling: SI 2002/1877, SI 2003/2047, SI 2004/1434, SI 2004/3340

s.76, repealed: 2004 c.5 Sch.6 para.4, Sch.9

s.76A, added: 2004 c.5 s.44

s.76B, added: 2004 c.5 s.44

s.77, see *R. (on the application of Adlard) v Secretary of State for Transport, Local Government and the Regions* [2002] EWHC 7, Daily Telegraph, January 24, 2002 (QBD (Admin Ct)), Collins, J.; see *R. (on the application of Friends Provident Life Office) v Secretary of State for the Environment, Transport and the Regions* [2001] EWHC Admin 820, [2002] 1 W.L.R. 1450 (QBD (Admin Ct)), Forbes, J.; see *R. (on the application of Hadfield) v Secretary of State for Transport, Local Government and the Regions* [2002] EWHC 1266, [2002] 26 E.G.C.S. 137 (QBD (Admin Ct)), Sullivan, J.; see *R. (on the application of Trustees of the Friends of the Lake District) v Secretary of State for the Environment, Transport and the Regions* [2001] EWHC Admin 281, [2002] 1 P. & C.R. 23 (QBD (Admin Ct)), Harrison, J.

s.77, amended: 2004 c.5 s.40

s.77, applied: SI 2002/1223 r.3, SI 2003/1266 r.3, SI 2003/1271 r.3, 2004 c.5 Sch.2 para.1

s.77, enabling: SI 2002/1877

s.78, see *Jory v Secretary of State forTransport, Local Government and the Regions* [2002] EWHC 2724, Times, December 3, 2002 (QBD (Admin Ct)), Sullivan, J.

s.78, amended: 2004 c.5 s.40, s.43

s.78, applied: SI 2002/1223 r.3, SI 2003/1266 r.3, SI 2003/1267 r.3, SI 2003/1271 r.3, 2004 c.5 Sch.2 para.1, Sch.4 para.5, SI 2004/932 Art.6

s.78, referred to: 2004 c.5 s.50

s.78, enabling: SI 2002/1877, SI 2003/2047, SI 2004/1434, SI 2004/3340

s.78A, added: 2004 c.5 s.50

1990–cont.

8. Town and Country Planning Act 1990– *cont.*

s.79, enabling: SI 2002/1877

s.83, amended: 2004 c.5 s.45

s.83, repealed (in part): 2004 c.5 s.45, Sch.9

s.85, amended: 2004 c.5 s.45

s.88, amended: 2004 c.5 s.40

s.90, see *Jory v Secretary of State for Transport, Local Government and the Regions* [2002] EWHC 2724, Times, December 3, 2002 (QBD (Admin Ct)), Sullivan, J.

s.90, applied: SI 2002/412 Art.14, SI 2002/1066 Art.17, SI 2002/1327 Art.14, SI 2003/1075 Art.36, SI 2004/389 Art.34, SI 2004/757 Art.20

s.91, see *R. (on the application of Murray) v Hampshire CC (No.1)* [2002] EWHC 1401, [2003] J.P.L. 224 (QBD (Admin Ct)), Burton, J.; see *R. (on the application of Murray) v Hampshire CC (No.2)* [2003] EWCA Civ 760, [2003] J.P.L. 1602 (CA), Carnwath, L.J.

s.91, amended: 2004 c.5 s.40, s.51

s.92, see *R. (on the application of Murray) v Hampshire CC (No.1)* [2002] EWHC 1401, [2003] J.P.L. 224 (QBD (Admin Ct)), Burton, J.; see *R. (on the application of Murray) v Hampshire CC (No.2)* [2003] EWCA Civ 760, [2003] J.P.L. 1602 (CA), Carnwath, L.J.

s.92, amended: 2004 c.5 s.51

s.92, repealed (in part): 2004 c.5 s.51

s.100, see *Redrow Homes Ltd v First Secretary of State* [2003] EWHC 3094, [2004] J.P.L. 1273 (QBD (Admin Ct)), Sullivan, J.

s.100, applied: SI 2004/932 Art.7

s.104, applied: SI 2004/932 Art.7

s.106, see *Kebbell Development Ltd v First Secretary of State* [2003] EWCA Civ 1855, [2004] J.P.L. 1710 (CA), Keene, L.J.; see *Kebbell Development Ltd v First Secretary of State* [2003] EWHC 902, [2004] J.P.L. 353 (QBD (Admin Ct)), Sir Richard Tucker; see *R. (on the application of Batchelor Enterprises Ltd) v North Dorset DC* [2003] EWHC 3006, [2004] J.P.L. 1222 (QBD (Admin Ct)), Sullivan, J.; see *R. (on the application of Burkett) v Hammersmith and Fulham LBC (No.1)* [2002] UKHL 23, [2002] 1 W.L.R. 1593 (HL), Lord Steyn; see *R. (on the application of Portland Port Ltd) v Weymouth and Portland BC* [2001] EWHC Admin 1171, [2002] 2 P. & C.R. 29 (QBD (Admin Ct)), Harrison, J.; see *R. (on the application of Prokopp) v London Underground Ltd* [2003] EWHC 960, [2003] 19 E.G.C.S. 119 (QBD (Admin Ct)), Collins, J.; see *R. (on the application of The Garden and Leisure Group Ltd) v North Somerset Council* [2003] EWHC

1990–cont.
8. Town and Country Planning Act 1990– cont.

s.106–cont.

1605, [2004] 1 P. & C.R. 39 (QBD (Admin Ct)), Richards, J.; see *Wrexham Mining Ltd v Flintshire CC* [2003] R.V.R. 305 (LandsTr), PR Francis FRICS; see *Younger Homes (Northern) Ltd v First Secretary of State* [2003] EWHC 3058, [2004] J.P.L. 950 (QBD (Admin Ct)), Ouseley, J.

s.106, repealed: 2004 c.5 Sch.6 para.5, Sch.9

s.106A, see *R. (on the application of Batchelor Enterprises Ltd) v North Dorset DC* [2003] EWHC 3006, [2004] J.P.L. 1222 (QBD (Admin Ct)), Sullivan, J.; see *R. (on the application of The Garden and Leisure Group Ltd) v North Somerset Council* [2003] EWHC 1605, [2004] 1 P. & C.R. 39 (QBD (Admin Ct)), Richards, J.

s.106A, repealed: 2004 c.5 Sch.6 para.5, Sch.9

s.106B, repealed: 2004 c.5 Sch.6 para.5, Sch.9

s.107, see *Redrow Homes Ltd v First Secretary of State* [2003] EWHC 3094, [2004] J.P.L. 1273 (QBD (Admin Ct)), Sullivan, J.

s.108, amended: 2004 c.5 s.40, Sch.6 para.6

s.109, amended: 2004 c.5 s.40

s.118, applied: 2003 c.21 Sch.4 para.6

s.137A, added: 2004 c.5 Sch.3 para.1

s.139, varied: SI 2004/932 Sch.1 para.1

s.140, varied: SI 2004/932 Sch.1 para.2

s.141, varied: SI 2004/932 Sch.1 para.3

s.143, varied: SI 2004/932 Sch.1 para.4

s.148, amended: 2003 c.21 Sch.17 para.102

s.148, varied: SI 2004/932 Sch.1 para.5

s.171A, see *St Anselm Development Co Ltd v First Secretary of State* [2003] EWHC 1592, [2004] R.T.R. 10 (QBD (Admin Ct)), Sullivan, J.

s.171A, referred to: SI 2002/2682 Reg.5, SI 2003/394 Reg.4

s.171B, see *Beach v Secretary of State for the Environment, Transport and the Regions* [2001] EWHC Admin 381, [2002] J.P.L. 185 (QBD (Admin Ct)), Ouseley, J.; see *Brown v First Secretary of State* [2003] EWHC 2800, [2004] J.P.L. 1074 (QBD (Admin Ct)), McCombe, J.; see *Conwy BC v Jones* [2002] EWHC 2393, [2003] A.C.D. 28 (QBD (Admin Ct)), Kennedy, L.J.; see *Fidler v First Secretary of State* [2003] EWHC 2003, [2004] J.P.L. 630 (QBD (Admin Ct)), Richards, J.; see *North Devon DC v First Secretary of State* [2004] EWHC 578, [2004] J.P.L. 1396 (QBD (Admin Ct)), Sullivan, J.; see *Sage v Secretary of State for the Environment, Transport and the Regions* [2001] EWCA Civ 1100, [2002] 1 P. & C.R. 38 (CA), Keene, L.J.; see *Sage v Secretary of State for the Environment, Transport and the*

1990–cont.
8. Town and Country Planning Act 1990– cont.

s.171B–cont.

Regions [2003] UKHL 22, [2003] 1 W.L.R. 983 (HL), Lord Hobhouse of Woodborough; see *St Anselm Development Co Ltd v First Secretary of State* [2003] EWHC 1592, [2004] R.T.R. 10 (QBD (Admin Ct)), Sullivan, J.; see *Thurrock BC v Secretary of State for the Environment, Transport and the Regions (No.2)* [2002] EWCA Civ 226, [2002] J.P.L. 1278 (CA), Schiemann, L.J.

s.171B, referred to: SI 2002/2682 Reg.5, SI 2003/394 Reg.4

s.171C, amended: SI 2003/956 Art.5

s.172, see *R. (on the application of Mid-Devon DC) v First Secretary of State* [2004] EWHC 814, [2004] 2 P. & C.R. 28 (QBD (Admin Ct)), Keith, J.; see *St Anselm Development Co Ltd v First Secretary of State* [2003] EWHC 1592, [2004] R.T.R. 10 (QBD (Admin Ct)), Sullivan, J.

s.172, applied: SI 2002/2682 Reg.4, Reg.5, Reg.8, SI 2002/2683 Reg.5, SI 2003/394 Reg.3, Reg.4, Reg.7, SI 2003/395 Reg.5

s.172, referred to: SI 2002/2682 Reg.5, SI 2003/394 Reg.4

s.173, see *Fidler v First Secretary of State* [2003] EWHC 2003, [2004] J.P.L. 630 (QBD (Admin Ct)), Richards, J.; see *St Anselm Development Co Ltd v First Secretary of State* [2003] EWHC 1592, [2004] R.T.R. 10 (QBD (Admin Ct)), Sullivan, J.; see *Wyatt Bros (Oxford) Ltd v Secretary of State for the Environment, Transport and the Regions* [2001] EWCA Civ 1560, [2002] P.L.C.R. 18 (CA), Kennedy, L.J.

s.173, referred to: SI 2002/2682 Reg.5, SI 2003/394 Reg.4

s.173, enabling: SI 2002/2682, SI 2003/394

s.173A, referred to: SI 2002/2682 Reg.5, SI 2003/394 Reg.4

s.174, see *R. (on the application of MDJ Light Bros (SP) Ltd) v First Secretary of State* [2003] EWHC 1287, [2004] J.P.L. 1596 (QBD (Admin Ct)), Sullivan, J.; see *St Anselm Development Co Ltd v First Secretary of State* [2003] EWHC 1592, [2004] R.T.R. 10 (QBD (Admin Ct)), Sullivan, J.; see *Wandsworth LBC v Secretary of State for Transport, Local Government and the Regions* [2003] EWHC 622, [2004] 1 P. & C.R. 32 (QBD (Admin Ct)), Sullivan, J.; see *Wyatt Bros (Oxford) Ltd v Secretary of State for the Environment, Transport and the Regions* [2001] EWCA Civ 1560, [2002] P.L.C.R. 18 (CA), Kennedy, L.J.

s.174, amended: SI 2003/956 Art.3

1990–cont.

8. Town and Country Planning Act 1990–
cont.

s.174, applied: SI 2002/2682 Reg.5, Reg.6, SI 2002/2683 Reg.3, Reg.4, Reg.5, SI 2002/2684 r.3, SI 2002/2685 r.3, SI 2002/2686 r.3, SI 2003/394 Reg.4, Reg.5, SI 2003/395 Reg.3, Reg.4, Reg.5, SI 2003/1268 r.3, SI 2003/1269 r.3, SI 2003/1270 r.3

s.174, referred to: SI 2002/2682 Reg.5, SI 2003/394 Reg.4

s.174, enabling: SI 2002/2682, SI 2003/394

s.175, referred to: SI 2002/2682 Reg.5, SI 2003/394 Reg.4

s.175, enabling: SI 2002/2682, SI 2002/2683, SI 2003/394, SI 2003/395

s.176, see *Wyatt Bros (Oxford) Ltd v Secretary of State for the Environment, Transport and the Regions* [2001] EWCA Civ 1560, [2002] P.L.C.R.18 (CA), Kennedy, L.J.

s.176, referred to: SI 2002/2682 Reg.5, SI 2003/394 Reg.4

s.177, referred to: SI 2002/2682 Reg.5, SI 2003/394 Reg.4, 2004 c.5 s.58

s.178, see *Buckinghamshire CC v Briar* [2002] EWHC 2821, [2003] Env. L.R. 25 (Ch D), Lawrence Collins, J.; see *R. (on the application of Lee) v Nuneaton and Bedworth BC* [2004] EWHC 950, [2004] J.P.L.1698 (QBD (Admin Ct)), Collins, J.

s.179, see *R. (on the application of Lynes) v West Berkshire DC* [2002] EWHC 1828, [2003] J.P.L. 1137 (QBD (Admin Ct)), Harrison, J.; see *R. v Clarke (Thomas George)* [2002] EWCA Crim 753, [2002] J.P.L.1372 (CA (Crim Div)), Cooke, J.; see *R. v Wood (David)* [2001] EWCA Crim 1395, [2002] J.P.L. 219 (CA (Crim Div)), Mantell, L.J.; see *Thompson v East Lindsey DC* [2002] EWHC 416, [2002] J.P.L.1269 (QBD (Admin Ct)), Richards, J.

s.182, applied: SI 2002/2682 Reg.11, SI 2003/394 Reg.10

s.186, see *International Ferry Traders Ltd v Adur DC* [2004] EWCA Civ 288, [2004] 2 E.G.L.R. 89 (CA), Pill, L.J.

s.187A, see *McGahan v Windsor and Maidenhead RBC* [2002] EWHC 1551, Times, July 30, 2002 (QBD (Admin Ct)), Harrison, J.

s.187B, see *Buckinghamshire CC v North West Estates Plc* [2002] EWHC 1088, Times, June 24, 2002 (Ch D), Jacob, J.; see *R. (on the application of Lee) v Nuneaton and Bedworth BC* [2004] EWHC 950, [2004] J.P.L. 1698 (QBD (Admin Ct)), Collins, J.; see *Salisbury DC v Le Roi* [2001] EWCA Civ 1490, [2002] 1 P. & C.R. 39 (CA), Buxton, L.J.; see *South Buckinghamshire DC v Flanagan* [2002] EWCA Civ 690, [2002] 1 W.L.R. 2601 (CA), Keene, L.J.; see *South Buckinghamshire DC v Porter (No.2)* [2001] EWCA Civ 1549, [2002] 1

1990–cont.

8. Town and Country Planning Act 1990–
cont.

s.187B–*cont.*

W.L.R. 1359 (CA), Simon Brown, L.J.; see *South Buckinghamshire DC v Porter (No.2)* [2003] UKHL 26, [2003] 2 A.C. 558 (HL), Lord Bingham of Cornhill; see *Stratford upon Avon DC v Hitchman* [2002] Env. L.R. 7 (QBD), Judge Peter Clark; see *Tonbridge and Malling BC v Davis* [2003] EWHC 1069, [2003] N.P.C. 63 (QBD), Stanley Burnton, J.

s.188, enabling: SI 2002/1877

s.191, see *Commercial Land Ltd v Secretary of State for Transport, Local Government and the Regions* [2002] EWHC 1264, [2003] J.P.L. 358 (QBD (Admin Ct)), Ouseley, J.; see *R. (on the application of Philcox) v Epping Forest DC* [2002] Env. L.R. 2 (CA), Pill, L.J.

s.191, applied: 2003 c.iii s.16

s.192, see *Eastleigh BC v First Secretary of State* [2004] EWHC 1408, [2004] 24 E.G.C.S. 149 (QBD (Admin Ct)), Collins, J.; see *Harrods Ltd v Secretary of State for the Environment, Transport and the Regions* [2002] EWCA Civ 412, Times, April 3, 2002 (CA), Schiemann, L.J.; see *R. (on the application of Bennett Fergusson Coal Ltd) v First Secretary of State* [2003] EWHC 1858, [2004] 1 P. & C.R. 30 (QBD (Admin Ct)), Blackburne, J.; see *R. (on the application of Newsum) v Welsh Assembly* [2004] EWHC 50, [2004] Env. L.R. 39 (QBD (Admin Ct)), Pitchford, J.; see *R. (on the application of Tapp) v Thanet DC* [2001] EWCA Civ 559, [2002] 1 P. & C.R. 7 (CA), Buxton, L.J.; see *Rugby Football Union v Secretary of State for Transport, Local Government and the Regions* [2002] EWCA Civ 1169, Times, August 13, 2002 (CA), Schiemann, L.J.; see *Waltham Forest LBC v Secretary of State for the Environment, Transport and the Regions* [2001] EWHC Admin 817, [2002] J.P.L. 727 (QBD (Admin Ct)), Sullivan, J.; see *Waltham Forest LBC v Secretary of State for Transport, Local Government and the Regions* [2002] EWCA Civ 330, Independent, March 22, 2002 (CA), Schiemann, L.J.

s.192, applied: 2004 c.5 s.49

s.192, see *Eastleigh BC v First Secretary of State* [2004] EWHC 1408, [2004] 24 E.G.C.S. 149 (QBD (Admin Ct)), Collins, J.; see *Harrods Ltd v Secretary of State for the Environment, Transport and the Regions* [2002] EWCA Civ 412, Times, April 3, 2002 (CA), Schiemann, L.J.; see *R. (on the application of Bennett Fergusson Coal Ltd) v First Secretary of State* [2003] EWHC 1858, [2004] 1 P. & C.R. 30 (QBD (Admin Ct)), Blackburne, J.; see *R. (on the*

1990–cont.
8. Town and Country Planning Act 1990–
cont.
  s.192–*cont.*
  application of Newsum) v Welsh Assembly
  [2004] EWHC 50, [2004] Env. L.R. 39
  (QBD (Admin Ct)), Pitchford, J.; see *R.*
  (on the application of Tapp) v Thanet DC
  [2001] EWCA Civ 559, [2002] 1 P. & C.R.
  7 (CA), Buxton, L.J.; see *Rugby Football*
  Union v Secretary of State for Transport, Lo-
  cal Government and the Regions [2002]
  EWCA Civ 1169, Times, August 13, 2002
  (CA), Schiemann, L.J.; see *Waltham Forest*
  LBC v Secretary of State for the Environ-
  ment, Transport and the Regions [2001]
  EWHC Admin 817, [2002] J.P.L. 727
  (QBD (Admin Ct)), Sullivan, J.; see *Wal-*
  tham Forest LBC v Secretary of State for
  Transport, Local Government and the Re-
  gions [2002] EWCA Civ 330, Independent,
  March 22, 2002 (CA), Schiemann, L.J.
  s.192, applied: 2003 c.iii s.16, 2004 c.5 s.49
  s.193, enabling: SI 2002/1877
  s.195, applied: SI 2002/2684 r.3, SI 2002/
  2685 r.3, r.11, r.25, SI 2002/2686 r.3, r.13,
  r.26, SI 2003/1268 r.3, r.9, SI 2003/1269
  r.3, r.13, SI 2003/1270 r.3, r.11, r.25
  s.196, enabling: SI 2002/1877
  s.198, see *Robinson v East Riding of Yorkshire*
  Council [2002] EWCA Civ 1660, [2003]
  J.P.L. 894 (CA), Scott Baker, L.J.
  s.198, amended: 2004 c.5 s.42
  s.198, applied: SI 2002/1066 Art.34, SI
  2004/757 Art.39
  s.198, disapplied: SI 2002/412 Art.28
  s.200, substituted: 2004 c.5 s.85
  s.208, applied: SI 2003/1266 r.3, SI 2003/
  1267 r.3, SI 2003/1271 r.3, 2004 c.5 s.59
  s.211, amended: 2004 c.5 s.86
  s.211, disapplied: SI 2002/412 Art.28
  s.217, amended: 2003 c.39 Sch.8 para.343,
  Sch.10
  s.220, amended: 2004 c.5 s.42, Sch.9
  s.220, applied: SI 2003/2253 Art.8
  s.221, applied: SI 2003/2253 Art.8
  s.224, see *Westminster City Council v Haw*
  [2002] EWHC 2073, (2002) 146 S.J.L.B.
  221 (QBD), Gray, J.
  s.224, amended: 2003 c.38 s.53
  s.224, applied: SI 2003/2253 Art.8, 2004 c.i
  Sch.2
  s.224, varied: 2004 c.i s.25
  s.226, amended: 2004 c.5 s.99, Sch.3 para.3,
  Sch.9
  s.226, repealed (in part): 2004 c.5 Sch.9
  s.228, amended: SI 2002/2626 Sch.2
  para.15, 2004 c.5 Sch.3 para.4
  s.228, applied: 2003 c.39 s.3
  s.236, amended: 2003 c.21 Sch.17 para.103
  s.237, amended: 2003 c.21 Sch.17 para.103
  s.238, varied: 2003 c.43 Sch.4 para.86
  s.239, varied: 2003 c.43 Sch.4 para.86

1990–cont.
8. Town and Country Planning Act 1990–
cont.
  s.240, varied: 2003 c.43 Sch.4 para.86
  s.245, amended: SI 2002/2626 Sch.2
  para.15
  s.245, repealed (in part): 2004 c.5 Sch.9
  s.249, varied: SI 2004/932 Sch.1 para.6
  s.251, varied: SI 2004/932 Sch.1 para.7
  s.253, amended: 2004 c.5 s.40
  s.256, amended: 2003 c.21 Sch.17 para.103
  s.258, varied: SI 2004/932 Sch.1 para.8
  s.260, amended: 2003 c.21 Sch.17 para.103
  s.262, applied: SI 2002/412 Art.34
  s.264, amended: SI 2003/1615 Sch.1 para.14,
  2004 c.5 s.40
  s.264, applied: SI 2002/412 Art.14, SI 2002/
  1066 Art.17, SI 2002/1327 Art.14, SI 2002/
  1943 Art.12, SI 2003/1075 Art.36, SI
  2004/389 Art.34, SI 2004/757 Art.20
  s.265, amended: SI 2002/2626 Sch.2
  para.15
  s.265, applied: SI 2002/794 Art.3, SI 2002/
  2626 Art.6
  s.271, applied: SI 2002/1064 Art.19, Sch.3
  para.1, SI 2002/1065 Art.19, Sch.6 para.1,
  Sch.6 para.3, SI 2002/1066 Art.31,
  Sch.10 para.1, SI 2002/1327 Art.26, Sch.5
  para.1, SI 2002/1943 Art.8, SI 2003/1075
  Art.33, Sch.12 para.1, Sch.13 para.42, SI
  2003/3364 Art.20, Sch.6 para.1, SI
  2004/389 Sch.12 para.1, SI 2004/757
  Art.35, Sch.12 para.1, Sch.13 para.4
  s.271, disapplied: SI 2002/412 Art.22, Sch.6
  para.2, SI 2002/1064 Sch.3 para.1, SI
  2002/1066 Sch.11 para.2, SI 2002/1327
  Sch.5 para.1, SI 2004/389 Sch.13 para.42,
  SI 2004/757 Sch.12 para.1
  s.271, referred to: SI 2004/389 Art.31
  s.271, varied: SI 2002/1065 Sch.6 para.1, SI
  2004/389 Sch.12 para.1
  s.272, amended: 2003 c.21 Sch.17 para.103
  s.272, applied: SI 2002/1064 Art.19, Sch.3
  para.1, SI 2002/1065 Art.19, Sch.6 para.1,
  Sch.6 para.3, SI 2002/1066 Art.31,
  Sch.10 para.1, SI 2002/1327 Art.26, Sch.5
  para.1, SI 2002/1943 Art.8, SI 2003/1075
  Art.33, Sch.12 para.1, Sch.13 para.42, SI
  2003/3364 Art.20, Sch.6 para.1, SI
  2004/389 Sch.12 para.1, SI 2004/757
  Art.35, Sch.12 para.1, Sch.13 para.4
  s.272, disapplied: SI 2002/412 Art.22, Sch.6
  para.2, SI 2002/1064 Sch.3 para.1, SI
  2002/1066 Sch.11 para.2, SI 2002/1327
  Sch.5 para.1, SI 2004/389 Sch.13 para.42,
  SI 2004/757 Sch.12 para.1
  s.272, referred to: SI 2004/389 Art.31
  s.272, varied: SI 2002/1065 Sch.6 para.1, SI
  2004/389 Sch.12 para.1
  s.273, amended: 2003 c.21 Sch.17 para.103
  s.273, applied: SI 2002/1064 Sch.3 para.1, SI
  2002/1065 Sch.6 para.3, SI 2002/1066
  Sch.10 para.1, SI 2002/1327 Sch.5 para.1,

1990–cont.

8. Town and Country Planning Act 1990–
cont.

s.273, applied:–cont.
SI 2003/1075 Sch.12 para.1, SI 2003/3364 Sch.6 para.1, SI 2004/389 Sch.12 para.1, SI 2004/757 Sch.12 para.1

s.273, disapplied: SI 2002/1064 Sch.3 para.1, SI 2002/1327 Sch.5 para.1, SI 2004/757 Sch.12 para.1

s.273, varied: SI 2002/1065 Sch.6 para.1, SI 2004/389 Sch.12 para.1

s.274, amended: 2003 c.21 Sch.17 para.103

s.274, applied: SI 2002/1064 Sch.3 para.1, SI 2002/1066 Sch.10 para.1, SI 2002/1327 Sch.5 para.1, SI 2003/3364 Sch.6 para.1, SI 2004/757 Sch.12 para.1

s.274, disapplied: SI 2002/1064 Sch.3 para.1, SI 2002/1327 Sch.5 para.1, SI 2004/757 Sch.12 para.1

s.274, varied: SI 2002/1065 Sch.6 para.1, SI 2004/389 Sch.12 para.1

s.275, applied: SI 2002/1066 Sch.10 para.1, SI 2002/1327 Sch.5 para.1, SI 2003/1075 Sch.12 para.1, SI 2003/3364 Sch.6 para.1, SI 2004/389 Sch.12 para.1, SI 2004/757 Sch.12 para.1

s.275, disapplied: SI 2002/1327 Sch.5 para.1, SI 2004/757 Sch.12 para.1

s.275, referred to: SI 2002/1064 Sch.3 para.1, SI 2002/1065 Sch.6 para.1

s.276, applied: SI 2002/1066 Sch.10 para.1, SI 2002/1327 Sch.5 para.1, SI 2003/1075 Sch.12 para.1, SI 2003/3364 Sch.6 para.1, SI 2004/389 Sch.12 para.1, SI 2004/757 Sch.12 para.1

s.276, disapplied: SI 2002/1327 Sch.5 para.1, SI 2004/757 Sch.12 para.1

s.276, referred to: SI 2002/1064 Sch.3 para.1, SI 2002/1065 Sch.6 para.1

s.277, applied: SI 2002/1066 Sch.10 para.1, SI 2002/1327 Sch.5 para.1, SI 2003/1075 Sch.12 para.1, SI 2003/3364 Sch.6 para.1, SI 2004/389 Sch.12 para.1, SI 2004/757 Sch.12 para.1

s.277, disapplied: SI 2002/1327 Sch.5 para.1, SI 2004/757 Sch.12 para.1

s.277, referred to: SI 2002/1064 Sch.3 para.1, SI 2002/1065 Sch.6 para.1

s.278, applied: SI 2002/1066 Sch.10 para.1, SI 2002/1327 Sch.5 para.1, SI 2003/1075 Sch.12 para.1, SI 2003/3364 Sch.6 para.1, SI 2004/389 Sch.12 para.1, SI 2004/757 Sch.12 para.1

s.278, disapplied: SI 2002/1327 Sch.5 para.1, SI 2004/757 Sch.12 para.1

s.278, referred to: SI 2002/1064 Sch.3 para.1, SI 2002/1065 Sch.6 para.1

s.279, amended: 2003 c.21 Sch.17 para.103, 2004 c.5 s.40

s.279, applied: SI 2002/1065 Sch.6 para.1, SI 2002/1066 Sch.10 para.1, SI 2002/1327 Sch.5 para.1, SI 2003/1075 Sch.12 para.1,

1990–cont.

8. Town and Country Planning Act 1990–
cont.

s.279, applied:–cont.
SI 2003/3364 Sch.6 para.1, SI 2004/389 Sch.12 para.1, SI 2004/757 Sch.12 para.1

s.279, disapplied: SI 2002/1327 Sch.5 para.1, SI 2004/757 Sch.12 para.1

s.279, referred to: SI 2002/1064 Sch.3 para.1

s.280, amended: 2003 c.21 Sch.17 para.104

s.280, applied: SI 2002/1065 Sch.6 para.1, SI 2002/1066 Sch.10 para.1, SI 2002/1327 Sch.5 para.1, SI 2003/1075 Sch.12 para.1, SI 2003/3364 Sch.6 para.1, SI 2004/389 Sch.12 para.1, SI 2004/757 Sch.12 para.1

s.280, disapplied: SI 2002/1327 Sch.5 para.1, SI 2004/757 Sch.12 para.1

s.280, referred to: SI 2002/1064 Sch.3 para.1

s.282, applied: SI 2002/1065 Sch.6 para.1, SI 2002/1066 Sch.10 para.1, SI 2002/1327 Sch.5 para.1, SI 2003/1075 Sch.12 para.1, SI 2003/3364 Sch.6 para.1, SI 2004/389 Sch.12 para.1, SI 2004/757 Sch.12 para.1

s.282, disapplied: SI 2002/1327 Sch.5 para.1, SI 2004/757 Sch.12 para.1

s.282, referred to: SI 2002/1064 Sch.3 para.1

s.284, amended: 2004 c.5 s.82

s.284, applied: 2004 c.5 s.59

s.284, repealed (in part): 2004 c.5 Sch.6 para.8, Sch.9

s.287, see *Fairfield Partnership v Huntingdonshire DC* [2003] EWHC 2430, (2003) 147 S.J.L.B. 1273 (QBD (Admin Ct)), Lindsay, J.; see *First Corporate Shipping Ltd (t/a Bristol Port Co) v North Somerset Council* [2001] EWCA Civ 693, [2002] P.L.C.R. 7 (CA), Buxton, L.J.; see *JS Bloor Ltd v Swindon BC* [2001] EWHC Admin 966, [2002] P.L.C.R. 22 (QBD (Admin Ct)), Ouseley, J.; see *Test Valley BC v Hampshire CC* [2002] P.L.C.R. 2 (QBD (Admin Ct)), Jack Beatson, Q.C.

s.287, amended: 2004 c.5 Sch.6 para.9, Sch.9

s.287, repealed (in part): 2004 c.5 Sch.6 para.9, Sch.9

s.288, see *Downderry Construction Ltd v Secretary of State for Transport, Local Government and the Regions* [2002] EWHC 2, [2002] A.C.D. 62 (QBD (Admin Ct)), Richards, J.; see *Evans v First Secretary of State* [2003] EWCA Civ 1523, [2004] Env. L.R. 17 (CA), Simon Brown, L.J.; see *Kebbell Development Ltd v First Secretary of State* [2003] EWCA Civ 1855, [2004] J.P.L. 1710 (CA), Keene, L.J.; see *Lough v First Secretary of State* [2004] EWCA Civ 905, [2004] 1 W.L.R. 2557 (CA), Pill, L.J.; see *Matthews v Secretary of State for the Environment, Transport and the Regions* [2001] EWHC Admin 815, [2002] 2 P. & C.R. 34 (QBD (Admin Ct)), Sullivan, J.; see *Monmouthshire CC v*

CAP.

1990–cont.

8. Town and Country Planning Act 1990–
cont.

s.288–cont.

National Assembly for Wales [2003] EWHC 1419, [2003] N.P.C. 69 (QBD (Admin Ct)), Mackay, J.; see *R. (on the application of Gosbee) v First Secretary of State* [2003] EWHC 770, [2004] 1 P. & C.R. 22 (QBD (Admin Ct)), Elias, J.; see *R. (on the application of Imperial Resources SA) v First Secretary of State* [2003] EWHC 658, (2003) 100(12) L.S.G. 33 (QBD (Admin Ct)), Sullivan, J.; see *R. (on the application of Redditch BC) v First Secretary of State* [2003] EWHC 650, [2003] 2 P. & C.R. 25 (QBD (Admin Ct)), Wilson, J.; see *R. (on the application of Waveney DC) v Secretary of State for Transport, Local Government and the Regions* [2002] EWHC 2397, [2003] J.P.L. 1058 (QBD (Admin Ct)), Sullivan, J.; see *Redrow Homes Ltd v First Secretary of State* [2003] EWHC 3094, [2004] J.P.L. 1273 (QBD (Admin Ct)), Sullivan, J.; see *Robinson v East Riding of Yorkshire Council* [2002] EWCA Civ 1660, [2003] J.P.L. 894 (CA), Scott Baker, L.J.; see *South Buckinghamshire DC v Porter (No.2)* [2003] EWCA Civ 687, [2004] 1 P. & C.R. 8 (CA), Pill, L.J.; see *St Leger Davey v First Secretary of State* [2004] EWHC 512, [2004] J.P.L. 1581 (QBD (Admin Ct)), Sullivan, J.; see *Trevett v Secretary of State for Transport, Local Government and the Regions* [2002] EWHC 2696, [2003] Env. L.R. D10 (QBD (Admin Ct)), Sullivan, J.; see *Wandsworth LBC v Secretary of State for Transport, Local Government and the Regions* [2003] EWCA Civ 142, [2003] 9 E.G.C.S. 196 (CA), Jonathan Parker, L.J.; see *Wheeler v First Secretary of State* [2003] EWHC 1194, [2004] 1 P. & C.R. 40 (QBD (Admin Ct)), Harrison, J.; see *Younger Homes (Northern) Ltd v First Secretary of State* [2003] EWHC 3058, [2004] J.P.L. 950 (QBD (Admin Ct)), Ouseley, J.

s.288, applied: 2004 c.5 s.58

s.289, see *Brown v First Secretary of State* [2003] EWHC 2800, [2004] J.P.L. 1074 (QBD (Admin Ct)), McCombe, J.; see *Ceredigion CC v National Assembly for Wales* [2001] EWHC Admin 694, [2002] 2 P. & C.R. 6 (QBD (Admin Ct)), Richards, J.; see *Hattingh v Secretary of State for the Environment, Transport and the Regions* [2001] EWHC Admin 539, [2002] P.L.C.R. 10 (QBD (Admin Ct)), Harrison, J.; see *R. (on the application of Waveney DC) v Secretary of State for Transport, Local Government and the Regions* [2002] EWHC 2397, [2003] J.P.L. 1058 (QBD (Admin Ct)), Sullivan, J.; see *Wheeler v First Secretary of State* [2003]

CAP.

1990–cont.

8. Town and Country Planning Act 1990–
cont.

s.289–cont.

EWHC 1194, [2004] 1 P. & C.R. 40 (QBD (Admin Ct)), Harrison, J.

s.289, applied: 2004 c.5 s.58

s.292A, added: 2004 c.5 s.79

s.293, amended: 2004 c.5 Sch.3 para.6

s.293, applied: 2004 c.5 s.47

s.293, repealed (in part): 2004 c.5 Sch.3 para.22, Sch.9

s.293A, added: 2004 c.5 s.82

s.294, see *R. (on the application of Cherwell DC) v First Secretary of State* [2004] EWHC 724, [2004] 2 P. & C.R. 27 (QBD (Admin Ct)), Collins, J.; see *R. (on the application of Mid-Devon DC) v First Secretary of State* [2004] EWHC 814, [2004] 2 P. & C.R. 28 (QBD (Admin Ct)), Keith, J.

s.294, repealed: 2004 c.5 Sch.3 para.9, Sch.9

s.295, repealed: 2004 c.5 Sch.3 para.9, Sch.9

s.296, amended: 2004 c.5 Sch.6 para.10

s.296, repealed: 2004 c.5 s.84, Sch.9

s.296A, added: 2004 c.5 s.84

s.296A, repealed: 2004 c.5 Sch.9

s.296B, added: 2004 c.5 s.84

s.296B, repealed: 2004 c.5 Sch.9

s.297, repealed: 2004 c.5 Sch.3 para.23, Sch.9

s.298, amended: 2004 c.5 Sch.3 para.24

s.298, repealed (in part): 2004 c.5 Sch.3 para.24, Sch.9

s.298A, added: 2004 c.5 Sch.3 para.10

s.299, applied: 2004 c.5 Sch.3 para.10

s.299, repealed: 2004 c.5 Sch.3 para.10, Sch.9

s.299A, repealed: 2004 c.5 Sch.3 para.25, Sch.9

s.300, applied: 2004 c.5 Sch.3 para.26

s.300, repealed: 2004 c.5 Sch.3 para.26, Sch.9

s.301, referred to: 2004 c.5 Sch.3 para.27

s.301, repealed: 2004 c.5 Sch.3 para.27, Sch.9

s.303, amended: 2004 c.5 s.53

s.303, repealed (in part): 2004 c.5 s.53, Sch.9

s.303, enabling: SI 2002/768, SI 2002/1876, SI 2002/2258, SI 2004/2736

s.303A, amended: 2004 c.5 Sch.6 para.11, Sch.9

s.303A, applied: SI 2002/452 Reg.3, SI 2002/2801 Reg.2, Reg.3, SI 2003/464 Reg.3, SI 2003/1179 Reg.3, Reg.4, Reg.5, SI 2003/2948 Reg.3, Reg.4, Reg.5, SI 2004/421 Reg.3, SI 2004/1716 Reg.3, Reg.4, Reg.5

s.303A, referred to: SI 2002/452 Reg.2, SI 2003/464 Reg.2, SI 2004/421 Reg.2

1990–cont.

8. Town and Country Planning Act 1990–
cont.

s.303A, repealed (in part): 2004 c.5 Sch.6 para.11, Sch.9

s.303A, enabling: SI 2002/452, SI 2002/2801, SI 2003/464, SI 2003/1179, SI 2003/2948, SI 2004/421, SI 2004/1716

s.304A, added: 2004 c.5 s.115

s.306, amended: 2004 c.5 Sch.6 para.12

s.321, amended: 2004 c.5 s.80

s.321A, added: 2004 c.5 s.80

s.321B, added: 2004 c.5 s.81

s.322A, applied: SI 2002/2127 Reg.15

s.323, enabling: SI 2002/2683, SI 2003/390, SI 2003/395

s.324, amended: 2004 c.5 Sch.6 para.13

s.324, applied: 2003 c.21 Sch.4 para.6

s.324, varied: 2003 c.21 Sch.4 para.6

s.325, applied: 2003 c.21 Sch.4 para.6

s.325, varied: 2003 c.21 Sch.4 para.6

s.325A, added: 2004 c.5 Sch.3 para.13

s.327A, added: 2004 c.5 s.42

s.329, amended: SI 2003/956 Art.4

s.329A, added: 2004 c.5 Sch.3 para.16

s.330, amended: SI 2003/956 Art.5

s.330, varied: SI 2004/932 Sch.1 para.9

s.330A, added: 2004 c.5 Sch.3 para.17

s.333, amended: 2004 c.5 s.40, Sch.6 para.14

s.333, enabling: SI 2002/828, SI 2002/1875, SI 2002/1877, SI 2002/1878, SI 2003/390, SI 2003/395, SI 2003/2047, SI 2004/1231, SI 2004/1434, SI 2004/2355, SI 2004/3340

s.334, repealed: 2003 c.17 Sch.6 para.109, Sch.7

s.336, see *Buckinghamshire CC v Briar* [2002] EWHC 2821, [2003] Env. L.R. 25 (Ch D), Lawrence Collins, J.; see *Kensington and Chelsea RLBC v Harvey Nichols & Co Ltd* [2001] EWCA Civ 702, [2002] 1 P. & C.R. 29 (CA), Dyson, L.J.

s.336, amended: SI 2003/956 Art.6, 2004 c.5 Sch.6 para.15, 2004 c.21 Sch.1 para.72

s.336, enabling: SI 2003/394

Sch.1 para.1, applied: SI 2003/1033 Reg.2, 2004 c.5 s.14, s.17

Sch.1 para.1, disapplied: 2004 c.5 s.14

Sch.1 para.1, enabling: SI 2003/1033

Sch.1 para.2, repealed (in part): 2004 c.5 Sch.6 para.16, Sch.9

Sch.1 para.3, amended: 2004 c.5 Sch.6 para.16, Sch.9

Sch.1 para.3, repealed (in part): 2004 c.5 Sch.9

Sch.1 para.5, enabling: SI 2002/1877

Sch.1 para.6, enabling: SI 2002/1877

Sch.1 para.7, substituted: 2004 c.5 Sch.6 para.16

Sch.1 para.7, enabling: SI 2002/1877

Sch.1 para.8, enabling: SI 2002/1877

1990–cont.

8. Town and Country Planning Act 1990–
cont.

Sch.2, applied: 2004 c.5 Sch.8 para.17

Sch.2 Part I para.1, repealed (in part): 2004 c.5 Sch.6 para.17, Sch.9

Sch.2 Part I para.2, repealed (in part): 2004 c.5 Sch.6 para.17, Sch.9

Sch.2 Part I para.3, repealed (in part): 2004 c.5 Sch.6 para.17, Sch.9

Sch.2 Part I para.4, repealed (in part): 2004 c.5 Sch.6 para.17, Sch.9

Sch.2 Part I para.5, repealed (in part): 2004 c.5 Sch.6 para.17, Sch.9

Sch.2 Part I para.6, repealed (in part): 2004 c.5 Sch.6 para.17, Sch.9

Sch.2 Part II para.1, repealed (in part): 2004 c.5 Sch.6 para.17, Sch.9

Sch.2 Part II para.2, repealed (in part): 2004 c.5 Sch.6 para.17, Sch.9

Sch.2 Part II para.3, repealed (in part): 2004 c.5 Sch.6 para.17, Sch.9

Sch.2 Part II para.4, repealed (in part): 2004 c.5 Sch.6 para.17, Sch.9

Sch.2 Part II para.5, repealed (in part): 2004 c.5 Sch.6 para.17, Sch.9

Sch.2 Part II para.6, repealed (in part): 2004 c.5 Sch.6 para.17, Sch.9

Sch.2 Part II para.7, repealed (in part): 2004 c.5 Sch.6 para.17, Sch.9

Sch.2 Part II para.8, repealed (in part): 2004 c.5 Sch.6 para.17, Sch.9

Sch.2 Part II para.9, repealed (in part): 2004 c.5 Sch.6 para.17, Sch.9

Sch.2 Part II para.10, repealed (in part): 2004 c.5 Sch.6 para.17, Sch.9

Sch.2 Part II para.11, repealed (in part): 2004 c.5 Sch.6 para.17, Sch.9

Sch.2 Part II para.12, repealed (in part): 2004 c.5 Sch.6 para.17, Sch.9

Sch.2 Part II para.13, repealed (in part): 2004 c.5 Sch.6 para.17, Sch.9

Sch.2 Part II para.14, repealed (in part): 2004 c.5 Sch.6 para.17, Sch.9

Sch.2 Part II para.15, repealed (in part): 2004 c.5 Sch.6 para.17, Sch.9

Sch.2 Part II para.16, repealed (in part): 2004 c.5 Sch.6 para.17, Sch.9

Sch.2 Part II para.17, repealed (in part): 2004 c.5 Sch.6 para.17, Sch.9

Sch.2 Part II para.18, repealed (in part): 2004 c.5 Sch.6 para.17, Sch.9

Sch.2 Part III para.1, repealed (in part): 2004 c.5 Sch.6 para.17, Sch.9

Sch.2 Part III para.2, repealed (in part): 2004 c.5 Sch.6 para.17, Sch.9

Sch.2 Part III para.3, repealed (in part): 2004 c.5 Sch.6 para.17, Sch.9

Sch.2 Part III para.4, applied: 2004 c.5 Sch.8 para.1

Sch.2 Part III para.4, repealed (in part): 2004 c.5 Sch.6 para.17, Sch.9

CAP.

1990–cont.

8. Town and Country Planning Act 1990–
cont.

Sch.2 Part III para.5, repealed (in part): 2004 c.5 Sch.6 para.17, Sch.9

Sch.2 Part III para.6, repealed (in part): 2004 c.5 Sch.6 para.17, Sch.9

Sch.2 Part III para.7, repealed (in part): 2004 c.5 Sch.6 para.17, Sch.9

Sch.2 Part III para.8, repealed (in part): 2004 c.5 Sch.6 para.17, Sch.9

Sch.2 Part III para.9, repealed (in part): 2004 c.5 Sch.6 para.17, Sch.9

Sch.2 Part III para.10, repealed (in part): 2004 c.5 Sch.6 para.17, Sch.9

Sch.4A para.1, added: 2004 c.5 Sch.1

Sch.4A para.2, added: 2004 c.5 Sch.1

Sch.4A para.3, added: 2004 c.5 Sch.1

Sch.4A para.4, added: 2004 c.5 Sch.1

Sch.4A para.4, enabling: SI 2004/2204

Sch.4A para.5, added: 2004 c.5 Sch.1

Sch.6 para.8, amended: SI 2002/2626 Sch.2 para.15

Sch.7 para.2, amended: 2004 c.5 s.45

Sch.7 para.3, repealed: 2004 c.5 s.45, Sch.9

Sch.7 para.4, repealed: 2004 c.5 s.45, Sch.9

Sch.7 para.12, amended: 2004 c.5 s.45

Sch.13 para.1, see *Halliday v Secretary of State for Transport, Local Government and the Regions* [2003] R.V.R. 12 (Lands Tr), George Bartlett Q.C. (President)

Sch.13 para.1, amended: 2003 c.21 Sch.17 para.105

Sch.13 para.1, referred to: 2004 c.5 Sch.8 para.16

Sch.13 para.1, repealed (in part): 2004 c.5 Sch.6 para.18, Sch.9

Sch.13 para.1A, added: 2004 c.5 Sch.6 para.18

Sch.13 para.1A, referred to: 2004 c.5 Sch.8 para.16

Sch.13 para.1A, repealed (in part): 2004 c.5 Sch.6 para.18, Sch.9

Sch.13 para.2, referred to: 2004 c.5 Sch.8 para.16

Sch.13 para.2, repealed (in part): 2004 c.5 Sch.6 para.18, Sch.9

Sch.13 para.3, referred to: 2004 c.5 Sch.8 para.16

Sch.13 para.3, repealed (in part): 2004 c.5 Sch.6 para.18, Sch.9

Sch.13 para.4, referred to: 2004 c.5 Sch.8 para.16

Sch.13 para.4, repealed (in part): 2004 c.5 Sch.6 para.18, Sch.9

Sch.13 para.5, amended: 2004 c.5 Sch.6 para.18

Sch.13 para.5, substituted: 2004 c.5 Sch.6 para.18

Sch.13 para.6, amended: 2004 c.5 Sch.6 para.18

CAP.

1990–cont.

8. Town and Country Planning Act 1990–
cont.

Sch.13 para.6, substituted: 2004 c.5 Sch.6 para.18

Sch.13 para.13, amended: 2004 c.5 Sch.6 para.18

Sch.13 para.13, substituted: 2004 c.5 Sch.6 para.18

Sch.15 para.14, amended: 2003 c.44 Sch.37 Part 9

Sch.15 para.14, disapplied: 2003 c.44 Sch.25 para.86

9. Planning (Listed Buildings and Conservation Areas) Act 1990

applied: SI 2003/390 Reg.5, 2004 c.5 s.43, s.51, Sch.4 para.9, Sch.4 para.10, Sch.4 para.12, SI 2004/932 Art.5

varied: 2004 c.5 Sch.4 para.12

s.1, see *Customs and Excise Commissioners v Zielinski Baker & Partners Ltd* [2002] EWCA Civ 692, [2002] S.T.C. 829 (CA), Aldous, L.J.; see *Customs and Excise Commissioners v Zielinski Baker & Partners Ltd* [2004] UKHL 7, [2004] 1 W.L.R. 707 (HL), Lord Nicholls of Birkenhead; see *Morris v Wrexham CBC* [2001] EWHC Admin 697, [2002] 2 P. & C.R. 7 (QBD (Admin Ct)), Jackson, J.; see *R. (on the application of Westminster City Council) v Secretary of State for the Environment, Transport and the Regions* [2001] EWHC Admin 270, [2002] 1 P. & C.R. 8 (QBD (Admin Ct)), Jackson, J.

s.9, see *Braun v Secretary of State for Transport, Local Government and the Regions* [2003] EWCA Civ 665, [2004] 1 P. & C.R. 15 (CA), Simon Brown, L.J.

s.10, amended: 2004 c.5 s.42, Sch.6 para.20, Sch.9

s.10, enabling: SI 2003/2048, SI 2004/2210

s.12, applied: SI 2002/1223 r.3, SI 2003/1266 r.3, SI 2003/1271 r.3

s.14, applied: SI 2002/1223 r.4, r.13

s.15, applied: SI 2002/2685 r.11, SI 2002/2686 r.13, SI 2003/1269 r.13, SI 2003/1270 r.11

s.18, amended: 2004 c.5 s.51

s.19, amended: 2004 c.5 s.51

s.19, applied: SI 2002/1223 r.3, SI 2003/1266 r.3, SI 2003/1271 r.3

s.20, applied: SI 2002/1223 r.3, SI 2003/1266 r.3, SI 2003/1267 r.3, SI 2003/1271 r.3, 2004 c.5 Sch.4 para.11

s.20, referred to: 2004 c.5 s.50

s.20A, added: 2004 c.5 s.50

s.21, enabling: SI 2003/2048, SI 2004/3341

s.23, amended: 2004 c.5 Sch.6 para.21

s.26, amended: 2004 c.5 Sch.6 para.22

s.32A, added: 2004 c.5 Sch.3 para.2

s.33, varied: SI 2004/932 Sch.1 para.10

s.34, varied: SI 2004/932 Sch.1 para.11

s.35, varied: SI 2004/932 Sch.1 para.12

1990–cont.

9. **Planning (Listed Buildings and Conservation Areas) Act 1990**–cont.

s.36, varied: SI 2004/932 Sch.1 para.13

s.38, see *Braun v Secretary of State for Transport, Local Government and the Regions* [2003] EWCA Civ 665, [2004] 1 P. & C.R. 15 (CA), Simon Brown, L.J.

s.38, applied: SI 2002/2682 Reg.8, SI 2002/2685 r.11, SI 2002/2686 r.13, SI 2003/394 Reg.7, SI 2003/1269 r.13, SI 2003/1270 r.11

s.39, amended: SI 2003/956 Art.7

s.39, applied: SI 2002/2682 Reg.6, SI 2002/2683 Reg.3, Reg.4, Reg.5, SI 2002/2684 r.3, SI 2002/2685 r.3, SI 2002/2686 r.3, SI 2003/394 Reg.5, SI 2003/395 Reg.3, Reg.4, Reg.5, SI 2003/1268 r.3, SI 2003/1269 r.3, SI 2003/1270 r.3, 2004 c.5 s.59

s.39, enabling: SI 2002/2682, SI 2003/394

s.40, enabling: SI 2002/2682, SI 2003/394, SI 2003/395

s.42, enabling: SI 2002/2682, SI 2003/394

s.46, applied: SI 2002/2682 Reg.11, SI 2003/394 Reg.10

s.47, amended: 2003 c.39 Sch.8 para.344, Sch.10, 2004 c.5 Sch.3 para.5

s.47, applied: SI 2004/2595 Reg.4, SI 2004/2732 Reg.4

s.50, amended: 2003 c.39 Sch.8 para.345, Sch.10

s.50, applied: SI 2004/2595 Reg.4, SI 2004/2732 Reg.4

s.51, amended: 2003 c.21 Sch.17 para.106

s.54, applied: SI 2004/1777 Art.25, SI 2004/1778 Art.25

s.55, applied: SI 2004/1777 Art.25, SI 2004/1778 Art.25

s.57, applied: SI 2004/1777 Art.25, SI 2004/1778 Art.25

s.58, applied: SI 2004/1777 Art.25, SI 2004/1778 Art.25

s.62, amended: 2004 c.5 s.83

s.62, referred to: 2004 c.5 s.59

s.63, applied: 2004 c.5 s.58

s.66, see *Ryan v Secretary of State for the Environment, Transport and the Regions* [2001] EWHC Admin 722, [2002] J.P.L. 711 (QBD (Admin Ct)), Judge Rich Q.C.

s.67, amended: 2004 c.5 Sch.6 para.23

s.67, repealed (in part): 2004 c.5 Sch.9

s.67, enabling: SI 2004/2210

s.72, see *R. (on the application of Waveney DC) v Secretary of State for Transport, Local Government and the Regions* [2002] EWHC 2397, [2003] J.P.L. 1058 (QBD (Admin Ct)), Sullivan, J.; see *Ryan v Secretary of State for the Environment, Transport and the Regions* [2001] EWHC Admin 722, [2002] J.P.L. 711 (QBD (Admin Ct)), Judge Rich Q.C.

s.73, amended: 2004 c.5 Sch.6 para.24

s.73, enabling: SI 2004/2210

1990–cont.

9. **Planning (Listed Buildings and Conservation Areas) Act 1990**–cont.

s.74, applied: SI 2002/1223 r.3, SI 2002/2684 r.3, SI 2002/2685 r.3, SI 2002/2686 r.3, SI 2003/1266 r.3, SI 2003/1267 r.3, SI 2003/1268 r.3, SI 2003/1270 r.3, SI 2003/1271 r.3, 2004 c.5 s.50, s.59

s.74, referred to: SI 2003/1269 r.3

s.82, enabling: SI 2003/2048

s.82A, added: 2004 c.5 s.79

s.82B, added: 2004 c.5 s.83

s.82C, added: 2004 c.5 Sch.3 para.7

s.82D, added: 2004 c.5 s.84

s.82E, added: 2004 c.5 s.84

s.82F, added: 2004 c.5 Sch.3 para.11

s.83, repealed: 2004 c.5 Sch.3 para.18, Sch.9

s.84, applied: 2004 c.5 Sch.3 para.18

s.84, repealed: 2004 c.5 Sch.3 para.18, Sch.9

s.84, enabling: SI 2003/2048

s.88C, added: 2004 c.5 Sch.3 para.14

s.89, amended: SI 2003/956 Art.8, 2004 c.5 s.42, Sch.3 para.19

s.89, enabling: SI 2003/390, SI 2003/395

s.91, amended: 2003 c.21 Sch.17 para.106, SI 2003/956 Art.9, 2004 c.5 Sch.6 para.25, Sch.9

s.91, varied: SI 2004/932 Sch.1 para.14

s.91, enabling: SI 2002/2682, SI 2003/390, SI 2003/394, SI 2003/395, SI 2004/3341

s.92, repealed (in part): 2004 c.5 Sch.9

s.93, amended: 2004 c.5 Sch.6 para.26

s.93, enabling: SI 2003/390, SI 2003/395, SI 2003/2048, SI 2004/2210, SI 2004/3341

s.94, applied: SI 2004/1777 Art.25

Sch.3, added: 2004 c.5 s.81

Sch.3 para.6A, added: 2004 c.5 s.80

Sch.3 para.7, amended: SI 2002/2626 Sch.2 para.16

10. **Planning (Hazardous Substances) Act 1990**

s.17, amended: 2004 c.5 Sch.3 para.20

s.20, applied: 2004 c.5 s.58, s.59

s.21, applied: 2004 c.5 s.58, s.59

s.22, applied: 2004 c.5 s.58

s.30A, added: 2004 c.5 s.79

s.30B, added: 2004 c.5 s.79

s.30B, referred to: 2004 c.5 s.119

s.30C, added: 2004 c.5 s.84

s.30D, added: 2004 c.5 s.84

s.31, amended: 2004 c.5 Sch.3 para.8

s.31, repealed (in part): 2004 c.5 Sch.9

s.31A, added: 2004 c.5 Sch.3 para.12

s.32, repealed: 2004 c.5 Sch.9

s.36C, added: 2004 c.5 Sch.3 para.15

s.37, amended: 2004 c.5 Sch.3 para.21

s.40, amended: 2004 c.5 Sch.6 para.27

Sch.1, added: 2004 c.5 s.81

Sch.1 para.6A, added: 2004 c.5 s.80

Sch.1 para.7, amended: SI 2002/2626 Sch.2 para.17

CAP.

1990–cont.

11. Planning (Consequential Provisions) Act 1990

Sch.2 para.63, repealed: 2003 c.21 Sch.19

14. Pakistan Act 1990

Sch.1 para.1, repealed: 2002 c.39 Sch.3

16. Food Safety Act 1990

see *Monks v East Northamptonshire DC* [2002] EWHC 473, (2002) 166 J.P. 592 (QBD (Admin Ct)), Silber, J.; see *Wei Hai Restaurant Ltd v Kingston upon Hull City Council* [2001] EWHC Admin 490, (2002) 166 J.P. 185 (QBD (Admin Ct)), Forbes, J.

applied: SI 2002/774 Reg.4, SI 2002/1281 Reg.3, SI 2002/2296 Reg.4, SI 2003/1119 Reg.4, SI 2003/1722 Reg.4, SI 2003/1774 Sch.1 para.1, SI 2003/1895 Sch.1 para.1, SI 2003/1940 Reg.4, SI 2003/1956 Reg.4, SI 2003/2074 Reg.4, SI 2003/2254 Reg.4, SI 2003/2288 Reg.4, SI 2003/2455 Reg.4, SI 2003/2910 Reg.4, SSI 2002/424 Reg.4, SSI 2003/382 Reg.5, SSI 2003/396 Reg.4

varied: SI 2002/1886 Reg.7

Part II, applied: SI 2003/1774 Sch.1 para.2, SI 2003/1895 Sch.1 para.2

s.1, amended: SI 2004/2990 Reg.3

s.1, applied: SI 2002/1689 Reg.3

s.1, enabling: SI 2003/1774, SI 2003/1895

s.2, applied: SI 2002/333 Reg.6, SI 2002/821 Reg.5, SI 2002/890 Reg.7, SI 2002/1817 Reg.9, SI 2002/1886 Reg.7, SSI 2002/50 Reg.6, SSI 2002/148 Reg.5, SSI 2002/267 Reg.7

s.2, varied: SI 2002/773 Reg.5, SI 2002/774 Reg.5, SI 2002/820 Reg.5, SI 2002/931 Reg.5, SI 2002/1090 Reg.5, SI 2002/1614 Reg.5, SI 2002/1798 Reg.5, SI 2002/2939 Reg.9, SI 2002/3157 Reg.5, SI 2002/3169 Reg.5, SI 2003/1387 Reg.11, SI 2003/1563 Reg.9, SI 2003/1564 Reg.9, SI 2003/1596 Reg.9, SI 2003/1659 Reg.10, SI 2003/1719 Reg.11, SI 2003/2075 Reg.8, SI 2003/2243 Reg.9, SI 2003/3037 Reg.10, SI 2003/3041 Reg.9, SI 2003/3044 Reg.9, SI 2003/3047 Reg.9, SI 2003/3053 Reg.9, SI 2003/3120 Reg.9, SI 2003/3207 Reg.12, SI 2004/314 Reg.12, SI 2004/553 Reg.9, SI 2004/1396 Reg.8, SSI 2002/50 Reg.6, SSI 2002/149 Reg.5, SSI 2002/179 Reg.6, SSI 2002/300 Reg.5, SSI 2002/397 Reg.8, SSI 2002/523 Reg.5, SSI 2003/291 Reg.11, SSI 2003/293 Reg.10, SSI 2003/311 Reg.10, SSI 2003/527 Reg.9, SSI 2003/569 Reg.10, SSI 2004/6 Reg.9, SSI 2004/8 Reg.12, SSI 2004/133 Reg.10, SSI 2004/187 Reg.6

s.3, applied: SI 2002/333 Reg.6, SI 2002/402 Art.5, SI 2002/1817 Reg.9, SI 2002/1886 Reg.7, SI 2004/2335 Reg.6, SSI 2002/50 Reg.6, SSI 2002/267 Reg.7

CAP.

1990–cont.

16. Food Safety Act 1990–*cont.*

s.3, varied: SI 2002/334 Art.5, SI 2002/890 Reg.7, SI 2002/2939 Reg.9, SI 2002/3157 Reg.5, SI 2002/3169 Reg.5, SI 2003/461 Reg.10, SI 2003/1387 Reg.11, SI 2003/1478 Reg.7, SI 2003/1563 Reg.9, SI 2003/1564 Reg.9, SI 2003/1596 Reg.9, SI 2003/1635 Reg.10, SI 2003/1659 Reg.10, SI 2003/1719 Reg.11, SI 2003/1721 Reg.7, SI 2003/2075 Reg.8, SI 2003/2243 Reg.9, SI 2003/3037 Reg.10, SI 2003/3041 Reg.9, SI 2003/3044 Reg.9, SI 2003/3047 Reg.9, SI 2003/3053 Reg.9, SI 2003/3120 Reg.9, SI 2003/3207 Reg.12, SI 2004/314 Reg.12, SI 2004/553 Reg.9, SI 2004/1396 Reg.8, SSI 2002/50 Reg.6, SSI 2002/64 Art.5, SSI 2002/397 Reg.8, SSI 2002/523 Reg.5, SSI 2003/145 Reg.10, SSI 2003/289 Reg.7, SSI 2003/291 Reg.11, SSI 2003/293 Reg.10, SSI 2003/311 Reg.10, SSI 2003/527 Reg.9, SSI 2003/569 Reg.10, SSI 2004/6 Reg.9, SSI 2004/8 Reg.12, SSI 2004/133 Reg.10, SSI 2004/432 Reg.6

s.5, applied: SI 2002/3170 Art.3, SI 2003/2577 Reg.3, SI 2004/2412 Reg.4, SSI 2004/432 Reg.6, SSI 2004/438 Reg.3

s.5, referred to: SI 2003/1387 Reg.8

s.6, amended: SI 2002/794 Sch.2

s.6, enabling: SI 2004/313, SI 2004/314, SSI 2002/50, SSI 2002/64, SSI 2002/234, SSI 2002/267, SSI 2002/283, SSI 2002/284, SSI 2002/349, SSI 2002/397, SSI 2002/498, SSI 2002/523, SSI 2002/524, SSI 2003/9, SSI 2003/53, SSI 2003/139, SSI 2003/145, SSI 2003/278, SSI 2003/289, SSI 2003/291, SSI 2003/293, SSI 2003/311, SSI 2003/527, SSI 2003/569, SSI 2004/6, SSI 2004/7, SSI 2004/8, SSI 2004/133, SSI 2004/269, SSI 2004/432, SSI 2004/525

s.8, applied: SI 2002/843 Reg.77, SI 2002/1416 Reg.77, SI 2002/3157 Reg.5, SI 2002/3169 Reg.5, SI 2003/461 Reg.10, SI 2003/1635 Reg.10, SI 2003/1659 Reg.10, SI 2003/1719 Reg.11, SI 2003/3037 Reg.10, SI 2003/3207 Reg.12, SI 2004/314 Reg.12, SI 2004/553 Reg.9, SI 2004/2335 Reg.6, SSI 2002/255 Reg.76, SSI 2002/267 Reg.7, SSI 2002/523 Reg.5, SSI 2003/145 Reg.10, SSI 2003/289 Reg.7, SSI 2003/291 Reg.11, SSI 2003/569 Reg.10, SSI 2004/6 Reg.9

s.8, referred to: SSI 2002/267 Reg.7, SSI 2002/397 Reg.8

s.8, varied: SI 2004/2335 Reg.7, SSI 2004/432 Reg.6

s.9, see *R. (on the application of Food Standards Agency) v Brent Justices* [2004] EWHC 459, (2004) 168 J.P. 241 (QBD (Admin Ct)), Stanley Burnton, J.

1990–cont.

16. Food Safety Act 1990–*cont.*

s.9, applied: SI 2002/821 Reg.5, SI 2002/
843 Reg.47, Reg.77, SI 2002/890 Reg.3,
SI 2002/1090 Reg.5, SI 2002/1416
Reg.47, Reg.77, SI 2002/1886 Reg.3, SI
2002/3169 Reg.5, SI 2003/1721 Reg.3,
SSI 2002/148 Reg.5, SSI 2002/255
Reg.76, SSI 2002/267 Reg.3, SSI 2002/
523 Reg.5, SSI 2003/289 Reg.3

s.9, referred to: SI 2002/821 Reg.5, SI 2002/
890 Reg.7, SI 2002/1798 Reg.5, SI 2002/
1886 Reg.7, SSI 2002/148 Reg.5, SSI
2002/149 Reg.5, SSI 2002/267 Reg.7,
SSI 2003/289 Reg.7

s.9, varied: SI 2002/183 Reg.6, SI 2002/203
Reg.6, SI 2002/334 Art.5, SI 2002/402
Art.5, SI 2002/773 Reg.5, SI 2002/774
Reg.5, SI 2002/820 Reg.5, SI 2002/821
Reg.5, SI 2002/843 Reg.77, SI 2002/890
Reg.7, SI 2002/931 Reg.5, SI 2002/1090
Reg.5, SI 2002/1416 Reg.77, SI 2002/
1614 Reg.5, SI 2002/1798 Reg.5, SI
2002/1886 Reg.7, SI 2002/3157 Reg.5,
SI 2003/1478 Reg.7, SI 2003/1721 Reg.7,
SI 2004/2335 Reg.7, SSI 2002/36 Reg.6,
SSI 2002/64 Art.5, SSI 2002/148 Reg.5,
SSI 2002/149 Reg.5, SSI 2002/255
Reg.76, SSI 2002/267 Reg.7, SSI 2002/
300 Reg.5, SSI 2003/289 Reg.7, SSI
2004/432 Reg.6

s.11, applied: SI 2003/1774 Sch.1 para.2, SI
2003/1895 Sch.1 para.2

s.12, applied: SI 2003/1774 Sch.1 para.2, SI
2003/1895 Sch.1 para.2

s.13, applied: SI 2002/334 Art.4, SI 2002/
402 Art.4, SSI 2002/64 Art.4, SSI 2002/
148 Reg.4, SSI 2002/149 Reg.4

s.13, enabling: SI 2002/334, SI 2002/402, SI
2002/602, SI 2003/2338, SI 2003/2661,
SSI 2002/64, SSI 2003/437

s.14, see *Nottingham City Council v
Wolverhampton and Dudley Breweries Plc*
[2003] EWHC 2847, [2004] Q.B. 1274
(QBD (Admin Ct)), Kennedy, L.J.

s.14, applied: SI 2002/843 Reg.77, SI 2002/
1416 Reg.77, SI 2002/3169 Reg.5, 2003
c.17 Sch.4 para.15, SI 2003/461 Reg.10, SI
2003/1635 Reg.10, SI 2003/1659 Reg.10,
SI 2003/1719 Reg.11, SI 2003/3037
Reg.10, SI 2003/3207 Reg.12, SI 2004/
314 Reg.12, SI 2004/553 Reg.9, SI 2004/
2335 Reg.6, SSI 2002/255 Reg.76, SSI
2002/267 Reg.7, SSI 2002/523 Reg.5,
SSI 2003/145 Reg.10, SSI 2003/289
Reg.7, SSI 2003/291 Reg.11, SSI 2003/
569 Reg.10, SSI 2004/6 Reg.9

s.14, referred to: SSI 2002/267 Reg.7, SSI
2002/397 Reg.8

s.15, applied: SI 2002/843 Reg.77, SI 2002/
1416 Reg.77, SI 2002/3169 Reg.5, 2003
c.17 Sch.4 para.15, SI 2003/461 Reg.10, SI
2003/1635 Reg.10, SI 2003/1659 Reg.10,
SI 2003/1719 Reg.11, SI 2003/3037

1990–cont.

16. Food Safety Act 1990–*cont.*

s.15, applied:–*cont.*

Reg.10, SI 2003/3207 Reg.12, SI 2004/
314 Reg.12, SI 2004/553 Reg.9, SI 2004/
2335 Reg.6, SSI 2002/255 Reg.76, SSI
2002/267 Reg.7, SSI 2002/523 Reg.5,
SSI 2003/145 Reg.10, SSI 2003/289
Reg.7, SSI 2003/291 Reg.11, SSI 2003/
569 Reg.10, SSI 2004/6 Reg.9

s.15, referred to: SSI 2002/267 Reg.7, SSI
2002/397 Reg.8

s.16, enabling: SI 2002/47, SI 2002/329, SI
2002/330, SI 2002/379, SI 2002/889, SI
2002/890, SI 2002/1472, SI 2002/1476,
SI 2002/1619, SI 2002/1817, SI 2002/
1886, SI 2002/1922, SI 2002/1923, SI
2002/2364, SI 2002/2834, SI 2002/
2939, SI 2002/3008, SI 2002/3157, SI
2002/3169, SI 2002/3231, SI 2003/302,
SI 2003/461, SI 2003/474, SI 2003/666,
SI 2003/832, SI 2003/945, SI 2003/
1008, SI 2003/1182, SI 2003/1387, SI
2003/1478, SI 2003/1484, SI 2003/
1563, SI 2003/1564, SI 2003/1596, SI
2003/1635, SI 2003/1659, SI 2003/
1713, SI 2003/1719, SI 2003/1721, SI
2003/1849, SI 2003/2075, SI 2003/
2243, SI 2003/2647, SI 2003/2754, SI
2003/2755, SI 2003/3037, SI 2003/
3041, SI 2003/3042, SI 2003/3044, SI
2003/3047, SI 2003/3053, SI 2003/
3120, SI 2003/3207, SI 2003/3208, SI
2003/3295, SI 2004/249, SI 2004/313,
SI 2004/314, SI 2004/455, SI 2004/553,
SI 2004/554, SI 2004/649, SI 2004/656,
SI 2004/1012, SI 2004/1396, SI 2004/
1509, SI 2004/1512, SI 2004/2335, SI
2004/2558, SI 2004/2601, SI 2004/
2824, SI 2004/3022, SI 2004/3062, SI
2004/3113, SI 2004/3220, SI 2004/
3279, SI 2004/3344, SI 2004/3348, SSI
2002/61, SSI 2002/87, SSI 2002/234,
SSI 2002/267, SSI 2002/283, SSI 2002/
284, SSI 2002/349, SSI 2002/397, SSI
2002/498, SSI 2002/523, SSI 2002/
524, SSI 2003/9, SSI 2003/53, SSI
2003/132, SSI 2003/139, SSI 2003/145,
SSI 2003/274, SSI 2003/278, SSI 2003/
289, SSI 2003/291, SSI 2003/293, SSI
2003/311, SSI 2003/527, SSI 2003/569,
SSI 2003/578, SSI 2003/599, SSI 2003/
6, SSI 2004/7, SSI 2004/8, SSI 2004/90,
SSI 2004/132, SSI 2004/133, SSI 2004/
244, SSI 2004/269, SSI 2004/413, SSI
2004/432, SSI 2004/472, SSI 2004/524,
SSI 2004/525, SSI 2004/548

s.17, enabling: SI 2002/47, SI 2002/329, SI
2002/330, SI 2002/333, SI 2002/379, SI
2002/890, SI 2002/1476, SI 2002/1817,
SI 2002/1886, SI 2002/1922, SI 2002/
1923, SI 2002/2364, SI 2002/2834, SI
2002/2939, SI 2002/3008, SI 2003/
302, SI 2003/461, SI 2003/474, SI 2003/

1990–cont.

16. Food Safety Act 1990–*cont.*
  s.17, enabling:–*cont.*

666, SI 2003/832, SI 2003/945, SI 2003/1008, SI 2003/1182, SI 2003/1387, SI 2003/1478, SI 2003/1563, SI 2003/1564, SI 2003/1596, SI 2003/1635, SI 2003/1659, SI 2003/1713, SI 2003/1719, SI 2003/1721, SI 2003/2243, SI 2003/2647, SI 2003/3037, SI 2003/3041, SI 2003/3042, SI 2003/3044, SI 2003/3047, SI 2003/3053, SI 2003/3120, SI 2003/3207, SI 2003/3208, SI 2003/3295, SI 2004/249, SI 2004/313, SI 2004/314, SI 2004/553, SI 2004/554, SI 2004/649, SI 2004/656, SI 2004/1012, SI 2004/1509, SI 2004/1512, SI 2004/2335, SI 2004/2558, SI 2004/2601, SI 2004/2824, SI 2004/3022, SI 2004/3062, SI 2004/3113, SI 2004/3220, SI 2004/3279, SI 2004/3344, SI 2004/3348, SSI 2002/50, SSI 2002/61, SSI 2002/87, SSI 2002/234, SSI 2002/267, SSI 2002/284, SSI 2002/349, SSI 2002/397, SSI 2002/498, SSI 2002/524, SSI 2003/9, SSI 2003/132, SSI 2003/139, SSI 2003/145, SSI 2003/274, SSI 2003/278, SSI 2003/289, SSI 2003/291, SSI 2003/293, SSI 2003/311, SSI 2003/492, SSI 2003/527, SSI 2003/569, SSI 2003/578, SSI 2003/599, SSI 2004/7, SSI 2004/8, SSI 2004/90, SSI 2004/132, SSI 2004/133, SSI 2004/269, SSI 2004/413, SSI 2004/432, SSI 2004/472, SSI 2004/524, SSI 2004/525, SSI 2004/548

  s.18, enabling: SI 2002/1922, SI 2002/3157, SI 2002/3169, SI 2003/2755, SI 2004/455, SI 2004/2335, SI 2004/3220, SSI 2002/284, SSI 2002/523, SSI 2004/244, SSI 2004/432

  s.19, enabling: SI 2002/47, SI 2002/1922, SSI 2002/87, SSI 2002/284

  s.20, applied: SI 2002/183 Reg.6, SI 2002/333 Reg.6, SI 2002/402 Art.5, SI 2002/1817 Reg.9, SI 2002/1886 Reg.7, SI 2004/2335 Reg.6, SSI 2002/50 Reg.6, SSI 2002/267 Reg.7, SSI 2002/424 Reg.5

  s.20, varied: SI 2002/203 Reg.6, SI 2002/334 Art.5, SI 2002/773 Reg.5, SI 2002/774 Reg.5, SI 2002/820 Reg.5, SI 2002/821 Reg.5, SI 2002/890 Reg.7, SI 2002/931 Reg.5, SI 2002/1090 Reg.5, SI 2002/1614 Reg.5, SI 2002/1798 Reg.5, SI 2002/2295 Reg.5, SI 2002/2296 Reg.5, SI 2002/2350 Reg.5, SI 2002/2351 Reg.5, SI 2002/2939 Reg.9, SI 2002/3157 Reg.5, SI 2002/3169 Reg.5, SI 2003/461 Reg.10, SI 2003/1119 Reg.5, SI 2003/1387 Reg.11, SI 2003/1478 Reg.7, SI 2003/1563 Reg.9, SI 2003/1564 Reg.9, SI 2003/1596 Reg.9, SI 2003/1635 Reg.10, SI 2003/1659 Reg.10, SI 2003/1719 Reg.11, SI 2003/1721 Reg.7, SI 2003/1722 Reg.5, SI 2003/1940 Reg.5, SI 2003/1956 Reg.5, SI

1990–cont.

16. Food Safety Act 1990–*cont.*
  s.20, varied:–*cont.*

2003/2074 Reg.5, SI 2003/2075 Reg.8, SI 2003/2243 Reg.9, SI 2003/2254 Reg.5, SI 2003/2288 Reg.5, SI 2003/2455 Reg.5, SI 2003/2910 Reg.5, SI 2003/3037 Reg.10, SI 2003/3041 Reg.9, SI 2003/3044 Reg.9, SI 2003/3047 Reg.9, SI 2003/3053 Reg.9, SI 2003/3120 Reg.9, SI 2003/3207 Reg.12, SI 2004/314 Reg.12, SI 2004/553 Reg.9, SI 2004/1396 Reg.8, SSI 2002/36 Reg.6, SSI 2002/50 Reg.6, SSI 2002/64 Art.5, SSI 2002/148 Reg.5, SSI 2002/149 Reg.5, SSI 2002/179 Reg.6, SSI 2002/300 Reg.5, SSI 2002/397 Reg.8, SSI 2002/425 Reg.5, SSI 2002/523 Reg.5, SSI 2003/145 Reg.10, SSI 2003/289 Reg.7, SSI 2003/291 Reg.11, SSI 2003/293 Reg.10, SSI 2003/311 Reg.10, SSI 2003/382 Reg.6, SSI 2003/396 Reg.5, SSI 2003/414 Reg.5, SSI 2003/418 Reg.5, SSI 2003/527 Reg.9, SSI 2003/569 Reg.10, SSI 2004/6 Reg.9, SSI 2004/8 Reg.12, SSI 2004/56 Reg.6, SSI 2004/133 Reg.10, SSI 2004/187 Reg.6, SSI 2004/432 Reg.6

  s.21, see *Kilhey Court Hotels Ltd v Wigan MBC* [2004] EWCA 2890 (QBD (Admin)), Forbes, J.

  s.21, applied: SI 2002/333 Reg.6, SI 2002/1817 Reg.9, SI 2002/1886 Reg.7, SI 2004/2335 Reg.6, SSI 2002/50 Reg.6, SSI 2002/267 Reg.7

  s.21, varied: SI 2002/890 Reg.7, SI 2002/2939 Reg.9, SI 2002/3157 Reg.5, SI 2002/3169 Reg.5, SI 2003/461 Reg.10, SI 2003/1387 Reg.11, SI 2003/1478 Reg.7, SI 2003/1563 Reg.9, SI 2003/1564 Reg.9, SI 2003/1596 Reg.9, SI 2003/1635 Reg.10, SI 2003/1659 Reg.10, SI 2003/1719 Reg.11, SI 2003/1721 Reg.7, SI 2003/2075 Reg.8, SI 2003/2243 Reg.9, SI 2003/3037 Reg.10, SI 2003/3041 Reg.9, SI 2003/3044 Reg.9, SI 2003/3047 Reg.9, SI 2003/3053 Reg.9, SI 2003/3120 Reg.9, SI 2003/3207 Reg.12, SI 2004/314 Reg.12, SI 2004/553 Reg.9, SI 2004/1396 Reg.8, SSI 2002/50 Reg.6, SSI 2002/397 Reg.8, SSI 2002/523 Reg.5, SSI 2003/145 Reg.10, SSI 2003/289 Reg.7, SSI 2003/291 Reg.11, SSI 2003/293 Reg.10, SSI 2003/311 Reg.10, SSI 2003/527 Reg.9, SSI 2003/569 Reg.10, SSI 2004/6 Reg.9, SSI 2004/8 Reg.12, SSI 2004/133 Reg.10, SSI 2004/432 Reg.6

  s.22, applied: SI 2002/333 Reg.6, SI 2002/1817 Reg.9, SI 2004/2335 Reg.6, SSI 2002/50 Reg.6

  s.22, varied: SI 2002/2939 Reg.9, SI 2002/3157 Reg.5, SI 2002/3169 Reg.5, SI 2003/1387 Reg.11, SI 2003/1563 Reg.9, SI

1990–cont.

16. Food Safety Act 1990–*cont.*

s.22, varied:–*cont.*

2003/1564 Reg.9, SI 2003/1596 Reg.9, SI 2003/1659 Reg.10, SI 2003/1719 Reg.11, SI 2003/2075 Reg.8, SI 2003/2243 Reg.9, SI 2003/3037 Reg.10, SI 2003/3041 Reg.9, SI 2003/3044 Reg.9, SI 2003/3047 Reg.9, SI 2003/3053 Reg.9, SI 2003/3120 Reg.9, SI 2003/3207 Reg.12, SI 2004/314 Reg.12, SI 2004/553 Reg.9, SI 2004/1396 Reg.8, SSI 2002/50 Reg.6, SSI 2002/397 Reg.8, SSI 2002/523 Reg.5, SSI 2003/291 Reg.11, SSI 2003/293 Reg.10, SSI 2003/311 Reg.10, SSI 2003/527 Reg.9, SSI 2003/569 Reg.10, SSI 2004/6 Reg.9, SSI 2004/8 Reg.12, SSI 2004/133 Reg.10, SSI 2004/432 Reg.6

s.26, enabling: SI 2002/47, SI 2002/329, SI 2002/330, SI 2002/333, SI 2002/379, SI 2002/890, SI 2002/1472, SI 2002/1619, SI 2002/1817, SI 2002/1886, SI 2002/1922, SI 2002/1923, SI 2002/2364, SI 2002/2834, SI 2002/2939, SI 2002/3008, SI 2002/3157, SI 2002/3169, SI 2002/3231, SI 2003/302, SI 2003/461, SI 2003/474, SI 2003/666, SI 2003/832, SI 2003/945, SI 2003/1008, SI 2003/1182, SI 2003/1387, SI 2003/1478, SI 2003/1484, SI 2003/1563, SI 2003/1564, SI 2003/1596, SI 2003/1635, SI 2003/1659, SI 2003/1713, SI 2003/1719, SI 2003/1721, SI 2003/1849, SI 2003/2243, SI 2003/2647, SI 2003/2754, SI 2003/2755, SI 2003/3037, SI 2003/3041, SI 2003/3042, SI 2003/3044, SI 2003/3047, SI 2003/3053, SI 2003/3120, SI 2003/3207, SI 2003/3208, SI 2003/3295, SI 2004/249, SI 2004/313, SI 2004/314, SI 2004/455, SI 2004/553, SI 2004/554, SI 2004/649, SI 2004/656, SI 2004/1012, SI 2004/1396, SI 2004/1509, SI 2004/1512, SI 2004/2335, SI 2004/2558, SI 2004/2601, SI 2004/2824, SI 2004/3022, SI 2004/3062, SI 2004/3113, SI 2004/3220, SI 2004/3279, SI 2004/3344, SI 2004/3348, SSI 2002/50, SSI 2002/87, SSI 2002/234, SSI 2002/267, SSI 2002/283, SSI 2002/284, SSI 2002/349, SSI 2002/397, SSI 2002/498, SSI 2002/523, SSI 2002/524, SSI 2003/9, SSI 2003/53, SSI 2003/132, SSI 2003/139, SSI 2003/145, SSI 2003/274, SSI 2003/278, SSI 2003/289, SSI 2003/291, SSI 2003/293, SSI 2003/311, SSI 2003/527, SSI 2003/569, SSI 2003/578, SSI 2003/599, SSI 2004/6, SSI 2004/7, SSI 2004/8, SSI 2004/90, SSI 2004/132, SSI 2004/133, SSI 2004/244, SSI 2004/269, SSI 2004/413, SSI 2004/432, SSI 2004/472, SSI 2004/524, SSI 2004/525, SSI 2004/548

s.29, amended: SSI 2002/424 Reg.5

1990–cont.

16. Food Safety Act 1990–*cont.*

s.29, applied: SI 2002/773 Reg.5, SI 2002/774 Reg.5, SI 2002/820 Reg.5, SI 2002/821 Reg.5, SI 2002/890 Reg.5, SI 2002/931 Reg.4, SI 2002/1090 Reg.4, SI 2002/1614 Reg.5, SI 2002/1798 Reg.5, SI 2002/1886 Reg.5, SI 2002/2295 Reg.5, SI 2002/2296 Reg.5, SI 2002/2350 Reg.5, SI 2002/2351 Reg.5, SI 2003/1119 Reg.5, SI 2003/1478 Reg.5, SI 2003/1722 Reg.5, SI 2003/1940 Reg.5, SI 2003/1956 Reg.5, SI 2003/2074 Reg.5, SI 2003/2254 Reg.5, SI 2003/2288 Reg.5, SI 2003/2455 Reg.5, SI 2003/2910 Reg.5, SSI 2002/148 Reg.5, SSI 2002/149 Reg.5, SSI 2002/179 Reg.4, SSI 2002/267 Reg.5, SSI 2002/424 Reg.5, SSI 2002/425 Reg.5, SSI 2003/289 Reg.5, SSI 2003/382 Reg.6, SSI 2003/396 Reg.5, SSI 2003/414 Reg.5, SSI 2003/418 Reg.5, SSI 2004/56 Reg.6, SSI 2004/187 Reg.4

s.29, referred to: SSI 2002/179 Reg.4

s.29, repealed (in part): SSI 2002/424 Reg.5

s.29, varied: SI 2002/773 Reg.5, SI 2002/774 Reg.5, SI 2002/820 Reg.5, SI 2002/821 Reg.5, SI 2002/890 Reg.5, SI 2002/931 Reg.5, SI 2002/1090 Reg.5, SI 2002/1614 Reg.5, SI 2002/1798 Reg.5, SI 2002/1886 Reg.5, SI 2002/2295 Reg.5, SI 2002/2296 Reg.5, SI 2002/2350 Reg.5, SI 2002/2351 Reg.5, SI 2003/1119 Reg.5, SI 2003/1478 Reg.5, SI 2003/1596 Reg.9, SI 2003/1721 Reg.5, SI 2003/1722 Reg.5, SI 2003/1940 Reg.5, SI 2003/1956 Reg.5, SI 2003/2074 Reg.5, SI 2003/2254 Reg.5, SI 2003/2288 Reg.5, SI 2003/2455 Reg.5, SI 2003/2910 Reg.5, SI 2003/3053 Reg.9, SSI 2002/148 Reg.5, SSI 2002/149 Reg.5, SSI 2002/179 Reg.6, SSI 2002/267 Reg.5, SSI 2002/300 Reg.5, SSI 2002/424 Reg.5, SSI 2002/425 Reg.5, SSI 2003/289 Reg.5, SSI 2003/311 Reg.10, SSI 2003/382 Reg.6, SSI 2003/396 Reg.5, SSI 2003/414 Reg.5, SSI 2003/418 Reg.5, SSI 2004/56 Reg.6, SSI 2004/187 Reg.6, SSI 2004/432 Reg.6

s.30, applied: SI 2002/333 Reg.6, SI 2002/1817 Reg.9, SI 2002/1886 Reg.7, SI 2002/3170 Art.3, SI 2003/1478 Reg.5, SI 2003/1721 Reg.5, SI 2003/2455 Reg.5, SI 2004/2335 Reg.6, SSI 2002/50 Reg.6, SSI 2002/267 Reg.7, SSI 2003/289 Reg.5, SSI 2003/382 Reg.6, SSI 2004/56 Reg.6

s.30, varied: SI 2002/843 Reg.77, SI 2002/890 Reg.7, SI 2002/931 Reg.5, SI 2002/1090 Reg.5, SI 2002/1416 Reg.77, SI 2002/2939 Reg.9, SI 2002/3157 Reg.5, SI 2002/3169 Reg.5, SI 2003/461 Reg.10, SI 2003/1387 Reg.11, SI 2003/1478 Reg.7, SI 2003/1563 Reg.9, SI 2003/1564 Reg.9, SI 2003/1596 Reg.9, SI 2003/1635 Reg.10, SI 2003/1659 Reg.10, SI 2003/

1990-cont.

16. Food Safety Act 1990-cont.

s.30, varied:-cont.

1719 Reg.11, SI 2003/1721 Reg.7, SI 2003/
1940 Reg.5, SI 2003/2075 Reg.8, SI
2003/2243 Reg.9, SI 2003/2455 Reg.5,
SI 2003/3037 Reg.10, SI 2003/3041
Reg.9, SI 2003/3044 Reg.9, SI 2003/
3047 Reg.9, SI 2003/3053 Reg.9, SI
2003/3120 Reg.9, SI 2003/3207 Reg.12,
SI 2004/314 Reg.12, SI 2004/553 Reg.9,
SI 2004/1396 Reg.8, SSI 2002/50 Reg.6,
SSI 2002/179 Reg.6, SSI 2002/255
Reg.76, SSI 2002/300 Reg.5, SSI 2002/
397 Reg.8, SSI 2002/523 Reg.5, SSI
2003/145 Reg.10, SSI 2003/289 Reg.7,
SSI 2003/291 Reg.11, SSI 2003/293
Reg.10, SSI 2003/311 Reg.10, SSI 2003/
382 Reg.6, SSI 2003/527 Reg.9, SSI
2003/569 Reg.10, SSI 2004/6 Reg.9, SSI
2004/8 Reg.12, SSI 2004/56 Reg.6, SSI
2004/133 Reg.10, SSI 2004/187 Reg.6,
SSI 2004/432 Reg.6

s.31, enabling: SI 2002/2364, SI 2002/2834,
SI 2002/3008, SI 2003/302, SI 2003/
666, SI 2003/3042, SI 2004/656, SI
2004/1509, SSI 2002/498, SSI 2003/9,
SSI 2003/139, SSI 2004/132

s.32, applied: SI 2002/183 Reg.5, SI 2002/
203 Reg.5, SI 2002/773 Reg.4, SI 2002/
820 Reg.4, SI 2002/821 Reg.4, SI 2002/
931 Reg.4, SI 2002/1090 Reg.4, SI 2002/
1614 Reg.4, SI 2002/1798 Reg.4, SI 2002/
2295 Reg.4, SI 2002/2296 Reg.4, SI
2002/2350 Reg.4, SI 2003/1119 Reg.4,
SI 2003/1722 Reg.4, SI 2003/1940
Reg.4, SI 2003/1956 Reg.4, SI 2003/
2074 Reg.4, SI 2003/2254 Reg.4, SI
2003/2288 Reg.4, SI 2003/2455 Reg.4,
SI 2003/2910 Reg.4, SSI 2002/36 Reg.5,
SSI 2002/179 Reg.4, SSI 2002/300 Reg.4,
SSI 2002/424 Reg.4, SSI 2002/425 Reg.4,
SSI 2003/382 Reg.5, SSI 2003/396
Reg.4, SSI 2003/414 Reg.4, SSI 2003/
418 Reg.4, SSI 2004/56 Reg.5, SSI
2004/187 Reg.4

s.32, referred to: SI 2002/774 Reg.4, SI
2002/2351 Reg.4, SSI 2002/148 Reg.4,
SSI 2002/149 Reg.4

s.32, varied: SI 2003/461 Reg.10, SI 2003/
1635 Reg.10, SSI 2003/145 Reg.10, SSI
2004/432 Reg.6

s.33, applied: SI 2002/183 Reg.6, SI 2002/
333 Reg.6, SI 2002/334 Art.5, SI 2002/
402 Art.5, SI 2002/774 Reg.5, SI 2002/
890 Reg.7, SI 2002/931 Reg.5, SI 2002/
1090 Reg.5, SI 2002/1798 Reg.5, SI
2002/1817 Reg.9, SI 2002/1886 Reg.7,
SI 2002/2296 Reg.5, SI 2002/3169
Reg.5, SI 2003/461 Reg.10, SI 2003/1387
Reg.11, SI 2003/1635 Reg.10, SI 2003/
1659 Reg.10, SI 2003/1719 Reg.11, SI
2003/3037 Reg.10, SI 2003/3207
Reg.12, SI 2004/2335 Reg.6, SSI 2002/

1990-cont.

16. Food Safety Act 1990-cont.

s.33, applied:-cont.

50 Reg.6, SSI 2002/148 Reg.5, SSI 2002/
267 Reg.7, SSI 2002/300 Reg.5, SSI
2002/424 Reg.5, SSI 2002/523 Reg.5,
SSI 2003/145 Reg.10, SSI 2003/289
Reg.7, SSI 2003/291 Reg.11, SSI 2003/
293 Reg.10, SSI 2004/6 Reg.9, SSI
2004/56 Reg.6, SSI 2004/432 Reg.6

s.33, referred to: SI 2002/1090 Reg.5, SI
2002/1798 Reg.5, SI 2002/2295 Reg.5,
SI 2002/2296 Reg.5, SI 2002/2350
Reg.5, SI 2002/2351 Reg.5, SI 2002/
3169 Reg.5, SSI 2002/397 Reg.8, SSI
2002/425 Reg.5

s.33, varied: SI 2002/203 Reg.6, SI 2002/
334 Art.5, SI 2002/773 Reg.5, SI 2002/
774 Reg.5, SI 2002/820 Reg.5, SI 2002/
821 Reg.5, SI 2002/890 Reg.7, SI 2002/
931 Reg.5, SI 2002/1090 Reg.5, SI 2002/
1614 Reg.5, SI 2002/1798 Reg.5, SI 2002/
1886 Reg.7, SI 2002/2295 Reg.5, SI
2002/2296 Reg.5, SI 2002/2350 Reg.5,
SI 2002/2351 Reg.5, SI 2002/2939
Reg.9, SI 2002/3157 Reg.5, SI 2002/
3169 Reg.5, SI 2003/461 Reg.10, SI
2003/1119 Reg.5, SI 2003/1387 Reg.11,
SI 2003/1478 Reg.7, SI 2003/1563
Reg.9, SI 2003/1564 Reg.9, SI 2003/
1596 Reg.9, SI 2003/1635 Reg.10, SI
2003/1659 Reg.10, SI 2003/1719 Reg.11,
SI 2003/1721 Reg.7, SI 2003/1722 Reg.5,
SI 2003/1940 Reg.5, SI 2003/1956 Reg.5,
SI 2003/2074 Reg.5, SI 2003/2075 Reg.8,
SI 2003/2243 Reg.9, SI 2003/2254
Reg.5, SI 2003/2288 Reg.5, SI 2003/
2455 Reg.5, SI 2003/2910 Reg.5, SI
2003/3037 Reg.10, SI 2003/3041 Reg.9,
SI 2003/3044 Reg.9, SI 2003/3047
Reg.9, SI 2003/3053 Reg.9, SI 2003/
3120 Reg.9, SI 2003/3207 Reg.12, SI
2004/314 Reg.12, SI 2004/553 Reg.9, SI
2004/1396 Reg.8, SI 2004/2335 Reg.6,
SSI 2002/36 Reg.6, SSI 2002/50 Reg.6,
SSI 2002/64 Art.5, SSI 2002/148 Reg.5,
SSI 2002/149 Reg.5, SSI 2002/179
Reg.6, SSI 2002/300 Reg.5, SSI 2002/
397 Reg.8, SSI 2002/425 Reg.5, SSI
2002/523 Reg.5, SSI 2003/145 Reg.10,
SSI 2003/289 Reg.7, SSI 2003/291
Reg.11, SSI 2003/293 Reg.10, SSI 2003/
311 Reg.10, SSI 2003/382 Reg.6, SSI
2003/396 Reg.5, SSI 2003/414 Reg.5,
SSI 2003/418 Reg.5, SSI 2003/527
Reg.9, SSI 2003/569 Reg.10, SSI 2004/6
Reg.9, SSI 2004/8 Reg.12, SSI 2004/56
Reg.6, SSI 2004/133 Reg.10, SSI 2004/
187 Reg.6, SSI 2004/432 Reg.6

s.34, applied: SI 2004/2335 Reg.6, SSI
2004/432 Reg.6

s.35, amended: 2003 c.44 Sch.26 para.42

1990–cont.

16. Food Safety Act 1990–*cont.*

s.35, applied: SI 2002/183 Reg.6, SI 2002/
333 Reg.6, SI 2002/334 Art.5, SI 2002/
402 Art.5, SI 2002/1817 Reg.9, SI 2002/
1886 Reg.7, SI 2004/2335 Reg.6, SSI
2002/50 Reg.6, SSI 2002/267 Reg.7, SSI
2002/424 Reg.5, SSI 2004/432 Reg.6

s.35, varied: SI 2002/203 Reg.6, SI 2002/
334 Art.5, SI 2002/773 Reg.5, SI 2002/
774 Reg.5, SI 2002/820 Reg.5, SI 2002/
821 Reg.5, SI 2002/890 Reg.7, SI 2002/
931 Reg.5, SI 2002/1090 Reg.5, SI 2002/
1614 Reg.5, SI 2002/1798 Reg.5, SI 2002/
2295 Reg.5, SI 2002/2296 Reg.5, SI
2002/2350 Reg.5, SI 2002/2351 Reg.5,
SI 2002/2939 Reg.9, SI 2002/3157
Reg.5, SI 2002/3169 Reg.5, SI 2003/461
Reg.10, SI 2003/1119 Reg.5, SI 2003/1387
Reg.11, SI 2003/1478 Reg.7, SI 2003/1563
Reg.9, SI 2003/1564 Reg.9, SI 2003/1596
Reg.9, SI 2003/1635 Reg.10, SI 2003/
1659 Reg.10, SI 2003/1719 Reg.11, SI
2003/1721 Reg.7, SI 2003/1722 Reg.5, SI
2003/1940 Reg.5, SI 2003/1956 Reg.5, SI
2003/2074 Reg.5, SI 2003/2075 Reg.8, SI
2003/2243 Reg.9, SI 2003/2254 Reg.5,
SI 2003/2288 Reg.5, SI 2003/2455
Reg.5, SI 2003/2910 Reg.5, SI 2003/
3037 Reg.10, SI 2003/3041 Reg.9, SI
2003/3044 Reg.9, SI 2003/3047 Reg.9,
SI 2003/3053 Reg.9, SI 2003/3120
Reg.9, SI 2003/3207 Reg.12, SI 2004/
314 Reg.12, SI 2004/553 Reg.9, SI 2004/
1396 Reg.8, SSI 2002/36 Reg.6, SSI
2002/50 Reg.6, SSI 2002/64 Art.5, SSI
2002/148 Reg.5, SSI 2002/149 Reg.5,
SSI 2002/179 Reg.6, SSI 2002/300
Reg.5, SSI 2002/397 Reg.8, SSI 2002/
425 Reg.5, SSI 2002/523 Reg.5, SSI
2003/145 Reg.10, SSI 2003/289 Reg.7,
SSI 2003/291 Reg.11, SSI 2003/293
Reg.10, SSI 2003/311 Reg.10, SSI 2003/
382 Reg.6, SSI 2003/396 Reg.5, SSI
2003/414 Reg.5, SSI 2003/418 Reg.5,
SSI 2003/527 Reg.9, SSI 2003/569
Reg.10, SSI 2004/6 Reg.9, SSI 2004/8
Reg.12, SSI 2004/56 Reg.6, SSI 2004/
133 Reg.10, SSI 2004/187 Reg.6, SSI
2004/432 Reg.6

s.36, applied: SI 2002/333 Reg.6, SI 2002/
334 Art.5, SI 2002/1817 Reg.9, SI 2002/
1886 Reg.7, SI 2004/2335 Reg.6, SSI
2002/50 Reg.6, SSI 2002/267 Reg.7, SSI
2002/424 Reg.5

s.36, varied: SI 2002/773 Reg.5, SI 2002/
774 Reg.5, SI 2002/820 Reg.5, SI 2002/
821 Reg.5, SI 2002/890 Reg.7, SI 2002/
931 Reg.5, SI 2002/1090 Reg.5, SI 2002/
1614 Reg.5, SI 2002/1798 Reg.5, SI 2002/
2295 Reg.5, SI 2002/2296 Reg.5, SI
2002/2350 Reg.5, SI 2002/2351 Reg.5,
SI 2002/2939 Reg.9, SI 2002/3157
Reg.5, SI 2002/3169 Reg.5, SI 2003/461

1990–cont.

16. Food Safety Act 1990–*cont.*

s.36, varied:–*cont.*

Reg.10, SI 2003/1119 Reg.5, SI 2003/1387
Reg.11, SI 2003/1478 Reg.7, SI 2003/1563
Reg.9, SI 2003/1564 Reg.9, SI 2003/1596
Reg.9, SI 2003/1635 Reg.10, SI 2003/
1659 Reg.10, SI 2003/1719 Reg.11, SI
2003/1721 Reg.7, SI 2003/1722 Reg.5, SI
2003/1940 Reg.5, SI 2003/1956 Reg.5, SI
2003/2074 Reg.5, SI 2003/2075 Reg.8, SI
2003/2243 Reg.9, SI 2003/2254 Reg.5,
SI 2003/2288 Reg.5, SI 2003/2455
Reg.5, SI 2003/2910 Reg.5, SI 2003/
3037 Reg.10, SI 2003/3041 Reg.9, SI
2003/3044 Reg.9, SI 2003/3047 Reg.9,
SI 2003/3053 Reg.9, SI 2003/3120
Reg.9, SI 2003/3207 Reg.12, SI 2004/
314 Reg.12, SI 2004/553 Reg.9, SI 2004/
1396 Reg.8, SSI 2002/50 Reg.6, SSI
2002/148 Reg.5, SSI 2002/149 Reg.5,
SSI 2002/179 Reg.6, SSI 2002/300
Reg.5, SSI 2002/397 Reg.8, SSI 2002/
425 Reg.5, SSI 2002/523 Reg.5, SSI
2003/145 Reg.10, SSI 2003/289 Reg.7,
SSI 2003/291 Reg.11, SSI 2003/293
Reg.10, SSI 2003/311 Reg.10, SSI 2003/
382 Reg.6, SSI 2003/396 Reg.5, SSI
2003/414 Reg.5, SSI 2003/418 Reg.5,
SSI 2003/527 Reg.9, SSI 2003/569
Reg.10, SSI 2004/6 Reg.9, SSI 2004/8
Reg.12, SSI 2004/56 Reg.6, SSI 2004/
133 Reg.10, SSI 2004/187 Reg.6, SSI
2004/432 Reg.6

s.36A, applied: SSI 2002/50 Reg.6, SSI
2002/267 Reg.7, SSI 2002/424 Reg.5

s.36A, varied: SSI 2002/50 Reg.6, SSI
2002/148 Reg.5, SSI 2002/149 Reg.5,
SSI 2002/179 Reg.6, SSI 2002/300
Reg.5, SSI 2002/397 Reg.8, SSI 2002/
425 Reg.5, SSI 2002/523 Reg.5, SSI
2003/145 Reg.10, SSI 2003/289 Reg.7,
SSI 2003/291 Reg.11, SSI 2003/293
Reg.10, SSI 2003/311 Reg.10, SSI 2003/
382 Reg.6, SSI 2003/396 Reg.5, SSI
2003/414 Reg.5, SSI 2003/418 Reg.5,
SSI 2003/527 Reg.9, SSI 2003/569
Reg.10, SSI 2004/6 Reg.9, SSI 2004/8
Reg.12, SSI 2004/56 Reg.6, SSI 2004/
133 Reg.10, SSI 2004/187 Reg.6, SSI
2004/432 Reg.6

s.37, applied: SI 2003/1736 Reg.7, SI 2003/
3003 Reg.9, SI 2003/3229 Reg.7, SSI
2003/299 Reg.7, SSI 2003/568 Reg.7

s.40, amended: SI 2004/2990 Reg.4

s.40, varied: SI 2002/931 Reg.5

s.43, amended: 2004 c.33 Sch.27 para.136

s.44, applied: SI 2002/183 Reg.6, SI 2002/
333 Reg.6, SI 2002/334 Art.5, SI 2002/
402 Art.5, SI 2002/1817 Reg.9, SI 2002/
1886 Reg.7, SI 2004/2335 Reg.6, SSI
2002/50 Reg.6, SSI 2002/267 Reg.7, SSI
2002/424 Reg.5

1990–cont.

16. Food Safety Act 1990–*cont.*

s.44, varied: SI 2002/203 Reg.6, SI 2002/
334 Art.5, SI 2002/773 Reg.5, SI 2002/
774 Reg.5, SI 2002/820 Reg.5, SI 2002/
821 Reg.5, SI 2002/843 Reg.77, SI 2002/
890 Reg.7, SI 2002/1090 Reg.5, SI 2002/
1416 Reg.77, SI 2002/1614 Reg.5, SI
2002/1798 Reg.5, SI 2002/2295 Reg.5,
SI 2002/2296 Reg.5, SI 2002/2350
Reg.5, SI 2002/2351 Reg.5, SI 2002/
2939 Reg.9, SI 2002/3169 Reg.5, SI
2003/461 Reg.10, SI 2003/1119 Reg.5, SI
2003/1387 Reg.11, SI 2003/1478 Reg.7,
SI 2003/1563 Reg.9, SI 2003/1564
Reg.9, SI 2003/1596 Reg.9, SI 2003/
1635 Reg.10, SI 2003/1659 Reg.10, SI
2003/1719 Reg.11, SI 2003/1721 Reg.7, SI
2003/1722 Reg.5, SI 2003/1940 Reg.5, SI
2003/1956 Reg.5, SI 2003/2074 Reg.5, SI
2003/2075 Reg.8, SI 2003/2243 Reg.9,
SI 2003/2254 Reg.5, SI 2003/2288
Reg.5, SI 2003/2455 Reg.5, SI 2003/
2910 Reg.5, SI 2003/3037 Reg.10, SI
2003/3041 Reg.9, SI 2003/3044 Reg.9,
SI 2003/3047 Reg.9, SI 2003/3053
Reg.9, SI 2003/3120 Reg.9, SI 2003/
3207 Reg.12, SI 2004/314 Reg.12, SI
2004/553 Reg.9, SI 2004/1396 Reg.8,
SSI 2002/36 Reg.6, SSI 2002/50 Reg.6,
SSI 2002/64 Art.5, SSI 2002/148 Reg.5,
SSI 2002/149 Reg.5, SSI 2002/179
Reg.6, SSI 2002/255 Reg.76, SSI 2002/
300 Reg.5, SSI 2002/397 Reg.8, SSI
2002/425 Reg.5, SSI 2002/523 Reg.5,
SSI 2003/145 Reg.10, SSI 2003/289
Reg.7, SSI 2003/291 Reg.11, SSI 2003/
293 Reg.10, SSI 2003/311 Reg.10, SSI
2003/382 Reg.6, SSI 2003/396 Reg.5,
SSI 2003/414 Reg.5, SSI 2003/418
Reg.5, SSI 2003/527 Reg.9, SSI 2003/
569 Reg.10, SSI 2004/6 Reg.9, SSI
2004/8 Reg.12, SSI 2004/56 Reg.6, SSI
2004/133 Reg.10, SSI 2004/187 Reg.6,
SSI 2004/432 Reg.6

s.45, enabling: SI 2002/1922, SI 2004/1697,
SI 2004/1871

s.48, amended: SI 2004/2990 Reg.5

s.48, applied: SI 2002/47, SI 2002/329, SI
2002/330, SI 2002/333, SI 2002/334, SI
2002/379, SI 2002/402, SI 2002/602, SI
2002/889, SI 2002/890, SI 2002/1472, SI
2002/1476, SI 2002/1619, SI 2002/1817,
SI 2002/1886, SI 2002/1922, SI 2002/
1923, SI 2002/2364, SI 2002/2834, SI
2002/2939, SI 2002/3157, SI 2002/
3169, SI 2002/3231, SI 2003/302, SI
2003/461, SI 2003/474, SI 2003/666, SI
2003/832, SI 2003/945, SI 2003/1008,
SI 2003/1182, SI 2003/1387, SI 2003/
1478, SI 2003/1484, SI 2003/1563, SI
2003/1564, SI 2003/1596, SI 2003/
1635, SI 2003/1659, SI 2003/1713, SI
2003/1719, SI 2003/1721, SI 2003/1774,

1990–cont.

16. Food Safety Act 1990–*cont.*

s.48, applied:–*cont.*

SI 2003/1849, SI 2003/1895, SI 2003/
2075, SI 2003/2243, SI 2003/2338, SI
2003/2647, SI 2003/2661, SI 2003/
2754, SI 2003/2755, SI 2003/3037, SI
2003/3041, SI 2003/3042, SI 2003/
3044, SI 2003/3047, SI 2003/3053, SI
2003/3120, SI 2003/3207, SI 2003/
3208, SI 2003/3295, SI 2004/249, SI
2004/313, SI 2004/314, SI 2004/455, SI
2004/553, SI 2004/554, SI 2004/649,
SI 2004/656, SI 2004/1012, SI 2004/
1396, SI 2004/1512, SI 2004/1697, SI
2004/2335, SI 2004/2558, SI 2004/
2601, SI 2004/2824, SI 2004/3022, SSI
2002/50, SSI 2002/61, SSI 2002/64, SSI
2002/87, SSI 2002/234, SSI 2002/267,
SSI 2002/283, SSI 2002/284, SSI 2002/
349, SSI 2002/397, SSI 2002/498, SSI
2002/523, SSI 2002/524, SSI 2003/9,
SSI 2003/53, SSI 2003/132, SSI 2003/
139, SSI 2003/145, SSI 2003/274, SSI
2003/289, SSI 2003/293, SSI 2003/311,
SSI 2003/437, SSI 2003/527, SSI 2003/
569, SSI 2003/599, SSI 2004/6, SSI
2004/7, SSI 2004/8, SSI 2004/90, SSI
2004/133, SSI 2004/269, SSI 2004/413,
SSI 2004/432, SSI 2004/472

s.48, enabling: SI 2002/47, SI 2002/329, SI
2002/330, SI 2002/333, SI 2002/334, SI
2002/379, SI 2002/402, SI 2002/602, SI
2002/890, SI 2002/1472, SI 2002/1619,
SI 2002/1817, SI 2002/1886, SI 2002/
1922, SI 2002/1923, SI 2002/2364, SI
2002/2834, SI 2002/2939, SI 2002/
3008, SI 2002/3157, SI 2002/3169, SI
2002/3231, SI 2003/302, SI 2003/461,
SI 2003/474, SI 2003/666, SI 2003/832,
SI 2003/945, SI 2003/1008, SI 2003/
1182, SI 2003/1387, SI 2003/1478, SI
2003/1484, SI 2003/1563, SI 2003/
1564, SI 2003/1596, SI 2003/1635, SI
2003/1659, SI 2003/1713, SI 2003/1719,
SI 2003/1721, SI 2003/1774, SI 2003/
1849, SI 2003/1895, SI 2003/2243, SI
2003/2338, SI 2003/2647, SI 2003/
2661, SI 2003/2754, SI 2003/2755, SI
2003/3037, SI 2003/3041, SI 2003/
3042, SI 2003/3044, SI 2003/3047, SI
2003/3053, SI 2003/3120, SI 2003/
3207, SI 2003/3208, SI 2003/3295, SI
2004/249, SI 2004/313, SI 2004/314, SI
2004/455, SI 2004/553, SI 2004/554, SI
2004/649, SI 2004/656, SI 2004/1012, SI
2004/1396, SI 2004/1509, SI 2004/1512,
SI 2004/1697, SI 2004/1871, SI 2004/
2335, SI 2004/2558, SI 2004/2601, SI
2004/2824, SI 2004/3022, SI 2004/
3062, SI 2004/3113, SI 2004/3220, SI
2004/3279, SI 2004/3344, SI 2004/
3348, SSI 2002/50, SSI 2002/61, SSI
2002/64, SSI 2002/87, SSI 2002/234,

CAP.

1990–cont.

16. Food Safety Act 1990–*cont.*

s.48, enabling:–*cont.*

SSI 2002/267, SSI 2002/283, SSI 2002/284, SSI 2002/349, SSI 2002/397, SSI 2002/498, SSI 2002/523, SSI 2002/524, SSI 2003/9, SSI 2003/53, SSI 2003/132, SSI 2003/139, SSI 2003/145, SSI 2003/274, SSI 2003/278, SSI 2003/289, SSI 2003/291, SSI 2003/293, SSI 2003/311, SSI 2003/437, SSI 2003/492, SSI 2003/527, SSI 2003/569, SSI 2003/578, SSI 2003/599, SSI 2004/6, SSI 2004/7, SSI 2004/8, SSI 2004/90, SSI 2004/132, SSI 2004/133, SSI 2004/244, SSI 2004/269, SSI 2004/413, SSI 2004/432, SSI 2004/472, SSI 2004/524, SSI 2004/525, SSI 2004/548

s.48A, applied: SI 2002/1472, SI 2003/461, SI 2004/1509, SI 2004/1871, SSI 2003/139, SSI 2003/578, SSI 2004/244

s.53, see *Greene King Plc v Harlow DC* [2003] EWHC 2852, [2004] 1 W.L.R. 2338 (QBD (Admin Ct)), Goldring, J.

s.53, amended: SI 2004/2990 Reg.6

s.56, amended: 2002 asp 3 Sch.7 para.19

s.58, varied: SI 2002/3157 Reg.5

s34., see *Tesco Stores Ltd v Harrow LBC* [2003] EWHC 2919, (2003) 167 J.P. 657 (QBD (Admin Ct)), Newman, J.

s8., see*Tesco Stores Ltd v Harrow LBC* [2003] EWHC 2919, (2003) 167 J.P. 657 (QBD (Admin Ct)), Newman, J.

Sch.1 para.1, enabling: SI 2002/329, SI 2002/330, SI 2002/379, SI 2002/1922, SI 2003/666, SI 2003/945, SI 2003/1008, SI 2003/1182, SI 2003/1713, SI 2003/3295, SI 2004/554, SI 2004/656, SI 2004/1509, SI 2004/2601, SI 2004/3348, SSI 2002/61, SSI 2002/284, SSI 2003/132, SSI 2003/274, SSI 2003/599, SSI 2004/132, SSI 2004/413, SSI 2004/548

Sch.1 para.3, enabling: SI 2002/1472, SI 2002/1619, SI 2002/3231, SI 2003/1484, SI 2003/1849, SI 2003/2754, SSI 2002/283, SSI 2003/53

Sch.1 para.4, enabling: SI 2002/1922, SSI 2002/284

Sch.1 para.5, enabling: SI 2002/47, SSI 2002/87

Sch.1 para.6, enabling: SI 2002/47, SSI 2002/87

Sch.2 para.13, repealed (in part): SI 2003/1281 Art.5

Sch.3 para.15, repealed: 2004 c.14 Sch.1 Part 2

18. Computer Misuse Act 1990

s.2, see *R. v Delamare (Ian)* [2003] EWCA Crim 424, [2003] 2 Cr. App. R. (S.) 80 (CA (Crim Div)), Jackson, J.

s.3, see *R. v Lindesay (Victor)* [2001] EWCA Crim 1720, [2002] 1 Cr. App. R. (S.) 86 (CA (Crim Div)), Judge Beaumont Q.C.; see *R. v*

CAP.

1990–cont.

18. Computer Misuse Act 1990–*cont.*

s.3–*cont.*

Vallor (Simon Lee) [2003] EWCA Crim 2288, [2004] 1 Cr. App. R. (S.) 54 (CA (Crim Div)), Penry-Davey, J.; see *Zezev v Governor of Brixton Prison* [2002] EWHC 589, [2002] 2 Cr. App. R. 33 (QBD (Admin Ct)), Lord Woolf of Barnes, L.C.J.

s.11, repealed (in part): 2003 c.39 Sch.8 para.346, Sch.10

s.14, amended: 2003 c.39 Sch.4 para.7

s.15, repealed: 2003 c.41 Sch.3 para.7, Sch.4

s.16, amended: 2003 c.39 Sch.8 para.347, Sch.10

s.17, see *Zezev v Governor of Brixton Prison* [2002] EWHC 589, [2002] 2 Cr. App. R. 33 (QBD (Admin Ct)), Lord Woolf of Barnes, L.C.J.

19. National Health Service and Community Care Act 1990

applied: SI 2002/2375 Reg.9, Reg.10, Reg.11, SI 2004/627 Sch.5 para.98

referred to: 2003 c.43 Sch.4 para.83

Part I, applied: SI 2004/118 Art.2

s.4, amended: 2002 c.17 Sch.1 para.40, Sch.5 para.31, 2003 c.4 Sch.3 para.6, 2003 c.43 Sch.14 Part 4, 2004 c.17 Sch.3 para.11

s.4, applied: 2004 c.34 Sch.14 para.2, SI 2004/291 Reg.9, Reg.10, Sch.6 para.101, Sch.6 para.102, SI 2004/433 Art.4, Art.6, Art.7, Art.10, Art.14, Art.43, SI 2004/477 Art.6, Art.7, Art.10, Art.14, Art.43, SI 2004/478 Reg.9, Reg.10, Sch.6 para.99, Sch.6 para.100, SI 2004/627 Reg.8, Reg.9, Sch.5 para.95, Sch.5 para.96, SI 2004/865 Art.42, Art.69, SI 2004/1016 Art.39

s.4, referred to: SI 2004/477 Art.4

s.4, repealed (in part): 2003 c.43 Sch.13 para.6, Sch.14 Part 7

s.4, varied: SI 2004/433 Art.43, SI 2004/477 Art.43

s.4, enabling: SI 2004/291, SI 2004/478, SI 2004/627, SI 2004/2694

s.4A, amended: 2002 c.17 Sch.1 para.41, Sch.2 para.54

s.5, applied: SI 2002/308, SI 2002/308 Art.3, SI 2002/442, SI 2002/647, SI 2002/731, SI 2002/891, SI 2002/1234, SI 2002/1243, SI 2002/1244, SI 2002/1251, SI 2002/1295, SI 2002/1296, SI 2002/1297, SI 2002/1313, SI 2002/1313 Art.3, SI 2002/1322, SI 2002/1322 Art.3, SI 2002/1324, SI 2002/1324 Art.3, SI 2002/1337, SI 2002/1338, SI 2002/1341, SI 2002/1341 Art.3, SI 2002/1360, SI 2002/1361, SI 2002/1362, SI 2002/1363, SI 2002/1363 Art.3, SI 2002/1364, SI 2002/1437, SI 2002/1490, SI 2002/1491, SI 2002/1495, SI 2002/1498, SI 2002/1615, SI 2002/1690, SI 2002/1791, SI 2002/2025, SI 2002/2025 Art.3, SI

CAP.

1990–cont.

19. National Health Service and Community Care Act 1990–*cont.*

s.5, applied:–*cont.*
2002/2073, SI 2002/2073 Art.3, SI 2002/2199, SI 2002/2419, SI 2002/2419 Art.3, SI 2002/2420, SI 2002/2420 Art.3, SI 2002/2616, SI 2002/2819 Reg.2, 2003 c.14 s.61, s.66, SI 2003/216, SI 2003/617, SI 2003/759, SI 2003/2346, SI 2003/2346 Art.3, SI 2003/3171 Sch.1 Part II, SI 2003/3172 Sch.2 Part I, Sch.2 Part II, 2004 c.28 s.9, 2004 c.36 Sch.1 Part 1

s.5, referred to: SI 2002/647 Art.3, SI 2002/1243 Art.3, SI 2002/1244 Art.3, SI 2002/1251 Art.3, SI 2002/1337 Art.3, SI 2002/1362 Art.3, SI 2002/1364 Art.3, SI 2003/216 Art.3, SI 2003/617 Art.3, SI 2003/759 Art.3

s.5, enabling: SI 2002/308, SI 2002/442, SI 2002/647, SI 2002/731, SI 2002/891, SI 2002/1234, SI 2002/1243, SI 2002/1244, SI 2002/1251, SI 2002/1293, SI 2002/1294, SI 2002/1295, SI 2002/1296, SI 2002/1297, SI 2002/1313, SI 2002/1322, SI 2002/1323, SI 2002/1335, SI 2002/1337, SI 2002/1338, SI 2002/1341, SI 2002/1342, SI 2002/1360, SI 2002/1361, SI 2002/1362, SI 2002/1363, SI 2002/1364, SI 2002/1437, SI 2002/1489, SI 2002/1490, SI 2002/1491, SI 2002/1492, SI 2002/1494, SI 2002/1495, SI 2002/1496, SI 2002/1497, SI 2002/1498, SI 2002/1499, SI 2002/1500, SI 2002/1615, SI 2002/1690, SI 2002/1791, SI 2002/2025, SI 2002/2073, SI 2002/2199, SI 2002/2397, SI 2002/2419, SI 2002/2420, SI 2002/2616, SI 2002/2617, SI 2003/216, SI 2003/617, SI 2003/759, SI 2003/760, SI 2003/791, SI 2003/792, SI 2003/817, SI 2003/834, SI 2003/844, SI 2003/866, SI 2003/868, SI 2003/1063, SI 2003/1276, SI 2003/1496, SI 2003/1499, SI 2003/1500, SI 2003/2149, SI 2003/2150, SI 2003/2344, SI 2003/2345, SI 2003/2346, SI 2003/2427, SI 2003/2434, SI 2004/19, SI 2004/75, SI 2004/469, SI 2004/487, SI 2004/766, SI 2004/864, SI 2004/1624, SI 2004/1626, SI 2004/2391, SI 2004/2394, SI 2004/2397, SI 2004/2893, SI 2004/2894, SI 2004/2895, SI 2004/2896, SI 2004/2897, SI 2004/2898, SI 2004/3365

s.6, see *Preston v Wolverhampton Healthcare NHS Trust (No.3)* [2002] O.P.L.R. 323 (ET), JK Macmillan

s.6, applied: SI 2002/2819 Reg.2, Reg.5

s.8, amended: 2002 c.17 Sch.1 para.42, Sch.5 para.32

s.9, applied: 2003 c.43 s.13

s.9, enabling: SI 2002/1336, SI 2003/914, SI 2004/588

s.11, applied: 2003 c.43 s.22

CAP.

1990–cont.

19. National Health Service and Community Care Act 1990–*cont.*

s.11, referred to: SI 2003/1093 Art.2, SI 2004/435 Art.2

s.11, enabling: SI 2003/622, SI 2003/1093, SI 2003/1096, SI 2004/435

s.12, amended: 2002 c.17 Sch.9 Part 3

s.18, amended: 2002 c.17 Sch.2 para.55, 2003 c.43 Sch.11 para.56

s.18, repealed (in part): 2003 c.43 Sch.14 Part 4

s.18, substituted: 2003 c.43 Sch.11 para.56

s.18, varied: SI 2004/865 Art.115, SI 2004/1016 Art.91

s.21, amended: 2002 c.17 Sch.1 para.43, Sch.5 para.33, 2003 c.43 Sch.4 para.84, 2004 c.17 Sch.3 para.11

s.21, repealed (in part): 2003 c.43 Sch.13 para.6, Sch.14 Part 7

s.21, enabling: SI 2002/1073

s.23, repealed (in part): 2003 c.43 Sch.14 Part 4

s.24, repealed: 2003 c.43 Sch.14 Part 4

s.29, repealed (in part): 2004 asp 7 Sch.2

s.31, repealed: 2004 asp 7 Sch.2

s.32, repealed: 2004 asp 7 Sch.2

s.33, repealed: 2004 asp 7 Sch.2

s.39, repealed (in part): 2003 asp 4 Sch.4 para.11

s.46, amended: SI 2003/154 Sch.1 para.4

s.46, applied: SI 2003/154 Reg.7, SI 2003/762 Reg.4

s.46, disapplied: SI 2003/1716 Art.2

s.46, referred to: SI 2003/1716(a), SI 2003/154 Sch.1 para.3

s.47, see *Crookdake v Drury* [2003] EWHC 1938, (2004) 76 B.M.L.R. 99 (QBD), Owen, J.; see *R. (on the application of AA) v Lambeth LBC* [2001] EWHC Admin 741, (2002) 5 C.C.L. Rep. 36 (QBD (Admin Ct)), Forbes, J.; see *R. (on the application of Khan) v Oxfordshire CC* [2004] EWCA Civ 309, [2004] H.L.R. 41 (CA), Ward, L.J.; see *R. (on the application of Khana) v Southwark LBC* [2001] EWCA Civ 999, [2002] H.L.R. 31 (CA), Mance, L.J.

s.47, amended: 2002 c.17 Sch.2 para.56

s.47, applied: 2003 c.5 s.4

s.49, amended: 2002 c.17 Sch.1 para.44, Sch.2 para.57, Sch.5 para.34

s.60, amended: 2002 c.17 Sch.1 para.45

s.60, repealed (in part): 2003 c.43 Sch.13 para.6, Sch.14 Part 4, Sch.14 Part 7

s.61, amended: 2002 c.17 Sch.5 para.35

s.61, applied: 2003 c.43 s.33

s.61A, added: SI 2003/2867 Sch.1 para.15

Sch.2, applied: 2003 c.43 Sch.4 para.85

Sch.2 Part I para.1, enabling: SI 2002/308, SI 2002/647, SI 2002/1243, SI 2002/1244, SI 2002/1296, SI 2002/1313, SI 2002/1324, SI 2002/1337, SI 2002/1341, SI

CAP.

CAP.

1990–cont.

19. National Health Service and Community Care Act 1990–*cont.*

Sch.2 Part I para.1, enabling:–*cont.*

2002/1362, SI 2002/1363, SI 2002/1364, SI 2002/1690, SI 2002/2025, SI 2002/2073, SI 2002/2397, SI 2002/2419, SI 2002/2420, SI 2002/2616, SI 2002/2617, SI 2003/216, SI 2003/617, SI 2003/759, SI 2003/760, SI 2003/791, SI 2003/792, SI 2003/834, SI 2003/844, SI 2003/866, SI 2003/868, SI 2003/1063, SI 2003/1276, SI 2003/1496, SI 2003/1499, SI 2003/1500

Sch.2 Part I para.3, applied: SI 2002/308 Art.3, SI 2002/647 Art.3, SI 2002/1251 Art.3, SI 2002/1364 Art.3, SI 2003/759 Art.4

Sch.2 Part I para.3, enabling: SI 2002/308, SI 2002/647, SI 2002/1243, SI 2002/1244, SI 2002/1251, SI 2002/1296, SI 2002/1313, SI 2002/1322, SI 2002/1324, SI 2002/1337, SI 2002/1341, SI 2002/1362, SI 2002/1363, SI 2002/1364, SI 2002/1690, SI 2002/2025, SI 2002/2073, SI 2002/2397, SI 2002/2419, SI 2002/2420, SI 2002/2617, SI 2003/216, SI 2003/617, SI 2003/759, SI 2003/760, SI 2003/791, SI 2003/792, SI 2003/834, SI 2003/844, SI 2003/866, SI 2003/1063, SI 2003/1276, SI 2003/1496, SI 2003/1499, SI 2003/1500, SI 2003/2149, SI 2003/2150, SI 2003/2344, SI 2003/2345, SI 2003/2346, SI 2003/2427, SI 2003/2434, SI 2004/75, SI 2004/469, SI 2004/487, SI 2004/766, SI 2004/864, SI 2004/1625, SI 2004/1626, SI 2004/2391, SI 2004/2394, SI 2004/2397, SI 2004/2893, SI 2004/2894, SI 2004/2895, SI 2004/2896, SI 2004/2897, SI 2004/2898

Sch.2 Part I para.4, amended: 2002 c.17 Sch.1 para.46, Sch.5 para.36

Sch.2 Part I para.4, enabling: SI 2002/308, SI 2002/647, SI 2002/1244, SI 2002/1251, SI 2002/1322, SI 2002/2073, SI 2002/2419

Sch.2 Part I para.5, amended: 2002 c.17 Sch.1 para.46

Sch.2 Part I para.5, enabling: SI 2002/308, SI 2002/647, SI 2002/1244, SI 2002/1293, SI 2002/1495, SI 2002/1496, SI 2002/1497, SI 2002/1498, SI 2002/1499, SI 2002/1500, SI 2002/2073, SI 2002/2419

Sch.2 Part II para.7, amended: 2004 c.23 Sch.2 para.14

Sch.2 Part II para.10, applied: SI 2002/2375 Reg.8

Sch.2 Part II para.13, amended: 2002 c.17 Sch.1 para.46, Sch.5 para.36

Sch.2 Part II para.13, applied: SI 2002/1792 Reg.4, SI 2003/2382 Reg.10

Sch.2 Part II para.15A, added: SI 2002/2759 Reg.4

1990–cont.

19. National Health Service and Community Care Act 1990–*cont.*

Sch.2 Part II para.16, referred to: 2003 c.43 s.4

Sch.2 Part II para.16, enabling: SI 2004/3365

Sch.2 Part II para.17, applied: SI 2002/1311 Reg.5

Sch.2 Part III para.21, repealed: 2003 c.43 Sch.14 Part 1

Sch.2 Part III para.25, repealed (in part): 2003 c.43 Sch.14 Part 1

Sch.2 Part IV, referred to: 2003 c.43 s.28

Sch.2 Part IV para.29, applied: SI 2002/308, SI 2002/647, SI 2002/1243, SI 2002/1244, SI 2002/1293, SI 2002/1294, SI 2002/1296, SI 2002/1313, SI 2002/1322, SI 2002/1323, SI 2002/1324, SI 2002/1335, SI 2002/1337, SI 2002/1341, SI 2002/1342, SI 2002/1362, SI 2002/1363, SI 2002/1364, SI 2002/1489, SI 2002/1492, SI 2002/1496, SI 2002/1497, SI 2002/1499, SI 2002/1500, SI 2002/1690, SI 2002/2025, SI 2002/2073, SI 2002/2419, SI 2002/2420, SI 2002/2616, SI 2003/216, SI 2003/617, SI 2003/759, SI 2003/817, SI 2003/868, SI 2003/2346

Sch.2 Part IV para.29, enabling: SI 2002/308, SI 2002/647, SI 2002/1243, SI 2002/1244, SI 2002/1293, SI 2002/1294, SI 2002/1296, SI 2002/1313, SI 2002/1322, SI 2002/1323, SI 2002/1324, SI 2002/1335, SI 2002/1337, SI 2002/1341, SI 2002/1342, SI 2002/1362, SI 2002/1363, SI 2002/1364, SI 2002/1489, SI 2002/1492, SI 2002/1496, SI 2002/1497, SI 2002/1499, SI 2002/1500, SI 2002/2025, SI 2002/2073, SI 2002/2419, SI 2002/2420, SI 2002/2616, SI 2003/216, SI 2003/617, SI 2003/759, SI 2003/868, SI 2003/2346

Sch.2 Part IV para.30, see *R. v Pennine Acute Hospitals NHS Trust (formerly Rochdale Healthcare NHS Trust)* [2003] EWCA Crim 3436, [2004] 1 All E.R. 1324 (CA (Crim Div)), Tuckey, L.J.

Sch.2 Part IV para.30, amended: 2002 c.17 Sch.1 para.46, Sch.5 para.36, 2003 c.43 Sch.4 para.85

Sch.2 Part IV para.30, applied: SI 2002/2616

Sch.2 Part IV para.30, enabling: SI 2002/2616

Sch.2 Part IV para.31, amended: 2002 c.17 Sch.1 para.46, Sch.2 para.58

Sch.2 Part IV para.32, amended: 2003 c.43 Sch.4 para.85

Sch.3 para.1, amended: 2003 c.43 s.191, Sch.14 Part 6

Sch.5 para.13, repealed: 2003 asp 13 Sch.5 Part 1

Sch.6, repealed: 2004 asp 7 Sch.2

CAP.

1990–cont.

19. National Health Service and Community Care Act 1990–*cont.*

Sch.8 Part III para.15, amended: 2004 c.21 Sch.1 para.73

Sch.9 para.7, repealed (in part): 2003 c.43 Sch.14 Part 1, 2004 c.30 Sch.7 Part 1

Sch.9 para.13, repealed (in part): 2003 c.43 Sch.14 Part 1

Sch.9 para.17, repealed: 2002 c.38 Sch.5

Sch.9 para.18, amended: 2003 c.43 Sch.14 Part 1

Sch.9 para.18, repealed (in part): 2003 c.4 Sch.4

Sch.9 para.19, repealed (in part): SSI 2002/176 Art.5, 2003 asp 4 Sch.4 para.11, 2004 asp 7 Sch.2

Sch.9 para.21, repealed: 2002 c.1 Sch.4

Sch.9 para.26, repealed (in part): SI 2002/2469 Sch.13

Sch.9 para.28, repealed: 2003 asp 13 Sch.5 Part 1

Sch.9 para.36, repealed (in part): 2003 c.43 Sch.14 Part 1

20. Entertainments (Increased Penalties) Act 1990

s.1, repealed: 2003 c.17 Sch.7

21. Licensing (Low Alcohol Drinks) Act 1990

s.1, repealed: 2003 c.17 Sch.7

23. Access to Health Records Act 1990

applied: 2003 c.43 Sch.4 para.87

s.1, amended: 2002 c.17 Sch.2 para.59, 2003 c.43 Sch.11 para.57, SSI 2004/167 Sch.1 para.3

s.1, varied: SI 2004/865 Art.109, SI 2004/1016 Art.85, SSI 2004/163 Art.96

s.7, amended: 2002 c.17 Sch.2 para.59, 2003 c.43 Sch.11 para.57, Sch.14 Part 4

s.7, repealed (in part): 2003 c.43 Sch.11 para.57, Sch.14 Part 4, SSI 2004/167 Sch.1 para.3

s.11, amended: SI 2002/2469 Sch.1 para.17, 2003 c.43 Sch.4 para.88, Sch.11 para.57, Sch.14 Part 1, SSI 2004/167 Sch.1 para.3

s.11, repealed (in part): 2003 asp 13 Sch.5 Part 1, SSI 2004/167 Sch.1 para.3

27. Social Security Act 1990

s.15, enabling: SI 2002/115, SI 2003/1017, SI 2003/2263, SI 2004/2430, SSI 2003/284, SSI 2003/529, SSI 2004/188

29. Finance Act 1990

referred to: 2003 c.1 Sch.6 para.165

s.21, repealed: 2003 c.1 Sch.8 Part 1

s.25, amended: 2002 c.23 Sch.17 para.4, Sch.40 Part 3, 2003 c.1 Sch.6 para.166, 2004 c.12 s.83, Sch.17 para.5, Sch.35 para.37

s.25, applied: 2002 c.23 s.98, SI 2002/2006 Reg.3, 2004 c.12 s.83

s.25, referred to: 2002 c.23 s.98, 2004 c.12 s.83

CAP.

1990–cont.

29. Finance Act 1990–*cont.*

s.25, varied: 2002 c.23 s.98, Sch.18 para.9

s.43, repealed: 2003 c.14 Sch.43 Part 3

s.44, repealed: 2004 c.12 Sch.42 Part 2

s.45, repealed (in part): 2003 c.14 Sch.43 Part 3

s.77, repealed: 2003 c.1 Sch.8 Part 1

s.79, repealed: 2003 c.1 Sch.8 Part 1

s.81, repealed (in part): 2002 c.23 Sch.40 Part 3

s.108, amended: 2003 c.14 Sch.20 para.5

s.125, amended: 2003 c.14 Sch.43 Part 5

s.125, repealed (in part): 2003 c.14 Sch.43 Part 5

s.128, applied: SI 2004/3114 Art.7, SI 2004/3121 Art.8

s.128, enabling: SI 2002/770, SI 2003/165, SI 2003/646, SI 2003/647, SI 2003/648, SI 2003/1960, SI 2003/2258, SI 2004/2106, SI 2004/3114, SI 2004/3120, SI 2004/3121

Sch.7 para.1, repealed: 2004 c.12 Sch.42 Part 2

Sch.14 Part I para.4, amended: 2003 c.1 Sch.6 para.167

Sch.14 Part I para.4, repealed (in part): 2003 c.1 Sch.8 Part 1

31. Aviation and Maritime Security Act 1990

s.1, see *R. v Lees (Shaun)* [2003] EWCA Crim 243, [2003] 2 Cr. App. R. (S.) 47 (CA (Crim Div)), Gray, J.

s.1, applied: 2003 c.42 Sch.5 para.51, Sch.5 para.94, Sch.5 para.158, 2003 c.44 Sch.15 para.50, Sch.17 para.46, SI 2004/1910 Sch.1

s.3, repealed (in part): 2004 c.14 Sch.1 Part 4

s.9, applied: 2003 c.42 Sch.5 para.52, Sch.5 para.95, Sch.5 para.159, 2003 c.44 Sch.4 para.34, Sch.15 para.51, Sch.17 para.47, SI 2004/1500 Sch.2 para.26, SI 2004/1910 Sch.1

s.10, applied: 2003 c.42 Sch.5 para.53, Sch.5 para.96, Sch.5 para.160, 2003 c.44 Sch.4 para.35, Sch.15 para.52, Sch.17 para.48, SI 2004/1500 Sch.2 para.27

s.11, applied: 2003 c.42 Sch.5 para.54, Sch.5 para.97, Sch.5 para.161, 2003 c.44 Sch.4 para.36, Sch.15 para.53, Sch.17 para.49, SI 2004/1500 Sch.2 para.28

s.12, applied: 2003 c.42 Sch.5 para.55, Sch.5 para.98, Sch.5 para.162, 2003 c.44 Sch.15 para.54, Sch.17 para.50

s.13, applied: 2003 c.42 Sch.5 para.56, Sch.5 para.99, Sch.5 para.163, 2003 c.44 Sch.15 para.55, Sch.17 para.51, SI 2004/1910 Sch.1

s.17, amended: 2002 c.8 s.2

s.22, amended: 2002 c.30 Sch.7 para.13

s.36A, added: 2003 c.20 s.113

s.46, applied: 2004 c.36 Sch.1 para.27, Sch.1 para.37

CAP.

CAP.

1990–cont.

31. Aviation and Maritime Security Act 1990–*cont.*

s.49, repealed: 2003 c.41 Sch.3 para.8, Sch.4

s.54, repealed (in part): 2004 c.14 Sch.1 Part 4

Sch.2 para.5, amended: 2003 asp 9 Sch.15

Sch.3 para.3, repealed: 2004 c.14 Sch.1 Part 4

34. British Nationality (Hong Kong) Act 1990

s.1, repealed (in part): 2002 c.41 s.7, Sch.9

s.2, amended: 2002 c.8 s.2, SI 2003/1016 Sch.1 para.4

Sch.1 para.4, amended: 2002 c.8 s.2

35. Enterprise and New Towns (Scotland) Act 1990

applied: SSI 2002/62 Sch.1

s.2, applied: SI 2002/1792 Sch.2 para.14, SI 2002/2005 Reg.9, SI 2002/2006 Reg.19, SI 2003/1660 Reg.19, SI 2004/959 Reg.4

s.2, referred to: SI 2003/1661 Reg.19

s.8, amended: 2003 asp 9 s.113

s.9, amended: SI 2003/2155 Sch.1 para.12

s.19, applied: 2002 asp 11 Sch.2 para.27, SSI 2002/77 Sch.1, SSI 2002/78 Sch.1, Sch.2

s.21, applied: SI 2003/2261 Sch.1 para.3

s.25, applied: 2003 asp 6 Sch.5, 2004 asp 2 Sch.5

s.25, referred to: 2002 asp 7 Sch.5

s.26, applied: 2003 asp 6 Sch.5, 2004 asp 2 Sch.5

s.26, referred to: 2002 asp 7 Sch.5

s.32, amended: 2003 asp 9 s.113, Sch.15

Sch.4 para.10, repealed: 2004 c.14 Sch.1 Part 2

36. Contracts (Applicable Law) Act 1990

see *Kenburn Waste Management Ltd v Bergmann* [2002] EWCA Civ 98, [2002] C.L.C 644 (CA), Robert Walker, L.J.; see *Shamil Bank of Bahrain EC v Beximco Pharmaceuticals Ltd* [2004] EWCA Civ 19, [2004] 1 W.L.R. 1784 (CA), Potter, L.J.

Sch.1, see *Kenburn Waste Management Ltd v Bergmann* [2002] F.S.R. 44 (Ch D), Pumfrey, J.

Sch.1 Art.4, see *Iran Continental Shelf Oil Co v IRI International Corp* [2002] C.L.C. 372 (QBD), McCombe, J.

37. Human Fertilisation and Embryology Act 1990

see *Centre for Reproductive Medicine v U* [2002] EWCA Civ 565, [2002] Lloyd's Rep. Med. 259 (CA), Hale, L.J.

referred to: 2002 c.38 Sch.3 para.76

s.1, see *R. (on the application of Quintavalle) v Secretary of State for Health* [2002] EWCA Civ 29, [2002] Q.B. 628 (CA), Lord Phillips of Worth Matravers, M.R.; see *R. (on the application of Quintavalle) v Secretary of State for Health* [2003] UKHL 13, [2003] 2 A.C. 687 (HL), Lord Bingham of Cornhill

s.1, applied: 2004 c.30 s.54

1990–cont.

37. Human Fertilisation and Embryology Act 1990–*cont.*

s.2, see *R. (on the application of Quintavalle) v Human Fertilisation and Embryology Authority* [2002] EWHC 2785, [2003] 2 All E.R. 105 (QBD (Admin Ct)), Maurice Kay, J.; see *R. (on the application of Quintavalle) v Human Fertilisation and Embryology Authority* [2003] EWCA Civ 667, [2004] Q.B. 168 (CA), Lord Phillips of Worth Matravers, M.R.

s.3, see *Attorney General's Reference (No.2 of 2003), Re* [2004] EWCA Crim 785, [2004] 1 W.L.R. 2062 (CA (Crim Div)), Judge, L.J.; see *R. (on the application of Quintavalle) v Human Fertilisation and Embryology Authority* [2002] EWHC 2785, [2003] 2 All E.R. 105 (QBD (Admin Ct)), Maurice Kay, J.; see *R. (on the application of Quintavalle) v Secretary of State for Health* [2003] UKHL 13, [2003] 2 A.C. 687 (HL), Lord Bingham of Cornhill

s.8, see *R. (on the application of Rose) v Secretary of State for Health* [2002] EWHC 1593, [2002] 2 F.L.R. 962 (QBD (Admin Ct)), Scott Baker, J.

s.27, amended: 2002 c.38 Sch.3 para.77

s.28, see *L Teaching Hospitals NHS Trust v A (Preliminary Hearing)* [2003] 1 F.L.R. 412 (QBD), Dame Elizabeth Butler-Sloss (President); see *R (A Child) (Contact: Human Fertilisation and Embryology Act 1990) (No.2), Re* [2003] EWCA Civ 182, [2003] Fam 129 (CA), Hale, L.J.

s.28, amended: 2002 c.38 Sch.3 para.78, 2003 c.24 s.1, Sch.1 para.13, Sch.1 para.14, Sch.1 para.15

s.28, applied: 2002 c.38 s.51

s.28, varied: 2003 c.24 s.2

s.29, amended: 2003 c.24 s.1, Sch.1 para.16

s.30, see *C (Surrogacy: Payments), Re* [2002] EWHC 157, [2002] 1 F.L.R. 909 (Fam Div), Wall, J.

s.30, amended: 2002 c.38 Sch.3 para.79

s.30, applied: SI 2002/79 Reg.3, SR 2002/14 Reg.3

s.30, varied: 2003 c.24 Sch.1 para.17

s.31, see *R. (on the application of Rose) v Secretary of State for Health* [2002] EWHC 1593, [2002] 2 F.L.R. 962 (QBD (Admin Ct)), Scott Baker, J.

s.31, applied: SI 2004/1511 Reg.2

s.31, enabling: SI 2004/1511

s.33, applied: SI 2002/325 Sch.3 para.2

s.41, see *Attorney General's Reference (No.2 of 2003), Re* [2004] EWCA Crim 785, [2004] 1 W.L.R. 2062 (CA (Crim Div)), Judge, L.J.

s.45, enabling: SI 2004/1511

Sch.2 para.1, see *R. (on the application of Quintavalle) v Human Fertilisation and Embryology Authority* [2002] EWHC

1990–cont.

37. Human Fertilisation and Embryology Act 1990–*cont.*

Sch.2 para.1–*cont.*

2785, [2003] 2 All E.R. 105 (QBD (Admin Ct)), Maurice Kay, J.; see *R. (on the application of Quintavalle) v Human Fertilisation and Embryology Authority* [2003] EWCA Civ 667, [2004] Q.B. 168 (CA), Lord Phillips of Worth Matravers, M.R.

Sch.2 para.1, applied: SI 2002/325 Reg.3

Sch.3, see *Evans v Amicus Healthcare Ltd* [2004] EWCA Civ 727, [2004] 3 W.L.R. 681 (CA), Thorpe, L.J.

Sch.3 para.4, see *Evans v Amicus Healthcare Ltd* [2003] EWHC 2161, [2003] 4 All E.R. 903 (Fam Div), Wall, J.; see *Evans v Amicus Healthcare Ltd* [2004] EWCA Civ 727, [2004] 3 W.L.R. 681 (CA), Thorpe, L.J.

Sch.3 para.6, see *Evans v Amicus Healthcare Ltd* [2004] EWCA Civ 727, [2004] 3 W.L.R. 681 (CA), Thorpe, L.J.

Sch.4 para.4, repealed: 2002 c.38 Sch.5

Sch.4 para.8, repealed (in part): 2004 c.30 Sch.7 Part 1

Sch.4 para.9, repealed (in part): 2004 c.30 Sch.7 Part 1

40. Law Reform (Miscellaneous Provisions) (Scotland) Act 1990

Commencement Orders: 2003 asp 4 Sch.4 para.12; SSI 2004/382 Art.2

applied: SSI 2004/157 Art.2

s.1, applied: SSI 2002/318 Art.4, 2004 c.27 s.54

s.1, referred to: 2004 c.27 s.26

s.7, applied: SI 2002/2376 Reg.2, SI 2002/2978 Sch.1 para.5, SI 2002/3038 Reg.5, SI 2002/3040 Reg.3, SI 2002/3177 Sch.1 para.5, SI 2003/348 Sch.6 para.8, SI 2003/506 Reg.3, SI 2003/1558 Sch.2 para.7, SI 2003/2773 Reg.3, SI 2003/3060 Reg.3, SI 2003/3190 Reg.4, SI 2003/3279 Reg.4, SI 2004/215 Sch.1, SI 2004/291 Reg.5, Sch.6 para.113, SI 2004/478 Reg.5, Sch.6 para.111, SI 2004/570 Reg.3, SI 2004/627 Reg.5, Sch.5 para.105, SI 2004/668 Reg.3, SI 2004/1742 Reg.5, SSI 2004/115 Sch.5 para.101, SSI 2004/116 Reg.3, Sch.1 para.66

s.8, amended: SI 2004/1941 Sch.1 para.4

s.12, applied: 2002 asp 13 Sch.1 para.79

s.16, substituted: 2003 asp 4 Sch.4 para.12

s.17, amended: 2003 asp 4 Sch.4 para.12

s.17, repealed (in part): 2003 asp 4 Sch.4 para.12

s.18, amended: 2003 asp 4 Sch.4 para.12

s.18, repealed (in part): 2003 asp 4 Sch.4 para.12

s.19, repealed: 2003 asp 4 Sch.4 para.12

s.20, amended: 2003 asp 4 Sch.4 para.12

s.20, repealed (in part): 2003 asp 4 Sch.4 para.12

s.20A, added: 2003 asp 4 Sch.4 para.12

1990–cont.

40. Law Reform (Miscellaneous Provisions) (Scotland) Act 1990–*cont.*

s.21, amended: 2003 asp 4 Sch.4 para.12

s.21A, added: 2003 asp 4 Sch.4 para.12

s.21B, added: 2003 asp 4 Sch.4 para.12

s.21C, added: 2003 asp 4 Sch.4 para.12

s.22, amended: 2003 asp 4 Sch.4 para.12

s.22, repealed (in part): 2003 asp 4 Sch.4 para.12

s.23, amended: 2003 asp 4 Sch.4 para.12

s.33, amended: 2003 asp 4 Sch.4 para.12

s.33, repealed (in part): 2003 asp 4 Sch.4 para.12

s.33, varied: SSI 2004/383 Reg.16

s.34, amended: 2003 asp 4 Sch.4 para.12

s.34, applied: SI 2003/409 Sch.1 Part I

s.34, repealed (in part): 2003 asp 4 Sch.4 para.12

s.34, varied: SSI 2004/383 Reg.16

s.34A, applied: SSI 2002/32 Art.2

s.34A, enabling: SSI 2002/32

s.40, amended: 2003 asp 4 Sch.4 para.12

s.40, repealed (in part): 2003 asp 4 Sch.4 para.12

s.41, repealed (in part): SI 2003/1398 Sch.1 para.12

s.41A, added: SI 2003/1398 Sch.1 para.12

s.41B, added: SI 2003/1398 Sch.1 para.12

s.42, amended: 2003 asp 4 Sch.4 para.12

s.49, referred to: SSI 2004/157 Sch.1 Part II

s.75, enabling: SSI 2004/382

Sch.1 Part I para.1, repealed: 2003 asp 4 Sch.4 para.12

Sch.1 Part I para.2, repealed: 2003 asp 4 Sch.4 para.12

Sch.1 Part I para.3, repealed: 2003 asp 4 Sch.4 para.12

Sch.1 Part I para.4, repealed: 2003 asp 4 Sch.4 para.12

Sch.1 Part I para.5, repealed: 2003 asp 4 Sch.4 para.12

Sch.1 Part I para.6, repealed: 2003 asp 4 Sch.4 para.12

Sch.1 Part I para.7, repealed: 2003 asp 4 Sch.4 para.12

Sch.1 Part I para.8, repealed: 2003 asp 4 Sch.4 para.12

Sch.1 Part I para.9, repealed: 2003 asp 4 Sch.4 para.12

Sch.1 Part I para.10, repealed: 2003 asp 4 Sch.4 para.12

Sch.1 Part I para.11, repealed: 2003 asp 4 Sch.4 para.12

Sch.1 Part I para.12, repealed: 2003 asp 4 Sch.4 para.12

Sch.1 Part I para.13, repealed: 2003 asp 4 Sch.4 para.12

Sch.1 Part I para.14, repealed: 2003 asp 4 Sch.4 para.12

Sch.1 Part I para.15, repealed: 2003 asp 4 Sch.4 para.12

1990–cont.

40. Law Reform (Miscellaneous Provisions) (Scotland) Act 1990–cont.

Sch.1 Part I para.16, repealed: 2003 asp 4 Sch.4 para.12

Sch.1 Part I para.17, repealed: 2003 asp 4 Sch.4 para.12

Sch.1 Part II para.18, repealed: 2003 asp 4 Sch.4 para.12

Sch.1 Part II para.19, repealed: 2003 asp 4 Sch.4 para.12

Sch.1 Part II para.20, repealed: 2003 asp 4 Sch.4 para.12

Sch.5 para.9, applied: SI 2003/2773 Reg.10

Sch.6 para.8, repealed (in part): 2004 asp 8 Sch.5

41. Courts and Legal Services Act 1990

Commencement Orders: 2002 c.40 Sch.26; 2004 c.14 Sch.1 Part 1; SI 2004/2950 Art.2

see *Designers Guild Ltd v Russell Williams (Textiles) Ltd (t/a Washington DC) (Costs) (No.1)* [2003] 1 Costs L.R. 128 (HL), Judge not specified

applied: 2002 c.40 Sch.15, 2003 c.3 s.3, s.5, SI 2004/2326 Reg.52

Part II, applied: 2003 c.39 s.70, s.77, SI 2003/1887 Sch.1

Part IV, applied: SI 2003/1887 Sch.1

s.1, applied: 2002 c.15 s.66, 2004 c.25 s.9

s.1, repealed (in part): 2003 c.39 Sch.8 para.348, Sch.10

s.2, repealed (in part): 2004 c.14 Sch.1 Part 1

s.4, see *Brown v Bennett (Wasted Costs) (No.1)* [2002] 1 W.L.R. 713 (Ch D), Neuberger, J.; see *Byrne v Sefton HA* [2001] EWCA Civ 1904, [2002] 1 W.L.R. 775 (CA), Chadwick, L.J.; see *Medcalf v Mardell (Wasted Costs Order)* [2002] UKHL 27, [2003] 1 A.C. 120 (HL), Lord Bingham of Cornhill

s.8, see *Kiam v MGN Ltd* [2002] EWCA Civ 43, [2003] Q.B. 281 (CA), Simon Brown, L.J.

s.9, see *Practice Direction (Fam Div: Lord Chancellor's Direction: Allocations to Judiciary (Amendments) 2002)* [2002] 2 F.L.R. 692 (Fam Div), Lord Irvine of Lairg, L.C.

s.10, amended: 2003 c.39 Sch.8 para.349, 2004 c.33 Sch.27 para.137

s.12, repealed: 2004 c.14 Sch.1 Part 1

s.14, repealed: 2004 c.14 Sch.1 Part 1

s.15, repealed (in part): 2003 c.39 Sch.10

s.16, repealed: 2004 c.14 Sch.1 Part 1

s.18, amended: SI 2003/1887 Sch.2 para.8

s.18A, amended: SI 2003/1887 Sch.2 para.8

s.21, amended: SI 2003/1887 Sch.2 para.8

s.21, applied: SI 2004/2757 Reg.3

s.21, varied: SI 2004/2757 Reg.4

s.22, amended: SI 2003/1887 Sch.2 para.8

s.22, applied: SI 2004/2757 Reg.3

s.22, disapplied: SI 2004/2757 Reg.4

1990–cont.

41. Courts and Legal Services Act 1990–cont.

s.22, varied: SI 2004/2757 Reg.4

s.23, applied: SI 2004/2757 Reg.3

s.23, varied: SI 2004/2757 Reg.4

s.24, applied: SI 2004/2757 Reg.3

s.24, varied: SI 2004/2757 Reg.4

s.25, applied: SI 2004/2757 Reg.3

s.25, varied: SI 2004/2757 Reg.4

s.26, amended: SI 2003/1887 Sch.2 para.8

s.26, enabling: SI 2004/2757

s.27, see *Ahmed v Powell* [2003] P.N.L.R. 22 (Sup Ct Costs Office), Chief Master Hurst; see *Gregory v Turner* [2003] EWCA Civ 183, [2003] 1 W.L.R. 1149 (CA), Brooke, L.J.; see *Izzo v Philip Ross & Co* [2002] B.P.I.R. 310 (Ch D), Neuberger, J.; see *Official Receiver v Broad (Rights of Audience)* [2003] EWCA Civ 404, [2003] C.P. Rep. 59 (CA), Jonathan Parker, L.J.

s.27, amended: SI 2003/1887 Sch.2 para.8

s.27, applied: 2003 c.39 s.77, 2004 c.31 s.37

s.28, see *Gregory v Turner* [2003] EWCA Civ 183, [2003] 1 W.L.R. 1149 (CA), Brooke, L.J.; see *Official Receiver v Broad (Rights of Audience)* [2003] EWCA Civ 404, [2003] C.P. Rep. 59 (CA), Jonathan Parker, L.J.

s.28, applied: 2003 c.39 s.77, 2004 c.31 s.37

s.34, amended: SI 2003/1887 Sch.2 para.8

s.35, amended: SI 2003/1887 Sch.2 para.8

s.37, amended: SI 2003/1887 Sch.2 para.8

s.39, amended: SI 2003/1887 Sch.2 para.8

s.40, amended: SI 2003/1887 Sch.2 para.8

s.41, amended: SI 2003/1887 Sch.2 para.8

s.43, amended: SI 2003/1887 Sch.2 para.8

s.44, amended: SI 2003/1887 Sch.2 para.8

s.45, amended: 2002 c.40 Sch.25 para.23, SI 2003/1887 Sch.2 para.8

s.45, substituted: 2002 c.40 Sch.25 para.23

s.46, amended: 2002 c.40 Sch.25 para.23

s.46, repealed (in part): 2002 c.40 Sch.26

s.46A, added: 2002 c.40 Sch.25 para.23

s.46B, added: 2002 c.40 Sch.25 para.23

s.48, amended: SI 2003/1887 Sch.2 para.8

s.50, amended: 2002 c.40 Sch.25 para.23, SI 2003/1398 Sch.1 para.13, SI 2003/1887 Sch.2 para.8, 2004 c.35 Sch.4 para.21

s.50, repealed (in part): SI 2003/1887 Sch.2 para.8

s.53, amended: SI 2003/1887 Sch.2 para.8

s.54, amended: SI 2003/1887 Sch.2 para.8

s.55, amended: SI 2003/1887 Sch.2 para.8

s.55, applied: SI 2004/2757 Reg.4, SI 2004/2951 Reg.3, Reg.4

s.55, enabling: SI 2004/2951

s.58, see *Benaim UK Ltd v Davies Middleton & Davies Ltd* [2004] EWHC 737, (2004) 154 N.L.J. 617 (QBD (T&CC)), Judge Rich Q.C.; see *Denton v Denton* [2004]

CAP.

1990–cont.

41. Courts and Legal Services Act 1990–
cont.

s.58–*cont.*

EWHC 1308, [2004] 2 F.L.R. 594 (Fam Div), Baron, J.; see *Hollins v Russell* [2003] EWCA Civ 718, [2003] 1 W.L.R. 2487 (CA), Brooke, L.J.; see *Myler v Williams* [2003] EWHC 1587, [2003] 4 Costs L.R. 566 (QBD), Crane, J.; see *Thornley v Lang* [2003] EWCA Civ 1484, [2004] 1 W.L.R. 378 (CA), Lord Phillips of Worth Matravers, M.R.

s.58, amended: SI 2003/1887 Sch.2 para.8

s.58, enabling: SI 2003/1240, SI 2003/3344

s.58A, amended: 2002 c.38 Sch.3 para.80, SI 2003/1887 Sch.2 para.8, 2004 c.33 Sch.27 para.138, Sch.30

s.58A, applied: 2002 c.38 Sch.4 para.22

s.58A, enabling: SI 2003/1240, SI 2003/3344

s.60, amended: SI 2003/1887 Sch.2 para.8

s.62, repealed: 2004 c.14 Sch.1 Part 1

s.69, amended: 2002 c.40 Sch.25 para.23, SI 2003/1887 Sch.2 para.8

s.71, applied: 2002 c.9 s.107, Sch.9 para.4, 2002 c.41 s.81, Sch.5 para.11, SI 2002/253 Art.34, SI 2002/254 Art.34, 2003 c.39 s.107, 2003 c.3 s.21, SI 2003/1372 r.4, 2004 c.7 Sch.1 para.1, 2004 c.18 s.81, 2004 c.35 Sch.4 para.1, Sch.4 para.2, SI 2004/652 Reg.4, SI 2004/1861 Reg.4, Reg.8, Sch.1 para.38, Sch.2 para.8, SI 2004/1937 Art.3, SSI 2004/155 Reg.2, SSI 2004/286 Reg.2, SSI 2004/292 Reg.4

s.74, applied: SI 2003/2342 Reg.2

s.78, repealed (in part): 2004 c.14 Sch.1 Part 1

s.84, repealed: 2004 c.14 Sch.1 Part 1

s.89, amended: SI 2003/1887 Sch.2 para.8

s.90, applied: SI 2003/1250 Art.21

s.93, repealed (in part): 2004 c.14 Sch.1 Part 1

s.105, amended: 2002 c.40 Sch.25 para.23

s.107, amended: 2002 c.40 Sch.25 para.23

s.109, repealed (in part): 2002 c.26 Sch.13, 2004 c.14 Sch.1 Part 1

s.113, amended: SI 2003/1887 Sch.2 para.8

s.113, applied: SI 2003/1887 Sch.1

s.114, repealed: 2004 c.14 Sch.1 Part 1

s.119, see *Byrne v Sefton HA* [2001] EWCA Civ 1904, [2002] 1 W.L.R. 775 (CA), Chadwick, L.J.

s.119, amended: 2002 c.40 Sch.25 para.23, Sch.26

s.119, enabling: SI 2003/1240, SI 2003/3344

s.120, applied: SI 2004/2757

s.120, enabling: SI 2004/2757

s.124, applied: SI 2003/1887 Sch.1

s.124, enabling: SI 2004/2950

s.125, amended: SI 2003/1887 Sch.2 para.8

s.125, applied: SI 2003/1887 Sch.1

Sch.3 para.1, amended: SI 2003/1887 Sch.2 para.8

CAP.

1990–cont.

41. Courts and Legal Services Act 1990–
cont.

Sch.3 para.2, amended: SI 2003/1887 Sch.2 para.8

Sch.3 para.3, amended: SI 2003/1887 Sch.2 para.8

Sch.3 para.4, amended: SI 2003/1887 Sch.2 para.8

Sch.3 para.5, amended: SI 2003/1887 Sch.2 para.8

Sch.3 para.6, amended: SI 2003/1887 Sch.2 para.8

Sch.3 para.7, amended: SI 2003/1887 Sch.2 para.8

Sch.3 para.8, amended: SI 2003/1887 Sch.2 para.8

Sch.3 para.9, amended: SI 2003/1887 Sch.2 para.8

Sch.4 Part I para.1, amended: SI 2003/1887 Sch.2 para.8

Sch.4 Part I para.2, amended: SI 2003/1887 Sch.2 para.8

Sch.4 Part I para.3, amended: SI 2003/1887 Sch.2 para.8

Sch.4 Part I para.4, amended: SI 2003/1887 Sch.2 para.8

Sch.4 Part I para.4, applied: SI 2003/1372 r.4

Sch.4 Part I para.5, amended: SI 2003/1887 Sch.2 para.8

Sch.4 Part I para.5, applied: SI 2003/1372 r.4

Sch.4 Part II para.6, amended: SI 2003/1887 Sch.2 para.8

Sch.4 Part II para.7, amended: SI 2003/1887 Sch.2 para.8

Sch.4 Part II para.8, amended: SI 2003/1887 Sch.2 para.8

Sch.4 Part II para.9, amended: SI 2003/1887 Sch.2 para.8

Sch.4 Part II para.10, amended: SI 2003/1887 Sch.2 para.8

Sch.4 Part II para.11, amended: SI 2003/1887 Sch.2 para.8

Sch.4 Part III para.12, amended: SI 2003/1887 Sch.2 para.8

Sch.4 Part III para.13, amended: SI 2003/1887 Sch.2 para.8

Sch.4 Part III para.14, amended: SI 2003/1887 Sch.2 para.8

Sch.4 Part III para.15, amended: SI 2003/1887 Sch.2 para.8

Sch.4 Part III para.16, amended: SI 2003/1887 Sch.2 para.8

Sch.4 Part III para.17, amended: SI 2003/1887 Sch.2 para.8

Sch.4 Part III para.18, amended: SI 2003/1887 Sch.2 para.8

Sch.4 Part III para.19, amended: SI 2003/1887 Sch.2 para.8

Sch.4 Part III para.20, amended: SI 2003/1887 Sch.2 para.8

1990–cont.

41. Courts and Legal Services Act 1990–
cont.

Sch.4 Part III para.21, amended: SI 2003/
1887 Sch.2 para.8

Sch.4 Part III para.22, amended: SI 2003/
1887 Sch.2 para.8

Sch.4 Part III para.23, amended: SI 2003/
1887 Sch.2 para.8

Sch.4 Part III para.24, amended: SI 2003/
1887 Sch.2 para.8

Sch.4 Part III para.28, amended: SI 2003/
1887 Sch.2 para.8

Sch.4i Part I, amended: 2002 c.40 Sch.25
para.23

Sch.4i Part I para.1, amended: 2002 c.40
Sch.25 para.23, SI 2003/1887 Sch.2
para.8

Sch.4i Part I para.2, amended: 2002 c.40
Sch.25 para.23, SI 2003/1887 Sch.2
para.8

Sch.4i Part I para.3, amended: 2002 c.40
Sch.25 para.23, SI 2003/1887 Sch.2
para.8

Sch.4i Part I para.4, amended: 2002 c.40
Sch.25 para.23, SI 2003/1887 Sch.2
para.8

Sch.4i Part I para.5, amended: 2002 c.40
Sch.25 para.23, SI 2003/1887 Sch.2
para.8

Sch.4i Part I para.6, amended: 2002 c.40
Sch.25 para.23, SI 2003/1887 Sch.2
para.8

Sch.4i Part I para.7, amended: 2002 c.40
Sch.25 para.23, SI 2003/1887 Sch.2
para.8

Sch.4i Part II, amended: 2002 c.40 Sch.25
para.23

Sch.4i Part II para.8, amended: 2002 c.40
Sch.25 para.23, SI 2003/1887 Sch.2
para.8

Sch.4i Part II para.9, amended: 2002 c.40
Sch.25 para.23, SI 2003/1887 Sch.2
para.8

Sch.4i Part II para.10, amended: 2002 c.40
Sch.25 para.23, SI 2003/1887 Sch.2
para.8

Sch.4i Part II para.11, amended: 2002 c.40
Sch.25 para.23, SI 2003/1887 Sch.2
para.8

Sch.4i Part II para.12, amended: 2002 c.40
Sch.25 para.23, SI 2003/1887 Sch.2
para.8

Sch.4i Part II para.13, amended: 2002 c.40
Sch.25 para.23, SI 2003/1887 Sch.2
para.8

Sch.4i Part II para.14, amended: 2002 c.40
Sch.25 para.23, SI 2003/1887 Sch.2
para.8

Sch.4i Part II para.15, amended: 2002 c.40
Sch.25 para.23, SI 2003/1887 Sch.2
para.8

1990–cont.

41. Courts and Legal Services Act 1990–
cont.

Sch.4i Part II para.16, amended: 2002 c.40
Sch.25 para.23, SI 2003/1887 Sch.2
para.8

Sch.4i Part III, amended: 2002 c.40 Sch.25
para.23

Sch.4i Part III para.17, amended: 2002 c.40
Sch.25 para.23, SI 2003/1887 Sch.2
para.8

Sch.4i Part III para.18, amended: 2002 c.40
Sch.25 para.23, SI 2003/1887 Sch.2
para.8

Sch.4i Part III para.19, amended: 2002 c.40
Sch.25 para.23, SI 2003/1887 Sch.2
para.8

Sch.4i Part III para.20, amended: 2002 c.40
Sch.25 para.23, SI 2003/1887 Sch.2
para.8

Sch.4i Part III para.21, amended: 2002 c.40
Sch.25 para.23, SI 2003/1887 Sch.2
para.8

Sch.4i Part III para.22, amended: 2002 c.40
Sch.25 para.23, SI 2003/1887 Sch.2
para.8

Sch.4i Part III para.23, amended: 2002 c.40
Sch.25 para.23, SI 2003/1887 Sch.2
para.8

Sch.4i Part III para.24, amended: 2002 c.40
Sch.25 para.23, SI 2003/1887 Sch.2
para.8

Sch.4i Part IV, amended: 2002 c.40 Sch.25
para.23

Sch.4i Part IV para.25, amended: 2002 c.40
Sch.25 para.23, SI 2003/1887 Sch.2
para.8

Sch.4i Part IV para.26, amended: 2002 c.40
Sch.25 para.23, SI 2003/1887 Sch.2
para.8

Sch.4i Part IV para.27, amended: 2002 c.40
Sch.25 para.23, SI 2003/1887 Sch.2
para.8

Sch.4i Part IV para.28, amended: 2002 c.40
Sch.25 para.23, SI 2003/1887 Sch.2
para.8

Sch.4i Part IV para.29, amended: 2002 c.40
Sch.25 para.23, SI 2003/1887 Sch.2
para.8

Sch.4i Part IV para.30, amended: 2002 c.40
Sch.25 para.23, SI 2003/1887 Sch.2
para.8

Sch.4i Part IV para.31, amended: 2002 c.40
Sch.25 para.23, SI 2003/1887 Sch.2
para.8

Sch.4i Part IV para.32, amended: 2002 c.40
Sch.25 para.23, SI 2003/1887 Sch.2
para.8

Sch.4i Part IV para.33, amended: 2002 c.40
Sch.25 para.23, SI 2003/1887 Sch.2
para.8

Sch.5 para.1, amended: SI 2003/1887 Sch.2
para.8

1990–cont.

41. Courts and Legal Services Act 1990–
cont.

Sch.5 para.2, amended: SI 2003/1887 Sch.2 para.8

Sch.5 para.3, amended: SI 2003/1887 Sch.2 para.8

Sch.5 para.4, amended: SI 2003/1887 Sch.2 para.8

Sch.5 para.5, amended: SI 2003/1887 Sch.2 para.8

Sch.5 para.6, amended: SI 2003/1887 Sch.2 para.8

Sch.5 para.7, amended: SI 2003/1887 Sch.2 para.8

Sch.5 para.8, amended: SI 2003/1887 Sch.2 para.8

Sch.5 para.9, amended: SI 2003/1887 Sch.2 para.8

Sch.5 para.10, amended: SI 2003/1887 Sch.2 para.8

Sch.5 para.11, amended: SI 2003/1887 Sch.2 para.8

Sch.6 para.1, amended: SI 2003/1887 Sch.2 para.8

Sch.6 para.2, amended: SI 2003/1887 Sch.2 para.8

Sch.6 para.3, amended: SI 2003/1887 Sch.2 para.8

Sch.8 Part I para.1, amended: SI 2003/1887 Sch.2 para.8

Sch.8 Part I para.2, amended: SI 2003/1887 Sch.2 para.8

Sch.8 Part I para.3, amended: SI 2003/1887 Sch.2 para.8

Sch.8 Part I para.4, amended: SI 2003/1887 Sch.2 para.8

Sch.8 Part I para.5, amended: SI 2003/1887 Sch.2 para.8

Sch.8 Part I para.6, amended: SI 2003/1887 Sch.2 para.8

Sch.8 Part I para.7, amended: SI 2003/1887 Sch.2 para.8

Sch.8 Part I para.8, amended: SI 2003/1887 Sch.2 para.8

Sch.8 Part I para.9, amended: SI 2003/1887 Sch.2 para.8

Sch.8 Part I para.10, amended: SI 2003/1887 Sch.2 para.8

Sch.8 Part I para.11, amended: SI 2003/1887 Sch.2 para.8

Sch.8 Part II para.12, amended: SI 2003/1887 Sch.2 para.8

Sch.8 Part II para.13, amended: SI 2003/1887 Sch.2 para.8

Sch.8 Part II para.14, amended: SI 2003/1887 Sch.2 para.8

Sch.8 Part II para.15, amended: SI 2003/1887 Sch.2 para.8

Sch.8 Part II para.16, amended: SI 2003/1887 Sch.2 para.8

1990–cont.

41. Courts and Legal Services Act 1990–
cont.

Sch.8 Part II para.17, amended: SI 2003/1887 Sch.2 para.8

Sch.8 Part II para.18, amended: SI 2003/1887 Sch.2 para.8

Sch.8 Part II para.19, amended: SI 2003/1887 Sch.2 para.8

Sch.8 Part II para.20, amended: SI 2003/1887 Sch.2 para.8

Sch.8 Part II para.21, amended: SI 2003/1887 Sch.2 para.8

Sch.8 Part II para.22, amended: SI 2003/1887 Sch.2 para.8

Sch.8 Part II para.23, amended: SI 2003/1887 Sch.2 para.8

Sch.8 Part II para.24, amended: SI 2003/1887 Sch.2 para.8

Sch.9 para.1, amended: SI 2003/1887 Sch.2 para.8

Sch.9 para.2, amended: SI 2003/1887 Sch.2 para.8

Sch.9 para.3, amended: SI 2003/1887 Sch.2 para.8

Sch.9 para.4, amended: SI 2003/1887 Sch.2 para.8

Sch.9 para.5, amended: SI 2003/1887 Sch.2 para.8

Sch.9 para.6, amended: SI 2003/1887 Sch.2 para.8

Sch.9 para.7, amended: SI 2003/1887 Sch.2 para.8

Sch.9 para.8, amended: SI 2003/1887 Sch.2 para.8

Sch.9 para.9, amended: SI 2003/1887 Sch.2 para.8

Sch.9 para.10, amended: SI 2003/1887 Sch.2 para.8

Sch.9 para.11, amended: SI 2003/1887 Sch.2 para.8

Sch.10 para.3, repealed: 2002 c.9 Sch.13

Sch.10 para.8, repealed: 2003 c.21 Sch.19

Sch.11, amended: 2002 c.41 Sch.7 para.16, 2004 c.19 Sch.2 para.6

Sch.16 Part I para.7, repealed: 2002 c.38 Sch.5

Sch.16 Part I para.14, amended: 2003 c.43 Sch.14 Part 1

Sch.16 Part I para.20, repealed: 2003 c.43 Sch.14 Part 1

Sch.17 para.1, repealed: 2004 c.14 Sch.1 Part 1

Sch.17 para.2, repealed: 2002 c.9 Sch.13

Sch.17 para.3, repealed: 2004 c.14 Sch.1 Part 1

Sch.17 para.7, repealed: 2003 c.44 Sch.37 Part 10

Sch.17 para.9, repealed: 2004 c.14 Sch.1 Part 1

Sch.17 para.14, repealed: 2003 c.39 Sch.10

Sch.17 para.18, repealed: 2004 c.14 Sch.1 Part 1

1990–cont.

41. Courts and Legal Services Act 1990–
cont.

Sch.18 para.4, repealed: 2002 c.40 Sch.26

Sch.18 para.5, repealed: 2003 c.44 Sch.37 Part 10

Sch.18 para.6, repealed: 2002 c.40 Sch.26

Sch.18 para.22, repealed: 2002 c.40 Sch.26

Sch.18 para.23, repealed: 2002 c.40 Sch.26

Sch.18 para.25, repealed (in part): 2003 c.44 Sch.37 Part 4

Sch.18 para.50, repealed: 2003 c.39 Sch.10

Sch.19 para.7, repealed: 2003 c.39 Sch.10

Sch.19 para.17, amended: SI 2003/1887 Sch.2 para.8

42. Broadcasting Act 1990

applied: 2002 c.40 Sch.15, SI 2002/2779 Art.60, 2003 c.17 Sch.1 para.8, 2003 c.21 s.198, s.211, s.212, s.220, s.235, s.240, s.245, s.246, s.251, s.263, s.270, s.296, s.317, s.343, s.390, s.393, s.394, Sch.10 para.9, Sch.10 para.10, Sch.10 para.12, SI 2003/284 Art.65, SI 2004/293 Reg.64, SI 2004/1975 Art.8, Art.9

disapplied: 2003 c.21 s.293

referred to: 2003 c.21 s.127, s.244, s.262, s.393, Sch.1 para.9, SI 2003/1374 Sch.1, SI 2004/870 Reg.5

varied: 2003 c.21 s.224

Part I, applied: SI 2002/2779 Art.39, Art.55, 2003 c.21 s.13, s.212, s.214, s.215, s.221, s.231, s.235, s.237, s.238, s.240, s.346, s.359, s.400, Sch.1 para.3, SI 2003/284 Art.44, Art.61, SI 2003/1900 Art.4, SI 2003/1902 Sch.1 para.1, SI 2004/293 Reg.46, Reg.60, SI 2004/1267 Reg.42, Reg.55

Part I, referred to: 2002 c.36 s.12, 2003 c.21 s.244, Sch.10 para.15

Part II, applied: 2003 c.21 s.213

Part III, applied: SI 2002/2779 Art.39, Art.55, 2003 c.21 s.13, s.246, s.250, s.251, s.346, s.359, s.400, Sch.1 para.5, SI 2003/284 Art.44, Art.61, SI 2003/1902 Sch.1 para.1, SI 2004/293 Reg.46, Reg.60, SI 2004/1267 Reg.42, Reg.55

Part III, referred to: 2002 c.36 s.12, 2003 c.21 s.262

s.1, repealed: 2003 c.21 Sch.19

s.2, amended: 2002 c.40 Sch.25 para.24

s.2, disapplied: 2002 c.36 s.12

s.2, repealed: 2003 c.21 Sch.19

s.3, amended: 2003 c.21 Sch.15 para.1

s.3, applied: 2003 c.21 s.235, s.240, s.278, s.279, s.286, s.287, s.288, s.296, s.352, s.354

s.4, amended: 2003 c.21 Sch.15 para.2, Sch.19

s.4, applied: 2003 c.21 s.217, s.347, Sch.10 para.7

s.4, varied: SI 2004/1975 Art.10

s.5, amended: 2003 c.21 s.350, Sch.15 para.3

1990–cont.

42. Broadcasting Act 1990–*cont.*

s.5, applied: 2003 c.21 s.235

s.5, repealed (in part): 2003 c.21 Sch.19

s.5, varied: SI 2003/1900 Art.5

s.6, see *R. (on the application of ProLife Alliance) v BBC* [2003] UKHL 23, [2004] 1 A.C.185 (HL), Lord Nicholls of Birkenhead

s.6, repealed: 2003 c.21 Sch.19

s.6, varied: 2003 c.21 Sch.18 para.41, Sch.18 para.43

s.7, repealed: 2003 c.21 Sch.19

s.7, varied: 2003 c.21 Sch.18 para.41, Sch.18 para.43

s.7A, repealed: 2003 c.21 Sch.19

s.7A, varied: 2003 c.21 Sch.18 para.41

s.8, repealed: 2003 c.21 Sch.19

s.8, varied: 2003 c.21 Sch.18 para.41

s.9, repealed: 2003 c.21 Sch.19

s.9, varied: 2003 c.21 Sch.18 para.41, Sch.18 para.43

s.10, repealed: 2003 c.21 Sch.19

s.10, varied: 2003 c.21 Sch.18 para.41

s.11, repealed: 2003 c.21 Sch.19

s.11, varied: 2003 c.21 Sch.18 para.41

s.12, repealed: 2003 c.21 Sch.19

s.12, varied: 2003 c.21 Sch.18 para.41

s.13, amended: 2003 c.21 Sch.15 para.5

s.13, applied: 2003 c.21 s.219, s.235

s.13, disapplied: 2003 c.21 s.241

s.14, amended: 2003 c.21 Sch.15 para.6

s.14, referred to: 2003 c.21 s.351

s.14, varied: 2003 c.21 Sch.18 para.31

s.15, amended: 2003 c.21 Sch.15 para.7

s.15, applied: 2003 c.21 s.217, s.227, s.230, s.292

s.15, disapplied: 2003 c.21 s.215

s.15, referred to: 2003 c.21 s.290

s.15, repealed (in part): 2003 c.21 Sch.19

s.16, amended: 2003 c.21 Sch.15 para.8, Sch.19

s.16, applied: SI 2003/1672

s.16, disapplied: 2003 c.21 s.215

s.16, repealed (in part): 2003 c.21 Sch.19

s.16, varied: 2003 c.21 Sch.18 para.34

s.16, enabling: SI 2003/1672

s.17, amended: 2003 c.21 Sch.15 para.9

s.17, applied: 2003 c.21 Sch.10 para.6

s.17, disapplied: 2003 c.21 s.215

s.17, referred to: 2003 c.21 s.216, s.222

s.17, varied: 2003 c.21 s.216, s.222, Sch.10 para.5

s.17A, amended: 2003 c.21 Sch.15 para.10

s.17A, disapplied: 2003 c.21 s.215

s.17A, varied: 2003 c.21 Sch.10 para.5

s.18, amended: 2003 c.21 Sch.13 para.2, Sch.15 para.10

s.18, referred to: 2003 c.21 Sch.13 para.9

s.19, amended: 2003 c.21 Sch.15 para.10

s.19, applied: 2003 c.21 s.227

s.19, varied: 2003 c.21 s.237, Sch.9 para.8

1990–cont.

42. Broadcasting Act 1990–*cont.*

s.20, repealed: 2003 c.21 Sch.19

s.21, amended: 2003 c.21 Sch.15 para.11

s.21A, repealed: 2003 c.21 Sch.19

s.22, amended: 2003 c.21 Sch.15 para.12

s.23, amended: 2003 c.21 Sch.15 para.13

s.23, applied: 2003 c.21 Sch.1 para.4

s.24, amended: 2003 c.21 Sch.15 para.14

s.24, applied: 2003 c.21 s.231

s.24, repealed (in part): 2003 c.21 Sch.19

s.25, repealed: 2003 c.21 Sch.19

s.26, repealed: 2003 c.21 Sch.19

s.27, repealed: 2003 c.21 Sch.19

s.28, amended: 2003 c.21 Sch.15 para.15

s.28, varied: 2003 c.21 Sch.18 para.31

s.29, amended: 2003 c.21 Sch.15 para.16

s.29, repealed (in part): 2003 c.21 Sch.19

s.30, repealed: 2003 c.21 Sch.19

s.31, repealed: 2003 c.21 Sch.19

s.31, varied: 2003 c.21 Sch.18 para.35

s.31A, repealed: 2003 c.21 Sch.19

s.32, repealed: 2003 c.21 Sch.19

s.33, repealed: 2003 c.21 Sch.19

s.34, repealed: 2003 c.21 Sch.19

s.35, repealed: 2003 c.21 Sch.19

s.36, repealed: 2003 c.21 Sch.19

s.36, varied: 2003 c.21 Sch.18 para.38

s.37, amended: 2003 c.21 Sch.15 para.17

s.38, repealed: 2003 c.21 Sch.19

s.39, amended: 2002 c.40 Sch.25 para.24

s.39, repealed: 2003 c.21 Sch.19

s.39, varied: 2003 c.21 Sch.18 para.36

s.40, amended: 2003 c.21 s.344, Sch.15 para.18

s.40, applied: 2003 c.21 Sch.10 para.8, SI 2004/1975 Sch.1 para.2

s.41, amended: 2003 c.21 Sch.13 para.3, Sch.15 para.18

s.41, applied: SI 2004/1975 Sch.1 para.3

s.42, amended: 2003 c.21 Sch.15 para.18

s.42, applied: 2003 c.21 Sch.10 para.11, SI 2004/1975 Sch.1 para.3

s.42A, repealed (in part): 2003 c.21 Sch.19

s.42B, amended: 2003 c.21 Sch.13 para.4, Sch.15 para.19

s.42B, referred to: 2003 c.21 Sch.13 para.9

s.43, referred to: 2003 c.21 s.240

s.43, repealed: 2003 c.21 Sch.19

s.44, repealed: 2003 c.21 Sch.19

s.45, repealed: 2003 c.21 Sch.19

s.45A, repealed: 2003 c.21 Sch.19

s.46, referred to: 2003 c.21 s.240

s.46, repealed: 2003 c.21 Sch.19

s.46, varied: 2003 c.21 Sch.18 para.26

s.47, repealed: 2003 c.21 Sch.19

s.48, amended: 2003 c.21 Sch.15 para.20

s.48, applied: 2003 c.21 s.218

s.48, disapplied: 2002 c.36 s.12

s.48, repealed (in part): 2003 c.21 Sch.19

s.48, varied: 2003 c.21 Sch.18 para.26

1990–cont.

42. Broadcasting Act 1990–*cont.*

s.49, amended: 2003 c.21 Sch.15 para.21

s.49, varied: 2003 c.21 Sch.18 para.5

s.50, amended: 2003 c.21 Sch.15 para.22, Sch.19

s.50, repealed (in part): 2003 c.21 Sch.19

s.51, amended: 2003 c.21 Sch.15 para.23

s.51, repealed (in part): 2003 c.21 Sch.19

s.51, varied: 2003 c.21 Sch.18 para.26

s.52, amended: 2003 c.21 Sch.15 para.24

s.53, amended: 2003 c.21 Sch.15 para.25, Sch.19

s.53, varied: 2003 c.21 Sch.18 para.50

s.54, amended: 2003 c.21 Sch.15 para.26

s.54, repealed (in part): 2003 c.21 Sch.19

s.55, amended: 2003 c.21 Sch.13 para.5, Sch.15 para.27

s.55, applied: SI 2004/1975 Sch.1 para.3

s.56, amended: 2003 c.21 Sch.19

s.56, referred to: 2002 c.36 s.12

s.57, applied: 2003 c.21 s.204

s.57, repealed: 2003 c.21 Sch.19

s.58, amended: 2003 c.21 Sch.15 para.28

s.59, repealed: 2003 c.21 Sch.19

s.60, repealed (in part): 2003 c.21 Sch.19

s.61, amended: 2003 c.21 s.207

s.61A, amended: 2003 c.21 s.207, Sch.19

s.61A, repealed (in part): 2003 c.21 Sch.19

s.62, repealed: 2003 c.21 Sch.19

s.65, repealed: 2003 c.21 Sch.19

s.66, amended: 2003 c.21 Sch.15 para.29

s.66A, amended: 2003 c.21 Sch.15 para.30

s.66A, repealed (in part): 2003 c.21 Sch.19

s.68, repealed: 2003 c.21 Sch.19

s.69, repealed: 2003 c.21 Sch.19

s.69, varied: SI 2003/3197 Sch.2 para.106

s.70, repealed: 2003 c.21 Sch.19

s.71, amended: 2003 c.21 Sch.15 para.31, Sch.19

s.72, disapplied: 2002 c.36 s.12

s.72, repealed: 2003 c.21 Sch.19

s.72, varied: 2003 c.21 Sch.18 para.26

s.73, repealed: 2003 c.21 Sch.19

s.74, repealed: 2003 c.21 Sch.19

s.75, repealed: 2003 c.21 Sch.19

s.75, varied: 2003 c.21 Sch.18 para.26

s.76, repealed: 2003 c.21 Sch.19

s.76A, repealed: 2003 c.21 Sch.19

s.77, repealed: 2003 c.21 Sch.19

s.78, repealed: 2003 c.21 Sch.19

s.78A, repealed: 2003 c.21 Sch.19

s.79, repealed: 2003 c.21 Sch.19

s.80, repealed: 2003 c.21 Sch.19

s.81, repealed: 2003 c.21 Sch.19

s.82, repealed: 2003 c.21 Sch.19

s.83, repealed: 2003 c.21 Sch.19

s.84, disapplied: 2002 c.36 s.12

s.84, referred to: 2003 c.21 s.251

s.84, repealed: 2003 c.21 Sch.19

1990–cont.

42. Broadcasting Act 1990–*cont.*

s.85, amended: 2002 c.40 Sch.25 para.24, 2003 c.21 Sch.15 para.32

s.85, repealed (in part): 2003 c.21 Sch.19

s.86, amended: 2003 c.21 s.252, Sch.15 para.33

s.86, applied: 2003 c.21 s.251, s.356

s.86, varied: SI 2004/1944 Sch.1 para.2

s.87, amended: 2003 c.21 Sch.15 para.34, Sch.19

s.87, applied: 2003 c.21 s.347

s.87, repealed (in part): 2003 c.21 Sch.19

s.87, varied: SI 2004/1975 Art.10

s.88, amended: 2003 c.21 s.350, Sch.15 para.35

s.88, repealed (in part): 2003 c.21 Sch.19

s.88, varied: 2003 c.21 Sch.18 para.39, SI 2003/1900 Art.5

s.89, amended: 2003 c.21 Sch.15 para.36

s.89, repealed (in part): 2003 c.21 Sch.19

s.90, repealed: 2003 c.21 Sch.19

s.90, varied: 2003 c.21 Sch.18 para.42, Sch.18 para.43

s.91, repealed: 2003 c.21 Sch.19

s.91, varied: 2003 c.21 Sch.18 para.42, Sch.18 para.43

s.92, repealed: 2003 c.21 Sch.19

s.92, varied: 2003 c.21 Sch.18 para.42

s.93, repealed: 2003 c.21 Sch.19

s.93, varied: 2003 c.21 Sch.18 para.42, Sch.18 para.43

s.94, repealed: 2003 c.21 Sch.19

s.94, varied: 2003 c.21 Sch.18 para.40, Sch.18 para.42

s.95, repealed: 2003 c.21 Sch.19

s.95, varied: 2003 c.21 Sch.18 para.42

s.96, repealed: 2003 c.21 Sch.19

s.96, varied: 2003 c.21 Sch.18 para.42

s.97, amended: 2003 c.21 Sch.15 para.37

s.97, applied: 2003 c.21 s.250

s.97, disapplied: 2003 c.21 s.258

s.98, amended: 2003 c.21 s.257, Sch.15 para.38, Sch.19

s.98, applied: 2003 c.21 s.245, s.253

s.98, repealed (in part): 2003 c.21 Sch.19

s.98, varied: 2003 c.21 Sch.18 para.44

s.99, amended: 2003 c.21 Sch.15 para.39, Sch.19

s.99, repealed (in part): 2003 c.21 Sch.19

s.99, varied: 2003 c.21 Sch.18 para.44

s.100, amended: 2003 c.21 s.257, Sch.15 para.40

s.100, varied: 2003 c.21 Sch.18 para.44

s.100A, added: 2003 c.21 s.257

s.100A, varied: 2003 c.21 Sch.18 para.44

s.101, amended: 2003 c.21 Sch.13 para.6, Sch.15 para.41

s.101, applied: 2003 c.21 Sch.13 para.6

s.101, referred to: 2003 c.21 Sch.13 para.9

s.101, varied: 2003 c.21 Sch.18 para.44

1990–cont.

42. Broadcasting Act 1990–*cont.*

s.102, amended: 2003 c.21 Sch.15 para.42

s.102, applied: 2003 c.21 s.253

s.102, varied: 2003 c.21 Sch.18 para.44

s.103, amended: 2003 c.21 Sch.15 para.43

s.103, varied: 2003 c.21 Sch.18 para.44

s.103A, amended: 2003 c.21 Sch.15 para.44, Sch.19

s.103A, repealed (in part): 2003 c.21 Sch.19

s.103A, varied: 2003 c.21 Sch.18 para.44, Sch.18 para.50

s.104, amended: 2003 c.21 Sch.15 para.45

s.104, applied: 2003 c.21 s.253

s.104, varied: 2003 c.21 Sch.18 para.44, SI 2004/1944 Sch.1 para.3

s.104A, amended: 2003 c.21 s.254, Sch.15 para.46, Sch.19

s.104A, varied: 2003 c.21 Sch.18 para.44, Sch.18 para.50, SI 2004/1944 Sch.1 para.4

s.104B, amended: 2003 c.21 s.255, Sch.15 para.47

s.104B, repealed (in part): 2003 c.21 Sch.19

s.104B, varied: 2003 c.21 Sch.18 para.44, SI 2004/1944 Sch.1 para.4

s.105, amended: 2003 c.21 Sch.15 para.48

s.105, varied: 2003 c.21 Sch.18 para.44, SI 2004/1944 Sch.1 para.5

s.106, amended: 2003 c.21 s.312, Sch.15 para.49, Sch.19

s.106, applied: 2003 c.21 s.253

s.106, varied: SI 2004/1944 Sch.1 para.6

s.106A, repealed: 2003 c.21 Sch.19

s.106ZA, added: 2003 c.21 s.313

s.107, repealed: 2003 c.21 Sch.19

s.107, varied: 2003 c.21 Sch.18 para.38

s.108, repealed: 2003 c.21 Sch.19

s.109, amended: 2003 c.21 s.344, Sch.15 para.50

s.109, applied: SI 2004/1975 Sch.1 para.2

s.109, varied: 2003 c.21 s.250

s.110, amended: 2003 c.21 Sch.13 para.7, Sch.15 para.50

s.110, applied: SI 2004/1975 Sch.1 para.3

s.110, referred to: 2003 c.21 Sch.13 para.9

s.110, repealed (in part): 2003 c.21 Sch.19

s.110, varied: 2003 c.21 s.250

s.111, amended: 2003 c.21 Sch.15 para.50

s.111, applied: SI 2004/1975 Sch.1 para.3

s.111, varied: 2003 c.21 s.250

s.111A, amended: 2003 c.21 Sch.15 para.50

s.111A, varied: 2003 c.21 s.250

s.111B, amended: 2003 c.21 Sch.15 para.51

s.111B, varied: 2003 c.21 Sch.18 para.45

s.112, referred to: 2003 c.21 s.251

s.112, repealed: 2003 c.21 Sch.19

s.112, varied: 2003 c.21 Sch.18 para.26

s.113, repealed: 2003 c.21 Sch.19

s.114, amended: 2003 c.21 Sch.15 para.52

s.114, repealed (in part): 2003 c.21 Sch.19

s.114, varied: 2003 c.21 Sch.18 para.26

1990–cont.

42. Broadcasting Act 1990–*cont.*
s.115, amended: 2003 c.21 Sch.15 para.53
s.116, amended: 2003 c.21 Sch.15 para.54, Sch.19
s.117, amended: 2003 c.21 Sch.15 para.55
s.117, repealed (in part): 2003 c.21 Sch.19
s.117, varied: 2003 c.21 Sch.18 para.26
s.118, amended: 2003 c.21 Sch.15 para.56
s.119, amended: 2003 c.21 Sch.15 para.57
s.119, repealed (in part): 2003 c.21 Sch.19
s.120, amended: 2003 c.21 Sch.13 para.8, Sch.15 para.58
s.120, applied: SI 2004/1975 Sch.1 para.3
s.122, repealed: 2003 c.21 Sch.19
s.123, repealed: 2003 c.21 Sch.19
s.124, repealed: 2003 c.21 Sch.19
s.125, repealed: 2003 c.21 Sch.19
s.126, amended: 2003 c.21 s.256, Sch.15 para.59, Sch.19
s.126, varied: SI 2004/1944 Sch.1 para.7
s.127, enabling: SI 2003/2554
s.128, repealed (in part): 2004 c.14 Sch.1 Part 5
s.134, repealed: 2003 c.21 Sch.19
s.168, varied: SI 2003/3196 Art.3
s.169, varied: SI 2003/3196 Art.3
s.170, varied: SI 2003/3196 Art.3
s.171, varied: SI 2003/3196 Art.3
s.172, varied: SI 2003/3196 Art.3, Sch.1 para.2
s.173, varied: SI 2003/3196 Art.3, Sch.1 para.3
s.176, amended: 2003 c.21 Sch.15 para.60
s.177, amended: 2003 c.21 Sch.15 para.61, Sch.19
s.177, applied: 2003 c.21 Sch.1 para.6
s.180, repealed (in part): 2003 c.21 Sch.19
s.181, repealed: 2003 c.21 Sch.19
s.181, varied: 2003 c.21 Sch.18 para.26, SI 2003/3142 Art.10
s.183, amended: 2003 c.21 s.208, Sch.15 para.62, Sch.19
s.183, applied: 2003 c.21 s.208
s.183, repealed (in part): 2003 c.21 Sch.19
s.183A, added: 2003 c.21 s.209
s.184, amended: 2003 c.21 Sch.15 para.63
s.184, applied: 2003 c.21 Sch.1 para.7
s.185, amended: 2003 c.21 s.297, Sch.15 para.64, Sch.19
s.185, applied: 2003 c.21 Sch.1 para.8
s.185, varied: 2003 c.21 Sch.18 para.46
s.186, amended: 2002 c.40 Sch.25 para.24
s.186, applied: SI 2003/1672
s.186, repealed: 2003 c.21 Sch.19
s.187, amended: 2002 c.40 Sch.25 para.24
s.187, repealed (in part): 2002 c.40 Sch.26, 2003 c.21 Sch.19
s.188, repealed (in part): 2003 c.21 Sch.19
s.189, applied: 2002 c.40 s.128, s.234
s.189, repealed: 2003 c.21 Sch.19

1990–cont.

42. Broadcasting Act 1990–*cont.*
s.190, repealed: 2003 c.21 Sch.19
s.191, repealed: 2003 c.21 Sch.19
s.192, repealed: 2002 c.40 Sch.26
s.193, amended: 2003 c.21 Sch.15 para.65
s.193, substituted: 2002 c.40 Sch.9 para.6
s.193, varied: SI 2003/1592 Sch.4 para.9
s.194A, amended: 2002 c.40 Sch.25 para.24, Sch.26, 2003 c.21 s.372
s.194A, referred to: 2003 c.21 s.283
s.196, amended: 2003 c.21 Sch.15 para.66, Sch.19
s.196, applied: 2003 c.21 s.393, Sch.1 para.9
s.196, repealed (in part): 2003 c.21 Sch.19
s.197, amended: 2002 c.40 Sch.25 para.24
s.197, repealed (in part): SI 2003/1398 Sch.1 para.14
s.199, amended: 2003 c.21 Sch.15 para.67
s.201, amended: 2003 c.21 s.360, Sch.19
s.202, amended: 2003 c.21 Sch.15 para.68, Sch.19
s.204, applied: SI 2004/308, SI 2004/309, SI 2004/715, SI 2004/716
s.204, enabling: SI 2003/3192, SI 2003/3193, SI 2003/3196, SI 2003/3203, SI 2004/308, SI 2004/309, SI 2004/715, SI 2004/716
Sch.1 para.1, repealed: 2003 c.21 Sch.19
Sch.1 para.2, repealed: 2003 c.21 Sch.19
Sch.1 para.3, repealed: 2003 c.21 Sch.19
Sch.1 para.4, repealed: 2003 c.21 Sch.19
Sch.1 para.5, repealed: 2003 c.21 Sch.19
Sch.1 para.6, repealed: 2003 c.21 Sch.19
Sch.1 para.7, repealed: 2003 c.21 Sch.19
Sch.1 para.8, repealed: 2003 c.21 Sch.19
Sch.1 para.9, repealed: 2003 c.21 Sch.19
Sch.1 para.10, repealed: 2003 c.21 Sch.19
Sch.1 para.11, repealed: 2003 c.21 Sch.19
Sch.1 para.12, repealed: 2003 c.21 Sch.19
Sch.1 para.13, repealed: 2003 c.21 Sch.19
Sch.1 para.14, repealed: 2003 c.21 Sch.19
Sch.1 para.15, repealed: 2003 c.21 Sch.19
Sch.1 para.16, repealed: 2003 c.21 Sch.19
Sch.2, applied: 2003 c.21 s.355, s.359, Sch.10 para.12, SI 2003/1900 Art.5, SI 2004/1944 Art.2
Sch.2, referred to: 2003 c.21 s.391
Sch.2 Part I, applied: 2003 c.21 s.353, Sch.14 para.18, SI 2003/3299 Art.3
Sch.2 Part I, referred to: 2003 c.21 s.351
Sch.2 Part I para.1, amended: 2003 c.21 s.357, Sch.15 para.69, Sch.19, 2004 c.33 Sch.27 para.139
Sch.2 Part I para.1, applied: 2003 c.21 s.357
Sch.2 Part I para.1, repealed (in part): 2003 c.21 Sch.19
Sch.2 Part I para.1, varied: 2004 c.33 Sch.21 para.34
Sch.2 Part I para.3A, repealed: 2003 c.21 Sch.19

1990–cont.

42. Broadcasting Act 1990–*cont.*

Sch.2 Part I para.3B, repealed: 2003 c.21 Sch.19

Sch.2 Part I para.4, repealed: 2003 c.21 Sch.19

Sch.2 Part II, applied: 2003 c.21 s.281

Sch.2 Part II, referred to: 2003 c.21 Sch.14 para.18

Sch.2 Part II para.1, amended: 2003 c.21 s.349, Sch.15 para.69, Sch.19

Sch.2 Part II para.1, repealed (in part): 2003 c.21 Sch.19

Sch.2 Part II para.1, varied: SI 2004/1944 Art.6, Sch.1 para.8

Sch.2 Part II para.2, amended: 2003 c.21 s.348, Sch.15 para.69

Sch.2 Part II para.2, referred to: 2003 c.21 s.348, Sch.14 para.15

Sch.2 Part II para.2, varied: 2003 c.21 Sch.18 para.54, SI 2004/1944 Art.6

Sch.2 Part II para.3, amended: 2003 c.21 Sch.15 para.69

Sch.2 Part II para.3, varied: SI 2004/1944 Art.6, Sch.1 para.8

Sch.2 Part II para.4, amended: 2003 c.21 s.348, Sch.15 para.69

Sch.2 Part II para.4, varied: SI 2004/1944 Art.6, Sch.1 para.8

Sch.2 Part II para.5, amended: 2003 c.21 Sch.15 para.69

Sch.2 Part II para.5, varied: SI 2004/1944 Art.6

Sch.2 Part II para.5A, amended: 2003 c.21 Sch.15 para.69, Sch.19

Sch.2 Part II para.5A, repealed (in part): 2003 c.21 Sch.19

Sch.2 Part II para.5A, varied: SI 2004/1944 Art.6

Sch.2 Part II para.6, amended: 2003 c.21 Sch.15 para.69

Sch.2 Part II para.6, varied: SI 2004/1944 Art.6

Sch.2 Part III, applied: 2003 c.21 s.350, Sch.14 para.14, SI 2003/1900 Art.5

Sch.2 Part III para.1, repealed: 2003 c.21 Sch.19

Sch.2 Part III para.1, varied: 2003 c.21 Sch.18 para.54

Sch.2 Part III para.2, repealed: 2003 c.21 Sch.19

Sch.2 Part III para.2, varied: 2003 c.21 Sch.18 para.54

Sch.2 Part III para.3, repealed: 2003 c.21 Sch.19

Sch.2 Part III para.3, varied: 2003 c.21 Sch.18 para.54

Sch.2 Part III para.4, repealed: 2003 c.21 Sch.19

Sch.2 Part III para.4, varied: 2003 c.21 Sch.18 para.54

1990–cont.

42. Broadcasting Act 1990–*cont.*

Sch.2 Part III para.5, repealed: 2003 c.21 Sch.19

Sch.2 Part III para.5, varied: 2003 c.21 Sch.18 para.54

Sch.2 Part III para.6, repealed: 2003 c.21 Sch.19

Sch.2 Part III para.6, varied: 2003 c.21 Sch.18 para.54

Sch.2 Part III para.7, repealed: 2003 c.21 Sch.19

Sch.2 Part III para.7, varied: 2003 c.21 Sch.18 para.54

Sch.2 Part III para.8, repealed: 2003 c.21 Sch.19

Sch.2 Part III para.8, varied: 2003 c.21 Sch.18 para.54

Sch.2 Part III para.9, repealed: 2003 c.21 Sch.19

Sch.2 Part III para.9, varied: 2003 c.21 Sch.18 para.54

Sch.2 Part III para.10, repealed: 2003 c.21 Sch.19

Sch.2 Part III para.10, varied: 2003 c.21 Sch.18 para.54

Sch.2 Part III para.11, applied: 2003 c.21 Sch.14 para.8

Sch.2 Part III para.11, repealed: 2003 c.21 Sch.19

Sch.2 Part III para.11, varied: 2003 c.21 Sch.18 para.54

Sch.2 Part III para.12, repealed: 2003 c.21 Sch.19

Sch.2 Part III para.12, varied: 2003 c.21 Sch.18 para.54

Sch.2 Part III para.13, repealed: 2003 c.21 Sch.19

Sch.2 Part III para.13, varied: 2003 c.21 Sch.18 para.54

Sch.2 Part III para.14, repealed: 2003 c.21 Sch.19

Sch.2 Part III para.14, varied: 2003 c.21 Sch.18 para.54

Sch.2 Part III para.15, repealed: 2003 c.21 Sch.19

Sch.2 Part III para.15, varied: 2003 c.21 Sch.18 para.54

Sch.2 Part III para.16, repealed: 2003 c.21 Sch.19

Sch.2 Part III para.16, varied: 2003 c.21 Sch.18 para.54

Sch.2 Part III para.17, repealed: 2003 c.21 Sch.19

Sch.2 Part III para.17, varied: 2003 c.21 Sch.18 para.54

Sch.2 Part IV, applied: 2003 c.21 s.350, Sch.14 para.14, SI 2003/1900 Art.5

Sch.2 Part IV para.1, repealed: 2003 c.21 Sch.19

Sch.2 Part IV para.1, varied: 2003 c.21 Sch.18 para.54

1990–cont.

42. Broadcasting Act 1990–cont.

Sch.2 Part IV para.2, repealed: 2003 c.21 Sch.19

Sch.2 Part IV para.2, varied: 2003 c.21 Sch.18 para.54

Sch.2 Part IV para.3, repealed: 2003 c.21 Sch.19

Sch.2 Part IV para.3, varied: 2003 c.21 Sch.18 para.54

Sch.2 Part IV para.4, repealed: 2003 c.21 Sch.19

Sch.2 Part IV para.4, varied: 2003 c.21 Sch.18 para.54

Sch.2 Part IV para.5, repealed: 2003 c.21 Sch.19

Sch.2 Part IV para.5, varied: 2003 c.21 Sch.18 para.54

Sch.2 Part IV para.6, repealed: 2003 c.21 Sch.19

Sch.2 Part IV para.6, varied: 2003 c.21 Sch.18 para.54

Sch.2 Part IV para.7, repealed: 2003 c.21 Sch.19

Sch.2 Part IV para.7, varied: 2003 c.21 Sch.18 para.54

Sch.2 Part IV para.8, repealed: 2003 c.21 Sch.19

Sch.2 Part IV para.8, varied: 2003 c.21 Sch.18 para.54

Sch.2 Part IV para.9, repealed: 2003 c.21 Sch.19

Sch.2 Part IV para.9, varied: 2003 c.21 Sch.18 para.54

Sch.2 Part IV para.10, repealed: 2003 c.21 Sch.19

Sch.2 Part IV para.10, varied: 2003 c.21 Sch.18 para.54

Sch.2 Part IV para.11, repealed: 2003 c.21 Sch.19

Sch.2 Part IV para.11, varied: 2003 c.21 Sch.18 para.54

Sch.2 Part IV para.12, repealed: 2003 c.21 Sch.19

Sch.2 Part IV para.12, varied: 2003 c.21 Sch.18 para.54

Sch.2 Part IV para.13, repealed: 2003 c.21 Sch.19

Sch.2 Part IV para.13, varied: 2003 c.21 Sch.18 para.54

Sch.2 Part IV para.14, repealed: 2003 c.21 Sch.19

Sch.2 Part IV para.14, varied: 2003 c.21 Sch.18 para.54

Sch.2 Part IV para.15, repealed: 2003 c.21 Sch.19

Sch.2 Part IV para.15, varied: 2003 c.21 Sch.18 para.54

Sch.2 Part V, applied: SI 2003/1900 Art.5

Sch.2 Part V, repealed: 2003 c.21 Sch.19

Sch.2 Part V, varied: 2003 c.21 Sch.18 para.26, Sch.18 para.54

1990–cont.

42. Broadcasting Act 1990–cont.

Sch.3, applied: 2003 c.21 Sch.1 para.4

Sch.3 para.1, amended: 2003 c.21 s.199, Sch.15 para.70

Sch.3 para.2, amended: 2003 c.21 Sch.15 para.70

Sch.3 para.3, amended: 2003 c.21 s.200, Sch.15 para.70

Sch.3 para.4, amended: 2003 c.21 Sch.15 para.70

Sch.3 para.5, amended: 2003 c.21 Sch.15 para.70

Sch.3 para.6, amended: 2003 c.21 Sch.15 para.70

Sch.3 para.7, amended: 2003 c.21 Sch.15 para.70

Sch.3 para.8, amended: 2003 c.21 Sch.15 para.70

Sch.3 para.9, amended: 2003 c.21 Sch.15 para.70

Sch.3 para.10, amended: 2003 c.21 Sch.15 para.70

Sch.3 para.11, amended: 2003 c.21 Sch.15 para.70

Sch.3 para.12, amended: 2003 c.21 Sch.15 para.70

Sch.3 para.12, applied: 2003 c.21 Sch.9 para.2

Sch.3 para.13, amended: 2003 c.21 Sch.15 para.70

Sch.4, amended: 2002 c.40 Sch.25 para.24

Sch.4, applied: SI 2003/1397 Art.8

Sch.4, amended: 2002 c.40 Sch.25 para.24

Sch.4 para.1, amended: 2002 c.40 Sch.25 para.24

Sch.4 para.1, repealed: 2003 c.21 Sch.19

Sch.4 para.1, varied: 2003 c.21 Sch.18 para.36

Sch.4 para.2, amended: 2002 c.40 Sch.25 para.24

Sch.4 para.2, repealed: 2003 c.21 Sch.19

Sch.4 para.2, varied: 2003 c.21 Sch.18 para.36

Sch.4 para.3, amended: 2002 c.40 Sch.25 para.24

Sch.4 para.3, repealed: 2003 c.21 Sch.19

Sch.4 para.3, varied: 2003 c.21 Sch.18 para.36

Sch.4 para.4, amended: 2002 c.40 Sch.25 para.24

Sch.4 para.4, repealed (in part): 2002 c.40 Sch.26, 2003 c.21 Sch.19

Sch.4 para.4, varied: 2003 c.21 Sch.18 para.36

Sch.4 para.4A, added: 2002 c.40 Sch.25 para.24

Sch.4 para.4A, referred to: SI 2003/1371

Sch.4 para.4A, repealed: 2003 c.21 Sch.19

Sch.4 para.4A, varied: 2003 c.21 Sch.18 para.36

Sch.4 para.4A, enabling: SI 2003/1371

1990–cont.

42. Broadcasting Act 1990–*cont.*

Sch.4 para.5, amended: 2002 c.40 Sch.25 para.24

Sch.4 para.5, repealed (in part): 2002 c.40 Sch.26, 2003 c.21 Sch.19

Sch.4 para.5, varied: 2003 c.21 Sch.18 para.36

Sch.4 para.5A, added: 2002 c.40 Sch.25 para.24

Sch.4 para.5A, repealed: 2003 c.21 Sch.19

Sch.4 para.5A, varied: 2003 c.21 Sch.18 para.36

Sch.4 para.5B, added: 2002 c.40 Sch.25 para.24

Sch.4 para.5B, repealed: 2003 c.21 Sch.19

Sch.4 para.5B, varied: 2003 c.21 Sch.18 para.36

Sch.4 para.5C, added: 2002 c.40 Sch.25 para.24

Sch.4 para.5C, repealed: 2003 c.21 Sch.19

Sch.4 para.5C, varied: 2003 c.21 Sch.18 para.36

Sch.4 para.5D, added: 2002 c.40 Sch.25 para.24

Sch.4 para.5D, repealed: 2003 c.21 Sch.19

Sch.4 para.5D, varied: 2003 c.21 Sch.18 para.36

Sch.4 para.5E, added: 2002 c.40 Sch.25 para.24

Sch.4 para.5E, repealed: 2003 c.21 Sch.19

Sch.4 para.5E, varied: 2003 c.21 Sch.18 para.36

Sch.4 para.5F, added: 2002 c.40 Sch.25 para.24

Sch.4 para.5F, repealed: 2003 c.21 Sch.19

Sch.4 para.5F, varied: 2003 c.21 Sch.18 para.36

Sch.4 para.5G, added: 2002 c.40 Sch.25 para.24

Sch.4 para.5G, repealed: 2003 c.21 Sch.19

Sch.4 para.5G, varied: 2003 c.21 Sch.18 para.36

Sch.4 para.6, amended: 2002 c.40 Sch.25 para.24

Sch.4 para.6, repealed: 2003 c.21 Sch.19

Sch.4 para.6, varied: 2003 c.21 Sch.18 para.36

Sch.4 para.7, amended: 2002 c.40 Sch.25 para.24

Sch.4 para.7, repealed: 2003 c.21 Sch.19

Sch.4 para.7, varied: 2003 c.21 Sch.18 para.36

Sch.4 para.8, amended: 2002 c.40 Sch.25 para.24

Sch.4 para.8, repealed (in part): 2002 c.40 Sch.26, 2003 c.21 Sch.19

Sch.4 para.8, varied: 2003 c.21 Sch.18 para.36

Sch.4 para.8A, repealed: 2003 c.21 Sch.19

Sch.4 para.8A, varied: 2003 c.21 Sch.18 para.36

1990–cont.

42. Broadcasting Act 1990–*cont.*

Sch.4 para.8A, added: 2002 c.40 Sch.25 para.24, SI 2003/1398 Sch.1 para.14

Sch.4 para.8A, repealed: 2003 c.21 Sch.19

Sch.4 para.8A, varied: 2003 c.21 Sch.18 para.36

Sch.4 para.8B, repealed: 2003 c.21 Sch.19

Sch.4 para.8B, varied: 2003 c.21 Sch.18 para.36

Sch.4 para.8B, added: 2002 c.40 Sch.25 para.24

Sch.4 para.8B, repealed: 2003 c.21 Sch.19

Sch.4 para.8B, varied: 2003 c.21 Sch.18 para.36

Sch.4 para.8C, repealed: 2003 c.21 Sch.19

Sch.4 para.8C, varied: 2003 c.21 Sch.18 para.36

Sch.4 para.8C, added: 2002 c.40 Sch.25 para.24

Sch.4 para.8C, repealed: 2003 c.21 Sch.19

Sch.4 para.8C, varied: 2003 c.21 Sch.18 para.36

Sch.4 para.9, amended: 2002 c.40 Sch.25 para.24

Sch.4 para.9, repealed: 2003 c.21 Sch.19

Sch.4 para.9, varied: 2003 c.21 Sch.18 para.36

Sch.4 para.10, amended: 2002 c.40 Sch.25 para.24, Sch.26

Sch.4 para.10, repealed: 2003 c.21 Sch.19

Sch.4 para.10, varied: 2003 c.21 Sch.18 para.36

Sch.5 para.1, repealed: 2003 c.21 Sch.19

Sch.5 para.2, repealed: 2003 c.21 Sch.19

Sch.5 para.3, repealed: 2003 c.21 Sch.19

Sch.5 para.4, repealed: 2003 c.21 Sch.19

Sch.5 para.5, repealed: 2003 c.21 Sch.19

Sch.5 para.6, repealed: 2003 c.21 Sch.19

Sch.5 para.7, repealed: 2003 c.21 Sch.19

Sch.6 para.1, amended: 2003 c.21 s.206

Sch.6 para.2, amended: 2003 c.21 Sch.15 para.71

Sch.6 para.2, repealed (in part): 2003 c.21 Sch.19

Sch.6 para.12, amended: 2003 c.21 Sch.15 para.71

Sch.6 para.13, amended: 2003 c.21 s.342, Sch.19

Sch.7 Part I, applied: 2003 c.21 s.227, Sch.10 para.15

Sch.7 Part I para.1, amended: 2003 c.21 Sch.15 para.72

Sch.7 Part I para.1, varied: 2003 c.21 s.237, Sch.9 para.8, Sch.18 para.37

Sch.7 Part I para.2, amended: 2003 c.21 Sch.15 para.72

Sch.7 Part I para.2, varied: 2003 c.21 s.237, Sch.9 para.8, Sch.18 para.37

Sch.7 Part II para.1, amended: 2003 c.21 Sch.15 para.72

1990–cont.

42. Broadcasting Act 1990–*cont.*

Sch.7 Part II para.1, varied: 2003 c.21 Sch.18 para.37

Sch.7 Part II para.2, amended: 2003 c.21 Sch.15 para.72

Sch.7 Part II para.2, varied: 2003 c.21 Sch.18 para.37

Sch.8 para.1, repealed: 2003 c.21 Sch.19

Sch.8 para.2, repealed: 2003 c.21 Sch.19

Sch.8 para.3, repealed: 2003 c.21 Sch.19

Sch.8 para.4, repealed: 2003 c.21 Sch.19

Sch.8 para.5, repealed: 2003 c.21 Sch.19

Sch.8 para.6, repealed: 2003 c.21 Sch.19

Sch.8 para.7, repealed: 2003 c.21 Sch.19

Sch.8 para.8, repealed: 2003 c.21 Sch.19

Sch.8 para.9, repealed: 2003 c.21 Sch.19

Sch.8 para.10, repealed: 2003 c.21 Sch.19

Sch.8 para.11, repealed: 2003 c.21 Sch.19

Sch.8 para.12, repealed: 2003 c.21 Sch.19

Sch.8 para.13, repealed: 2003 c.21 Sch.19

Sch.8 para.14, repealed: 2003 c.21 Sch.19

Sch.8 para.15, repealed: 2003 c.21 Sch.19

Sch.8 para.16, repealed: 2003 c.21 Sch.19

Sch.10 para.4, repealed: 2004 c.14 Sch.1 Part 5

Sch.12 Part I para.1, repealed: 2003 c.21 Sch.19

Sch.12 Part I para.2, repealed: 2003 c.21 Sch.19

Sch.12 Part II para.1, repealed: 2003 c.21 Sch.19

Sch.12 Part II para.2, repealed: 2003 c.21 Sch.19

Sch.12 Part II para.3, repealed: 2003 c.21 Sch.19

Sch.12 Part II para.4, repealed: 2003 c.21 Sch.19

Sch.12 Part II para.4A, repealed: 2003 c.21 Sch.19

Sch.12 Part II para.5, repealed: 2003 c.21 Sch.19

Sch.12 Part II para.6, repealed: 2003 c.21 Sch.19

Sch.12 Part II para.7, repealed: 2003 c.21 Sch.19

Sch.12 Part II para.8, repealed: 2003 c.21 Sch.19

Sch.12 Part II para.9, repealed: 2003 c.21 Sch.19

Sch.12 Part II para.10, repealed: 2003 c.21 Sch.19

Sch.12 Part II para.11, repealed: 2003 c.21 Sch.19

Sch.12 Part II para.12, repealed: 2003 c.21 Sch.19

Sch.12 Part III para.1, repealed: 2003 c.21 Sch.19

Sch.12 Part III para.2, repealed: 2003 c.21 Sch.19

Sch.12 Part III para.3, repealed: 2003 c.21 Sch.19

1990–cont.

42. Broadcasting Act 1990–*cont.*

Sch.12 Part III para.4, repealed: 2003 c.21 Sch.19

Sch.12 Part III para.4A, repealed: 2003 c.21 Sch.19

Sch.12 Part III para.5, repealed: 2003 c.21 Sch.19

Sch.12 Part III para.6, repealed: 2003 c.21 Sch.19

Sch.12 Part III para.7, repealed: 2003 c.21 Sch.19

Sch.18 Part I para.1, repealed (in part): 2003 c.21 Sch.19

Sch.18 Part I para.2, repealed (in part): 2003 c.21 Sch.19

Sch.18 Part I para.4, repealed: 2003 c.21 Sch.19

Sch.18 Part II para.1, repealed (in part): 2003 c.21 Sch.19

Sch.18 Part II para.5, repealed: 2003 c.21 Sch.19

Sch.19, applied: 2003 c.21 Sch.1 para.7

Sch.19 para.1, amended: 2003 c.21 Sch.15 para.73

Sch.19 para.2, amended: 2003 c.21 s.210, Sch.15 para.73

Sch.19 para.3, amended: 2003 c.21 Sch.15 para.73

Sch.19 para.4, amended: 2003 c.21 Sch.15 para.73

Sch.19 para.5, amended: 2003 c.21 Sch.15 para.73

Sch.19 para.6, amended: 2003 c.21 Sch.15 para.73

Sch.19 para.7, amended: 2003 c.21 s.210, Sch.15 para.73

Sch.19 para.8, amended: 2003 c.21 Sch.15 para.73, Sch.19

Sch.19 para.8A, added: 2003 c.21 s.210

Sch.19 para.8A, amended: 2003 c.21 Sch.15 para.73

Sch.19 para.9, amended: 2003 c.21 Sch.15 para.73

Sch.19 para.10, amended: 2003 c.21 Sch.15 para.73

Sch.19 para.11, amended: 2003 c.21 Sch.15 para.73, Sch.19

Sch.19 para.12, amended: 2003 c.21 s.210, Sch.15 para.73

Sch.20 para.7, repealed: 2003 c.17 Sch.7

Sch.20 para.8, repealed: 2003 c.17 Sch.7

Sch.20 para.9, repealed: 2003 c.21 Sch.19

Sch.20 para.20, repealed: 2002 c.40 Sch.26

Sch.20 para.24, repealed (in part): 2003 c.21 Sch.19

Sch.20 para.28, repealed: 2002 c.40 Sch.26

Sch.20 para.29, repealed (in part): 2003 c.44 Sch.37 Part 4

Sch.20 para.38, repealed: 2003 c.21 Sch.19

Sch.20 para.54, repealed: 2003 c.21 Sch.19

Sch.22 para.1, repealed: 2003 c.21 Sch.19

CAP.

CAP.

1990–cont.

42. Broadcasting Act 1990–*cont.*
Sch.22 para.2, repealed: 2003 c.21 Sch.19
Sch.22 para.3, repealed: 2003 c.21 Sch.19
Sch.22 para.4, amended: 2003 c.21 Sch.19
Sch.22 para.5, repealed: 2003 c.21 Sch.19

43. Environmental Protection Act 1990
see *Brent LBC v Reynolds* [2001] EWCA Civ
1843, [2002] H.L.R.15 (CA), Buxton, L.J.;
see *Environment Agency v R Newcomb &
Sons Ltd* [2002] EWHC 2095, [2003] Env.
L.R.12 (QBD (Admin Ct)), Newman, J.; see
*R. (on the application of United Kingdom
Renderers Association Ltd) v Secretary of
State for the Environment, Transport and
the Regions* [2001] EWHC Admin 675,
[2002] Env. L.R. 21 (QBD (Admin Ct)),
Ouseley, J.; see *Woods v Sevenoaks DC*
[2004] EWHC 1511, [2004] N.P.C. 97
(QBD (Admin Ct)), McCombe, J.
applied: SI 2002/843 Reg.68, SI 2002/1416
Reg.68, SI 2002/3188 Reg.15, Reg.17,
Reg.21, Reg.24, Reg.26, SSI 2002/255
Reg.67, Sch.5, SSI 2002/541 Reg.2,
Reg.20, Reg.23, 2004 asp 8 s.60
referred to: 2003 c.38 s.55, s.56
Part I, applied: SI 2002/2688 Reg.5, SSI
2002/493 Reg.5
Part II, added: 2003 asp 1 s.34
Part IV, applied: 2003 c.26 s.119
Part VI, applied: SI 2002/2443 Reg.5, SI
2002/3188 Reg.38, SI 2004/2412 Reg.4,
SI 2004/2692 Reg.5, SSI 2002/541
Reg.5, SSI 2004/438 Reg.3
Part VI, referred to: SSI 2002/541 Reg.2,
Reg.34
s.3, repealed (in part): SI 2002/3153 Sch.6
Part I
s.6, see *R. (on the application of Furness) v
Environment Agency* [2001] EWHC
Admin 1058, [2002] Env. L.R. 26 (QBD
(Admin Ct)), Turner, J.
s.11, applied: SI 2002/2980 Reg.3, SI 2004/
107 Reg.3, SSI 2003/170 Reg.3, SSI 2004/
26 Reg.3, Reg.5
s.23, see *R. v Clutton Agriculture Ltd* [2001]
EWCA Crim 2710, [2002] Env. L.R.19 (CA
(Crim Div)), Judge Openshaw Q.C.
s.23, amended: 2004 asp 8 Sch.2 para.4
s.29, enabling: SI 2002/674, SI 2002/1087,
SI 2004/70, SSI 2004/275
s.33, see *Environment Agency v ME Foley
Contractors Ltd* [2002] EWHC 258,
[2002] 1 W.L.R. 1754 (QBD (Admin Ct)),
Auld, L.J.; see *Environment Agency v
Melland* [2002] EWHC 904, [2002]
R.T.R. 25 (QBD (Admin Ct)), Harrison, J.;
see *R. (on the application of Philcox) v
Epping Forest DC* [2002] Env. L.R. 2
(CA), Pill, L.J.
s.33, amended: 2004 asp 8 Sch.2 para.4
s.33, applied: SI 2003/780, SSI 2004/426
Art.2

1990–cont.

43. Environmental Protection Act 1990–
cont.
s.33, referred to: SI 2003/595, SI 2003/780
s.33, enabling: SI 2003/595, SI 2003/780,
SSI 2004/275
s.33A, added: 2004 asp 8 s.55
s.33A, enabling: SSI 2004/426
s.34, see *Gateway Professional Services
(Management) Ltd v Kingston upon Hull
City Council* [2004] EWHC 597, [2004]
Env. L.R. 42 (QBD (Admin Ct)), Laws, L.J.
s.34, enabling: SI 2003/63, SI 2003/1720,
SSI 2003/533
s.35, applied: SI 2002/843 Reg.64, Reg.68,
SI 2002/1416 Reg.64, Reg.68, SSI 2002/
255 Reg.63, Reg.67
s.36, amended: 2004 asp 6 Sch.7 para.7
s.36, referred to: SI 2003/2635 Reg.49, SSI
2003/593 Reg.8
s.37, disapplied: SI 2003/2635 Reg.44,
Reg.46, SSI 2003/593 Reg.3, Reg.5
s.37A, disapplied: SI 2003/2635 Reg.44,
Reg.46, SSI 2003/593 Reg.3, Reg.5
s.44A, applied: 2003 c.33 s.17, s.19
s.45, amended: 2002 asp 3 Sch.7 para.20
s.45A, added: 2003 c.29 s.1
s.45B, added: 2003 c.29 s.2
s.47A, added: 2003 c.29 s.3
s.48, amended: 2003 c.33 s.31
s.49, referred to: 2003 c.33 s.35
s.49, repealed (in part): 2003 asp1 s.34, 2003
c.33 s.35
s.51, see *Durham CC v Darlington BC* [2003]
EWHC 2598, [2004] B.L.G.R. 311 (QBD
(Admin Ct)), Stanley Burnton, J.; see *R. v
Brighton and Hove Council Ex p. Rayson*
[2003] Env. L.R.14 (QBD), Sullivan, J.
s.51, amended: 2003 c.33 s.31
s.52, applied: SI 2004/639 Reg.3
s.52, enabling: SI 2002/531, SI 2003/596, SI
2004/639
s.52A, added: 2003 c.33 s.31
s.53, amended: 2002 asp 3 Sch.7 para.20
s.53, repealed (in part): 2002 asp 3 Sch.7
para.20
s.59A, added: 2003 c.38 s.55
s.64, enabling: SI 2004/70
s.71, amended: 2003 c.38 s.55
s.74, enabling: SI 2003/171, SI 2003/595, SI
2003/780, SSI 2004/275
s.75, applied: SI 2003/2454 Sch.3, SI 2003/
2761 Sch.3
s.77, repealed (in part): 2004 c.14 Sch.1 Part
13
s.78A, amended: 2003 c.37 s.86
s.78A, repealed (in part): 2003 c.37 s.86,
Sch.9 Part 3
s.78C, amended: 2003 c.37 s.86
s.78E, amended: 2003 c.37 s.86
s.78K, amended: 2003 c.37 s.86
s.78X, amended: 2003 c.37 s.86

1990–cont.

43. Environmental Protection Act 1990– *cont.*

s.78YB, amended: 2003 c.37 s.86

s.79, see *Hounslow LBC v Thames Water Utilities Ltd* [2003] EWHC 1197, [2004] Q.B. 212 (QBD (Admin Ct)), Pitchford, J.; see *R. (on the application of Anne) v Test Valley BC* [2001] EWHC Admin 1019, [2002] Env. L.R. 22 (QBD (Admin Ct)), Forbes, J.; see *Robb v Dundee City Council* 2002 S.C. 301 (Ex Div), Lord Cameron of Lochbroom, Lord Johnston, Lady Paton; see *Tee-Hillman v Southampton Crown Court* [2003] EWHC 237, [2003] E.H.L.R.14 (QBD (Admin Ct)), Henriques, J.; see *Tewkesbury BC v Deacon* [2003] EWHC 2544, [2004] Env. L.R. 22 (QBD (Admin Ct)), Evans-Lombe, J.

s.79, applied: SI 2003/1075 Art.35, SI 2004/ 389 Art.33, SI 2004/757 Art.50

s.79, referred to: SI 2002/1066 Art.43

s.80, see *Bradford MDC v Yorkshire Water Services Ltd* [2001] EWHC Admin 687, [2002] Env. L.R. 16 (QBD (Admin Ct)), Brooke, L.J.; see *Camden LBC v Easynet Ltd* [2002] EWHC 2929, [2003] E.H.L.R. 5 (QBD (Admin Ct)), Stanley Burnton, J.; see *Lewisham LBC v Hall* [2002] EWHC 960, [2002] E.H.L.R. Dig. 9 (QBD (Admin Ct)), Moses, J.; see *Stratford upon Avon DC v Hitchman* [2002] Env. L.R. 7 (QBD), Judge Peter Clark; see *Tee-Hillman v Southampton Crown Court* [2003] EWHC 237, [2003] E.H.L.R. 14 (QBD (Admin Ct)), Henriques, J.; see *Tewkesbury BC v Deacon* [2003] EWHC 2544, [2004] Env. L.R. 22 (QBD (Admin Ct)), Evans-Lombe, J.

s.80, amended: 2004 asp 8 Sch.2 para.4

s.80, applied: 2004 c.i Sch.2

s.81, amended: 2004 asp 8 Sch.4 para.3

s.82, see *Jones v Walsall MBC* [2002] EWHC 1232, [2003] Env. L.R. 5 (QBD (Admin Ct)), Michael Supperstone Q.C.; see *R. (on the application of Islington LBC) v Inner London Crown Court* [2003] EWHC 2500, [2004] Env. L.R. 20 (QBD (Admin Ct)), Brooke, L.J.; see *Robb v Dundee City Council* 2002 S.C. 301 (Ex Div), Lord Cameron of Lochbroom, Lord Johnston, Lady Paton

s.82, applied: SI 2002/1066 Art.43, SI 2003/ 1075 Art.35, SI 2004/389 Art.33, SI 2004/ 757 Art.50

s.86, referred to: SI 2002/757 Sch.5

s.87, applied: SI 2002/1837 Sch.1 Part II, SSI 2004/427 Art.2

s.88, amended: SI 2002/424 Art.2, SI 2004/ 909 Art.2, SSI 2003/268 Art.2, 2004 asp 8 s.56

1990–cont.

43. Environmental Protection Act 1990– *cont.*

s.88, applied: 2002 c.30 Sch.4 para.1, Sch.5 para.1, 2003 c.26 s.119, SI 2004/915 Sch.1 para.1

s.88, repealed (in part): 2003 c.26 Sch.8 Part 1

s.88, substituted: SI 2004/909 Art.2

s.88, varied: SI 2002/425 Art.2, 2004 c.i s.28

s.88, enabling: SI 2002/424, SI 2002/425, SI 2004/909, SSI 2003/268, SSI 2004/427

s.89, amended: 2004 asp 8 s.57

s.91, amended: 2004 asp 8 s.57

s.92, amended: 2003 c.38 s.56, 2004 asp 8 s.57

s.98, amended: 2002 c.32 Sch.7 para.2

s.98, repealed (in part): 2002 c.32 Sch.21 para.10, Sch.22 Part 3

s.106, amended: SI 2002/2443 Reg.3, SI 2002/3188 Reg.4, SSI 2002/541 Reg.3

s.106, applied: SI 2002/2443 Reg.5, SI 2002/3188 Reg.6, SSI 2002/541 Reg.5

s.106, repealed (in part): SI 2002/2443 Reg.3, SI 2002/3188 Reg.4, SSI 2002/ 541 Reg.3

s.106, substituted: SI 2002/2443 Reg.3

s.106, varied: SI 2002/3188 Reg.6

s.106, enabling: SI 2002/3188

s.107, amended: SI 2002/2443 Reg.4, SI 2002/3188 Reg.5, SSI 2002/541 Reg.4

s.107, varied: SI 2002/3188 Reg.6

s.107, enabling: SI 2002/3188

s.108, applied: SI 2002/2443 Reg.15, SI 2002/3188 Reg.16, SSI 2002/541 Reg.15

s.108, disapplied: SI 2002/2443 Reg.17A, SSI 2002/541 Reg.17A

s.108, referred to: SI 2002/2443 Reg.15

s.108, varied: SI 2002/3188 Reg.6

s.108, enabling: SI 2002/2443

s.109, varied: SI 2002/3188 Reg.6

s.110, applied: SI 2002/2443 Reg.32, Reg.34, SI 2002/3188 Reg.33, Reg.35, SSI 2002/541 Reg.32, Reg.34

s.110, varied: SI 2002/3188 Reg.6

s.111, amended: SI 2002/2443 Reg.19, SI 2002/3188 Reg.20, SSI 2002/541 Reg.19

s.111, applied: SI 2002/2443 Reg.8, Reg.9, Reg.14, Reg.15, Reg.16, Reg.18, Reg.19, Reg.21, Reg.22, Reg.23, Reg.28, Reg.31, Reg.32, Reg.34, SI 2002/3188 Reg.9, Reg.10, Reg.16, Reg.17, Reg.19, Reg.20, Reg.22, Reg.23, Reg.24, Reg.29, Reg.32, Reg.33, Reg.35, SSI 2002/541 Reg.8, Reg.9, Reg.14, Reg.15, Reg.16, Reg.18, Reg.19, Reg.21, Reg.22, Reg.23, Reg.28, Reg.31, Reg.34

s.111, disapplied: SI 2002/2443 Reg.17A, SSI 2002/541 Reg.17A

s.111, referred to: SI 2002/800 Sch.1, SI 2002/2443 Reg.9, Reg.15

s.111, varied: SI 2002/3188 Reg.6

1990–cont.

43. Environmental Protection Act 1990–
cont.

s.111, enabling: SI 2002/2443, SI 2002/3188

s.112, amended: SI 2002/2443 Reg.29, SI 2002/3188 Reg.30, SSI 2002/541 Reg.29

s.112, applied: SI 2002/2443 Reg.34, SI 2002/3188 Reg.35, SSI 2002/541 Reg.34

s.112, repealed (in part): SI 2002/2443 Reg.29, SI 2002/3188 Reg.30, SSI 2002/541 Reg.29

s.112, varied: SI 2002/3188 Reg.6

s.113, varied: SI 2002/3188 Reg.6

s.114, varied: SI 2002/3188 Reg.6

s.115, varied: SI 2002/3188 Reg.6

s.116, varied: SI 2002/3188 Reg.6

s.117, varied: SI 2002/3188 Reg.6

s.118, amended: 2003 c.44 Sch.37 Part 9

s.118, applied: SI 2002/2443 Reg.34, SI 2002/3188 Reg.35, SSI 2002/541 Reg.34

s.118, disapplied: 2003 c.44 Sch.25 para.87

s.118, varied: SI 2002/3188 Reg.6

s.119, amended: SI 2002/2443 Reg.30, SI 2002/3188 Reg.31, SSI 2002/541 Reg.30

s.119, varied: SI 2002/3188 Reg.6

s.120, applied: SI 2002/2443 Reg.34, SI 2002/3188 Reg.35, SSI 2002/541 Reg.34

s.120, varied: SI 2002/3188 Reg.6

s.121, varied: SI 2002/3188 Reg.6

s.122, applied: SSI 2002/541 Reg.34

s.122, referred to: SI 2002/800 Sch.1

s.122, varied: SI 2002/3188 Reg.6

s.122, enabling: SI 2002/2443, SI 2002/3188

s.123, amended: SI 2002/2443 Reg.33, SI 2002/3188 Reg.34, SSI 2002/541 Reg.33

s.123, applied: SI 2002/2443 Reg.33, SI 2002/3188 Reg.34, SSI 2002/541 Reg.33

s.123, referred to: SI 2002/800 Sch.1

s.123, repealed (in part): SI 2002/2443 Reg.33, SI 2002/3188 Reg.34, SSI 2002/541 Reg.33

s.123, varied: SI 2002/3188 Reg.6

s.123, enabling: SI 2002/2443, SI 2002/3188

s.124, varied: SI 2002/3188 Reg.6

s.125, varied: SI 2002/3188 Reg.6

s.126, applied: SI 2002/2443, SI 2002/2443 Reg.32, SI 2002/3188, SSI 2002/541 Reg.32

s.126, varied: SI 2002/3188 Reg.6

s.126, enabling: SI 2002/3188

s.127, amended: SI 2002/2443 Reg.38, SI 2002/3188 Reg.40

s.127, varied: SI 2002/3188 Reg.6

s.140, applied: SI 2002/2102(a), SI 2002/528, SI 2002/528 Reg.4, SI 2002/1730, SI 2003/2512(a), SI 2003/409 Sch.1 Part I, SSI 2004/289, SSI 2004/358

s.140, enabling: SI 2002/528, SI 2002/1730, SI 2002/2102, SI 2003/2512, SSI 2004/289, SSI 2004/358

1990–cont.

43. Environmental Protection Act 1990–
cont.

s.141, amended: 2003 c.44 Sch.27 para.6

s.153, amended: SI 2002/1686 Art.2, SI 2002/2021 Art.2, SI 2003/714 Art.2, SI 2003/2119 Art.2, SSI 2002/83 Art.2

s.153, varied: SSI 2003/173 Art.2

s.153, enabling: SI 2002/1686, SI 2002/2021, SI 2003/714, SI 2003/2119, SSI 2002/83, SSI 2003/173

s.156, enabling: SI 2002/2443

s.157, applied: 2003 asp 3 Sch.2 para.15

s.158, applied: 2003 asp 3 Sch.2 para.15

s.160, applied: 2003 asp 3 Sch.2 para.15, 2004 asp 8 s.60

s.160, varied: 2003 c.38 s.48, s.49

s.163A, added: SI 2002/2443 Reg.39

s.163A, repealed (in part): SI 2002/3188 Reg.41

s.164, amended: SI 2002/3153 Sch.6 Part I, 2003 c.29 s.4

s79., see *Jones v Walsall MBC* [2002] EWHC 1232, [2003] Env. L.R. 5 (QBD (Admin Ct)), Michael Supperstone Q.C.

Sch.13 Part I para.2, repealed (in part): 2004 c.14 Sch.1 Part 13

Sch.13 Part I para.6, repealed: 2004 c.14 Sch.1 Part 13

Sch.15 para.21, repealed: 2004 c.14 Sch.1 Part 13

1991

xix. City of Edinburgh District Council Order Confirmation Act 1991

Sch.1, disapplied: 2003 asp 16 s.1

Criminal Law (Measures) Act (Bahamas) 1991

see *Pinder v Queen, The* [2002] UKPC 46, [2003] 1 A.C. 620 (PC (Bah)), Lord Millett

xvi. Greater Manchester (Light Rapid Transit System) Act 1991

applied: SI 2003/2907 Art.3

s.4, amended: SI 2003/2907 Art.3

s.4, referred to: SI 2003/2907 Art.3

vii. Heathrow Express Railway Act 1991

referred to: SI 2002/1064 Art.17, SI 2002/1065 Art.21

s.43, repealed (in part): SI 2002/1064 Art.33

xii. Highland Regional Council (Harbours) Order Confirmation Act 1991. 1991

applied: SSI 2004/171 Art.3

s.3, varied: SSI 2004/171 Art.3

s.59, disapplied: SSI 2004/171 Art.3

s.62, disapplied: SSI 2004/171 Art.3

s.64, disapplied: SSI 2004/171 Art.3

Sch.1, varied: SSI 2004/171 Art.3

xiii. London Local Authorities Act 1991

referred to: 2003 c.43 Sch.4 para.91

s.2, amended: 2004 c.i Sch.5

CAP.

1991–cont.

xiii. London Local Authorities Act 1991– cont.

s.4, amended: SI 2002/254 Sch.4 para.5, 2003 c.43 Sch.4 para.92

s.15, amended: 2004 c.i s.21

s.18, repealed: 2003 c.17 Sch.7

s.19, repealed: 2003 c.17 Sch.7

s.20, repealed: 2003 c.17 Sch.7

s.21, repealed: 2003 c.17 Sch.7

1. Care of Churches and Ecclesiastical Jurisdiction Measure 1991

s.13, applied: SI 2002/1892 Sch.1 Part TABLE, SI 2003/1933 Sch.1 Part I, SI 2004/1888 Sch.1 Part TABLE

s.22, applied: SI 2002/1893 para.4, SI 2003/1936 para.4

s.25, amended: 2003 c.3 s.45

s.26, amended: 2003 c.3 s.45

2. Diocesan Boards of Education Measure 1991

s.3, amended: 2002 c.32 Sch.4 para.13

s.3, applied: SI 2003/1377 Reg.17, SI 2003/1558 Reg.49

s.10, amended: 2002 c.32 Sch.7 para.3

4. Namibia Act 1991

Sch.1 para.1, repealed: 2002 c.39 Sch.3

5. Ministerial and other Pensions and Salaries Act 1991

applied: 2003 c.1 s.291

s.1, repealed (in part): 2004 c.14 Sch.1 Part 11

s.7, repealed (in part): 2004 c.14 Sch.1 Part 11

9. Community Charges (General Reduction) Act 1991

repealed: 2004 c.14 Sch.1 Part 10

16. Oversea Superannuation Act 1991

s.2, repealed: 2003 c.1 Sch.8 Part 1

17. Maintenance Enforcement Act 1991

Sch.2 para.11, repealed (in part): 2003 c.39 Sch.10

19. Football (Offences) Act 1991

applied: SI 2004/2410 Art.3

s.1, enabling: SI 2004/2410

s.3, see *DPP v Stoke on Trent Magistrates Court* [2003] EWHC 1593, [2003] 3 All E.R. 1086 (QBD (Admin Ct)), Auld, L.J.

21. Disability Living Allowance and Disability Working Allowance Act 1991

Sch.2 para.18, repealed: 2003 c.1 Sch.8 Part 1

Sch.3 Part II para.9, repealed: 2002 c.21 Sch.6

Sch.3 Part II para.10, repealed: 2002 c.21 Sch.6

Sch.3 Part II para.11, repealed: 2002 c.21 Sch.6

Sch.3 Part II para.12, repealed: 2002 c.21 Sch.6

Sch.3 Part II para.13, repealed: 2002 c.21 Sch.6

Sch.3 Part II para.14, repealed: 2002 c.21 Sch.6

CAP.

1991–cont.

21. Disability Living Allowance and Disability Working Allowance Act 1991– cont.

Sch.3 Part II para.15, repealed: 2002 c.21 Sch.6

22. New Roads and Street Works Act 1991

Commencement Orders: SI 2004/1780 Art.2; SI 2002/3267 Art.2

applied: SI 2002/1066 Art.3, 2004 c.18 s.40

referred to: SI 2004/389 Art.12

Part III, see *Road Management Services (A13) Plc v London Power Networks Plc* [2003] B.L.R. 303 (QBD (T&CC)), Forbes, J.

Part III, applied: SI 2002/412 Art.3, Art.10, Sch.5 para.5, SI 2002/1065 Sch.6 para.5, SI 2002/1066 Art.3, Sch.10 para.1, Sch.10 para.2, SI 2002/1327 Sch.5 para.1, Sch.5 para.2, SI 2003/1075 Art.15, Sch.12 para.1, Sch.12 para.2, Sch.12 para.3, Sch.13 para.9, Sch.13 para.16, Sch.13 para.21, SI 2003/3364 Sch.6 para.2, Sch.6 para.3, SI 2004/389 Sch.12 para.1, Sch.12 para.2, Sch.12 para.3, Sch.13 para.9, Sch.13 para.21, SI 2004/757 Art.3, Sch.12 para.1, Sch.12 para.2, Sch.16 para.5

Part III, referred to: SI 2002/366 Sch.2 para.9, SI 2002/1064 Sch.3 para.1

Part III, see *Road Management Services (A13) Plc v London Power Networks Plc* [2003] B.L.R. 303 (QBD (T&CC)), Forbes, J.

Part III, added: 2004 c.18 s.59

Part IV, applied: 2004 asp 10 s.12

s.10, amended: SI 2003/1398 Sch.1 para.18

s.10, repealed (in part): SI 2003/1398 Sch.1 para.18

s.14, enabling: SI 2003/2186

s.15, applied: SI 2003/2186 Reg.5

s.15, enabling: SI 2003/2186

s.33, amended: SI 2003/1398 Sch.1 para.18

s.33, repealed (in part): SI 2003/1398 Sch.1 para.18

s.48, see *Thames Water Utilities Ltd v London Underground Ltd* [2004] EWCA Civ 615, (2004) 148 S.J.L.B. 633 (CA), Brooke, L.J.

s.48, varied: SI 2002/412 Art.3

s.49, varied: SI 2002/412 Art.3

s.50, applied: SI 2002/2091 Reg.8

s.50, varied: SI 2002/412 Art.3

s.51, amended: 2004 c.18 Sch.1

s.51, varied: SI 2002/412 Art.3

s.52, varied: SI 2002/412 Art.3

s.53, amended: 2004 c.18 s.45

s.53, varied: SI 2002/412 Art.3

s.53A, added: 2004 c.18 s.48

s.53A, varied: SI 2002/412 Art.3

s.54, amended: 2004 c.18 s.49, Sch.1

s.54, applied: SI 2002/1327 Art.3, SI 2003/1075 Art.13, SI 2004/389 Art.12, SI 2004/757 Art.3

1991–cont.

22. New Roads and Street Works Act 1991–*cont.*

s.54, varied: SI 2002/412 Art.3, Art.9, SI 2002/1066 Art.3

s.55, amended: 2004 c.18 s.49, s.51, Sch.1

s.55, applied: SI 2002/1327 Art.3, SI 2003/1075 Art.13, SI 2004/389 Art.12, SI 2004/757 Art.3

s.55, varied: SI 2002/412 Art.3, Art.9, SI 2002/1066 Art.3

s.56, amended: 2004 c.18 s.43, Sch.1

s.56, disapplied: SI 2002/1066 Art.3, SI 2002/1327 Art.3, SI 2004/757 Art.3

s.56, varied: SI 2002/412 Art.3

s.56A, added: 2004 c.18 s.44

s.56A, varied: SI 2002/412 Art.3

s.57, amended: 2004 c.18 s.52, Sch.1

s.57, applied: SI 2002/1327 Art.3, SI 2004/757 Art.3

s.57, varied: SI 2002/412 Art.3, SI 2002/1066 Art.3

s.58, amended: 2004 c.18 s.51, Sch.1

s.58, disapplied: SI 2002/1066 Art.3, SI 2002/1327 Art.3, SI 2004/757 Art.3

s.58, varied: SI 2002/412 Art.3

s.58A, added: 2004 c.18 s.52

s.58A, varied: SI 2002/412 Art.3

s.59, amended: 2004 c.18 s.42

s.59, applied: SI 2002/1327 Art.3, SI 2003/1075 Art.13, SI 2004/389 Art.12, SI 2004/757 Art.3

s.59, varied: SI 2002/412 Art.3, Art.9, SI 2002/1066 Art.3

s.60, amended: 2004 c.18 Sch.1

s.60, applied: SI 2002/1327 Art.3, SI 2003/1075 Art.13, SI 2004/389 Art.12, SI 2004/757 Art.3

s.60, varied: SI 2002/412 Art.3, Art.9, SI 2002/1066 Art.3

s.61, varied: SI 2002/412 Art.3

s.62, varied: SI 2002/412 Art.3

s.63, varied: SI 2002/412 Art.3

s.64, amended: 2004 c.18 s.52

s.64, varied: SI 2002/412 Art.3

s.65, amended: 2004 c.18 Sch.1

s.65, varied: SI 2002/412 Art.3

s.66, amended: 2004 c.18 Sch.1

s.66, varied: SI 2002/412 Art.3

s.67, amended: 2004 c.18 s.50, Sch.1

s.67, varied: SI 2002/412 Art.3

s.68, amended: 2004 c.18 Sch.1

s.68, applied: SI 2002/1327 Art.3, SI 2004/757 Art.3

s.68, varied: SI 2002/412 Art.3, SI 2002/1066 Art.3

s.69, amended: 2004 c.18 Sch.1

s.69, applied: SI 2002/1327 Art.3, SI 2003/1075 Art.13, SI 2004/389 Art.12, SI 2004/757 Art.3

s.69, varied: SI 2002/412 Art.3, Art.9, SI 2002/1066 Art.3

1991–cont.

22. New Roads and Street Works Act 1991–*cont.*

s.70, amended: 2004 c.18 s.40, s.54

s.70, varied: SI 2002/412 Art.3

s.71, amended: 2004 c.18 Sch.1

s.71, varied: SI 2002/412 Art.3

s.71, enabling: SI 2002/1487

s.72, amended: 2004 c.18 s.53, s.58

s.72, varied: SI 2002/412 Art.3

s.73, varied: SI 2002/412 Art.3

s.73A, added: 2004 c.18 s.55

s.73A, varied: SI 2002/412 Art.3

s.73B, added: 2004 c.18 s.55

s.73B, varied: SI 2002/412 Art.3

s.73C, added: 2004 c.18 s.55

s.73C, varied: SI 2002/412 Art.3

s.73D, added: 2004 c.18 s.56

s.73D, varied: SI 2002/412 Art.3

s.73E, added: 2004 c.18 s.56

s.73E, varied: SI 2002/412 Art.3

s.73F, varied: SI 2002/412 Art.3

s.74, amended: 2004 c.18 s.40, s.52

s.74, varied: SI 2002/412 Art.3

s.74A, amended: 2004 c.18 s.40

s.74A, varied: SI 2002/412 Art.3

s.74A, enabling: SI 2004/2175

s.74B, varied: SI 2002/412 Art.3

s.75, applied: SI 2002/1327 Art.3, SI 2004/757 Art.3

s.75, substituted: 2004 c.18 s.58

s.75, varied: SI 2002/412 Art.3, SI 2002/1066 Art.3

s.75, enabling: SI 2002/2092, SI 2002/3181, SI 2004/572, SI 2004/1809

s.76, applied: SI 2002/1327 Art.3, SI 2003/1075 Art.13, SI 2004/389 Art.12, SI 2004/757 Art.3

s.76, varied: SI 2002/412 Art.3, Art.9, SI 2002/1066 Art.3

s.77, applied: SI 2002/1327 Art.3, SI 2003/1075 Art.13, SI 2004/389 Art.12, SI 2004/757 Art.3

s.77, varied: SI 2002/412 Art.3, Art.9, SI 2002/1066 Art.3

s.78, varied: SI 2002/412 Art.3

s.78A, added: 2004 c.18 s.57

s.78A, varied: SI 2002/412 Art.3

s.79, amended: 2004 c.18 s.46, Sch.1

s.79, applied: SI 2002/3217 Reg.4

s.79, disapplied: SI 2002/3217 Reg.5

s.79, varied: SI 2002/412 Art.3

s.79, enabling: SI 2002/3217

s.80, amended: 2004 c.18 s.47, Sch.1

s.80, varied: SI 2002/412 Art.3

s.81, varied: SI 2002/412 Art.3

s.82, varied: SI 2002/412 Art.3

s.83, amended: 2004 c.18 Sch.1

s.83, varied: SI 2002/412 Art.3

1991–cont.

22. New Roads and Street Works Act 1991–cont.

s.84, see *British Telecommunications Plc v Gwynedd Council* [2004] EWCA Civ 942, [2004] 4 All E.R. 975 (CA), Auld, L.J.

s.84, varied: SI 2002/412 Art.3

s.85, see *British Telecommunications Plc v Gwynedd Council* [2004] EWCA Civ 942, [2004] 4 All E.R. 975 (CA), Auld, L.J.; see *Thames Water Utilities Ltd v London Underground Ltd* [2004] EWCA Civ 615, (2004) 148 S.J.L.B. 633 (CA), Brooke, L.J.

s.85, applied: SI 2002/1066 Art.25, Sch.10 para.2, SI 2002/1327 Sch.5 para.2, SI 2003/1075 Sch.12 para.2, Sch.13 para.9, Sch.13 para.21, SI 2003/3364 Sch.6 para.2, SI 2004/389 Sch.12 para.2, Sch.13 para.9, Sch.13 para.21, SI 2004/757 Art.29, Sch.12 para.2

s.85, varied: SI 2002/412 Art.3

s.86, referred to: SI 2002/412 Art.3, SI 2002/1066 Art.3, SI 2004/757 Art.3

s.86, varied: SI 2002/412 Art.3

s.87, applied: SI 2002/412 Art.10, SI 2003/1075 Art.15

s.87, referred to: SI 2002/1066 Art.3, SI 2004/757 Art.3

s.87, varied: SI 2002/412 Art.3

s.88, amended: 2004 c.18 s.40, s.52

s.88, varied: SI 2002/412 Art.3

s.89, amended: 2004 c.18 s.52

s.89, varied: SI 2002/412 Art.3

s.90, amended: 2004 c.18 s.53

s.90, varied: SI 2002/412 Art.3

s.91, see *Thames Water Utilities Ltd v London Underground Ltd* [2004] EWCA Civ 615, (2004) 148 S.J.L.B. 633 (CA), Brooke, L.J.

s.91, varied: SI 2002/412 Art.3

s.92, amended: 2004 c.18 Sch.1

s.92, varied: SI 2002/412 Art.3

s.93, amended: 2004 c.18 s.49

s.93, varied: SI 2002/412 Art.3

s.94, varied: SI 2002/412 Art.3

s.95, varied: SI 2002/412 Art.3

s.95A, added: 2004 c.18 s.41

s.95A, varied: SI 2002/412 Art.3

s.96, see *Road Management Services (A13) Plc v London Power Networks Plc* [2003] B.L.R. 303 (QBD (T&CC)), Forbes, J.

s.96, amended: 2004 c.18 s.57

s.96, varied: SI 2002/412 Art.3

s.96, enabling: SI 2002/2091

s.97, amended: 2004 c.18 s.64

s.97, varied: SI 2002/412 Art.3

s.98, varied: SI 2002/412 Art.3

s.99, varied: SI 2002/412 Art.3

s.100, varied: SI 2002/412 Art.3

s.101, see *Thames Water Utilities Ltd v London Underground Ltd* [2004] EWCA Civ 615, (2004) 148 S.J.L.B. 633 (CA), Brooke, L.J.

1991–cont.

22. New Roads and Street Works Act 1991–cont.

s.101, varied: SI 2002/412 Art.3

s.102, varied: SI 2002/412 Art.3

s.103, varied: SI 2002/412 Art.3

s.104, varied: SI 2002/412 Art.3

s.104, enabling: SI 2002/1487, SI 2002/2091, SI 2002/2092, SI 2002/3181, SI 2002/3217, SI 2004/572, SI 2004/1809

s.105, varied: SI 2002/412 Art.3

s.106, amended: 2004 c.18 s.41, s.55

s.106, varied: SI 2002/412 Art.3

s.108, amended: 2002 asp 3 Sch.7 para.21

s.109, amended: 2002 asp 3 Sch.7 para.21

s.109, applied: SSI 2003/415 Reg.3, SSI 2003/416 Reg.8, SSI 2003/509 Reg.9

s.117, amended: 2002 asp 3 Sch.7 para.21

s.120, applied: SSI 2003/509 Reg.9

s.121, applied: SSI 2003/509 Reg.9

s.130, enabling: SSI 2003/417, SSI 2003/512

s.134, enabling: SSI 2002/13, SSI 2003/415, SSI 2004/84

s.144, enabling: SSI 2003/509

s.148, amended: 2002 asp 3 Sch.7 para.21

s.149, amended: 2002 asp 3 Sch.7 para.21

s.155, enabling: SSI 2003/416

s.163, enabling: SSI 2002/13, SSI 2003/415, SSI 2003/416, SSI 2003/417, SSI 2003/509, SSI 2003/512, SSI 2004/84

s.164, amended: 2002 asp 3 Sch.7 para.21

s.170, enabling: SI 2002/3267, SI 2004/1780

Sch.3 para.5, amended: 2004 c.18 Sch.1

Sch.3A para.1, added: 2004 c.18 Sch.4

Sch.3A para.2, added: 2004 c.18 Sch.4

Sch.3A para.3, added: 2004 c.18 Sch.4

Sch.3A para.4, added: 2004 c.18 Sch.4

Sch.3A para.5, added: 2004 c.18 Sch.4

Sch.3A para.6, added: 2004 c.18 Sch.4

Sch.4A, added: 2004 c.18 Sch.2

Sch.4B, applied: 2004 c.18 s.37

Sch.4 para.6, amended: 2004 c.18 Sch.1

Sch.4 para.7, amended: 2003 c.21 Sch.17 para.108, Sch.19

Sch.4 para.12, amended: 2004 c.18 Sch.1

Sch.4 para.13, amended: 2004 c.18 Sch.1

Sch.4B para.1, added: 2004 c.18 Sch.3

Sch.4B para.2, added: 2004 c.18 Sch.3

Sch.4B para.3, added: 2004 c.18 Sch.3

Sch.4B para.4, added: 2004 c.18 Sch.3

Sch.4B para.5, added: 2004 c.18 Sch.3

Sch.4B para.6, added: 2004 c.18 Sch.3

Sch.4B para.7, added: 2004 c.18 Sch.3

Sch.4B para.8, added: 2004 c.18 Sch.3

Sch.4B para.9, added: 2004 c.18 Sch.3

Sch.6 para.7, amended: 2002 asp 3 Sch.7 para.21, 2003 c.21 Sch.17 para.108, Sch.19

Sch.6 para.9, amended: 2002 asp 3 Sch.7 para.21

CAP.

1991-cont.

23. Children and Young Persons (Protection from Tobacco) Act 1991
s.4, applied: SI 2003/1376 Sch.1

25. Criminal Procedure (Insanity and Unfitness to Plead) Act 1991
see *R. (on the application of South West Yorkshire Mental Health NHS Trust) v Bradford Crown Court* [2003] EWCA Civ 1857, [2004] 1 W.L.R. 1664 (CA), Pill, L.J.; see *R. v Grant (Heather)* [2001] EWCA Crim 2611, [2002] Q.B. 1030 (CA (Crim Div)), Richards, J.
s.3, repealed: 2004 c.28 Sch.11
s.5, repealed: 2004 c.28 s.24, Sch.11
s.6, amended: 2004 c.28 Sch.11
s.6, repealed (in part): 2004 c.28 Sch.11
Sch.1, see *R. (on the application of South West Yorkshire Mental Health NHS Trust) v Bradford Crown Court* [2003] EWHC 640, [2003] A.C.D. 68 (QBD (Admin Ct)), Newman, J.
Sch.1 para.1, repealed: 2004 c.28 s.24, Sch.11
Sch.1 para.2, repealed: 2004 c.28 s.24, Sch.11
Sch.1 para.3, repealed: 2004 c.28 s.24, Sch.11
Sch.1 para.4, repealed: 2004 c.28 s.24, Sch.11
Sch.2 Part I, applied: SI 2003/762 Reg.2, SI 2004/1748 Sch.1, SSI 2003/243 Reg.2
Sch.2 Part I para.1, repealed: 2004 c.28 s.24, Sch.11
Sch.2 Part II para.2, repealed: 2004 c.28 s.24, Sch.11
Sch.2 Part II para.3, repealed: 2004 c.28 s.24, Sch.11
Sch.2 Part II para.4, repealed: 2004 c.28 s.24, Sch.11
Sch.2 Part II para.5, repealed: 2004 c.28 s.24, Sch.11
Sch.2 Part III para.6, repealed: 2004 c.28 s.24, Sch.11
Sch.2 Part III para.7, repealed: 2004 c.28 s.24, Sch.11
Sch.2 Part III para.8, repealed: 2004 c.28 s.24, Sch.11
Sch.2 Part III para.9, repealed: 2004 c.28 s.24, Sch.11
Sch.2 Part III para.10, repealed: 2004 c.28 s.24, Sch.11
Sch.2 Part III para.11, repealed: 2004 c.28 s.24, Sch.11

27. Radioactive Material (Road Transport) Act 1991
s.1, applied: SI 2004/568 Reg.24
s.1, enabling: SI 2002/1092
s.2, enabling: SI 2002/1093, SI 2003/1867

28. Natural Heritage (Scotland) Act 1991
s.1, applied: SSI 2002/541 Reg.12
s.5, applied: SI 2003/2261 Sch.3 Part I, Sch.4 para.3

CAP.

1991-cont.

28. Natural Heritage (Scotland) Act 1991- *cont.*
s.6, applied: 2002 asp 3 s.54
s.6, repealed: 2004 asp 6 Sch.7 para.8
s.10, applied: 2004 asp 6 s.28
s.12, applied: 2004 asp 6 Sch.5 para.7
s.12, repealed: 2004 asp 6 Sch.7 para.8
s.20, amended: 2002 asp 3 Sch.7 para.22
s.22, amended: 2002 asp 3 Sch.7 para.22
s.24, amended: 2002 asp 3 Sch.7 para.22
Sch.7 para.3, amended: 2002 asp 3 Sch.7 para.22
Sch.7 para.5, amended: 2002 asp 3 Sch.7 para.22
Sch.7 para.6, amended: 2002 asp 3 Sch.7 para.22
Sch.7 para.7, amended: 2002 asp 3 Sch.7 para.22
Sch.8 para.1, repealed (in part): 2002 asp 3 Sch.7 para.22
Sch.9 para.1, amended: 2002 asp 3 Sch.7 para.22

29. Property Misdescriptions Act 1991
applied: 2002 c.40 Sch.14, Sch.15, SI 2003/1376 Sch.1, SI 2003/1593 Sch.1 Part I
s.5, amended: SI 2003/1400 Sch.5
Sch.1 para.2, repealed: 2002 c.40 Sch.26
Sch.1 para.7, repealed: 2002 c.40 Sch.26

31. Finance Act 1991
s.19, repealed: 2004 c.14 Sch.1 Part 9
s.20, repealed: 2004 c.14 Sch.1 Part 9
s.34, repealed: 2004 c.12 Sch.42 Part 3
s.35, repealed: 2004 c.12 Sch.42 Part 3
s.36, repealed: 2004 c.12 Sch.42 Part 3
s.38, amended: 2003 c.1 Sch.6 para.168
s.38, repealed (in part): 2003 c.1 Sch.8 Part 1
s.39, repealed: 2003 c.1 Sch.8 Part 1
s.40, repealed: 2003 c.1 Sch.8 Part 1
s.44, repealed: 2003 c.1 Sch.8 Part 1
s.47, repealed: 2004 c.12 Sch.42 Part 2
s.69, repealed: 2003 c.1 Sch.8 Part 1
s.72, amended: 2002 c.23 s.48
s.72, applied: 2002 c.23 s.48, 2004 c.12 s.121, s.128
s.111, amended: 2003 c.14 Sch.20 para.3
s.116, enabling: SI 2003/2078, SI 2004/3218
s.117, enabling: SI 2003/2078, SI 2004/3218
s.120, repealed: 2004 c.14 Sch.1 Part 9
Sch.2 para.1, amended: 2003 c.17 Sch.7
Sch.2 para.21A, repealed: 2002 c.40 Sch.26
Sch.2 para.22, repealed: 2002 c.40 Sch.26
Sch.6 para.1, repealed: 2003 c.1 Sch.8 Part 1
Sch.6 para.3, repealed: 2003 c.1 Sch.8 Part 1
Sch.7 para.1, amended: 2003 c.14 Sch.43 Part 3
Sch.7 para.11, repealed: 2003 c.14 Sch.43 Part 3
Sch.7 para.13, repealed (in part): 2004 c.12 Sch.42 Part 2

1991–cont.

31. Finance Act 1991–*cont.*

Sch.7 para.16, amended: 2003 c.14 Sch.33 para.6, SI 2004/2310 Sch.1 para.47

34. Planning and Compensation Act 1991

see *R. (on the application of Wells) v Secretary of State for Transport, Local Government and the Regions (C201/02)* [2004] 1 C.M.L.R. 31 (ECJ), Judge Jann (President)

s.17, repealed (in part): 2004 c.5 Sch.9

s.22, see *Earthline Ltd v Secretary of State for Transport, Local Government and the Regions* [2002] EWCA Civ 1599, [2003] 1 P. & C.R. 24 (CA), Brooke, L.J.

s.22, applied: 2004 c.5 s.87

s.22, varied: 2004 c.5 s.87

s.27, see *JS Bloor Ltd v Swindon BC* [2001] EWHC Admin 966, [2002] P.L.C.R. 22 (QBD (Admin Ct)), Ouseley, J.

s.80, see *Matthews v Environment Agency* [2002] 3 E.G.L.R. 168 (Lands Tr), NJ Rose, FRICS

s.80, enabling: SI 2002/116, SSI 2003/175

Sch.2, see *Earthline Ltd v Secretary of State for Transport, Local Government and the Regions* [2002] EWCA Civ 1599, [2003] 1 P. & C.R. 24 (CA), Brooke, L.J.

Sch.2, applied: 2004 c.5 s.87

Sch.2 para.1, varied: 2004 c.5 s.87

Sch.4 Part I, see *JS Bloor Ltd v Swindon BC* [2001] EWHC Admin 966, [2002] P.L.C.R. 22 (QBD (Admin Ct)), Ouseley, J.

Sch.4 Part III para.40, repealed (in part): 2004 c.5 Sch.7 para.16, Sch.9

Sch.4 Part III para.41, repealed (in part): 2004 c.5 Sch.7 para.16, Sch.9

Sch.4 Part III para.42, repealed (in part): 2004 c.5 Sch.7 para.16, Sch.9

Sch.4 Part III para.43, repealed (in part): 2004 c.5 Sch.7 para.16, Sch.9

Sch.4 Part III para.44, repealed (in part): 2004 c.5 Sch.7 para.16, Sch.9

Sch.4 Part III para.45, repealed (in part): 2004 c.5 Sch.7 para.16, Sch.9

Sch.4 Part III para.46, repealed (in part): 2004 c.5 Sch.7 para.16, Sch.9

Sch.4 Part III para.47, repealed (in part): 2004 c.5 Sch.7 para.16, Sch.9

Sch.4 Part III para.48, repealed (in part): 2004 c.5 Sch.7 para.16, Sch.9

Sch.4 Part III para.49, repealed (in part): 2004 c.5 Sch.7 para.16, Sch.9

Sch.4 Part III para.50, repealed (in part): 2004 c.5 Sch.7 para.16, Sch.9

Sch.4 Part III para.51, repealed (in part): 2004 c.5 Sch.7 para.16, Sch.9

Sch.18 Part I, amended: SI 2002/116 Art.2, SSI 2003/175 Art.2

Sch.18 Part II, amended: 2004 c.5 Sch.9

37. Smoke Detectors Act 1991

s.2, amended: 2004 c.21 Sch.1 para.74

1991–cont.

40. Road Traffic Act 1991

Part II, applied: SI 2002/3113 Reg.4, 2003 c.iii Sch.1 para.6, 2004 c.i s.7

Part II, referred to: 2003 c.iii s.20, SI 2004/1608 Art.5

s.31, repealed: 2004 c.14 Sch.1 Part 14

s.43, repealed (in part): 2004 c.18 Sch.12 Part 1

s.46, varied: SI 2002/1484 Sch.2 para.1

s.49, repealed: 2004 c.14 Sch.1 Part 14

s.58, applied: SI 2003/1615 Art.5

s.65, repealed (in part): 2004 c.18 Sch.12 Part 1

s.66, amended: SI 2003/251 Sch.1 para.1

s.66, applied: SI 2002/37 Art.5, SI 2002/421 Art.5, SI 2002/422 Art.5, SI 2002/1484 Art.5, SI 2002/1485 Art.5, SI 2002/2012 Art.5, SI 2002/2183 Art.5, SI 2002/2188 Art.5, SI 2002/3265 Art.6, SI 2002/3266 Art.5, SSI 2002/400 Reg.4, 2003 c.iii s.15, SI 2003/95 Art.5, SI 2003/251 Art.5, SI 2003/634 Art.5, SI 2003/635 Art.5, SI 2003/898 Art.5, SI 2003/1261 Art.5, SI 2003/1984 Art.5, SI 2003/2334 Art.5, SI 2003/2336 Art.5, SI 2003/2677 Art.5, SI 2003/2711 Art.5, SI 2004/914 Art.5, SI 2004/1278 Art.5, SI 2004/1285 Art.5, SI 2004/1305 Art.5, SI 2004/1402 Art.5, SI 2004/2028 Art.5, SI 2004/2111 Art.5, SI 2004/2188 Art.5, SI 2004/2193 Art.5, SI 2004/2194 Art.5, SI 2004/2212 Art.5, SI 2004/2260 Art.5, SI 2004/2424 Art.5, SI 2004/2616 Art.5, SSI 2002/398 Art.4, SSI 2003/71 Reg.4, SSI 2003/72 Reg.2, SSI 2004/86 Reg.4, SSI 2004/87 Art.4

s.66, referred to: SSI 2002/399 Reg.2, SSI 2004/85 Reg.2

s.66, repealed (in part): 2004 c.18 Sch.12 Part 1

s.66, varied: SI 2002/37 Sch.1 para.1, SI 2002/126 Sch.1 para.1, SI 2002/276 Sch.1 para.1, SI 2002/421 Sch.1 para.1, SI 2002/422 Sch.1 para.1, SI 2002/1351 Sch.1 para.1, SI 2002/1352 Sch.1 para.1, SI 2002/1353 Sch.1 para.1, SI 2002/1484 Sch.1 para.1, SI 2002/1485 Sch.1 para.1, SI 2002/1486 Sch.1 para.1, SI 2002/1504 Sch.1 para.1, SI 2002/1621 Sch.1 para.1, SI 2002/2012 Sch.1 para.1, SI 2002/2183 Sch.1 para.1, SI 2002/2184 Sch.1 para.1, SI 2002/2185 Sch.1 para.1, SI 2002/2186 Sch.1 para.1, SI 2002/2187 Sch.1 para.1, SI 2002/2188 Sch.1 para.1, SI 2002/2520 Sch.1 para.1, SI 2002/2705 Sch.1 para.1, SI 2002/3265 Sch.1 para.1, SI 2002/3266 Sch.1 para.1, SI 2003/95 Sch.1 para.1, SI 2003/251 Sch.1 para.1, SI 2003/634 Sch.1 para.1, SI 2003/635 Sch.1 para.1, SI 2003/1261 Sch.1 para.1, SI 2003/1262 Art.5, Sch.1 para.1, SI 2003/1924 Sch.1 para.1, SI 2003/1984 Sch.1 para.1, SI 2003/2152 Sch.1 para.1, SI 2003/2153 Sch.1 para.1, SI

1991–cont.

40. Road Traffic Act 1991–*cont.*

s.66, varied:–*cont.*

2003/2326 Sch.1 para.1, SI 2003/2334 Sch.1 para.1, SI 2003/2336 Sch.1 para.1, SI 2003/2440 Sch.1 para.1, SI 2003/2677 Sch.1 para.1, SI 2003/2711 Sch.1 para.1, SI 2004/13 Art.5, Sch.1 para.1, SI 2004/104 Sch.1 para.1, SI 2004/914 Sch.1 para.1, SI 2004/1278 Sch.1 para.1, SI 2004/1285 Sch.1 para.1, SI 2004/1305 Sch.1 para.1, SI 2004/1402 Sch.1 para.1, SI 2004/1608 Sch.1 para.1, SI 2004/2028 Sch.2 para.1, SI 2004/2111 Sch.1 para.1, SI 2004/2188 Sch.1 para.1, SI 2004/2193 Sch.1 para.1, SI 2004/2194 Sch.1 para.1, SI 2004/2212 Sch.1 para.1, SI 2004/2260 Sch.1 para.1, SI 2004/2424 Sch.2 para.1, SI 2004/2616 Sch.1 para.1, SSI 2002/398 Sch.2 para.1, SSI 2003/70 Sch.2 para.1, SSI 2004/87 Sch.2 para.1

s.67, repealed (in part): 2004 c.18 Sch.12 Part 1

s.68, repealed (in part): 2004 c.18 Sch.12 Part 1

s.69, applied: SI 2002/37 Art.5, SI 2002/421 Art.5, SI 2002/422 Art.5, SI 2002/1484 Art.5, SI 2002/1485 Art.5, SI 2002/2012 Art.5, SI 2002/2183 Art.5, SI 2002/2188 Art.5, SI 2002/3265 Art.6, SI 2002/3266 Art.5, SI 2003/95 Art.5, SI 2003/251 Art.5, SI 2003/634 Art.5, SI 2003/635 Art.5, SI 2003/898 Art.5, SI 2003/1261 Art.5, SI 2003/1984 Art.5, SI 2003/2334 Art.5, SI 2003/2336 Art.5, SI 2003/2711 Art.5, SI 2004/914 Art.5, SI 2004/1278 Art.5, SI 2004/1285 Art.5, SI 2004/1305 Art.5, SI 2004/1402 Art.5, SI 2004/2028 Art.5, SI 2004/2111 Art.5, SI 2004/2188 Art.5, SI 2004/2193 Art.5, SI 2004/2194 Art.5, SI 2004/2212 Art.5, SI 2004/2260 Art.5, SI 2004/2424 Art.5, SI 2004/2616 Art.5, SSI 2002/398 Art.4, SSI 2003/72 Reg.2, SSI 2004/87 Art.4

s.69, referred to: SSI 2002/399 Reg.2, SSI 2004/85 Reg.2

s.69, repealed (in part): 2004 c.18 Sch.12 Part 1

s.69, varied: SI 2002/37 Sch.1 para.2, SI 2002/126 Sch.1 para.2, SI 2002/276 Sch.1 para.2, SI 2002/421 Sch.1 para.2, SI 2002/422 Sch.1 para.2, SI 2002/1351 Sch.1 para.2, SI 2002/1352 Sch.1 para.2, SI 2002/1353 Sch.1 para.2, SI 2002/1484 Sch.1 para.2, SI 2002/1485 Sch.1 para.2, SI 2002/1486 Sch.1 para.2, SI 2002/1504 Sch.1 para.2, SI 2002/1621 Sch.1 para.2, SI 2002/2012 Sch.1 para.2, SI 2002/2183 Sch.1 para.2, SI 2002/2184 Sch.1 para.2, SI 2002/2185 Sch.1 para.2, SI 2002/2186 Sch.1 para.2, SI 2002/2187 Sch.1 para.2, SI 2002/2188 Sch.1 para.2, SI 2002/2520 Sch.1 para.2, SI 2002/2705 Sch.1 para.2, SI 2002/3265 Sch.1 para.2, SI

1991–cont.

40. Road Traffic Act 1991–*cont.*

s.69, varied:–*cont.*

2002/3266 Sch.1 para.2, SI 2003/95 Sch.1 para.2, SI 2003/251 Sch.1 para.2, SI 2003/634 Sch.1 para.2, SI 2003/635 Sch.1 para.2, SI 2003/898 Sch.1 para.2, SI 2003/1261 Sch.1 para.2, SI 2003/1262 Art.5, Sch.1 para.2, SI 2003/1924 Sch.1 para.2, SI 2003/1984 Sch.1 para.2, SI 2003/2152 Sch.1 para.2, SI 2003/2153 Sch.1 para.2, SI 2003/2326 Sch.1 para.2, SI 2003/2334 Sch.1 para.2, SI 2003/2336 Sch.1 para.2, SI 2003/2440 Sch.1 para.2, SI 2003/2711 Sch.1 para.2, SI 2004/13 Art.5, Sch.1 para.2, SI 2004/104 Sch.1 para.2, SI 2004/914 Sch.1 para.2, SI 2004/1278 Sch.1 para.2, SI 2004/1285 Sch.1 para.2, SI 2004/1305 Sch.1 para.2, SI 2004/1402 Sch.1 para.2, SI 2004/1608 Sch.1 para.2, SI 2004/2028 Sch.2 para.2, SI 2004/2111 Sch.1 para.2, SI 2004/2188 Sch.1 para.2, SI 2004/2193 Sch.1 para.2, SI 2004/2194 Sch.1 para.2, SI 2004/2212 Sch.1 para.2, SI 2004/2260 Sch.1 para.2, SI 2004/2424 Sch.2 para.2, SI 2004/2616 Sch.1 para.2, SSI 2002/398 Sch.2 para.2, SSI 2003/70 Sch.2 para.2, SSI 2004/87 Sch.2 para.2

s.70, applied: SI 2002/37 Art.5, SI 2002/421 Art.5, SI 2002/1484 Art.5, SI 2002/1485 Art.5, SI 2002/2012 Art.5, SI 2002/2183 Art.5, SI 2002/2188 Art.5, SI 2002/3265 Art.6, SI 2002/3266 Art.5, SI 2003/95 Art.5, SI 2003/251 Art.5, SI 2003/634 Art.5, SI 2003/635 Art.5, SI 2003/898 Art.5, SI 2003/1261 Art.5, SI 2003/1984 Art.5, SI 2003/2334 Art.5, SI 2003/2336 Art.5, SI 2003/2711 Art.5, SI 2004/914 Art.5, SI 2004/1278 Art.5, SI 2004/1285 Art.5, SI 2004/1305 Art.5, SI 2004/1402 Art.5, SI 2004/2028 Art.5, SI 2004/2111 Art.5, SI 2004/2188 Art.5, SI 2004/2193 Art.5, SI 2004/2194 Art.5, SI 2004/2212 Art.5, SI 2004/2260 Art.5, SI 2004/2424 Art.5, SI 2004/2616 Art.5, SSI 2002/398 Art.4, SSI 2004/87 Art.4

s.70, repealed (in part): 2004 c.18 Sch.12 Part 1

s.70, varied: SI 2003/1262 Art.5, SI 2004/13 Art.5, SI 2004/2684 Art.5

s.71, applied: SI 2002/37 Art.5, SI 2002/421 Art.5, SI 2002/1484 Art.5, SI 2002/1485 Art.5, SI 2002/2012 Art.5, SI 2002/2183 Art.5, SI 2002/2188 Art.5, SI 2002/3265 Art.6, SI 2002/3266 Art.5, SI 2003/95 Art.5, SI 2003/251 Art.5, SI 2003/634 Art.5, SI 2003/635 Art.5, SI 2003/898 Art.5, SI 2003/1261 Art.5, SI 2003/1984 Art.5, SI 2003/2334 Art.5, SI 2003/2336 Art.5, SI 2003/2677 Art.5, SI 2003/2711 Art.5, SI 2004/914 Art.5, SI 2004/1278 Art.5, SI 2004/1285 Art.5, SI 2004/1305 Art.5, SI 2004/1402 Art.5, SI 2004/2028

1991-cont.

40. Road Traffic Act 1991-*cont.*

s.71, applied:–*cont.*

Art.5, SI 2004/2111 Art.5, SI 2004/2188 Art.5, SI 2004/2193 Art.5, SI 2004/2194 Art.5, SI 2004/2212 Art.5, SI 2004/2260 Art.5, SI 2004/2424 Art.5, SI 2004/2616 Art.5, SSI 2002/398 Art.4, SSI 2002/400 Reg.4, SSI 2003/71 Reg.4, SSI 2004/86 Reg.4, SSI 2004/87 Art.4

s.71, repealed (in part): 2004 c.18 Sch.12 Part 1

s.71, varied: SI 2002/37 Sch.1 para.3, SI 2002/126 Sch.1 para.3, SI 2002/276 Sch.1 para.3, SI 2002/421 Sch.1 para.3, SI 2002/422 Sch.1 para.3, SI 2002/1351 Sch.1 para.3, SI 2002/1352 Sch.1 para.3, SI 2002/1353 Sch.1 para.3, SI 2002/1484 Sch.1 para.3, SI 2002/1485 Sch.1 para.3, SI 2002/1486 Sch.1 para.3, SI 2002/1504 Sch.1 para.3, SI 2002/1621 Sch.1 para.3, SI 2002/2012 Sch.1 para.3, SI 2002/2183 Sch.1 para.3, SI 2002/2184 Sch.1 para.3, SI 2002/2185 Sch.1 para.3, SI 2002/2186 Sch.1 para.3, SI 2002/2187 Sch.1 para.3, SI 2002/2188 Sch.1 para.3, SI 2002/2520 Sch.1 para.3, SI 2002/2705 Sch.1 para.3, SI 2002/3265 Sch.1 para.3, SI 2002/3266 Sch.1 para.3, SI 2003/95 Sch.1 para.3, SI 2003/251 Sch.1 para.3, SI 2003/634 Sch.1 para.3, SI 2003/635 Sch.1 para.3, SI 2003/898 Sch.1 para.3, SI 2003/1261 Sch.1 para.3, SI 2003/1262 Art.5, Sch.1 para.3, SI 2003/1924 Sch.1 para.3, SI 2003/1984 Sch.1 para.3, SI 2003/2152 Sch.1 para.3, SI 2003/2153 Sch.1 para.3, SI 2003/2326 Sch.1 para.3, SI 2003/2334 Sch.1 para.3, SI 2003/2336 Sch.1 para.3, SI 2003/2440 Sch.1 para.3, SI 2003/2677 Sch.1 para.2, SI 2003/2711 Sch.1 para.3, SI 2004/13 Art.5, Sch.1 para.3, SI 2004/104 Sch.1 para.3, SI 2004/914 Sch.1 para.3, SI 2004/1278 Sch.1 para.3, SI 2004/1285 Sch.1 para.3, SI 2004/1305 Sch.1 para.3, SI 2004/1402 Sch.1 para.3, SI 2004/1608 Sch.1 para.3, SI 2004/2028 Sch.2 para.3, SI 2004/2111 Sch.1 para.3, SI 2004/2188 Sch.1 para.3, SI 2004/2193 Sch.1 para.3, SI 2004/2194 Sch.1 para.3, SI 2004/2212 Sch.1 para.3, SI 2004/2260 Sch.1 para.3, SI 2004/2424 Sch.2 para.3, SI 2004/2616 Sch.1 para.3, SI 2004/2684 Art.5, SSI 2002/398 Sch.2 para.3, SSI 2003/70 Sch.2 para.3, SSI 2004/87 Sch.2 para.3

s.72, applied: SI 2002/37 Art.5, SI 2002/421 Art.5, SI 2002/1484 Art.5, SI 2002/1485 Art.5, SI 2002/2012 Art.5, SI 2002/2183 Art.5, SI 2002/2188 Art.5, SI 2002/3265 Art.6, SI 2002/3266 Art.5, SI 2003/95 Art.5, SI 2003/251 Art.5, SI 2003/634 Art.5, SI 2003/635 Art.5, SI 2003/898 Art.5, SI 2003/1261 Art.5, SI 2003/1984 Art.5, SI 2003/2334 Art.5, SI 2003/2336

1991-cont.

40. Road Traffic Act 1991-*cont.*

s.72, applied:–*cont.*

Art.5, SI 2003/2677 Art.5, SI 2003/2711 Art.5, SI 2004/914 Art.5, SI 2004/1278 Art.5, SI 2004/1285 Art.5, SI 2004/1305 Art.5, SI 2004/1402 Art.5, SI 2004/2028 Art.5, SI 2004/2111 Art.5, SI 2004/2188 Art.5, SI 2004/2193 Art.5, SI 2004/2194 Art.5, SI 2004/2212 Art.5, SI 2004/2260 Art.5, SI 2004/2424 Art.5, SI 2004/2616 Art.5, SSI 2002/398 Art.4, SSI 2002/400 Reg.14, SSI 2003/71 Reg.14, SSI 2004/86 Reg.14, SSI 2004/87 Art.4

s.72, referred to: SSI 2002/400 Reg.3, SSI 2003/71 Reg.3, SSI 2004/86 Reg.3

s.72, repealed (in part): 2004 c.18 Sch.12 Part 1

s.72, varied: SI 2003/1262 Art.5, SI 2004/13 Art.5

s.73, amended: SI 2003/251 Sch.1 para.4

s.73, applied: SI 2002/37 Art.5, SI 2002/421 Art.5, SI 2002/1484 Art.5, SI 2002/1485 Art.5, SI 2002/2012 Art.5, SI 2002/2183 Art.5, SI 2002/2188 Art.5, SI 2002/3265 Art.6, SI 2002/3266 Art.5, SSI 2002/398 Art.6, SSI 2002/400 Reg.6, Reg.9, 2003 c.iii Sch.1 para.10, SI 2003/95 Art.5, SI 2003/251 Art.5, SI 2003/634 Art.5, SI 2003/635 Art.5, SI 2003/898 Art.5, SI 2003/1261 Art.5, SI 2003/1984 Art.5, SI 2003/2334 Art.5, SI 2003/2336 Art.5, SI 2003/2677 Art.5, SI 2003/2711 Art.5, SSI 2003/70 Art.6, SSI 2003/71 Reg.6, Reg.9, 2004 c.18 s.81, SI 2004/914 Art.5, SI 2004/1278 Art.5, SI 2004/1285 Art.5, SI 2004/1305 Art.5, SI 2004/1402 Art.5, SI 2004/2028 Art.5, SI 2004/2111 Art.5, SI 2004/2188 Art.5, SI 2004/2193 Art.5, SI 2004/2194 Art.5, SI 2004/2212 Art.5, SI 2004/2260 Art.5, SI 2004/2424 Art.5, SI 2004/2616 Art.5, SSI 2002/398 Art.4, SSI 2004/86 Reg.6, Reg.9, SSI 2004/87 Art.4, Art.6

s.73, disapplied: 2003 c.iii Sch.1 para.10

s.73, referred to: SSI 2002/398 Art.6, 2003 c.iii Sch.1 para.10

s.73, repealed (in part): 2004 c.18 Sch.12 Part 1

s.73, varied: SI 2002/37 Sch.1 para.4, SI 2002/126 Sch.1 para.4, SI 2002/276 Sch.1 para.4, SI 2002/421 Sch.1 para.4, SI 2002/422 Sch.1 para.4, SI 2002/1351 Sch.1 para.4, SI 2002/1352 Sch.1 para.4, SI 2002/1353 Sch.1 para.4, SI 2002/1484 Sch.1 para.4, SI 2002/1485 Sch.1 para.4, SI 2002/1486 Sch.1 para.4, SI 2002/1504 Sch.1 para.4, SI 2002/1621 Sch.1 para.4, SI 2002/2012 Sch.1 para.4, SI 2002/2183 Sch.1 para.4, SI 2002/2184 Sch.1 para.4, SI 2002/2185 Sch.1 para.4, SI 2002/2186 Sch.1 para.4, SI 2002/2187 Sch.1 para.4, SI 2002/2188 Sch.1 para.4, SI 2002/2520 Sch.1 para.4, SI 2002/2705 Sch.1 para.4,

1991–cont.

40. Road Traffic Act 1991–*cont.*

s.73, varied:–*cont.*

SI 2002/3265 Sch.1 para.4, SI 2002/3266 Sch.1 para.4, SI 2003/95 Sch.1 para.4, SI 2003/251 Sch.1 para.4, SI 2003/634 Sch.1 para.4, SI 2003/635 Sch.1 para.4, SI 2003/898 Sch.1 para.4, SI 2003/1261 Sch.1 para.4, SI 2003/1262 Art.5, Sch.1 para.4, SI 2003/1924 Sch.1 para.4, SI 2003/1984 Sch.1 para.4, SI 2003/2152 Sch.1 para.4, SI 2003/2153 Sch.1 para.4, SI 2003/2326 Sch.1 para.4, SI 2003/2334 Sch.1 para.4, SI 2003/2336 Sch.1 para.4, SI 2003/2440 Sch.1 para.4, SI 2003/2677 Sch.1 para.3, SI 2003/2711 Sch.1 para.4, SI 2004/13 Art.5, Sch.1 para.4, SI 2004/104 Sch.1 para.4, SI 2004/914 Sch.1 para.4, SI 2004/1278 Sch.1 para.4, SI 2004/1285 Sch.1 para.4, SI 2004/1305 Sch.1 para.4, SI 2004/1402 Sch.1 para.4, SI 2004/1608 Sch.1 para.4, SI 2004/2028 Sch.2 para.4, SI 2004/2111 Sch.1 para.4, SI 2004/2188 Sch.1 para.4, SI 2004/2193 Sch.1 para.4, SI 2004/2194 Sch.1 para.4, SI 2004/2212 Sch.1 para.4, SI 2004/2260 Sch.1 para.4, SI 2004/2424 Sch.2 para.4, SI 2004/2616 Sch.1 para.4, SSI 2002/398 Sch.2 para.4, SSI 2003/70 Sch.2 para.4, SSI 2004/87 Sch.2 para.4

s.73, enabling: SSI 2002/400, SSI 2003/71, SSI 2004/86

s.74, applied: SI 2002/37 Art.5, SI 2002/421 Art.5, SI 2002/422 Art.5, SI 2002/1484 Art.5, SI 2002/1485 Art.5, SI 2002/2012 Art.5, SI 2002/2183 Art.5, SI 2002/2188 Art.5, SI 2002/3265 Art.6, SI 2002/3266 Art.5, 2003 c.iii s.4, s.10, SI 2003/95 Art.5, SI 2003/251 Art.5, SI 2003/634 Art.5, SI 2003/635 Art.5, SI 2003/898 Art.5, SI 2003/1261 Art.5, SI 2003/1984 Art.5, SI 2003/2334 Art.5, SI 2003/2336 Art.5, SI 2003/2677 Art.5, SI 2003/2711 Art.5, SI 2004/914 Art.5, SI 2004/1278 Art.5, SI 2004/1285 Art.5, SI 2004/1305 Art.5, SI 2004/1402 Art.5, SI 2004/2028 Art.5, SI 2004/2111 Art.5, SI 2004/2188 Art.5, SI 2004/2193 Art.5, SI 2004/2194 Art.5, SI 2004/2212 Art.5, SI 2004/2260 Art.5, SI 2004/2424 Art.5, SI 2004/2616 Art.5, SSI 2002/398 Art.4, SSI 2004/87 Art.4

s.74, repealed (in part): 2004 c.18 Sch.12 Part 1

s.74, varied: SI 2002/37 Sch.1 para.5, SI 2002/126 Sch.1 para.5, SI 2002/276 Sch.1 para.5, SI 2002/421 Sch.1 para.5, SI 2002/422 Sch.1 para.5, SI 2002/1351 Sch.1 para.5, SI 2002/1352 Sch.1 para.5, SI 2002/1353 Sch.1 para.5, SI 2002/1484 Sch.1 para.5, SI 2002/1485 Sch.1 para.5, SI 2002/1486 Sch.1 para.5, SI 2002/1504 Sch.1 para.5, SI 2002/1621 Sch.1 para.5, SI 2002/2012 Sch.1 para.5, SI 2002/2183 Sch.1 para.5, SI 2002/2184 Sch.1 para.5,

1991–cont.

40. Road Traffic Act 1991–*cont.*

s.74, varied:–*cont.*

SI 2002/2185 Sch.1 para.5, SI 2002/2186 Sch.1 para.5, SI 2002/2187 Sch.1 para.5, SI 2002/2188 Sch.1 para.5, SI 2002/2520 Sch.1 para.5, SI 2002/2705 Sch.1 para.5, SI 2002/3265 Sch.1 para.5, SI 2002/3266 Sch.1 para.5, SI 2003/95 Sch.1 para.5, SI 2003/251 Sch.1 para.5, SI 2003/634 Sch.1 para.5, SI 2003/635 Sch.1 para.5, SI 2003/898 Sch.1 para.5, SI 2003/1261 Sch.1 para.5, SI 2003/1262 Art.5, Sch.1 para.5, SI 2003/1924 Sch.1 para.5, SI 2003/1984 Sch.1 para.5, SI 2003/2152 Sch.1 para.5, SI 2003/2153 Sch.1 para.5, SI 2003/2326 Sch.1 para.5, SI 2003/2334 Sch.1 para.5, SI 2003/2336 Sch.1 para.5, SI 2003/2440 Sch.1 para.5, SI 2003/2677 Sch.1 para.4, SI 2003/2711 Sch.1 para.5, SI 2004/13 Art.5, Sch.1 para.5, SI 2004/104 Sch.1 para.5, SI 2004/914 Sch.1 para.5, SI 2004/1278 Sch.1 para.5, SI 2004/1285 Sch.1 para.5, SI 2004/1305 Sch.1 para.5, SI 2004/1402 Sch.1 para.5, SI 2004/1608 Sch.1 para.5, SI 2004/2028 Sch.2 para.5, SI 2004/2111 Sch.1 para.5, SI 2004/2188 Sch.1 para.5, SI 2004/2193 Sch.1 para.5, SI 2004/2194 Sch.1 para.5, SI 2004/2212 Sch.1 para.5, SI 2004/2260 Sch.1 para.5, SI 2004/2424 Sch.2 para.5, SI 2004/2616 Sch.1 para.5, SI 2004/2684 Art.5, SSI 2002/398 Sch.2 para.5, SSI 2003/70 Sch.2 para.5, SSI 2004/87 Sch.2 para.5

s.74A, applied: 2003 c.iii s.4

s.74A, repealed (in part): 2004 c.18 Sch.12 Part 1

s.76, amended: SI 2003/859 Art.2

s.76, applied: SI 2003/859, 2004 c.18 Sch.8 para.2, Sch.10 para.1, SI 2004/2684

s.76, repealed (in part): 2004 c.18 Sch.12 Part 1

s.76, enabling: SI 2003/859, SI 2004/2684

s.76A, applied: 2004 c.18 Sch.8 para.3, Sch.10 para.2

s.76A, repealed (in part): 2004 c.18 Sch.12 Part 1

s.77, applied: 2003 c.iii s.4

s.77, repealed (in part): 2004 c.18 Sch.12 Part 1

s.77, enabling: SI 2004/2684

s.78, applied: SI 2002/37 Art.5, SI 2002/421 Art.5, SI 2002/422 Art.5, SI 2002/1484 Art.5, SI 2002/1485 Art.5, SI 2002/2012 Art.5, SI 2002/2183 Art.5, SI 2002/2188 Art.5, SI 2002/3265 Art.6, SI 2002/3266 Art.5, SI 2003/95 Art.5, SI 2003/251 Art.5, SI 2003/634 Art.5, SI 2003/635 Art.5, SI 2003/898 Art.5, SI 2003/1261 Art.5, SI 2003/1984 Art.5, SI 2003/2334 Art.5, SI 2003/2336 Art.5, SI 2003/2677 Art.5, SI 2003/2711 Art.5, 2004 c.18 s.82, s.83, SI

1991–cont.

40. Road Traffic Act 1991–cont.

s.78, applied:–cont.

2004/914 Art.5, SI 2004/1278 Art.5, SI 2004/1285 Art.5, SI 2004/1305 Art.5, SI 2004/1402 Art.5, SI 2004/2028 Art.5, SI 2004/2111 Art.5, SI 2004/2188 Art.5, SI 2004/2193 Art.5, SI 2004/2194 Art.5, SI 2004/2212 Art.5, SI 2004/2260 Art.5, SI 2004/2424 Art.5, SI 2004/2616 Art.5

s.78, repealed (in part): 2004 c.18 Sch.12 Part 1

s.78, varied: SI 2002/37 Sch.1 para.6, SI 2002/126 Sch.1 para.6, SI 2002/276 Sch.1 para.6, SI 2002/421 Sch.1 para.6, SI 2002/422 Sch.1 para.6, SI 2002/1351 Sch.1 para.6, SI 2002/1352 Sch.1 para.6, SI 2002/1353 Sch.1 para.6, SI 2002/1484 Sch.1 para.6, SI 2002/1485 Sch.1 para.6, SI 2002/1486 Sch.1 para.6, SI 2002/1504 Sch.1 para.6, SI 2002/1621 Sch.1 para.6, SI 2002/2012 Sch.1 para.6, SI 2002/2183 Sch.1 para.6, SI 2002/2184 Sch.1 para.6, SI 2002/2185 Sch.1 para.6, SI 2002/2186 Sch.1 para.6, SI 2002/2187 Sch.1 para.6, SI 2002/2188 Sch.1 para.6, SI 2002/2520 Sch.1 para.6, SI 2002/2705 Sch.1 para.6, SI 2002/3265 Sch.1 para.6, SI 2002/3266 Sch.1 para.6, 2003 c.iii Sch.1 para.6, SI 2003/95 Sch.1 para.6, SI 2003/251 Sch.1 para.6, SI 2003/634 Sch.1 para.6, SI 2003/635 Sch.1 para.6, SI 2003/898 Sch.1 para.6, SI 2003/1261 Sch.1 para.6, SI 2003/1262 Art.5, Sch.1 para.6, SI 2003/1924 Sch.1 para.6, SI 2003/1984 Sch.1 para.6, SI 2003/2152 Sch.1 para.6, SI 2003/2153 Sch.1 para.6, SI 2003/2326 Sch.1 para.6, SI 2003/2334 Sch.1 para.6, SI 2003/2336 Sch.1 para.6, SI 2003/2440 Sch.1 para.6, SI 2003/2677 Sch.1 para.5, SI 2003/2711 Sch.1 para.6, SI 2004/13 Art.5, Sch.1 para.6, SI 2004/104 Sch.1 para.6, SI 2004/914 Sch.1 para.6, SI 2004/1278 Sch.1 para.6, SI 2004/1285 Sch.1 para.6, SI 2004/1305 Sch.1 para.6, SI 2004/1402 Sch.1 para.6, SI 2004/1608 Sch.1 para.6, SI 2004/2028 Sch.2 para.6, SI 2004/2111 Sch.1 para.6, SI 2004/2188 Sch.1 para.6, SI 2004/2193 Sch.1 para.6, SI 2004/2194 Sch.1 para.6, SI 2004/2212 Sch.1 para.6, SI 2004/2260 Sch.1 para.6, SI 2004/2424 Sch.2 para.6, SI 2004/2616 Sch.1 para.6

s.78, enabling: SI 2003/1857

s.79, applied: SI 2002/37 Art.5, SI 2002/421 Art.5, SI 2002/422 Art.5, SI 2002/1484 Art.5, SI 2002/1485 Art.5, SI 2002/2012 Art.5, SI 2002/2183 Art.5, SI 2002/2188 Art.5, SI 2002/3265 Art.6, SI 2002/3266 Art.5, SI 2003/95 Art.5, SI 2003/251 Art.5, SI 2003/634 Art.5, SI 2003/635 Art.5, SI 2003/898 Art.5, SI 2003/1261 Art.5, SI 2003/1984 Art.5, SI 2003/2334 Art.5, SI 2003/2336 Art.5, SI 2003/2677 Art.5, SI

1991–cont.

40. Road Traffic Act 1991–cont.

s.79, applied:–cont.

2003/2711 Art.5, SI 2004/914 Art.5, SI 2004/1278 Art.5, SI 2004/1285 Art.5, SI 2004/1305 Art.5, SI 2004/2028 Art.5, SI 2004/2111 Art.5, SI 2004/2188 Art.5, SI 2004/2193 Art.5, SI 2004/2194 Art.5, SI 2004/2212 Art.5, SI 2004/2260 Art.5, SI 2004/2424 Art.5, SI 2004/2616 Art.5, SSI 2002/398 Art.4, SSI 2003/70 Art.4, SSI 2004/87 Art.4

s.79, repealed (in part): 2004 c.18 Sch.12 Part 1

s.79, varied: SI 2003/1262 Art.5, SI 2003/2677 Sch.1 para.6, SI 2004/13 Art.5, SI 2004/2684 Art.5

s.82, applied: SI 2002/37 Art.5, SI 2002/421 Art.5, SI 2002/422 Art.5, SI 2002/1484 Art.5, SI 2002/1485 Art.5, SI 2002/2012 Art.5, SI 2002/2183 Art.5, SI 2002/2188 Art.5, SI 2002/3265 Art.6, SI 2002/3266 Art.5, SI 2003/95 Art.5, SI 2003/251 Art.5, SI 2003/634 Art.5, SI 2003/635 Art.5, SI 2003/898 Art.5, SI 2003/1261 Art.5, SI 2003/1984 Art.5, SI 2003/2334 Art.5, SI 2003/2336 Art.5, SI 2003/2677 Art.5, SI 2003/2711 Art.5, SI 2004/914 Art.5, SI 2004/1278 Art.5, SI 2004/1285 Art.5, SI 2004/1305 Art.5, SI 2004/1402 Art.5, SI 2004/2028 Art.5, SI 2004/2111 Art.5, SI 2004/2188 Art.5, SI 2004/2193 Art.5, SI 2004/2212 Art.5, SI 2004/2260 Art.5, SI 2004/2424 Art.5, SI 2004/2616 Art.5, SSI 2002/398 Art.4, SSI 2003/70 Art.4, SSI 2004/87 Art.4

s.82, varied: SI 2002/37 Sch.1 para.7, SI 2002/126 Sch.1 para.7, SI 2002/276 Sch.1 para.7, SI 2002/421 Sch.1 para.7, SI 2002/422 Sch.1 para.7, SI 2002/1351 Sch.1 para.7, SI 2002/1352 Sch.1 para.7, SI 2002/1353 Sch.1 para.7, SI 2002/1484 Sch.1 para.7, SI 2002/1485 Sch.1 para.7, SI 2002/1486 Sch.1 para.7, SI 2002/1504 Sch.1 para.7, SI 2002/1621 Sch.1 para.7, SI 2002/2012 Sch.1 para.7, SI 2002/2183 Sch.1 para.7, SI 2002/2184 Sch.1 para.7, SI 2002/2185 Sch.1 para.7, SI 2002/2186 Sch.1 para.7, SI 2002/2187 Sch.1 para.7, SI 2002/2188 Sch.1 para.7, SI 2002/2520 Sch.1 para.7, SI 2002/2705 Sch.1 para.7, SI 2002/3265 Sch.1 para.7, SI 2002/3266 Sch.1 para.7, SI 2003/95 Sch.1 para.7, SI 2003/251 Sch.1 para.7, SI 2003/634 Sch.1 para.7, SI 2003/635 Sch.1 para.7, SI 2003/898 Sch.1 para.7, SI 2003/1261 Sch.1 para.7, SI 2003/1262 Art.5, Sch.1 para.7, SI 2003/1924 Sch.1 para.7, SI 2003/1984 Sch.1 para.7, SI 2003/2152 Sch.1 para.7, SI 2003/2153 Sch.1 para.7, SI 2003/2326 Sch.1 para.7, SI 2003/2334 Sch.1 para.7, SI 2003/2336 Sch.1 para.7, SI 2003/2440 Sch.1 para.7, SI 2003/2677 Sch.1 para.7, SI 2003/2711 Sch.1 para.7, SI

1991–cont.

40. Road Traffic Act 1991–cont.

s.82, varied:–cont.

2004/13 Art.5, Sch.1 para.7, SI 2004/104
Sch.1 para.7, SI 2004/914 Sch.1 para.7, SI
2004/1278 Sch.1 para.7, SI 2004/1285
Sch.1 para.7, SI 2004/1305 Sch.1 para.7, SI
2004/1402 Sch.1 para.7, SI 2004/1608
Sch.1 para.7, SI 2004/2028 Sch.2 para.7,
SI 2004/2111 Sch.1 para.7, SI 2004/2188
Sch.1 para.7, SI 2004/2193 Sch.1 para.7, SI
2004/2194 Sch.1 para.7, SI 2004/2212
Sch.1 para.7, SI 2004/2260 Sch.1 para.7,
SI 2004/2424 Sch.2 para.7, SI 2004/
2616 Sch.1 para.7, SSI 2002/398 Sch.2
para.6, SSI 2003/70 Sch.2 para.6, SSI
2004/87 Sch.2 para.6

Sch.1 para.3, applied: SI 2002/1621

Sch.2, referred to: SI 2002/2012 Art.6

Sch.2 para.3, applied: SI 2002/1621

Sch.3, applied: SI 2002/3113 Reg.4, 2004
c.18 s.88

Sch.3, referred to: SI 2002/1485 Art.6

Sch.3 para.1, applied: SI 2002/37, SI 2002/
126, SI 2002/276, SI 2002/421, SI 2002/
422, SI 2002/1351, SI 2002/1352, SI
2002/1353, SI 2002/1484, SI 2002/
1485, SI 2002/1486, SI 2002/1504, SI
2002/2012, SI 2002/2183, SI 2002/
2184, SI 2002/2185, SI 2002/2186, SI
2002/2187, SI 2002/2188, SI 2002/
2440, SI 2002/2520, SI 2002/2705, SI
2002/3265, SI 2002/3266, SI 2003/95,
SI 2003/251, SI 2003/634, SI 2003/635,
SI 2003/898, SI 2003/1261, SI 2003/
1262, SI 2003/1984, SI 2003/2152, SI
2003/2153, SI 2003/2326, SI 2003/
2334, SI 2003/2336, SI 2003/2440, SI
2003/2677, SI 2003/2711, SI 2004/13, SI
2004/538, SI 2004/914, SI 2004/1278, SI
2004/1285, SI 2004/1305, SI 2004/1608,
SI 2004/2424, SI 2004/2616, SSI 2002/
187, SSI 2002/188, SSI 2002/398, SSI
2003/70, 2004 c.18 Sch.8 para.8, SI
2004/104, SI 2004/1402, SI 2004/2028,
SI 2004/2111, SI 2004/2188, SI 2004/
2193, SI 2004/2194, SI 2004/2212, SI
2004/2260, SSI 2004/87

Sch.3 para.1, repealed (in part): 2004 c.18
Sch.12 Part 1

Sch.3 para.1, varied: SI 2002/1485 Sch.2
para.7, SI 2002/1486 Sch.2 para.7, SSI
2002/398 Sch.3 Part II, SSI 2003/70
Sch.3 Part II, SSI 2004/87 Sch.3 Part II

Sch.3 para.1, enabling: SI 2002/37, SI 2002/
126, SI 2002/276, SI 2002/421, SI 2002/
422, SI 2002/1351, SI 2002/1352, SI
2002/1353, SI 2002/1484, SI 2002/
1485, SI 2002/1486, SI 2002/1504, SI
2002/1621, SI 2002/2012, SI 2002/2183,
SI 2002/2184, SI 2002/2185, SI 2002/
2186, SI 2002/2187, SI 2002/2188, SI
2002/2440, SI 2002/2520, SI 2002/
2705, SI 2002/3265, SI 2002/3266, SI

1991–cont.

40. Road Traffic Act 1991–cont.

Sch.3 para.1, enabling:–cont.

2003/95, SI 2003/251, SI 2003/634, SI
2003/635, SI 2003/898, SI 2003/1261,
SI 2003/1262, SI 2003/1924, SI 2003/
1984, SI 2003/2152, SI 2003/2153, SI
2003/2326, SI 2003/2334, SI 2003/
2336, SI 2003/2440, SI 2003/2677, SI
2003/2711, SI 2004/13, SI 2004/104, SI
2004/538, SI 2004/914, SI 2004/1278,
SI 2004/1285, SI 2004/1305, SI 2004/
1402, SI 2004/1608, SI 2004/2028, SI
2004/2111, SI 2004/2188, SI 2004/2193,
SI 2004/2194, SI 2004/2212, SI 2004/
2260, SI 2004/2263, SI 2004/2424, SI
2004/2616, SI 2004/3246, SI 2004/
3310, SSI 2002/187, SSI 2002/188, SSI
2002/398, SSI 2003/70, SSI 2004/87

Sch.3 para.2, amended: SI 2003/859 Art.2,
SSI 2003/508 Art.2

Sch.3 para.2, applied: SI 2002/37, SI 2002/
126, SI 2002/276, SI 2002/421, SI 2002/
422, SI 2002/1351, SI 2002/1352, SI
2002/1353, SI 2002/1484, SI 2002/
1485, SI 2002/1486, SI 2002/1504, SI
2002/2012, SI 2002/2183, SI 2002/
2184, SI 2002/2185, SI 2002/2186, SI
2002/2187, SI 2002/2188, SI 2002/
2440, SI 2002/2520, SI 2002/2705, SI
2002/3265, SI 2002/3266, SI 2003/95,
SI 2003/251, SI 2003/634, SI 2003/635,
SI 2003/859, SI 2003/898, SI 2003/1261,
SI 2003/1262, SI 2003/1984, SI 2003/
2152, SI 2003/2153, SI 2003/2326, SI
2003/2334, SI 2003/2336, SI 2003/
2440, SI 2003/2677, SI 2003/2711, SI
2004/13, SI 2004/538, SI 2004/914, SI
2004/1278, SI 2004/1285, SI 2004/
1305, SI 2004/1608, SI 2004/2424, SI
2004/2616, SSI 2002/187, SSI 2002/
188, SSI 2002/398, SSI 2003/70, SSI
2003/508, 2004 c.18 Sch.8 para.8,
Sch.10 para.3, SI 2004/104, SI 2004/
1402, SI 2004/2028, SI 2004/2111, SI
2004/2188, SI 2004/2193, SI 2004/
2194, SI 2004/2212, SI 2004/2260, SSI
2004/87

Sch.3 para.2, repealed (in part): 2004 c.18
Sch.12 Part 1

Sch.3 para.2, varied: SI 2002/1486 Sch.2
para.7

Sch.3 para.2, enabling: SI 2002/37, SI 2002/
126, SI 2002/276, SI 2002/421, SI 2002/
422, SI 2002/1351, SI 2002/1352, SI
2002/1353, SI 2002/1484, SI 2002/
1485, SI 2002/1486, SI 2002/1504, SI
2002/1621, SI 2002/2012, SI 2002/2183,
SI 2002/2184, SI 2002/2185, SI 2002/
2186, SI 2002/2187, SI 2002/2188, SI
2002/2440, SI 2002/2520, SI 2002/
2705, SI 2002/3265, SI 2002/3266, SI
2003/95, SI 2003/251, SI 2003/634, SI
2003/635, SI 2003/859, SI 2003/898,

CAP.

1991–cont.

40. Road Traffic Act 1991–*cont.*

Sch.3 para.2, enabling:–*cont.*

SI 2003/1261, SI 2003/1262, SI 2003/1924, SI 2003/1984, SI 2003/2152, SI 2003/2153, SI 2003/2326, SI 2003/2334, SI 2003/2336, SI 2003/2440, SI 2003/2677, SI 2003/2711, SI 2004/13, SI 2004/104, SI 2004/538, SI 2004/914, SI 2004/1278, SI 2004/1285, SI 2004/1305, SI 2004/1402, SI 2004/1608, SI 2004/2028, SI 2004/2111, SI 2004/2188, SI 2004/2193, SI 2004/2194, SI 2004/2212, SI 2004/2260, SI 2004/2263, SI 2004/2424, SI 2004/2616, SI 2004/3246, SI 2004/3310, SSI 2002/187, SSI 2002/188, SSI 2002/398, SSI 2003/70, SSI 2003/508, SSI 2004/87

Sch.3 para.3, applied: SI 2002/1353

Sch.3 para.3, repealed (in part): 2004 c.18 Sch.12 Part 1

Sch.3 para.3, varied: SI 2002/1486 Sch.2 para.7

Sch.3 para.3, enabling: SI 2002/37, SI 2002/126, SI 2002/276, SI 2002/422, SI 2002/1351, SI 2002/1352, SI 2002/1353, SI 2002/1484, SI 2002/1485, SI 2002/1486, SI 2002/1504, SI 2002/1621, SI 2002/2012, SI 2002/2183, SI 2002/2184, SI 2002/2185, SI 2002/2186, SI 2002/2187, SI 2002/2188, SI 2002/2440, SI 2002/2520, SI 2002/2705, SI 2002/3265, SI 2002/3266, SI 2003/95, SI 2003/251, SI 2003/634, SI 2003/635, SI 2003/898, SI 2003/1261, SI 2003/1262, SI 2003/1924, SI 2003/1984, SI 2003/2152, SI 2003/2153, SI 2003/2326, SI 2003/2334, SI 2003/2336, SI 2003/2440, SI 2003/2677, SI 2003/2711, SI 2004/13, SI 2004/104, SI 2004/538, SI 2004/914, SI 2004/1278, SI 2004/1285, SI 2004/1305, SI 2004/1402, SI 2004/1608, SI 2004/2028, SI 2004/2111, SI 2004/2188, SI 2004/2193, SI 2004/2194, SI 2004/2212, SI 2004/2260, SI 2004/2263, SI 2004/2424, SI 2004/2616, SI 2004/3246, SI 2004/3310, SSI 2002/187, SSI 2002/188, SSI 2002/398, SSI 2003/70, SSI 2004/87

Sch.3 para.4, repealed (in part): 2004 c.18 Sch.12 Part 1

Sch.3 para.4, varied: SI 2002/1486 Sch.2 para.7

Sch.6, applied: SI 2002/421 Art.5, SI 2002/422 Art.5, SI 2002/1484 Art.5, SI 2002/1485 Art.5, SI 2002/2012 Art.5, SI 2002/2183 Art.5, SI 2002/2188 Art.5, SI 2002/3265 Art.6, SI 2002/3266 Art.5, SI 2003/251 Art.5, SI 2003/634 Art.5, SI 2003/635 Art.5, SI 2003/898 Art.5, SI 2003/1261 Art.5, SI 2003/1984 Art.5, SI 2003/2334 Art.5, SI 2003/2336 Art.5, SI 2003/2677 Art.5, SI 2003/2711 Art.5, SI 2004/914 Art.5, SI 2004/1278 Art.5, SI 2004/1285

CAP.

1991–cont.

40. Road Traffic Act 1991–*cont.*

Sch.6, applied:–*cont.*

Art.5, SI 2004/1305 Art.5, SI 2004/1402 Art.5, SI 2004/2028 Art.5, SI 2004/2111 Art.5, SI 2004/2188 Art.5, SI 2004/2193 Art.5, SI 2004/2194 Art.5, SI 2004/2212 Art.5, SI 2004/2260 Art.5, SI 2004/2424 Art.5, SI 2004/2616 Art.5, SSI 2002/398 Art.4, SSI 2003/70 Art.4, SSI 2004/87 Art.4

Sch.6 para.1, repealed (in part): 2004 c.18 Sch.12 Part 1

Sch.6 para.1, varied: SI 2002/37 Sch.1 para.8, SI 2002/126 Sch.1 para.8, SI 2002/276 Sch.1 para.8, SI 2002/421 Sch.1 para.8, SI 2002/422 Sch.1 para.8, SI 2002/1351 Sch.1 para.8, SI 2002/1352 Sch.1 para.8, SI 2002/1353 Sch.1 para.8, SI 2002/1484 Sch.1 para.8, SI 2002/1485 Sch.1 para.8, SI 2002/1486 Sch.1 para.8, SI 2002/1504 Sch.1 para.8, SI 2002/1621 Sch.1 para.8, SI 2002/2012 Sch.1 para.8, SI 2002/2183 Sch.1 para.8, SI 2002/2184 Sch.1 para.8, SI 2002/2185 Sch.1 para.8, SI 2002/2186 Sch.1 para.8, SI 2002/2187 Sch.1 para.8, SI 2002/2188 Sch.1 para.8, SI 2002/2520 Sch.1 para.8, SI 2002/2705 Sch.1 para.8, SI 2002/3265 Sch.1 para.8, SI 2002/3266 Sch.1 para.8, SI 2003/95 Sch.1 para.8, SI 2003/251 Sch.1 para.8, SI 2003/634 Sch.1 para.8, SI 2003/635 Sch.1 para.8, SI 2003/898 Sch.1 para.8, SI 2003/1261 Sch.1 para.8, SI 2003/1262 Art.5, Sch.1 para.8, SI 2003/1924 Sch.1 para.8, SI 2003/1984 Sch.1 para.8, SI 2003/2152 Sch.1 para.8, SI 2003/2153 Sch.1 para.8, SI 2003/2326 Sch.1 para.8, SI 2003/2334 Sch.1 para.8, SI 2003/2336 Sch.1 para.8, SI 2003/2440 Sch.1 para.8, SI 2003/2677 Sch.1 para.8, SI 2003/2711 Sch.1 para.8, SI 2004/13 Art.5, Sch.1 para.8, SI 2004/104 Sch.1 para.8, SI 2004/914 Sch.1 para.8, SI 2004/1278 Sch.1 para.8, SI 2004/1285 Sch.1 para.8, SI 2004/1305 Sch.1 para.8, SI 2004/1402 Sch.1 para.8, SI 2004/1608 Sch.1 para.8, SI 2004/2028 Sch.2 para.8, SI 2004/2111 Sch.1 para.8, SI 2004/2188 Sch.1 para.8, SI 2004/2193 Sch.1 para.8, SI 2004/2194 Sch.1 para.8, SI 2004/2212 Sch.1 para.8, SI 2004/2260 Sch.1 para.8, SI 2004/2424 Sch.2 para.8, SI 2004/2616 Sch.1 para.8, SSI 2002/398 Sch.2 para.7, SSI 2003/70 Sch.2 para.7, SSI 2004/87 Sch.2 para.7

Sch.6 para.2, see *R. (on the application of Westminster City Council) v Parking Adjudicator* [2002] EWHC 1007, [2003] R.T.R. 1 (QBD (Admin Ct)), Elias, J.

Sch.6 para.2, applied: SSI 2002/400 Reg.4, SSI 2003/71 Reg.4, SSI 2004/86 Reg.4

Sch.6 para.2, repealed (in part): 2004 c.18 Sch.12 Part 1

1991–cont.

40. Road Traffic Act 1991–*cont.*

Sch.6 para.2, varied: SI 2002/37 Sch.1 para.8, SI 2002/126 Sch.1 para.8, SI 2002/276 Sch.1 para.8, SI 2002/421 Sch.1 para.8, SI 2002/422 Sch.1 para.8, SI 2002/1351 Sch.1 para.8, SI 2002/1352 Sch.1 para.8, SI 2002/1353 Sch.1 para.8, SI 2002/1484 Sch.1 para.8, SI 2002/1485 Sch.1 para.8, SI 2002/1486 Sch.1 para.8, SI 2002/1504 Sch.1 para.8, SI 2002/1621 Sch.1 para.8, SI 2002/2012 Sch.1 para.8, SI 2002/2183 Sch.1 para.8, SI 2002/2184 Sch.1 para.8, SI 2002/2185 Sch.1 para.8, SI 2002/2186 Sch.1 para.8, SI 2002/2187 Sch.1 para.8, SI 2002/2188 Sch.1 para.8, SI 2002/2520 Sch.1 para.8, SI 2002/2705 Sch.1 para.8, SI 2002/3265 Sch.1 para.8, SI 2002/3266 Sch.1 para.8, SI 2003/95 Sch.1 para.8, SI 2003/251 Sch.1 para.8, SI 2003/634 Sch.1 para.8, SI 2003/635 Sch.1 para.8, SI 2003/898 Sch.1 para.8, SI 2003/1261 Sch.1 para.8, SI 2003/1262 Art.5, Sch.1 para.8, SI 2003/1924 Sch.1 para.8, SI 2003/1984 Sch.1 para.8, SI 2003/2152 Sch.1 para.8, SI 2003/2153 Sch.1 para.8, SI 2003/2326 Sch.1 para.8, SI 2003/2334 Sch.1 para.8, SI 2003/2336 Sch.1 para.8, SI 2003/2440 Sch.1 para.8, SI 2003/2711 Sch.1 para.8, SI 2004/13 Art.5, Sch.1 para.8, SI 2004/104 Sch.1 para.8, SI 2004/914 Sch.1 para.8, SI 2004/1278 Sch.1 para.8, SI 2004/1285 Sch.1 para.8, SI 2004/1305 Sch.1 para.8, SI 2004/1402 Sch.1 para.8, SI 2004/1608 Sch.1 para.8, SI 2004/2028 Sch.2 para.8, SI 2004/2111 Sch.1 para.8, SI 2004/2188 Sch.1 para.8, SI 2004/2193 Sch.1 para.8, SI 2004/2194 Sch.1 para.8, SI 2004/2212 Sch.1 para.8, SI 2004/2260 Sch.1 para.8, SI 2004/2424 Sch.2 para.8, SI 2004/2616 Sch.1 para.8, SI 2004/2684 Art.5, SSI 2002/398 Sch.2 para.7, SSI 2003/70 Sch.2 para.7, SSI 2004/87 Sch.2 para.7

Sch.6 para.3, repealed (in part): 2004 c.18 Sch.12 Part 1

Sch.6 para.3, varied: SI 2002/37 Sch.1 para.8, SI 2002/126 Sch.1 para.8, SI 2002/276 Sch.1 para.8, SI 2002/421 Sch.1 para.8, SI 2002/422 Sch.1 para.8, SI 2002/1351 Sch.1 para.8, SI 2002/1352 Sch.1 para.8, SI 2002/1353 Sch.1 para.8, SI 2002/1484 Sch.1 para.8, SI 2002/1485 Sch.1 para.8, SI 2002/1486 Sch.1 para.8, SI 2002/1504 Sch.1 para.8, SI 2002/1621 Sch.1 para.8, SI 2002/2012 Sch.1 para.8, SI 2002/2183 Sch.1 para.8, SI 2002/2184 Sch.1 para.8, SI 2002/2185 Sch.1 para.8, SI 2002/2186 Sch.1 para.8, SI 2002/2187 Sch.1 para.8, SI 2002/2520 Sch.1 para.8, SI 2002/2705 Sch.1 para.8, SI 2002/3265 Sch.1 para.8, SI 2002/3266 Sch.1 para.8, SI 2003/95 Sch.1 para.8, SI 2003/251 Sch.1

1991–cont.

40. Road Traffic Act 1991–*cont.*

Sch.6 para.3, varied:–*cont.*

para.8, SI 2003/634 Sch.1 para.8, SI 2003/635 Sch.1 para.8, SI 2003/898 Sch.1 para.8, SI 2003/1261 Sch.1 para.8, SI 2003/1262 Art.5, Sch.1 para.8, SI 2003/1924 Sch.1 para.8, SI 2003/1984 Sch.1 para.8, SI 2003/2152 Sch.1 para.8, SI 2003/2153 Sch.1 para.8, SI 2003/2326 Sch.1 para.8, SI 2003/2334 Sch.1 para.8, SI 2003/2336 Sch.1 para.8, SI 2003/2440 Sch.1 para.8, SI 2003/2677 Sch.1 para.8, SI 2003/2711 Sch.1 para.8, SI 2004/13 Art.5, Sch.1 para.8, SI 2004/104 Sch.1 para.8, SI 2004/914 Sch.1 para.8, SI 2004/1278 Sch.1 para.8, SI 2004/1285 Sch.1 para.8, SI 2004/1305 Sch.1 para.8, SI 2004/1402 Sch.1 para.8, SI 2004/1608 Sch.1 para.8, SI 2004/2028 Sch.2 para.8, SI 2004/2111 Sch.1 para.8, SI 2004/2188 Sch.1 para.8, SI 2004/2193 Sch.1 para.8, SI 2004/2194 Sch.1 para.8, SI 2004/2212 Sch.1 para.8, SI 2004/2260 Sch.1 para.8, SI 2004/2424 Sch.2 para.8, SI 2004/2616 Sch.1 para.8, SSI 2002/398 Sch.2 para.7, SSI 2003/70 Sch.2 para.7, SSI 2004/87 Sch.2 para.7

Sch.6 para.4, repealed (in part): 2004 c.18 Sch.12 Part 1

Sch.6 para.4, varied: SI 2002/37 Sch.1 para.8, SI 2002/126 Sch.1 para.8, SI 2002/276 Sch.1 para.8, SI 2002/421 Sch.1 para.8, SI 2002/422 Sch.1 para.8, SI 2002/1351 Sch.1 para.8, SI 2002/1352 Sch.1 para.8, SI 2002/1353 Sch.1 para.8, SI 2002/1484 Sch.1 para.8, SI 2002/1485 Sch.1 para.8, SI 2002/1486 Sch.1 para.8, SI 2002/1504 Sch.1 para.8, SI 2002/1621 Sch.1 para.8, SI 2002/2012 Sch.1 para.8, SI 2002/2183 Sch.1 para.8, SI 2002/2184 Sch.1 para.8, SI 2002/2185 Sch.1 para.8, SI 2002/2186 Sch.1 para.8, SI 2002/2187 Sch.1 para.8, SI 2002/2520 Sch.1 para.8, SI 2002/2705 Sch.1 para.8, SI 2002/3265 Sch.1 para.8, SI 2002/3266 Sch.1 para.8, SI 2003/95 Sch.1 para.8, SI 2003/251 Sch.1 para.8, SI 2003/634 Sch.1 para.8, SI 2003/635 Sch.1 para.8, SI 2003/898 Sch.1 para.8, SI 2003/1261 Sch.1 para.8, SI 2003/1262 Art.5, Sch.1 para.8, SI 2003/1924 Sch.1 para.8, SI 2003/1984 Sch.1 para.8, SI 2003/2152 Sch.1 para.8, SI 2003/2153 Sch.1 para.8, SI 2003/2326 Sch.1 para.8, SI 2003/2334 Sch.1 para.8, SI 2003/2336 Sch.1 para.8, SI 2003/2440 Sch.1 para.8, SI 2003/2677 Sch.1 para.8, SI 2003/2711 Sch.1 para.8, SI 2004/13 Art.5, Sch.1 para.8, SI 2004/104 Sch.1 para.8, SI 2004/914 Sch.1 para.8, SI 2004/1278 Sch.1 para.8, SI 2004/1285 Sch.1 para.8, SI 2004/1305 Sch.1 para.8, SI 2004/1402 Sch.1 para.8, SI 2004/1608 Sch.1 para.8, SI 2004/2028 Sch.2 para.8,

1991—cont.

40. Road Traffic Act 1991—*cont.*

Sch.6 para.4, varied:—*cont.*

SI 2004/2111 Sch.1 para.8, SI 2004/2188 Sch.1 para.8, SI 2004/2193 Sch.1 para.8, SI 2004/2194 Sch.1 para.8, SI 2004/2212 Sch.1 para.8, SI 2004/2260 Sch.1 para.8, SI 2004/2424 Sch.2 para.8, SI 2004/2616 Sch.1 para.8, SSI 2002/398 Sch.2 para.7, SSI 2003/70 Sch.2 para.7, SSI 2004/87 Sch.2 para.7

Sch.6 para.5, applied: SSI 2002/400 Reg.14, SSI 2003/71 Reg.14, SSI 2004/86 Reg.14

Sch.6 para.5, referred to: SSI 2002/400 Reg.3, SSI 2003/71 Reg.3, SSI 2004/86 Reg.3

Sch.6 para.5, repealed (in part): 2004 c.18 Sch.12 Part 1

Sch.6 para.5, varied: SI 2002/37 Sch.1 para.8, SI 2002/126 Sch.1 para.8, SI 2002/276 Sch.1 para.8, SI 2002/421 Sch.1 para.8, SI 2002/422 Sch.1 para.8, SI 2002/1351 Sch.1 para.8, SI 2002/1352 Sch.1 para.8, SI 2002/1353 Sch.1 para.8, SI 2002/1484 Sch.1 para.8, SI 2002/1485 Sch.1 para.8, SI 2002/1486 Sch.1 para.8, SI 2002/1504 Sch.1 para.8, SI 2002/1621 Sch.1 para.8, SI 2002/2012 Sch.1 para.8, SI 2002/2183 Sch.1 para.8, SI 2002/2184 Sch.1 para.8, SI 2002/2185 Sch.1 para.8, SI 2002/2186 Sch.1 para.8, SI 2002/2187 Sch.1 para.8, SI 2002/2520 Sch.1 para.8, SI 2002/2705 Sch.1 para.8, SI 2002/3265 Sch.1 para.8, SI 2002/3266 Sch.1 para.8, SI 2003/95 Sch.1 para.8, SI 2003/251 Sch.1 para.8, SI 2003/634 Sch.1 para.8, SI 2003/635 Sch.1 para.8, SI 2003/898 Sch.1 para.8, SI 2003/1261 Sch.1 para.8, SI 2003/1262 Art.5, Sch.1 para.8, SI 2003/1924 Sch.1 para.8, SI 2003/1984 Sch.1 para.8, SI 2003/2152 Sch.1 para.8, SI 2003/2153 Sch.1 para.8, SI 2003/2326 Sch.1 para.8, SI 2003/2334 Sch.1 para.8, SI 2003/2336 Sch.1 para.8, SI 2003/2440 Sch.1 para.8, SI 2003/2677 Sch.1 para.8, SI 2003/2711 Sch.1 para.8, SI 2004/13 Art.5, Sch.1 para.8, SI 2004/104 Sch.1 para.8, SI 2004/914 Sch.1 para.8, SI 2004/1278 Sch.1 para.8, SI 2004/1285 Sch.1 para.8, SI 2004/1305 Sch.1 para.8, SI 2004/1402 Sch.1 para.8, SI 2004/1608 Sch.1 para.8, SI 2004/2028 Sch.2 para.8, SI 2004/2111 Sch.1 para.8, SI 2004/2188 Sch.1 para.8, SI 2004/2193 Sch.1 para.8, SI 2004/2194 Sch.1 para.8, SI 2004/2212 Sch.1 para.8, SI 2004/2260 Sch.1 para.8, SI 2004/2424 Sch.2 para.8, SI 2004/2616 Sch.1 para.8, SSI 2002/398 Sch.2 para.7, SSI 2003/70 Sch.2 para.7, SSI 2004/87 Sch.2 para.7

Sch.6 para.6, repealed (in part): 2004 c.18 Sch.12 Part 1

1991—cont.

40. Road Traffic Act 1991—*cont.*

Sch.6 para.6, varied: SI 2002/37 Sch.1 para.8, SI 2002/126 Sch.1 para.8, SI 2002/276 Sch.1 para.8, SI 2002/421 Sch.1 para.8, SI 2002/422 Sch.1 para.8, SI 2002/1351 Sch.1 para.8, SI 2002/1352 Sch.1 para.8, SI 2002/1353 Sch.1 para.8, SI 2002/1484 Sch.1 para.8, SI 2002/1485 Sch.1 para.8, SI 2002/1486 Sch.1 para.8, SI 2002/1504 Sch.1 para.8, SI 2002/1621 Sch.1 para.8, SI 2002/2012 Sch.1 para.8, SI 2002/2183 Sch.1 para.8, SI 2002/2184 Sch.1 para.8, SI 2002/2185 Sch.1 para.8, SI 2002/2186 Sch.1 para.8, SI 2002/2187 Sch.1 para.8, SI 2002/2520 Sch.1 para.8, SI 2002/2705 Sch.1 para.8, SI 2002/3265 Sch.1 para.8, SI 2002/3266 Sch.1 para.8, SI 2003/95 Sch.1 para.8, SI 2003/251 Sch.1 para.8, SI 2003/634 Sch.1 para.8, SI 2003/635 Sch.1 para.8, SI 2003/898 Sch.1 para.8, SI 2003/1261 Sch.1 para.8, SI 2003/1262 Art.5, Sch.1 para.8, SI 2003/1924 Sch.1 para.8, SI 2003/1984 Sch.1 para.8, SI 2003/2152 Sch.1 para.8, SI 2003/2153 Sch.1 para.8, SI 2003/2326 Sch.1 para.8, SI 2003/2334 Sch.1 para.8, SI 2003/2336 Sch.1 para.8, SI 2003/2440 Sch.1 para.8, SI 2003/2677 Sch.1 para.8, SI 2003/2711 Sch.1 para.8, SI 2004/13 Art.5, Sch.1 para.8, SI 2004/104 Sch.1 para.8, SI 2004/914 Sch.1 para.8, SI 2004/1278 Sch.1 para.8, SI 2004/1285 Sch.1 para.8, SI 2004/1305 Sch.1 para.8, SI 2004/1402 Sch.1 para.8, SI 2004/1608 Sch.1 para.8, SI 2004/2028 Sch.2 para.8, SI 2004/2111 Sch.1 para.8, SI 2004/2188 Sch.1 para.8, SI 2004/2193 Sch.1 para.8, SI 2004/2194 Sch.1 para.8, SI 2004/2212 Sch.1 para.8, SI 2004/2260 Sch.1 para.8, SI 2004/2424 Sch.2 para.8, SI 2004/2616 Sch.1 para.8, SSI 2002/398 Sch.2 para.7, SSI 2003/70 Sch.2 para.7, SSI 2004/87 Sch.2 para.7

Sch.6 para.7, repealed (in part): 2004 c.18 Sch.12 Part 1

Sch.6 para.7, varied: SI 2002/37 Sch.1 para.8, SI 2002/126 Sch.1 para.8, SI 2002/276 Sch.1 para.8, SI 2002/421 Sch.1 para.8, SI 2002/422 Sch.1 para.8, SI 2002/1351 Sch.1 para.8, SI 2002/1352 Sch.1 para.8, SI 2002/1353 Sch.1 para.8, SI 2002/1484 Sch.1 para.8, SI 2002/1485 Sch.1 para.8, SI 2002/1486 Sch.1 para.8, SI 2002/1504 Sch.1 para.8, SI 2002/1621 Sch.1 para.8, SI 2002/2012 Sch.1 para.8, SI 2002/2183 Sch.1 para.8, SI 2002/2184 Sch.1 para.8, SI 2002/2185 Sch.1 para.8, SI 2002/2186 Sch.1 para.8, SI 2002/2187 Sch.1 para.8, SI 2002/2520 Sch.1 para.8, SI 2002/2705 Sch.1 para.8, SI 2002/3265 Sch.1 para.8, SI 2002/3266 Sch.1 para.8, SI 2003/95 Sch.1 para.8, SI 2003/251 Sch.1 para.8, SI 2003/634 Sch.1 para.8, SI 2003/

1991-cont.

40. Road Traffic Act 1991-*cont.*
  Sch.6 para.7, varied:-*cont.*

    635 Sch.1 para.8, SI 2003/898 Sch.1 para.8, SI 2003/1261 Sch.1 para.8, SI 2003/1262 Art.5, Sch.1 para.8, SI 2003/1924 Sch.1 para.8, SI 2003/1984 Sch.1 para.8, SI 2003/2152 Sch.1 para.8, SI 2003/2153 Sch.1 para.8, SI 2003/2326 Sch.1 para.8, SI 2003/2334 Sch.1 para.8, SI 2003/2336 Sch.1 para.8, SI 2003/2440 Sch.1 para.8, SI 2003/2677 Sch.1 para.8, SI 2003/2711 Sch.1 para.8, SI 2004/13 Art.5, Sch.1 para.8, SI 2004/104 Sch.1 para.8, SI 2004/914 Sch.1 para.8, SI 2004/1278 Sch.1 para.8, SI 2004/1285 Sch.1 para.8, SI 2004/1305 Sch.1 para.8, SI 2004/1402 Sch.1 para.8, SI 2004/1608 Sch.1 para.8, SI 2004/2028 Sch.2 para.8, SI 2004/2111 Sch.1 para.8, SI 2004/2188 Sch.1 para.8, SI 2004/2193 Sch.1 para.8, SI 2004/2194 Sch.1 para.8, SI 2004/2212 Sch.1 para.8, SI 2004/2260 Sch.1 para.8, SI 2004/2424 Sch.2 para.8, SI 2004/2616 Sch.1 para.8, SSI 2002/398 Sch.2 para.7, SSI 2003/70 Sch.2 para.7, SSI 2004/87 Sch.2 para.7

  Sch.6 para.8, applied: 2003 c.iii s.15

  Sch.6 para.8, repealed (in part): 2004 c.18 Sch.12 Part 1

  Sch.6 para.8, varied: SI 2002/37 Sch.1 para.8, SI 2002/126 Sch.1 para.8, SI 2002/276 Sch.1 para.8, SI 2002/421 Sch.1 para.8, SI 2002/422 Sch.1 para.8, SI 2002/1351 Sch.1 para.8, SI 2002/1352 Sch.1 para.8, SI 2002/1353 Sch.1 para.8, SI 2002/1484 Sch.1 para.8, SI 2002/1485 Sch.1 para.8, SI 2002/1486 Sch.1 para.8, SI 2002/1504 Sch.1 para.8, SI 2002/1621 Sch.1 para.8, SI 2002/2012 Sch.1 para.8, SI 2002/2183 Sch.1 para.8, SI 2002/2184 Sch.1 para.8, SI 2002/2185 Sch.1 para.8, SI 2002/2186 Sch.1 para.8, SI 2002/2187 Sch.1 para.8, SI 2002/2520 Sch.1 para.8, SI 2002/2705 Sch.1 para.8, SI 2002/3265 Sch.1 para.8, SI 2002/3266 Sch.1 para.8, 2003 c.iii s.15, SI 2003/95 Sch.1 para.8, SI 2003/251 Sch.1 para.8, SI 2003/634 Sch.1 para.8, SI 2003/635 Sch.1 para.8, SI 2003/898 Sch.1 para.8, SI 2003/1261 Sch.1 para.8, SI 2003/1262 Art.5, Sch.1 para.8, SI 2003/1924 Sch.1 para.8, SI 2003/1984 Sch.1 para.8, SI 2003/2152 Sch.1 para.8, SI 2003/2153 Sch.1 para.8, SI 2003/2326 Sch.1 para.8, SI 2003/2334 Sch.1 para.8, SI 2003/2336 Sch.1 para.8, SI 2003/2440 Sch.1 para.8, SI 2003/2677 Sch.1 para.8, SI 2003/2711 Sch.1 para.8, SI 2004/13 Art.5, Sch.1 para.8, SI 2004/104 Sch.1 para.8, SI 2004/914 Sch.1 para.8, SI 2004/1278 Sch.1 para.8, SI 2004/1285 Sch.1 para.8, SI 2004/1305 Sch.1 para.8, SI 2004/1402 Sch.1 para.8, SI 2004/1608 Sch.1 para.8, SI

1991-cont.

40. Road Traffic Act 1991-*cont.*
  Sch.6 para.8, varied:-*cont.*

    2004/2028 Sch.2 para.8, SI 2004/2111 Sch.1 para.8, SI 2004/2188 Sch.1 para.8, SI 2004/2193 Sch.1 para.8, SI 2004/2194 Sch.1 para.8, SI 2004/2212 Sch.1 para.8, SI 2004/2260 Sch.1 para.8, SI 2004/2424 Sch.2 para.8, SI 2004/2616 Sch.1 para.8, SSI 2002/398 Sch.2 para.7, SSI 2003/70 Sch.2 para.7, SSI 2004/87 Sch.2 para.7

  Sch.6 para.9, repealed (in part): 2004 c.18 Sch.12 Part 1

  Sch.6 para.9, varied: SI 2002/276 Sch.1 para.8, SI 2002/422 Sch.1 para.8, SI 2002/1351 Sch.1 para.8, SI 2002/1352 Sch.1 para.8, SI 2002/1353 Sch.1 para.8, SI 2002/1484 Sch.1 para.8, SI 2002/1485 Sch.1 para.8, SI 2002/1486 Sch.1 para.8, SI 2002/1621 Sch.1 para.8, SI 2002/2012 Sch.1 para.8, SI 2002/2183 Sch.1 para.8, SI 2002/2184 Sch.1 para.8, SI 2002/2185 Sch.1 para.8, SI 2002/2520 Sch.1 para.8, SI 2002/2705 Sch.1 para.8, SI 2002/3265 Sch.1 para.8, SI 2002/3266 Sch.1 para.8, SI 2003/95 Sch.1 para.8, SI 2003/1262 Art.5, SI 2003/2152 Sch.1 para.8, SI 2003/2153 Sch.1 para.8, SI 2004/13 Art.5, SI 2004/104 Sch.1 para.8, SI 2004/1608 Sch.1 para.8, SSI 2002/398 Sch.2 para.7

  Sch.6 para.10, repealed (in part): 2004 c.18 Sch.12 Part 1

  Sch.6 para.10, varied: SI 2002/276 Sch.1 para.8, SI 2002/422 Sch.1 para.8, SI 2002/1351 Sch.1 para.8, SI 2002/1352 Sch.1 para.8, SI 2002/1353 Sch.1 para.8, SI 2002/1484 Sch.1 para.8, SI 2002/1485 Sch.1 para.8, SI 2002/1486 Sch.1 para.8, SI 2002/1621 Sch.1 para.8, SI 2002/2012 Sch.1 para.8, SI 2002/2183 Sch.1 para.8, SI 2002/2184 Sch.1 para.8, SI 2002/2185 Sch.1 para.8, SI 2002/2520 Sch.1 para.8, SI 2002/2705 Sch.1 para.8, SI 2002/3265 Sch.1 para.8, SI 2002/3266 Sch.1 para.8, SI 2003/95 Sch.1 para.8, SI 2003/1262 Art.5, SI 2003/2152 Sch.1 para.8, SI 2003/2153 Sch.1 para.8, SI 2004/13 Art.5, SI 2004/104 Sch.1 para.8, SI 2004/1608 Sch.1 para.8, SSI 2002/398 Sch.2 para.7

41. Arms Control and Disarmament (Inspections) Act 1991
  amended: 2003 c.34 Sch.1 para.3
  s.1, amended: 2003 c.34 Sch.1 para.2
  s.1, repealed (in part): 2003 c.34 Sch.2
  s.2, amended: 2003 c.34 Sch.1 para.4, Sch.2
  s.3, amended: 2003 c.34 Sch.1 para.5, Sch.2
  s.6, applied: 2003 c.34 s.3
  Sch.1, repealed: 2003 c.34 Sch.1 para.6

CAP.

1991–cont.

45. Coal Mining Subsidence Act 1991
s.40, see *Langley v Coal Authority (No.1)* [2002] R.V.R. 216 (Lands Tr), Judge Levy Q.C.
s.50, enabling: SI 2004/2241
s.52, amended: 2003 c.21 Sch.17 para.109

47. Mental Health (Detention) (Scotland) Act 1991
repealed: 2003 asp 13 Sch.5 Part 1

48. Child Support Act 1991
see *R. (on the application of Kehoe) v Secretary of State for Work and Pensions* [2003] EWHC 1021, [2003] 2 F.L.R. 578 (QBD (Admin Ct)), Wall, J.; see *R. (on the application of Kehoe) v Secretary of State for Work and Pensions* [2004] EWCA Civ 225, [2004] Q.B. 1378 (CA), Ward, L.J.; see *Secretary of State for Work and Pensions v Jones* [2003] EWHC 2163, [2004] 1 F.L.R. 282 (Fam Div), Dame Elizabeth Butler-Sloss (President)
applied: SI 2003/1325 Art.2, SSI 2002/132 Sch.1 para.33.2, SSI 2002/494 Reg.33, 2004 c.33 Sch.5 para.49, Sch.6 para.27
s.3, applied: SSI 2002/132 Sch.1 para.33.2
s.4, applied: SI 2003/194 Reg.2
s.4, enabling: SI 2003/194
s.6, applied: SI 2003/192 Art.4
s.7, applied: SI 2003/194 Reg.2
s.7, enabling: SI 2003/194
s.8, see *Otto v Otto* 2002 Fam. L.R. 95 (Sh Ct (Grampian, Highland and Islands)), AL MacFadyen
s.8, amended: 2004 c.33 Sch.24 para.1, Sch.30
s.8, applied: SSI 2002/132 Sch.1 para.33.2, 2004 c.33 Sch.5 para.49, Sch.6 para.27
s.10, applied: SSI 2002/132 Sch.1 para.33.3, 2004 c.33 Sch.5 para.62, Sch.6 para.33
s.10, varied: SSI 2003/96 Art.3
s.12, enabling: SI 2003/2779
s.14, enabling: SI 2002/1204, SI 2003/3206, SI 2004/2415
s.15, amended: 2004 c.33 Sch.24 para.2
s.16, applied: SI 2002/1204 Reg.1
s.16, referred to: SI 2003/129 Reg.1, Reg.2
s.16, enabling: SI 2002/1204, SI 2003/129, SI 2003/2779, SI 2004/2415
s.16A, applied: SI 2002/1204 Reg.1
s.17, applied: SI 2002/1204 Reg.1
s.17, enabling: SI 2002/1204, SI 2003/328, SI 2003/1050, SI 2003/2779, SI 2004/2415
s.20, applied: SI 2002/1204 Reg.1, SI 2002/1915 Art.3, Art.4, SSI 2003/96 Art.2
s.20, enabling: SI 2002/1204, SI 2002/1379, SI 2004/3368
s.23, amended: 2002 c.26 Sch.3 para.21
s.26, amended: 2002 c.38 Sch.3 para.81
s.28B, enabling: SI 2002/1204, SI 2003/328, SI 2004/2415
s.28E, applied: SI 2003/2779 Reg.2

CAP.

1991–cont.

48. Child Support Act 1991–*cont.*
s.28E, enabling: SI 2002/1204, SI 2003/328, SI 2003/2779
s.28G, enabling: SI 2002/1204
s.31, enabling: SI 2003/328
s.33, see *R. (on the application of Denson) v Child Support Agency* [2002] EWHC 154, [2002] 1 F.L.R. 938 (QBD (Admin Ct)), Munby, J.
s.38, amended: 2002 asp 17 Sch.3 para.20
s.42, enabling: SI 2003/328, SI 2003/2779
s.43, enabling: SI 2002/1950
s.45, enabling: SI 2002/1915, SSI 2003/96
s.46, applied: SI 2003/192 Art.4
s.46, enabling: SI 2002/1204, SI 2003/328, SI 2003/2779
s.47, amended: 2002 c.21 Sch.3 para.22
s.51, applied: SI 2002/1204 Reg.1
s.51, enabling: SI 2002/1204, SI 2003/328, SI 2003/2779, SI 2003/3206, SI 2004/2415
s.52, applied: SI 2002/1204, SI 2003/328, SI 2003/2779, SI 2004/2415, SSI 2003/96
s.52, enabling: SI 2002/1204, SI 2003/129, SI 2003/328, SI 2003/1195, SI 2003/2779, SI 2003/3206, SI 2004/2415
s.54, amended: 2002 c.21 Sch.6
s.54, applied: SI 2002/1204 Reg.1
s.54, referred to: SI 2003/495 Reg.6
s.54, enabling: SI 2002/1204, SI 2003/129, SI 2003/194, SI 2003/328, SI 2003/1050, SI 2003/1195, SI 2003/2779, SI 2003/3206, SI 2004/2415
s.55, amended: 2004 c.33 Sch.24 para.3
s.55, applied: SSI 2002/132 Sch.1 para.33.2
s.57, enabling: SI 2002/1204, SI 2003/3206
s.58, enabling: SSI 2003/96
Sch.1 Part I para.4, enabling: SI 2002/2497
Sch.1 Part I para.4, enabling: SI 2003/2779
Sch.1 Part I para.5, enabling: SI 2002/1204, SI 2003/328, SI 2003/1195, SI 2004/2415
Sch.1 Part I para.5, enabling: SI 2003/2779
Sch.1 Part I para.6, amended: 2004 c.33 Sch.24 para.4, Sch.24 para.5
Sch.1 Part I para.6, enabling: SI 2003/328, SI 2004/2415
Sch.1 Part I para.6, enabling: SI 2003/2779
Sch.1 Part I para.7, enabling: SI 2003/328
Sch.1 Part I para.9, enabling: SI 2004/2415
Sch.1 Part I para.10, enabling: SI 2002/1204, SI 2003/328, SI 2004/2415
Sch.1 Part I para.10, enabling: SI 2003/2779
Sch.1 Part I para.10C, amended: 2004 c.33 Sch.24 para.6
Sch.1 Part II para.11, enabling: SI 2002/1204, SI 2003/328, SI 2003/2779, SI 2004/2415
Sch.4 para.8, amended: 2002 c.26 Sch.3 para.22, Sch.12 para.47
Sch.4A para.1, enabling: SI 2004/2415
Sch.4A para.2, enabling: SI 2004/2415

1991–cont.

48. Child Support Act 1991–*cont.*

Sch.4B Part I para.2, enabling: SI 2003/328, SI 2003/2779

Sch.4B Part I para.3, enabling: SI 2002/1204, SI 2003/2779

Sch.4B Part I para.4, enabling: SI 2002/1204, SI 2003/2779

Sch.4B Part I para.5, enabling: SI 2002/1204, SI 2003/328, SI 2003/2779, SI 2004/2415

Sch.4B Part II para.6, enabling: SI 2004/2415

49. School Teachers Pay and Conditions Act 1991

applied: SI 2002/2103 Art.3

repealed: 2002 c.32 Sch.22 Part 1

s.1, applied: 2002 c.32 s.119, Sch.11 para.15, SI 2002/838, SI 2002/2223, SI 2003/769, SI 2003/2169, SI 2004/2142

s.1, repealed: 2002 c.32 Sch.22 Part 1

s.2, applied: SI 2002/377 Sch.2 para.19, Sch.2 para.20, SI 2002/838, SI 2002/2223, SI 2003/453 Sch.1 para.19, Sch.1 para.20, SI 2003/769, SI 2003/3247 Sch.1 para.19, Sch.1 para.20

s.2, enabling: SI 2002/838, SI 2002/2223, SI 2003/769

s.5, applied: SI 2002/838 Art.2

s.5, referred to: SI 2002/2223 Art.2, SI 2003/769 Art.2

s.5, enabling: SI 2002/838, SI 2002/2103, SI 2002/2223, SI 2003/769

Sch.1 para.1, repealed: 2002 c.32 Sch.22 Part 1

Sch.1 para.2, repealed: 2002 c.32 Sch.22 Part 1

Sch.1 para.3, repealed: 2002 c.32 Sch.22 Part 1

Sch.1 para.4, repealed: 2002 c.32 Sch.22 Part 1

Sch.1 para.5, repealed: 2002 c.32 Sch.22 Part 1

52. Ports Act 1991

s.29, repealed: 2003 c.26 Sch.8 Part 1

s.36A, added: SI 2003/2867 Sch.1 para.16

Sch.2 para.11, amended: 2003 c.14 Sch.20 para.3

53. Criminal Justice Act 1991

see *R. (on the application of Uttley) v Secretary of State for the Home Department* [2004] UKHL 38, [2004] 1 W.L.R. 2278 (HL), Lord Steyn; see *R. v Matthews (Jonathan Edward)* [2002] EWCA Crim 677, [2002] 1 W.L.R. 2578 (CA (Crim Div)), Johnson, J.; see *R. v R (Sentencing: Extended Licences)* [2003] EWCA Crim 2199, [2004] 1 W.L.R. 490 (CA (Crim Div)), Pitchers, J.

s.2, see *R. (on the application of Giles) v Parole Board* [2001] EWHC Admin 834, [2002] 1 W.L.R. 654 (QBD (Admin Ct)), Elias, J.; see *R. (on the application of Giles) v Parole Board* [2002] EWCA Civ 951, [2003] 2

1991–cont.

53. Criminal Justice Act 1991–*cont.*

s.2–*cont.*

W.L.R. 196 (CA), Kennedy, L.J.; see *R. (on the application of Giles) v Parole Board* [2003] UKHL 42, [2004] 1 A.C. 1 (HL), Lord Bingham of Cornhill; see *R. v Brown (Graham)* [2001] EWCA Crim 724, [2002] 1 Cr. App. R. (S.) 1 (CA (Crim Div)), Rougier, J.; see *R. v Everleigh (Martyn Latham)* [2001] EWCA Crim 1276, [2002] 1 Cr. App. R. (S.) 32 (CA (Crim Div)), Rose, L.J.

s.20A, amended: 2003 c.39 s.95, Sch.8 para.350

s.20A, applied: 2003 c.44 s.164

s.20A, disapplied: 2003 c.44 Sch.25 para.88

s.24, amended: 2002 c.16 Sch.2 para.31, 2003 c.39 s.96, 2004 c.28 Sch.10 para.30

s.24, applied: 2003 c.39 Sch.6 para.2

s.24, enabling: SI 2003/1360, SI 2004/2889

s.26, repealed (in part): 2003 c.44 Sch.37 Part 9

s.32, see *R. (on the application of Roberts) v Parole Board* [2004] EWCA Civ 1031, [2004] 4 All E.R. 1136 (CA (Civ Div)), Tuckey, L.J.

s.32, repealed: 2003 c.44 s.303, Sch.37 Part 7

s.33, see *R. (on the application of Uttley) v Secretary of State for the Home Department* [2003] EWCA Civ 1130, [2003] 1 W.L.R. 2590 (CA), Pill, L.J.

s.33, repealed: 2003 c.44 s.303, Sch.37 Part 7

s.33A, repealed: 2003 c.44 s.303, Sch.37 Part 7

s.34, see *R. v Royal (Carl Christopher)* [2003] EWCA Crim 1152, [2004] 1 Cr. App. R. (S.) 2 (CA (Crim Div)), Laws, L.J.

s.34, repealed: 2003 c.44 s.303, Sch.37 Part 7

s.34A, amended: SI 2002/2933 Art.2, 2003 c.42 Sch.6 para.30, SI 2003/1602 Art.3, SI 2003/1691 Art.2

s.34A, applied: SI 2003/1691

s.34A, repealed: 2003 c.44 s.303, Sch.37 Part 7

s.34A, enabling: SI 2002/2933, SI 2003/1602, SI 2003/1691

s.35, see *R. (on the application of Clift) v Secretary of State for the Home Department* [2004] EWCA Civ 514, [2004] 1 W.L.R. 2223 (CA), Lord Woolf of Barnes, L.C.J.; see *Stafford v United Kingdom (46295/99)* (2002) 35 E.H.R.R. 32 (ECHR), L Wildhaber (President)

s.35, repealed: 2003 c.44 s.303, Sch.37 Part 7

s.36, repealed: 2003 c.44 s.303, Sch.37 Part 7

1991–cont.

53. Criminal Justice Act 1991–*cont.*

s.37, see *R. (on the application of Uttley) v Secretary of State for the Home Department* [2003] EWCA Civ 1130, [2003] 1 W.L.R. 2590 (CA), Pill, L.J.

s.37, applied: SI 2003/762 Reg.2, SI 2004/1748 Sch.1, SSI 2003/243 Reg.2

s.37, repealed: 2003 c.44 s.303, Sch.37 Part 7

s.37A, repealed: 2003 c.44 s.303, Sch.37 Part 7

s.38, repealed: 2003 c.44 s.303, Sch.37 Part 7

s.38A, repealed: 2003 c.44 s.303, Sch.37 Part 7

s.39, see *R. (on the application of Biggs) v Secretary of State for the Home Department* [2002] EWHC 1012, (2002) 99(26) L.S.G. 38 (QBD (Admin Ct)), Richards, J.; see *R. (on the application of S) v Secretary of State for the Home Department* [2002] EWHC 2424, Times, November 13, 2002 (QBD (Admin Ct)), Maurice Kay, J.; see *R. (on the application of Uttley) v Secretary of State for the Home Department* [2003] EWCA Civ 1130, [2003] 1 W.L.R. 2590 (CA), Pill, L.J.; see *R. v Stocker (David Paul)* [2003] EWCA Crim 121, [2003] 2 Cr. App. R. (S.) 54 (CA (Crim Div)), Judge Fawcus; see *R. v Teasdale (Steven Mark) (Appeal against Sentence)* [2003] EWCA Crim 1641, [2004] 1 Cr. App. R. (S.) 6 (CA (Crim Div)), Moses, J.

s.39, repealed: 2003 c.44 s.303, Sch.37 Part 7

s.40, repealed: 2003 c.44 s.303, Sch.37 Part 7

s.40A, repealed: 2003 c.44 s.303, Sch.37 Part 7

s.41, repealed: 2003 c.44 s.303, Sch.37 Part 7

s.42, see *Ezeh v United Kingdom (39665/98)* (2004) 39 E.H.R.R. 1 (ECHR (Grand Chamber)), Judge Wildhaber (President); see *R. (on the application of Carroll) v Secretary of State for the Home Department* [2001] EWCA Civ 1224, [2002] 1 W.L.R. 545 (CA), Lord Woolf of Barnes, L.C.J.

s.42, amended: 2003 c.44 Sch.20 para.2

s.42, repealed: 2003 c.44 s.303, Sch.37 Part 7

s.43, amended: 2004 c.31 Sch.5 Part 4

s.43, repealed: 2003 c.44 s.303, Sch.37 Part 7

s.44, see *R. v Massie (Raymond)* [2002] EWCA Crim 1871, [2003] 1 Cr. App. R. (S.) 80 (CA (Crim Div)), Wright, J.

s.44, repealed: 2003 c.44 s.303, Sch.37 Part 7

1991–cont.

53. Criminal Justice Act 1991–*cont.*

s.44A, see *R. (on the application of Sim) v Parole Board* [2003] EWCA Civ 1845, [2004] Q.B. 1288 (CA), Ward, L.J.; see *R. (on the application of Sim) v Parole Board* [2003] EWHC 152, [2003] 2 W.L.R. 1374 (QBD (Admin Ct)), Elias, J.

s.44A, repealed: 2003 c.44 s.303, Sch.37 Part 7

s.45, repealed: 2003 c.44 s.303, Sch.37 Part 7

s.46, amended: 2003 c.44 Sch.20 para.3

s.46, repealed: 2003 c.44 s.303, Sch.37 Part 7

s.46A, added: 2003 c.44 Sch.20 para.4

s.46A, repealed: 2003 c.44 s.303, Sch.37 Part 7

s.46B, added: 2003 c.44 Sch.20 para.4

s.46B, repealed: 2003 c.44 s.303, Sch.37 Part 7

s.47, repealed (in part): 2003 c.41 Sch.4, 2003 c.44 s.303, Sch.37 Part 7

s.48, repealed: 2003 c.44 s.303, Sch.37 Part 7

s.49, repealed: 2003 c.44 s.303, Sch.37 Part 7

s.50, repealed: 2003 c.44 s.303, Sch.37 Part 7

s.51, see *R. v Whitfield (Lee David)* [2001] EWCA Crim 3043, [2002] 2 Cr. App. R. (S.) 44 (CA (Crim Div)), Gross, J.

s.51, repealed: 2003 c.44 s.303, Sch.37 Part 7

s.53, applied: SI 2002/1688 r.2

s.53, repealed: 2003 c.44 Sch.37 Part 4, Sch.3 para.62

s.55, repealed (in part): 2003 c.44 Sch.37 Part 4, SI 2004/2035 Sch.1 para.33

s.65, amended: 2003 c.44 Sch.38 para.5, 2004 c.31 Sch.5 Part 4

s.65, repealed: 2003 c.44 Sch.32 para.63, Sch.37 Part 7

s.76, repealed: 2003 c.39 Sch.8 para.351, Sch.10

s.77, repealed: 2003 c.39 Sch.8 para.351, Sch.10

s.78, repealed: 2003 c.39 Sch.8 para.351, Sch.10

s.92, amended: 2003 c.39 Sch.8 para.352, Sch.10

s.92, repealed (in part): 2003 c.39 Sch.8 para.352, Sch.10

s.95, amended: 2003 c.44 s.175

Sch.3 Part III para.10, amended: 2003 c.44 Sch.32 para.64

Sch.3 Part III para.11, amended: 2003 c.44 Sch.32 para.64

Sch.5 para.1, repealed: 2003 c.44 Sch.37 Part 7

Sch.5 para.2, repealed: 2003 c.44 Sch.37 Part 7

1991-cont.

53. Criminal Justice Act 1991-*cont.*

Sch.5 para.3, repealed: 2003 c.44 Sch.37 Part 7

Sch.5 para.4, repealed: 2003 c.44 Sch.37 Part 7

Sch.5 para.5, repealed: 2003 c.44 Sch.37 Part 7

Sch.5 para.6, repealed: 2003 c.44 Sch.37 Part 7

Sch.5 para.7, repealed: 2003 c.44 Sch.37 Part 7

Sch.5 para.8, repealed: 2003 c.44 Sch.37 Part 7

Sch.5 para.9, repealed: 2003 c.44 Sch.37 Part 7

Sch.5 para.10, repealed: 2003 c.44 Sch.37 Part 7

Sch.5 para.11, repealed: 2003 c.44 Sch.37 Part 7

Sch.6 para.1, repealed: 2003 c.44 Sch.37 Part 4, Sch.3 para.62

Sch.6 para.2, repealed: 2003 c.44 Sch.37 Part 4, Sch.3 para.62

Sch.6 para.3, repealed: 2003 c.44 Sch.37 Part 4, Sch.3 para.62

Sch.6 para.4, repealed: 2003 c.44 Sch.37 Part 4, Sch.3 para.62

Sch.6 para.5, amended: SI 2004/2035 Sch.1 para.34

Sch.6 para.5, repealed: 2003 c.44 Sch.37 Part 4, Sch.3 para.62

Sch.6 para.6, repealed: 2003 c.44 Sch.37 Part 4, Sch.3 para.62

Sch.6 para.7, repealed: 2003 c.44 Sch.37 Part 4, Sch.3 para.62

Sch.6 para.8, repealed: 2003 c.44 Sch.37 Part 4, Sch.3 para.62

Sch.6 para.9, repealed: 2003 c.44 Sch.37 Part 4, Sch.3 para.62

Sch.11 para.18, repealed: 2003 c.44 Sch.37 Part 10

Sch.11 para.22, amended: 2003 c.44 Sch.37 Part 2

Sch.11 para.25, repealed: 2003 c.44 Sch.37 Part 4

Sch.11 para.40, amended: 2003 c.39 Sch.10

Sch.11 para.41, repealed (in part): 2003 c.39 Sch.10

Sch.12 para.8, repealed (in part): 2003 c.44 Sch.37 Part 7

Sch.12 para.9, repealed (in part): 2003 c.44 Sch.37 Part 7

54. Deer Act 1991

s.7, amended: SI 2002/794 Sch.1 para.34

s.9, amended: 2003 c.44 Sch.26 para.43

s.10, amended: 2003 c.44 Sch.37 Part 9

s.10, disapplied: 2003 c.44 Sch.25 para.89

55. Agricultural Holdings (Scotland) Act 1991

applied: 2003 asp 11 s.1, s.38, s.70, s.84, s.85, s.86, s.87, s.88, s.89

1991-cont.

55. Agricultural Holdings (Scotland) Act 1991-*cont.*

disapplied: 2003 asp 11 s.1

referred to: 2003 asp 11 s.1

Part IV, applied: 2003 asp 11 s.2

Part IV, referred to: SSI 2003/548 Sch.1 para.6

Part V, referred to: SSI 2003/548 Sch.1 para.6

s.1, applied: SSI 2002/110 Sch.2 para.1, 2004 c.33 s.104

s.1, referred to: 2003 asp 9 Sch.11 para.3

s.2, referred to: SSI 2003/548, SSI 2003/548 Sch.1 para.2

s.2, repealed: 2003 asp 11 s.1

s.4, amended: 2003 asp 11 Sch.1 para.12

s.5, amended: 2003 asp 11 s.60

s.5, applied: 2003 asp 11 s.13

s.5, repealed (in part): 2003 asp 11 s.60, Sch.1 para.13

s.7, amended: 2003 asp 11 s.62

s.7, referred to: SSI 2003/548 Sch.1 para.3

s.7, varied: 2003 asp 11 s.14

s.8, amended: 2003 asp 11 s.61

s.8, referred to: SSI 2003/548 Sch.1 para.4

s.9, amended: 2003 asp 11 Sch.1 para.14

s.9, applied: 2003 asp 11 s.58

s.9, varied: 2003 asp 11 s.15

s.10A, added: 2003 asp 11 s.66

s.11, applied: SSI 2004/143 Reg.16

s.11, varied: 2003 asp 11 s.21, 2004 c.33 Sch.21 para.35

s.12, applied: SSI 2004/143 Reg.16

s.12, varied: 2003 asp 11 s.22

s.13, amended: 2003 asp 11 s.63, Sch.1 para.15

s.14, substituted: 2003 asp 11 Sch.1 para.16

s.15, repealed (in part): 2003 asp 11 Sch.1 para.17

s.15A, added: 2003 asp 11 s.64

s.16A, added: 2003 asp 11 s.65

s.19, repealed (in part): 2003 asp 11 Sch.1 para.18

s.20, amended: 2003 asp 11 Sch.1 para.19

s.20, repealed (in part): 2003 asp 11 Sch.1 para.19

s.21, see *Hoy Trust v Thomson* 2003 S.L.T. (Sh Ct) 20 (Sh Pr), Sir SST Young Q.C., Sheriff Principal

s.21, amended: 2003 asp 11 Sch.1 para.20

s.21, applied: SSI 2002/132 Sch.1 para.30.5, 2003 asp 11 s.73, SSI 2004/143 Reg.16

s.21, disapplied: 2003 asp 11 s.2, s.73

s.21, referred to: SSI 2003/548 Sch.1 para.5

s.22, amended: 2003 asp 11 s.67

s.22, applied: SSI 2003/209 Art.6, SSI 2004/143 Reg.16

s.22, referred to: SSI 2003/548 Sch.1 para.5

s.23, see *Viscount Reidhaven v MacDonald-Grant* 2002 S.L.C.R. 33 (Land Ct (Full Ct)), Lord McGhie, DJ Houston, J Kinloch

s.23, amended: 2003 asp 11 Sch.1 para.21

1991–cont.

55. Agricultural Holdings (Scotland) Act 1991–*cont.*

s.24, amended: 2003 asp 11 s.67

s.24, applied: SSI 2003/209 Art.6

s.24, referred to: SSI 2004/143 Reg.16

s.25, see *Viscount Reidhaven v MacDonald-Grant* 2002 S.L.C.R. 33 (Land Ct (Full Ct)), Lord McGhie, DJ Houston, J Kinloch

s.29, referred to: 2003 asp 11 s.17

s.29A, added: 2003 asp 11 s.68

s.31, amended: 2003 asp 11 Sch.1 para.22

s.32, amended: 2003 asp 11 Sch.1 para.23

s.33A, added: 2003 asp 11 s.43

s.34, amended: 2003 asp 11 Sch.1 para.24

s.34, repealed (in part): 2003 asp 11 s.43

s.35, varied: 2003 asp 11 s.46

s.36, amended: 2003 asp 11 s.44, Sch.1 para.25

s.37, amended: 2003 asp 11 Sch.1 para.26

s.37, repealed (in part): 2003 asp 11 s.43

s.38, amended: 2003 asp 11 s.43

s.38, repealed (in part): 2003 asp 11 s.43

s.39, applied: 2003 asp 11 s.10

s.39, varied: 2003 asp 11 s.49

s.41, amended: 2003 asp 11 Sch.1 para.27

s.43, amended: 2003 asp 11 Sch.1 para.28

s.43, repealed (in part): 2003 asp 11 s.50

s.43, varied: 2003 asp 11 s.52

s.44, varied: 2003 asp 11 s.53

s.45A, added: 2003 asp 11 s.51

s.45A, applied: 2003 asp 11 s.2

s.45A, varied: 2003 asp 11 s.53

s.46, amended: 2003 asp 11 Sch.1 para.29

s.47, amended: 2003 asp 11 s.51

s.47, applied: 2003 asp 11 s.53

s.49, amended: 2003 asp 11 Sch.1 para.30

s.50, amended: 2003 asp 11 Sch.1 para.31

s.52, amended: 2003 asp 11 s.50, Sch.1 para.32

s.52, applied: 2003 asp 11 s.53

s.52, referred to: SSI 2003/548 Sch.1 para.6

s.55, amended: 2003 asp 11 Sch.1 para.33

s.60, see *Hiskett v Wilson* 2003 S.L.T. 58 (OH), Lord Macfadyen

s.60, referred to: 2003 asp 11 s.83, SSI 2003/548 Sch.1 para.7

s.60, substituted: 2003 asp 11 s.75

s.61, referred to: 2003 asp 11 s.83

s.61, substituted: 2003 asp 11 s.76

s.61A, applied: 2003 asp 11 s.90

s.62, amended: 2003 asp 11 Sch.1 para.34

s.62, applied: 2003 asp 11 s.80

s.63, referred to: SSI 2003/548 Sch.1 para.7

s.63, repealed: 2003 asp 11 Sch.1 para.35

s.64, repealed: 2003 asp 11 Sch.1 para.35

s.65, applied: 2003 asp 11 s.80

s.66, amended: 2003 asp 11 Sch.1 para.36

s.66, applied: 2003 asp 11 s.80

s.68, amended: 2003 asp 11 Sch.1 para.37

s.68, referred to: SSI 2003/548 Sch.1 para.8

1991–cont.

55. Agricultural Holdings (Scotland) Act 1991–*cont.*

s.68, repealed (in part): 2003 asp 11 Sch.1 para.37

s.69, repealed: 2003 asp 11 Sch.1 para.38

s.70, repealed: 2003 asp 11 Sch.1 para.38

s.71, amended: 2003 asp 11 Sch.1 para.39

s.72, repealed (in part): 2003 asp 11 Sch.1 para.40

s.80, amended: 2003 asp 11 s.61

s.80, repealed (in part): 2003 asp 11 Sch.1 para.41

s.85, amended: 2003 asp 11 s.69, Sch.1 para.42

s.85, applied: SI 2002/302 Art.4, SI 2002/303 Art.4, SI 2003/285 Art.4, SI 2003/286 Art.4, SI 2004/368 Art.4, SI 2004/369 Art.4

s.86, amended: 2003 asp 11 Sch.1 para.43

Sch.1, applied: 2003 asp 11 s.13

Sch.1, referred to: 2003 asp 11 s.13

Sch.2, see *Viscount Reidhaven v MacDonald-Grant* 2002 S.L.C.R. 33 (Land Ct (Full Ct)), Lord McGhie, DJ Houston, J Kinloch

Sch.5, applied: 2003 asp 11 s.46, s.49

Sch.5, referred to: 2003 asp 11 s.10, s.45

Sch.5 Part I, referred to: 2003 asp 11 s.48

Sch.5 Part II, referred to: 2003 asp 11 s.49

Sch.5 Part III, referred to: 2003 asp 11 s.58

Sch.5 Part III para.32, referred to: 2003 asp 11 s.45

Sch.7 para.1, referred to: SSI 2003/548 Sch.1 para.7

Sch.7 para.1, repealed: 2003 asp 11 Sch.1 para.44

Sch.7 para.2, repealed: 2003 asp 11 Sch.1 para.44

Sch.7 para.3, repealed: 2003 asp 11 Sch.1 para.44

Sch.7 para.4, repealed: 2003 asp 11 Sch.1 para.44

Sch.7 para.5, repealed: 2003 asp 11 Sch.1 para.44

Sch.7 para.6, repealed: 2003 asp 11 Sch.1 para.44

Sch.7 para.7, repealed: 2003 asp 11 Sch.1 para.44

Sch.7 para.8, repealed: 2003 asp 11 Sch.1 para.44

Sch.7 para.9, repealed: 2003 asp 11 Sch.1 para.44

Sch.7 para.10, repealed: 2003 asp 11 Sch.1 para.44

Sch.7 para.11, repealed: 2003 asp 11 Sch.1 para.44

Sch.7 para.12, repealed: 2003 asp 11 Sch.1 para.44

Sch.7 para.13, repealed: 2003 asp 11 Sch.1 para.44

Sch.7 para.14, repealed: 2003 asp 11 Sch.1 para.44

1991–cont.

55. Agricultural Holdings (Scotland) Act 1991–*cont.*

Sch.7 para.15, repealed: 2003 asp 11 Sch.1 para.44

Sch.7 para.16, repealed: 2003 asp 11 Sch.1 para.44

Sch.7 para.17, repealed: 2003 asp 11 Sch.1 para.44

Sch.7 para.18, repealed: 2003 asp 11 Sch.1 para.44

Sch.7 para.19, repealed: 2003 asp 11 Sch.1 para.44

Sch.7 para.20, repealed: 2003 asp 11 Sch.1 para.44

Sch.7 para.21, repealed: 2003 asp 11 Sch.1 para.44

Sch.7 para.22, repealed: 2003 asp 11 Sch.1 para.44

Sch.7 para.23, repealed: 2003 asp 11 Sch.1 para.44

Sch.7 para.24, repealed: 2003 asp 11 Sch.1 para.44

Sch.7 para.25, repealed: 2003 asp 11 Sch.1 para.44

Sch.8 para.1, varied: 2003 asp 11 s.54

Sch.8 para.2, amended: 2003 asp 11 Sch.1 para.45

Sch.8 para.2, varied: 2003 asp 11 s.54

Sch.8 para.3, amended: 2003 asp 11 Sch.1 para.45

Sch.8 para.3, varied: 2003 asp 11 s.54

Sch.8 para.4, varied: 2003 asp 11 s.54

Sch.8 para.5, varied: 2003 asp 11 s.54

Sch.8 para.6, varied: 2003 asp 11 s.54

Sch.9 Part I para.1, amended: 2003 asp 11 Sch.1 para.46

Sch.9 Part I para.4, amended: 2003 asp 11 Sch.1 para.46

Sch.10 Part I para.1, amended: 2003 asp 11 Sch.1 para.47

Sch.10 Part I para.4, amended: 2003 asp 11 Sch.1 para.47

56. Water Industry Act 1991

see *Marcic v Thames Water Utilities Ltd* [2003] UKHL 66, [2004] 2 A.C. 42 (HL), Lord Nicholls of Birkenhead

applied: 2002 c.40 Sch.15, 2003 c.37 s.52, 2003 c.43 Sch.4 para.89, SI 2003/419 Art.63

referred to: SI 2002/808 Art.2, 2003 c.37 Sch.8 para.2

varied: SI 2004/641 Sch.3 para.7

Part II c.I, applied: 2002 c.40 s.249, 2003 c.37 Sch.4 para.4

Part II c.IA, applied: 2003 c.37 s.103

Part II c.II, added: 2003 c.37 s.48

Part II c.III, added: 2003 c.37 s.50

Part III c.II, added: 2003 c.37 Sch.8 para.17

Part III c.III, amended: 2003 c.37 Sch.8 para.18

s.1, repealed: 2003 c.37 s.34, Sch.9 Part 2

1991–cont.

56. Water Industry Act 1991–*cont.*

s.1A, added: 2003 c.37 s.34

s.2, amended: 2002 c.40 Sch.25 para.25, 2003 c.37 s.39

s.2A, added: 2003 c.37 s.40

s.3, amended: 2003 c.37 s.82

s.3, repealed (in part): SI 2002/794 Sch.2

s.5, amended: SI 2002/794 Sch.2

s.6, amended: 2003 c.37 Sch.8 para.3

s.6, applied: SI 2004/71 Sch.1

s.7, applied: SI 2004/71 Sch.1

s.12, amended: 2002 c.40 Sch.25 para.25, 2003 c.37 s.54

s.12, applied: SI 2003/1397 Art.8

s.12, repealed (in part): 2003 c.37 Sch.9 Part 2

s.14, amended: 2003 c.37 s.55

s.14, applied: 2003 c.37 s.53, SI 2003/1397 Art.8

s.14, repealed (in part): 2002 c.40 Sch.26, 2003 c.37 Sch.9 Part 2

s.14A, added: 2002 c.40 Sch.25 para.25

s.14B, added: 2002 c.40 Sch.25 para.25

s.14B, referred to: SI 2003/1371

s.14B, enabling: SI 2003/1371

s.15, amended: 2002 c.40 Sch.25 para.25

s.16, amended: 2003 c.37 s.55

s.16A, added: 2003 c.37 s.55

s.16B, added: 2003 c.37 s.55

s.17, amended: 2002 c.40 Sch.9 para.7

s.17, varied: SI 2003/1592 Sch.4 para.10

s.17A, added: 2003 c.37 Sch.4 para.2

s.17B, added: 2003 c.37 Sch.4 para.2

s.17C, added: 2003 c.37 Sch.4 para.2

s.17D, added: 2003 c.37 Sch.4 para.2

s.17E, added: 2003 c.37 Sch.4 para.2

s.17F, added: 2003 c.37 Sch.4 para.2

s.17G, added: 2003 c.37 Sch.4 para.2

s.17H, added: 2003 c.37 Sch.4 para.2

s.17I, added: 2003 c.37 Sch.4 para.2

s.17J, added: 2003 c.37 Sch.4 para.2

s.17K, added: 2003 c.37 Sch.4 para.2

s.17L, added: 2003 c.37 Sch.4 para.2

s.17M, added: 2003 c.37 Sch.4 para.2

s.17N, added: 2003 c.37 Sch.4 para.2

s.17O, added: 2003 c.37 Sch.4 para.2

s.17P, added: 2003 c.37 Sch.4 para.2

s.17Q, added: 2003 c.37 Sch.4 para.2

s.17R, added: 2003 c.37 Sch.4 para.2

s.18, amended: 2003 c.37 s.49, Sch.8 para.4

s.18, applied: 2004 c.21 s.39, s.42

s.19, amended: 2003 c.37 Sch.8 para.5

s.20, amended: 2003 c.37 s.49, Sch.8 para.6

s.20, applied: 2003 c.37 s.49

s.22, amended: 2003 c.37 Sch.8 para.7

s.22A, added: 2003 c.37 s.48

s.22B, added: 2003 c.37 s.48

s.22C, added: 2003 c.37 s.48

s.22D, added: 2003 c.37 s.48

s.22E, added: 2003 c.37 s.48

1991–cont.

56. Water Industry Act 1991–*cont.*
s.22F, added: 2003 c.37 s.48
s.23, amended: 2003 c.37 Sch.8 para.8
s.24, amended: 2003 c.37 Sch.8 para.9
s.25, amended: 2003 c.37 Sch.8 para.10
s.26, amended: 2003 c.37 Sch.8 para.11
s.27, amended: 2002 c.40 Sch.25 para.25, 2003 c.37 Sch.8 para.12
s.27A, added: 2003 c.37 s.35
s.27A, referred to: SI 2004/2528 Sch.1 para.3
s.27B, added: 2003 c.37 s.35
s.27C, added: 2003 c.37 s.43
s.27D, added: 2003 c.37 s.43
s.27E, added: 2003 c.37 s.43
s.27F, added: 2003 c.37 s.43
s.27G, added: 2003 c.37 s.43
s.27H, added: 2003 c.37 s.44
s.27I, added: 2003 c.37 s.44
s.27J, added: 2003 c.37 s.44
s.27K, added: 2003 c.37 s.44
s.28, applied: 2003 c.37 s.37
s.28, referred to: 2003 c.37 s.35
s.28, repealed: 2003 c.37 s.35, Sch.9 Part 2
s.29, substituted: 2003 c.37 s.46
s.29A, added: 2003 c.37 s.47
s.30, repealed: 2003 c.37 s.46, Sch.9 Part 2
s.30ZA, added: 2003 c.37 s.43
s.30ZB, added: 2003 c.37 s.43
s.31, amended: 2002 c.40 Sch.9 para.19, Sch.25 para.25, Sch.26, SI 2004/1261 Sch.2 para.4
s.31, repealed (in part): 2002 c.40 Sch.25 para.25, Sch.26
s.32, applied: 2002 c.40 s.121, SI 2003/1397 Art.3, SI 2003/1398 Art.3, SI 2003/3180 Art.3, SI 2004/3233 Art.4
s.32, referred to: SI 2003/1397 Art.3
s.32, substituted: 2002 c.40 s.70
s.33, applied: 2002 c.40 s.121
s.33, referred to: SI 2003/1397 Art.3
s.33, substituted: 2002 c.40 s.70
s.33, enabling: SI 2004/3206
s.34, applied: 2002 c.40 s.121
s.34, referred to: SI 2003/1397 Art.3
s.34, substituted: 2002 c.40 s.70
s.35, amended: 2003 c.37 Sch.7 para.27
s.35, referred to: SI 2003/1397 Art.3
s.35, substituted: 2002 c.40 s.70
s.35, varied: SI 2003/1397 Art.3, SI 2004/3233 Art.5
s.35A, applied: SI 2004/2528 Sch.1 para.4
s.36, amended: 2002 c.40 Sch.9 para.8, Sch.26, 2003 c.37 s.97
s.37A, added: 2003 c.37 s.62
s.37B, added: 2003 c.37 s.62
s.37C, added: 2003 c.37 s.62
s.37D, added: 2003 c.37 s.62
s.38B, added: 2003 c.37 s.45
s.39, amended: 2003 c.37 s.41, Sch.9 Part 2
s.39A, amended: 2003 c.37 Sch.8 para.13

1991–cont.

56. Water Industry Act 1991–*cont.*
s.39B, added: 2003 c.37 s.63
s.39C, added: 2003 c.37 s.63
s.41, applied: 2003 c.37 s.90, s.91
s.42, amended: 2003 c.37 s.90
s.42, applied: 2003 c.37 s.91
s.43, amended: 2003 c.37 s.91, Sch.8 para.14
s.43, referred to: 2003 c.37 s.90, s.91
s.43A, added: 2003 c.37 s.91
s.44, amended: 2003 c.37 s.91, Sch.9 Part 3
s.45, amended: 2003 c.37 s.92
s.47, amended: 2003 c.37 s.92
s.51A, added: 2003 c.37 s.92
s.51B, added: 2003 c.37 s.92
s.51C, added: 2003 c.37 s.92
s.51D, added: 2003 c.37 s.92
s.51E, added: 2003 c.37 s.92
s.52, amended: 2003 c.37 Sch.8 para.15
s.55, amended: 2003 c.37 Sch.8 para.16
s.57, amended: 2003 c.37 s.84, 2004 c.21 Sch.1 para.76
s.57, repealed (in part): 2004 c.21 Sch.2
s.58, amended: 2003 c.37 s.84
s.66A, added: 2003 c.37 Sch.4 para.3
s.66B, added: 2003 c.37 Sch.4 para.3
s.66C, added: 2003 c.37 Sch.4 para.3
s.66D, added: 2003 c.37 Sch.4 para.3
s.66E, added: 2003 c.37 Sch.4 para.3
s.66F, added: 2003 c.37 Sch.4 para.3
s.66G, added: 2003 c.37 Sch.4 para.3
s.66H, added: 2003 c.37 Sch.4 para.3
s.66I, added: 2003 c.37 Sch.4 para.3
s.66J, added: 2003 c.37 Sch.4 para.3
s.66K, added: 2003 c.37 Sch.4 para.3
s.66L, added: 2003 c.37 Sch.4 para.3
s.68, amended: 2003 c.37 Sch.8 para.18
s.69, amended: 2003 c.37 Sch.8 para.19, Sch.9 Part 3
s.70, see *Secretary of State for the Environment, Transport and the Regions v Yorkshire Water Services Ltd* [2001] EWCA Crim 2635, [2002] 2 Cr. App. R. (S.) 13 (CA (Crim Div)), Rougier, J.
s.70, amended: 2003 c.37 s.61, Sch.8 para.20
s.72, amended: 2003 c.37 Sch.8 para.21
s.73, amended: 2003 c.37 Sch.8 para.22
s.74, amended: 2003 c.37 Sch.8 para.23
s.75, amended: 2003 c.37 Sch.8 para.24
s.76, amended: 2003 c.37 Sch.8 para.25
s.78, amended: 2003 c.37 Sch.8 para.26
s.86, amended: 2003 c.37 s.57, Sch.8 para.27, Sch.9 Part 3
s.86A, amended: 2003 c.37 Sch.7 para.27
s.87, amended: SI 2002/2469 Sch.1 para.18
s.87, applied: 2003 c.37 s.58
s.87, referred to: SI 2002/2375 Sch.3
s.87, substituted: 2003 c.37 s.58
s.88, amended: 2003 c.37 s.58
s.88A, added: 2003 c.37 s.58
s.89, amended: SI 2002/2469 Sch.1 para.18

1991–cont.

56. Water Industry Act 1991–*cont.*
s.89, substituted: 2003 c.37 s.58
s.90, substituted: 2003 c.37 s.58
s.91, substituted: 2003 c.37 s.58
s.93, amended: 2003 c.37 Sch.8 para.28
s.93A, amended: 2003 c.37 Sch.8 para.29
s.93B, amended: 2003 c.37 Sch.8 para.30
s.93C, amended: 2003 c.37 Sch.8 para.31
s.93D, amended: 2003 c.37 Sch.8 para.32
s.94, see *British Waterways Board v Severn Trent Water Ltd* [2001] EWCA Civ 276, [2002] Ch. 25 (CA), Peter Gibson, L.J.
s.94, amended: 2003 c.37 s.88, s.97
s.95B, added: 2003 c.37 s.45
s.96, amended: 2003 c.37 s.42, Sch.9 Part 2
s.98, amended: 2003 c.37 s.95, Sch.9 Part 3
s.98, applied: 2003 c.37 s.95
s.99, amended: 2003 c.37 s.93, s.95
s.100, amended: 2003 c.37 s.93
s.100, applied: 2003 c.37 s.93
s.100, referred to: 2003 c.37 s.93
s.100A, added: 2003 c.37 s.93
s.101, referred to: 2003 c.37 s.95
s.101, substituted: 2003 c.37 s.95
s.101A, see *R. (on the application of Anglian Water Services Ltd) v Environment Agency (No.1)* [2002] EWCA Civ 5, Times, February 18, 2002 (CA), Laws, L.J.; see *R. (on the application of Anglian Water Services Ltd) v Environment Agency (No.2)* [2003] EWHC 1506, [2004] Env. L.R. 15 (QBD (Admin Ct)), Owen, J.
s.101A, amended: 2003 c.37 Sch.9 Part 3
s.101A, applied: 2003 c.37 s.95
s.101B, added: 2003 c.37 s.95
s.101B, disapplied: 2003 c.37 s.95
s.102, amended: 2003 c.37 s.96, Sch.9 Part 3
s.102, referred to: 2003 c.37 s.96
s.103, amended: 2003 c.37 s.96, Sch.9 Part 3
s.103, referred to: 2003 c.37 s.96
s.104, amended: 2003 c.37 s.96
s.104, repealed (in part): 2003 c.37 Sch.9 Part 3
s.105, amended: 2003 c.37 s.96
s.105A, added: 2003 c.37 s.98
s.105B, added: 2003 c.37 s.98
s.105C, added: 2003 c.37 s.98
s.106, amended: 2003 c.37 s.99
s.111, amended: 2003 c.37 Sch.7 para.39
s.116A, amended: 2003 c.37 Sch.7 para.27
s.119, amended: 2003 c.37 s.89
s.121, amended: 2003 c.37 s.89
s.138, repealed (in part): 2003 c.37 s.88, Sch.9 Part 3
s.139, substituted: 2003 c.37 s.88
s.141, amended: 2003 c.37 s.88
s.143A, enabling: SI 2003/552
s.144A, applied: SI 2004/701 Reg.2
s.144A, enabling: SI 2004/701
s.144B, applied: SI 2004/701 Reg.2

1991–cont.

56. Water Industry Act 1991–*cont.*
s.144B, enabling: SI 2004/701
s.146, see *Thames Water Utilities Ltd v Hampstead Homes (London) Ltd* [2002] EWCA Civ 1487, [2003] 1 W.L.R. 198 (CA), May, L.J.
s.147, amended: 2004 c.21 Sch.1 para.77
s.147, applied: 2004 c.21 s.38, s.39
s.147, repealed (in part): 2004 c.21 Sch.2
s.148, amended: 2003 c.37 Sch.8 para.33
s.150, amended: 2003 c.37 s.59, Sch.8 para.34
s.152, amended: 2003 c.37 Sch.8 para.35
s.157, enabling: SI 2003/757, SI 2004/1106
s.158, amended: 2003 c.37 s.97, Sch.8 para.36
s.159, see *British Waterways Board v Severn Trent Water Ltd* [2001] EWCA Civ 276, [2002] Ch. 25 (CA), Peter Gibson, L.J.
s.159, amended: 2003 c.37 s.97
s.162, amended: 2003 c.37 Sch.8 para.37
s.163, amended: 2003 c.37 Sch.8 para.38
s.165, see *British Waterways Board v Severn Trent Water Ltd* [2001] EWCA Civ 276, [2002] Ch. 25 (CA), Peter Gibson, L.J.
s.171, amended: 2003 c.37 s.88, s.97
s.174, amended: 2003 c.37 Sch.8 para.39
s.175, amended: 2003 c.37 Sch.8 para.40
s.179, amended: 2003 c.37 s.92, s.97, Sch.8 para.41
s.179, applied: SI 2002/366 Sch.2 para.9
s.181, amended: 2003 c.37 Sch.7 para.27
s.192A, added: 2003 c.37 s.38
s.192A, disapplied: SI 2004/2528 Sch.1 para.3
s.192A, varied: SI 2004/2528 Sch.1 para.3
s.192B, added: 2003 c.37 s.38
s.192B, disapplied: SI 2004/2528 Sch.1 para.2, Sch.1 para.3
s.192B, varied: SI 2004/2528 Sch.1 para.3
s.193, repealed: 2003 c.37 Sch.9 Part 2
s.194, repealed: 2003 c.37 s.38, Sch.9 Part 2
s.195, amended: 2003 c.37 s.48, Sch.8 para.42, Sch.9 Part 2
s.195A, added: 2003 c.37 s.51
s.198, amended: 2003 c.37 s.92
s.199, amended: 2003 c.37 s.97
s.201, amended: 2002 c.40 Sch.25 para.25, 2003 c.37 Sch.8 para.43
s.202, amended: 2003 c.37 Sch.8 para.44
s.203, amended: 2003 c.37 Sch.8 para.45
s.205, amended: 2003 c.37 Sch.8 para.46
s.206, amended: 2002 c.40 Sch.25 para.25, 2003 c.37 Sch.7 para.27, Sch.8 para.47, 2003 c.44 Sch.37 Part 9
s.206, applied: SI 2003/419 Art.63
s.206, disapplied: 2003 c.44 Sch.25 para.90
s.206, referred to: 2003 c.20 s.115
s.207, amended: SI 2002/794 Sch.2
s.208, amended: 2003 c.37 Sch.7 para.27, Sch.8 para.48

1991–cont.

56. Water Industry Act 1991–*cont.*

s.209, see *Thames Water Utilities Ltd v Digginwell Plant & Construction Ltd* [2002] EWHC 1171, [2003] Env. L.R. 21 (QBD (T&CC)), Judge Richard Seymour Q.C.

s.213, amended: 2003 c.37 s.58, Sch.7 para.39, Sch.8 para.49

s.213, enabling: SI 2003/552, SI 2004/701, SI 2004/3202, SI 2004/3206

s.219, amended: 2002 c.40 Sch.25 para.25, 2003 c.21 Sch.17 para.110, 2003 c.37 s.57, s.92, s.97, s.99, Sch.7 para.27, Sch.8 para.50, Sch.9 Part 3, SI 2003/1615 Sch.1 para.15

Sch.1 para.1, repealed: 2003 c.37 s.34, Sch.9 Part 2

Sch.1 para.2, repealed: 2003 c.37 s.34, Sch.9 Part 2

Sch.1 para.3, repealed: 2003 c.37 s.34, Sch.9 Part 2

Sch.1 para.4, repealed: 2003 c.37 s.34, Sch.9 Part 2

Sch.1 para.5, repealed: 2003 c.37 s.34, Sch.9 Part 2

Sch.1A para.1, added: 2003 c.37 Sch.1

Sch.1A para.2, added: 2003 c.37 Sch.1

Sch.1A para.3, added: 2003 c.37 Sch.1

Sch.1A para.4, added: 2003 c.37 Sch.1

Sch.1A para.5, added: 2003 c.37 Sch.1

Sch.1A para.6, added: 2003 c.37 Sch.1

Sch.1A para.6, applied: 2004 c.36 Sch.1 para.21

Sch.1A para.7, added: 2003 c.37 Sch.1

Sch.1A para.8, added: 2003 c.37 Sch.1

Sch.1A para.9, added: 2003 c.37 Sch.1

Sch.1A para.10, added: 2003 c.37 Sch.1

Sch.1A para.11, added: 2003 c.37 Sch.1

Sch.1A para.12, added: 2003 c.37 Sch.1

Sch.2 para.1, amended: 2003 c.37 Sch.8 para.51

Sch.2 para.2, amended: 2003 c.37 Sch.8 para.51

Sch.2 para.3, amended: 2003 c.37 Sch.8 para.51

Sch.2 para.4A, added: 2003 c.37 Sch.8 para.51

Sch.2 para.5, amended: 2003 c.37 Sch.8 para.51

Sch.2 para.6, amended: 2003 c.37 Sch.8 para.51

Sch.3 Part I para.4, amended: 2003 c.37 Sch.8 para.52

Sch.3 Part I para.10, amended: 2003 c.37 Sch.8 para.52

Sch.3A para.1, added: 2003 c.37 Sch.2

Sch.3A para.2, added: 2003 c.37 Sch.2

Sch.3A para.3, added: 2003 c.37 Sch.2

Sch.3A para.4, added: 2003 c.37 Sch.2

Sch.3A para.5, added: 2003 c.37 Sch.2

Sch.3A para.6, added: 2003 c.37 Sch.2

1991–cont.

56. Water Industry Act 1991–*cont.*

Sch.3A para.7, added: 2003 c.37 Sch.2

Sch.3A para.8, added: 2003 c.37 Sch.2

Sch.3A para.9, added: 2003 c.37 Sch.2

Sch.3A para.10, added: 2003 c.37 Sch.2

Sch.3A para.11, added: 2003 c.37 Sch.2

Sch.3A para.12, added: 2003 c.37 Sch.2

Sch.3A para.13, added: 2003 c.37 Sch.2

Sch.3A para.14, added: 2003 c.37 Sch.2

Sch.3A para.15, added: 2003 c.37 Sch.2

Sch.3A para.16, added: 2003 c.37 Sch.2

Sch.3A para.17, added: 2003 c.37 Sch.2

Sch.3A para.18, added: 2003 c.37 Sch.2

Sch.3A para.19, added: 2003 c.37 Sch.2

Sch.3A para.20, added: 2003 c.37 Sch.2

Sch.3A para.21, added: 2003 c.37 Sch.2

Sch.4ZA, applied: 2002 c.40 s.121

Sch.4 para.1, repealed: 2003 c.37 s.35, Sch.9 Part 2

Sch.4 para.1, varied: 2003 c.37 s.36

Sch.4 para.2, repealed: 2003 c.37 s.35, Sch.9 Part 2

Sch.4 para.2, varied: 2003 c.37 s.36

Sch.4 para.3, repealed: 2003 c.37 s.35, Sch.9 Part 2

Sch.4 para.3, varied: 2003 c.37 s.36

Sch.4 para.4, repealed: 2003 c.37 s.35, Sch.9 Part 2

Sch.4 para.4, varied: 2003 c.37 s.36

Sch.4 para.5, repealed: 2003 c.37 s.35, Sch.9 Part 2

Sch.4 para.5, varied: 2003 c.37 s.36

Sch.4A para.2, amended: 2004 c.34 Sch.15 para.36

Sch.4A para.7, substituted: 2003 c.43 Sch.11 para.58

Sch.4A para.7, varied: SI 2004/288 Art.7, SI 2004/480 Art.6

Sch.4A para.13, amended: 2002 c.41 s.66, SI 2003/1016 Sch.1 para.5

Sch.4A para.15, amended: 2004 c.21 Sch.1 para.78

Sch.4A para.15, substituted: 2004 c.21 Sch.1 para.78

Sch.4A para.16, amended: 2003 c.43 Sch.4 para.90

Sch.4ZA para.1, added: 2002 c.40 s.70, Sch.6

Sch.4ZA para.1, enabling: SI 2004/3202

Sch.4ZA para.2, added: 2002 c.40 s.70, Sch.6

Sch.4ZA para.2, enabling: SI 2004/3202

Sch.4ZA para.3, added: 2002 c.40 s.70, Sch.6

Sch.4ZA para.4, added: 2002 c.40 s.70, Sch.6

Sch.4ZA para.5, added: 2002 c.40 s.70, Sch.6

Sch.4ZA para.6, added: 2002 c.40 s.70, Sch.6

Sch.4ZA para.7, added: 2002 c.40 s.70, Sch.6

1991–cont.

56. Water Industry Act 1991–cont.

Sch.6 Part I para.5, amended: 2003 c.44 Sch.32 para.159, Sch.37 Part 9

Sch.6 Part I para.5, disapplied: 2003 c.44 Sch.25 para.91

Sch.6 Part II para.7, see *Severn Trent Water Ltd v Slack* [2001] EWHC Admin 1094, [2002] E.H.L.R. 12 (QBD (Admin Ct)), Elias, J.

Sch.6 Part II para.7, applied: SI 2003/3341 Art.2

Sch.6 Part II para.8, applied: SI 2003/3341 Art.2

Sch.6 Part II para.9, applied: SI 2003/3341 Art.2

Sch.6 Part II para.10, applied: SI 2003/3341 Art.2

Sch.6 Part II para.12, applied: SI 2003/3341 Art.2

Sch.6 Part II para.13, applied: SI 2003/3341 Art.2

Sch.7 para.1, amended: SI 2002/2469 Sch.1 para.18

Sch.7 para.1, repealed: 2003 c.37 s.58, Sch.9 Part 3

Sch.7 para.2, amended: SI 2002/2469 Sch.1 para.18

Sch.7 para.2, repealed: 2003 c.37 s.58, Sch.9 Part 3

Sch.7 para.3, amended: SI 2002/2469 Sch.1 para.18

Sch.7 para.3, repealed: 2003 c.37 s.58, Sch.9 Part 3

Sch.12, see *Davies v Hyder Plc (formerly Welsh Water)* [2003] R.V.R. 37 (Lands Tr), NJ Rose, FRICS

Sch.12 para.2, see *Hodder v Southern Water Services Ltd* [2002] R.V.R. 365 (Lands Tr), NJ Rose, FRICS

Sch.12 para.4, amended: 2003 c.37 s.97

Sch.13 Part I para.1, amended: 2003 c.21 Sch.17 para.111, 2004 c.20 Sch.19 para.17

Sch.13 Part I para.4, amended: 2003 c.21 Sch.17 para.111

Sch.15 Part I, amended: 2002 c.40 Sch.25 para.25, 2003 c.20 Sch.2 para.19, 2003 c.21 Sch.17 para.112

Sch.15 Part II, amended: 2002 c.40 Sch.25 para.25, 2003 c.20 Sch.2 para.19, 2003 c.21 Sch.17 para.112

57. Water Resources Act 1991

applied: 2002 c.40 Sch.15, SI 2002/1384 Art.10, SI 2002/3127 Art.16, 2003 c.37 s.103, SI 2003/1075 Art.21, SI 2004/757 Art.18, SI 2004/933 Art.19, SI 2004/1280 Art.15

referred to: SI 2002/412 Art.12, SI 2002/1064 Art.6, SI 2003/2829 Art.20, SI 2003/2830 Sch.2 para.13, SI 2003/2831 Art.19, SI 2004/757 Art.18

Part II, applied: 2003 c.37 s.33

1991–cont.

57. Water Resources Act 1991–cont.

Part II c.II, applied: 2003 c.37 s.10, s.102, s.103, SI 2003/1075 Sch.13 para.39, SI 2003/3364 Sch.8 para.11, SI 2004/389 Sch.13 para.39

Part II c.II, applied: 2003 c.37 s.10

Part II c.II, added: 2003 c.37 s.23

Part III c.I, applied: SI 2003/1238 Reg.2

s.20, amended: 2003 c.37 Sch.7 para.28

s.20A, added: 2003 c.37 s.28

s.20B, added: 2003 c.37 s.29

s.20C, added: 2003 c.37 s.31

s.21, amended: SI 2002/2626 Sch.2 para.18, 2003 c.37 s.8, Sch.9 Part 1

s.24, amended: 2003 c.37 s.60

s.24, applied: 2003 c.37 s.10

s.24A, added: 2003 c.37 s.1

s.25, amended: 2003 c.37 s.2, s.60, Sch.9 Part 1

s.25, applied: 2003 c.37 s.2, s.3

s.25, disapplied: 2003 c.37 s.3

s.25, referred to: 2003 c.37 s.3

s.25A, added: 2003 c.37 s.30

s.25A, applied: 2003 c.37 s.4

s.25B, added: 2003 c.37 s.30

s.25C, added: 2003 c.37 s.30

s.26, substituted: 2003 c.37 s.5

s.27, applied: 2003 c.37 s.10

s.27, substituted: 2003 c.37 s.6

s.27A, added: 2003 c.37 s.6

s.28, repealed: 2003 c.37 s.6, Sch.9 Part 1

s.29, amended: 2003 c.37 s.7

s.29, repealed (in part): 2003 c.37 s.7, Sch.9 Part 1

s.30, applied: SI 2003/1075 Sch.13 para.39, SI 2003/3364 Sch.8 para.11, SI 2004/389 Sch.13 para.39

s.30, repealed: 2003 c.37 s.8, Sch.9 Part 1

s.31, repealed: 2003 c.37 s.8, Sch.9 Part 1

s.32, amended: 2004 c.21 Sch.1 para.79

s.33, applied: 2003 c.37 s.10

s.33, disapplied: 2003 c.37 s.10

s.33, referred to: 2003 c.37 s.10

s.33, repealed: 2003 c.37 Sch.9 Part 1

s.33A, applied: 2003 c.37 s.10

s.34, amended: 2003 c.37 Sch.7 para.2

s.35, amended: 2003 c.37 s.11

s.36, repealed: 2003 c.37 s.12, Sch.9 Part 1

s.36A, added: 2003 c.37 s.13

s.37, substituted: 2003 c.37 s.14

s.37A, added: 2003 c.37 s.14

s.38, amended: 2003 c.37 s.14, s.15, s.31

s.38, varied: SI 2004/641 Sch.3 para.2

s.39, amended: 2003 c.37 s.16

s.39, applied: 2003 c.37 s.3

s.39, disapplied: 2003 c.37 s.102

s.39, repealed (in part): 2003 c.37 s.16, Sch.9 Part 1

s.39A, added: 2003 c.37 s.17

s.39B, added: 2003 c.37 s.18

CAP.

1991–cont.

57. Water Resources Act 1991–*cont.*

s.40, amended: 2003 c.37 Sch.7 para.3

s.41, amended: 2003 c.37 s.13

s.42, amended: 2003 c.37 s.14, s.16

s.42, disapplied: 2003 c.37 s.102

s.42, varied: SI 2003/164 Reg.13

s.43, amended: 2003 c.37 s.14

s.43, applied: SI 2003/164 Reg.8

s.44, amended: 2003 c.37 s.16

s.44, disapplied: 2003 c.37 s.102

s.45, amended: 2003 c.37 s.13

s.46, amended: 2003 c.37 s.19

s.46A, added: 2003 c.37 s.20

s.46A, varied: SI 2004/641 Sch.3 para.2

s.47, amended: 2003 c.37 s.19, s.23, Sch.9 Part 1

s.47, repealed (in part): 2003 c.37 s.23, Sch.9 Part 1

s.48, amended: 2003 c.37 s.24

s.48, applied: 2003 c.37 s.102

s.48, varied: 2003 c.37 s.24

s.48A, added: 2003 c.37 s.24

s.48A, disapplied: 2003 c.37 s.24

s.48A, varied: SI 2004/641 Sch.3 para.4

s.49, referred to: 2003 c.37 s.23

s.49, repealed: 2003 c.37 s.23, Sch.9 Part 1

s.50, referred to: 2003 c.37 s.23

s.50, repealed: 2003 c.37 s.23, Sch.9 Part 1

s.51, amended: 2003 c.37 s.21, Sch.7 para.4

s.52, amended: 2003 c.37 s.22

s.52, applied: SI 2003/164 Reg.14, Reg.15

s.52, repealed (in part): 2003 c.37 s.22, Sch.9 Part 1

s.54, applied: 2003 c.37 s.27

s.56, applied: 2003 c.37 s.27

s.57, amended: 2003 c.37 Sch.7 para.5

s.61, amended: 2003 c.37 s.25, Sch.7 para.6

s.61, applied: 2003 c.37 s.25, s.27

s.61, referred to: 2003 c.37 s.3

s.61, varied: 2003 c.37 s.3

s.61A, added: 2003 c.37 s.26

s.61A, referred to: SI 2004/2528 Sch.1 para.1

s.64, amended: 2003 c.37 s.2

s.66, amended: 2003 c.37 s.14

s.66, repealed (in part): 2003 c.37 Sch.7 para.7, Sch.9 Part 3

s.67, amended: 2003 c.37 s.2, Sch.7 para.8

s.70, amended: 2003 c.37 s.8

s.71, amended: 2003 c.37 Sch.7 para.9, Sch.9 Part 3

s.72, amended: 2003 c.37 s.1, s.2, s.17

s.73, applied: SI 2003/3341 (b)

s.73, enabling: SI 2003/3341

s.74, enabling: SI 2003/3341

s.77, repealed (in part): 2003 c.37 Sch.9 Part 3

s.78, enabling: SI 2003/3341

s.79, amended: 2003 c.37 s.64

s.79A, amended: 2003 c.37 s.64

CAP.

1991–cont.

57. Water Resources Act 1991–*cont.*

s.79A, repealed (in part): 2003 c.37 Sch.9 Part 3

s.82, enabling: SI 2003/1053, SI 2003/1238

s.85, see *Express Ltd (t/a Express Dairies Distribution) v Environment Agency* [2003] EWHC 448, [2004] 1 W.L.R. 579 (QBD (Admin Ct)), Hale, L.J.; see *R. v Anglian Water Services Ltd* [2003] EWCA Crim 2243, [2004] Env. L.R. 10 (CA (Crim Div)), Scott Baker, L.J.

s.85, applied: SI 2002/412 Art.12, SI 2002/1327 Art.13, SI 2003/1075 Art.21, SI 2003/3364 Art.10, SI 2004/389 Art.19, SI 2004/757 Art.18

s.85, referred to: SI 2002/1064 Art.6, SI 2002/1065 Art.6, SI 2002/1066 Art.15

s.89, see *Express Ltd (t/a Express Dairies Distribution) v Environment Agency* [2003] EWHC 448, [2004] 1 W.L.R. 579 (QBD (Admin Ct)), Hale, L.J.

s.102, enabling: SI 2003/1238

s.104, varied: SI 2003/1238 Reg.2

s.109, applied: SI 2002/366 Sch.2 para.2, SI 2002/1064 Sch.3 para.3, SI 2002/1066 Sch.13 para.2, SI 2002/1384 Art.10, SI 2003/1075 Sch.13 para.39, SI 2003/3364 Sch.8 para.11, SI 2004/389 Sch.13 para.39, SI 2004/1280 Art.15

s.109, disapplied: SI 2004/757 Art.4

s.109, referred to: SI 2002/412 Sch.6 para.2, SI 2002/1065 Sch.6 para.7, SI 2002/3127 Art.16

s.113, applied: SI 2002/366 Sch.2 para.3, SI 2002/412 Sch.6 para.3, SI 2002/1066 Sch.13 para.9

s.114, applied: 2003 c.37 s.3

s.120, varied: 2003 c.37 s.33

s.125, repealed (in part): 2003 c.37 Sch.7 para.10, Sch.9 Part 3

s.134, applied: SI 2004/388 Art.2

s.135, enabling: SI 2004/388

s.147, repealed (in part): 2003 c.37 s.69, Sch.9 Part 3

s.148, repealed (in part): 2003 c.37 s.69, Sch.9 Part 3

s.149, repealed (in part): 2003 c.37 s.69, Sch.9 Part 3

s.158, amended: 2002 c.9 Sch.11 para.25

s.158, varied: 2003 c.37 s.33

s.161A, see *Eastern Counties Leather Plc v Eastern Counties Leather Group Ltd* [2002] EWHC 494, [2002] Env. L.R. 34 (Ch D), Blackburne, J.

s.161B, applied: 2003 c.37 s.4

s.161C, applied: 2003 c.37 s.4

s.163, amended: SI 2003/1615 Sch.1 para.16

s.165, amended: 2003 c.37 s.69

s.166, amended: 2003 c.37 s.69

s.169, amended: 2003 c.37 s.71

s.189, amended: 2003 c.37 s.23

1991–cont.

57. Water Resources Act 1991–*cont.*

s.189, applied: SI 2003/164 Reg.16

s.199, amended: 2003 c.37 s.8

s.199A, added: 2003 c.37 s.8

s.201, substituted: 2003 c.37 s.70

s.201, varied: 2003 c.37 s.33

s.202, varied: SI 2003/3242 Reg.19, SI 2004/99 Sch.1 para.15

s.203, amended: 2003 c.37 Sch.8 para.53

s.204, amended: 2003 c.37 Sch.7 para.28, Sch.8 para.53

s.204, referred to: 2003 c.20 s.115

s.205, amended: 2003 c.44 Sch.32 para.160

s.206, amended: 2003 c.37 Sch.7 para.11

s.210, applied: SI 2002/1998 Art.17

s.211, disapplied: SI 2002/1998 Art.32

s.216, varied: 2003 c.37 s.33

s.217, amended: 2003 c.37 Sch.7 para.12

s.219, amended: 2003 c.37 Sch.7 para.28

s.219, enabling: SI 2003/1053, SI 2003/ 1238

s.220, varied: 2003 c.37 s.33

s.221, amended: 2003 c.21 Sch.17 para.113, 2003 c.37 Sch.9 Part 3

s.221, applied: 2003 c.37 s.27

s.222, amended: 2003 c.37 Sch.7 para.13

s.222, varied: 2003 c.37 s.33

s.223, repealed: 2003 c.37 s.32, Sch.9 Part 1

Sch.2 para.8, amended: SI 2003/2867 Sch.1 para.17

Sch.5 para.2, amended: SI 2002/2626 Sch.2 para.18

Sch.6, disapplied: 2003 c.37 s.10

Sch.6 para.1, amended: SI 2002/2626 Sch.2 para.18

Sch.6 para.1, substituted: 2003 c.37 Sch.7 para.14

Sch.6 para.2, substituted: 2003 c.37 Sch.7 para.14

Sch.6 para.2, amended: SI 2002/2626 Sch.2 para.18

Sch.6 para.3, substituted: 2003 c.37 Sch.7 para.14

Sch.6 para.4, substituted: 2003 c.37 Sch.7 para.14

Sch.7 para.1, varied: 2003 c.37 s.24

Sch.7 para.2, varied: 2003 c.37 s.24

Sch.8 para.2, amended: 2003 c.37 s.65

Sch.8 para.2, applied: SI 2003/3341 (c), SI 2003/3341 (d)

Sch.8 para.2, enabling: SI 2003/3341

Sch.10 para.11, amended: 2003 c.37 s.87, Sch.9 Part 3

Sch.10 para.11, applied: SI 2004/2528 Sch.1 para.6

Sch.10 para.11, repealed (in part): 2003 c.37 Sch.9 Part 3

Sch.21 para.5, see *Matthews v Environment Agency* [2002] 3 E.G.L.R. 168 (Lands Tr), NJ Rose, FRICS

1991–cont.

57. Water Resources Act 1991–*cont.*

Sch.22 para.1, amended: 2003 c.21 Sch.17 para.114, 2004 c.20 Sch.19 para.18

Sch.22 para.5, amended: 2003 c.21 Sch.17 para.114

Sch.22 para.6, amended: SI 2003/1615 Sch.1 para.16

Sch.24 Part I, amended: 2002 c.40 Sch.25 para.26, 2003 c.20 Sch.2 para.19, 2003 c.21 Sch.17 para.115

Sch.24 Part II, amended: 2002 c.40 Sch.25 para.26, 2003 c.20 Sch.2 para.19, 2003 c.21 Sch.17 para.115

Sch.25, applied: SI 2002/1998 Art.17, Art.34

Sch.25 para.1, applied: SI 2002/1998 Art.4, Art.30, Art.32

Sch.25 para.1, varied: SI 2002/1998 Art.32

Sch.26, applied: SI 2002/1998 Art.17

58. Statutory Water Companies Act 1991

applied: 2002 c.40 Sch.15

59. Land Drainage Act 1991

applied: 2002 c.40 Sch.15, SI 2002/366 Sch.2 para.2, SI 2002/1384 Art.10, SI 2002/3127 Art.16, SI 2004/933 Art.19, SI 2004/1280 Art.15, SI 2004/2190 Art.19

referred to: SI 2002/412 Sch.6 para.2, SI 2003/2829 Art.20, SI 2003/2830 Sch.2 para.13, SI 2003/2831 Art.19

s.1, applied: SI 2004/344 Art.2

s.3, applied: SI 2004/344 Art.2, SI 2004/ 1657

s.3, enabling: SI 2004/1657

s.4, applied: SI 2004/344 Art.2

s.5, applied: SI 2004/344 Art.2

s.14, see *R. (on the application of MWH&H Ward Estates Ltd) v Monmouthshire CC* [2002] EWCA Civ 1915, [2003] E.H.L.R. 10 (CA), Laws, L.J.; see *R. (on the application of MWH&H Ward Estates Ltd) v Monmouthshire CC* [2002] EWHC 229, [2002] E.H.L.R. 14 (QBD (Admin Ct)), Richards, J.

s.16, amended: 2003 c.37 Sch.7 para.40

s.23, disapplied: SI 2004/757 Art.4

s.35, amended: SI 2002/2626 Sch.2 para.19

s.55, amended: 2003 c.37 Sch.7 para.40

s.64, see *R. (on the application of MWH&H Ward Estates Ltd) v Monmouthshire CC* [2002] EWCA Civ 1915, [2003] E.H.L.R. 10 (CA), Laws, L.J.; see *R. (on the application of MWH&H Ward Estates Ltd) v Monmouthshire CC* [2002] EWHC 229, [2002] E.H.L.R. 14 (QBD (Admin Ct)), Richards, J.

s.69, applied: SI 2002/2780 Reg.2

Sch.3, enabling: SI 2004/1657

Sch.3 para.2, applied: SI 2004/1657

Sch.3 para.2, referred to: SI 2004/1657

Sch.3 para.5, applied: SI 2004/1657 Art.1

Sch.6 para.1, amended: 2003 c.21 Sch.17 para.116, 2004 c.20 Sch.19 para.19

CAP.

1991–cont.

59. Land Drainage Act 1991–*cont.*
Sch.6 para.4, amended: SI 2003/1615 Sch.1 para.17

60. Water Consolidation (Consequential Provisions) Act 1991
applied: 2002 c.40 Sch.15
Sch.1 para.10, repealed: 2003 c.37 Sch.7 para.29, Sch.9 Part 3
Sch.1 para.24, repealed: 2002 c.40 Sch.26
Sch.1 para.26, repealed: 2002 c.40 Sch.26
Sch.1 para.28, repealed (in part): 2003 c.37 Sch.7 para.29, Sch.9 Part 3
Sch.1 para.29, repealed (in part): 2003 c.37 Sch.7 para.29, Sch.9 Part 3
Sch.1 para.33, repealed: 2002 c.40 Sch.26
Sch.1 para.34, repealed: 2002 c.40 Sch.26
Sch.1 para.52, repealed: 2002 c.40 Sch.26
Sch.2 Part I para.8, amended: 2003 c.37 Sch.7 para.29
Sch.2 Part I para.10, amended: 2003 c.37 Sch.7 para.29

65. Dangerous Dogs Act 1991
s.3, see *R. v Cox (Jacqueline)* [2004] EWCA Crim 282, [2004] 2 Cr. App. R. (S.) 54 (CA (Crim Div)), Lord Woolf of Barnes, L.C.J.; see *R. v Haynes (Rodney)* [2003] EWCA Crim 3247, [2004] 2 Cr. App. R. (S.) 9 (CA (Crim Div)), Judge Jeremy Roberts Q.C.; see *R. v Holland (Elizabeth)* [2002] EWCA Crim 1585, [2003] 1 Cr. App. R. (S.) 60 (CA (Crim Div)), Pitchford, J.
s.4, see *R. v Haynes (Rodney)* [2003] EWCA Crim 3247, [2004] 2 Cr. App. R. (S.) 9 (CA (Crim Div)), Judge Jeremy Roberts Q.C.; see *R. v Holland (Elizabeth)* [2002] EWCA Crim 1585, [2003] 1 Cr. App. R. (S.) 60 (CA (Crim Div)), Pitchford, J.
s.4, amended: 2003 c.39 Sch.8 para.353
s.10, see *DPP v Zhao* [2003] EWHC 1724, (2003) 167 J.P. 521 (QBD (Admin Ct)), Owen, J.

66. British Technology Group Act 1991
s.1, repealed (in part): 2004 c.14 Sch.1 Part 16
s.2, repealed: 2004 c.14 Sch.1 Part 16
s.3, repealed: 2004 c.14 Sch.1 Part 16
s.4, repealed: 2004 c.14 Sch.1 Part 16
s.5, repealed: 2004 c.14 Sch.1 Part 16
s.6, repealed: 2004 c.14 Sch.1 Part 16
s.7, repealed: 2004 c.14 Sch.1 Part 16
s.8, amended: 2004 c.14 Sch.1 Part 16
s.8, repealed (in part): 2004 c.14 Sch.1 Part 16
s.9, repealed: 2004 c.14 Sch.1 Part 16
s.13, repealed: 2004 c.14 Sch.1 Part 16
s.14, amended: 2004 c.14 Sch.1 Part 16
Sch.1 para.1, repealed: 2004 c.14 Sch.1 Part 16

67. Export and Investment Guarantees Act 1991
s.1, applied: 2004 c.35 Sch.3, Sch.8
s.2, applied: 2004 c.35 Sch.3, Sch.8
s.3, applied: 2004 c.35 Sch.3, Sch.8
s.4, applied: 2004 c.35 Sch.3, Sch.8

CAP.

1991–cont.

67. Export and Investment Guarantees Act 1991–*cont.*
s.7, applied: 2004 c.35 Sch.3, Sch.8
s.7, repealed (in part): 2004 c.14 Sch.1 Part 16
s.15, repealed (in part): 2004 c.14 Sch.1 Part 16

1992

iii. London Underground Act 1992
see *Thames Water Utilities Ltd v London Underground Ltd* [2004] EWCA Civ 615, (2004) 148 S.J.L.B. 633 (CA), Brooke, L.J.

Offences Against the Person (Amendment) Act (Jamaica) 1992
see *Watson (Lambert) v Queen, The* [2004] UKPC 34, [2004] 3 W.L.R. 841 (PC (Jam)), Lord Bingham of Cornhill

xii. Peterhead Harbours Order Confirmation Act 1992
applied: SSI 2002/504 Art.10
Sch.1, amended: SSI 2002/504 Art.15
Sch.1, applied: SSI 2002/504 Art.10
Sch.1, repealed: SSI 2002/504 Art.16

1. Church of England (Miscellaneous Provisions) Measure 1992
applied: SI 2003/1932 Sch.1 para.10
referred to: SI 2002/1894 Sch.1 para.10, SI 2004/1890 Sch.1 para.10

2. Stamp Duty (Temporary Provisions) Act 1992
s.1, amended: 2003 c.14 Sch.20 para.3

3. Severn Bridges Act 1992
s.8, amended: 2004 c.21 Sch.1 para.80
s.8, referred to: SI 2002/3004 Art.2, SI 2003/3276 Art.2
s.9, applied: SI 2002/3004 Art.1, SI 2003/3276 Art.1
s.9, enabling: SI 2002/3004, SI 2003/3276

4. Social Security Contributions and Benefits Act 1992
see *FS Consulting Ltd v McCaul (Inspector of Taxes)* [2002] S.T.C. (S.C.D.) 138 (Sp Comm), Nuala Brice; see *Synaptek Ltd v Young (Inspector of Taxes)* [2003] EWHC 645, [2003] S.T.C. 543 (Ch D), Hart, J.
applied: 2002 c.21 s.50, Sch.5 para.7, 2002 c.22 s.45, SI 2002/36 Art.2, SI 2002/1792 Reg.17, SI 2002/1888 Art.3, SI 2002/2006 Reg.7, SI 2002/2822 Reg.32, SI 2002/3047 Reg.5, SI 2002/3200 Sch.3 para.1, SI 2003/324 Art.2, SI 2003/492 Reg.1, Reg.12, Reg.20, Reg.23, Reg.35, Reg.36, Reg.42, SI 2003/495 Reg.10, SI 2003/526 Art.1, Art.6, SI 2003/527 Reg.31, SI 2003/916 Reg.21, SI 2003/1325 Art.2, 2004 c.12 Sch.28 para.2, Sch.28 para.16, 2004 c.33 s.254, SI 2004/263 Art.2, SI 2004/291 Sch.4, SI 2004/478 Sch.4, SI 2004/552 Art.1, Art.6, SI 2004/627 Sch.2, SI 2004/3114 Art.3, SI 2004/3121 Art.4, SR 2003/28

1992–cont.

4. **Social Security Contributions and Benefits Act 1992**–*cont.*

applied: 2002 c.21 s.50–*cont.*

Reg.17, SSI 2002/494 Sch.2 para.9, SSI 2004/115 Sch.3, SSI 2004/257 Reg.31

referred to: 2003 c.1 Sch.6 para.169, SI 2003/492 Reg.31, SI 2003/916 Reg.27

Part I, applied: 2002 c.29 s.323, SI 2002/830, SI 2003/963, SSI 2003/176 Art.4, SSI 2003/461 Reg.11, 2004 c.12 Sch.11 para.4, Sch.11 para.12

Part I, referred to: SI 2004/889

Part II, applied: SI 2002/427 Reg.3, Reg.5, Reg.12, Reg.14, SI 2002/836 Reg.3, Reg.5, Reg.12, Reg.14, SI 2003/601 Reg.2, SR 2002/127 Reg.3, Reg.5, SSI 2003/176 Art.4, 2004 c.7 Sch.5 para.2

Part III, applied: SI 2003/601 Reg.2, SSI 2003/176 Art.4

Part IV, applied: SI 2002/1792 Reg.15, SI 2003/601 Reg.2, SSI 2003/176 Art.4

Part V, applied: SI 2003/601 Reg.2, SSI 2003/176 Art.4

Part VI, applied: SR 2002/224 Sch.3 para.1, SSI 2003/176 Art.4

Part VII, applied: SI 2002/195 Reg.30, Sch.3 para.1, SI 2002/1330 Sch.3 para.1, SI 2002/2005 Reg.13, SI 2002/2008 Reg.4, SI 2002/3200 Reg.29, Sch.3 para.1, SI 2003/1994 Sch.3 para.1, SI 2003/2098 Reg.8, SI 2003/2382 Reg.17, SI 2004/683 Reg.8, SR 2002/265 Sch.7 para.1, SSI 2003/140 Sch.1 para.5, SSI 2003/376 Sch.1 para.3, SSI 2003/460 Sch.1 para.3

Part VII, disapplied: SI 2002/195 Sch.3 para.1

Part VIII, applied: SI 2002/1792 Reg.15, Sch.2 para.4

Part IX, applied: 2002 c.21 s.49, SI 2002/1330 Sch.3 para.1, SI 2002/1792 Reg.15, Sch.1 para.2, SI 2002/3200 Reg.15, Sch.3 para.1, SI 2003/493 Reg.5, Reg.34, Reg.35, SI 2003/916 Sch.2 para.1, SI 2003/1994 Sch.3 para.1

Part IX, disapplied: SI 2002/195 Reg.15, Sch.3 para.1

Part X, applied: SI 2002/1792 Reg.15

Part XI, applied: SI 2002/2005 Reg.9, SI 2002/2822 Reg.18, Reg.27, SSI 2003/461 Reg.10

Part XII, applied: SSI 2003/461 Reg.10

Part XIIZA, applied: SI 2002/1792 Reg.17A, Reg.15, SI 2002/2819 Reg.2, Reg.4, SI 2002/2821 Reg.2, Reg.3, Reg.4, Reg.7, Reg.8, SI 2002/2822 Reg.3, Reg.24, Reg.31, Reg.32, Reg.34, Reg.38, Reg.40, Reg.46, SI 2003/500 Reg.4, Reg.15, SI 2003/1194 Reg.4, Reg.15

Part XIIZA, referred to: 2002 c.22 s.55, SI 2003/500 Reg.2, Reg.3

1992–cont.

4. **Social Security Contributions and Benefits Act 1992**–*cont.*

Part XIIZB, applied: SI 2002/1792 Reg.17A, Reg.15, SI 2002/2819 Reg.2, Reg.4, SI 2002/2821 Reg.2, Reg.3, Reg.4, Reg.7, Reg.8, SI 2002/2822 Reg.3, Reg.15, Reg.31, Reg.32, Reg.34, Reg.38, Reg.40, Reg.46, SI 2003/500 Reg.4, Reg.9, SI 2003/1194 Reg.4, Reg.9

Part XIIZB, referred to: 2002 c.22 s.55, SI 2003/500 Reg.2, Reg.3

s.1, amended: 2002 c.22 s.6, 2003 c.1 Sch.6 para.170

s.2, see *Rashid v Garcia (Status Inspector)* [2003] S.T.C. (S.C.D.) 36 (Sp Comm), John F Avery Jones; see *RCI (Europe) Ltd v Woods (Inspector of Taxes)* [2003] S.T.C. (S.C.D.) 128 (Sp Comm), John F Avery Jones

s.2, amended: 2003 c.1 Sch.6 para.171

s.2, enabling: SI 2003/736, SI 2004/770

s.3, applied: SI 2004/173

s.3, enabling: SI 2002/307, SI 2002/842, SI 2002/2366, SI 2002/2823, SI 2002/2924, SI 2002/3019, SI 2002/3197, SI 2003/193, SI 2003/964, SI 2003/1059, SI 2003/2085, SI 2003/2340, SI 2003/2958, SI 2004/173, SI 2004/770, SI 2004/2096

s.4, see *RCI (Europe) Ltd v Woods (Inspector of Taxes)* [2003] EWHC 3129, [2004] S.T.C. 315 (Ch D), Lightman, J.

s.4, amended: 2002 c.22 Sch.7 para.3, 2003 c.14 Sch.22 para.48, 2003 c.1 Sch.6 para.172

s.4, enabling: SI 2002/307, SI 2003/2085, SI 2004/770

s.4A, amended: SI 2003/1874 Art.3, Art.4

s.4A, enabling: SI 2002/703, SI 2003/1874, SI 2003/2079, SI 2004/770

s.5, enabling: SI 2002/238, SI 2003/193, SI 2004/220

s.6, applied: SI 2002/2821 Reg.4

s.7, amended: 2003 c.1 Sch.6 para.173

s.7, enabling: SI 2003/736, SI 2003/2420

s.8, applied: SI 2002/2822 Reg.42

s.8, substituted: 2002 c.19 s.1

s.9, amended: 2002 c.19 s.2, SI 2002/830 Art.2

s.10, amended: 2002 c.19 Sch.1 para.2, 2003 c.1 Sch.6 para.174

s.10, repealed (in part): 2003 c.1 Sch.8 Part 1

s.10, enabling: SI 2003/2085, SI 2004/770

s.10A, amended: 2002 c.19 Sch.1 para.3, 2003 c.1 Sch.6 para.177, 2004 c.3 Sch.1 para.1

s.10A, applied: SI 2002/2822 Reg.39

s.10A, enabling: SI 2004/770

s.10ZA, amended: 2003 c.1 Sch.6 para.175

s.10ZB, amended: 2003 c.1 Sch.6 para.176

1992–cont.

4. **Social Security Contributions and Benefits Act 1992**–*cont.*
s.11, amended: SI 2002/830 Art.3, SI 2003/ 963 Art.2, SI 2004/889 Art.2
s.12ZA, applied: SI 2003/499 Reg.2
s.12ZB, applied: SI 2003/499 Reg.3
s.13, amended: SI 2002/830 Art.4, SI 2003/ 963 Art.3, SI 2004/889 Art.3
s.13, enabling: SI 2004/1362
s.14, enabling: SI 2003/193
s.15, amended: 2002 c.19 s.3, SI 2002/830 Art.5, SI 2004/889 Art.4
s.16, repealed (in part): 2002 c.19 Sch.2
s.17, amended: 2002 c.19 Sch.1 para.4
s.17, repealed (in part): 2002 c.19 Sch.2
s.17, enabling: SI 2002/2366, SI 2003/193, SI 2003/2958
s.18, amended: 2002 c.19 s.3, Sch.2, SI 2002/830 Art.5, 2004 c.3 Sch.1 para.1, SI 2004/889 Art.4
s.18, enabling: SI 2004/770
s.19, amended: 2002 c.19 Sch.1 para.5
s.19, applied: SI 2003/527 Reg.31, SSI 2004/ 257 Reg.31
s.19, enabling: SI 2003/193, SI 2003/964, SI 2004/770
s.20, amended: 2002 c.21 Sch.6, 2004 c.33 Sch.24 para.13
s.21, amended: 2002 c.19 Sch.1 para.6, 2002 c.21 Sch.6
s.22, amended: 2002 c.19 Sch.1 para.7
s.22, enabling: SI 2002/490, SI 2002/2497, SI 2003/455, SI 2003/521
s.23, amended: 2002 c.19 Sch.1 para.8
s.23, enabling: SI 2003/608
s.24, amended: 2002 c.19 Sch.1 para.9
s.30A, amended: 2004 c.33 Sch.24 para.14
s.30A, applied: SI 2002/1792 Sch.6 para.4, SI 2002/2005 Reg.6, Reg.13, 2003 c.1 s.660, SI 2003/493 Reg.10, SSI 2003/ 176 Art.4, SSI 2004/83 Reg.3
s.30A, varied: SI 2003/737 Reg.2
s.30A, enabling: SI 2002/2311
s.30B, amended: 2002 c.21 Sch.6, 2004 c.33 Sch.24 para.15
s.30B, applied: SI 2002/668 Art.6, SI 2002/ 2005 Reg.6, 2003 c.1 s.664, SI 2003/526 Art.6, SI 2004/552 Art.6
s.30C, amended: 2002 c.21 Sch.3 para.25
s.30C, applied: SI 2002/491 Reg.6, SI 2002/ 2005 Reg.6
s.30C, varied: SI 2003/962 Art.5
s.30D, applied: SI 2002/2005 Reg.6
s.30D, varied: SI 2003/737 Reg.3
s.30D, enabling: SI 2003/1068
s.30DD, applied: SI 2002/1792 Reg.15, SI 2002/2005 Reg.6
s.30E, applied: SI 2002/1792 Reg.15, SI 2002/2005 Reg.6
s.30E, enabling: SI 2002/684, SI 2002/2311, SI 2003/2262, SI 2004/2301

1992–cont.

4. **Social Security Contributions and Benefits Act 1992**–*cont.*
s.35, amended: 2002 c.22 Sch.7 para.4
s.35, applied: 2003 c.1 s.677
s.35, enabling: SI 2002/2690
s.35A, amended: 2002 c.22 s.48, Sch.7 para.5
s.35A, varied: 2002 c.22 s.48
s.35A, enabling: SI 2002/2690, SI 2003/ 659
s.36, see *Hooper v Secretary of State for Work and Pensions* [2002] EWHC 191, [2002] U.K.H.R.R. 785 (QBD (Admin Ct)), Moses, J.; see *Hooper v Secretary of State for Work and Pensions* [2003] EWCA Civ 813, [2003] 1 W.L.R. 2623 (CA), Lord Phillips of Worth Matravers, M.R.
s.36, amended: 2004 c.33 Sch.24 para.16
s.36, applied: 2003 c.1 s.677
s.36A, amended: 2004 c.33 Sch.24 para.17
s.37, see *Hooper v Secretary of State for Work and Pensions* [2002] EWHC 191, [2002] U.K.H.R.R. 785 (QBD (Admin Ct)), Moses, J.; see *Hooper v Secretary of State for Work and Pensions* [2003] EWCA Civ 813, [2003] 1 W.L.R. 2623 (CA), Lord Phillips of Worth Matravers, M.R.
s.37, amended: 2002 c.21 Sch.3 para.26, 2004 c.33 Sch.24 para.18, Sch.30
s.37, applied: SI 2002/1792 Sch.4 para.7A, 2004 c.7 Sch.5 para.3
s.37, varied: SI 2003/938 Art.4
s.37ZB, applied: SI 2002/1792 Sch.1 para.1
s.38, see *Hooper v Secretary of State for Work and Pensions* [2003] EWCA Civ 813, [2003] 1 W.L.R. 2623 (CA), Lord Phillips of Worth Matravers, M.R.
s.38, amended: 2004 c.33 Sch.24 para.19, Sch.30
s.38, applied: 2004 c.7 Sch.5 para.4
s.39, amended: 2002 c.21 Sch.3 para.27
s.39A, amended: 2002 c.21 Sch.3 para.28, 2004 c.33 Sch.24 para.20, Sch.30
s.39A, applied: SI 2002/1792 Sch.4 para.7, 2004 c.7 Sch.5 para.3, Sch.5 para.5
s.39A, varied: SI 2003/938 Art.4
s.39B, amended: 2004 c.33 Sch.24 para.21, Sch.30
s.39B, applied: 2003 c.1 s.660
s.39C, amended: 2002 c.21 Sch.3 para.29, 2004 c.33 Sch.24 para.22
s.40, applied: SI 2002/2005 Reg.13, 2003 c.1 s.660, SSI 2003/176 Art.4, 2004 c.7 Sch.5 para.6
s.40, referred to: SI 2003/962 Art.5
s.41, applied: SI 2002/2005 Reg.13, 2003 c.1 s.660, SSI 2003/176 Art.4, 2004 c.7 Sch.5 para.6
s.41, referred to: SI 2003/962 Art.5
s.42, amended: 2002 c.21 Sch.3 para.30
s.42, varied: SI 2003/962 Art.5

CAP.

1992–cont.

4. **Social Security Contributions and Benefits Act 1992**–*cont.*

s.43, see *Secretary of State for Work and Pensions v Nelligan* [2003] EWCA Civ 555, [2004] 1 W.L.R. 894 (CA), Scott Baker, L.J.

s.43, amended: 2004 c.35 s.296

s.44, amended: 2002 c.19 Sch.1 para.10, SI 2002/668 Art.4, SI 2003/526 Art.4, SI 2004/552 Art.4

s.44, applied: 2004 c.7 Sch.5 para.7

s.44, referred to: SI 2002/1792 Sch.3 para.2, SI 2002/3019 Reg.36

s.44A, amended: 2002 c.19 Sch.1 para.11, SI 2002/1457 Sch.1 para.2

s.45A, repealed: 2002 c.21 Sch.6

s.46, amended: 2004 c.33 Sch.24 para.23

s.47, applied: SI 2002/668 Art.6, SI 2003/526 Art.6, SI 2004/552 Art.6

s.48, amended: 2004 c.33 Sch.24 para.24

s.48A, amended: 2004 c.33 Sch.24 para.25

s.48A, applied: 2004 c.7 Sch.5 para.8

s.48B, amended: 2004 c.33 Sch.24 para.26

s.48B, applied: 2004 c.7 Sch.5 para.8

s.48BB, amended: 2002 c.21 Sch.3 para.31, 2004 c.33 Sch.24 para.27

s.48BB, applied: 2004 c.7 Sch.5 para.8

s.48C, applied: SI 2002/668 Art.6, SI 2003/526 Art.6, SI 2004/552 Art.6

s.51, amended: 2002 c.21 Sch.3 para.32, 2004 c.33 Sch.24 para.28

s.51, applied: 2004 c.7 Sch.5 para.8

s.51A, amended: 2004 c.33 Sch.24 para.29

s.51A, applied: 2004 c.7 Sch.5 para.8

s.52, amended: 2004 c.33 Sch.24 para.30

s.52, applied: 2004 c.7 Sch.5 para.8

s.55, substituted: 2004 c.35 s.297

s.55A, applied: SI 2002/668 Art.4, SI 2003/526 Art.4, 2004 c.7 Sch.5 para.9

s.55A, varied: SI 2004/552 Art.4

s.55C, applied: SI 2002/668 Art.4, SI 2003/526 Art.4

s.55C, substituted: 2004 c.35 s.297

s.55C, varied: SI 2004/552 Art.4

s.56, amended: 2002 c.21 Sch.6

s.56, applied: SI 2002/1792 Reg.15, 2003 c.1 s.677

s.60, amended: 2002 c.21 Sch.3 para.33, 2004 c.33 Sch.24 para.31

s.60, repealed (in part): 2002 c.21 Sch.6

s.60, enabling: SI 2003/937

s.61, amended: 2002 c.21 Sch.6

s.61A, amended: 2004 c.33 Sch.24 para.32

s.62, amended: 2004 c.33 Sch.24 para.33, 2004 c.35 Sch.11 para.17

s.63, amended: 2002 c.21 Sch.6, SI 2002/1457 Sch.1 para.2

s.64, applied: SI 2002/1792 Reg.15, SI 2002/2005 Reg.13, SSI 2002/494 Sch.2 para.7, 2003 c.1 s.677, SSI 2003/176 Art.4

s.65, applied: SI 2002/2005 Reg.17

CAP.

1992–cont.

4. **Social Security Contributions and Benefits Act 1992**–*cont.*

s.67, enabling: SI 2002/208, SI 2002/1406, SI 2003/2259

s.68, applied: SI 2002/1792 Sch.6 para.4, SI 2002/2005 Reg.13, 2003 c.1 s.677, SSI 2003/176 Art.4

s.70, see *Flemming v Secretary of State for Work and Pensions* [2002] EWCA Civ 641, [2002] 1 W.L.R. 2322 (CA), Pill, L.J.; see *Pridding v Secretary of State for Work and Pensions* [2002] EWCA Civ 306, [2002] C.P.L.R. 315 (CA), Keene, L.J.

s.70, amended: SI 2002/1457 Art.3, Sch.1 para.2

s.70, applied: 2002 c.16 s.2, SI 2002/1457 Art.4, SI 2002/1792 Reg.6, Sch.1 para.1, Sch.1 para.4, Sch.1 para.5, Sch.3 para.1, 2003 c.1 s.660, SSI 2004/83 Reg.3

s.70, repealed (in part): SI 2002/1457 Art.3

s.70, enabling: SI 2002/2497

s.71, applied: SI 2002/1792 Sch.6 para.4, SI 2002/2005 Reg.13, SI 2002/2779 Sch.3 para.2, SI 2003/284 Sch.2 para.2, SSI 2002/494 Sch.2 para.7, 2003 c.1 s.677, SSI 2003/176 Art.4

s.72, see *Moyna v Secretary of State for Work and Pensions* [2003] UKHL 44, [2003] 1 W.L.R. 1929 (HL), Lord Hoffmann

s.72, applied: SI 2002/1792 Sch.1 para.1, Sch.1 para.2, Sch.3 para.1, Sch.6 para.4, SI 2002/2005 Reg.17, SI 2002/2007 Reg.8, SSI 2003/176 Art.4

s.72, enabling: SI 2002/208, SI 2002/1406, SI 2003/2259

s.73, applied: SI 2002/1792 Sch.6 para.4, SI 2002/2779 Sch.3 para.2, SI 2003/284 Sch.2 para.2, SI 2004/293 Sch.2 para.16

s.73, enabling: SI 2002/648

s.74, applied: SI 2002/1792 Sch.6 para.4

s.75, applied: SI 2002/1792 Sch.6 para.4

s.76, applied: SI 2002/1792 Sch.6 para.4

s.77, amended: 2002 c.21 Sch.6, 2004 c.33 Sch.24 para.34

s.77, applied: 2002 c.21 s.49, SI 2002/1330 Sch.3 para.1, SI 2002/1792 Reg.15, SI 2002/3200 Reg.15, Sch.3 para.1, 2003 c.1 s.677, SI 2003/495 Reg.7, Reg.8, Reg.10, SI 2003/1994 Sch.3 para.1

s.77, disapplied: SI 2002/195 Reg.15, Sch.3 para.1

s.77, varied: SI 2003/495 Reg.4, Reg.5, Reg.6

s.77, enabling: SI 2002/492, SI 2003/495

s.78, amended: 2002 c.21 Sch.6

s.78, applied: 2004 c.7 Sch.5 para.11

s.79, applied: SI 2002/668 Art.3

s.79, enabling: SI 2002/2497

s.80, amended: SI 2002/668 Art.8, SI 2003/526 Art.8

s.80, applied: 2002 c.21 s.1

s.80, repealed: 2002 c.21 Sch.6

CAP.

1992–cont.

4. Social Security Contributions and Benefits Act 1992–*cont.*

s.80, varied: SI 2004/552 Art.8

s.81, repealed: 2002 c.21 Sch.6

s.82, amended: 2004 c.33 Sch.24 para.35

s.83A, amended: 2004 c.33 Sch.24 para.36

s.85, amended: 2004 c.33 Sch.24 para.37

s.85, repealed (in part): 2004 c.33 Sch.24 para.37, Sch.30

s.86A, enabling: SI 2003/937

s.89, amended: 2002 c.21 Sch.6

s.90, amended: 2002 c.21 Sch.6, SI 2002/1457 Sch.1 para.2

s.90, applied: 2002 c.21 s.1

s.90, enabling: SI 2002/684, SI 2002/2497, SI 2003/601, SI 2004/583

s.91, amended: 2002 c.21 Sch.6

s.94, see *Mullen v Secretary of State for Work and Pensions* 2002 S.C. 251 (2 Div), Lord Gill L.J.C., Lord Bonomy, Lord Eassie

s.94, applied: 2003 c.1 s.677

s.104, applied: SI 2002/1792 Reg.15, Sch.5 para.20, SI 2002/2005 Reg.13, SSI 2002/494 Sch.2 para.7, SSI 2003/176 Art.4

s.105, applied: SI 2002/1792 Reg.15, Sch.5 para.20

s.107, applied: SI 2002/668 Art.6, SI 2003/526 Art.6, SI 2004/552 Art.6

s.108, see *R. (on the application of National Association of Colliery Overmen Deputies and Shotfirers) v Secretary of State for Work and Pensions* [2003] EWHC 607, [2004] A.C.D. 14 (QBD (Admin Ct)), Pitchford, J.

s.108, referred to: SI 2003/2190

s.108, enabling: SI 2003/270, SI 2003/2190

s.109, enabling: SI 2002/1717, SI 2003/270, SI 2003/2190

s.112, applied: SSI 2003/461 Reg.10

s.113, amended: 2004 c.33 Sch.24 para.38

s.113, applied: SI 2002/2005 Reg.17, SI 2002/2007 Reg.8

s.113, enabling: SI 2002/684, SI 2002/2497, SI 2003/601, SI 2004/565, SI 2004/583, SI 2004/960

s.114, amended: 2002 c.21 Sch.3 para.34, 2004 c.33 Sch.24 para.39

s.114, enabling: SI 2003/937

s.116, enabling: SI 2003/737

s.117, enabling: SI 2004/944

s.118, enabling: SI 2003/964

s.119, enabling: SI 2002/2366

s.121, amended: 2004 c.33 Sch.24 para.40

s.122, amended: 2002 c.19 Sch.1 para.12, Sch.2, 2002 c.21 Sch.6, 2003 c.1 Sch.6 para.178, 2004 c.33 Sch.24 para.41, 2004 c.35 Sch.11 para.18

s.122, enabling: SI 2002/490, SI 2002/492, SI 2002/684, SI 2002/703, SI 2002/1717, SI 2002/2311, SI 2003/270, SI 2003/455, SI 2003/521, SI 2003/601, SI 2003/659,

CAP.

1992–cont.

4. Social Security Contributions and Benefits Act 1992–*cont.*

s.122, enabling:–*cont.*

SI 2003/937, SI 2003/1068, SI 2003/1767, SI 2003/2190, SI 2003/2262, SI 2004/220, SI 2004/583, SI 2004/770, SI 2004/960, SI 2004/1361, SI 2004/2301

s.123, amended: SI 2002/1397 Sch.1 para.7

s.123, repealed (in part): 2002 c.21 Sch.6

s.123, enabling: SI 2002/105, SI 2002/338, SI 2002/398, SI 2002/490, SI 2002/499, SI 2002/525, SI 2002/841, SI 2002/1411, SI 2002/1589, SI 2002/1763, SI 2002/2019, SI 2002/2020, SI 2002/2207, SI 2002/2314, SI 2002/2322, SI 2002/2380, SI 2002/2402, SI 2002/2442, SI 2002/2689, SI 2003/308, SI 2003/325, SI 2003/363, SI 2003/455, SI 2003/511, SI 2003/770, SI 2003/1121, SI 2003/1195, SI 2003/1338, SI 2003/1589, SI 2003/1701, SI 2003/1731, SI 2003/1914, SI 2003/2275, SI 2003/2279, SI 2003/2325, SI 2003/2379, SI 2003/2399, SI 2003/2439, SI 2003/2634, SI 2003/2693, SI 2004/14, SI 2004/98, SI 2004/154, SI 2004/319, SI 2004/440, SI 2004/565, SI 2004/781, SI 2004/963, SI 2004/1141, SI 2004/1232, SI 2004/1520, SI 2004/1708, SI 2004/1869, SI 2004/2174, SI 2004/2303, SI 2004/2308, SI 2004/2327, SI 2004/2825, SI 2004/2984

s.124, amended: 2002 c.16 Sch.2 para.2, Sch.3, 2004 c.33 Sch.24 para.42

s.124, applied: SI 2002/1015 Reg.3, SI 2002/2022 Reg.3, SSI 2002/76 Reg.2, SSI 2002/289 Reg.3, SSI 2002/494 Reg.33, Sch.2 para.5, Sch.3 para.7, 2003 c.1 s.660, SSI 2004/83 Reg.3

s.124, enabling: SI 2003/455, SI 2003/1731

s.126, amended: SI 2002/668 Art.18, 2003 c.1 Sch.6 para.179, SI 2003/526 Art.19, 2004 c.33 Sch.24 para.43, SI 2004/552 Art.18

s.126, applied: 2003 c.1 s.665

s.127, amended: 2004 c.33 Sch.24 para.44

s.128, applied: SSI 2002/494 Reg.33, Sch.3 para.8

s.128, referred to: 2003 c.1 Sch.7 para.88

s.128, repealed: 2002 c.21 Sch.6

s.128, enabling: SI 2002/14, SI 2002/525, SI 2002/1333, SI 2002/1334, SI 2002/1696, SI 2003/44

s.129, see *Taylor v Inland Revenue Commissioners* [2004] EWCA Civ 174, [2004] S.T.C. 683 (CA), Peter Gibson, L.J.

s.129, applied: SSI 2002/494 Reg.33, SSI 2003/176 Art.4

s.129, repealed: 2002 c.21 Sch.6

s.129, enabling: SI 2002/14, SI 2002/525, SI 2002/1333, SI 2002/1334, SI 2003/44, SI 2003/963

CAP.

1992–cont.

4. Social Security Contributions and Benefits Act 1992–*cont.*

s.130, see *Secretary of State for Work and Pensions v Robinson* [2004] EWCA Civ 342, [2004] H.L.R. 39 (CA), Ward, L.J.

s.130, applied: SSI 2002/494 Reg.33, 2003 c.1 s.677

s.130, enabling: SI 2002/1589, SI 2002/2322, SI 2003/48, SI 2003/325, SI 2003/363, SI 2003/1195, SI 2003/1338, SI 2003/1589, SI 2003/2275, SI 2003/2279, SI 2003/2399, SI 2004/14, SI 2004/319, SI 2004/781, SI 2004/2327, SI 2004/2984

s.131, applied: 2003 c.1 s.677

s.131, enabling: SI 2002/1763, SI 2003/325, SI 2003/1195, SI 2003/1338, SI 2003/1589, SI 2003/2275, SI 2004/14, SI 2004/154, SI 2004/319, SI 2004/781, SI 2004/1232, SI 2004/2303, SI 2004/2327

s.132, amended: 2004 c.33 Sch.24 para.45

s.133, enabling: SI 2003/45

s.134, enabling: SI 2003/325

s.135, amended: 2002 c.21 Sch.6

s.135, enabling: SI 2002/105, SI 2002/338, SI 2002/398, SI 2002/490, SI 2002/841, SI 2002/2019, SI 2002/2020, SI 2002/2402, SI 2002/2497, SI 2003/325, SI 2003/455, SI 2003/1121, SI 2003/1195, SI 2003/1589, SI 2003/1731, SI 2003/2275, SI 2003/2279, SI 2003/2325, SI 2003/2379, SI 2003/2693, SI 2004/14, SI 2004/319, SI 2004/440, SI 2004/1141, SI 2004/1232, SI 2004/1520, SI 2004/2174, SI 2004/2327, SI 2004/2825

s.136, enabling: SI 2002/14, SI 2002/499, SI 2002/525, SI 2002/841, SI 2002/1333, SI 2002/1411, SI 2002/1589, SI 2002/1696, SI 2002/2207, SI 2002/2314, SI 2002/2380, SI 2002/2402, SI 2002/2442, SI 2002/2497, SI 2002/2689, SI 2003/44, SI 2003/308, SI 2003/325, SI 2003/455, SI 2003/511, SI 2003/770, SI 2003/1589, SI 2003/1701, SI 2003/1731, SI 2003/1914, SI 2003/2275, SI 2003/2279, SI 2003/2439, SI 2004/14, SI 2004/98, SI 2004/290, SI 2004/319, SI 2004/565, SI 2004/963, SI 2004/1141, SI 2004/1708, SI 2004/2308, SI 2004/2327

s.136A, added: 2002 c.16 Sch.2 para.3

s.136A, enabling: SI 2003/325, SI 2003/1338, SI 2003/2275, SI 2003/2634, SI 2004/14, SI 2004/290, SI 2004/2327

s.137, amended: 2002 c.16 Sch.2 para.4, 2004 c.33 Sch.24 para.46, Sch.30

s.137, enabling: SI 2002/14, SI 2002/105, SI 2002/338, SI 2002/398, SI 2002/490, SI 2002/499, SI 2002/525, SI 2002/841, SI 2002/1333, SI 2002/1334, SI 2002/1411, SI 2002/1589, SI 2002/1696, SI 2002/1763, SI 2002/2019, SI 2002/2020, SI 2002/2207, SI 2002/2314, SI 2002/

CAP.

1992–cont.

4. Social Security Contributions and Benefits Act 1992–*cont.*

s.137, enabling:–*cont.*
2322, SI 2002/2380, SI 2002/2402, SI 2002/2442, SI 2002/2689, SI 2003/44, SI 2003/308, SI 2003/325, SI 2003/455, SI 2003/511, SI 2003/770, SI 2003/1121, SI 2003/1195, SI 2003/1338, SI 2003/1589, SI 2003/1701, SI 2003/1731, SI 2003/1914, SI 2003/2275, SI 2003/2279, SI 2003/2325, SI 2003/2379, SI 2003/2399, SI 2003/2439, SI 2003/2634, SI 2003/2693, SI 2004/14, SI 2004/98, SI 2004/154, SI 2004/290, SI 2004/319, SI 2004/440, SI 2004/565, SI 2004/781, SI 2004/963, SI 2004/1141, SI 2004/1232, SI 2004/1520, SI 2004/1708, SI 2004/1869, SI 2004/2174, SI 2004/2303, SI 2004/2308, SI 2004/2327, SI 2004/2825, SI 2004/2984

s.138, applied: SSI 2002/494 Reg.33, Sch.2 para.7, 2003 c.1 s.677

s.138, enabling: SI 2002/79, SI 2002/470, SI 2002/2323, SI 2002/2497, SI 2002/2524, SI 2002/2660, SI 2002/3019, SI 2003/455, SI 2003/471, SI 2003/1121, SI 2003/1570, SI 2003/1731, SI 2003/1737, SI 2003/2192, SI 2003/2605, SI 2003/3023, SI 2004/1141, SI 2004/2154, SI 2004/2536, SI 2004/2600

s.139, applied: SSI 2004/468 Reg.35

s.141, applied: 2003 c.1 s.677

s.142, applied: SI 2003/493 Reg.6, Reg.7, Reg.8, Reg.9, Reg.10

s.142, disapplied: 2002 c.21 s.49

s.142, enabling: SI 2003/493, SI 2004/761

s.143, amended: 2004 c.33 Sch.24 para.47

s.143, applied: SI 2003/493 Reg.2, Reg.3, Reg.4, Reg.36

s.143, disapplied: SI 2003/493 Reg.36

s.143, enabling: SI 2003/493

s.144, see *R. (on the application of Barber) v Secretary of State for Work and Pensions* [2002] EWHC 1915, [2002] 2 F.L.R. 1181 (QBD (Admin Ct)), Sir Richard Tucker

s.144, applied: SI 2003/493 Reg.9, Reg.10

s.144, enabling: SI 2003/493, SI 2003/937

s.145, repealed (in part): 2002 c.21 Sch.6

s.145A, added: 2002 c.21 s.55

s.145A, amended: 2004 c.33 Sch.24 para.48

s.145A, applied: SI 2003/493 Reg.20

s.145A, enabling: SI 2003/493

s.146, applied: SI 2003/493 Reg.21, Reg.24, Reg.27, Reg.30, Reg.31, Reg.32

s.146, substituted: 2002 c.21 s.56

s.146, enabling: SI 2003/493, SI 2004/1244

s.147, applied: SI 2003/493 Reg.36, Reg.37

s.147, varied: SI 2003/493 Reg.19

s.147, enabling: SI 2003/493, SI 2003/937, SI 2004/1244

s.148, amended: 2002 c.16 Sch.2 para.5

1992–cont.
4. Social Security Contributions and Benefits Act 1992–*cont.*

s.148, applied: 2003 c.1 s.677

s.148, repealed (in part): 2002 c.16 Sch.2 para.5, Sch.3

s.149, amended: 2002 c.16 Sch.2 para.6

s.150, amended: 2002 c.16 Sch.2 para.7, SI 2002/1457 Sch.1 para.2, 2003 c.1 Sch.6 para.180, 2004 c.33 Sch.24 para.49

s.150, applied: SI 2002/668 Art.4

s.150, repealed (in part): 2003 c.1 Sch.8 Part 1

s.151, applied: SI 2002/2822 Reg.39, 2003 c.1 s.660

s.153, enabling: SI 2002/2690

s.157, amended: SI 2002/668 Art.9, SI 2003/526 Art.9, SI 2004/552 Art.9

s.163, amended: 2003 c.1 Sch.6 para.181

s.163, enabling: SI 2002/2690

s.164, amended: 2002 c.22 s.20, Sch.7 para.6, Sch.8 Part 1

s.164, applied: 2003 c.1 s.660

s.164, enabling: SI 2002/2690

s.165, amended: 2002 c.22 s.18

s.165, enabling: SI 2002/2690

s.166, referred to: 2002 c.22 s.48

s.166, substituted: 2002 c.22 s.19

s.166, enabling: SI 2002/2690

s.167, applied: 2002 c.22 s.7, SI 2002/2820 Reg.3

s.167, substituted: 2002 c.22 s.21

s.167, enabling: SI 2002/225, SI 2003/672, SI 2004/698

s.171, amended: 2003 c.1 Sch.6 para.182

s.171, enabling: SI 2002/225, SI 2002/238, SI 2002/2690, SI 2003/45, SI 2003/672, SI 2003/964, SI 2004/698, SI 2004/770

s.171D, enabling: SI 2002/491, SI 2002/684, SI 2002/2311, SI 2003/2262, SI 2004/1869, SI 2004/2301

s.171E, applied: SI 2002/1792 Sch.2 para.1

s.171G, enabling: SI 2002/491, SI 2002/684, SI 2002/2311, SI 2003/2262, SI 2004/1869, SI 2004/2301

s.171ZA, added: 2002 c.22 s.2

s.171ZA, applied: SI 2002/2820 Reg.11, SI 2002/2821 Reg.5, SI 2002/2822 Reg.4, Reg.9, Reg.33, 2003 c.1 s.660

s.171ZA, varied: SI 2002/2822 Reg.5, SI 2003/1194 Reg.2, Reg.3

s.171ZA, enabling: SI 2002/2822

s.171ZB, added: 2002 c.22 s.2

s.171ZB, applied: SI 2002/2820 Reg.11, SI 2002/2821 Reg.5, SI 2002/2822 Reg.11, Reg.15, Reg.33, 2003 c.1 s.660, SI 2003/500 Reg.5, Reg.9, SI 2003/1194 Reg.5, Reg.9

s.171ZB, referred to: SI 2003/499 Reg.2

s.171ZB, varied: SI 2003/499 Sch.1, SI 2003/1194 Reg.2, Reg.3

s.171ZB, enabling: SI 2002/2822, SI 2003/500, SI 2003/1194, SI 2004/488

1992–cont.
4. Social Security Contributions and Benefits Act 1992–*cont.*

s.171ZC, added: 2002 c.22 s.2

s.171ZC, applied: SI 2002/2820 Reg.9, Reg.11, SI 2002/2822 Reg.6, Reg.7, Reg.12, Reg.13, SI 2003/500 Reg.6, Reg.7, SI 2003/1194 Reg.6

s.171ZC, varied: SI 2003/1194 Reg.2, Reg.3

s.171ZC, enabling: SI 2002/2822, SI 2003/500, SI 2003/1194

s.171ZD, added: 2002 c.22 s.2

s.171ZD, disapplied: SI 2002/2822 Reg.43

s.171ZD, varied: SI 2003/1194 Reg.2, Reg.3

s.171ZD, enabling: SI 2002/2822, SI 2003/500, SI 2003/1194, SI 2004/1869

s.171ZE, added: 2002 c.22 s.2

s.171ZE, applied: SI 2002/2822 Reg.8, Reg.9, Reg.14, Reg.15, SI 2003/500 Reg.8, Reg.9, SI 2003/1194 Reg.8, Reg.9

s.171ZE, referred to: SI 2003/499 Reg.2

s.171ZE, varied: SI 2003/499 Sch.1, SI 2003/1194 Reg.2, Reg.3

s.171ZE, enabling: SI 2002/2818, SI 2002/2822, SI 2003/500, SI 2003/1194, SI 2004/925

s.171ZF, added: 2002 c.22 s.2

s.171ZF, varied: SI 2003/1194 Reg.2, Reg.3

s.171ZG, added: 2002 c.22 s.2

s.171ZG, applied: SI 2002/2822 Reg.19

s.171ZG, varied: SI 2003/1194 Reg.2, Reg.3

s.171ZG, enabling: SI 2002/2822, SI 2003/500, SI 2003/1194, SI 2004/1869

s.171ZH, added: 2002 c.22 s.2

s.171ZH, varied: SI 2003/1194 Reg.2, Reg.3

s.171ZI, added: 2002 c.22 s.2

s.171ZI, varied: SI 2003/1194 Reg.2, Reg.3

s.171ZI, enabling: SI 2002/2821, SI 2003/1193

s.171ZJ, added: 2002 c.22 s.2

s.171ZJ, amended: 2003 c.1 Sch.6 para.183

s.171ZJ, applied: SI 2002/2822 Reg.39, Reg.40

s.171ZJ, referred to: SI 2003/499 Reg.2

s.171ZJ, varied: SI 2003/499 Sch.1, SI 2003/1194 Reg.2, Reg.3

s.171ZJ, enabling: SI 2002/2819, SI 2002/2821, SI 2002/2822, SI 2003/500, SI 2003/1193, SI 2003/1194, SI 2004/488

s.171ZK, added: 2002 c.22 s.2

s.171ZK, varied: SI 2003/1194 Reg.2, Reg.3

s.171ZK, enabling: SI 2003/499, SI 2004/488

s.171ZL, added: 2002 c.22 s.4

s.171ZL, amended: 2004 c.33 Sch.24 para.50

s.171ZL, applied: SI 2002/2820 Reg.9, Reg.11, SI 2002/2821 Reg.6, SI 2002/2822 Reg.21, Reg.23, Reg.33, 2003 c.1 s.660, SI 2003/500 Reg.12, Reg.14, SI 2003/1194 Reg.12, Reg.14

s.171ZL, referred to: SI 2002/2822 Reg.29, SI 2003/499 Reg.3

1992–cont.

4. Social Security Contributions and Benefits Act 1992–*cont.*

s.171ZL, varied: SI 2003/499 Sch.2, SI 2003/1194 Reg.2, Reg.3

s.171ZL, enabling: SI 2002/2822, SI 2003/500, SI 2003/1194

s.171ZM, added: 2002 c.22 s.4

s.171ZM, applied: SI 2003/500 Reg.17, SI 2003/1194 Reg.17

s.171ZM, disapplied: SI 2002/2822 Reg.43, Reg.44, SI 2003/500 Reg.17, SI 2003/1194 Reg.17

s.171ZM, varied: SI 2003/1194 Reg.2, Reg.3

s.171ZM, enabling: SI 2002/2822, SI 2003/500, SI 2003/1194

s.171ZN, added: 2002 c.22 s.4

s.171ZN, varied: SI 2003/1194 Reg.2, Reg.3

s.171ZN, enabling: SI 2002/2818, SI 2002/2822, SI 2003/500, SI 2003/1194

s.171ZO, added: 2002 c.22 s.4

s.171ZO, varied: SI 2003/1194 Reg.2, Reg.3

s.171ZP, added: 2002 c.22 s.4

s.171ZP, applied: SI 2002/2822 Reg.28

s.171ZP, varied: SI 2003/1194 Reg.2, Reg.3

s.171ZP, enabling: SI 2002/2690, SI 2002/2822, SI 2003/500, SI 2003/1194

s.171ZQ, added: 2002 c.22 s.4

s.171ZQ, varied: SI 2003/1194 Reg.2, Reg.3

s.171ZR, added: 2002 c.22 s.4

s.171ZR, varied: SI 2003/1194 Reg.2, Reg.3

s.171ZR, enabling: SI 2002/2821, SI 2003/1193

s.171ZS, added: 2002 c.22 s.4

s.171ZS, amended: 2003 c.1 Sch.6 para.184

s.171ZS, applied: SI 2002/2822 Reg.39, Reg.40

s.171ZS, referred to: SI 2003/499 Reg.3

s.171ZS, varied: SI 2003/499 Sch.2, SI 2003/1194 Reg.2, Reg.3

s.171ZS, enabling: SI 2002/2690, SI 2002/2819, SI 2002/2821, SI 2002/2822, SI 2003/500, SI 2003/1193, SI 2003/1194, SI 2004/488

s.171ZT, added: 2002 c.22 s.4

s.171ZT, varied: SI 2003/1194 Reg.2, Reg.3

s.171ZT, enabling: SI 2003/499, SI 2004/488

s.172, applied: 2002 c.16 s.17

s.173, applied: 2002 c.16 s.17

s.175, amended: 2002 c.21 Sch.6

s.175, applied: SI 2003/325 Sch.1, 2004 c.33 s.254, SI 2004/173

s.175, repealed (in part): 2002 c.21 Sch.6

s.175, varied: 2002 c.16 s.19

s.175, enabling: SI 2002/14, SI 2002/79, SI 2002/105, SI 2002/208, SI 2002/225, SI 2002/238, SI 2002/338, SI 2002/398, SI 2002/470, SI 2002/490, SI 2002/491, SI 2002/492, SI 2002/499, SI 2002/525, SI 2002/550, SI 2002/648, SI 2002/683, SI 2002/684, SI 2002/703, SI 2002/841, SI 2002/842, SI 2002/1333, SI 2002/1334,

1992–cont.

4. Social Security Contributions and Benefits Act 1992–*cont.*

s.175, enabling:–*cont.*

SI 2002/1406, SI 2002/1411, SI 2002/1589, SI 2002/1696, SI 2002/1717, SI 2002/1763, SI 2002/1792, SI 2002/2019, SI 2002/2020, SI 2002/2207, SI 2002/2311, SI 2002/2314, SI 2002/2322, SI 2002/2323, SI 2002/2380, SI 2002/2402, SI 2002/2442, SI 2002/2497, SI 2002/2524, SI 2002/2660, SI 2002/2689, SI 2002/2690, SI 2002/2822, SI 2002/3019, SI 2002/3197, SI 2003/44, SI 2003/193, SI 2003/270, SI 2003/308, SI 2003/325, SI 2003/363, SI 2003/455, SI 2003/471, SI 2003/493, SI 2003/500, SI 2003/511, SI 2003/521, SI 2003/601, SI 2003/608, SI 2003/659, SI 2003/672, SI 2003/702, SI 2003/737, SI 2003/770, SI 2003/937, SI 2003/964, SI 2003/1059, SI 2003/1068, SI 2003/1121, SI 2003/1194, SI 2003/1195, SI 2003/1338, SI 2003/1570, SI 2003/1589, SI 2003/1701, SI 2003/1731, SI 2003/1737, SI 2003/1767, SI 2003/1864, SI 2003/1914, SI 2003/2079, SI 2003/2085, SI 2003/2190, SI 2003/2192, SI 2003/2259, SI 2003/2262, SI 2003/2275, SI 2003/2279, SI 2003/2325, SI 2003/2379, SI 2003/2399, SI 2003/2420, SI 2003/2439, SI 2003/2605, SI 2003/2634, SI 2003/2693, SI 2003/3023, SI 2004/14, SI 2004/98, SI 2004/154, SI 2004/173, SI 2004/220, SI 2004/319, SI 2004/440, SI 2004/488, SI 2004/565, SI 2004/583, SI 2004/647, SI 2004/698, SI 2004/723, SI 2004/770, SI 2004/781, SI 2004/944, SI 2004/960, SI 2004/963, SI 2004/1141, SI 2004/1232, SI 2004/1361, SI 2004/1362, SI 2004/1520, SI 2004/1708, SI 2004/1869, SI 2004/2096, SI 2004/2154, SI 2004/2174, SI 2004/2301, SI 2004/2303, SI 2004/2308, SI 2004/2311, SI 2004/2327, SI 2004/2536, SI 2004/2600, SI 2004/2825, SI 2004/2984

s.176, amended: 2002 c.22 Sch.7 para.7, 2004 c.35 Sch.11 para.19

s.176, applied: SI 2002/2818, SI 2003/964, SI 2004/925

s.176, enabling: SI 2003/964

Sch.1 para.1, amended: 2002 c.19 Sch.1 para.13

Sch.1 para.2, enabling: SI 2002/2366

Sch.1 para.3, amended: 2002 c.19 Sch.1 para.13, 2004 c.3 s.1, Sch.2 Part 1

Sch.1 para.3, enabling: SI 2003/193, SI 2003/1337, SI 2004/770, SI 2004/2246

Sch.1 para.3A, amended: 2004 c.3 s.3

Sch.1 para.3A, applied: 2003 c.14 Sch.23 para.15, Sch.23 para.21, 2003 c.1 s.428A, s.442A, s.481

Sch.1 para.3B, amended: 2004 c.3 s.3

1992–cont.

4. Social Security Contributions and Benefits Act 1992–cont.

Sch.1 para.3B, applied: 2003 c.1 s.428A, s.442A, s.482, 2003 c.14 Sch.23 para.15, Sch.23 para.21, 2003 c.1 s.481, SI 2003/2682 Reg.70

Sch.1 para.3B, repealed (in part): 2004 c.3 Sch.2 Part 1

Sch.1 para.3B, enabling: SI 2004/2096

Sch.1 para.4, enabling: SI 2002/2366

Sch.1 para.6, amended: 2003 c.14 s.147, 2003 c.1 Sch.6 para.185

Sch.1 para.6, enabling: SI 2002/2929, SI 2003/193, SI 2003/1337, SI 2003/2085, SI 2004/770, SI 2004/2096

Sch.1 para.7, amended: 2003 c.1 Sch.6 para.185, 2004 c.12 Sch.12 para.13

Sch.1 para.7B, amended: 2003 c.1 Sch.6 para.185

Sch.1 para.7B, enabling: SI 2004/770

Sch.1 para.7BZA, added: 2004 c.3 s.5

Sch.1 para.8, enabling: SI 2002/2366, SI 2003/2958, SI 2004/770, SI 2004/1361, SI 2004/2096

Sch.3 Part I para.2, amended: 2002 c.19 Sch.1 para.14

Sch.3 Part I para.2, varied: SI 2003/737 Reg.4

Sch.3 Part I para.2, enabling: SI 2002/2497

Sch.3 Part I para.4, amended: 2002 c.19 Sch.1 para.14

Sch.3 Part I para.5, amended: 2002 c.19 Sch.1 para.14

Sch.3 Part I para.5, enabling: SI 2003/1767

Sch.3 Part II para.7, amended: 2002 c.19 Sch.1 para.14

Sch.4, substituted: SI 2003/526 Sch.1

Sch.4 Part I, disapplied: SI 2003/526 Art.3

Sch.4 Part I, referred to: SI 2002/668 Art.3, SI 2003/526 Art.3, SI 2004/552 Art.3

Sch.4 Part I, substituted: SI 2003/526 Sch.1, SI 2004/552 Sch.1

Sch.4 Part II, substituted: SI 2003/526 Sch.1, SI 2004/552 Sch.1

Sch.4 Part III, amended: SI 2002/1457 Sch.1 para.2, SI 2004/552 Sch.1, SI 2004/942 Art.2

Sch.4 Part III, disapplied: SI 2003/526 Art.3

Sch.4 Part III, referred to: SI 2002/668 Art.3, SI 2003/526 Art.3

Sch.4 Part III, substituted: SI 2003/526 Sch.1

Sch.4 Part IV, amended: 2002 c.21 Sch.6, SI 2002/1457 Sch.1 para.2

Sch.4 Part IV, disapplied: SI 2003/526 Art.3

Sch.4 Part IV, referred to: SI 2002/668 Art.3, SI 2003/526 Art.3

Sch.4 Part IV, substituted: SI 2003/526 Sch.1, SI 2004/552 Sch.1

Sch.4 Part V, disapplied: SI 2003/526 Art.3

Sch.4 Part V, referred to: SI 2002/668 Art.3, SI 2003/526 Art.3

1992–cont.

4. Social Security Contributions and Benefits Act 1992–cont.

Sch.4 Part V, substituted: SI 2003/526 Sch.1, SI 2004/552 Sch.1

Sch.4A Part I para.1, amended: 2004 c.33 Sch.24 para.51

Sch.5, applied: SI 2002/668 Art.4, SI 2003/526 Art.4

Sch.5, amended: 2004 c.35 Sch.11 para.13

Sch.5 paraA.1, added: 2004 c.35 Sch.11 para.4

Sch.5 paraA.1, amended: 2004 c.35 Sch.11 para.3

Sch.5 paraA.1, varied: SI 2004/552 Art.4

Sch.5 para.1, amended: 2004 c.35 Sch.11 para.3

Sch.5 para.1, substituted: 2004 c.35 Sch.11 para.5

Sch.5 para.1, varied: SI 2004/552 Art.4

Sch.5 para.2, amended: 2002 c.21 Sch.6, 2004 c.35 Sch.11 para.3, Sch.11 para.6

Sch.5 para.2, varied: 2004 c.35 Sch.11 para.6, SI 2004/552 Art.4

Sch.5 para.2A, added: 2004 c.35 Sch.11 para.7

Sch.5 para.2A, amended: 2004 c.35 Sch.11 para.3

Sch.5 para.2A, varied: SI 2004/552 Art.4

Sch.5 para.3, amended: 2004 c.35 Sch.11 para.3

Sch.5 para.3, varied: SI 2004/552 Art.4

Sch.5 para.3A, added: 2004 c.35 Sch.11 para.8

Sch.5 para.3A, amended: 2004 c.35 Sch.11 para.3

Sch.5 para.3A, varied: SI 2004/552 Art.4

Sch.5 para.3B, added: 2004 c.35 Sch.11 para.8

Sch.5 para.3B, amended: 2004 c.35 Sch.11 para.3

Sch.5 para.3B, varied: 2004 c.35 Sch.11 para.8, SI 2004/552 Art.4

Sch.5 para.3C, added: 2004 c.35 Sch.11 para.9

Sch.5 para.3C, amended: 2004 c.35 Sch.11 para.3

Sch.5 para.3C, varied: SI 2004/552 Art.4

Sch.5 para.4, amended: 2004 c.35 Sch.11 para.3, Sch.11 para.10

Sch.5 para.4, varied: SI 2004/552 Art.4

Sch.5 para.5, amended: 2004 c.35 Sch.11 para.3

Sch.5 para.5, varied: SI 2004/552 Art.4

Sch.5 para.5A, amended: 2004 c.35 Sch.11 para.3

Sch.5 para.5A, varied: SI 2004/552 Art.4

Sch.5 para.6, amended: 2004 c.35 Sch.11 para.3

Sch.5 para.6, varied: SI 2004/552 Art.4

Sch.5 para.7, amended: 2004 c.35 Sch.11 para.3

1992–cont.

4. **Social Security Contributions and Benefits Act 1992**–*cont.*

Sch.5 para.7, varied: SI 2004/552 Art.4

Sch.5 para.7A, added: 2004 c.35 Sch.11 para.11

Sch.5 para.7A, amended: 2004 c.35 Sch.11 para.3

Sch.5 para.7A, varied: SI 2004/552 Art.4

Sch.5 para.7B, added: 2004 c.35 Sch.11 para.11

Sch.5 para.7B, amended: 2004 c.35 Sch.11 para.3

Sch.5 para.7B, varied: 2004 c.35 Sch.11 para.11, SI 2004/552 Art.4

Sch.5 para.7C, added: 2004 c.35 Sch.11 para.12

Sch.5 para.7C, amended: 2004 c.35 Sch.11 para.3

Sch.5 para.7C, varied: SI 2004/552 Art.4

Sch.5 para.8, amended: 2004 c.35 Sch.11 para.3, Sch.11 para.14

Sch.5 para.8, varied: SI 2004/552 Art.4

Sch.5 para.9, amended: 2004 c.35 Sch.11 para.3

Sch.5 para.9, varied: SI 2004/552 Art.4

Sch.5A para.1, added: 2004 c.35 Sch.11 para.15

Sch.5A para.2, added: 2004 c.35 Sch.11 para.15

Sch.5A para.3, added: 2004 c.35 Sch.11 para.15

Sch.5A para.4, added: 2004 c.35 Sch.11 para.15

Sch.5A para.5, added: 2004 c.35 Sch.11 para.15

Sch.6 para.1, enabling: SI 2002/1717

Sch.7 Part I, applied: SSI 2003/176 Art.4

Sch.7 Part I para.2, enabling: SI 2002/684, SI 2002/2311, SI 2003/2262, SI 2004/2301

Sch.7 Part I para.4, amended: SI 2002/683 Art.2, SI 2003/600 Art.2, 2004 c.33 Sch.24 para.52

Sch.7 Part I para.4, enabling: SI 2002/683, SI 2003/600, SI 2004/578

Sch.7 Part I para.5, amended: 2004 c.33 Sch.24 para.52

Sch.7 Part I para.6, amended: 2004 c.33 Sch.24 para.52

Sch.7 Part II para.9, applied: SI 2002/668 Art.6, SI 2003/526 Art.6, SI 2004/552 Art.6

Sch.7 Part V para.13, applied: SI 2002/668 Art.4, Art.6, SI 2003/526 Art.4, Art.6, SI 2004/552 Art.6

Sch.7 Part V para.13, varied: SI 2004/552 Art.4

Sch.7 Part VI para.15, amended: 2004 c.33 Sch.24 para.52

Sch.8 Part I para.2, amended: SI 2002/668 Art.7, SI 2003/526 Art.7, SI 2004/552 Art.7

1992–cont.

4. **Social Security Contributions and Benefits Act 1992**–*cont.*

Sch.8 Part I para.2, enabling: SI 2002/718, SI 2003/656, SI 2004/582

Sch.8 Part I para.4, applied: SI 2002/1792 Reg.15

Sch.8 Part I para.6, amended: SI 2002/668 Art.7, SI 2003/526 Art.7, 2004 c.33 Sch.24 para.53, SI 2004/552 Art.7

Sch.8 Part II para.7, applied: SI 2002/1792 Reg.15

Sch.8 Part III para.8, amended: 2004 c.33 Sch.24 para.53

Sch.9 para.1, applied: SI 2003/493 Reg.17, Reg.18, Reg.36, 2004 c.6 s.2, s.10, s.16

Sch.9 para.1, disapplied: SI 2003/493 Reg.16, Reg.17

Sch.9 para.1, enabling: SI 2003/493

Sch.9 para.2, applied: SI 2003/493 Reg.11

Sch.9 para.2, enabling: SI 2003/493

Sch.9 para.3, amended: 2004 c.33 Sch.24 para.54

Sch.9 para.3, applied: SI 2003/493 Reg.13

Sch.9 para.3, enabling: SI 2003/493

Sch.9 para.4, repealed: 2002 c.21 Sch.6

Sch.10, applied: SI 2003/493 Reg.14

Sch.10 para.1, varied: SI 2003/493 Reg.15

Sch.10 para.2, varied: SI 2003/493 Reg.15

Sch.10 para.3, varied: SI 2003/493 Reg.15

Sch.10 para.4, varied: SI 2003/493 Reg.15

Sch.10 para.5, applied: 2002 c.21 s.49

Sch.10 para.5, varied: SI 2003/493 Reg.15

Sch.10 para.6, applied: 2002 c.21 s.49

Sch.10 para.6, varied: SI 2003/493 Reg.15

Sch.10 para.6, enabling: SI 2003/493

Sch.11 para.1, enabling: SI 2002/2690

Sch.11 para.1A, enabling: SI 2002/2690

Sch.11 para.2, repealed (in part): SI 2002/2034 Sch.2 para.1

Sch.11 para.3, referred to: SI 2002/2034 Sch.2 para.4

Sch.11 para.4, repealed: SI 2002/2034 Sch.2 para.1

Sch.13 para.2, enabling: SI 2002/2690

5. **Social Security Administration Act 1992**

applied: 2002 c.21 s.50, Sch.5 para.7, SI 2002/1888 Art.3, SI 2002/3047 Reg.5, SI 2004/291 Sch.4, SI 2004/478 Sch.4, SI 2004/627 Sch.2, SSI 2004/115 Sch.3

referred to: 2003 c.1 Sch.6 para.186, 2003 c.26 Sch.7 para.34, SI 2003/916 Reg.27

Part X, applied: 2002 c.21 s.49, SI 2003/916 Sch.2 para.3

Part XIII, disapplied: 2002 c.21 s.50

s.1, see *Secretary of State for Work and Pensions v Nelligan* [2003] EWCA Civ 555, [2004] 1 W.L.R. 894 (CA), Scott Baker, L.J.

s.1, amended: 2002 c.16 Sch.1 para.2

s.1, disapplied: 2004 c.7 Sch.5 para.3

1992–cont.

5. **Social Security Administration Act 1992**–*cont.*

s.1, referred to: 2004 c.7 Sch.5 para.3, Sch.5 para.5

s.1, enabling: SI 2002/1696, SI 2003/48, SI 2003/455, SI 2003/937, SI 2003/1589

s.2A, amended: SI 2002/1457 Sch.1 para.3

s.2A, enabling: SI 2002/670, SI 2002/1703, SI 2002/2497, SI 2003/400, SI 2003/2439, SI 2004/565, SI 2004/959, SI 2004/2244

s.2AA, added: 2002 c.22 s.49

s.2AA, amended: 2004 c.33 Sch.24 para.55

s.2AA, applied: SI 2003/1886

s.2AA, enabling: SI 2003/1886, SI 2004/959

s.2B, amended: 2002 c.22 Sch.7 para.9, Sch.8 Part 1

s.2B, applied: SI 2002/1703 Reg.11, SI 2003/1886 Reg.10, SI 2003/2439 Reg.9, SI 2004/959 Reg.11, SI 2004/2244 Reg.6

s.2B, enabling: SI 2002/1703, SI 2003/1886, SI 2003/2439, SI 2004/565, SI 2004/959, SI 2004/2244

s.2C, amended: 2002 c.22 Sch.7 para.10

s.2C, enabling: SI 2004/565

s.3, amended: 2002 c.21 Sch.6, 2004 c.33 Sch.24 para.56

s.5, amended: 2002 c.16 Sch.1 para.3, 2002 c.22 Sch.7 para.11

s.5, applied: 2002 c.21 s.58

s.5, repealed (in part): 2002 c.21 Sch.6

s.5, enabling: SI 2002/398, SI 2002/428, SI 2002/1696, SI 2002/1703, SI 2002/1950, SI 2002/2441, SI 2002/2497, SI 2002/2660, SI 2002/2690, SI 2002/2818, SI 2002/2822, SI 2002/3019, SI 2002/3197, SI 2003/48, SI 2003/325, SI 2003/492, SI 2003/500, SI 2003/916, SI 2003/1050, SI 2003/1189, SI 2003/1194, SI 2003/1338, SI 2003/1589, SI 2003/1632, SI 2003/1945, SI 2003/2106, SI 2003/2107, SI 2003/2274, SI 2003/2275, SI 2003/2325, SI 2003/2399, SI 2003/3209, SI 2004/14, SI 2004/319, SI 2004/576, SI 2004/761, SI 2004/1240, SI 2004/1821, SI 2004/2283, SI 2004/2303, SI 2004/2308, SI 2004/2327, SI 2004/3368

s.6, enabling: SI 2002/1703, SI 2003/48, SI 2003/325, SI 2003/1338, SI 2003/1589, SI 2003/1632, SI 2003/2275, SI 2004/14, SI 2004/319, SI 2004/2303, SI 2004/2308, SI 2004/3368

s.7, enabling: SI 2003/492

s.7A, amended: 2002 c.22 Sch.7 para.12

s.7A, enabling: SI 2002/1132, SI 2002/1703, SI 2002/2497, SI 2002/3019, SI 2003/48, SI 2003/1632

s.11, repealed: 2002 c.21 Sch.6

s.12, enabling: SI 2002/2323

s.13, applied: SI 2003/493 Reg.38

1992–cont.

5. **Social Security Administration Act 1992**–*cont.*

s.13, disapplied: SI 2003/493 Reg.37

s.15A, amended: 2002 c.16 Sch.2 para.9, SI 2002/1555 Art.17, 2004 c.33 Sch.24 para.57

s.15A, enabling: SI 2002/355, SI 2002/2441, SI 2002/3019, SI 2002/3197, SI 2003/470, SI 2004/576

s.63, see *R. (on the application of Bewry) v Norwich City Council* [2001] EWHC Admin 657, [2002] H.R.L.R. 2 (QBD (Admin Ct)), Moses, J.

s.71, see *Hinchy v Secretary of State for Work and Pensions* [2003] EWCA Civ 138, [2003] 1 W.L.R. 2018 (CA), Aldous, L.J.

s.71, amended: 2002 c.16 Sch.2 para.10, 2002 c.21 Sch.4 para.2, 2004 c.33 Sch.24 para.58

s.71, applied: SI 2002/3019 Reg.36, SI 2003/492 Reg.37, Reg.40, Reg.42, SI 2003/916 Reg.18, Reg.27

s.71, disapplied: SI 2003/492 Reg.36

s.71, referred to: 2003 c.1 Sch.6 para.241

s.71, repealed (in part): 2002 c.21 Sch.6

s.71, enabling: SI 2002/2441, SI 2003/492

s.73, amended: 2004 c.33 Sch.24 para.59

s.73, applied: SI 2002/668 Art.6, SI 2003/526 Art.6, SI 2004/552 Art.6

s.73, enabling: SI 2002/685, SI 2002/2497, SI 2003/136, SI 2003/937, SI 2003/1195, SI 2004/101, SI 2004/565

s.74, amended: 2002 c.16 Sch.2 para.11

s.74A, amended: 2004 c.33 Sch.24 para.60, Sch.30

s.75, see *Secretary of State for Work and Pensions v Chiltern DC* [2003] EWCA Civ 508, [2003] H.L.R. 67 (CA), Hale, L.J.

s.75, enabling: SI 2003/325, SI 2003/1338, SI 2004/14

s.76, enabling: SI 2003/325, SI 2003/1338, SI 2004/14

s.78, amended: 2004 c.33 Sch.24 para.61

s.78, enabling: SI 2002/2497, SI 2003/937, SI 2003/1589

s.80, applied: 2002 c.21 s.49

s.105, amended: 2003 c.44 Sch.37 Part 9, 2004 c.33 Sch.24 para.62

s.105, disapplied: 2003 c.44 Sch.25, Sch.25 para.92

s.107, amended: 2003 c.39 Sch.8 para.354, 2004 c.33 Sch.24 para.63

s.107, enabling: SI 2002/2497

s.109B, amended: SI 2002/817 Art.2, Art.3, 2004 c.33 Sch.24 para.64

s.109B, varied: SI 2004/1822 Sch.1 para.16

s.109B, enabling: SI 2002/817

s.110A, applied: SI 2002/1888 Art.3

s.110AA, applied: SI 2002/1888 Art.3

s.110ZA, substituted: 2004 c.3 s.7

s.111, amended: 2004 c.3 Sch.1 para.3

1992–cont.

5. Social Security Administration Act 1992–*cont.*

s.111, repealed (in part): 2004 c.3 Sch.1 para.3, Sch.2 Part 1

s.111A, applied: SI 2003/492 Reg.4

s.111A, enabling: SI 2003/492, SI 2003/3209

s.112, see *Fairbank v Lambeth Magistrates Court* [2002] EWHC 785, [2003] H.L.R. 7 (QBD (Admin Ct)), Kennedy, L.J.

s.112, amended: 2003 c.44 Sch.26 para.44

s.112, applied: SI 2003/492 Reg.4

s.112, enabling: SI 2003/492, SI 2003/3209

s.113, amended: 2004 c.3 s.9, Sch.2 Part 1

s.113A, added: 2004 c.3 s.9

s.113B, added: 2004 c.3 s.9

s.115, applied: SI 2004/1020 Reg.4

s.115A, applied: SI 2003/250 Reg.4, Reg.9, SI 2003/2644 Reg.4, Reg.9, SI 2004/585 Reg.4, Reg.9, SI 2004/1020 Reg.9, SSI 2004/114 Sch.1 para.2, Sch.1 para.3

s.116, applied: SI 2002/1888 Art.3

s.121, amended: 2003 c.39 Sch.8 para.355

s.121A, amended: 2004 c.3 s.5

s.121B, amended: 2002 asp 17 Sch.3 para.21, 2004 c.3 s.5

s.121C, amended: 2004 c.3 s.5

s.121DA, amended: 2002 c.16 Sch.2 para.12, 2002 c.21 Sch.6

s.121E, amended: 2002 c.22 Sch.6 para.11

s.121F, amended: 2002 c.22 Sch.6 para.13

s.122, amended: 2002 c.21 Sch.5 para.12, 2002 c.22 Sch.6 para.5, Sch.8 Part 1

s.122AA, amended: 2002 c.22 Sch.7 para.13, 2004 c.35 Sch.12 para.7

s.122C, amended: 2002 c.22 Sch.6 para.2

s.122D, amended: 2002 c.22 Sch.6 para.3, 2004 c.35 Sch.10 para.3

s.122E, enabling: SI 2004/574

s.122ZA, added: 2002 c.22 Sch.6 para.6

s.123, amended: SI 2004/1823 Art.12

s.123, referred to: SI 2002/2264 Art.5

s.123, repealed (in part): SI 2004/1823 Art.12

s.124, amended: 2002 c.16 Sch.2 para.13, 2002 c.21 Sch.6, SI 2002/3076 Sch.1, SSI 2002/389 Sch.1

s.125, amended: 2002 c.16 Sch.2 para.14

s.126, amended: 2002 c.16 Sch.2 para.15

s.128A, enabling: SI 2003/1338, SI 2003/1589, SI 2004/14

s.130, amended: 2004 c.3 s.9

s.132, amended: 2004 c.3 s.9

s.132, enabling: SI 2002/2690

s.134, amended: 2003 c.26 Sch.7 para.35

s.134, applied: 2004 c.34 s.237

s.134, enabling: SI 2002/841

s.139, amended: 2003 c.1 Sch.6 para.187, 2004 c.33 Sch.24 para.65

s.139, enabling: SI 2002/841

s.139D, amended: 2004 c.23 Sch.2 para.15

s.139D, applied: SI 2002/1888 Art.3

s.139E, applied: SI 2002/1888 Art.3

1992–cont.

5. Social Security Administration Act 1992–*cont.*

s.139F, applied: SI 2002/1888 Art.3

s.139G, applied: SI 2002/1888 Art.3

s.139H, applied: SI 2002/1888 Art.3

s.140B, amended: 2003 c.26 Sch.8 Part 1

s.140B, repealed (in part): 2003 c.26 Sch.8 Part 1

s.140B, enabling: SI 2002/1859, SI 2002/3116, SI 2003/3179, SI 2004/646, SI 2004/2329

s.140C, see *R. (on the application of Isle of Anglesey CC) v Secretary of State for Work and Pensions* [2003] EWHC 2518, [2004] B.L.G.R. 614 (QBD (Admin Ct)), Lindsay, J.

s.140C, amended: 2003 c.26 Sch.7 para.37

s.140C, enabling: SI 2003/3179, SI 2004/646, SI 2004/2329

s.140D, repealed (in part): 2003 c.26 Sch.8 Part 1

s.140EE, amended: 2003 c.26 Sch.8 Part 1

s.140F, enabling: SI 2002/1859, SI 2002/3116, SI 2003/3179, SI 2004/646

s.140G, repealed (in part): 2003 c.26 Sch.8 Part 1

s.141, amended: 2002 c.19 Sch.1 para.16

s.141, applied: SI 2002/830, SI 2003/963, SI 2004/889, SI 2004/944

s.141, enabling: SI 2002/830, SI 2003/963, SI 2004/889

s.142, enabling: SI 2002/830, SI 2003/963, SI 2004/889

s.143, amended: 2002 c.19 Sch.1 para.17

s.143, applied: SI 2002/830

s.143, repealed (in part): 2002 c.19 Sch.2

s.143, enabling: SI 2002/830, SI 2004/889

s.144, enabling: SI 2002/830, SI 2004/889

s.145, amended: 2002 c.19 Sch.1 para.18

s.148, applied: SI 2002/519, SI 2003/517, SR 2002/89, SR 2003/146, 2004 c.35 Sch.7 para.27, SI 2004/262

s.148, enabling: SI 2002/519, SI 2003/517, SI 2004/262

s.148A, applied: SI 2003/324, SR 2002/57, SR 2003/85

s.148A, enabling: SI 2002/36, SI 2003/324, SI 2004/263

s.150, amended: 2002 c.16 Sch.2 para.16, 2002 c.21 Sch.3 para.35, Sch.6, 2002 c.22 Sch.7 para.14, 2004 c.35 Sch.11 para.21

s.150, applied: SI 2002/668, SI 2002/684, SI 2002/699, SI 2002/829, SI 2002/1792 Reg.10, SI 2003/526, SI 2003/526 Art.4, SI 2003/601, SI 2003/681, SI 2004/552, SI 2004/583, SI 2004/758, SI 2004/942, SI 2004/943, SR 2002/99, SR 2003/155

s.150, referred to: SI 2002/699, SI 2003/681, SI 2004/758

s.150, repealed (in part): 2002 c.21 Sch.6

s.150, varied: SI 2004/552 Art.4

CAP.

CAP.

1992–cont.

5. Social Security Administration Act 1992–*cont.*

s.150, enabling: SI 2002/668, SI 2002/829, SI 2003/526, SI 2004/552, SI 2004/942

s.151, amended: 2004 c.35 Sch.11 para.22

s.151, applied: SI 2002/699, SI 2002/1792 Reg.10, SI 2003/681, SI 2004/758, SR 2003/155

s.151, enabling: SI 2002/668, SI 2003/526, SI 2004/552

s.154, repealed (in part): 2002 c.21 Sch.6

s.154, varied: SI 2003/938 Art.5

s.155, disapplied: SI 2002/684 Reg.2, SI 2003/601 Reg.2, SI 2004/960 Reg.2

s.155, varied: SI 2004/583 Reg.2

s.155, enabling: SI 2002/684, SI 2003/601, SI 2004/583, SI 2004/960

s.156, amended: 2004 c.33 Sch.24 para.66

s.159B, added: 2002 c.16 Sch.2 para.17

s.159B, amended: 2003 c.1 Sch.6 para.188

s.159B, enabling: SI 2002/3019

s.162, amended: 2002 c.19 s.4, Sch.1 para.19, Sch.2, 2003 c.1 Sch.6 para.189, 2004 c.3 Sch.1 para.3

s.162, repealed (in part): 2002 c.19 Sch.2, 2004 c.3 Sch.1 para.3, Sch.2 Part 1

s.163, amended: 2002 c.22 s.6

s.163, repealed (in part): 2002 c.21 Sch.6

s.163, enabling: SI 2003/672

s.165, amended: 2002 c.16 Sch.2 para.18, 2002 c.22 s.6

s.169, amended: 2002 c.16 Sch.2 para.19

s.170, amended: 2002 c.16 Sch.2 para.20, 2004 c.10 s.7, SI 2004/1987 Art.9

s.171, enabling: SI 2003/672

s.172, see *Howker v Secretary of State for Work and Pensions* [2002] EWCA Civ 1623, [2003] I.C.R. 405 (CA), Peter Gibson, L.J.

s.179, amended: 2002 c.16 Sch.2 para.21

s.179, applied: SI 2003/916 Sch.2 para.9, 2004 c.35 s.299

s.179, repealed (in part): 2002 c.21 Sch.6

s.180, amended: 2002 c.16 Sch.2 para.22

s.180, applied: SI 2003/916 Sch.2 para.2

s.180A, applied: SI 2003/916 Sch.2 para.2

s.181, amended: SI 2002/1397 Sch.1 para.8

s.182, amended: SI 2002/1397 Sch.1 para.8, 2003 c.44 Sch.37 Part 9

s.182, disapplied: 2003 c.44 Sch.25, Sch.25 para.93

s.187, amended: 2002 c.16 Sch.2 para.23

s.189, amended: 2002 c.21 Sch.4 para.3, Sch.6

s.189, applied: SR 2002/89, SR 2002/99, SR 2003/146, SR 2003/155

s.189, enabling: SI 2002/355, SI 2002/398, SI 2002/519, SI 2002/668, SI 2002/670, SI 2002/684, SI 2002/685, SI 2002/817, SI 2002/829, SI 2002/830, SI 2002/1132, SI 2002/1696, SI 2002/1703, SI 2002/1859, SI 2002/1950, SI 2002/2323, SI

1992–cont.

5. Social Security Administration Act 1992–*cont.*

s.189, enabling:–*cont.*

2002/2441, SI 2002/2497, SI 2002/2660, SI 2002/2690, SI 2002/3019, SI 2002/3116, SI 2002/3197, SI 2003/48, SI 2003/136, SI 2003/325, SI 2003/400, SI 2003/455, SI 2003/470, SI 2003/492, SI 2003/517, SI 2003/526, SI 2003/601, SI 2003/937, SI 2003/963, SI 2003/1050, SI 2003/1189, SI 2003/1195, SI 2003/1338, SI 2003/1589, SI 2003/1632, SI 2003/1886, SI 2003/1945, SI 2003/2106, SI 2003/2107, SI 2003/2274, SI 2003/2275, SI 2003/2325, SI 2003/2399, SI 2003/2439, SI 2003/3179, SI 2003/3209, SI 2004/14, SI 2004/101, SI 2004/262, SI 2004/319, SI 2004/552, SI 2004/565, SI 2004/574, SI 2004/576, SI 2004/583, SI 2004/646, SI 2004/761, SI 2004/942, SI 2004/959, SI 2004/960, SI 2004/1821, SI 2004/2244, SI 2004/2283, SI 2004/2303, SI 2004/2327, SI 2004/2329, SI 2004/3368

s.190, amended: 2002 c.22 Sch.7 para.15

s.190, applied: SI 2002/668, SI 2002/699, SI 2002/817, SI 2002/829, SI 2002/830, SI 2003/526, SI 2003/681, SI 2003/963, SI 2003/1886, SI 2004/552, SI 2004/758, SI 2004/889, SI 2004/942, SI 2004/943

s.191, amended: 2002 c.16 Sch.2 para.24, 2002 c.22 Sch.7 para.16

s.191, repealed (in part): 2002 c.21 Sch.6

s.191, enabling: SI 2002/428, SI 2002/670, SI 2002/684, SI 2002/685, SI 2002/1132, SI 2002/1703, SI 2002/2323, SI 2002/2441, SI 2002/2690, SI 2002/3197, SI 2003/48, SI 2003/400, SI 2003/492, SI 2003/601, SI 2003/937, SI 2003/1050, SI 2003/1189, SI 2003/1589, SI 2003/1632, SI 2003/1886, SI 2003/2274, SI 2003/2325, SI 2003/2399, SI 2003/2439, SI 2003/3209, SI 2004/14, SI 2004/319, SI 2004/565, SI 2004/574, SI 2004/576, SI 2004/583, SI 2004/761, SI 2004/959, SI 2004/960, SI 2004/1821, SI 2004/2244, SI 2004/2283, SI 2004/2303, SI 2004/2327, SI 2004/3368

Sch.4 Part I, amended: SI 2002/1397 Sch.1 para.8

Sch.4 Part II para.1, substituted: SI 2002/1397 Sch.1 para.8

Sch.4 Part II para.1A, substituted: SI 2002/1397 Sch.1 para.8

Sch.4 Part II para.2, substituted: SI 2002/1397 Sch.1 para.8

Sch.8 para.1, enabling: SI 2002/718

Sch.9 para.1, enabling: SI 2002/718, SI 2003/656, SI 2004/582

6. Social Security (Consequential Provisions) Act 1992

s.5, enabling: SI 2002/2497

CAP.

6. Social Security (Consequential Provisions) Act 1992–*cont.*

Sch.2 para.73, repealed: 2002 c.40 Sch.26

Sch.2 para.93, repealed: 2003 c.1 Sch.8 Part 1

Sch.3 Part II para.12, enabling: SI 2002/2497

Sch.3 Part II para.15, applied: 2004 c.7 Sch.5 para.12, Sch.5 para.16

7. Social Security Contributions and Benefits (Northern Ireland) Act 1992

applied: 2002 c.11 (NI) s.6, 2002 c.21 s.50, 2002 c.22 s.46, 2002 c.29 s.323, SI 2002/1792 Reg.17, SI 2003/492 Reg.1, Reg.12, Reg.20, Reg.23, Reg.35, Reg.36, Reg.42, SI 2003/495 Reg.10, SR 2002/224 Sch.3 para.1, SR 2002/352 Reg.16, Reg.17, SR 2003/28 Reg.17, SR 2003/85 Art.2, SR 2003/155 Art.1, Art.6, SR 2003/212 Art.2, SSI 2003/461 Reg.13, Reg.16

referred to: 2002 c.14 (NI) Sch.2 para.1

Part I, applied: 2002 c.29 s.323, 2004 c.12 Sch.11 para.4, Sch.11 para.12

Part II, applied: SI 2002/427 Reg.3, Reg.5, Reg.12, Reg.14, SI 2002/836 Reg.3, Reg.5, Reg.12, Reg.14, SR 2002/127 Reg.3, Reg.5, SR 2003/156 Reg.2, 2004 c.7 Sch.5 para.2

Part II, referred to: SR 2002/108 Reg.2

Part III, applied: SR 2003/156 Reg.2

Part III, referred to: SR 2002/108 Reg.2

Part III, amended: SR 2002/321 Art.2

Part IV, applied: SR 2003/28 Reg.15, SR 2003/156 Reg.2

Part IV, referred to: SR 2002/108 Reg.2

Part V, applied: SR 2003/156 Reg.2

Part V, referred to: SR 2002/108 Reg.2

Part VII, applied: SR 2002/56 Reg.4, SR 2002/224 Reg.31, SR 2002/265 Sch.7 para.1

Part VIII, applied: SR 2003/28 Reg.15

Part IX, applied: 2002 c.21 s.49, SI 2003/493 Reg.5, Reg.34, Reg.35, SR 2002/265 Sch.7 para.1, SR 2003/28 Reg.15, Sch.1 para.2

Part X, applied: SR 2003/28 Reg.15

Part XI, applied: SR 2002/378 Reg.18, Reg.27

Part XIIZA, applied: SR 2002/378 Reg.3, Reg.24, Reg.31, Reg.32, Reg.34, Reg.38, Reg.39, Reg.40, Reg.46, SR 2002/382 Reg.2, Reg.3, Reg.4, Reg.7, Reg.8, Reg.9, SR 2003/28 Reg.15, SR 2003/223 Reg.4, Reg.15

Part XIIZA, referred to: SR 2003/221 Reg.2, SR 2003/223 Reg.2

Part XIIZB, applied: SR 2002/378 Reg.3, Reg.31, Reg.32, Reg.34, Reg.38, Reg.39, Reg.40, Reg.46, SR 2002/382 Reg.2, Reg.3, Reg.4, Reg.7, Reg.8, Reg.9, SR 2003/28 Reg.15, SR 2003/223 Reg.4, Reg.9

Part XIIZB, disapplied: SR 2002/378 Reg.15

CAP.

7. Social Security Contributions and Benefits (Northern Ireland) Act 1992–*cont.*

Part XIIZB, referred to: SR 2003/221 Reg.3, SR 2003/223 Reg.2

Part XIII, applied: SR 2003/28 Sch.2 para.4

s.1, amended: SI 2002/2836 Art.7

s.2, enabling: SI 2003/733

s.3, enabling: SI 2002/307, SI 2002/2366, SI 2002/2925, SI 2003/193, SI 2003/964, SI 2003/1059, SI 2003/2085, SI 2003/2175, SI 2003/2958, SI 2004/173, SI 2004/2096

s.4, amended: SI 2002/2836 Sch.2 para.1

s.4, enabling: SI 2002/307, SI 2003/2085

s.4A, amended: SI 2003/1884 Art.3, Art.4

s.4A, enabling: SI 2002/705, SI 2003/1884, SI 2003/2080

s.5, applied: SR 2002/378 Reg.5

s.5, enabling: SI 2002/238, SI 2003/193, SI 2004/220

s.6, applied: SR 2002/382 Reg.4

s.7, enabling: SI 2003/733, SI 2003/2421

s.8, substituted: 2002 c.19 s.1

s.9, amended: 2002 c.19 s.2, SI 2002/830 Art.2

s.10, amended: 2002 c.19 Sch.1 para.21

s.10, repealed (in part): 2003 c.1 Sch.8 Part 1

s.10, enabling: SI 2003/2085

s.10A, amended: 2002 c.19 Sch.1 para.22, 2004 c.3 Sch.1 para.2

s.11, amended: SI 2002/830 Art.3, SI 2003/963 Art.2

s.11, applied: SSI 2003/461 Reg.14

s.13, amended: SI 2002/830 Art.4, SI 2003/963 Art.3

s.13, enabling: SI 2004/1362

s.14, enabling: SI 2003/193

s.15, amended: 2002 c.19 s.3, SI 2002/830 Art.5

s.15, applied: SSI 2003/461 Reg.14

s.16, repealed: 2002 c.19 Sch.2

s.17, amended: 2002 c.19 Sch.1 para.23

s.17, repealed (in part): 2002 c.19 Sch.2

s.17, enabling: SI 2002/2366, SI 2003/193, SI 2003/2958

s.18, amended: 2002 c.19 s.3, Sch.2, SI 2002/830 Art.5, 2004 c.3 Sch.1 para.2

s.18, enabling: SI 2004/770

s.19, amended: 2002 c.19 Sch.1 para.24

s.19, enabling: SI 2003/193, SI 2003/964

s.20, amended: 2002 c.21 Sch.6

s.21, amended: 2002 c.19 Sch.1 para.25, 2002 c.21 Sch.6

s.22, amended: 2002 c.19 Sch.1 para.26

s.22, enabling: SR 2002/80, SR 2002/323, SR 2003/151, SR 2003/195

s.23, amended: 2002 c.19 Sch.1 para.27

s.23, enabling: SR 2003/161

s.24, amended: 2002 c.19 Sch.1 para.28

1992–cont.

7. **Social Security Contributions and Benefits (Northern Ireland) Act 1992–** cont.

s.30A, applied: SI 2003/493 Reg.10, SR 2003/28 Sch.6 para.4

s.30A, varied: SI 2003/735 Reg.2

s.30A, enabling: SR 2002/276

s.30B, amended: 2002 c.21 Sch.6

s.30B, applied: SR 2002/99 Art.6, SR 2003/155 Art.6

s.30C, amended: 2002 c.21 Sch.3 para.37

s.30C, varied: SI 2003/962 Art.5

s.30D, varied: SI 2003/735 Reg.3

s.30D, enabling: SR 2003/231

s.30DD, applied: SR 2003/28 Reg.15

s.30E, enabling: SR 2002/276

s.35, amended: 2002 c.10 (NI) Sch.1 para.2

s.35, enabling: SR 2002/354

s.35A, amended: 2002 c.10 (NI) s.4, (NI) Sch.1 para.3

s.35A, applied: SR 2002/99 Art.1

s.35A, repealed (in part): 2002 c.10 (NI) s.4, (NI) Sch.1 para.3

s.35A, varied: 2002 c.10 (NI) s.4

s.35A, enabling: SR 2002/354, SR 2002/359, SR 2003/168

s.36, applied: SR 2002/79 Reg.19

s.37, amended: 2002 c.21 Sch.3 para.38

s.37, applied: 2004 c.7 Sch.5 para.3

s.37, varied: SR 2003/212 Art.3

s.38, applied: 2004 c.7 Sch.5 para.4

s.39, amended: 2002 c.21 Sch.3 para.39

s.39A, amended: 2002 c.21 Sch.3 para.40

s.39A, applied: SR 2003/28 Sch.4 para.7, 2004 c.7 Sch.5 para.3, Sch.5 para.5

s.39A, varied: SR 2003/212 Art.3

s.39C, amended: 2002 c.21 Sch.3 para.41

s.40, applied: 2004 c.7 Sch.5 para.6

s.40, referred to: SI 2003/962 Art.5

s.41, applied: 2004 c.7 Sch.5 para.6

s.41, referred to: SI 2003/962 Art.5

s.42, amended: 2002 c.21 Sch.3 para.42

s.42, varied: SI 2003/962 Art.5

s.44, amended: 2002 c.19 Sch.1 para.29, SR 2002/99 Art.4, SR 2003/155 Art.4

s.44, applied: 2004 c.7 Sch.5 para.7

s.44, referred to: SR 2003/28 Sch.3 para.2, SR 2003/191 Reg.34

s.44A, amended: 2002 c.19 Sch.1 para.30, SR 2002/57 Art.2, SR 2002/321 Art.2

s.45, applied: SSI 2003/461 Reg.19

s.45A, repealed: 2002 c.21 Sch.6

s.47, applied: SR 2002/99 Art.6, SR 2003/155 Art.6

s.48A, applied: 2004 c.7 Sch.5 para.8

s.48B, applied: 2004 c.7 Sch.5 para.8

s.48BB, amended: 2002 c.21 Sch.3 para.43

s.48BB, applied: 2004 c.7 Sch.5 para.8

s.48C, applied: SR 2002/99 Art.6, SR 2003/155 Art.6

1992–cont.

7. **Social Security Contributions and Benefits (Northern Ireland) Act 1992–** cont.

s.51, amended: 2002 c.21 Sch.3 para.44

s.51, applied: 2004 c.7 Sch.5 para.8

s.51A, applied: 2004 c.7 Sch.5 para.8

s.52, applied: 2004 c.7 Sch.5 para.8

s.55A, applied: 2004 c.7 Sch.5 para.9

s.55A, varied: SR 2002/99 Art.4, SR 2003/155 Art.4

s.55C, varied: SR 2002/99 Art.4, SR 2003/155 Art.4

s.56, amended: 2002 c.21 Sch.6

s.56, applied: SR 2003/28 Reg.15

s.60, amended: 2002 c.21 Sch.3 para.45

s.60, repealed (in part): 2002 c.21 Sch.6

s.60, enabling: SR 2003/213

s.61, amended: 2002 c.21 Sch.6

s.63, amended: 2002 c.21 Sch.6, SR 2002/321 Art.2

s.64, applied: SR 2002/56 Reg.4, SR 2003/28 Reg.15

s.67, enabling: SR 2002/31, SR 2002/132

s.68, applied: SR 2003/28 Sch.6 para.4

s.70, amended: SR 2002/321 Art.2, Reg.3

s.70, applied: 2002 c.14 (NI) s.2, SR 2003/28 Sch.1 para.1, Sch.1 para.4, Sch.1 para.5, Sch.3 para.1

s.70, repealed (in part): SR 2002/321 Reg.3

s.70, enabling: SR 2002/323

s.71, applied: SR 2002/56 Reg.4, SR 2003/28 Sch.6 para.4

s.72, applied: SR 2002/79 Reg.5, Reg.11, SR 2003/28 Sch.1 para.1, Sch.1 para.2, Sch.3 para.1, Sch.6 para.4

s.72, enabling: SR 2002/31, SR 2002/132

s.73, applied: SI 2004/1267 Sch.2 para.4, SR 2003/28 Sch.6 para.4

s.73, enabling: SR 2002/97

s.74, applied: SR 2003/28 Sch.6 para.4

s.75, applied: SR 2003/28 Sch.6 para.4

s.76, applied: SR 2003/28 Sch.6 para.4

s.77, amended: 2002 c.21 Sch.6

s.77, applied: 2002 c.21 s.49, SI 2003/495 Reg.7, Reg.8, Reg.10, SR 2002/224 Reg.16, Sch.3 para.1, SR 2002/265 Sch.7 para.1, SR 2003/28 Reg.15

s.77, varied: SI 2003/495 Reg.4, Reg.5, Reg.6

s.77, enabling: SI 2003/495, SR 2002/87

s.78, amended: 2002 c.21 Sch.6

s.78, applied: 2004 c.7 Sch.5 para.11

s.79, applied: SR 2002/99 Art.3

s.79, enabling: SR 2002/323

s.80, amended: SR 2002/99 Art.8, SR 2003/155 Art.8

s.80, applied: 2002 c.21 s.1, SR 2002/99 Art.8, SR 2003/155 Art.8

s.80, repealed: 2002 c.21 Sch.6

s.81, repealed: 2002 c.21 Sch.6

s.86A, enabling: SR 2003/213

1992–cont.

7. **Social Security Contributions and Benefits (Northern Ireland) Act 1992–**cont.

s.89, amended: 2002 c.21 Sch.6

s.90, amended: 2002 c.21 Sch.6, SR 2002/321 Art.2

s.90, applied: 2002 c.21 s.1

s.90, enabling: SR 2002/108, SR 2002/323, SR 2003/156

s.91, amended: 2002 c.21 Sch.6

s.103, applied: SR 2002/56 Reg.4, SR 2002/79 Reg.19

s.104, applied: SR 2002/56 Reg.4, SR 2002/79 Reg.19, SR 2003/28 Reg.15

s.105, applied: SR 2002/56 Reg.4, SR 2002/79 Reg.19, SR 2003/28 Reg.15

s.107, applied: SR 2002/99 Art.6, SR 2003/155 Art.6

s.108, enabling: SR 2003/63

s.109, enabling: SR 2002/237, SR 2003/63

s.113, enabling: SI 2004/960, SR 2002/108, SR 2002/323, SR 2003/156

s.114, amended: 2002 c.21 Sch.3 para.46

s.114, enabling: SR 2003/213

s.116, enabling: SI 2003/735

s.117, enabling: SI 2004/944

s.118, enabling: SI 2003/964

s.119, enabling: SI 2002/2366

s.121, amended: 2002 c.19 Sch.1 para.31, Sch.2, 2002 c.21 Sch.6

s.121, enabling: SI 2002/705, SI 2004/220, SI 2004/960

s.122, applied: SR 2002/224 Sch.3 para.1, SR 2002/242 Art.3, SR 2002/265 Sch.7 para.1

s.122, repealed (in part): 2002 c.21 Sch.6

s.122, enabling: SI 2002/524, SR 2002/16, SR 2002/58, SR 2002/80, SR 2002/128, SR 2002/132, SR 2002/203, SR 2002/222, SR 2002/243, SR 2002/267, SR 2002/270, SR 2002/275, SR 2002/280, SR 2002/295, SR 2002/299, SR 2002/322, SR 2002/323, SR 2002/332, SR 2002/363, SR 2003/1, SR 2003/108, SR 2003/154, SR 2003/187, SR 2003/189, SR 2003/195, SR 2003/196, SR 2003/261, SR 2003/267, SR 2003/351

s.123, amended: 2002 c.14 (NI) Sch.2 para.2, (NI) Sch.3

s.123, applied: SR 2002/79 Reg.11, SR 2002/136 Reg.2

s.123, enabling: SR 2002/80, SR 2002/132, SR 2002/323, SR 2002/332, SR 2002/363, SR 2003/195

s.125, amended: SR 2002/99 Art.18, SR 2003/155 Art.19

s.127, repealed: 2002 c.21 Sch.6

s.127, enabling: SI 2002/1339, SI 2002/1340, SI 2002/1697, SI 2003/45

s.128, repealed: 2002 c.21 Sch.6

1992–cont.

7. **Social Security Contributions and Benefits (Northern Ireland) Act 1992–**cont.

s.128, enabling: SI 2002/1339, SI 2002/1340, SI 2003/45

s.129, amended: SI 2002/3154 Art.8

s.129, enabling: SR 2002/222, SR 2002/280, SR 2003/80, SR 2003/108, SR 2003/187, SR 2003/189, SR 2003/261

s.131, amended: 2002 c.21 Sch.6

s.131, applied: 2002 c.5 (NI) s.3

s.131, repealed (in part): 2002 c.5 (NI) Sch.1

s.131, enabling: SR 2002/16, SR 2002/58, SR 2002/80, SR 2002/128, SR 2002/132, SR 2002/267, SR 2002/322, SR 2002/323, SR 2003/1, SR 2003/195, SR 2003/261, SR 2003/267

s.132, enabling: SI 2002/524, SI 2002/1340, SI 2003/45, SR 2002/128, SR 2002/132, SR 2002/203, SR 2002/222, SR 2002/270, SR 2002/275, SR 2002/295, SR 2002/299, SR 2002/323, SR 2002/363, SR 2003/1, SR 2003/154, SR 2003/189, SR 2003/195, SR 2003/196, SR 2003/351

s.132A, added: 2002 c.14 (NI) Sch.2 para.3

s.133, amended: 2002 c.14 (NI) Sch.2 para.4

s.133, enabling: SI 2002/524, SI 2002/1339, SI 2002/1340, SI 2003/45, SR 2002/132, SR 2002/243, SR 2002/363, SR 2003/1

s.134, see *Kerr v Department for Social Development* [2004] UKHL 23, [2004] 1 W.L.R. 1372 (HL (NI)), Lord Steyn

s.134, enabling: SR 2002/14, SR 2002/90, SR 2002/284, SR 2002/315, SR 2002/323, SR 2002/327, SR 2003/117, SR 2003/191, SR 2003/195, SR 2003/264, SR 2003/267, SR 2003/308, SR 2003/349

s.137, applied: SR 2002/56 Reg.4

s.138, applied: SI 2003/493 Reg.6, Reg.7, Reg.8, Reg.9, Reg.10

s.138, disapplied: 2002 c.21 s.49

s.138, enabling: SI 2003/493, SI 2004/761

s.139, applied: SI 2003/493 Reg.2, Reg.3, Reg.4, Reg.36

s.139, disapplied: SI 2003/493 Reg.36

s.139, enabling: SI 2003/493

s.140, applied: SI 2003/493 Reg.9, Reg.10

s.140, enabling: SI 2003/493, SR 2003/213

s.141, repealed (in part): 2002 c.21 Sch.6

s.141, enabling: SI 2003/493

s.141A, added: 2002 c.21 s.55

s.141A, applied: SI 2003/493 Reg.20

s.142, applied: SI 2003/493 Reg.23, Reg.25, Reg.28

s.142, substituted: 2002 c.21 s.56

s.142, enabling: SI 2003/493, SI 2004/1244

s.143, applied: SI 2003/493 Reg.36, Reg.37

s.143, varied: SI 2003/493 Reg.19

s.143, enabling: SI 2003/493, SI 2004/1244

1992–cont.

7. **Social Security Contributions and Benefits (Northern Ireland) Act 1992–** *cont.*

s.144, amended: 2002 c.14 (NI) Sch.2 para.5

s.144, repealed (in part): 2002 c.14 (NI) Sch.2 para.5, (NI) Sch.3

s.145, amended: 2002 c.14 (NI) Sch.2 para.6

s.146, amended: 2002 c.14 (NI) Sch.2 para.7, SR 2002/321 Art.2

s.146, applied: SR 2002/56 Reg.4

s.146, repealed (in part): 2003 c.1 Sch.8 Part1

s.147, see *Woodbury Investments Ltd v McKeever (Inspector of Taxes)* [2004] S.T.C. (S.C.D.) 336 (Sp Comm), BMF O'Brien

s.147, applied: 2002 c.29 s.323

s.149, enabling: SR 2002/354

s.153, amended: SR 2002/99 Art.9, SR 2003/155 Art.9

s.159, enabling: SR 2002/359

s.160, amended: 2002 c.10 (NI) s.3, (NI) Sch.1 para.4, (NI) Sch.2

s.160, applied: 2002 c.29 s.323

s.160, enabling: SR 2002/354, SR 2002/359

s.161, amended: 2002 c.10 (NI) s.1

s.161, enabling: SR 2002/354

s.162, referred to: SR 2002/354 Reg.7

s.162, substituted: 2002 c.10 (NI) s.2

s.162, enabling: SR 2002/354

s.163, applied: SI 2002/2836 Art.8, SR 2002/379 Reg.3

s.163, substituted: 2002 c.22 s.21

s.163, enabling: SI 2002/225, SI 2004/698

s.167, enabling: SI 2004/698, SR 2002/354, SR 2002/359

s.167D, enabling: SR 2002/86, SR 2002/276

s.167E, applied: SR 2003/28 Sch.2 para.1

s.167ZA, added: SI 2002/2836 Art.5

s.167ZA, applied: SR 2002/378 Reg.4, Reg.9, Reg.33, SR 2002/379 Reg.11, SR 2002/381 Reg.2, SR 2002/382 Reg.5

s.167ZA, referred to: SR 2002/378 Reg.5

s.167ZA, enabling: SR 2002/378

s.167ZB, added: SI 2002/2836 Art.5

s.167ZB, applied: SR 2002/378 Reg.11, Reg.15, Reg.33, SR 2002/379 Reg.11, SR 2002/381 Reg.2, SR 2002/382 Reg.5, SR 2003/223 Reg.5, Reg.9

s.167ZB, referred to: SR 2003/221 Reg.2

s.167ZB, varied: SR 2003/221 Sch.1

s.167ZB, enabling: SR 2002/378, SR 2003/223

s.167ZC, added: SI 2002/2836 Art.5

s.167ZC, applied: SR 2002/378 Reg.6, Reg.7, Reg.12, Reg.13, SR 2002/379 Reg.9, Reg.11, SR 2003/223 Reg.6, Reg.7

s.167ZC, enabling: SR 2002/378, SR 2003/223

s.167ZD, added: SI 2002/2836 Art.5

s.167ZD, disapplied: SR 2002/378 Reg.43

1992–cont.

7. **Social Security Contributions and Benefits (Northern Ireland) Act 1992–** *cont.*

s.167ZD, enabling: SR 2002/378, SR 2003/223

s.167ZE, added: SI 2002/2836 Art.5

s.167ZE, applied: SR 2002/378 Reg.8, Reg.9, Reg.14, Reg.15, SR 2003/223 Reg.8, Reg.9

s.167ZE, referred to: SR 2003/221 Reg.2

s.167ZE, varied: SR 2003/221 Sch.1

s.167ZE, enabling: SR 2002/378, SR 2002/380, SR 2003/223

s.167ZG, added: SI 2002/2836 Art.5

s.167ZG, applied: SR 2002/378 Reg.19

s.167ZG, enabling: SR 2002/378, SR 2003/223

s.167ZI, added: SI 2002/2836 Art.5

s.167ZI, enabling: SR 2002/382, SR 2003/277

s.167ZJ, added: SI 2002/2836 Art.5

s.167ZJ, applied: SR 2002/378 Reg.39, Reg.40

s.167ZJ, referred to: SR 2003/221 Reg.2

s.167ZJ, varied: SR 2003/221 Sch.1

s.167ZJ, enabling: SR 2002/378, SR 2002/381, SR 2003/223

s.167ZK, added: SI 2002/2836 Art.5

s.167ZK, enabling: SR 2003/221

s.167ZL, added: SI 2002/2836 Art.6

s.167ZL, applied: SR 2002/378 Reg.21, Reg.23, Reg.33, SR 2002/379 Reg.9, Reg.11, SR 2002/382 Reg.6, SR 2003/223 Reg.12, Reg.14

s.167ZL, disapplied: SR 2002/378 Reg.29

s.167ZL, referred to: SR 2003/221 Reg.3

s.167ZL, varied: SR 2003/221 Sch.2

s.167ZL, enabling: SR 2002/378, SR 2003/223

s.167ZM, added: SI 2002/2836 Art.6

s.167ZM, applied: SR 2003/223 Reg.17

s.167ZM, disapplied: SR 2002/378 Reg.43, Reg.44, SR 2003/223 Reg.17

s.167ZM, enabling: SR 2002/378, SR 2003/223

s.167ZN, added: SI 2002/2836 Art.6

s.167ZN, enabling: SR 2002/378, SR 2002/380, SR 2003/223

s.167ZP, added: SI 2002/2836 Art.6

s.167ZP, applied: SR 2002/378 Reg.28

s.167ZP, enabling: SR 2002/359, SR 2002/378, SR 2003/223

s.167ZR, added: SI 2002/2836 Art.6

s.167ZR, enabling: SR 2002/382, SR 2003/277

s.167ZS, added: SI 2002/2836 Art.6

s.167ZS, applied: SR 2002/378 Reg.39, Reg.40

s.167ZS, referred to: SR 2003/221 Reg.3

s.167ZS, varied: SR 2003/221 Sch.2

s.167ZS, enabling: SR 2002/378, SR 2002/381, SR 2003/223

CAP.

1992–cont.

7. **Social Security Contributions and Benefits (Northern Ireland) Act 1992–** *cont.*

s.167ZT, added: SI 2002/2836 Art.6

s.167ZT, enabling: SR 2003/221

s.168, applied: 2002 c.14 (NI) s.17

s.169, applied: 2002 c.14 (NI) s.17

s.170, amended: SI 2002/2836 Sch.2 para.1

s.171, amended: 2002 c.21 Sch.4 para.5

s.171, applied: 2002 c.11 (NI) s.6, SI 2004/ 770

s.171, enabling: SI 2002/225, SI 2002/238, SI 2002/524, SI 2002/705, SI 2002/ 1339, SI 2002/1340, SI 2003/45, SI 2003/193, SI 2003/493, SI 2003/735, SI 2003/964, SI 2003/1059, SI 2003/2080, SI 2003/2085, SI 2003/2175, SI 2003/ 2421, SI 2004/173, SI 2004/220, SI 2004/698, SI 2004/770, SI 2004/944, SI 2004/960, SI 2004/1362, SI 2004/ 2096, SR 2002/14, SR 2002/16, SR 2002/31, SR 2002/58, SR 2002/80, SR 2002/83, SR 2002/86, SR 2002/87, SR 2002/90, SR 2002/97, SR 2002/107, SR 2002/108, SR 2002/114, SR 2002/128, SR 2002/132, SR 2002/203, SR 2002/ 222, SR 2002/237, SR 2002/243, SR 2002/267, SR 2002/270, SR 2002/275, SR 2002/276, SR 2002/280, SR 2002/ 284, SR 2002/295, SR 2002/299, SR 2002/315, SR 2002/322, SR 2002/323, SR 2002/327 Reg.3, SR 2002/332, SR 2002/354, SR 2002/359, SR 2002/363, SR 2002/378, SR 2003/1, SR 2003/28, SR 2003/63, SR 2003/108, SR 2003/ 117, SR 2003/151, SR 2003/154, SR 2003/156, SR 2003/157, SR 2003/161, SR 2003/164, SR 2003/168, SR 2003/ 187, SR 2003/189, SR 2003/191, SR 2003/195, SR 2003/196, SR 2003/202, SR 2003/213, SR 2003/223, SR 2003/ 231, SR 2003/261, SR 2003/264, SR 2003/267, SR 2003/308, SR 2003/349, SR 2003/351

s.172, amended: 2002 c.21 Sch.4 para.6, Sch.6, SI 2002/2836 Sch.2 para.1

s.172, applied: SI 2003/964

Sch.1 para.1, amended: 2002 c.19 Sch.1 para.32

Sch.1 para.2, enabling: SI 2002/2366

Sch.1 para.3, amended: 2002 c.19 Sch.1 para.32, 2004 c.3 s.2, Sch.2 Part 1

Sch.1 para.3, enabling: SI 2003/193, SI 2003/ 1337, SI 2004/770, SI 2004/2246

Sch.1 para.3A, amended: 2004 c.3 s.4

Sch.1 para.3B, amended: 2004 c.3 s.4

Sch.1 para.3B, repealed (in part): 2004 c.3 s.4, Sch.2 Part 1

Sch.1 para.3B, enabling: SI 2004/2096

Sch.1 para.4, enabling: SI 2002/2366

Sch.1 para.6, amended: 2003 c.14 s.147

CAP.

1992–cont.

7. **Social Security Contributions and Benefits (Northern Ireland) Act 1992–** *cont.*

Sch.1 para.6, enabling: SI 2002/2929, SI 2003/193, SI 2003/1337, SI 2003/2085, SI 2004/770, SI 2004/2096

Sch.1 para.7, amended: 2004 c.12 Sch.12 para.14

Sch.1 para.7BZA, added: 2004 c.3 s.6

Sch.1 para.8, enabling: SI 2002/2366, SI 2003/2958, SI 2004/2096

Sch.3 Part I para.2, amended: 2002 c.19 Sch.1 para.33

Sch.3 Part I para.2, varied: SI 2003/735 Reg.4

Sch.3 Part I para.2, enabling: SR 2002/323

Sch.3 Part I para.4, amended: 2002 c.19 Sch.1 para.33

Sch.3 Part I para.5, amended: 2002 c.19 Sch.1 para.33

Sch.3 Part II para.7, amended: 2002 c.19 Sch.1 para.33

Sch.4, referred to: SR 2003/155 Art.3

Sch.4, substituted: SR 2003/155 Sch.1

Sch.4 Part I, applied: SR 2002/99 Art.3

Sch.4 Part I, referred to: SR 2003/155 Art.3

Sch.4 Part I, substituted: SR 2002/99 Sch.1, SR 2003/155 Sch.1

Sch.4 Part II, substituted: SR 2002/99 Sch.1, SR 2003/155 Sch.1

Sch.4 Part III, amended: SR 2002/321 Art.2

Sch.4 Part III, applied: SR 2002/99 Art.3

Sch.4 Part III, referred to: SR 2003/155 Art.3

Sch.4 Part III, substituted: SR 2002/99 Sch.1, SR 2003/155 Sch.1

Sch.4 Part IV, amended: 2002 c.21 Sch.6, SR 2002/321 Art.2

Sch.4 Part IV, applied: SR 2002/99 Art.3

Sch.4 Part IV, referred to: SR 2003/155 Art.3

Sch.4 Part IV, substituted: SR 2002/99 Sch.1, SR 2003/155 Sch.1

Sch.4 Part V, applied: SR 2002/99 Art.3

Sch.4 Part V, referred to: SR 2003/155 Art.3

Sch.4 Part V, substituted: SR 2002/99 Sch.1, SR 2003/155 Sch.1

Sch.5 para.1, varied: SR 2002/99 Art.4, SR 2003/155 Art.4

Sch.5 para.2, amended: 2002 c.21 Sch.6

Sch.5 para.2, varied: SR 2002/99 Art.4, SR 2003/155 Art.4

Sch.5 para.3, varied: SR 2002/99 Art.4, SR 2003/155 Art.4

Sch.5 para.4, varied: SR 2002/99 Art.4, SR 2003/155 Art.4

Sch.5 para.5, varied: SR 2002/99 Art.4, SR 2003/155 Art.4

Sch.5 para.6, varied: SR 2002/99 Art.4, SR 2003/155 Art.4

Sch.5 para.7, varied: SR 2002/99 Art.4, SR 2003/155 Art.4

CAP.

1992–cont.

7. Social Security Contributions and Benefits (Northern Ireland) Act 1992– *cont.*

Sch.5 para.8, varied: SR 2002/99 Art.4, SR 2003/155 Art.4

Sch.5 para.9, varied: SR 2002/99 Art.4, SR 2003/155 Art.4

Sch.5 para.10, varied: SR 2002/99 Art.4, SR 2003/155 Art.4

Sch.6 para.1, enabling: SR 2002/237

Sch.7 Part I para.2, enabling: SR 2002/276

Sch.7 Part I para.4, amended: SR 2002/107 Art.2, SR 2003/157 Art.2

Sch.7 Part I para.4, enabling: SR 2002/107, SR 2003/157

Sch.7 Part II para.9, applied: SR 2002/99 Art.6, SR 2003/155 Art.6

Sch.7 Part V para.13, applied: SR 2002/99 Art.6, SR 2003/155 Art.6

Sch.7 Part V para.13, varied: SR 2002/99 Art.4, SR 2003/155 Art.4

Sch.8 Part I para.2, amended: SR 2002/99 Art.7, SR 2003/155 Art.7

Sch.8 Part I para.2, enabling: SR 2002/114, SR 2003/164

Sch.8 Part II para.4, applied: SR 2002/56 Reg.4, SR 2003/28 Reg.15

Sch.9 para.1, amended: 2002 c.26 Sch.12 para.48

Sch.9 para.1, applied: SI 2003/493 Reg.17, Reg.18, Reg.36, 2004 c.6 s.2, s.10, s.16

Sch.9 para.1, disapplied: SI 2003/493 Reg.16, Reg.17

Sch.9 para.1, enabling: SI 2003/493

Sch.9 para.2, applied: SI 2003/493 Reg.11

Sch.9 para.2, enabling: SI 2003/493

Sch.9 para.3, applied: SI 2003/493 Reg.13

Sch.9 para.3, enabling: SI 2003/493

Sch.9 para.4, repealed: 2002 c.21 s.57, Sch.6

Sch.10, applied: SI 2003/493 Reg.14

Sch.10 para.1, varied: SI 2003/493 Reg.15

Sch.10 para.2, varied: SI 2003/493 Reg.15

Sch.10 para.3, varied: SI 2003/493 Reg.15

Sch.10 para.4, varied: SI 2003/493 Reg.15

Sch.10 para.5, applied: 2002 c.21 s.49

Sch.10 para.5, varied: SI 2003/493 Reg.15

Sch.10 para.6, applied: 2002 c.21 s.49

Sch.10 para.6, varied: SI 2003/493 Reg.15

Sch.10 para.6, enabling: SI 2003/493

Sch.11 para.1, enabling: SR 2002/354

Sch.11 para.1A, enabling: SR 2002/354

Sch.11 para.2, repealed (in part): SR 2002/298 Sch.2 para.1

Sch.11 para.3, referred to: SR 2002/298 Sch.2 para.4

Sch.11 para.4, repealed: SR 2002/298 Sch.2 para.1

Sch.13 para.2, enabling: SR 2002/359

8. Social Security Administration (Northern Ireland) Act 1992

applied: 2002 c.21 s.50

CAP.

1992–cont.

8. Social Security Administration (Northern Ireland) Act 1992–*cont.*

referred to: 2002 c.14 (NI) Sch.2 para.8, 2002 c.22 s.55

Part I, referred to: 2002 c.14 (NI) Sch.1 para.1

Part XII, disapplied: 2002 c.21 s.50

s.1, amended: 2002 c.14 (NI) Sch.1 para.2

s.1, disapplied: 2004 c.7 Sch.5 para.3

s.1, referred to: SR 2003/213 Reg.2, 2004 c.7 Sch.5 para.3, Sch.5 para.5

s.1, enabling: SR 2003/80, SR 2003/189, SR 2003/195, SR 2003/213

s.2A, amended: SR 2002/321 Art.2

s.2A, enabling: SR 2002/105, SR 2002/323, SR 2003/107

s.2AA, added: 2002 c.10 (NI) s.5

s.2AA, amended: SR 2002/321 Art.2

s.2B, amended: 2002 c.10 (NI) Sch.1 para.6

s.2C, amended: 2002 c.10 (NI) Sch.1 para.7

s.3, amended: 2002 c.21 Sch.6

s.5, amended: 2002 c.14 (NI) Sch.1 para.3, SI 2002/2836 Sch.2 para.2

s.5, applied: 2002 c.21 s.58, SR 2002/79 Reg.20

s.5, repealed (in part): 2002 c.21 Sch.6

s.5, enabling: SI 2002/527, SI 2003/492, SI 2003/916, SI 2003/1945, SI 2003/2106, SI 2003/2107, SI 2004/761, SI 2004/1240, SR 2002/67, SR 2002/132, SR 2002/254, SR 2002/297, SR 2002/323, SR 2002/327 Reg.3, SR 2002/354, SR 2002/378, SR 2002/380, SR 2003/80, SR 2003/189, SR 2003/191, SR 2003/223, SR 2003/224

s.5A, amended: 2002 c.10 (NI) Sch.1 para.8

s.5A, enabling: SR 2002/323, SR 2003/80, SR 2003/191

s.9, repealed: 2002 c.21 Sch.6

s.10, enabling: SR 2002/284

s.11, applied: SI 2003/493 Reg.38

s.11, disapplied: SI 2003/493 Reg.37

s.13A, amended: 2002 c.14 (NI) Sch.2 para.9, SI 2002/1555 Art.18

s.13A, repealed (in part): SI 2002/1555 Art.18

s.13A, enabling: SR 2002/59, SR 2003/118, SR 2003/191

s.22, applied: SR 2003/18 Reg.27

s.22, enabling: SR 2003/18

s.50, amended: 2002 c.26 Sch.3 para.19

s.69, amended: 2002 c.14 (NI) Sch.2 para.10, 2002 c.21 Sch.4 para.8

s.69, applied: SI 2003/492 Reg.37, Reg.40, Reg.42, SR 2003/191 Reg.34

s.69, disapplied: SI 2003/492 Reg.36

s.69, repealed (in part): 2002 c.21 Sch.6

s.69, enabling: SI 2003/492, SR 2003/191

s.71, applied: SR 2002/99 Art.6, SR 2003/155 Art.6

s.71, enabling: SR 2002/106, SR 2002/323, SR 2003/44, SR 2003/213, SR 2003/261

s.72, amended: 2002 c.14 (NI) Sch.2 para.11

1992–cont.

8. **Social Security Administration (Northern Ireland) Act 1992**–*cont.*
s.72, enabling: SR 2003/191, SR 2003/256
s.74, enabling: SR 2002/323, SR 2003/213
s.76, applied: 2002 c.21 s.49
s.101, applied: SI 2003/435 Sch.2 para.2
s.102, enabling: SR 2002/323
s.103, amended: SI 2003/435 Sch.4 para.10
s.103B, amended: SR 2002/408 Art.2
s.103B, enabling: SR 2002/408
s.104ZA, substituted: 2004 c.3 s.8
s.105, amended: 2004 c.3 Sch.1 para.4
s.105, repealed (in part): 2004 c.3 Sch.1
   para.4, Sch.2 Part 1
s.105A, applied: SI 2003/492 Reg.4
s.105A, enabling: SI 2003/492
s.106, applied: SI 2003/492 Reg.4
s.106, enabling: SI 2003/492
s.107, amended: 2004 c.3 s.10, Sch.2 Part 1
s.107A, added: 2004 c.3 s.10
s.107B, added: 2004 c.3 s.10
s.115A, substituted: 2004 c.3 s.6
s.115A, enabling: SI 2004/2247
s.115B, amended: 2004 c.3 s.6
s.115CA, amended: 2002 c.14 (NI) Sch.2
   para.12, 2002 c.21 Sch.6
s.116, amended: 2002 c.21 Sch.5 para.12,
   2002 c.22 Sch.8 Part 1
s.116AA, amended: SI 2002/2836 Sch.2
   para.2
s.116C, amended: 2002 c.10 (NI) s.6
s.116C, repealed (in part): 2002 c.10 (NI) s.6,
   (NI) Sch.2
s.116D, amended: 2002 c.10 (NI) s.6
s.117, amended: SI 2004/1823 Art.13
s.117, applied: 2002 c.5 (NI) s.2
s.117, referred to: SI 2002/3154 Art.7
s.117, repealed (in part): SI 2003/418 Sch.3
s.118, amended: 2002 c.14 (NI) Sch.2 para.13
s.119, amended: 2002 c.14 (NI) Sch.2 para.14
s.122, amended: 2004 c.3 s.10
s.124, amended: 2004 c.3 s.10
s.124, enabling: SR 2002/354
s.128D, amended: SI 2003/418 Sch.2 para.4
s.129, applied: SI 2002/830, SI 2003/963, SI
   2004/944
s.129, enabling: SI 2002/830, SI 2003/963,
   SI 2004/889
s.130, enabling: SR 2002/89, SR 2003/146
s.130A, enabling: SR 2002/57, SR 2003/85
s.132, amended: 2002 c.21 Sch.4 para.9
s.132, applied: 2002 c.21 s.49, SI 2004/943,
   SR 2002/102, SR 2002/108, SR 2003/28
   Reg.10, SR 2003/156, SR 2003/169
s.132, varied: SR 2002/99 Art.4, SR 2003/
   155 Art.4
s.132, enabling: SI 2002/829, SI 2004/943,
   SR 2002/99, SR 2003/155
s.133, amended: 2002 c.21 Sch.4 para.9
s.133, applied: 2002 c.21 s.49

1992–cont.

8. **Social Security Administration (Northern Ireland) Act 1992**–*cont.*
s.134, applied: 2002 c.21 s.49
s.134, repealed (in part): 2002 c.21 Sch.6
s.134, varied: SR 2003/212 Art.4
s.135, disapplied: SI 2004/960 Reg.2, SR
   2002/108 Reg.2, SR 2003/156 Reg.2
s.135, enabling: SI 2004/960, SR 2002/108,
   SR 2003/156
s.139B, added: 2002 c.14 (NI) Sch.2 para.15
s.139B, enabling: SR 2003/191
s.142, amended: 2002 c.19 s.5, Sch.1 para.34,
   Sch.2, 2004 c.3 Sch.1 para.4
s.142, repealed (in part): 2002 c.19 Sch.2,
   2004 c.3 Sch.1 para.4, Sch.2 Part 1
s.143, amended: SI 2002/2836 Art.7
s.145, amended: 2002 c.14 (NI) Sch.2
   para.16, SI 2002/2836 Art.7
s.148, amended: 2002 c.14 (NI) Sch.2 para.17
s.149, amended: 2002 c.14 (NI) Sch.2
   para.18, SI 2004/1987 Art.9
s.155, amended: 2002 c.14 (NI) Sch.2
   para.19, (NI) Sch.3
s.155, repealed (in part): 2002 c.21 Sch.6
s.156, amended: 2002 c.14 (NI) Sch.2
   para.20
s.161, enabling: SR 2002/59
s.163, amended: 2002 c.14 (NI) Sch.2
   para.21
s.165, amended: 2002 c.21 Sch.4 para.10
s.165, enabling: SI 2002/830, SI 2003/492,
   SI 2003/963, SI 2003/1945, SI 2003/
   2106, SI 2003/2107, SI 2004/761, SI
   2004/889, SI 2004/943, SI 2004/960,
   SR 2002/89, SR 2002/99, SR 2002/105,
   SR 2002/106, SR 2002/108, SR 2002/
   132, SR 2002/254, SR 2002/284, SR
   2002/297, SR 2002/323, SR 2002/327
   Reg.3, SR 2002/354, SR 2002/408, SR
   2003/18, SR 2003/44, SR 2003/80, SR
   2003/107, SR 2003/118, SR 2003/146,
   SR 2003/155, SR 2003/156, SR 2003/
   189, SR 2003/191, SR 2003/195, SR
   2003/213, SR 2003/261
s.166, amended: 2002 c.10 (NI) Sch.1 para.9,
   2002 c.21 Sch.4 para.11
s.166, applied: SI 2002/830, SI 2003/963, SI
   2004/943
s.167, amended: 2002 c.10 (NI) s.6, 2002 c.14
   (NI) Sch.2 para.22
s.167, repealed (in part): 2002 c.21 Sch.6
s.167, enabling: SI 2002/527, SI 2003/492,
   SI 2004/761, SI 2004/960
Sch.2 para.1, repealed (in part): 2002 c.26
   Sch.13
Sch.4 Part III para.5, amended: SI 2004/943
   Art.2
Sch.6 para.1, enabling: SR 2002/114, SR
   2003/164

1992–cont.

9. Social Security (Consequential Provisions) (Northern Ireland) Act 1992
s.5, enabling: SR 2002/323
Sch.2 para.4, repealed: SI 2003/413 Sch.1
Sch.2 para.24, repealed: SI 2003/435 Sch.5
Sch.2 para.33, repealed: 2003 c.1 Sch.8 Part 1
Sch.3 Part II para.12, enabling: SR 2002/323
Sch.3 Part II para.15, applied: 2004 c.7 Sch.5 para.13, Sch.5 para.17

10. Bingo Act 1992
s.1, repealed (in part): 2004 c.14 Sch.1 Part 17

11. Aggravated Vehicle-Taking Act 1992
s.1, amended: 2003 c.44 Sch.32 para.65

12. Taxation of Chargeable Gains Act 1992
applied: 2002 c.23 s.81, Sch.16 para.49, Sch.18 para.10, Sch.26 para.16, Sch.26 para.37, Sch.26 para.45, Sch.28 para.4, Sch.29 para.124, Sch.29 para.130, Sch.29 para.131, Sch.29 para.132, SI 2002/1970 Reg.4, Reg.8, Reg.9, Reg.11, 2003 c.1 Sch.2 para.92, 2004 c.12 s.133, Sch.10 para.9, Sch.10 para.11, Sch.36 para.2, 2004 c.20 Sch.9 para.3, Sch.9 para.4, Sch.9 para.18, Sch.9 para.29, Sch.9 para.32, 2004 c.35 Sch.3, Sch.8
disapplied: 2003 c.14 s.195
referred to: 2002 c.23 Sch.29 para.130, 2003 c.1 s.515, Sch.6 para.207, 2004 c.12 s.107, 2004 c.20 Sch.9 para.28
varied: 2004 c.20 Sch.9 para.6, Sch.9 para.20
Part IV c.I, applied: 2002 c.23 Sch.16 para.47
Part IV c.II, applied: 2002 c.23 Sch.16 para.40, Sch.16 para.41, 2003 c.1 Sch.2 para.87
Part IV c.II, amended: 2002 c.23 Sch.40 Part 3
Part V c.II, added: 2004 c.12 Sch.21 para.4
Part VI c.I, added: 2002 c.23 s.44
s.1, see *Strand Options & Futures Ltd v Vojak (Inspector of Taxes)* [2003] EWHC 67, [2003] S.T.C. 331 (Ch D), Etherton, J.
s.2, amended: 2002 c.23 Sch.11 para.2, Sch.40 Part 3
s.2, referred to: 2004 c.12 s.109
s.2A, amended: 2002 c.23 s.46, Sch.40 Part 3
s.3, amended: SI 2002/702 Art.2, 2003 c.14 Sch.28 para.3
s.3, applied: SI 2003/842, SI 2003/842 Art.2, SI 2004/774 Art.2
s.3, referred to: 2004 c.12 s.109
s.3, repealed (in part): 2003 c.14 Sch.43 Part 3
s.3, enabling: SI 2002/702, SI 2003/842, SI 2004/774
s.3A, added: 2003 c.14 Sch.28 para.1
s.8, see *Taylor (Inspector of Taxes) v MEPC Holdings Ltd* [2002] EWCA Civ 883, [2002] S.T.C. 997 (CA), Chadwick, L.J.
s.8, applied: 2004 c.12 s.133, 2004 c.20 s.44

1992–cont.

12. Taxation of Chargeable Gains Act 1992–*cont.*
s.9, amended: 2003 c.1 Sch.6 para.208
s.9, applied: 2003 c.1 Sch.7 para.12
s.10, amended: 2003 c.14 Sch.43 Part 3
s.10, applied: 2002 c.23 Sch.29 para.130
s.10, repealed (in part): 2003 c.14 Sch.43 Part 3
s.10A, applied: 2003 c.14 s.162
s.10A, referred to: 2002 c.23 Sch.11 para.7
s.10B, added: 2003 c.14 s.149
s.11, amended: 2003 c.1 Sch.6 para.209
s.13, amended: 2002 c.23 Sch.40 Part 3, 2003 c.14 Sch.27 para.2, 2004 c.12 Sch.35 para.39
s.13, applied: SI 2002/2848 Sch.1 Part III
s.15, varied: 2002 c.29 Sch.10 para.3
s.16, referred to: SI 2004/2199 Reg.5
s.16, varied: 2002 c.29 Sch.10 para.3
s.17, see *Langham (Inspector of Taxes) v Veltema* [2002] EWHC 2689, [2002] S.T.C. 1557 (Ch D), Park, J.; see *Mansworth (Inspector of Taxes) v Jelley* [2002] EWHC 442, [2002] S.T.C. 1013 (Ch D), Lightman, J.
s.17, varied: 2002 c.29 Sch.10 para.3
s.18, applied: 2004 c.12 s.133
s.18, referred to: SI 2002/1970 Reg.5
s.18, varied: 2002 c.29 Sch.10 para.3
s.19, varied: 2002 c.29 Sch.10 para.3
s.20, varied: 2002 c.29 Sch.10 para.3
s.24, applied: 2002 c.23 Sch.16 para.28
s.25, amended: 2003 c.14 Sch.27 para.2
s.25, varied: 2003 c.14 s.153
s.26, amended: 2003 c.14 Sch.20 para.3
s.28, see *Jerome v Kelly (Inspector of Taxes)* [2002] EWHC 604, [2002] S.T.C. 609 (Ch D), Park, J.
s.30, applied: SI 2002/653 Art.6
s.31, amended: 2002 c.23 Sch.9 para.5
s.33A, added: 2002 c.23 Sch.30 para.6
s.34, amended: 2002 c.23 Sch.9 para.5
s.35, amended: 2004 c.20 Sch.9 para.36
s.37, see *Strand Options & Futures Ltd v Vojak (Inspector of Taxes)* [2002] S.T.C. (S.C.D.) 398 (Sp Comm), John F Avery Jones
s.37, applied: 2004 c.12 s.133
s.37, repealed (in part): SI 2004/2310 Sch.1 para.48
s.38, amended: 2003 c.14 Sch.18 para.5
s.38, applied: 2002 c.23 Sch.26 para.45H, Sch.29 para.130, SI 2002/653 Art.4, 2004 c.20 Sch.9 para.4
s.39, see *Fullarton v Inland Revenue Commissioners* [2004] S.T.C. (S.C.D.) 207 (Sp Comm), T Gordon Coutts Q.C.
s.39, applied: 2004 c.12 s.133
s.40, amended: 2002 c.23 Sch.25 para.60
s.41, see *Fullarton v Inland Revenue Commissioners* [2004] S.T.C. (S.C.D.) 207 (Sp Comm), T Gordon Coutts Q.C.

1992–cont.

12. Taxation of Chargeable Gains Act 1992–cont.

s.42, referred to: 2002 c.23 Sch.26 para.45H

s.50, see *Wardhaugh (Inspector of Taxes) v Penrith Rugby Union Football Club* [2002] EWHC 918, [2002] S.T.C. 776 (Ch D), Ferris, J.

s.62, amended: 2002 c.23 s.52

s.77, see *West (Inspector of Taxes) v Trennery* [2002] S.T.C. (S.C.D.) 370 (Sp Comm), John F Avery Jones; see *West (Inspector of Taxes) v Trennery* [2003] EWCA Civ 1792, [2004] S.T.C. 170 (CA), Jonathan Parker, L.J.; see *West (Inspector of Taxes) v Trennery* [2003] EWHC 676, [2003] S.T.C. 580 (Ch D), Peter Smith, J.

s.77, amended: 2002 c.23 Sch.11 para.3

s.77, applied: 2002 c.23 Sch.11 para.7, SI 2002/2848 Sch.1 Part III, 2004 c.12 Sch.15 para.9

s.77, referred to: 2004 c.12 s.109

s.77, repealed (in part): 2002 c.23 Sch.40 Part 3

s.78, applied: 2002 c.23 Sch.11 para.8

s.79, amended: 2004 c.12 Sch.21 para.2

s.79, referred to: 2004 c.12 s.116

s.80, varied: 2003 c.14 s.153

s.85A, substituted: 2003 c.14 s.163

s.86, amended: 2002 c.23 Sch.11 para.4

s.86, applied: 2002 c.23 Sch.11 para.7, SI 2002/2848 Sch.1 Part III, 2004 c.12 Sch.15 para.9

s.86, repealed (in part): 2002 c.23 Sch.40 Part 3

s.86A, amended: 2002 c.23 Sch.11 para.5, Sch.40 Part 3

s.87, amended: 2002 c.23 Sch.11 para.6

s.90, amended: 2003 c.14 s.163

s.99, amended: 2004 c.12 s.118

s.99A, added: 2004 c.12 s.118

s.99A, repealed (in part): 2004 c.12 Sch.42 Part 3

s.100, varied: SI 2004/2199 Reg.5

s.102, amended: 2002 c.23 Sch.9 para.5

s.104, disapplied: 2002 c.23 Sch.16 para.47

s.105, disapplied: 2002 c.23 Sch.16 para.47

s.105A, added: 2002 c.23 s.50

s.105A, disapplied: 2002 c.23 Sch.16 para.47

s.105B, added: 2002 c.23 s.50

s.105B, disapplied: 2002 c.23 Sch.16 para.47

s.106, amended: 2003 c.14 Sch.27 para.2

s.106, disapplied: 2002 c.23 Sch.16 para.47

s.106A, disapplied: 2002 c.23 Sch.16 para.47

s.107, disapplied: 2002 c.23 Sch.16 para.47

s.116, applied: 2002 c.23 Sch.16 para.40, Sch.16 para.41, SI 2002/1970 Reg.7, Reg.9

s.116, disapplied: 2002 c.23 Sch.16 para.40

s.116, referred to: SI 2002/1970 Reg.9, Reg.10

s.117, amended: 2002 c.23 Sch.40 Part 3

s.117A, repealed: 2002 c.23 Sch.40 Part 3

s.117B, repealed: 2002 c.23 Sch.40 Part 3

1992–cont.

12. Taxation of Chargeable Gains Act 1992–cont.

s.119A, added: 2003 c.14 Sch.22 para.50

s.119A, amended: 2004 c.12 Sch.16 para.6

s.119A, repealed (in part): 2004 c.12 Sch.16 para.6, Sch.42 Part 2

s.120, amended: 2003 c.14 Sch.22 para.51, 2003 c.1 Sch.6 para.210

s.120, repealed (in part): 2003 c.1 Sch.8 Part 1

s.126, see *Unilever (UK) Holdings Ltd v Smith (Inspector of Taxes)* [2002] S.T.C. 113 (Ch D), Burton, J.

s.126, applied: 2003 c.14 s.195

s.126, referred to: 2002 c.23 Sch.16 para.40, SI 2002/2661 Reg.4, 2003 c.14 s.195, SI 2004/1450 Reg.36

s.126 to s.131, see *Unilever (UK) Holdings Ltd v Smith (Inspector of Taxes)* [2002] EWCA Civ 1787, [2003] S.T.C. 15 (CA), Jonathan Parker, L.J.

s.127, see *Unilever (UK) Holdings Ltd v Smith (Inspector of Taxes)* [2002] S.T.C. 113 (Ch D), Burton, J.

s.127, applied: 2002 c.23 Sch.16 para.47, SI 2002/1970 Reg.10, Reg.11, Reg.12, 2003 c.1 s.462, s.702

s.127, disapplied: 2002 c.23 Sch.16 para.40, 2003 c.1 Sch.2 para.88, SI 2004/1450 Reg.36

s.127, referred to: SI 2002/1970 Reg.11, 2003 c.14 s.195

s.128, see *Unilever (UK) Holdings Ltd v Smith (Inspector of Taxes)* [2002] S.T.C. 113 (Ch D), Burton, J.

s.128, applied: 2003 c.1 s.462, s.702

s.128, disapplied: 2002 c.23 Sch.16 para.40, 2003 c.1 Sch.2 para.88, SI 2004/1450 Reg.36

s.128, referred to: 2003 c.1 s.462, 2003 c.14 s.195

s.129, applied: 2003 c.1 s.462, s.702

s.129, disapplied: 2002 c.23 Sch.16 para.40, 2003 c.1 Sch.2 para.88, SI 2004/1450 Reg.36

s.129, referred to: 2003 c.14 s.195

s.130, applied: 2003 c.1 s.462, s.702

s.130, disapplied: 2002 c.23 Sch.16 para.40, 2003 c.1 Sch.2 para.88, SI 2004/1450 Reg.36

s.130, referred to: 2003 c.14 s.195

s.131, disapplied: SI 2004/1450 Reg.36

s.131, referred to: 2003 c.14 s.195

s.135, applied: 2002 c.23 Sch.9 para.7

s.135, disapplied: 2002 c.23 Sch.16 para.41

s.135, referred to: 2002 c.23 s.45, SI 2002/2661 Reg.5

s.135, substituted: 2002 c.23 Sch.9 para.1

s.136, applied: 2002 c.23 Sch.9 para.7, Sch.16 para.48

s.136, disapplied: 2002 c.23 Sch.16 para.41

1992–cont.

12. Taxation of Chargeable Gains Act 1992–*cont.*

s.136, referred to: 2002 c.23 s.45, SI 2002/ 2661 Reg.6

s.136, substituted: 2002 c.23 Sch.9 para.2

s.137, amended: 2002 c.23 Sch.9 para.5

s.137, applied: 2002 c.23 Sch.16 para.48

s.138, amended: 2002 c.23 Sch.9 para.5

s.138, applied: SI 2004/1864 Reg.5

s.138A, amended: 2003 c.14 s.161

s.138A, applied: 2003 c.14 s.162

s.138A, repealed (in part): 2003 c.14 Sch.43 Part 3

s.139, amended: 2002 c.23 Sch.9 para.5, Sch.40 Part 3, 2003 c.14 Sch.27 para.2

s.139, applied: 2002 c.23 Sch.29 para.127, SI 2004/1864 Reg.5

s.140, amended: 2003 c.14 s.153

s.140A, amended: 2003 c.14 Sch.27 para.2

s.140A, applied: 2002 c.23 Sch.29 para.127

s.140B, applied: SI 2004/1864 Reg.5

s.140C, amended: 2003 c.14 s.153

s.140D, applied: SI 2004/1864 Reg.5

s.143, applied: 2002 c.23 Sch.26 para.37, Sch.26 para.45, Sch.28 para.4

s.144ZA, added: 2003 c.14 s.158

s.147, amended: 2002 c.23 Sch.9 para.5

s.149AA, added: 2003 c.14 Sch.22 para.52

s.149B, amended: 2003 c.14 Sch.22 para.53, 2003 c.1 Sch.6 para.211

s.149C, added: 2003 c.1 Sch.6 para.212

s.151, enabling: SI 2002/1974, SI 2002/3158, SI 2003/2747, SI 2003/2748, SI 2004/ 1676, SI 2004/1677, SI 2004/2996

s.151A, applied: SI 2004/2199 Reg.13

s.151A, referred to: SI 2004/2199 Reg.6

s.151A, repealed (in part): 2004 c.12 Sch.42 Part 2

s.151A, varied: SI 2004/2199 Reg.6

s.151B, amended: 2002 c.23 Sch.9 para.5

s.151B, applied: 2004 c.12 Sch.19 para.7, SI 2004/2199 Reg.13

s.151B, referred to: SI 2004/2199 Reg.6

s.151B, varied: SI 2004/2199 Reg.6

s.152, see *Inland Revenue Commissioners v Richmond* [2003] EWHC 999, [2003] S.T.C. 1394 (Ch D (Companies Court)), Etherton, J.; see *R. (on the application of Barnett) v Inland Revenue Commissioners* [2003] EWHC 2581, [2004] S.T.C. 763 (QBD (Admin Ct)), Davis, J.; see *Wardhaugh (Inspector of Taxes) v Penrith Rugby Union Football Club* [2002] EWHC 918, [2002] S.T.C. 776 (Ch D), Ferris, J.

s.152, applied: 2002 c.23 Sch.29 para.132

s.152, referred to: 2002 c.23 Sch.29 para.132

s.153, applied: 2002 c.23 Sch.29 para.132

s.155, applied: 2002 c.23 Sch.29 para.132

s.155, repealed (in part): 2002 c.23 Sch.29 para.132

s.159, amended: 2003 c.14 Sch.27 para.2

1992–cont.

12. Taxation of Chargeable Gains Act 1992–*cont.*

s.161, see *New Angel Court Ltd v Adam (Inspector of Taxes)* [2003] EWHC 1876, [2003] S.T.C. 1172 (Ch D), Lawrence Collins, J.

s.161, amended: 2002 c.23 Sch.40 Part 3

s.161, referred to: 2002 c.23 Sch.26 para.45

s.162A, added: 2002 c.23 s.49

s.164L, see *Inwards v Williamson (Inspector of Taxes)* [2003] S.T.C. (S.C.D.) 355 (Sp Comm), Julian Ghosh

s.165, amended: 2004 c.12 Sch.21 para.3

s.165, applied: 2004 c.12 s.116

s.169B, referred to: 2004 c.12 Sch.21 para.10

s.169C, referred to: 2004 c.12 Sch.21 para.10

s.170, applied: 2002 c.23 Sch.26 para.28, Sch.29 para.54, 2003 asp 2 s.40, s.41, 2003 asp 11 s.27, 2004 c.12 s.51, 2004 c.20 Sch.9 para.28, Sch.9 para.35

s.170, varied: 2004 c.12 s.307, SI 2004/1865 Reg.2

s.171, amended: 2002 c.23 Sch.9 para.5, 2003 c.14 Sch.27 para.2

s.171, applied: 2002 c.23 Sch.29 para.54, 2003 asp 2 s.40, s.41, 2003 asp 11 s.27, 2004 c.20 Sch.9 para.35, SI 2004/1865 Reg.2

s.171, disapplied: 2002 c.23 Sch.29 para.86, SI 2004/2199 Reg.12

s.171A, amended: 2003 c.14 Sch.33 para.17

s.171A, applied: 2002 c.23 Sch.29 para.54, 2003 asp 2 s.40, s.41, 2003 asp 11 s.27, 2004 c.20 Sch.9 para.35, SI 2004/1865 Reg.2

s.172, applied: 2002 c.23 Sch.29 para.54, 2003 asp 2 s.40, s.41, 2003 asp 11 s.27, 2004 c.20 Sch.9 para.35, SI 2004/1865 Reg.2

s.173, see *New Angel Court Ltd v Adam (Inspector of Taxes)* [2003] S.T.C. (S.C.D.) 233 (Sp Comm), John F Avery Jones; see *New Angel Court Ltd v Adam (Inspector of Taxes)* [2004] EWCA Civ 242, [2004] 1 W.L.R. 1988 (CA), Lord Phillips of Worth Matravers, M.R.

s.173, amended: 2003 c.14 s.153

s.173, applied: 2002 c.23 Sch.29 para.54, 2003 asp 2 s.40, s.41, 2003 asp 11 s.27, 2004 c.20 Sch.9 para.35, SI 2004/1865 Reg.2

s.174, applied: 2002 c.23 Sch.29 para.54, 2003 asp 2 s.40, s.41, 2003 asp 11 s.27, 2004 c.20 Sch.9 para.35, SI 2004/1865 Reg.2

s.175, amended: 2003 c.14 s.153, Sch.27 para.2

s.175, applied: 2002 c.23 Sch.29 para.54, 2003 asp 2 s.40, s.41, 2003 asp 11 s.27, 2004 c.20 Sch.9 para.35, SI 2004/1865 Reg.2

1992–cont.

12. Taxation of Chargeable Gains Act 1992–cont.

s.176, applied: 2002 c.23 Sch.29 para.54, 2003 asp 2 s.40, s.41, 2003 asp 11 s.27, 2004 c.20 Sch.9 para.35, SI 2004/1865 Reg.2

s.177, applied: 2002 c.23 Sch.29 para.54, 2003 asp 2 s.40, s.41, 2003 asp 11 s.27, 2004 c.20 Sch.9 para.35, SI 2004/1865 Reg.2

s.177A, applied: 2002 c.23 Sch.29 para.54, 2003 asp 2 s.40, s.41, 2003 asp 11 s.27, 2004 c.20 Sch.9 para.35, SI 2004/1865 Reg.2

s.177B, applied: 2002 c.23 Sch.29 para.54, 2003 asp 2 s.40, s.41, 2003 asp 11 s.27, 2004 c.20 Sch.9 para.35, SI 2004/1865 Reg.2

s.178, applied: 2002 c.23 Sch.29 para.54, 2003 asp 2 s.40, s.41, 2003 asp 11 s.27, 2004 c.20 Sch.9 para.35, SI 2004/1865 Reg.2

s.179, amended: 2002 c.23 Sch.8 para.2, 2003 c.14 Sch.27 para.2

s.179, applied: 2002 c.23 Sch.29 para.54, Sch.29 para.131, 2003 asp 2 s.40, s.41, 2003 asp 11 s.27, 2004 c.20 Sch.9 para.5, Sch.9 para.35, SI 2004/1865 Reg.2

s.179, disapplied: 2004 c.20 Sch.9 para.19

s.179, varied: 2004 c.20 Sch.9 para.5, Sch.9 para.19

s.179A, added: 2002 c.23 s.42

s.179A, applied: 2002 c.23 Sch.29 para.54, 2003 asp 2 s.40, s.41, 2003 asp 11 s.27, 2004 c.20 Sch.9 para.35, SI 2004/1865 Reg.2

s.179B, added: 2002 c.23 s.43

s.179B, applied: 2002 c.23 Sch.29 para.54, 2003 asp 2 s.40, s.41, 2003 asp 11 s.27, 2004 c.20 Sch.9 para.35, SI 2004/1865 Reg.2

s.180, applied: 2002 c.23 Sch.29 para.54, 2003 asp 2 s.40, s.41, 2003 asp 11 s.27, 2004 c.20 Sch.9 para.35, SI 2004/1865 Reg.2

s.181, applied: 2002 c.23 Sch.29 para.54, 2003 asp 2 s.40, s.41, 2003 asp 11 s.27, 2004 c.20 Sch.9 para.35

s.185, amended: 2003 c.14 s.153

s.190, amended: 2003 c.14 Sch.27 para.2

s.199, amended: 2003 c.14 Sch.27 para.2

s.199, varied: 2003 c.14 s.153

s.204, amended: 2003 c.14 Sch.43 Part 3

s.210, substituted: 2003 c.14 s.157

s.210A, added: 2003 c.14 Sch.33 para.14

s.210A, amended: 2004 c.12 Sch.7 para.6, Sch.7 para.9

s.210A, applied: 2003 c.14 Sch.33 para.6

s.210B, added: 2003 c.14 Sch.33 para.15

s.211, amended: 2002 c.23 Sch.9 para.5, Sch.40 Part 3

1992–cont.

12. Taxation of Chargeable Gains Act 1992–cont.

s.211, repealed (in part): 2003 c.14 Sch.43 Part 3

s.211A, added: 2002 c.23 s.85

s.211ZA, added: 2003 c.14 Sch.33 para.21

s.211ZA, amended: 2004 c.12 Sch.7 para.9

s.212, amended: 2003 c.14 Sch.43 Part 3, 2004 c.12 Sch.26 para.11

s.212, varied: SI 2004/2680 Reg.19

s.213, amended: 2003 c.14 s.153, Sch.33 para.16, 2004 c.12 Sch.7 para.9

s.213, repealed (in part): 2003 c.14 Sch.43 Part 3

s.214BA, added: 2003 c.14 Sch.33 para.32

s.214C, amended: 2002 c.23 Sch.40 Part 3

s.222, amended: 2003 c.1 Sch.6 para.213, 2004 c.12 Sch.22 para.1

s.223, amended: 2004 c.12 Sch.22 para.2, Sch.42 Part 2

s.223, applied: 2004 c.12 Sch.22 para.8

s.224, amended: 2004 c.12 Sch.22 para.3

s.225, amended: 2004 c.12 Sch.22 para.4

s.225A, added: 2004 c.12 Sch.22 para.5

s.226A, added: 2004 c.12 Sch.22 para.6

s.226A, applied: 2004 c.12 Sch.22 para.7

s.226A, referred to: 2004 c.12 Sch.22 para.7, Sch.22 para.8

s.226A, varied: 2004 c.12 Sch.22 para.8

s.226B, added: 2004 c.12 Sch.22 para.6

s.228, amended: 2003 c.14 Sch.27 para.2

s.236A, amended: 2003 c.1 Sch.6 para.214

s.238, amended: 2003 c.1 Sch.6 para.215

s.238A, added: 2003 c.1 Sch.6 para.216

s.239A, substituted: 2004 c.12 Sch.35 para.40

s.239B, substituted: 2004 c.12 Sch.35 para.40

s.241, see *Patel v Maidment (Inspector of Taxes)* [2004] S.T.C. (S.C.D.) 41 (Sp Comm), John F Avery Jones

s.241, amended: 2002 c.23 Sch.8 para.3

s.251, amended: 2002 c.23 Sch.9 para.5

s.251, applied: 2004 c.20 Sch.9 para.6, Sch.9 para.20

s.253, see *Crosby v Broadhurst (Inspector of Taxes)* [2004] S.T.C. (S.C.D.) 348 (Sp Comm), Colin Bishopp; see *Robson v Mitchell (Inspector of Taxes)* [2004] EWHC 1596, [2004] S.T.C. 1544 (Ch D), Patten, J.

s.257, varied: 2002 c.23 Sch.18 para.9

s.260, see *Two Settlors v Inland Revenue Commissioners* [2004] S.T.C. (S.C.D.) 45 (Sp Comm), John F Avery Jones

s.260, amended: 2004 c.12 Sch.21 para.5

s.260, applied: 2004 c.12 s.116

s.260, repealed (in part): 2004 c.12 Sch.42 Part 2

s.263B, applied: SI 2004/1863 Sch.1 para.7

s.263D, added: 2004 c.12 Sch.24 para.3

1992–cont.

12. Taxation of Chargeable Gains Act 1992–*cont.*

s.263ZA, added: 2003 c.1 Sch.6 para.217

s.263ZA, referred to: 2003 c.1 s.555

s.271, amended: 2003 c.1 Sch.6 para.218, 2004 c.12 s.187, Sch.42 Part 3, SI 2004/2744 Sch.1 para.3

s.271, repealed (in part): 2004 c.12 s.187, Sch.42 Part 3

s.272, applied: 2004 c.12 s.278

s.276, varied: 2003 c.14 s.153

s.277, amended: 2002 c.23 s.88, 2004 c.12 s.112

s.278, amended: 2002 c.23 s.88, 2004 c.12 s.115

s.279A, added: 2003 c.14 s.162

s.279A, applied: 2003 c.14 s.162

s.279B, added: 2003 c.14 s.162

s.279C, added: 2003 c.14 s.162

s.279C, applied: 2003 c.14 s.162

s.279C, disapplied: 2003 c.14 s.162

s.279D, added: 2003 c.14 s.162

s.281, amended: 2004 c.12 Sch.21 para.6, Sch.42 Part 2

s.281, referred to: 2004 c.12 s.116

s.282, amended: 2004 c.12 Sch.21 para.7

s.283, referred to: 2004 c.12 s.109

s.288, amended: 2002 c.23 s.103, 2003 c.14 s.148, Sch.22 para.54, 2003 c.1 Sch.6 para.219, 2004 c.12 s.118, Sch.35 para.41, SI 2004/2744 Sch.1 para.3

Sch.A1 para.5, amended: 2003 c.14 s.160

Sch.A1 para.5, referred to: 2002 c.23 Sch.10 para.8

Sch.A1 para.6A, referred to: 2002 c.23 Sch.10 para.8

Sch.A1 para.9, amended: 2003 c.14 s.160

Sch.A1 para.11, referred to: 2002 c.23 Sch.10 para.8

Sch.A1 para.11, repealed: 2002 c.23 Sch.40 Part 3

Sch.A1 para.11A, added: 2002 c.23 Sch.10 para.3

Sch.A1 para.11A, referred to: 2002 c.23 Sch.10 para.8

Sch.A1 para.12, referred to: 2002 c.23 Sch.10 para.8

Sch.A1 para.15, amended: 2003 c.14 s.160

Sch.A1 para.16, amended: 2004 c.12 Sch.21 para.8

Sch.A1 para.18, amended: 2002 c.23 Sch.9 para.5

Sch.A1 para.18, referred to: 2002 c.23 Sch.10 para.8

Sch.A1 para.19, amended: 2003 c.14 s.160

Sch.A1 para.22, amended: 2002 c.23 Sch.10 para.4, Sch.10 para.5, Sch.10 para.6, Sch.10 para.7, Sch.10 para.8, Sch.10 para.9, Sch.10 para.10, Sch.40 Part 3

Sch.A1 para.22, referred to: 2002 c.23 Sch.10 para.8

1992–cont.

12. Taxation of Chargeable Gains Act 1992–*cont.*

Sch.A1 para.22A, added: 2002 c.23 Sch.10 para.9

Sch.A1 para.22B, added: 2002 c.23 Sch.10 para.10

Sch.A1 para.23, amended: 2002 c.23 Sch.10 para.6, Sch.10 para.11, Sch.40 Part 3

Sch.A1 para.23, repealed (in part): 2002 c.23 Sch.40 Part 3

Sch.A1 para.24, amended: 2002 c.23 Sch.10 para.12

Sch.A1 para.24, repealed (in part): 2002 c.23 Sch.40 Part 3

Sch.1 para.1, amended: 2003 c.14 Sch.28 para.2, Sch.28 para.4

Sch.1 para.2, amended: 2003 c.14 Sch.28 para.2, Sch.28 para.5, 2004 c.12 Sch.35 para.42

Sch.1 para.2, repealed (in part): 2003 c.14 Sch.43 Part 3, 2004 c.12 Sch.35 para.42, Sch.42 Part 3

Sch.2 para.19, see *Unilever (UK) Holdings Ltd v Smith (Inspector of Taxes)* [2002] EWCA Civ 1787, [2003] S.T.C. 15 (CA), Jonathan Parker, L.J.

Sch.4B, applied: 2003 c.14 s.163

Sch.4C, applied: 2003 c.14 s.163

Sch.4C, referred to: 2003 c.14 s.163

Sch.4C para.1, applied: 2003 c.14 s.163

Sch.4C para.1, referred to: 2003 c.14 s.163

Sch.4C para.1, substituted: 2003 c.14 Sch.29 para.2

Sch.4C para.1, varied: 2003 c.14 s.163

Sch.4C para.2, substituted: 2003 c.14 Sch.29 para.2

Sch.4C para.2, varied: 2003 c.14 s.163

Sch.4C para.3, varied: 2003 c.14 s.163

Sch.4C para.4, varied: 2003 c.14 s.163

Sch.4C para.5, varied: 2003 c.14 s.163

Sch.4C para.6, amended: 2003 c.14 Sch.29 para.5

Sch.4C para.6, varied: 2003 c.14 s.163

Sch.4C para.7, varied: 2003 c.14 s.163

Sch.4C para.7A, added: 2003 c.14 Sch.29 para.3

Sch.4C para.7A, varied: 2003 c.14 s.163

Sch.4C para.7B, added: 2003 c.14 Sch.29 para.3

Sch.4C para.7B, varied: 2003 c.14 s.163

Sch.4C para.8, substituted: 2003 c.14 Sch.29 para.4

Sch.4C para.8, varied: 2003 c.14 s.163

Sch.4C para.8A, applied: 2003 c.14 s.163

Sch.4C para.8A, substituted: 2003 c.14 Sch.29 para.4

Sch.4C para.8A, varied: 2003 c.14 s.163

Sch.4C para.8B, substituted: 2003 c.14 Sch.29 para.4

Sch.4C para.8B, varied: 2003 c.14 s.163

1992–cont.

12. **Taxation of Chargeable Gains Act 1992**–*cont.*

Sch.4C para.8C, substituted: 2003 c.14 Sch.29 para.4

Sch.4C para.8C, varied: 2003 c.14 s.163

Sch.4C para.9, substituted: 2003 c.14 Sch.29 para.4

Sch.4C para.9, varied: 2003 c.14 s.163

Sch.4C para.10, amended: 2003 c.14 Sch.29 para.6

Sch.4C para.10, varied: 2003 c.14 s.163

Sch.4C para.11, varied: 2003 c.14 s.163

Sch.4C para.12, amended: 2003 c.14 Sch.29 para.6

Sch.4C para.12, varied: 2003 c.14 s.163

Sch.4C para.12A, added: 2003 c.14 Sch.29 para.4

Sch.4C para.12A, varied: 2003 c.14 s.163

Sch.4C para.13, amended: 2003 c.14 Sch.29 para.6

Sch.4C para.13, varied: 2003 c.14 s.163

Sch.4C para.13A, added: 2003 c.14 Sch.29 para.6

Sch.4C para.13A, varied: 2003 c.14 s.163

Sch.4C para.14, varied: 2003 c.14 s.163

Sch.5B, applied: 2002 c.23 s.50

Sch.5B, referred to: 2004 c.12 Sch.27 para.4, SI 2004/712 Reg.1

Sch.5C, applied: 2002 c.23 Sch.33 para.5, Sch.33 para.9, SI 2004/2199 Reg.13

Sch.5C, referred to: 2004 c.12 Sch.19 para.7

Sch.5 para.6, applied: 2002 c.23 Sch.11 para.8

Sch.5AA para.1, added: 2002 c.23 Sch.9 para.3

Sch.5AA para.2, added: 2002 c.23 Sch.9 para.3

Sch.5AA para.3, added: 2002 c.23 Sch.9 para.3

Sch.5AA para.4, added: 2002 c.23 Sch.9 para.3

Sch.5AA para.5, added: 2002 c.23 Sch.9 para.3

Sch.5AA para.6, added: 2002 c.23 Sch.9 para.3

Sch.5AA para.7, added: 2002 c.23 Sch.9 para.3

Sch.5AA para.8, added: 2002 c.23 Sch.9 para.3

Sch.5B para.1, amended: 2004 c.12 Sch.18 para.13, Sch.42 Part 2

Sch.5B para.1A, amended: 2004 c.12 Sch.18 para.14

Sch.5B para.2, amended: 2004 c.12 Sch.42 Part 2

Sch.5B para.6, referred to: SI 2004/1863 Sch.1 para.3

Sch.5B para.10, amended: 2004 c.12 Sch.18 para.15

Sch.5B para.10, applied: 2004 c.12 Sch.18 para.15

1992–cont.

12. **Taxation of Chargeable Gains Act 1992**–*cont.*

Sch.5B para.13, amended: 2004 c.12 Sch.18 para.16

Sch.5B para.14, amended: 2004 c.12 Sch.18 para.17

Sch.5B para.14A, applied: 2004 c.12 Sch.18 para.17, Sch.18 para.18

Sch.5B para.14A, repealed (in part): 2004 c.12 Sch.42 Part 2

Sch.5B para.16, amended: 2004 c.12 Sch.18 para.19

Sch.5B para.19, amended: 2004 c.12 Sch.18 para.20

Sch.5C para.1, repealed: 2004 c.12 Sch.42 Part 2

Sch.5C para.2, applied: SI 2004/2199 Reg.13

Sch.5C para.2, repealed: 2004 c.12 Sch.42 Part 2

Sch.5C para.3, repealed: 2004 c.12 Sch.42 Part 2

Sch.5C para.3, varied: SI 2004/2199 Reg.7

Sch.5C para.4, repealed: 2004 c.12 Sch.42 Part 2

Sch.5C para.5, repealed: 2004 c.12 Sch.42 Part 2

Sch.5C para.5, varied: SI 2004/2199 Reg.7

Sch.5C para.6, repealed: 2004 c.12 Sch.42 Part 2

Sch.6 Part I para.2, amended: 2002 c.23 Sch.9 para.5

Sch.7AB, referred to: 2002 c.23 s.44

Sch.7AC, referred to: 2002 c.23 s.44

Sch.7 Part I para.2, amended: 2004 c.12 Sch.21 para.9

Sch.7AB para.1, added: 2002 c.23 Sch.7

Sch.7AB para.2, added: 2002 c.23 Sch.7

Sch.7AB para.3, added: 2002 c.23 Sch.7

Sch.7AB para.4, added: 2002 c.23 Sch.7

Sch.7AB para.5, added: 2002 c.23 Sch.7

Sch.7AB para.6, added: 2002 c.23 Sch.7

Sch.7AB para.7, added: 2002 c.23 Sch.7

Sch.7AB para.8, added: 2002 c.23 Sch.7

Sch.7AB para.9, added: 2002 c.23 Sch.7

Sch.7AB para.10, added: 2002 c.23 Sch.7

Sch.7AC Part I, applied: SI 2002/1970 Reg.4, Reg.7

Sch.7AC Part I para.1, added: 2002 c.23 Sch.8 para.1

Sch.7AC Part I para.2, added: 2002 c.23 Sch.8 para.1

Sch.7AC Part I para.2, applied: 2002 c.23 Sch.26 para.45A

Sch.7AC Part I para.3, added: 2002 c.23 Sch.8 para.1

Sch.7AC Part I para.4, added: 2002 c.23 Sch.8 para.1

Sch.7AC Part I para.5, added: 2002 c.23 Sch.8 para.1

Sch.7AC Part I para.6, added: 2002 c.23 Sch.8 para.1

1992–cont.

12. **Taxation of Chargeable Gains Act 1992**–*cont.*

Sch.7AC Part II para.7, added: 2002 c.23 Sch.8 para.1

Sch.7AC Part II para.8, added: 2002 c.23 Sch.8 para.1

Sch.7AC Part II para.9, added: 2002 c.23 Sch.8 para.1

Sch.7AC Part II para.10, added: 2002 c.23 Sch.8 para.1

Sch.7AC Part II para.11, added: 2002 c.23 Sch.8 para.1

Sch.7AC Part II para.12, added: 2002 c.23 Sch.8 para.1

Sch.7AC Part II para.12, amended: 2003 c.14 Sch.38 para.9

Sch.7AC Part II para.13, added: 2002 c.23 Sch.8 para.1

Sch.7AC Part II para.14, added: 2002 c.23 Sch.8 para.1

Sch.7AC Part II para.15, added: 2002 c.23 Sch.8 para.1

Sch.7AC Part II para.16, added: 2002 c.23 Sch.8 para.1

Sch.7AC Part II para.17, added: 2002 c.23 Sch.8 para.1

Sch.7AC Part III para.18, added: 2002 c.23 Sch.8 para.1

Sch.7AC Part III para.18, amended: 2003 c.14 Sch.20 para.3

Sch.7AC Part III para.19, added: 2002 c.23 Sch.8 para.1

Sch.7AC Part III para.19, amended: 2003 c.14 Sch.20 para.3

Sch.7AC Part III para.20, added: 2002 c.23 Sch.8 para.1

Sch.7AC Part III para.21, added: 2002 c.23 Sch.8 para.1

Sch.7AC Part III para.22, added: 2002 c.23 Sch.8 para.1

Sch.7AC Part III para.23, added: 2002 c.23 Sch.8 para.1

Sch.7AC Part III para.24, added: 2002 c.23 Sch.8 para.1

Sch.7AC Part III para.25, added: 2002 c.23 Sch.8 para.1

Sch.7AC Part IV para.26, added: 2002 c.23 Sch.8 para.1

Sch.7AC Part IV para.27, added: 2002 c.23 Sch.8 para.1

Sch.7AC Part IV para.28, added: 2002 c.23 Sch.8 para.1

Sch.7AC Part IV para.29, added: 2002 c.23 Sch.8 para.1

Sch.7AC Part IV para.30, added: 2002 c.23 Sch.8 para.1

Sch.7AC Part IV para.31, added: 2002 c.23 Sch.8 para.1

Sch.7AC Part V para.32, added: 2002 c.23 Sch.8 para.1

1992–cont.

12. **Taxation of Chargeable Gains Act 1992**–*cont.*

Sch.7AC Part V para.33, added: 2002 c.23 Sch.8 para.1

Sch.7AC Part V para.34, added: 2002 c.23 Sch.8 para.1

Sch.7AC Part V para.35, added: 2002 c.23 Sch.8 para.1

Sch.7AC Part V para.36, added: 2002 c.23 Sch.8 para.1

Sch.7AC Part V para.37, added: 2002 c.23 Sch.8 para.1

Sch.7AC Part V para.38, added: 2002 c.23 Sch.8 para.1

Sch.7AC Part V para.39, added: 2002 c.23 Sch.8 para.1

Sch.7AD para.1, added: 2002 c.23 Sch.31

Sch.7AD para.2, added: 2002 c.23 Sch.31

Sch.7AD para.3, added: 2002 c.23 Sch.31

Sch.7AD para.4, added: 2002 c.23 Sch.31

Sch.7AD para.5, added: 2002 c.23 Sch.31

Sch.7AD para.6, added: 2002 c.23 Sch.31

Sch.7AD para.7, added: 2002 c.23 Sch.31

Sch.7AD para.8, added: 2002 c.23 Sch.31

Sch.7AD para.9, added: 2002 c.23 Sch.31

Sch.7AD para.10, added: 2002 c.23 Sch.31

Sch.7AD para.10, amended: 2003 c.14 Sch.43 Part 3

Sch.7AD para.11, added: 2002 c.23 Sch.31

Sch.7AD para.12, added: 2002 c.23 Sch.31

Sch.7AD para.13, added: 2002 c.23 Sch.31

Sch.7A para.1, amended: 2003 c.14 Sch.27 para.2

Sch.7B para.1, amended: 2003 c.14 Sch.43 Part 3

Sch.7B para.1, varied: SI 2004/2200 Reg.7

Sch.7B para.1A, varied: SI 2004/2200 Reg.7

Sch.7B para.2, varied: SI 2004/2200 Reg.7

Sch.7B para.3, varied: SI 2004/2200 Reg.7

Sch.7B para.4, varied: SI 2004/2200 Reg.7

Sch.7B para.5, varied: SI 2004/2200 Reg.7

Sch.7B para.6, varied: SI 2004/2200 Reg.7

Sch.7B para.6A, varied: SI 2004/2200 Reg.7

Sch.7B para.6B, varied: SI 2004/2200 Reg.7

Sch.7B para.7, varied: SI 2004/2200 Reg.7

Sch.7B para.7A, added: 2002 c.23 s.42

Sch.7B para.7A, varied: SI 2004/2200 Reg.7

Sch.7B para.8, varied: SI 2004/2200 Reg.7

Sch.7B para.9, varied: SI 2004/2200 Reg.7

Sch.7B para.9A, varied: SI 2004/2200 Reg.7

Sch.7B para.10, varied: SI 2004/2200 Reg.7004/2200 Reg.7

Sch.7B para.12, varied: SI 2004/2200 Reg.7

Sch.7B para.13, varied: SI 2004/2200 Reg.7

Sch.7B para.14, varied: SI 2004/2200 Reg.7

Sch.7B para.15, varied: SI 2004/2200 Reg.7

Sch.7B para.16, added: 2002 c.23 Sch.8 para.4

Sch.7B para.16, varied: SI 2004/2200 Reg.7

1992–cont.

12. Taxation of Chargeable Gains Act 1992–*cont.*

Sch.7C para.1, amended: 2003 c.1 Sch.6 para.220

Sch.7C para.2, amended: 2003 c.1 Sch.6 para.220

Sch.7D Part 1, applied: 2003 c.1 Sch.2 para.87

Sch.7D Part 1, referred to: 2003 c.1 s.515

Sch.7D Part 1 para.1, added: 2003 c.1 Sch.6 para.221

Sch.7D Part 1 para.2, added: 2003 c.1 Sch.6 para.221

Sch.7D Part 1 para.2, applied: 2003 c.1 Sch.7 para.86

Sch.7D Part 1 para.3, added: 2003 c.1 Sch.6 para.221

Sch.7D Part 1 para.4, added: 2003 c.1 Sch.6 para.221

Sch.7D Part 1 para.5, added: 2003 c.1 Sch.6 para.221

Sch.7D Part 1 para.6, added: 2003 c.1 Sch.6 para.221

Sch.7D Part 1 para.6, applied: 2003 c.1 s.512

Sch.7D Part 1 para.7, added: 2003 c.1 Sch.6 para.221

Sch.7D Part 1 para.8, added: 2003 c.1 Sch.6 para.221

Sch.7D Part 2 para.9, added: 2003 c.1 Sch.6 para.221

Sch.7D Part 2 para.9, varied: 2003 c.1 Sch.7 para.72

Sch.7D Part 2 para.10, added: 2003 c.1 Sch.6 para.221

Sch.7D Part 2 para.10, varied: 2003 c.1 Sch.7 para.72

Sch.7D Part 3, applied: 2003 c.1 Sch.7 para.76

Sch.7D Part 3 para.11, added: 2003 c.1 Sch.6 para.221

Sch.7D Part 3 para.11, varied: 2003 c.1 Sch.7 para.74

Sch.7D Part 3 para.12, added: 2003 c.1 Sch.6 para.221

Sch.7D Part 3 para.12, varied: 2003 c.1 Sch.7 para.74

Sch.7D Part 3 para.13, added: 2003 c.1 Sch.6 para.221

Sch.7D Part 3 para.13, varied: 2003 c.1 Sch.7 para.74

Sch.7D Part 4, referred to: 2003 c.1 s.527, SI 2004/712 Reg.1

Sch.7D Part 4 para.14, added: 2003 c.1 Sch.6 para.221

Sch.7D Part 4 para.15, added: 2003 c.1 Sch.6 para.221

Sch.7D Part 4 para.16, added: 2003 c.1 Sch.6 para.221

Sch.9, applied: SI 2002/2849 Art.2, SI 2004/438 Art.2

Sch.9 Part I para.1, enabling: SI 2002/2849, SI 2004/438

1992–cont.

12. Taxation of Chargeable Gains Act 1992–*cont.*

Sch.10 para.7, repealed: 2003 c.21 Sch.19

Sch.10 para.14, repealed (in part): 2003 c.1 Sch.8 Part 1, 2004 c.12 Sch.42 Part 2, Sch.42 Part 3

Sch.10 para.16, repealed (in part): 2003 c.1 Sch.8 Part 1

13. Further and Higher Education Act 1992

applied: SI 2002/2523 Sch.1 para.1

referred to: 2004 c.8 s.29

s.6, applied: SI 2002/1663 Reg.3

s.16, applied: SI 2002/2522, SI 2003/507 Reg.11, SI 2003/510

s.16, enabling: SI 2002/2522, SI 2003/510, SI 2004/3108

s.17, applied: 2003 c.14 Sch.4 para.17

s.17, enabling: SI 2002/2522, SI 2003/510, SI 2004/3108

s.18, amended: 2002 c.32 Sch.21 para.11

s.20, enabling: SI 2002/2523, SI 2003/514, SI 2004/3109

s.21, amended: 2002 c.32 Sch.21 para.12

s.21, enabling: SI 2002/1094, SI 2002/2523, SI 2003/514, SI 2004/3109

s.23, amended: 2002 c.32 Sch.22 Part 3

s.23, repealed (in part): 2002 c.32 Sch.22 Part 3

s.26, applied: SI 2002/2996, SI 2002/2996 Art.2, SI 2003/516 Art.3, SI 2003/1293 Art.3, SI 2003/1610 Art.3, SI 2003/1611 Art.3

s.26, referred to: SI 2002/2996, SI 2002/2996 Art.3

s.26, repealed (in part): 2002 c.32 Sch.22 Part 1

s.26, varied: SI 2002/243 Art.3, SI 2002/244 Art.3, SI 2002/245 Art.3, SI 2002/246 Art.3, SI 2002/1402, SI 2002/1695 Art.3, SI 2002/1714 Art.3, SI 2003/2442 Art.3, SI 2003/2918 Art.3, SI 2004/1598 Art.3, SI 2004/1681 Art.3, SI 2004/2024 Art.3

s.26, enabling: SI 2002/2996

s.27, applied: SI 2002/243, SI 2002/244, SI 2002/245, SI 2002/246, SI 2002/1402, SI 2003/507 Reg.11, SI 2003/516, SI 2003/1293, SI 2003/1611, SI 2003/2918, SI 2004/2024

s.27, enabling: SI 2002/243, SI 2002/244, SI 2002/245, SI 2002/246, SI 2002/1402, SI 2002/1695, SI 2002/1714, SI 2003/516, SI 2003/1293, SI 2003/1610, SI 2003/1611, SI 2003/2442, SI 2003/2918, SI 2004/1598, SI 2004/1681, SI 2004/2024

s.37, repealed (in part): 2002 c.32 Sch.21 para.15, Sch.22 Part 3

s.39, repealed (in part): 2002 c.32 Sch.22 Part 3

s.40, repealed (in part): 2002 c.32 Sch.22 Part 3

1992–cont.

13. Further and Higher Education Act 1992–cont.

s.41, repealed (in part): 2002 c.32 Sch.22 Part 3

s.42, repealed (in part): 2002 c.32 Sch.22 Part 3

s.43, amended: 2002 c.32 Sch.21 para.17

s.48, repealed: 2002 c.32 Sch.22 Part 1

s.50, enabling: SI 2003/51

s.51, applied: SI 2002/243, SI 2002/244, SI 2002/245, SI 2002/246, SI 2002/1402, SI 2002/1695, SI 2002/1714, SI 2002/2522, SI 2003/507 Reg.11, SI 2003/510, SI 2003/516, SI 2003/1293, SI 2003/2442, SI 2003/2918, SI 2004/1598, SI 2004/1681, SI 2004/2024

s.51, enabling: SI 2002/2522, SI 2004/1681

s.52A, amended: 2002 c.32 Sch.21 para.19

s.54, amended: 2002 c.32 Sch.7 para.4, Sch.21 para.20

s.55, applied: SI 2002/928 Sch.3

s.60, repealed (in part): 2002 c.32 Sch.22 Part 3

s.64, repealed: 2004 c.14 Sch.1 Part 5

s.65, applied: SI 2002/195 Reg.5, Reg.11, SI 2002/1330 Sch.3 para.1, SI 2002/3200 Reg.5, Reg.11, Sch.3 para.1, SI 2003/1994 Sch.3 para.1, SR 2002/224 Reg.5, Reg.11, Sch.3 para.1, SR 2002/265 Sch.7 para.1, 2004 c.8 s.23, s.24, s.27, s.28, s.34

s.65, disapplied: SI 2002/195 Sch.3 para.1

s.68, applied: 2004 c.8 s.23, s.27

s.80, repealed: 2004 c.14 Sch.1 Part 5

s.85, disapplied: 2004 c.31 s.18

s.85A, added: 2002 c.32 Sch.20 para.2

s.85A, applied: SI 2003/348 Sch.6 para.10

s.88A, added: SI 2003/2867 Sch.1 para.18

s.89, enabling: SI 2002/2523, SI 2003/514, SI 2004/3109

s.90, applied: SI 2002/2978 Reg.5, SI 2002/3177 Reg.5, 2003 c.14 Sch.4 para.17

s.91, applied: SI 2002/324 Reg.3, SI 2002/327 Reg.3, 2003 c.14 Sch.4 para.17, SI 2003/1660 Reg.20, SI 2003/1661 Reg.20, SI 2004/118 Art.2

s.91, referred to: SI 2004/118 Art.3, SSI 2003/176 Sch.3 para.7

Sch.4, enabling: SI 2002/2523, SI 2003/514, SI 2004/3109

Sch.5 para.6, amended: 2002 c.9 Sch.11 para.27

Sch.5 para.7, amended: 2003 c.14 Sch.20 para.3

Sch.8 Part I para.37, repealed: 2004 c.14 Sch.1 Part 5

Sch.8 Part I para.46, repealed (in part): 2002 c.32 Sch.22 Part 3

Sch.8 Part I para.47, repealed (in part): 2002 c.32 Sch.22 Part 3

Sch.8 Part I para.49, repealed: 2002 c.32 Sch.22 Part 3

1992–cont.

13. Further and Higher Education Act 1992–cont.

Sch.8 Part II para.83, repealed: 2002 c.32 Sch.22 Part 3

Sch.8 Part II para.90, repealed (in part): 2002 c.32 Sch.22 Part 3

14. Local Government Finance Act 1992

applied: SI 2004/291 Sch.4, SI 2004/478 Sch.4, SI 2004/627 Sch.2

referred to: SI 2002/808 Art.2, 2003 c.26 Sch.7 para.40

Part I, applied: SI 2003/2382 Reg.17, SI 2003/2613 Sch.1 para.17, SSI 2003/376 Sch.1 para.3, SSI 2003/460 Sch.1 para.3, 2004 c.34 s.237

Part I, disapplied: SSI 2003/147 Reg.2

Part I c.II, applied: 2002 c.21 s.63

Part II, applied: 2002 asp 3 s.36, s.37, s.62, SSI 2003/376 Sch.1 para.3, SSI 2003/460 Sch.1 para.3

Part II, disapplied: SSI 2003/147 Reg.2

Pt.II, see *Scottish Water v Clydecare Ltd* 2003 S.C. 330 (Ex Div), Lord Osborne, Lord Macfadyen, Lord Sutherland

s.3, enabling: SI 2003/3121, SI 2004/2921

s.4, enabling: SI 2003/3121, SI 2004/2921

s.5, amended: 2003 c.26 s.78, SI 2003/3046 Art.2

s.5, enabling: SI 2003/3046

s.6, see *Bennett v Copeland BC* [2004] EWCA Civ 672, [2004] R.A. 171 (CA), Peter Gibson, L.J.; see *R. (on the application of Clark) v Bracknell Forest BC* [2003] EWHC 3095, [2004] R.V.R. 30 (QBD (Admin Ct)), Munby, J.; see *R. (on the application of Navabi) v Chester le Street DC* [2001] EWHC Admin 796, [2002] R.V.R. 10 (QBD (Admin Ct)), Elias, J.; see *Williams v Horsham DC* [2003] EWHC 1862, [2003] R.V.R. 298 (QBD (Admin Ct)), McCombe, J.; see *Williams v Horsham DC* [2004] EWCA Civ 39, [2004] 1 W.L.R. 1137 (CA), Lord Phillips of Worth Matravers, M.R.

s.6, amended: 2003 c.26 s.74

s.8, enabling: SI 2003/3125, SI 2004/2920

s.9, amended: 2003 c.26 s.74, 2004 c.33 Sch.27 para.140

s.11, see *R. (on the application of Clark) v Bracknell Forest BC* [2003] EWHC 3095, [2004] R.V.R. 30 (QBD (Admin Ct)), Munby, J.; see *Williams v Horsham DC* [2004] EWCA Civ 39, [2004] 1 W.L.R. 1137 (CA), Lord Phillips of Worth Matravers, M.R.

s.11, amended: 2003 c.26 Sch.7 para.41, Sch.8 Part 1

s.11, applied: SI 2003/2613 Sch.1 para.17

s.11, referred to: SI 2003/2613 Sch.1 para.9

s.11A, added: 2003 c.26 s.75

CAP.

1992–cont.

14. Local Government Finance Act 1992–
cont.

s.11A, applied: SI 2003/2613 Sch.1 para.9, Sch.1 para.10, Sch.1 para.17, SI 2003/3011 Reg.3

s.11A, enabling: SI 2003/3011, SI 2004/926

s.12, substituted: 2003 c.26 s.75

s.12, enabling: SI 2004/452, SI 2004/3094

s.13, amended: 2003 c.26 Sch.7 para.42

s.13, enabling: SI 2004/3142

s.13A, added: 2003 c.26 s.76

s.13A, applied: SI 2003/2613 Sch.1 para.9, Sch.1 para.17

s.13B, added: 2003 c.26 s.79

s.13B, enabling: SI 2004/3142

s.14, varied: SI 2002/1129 Art.5

s.14, enabling: SI 2003/1715

s.16, referred to: SI 2003/2613 Sch.1 para.17

s.17, amended: 2003 c.26 Sch.7 para.43

s.17, applied: SSI 2002/33 Art.8, 2003 c.26 Sch.7 para.43

s.18, amended: 2004 c.33 Sch.27 para.140

s.19, repealed (in part): 2003 c.39 Sch.8 para.356, Sch.10

s.21, amended: 2003 c.26 Sch.7 para.44

s.22, amended: 2003 c.26 Sch.7 para.45

s.22B, added: 2003 c.26 s.77

s.22B, applied: SI 2003/2613 Reg.1

s.24, amended: 2003 c.26 Sch.7 para.46

s.25, referred to: 2003 c.26 s.128

s.25, repealed: 2003 c.26 Sch.8 Part 1

s.27, amended: 2003 c.44 Sch.37 Part 9

s.27, disapplied: 2003 c.44 Sch.25 para.94

s.28, amended: 2003 c.26 Sch.7 para.48

s.30, see *Regentford Ltd v Thanet DC* [2004] EWHC 246, [2004] R.A. 113 (QBD (Admin Ct)), Lightman, J.

s.30, applied: SI 2003/2613 Sch.1 para.6

s.30, varied: SI 2002/1129 Art.5

s.31, applied: SI 2003/2613 Reg.5

s.31, varied: SI 2002/1129 Art.5

s.32, amended: SI 2002/328 Reg.2

s.32, applied: SI 2002/1129 Art.5, 2003 c.26 s.25, s.26, s.27, s.28, SI 2003/2613 Sch.1 para.8A, Sch.1 para.8, Sch.3 para.2, Sch.3 para.3

s.32, repealed (in part): 2003 c.26 Sch.8 Part 1

s.32, varied: SI 2002/155 Reg.2, SI 2002/1129 Art.5, SI 2003/195 Reg.2, SI 2004/243 Reg.2

s.32, enabling: SI 2002/155, SI 2002/328, SI 2003/195, SI 2004/243

s.33, applied: 2004 c.i s.23

s.33, varied: SI 2002/155 Reg.3, SI 2002/1129 Art.5, SI 2003/195 Reg.3, SI 2004/243 Reg.3

s.33, enabling: SI 2002/155, SI 2002/328, SI 2003/195, SI 2003/3012, SI 2004/243, SI 2004/3094

s.34, varied: SI 2002/1129 Art.5

CAP.

1992–cont.

14. Local Government Finance Act 1992–
cont.

s.34, enabling: SI 2003/3012, SI 2003/3181, SI 2004/3094

s.35, referred to: SI 2002/1129 Art.5

s.35, varied: SI 2002/1129 Art.5

s.35, enabling: SI 2003/3181

s.36, applied: SI 2003/2613 Sch.1 para.6

s.36, varied: SI 2002/1129 Art.5

s.37, varied: SI 2002/1129 Art.5

s.38, varied: SI 2002/1129 Art.5

s.39, amended: 2003 c.26 s.83, 2004 c.21 Sch.1 para.81

s.39, referred to: 2003 c.26 s.83

s.40, applied: SI 2003/2613 Sch.1 para.6, 2004 c.21 s.3

s.41, applied: SI 2002/1129 Art.5, SI 2003/2613 Sch.1 para.8

s.41, varied: SI 2002/1129 Art.5

s.43, applied: 2003 c.26 s.25, s.26, s.27, s.28, SI 2003/2613 Reg.5, Sch.1 para.8A, Sch.3 para.2, Sch.3 para.3, 2004 c.21 s.3

s.43, repealed (in part): 2003 c.26 Sch.8 Part 1

s.43, varied: SI 2002/155 Reg.4, SI 2003/195 Reg.4, SI 2004/243 Reg.4, SI 2004/451 Reg.2

s.43, enabling: SI 2002/155, SI 2003/195, SI 2004/243, SI 2004/451

s.44, varied: SI 2002/155 Reg.5, SI 2003/195 Reg.5, SI 2004/243 Reg.5, SI 2004/451 Reg.3

s.44, enabling: SI 2002/155, SI 2003/195, SI 2003/3012, SI 2004/243, SI 2004/451, SI 2004/3094

s.45, enabling: SI 2003/3012, SI 2004/3094

s.47, applied: SI 2003/2613 Sch.1 para.6

s.48, enabling: SI 2003/3012, SI 2004/3094

s.50, applied: SI 2003/2613 Reg.5, Sch.3 para.2, Sch.3 para.3

s.50, referred to: SI 2002/1129 Art.5

s.50, repealed (in part): 2003 c.26 Sch.8 Part 1

s.52B, applied: SI 2004/1908

s.52D, applied: SI 2004/1908

s.52D, enabling: SI 2004/1908

s.52E, applied: SI 2004/1908

s.52F, enabling: SI 2004/1908

s.52Z, repealed (in part): 2003 c.26 Sch.8 Part 1

s.54, varied: SI 2002/1129 Art.5

s.66, amended: 2003 c.26 Sch.7 para.49

s.67, amended: 2003 c.26 s.84, Sch.7 para.50

s.69, amended: 2003 c.26 Sch.7 para.51, Sch.8 Part 1

s.69, applied: 2003 c.26 s.23

s.69, repealed (in part): 2003 c.26 Sch.8 Part 1

s.70, applied: 2002 asp 3 s.36

s.72, enabling: SSI 2002/101, SSI 2002/102

CAP.

1992–cont.

14. Local Government Finance Act 1992– *cont.*

s.75, applied: 2002 asp 3 s.36

s.76, applied: 2002 asp 3 s.36

s.76, enabling: SSI 2003/137

s.77, applied: 2002 asp 3 s.36

s.77A, added: 2004 c.33 s.133

s.79, applied: SSI 2002/33 Art.9, 2003 asp 1 s.33

s.79, referred to: 2003 asp 1 s.33

s.81, applied: SSI 2002/33 Art.12

s.93, amended: 2003 asp 1 s.41, SSI 2003/567 Art.2

s.93, applied: SSI 2003/580 Reg.2

s.93, enabling: SSI 2003/580

s.99, applied: 2002 asp 3 s.62

s.99, referred to: SSI 2002/494 Sch.2 para.10

s.99, enabling: SSI 2002/102

s.113, amended: 2003 c.26 Sch.7 para.52

s.113, enabling: SI 2002/155, SI 2003/195, SI 2003/522, SI 2003/768, SI 2003/1715, SI 2003/2613, SI 2003/3081, SI 2003/3121, SI 2003/3125, SI 2004/243, SI 2004/451, SI 2004/452, SI 2004/460, SI 2004/785, SI 2004/927, SI 2004/1013, SI 2004/2920, SI 2004/2921, SI 2004/3142, SI 2004/3143, SSI 2003/176

s.116, enabling: SI 2003/2613, SI 2003/3012, SI 2003/3081, SI 2003/3181, SI 2004/460, SI 2004/3094, SI 2004/3143, SSI 2002/102, SSI 2003/137, SSI 2003/147

Sch.1 para.1, applied: SSI 2003/176 Art.3

Sch.1 para.1, enabling: SSI 2003/176

Sch.1 para.2, applied: SSI 2003/176 Art.4, SSI 2004/115 Sch.3

Sch.1 para.2, enabling: SSI 2003/176

Sch.1 para.4, applied: SI 2003/673 Art.3, SSI 2003/176 Art.5, Art.6, Art.7, Art.8

Sch.1 para.4, enabling: SI 2003/673, SSI 2003/176

Sch.1 para.5, applied: SSI 2003/176 Art.9

Sch.1 para.5, enabling: SSI 2003/176

Sch.1 para.7, enabling: SI 2003/3121, SI 2004/2921

Sch.1 para.8, see *Scottish Water v Clydecare Ltd* 2003 S.C. 330 (Ex Div), Lord Osborne, Lord Macfadyen, Lord Sutherland

Sch.2 para.1, enabling: SI 2003/2613, SI 2003/3081, SI 2004/460, SI 2004/785, SI 2004/927, SI 2004/3143, SSI 2003/147

Sch.2 para.2, enabling: SI 2003/2613, SI 2003/3081, SI 2004/460, SI 2004/3143

Sch.2 para.4, enabling: SI 2003/2613, SI 2003/3081, SI 2004/460, SI 2004/785, SI 2004/927

Sch.2 para.8, amended: 2003 c.26 Sch.7 para.53

Sch.2 para.14, enabling: SI 2003/2613, SI 2004/460

CAP.

1992–cont.

14. Local Government Finance Act 1992– *cont.*

Sch.2 para.17, enabling: SSI 2003/147

Sch.2 para.18A, added: 2003 c.26 s.85

Sch.2 para.21, added: 2003 c.26 Sch.7 para.53

Sch.2 para.21, enabling: SI 2003/3081, SI 2004/927

Sch.3 para.6, enabling: SI 2003/2613, SI 2003/3081, SI 2004/460

Sch.4 para.1, enabling: SI 2003/522, SI 2003/768, SI 2003/1715, SI 2004/785, SI 2004/927, SI 2004/1013

Sch.4 para.2, enabling: SI 2003/1715

Sch.4 para.3, enabling: SI 2003/1715, SI 2004/785, SI 2004/927

Sch.4 para.5, amended: 2003 c.26 s.80

Sch.4 para.5, enabling: SI 2003/522, SI 2003/768, SI 2004/785, SI 2004/927

Sch.4 para.6, amended: 2002 c.16 Sch.2 para.33

Sch.4 para.7, amended: 2003 c.26 s.80

Sch.4 para.7, enabling: SI 2004/1013

Sch.4 para.8, enabling: SI 2003/1715

Sch.4 para.11A, added: 2003 c.26 s.81

Sch.4 para.11A, enabling: SI 2004/785, SI 2004/927

Sch.4 para.12, amended: 2002 c.16 Sch.2 para.34

Sch.4 para.12A, added: 2003 c.26 s.82

Sch.4 para.12A, enabling: SI 2004/785, SI 2004/927

Sch.4 para.20, added: 2003 c.26 Sch.7 para.54

Sch.4 para.20, enabling: SI 2004/785, SI 2004/927

Sch.5 para.2, applied: SSI 2002/91 Reg.9, Reg.10, SSI 2003/160 Reg.9, Reg.10

Sch.8 para.2, amended: 2002 asp 17 Sch.3 para.22

Sch.8 para.2, enabling: SSI 2002/560

Sch.8 para.4, amended: 2002 asp 17 Sch.3 para.22

Sch.8 para.6, amended: 2002 c.16 Sch.2 para.35

Sch.9 para.1, applied: SI 2003/2275 Sch.1

Sch.9 para.1, referred to: SI 2003/325 Sch.1

Sch.9 para.2, repealed: 2002 c.21 Sch.6

Sch.9 para.4, referred to: SI 2003/325 Sch.1

Sch.9 para.8, repealed: 2002 c.21 Sch.6

Sch.9 para.12, applied: SI 2003/2275 Sch.1

Sch.9 para.12, referred to: SI 2003/325 Sch.1

Sch.10 Part I para.6, repealed (in part): 2003 c.26 Sch.8 Part 1

Sch.12 Part I para.1, enabling: SSI 2002/70, SSI 2002/230, SSI 2003/42, SSI 2004/14

Sch.12 Part I para.2, applied: SSI 2002/70, SSI 2002/230, SSI 2003/42

Sch.12 Part II para.6, amended: SSI 2002/176 Art.6

1992–cont.

14. Local Government Finance Act 1992– *cont.*

Sch.12 Part II para.9, applied: SSI 2002/70 Art.3, SSI 2002/230 Art.4, SSI 2003/42 Art.2, SSI 2004/14 Art.3

Sch.12 Part II para.9, enabling: SSI 2002/70, SSI 2002/230, SSI 2003/42, SSI 2004/14

Sch.13 para.6, repealed: 2004 c.36 Sch.3

Sch.13 para.80, amended: 2003 c.26 Sch.7 para.55

Sch.13 para.80, referred to: 2003 c.26 s.128

Sch.13 para.80, repealed (in part): 2003 c.26 Sch.8 Part 1

Sch.13 para.84, repealed (in part): 2003 c.26 Sch.8 Part 1

Sch.13 para.90, repealed (in part): 2003 c.26 Sch.8 Part 1

15. Offshore Safety Act 1992

s.1, enabling: SI 2002/2175

19. Local Government Act 1992

Commencement Orders: 2003 asp 1 s.60

see *Bogdal v Kingston upon Hull City Council* [2002] R.A. 145 (CA), Stuart-Smith, L.J.

applied: 2003 c.ii, 2003 c.iv, SI 2003/527 Reg.2

referred to: 2003 c.10 s.18

Part II, applied: 2003 c.10 s.2, SI 2003/2613 Sch.1 para.8, 2004 c.21 s.2, s.4

Part II, referred to: 2003 c.10 s.18

s.1, amended: 2003 asp 1 s.13, s.17

s.1, applied: 2003 asp 1 s.13, SSI 2003/286 Reg.2

s.1A, repealed (in part): 2003 asp 1 s.60

s.2, amended: 2003 asp 1 s.13

s.5, repealed (in part): 2003 asp 1 s.5

s.6, repealed (in part): 2003 asp 1 s.5

s.8, repealed (in part): 2003 asp 1 s.60

s.9, repealed (in part): 2003 asp 1 s.60

s.10, repealed (in part): 2003 asp 1 s.60

s.11, repealed (in part): 2003 asp 1 s.60

s.14, repealed (in part): 2004 c.5 Sch.7 para.17, Sch.9

s.14, varied: 2003 c.10 s.15

s.15, applied: SI 2002/48, SI 2002/49, SI 2002/187, SI 2002/1031, SI 2002/1032, SI 2002/1033, SI 2002/1034, SI 2002/1035, SI 2002/1036, SI 2002/1781, SI 2002/1783, SI 2002/1784, SI 2002/1785, SI 2002/1786, SI 2002/1787, SI 2002/1788, SI 2002/2234, SI 2002/2235, SI 2002/2236, SI 2002/2237, SI 2002/2238, SI 2002/2239, SI 2002/2240, SI 2002/2241, SI 2002/2242, SI 2002/2243, SI 2002/2368, SI 2002/2370, SI 2002/2371, SI 2002/2372, SI 2002/2373, SI 2002/2374, SI 2002/2593, SI 2002/2594, SI 2002/2595, SI 2002/2596, SI 2002/2597, SI 2002/2598, SI 2002/2599, SI 2002/2600, SI 2002/2601, SI 2002/2602, SI 2002/2603, SI 2002/2604, SI 2002/2882, SI 2002/

1992–cont.

19. Local Government Act 1992– *cont.*

s.15, applied:–*cont.*

2883, SI 2002/2884, SI 2002/2885, SI 2002/2886, SI 2002/2887, SI 2002/2888, SI 2002/2889, SI 2002/2890, SI 2002/2891, SI 2002/2892, SI 2002/2985, SI 2002/2986, SI 2002/2987, SI 2002/2988, SI 2002/2989, SI 2002/2990, SI 2002/2991, SI 2002/3218, SI 2002/3221, SI 2002/3222, SI 2002/3223, SI 2002/3224, SI 2002/3225, SI 2002/3227, SI 2002/3228, SI 2003/157, SI 2003/158, SI 2003/159, SI 2003/160, SI 2003/161, SI 2003/162, SI 2003/322, SI 2003/1088, SI 2003/1977, SI 2003/1979, SI 2003/1980, SI 2003/2156, SI 2003/2505, SI 2003/2506, SI 2003/2507, SI 2003/2508, SI 2003/2509, SI 2003/2510, SI 2003/2511, SI 2003/2767, SI 2003/3087, SI 2003/3088, SI 2003/3089, SI 2003/3090, SI 2003/3091, SI 2004/120, SI 2004/121, SI 2004/122, SI 2004/123, SI 2004/124, SI 2004/125, SI 2004/126, SI 2004/356, SI 2004/357, SI 2004/358, SI 2004/359, SI 2004/360, SI 2004/361, SI 2004/362, SI 2004/363, SI 2004/364, SI 2004/365, SI 2004/720, SI 2004/2811, SI 2004/2812, SI 2004/2813, SI 2004/2814, SI 2004/2815, SI 2004/2816, SI 2004/2817, SI 2004/2818, SI 2004/2819, SI 2004/2820, SI 2004/2821

s.15, varied: 2003 c.10 s.15

s.15, enabling: SI 2002/48, SI 2002/49, SI 2002/187, SI 2002/1031, SI 2002/1032, SI 2002/1033, SI 2002/1034, SI 2002/1035, SI 2002/1036, SI 2002/1781, SI 2002/1783, SI 2002/1784, SI 2002/1785, SI 2002/1786, SI 2002/1787, SI 2002/1788, SI 2002/2368, SI 2002/2369, SI 2002/2370, SI 2002/2371, SI 2002/2372, SI 2002/2373, SI 2002/2374, SI 2002/2593, SI 2002/2594, SI 2002/2595, SI 2002/2596, SI 2002/2597, SI 2002/2598, SI 2002/2599, SI 2002/2600, SI 2002/2601, SI 2002/2602, SI 2002/2603, SI 2002/2604, SI 2002/2890, SI 2002/2892, SI 2002/2984, SI 2002/2986, SI 2002/2987, SI 2002/2988, SI 2002/2989, SI 2002/2990, SI 2002/2991, SI 2002/3218, SI 2002/3221, SI 2002/3222, SI 2002/3223, SI 2002/3224, SI 2002/3225, SI 2002/3227, SI 2002/3228, SI 2003/157, SI 2003/158, SI 2003/159, SI 2003/160, SI 2003/162, SI 2003/322, SI 2003/1088, SI 2003/1977, SI 2003/1979, SI 2003/1980, SI 2003/2156, SI 2003/2505, SI 2003/2506, SI 2003/2507, SI 2003/2508, SI 2003/2509, SI 2003/2510, SI 2003/2511, SI 2003/2767, SI 2003/2769, SI 2004/120, SI 2004/121, SI 2004/122, SI 2004/123, SI 2004/124, SI 2004/125, SI 2004/126, SI 2004/2811, SI

CAP.

CAP.

1992–cont.

19. Local Government Act 1992–*cont.*
  s.15, enabling:–*cont.*
    2004/2812, SI 2004/2813, SI 2004/2814,
    SI 2004/2815, SI 2004/2816, SI 2004/
    2817, SI 2004/2818, SI 2004/2819, SI
    2004/3245, SI 2004/3247, SI 2004/
    3248, SI 2004/3250, SI 2004/3251, SI
    2004/3252
  s.15A, varied: 2003 c.10 s.15
  s.16, varied: 2003 c.10 s.15
  s.17, applied: SI 2003/533 Reg.9, SI 2003/
    2604 Art.1, SI 2003/3052 Art.1
  s.17, varied: 2003 c.10 s.17
  s.17, enabling: SI 2002/48, SI 2002/49, SI
    2002/187, SI 2002/1031, SI 2002/1032,
    SI 2002/1033, SI 2002/1034, SI 2002/
    1035, SI 2002/1036, SI 2002/1781, SI
    2002/1783, SI 2002/1784, SI 2002/1785,
    SI 2002/1786, SI 2002/1787, SI 2002/
    1788, SI 2002/2234, SI 2002/2235, SI
    2002/2236, SI 2002/2237, SI 2002/
    2238, SI 2002/2239, SI 2002/2240, SI
    2002/2241, SI 2002/2242, SI 2002/
    2243, SI 2002/2368, SI 2002/2369, SI
    2002/2370, SI 2002/2371, SI 2002/
    2372, SI 2002/2373, SI 2002/2374, SI
    2002/2593, SI 2002/2594, SI 2002/
    2595, SI 2002/2596, SI 2002/2597, SI
    2002/2598, SI 2002/2599, SI 2002/
    2600, SI 2002/2601, SI 2002/2602, SI
    2002/2603, SI 2002/2604, SI 2002/
    2882, SI 2002/2883, SI 2002/2884, SI
    2002/2885, SI 2002/2886, SI 2002/
    2887, SI 2002/2888, SI 2002/2889, SI
    2002/2890, SI 2002/2891, SI 2002/
    2892, SI 2002/2982, SI 2002/2983, SI
    2002/2984, SI 2002/2985, SI 2002/
    2986, SI 2002/2987, SI 2002/2988, SI
    2002/2989, SI 2002/2990, SI 2002/
    2991, SI 2002/2992, SI 2002/3218, SI
    2002/3221, SI 2002/3222, SI 2002/
    3223, SI 2002/3224, SI 2002/3225, SI
    2002/3227, SI 2002/3228, SI 2003/157,
    SI 2003/158, SI 2003/159, SI 2003/160,
    SI 2003/161, SI 2003/162, SI 2003/322,
    SI 2003/711, SI 2003/1088, SI 2003/
    1089, SI 2003/1090, SI 2003/1091, SI
    2003/1977, SI 2003/1979, SI 2003/1980,
    SI 2003/2156, SI 2003/2505, SI 2003/
    2506, SI 2003/2507, SI 2003/2508, SI
    2003/2509, SI 2003/2510, SI 2003/
    2511, SI 2003/2767, SI 2003/2769, SI
    2003/3087, SI 2003/3088, SI 2003/
    3089, SI 2003/3090, SI 2003/3091, SI
    2004/120, SI 2004/121, SI 2004/122, SI
    2004/123, SI 2004/124, SI 2004/125, SI
    2004/126, SI 2004/127, SI 2004/128, SI
    2004/356, SI 2004/357, SI 2004/358, SI
    2004/359, SI 2004/360, SI 2004/361, SI
    2004/362, SI 2004/363, SI 2004/364, SI
    2004/365, SI 2004/720, SI 2004/721, SI
    2004/1073, SI 2004/2677, SI 2004/2678,
    SI 2004/2811, SI 2004/2812, SI 2004/

1992–cont.

19. Local Government Act 1992–*cont.*
  s.17, enabling:–*cont.*
    2813, SI 2004/2814, SI 2004/2815, SI
    2004/2816, SI 2004/2817, SI 2004/
    2818, SI 2004/2819, SI 2004/2820, SI
    2004/2821, SI 2004/3106, SI 2004/
    3245, SI 2004/3247, SI 2004/3248, SI
    2004/3250, SI 2004/3251, SI 2004/
    3252, SI 2004/3253
  s.18, amended: 2004 c.21 Sch.1 para.82
  s.18, repealed (in part): 2004 c.21 Sch.1
    para.82, Sch.2
  s.18, varied: 2003 c.10 s.18
  s.19, applied: SI 2003/533 Reg.9
  s.21, varied: 2003 c.10 s.18
  s.23, repealed: 2004 c.14 Sch.1 Part 10
  s.24, repealed: 2004 c.14 Sch.1 Part 10
  s.26, varied: 2003 c.10 s.18
  s.26, enabling: SI 2002/48, SI 2002/49, SI
    2002/187, SI 2002/1032, SI 2002/1033,
    SI 2002/1034, SI 2002/1035, SI 2002/
    1036, SI 2002/1781, SI 2002/1783, SI
    2002/1784, SI 2002/1785, SI 2002/1786,
    SI 2002/1787, SI 2002/1788, SI 2002/
    2234, SI 2002/2235, SI 2002/2236, SI
    2002/2237, SI 2002/2238, SI 2002/
    2239, SI 2002/2240, SI 2002/2241, SI
    2002/2242, SI 2002/2243, SI 2002/
    2368, SI 2002/2369, SI 2002/2370, SI
    2002/2371, SI 2002/2372, SI 2002/
    2373, SI 2002/2374, SI 2002/2593, SI
    2002/2594, SI 2002/2595, SI 2002/
    2596, SI 2002/2597, SI 2002/2598, SI
    2002/2599, SI 2002/2600, SI 2002/
    2601, SI 2002/2602, SI 2002/2603, SI
    2002/2604, SI 2002/2882, SI 2002/
    2883, SI 2002/2884, SI 2002/2885, SI
    2002/2886, SI 2002/2887, SI 2002/
    2888, SI 2002/2889, SI 2002/2890, SI
    2002/2891, SI 2002/2892, SI 2002/
    2982, SI 2002/2983, SI 2002/2984, SI
    2002/2985, SI 2002/2986, SI 2002/
    2987, SI 2002/2988, SI 2002/2989, SI
    2002/2990, SI 2002/2991, SI 2002/
    2992, SI 2002/3218, SI 2002/3221, SI
    2002/3222, SI 2002/3223, SI 2002/
    3224, SI 2002/3225, SI 2002/3227, SI
    2002/3228, SI 2003/157, SI 2003/158,
    SI 2003/159, SI 2003/160, SI 2003/161,
    SI 2003/162, SI 2003/322, SI 2003/711,
    SI 2003/1088, SI 2003/1089, SI 2003/
    1090, SI 2003/1091, SI 2003/1977, SI
    2003/1979, SI 2003/1980, SI 2003/
    2156, SI 2003/2505, SI 2003/2506, SI
    2003/2507, SI 2003/2508, SI 2003/
    2509, SI 2003/2510, SI 2003/2511, SI
    2003/2767, SI 2003/2769, SI 2003/
    3087, SI 2003/3088, SI 2003/3089, SI
    2003/3090, SI 2003/3091, SI 2004/120,
    SI 2004/121, SI 2004/122, SI 2004/123, SI
    2004/124, SI 2004/125, SI 2004/126, SI
    2004/127, SI 2004/128, SI 2004/356, SI
    2004/357, SI 2004/358, SI 2004/359, SI

1992–cont.

19. Local Government Act 1992–*cont.*

s.26, enabling:–*cont.*

2004/360, SI 2004/361, SI 2004/362, SI 2004/363, SI 2004/364, SI 2004/365, SI 2004/720, SI 2004/721, SI 2004/1073, SI 2004/2677, SI 2004/2678, SI 2004/2811, SI 2004/2812, SI 2004/2813, SI 2004/2814, SI 2004/2815, SI 2004/2816, SI 2004/2817, SI 2004/2818, SI 2004/2819, SI 2004/2820, SI 2004/2821, SI 2004/3106, SI 2004/3245, SI 2004/3247, SI 2004/3248, SI 2004/3250, SI 2004/3251, SI 2004/3252, SI 2004/3253

Sch.1 para.1, repealed (in part): 2003 asp 1 s.60

Sch.1 para.2, repealed (in part): 2003 asp 1 s.60

Sch.1 para.3, repealed (in part): 2003 asp 1 s.60

Sch.1 para.4, repealed (in part): 2003 asp 1 s.60

Sch.1 para.5, repealed (in part): 2003 asp 1 s.60

Sch.1 para.6, repealed (in part): 2003 asp 1 s.60

Sch.1 para.7, repealed (in part): 2003 asp 1 s.60

Sch.1 para.8, repealed (in part): 2003 asp 1 s.60

Sch.1 para.9, repealed (in part): 2003 asp 1 s.60

Sch.1 para.10, repealed (in part): 2003 asp 1 s.60

Sch.1 para.11, repealed (in part): 2003 asp 1 s.60

Sch.1 para.12, repealed (in part): 2003 asp 1 s.60

Sch.1 para.13, repealed (in part): 2003 asp 1 s.60

Sch.1 para.14, repealed (in part): 2003 asp 1 s.60

20. Finance Act 1992

s.8, repealed: 2004 c.14 Sch.1 Part 9

23. Access to Neighbouring Land Act 1992

applied: SI 2003/1417 r.80

s.4, amended: 2002 c.9 Sch.11 para.26

s.5, amended: 2002 c.9 Sch.11 para.26

s.5, repealed (in part): 2002 c.9 Sch.13

25. Prison Security Act 1992

s.1, see *R. v Whiteman (Mark)* [2004] EWCA Crim 569, [2004] 2 Cr. App. R. (S.) 59 (CA (Crim Div)), Kay, L.J.

29. Still-Birth (Definition) Act 1992

s.2, repealed (in part): 2004 c.14 Sch.1 Part 17

34. Sexual Offences (Amendment) Act 1992

s.2, amended: 2003 c.42 Sch.6 para.31, SI 2003/1247 Sch.1 para.12

s.4, amended: SI 2003/1247 Sch.1 para.13

1992–cont.

34. Sexual Offences (Amendment) Act 1992–*cont.*

s.6, amended: 2003 c.44 Sch.3 para.63, SI 2003/1247 Sch.1 para.14

35. Timeshare Act 1992

applied: 2002 c.40 Sch.14, Sch.15, SI 2003/1376 Sch.1, SI 2003/1593 Sch.1 Part I

referred to: SI 2003/1374 Sch.1, SI 2003/1922 Reg.2

s.1, amended: SI 2003/1922 Sch.1 para.1

s.1A, amended: SI 2003/1922 Sch.1 para.2

s.2, amended: SI 2003/1922 Sch.1 para.3

s.2, applied: SI 2003/2579 Art.3, Art.6

s.2, repealed (in part): SI 2003/1922 Sch.1 para.3

s.2, substituted: SI 2003/1922 Sch.1 para.3

s.3, amended: SI 2003/1922 Sch.1 para.4

s.3, applied: SI 2003/2579 Art.4, Art.6

s.3, substituted: SI 2003/1922 Sch.1 para.4

s.4, amended: SI 2003/1922 Sch.1 para.5

s.4, enabling: SI 2003/2579

s.5, amended: SI 2003/1922 Sch.1 para.6

s.5, repealed (in part): SI 2003/1922 Sch.1 para.6

s.5A, amended: SI 2003/1922 Sch.1 para.7

s.6, amended: SI 2003/1922 Sch.1 para.8

s.6A, applied: SI 2004/2095 Reg.11

s.10A, amended: SI 2003/1922 Sch.1 para.9

s.11, amended: SI 2003/1400 Sch.5

s.12, enabling: SI 2003/2579

Sch.1i, repealed (in part): SI 2003/1922 Sch.1 para.10

Sch.2 para.2, repealed (in part): 2002 c.40 Sch.26

Sch.2 para.5, repealed: 2002 c.40 Sch.26

37. Further and Higher Education (Scotland) Act 1992

applied: SI 2003/409 Sch.1 Part I

Part I, applied: SI 2003/1660 Reg.20, SI 2003/1661 Reg.20, SSI 2002/314 Reg.2

Part II, applied: SI 2003/1660 Reg.20, SI 2003/1661 Reg.20, SSI 2002/62 Sch.2 Part II

s.1, applied: SI 2003/1660 Reg.20, SI 2003/1661 Reg.20

s.3, enabling: SSI 2003/297, SSI 2004/274

s.5, applied: SSI 2004/274

s.12, amended: SSI 2003/487 Art.2

s.12, applied: SI 2002/2006 Reg.19, SSI 2003/487

s.12, enabling: SSI 2003/487

s.23, repealed: 2004 asp 4 Sch.3 para.7

s.36, applied: 2002 asp 13 Sch.1 para.47, SI 2003/1660 Reg.20, SI 2003/1661 Reg.20, SSI 2002/62 Sch.2 Part II

s.44, applied: SSI 2002/77 Sch.1, SSI 2002/78 Sch.1, Sch.2

s.56, applied: SSI 2002/314 Reg.2

s.58A, added: SI 2003/2867 Sch.1 para.19

Sch.2 para.9, amended: SSI 2003/199 Sch.1

1992–cont.

37. Further and Higher Education (Scotland) Act 1992–cont.

Sch.2 para.9, repealed (in part): SSI 2003/199 Sch.1

Sch.2 para.11, amended: SSI 2003/199 Sch.1

Sch.2 para.14, repealed: SSI 2003/199 Sch.1

Sch.2 para.15, repealed: SSI 2003/199 Sch.1

Sch.3 para.1, amended: 2003 asp 9 Sch.14 para.10

Sch.3 para.2, amended: 2003 asp 9 Sch.15

Sch.3 para.4, amended: 2003 asp 9 Sch.14 para.10

Sch.9 para.7, repealed (in part): 2004 asp 4 Sch.3 para.7

Sch.9 para.9, repealed: 2003 asp 13 Sch.5 Part 1

39. Army Act 1992

s.1, applied: SR 2003/28 Sch.6 para.2

40. Friendly Societies Act 1992

applied: 2002 c.23 Sch.29 para.46, 2002 c.40 s.255, SI 2002/3150 Art.25, SI 2003/1102 Reg.2

referred to: SI 2002/3150 Art.25, SI 2004/353 Reg.2

s.24, applied: SI 2003/1102 Reg.34, Reg.36, SI 2004/353 Reg.34, Reg.36

s.65, applied: SI 2003/3075 Reg.26

s.66, applied: SI 2003/3075 Reg.26

s.77, amended: 2004 c.33 Sch.27 para.141

s.77, varied: 2004 c.33 Sch.21 para.36

s.105A, added: SI 2003/2867 Sch.1 para.20

s.110, substituted: 2003 c.39 Sch.8 para.357

s.116, applied: 2003 c.17 s.65

s.119A, amended: 2004 c.33 Sch.27 para.142

s.119A, varied: 2004 c.33 Sch.21 para.37

Sch.2 paraA, amended: 2004 c.33 Sch.27 para.143

Sch.16 para.44, repealed: 2003 c.39 Sch.10

Sch.18, applied: 2002 c.23 Sch.29 para.53

Sch.21 Part I para.7, repealed: 2004 c.27 Sch.8

41. Charities Act 1992

s.60, amended: 2003 c.21 Sch.17 para.118, Sch.19

s.60, applied: SI 2003/1376 Sch.1, SI 2003/1593 Sch.1 Part I

s.61, applied: SI 2003/1593 Sch.1 Part I

s.63, applied: SI 2003/1376 Sch.1, SI 2003/1593 Sch.1 Part I

s.65, varied: 2002 c.i s.21

s.66, varied: 2002 c.i s.21

s.67, varied: 2002 c.i s.21

s.68, varied: 2002 c.i s.21

s.69, varied: 2002 c.i s.21

s.70, varied: 2002 c.i s.21

s.71, amended: 2003 c.39 Sch.8 para.358, Sch.10

s.71, varied: 2002 c.i s.21

s.73, varied: 2002 c.i s.21

s.74, varied: 2002 c.i s.21

1992–cont.

42. Transport and Works Act 1992

s.1, applied: SI 2002/366, SI 2002/412, SI 2002/1065, SI 2002/1066, SI 2002/1327, SI 2002/1943, SI 2002/1997, SI 2002/2398, SI 2003/1075, SI 2003/2907, SI 2003/3364, 2004 c.5 s.106, s.107, SI 2004/389, SI 2004/1817

s.1, enabling: SI 2002/366, SI 2002/412, SI 2002/1064, SI 2002/1065, SI 2002/1066, SI 2002/1327, SI 2002/1943, SI 2002/1997, SI 2002/2398, SI 2003/1075, SI 2003/2907, SI 2003/3364, SI 2004/389, SI 2004/757, SI 2004/1817, SI 2004/3126

s.3, applied: SI 2002/1998, SI 2003/2829, SI 2003/2830, SI 2003/2831, 2004 c.5 s.106, s.107, SI 2004/933

s.3, enabling: SI 2002/1998, SI 2003/2829, SI 2003/2830, SI 2003/2831, SI 2004/757, SI 2004/933, SI 2004/3054

s.5, applied: SI 2002/366, SI 2002/412, SI 2002/1066, SI 2002/1327, SI 2002/1998, SI 2003/1075, SI 2003/2829, SI 2003/2830, SI 2003/2907, SI 2003/3364, SI 2004/389, SI 2004/933, SI 2004/1817

s.5, enabling: SI 2002/366, SI 2002/412, SI 2002/1064, SI 2002/1065, SI 2002/1066, SI 2002/1327, SI 2002/1943, SI 2002/1997, SI 2002/1998, SI 2002/2398, SI 2003/1075, SI 2003/2829, SI 2003/2830, SI 2003/2831, SI 2003/2907, SI 2003/3364, SI 2004/389, SI 2004/757, SI 2004/933, SI 2004/1817, SI 2004/3054, SI 2004/3126

s.6, applied: SI 2002/366, SI 2002/412, SI 2002/1064, SI 2002/1065, SI 2002/1066, SI 2002/1327, SI 2002/1943, SI 2002/1997, SI 2002/1998, SI 2002/2398, SI 2003/1075, SI 2003/2829, SI 2003/2830, SI 2003/2831, SI 2003/2907, SI 2003/3364, SI 2004/389, SI 2004/757, SI 2004/933, SI 2004/1817

s.6, enabling: SI 2002/1965, SI 2003/2907

s.6A, applied: SI 2002/1065, SI 2002/1327, SI 2002/1943, SI 2002/1997, SI 2002/1998, SI 2002/2398, SI 2003/2829, SI 2003/2830, SI 2003/2831, SI 2003/2907, SI 2004/389, SI 2004/757, SI 2004/933, SI 2004/1817

s.6A, enabling: SI 2003/2907

s.7, applied: SI 2002/366, SI 2002/412, SI 2002/1064, SI 2002/1065, SI 2002/1066, SI 2002/1327, SI 2002/1943, SI 2002/1997, SI 2002/1998, SI 2002/2398, SI 2003/1075, SI 2003/2829, SI 2003/2830, SI 2003/2831, SI 2003/2907, SI 2003/3364, 2004 c.5 s.106, s.107, SI 2004/389, SI 2004/757, SI 2004/933, SI 2004/1817

s.7, enabling: SI 2003/2907

s.9, applied: SI 2004/2018 r.4, r.15, r.20

1992–cont.

42. Transport and Works Act 1992–*cont.*

s.10, applied: SI 2002/366, SI 2002/412, SI 2002/1064, SI 2002/1065, SI 2002/1066, SI 2002/1327, SI 2002/1943, SI 2002/1997, SI 2002/1998, SI 2002/2398, SI 2003/1075, SI 2003/2829, SI 2003/2830, SI 2003/2831, SI 2003/2907, SI 2003/3364, SI 2004/389, SI 2004/757, SI 2004/933, SI 2004/1817

s.10, enabling: SI 2003/2907

s.11, applied: SI 2002/412, SI 2002/1064, SI 2002/1065, SI 2002/1066, SI 2002/1327, SI 2002/1998, SI 2003/1075, SI 2003/3364, SI 2004/389, SI 2004/757, SI 2004/2018 r.3

s.11, enabling: SI 2003/1075, SI 2004/389, SI 2004/757, SI 2004/3054

s.13, applied: SI 2003/3364

s.14, applied: SI 2004/2018 r.21

s.20, repealed (in part): SI 2003/1615 Sch.1 para.18

s.23, amended: SI 2002/2626 Sch.2 para.20

s.31, amended: 2002 c.30 s.58

s.31, applied: SI 2003/2462 Art.2

s.31, enabling: SI 2003/2462

s.31A, added: 2002 c.30 s.58

s.33, amended: 2002 c.30 s.58

s.34, amended: 2002 c.30 s.58

s.35, amended: 2002 c.30 s.58

s.38, amended: 2002 c.30 s.58

s.38, applied: SI 2003/2462 Art.2

s.38, enabling: SI 2003/2462

s.41, applied: SI 2002/412 Art.25, SI 2002/1066 Art.33, SI 2002/1997 Art.6, SI 2002/2398 Art.7, SI 2003/1075 Art.37, SI 2003/3364 Art.23, SI 2004/389 Art.35, SI 2004/757 Art.38, SI 2004/1817 Art.6

s.42, applied: SSI 2003/359 Art.9

s.50, repealed: 2004 c.14 Sch.1 Part 14

Sch.1 para.1, enabling: SI 2002/366, SI 2002/412, SI 2002/1064, SI 2002/1065, SI 2002/1066, SI 2002/1327, SI 2002/1943, SI 2002/1997, SI 2002/1998, SI 2002/2398, SI 2003/1075, SI 2003/2829, SI 2003/2830, SI 2003/2831, SI 2003/2907, SI 2003/3364, SI 2004/389, SI 2004/757, SI 2004/933, SI 2004/1817, SI 2004/3054, SI 2004/3126

Sch.1 para.2, enabling: SI 2002/412, SI 2002/1064, SI 2002/1065, SI 2002/1066, SI 2002/1327, SI 2002/1943, SI 2002/1998, SI 2003/1075, SI 2003/2829, SI 2003/2830, SI 2003/2831, SI 2003/2907, SI 2003/3364, SI 2004/389, SI 2004/757, SI 2004/933, SI 2004/3054

Sch.1 para.3, enabling: SI 2002/412, SI 2002/1064, SI 2002/1065, SI 2002/1066, SI 2002/1327, SI 2002/1943, SI 2002/2398, SI 2003/1075, SI 2003/3364, SI 2004/389, SI 2004/757, SI 2004/3054, SI 2004/3126

1992–cont.

42. Transport and Works Act 1992–*cont.*

Sch.1 para.4, enabling: SI 2002/412, SI 2002/1064, SI 2002/1065, SI 2002/1066, SI 2002/1327, SI 2002/1943, SI 2002/1998, SI 2003/1075, SI 2003/2829, SI 2003/2830, SI 2003/2831, SI 2003/3364, SI 2004/389, SI 2004/757, SI 2004/933, SI 2004/3054

Sch.1 para.5, enabling: SI 2002/412, SI 2002/1064, SI 2002/1065, SI 2003/1075, SI 2003/3364, SI 2004/389, SI 2004/3054

Sch.1 para.6, enabling: SI 2003/3364

Sch.1 para.7, enabling: SI 2002/366, SI 2002/412, SI 2002/1064, SI 2002/1065, SI 2002/1066, SI 2002/1327, SI 2002/1943, SI 2002/1998, SI 2003/1075, SI 2003/2829, SI 2003/2830, SI 2003/2831, SI 2003/3364, SI 2004/389, SI 2004/757, SI 2004/933, SI 2004/3054

Sch.1 para.8, enabling: SI 2002/412, SI 2002/1064, SI 2002/1066, SI 2002/1327, SI 2002/1943, SI 2002/1998, SI 2002/2398, SI 2003/1075, SI 2003/2829, SI 2003/2830, SI 2003/2831, SI 2003/3364, SI 2004/389, SI 2004/757, SI 2004/933, SI 2004/1817, SI 2004/3054, SI 2004/3126

Sch.1 para.9, enabling: SI 2002/412, SI 2002/1064, SI 2002/1327

Sch.1 para.10, enabling: SI 2002/412, SI 2002/1064, SI 2002/1065, SI 2002/1066, SI 2002/1327, SI 2002/1943, SI 2003/1075, SI 2003/2829, SI 2003/2830, SI 2003/2831, SI 2003/3364, SI 2004/389, SI 2004/757, SI 2004/933, SI 2004/3054

Sch.1 para.11, enabling: SI 2002/412, SI 2002/1064, SI 2002/1065, SI 2002/1066, SI 2002/1327, SI 2002/1943, SI 2003/1075, SI 2003/3364, SI 2004/389, SI 2004/757, SI 2004/3054

Sch.1 para.12, enabling: SI 2002/412, SI 2002/1327, SI 2002/1998

Sch.1 para.13, enabling: SI 2002/412, SI 2002/1064, SI 2002/1327, SI 2002/1998

Sch.1 para.15, enabling: SI 2002/412, SI 2002/1064, SI 2002/1065, SI 2002/1066, SI 2002/1327, SI 2002/1943, SI 2002/1997, SI 2002/2398, SI 2003/2829, SI 2003/2830, SI 2003/2831, SI 2003/3364, SI 2004/757, SI 2004/933, SI 2004/1817, SI 2004/3054, SI 2004/3126

Sch.1 para.16, enabling: SI 2002/366, SI 2002/412, SI 2002/1064, SI 2002/1065, SI 2002/1066, SI 2002/1327, SI 2002/1943, SI 2002/1998, SI 2003/1075, SI 2003/3364, SI 2004/389, SI 2004/757, SI 2004/3054

Sch.1 para.17, enabling: SI 2002/366, SI 2002/412, SI 2002/1065, SI 2002/1066, SI 2002/1327, SI 2002/1943, SI 2002/2398, SI 2003/1075, SI 2003/2829, SI

1992–cont.

42. Transport and Works Act 1992–*cont.*

Sch.1 para.17, enabling:–*cont.*

2003/2830, SI 2003/2831, SI 2003/3364, SI 2004/389, SI 2004/757, SI 2004/933, SI 2004/1817, SI 2004/3054, SI 2004/3126

43. Competition and Service (Utilities) Act 1992

s.1, repealed: 2003 c.21 Sch.19

s.2, repealed: 2003 c.21 Sch.19

s.3, repealed: 2003 c.21 Sch.19

s.4, repealed: 2003 c.21 Sch.19

s.5, repealed: 2003 c.21 Sch.19

s.6, repealed: 2003 c.21 Sch.19

s.7, repealed: 2003 c.21 Sch.19

s.8, repealed: 2003 c.21 Sch.19

s.9, repealed: 2003 c.21 Sch.19

s.10, repealed: 2003 c.21 Sch.19

s.49, repealed: 2003 c.21 Sch.19

s.50, repealed: 2003 c.37 Sch.7 para.30, Sch.9 Part 3

Sch.1 para.1, repealed: 2003 c.21 Sch.19

Sch.1 para.2, repealed: 2003 c.21 Sch.19

Sch.1 para.3, repealed (in part): 2003 c.21 Sch.19

Sch.1 para.4, repealed: 2003 c.21 Sch.19

44. Museums and Galleries Act 1992

s.8A, added: SI 2003/2867 Sch.1 para.21

48. Finance (No.2) Act 1992

s.1, enabling: SI 2002/501, SI 2002/2692, SI 2004/1003, SI 2004/2065

s.2, enabling: SI 2004/1003

s.35, repealed (in part): 2002 c.23 Sch.40 Part 3

s.37, repealed: 2003 c.1 Sch.8 Part 1

s.40A, applied: 2004 c.12 s.123

s.40B, applied: 2004 c.12 s.123

s.40C, applied: 2004 c.12 s.123

s.40D, applied: 2002 c.23 s.99, 2004 c.12 s.123

s.41, applied: 2002 c.23 s.99, 2004 c.12 s.123

s.42, applied: 2002 c.23 s.99, 2004 c.12 s.123

s.43, applied: 2004 c.12 s.123

s.54, repealed: 2003 c.1 Sch.8 Part 1

s.65, varied: SI 2004/2200 Reg.8

Sch.10 para.9, applied: SI 2002/2006 Reg.11, Reg.19

Sch.10 para.11, applied: SI 2002/2006 Reg.11

Sch.12 para.3, amended: 2002 c.23 s.107

Sch.12 para.3, repealed (in part): 2002 c.23 s.107, Sch.40 Part 3

Sch.12 para.4, repealed (in part): 2002 c.23 s.107, Sch.40 Part 3

see *Peakviewing (Interactive) Ltd v Secretary of State for Culture, Media and Sport* [2002] EWHC 1531, [2002] S.T.C. 1226 (QBD (Admin Ct)), Lawrence Collins, J.

50. Carriage of Goods by Sea Act 1992

s.1, amended: 2003 c.21 Sch.17 para.119

1992–cont.

50. Carriage of Goods by Sea Act 1992–*cont.*

s.2, see *East West Corp v DKBS 1912* [2002] EWHC 83, [2002] 1 All E.R. (Comm) 676 (QBD (Comm Ct)), Thomas, J.; see *East West Corp v DKBS 1912* [2003] EWCA Civ 83, [2003] Q.B.1509 (CA), Mance, L.J.

s.3, see *Borealis AB (formerly Borealis Petrokemi AB and Statoil Petrokemi AB) v Stargas Ltd (The Berge Sisar)* [2001] UKHL 17, [2002] 2 A.C. 205 (HL), Lord Hobhouse of Woodborough

s.5, see *East West Corp v DKBS 1912* [2002] EWHC 83, [2002] 1 All E.R. (Comm) 676 (QBD (Comm Ct)), Thomas, J.; see *East West Corp v DKBS 1912* [2003] EWCA Civ 83, [2003] Q.B.1509 (CA), Mance, L.J.

s.5, amended: 2003 c.21 Sch.19

51. Protection of Badgers Act 1992

s.1, amended: 2004 asp 6 Sch.6 para.26

s.1, repealed (in part): 2004 asp 6 Sch.6 para.26

s.6, amended: 2004 asp 6 Sch.6 para.26

s.8, amended: 2004 asp 6 Sch.6 para.26

s.8, repealed (in part): 2002 asp 6 Sch.1 para.5, 2004 c.37 Sch.3

s.9, amended: 2004 asp 6 Sch.6 para.26

s.10, amended: SI 2002/794 Sch.1 para.35

s.11, substituted: 2004 asp 6 Sch.6 para.26

s.11A, added: 2004 asp 6 Sch.6 para.26

s.12, amended: 2004 asp 6 Sch.6 para.26

s.12A, added: 2004 asp 6 Sch.6 para.26

s.12B, added: 2004 asp 6 Sch.6 para.26

s.13, amended: 2003 c.39 Sch.8 para.359, 2004 asp 6 Sch.6 para.26

52. Trade Union and Labour Relations (Consolidation) Act 1992

applied: 2002 c.22 s.45, SI 2003/722 Art.5, SI 2003/1660 Reg.33, SI 2003/1661 Reg.33, 2004 c.35 s.261, SI 2004/1168 Art.5

referred to: 2004 c.24 s.42

Part IV c.II, applied: SI 2002/377 Sch.1 para.36, SI 2002/3199 Sch.2 para.20, SI 2003/3118 Sch.2 para.20, SI 2003/3170 Sch.3 para.20, SI 2004/753 Sch.1 para.147

s.1, applied: 2003 c.20 s.30, SI 2004/753 Sch.1 para.147

s.5, applied: SI 2004/753 Sch.1 para.147

s.9, amended: 2004 c.24 s.51

s.9, repealed (in part): 2004 c.24 s.51, Sch.2

s.19, repealed (in part): 2004 c.24 Sch.1 para.3, Sch.2

s.23, amended: 2004 c.33 Sch.27 para.144

s.34, repealed (in part): 2004 c.24 s.53, Sch.2

s.36, amended: 2004 c.24 s.53

s.37, amended: 2004 c.24 s.53

s.41, amended: 2004 c.24 Sch.1 para.4

s.46, amended: 2004 c.24 s.52, Sch.2

s.49, enabling: SI 2002/2267

CAP.

1992–cont.

52. Trade Union and Labour Relations (Consolidation) Act 1992–*cont.*

s.54, amended: 2004 c.24 Sch.1 para.5
s.62, amended: 2004 c.24 s.24, Sch.2
s.67, amended: 2004 c.24 s.34, Sch.2
s.67, applied: SI 2002/2927 Art.4
s.67, repealed (in part): 2004 c.24 s.34, Sch.2
s.68, applied: SI 2004/1861 Sch.1 para.22
s.70C, applied: SI 2002/2927 Art.4
s.75, enabling: SI 2002/2267
s.82, amended: 2004 c.24 Sch.1 para.6
s.98, amended: 2004 c.24 s.50
s.100A, enabling: SI 2002/2267
s.101A, added: 2004 c.24 s.50
s.101B, added: 2004 c.24 s.50
s.103, amended: 2004 c.24 Sch.1 para.7
s.116A, added: 2004 c.24 s.55
s.118, amended: 2004 c.24 s.55
s.126, amended: 2004 c.24 s.51
s.126, repealed (in part): 2004 c.24 s.51, Sch.2
s.127, repealed (in part): SI 2002/3203 Art.4
s.133, amended: 2004 c.24 s.50, Sch.2
s.137, applied: SI 2002/2927 Art.4
s.138, applied: SI 2002/2927 Art.4
s.139, applied: SI 2002/2927 Art.4
s.145A, added: 2004 c.24 s.29
s.145A, applied: 2002 c.22 Sch.3, Sch.4, Sch.5
s.145B, added: 2004 c.24 s.29
s.145B, applied: 2002 c.22 Sch.3, Sch.4, Sch.5
s.145C, added: 2004 c.24 s.29
s.145D, added: 2004 c.24 s.29
s.145E, added: 2004 c.24 s.29
s.145F, added: 2004 c.24 s.29
s.146, amended: 2004 c.24 s.30, s.31, Sch.1 para.8, Sch.2
s.146, applied: 2002 c.22 Sch.3, Sch.4, Sch.5
s.146, varied: SI 2003/1964 Sch.1
s.147, varied: SI 2003/1964 Sch.1
s.148, amended: 2004 c.24 Sch.1 para.9
s.148, repealed (in part): 2004 c.24 Sch.2
s.150, amended: 2004 c.24 Sch.1 para.10
s.151, amended: 2004 c.24 s.30, s.31, Sch.2
s.152, amended: 2004 c.24 s.30, s.32, Sch.2
s.152, applied: SI 2002/10 Sch.1, SI 2003/3038 Sch.1
s.152, varied: SI 2003/1964 Sch.1
s.153, applied: SI 2002/10 Sch.1, SI 2003/3038 Sch.1
s.153, varied: SI 2003/1964 Sch.1
s.154, substituted: 2004 c.24 s.35
s.154, varied: SI 2003/1964 Sch.1
s.155, amended: 2004 c.24 Sch.1 para.11, Sch.2
s.155, disapplied: SI 2004/753 Sch.1 para.152, Sch.1 para.160
s.156, amended: SI 2002/10 Sch.1, SI 2002/2927 Sch.1, SI 2003/3038 Sch.1

CAP.

1992–cont.

52. Trade Union and Labour Relations (Consolidation) Act 1992–*cont.*

s.156, referred to: SI 2004/753 Sch.1 para.148
s.161, see *Dowling v Ilic (t/a ME Ilic Haulage)* [2004] I.C.R. 1176 (EAT), Burton, J.
s.161, amended: 2004 c.24 Sch.1 para.12
s.161, applied: SI 2004/1861 Sch.1 para.18
s.164, see *Dowling v Ilic (t/a ME Ilic Haulage)* [2004] I.C.R. 1176 (EAT), Burton, J.
s.168, applied: SI 2002/377 Sch.1 para.36, SI 2002/3199 Sch.2 para.20, SI 2002/3207 Reg.14, SI 2003/3118 Sch.2 para.20, SI 2003/3170 Sch.3 para.20, SI 2004/1861 Sch.1 para.22
s.168, referred to: SI 2002/3207 Reg.14
s.168A, added: 2002 c.22 s.43
s.169, amended: 2002 c.22 s.43
s.169, applied: SI 2002/3207 Reg.14, SI 2004/1861 Sch.1 para.22
s.170, amended: 2002 c.22 s.43
s.170, applied: SI 2002/377 Sch.1 para.36, SI 2002/3199 Sch.2 para.20, SI 2003/3118 Sch.2 para.20, SI 2003/3170 Sch.3 para.20, SI 2004/1861 Sch.1 para.22
s.171, amended: 2002 c.22 Sch.7 para.19
s.171, applied: SI 2002/3207 Reg.14
s.172, amended: 2002 c.22 Sch.7 para.20
s.172, applied: SI 2002/3207 Reg.14
s.173, amended: 2002 c.22 s.43, Sch.7 para.21
s.173, applied: SI 2002/3207 Reg.14
s.174, amended: 2004 c.24 s.33
s.174, applied: SI 2002/10 Sch.1, SI 2003/3038 Sch.1
s.174, referred to: 2004 c.24 s.33
s.176, amended: SI 2002/10 Sch.1, SI 2002/2927 Sch.1, SI 2003/3038 Sch.1, 2004 c.24 s.33, s.34, Sch.2
s.176, applied: SI 2002/2927 Art.4
s.176, referred to: 2004 c.24 s.33
s.178, see *Prison Service v Bewley* [2004] I.C.R. 422 (EAT), Judge Peter Clark; see *Transport and General Workers Union v Asda* [2004] I.R.L.R. 836 (Central Arbitration Committee), Professor Kenny Miller (Deputy Chairman)
s.178, referred to: SI 2004/1861 Sch.1 para.16
s.181, varied: SI 2003/1964 Sch.1
s.182, varied: SI 2003/1964 Sch.1
s.183, varied: SI 2003/1964 Sch.1
s.184, varied: SI 2003/1964 Sch.1
s.185, varied: SI 2003/1964 Sch.1
s.188, see *GMB v Amicus (AEEU & MSF)* [2003] I.C.R. 1396 (EAT), Mitting, J.; see *Middlesbrough BC v TGWU* [2002] I.R.L.R. 332 (EAT), Judge Peter Clark; see *MSF v Refuge Assurance Plc* [2002] 2 C.M.L.R. 27 (EAT), Lindsay, J. (President); see *Securicor Omega Express Ltd v GMB (A Trade Union)* [2004] I.R.L.R. 9 (EAT), Burton, J.; see *Susie Radin Ltd v GMB*

CAP.

1992–cont.

52. Trade Union and Labour Relations (Consolidation) Act 1992–*cont.*

s.188–*cont.*

[2004] EWCA Civ 180, [2004] 2 All E.R. 279 (CA), Peter Gibson, L.J.

s.188, applied: SI 2004/752 Reg.4

s.189, see *Susie Radin Ltd v GMB* [2004] EWCA Civ 180, [2004] 2 All E.R. 279 (CA), Peter Gibson, L.J.

s.189, applied: SI 2002/2822 Reg.39

s.192, applied: SI 2004/1861 Sch.1 para.22

s.196, applied: SI 2002/377 Sch.1 para.36

s.196, referred to: SI 2002/3199 Sch.2 para.20, SI 2003/3118 Sch.2 para.20, SI 2003/3170 Sch.3 para.20

s.199, amended: 2002 c.22 s.43

s.199, applied: SI 2004/2356

s.199, referred to: SI 2003/1191

s.199, enabling: SI 2004/2356

s.200, amended: 2002 c.22 s.43

s.200, applied: SI 2003/1191, SI 2004/2356, SI 2004/2356 Art.2

s.200, enabling: SI 2003/1191, SI 2004/2356

s.201, enabling: SI 2003/1191

s.203, amended: 2002 c.22 s.43

s.210A, added: 2004 c.24 s.21

s.211, applied: SI 2003/1660 Sch.4 para.2, SI 2003/1661 Sch.4 para.2

s.212A, amended: 2002 c.22 Sch.7 para.22

s.212A, applied: SI 2003/694, SI 2003/694 Sch.1 para.1, SI 2003/1660 Sch.4 para.2, SI 2003/1661 Sch.4 para.2, SI 2004/753, SI 2004/753 Sch.1 para.1, SI 2004/2333, SI 2004/2333 Sch.1 para.1

s.212A, enabling: SI 2003/694, SI 2004/753, SI 2004/2333

s.219, see *British Telecommunications Plc v Communication Workers Union* [2003] EWHC 937, [2004] I.R.L.R. 58 (QBD), Stanley Burnton, J.

s.219, referred to: SI 2003/1964 Art.5

s.220, applied: 2003 c.38 s.30, 2004 asp 8 s.21

s.226, see *P v National Association of School Masters Union of Women Teachers (NASUWT)* [2003] UKHL 8, [2003] 2 A.C. 663 (HL), Lord Bingham of Cornhill

s.226A, see *British Telecommunications Plc v Communication Workers Union* [2003] EWHC 937, [2004] I.R.L.R. 58 (QBD), Stanley Burnton, J.

s.226A, amended: 2004 c.24 s.22

s.226A, repealed (in part): 2004 c.24 s.22, Sch.2

s.226B, enabling: SI 2002/2267

s.227, see *P v National Association of School Masters Union of Women Teachers (NASUWT)* [2003] UKHL 8, [2003] 2 A.C. 663 (HL), Lord Bingham of Cornhill

s.227, amended: 2004 c.24 s.23

CAP.

1992–cont.

52. Trade Union and Labour Relations (Consolidation) Act 1992–*cont.*

s.228, see *P v National Association of School Masters Union of Women Teachers (NASUWT)* [2003] UKHL 8, [2003] 2 A.C. 663 (HL), Lord Bingham of Cornhill

s.229, see *P v National Association of School Masters Union of Women Teachers (NASUWT)* [2003] UKHL 8, [2003] 2 A.C. 663 (HL), Lord Bingham of Cornhill

s.229, amended: 2004 c.24 Sch.1 para.13

s.230, see *P v National Association of School Masters Union of Women Teachers (NASUWT)* [2003] UKHL 8, [2003] 2 A.C. 663 (HL), Lord Bingham of Cornhill

s.232, see *P v National Association of School Masters Union of Women Teachers (NASUWT)* [2003] UKHL 8, [2003] 2 A.C. 663 (HL), Lord Bingham of Cornhill

s.232B, amended: 2004 c.24 s.24

s.233, amended: 2004 c.24 Sch.1 para.14

s.234A, see *British Telecommunications Plc v Communication Workers Union* [2003] EWHC 937, [2004] I.R.L.R. 58 (QBD), Stanley Burnton, J.

s.234A, amended: 2004 c.24 s.25

s.234A, repealed (in part): 2004 c.24 s.25, Sch.2

s.237, see *Balfour Kilpatrick Ltd v Acheson* [2003] I.R.L.R. 683 (EAT), Elias, J.

s.237, amended: 2004 c.24 s.40, s.41

s.237, applied: SI 2003/3319 Reg.7

s.238, amended: 2004 c.24 s.40, s.41

s.238, applied: SI 2004/752 Reg.4

s.238A, amended: 2004 c.24 s.26, s.27, s.28

s.238A, applied: SI 2004/752 Reg.4, SI 2004/1861 Sch.1 para.55

s.238B, added: 2004 c.24 s.28

s.240, amended: 2003 c.44 Sch.37 Part 9 Sch.25 para.95

s.241, amended: 2004 c.33 Sch.27 para.145

s.244, see *British Telecommunications Plc v Communication Workers Union* [2003] EWHC 937, [2004] I.R.L.R. 58 (QBD), Stanley Burnton, J.; see *P v National Association of School Masters Union of Women Teachers (NASUWT)* [2003] UKHL 8, [2003] 2 A.C. 663 (HL), Lord Bingham of Cornhill; see *UNISON v United Kingdom (Admissibility) (53574/99)* [2002] I.R.L.R. 497 (ECHR), G Ress (President)

s.244, referred to: SI 2003/1964 Art.5

s.256A, repealed (in part): 2004 c.24 s.49, Sch.2

s.256ZA, added: 2004 c.24 s.48

s.263A, amended: 2004 c.24 Sch.1 para.15

s.279, amended: 2002 c.17 Sch.2 para.60, Sch.3 para.13, 2003 c.43 Sch.11 para.59, Sch.14 Part 4, SI 2004/957 Sch.1 para.7

s.279, referred to: SI 2004/865 Art.112

1992–cont.

52. Trade Union and Labour Relations (Consolidation) Act 1992–*cont.*

s.279, varied: SI 2004/288 Art.7, SI 2004/480 Art.6, SI 2004/865 Art.109, Art.112, SI 2004/1016 Art.85, Art.88, SSI 2004/163 Art.96, Art.99

s.280, varied: 2002 c.30 Sch.3 para.19

s.284, amended: 2004 c.24 Sch.1 para.16

s.285, amended: 2004 c.24 Sch.1 para.17

s.286, amended: 2004 c.24 Sch.1 para.18

s.288, applied: SI 2004/754 Art.2, Art.3

s.288, repealed (in part): 2004 c.24 Sch.1 para.19, Sch.2

s.288, enabling: SI 2004/754, SI 2004/2515

s.292, amended: 2004 c.24 Sch.1 para.20, 2004 c.33 Sch.27 para.146

s.292, repealed (in part): 2004 c.24 Sch.1 para.20, Sch.2

s.296, see *R. (on the application of BBC) v Central Arbitration Committee* [2003] EWHC 1375, [2003] I.C.R. 1542 (QBD (Admin Ct)), Moses, J.

s.296, amended: 2004 c.24 Sch.1 para.21

s.298, amended: 2004 c.24 s.50

s.299, amended: 2004 c.24 s.50, Sch.1 para.22, Sch.2

Sch.A1, see *Transport and General Workers Union v Asda* [2004] I.R.L.R. 836 (Central Arbitration Committee), Professor Kenny Miller (Deputy Chairman)

Sch.A1 Part I para.1, see *R. (on the application of BBC) v Central Arbitration Committee* [2003] EWHC 1375, [2003] I.C.R. 1542 (QBD (Admin Ct)), Moses, J.

Sch.A1 Part I para.2, amended: 2004 c.24 Sch.1 para.23

Sch.A1 Part I para.6, amended: 2004 c.24 s.50

Sch.A1 Part I para.11, amended: 2004 c.24 s.1

Sch.A1 Part I para.12, amended: 2004 c.24 s.1

Sch.A1 Part I para.16, amended: 2004 c.24 Sch.1 para.23

Sch.A1 Part I para.17, amended: 2004 c.24 Sch.1 para.23

Sch.A1 Part I para.18, amended: 2004 c.24 s.2

Sch.A1 Part I para.18A, added: 2004 c.24 s.3

Sch.A1 Part I para.19, substituted: 2004 c.24 s.4

Sch.A1 Part I para.19C, added: 2004 c.24 s.5

Sch.A1 Part I para.19D, added: 2004 c.24 s.5

Sch.A1 Part I para.19E, added: 2004 c.24 s.5

Sch.A1 Part I para.19F, added: 2004 c.24 s.5

Sch.A1 Part I para.20, amended: 2004 c.24 Sch.1 para.23

Sch.A1 Part I para.21, amended: 2004 c.24 Sch.1 para.23

Sch.A1 Part I para.22, amended: 2004 c.24 s.5, s.6, s.7

Sch.A1 Part I para.23, amended: 2004 c.24 s.5

1992–cont.

52. Trade Union and Labour Relations (Consolidation) Act 1992–*cont.*

Sch.A1 Part I para.25, amended: 2004 c.24 s.8

Sch.A1 Part I para.25, enabling: SI 2002/2268

Sch.A1 Part I para.26, amended: 2004 c.24 s.5, s.9

Sch.A1 Part I para.27, amended: 2004 c.24 s.9

Sch.A1 Part I para.27A, added: 2004 c.24 s.10

Sch.A1 Part I para.27B, added: 2004 c.24 s.10

Sch.A1 Part I para.27C, added: 2004 c.24 s.10

Sch.A1 Part I para.27D, added: 2004 c.24 s.10

Sch.A1 Part I para.27E, added: 2004 c.24 s.10

Sch.A1 Part I para.27F, added: 2004 c.24 s.10

Sch.A1 Part I para.28, amended: 2004 c.24 Sch.1 para.23

Sch.A1 Part I para.29, amended: 2004 c.24 s.10

Sch.A1 Part I para.32, amended: 2004 c.24 Sch.1 para.23

Sch.A1 Part I para.35, amended: 2004 c.24 s.11, s.50

Sch.A1 Part I para.37, amended: 2004 c.24 Sch.1 para.23

Sch.A1 Part I para.38, amended: 2004 c.24 Sch.1 para.23

Sch.A1 Part I para.40, amended: 2004 c.24 Sch.1 para.23

Sch.A1 Part I para.41, amended: 2004 c.24 Sch.1 para.23

Sch.A1 Part I para.44, amended: 2004 c.24 s.11, s.50

Sch.A1 Part I para.46, amended: 2004 c.24 Sch.1 para.23

Sch.A1 Part I para.48, amended: 2004 c.24 Sch.1 para.23

Sch.A1 Part I para.49, amended: 2004 c.24 Sch.1 para.23

Sch.A1 Part I para.51, amended: 2004 c.24 Sch.1 para.23

Sch.A1 Part II para.52, amended: 2004 c.24 Sch.1 para.23

Sch.A1 Part II para.60, amended: 2004 c.24 s.50

Sch.A1 Part III para.83, amended: 2004 c.24 Sch.1 para.23

Sch.A1 Part III para.87, amended: 2004 c.24 s.6

Sch.A1 Part III para.89, amended: 2004 c.24 Sch.1 para.23

Sch.A1 Part III para.93, amended: 2004 c.24 Sch.1 para.23

Sch.A1 Part IV para.99, amended: 2004 c.24 s.12

Sch.A1 Part IV para.99A, added: 2004 c.24 s.12

Sch.A1 Part IV para.100, amended: 2004 c.24 s.12

1992–cont.

52. Trade Union and Labour Relations (Consolidation) Act 1992–*cont.*

Sch.A1 Part IV para.101, repealed (in part): 2004 c.24 s.12, Sch.2

Sch.A1 Part IV para.103, amended: 2004 c.24 s.12

Sch.A1 Part IV para.109, amended: 2004 c.24 s.12

Sch.A1 Part IV para.109, repealed (in part): 2004 c.24 s.12, Sch.2

Sch.A1 Part IV para.113, amended: 2004 c.24 s.12

Sch.A1 Part IV para.113, repealed (in part): 2004 c.24 s.12, Sch.2

Sch.A1 Part IV para.117, amended: 2004 c.24 s.8

Sch.A1 Part IV para.117, enabling: SI 2002/2268

Sch.A1 Part IV para.118, amended: 2004 c.24 s.9

Sch.A1 Part IV para.119, amended: 2004 c.24 s.9

Sch.A1 Part IV para.119, repealed (in part): 2004 c.24 Sch.1 para.23, Sch.2

Sch.A1 Part IV para.119A, added: 2004 c.24 s.13

Sch.A1 Part IV para.119B, added: 2004 c.24 s.13

Sch.A1 Part IV para.119C, added: 2004 c.24 s.13

Sch.A1 Part IV para.119D, added: 2004 c.24 s.13

Sch.A1 Part IV para.119E, added: 2004 c.24 s.13

Sch.A1 Part IV para.119F, added: 2004 c.24 s.13

Sch.A1 Part IV para.119G, added: 2004 c.24 s.13

Sch.A1 Part IV para.119H, added: 2004 c.24 s.13

Sch.A1 Part IV para.119I, added: 2004 c.24 s.13

Sch.A1 Part IV para.120, repealed (in part): 2004 c.24 Sch.1 para.23

Sch.A1 Part IV para.121, amended: 2004 c.24 s.13

Sch.A1 Part V para.122, amended: 2004 c.24 Sch.1 para.23

Sch.A1 Part V para.123, amended: 2004 c.24 Sch.1 para.23

Sch.A1 Part V para.130, amended: 2004 c.24 s.12

Sch.A1 Part V para.130, repealed (in part): 2004 c.24 s.12, Sch.2

Sch.A1 Part V para.133, amended: 2004 c.24 Sch.1 para.23

Sch.A1 Part VI para.134, amended: 2004 c.24 s.50

Sch.A1 Part VI para.138, amended: 2004 c.24 s.50

1992–cont.

52. Trade Union and Labour Relations (Consolidation) Act 1992–*cont.*

Sch.A1 Part VI para.147, amended: 2004 c.24 Sch.1 para.23

Sch.A1 Part VIII para.156, applied: 2002 c.22 Sch.3, Sch.4, Sch.5

Sch.A1 Part IX para.165A, added: 2004 c.24 s.14

Sch.A1 Part IX para.166, amended: 2004 c.24 s.15, SI 2004/3342 Art.6

Sch.A1 Part IX para.166A, added: 2004 c.24 s.16

Sch.A1 Part IX para.166B, added: 2004 c.24 s.17

Sch.A1 Part IX para.169A, added: 2004 c.24 s.18

Sch.A1 Part IX para.169B, added: 2004 c.24 s.18

Sch.A1 Part IX para.169C, added: 2004 c.24 s.18

Sch.A1 Part IX para.170A, added: 2004 c.24 s.19

Sch.A1 Part IX para.171A, added: 2004 c.24 s.20

Sch.A1 para.11, see *R. (on the application of Kwik-Fit Ltd) v Central Arbitration Committee* [2002] EWCA Civ 512, [2002] I.C.R. 1212 (CA), Buxton, L.J.

Sch.A1 para.19, see *R. (on the application of Kwik-Fit Ltd) v Central Arbitration Committee* [2002] EWCA Civ 512, [2002] I.C.R. 1212 (CA), Buxton, L.J.

Sch.A1 para.22, see *Fullarton Computer Industries Ltd v Central Arbitration Committee* 2002 S.L.T. 13 (OH), Lord Johnston

Sch.2 para.27, repealed: 2004 c.14 Sch.1 Part 2

53. Tribunals and Inquiries Act 1992

applied: 2004 c.5 s.114

disapplied: SI 2003/956

s.1, applied: 2004 c.5 s.8

s.2, amended: SI 2004/1823 Art.14

s.7, amended: 2004 c.35 Sch.12 para.8

s.7, repealed (in part): 2004 c.19 Sch.2 para.7, Sch.4

s.8, applied: SI 2002/37, SI 2002/126, SI 2002/247, SI 2002/276, SI 2002/422, SI 2002/529, SI 2002/553, SI 2002/643, SI 2002/770, SI 2002/1204, SI 2002/1351, SI 2002/1352, SI 2002/1353, SI 2002/1379, SI 2002/1484, SI 2002/1485, SI 2002/1486, SI 2002/1504, SI 2002/1621, SI 2002/1703, SI 2002/1921, SI 2002/1985, SI 2002/2012, SI 2002/2183, SI 2002/2184, SI 2002/2185, SI 2002/2186, SI 2002/2187, SI 2002/2188, SI 2002/2440, SI 2002/2520, SI 2002/2550, SI 2002/2705, SI 2002/2722, SI 2002/2787, SI 2002/2851, SI 2002/2972, SI 2002/2976, SI 2002/3176, SI 2002/3178, SI 2002/3179, SI

CAP.

1992–cont.

53. Tribunals and Inquiries Act 1992–*cont.*
s.8, applied:–*cont.*
2002/3196, SI 2002/3198, SI 2002/3237, SI 2002/3265, SI 2002/3266, SI 2003/95, SI 2003/287, SI 2003/463, SI 2003/512, SI 2003/626, SI 2003/634, SI 2003/635, SI 2003/652, SI 2003/801, SI 2003/898, SI 2003/916, SI 2003/968, SI 2003/1060, SI 2003/1261, SI 2003/1262, SI 2003/1372, SI 2003/1581, SI 2003/1735, SI 2003/1886, SI 2003/1924, SI 2003/1984, SI 2003/2043, SI 2003/2152, SI 2003/2153, SI 2003/2171, SI 2003/2334, SI 2003/2336, SI 2003/2439, SI 2003/2440, SI 2003/2597, SI 2003/2677, SI 2003/2711, SI 2003/2757, SI 2003/2945, SI 2003/3227, SI 2003/3246, SI 2004/104, SI 2004/402, SI 2004/565, SI 2004/664, SI 2004/914, SI 2004/947, SI 2004/948, SI 2004/959, SI 2004/1032, SI 2004/1278, SI 2004/1285, SI 2004/1305, SI 2004/1402, SI 2004/1608, SI 2004/1805, SI 2004/1861, SI 2004/1891, SI 2004/2028, SI 2004/2073, SI 2004/2111, SI 2004/2188, SI 2004/2193, SI 2004/2194, SI 2004/2212, SI 2004/2244, SI 2004/2260, SI 2004/2351, SI 2004/2424, SI 2004/2616, SI 2004/2682, SI 2004/3052, SSI 2002/63, SSI 2002/400, SSI 2003/71, SSI 2003/452, SSI 2003/521, SSI 2004/38, SSI 2004/86, SSI 2004/122, SSI 2004/271, SSI 2004/480

s.8, enabling: SI 2002/3198, SI 2003/513, SI 2004/948, SI 2004/3205

s.9, applied: SI 2003/394 Reg.8

s.9, enabling: SI 2002/1223, SI 2002/2684, SI 2002/2685, SI 2002/2686, SI 2003/1266, SI 2003/1267, SI 2003/1268, SI 2003/1269, SI 2003/1270, SI 2003/1271, SI 2004/2018

s.10, repealed (in part): 2004 c.35 Sch.13 Part 1

s.11, see *R. (on the application of S (A Child)) v Oxfordshire CC* [2004] EWHC 133, [2004] E.L.R. 489 (QBD (Admin Ct)), Andrew Nicol Q.C.; see *R. (on the application of Wolters (London) Ltd) v London Rent Assessment Committee* [2003] EWHC 1465, [2003] 3 E.G.L.R. 17 (QBD (Admin Ct)), Harrison, J.; see *Southampton City Council v G* [2002] EWHC 1516, [2002] E.L.R. 698 (QBD (Admin Ct)), Sullivan, J.

s.11, amended: 2002 c.40 Sch.25 para.27

s.11, applied: 2002 c.15 s.175, SSI 2004/38 Reg.21, Reg.23, Reg.25

s.11, disapplied: 2004 c.34 s.231

s.13, enabling: SI 2003/756, SI 2004/594, SSI 2004/119

s.14, amended: 2002 c.40 Sch.25 para.27, 2004 c.35 Sch.12 para.8

Sch.1 Part I, added: 2002 c.9 Sch.9 para.8

CAP.

1992–cont.

53. Tribunals and Inquiries Act 1992–*cont.*
Sch.1 Part I, amended: 2002 c.32 Sch.18 para.15, 2002 c.41 Sch.7 para.17, SI 2002/2469 Sch.1 para.19, 2003 c.21 Sch.19, 2003 c.39 Sch.8 para.360, Sch.10, SI 2003/756 Art.2, 2004 c.7 Sch.1 para.9, 2004 c.19 Sch.2 para.7, 2004 c.35 Sch.12 para.8, Sch.13 Part 1

Sch.1 Part I, substituted: 2002 c.32 Sch.21 para.22, 2002 c.40 Sch.25 para.27, 2004 c.18 Sch.11 para.5, SI 2004/594 Art.2

Sch.1 Part I, varied: SSI 2002/398 Art.6, SSI 2003/70 Art.6, SSI 2004/87 Art.6

Sch.1 Part II, added: 2004 asp 4 Sch.3 para.8

Sch.1 Part II, amended: 2003 asp 11 Sch.1 para.48, 2003 asp 13 Sch.4 para.5, SSI 2004/119 Art.2

Sch.1 Part II, repealed: 2003 c.43 Sch.14 Part 3

Sch.3 para.13, repealed (in part): 2002 c.15 Sch.14

57. Sporting Events (Control of Alcohol etc.) (Amendment) Act 1992
repealed: 2003 c.17 Sch.7

58. Car Tax (Abolition) Act 1992
repealed: 2004 c.14 Sch.1 Part 9

1993

Asylum and Immigration Act 1993
Sch.2 para.5, see *Secretary of State for the Home Department v Vairavanathan* [2002] EWCA Civ 1310, [2003] Imm. A.R. 81 (CA), Schiemann, L.J.

ix. London Underground (Jubilee) Act 1993
see *Thames Water Utilities Ltd v London Underground Ltd* [2004] EWCA Civ 615, (2004) 148 S.J.L.B. 633 (CA), Brooke, L.J.

1. Incumbents (Vacation of Benefices) (Amendment) Measure 1993
applied: SI 2002/1893 para.4, SI 2003/1936 para.4

3. Social Security Act 1993
s.2, applied: SI 2002/830, SI 2003/963, SI 2003/963 Art.4
s.2, varied: SI 2004/889 Art.5
s.2, enabling: SI 2002/830, SI 2003/963, SI 2004/889

8. Judicial Pensions and Retirement Act 1993
applied: 2002 c.9 Sch.9 para.2
referred to: SI 2003/2916 Reg.2
Part I, applied: 2003 asp 13 Sch.2 para.6
s.1, enabling: SI 2002/1347, SI 2002/3083, SI 2003/1311, SI 2003/2589, SI 2003/2775
s.13, applied: SI 2003/2916 Reg.2
s.13, varied: SI 2003/2916 Reg.4
s.25, repealed (in part): SI 2004/1823 Art.15
s.26, applied: 2002 c.9 Sch.9 para.1, 2002 c.41 Sch.4 para.1, Sch.5 para.2

CAP.

1993-cont.

8. Judicial Pensions and Retirement Act 1993-*cont.*
s.26, repealed (in part): 2003 c.21 Sch.19

Sch.1 Part II, amended: 2002 c.41 Sch.7 para.18, SI 2002/1347 Art.3, SI 2002/3083 Art.2, 2003 c.39 Sch.10, SI 2003/1311 Art.2, SI 2003/2589 Art.2, SI 2003/2775 Art.2, 2004 c.19 Sch.2 para.8, 2004 c.35 Sch.4 para.17

Sch.5, amended: 2002 c.9 Sch.11 para.28, 2002 c.32 Sch.22 Part 3, 2002 c.41 Sch.7 para.19, 2003 c.21 Sch.19, 2003 c.39 s.89, Sch.10, 2004 c.19 Sch.2 para.8, 2004 c.35 Sch.4 para.17

Sch.6 para.14, repealed (in part): 2003 c.39 Sch.10

Sch.6 para.58, repealed: 2003 c.21 Sch.19

Sch.7 para.5, repealed (in part): 2002 c.32 Sch.22 Part 3, 2003 c.21 Sch.19

9. Prisoners and Criminal Proceedings (Scotland) Act 1993
applied: 2003 asp 7 s.16

disapplied: 2003 asp 7 s.27

referred to: SSI 2003/184 Reg.7

Part I, applied: 2003 asp 5 s.14, 2003 asp 7 s.40, 2003 asp 13 s.217

s.1, amended: 2003 asp 7 s.28

s.1, applied: SI 2003/762 Reg.2, SI 2004/1748 Sch.1, SSI 2003/243 Reg.2, SSI 2003/287 Art.2

s.1, referred to: 2003 asp 7 s.28, SSI 2003/287 Art.2

s.1A, amended: 2003 asp 7 Sch.4 para.2

s.1A, substituted: 2003 asp 7 s.30

s.2, see *Ansari (Yusuf) v HM Advocate* 2003 J.C. 105 (HCJ), Lord Gill L.J.C., Lord Kirkwood, Lord Marnoch, Lord McCluskey, Lord Reed; see *McWilliam, Petitioner* 2002 S.L.T. 972 (HCJ Appeal), Lord Hamilton, Lord Reed, Lord Drummond Young; see *Wright (Gavin Raymond) v HM Advocate* 2003 J.C. 135 (HCJ), Lord Gill L.J.C., Lord Kirkwood, Lord Marnoch, Lord McCluskey, Lord Reed

s.2, amended: 2003 asp 7 s.29, Sch.1 para.1, Sch.5

s.3A, amended: 2003 asp 7 s.31

s.4, amended: 2003 asp 13 Sch.4 para.6

s.4, repealed (in part): 2003 asp 13 Sch.5 Part 1

s.5, amended: 2003 asp 7 s.29, s.36

s.7, amended: 2003 asp 7 s.38

s.7, applied: 2003 asp 7 s.40, SSI 2003/287 Art.2

s.7, referred to: SSI 2003/287 Art.2

s.7, repealed (in part): 2003 asp 7 s.38

s.10, amended: 2003 asp 7 Sch.4 para.2, 2003 c.44 Sch.32 para.66

s.10, applied: SSI 2003/179 Reg.3, Reg.9

s.10, repealed (in part): 2003 c.44 Sch.32 para.66, Sch.37 Part 7

CAP.

1993-cont.

9. Prisoners and Criminal Proceedings (Scotland) Act 1993-*cont.*
s.12, amended: 2003 asp 7 s.28, s.35

s.12, applied: 2003 asp 7 s.40, SSI 2003/287 Art.2

s.12, referred to: SSI 2003/287 Art.2

s.12A, added: 2003 asp 7 s.35

s.12B, added: 2003 asp 7 s.35

s.15, amended: 2003 asp 7 s.60

s.16, repealed (in part): 2003 asp 7 s.36

s.17, amended: 2003 asp 7 s.36

s.18, amended: 2003 asp 7 s.60

s.20, repealed (in part): 2003 asp 7 s.28

s.26A, amended: 2003 asp 7 s.37

s.26B, added: 2003 asp 7 s.41

s.27, amended: 2003 asp 7 s.32, Sch.1 para.1

s.45, amended: 2003 asp 7 Sch.4 para.2

s.47, applied: 2003 asp 7 s.27

Sch.1 para.2, substituted: 2003 asp 7 s.32

Sch.1 para.3, repealed: 2003 asp 7 s.32

Sch.1 para.4, repealed: 2003 asp 7 s.32

Sch.2 para.3D, enabling: SSI 2003/184

Sch.2 para.6B, applied: SSI 2003/184

Sch.5 para.2, repealed: 2003 asp 13 Sch.5 Part 1

Sch.6, applied: 2003 asp 7 s.34, Sch.4 para.1

Sch.6 para.1, amended: 2003 asp 7 s.33

Sch.6 para.2, applied: 2003 asp 7 s.27

10. Charities Act 1993
applied: SI 2002/1714 Art.4, SI 2002/1792 Sch.5 para.28, SI 2003/1881 Art.2, 2004 c.35 Sch.3, Sch.8, SI 2004/1995 Art.2, SI 2004/2042 Reg.31, SR 2003/28 Sch.5 para.28, 2004 c.iv s.11

Part VII, applied: SI 2003/1417 r.177

s.3, applied: 2003 c.ii s.7

s.3, enabling: SI 2002/1598

s.13, see *Attorney General v Hyde* [2002] W.T.L.R. 1419 (Ch D), Lawrence Collins, J.

s.15, applied: SI 2004/1986

s.15, enabling: SI 2004/1986

s.16, applied: SI 2003/1417 r.178

s.17, applied: SI 2003/1688, SI 2004/160

s.17, referred to: SI 2004/160

s.17, enabling: SI 2003/1688, SI 2004/160

s.18, applied: SI 2003/1417 r.178

s.20, applied: SI 2003/1688, SI 2004/160

s.21, applied: SI 2003/1417 r.178

s.36, see *Barnes v Derby Diocesan Board of Finance* [2002] EWHC 2940, [2003] 5 Ch. 239 (Ch D), Etherton, J.; see *Bayoumi v Women's Total Abstinence Educational Union Ltd* [2003] EWCA Civ 1548, [2004] Ch. 46 (CA), Chadwick, L.J.; see *Bayoumi v Women's Total Abstinence Educational Union Ltd* [2003] EWHC 212, [2003] 5 Ch. 283 (Ch D), Simon Berry Q.C.

s.37, see *Bayoumi v Women's Total Abstinence Educational Union Ltd* [2003] EWCA Civ 1548, [2004] Ch. 46 (CA), Chadwick,

1993–cont.

10. Charities Act 1993–cont.
s.37–cont.
L.J.; see *Bayoumi v Women's Total Absti-nence Educational Union Ltd* [2003] EWHC 212, [2003] 5 Ch. 283 (Ch D), Si-mon Berry Q.C.
s.37, amended: 2002 c.9 Sch.11 para.29
s.37, applied: SI 2003/1417 r.176, r.179, r.180
s.37, enabling: SI 2003/1417
s.39, amended: 2002 c.9 Sch.11 para.29
s.39, applied: SI 2003/1417 r.176, r.180
s.39, enabling: SI 2003/1417
s.50, applied: SI 2003/1417 r.177
s.65, see *Bayoumi v Women's Total Abstinence Educational Union Ltd* [2003] EWCA Civ 1548, [2004] Ch. 46 (CA), Chadwick, L.J.
s.72, amended: SI 2004/1941 Sch.1 para.5
s.99, repealed: 2004 c.14 Sch.1 Part 17
Sch.1 para.2, applied: 2004 c.27 Sch.3 para.4
Sch.2, enabling: SI 2002/1626, SI 2003/1881, SI 2004/1995
Sch.5 para.1, amended: 2004 c.33 Sch.27 para.147
Sch.5 para.2, varied: 2004 c.33 Sch.21 para.38
Sch.6 para.27, repealed: 2003 c.17 Sch.7
Sch.8 Part I para.1, repealed: 2004 c.14 Sch.1 Part 17
Sch.8 Part I para.2, repealed: 2004 c.14 Sch.1 Part 17
Sch.8 Part II, repealed: 2004 c.14 Sch.1 Part 17

11. Clean Air Act 1993
applied: 2002 c.40 Sch.14, Sch.15, SSI 2003/129 Sch.2 para.4
referred to: SSI 2004/70 Sch.2 para.4
s.16, amended: 2003 asp 8 Sch.6 para.20
s.16, applied: 2003 asp 8 Sch.6 para.20
s.20, applied: SSI 2003/436 Sch.1
s.20, disapplied: SI 2003/2328 Art.2, SI 2003/2727 Art.2
s.20, enabling: SI 2002/3046, SI 2002/3160, SSI 2002/527
s.21, enabling: SI 2003/2328, SI 2003/2727, SSI 2003/436
s.30, amended: 2004 c.14 Sch.1 Part 13
s.30, applied: SI 2003/3078
s.30, enabling: SI 2003/3078
s.63, enabling: SI 2002/3046, SI 2002/3160, SI 2003/3078, SSI 2002/527
s.68, repealed (in part): 2004 c.14 Sch.1 Part 13

12. Radioactive Substances Act 1993
applied: SR 2003/208 Reg.3
s.2, referred to: SI 2003/2454 Sch.3, SI 2003/2761 Sch.3
s.7, applied: SI 2002/1177 Art.2, SR 2003/95 Art.3, 2004 c.20 s.10
s.8, enabling: SI 2002/1177, SR 2003/95
s.13, see *R. (on the application of Marchiori) v Environment Agency* [2002] EWCA Civ 3, [2002] Eu. L.R. 225 (CA), Laws, L.J.

1993–cont.

12. Radioactive Substances Act 1993–cont.
s.13, applied: SR 2003/46 Sch.1 Part 1, 2004 c.20 s.10
s.13, disapplied: SI 2002/1177 Art.3, SR 2003/95 Art.4
s.14, applied: 2004 c.20 s.10
s.14, disapplied: SI 2002/1177 Art.3, SR 2003/95 Art.4
s.15, amended: SR 2003/208 Reg.4
s.15, enabling: SI 2002/1177, SR 2003/95
s.16, amended: 2004 c.20 Sch.15 para.2
s.16A, added: 2004 c.20 s.72
s.17, amended: 2004 c.20 s.73
s.17A, added: 2004 c.20 s.74
s.19, amended: 2004 c.20 Sch.15 para.3
s.20, amended: 2004 c.20 Sch.15 para.4
s.21, amended: 2004 c.20 Sch.15 para.5
s.22, amended: 2004 c.20 Sch.15 para.6
s.23, amended: 2004 c.20 Sch.15 para.7
s.24, amended: 2004 c.20 Sch.15 para.8
s.25, amended: 2004 c.20 Sch.15 para.9
s.26, amended: 2004 c.20 Sch.15 para.10
s.32, amended: 2004 c.20 Sch.15 para.11 h.15 para.12
s.38, repealed (in part): 2002 c.26 Sch.13
s.47, amended: 2004 c.20 Sch.15 para.13
s.47, varied: SI 2004/1822 Sch.1 para.17
Sch.5 Part II para.8, repealed: 2004 c.14 Sch.1 Part 16

14. Disability (Grants) Act 1993
applied: SI 2003/1325 Art.2

19. Trade Union Reform and Employment Rights Act 1993
s.34, repealed (in part): 2004 c.14 Sch.1 Part 8
s.35, repealed: 2004 c.14 Sch.1 Part 8
Sch.8 para.33, repealed: 2004 c.14 Sch.1 Part 2
Sch.8 para.68, repealed: 2004 c.14 Sch.1 Part 8
Sch.9 para.2, repealed: 2004 c.14 Sch.1 Part 8

21. Osteopaths Act 1993
Commencement Orders: SI 2002/500 Art.2
applied: SI 2002/2376 Reg.4
s.10, amended: 2002 c.17 s.33
s.10, applied: SI 2003/833 Art.4
s.10, repealed (in part): 2002 c.17 Sch.9 Part 2
s.22, amended: 2002 c.17 s.33
s.22, applied: 2002 c.17 s.29
s.23, amended: 2002 c.17 s.33
s.29, amended: 2002 c.17 s.33
s.29, applied: SI 2003/833 Art.4
s.31, amended: 2002 c.17 s.33
s.31, applied: SI 2003/833 Art.4
s.31, repealed (in part): 2002 c.17 Sch.9 Part 2
s.33, amended: 2002 c.40 Sch.25 para.29
s.35, applied: SI 2002/827
s.35, referred to: SI 2002/827
s.35, repealed (in part): 2002 c.17 Sch.9 Part 2

CAP.

1993–cont.

21. **Osteopaths Act 1993**–*cont.*
s.36, enabling: SI 2002/827
s.41, applied: SR 2002/386 Reg.4
s.42, enabling: SI 2002/500
Sch.1 Part I para.10, applied: SI 2002/827
Sch.1 Part I para.11A, added: 2003 c.43 Sch.12 para.5
Sch.1 Part I para.14, applied: SI 2002/827

22. **Merchant Shipping (Registration, etc.) Act 1993**
varied: SI 2004/1284 Art.3

23. **Asylum and Immigration Appeals Act 1993**
applied: 2002 c.41 s.67, s.77, s.78
referred to: SI 2003/754 Sch.2 para.4
s.8, see *R. (on the application of Secretary of State for the Home Department) v Immigration Appeal Tribunal* [2001] EWHC Admin 1067, [2002] Imm. A.R. 491 (QBD (Admin Ct)), Schiemann, L.J.; see *Saad v Secretary of State for the Home Department* [2001] EWCA Civ 2008, [2002] Imm. A.R. 471 (CA), Lord Phillips of Worth Matravers, M.R.
s.8, applied: SI 2003/754 Sch.2 para.4
s.9, see *Suarez v Secretary of State for the Home Department* [2002] EWCA Civ 722, [2002] 1 W.L.R. 2663 (CA), Potter, L.J.
s.9, referred to: SI 2003/754 Sch.2 para.4
s.9A, amended: SI 2003/1016 Sch.1 para.6
s.9A, applied: 2002 c.41 s.68
s.9A, disapplied: SI 2003/754 Sch.2 para.4
s.9A, repealed: 2004 c.19 Sch.2 para.9, Sch.4
s.9A, varied: SI 2003/754 Sch.2 para.4
Sch.2, applied: SI 2003/754 Sch.2 para.2, Sch.2 para.4
Sch.2 para.4, applied: SI 2003/754 Sch.2 para.2
Sch.2 para.5, see *R. (on the application of Gaviria) v Secretary of State for the Home Department* [2001] EWHC Admin 250, [2002] 1 W.L.R. 65 (QBD (Admin Ct)), Stanley Burnton, J.; see *R. (on the application of Javed) v Secretary of State for the Home Department* [2001] EWCA Civ 789, [2002] Q.B. 129 (CA), Lord Phillips of Worth Matravers, M.R.; see *R. (on the application of Vallaj) v Special Adjudicator* [2002] Imm. A.R. 16 (QBD), Dyson, J.; see *Singh (Jijar) v Secretary of State for the Home Department* 2002 S.L.T. 73 (OH), Lord Dawson
Sch.2 para.5, varied: SI 2003/754 Sch.2 para.4
Sch.2 para.9, applied: SI 2003/754 Sch.2 para.2

25. **Local Government (Overseas Assistance) Act 1993**
s.1, amended: 2004 c.21 Sch.1 para.83, 2004 c.36 Sch.2 para.10

CAP.

1993–cont.

26. **Bail (Amendment) Act 1993**
s.1, see *R. (on the application of Jeffrey) v Warwick Crown Court* [2002] EWHC 2469, [2003] Crim. L.R. 190 (QBD (Admin Ct)), Hooper, J.
s.1, amended: 2003 c.41 s.200, Sch.4, 2003 c.44 s.18

28. **Leasehold Reform, Housing and Urban Development Act 1993**
applied: SI 2002/367 (a)
Part 1, see *Etzin v Reece* [2003] 1 P. & C.R. D9 (Ch D), L Henderson Q.C.
Part I, see *Earl Cadogan v Search Guarantees Plc* [2004] EWCA Civ 969, [2004] 1 W.L.R. 2768 (CA), Jonathan Parker, L.J.
Part I c.I, applied: 2002 c.15 s.114, s.159, SI 2003/1417 r.196
Part I c.IV, applied: 2002 c.15 s.159, SI 2003/2099 Sch.1 para.3, SI 2004/681 Sch.1 para.3
Part I c.V, applied: 2002 c.15 s.172
s.1, see *Shortdean Place (Eastbourne) Residents Association Ltd v Lynari Properties Ltd* [2003] 3 E.G.L.R. 147 (Lands Tr), Peter H Clarke FRICS
s.1, amended: 2002 c.15 Sch.8 para.3
s.2, amended: 2002 c.15 Sch.8 para.4, Sch.14
s.4, amended: 2002 c.15 s.115, s.116
s.4A, added: 2002 c.15 s.122
s.4B, added: 2002 c.15 s.122
s.4C, added: 2002 c.15 s.122
s.5, amended: 2002 c.15 Sch.14
s.6, repealed (in part): 2002 c.15 Sch.14
s.7, amended: 2002 c.15 Sch.14, 2004 c.33 Sch.8 para.47
s.8, repealed (in part): 2002 c.15 Sch.14
s.8A, repealed (in part): 2002 c.15 Sch.14
s.10, see *Slamon v Planchon* [2004] EWCA Civ 799, [2004] 4 All E.R. 407 (CA), Peter Gibson, L.J.
s.10, amended: 2002 c.15 s.118, Sch.14, 2004 c.33 Sch.8 para.48
s.10, repealed (in part): 2002 c.15 Sch.14
s.10, varied: 2004 c.33 Sch.21 para.39
s.11, amended: 2002 c.15 Sch.8 para.5, Sch.14
s.12, repealed (in part): 2002 c.15 Sch.14
s.12A, added: 2002 c.15 s.123
s.13, see *Penman v Upavon Enterprises Ltd* [2001] EWCA Civ 956, [2002] L. & T.R. 10 (CA), Arden, L.J.; see *Raymere Ltd v Belle Vue Gardens Ltd* [2003] EWCA Civ 996, [2004] Ch. 29 (CA), Brooke, L.J.; see *West Hampstead Management Co Ltd v Pearl Property Ltd* [2002] EWCA Civ 1372, [2002] 3 E.G.L.R. 55 (CA), Arden, L.J.
s.13, amended: 2002 c.15 s.121, s.123, Sch.8 para.6, Sch.14
s.13, applied: SI 2002/3012 Sch.2 para.1, SI 2003/1990 Reg.2, SI 2004/670 Reg.2
s.13, referred to: SI 2002/3012 Sch.2 para.2

1993—cont.

28. Leasehold Reform, Housing and Urban Development Act 1993—cont.

s.13, repealed (in part): 2002 c.15 Sch.14

s.14, referred to: SI 2002/3012 Sch.2 para.2

s.14, repealed: 2002 c.15 Sch.14

s.15, repealed: 2002 c.15 Sch.14

s.16, repealed: 2002 c.15 Sch.14

s.17, amended: 2002 c.15 s.125, Sch.8 para.7

s.18, amended: 2002 c.15 s.126, Sch.8 para.8, Sch.14

s.18, repealed (in part): 2002 c.15 Sch.14

s.20, see *Raymere Ltd v Belle Vue Gardens Ltd* [2003] EWCA Civ 996, [2004] Ch. 29 (CA), Brooke, L.J.

s.20, amended: 2002 c.15 Sch.8 para.9

s.21, see *Raymere Ltd v Belle Vue Gardens Ltd* [2003] EWCA Civ 996, [2004] Ch. 29 (CA), Brooke, L.J.

s.21, amended: 2002 c.15 Sch.8 para.10

s.21, applied: SI 2002/3208 Reg.4, Reg.5, SI 2003/990 Reg.4, Reg.5

s.22, amended: 2002 c.15 Sch.8 para.11

s.23, amended: 2002 c.15 Sch.8 para.12, Sch.8 para.13

s.24, see *Castlegroom Ltd v Enoch* [2003] 2 E.G.L.R. 54 (CC (Bromley)), Judge Hallon; see *Penman v Upavon Enterprises Ltd* [2001] EWCA Civ 956, [2002] L. & T.R. 10 (CA), Arden, L.J.

s.24, amended: 2002 c.15 Sch.8 para.13

s.24, applied: SI 2003/2099 Sch.1 para.1, SI 2004/681 Sch.1 para.1

s.25, amended: 2002 c.15 Sch.8 para.14

s.25, applied: SI 2003/2099 Sch.1 para.1, SI 2004/681 Sch.1 para.1

s.26, amended: 2002 c.15 Sch.8 para.15

s.26, applied: SI 2002/3012 Sch.2 para.1, SI 2003/1417 r.93

s.27, amended: 2002 c.15 Sch.8 para.16

s.27, applied: SI 2003/2099 Sch.1 para.1, SI 2004/681 Sch.1 para.1

s.28, amended: 2002 c.15 Sch.8 para.17, Sch.14

s.28, repealed (in part): 2002 c.15 Sch.14

s.29, amended: 2002 c.15 Sch.8 para.18, SI 2003/2096 Sch.1 para.20

s.29, repealed (in part): 2002 c.15 Sch.14

s.30, amended: 2002 c.15 Sch.8 para.19

s.31, amended: 2002 c.15 Sch.8 para.20

s.32, see *Castlegroom Ltd v Enoch* [2003] 2 E.G.L.R. 54 (CC (Bromley)), Judge Hallon

s.32, amended: 2002 c.15 Sch.8 para.21

s.33, see *Blendcrown Ltd v Church Commissioners for England* [2004] 1 E.G.L.R. 143 (Lands Tr), PH Clarke, FRICS

s.33, amended: 2002 c.15 Sch.8 para.22, Sch.14

s.33, repealed (in part): 2002 c.15 Sch.14

s.34, amended: 2002 c.9 Sch.11 para.30, 2002 c.15 Sch.8 para.23

s.34, applied: SI 2003/1417 r.196

1993—cont.

28. Leasehold Reform, Housing and Urban Development Act 1993—cont.

s.34, enabling: SI 2003/1417

s.35, amended: 2002 c.15 Sch.8 para.24

s.36, amended: 2002 c.15 Sch.8 para.25

s.37A, amended: 2002 c.15 Sch.8 para.26, Sch.14

s.37A, repealed (in part): 2002 c.15 Sch.14

s.38, amended: 2002 c.15 Sch.8 para.27, Sch.14

s.39, amended: 2002 c.15 s.130, s.132

s.39, repealed (in part): 2002 c.15 Sch.14

s.41, see *Wellcome Trust Ltd v Bellhurst Ltd* [2002] EWCA Civ 790, [2003] H.L.R. 10 (CA), Robert Walker, L.J.

s.41, amended: 2002 c.15 Sch.8 para.28

s.42, see *Bishopsgate Foundation v Curtis* [2004] 46 E.G. 152 (CC (Central London)), Judge Roger Cooke; see *Burman v Mount Cook Land Ltd* [2001] EWCA Civ 1712, [2002] Ch. 256 (CA), Chadwick, L.J.; see *Green v Alexander Johnson (A Firm)* [2004] EWHC 1205, [2004] P.N.L.R. 40 (Ch D), Peter Smith, J.; see *Latifi v Colherne Court Freehold Ltd* [2002] EWHC 2873, [2003] 1 E.G.L.R. 78 (QBD), Cooke, J.; see *Lay v Ackerman* [2004] EWCA Civ 184, [2004] H.L.R. 40 (CA), Arden, L.J.; see *Money v Westholme Investments Ltd* [2003] EWCA Civ 1659, (2003) 147 S.J.L.B. 357 (CA), Clarke, L.J.; see *Mount Cook Land Ltd v Rosen* [2003] 1 E.G.L.R. 75 (CC (Central London)), Judge Knight Q.C.; see *St Ermins Property Co Ltd v Tingay* [2002] EWHC 1673, [2003] L. & T.R. 6 (Ch D), Lloyd, J.

s.42, amended: 2002 c.15 s.132

s.42, applied: SI 2002/3012 Sch.2 para.4, SI 2003/1990 Reg.2, SI 2004/670 Reg.2

s.42, repealed (in part): 2002 c.15 Sch.14

s.45, see *Bishopsgate Foundation v Curtis* [2004] 46 E.G. 152 (CC (Central London)), Judge Roger Cooke; see *Burman v Mount Cook Land Ltd* [2001] EWCA Civ 1712, [2002] Ch. 256 (CA), Chadwick, L.J.; see *Lay v Ackerman* [2004] EWCA Civ 184, [2004] H.L.R. 40 (CA), Arden, L.J.

s.45, amended: 2002 c.15 Sch.14

s.46, see *Bishopsgate Foundation v Curtis* [2004] 46 E.G. 152 (CC (Central London)), Judge Roger Cooke

s.48, applied: SI 2003/2099 Sch.1 para.1, SI 2004/681 Sch.1 para.1

s.49, see *Burman v Mount Cook Land Ltd* [2001] EWCA Civ 1712, [2002] Ch. 256 (CA), Chadwick, L.J.

s.50, applied: SI 2002/3012 Sch.2 para.4, SI 2003/1417 r.93

s.51, applied: SI 2003/2099 Sch.1 para.1, SI 2004/681 Sch.1 para.1

CAP.

1993–cont.

28. Leasehold Reform, Housing and Urban Development Act 1993–cont.

s.54, amended: 2002 c.15 Sch.8 para.29

s.56, applied: SI 2003/1417 r.196

s.57, amended: 2002 c.9 Sch.11 para.30

s.57, applied: SI 2003/1417 r.196

s.57, enabling: SI 2003/1417

s.62, repealed (in part): 2002 c.15 Sch.14

s.69, see *Malone v Bircham & Co Nominees (No.2) Ltd* [2003] EWHC 3173, [2003] N.P.C.166 (Ch D), Lawrence Collins, J.

s.69, amended: 2002 c.15 s.117

s.70, amended: 2002 c.15 Sch.13 para.13

s.70, applied: SI 2002/3208 Reg.4, SI 2003/990 Reg.4, SI 2003/2099 Sch.2 para.3, SI 2004/681 Sch.2 para.3

s.71, applied: SI 2003/2099 Sch.2 para.3, SI 2004/681 Sch.2 para.3

s.72, applied: SI 2003/2099 Sch.2 para.3, SI 2004/681 Sch.2 para.3

s.73, applied: SI 2003/2099 Sch.2 para.3, SI 2004/681 Sch.2 para.3

s.74, amended: 2002 c.15 Sch.8 para.30

s.75, repealed (in part): 2002 c.15 Sch.14

s.76, referred to: 2002 c.15 Sch.7 para.14

s.76, varied: 2002 c.15 Sch.7 para.14

s.77, varied: 2002 c.15 Sch.7 para.14

s.78, varied: 2002 c.15 Sch.7 para.14

s.79, varied: 2002 c.15 Sch.7 para.14

s.80, amended: 2002 c.15 Sch.10 para.17

s.80, varied: 2002 c.15 Sch.7 para.14

s.81, varied: 2002 c.15 Sch.7 para.14

s.82, amended: 2002 c.15 Sch.10 para.19

s.82, varied: 2002 c.15 Sch.7 para.14

s.83, varied: 2002 c.15 Sch.7 para.14

s.84, amended: 2002 c.15 Sch.9 para.10

s.84, varied: 2002 c.15 Sch.7 para.14

s.87, amended: 2002 c.15 Sch.9 para.11

s.87, applied: SI 2004/1802 Art.4

s.87, enabling: SI 2004/1802

s.88, amended: 2002 c.15 Sch.13 para.14, Sch.14

s.88, applied: SI 2003/2099 Sch.1 para.1, SI 2004/681 Sch.1 para.1

s.88, repealed (in part): 2002 c.15 Sch.14

s.90, see *Goldstein v Conley* [2001] EWCA Civ 637, [2002] 1 W.L.R. 281 (CA), Clarke, L.J.

s.91, see *Goldstein v Conley* [2001] EWCA Civ 637, [2002] 1 W.L.R. 281 (CA), Clarke, L.J.

s.91, amended: 2002 c.15 Sch.8 para.31, Sch.13 para.15, Sch.14

s.91, applied: SI 2003/2099 Sch.1 para.1, SI 2004/681 Sch.1 para.1

s.91, repealed (in part): 2002 c.15 Sch.14

s.93, amended: 2002 c.15 Sch.8 para.32, Sch.14

s.93A, amended: 2002 c.15 Sch.8 para.33

s.94, amended: 2002 c.15 s.133, Sch.14

CAP.

1993–cont.

28. Leasehold Reform, Housing and Urban Development Act 1993–cont.

s.94, applied: 2002 c.15 s.159, SI 2003/2099 Sch.1 para.1, SI 2004/681 Sch.1 para.1

s.94, repealed (in part): 2002 c.15 Sch.14

s.97, amended: 2002 c.9 Sch.11 para.30, 2002 c.15 Sch.8 para.34

s.97, repealed (in part): 2002 c.9 Sch.13

s.98, amended: 2002 c.15 Sch.8 para.35

s.98, enabling: SI 2003/1990, SI 2004/670

s.99, see *St Ermins Property Co Ltd v Tingay* [2002] EWHC1673, [2003] L. & T.R. 6 (Ch D), Lloyd, J.

s.99, amended: 2002 c.15 Sch.14

s.99, enabling: SI 2002/3208, SI 2003/990

s.100, enabling: SI 2004/1802

s.101, amended: 2002 c.15 Sch.14

s.135, amended: SI 2002/367 Art.2

s.135, repealed (in part): SI 2002/367 Art.2

s.136, amended: SI 2004/533 Art.5

s.136, applied: SI 2003/3146 Reg.25

s.136, repealed (in part): SI 2004/533 Art.5

s.170, enabling: SI 2004/932

s.171, enabling: SI 2004/932

Sch.3 Part I, amended: 2002 c.15 Sch.14

Sch.3 Part I para.1, amended: 2002 c.15 Sch.8 para.37

Sch.3 Part I para.2, amended: 2002 c.15 Sch.8 para.37

Sch.3 Part I para.3, amended: 2002 c.15 Sch.8 para.37

Sch.3 Part I para.4, amended: 2002 c.15 Sch.8 para.37

Sch.3 Part I para.5, amended: 2002 c.15 Sch.8 para.37

Sch.3 Part I para.6, amended: 2002 c.15 Sch.8 para.37

Sch.3 Part I para.8, repealed (in part): 2002 c.15 Sch.14

Sch.3 Part I para.9, repealed (in part): 2002 c.15 Sch.14

Sch.3 Part I para.10, amended: 2002 c.15 Sch.14

Sch.3 Part II, amended: 2002 c.15 Sch.8 para.37

Sch.3 Part II para.12, amended: 2002 c.15 Sch.8 para.37

Sch.3 Part II para.13, amended: 2002 c.15 Sch.8 para.37

Sch.3 Part III para.15, amended: 2002 c.15 Sch.8 para.37

Sch.3 Part III para.16, substituted: 2002 c.15 Sch.8 para.37

Sch.4 para.1, amended: 2002 c.15 Sch.8 para.38

Sch.4 para.2, amended: 2002 c.15 Sch.8 para.38

Sch.4 para.3, amended: 2002 c.15 Sch.8 para.38

1993–cont.

28. **Leasehold Reform, Housing and Urban Development Act 1993**–*cont.*

Sch.5., see *Castlegroom Ltd v Enoch* [2003] 2 E.G.L.R. 54 (CC (Bromley)), Judge Hallon

Sch.5 para.5, repealed (in part): 2002 c.15 Sch.14

Sch.6, see *West Hampstead Management Co Ltd v Pearl Property Ltd* [2002] EWCA Civ 1372, [2002] 3 E.G.L.R. 55 (CA), Arden, L.J.

Sch.6 Part I para.1, amended: 2002 c.15 s.126, Sch.14

Sch.6 Part II para.2, amended: 2002 c.15 s.126

Sch.6 Part II para.3, amended: 2002 c.15 s.126, Sch.8 para.40

Sch.6 Part II para.4, amended: 2002 c.15 s.126, s.127, s.128

Sch.6 Part II para.4, varied: SI 2002/3012 Sch.2 para.3, SI 2004/3056 Art.4, SI 2004/3056art4(1)

Sch.6 Part II para.5, amended: 2002 c.15 s.126

Sch.6 Part II para.5A, amended: 2002 c.15 s.126

Sch.6 Part II para.5B, amended: 2002 c.15 s.126

Sch.6 Part II para.5C, amended: 2002 c.15 s.126

Sch.6 Part III para.6, amended: 2002 c.15 s.126

Sch.6 Part III para.7, amended: 2002 c.15 s.126

Sch.6 Part III para.8, amended: 2002 c.15 s.126

Sch.6 Part III para.9, amended: 2002 c.15 s.126

Sch.6 Part III para.9A, amended: 2002 c.15 s.126

Sch.6 Part IV para.10, amended: 2002 c.15 s.126, Sch.8 para.40

Sch.6 Part IV para.11, amended: 2002 c.15 s.126

Sch.6 Part IV para.12, amended: 2002 c.15 s.126

Sch.6 Part IV para.13, amended: 2002 c.15 s.126

Sch.6 Part V para.14, amended: 2002 c.15 s.126

Sch.6 Part V para.15, amended: 2002 c.15 s.126

Sch.6 Part V para.16, amended: 2002 c.15 s.126

Sch.6 Part V para.17, amended: 2002 c.15 s.126

Sch.6 Part VI para.18, amended: 2002 c.15 s.126

Sch.6 Part VI para.19, amended: 2002 c.15 s.126

Sch.6 Part VI para.20, amended: 2002 c.15 s.126

1993–cont.

28. **Leasehold Reform, Housing and Urban Development Act 1993**–*cont.*

Sch.6 Part VI para.21, amended: 2002 c.15 s.126

Sch.8 para.1, amended: 2002 c.15 Sch.8 para.42

Sch.8 para.2, amended: 2002 c.15 Sch.8 para.42

Sch.8 para.3, amended: 2002 c.15 Sch.8 para.42

Sch.8 para.4, amended: 2002 c.15 Sch.8 para.42

Sch.8 para.5, amended: 2002 c.15 Sch.8 para.42

Sch.9 Part I para.1, amended: 2002 c.15 Sch.8 para.43

Sch.9 Part II para.2, amended: 2002 c.15 Sch.8 para.43

Sch.9 Part II para.3, amended: 2002 c.15 Sch.8 para.43

Sch.9 Part II para.3, applied: 2004 c.34 s.202

Sch.9 Part II para.4, amended: 2002 c.15 Sch.8 para.43

Sch.9 Part III para.5, amended: 2002 c.15 Sch.8 para.43

Sch.9 Part III para.6, amended: 2002 c.15 Sch.8 para.43

Sch.9 Part III para.7, amended: 2002 c.15 Sch.8 para.43

Sch.9 Part IV para.8, amended: 2002 c.15 Sch.8 para.43

Sch.9 Part IV para.9, amended: 2002 c.15 Sch.8 para.43

Sch.9 Part IV para.9A, amended: 2002 c.15 Sch.8 para.43

Sch.9 Part IV para.10, amended: 2002 c.15 Sch.8 para.43

Sch.9 Part IV para.11, amended: 2002 c.15 Sch.8 para.43

Sch.9 Part IV para.12, amended: 2002 c.15 Sch.8 para.43

Sch.9 Part IV para.13, amended: 2002 c.15 Sch.8 para.43

Sch.9 Part IV para.14, amended: 2002 c.15 Sch.8 para.43

Sch.9 Part IV para.15, amended: 2002 c.15 Sch.8 para.43

Sch.9 Part IV para.16, amended: 2002 c.15 Sch.8 para.43

Sch.9 Part IV para.17, amended: 2002 c.15 Sch.8 para.43

Sch.9 Part IV para.18, amended: 2002 c.15 Sch.8 para.43

Sch.11 Part 1 para.4, see *Wellcome Trust Ltd v Bellhurst Ltd* [2002] EWCA Civ 790, [2003] H.L.R. 10 (CA), Robert Walker, L.J.

Sch.13 Part I para.1, amended: 2002 c.15 s.134, Sch.14

Sch.13 Part II para.2, amended: 2002 c.15 s.134

1993–cont.

28. Leasehold Reform, Housing and Urban Development Act 1993–cont.

Sch.13 Part II para.3, amended: 2002 c.15 s.134

Sch.13 Part II para.4, amended: 2002 c.15 s.134, s.135, s.136

Sch.13 Part II para.4A, amended: 2002 c.15 s.134

Sch.13 Part II para.4B, amended: 2002 c.15 s.134

Sch.13 Part II para.5, amended: 2002 c.15 s.134

Sch.13 Part III para.6, amended: 2002 c.15 s.134

Sch.13 Part III para.7, amended: 2002 c.15 s.134

Sch.13 Part III para.8, amended: 2002 c.15 s.134

Sch.13 Part III para.9, amended: 2002 c.15 s.134

Sch.13 Part III para.10, amended: 2002 c.15 s.134

Sch.14 para.2, applied: SI 2003/2099 Sch.1 para.1, SI 2004/681 Sch.1 para.1

Sch.18 para.9, amended: SI 2003/1326 Art.18

Sch.18 para.10, amended: SI 2003/1326 Art.18

Sch.18 para.12, amended: SI 2003/1326 Art.18

Sch.20 Part I para.1, amended: 2004 c.5 Sch.7 para.18

Sch.20 Part I para.2, repealed: 2004 c.5 Sch.9

Sch.20 Part II para.4, amended: 2003 c.21 Sch.17 para.123

Sch.20 Part II para.5, amended: 2003 c.21 Sch.17 para.123

Sch.20 Part II para.11, amended: 2003 c.21 Sch.17 para.123

Sch.20 Part II para.12, amended: 2003 c.21 Sch.17 para.123

Sch.20 Part II para.14, amended: 2003 c.21 Sch.17 para.123

Sch.20 Part II para.19, repealed (in part): 2003 c.21 Sch.19

Sch.21 para.1, repealed: 2002 c.9 Sch.13

34. Finance Act 1993

referred to: 2004 c.12 Sch.25 para.1

Part II c.II, applied: 2002 c.23 Sch.23 para.26, Sch.28 para.3

Part II Ch.II, see *Finance Ltd v Inspector of Taxes* [2003] S.T.C. (S.C.D.) 344 (Sp Comm), AN Brice (Chairman)

s.10, amended: 2002 c.23 s.7, 2004 c.12 s.14

s.22, repealed: 2003 c.14 Sch.43 Part 5

s.24, repealed (in part): 2004 c.14 Sch.1 Part 17

s.24, enabling: SI 2002/2354, SI 2002/2355

s.28, enabling: SI 2002/2354

s.36, repealed (in part): 2002 c.40 Sch.26

1993–cont.

34. Finance Act 1993–cont.

s.38, enabling: SI 2002/2354, SI 2002/2355

s.39, repealed (in part): 2002 c.23 Sch.40 Part 1

s.60, repealed: 2002 c.23 Sch.40 Part 3

s.68, repealed: 2003 c.1 Sch.8 Part 1

s.73, repealed: 2003 c.1 Sch.8 Part 1

s.74, repealed: 2003 c.1 Sch.8 Part 1

s.75, repealed: 2003 c.1 Sch.8 Part 1

s.76, repealed: 2003 c.1 Sch.8 Part 1

s.86, amended: 2002 c.23 s.43

s.92, amended: 2002 c.23 Sch.24 para.2

s.92, applied: 2002 c.23 Sch.24 para.7

s.92, referred to: 2002 c.23 Sch.24 para.7

s.92, substituted: 2004 c.12 Sch.10 para.77

s.92A, applied: 2002 c.23 Sch.24 para.7

s.92A, referred to: 2002 c.23 Sch.24 para.7

s.92A, substituted: 2004 c.12 Sch.10 para.77

s.92B, applied: 2002 c.23 Sch.24 para.7

s.92B, referred to: 2002 c.23 Sch.24 para.7

s.92B, substituted: 2004 c.12 Sch.10 para.77

s.92C, applied: 2002 c.23 Sch.24 para.7

s.92C, referred to: 2002 c.23 Sch.24 para.7

s.92C, substituted: 2004 c.12 Sch.10 para.77

s.92D, applied: 2002 c.23 Sch.24 para.7

s.92D, referred to: 2002 c.23 Sch.24 para.7

s.92D, substituted: 2004 c.12 Sch.10 para.77

s.92E, applied: 2002 c.23 Sch.24 para.7

s.92E, referred to: 2002 c.23 Sch.24 para.7

s.92E, substituted: 2004 c.12 Sch.10 para.77

s.93, amended: 2002 c.23 s.103, Sch.24 para.3, Sch.40 Part 3, 2003 c.14 Sch.27 para.3

s.93, applied: 2002 c.23 Sch.24 para.7

s.93, referred to: 2002 c.23 Sch.24 para.7

s.93, repealed (in part): 2002 c.23 Sch.40 Part 3

s.93, substituted: 2004 c.12 Sch.10 para.77

s.93A, added: 2002 c.23 Sch.24 para.4

s.93A, amended: 2003 c.14 Sch.27 para.3

s.93A, applied: 2002 c.23 Sch.24 para.7, Sch.26 para.16

s.93A, referred to: 2002 c.23 Sch.24 para.7

s.93A, substituted: 2004 c.12 Sch.10 para.77

s.94, applied: 2002 c.23 Sch.24 para.7

s.94, referred to: 2002 c.23 Sch.24 para.7

s.94, substituted: 2002 c.23 Sch.24 para.5, 2004 c.12 Sch.10 para.77

s.94A, referred to: 2002 c.23 Sch.24 para.7

s.94AA, applied: 2002 c.23 Sch.24 para.7

s.94AA, referred to: 2002 c.23 Sch.24 para.7

s.94AA, substituted: 2004 c.12 Sch.10 para.77

s.94AB, added: 2002 c.23 Sch.24 para.6

s.94AB, applied: 2002 c.23 Sch.24 para.7

s.94AB, referred to: 2002 c.23 Sch.24 para.7

s.94AB, substituted: 2004 c.12 Sch.10 para.77

s.95, referred to: 2002 c.23 Sch.24 para.7

s.105, repealed (in part): 2003 c.1 Sch.8 Part 1

1993–cont.

34. Finance Act 1993–cont.

s.106, repealed: 2004 c.12 Sch.42 Part 3

s.107, repealed (in part): 2004 c.12 Sch.42 Part 3

s.112, repealed: 2004 c.12 Sch.42 Part 3

s.118, applied: SI 2002/2848 Sch.1 Part III

s.124, repealed: 2003 c.1 Sch.8 Part 1

s.125, repealed: 2002 c.23 s.79

s.126, repealed (in part): 2002 c.23 s.79, Sch.24 para.7

s.127, repealed: 2002 c.23 s.79

s.128, applied: 2002 c.23 Sch.23 para.25

s.128, repealed: 2002 c.23 s.79

s.129, repealed: 2002 c.23 s.79

s.130, applied: 2002 c.23 Sch.23 para.25

s.130, repealed: 2002 c.23 s.79

s.131, repealed: 2002 c.23 s.79

s.132, repealed: 2002 c.23 s.79

s.133, repealed: 2002 c.23 s.79

s.134, repealed: 2002 c.23 s.79

s.135, repealed: 2002 c.23 s.79

s.135A, repealed: 2002 c.23 s.79

s.136, referred to: 2002 c.23 Sch.23 para.21

s.136, repealed: 2002 c.23 s.79

s.136A, referred to: 2002 c.23 Sch.23 para.21

s.136A, repealed: 2002 c.23 s.79

s.137, disapplied: 2002 c.23 Sch.28 para.3

s.137, repealed: 2002 c.23 s.79

s.138, repealed: 2002 c.23 s.79

s.139, applied: 2002 c.23 Sch.23 para.26

s.139, referred to: 2002 c.23 Sch.23 para.26

s.139, repealed: 2002 c.23 s.79

s.140, referred to: 2002 c.23 Sch.23 para.26

s.140, repealed: 2002 c.23 s.79

s.141, referred to: 2002 c.23 Sch.23 para.26

s.141, repealed: 2002 c.23 s.79

s.142, referred to: 2002 c.23 Sch.23 para.26

s.142, repealed: 2002 c.23 s.79

s.143, referred to: 2002 c.23 Sch.23 para.26

s.143, repealed: 2002 c.23 s.79

s.144, repealed: 2002 c.23 s.79

s.145, repealed: 2002 c.23 s.79

s.146, repealed: 2002 c.23 s.79

s.147, repealed: 2002 c.23 s.79

s.148, repealed: 2002 c.23 s.79

s.149, repealed: 2002 c.23 s.79

s.150, amended: 2002 c.23 s.103

s.150, repealed: 2002 c.23 s.79

s.151, repealed: 2002 c.23 s.79

s.152, repealed: 2002 c.23 s.79

s.153, repealed: 2002 c.23 s.79

s.154, amended: 2002 c.23 s.103

s.154, repealed: 2002 c.23 s.79

s.155, amended: 2002 c.23 s.103

s.155, repealed: 2002 c.23 s.79

s.156, amended: 2002 c.23 s.103

s.156, repealed: 2002 c.23 s.79

s.157, repealed: 2002 c.23 s.79

s.158, repealed: 2002 c.23 s.79

s.159, amended: 2002 c.23 s.103

1993–cont.

34. Finance Act 1993–cont.

s.159, repealed: 2002 c.23 s.79

s.160, repealed: 2002 c.23 s.79

s.161, repealed: 2002 c.23 s.79

s.162, repealed: 2002 c.23 s.79

s.163, repealed: 2002 c.23 s.79

s.164, referred to: SI 2002/1969 Reg.2, Reg.12, Reg.28

s.164, repealed: 2002 c.23 s.79

s.165, applied: 2002 c.23 Sch.23 para.22

s.165, referred to: SI 2002/1969 Part 2, Reg.2

s.165, repealed: 2002 c.23 s.79

s.166, repealed: 2002 c.23 s.79

s.167, referred to: SI 2002/1969 Part 2, Reg.2, Reg.12, Reg.18, Reg.28

s.167, repealed: 2002 c.23 s.79

s.168, referred to: SI 2002/1969 Reg.18

s.168, repealed: 2002 c.23 s.79

s.168A, repealed: 2002 c.23 s.79

s.169, repealed: 2002 c.23 s.79

s.178, amended: 2002 c.23 Sch.32 para.2, Sch.32 para.3, Sch.32 para.4

s.179B, added: 2004 c.12 Sch.25 para.2

s.184, amended: 2002 c.23 Sch.32 para.5

s.202, amended: 2003 c.14 Sch.20 para.3

s.203, amended: 2003 c.14 Sch.20 para.3

Sch.3 para.1, repealed: 2003 c.1 Sch.8 Part 1

Sch.3 para.2, repealed: 2003 c.1 Sch.8 Part 1

Sch.3 para.3, repealed: 2003 c.1 Sch.8 Part 1

Sch.3 para.4, repealed: 2003 c.1 Sch.8 Part 1

Sch.3 para.5, repealed: 2003 c.1 Sch.8 Part 1

Sch.3 para.6, repealed: 2003 c.1 Sch.8 Part 1

Sch.3 para.7, repealed: 2003 c.1 Sch.8 Part 1

Sch.4 para.1, repealed: 2003 c.1 Sch.8 Part 1

Sch.4 para.2, repealed: 2003 c.1 Sch.8 Part 1

Sch.4 para.3, repealed: 2003 c.1 Sch.8 Part 1

Sch.4 para.4, repealed: 2003 c.1 Sch.8 Part 1

Sch.4 para.5, repealed: 2003 c.1 Sch.8 Part 1

Sch.4 para.6, repealed: 2003 c.1 Sch.8 Part 1

Sch.4 para.7, repealed: 2003 c.1 Sch.8 Part 1

Sch.4 para.8, repealed: 2003 c.1 Sch.8 Part 1

Sch.5 para.1, repealed: 2003 c.1 Sch.8 Part 1

Sch.5 para.2, repealed: 2003 c.1 Sch.8 Part 1

Sch.15, referred to: SI 2002/1969 Reg.12, Reg.28

Sch.15 para.1, repealed: 2002 c.23 Sch.40 Part 3

Sch.15 para.2, repealed: 2002 c.23 Sch.40 Part 3

Sch.15 para.3, repealed: 2002 c.23 Sch.40 Part 3

Sch.15 para.4, applied: 2002 c.23 Sch.23 para.26

Sch.15 para.4, repealed: 2002 c.23 Sch.40 Part 3

Sch.15 para.4A, repealed: 2002 c.23 Sch.40 Part 3

Sch.15 para.5, repealed: 2002 c.23 Sch.40 Part 3

CAP.

1993–cont.

34. Finance Act 1993–*cont.*

Sch.15 para.5A, repealed: 2002 c.23 Sch.40 Part 3

Sch.15 para.6, repealed: 2002 c.23 Sch.40 Part 3

Sch.15 para.7, repealed: 2002 c.23 Sch.40 Part 3

Sch.15 para.8, repealed: 2002 c.23 Sch.40 Part 3

Sch.15 para.9, repealed: 2002 c.23 Sch.40 Part 3

Sch.16, referred to: SI 2002/1969 Reg.2, Reg.28

Sch.16 para.1, repealed: 2002 c.23 Sch.40 Part 3

Sch.16 para.2, repealed: 2002 c.23 Sch.40 Part 3

Sch.16 para.3, referred to: SI 2002/1969 Part 2

Sch.16 para.3, repealed: 2002 c.23 Sch.40 Part 3

Sch.16 para.4, repealed: 2002 c.23 Sch.40 Part 3

Sch.16 para.5, repealed: 2002 c.23 Sch.40 Part 3

Sch.16 para.6, repealed: 2002 c.23 Sch.40 Part 3

Sch.17 para.1, repealed: 2002 c.23 Sch.40 Part 3

Sch.17 para.2, repealed: 2002 c.23 Sch.40 Part 3

Sch.17 para.3, repealed: 2002 c.23 Sch.40 Part 3

Sch.17 para.4, repealed: 2002 c.23 Sch.40 Part 3

Sch.17 para.5, repealed: 2002 c.23 Sch.40 Part 3

Sch.17 para.6, repealed: 2002 c.23 Sch.40 Part 3

Sch.17 para.7, repealed: 2002 c.23 Sch.40 Part 3

Sch.17 para.8, repealed: 2002 c.23 Sch.40 Part 3

Sch.18 para.2, repealed: 2002 c.23 Sch.40 Part 3

Sch.20A Part I para.1, added: 2004 c.12 Sch.25 para.3

Sch.20A Part I para.2, added: 2004 c.12 Sch.25 para.3

Sch.20A Part I para.3, added: 2004 c.12 Sch.25 para.3

Sch.20A Part I para.4, added: 2004 c.12 Sch.25 para.3

Sch.20A Part I para.5, added: 2004 c.12 Sch.25 para.3

Sch.20A Part II para.6, added: 2004 c.12 Sch.25 para.3

Sch.20A Part II para.7, added: 2004 c.12 Sch.25 para.3

Sch.20A Part II para.8, added: 2004 c.12 Sch.25 para.3

CAP.

1993–cont.

34. Finance Act 1993–*cont.*

Sch.20A Part III para.9, added: 2004 c.12 Sch.25 para.3

Sch.20A Part III para.10, added: 2004 c.12 Sch.25 para.3

Sch.20A Part III para.11, added: 2004 c.12 Sch.25 para.3

36. Criminal Justice Act 1993

see *R. v Sekhon (Daljit Singh)* [2002] EWCA Crim 2954, [2003] 1 W.L.R. 1655 (CA (Crim Div)), Lord Woolf of Barnes, L.C.J.; see *R. v Smith (John)* [2002] EWCA Crim 2561, [2003] 2 Cr. App. R. (S.) 4 (CA (Crim Div)), Longmore, L.J.

Part 3, see *R. v Levin (David)* [2004] EWCA Crim 408, [2004] 2 Cr. App. R. (S.) 61 (CA (Crim Div)), Rose, L.J.

s.21, repealed (in part): 2002 c.29 Sch.12

s.27, repealed: 2002 c.29 Sch.12

s.28, repealed: 2002 c.29 Sch.12

s.29, repealed: 2002 c.29 Sch.12

s.30, repealed: 2002 c.29 Sch.12

s.31, repealed: 2002 c.29 Sch.12

s.32, repealed: 2002 c.29 Sch.12

s.33, repealed: 2002 c.29 Sch.12

s.34, repealed: 2002 c.29 Sch.12

s.35, repealed: 2002 c.29 Sch.12

s.60, enabling: SI 2002/1874

s.62, enabling: SI 2002/1874

s.64, applied: SI 2002/1874

s.64, enabling: SI 2002/1874

s.67, repealed (in part): 2003 c.44 Sch.37 Part 7

s.72, repealed: 2003 c.41 Sch.4

s.79, repealed (in part): 2003 c.41 Sch.4

Sch.2 para.2, varied: SI 2003/1633 Sch.2 para.8

Sch.4 para.3, repealed: 2002 c.29 Sch.12

Sch.5 Part I para.14, repealed: 2002 c.29 Sch.12

Sch.5 Part II para.21, repealed: SI 2002/3150 Sch.4

37. Agriculture Act 1993

s.14, applied: SI 2002/128

s.14, enabling: SI 2002/128, SSI 2003/534

s.21, repealed (in part): 2004 c.14 Sch.1 Part 2

s.25, repealed: 2004 c.14 Sch.1 Part 2

s.26, repealed: 2004 c.14 Sch.1 Part 2

s.27, repealed: 2004 c.14 Sch.1 Part 2

s.28, repealed: 2004 c.14 Sch.1 Part 2

s.29, repealed: 2004 c.14 Sch.1 Part 2

s.30, repealed: 2004 c.14 Sch.1 Part 2

s.31, repealed: 2004 c.14 Sch.1 Part 2

s.32, repealed: 2004 c.14 Sch.1 Part 2

s.33, repealed: 2004 c.14 Sch.1 Part 2

s.34, repealed: 2004 c.14 Sch.1 Part 2

s.35, repealed: 2004 c.14 Sch.1 Part 2

s.37, repealed: 2004 c.14 Sch.1 Part 2

s.38, repealed: 2004 c.14 Sch.1 Part 2

s.39, repealed: 2004 c.14 Sch.1 Part 2

1993–cont.

37. Agriculture Act 1993–cont.
s.40, repealed: 2004 c.14 Sch.1 Part 2
s.41, repealed: 2004 c.14 Sch.1 Part 2
s.42, repealed: 2004 c.14 Sch.1 Part 2
s.43, repealed: 2004 c.14 Sch.1 Part 2
s.44, repealed: 2004 c.14 Sch.1 Part 2
s.45, repealed: 2004 c.14 Sch.1 Part 2
s.47, repealed: 2004 c.14 Sch.1 Part 2
s.59, repealed: 2004 c.14 Sch.1 Part 2
s.62, repealed (in part): 2004 c.14 Sch.1 Part 2
s.64, repealed (in part): 2004 c.14 Sch.1 Part 2
Sch.3 para.1, repealed: 2004 c.14 Sch.1 Part 2
Sch.3 para.2, repealed: 2004 c.14 Sch.1 Part 2
Sch.3 para.3, repealed: 2004 c.14 Sch.1 Part 2
Sch.3 para.4, repealed: 2004 c.14 Sch.1 Part 2
Sch.3 para.5, repealed: 2004 c.14 Sch.1 Part 2
Sch.3 para.6, repealed: 2004 c.14 Sch.1 Part 2
Sch.3 para.7, repealed: 2004 c.14 Sch.1 Part 2
Sch.3 para.8, repealed: 2004 c.14 Sch.1 Part 2
Sch.3 para.9, repealed: 2004 c.14 Sch.1 Part 2
Sch.3 para.10, repealed: 2004 c.14 Sch.1 Part 2

38. Welsh Language Act 1993
applied: SI 2003/694 Sch.1 para.81, SI 2004/753 Sch.1 para.96, SI 2004/2333 Sch.1 para.96
Part II, applied: SI 2002/1441 Art.2, SI 2004/71 Art.2
s.6, amended: 2002 c.17 Sch.5 para.37, 2003 c.4 Sch.3 para.7, Sch.3 para.8, 2004 c.21 Sch.1 para.84
s.6, enabling: SI 2002/1441, SI 2004/71
s.26, applied: 2002 c.24 s.7, SI 2002/2799, SI 2002/2800, SI 2003/61, SI 2003/62, SI 2003/117, SI 2003/284 Sch.5 para.4, Sch.5 para.6, SI 2003/3048, SI 2003/3096 Art.28
s.26, enabling: SI 2002/122, SI 2002/1838, SI 2002/2312, SI 2003/414, SI 2003/1255, SI 2004/675, SI 2004/678, SI 2004/870, SI 2004/1233, SI 2004/1234, SI 2004/1373, SI 2004/1508, SI 2004/3169
s.27, enabling: SI 2004/1373
s.35, consolidated: 2002 c.24 s.7
s.35, repealed (in part): 2002 c.24 Sch.4

39. National Lottery etc Act 1993
Part I, applied: SSI 2003/231 Sch.1 para.14, Sch.3 para.9
s.4, varied: 2004 c.25 s.34
s.5, amended: 2004 c.25 s.34
s.5, applied: SI 2002/1889 Art.2, Art.3, 2004 c.25 s.21, s.24, s.26, s.28, s.32
s.5, referred to: 2004 c.25 s.34
s.6, applied: SI 2002/1889 Art.2, Art.3, 2004 c.25 s.21, s.22
s.7, applied: SI 2002/1889 Art.2, Art.3
s.7, enabling: SI 2002/3124, SI 2003/2771
s.8, applied: SI 2002/1889 Art.2, Art.3
s.9, amended: 2004 c.25 s.34

1993–cont.

39. National Lottery etc Act 1993–cont.
s.9, applied: SI 2002/1889 Art.2, Art.3, 2004 c.25 s.24
s.10, applied: SI 2002/1889 Art.2, Art.3
s.10A, amended: 2004 c.25 s.34
s.11, varied: 2004 c.25 s.34
s.13, applied: SI 2003/1376 Sch.1, SI 2003/1593 Sch.1 Part I
s.16, applied: SI 2003/1376 Sch.1, SI 2003/1593 Sch.1 Part I
s.17, repealed: 2004 c.25 Sch.2 para.21, Sch.6
s.21, repealed (in part): 2004 c.25 s.34, Sch.6
s.22, amended: 2003 c.23 s.1, 2004 c.25 s.34
s.22, applied: SI 2003/235 Art.2
s.22, referred to: 2004 c.25 s.25
s.22, repealed (in part): 2004 c.25 s.34, Sch.6
s.23, applied: SI 2003/235, 2004 c.25 s.26, s.28, s.32
s.23, referred to: 2004 c.25 s.25, s.26, s.28, s.32
s.25, amended: 2003 c.23 s.1
s.25, applied: SI 2002/638 Sch.1 para.4, Sch.1 para.5, SI 2003/664 Sch.1 para.4, Sch.1 para.5, SI 2004/691 Sch.1 para.4, Sch.1 para.5
s.25A, applied: 2004 c.25 Sch.5 para.13
s.25B, amended: 2003 c.23 s.1
s.30, repealed: 2004 c.25 s.34, Sch.6
s.33, varied: 2004 c.25 s.34
s.38, amended: 2003 c.23 s.1
s.40, see *R. (on the application of Asha Foundation) v Millennium Commission* [2002] EWHC 916, Times, June 6, 2002 (QBD (Admin Ct)), Lightman, J.
s.41, amended: 2003 c.23 s.1
s.41, see *R. (on the application of Asha Foundation) v Millennium Commission* [2002] EWHC 916, Times, June 6, 2002 (QBD (Admin Ct)), Lightman, J.
s.43B, amended: 2003 c.23 s.1
s.43B, applied: SI 2004/143 Art.2
s.43B, enabling: SI 2004/143
s.43C, applied: SI 2004/143
s.43C, enabling: SI 2004/143
s.44, amended: 2003 c.23 s.1
s.44, applied: SI 2002/638 Sch.1 para.2, SI 2003/664 Sch.1 para.2, SI 2004/691 Sch.1 para.2
s.49, applied: SI 2002/639 Art.5
s.60, applied: SI 2004/143
s.60, enabling: SI 2002/3124, SI 2003/2771
Sch.2A para.10, applied: 2004 c.25 s.26
Sch.3 Part I para.3, amended: SI 2003/2096 Sch.1 para.21
Sch.3A para.2, enabling: SI 2002/638, SI 2003/664, SI 2004/691
Sch.3A para.3, applied: SI 2002/638 Art.2, SI 2003/664 Art.2, SI 2004/691 Art.2

CAP.

1993–cont.

39. National Lottery etc Act 1993–*cont.*

Sch.3A para.3, enabling: SI 2002/638, SI 2003/664, SI 2004/691

Sch.3A para.6, enabling: SI 2003/664, SI 2004/691

Sch.6 para.1, amended: SI 2003/3033 Art.2

Sch.6 para.2, enabling: SI 2003/3033

Sch.6A para.1, amended: SI 2003/2869 Art.2

Sch.6A para.1, enabling: SI 2003/2869

41. European Parliamentary Elections Act 1993

s.3, consolidated: 2002 c.24 Sch.3 para.1

s.3, repealed: 2002 c.24 Sch.4

42. Cardiff Bay Barrage Act 1993

see *Waters v Welsh Development Agency* [2004] UKHL 19, [2004] 1 W.L.R. 1304 (HL), Lord Nicholls of Birkenhead

Sch.2 para.1, amended: 2003 c.21 Sch.17 para.124

Sch.2 para.16, amended: 2003 c.21 Sch.17 para.124

Sch.4 para.3, amended: 2003 c.21 Sch.17 para.125, Sch.19

Sch.7 para.21, amended: 2003 c.21 Sch.17 para.126

Sch.7 para.21, repealed (in part): 2003 c.21 Sch.19

43. Railways Act 1993

applied: 2002 c.40 Sch.15, SI 2003/409 Sch.1 Part I

referred to: 2003 c.20 Sch.2 para.1, SI 2003/1325 Art.3

Part I, applied: SI 2003/1075 Art.40, SI 2003/1594 Art.2, SI 2003/3364 Art.31, SI 2004/389 Art.38

Part I, referred to: SI 2002/2398 Art.5

Part II, applied: SI 2003/409 Sch.1 Part I

s.1, repealed: 2003 c.20 Sch.8

s.3, repealed (in part): 2004 c.14 Sch.1 Part 5

s.4, see *R. (on the application of London & Continental Stations & Property Ltd) v Rail Regulator* [2003] EWHC 2607, [2004] A.C.D. 13 (QBD (Admin Ct)), Moses, J.; see *Railtrack Plc (In Administration) (No.2), Re* [2002] EWCA Civ 955, [2002] 1 W.L.R. 3002 (CA), Lord Woolf of Barnes, L.C.J.

s.4, amended: 2002 c.40 Sch.25 para.30, Sch.26, 2003 c.20 Sch.2 para.3, Sch.8

s.4, repealed (in part): 2002 c.40 Sch.26

s.6, amended: 2003 c.20 Sch.2 para.3

s.6, applied: SI 2003/1695 Art.5

s.6, referred to: SI 2004/1072 Art.3

s.7, amended: 2003 c.20 Sch.2 para.3, Sch.2 para.4

s.7, applied: SI 2003/1695 Art.5

s.7, enabling: SI 2004/1072

s.7A, amended: 2003 c.20 Sch.2 para.3

s.8, amended: 2003 c.20 Sch.2 para.3, Sch.2 para.5

CAP.

1993–cont.

43. Railways Act 1993–*cont.*

s.8, applied: 2004 c.36 Sch.1 para.23, Sch.1 para.24, Sch.1 para.34, Sch.1 para.35, SI 2004/1522 Art.2

s.9, amended: 2003 c.20 Sch.2 para.3, Sch.2 para.6

s.11, amended: 2003 c.20 Sch.2 para.3

s.12, amended: 2003 c.20 Sch.2 para.3

s.13, amended: 2002 c.40 Sch.25 para.30, 2003 c.20 Sch.2 para.3

s.13, applied: SI 2003/1397 Art.8

s.13, repealed (in part): 2002 c.40 Sch.26

s.13A, added: 2002 c.40 Sch.25 para.30

s.13B, added: 2002 c.40 Sch.25 para.30

s.13B, amended: 2003 c.21 Sch.16 para.4

s.13B, referred to: SI 2003/1371

s.13B, enabling: SI 2003/1371

s.14, amended: 2002 c.40 Sch.25 para.30, 2003 c.20 Sch.2 para.3

s.15, amended: 2003 c.20 Sch.2 para.3, Sch.8

s.15A, amended: 2003 c.20 Sch.2 para.3

s.15B, amended: 2003 c.20 Sch.2 para.3

s.15C, amended: 2002 c.40 Sch.25 para.30, 2003 c.20 Sch.2 para.3, Sch.2 para.8, Sch.8, 2003 c.21 Sch.16 para.4

s.15C, referred to: SI 2003/1371

s.15C, enabling: SI 2003/1371

s.16, amended: 2002 c.40 Sch.9 para.10, 2003 c.20 Sch.2 para.3

s.16, varied: SI 2003/1592 Sch.4 para.12

s.16A, amended: 2003 c.20 Sch.2 para.3

s.16B, amended: 2003 c.20 Sch.2 para.3

s.16C, amended: 2003 c.20 Sch.2 para.3

s.16D, amended: 2003 c.20 Sch.2 para.3

s.16E, amended: 2003 c.20 Sch.2 para.3

s.16F, amended: 2003 c.20 Sch.2 para.3

s.16G, amended: 2003 c.20 Sch.2 para.3

s.16H, amended: 2003 c.20 Sch.2 para.3

s.16I, amended: 2003 c.20 Sch.2 para.3

s.17, see *R. (on the application of London & Continental Stations & Property Ltd) v Rail Regulator* [2003] EWHC 2607, [2004] A.C.D. 13 (QBD (Admin Ct)), Moses, J.; see *Railtrack Plc (In Administration) (No.2), Re* [2002] EWCA Civ 955, [2002] 1 W.L.R. 3002 (CA), Lord Woolf of Barnes, L.C.J.

s.17, amended: 2003 c.20 Sch.2 para.3

s.17, referred to: SI 2004/1072 Art.4

s.18, amended: 2003 c.20 Sch.2 para.3

s.18, referred to: SI 2004/1072 Art.4

s.19, amended: 2003 c.20 Sch.2 para.3

s.19A, amended: 2003 c.20 Sch.2 para.3

s.20, amended: 2003 c.20 Sch.2 para.3, Sch.2 para.9

s.20, enabling: SI 2004/1072

s.21, amended: 2003 c.20 Sch.2 para.3, Sch.2 para.10, Sch.8

s.22, amended: 2002 c.40 Sch.25 para.30, 2003 c.20 Sch.2 para.3

1993–cont.

43. Railways Act 1993–*cont.*

s.22A, amended: 2003 c.20 Sch.2 para.3

s.22A, referred to: SI 2004/1072 Art.4

s.22B, amended: 2003 c.20 Sch.2 para.3

s.22C, amended: 2003 c.20 Sch.2 para.3

s.23, applied: SI 2002/1946 Art.3, SI 2004/1072 Art.5

s.24, amended: 2003 c.20 Sch.2 para.3

s.24, applied: SI 2002/1946

s.24, enabling: SI 2002/1946, SI 2004/1072

s.26, amended: 2003 c.20 Sch.2 para.3

s.37, disapplied: SI 2002/1946 Art.4, SI 2004/1072 Art.6

s.39, disapplied: SI 2002/1946 Art.4, SI 2004/1072 Art.7, Art.11

s.41, disapplied: SI 2002/1946 Art.4, SI 2004/1072 Art.8

s.43, amended: 2003 c.20 Sch.2 para.3

s.46, amended: 2003 c.20 Sch.2 para.3

s.46A, amended: 2003 c.20 Sch.2 para.3

s.46B, amended: 2003 c.20 Sch.2 para.3

s.49, enabling: SI 2002/1946, SI 2002/2703, SI 2004/1072

s.55, amended: 2003 c.20 Sch.2 para.3, Sch.2 para.11

s.56, amended: 2003 c.20 Sch.2 para.3

s.57A, amended: 2003 c.20 Sch.2 para.3, Sch.2 para.12

s.57B, amended: 2003 c.20 Sch.2 para.3, Sch.8

s.57C, amended: 2003 c.20 Sch.2 para.3

s.59, see *Railtrack Plc (In Administration) (No.2), Re* [2002] EWCA Civ 955, [2002] 1 W.L.R. 3002 (CA), Lord Woolf of Barnes, L.C.J.

s.59, applied: 2002 c.40 s.249

s.63, applied: 2002 c.18 Sch.2 Part 2, Sch.2 Part 9, 2003 c.13 Sch.2 Part 2, Sch.2 Part 3, Sch.2 Part 10, 2004 c.9 Sch.2 Part 2, Sch.2 Part 9

s.66, amended: 2002 c.40 Sch.25 para.30

s.66, repealed (in part): 2002 c.40 Sch.26, SI 2003/1398 Sch.1 para.21

s.66, varied: SI 2003/1592 Sch.4 para.12

s.67, amended: 2002 c.40 Sch.9 para.21, Sch.25 para.30, Sch.26, 2003 c.20 Sch.2 para.3, SI 2003/1398 Sch.1 para.21, SI 2004/1261 Sch.2 para.6

s.67, repealed (in part): 2002 c.40 Sch.25 para.30, Sch.26

s.68, amended: 2003 c.20 Sch.2 para.3

s.69, amended: 2002 c.40 Sch.25 para.30, 2003 c.20 Sch.2 para.3

s.71, amended: 2002 c.40 Sch.25 para.30, 2003 c.20 Sch.2 para.3

s.72, amended: 2003 c.20 Sch.2 para.3

s.73, amended: 2003 c.20 Sch.2 para.3

s.74, amended: 2002 c.40 Sch.25 para.30, 2003 c.20 Sch.2 para.3, Sch.2 para.14, Sch.8

s.75, amended: 2003 c.20 Sch.2 para.3

1993–cont.

43. Railways Act 1993–*cont.*

s.76, amended: 2003 c.20 Sch.2 para.3, Sch.2 para.15

s.76, applied: SI 2003/1695 Art.3

s.76, varied: SI 2003/1696 Art.3

s.76, enabling: SI 2003/1695, SI 2003/1696

s.77, amended: 2003 c.20 Sch.2 para.3, Sch.2 para.16

s.77, applied: SI 2003/1695 Art.4

s.77, varied: SI 2003/1696 Art.4

s.77, enabling: SI 2003/1695, SI 2003/1696

s.79, amended: 2003 c.20 Sch.2 para.3

s.83, amended: 2002 c.40 Sch.25 para.30, Sch.26

s.83, referred to: SI 2002/2977 Sch.1 para.4

s.92, see *Manchester City Council v Railtrack Plc* [2002] EWHC 2719, [2003] E.H.L.R. 8 (QBD (Admin Ct)), Silber, J.

s.95, amended: 2003 c.20 Sch.2 para.3

s.118, amended: 2003 c.20 Sch.2 para.3

s.121A, added: 2003 c.20 s.106

s.122, referred to: SI 2002/1066 Art.43, SI 2004/757 Art.50

s.132, repealed: 2003 c.20 Sch.8

s.133, applied: SI 2004/1573 Art.11

s.133, repealed: 2003 c.20 Sch.8

s.136, amended: SI 2003/1615 Sch.1 para.19

s.143, enabling: SI 2002/2703

s.145, amended: 2002 c.40 Sch.25 para.30, 2003 c.20 Sch.2 para.3, 2003 c.21 Sch.17 para.127

s.145, referred to: 2003 c.20 s.115

s.151, amended: 2003 c.20 Sch.8

s.151, enabling: SI 2002/1946, SI 2002/2703, SI 2004/1072

Sch.1 para.1, repealed: 2003 c.20 Sch.8

Sch.1 para.2, repealed: 2003 c.20 Sch.8

Sch.1 para.3, repealed: 2003 c.20 Sch.8

Sch.1 para.4, repealed: 2003 c.20 Sch.8

Sch.1 para.5, repealed: 2003 c.20 Sch.8

Sch.1 para.6, repealed: 2003 c.20 Sch.8

Sch.1 para.7, repealed: 2003 c.20 Sch.8

Sch.1 para.8, repealed: 2003 c.20 Sch.8

Sch.2 para.1, amended: 2003 c.20 Sch.2 para.3

Sch.2 para.2, amended: 2003 c.20 Sch.2 para.3

Sch.2 para.2A, amended: 2003 c.20 Sch.2 para.3

Sch.2 para.3, amended: 2003 c.20 Sch.2 para.3

Sch.2 para.4, amended: 2003 c.20 Sch.2 para.3

Sch.2 para.5, amended: 2003 c.20 Sch.2 para.3

Sch.2 para.6, amended: 2003 c.20 Sch.2 para.3

Sch.2 para.7, amended: 2003 c.20 Sch.2 para.3

Sch.2 para.8, amended: 2003 c.20 Sch.2 para.3

1993–cont.

43. Railways Act 1993–*cont.*

Sch.2 para.9, amended: 2003 c.20 Sch.2 para.3

Sch.2 para.10, amended: 2003 c.20 Sch.2 para.3

Sch.3 para.1, amended: 2003 c.20 Sch.2 para.3

Sch.3 para.2, amended: 2003 c.20 Sch.2 para.3

Sch.3 para.3, amended: 2003 c.20 Sch.2 para.3

Sch.3 para.4, amended: 2003 c.20 Sch.2 para.3

Sch.3 para.5, amended: 2003 c.20 Sch.2 para.3

Sch.3 para.6, amended: 2003 c.20 Sch.2 para.3

Sch.3 para.7, amended: 2003 c.20 Sch.2 para.3

Sch.3 para.8, amended: 2003 c.20 Sch.2 para.3

Sch.3 para.9, amended: 2003 c.20 Sch.2 para.3

Sch.4A, applied: SI 2003/1397 Art.8

Sch.4 para.1, amended: 2003 c.20 Sch.2 para.3

Sch.4 para.2, amended: 2003 c.20 Sch.2 para.3

Sch.4 para.3, amended: 2003 c.20 Sch.2 para.3

Sch.4 para.4, amended: 2003 c.20 Sch.2 para.3

Sch.4 para.5, amended: 2003 c.20 Sch.2 para.3

Sch.4 para.6, amended: 2003 c.20 Sch.2 para.3

Sch.4 para.7, amended: 2003 c.20 Sch.2 para.3

Sch.4A para.1, amended: 2003 c.20 Sch.2 para.3

Sch.4A para.2, amended: 2003 c.20 Sch.2 para.3

Sch.4A para.3, amended: 2003 c.20 Sch.2 para.3

Sch.4A para.4, amended: 2003 c.20 Sch.2 para.3

Sch.4A para.5, amended: 2003 c.20 Sch.2 para.3

Sch.4A para.6, amended: 2003 c.20 Sch.2 para.3

Sch.4A para.7, amended: 2003 c.20 Sch.2 para.3

Sch.4A para.8, amended: 2003 c.20 Sch.2 para.3

Sch.4A para.9, amended: 2003 c.20 Sch.2 para.3

Sch.4A para.10, amended: 2003 c.20 Sch.2 para.3

Sch.4A para.10, substituted: 2002 c.40 Sch.25 para.30

1993–cont.

43. Railways Act 1993–*cont.*

Sch.4A para.10, amended: 2003 c.20 Sch.2 para.3

Sch.4A para.10A, amended: 2003 c.20 Sch.2 para.3, 2003 c.21 Sch.16 para.4

Sch.4A para.10A, referred to: SI 2003/1371

Sch.4A para.10A, enabling: SI 2003/1371

Sch.4A para.11, amended: 2002 c.40 Sch.25 para.30, 2003 c.20 Sch.2 para.3

Sch.4A para.12, amended: 2003 c.20 Sch.2 para.3

Sch.4A para.13, amended: 2003 c.20 Sch.2 para.3

Sch.4A para.14, amended: 2003 c.20 Sch.2 para.3

Sch.4A para.15, amended: 2002 c.40 Sch.25 para.30, 2003 c.20 Sch.2 para.3, 2003 c.21 Sch.16 para.4

Sch.4A para.15, referred to: SI 2003/1371

Sch.4A para.15, enabling: SI 2003/1371

Sch.4A para.16, amended: 2003 c.20 Sch.2 para.3

Sch.5, applied: SI 2002/1946 Art.5

Sch.5, disapplied: SI 2004/1072 Art.9

Sch.6 Part I para.1, amended: 2003 c.20 Sch.2 para.18

Sch.6 Part I para.2, amended: 2003 c.20 Sch.2 para.18

Sch.6 Part I para.3, amended: 2003 c.20 Sch.2 para.18

Sch.6 Part I para.4, amended: 2003 c.20 Sch.2 para.18

Sch.6 Part I para.5, amended: 2003 c.20 Sch.2 para.18

Sch.6 Part I para.6, amended: 2003 c.20 Sch.2 para.18

Sch.6 Part I para.7, amended: 2003 c.20 Sch.2 para.18

Sch.6 Part I para.8, amended: 2003 c.20 Sch.2 para.18

Sch.6 Part I para.9, amended: 2003 c.20 Sch.2 para.18

Sch.6 Part I para.10, amended: 2003 c.20 Sch.2 para.18

Sch.6 Part I para.11, amended: 2003 c.20 Sch.2 para.18

Sch.8 para.14, amended: 2003 c.14 Sch.20 para.3

Sch.10 para.1, repealed: 2003 c.20 Sch.8

Sch.10 para.2, repealed: 2003 c.20 Sch.8

Sch.10 para.3, repealed: 2003 c.20 Sch.8

Sch.11, applied: 2003 c.20 Sch.4 para.24

Sch.12 para.7, repealed: 2002 c.40 Sch.26

Sch.12 para.8, repealed: 2002 c.40 Sch.26

Sch.12 para.11, repealed: 2002 c.40 Sch.26

Sch.12 para.12, repealed (in part): 2002 c.40 Sch.26

Sch.12 para.26, repealed: 2002 c.40 Sch.26

44. Crofters Act 1993

s.23, see *MacPherson v Walker (No.1)* 2003 S.L.C.R. 76 (Land Ct (Div Ct)), DJ Houston

1993–cont.

44. Crofters (Scotland) Act 1993

applied: SSI 2002/201 Art.15, 2003 asp 2 s.65, s.96, 2003 asp 9 Sch.11 para.3, SSI 2003/1 Art.15, SSI 2003/209 Art.5

s.1, applied: SI 2003/409 Sch.1 Part I, SSI 2004/474 Sch.1

s.3, applied: SSI 2002/110 Sch.2 para.1

s.3, referred to: SSI 2003/1 Art.15

s.6, see *MacGillivray v MacColl's Executor* 2002 S.L.C.R. 133 (Land Ct (Div Ct)), DJ Houston

s.12, see *Crofters Commission v Scottish Ministers* 2002 S.L.T. (Land Ct) 19 (Land Ct (Full Ct)), Lord McGhie, DJ Houston, DM MacDonald

s.12, applied: 2003 asp 2 s.65, s.84

s.16, amended: 2003 asp 9 Sch.14 para.11

s.20, applied: SSI 2003/209 Art.6, SSI 2004/143 Reg.16

s.29, amended: 2003 asp 11 Sch.1 para.49

s.30, amended: 2003 asp 11 Sch.1 para.49

s.42, applied: SSI 2004/117 Sch.3 para.4

s.47, applied: SSI 2002/34 Art.4, SSI 2002/201 Art.15, SSI 2003/1 Art.15

s.61, amended: 2004 c.33 Sch.28 para.58

s.61, varied: 2004 c.33 Sch.21 para.40

Sch.2 para.11, amended: 2003 asp 11 Sch.1 para.49

45. Scottish Land Court Act 1993

applied: SSI 2002/110 Sch.2 para.25

s.1, amended: 2003 asp 2 s.97, 2003 asp 11 s.82, 2004 asp 6 Sch.7 para.9

s.1, applied: 2003 asp 2 s.97, SSI 2004/278 Reg.11, SSI 2004/381 Reg.12

Sch.1 para.6, amended: 2003 asp 11 s.82

Sch.1 para.6, disapplied: 2003 asp 2 s.97

46. Health Service Commissioners Act 1993

applied: 2002 asp 11 s.21, SI 2002/553 Art.10, SSI 2002/103 Sch.1 Part II, SSI 2002/305 Sch.1 Part II, SSI 2002/534 Sch.1 Part II, 2003 c.43 s.113

referred to: 2002 asp 11 Sch.7 para.1, 2003 c.43 Sch.4 para.93, Sch.11 para.60

repealed (in part): 2002 asp 11 Sch.6 para.14

s.1, amended: SI 2004/1823 Art.17

s.1, applied: 2002 asp 11 Sch.7 para.1

s.1, repealed (in part): SI 2004/1823 Art.17

s.2, amended: 2002 c.17 Sch.1 para.47, Sch.5 para.38, Sch.9 Part 1, 2003 c.43 Sch.4 para.94, Sch.11 para.61

s.2, applied: SI 2003/1520 Art.2, SI 2004/1119 Art.2

s.2, repealed (in part): 2003 c.43 Sch.13 para.7, Sch.14 Part 4, Sch.14 Part 7, SI 2004/1823 Art.17

s.2, enabling: SI 2003/1520, SI 2004/1119

s.2A, amended: SI 2002/2861 Reg.26, 2003 c.43 Sch.11 para.62, SI 2004/1823 Art.17

s.2A, referred to: SI 2004/865 Art.113

s.2A, repealed (in part): SI 2004/1823 Art.17

1993–cont.

46. Health Service Commissioners Act 1993–*cont.*

s.2A, varied: SI 2004/288 Art.7, SI 2004/480 Art.6, SI 2004/865 Art.109, Art.113, SI 2004/1016 Art.85, Art.89

s.2B, amended: SI 2004/1823 Art.17

s.2B, repealed (in part): SI 2004/1823 Art.17

s.3, amended: 2003 c.43 s.118

s.4, amended: 2003 c.43 Sch.9 para.11

s.4, repealed (in part): 2003 c.43 Sch.14 Part 2

s.6, amended: 2002 c.17 Sch.2 para.61, 2003 c.43 Sch.11 para.63, Sch.14 Part 4

s.6, referred to: SI 2004/865 Art.113

s.6, varied: SI 2004/288 Art.7, SI 2004/480 Art.6, SI 2004/865 Art.113, SI 2004/1016 Art.89

s.7, amended: SI 2004/1823 Art.17

s.10, applied: 2003 c.43 s.113, SI 2004/1768 Reg.16

s.11, amended: 2003 c.43 Sch.9 para.11, SI 2004/1823 Art.17

s.12, amended: 2003 c.43 Sch.9 para.11

s.14, amended: 2003 c.43 Sch.9 para.11, SI 2004/1823 Art.17

s.14A, amended: 2003 c.43 Sch.9 para.11

s.14B, amended: 2003 c.43 Sch.9 para.11

s.17, amended: SI 2004/2359 Art.3

s.18, amended: 2003 c.43 Sch.11 para.64, 2004 c.34 Sch.15 para.37, Sch.16, SI 2004/1823 Art.17

s.19, amended: SI 2004/1823 Art.17

Sch.1, amended: SI 2004/1823 Art.17

Sch.1 para.A.1, amended: SI 2004/1823 Art.17

Sch.1 para.1, amended: SI 2004/1823 Art.17

Sch.1 para.1, repealed (in part): SI 2004/1823 Art.17

Sch.1 para.2, amended: SI 2004/1823 Art.17

Sch.1 para.3, amended: SI 2004/1823 Art.17

Sch.1 para.3A, amended: SI 2004/1823 Art.17

Sch.1 para.4, amended: SI 2004/1823 Art.17

Sch.1 para.4, repealed (in part): SI 2004/1823 Art.17

Sch.1 para.5, amended: SI 2004/1823 Art.17

Sch.1 para.6, amended: SI 2004/1823 Art.17

Sch.1 para.6, repealed (in part): SI 2004/1823 Art.17

Sch.1 para.7, amended: SI 2004/1823 Art.17

Sch.1 para.8, amended: SI 2004/1823 Art.17

Sch.1 para.9, amended: SI 2004/1823 Art.17

Sch.1 para.10, amended: SI 2004/1823 Art.17

Sch.1 para.11, amended: SI 2004/1823 Art.17

Sch.1 para.12, amended: SI 2004/1823 Art.17

Sch.1 para.13, amended: SI 2004/1823 Art.17

Sch.1 para.14, amended: SI 2004/1823 Art.17

Sch.1 para.15, amended: SI 2004/1823 Art.17

Sch.1A para.5, amended: SI 2004/1823 Art.17

Sch.1A para.6, amended: SI 2004/1823 Art.17

CAP.

1993–cont.

46. Health Service Commissioners Act 1993–*cont.*
Sch.1A para.13, repealed (in part): 2004 c.23 Sch.2 para.16, Sch.4
Sch.2 para.5, repealed: SI 2004/1823 Art.17
Sch.2 para.6, repealed: SI 2004/1823 Art.17

47. Probation Service Act 1993
s.27, applied: SI 2002/1792 Sch.2 para.4
Sch.3 para.5, repealed: 2003 c.44 Sch.37 Part 10

48. Pension Schemes Act 1993
applied: 2002 c.29 s.275, SI 2003/526 Art.1, Art.6, 2004 c.12 s.202, 2004 c.35 s.7, s.19, s.21, s.87, s.165, s.201, s.321, Sch.3, SI 2004/552 Art.1, Art.6
referred to: 2004 c.35 s.322
Part III, applied: 2002 c.22 s.15, SI 2002/519 Art.2, 2003 c.20 Sch.4 para.24, SI 2003/517 Art.2, 2004 c.35 Sch.3, Sch.8, SI 2004/262 Art.2
Part IV c.I, applied: 2004 c.35 s.318
Part IV c.III, applied: 2004 c.7 Sch.5 para.14
Part IV c.IV, applied: SI 2002/819 Reg.4, Sch.1 Part 2
Part IV c.IV, referred to: 2004 c.35 s.24, s.73
Part IV c.V, applied: 2004 c.35 s.135, s.138, Sch.7 para.20, Sch.7 para.32
Part IV c.V, referred to: 2004 c.35 s.24, s.73
Part IV c.V, added: 2004 c.35 s.264
Part IVA c.II, referred to: 2004 c.35 s.73
Part X, see *R. (on the application of Britannic Asset Management Ltd) v Pensions Ombudsman* [2002] EWCA Civ 1405, [2002] 4 All E.R. 860 (CA), Chadwick, L.J.
Part X, applied: SI 2003/1660 Reg.27, SI 2003/1661 Reg.27, 2004 c.35 s.275
s.1, amended: 2004 c.35 s.239
s.1, applied: SSI 2002/494 Sch.2 para.8
s.6, applied: SI 2002/459 Reg.10, SR 2002/74 Reg.9
s.6, repealed: 2004 c.35 Sch.13 Part 1
s.8, applied: 2004 c.12 s.188, s.190, s.196, s.232, s.233, s.236, Sch.36 para.14
s.8, enabling: SI 2002/681
s.9, amended: 2004 c.35 s.283
s.9, applied: 2004 c.35 s.257
s.9, enabling: SI 2002/681
s.10, amended: 2002 c.29 Sch.11 para.22
s.11, enabling: SI 2002/681
s.12A, applied: 2004 c.35 s.258
s.13, applied: 2004 c.7 Sch.5 para.14
s.14, amended: 2002 c.29 Sch.11 para.22
s.14, referred to: 2004 c.7 Sch.5 para.14
s.14, enabling: SI 2003/608
s.15, applied: SI 2002/668 Art.5, SI 2003/526 Art.5, 2004 c.7 Sch.5 para.14, SI 2004/552 Art.5
s.15, varied: SI 2003/526 Art.5, SI 2004/552 Art.5
s.16, applied: 2004 c.7 Sch.5 para.14
s.17, amended: 2004 c.35 s.284

CAP.

1993–cont.

48. Pension Schemes Act 1993–*cont.*
s.17, applied: SI 2002/668 Art.5, SI 2003/526 Art.5, SI 2004/552 Art.5
s.19, applied: 2004 c.7 Sch.5 para.14
s.21, amended: 2004 c.35 s.284
s.21, enabling: SI 2002/681
s.28, amended: 2004 c.35 s.284, Sch.13 Part 1
s.28, repealed (in part): 2004 c.35 s.284, Sch.13 Part 1
s.28, enabling: SI 2002/681
s.28A, enabling: SI 2002/681
s.29, amended: 2004 c.35 s.284, Sch.13 Part 1
s.32, enabling: SI 2002/681
s.32A, enabling: SI 2002/681
s.34, amended: 2004 c.35 Sch.13 Part 1
s.34, enabling: SI 2002/681
s.41, amended: 2002 c.19 Sch.1 para.36
s.41, varied: 2004 c.12 s.202
s.42A, amended: 2002 c.19 Sch.1 para.37
s.42A, applied: 2004 c.12 s.188
s.43, amended: 2002 c.19 Sch.1 para.38
s.43, applied: 2004 c.12 s.188, s.202
s.45, varied: 2004 c.12 s.202
s.47, amended: 2002 c.16 s.18, 2002 c.29 Sch.11 para.22, 2004 c.35 s.165
s.48A, amended: 2002 c.19 Sch.1 para.39
s.53, amended: 2004 c.35 Sch.12 para.10
s.55, enabling: SI 2002/681
s.56, amended: 2004 c.35 Sch.12 para.11
s.56, enabling: SI 2002/681
s.57, enabling: SI 2002/681
s.61, amended: 2004 c.35 Sch.12 para.12
s.67, see *Merchant Navy Ratings Pension Fund Trustees Ltd v Chambers* [2002] I.C.R. 359 (Ch D), Blackburne, J.
s.68, amended: 2003 c.39 Sch.8 para.361
s.68B, amended: 2002 c.29 Sch.11 para.22
s.71, amended: 2004 c.35 s.263
s.71, applied: 2004 c.12 Sch.29 para.5
s.72, amended: 2004 c.35 s.263
s.84, amended: 2004 c.35 s.281
s.93A, applied: 2004 c.35 s.23
s.94, amended: 2004 c.35 Sch.12 para.13
s.94, applied: 2004 c.35 s.18
s.97, enabling: SI 2003/1727, SI 2004/1140
s.99, amended: 2004 c.35 Sch.12 para.14
s.99, applied: 2004 c.35 s.10, s.96, Sch.2 para.1
s.99, repealed (in part): 2004 c.35 Sch.13 Part 1
s.101, applied: 2004 c.35 s.96
s.101AA, added: 2004 c.35 s.264
s.101AA, applied: 2004 c.35 Sch.7 para.20, Sch.7 para.32
s.101AB, added: 2004 c.35 s.264
s.101AB, applied: 2004 c.35 s.18
s.101AC, added: 2004 c.35 s.264
s.101AD, added: 2004 c.35 s.264

1993–cont.

48. Pension Schemes Act 1993–*cont.*
s.101AE, added: 2004 c.35 s.264
s.101AF, added: 2004 c.35 s.264
s.101AH, added: 2004 c.35 s.264
s.101AI, added: 2004 c.35 s.264
s.101B, see *R. (on the application of Smith) v Secretary of State for Defence* [2004] EWHC 1797, [2004] Pens. L.R. 323 (QBD (Admin Ct)), Wilson, J.
s.101C, see *R. (on the application of Smith) v Secretary of State for Defence* [2004] EWHC 1797, [2004] Pens. L.R. 323 (QBD (Admin Ct)), Wilson, J.
s.101E, amended: 2004 c.33 Sch.27 para.148
s.101F, applied: 2004 c.35 s.18
s.101I, enabling: SI 2003/1727
s.101J, amended: 2004 c.35 Sch.12 para.15
s.101J, applied: 2004 c.35 s.10, s.96, Sch.2 para.2
s.101J, repealed (in part): 2004 c.35 Sch.13 Part 1
s.101L, enabling: SI 2003/1727
s.109, see *Hearn v Younger* [2002] EWHC 963, [2003] O.P.L.R. 45 (Ch D), Etherton, J.
s.109, applied: SI 2002/649 Art.2, SI 2003/524 Art.2, SI 2004/537 Art.2, SR 2002/98, SR 2003/150
s.109, enabling: SI 2002/649, SI 2003/524, SI 2004/537
s.111, repealed: 2004 c.35 s.267, Sch.13 Part 1
s.111A, amended: 2004 c.35 s.268
s.111A, applied: 2004 c.35 s.74, s.90
s.111A, repealed (in part): 2004 c.35 Sch.12 para.16, Sch.13 Part 1
s.111B, repealed: 2004 c.35 Sch.13 Part 1
s.113, amended: 2004 c.35 Sch.12 para.17
s.113, referred to: 2004 c.35 s.73
s.113, enabling: SI 2002/459, SI 2002/1383
s.113A, added: 2004 c.35 Sch.12 para.18
s.123, amended: SI 2003/2096 Sch.1 para.22, 2004 c.35 Sch.12 para.19, Sch.13 Part 1
s.123, repealed (in part): 2004 c.35 Sch.12 para.19, Sch.13 Part 1
s.124, amended: 2004 c.35 Sch.12 para.20
s.129, amended: 2004 c.35 Sch.12 para.21, Sch.13 Part 1
s.129, applied: 2004 c.35 s.318
s.129, repealed (in part): 2004 c.35 Sch.13 Part 1
s.130, amended: 2004 c.35 Sch.12 para.22
s.131, amended: 2004 c.35 Sch.13 Part 1
s.132, amended: 2004 c.35 s.267, Sch.13 Part 1
s.145, amended: 2004 c.35 s.274, Sch.12 para.23
s.145A, added: 2004 c.35 s.274
s.146, see *R. (on the application of Britannic Asset Management Ltd) v Pensions Ombudsman* [2002] EWHC 441, [2002]

1993–cont.

48. Pension Schemes Act 1993–*cont.*
s.146–*cont.*
O.P.L.R. 175 (QBD (Admin Ct)), Lightman, J.
s.146, amended: 2004 c.35 s.275, Sch.12 para.24
s.146, applied: 2004 c.35 s.275
s.148, referred to: 2004 c.35 s.276
s.148, repealed (in part): 2004 c.35 s.276, Sch.13 Part 1
s.149, amended: 2004 c.35 Sch.12 para.25, Sch.13 Part 1
s.149, referred to: 2004 c.35 s.276
s.149, repealed (in part): 2004 c.35 s.276, Sch.13 Part 1
s.151, see *Legal & General Assurance Society Ltd v CCA Stationery Ltd* [2003] EWHC 1491, [2003] Pens. L.R. 261 (Ch D), Etherton, J.; see *Newham LBC v Skingle* [2003] EWCA Civ 280, [2003] 2 All E.R. 761 (CA), Jonathan Parker, L.J.; see *NUS Officials and Employees Superannuation Fund Trustees v Pensions Ombudsman* [2002] O.P.L.R. 17 (Ch D), Lightman, J.
s.151, amended: 2004 c.35 s.276, Sch.13 Part 1
s.151, referred to: 2004 c.35 s.276
s.151, repealed (in part): 2004 c.35 s.276, Sch.13 Part 1
s.156, enabling: SI 2002/681
s.158, amended: SI 2002/1397 Sch.1 para.9, 2004 c.35 Sch.13 Part 1
s.158, repealed (in part): 2004 c.35 Sch.13 Part 1
s.158A, amended: SI 2002/1397 Sch.1 para.9, 2004 c.35 Sch.12 para.26
s.159, disapplied: 2002 c.29 s.273
s.168, amended: 2004 c.35 Sch.12 para.27
s.168, applied: 2004 c.35 s.76, s.78, s.256, s.310, Sch.2 para.3
s.168A, repealed: 2004 c.35 Sch.13 Part 1
s.175, amended: 2004 c.35 Sch.1 para.26, Sch.12 para.28, Sch.13 Part 1
s.175, referred to: 2004 c.35 s.73
s.175, repealed (in part): 2004 c.35 Sch.13 Part 1
s.177, repealed (in part): 2004 c.35 Sch.13 Part 1
s.178, amended: 2004 c.35 Sch.12 para.29
s.179, amended: 2004 c.35 Sch.12 para.30
s.180, see *Universities Superannuation Scheme Ltd v Simpson* [2004] EWHC 935, [2004] I.C.R. 1426 (Ch D), Lloyd, J.
s.181, amended: 2002 c.29 Sch.11 para.22, 2003 c.1 Sch.6 para.222, 2004 c.35 s.7, s.267, s.282, Sch.12 para.31, Sch.13 Part 1
s.181, enabling: SI 2002/681, SI 2002/1383, SI 2003/608, SI 2003/1727, SI 2003/2916, SI 2004/1140

CAP.

1993–cont.

48. Pension Schemes Act 1993–*cont.*

s.182, enabling: SI 2002/681, SI 2002/1383, SI 2003/608, SI 2003/1727, SI 2003/2916, SI 2004/1140

s.183, amended: 2004 c.35 Sch.12 para.32

s.183, enabling: SI 2002/681, SI 2002/1383, SI 2003/1727

s.185, enabling: SI 2003/1727

s.192, amended: 2004 c.35 Sch.12 para.33, Sch.13 Part 1

Sch.3 para.2, applied: SI 2002/2951 Art.2, SI 2003/3002 Art.2, SI 2004/2948 Art.2, SR 2002/369

Sch.3 para.2, enabling: SI 2002/2951, SI 2003/3002, SI 2004/2948

Sch.6 Part II para.17, enabling: SI 2003/2916

Sch.8 para.19, repealed: 2004 c.14 Sch.1 Part 5

Sch.8 para.20, repealed: 2004 c.12 Sch.42 Part 3

Sch.9 para.5, repealed: 2004 c.35 Sch.13 Part 1

Sch.9 para.7, repealed (in part): 2004 c.35 Sch.13 Part 1

49. Pension Schemes (Northern Ireland) Act 1993

applied: 2002 c.29 s.275, SR 2002/352 Reg.37, Reg.105, Reg.136, SR 2003/155 Art.1, Art.6, 2004 c.12 s.202, 2004 c.35 Sch.3, Sch.8

Part III, applied: 2002 c.22 s.15, SR 2002/89 Art.2, 2003 c.20 Sch.4 para.24, SR 2003/146 Art.2, 2004 c.35 Sch.3, Sch.8

Part III c.III, enabling: SR 2003/256

Part IV c.III, applied: SR 2002/352 Reg.91, 2004 c.7 Sch.5 para.15

Part IV c.IV, applied: SR 2002/352 Reg.118, Reg.119, Reg.120, Reg.122, Reg.125, SR 2002/353 Reg.18

Part IVA c.II, applied: SR 2002/352 Reg.144

s.1, applied: SR 2002/352 Reg.4

s.2, applied: SR 2002/369 Reg.2

s.4, applied: 2004 c.12 s.188, s.190, s.196, s.232, s.233, s.236, Sch.36 para.14

s.4, enabling: SR 2002/109

s.5, enabling: SR 2002/109, SR 2003/256

s.6, amended: 2002 c.29 Sch.11 para.23

s.7, enabling: SR 2002/109

s.8C, applied: SR 2002/352 Reg.61, Reg.119

s.9, applied: 2004 c.7 Sch.5 para.15

s.10, amended: 2002 c.29 Sch.11 para.23

s.10, applied: SR 2002/352 Reg.39, Reg.40

s.10, referred to: SR 2002/352 Reg.40, 2004 c.7 Sch.5 para.15

s.11, applied: SR 2003/155 Art.5

s.11, referred to: 2004 c.7 Sch.5 para.15

s.11, varied: SR 2002/99 Art.5, SR 2003/155 Art.5

s.12, applied: SR 2002/352 Reg.40, 2004 c.7 Sch.5 para.15

s.13, applied: SR 2003/155 Art.5

CAP.

1993–cont.

49. Pension Schemes (Northern Ireland) Act 1993–*cont.*

s.15, applied: SR 2002/352 Reg.61, Reg.119, 2004 c.7 Sch.5 para.15

s.15, enabling: SR 2003/256

s.16, applied: SR 2002/352 Reg.119

s.17, applied: SR 2002/352 Reg.61

s.17, enabling: SR 2002/109

s.19, applied: SR 2002/352 Reg.124

s.22, enabling: SR 2003/256

s.24, enabling: SR 2002/109

s.24A, enabling: SR 2002/109

s.25, enabling: SR 2003/256

s.26, enabling: SR 2003/256

s.28, enabling: SR 2002/109

s.28A, enabling: SR 2002/109, SR 2003/256

s.30, enabling: SR 2002/109

s.37, amended: 2002 c.19 Sch.1 para.41

s.38A, amended: 2002 c.19 Sch.1 para.42

s.38A, applied: 2004 c.12 s.188

s.38A, enabling: SI 2002/681

s.39, amended: 2002 c.19 Sch.1 para.43

s.39, applied: 2004 c.12 s.188, s.202

s.43, amended: 2002 c.14 (NI) s.18, 2002 c.29 Sch.11 para.23, SI 2002/1555 Art.20

s.43, referred to: 2002 c.14 (NI)

s.44A, amended: 2002 c.19 Sch.1 para.44

s.51, applied: SR 2002/352 Reg.93, Reg.121

s.51, enabling: SI 2002/681

s.52, enabling: SI 2002/681

s.53, enabling: SI 2002/681

s.57, applied: SR 2002/352 Reg.93

s.64A, applied: SR 2002/352 Reg.136

s.64B, amended: 2002 c.29 Sch.11 para.23

s.73, applied: SR 2002/352 Reg.61

s.89A, applied: SR 2002/353 Reg.11

s.97D, enabling: SR 2003/256

s.97L, enabling: SR 2003/256

s.105, applied: SR 2002/98 Art.2, SR 2003/150 Art.2

s.105, enabling: SR 2002/98, SR 2003/150

s.107, applied: SR 2002/352 Sch.6 para.31

s.109, enabling: SR 2002/74, SR 2002/410, SR 2003/256

s.142, enabling: SR 2003/256

s.147A, enabling: SR 2003/256

s.152, enabling: SR 2002/109

s.155, disapplied: 2002 c.29 s.273

s.165, amended: SI 2002/1555 Art.21

s.176, amended: 2002 c.29 Sch.11 para.23, SI 2002/1555 Art.22

s.177, enabling: SI 2002/681, SR 2002/109, SR 2002/410

s.178, enabling: SI 2002/681, SR 2002/109, SR 2002/410

Sch.3 para.2, enabling: SR 2002/369

1994

xi. **CroydonTramlink Act 1994**
s.45, repealed: SI 2003/1614 Art.3

xiii. **London Docklands Development Corporation Act 1994**
s.13, disapplied: SI 2004/757 Art.4

xii. **London Local Authorities Act 1994**
s.2, amended: 2004 c.i Sch.5
s.4, amended: SI 2003/1615 Sch.1 para.35
s.5, repealed: 2003 c.17 Sch.7

Value Added Taxes Act 1994
Sch 9., see *Messenger Leisure Developments Ltd v Customs and Excise Commissioners* [2004] EWHC 1761, [2004] S.T.C. 1563 (Ch D), Hart, J.

VAT Act 1994
s.30, see *R. (on the application ofTeleos Plc) v Customs and Excise Commissioners* [2004] EWHC 1035, [2004] Eu. L.R. 798 (QBD (Admin Ct)), Moses, J.

2. **Care of Cathedrals (Supplementary Provisions) Measure 1994**
applied: SI 2002/1893 para.4, SI 2003/1936 para.4
s.4, applied: SI 2002/1892 Sch.1 PartTABLE, SI 2003/1933 Sch.1 Part I, SI 2004/1888 Sch.1 PartTABLE

3. **Church of England (Legal Aid) Measure 1994**
s.1, applied: SI 2002/1893 para.1, SI 2003/1936 para.1
Sch.1, amended: 2003 c.3 s.44

6. **Mental Health (Amendment) Act 1994**
repealed: 2004 c.14 Sch.1 Part 17

9. **Finance Act 1994**
Part I c.II, applied: SI 2003/2758 Art.4
Part III, applied: 2003 c.14 s.194
Part IV c.II, applied: 2002 c.23 Sch.28 para.2, Sch.28 para.3, Sch.28 para.4, Sch.28 para.5, Sch.28 para.6, Sch.29 para.75
Part IV c.V, applied: 2002 c.23 Sch.29 para.129
s.8, applied: SSI 2003/179 Reg.3
s.9, see *Tyler v Customs and Excise Commissioners* [2003] V. & D.R. 358 (VAT and Duties Tribunal (London)), John Walters Q.C. (Chairman)
s.9, applied: SI 2002/501 Reg.25, SI 2002/1773 Reg.15
s.10, see *Tyler v Customs and Excise Commissioners* [2003] V. & D.R. 358 (VAT and Duties Tribunal (London)), John Walters Q.C. (Chairman)
s.12, see *Anglo-German Breweries Ltd, Re* [2002] EWHC 2458, [2003] B.T.C. 5021 (Ch D (Companies Court)), Lawrence Collins, J.; see *Dave v Customs and Excise Commissioners (Costs)* [2002] EWHC 969, [2002] S.T.C. 900 (Ch D), Burton, J.
s.12, amended: 2004 c.12 s.4
s.12A, amended: 2002 c.23 Sch.1 para.4
s.12B, amended: 2002 c.23 Sch.1 para.4

1994–cont.

9. **Finance Act 1994**–*cont.*
s.14, see *Angliss v Customs and Excise Commissioners* [2002] EWHC 1311, [2002] V. & D.R. 274 (Ch D), Laddie, J.; see *Customs and Excise Commissioners v Alzitrans SL* [2003] EWHC 75, [2003] V. & D.R. 369 (Ch D), Blackburne, J.
s.14, amended: 2002 c.23 s.21, Sch.1 para.4, 2004 c.12 s.4
s.15, see *Customs and Excise Commissioners v Alzitrans SL* [2003] EWHC 75, [2003] V. & D.R. 369 (Ch D), Blackburne, J.; see *Dave v Customs and Excise Commissioners (Costs)* [2002] EWHC 969, [2002] S.T.C. 900 (Ch D), Burton, J.
s.16, see *Angliss v Customs and Excise Commissioners* [2002] EWHC 1311, [2002] V. & D.R. 274 (Ch D), Laddie, J.; see *Customs and Excise Commissioners v Dickinson* [2003] EWHC 2358, [2004] 1 W.L.R. 1160 (Ch D), Peter Smith, J.; see *Dave v Customs and Excise Commissioners (Costs)* [2002] EWHC 969, [2002] S.T.C. 900 (Ch D), Burton, J.; see *Gora v Customs and Excise Commissioners* [2003] EWCA Civ 525, [2004] Q.B. 93 (CA), Pill, L.J.; see *Kett v Customs and Excise Commissioners* [2003] V. & D.R. 363 (VAT and Duties Tribunal (London)), Theodore Wallace (Chairman)
s.20, referred to: SI 2003/3113 Sch.1
s.22, repealed (in part): 2003 c.44 Sch.37 Part 6, SI 2004/1501 Sch.2
s.23, applied: SI 2003/3113 Sch.1
s.30, amended: 2002 c.23 s.121, Sch.40 Part 4
s.62, amended: SI 2003/2096 Sch.1 para.23
s.88, repealed: 2003 c.1 Sch.8 Part 1
s.89, repealed: 2003 c.1 Sch.8 Part 1
s.103, repealed: 2004 c.12 Sch.42 Part 3
s.104, repealed: 2004 c.12 Sch.42 Part 3
s.105, repealed: 2004 c.12 Sch.42 Part 3
s.106, repealed: 2004 c.12 Sch.42 Part 3
s.107, repealed: 2004 c.12 Sch.42 Part 3
s.108, repealed (in part): 2003 c.1 Sch.8 Part 1
s.109, repealed: 2003 c.1 Sch.8 Part 1
s.110, repealed: 2003 c.1 Sch.8 Part 1
s.114, repealed: 2002 c.23 Sch.40 Part 3
s.115, repealed: 2002 c.23 Sch.40 Part 3
s.116, repealed: 2002 c.23 Sch.40 Part 3
s.125, repealed: 2003 c.1 Sch.8 Part 1
s.126, repealed: 2003 c.1 Sch.8 Part 1
s.127, repealed: 2003 c.1 Sch.8 Part 1
s.128, repealed: 2003 c.1 Sch.8 Part 1
s.129, repealed: 2003 c.1 Sch.8 Part 1
s.130, repealed: 2003 c.1 Sch.8 Part 1
s.131, repealed: 2003 c.1 Sch.8 Part 1
s.132, repealed: 2003 c.1 Sch.8 Part 1
s.139, repealed (in part): 2002 c.21 Sch.6, 2003 c.1 Sch.8 Part 1

1994–cont.

9. Finance Act 1994–*cont.*

s.147, see *Scottish Provident Institution v Inland Revenue Commissioners* [2004] UKHL 52, [2004] 1 W.L.R. 3172 (HL), Lord Nicholls of Birkenhead

s.147, referred to: 2002 c.23 Sch.29 para.75

s.147, repealed: 2002 c.23 Sch.40 Part 3

s.147A, see *Scottish Provident Institution v Inland Revenue Commissioners* [2003] S.T.C. 1035 (1 Div), Lord Cullen L.P., Lady Cosgrove, Lord Eassie

s.147A, referred to: 2002 c.23 Sch.29 para.75

s.147A, repealed: 2002 c.23 Sch.40 Part 3

s.148, referred to: 2002 c.23 Sch.29 para.75

s.148, repealed: 2002 c.23 Sch.40 Part 3

s.149, repealed: 2002 c.23 Sch.40 Part 3

s.150, repealed: 2002 c.23 Sch.40 Part 3

s.150A, see *Scottish Provident Institution v Inland Revenue Commissioners* [2003] S.T.C. 1035 (1 Div), Lord Cullen L.P., Lady Cosgrove, Lord Eassie; see *Scottish Provident Institution v Inland Revenue Commissioners* [2004] UKHL 52, [2004] 1 W.L.R. 3172 (HL), Lord Nicholls of Birkenhead

s.150A, repealed: 2002 c.23 Sch.40 Part 3

s.151, repealed: 2002 c.23 Sch.40 Part 3

s.152, repealed: 2002 c.23 Sch.40 Part 3

s.153, amended: 2002 c.23 s.70

s.153, repealed: 2002 c.23 Sch.40 Part 3

s.154, repealed: 2002 c.23 Sch.40 Part 3

s.155, see *Scottish Provident Institution v Inland Revenue Commissioners* [2003] S.T.C. 1035 (1 Div), Lord Cullen L.P., Lady Cosgrove, Lord Eassie

s.155, repealed: 2002 c.23 Sch.40 Part 3

s.156, see *Scottish Provident Institution v Inland Revenue Commissioners* [2003] S.T.C. 1035 (1 Div), Lord Cullen L.P., Lady Cosgrove, Lord Eassie

s.156, amended: 2002 c.23 s.103

s.156, repealed: 2002 c.23 Sch.40 Part 3

s.157, repealed: 2002 c.23 Sch.40 Part 3

s.158, repealed: 2002 c.23 Sch.40 Part 3

s.159, applied: 2002 c.23 Sch.28 para.1

s.159, repealed: 2002 c.23 Sch.40 Part 3

s.160, applied: 2002 c.23 Sch.28 para.1

s.160, repealed: 2002 c.23 Sch.40 Part 3

s.161, repealed: 2002 c.23 Sch.40 Part 3

s.162, repealed: 2002 c.23 Sch.40 Part 3

s.163, repealed: 2002 c.23 Sch.40 Part 3

s.164, repealed: 2002 c.23 Sch.40 Part 3

s.165, disapplied: 2002 c.23 Sch.28 para.3

s.165, repealed: 2002 c.23 Sch.40 Part 3

s.166, disapplied: 2002 c.23 Sch.28 para.3

s.166, repealed: 2002 c.23 Sch.40 Part 3

s.167, disapplied: 2002 c.23 Sch.28 para.3

s.167, repealed: 2002 c.23 Sch.40 Part 3

s.168, disapplied: 2002 c.23 Sch.28 para.3

s.168, repealed: 2002 c.23 Sch.40 Part 3

s.168A, added: 2002 c.23 s.69

1994–cont.

9. Finance Act 1994–*cont.*

s.168A, applied: 2002 c.23 s.69

s.168A, disapplied: 2002 c.23 Sch.28 para.3

s.168A, referred to: 2002 c.23 s.69

s.168A, repealed: 2002 c.23 Sch.40 Part 3

s.168A, varied: 2002 c.23 s.69

s.169, repealed: 2002 c.23 Sch.40 Part 3

s.170, repealed: 2002 c.23 Sch.40 Part 3

s.171, repealed: 2002 c.23 Sch.40 Part 3

s.172, repealed: 2002 c.23 Sch.40 Part 3

s.173, repealed: 2002 c.23 Sch.40 Part 3

s.174, repealed: 2002 c.23 Sch.40 Part 3

s.175, repealed: 2002 c.23 Sch.40 Part 3

s.177, repealed: 2002 c.23 Sch.40 Part 3

s.219, amended: 2003 c.14 Sch.43 Part 3

s.225, amended: 2002 c.23 Sch.32 para.7, Sch.32 para.8, Sch.32 para.9

s.226, amended: 2002 c.23 Sch.27 para.16

s.226, repealed (in part): 2002 c.23 Sch.40 Part 3

s.230, amended: 2002 c.23 Sch.32 para.10

s.240, referred to: 2003 c.14 Sch.19 para.8

s.241, amended: 2003 c.14 Sch.20 para.3

s.242, amended: 2003 c.14 Sch.20 para.3

s.244, applied: 2003 c.14 Sch.10 para.1

s.245, amended: SI 2003/2867 Sch.1 para.22

s.249, applied: 2002 c.23 s.90

Sch.5 para.2, see *Gora v Customs and Excise Commissioners* [2003] EWCA Civ 525, [2004] Q.B. 93 (CA), Pill, L.J.

Sch.5 para.6, amended: 2002 c.23 Sch.4 para.12

Sch.6 para.13, repealed (in part): 2002 c.40 Sch.26

Sch.6A para.2, see *National Insurance & Guarantee Corp Ltd v Customs and Excise Commissioners* [2002] V. & D.R. 249 (V&DTr (London)), Theodore Wallace (Chairman)

Sch.6A Part II para.3A, added: 2003 c.14 s.194

Sch.7 Part I para.1, repealed (in part): 2003 c.44 Sch.37 Part 6, SI 2004/1501 Sch.2

Sch.7 Part III para.7, repealed (in part): 2002 c.40 Sch.26

Sch.7 Part VI para.25, disapplied: SI 2004/674 Sch.2 para.4

Sch.7 Part VI para.25, varied: SI 2004/674 Sch.2 para.4

Sch.7 Part VI para.28B, added: SI 2004/355 Art.4

Sch.7A Part I para.3, amended: SI 2002/1397 Sch.1 para.10

Sch.17 para.5, repealed: 2004 c.12 Sch.42 Part 2

Sch.18 para.1, repealed: 2002 c.23 Sch.40 Part 3

Sch.18 para.1A, repealed: 2002 c.23 Sch.40 Part 3

1994–cont.

9. Finance Act 1994–*cont.*

Sch.18 para.2, repealed: 2002 c.23 Sch.40 Part 3

Sch.18 para.3, repealed: 2002 c.23 Sch.40 Part 3

Sch.18 para.4, repealed: 2002 c.23 Sch.40 Part 3

Sch.20 para.2, see *Lyons v Kelly (Inspector of Taxes)* [2002] S.T.C. (S.C.D.) 455 (Sp Comm), Nuala Brice

Sch.24 para.27, amended: 2003 c.1 Sch.6 para.224

15. Antarctic Act 1994

applied: SI 2003/409 Sch.1 Part I

s.9, enabling: SI 2002/2054, SI 2003/323, SI 2004/2782

s.10, enabling: SI 2002/2054, SI 2004/2782

s.25, enabling: SI 2002/2054, SI 2003/323, SI 2004/2782

s.31, amended: 2002 c.8 s.2

s.32, enabling: SI 2002/2054, SI 2003/323, SI 2004/2782

16. State Hospitals (Scotland) Act 1994

s.2, repealed (in part): 2003 asp 13 Sch.5 Part 1

17. Chiropractors Act 1994

Commencement Orders: SI 2002/312 Art.2; SI 2004/1521 Art.2

applied: SI 2002/2376 Reg.4

s.3, applied: SI 2002/2704, SI 2002/2704 Sch.1

s.3, enabling: SI 2002/2704

s.6, applied: SI 2002/2704, SI 2002/2704 Sch.1, SI 2004/1877 Sch.1

s.6, enabling: SI 2002/2704, SI 2004/1877

s.10, amended: 2002 c.17 s.34

s.10, applied: SI 2003/833 Art.4

s.10, repealed (in part): 2002 c.17 Sch.9 Part 2

s.14, applied: SI 2002/2704, SI 2002/2704 Sch.1, Sch.1 para.4, Sch.1 para.9

s.14, referred to: SI 2002/2704 Sch.1 para.13

s.14, enabling: SI 2002/2704

s.17, applied: SI 2004/1877 Sch.1

s.17, enabling: SI 2004/1877

s.20, applied: SI 2004/1877 Sch.1

s.22, amended: 2002 c.17 s.34

s.22, applied: 2002 c.17 s.29, SI 2004/1877 Sch.1

s.23, amended: 2002 c.17 s.34

s.23, applied: SI 2004/1877 Sch.1

s.29, amended: 2002 c.17 s.34

s.29, applied: SI 2003/833 Art.4, SI 2004/1877 Sch.1

s.31, amended: 2002 c.17 s.34

s.31, applied: SI 2003/833 Art.4

s.31, repealed (in part): 2002 c.17 Sch.9 Part 2

s.33, amended: 2002 c.40 Sch.25 para.31

s.35, applied: SI 2002/2704, SI 2002/2704 Sch.1

s.35, referred to: SI 2002/1263, SI 2004/1877

1994–cont.

17. Chiropractors Act 1994–*cont.*

s.35, repealed (in part): 2002 c.17 Sch.9 Part 2

s.35, enabling: SI 2002/1263, SI 2002/2704, SI 2004/1877

s.36, applied: SI 2002/2704

s.36, referred to: SI 2002/1263, SI 2004/1877

s.43, applied: SR 2002/386 Reg.4

s.44, enabling: SI 2002/312, SI 2004/1521

Sch.1 Part I para.10, enabling: SI 2002/1263

Sch.1 Part I para.11A, added: 2003 c.43 Sch.12 para.6

Sch.1 Part I para.14, enabling: SI 2002/1263

18. Social Security (Incapacity for Work) Act 1994

applied: SI 2003/527 Reg.31, SI 2003/1325 Art.2, SSI 2004/257 Reg.31

s.2, repealed (in part): 2002 c.21 Sch.6

s.4, enabling: SI 2002/491

s.10, repealed: 2002 c.21 Sch.6

Sch.1 Part I para.32, repealed: 2002 c.21 Sch.6

Sch.1 Part I para.36, referred to: SI 2003/325 Sch.1

19. Local Government (Wales) Act 1994

referred to: 2003 c.26 Sch.7 para.56

s.3, applied: SI 2003/1082 Reg.11

s.6, repealed: 2004 c.14 Sch.1 Part 10

s.26, repealed: 2004 c.14 Sch.1 Part 10

s.32, repealed: 2004 c.14 Sch.1 Part 10

s.38, amended: 2003 c.26 s.70

s.40, repealed: 2004 c.14 Sch.1 Part 10

s.51, amended: 2003 c.26 Sch.7 para.57, Sch.8 Part 1

s.51, repealed (in part): 2003 c.26 Sch.8 Part 1

s.63, amended: 2003 c.26 Sch.7 para.58

Sch.2 para.2, repealed: 2003 c.17 Sch.7

Sch.7 Part II para.43, repealed (in part): 2004 c.18 Sch.12 Part 1

Sch.8 para.3, repealed (in part): SI 2003/973 Art.13

Sch.10 para.9, repealed: 2002 c.38 Sch.5

Sch.10 para.11, repealed (in part): 2002 c.17 Sch.8 para.19, Sch.9 Part 3

Sch.14 para.1, repealed: 2004 c.14 Sch.1 Part 10

Sch.14 para.2, repealed: 2004 c.14 Sch.1 Part 10

Sch.14 para.3, repealed: 2004 c.14 Sch.1 Part 10

Sch.14 para.4, repealed: 2004 c.14 Sch.1 Part 10

Sch.14 para.5, repealed: 2004 c.14 Sch.1 Part 10

Sch.14 para.6, repealed: 2004 c.14 Sch.1 Part 10

Sch.14 para.7, repealed: 2004 c.14 Sch.1 Part 10

1994–cont.

19. Local Government (Wales) Act 1994–
cont.

Sch.14 para.8, repealed: 2004 c.14 Sch.1 Part 10

Sch.14 para.9, repealed: 2004 c.14 Sch.1 Part 10

Sch.14 para.10, repealed: 2004 c.14 Sch.1 Part 10

Sch.14 para.11, repealed: 2004 c.14 Sch.1 Part 10

Sch.14 para.12, repealed: 2004 c.14 Sch.1 Part 10

Sch.14 para.13, repealed: 2004 c.14 Sch.1 Part 10

Sch.15 para.30, referred to: 2003 c.26 s.128

Sch.15 para.30, repealed: 2003 c.26 Sch.8 Part 1

Sch.16 para.41, repealed: 2003 c.17 Sch.7

Sch.16 para.22, repealed: 2003 c.17 Sch.7

Sch.16 para.29, repealed: 2003 c.17 Sch.7

Sch.16 para.32, repealed: 2003 c.17 Sch.7

Sch.16 para.36, repealed: 2003 c.17 Sch.7

Sch.16 para.69, repealed: 2003 c.17 Sch.7

Sch.16 para.72, repealed: 2003 c.21 Sch.19

Sch.16 para.73, repealed: 2003 c.17 Sch.7

Sch.16 para.88, repealed (in part): 2003 c.26 Sch.8 Part 1

Sch.16 para.96, referred to: 2003 c.26 s.128

Sch.16 para.96, repealed: 2003 c.26 Sch.8 Part 1

Sch.16 para.97, referred to: 2003 c.26 s.128

Sch.16 para.97, repealed: 2003 c.26 Sch.8 Part 1

20. Sunday Trading Act 1994

applied: 2004 c.26 s.3

Sch.1, amended: SI 2004/470 Art.2

Sch.1 para.1, amended: 2003 c.17 Sch.6 para.110

Sch.1 para.2, amended: 2004 c.26 s.4, SI 2004/470 Art.2

Sch.1 para.3, amended: 2003 c.17 Sch.6 para.110

Sch.1 para.3, referred to: 2004 c.26 s.1

Sch.1 para.3, varied: 2004 c.26 s.1

Sch.1 para.4, repealed: SI 2004/470 Art.2

Sch.1 para.5, repealed: SI 2004/470 Art.2

Sch.1 para.6, amended: SI 2004/470 Art.2

Sch.1 para.8, substituted: SI 2004/470 Art.2

Sch.1 para.9, repealed: SI 2004/470 Art.2

Sch.2 Part I para.2, applied: 2004 c.26 s.3

Sch.2 Part I para.3, applied: 2004 c.26 s.3

Sch.2 Part I para.3, varied: 2004 c.26 s.3

Sch.2 Part I para.4, applied: 2004 c.26 s.3

Sch.2 Part I para.5, applied: 2004 c.26 s.3

Sch.2 Part I para.6, applied: 2004 c.26 s.3

Sch.2 Part I para.7, applied: 2004 c.26 s.3

Sch.3, added: 2004 c.26 s.4

Sch.3 para.1, amended: SI 2004/470 Art.2

Sch.3 para.3, applied: 2004 c.26 s.2

Sch.3 para.4, applied: 2004 c.26 s.2

1994–cont.

20. Sunday Trading Act 1994–*cont.*

Sch.3 para.5, applied: 2004 c.26 s.2

Sch.3 para.6, applied: 2004 c.26 s.2

Sch.3 para.6, varied: 2004 c.26 s.2

Sch.3 para.7, applied: 2004 c.26 s.2

Sch.3 para.7, varied: 2004 c.26 s.2

Sch.3 para.8, applied: 2004 c.26 s.2

21. Coal Industry Act 1994

Commencement Orders: SI 2004/144 Art.2, Sch.1

applied: 2002 c.40 Sch.15, 2003 c.17 s.66

s.4A, added: 2003 c.37 s.85

s.4B, added: 2003 c.37 s.85

s.4C, added: 2003 c.37 s.85

s.23, enabling: SI 2004/144

s.24, repealed: 2004 c.14 Sch.1 Part 5

s.36, amended: 2002 c.40 Sch.17 para.48

s.38, applied: 2002 c.9 s.33, Sch.1 para.7, Sch.3 para.7

s.46, enabling: SI 2004/2241

s.49, applied: 2002 c.9 s.33, Sch.1 para.7, Sch.3 para.7

s.51, applied: 2002 c.9 s.33, Sch.1 para.7, Sch.3 para.7

s.59, amended: 2002 c.40 Sch.25 para.32, SI 2002/1555 Art.23, 2003 c.37 Sch.7 para.31

s.68, amended: 2003 c.37 s.85

s.68, enabling: SI 2004/144

Sch.1A, referred to: 2003 c.37 s.85

Sch.1B, referred to: 2003 c.37 s.85

Sch.1A para.1, added: 2003 c.37 Sch.5

Sch.1A para.2, added: 2003 c.37 Sch.5

Sch.1A para.3, added: 2003 c.37 Sch.5

Sch.1A para.4, added: 2003 c.37 Sch.5

Sch.1A para.5, added: 2003 c.37 Sch.5

Sch.1B para.1, added: 2003 c.37 Sch.6

Sch.1B para.2, added: 2003 c.37 Sch.6

Sch.1B para.3, added: 2003 c.37 Sch.6

Sch.1B para.4, added: 2003 c.37 Sch.6

Sch.1B para.5, added: 2003 c.37 Sch.6

Sch.1B para.6, added: 2003 c.37 Sch.6

Sch.1B para.7, added: 2003 c.37 Sch.6

Sch.1B para.8, added: 2003 c.37 Sch.6

Sch.9 para.1, repealed: 2002 c.9 Sch.13

Sch.9 para.14, repealed: 2002 c.40 Sch.26

Sch.9 para.15, repealed: 2002 c.40 Sch.26

Sch.9 para.21, repealed: 2002 c.40 Sch.26

Sch.9 para.23, repealed: 2002 c.40 Sch.26

Sch.9 para.24, repealed: 2002 c.1 Sch.4

22. Vehicle Excise and Registration Act 1994

applied: 2002 c.23 s.19, SI 2002/1808 Reg.11, Reg.14, SI 2002/2742 Reg.9A, Reg.33, Reg.46, Sch.2 para.4, SI 2002/3049 Reg.7, 2003 c.1 s.140, s.142, s.171, 2003 c.39 Sch.5 para.38, 2003 c.iii s.2, SI 2003/37 Reg.3, SI 2003/300 Reg.11, Reg.14, SI 2003/1959 Reg.14, Sch.1 para.4, SI 2003/1998 Sch.11 para.3, SI

1994–cont.

22. Vehicle Excise and Registration Act 1994–cont.

applied: 2002 c.23 s.19–cont.

2003/2994 Art.2, 2004 c.18 s.90, SI 2004/176 Reg.19, Reg.24, SI 2004/242 Reg.3, SI 2004/1896 Reg.3, SI 2004/2577 Reg.3, SR 2003/303 Reg.20, SSI 2003/212 Reg.15

referred to: 2003 c.43 Sch.4 para.95

s.1, amended: 2002 c.23 Sch.5 para.2

s.2, amended: 2002 c.23 Sch.5 para.3

s.7, amended: 2002 c.23 Sch.5 para.4

s.7, applied: SI 2002/2742 Reg.30, Reg.33

s.7, referred to: SI 2002/2742 Reg.10, SI 2003/2994 Art.2

s.7, enabling: SI 2002/2742, SI 2004/238

s.7A, added: 2002 c.23 Sch.5 para.5

s.7A, applied: SI 2003/2981

s.7A, enabling: SI 2003/2981

s.7B, added: 2002 c.23 Sch.5 para.5

s.7B, enabling: SI 2003/3073

s.10, applied: SI 2002/2742 Sch.4 para.3, Sch.4 para.5, Sch.4 para.7, Sch.4 para.9

s.10, enabling: SI 2002/2742

s.11, applied: SR 2003/303 Reg.6

s.11, referred to: SI 2002/2742 Sch.6 para.6, Sch.6 para.9

s.11, enabling: SI 2002/2742

s.12, enabling: SI 2002/2742

s.13, amended: 2002 c.23 s.18

s.14, applied: SI 2002/2742 Reg.36

s.14, enabling: SI 2002/2742

s.15A, added: 2003 c.14 s.16

s.16, repealed: 2003 c.14 Sch.43 Part 1

s.19, applied: SI 2002/2742 Reg.9, Reg.46

s.19C, added: 2004 c.12 s.18

s.21, applied: SI 2002/2742 Reg.10

s.21, referred to: SI 2003/2994 Art.2

s.21, enabling: SI 2002/2742, SI 2003/3110

s.22, amended: 2002 c.23 Sch.5 para.6

s.22, referred to: SI 2003/2994 Art.2

s.22, enabling: SI 2002/2381, SI 2002/2382, SI 2002/2742, SI 2003/2154, SI 2003/3073, SI 2004/238, SI 2004/1773, SI 2004/2099, SI 2004/3298

s.22A, applied: SI 2003/2994 Art.2

s.22A, enabling: SI 2002/2381, SI 2002/2382, SI 2002/2742, SI 2004/2099

s.22ZA, added: 2002 c.23 s.17

s.22ZA, amended: 2003 c.14 s.15

s.23, applied: SI 2002/2742 Reg.30

s.23, enabling: SI 2002/2687, SI 2002/2742

s.25, enabling: SI 2002/2742

s.27, applied: SI 2002/2977 Sch.1 Part II

s.29, amended: 2002 c.23 Sch.5 para.7

s.30, enabling: SI 2002/2742 Reg.46

s.31A, substituted: 2002 c.23 Sch.5 para.8

s.31B, applied: SI 2002/2742 Reg.26A

s.31B, substituted: 2002 c.23 Sch.5 para.8

s.31B, enabling: SI 2003/3073

1994–cont.

22. Vehicle Excise and Registration Act 1994–cont.

s.31C, substituted: 2002 c.23 Sch.5 para.8

s.32, amended: 2002 c.23 Sch.5 para.9, SI 2003/1247 Sch.1 para.15, Sch.2

s.33, amended: 2002 c.23 Sch.5 para.10

s.33, applied: SI 2002/2742 Reg.6, Reg.42

s.33, enabling: SI 2002/2742

s.34, amended: 2002 c.23 Sch.5 para.11

s.35A, amended: 2002 c.23 s.18

s.36, amended: 2002 c.23 s.18

s.47, amended: 2002 c.23 Sch.5 para.12

s.48, amended: 2002 c.23 Sch.5 para.13

s.51, amended: 2003 c.39 Sch.8 para.362

s.52, applied: SI 2002/2742 Reg.46

s.52, enabling: SI 2002/2742

s.53, amended: 2002 c.23 Sch.5 para.14

s.54, amended: 2002 c.23 Sch.5 para.15

s.55, amended: 2003 c.39 Sch.8 para.362

s.57, amended: 2002 c.23 Sch.5 para.16

s.57, repealed (in part): 2002 c.23 Sch.40 Part 1

s.57, enabling: SI 2002/745, SI 2002/2381, SI 2002/2382, SI 2002/2687, SI 2002/2742, SI 2003/1814, SI 2003/2154, SI 2003/2335, SI 2003/2981, SI 2003/3073, SI 2004/1773, SI 2004/1872

s.58, amended: 2004 c.12 s.18

s.59, applied: SI 2002/2742 Reg.47

s.59, enabling: SI 2002/2742, SI 2003/2154

s.61A, enabling: SI 2002/2742

s.61B, enabling: SI 2002/2742, SI 2003/1814, SI 2003/2335, SI 2004/1872

s.62, amended: 2002 c.23 Sch.5 para.17

s.62, applied: SI 2002/2742 Reg.35

s.62, referred to: SR 2003/303 Reg.6

s.62, enabling: SI 2002/2742

Sch.1, applied: SI 2002/2742 Reg.43

Sch.1, referred to: SI 2002/2742 Reg.5

Sch.1 Part I para.1, amended: 2002 c.23 s.20, 2003 c.14 s.14

Sch.1 Part I para.1, enabling: SI 2002/2742

Sch.1 Part IA para.1B, amended: 2002 c.23 s.15, 2003 c.14 s.14

Sch.1 Part IB para.1J, amended: 2003 c.14 s.14

Sch.1 Part IB para.1J, substituted: 2002 c.23 s.16

Sch.1 Part II para.2, amended: 2002 c.23 s.18

Sch.1 Part II para.2, applied: SI 2002/2742 Reg.40

Sch.1 Part II para.2, repealed (in part): 2002 c.23 Sch.40 Part 1

Sch.1 Part III, applied: SI 2002/2742 Reg.44, 2003 c.1 s.242

Sch.1 Part III para.3, referred to: SI 2002/2742 Reg.5

Sch.1 Part III para.3, enabling: SI 2002/2742

Sch.1 Part IV, applied: SI 2003/1998 Sch.2 para.2

Sch.1 Part IV para.4, referred to: SI 2002/2742 Reg.42

CAP.

1994–cont.

22. Vehicle Excise and Registration Act 1994–*cont.*

Sch.1 Part V, applied: SI 2003/1998 Sch.4 para.1

Sch.1 Part V para.5, applied: SI 2002/2742 Reg.45

Sch.1 Part V para.5, referred to: SI 2002/2742 Sch.7 para.3, Sch.7 para.4

Sch.1 Part V para.5, enabling: SI 2002/2742

Sch.1 Part VI para.6, referred to: SI 2002/2742 Reg.5

Sch.1 Part VII para.7, referred to: SI 2002/2742 Reg.5

Sch.1 Part VIII para.9A, referred to: SI 2002/2742 Reg.5

Sch.1 Part VIII para.11A, referred to: SI 2002/2742 Reg.5

Sch.1 Part VIII para.18, enabling: SI 2002/1072

Sch.2A, applied: SI 2002/2742 Reg.46

Sch.2 para.2, referred to: SI 2002/2742 Sch.4 para.1

Sch.2 para.2A, applied: SI 2002/2742 Reg.4

Sch.2 para.2A, referred to: SI 2002/2742 Sch.4 para.1

Sch.2 para.2A, enabling: SI 2002/2742

Sch.2 para.3, referred to: SI 2002/2742 Sch.4 para.1

Sch.2 para.4, amended: 2004 c.21 Sch.1 para.85

Sch.2 para.4, applied: SI 2002/1040 Sch.4

Sch.2 para.5, amended: 2004 c.21 Sch.1 para.85

Sch.2 para.5, applied: SI 2002/1040 Sch.4

Sch.2 para.6, applied: SI 2002/1040 Sch.4

Sch.2 para.7, amended: 2002 c.17 Sch.5 para.39, 2003 c.43 Sch.4 para.96

Sch.2 para.7, applied: SI 2002/1040 Sch.4

Sch.2 para.18, applied: SI 2002/1040 Sch.4, SI 2002/2742 Reg.10

Sch.2 para.19, applied: SI 2002/1040 Sch.4, SI 2002/2742 Reg.10, Reg.33

Sch.2 para.20, applied: SI 2002/1040 Sch.4

Sch.2 para.23, referred to: SI 2002/2742 Sch.4 para.1

Sch.2 para.24, referred to: SI 2002/2742 Sch.4 para.1

Sch.2 para.24, enabling: SI 2002/2742, SI 2003/2154

Sch.2A para.3, enabling: SI 2002/745

Sch.3 para.3, repealed (in part): 2003 c.21 Sch.19

Sch.3 para.22, repealed: 2003 c.1 Sch.8 Part 1

Sch.4 para.7, applied: SI 2002/2742 Reg.33

23. Value Added Tax Act 1994

see *University of Bristol v Customs and Excise Commissioners* [2002] S.T.I. 125 (V&DTr), JC Gort (Chairman)

applied: 2002 c.40 Sch.14, 2004 c.20 s.86, SI 2004/674 Sch.1 Part 1, SI 2004/1929 Reg.4, SI 2004/1933 Art.2

CAP.

1994–cont.

23. Value Added Tax Act 1994–*cont.*

referred to: 2003 c.43 Sch.4 para.97

Part IV, added: 2004 c.12 Sch.2 para.1

s.2, see *Oval (717) Ltd v Customs and Excise Commissioners* [2002] V. & D.R. 581, [2003] S.T.I. 608 (V&DTr), Nuala Brice (Chairman)

s.3, enabling: SI 2004/1675

s.3A, added: 2003 c.14 Sch.2 para.2

s.4, see *Isle of Wight Council v Customs and Excise Commissioners* [2004] B.V.C. 2181 (V&DTr), Stephen Oliver Q.C. (Chairman)

s.5, enabling: SI 2002/1280, SI 2003/1055, SI 2004/779, SI 2004/3084, SI 2004/3085, SI 2004/3150

s.6, see *Cumbernauld Development Corp v Customs and Excise Commissioners* [2002] S.T.C. 226 (2 Div), Lord Gill L.J.C., Lord Coulsfield, Lord MacLean

s.6, amended: 2002 c.23 s.24

s.6, applied: SI 2002/1280 Art.1, SI 2004/1933 Sch.2 para.4

s.6, repealed (in part): 2002 c.23 s.24, Sch.40 Part 2

s.6, enabling: SI 2002/2918, SI 2003/1069, SI 2003/2318, SI 2003/3220

s.7, applied: SI 2004/1933 Sch.2 para.6

s.7, enabling: SI 2003/862, SI 2004/3148

s.8, enabling: SI 2003/863, SI 2004/3149

s.9A, added: 2004 c.12 s.21

s.9A, enabling: SI 2004/3140, SI 2004/3148

s.12, enabling: SI 2003/3220

s.14, see *Musashi Autoparts Europe Ltd (formerly TAP Manufacturing Ltd) v Customs and Excise Commissioners* [2003] EWHC 343, [2003] S.T.C. 449 (Ch D), Lightman, J.

s.14, enabling: SI 2004/1082

s.16, enabling: SI 2003/2318, SI 2004/1082

s.19, see *Customs and Excise Commissioners v Ping (Europe) Ltd* [2002] EWCA Civ 1115, [2002] S.T.C. 1186 (CA), Robert Walker, L.J.

s.23, amended: 2003 c.14 s.10

s.24, see *BUPA Purchasing Ltd v Customs and Excise Commissioners* [2003] EWHC 1957, [2003] S.T.C. 1203 (Ch D), Park, J.

s.24, amended: 2003 c.14 s.17

s.24, enabling: SI 2003/1114

s.25, enabling: SI 2002/1142, SI 2003/1069, SI 2004/767, SI 2004/1082, SI 2004/1675

s.26, see *Water Hall Group Plc v Customs and Excise Commissioners* [2003] V. & D.R. 257 (V&DTr), Peter H Lawson (Chairman); see *WHA Ltd v Customs and Excise Commissioners* [2003] EWHC 305, [2003] S.T.C. 648 (Ch D), Lloyd, J.; see *WHA Ltd v Customs and Excise Commissioners* [2004] EWCA Civ 559, [2004] S.T.C. 1081 (CA), Waller, L.J.

1994–cont.

23. Value Added Tax Act 1994–*cont.*

s.26, enabling: SI 2002/1074, SI 2003/3220, SI 2004/3140

s.26A, added: 2002 c.23 s.22

s.26A, enabling: SI 2002/3027, SI 2003/532

s.26B, added: 2002 c.23 s.23

s.26B, enabling: SI 2002/1142, SI 2003/1069, SI 2003/3220, SI 2004/767

s.29A, enabling: SI 2002/1100, SI 2004/777

s.30, see *Beynon v Customs and Excise Commissioners* [2002] EWCA Civ 1870, [2003] S.T.C. 169 (CA), Aldous, L.J.; see *Customs and Excise Commissioners v Zielinski Baker & Partners Ltd* [2002] EWCA Civ 692, [2002] S.T.C. 829 (CA), Aldous, L.J.; see *Simply Travel Ltd v Customs and Excise Commissioners* [2002] S.T.C. 194 (Ch D), Lightman, J.; see *Talacre Beach Caravan Sales Ltd v Customs and Excise Commissioners* [2004] EWHC 165, [2004] S.T.C. 817 (Ch D), Lindsay, J.

s.30, enabling: SI 2002/456, SI 2002/1101, SI 2002/1173, SI 2002/2813, SI 2003/1485, SI 2004/3343

s.31, enabling: SI 2002/762, SI 2003/24, SI 2003/1568, SI 2003/1569, SI 2004/3083

s.33, see *City of London Corp v Customs and Excise Commissioners* [2003] B.V.C. 2192 (V&DTr), Paul Heim (Chairman); see *R. (on the application of Cardiff City Council) v Customs and Excise Commissioners* [2002] EWHC 2085, [2002] S.T.C. 1318 (QBD (Admin Ct)), Stanley Burnton, J.; see *R. (on the application of Cardiff City Council) v Customs and Excise Commissioners* [2003] EWCA Civ 1456, [2004] S.T.C. 356 (CA), Schiemann, L.J.

s.33, amended: 2003 c.21 Sch.17 para.129

s.33A, enabling: SI 2004/1709

s.35, see *Blom-Cooper v Customs and Excise Commissioners* [2002] EWHC 1421, [2002] S.T.C. 1061 (Ch D), Peter Smith, J.; see *Blom-Cooper v Customs and Excise Commissioners* [2003] EWCA Civ 493, [2003] S.T.C. 669 (CA), Chadwick, L.J.; see *Jacobs v Customs and Excise Commissioners* [2004] EWHC 2358, [2004] S.T.C. 1662 (Ch D), Evans-Lombe, J.; see *Jacobs v Customs and Excise Commissioners* [2004] V. & D.R. 80 (V&DTr), Lady Mitting (Chairman)

s.36, see *General Motors Acceptance Corp (UK) Plc v Customs and Excise Commissioners* [2004] EWHC 192, [2004] S.T.C. 577 (Ch D), Field, J.

s.36, repealed (in part): 2002 c.23 Sch.40 Part 2

s.36, enabling: SI 2002/3027, SI 2003/3220

s.36A, added: 2002 c.23 s.25

s.36A, enabling: SI 2002/1935

s.37, enabling: SI 2004/3147

1994–cont.

23. Value Added Tax Act 1994–*cont.*

s.39, enabling: SI 2004/3140

s.41, amended: 2002 c.17 Sch.5 para.40, 2003 c.43 s.33

s.41, applied: 2002 asp 7 s.1, s.2, 2003 asp 6 s.1, s.2, 2004 asp 2 s.1, s.2

s.43, see *J&W Waste Management Ltd v Customs and Excise Commissioners* [2003] V. & D.R. 350 (VAT and Duties Tribunal (London)), Paul Heim

s.43, amended: 2004 c.12 s.20

s.43, applied: SI 2004/1933 Sch.1

s.43, enabling: SI 2002/1280

s.43A, referred to: SI 2004/1931 Art.2

s.43A, varied: SI 2004/1931 Art.2

s.43AA, added: 2004 c.12 s.20

s.43AA, enabling: SI 2004/1931

s.43B, amended: 2004 c.12 s.20

s.43C, amended: 2004 c.12 s.20

s.43D, added: 2004 c.12 s.20

s.45, see *Jamieson v Customs and Excise Commissioners* [2002] S.T.C. 1418 (Ch D), Peter Leaver Q.C.

s.46, amended: SI 2003/2096 Sch.1 para.25

s.47, see *United Utilities Plc v Customs and Excise Commissioners* [2004] EWCA Civ 245, [2004] S.T.C. 727 (CA), Auld, L.J.

s.48, amended: 2003 c.14 s.197, SI 2003/3092 Art.2

s.48, enabling: SI 2003/3092

s.49, enabling: SI 2004/1675

s.50A, enabling: SI 2002/1502, SI 2002/1503

s.51, enabling: SI 2002/1102, SI 2004/778

s.51B, added: 2003 c.14 Sch.1 para.1

s.53, see *Customs and Excise Commissioners v First Choice Holidays Plc* [2004] EWCA Civ 1044, [2004] S.T.C. 1407 (CA), Mummery, L.J.

s.57, amended: SI 2002/1099 Art.2, SI 2003/1057 Art.2, SI 2004/776 Art.2

s.57, enabling: SI 2002/1099, SI 2003/1057, SI 2004/776

s.58, enabling: SI 2004/1675

s.60, see *Akbar (t/a Mumtaz Paan House) v Customs and Excise Commissioners (Human Rights)* [2002] B.P.I.R. 62 (Ch D), Judge Behrens Q.C.; see *Storey v Customs and Excise Commissioners* [2003] S.T.I. 313 (V&DTr), Stephen Oliver Q.C. (Chairman)

s.60, applied: SSI 2003/179 Reg.3

s.62, applied: 2003 c.14 s.27

s.63, applied: 2003 c.14 s.27

s.64, applied: 2003 c.14 s.27

s.65, applied: 2003 c.14 s.27

s.66, applied: 2003 c.14 s.27

s.67, applied: 2003 c.14 s.27

s.68, applied: 2003 c.14 s.27

s.69, applied: 2003 c.14 s.27

s.69A, applied: 2003 c.14 s.27

CAP.

1994–cont.

23. Value Added Tax Act 1994–cont.

s.70, see *Ball v Customs and Excise Commissioners* [2002] S.T.I. 1527 (V&DTr), CP Bishopp (Chairman)

s.70, amended: 2004 c.12 Sch.2 para.3

s.72, amended: 2003 c.14 s.17

s.73, see *Courts Plc v Customs and Excise Commissioners* [2003] EWHC 2541, [2004] S.T.C. 690 (Ch D), Blackburne, J.; see *Customs and Excise Commissioners v D&D Marketing (UK) Ltd* [2002] EWHC 660, [2003] B.P.I.R. 539 (Ch D), Evans-Lombe, J.; see *Customs and Excise Commissioners v DFS Furniture Co Plc (No.2)* [2004] EWCA Civ 243, [2004] 1 W.L.R. 2159 (CA), Lord Phillips of Worth Matravers, M.R.; see *Hindle (t/a DJ Baker Bar) v Customs and Excise Commissioners* [2003] EWHC1665, [2004] S.T.C. 412 (Ch D), Neuberger, J.; see *Hossain v Customs and Excise Commissioners* [2004] EWHC 1898, [2004] S.T.C. 1572 (Ch D), Hart, J.; see *Laura Ashley Ltd v Customs and Excise Commissioners* [2003] EWHC 2832, [2004] S.T.C. 635 (Ch D), David Richards, J; see *Musashi Autoparts Europe Ltd (formerly TAP Manufacturing Ltd) v Customs and Excise Commissioners* [2003] EWCA Civ1738, [2004] S.T.C. 220 (CA), Pill, L.J.; see *Musashi Autoparts Europe Ltd (formerly TAP Manufacturing Ltd) v Customs and Excise Commissioners* [2003] EWHC 343, [2003] S.T.C. 449 (Ch D), Lightman, J.; see *Pegasus Birds Ltd v Customs and Excise Commissioners* [2003] EWHC 2552, [2004] S.T.C. 262 (Ch D), Patten, J.; see *Pegasus Birds Ltd v Customs and Excise Commissioners* [2004] EWCA Civ 1015, [2004] S.T.C. 1509 (CA), Waller, L.J.; see *R. (on the application of Freeserve.com Plc) v Customs and Excise Commissioners* [2003] EWHC 2736, [2004] S.T.C. 187 (QBD (Admin Ct)), Evans-Lombe, J.; see *Rowe (t/a Cheshire Hearing Centre) v Customs and Excise Commissioners* [2002] V. & D.R. 156 (V&DTr (Manchester)), Colin Bishopp (Chairman); see *University Court of the University of Glasgow v Customs and Excise Commissioners* [2003] S.T.C. 495 (1 Div), Lord Hamilton, Lord Cullen L.P., Lord Marnoch; see *University of Huddersfield Higher Education Corp v Customs and Excise Commissioners* [2003] B.V.C. 2163 (VAT and Duties Tribunal (Manchester)), JD Demack (Chairman)

s.76, disapplied: SI 2004/674 Sch.2 para.3

s.76, varied: SI 2004/674 Sch.2 para.3

s.77, see *Laura Ashley Ltd v Customs and Excise Commissioners* [2003] EWHC 2832, [2004] S.T.C. 635 (Ch D), David Richards, J

CAP.

1994–cont.

23. Value Added Tax Act 1994–cont.

s.77A, see *R. (on the application of Federation of Technological Industries) v Customs and Excise Commissioners* [2004] EWCA Civ 1020, [2004] S.T.C. 1424 (CA), Ward, L.J.; see *R. (on the application of Federation of Technological Industries) v Customs and Excise Commissioners* [2004] EWHC 254, [2004] S.T.C. 1008 (QBD (Admin Ct)), Lightman, J.

s.77A, added: 2003 c.14 s.18

s.78A, see *Customs and Excise Commissioners v DFS Furniture Co Plc (No.2)* [2003] EWHC 857, [2003] S.T.C. 739 (Ch D), Sir Andrew Morritt V.C.; see *Customs and Excise Commissioners v DFS Furniture Co Plc (No.2)* [2004] EWCA Civ 243, [2004] 1 W.L.R. 2159 (CA), Lord Phillips of Worth Matravers, M.R.

s.79, see *Anglo-German Breweries Ltd, Re* [2002] EWHC 2458, [2003] B.T.C. 5021 (Ch D (Companies Court)), Lawrence Collins, J.

s.80, see *Customs and Excise Commissioners v DFS Furniture Co Plc (No.2)* [2003] EWHC 857, [2003] S.T.C. 739 (Ch D), Sir Andrew Morritt V.C.; see *Customs and Excise Commissioners v DFS Furniture Co Plc (No.2)* [2004] EWCA Civ 243, [2004] 1 W.L.R. 2159 (CA), Lord Phillips of Worth Matravers, M.R.; see *Isle of Wight Council v Customs and Excise Commissioners* [2004] EWHC 2541, [2004] 48 E.G.C.S. 132 (Ch D), Pumfrey, J.; see *King (t/a Barbury Shooting School) v Customs and Excise Commissioners* [2003] S.T.I. 510 (V&DTr), R Barlow (Chairman); see *Marks & Spencer Plc v Customs and Excise Commissioners (No.5)* [2003] EWCA Civ 1448, [2004] S.T.C. 1 (CA), Auld, L.J.; see *R. (on the application of Cardiff City Council) v Customs and Excise Commissioners* [2002] EWHC 2085, [2002] S.T.C. 1318 (QBD (Admin Ct)), Stanley Burnton, J.; see *R. (on the application of DFS Furniture Co Plc) v Customs and Excise Commissioners (No.1)* [2002] EWHC 807, [2002] S.T.C. 760 (QBD (Admin Ct)), Moses, J.; see *Shendish Manor Ltd v Customs and Excise Commissioners* [2004] V. & D.R. 64 (V&DTr), Theodore Wallace (Chairman)

s.81, amended: SI 2003/2096 Sch.1 para.26

s.82, amended: 2003 c.39 Sch.8 para.363

s.82, applied: 2003 c.39 Sch.9 para.2

s.83, see *Daniels (t/a Homeforce) v Customs and Excise Commissioners* [2002] V. & D.R. 591 (V&DTr), John Walters Q.C. (Chairman); see *J&W Waste Management Ltd v Customs and Excise Commissioners* [2003] V. & D.R. 350 (VAT and Duties Tribunal (London)), Paul Heim; see *National Westminster Bank Plc v Customs*

1994–cont.
23. Value Added Tax Act 1994–*cont.*

s.83–*cont.*

and Excise Commissioners (Unjust Enrich-ment) [2003] EWHC 1822, [2003] S.T.C. 1072 (Ch D), Jacob, J.; see *Pegasus Birds Ltd v Customs and Excise Commissioners* [2003] EWHC 2552, [2004] S.T.C. 262 (Ch D), Patten, J.; see *Pegasus Birds Ltd v Customs and Excise Commissioners* [2004] EWCA Civ 1015, [2004] S.T.C. 1509 (CA), Waller, L.J.; see *Rahman (t/a Khayam Restaurant) v Customs and Excise Commissioners (No.2)* [2002] EWCA Civ 1881, [2003] S.T.C. 150 (CA), Chadwick, L.J.

s.83, amended: 2002 c.23 s.23, s.24, 2003 c.14 s.17, s.18, SI 2003/3075 Sch.2 para.1, 2004 c.12 s.22, Sch.2 para.4

s.83, referred to: SI 2003/3102 Reg.13

s.84, see *Customs and Excise Commissioners v D&D Marketing (UK) Ltd* [2002] EWHC 660, [2003] B.P.I.R. 539 (Ch D), Evans-Lombe, J.; see *Daniels (t/a Homeforce) v Customs and Excise Commissioners* [2002] V. & D.R. 591 (V&DTr), John Walters Q.C. (Chairman); see *National Westminster Bank Plc v Customs and Excise Commissioners (Unjust Enrichment)* [2003] EWHC 1822, [2003] S.T.C. 1072 (Ch D), Jacob, J.; see *Rahman (t/a Khayam Restaurant) v Customs and Excise Commissioners (No.2)* [2002] EWCA Civ 1881, [2003] S.T.C. 150 (CA), Chadwick, L.J.; see *University Court of the University of Glasgow v Customs and Excise Commissioners* [2003] S.T.C. 495 (1 Div), Lord Hamilton, Lord Cullen L.P., Lord Marnoch

s.84, amended: 2002 c.23 s.23, 2003 c.14 s.17, s.18, 2004 c.12 Sch.2 para.5

s.84, referred to: 2004 c.12 Sch.2 para.5

s.85, see *R. (on the application of DFS Furniture Co Plc) v Customs and Excise Commissioners (No.1)* [2002] EWHC 807, [2002] S.T.C. 760 (QBD (Admin Ct)), Moses, J.; see *Specsavers Optical Group v Customs and Excise Commissioners* [2003] B.V.C. 2392 (V&DTr), John Clark (Chairman)

s.85, varied: 2003 c.14 s.37, SI 2003/3102 Reg.13

s.87, varied: 2003 c.14 s.37, SI 2003/3102 Reg.13

s.88, amended: 2002 c.23 s.24

s.88, enabling: SI 2003/1485, SI 2004/3140

s.93, enabling: SI 2004/1082

s.94, see *Isle of Wight Council v Customs and Excise Commissioners* [2004] EWHC 2541, [2004] 48 E.G.C.S. 132 (Ch D), Pumfrey, J.; see *Yarburgh Childrens Trust v Customs and Excise Commissioners* [2002] S.T.C. 207 (Ch D), Patten, J.

1994–cont.
23. Value Added Tax Act 1994–*cont.*

s.96, see *Cumbernauld Development Corp v Customs and Excise Commissioners* [2002] S.T.C. 226 (2 Div), Lord Gill L.J.C., Lord Coulsfield, Lord MacLean

s.96, amended: 2003 c.14 s.20

s.96, enabling: SI 2002/1173, SI 2002/2813, SI 2003/1568, SI 2003/1569, SI 2004/3343

s.97, amended: 2004 c.12 s.20, s.22, Sch.2 para.6

Sch.A1 para.1, see *Oval (717) Ltd v Customs and Excise Commissioners* [2002] V. & D.R. 581, [2003] S.T.I. 608 (V&DTr), Nuala Brice (Chairman)

Sch.A1 para.2, see *Oval (717) Ltd v Customs and Excise Commissioners* [2002] V. & D.R. 581, [2003] S.T.I. 608 (V&DTr), Nuala Brice (Chairman)

Sch.A1 para.3, see *Oval (717) Ltd v Customs and Excise Commissioners* [2002] V. & D.R. 581, [2003] S.T.I. 608 (V&DTr), Nuala Brice (Chairman)

Sch.1 para.1, amended: SI 2002/1098 Art.2, SI 2003/1058 Art.2, SI 2004/775 Art.2

Sch.1 para.4, amended: SI 2002/1098 Art.2, SI 2003/1058 Art.2, SI 2004/775 Art.2

Sch.1 para.13, amended: 2003 c.14 Sch.2 para.3

Sch.1 para.15, enabling: SI 2002/1098, SI 2003/1058, SI 2004/775

Sch.1 para.17, enabling: SI 2004/1675

Sch.2 para.9, enabling: SI 2004/1675

Sch.3 para.1, amended: SI 2002/1098 Art.3, SI 2003/1058 Art.3, SI 2004/775 Art.3

Sch.3 para.2, amended: SI 2002/1098 Art.3, SI 2003/1058 Art.3, SI 2004/775 Art.3

Sch.3 para.9, enabling: SI 2002/1098, SI 2003/1058, SI 2004/775

Sch.3 para.10, enabling: SI 2004/1675

Sch.3A para.8, enabling: SI 2004/1675

Sch.3B Part 1 para.1, added: 2003 c.14 Sch.2 para.4

Sch.3B Part 1 para.2, added: 2003 c.14 Sch.2 para.4

Sch.3B Part 1 para.3, added: 2003 c.14 Sch.2 para.4

Sch.3B Part 1 para.4, added: 2003 c.14 Sch.2 para.4

Sch.3B Part 1 para.5, added: 2003 c.14 Sch.2 para.4

Sch.3B Part 1 para.6, added: 2003 c.14 Sch.2 para.4

Sch.3B Part 1 para.7, added: 2003 c.14 Sch.2 para.4

Sch.3B Part 1 para.8, added: 2003 c.14 Sch.2 para.4

Sch.3B Part 1 para.9, added: 2003 c.14 Sch.2 para.4

Sch.3B Part 2 para.10, added: 2003 c.14 Sch.2 para.4

1994–cont.

23. Value Added Tax Act 1994–*cont.*

Sch.3B Part 2 para.11, added: 2003 c.14 Sch.2 para.4

Sch.3B Part 2 para.12, added: 2003 c.14 Sch.2 para.4

Sch.3B Part 2 para.13, added: 2003 c.14 Sch.2 para.4

Sch.3B Part 2 para.14, added: 2003 c.14 Sch.2 para.4

Sch.3B Part 2 para.15, added: 2003 c.14 Sch.2 para.4

Sch.3B Part 3 para.16, added: 2003 c.14 Sch.2 para.4

Sch.3B Part 4 para.17, added: 2003 c.14 Sch.2 para.4

Sch.3B Part 4 para.18, added: 2003 c.14 Sch.2 para.4

Sch.3B Part 4 para.19, added: 2003 c.14 Sch.2 para.4

Sch.3B Part 4 para.20, added: 2003 c.14 Sch.2 para.4

Sch.3B Part 4 para.21, added: 2003 c.14 Sch.2 para.4

Sch.3B Part 4 para.22, added: 2003 c.14 Sch.2 para.4

Sch.3B Part 5 para.23, added: 2003 c.14 Sch.2 para.4

Sch.4 para.1, see *Beynon v Customs and Excise Commissioners* [2002] EWCA Civ 1870, [2003] S.T.C. 169 (CA), Aldous, L.J.; see *Stewart (t/a GT Shooting) v Customs and Excise Commissioners* [2001] EWCA Civ 1988, [2002] S.T.C. 255 (CA), Laws, L.J.

Sch.4 para.5, see *Supanet Ltd v Customs and Excise Commissioners* [2002] S.T.I. 1678 (V&DTr), Colin Bishopp (Chairman)

Sch.4 para.5, amended: 2003 c.14 s.21, s.22

Sch.4 para.5, referred to: 2003 c.14 s.22, 2004 c.12 s.22

Sch.4 para.6, disapplied: SI 2004/3150 Art.2

Sch.5 para.5A, added: SI 2004/3149 Art.3

Sch.5 para.7A, substituted: SI 2003/863 Art.2

Sch.5 para.7B, added: SI 2003/863 Art.2

Sch.5 para.7C, added: SI 2003/863 Art.2

Sch.5 para.8, amended: SI 2003/863 Art.2

Sch.6 para.1A, added: 2004 c.12 s.22

Sch.6 para.5, see *Hartwell Plc v Customs and Excise Commissioners* [2002] S.T.C. 22 (Ch D), Patten, J.; see *Tesco Plc v Customs and Excise Commissioners* [2002] EWHC 2131, [2002] S.T.C. 1332 (Ch D), Ferris, J.; see *Tesco Plc v Customs and Excise Commissioners* [2003] EWCA Civ 1367, [2003] S.T.C. 1561 (CA), Jonathan Parker, L.J.

Sch.6 para.5, repealed: 2003 c.14 Sch.43 Part 2

Sch.7A Part II, added: SI 2002/1100 Art.3, Art.4, Art.5

1994–cont.

23. Value Added Tax Act 1994–*cont.*

Sch.7A Part II, amended: 2002 c.21 Sch.3 para.48, SI 2002/1100 Art.3, Art.4, Art.5, SI 2004/777 Art.3

Sch.7A Part II, repealed: SI 2002/1100 Art.4

Sch.7A Part II, substituted: SI 2002/1100 Art.4, Art.5

Sch.8, see *Beynon v Customs and Excise Commissioners* [2002] EWCA Civ 1870, [2003] S.T.C. 169 (CA), Aldous, L.J.; see *Cantrell (t/a Foxearth Lodge Nursing Home) v Customs and Excise Commissioners* [2003] EWHC 404, [2003] S.T.C. 486 (Ch D), Sir Andrew Morritt V.C.

Sch.8 Part II, added: SI 2002/456 Art.2

Sch.8 Part II, amended: 2002 c.21 Sch.3 para.49, SI 2002/456 Art.2, SI 2002/1101 Art.2, SI 2002/1173 Art.2, SI 2002/1397 Sch.1 para.11, SI 2002/2813 Art.3, Art.4, 2003 c.43 Sch.4 para.98

Sch.8 Part II, applied: SI 2004/1933 Sch.1

Sch.8 Part II, substituted: SI 2002/1173 Art.2

Sch.8 Part II Group 5 Item 2 Note 6, see *Yarburgh Childrens Trust v Customs and Excise Commissioners* [2002] S.T.C. 207 (Ch D), Patten, J.

Sch.8 Part II Group 6, see *Customs and Excise Commissioners v Zielinski Baker & Partners Ltd* [2002] EWCA Civ 692, [2002] S.T.C. 829 (CA), Aldous, L.J.

Sch.8 Part II Group 8 Note, see *Cairngorm Mountain v Customs and Excise Commissioners* [2002] S.T.I. 1674 (V&DTr), T Gordon Coutts Q.C. (Chairman)

Sch.8 Part II Group 8 Item 4, see *Cairngorm Mountain v Customs and Excise Commissioners* [2002] S.T.I. 1674 (V&DTr), T Gordon Coutts Q.C. (Chairman)

Sch.8 Part II Group 11 Item 1, see *Royal Bank of Scotland Group Plc v Customs and Excise Commissioners (Reciprocity Fees)* [2002] S.T.C. 575 (2 Div), Lord Gill L.J.C., Lord Coulsfield, Lord Sutherland

Sch.8 Part II Group 15 Item 5, see *Royal Midland Counties Home for Disabled People v Customs and Excise Commissioners* [2002] S.T.C. 395 (Ch D), Neuberger, J.

Sch.8 Part II Group 15 Note 3, see *Royal Midland Counties Home for Disabled People v Customs and Excise Commissioners* [2002] S.T.C. 395 (Ch D), Neuberger, J.

Sch.8 Grp.3 Item 1, see *College of Estate Management v Customs and Excise Commissioners* [2003] V. & D.R. 165 (V&DTr), Rodney P Huggins (Chairman)

Sch.8 Group.3 Item 2, see *Telewest Communications Plc v Customs and Excise Commissioners* [2003] B.V.C. 2296

1994–cont.

23. Value Added Tax Act 1994–*cont.*

Sch.8 Group.3 Item 2–*cont.*

(VAT and Duties Tribunal (London)), Nuala Brice (Chairman)

Sch.8 Grp.5 Item 2, see *Wallis Ltd v Customs and Excise Commissioners* [2003] V. & D.R. 151 (VAT and Duties Tribunal (London)), Theodore Wallace (Chairman)

Sch.8 Grp.5 Note 4, see *Wallis Ltd v Customs and Excise Commissioners* [2003] V. & D.R. 151 (VAT and Duties Tribunal (London)), Theodore Wallace (Chairman)

Sch.8 Grp.5 Note 16, see *Wallis Ltd v Customs and Excise Commissioners* [2003] V. & D.R. 151 (VAT and Duties Tribunal (London)), Theodore Wallace (Chairman)

Sch.8 Group.8 Item 10, see *Societe Internationale de Telecommunications Aeronautiques SC (SITA) v Customs and Excise Commissioners* [2003] B.V.C. 2375 (VAT and Duties Tribunal (London)), Stephen Oliver Q.C. (Chairman)

Sch.8 Group 1, see *Happy Place Ltd (t/a The Munch Box) v Customs and Excise Commissioners* [2002] S.T.I. 1529 (V&DTr), JF Avery Jones CBE (Chairman); see *Leach (t/a Carlton Catering) v Customs and Excise Commissioners* [2003] S.T.I. 308 (VAT Tr (London)), JC Gort (Chairman)

Sch.8 Group 3 Item 1, see *College of Estate Management v Customs and Excise Commissioners* [2003] EWHC 2712, [2004] S.T.C. 235 (Ch D), Lightman, J.

Sch.8 Group 5, see *Jacobs v Customs and Excise Commissioners* [2004] V. & D.R. 80 (V&DTr), Lady Mitting (Chairman)

Sch.8 Group 5 Item 1, see *Jacobs v Customs and Excise Commissioners* [2004] EWHC 2358, [2004] S.T.C. 1662 (Ch D), Evans-Lombe, J.

Sch.8 Group 5 Item 1 Note 6, see *Southwick Community Association v Customs and Excise Commissioners* [2002] V. & D.R. 288 (V&DTr), Rodney P Huggins (Chairman)

Sch.8 Group 5 Item 2, see *Southwick Community Association v Customs and Excise Commissioners* [2002] V. & D.R. 288 (V&DTr), Rodney P Huggins (Chairman)

Sch.8 Group 5 item 2 note 6, see *Customs and Excise Commissioners v St Paul's Community Project Ltd* [2004] EWHC 2490, [2004] B.T.C. 5803 (Ch D), Evans-Lombe, J.

Sch.8 Group 6 Item 2, see *Customs and Excise Commissioners v Zielinski Baker & Partners Ltd* [2004] UKHL 7, [2004] 1 W.L.R. 707 (HL), Lord Nicholls of Birkenhead

1994–cont.

23. Value Added Tax Act 1994–*cont.*

Sch.8 Group 8 Item 10, see *Societe Internationale de Telecommunications Aeronautiques SC (SITA) v Customs and Excise Commissioners* [2003] EWHC 3039, [2004] S.T.C. 950 (Ch D), Sir Andrew Morritt V.C.

Sch.8 Group 8 item 12, see *Simply Travel Ltd v Customs and Excise Commissioners* [2002] S.T.C. 194 (Ch D), Lightman, J.

Sch.8 Group 9, see *Talacre Beach Caravan Sales Ltd v Customs and Excise Commissioners* [2004] EWCA Civ 682, [2004] 2 C.M.L.R. 52 (CA), Peter Gibson, L.J.

Sch.8 Group 9 Item 3 Note, see *Talacre Beach Caravan Sales Ltd v Customs and Excise Commissioners* [2004] EWHC 165, [2004] S.T.C. 817 (Ch D), Lindsay, J.

Sch.8 Group 12 Item 1A, see *Beynon v Customs and Excise Commissioners* [2004] UKHL 53, [2004] 4 All E.R. 1091 (HL), Lord Nicholls of Birkenhead

Sch.9, see *Winterthur Life UK Ltd v Customs and Excise Commissioners (No.3)* [2002] Pens L.R. 203 (V&DTr), Paul Heim

Sch.9 Part II, see *WHA Ltd v Customs and Excise Commissioners* [2004] EWCA Civ 559, [2004] S.T.C. 1081 (CA), Waller, L.J.

Sch.9 Part II, amended: SI 2002/253 Sch.5 para.12, SI 2002/254 Sch.4 para.6, SI 2002/762 Art.3, Art.5, Art.6, 2003 c.14 s.10, 2003 c.21 Sch.17 para.129, SI 2003/24 Art.3, SI 2003/1569 Art.2, SI 2004/3083 Art.3, Art.4, Art.6

Sch.9 Part II, referred to: SI 2003/24 Art.2

Sch.9 Part II, repealed (in part): SI 2003/1568 Art.2, SI 2003/1569 Art.2, SI 2004/3083 Art.5

Sch.9 Part II, substituted: SI 2002/762 Art.4

Sch.9 Part II Group 1, see *Colaingrove Ltd v Customs and Excise Commissioners* [2004] EWCA Civ 146, [2004] S.T.C. 712 (CA), Thorpe, L.J.

Sch.9 Part II Group 5 Item 1, see *Royal Bank of Scotland Group Plc v Customs and Excise Commissioners (Reciprocity Fees)* [2002] S.T.C. 575 (2 Div), Lord Gill L.J.C., Lord Coulsfield, Lord Sutherland

Sch.9 Part II Group 12, see *New Forest Agricultural Show Society v Customs and Excise Commissioners* [2002] S.T.I. 1361 (V&DTr), Angus Nicol (Chairman)

Sch.9 Group.2 Note 7, see *Teletech UK Ltd v Customs and Excise Commissioners* [2003] B.V.C. 2514 (VAT and Duties Tribunal (Edinburgh)), T Gordon Coutts Q.C. (Chairman)

Sch.9 Group.5 Item 1, see *Rugby Football Union v Customs and Excise Commissioners* [2003] B.V.C. 2506 (VAT

CAP.

1994–cont.
23. Value Added Tax Act 1994–*cont.*

Sch.9 Group.5 Item 1–*cont.*

and DutiesTribunal (London)), Stephen Oliver Q.C. (Chairman)

Sch.9 Group. 5 Item 6, see *Rugby Football Union v Customs and Excise Commissioners* [2003] B.V.C. 2506 (VAT and Duties Tribunal (London)), Stephen Oliver Q.C. (Chairman)

Sch.9 Grp.6 Item 1, see *College of Estate Management v Customs and Excise Commissioners* [2003] V. & D.R. 165 (V&DTr), Rodney P Huggins (Chairman)

Sch.9 Grp.6 Item 3, see *College of Estate Management v Customs and Excise Commissioners* [2003] V. & D.R. 165 (V&DTr), Rodney P Huggins (Chairman)

Sch.9 Grp.7, see *Kingscrest Associates Ltd (t/a Kingscrest Residential Care Homes) v Customs and Excise Commissioners* [2003] B.V.C. 2592 (V&DTr), Adrian Shipwright (Chairman)

Sch.9 Group 1, see *Latchmere Properties Ltd v Customs and Excise Commissioners* [2004] B.V.C. 2132 (V&DTr), Theodore Wallace (Chairman)

Sch.9 Group 1 Item 1, see *Centralan Property Ltd v Customs and Excise Commissioners* [2003] EWHC 44, [2003] S.T.C. 290 (Ch D), Sir Andrew Morritt V.C.; see *Colaingrove Ltd v Customs and Excise Commissioners* [2003] EWHC 821, [2003] S.T.C. 680 (Ch D), Jacob, J.; see *Venuebest Ltd v Customs and Excise Commissioners* [2002] EWHC 2870, [2003] S.T.C. 433 (Ch D), Sir Andrew Morritt V.C.

Sch.9 Group 2 Item 1, see *CR Smith Glaziers (Dunfermline) Ltd v Customs and Excise Commissioners* [2003] UKHL 7, [2003] 1 W.L.R. 656 (HL), Lord Hoffmann

Sch.9 Group 4 Item 1, see *United Utilities Plc v Customs and Excise Commissioners* [2002] EWHC 2811, [2003] S.T.C. 223 (Ch D), Ferris, J.

Sch.9 Group 5 item 2, see *BAA Plc v Customs and Excise Commissioners* [2002] EWHC 196, [2002] S.T.C. 327 (Ch D), Etherton, J.

Sch.9 Group 5 Item 5, see *BAA Plc v Customs and Excise Commissioners* [2002] EWCA Civ 1814, [2003] S.T.C. 35 (CA), Sir Andrew Morritt V.C.; see *BAA Plc v Customs and Excise Commissioners* [2002] EWHC 196, [2002] S.T.C. 327 (Ch D), Etherton, J.; see *Institute of Directors v Customs and Excise Commissioners* [2002] B.V.C. 2065 (V&DTr), JC Gort (Chairman)

Sch.9 Group 5 Item 8, see *National Westminster Bank Plc v Customs and Excise Commissioners (V&DTr 17687)* [2003] B.V.C. 2003 (V&DTr), Rodney P Huggins (Chairman)

CAP.

1994–cont.
23. Value Added Tax Act 1994–*cont.*

Sch.9 Group 6 Item 1, see *Cooke (t/a Surrey Language Centre) v Customs and Excise Commissioners* [2002] V. & D.R. 357 (V&DTr), Jill Gort (Chairman)

Sch.9 Group 6 Item 3, see *College of Estate Management v Customs and Excise Commissioners* [2003] EWHC 2712, [2004] S.T.C. 235 (Ch D), Lightman, J.

Sch.9 Group 6 Item 4, see *College of Estate Management v Customs and Excise Commissioners* [2003] EWHC 2712, [2004] S.T.C. 235 (Ch D), Lightman, J.; see *Customs and Excise Commissioners v Leicester University Students Union* [2001] EWCA Civ 1972, [2002] S.T.C. 147 (CA), Peter Gibson, L.J.

Sch.9 Group 7, see *Gambro Hospal Ltd v Customs and Excise Commissioners* [2004] B.V.C. 2191 (V&DTr), Richard Barlow (Chairman); see *Kingscrest Associates Ltd v Customs and Excise Commissioners* [2002] EWHC 410, [2002] S.T.C. 490 (Ch D), Pumfrey, J.

Sch.9 Group 7 Item 1, see *Leightons Ltd v Customs and Excise Commissioners* [2002] B.V.C. 2027 (V&DTr), Nuala Brice (Chairman)

Sch.9 Group 7 Item 4, see *Rowe (t/a Cheshire Hearing Centre) v Customs and Excise Commissioners* [2002] V. & D.R. 156 (V&DTr (Manchester)), Colin Bishopp (Chairman)

Sch.9 Group 9 item 1, see *Expert Witness Institute v Customs and Excise Commissioners* [2001] EWCA Civ 1882, [2002] 1 W.L.R. 1674 (CA), Chadwick, L.J.; see *Game Conservancy Trust v Customs and Excise Commissioners* [2002] B.V.C. 2003 (V&DTr), Stephen Oliver Q.C. (Chairman)

Sch.10 para.1, amended: SI 2002/1102 Art.2

Sch.10 para.2, see *Brambletye School Trust Ltd v Customs and Excise Commissioners* [2003] B.V.C. 2015 (V&DTr (London)), Nuala Brice (Chairman); see *Centralan Property Ltd v Customs and Excise Commissioners* [2003] EWHC 44, [2003] S.T.C. 290 (Ch D), Sir Andrew Morritt V.C.; see *Customs and Excise Commissioners v Southern Primary Housing Association Ltd* [2003] EWCA Civ 1662, [2004] S.T.C. 209 (CA), Jacob, L.J.; see *Foreign Property APS v Secretary of State for Health* [2003] EWCA Civ 1541, [2004] 2 P. & C.R. 5 (CA), Simon Brown, L.J.

Sch.10 para.2, amended: SI 2004/778 Art.3, Art.4

Sch.10 para.2, applied: 2003 c.14 Sch.4 para.2

Sch.10 para.3A, see *Brambletye School Trust Ltd v Customs and Excise Commissioners* [2003] B.V.C. 2015 (V&DTr (London)),

CAP.

1994–cont.

23. Value Added Tax Act 1994–*cont.*

Sch.10 para.3A–*cont.*

Nuala Brice (Chairman); see *Centralan Property Ltd v Customs and Excise Commissioners* [2003] EWHC 44, [2003] S.T.C. 290 (Ch D), Sir Andrew Morritt V.C.

Sch.10 para.3A, amended: SI 2004/778 Art.5

Sch.10A para.1, added: 2003 c.14 Sch.1 para.2

Sch.10A para.2, added: 2003 c.14 Sch.1 para.2

Sch.10A para.3, added: 2003 c.14 Sch.1 para.2

Sch.10A para.4, added: 2003 c.14 Sch.1 para.2

Sch.10A para.5, added: 2003 c.14 Sch.1 para.2

Sch.10A para.6, added: 2003 c.14 Sch.1 para.2

Sch.10A para.7, added: 2003 c.14 Sch.1 para.2

Sch.10A para.8, added: 2003 c.14 Sch.1 para.2

Sch.11, amended: 2002 c.23 s.24

Sch.11 para.2, amended: 2002 c.23 s.24, Sch.40 Part 2

Sch.11 para.2, repealed (in part): 2002 c.23 s.24, Sch.40 Part 2

Sch.11 para.2, enabling: SI 2002/1142, SI 2003/1069, SI 2003/1485, SI 2003/3220, SI 2004/767, SI 2004/1082, SI 2004/1675

Sch.11 para.2A, added: 2002 c.23 s.24

Sch.11 para.2A, enabling: SI 2003/3220, SI 2004/1082

Sch.11 para.2B, added: 2002 c.23 s.24

Sch.11 para.2B, enabling: SI 2003/3220

Sch.11 para.3, substituted: 2002 c.23 s.24

Sch.11 para.3, enabling: SI 2003/3220

Sch.11 para.4, see *R. (on the application of Federation of Technological Industries) v Customs and Excise Commissioners* [2004] EWHC 254, [2004] S.T.C. 1008 (QBD (Admin Ct)), Lightman, J.

Sch.11 para.4, amended: 2003 c.14 s.17

Sch.11 para.6, repealed (in part): SI 2004/1501 Sch.2

Sch.11 para.6, enabling: SI 2003/3220

Sch.11 para.7, see *Interleasing Ltd v Customs and Excise Commissioners* [2003] B.V.C. 2142 (V&DTr), Colin Bishopp (Chairman)

Sch.11 para.7, enabling: SI 2004/1675

Sch.11 para.10, see *R. (on the application of Paul Da Costa & Co) v Thames Magistrates Court* [2002] EWHC 40, [2002] S.T.C. 267 (QBD (Admin Ct)), Kennedy, L.J.

Sch.11A para.1, added: 2004 c.12 Sch.2 para.2

Sch.11A para.2, added: 2004 c.12 Sch.2 para.2

Sch.11A para.3, added: 2004 c.12 Sch.2 para.2

CAP.

1994–cont.

23. Value Added Tax Act 1994–*cont.*

Sch.11A para.3, applied: SI 2004/1933 Art.3

Sch.11A para.3, enabling: SI 2004/1933

Sch.11A para.4, added: 2004 c.12 Sch.2 para.2

Sch.11A para.4, applied: SI 2004/1929 Reg.4, SI 2004/1933 Art.3

Sch.11A para.4, enabling: SI 2004/1933

Sch.11A para.5, added: 2004 c.12 Sch.2 para.2

Sch.11A para.6, added: 2004 c.12 Sch.2 para.2

Sch.11A para.6, applied: SI 2004/1929 Reg.2, Reg.3, Reg.4

Sch.11A para.6, enabling: SI 2004/1929

Sch.11A para.7, added: 2004 c.12 Sch.2 para.2

Sch.11A para.8, added: 2004 c.12 Sch.2 para.2

Sch.11A para.9, added: 2004 c.12 Sch.2 para.2

Sch.11A para.9, applied: SI 2004/1929 Reg.4

Sch.11A para.9, enabling: SI 2004/1929

Sch.11A para.10, added: 2004 c.12 Sch.2 para.2

Sch.11A para.11, added: 2004 c.12 Sch.2 para.2

Sch.11A para.12, added: 2004 c.12 Sch.2 para.2

Sch.11A para.13, added: 2004 c.12 Sch.2 para.2

Sch.11A para.13, enabling: SI 2004/1929

Sch.12 para.9, applied: 2003 c.14 s.37

Sch.12 para.9, referred to: SI 2003/3102 Reg.13

Sch.12 para.9, enabling: SI 2002/2851, SI 2003/2757, SI 2004/1032

Sch.14 para.8, repealed: 2002 c.40 Sch.26

26. Trade Marks Act 1994

see *ST Dupont v El du Pont de Nemours & Co (Trade Marks: Distinctiveness)* [2002] EWHC 2455, Times, November 28, 2002 (Ch D), Neuberger, J.

applied: 2002 c.40 Sch.14, Sch.15, SI 2003/409 Sch.1 Part I

s.1, see *CYCLING IS.. Trade Mark* [2002] R.P.C. 37 (Appointed Person), Geoffrey Hobbs Q.C.; see *Duckham & Co's Trade Mark Application (No.2154506)* [2004] R.P.C. 28 (TMR), Allan James; see *West (t/a Eastenders) v Fuller Smith & Turner Plc* [2003] EWCA Civ 48, [2003] F.S.R. 44 (CA), Pumfrey, J.

s.2, see *Inter Lotto (UK) Ltd v Camelot Group Plc* [2003] EWCA Civ 1132, [2004] 1 W.L.R. 955 (CA), Carnwath, L.J.; see *Inter Lotto (UK) Ltd v Camelot Group Plc* [2003] EWHC 1256, [2003] 3 All E.R. 191 (Ch D), Laddie, J.

CAP.

1994–cont.

26. Trade Marks Act 1994–*cont.*

s.3, see *Besnier SA's Trade Mark Application* [2002] R.P.C. 7 (Appointed Person), Simon Thorley Q.C.; see *Byford v Oliver* [2003] EWHC 295, [2003] E.M.L.R. 20 (Ch D), Laddie, J.; see *CDW Graphic Design Ltd's Trade Mark Application* [2003] R.P.C. 30 (TMR), Allan James; see *CYCLING IS.. Trade Mark* [2002] R.P.C. 37 (Appointed Person), Geoffrey Hobbs Q.C.; see *DAAWAT Trade Mark* [2002] R.P.C. 12 (TMR), Allan James; see *DAAWAT Trade Mark* [2003] R.P.C. 11 (Appointed Person), Geoffrey Hobbs Q.C.; see *Duckham & Co's Trade Mark Application (No.2154506)* [2004] R.P.C. 28 (TMR), Allan James; see *Dyson Ltd v Registrar of Trade Marks* [2003] EWHC 1062, [2003] 1 W.L.R. 2406 (Ch D), Patten, J.; see *ELIZABETH EMANUEL Trade Mark* [2004] R.P.C.15 (Appointed Person), David Kitchin Q.C.; see *Ferrero SpA's Trade Marks* [2004] R.P.C. 29 (Appointed Person), David Kitchin Q.C.; see *Ghazilian's Trade Mark Application* [2002] E.T.M.R. 56 (TMR), Janet Folwell; see *Ghazilian's Trade Mark Application* [2002] E.T.M.R. 57 (Appointed Person), Simon Thorley Q.C.; see *Harrison v Teton Valley Trading Co Ltd* [2002] EWHC 3009, [2004] F.S.R. 13 (Pat Ct), Pumfrey, J.; see *Harrison v Teton Valley Trading Co Ltd* [2004] EWCA Civ 1028, [2004] 1 W.L.R. 2577 (CA (Civ Div)), Pill, L.J.; see *Inter Lotto (UK) Ltd v National Lottery Commission (Leave to Amend Particulars of Objection)* [2004] EWHC 689, [2004] R.P.C. 42 (Ch D), Patten, J.; see *Mary Wilson Enterprises Inc's Trade Mark Application* [2003] E.M.L.R. 14 (Appointed Person), Geoffrey Hobbs Q.C.; see *Societe des Produits Nestle SA v Mars UK Ltd* [2002] EWHC 2533, [2003] F.S.R. 37 (Ch D), Rimer, J.; see *Societe des Produits Nestle SA v Mars UK Ltd* [2003] EWCA Civ 1072, [2003] E.T.M.R. 101 (CA), Sir Andrew Morritt V.C.; see *Telewest Communications Plc's Trade Mark Application* [2003] R.P.C. 26 (Appointed Person), Geoffrey Hobbs Q.C.; see *West (t/a Eastenders) v Fuller Smith & Turner Plc* [2003] EWCA Civ 48, [2003] F.S.R. 44 (CA), Pumfrey, J.

s.5, see *Byford v Oliver* [2003] EWHC 295, [2003] E.M.L.R. 20 (Ch D), Laddie, J.; see *Duckham & Co's Trade Mark Application (No.2154506)* [2004] R.P.C. 28 (TMR), Allan James; see *Harrison v Teton Valley Trading Co Ltd* [2002] EWHC 3009, [2004] F.S.R. 13 (Pat Ct), Pumfrey, J.; see *IDG Communications Ltd's Trade Mark Application* [2002] R.P.C. 10 (TMR), SP Rowan; see *Intel Corp v Sihra* [2003] EWHC 17, [2004] E.T.M.R. 44 (Ch D),

CAP.

1994–cont.

26. Trade Marks Act 1994–*cont.*

s.5–*cont.*

Patten, J.; see *Mary Wilson Enterprises Inc's Trade Mark Application* [2003] E.M.L.R. 14 (Appointed Person), Geoffrey Hobbs Q.C.; see *REEF Trade Mark* [2002] EWCA Civ 763, [2003] R.P.C. 5 (CA), Robert Walker, L.J.; see *REEF Trade Mark* [2002] R.P.C.19 (Ch D), Pumfrey, J.; see *SC Prodal 94 Srl v Spirits International NV* [2003] EWHC 2756, (2004) 27(2) I.P.D. 27016 (Ch D), Laddie, J.; see *Silver Spring Mineral Water Co Ltd's Trade Mark Application (No.2)* [2004] R.P.C. 13 (TMR), Mike Knight; see *ST Dupont v El Du Pont de Nemours & Co (Trade Marks: Distinctiveness)* [2003] EWCA Civ 1368, [2004] F.S.R. 15 (CA), Aldous, L.J.

s.5, amended: SI 2004/2332 Reg.3

s.5, repealed (in part): SI 2004/946 Reg.7

s.6, amended: SI 2004/2332 Reg.4

s.6A, added: SI 2004/946 Reg.4

s.10, see *AAH Pharmaceuticals Ltd v Vantagemax Plc* [2002] EWHC 990, [2003] E.T.M.R. 18 (Ch D), Pumfrey, J.; see *Asprey & Garrard Ltd v WRA (Guns) Ltd (t/a William R Asprey Esquire)* [2001] EWCA Civ 1499, [2002] E.T.M.R. 47 (CA), Peter Gibson, L.J.; see *Asprey & Garrard Ltd v WRA (Guns) Ltd (t/a William R Asprey Esquire)* [2002] F.S.R. 30 (Ch D), Jacob, J.; see *Compass Publishing BV v Compass Logistics Ltd* [2004] EWHC 520, [2004] R.P.C. 41 (Ch D), Laddie, J.; see *Gleneagles Hotels Ltd v Quillco 100 Ltd* 2003 S.L.T. 812 (OH), Lord Nimmo Smith; see *Harding v Smilecare Ltd* [2002] F.S.R. 37 (Ch D), PW Smith Q.C.; see *Levi Strauss & Co v Tesco Stores Ltd* [2002] EWHC 1625, [2002] 3 C.M.L.R. 11 (Ch D), Pumfrey, J.; see *Musical Fidelity Ltd v Vickers (t/a Vickers Hi-Fi)* [2002] EWHC 1000, (2002) 25(8) I.P.D. 25054 (Ch D), Rimer, J.; see *PAG Ltd v Hawk-Woods Ltd* [2002] E.T.M.R. 70 (Ch D), Pumfrey, J.; see *Premier Luggage & Bags Ltd v Premier Co (UK) Ltd* [2002] EWCA Civ 387, [2002] E.T.M.R. 69 (CA), Chadwick, L.J.; see *R. v Isaac (James Rupert)* [2004] EWCA Crim 1082, (2004) 168 J.P. 417 (CA (Crim Div)), Pill, L.J.; see *Reed Executive Plc v Reed Business Information Ltd* [2002] EWHC 1015, [2003] Info. T.L.R. 7 (Ch D), Pumfrey, J.; see *Reed Executive Plc v Reed Business Information Ltd* [2004] EWCA Civ 159, [2004] E.T.M.R. 56 (CA), Auld, L.J.; see *Thomson Holidays Ltd v Norwegian Cruise Line Ltd* [2002] EWCA Civ 1828, [2003] R.P.C. 32 (CA), Aldous, L.J.

s.10, amended: SI 2004/946 Reg.7

s.10, repealed (in part): SI 2004/946 Reg.7

1994–cont.
26. Trade Marks Act 1994–cont.

s.11, see *Asprey & Garrard Ltd v WRA (Guns) Ltd (t/a William R Asprey Esquire)* [2001] EWCA Civ 1499, [2002] E.T.M.R. 47 (CA), Peter Gibson, L.J.; see *CYCLING IS.. Trade Mark* [2002] R.P.C. 37 (Appointed Person), Geoffrey Hobbs Q.C.; see *D Green & Co (Stoke Newington) Ltd v Regalzone Ltd* [2001] EWCA Civ 639, [2002] E.T.M.R. 22 (CA), Chadwick, L.J.; see *Reed Executive Plc v Reed Business Information Ltd* [2004] EWCA Civ 159, [2004] E.T.M.R. 56 (CA), Auld, L.J.; see *West (t/a Eastenders) v Fuller Smith & Turner Plc* [2002] EWHC 122, [2003] E.T.M.R. 30 (Ch D), Christopher Floyd Q.C.

s.13, see *Mars UK Ltd v Societe des Produits Nestle SA* [2003] EWHC 3052, [2004] R.P.C. 27 (Ch D), Lloyd, J.

s.16, see *Miller Brewing Co v Ruhi Enterprises Ltd* [2003] EWHC 1606, [2004] F.S.R. 5 (Ch D), Neuberger, J.

s.19, see *Miller Brewing Co v Ruhi Enterprises Ltd* [2003] EWHC 1606, [2004] F.S.R. 5 (Ch D), Neuberger, J.

s.21, see *Reckitt Benkiser (UK) Ltd v Home Pairfum Ltd* [2004] EWHC 302, [2004] F.S.R. 37 (Ch D), Laddie, J.

s.32, see *Ferrero SpA's Trade Marks* [2004] R.P.C. 29 (Appointed Person), David Kitchin Q.C.; see *Robert McBride Ltd's Trade Mark Application* [2003] R.P.C. 19 (Appointed Person), Geoffrey Hobbs, Q.C.

s.34, see *Altecnic Ltd's Trade Mark Application (No.2126884)* [2001] EWCA Civ 1928, [2002] R.P.C. 34 (CA), Mummery, L.J.

s.37, see *Digeo Broadband Inc's Trade Mark Application (No.2230395)* [2004] R.P.C. 32 (Appointed Person), Geoffrey Hobbs Q.C.; see *Inter Lotto (UK) Ltd v National Lottery Commission (Leave to Amend Particulars of Objection)* [2004] EWHC 689, [2004] R.P.C. 42 (Ch D), Patten, J.; see *Nettec Solutions Ltd's Trade Mark Application* [2003] R.P.C. 17 (Appointed Person), Ruth Annand

s.38, enabling: SI 2004/947

s.39, see *Altecnic Ltd's Trade Mark Application (No.2126884)* [2001] EWCA Civ 1928, [2002] R.P.C. 34 (CA), Mummery, L.J.; see *Duckham & Co's Trade Mark Application (No.2154506)* [2004] R.P.C. 28 (TMR), Allan James

s.39, enabling: SI 2004/947

s.40, see *Nettec Solutions Ltd's Trade Mark Application* [2003] R.P.C. 17 (Appointed Person), Ruth Annand

s.40, amended: SI 2004/946 Reg.5

s.41, see *Digeo Broadband Inc's Trade Mark Application (No.2230395)* [2004] R.P.C. 32 (Appointed Person), Geoffrey Hobbs Q.C.

1994–cont.
26. Trade Marks Act 1994–cont.

s.41, enabling: SI 2004/947

s.44, enabling: SI 2004/947

s.46, see *Anheuser Busch Inc v Budejovicky Budvar Narodni Podnik (Application for Revocation)* [2002] EWCA Civ 1534, [2003] R.P.C. 25 (CA), Sir Martin Nourse; see *Anheuser Busch Inc v Budejovicky Budvar Narodni Podnik (Application for Revocation)* [2002] R.P.C. 38 (Ch D), Simon Thorley Q.C.; see *Geoffrey Inc's Trade Mark Application (No.12244)* [2004] R.P.C. 30 (TMR), John MacGillivray; see *H Young (Operations) Ltd v Medici Ltd* [2003] EWHC 1589, [2004] F.S.R. 19 (Ch D), Jacob, J.; see *La Mer Technology Inc v Laboratoires Goemar SA (C259/02)* [2004] E.T.M.R. 47 (ECJ), Judge Cunha Rodrigues (President); see *Philosophy Inc v Ferretti Studio Srl* [2002] EWCA Civ 921, [2003] E.T.M.R. 8 (CA), Peter Gibson, L.J.; see *RIVERIA Trade Mark* [2003] R.P.C. 50 (TMR), Allan James; see *SAFARI Trade Mark* [2002] R.P.C. 23 (TMR), Allan James; see *Thomson Holidays Ltd v Norwegian Cruise Line Ltd* [2002] EWCA Civ 1828, [2003] R.P.C. 32 (CA), Aldous, L.J.; see *West (t/a Eastenders) v Fuller Smith & Turner Plc* [2003] EWCA Civ 48, [2003] F.S.R. 44 (CA), Pumfrey, J.

s.47, amended: SI 2004/946 Reg.6

s.47, applied: SI 2004/946 Reg.9

s.52, enabling: SI 2004/949, SI 2004/2332

s.53, amended: SI 2004/2332 Reg.5

s.54, enabling: SI 2002/692, SI 2004/948

s.65, enabling: SI 2004/947

s.72, see *FIRETRACE Trade Mark* [2002] R.P.C.15 (TMR), Mike Knight

s.75, see *Minsterstone Ltd v Be Modern Ltd* [2002] F.S.R. 53 (CC (Central London)), Judge Fysh Q.C.

s.76, see *ELIZABETH EMANUEL Trade Mark* [2004] R.P.C. 15 (Appointed Person), David Kitchin Q.C.

s.76, enabling: SI 2004/947

s.78, enabling: SI 2004/947

s.89, amended: SI 2004/1473 Reg.13

s.92, see *R. v Gleeson (John Vincent)* [2001] EWCA Crim 2023, [2002] 1 Cr. App. R. (S.) 112 (CA (Crim Div)), Rose, L.J.; see *R. v Isaac (James Rupert)* [2004] EWCA Crim 1082, (2004) 168 J.P. 417 (CA (Crim Div)), Pill, L.J.; see *R. v Johnstone (Robert Alexander)* [2002] EWCA Crim 194, [2003] E.T.M.R. 1 (CA (Crim Div)), Tuckey, L.J.; see *R. v Johnstone (Robert Alexander)* [2003] UKHL 28, [2003] 1 W.L.R. 1736 (HL), Lord Nicholls of Birkenhead; see *R. v Passley (Allen Martin)* [2003] EWCA Crim 2727, [2004] 1 Cr.App.R.(S.) 70 (CA (Crim Div)), Henriques, J.; see *R. v S*

1994–cont.

26. Trade Marks Act 1994–cont.

s.92–cont.

(Trademark Defence) [2002] EWCA Crim 2558, [2003] 1 Cr. App. R. 35 (CA (Crim Div)), Rose, L.J.; see R. v Wakefield (Mark) [2004] EWCA Crim 2278, (2004) 168 J.P. 505 (CA (Crim Div)), Latham, L.J.; see R. v Zaman (Qamar) [2002] EWCA Crim 1862, [2003] F.S.R. 13 (CA (Crim Div)), Longmore, L.J.

s.92, applied: 2002 c.29 Sch.2 para.7, Sch.4 para.7, Sch.5 para.7, 2003 c.17 Sch.4 para.16, SI 2003/1376 Sch.1, SI 2003/1593 Sch.1 Part I

s.92A, added: 2002 c.25 s.6

s.101, see R. v Wakefield (Mark) [2004] EWCA Crim 2278, (2004) 168 J.P. 505 (CA (Crim Div)), Latham, L.J.

s.104, amended: SI 2004/2332 Reg.6

s.108, enabling: SI 2002/3148, SI 2004/1497

Sch.3, see Ferrero SpA's Trade Marks [2004] R.P.C. 29 (Appointed Person), David Kitchin Q.C.

Sch.4 para.1, amended: 2004 c.14 Sch.1 Part 2

29. Police and Magistrates Courts Act 1994

referred to: SI 2003/527 Reg.2

s.30, repealed (in part): 2003 c.26 Sch.8 Part 1

Sch.8 Part II para.28, repealed: 2003 c.44 Sch.37 Part 10

Sch.8 Part II para.29, repealed: 2003 c.39 Sch.10

Sch.8 Part II para.30, repealed: 2003 c.39 Sch.10

Sch.8 Part II para.32, repealed: 2003 c.39 Sch.10

Sch.8 Part II para.33, repealed: 2003 c.39 Sch.10

Sch.8 Part II para.34, repealed: 2003 c.39 Sch.10

30. Education Act 1994

referred to: 2004 c.8 s.29

Part I, applied: SI 2002/479 Art.2, SI 2002/2713 Art.2, SI 2002/3003 Art.2, SI 2003/271 Art.2, SI 2003/2636 Art.2, SI 2003/3278 Art.2

s.1, varied: SI 2002/3003 Art.3

s.2, varied: SI 2002/3003 Art.3

s.3, varied: SI 2002/3003 Art.3

s.4, referred to: SI 2002/1330 Reg.10, SI 2003/1994 Reg.10

s.4, repealed (in part): 2002 c.32 Sch.21 para.23, Sch.22 Part 3

s.4, varied: SI 2002/3003 Art.3

s.4, enabling: SI 2002/479, SI 2002/2713, SI 2002/3003, SI 2003/271, SI 2003/2636, SI 2003/3278

s.5, applied: SI 2002/1330 Sch.3 para.1, SI 2002/3200 Sch.3 para.1, SI 2003/1994 Sch.3 para.1, SR 2002/224 Sch.3 para.1,

1994–cont.

30. Education Act 1994–cont.

s.5, applied:–cont.

SR 2002/265 Sch.7 para.1, 2004 c.8 s.23, s.24, s.27, s.28, s.34

s.5, disapplied: SI 2002/195 Sch.3 para.1

s.5, varied: SI 2002/3003 Art.3

s.6, varied: SI 2002/3003 Art.3

s.7, applied: 2004 c.8 s.23, s.27

s.7, varied: SI 2002/3003 Art.3

s.8, varied: SI 2002/3003 Art.3

s.9, varied: SI 2002/3003 Art.3

s.10, varied: SI 2002/3003 Art.3

s.11, varied: SI 2002/3003 Art.3

s.11A, varied: SI 2002/3003 Art.3

s.12, varied: SI 2002/3003 Art.3

s.13, varied: SI 2002/3003 Art.3

s.14, repealed (in part): 2002 c.32 Sch.21 para.24, Sch.22 Part 3

s.14, varied: SI 2002/3003 Art.3

s.15, varied: SI 2002/3003 Art.3

s.16, applied: SI 2002/507, SI 2002/2513, SI 2003/2038, SI 2003/2564

s.16, varied: SI 2002/3003 Art.3

s.16, enabling: SI 2002/507, SI 2002/2513, SI 2003/2038, SI 2003/2564rt.3

s.18, varied: SI 2002/3003 Art.3

s.18A, varied: SI 2002/3003 Art.3

s.19, amended: 2002 c.32 Sch.21 para.25

s.19, varied: SI 2002/3003 Art.3

s.23, enabling: SI 2002/507, SI 2002/2513, SI 2003/2038, SI 2003/2564

Sch.2 para.8, repealed (in part): 2002 c.32 Sch.22 Part 3

33. Criminal Justice and Public Order Act 1994

Commencement Orders: SI 2002/447 Art.2

see R. v Collins (Jamie Lee) [2004] EWCA Crim 83, [2004] 1 W.L.R. 1705 (CA (Crim Div)), Thomas, L.J.

referred to: 2003 asp 2 Sch.2 para.10

s.7, enabling: SI 2003/3005

s.25, see R. (on the application of O) v Harrow Crown Court [2003] EWHC 868, [2003] 1 W.L.R. 2756 (QBD (Admin Ct)), Kennedy, L.J.; see SBC v United Kingdom (39360/98) (2002) 34 E.H.R.R. 21 (ECHR), J-P Costa (President)

s.25, amended: 2003 c.42 Sch.6 para.32, 2003 c.44 Sch.32 para.67, Sch.37 Part 7

s.26, repealed: 2003 c.44 Sch.37 Part 2

s.29, repealed (in part): 2003 c.44 Sch.37 Part 1

s.31, repealed: 2003 c.44 Sch.37 Part 5

s.34, see R. v Daly (Andrew) [2001] EWCA Crim 2643, [2002] 2 Cr. App. R. 14 (CA (Crim Div)), Kennedy, L.J.; see R. v Gowland-Wynn (Geoffrey) [2001] EWCA Crim 2715, [2002] 1 Cr. App. R. 41 (CA (Crim Div)), Lord Woolf of Barnes, L.C.J.; see R. v Knight (Philip) [2003] EWCA Crim 1977, [2004] 1 W.L.R. 340 (CA

1994–cont.

33. Criminal Justice and Public Order Act 1994–*cont.*

s.34–*cont.*

(Crim Div)), Laws, L.J.; see *R. v Parchment (Jamal Sky)* [2003] EWCA Crim 2428, (2003) 147 S.J.L.B. 1088 (CA (Crim Div)), Mantell, L.J.; see *R. v Petkar (Rafiq)* [2003] EWCA Crim 2668, [2004] 1 Cr. App. R. 22 (CA (Crim Div)), Rix, L.J.; see *R. v Turner (Dwaine)* [2003] EWCA Crim 3108, [2004] 1 All E.R. 1025 (CA (Crim Div)), Scott Baker, L.J.; see *R. v Webber (Robert)* [2004] UKHL 1, [2004] 1 W.L.R. 404 (HL), Lord Bingham of Cornhill

s.34, amended: 2003 c.44 Sch.3 para.64

s.34, applied: 2002 c.30 s.36

s.34, repealed (in part): 2003 c.44 Sch.37 Part 4, Sch.3 para.64

s.35, see *R. v Gough (Steven Robert)* [2001] EWCA Crim 2545, [2002] 2 Cr. App. R. 8 (CA (Crim Div)), Kennedy, L.J.

s.35, amended: 2003 c.44 Sch.36 para.63

s.35, applied: 2004 c.28 s.6

s.36, amended: 2003 c.44 Sch.3 para.64

s.36, repealed (in part): 2003 c.44 Sch.37 Part 4, Sch.3 para.64

s.36, varied: 2002 c.30 Sch.4 para.21

s.37, amended: 2003 c.44 Sch.3 para.64

s.37, repealed (in part): 2003 c.44 Sch.37 Part 4, Sch.3 para.64

s.40, repealed: 2003 c.44 Sch.37 Part 10

s.42, repealed: 2003 c.44 Sch.37 Part 10

s.51, see *Attorney General's Reference (No.1 of 2004), Re* [2004] EWCA Crim 1025, [2004] 1 W.L.R. 2111 (CA (Crim Div)), Lord Woolf of Barnes, L.C.J.; see *R. v Atkin (Suzanne Marie)* [2002] EWCA Crim 3195, [2003] 2 Cr. App. R. (S.) 40 (CA (Crim Div)), Silber, J.; see *R. v Baxter (Robert Peter)* [2002] EWCA Crim 1516, [2003] 1 Cr. App. R. (S.) 50 (CA (Crim Div)), Davis, J.; see *R. v Chinery (Andrew John)* [2002] EWCA Crim 32, [2002] 2 Cr. App. R. (S.) 55 (CA (Crim Div)), Bennett, J.; see *R. v Patrascu (Andrew)* [2004] EWCA Crim 2417, [2004] 4 All E.R. 1066 (CA (Crim Div)), May, L.J.

s.51, amended: 2003 c.44 Sch.36 para.11, Sch.36 para.64

s.52, repealed (in part): 2003 c.39 Sch.10

s.53, repealed: SI 2003/435 Sch.5

s.54, repealed (in part): 2002 c.30 Sch.8

s.60, see *DPP v Avery* [2001] EWHC Admin 748, [2002] 1 Cr. App. R. 31 (QBD (Admin Ct)), Newman, J.

s.60, amended: 2003 c.20 Sch.5 para.4, 2003 c.44 Sch.26 para.45, SI 2004/1573 Art.12

s.60, applied: SI 2002/1372 Reg.5

s.60, varied: 2003 c.20 Sch.5 para.4

s.60A, enabling: SI 2002/1372

1994–cont.

33. Criminal Justice and Public Order Act 1994–*cont.*

s.60AA, amended: 2003 c.20 Sch.5 para.4, 2003 c.44 Sch.26 para.45

s.60AA, applied: SI 2002/1372 Reg.5

s.60AA, varied: 2003 c.20 Sch.5 para.4

s.61, see *R. (on the application of Fuller) v Chief Constable of Dorset* [2001] EWHC Admin 1057, [2003] Q.B. 480 (QBD (Admin Ct)), Stanley Burnton, J.

s.61, amended: 2003 asp 2 Sch.2 para.11, 2003 c.44 Sch.26 para.45

s.62A, added: 2003 c.38 s.60

s.62B, added: 2003 c.38 s.61

s.62B, amended: 2003 c.44 Sch.26 para.45

s.62C, added: 2003 c.38 s.62

s.62D, added: 2003 c.38 s.63

s.62E, added: 2003 c.38 s.64

s.63, amended: 2003 c.17 Sch.6 para.111, Sch.7, 2003 c.38 s.58, Sch.3, 2003 c.44 Sch.26 para.45

s.63, repealed (in part): 2003 c.17 Sch.7

s.63, substituted: 2003 c.38 s.58

s.64, amended: 2003 asp 2 Sch.2 para.12

s.66, applied: SI 2003/336 Sch.1 Part 2, SSI 2003/179 Reg.3

s.67, amended: 2003 c.38 s.62

s.68, see *DPP v Bayer* [2003] EWHC 2567, [2004] 1 W.L.R. 2856 (QBD (Admin Ct)), Brooke, L.J.; see *DPP v Tilly* [2001] EWHC Admin 821, (2002) 166 J.P. 22 (QBD (Admin Ct)), Rafferty, J.

s.68, amended: 2003 asp 2 Sch.2 para.13, 2003 c.38 Sch.3, 2003 c.44 Sch.26 para.45

s.69, amended: 2003 c.38 Sch.3, 2003 c.44 Sch.26 para.45

s.77, see *R. (on the application of Ward) v Hillingdon LBC* [2001] EWHC Admin 91, [2002] E.H.L.R. 4 (QBD (Admin Ct)), Stanley Burnton, J.

s.92, repealed: 2003 c.21 Sch.19

s.102, amended: 2003 asp 7 s.76

s.106, amended: 2003 asp 11 Sch.1 para.50

s.120, enabling: SI 2004/1408

s.123, applied: SI 2004/702 Sch.4 para.7

s.123, repealed (in part): SI 2004/702 Sch.8

s.134, repealed (in part): 2003 asp 7 Sch.5

s.139, amended: 2002 c.29 Sch.11 para.24

s.142, see *R. v Hinds (Gary David)* [2003] EWCA Crim 532, [2003] 2 Cr. App. R. (S.) 76 (CA (Crim Div)), Ian Kennedy, J.

s.142, repealed: 2003 c.42 Sch.7

s.143, repealed: 2003 c.42 Sch.7

s.144, repealed: 2003 c.42 Sch.7

s.157, repealed (in part): SI 2004/702 Sch.8

s.158, repealed: 2003 c.41 Sch.4

s.159, repealed: 2003 c.41 Sch.4

s.163, amended: 2003 c.21 Sch.17 para.130

s.164, repealed (in part): 2003 c.32 Sch.6

s.172, enabling: SI 2002/447

CAP.

1994–cont.

33. Criminal Justice and Public Order Act 1994–*cont.*

Sch.8 Part III, amended: SI 2004/702 Sch.8

Sch.9 para.12, repealed: 2003 c.44 Sch.37 Part 4

Sch.9 para.17, repealed (in part): 2003 c.44 Sch.37 Part 4

Sch.9 para.18, repealed (in part): 2003 c.44 Sch.37 Part 4

Sch.9 para.25, repealed: 2003 c.44 Sch.37 Part 4

Sch.9 para.27, repealed: 2003 c.44 Sch.37 Part 4

Sch.9 para.29, repealed: 2003 c.44 Sch.37 Part 4

Sch.9 para.31, repealed: 2003 c.44 Sch.37 Part 6

Sch.9 para.36, repealed: 2002 c.29 Sch.12

Sch.9 para.49, repealed: 2003 c.44 Sch.37 Part 4

Sch.10 para.15, repealed: 2003 c.44 Sch.37 Part 2

Sch.10 para.26, repealed: 2003 c.42 Sch.6 para.32, Sch.7

Sch.10 para.29, repealed: 2003 c.44 Sch.37 Part 10

Sch.10 para.34, repealed: 2003 c.44 Sch.37 Part 2

Sch.10 para.35, repealed (in part): 2003 c.42 Sch.6 para.32, Sch.7

Sch.10 para.40, repealed: 2003 c.44 Sch.37 Part 4

Sch.10 para.71, repealed: 2003 c.44 Sch.37 Part 4

35. Sale and Supply of Goods Act 1994

see *Clegg v Andersson (t/a Nordic Marine)* [2003] EWCA Civ 320, [2003] 1 All E.R. (Comm) 721 (CA), Sir Robert Andrew Morritt V.C.

36. Law of Property (Miscellaneous Provisions) Act 1994

applied: SI 2003/1417 r.8

Part I, applied: 2002 c.9 Sch.10 para.3, SI 2003/1417 r.67, r.68

s.4, applied: SI 2003/1417 r.67

s.5, amended: 2002 c.15 Sch.5 para.7

s.6, amended: 2002 c.9 Sch.11 para.31

s.8, referred to: SI 2003/1417 r.67

s.9, amended: 2004 c.14 Sch.1 Part 12

s.11, applied: SI 2003/1417 r.67

s.17, amended: 2002 c.9 Sch.11 para.31

s.19, amended: 2002 c.35 s.2

Sch.1 para.2, repealed: 2002 c.9 Sch.13

37. Drug Trafficking Act 1994

see *Hughes v Customs and Excise Commissioners* [2002] EWCA Civ 734, [2003] 1 W.L.R. 177 (CA), Simon Brown, L.J.; see *R. v Johannes (Karl Christopher)* [2001] EWCA Crim 2825, [2002] 2 Cr. App. R. (S.) 30 (CA (Crim Div)), Pitchford, J.

CAP.

1994–cont.

37. Drug Trafficking Act 1994–*cont.*

applied: 2002 c.29 s.118

Part I, applied: 2002 c.29 s.8, s.94, s.158

s.1, repealed: 2002 c.29 Sch.12

s.2, see *R. v Benjafield (Karl Robert) (Confiscation Order)* [2002] UKHL 2, [2003] 1 A.C. 1099 (HL), Lord Steyn; see *R. v Davies (Steven) (Confiscation Order)* [2001] EWCA Crim 2902, [2002] 1 W.L.R. 1806 (CA (Crim Div)), Pitchford, J.; see *R. v Deprince (Jahvad John)* [2004] EWCA Crim 524, [2004] 2 Cr. App. R. (S.) 91 (CA (Crim Div)), Mantell, L.J.; see *R. v Phillips (Richard William)* [2001] EWCA Crim 2790, [2002] 2 Cr. App. R. (S.) 16 (CA (Crim Div)), Wright, J.

s.2, repealed: 2002 c.29 Sch.12

s.3, see *R. v Copeland (Alphonso)* [2002] EWCA Crim 736, [2002] 2 Cr. App. R. (S.) 111 (CA (Crim Div)), Sir Richard Tucker; see *R. v Davies (Steven) (Confiscation Order)* [2001] EWCA Crim 2902, [2002] 1 W.L.R. 1806 (CA (Crim Div)), Pitchford, J.; see *R. v Jagdev (Menohar Singh)* [2002] EWCA Crim 1326, [2002] 1 W.L.R. 3017 (CA (Crim Div)), Hedley, J.; see *R. v Phillips (Richard William)* [2001] EWCA Crim 2790, [2002] 2 Cr. App. R. (S.) 16 (CA (Crim Div)), Wright, J.; see *R. v Pisciotto (Frank)* [2002] EWCA Crim 1592, [2003] 1 Cr. App. R. 4 (CA (Crim Div)), Keene, L.J.; see *R. v Zelzele (Behcet)* [2001] EWCA Crim 1763, [2002] 1 Cr. App. R. (S.) 62 (CA (Crim Div)), Tomlinson, J

s.3, repealed: 2002 c.29 Sch.12

s.4, see *R. v Benjafield (Karl Robert) (Confiscation Order)* [2002] UKHL 2, [2003] 1 A.C. 1099 (HL), Lord Steyn; see *R. v Walls (Andrew)* [2002] EWCA Crim 2456, [2003] 1 W.L.R. 731 (CA (Crim Div)), Judge David Clarke Q.C.

s.4, repealed: 2002 c.29 Sch.12

s.5, repealed: 2002 c.29 Sch.12

s.6, repealed: 2002 c.29 Sch.12

s.7, see *R. v Walls (Andrew)* [2002] EWCA Crim 2456, [2003] 1 W.L.R. 731 (CA (Crim Div)), Judge David Clarke Q.C.

s.7, repealed: 2002 c.29 Sch.12

s.8, repealed: 2002 c.29 Sch.12

s.9, repealed: 2002 c.29 Sch.12

s.10, repealed: 2002 c.29 Sch.12

s.11, see *R. v Copeland (Alphonso)* [2002] EWCA Crim 736, [2002] 2 Cr. App. R. (S.) 111 (CA (Crim Div)), Sir Richard Tucker

s.11, repealed: 2002 c.29 Sch.12

s.12, repealed: 2002 c.29 Sch.12

s.13, see *R. v Phillips (Richard William)* [2001] EWCA Crim 2790, [2002] 2 Cr. App. R. (S.) 16 (CA (Crim Div)), Wright, J.

s.13, repealed: 2002 c.29 Sch.12

s.14, repealed: 2002 c.29 Sch.12

1994–cont.

37. Drug Trafficking Act 1994–*cont.*
s.15, repealed: 2002 c.29 Sch.12
s.16, repealed: 2002 c.29 Sch.12
s.17, see *R. v Briggs (James)* [2003] EWCA Crim 3298, [2004] 2 Cr. App. R. (S.) 7 (CA (Crim Div)), Poole, J.
s.17, repealed: 2002 c.29 Sch.12
s.18, repealed: 2002 c.29 Sch.12
s.19, repealed: 2002 c.29 Sch.12
s.20, repealed: 2002 c.29 Sch.12
s.21, repealed: 2002 c.29 Sch.12
s.22, repealed: 2002 c.29 Sch.12
s.23, repealed: 2002 c.29 Sch.12
s.24, repealed: 2002 c.29 Sch.12
s.25, repealed: 2002 c.29 Sch.12
s.26, see *DPP v Compton* [2002] EWCA Civ 1720, Times, December 11, 2002 (CA), Simon Brown, L.J.
s.26, amended: 2002 c.9 Sch.11 para.32
s.26, repealed (in part): 2002 c.9 Sch.13, 2002 c.29 Sch.12
s.27, applied: 2002 c.29 s.41, s.49, s.51, s.53, s.79, s.120, s.125, s.128, s.145, s.190, s.197, s.199, s.201, s.227
s.27, repealed: 2002 c.29 Sch.12
s.28, amended: 2002 c.9 Sch.11 para.32
s.28, repealed: 2002 c.29 Sch.12
s.29, see *Customs and Excise Commissioners v A* [2002] EWCA Civ 1039, [2003] Fam. 55 (CA), Schiemann, L.J.
s.29, repealed: 2002 c.29 Sch.12
s.30, repealed: 2002 c.29 Sch.12
s.31, see *Customs and Excise Commissioners v A* [2002] EWHC 611, [2002] 2 F.L.R. 274 (QBD (Admin Ct)), Munby, J.
s.31, repealed: 2002 c.29 Sch.12
s.32, see *DPP v Compton* [2002] EWCA Civ 1720, Times, December 11, 2002 (CA), Simon Brown, L.J.
s.32, repealed: 2002 c.29 Sch.12
s.33, repealed: 2002 c.29 Sch.12
s.34, repealed: 2002 c.29 Sch.12
s.35, repealed: 2002 c.29 Sch.12
s.36, repealed: 2002 c.29 Sch.12
s.37, repealed: 2002 c.29 Sch.12
s.38, repealed: 2002 c.29 Sch.12
s.39, applied: SI 2002/2846 Art.2
s.39, repealed: 2002 c.29 Sch.12
s.39, enabling: SI 2002/257, SI 2002/2846
s.40, applied: SI 2002/2846 Art.2
s.40, repealed: 2002 c.29 Sch.12
s.41, repealed: 2002 c.29 Sch.12
s.42, see *Customs and Excise Commissioners v Duffy* [2002] EWHC 425, (2002) 166 J.P. 221 (QBD (Admin Ct)), Kennedy, L.J.
s.42, applied: SI 2002/3015 Art.3
s.42, repealed: 2002 c.29 Sch.12
s.43, see *Butt v Customs and Excise Commissioners* [2001] EWHC Admin 1066, (2002) 166 J.P. 173 (QBD (Admin Ct)), Hallett, J.

1994–cont.

37. Drug Trafficking Act 1994–*cont.*
s.43, applied: SI 2002/3015 Art.3, SI 2003/336 Sch.1 Part 2
s.43, repealed: 2002 c.29 Sch.12
s.44, applied: SI 2002/3015 Art.3
s.44, repealed: 2002 c.29 Sch.12
s.45, applied: SI 2002/3015 Art.3
s.45, repealed: 2002 c.29 Sch.12
s.46, applied: SI 2002/3015 Art.3
s.46, repealed: 2002 c.29 Sch.12
s.47, applied: SI 2002/3015 Art.3
s.47, repealed: 2002 c.29 Sch.12
s.48, applied: SI 2002/3015 Art.3
s.48, repealed: 2002 c.29 Sch.12
s.49, see *R. v Hussain (Akhtar)* [2002] EWCA Crim 6, [2002] 2 Cr. App. R. 26 (CA (Crim Div)), May, L.J.; see *R. v Montila (Steven William)* [2003] EWCA Crim 3082, [2004] 1 W.L.R. 624 (CA (Crim Div)), Scott Baker, L.J.; see *R. v Montila (Steven William)* [2004] UKHL 50, [2004] 1 W.L.R. 3141 (HL), Lord Bingham of Cornhill
s.49, repealed: 2002 c.29 Sch.12
s.50, repealed: 2002 c.29 Sch.12
s.51, repealed: 2002 c.29 Sch.12
s.52, see *R. v Duff (Jonathan Michael)* [2002] EWCA Crim 2117, [2003] 1 Cr. App. R. (S.) 88 (CA (Crim Div)), McCombe, J.
s.52, repealed: 2002 c.29 Sch.12
s.53, applied: SI 2003/120 Art.5
s.53, referred to: SI 2003/120 Art.5
s.53, repealed: 2002 c.29 Sch.12
s.54, repealed: 2002 c.29 Sch.12
s.55, amended: 2002 c.29 Sch.12, 2003 c.39 Sch.8 para.364
s.55, applied: SI 2003/120 Art.6
s.56, amended: 2002 c.29 Sch.12
s.56, applied: SI 2003/120 Art.6
s.57, applied: SI 2003/120 Art.6
s.58, applied: SI 2003/120 Art.5
s.59, amended: 2002 c.29 Sch.11 para.25, Sch.12
s.59, applied: SI 2003/120 Art.6
s.59, repealed (in part): 2002 c.29 Sch.12
s.59A, added: 2002 c.29 Sch.11 para.25
s.59A, applied: SI 2003/120 Art.6
s.60, amended: 2002 c.29 Sch.11 para.25, Sch.12, 2003 c.44 Sch.36 para.12
s.60, applied: SI 2003/120 Art.6
s.60, repealed (in part): 2002 c.29 Sch.12
s.61, amended: 2002 c.29 Sch.11 para.25
s.61, applied: SI 2003/120 Art.6
s.61, repealed (in part): 2002 c.29 Sch.12
s.62, repealed: 2002 c.29 Sch.12
s.63, repealed (in part): 2002 c.29 Sch.12
s.64, repealed: 2002 c.29 Sch.12
s.68, amended: 2002 c.29 Sch.11 para.25, Sch.12
s.68, repealed (in part): 2002 c.29 Sch.12

1994–cont.

37. Drug Trafficking Act 1994–*cont.*
Sch.1 para.1, repealed: 2002 c.9 Sch.13
Sch.1 para.3, repealed: 2002 c.29 Sch.12
Sch.1 para.4, repealed (in part): 2002 c.29 Sch.12
Sch.1 para.8, repealed: 2002 c.29 Sch.12
Sch.1 para.21, repealed: 2002 c.29 Sch.12
Sch.1 para.26, repealed: 2002 c.29 Sch.12

39. Local Government etc (Scotland) Act 1994
applied: SI 2002/2005 Sch.1 para.9
referred to: SI 2002/2007 Reg.8, SSI 2004/257 Reg.2
s.1, applied: SSI 2002/398 Sch.1, SSI 2002/473 Art.1
s.2, applied: 2002 asp 13 Sch.1 para.21, 2002 c.38 s.63, s.65, Sch.2 para.2, SI 2002/2779 Sch.1 para.1, 2003 c.14 s.61, s.66, Sch.9 para.1, 2003 c.44 Sch.9 para.1, Sch.9 para.2, SI 2003/1082 Reg.11, SI 2003/3172 Sch.2 Part I, Sch.2 Part II, SSI 2002/62 Sch.1, SSI 2002/167 Reg.6, 2004 c.36 Sch.1 para.13
s.4, amended: 2002 asp 1 s.4
s.5, amended: 2002 asp 1 s.1, s.4
s.5, repealed (in part): 2004 asp 9 s.5
s.18, applied: SI 2003/409 Sch.1 Part I
s.27, amended: 2003 asp 1 s.32
s.27, applied: 2002 asp 13 Sch.1 para.20
s.29, applied: 2002 asp 3 s.37
s.40, applied: SSI 2003/128
s.40, enabling: SSI 2003/128
s.62, applied: SSI 2002/62 Sch.1
s.62, repealed: 2002 asp 3 Sch.7 para.23
s.63, repealed: 2002 asp 3 Sch.7 para.23
s.64, repealed: 2002 asp 3 Sch.7 para.23
s.65, repealed (in part): 2002 asp 3 Sch.7 para.23
s.66, applied: SSI 2002/166 Art.5
s.66, repealed: 2002 asp 3 Sch.7 para.23
s.67A, repealed: 2002 asp 3 Sch.7 para.23
s.68, repealed: 2002 asp 3 Sch.7 para.23
s.69, repealed: 2002 asp 3 Sch.7 para.23
s.70, repealed: 2002 asp 3 Sch.7 para.23
s.71, repealed: 2002 asp 3 Sch.7 para.23
s.72, repealed: 2002 asp 3 Sch.7 para.23
s.73, repealed: 2002 asp 3 Sch.7 para.23
s.74, see *Scottish Water v Clydecare Ltd* 2003 S.C. 330 (Ex Div), Lord Osborne, Lord Macfadyen, Lord Sutherland
s.74, repealed: 2002 asp 3 Sch.7 para.23
s.75, repealed: 2002 asp 3 Sch.7 para.23
s.75A, repealed: 2002 asp 3 Sch.7 para.23
s.76, repealed: 2002 asp 3 Sch.7 para.23
s.76, varied: SSI 2002/166 Art.4
s.77, repealed: 2002 asp 3 Sch.7 para.23
s.78, repealed: 2002 asp 3 Sch.7 para.23
s.79, see *Scottish Water v Clydecare Ltd* 2003 S.C. 330 (Ex Div), Lord Osborne, Lord Macfadyen, Lord Sutherland
s.79, applied: SSI 2002/166 Art.3

1994–cont.

39. Local Government etc (Scotland) Act 1994–*cont.*
s.79, repealed: 2002 asp 3 Sch.7 para.23
s.79, enabling: SSI 2002/33
s.80, repealed: 2002 asp 3 Sch.7 para.23
s.81, repealed: 2002 asp 3 Sch.7 para.23
s.81, enabling: SSI 2002/47
s.82, repealed: 2002 asp 3 Sch.7 para.23
s.83, repealed: 2002 asp 3 Sch.7 para.23
s.84, applied: SSI 2002/118 Art.3
s.84, referred to: 2002 asp 7 Sch.5
s.84, repealed: 2002 asp 3 Sch.7 para.23
s.85, repealed: 2002 asp 3 Sch.7 para.23
s.86, repealed: 2002 asp 3 Sch.7 para.23
s.87, applied: SSI 2002/118 Art.3
s.87, repealed: 2002 asp 3 Sch.7 para.23
s.88, applied: SSI 2002/118 Art.3
s.88, repealed: 2002 asp 3 Sch.7 para.23
s.89, repealed: 2002 asp 3 Sch.7 para.23
s.90, repealed: 2002 asp 3 Sch.7 para.23
s.91, repealed: 2002 asp 3 Sch.7 para.23
s.92, repealed: 2002 asp 3 Sch.7 para.23
s.93, repealed: 2002 asp 3 Sch.7 para.23
s.94, repealed: 2002 asp 3 Sch.7 para.23
s.95, repealed: 2002 asp 3 Sch.7 para.23
s.96, repealed: 2002 asp 3 Sch.7 para.23
s.97, repealed: 2002 asp 3 Sch.7 para.23
s.98, repealed: 2002 asp 3 Sch.7 para.23
s.99, repealed: 2002 asp 3 Sch.7 para.23
s.100, repealed: 2002 asp 3 Sch.7 para.23
s.116, repealed: 2002 asp 3 Sch.7 para.23
s.117, repealed: 2002 asp 3 Sch.7 para.23
s.118, repealed: 2002 asp 3 Sch.7 para.23
s.119, repealed: 2002 asp 3 Sch.7 para.23
s.120, repealed: 2002 asp 3 Sch.7 para.23
s.121, repealed: 2002 asp 3 Sch.7 para.23
s.122, repealed: 2002 asp 3 Sch.7 para.23
s.123, repealed: 2002 asp 3 Sch.7 para.23
s.124, repealed: 2002 asp 3 Sch.7 para.23
s.125, repealed: 2002 asp 3 Sch.7 para.23
s.125A, repealed: 2002 asp 3 Sch.7 para.23
s.126, repealed: 2002 asp 3 Sch.7 para.23
s.128, applied: SSI 2003/231 Sch.4 para.20
s.151, see *Drummond Estates v Central Scotland Assessor* [2004] R.A. 145 (Lands Tr (Scot)), Lord McGhie, AR MacLeary, FRICS
s.153, enabling: SSI 2002/91, SSI 2003/160, SSI 2004/92
s.172, applied: 2002 asp 13 Sch.1 para.56, SSI 2004/396 Sch.1 para.9, SSI 2004/397 Sch.1 para.9
s.172, referred to: SSI 2004/396 Sch.1 para.8, SSI 2004/397 Sch.1 para.8
s.172, enabling: SSI 2004/396, SSI 2004/397
s.173, applied: SSI 2004/396, SSI 2004/396 Sch.1 para.9, SSI 2004/397, SSI 2004/397 Sch.1 para.9, SSI 2004/464, SSI 2004/465

1994–cont.

39. Local Government etc (Scotland) Act 1994–cont.

s.173, enabling: SSI 2004/396, SSI 2004/397, SSI 2004/464, SSI 2004/465

s.174, applied: SSI 2004/396 Sch.1 para.9, SSI 2004/397 Sch.1 para.9

Sch.1, applied: SSI 2002/398 Sch.1

Sch.1 Part I, applied: SSI 2002/473 Art.1

Sch.5, enabling: SSI 2003/128

Sch.5 Part II para.7, amended: 2003 asp1 s.48

Sch.7 para.1, repealed: 2002 asp 3 Sch.7 para.23

Sch.7 para.2, repealed: 2002 asp 3 Sch.7 para.23

Sch.7 para.3, repealed: 2002 asp 3 Sch.7 para.23

Sch.7 para.4, repealed: 2002 asp 3 Sch.7 para.23

Sch.7 para.5, repealed: 2002 asp 3 Sch.7 para.23

Sch.7 para.6, repealed: 2002 asp 3 Sch.7 para.23

Sch.7 para.7, repealed: 2002 asp 3 Sch.7 para.23

Sch.7 para.8, repealed: 2002 asp 3 Sch.7 para.23

Sch.7 para.9, repealed: 2002 asp 3 Sch.7 para.23

Sch.7 para.10, repealed: 2002 asp 3 Sch.7 para.23

Sch.7 para.11, repealed: 2002 asp 3 Sch.7 para.23

Sch.7 para.12, repealed: 2002 asp 3 Sch.7 para.23

Sch.7 para.13, repealed: 2002 asp 3 Sch.7 para.23

Sch.7 para.14, repealed: 2002 asp 3 Sch.7 para.23

Sch.7 para.15, repealed: 2002 asp 3 Sch.7 para.23

Sch.7 para.16, repealed: 2002 asp 3 Sch.7 para.23

Sch.7 para.17, repealed: 2002 asp 3 Sch.7 para.23

Sch.7 para.18, repealed: 2002 asp 3 Sch.7 para.23

Sch.8, repealed: 2002 asp 3 Sch.7 para.23

Sch.9A Part I para.1, repealed: 2002 asp 3 Sch.7 para.23

Sch.9A Part I para.2, repealed: 2002 asp 3 Sch.7 para.23

Sch.9A Part I para.3, repealed: 2002 asp 3 Sch.7 para.23

Sch.9A Part I para.3A, repealed: 2002 asp 3 Sch.7 para.23

Sch.9A Part II para.4, repealed: 2002 asp 3 Sch.7 para.23

Sch.9A Part II para.5, repealed: 2002 asp 3 Sch.7 para.23

Sch.9A Part II para.6, repealed: 2002 asp 3 Sch.7 para.23

1994–cont.

39. Local Government etc (Scotland) Act 1994–cont.

Sch.10 para.1, repealed: 2002 asp 3 Sch.7 para.23

Sch.10 para.2, amended: 2002 asp 17 Sch.3 para.23

Sch.10 para.2, repealed: 2002 asp 3 Sch.7 para.23

Sch.10 para.2, enabling: SSI 2002/560

Sch.10 para.3, repealed: 2002 asp 3 Sch.7 para.23

Sch.10 para.4, amended: 2002 asp 17 Sch.3 para.23

Sch.10 para.4, repealed: 2002 asp 3 Sch.7 para.23

Sch.11 para.1, repealed: 2002 asp 3 Sch.7 para.23

Sch.11 para.2, repealed: 2002 asp 3 Sch.7 para.23

Sch.11 para.3, repealed: 2002 asp 3 Sch.7 para.23

Sch.11 para.4, repealed: 2002 asp 3 Sch.7 para.23

Sch.11 para.5, repealed: 2002 asp 3 Sch.7 para.23

Sch.11 para.6, repealed: 2002 asp 3 Sch.7 para.23

Sch.11 para.7, repealed: 2002 asp 3 Sch.7 para.23

Sch.11 para.8, repealed: 2002 asp 3 Sch.7 para.23

Sch.11 para.9, repealed: 2002 asp 3 Sch.7 para.23

Sch.11 para.10, repealed: 2002 asp 3 Sch.7 para.23

Sch.11 para.11, repealed: 2002 asp 3 Sch.7 para.23

Sch.11 para.12, repealed: 2002 asp 3 Sch.7 para.23

Sch.13 para.24, repealed: 2004 c.36 Sch.3

Sch.13 para.38, repealed (in part): 2002 asp 3 Sch.7 para.23

Sch.13 para.52, repealed: 2003 asp 8 Sch.6 para.21

Sch.13 para.56, repealed (in part): 2002 asp 3 Sch.7 para.23

Sch.13 para.66, repealed (in part): 2002 asp 3 Sch.7 para.23

Sch.13 para.72, repealed (in part): 2002 asp 3 Sch.7 para.23

Sch.13 para.75, repealed (in part): 2002 asp 3 Sch.7 para.23

Sch.13 para.92, repealed (in part): 2002 asp 3 Sch.7 para.23

Sch.13 para.100, repealed (in part): 2002 asp 11 Sch.6 para.15

Sch.13 para.119, repealed (in part): 2002 asp 3 Sch.7 para.23

Sch.13 para.128, repealed (in part): 2002 asp 3 Sch.7 para.23

CAP.

1994–cont.

39. Local Government etc (Scotland) Act 1994–*cont.*

Sch.13 para.133, repealed (in part): 2002 asp 3 Sch.7 para.23

Sch.13 para.135, repealed (in part): 2002 asp 3 Sch.7 para.23

Sch.13 para.137, repealed (in part): 2002 asp 3 Sch.7 para.23

Sch.13 para.152, repealed (in part): 2002 asp 3 Sch.7 para.23

Sch.13 para.167, repealed (in part): 2002 asp 3 Sch.7 para.23

Sch.13 para.168, repealed (in part): 2002 asp 3 Sch.7 para.23

Sch.13 para.181, repealed (in part): 2002 asp 3 Sch.7 para.23

40. Deregulation and Contracting Out Act 1994

referred to: SI 2002/808 Art.2

s.1, enabling: SI 2002/367, SI 2002/460, SI 2002/493, SI 2002/1419

s.3, applied: SI 2002/367(b), SI 2002/460(d), SI 2002/1419(d), SI 2002/367(d), SI 2002/493

s.4, applied: SI 2002/367(d), SI 2002/460(d), SI 2002/493

s.7, repealed (in part): 2002 c.40 Sch.26

s.8, repealed: 2003 c.21 Sch.19

s.9, repealed: 2002 c.40 Sch.26

s.14, repealed: 2004 c.14 Sch.1 Part 16

s.18, repealed (in part): 2003 c.17 Sch.7

s.19, repealed: 2003 c.17 Sch.7

s.21, repealed: 2003 c.17 Sch.6 para.112, Sch.7

s.23, repealed: 2004 c.14 Sch.1 Part 16

s.24, repealed: 2004 c.14 Sch.1 Part 16

s.62, repealed (in part): 2004 c.14 Sch.1 Part 16

s.64, repealed: 2004 c.14 Sch.1 Part 16

s.69, applied: SI 2002/3052

s.69, referred to: SI 2004/1975

s.69, varied: 2003 c.21 s.1, Sch.18 para.6, SI 2004/1777 Art.34, SI 2004/1778 Art.34, SI 2004/1975

s.69, enabling: SI 2002/445, SI 2002/1888, SI 2002/3052, SI 2003/1668, SI 2003/1908, SI 2004/1975

s.70, applied: 2002 c.32 s.183, SI 2002/928, SI 2002/1888, SI 2003/2704

s.70, referred to: SI 2002/1888 Art.3

s.70, varied: 2003 c.21 s.1, Sch.18 para.6, SI 2004/1777 Art.34, SI 2004/1778 Art.34, SI 2004/1975

s.70, enabling: SI 2002/928, SI 2002/1888, SI 2003/2704

s.71, amended: 2003 c.26 Sch.7 para.59

s.71, referred to: SI 2002/1888 Art.3

s.71, varied: 2003 c.21 s.1, Sch.18 para.6, SI 2004/1777 Art.34, SI 2004/1778 Art.34, SI 2004/1975

CAP.

1994–cont.

40. Deregulation and Contracting Out Act 1994–*cont.*

s.72, varied: 2003 c.21 s.1, Sch.18 para.6, SI 2004/1777 Art.34, SI 2004/1778 Art.34, SI 2004/1975

s.73, varied: 2003 c.21 s.1, Sch.18 para.6, SI 2004/1777 Art.34, SI 2004/1778 Art.34, SI 2004/1975

s.74, varied: 2003 c.21 s.1, Sch.18 para.6, SI 2004/1777 Art.34, SI 2004/1778 Art.34, SI 2004/1975

s.75, varied: 2003 c.21 s.1, Sch.18 para.6, SI 2004/1777 Art.34, SI 2004/1778 Art.34, SI 2004/1975

s.76, varied: 2003 c.21 s.1, Sch.18 para.6, SI 2004/1777 Art.34, SI 2004/1778 Art.34, SI 2004/1975

s.77, applied: SI 2002/445, SI 2002/928, SI 2002/1888, SI 2002/3052, SI 2003/1668, SI 2003/1908, SI 2003/2704, SI 2004/1975

s.77, varied: 2003 c.21 s.1, Sch.18 para.6, SI 2004/1777 Art.34, SI 2004/1778 Art.34, SI 2004/1975

s.77, enabling: SI 2002/445, SI 2002/928, SI 2002/1888, SI 2002/3052, SI 2003/1668, SI 2003/1908, SI 2004/1975

s.78, varied: 2003 c.21 s.1, Sch.18 para.6, SI 2004/1777 Art.34, SI 2004/1778 Art.34, SI 2004/1975

s.79, amended: SI 2004/1823 Art.18

s.79, varied: 2003 c.21 s.1, Sch.18 para.6, SI 2004/1777 Art.34, SI 2004/1778 Art.34, SI 2004/1975

s.79, enabling: SI 2002/3052

s.82, amended: SI 2003/1398 Sch.1 para.22

s.82, repealed (in part): 2004 c.14 Sch.1 Part 16

Sch.2 para.1, amended: 2003 c.20 Sch.2 para.19

Sch.2 para.1, repealed: 2002 c.40 Sch.26

Sch.2 para.2, amended: 2003 c.20 Sch.2 para.19

Sch.2 para.2, repealed: 2002 c.40 Sch.26

Sch.2 para.3, amended: 2003 c.20 Sch.2 para.19

Sch.2 para.3, repealed: 2002 c.40 Sch.26

Sch.2 para.4, amended: 2003 c.20 Sch.2 para.19

Sch.2 para.4, repealed: 2002 c.40 Sch.26

Sch.2 para.5, amended: 2003 c.20 Sch.2 para.19

Sch.2 para.5, repealed: 2002 c.40 Sch.26

Sch.2 para.6, amended: 2003 c.20 Sch.2 para.19

Sch.2 para.6, repealed: 2002 c.40 Sch.26

Sch.2 para.7, amended: 2003 c.20 Sch.2 para.19

Sch.2 para.7, repealed: 2002 c.40 Sch.26

Sch.2 para.8, amended: 2003 c.20 Sch.2 para.19

1994–cont.

40. Deregulation and Contracting Out Act 1994–cont.

Sch.2 para.8, repealed: 2002 c.40 Sch.26

Sch.2 para.9, amended: 2003 c.20 Sch.2 para.19

Sch.2 para.9, repealed: 2002 c.40 Sch.26

Sch.2 para.10, amended: 2003 c.20 Sch.2 para.19

Sch.2 para.10, repealed: 2002 c.40 Sch.26

Sch.2 para.11, amended: 2003 c.20 Sch.2 para.19

Sch.2 para.11, repealed: 2002 c.40 Sch.26

Sch.2 para.12, amended: 2003 c.20 Sch.2 para.19

Sch.2 para.12, repealed: 2002 c.40 Sch.26

Sch.2 para.13, amended: 2003 c.20 Sch.2 para.19

Sch.2 para.13, repealed: 2002 c.40 Sch.26

Sch.2 para.14, amended: 2003 c.20 Sch.2 para.19

Sch.2 para.14, repealed: 2002 c.40 Sch.26

Sch.2 para.15, amended: 2003 c.20 Sch.2 para.19

Sch.2 para.15, repealed: 2002 c.40 Sch.26

Sch.4 para.2, repealed: 2002 c.40 Sch.26

Sch.4 para.3, repealed (in part): 2003 c.21 Sch.19

Sch.4 para.4, amended: 2003 c.20 Sch.2 para.19

Sch.4 para.5, repealed: 2004 c.14 Sch.1 Part 16

Sch.4 para.6, repealed: 2004 c.14 Sch.1 Part 16

Sch.4 para.7, repealed: 2004 c.14 Sch.1 Part 16

Sch.4 para.8, repealed: 2004 c.14 Sch.1 Part 16

Sch.7, repealed: 2003 c.17 Sch.7

Sch.10 Part I para.1, repealed (in part): 2004 c.14 Sch.1 Part 16

Sch.10 Part I para.2, repealed (in part): 2004 c.14 Sch.1 Part 16

Sch.10 Part II para.3, repealed: 2004 c.14 Sch.1 Part 16

Sch.10 Part II para.4, repealed: 2004 c.14 Sch.1 Part 16

Sch.10 Part II para.5, repealed: 2004 c.14 Sch.1 Part 16

Sch.11 para.1, repealed: 2003 c.17 Sch.7

Sch.11 para.2, repealed (in part): 2002 c.40 Sch.26, SI 2003/3180 Sch.1 para.5

Sch.11 para.4, repealed (in part): 2002 c.40 Sch.26, 2004 c.14 Sch.1 Part 16

Sch.11 para.7, repealed (in part): 2004 c.14 Sch.1 Part 16

Sch.11 para.8, repealed: 2004 c.14 Sch.1 Part 16

Sch.11 para.9, repealed: 2004 c.14 Sch.1 Part 16

Sch.11 para.10, repealed: SI 2002/3150 Sch.4

1994–cont.

40. Deregulation and Contracting Out Act 1994–cont.

Sch.11 para.11, repealed: 2004 c.14 Sch.1 Part 16

Sch.11 para.12, repealed (in part): 2004 c.14 Sch.1 Part 16

Sch.16 para.2, repealed: 2003 c.39 Sch.10

1995

i. British Waterways Act 1995

s.3, amended: 2003 c.21 Sch.17 para.134

x. London Local Authorities Act 1995

s.2, amended: 2004 c.18 Sch.11 para.6, 2004 c.21 Sch.1 para.86, 2004 c.i Sch.5

s.4, repealed: 2004 c.18 Sch.12 Part 1

s.5, amended: 2004 c.21 Sch.1 para.86

s.5, repealed: 2004 c.18 Sch.12 Part 1

s.7, repealed: 2004 c.18 Sch.12 Part 1

s.8, repealed: 2004 c.18 Sch.12 Part 1

s.9, amended: 2004 c.18 Sch.11 para.6

s.11, see *R. (on the application of Maiden Outdoor Advertising Ltd) v Lambeth LBC* [2003] EWHC 1224, [2004] J.P.L. 820 (QBD (Admin Ct)), Collins, J.

s.12, amended: 2004 c.i s.12

s.12, applied: 2004 c.i s.13

s.12, disapplied: 2004 c.i s.14

s.13, amended: SI 2003/1615 Sch.1 para.36

s.14, amended: 2003 c.17 Sch.6 para.113, Sch.7

s.14, applied: 2003 c.17 Sch.2 para.4

s.14, repealed (in part): 2003 c.17 Sch.6 para.113, Sch.7

s.16, applied: 2003 c.17 Sch.2 para.4

s.17, amended: 2004 c.21 Sch.1 para.86

s.22, amended: 2004 c.21 Sch.1 para.86

s.24, amended: 2003 c.44 Sch.26 para.46

s.25, amended: 2004 c.21 Sch.1 para.86

s.28, repealed: 2003 c.17 Sch.7

s.39, amended: SI 2004/916 Art.3, SI 2004/1268 Art.3

s.45, repealed: 2003 c.17 Sch.7

s.46, repealed: 2003 c.17 Sch.7

Value Added Tax Act 1995

s.84, see *Tricell UK Ltd v Customs and Excise Commissioners* [2003] V. & D.R. 333 (VAT and Duties Tribunal (Manchester)), Colin Bishopp (Chairman)

Sch.9 Group 5 Item 6, see *Southampton Leisure Holdings Plc v Customs and Excise Commissioners* [2002] V. & D.R. 235 (V&DTr (London)), Nuala Brice (Chairman)

3. South Africa Act 1995

Sch.1 para.1, repealed: 2002 c.39 Sch.3

4. Finance Act 1995

referred to: 2003 c.1 Sch.6 para.225

s.5, applied: 2003 c.17 Sch.8 para.30

s.17, amended: 2002 c.40 Sch.26

s.43, repealed: 2003 c.1 Sch.8 Part 1

s.44, repealed: 2003 c.1 Sch.8 Part 1

1995–cont.

4. Finance Act 1995–*cont.*

s.45, repealed: 2003 c.1 Sch.8 Part 1

s.52, repealed (in part): 2002 c.23 Sch.40 Part 3

s.58, repealed: 2004 c.12 Sch.42 Part 3

s.59, repealed: 2004 c.12 Sch.42 Part 3

s.60, repealed: 2004 c.12 Sch.42 Part 3

s.61, repealed: 2004 c.12 Sch.42 Part 3

s.72, repealed (in part): 2004 c.12 Sch.42 Part 2

s.73, varied: 2002 c.23 Sch.33 para.14

s.87, repealed (in part): 2004 c.12 Sch.42 Part 2

s.91, repealed: 2003 c.1 Sch.8 Part 1

s.92, repealed: 2003 c.1 Sch.8 Part 1

s.93, repealed: 2003 c.1 Sch.8 Part 1

s.108, repealed: 2003 c.1 Sch.8 Part 1

s.108, restored: 2004 c.12 Sch.17 para.6

s.111, repealed: 2003 c.1 Sch.8 Part 1

s.126, amended: 2003 c.14 Sch.27 para.4, Sch.43 Part 3

s.126, repealed (in part): 2003 c.14 Sch.43 Part 3

s.127, amended: 2003 c.14 Sch.27 para.5, Sch.43 Part 3

s.127, applied: SI 2003/2172 Reg.2

s.127, referred to: SI 2003/2172 Reg.2

s.127, repealed (in part): 2003 c.14 Sch.43 Part 3

s.127, enabling: SI 2003/2172

s.128, amended: 2003 c.14 Sch.27 para.6, 2003 c.1 Sch.6 para.226

s.129, repealed: 2003 c.14 Sch.43 Part 3

s.131, repealed: 2002 c.23 Sch.40 Part 3

s.132, repealed: 2002 c.23 Sch.40 Part 3

s.134, repealed (in part): 2004 c.12 Sch.42 Part 2

s.137, amended: 2003 c.1 Sch.6 para.227

s.137, repealed (in part): 2003 c.1 Sch.8 Part 1

s.139, repealed: 2004 c.12 Sch.42 Part 2

s.141, repealed: 2003 c.1 Sch.8 Part 1

s.152, enabling: SI 2002/1973, SI 2003/1831

Sch.3 para.8, repealed (in part): 2002 c.23 Sch.40 Part 1

Sch.4 Part III para.7, repealed: 2002 c.23 Sch.40 Part 1

Sch.8 Part I para.4, repealed (in part): 2004 c.12 Sch.42 Part 3

Sch.8 Part I para.7, repealed: 2004 c.12 Sch.42 Part 2

Sch.8 Part I para.23, repealed (in part): 2004 c.12 Sch.42 Part 2

Sch.8 Part III para.58, enabling: SI 2003/1828, SI 2003/2573, SI 2003/2642, SI 2004/2189, SI 2004/2257

Sch.8 para.55, see *Royal London Mutual Insurance Society Ltd v Barrett (Inspector of Taxes)* [2002] EWHC 1416, [2002] S.T.C. 1020 (Ch D), Peter Smith, J.; see *Royal London Mutual Insurance Society Ltd v Barrett (Inspector of Taxes)* [2002]

1995–cont.

4. Finance Act 1995–*cont.*

Sch.8 para.55–*cont.*

S.T.C. (S.C.D.) 61 (Sp Comm), Nuala Brice; see *Royal London Mutual Insurance Society Ltd v Barrett (Inspector of Taxes)* [2003] EWCA Civ 789, [2003] S.T.C. 1129 (CA), Arden, L.J.

Sch.8 para.57, see *Royal London Mutual Insurance Society Ltd v Barrett (Inspector of Taxes)* [2003] EWCA Civ 789, [2003] S.T.C. 1129 (CA), Arden, L.J.

Sch.11 para.1, repealed: 2004 c.12 Sch.42 Part 3

Sch.11 para.2, repealed: 2004 c.12 Sch.42 Part 3

Sch.11 para.3, repealed: 2004 c.12 Sch.42 Part 3

Sch.11 para.4, repealed: 2004 c.12 Sch.42 Part 3

Sch.11 para.5, repealed: 2004 c.12 Sch.42 Part 3

Sch.11 para.6, repealed: 2004 c.12 Sch.42 Part 3

Sch.11 para.7, repealed: 2004 c.12 Sch.42 Part 3

Sch.11 para.8, repealed: 2004 c.12 Sch.42 Part 3

Sch.11 para.9, repealed: 2004 c.12 Sch.42 Part 3

Sch.11 para.10, repealed: 2004 c.12 Sch.42 Part 3

Sch.11 para.11, repealed: 2004 c.12 Sch.42 Part 3

Sch.11 para.12, repealed: 2004 c.12 Sch.42 Part 3

Sch.13 para.4, repealed (in part): 2004 c.12 Sch.42 Part 2

Sch.16, repealed: 2004 c.12 Sch.42 Part 2

Sch.24 Part I para.1, repealed: 2002 c.23 Sch.40 Part 3

Sch.24 Part I para.2, repealed: 2002 c.23 Sch.40 Part 3

Sch.24 Part I para.3, repealed: 2002 c.23 Sch.40 Part 3

Sch.24 Part II para.7, amended: 2002 c.23 Sch.23 para.22

Sch.25 para.6, repealed (in part): 2002 c.23 Sch.40 Part 3

Sch.25 para.7, repealed: 2002 c.23 Sch.40 Part 3

Sch.27 para.1, repealed: 2004 c.12 Sch.42 Part 2

Sch.27 para.2, repealed: 2004 c.12 Sch.42 Part 2

Sch.27 para.3, repealed: 2004 c.12 Sch.42 Part 2

Sch.27 para.4, repealed: 2004 c.12 Sch.42 Part 2

Sch.27 para.5, repealed: 2004 c.12 Sch.42 Part 2

1995–cont.

4. Finance Act 1995–*cont.*
Sch.27 para.6, repealed: 2004 c.12 Sch.42 Part 2
Sch.27 para.7, repealed: 2004 c.12 Sch.42 Part 2
Sch.27 para.8, repealed: 2004 c.12 Sch.42 Part 2
Sch.27 para.9, repealed: 2004 c.12 Sch.42 Part 2
6. Civil Evidence (Family Mediation) (Scotland) Act 1995
s.1, amended: 2004 c.33 Sch.28 para.59
7. Requirements of Writing (Scotland) Act 1995
see *Howgate Shopping Centre Ltd v GLS 164 Ltd* 2002 S.L.T. 820 (OH), Lord Macfadyen
s.2, applied: 2003 asp 9 s.84
s.3, applied: SI 2002/427 Reg.15, SI 2002/836 Reg.15
s.9, applied: 2003 asp 4 s.14, SI 2004/1611 Reg.27
s.13, repealed (in part): 2003 asp 9 Sch.15
Sch.2 para.6, applied: SSI 2002/103 Art.4, Sch.1 Part II, SSI 2002/305 Art.4, Sch.1 Part II, SSI 2002/534 Art.4, Sch.1 Part II
8. Agricultural Tenancies Act 1995
applied: 2002 c.15 Sch.2 para.2
s.7, amended: 2004 c.33 Sch.8 para.49
s.9, see *Barclays Bank Plc v Bean* [2004] 41 E.G. 152 (Ch D), Judge Langan
10. Home Energy Conservation Act 1995
disapplied: 2003 c.30 s.4
s.1, amended: 2004 c.34 Sch.15 para.38
11. Proceeds of Crime Act 1995
see *R. v Brown (Peter John) (Appeal against Sentence)* [2001] EWCA Crim 2761, [2002] 2 Cr. App. R. (S.) 34 (CA (Crim Div)), Mantell, L.J.; see *R. v Palmer (John)* [2002] EWCA Crim 2202, [2003] 1 Cr. App. R. (S.) 112 (CA (Crim Div)), Rix, L.J.; see *R. v Simpson (Ian McDonald)* [2003] EWCA Crim 1499, [2004] Q.B. 118 (CA (Crim Div)), Lord Woolf of Barnes, L.C.J.; see *R. v Smith (John)* [2002] EWCA Crim 2561, [2003] 2 Cr. App. R. (S.) 4 (CA (Crim Div)), Longmore, L.J.
s.1, repealed: 2002 c.29 Sch.12
s.2, repealed: 2002 c.29 Sch.12
s.3, repealed: 2002 c.29 Sch.12
s.4, repealed: 2002 c.29 Sch.12
s.5, repealed: 2002 c.29 Sch.12
s.6, repealed: 2002 c.29 Sch.12
s.7, repealed: 2002 c.29 Sch.12
s.8, repealed: 2002 c.29 Sch.12
s.9, repealed: 2002 c.29 Sch.12
s.10, repealed: 2002 c.29 Sch.12
s.11, repealed: 2002 c.29 Sch.12
s.12, repealed: 2002 c.29 Sch.12
s.13, repealed: 2002 c.29 Sch.12
s.15, repealed (in part): 2002 c.29 Sch.12

1995–cont.

11. Proceeds of Crime Act 1995–*cont.*
s.16, repealed (in part): 2002 c.29 Sch.12
Sch.1 para.1, repealed: 2002 c.29 Sch.12
Sch.1 para.2, repealed: 2002 c.29 Sch.12
Sch.1 para.3, repealed: 2002 c.29 Sch.12
12. Carers (Recognition and Services) Act 1995
s.1, amended: 2004 c.15 s.1, s.2
s.1, referred to: 2004 c.15 s.3
13. Road Traffic (New Drivers) Act 1995
referred to: 2003 c.32 Sch.5 para.45
s.2, amended: 2003 c.32 Sch.5 para.46
s.3, amended: 2003 c.32 Sch.5 para.47
s.4, amended: 2003 c.32 Sch.5 para.48
s.5, amended: 2003 c.32 Sch.5 para.49
s.7, amended: 2003 c.32 Sch.5 para.50
s.9, amended: 2003 c.32 Sch.5 para.51
Sch.1, referred to: 2003 c.32 Sch.5 para.52
Sch.1 Part I para.1, amended: 2003 c.32 Sch.5 para.53
Sch.1 Part I para.2, amended: 2003 c.32 Sch.5 para.54
Sch.1 Part II para.3, amended: 2003 c.39 Sch.8 para.365
Sch.1 Part III para.5, amended: 2003 c.32 Sch.5 para.55
Sch.1 Part III para.6, amended: 2003 c.32 Sch.5 para.56
Sch.1 Part IV para.8, amended: 2003 c.32 Sch.5 para.57
Sch.1 Part IV para.9, amended: 2003 c.32 Sch.5 para.58
Sch.1 Part V para.10, amended: 2003 c.32 Sch.5 para.59
Sch.1 Part V para.11, amended: 2003 c.32 Sch.5 para.60
15. Activity Centres (Young Persons Safety) Act 1995
s.1, applied: 2002 asp 11 Sch.2 para.76
s.1, enabling: SI 2004/1309
s.2, enabling: SI 2004/1309
s.3, applied: SI 2004/1309
s.3, enabling: SI 2004/1309
16. Prisoners (Return to Custody) Act 1995
s.1, amended: 2003 c.44 s.186
s.1, applied: 2003 c.44 s.246, s.260
17. Health Authorities Act 1995
s.1, repealed: 2002 c.17 Sch.9 Part 3
Sch.1 Part I para.11, repealed (in part): 2003 c.4 Sch.4
Sch.1 Part I para.18, repealed (in part): 2003 c.43 Sch.14 Part 4
Sch.1 Part I para.19, repealed (in part): 2003 c.43 Sch.14 Part 4
Sch.1 Part I para.20, repealed (in part): 2003 c.43 Sch.14 Part 4
Sch.1 Part I para.21, repealed (in part): 2003 c.43 Sch.14 Part 4
Sch.1 Part I para.22, repealed (in part): 2003 c.43 Sch.14 Part 4

CAP.

1995–cont.

17. Health Authorities Act 1995–*cont.*

Sch.1 Part I para.23, repealed (in part): 2003 c.43 Sch.14 Part 4

Sch.1 Part I para.24, repealed: 2003 c.43 Sch.14 Part 4

Sch.1 Part I para.25, repealed: 2003 c.43 Sch.14 Part 4

Sch.1 Part I para.26, repealed: 2003 c.43 Sch.14 Part 4

Sch.1 Part I para.32, repealed (in part): 2002 c.17 Sch.9 Part 3

Sch.1 Part I para.50, repealed (in part): 2003 c.4 Sch.4

Sch.1 Part I para.53, repealed: 2002 c.17 Sch.9 Part 3

Sch.1 Part I para.62, repealed (in part): 2003 c.4 Sch.4

Sch.1 Part III para.92, repealed (in part): 2004 c.30 Sch.7 Part 1

Sch.1 Part III para.97, repealed (in part): 2004 c.14 Sch.1 Part 10

Sch.1 Part III para.101, repealed: 2002 c.38 Sch.5

Sch.1 Part III para.102, repealed (in part): 2004 asp 7 Sch.2

Sch.1 Part III para.105, repealed: 2002 c.1 Sch.4

Sch.1 Part III para.107, repealed (in part): 2002 c.17 Sch.9 Part 3

Sch.1 Part III para.108, repealed (in part): SI 2002/2469 Sch.13

Sch.1 Part III para.109, repealed: 2003 c.43 Sch.14 Part 2

Sch.1 Part III para.111, repealed (in part): SI 2002/2469 Sch.13

Sch.1 Part III para.120, repealed: 2003 c.37 Sch.7 para.41, Sch.9 Part 3

Sch.2 para.2, amended: 2002 c.17 Sch.2 para.62, SI 2002/2469 Sch.1 para.20

Sch.2 para.5, amended: SI 2003/2867 Sch.1 para.23

18. Jobseekers Act 1995

applied: 2002 c.21 Sch.5 para.7, SI 2002/1015 Reg.3, SI 2002/2006 Reg.7, SI 2002/2022 Reg.3, SI 2003/1325 Art.2, SI 2004/3114 Art.3, SI 2004/3121 Art.4, SSI 2002/289 Reg.3, SSI 2002/494 Reg.33, Sch.2 para.5, Sch.3 para.7, Sch.3 para.8, SSI 2003/140 Sch.1 para.5

referred to: 2003 c.1 Sch.6 para.228

Part I, applied: SI 2002/3200 Reg.29, SI 2003/492 Reg.19, SSI 2004/83 Reg.3

s.1, amended: 2004 c.33 Sch.24 para.118

s.1, applied: SI 2002/1792 Reg.13B, Reg.9, SI 2002/2007 Reg.5, 2003 c.1 s.660, SI 2003/493 Reg.10, SI 2003/2098 Reg.8, SI 2004/683 Reg.8, SI 2004/934 Reg.6

s.1, disapplied: SI 2004/934 Reg.6

s.1, referred to: SI 2002/1701 Reg.2, SI 2002/1703 Reg.8, SI 2004/934 Reg.6, SI 2004/959 Reg.20

CAP.

1995–cont.

18. Jobseekers Act 1995–*cont.*

s.1, varied: SI 2003/2438 Reg.5

s.1, enabling: SI 2002/1701, SI 2002/2689

s.2, amended: 2002 c.19 Sch.1 para.45

s.3, amended: 2002 c.16 Sch.2 para.37, 2004 c.33 Sch.24 para.119

s.3A, amended: 2002 c.16 Sch.2 para.38

s.4, enabling: SI 2002/398, SI 2002/841, SI 2002/2019, SI 2002/2020, SI 2002/2380, SI 2003/455, SI 2003/511, SI 2003/1121, SI 2003/1195, SI 2003/1731, SI 2003/2279, SI 2004/565, SI 2004/1232, SI 2004/2327, SI 2004/2825

s.5, enabling: SI 2002/490

s.6, enabling: SI 2002/1763, SI 2002/3072, SI 2004/1869

s.7, enabling: SI 2004/1008, SI 2004/1869

s.8, enabling: SI 2002/3072

s.12, enabling: SI 2002/841, SI 2002/1411, SI 2002/1589, SI 2002/2207, SI 2002/2314, SI 2002/2380, SI 2002/2402, SI 2002/2442, SI 2002/2689, SI 2003/455, SI 2003/511, SI 2003/1701, SI 2003/1731, SI 2003/1914, SI 2003/2279, SI 2003/2439, SI 2004/98, SI 2004/565, SI 2004/963, SI 2004/1141, SI 2004/1708, SI 2004/2308

s.13, enabling: SI 2003/455, SI 2003/1731

s.14, applied: 2003 c.1 s.673, SI 2003/2682 Reg.64

s.15, amended: 2003 c.1 Sch.6 para.229, 2004 c.33 Sch.24 para.120

s.15A, amended: 2004 c.33 Sch.24 para.121

s.19, applied: SI 2003/2438 Reg.7, SI 2004/934 Reg.7, SI 2004/959 Reg.21

s.19, enabling: SI 2002/2314, SI 2003/2438, SI 2004/867, SI 2004/868, SI 2004/869, SI 2004/934, SI 2004/959, SI 2004/1008, SI 2004/1043

s.20A, applied: SI 2003/2438 Reg.7, SI 2004/934 Reg.7, SI 2004/959 Reg.21

s.23, amended: 2004 c.33 Sch.24 para.122

s.26, amended: 2003 c.1 Sch.6 para.230

s.26, applied: 2003 c.1 s.677

s.26, enabling: SI 2002/490, SI 2002/2497, SI 2002/3197, SI 2003/1589, SI 2004/1655

s.29, applied: SI 2004/934

s.29, repealed (in part): 2002 c.21 Sch.6

s.29, enabling: SI 2004/867, SI 2004/868, SI 2004/869, SI 2004/934

s.31, amended: 2004 c.33 Sch.24 para.123

s.31, enabling: SI 2002/1379

s.35, amended: 2004 c.33 Sch.24 para.124, Sch.30

s.35, applied: SI 2002/2822 Reg.35

s.35, enabling: SI 2002/398, SI 2002/490, SI 2002/841, SI 2002/1379, SI 2002/1411, SI 2002/1589, SI 2002/1701, SI 2002/1763, SI 2002/2019, SI 2002/2020, SI 2002/2207, SI 2002/2314, SI 2002/2380, SI

1995–cont.

18. Jobseekers Act 1995–*cont.*

s.35, enabling:–*cont.*

2002/2402, SI 2002/2442, SI 2002/2689, SI 2002/3072, SI 2002/3197, SI 2003/455, SI 2003/511, SI 2003/1121, SI 2003/1589, SI 2003/1701, SI 2003/1731, SI 2003/1914, SI 2003/2279, SI 2003/2439, SI 2004/98, SI 2004/565, SI 2004/867, SI 2004/868, SI 2004/869, SI 2004/963, SI 2004/1008, SI 2004/1141, SI 2004/1232, SI 2004/1655, SI 2004/1708, SI 2004/1869, SI 2004/2308, SI 2004/2327, SI 2004/2825

s.36, enabling: SI 2002/398, SI 2002/490, SI 2002/841, SI 2002/1411, SI 2002/1589, SI 2002/1701, SI 2002/1763, SI 2002/2019, SI 2002/2020, SI 2002/2207, SI 2002/2314, SI 2002/2380, SI 2002/2402, SI 2002/2442, SI 2002/2689, SI 2002/3072, SI 2002/3197, SI 2003/455, SI 2003/511, SI 2003/1121, SI 2003/1195, SI 2003/1589, SI 2003/1701, SI 2003/1731, SI 2003/1914, SI 2003/2279, SI 2003/2439, SI 2004/98, SI 2004/565, SI 2004/867, SI 2004/868, SI 2004/869, SI 2004/934, SI 2004/963, SI 2004/1008, SI 2004/1141, SI 2004/1232, SI 2004/1655, SI 2004/1708, SI 2004/1869, SI 2004/2308, SI 2004/2825

s.37, applied: SI 2002/1763, SI 2002/3072, SI 2004/867, SI 2004/868, SI 2004/869, SI 2004/934, SI 2004/1008, SI 2004/1869

s.40, enabling: SI 2002/2497

Sch.1 para.1, enabling: SI 2002/2689, SI 2003/511, SI 2004/963

Sch.1 para.3, enabling: SI 2002/2314, SI 2003/511

Sch.1 para.4, enabling: SI 2002/1379, SI 2003/511

Sch.1 para.5, enabling: SI 2003/511

Sch.1 para.8A, enabling: SI 2003/511

Sch.1 para.9C, amended: 2004 c.33 Sch.24 para.125

Sch.1 para.11, enabling: SI 2004/1869

Sch.1 para.13, enabling: SI 2002/2402

Sch.2 para.4, repealed: 2003 c.39 Sch.10

Sch.2 para.9, repealed: 2002 c.21 Sch.6

Sch.2 para.12, repealed: 2003 c.1 Sch.8 Part 1

Sch.2 para.14, repealed: 2003 c.1 Sch.8 Part 1

Sch.2 para.16, repealed: 2003 c.1 Sch.8 Part 1

Sch.2 para.33, repealed: 2002 c.21 Sch.6

Sch.2 para.34, repealed: 2002 c.21 Sch.6

Sch.2 para.35, applied: SI 2003/2275 Sch.1

Sch.2 para.74, repealed: SI 2002/1397 Sch.1 para.12

21. Merchant Shipping Act 1995

see *CMA CGM SA v Classica Shipping Co Ltd (The CMA Djakarta)* [2003] EWHC 641, [2003] 2 All E.R. (Comm) 21 (QBD (Comm Ct)), David Steel, J.; see *CMA CGM SA v Classica Shipping Co Ltd (The*

1995–cont.

21. Merchant Shipping Act 1995–*cont.*

see–*cont.*

CMA Djakarta) [2004] EWCA Civ 114, [2004] 1 All E.R. (Comm) 865 (CA), Waller, L.J.

applied: 2004 c.20 s.86, SI 2004/568 Sch.2 para.10, SI 2004/757 Art.15, SI 2004/1713 Reg.16, SR 2002/1 Reg.8, Reg.21, SSI 2002/410 Art.26, Art.33, 2003 asp 19 s.3, s.4

Part I, applied: SI 2003/1902 Sch.7 para.5

Part II, applied: SI 2003/1535 Art.6, SI 2004/398 Art.6, SSI 2002/410 Art.26, SSI 2002/504 Art.6

Part IX, applied: SI 2004/2190 Art.8, SI 2004/2469 Art.6, SSI 2002/410 Art.6, Art.25, Art.27

Part XI, applied: SI 2002/1587 Reg.17

s.8, applied: SI 2002/790 Art.2

s.15, amended: SI 2002/794 Sch.1 para.36, Sch.2

s.18, applied: SI 2003/1248 Art.4

s.18, referred to: SI 2003/1248 Sch.1

s.18, enabling: SI 2003/1248

s.43, enabling: SI 2002/2201

s.47, enabling: SI 2004/302

s.53, amended: SI 2002/3135 Sch.1 para.12

s.55, amended: SI 2002/2125 Sch.2 para.1

s.57, amended: 2003 c.44 Sch.37 Part 9

s.57, disapplied: 2003 c.44 Sch.25 para.96

s.57, repealed (in part): 2003 c.44 Sch.37 Part 9

s.68, amended: 2003 c.39 Sch.8 para.366

s.73, amended: 2002 c.8 s.2

s.77, enabling: SI 2002/1473

s.82, enabling: SI 2003/2861

s.85, see *Ziemniak v ETPM Deep Sea Ltd* [2003] EWCA Civ 636, [2003] 2 All E.R. (Comm) 283 (CA), Kay, L.J.

s.85, amended: 2002 c.8 s.2

s.85, referred to: SI 2002/1473 Sch.3 para.5, SI 2003/2950 Reg.5, SI 2004/302 Reg.6, SI 2004/2884 Reg.4

s.85, enabling: SI 2002/1473, SI 2002/1650, SI 2002/2055, SI 2002/2125, SI 2002/2201, SI 2003/771, SI 2003/1112, SI 2003/1636, SI 2003/2002, SI 2003/2950, SI 2003/2951, SI 2003/3049, SI 2004/302, SI 2004/303, SI 2004/929, SI 2004/930, SI 2004/1107, SI 2004/1266, SI 2004/1469, SI 2004/1713, SI 2004/2110, SI 2004/2151, SI 2004/2169, SI 2004/2259, SI 2004/2883, SI 2004/2884

s.86, applied: SI 2002/1473, SI 2002/2201, SI 2003/1636, SI 2003/2002, SI 2003/3049, SI 2004/303, SI 2004/930, SI 2004/1469

s.86, referred to: SI 2002/1650, SI 2002/2055, SI 2003/771, SI 2003/1112, SI 2003/2950, SI 2003/2951, SI 2004/302, SI 2004/929, SI 2004/1107, SI 2004/

CAP.

1995–cont.

21. Merchant Shipping Act 1995–*cont.*
s.86, referred to:–*cont.*
1266, SI 2004/2151, SI 2004/2259, SI 2004/2883, SI 2004/2884
s.86, enabling: SI 2002/1473, SI 2002/1650, SI 2002/2055, SI 2002/2125, SI 2002/2201, SI 2003/771, SI 2003/1112, SI 2003/1636, SI 2003/2002, SI 2003/2950, SI 2003/2951, SI 2003/3049, SI 2004/302, SI 2004/303, SI 2004/929, SI 2004/930, SI 2004/1107, SI 2004/1266, SI 2004/1469, SI 2004/1713, SI 2004/2151, SI 2004/2169, SI 2004/2259, SI 2004/2883, SI 2004/2884
s.88, enabling: SI 2002/1587
s.91, amended: SI 2002/1473 Sch.1 para.1, Sch.2 para.1, 2003 c.21 Sch.17 para.132
s.91, repealed (in part): SI 2002/1473 Sch.1 para.1
s.95, applied: SI 2002/2125 Reg.18, SI 2002/2201 Reg.12, SI 2003/1809 Reg.23, SI 2004/1713 Reg.17
s.96, applied: SI 2002/2201 Reg.12
s.96, varied: SI 2002/2055 Reg.16, SI 2002/2125 Reg.18, SI 2003/1809 Reg.23, SI 2004/1713 Reg.17
s.97, applied: SI 2002/2201 Reg.12
s.97, varied: SI 2002/2055 Reg.16, SI 2002/2125 Reg.18, SI 2003/1809 Reg.23, SI 2004/1713 Reg.17
s.100C, repealed: 2003 c.16 Sch.3
s.100D, repealed: 2003 c.16 Sch.3
s.100E, repealed: 2003 c.16 Sch.3
s.108A, added: 2003 c.16 s.1
s.117, repealed: 2003 c.20 Sch.8
s.121, see *Todd v Adams (t/a Trelawney Fishing Co) (The Maragetha Maria)* [2002] EWCA Civ 509, [2002] 2 All E.R. (Comm) 97 (CA), Neuberger, J.
s.122, see *Todd v Adams (t/a Trelawney Fishing Co) (The Maragetha Maria)* [2002] EWCA Civ 509, [2002] 2 All E.R. (Comm) 97 (CA), Neuberger, J.
s.123, see *Todd v Adams (t/a Trelawney Fishing Co) (The Maragetha Maria)* [2002] EWCA Civ 509, [2002] 2 All E.R. (Comm) 97 (CA), Neuberger, J.
s.124, see *Todd v Adams (t/a Trelawney Fishing Co) (The Maragetha Maria)* [2002] EWCA Civ 509, [2002] 2 All E.R. (Comm) 97 (CA), Neuberger, J.
s.125, see *Todd v Adams (t/a Trelawney Fishing Co) (The Maragetha Maria)* [2002] EWCA Civ 509, [2002] 2 All E.R. (Comm) 97 (CA), Neuberger, J.
s.128, enabling: SI 2002/3147
s.130A, applied: SI 2003/1809
s.130A, enabling: SI 2003/1809
s.130B, enabling: SI 2003/1809
s.130C, enabling: SI 2003/1809
s.130D, enabling: SI 2003/1809
s.135, amended: 2004 c.21 Sch.1 para.87

CAP.

1995–cont.

21. Merchant Shipping Act 1995–*cont.*
s.136A, amended: SI 2002/3153 Sch.5 para.4
s.137, repealed: 2003 c.16 Sch.3
s.138, repealed: 2003 c.16 Sch.3
s.138A, repealed: 2003 c.16 Sch.3
s.139, repealed: 2003 c.16 Sch.3
s.140, repealed: 2003 c.16 Sch.3
s.141, repealed: 2003 c.16 Sch.3
s.141, enabling: SI 2002/3147
s.145, amended: 2003 c.44 Sch.36 para.13
s.145, substituted: 2003 c.44 Sch.36 para.13
s.147, enabling: SI 2002/3147
s.157, amended: SI 2003/2559 Art.2
s.157, enabling: SI 2003/2559
s.170, see *Alegrete Shipping Co Inc v International Oil Pollution Compensation Fund 1971* [2002] EWHC 1095, [2002] 2 All E.R. (Comm) 416 (QBD (Adm Ct)), David Steel, J.
s.176, enabling: SI 2003/2559
s.183, see *Lee v Airtours Holidays Ltd* [2004] 1 Lloyd's Rep. 683 (CC (Central London)), Judge Hallgarten Q.C.; see *Norfolk v My Travel Group Plc* [2004] 1 Lloyd's Rep. 106 (CC (Plymouth)), Judge Overend
s.185, see *Todd v Adams (t/a Trelawney Fishing Co) (The Maragetha Maria)* [2002] EWCA Civ 509, [2002] 2 All E.R. (Comm) 97 (CA), Neuberger, J.
s.185, applied: SI 2004/1273
s.185, enabling: SI 2004/1273
s.190, see *Sweet v Royal National Lifeboat Institution (The Edward Duke of Windsor)* [2002] EWHC 117, Times, February 22, 2002 (QBD (Adm Ct)), Tomlinson, J
s.193, referred to: SSI 2004/171 Art.3
s.205, enabling: SI 2002/504, SI 2004/610
s.221, amended: SI 2003/2867 Sch.1 para.24
s.252, applied: SSI 2002/410 Art.24, Art.25
s.252, referred to: SSI 2002/410 Art.25
s.253, applied: SSI 2002/410 Art.24, Art.25
s.255, applied: SI 2002/2618 Art.8
s.256, applied: SI 2003/2496 Art.10
s.267, applied: 2003 c.20 s.89
s.267, varied: SI 2002/1587 Reg.17
s.267, enabling: SI 2004/1266
s.268, varied: SI 2002/1587 Reg.17
s.284, applied: 2003 c.20 s.84, SI 2003/1809 Reg.23, SI 2004/1713 Reg.17
s.284, varied: SI 2002/1473 Reg.11, SI 2002/2055 Reg.15, SI 2002/2125 Reg.17, SI 2002/2201 Reg.11, SI 2003/1809 Reg.22, SI 2003/2950 Reg.9, SI 2004/302 Reg.11, SI 2004/1713 Reg.16, SI 2004/2110 Reg.21, SI 2004/2884 Reg.10
s.302, applied: SI 2002/2055 Reg.7
s.302, enabling: SI 2003/788, SI 2004/302, SI 2004/1977
s.306, applied: SI 2002/2201

CAP.

1995–cont.

21. Merchant Shipping Act 1995–*cont.*
s.306, referred to: SI 2003/1809, SI 2004/302

s.307, enabling: SI 2002/2201

s.308, referred to: SSI 2002/410 Art.25

s.311, repealed: 2003 c.20 Sch.8

s.313, applied: 2003 c.20 s.89

s.313A, amended: 2002 c.8 s.2

s.314, varied: SI 2004/1284 Art.3

s.315, enabling: SI 2002/3147, SI 2004/1284, SI 2004/3041, SI 2004/3042

Sch.2, enabling: SI 2002/1587

Sch.3A para.1, added: 2003 c.16 Sch.1

Sch.3A para.1, amended: SI 2004/2110 Reg.22

Sch.3A para.2, added: 2003 c.16 Sch.1

Sch.3A para.3, added: 2003 c.16 Sch.1

Sch.3A para.4, added: 2003 c.16 Sch.1

Sch.3A para.5, added: 2003 c.16 Sch.1

Sch.3A para.6, added: 2003 c.16 Sch.1

Sch.3A para.7, added: 2003 c.16 Sch.1

Sch.3A para.8, added: 2003 c.16 Sch.1

Sch.3A para.9, added: 2003 c.16 Sch.1

Sch.3A para.10, added: 2003 c.16 Sch.1

Sch.3A para.11, added: 2003 c.16 Sch.1

Sch.3A para.12, added: 2003 c.16 Sch.1

Sch.3A para.13, added: 2003 c.16 Sch.1

Sch.3A para.14, added: 2003 c.16 Sch.1

Sch.3A para.15, added: 2003 c.16 Sch.1

Sch.3A para.16, added: 2003 c.16 Sch.1

Sch.3A para.17, added: 2003 c.16 Sch.1

Sch.3A para.18, added: 2003 c.16 Sch.1

Sch.3A para.19, added: 2003 c.16 Sch.1

Sch.3A para.20, added: 2003 c.16 Sch.1

Sch.3A para.21, added: 2003 c.16 Sch.1

Sch.3A para.22, added: 2003 c.16 Sch.1

Sch.3A para.23, added: 2003 c.16 Sch.1

Sch.3A para.24, added: 2003 c.16 Sch.1

Sch.4, see *Alegrete Shipping Co Inc v International Oil Pollution Compensation Fund 1971* [2003] EWCA Civ 65, [2003] 2 All E.R. (Comm) 1 (CA), Mance, L.J.

Sch.4 s.175, see *Alegrete Shipping Co Inc v International Oil Pollution Compensation Fund 1971* [2003] EWCA Civ 65, [2003] 2 All E.R. (Comm) 1 (CA), Mance, L.J.

Sch.5 Part I, amended: SI 2003/2559 Art.2

Sch.7 Part I, applied: SI 2003/3135 Art.2

Sch.7 Part I Art.4, see *Margolle v Delta Maritime Co Ltd* [2002] EWHC 2452, [2003] 1 All E.R. (Comm) 102 (QBD (Adm Ct)), Gross, J.

Sch.7 Part II para.2A, repealed: SI 2004/1273 Art.2

Sch.7 Part II para.8, enabling: SI 2003/3135, SI 2003/3136, SI 2004/931

Sch.12, varied: SI 2004/1284 Art.3

23. Goods Vehicles (Licensing of Operators) Act 1995
s.13, applied: SI 2004/1878 Reg.3

CAP.

1995–cont.

23. Goods Vehicles (Licensing of Operators) Act 1995–*cont.*
s.17, applied: SI 2004/1878 Reg.3

s.24, applied: SI 2004/1878 Reg.3

s.25, applied: SI 2004/1878 Reg.3

s.27, see *Crompton (t/a David Crompton Haulage) v Department of Transport North Western Area* [2003] EWCA Civ 64, [2003] R.T.R. 34 (CA), Kennedy, L.J.

s.45, enabling: SI 2002/2778, SI 2004/1878

s.56, repealed: 2004 c.14 Sch.1 Part 14

s.57, applied: SI 2002/2778, SI 2004/462, SI 2004/1878

s.57, enabling: SI 2002/2778, SI 2004/462, SI 2004/1878

s.58, enabling: SI 2002/2778

Sch.3 para.3, amended: 2003 c.44 Sch.32 para.68

Sch.6 para.6, repealed: 2004 c.14 Sch.1 Part 14

Sch.7 para.2, repealed: 2004 c.14 Sch.1 Part 14

Sch.7 para.4, repealed: 2004 c.14 Sch.1 Part 14

Sch.7 para.13, repealed: 2004 c.14 Sch.1 Part 14

Sch.7 para.14, repealed: 2004 c.14 Sch.1 Part 14

25. Environment Act 1995
Commencement Orders: SSI 2004/541 Art.2; SSI 2003/206 Art.2; 2002 asp 3 Sch.7 para.24

applied: SSI 2004/143 Reg.24

referred to: SI 2003/300 Reg.2, SSI 2003/212 Reg.2

s.1, applied: SI 2004/1818 Reg.3

s.2, repealed (in part): 2004 c.14 Sch.1 Part 13

s.3, repealed (in part): 2004 c.14 Sch.1 Part 13

s.6, amended: 2003 c.37 s.72, s.73, Sch.7 para.15

s.11, applied: SI 2002/784

s.11, repealed: SI 2002/784 Art.2

s.14, applied: SI 2003/409 Sch.1 Part I

s.14, enabling: SI 2004/3163

s.16, enabling: SI 2004/3163, SI 2004/3164, SI 2004/3165

s.16A, added: 2003 c.37 s.67

s.16B, added: 2003 c.37 s.67

s.17, amended: 2003 c.37 s.66

s.18A, added: 2003 c.37 s.66

s.18A, enabling: SI 2004/3163, SI 2004/3164, SI 2004/3165

s.20, applied: SSI 2004/474 Sch.1

s.21, repealed (in part): 2004 c.14 Sch.1 Part 13

s.22, repealed (in part): 2004 c.14 Sch.1 Part 13

s.33A, added: 2003 c.37 s.9

s.35, repealed (in part): 2004 asp 6 Sch.7 para.10

1995–cont.

25. Environment Act 1995–*cont.*

s.36, amended: 2002 asp 3 Sch.7 para.24, 2004 asp 6 Sch.7 para.10

s.36, repealed (in part): SSI 2003/331 Sch.1 para.7

s.40, varied: SI 2003/3242 Reg.20, SI 2004/99 Sch.1 para.16

s.41, amended: SSI 2003/235 Sch.6 para.1

s.41, applied: SI 2003/2635 Reg.49, SSI 2003/593 Reg.8

s.41, disapplied: SI 2003/2635 Reg.49

s.43, varied: SI 2002/1998 Art.24

s.46, amended: SI 2003/1326 Art.19

s.48, applied: 2003 asp 6 Sch.5, 2004 asp 2 Sch.5

s.48, referred to: 2002 asp 7 Sch.5

s.56, amended: SSI 2003/171 Reg.2, SSI 2004/275 Reg.2

s.67, repealed (in part): 2004 c.5 Sch.7 para.19, Sch.9

s.73, repealed (in part): 2003 c.26 Sch.8 Part 1

s.80, applied: SI 2002/3153 Art.10

s.82, applied: SI 2002/1808 Reg.3, SI 2003/300 Reg.3

s.83, applied: SI 2002/1808 Reg.3, Reg.4, SI 2003/300 Reg.3, Reg.4

s.85, applied: SI 2003/2121 Reg.14

s.87, applied: SI 2002/1808, SI 2002/3043, SI 2002/3182, SI 2003/300, SSI 2002/297, SSI 2003/212

s.87, enabling: SI 2002/1808, SI 2002/3043, SI 2002/3182, SI 2003/300, SSI 2002/297, SSI 2003/212

s.88, applied: SI 2002/1808 Reg.5, SI 2003/300 Reg.5, SSI 2003/212 Reg.5

s.91, enabling: SI 2002/3043, SSI 2002/297

s.93, applied: SI 2002/732, SI 2002/813, SI 2003/3238, SI 2003/3294, SSI 2002/147, SSI 2003/613

s.93, referred to: SI 2002/732, SI 2002/813, SI 2003/3238, SSI 2003/613

s.93, enabling: SI 2002/732, SI 2002/813, SI 2003/3238, SI 2003/3294, SSI 2002/147, SSI 2003/613

s.94, referred to: SI 2003/3238, SI 2003/3294

s.94, repealed (in part): SI 2004/1261 Sch.2 para.7

s.94, enabling: SI 2002/732, SI 2002/813, SI 2003/3238, SI 2003/3294, SSI 2002/147, SSI 2003/613

s.94A, repealed: SI 2004/1261 Sch.2 para.7

s.95, enabling: SI 2003/3238, SI 2003/3294, SSI 2003/613

s.96, see *R. (on the application of Payne) v Caerphilly CBC* [2002] EWHC 866, [2002] P.L.C.R. 25 (QBD (Admin Ct)), Sullivan, J.

1995–cont.

25. Environment Act 1995–*cont.*

s.98, enabling: SI 2003/838, SI 2004/114, SSI 2003/177, SSI 2003/303, SSI 2004/109, SSI 2004/113

s.99, applied: SI 2003/838

s.101, repealed (in part): 2003 c.37 Sch.9 Part 3

s.108, amended: 2003 c.38 s.55

s.108, applied: SI 2003/3310 Reg.8, SI 2003/3311 Reg.3, SI 2004/1769 Sch.1 para.1

s.108, referred to: 2003 asp 3 Sch.2 para.10

s.108, varied: SI 2003/3310 Reg.8, SI 2004/1769 Sch.1 para.2

s.111, repealed (in part): 2004 c.14 Sch.1 Part 13

s.113, referred to: 2003 c.33 s.14

s.114, amended: 2003 c.37 s.3, s.8, s.13, s.21

s.114, applied: SSI 2003/168 Reg.6

s.118, repealed (in part): 2004 c.14 Sch.1 Part 13

s.122, varied: SI 2003/3242 Reg.20, SI 2004/99 Sch.1 para.16

s.123, applied: SSI 2004/143 Reg.24

s.125, enabling: SSI 2003/206

Sch.4, enabling: SI 2004/3163

Sch.4 para.1, amended: 2003 c.37 s.68, Sch.9 Part 3

Sch.4 para.1, repealed (in part): 2003 c.37 Sch.9 Part 3

Sch.4 para.1, enabling: SI 2004/3163

Sch.4 para.3, enabling: SI 2004/3163, SI 2004/3164, SI 2004/3165

Sch.7 para.2, applied: SI 2002/975 Reg.2

Sch.8 para.8, repealed (in part): 2003 c.26 Sch.8 Part 1

Sch.10 para.31, repealed (in part): 2003 c.26 Sch.8 Part 1

Sch.11 para.5, enabling: SI 2002/1808, SI 2003/300, SSI 2003/212

Sch.13, see *R. (on the application of Payne) v Caerphilly CBC* [2003] EWCA Civ 71, [2003] Env. L.R. 31 (CA), Dyson, L.J.

Sch.13 para.1, amended: SI 2003/956 Art.10

Sch.13 para.9, see *R. (on the application of Payne) v Caerphilly CBC* [2002] EWHC 866, [2002] P.L.C.R. 25 (QBD (Admin Ct)), Sullivan, J.

Sch.13 para.9, amended: SI 2003/956 Art.10

Sch.13 para.19, see *R. (on the application of Payne) v Caerphilly CBC* [2003] EWCA Civ 71, [2003] Env. L.R. 31 (CA), Dyson, L.J.

Sch.14 para.2, amended: SI 2003/956 Art.10, 2004 c.5 Sch.7 para.19

Sch.14 para.3A, added: 2004 c.5 Sch.7 para.19

Sch.14 para.6, amended: SI 2003/956 Art.10

Sch.18, applied: SI 2004/1769 Sch.1 para.3

Sch.18 para.1, varied: SI 2004/1769 Sch.1 para.3

1995–cont.

25. Environment Act 1995–*cont.*

Sch.18 para.2, varied: SI 2004/1769 Sch.1 para.3

Sch.18 para.3, varied: SI 2004/1769 Sch.1 para.3

Sch.18 para.4, varied: SI 2004/1769 Sch.1 para.3

Sch.18 para.5, varied: SI 2004/1769 Sch.1 para.3

Sch.18 para.6, varied: SI 2004/1769 Sch.1 para.3

Sch.20, referred to: 2003 c.38 s.72

Sch.21 Part II para.6, repealed: 2002 asp 3 Sch.7 para.24

Sch.22 para.1, repealed (in part): 2004 c.14 Sch.1 Part 13

Sch.22 para.3, repealed (in part): 2004 c.14 Sch.1 Part 13

Sch.22 para.11, repealed (in part): 2004 c.14 Sch.1 Part 13

Sch.22 para.12, repealed (in part): 2004 c.14 Sch.1 Part 13

Sch.22 para.19, repealed (in part): 2004 c.14 Sch.1 Part 13

Sch.22 para.25, repealed: 2004 c.14 Sch.1 Part 13

Sch.22 para.29, repealed (in part): 2004 c.14 Sch.1 Part 13

Sch.22 para.34, repealed (in part): 2004 c.14 Sch.1 Part 13

Sch.22 para.37, repealed (in part): 2004 c.14 Sch.1 Part 13

Sch.22 para.63, repealed: 2004 c.14 Sch.1 Part 13

Sch.22 para.75, repealed: 2004 c.14 Sch.1 Part 13

Sch.22 para.78, repealed: 2004 c.14 Sch.1 Part 13

Sch.22 para.84, repealed: 2004 c.14 Sch.1 Part 13

Sch.22 para.85, repealed: 2004 c.14 Sch.1 Part 13

Sch.22 para.87, repealed: 2004 c.14 Sch.1 Part 13

Sch.22 para.90, repealed: 2004 c.14 Sch.1 Part 13

Sch.22 para.94, repealed: 2004 c.14 Sch.1 Part 13

Sch.22 para.116, repealed: 2004 c.14 Sch.1 Part 13

Sch.22 para.129, repealed: 2004 c.14 Sch.1 Part 13

Sch.22 para.131, repealed: 2004 c.14 Sch.1 Part 13

Sch.22 para.136, repealed: 2004 c.14 Sch.1 Part 13

Sch.22 para.137, repealed: 2004 c.14 Sch.1 Part 13

Sch.22 para.138, repealed: 2004 c.14 Sch.1 Part 13

1995–cont.

25. Environment Act 1995–*cont.*

Sch.22 para.146, repealed: 2004 c.14 Sch.1 Part 13

Sch.22 para.148, repealed: 2004 c.14 Sch.1 Part 13

Sch.22 para.149, repealed: 2004 c.14 Sch.1 Part 13

Sch.22 para.152, repealed: 2004 c.14 Sch.1 Part 13

Sch.22 para.153, repealed: 2004 c.14 Sch.1 Part 13

Sch.22 para.154, repealed: 2004 c.14 Sch.1 Part 13

Sch.22 para.155, repealed: 2004 c.14 Sch.1 Part 13

Sch.22 para.156, repealed: 2004 c.14 Sch.1 Part 13

Sch.22 para.168, repealed: 2004 c.14 Sch.1 Part 13

Sch.22 para.171, repealed: 2004 c.14 Sch.1 Part 13

Sch.22 para.174, repealed: 2004 c.14 Sch.1 Part 13

Sch.22 para.175, repealed: 2004 c.14 Sch.1 Part 13

Sch.22 para.176, repealed: 2004 c.14 Sch.1 Part 13

Sch.22 para.178, repealed: 2004 c.14 Sch.1 Part 13

Sch.22 para.179, repealed: 2004 c.14 Sch.1 Part 13

Sch.22 para.181, repealed: 2003 c.37 Sch.7 para.15, Sch.9 Part 3

Sch.22 para.201, repealed: 2004 c.14 Sch.1 Part 13

Sch.22 para.207, repealed: 2004 c.14 Sch.1 Part 13

Sch.22 para.216, repealed: 2004 c.14 Sch.1 Part 13

Sch.22 para.218, repealed: 2004 c.14 Sch.1 Part 13

Sch.22 para.221, repealed: 2004 c.14 Sch.1 Part 13

Sch.22 para.225, repealed: 2004 c.14 Sch.1 Part 13

Sch.22 para.226, repealed: 2004 c.14 Sch.1 Part 13

Sch.22 para.229, repealed: 2004 c.14 Sch.1 Part 13

Sch.23 Part I para.5, repealed: 2004 c.14 Sch.1 Part 13

26. Pensions Act 1995

applied: SI 2003/1325 Art.2, 2004 c.35 s.7, s.80, s.87, s.201, s.231, s.321, s.322

referred to: 2004 c.35 s.322

Part I, applied: 2004 c.35 s.233, s.314

s.1, repealed: 2004 c.35 Sch.13 Part 1

s.2, repealed: 2004 c.35 Sch.13 Part 1

s.3, applied: 2004 c.35 s.10, s.66, s.78, s.96, s.97, s.101, Sch.2 para.4, Sch.2 para.5, Sch.2 para.9

1995–cont.

26. Pensions Act 1995–*cont.*

s.3, substituted: 2004 c.35 s.33

s.4, amended: 2004 c.35 s.34, Sch.12 para.35

s.4, applied: 2004 c.35 s.10, s.96, s.97, s.101, Sch.2 para.6, Sch.2 para.7, Sch.2 para.8

s.5, repealed: 2004 c.35 Sch.13 Part 1

s.7, amended: 2004 c.35 s.35, Sch.12 para.36, Sch.13 Part 1

s.7, applied: 2004 c.35 s.10, s.96, s.97, Sch.1 para.20, Sch.2 para.9

s.7, repealed (in part): 2004 c.35 s.35, Sch.13 Part 1

s.8, amended: 2004 c.35 s.35

s.9, amended: 2004 c.35 Sch.12 para.37

s.9, applied: 2004 c.35 s.96, s.97, Sch.2 para.10

s.10, amended: 2004 c.35 Sch.12 para.38, Sch.13 Part 1

s.10, applied: SI 2002/459 Reg.13, 2004 c.35 s.13, s.14, s.20, s.21, s.24, s.28, s.30, s.31, s.41, s.50, s.62, s.64, s.69, s.70, s.71, s.76, s.78, s.133, s.134, s.135, s.138, s.140, s.153, s.154, s.157, s.219, s.223, s.224, s.225, s.226, s.227, s.228, s.229, s.230, s.238, s.242, s.252, s.253, s.255, s.256, s.287, s.291, s.292, s.293, s.310, s.314, Sch.2 para.11

s.10, referred to: SI 2002/459 Reg.7

s.10, enabling: SI 2002/459

s.11, amended: 2004 c.35 s.22

s.11, applied: 2004 c.35 s.23, s.24, s.27, s.28, s.30, s.97, s.135, s.139, s.219, Sch.2 para.12

s.11, repealed (in part): 2004 c.35 s.22, Sch.13 Part 1

s.13, repealed: 2004 c.35 Sch.13 Part 1

s.15, amended: 2004 c.35 Sch.12 para.39

s.15, applied: 2004 c.35 Sch.2 para.13

s.16, see *Bain, Petitioner* 2002 S.L.T. 1112 (Court of Session (Inner House, Extra Division)), Lord Cameron of Lochbroom, Lord Johnston, Lord Wheatley

s.16, repealed: 2004 c.35 Sch.13 Part 1

s.17, repealed: 2004 c.35 Sch.13 Part 1

s.17, enabling: SI 2002/2327

s.18, repealed: 2004 c.35 Sch.13 Part 1

s.18A, repealed: 2004 c.35 Sch.13 Part 1

s.19, repealed: 2004 c.35 Sch.13 Part 1

s.19, enabling: SI 2002/2327

s.20, repealed: 2004 c.35 Sch.13 Part 1

s.21, repealed: 2004 c.35 Sch.13 Part 1

s.21, enabling: SI 2002/2327

s.22, amended: 2004 c.35 s.36, Sch.12 para.40, Sch.13 Part 1

s.22, referred to: SI 2002/459 Reg.3, Reg.4

s.23, applied: SI 2002/459 Reg.3, Reg.10, 2004 c.35 s.96, s.97, Sch.1 para.20

s.23, substituted: 2004 c.35 s.36

s.23, enabling: SI 2002/459

s.24, substituted: 2004 c.35 s.36

1995–cont.

26. Pensions Act 1995–*cont.*

s.25, amended: 2004 c.35 s.36, Sch.12 para.41, Sch.13 Part 1

s.26, amended: 2004 c.35 Sch.12 para.42

s.26A, applied: SI 2002/459 Reg.7

s.26A, disapplied: SI 2002/459 Reg.6

s.26A, referred to: SI 2002/459 Reg.3, Reg.5

s.26A, repealed: 2004 c.35 Sch.12 para.43, Sch.13 Part 1

s.26A, varied: SI 2002/459 Reg.3

s.26B, applied: SI 2002/459 Reg.4, Reg.7

s.26B, disapplied: SI 2002/459 Reg.6

s.26B, referred to: SI 2002/459 Reg.4, Reg.5

s.26B, repealed: 2004 c.35 Sch.12 para.43, Sch.13 Part 1

s.26B, varied: SI 2002/459 Reg.4

s.26C, applied: SI 2002/459 Reg.5

s.26C, repealed: 2004 c.35 Sch.12 para.43, Sch.13 Part 1

s.28, repealed (in part): 2004 c.35 Sch.12 para.44, Sch.13 Part 1

s.29, amended: 2004 c.35 Sch.12 para.45, Sch.13 Part 1, SI 2004/1941 Sch.1 para.6

s.29, applied: 2004 c.35 s.10, s.96, s.97, Sch.2 para.14, Sch.2 para.15

s.29, repealed (in part): 2004 c.35 Sch.13 Part 1

s.30, amended: 2004 c.35 s.37, Sch.12 para.46

s.30, applied: 2004 c.35 s.96, s.97, Sch.2 para.15

s.30, repealed (in part): 2004 c.35 Sch.12 para.46, Sch.13 Part 1

s.30A, repealed: 2004 c.35 Sch.12 para.47, Sch.13 Part 1

s.31, repealed: 2004 c.35 Sch.13 Part 1

s.32, amended: 2004 c.35 Sch.12 para.48

s.34, amended: 2004 c.35 Sch.12 para.49

s.34, applied: 2004 c.35 s.249

s.35, see *Pitmans Trustees Ltd v Telecommunications Group Plc* [2004] EWHC 181, [2004] Pens. L.R. 213 (Ch D), Sir Andrew Morritt V.C.

s.35, applied: 2004 c.35 s.248

s.35, referred to: 2004 c.35 s.247

s.35, substituted: 2004 c.35 s.244

s.36, amended: 2004 c.35 s.245

s.36, repealed (in part): 2004 c.35 s.245, Sch.13 Part 1

s.36A, added: 2004 c.35 s.246

s.37, applied: 2004 c.35 s.251

s.37, referred to: 2004 c.35 s.251

s.37, substituted: 2004 c.35 s.250

s.38, amended: 2004 c.35 Sch.12 para.50, Sch.13 Part 1

s.40, amended: 2004 c.35 Sch.12 para.51, SI 2004/355 Art.5

s.40, enabling: SI 2002/681

s.41, amended: 2004 c.35 Sch.12 para.52

s.41, repealed (in part): 2004 c.35 Sch.13 Part 1

CAP.

CAP.

1995–cont.

1995–cont.

26. Pensions Act 1995–*cont.*

s.47, amended: 2004 c.35 Sch.12 para.53

s.47, applied: SI 2002/459 Reg.8, Reg.10

s.48, repealed: 2004 c.35 Sch.13 Part 1

s.49, amended: 2004 c.35 s.269, Sch.12 para.54

s.49, applied: 2004 c.35 s.24, s.90, s.133

s.49, repealed (in part): 2004 c.35 Sch.12 para.54, Sch.13 Part 1

s.49A, applied: SI 2002/459 Reg.8, Reg.13

s.49A, disapplied: SI 2002/459 Reg.13

s.49A, referred to: SI 2002/459 Reg.13

s.49A, repealed (in part): 2004 c.35 Sch.12 para.55, Sch.13 Part 1

s.50, substituted: 2004 c.35 s.273

s.51, amended: 2004 c.35 s.278, Sch.13 Part 1

s.51ZA, added: 2004 c.35 s.278

s.54, amended: 2004 c.35 s.278, Sch.13 Part 1

s.56, repealed: 2004 c.35 Sch.13 Part 1

s.56, enabling: SI 2002/380, SI 2004/3031

s.57, repealed: 2004 c.35 Sch.13 Part 1

s.57, enabling: SI 2002/380, SI 2004/3031

s.58, repealed: 2004 c.35 Sch.13 Part 1

s.58, enabling: SI 2002/380

s.59, repealed: 2004 c.35 Sch.13 Part 1

s.59, enabling: SI 2002/380

s.60, amended: SI 2002/380 Reg.5

s.60, repealed: 2004 c.35 Sch.13 Part 1

s.61, repealed: 2004 c.35 Sch.13 Part 1

s.61, enabling: SI 2002/380

s.62, see *Ford Motor Co Ltd v Carr* [2002] O.P.L.R. 315 (EAT), Maurice Kay, J.

s.63, amended: 2004 c.35 Sch.13 Part 1

s.67, applied: 2003 c.20 Sch.4 para.24, 2004 c.35 s.90

s.67, substituted: 2004 c.35 s.262

s.67, enabling: SI 2002/681

s.67A, applied: 2004 c.35 s.90

s.67A, substituted: 2004 c.35 s.262

s.67G, applied: 2004 c.35 s.90, s.97, Sch.2 para.16

s.67G, substituted: 2004 c.35 s.262

s.67H, applied: 2004 c.35 s.90, s.97, Sch.2 para.17

s.67H, substituted: 2004 c.35 s.262

s.67I, applied: 2004 c.35 s.90

s.67I, substituted: 2004 c.35 s.262

s.68, amended: 2004 c.35 Sch.12 para.56

s.69, see *Law Debenture Trust Corp Plc v Lonrho Africa Trade & Finance Ltd* [2002] EWHC 2732, [2003] O.P.L.R. 167 (Ch D), Patten, J.

s.69, amended: 2004 c.35 Sch.12 para.57, Sch.13 Part 1

s.69, applied: 2004 c.35 s.10, Sch.1 para.25, Sch.2 para.18

s.69, repealed (in part): 2004 c.35 Sch.12 para.57, Sch.13 Part 1

26. Pensions Act 1995–*cont.*

s.71A, amended: 2004 c.35 Sch.12 para.58

s.71A, applied: SI 2002/459 Reg.8, 2004 c.35 s.10, Sch.2 para.19

s.71A, repealed (in part): 2004 c.35 Sch.13 Part 1

s.71A, enabling: SI 2002/459

s.72, enabling: SI 2002/346

s.72A, applied: SI 2002/459 Reg.9, Reg.10, Reg.11, Reg.14

s.72A, repealed (in part): 2004 c.35 Sch.12 para.59, Sch.13 Part 1

s.72B, applied: SI 2002/459 Reg.14, 2004 c.35 s.96, Sch.1 para.20

s.72B, repealed (in part): 2004 c.35 Sch.13 Part 1

s.72B, enabling: SI 2002/459

s.72C, repealed (in part): 2004 c.35 Sch.12 para.60, Sch.13 Part 1

s.73, applied: SI 2002/459 Reg.12, 2004 c.35 s.150

s.73, repealed (in part): 2004 c.35 Sch.12 para.61, Sch.13 Part 1

s.73, substituted: 2004 c.35 s.270

s.73, enabling: SI 2002/380, SI 2004/403, SI 2004/1140

s.73A, applied: SI 2002/459 Reg.12, 2004 c.35 s.150

s.73B, applied: SI 2002/459 Reg.12, 2004 c.35 s.150

s.74, amended: 2004 c.35 s.270, Sch.13 Part 1

s.74, applied: SI 2002/459 Reg.12

s.74, repealed (in part): 2004 c.35 s.270, Sch.13 Part 1

s.75, see *Bradstock Group Pension Scheme Trustees Ltd v Bradstock Group Plc* [2002] EWHC 651, [2002] I.C.R. 1427 (Ch D), Charles Aldous Q.C.; see *Pitmans Trustees Ltd v Telecommunications Group Plc* [2004] EWHC 181, [2004] Pens. L.R. 213 (Ch D), Sir Andrew Morritt V.C.; see *T&N Ltd, Re* [2004] EWHC 1680, [2004] Pens. L.R. 351 (Ch D (Companies Ct)), David Richards, J.

s.75, amended: 2004 c.35 s.271

s.75, applied: 2004 c.12 s.199, 2004 c.35 s.38, s.39, s.40, s.41, s.44, s.45, s.48, s.49, s.50, s.51, s.137, s.143, SI 2004/403 Reg.1

s.75, referred to: 2004 c.35 s.38

s.75, repealed (in part): 2004 c.35 s.271, Sch.13 Part 1

s.75, enabling: SI 2002/380, SI 2004/403

s.75A, added: 2004 c.35 s.272

s.76, amended: 2004 c.35 Sch.12 para.62

s.76, repealed (in part): 2004 c.35 Sch.12 para.62, Sch.13 Part 1

s.77, amended: 2004 c.35 Sch.12 para.63

s.77, repealed (in part): 2004 c.35 Sch.12 para.63, Sch.13 Part 1

s.78, repealed: 2004 c.35 Sch.13 Part 1

1995–cont.

26. Pensions Act 1995–*cont.*

s.79, repealed: 2004 c.35 Sch.13 Part 1

s.80, amended: 2004 c.35 s.277

s.80, repealed: 2004 c.35 Sch.13 Part 1

s.81, repealed (in part): 2004 c.35 s.277, Sch.13 Part 1

s.82, repealed: 2004 c.35 Sch.13 Part 1

s.83, amended: 2004 c.35 s.277

s.83, repealed: 2004 c.35 Sch.13 Part 1

s.83, varied: SI 2004/3350 Art.4

s.84, repealed: 2004 c.35 Sch.13 Part 1

s.85, repealed: 2004 c.35 Sch.13 Part 1

s.86, repealed: 2004 c.35 Sch.13 Part 1

s.87, repealed (in part): 2004 c.35 Sch.12 para.64, Sch.13 Part 1

s.88, amended: 2004 c.35 s.269

s.88, applied: 2004 c.35 s.90

s.88, repealed (in part): 2004 c.35 Sch.12 para.65, Sch.13 Part 1

s.89, amended: 2004 c.35 Sch.12 para.66, Sch.13 Part 1

s.91, see *Fisher v Harrison* [2003] EWCA Civ 1047, [2003] B.P.I.R. 1322 (CA), Mance, L.J.

s.91, amended: 2004 c.35 s.266

s.91, disapplied: 2002 c.29 s.273

s.91, enabling: SI 2002/681

s.92, enabling: SI 2002/681

s.96, repealed: 2004 c.35 Sch.13 Part 1

s.97, repealed: 2004 c.35 Sch.13 Part 1

s.98, repealed: 2004 c.35 Sch.13 Part 1

s.99, repealed: 2004 c.35 Sch.13 Part 1

s.100, repealed: 2004 c.35 Sch.13 Part 1

s.101, repealed: 2004 c.35 Sch.13 Part 1

s.102, repealed: 2004 c.35 Sch.13 Part 1

s.103, repealed: 2004 c.35 Sch.13 Part 1

s.104, repealed: 2004 c.35 Sch.13 Part 1

s.105, repealed: 2004 c.35 Sch.13 Part 1

s.106, repealed: 2004 c.35 Sch.13 Part 1

s.107, repealed: 2004 c.35 Sch.13 Part 1

s.108, repealed: 2004 c.35 Sch.13 Part 1

s.109, repealed: 2004 c.35 Sch.13 Part 1

s.110, repealed: 2004 c.35 Sch.13 Part 1

s.111, repealed: 2004 c.35 Sch.13 Part 1

s.112, repealed: 2004 c.35 Sch.13 Part 1

s.113, repealed: 2004 c.35 Sch.13 Part 1

s.114, applied: 2004 c.35 s.302

s.114, repealed: 2004 c.35 Sch.13 Part 1

s.116, applied: 2004 c.35 s.314

s.117, applied: 2004 c.35 s.318

s.117, repealed (in part): 2004 c.35 Sch.13 Part 1

s.118, amended: 2004 c.35 Sch.12 para.67

s.118, referred to: SI 2002/459 Reg.4

s.118, repealed (in part): 2004 c.35 Sch.12 para.67, Sch.13 Part 1

s.118, enabling: SI 2002/459

s.119, amended: 2004 c.35 Sch.12 para.68, Sch.13 Part 1

s.120, enabling: SI 2002/380

1995–cont.

26. Pensions Act 1995–*cont.*

s.124, amended: 2004 c.35 s.7, Sch.12 para.69, Sch.13 Part 1

s.124, applied: SI 2002/346, SI 2002/3202 Reg.4, SI 2004/403 Reg.1

s.124, disapplied: SI 2002/459 Reg.12

s.124, enabling: SI 2002/380, SI 2002/459, SI 2002/681, SI 2002/2327, SI 2004/403, SI 2004/1140, SI 2004/3031

s.125, amended: 2004 c.35 s.240

s.125, enabling: SI 2002/380

s.127, repealed: 2002 c.21 Sch.6

s.134, referred to: 2004 c.35 s.322

s.134, repealed (in part): 2004 c.35 Sch.13 Part 1

s.142, repealed (in part): 2004 c.35 Sch.13 Part 1

s.150, repealed: 2004 c.14 Sch.1 Part 5

s.157, see *R. (on the application of Britannic Asset Management Ltd) v Pensions Ombudsman* [2002] EWHC 441, [2002] O.P.L.R. 175 (QBD (Admin Ct)), Lightman, J.

s.162, amended: 2004 c.35 s.279, Sch.13 Part 1

s.163, amended: 2004 c.35 s.279

s.174, enabling: SI 2002/346, SI 2002/380, SI 2002/459, SI 2002/681, SI 2004/403, SI 2004/1140, SI 2004/3031

s.175, amended: 2004 c.35 s.240, Sch.13 Part 1

s.175, enabling: SI 2002/380

s.178, amended: 2004 c.14 Sch.1 Part 5, 2004 c.35 Sch.13 Part 1

Sch.1 para.1, repealed: 2004 c.35 Sch.13 Part 1

Sch.1 para.2, repealed: 2004 c.35 Sch.13 Part 1

Sch.1 para.3, repealed: 2004 c.35 Sch.13 Part 1

Sch.1 para.4, repealed: 2004 c.35 Sch.13 Part 1

Sch.1 para.5, repealed: 2004 c.35 Sch.13 Part 1

Sch.1 para.6, repealed: 2004 c.35 Sch.13 Part 1

Sch.1 para.7, repealed: 2004 c.35 Sch.13 Part 1

Sch.1 para.8, repealed: 2004 c.35 Sch.13 Part 1

Sch.1 para.9, repealed: 2004 c.35 Sch.13 Part 1

Sch.1 para.10, repealed: 2004 c.35 Sch.13 Part 1

Sch.1 para.11, repealed: 2004 c.35 Sch.13 Part 1

Sch.1 para.12, repealed: 2004 c.35 Sch.13 Part 1

Sch.1 para.13, repealed: 2004 c.35 Sch.13 Part 1

1995–cont.

26. Pensions Act 1995–cont.

Sch.1 para.14, repealed: 2004 c.35 Sch.13 Part 1

Sch.1 para.15, repealed: 2004 c.35 Sch.13 Part 1

Sch.1 para.16, repealed: 2004 c.35 Sch.13 Part 1

Sch.1 para.17, repealed: 2004 c.35 Sch.13 Part 1

Sch.1 para.18, repealed: 2004 c.35 Sch.13 Part 1

Sch.1 para.19, repealed: 2004 c.35 Sch.13 Part 1

Sch.1 para.20, repealed: 2004 c.35 Sch.13 Part 1

Sch.2 para.1, repealed: 2004 c.35 Sch.13 Part 1

Sch.2 para.2, repealed: 2004 c.35 Sch.13 Part 1

Sch.2 para.3, repealed: 2004 c.35 Sch.13 Part 1

Sch.2 para.4, repealed: 2004 c.35 Sch.13 Part 1

Sch.2 para.5, repealed: 2004 c.35 Sch.13 Part 1

Sch.2 para.6, repealed: 2004 c.35 Sch.13 Part 1

Sch.2 para.7, repealed: 2004 c.35 Sch.13 Part 1

Sch.2 para.8, repealed: 2004 c.35 Sch.13 Part 1

Sch.2 para.9, repealed: 2004 c.35 Sch.13 Part 1

Sch.2 para.10, repealed: 2004 c.35 Sch.13 Part 1

Sch.2 para.11, repealed: 2004 c.35 Sch.13 Part 1

Sch.2 para.12, repealed: 2004 c.35 Sch.13 Part 1

Sch.2 para.13, repealed: 2004 c.35 Sch.13 Part 1

Sch.2 para.14, repealed: 2004 c.35 Sch.13 Part 1

Sch.2 para.15, repealed: 2004 c.35 Sch.13 Part 1

Sch.2 para.16, repealed: 2004 c.35 Sch.13 Part 1

Sch.2 para.17, repealed: 2004 c.35 Sch.13 Part 1

Sch.2 para.18, repealed: 2004 c.35 Sch.13 Part 1

Sch.2 para.19, repealed: 2004 c.35 Sch.13 Part 1

Sch.2 para.20, repealed: 2004 c.35 Sch.13 Part 1

Sch.3 para.12, repealed: 2004 c.27 Sch.8, 2004 c.35 Sch.13 Part 1

Sch.3 para.21, repealed: 2004 c.35 Sch.13 Part 1

Sch.3 para.23, repealed: 2004 c.35 Sch.13 Part 1

1995–cont.

26. Pensions Act 1995–cont.

Sch.3 para.44, repealed (in part): 2004 c.35 Sch.13 Part 1

Sch.4 Part I para.1, amended: 2002 c.16 Sch.2 para.39

Sch.4 Part I para.1, applied: 2003 asp 1 s.44

Sch.4 Part II para.6, amended: 2004 c.35 s.297

Sch.4 Part III para.21, referred to: 2004 c.35 s.322

Sch.4 Part III para.21, repealed (in part): 2004 c.35 Sch.13 Part 1

Sch.5 para.12, repealed: 2004 c.12 Sch.42 Part 3

Sch.5 para.20, repealed: 2004 c.35 Sch.13 Part 1

Sch.5 para.77, repealed (in part): 2004 c.35 Sch.13 Part 1

Sch.6 para.6, repealed (in part): 2004 c.35 Sch.13 Part 1

27. Geneva Conventions (Amendment) Act 1995

applied: SI 2002/1076 Sch.1

referred to: SI 2002/1076

s.1, varied: SI 2002/1076 Sch.2 para.1, Sch.2 para.2

s.2, varied: SI 2002/1076 Sch.2 para.3

s.3, varied: SI 2002/1076 Sch.2 para.4

s.4, varied: SI 2002/1076 Sch.2 para.5

s.5, varied: SI 2002/1076 Sch.2 para.6

s.7, applied: SI 2002/1076

s.7, varied: SI 2002/1076 Sch.2 para.7

30. Landlord and Tenant (Covenants) Act 1995

s.1, applied: 2002 c.9 Sch.12 para.20

s.3, amended: 2002 c.9 Sch.11 para.33

s.8, see *BHP Petroleum Great Britain Ltd v Chesterfield Properties Ltd* [2001] EWCA Civ 1797, [2002] Ch. 194 (CA), Jonathan Parker, L.J.

s.15, amended: 2002 c.9 Sch.11 para.33

s.20, amended: 2002 c.9 Sch.11 para.33

s.28, see *BHP Petroleum Great Britain Ltd v Chesterfield Properties Ltd* [2002] Ch. 12 (Ch D), Lightman, J.

32. Olympic Symbol etc (Protection) Act 1995

referred to: SI 2003/2500 Sch.1 Part 1

s.4, amended: SI 2003/2498 Sch.1 para.20

33. Licensing (Sunday Hours) Act 1995

repealed: 2003 c.17 Sch.7

34. Child Support Act 1995

s.10, amended: 2003 c.1 Sch.6 para.231, 2004 c.33 Sch.24 para.126, Sch.24 para.127, Sch.30

s.10, applied: 2003 c.1 s.666, s.670

s.10, enabling: SI 2002/2497, SI 2002/3197

s.24, applied: 2003 c.1 s.677

s.26, enabling: SI 2002/2497, SI 2002/3197

Sch.3 para.1, repealed: 2003 c.1 Sch.8 Part 1

CAP.

1995–cont.

35. Criminal Appeal Act 1995

see *R. (on the application of Christofides) v Secretary of State for the Home Department* [2002] EWHC 1083, [2002] 1 W.L.R. 2769 (QBD (Admin Ct)), Sedley, L.J.

s.9, amended: 2004 c.28 Sch.10 para.31

s.9, applied: 2003 c.44 s.51

s.10, amended: 2004 c.28 Sch.10 para.32

s.10, applied: SI 2004/1500 Art.10

s.11, applied: 2003 c.44 s.51

s.12, applied: SI 2004/1500 Art.10

s.13, see *R. v Thomas (Ian James)* [2002] EWCA Crim 941, [2003] 1 Cr. App. R. 11 (CA (Crim Div)), Auld, L.J.

s.14, see *R. v Smith (Wallace Duncan) (No.3)* [2002] EWCA Crim 2907, [2003] 1 W.L.R. 1647 (CA (Crim Div)), Buxton, L.J.; see *R. v Smith (Wallace Duncan) (No.4)* [2004] EWCA Crim 631, [2004] Q.B. 1418 (CA (Crim Div)), Lord Woolf of Barnes, L.C.J.

s.14, amended: 2003 c.44 s.315

s.15, amended: 2003 c.44 Sch.36 para.97

s.22, amended: 2002 c.26 Sch.12 para.49

s.22, repealed (in part): 2003 c.39 Sch.8 para.367, Sch.10

Sch.2 para.8, repealed: 2003 c.44 Sch.37 Part 10

36. Children (Scotland) Act 1995

Commencement Orders: SSI 2002/12 Art.2

see *Edinburgh City Council v W* 2002 Fam. L.R. 67 (Sh Pr), CGB Nicholson Q.C., Sheriff Principal

applied: 2002 c.38 s.46, 2003 asp 7 s.14, SI 2004/1611 Reg.25, SSI 2004/115 Sch.5 para.15, Sch.5 para.83, SSI 2004/116 Sch.1 para.8, Sch.1 para.48, Sch.2 para.9

Part II, applied: SI 2002/2007 Reg.3, SI 2003/493 Reg.18

Part II c.3, applied: 2002 c.21 Sch.5 para.10A

Part II c.3, added: 2004 asp 8 s.137

s.1, see *G v Edinburgh City Council (Adoption: Paternal Rights)* 2002 S.C. 440 (Ex Div), Lord Coulsfield, Lord Caplan, Lady Cosgrove; see *G v Edinburgh City Council (Adoption: Paternal Rights)* 2002 S.L.T. (Sh Ct) 58 (Sh Pr), CGB Nicholson Q.C., Sheriff Principal

s.1, applied: SI 2004/1309 Reg.3

s.4, see *West Lothian Council v M* 2002 S.C. 411 (2 Div), Lord Gill L.J.C., Lord Hamilton, Lord Reed

s.6, see *West Lothian Council v M* 2002 S.C. 411 (2 Div), Lord Gill L.J.C., Lord Hamilton, Lord Reed

s.9, see *I v Argyll and Clyde Health Board* 2003 S.L.T. 231 (OH), Lord Carloway

s.11, see *G v Edinburgh City Council (Adoption: Paternal Rights)* 2002 S.C. 440 (Ex Div), Lord Coulsfield, Lord Caplan, Lady Cosgrove; see *G v Edinburgh City Council (Adoption:*

CAP.

1995–cont.

36. Children (Scotland) Act 1995–*cont.*

s.11–*cont.*

Paternal Rights) 2002 S.L.T. (Sh Ct) 58 (Sh Pr), CGB Nicholson Q.C., Sheriff Principal; see *Orr v K* 2003 S.L.T. (Sh Ct) 70 (Sh Ct (Tayside, Central and Fife)), Sheriff FR Crowe; see *Shields v Shields* 2002 S.C. 246 (Ex Div), Lord Marnoch, Lady Cosgrove, Lord Dawson; see *X v Y (Parental Rights: Insemination)* 2002 S.L.T. (Sh Ct) 161 (Sh Ct (Glasgow and Strathkelvin)), ALA Duncan

s.11, applied: SSI 2002/132 Sch.1 para.26.5, SSI 2002/494 Reg.18

s.12, amended: 2004 c.33 Sch.28 para.60

s.13, see *I v Argyll and Clyde Health Board* 2003 S.L.T. 231 (OH), Lord Carloway

s.13, applied: SSI 2002/132 Sch.1 para.26.5

s.15, referred to: SSI 2003/19 Reg.24, Reg.26

s.16, see *S v Proudfoot* 2002 S.L.T. 743 (OH), Lord Menzies

s.17, see *S v N* 2002 S.L.T. 589 (Ex Div), Lord Emslie, Lord Cameron of Lochbroom, Lord Reed

s.17, applied: 2003 c.14 Sch.36 para.4, SSI 2003/608 Reg.6

s.17, enabling: SSI 2003/608

s.22, amended: 2002 c.21 Sch.3 para.50, Sch.6

s.22, applied: 2002 c.41 Sch.3 para.1, SSI 2003/243 Reg.2

s.23, amended: 2002 asp 5 s.10, 2003 asp 13 s.227, Sch.4 para.7

s.23, applied: 2003 asp 13 s.62

s.24, amended: 2002 asp 5 s.11

s.24, applied: 2002 asp 5 s.12

s.24A, added: 2002 asp 5 s.11

s.25, see *Aberdeen City Council v Molina* 2002 Hous. L.R. 98 (Sh Pr), Sir SST Young Q.C., Sheriff Principal

s.26, applied: SI 2002/2007 Reg.3, SI 2003/493 Reg.16

s.29, applied: 2002 c.41 Sch.3 para.1, SSI 2003/608 Reg.8, Reg.9, Reg.11, Reg.16

s.29, referred to: SI 2004/747 Reg.2, SSI 2003/608 Reg.11, Reg.16

s.30, applied: 2002 c.41 Sch.3 para.1

s.39, applied: 2003 asp 5 Sch.2 para.6

s.41, applied: SSI 2002/63 r.3

s.42, enabling: SSI 2002/30, SSI 2002/63

s.44, amended: 2003 asp 7 s.52

s.51, see *C v Miller* 2003 S.L.T. 1379 (Court of Session (Inner House, Extra Division)), Lord Osborne, Lord Carloway, Lord Hamilton; see *M, Appellant* 2003 S.L.T. (Sh Ct) 112 (Sh Ct (Tayside, Central and Fife)), Sheriff IC Simpson; see *S v N* 2002 S.L.T. 589 (Ex Div), Lord Emslie, Lord Cameron of Lochbroom, Lord Reed; see *S v Proudfoot* 2002 S.L.T. 743 (OH), Lord Menzies

s.51, amended: 2004 asp 8 Sch.4 para.4

1995–cont.

36. Children (Scotland) Act 1995–*cont.*

s.52, see *C v Miller* 2003 S.L.T.1379 (Court of Session (Inner House, Extra Division)), Lord Osborne, Lord Carloway, Lord Hamilton; see *Walker v C (No.2)* 2003 S.C. 570 (1 Div), Lord Cullen L.P., Lord McCluskey, Lord Philip

s.52, amended: 2004 asp 8 s.12

s.54, amended: 2004 c.33 Sch.28 para.61

s.56, amended: 2004 asp 8 s.137

s.57, applied: SI 2004/2695 Sch.1 para.22

s.58, see *K and F, Applicants* 2002 S.L.T. (Sh Ct) 38 (Sh Pr), CGB Nicholson Q.C., Sheriff Principal

s.64, applied: SSI 2002/63 r.3

s.65, see *Walker v C (No.1)* 2003 S.L.T. (Sh Ct) 31 (Sh Pr), Sir SST Young, Sheriff Principal; see *Walker v C (No.2)* 2003 S.C. 570 (1 Div), Lord Cullen L.P., Lord McCluskey, Lord Philip

s.65, amended: 2004 asp 8 s.12

s.66, amended: 2004 asp 8 Sch.4 para.4

s.68, see *Walker v C (No.2)* 2003 S.C. 570 (1 Div), Lord Cullen L.P., Lord McCluskey, Lord Philip

s.68, amended: 2004 asp 8 Sch.4 para.4

s.68A, added: 2004 asp 3 s.23

s.68B, added: 2004 asp 3 s.23

s.69, amended: 2004 asp 8 Sch.4 para.4

s.70, see *Walker v C (No.1)* 2003 S.L.T. (Sh Ct) 31 (Sh Pr), Sir SST Young, Sheriff Principal

s.70, amended: 2004 asp 8 s.135, s.136

s.70, applied: SI 2002/635 Reg.2, SI 2002/896 Sch.1 para.3, 2003 c.14 Sch.36 para.4, SI 2004/2695 Sch.1 para.23, SSI 2003/231 Sch.3 para.6

s.70, referred to: SSI 2002/63 r.3

s.71, amended: 2004 asp 8 s.136

s.71A, added: 2004 asp 8 s.136

s.73, see *S v Proudfoot* 2002 S.L.T. 743 (OH), Lord Menzies

s.73, amended: 2004 asp 8 s.12

s.75A, added: 2004 asp 8 s.116

s.76, see *Glasgow City Council v H* 2003 S.L.T. (Sh Ct) 61 (Sh Pr), EF Bowen Q.C., Sheriff Principal

s.76, applied: SI 2004/2695 Sch.1 para.22

s.76, repealed (in part): SSI 2003/583 Sch.1 para.12

s.81, applied: SI 2002/896 Sch.1 para.64, SI 2004/2695 Sch.1 para.10

s.83, applied: SI 2002/635 Sch.1 para.2, SI 2002/896 Sch.1 para.64, SI 2004/2695 Sch.1 para.10

s.86, see *Glasgow City Council v H* 2003 S.L.T. (Sh Ct) 61 (Sh Pr), EF Bowen Q.C., Sheriff Principal

s.86, amended: 2002 c.38 Sch.3 para.83, Sch.3 para.84

1995–cont.

36. Children (Scotland) Act 1995–*cont.*

s.86, applied: 2002 c.38 Sch.4 para.23, SI 2002/635 Reg.2, SI 2002/896 Sch.1 para.4, 2003 asp 13 s.252, SI 2004/2695 Sch.1 para.24, SSI 2002/494 Reg.18

s.86, referred to: 2002 c.38 Sch.3 para.82

s.89, applied: SI 2002/635 Sch.1 para.2, SI 2002/896 Sch.1 para.64, SI 2004/2695 Sch.1 para.10

s.91, enabling: SSI 2003/44

s.93, see *S v N* 2002 S.L.T. 589 (Ex Div), Lord Emslie, Lord Cameron of Lochbroom, Lord Reed

s.93, amended: 2003 asp 7 s.52, 2004 asp 8 s.137, Sch.4 para.4

s.101, applied: SSI 2003/231 Sch.4 para.21

s.103, enabling: SSI 2002/63

s.105, enabling: SSI 2002/12

Sch.1 para.3, applied: 2002 asp 11 Sch.2 para.15

Sch.1 para.8, applied: 2002 asp 11 Sch.2 para.15, 2003 asp 5 Sch.2 para.6

Sch.4 para.25, repealed: 2002 asp 11 Sch.6 para.16

Sch.4 para.28, repealed (in part): 2004 asp 4 Sch.3 para.9

Sch.4 para.33, repealed: 2003 asp 13 Sch.5 Part 1

37. Atomic Energy Authority Act 1995

s.1, repealed: 2004 c.20 Sch.23 Part 1

s.2, repealed: 2004 c.20 Sch.23 Part 1

s.3, repealed: 2004 c.20 Sch.23 Part 1

s.4, repealed: 2004 c.20 Sch.23 Part 1

s.5, repealed: 2004 c.20 Sch.23 Part 1

s.6, repealed: 2004 c.20 Sch.23 Part 1

s.7, repealed: 2004 c.20 Sch.23 Part 1

s.8, repealed: 2004 c.20 Sch.23 Part 1

s.9, repealed: 2004 c.20 Sch.23 Part 1

s.10, repealed: 2004 c.20 Sch.23 Part 1

s.12, repealed: 2004 c.20 Sch.23 Part 1

s.13, repealed: 2004 c.20 Sch.23 Part 1

Sch.1 para.1, repealed: 2004 c.20 Sch.23 Part 1

Sch.1 para.2, repealed: 2004 c.20 Sch.23 Part 1

Sch.1 para.3, repealed: 2004 c.20 Sch.23 Part 1

Sch.1 para.4, repealed: 2004 c.20 Sch.23 Part 1

Sch.1 para.5, repealed: 2004 c.20 Sch.23 Part 1

Sch.1 para.6, repealed: 2004 c.20 Sch.23 Part 1

Sch.1 para.7, repealed: 2004 c.20 Sch.23 Part 1

Sch.1 para.8, repealed: 2004 c.20 Sch.23 Part 1

Sch.1 para.9, repealed: 2004 c.20 Sch.23 Part 1

Sch.1 para.10, repealed: 2004 c.20 Sch.23 Part 1

1995–cont.

37. Atomic Energy Authority Act 1995– *cont.*

Sch.2 para.1, repealed: 2004 c.20 Sch.23 Part 1

Sch.2 para.2, repealed: 2004 c.20 Sch.23 Part 1

Sch.2 para.3, repealed: 2004 c.20 Sch.23 Part 1

Sch.2 para.4, repealed: 2004 c.20 Sch.23 Part 1

Sch.2 para.5, repealed: 2004 c.20 Sch.23 Part 1

Sch.2 para.6, repealed: 2004 c.20 Sch.23 Part 1

Sch.2 para.7, repealed: 2004 c.20 Sch.23 Part 1

Sch.2 para.8, repealed: 2004 c.20 Sch.23 Part 1

Sch.2 para.9, repealed: 2004 c.20 Sch.23 Part 1

Sch.2 para.10, repealed: 2004 c.20 Sch.23 Part 1

Sch.2 para.11, repealed: 2004 c.20 Sch.23 Part 1

Sch.2 para.12, repealed: 2004 c.20 Sch.23 Part 1

Sch.2 para.13, repealed: 2004 c.20 Sch.23 Part 1

Sch.2 para.14, repealed: 2004 c.20 Sch.23 Part 1

Sch.2 para.15, repealed: 2004 c.20 Sch.23 Part 1

Sch.3 Part I para.1, repealed: 2004 c.20 Sch.23 Part 1

Sch.3 Part I para.2, repealed: 2004 c.20 Sch.23 Part 1

Sch.3 Part I para.3, repealed: 2004 c.20 Sch.23 Part 1

Sch.3 Part I para.4, repealed: 2004 c.20 Sch.23 Part 1

Sch.3 Part I para.5, repealed: 2004 c.20 Sch.23 Part 1

Sch.3 Part I para.6, repealed: 2004 c.20 Sch.23 Part 1

Sch.3 Part I para.7, repealed: 2004 c.20 Sch.23 Part 1

Sch.3 Part I para.8, repealed: 2004 c.20 Sch.23 Part 1

Sch.3 Part I para.9, repealed: 2004 c.20 Sch.23 Part 1

Sch.3 Part I para.10, repealed: 2004 c.20 Sch.23 Part 1

Sch.3 Part I para.11, repealed: 2004 c.20 Sch.23 Part 1

Sch.3 Part I para.12, repealed: 2004 c.20 Sch.23 Part 1

Sch.3 Part I para.13, repealed: 2004 c.20 Sch.23 Part 1

Sch.3 Part II para.14, repealed: 2004 c.20 Sch.23 Part 1

1995–cont.

37. Atomic Energy Authority Act 1995– *cont.*

Sch.3 Part II para.15, repealed: 2004 c.20 Sch.23 Part 1

Sch.3 Part II para.16, repealed: 2004 c.20 Sch.23 Part 1

Sch.3 Part II para.17, repealed: 2004 c.20 Sch.23 Part 1

Sch.3 Part II para.18, repealed: 2004 c.20 Sch.23 Part 1

Sch.3 Part II para.19, repealed: 2004 c.20 Sch.23 Part 1

Sch.3 Part II para.20, repealed: 2004 c.20 Sch.23 Part 1

Sch.3 Part II para.21, repealed: 2004 c.20 Sch.23 Part 1

Sch.3 Part II para.22, repealed: 2004 c.20 Sch.23 Part 1

Sch.3 Part III para.23, repealed: 2004 c.20 Sch.23 Part 1

Sch.3 Part III para.24, repealed: 2004 c.20 Sch.23 Part 1

Sch.3 Part III para.25, repealed: 2004 c.20 Sch.23 Part 1

Sch.4 para.1, repealed: 2004 c.20 Sch.23 Part 1

Sch.4 para.2, repealed: 2004 c.20 Sch.23 Part 1

Sch.4 para.3, repealed: 2004 c.20 Sch.23 Part 1

Sch.4 para.4, repealed: 2004 c.20 Sch.23 Part 1

Sch.4 para.5, repealed: 2004 c.20 Sch.23 Part 1

Sch.4 para.6, repealed: 2004 c.20 Sch.23 Part 1

Sch.4 para.7, repealed: 2004 c.20 Sch.23 Part 1

38. Civil Evidence Act 1995

see *Chase v News Group Newspapers Ltd* [2002] EWCA Civ 1772, [2003] E.M.L.R. 11 (CA), Brooke, L.J.; see *R. (on the application of McCann) v Manchester Crown Court* [2002] UKHL 39, [2003] 1 A.C. 787 (HL), Lord Steyn; see *Sunley v Gowland White (Surveyors & Estate Agents) Ltd* [2003] EWCA Civ 240, [2004] P.N.L.R. 15 (CA), Clarke, L.J.

s.2, applied: 2002 c.29 s.46

s.2, disapplied: SI 2003/421 r.39

s.3, see *Tsavliris Russ (Worldwide Salvage & Towage) Ltd v RL Baron Shipping Co SA (The Green Opal)* [2003] 1 Lloyd's Rep. 523 (QBD (Adm Ct)), Tomlinson, J.

s.3, applied: 2002 c.29 s.46

s.4, applied: 2002 c.29 s.46

s.7, referred to: 2004 c.33 s.84

Sch.1 para.12, repealed: 2003 c.44 Sch.37 Part 6

1995–cont.

39. Criminal Law (Consolidation) (Scotland) Act 1995

referred to: 2003 c.32 Sch.5 para.61

Part II, applied: SSI 2004/356 Art.2

Part VI, added: 2003 c.32 s.89

s.1, applied: 2003 asp 5 Sch.1 para.2, 2003 c.42 Sch.3 para.49, 2003 c.44 Sch.16 para.12, SI 2003/1184 Sch.2 para.15, SSI 2003/441 Sch.1 para.15, SSI 2004/411 Sch.1 para.19

s.2, applied: 2003 asp 5 Sch.1 para.1, 2003 c.42 Sch.3 para.50, 2003 c.44 Sch.16 para.13, SI 2003/1184 Sch.2 para.16, SSI 2003/441 Sch.1 para.15, SSI 2004/411 Sch.1 para.19

s.2, varied: 2004 c.33 Sch.21 para.41

s.3, applied: 2003 asp 5 Sch.1 para.1, 2003 c.42 Sch.3 para.51, 2003 c.44 Sch.16 para.14, SI 2003/1184 Sch.2 para.17, SI 2004/1910 Sch.3, SSI 2003/441 Sch.1 para.15, SSI 2004/411 Sch.1 para.19

s.4, varied: 2003 asp 13 s.319

s.5, amended: 2003 c.42 Sch.6 para.33

s.5, applied: SI 2002/57 Sch.4 para.2, 2003 asp 5 Sch.1 para.1, 2003 c.42 Sch.3 para.52, 2003 c.44 Sch.16 para.15, SI 2003/1184 Sch.2 para.18, SI 2004/1910 Sch.3, SSI 2003/441 Sch.1 para.15, SSI 2004/411 Sch.1 para.19

s.5, disapplied: SSI 2003/19 Sch.5 para.9

s.5, referred to: SI 2003/237 Sch.4 para.2

s.6, applied: 2003 asp 5 Sch.1 para.1, 2003 c.42 Sch.3 para.53, 2003 c.44 Sch.16 para.16, SI 2003/1184 Sch.2 para.19, SI 2004/1910 Sch.3, SSI 2003/441 Sch.1 para.15, SSI 2004/411 Sch.1 para.19

s.7, applied: 2003 asp 5 Sch.1 para.2, 2003 c.42 Sch.5 para.101, SSI 2003/441 Sch.1 para.15

s.8, applied: 2003 asp 5 Sch.1 para.1, 2003 c.42 Sch.3 para.54, 2003 c.44 Sch.16 para.17, SSI 2003/441 Sch.1 para.15

s.8, repealed (in part): 2003 asp 7 s.19

s.9, applied: 2003 asp 5 Sch.1 para.1, 2003 c.42 Sch.5 para.102

s.10, applied: 2003 asp 5 Sch.1 para.1, 2003 c.42 Sch.3 para.55, 2003 c.44 Sch.16 para.18, SSI 2003/441 Sch.1 para.15

s.11, applied: 2002 c.29 Sch.4 para.8, 2003 asp 5 Sch.1 para.2, 2003 c.42 Sch.5 para.103

s.12, applied: 2003 asp 5 Sch.1 para.1, 2003 c.42 Sch.5 para.104

s.13, applied: 2003 asp 5 Sch.1 para.1, Sch.1 para.2, 2003 c.42 Sch.3 para.56, Sch.5 para.105, 2003 c.44 Sch.16 para.19, SI 2003/1184 Sch.2 para.20, SSI 2003/441 Sch.1 para.15

s.13, repealed (in part): 2003 asp 13 Sch.5 Part 1

s.15, repealed: 2003 asp 7 s.19

s.16B, amended: 2003 asp 7 s.19

1995–cont.

39. Criminal Law (Consolidation) (Scotland) Act 1995–*cont.*

s.16B, applied: SI 2002/635 Sch.1 para.4, SI 2002/896 Sch.1 para.81, SI 2004/2695 Sch.1 para.19

s.16B, referred to: 2003 c.42 s.142

s.18, enabling: SSI 2002/382, SSI 2004/356

s.24, see *Hoekstra v HM Advocate (No.7)* 2002 S.L.T. 599 (HCJ Appeal), Lord Cullen L.J.G., Lord Coulsfield, Lord Osborne

s.27, amended: 2003 c.32 Sch.5 para.62

s.27, applied: 2003 c.32 s.15

s.28, amended: 2003 c.32 Sch.5 para.63

s.28, repealed (in part): 2003 c.32 Sch.6

s.31, applied: SI 2003/120 Art.6, SSI 2003/179 Reg.3

s.31, repealed: 2002 c.29 Sch.12

s.32, applied: SI 2003/120 Art.6

s.32, repealed: 2002 c.29 Sch.12

s.33, applied: SI 2003/120 Art.6

s.33, repealed: 2002 c.29 Sch.12

s.34, applied: SI 2003/120 Art.6

s.34, repealed: 2002 c.29 Sch.12

s.35, applied: SI 2003/120 Art.6

s.35, repealed: 2002 c.29 Sch.12

s.36, applied: SI 2003/120 Art.5

s.36, repealed: 2002 c.29 Sch.12

s.37, repealed: 2002 c.29 Sch.12

s.38, repealed: 2002 c.29 Sch.12

s.39, repealed: 2002 c.29 Sch.12

s.40, applied: SI 2003/120 Art.5

s.40, referred to: SI 2003/120 Art.5

s.40, repealed: 2002 c.29 Sch.12

s.41, referred to: SSI 2003/210 Art.7

s.41, repealed: 2002 c.29 Sch.12

s.42, applied: SI 2003/120 Art.6

s.42, repealed: 2002 c.29 Sch.12

s.43, referred to: SSI 2003/210 Art.7

s.43, repealed: 2002 c.29 Sch.12

s.44, applied: 2002 c.29 Sch.6 para.2, 2002 c.38 s.41, 2003 c.32 s.30, s.31, 2004 c.27 Sch.7 para.3

s.45, applied: 2003 c.32 s.30, s.31

s.46, applied: 2003 c.32 s.30, s.31

s.49., see *McAuley v Brown* 2003 S.L.T. 736 (HCJ), Lord Macfadyen, Lord Carloway, Temporary Judge Sir GH Gordon Q.C.; see *McGuire v Higson* 2003 S.L.T. 890 (HCJ), Lord Osborne, Temporary Judge CGB Nicholson Q.C., Lady Paton; see *Robertson v Higson* 2003 S.L.T. 1276 (HCJ), Lord Marnoch, Lord Clarke, Lord Hamilton

s.50A, applied: 2003 c.42 Sch.5 para.106, SI 2004/1910 Sch.3, SSI 2003/441 Sch.1 para.19, SSI 2004/411 Sch.1 para.27

s.52, applied: SI 2004/1910 Sch.3

1995–cont.

40. Criminal Procedure (Consequential Provisions) (Scotland) Act 1995

Sch.3 Part II para.4, repealed (in part): 2002 c.29 Sch.12

Sch.4 para.11, repealed: 2003 asp 15 Sch.4 Part 2

Sch.4 para.30, repealed: 2004 asp 8 Sch.5

Sch.4 para.46, repealed: 2004 c.14 Sch.1 Part 16

Sch.4 para.47, repealed: 2004 c.14 Sch.1 Part 9

Sch.4 para.48, repealed (in part): 2003 c.21 Sch.19

Sch.4 para.50, repealed: 2003 asp 13 Sch.5 Part 1

Sch.4 para.69, repealed: 2002 c.29 Sch.12

Sch.4 para.94, repealed: 2002 c.29 Sch.12

Sch.4 para.98, repealed: 2004 c.35 Sch.13 Part 1

42. Private International Law (Miscellaneous Provisions) Act 1995

s.4, repealed (in part): 2002 c.29 Sch.12

s.11, see *Morin v Bonhams & Brooks Ltd* [2003] EWCA Civ 1802, [2004] 1 All E.R. (Comm) 880 (CA), Mance, L.J.; see *Morin v Bonhams & Brooks Ltd* [2003] EWHC 467, [2003] 2 All E.R. (Comm) 36 (QBD (Comm Ct)), Jonathan Hirst, Q.C.

s.12, see *Roerig v Valiant Trawlers Ltd* [2002] EWCA Civ 21, [2002] 1 W.L.R. 2304 (CA), Waller, L.J.

43. Proceeds of Crime (Scotland) Act 1995

applied: SSI 2003/120 r.3, SSI 2003/210 Art.7

Part I, applied: 2002 c.29 s.8, s.94, s.158

Part II, applied: 2002 asp 6 s.7, 2002 c.29 s.82, s.97, s.148, s.230

s.1, see *HM Advocate v Urquhart (Robert David)* 2002 S.L.T. 1143 (HCJ), Lord Mackay of Drumadoon

s.1, repealed: 2002 c.29 Sch.12

s.2, repealed (in part): 2002 c.29 Sch.12

s.3, see *HM Advocate v McIntosh (Robert) (No.1)* [2001] UKPC D1, [2003] 1 A.C. 1078 (PC), Lord Bingham of Cornhill, L.C.J.

s.3, repealed: 2002 c.29 Sch.12

s.4, repealed: 2002 c.29 Sch.12

s.5, applied: SSI 2003/179 Reg.5

s.5, repealed: 2002 c.29 Sch.12

s.6, see *HM Advocate v McIntosh (Robert) (No.2)* 2002 S.C.C.R. 287 (HCJ), Lord Eassie; see *HM Advocate v Urquhart (Robert David)* 2002 S.L.T. 1143 (HCJ), Lord Mackay of Drumadoon

s.6, applied: SSI 2003/179 Reg.5

s.6, repealed: 2002 c.29 Sch.12

s.7, repealed: 2002 c.29 Sch.12

s.8, repealed: 2002 c.29 Sch.12

s.9, repealed: 2002 c.29 Sch.12

s.10, repealed: 2002 c.29 Sch.12

1995–cont.

43. Proceeds of Crime (Scotland) Act 1995–*cont.*

s.11, repealed: 2002 c.29 Sch.12

s.12, repealed: 2002 c.29 Sch.12

s.13, repealed: 2002 c.29 Sch.12

s.14, repealed: 2002 c.29 Sch.12

s.15, repealed: 2002 c.29 Sch.12

s.16, repealed: 2002 c.29 Sch.12

s.17, repealed: 2002 c.29 Sch.12

s.18, applied: SSI 2003/179 Reg.5

s.18, repealed: 2002 c.29 Sch.12

s.19, repealed: 2002 c.29 Sch.12

s.20, repealed: 2002 c.29 Sch.12

s.22, applied: SI 2003/336 Sch.1 Part 2

s.24, applied: SI 2003/336 Sch.1 Part 2

s.25, applied: SSI 2003/179 Reg.5

s.26, applied: SI 2003/336 Sch.1 Part 2, SSI 2003/179 Reg.5

s.27, applied: SSI 2003/179 Reg.5

s.28, amended: 2002 c.29 Sch.11 para.28, Sch.12

s.28, repealed (in part): 2002 c.29 Sch.12

s.29, repealed: 2002 c.29 Sch.12

s.31, amended: 2002 c.29 Sch.12

s.31, repealed (in part): 2002 c.29 Sch.12

s.35, repealed: 2002 c.29 Sch.12

s.36, repealed: 2002 c.29 Sch.12

s.37, repealed: 2002 c.29 Sch.12

s.38, repealed: 2002 c.29 Sch.12

s.39, repealed: 2002 c.29 Sch.12

s.40, repealed (in part): 2002 c.29 Sch.12

s.42, amended: 2002 c.29 Sch.11 para.28

s.42, repealed (in part): 2002 c.29 Sch.12

s.43, amended: 2002 c.29 Sch.11 para.28, Sch.12

s.43, repealed (in part): 2002 c.29 Sch.11 para.28, Sch.12

s.45, applied: SSI 2003/179 Reg.5

s.45, repealed (in part): 2002 c.29 Sch.12

s.47, repealed: 2002 c.29 Sch.12

s.49, amended: 2002 c.29 Sch.12

s.49, repealed (in part): 2002 c.29 Sch.12

Sch.1 para.1, amended: 2002 c.29 Sch.12

Sch.1 para.1, repealed (in part): 2002 c.29 Sch.12

Sch.1 para.2, amended: 2002 c.29 Sch.12

Sch.1 para.4, repealed: 2002 c.29 Sch.12

Sch.1 para.5, amended: 2002 c.29 Sch.12

Sch.1 para.7, amended: 2002 asp 17 Sch.3 para.24

Sch.1 para.8, amended: 2002 c.29 Sch.12

Sch.1 para.10, amended: 2002 c.29 Sch.12

Sch.1 para.10, repealed (in part): 2002 c.29 Sch.12

Sch.1 para.12, amended: 2002 c.29 Sch.12

Sch.2 para.1, amended: 2002 c.29 Sch.12

Sch.2 para.2, amended: 2002 c.29 Sch.12

Sch.2 para.2, repealed (in part): 2002 c.29 Sch.12

Sch.2 para.3, amended: 2002 c.29 Sch.12

CAP.

CAP.

1995–cont.

1995–cont.

43. Proceeds of Crime (Scotland) Act 1995–*cont.*

Sch.2 para.3, repealed (in part): 2002 c.29 Sch.12

Sch.2 para.4, amended: 2002 c.29 Sch.12

Sch.2 para.6, repealed (in part): 2002 c.29 Sch.12

45. Gas Act 1995

applied: 2002 c.40 Sch.15, 2004 c.20 s.188

Sch.4 para.2, amended: 2004 c.34 Sch.15 para.39

Sch.4 para.2, repealed (in part): 2004 c.36 Sch.3

46. Criminal Procedure (Scotland) Act 1995

applied: SI 2002/1792 Reg.5, 2003 asp 13 s.8, s.11, s.13, s.227, s.237, s.238, s.239, s.240, s.241, s.242, s.243, s.244, s.255, s.260, s.261, s.262, s.263, s.276, s.278, s.289, s.290, s.291, s.299, s.310, 2003 c.41 s.142, 2003 c.42 Sch.3 para.98, SSI 2004/115 Sch.3, SSI 2004/405 Art.3

disapplied: SSI 2004/405 Art.4

referred to: 2003 asp 7 s.87, 2003 c.32 Sch.5 para.64, 2004 asp 5 Sch.1 para.1, SSI 2004/405 Art.3

Part VII, added: 2004 asp 5 s.15

Part VII, added: 2004 asp 5 s.5

Part VII, added: 2004 asp 5 s.11

Part VIII, applied: 2003 asp 5 s.7

Part XI, added: 2004 asp 8 s.120

Pt.XA, see *McWilliam, Petitioner* 2002 S.L.T. 972 (HCJ Appeal), Lord Hamilton, Lord Reed, Lord Drummond Young

s.1, see *Stevens (Andrew) v HM Advocate* 2002 S.L.T. 1249 (HCJ), Lady Paton

s.1, referred to: SSI 2003/19 Sch.5 para.9

s.2, amended: 2004 asp 5 Sch.1 para.2

s.5, see *Marshall v Stott* 2002 S.L.T. 1353 (HCJ), Lord Hardie, Lord MacLean; see *Paterson v Webster* 2002 S.L.T. 1120 (HCJ), Lord Macfadyen, Lord MacLean, Lord McCluskey

s.6, see *Clarke v Fraser* 2002 S.L.T. 745 (HCJ), Lord Marnoch, Lord Macfadyen, Lord Osborne

s.8, applied: 2004 c.33 s.116

s.9A, added: 2003 asp 7 s.59

s.11, varied: 2003 asp 7 s.69

s.14, see *Mallin v Clark* 2002 S.L.T. 1202 (HCJ), Lord McCluskey, Lord Cullen L.J.G., Lord Hamilton

s.15, applied: 2004 c.33 s.116

s.17A, added: 2002 asp 9 Sch.1 para.2

s.17A, amended: 2003 asp 7 Sch.4 para.3, 2004 asp 5 Sch.1 para.3

s.18, amended: 2003 asp 7 s.55

s.18, applied: SSI 2004/257 Reg.19

s.18, referred to: 2003 asp 7 s.56

s.18, repealed (in part): 2003 asp 7 s.55

s.19, amended: 2003 asp 7 s.55

46. Criminal Procedure (Scotland) Act 1995–*cont.*

s.19, applied: SSI 2004/257 Reg.19

s.19A, amended: 2003 asp 7 s.55

s.19A, applied: SSI 2004/257 Reg.19

s.19B, substituted: 2003 asp 7 s.55

s.22A, referred to: 2003 asp 7 s.80

s.23A, amended: 2004 asp 5 Sch.1 para.4

s.24, amended: 2002 asp 9 s.5, 2004 asp 5 Sch.1 para.5

s.24A, added: 2003 c.41 s.199

s.24AZ, added: 2004 asp 5 s.17

s.24B, added: 2004 asp 5 s.17

s.24C, added: 2004 asp 5 s.17

s.24D, added: 2004 asp 5 s.17

s.24E, added: 2004 asp 5 s.17

s.25, amended: 2004 asp 5 s.18, Sch.1 para.6

s.25A, added: 2004 asp 5 Sch.1 para.7

s.27, see *HM Advocate v M* 2003 S.L.T. 1151 (HCJ), Lord Hamilton, Lord Cameron of Lochbroom, Lord Cullen L.J.G.

s.27, amended: 2004 asp 5 Sch.1 para.8

s.28, amended: 2004 asp 5 Sch.1 para.9

s.30, amended: 2004 asp 5 s.18

s.31, amended: 2004 asp 5 s.18, Sch.1 para.10

s.32, amended: 2004 asp 5 Sch.1 para.11

s.34, applied: 2003 asp 7 s.80

s.35, amended: 2002 asp 9 Sch.1 para.3, 2003 asp 7 Sch.4 para.3, 2004 asp 5 Sch.1 para.12

s.44, amended: 2004 asp 8 s.10

s.44, applied: 2003 c.42 s.131

s.47, applied: 2004 asp 8 s.111

s.49, amended: 2003 c.44 s.290

s.49, applied: 2003 c.44 s.291

s.51, amended: 2003 asp 7 s.23

s.52, repealed (in part): 2003 asp 13 Sch.5 Part 1

s.52A, added: 2003 asp 13 s.130

s.52B, added: 2003 asp 13 s.130

s.52C, added: 2003 asp 13 s.130

s.52D, added: 2003 asp 13 s.130

s.52D, applied: 2003 asp 13 s.136

s.52E, added: 2003 asp 13 s.130

s.52F, added: 2003 asp 13 s.130

s.52F, applied: 2003 asp 13 s.287

s.52G, added: 2003 asp 13 s.130

s.52H, added: 2003 asp 13 s.130

s.52J, added: 2003 asp 13 s.130

s.52K, added: 2003 asp 13 s.130

s.52L, added: 2003 asp 13 s.130

s.52L, applied: 2003 asp 13 s.287

s.52M, added: 2003 asp 13 s.130

s.52M, applied: 2003 asp 13 s.136

s.52N, added: 2003 asp 13 s.130

s.52P, added: 2003 asp 13 s.130

s.52P, applied: 2003 asp 13 s.287

s.52Q, added: 2003 asp 13 s.130

s.52R, added: 2003 asp 13 s.130

s.52S, added: 2003 asp 13 s.130

1995–cont.

46. Criminal Procedure (Scotland) Act 1995–cont.

s.52T, added: 2003 asp 13 s.130
s.52U, added: 2003 asp 13 s.130
s.53, applied: 2003 asp 13 s.136
s.53, substituted: 2003 asp 13 s.131
s.54, see *Hughes (Brian Andrew) v HM Advocate* 2002 J.C. 23 (HCJ Appeal), Lord Rodger L.J.G, Lord Cameron of Lochbroom, Lady Paton
s.54, amended: 2003 asp 13 Sch.4 para.8, 2004 asp 5 Sch.1 para.13
s.54, applied: 2003 asp 13 s.136, s.310
s.55, applied: 2003 asp 5 s.10
s.56, amended: 2004 asp 5 Sch.1 para.14
s.56, repealed (in part): 2004 asp 5 Sch.1 para.14
s.57, amended: 2003 asp 7 s.2, 2003 asp 13 Sch.4 para.8
s.57, applied: 2003 asp 13 s.136, SI 2003/495 Reg.7, SI 2003/762 Reg.2, SI 2004/1748 Sch.1, SSI 2003/243 Reg.2
s.57, referred to: 2003 asp 5 s.10
s.57A, added: 2003 asp 13 s.133
s.57A, applied: 2003 asp 13 s.1, s.136, s.289, SI 2003/495 Reg.7
s.57A, referred to: 2003 asp 13 s.137
s.57B, added: 2003 asp 13 s.133
s.57B, applied: SI 2003/495 Reg.7
s.57C, added: 2003 asp 13 s.133
s.57C, applied: SI 2003/495 Reg.7
s.57D, added: 2003 asp 13 s.133
s.57D, applied: SI 2003/495 Reg.7
s.58, amended: 2003 asp 13 Sch.4 para.8, Sch.5 Part 1
s.58, applied: 2003 asp 7 s.7, SI 2003/495 Reg.7, SI 2003/762 Reg.2, SI 2004/1748 Sch.1
s.58, repealed (in part): 2003 asp 13 Sch.5 Part 1
s.59, amended: 2003 asp 13 Sch.4 para.8
s.59, applied: SI 2003/762 Reg.2, SI 2004/1748 Sch.1
s.59, repealed (in part): 2003 asp 13 Sch.5 Part 1
s.59A, applied: 2003 asp 7 s.7, SI 2003/495 Reg.7
s.59A, substituted: 2003 asp 13 Sch.4 para.8
s.60, amended: 2003 asp 13 Sch.4 para.8
s.60A, amended: 2003 asp 13 Sch.4 para.8
s.60B, amended: 2003 asp 13 Sch.4 para.8
s.60C, added: 2003 asp 13 s.134
s.60D, added: 2003 asp 13 s.134
s.61, amended: 2003 asp 13 Sch.4 para.8
s.65, see *Cunningham (Robert John) v HM Advocate* 2002 S.C.C.R. 499 (HCJ Appeal), Lord MacLean, Lord Coulsfield, Lord Sutherland; see *Farrell (Paul Michael) v HM Advocate* 2002 J.C. 50 (HCJ Appeal), Lord Hamilton; see *Gardner (James Scott) v HM Advocate*

1995–cont.

46. Criminal Procedure (Scotland) Act 1995–cont.

s.65–cont.
2003 S.C.C.R. 74 (HCJ), Lord Osborne, Lord Cameron of Lochbroom, Lord Hamilton; see *Goldie (Raymond) v HM Advocate* 2003 S.L.T. 1078 (HCJ), Lord Osborne, Lord Gill L.J.C., Lord Kirkwood; see *HM Advocate v Fitzpatrick (Ian Irwin)* 2002 S.C.C.R. 758 (HCJ), Lord Gill L.J.C., Lord Kirkwood, Lord Osborne; see *Hogg (Steven Kenneth) v HM Advocate* 2002 S.L.T. 639 (HCJ Appeal), Lord Rodger L.J.G., Lord Carloway, Lord Hamilton; see *Kelly (Peter David) v HM Advocate* 2002 S.L.T. 43 (HCJ Appeal), Lord Rodger L.J.G., Lord Osborne, Lord Nimmo Smith; see *Palmer (Jason) v HM Advocate* 2002 S.C.C.R. 908 (HCJ), Lord MacLean, Lord Gill L.J.C., Lord Kingarth; see *Riaviz (Loreno Carlo) v HM Advocate* 2003 S.L.T. 1110 (HCJ), Lord Gill L.J.C., Lord Kirkwood, Lord MacLean
s.65, amended: 2004 asp 5 s.6
s.65, applied: 2002 c.29 s.151
s.65, referred to: SSI 2004/405 Art.3
s.65, repealed (in part): 2004 asp 5 s.6
s.66, see *Bryceland, Petitioner* 2003 S.L.T. 54 (HCJ), Lord Cullen L.J.G., Lord Kirkwood, Lord McCluskey
s.66, amended: 2002 asp 9 Sch.1 para.4, 2003 asp 7 s.61, Sch.4 para.3, 2004 asp 5 s.1, s.7, s.10, Sch.1 para.15
s.66, applied: SSI 2004/176 Art.3
s.66, repealed (in part): 2004 asp 5 s.1, s.7, Sch.1 para.15
s.67, amended: 2004 asp 5 Sch.1 para.16
s.67A, repealed: 2004 asp 5 Sch.1 para.17
s.68, amended: 2004 asp 5 Sch.1 para.18
s.69, amended: 2003 asp 7 Sch.1 para.2, 2004 asp 5 Sch.1 para.19
s.70, amended: 2004 asp 5 s.10
s.70, applied: 2004 c.11 s.21, s.22
s.71, amended: 2002 asp 9 s.8, Sch.1 para.5, 2004 asp 3 s.2, s.7, 2004 asp 5 s.14, s.19, Sch.1 para.20
s.71, applied: 2004 asp 8 s.9
s.71, repealed (in part): 2004 asp 5 Sch.1 para.20
s.71A, added: 2002 asp 9 Sch.1 para.6
s.71A, amended: 2004 asp 3 s.7
s.71A, repealed: 2004 asp 5 Sch.1 para.21
s.72, added: 2004 asp 5 s.1
s.72, amended: 2002 asp 9 s.8
s.72, applied: 2004 asp 8 s.9
s.72, substituted: 2004 asp 5 s.1
s.72A, added: 2002 asp 9 Sch.1 para.7, 2004 asp 5 s.1
s.72A, amended: 2004 asp 3 s.7
s.72A, substituted: 2004 asp 5 s.1
s.72B, added: 2004 asp 5 s.1

1995-cont.

46. Criminal Procedure (Scotland) Act 1995-*cont.*

s.72B, amended: 2004 asp 5 s.1

s.72B, substituted: 2004 asp 5 s.1

s.72C, added: 2004 asp 5 s.1

s.72C, substituted: 2004 asp 5 s.1

s.72D, added: 2004 asp 5 s.1

s.72D, amended: 2004 asp 5 s.1

s.72D, substituted: 2004 asp 5 s.1

s.72E, added: 2004 asp 5 s.1, s.2

s.72E, substituted: 2004 asp 5 s.1

s.72F, added: 2004 asp 5 s.1, s.8

s.72F, substituted: 2004 asp 5 s.1

s.72G, added: 2004 asp 5 s.1, s.12

s.72G, substituted: 2004 asp 5 s.1

s.73, added: 2004 asp 5 s.1

s.73, amended: 2002 asp 9 s.8, 2004 asp 3 s.2, 2004 asp 5 s.1

s.73, substituted: 2004 asp 5 s.1

s.73A, added: 2004 asp 3 s.2, 2004 asp 5 s.1

s.73A, substituted: 2004 asp 5 s.1

s.74, amended: 2004 asp 3 s.2, 2004 asp 5 s.3, Sch.1 para.22

s.75, amended: 2004 asp 5 Sch.1 para.23

s.76, see *Du Plooy (Devonne) v HM Advocate (No.1)* 2003 S.L.T. 1237 (HCJ), Lord Cullen L.J.G., Lord MacLean, Lord Osborne; see *HM Advocate v Millbank (Joseph) (Sentencing)* 2002 S.L.T. 1116 (HCJ Appeal), Lord Gill L.C.J., Lord Kirkwood, Lord MacLean

s.76, amended: 2004 asp 5 Sch.1 para.24

s.76, applied: SSI 2004/176 Art.3

s.78, amended: 2002 asp 9 s.6, 2004 asp 5 Sch.1 para.25

s.79, amended: 2004 asp 8 Sch.4 para.5

s.79, substituted: 2004 asp 5 s.13

s.79A, added: 2004 asp 5 s.14

s.80, repealed: 2004 asp 5 Sch.1 para.26

s.81, applied: SSI 2004/176 Art.3

s.81, substituted: 2004 asp 5 s.9

s.81, varied: SSI 2004/405 Art.4

s.82, amended: 2004 asp 5 Sch.1 para.27

s.83, amended: 2003 asp 7 s.58, 2004 asp 5 Sch.1 para.28

s.83, repealed (in part): 2004 asp 5 Sch.1 para.28

s.83A, referred to: SSI 2004/405 Art.4

s.84, amended: 2004 asp 5 Sch.1 para.29

s.84, repealed (in part): 2004 asp 5 Sch.1 para.29

s.85, amended: 2004 asp 5 Sch.1 para.30

s.85, applied: 2003 asp 7 s.78

s.87, amended: 2004 asp 5 Sch.1 para.31

s.87A, added: 2004 asp 5 s.13

s.90B, added: 2004 asp 5 s.11

s.90C, amended: 2004 asp 5 s.11

s.92, see *Drummond (Andrew Page) v HM Advocate* 2003 S.L.T. 295 (HCJ), Lord Marnoch, Lord Cameron of Lochbroom, Lord Cullen L.J.G.

1995-cont.

46. Criminal Procedure (Scotland) Act 1995-*cont.*

s.92, amended: 2004 asp 5 s.10

s.93, applied: 2003 asp 7 s.21

s.94, amended: 2003 asp 7 s.65

s.99, amended: 2003 asp 7 s.79

s.101, amended: 2002 asp 9 s.10, 2003 asp 7 s.57, Sch.1 para.2

s.103, amended: 2003 asp 7 s.66

s.105, amended: 2003 asp 7 s.66

s.105A, added: 2003 asp 7 s.66

s.106, see *Arthur (Alexander) v HM Advocate (No.1)* 2002 S.C.C.R. 796 (HCJ Appeal), Lord Hamilton, Lord Carloway, Lord Kingarth; see *Binnie (William Smart) v HM Advocate* 2002 S.L.T. 994 (HCJ), Lord Gill L.J.C., Lord Kirkwood, Lord MacLean; see *E v HM Advocate* 2002 J.C. 215 (HCJ Appeal), Lord Gill L.J.C.; see *HM Advocate v Al-Megrahi (No.4)* 2002 J.C. 99 (HCJ Appeal), Lord Cullen L.J.G., Lord Kirkwood, Lord Macfadyen, Lord Nimmo Smith, Lord Osborne; see *Holland (James) v HM Advocate (No.1)* 2003 S.L.T. 1119 (HCJ), Lord Abernethy, Lord Osborne; see *Lyon (Edward) v HM Advocate* 2003 S.C.C.R. 692 (HCJ), Lord McCluskey, Lord Gill L.J.C., Lord Osborne

s.106, amended: 2003 asp 5 s.16, 2003 asp 7 Sch.1 para.2

s.106, applied: 2002 c.29 s.100, 2003 asp 5 s.10, SSI 2003/387 Art.4

s.107, see *Ryan, Petitioner* 2002 S.L.T. 275 (HCJ Appeal), Lord Gill L.J.C., Lady Cosgrove, Lord Marnoch, Lady Paton, Lord Reed

s.107, amended: 2003 asp 7 s.62

s.108, amended: 2002 c.29 s.115

s.108, applied: 2002 c.29 s.151, SSI 2003/387 Art.4

s.109, amended: 2002 c.29 Sch.11 para.29

s.109, applied: 2002 c.29 s.100

s.109, referred to: SSI 2003/210 Art.7

s.110, see *HM Advocate v Al-Megrahi (No.5)* 2002 J.C. 38 (HCJ Appeal), Lord Kirkwood, Lord Carloway, Lord Hamilton, Lord Nimmo Smith, Lord Wheatley

s.110, amended: SSI 2002/387 Art.2, 2004 asp 5 s.24

s.111, amended: 2004 asp 5 s.24

s.112, amended: 2003 asp 7 s.66

s.113, see *HM Advocate v Al-Megrahi (No.5)* 2002 J.C. 38 (HCJ Appeal), Lord Kirkwood, Lord Carloway, Lord Hamilton, Lord Nimmo Smith, Lord Wheatley

s.114, amended: SSI 2003/387 Art.2

s.115, amended: SSI 2003/387 Art.2

s.116, amended: 2003 asp 5 s.16

s.118, see *Cochrane (Ronald) v HM Advocate* 2002 S.L.T. 1424 (HCJ), Lord Gill L.J.C., Lord Kirkwood, Lord Osborne; see *Dunn*

CAP.

1995–cont.

46. Criminal Procedure (Scotland) Act 1995–*cont.*

s.118–*cont.*

(Kevin Joseph) v HM Advocate 2003 S.L.T. 269 (HCJ), Lord MacLean, Lord Kirkwood, Lady Paton; see *HM Advocate v Hemphill (John)* 2002 S.L.T. 754 (HCJ), Lord Prosser

s.118, amended: 2003 asp 5 s.16, 2003 asp 13 Sch.4 para.8

s.118, applied: 2003 asp 13 s.136

s.119, see *HM Advocate v Chalmers (Michael John)* 2003 S.C.C.R. 248 (HCJ), Lord Osborne; see *HM Advocate v Hemphill (John)* 2002 S.L.T. 754 (HCJ), Lord Prosser

s.119, amended: 2004 asp 5 Sch.1 para.32

s.121A, amended: 2003 asp 5 s.16

s.123, see *Lord Advocate's Reference (No.1 of 2001)* 2002 S.L.T. 466 (HCJ), Lord Cullen L.J.G., Lady Cosgrove, Lord Marnoch, Lord McCluskey, Lord Menzies, Lord Nimmo Smith, Lord Wheatley

s.134, applied: 2003 asp 7 s.82, 2003 c.32 s.18, 2003 c.44 Sch.11 para.24, Sch.13 para.22

s.136, see *Shaw v Dyer* 2002 S.L.T. 826 (HCJ Appeal), Lord Marnoch, Lord Macfadyen, Lord Osborne

s.136, applied: SSI 2002/139 Reg.20, SSI 2002/278 Reg.15, SSI 2003/129 Reg.22, 2004 c.33 s.100, SSI 2004/70 Reg.21

s.136, disapplied: SI 2002/111 Art.20, SI 2002/2628 Art.16, SI 2003/1519 Art.20, SI 2004/348 Art.15

s.137A, added: 2003 asp 7 s.58

s.137B, added: 2003 asp 7 s.58

s.140, amended: 2002 asp 9 Sch.1 para.8, 2003 asp 7 s.61, Sch.4 para.3

s.140, repealed (in part): 2004 asp 5 Sch.1 para.33

s.141, amended: 2003 asp 7 s.61

s.143, applied: 2004 c.11 s.21, s.22

s.144, see *Shaw v Dyer* 2002 S.L.T. 826 (HCJ Appeal), Lord Marnoch, Lord Macfadyen, Lord Osborne

s.144, amended: 2002 asp 9 Sch.1 para.9, 2003 asp 7 s.63, Sch.4 para.3

s.145, amended: 2003 asp 7 s.63

s.145A, added: 2003 asp 7 s.63

s.146, amended: 2002 asp 9 Sch.1 para.10, 2003 asp 7 Sch.4 para.3

s.147, applied: 2002 c.29 s.151

s.148, amended: 2002 asp 9 s.8, 2004 asp 3 s.2

s.148A, added: 2002 asp 9 Sch.1 para.11

s.148B, added: 2004 asp 3 s.9

s.149A, added: 2002 asp 9 s.6

s.150, see *Reynolds v Dyer* 2002 S.L.T. 295 (HCJ Appeal), Lord Kirkwood, Lord Nimmo Smith, Lord Weir

CAP.

1995–cont.

46. Criminal Procedure (Scotland) Act 1995–*cont.*

s.150, amended: 2002 asp 4 s.1, 2002 asp 9 Sch.1 para.12

s.151, see *Clarke v Fraser* 2002 S.L.T. 745 (HCJ), Lord Marnoch, Lord Macfadyen, Lord Osborne

s.155, see *Mair (Bryan), Petitioner* 2002 S.L.T. (Sh Ct) 2 (Sh Ct (South Strathclyde, Dumfries and Galloway)), Sheriff IC Simpson

s.156, amended: 2004 asp 5 Sch.1 para.34

s.156, applied: 2003 c.32 Sch.1 para.2, Sch.2 para.2

s.157, see *Higson v Clark* 2003 S.L.T. 253 (HCJ), Lord Marnoch, Lady Cosgrove, Lord Hamilton

s.157, amended: 2002 asp 9 s.8

s.166, see *Clampett v Stott* 2002 J.C. 89 (HCJ Appeal), Lord Cameron of Lochbroom, Lord Marnoch, Lord McCluskey

s.166, amended: 2002 asp 9 s.10

s.167, amended: 2003 asp 7 s.26

s.173, amended: 2003 asp 5 s.16

s.174, applied: SSI 2003/179 Reg.6

s.175, amended: 2002 c.29 s.115, 2003 asp 5 s.16

s.175, applied: 2002 c.29 s.100, s.151, 2003 asp 5 s.10, SSI 2003/387 Art.4

s.176, varied: 2002 c.29 s.100

s.181, amended: 2004 asp 5 s.24

s.186, amended: 2003 asp 5 s.16, 2004 asp 5 s.24

s.187, amended: 2003 asp 5 s.16

s.189, amended: 2003 asp 5 s.16

s.190, amended: 2003 asp 13 Sch.4 para.8

s.190, applied: 2003 asp 13 s.136

s.191, applied: 2003 asp 5 s.7

s.193A, amended: 2003 asp 5 s.16, 2004 asp 8 Sch.4 para.5

s.195, see *Phillips v Houston* 2003 S.C.C.R. 653 (HCJ), Lord Marnoch, Lord Clarke, Lord Hamilton

s.195, amended: 2003 asp 7 Sch.1 para.2

s.196, see *Du Plooy (Devonne) v HM Advocate (No.1)* 2003 S.L.T. 1237 (HCJ), Lord Cullen L.J.G., Lord MacLean, Lord Osborne; see *McIntyre (Joseph Michael) v HM Advocate (Sentencing)* 2003 S.L.T. 229 (HCJ), Lord Gill L.J.C., Lord Kirkwood, Lord Osborne

s.196, amended: 2004 asp 5 s.20

s.198, see *Steele (Robert) v HM Advocate* 2002 S.L.T. 868 (HCJ Appeal), Lord Osborne, Lord Kirkwood, Lord Sutherland

s.200, amended: 2003 asp 13 s.132, Sch.4 para.8, Sch.5 Part 1

s.201, amended: 2003 asp 7 s.21, s.67

s.201, applied: 2002 c.29 s.100

s.201, varied: 2003 asp 7 s.21

s.202, applied: 2002 c.29 s.100

1995–cont.

46. Criminal Procedure (Scotland) Act 1995–cont.

s.204, amended: 2003 asp 7 Sch.1 para.2

s.204B, added: 2003 asp 7 s.26

s.205, see *Stewart (William) v HM Advocate (Sentencing)* 2002 S.L.T. 1307 (HCJ Appeal), Lord Cullen L.J.G., Lord Hamilton, Lord Marnoch

s.205, applied: 2003 asp 7 s.16

s.205B, amended: 2002 c.29 Sch.11 para.29

s.205B, referred to: SSI 2003/210 Art.7

s.207, see *Ross (Scott Andrew) v HM Advocate (Sentencing)* 2002 J.C. 84 (HCJ Appeal), Lord Coulsfield, Judge EF Bowen Q.C.

s.208, amended: 2004 asp 8 s.10

s.208, applied: 2003 asp 7 s.7, s.16, 2003 c.42 s.131, 2003 c.44 s.291

s.208, substituted: 2003 c.44 s.290, 2004 asp 8 s.10

s.209, see *Hepburn (Neil Alexander) v HM Advocate (Sentencing)* 2002 S.C.C.R. 934 (HCJ), Lord Coulsfield, Lord Hamilton

s.209, applied: 2003 asp 5 s.14

s.210, amended: 2003 asp 13 Sch.4 para.8, Sch.5 Part 1, 2003 c.32 Sch.5 para.65

s.210A, see *HM Advocate v Millbank (Joseph) (Sentencing)* 2002 S.L.T. 1116 (HCJ Appeal), Lord Gill L.C.J., Lord Kirkwood, Lord MacLean; see *McGovaney (Stephen) v HM Advocate (Sentencing)* 2002 S.C.C.R. 762 (HCJ), Lord Gill L.J.C., Lord MacLean, Lord Osborne; see *O'Hare v HM Advocate (Sentencing)* 2002 S.L.T. 925 (Note) (HCJ Appeal), Lord Bonomy, Lord Penrose

s.210A, amended: 2003 asp 13 s.312, SSI 2003/48 Art.2, 2004 asp 5 s.21

s.210A, applied: SSI 2003/48

s.210A, referred to: 2003 asp 7 s.21

s.210A, enabling: SSI 2003/48

s.210AA, added: 2003 asp 7 s.20

s.210B, added: 2003 asp 7 s.1

s.210C, added: 2003 asp 7 s.1

s.210D, added: 2003 asp 7 s.1

s.210E, added: 2003 asp 7 s.1

s.210F, added: 2003 asp 7 s.1

s.210F, applied: 2003 asp 7 s.6, 2003 c.42 s.82

s.210G, added: 2003 asp 7 s.1

s.210H, added: 2003 asp 7 s.1

s.211, applied: 2002 c.29 s.130, s.131

s.211, varied: 2002 c.29 s.118

s.214, varied: 2002 c.29 s.118

s.216, varied: 2002 c.29 s.118

s.217, varied: 2002 c.29 s.118

s.218, varied: 2002 c.29 s.118

s.219, amended: 2002 c.29 Sch.11 para.29, 2004 asp 8 Sch.4 para.5

s.219, applied: 2002 c.29 s.118

s.219, referred to: SSI 2003/210 Art.7

1995–cont.

46. Criminal Procedure (Scotland) Act 1995–cont.

s.219, varied: 2002 c.29 s.118

s.220, amended: 2003 asp 7 Sch.4 para.3

s.220, varied: 2002 c.29 s.118

s.221, amended: 2002 asp 17 Sch.3 para.25

s.221, applied: 2002 asp 10 s.3, 2002 c.29 s.118, 2004 asp 6 s.47, SSI 2004/289 Reg.8

s.221, referred to: SSI 2002/51 Art.6, SSI 2003/56 Art.13, SSI 2003/88 Art.6, SSI 2004/44 Art.16, SSI 2004/209 Art.7, SSI 2004/392 Art.11

s.221, varied: 2002 c.29 s.118

s.222, applied: SI 2002/272 Art.5, SI 2004/1237 Art.6, SSI 2002/51 Art.6, SSI 2003/56 Art.13, SSI 2003/88 Art.6, SSI 2004/44 Art.16, SSI 2004/209 Art.7, SSI 2004/392 Art.11

s.222, varied: 2002 c.29 s.118, SI 2003/772 Art.5

s.223, varied: 2002 c.29 s.118

s.224, varied: 2002 c.29 s.118

s.228, amended: 2003 asp 7 s.42

s.228, applied: 2003 asp 13 s.299, 2003 c.44 Sch.9 para.1, SI 2003/762 Reg.2, SI 2004/1748 Sch.1

s.229, see *Lynn v Howdle* 2002 S.L.T. 970 (HCJ), Lord Kirkwood, Lord Marnoch, Lord Sutherland

s.229, applied: SI 2003/762 Reg.2, SI 2004/1748 Sch.1

s.230, amended: 2003 asp 13 s.135, Sch.4 para.8, Sch.5 Part 1

s.230, applied: 2003 asp 13 s.299, SI 2003/762 Reg.2, SI 2004/1748 Sch.1

s.230A, added: 2003 asp 7 s.46

s.232, amended: 2003 asp 7 s.42, s.46, s.60

s.232, applied: 2003 asp 7 s.42, SSI 2003/179 Reg.4

s.233, amended: 2003 asp 7 s.60

s.233, applied: 2003 asp 7 s.42, SSI 2003/179 Reg.4

s.234, amended: 2003 c.44 Sch.32 para.70, Sch.37 Part 7

s.234, repealed (in part): 2003 c.44 Sch.32 para.70, Sch.37 Part 7

s.234A, amended: 2003 asp 7 s.49

s.234A, applied: SSI 2003/179 Reg.4

s.234AA, added: 2004 asp 8 s.118

s.234AB, added: 2004 asp 8 s.118

s.234AB, applied: 2004 asp 8 s.119

s.234B, applied: SI 2003/762 Reg.2, SI 2004/1748 Sch.1, SSI 2003/243 Reg.2

s.234CA, added: 2003 asp 7 s.47

s.234D, amended: 2003 asp 7 s.42

s.234E, amended: 2003 asp 7 s.47, s.60

s.234E, applied: SSI 2003/179 Reg.4

s.234F, amended: 2003 asp 7 s.64

s.234F, applied: SSI 2003/179 Reg.4

1995–cont.

46. Criminal Procedure (Scotland) Act 1995–cont.

s.234G, see *Tweedie v Higson* 2002 S.L.T. 443 (HCJ Appeal), Lord Cameron of Lochbroom, Sir Gerald Gordon Q.C.

s.234G, amended: 2003 asp 7 s.47, s.60

s.234G, applied: 2003 asp 7 s.42, SSI 2003/179 Reg.4

s.234H, amended: 2003 asp 7 s.42

s.234H, applied: 2003 asp 7 s.42

s.235, amended: 2003 asp 7 s.50, 2004 asp 8 Sch.4 para.5

s.235, applied: SSI 2004/194 Art.3

s.235, enabling: SSI 2004/194

s.236, amended: 2003 asp 7 s.50

s.238, see *McCusker v Spiers* 2003 S.L.T. 1263 (HCJ), Lord Macfadyen, Lord Carloway, Temporary Judge Sir Gerald Gordon Q.C.

s.238, applied: 2003 asp 7 s.42

s.239, see *Lynn v Howdle* 2002 S.L.T. 970 (HCJ), Lord Kirkwood, Lord Marnoch, Lord Sutherland

s.239, amended: 2003 asp 7 s.60, 2004 asp 8 Sch.4 para.5

s.239, applied: 2003 c.44 Sch.9 para.2, SSI 2003/179 Reg.4

s.240, amended: 2003 asp 7 s.60

s.240, applied: 2003 c.44 Sch.9 para.2, SSI 2003/179 Reg.4

s.241, applied: 2003 c.44 Sch.9 para.2

s.242, amended: 2003 c.44 Sch.32 para.71

s.242, applied: 2003 c.44 Sch.9 para.2

s.243, applied: 2003 c.44 Sch.9 para.2

s.244, amended: 2002 c.26 Sch.4 para.37, 2003 c.44 Sch.32 para.72

s.244, applied: 2003 c.44 Sch.9 para.2

s.245, applied: 2003 c.44 Sch.9 para.2

s.245A, amended: 2003 asp 7 s.43, s.50, 2004 asp 5 Sch.1 para.35, 2004 asp 8 s.121, Sch.5

s.245A, enabling: SSI 2002/119

s.245C, amended: 2004 asp 5 Sch.1 para.36

s.245C, applied: SSI 2002/119 Reg.5, 2003 asp 7 s.40

s.245C, varied: 2003 c.44 Sch.11 para.23, Sch.13 para.21

s.245C, enabling: SSI 2002/119

s.245D, amended: 2004 asp 8 Sch.4 para.5

s.245E, amended: 2003 asp 7 s.43, s.60, 2004 asp 5 Sch.1 para.37, 2004 asp 8 Sch.4 para.5

s.245E, applied: SSI 2003/179 Reg.4

s.245F, amended: 2003 asp 7 s.43, s.60

s.245F, applied: 2003 c.44 Sch.13 para.14, SSI 2003/179 Reg.4

s.245G, amended: 2004 asp 8 Sch.4 para.5

s.245H, amended: 2004 asp 8 Sch.4 para.5

s.245H, applied: 2003 c.44 Sch.13 para.14

s.245J, added: 2003 asp 7 s.48

s.246, applied: 2003 c.41 s.153

1995–cont.

46. Criminal Procedure (Scotland) Act 1995–cont.

s.247, applied: 2003 c.42 s.134

s.249, applied: 2002 c.29 s.97, s.99, s.100, s.104, s.105, s.106, s.107, s.308, 2003 c.43 Sch.10 para.1

s.249, disapplied: 2002 c.29 s.97

s.255, amended: 2004 asp 5 Sch.1 para.38

s.255A, amended: 2004 asp 5 Sch.1 para.39

s.257, amended: 2004 asp 5 Sch.1 para.40

s.258, amended: 2004 asp 5 s.16, Sch.1 para.41

s.259, see *Daly (James Joseph) v HM Advocate* 2003 S.L.T. 773 (HCJ), Lord Hamilton, Lord Gill L.J.C., Lord MacLean; see *Goldie (Raymond) v HM Advocate* 2003 S.L.T. 1078 (HCJ), Lord Osborne, Lord Gill L.J.C., Lord Kirkwood; see *HM Advocate v Bain (David)* 2002 S.L.T. 340 (HCJ Appeal), Lord Reed; see *HM Advocate v Beggs (No.3)* 2002 S.L.T. 153 (HCJ), Lord Osborne; see *HM Advocate v M* 2003 S.L.T. 1151 (HCJ), Lord Hamilton, Lord Cameron of Lochbroom, Lord Cullen L.J.G.; see *McKenna (Michael) v HM Advocate* 2003 S.L.T. 769 (HCJ), Lord MacLean, Lord Gill L.J.C., Lord Hamilton; see *McPhee (William McAllister) v HM Advocate* 2002 S.L.T. 90 (HCJ Appeal), Lord Rodger L.J.G., Lord Cowie, Lord Marnoch; see *N v HM Advocate* 2003 J.C. 140 (HCJ), Lord Gill L.J.C., Lord Hamilton, Lord MacLean

s.259, amended: 2004 asp 5 Sch.1 para.42

s.260, amended: 2004 asp 5 s.23

s.263, see *Kerr v HM Advocate (Identification Evidence)* 2002 S.L.T. 582 (HCJ), Lord McCluskey, Lord Cameron of Lochbroom, Lord Cullen L.J.G; see *Leckie (Dennis) v HM Advocate* 2002 S.L.T. 595 (HCJ Appeal), Lord Clarke, Lord Bonomy, Lord Marnoch

s.266, see *Robertson (Arthur) v HM Advocate* 2003 S.L.T. 127 (HCJ Appeal), Lord Coulsfield, Lord Osborne, Lord Weir

s.266, amended: 2002 asp 9 s.10

s.267A, added: 2004 asp 5 s.22

s.268, see *Kerr v HM Advocate (Identification Evidence)* 2002 S.L.T. 582 (HCJ), Lord McCluskey, Lord Cameron of Lochbroom, Lord Cullen L.J.G

s.271, see *Hampson (Stewart) v HM Advocate* 2003 S.L.T. 94 (HCJ), Lord Cullen L.J.G., Lord Cameron of Lochbroom, Lord Marnoch

s.271, substituted: 2004 asp 3 s.1

s.271A, amended: 2004 asp 5 Sch.1 para.43

s.271A, repealed (in part): 2004 asp 5 Sch.1 para.43

s.271C, amended: 2004 asp 5 Sch.1 para.44

s.273, referred to: 2003 c.32 s.29

s.274, substituted: 2002 asp 9 s.7

1995–cont.

46. Criminal Procedure (Scotland) Act 1995–cont.

s.275, see *Cumming (Hugh Leishman) v HM Advocate* 2003 S.C.C.R. 261 (HCJ), Lord Cullen L.J.G., Lord McCluskey, Lord Osborne; see *Kinnin (David Henderson) v HM Advocate* 2003 S.C.C.R. 295 (HCJ), Lord Cullen L.J.G., Lord McCluskey, Lord Osborne

s.275, substituted: 2002 asp 9 s.8

s.275A, added: 2002 asp 9 s.10

s.275B, added: 2002 asp 9 s.10

s.275B, amended: 2004 asp 5 Sch.1 para.45

s.275C, added: 2004 asp 3 s.5

s.277, amended: 2004 asp 5 Sch.1 para.46

s.278, amended: 2004 asp 5 Sch.1 para.47

s.279, see *HM Advocate v Al-Megrahi (No.4)* 2002 J.C. 99 (HCJ Appeal), Lord Cullen L.J.G., Lord Kirkwood, Lord Macfadyen, Lord Nimmo Smith, Lord Osborne

s.280, amended: 2004 asp 5 Sch.1 para.48

s.281, see *Dass (Harpitt Singh) v HM Advocate* 2003 S.L.T. 407 (HCJ), Lord Gill L.J.C., Lord Kirkwood, Lord MacLean

s.281, amended: 2004 asp 5 Sch.1 para.49

s.281A, added: 2004 asp 3 s.4

s.281A, amended: 2004 asp 5 Sch.1 para.50

s.282, amended: 2004 asp 5 Sch.1 para.51

s.283, amended: 2004 asp 5 Sch.1 para.52

s.284, amended: 2003 asp 7 s.54, 2004 asp 5 Sch.1 para.53

s.286, amended: 2003 asp 7 s.57, 2004 asp 5 Sch.1 para.54

s.286A, added: 2003 asp 7 s.57

s.288C, added: 2002 asp 9 s.1

s.288C, amended: 2003 asp 7 s.15, 2004 asp 5 s.4, Sch.1 para.55

s.288D, added: 2002 asp 9 s.2

s.288D, amended: 2003 asp 7 s.15, 2004 asp 5 s.4, Sch.1 para.56

s.288E, added: 2004 asp 3 s.6

s.288E, amended: 2004 asp 5 s.4

s.288F, added: 2004 asp 3 s.6

s.288F, amended: 2004 asp 5 s.4

s.288G, added: 2004 asp 3 s.10

s.291, amended: 2002 asp 9 s.4, 2004 asp 3 s.8

s.293, applied: SI 2004/1910 Sch.3

s.294, referred to: 2003 asp 15 s.1, s.2, s.5, s.6, s.8, s.12

s.295, amended: 2003 asp 7 s.24

s.302, amended: 2003 c.21 Sch.17 para.133

s.302, applied: SI 2003/250 Reg.4, Reg.9, SI 2003/2644 Reg.4, Reg.9, SI 2004/585 Reg.4, Reg.9, SI 2004/1020 Reg.4, Reg.9, SSI 2004/114 Sch.1 para.2, Sch.1 para.3

s.305, applied: 2002 c.29 s.386, s.396, s.403, s.408, SSI 2003/387

s.305, enabling: SSI 2002/136, SSI 2002/137, SSI 2002/387, SSI 2002/454, SSI 2002/517, SSI 2003/120, SSI 2003/387,

1995–cont.

46. Criminal Procedure (Scotland) Act 1995–cont.

s.305, enabling:–cont.
SSI 2003/468, SSI 2004/195, SSI 2004/206, SSI 2004/346, SSI 2004/434, SSI 2004/481

s.307, amended: 2003 asp 7 s.57, s.60, s.76, Sch.1 para.2, 2003 asp 13 Sch.4 para.8, Sch.5 Part 1, 2004 asp 3 s.1, 2004 asp 5 Sch.1 para.57

s.307, applied: 2003 asp 7 s.87, SI 2003/495 Reg.7

Sch.1, applied: SI 2002/635 Sch.1 para.2, SI 2002/896 Sch.1 para.57, SI 2004/478 Sch.6 para.111

Sch.1, referred to: SI 2002/57 Sch.4 para.2, SI 2003/237 Sch.4 para.2, SI 2004/291 Reg.5, Sch.6 para.113, SI 2004/478 Reg.5, SI 2004/627 Reg.5, SI 2004/2695 Sch.1 para.6, SSI 2004/115 Reg.5, Sch.5 para.101, SSI 2004/116 Reg.3, Sch.1 para.66

Sch.3 para.2, see *HM Advocate v Chalmers (Michael John)* 2003 S.C.C.R. 248 (HCJ), Lord Osborne

Sch.3 para.10, referred to: 2003 asp 15 s.1, s.2, s.5, s.6, s.8, s.12

Sch.6 para.3, amended: 2003 asp 7 s.46

Sch.6 para.5, amended: 2003 asp 7 s.60

Sch.7 para.3, amended: 2004 asp 8 Sch.4 para.5

Sch.7 para.4, amended: 2003 asp 7 s.50

Sch.7 para.4, applied: SSI 2003/179 Reg.4

Sch.7 para.5, amended: 2003 asp 7 s.50

Sch.7 para.5, applied: SSI 2003/179 Reg.4

Sch.7 para.5A, added: 2003 asp 7 s.60

Sch.8 para.2, see *HM Advocate v Al-Megrahi (No.4)* 2002 J.C. 99 (HCJ Appeal), Lord Cullen L.J.G., Lord Kirkwood, Lord Macfadyen, Lord Nimmo Smith, Lord Osborne

Sch.9, amended: 2003 asp 8 Sch.6 para.22, 2003 c.21 Sch.17 para.133, Sch.19, 2004 asp 5 Sch.1 para.58, 2004 asp 8 Sch.4 para.5

50. Disability Discrimination Act 1995

Commencement Orders: SI 2003/215 Art.1, Art.2

see *Catherall v Michelin Tyre Plc* [2003] I.C.R. 28 (EAT), Nelson, J.; see *Cruickshank v VAW Motorcast Ltd* [2002] I.C.R. 729 (EAT), Judge Altman; see *Kirton v Tetrosyl Ltd* [2003] I.C.R. 37 (EAT), Judge JR Reid Q.C.; see *Law Hospital NHS Trust v Rush* 2002 S.C. 24 (Ex Div), Lord Kirkwood, Lord Cowie, Lord Nimmo Smith; see *Mackay-Ludgate v Lord Advocate* 2002 S.C.L.R. 109 (OH), Lord Philip; see *Power v Panasonic UK Ltd* [2003] I.R.L.R. 151 (EAT), Recorder Slade Q.C.; see *Quinn v Schwarzkopf Ltd* [2002] I.R.L.R. 602 (IH), Lord Coulsfield; see *R. (on the*

CAP.

1995–cont.

50. Disability Discrimination Act 1995–
cont.

see–cont.

application of Longstaff) v Newcastle upon Tyne NHS Primary Care Trust [2003] EWHC 3252, [2004] Lloyd's Rep. Med. 400 (QBD (Admin Ct)), Charles, J.; see Rhys-Harper v Relaxion Group Plc [2003] UKHL 33, [2003] 4 All E.R. 1113 (HL), Lord Nicholls of Birkenhead; see Wilding v British Telecommunications Plc [2002] EWCA Civ 349, [2002] I.C.R. 1079 (CA), Potter, L.J.

applied: 2002 asp 13 s.12, SI 2002/1596 Reg.3, SI 2002/1985 Reg.1, Reg.42, SI 2002/3199 Sch.1 para.21, 2003 c.1 s.439, s.477, SI 2003/439 Art.3, SI 2003/712 Reg.3, SI 2003/3118 Sch.1 para.19, SI 2003/3170 Sch.1 para.21, 2004 asp 4 s.5, SI 2004/753 Sch.1 para.168, SI 2004/1861 Sch.1 para.50, Sch.1 para.61

referred to: SI 2002/757 Sch.1, Sch.10, SI 2003/530 Sch.1, SR 2002/120 Sch.1

Part II, added: SI 2003/1673 Reg.4

Part II, applied: SI 2003/3139 Reg.6, SI 2004/1861 Sch.1 para.22, SI 2004/2300 Art.3, SI 2004/2302 Art.3, SI 2004/2733 Reg.6

Part II, added: SI 2003/2770 Reg.3

Part II, added: SI 2003/1673 Reg.6

Part II, added: SI 2003/1673 Reg.8

Part II, added: SI 2003/1673 Reg.15

Part II, amended: SI 2003/1673 Reg.15

Part II, added: SI 2003/1673 Reg.17

Part III, see Woodrup v Southwark LBC [2002] EWCA Civ 1716, [2003] I.R.L.R. 111 (CA), Simon Brown, L.J.

Part IV, applied: SI 2002/1459 Art.2

Part IV c.001, applied: SI 2002/2216 Sch.1

Part IV c.002, applied: SI 2002/2216 Sch.1

s.1, see College of Ripon and York St John v Hobbs [2002] I.R.L.R.185 (EAT), Lindsay, J. (President); see Hewett v Motorola Ltd [2004] I.R.L.R. 545 (EAT), Judge Ansell; see Johnson & Johnson Medical Ltd v Filmer (No.1) [2002] I.C.R 292 (EAT), Judge Peter Clark; see Latchman v Reed Business Information Ltd [2002] I.C.R. 1453 (EAT), Lindsay, J. (President); see McNicol v Balfour Beatty Rail Maintenance Ltd [2002] EWCA Civ 1074, [2002] I.C.R. 1498 (CA), Mummery, L.J.; see McNicol v Balfour Beatty Rail Maintenance Ltd [2002] I.C.R. 381 (EAT), Commissioner Howell Q.C.; see Morgan v Staffordshire University [2002] I.C.R. 475 (EAT), Lindsay, J. (President); see Murray v Newham Citizens Advice Bureau Ltd [2003] I.C.R. 643 (EAT), Judge Serota Q.C.; see Paul v National Probation Service [2004] I.R.L.R.190 (EAT), Cox, J.; see Swift v Chief Constable of Wiltshire

CAP.

1995–cont.

50. Disability Discrimination Act 1995–
cont.

s.1–cont.

[2004] I.C.R. 909 (EAT), Judge Richardson

s.3A, amended: SI 2003/1673 Reg.4

s.3B, amended: SI 2003/1673 Reg.4

s.4, see Archibald v Fife Council [2004] UKHL 32, [2004] 4 All E.R. 1113 (HL), Lord Nicholls of Birkenhead; see Jones v 3M Healthcare Ltd [2002] EWCA Civ 304, [2002] I.C.R. 1124 (CA), Mummery, L.J.; see Mallon v Corus Constructions & Industrial (2003) 147 S.J.L.B. 1150 (EAT), Judge Burke Q.C.; see Meikle v Nottinghamshire CC [2004] EWCA Civ 859, [2004] 4 All E.R. 97 (CA), Thorpe, L.J.; see Mid Staffordshire General Hospitals NHS Trust v Cambridge [2003] I.R.L.R. 566 (EAT), Keith, J.; see Ree v Redrow Homes (Yorkshire) Ltd (2003) 153 N.L.J. 718 (EAT), Judge Prophet

s.4, amended: SI 2003/1673 Reg.4

s.4, substituted: SI 2003/1673 Reg.5

s.4, varied: SI 2003/1964 Sch.1

s.4, see Archibald v Fife Council [2004] UKHL 32, [2004] 4 All E.R. 303 (HL), Lord Nicholls of Birkenhead; see Jones v 3M Healthcare Ltd [2002] EWCA Civ 304, [2002] I.C.R. 1124 (CA), Mummery, L.J.; see Mallon v Corus Constructions & Industrial (2003) 147 S.J.L.B. 1150 (EAT), Judge Burke Q.C.; see Meikle v Nottinghamshire CC [2004] EWCA Civ 859, [2004] 4 All E.R. 97 (CA), Thorpe, L.J.; see Mid Staffordshire General Hospitals NHS Trust v Cambridge [2003] I.R.L.R. 566 (EAT), Keith, J.; see Ree v Redrow Homes (Yorkshire) Ltd (2003) 153 N.L.J. 718 (EAT), Judge Prophet

s.4, amended: SI 2003/1673 Reg.4

s.4A, amended: SI 2003/1673 Reg.4

s.4B, amended: SI 2003/1673 Reg.4

s.4C, amended: SI 2003/1673 Reg.4

s.4D, amended: SI 2003/1673 Reg.4

s.4E, amended: SI 2003/1673 Reg.4

s.4F, amended: SI 2003/1673 Reg.4

s.4G, amended: SI 2003/1673 Reg.4

s.4H, amended: SI 2003/1673 Reg.4

s.4I, amended: SI 2003/1673 Reg.4

s.4J, amended: SI 2003/1673 Reg.4

s.4K, amended: SI 2003/1673 Reg.4

s.5, see Archibald v Fife Council [2004] UKHL 32, [2004] 4 All E.R. 303 (HL), Lord Nicholls of Birkenhead; see Collins v Royal National Theatre Board Ltd [2004] EWCA Civ 144, [2004] 2 All E.R. 851 (CA), Brooke, L.J.; see Jangra v Gate Gourmet London Ltd (2002) 99(46) L.S.G. 32 (EAT), Judge Burke Q.C.; see Lane Group Plc v Farmiloe [2004] P.I.Q.R. P22 (EAT), Judge Peter Clark; see Mallon v

1995–cont.

50. Disability Discrimination Act 1995– cont.

s.5–*cont.*

Corus Constructions & Industrial (2003) 147 S.J.L.B. 1150 (EAT), Judge Burke Q.C.; see *Meikle v Nottinghamshire CC* [2004] EWCA Civ 859, [2004] 4 All E.R. 97 (CA),Thorpe, L.J.; see *Mid Staffordshire General Hospitals NHS Trust v Cambridge* [2003] I.R.L.R. 566 (EAT), Keith, J.; see *Murphy v Slough BC* [2004] I.C.R. 1163 (EAT), Silber, J.; see *Murray v Newham Citizens Advice Bureau Ltd* [2003] I.C.R. 643 (EAT), Judge Serota Q.C.; see *Paul v National Probation Service* [2004] I.R.L.R. 190 (EAT), Cox, J.; see *Ree v Redrow Homes (Yorkshire) Ltd* (2003) 153 N.L.J. 718 (EAT), Judge Prophet; see *Rowden v Dutton Gregory* [2002] I.C.R. 971 (EAT), Lindsay, J. (President)

s.5, amended: SI 2003/1673 Reg.4

s.5, substituted: SI 2003/1673 Reg.5

s.5, varied: SI 2003/1964 Sch.1

s.5, enabling: SI 2004/153

s.6, see *Archibald v Fife Council* [2004] UKHL 32, [2004] 4 All E.R. 303 (HL), Lord Nicholls of Birkenhead; see *Collins v Royal National Theatre Board Ltd* [2004] EWCA Civ 144, [2004] 2 All E.R. 851 (CA), Brooke, L.J.; see *Jangra v Gate Gourmet London Ltd* (2002) 99(46) L.S.G. 32 (EAT), Judge Burke Q.C.; see *Johnson & Johnson Medical Ltd v Filmer (No.1)* [2002] I.C.R 292 (EAT), Judge Peter Clark; see *Lane Group Plc v Farmiloe* [2004] P.I.Q.R. P22 (EAT), Judge Peter Clark; see *Mallon v Corus Constructions & Industrial* (2003) 147 S.J.L.B. 1150 (EAT), Judge Burke Q.C.; see *Meikle v Nottinghamshire CC* [2004] EWCA Civ 859, [2004] 4 All E.R. 97 (CA), Thorpe, L.J.; see *Mid Staffordshire General Hospitals NHS Trust v Cambridge* [2003] I.R.L.R. 566 (EAT), Keith, J.; see *Murphy v Slough BC* [2004] I.C.R. 1163 (EAT), Silber, J.; see *Paul v National Probation Service* [2004] I.R.L.R. 190 (EAT), Cox, J.; see *Prison Service v Beart* [2003] EWCA Civ 119, [2003] I.C.R. 1068 (CA), Peter Gibson, L.J.; see *Rowden v Dutton Gregory* [2002] I.C.R. 971 (EAT), Lindsay, J. (President); see *Swift v Chief Constable of Wiltshire* [2004] I.C.R. 909 (EAT), Judge Richardson

s.6, amended: SI 2003/1673 Reg.4

s.6, substituted: SI 2003/1673 Reg.5

s.6, varied: SI 2003/1964 Sch.1

s.6, enabling: SI 2004/153

s.6A, amended: SI 2003/1673 Reg.4

s.6B, amended: SI 2003/1673 Reg.4

s.6C, amended: SI 2003/1673 Reg.4

1995–cont.

50. Disability Discrimination Act 1995– cont.

s.7, see *South East Sheffield Citizens Advice Bureau v Grayson* [2004] I.C.R. 1138 (EAT), Rimer, J.; see *Whittaker v P&D Watson (t/a P&M Watson Haulage)* [2002] I.C.R. 1244 (EAT), Lindsay, J. (President)

s.7, amended: SI 2003/1673 Reg.4

s.7, referred to: SI 2003/1964 Art.3

s.7, repealed: SI 2003/1673 Reg.7

s.7A, amended: SI 2003/1673 Reg.4

s.7B, amended: SI 2003/1673 Reg.4

s.7C, amended: SI 2003/1673 Reg.4

s.7D, amended: SI 2003/1673 Reg.4

s.8, amended: SI 2003/1673 Reg.4

s.8, applied: 2002 c.22 Sch.3, Sch.4, Sch.5, SI 2003/2902 Sch.2, Sch.3, Sch.4

s.8, substituted: SI 2003/1673 Reg.9

s.9, amended: SI 2003/1673 Reg.4

s.9, applied: SI 2004/754 Art.2, Art.3

s.9, repealed: SI 2003/1673 Reg.10

s.9, enabling: SI 2004/754, SI 2004/2515

s.10, amended: SI 2003/1673 Reg.4

s.10, substituted: SI 2003/1673 Reg.11

s.11, amended: SI 2003/1673 Reg.4

s.11, repealed: SI 2003/1673 Reg.12

s.11, varied: SI 2003/1964 Sch.1

s.12, amended: SI 2003/1673 Reg.4

s.12, repealed: SI 2003/1673 Reg.12

s.12, varied: SI 2003/1964 Sch.1

s.12, enabling: SI 2004/153

s.13, see *1 Pump Court Chambers v Horton* [2004] EWCA Civ 941, [2004] 3 All E.R. 852 (CA), Peter Gibson, L.J.; see *Cox v General Medical Council* (2003) 70 B.M.L.R. 31 (EAT), Holland, J.

s.13, amended: SI 2003/1673 Reg.4

s.13, substituted: SI 2003/1673 Reg.13

s.13, see *1 Pump Court Chambers v Horton* [2004] EWCA Civ 941, [2004] 3 All E.R. 852 (CA), Peter Gibson, L.J.; see *Cox v General Medical Council* (2003) 70 B.M.L.R. 31 (EAT), Holland, J.

s.13, amended: SI 2003/1673 Reg.4

s.14, amended: SI 2003/1673 Reg.4

s.14, substituted: SI 2003/1673 Reg.13

s.14, amended: SI 2003/1673 Reg.4

s.14A, amended: SI 2003/1673 Reg.4

s.14B, amended: SI 2003/1673 Reg.4

s.14C, amended: SI 2003/1673 Reg.4

s.14D, amended: SI 2003/1673 Reg.4

s.15, amended: SI 2003/1673 Reg.4

s.15, substituted: SI 2003/1673 Reg.13

s.16, amended: SI 2003/1673 Reg.4

s.16, substituted: SI 2003/1673 Reg.14

s.16, varied: SI 2003/1964 Sch.1

s.16, enabling: SI 2004/153

s.16A, amended: SI 2003/1673 Reg.4

s.16B, amended: SI 2003/1673 Reg.4

1995–cont.

50. Disability Discrimination Act 1995–
cont.

s.16C, amended: SI 2003/1673 Reg.4

s.17, amended: SI 2003/1673 Reg.4

s.17, repealed: SI 2003/2770 Reg.4

s.17A, amended: SI 2003/1673 Reg.4, Reg.9

s.17A, applied: 2002 c.22 Sch.3, Sch.4, Sch.5, SI 2003/1673 Reg.2, SI 2004/1861 Sch.1 para.22, Sch.1 para.50, SI 2004/2302 Art.3

s.17B, added: SI 2003/1673 Reg.16

s.17B, amended: SI 2003/1673 Reg.4

s.17C, added: SI 2003/1673 Reg.16

s.17C, amended: SI 2003/1673 Reg.4

s.18, amended: SI 2003/1673 Reg.4

s.18A, amended: SI 2003/1673 Reg.4, Reg.14

s.18A, applied: SI 2004/153 Reg.4, Reg.5, Reg.6, Reg.7, Reg.8

s.18A, varied: SI 2004/153 Reg.9

s.18B, added: SI 2003/1673 Reg.17

s.18B, amended: SI 2003/1673 Reg.4

s.18C, amended: SI 2003/1673 Reg.4

s.18D, added: SI 2003/1673 Reg.18

s.18D, amended: SI 2003/1673 Reg.4, SI 2003/2770 Reg.4

s.19, enabling: SI 2002/1980

s.21, applied: 2002 asp 13 s.11, SR 2003/109 Reg.3, Reg.7

s.21, enabling: SI 2004/1429, SR 2003/109

s.21A, added: SI 2003/1673 Reg.19

s.22, see *Manchester City Council v Romano* [2004] EWCA Civ 834, [2004] 4 All E.R. 21 (CA), Brooke, L.J.; see *North Devon Homes Ltd v Brazier* [2003] EWHC 574, [2003] H.L.R. 59 (QBD), David Steel, J.

s.23, amended: 2004 c.33 Sch.27 para.150

s.24, see *Manchester City Council v Romano* [2004] EWCA Civ 834, [2004] 4 All E.R. 21 (CA), Brooke, L.J.; see *North Devon Homes Ltd v Brazier* [2003] EWHC 574, [2003] H.L.R. 59 (QBD), David Steel, J.

s.25, see *Purves v Joydisc Ltd* 2003 S.L.T. (Sh Ct) 64 (Sh Pr), ID Macphail Q.C., Sheriff Principal

s.25, amended: SI 2003/1673 Reg.19

s.25, applied: SI 2004/1861 Sch.1 para.22, Sch.1 para.50

s.26, amended: SI 2003/1673 Reg.19

s.27, applied: SR 2003/109 Reg.4, Reg.5, Reg.6, Reg.7, Reg.8

s.27, varied: SR 2003/109 Reg.9

s.27, enabling: SR 2003/109

s.28C, applied: SI 2002/928 Sch.3

s.28D, amended: 2002 c.32 Sch.21 para.26

s.28D, applied: SI 2002/1981 Reg.2, Reg.3, SI 2003/2531 Reg.2, Reg.3, Reg.4

s.28D, repealed (in part): 2004 c.31 Sch.5 Part 3

s.28D, varied: SI 2002/928 Sch.3

s.28D, enabling: SI 2002/1981, SI 2003/2531

1995–cont.

50. Disability Discrimination Act 1995–
cont.

s.28E, amended: 2002 c.32 Sch.7 para.5

s.28H, amended: 2002 c.32 Sch.18 para.8

s.28I, amended: 2002 c.32 Sch.18 para.9

s.28J, amended: 2002 c.32 Sch.18 para.10

s.28J, applied: SI 2002/1985, SI 2002/1985 Reg.26, Reg.40

s.28J, repealed (in part): 2002 c.32 Sch.22 Part 2

s.28J, enabling: SI 2002/1985

s.28K, amended: 2002 c.32 Sch.7 para.5

s.28L, see *McAuley Catholic High School v CC* [2003] EWHC 3045, [2004] 2 All E.R. 436 (QBD (Admin Ct)), Silber, J.

s.28L, amended: 2002 c.32 Sch.7 para.5, Sch.21 para.27

s.28M, amended: 2002 c.32 Sch.18 para.11

s.28Q, amended: 2002 c.32 Sch.21 para.28

s.28Q, repealed (in part): 2002 c.32 Sch.7 para.5, Sch.22 Part 3

s.28R, applied: SI 2002/1459, SI 2002/1459 Art.2

s.28R, enabling: SI 2002/1459

s.28T, applied: SI 2002/928 Sch.3

s.28T, referred to: SI 2002/1458 Reg.3

s.28T, varied: SI 2002/2217 Sch.2

s.28U, applied: SI 2002/2217 Art.6

s.28W, applied: SI 2002/1458 Reg.3, Reg.4, Reg.5, Reg.6

s.37A, added: 2002 c.37 s.1

s.37A, amended: 2002 c.37 s.1

s.37A, applied: SI 2003/3122 Reg.2, Reg.3

s.37A, enabling: SI 2003/3122

s.38, amended: 2002 c.37 s.3, 2003 c.39 Sch.8 para.368

s.38, repealed (in part): 2003 c.39 Sch.8 para.368, Sch.10

s.40, applied: SR 2003/37

s.40, enabling: SI 2002/2981, SR 2003/37

s.41, applied: SR 2003/37 Reg.6, Reg.19

s.41, enabling: SR 2003/37

s.42, applied: SR 2003/37 Reg.9, Reg.13, Reg.15, Reg.19

s.42, enabling: SR 2003/37

s.44, applied: SR 2003/37 Reg.19

s.44, enabling: SR 2003/37

s.45, applied: SI 2003/1818, SI 2004/1881, SR 2003/37

s.45, enabling: SI 2003/1818, SI 2004/1881, SR 2003/37

s.47, applied: SI 2002/285, SI 2002/656, SI 2002/657, SI 2002/1166 Reg.13, Reg.22, SI 2002/1188, SI 2002/1694, SI 2002/1762, SI 2002/2873, SI 2002/3001, SI 2002/3002, SI 2003/1436, SI 2003/1562, SI 2003/1687, SI 2003/2408, SI 2004/954, SI 2004/1302, SI 2004/1410, SI 2004/2149, SI 2004/2150

1995–cont.

50. Disability Discrimination Act 1995– cont.

s.47, enabling: SI 2002/285, SI 2002/656, SI 2002/657, SI 2002/1188, SI 2002/1617, SI 2002/1694, SI 2002/1699, SI 2002/1762, SI 2002/2873, SI 2002/3001, SI 2002/3002, SI 2003/1436, SI 2003/1562, SI 2003/1687, SI 2003/1704, SI 2003/2408, SI 2004/954, SI 2004/955, SI 2004/1205, SI 2004/1302, SI 2004/1410, SI 2004/2149, SI 2004/2150, SI 2004/2180, SI 2004/3139, SI 2004/3198

s.49, amended: 2002 c.37 s.4

s.52, enabling: SI 2002/721

s.53, applied: SI 2004/2300 Art.3

s.53A, amended: SI 2003/1673 Reg.20

s.53A, applied: SI 2002/720 Art.2, SI 2003/1673 Reg.1, SI 2004/2302 Art.2

s.53A, disapplied: SI 2004/2302 Art.3

s.53A, enabling: SI 2002/720, SI 2002/2216, SI 2004/2302

s.54, enabling: SI 2004/2300

s.55, amended: SI 2003/1673 Reg.21, SI 2003/2770 Reg.4

s.55, varied: SI 2003/1964 Sch.1

s.56, amended: SI 2003/1673 Reg.22

s.56, applied: SI 2004/1168 Art.3, Art.4, Sch.1, Sch.2

s.56, referred to: SI 2004/752 Reg.14

s.56, enabling: SI 2004/1168

s.57, see *Lane Group Plc v Farmiloe* [2004] P.I.Q.R. P22 (EAT), Judge Peter Clark

s.57, varied: SI 2003/1964 Sch.1

s.58, see *Ree v Redrow Homes (Yorkshire) Ltd* (2003) 153 N.L.J. 718 (EAT), Judge Prophet

s.58, varied: SI 2003/1964 Sch.1

s.59, amended: SI 2003/1673 Reg.23

s.64, amended: 2003 c.20 Sch.5 para.4, SI 2003/1673 Reg.24

s.64, repealed (in part): SI 2003/1673 Reg.24

s.64, varied: 2003 c.20 Sch.5 para.4

s.64A, added: SI 2003/1673 Reg.25

s.66, repealed: SI 2003/1673 Reg.26

s.67, enabling: SI 2002/1980, SI 2002/1981, SI 2002/1985, SI 2002/2216, SI 2002/2981, SI 2003/712, SI 2003/1818, SI 2003/2531, SI 2003/3122, SI 2004/153, SI 2004/1168, SI 2004/1429, SI 2004/1881, SI 2004/2300, SI 2004/2302, SR 2003/109

s.68, see *Burton v Higham (t/a Ace Appointments)* [2003] I.R.L.R. 257 (EAT), Judge McMullen Q.C.; see *South East Sheffield Citizens Advice Bureau v Grayson* [2004] I.C.R. 1138 (EAT), Rimer, J.

s.68, amended: 2002 c.37 s.5, SI 2003/1673 Reg.27

s.68, repealed (in part): SI 2003/1673 Reg.27

s.68, enabling: SI 2002/1980, SI 2002/1981, SI 2002/1985

1995–cont.

50. Disability Discrimination Act 1995– cont.

s.70, amended: SI 2003/1673 Reg.28

s.70, enabling: SI 2003/215, SR 2003/24

Sch.1 para.1, see *Murray v Newham Citizens Advice Bureau Ltd* [2003] I.C.R. 643 (EAT), Judge Serota Q.C.

Sch.1 para.2, see *Latchman v Reed Business Information Ltd* [2002] I.C.R. 1453 (EAT), Lindsay, J. (President); see *Swift v Chief Constable of Wiltshire* [2004] I.C.R. 909 (EAT), Judge Richardson

Sch.1 para.6, see *Woodrup v Southwark LBC* [2002] EWCA Civ 1716, [2003] I.R.L.R. 111 (CA), Simon Brown, L.J.

Sch.1 para.7, enabling: SI 2003/712

Sch.1 para.8, see *Kirton v Tetrosyl Ltd* [2003] EWCA Civ 619, [2003] I.C.R. 1237 (CA), Pill, L.J.; see *Mowat-Brown v University of Surrey* [2002] I.R.L.R. 235 (EAT), Judge Reid Q.C.

Sch.2 para.2C, added: SI 2003/1673 Reg.29

Sch.2 para.3, amended: SI 2003/2770 Reg.4

Sch.2 para.3, substituted: SI 2003/1673 Reg.29

Sch.2 para.4, amended: SI 2003/2770 Reg.4

Sch.2 para.4, substituted: SI 2003/1673 Reg.29

Sch.3 Part I para.1, amended: SI 2003/1673 Reg.29

Sch.3 Part I para.2, amended: SI 2003/1673 Reg.29, SI 2003/2770 Reg.4

Sch.3 Part I para.3, amended: SI 2003/1673 Reg.29

Sch.3 Part I para.3, applied: SI 2004/1168 Art.4

Sch.3 Part I para.4, amended: SI 2003/1673 Reg.29

Sch.3 Part II para.5, amended: SI 2003/1673 Reg.29

Sch.3 Part II para.6, amended: SI 2003/1673 Reg.29

Sch.3 Part II para.7, amended: SI 2003/1673 Reg.29

Sch.3 Part II para.8, amended: SI 2003/1673 Reg.29

Sch.3 Part III para.9, amended: SI 2003/1673 Reg.29

Sch.3 Part III para.10, amended: 2002 c.32 Sch.18 para.12, SI 2003/1673 Reg.29

Sch.3 Part III para.10, applied: SI 2002/1985 Reg.7, Reg.39

Sch.3 Part III para.11, amended: SI 2003/1673 Reg.29

Sch.3 Part IV para.12, amended: SI 2003/1673 Reg.29

Sch.3 Part IV para.13, amended: SI 2003/1673 Reg.29, 2004 c.8 s.19

Sch.3 Part IV para.14, amended: SI 2003/1673 Reg.29

1995–cont.

50. Disability Discrimination Act 1995– cont.

Sch.3 Part IV para.15, amended: SI 2003/ 1673 Reg.29

Sch.3A Part I para.1, added: SI 2003/1673 Sch.1

Sch.3A Part I para.2, added: SI 2003/1673 Sch.1

Sch.3A Part I para.3, added: SI 2003/1673 Sch.1

Sch.3A Part II para.4, added: SI 2003/1673 Sch.1

Sch.3A Part II para.5, added: SI 2003/1673 Sch.1

Sch.3A Part II para.6, added: SI 2003/1673 Sch.1

Sch.3A Part II para.7, added: SI 2003/1673 Sch.1

Sch.3A Part II para.8, added: SI 2003/1673 Sch.1

Sch.3A Part II para.9, added: SI 2003/1673 Sch.1

Sch.3A Part III para.10, added: SI 2003/1673 Sch.1

Sch.3A Part III para.11, added: SI 2003/1673 Sch.1

Sch.4 Part I, applied: SI 2004/153 Reg.4, Reg.5, Reg.6, Reg.7

Sch.4 Part I, amended: SI 2003/1673 Reg.29

Sch.4 Part I para.1, amended: SI 2003/1673 Reg.29

Sch.4 Part I para.2, amended: SI 2003/1673 Reg.29

Sch.4 Part I para.2, varied: SI 2004/153 Reg.9

Sch.4 Part I para.3, amended: SI 2003/1673 Reg.29

Sch.4 Part I para.3, enabling: SI 2004/153

Sch.4 Part I para.4, amended: SI 2003/1673 Reg.29

Sch.4 Part I para.4, enabling: SI 2004/153

Sch.4 Part II, applied: SR 2003/109 Reg.5, Reg.6, Reg.7, Reg.8

Sch.4 Part II para.5, amended: SI 2003/1673 Reg.29

Sch.4 Part II para.5, varied: SR 2003/109 Reg.9

Sch.4 Part II para.6, amended: SI 2003/1673 Reg.29

Sch.4 Part II para.6, varied: SR 2003/109 Reg.9

Sch.4 Part II para.7, amended: SI 2003/1673 Reg.29

Sch.4 Part II para.7, varied: SR 2003/109 Reg.9

Sch.4 Part II para.8, amended: SI 2003/1673 Reg.29

Sch.4 Part II para.8, enabling: SR 2003/109

Sch.4 Part II para.9, amended: SI 2003/1673 Reg.29

Sch.4 Part II para.9, enabling: SR 2003/109

1995–cont.

50. Disability Discrimination Act 1995– cont.

Sch.4 Part III, applied: SI 2002/1458 Reg.3, Reg.4, Reg.5, Reg.6

Sch.4 Part III para.10, amended: SI 2003/ 1673 Reg.29

Sch.4 Part III para.10, substituted: SI 2002/ 1458 Reg.7

Sch.4 Part III para.11, amended: SI 2003/1673 Reg.29

Sch.4 Part III para.12, amended: SI 2003/ 1673 Reg.29

Sch.4 Part III para.13, amended: SI 2003/ 1673 Reg.29

Sch.4 Part III para.13, enabling: SI 2002/1458

Sch.4 Part III para.14, amended: SI 2003/ 1673 Reg.29

Sch.4A para.1, amended: 2002 c.32 Sch.21 para.29

Sch.4A para.1, repealed (in part): 2002 c.32 Sch.22 Part 3

Sch.4A para.3, repealed (in part): 2002 c.32 Sch.21 para.29

Sch.4C Part I para.2, applied: SI 2002/2217 Art.6

Sch.4C Part II para.6, applied: SI 2002/2217 Art.6

Sch.8 para.21A, added: 2002 c.37 s.1

51. Medical (Professional Performance) Act 1995

Sch.1 para.28, repealed (in part): 2003 c.43 Sch.14 Part 4

52. Mental Health (Patients in the Community) Act 1995

s.4, repealed: 2003 asp 13 Sch.5 Part 1

s.5, repealed: 2003 asp 13 Sch.5 Part 1

s.6, repealed: 2003 asp 13 Sch.5 Part 1

Sch.2 para.1, repealed: 2003 asp 13 Sch.5 Part 1

Sch.2 para.2, repealed: 2003 asp 13 Sch.5 Part 1

Sch.2 para.3, repealed: 2003 asp 13 Sch.5 Part 1

Sch.2 para.4, repealed: 2003 asp 13 Sch.5 Part 1

Sch.2 para.5, repealed: 2003 asp 13 Sch.5 Part 1

Sch.2 para.6, repealed: 2003 asp 13 Sch.5 Part 1

Sch.2 para.7, repealed: 2003 asp 13 Sch.5 Part 1

Sch.2 para.8, repealed: 2003 asp 13 Sch.5 Part 1

Sch.2 para.9, repealed: 2003 asp 13 Sch.5 Part 1

Sch.2 para.10, repealed: 2003 asp 13 Sch.5 Part 1

53. Criminal Injuries Compensation Act 1995

s.5, applied: 2002 asp 11 Sch.4 para.5, SI 2003/409 Sch.1 Part I

CAP.

1995–cont.

53. Criminal Injuries Compensation Act 1995–*cont.*
s.7A, added: 2004 c.28 s.57
s.7B, added: 2004 c.28 s.57
s.7C, added: 2004 c.28 s.57
s.7D, added: 2004 c.28 s.57
s.9, amended: 2004 c.28 s.57
s.11, amended: 2003 c.42 Sch.6 para.34, 2004 c.28 s.57

1996

viii. City of Westminster Act 1996
s.2, amended: 2004 c.i Sch.5

Crimes Amendment (Controlled Operations) Act 1996
s.15X, see *Nicholas v Australia (1080/2002)* (2004) 11 I.H.R.R. 933 (UN Human Rights Committee), Judge not specified

Criminal Procedure and Investigation Act 1996
s.3, see *R. v G* [2004] EWCA Crim 1368, [2004] 1 W.L.R. 2932 (CA (Crim Div)), Rose, L.J.
s.7, see *R. v G* [2004] EWCA Crim 1368, [2004] 1 W.L.R. 2932 (CA (Crim Div)), Rose, L.J.

Industrial Tribunals Act 1996
s.6, see *Dispatch Management Services (UK) Ltd v Douglas* [2002] I.R.L.R. 389 (EAT), Wall, J.

ix. London Local Authorities Act 1996
Part II, applied: 2004 c.i s.7
Part II, referred to: 2003 c.iii s.20
s.2, amended: 2004 c.i Sch.5
s.20, repealed: 2003 c.17 Sch.7
s.21, repealed: 2003 c.17 Sch.7
s.22, repealed: 2003 c.17 Sch.7
s.23, repealed: 2003 c.17 Sch.7

xii. Scottish Borders Council (Jim Clark Memorial Rally) Order Confirmation Act 1996
s.2, amended: SI 2003/1542 Sch.1 para.2, Sch.2
s.12, amended: SI 2003/1542 Sch.1 para.2

2. Hong Kong (Overseas Public Servants) Act 1996
s.2, repealed: 2004 c.14 Sch.1 Part 11
s.3, repealed: 2004 c.14 Sch.1 Part 11
s.5, repealed (in part): 2004 c.14 Sch.1 Part 11
s.6, repealed (in part): 2004 c.14 Sch.1 Part 11

3. Wild Mammals (Protection) Act 1996
s.2, amended: 2002 asp 6 Sch.1 para.6
s.2, applied: 2004 c.37 Sch.2 para.5

6. Chemical Weapons Act 1996
s.2, applied: 2002 c.26 Sch.7 para.34, SI 2004/1910 Sch.1
s.2, enabling: SI 2004/2406
s.3, amended: 2002 c.8 s.2
s.11, applied: 2002 c.26 Sch.7 para.34, SI 2004/1910 Sch.1

CAP.

1996–cont.

6. Chemical Weapons Act 1996–*cont.*
s.23, enabling: SI 2004/2406
s.31, amended: 2002 c.26 Sch.7 para.34

8. Finance Act 1996
see *Scottish Provident Institution v Inland Revenue Commissioners* [2002] S.T.C. (S.C.D.) 252 (Sp Comm), J Gordon Reid Q.C.
applied: SI 2002/1970 Reg.6
Part IV c.II, applied: 2002 c.23 s.71, s.81, Sch.23 para.17, Sch.23 para.25, Sch.25 para.63, Sch.26 para.45F, Sch.26 para.45I, Sch.26 para.14, Sch.26 para.19, Sch.26 para.39, Sch.26 para.40, Sch.26 para.42, Sch.26 para.48, Sch.28 para.4, Sch.28 para.5, Sch.28 para.6, Sch.29 para.75, 2002 c.29 Sch.10 para.9, 2004 c.20 s.27, Sch.9 para.33
Part IV c.II, referred to: 2002 c.23 Sch.23 para.26
Part IV c.II, applied: 2002 c.23 Sch.26 para.42
s.30, see *Blom-Cooper v Customs and Excise Commissioners* [2002] EWHC 1421, [2002] S.T.C.1061 (Ch D), Peter Smith, J.
s.38, repealed (in part): 2002 c.23 Sch.40 Part 2
s.40, see *Parkwood Landfill Ltd v Customs and Excise Commissioners* [2002] EWCA Civ 1707, [2003] 1 W.L.R. 697 (CA), Aldous, L.J.; see *Parkwood Landfill Ltd v Customs and Excise Commissioners* [2002] EWHC 47, [2002] S.T.C. 417 (Ch D), Sir Robert Andrew Morritt V.C.
s.42, amended: 2002 c.23 s.122, 2003 c.14 s.187
s.43C, see *Customs and Excise Commissioners v Ebbcliff Ltd* [2003] EWHC 3181, [2004] S.T.C. 391 (Ch D), Etherton, J.; see *Customs and Excise Commissioners v Ebbcliff Ltd* [2003] V. & D.R. 291 (V&DTr), Nuala Brice (Chairman); see *Customs and Excise Commissioners v Ebbcliff Ltd* [2004] EWCA Civ 1071, [2004] S.T.C. 1496 (CA), Peter Gibson, L.J.
s.51, enabling: SI 2002/1, SI 2003/605, SI 2003/2313, SI 2004/769
s.52, enabling: SI 2004/769
s.53, enabling: SI 2002/1, SI 2003/605, SI 2003/2313, SI 2004/769
s.58, amended: SI 2003/2096 Sch.1 para.28
s.62, see *Customs and Excise Commissioners v Ebbcliff Ltd* [2004] EWCA Civ 1071, [2004] S.T.C.1496 (CA), Peter Gibson, L.J.
s.62, enabling: SI 2002/1
s.64, see *Parkwood Landfill Ltd v Customs and Excise Commissioners* [2002] EWHC 47, [2002] S.T.C. 417 (Ch D), Sir Robert Andrew Morritt V.C.
s.66, amended: SI 2002/3153 Sch.5 para.5
s.72, repealed (in part): 2004 c.12 Sch.42 Part 2

1996–cont.

8. Finance Act 1996–*cont.*

s.80, applied: 2002 c.23 Sch.26 para.42

s.80, varied: 2004 c.20 Sch.9 para.11, Sch.9 para.23

s.81, see *HSBC Life (UK) Ltd v Stubbs (Inspector of Taxes)* [2002] S.T.C. (S.C.D.) 9 (Sp Comm), Malachy Cornwell-Kelly

s.81, amended: 2002 c.23 Sch.25 para.2

s.81, referred to: 2002 c.23 Sch.29 para.75

s.81, varied: 2004 c.20 Sch.9 para.11, Sch.9 para.23

s.82, applied: 2002 c.23 Sch.23 para.26, Sch.26 para.42

s.82, varied: 2004 c.20 Sch.9 para.11, Sch.9 para.23

s.83, amended: 2002 c.23 Sch.25 para.3, Sch.40 Part 3

s.83, applied: 2002 c.23 Sch.25 para.61A, 2004 c.20 s.44

s.83, referred to: 2004 c.20 s.44

s.83, repealed (in part): 2002 c.23 Sch.25 para.3, Sch.40 Part 3

s.83, varied: 2004 c.20 Sch.9 para.11, Sch.9 para.23

s.84, amended: 2002 c.23 s.103, Sch.23 para.2, Sch.25 para.4, 2004 c.12 Sch.10 para.1, Sch.42 Part 2

s.84, applied: 2002 c.23 Sch.25 para.9, 2002 c.29 Sch.10 para.9

s.84, repealed (in part): 2004 c.12 Sch.42 Part 2

s.84, varied: 2004 c.20 Sch.9 para.11, Sch.9 para.23

s.84A, added: 2002 c.23 Sch.23 para.3

s.84A, amended: 2004 c.12 Sch.10 para.2

s.84A, applied: 2002 c.23 Sch.23 para.26, SI 2002/1970 Reg.3, Reg.7, Reg.13

s.84A, referred to: SI 2002/1970 Reg.3, Reg.6, Reg.7, Reg.13

s.84A, repealed (in part): 2004 c.12 Sch.42 Part 2

s.84A, varied: 2004 c.20 Sch.9 para.11, Sch.9 para.23

s.84A, enabling: SI 2002/1970, SI 2004/ 3256, SI 2004/3259

s.85, amended: 2002 c.23 s.103, Sch.23 para.4, Sch.25 para.5, Sch.40 Part 3

s.85, substituted: 2004 c.12 Sch.10 para.3

s.85, varied: 2004 c.20 Sch.9 para.11, Sch.9 para.23

s.85A, varied: 2004 c.20 Sch.9 para.11, Sch.9 para.23

s.85B, varied: 2004 c.20 Sch.9 para.11, Sch.9 para.23

s.85B, enabling: SI 2004/3256, SI 2004/ 3271, SI 2004/3347

s.86, amended: 2002 c.23 Sch.25 para.6, Sch.25 para.7

s.86, applied: 2002 c.23 Sch.26 para.19

s.86, substituted: 2004 c.12 Sch.10 para.3

1996–cont.

8. Finance Act 1996–*cont.*

s.86, varied: 2004 c.20 Sch.9 para.11, Sch.9 para.23

s.87, amended: 2002 c.23 Sch.25 para.7, 2004 c.12 Sch.10 para.4

s.87, applied: 2002 c.23 s.73, Sch.26 para.45E, Sch.26 para.6, Sch.26 para.7, Sch.26 para.26

s.87, repealed (in part): 2002 c.23 Sch.40 Part 3

s.87, varied: 2004 c.20 Sch.9 para.11, Sch.9 para.23

s.87A, added: 2002 c.23 Sch.25 para.8

s.87A, applied: 2002 c.23 Sch.26 para.6, Sch.26 para.7, Sch.26 para.26

s.87A, varied: 2004 c.20 Sch.9 para.11, Sch.9 para.23

s.88, disapplied: 2002 c.23 Sch.26 para.6, Sch.26 para.7, Sch.26 para.26

s.88, repealed (in part): 2004 c.12 Sch.42 Part 2

s.88, varied: 2004 c.20 Sch.9 para.11, Sch.9 para.23

s.88A, added: 2002 c.23 s.71

s.88A, amended: 2004 c.12 Sch.10 para.6

s.88A, applied: 2002 c.23 s.71

s.88A, repealed (in part): 2004 c.12 Sch.42 Part 2

s.88A, varied: 2004 c.20 Sch.9 para.11, Sch.9 para.23

s.89, repealed: 2002 c.23 Sch.40 Part 3

s.89, varied: 2004 c.20 Sch.9 para.11, Sch.9 para.23

s.90, amended: 2002 c.23 Sch.25 para.10

s.90, repealed: 2004 c.12 Sch.42 Part 2

s.90, varied: 2004 c.20 Sch.9 para.11, Sch.9 para.23

s.90A, added: 2004 c.12 Sch.10 para.8

s.90A, varied: 2004 c.20 Sch.9 para.11, Sch.9 para.23

s.90A, enabling: SI 2004/3271

s.91, repealed: 2002 c.23 Sch.40 Part 3

s.91, varied: 2004 c.20 Sch.9 para.11, Sch.9 para.23

s.92, amended: 2002 c.23 s.72, s.73, Sch.23 para.5, Sch.40 Part 3

s.92, applied: 2002 c.23 s.72, s.73, Sch.26 para.4, Sch.26 para.5, Sch.26 para.6, Sch.26 para.7, Sch.26 para.8, Sch.26 para.45, SI 2002/1970 Reg.6

s.92, disapplied: 2002 c.23 s.72, s.73

s.92, repealed: 2004 c.12 Sch.42 Part 2

s.92, varied: 2004 c.20 Sch.9 para.11, Sch.9 para.23

s.92A, added: 2002 c.23 s.74

s.92A, applied: 2002 c.23 Sch.26 para.6, SI 2002/1970 Reg.6

s.92A, repealed: 2004 c.12 Sch.42 Part 2

s.92A, varied: 2004 c.20 Sch.9 para.11, Sch.9 para.23

s.93, amended: 2002 c.23 s.75

1996–cont.

8. Finance Act 1996–*cont.*

s.93, applied: 2002 c.23 s.75, s.77, Sch.26 para.4, Sch.26 para.5, Sch.26 para.6, Sch.26 para.7, Sch.26 para.8, Sch.26 para.45, SI 2002/1970 Reg.6, Reg.7

s.93, repealed (in part): 2002 c.23 Sch.40 Part 3, 2004 c.12 Sch.42 Part 2

s.93, varied: 2004 c.20 Sch.9 para.11, Sch.9 para.23

s.93A, added: 2002 c.23 s.76

s.93A, amended: 2002 c.23 Sch.27 para.18

s.93A, applied: 2002 c.23 Sch.26 para.6, Sch.26 para.7

s.93A, repealed (in part): 2002 c.23 Sch.40 Part 3, 2004 c.12 Sch.42 Part 2

s.93A, varied: 2004 c.20 Sch.9 para.11, Sch.9 para.23

s.93B, added: 2002 c.23 s.77

s.93B, repealed: 2004 c.12 Sch.42 Part 2

s.93B, varied: 2004 c.20 Sch.9 para.11, Sch.9 para.23

s.94, amended: 2002 c.23 Sch.25 para.12

s.94, repealed: 2004 c.12 Sch.42 Part 2

s.94, varied: 2004 c.20 Sch.9 para.11, Sch.9 para.23

s.94A, added: 2004 c.12 Sch.10 para.13

s.94A, applied: 2002 c.23 Sch.26 para.45A, Sch.26 para.45F

s.94A, referred to: 2002 c.23 Sch.26 para.45I, Sch.26 para.45D

s.94A, varied: 2004 c.20 Sch.9 para.11, Sch.9 para.23

s.95, amended: 2004 c.12 Sch.10 para.14

s.95, varied: 2004 c.20 Sch.9 para.11, Sch.9 para.23

s.96, repealed (in part): 2004 c.12 Sch.42 Part 2

s.96, varied: 2004 c.20 Sch.9 para.11, Sch.9 para.23

s.97, amended: 2002 c.23 Sch.25 para.13

s.97, varied: 2004 c.20 Sch.9 para.11, Sch.9 para.23

s.98, varied: 2004 c.20 Sch.9 para.11, Sch.9 para.23

s.99, varied: 2004 c.20 Sch.9 para.11, Sch.9 para.23

s.100, amended: 2003 c.14 Sch.38 para.14, SI 2004/2310 Sch.1 para.49

s.100, substituted: 2002 c.23 Sch.23 para.6

s.100, varied: 2004 c.20 Sch.9 para.11, Sch.9 para.23

s.101, amended: 2002 c.23 Sch.27 para.19, 2004 c.12 Sch.10 para.16

s.101, repealed (in part): 2002 c.23 Sch.40 Part 3

s.101, varied: 2004 c.20 Sch.9 para.11, Sch.9 para.23

s.102, varied: 2004 c.20 Sch.9 para.11, Sch.9 para.23

1996–cont.

8. Finance Act 1996–*cont.*

s.103, see *HSBC Life (UK) Ltd v Stubbs (Inspector of Taxes)* [2002] S.T.C. (S.C.D.) 9 (Sp Comm), Malachy Cornwell-Kelly

s.103, amended: 2002 c.23 Sch.23 para.7, Sch.25 para.14, Sch.25 para.15, Sch.25 para.16, 2004 c.12 Sch.10 para.17, Sch.42 Part 2

s.103, repealed (in part): 2004 c.12 Sch.42 Part 2

s.103, varied: 2004 c.20 Sch.9 para.11, Sch.9 para.23

s.104, varied: 2004 c.20 Sch.9 para.11, Sch.9 para.23

s.105, varied: 2004 c.20 Sch.9 para.11, Sch.9 para.23

s.106, repealed: 2003 c.1 Sch.8 Part 1

s.107, repealed: 2003 c.1 Sch.8 Part 1

s.108, repealed: 2003 c.1 Sch.8 Part 1

s.109, repealed: 2003 c.1 Sch.8 Part 1

s.110, repealed: 2003 c.1 Sch.8 Part 1

s.113, repealed: 2003 c.1 Sch.8 Part 1

s.114, repealed: 2003 c.1 Sch.8 Part 1

s.115, applied: 2003 c.1 Sch.7 para.76

s.115, repealed: 2003 c.1 Sch.8 Part 1

s.120, repealed (in part): 2003 c.1 Sch.8 Part 1

s.148, amended: 2004 c.12 Sch.35 para.44

s.151, referred to: 2003 c.1 s.655

s.151, enabling: SI 2003/2339, SI 2004/575

s.152, repealed: 2003 c.1 Sch.8 Part 1

s.164, repealed (in part): 2004 c.12 Sch.42 Part 2

s.172, repealed: 2004 c.12 Sch.42 Part 3

s.178, repealed: 2004 c.12 Sch.42 Part 2

s.190, amended: 2003 c.14 Sch.20 para.3

s.197, applied: SI 2004/674 Reg.24

s.197, enabling: SI 2003/230

Sch.5 Part I para.2, repealed (in part): 2003 c.44 Sch.37 Part 6, SI 2004/1501 Sch.2

Sch.5 Part I para.2, enabling: SI 2004/769

Sch.5 Part III para.12, repealed (in part): 2002 c.40 Sch.26

Sch.5 Part III para.13, enabling: SSI 2002/560

Sch.6 para.26, repealed: 2003 c.14 Sch.43 Part 3

Sch.7 para.5, repealed: 2003 c.1 Sch.8 Part 1

Sch.7 para.17, repealed: 2003 c.14 Sch.43 Part 5

Sch.8 para.1, amended: 2002 c.23 Sch.25 para.19

Sch.8 para.2, amended: 2002 c.23 Sch.25 para.19

Sch.8 para.2, repealed: 2002 c.23 Sch.40 Part 3

Sch.8 para.3, amended: 2002 c.23 Sch.25 para.18, Sch.25 para.19, SI 2004/2310 Sch.1 para.50

Sch.8 para.4, amended: 2002 c.23 Sch.25 para.19

Sch.8 para.5, amended: 2002 c.23 Sch.25 para.19

1996–cont.

8. Finance Act 1996–*cont.*

Sch.9, referred to: 2004 c.12 Sch.5 para.5, Sch.8 para.1

Sch.9, amended: 2004 c.12 Sch.10 para.20

Sch.9, amended: 2004 c.12 Sch.10 para.22

Sch.9, amended: 2004 c.12 Sch.10 para.23

Sch.9, amended: 2004 c.12 Sch.10 para.24

Sch.9, amended: 2004 c.12 Sch.10 para.25

Sch.9, added: 2004 c.12 Sch.10 para.36

Sch.9 para.1, substituted: 2002 c.23 Sch.25 para.20

Sch.9 para.1A, added: 2002 c.23 Sch.25 para.21

Sch.9 para.2, amended: 2002 c.23 Sch.25 para.22, 2003 c.14 Sch.37 para.2, Sch.43 Part 3, 2004 c.12 Sch.8 para.2, Sch.35 para.45

Sch.9 para.3, amended: 2004 c.12 Sch.10 para.19

Sch.9 para.4, repealed: 2002 c.23 Sch.40 Part 3

Sch.9 para.5, amended: 2002 c.23 Sch.23 para.8, 2004 c.12 Sch.8 para.3, Sch.10 para.20

Sch.9 para.5, repealed (in part): 2004 c.12 Sch.42 Part 2

Sch.9 para.5A, added: 2002 c.23 Sch.25 para.23

Sch.9 para.5A, amended: 2004 c.12 Sch.10 para.21, Sch.42 Part 2

Sch.9 para.6, amended: 2002 c.23 Sch.23 para.9, Sch.25 para.24, 2004 c.12 Sch.10 para.22, Sch.42 Part 2

Sch.9 para.6A, added: 2002 c.23 Sch.25 para.25

Sch.9 para.6A, amended: 2003 c.14 Sch.41 para.4, SI 2003/2096 Sch.1 para.29, 2004 c.12 Sch.8 para.4, Sch.10 para.23

Sch.9 para.6A, repealed: 2004 c.12 Sch.8 para.4

Sch.9 para.6B, added: 2002 c.23 Sch.25 para.26

Sch.9 para.6B, amended: 2004 c.12 Sch.10 para.24

Sch.9 para.6C, added: 2002 c.23 Sch.25 para.27

Sch.9 para.6C, amended: 2004 c.12 Sch.10 para.25, Sch.42 Part 2

Sch.9 para.8, amended: 2004 c.12 Sch.10 para.26

Sch.9 para.9, amended: 2004 c.12 Sch.10 para.27, Sch.42 Part 2

Sch.9 para.10, amended: 2002 c.23 Sch.25 para.28, 2004 c.12 Sch.10 para.28

Sch.9 para.10A, added: 2004 c.12 Sch.8 para.5

Sch.9 para.10A, repealed (in part): 2004 c.12 Sch.42 Part 2

Sch.9 para.11, amended: 2002 c.23 Sch.23 para.10, 2004 c.12 Sch.5 para.6, Sch.10 para.30

1996–cont.

8. Finance Act 1996–*cont.*

Sch.9 para.11, repealed (in part): 2002 c.23 Sch.40 Part 3

Sch.9 para.11A, added: 2002 c.23 Sch.23 para.11

Sch.9 para.11A, amended: 2004 c.12 s.34, Sch.42 Part 2

Sch.9 para.11A, repealed (in part): 2004 c.12 Sch.42 Part 2

Sch.9 para.12, amended: 2002 c.23 Sch.23 para.12, Sch.25 para.29, 2003 c.14 Sch.37 para.3, 2004 c.12 Sch.5 para.7, Sch.10 para.31, SI 2004/2200 Reg.9

Sch.9 para.12, repealed (in part): 2004 c.12 Sch.42 Part 2

Sch.9 para.13, amended: 2002 c.23 Sch.23 para.13, Sch.25 para.30, Sch.40 Part 3, 2004 c.12 Sch.42 Part 2

Sch.9 para.14, amended: 2002 c.23 s.103, Sch.25 para.31, 2004 c.12 Sch.10 para.33, Sch.42 Part 2

Sch.9 para.15, amended: 2002 c.23 Sch.25 para.32, Sch.40 Part 3, 2003 c.14 Sch.38 para.18, Sch.43 Part 3

Sch.9 para.16, amended: 2004 c.12 Sch.42 Part 2

Sch.9 para.16, substituted: 2004 c.12 Sch.5 para.8

Sch.9 para.17, amended: 2002 c.23 Sch.25 para.33, Sch.40 Part 3, 2003 c.14 Sch.37 para.4

Sch.9 para.17, referred to: 2003 c.14 Sch.37 para.4

Sch.9 para.17, repealed (in part): 2002 c.23 Sch.40 Part 3

Sch.9 para.17, varied: 2002 c.23 Sch.25 para.62

Sch.9 para.18, amended: 2002 c.23 Sch.25 para.34, Sch.40 Part 3, 2003 c.14 Sch.37 para.5, 2004 c.12 Sch.8 para.6

Sch.9 para.18, applied: 2002 c.23 Sch.25 para.63

Sch.9 para.18, referred to: 2003 c.14 Sch.37 para.5

Sch.9 para.18, repealed (in part): 2004 c.12 Sch.42 Part 2

Sch.9 para.18, varied: 2002 c.23 Sch.25 para.63

Sch.9 para.19, added: 2002 c.23 Sch.25 para.35

Sch.9 para.19, amended: 2004 c.12 Sch.10 para.35

Sch.9 para.19, repealed (in part): 2004 c.12 Sch.42 Part 2

Sch.9 para.19B, enabling: SI 2004/3271, SI 2004/3347

Sch.9 para.20, added: 2002 c.23 Sch.25 para.36

Sch.9 para.20, repealed (in part): 2004 c.12 Sch.42 Part 2

Sch.10, substituted: 2002 c.23 Sch.25 para.38

1996–cont.

8. **Finance Act 1996**–*cont.*

Sch.10, amended: 2004 c.12 Sch.10 para.40

Sch.10 para.1, amended: 2002 c.23 s.103

Sch.10 para.1, substituted: 2002 c.23 Sch.25 para.37

Sch.10 para.1A, substituted: 2004 c.12 Sch.10 para.38

Sch.10 para.2A, amended: 2004 c.12 Sch.10 para.39, Sch.42 Part 2

Sch.10 para.2B, amended: 2004 c.12 Sch.10 para.40, Sch.42 Part 2

Sch.10 para.3, repealed: 2004 c.12 Sch.26 para.1, Sch.42 Part 2

Sch.10 para.3, substituted: 2002 c.23 Sch.25 para.39

Sch.10 para.3, varied: SI 2004/2572 Reg.6, Reg.7

Sch.10 para.4, amended: 2004 c.12 Sch.10 para.41

Sch.10 para.7, amended: 2004 c.12 Sch.26 para.12

Sch.10 para.8, amended: 2002 c.23 Sch.27 para.20, 2004 c.12 Sch.26 para.12

Sch.11 Part I para.1, amended: 2002 c.23 Sch.23 para.14, Sch.25 para.40, 2004 c.12 Sch.10 para.42

Sch.11 Part I para.1, varied: 2002 c.23 Sch.26 para.42

Sch.11 Part I para.2, amended: 2003 c.14 Sch.33 para.3

Sch.11 Part I para.2, varied: 2002 c.23 Sch.26 para.42

Sch.11 Part I para.3, varied: 2002 c.23 Sch.26 para.42

Sch.11 Part I para.3A, amended: 2002 c.23 Sch.23 para.15, Sch.40 Part 3

Sch.11 Part I para.3A, varied: 2002 c.23 Sch.26 para.42

Sch.11 Part I para.4, amended: 2003 c.14 Sch.43 Part 3, 2004 c.12 Sch.6 para.9, Sch.42 Part 2

Sch.11 Part I para.4, varied: 2002 c.23 Sch.26 para.42

Sch.11 Part I para.5, varied: 2002 c.23 Sch.26 para.42

Sch.11 Part I para.6, varied: 2002 c.23 Sch.26 para.42

Sch.12, applied: 2002 c.29 Sch.10 para.5

Sch.12, repealed: 2002 c.23 Sch.40 Part 3

Sch.13, applied: SI 2004/1450 Reg.24

Sch.13, substituted: 2003 c.14 Sch.39 para.5

Sch.13 para.1, amended: 2003 c.14 Sch.39 para.1, Sch.43 Part 3

Sch.13 para.1, referred to: SI 2002/2006 Reg.14

Sch.13 para.1, repealed (in part): 2003 c.14 Sch.43 Part 3

Sch.13 para.2, see *Campbell v Inland Revenue Commissioners* [2004] S.T.C. (S.C.D.) 396 (Sp Comm), Theodore Wallace

1996–cont.

8. **Finance Act 1996**–*cont.*

Sch.13 para.2, repealed: 2003 c.14 Sch.43 Part 3

Sch.13 para.3A, added: 2002 c.23 s.104

Sch.13 para.6, amended: 2003 c.14 Sch.39 para.5

Sch.13 para.6, applied: 2003 c.14 Sch.39 para.6

Sch.13 para.6, repealed (in part): 2003 c.14 Sch.43 Part 3

Sch.13 para.7, repealed: 2003 c.14 Sch.43 Part 3

Sch.13 para.8, amended: 2004 c.12 s.138

Sch.13 para.9, amended: 2004 c.12 s.138

Sch.13 para.9A, added: 2002 c.23 s.104

Sch.13 para.9A, repealed: 2003 c.14 Sch.43 Part 3

Sch.13 para.11, repealed: 2003 c.14 Sch.43 Part 3

Sch.13 para.14, amended: 2003 c.14 Sch.43 Part 3, 2004 c.12 s.138

Sch.13 para.14, referred to: 2004 c.12 s.138

Sch.13 para.14A, added: 2003 c.14 Sch.39 para.3

Sch.13 para.14B, added: 2004 c.12 s.138

Sch.13 para.14C, added: 2004 c.12 s.138

Sch.13 para.14D, added: 2004 c.12 s.138

Sch.13 para.14E, added: 2004 c.12 s.138

Sch.13 para.15, amended: 2003 c.14 Sch.39 para.4, 2004 c.12 s.138

Sch.14 para.8, repealed: 2004 c.12 Sch.42 Part 2

Sch.14 para.67, repealed: 2002 c.23 Sch.40 Part 3

Sch.14 para.68, repealed: 2002 c.23 Sch.40 Part 3

Sch.14 para.69, repealed: 2002 c.23 Sch.40 Part 3

Sch.14 para.70, repealed: 2002 c.23 Sch.40 Part 3

Sch.14 para.71, repealed: 2002 c.23 Sch.40 Part 3

Sch.14 para.72, repealed: 2002 c.23 Sch.40 Part 3

Sch.14 para.73, repealed: 2002 c.23 Sch.40 Part 3

Sch.14 para.74, repealed: 2002 c.23 Sch.40 Part 3

Sch.14 para.75, repealed: 2002 c.23 Sch.40 Part 3

Sch.14 para.76, repealed: 2002 c.23 Sch.40 Part 3

Sch.14 para.77, repealed: 2002 c.23 Sch.40 Part 3

Sch.14 para.78, repealed: 2002 c.23 Sch.40 Part 3

Sch.14 para.79, repealed: 2002 c.23 Sch.40 Part 3

Sch.15 Part I para.8, amended: 2003 c.14 Sch.27 para.8

CAP.

CAP.

1996–cont.

8. Finance Act 1996–*cont.*

Sch.15 Part I para.11, amended: 2002 c.23 Sch.25 para.41

Sch.15 Part I para.11A, added: 2002 c.23 Sch.25 para.42

Sch.15 Part I para.22, repealed: 2002 c.23 Sch.40 Part 3

Sch.15 Part I para.23, repealed: 2002 c.23 Sch.40 Part 3

Sch.15 Part I para.24, repealed: 2002 c.23 Sch.40 Part 3

Sch.15 Part I para.25, repealed: 2002 c.23 Sch.40 Part 3

Sch.16 para.1, repealed: 2003 c.1 Sch.8 Part 1

Sch.16 para.2, applied: 2003 c.1 Sch.7 para.75

Sch.16 para.2, repealed: 2003 c.1 Sch.8 Part 1

Sch.16 para.3, applied: 2003 c.1 Sch.7 para.75

Sch.16 para.3, repealed: 2003 c.1 Sch.8 Part 1

Sch.16 para.4, repealed: 2003 c.1 Sch.8 Part 1

Sch.16 para.5, repealed: 2003 c.1 Sch.8 Part 1

Sch.20 para.6, repealed: 2003 c.1 Sch.8 Part 1

Sch.20 para.7, repealed: 2003 c.1 Sch.8 Part 1

Sch.20 para.8, repealed: 2003 c.1 Sch.8 Part 1

Sch.20 para.9, repealed: 2003 c.1 Sch.8 Part 1

Sch.20 para.10, repealed: 2003 c.1 Sch.8 Part 1

Sch.20 para.41, repealed: 2003 c.1 Sch.8 Part 1

Sch.20 para.42, repealed: 2003 c.1 Sch.8 Part 1

Sch.20 para.68, repealed: 2002 c.23 Sch.40 Part 3

Sch.20 para.69, repealed: 2002 c.23 Sch.40 Part 3

Sch.20 para.70, repealed: 2002 c.23 Sch.40 Part 3

Sch.20 para.71, repealed: 2002 c.23 Sch.40 Part 3

Sch.21 para.17, repealed: 2004 c.12 Sch.42 Part 3

Sch.31 para.3, repealed (in part): 2004 c.12 Sch.42 Part 2

Sch.39 Part I para.2, repealed: 2004 c.12 Sch.42 Part 3

14. Reserve Forces Act 1996

referred to: 2003 c.44 s.337

Part I, applied: 2003 c.13 Sch.2 Part 23, 2004 c.9 Sch.2 Part 22

Part III, applied: 2003 c.13 Sch.2 Part 23, 2004 c.9 Sch.2 Part 22

Part IV, applied: 2003 c.13 Sch.2 Part 23, 2004 c.9 Sch.2 Part 22

Part V, applied: 2003 c.13 Sch.2 Part 23, 2004 c.9 Sch.2 Part 22

Part XI, applied: SI 2002/2034 Reg.14, SR 2002/298 Reg.14

1996–cont.

14. Reserve Forces Act 1996–*cont.*

s.1, applied: SI 2002/377 Sch.1 para.36, SI 2002/3199 Sch.2 para.20, SI 2003/3170 Sch.3 para.20

s.1, referred to: SI 2003/3118 Sch.2 para.20

s.24, applied: 2003 c.13 Sch.2 Part 2

s.75, amended: 2003 c.44 Sch.37 Part 9

s.75, disapplied: 2003 c.44 Sch.25 para.97

s.78, applied: 2003 c.44 Sch.25 para.98

s.79, applied: 2003 c.44 Sch.25 para.98

s.82, amended: 2003 c.44 Sch.37 Part 9

s.82, disapplied: 2003 c.44 Sch.25 para.98

s.87, amended: 2003 c.44 Sch.37 Part 9

s.87, disapplied: 2003 c.44 Sch.25 para.99

s.99, amended: 2003 c.44 Sch.37 Part 9

s.99, disapplied: 2003 c.44 Sch.25 para.100

Sch.1 para.5, amended: 2003 c.44 Sch.32 para.162, Sch.37 Part 9

Sch.1 para.5, disapplied: 2003 c.44 Sch.25 para.101

Sch.2 para.3, amended: 2003 c.44 Sch.3 para.65

Sch.2 para.7, amended: 2003 c.39 Sch.8 para.369

Sch.3 para.9, amended: 2003 c.39 Sch.8 para.370

15. National Health Service (Residual Liabilities) Act 1996

s.1, see *R. v Pennine Acute Hospitals NHS Trust (formerly Rochdale Healthcare NHS Trust)* [2003] EWCA Crim 3436, [2004] 1 All E.R. 1324 (CA (Crim Div)), Tuckey, L.J.

s.2, repealed (in part): 2004 asp 7 Sch.2

16. Police Act 1996

applied: SI 2002/325 Sch.2 para.8, SI 2002/327 Sch.2 para.7, SI 2002/812 Sch.2 para.7, SI 2002/919 Sch.2 para.9A, Sch.3 para.13A, Sch.8 para.9, Sch.8 para.9A, 2003 c.20 s.21, s.22, s.23, SI 2003/527 Reg.2, SI 2003/781 Sch.2 para.7, 2004 c.20 s.66

Part IV c.I, applied: SI 2003/2601 Reg.4, SI 2004/671 Art.2, Art.4

Part IV c.I, disapplied: 2002 c.30 s.26

Part IV c.I, referred to: SI 2003/2601 Reg.3

Part IV c.I, applied: 2002 c.30 s.28

s.2, applied: SI 2003/527 Reg.11, SI 2003/3171 Sch.1 Part 1, SI 2003/3172 Sch.1

s.3, applied: SI 2002/695 Art.3, 2003 c.26 s.23, s.33, s.103, 2003 c.39 Sch.2 para.1, 2004 c.34 Sch.14 para.2

s.5, amended: 2003 c.39 Sch.8 para.371

s.5, repealed (in part): 2003 c.39 Sch.8 para.371, Sch.8 para.372, Sch.10

s.5B, applied: 2004 c.34 Sch.14 para.2

s.5C, amended: 2003 c.39 Sch.8 para.372

s.5C, repealed (in part): 2003 c.39 Sch.10

s.6A, amended: 2002 c.30 s.92

s.6A, applied: SI 2002/2526 Reg.2, 2003 c.20 s.55

s.6A, enabling: SI 2002/2526

1996–cont.

16. Police Act 1996–*cont.*

s.8, applied: 2002 c.30 s.40
s.8, amended: 2002 c.30 s.92, Sch.7 para.14
s.8, applied: 2003 c.20 s.52
s.9, amended: 2002 c.30 s.92
s.9E, amended: 2002 c.30 s.30, s.31, s.32
s.9F, amended: 2002 c.30 s.32
s.9FA, amended: 2002 c.30 s.32
s.9G, amended: 2002 c.30 s.32
s.11, amended: 2002 c.30 s.30, s.31, s.32
s.11, applied: SI 2003/527 Reg.11
s.11A, amended: 2002 c.30 s.32
s.12, amended: 2002 c.30 s.32
s.12A, applied: SI 2004/645 Reg.43
s.15, applied: SI 2003/527 Reg.24
s.18, substituted: 2002 c.30 s.101
s.23, amended: 2004 c.20 Sch.14 para.7, SI 2004/1573 Art.12
s.23, varied: 2003 c.20 Sch.5 para.4
s.24, amended: SI 2004/1573 Art.12
s.24, applied: 2002 c.30 s.16
s.24, varied: 2003 c.20 Sch.5 para.4
s.25, amended: SI 2004/1573 Art.12
s.25, varied: 2003 c.20 Sch.5 para.4
s.26, amended: 2002 c.1 Sch.4
s.29, applied: 2004 c.20 s.55
s.29, varied: 2003 c.20 s.24, s.25
s.30, varied: 2003 c.20 Sch.5 para.4
s.32, applied: SI 2003/527 Reg.21
s.36A, added: 2002 c.30 s.1
s.36A, applied: 2004 c.20 Sch.12 para.1
s.36A, referred to: 2003 c.20 s.75
s.37, applied: SI 2002/695, 2003 c.20 s.50, SI 2003/830, 2004 c.20 Sch.12 para.1
s.37, enabling: SI 2002/695, SI 2003/830
s.39, applied: 2003 c.20 s.47
s.39A, added: 2002 c.30 s.2
s.39A, applied: 2003 c.20 s.48
s.40, substituted: 2002 c.30 s.4
s.41A, added: 2002 c.30 s.5
s.41B, added: 2002 c.30 s.5
s.42, amended: 2002 c.30 s.33
s.42, repealed (in part): 2002 c.30 Sch.8
s.42A, added: 2002 c.30 s.34
s.50, applied: 2002 c.30 s.36, s.82, 2003 c.20 s.36, s.42, 2004 c.20 s.58, Sch.13 para.3
s.50, referred to: 2003 c.20 s.42
s.50, enabling: SI 2002/767, SI 2002/1758, SI 2002/2529, SI 2002/3162, SI 2002/3180, SI 2003/527, SI 2003/528, SI 2003/2594, SI 2003/2595, SI 2003/2596, SI 2003/2599, SI 2003/2600, SI 2004/645, SI 2004/3216
s.51, amended: 2002 c.30 s.35
s.51, applied: 2002 c.30 s.36, s.82, 2003 c.20 s.37, s.42
s.51, enabling: SI 2002/3180, SI 2004/645
s.52, applied: 2003 c.20 s.38, s.42
s.53, amended: 2002 c.30 s.6

1996–cont.

16. Police Act 1996–*cont.*

s.53, applied: 2003 c.20 s.44
s.53A, added: 2002 c.30 s.7
s.53A, applied: 2003 c.20 s.45
s.53A, varied: 2003 c.20 s.45
s.54, amended: 2002 c.30 s.3, s.84, Sch.7 para.15
s.54, applied: 2003 c.20 s.67, SI 2003/409 Sch.1 Part I
s.55, applied: 2003 c.20 s.63
s.57, applied: SI 2002/534 Art.2, SI 2004/2409 Art.5
s.59, referred to: 2004 c.20 s.64, s.65
s.59, varied: 2002 c.30 s.90, s.91
s.60, applied: 2003 c.20 s.39, s.42
s.60, enabling: SI 2004/2660
s.61, referred to: SI 2003/527 Reg.46, SSI 2004/257 Reg.46
s.62, amended: 2002 c.30 s.90, s.91, Sch.7 para.16, Sch.8
s.62, applied: SI 2002/1758, SI 2002/2529, SI 2003/527, SI 2003/527 Reg.46, SI 2003/2594, SI 2003/2717, SR 2002/95, SR 2002/100, SR 2003/184, SSI 2003/220, SSI 2004/121, SSI 2004/257
s.62, referred to: SSI 2004/257 Reg.46
s.63, amended: 2002 c.30 s.90, s.91, Sch.7 para.17
s.63, applied: SI 2002/1758, SI 2002/2529, SI 2002/3162, SI 2003/527, SI 2003/528, SI 2003/2594, SI 2003/2595, SI 2003/2596, SI 2003/2599, SI 2003/2600, SI 2003/2601, SI 2003/2602, SI 2004/643, SI 2004/645
s.63, repealed (in part): 2002 c.30 Sch.8
s.64, referred to: 2004 c.20 s.64, s.65
s.65, repealed: 2002 c.30 Sch.8
s.65, varied: SI 2004/671 Art.2
s.66, repealed: 2002 c.30 Sch.8
s.66, varied: SI 2004/671 Art.2
s.67, applied: SI 2004/671 Art.4
s.67, repealed: 2002 c.30 Sch.8
s.67, varied: SI 2004/671 Art.2
s.68, applied: SI 2004/671 Art.4
s.68, repealed: 2002 c.30 Sch.8
s.68, varied: SI 2004/671 Art.2
s.69, repealed: 2002 c.30 Sch.8
s.69, varied: SI 2004/671 Art.2
s.70, repealed: 2002 c.30 Sch.8
s.70, varied: SI 2004/671 Art.2
s.71, applied: SI 2004/671 Art.2
s.71, repealed: 2002 c.30 Sch.8
s.71, varied: SI 2004/671 Art.2
s.72, repealed: 2002 c.30 Sch.8
s.72, varied: SI 2004/671 Art.2
s.73, repealed: 2002 c.30 Sch.8
s.73, varied: SI 2004/671 Art.2
s.74, applied: SI 2004/671 Art.4
s.74, repealed: 2002 c.30 Sch.8
s.74, varied: SI 2004/671 Art.2

1996–cont.

16. Police Act 1996–*cont.*

s.75, applied: SI 2003/2601 Sch.1 para.3, SI 2004/671 Art.4

s.75, repealed: 2002 c.30 Sch.8

s.75, varied: SI 2004/671 Art.2

s.76, repealed: 2002 c.30 Sch.8

s.76, varied: SI 2004/671 Art.2

s.77, repealed: 2002 c.30 Sch.8

s.77, varied: SI 2004/671 Art.2

s.78, applied: 2002 c.30 s.9, s.26

s.78, repealed: 2002 c.30 Sch.8

s.78, varied: SI 2004/671 Art.2

s.79, repealed: 2002 c.30 Sch.8

s.79, varied: SI 2004/671 Art.2

s.80, see *R. (on the application of Green) v Police Complaints Authority* [2001] EWHC Admin 1160, [2002] U.K.H.R.R. 293 (QBD (Admin Ct)), Moses, J.; see *R. (on the application of Green) v Police Complaints Authority* [2004] UKHL 6, [2004] 1 W.L.R. 725 (HL), Lord Bingham of Cornhill

s.80, repealed: 2002 c.30 Sch.8

s.80, varied: SI 2004/671 Art.2

s.81, repealed: 2002 c.30 Sch.8

s.81, varied: SI 2004/671 Art.2

s.81, enabling: SI 2003/2602

s.82, repealed: 2002 c.30 Sch.8

s.82, varied: SI 2004/671 Art.2

s.83, repealed: 2002 c.30 Sch.8

s.83, varied: SI 2004/671 Art.2

s.84, applied: 2003 c.20 s.36, s.42, SI 2004/645 Reg.17, Reg.35

s.85, applied: 2003 c.20 s.36, s.42, SI 2004/645 Reg.34

s.85, enabling: SI 2003/2597

s.86, repealed: 2002 c.30 Sch.8

s.87, amended: 2002 c.30 Sch.7 para.18

s.88, see *Weir v Bettison (Sued as Chief Constable of Merseyside)* [2003] EWCA Civ 111, [2003] I.C.R. 708 (CA), Sir Denis Henry

s.88, amended: 2002 c.30 s.102, s.103

s.88, applied: SI 2004/1127 Art.2

s.88, varied: 2003 c.20 s.25

s.88, enabling: SI 2004/1127

s.89, see *Hobson v Chief Constable of Cheshire* [2003] EWHC 3011, (2004) 168 J.P. 111 (QBD (Admin Ct)), Maurice Kay, J.

s.89, amended: 2002 c.30 s.104, 2003 c.44 Sch.26 para.47

s.89, applied: 2003 c.20 s.68, SI 2004/1127 Art.2

s.89, varied: 2003 c.32 s.84, 2004 c.20 s.68

s.89, enabling: SI 2004/1127

s.90, applied: 2003 c.20 s.68

s.90, referred to: 2003 c.20 Sch.5 para.3

s.90, varied: 2003 c.20 s.68, 2004 c.20 s.68

s.91, amended: 2004 c.20 s.68

s.91, varied: 2003 c.20 Sch.5 para.4

1996–cont.

16. Police Act 1996–*cont.*

s.97, amended: 2002 c.1 Sch.3 para.11, Sch.4, 2002 c.29 Sch.11 para.30, 2002 c.30 s.102, Sch.7 para.19

s.97, applied: 2002 c.30 s.29, Sch.3 para.19, SI 2003/527 Reg.24

s.97, referred to: 2003 c.20 s.49

s.97, varied: SI 2003/527 Reg.40

s.101, amended: 2003 c.20 Sch.5 para.4

s.101, applied: 2003 c.14 Sch.9 para.1, 2003 c.20 Sch.4 para.7, 2004 c.36 Sch.1 para.3

s.101, varied: 2003 c.20 Sch.5 para.4

s.105, amended: 2002 c.30 Sch.8

Sch.1, referred to: 2003 c.39 s.4, SI 2004/1192

Sch.2 para.1, amended: 2003 c.39 Sch.8 para.373

Sch.2 para.7, substituted: 2003 c.39 Sch.8 para.373

Sch.2 para.8, substituted: 2003 c.39 Sch.8 para.373

Sch.2 para.11, amended: SI 2004/1941 Sch.1 para.7

Sch.2 para.14, amended: 2003 c.39 Sch.8 para.373

Sch.2 para.18, amended: 2003 c.39 Sch.8 para.373

Sch.2 para.19, amended: 2003 c.39 Sch.8 para.373, Sch.10

Sch.2 para.25, repealed: 2002 c.30 s.94, Sch.8

Sch.2 para.25A, amended: 2002 c.30 s.94

Sch.2 para.27, substituted: 2003 c.39 Sch.8 para.373

Sch.2A para.1, amended: 2003 c.39 Sch.8 para.374

Sch.2A para.5, substituted: 2003 c.39 Sch.8 para.374

Sch.2A para.7, amended: SI 2004/1941 Sch.1 para.7

Sch.2A para.9, amended: 2003 c.39 Sch.8 para.374

Sch.2A para.13, amended: 2003 c.39 Sch.8 para.374

Sch.2A para.14, amended: 2003 c.39 Sch.8 para.374, Sch.10

Sch.2A para.20, repealed: 2002 c.30 s.94, Sch.8

Sch.2A para.20A, amended: 2002 c.30 s.94

Sch.2A para.22, substituted: 2003 c.39 Sch.8 para.374

Sch.3 para.1, amended: 2003 c.39 Sch.8 para.375

Sch.3 para.3, disapplied: SI 2004/671 Art.4

Sch.3 para.11, enabling: SI 2002/1282

Sch.3A para.1, added: 2003 c.39 Sch.8 para.376

Sch.3A para.2, added: 2003 c.39 Sch.8 para.376

Sch.3A para.3, added: 2003 c.39 Sch.8 para.376

CAP.

1996–cont.

16. Police Act 1996–*cont.*

Sch.3A para.4, added: 2003 c.39 Sch.8 para.376

Sch.3A para.5, added: 2003 c.39 Sch.8 para.376

Sch.3A para.6, added: 2003 c.39 Sch.8 para.376

Sch.4, applied: SI 2002/2312 Art.2

Sch.4, substituted: 2002 c.30 s.83

Sch.5 para.1, repealed: 2002 c.30 Sch.8

Sch.5 para.2, repealed: 2002 c.30 Sch.8

Sch.5 para.3, repealed: 2002 c.30 Sch.8

Sch.5 para.4, repealed: 2002 c.30 Sch.8

Sch.5 para.5, repealed: 2002 c.30 Sch.8

Sch.5 para.6, repealed: 2002 c.30 Sch.8

Sch.5 para.7, repealed: 2002 c.30 Sch.8

Sch.5 para.8, repealed: 2002 c.30 Sch.8

Sch.5 para.9, repealed: 2002 c.30 Sch.8

Sch.5 para.10, repealed: 2002 c.30 Sch.8

Sch.5 para.11, repealed: 2002 c.30 Sch.8

Sch.5 para.12, repealed: 2002 c.30 Sch.8

Sch.5 para.13, repealed: 2002 c.30 Sch.8

Sch.7 Part I para.1, amended: 2003 c.26 Sch.8 Part 1

Sch.7 Part II para.23, repealed: 2003 c.44 Sch.37 Part 10

Sch.8 Part III para.13, applied: 2002 c.30 s.26

17. Employment Tribunals Act 1996

see *Johnston v Miller Bros & FP Butler Ltd* [2002] I.C.R. 744 (EAT), Recorder Langstaff Q.C.

applied: SI 2003/694 Sch.1 para.21, 2004 c.35 s.261

referred to: SI 2003/1964 Art.6, 2004 c.24 s.42

s.1, referred to: SI 2003/1964 Art.6

s.1, enabling: SI 2004/1861

s.3, see *Thorpe v Dul* [2003] I.C.R. 1556 (EAT), Wall, J.

s.3, applied: SI 2004/1861 Sch.1 para.22

s.4, applied: SI 2004/1861 Sch.1 para.18, Sch.1 para.26

s.4, varied: SI 2004/1861 Reg.12

s.4, enabling: SI 2004/1861, SI 2004/2351

s.5, applied: SI 2004/1861 Sch.1 para.38, Sch.1 para.48

s.7, amended: 2002 c.22 s.24, s.25, s.26

s.7, applied: 2002 c.22 s.32, SI 2004/1861 Sch.1 para.10

s.7, enabling: SI 2002/2972, SI 2004/1861, SI 2004/2351

s.7A, added: 2002 c.22 s.27

s.7A, enabling: SI 2004/1861

s.9, amended: 2002 c.22 s.28

s.9, enabling: SI 2004/1861, SI 2004/2351

s.10, amended: 2004 c.24 s.36, Sch.1 para.24

s.10, enabling: SI 2004/1861, SI 2004/2351

s.10A, enabling: SI 2004/1861

s.11, enabling: SI 2004/1861

s.12, amended: SI 2003/1673 Reg.31

CAP.

1996–cont.

17. Employment Tribunals Act 1996–*cont.*

s.12, enabling: SI 2004/1861

s.13, amended: 2002 c.22 s.22

s.13, enabling: SI 2004/1861

s.13A, added: 2002 c.22 s.22

s.13A, enabling: SI 2004/1861

s.18, amended: 2002 c.22 s.24, Sch.7 para.23, SI 2002/2034 Sch.2 para.2, SI 2003/1660 Sch.5 para.1, SI 2003/1661 Sch.5 para.1, SI 2003/1673 Reg.31, SI 2003/3049 Sch.2 para.2, 2004 c.24 Sch.1 para.25, SI 2004/1713 Sch.2 para.1, SI 2004/2326 Reg.46

s.18, applied: SI 2002/2822 Reg.34, SI 2003/694 Sch.1 para.21, SI 2003/3049 Reg.19, SI 2004/753 Sch.1 para.26, SI 2004/1713 Reg.20, SI 2004/2326 Reg.52, SI 2004/2333 Sch.1 para.26

s.18, referred to: SI 2004/1713 Reg.20

s.19, amended: 2002 c.22 Sch.7 para.23

s.19, repealed (in part): 2002 c.22 s.24, Sch.8 Part 1

s.19, substituted: 2002 c.22 s.24

s.19, enabling: SI 2004/1861

s.20, amended: SI 2004/2326 Reg.48

s.21, amended: SI 2002/2034 Sch.2 para.2, SI 2003/1660 Sch.5 para.1, SI 2003/1661 Sch.5 para.1, SI 2003/3049 Sch.2 para.2, 2004 c.24 s.38, SI 2004/1713 Sch.2 para.1, SI 2004/2326 Reg.49

s.21, disapplied: SI 2004/2326 Reg.48

s.21, repealed (in part): 2002 c.21 Sch.6

s.28, see *De Haney v Brent MIND* [2003] EWCA Civ 1637, [2004] I.C.R. 348 (CA), Carnwath, L.J.

s.30, see *Miriki v General Council of the Bar* [2001] EWCA Civ 1973, [2002] I.C.R. 505 (CA), Peter Gibson, L.J.

s.30, repealed (in part): 2004 c.24 Sch.1 para.26, Sch.2

s.30, enabling: SI 2004/2526

s.31, enabling: SI 2004/2526

s.32, enabling: SI 2004/2526

s.33, amended: 2004 c.24 s.49

s.34, substituted: 2002 c.22 s.23

s.34, enabling: SI 2004/2526

s.35, see *Tran v Greenwich Vietnam Community Project* [2002] EWCA Civ 553, [2002] I.C.R. 1101 (CA), Sedley, L.J.

s.36, repealed (in part): 2004 c.24 Sch.1 para.27, Sch.2

s.41, enabling: SI 2004/1861, SI 2004/2351, SI 2004/2526

s.42, amended: 2004 c.24 s.49

18. Employment Rights Act 1996

see *Secretary of State for Trade and Industry v Frid* [2002] B.P.I.R. 1040 (Ch D (Bankruptcy Ct)), Registrar Jaques

applied: 2002 c.22 s.45, 2002 c.40 Sch.3 para.15, SI 2002/1311 Reg.5, SI 2002/2788 Reg.29, Reg.30, SI 2002/2822

CAP.

1996–cont.

18. Employment Rights Act 1996–*cont.*
applied: 2002 c.22 s.45–*cont.*
  Reg.39, 2003 asp 5 s.18, 2003 c.1 Sch.3 para.34, 2003 c.26 Sch.5 para.8, 2003 c.37 Sch.3 para.9, 2003 c.43 Sch.8 para.3, 2004 c.35 s.261, SI 2004/753 Sch.1 para.26, SI 2004/2333 Sch.1 para.26, SSI 2003/344 Reg.5
  referred to: SI 2002/808 Art.2, SI 2002/3207 Reg.16, 2003 c.43 Sch.4 para.99, 2004 c.24 s.42
  Part I, applied: SI 2003/3319 Reg.14
  Part IVA, see *Street v Derbyshire Unemployed Workers Centre* [2004] EWCA Civ 964, [2004] 4 All E.R. 839 (CA), Auld, L.J.
  Part IVA, applied: 2002 c.22 Sch.2 para.15
  Part IVA, referred to: SI 2004/753 Sch.1 para.166
  Part IX, applied: SI 2004/1964 Sch.6 para.10
  Part X, see *Eastwood v Magnox Electric Plc* [2002] EWCA Civ 463, [2003] I.C.R. 520 (CA), Peter Gibson, L.J.; see *Johnson v Unisys Ltd* [2001] UKHL 13, [2003] 1 A.C. 518 (HL), Lord Hoffmann
  Part X, applied: SI 2002/2034 Reg.6, SI 2002/2788 Reg.28, Reg.29, SI 2002/3207 Reg.16, SI 2004/752 Reg.4, SI 2004/753, SI 2004/753 Sch.1 para.113, SI 2004/2326 Reg.42
  Part X, disapplied: 2002 c.40 Sch.3 para.15
  Part X, referred to: SI 2004/753 Sch.1 para.9, Sch.1 para.18
  Part XI, applied: SI 2002/221 Sch.5 para.11, 2003 c.26 Sch.5 para.8, 2003 c.43 Sch.8 para.3, 2004 c.17 Sch.2 para.3, 2004 c.23 Sch.3 para.3, SI 2004/753 Sch.1 para.149, Sch.1 para.157, SI 2004/1573 Art.6
  Part XI, disapplied: SI 2004/753 Sch.1 para.161
  Part XI, referred to: SI 2004/753 Sch.1 para.150, Sch.1 para.155
  Part XII, see *Benson v Secretary of State for Trade and Industry* [2003] I.C.R. 1082 (EAT), Burton, J.; see *Secretary of State for Trade and Industry v Frid* [2003] 2 B.C.L.C. 284 (Ch D (Companies Court)), David Mackie Q.C.
  Part XII, applied: SI 2002/10 Sch.1, SI 2003/3038 Sch.1
  Part XIV c.I, applied: SI 2002/2034 Reg.8, SI 2002/2788 Reg.2, SI 2002/3236 Reg.3, 2003 c.43 Sch.1 para.3, SI 2004/753 Sch.1 para.141
  Part XIV c.II, applied: 2002 c.22 s.38, SI 2002/2788 Reg.31, SI 2002/3207 Reg.15, SI 2003/694 Sch.1 para.99, SI 2004/753 Sch.1 para.143, SI 2004/2326 Reg.40, SI 2004/2333 Sch.1 para.120
  s.1, applied: 2002 c.22 s.38
  s.3, amended: 2002 c.22 s.35
  s.3, repealed (in part): 2002 c.22 s.36, Sch.8 Part 1

CAP.

1996–cont.

18. Employment Rights Act 1996–*cont.*
  s.4, applied: 2002 c.22 s.38
  s.7A, added: 2002 c.22 s.37
  s.7B, added: 2002 c.22 s.37
  s.11, applied: SI 2004/1861 Reg.14
  s.13, see *Gill v Ford Motor Co Ltd* [2004] I.R.L.R. 840 (EAT), Beatson, J.; see *Jowitt v Pioneer Technology (UK) Ltd* [2002] I.R.L.R. 790 (EAT), Judge DM Levy Q.C.; see *Langshaw v Plume School Governing Body* [2003] E.L.R. 97 (EAT), Judge Peter Clark; see *Silva v Albion Hotel (Freshwater) Ltd* [2002] I.R.L.R. 200 (EAT), Judge Serota Q.C.
  s.13, applied: SI 2004/1861 Sch.1 para.22
  s.14, see *Gill v Ford Motor Co Ltd* [2004] I.R.L.R. 840 (EAT), Beatson, J.
  s.14, applied: SI 2004/1861 Sch.1 para.22
  s.15, applied: SI 2004/1861 Sch.1 para.22
  s.16, applied: SI 2004/1861 Sch.1 para.22
  s.17, applied: SI 2004/1861 Sch.1 para.22
  s.18, applied: SI 2004/1861 Sch.1 para.22
  s.19, applied: SI 2004/1861 Sch.1 para.22
  s.20, applied: SI 2004/1861 Sch.1 para.22
  s.21, applied: SI 2004/1861 Sch.1 para.22
  s.22, applied: SI 2004/1861 Sch.1 para.22
  s.23, see *List Design Group Ltd v Douglas* [2002] I.C.R. 686 (EAT), Bell, J.
  s.23, applied: 2002 c.22 Sch.3, Sch.4, Sch.5, SI 2004/1861 Sch.1 para.22
  s.24, applied: SI 2004/1861 Sch.1 para.22
  s.25, applied: SI 2004/1861 Sch.1 para.22
  s.26, applied: SI 2004/1861 Sch.1 para.22
  s.27, see *Campbell v Union Carbide Ltd* [2002] Emp. L.R. 1267 (EAT), Judge Peter Clark; see *Canada Life Ltd v Gray* [2004] I.C.R. 673 (EAT), Judge Peter Clark
  s.27, amended: 2002 c.22 Sch.7 para.25
  s.27, applied: SI 2004/1861 Sch.1 para.22
  s.28, applied: SI 2002/2927 Art.4, SI 2004/1861 Sch.1 para.22
  s.29, repealed (in part): SI 2002/2034 Sch.2 para.3
  s.31, amended: SI 2002/10 Sch.1, SI 2002/2927 Sch.1, SI 2003/3038 Sch.1
  s.35, amended: SI 2002/794 Sch.1 para.37
  s.36, amended: 2003 c.18 s.1
  s.43A, applied: SI 2004/2326 Reg.42, Reg.44
  s.43B, see *Bladon v ALM Medical Services Ltd* [2002] EWCA Civ 1085, [2002] I.C.R. 1444 (CA), Mummery, L.J.; see *Kraus v Penna Plc* [2004] I.R.L.R. 260 (EAT), Cox, J.; see *Parkins v Sodexho Ltd* [2002] I.R.L.R. 109 (EAT), Judge J Altman; see *Street v Derbyshire Unemployed Workers Centre* [2004] EWCA Civ 964, [2004] 4 All E.R. 839 (CA), Auld, L.J.

1996–cont.

18. **Employment Rights Act 1996**–*cont.*

s.43C, see *Street v Derbyshire Unemployed Workers Centre* [2004] EWCA Civ 964, [2004] 4 All E.R. 839 (CA), Auld, L.J.

s.43C, enabling: SI 2002/2788

s.43F, see *Miklaszewicz v Stolt Offshore Ltd* 2002 S.C. 232 (Ex Div), Lord Nimmo Smith, Lord Marnoch, Lord Weir

s.43F, enabling: SI 2003/1993, SI 2004/3265

s.43G, see *Street v Derbyshire Unemployed Workers Centre* [2004] EWCA Civ 964, [2004] 4 All E.R. 839 (CA), Auld, L.J.; see *Street v Derbyshire Unemployed Workers Centre* [2004] I.C.R. 213 (EAT), Judge J McMullen Q.C.

s.43K, amended: 2002 c.17 Sch.2 para.63, 2003 c.43 Sch.11 para.65, Sch.14 Part 4, SI 2004/957 Sch.1 para.8

s.43K, repealed (in part): 2003 c.43 Sch.14 Part 4

s.43K, varied: SI 2004/288 Art.7, SI 2004/480 Art.6, SI 2004/865 Art.109, SI 2004/1016 Art.85, SSI 2004/163 Art.96

s.43KA, added: 2002 c.30 s.37

s.45A, amended: SI 2003/3049 Sch.2 para.3, SI 2004/1713 Sch.2 para.2

s.47B, see *Edgar v Meteorological Office* [2002] I.C.R. 149 (EAT), Judge Peter Clark; see *Knight v Harrow LBC* [2003] I.R.L.R. 140 (EAT), Recorder Underhill Q.C.

s.47B, applied: SI 2004/1861 Sch.1 para.22

s.47C, see *South Central Trains Ltd v Rodway* [2004] I.R.L.R. 777 (EAT), Judge Birtles

s.47C, amended: 2002 c.22 Sch.7 para.26

s.47C, applied: SI 2002/2788 Reg.28

s.47C, enabling: SI 2002/2788, SI 2002/2789, SI 2003/921

s.47D, added: 2002 c.21 Sch.1 para.1

s.47E, added: 2002 c.22 s.47

s.48, amended: 2002 c.21 Sch.1 para.1, 2002 c.22 Sch.7 para.27, 2004 c.24 s.40, s.41

s.48, applied: 2002 c.22 Sch.3, Sch.4, Sch.5, SI 2002/3207 Reg.16, SI 2004/2326 Reg.45

s.49, see *Virgo Fidelis Senior School v Boyle* [2004] I.C.R. 1210 (EAT), Judge Ansell

s.49, amended: 2002 c.21 Sch.1 para.1

s.49, applied: SI 2004/2326 Reg.45

s.49A, amended: 2002 c.30 s.95

s.50, see *Riley-Williams v Argos Ltd* (2003) 147 S.J.L.B. 695 (EAT), Judge McMullen Q.C.

s.50, amended: SI 2002/2469 Sch.1 para.22, 2003 c.43 Sch.4 para.100

s.50, applied: SI 2002/377 Sch.1 para.36, SI 2002/3199 Sch.2 para.20, SI 2003/3118 Sch.2 para.20, SI 2003/3170 Sch.3 para.20, SI 2004/1861 Sch.1 para.22

s.50, varied: SI 2004/1822 Sch.1 para.18

s.52, applied: SI 2004/1861 Sch.1 para.22

1996–cont.

18. **Employment Rights Act 1996**–*cont.*

s.53, applied: SI 2004/1861 Sch.1 para.22

s.55, amended: SI 2002/253 Sch.5 para.13, SI 2004/1771 Sch.1 para.3

s.55, applied: SI 2002/377 Sch.1 para.36, SI 2002/3199 Sch.2 para.20, SI 2003/3118 Sch.2 para.20, SI 2003/3170 Sch.3 para.20, SI 2004/1861 Sch.1 para.22

s.56, applied: SI 2004/1861 Sch.1 para.22

s.57A, see *Forster v Cartwright Black* [2004] I.R.L.R. 781 (EAT), Beatson, J.; see *Qua v John Ford Morrison Solicitors* [2003] I.C.R. 482 (EAT), Recorder Cox Q.C.

s.57A, amended: 2004 c.33 Sch.27 para.151

s.58, amended: 2004 c.35 Sch.13 Part 1

s.62, applied: SI 2004/2326 Reg.40

s.64, applied: SI 2004/1861 Sch.1 para.22

s.65, repealed (in part): SI 2002/2034 Sch.2 para.3

s.66, varied: SI 2003/1964 Sch.1

s.67, varied: SI 2003/1964 Sch.1

s.68, applied: SI 2004/1861 Sch.1 para.22

s.68, varied: SI 2003/1964 Sch.1

s.70, varied: SI 2003/1964 Sch.1

s.71, applied: SI 2002/509 Reg.6

s.71, enabling: SI 2002/2789

s.71, amended: 2002 c.22 s.17

s.71, applied: SI 2002/2005 Reg.5, SI 2003/3111 Reg.5

s.71, varied: SI 2003/1964 Sch.1

s.73, applied: SI 2002/509 Reg.6

s.73, enabling: SI 2002/2789

s.73, amended: 2002 c.22 s.17

s.73, applied: SI 2003/3111 Reg.5

s.74, enabling: SI 2002/2789

s.74, amended: 2002 c.22 s.17

s.75, enabling: SI 2002/2789

s.75A, added: 2002 c.22 s.3

s.75A, applied: SI 2002/2005 Reg.5, SI 2002/2788 Reg.19, SI 2003/3111 Reg.5

s.75A, enabling: SI 2002/2788, SI 2003/921, SI 2004/923

s.75B, added: 2002 c.22 s.3

s.75B, applied: SI 2003/3111 Reg.5

s.75B, enabling: SI 2002/2788, SI 2003/921, SI 2004/923

s.75C, added: 2002 c.22 s.3

s.75C, enabling: SI 2002/2788, SI 2003/921

s.75D, added: 2002 c.22 s.3

s.75D, enabling: SI 2002/2788, SI 2003/921, SI 2004/923

s.76, applied: SI 2002/509 Reg.6

s.76, enabling: SI 2002/2789

s.76, applied: SI 2003/3111 Reg.5

s.78, amended: 2002 c.22 Sch.7 para.28

s.80A, added: 2002 c.22 s.1

s.80A, applied: SI 2002/2005 Reg.5, SI 2003/3111 Reg.5

s.80A, enabling: SI 2002/2788

s.80B, added: 2002 c.22 s.1

CAP.

1996–cont.

18. Employment Rights Act 1996–*cont.*

s.80B, applied: SI 2003/3111 Reg.5

s.80B, varied: SI 2003/920 Sch.1

s.80B, enabling: SI 2002/2788, SI 2003/920, SI 2003/921

s.80C, added: 2002 c.22 s.1

s.80C, applied: SI 2002/2788 Reg.12

s.80C, enabling: SI 2002/2788, SI 2003/921

s.80D, added: 2002 c.22 s.1

s.80D, enabling: SI 2002/2788, SI 2003/921

s.80E, added: 2002 c.22 s.1

s.80E, enabling: SI 2002/2788, SI 2003/921

s.80F, added: 2002 c.22 s.47

s.80F, applied: SI 2003/694 Sch.1 para.2, Sch.1 para.70, Sch.1 para.96, SI 2004/2333 Sch.1 para.2, Sch.1 para.85, Sch.1 para.117

s.80F, referred to: SI 2003/694 Sch.1 para.11

s.80F, enabling: SI 2002/3236

s.80G, added: 2002 c.22 s.47

s.80G, applied: SI 2003/694, SI 2003/694 Sch.1 para.97, SI 2004/2333, SI 2004/2333 Sch.1 para.19, Sch.1 para.118

s.80G, referred to: SI 2002/3207 Reg.5, SI 2003/694 Sch.1 para.11, Sch.1 para.14

s.80G, enabling: SI 2002/3207

s.80H, added: 2002 c.22 s.47

s.80H, applied: SI 2002/3236 Reg.6, Reg.7, SI 2003/694, SI 2003/694 Sch.1 para.97, SI 2004/2333, SI 2004/2333 Sch.1 para.19, Sch.1 para.118

s.80H, referred to: SI 2003/694 Sch.1 para.8, Sch.1 para.14

s.80H, enabling: SI 2002/3236

s.80I, added: 2002 c.22 s.47

s.80I, applied: SI 2002/3236 Reg.7

s.80I, enabling: SI 2002/3236

s.86, see *Budd v Scotts Co (UK) Ltd* [2004] I.C.R. 299 (EAT), Judge Burke Q.C.; see *Hardy v Polk Ltd* [2004] I.R.L.R. 420 (EAT), Burton, J.; see *Virgin Net Ltd v Harper* 9[2004] EWCA Civ 271, [2004] I.R.L.R. 390 (CA), Brooke, L.J.

s.86, applied: SI 2004/753 Sch.1 para.140

s.86, repealed (in part): SI 2002/2034 Sch.2 para.3

s.87, see *Budd v Scotts Co (UK) Ltd* [2004] I.C.R. 299 (EAT), Judge Burke Q.C.

s.88, amended: 2002 c.22 Sch.7 para.29

s.89, amended: 2002 c.22 Sch.7 para.30

s.92, see *Health Development Agency v Parish* [2004] I.R.L.R. 550 (EAT), Judge Richardson

s.92, amended: 2002 c.22 Sch.7 para.31, SI 2002/2034 Sch.2 para.3, 2004 c.24 Sch.1 para.28

s.92, applied: SI 2002/2034 Reg.5

s.92, varied: SI 2003/1964 Art.4, Sch.1

s.93, varied: SI 2003/1964 Sch.1

CAP.

1996–cont.

18. Employment Rights Act 1996–*cont.*

s.94, see *Green v Victoria Road Primary School Governing Body* [2003] I.C.R. 713 (EAT), Judge Ansell; see *Lawson v Serco Ltd* [2004] EWCA Civ 12, [2004] 2 All E.R. 200 (CA), Pill, L.J.; see *Rutherford v Secretary of State for Trade and Industry* [2004] EWCA Civ 1186, [2004] 3 C.M.L.R. 53 (CA (Civ Div)), Potter, L.J.; see *Street v Derbyshire Unemployed Workers Centre* [2004] I.C.R. 213 (EAT), Judge J McMullen Q.C.

s.94, varied: SI 2003/1964 Art.4, Sch.1

s.95, see *Green v Victoria Road Primary School Governing Body* [2003] I.C.R. 713 (EAT), Judge Ansell; see *Rossiter v Pendragon Plc* [2002] EWCA Civ 745, [2002] 2 C.M.L.R. 43 (CA), Peter Gibson, L.J.

s.95, amended: SI 2002/2034 Sch.2 para.3, 2004 c.24 Sch.1 para.29, Sch.2

s.95, varied: SI 2003/1964 Art.4, Sch.1

s.96, varied: SI 2003/1964 Art.4, Sch.1

s.97, see *Fitzgerald v University of Kent at Canterbury* [2004] EWCA Civ 143, [2004] I.C.R. 737 (CA), Brooke, L.J.; see *Johnston v Miller Bros & FP Butler Ltd* [2002] I.C.R. 744 (EAT), Recorder Langstaff Q.C.; see *Virgin Net Ltd v Harper* 9[2004] EWCA Civ 271, [2004] I.R.L.R. 390 (CA), Brooke, L.J.

s.97, amended: SI 2002/2034 Sch.2 para.3

s.97, applied: SI 2002/2788 Reg.3, SI 2002/2927 Art.4, SI 2004/2566 Art.7

s.97, referred to: 2002 c.22 s.38

s.97, varied: SI 2003/1964 Art.4, Sch.1

s.98, see *Cobley v Forward Technology Industries Plc* [2003] EWCA Civ 646, [2003] I.C.R. 1050 (CA), Mummery, L.J.; see *London Underground Ltd v Strouthos* [2004] EWCA Civ 402, [2004] I.R.L.R. 636 (CA), Pill, L.J.; see *R. (on the application of George) v General Medical Council* [2003] EWHC 1124, [2004] Lloyd's Rep. Med. 33 (QBD (Admin Ct)), Collins, J.; see *Riley-Williams v Argos Ltd* (2003) 147 S.J.L.B. 695 (EAT), Judge McMullen Q.C.; see *Sainsbury's Supermarkets Ltd v Hitt* [2002] EWCA Civ 1588, [2003] I.C.R. 111 (CA), Mummery, L.J.; see *Street v Derbyshire Unemployed Workers Centre* [2004] I.C.R. 213 (EAT), Judge J McMullen Q.C.; see *Thomas v Hillingdon LBC* Times, October 4, 2002 (EAT), Recorder Elizabeth Slade, Q.C.; see *Thorpe v Dul* [2003] I.C.R. 1556 (EAT), Wall, J.; see *X v Y (Employment: Sex Offender)* [2003] I.C.R. 1138 (EAT), Judge Peter Clark; see *X v Y (Employment: Sex Offender)* [2004] EWCA Civ 662, [2004] I.R.L.R. 625 (CA), Brooke, L.J.

s.98, amended: 2002 c.22 Sch.7 para.32, 2004 c.24 Sch.1 para.30

1996–cont.

18. Employment Rights Act 1996–*cont.*
s.98, varied: SI 2003/1964 Art.4, Sch.1
s.98A, added: 2002 c.22 s.34
s.98A, varied: SI 2003/1964 Art.4, Sch.1
s.98B, added: 2004 c.24 s.40
s.98B, varied: SI 2003/1964 Art.4, Sch.1
s.99, see *Forster v Cartwright Black* [2004] I.R.L.R. 781 (EAT), Beatson, J.; see *Visa International Service Association v Paul* [2004] I.R.L.R. 42 (EAT), Judge Peter Clark
s.99, amended: 2002 c.22 Sch.7 para.33
s.99, applied: SI 2002/2788 Reg.29
s.99, varied: SI 2003/1964 Art.4, Sch.1
s.99, enabling: SI 2002/2788, SI 2002/2789, SI 2003/921
s.100, see *Balfour Kilpatrick Ltd v Acheson* [2003] I.R.L.R. 683 (EAT), Elias, J.
s.100, applied: SI 2002/10 Sch.1, SI 2003/3038 Sch.1, SI 2004/753 Sch.1 para.166
s.100, varied: SI 2003/1964 Art.4, Sch.1
s.101, varied: SI 2003/1964 Art.4, Sch.1
s.101A, amended: SI 2004/1713 Sch.2 para.2
s.101A, applied: SI 2002/10 Sch.1, SI 2003/3038 Sch.1
s.101A, substituted: SI 2003/3049 Sch.2 para.3
s.101A, varied: SI 2003/1964 Art.4, Sch.1
s.102, applied: SI 2002/10 Sch.1, SI 2003/3038 Sch.1
s.102, varied: SI 2003/1964 Art.4, Sch.1
s.103, applied: SI 2002/10 Sch.1, SI 2003/3038 Sch.1
s.103, varied: SI 2003/1964 Art.4, Sch.1
s.103A, see *Bladon v ALM Medical Services Ltd* [2002] EWCA Civ 1085, [2002] I.C.R. 1444 (CA), Mummery, L.J.; see *Darnton v University of Surrey* [2003] I.C.R. 615 (EAT), Judge Serota Q.C.; see *Street v Derbyshire Unemployed Workers Centre* [2004] EWCA Civ 964, [2004] 4 All E.R. 839 (CA), Auld, L.J.; see *Street v Derbyshire Unemployed Workers Centre* [2004] I.C.R. 213 (EAT), Judge J McMullen Q.C.
s.103A, applied: SI 2004/1861 Sch.1 para.22
s.103A, varied: SI 2003/1964 Art.4, Sch.1
s.104, amended: 2002 c.22 Sch.7 para.34, SI 2003/3049 Sch.2 para.3, 2004 c.24 Sch.1 para.31, SI 2004/1713 Sch.2 para.2
s.104, varied: SI 2003/1964 Art.4, Sch.1
s.104A, varied: SI 2003/1964 Art.4, Sch.1
s.104B, substituted: 2002 c.21 Sch.1 para.3
s.104B, varied: SI 2003/1964 Art.4, Sch.1
s.104C, added: 2002 c.22 s.47
s.104C, varied: SI 2003/1964 Art.4, Sch.1
s.105, amended: 2002 c.21 Sch.1 para.3, SI 2002/2034 Sch.2 para.3, 2004 c.24 s.40, s.41, SI 2004/2326 Reg.43
s.105, applied: SI 2004/753 Sch.1 para.166, SI 2004/1861 Sch.1 para.22

1996–cont.

18. Employment Rights Act 1996–*cont.*
s.105, varied: SI 2003/1964 Art.4, Sch.1
s.106, amended: 2002 c.22 Sch.7 para.35
s.106, varied: SI 2003/1964 Art.4, Sch.1
s.107, varied: SI 2003/1964 Art.4, Sch.1
s.108, see *Virgin Net Ltd v Harper* [2003] I.R.L.R. 831 (EAT), Judge Peter Clark; see *Virgin Net Ltd v Harper* 9[2004] EWCA Civ 271, [2004] I.R.L.R. 390 (CA), Brooke, L.J.
s.108, amended: 2002 c.21 Sch.1 para.3, SI 2002/2034 Sch.2 para.3, 2004 c.24 s.40, s.41, Sch.1 para.32, SI 2004/2326 Reg.43
s.108, disapplied: SI 2002/3207 Reg.16
s.108, varied: SI 2003/1964 Art.4, Sch.1
s.109, see *Gidella v Wandsworth LBC* [2002] 3 C.M.L.R. 37 (EAT), Lindsay, J. (President); see *Jayawardane v Customs and Excise Commissioners* [2003] Pens. L.R. 1 (EAT), Wall, J.; see *Rutherford v Secretary of State for Trade and Industry* [2003] 3 C.M.L.R. 27 (EAT), Wall, J.; see *Rutherford v Secretary of State for Trade and Industry* [2004] EWCA Civ 1186, [2004] 3 C.M.L.R. 53 (CA (Civ Div)), Potter, L.J.; see *Wall v British Compressed Air Society* [2003] EWCA Civ 1762, [2004] I.C.R. 408 (CA), Simon Brown, L.J.; see *Wall v British Compressed Air Society* [2003] I.R.L.R. 836 (EAT), Rimer, J.
s.109, amended: SI 2002/2034 Sch.2 para.3, 2004 c.24 s.40, s.41, Sch.1 para.33, SI 2004/2326 Reg.43
s.109, disapplied: SI 2002/3207 Reg.16
s.109, varied: SI 2003/1964 Art.4, Sch.1
s.110, amended: 2002 c.22 s.44
s.110, applied: SI 2002/2822 Reg.34, SI 2004/752 Reg.4, SI 2004/753 Sch.1 para.154
s.110, varied: SI 2003/1964 Art.4, Sch.1
s.111, see *Consignia Plc v Sealy* [2002] EWCA Civ 878, [2002] 3 All E.R. 801 (CA), Hart, J.; see *Rai v Somerfield Stores Ltd* [2004] I.C.R. 656 (EAT), Judge Burke Q.C.; see *Street v Derbyshire Unemployed Workers Centre* [2004] I.C.R. 213 (EAT), Judge J McMullen Q.C.
s.111, applied: 2002 c.22 Sch.3, Sch.4, Sch.5, SI 2002/2822 Reg.34, SI 2002/2927 Art.4, SI 2004/1861 Sch.1 para.55
s.111, varied: SI 2002/3207 Reg.16, SI 2003/1964 Art.4, Sch.1
s.112, amended: 2002 c.22 s.34, Sch.7 para.36
s.112, applied: SSI 2003/461 Reg.10
s.112, varied: SI 2002/3207 Reg.16, SI 2003/1964 Art.4, Sch.1
s.113, varied: SI 2002/3207 Reg.16, SI 2003/1964 Art.4, Sch.1
s.114, applied: SI 2002/2927 Art.4
s.114, varied: SI 2002/3207 Reg.16, SI 2003/1964 Art.4, Sch.1

1996–cont.

18. Employment Rights Act 1996–cont.

s.115, applied: SI 2002/2927 Art.4

s.115, varied: SI 2002/3207 Reg.16, SI 2003/1964 Art.4, Sch.1

s.116, varied: SI 2002/3207 Reg.16, SI 2003/1964 Art.4, Sch.1

s.117, amended: 2002 c.22 s.34, Sch.7 para.37

s.117, applied: SI 2002/2927 Art.4, SI 2004/753 Sch.1 para.185, SSI 2003/461 Reg.10

s.117, varied: SI 2002/3207 Reg.16, SI 2003/1964 Art.4, Sch.1, SI 2004/753 Art.6

s.118, amended: 2002 c.22 Sch.7 para.38

s.118, applied: SI 2002/2927 Art.4

s.118, repealed (in part): 2002 c.22 Sch.8 Part 1

s.118, varied: SI 2002/3207 Reg.16, SI 2003/1964 Art.4, Sch.1

s.119, varied: SI 2002/3207 Reg.16, SI 2003/1964 Art.4, Sch.1

s.120, amended: 2002 c.22 s.34, SI 2002/10 Sch.1, SI 2002/2927 Sch.1, SI 2003/3038 Sch.1

s.120, referred to: SI 2004/753 Sch.1 para.148

s.120, varied: SI 2002/3207 Reg.16, SI 2003/1964 Art.4, Sch.1

s.121, varied: SI 2002/3207 Reg.16, SI 2003/1964 Art.4, Sch.1

s.122, varied: SI 2002/3207 Reg.16, SI 2003/1964 Art.4, Sch.1

s.123, see *Dunnachie v Kingston upon Hull City Council* [2003] I.C.R. 1294 (EAT), Burton, J.; see *Dunnachie v Kingston upon Hull City Council* [2004] EWCA Civ 84, [2004] 2 All E.R. 501 (CA), Brooke, L.J.; see *Dunnachie v Kingston upon Hull City Council* [2004] UKHL 36, [2004] 3 W.L.R. 310 (HL), Lord Nicholls of Birkenhead; see *Elkouil v Coney Island Ltd* [2002] I.R.L.R. 174 (EAT), Judge JR Reid Q.C.; see *Kingston Upon Hull City Council v Dunnachie (No.3)* [2004] I.C.R. 227 (EAT), Burton, J.

s.123, amended: 2002 c.22 s.34, Sch.7 para.39

s.123, varied: SI 2002/3207 Reg.16, SI 2003/1964 Art.4, Sch.1

s.124, amended: SI 2002/10 Sch.1, SI 2002/2927 Sch.1, SI 2003/3038 Sch.1

s.124, referred to: SI 2004/753 Sch.1 para.166

s.124, varied: SI 2002/3207 Reg.16, SI 2003/1964 Art.4, Sch.1

s.124A, added: 2002 c.22 s.39

s.124A, varied: SI 2002/3207 Reg.16, SI 2003/1964 Art.4, Sch.1

s.125, varied: SI 2002/3207 Reg.16, SI 2003/1964 Art.4, Sch.1

s.126, amended: SI 2003/1660 Sch.5 para.2, SI 2003/1661 Sch.5 para.2

s.126, varied: SI 2002/3207 Reg.16, SI 2003/1964 Art.4, Sch.1

1996–cont.

18. Employment Rights Act 1996–cont.

s.127, varied: SI 2002/3207 Reg.16, SI 2003/1964 Art.4, Sch.1

s.127A, repealed: 2002 c.22 Sch.7 para.40, Sch.8 Part 1

s.127A, varied: SI 2002/3207 Reg.16, SI 2003/1964 Art.4, Sch.1

s.127B, varied: SI 2002/3207 Reg.16, SI 2003/1964 Art.4, Sch.1

s.128, applied: SI 2002/3207 Reg.16, SI 2004/752 Reg.5, SI 2004/1861 Sch.1 para.18

s.128, varied: SI 2002/3207 Reg.16, SI 2003/1964 Art.4, Sch.1

s.129, applied: SI 2002/3207 Reg.16

s.129, varied: SI 2002/3207 Reg.16, SI 2003/1964 Art.4, Sch.1

s.130, applied: SI 2002/3207 Reg.16

s.130, varied: SI 2002/3207 Reg.16, SI 2003/1964 Art.4, Sch.1

s.131, applied: SI 2002/3207 Reg.16

s.131, varied: SI 2002/3207 Reg.16, SI 2003/1964 Art.4, Sch.1

s.132, applied: SI 2002/3207 Reg.16

s.132, varied: SI 2002/3207 Reg.16, SI 2003/1964 Art.4, Sch.1

s.133, varied: SI 2003/1964 Art.4, Sch.1

s.134, amended: 2002 c.32 Sch.21 para.30

s.134, varied: SI 2003/1964 Art.4, Sch.1

s.134A, amended: 2002 c.30 s.95

s.134A, varied: SI 2003/1964 Art.4, Sch.1

s.135, see *Rutherford v Secretary of State for Trade and Industry* [2004] EWCA Civ 1186, [2004] 3 C.M.L.R. 53 (CA (Civ Div)), Potter, L.J.

s.135, applied: SI 2002/2927 Art.4

s.136, amended: SI 2002/2034 Sch.2 para.3

s.138, applied: SI 2004/753 Sch.1 para.149

s.139, see *Pitman v Foreign and Commonwealth Office* [2003] I.C.R. 699 (EAT), Elias, J.

s.139, amended: 2002 c.32 Sch.21 para.31

s.139, applied: 2002 c.32 s.37

s.139, referred to: SI 2004/753 Sch.1 para.150

s.141, applied: SI 2004/753 Sch.1 para.149

s.145, amended: SI 2002/2034 Sch.2 para.3

s.145, applied: SI 2002/2034 Sch.2 para.5, SI 2002/2927 Art.4

s.153, applied: SI 2002/2927 Art.4

s.156, see *Rutherford v Secretary of State for Trade and Industry* [2003] 3 C.M.L.R. 27 (EAT), Wall, J.; see *Rutherford v Secretary of State for Trade and Industry* [2004] EWCA Civ 1186, [2004] 3 C.M.L.R. 53 (CA (Civ Div)), Potter, L.J.

s.161, varied: 2004 c.33 Sch.21 para.42

s.163, applied: 2002 c.22 Sch.3, Sch.4, Sch.5, SI 2004/1861 Sch.1 para.22

s.164, applied: SI 2004/1861 Sch.1 para.22

CAP.

1996–cont.

18. Employment Rights Act 1996–*cont.*

s.166, see *Secretary of State for Trade and Industry v Frid* [2004] UKHL 24, [2004] 2 A.C. 506 (HL), Lord Nicholls of Birkenhead; see *Secretary of State for Trade and Industry v Key* [2004] B.P.I.R. 214 (EAT), Judge Peter Clark

s.166, amended: 2002 c.40 Sch.17 para.49, Sch.26

s.167, see *Secretary of State for Trade and Industry v Frid* [2003] 2 B.C.L.C. 284 (Ch D (Companies Court)), David Mackie Q.C.; see *Secretary of State for Trade and Industry v Frid* [2004] UKHL 24, [2004] 2 A.C. 506 (HL), Lord Nicholls of Birkenhead

s.170, applied: SI 2004/1861 Sch.1 para.61

s.182, applied: SI 2002/2927 Art.4

s.183, see *Secretary of State for Trade and Industry v Key* [2004] B.P.I.R. 214 (EAT), Judge Peter Clark

s.183, amended: 2002 c.40 Sch.17 para.49, Sch.26

s.184, see *Benson v Secretary of State for Trade and Industry* [2003] I.C.R. 1082 (EAT), Burton, J.; see *Titchener v Secretary of State for Trade and Industry* [2002] I.C.R. 225 (EAT), Recorder Cox Q.C.

s.184, applied: SI 2004/753 Art.7

s.185, applied: SI 2002/2927 Art.4

s.186, see *Titchener v Secretary of State for Trade and Industry* [2002] I.C.R. 225 (EAT), Recorder Cox Q.C.

s.186, amended: SI 2002/10 Sch.1, SI 2002/2927 Sch.1, SI 2003/3038 Sch.1

s.189, repealed (in part): 2002 c.40 Sch.26

s.191, amended: 2002 c.22 Sch.7 para.41, 2004 c.24 Sch.1 para.34, Sch.2

s.192, amended: 2002 c.21 Sch.1 para.1, 2002 c.22 Sch.7 para.42, 2004 c.24 Sch.1 para.35

s.192, repealed (in part): 2002 c.21 Sch.6

s.194, amended: 2002 c.21 Sch.1 para.1, 2002 c.22 Sch.7 para.43, 2004 c.24 s.41, Sch.1 para.36

s.194, applied: SI 2003/1660 Reg.38, SI 2003/1661 Reg.38

s.195, amended: 2002 c.21 Sch.1 para.1, 2002 c.22 Sch.7 para.43, 2004 c.24 s.41, Sch.1 para.37

s.195, applied: SI 2003/1660 Reg.37, SI 2003/1661 Reg.37

s.196, see *Jackson v Ghost Ltd* [2003] I.R.L.R. 824 (EAT), Judge Peter Clark; see *Lawson v Serco Ltd* [2004] EWCA Civ 12, [2004] 2 All E.R. 200 (CA), Pill, L.J.; see *Pitman v Foreign and Commonwealth Office* [2003] I.C.R. 699 (EAT), Elias, J.

s.197, applied: SI 2002/2034 Sch.2 para.5

s.197, repealed: SI 2002/2034 Sch.2 para.3

s.199, amended: 2002 c.22 Sch.7 para.44, 2004 c.24 s.41

CAP.

1996–cont.

18. Employment Rights Act 1996–*cont.*

s.199, repealed (in part): SI 2002/2034 Sch.2 para.3

s.200, amended: 2002 c.30 s.37, Sch.8, 2004 c.24 Sch.1 para.38

s.200, varied: 2002 c.30 Sch.3 para.19

s.202, amended: 2004 c.24 Sch.1 para.39

s.203, see *Fitzgerald v University of Kent at Canterbury* [2004] EWCA Civ 143, [2004] I.C.R. 737 (CA), Brooke, L.J.

s.203, amended: SI 2002/2034 Sch.2 para.3

s.203, applied: SI 2004/754 Art.2, Art.3

s.203, repealed (in part): SI 2002/2034 Sch.2 para.3

s.203, varied: SI 2002/2034 Reg.10

s.203, enabling: SI 2004/754, SI 2004/2515

s.209, enabling: SI 2002/532, SI 2004/1682

s.212, see *Curr v Marks & Spencer Plc* [2002] Emp. L.R. 705 (EAT), Judge Wilkie Q.C.; see *Curr v Marks & Spencer Plc* [2002] EWCA Civ 1852, [2003] I.C.R. 443 (CA), Peter Gibson, L.J.

s.218, see *Stevens v Bower* [2004] EWCA Civ 496, [2004] I.R.L.R. 957 (CA), Potter, L.J.

s.218, amended: 2002 c.32 Sch.21 para.32, SI 2002/2469 Sch.1 para.22, 2003 c.43 Sch.4 para.101, 2004 c.17 Sch.3 para.13

s.218, repealed (in part): 2003 c.43 Sch.13 para.8, Sch.14 Part 4, Sch.14 Part 7

s.221, see *Bamsey v Albon Engineering & Manufacturing Plc* [2004] EWCA Civ 359, [2004] 2 C.M.L.R. 59 (CA), Auld, L.J.; see *Evans v Malley Organisation Ltd (t/a First Business Support)* [2002] EWCA Civ 1834, [2003] I.C.R. 432 (CA), Pill, L.J.; see *Paggetti v Cobb* [2002] I.R.L.R. 861 (EAT), Judge Peter Clark

s.221, varied: SI 2003/3049 Reg.11, SI 2004/1713 Reg.11

s.222, varied: SI 2003/3049 Reg.11, SI 2004/1713 Reg.11

s.223, varied: SI 2003/3049 Reg.11, SI 2004/1713 Reg.11

s.224, see *Bamsey v Albon Engineering & Manufacturing Plc* [2004] EWCA Civ 359, [2004] 2 C.M.L.R. 59 (CA), Auld, L.J.

s.224, varied: SI 2003/3049 Reg.11, SI 2004/1713 Reg.11

s.225, amended: 2002 c.22 Sch.7 para.45

s.226, amended: 2002 c.22 Sch.7 para.46

s.227, amended: 2002 c.22 Sch.7 para.47, SI 2002/10 Sch.1, SI 2002/2927 Sch.1, SI 2003/3038 Sch.1

s.227, applied: SI 2002/769 Reg.11, SI 2002/3207 Reg.15

s.227, referred to: 2002 c.22 s.38, SI 2003/3049 Reg.11

s.228, referred to: SI 2003/3049 Reg.11

s.230, see *Dowling v Ilic (t/a ME Ilic Haulage)* [2004] I.C.R. 1176 (EAT), Burton, J.; see *Essex Strategic HA (formerly North Essex HA) v David-John* [2004] I.C.R. 112

1996–cont.

18. Employment Rights Act 1996–*cont.*

s.230–*cont.*

(EAT), Judge DM Levy Q.C.; see *Franks v Reuters Ltd* [2003] EWCA Civ 417, [2003] I.C.R. 1166 (CA), Mummery, L.J.; see *Thorpe v Dul* [2003] I.C.R. 1556 (EAT), Wall, J.

s.230, applied: SI 2003/3319 Reg.24

s.231, applied: SI 2002/2822 Reg.36

s.232, amended: 2003 c.17 Sch.6 para.114, 2003 c.18 s.1

s.233, amended: 2003 c.18 s.1

s.234, see *Bamsey v Albon Engineering & Manufacturing Plc* [2003] I.C.R. 1224 (EAT), Judge Ansell; see *Bamsey v Albon Engineering & Manufacturing Plc* [2004] EWCA Civ 359, [2004] 2 C.M.L.R. 59 (CA), Auld, L.J.

s.235, amended: 2002 c.22 Sch.7 para.48, SI 2002/2034 Sch.2 para.3

s.236, amended: 2002 c.22 Sch.7 para.49

s.236, applied: SI 2002/2788, SI 2002/2789, SI 2002/3207, SI 2003/920, SI 2003/921, SI 2004/923

s.236, enabling: SI 2002/532

s.244, amended: 2003 c.18 s.1

Sch.1 para.17, repealed: 2004 c.14 Sch.1 Part 2

Sch.2 Part II para.15, repealed: 2004 c.14 Sch.1 Part 8

19. Law Reform (Year and a Day Rule) Act 1996

s.2, amended: 2004 c.28 Sch.10 para.33, Sch.11

20. Dogs (Fouling of Land) Act 1996

applied: 2003 c.26 s.119

s.4, applied: 2002 c.30 Sch.4 para.1, Sch.5 para.1, SI 2002/425, SI 2002/425 Art.2, 2003 c.26 s.119, SI 2004/909, SI 2004/915 Sch.1 para.1

23. Arbitration Act 1996

see *Atlanska Plovidba v Consignaciones Asturianas SA (The Lapad)* [2004] EWHC 1273, [2004] 2 Lloyd's Rep. 109 (QBD (Adm Ct)), Moore-Bick, J.; see *Nagusina Naviera v Allied Maritime Inc* [2002] C.L.C. 385 (QBD (Comm Ct)), Andrew Smith, J.

applied: SI 2002/1711 Reg.12, SI 2003/473 Art.8, SI 2003/694 Sch.1 para.110, SI 2004/248 Reg.12, SI 2004/753 Sch.1 para.181EW, SI 2004/2333 Sch.1 para.133, SR 2002/293 Reg.6, SR 2002/307 Reg.6, SR 2003/353 Reg.6, SR 2003/360 Reg.6

disapplied: SI 2002/457 Sch.1 para.34, SI 2002/897 Sch.1 para.34

Part I, see *Reliance Industries Ltd v Enron Oil and Gas India Ltd* [2002] 1 All E.R. (Comm) 59 (QBD (Comm Ct)), Aikens, J.

Part I, disapplied: SI 2003/431 Art.44

Part I, referred to: SI 2004/2333 Art.4

1996–cont.

23. Arbitration Act 1996–*cont.*

s.1, see *Hiscox Underwriting Ltd v Dickson Manchester & Co Ltd* [2004] EWHC 479, [2004] 1 All E.R. (Comm) 753 (QBD (Comm Ct)), Cooke, J.

s.1, varied: SR 2002/88 Sch.1 para.2

s.2, varied: SR 2002/88 Sch.1 para.2

s.3, varied: SR 2002/88 Sch.1 para.2

s.4, varied: SR 2002/88 Sch.1 para.2

s.5, see *Dardana Ltd v Yukos Oil Co (No.1)* [2002] 1 Lloyd's Rep. 225 (QBD (Comm Ct)), Judge Chambers Q.C.; see *Flight Training International Inc v International Fire Training Equipment Ltd* [2004] EWHC 721, [2004] 2 All E.R. (Comm) 568 (QBD (Comm Ct)), Cresswell, J.; see *Whiting v Halverson* [2003] EWCA Civ 403, (2003) 147 S.J.L.B. 541 (CA), Brooke, L.J.

s.5, varied: SR 2002/88 Sch.1 para.2

s.6, see *Flight Training International Inc v International Fire Training Equipment Ltd* [2004] EWHC 721, [2004] 2 All E.R. (Comm) 568 (QBD (Comm Ct)), Cresswell, J.

s.6, varied: SR 2002/88 Sch.1 para.2

s.7, varied: SR 2002/88 Sch.1 para.2

s.8, varied: SR 2002/88 Sch.1 para.2

s.9, see *Capital Trust Investments Ltd v Radio Design TJ AB* [2002] EWCA Civ 135, [2002] 2 All E.R. 159 (CA), Jacob, J; see *Cigna Life Insurance Co of Europe SA NV v Intercaser SA de Seguros y Reaseguros* [2002] 1 All E.R. (Comm) 235 (QBD (Comm Ct)), Morison, J.; see *Downing v Al Tameer Establishment* [2002] EWCA Civ 721, [2002] 2 All E.R. (Comm) 545 (CA), Potter, L.J.; see *El Nasharty v J Sainsbury Plc* [2003] EWHC 2195, [2004] 1 All E.R. (Comm) 728 (QBD (Comm Ct)), Julian Flaux Q.C.; see *Exeter City AFC Ltd v Football Conference Ltd* [2004] EWHC 831, [2004] 1 W.L.R. 2910 (Ch D), Judge Weeks Q.C.; see *Road Management Services (A13) Plc v London Power Networks Plc* [2003] B.L.R. 303 (QBD (T&CC)), Forbes, J.; see *Shalson v DF Keane Ltd* [2003] EWHC 599, [2003] B.P.I.R. 1045 (Ch D), Blackburne, J.; see *Sun Life Assurance Co of Canada v CX Reinsurance Co Ltd (formerly CNA Reinsurance Co Ltd)* [2003] EWCA Civ 283, [2004] Lloyd's Rep. I.R. 58 (CA), Potter, L.J.; see *T&N Ltd v Royal & Sun Alliance Plc* [2002] EWHC 2420, [2002] C.L.C. 1342 (Ch D), Lloyd, J.

s.9, varied: SR 2002/88 Sch.1 para.2

s.10, varied: SR 2002/88 Sch.1 para.2

s.11, varied: SR 2002/88 Sch.1 para.2

s.12, see *Monella v Pizza Express (Restaurants) Ltd* [2003] EWHC 2966, [2004] 1 E.G.L.R. 43 (Ch D), Sir Andrew Morritt V.C.

1996–cont.

23. Arbitration Act 1996–*cont.*

s.12, varied: SR 2002/88 Sch.1 para.2

s.13, varied: SR 2002/88 Sch.1 para.2

s.14, varied: SR 2002/88 Sch.1 para.2

s.15, varied: SR 2002/88 Sch.1 para.2

s.16, varied: SR 2002/88 Sch.1 para.2

s.17, see *Minermet SpA Milan v Luckyfield Shipping Corp SA* [2004] EWHC 729, [2004] 2 Lloyd's Rep. 348 (QBD (Comm Ct)), Cooke, J.

s.17, varied: SR 2002/88 Sch.1 para.2

s.18, varied: SR 2002/88 Sch.1 para.2

s.19, varied: SR 2002/88 Sch.1 para.2

s.20, varied: SR 2002/88 Sch.1 para.2

s.21, varied: SR 2002/88 Sch.1 para.2

s.22, varied: SR 2002/88 Sch.1 para.2

s.23, varied: SR 2002/88 Sch.1 para.2

s.24, see *Kalmneft JSC v Glencore International AG* [2002] 1 All E.R. 76 (QBD (Comm Ct)), Colman, J.

s.24, applied: SI 2003/694 Sch.1 para.41, SI 2004/2333 Sch.1 para.52EW, SR 2002/120 Sch.1

s.24, referred to: SI 2004/753 Sch.1 para.47EW, SI 2004/2333 Sch.1 para.47EW, SR 2002/120 Sch.1

s.24, varied: SI 2003/694 Sch.1 para.43, SI 2004/753 Sch.1 para.52EW, SI 2004/2333 Sch.1 para.52EW, SR 2002/88 Sch.1 para.2

s.25, varied: SR 2002/88 Sch.1 para.2

s.26, varied: SR 2002/88 Sch.1 para.2

s.27, varied: SR 2002/88 Sch.1 para.2

s.28, see *Agrimex Ltd v Tradigrain SA* [2003] EWHC 1656, [2003] 2 Lloyd's Rep. 537 (QBD (Comm Ct)), Thomas, J.

s.28, varied: SR 2002/88 Sch.1 para.2

s.29, varied: SR 2002/88 Sch.1 para.2

s.30, varied: SR 2002/88 Sch.1 para.2

s.31, see *Kalmneft JSC v Glencore International AG* [2002] 1 All E.R. 76 (QBD (Comm Ct)), Colman, J.

s.31, varied: SR 2002/88 Sch.1 para.2

s.32, see *Peterson Farms Inc v C&M Farming Ltd (Payment into Court)* [2003] EWHC 2298, [2004] 1 Lloyd's Rep. 614 (QBD (Comm Ct)), Tomlinson, J.

s.32, varied: SR 2002/88 Sch.1 para.2

s.33, see *Kalmneft JSC v Glencore International AG* [2002] 1 All E.R. 76 (QBD (Comm Ct)), Colman, J.; see *Minermet SpA Milan v Luckyfield Shipping Corp SA* [2004] EWHC 729, [2004] 2 Lloyd's Rep. 348 (QBD (Comm Ct)), Cooke, J.; see *Warborough Investments Ltd v S Robinson & Sons (Holdings) Ltd* [2003] EWCA Civ 751, [2004] 2 P. & C.R. 6 (CA), Jonathan Parker, L.J.

s.33, varied: SR 2002/88 Sch.1 para.2

s.34, varied: SR 2002/88 Sch.1 para.2

1996–cont.

23. Arbitration Act 1996–*cont.*

s.35, varied: SR 2002/88 Sch.1 para.2

s.36, varied: SR 2002/88 Sch.1 para.2

s.37, varied: SR 2002/88 Sch.1 para.2

s.38, applied: SR 2003/138 r.9

s.38, varied: SR 2002/88 Sch.1 para.2

s.39, see *Kastner v Jason* [2004] EWHC 592, [2004] 2 Lloyd's Rep. 233 (Ch D), Lightman, J.

s.39, varied: SR 2002/88 Sch.1 para.2

s.40, see *Al Hadha Trading Co v Tradigrain SA* [2002] 2 Lloyd's Rep. 512 (QBD (Merc Ct)), Judge Havelock-Allan Q.C.

s.40, varied: SR 2002/88 Sch.1 para.2

s.41, see *Al Hadha Trading Co v Tradigrain SA* [2002] 2 Lloyd's Rep. 512 (QBD (Merc Ct)), Judge Havelock-Allan Q.C.

s.41, varied: SR 2002/88 Sch.1 para.2

s.42, varied: SR 2002/88 Sch.1 para.2

s.43, applied: SR 2003/138 r.9

s.43, varied: SR 2002/88 Sch.1 para.2

s.44, see *Commerce & Industry Insurance Co (Canada) v Lloyd's Underwriters* [2002] 1 W.L.R. 1323 (QBD (Comm Ct)), Moore-Bick, J.; see *Hiscox Underwriting Ltd v Dickson Manchester & Co Ltd* [2004] EWHC 479, [2004] 1 All E.R. (Comm) 753 (QBD (Comm Ct)), Cooke, J.; see *Petroleum Investment Co Ltd v Kantupan Holdings Co Ltd* [2002] 1 All E.R. (Comm) 124 (QBD (Comm Ct)), Toulson, J.

s.44, varied: SR 2002/88 Sch.1 para.2

s.45, varied: SI 2003/694 Sch.1 para.93, SI 2004/753 Sch.1 para.110EW, SI 2004/2333 Sch.1 para.108EW, SR 2002/88 Sch.1 para.2

s.46, applied: SR 2002/120 Art.4

s.46, varied: SI 2003/694 Art.4, SI 2004/753 Art.5, SI 2004/2333 Art.5, SR 2002/88 Sch.1 para.2, SR 2002/120 Art.4

s.47, varied: SR 2002/88 Sch.1 para.2

s.48, see *Hiscox Underwriting Ltd v Dickson Manchester & Co Ltd* [2004] EWHC 479, [2004] 1 All E.R. (Comm) 753 (QBD (Comm Ct)), Cooke, J.; see *Kastner v Jason* [2004] EWHC 592, [2004] 2 Lloyd's Rep. 233 (Ch D), Lightman, J.; see *Lesotho Highlands Development Authority v Impregilo SpA* [2003] EWCA Civ 1159, [2004] 1 All E.R. (Comm) 97 (CA), Brooke, L.J.

s.48, varied: SR 2002/88 Sch.1 para.2

s.49, see *Durham CC v Darlington BC* [2003] EWHC 2598, [2004] B.L.G.R. 311 (QBD (Admin Ct)), Stanley Burnton, J.; see *Lesotho Highlands Development Authority v Impregilo SpA* [2003] EWCA Civ 1159, [2004] 1 All E.R. (Comm) 97 (CA), Brooke, L.J.

s.49, varied: SR 2002/88 Sch.1 para.2

s.50, varied: SR 2002/88 Sch.1 para.2

s.51, varied: SR 2002/88 Sch.1 para.2

1996–cont.

23. Arbitration Act 1996–*cont.*

s.52, varied: SR 2002/88 Sch.1 para.2

s.53, varied: SR 2002/88 Sch.1 para.2

s.54, varied: SR 2002/88 Sch.1 para.2

s.55, varied: SR 2002/88 Sch.1 para.2

s.56, varied: SR 2002/88 Sch.1 para.2

s.57, see *Gannet Shipping Ltd v Eastrade Commodities Inc* [2002] 1 All E.R. (Comm) 297 (QBD (Comm Ct)), Langley, J.; see *Torch Offshore LLC v Cable Shipping Inc* [2004] EWHC 787, [2004] 2 All E.R. (Comm) 365 (QBD (Comm Ct)), Cooke, J.

s.57, varied: SR 2002/88 Sch.1 para.2

s.58, varied: SR 2002/88 Sch.1 para.2

s.59, varied: SR 2002/88 Sch.1 para.2

s.60, varied: SR 2002/88 Sch.1 para.2

s.61, varied: SR 2002/88 Sch.1 para.2

s.62, varied: SR 2002/88 Sch.1 para.2

s.63, varied: SR 2002/88 Sch.1 para.2

s.64, varied: SR 2002/88 Sch.1 para.2

s.65, varied: SR 2002/88 Sch.1 para.2

s.66, see *Goldstein v Conley* [2001] EWCA Civ 637, [2002] 1 W.L.R. 281 (CA), Clarke, L.J.

s.66, varied: SI 2003/694 Sch.1 para.111, SI 2004/753 Sch.1 para.183EW, SI 2004/2333 Sch.1 para.135EW, SR 2002/88 Sch.1 para.2

s.67, see *Athletic Union of Constantinople (AEK) v National Basketball Association (Application to Strike Out)* [2002] EWCA Civ 830, [2002] 1 W.L.R. 2863 (CA), Lord Phillips of Worth Matravers, M.R.; see *Athletic Union of Constantinople (AEK) v National Basketball Association* [2002] 1 All E.R. (Comm) 70 (QBD (Comm Ct)), Richard Field Q.C.; see *Electrosteel Castings Ltd v Scan Trans Shipping & Chartering Sdn Bhd* [2002] EWHC 1993, [2002] 2 All E.R. (Comm) 1064 (QBD (Comm Ct)), Gross, J.; see *Equatorial Traders Ltd v Louis Dreyfus Trading Ltd* [2002] EWHC 2023, [2002] 2 Lloyd's Rep. 638 (QBD (Comm Ct)); see *Hussmann (Europe) Ltd v Pharaon* [2003] EWCA Civ 266, [2003] 1 All E.R. (Comm) 879 (CA), Rix, L.J.; see *JSC Zestafoni G Nikoladze Ferroalloy Plant v Ronly Holdings Ltd* [2004] EWHC 245, [2004] 2 Lloyd's Rep. 335 (QBD (Comm Ct)), Colman, J.; see *Kalmneft JSC v Glencore International AG* [2002] 1 All E.R. 76 (QBD (Comm Ct)), Colman, J.; see *Lesotho Highlands Development Authority v Impregilo SpA* [2002] EWHC 2435, [2003] 1 All E.R. (Comm) 22 (QBD (Comm Ct)), Morison, J.; see *Peoples Insurance Co of China (Hebei Branch) v Vysanthi Shipping Co Ltd (The Joanna V)* [2003] EWHC 1655, [2003] 2 Lloyd's Rep. 617 (QBD (Comm Ct)), Thomas, J.; see *Peterson Farms Inc v*

1996–cont.

23. Arbitration Act 1996–*cont.*

s.67–*cont.*

C&M Farming Ltd (Payment into Court) [2003] EWHC 2298, [2004] 1 Lloyd's Rep. 614 (QBD (Comm Ct)), Tomlinson, J.; see *Peterson Farms Inc v C&M Farming Ltd* [2004] EWHC 121, [2004] 1 Lloyd's Rep. 603 (QBD (Comm Ct)), Langley, J.

s.67, varied: SI 2003/694 Sch.1 para.113, SI 2004/753 Sch.1 para.187EW, SI 2004/2333 Sch.1 para.138EW, SR 2002/88 Sch.1 para.2

s.68, see *Al Hadha Trading Co v Tradigrain SA* [2002] 2 Lloyd's Rep. 512 (QBD (Merc Ct)), Judge Havelock-Allan Q.C.; see *Ascot Commodities NV v Olam International Ltd* [2002] C.L.C. 277 (QBD (Comm Ct)), Toulson, J.; see *Checkpoint Ltd v Strathclyde Pension Fund* [2002] EWHC 439, [2002] 2 E.G.L.R. 97 (Ch D), Park, J.; see *Checkpoint Ltd v Strathclyde Pension Fund* [2003] EWCA Civ 84, [2003] 1 E.G.L.R. 1 (CA), Ward, L.J.; see *Department of Economic Policy and Development of the City of Moscow v Bankers Trust Co* [2004] EWCA Civ 314, [2004] 3 W.L.R. 533 (CA), Sir Andrew Morritt V.C.; see *Equatorial Traders Ltd v Louis Dreyfus Trading Ltd* [2002] EWHC 2023, [2002] 2 Lloyd's Rep. 638 (QBD (Comm Ct)), Judge Chambers Q.C.; see *Guardcliffe Properties Ltd v City & St James* [2003] EWHC 215, [2003] 2 E.G.L.R. 16 (Ch D), Etherton, J.; see *Kalmneft JSC v Glencore International AG* [2002] 1 All E.R. 76 (QBD (Comm Ct)), Colman, J.; see *Lesotho Highlands Development Authority v Impregilo SpA* [2002] EWHC 2435, [2003] 1 All E.R. (Comm) 22 (QBD (Comm Ct)), Morison, J.; see *Margulead Ltd v Exide Technologies* [2004] EWHC 1019, [2004] 2 All E.R. (Comm) 727 (QBD (Comm Ct)), Colman, J.; see *Marklands Ltd v Virgin Retail Ltd* [2003] EWHC 3428, [2004] 2 E.G.L.R. 43 (Ch D), Lewison, J.; see *Peterson Farms Inc v C&M Farming Ltd (Payment into Court)* [2003] EWHC 2298, [2004] 1 Lloyd's Rep. 614 (QBD (Comm Ct)), Tomlinson, J.; see *Ronly Holdings Ltd v JSC Zestafoni G Nikoladze Ferroalloy Plant* [2004] EWHC 1354, [2004] 1 C.L.C. 1168 (QBD (Comm Ct)), Gross, J.; see *Tame Shipping Ltd v Easy Navigation Ltd (The Easy Rider)* [2004] EWHC 1862, [2004] 2 All E.R. (Comm) 521 (QBD (Comm)), Moore-Bick, J.; see *Torch Offshore LLC v Cable Shipping Inc* [2004] EWHC 787, [2004] 2 All E.R. (Comm) 365 (QBD (Comm Ct)), Cooke, J.; see *Warborough Investments Ltd v S Robinson & Sons (Holdings) Ltd* [2003] EWCA Civ 751, [2004] 2 P. & C.R. 6

1996–cont.

23. Arbitration Act 1996–*cont.*

s.68–*cont.*

(CA), Jonathan Parker, L.J.; see *Westland Helicopters Ltd v Al-Hejailan* [2004] EWHC 1625, [2004] 2 Lloyd's Rep. 523 (QBD (Comm Ct)), Colman, J.

s.68, varied: SI 2003/694 Sch.1 para.114, SI 2004/753 Sch.1 para.194EW, SI 2004/2333 Sch.1 para.145EW, SR 2002/88 Sch.1 para.2

s.69, see *Al Hadha Trading Co v Tradigrain SA* [2002] 2 Lloyd's Rep. 512 (QBD (Merc Ct)), Judge Havelock-Allan Q.C.; see *BLCT (13096) Ltd v J Sainsbury Plc* [2003] EWCA Civ 884, [2004] 1 C.L.C. 24 (CA), Arden, L.J.; see *Checkpoint Ltd v Strathclyde Pension Fund* [2002] EWHC 439, [2002] 2 E.G.L.R. 97 (Ch D), Park, J.; see *CMA CGM SA v Beteiligungs KG MS Northern Pioneer Schiffahrtsgesellschaft mbH & Co* [2002] EWCA Civ 1878, [2003] 1 W.L.R. 1015 (CA), Lord Phillips of Worth Matravers, M.R.; see *Glencore Grain Ltd v Goldbeam Shipping Inc (The Mass Glory)* [2002] EWHC 27, [2002] 2 Lloyd's Rep. 244 (QBD (Comm Ct)), Moore-Bick, J.; see *Icon Navigation Corp v Sinochem International Petroleum (Bahamas) Co Ltd* [2002] EWHC 2812, [2003] 1 All E.R. (Comm) 405 (QBD (Comm Ct)), Moore-Bick, J.; see *Kalmneft JSC v Glencore International AG* [2002] 1 All E.R. 76 (QBD (Comm Ct)), Colman, J.; see *Louis Dreyfus Trading Ltd v Reliance Trading Ltd* [2004] EWHC 525, [2004] 2 Lloyd's Rep. 243 (QBD (Comm Ct)), Andrew Smith, J.; see *Marklands Ltd v Virgin Retail Ltd* [2003] EWHC 3428, [2004] 2 E.G.L.R. 43 (Ch D), Lewison, J.; see *Mousaka Inc v Golden Seagull Maritime Inc* [2002] 1 W.L.R. 395 (QBD (Comm Ct)), David Steel, J.; see *North Range Shipping Ltd v Seatrans Shipping Corp (The Western Triumph)* [2002] EWCA Civ 405, [2002] 1 W.L.R. 2397 (CA), Tuckey, L.J.; see *Peterson Farms Inc v C&M Farming Ltd (Payment into Court)* [2003] EWHC 2298, [2004] 1 Lloyd's Rep. 614 (QBD (Comm Ct)), Tomlinson, J.; see *Reliance Industries Ltd v Enron Oil and Gas India Ltd* [2002] 1 All E.R. (Comm) 59 (QBD (Comm Ct)), Aikens, J.

s.69, varied: SI 2003/694 Sch.1 para.115, SI 2004/753 Sch.1 para.200EW, SI 2004/2333 Sch.1 para.151EW, SR 2002/88 Sch.1 para.2

s.70, see *Peoples Insurance Co of China (Hebei Branch) v Vysanthi Shipping Co Ltd (The Joanna V)* [2003] EWHC 1655, [2003] 2 Lloyd's Rep. 617 (QBD (Comm Ct)), Thomas, J.; see *Peterson Farms Inc v C&M Farming Ltd (Payment into Court)* [2003] EWHC 2298, [2004] 1 Lloyd's

1996–cont.

23. Arbitration Act 1996–*cont.*

s.70–*cont.*

Rep. 614 (QBD (Comm Ct)), Tomlinson, J.; see *Torch Offshore LLC v Cable Shipping Inc* [2004] EWHC 787, [2004] 2 All E.R. (Comm) 365 (QBD (Comm Ct)), Cooke, J.

s.70, varied: SI 2003/694 Sch.1 para.116, SI 2004/753 Sch.1 para.205EW, SI 2004/2333 Sch.1 para.156EW, SR 2002/88 Sch.1 para.2

s.71, varied: SI 2003/694 Sch.1 para.118, SI 2004/753 Sch.1 para.212EW, SI 2004/2333 Sch.1 para.163EW, SR 2002/88 Sch.1 para.2

s.72, see *Peterson Farms Inc v C&M Farming Ltd (Payment into Court)* [2003] EWHC 2298, [2004] 1 Lloyd's Rep. 614 (QBD (Comm Ct)), Tomlinson, J.

s.72, varied: SR 2002/88 Sch.1 para.2

s.73, see *Athletic Union of Constantinople (AEK) v National Basketball Association* [2002] 1 All E.R. (Comm) 70 (QBD (Comm Ct)), Richard Field Q.C.; see *JSC Zestafoni G Nikoladze Ferroalloy Plant v Ronly Holdings Ltd* [2004] EWHC 245, [2004] 2 Lloyd's Rep. 335 (QBD (Comm Ct)), Colman, J.

s.73, varied: SR 2002/88 Sch.1 para.2

s.74, varied: SR 2002/88 Sch.1 para.2

s.75, varied: SR 2002/88 Sch.1 para.2

s.76, varied: SR 2002/88 Sch.1 para.2

s.77, varied: SI 2003/694 Sch.1 para.128, SI 2004/753 Sch.1 para.223EW, SI 2004/2333 Sch.1 para.174EW, SR 2002/88 Sch.1 para.2

s.78, applied: SI 2004/2333 Sch.1 para.175EW

s.78, varied: SI 2003/694 Sch.1 para.129, SI 2004/753 Sch.1 para.224EW, SI 2004/2333 Sch.1 para.175EW, SR 2002/88 Sch.1 para.2

s.79, see *Equatorial Traders Ltd v Louis Dreyfus Trading Ltd* [2002] EWHC 2023, [2002] 2 Lloyd's Rep. 638 (QBD (Comm Ct)), Judge Chambers Q.C.; see *Minermet SpA Milan v Luckyfield Shipping Corp SA* [2004] EWHC 729, [2004] 2 Lloyd's Rep. 348 (QBD (Comm Ct)), Cooke, J.; see *Peoples Insurance Co of China (Hebei Branch) v Vysanthi Shipping Co Ltd (The Joanna V)* [2003] EWHC 1655, [2003] 2 Lloyd's Rep. 617 (QBD (Comm Ct)), Thomas, J.

s.79, varied: SR 2002/88 Sch.1 para.2

s.80, see *Kalmneft JSC v Glencore International AG* [2002] 1 All E.R. 76 (QBD (Comm Ct)), Colman, J.; see *Peoples Insurance Co of China (Hebei Branch) v Vysanthi Shipping Co Ltd (The Joanna V)* [2003] EWHC 1655, [2003] 2 Lloyd's Rep. 617 (QBD (Comm Ct)), Thomas, J.

CAP.

1996–cont.

23. Arbitration Act 1996–cont.

s.80, applied: SI 2004/2333 Sch.1 para.168EW, SR 2002/120 Sch.1

s.80, varied: SI 2003/694 Sch.1 para.122, SI 2004/753 Sch.1 para.217EW, SI 2004/2333 Sch.1 para.168EW, SR 2002/88 Sch.1 para.2

s.81, applied: SI 2004/2333 Sch.1 para.160EW, SR 2002/120 Sch.1

s.81, varied: SI 2003/694 Sch.1 para.117, SI 2004/753 Sch.1 para.209EW, SR 2002/88 Sch.1 para.2

s.82, see *Reliance Industries Ltd v Enron Oil and Gas India Ltd* [2002] 1 All E.R. (Comm) 59 (QBD (Comm Ct)), Aikens, J.

s.82, varied: SR 2002/88 Sch.1 para.2

s.83, varied: SR 2002/88 Sch.1 para.2

s.84, varied: SR 2002/88 Sch.1 para.2

s.85, varied: SR 2002/88 Sch.1 para.2

s.86, varied: SR 2002/88 Sch.1 para.2

s.87, varied: SR 2002/88 Sch.1 para.2

s.88, varied: SR 2002/88 Sch.1 para.2

s.89, varied: SR 2002/88 Sch.1 para.2

s.90, varied: SR 2002/88 Sch.1 para.2

s.91, varied: SR 2002/88 Sch.1 para.2

s.92, varied: SR 2002/88 Sch.1 para.2

s.93, applied: SI 2004/3121 Sch.1

s.93, varied: SR 2002/88 Sch.1 para.2

s.94, varied: SR 2002/88 Sch.1 para.2

s.95, varied: SR 2002/88 Sch.1 para.2

s.96, varied: SR 2002/88 Sch.1 para.2

s.97, varied: SR 2002/88 Sch.1 para.2

s.98, varied: SR 2002/88 Sch.1 para.2

s.103, see *Dardana Ltd v Yukos Oil Co (No.1)* [2002] 1 Lloyd's Rep. 225 (QBD (Comm Ct)), Judge Chambers Q.C.; see *Dardana Ltd v Yukos Oil Co (No.1)* [2002] EWCA Civ 543, [2002] 1 All E.R. (Comm) 819 (CA), Mance, L.J.

s.105, varied: SR 2002/88 Sch.1 para.2

s.106, varied: SR 2002/88 Sch.1 para.2

s.107, varied: SR 2002/88 Sch.1 para.2

s.108, varied: SR 2002/88 Sch.1 para.2

s.109, varied: SR 2002/88 Sch.1 para.2

s.110, varied: SR 2002/88 Sch.1 para.2

Sch.3 para.3, repealed: 2004 c.14 Sch.1 Part 6

Sch.3 para.7, repealed: 2003 c.21 Sch.19

Sch.3 para.58, repealed: SI 2003/431 Sch.5

24. Treasure Act 1996

s.2, applied: SI 2002/2666, SI 2002/2666 Art.3

s.2, enabling: SI 2002/2666

s.8, amended: 2003 c.44 Sch.26 para.48

25. Criminal Procedure and Investigations Act 1996

see *R. v Patel (Atul)* [2001] EWCA Crim 2505, [2002] Crim. L.R. 304 (CA (Crim Div)), Longmore, L.J.

Part III, applied: 2003 c.44 s.45

CAP.

1996–cont.

25. Criminal Procedure and Investigations Act 1996–cont.

s.1, amended: 2002 c.26 Sch.13, 2003 c.44 Sch.37 Part 4, Sch.3 para.66, SI 2003/1247 Sch.1 para.16

s.1, repealed (in part): 2003 c.44 Sch.37 Part 4, Sch.3 para.66

s.3, see *R. v Cairns (Alison Louise)* [2002] EWCA Crim 2838, [2003] 1 W.L.R. 796 (CA (Crim Div)), Keene, L.J.

s.3, amended: 2003 c.44 s.32, Sch.36 para.21

s.3, applied: SI 2003/1247 Art.16

s.4, amended: 2003 c.44 Sch.36 para.22

s.4, applied: SI 2003/1247 Art.16, SI 2004/1988 Art.7

s.5, see *R. (on the application of Sullivan) v Maidstone Crown Court* [2002] EWHC 967, [2002] 1 W.L.R. 2747 (QBD (Admin Ct)), Kennedy, L.J.; see *R. v Cairns (Alison Louise)* [2002] EWCA Crim 2838, [2003] 1 W.L.R. 796 (CA (Crim Div)), Keene, L.J.; see *R. v Gleeson (John Vincent)* [2003] EWCA Crim 3357, [2004] 1 Cr. App. R. 29 (CA (Crim Div)), Auld, L.J.

s.5, amended: 2003 c.44 s.33, Sch.3 para.66

s.5, applied: SI 2003/1247 Art.16

s.5, repealed (in part): 2003 c.44 Sch.36 para.23, Sch.37 Part 3, Sch.37 Part 4, Sch.3 para.66

s.6, applied: SI 2003/1247 Art.16

s.6, repealed (in part): 2003 c.44 Sch.36 para.24, Sch.37 Part 3

s.6A, added: 2003 c.44 s.33

s.6B, added: 2003 c.44 s.33

s.6C, added: 2003 c.44 s.34

s.6D, added: 2003 c.44 s.35

s.6E, added: 2003 c.44 s.36

s.7, see *Lewisham LBC v Elias* [2003] EWHC 1184, [2004] Env. L.R. 14 (QBD (Admin Ct)), Pitchford, J.; see *R. v Cairns (Alison Louise)* [2002] EWCA Crim 2838, [2003] 1 W.L.R. 796 (CA (Crim Div)), Keene, L.J.

s.7, applied: SI 2003/1247 Art.16

s.7, repealed: 2003 c.44 Sch.36 para.25, Sch.37 Part 3

s.7A, added: 2003 c.44 s.37

s.8, amended: 2003 c.44 s.38

s.9, applied: SI 2003/1247 Art.16

s.9, repealed: 2003 c.44 Sch.36 para.26, Sch.37 Part 3

s.10, amended: 2003 c.44 Sch.36 para.27

s.11, substituted: 2003 c.44 s.39

s.12, amended: 2003 c.44 Sch.36 para.28

s.13, amended: 2003 c.44 Sch.36 para.29

s.13, repealed (in part): 2003 c.44 Sch.37 Part 4, Sch.3 para.66

s.14, amended: 2003 c.44 Sch.36 para.30

s.15, amended: 2003 c.44 Sch.36 para.31

s.16, amended: 2003 c.44 Sch.36 para.32

1996–cont.

25. Criminal Procedure and Investigations Act 1996–*cont.*

s.17, amended: 2003 c.44 Sch.36 para.33

s.19, amended: 2003 c.39 Sch.8 para.377, 2003 c.44 Sch.36 para.34

s.20, amended: 2003 c.39 Sch.8 para.378, 2003 c.44 Sch.36 para.35

s.20, applied: 2003 c.44 s.127, SI 2004/1501 Art.31

s.20, repealed (in part): 2003 c.44 Sch.36 para.35, Sch.37 Part 3

s.21, amended: 2003 c.44 Sch.3 para.66

s.21A, added: 2003 c.44 s.40

s.28, amended: 2003 c.44 Sch.3 para.66

s.28, repealed (in part): 2003 c.44 Sch.37 Part 4, Sch.3 para.66

s.29, see *Attorney General's Reference (No.1 of 2004), Re* [2004] EWCA Crim 1025, [2004] 1 W.L.R. 2111 (CA (Crim Div)), Lord Woolf of Barnes, L.C.J.; see *Kanaris v Governor of Pentonville Prison* [2003] UKHL 2, [2003] 1 W.L.R. 443 (HL), Lord Hutton; see *R. v Claydon (Colette Dawn)* [2001] EWCA Crim 1359, [2004] 1 W.L.R. 1575 (CA (Crim Div)), Henry, L.J.; see *R. v Pennine Acute Hospitals NHS Trust (formerly Rochdale Healthcare NHS Trust)* [2003] EWCA Crim 3436, [2004] 1 All E.R. 1324 (CA (Crim Div)), Tuckey, L.J.; see *R. v Shayler (David Michael)* [2002] UKHL 11, [2003] 1 A.C. 247 (HL), Lord Bingham of Cornhill; see *R. v Ward (Roger)* [2003] EWCA Crim 814, [2003] 2 Cr. App. R. 20 (CA (Crim Div)), Kay, L.J.

s.29, amended: 2003 c.44 s.45, s.309, s.310, Sch.36 para.66

s.29, varied: 2004 c.28 s.18

s.31, see *Kanaris v Governor of Pentonville Prison* [2003] UKHL 2, [2003] 1 W.L.R. 443 (HL), Lord Hutton; see *R. v Shayler (David Michael)* [2002] UKHL 11, [2003] 1 A.C. 247 (HL), Lord Bingham of Cornhill; see *R. v Ward (Roger)* [2003] EWCA Crim 814, [2003] 2 Cr. App. R. 20 (CA (Crim Div)), Kay, L.J.

s.31, amended: 2003 c.44 s.310, Sch.36 para.67

s.31, repealed (in part): 2003 c.44 Sch.36 para.36, Sch.37 Part 3

s.33, amended: 2003 c.39 Sch.8 para.379

s.33, substituted: 2003 c.39 Sch.8 para.379

s.34, amended: 2003 c.44 Sch.36 para.68

s.35, see *R. v Claydon (Colette Dawn)* [2001] EWCA Crim 1359, [2004] 1 W.L.R. 1575 (CA (Crim Div)), Henry, L.J.; see *R. v E* [2004] EWCA Crim 1243, [2004] 1 W.L.R. 3279 (CA (Crim Div)), Rose, L.J.; see *R. v H (Assault of Child: Reasonable Chastisement)* [2001] EWCA Crim 1024, [2002] 1 Cr. App. R. 7 (CA (Crim Div)), Rose, L.J.; see *R. v K (Age of Consent: Reasonable Belief)* [2001] UKHL 41,

1996–cont.

25. Criminal Procedure and Investigations Act 1996–*cont.*

s.35–*cont.*

[2002] 1 A.C. 462 (HL), Lord Bingham of Cornhill; see *R. v Mokrecovas (Andrius)* [2001] EWCA Crim 1644, [2002] 1 Cr. App. R. 20 (CA (Crim Div)), Lord Woolf of Barnes, L.C.J.

s.35, amended: 2003 c.44 s.45, Sch.36 para.69

s.35, varied: 2004 c.28 s.18

s.36, amended: 2003 c.44 Sch.36 para.70

s.37, amended: 2003 c.44 s.311

s.38, amended: 2003 c.44 s.311

s.39, amended: 2002 c.26 Sch.13, 2003 c.44 Sch.36 para.71, Sch.3 para.66

s.40, see *R. v Ward (Roger)* [2003] EWCA Crim 814, [2003] 2 Cr. App. R. 20 (CA (Crim Div)), Kay, L.J.

s.41, amended: 2003 c.44 s.311

s.44, repealed (in part): 2003 c.44 Sch.37 Part 4

s.45, repealed: 2003 c.44 Sch.37 Part 4

s.49, repealed (in part): 2003 c.44 Sch.37 Part 4

s.56, repealed (in part): 2003 c.42 Sch.7

s.68, repealed: 2003 c.44 Sch.37 Part 4, Sch.3 para.66

s.77, amended: 2003 c.44 Sch.36 para.37

s.79, amended: 2003 c.44 s.311

Sch.1 Part I para.2, repealed: 2003 c.44 Sch.37 Part 4

Sch.1 Part I para.3, repealed: 2003 c.44 Sch.37 Part 4

Sch.1 Part I para.4, repealed: 2003 c.44 Sch.37 Part 4

Sch.1 Part I para.5, repealed: 2003 c.44 Sch.37 Part 4

Sch.1 Part I para.8, repealed: 2003 c.44 Sch.37 Part 4

Sch.1 Part I para.10, repealed: 2003 c.44 Sch.37 Part 4

Sch.1 Part I para.12, repealed: 2003 c.44 Sch.37 Part 4

Sch.1 Part I para.13, repealed: 2003 c.44 Sch.37 Part 4

Sch.1 Part II para.15, repealed: 2003 c.44 Sch.37 Part 4

Sch.1 Part II para.16, repealed: 2003 c.44 Sch.37 Part 4

Sch.1 Part II para.17, repealed: 2003 c.44 Sch.37 Part 4

Sch.1 Part II para.18, repealed: 2003 c.44 Sch.37 Part 4

Sch.1 Part II para.19, repealed: 2003 c.44 Sch.37 Part 4

Sch.1 Part II para.22, repealed (in part): 2003 c.44 Sch.37 Part 4

Sch.1 Part II para.24, repealed: 2003 c.44 Sch.37 Part 4

CAP.

1996–cont.

25. Criminal Procedure and Investigations Act 1996–*cont.*

Sch.1 Part II para.25, repealed: 2003 c.44 Sch.37 Part 4

Sch.1 Part II para.26, repealed: 2003 c.44 Sch.37 Part 4

Sch.1 Part II para.28, repealed: 2003 c.44 Sch.37 Part 4, Sch.37 Part 6

Sch.1 Part II para.29, repealed: 2003 c.44 Sch.37 Part 4, Sch.37 Part 6

Sch.1 Part II para.30, repealed: 2003 c.44 Sch.37 Part 4, Sch.37 Part 6

Sch.1 Part II para.31, repealed: 2003 c.44 Sch.37 Part 4, Sch.37 Part 6

Sch.1 Part II para.32, repealed: 2003 c.44 Sch.37 Part 4

Sch.1 Part II para.34, repealed: 2003 c.44 Sch.37 Part 4

Sch.1 Part II para.35, repealed: 2003 c.44 Sch.37 Part 4

Sch.1 Part II para.36, repealed: 2003 c.44 Sch.37 Part 4

Sch.1 Part II para.37, repealed: 2003 c.44 Sch.37 Part 4

Sch.1 Part II para.38, repealed: 2003 c.44 Sch.37 Part 4

Sch.2 para.1, repealed: 2003 c.44 Sch.37 Part 4, Sch.3 para.66

Sch.2 para.2, repealed: 2003 c.44 Sch.37 Part 4, Sch.3 para.66

Sch.2 para.3, repealed: 2003 c.44 Sch.37 Part 4, Sch.3 para.66

Sch.2 para.4, amended: 2003 c.39 Sch.8 para.380

Sch.2 para.4, repealed: 2003 c.44 Sch.37 Part 4, Sch.3 para.66

Sch.2 para.5, repealed: 2003 c.44 Sch.37 Part 4, Sch.3 para.66

Sch.2 para.6, repealed: 2003 c.44 Sch.37 Part 4, Sch.3 para.66

Sch.2 para.7, repealed: 2003 c.44 Sch.37 Part 4, Sch.3 para.66

Sch.3 para.8, amended: 2002 c.26 Sch.13

Sch.4 para.7, amended: 2003 c.44 Sch.36 para.38

Sch.4 para.11, repealed: SI 2003/435 Sch.5

Sch.4 para.13, amended: 2003 c.39 Sch.8 para.381

Sch.4 para.15, amended: 2003 c.44 Sch.36 para.72

Sch.4 para.15A, added: 2003 c.44 Sch.36 para.72

Sch.4 para.16, repealed: 2003 c.44 s.311, Sch.37 Part 12

Sch.4 para.19, repealed: SI 2003/435 Sch.5

27. Family Law Act 1996

see *A (A Child) (Abduction: Rights of Custody: Imprisonment), Re* [2004] 1 F.L.R. 1 (Fam Div), Dame Elizabeth Butler-Sloss (President); see *Chan Pui Chun v Leung Kam Ho* [2002] EWCA Civ 1075,

CAP.

1996–cont.

27. Family Law Act 1996–*cont.*

see–*cont.*

[2003] 1 F.L.R. 23 (CA), Jonathan Parker, L.J.

applied: SI 2003/165 Sch.4, SI 2003/1417 Sch.2 para.2, SI 2003/2092 Sch.4, SI 2004/595 Sch.4

referred to: 2002 c.38 Sch.3 para.85

Part IV, amended: 2004 c.33 Sch.9 para.1

Part IV, applied: 2004 c.33 Sch.9 para.25, SI 2004/3114 Sch.1

s.9, repealed (in part): 2002 c.27 s.1

s.22, amended: SI 2003/3191 Sch.1 para.2

s.22, varied: SI 2003/3191 Art.3

s.30, see *Moore v Moore* [2004] EWCA Civ 1243, [2004] 3 F.C.R. 461 (CA), Thorpe, L.J.

s.30, amended: 2004 c.33 Sch.9 para.1

s.30, applied: 2002 c.15 s.61

s.31, amended: 2002 c.9 Sch.11 para.34, 2004 c.33 Sch.9 para.2

s.31, applied: SI 2003/1417 r.82, SI 2003/1953 Art.20

s.31, repealed (in part): 2002 c.9 Sch.13

s.32, applied: SI 2003/1417 r.82

s.32, substituted: 2004 c.33 Sch.9 para.3

s.33, see *Chan Pui Chun v Leung Kam Ho* [2002] B.P.I.R. 723 (Ch D), Judge McGonigal; see *Moore v Moore* [2004] EWCA Civ 1243, [2004] 3 F.C.R. 461 (CA), Thorpe, L.J.

s.33, amended: 2004 c.33 Sch.9 para.4

s.33, applied: SI 2003/1953 Sch.1, 2004 c.33 s.46

s.34, amended: 2004 c.33 Sch.9 para.5

s.35, amended: 2004 c.33 Sch.9 para.6

s.36, see *Clibbery v Allan* [2002] EWCA Civ 45, [2002] Fam. 261 (CA), Dame Elizabeth Butler-Sloss (President)

s.36, amended: 2004 c.28 s.2, Sch.10 para.34, 2004 c.33 Sch.9 para.7

s.37, amended: 2004 c.33 Sch.9 para.8

s.37, applied: 2004 c.33 s.46

s.38, amended: 2004 c.28 Sch.10 para.35

s.41, repealed: 2004 c.28 s.2, Sch.11

s.42, see *Lomas v Parle* [2003] EWCA Civ 1804, [2004] 1 W.L.R. 1642 (CA), Thorpe, L.J.

s.42, amended: 2004 c.28 Sch.10 para.36, Sch.11, 2004 c.33 Sch.9 para.9

s.42A, added: 2004 c.28 s.1

s.42A, referred to: 2004 c.28 Sch.12 para.1

s.44, amended: 2004 c.33 Sch.9 para.10

s.46, amended: 2004 c.28 Sch.10 para.37

s.47, amended: 2004 c.28 Sch.10 para.38

s.47, repealed (in part): 2004 c.28 Sch.10 para.38, Sch.11

s.49, amended: 2004 c.28 Sch.10 para.39, Sch.11, 2004 c.33 Sch.9 para.11

s.54, amended: 2004 c.33 Sch.9 para.12

1996–cont.

27. Family Law Act 1996–*cont.*
s.56, applied: SI 2003/165 Sch.3 Part III, SI 2003/1417 r.158, SI 2003/2092 Sch.3 Part 3, SI 2004/595 Sch.3 Part 3
s.62, amended: 2002 c.38 Sch.3 para.86, Sch.3 para.87, 2004 c.28 s.3, s.4, Sch.10 para.40, 2004 c.33 Sch.9 para.13
s.63, amended: 2002 c.38 Sch.3 para.88, 2004 c.28 Sch.10 para.41, 2004 c.33 Sch.9 para.14, Sch.30
s.63, varied: 2004 c.33 Sch.21 para.43
s.64, amended: 2004 c.33 Sch.27 para.152, Sch.30
Sch.4, amended: 2004 c.33 Sch.9 para.15
Sch.4 para.2, amended: 2004 c.33 Sch.9 para.15
Sch.4 para.3, amended: 2004 c.33 Sch.9 para.15
Sch.4 para.4, amended: 2002 c.9 Sch.11 para.34, 2004 c.33 Sch.9 para.15
Sch.4 para.4, applied: SI 2003/1417 r.82
Sch.4 para.4, enabling: SI 2003/1417
Sch.4 para.5, amended: 2004 c.33 Sch.9 para.15
Sch.4 para.6, amended: 2004 c.33 Sch.9 para.15
Sch.7, applied: 2004 c.33 Sch.7 para.13
Sch.7 Part I para.1, amended: 2004 c.33 Sch.9 para.16
Sch.7 Part I para.2, amended: 2004 c.33 Sch.9 para.16
Sch.7 Part I para.3, amended: 2004 c.28 Sch.10 para.42
Sch.7 Part I para.4, amended: 2004 c.28 Sch.10 para.42, 2004 c.33 Sch.9 para.16, Sch.30
Sch.7 Part I para.5, amended: 2004 c.33 Sch.9 para.16
Sch.7 Part II para.6, amended: 2004 c.33 Sch.9 para.16
Sch.7 Part II para.7, amended: 2004 c.33 Sch.9 para.16
Sch.7 Part II para.7, repealed (in part): 2004 c.33 Sch.9 para.16, Sch.30
Sch.7 Part II para.8, amended: 2004 c.33 Sch.9 para.16
Sch.7 Part II para.9, amended: 2004 c.33 Sch.9 para.16
Sch.7 Part III para.10, amended: 2004 c.33 Sch.9 para.16
Sch.7 Part III para.10, applied: 2004 c.33 Sch.7 para.13
Sch.7 Part III para.11, amended: 2004 c.33 Sch.9 para.16
Sch.7 Part III para.11, applied: 2004 c.33 Sch.7 para.13
Sch.7 Part III para.12, substituted: 2004 c.33 Sch.9 para.16
Sch.7 Part III para.13, substituted: 2004 c.33 Sch.9 para.16

1996–cont.

27. Family Law Act 1996–*cont.*
Sch.7 Part III para.14, applied: 2004 c.33 Sch.7 para.13
Sch.7 Part III para.15, amended: 2004 c.33 Sch.9 para.16
Sch.8 Part I para.37, amended: 2002 c.8 s.1
Sch.8 Part III para.45, repealed: 2002 c.9 Sch.13
Sch.8 Part III para.48, repealed (in part): 2004 c.33 Sch.30
Sch.8 Part III para.53, repealed (in part): 2004 c.33 Sch.30
Sch.8 Part III para.59, repealed (in part): 2004 c.33 Sch.30

29. Sexual Offences (Conspiracy and Incitement) Act 1996
Sch.1 para.1, amended: 2003 c.42 Sch.6 para.35
Sch.1 para.1, repealed (in part): 2003 c.42 Sch.7
Sch.1 para.2, amended: SI 2003/1247 Sch.1 para.17
Sch.1 para.2, repealed (in part): SI 2003/1247 Sch.2

30. Community Care (Direct Payments) Act 1996
applied: SI 2002/2006 Reg.19, SSI 2002/494 Reg.33, Sch.2 para.5, Sch.3 para.8

31. Defamation Act 1996
referred to: SI 2002/808 Art.2, SI 2002/1057 Art.2
s.2, see *Abu v MGN Ltd* [2002] EWHC 2345, [2003] 1 W.L.R. 2201 (QBD), Eady, J.; see *Milne v Express Newspapers (No.1)* [2004] EWCA Civ 664, [2004] E.M.L.R. 24 (CA), May, L.J.
s.3, see *Abu v MGN Ltd* [2002] EWHC 2345, [2003] 1 W.L.R. 2201 (QBD), Eady, J.; see *Cleese v Clark* [2003] EWHC 137, [2004] E.M.L.R. 3 (QBD), Eady, J.; see *Milne v Express Newspapers (No.1)* [2004] EWCA Civ 664, [2004] E.M.L.R. 24 (CA), May, L.J.; see *Nail v News Group Newspapers Ltd* [2004] EWHC 647, [2004] E.M.L.R. 20 (QBD), Eady, J.; see *Rigg v Associated Newspapers Ltd* [2003] EWHC 710, [2004] E.M.L.R. 4 (QBD), Gray, J.
s.4, see *Abu v MGN Ltd* [2002] EWHC 2345, [2003] 1 W.L.R. 2201 (QBD), Eady, J.; see *Milne v Express Newspapers (No.1)* [2002] EWHC 2564, [2003] 1 W.L.R. 927 (QBD), Eady, J.; see *Milne v Express Newspapers (No.1)* [2004] EWCA Civ 664, [2004] E.M.L.R. 24 (CA), May, L.J.; see *Rigg v Associated Newspapers Ltd* [2003] EWHC 710, [2004] E.M.L.R. 4 (QBD), Gray, J.
s.8, see *Loutchansky v Times Newspapers Ltd (No.2)* [2001] EWCA Civ 1805, [2002] Q.B. 783 (CA), Lord Phillips of Worth Matravers, M.R.

CAP.

1996–cont.

37. Noise Act 1996
s.1, substituted: 2003 c.38 s.42
s.2, amended: 2003 c.38 s.42, Sch.3
s.9, amended: 2003 c.38 s.42
s.11, amended: 2003 c.38 s.42
Sch.1 para.3, applied: SI 2003/336 Sch.1 Part 2
Sch.1 para.4, applied: SI 2003/336 Sch.1 Part 2
Sch.1 para.5, see *R. (on the application of Wotton) v Central Devon Magistrates Court* [2003] EWHC 146, [2003] E.H.L.R. Dig. 6 (QBD (Admin Ct)), McCombe, J.

40. Party Wall etc Act 1996
s.3, see *Roadrunner Properties Ltd v Dean* [2003] EWCA Civ 1816, [2004] 1 E.G.L.R. 73 (CA), Chadwick, L.J.

41. Hong Kong (War Wives and Widows) Act 1996
s.2, amended: SI 2003/1016 Sch.1 para.8

42. Railway Heritage Act 1996
applied: SI 2002/655 Reg.21

43. Education (Scotland) Act 1996
applied: 2002 asp 14 s.1
s.1, amended: 2002 asp 14 s.1
s.1, repealed (in part): 2002 asp 14 s.1
s.4, amended: 2004 asp 4 Sch.3 para.10
s.7, amended: 2002 asp 14 s.5
s.33, amended: 2004 asp 4 Sch.3 para.10
Sch.1 para.2, amended: 2002 asp 14 s.1
Sch.1 para.3, repealed: 2002 asp 14 s.1
Sch.1 para.9, amended: 2002 asp 14 s.1
Sch.1 para.9, repealed (in part): 2002 asp 14 s.1
Sch.1 para.10, amended: 2002 asp 14 s.1, s.2
Sch.1 para.11, amended: 2002 asp 14 s.1

46. Armed Forces Act 1996
see *Cooper v United Kingdom (48843/99)* (2004) 39 E.H.R.R. 8 (ECHR), Judge Wildhaber (President)
s.8, repealed: 2004 c.28 Sch.11
s.29, repealed: SI 2004/702 Sch.8
Sch.2 para.1, repealed: 2004 c.28 Sch.11
Sch.2 para.2, repealed: 2004 c.28 Sch.11
Sch.2 para.3, repealed: 2004 c.28 Sch.11
Sch.2 para.4, repealed: 2004 c.28 Sch.11
Sch.2 para.5, repealed: 2004 c.28 Sch.11
Sch.2 para.6, repealed: 2004 c.28 Sch.11
Sch.2 para.7, repealed: 2004 c.28 Sch.11
Sch.2 para.8, repealed: 2004 c.28 Sch.11
Sch.2 para.9, repealed: 2004 c.28 Sch.11
Sch.2 para.10, repealed: 2004 c.28 Sch.11
Sch.2 para.11, repealed: 2004 c.28 Sch.11
Sch.2 para.12, repealed: 2004 c.28 Sch.11

47. Trusts of Land and Appointment of Trustees Act 1996
see *Owo-Samson v Barclays Bank Plc (No.1)* [2003] EWCA Civ 714, [2003] B.P.I.R. 1373 (CA), Carnwath, L.J.

CAP.

1996–cont.

47. Trusts of Land and Appointment of Trustees Act 1996–*cont.*
s.2, referred to: SI 2003/1417 Sch.7 para.16
s.6, applied: SI 2003/1417 r.93
s.7, amended: 2002 c.15 Sch.5 para.8
s.8, applied: SI 2003/1417 r.93, r.94
s.9, applied: SI 2003/1417 r.63
s.11, see *Notting Hill Housing Trust v Brackley* [2001] EWCA Civ 601, [2002] H.L.R. 10 (CA), Peter Gibson, L.J.
s.14, see *Chan Pui Chun v Leung Kam Ho* [2002] B.P.I.R. 723 (Ch D), Judge McGonigal; see *Lissimore v Downing* [2003] 2 F.L.R. 308 (Ch D), Judge Norris Q.C.; see *White v White* [2003] EWCA Civ 924, [2004] 2 F.L.R. 321 (CA), Thorpe, L.J.
s.15, see *White v White* [2003] EWCA Civ 924, [2004] 2 F.L.R. 321 (CA), Thorpe, L.J.
Sch.1 para.3, amended: 2004 c.33 Sch.27 para.153
Sch.3 para.5, repealed: 2002 c.9 Sch.13

48. Damages Act 1996
s.1, see *Cooke v United Bristol Healthcare NHS Trust* [2003] EWCA Civ 1370, [2004] 1 W.L.R. 251 (CA), Laws, L.J.; see *Warriner v Warriner* [2002] EWCA Civ 81, [2002] 1 W.L.R. 1703 (CA), Dyson, L.J.
s.1, referred to: SSI 2002/46 Art.3
s.1, enabling: SSI 2002/46
s.2, disapplied: 2003 c.39 s.101
s.2, substituted: 2003 c.39 s.100
s.4, substituted: 2003 c.39 s.101
s.6, amended: 2003 c.39 s.101
Sch.1 para.1, amended: 2003 c.39 s.101

49. Asylum and Immigration Act 1996
see *Dowling & Rutter v Abacus Frozen Foods Ltd (No.2)* 2002 S.L.T. 491 (OH), Lord Johnston
applied: 2002 c.41 s.67, s.77, s.78
s.2, see *R. (on the application of Benda) v Secretary of State for the Home Department (No.1)* [2002] EWHC 127, [2002] Imm. A.R. 314 (QBD (Admin Ct)), Maurice Kay, J.; see *R. (on the application of Gashi (Agim)) v Secretary of State for the Home Department* [2001] EWHC Admin 622, [2002] Imm. A.R. 82 (QBD (Admin Ct)), Scott Baker, J.; see *R. (on the application of Gashi (Agim)) v Secretary of the Home Department (Application for Permission to Appeal)* [2001] EWCA Civ 1850, [2002] Imm. A.R. 351 (CA), Dame Elizabeth Butler-Sloss (President); see *R. (on the application of Yogathas) v Secretary of State for the Home Department* [2002] UKHL 36, [2003] 1 A.C. 920 (HL), Lord Hope of Craighead; see *R. (on the application of Zeqiri) v Secretary of State for the Home Department* [2001] EWCA Civ 342, [2002] Imm. A.R. 42 (CA), Lord Phillips of Worth Matravers, M.R.

CAP.

1996–cont.

49. Asylum and Immigration Act 1996–
cont.
s.4, referred to: SI 2003/2900 Sch.1
s.5, repealed: 2002 c.41 Sch.9
s.7, referred to: SI 2003/2900 Sch.1
s.8, see *Addey and Stanhope School
Governing Body v Vakante* [2003] I.C.R.
290 (EAT), Judge Serota Q.C.
s.8, amended: 2002 c.41 s.147, 2004 c.19 s.6
s.8, applied: 2002 c.41 s.134, SI 2004/755
Art.3, Art.4
s.8, repealed (in part): 2004 c.19 Sch.4
s.8, enabling: SI 2004/755
Sch.2, referred to: SI 2003/2900 Sch.1
Sch.2 para.1, referred to: SI 2003/2900 Sch.1

50. Nursery Education and Grant-Maintained Schools Act 1996
repealed (in part): 2002 c.32 Sch.22 Part 3
s.1, repealed (in part): 2002 c.32 s.18
Sch.2 para.1, amended: SI 2002/1397 Sch.1
para.13

52. Housing Act 1996
applied: 2002 c.40 Sch.17 para.50, SI 2003/
1417 r.181, r.182, r.183
referred to: 2002 c.7 s.17, 2004 c.34 s.267
Part I, applied: 2002 c.40 s.255, 2003 c.26
s.128, 2004 c.34 s.79, Sch.14 para.2, SI
2004/118 Art.3
Part I c.III, added: 2004 c.34 s.220
Part IV, disapplied: SI 2003/239 Reg.3
Part V, see *Merton LBC v Williams* [2002]
EWCA Civ 980, [2003] H.L.R. 20 (CA),
Mance, L.J.
Part V c.III, applied: SI 2004/1306 r.20
Part VI, see *R. (on the application of Giles) v
Fareham BC* [2002] EWHC 2951, [2003]
H.L.R. 36 (QBD (Admin Ct)), M
Supperstone, Q.C.
Part VI, applied: 2002 c.7 s.7, SI 2004/1235
Reg.4
Part VI, disapplied: SI 2002/3264 Reg.3
Part VII, see *Begum (Runa) v Tower Hamlets
LBC* [2002] EWCA Civ 239, [2002] 1
W.L.R. 2491 (CA), Laws, L.J.; see *Begum
(Runa) v Tower Hamlets LBC* [2003] UKHL
5, [2003] 2 A.C. 430 (HL), Lord Hoffmann;
see *Kaya v Haringey LBC* [2001] EWCA Civ
677, [2002] H.L.R.1 (CA), Buxton, L.J.; see
*R. (on the application of B) v Southwark
LBC* [2003] EWHC 1678, [2004] H.L.R. 3
(QBD (Admin Ct)), Owen, J.; see *R. (on the
application of Morris) v Westminster City
Council (No.1)* [2003] EWHC 2266,
[2004] H.L.R. 18 (QBD (Admin Ct)),
Keith, J.
Part VII, applied: SI 2002/2051 Art.2, SI
2002/3264 Reg.4, SI 2003/3326 Art.1, SI
2004/1235 Reg.4
Part VII, referred to: 2002 c.7 s.20
s.8, applied: 2004 c.34 s.200

CAP.

1996–cont.

52. Housing Act 1996–cont.
s.9, see *R. (on the application of Clays Lane
Housing Cooperative Ltd) v Housing Corp*
[2004] EWHC 1084, [2004] H.L.R. 51
(QBD (Admin Ct)), Keith, J.
s.11, repealed (in part): 2002 c.9 Sch.13
s.11, substituted: 2004 c.34 s.199
s.11, varied: 2004 c.34 s.199
s.11A, substituted: 2004 c.34 s.199
s.11B, substituted: 2004 c.34 s.199
s.12, amended: 2004 c.34 s.199
s.12A, added: 2004 c.34 s.200
s.12B, added: 2004 c.34 s.200
s.13, amended: 2002 c.9 Sch.11 para.35,
2004 c.34 s.200
s.13, applied: SI 2003/1417 r.95
s.15, amended: 2004 c.33 Sch.8 para.50,
Sch.30
s.15A, added: 2004 c.34 s.201
s.16, amended: 2003 c.21 Sch.17 para.136,
2004 c.34 s.202
s.16, applied: 2004 c.34 s.202
s.16A, added: 2004 c.34 s.221
s.17, applied: 2002 c.15 s.76, SI 2002/1091
Art.2, SI 2003/54, SI 2003/54 Art.2, SI
2003/1147, 2004 c.34 s.192, s.194
s.17, enabling: SI 2002/1091, SI 2003/54, SI
2003/1147
s.18, amended: 2004 c.34 Sch.11 para.8,
Sch.16
s.20, amended: 2004 c.34 Sch.11 para.9,
Sch.16
s.20, applied: 2003 c.14 Sch.9 para.1
s.21, amended: 2004 c.34 Sch.11 para.10,
Sch.16
s.21, applied: 2003 c.14 Sch.9 para.1
s.28, amended: 2004 c.34 Sch.11 para.11
s.31, amended: 2004 c.34 Sch.11 para.12
s.36, amended: 2003 c.38 s.12, 2004 c.34
Sch.11 para.13
s.40, amended: 2002 c.40 Sch.17 para.51
s.41, amended: 2002 c.40 Sch.17 para.52
s.51, amended: 2004 c.34 s.228
s.51, applied: 2002 asp 11 s.21
s.51A, added: 2004 c.34 s.228
s.51B, added: 2004 c.34 s.228
s.51C, added: 2004 c.34 s.228
s.52, amended: 2004 c.34 Sch.15 para.41
s.54, amended: 2004 c.34 Sch.15 para.42
s.62, amended: 2004 c.33 Sch.8 para.51
s.62, varied: 2004 c.33 Sch.21 para.44
s.65, repealed: 2004 c.34 Sch.16
s.66, repealed: 2004 c.34 Sch.16
s.67, repealed: 2004 c.34 Sch.16
s.68, repealed: 2004 c.34 Sch.16
s.69, repealed: 2004 c.34 Sch.16
s.70, repealed: 2004 c.34 Sch.16
s.71, repealed: 2004 c.34 Sch.16
s.72, repealed: 2004 c.34 Sch.16
s.73, repealed: 2004 c.34 Sch.16

1996–cont.

52. Housing Act 1996–*cont.*

s.74, repealed: 2004 c.34 Sch.16

s.75, repealed: 2004 c.34 Sch.16

s.76, repealed: 2004 c.34 Sch.16

s.77, repealed: 2004 c.34 Sch.16

s.78, repealed: 2004 c.34 Sch.16

s.79, repealed: 2004 c.34 Sch.16

s.81, see *Mohammadi v Anston Investments Ltd* [2003] EWCA Civ 981, [2004] H.L.R. 8 (CA), May, L.J.

s.81, amended: 2002 c.15 s.170, Sch.13 para.16

s.81, applied: 2002 c.15 s.172

s.82, repealed (in part): 2002 c.15 Sch.14

s.83, repealed (in part): 2002 c.15 Sch.14

s.84, applied: 2002 c.15 s.172

s.84, varied: 2002 c.15 Sch.7 para.15

s.85, see *Maunder Taylor v Blaquiere* [2002] EWCA Civ 1633, [2003] 1 W.L.R. 379 (CA), Aldous, L.J.

s.86, repealed (in part): 2002 c.15 Sch.14

s.105, repealed (in part): 2002 c.15 Sch.14

s.111, repealed (in part): 2002 c.15 Sch.14

s.112, repealed (in part): 2002 c.15 Sch.14

s.119, repealed (in part): 2002 c.15 Sch.14

s.120, referred to: SI 2003/325 Sch.1

s.122, amended: 2003 c.26 Sch.7 para.60

s.122, enabling: SI 2002/2322, SI 2003/48, SI 2003/363, SI 2003/478, SI 2003/1338, SI 2003/2398, SI 2003/2399, SI 2004/14, SI 2004/781, SI 2004/2101, SI 2004/2984

s.124, see *R. (on the application of McLellan) v Bracknell Forest BC* [2001] EWCA Civ 1510, [2002] Q.B. 1129 (CA), Waller, L.J.

s.124, applied: 2004 c.34 s.124, Sch.7 para.4, Sch.7 para.12

s.125, amended: 2004 c.34 s.179

s.125A, added: 2004 c.34 s.179

s.125B, added: 2004 c.34 s.179

s.127, see *R. (on the application of McLellan) v Bracknell Forest BC* [2001] EWCA Civ 1510, [2002] Q.B. 1129 (CA), Waller, L.J.

s.128, see *Cardiff City Council v Stone* [2002] EWCA Civ 298, [2003] H.L.R. 47 (CA), Arden, L.J.; see *Forbes v Lambeth LBC* [2003] EWHC 222, [2003] H.L.R. 49 (QBD), Crane, J.; see *R. (on the application of McLellan) v Bracknell Forest BC* [2001] EWCA Civ 1510, [2002] Q.B. 1129 (CA), Waller, L.J.

s.129, see *Cardiff City Council v Stone* [2002] EWCA Civ 298, [2003] H.L.R. 47 (CA), Arden, L.J.

s.130, see *Salford City Council v Garner* [2004] EWCA Civ 364, [2004] H.L.R. 35 (CA), Chadwick, L.J.

s.132, amended: 2004 c.33 Sch.8 para.52

s.133, amended: 2004 c.33 Sch.8 para.53, Sch.30

1996–cont.

52. Housing Act 1996–*cont.*

s.134, amended: 2004 c.33 Sch.8 para.54, Sch.30

s.140, amended: 2004 c.33 Sch.8 para.51

s.140, varied: 2004 c.33 Sch.21 para.45

s.143A, added: 2003 c.38 Sch.1 para.1

s.143B, added: 2003 c.38 Sch.1 para.1

s.143C, added: 2003 c.38 Sch.1 para.1

s.143D, added: 2003 c.38 Sch.1 para.1

s.143E, added: 2003 c.38 Sch.1 para.1

s.143F, added: 2003 c.38 Sch.1 para.1

s.143F, applied: SI 2004/1679 Reg.2

s.143F, referred to: SI 2004/1679 Reg.4

s.143F, enabling: SI 2004/1679

s.143G, added: 2003 c.38 Sch.1 para.1

s.143H, added: 2003 c.38 Sch.1 para.1

s.143H, amended: 2004 c.33 Sch.8 para.55

s.143I, added: 2003 c.38 Sch.1 para.1

s.143I, amended: 2004 c.33 Sch.8 para.56

s.143J, added: 2003 c.38 Sch.1 para.1

s.143J, amended: 2004 c.33 Sch.8 para.57

s.143K, added: 2003 c.38 Sch.1 para.1

s.143K, amended: 2004 c.33 Sch.8 para.58

s.143L, added: 2003 c.38 Sch.1 para.1

s.143M, added: 2003 c.38 Sch.1 para.1

s.143N, added: 2003 c.38 Sch.1 para.1

s.143O, added: 2003 c.38 Sch.1 para.1

s.143P, added: 2003 c.38 Sch.1 para.1

s.143P, amended: 2004 c.33 Sch.8 para.59

s.143P, varied: 2004 c.33 Sch.21 para.46

s.152, see *G v Harrow LBC* [2004] EWHC 17, [2004] N.P.C. 4 (QBD), Roderick Evans, J.; see *Manchester City Council v Ali* [2003] H.L.R. 11 (QBD), Poole, J.; see *Manchester City Council v Lee* [2003] EWCA Civ 1256, [2004] 1 W.L.R. 349 (CA), Pill, L.J.; see *Nottingham City Council v Thames* [2002] EWCA Civ 1098, [2003] H.L.R. 14 (CA), Ward, L.J.; see *Stafford BC v Haynes* [2003] EWCA Civ 159, [2003] H.L.R. 46 (CA), Hale, L.J.

s.152, repealed (in part): 2003 c.38 s.13, Sch.3

s.153, repealed (in part): 2003 c.38 s.13, Sch.3

s.153A, added: 2003 c.38 s.13

s.153B, added: 2003 c.38 s.13

s.153C, added: 2003 c.38 s.13

s.153D, added: 2003 c.38 s.13

s.153E, added: 2003 c.38 s.13

s.154, amended: 2003 c.38 s.13

s.155, amended: 2003 c.38 s.13

s.157, amended: 2003 c.38 s.13

s.158, amended: 2003 c.38 s.13, Sch.3

s.158, repealed (in part): 2003 c.38 s.13, Sch.3

s.159, see *R. (on the application of Giles) v Fareham BC* [2002] EWHC 2951, [2003] H.L.R. 36 (QBD (Admin Ct)), M Supperstone, Q.C.

s.159, amended: 2002 c.7 s.13

1996–cont.

52. Housing Act 1996–*cont.*

s.160, amended: 2004 c.33 Sch.8 para.60, Sch.30

s.160, enabling: SI 2002/3264, SI 2003/239

s.160A, added: 2002 c.7 s.14

s.160A, applied: SI 2002/3264 Reg.4, Reg.5, SI 2003/239 Reg.4, Reg.5

s.160A, enabling: SI 2002/3264, SI 2003/239, SI 2004/1235

s.161, amended: 2002 c.7 Sch.1 para.3

s.161, repealed (in part): 2002 c.7 s.14, Sch.2

s.162, repealed (in part): 2002 c.7 s.14, Sch.2

s.163, repealed (in part): 2002 c.7 s.14, Sch.2

s.164, repealed (in part): 2002 c.7 s.14, Sch.2

s.165, repealed (in part): 2002 c.7 s.14, Sch.2

s.166, substituted: 2002 c.7 s.15

s.167, see *Kensington and Chelsea RLBC v O'Sullivan* [2003] EWCA Civ 371, [2003] 2 F.L.R. 459 (CA), Arden, L.J.; see *R. (on the application of Giles) v Fareham BC* [2002] EWHC 2951, [2003] H.L.R. 36 (QBD (Admin Ct)), M Supperstone, Q.C.; see *R. (on the application of Lindsay) v Lambeth LBC* [2002] EWCA Civ 1084, [2002] H.L.R. 57 (CA), Collins, J.; see *R. (on the application of Maali) v Lambeth LBC* [2003] EWHC 2231, [2004] H.L.R. 12 (QBD (Admin Ct)), Crane, J.

s.167, amended: 2002 c.7 s.16, 2004 c.34 s.223

s.168, amended: 2002 c.7 Sch.1 para.4

s.170, amended: 2002 c.7 Sch.1 para.5

s.172, enabling: SI 2002/3264, SI 2004/1235

s.174, amended: 2002 c.7 Sch.1 para.6, Sch.2

s.175, see *Higgs v Brighton and Hove City Council* [2003] EWCA Civ 895, [2003] 1 W.L.R. 2241 (CA), Kay, L.J.; see *Porteous v West Dorset DC* [2004] EWCA Civ 244, [2004] H.L.R. 30 (CA), Mantell, L.J.; see *R. (on the application of B) v Southwark LBC* [2003] EWHC 1678, [2004] H.L.R. 3 (QBD (Admin Ct)), Owen, J.; see *R. (on the application of Lee) v Nuneaton and Bedworth BC* [2004] EWHC 950, [2004] J.P.L. 1698 (QBD (Admin Ct)), Collins, J.

s.177, see *Bond v Leicester City Council* [2001] EWCA Civ 1544, [2002] 1 F.C.R. 566 (CA), Hale, L.J.

s.178, amended: 2002 c.38 Sch.3 para.90, Sch.3 para.91, Sch.3 para.92, 2004 c.33 Sch.8 para.61

s.178, referred to: 2002 c.38 Sch.3 para.89

s.178, varied: 2004 c.33 Sch.21 para.47

s.182, see *R. (on the application of Khatun) v Newham LBC* [2004] EWCA Civ 55, [2004] 3 W.L.R. 417 (CA), Auld, L.J.

s.184, see *Porteous v West Dorset DC* [2004] EWCA Civ 244, [2004] H.L.R. 30 (CA), Mantell, L.J.

1996–cont.

52. Housing Act 1996–*cont.*

s.185, see *R. (on the application of Morris) v Westminster City Council (No.1)* [2003] EWHC 2266, [2004] H.L.R. 18 (QBD (Admin Ct)), Keith, J.

s.185, amended: 2002 c.7 Sch.1 para.7

s.185, enabling: SI 2004/1235

s.188, see *Anufrijeva v Southwark LBC* [2002] EWHC 3163, (2003) 6 C.C.L. Rep. 25 (QBD), Newman, J.; see *Bernard v Enfield LBC* [2001] EWCA Civ 1831, [2002] H.L.R. 46 (CA), Mummery, L.J.

s.188, amended: 2002 c.7 Sch.1 para.8

s.188, applied: 2002 c.41 s.55, Sch.3 para.1, SI 2003/3326 Art.3

s.189, see *Ekinci v Hackney LBC* [2001] EWCA Civ 776, [2002] H.L.R. 2 (CA), Pill, L.J.; see *Griffin v Westminster City Council* [2004] EWCA Civ 108, [2004] H.L.R. 32 (CA), Kennedy, L.J.; see *Higgs v Brighton and Hove City Council* [2003] EWCA Civ 895, [2003] 1 W.L.R. 2241 (CA), Kay, L.J.

s.189, applied: SI 2002/2051

s.189, enabling: SI 2002/2051

s.190, see *R. (on the application of S) v Wandsworth LBC* [2001] EWHC Admin 709, [2002] 1 F.L.R. 469 (QBD (Admin Ct)), Jack Beatson Q.C.

s.190, amended: 2002 c.7 Sch.1 para.9, Sch.1 para.10

s.190, applied: SI 2003/3326 Art.3

s.191, see *Goodger v Ealing LBC* [2002] EWCA Civ 751, [2003] H.L.R. 6 (CA), Buxton, L.J.; see *Noh v Hammersmith and Fulham LBC* [2001] EWCA Civ 905, [2002] H.L.R. 54 (CA), Arden, L.J.; see *O'Connor v Kensington and Chelsea RLBC* [2004] EWCA Civ 394, [2004] H.L.R. 37 (CA), Waller, L.J.

s.191, repealed (in part): 2002 c.7 Sch.2

s.192, amended: 2002 c.7 s.5, Sch.1 para.11, Sch.1 para.12

s.193, see *Al-Ameri v Kensington and Chelsea RLBC* [2003] EWCA Civ 235, [2003] 1 W.L.R. 1289 (CA), Simon Brown, L.J.; see *Anufrijeva v Southwark LBC* [2002] EWHC 3163, (2003) 6 C.C.L. Rep. 25 (QBD), Newman, J.; see *Begum (Amirun) v Tower Hamlets LBC* [2002] EWHC 633, [2003] H.L.R. 8 (QBD (Admin Ct)), Stanley Burnton, J.; see *Begum (Runa) v Tower Hamlets LBC* [2003] UKHL 5, [2003] 2 A.C. 430 (HL), Lord Hoffmann; see *Porteous v West Dorset DC* [2004] EWCA Civ 244, [2004] H.L.R. 30 (CA), Mantell, L.J.; see *R. (on the application of Khatun) v Newham LBC* [2004] EWCA Civ 55, [2004] 3 W.L.R. 417 (CA), Auld, L.J.; see *Sharp v Brent LBC* [2003] EWCA Civ 779, [2003] H.L.R. 65 (CA), Laws, L.J.; see *Sheffield City Council v Smart* [2002]

1996–cont.

52. Housing Act 1996–cont.

s.193–cont.

EWCA Civ 4, [2002] H.L.R. 34 (CA), Laws, L.J.

s.193, amended: 2002 c.7 s.6, s.8, Sch.1 para.13, Sch.2

s.193, applied: 2002 c.7 s.6, SI 2003/3326 Art.3, Art.4, 2004 c.19 s.11

s.193, referred to: 2002 c.7 s.7, s.9

s.194, applied: 2002 c.7 s.6

s.194, repealed (in part): 2002 c.7 Sch.2

s.195, see *Hounslow LBC v Adjei* [2004] EWHC 207, [2004] 2 All E.R. 636 (Ch D), Pumfrey, J.

s.195, amended: 2002 c.7 s.5, Sch.1 para.14

s.195, applied: 2002 c.7 s.9, SI 2003/3326 Art.3

s.196, repealed (in part): 2002 c.7 Sch.2

s.197, applied: 2002 c.7 s.9

s.197, repealed (in part): 2002 c.7 Sch.2

s.198, see *Mohamed v Hammersmith and Fulham LBC* [2001] UKHL 57, [2002] 1 A.C. 547 (HL), Lord Slynn of Hadley

s.198, amended: 2002 c.7 Sch.2

s.199, see *Al-Ameri v Kensington and Chelsea RLBC* [2003] EWCA Civ 235, [2003] 1 W.L.R. 1289 (CA), Simon Brown, L.J.; see *Al-Ameri v Kensington and Chelsea RLBC* [2004] UKHL 4, [2004] 2 A.C. 159 (HL), Lord Bingham of Cornhill; see *Mohamed v Hammersmith and Fulham LBC* [2001] UKHL 57, [2002] 1 A.C. 547 (HL), Lord Slynn of Hadley

s.199, amended: 2004 c.19 s.11

s.199, applied: 2004 c.19 s.11

s.200, amended: 2002 c.7 Sch.2

s.200, applied: SI 2003/3326 Art.3, Art.4

s.202, see *Adan v Newham LBC* [2001] EWCA Civ 1916, [2002] 1 WL.R. 2120 (CA), Brooke, L.J.; see *Begum (Runa) v Tower Hamlets LBC* [2002] EWCA Civ 239, [2002] 1 W.L.R. 2491 (CA), Laws, L.J.; see *Francis v Kensington and Chelsea RLBC* [2003] EWCA Civ 443, [2003] 1 W.L.R. 2248 (CA), Simon Brown, L.J.; see *Hackney LBC v Sareen* [2003] EWCA Civ 351, [2003] H.L.R. 54 (CA), Auld, L.J.; see *R. (on the application of C) v Lewisham LBC* [2003] EWCA Civ 927, [2003] 3 All E.R. 1277 (CA), Ward, L.J.; see *Sharp v Brent LBC* [2003] EWCA Civ 779, [2003] H.L.R. 65 (CA), Laws, L.J.

s.202, amended: 2002 c.7 s.8, Sch.1 para.16

s.203, see *Adan v Newham LBC* [2001] EWCA Civ 1916, [2002] 1 WL.R. 2120 (CA), Brooke, L.J.; see *Bernard v Enfield LBC* [2001] EWCA Civ 1831, [2002] H.L.R. 46 (CA), Mummery, L.J.

s.204, see *Adan v Newham LBC* [2001] EWCA Civ 1916, [2002] 1 WL.R. 2120 (CA), Brooke, L.J.; see *Begum (Runa) v*

1996–cont.

52. Housing Act 1996–cont.

s.204–cont.

Tower Hamlets LBC [2002] EWCA Civ 239, [2002] 1 W.L.R. 2491 (CA), Laws, L.J.; see *Begum (Runa) v Tower Hamlets LBC* [2003] UKHL 5, [2003] 2 A.C. 430 (HL), Lord Hoffmann; see *Francis v Kensington and Chelsea RLBC* [2003] EWCA Civ 443, [2003] 1 W.L.R. 2248 (CA), Simon Brown, L.J.; see *Hackney LBC v Sareen* [2003] EWCA Civ 351, [2003] H.L.R. 54 (CA), Auld, L.J.; see *Sharp v Brent LBC* [2003] EWCA Civ 779, [2003] H.L.R. 65 (CA), Laws, L.J.; see *Van Aken v Camden LBC* [2002] EWCA Civ 1724, [2003] 1 W.L.R. 684 (CA), Jonathan Parker, L.J.

s.204, amended: 2002 c.7 Sch.1 para.17

s.204, applied: 2002 c.41 s.55, Sch.3 para.1

s.204A, see *Francis v Kensington and Chelsea RLBC* [2003] EWCA Civ 443, [2003] 1 W.L.R. 2248 (CA), Simon Brown, L.J.

s.204A, added: 2002 c.7 s.11

s.205, amended: 2002 c.7 Sch.1 para.18, Sch.2

s.207, repealed (in part): 2002 c.7 Sch.2

s.209, substituted: 2002 c.7 Sch.1 para.19

s.210, amended: 2004 c.34 Sch.15 para.43

s.210, enabling: SI 2003/3326

s.213A, added: 2002 c.7 s.12

s.215, enabling: SI 2003/239, SI 2003/3326, SI 2004/1235

s.216, disapplied: 2002 c.7 s.20

s.217, amended: 2002 c.7 Sch.1 para.20

s.218, amended: 2002 c.7 Sch.2

s.218A, added: 2003 c.38 s.12

Sch.1 Part I para.1, amended: 2004 c.34 Sch.11 para.14

Sch.1 Part II para.4, amended: SI 2004/1941 Sch.1 para.8

Sch.1 Part II para.15, amended: 2004 c.34 Sch.11 para.15

Sch.1 Part II para.15A, added: 2004 c.34 Sch.11 para.16

Sch.1 Part III para.16, amended: 2004 c.34 Sch.11 para.17

Sch.1 Part III para.16, repealed (in part): 2004 c.34 Sch.11 para.17, Sch.16

Sch.1 Part III para.16A, added: 2004 c.34 Sch.11 para.18

Sch.1 Part III para.17, substituted: 2004 c.34 Sch.11 para.19

Sch.1 Part III para.18, amended: 2004 c.34 Sch.11 para.20, Sch.16

Sch.1 Part III para.19, amended: 2004 c.34 Sch.11 para.22

Sch.1 Part III para.19, repealed (in part): 2004 c.34 Sch.11 para.22, Sch.16

Sch.1 Part III para.19A, added: 2004 c.34 Sch.11 para.23

Sch.1 Part III para.21A, added: 2004 c.34 Sch.11 para.21

1996–cont.

52. Housing Act 1996–*cont.*

Sch.1 Part IV para.20, amended: 2004 c.34 Sch.11 para.24

Sch.1 Part IV para.20A, added: 2004 c.34 Sch.11 para.25

Sch.1 Part IV para.21, amended: 2004 c.34 Sch.11 para.26

Sch.1 Part IV para.23, amended: 2003 c.44 Sch.37 Part 9

Sch.1 Part IV para.23, disapplied: 2003 c.44 Sch.25 para.102

Sch.1 Part IV para.24, amended: 2003 c.44 Sch.37 Part 9

Sch.1 Part IV para.24, disapplied: 2003 c.44 Sch.25 para.102

Sch.1 para.27, see *R. (on the application of Clays Lane Housing Cooperative Ltd) v Housing Corp* [2004] EWHC 1084, [2004] H.L.R. 51 (QBD (Admin Ct)), Keith, J.

Sch.3 para.1, amended: 2003 c.14 Sch.20 para.3

Sch.4, applied: 2002 c.15 s.172

Sch.4 para.1, varied: 2002 c.15 Sch.7 para.15

Sch.4 para.2, varied: 2002 c.15 Sch.7 para.15

Sch.4 para.3, varied: 2002 c.15 Sch.7 para.15

Sch.4 para.4, amended: 2002 c.15 Sch.9 para.12

Sch.4 para.4, varied: 2002 c.15 Sch.7 para.15

Sch.4 para.5, varied: 2002 c.15 Sch.7 para.15

Sch.4 para.6, varied: 2002 c.15 Sch.7 para.15

Sch.4 para.7, varied: 2002 c.15 Sch.7 para.15

Sch.4 para.8, varied: 2002 c.15 Sch.7 para.15

Sch.6 Part IV para.7, repealed (in part): 2002 c.15 Sch.14

Sch.6 Part IV para.8, repealed (in part): 2002 c.15 Sch.14

Sch.9 para.2, repealed (in part): 2002 c.15 Sch.14

Sch.9 para.3, repealed (in part): 2002 c.15 Sch.14

Sch.9 para.4, repealed (in part): 2002 c.15 Sch.14

Sch.9 para.5, repealed (in part): 2002 c.15 Sch.14

Sch.10 para.4, repealed (in part): 2002 c.15 Sch.14

Sch.10 para.18, repealed (in part): 2002 c.15 Sch.14

53. Housing Grants, Construction and Regeneration Act 1996

see *Atlas Ceiling & Partition Co Ltd v Crowngate Estates (Cheltenham) Ltd* (2002) 18 Const. L.J. 49 (QBD (T&CC)), Judge Thornton Q.C.; see *Construction Centre Group Ltd v Highland Council* 2003 S.C. 464 (Ex Div), Lord Hamilton, Lord Carloway, Lord Osborne; see *Ide Contracting Ltd v RG Carter Cambridge Ltd* [2004] B.L.R. 172 (QBD (T&CC)), Judge Havery Q.C.; see *Parsons Plastics*

1996–cont.

53. Housing Grants, Construction and Regeneration Act 1996–*cont.*

see–*cont.*

(Research & Development) Ltd v Purac Ltd [2002] EWCA Civ 459, [2002] B.L.R. 334 (CA), Pill, L.J.; see *RG Carter Ltd v Edmund Nuttall Ltd* [2002] B.L.R. 359 (QBD (T&CC)), Judge Bowsher Q.C.

applied: SI 2002/1860(a)

disapplied: 2004 c.34 s.224

referred to: 2003 c.43 Sch.4 para.102

Part I c.I, applied: SI 2002/1860(a)

s.1, amended: SI 2002/1860 Sch.3 para.2, 2004 c.34 s.224

s.1, applied: SI 2002/1860(a)

s.1, repealed (in part): SI 2002/1860 Sch.6

s.2, enabling: SI 2002/667, SI 2002/2799, SI 2003/2707, SI 2004/254

s.3, amended: SI 2002/2469 Sch.1 para.23, 2003 c.43 Sch.4 para.103

s.4, repealed: SI 2002/1860 Sch.6

s.5, repealed: SI 2002/1860 Sch.6

s.6, repealed: SI 2002/1860 Sch.6

s.7, repealed: SI 2002/1860 Sch.6

s.8, repealed: SI 2002/1860 Sch.6

s.9, repealed: SI 2002/1860 Sch.6

s.10, repealed: SI 2002/1860 Sch.6

s.11, repealed: SI 2002/1860 Sch.6

s.12, repealed: SI 2002/1860 Sch.6

s.13, repealed: SI 2002/1860 Sch.6

s.14, repealed: SI 2002/1860 Sch.6

s.15, repealed: SI 2002/1860 Sch.6

s.16, repealed: SI 2002/1860 Sch.6

s.17, repealed: SI 2002/1860 Sch.6

s.18, repealed: SI 2002/1860 Sch.6

s.19, amended: SI 2002/1860 Sch.3 para.4, Sch.6, 2004 c.34 s.224

s.20, amended: SI 2002/1860 Sch.6

s.21, amended: SI 2002/1860 Sch.6

s.22, amended: SI 2002/1860 Sch.6

s.22A, added: SI 2002/1860 Sch.3 para.6

s.22A, amended: 2004 c.34 s.224

s.23, see *R. (on the application of B) v Calderdale MBC* [2004] EWCA Civ 134, [2004] 1 W.L.R. 2017 (CA), Dame Elizabeth Butler-Sloss (President)

s.23, amended: SI 2002/1860 Sch.3 para.7, Sch.6, 2004 c.34 s.224

s.23, repealed (in part): SI 2002/1860 Sch.6

s.24, see *R. (on the application of B) v Calderdale MBC* [2004] EWCA Civ 134, [2004] 1 W.L.R. 2017 (CA), Dame Elizabeth Butler-Sloss (President)

s.24, amended: SI 2002/1860 Sch.3 para.8, Sch.6, 2004 c.34 s.224

s.24, repealed (in part): 2004 c.34 Sch.15 para.44, Sch.16

s.25, repealed: SI 2002/1860 Sch.6

s.26, repealed: SI 2002/1860 Sch.6

s.27, repealed: SI 2002/1860 Sch.6

s.28, repealed: SI 2002/1860 Sch.6

1996–cont.

53. Housing Grants, Construction and Regeneration Act 1996–*cont.*

s.29, amended: SI 2002/1860 Sch.3 para.10, Sch.6, 2004 c.34 s.224

s.29, repealed (in part): SI 2002/1860 Sch.6

s.30, amended: SI 2002/1860 Sch.6, 2004 c.33 Sch.8 para.62

s.30, repealed (in part): SI 2002/1860 Sch.6

s.30, enabling: SI 2002/530, SI 2002/2798, SI 2003/2504, SI 2004/253

s.31, amended: SI 2002/1860 Sch.3 para.12

s.31, repealed (in part): SI 2002/1860 Sch.6

s.32, repealed: SI 2002/1860 Sch.6

s.33, amended: SI 2002/1860 Sch.6

s.33, repealed (in part): SI 2002/1860 Sch.6

s.33, enabling: SI 2002/837

s.36, amended: SI 2002/1860 Sch.3 para.15

s.40, amended: SI 2002/1860 Sch.3 para.16, Sch.6

s.40, repealed (in part): SI 2002/1860 Sch.6

s.41, amended: SI 2002/1860 Sch.3 para.17, Sch.6, 2004 c.34 s.224

s.43, amended: SI 2002/1860 Sch.3 para.18, Sch.6

s.43, repealed (in part): SI 2002/1860 Sch.6

s.44, amended: SI 2002/1860 Sch.3 para.19

s.44, repealed (in part): SI 2002/1860 Sch.6

s.45, repealed: SI 2002/1860 Sch.6

s.46, repealed: SI 2002/1860 Sch.6

s.47, repealed: SI 2002/1860 Sch.6

s.48, repealed: SI 2002/1860 Sch.6

s.49, repealed: SI 2002/1860 Sch.6

s.50, repealed: SI 2002/1860 Sch.6

s.52, amended: SI 2002/1860 Sch.3 para.21, Sch.6

s.52, repealed (in part): SI 2002/1860 Sch.6

s.53, repealed: SI 2002/1860 Sch.6

s.54, repealed: SI 2002/1860 Sch.6

s.54, varied: 2004 c.33 Sch.8 para.63

s.55, amended: SI 2002/1860 Sch.6

s.55, repealed (in part): SI 2002/1860 Sch.6

s.57, amended: SI 2002/1860 Sch.3 para.24, 2004 c.34 s.224

s.57, repealed (in part): SI 2002/1860 Sch.6

s.58, amended: SI 2002/1860 Sch.3 para.25, Sch.6, 2004 c.34 s.224, Sch.16

s.59, amended: SI 2002/1860 Sch.3 para.26, Sch.6, 2004 c.34 s.224, Sch.16

s.60, repealed: SI 2002/1860 Sch.6

s.61, repealed: SI 2002/1860 Sch.6

s.62, repealed: SI 2002/1860 Sch.6

s.63, repealed: SI 2002/1860 Sch.6

s.64, amended: SI 2002/2469 Sch.1 para.23

s.64, repealed: SI 2002/1860 Sch.6

s.65, repealed: SI 2002/1860 Sch.6

s.66, repealed: SI 2002/1860 Sch.6

s.67, repealed: SI 2002/1860 Sch.6

s.68, repealed: SI 2002/1860 Sch.6

s.69, repealed: SI 2002/1860 Sch.6

s.70, repealed: SI 2002/1860 Sch.6

1996–cont.

53. Housing Grants, Construction and Regeneration Act 1996–*cont.*

s.71, repealed: SI 2002/1860 Sch.6

s.72, repealed: SI 2002/1860 Sch.6

s.73, repealed: SI 2002/1860 Sch.6

s.74, repealed: SI 2002/1860 Sch.6

s.75, repealed: SI 2002/1860 Sch.6

s.76, repealed: SI 2002/1860 Sch.6

s.77, amended: 2002 c.21 Sch.3 para.58

s.77, repealed: SI 2002/1860 Sch.6

s.78, repealed: SI 2002/1860 Sch.6

s.79, repealed: SI 2002/1860 Sch.6

s.80, repealed: SI 2002/1860 Sch.6

s.81, repealed: 2004 c.34 Sch.16

s.82, repealed: 2004 c.34 Sch.16

s.83, repealed: 2004 c.34 Sch.16

s.84, repealed: 2004 c.34 Sch.16

s.85, repealed: 2004 c.34 Sch.16

s.86, repealed: 2004 c.34 s.51, Sch.16

s.87, repealed: 2004 c.34 Sch.16

s.88, repealed: 2004 c.34 Sch.16

s.89, repealed: 2004 c.34 Sch.16

s.90, repealed: 2004 c.34 Sch.16

s.91, repealed: 2004 c.34 Sch.16

s.93, repealed (in part): SI 2002/1860 Sch.6

s.94, repealed (in part): SI 2002/1860 Sch.6

s.95, amended: SI 2002/1860 Sch.3 para.31

s.95, repealed (in part): SI 2002/1860 Sch.6

s.96, repealed: SI 2002/1860 Sch.6

s.97, repealed: 2004 c.34 Sch.16

s.98, repealed (in part): SI 2002/1860 Sch.6

s.101, amended: SI 2002/1860 Sch.3 para.34, Sch.6

s.102, amended: SI 2002/1860 Sch.3 para.35

s.104, see *Baldwins Industrial Services Plc v Barr Ltd* [2003] B.L.R. 176 (QBD (T&CC)), Judge Kirkham; see *Gillies Ramsay Diamond v PJW Enterprises Ltd* 2003 S.L.T. 162 (OH), Lady Paton

s.105, see *Baldwins Industrial Services Plc v Barr Ltd* [2003] B.L.R. 176 (QBD (T&CC)), Judge Kirkham; see *Comsite Projects Ltd v Andritz AG* [2003] EWHC 958, (2004) 20 Const. L.J. 24 (QBD (T&CC)), Judge Kirkham; see *Conor Engineering Ltd v Constructions Industrielles de la Mediterranee (CNIM) SA* [2004] EWHC 899, [2004] B.L.R. 212 (QBD (T&CC)), David Blunt Q.C.

s.105, amended: 2003 c.21 Sch.17 para.137

s.107, see *Carillion Construction Ltd v Devonport Royal Dockyard* [2003] B.L.R. 79 (QBD (T&CC)), Judge Bowsher Q.C.; see *Connex South Eastern Ltd v MJ Building Services Group Plc* [2004] EWHC 1518, [2004] B.L.R. 333 (QBD (T&CC)), Richard Havery Q.C.; see *Cowlin Construction Ltd v CFW Architects* [2003] B.L.R. 241 (QBD), Frances Kirkham, J.; see *Pegram Shopfitters Ltd v*

CAP.

CAP.

1996–cont.

53. Housing Grants, Construction and Regeneration Act 1996–cont.

s.107–cont.

Tally Weijl (UK) Ltd [2003] EWCA Civ 1750, [2004] 1 W.L.R. 2082 (CA), May, L.J.; see *Thomas-Fredric's (Construction) Ltd v Wilson* [2003] EWCA Civ 1494, [2004] B.L.R. 23 (CA), Simon Brown, L.J.

s.108, see *Barnes & Elliott Ltd v Taylor Woodrow Holdings Ltd* [2003] EWHC 3100, [2004] B.L.R. 111 (QBD (T&CC)), Judge Humphrey LLoyd Q.C.; see *Buxton Building Contractors Ltd v Durand Primary School Governors* [2004] EWHC 733, [2004] B.L.R. 374 (QBD (T&CC)), Judge Thornton Q.C.; see *Canary Riverside Development (Private) Ltd v Timtec International Ltd* (2003) 19 Const. L.J. 283 (QBD), DKR Oliver Q.C.; see *coA v B* 2003 S.L.T. 242 (OH), Lord Drummond Young; see *Connex South Eastern Ltd v MJ Building Services Group Plc* [2004] EWHC 1518, [2004] B.L.R. 333 (QBD (T&CC)), Richard Havery Q.C.; see *Construction Centre Group Ltd v Highland Council* 2002 S.L.T. 1274 (OH), Lord Macfadyen; see *David McLean Housing Contractors Ltd v Swansea Housing Association Ltd* [2002] B.L.R. 125 (QBD (T&CC)), Judge Humphrey Lloyd Q.C.; see *McAlpine PPS Pipeline Systems Joint Venture v Transco Plc* [2004] EWHC 2030, [2004] B.L.R. 352 (QBD (T&CC)), Judge Toulmin Q.C.; see *Pegram Shopfitters Ltd v Tally Weijl (UK) Ltd* [2003] EWCA Civ 1750, [2004] 1 W.L.R. 2082 (CA), May, L.J.; see *Pegram Shopfitters Ltd v Tally Weijl (UK) Ltd* [2003] EWHC 984, [2003] 1 W.L.R. 2990 (QBD (T&CC)), Judge Thornton Q.C.; see *Quality Street Properties (Trading) Ltd v Elmwood (Glasgow) Ltd* 2002 S.C.L.R. 1118 (Sh Pr), EF Bowen Q.C., Sheriff Principal; see *Simons Construction Ltd v Aardvark Developments Ltd* [2003] EWHC 2474, [2004] B.L.R. 117 (QBD (T&CC)), Judge Richard Seymour Q.C.; see *St Andrews Bay Development Ltd v HBG Management Ltd* 2003 S.L.T. 740 (OH), Lord Wheatley

s.108, see *Levolux AT Ltd v Ferson Contractors Ltd* [2003] EWCA Civ 11, [2003] 1 All E.R. (Comm) 385 (CA), Mantell, L.J.

s.109, see *Tim Butler Contractors Ltd v Merewood Homes Ltd* (2002) 18 Const. L.J. 74 (QBD (T&CC)), Judge Gilliland Q.C.

s.110, see *Karl Construction (Scotland) Ltd v Sweeney Civil Engineering (Scotland) Ltd* 2002 S.C.L.R. 766 (Ex Div), Lord Marnoch, Lord Clarke, Lord Dawson; see *SL Timber Systems Ltd v Carillion Construction Ltd* 2002 S.L.T. 997 (OH), Lord Macfadyen; see *Tim Butler Contractors Ltd v Merewood Homes Ltd*

1996–cont.

53. Housing Grants, Construction and Regeneration Act 1996–cont.

s.110–cont.

(2002) 18 Const. L.J. 74 (QBD (T&CC)), Judge Gilliland Q.C.

s.111, see *Clark Contracts Ltd v Burrell Co (Construction Management) Ltd (No.1)* 2002 S.L.T. (Sh Ct) 103 (Sh Ct (Glasgow and Strathkelvin)), JA Taylor; see *Conor Engineering Ltd v Constructions Industrielles de la Mediterranee (CNIM) SA* [2004] EWHC 899, [2004] B.L.R. 212 (QBD (T&CC)), David Blunt Q.C.; see *Construction Centre Group Ltd v Highland Council* 2002 S.L.T. 1274 (OH), Lord Macfadyen; see *Levolux AT Ltd v Ferson Contractors Ltd* [2002] B.L.R. 341 (QBD (T&CC)), Judge David Wilcox; see *Rupert Morgan Building Services (LLC) Ltd v Jervis* [2003] EWCA Civ 1563, [2004] 1 W.L.R. 1867 (CA), Schiemann, L.J.; see *Shimizu Europe Ltd v LBJ Fabrications Ltd* [2003] EWHC 1229, [2003] B.L.R. 381 (QBD (T&CC)), Judge Kirkham; see *SL Timber Systems Ltd v Carillion Construction Ltd* 2002 S.L.T. 997 (OH), Lord Macfadyen

s.113, amended: SI 2003/2096 Sch.1 para.30

s.131, repealed: SI 2002/1860 Sch.6

s.132, repealed: SI 2002/1860 Sch.6

s.132, enabling: SI 2002/666, SI 2002/2800

s.133, repealed: SI 2002/1860 Sch.6

s.134, repealed: SI 2002/1860 Sch.6

s.135, repealed: SI 2002/1860 Sch.6

s.136, repealed: SI 2002/1860 Sch.6

s.137, repealed: SI 2002/1860 Sch.6

s.138, repealed (in part): 2002 c.9 Sch.13, SI 2002/1860 Sch.6

s.139, repealed: SI 2002/1860 Sch.6

s.140, repealed: SI 2002/1860 Sch.6

s.146, enabling: SI 2002/530, SI 2002/666, SI 2002/667, SI 2002/837, SI 2002/2798, SI 2002/2799, SI 2002/2800, SI 2003/2504, SI 2003/2707, SI 2004/253, SI 2004/254

Sch.1 para.10, repealed: 2004 c.34 Sch.16

Sch.1 para.12, repealed: 2002 c.15 Sch.14

Sch.1 para.15, repealed (in part): SI 2002/1860 Sch.6

55. Broadcasting Act 1996

Commencement Orders: 2003 c.21 Sch.19

applied: 2002 c.40 Sch.15, 2003 c.21 s.198, s.205, s.211, s.212, s.245, s.246, s.263, s.270, s.317, s.343, s.390, s.393, s.394, Sch.10 para.9, Sch.10 para.10, Sch.10 para.12, SI 2004/1975 Art.8, Art.9

referred to: 2003 c.21 s.244, s.262, s.393, Sch.1 para.9, SI 2003/1374 Sch.1

varied: SI 2003/3192 Sch.1 para.1, SI 2003/3193 Sch.1 para.1, Sch.1 para.2

Part I, applied: SI 2002/2779 Art.39, Art.55, 2003 c.21 s.13, s.175, s.215, s.218, s.219, s.241, s.243, s.346, s.359, s.400, Sch.1

1996–cont.

55. Broadcasting Act 1996–*cont.*

Part I, applied:–*cont.*

para.3, SI 2003/284 Art.44, Art.61, SI 2003/1902 Sch.1 para.1, SI 2004/293 Reg.46, Reg.60, SI 2004/1267 Reg.42, Reg.55

Part I, referred to: 2002 c.36 s.12, 2003 c.21 s.241, s.244

Part II, applied: SI 2002/2779 Art.39, Art.55, 2003 c.21 s.13, s.175, s.258, s.346, s.359, s.400, Sch.1 para.5, SI 2003/284 Art.44, Art.61, SI 2003/1902 Sch.1 para.1, SI 2004/293 Reg.46, Reg.60, SI 2004/1267 Reg.42, Reg.55

Part II, referred to: 2002 c.36 s.12, 2003 c.21 s.262

Part III, applied: SI 2003/1902 Sch.1 para.1

Part IV, applied: 2003 c.21 s.358, Sch.1 para.13

Part V, applied: 2003 c.21 s.235, s.237, s.238, s.328, s.358, Sch.12 para.2, Sch.12 para.19, Sch.1 para.14, SI 2003/3142 Art.11

Part V, referred to: 2003 c.21 s.198, s.203

s.1, amended: 2003 c.21 Sch.15 para.74

s.1, applied: SI 2003/3203 Sch.1 para.2

s.1, repealed (in part): 2003 c.21 Sch.19

s.1, varied: 2003 c.21 Sch.18 para.33, SI 2003/3192 Art.2, Sch.1 para.2, Sch.1 para.3, SI 2003/3193 Art.2, Sch.1 para.3, SI 2003/3203 Art.2, Sch.1 para.2, Sch.1 para.3

s.2, amended: 2003 c.21 Sch.15 para.75

s.2, referred to: SI 2003/3197 Sch.2 para.108

s.2, repealed (in part): 2003 c.21 Sch.19

s.2, varied: 2003 c.21 Sch.18 para.33, SI 2003/3192 Art.2, Sch.1 para.4, SI 2003/3193 Art.2, Sch.1 para.4, SI 2003/3203 Art.2, Sch.1 para.4

s.3, amended: 2003 c.21 Sch.15 para.76

s.3, varied: 2003 c.21 Sch.18 para.33, SI 2003/3192 Art.2, Sch.1 para.5, SI 2003/3193 Art.2, Sch.1 para.5, SI 2003/3203 Art.2, Sch.1 para.5

s.4, amended: 2003 c.21 Sch.15 para.77, Sch.19

s.4, applied: 2003 c.21 s.347

s.4, varied: 2003 c.21 Sch.18 para.33, SI 2003/3192 Art.2, Sch.1 para.6, SI 2003/3193 Art.2, Sch.1 para.6, SI 2003/3203 Art.2, Sch.1 para.6, SI 2004/1975 Art.10

s.5, amended: 2003 c.21 s.350, Sch.15 para.78

s.5, repealed (in part): 2003 c.21 Sch.19

s.5, varied: 2003 c.21 Sch.18 para.33, SI 2003/1900 Art.5, SI 2003/3192 Art.2, Sch.1 para.7, SI 2003/3193 Art.2, SI 2003/3203 Art.2, Sch.1 para.7

s.6, repealed: 2003 c.21 Sch.19

s.6, varied: 2003 c.21 Sch.18 para.33, SI 2003/3192 Art.2, SI 2003/3193 Art.2, SI 2003/3203 Art.2

s.7, amended: 2003 c.21 Sch.15 para.79

1996–cont.

55. Broadcasting Act 1996–*cont.*

s.7, referred to: 2003 c.21 s.243

s.7, varied: 2003 c.21 Sch.18 para.33, SI 2003/3192 Art.2, Sch.1 para.8, SI 2003/3193 Art.2, SI 2003/3203 Art.2, Sch.1 para.8

s.8, amended: 2003 c.21 Sch.15 para.80

s.8, referred to: 2003 c.21 s.243

s.8, varied: 2003 c.21 Sch.18 para.33, SI 2003/3192 Art.2, Sch.1 para.9, SI 2003/3193 Art.2, SI 2003/3203 Art.2, Sch.1 para.9

s.9, amended: 2003 c.21 Sch.15 para.81

s.9, referred to: 2003 c.21 s.243

s.9, varied: 2003 c.21 Sch.18 para.33, SI 2003/3192 Art.2, SI 2003/3193 Art.2, SI 2003/3203 Art.2

s.10, amended: 2003 c.21 Sch.15 para.82

s.10, referred to: 2003 c.21 s.243

s.10, varied: 2003 c.21 Sch.18 para.33, SI 2003/3192 Art.2, SI 2003/3193 Art.2, SI 2003/3203 Art.2

s.11, amended: 2003 c.21 Sch.13 para.11, Sch.15 para.83, Sch.19

s.11, applied: 2003 c.21 Sch.13 para.11

s.11, referred to: 2003 c.21 s.243

s.11, varied: 2003 c.21 Sch.18 para.33, SI 2003/3192 Art.2, SI 2003/3193 Art.2, SI 2003/3203 Art.2

s.12, amended: 2003 c.21 s.242, Sch.15 para.84

s.12, applied: 2003 c.21 s.243, SI 2003/3203 Sch.1 para.2

s.12, referred to: 2003 c.21 s.243

s.12, repealed (in part): 2003 c.21 Sch.19

s.12, varied: 2003 c.21 Sch.18 para.33, SI 2003/3192 Art.2, Sch.1 para.2, Sch.1 para.10, SI 2003/3193 Art.2, SI 2003/3203 Art.2, Sch.1 para.2, Sch.1 para.10

s.13, amended: 2003 c.21 Sch.15 para.85

s.13, applied: SI 2003/3203 Sch.1 para.2

s.13, referred to: 2003 c.21 s.243

s.13, varied: 2003 c.21 Sch.18 para.33, SI 2003/3192 Art.2, Sch.1 para.2, Sch.1 para.11, SI 2003/3193 Art.2, SI 2003/3203 Art.2, Sch.1 para.2, Sch.1 para.11

s.14, amended: 2003 c.21 Sch.15 para.86

s.14, referred to: 2003 c.21 s.243

s.14, varied: 2003 c.21 Sch.18 para.33, SI 2003/3192 Art.2, SI 2003/3193 Art.2, SI 2003/3203 Art.2

s.15, amended: 2003 c.21 Sch.13 para.12, Sch.15 para.87

s.15, referred to: 2003 c.21 s.243

s.15, varied: 2003 c.21 Sch.18 para.33, SI 2003/3192 Art.2, SI 2003/3193 Art.2, SI 2003/3203 Art.2

s.16, amended: 2003 c.21 Sch.15 para.88, Sch.19

s.16, referred to: 2003 c.21 s.243

1996–cont.

55. Broadcasting Act 1996–*cont.*

s.16, varied: 2003 c.21 Sch.18 para.33, Sch.18 para.50, SI 2003/3192 Art.2, SI 2003/3193 Art.2, SI 2003/3203 Art.2

s.17, amended: 2003 c.21 Sch.13 para.13, Sch.15 para.89

s.17, applied: 2003 c.21 Sch.13 para.12, SI 2004/1975 Sch.1 para.4

s.17, varied: 2003 c.21 Sch.18 para.33, SI 2003/3192 Art.2, SI 2003/3193 Art.2, SI 2003/3203 Art.2

s.18, amended: 2003 c.21 Sch.15 para.90

s.18, referred to: 2003 c.21 s.243

s.18, repealed (in part): 2003 c.21 Sch.19

s.18, varied: 2003 c.21 Sch.18 para.33, SI 2003/3192 Art.2, SI 2003/3193 Art.2, SI 2003/3203 Art.2

s.19, amended: 2003 c.21 Sch.15 para.91

s.19, applied: SI 2003/3203 Sch.1 para.2

s.19, referred to: 2003 c.21 s.243

s.19, repealed (in part): 2003 c.21 Sch.19

s.19, varied: 2003 c.21 Sch.18 para.33, SI 2003/3192 Art.2, Sch.1 para.2, Sch.1 para.12, SI 2003/3193 Art.2, SI 2003/3203 Art.2, Sch.1 para.2, Sch.1 para.12

s.20, repealed: 2003 c.21 Sch.19

s.20, varied: 2003 c.21 Sch.18 para.33, SI 2003/3192 Art.2, Sch.1 para.2, SI 2003/3193 Art.2, SI 2003/3203 Art.2, Sch.1 para.2

s.21, applied: SI 2003/3203 Sch.1 para.2

s.21, repealed: 2003 c.21 Sch.19

s.21, varied: 2003 c.21 Sch.18 para.33, SI 2003/3192 Sch.1 para.13, SI 2003/3193 Art.2

s.22, repealed: 2003 c.21 Sch.19

s.22, varied: 2003 c.21 Sch.18 para.33, SI 2003/3192 Art.2, SI 2003/3193 Art.2, SI 2003/3203 Art.2

s.23, amended: 2003 c.21 Sch.13 para.14, Sch.15 para.92

s.23, applied: 2003 c.21 Sch.13 para.12, SI 2004/1975 Sch.1 para.4

s.23, varied: 2003 c.21 Sch.18 para.33, SI 2003/3192 Art.2, SI 2003/3193 Art.2, SI 2003/3203 Art.2

s.24, amended: 2003 c.21 Sch.15 para.93

s.24, applied: SI 2003/3203 Sch.1 para.2

s.24, varied: 2003 c.21 Sch.18 para.33, SI 2003/3192 Art.2, Sch.1 para.2, Sch.1 para.14, SI 2003/3193 Art.2, SI 2003/3203 Art.2, Sch.1 para.2, Sch.1 para.13

s.25, amended: 2003 c.21 Sch.15 para.94

s.25, repealed (in part): 2003 c.21 Sch.19

s.25, varied: 2003 c.21 Sch.18 para.33, SI 2003/3192 Art.2, Sch.1 para.15, SI 2003/3193 Art.2, Sch.1 para.7, SI 2003/3203 Art.2, Sch.1 para.14

s.26, amended: 2003 c.21 Sch.15 para.95

1996–cont.

55. Broadcasting Act 1996–*cont.*

s.26, varied: 2003 c.21 Sch.18 para.33, SI 2003/3192 Art.2, SI 2003/3193 Art.2, SI 2003/3203 Art.2

s.27, amended: 2003 c.21 Sch.13 para.15, Sch.15 para.96

s.27, applied: 2003 c.21 Sch.13 para.12, SI 2004/1975 Sch.1 para.4

s.27, varied: 2003 c.21 Sch.18 para.33, SI 2003/3192 Art.2, SI 2003/3193 Art.2, SI 2003/3203 Art.2

s.28, applied: 2003 c.21 Sch.1 para.10, SI 2003/3203 Sch.1 para.2

s.28, repealed: 2003 c.21 Sch.19

s.28, varied: 2003 c.21 Sch.18 para.33, SI 2003/3192 Art.2, Sch.1 para.2, Sch.1 para.16, SI 2003/3193 Art.2, SI 2003/3203 Art.2, Sch.1 para.2, Sch.1 para.15

s.29, amended: 2003 c.21 Sch.19

s.29, varied: 2003 c.21 Sch.18 para.33

s.30, applied: 2003 c.21 s.221

s.30, repealed: 2003 c.21 Sch.19

s.30, varied: 2003 c.21 Sch.18 para.33, SI 2003/3192 Art.2, SI 2003/3193 Art.2, SI 2003/3203 Art.2

s.31, repealed: 2003 c.21 Sch.19

s.31, varied: 2003 c.21 Sch.18 para.33, SI 2003/3192 Art.2, Sch.1 para.17, SI 2003/3193 Art.2, Sch.1 para.8, SI 2003/3203 Art.2, Sch.1 para.16

s.32, amended: 2003 c.21 Sch.15 para.97

s.32, varied: 2003 c.21 Sch.18 para.33

s.33, amended: 2003 c.21 Sch.15 para.98, Sch.19

s.33, applied: 2003 c.21 Sch.1 para.11

s.33, varied: 2003 c.21 Sch.18 para.33, SI 2003/3192 Art.2, Sch.1 para.18, SI 2003/3193 Art.2, Sch.1 para.9, SI 2003/3203 Art.2, Sch.1 para.17

s.34, repealed: 2003 c.21 Sch.19

s.34, varied: 2003 c.21 Sch.18 para.33, SI 2003/3192 Art.2, SI 2003/3193 Art.2, SI 2003/3203 Art.2

s.35, amended: 2003 c.21 Sch.15 para.99

s.35, varied: 2003 c.21 Sch.18 para.33, SI 2003/3192 Art.2, SI 2003/3193 Art.2, SI 2003/3203 Art.2

s.36, amended: 2003 c.21 Sch.13 para.16

s.36, applied: SI 2003/3203 Sch.1 para.2

s.36, varied: 2003 c.21 Sch.18 para.33, SI 2003/3192 Art.2, Sch.1 para.2, SI 2003/3193 Art.2, SI 2003/3203 Art.2

s.37, varied: 2003 c.21 Sch.18 para.33, SI 2003/3192 Art.2, SI 2003/3193 Art.2, SI 2003/3203 Art.2

s.38, repealed: 2003 c.21 Sch.19

s.38, varied: 2003 c.21 Sch.18 para.33, SI 2003/3192 Art.2, Sch.1 para.19, SI 2003/3193 Art.2, Sch.1 para.10, SI 2003/3203 Art.2, Sch.1 para.18

1996–cont.

55. Broadcasting Act 1996–*cont.*

s.39, amended: 2003 c.21 Sch.15 para.100, Sch.19

s.39, varied: 2003 c.21 Sch.18 para.33, SI 2003/3192 Art.2, Sch.1 para.20, SI 2003/3193 Art.2, Sch.1 para.11, SI 2003/3203 Art.2, Sch.1 para.19

s.40, amended: 2003 c.21 Sch.15 para.101, Sch.19

s.40, applied: SI 2003/3203 Sch.1 para.2

s.40, varied: 2003 c.21 s.258, SI 2003/3192 Art.2, Sch.1 para.2, Sch.1 para.21, SI 2003/ 3193 Art.2, Sch.1 para.12, SI 2003/3203 Art.2, Sch.1 para.2, Sch.1 para.20

s.41, amended: 2003 c.21 s.256

s.41, applied: SI 2003/3203 Sch.1 para.2

s.41, varied: 2003 c.21 s.258, SI 2003/3192 Art.2, Sch.1 para.2, Sch.1 para.22, SI 2003/ 3193 Art.2, SI 2003/3203 Art.2, Sch.1 para.2, Sch.1 para.21

s.42, amended: 2003 c.21 Sch.15 para.102

s.42, varied: 2003 c.21 s.258, SI 2003/3192 Art.2, Sch.1 para.23, SI 2003/3193 Art.2, Sch.1 para.13, SI 2003/3203 Art.2, Sch.1 para.22

s.43, amended: 2003 c.21 Sch.15 para.103, Sch.19

s.43, applied: 2003 c.21 s.347

s.43, repealed (in part): 2003 c.21 Sch.19

s.43, varied: 2003 c.21 s.258, SI 2003/3192 Art.2, SI 2003/3193 Art.2, SI 2003/3203 Art.2, SI 2004/1975 Art.10

s.44, amended: 2003 c.21 s.350, Sch.15 para.104

s.44, repealed (in part): 2003 c.21 Sch.19

s.44, varied: 2003 c.21 s.258, SI 2003/1900 Art.5, SI 2003/3192 Art.2, SI 2003/3193 Art.2, SI 2003/3203 Art.2

s.45, repealed: 2003 c.21 Sch.19

s.45, varied: 2003 c.21 s.258, SI 2003/3192 Art.2, SI 2003/3193 Art.2, Sch.1 para.14, SI 2003/3203 Art.2

s.46, amended: 2003 c.21 Sch.15 para.105

s.46, repealed (in part): 2003 c.21 Sch.19

s.46, varied: 2003 c.21 s.258, SI 2003/3192 Art.2, Sch.1 para.2, Sch.1 para.24, SI 2003/ 3193 Art.2, SI 2003/3203 Art.2, Sch.1 para.2, Sch.1 para.23

s.47, amended: 2003 c.21 Sch.15 para.106

s.47, repealed (in part): 2003 c.21 Sch.19

s.47, varied: 2003 c.21 s.258, SI 2003/3192 Art.2, Sch.1 para.25, SI 2003/3193 Art.2, SI 2003/3203 Art.2, Sch.1 para.24

s.48, amended: 2003 c.21 Sch.15 para.107

s.48, varied: 2003 c.21 s.258, Sch.18 para.48, SI 2003/3192 Art.2, SI 2003/3193 Art.2, SI 2003/3203 Art.2

s.49, amended: 2003 c.21 Sch.15 para.108

s.49, applied: 2003 c.21 Sch.1 para.12

1996–cont.

55. Broadcasting Act 1996–*cont.*

s.49, varied: 2003 c.21 s.258, SI 2003/3192 Art.2, Sch.1 para.26, SI 2003/3203 Art.2, Sch.1 para.25

s.50, amended: 2003 c.21 Sch.15 para.109

s.50, varied: 2003 c.21 s.258, SI 2003/3192 Art.2, Sch.1 para.27, SI 2003/3193 Art.2, Sch.1 para.15, SI 2003/3203 Art.2, Sch.1 para.26

s.51, amended: 2003 c.21 Sch.15 para.110

s.51, varied: 2003 c.21 s.258, SI 2003/3192 Art.2, SI 2003/3193 Art.2, Sch.1 para.16, SI 2003/3203 Art.2

s.52, amended: 2003 c.21 Sch.15 para.111

s.52, varied: 2003 c.21 s.258, SI 2003/3192 Art.2, SI 2003/3203 Art.2

s.53, amended: 2003 c.21 Sch.13 para.17, Sch.15 para.112

s.53, applied: 2003 c.21 Sch.13 para.17

s.53, varied: 2003 c.21 s.258, SI 2003/3192 Art.2, SI 2003/3193 Art.2, SI 2003/3203 Art.2

s.54, amended: 2003 c.21 s.259, s.315, Sch.15 para.113

s.54, applied: SI 2003/3203 Sch.1 para.2

s.54, repealed (in part): 2003 c.21 Sch.19

s.54, varied: 2003 c.21 s.258, SI 2003/3192 Art.2, Sch.1 para.2, Sch.1 para.28, SI 2003/ 3193 Art.2, Sch.1 para.17, SI 2003/3203 Art.2, Sch.1 para.2, Sch.1 para.27

s.55, amended: 2003 c.21 Sch.15 para.114

s.55, applied: SI 2003/3203 Sch.1 para.2

s.55, varied: 2003 c.21 s.258, SI 2003/3192 Art.2, Sch.1 para.29, SI 2003/3193 Art.2, SI 2003/3203 Art.2, Sch.1 para.28

s.56, amended: 2003 c.21 Sch.15 para.115, Sch.19

s.56, varied: 2003 c.21 s.258, SI 2003/3192 Art.2, SI 2003/3193 Art.2, SI 2003/3203 Art.2

s.57, amended: 2003 c.21 Sch.13 para.18, Sch.15 para.116

s.57, varied: 2003 c.21 s.258, SI 2003/3192 Art.2, SI 2003/3193 Art.2, SI 2003/3203 Art.2

s.58, amended: 2003 c.21 s.261, Sch.15 para.117, Sch.19

s.58, repealed (in part): 2003 c.21 Sch.19

s.58, varied: 2003 c.21 s.258, Sch.18 para.50, SI 2003/3192 Art.2, SI 2003/3193 Art.2, Sch.1 para.18, SI 2003/3203 Art.2

s.59, amended: 2003 c.21 Sch.13 para.19, Sch.15 para.118

s.59, applied: SI 2004/1975 Sch.1 para.4

s.59, varied: 2003 c.21 s.258, SI 2003/3192 Art.2, SI 2003/3193 Art.2, SI 2003/3203 Art.2

s.60, amended: 2003 c.21 s.260, Sch.15 para.119

s.60, repealed (in part): 2003 c.21 Sch.19

1996–cont.

55. Broadcasting Act 1996–*cont.*

s.60, varied: 2003 c.21 s.258, SI 2003/3192 Art.2, SI 2003/3193 Art.2, Sch.1 para.19, SI 2003/3203 Art.2

s.61, amended: 2003 c.21 Sch.15 para.120

s.61, repealed (in part): 2003 c.21 Sch.19

s.61, varied: 2003 c.21 s.258, SI 2003/3192 Art.2, SI 2003/3193 Art.2, SI 2003/3203 Art.2

s.62, amended: 2003 c.21 Sch.13 para.20, Sch.15 para.121

s.62, applied: SI 2004/1975 Sch.1 para.4

s.62, varied: 2003 c.21 s.258, SI 2003/3192 Art.2, SI 2003/3193 Art.2, Sch.1 para.20, SI 2003/3203 Art.2

s.63, amended: 2003 c.21 s.260

s.63, applied: 2002 c.36 s.12, SI 2003/3203 Sch.1 para.2

s.63, varied: 2003 c.21 s.258, SI 2003/3192 Art.2, Sch.1 para.2, Sch.1 para.30, SI 2003/3193 Art.2, Sch.1 para.21, SI 2003/3203 Art.2, Sch.1 para.2, Sch.1 para.29

s.64, amended: 2003 c.21 Sch.15 para.122

s.64, varied: 2003 c.21 s.258, SI 2003/3192 Art.2, SI 2003/3193 Art.2, SI 2003/3203 Art.2

s.65, amended: 2003 c.21 Sch.15 para.123

s.65, varied: 2003 c.21 s.258, SI 2003/3192 Art.2, SI 2003/3193 Art.2, SI 2003/3203 Art.2

s.66, amended: 2003 c.21 Sch.13 para.21, Sch.15 para.124

s.66, applied: SI 2004/1975 Sch.1 para.4

s.66, varied: 2003 c.21 s.258, SI 2003/3192 Art.2, SI 2003/3193 Art.2, SI 2003/3203 Art.2

s.67, amended: 2003 c.21 Sch.15 para.125

s.67, applied: 2003 c.21 Sch.1 para.11

s.67, varied: 2003 c.21 s.258, SI 2003/3192 Art.2, Sch.1 para.31, SI 2003/3193 Art.2, SI 2003/3203 Art.2, Sch.1 para.30

s.68, repealed: 2003 c.21 Sch.19

s.68, varied: 2003 c.21 s.258, SI 2003/3192 Art.2, SI 2003/3193 Art.2, SI 2003/3203 Art.2

s.69, amended: 2003 c.21 Sch.13 para.22

s.69, applied: SI 2003/3203 Sch.1 para.2

s.69, varied: 2003 c.21 s.258, SI 2003/3192 Art.2, Sch.1 para.2, SI 2003/3193 Art.2, SI 2003/3203 Art.2

s.70, varied: 2003 c.21 s.258, SI 2003/3192 Art.2, SI 2003/3193 Art.2, SI 2003/3203 Art.2

s.71, repealed: 2003 c.21 Sch.19

s.71, varied: 2003 c.21 s.258, SI 2003/3192 Art.2, Sch.1 para.32, SI 2003/3193 Art.2, Sch.1 para.22, SI 2003/3203 Art.2, Sch.1 para.31

s.72, amended: 2003 c.21 s.260, Sch.15 para.126, Sch.19

1996–cont.

55. Broadcasting Act 1996–*cont.*

s.72, varied: 2003 c.21 s.258, SI 2003/3192 Art.2, Sch.1 para.33, SI 2003/3193 Art.2, Sch.1 para.23, SI 2003/3203 Art.2, Sch.1 para.32

s.73, varied: SI 2003/3192 Art.2, SI 2003/3193 Art.2, SI 2003/3203 Art.2

s.74, repealed: 2003 c.21 Sch.19

s.74, varied: SI 2003/3192 Art.2, SI 2003/3193 Art.2, SI 2003/3203 Art.2

s.75, repealed: 2003 c.21 Sch.19

s.75, varied: SI 2003/3192 Art.2, SI 2003/3193 Art.2, SI 2003/3203 Art.2

s.76, repealed: 2003 c.21 Sch.19

s.76, varied: SI 2003/3192 Art.2, SI 2003/3193 Art.2, SI 2003/3203 Art.2

s.78, repealed: 2003 c.21 Sch.19

s.78, varied: SI 2003/3192 Art.2, SI 2003/3193 Art.2, SI 2003/3203 Art.2

s.79, repealed: 2003 c.21 Sch.19

s.79, varied: SI 2003/3192 Art.2, SI 2003/3193 Art.2, SI 2003/3203 Art.2

s.80, repealed (in part): 2003 c.21 Sch.19

s.82, repealed: 2003 c.21 Sch.19

s.82, varied: SI 2003/3192 Art.2, SI 2003/3193 Art.2, SI 2003/3203 Art.2

s.83, repealed: 2003 c.21 Sch.19

s.83, varied: SI 2003/3192 Art.2, SI 2003/3193 Art.2, SI 2003/3203 Art.2

s.84, repealed: 2003 c.21 Sch.19

s.84, varied: SI 2003/3192 Art.2, Sch.1 para.34, SI 2003/3193 Art.2, Sch.1 para.24, SI 2003/3203 Art.2, Sch.1 para.33

s.85, varied: SI 2003/3192 Art.2, SI 2003/3203 Art.2

s.86, repealed (in part): 2003 c.21 Sch.19

s.86, varied: SI 2003/3192 Art.2, Sch.1 para.35, SI 2003/3193 Art.2, Sch.1 para.25, SI 2003/3203 Art.2, Sch.1 para.34

s.87, repealed: 2003 c.21 Sch.19

s.87, varied: SI 2003/3192 Art.2, SI 2003/3193 Art.2, SI 2003/3203 Art.2

s.88, repealed: 2003 c.21 Sch.19

s.88, varied: SI 2003/3192 Art.2, Sch.1 para.36, SI 2003/3203 Art.2, Sch.1 para.35

s.89, repealed: 2003 c.21 Sch.19

s.89, varied: SI 2003/3192 Art.2, SI 2003/3203 Art.2

s.90, repealed: 2003 c.21 Sch.19

s.91, repealed: 2003 c.21 Sch.19

s.92, varied: SI 2003/3192 Art.2, SI 2003/3193 Art.2, SI 2003/3203 Art.2

s.93, repealed: 2003 c.21 Sch.19

s.93, varied: SI 2003/3192 Art.2, SI 2003/3203 Art.2

s.94, varied: SI 2003/3192 Art.2

s.95, repealed (in part): 2003 c.21 Sch.19

s.96, varied: SI 2003/3192 Art.2, SI 2003/3203 Art.2

s.97, amended: 2003 c.21 s.299, Sch.19

1996–cont.

55. Broadcasting Act 1996–*cont.*

s.97, varied: 2003 c.21 Sch.18 para.51, SI 2003/3142 Art.10, SI 2003/3192 Art.2, Sch.1 para.37, SI 2003/3193 Art.2, Sch.1 para.26, SI 2003/3203 Art.2, Sch.1 para.36

s.98, amended: 2003 c.21 Sch.15 para.127

s.98, applied: SI 2003/3203 Sch.1 para.2

s.98, varied: 2003 c.21 Sch.18 para.51, SI 2003/3192 Art.2, Sch.1 para.2, Sch.1 para.38, SI 2003/3193 Art.2, SI 2003/3203 Art.2, Sch.1 para.2, Sch.1 para.37

s.99, amended: 2003 c.21 s.300

s.99, varied: 2003 c.21 Sch.18 para.51, SI 2003/3192 Art.2, Sch.1 para.39, SI 2003/3193 Art.2, Sch.1 para.27, SI 2003/3203 Art.2, Sch.1 para.38

s.100, varied: 2003 c.21 Sch.18 para.51, SI 2003/3192 Art.2, Sch.1 para.40, SI 2003/3193 Art.2, SI 2003/3203 Art.2, Sch.1 para.39

s.101, amended: 2003 c.21 s.300, Sch.15 para.128

s.101, varied: 2003 c.21 Sch.18 para.51, SI 2003/3192 Art.2, Sch.1 para.41, SI 2003/3193 Art.2, SI 2003/3203 Art.2, Sch.1 para.40

s.101A, varied: 2003 c.21 Sch.18 para.51, SI 2003/3192 Art.2, SI 2003/3193 Art.2, SI 2003/3203 Art.2

s.101B, amended: 2003 c.21 Sch.15 para.128

s.101B, varied: 2003 c.21 Sch.18 para.51, SI 2003/3192 Art.2, SI 2003/3193 Art.2, SI 2003/3203 Art.2

s.102, amended: 2003 c.21 s.300, Sch.15 para.128

s.102, applied: SI 2003/3203 Sch.1 para.2

s.102, varied: 2003 c.21 Sch.18 para.51, SI 2003/3192 Art.2, Sch.1 para.2, Sch.1 para.42, SI 2003/3193 Art.2, SI 2003/3203 Art.2, Sch.1 para.2, Sch.1 para.41

s.103, amended: 2003 c.21 s.300, Sch.15 para.128

s.103, varied: 2003 c.21 Sch.18 para.51, SI 2003/3192 Art.2, Sch.1 para.43, SI 2003/3193 Art.2, Sch.1 para.28, SI 2003/3203 Art.2, Sch.1 para.42

s.104, amended: 2003 c.21 s.301, Sch.15 para.129, Sch.19

s.104, varied: 2003 c.21 Sch.18 para.51, SI 2003/3192 Art.2, Sch.1 para.44, SI 2003/3193 Art.2, Sch.1 para.29, SI 2003/3203 Art.2, Sch.1 para.43

s.104A, amended: 2003 c.21 Sch.15 para.130

s.104A, varied: 2003 c.21 Sch.18 para.51, SI 2003/3192 Art.2, SI 2003/3193 Art.2, SI 2003/3203 Art.2

s.104ZA, added: 2003 c.21 s.302

s.104ZA, varied: 2003 c.21 Sch.18 para.51, SI 2003/3192 Art.2, SI 2003/3193 Art.2, SI 2003/3203 Art.2

s.105, amended: 2003 c.21 s.302, Sch.19

1996–cont.

55. Broadcasting Act 1996–*cont.*

s.105, varied: 2003 c.21 Sch.18 para.51, SI 2003/3192 Art.2, SI 2003/3193 Art.2, SI 2003/3203 Art.2

s.106, repealed: 2003 c.21 Sch.19

s.106, varied: 2003 c.21 Sch.18 para.52, SI 2003/3192 Art.2, SI 2003/3193 Art.2, SI 2003/3203 Art.2

s.107, amended: 2003 c.21 Sch.15 para.132, Sch.15 para.133, Sch.19

s.107, applied: 2003 c.21 s.326, Sch.1 para.14

s.107, repealed (in part): 2003 c.21 Sch.19

s.107, varied: 2003 c.21 Sch.18 para.52, Sch.18 para.53, SI 2003/3192 Art.2, Sch.1 para.45, SI 2003/3193 Art.2, Sch.1 para.30, SI 2003/3203 Art.2, Sch.1 para.44

s.108, applied: SI 2003/3142 Art.11

s.108, repealed: 2003 c.21 Sch.19

s.108, varied: 2003 c.21 Sch.18 para.43, Sch.18 para.52, SI 2003/3192 Art.2, Sch.1 para.46, SI 2003/3193 Art.2, Sch.1 para.31, SI 2003/3203 Art.2, Sch.1 para.45

s.109, repealed: 2003 c.21 Sch.19

s.109, varied: 2003 c.21 Sch.18 para.52, SI 2003/3192 Art.2, Sch.1 para.47, SI 2003/3193 Art.2, SI 2003/3203 Art.2, Sch.1 para.46

s.110, amended: 2003 c.21 Sch.15 para.132, Sch.19

s.110, repealed (in part): 2003 c.21 Sch.19

s.110, varied: 2003 c.21 Sch.18 para.52, SI 2003/3192 Art.2, SI 2003/3193 Art.2, SI 2003/3203 Art.2

s.111, amended: 2003 c.21 Sch.15 para.132

s.111, varied: 2003 c.21 Sch.18 para.52, SI 2003/3192 Art.2, SI 2003/3193 Art.2, SI 2003/3203 Art.2

s.112, repealed: 2003 c.21 Sch.19

s.112, varied: 2003 c.21 Sch.18 para.52, SI 2003/3192 Art.2, SI 2003/3193 Art.2, SI 2003/3203 Art.2

s.113, repealed: 2003 c.21 Sch.19

s.113, varied: 2003 c.21 Sch.18 para.52, SI 2003/3192 Art.2, SI 2003/3193 Art.2, SI 2003/3203 Art.2

s.114, amended: 2003 c.21 Sch.15 para.132, Sch.19

s.114, varied: 2003 c.21 Sch.18 para.52, SI 2003/3192 Art.2, Sch.1 para.48, SI 2003/3193 Art.2, Sch.1 para.32, SI 2003/3203 Art.2, Sch.1 para.47

s.115, amended: 2003 c.21 s.327, Sch.15 para.132, Sch.15 para.134

s.115, repealed (in part): 2003 c.21 Sch.19

s.115, varied: 2003 c.21 Sch.18 para.52, SI 2003/3192 Art.2, SI 2003/3193 Art.2, SI 2003/3203 Art.2

s.116, repealed: 2003 c.21 Sch.19

s.116, varied: 2003 c.21 Sch.18 para.52, SI 2003/3192 Art.2, Sch.1 para.49, SI 2003/3193 Art.2, Sch.1 para.33, SI 2003/3203 Art.2, Sch.1 para.48

1996–cont.

55. Broadcasting Act 1996–cont.

s.117, amended: 2003 c.21 Sch.15 para.135

s.117, varied: 2003 c.21 Sch.18 para.52, SI 2003/3192 Art.2, Sch.1 para.50, SI 2003/3193 Art.2, Sch.1 para.34, SI 2003/3203 Art.2, Sch.1 para.49

s.118, amended: 2003 c.21 Sch.15 para.132, Sch.19

s.118, varied: 2003 c.21 Sch.18 para.52, SI 2003/3192 Art.2, SI 2003/3193 Art.2, SI 2003/3203 Art.2

s.119, amended: 2003 c.21 s.327, Sch.15 para.132, Sch.15 para.136, Sch.19

s.119, applied: 2003 c.21 s.341

s.119, repealed (in part): 2003 c.21 Sch.15 para.136, Sch.19

s.119, varied: 2003 c.21 Sch.18 para.52, SI 2003/3192 Art.2, Sch.1 para.51, SI 2003/3193 Art.2, Sch.1 para.35, SI 2003/3203 Art.2, Sch.1 para.50

s.120, amended: 2003 c.21 s.327, Sch.15 para.132, Sch.19

s.120, varied: 2003 c.21 Sch.18 para.52, SI 2003/3192 Art.2, SI 2003/3193 Art.2, SI 2003/3203 Art.2

s.121, amended: 2003 c.21 Sch.15 para.132

s.121, varied: 2003 c.21 Sch.18 para.52, SI 2003/3192 Art.2, SI 2003/3193 Art.2, SI 2003/3203 Art.2

s.122, repealed: 2003 c.21 Sch.19

s.122, varied: 2003 c.21 Sch.18 para.52, SI 2003/3192 Art.2, SI 2003/3193 Art.2, SI 2003/3203 Art.2

s.123, repealed: 2003 c.21 Sch.19

s.123, varied: 2003 c.21 Sch.18 para.52, SI 2003/3192 Art.2, SI 2003/3193 Art.2, SI 2003/3203 Art.2

s.124, repealed: 2003 c.21 Sch.19

s.124, varied: 2003 c.21 Sch.18 para.52, SI 2003/3192 Art.2, Sch.1 para.52, SI 2003/3193 Art.2, Sch.1 para.36, SI 2003/3203 Art.2, Sch.1 para.51

s.125, repealed: 2003 c.21 Sch.19

s.125, varied: 2003 c.21 Sch.18 para.52, SI 2003/3192 Art.2, Sch.1 para.53, SI 2003/3193 Art.2, Sch.1 para.37, SI 2003/3203 Art.2, Sch.1 para.52

s.126, repealed: 2003 c.21 Sch.19

s.126, varied: 2003 c.21 Sch.18 para.52, SI 2003/3192 Art.2, SI 2003/3193 Art.2, SI 2003/3203 Art.2

s.127, repealed: 2003 c.21 Sch.19

s.127, varied: 2003 c.21 Sch.18 para.52

s.128, repealed: 2003 c.21 Sch.19

s.128, varied: 2003 c.21 Sch.18 para.52, SI 2003/3192 Art.2, SI 2003/3193 Art.2, SI 2003/3203 Art.2

s.129, repealed: 2003 c.21 Sch.19

s.129, varied: 2003 c.21 Sch.18 para.52, SI 2003/3192 Art.2, SI 2003/3193 Art.2, SI 2003/3203 Art.2

1996–cont.

55. Broadcasting Act 1996–cont.

s.130, amended: 2003 c.21 Sch.15 para.137, Sch.19

s.130, repealed (in part): 2003 c.21 Sch.19

s.130, varied: 2003 c.21 Sch.18 para.52, SI 2003/3192 Art.2, Sch.1 para.54, SI 2003/3193 Art.2, Sch.1 para.38, SI 2003/3203 Art.2, Sch.1 para.53

s.131, varied: SI 2003/3193 Art.2

s.132, varied: SI 2003/3193 Art.2

s.133, varied: SI 2003/3193 Art.2

s.136, varied: SI 2003/3193 Art.2

s.137, amended: SI 2003/2498 Sch.1 para.21, Sch.2

s.142, amended: 2002 c.40 Sch.25 para.34

s.142, repealed: 2003 c.21 Sch.19

s.142, varied: SI 2003/3192 Art.2, Sch.1 para.55, SI 2003/3193 Art.2, Sch.1 para.39, SI 2003/3203 Art.2, Sch.1 para.54

s.143, amended: 2003 c.21 Sch.15 para.138

s.143, repealed (in part): 2003 c.21 Sch.19

s.143, varied: SI 2003/3192 Art.2, Sch.1 para.56, SI 2003/3193 Art.2, Sch.1 para.40, SI 2003/3203 Art.2, Sch.1 para.55

s.144, amended: 2003 c.21 Sch.15 para.139, 2003 c.44 Sch.37 Part 9

s.144, disapplied: 2003 c.44 Sch.25 para.103

s.144, repealed (in part): 2003 c.21 Sch.19

s.144, varied: SI 2003/3192 Art.2, Sch.1 para.57, SI 2003/3193 Art.2, Sch.1 para.41, SI 2003/3203 Art.2, Sch.1 para.56

s.145, amended: 2003 c.21 Sch.15 para.140, Sch.19, SI 2003/3299 Art.13

s.145, applied: 2003 c.21 s.281

s.145, varied: SI 2003/3192 Art.2, SI 2003/3193 Art.2, SI 2003/3203 Art.2

s.146, varied: SI 2003/3192 Art.2, Sch.1 para.58, SI 2003/3193 Art.2, Sch.1 para.42, SI 2003/3203 Art.2, Sch.1 para.57

s.147, amended: 2003 c.21 Sch.15 para.141

s.147, varied: SI 2003/3192 Art.2, SI 2003/3193 Art.2, SI 2003/3203 Art.2

s.148, varied: SI 2003/3192 Art.2, SI 2003/3193 Art.2, SI 2003/3203 Art.2

s.150, applied: SI 2003/3192, SI 2003/3193, SI 2003/3203, SI 2004/308, SI 2004/309, SI 2004/715, SI 2004/716

s.150, varied: SI 2003/3192 Sch.1 para.59, SI 2003/3193 Art.2, Sch.1 para.43, SI 2003/3203 Sch.1 para.58

s.150, enabling: SI 2003/3192, SI 2003/3193, SI 2003/3203, SI 2004/308, SI 2004/309, SI 2004/715, SI 2004/716

Sch.1 Part I para.1, amended: 2003 c.21 Sch.15 para.142

Sch.1 Part I para.1, varied: 2003 c.21 Sch.18 para.37, SI 2003/3192 Art.2, SI 2003/3193 Art.2, SI 2003/3203 Art.2

Sch.1 Part I para.2, amended: 2003 c.21 Sch.15 para.142

1996–cont.

55. Broadcasting Act 1996–cont.

Sch.1 Part I para.2, varied: 2003 c.21 Sch.18 para.37, SI 2003/3192 Art.2, SI 2003/3193 Art.2, SI 2003/3203 Art.2

Sch.1 Part II para.3, amended: 2003 c.21 Sch.15 para.142

Sch.1 Part II para.3, varied: 2003 c.21 Sch.18 para.37, SI 2003/3192 Art.2, SI 2003/3193 Art.2, SI 2003/3203 Art.2

Sch.1 Part II para.4, amended: 2003 c.21 Sch.15 para.142

Sch.1 Part II para.4, varied: 2003 c.21 Sch.18 para.37, SI 2003/3192 Art.2, SI 2003/3193 Art.2, SI 2003/3203 Art.2

Sch.2 Part I para.1, repealed (in part): 2003 c.21 Sch.19

Sch.2 Part I para.1, varied: SI 2003/3192 Art.2, SI 2003/3193 Art.2, SI 2003/3203 Art.2

Sch.2 Part I para.2, varied: SI 2003/3192 Art.2, SI 2003/3193 Art.2, SI 2003/3203 Art.2

Sch.2 Part I para.3, varied: SI 2003/3192 Art.2, SI 2003/3193 Art.2, SI 2003/3203 Art.2

Sch.2 Part I para.4, repealed: 2003 c.21 Sch.19

Sch.2 Part I para.4, varied: SI 2003/3192 Art.2, SI 2003/3193 Art.2, SI 2003/3203 Art.2

Sch.2 Part I para.5, repealed: 2003 c.21 Sch.19

Sch.2 Part I para.5, varied: SI 2003/3192 Art.2, SI 2003/3193 Art.2, SI 2003/3203 Art.2

Sch.2 Part II para.6, repealed (in part): 2003 c.21 Sch.19

Sch.2 Part II para.6, varied: SI 2003/3192 Art.2, SI 2003/3193 Art.2, SI 2003/3203 Art.2

Sch.2 Part II para.7, varied: SI 2003/3192 Art.2, SI 2003/3193 Art.2, SI 2003/3203 Art.2

Sch.2 Part II para.8, varied: SI 2003/3192 Art.2, SI 2003/3193 Art.2, SI 2003/3203 Art.2

Sch.2 Part II para.9, varied: SI 2003/3192 Art.2, SI 2003/3193 Art.2, SI 2003/3203 Art.2

Sch.2 Part III para.10, repealed: 2003 c.21 Sch.19

Sch.2 Part III para.10, varied: SI 2003/3192 Art.2, SI 2003/3193 Art.2, SI 2003/3203 Art.2

Sch.2 Part IV para.11, repealed: 2003 c.21 Sch.19

Sch.2 Part IV para.11, varied: SI 2003/3192 Art.2, SI 2003/3193 Art.2, SI 2003/3203 Art.2

Sch.2 Part V para.12, varied: SI 2003/3192 Art.2, SI 2003/3193 Art.2, SI 2003/3203 Art.2

1996–cont.

55. Broadcasting Act 1996–cont.

Sch.2 Part V para.13, varied: SI 2003/3192 Art.2, SI 2003/3193 Art.2, SI 2003/3203 Art.2

Sch.3 para.1, repealed: 2003 c.21 Sch.19

Sch.3 para.1, varied: SI 2003/3192 Art.2, Sch.1 para.60, SI 2003/3193 Art.2, SI 2003/3203 Art.2, Sch.1 para.59

Sch.3 para.2, repealed: 2003 c.21 Sch.19

Sch.3 para.2, varied: SI 2003/3192 Art.2, SI 2003/3193 Art.2, SI 2003/3203 Art.2

Sch.3 para.3, repealed: 2003 c.21 Sch.19

Sch.3 para.3, varied: SI 2003/3192 Art.2, Sch.1 para.60, SI 2003/3193 Art.2, SI 2003/3203 Art.2, Sch.1 para.59

Sch.3 para.4, repealed: 2003 c.21 Sch.19

Sch.3 para.4, varied: SI 2003/3192 Art.2, Sch.1 para.60, SI 2003/3193 Art.2, SI 2003/3203 Art.2, Sch.1 para.59

Sch.3 para.5, repealed: 2003 c.21 Sch.19

Sch.3 para.5, varied: SI 2003/3192 Art.2, Sch.1 para.60, SI 2003/3193 Art.2, SI 2003/3203 Art.2, Sch.1 para.59

Sch.3 para.6, repealed: 2003 c.21 Sch.19

Sch.3 para.6, varied: SI 2003/3192 Art.2, Sch.1 para.60, SI 2003/3193 Art.2, SI 2003/3203 Art.2, Sch.1 para.59

Sch.3 para.7, repealed: 2003 c.21 Sch.19

Sch.3 para.7, varied: SI 2003/3192 Art.2, Sch.1 para.60, SI 2003/3193 Art.2, SI 2003/3203 Art.2, Sch.1 para.59

Sch.3 para.8, repealed: 2003 c.21 Sch.19

Sch.3 para.8, varied: SI 2003/3192 Art.2, Sch.1 para.60, SI 2003/3193 Art.2, SI 2003/3203 Art.2, Sch.1 para.59

Sch.3 para.9, repealed: 2003 c.21 Sch.19

Sch.3 para.9, varied: SI 2003/3192 Art.2, Sch.1 para.60, SI 2003/3193 Art.2, SI 2003/3203 Art.2, Sch.1 para.59

Sch.3 para.10, repealed: 2003 c.21 Sch.19

Sch.3 para.10, varied: SI 2003/3192 Art.2, Sch.1 para.60, SI 2003/3193 Art.2, SI 2003/3203 Art.2, Sch.1 para.59

Sch.3 para.11, repealed: 2003 c.21 Sch.19

Sch.3 para.11, varied: SI 2003/3192 Art.2, Sch.1 para.60, SI 2003/3193 Art.2, SI 2003/3203 Art.2, Sch.1 para.59

Sch.3 para.12, repealed: 2003 c.21 Sch.19

Sch.3 para.12, varied: SI 2003/3192 Art.2, SI 2003/3193 Art.2, SI 2003/3203 Art.2

Sch.3 para.13, repealed: 2003 c.21 Sch.19

Sch.3 para.13, varied: SI 2003/3192 Art.2, SI 2003/3193 Art.2, SI 2003/3203 Art.2

Sch.3 para.14, repealed: 2003 c.21 Sch.19

Sch.3 para.14, varied: SI 2003/3192 Art.2, Sch.1 para.60, SI 2003/3193 Art.2, SI 2003/3203 Art.2, Sch.1 para.59

Sch.4 para.1, repealed: 2003 c.21 Sch.19

Sch.4 para.1, varied: SI 2003/3192 Art.2, SI 2003/3193 Art.2, SI 2003/3203 Art.2

Sch.4 para.2, repealed: 2003 c.21 Sch.19

1996–cont.

55. Broadcasting Act 1996–*cont.*

Sch.4 para.2, varied: SI 2003/3192 Art.2, SI 2003/3193 Art.2, SI 2003/3203 Art.2

Sch.4 para.3, repealed: 2003 c.21 Sch.19

Sch.4 para.3, varied: SI 2003/3192 Art.2, SI 2003/3193 Art.2, SI 2003/3203 Art.2

Sch.4 para.4, repealed: 2003 c.21 Sch.19

Sch.4 para.4, varied: SI 2003/3192 Art.2, SI 2003/3193 Art.2, SI 2003/3203 Art.2

Sch.4 para.5, repealed: 2003 c.21 Sch.19

Sch.4 para.5, varied: SI 2003/3192 Art.2, SI 2003/3193 Art.2, SI 2003/3203 Art.2

Sch.4 para.6, repealed: 2003 c.21 Sch.19

Sch.4 para.6, varied: SI 2003/3192 Art.2, SI 2003/3193 Art.2, SI 2003/3203 Art.2

Sch.4 para.7, repealed: 2003 c.21 Sch.19

Sch.4 para.7, varied: SI 2003/3192 Art.2, SI 2003/3193 Art.2, SI 2003/3203 Art.2

Sch.4 para.8, repealed: 2003 c.21 Sch.19

Sch.4 para.8, varied: SI 2003/3192 Art.2, SI 2003/3193 Art.2, SI 2003/3203 Art.2

Sch.5 para.1, varied: SI 2003/3193 Art.2

Sch.5 para.2, varied: SI 2003/3193 Art.2

Sch.5 para.3, varied: SI 2003/3193 Art.2

Sch.5 para.4, varied: SI 2003/3193 Art.2

Sch.5 para.5, varied: SI 2003/3193 Art.2

Sch.5 para.6, varied: SI 2003/3193 Art.2

Sch.5 para.7, varied: SI 2003/3193 Art.2

Sch.5 para.8, varied: SI 2003/3193 Art.2

Sch.5 para.9, varied: SI 2003/3193 Art.2

Sch.5 para.10, varied: SI 2003/3193 Art.2

Sch.7, substituted: SI 2003/2867 Sch.1 para.25

Sch.7 para.25, amended: SI 2003/2867 Sch.1 para.25

Sch.8 para.1, varied: SI 2003/3192 Art.2, SI 2003/3193 Art.2, SI 2003/3203 Art.2

Sch.8 para.2, varied: SI 2003/3192 Art.2, SI 2003/3193 Art.2, SI 2003/3203 Art.2

Sch.8 para.3, varied: SI 2003/3192 Art.2, SI 2003/3193 Art.2, SI 2003/3203 Art.2

Sch.8 para.4, repealed: 2003 c.21 Sch.19

Sch.8 para.4, varied: SI 2003/3192 Art.2, Sch.1 para.61, SI 2003/3193 Art.2, Sch.1 para.44, SI 2003/3203 Art.2, Sch.1 para.60

Sch.8 para.5, varied: SI 2003/3192 Art.2, SI 2003/3193 Art.2, SI 2003/3203 Art.2

Sch.8 para.6, varied: SI 2003/3192 Art.2, SI 2003/3193 Art.2, SI 2003/3203 Art.2

Sch.8 para.7, varied: SI 2003/3192 Art.2, SI 2003/3193 Art.2, SI 2003/3203 Art.2

Sch.8 para.8, varied: SI 2003/3192 Art.2, SI 2003/3193 Art.2, SI 2003/3203 Art.2

Sch.10 Part I para.1, repealed: 2003 c.21 Sch.19

Sch.10 Part I para.1, varied: SI 2003/3192 Art.2, SI 2003/3193 Art.2, SI 2003/3203 Art.2

Sch.10 Part I para.2, varied: SI 2003/3192 Art.2, SI 2003/3193 Art.2, SI 2003/3203 Art.2

1996–cont.

55. Broadcasting Act 1996–*cont.*

Sch.10 Part I para.3, repealed: 2003 c.21 Sch.19

Sch.10 Part I para.3, varied: SI 2003/3192 Art.2, SI 2003/3193 Art.2, SI 2003/3203 Art.2

Sch.10 Part I para.4, repealed: 2003 c.21 Sch.19

Sch.10 Part I para.4, varied: SI 2003/3192 Art.2, Sch.1 para.62, SI 2003/3193 Art.2, Sch.1 para.45, SI 2003/3203 Art.2, Sch.1 para.61

Sch.10 Part I para.5, repealed: 2003 c.21 Sch.19

Sch.10 Part I para.5, varied: SI 2003/3192 Art.2, SI 2003/3193 Art.2, SI 2003/3203 Art.2

Sch.10 Part I para.6, repealed: 2003 c.21 Sch.19

Sch.10 Part I para.6, varied: SI 2003/3192 Art.2, SI 2003/3193 Art.2, SI 2003/3203 Art.2

Sch.10 Part I para.7, varied: SI 2003/3192 Art.2, SI 2003/3193 Art.2, Sch.1 para.45, SI 2003/3203 Art.2

Sch.10 Part I para.8, repealed: 2003 c.21 Sch.19

Sch.10 Part I para.8, varied: SI 2003/3192 Art.2, Sch.1 para.62, SI 2003/3193 Art.2, Sch.1 para.45, SI 2003/3203 Art.2, Sch.1 para.61

Sch.10 Part I para.9, varied: SI 2003/3192 Art.2, SI 2003/3193 Art.2, SI 2003/3203 Art.2

Sch.10 Part I para.10, varied: SI 2003/3192 Art.2, Sch.1 para.62, SI 2003/3193 Art.2, Sch.1 para.45, SI 2003/3203 Art.2, Sch.1 para.61

Sch.10 Part I para.11, repealed: 2003 c.21 Sch.19

Sch.10 Part I para.11, varied: SI 2003/3192 Art.2, SI 2003/3193 Art.2, SI 2003/3203 Art.2

Sch.10 Part II para.12, repealed: 2003 c.21 Sch.19

Sch.10 Part II para.12, varied: SI 2003/3192 Art.2, SI 2003/3193 Art.2, SI 2003/3203 Art.2

Sch.10 Part II para.13, repealed: 2003 c.21 Sch.19

Sch.10 Part II para.13, varied: SI 2003/3192 Art.2, SI 2003/3193 Art.2, SI 2003/3203 Art.2

Sch.10 Part II para.14, repealed: 2003 c.21 Sch.19

Sch.10 Part II para.14, varied: SI 2003/3192 Art.2, SI 2003/3193 Art.2, SI 2003/3203 Art.2

Sch.10 Part II para.15, varied: SI 2003/3192 Art.2, SI 2003/3193 Art.2, Sch.1 para.45, SI 2003/3203 Art.2

CAP.

1996–cont.

55. Broadcasting Act 1996–*cont.*

Sch.10 Part II para.16, repealed: 2003 c.21 Sch.19

Sch.10 Part II para.16, varied: SI 2003/3192 Art.2, Sch.1 para.62, SI 2003/3193 Art.2, Sch.1 para.45, SI 2003/3203 Art.2, Sch.1 para.61

Sch.10 Part II para.17, varied: SI 2003/3192 Art.2, SI 2003/3193 Art.2, SI 2003/3203 Art.2

Sch.10 Part II para.18, repealed: 2003 c.21 Sch.19

Sch.10 Part II para.18, varied: SI 2003/3192 Art.2, Sch.1 para.62, SI 2003/3193 Art.2, Sch.1 para.45, SI 2003/3203 Art.2, Sch.1 para.61

Sch.10 Part II para.19, repealed: 2003 c.21 Sch.19

Sch.10 Part II para.19, varied: SI 2003/3192 Art.2, SI 2003/3193 Art.2, Sch.1 para.45, SI 2003/3203 Art.2

Sch.10 Part II para.20, repealed: 2003 c.21 Sch.19

Sch.10 Part II para.20, varied: SI 2003/3192 Art.2, Sch.1 para.62, SI 2003/3193 Art.2, SI 2003/3203 Art.2, Sch.1 para.61

Sch.10 Part II para.21, varied: SI 2003/3192 Art.2, Sch.1 para.62, SI 2003/3193 Art.2, Sch.1 para.45, SI 2003/3203 Art.2, Sch.1 para.61

Sch.10 Part II para.22, repealed: 2003 c.21 Sch.19

Sch.10 Part II para.22, varied: SI 2003/3192 Art.2, Sch.1 para.62, SI 2003/3193 Art.2, SI 2003/3203 Art.2, Sch.1 para.61

Sch.10 Part II para.23, repealed: 2003 c.21 Sch.19

Sch.10 Part II para.23, varied: SI 2003/3192 Art.2, Sch.1 para.62, SI 2003/3193 Art.2, SI 2003/3203 Art.2, Sch.1 para.61

Sch.10 Part II para.24, repealed: 2003 c.21 Sch.19

Sch.10 Part II para.24, varied: SI 2003/3192 Art.2, Sch.1 para.62, SI 2003/3193 Art.2, Sch.1 para.45, SI 2003/3203 Art.2, Sch.1 para.61

Sch.10 Part II para.25, repealed: 2003 c.21 Sch.19

Sch.10 Part II para.25, varied: SI 2003/3192 Art.2, Sch.1 para.62, SI 2003/3193 Art.2, SI 2003/3203 Art.2, Sch.1 para.61

Sch.10 Part II para.26, repealed (in part): 2003 c.21 Sch.19

Sch.10 Part II para.26, varied: SI 2003/3192 Art.2, Sch.1 para.62, SI 2003/3193 Art.2, Sch.1 para.45, SI 2003/3203 Art.2, Sch.1 para.61

Sch.10 Part III, varied: SI 2003/3192 Sch.1 para.62, SI 2003/3193 Sch.1 para.45, SI 2003/3203 Sch.1 para.61

Sch.10 Part III para.27, repealed (in part): 2003 c.21 Sch.19

CAP.

1996–cont.

55. Broadcasting Act 1996–*cont.*

Sch.10 Part III para.27, varied: SI 2003/3192 Art.2, SI 2003/3193 Art.2, SI 2003/3203 Art.2

Sch.10 Part III para.28, varied: SI 2003/3192 Art.2, SI 2003/3193 Art.2, SI 2003/3203 Art.2

Sch.10 Part III para.29, varied: SI 2003/3192 Art.2, SI 2003/3193 Art.2, SI 2003/3203 Art.2

Sch.10 Part III para.30, amended: 2002 c.24 Sch.3 para.5

Sch.10 Part III para.30, varied: SI 2003/3192 Art.2, SI 2003/3193 Art.2, SI 2003/3203 Art.2

Sch.10 Part III para.31, varied: SI 2003/3192 Art.2, SI 2003/3193 Art.2, SI 2003/3203 Art.2

Sch.10 Part III para.32, varied: SI 2003/3192 Art.2, SI 2003/3193 Art.2, SI 2003/3203 Art.2

Sch.11 Part I, varied: SI 2003/3192 Art.2, Sch.1 para.63, SI 2003/3193 Art.2, Sch.1 para.46, SI 2003/3203 Art.2, Sch.1 para.62

56. Education Act 1996

see *M v Worcestershire CC* [2002] EWHC 1292, [2003] E.L.R. 31 (QBD (Admin Ct)), Lawrence Collins, J.; see *R. (on the application of B (A Child)) v Alperton Community School Head Teacher and Governing Body* [2001] EWHC Admin 229, [2002] B.L.G.R. 132 (QBD (Admin Ct)), Newman, J.

applied: 2002 c.32 s.212, s.217, 2002 c.38 s.4, s.8, 2002 c.41 s.36, s.37, SI 2002/152 Reg.24, SI 2002/195 Reg.16, SI 2002/377 Reg.20, Reg.24, Reg.26, Sch.2 para.15, Sch.2 para.24, SI 2002/1330 Sch.2 para.14, SI 2002/1983 Reg.3, Reg.4, Reg.5, Reg.6, SI 2002/2903 Reg.8, SI 2002/2904 Reg.8, SI 2002/3199 Reg.1, SI 2002/3200 Reg.16, SI 2003/453 Reg.1, SI 2003/1994 Sch.2 para.14, SI 2003/3247 Reg.20, Reg.23, Reg.25, Sch.1 para.15, Sch.1 para.24, 2004 c.31 s.12, s.29, SI 2004/692 Sch.4 para.5, SI 2004/1011 Reg.7, SI 2004/2506 Reg.17, Sch.1 para.17, SSI 2003/176 Sch.3 para.6

referred to: SI 2002/808 Art.2, 2003 c.43 Sch.4 para.104

varied: SI 2003/2045 Reg.6

Part I, applied: SI 2002/816 Reg.3

Part III c.VI, applied: SI 2002/377 Sch.4 para.2

Part III c.VI, referred to: SI 2003/453 Sch.3 para.2, SI 2003/3247 Sch.3 para.2

Part IV, applied: 2002 c.32 Sch.18 para.17, SI 2002/152 Reg.23, SI 2002/1985 Reg.7, Reg.21

Part IV, referred to: SI 2002/152 Reg.5, SI 2002/1985 Reg.21

Part V c.II, applied: SI 2002/438 Sch.1 para.1

1996–cont.

56. Education Act 1996–*cont.*

Part V c.II, repealed (in part): 2002 c.32 Sch.22 Part 3

Part VI c.II, applied: SI 2002/377 Sch.1 para.19, SI 2002/3199 Sch.1 para.12, SI 2003/3118 Sch.1 para.12, SI 2003/3170 Sch.1 para.12

Part VI c.III, applied: 2002 c.32 s.27

Part VII, applied: SI 2002/1985 Reg.27

s.2, amended: 2002 c.32 s.156, s.177, Sch.7 para.6, Sch.21 para.33, Sch.22 Part 3

s.2, applied: 2002 c.32 s.177

s.2A, applied: SI 2002/152 Reg.19

s.3, amended: 2002 c.32 Sch.21 para.34

s.4, amended: 2002 c.32 Sch.22 Part 3

s.4, applied: SI 2004/118 Art.2

s.4, disapplied: 2002 c.41 s.36

s.5, amended: 2002 c.32 Sch.22 Part 3

s.5, enabling: SI 2002/1983

s.6, amended: 2002 c.32 s.156

s.8, applied: SI 2003/118 Reg.13, 2004 c.33 Sch.5 para.49, Sch.6 para.27

s.9, see *Oxfordshire CC v B* [2001] EWCA Civ 1358, [2002] B.L.G.R. 279 (CA), Sedley, L.J.; see *R. (on the application of C) v Special Educational Needs and Disability Tribunal* [2003] EWHC 1590, [2004] E.L.R. 111 (QBD (Admin Ct)), McCombe, J.; see *S v Hackney LBC* [2001] EWHC Admin 572, [2002] E.L.R. 45 (QBD (Admin Ct)), Collins, J.; see *S v S County Council* [2002] EWHC 1808, [2003] E.L.R. 78 (QBD (Admin Ct)), Sir Richard Tucker; see *Southampton City Council v G* [2002] EWHC 1516, [2002] E.L.R. 698 (QBD (Admin Ct)), Sullivan, J.; see *T v Special Educational Needs Tribunal* [2002] EWHC 1474, [2002] E.L.R. 704 (QBD (Admin Ct)), Richards, J.

s.13, applied: 2002 c.41 s.36

s.14, amended: 2002 c.32 s.194

s.15A, applied: SI 2002/3199 Sch.1 para.19, Sch.1 para.20, SI 2003/3118 Sch.1 para.17, Sch.1 para.18, SI 2003/3170 Sch.1 para.19, Sch.1 para.20

s.15B, applied: SI 2002/3199 Sch.1 para.19, SI 2003/3118 Sch.1 para.17, SI 2003/3170 Sch.1 para.19

s.15B, disapplied: 2004 c.31 s.18

s.18, applied: SI 2002/377 Sch.1 para.23, SI 2002/928 Sch.1, SI 2002/3199 Sch.2 para.18, SI 2003/3118 Sch.2 para.18, SI 2003/3170 Sch.3 para.18

s.19, see *R. (on the application of G (A Child)) v Westminster City Council* [2004] EWCA Civ 45, [2004] 1 W.L.R. 1113 (CA), Lord Phillips of Worth Matravers; see *R. (on the application of G) v Westminster City Council (Application for Permission for Judicial Review)* [2003] E.L.R. 734 (QBD (Admin Ct)), George Bartlett Q.C.; see *R. (on the application of S (A Child)) v C High*

1996–cont.

56. Education Act 1996–*cont.*

s.19–*cont.*

School Head Teacher [2001] EWHC Admin 513, [2002] E.L.R. 73 (QBD (Admin Ct)), Richards, J.

s.19, applied: SI 2002/377 Sch.1 para.12, SI 2002/3199 Sch.2 para.9, SI 2003/3118 Sch.2 para.7, SI 2003/3170 Sch.3 para.9

s.19, disapplied: 2002 c.41 s.36

s.29, repealed (in part): 2002 c.32 Sch.21 para.35, Sch.22 Part 3

s.29, enabling: SI 2002/157, SI 2002/2017, SI 2002/2897, SI 2003/190, SI 2003/2135, SI 2003/2694, SI 2004/1025

s.55A, see *Bournemouth BC v Meredith* [2003] E.L.R. 1 (EAT), Maurice Kay, J.

s.101, applied: SI 2002/377 Sch.4 para.1

s.101, referred to: SI 2003/453 Sch.3 para.1, SI 2003/3247 Sch.3 para.1

s.255, applied: SI 2002/377 Sch.4 para.23, SI 2003/453 Sch.3 para.23, SI 2003/3247 Sch.3 para.23

s.312, see *R. (on the application of S (A Child)) v Oxfordshire CC* [2004] EWHC 133, [2004] E.L.R. 489 (QBD (Admin Ct)), Andrew Nicol Q.C.; see *Wakefield MDC v E* [2001] EWHC Admin 508, [2002] E.L.R. 203 (QBD (Admin Ct)), Collins, J.

s.313, see *R. (on the application of Wilson) v Blaenau Gwent CBC* [2003] EWHC 2880, [2004] E.L.R. 152 (QBD (Admin Ct)), Owen, J.

s.313, amended: 2002 c.32 Sch.18 para.2, Sch.21 para.36

s.313, applied: SI 2002/377 Sch.1 para.8, SI 2002/3199 Sch.2 para.7, SI 2003/2453 Sch.1 para.8, SI 2003/3118 Sch.2 para.5, SI 2003/3170 Sch.3 para.7, SI 2003/3227 Reg.5, SI 2003/3237 Sch.1 para.11, SI 2003/3246 Reg.6, SI 2004/1026 Sch.1 para.2

s.314, applied: SI 2002/156 Art.2

s.314, enabling: SI 2002/156

s.315, see *R. (on the application of C) v Special Educational Needs and Disability Tribunal* [2003] EWHC 1590, [2004] E.L.R. 111 (QBD (Admin Ct)), McCombe, J.

s.315, amended: 2002 c.32 Sch.21 para.37

s.316, see *R. (on the application of MH) v Special Educational Needs and Disability Tribunal* [2004] EWCA Civ 770, [2004] B.L.G.R. 844 (CA), May, L.J.; see *Slough BC v C* [2004] EWHC 1759, [2004] E.L.R. 546 (QBD (Admin Ct)), Richards, J.

s.316, amended: 2002 c.32 Sch.7 para.6

s.316, applied: SI 2002/928 Sch.1

s.316, disapplied: 2002 c.41 s.36

s.316A, see *R. (on the application of MH) v Special Educational Needs and Disability Tribunal* [2004] EWCA Civ 770, [2004] B.L.G.R. 844 (CA), May, L.J.

1996–cont.

56. Education Act 1996–*cont.*

s.316A, amended: 2002 c.32 Sch.21 para.38, Sch.22 Part 3

s.316A, applied: SI 2002/152 Reg.13, SI 2002/928 Sch.1

s.316A, enabling: SI 2002/152

s.317, amended: 2002 c.32 Sch.21 para.39

s.317, applied: SI 2002/928 Sch.1

s.317, repealed (in part): 2002 c.32 Sch.22 Part 3

s.317, varied: SI 2004/657 Art.3, SI 2004/2683 Art.3, SI 2004/2810 Art.3

s.317A, amended: 2002 c.32 Sch.21 para.40

s.317A, applied: SI 2002/928 Sch.1

s.317A, varied: SI 2004/657 Art.3

s.318, amended: 2002 c.32 s.194, Sch.21 para.41

s.318, applied: SI 2002/928 Sch.1

s.318, repealed (in part): 2002 c.32 Sch.22 Part 3

s.319, see *R. (on the application of C) v Special Educational Needs and Disability Tribunal* [2003] EWHC 1590, [2004] E.L.R. 111 (QBD (Admin Ct)), McCombe, J.; see *T v Special Educational Needs Tribunal* [2002] EWHC 1474, [2002] E.L.R. 704 (QBD (Admin Ct)), Richards, J.

s.319, applied: SI 2002/152 Reg.17, SI 2002/928 Sch.1

s.320, applied: SI 2002/377 Reg.4, Sch.1 para.15, SI 2002/928 Sch.1, SI 2002/3199 Sch.2 para.11, SI 2003/3118 Sch.2 para.9, SI 2003/3170 Sch.3 para.11

s.321, amended: 2002 c.32 Sch.21 para.42

s.321, applied: SI 2002/377 Sch.1 para.4, SI 2002/928 Sch.1, SI 2002/3199 Sch.1 para.2, SI 2003/3118 Sch.1 para.2, SI 2003/3170 Sch.1 para.2

s.322, see *S v S County Council* [2002] EWHC 1808, [2003] E.L.R. 78 (QBD (Admin Ct)), Sir Richard Tucker

s.322, applied: SI 2002/377 Sch.1 para.4, SI 2002/928 Sch.1, SI 2002/3199 Sch.1 para.2, SI 2003/3118 Sch.1 para.2, SI 2003/3170 Sch.1 para.2

s.322, enabling: SI 2002/152

s.323, see *O v Harrow LBC* [2001] EWCA Civ 2046, [2002] 1 W.L.R. 928 (CA), Simon Brown, L.J.

s.323, applied: 2002 c.32 s.115, SI 2002/152 Reg.6, Reg.7, Reg.11, Reg.12, Reg.26, SI 2002/377 Sch.1 para.4, SI 2002/928 Sch.1, SI 2002/3199 Sch.1 para.2, SI 2003/3118 Sch.1 para.2, SI 2003/3170 Sch.1 para.2

s.324, see *E v Newham LBC* [2003] EWCA Civ 9, [2003] B.L.G.R. 547 (CA), Schiemann, L.J.; see *E v Rotherham MBC* [2001] EWHC Admin 432, [2002] E.L.R. 266 (QBD (Admin Ct)), Bell, J.; see *E v X LBC* [2002] EWHC 915, [2002] E.L.R. 453 (QBD (Admin Ct)), Stanley Burnton, J.; see

1996–cont.

56. Education Act 1996–*cont.*

s.324–*cont.*

O v Harrow LBC [2001] EWCA Civ 2046, [2002] 1 W.L.R. 928 (CA), Simon Brown, L.J.; see *R. (on the application of A) v Cambridgeshire CC* [2002] EWHC 2391, [2003] E.L.R. 464 (QBD (Admin Ct)), Pitchford, J.

s.324, amended: 2002 c.32 Sch.21 para.43

s.324, applied: 2002 c.32 s.92, s.94, s.113, s.115, 2002 c.41 s.36, SI 2002/152 Reg.7, SI 2002/327 Sch.3 para.13, SI 2002/377 Sch.1 para.4, SI 2002/928 Sch.1, SI 2002/1187 Reg.22, SI 2002/2071 Reg.4, SI 2002/2897 Sch.2 para.3, Sch.3 para.3, SI 2002/2952 Sch.1 para.2, SI 2002/3199 Sch.1 para.2, SI 2003/1041 Sch.1 para.1, SI 2003/1934 Sch.1 para.5, SI 2003/2453 Sch.1 para.8, SI 2003/3118 Sch.1 para.2, SI 2003/3170 Sch.1 para.2, SI 2003/3230 Sch.1 para.5, SI 2003/3246 Reg.6

s.324, varied: SI 2003/1041 Sch.1 para.2, Sch.1 para.3, Sch.1 para.4, Sch.1 para.5

s.324, enabling: SI 2002/152

s.325, see *O v Harrow LBC* [2001] EWCA Civ 2046, [2002] 1 W.L.R. 928 (CA), Simon Brown, L.J.

s.325, applied: SI 2002/152 Reg.13, Reg.17, Reg.26, SI 2002/377 Sch.1 para.4, SI 2002/928 Sch.1, SI 2002/3199 Sch.1 para.2, SI 2003/3118 Sch.1 para.2, SI 2003/3170 Sch.1 para.2

s.325, enabling: SI 2002/152

s.326, see *E v Rotherham MBC* [2001] EWHC Admin 432, [2002] E.L.R. 266 (QBD (Admin Ct)), Bell, J.

s.326, applied: 2002 c.41 s.36, SI 2002/152 Reg.17, SI 2002/377 Sch.1 para.4, SI 2002/928 Sch.1, SI 2002/3199 Sch.1 para.2, SI 2003/3118 Sch.1 para.2, SI 2003/3170 Sch.1 para.2

s.326A, amended: 2002 c.32 Sch.18 para.3

s.326A, applied: 2002 c.32 Sch.18 para.18, SI 2002/377 Sch.1 para.4, SI 2002/928 Sch.1, SI 2002/3199 Sch.1 para.2, SI 2003/3118 Sch.1 para.2, SI 2003/3170 Sch.1 para.2

s.327, amended: 2002 c.32 s.173

s.327, applied: SI 2002/377 Sch.1 para.4, SI 2002/3199 Sch.1 para.2, SI 2003/3118 Sch.1 para.2, SI 2003/3170 Sch.1 para.2

s.328, applied: SI 2002/152 Reg.6, Reg.12, Reg.20, Reg.21, Reg.22, Reg.23, Reg.26, SI 2002/377 Sch.1 para.4, SI 2002/928 Sch.1, SI 2002/3199 Sch.1 para.2, SI 2003/3118 Sch.1 para.2, SI 2003/3170 Sch.1 para.2

s.328, enabling: SI 2002/152

s.329, applied: SI 2002/152 Reg.6, Reg.12, Reg.17, Reg.26, SI 2002/377 Sch.1 para.4, SI 2002/928 Sch.1, SI 2002/3199 Sch.1 para.2, SI 2003/3118 Sch.1 para.2, SI 2003/3170 Sch.1 para.2

1996–cont.

56. Education Act 1996–*cont.*

s.329, enabling: SI 2002/152

s.329A, amended: 2002 c.32 Sch.21 para.44, Sch.22 Part 3

s.329A, applied: SI 2002/152 Reg.6, Reg.7, Reg.11, Reg.12, SI 2002/377 Sch.1 para.4, SI 2002/928 Sch.1, SI 2002/3199 Sch.1 para.2, SI 2003/3118 Sch.1 para.2, SI 2003/3170 Sch.1 para.2

s.329A, varied: 2002 c.41 s.36, SI 2004/657 Art.3

s.329A, enabling: SI 2002/152

s.330, applied: SI 2002/377 Sch.1 para.4, SI 2002/3199 Sch.1 para.2, SI 2003/3118 Sch.1 para.2, SI 2003/3170 Sch.1 para.2

s.331, applied: SI 2002/377 Sch.1 para.4, SI 2002/928 Sch.1, SI 2002/3199 Sch.1 para.2, SI 2003/3118 Sch.1 para.2, SI 2003/3170 Sch.1 para.2

s.332, amended: 2003 c.43 Sch.4 para.105

s.332A, applied: SI 2002/928 Sch.1

s.332B, applied: SI 2002/152 Reg.12, Reg.17, SI 2002/928 Sch.1

s.333, amended: 2002 c.32 Sch.18 para.4

s.333, applied: 2002 c.32 Sch.18 para.13, Sch.18 para.18

s.333, enabling: SI 2002/1985, SI 2002/2787

s.334, applied: 2002 c.32 Sch.18 para.18

s.334, enabling: SI 2002/1985, SI 2002/2787

s.335, applied: 2002 c.32 Sch.18 para.18

s.336, applied: 2002 c.32 Sch.18 para.18

s.336, enabling: SI 2002/1985, SI 2002/2787

s.336A, amended: 2002 c.32 Sch.18 para.6

s.336A, applied: 2002 c.32 Sch.18 para.18

s.336ZA, added: 2002 c.32 Sch.18 para.5

s.336ZA, applied: 2002 c.32 Sch.18 para.18

s.342, applied: SI 2002/152 Reg.18, SI 2003/1021 Reg.7, Reg.8

s.342, enabling: SI 2002/1982

s.347, amended: 2002 c.32 s.174

s.347, applied: SI 2002/152 Reg.17, SI 2003/1926 Reg.3, SI 2004/692 Sch.4 para.5

s.347, enabling: SI 2002/2072

s.348, applied: SI 2002/377 Reg.4, Sch.1 para.15, SI 2002/928 Sch.1, SI 2002/3199 Sch.2 para.11, SI 2003/3118 Sch.2 para.9, SI 2003/3170 Sch.3 para.11

s.350, repealed (in part): 2002 c.32 Sch.22 Part 3

s.351, repealed (in part): 2002 c.32 Sch.22 Part 3

s.352, repealed (in part): 2002 c.32 Sch.22 Part 3

s.353, applied: SI 2003/543 Reg.6

s.354, applied: SI 2003/543 Reg.6

s.356, applied: SI 2002/377 Sch.1 para.44, SI 2002/3199 Sch.1 para.24, SI 2003/3118 Sch.1 para.21

1996–cont.

56. Education Act 1996–*cont.*

s.356, referred to: SI 2002/45 Art.4, Art.8

s.356, enabling: SI 2002/45

s.362, applied: SI 2002/928 Sch.1

s.362, repealed (in part): 2002 c.32 Sch.22 Part 3

s.363, repealed (in part): 2002 c.32 Sch.22 Part 3

s.363, enabling: SI 2002/2048

s.364, repealed (in part): 2002 c.32 Sch.22 Part 3

s.365, repealed (in part): 2002 c.32 Sch.22 Part 3

s.366, repealed (in part): 2002 c.32 Sch.22 Part 3

s.367, repealed (in part): 2002 c.32 Sch.22 Part 3

s.368, applied: SI 2002/2048, SI 2003/252

s.368, repealed (in part): 2002 c.32 Sch.22 Part 3

s.368, enabling: SI 2002/2048

s.369, repealed (in part): 2002 c.32 Sch.22 Part 3

s.390, applied: SI 2002/377 Sch.1 para.28, SI 2002/928 Sch.1, SI 2002/3199 Sch.1 para.25, SI 2003/3118 Sch.1 para.22, SI 2003/3170 Sch.1 para.25

s.392, applied: SI 2002/928 Sch.1

s.402, amended: 2002 c.32 Sch.21 para.45

s.402, applied: SI 2002/2897 Reg.3, SI 2004/1025 Reg.2

s.403, applied: 2002 c.32 s.79, s.100

s.406, applied: SI 2002/928 Sch.1

s.407, applied: SI 2002/928 Sch.1

s.408, amended: 2002 c.32 Sch.21 para.46

s.408, applied: SI 2002/928 Sch.1, SI 2003/1006, SI 2004/1025, SI 2004/1026, SI 2004/1736

s.408, repealed (in part): 2002 c.32 Sch.22 Part 3

s.408, enabling: SI 2002/46, SI 2002/1680, SI 2002/2017, SI 2002/2897, SI 2003/1006, SI 2003/2135, SI 2003/2694, SI 2004/1025, SI 2004/1026, SI 2004/1076, SI 2004/1736, SI 2004/2141

s.409, amended: 2002 c.32 Sch.21 para.47, Sch.22 Part 3

s.409, applied: SI 2002/928 Sch.1

s.410, repealed (in part): 2002 c.32 s.205, Sch.22 Part 3

s.433, applied: SI 2002/928 Sch.1

s.434, see *R. (on the application of M) v BLBC* [2002] EWHC 2483, [2003] E.L.R. 144 (QBD (Admin Ct)), Jack Beatson, Q.C.

s.434, applied: SI 2002/377 Reg.13, SI 2003/453 Reg.10, SI 2003/3247 Reg.10, SI 2004/2506 Reg.9

s.435, applied: SI 2002/928 Sch.1

s.437, applied: SI 2002/928 Sch.1

s.438, applied: SI 2002/928 Sch.1

s.439, amended: 2002 c.32 Sch.4 para.14

1996–cont.

56. Education Act 1996–*cont.*

s.439, applied: SI 2002/928 Sch.1, SI 2003/ 1041 Sch.1 para.1

s.439, varied: SI 2003/1041 Sch.1 para.2, Sch.1 para.3, Sch.1 para.4, Sch.1 para.5

s.440, applied: SI 2002/928 Sch.1

s.441, applied: SI 2002/928 Sch.1

s.442, applied: SI 2002/928 Sch.1

s.444, see *Barnfather v Islington Education Authority* [2003] EWHC 418, [2003] 1 W.L.R. 2318 (QBD (Admin Ct)), Maurice Kay, J.; see *Graves v Islington LBC* [2003] EWHC 2817, [2004] E.L.R.1 (QBD (Admin Ct)), Beatson, J.; see *R. (on the application of H) v Brent LBC* [2002] EWHC 1105, [2002] E.L.R. 509 (QBD (Admin Ct)), Michael Supperstone Q.C.; see *R. (on the application of T) v Leeds City Council* [2002] E.L.R. 91 (QBD (Admin Ct)), Turner, J.

s.444, amended: 2003 c.44 Sch.26 para.49

s.444A, added: 2003 c.38 s.23

s.444A, applied: 2002 c.30 Sch.5 para.1, SI 2004/181, SI 2004/181 Reg.5, SI 2004/ 915 Sch.1 para.1

s.444A, referred to: 2003 c.38 s.23

s.444A, varied: 2003 c.38 s.23

s.444A, enabling: SI 2004/181, SI 2004/920

s.444B, added: 2003 c.38 s.23

s.444B, applied: SI 2004/181

s.444B, referred to: 2003 c.38 s.23

s.444B, varied: 2003 c.38 s.23

s.444B, enabling: SI 2004/181, SI 2004/920

s.447, see *Graves v Islington LBC* [2003] EWHC 2817, [2004] E.L.R. 1 (QBD (Admin Ct)), Beatson, J.

s.451, amended: 2002 c.32 Sch.21 para.48

s.453, applied: SI 2002/928 Sch.1

s.456, applied: SI 2002/928 Sch.1

s.457, amended: 2002 c.32 s.200

s.457, applied: SI 2002/2897 Sch.1 para.12, SI 2003/381 Reg.3, Reg.4, SI 2003/860 Reg.3, Reg.4

s.457, enabling: SI 2003/381, SI 2003/860

s.458, applied: SI 2002/928 Sch.1

s.463, applied: SI 2003/1934 Reg.6, SI 2003/3230 Reg.4, SI 2004/118 Art.2

s.463, substituted: 2002 c.32 s.172

s.464, repealed (in part): 2002 c.32 Sch.22 Part 3

s.465, applied: SI 2003/1926 Reg.3, SI 2003/3232 Reg.3

s.465, repealed (in part): 2002 c.32 Sch.22 Part 3

s.466, repealed (in part): 2002 c.32 Sch.22 Part 3

s.467, repealed (in part): 2002 c.32 Sch.22 Part 3

s.468, applied: SI 2003/1184 Reg.3

s.468, repealed (in part): 2002 c.32 Sch.22 Part 3

1996–cont.

56. Education Act 1996–*cont.*

s.468, varied: SI 2003/1184 Reg.3

s.469, repealed (in part): 2002 c.32 Sch.22 Part 3

s.470, applied: SI 2002/233 Reg.8, SI 2002/ 896 Sch.1 para.3, SI 2002/2978 Sch.1 para.7, SI 2002/3177 Sch.1 para.7, SI 2003/348 Sch.6 para.9, SI 2003/1558 Sch.2 para.8, SI 2004/2695 Sch.1 para.34

s.470, repealed (in part): 2002 c.32 Sch.22 Part 3

s.470, varied: SI 2003/1184 Reg.3

s.471, applied: SI 2002/233 Reg.8, SI 2002/ 896 Sch.1 para.3, SI 2002/2978 Sch.1 para.7, SI 2002/3177 Sch.1 para.7, SI 2003/348 Sch.6 para.9, SI 2003/1558 Sch.2 para.8, SI 2004/2695 Sch.1 para.34

s.471, repealed (in part): 2002 c.32 Sch.22 Part 3

s.471, varied: SI 2003/1184 Reg.3

s.472, repealed (in part): 2002 c.32 Sch.22 Part 3

s.473, repealed (in part): 2002 c.32 Sch.22 Part 3

s.473A, repealed (in part): 2002 c.32 Sch.22 Part 3

s.473B, repealed (in part): 2002 c.32 Sch.22 Part 3

s.474, repealed (in part): 2002 c.32 Sch.22 Part 3

s.475, repealed (in part): 2002 c.32 Sch.22 Part 3

s.476, repealed (in part): 2002 c.32 Sch.22 Part 3

s.477, repealed (in part): 2002 c.32 Sch.22 Part 3

s.478, repealed (in part): 2002 c.32 Sch.22 Part 3

s.482, applied: 2002 c.32 s.67, s.68, Sch.8 para.4, Sch.8 para.9, SI 2002/195 Reg.17, SI 2002/1330 Sch.2 para.15, 2003 c.14 Sch.4 para.17, SI 2003/507 Reg.19, SI 2003/1200 Reg.15

s.482, disapplied: 2002 c.32 Sch.8 para.9

s.482, substituted: 2002 c.32 s.65

s.483, amended: 2002 c.32 s.65

s.483, repealed (in part): 2002 c.32 Sch.22 Part 3

s.483A, amended: 2002 c.32 Sch.7 para.6

s.483A, repealed (in part): 2002 c.32 Sch.7 para.6, Sch.22 Part 3

s.483A, enabling: SI 2002/2071

s.484, amended: 2002 c.32 Sch.21 para.49, Sch.22 Part 3

s.484, applied: SI 2002/377 Reg.10, SI 2002/438 Reg.6, SI 2002/510 Reg.12, SI 2002/679 Reg.5, SI 2002/906 Art.15, SI 2002/3199 Sch.2 para.1, SI 2003/453 Reg.7, Reg.14, SI 2003/3118 Sch.2 para.1, SI 2003/3170 Sch.3 para.2, SSI 2003/ 176 Sch.3 para.6

1996–cont.

56. Education Act 1996–*cont.*

s.484, repealed (in part): 2002 c.32 Sch.21 para.49, Sch.22 Part 3

s.484, enabling: SI 2002/438, SI 2002/510, SI 2002/679, SI 2002/1738, SI 2002/1857, SI 2002/2814

s.485, enabling: SI 2002/2004, SI 2002/2064

s.486, repealed (in part): 2002 c.32 s.18, Sch.22 Part 3

s.487, repealed (in part): 2002 c.32 s.18, Sch.22 Part 3

s.488, repealed (in part): 2002 c.32 s.18, Sch.22 Part 3

s.489, enabling: SI 2002/438, SI 2002/510, SI 2002/679, SI 2002/1738, SI 2002/1857, SI 2002/2004, SI 2002/2064, SI 2002/2814

s.490, repealed (in part): 2002 c.32 s.18, Sch.22 Part 3

s.491, repealed (in part): 2002 c.32 s.18, Sch.22 Part 3

s.492, applied: SI 2002/377 Reg.4, SI 2002/535 Sch.1

s.492, repealed (in part): 2002 c.32 Sch.22 Part 3

s.493, amended: 2002 c.32 s.208

s.493, applied: SI 2002/377 Reg.4, SI 2002/535 Sch.1, SI 2002/3199 Sch.2 para.12, SI 2003/3118 Sch.2 para.10, SI 2003/3170 Sch.3 para.12

s.494, applied: 2002 c.32 s.208, SI 2002/377 Reg.4, SI 2002/535 Sch.1, SI 2002/3199 Sch.2 para.12, SI 2003/453 Reg.1, Reg.22, SI 2003/3118 Sch.2 para.10, SI 2003/3170 Sch.3 para.12, SI 2003/3247 Reg.22, Reg.23, SI 2004/2506 Reg.2, Reg.19

s.494, enabling: SI 2002/408, SI 2004/402

s.495, applied: 2002 c.32 s.34

s.496, see *R. (on the application of McNally) v Secretary of State for Education and Employment* [2001] EWCA Civ 332, [2002] I.C.R. 15 (CA), Kennedy, L.J.

s.496, applied: 2002 c.32 s.34, SI 2002/2903 Reg.8, SI 2002/2904 Reg.8

s.497, see *R. (on the application of McNally) v Secretary of State for Education and Employment* [2001] EWCA Civ 332, [2002] I.C.R. 15 (CA), Kennedy, L.J.

s.497, applied: 2002 c.32 s.34, SI 2002/2903 Reg.8, SI 2002/2904 Reg.8

s.497A, amended: 2002 c.32 s.60

s.497A, applied: 2002 c.32 s.34, 2004 c.31 s.50

s.497A, repealed (in part): 2002 c.32 s.60, Sch.22 Part 3

s.497A, substituted: 2002 c.32 s.60

s.497A, varied: 2004 c.31 s.50

s.497AA, added: 2002 c.32 s.61

s.497AA, applied: 2002 c.32 s.34, 2004 c.31 s.50

1996–cont.

56. Education Act 1996–*cont.*

s.497AA, varied: 2004 c.31 s.50

s.497B, amended: 2002 c.32 s.62

s.497B, applied: 2002 c.32 s.34, s.64, 2004 c.31 s.50

s.497B, substituted: 2002 c.32 s.62

s.497B, varied: 2004 c.31 s.50

s.498, applied: 2002 c.32 s.34

s.499, see *R. (on the application of Transport and General Workers Union) v Walsall MBC* [2001] EWHC Admin 452, [2002] E.L.R. 329 (QBD (Admin Ct)), Harrison, J.

s.499, amended: 2002 c.32 Sch.21 para.50

s.499, applied: SI 2002/928 Sch.1

s.499, enabling: SI 2003/2045

s.508, applied: SI 2002/3199 Sch.1 para.20, SI 2003/3118 Sch.1 para.18, SI 2003/3170 Sch.1 para.20

s.509, see *R. (on the application of T) v Leeds City Council* [2002] E.L.R. 91 (QBD (Admin Ct)), Turner, J.

s.509, amended: 2002 c.32 Sch.19 para.2, Sch.21 para.51

s.509, applied: SI 2002/377 Sch.1 para.19, SI 2002/535 Sch.1, SI 2002/928 Sch.1, SI 2002/1015 Reg.3, SI 2002/1016 Art.3, SI 2002/2022 Reg.3, SI 2002/2023 Art.3, SI 2002/3199 Sch.1 para.11, SI 2003/3118 Sch.1 para.11, SI 2003/3170 Sch.1 para.11

s.509, repealed (in part): 2002 c.32 Sch.22 Part 3

s.509A, amended: 2002 c.32 Sch.19 para.6

s.509A, applied: SI 2002/928 Sch.1

s.509A, repealed (in part): 2002 c.32 Sch.22 Part 3

s.509AA, added: 2002 c.32 Sch.19 para.3

s.509AA, applied: SI 2002/928 Sch.1, SI 2002/3199 Sch.1 para.11, SI 2003/3118 Sch.1 para.11, SI 2003/3170 Sch.1 para.11

s.509AB, added: 2002 c.32 Sch.19 para.4

s.509AB, applied: SI 2002/928 Sch.1, SI 2002/3199 Sch.1 para.11, SI 2003/3118 Sch.1 para.11, SI 2003/3170 Sch.1 para.11

s.509AC, added: 2002 c.32 Sch.19 para.5

s.509AC, applied: SI 2002/928 Sch.1, SI 2002/3199 Sch.1 para.11, SI 2003/3118 Sch.1 para.11, SI 2003/3170 Sch.1 para.11

s.510, applied: SI 2002/377 Sch.1 para.19, SI 2002/928 Sch.1, SI 2002/3199 Sch.1 para.11, SI 2003/3118 Sch.1 para.11, SI 2003/3170 Sch.1 para.11

s.511, applied: SI 2002/928 Sch.1, SI 2002/3199 Sch.1 para.11

s.512, see *R. (on the application of Transport and General Workers Union) v Walsall MBC* [2001] EWHC Admin 452, [2002] E.L.R. 329 (QBD (Admin Ct)), Harrison, J.

s.512, amended: 2002 c.32 s.201

s.512, applied: SI 2002/195 Reg.17, SI 2002/377 Sch.1 para.20, SI 2002/928 Sch.1, SI 2002/1330 Sch.2 para.15, SI 2002/3199

1996–cont.

56. Education Act 1996–*cont.*

s.512, applied:–*cont.*

Sch.1 para.11, Sch.2 para.15, SI 2003/382 Art.3, SI 2003/880 Art.3, SI 2003/3118 Sch.2 para.15, SI 2003/3170 Sch.3 para.15, SI 2003/3237 Sch.1 para.9, Sch.1 para.10, SI 2004/1026 Sch.1 para.1

s.512, disapplied: SI 2003/880 Art.4

s.512, referred to: SI 2003/1963 Reg.18

s.512, substituted: 2002 c.32 s.201

s.512, enabling: SI 2003/382, SI 2003/880

s.512A, amended: 2002 c.32 s.201, Sch.21 para.52

s.512A, applied: SI 2002/195 Reg.17, SI 2002/377 Sch.1 para.20, SI 2002/1330 Sch.2 para.15, SI 2002/3199 Sch.1 para.11, SI 2003/1963 Reg.18

s.512ZA, applied: SI 2002/195 Reg.17, SI 2002/377 Sch.1 para.20, SI 2002/1330 Sch.2 para.15, SI 2002/3199 Sch.1 para.11, Sch.2 para.15, SI 2003/3118 Sch.2 para.15, SI 2003/3170 Sch.3 para.15

s.512ZA, substituted: 2002 c.32 s.201

s.512ZA, varied: SI 2004/592 Art.2

s.512ZB, amended: 2002 c.32 s.201

s.512ZB, applied: SI 2002/195 Reg.17, SI 2002/377 Sch.1 para.20, SI 2002/1330 Sch.2 para.15, SI 2002/3199 Sch.1 para.11, Sch.2 para.15, SI 2003/383 Art.3, SI 2003/879 Art.3, SI 2003/3118 Sch.2 para.15, SI 2003/3170 Sch.3 para.15, SI 2003/3237 Sch.1 para.9, Sch.1 para.10, SI 2004/1026 Sch.1 para.1

s.512ZB, referred to: SI 2003/1963 Reg.18

s.512ZB, substituted: 2002 c.32 s.201

s.512ZB, enabling: SI 2003/383, SI 2003/879

s.513, applied: SI 2002/377 Sch.1 para.20, SI 2002/928 Sch.1, SI 2002/3199 Sch.1 para.11, Sch.2 para.15, SI 2003/3170 Sch.3 para.15

s.514, applied: SI 2002/377 Sch.1 para.19, SI 2002/928 Sch.1, SI 2002/3199 Sch.1 para.11, SI 2003/3118 Sch.1 para.11, SI 2003/3170 Sch.1 para.11

s.517, see *R. (on the application of C) v Special Educational Needs and Disability Tribunal* [2003] EWHC 1590, [2004] E.L.R. 111 (QBD (Admin Ct)), McCombe, J.

s.517, applied: SI 2002/928 Sch.1

s.518, applied: SI 2002/377 Reg.4, Sch.1 para.19, SI 2002/928 Sch.1, SI 2002/2006 Reg.19, SI 2002/3199 Sch.1 para.11, Sch.1 para.15, SI 2003/3118 Sch.1 para.11, Sch.1 para.15, SI 2003/3170 Sch.1 para.11, Sch.1 para.15

s.518, enabling: SI 2002/1841, SI 2002/1856, SI 2003/553, SI 2004/1006

s.519, applied: SI 2002/377 Sch.4 para.15, SI 2003/453 Sch.3 para.15, SI 2003/523 Reg.5, SI 2003/3247 Sch.3 para.15, SI 2004/2507 Sch.1 para.14

1996–cont.

56. Education Act 1996–*cont.*

s.519, enabling: SI 2003/523

s.520, amended: 2003 c.43 Sch.11 para.66

s.526, applied: SI 2002/928 Sch.1

s.527, applied: SI 2002/928 Sch.1

s.527A, applied: SI 2002/377 Sch.1 para.13, SI 2002/3199 Sch.1 para.6, Sch.2 para.10, SI 2003/3118 Sch.1 para.6, Sch.2 para.8, SI 2003/3170 Sch.1 para.6, Sch.3 para.10

s.527A, repealed: 2004 c.31 Sch.5 Part 1

s.527A, enabling: SI 2003/3082

s.528, applied: SI 2002/928 Sch.1

s.530, amended: 2002 c.32 Sch.8 para.9, Sch.21 para.53

s.532, amended: 2004 c.31 Sch.2 para.4

s.533, amended: 2002 c.32 Sch.21 para.54

s.537, amended: 2002 c.32 Sch.7 para.6

s.537, repealed (in part): 2002 c.32 Sch.22 Part 3

s.537, enabling: SI 2002/1172, SI 2002/1400, SI 2002/2017, SI 2002/2897, SI 2003/2135, SI 2004/1025, SI 2004/1076, SI 2004/1736

s.537A, applied: SI 2003/2453 Reg.4, SI 2003/3237 Reg.4, SI 2004/549 Reg.3

s.537A, enabling: SI 2002/2017, SI 2002/3112, SI 2003/2135, SI 2003/2453, SI 2003/3237, SI 2003/3277, SI 2004/549, SI 2004/1025, SI 2004/1377, SI 2004/2141

s.541, amended: 2002 c.32 Sch.7 para.6

s.542, applied: SI 2002/928 Sch.1

s.545, amended: 2002 c.32 Sch.22 Part 3

s.545, repealed (in part): 2002 c.32 Sch.21 para.55

s.547, amended: 2002 c.32 Sch.20 para.1

s.547, applied: SI 2003/348 Sch.6 para.10, SI 2003/1558 Sch.2 para.9

s.548, see *R. (on the application of Williamson) v Secretary of State for Education and Employment* [2001] EWHC Admin 960, [2002] 1 F.L.R. 493 (QBD (Admin Ct)), Elias, J.; see *R. (on the application of Williamson) v Secretary of State for Education and Employment* [2002] EWCA Civ 1926, [2003] Q.B. 1300 (CA), Buxton, L.J.

s.548, repealed (in part): 2002 c.32 Sch.22 Part 3

s.550B, amended: 2002 c.32 Sch.7 para.6

s.551, enabling: SI 2002/107, SI 2002/1556, SI 2003/3231

s.557, amended: 2002 c.32 s.69

s.559, amended: 2003 c.44 Sch.26 para.49

s.560, applied: SI 2002/928 Sch.1

s.562, amended: 2003 c.44 Sch.32 para.73

s.563, applied: SI 2002/928 Sch.1

s.563, enabling: SI 2002/1680, SI 2004/1026, SI 2004/1076

s.564, amended: SI 2002/3076 Sch.1

s.566, amended: 2004 c.31 Sch.2 para.4

1996–cont.

56. Education Act 1996–*cont.*

s.568, amended: 2002 c.32 Sch.22 Part 3

s.568, repealed (in part): 2002 c.32 Sch.22 Part 3

s.568, substituted: 2002 c.32 Sch.22 Part 3

s.568, enabling: SI 2002/45, SI 2003/382, SI 2003/383, SI 2003/879, SI 2003/880, SI 2004/1736

s.569, applied: SI 2004/181

s.569, enabling: SI 2002/46, SI 2002/107, SI 2002/152, SI 2002/157, SI 2002/408, SI 2002/438, SI 2002/510, SI 2002/679, SI 2002/1172, SI 2002/1400, SI 2002/1556, SI 2002/1680, SI 2002/1738, SI 2002/1841, SI 2002/1856, SI 2002/1857, SI 2002/1982, SI 2002/1985, SI 2002/2004, SI 2002/2017, SI 2002/2048, SI 2002/2064, SI 2002/2071, SI 2002/2072, SI 2002/2787, SI 2002/2814, SI 2002/2897, SI 2002/3112, SI 2003/190, SI 2003/381, SI 2003/523, SI 2003/553, SI 2003/860, SI 2003/2453, SI 2003/3082, SI 2003/3231, SI 2003/3237, SI 2004/181, SI 2004/402, SI 2004/549, SI 2004/920, SI 2004/1006, SI 2004/1025, SI 2004/1026, SI 2004/1076, SI 2004/1377, SI 2004/1736, SI 2004/2141

s.572, amended: 2003 c.38 s.23, SI 2004/2521 Art.3

s.572, applied: SI 2003/1377 Reg.4, SI 2003/1558 Reg.7

s.578, amended: 2002 c.32 Sch.22 Part 1, Sch.22 Part 3, 2004 c.8 s.54

s.578, applied: SI 2002/327 Reg.4

s.578, referred to: SI 2002/2523 Sch.2 para.2, SI 2003/514 Sch.2 para.2

s.579, see *Wakefield MDC v E* [2001] EWHC Admin 508, [2002] E.L.R. 203 (QBD (Admin Ct)), Collins, J.

s.579, amended: 2002 c.32 Sch.21 para.57, SI 2003/2045 Reg.3

s.579, applied: SI 2002/535 Reg.2, SI 2002/536 Reg.2

s.579, enabling: SI 2002/1982, SI 2002/1985, SI 2003/381

s.580, amended: 2002 c.32 Sch.7 para.6, Sch.22 Part 3

Sch.1 para.3, enabling: SI 2002/2550, SI 2003/287, SI 2003/3111

Sch.1 para.5, referred to: 2003 c.26 s.128

Sch.1 para.5, repealed: 2003 c.26 Sch.8 Part 1

Sch.1 para.6, amended: SI 2002/2953 Reg.2

Sch.1 para.6, varied: SI 2002/3184 Reg.5

Sch.1 para.7, applied: 2002 c.32 s.52

Sch.1 para.7, repealed (in part): 2002 c.32 Sch.22 Part 3, SI 2002/2953 Reg.2

Sch.7 para.11, amended: 2002 c.9 Sch.11 para.36

Sch.9 para.19, enabling: SI 2003/523

Sch.26 para.2, enabling: SI 2002/152

Sch.26 para.3, enabling: SI 2002/152

1996–cont.

56. Education Act 1996–*cont.*

Sch.27, applied: SI 2002/152 Reg.23

Sch.27 para.2, applied: SI 2002/152 Reg.14, Reg.17, Reg.26

Sch.27 para.2, enabling: SI 2002/152

Sch.27 para.2A, applied: SI 2002/152 Reg.14, Reg.15, Reg.17

Sch.27 para.2B, applied: SI 2002/152 Reg.14, Reg.15, Reg.17

Sch.27 para.2B, enabling: SI 2002/152

Sch.27 para.3, see *R. (on the application of MH) v Special Educational Needs and Disability Tribunal* [2004] EWCA Civ 770, [2004] B.L.G.R. 844 (CA), May, L.J.

Sch.27 para.3, applied: SI 2002/152 Reg.26

Sch.27 para.3, disapplied: 2002 c.41 s.36

Sch.27 para.3A, amended: 2002 c.32 Sch.21 para.58

Sch.27 para.4, applied: SI 2002/152 Reg.17

Sch.27 para.5, enabling: SI 2002/152

Sch.27 para.6, applied: SI 2002/152 Reg.17

Sch.27 para.6, enabling: SI 2002/152

Sch.27 para.7, enabling: SI 2002/152

Sch.27 para.8, see *Slough BC v C* [2004] EWHC 1759, [2004] E.L.R. 546 (QBD (Admin Ct)), Richards, J.

Sch.27 para.8, amended: 2002 c.32 Sch.21 para.58

Sch.27 para.8, applied: SI 2002/152 Reg.17

Sch.27 para.8, disapplied: 2002 c.41 s.36

Sch.27 para.8, enabling: SI 2002/152

Sch.27 para.10, applied: SI 2002/152 Reg.26

Sch.27 para.11, applied: SI 2002/152 Reg.17, Reg.26

Sch.27 para.11, enabling: SI 2002/152

Sch.31, applied: SI 2002/377 Sch.1 para.28, SI 2002/3199 Sch.1 para.25, SI 2003/3118 Sch.1 para.22, SI 2003/3170 Sch.1 para.25

Sch.34 para.1, repealed (in part): 2002 c.32 Sch.22 Part 3

Sch.34 para.2, repealed (in part): 2002 c.32 Sch.22 Part 3

Sch.34 para.3, repealed (in part): 2002 c.32 Sch.22 Part 3

Sch.34 para.4, repealed (in part): 2002 c.32 Sch.22 Part 3

Sch.34 para.5, repealed (in part): 2002 c.32 Sch.22 Part 3

Sch.35A para.1, added: 2002 c.32 Sch.7 para.1

Sch.35A para.2, added: 2002 c.32 Sch.7 para.1

Sch.35A para.3, added: 2002 c.32 Sch.7 para.1

Sch.35A para.4, added: 2002 c.32 Sch.7 para.1

Sch.35A para.5, added: 2002 c.32 Sch.7 para.1

Sch.35A para.6, added: 2002 c.32 Sch.7 para.1

CAP.

1996–cont.

56. Education Act 1996–*cont.*

Sch.35A para.7, added: 2002 c.32 Sch.7 para.1

Sch.35A para.8, added: 2002 c.32 Sch.7 para.1

Sch.35A para.9, added: 2002 c.32 Sch.7 para.1

Sch.35A para.10, added: 2002 c.32 Sch.7 para.1

Sch.35A para.11, added: 2002 c.32 Sch.7 para.1

Sch.35A para.12, added: 2002 c.32 Sch.7 para.1

Sch.35A para.13, added: 2002 c.32 Sch.7 para.1

Sch.37 Part I para.13, repealed (in part): 2002 c.32 Sch.22 Part 3

Sch.37 Part I para.26, repealed: SI 2003/ 1398 Sch.1 para.25

Sch.37 Part I para.49, repealed: 2004 c.14 Sch.1 Part 10

Sch.37 Part I para.53, repealed: 2004 c.14 Sch.1 Part 2

Sch.37 Part I para.55, repealed (in part): 2002 c.32 Sch.22 Part 3

Sch.37 Part I para.59, repealed: 2004 c.22 Sch.1

Sch.37 Part I para.65, repealed (in part): 2002 c.32 Sch.22 Part 3

Sch.37 Part I para.76, repealed: 2002 c.32 Sch.22 Part 3

Sch.37 Part I para.101, repealed: 2002 c.32 Sch.22 Part 1

Sch.37 Part I para.131, repealed (in part): 2002 c.32 Sch.22 Part 3

57. School Inspections Act 1996

applied: 2002 c.41 s.36

Part I, applied: SI 2002/432 Sch.2 para.7, Sch.2 para.14, SI 2002/3177 Reg.2, SI 2003/507 Sch.3 para.7, Sch.3 para.14, SI 2004/1576 Sch.3 para.8, Sch.3 para.18

s.1, applied: SI 2002/252, SI 2002/3156, SI 2003/1872

s.1, enabling: SI 2002/252, SI 2002/1821, SI 2002/3156, SI 2003/1872, SI 2004/713, SI 2004/1286, SI 2004/2032, SI 2004/ 2672

s.2, amended: 2002 c.32 s.179, Sch.16 para.1

s.2, applied: SI 2002/152 Reg.24, 2004 c.31 s.20

s.3, amended: 2002 c.32 s.179, Sch.22 Part 3

s.3, applied: SI 2002/152 Reg.24

s.4, applied: SI 2002/2632

s.4, enabling: SI 2002/260, SI 2002/1079, SI 2002/2632, SI 2003/3205

s.5, amended: 2002 c.32 s.179, Sch.16 para.2

s.6, amended: 2002 c.32 s.179, Sch.22 Part 3

s.9, applied: SI 2002/2953 Reg.6

s.10, amended: 2002 c.32 Sch.7 para.7, Sch.16 para.3, Sch.21 para.59

CAP.

1996–cont.

57. School Inspections Act 1996–*cont.*

s.10, applied: SI 2003/1921 Reg.5, SI 2003/ 3118 Sch.2 para.27

s.10, repealed (in part): 2002 c.32 Sch.22 Part 3

s.11, amended: 2002 c.32 Sch.7 para.7, Sch.21 para.60, Sch.22 Part 3

s.11, repealed (in part): 2002 c.32 Sch.21 para.60, Sch.22 Part 3

s.11, varied: SI 2004/657 Art.3

s.12, amended: 2002 c.32 Sch.16 para.4

s.13, referred to: SI 2003/530 Sch.3

s.15, amended: 2002 c.32 Sch.21 para.61, Sch.22 Part 3

s.15, varied: SI 2004/657 Art.3

s.15, enabling: SI 2004/784

s.16, amended: 2002 c.32 Sch.16 para.7, Sch.21 para.62, Sch.22 Part 3

s.16, applied: SI 2002/928 Sch.3

s.16, varied: SI 2004/657 Art.3

s.16A, added: 2002 c.32 s.54

s.16A, applied: SI 2002/928 Sch.3

s.16A, referred to: SI 2002/2113 Reg.4

s.17, amended: 2002 c.32 Sch.16 para.8, Sch.21 para.63

s.17, applied: SI 2002/928 Sch.3

s.17, disapplied: SI 2004/2683 Art.2, SI 2004/2810 Art.2

s.17, varied: SI 2004/657 Art.3

s.17, enabling: SI 2004/784

s.18, amended: 2002 c.32 Sch.21 para.64

s.18, applied: SI 2002/928 Sch.3

s.18, varied: SI 2004/657 Art.3

s.20, repealed (in part): 2002 c.32 Sch.22 Part 3

s.21, amended: 2002 c.32 Sch.21 para.65, Sch.22 Part 3

s.21, applied: SI 2002/928 Sch.3

s.21, repealed (in part): 2002 c.32 Sch.22 Part 3

s.21, varied: SI 2004/657 Art.3

s.21, enabling: SI 2004/784

s.23, amended: 2002 c.32 Sch.21 para.66

s.24, applied: SI 2002/928 Sch.3

s.25, applied: SI 2002/928 Sch.3

s.42, applied: 2002 c.32 s.159, s.164

s.45, enabling: SI 2004/784

Sch.1 para.1, amended: 2002 c.32 Sch.16 para.9

Sch.1 para.1, substituted: 2002 c.32 Sch.16 para.9

Sch.1 para.2, amended: 2002 c.32 Sch.16 para.9

Sch.2, applied: SI 2003/437 Sch.1 Part 1

Sch.2 para.2, applied: SI 2002/2953 Reg.6

Sch.2 para.3, applied: SI 2002/2953 Reg.6

Sch.3 para.1, amended: 2002 c.32 Sch.21 para.67, Sch.22 Part 3

Sch.3 para.1, repealed (in part): 2002 c.32 Sch.21 para.67, Sch.22 Part 3

Sch.3 para.1, varied: SI 2004/657 Art.3

1996–cont.

57. School Inspections Act 1996–*cont.*
Sch.3 para.3, amended: 2002 c.32 Sch.16 para.5
Sch.3 para.3, applied: 2002 c.32 s.164
Sch.3 para.3A, amended: 2002 c.32 Sch.16 para.6
Sch.3 para.3A, applied: 2002 c.32 s.164
Sch.3 para.7, amended: 2002 c.32 s.179
Sch.3 para.7, applied: SI 2002/152 Reg.24
Sch.4 para.2, enabling: SI 2004/784
Sch.4 para.3, amended: 2002 c.32 Sch.21 para.68
Sch.4 para.3, disapplied: SI 2004/2683 Art.2, SI 2004/2810 Art.2
Sch.4 para.3, enabling: SI 2004/784

58. Deer (Scotland) Act 1996
s.1, applied: SSI 2004/474 Sch.1
Sch.3, amended: 2004 asp 6 Sch.7 para.11

61. Channel Tunnel Rail Link Act 1996
applied: SI 2002/1943 Art.11
varied: SI 2002/1943 Art.15
Part I, applied: SI 2002/1943 Art.6, Art.14, Art.15
s.4, see *English Welsh and Scottish Railways Ltd v Secretary of State for Transport, Local Government and the Regions* [2002] EWHC 2641, [2002] N.P.C. 159 (QBD (Admin Ct)), Harrison, J.
s.4, applied: SI 2002/1943 Art.9
s.5, see *English Welsh and Scottish Railways Ltd v Secretary of State for Transport, Local Government and the Regions* [2002] EWHC 2641, [2002] N.P.C. 159 (QBD (Admin Ct)), Harrison, J.
s.8, applied: SI 2002/1943 Art.15
s.17, amended: 2003 c.20 Sch.2 para.19
s.19, applied: 2002 c.40 s.249
s.21, amended: 2002 c.40 Sch.25 para.35, 2003 c.20 Sch.2 para.19, Sch.2 para.22
s.22, amended: 2002 c.40 Sch.25 para.35, 2003 c.20 Sch.2 para.19, Sch.2 para.22, SI 2003/1398 Sch.1 para.24, SI 2004/1261 Sch.2 para.8
s.22, repealed (in part): 2002 c.40 Sch.25 para.26, Sch.26
s.24, repealed: SI 2003/1398 Sch.1 para.24
s.26, repealed: SI 2003/1398 Sch.1 para.24
s.29, amended: SI 2002/2626 Sch.2 para.21
s.34, applied: SI 2002/1943 Art.16
s.34, enabling: SI 2003/2306, SI 2003/2834
s.43, applied: SI 2002/1943 Art.15
s.50, amended: SI 2002/2626 Sch.2 para.21
s.54, applied: SI 2002/1943 Art.15
Sch.2 para.4, applied: SI 2002/1943 Art.15
Sch.2 para.9, applied: SI 2002/1943 Art.15
Sch.2 para.10, applied: SI 2002/1943 Art.15
Sch.3 para.2, amended: SI 2002/2626 Sch.2 para.21
Sch.6 Part II para.6, amended: 2003 c.21 Sch.17 para.138

1996–cont.

61. Channel Tunnel Rail Link Act 1996– *cont.*
Sch.6 Part III para.15, amended: 2003 c.21 Sch.17 para.138
Sch.7 para.5, amended: SI 2002/2626 Sch.2 para.21
Sch.10, applied: SI 2002/1943 Art.15
Sch.14 para.13, amended: SI 2002/2626 Sch.2 para.21
Sch.15 Part II, applied: SI 2002/1943 Art.15
Sch.15 Part II para.2, amended: SI 2002/2626 Sch.2 para.21
Sch.15 Part III, applied: SI 2002/1943 Art.15
Sch.15 Part IV, applied: SI 2002/1943 Art.15
Sch.15 Part IV para.1, amended: 2003 c.21 Sch.17 para.139, Sch.19
Sch.15 Part IV para.2, amended: 2003 c.21 Sch.17 para.139
Sch.15 Part IV para.3, amended: 2003 c.21 Sch.17 para.139
Sch.15 Part IV para.4, amended: 2003 c.21 Sch.17 para.139
Sch.15 Part IV para.5, amended: 2003 c.21 Sch.17 para.139

1997

1. Horserace Totalisator Board Act 1997
repealed: 2004 c.25 Sch.6

1. Pensions Measure 1997
s.4, amended: 2003 c.2 s.4
s.7, substituted: 2003 c.2 s.5

2. Land Registration Act 1997
s.1, repealed: 2002 c.9 Sch.13
s.2, repealed: 2002 c.9 Sch.13
s.3, repealed: 2002 c.9 Sch.13
s.5, repealed (in part): 2002 c.9 Sch.13
Sch.1 Part I para.1, repealed: 2002 c.9 Sch.13
Sch.1 Part I para.2, repealed: 2002 c.9 Sch.13
Sch.1 Part I para.3, repealed: 2002 c.9 Sch.13
Sch.1 Part I para.4, repealed: 2002 c.9 Sch.13
Sch.1 Part I para.5, repealed: 2002 c.9 Sch.13
Sch.1 Part I para.6, repealed: 2002 c.9 Sch.13

4. Telecommunications (Fraud) Act 1997
repealed: 2003 c.21 Sch.19

5. Firearms (Amendment) Act 1997
see *Evans v Chief Constable of Central Scotland* 2002 S.L.T. (Sh Ct) 152 (Sh Pr), CGB Nicholson Q.C., Sheriff Principal; see *Stewart (t/a GT Shooting) v Customs and Excise Commissioners* [2001] EWCA Civ 1988, [2002] S.T.C. 255 (CA), Laws, L.J.
applied: 2003 c.17 Sch.4 para.17

7. Northern Ireland Arms Decommissioning Act 1997
applied: 2002 c.6 s.1
s.2, amended: 2002 c.6 s.1
s.2, applied: SI 2003/426 Art.2, SI 2004/464 Art.2
s.2, enabling: SI 2003/426, SI 2004/464
s.10, amended: SI 2004/702 Sch.7 para.21

CAP.

1997–cont.

7. Northern Ireland Arms Decommissioning Act 1997–*cont.*
Sch.1 para.8, amended: SI 2004/702 Sch.7 para.22

8. Town and Country Planning (Scotland) Act 1997
applied: SSI 2002/410 Art.57, 2003 asp 2 s.7, 2003 asp 3 s.24, 2003 c.14 s.61, s.66, 2003 c.21 Sch.4 para.4, SSI 2003/235 Reg.5, SSI 2003/341 Reg.5, 2004 asp 10 s.33

referred to: 2004 c.5 s.121

Part II, applied: SSI 2002/201 Art.7

Part III, applied: SI 2003/409 Sch.1 Part I, SSI 2002/201 Art.7, 2004 asp 6 s.14, s.17, SSI 2004/219 Reg.5, Reg.6, SSI 2004/474 Art.2

Part IV, applied: SSI 2002/201 Art.7

Part V, applied: SSI 2002/201 Art.7

Part V c.II, applied: 2004 asp 10 s.34

Part VI, applied: SSI 2002/201 Art.7

Part VII, applied: SSI 2002/201 Art.7

Part VIII, applied: SSI 2002/201 Art.7

Part IX, applied: SSI 2002/201 Art.7

Part X, applied: SSI 2002/201 Art.7

Part XII, applied: SSI 2002/201 Art.7

Part XIII, applied: SSI 2002/201 Art.7

Part XIV, applied: SSI 2002/201 Art.7

s.4, varied: SSI 2003/1 Art.7

s.5, varied: SSI 2003/1 Art.7

s.6, varied: SSI 2003/1 Art.7

s.7, varied: SSI 2003/1 Art.7

s.8, varied: SSI 2003/1 Art.7

s.9, varied: SSI 2003/1 Art.7

s.10, see *SHBA Ltd v Scottish Ministers* 2002 S.L.T. 1321 (OH), Lord Macfadyen

s.10, varied: SSI 2003/1 Art.7

s.11, varied: SSI 2003/1 Art.7

s.12, varied: SSI 2003/1 Art.7

s.13, varied: SSI 2003/1 Art.7

s.14, varied: SSI 2003/1 Art.7

s.15, varied: SSI 2003/1 Art.7

s.16, varied: SSI 2003/1 Art.7

s.17, varied: SSI 2003/1 Art.7

s.18, varied: SSI 2003/1 Art.7

s.19, varied: SSI 2003/1 Art.7

s.20, varied: SSI 2003/1 Art.7

s.21, varied: SSI 2003/1 Art.7

s.22, varied: SSI 2003/1 Art.7

s.23, varied: SSI 2003/1 Art.7

s.24, varied: SSI 2003/1 Art.7

s.25, varied: SSI 2003/1 Art.7

s.26, amended: 2003 asp 3 s.24, SSI 2003/341 Reg.2, 2004 c.5 Sch.7 para.20

s.33, applied: SSI 2004/219 Sch.1 para.7

s.35, amended: 2003 asp 11 Sch.1 para.51

s.40, amended: 2003 asp 3 s.24

s.40, enabling: SSI 2002/324, SSI 2003/341

s.46, applied: SSI 2003/1 Art.7

s.46, referred to: SSI 2003/1 Art.7

CAP.

1997–cont.

8. Town and Country Planning (Scotland) Act 1997–*cont.*
s.47, applied: SSI 2004/219 Reg.7, Reg.8, Reg.10

s.54, amended: 2004 asp 6 Sch.7 para.12

s.88A, added: 2004 c.5 Sch.5 para.1

s.99, amended: SI 2003/2155 Sch.1 para.13

s.102, applied: SSI 2003/452 r.10

s.104, applied: SSI 2003/452 r.10

s.123, varied: SSI 2003/1 Art.7

s.124, varied: SSI 2003/1 Art.7

s.125, amended: SSI 2004/332 Art.5

s.125, varied: SSI 2003/1 Art.7

s.126, varied: SSI 2003/1 Art.7

s.127, varied: SSI 2003/1 Art.7

s.128, varied: SSI 2003/1 Art.7

s.129, varied: SSI 2003/1 Art.7

s.130, amended: SSI 2004/332 Art.3

s.130, applied: SSI 2004/219 Reg.11, Sch.1 para.8

s.130, varied: SSI 2003/1 Art.7

s.131, applied: SSI 2004/219 Reg.11

s.131, varied: SSI 2003/1 Art.7

s.132, applied: SSI 2004/219 Reg.11

s.132, varied: SSI 2003/1 Art.7

s.133, applied: SSI 2004/219 Reg.10, Reg.11, Reg.15, Sch.1 para.1, Sch.1 para.8, Sch.1 para.10

s.133, varied: SSI 2003/1 Art.7

s.134, varied: SSI 2003/1 Art.7

s.135, varied: SSI 2003/1 Art.7

s.136, varied: SSI 2003/1 Art.7

s.137, varied: SSI 2003/1 Art.7

s.138, varied: SSI 2003/1 Art.7

s.139, varied: SSI 2003/1 Art.7

s.140, varied: SSI 2003/1 Art.7

s.141, varied: SSI 2003/1 Art.7

s.142, varied: SSI 2003/1 Art.7

s.143, varied: SSI 2003/1 Art.7

s.144, varied: SSI 2003/1 Art.7

s.145, varied: SSI 2003/1 Art.7

s.146, varied: SSI 2003/1 Art.7

s.147, varied: SSI 2003/1 Art.7

s.148, varied: SSI 2003/1 Art.7

s.149, varied: SSI 2003/1 Art.7

s.150, applied: SSI 2004/219 Reg.1, Reg.11, Reg.12

s.150, varied: SSI 2003/1 Art.7

s.151, applied: SSI 2004/219 Reg.1, Reg.11, Reg.12

s.151, varied: SSI 2003/1 Art.7

s.152, varied: SSI 2003/1 Art.7

s.153, varied: SSI 2003/1 Art.7

s.154, applied: SSI 2004/219 Reg.11

s.154, varied: SSI 2003/1 Art.7

s.155, varied: SSI 2003/1 Art.7

s.156, varied: SSI 2003/1 Art.7

s.157, varied: SSI 2003/1 Art.7

s.158, varied: SSI 2003/1 Art.7

s.162, substituted: 2004 c.5 s.95

1997–cont.

8. **Town and Country Planning (Scotland) Act 1997**–cont.

s.172, amended: 2004 c.5 s.96

s.182, applied: 2003 asp 9 s.21, SI 2003/2253 Art.8

s.183, applied: SI 2003/2253 Art.8

s.184, applied: 2003 asp 9 s.21

s.186, applied: SI 2003/2253 Art.8

s.188, repealed (in part): 2003 asp 1 s.60

s.189, amended: 2004 c.5 Sch.5 para.3

s.189, applied: 2003 asp 11 s.54

s.189, repealed (in part): 2003 asp 1 s.60

s.190, amended: 2004 c.5 Sch.5 para.4

s.194, amended: SI 2003/2155 Sch.1 para.13

s.195, varied: SSI 2004/171 Art.26

s.196, amended: SI 2003/2155 Sch.1 para.13

s.197, varied: 2003 c.21 Sch.4 para.4

s.198, disapplied: 2004 asp 10 s.27

s.198, varied: 2003 c.21 Sch.4 para.4

s.205, amended: SI 2003/2155 Sch.1 para.13

s.208, amended: 2003 asp 2 Sch.2 para.17

s.208, applied: 2003 asp 2 s.20

s.211, disapplied: 2004 asp 10 s.27

s.212, amended: SI 2003/2155 Sch.1 para.13

s.224, applied: 2004 asp 10 s.22

s.224, varied: 2003 c.21 Sch.4 para.4

s.225, amended: SI 2003/2155 Sch.1 para.13

s.225, applied: 2004 asp 10 s.22

s.225, varied: 2003 c.21 Sch.4 para.4

s.226, amended: SI 2003/2155 Sch.1 para.13

s.226, varied: 2003 c.21 Sch.4 para.4

s.227, amended: SI 2003/2155 Sch.1 para.13

s.227, varied: 2003 c.21 Sch.4 para.4

s.232, amended: SI 2003/2155 Sch.1 para.13

s.233, amended: SI 2003/2155 Sch.1 para.13

s.237, see *Cala Management Ltd v Scottish Ministers* 2002 S.C. 42 (Court of Session (Inner House, Extra Division)), Lord Coulsfield, Lord Caplan, Lord Marnoch; see *Di Ciacca v Scottish Ministers* 2003 S.L.T. 1031 (OH), Lord Reed

s.237, amended: 2004 c.5 s.92

s.239, see *Cala Management Ltd v Scottish Ministers* 2002 S.C. 42 (Court of Session (Inner House, Extra Division)), Lord Coulsfield, Lord Caplan, Lord Marnoch; see *Di Ciacca v Scottish Ministers* 2003 S.L.T. 1031 (OH), Lord Reed

s.241A, added: 2004 c.5 s.90

s.242, amended: 2004 c.5 Sch.5 para.6

s.242, repealed (in part): 2004 c.5 Sch.5 para.23, Sch.9

s.242A, added: 2004 c.5 s.92

s.243, repealed: 2004 c.5 Sch.5 para.9, Sch.9

s.244, repealed: 2004 c.5 Sch.5 para.9, Sch.9

s.245, repealed: 2004 c.5 s.94, Sch.9

s.245A, added: 2004 c.5 s.94

s.245A, repealed: 2004 c.5 Sch.9

s.245B, added: 2004 c.5 s.94

1997–cont.

8. **Town and Country Planning (Scotland) Act 1997**–cont.

s.245B, repealed: 2004 c.5 Sch.9

s.246, repealed: 2004 c.5 Sch.5 para.23, Sch.9

s.247, repealed: 2004 c.5 Sch.9

s.247, substituted: 2004 c.5 Sch.5 para.24

s.247A, added: 2004 c.5 Sch.5 para.10

s.247A, repealed: 2004 c.5 Sch.9

s.248, applied: 2004 c.5 Sch.5 para.10

s.248, repealed: 2004 c.5 Sch.5 para.10, Sch.9

s.249, applied: 2004 c.5 Sch.5 para.25

s.249, repealed: 2004 c.5 Sch.5 para.25, Sch.9

s.250, referred to: 2004 c.5 Sch.5 para.26

s.250, repealed: 2004 c.5 Sch.5 para.26, Sch.9

s.252, applied: SSI 2002/122, SSI 2004/219

s.252, enabling: SSI 2002/122, SSI 2004/219

s.264, repealed: 2004 asp 6 Sch.7 para.12

s.265, see *Cannell v Scottish Ministers* 2002 S.L.T. 634 (OH), Lord Morison; see *Cannell v Scottish Ministers* 2003 S.C. 404 (Court of Session (Inner House, Extra Division)), Lord Macfadyen, Lord Marnoch, Lady Smith

s.265, applied: 2003 asp 2 s.11, s.18, SSI 2004/219 Reg.11

s.265A, added: 2004 c.5 s.91

s.269, applied: 2003 c.21 Sch.4 para.7

s.269, varied: 2003 c.21 Sch.4 para.7

s.270, applied: 2003 c.21 Sch.4 para.7

s.270, varied: 2003 c.21 Sch.4 para.7

s.270A, added: 2004 c.5 Sch.5 para.14

s.271, amended: SSI 2004/332 Art.4

s.271A, added: 2004 c.5 Sch.5 para.17

s.272, amended: SSI 2004/332 Art.5

s.272A, added: 2004 c.5 Sch.5 para.18

s.274, applied: 2003 asp 8 s.33

s.274, referred to: 2003 asp 8 s.33

s.275, amended: 2003 asp 3 s.24, 2004 c.5 Sch.7 para.20

s.275, enabling: SSI 2003/446

s.277, amended: SSI 2004/332 Art.6

Sch.4 para.8, amended: 2002 asp 11 Sch.6 para.17

Sch.6, applied: SI 2003/409 Sch.1 Part I

Sch.7, applied: SI 2003/409 Sch.1 Part I

Sch.7 para.3, amended: SI 2002/2626 Sch.2 para.22

Sch.7 para.8, amended: SI 2002/2626 Sch.2 para.22

Sch.8 Part I para.10, applied: 2004 c.5 s.97

Sch.8 Part I para.10, varied: 2004 c.5 s.97

Sch.8 Part II, applied: 2004 c.5 s.97

Sch.8 Part II para.13, varied: 2004 c.5 s.97

Sch.9 para.1, amended: SSI 2004/332 Art.7

Sch.9 para.9, amended: SSI 2004/332 Art.7

1997–cont.

8. **Town and Country Planning (Scotland) Act 1997**–cont.

Sch.10 para.2, amended: 2004 c.5 Sch.7 para.20, SSI 2004/332 Art.8

Sch.10 para.3A, added: 2004 c.5 Sch.7 para.20

Sch.10 para.6, amended: SSI 2004/332 Art.8

Sch.14 para.1, amended: SI 2003/2155 Sch.1 para.13

Sch.14 para.14, applied: 2004 asp 10 s.34

Sch.15, applied: SSI 2003/446 Reg.5, SSI 2004/171 Art.26

Sch.15 Part I para.1, applied: SSI 2003/446 Reg.5

Sch.15 Part I para.1, referred to: SSI 2003/446 Sch.1

Sch.15 Part I para.1, varied: SSI 2004/171 Art.26

Sch.15 Part I para.1, enabling: SSI 2003/446

Sch.15 Part I para.2, applied: SSI 2003/446 Reg.5, Sch.1

Sch.15 Part I para.2, referred to: SSI 2003/446 Sch.1

Sch.15 Part I para.2, varied: SSI 2004/171 Art.26

Sch.15 Part I para.2, enabling: SSI 2003/446

Sch.15 Part I para.3, referred to: SSI 2003/446 Sch.1

Sch.15 Part I para.3, varied: SSI 2004/171 Art.26

Sch.15 Part I para.4, applied: SSI 2003/446 Reg.5

Sch.15 Part I para.4, referred to: SSI 2003/446 Sch.1

Sch.15 Part I para.4, varied: SSI 2004/171 Art.26

Sch.15 Part I para.4, enabling: SSI 2003/446

Sch.15 Part I para.5, referred to: SSI 2003/446 Sch.1

Sch.15 Part I para.5, varied: SSI 2004/171 Art.26

Sch.15 Part I para.6, referred to: SSI 2003/446 Sch.1

Sch.15 Part I para.6, varied: SSI 2004/171 Art.26

Sch.15 Part I para.7, referred to: SSI 2003/446 Sch.1

Sch.15 Part I para.7, varied: SSI 2004/171 Art.26

Sch.15 Part I para.8, referred to: SSI 2003/446 Sch.1

Sch.15 Part I para.8, varied: SSI 2004/171 Art.26

Sch.15 Part I para.9, varied: SSI 2004/171 Art.26

Sch.15 Part I para.10, varied: SSI 2004/171 Art.26

Sch.15 Part I para.11, varied: SSI 2004/171 Art.26

Sch.15 Part I para.12, varied: SSI 2004/171 Art.26

1997–cont.

8. **Town and Country Planning (Scotland) Act 1997**–cont.

Sch.15 Part I para.13, varied: SSI 2004/171 Art.26

Sch.15 Part I para.14, varied: SSI 2004/171 Art.26

Sch.15 Part I para.15, varied: SSI 2004/171 Art.26

Sch.15 Part II para.16, varied: SSI 2004/171 Art.26

Sch.15 Part II para.17, varied: SSI 2004/171 Art.26

Sch.15 Part II para.18, varied: SSI 2004/171 Art.26

Sch.15 Part II para.19, varied: SSI 2004/171 Art.26

Sch.15 Part II para.20, varied: SSI 2004/171 Art.26

Sch.15 Part II para.21, varied: SSI 2004/171 Art.26

Sch.15 Part II para.22, varied: SSI 2004/171 Art.26

Sch.15 Part II para.23, varied: SSI 2004/171 Art.26

Sch.15 Part II para.24, varied: SSI 2004/171 Art.26

Sch.15 Part II para.25, varied: SSI 2004/171 Art.26

Sch.15 Part II para.26, varied: SSI 2004/171 Art.26

Sch.15 Part II para.27, varied: SSI 2004/171 Art.26

Sch.15 Part II para.28, varied: SSI 2004/171 Art.26

Sch.15 Part II para.29, varied: SSI 2004/171 Art.26

Sch.15 Part II para.30, varied: SSI 2004/171 Art.26

Sch.15 Part II para.31, varied: SSI 2004/171 Art.26

Sch.15 Part II para.32, varied: SSI 2004/171 Art.26

Sch.15 Part II para.33, varied: SSI 2004/171 Art.26

Sch.15 Part II para.34, varied: SSI 2004/171 Art.26

Sch.15 Part II para.35, varied: SSI 2004/171 Art.26

Sch.15 Part II para.36, varied: SSI 2004/171 Art.26

Sch.15 Part II para.37, varied: SSI 2004/171 Art.26

Sch.15 Part III para.38, varied: SSI 2004/171 Art.26

Sch.15 Part III para.39, varied: SSI 2004/171 Art.26

9. **Planning (Listed Buildings and Conservation Areas) (Scotland) Act 1997**

applied: SSI 2002/201 Art.7

referred to: 2004 c.5 s.121

s.1, applied: 2003 asp 8 s.35

1997–cont.

9. Planning (Listed Buildings and Conservation Areas) (Scotland) Act 1997–*cont.*
s.3, applied: 2003 asp 8 s.35
s.11, applied: SSI 2003/1 Art.7
s.11, referred to: SSI 2003/1 Art.7
s.28A, added: 2004 c.5 Sch.5 para.2
s.35, amended: SSI 2004/332 Art.9
s.42, see *Prestige Assets Ltd v Renfrewshire Council* 2003 S.C. 88 (OH), Lord Mackay of Drumadoon
s.42, amended: 2004 c.5 Sch.5 para.5
s.42, applied: SSI 2003/446 Reg.4
s.43, see *Prestige Assets Ltd v Renfrewshire Council* 2003 S.C. 88 (OH), Lord Mackay of Drumadoon
s.45, applied: SSI 2003/446 Reg.4
s.46, amended: SI 2003/2155 Sch.1 para.14
s.57, amended: 2004 c.5 s.93
s.58, see *County Properties Ltd v Scottish Ministers* 2002 S.C. 79 (Ex Div), Lord Prosser, Lord Kirkwood, Lord Mackay of Drumadoon
s.66, applied: 2003 asp 8 s.35
s.69, repealed (in part): 2003 asp 4 Sch.4 para.13
s.71, repealed (in part): 2003 asp 4 Sch.4 para.13
s.72, repealed (in part): 2003 asp 4 Sch.4 para.13
s.73A, added: 2004 c.5 s.90
s.73B, added: 2004 c.5 s.93
s.73C, added: 2004 c.5 Sch.5 para.7
s.73D, added: 2004 c.5 s.94
s.73E, added: 2004 c.5 s.94
s.73F, added: 2004 c.5 Sch.5 para.11
s.74, repealed: 2004 c.5 Sch.5 para.19, Sch.9
s.75, applied: 2004 c.5 Sch.5 para.19
s.75, repealed: 2004 c.5 Sch.5 para.19, Sch.9
s.78A, added: 2004 c.5 Sch.5 para.15
s.79, amended: 2004 c.5 Sch.5 para.20, SSI 2004/332 Art.10
s.81, amended: SI 2003/2155 Sch.1 para.14, SSI 2004/332 Art.11
Sch.3 para.6, amended: 2004 c.5 s.91
Sch.3 para.7, amended: 2002 asp 11 Sch.6 para.18

10. Planning (Hazardous Substances) (Scotland) Act 1997
applied: SSI 2002/201 Art.7
referred to: 2004 c.5 s.121
s.15, amended: 2004 c.5 Sch.5 para.21
s.18, applied: SSI 2003/1 Art.7
s.18, referred to: SSI 2003/1 Art.7
s.30A, added: 2004 c.5 s.90
s.30B, added: 2004 c.5 s.94
s.30C, added: 2004 c.5 s.94
s.31, amended: 2004 c.5 Sch.5 para.8
s.31, repealed (in part): 2004 c.5 Sch.5 para.8, Sch.9
s.32, repealed: 2004 c.5 Sch.5 para.12, Sch.9
s.32A, added: 2004 c.5 Sch.5 para.13

1997–cont.

10. Planning (Hazardous Substances) (Scotland) Act 1997–*cont.*
s.35A, added: 2004 c.5 Sch.5 para.16
s.36, amended: 2004 c.5 Sch.5 para.22
Sch.1 para.6, amended: 2004 c.5 s.91
Sch.1 para.7, amended: 2002 asp 11 Sch.6 para.19

11. Planning (Consequential Provisions) (Scotland) Act 1997
Sch.2 para.6, repealed: 2003 asp 8 Sch.6 para.23
Sch.2 para.37, repealed: 2003 c.21 Sch.19
Sch.2 para.58, repealed: 2002 asp 3 Sch.7 para.25

12. Civil Procedure Act 1997
s.1, amended: 2003 c.39 s.82
s.1, applied: SI 2002/2058, SI 2003/1242, SI 2004/2072
s.1, enabling: SI 2002/3219
s.2, amended: 2003 c.39 s.83
s.2, applied: SI 2002/2058, SI 2002/3219, SI 2003/1242, SI 2004/2072, SI 2004/3129
s.2, repealed (in part): 2003 c.39 s.85, Sch.10
s.2, enabling: SI 2002/2058, SI 2002/3219, SI 2003/364, SI 2003/1242, SI 2003/1329, SI 2003/2113, SI 2003/3261, SI 2004/1306, SI 2004/2072, SI 2004/3129
s.2A, added: 2003 c.39 s.84
s.3, substituted: 2003 c.39 s.85
s.4, enabling: SI 2002/439, SI 2003/490, SI 2004/1033
s.7, amended: 2004 c.33 Sch.27 para.154
Sch.2 para.3, repealed: 2003 c.39 Sch.10

13. United Nations Personnel Act 1997
referred to: 2003 c.32 Sch.5 para.66
s.5, amended: 2003 c.32 Sch.5 para.67
s.6, repealed: 2003 c.41 Sch.4

16. Finance Act 1997
s.10, amended: 2002 c.23 s.11
s.11, amended: 2002 c.23 s.10, 2003 c.14 s.13, 2004 c.12 s.16
s.12, enabling: SI 2002/2310, SI 2003/2247, SI 2004/2243
s.14, enabling: SI 2002/2310, SI 2003/2247, SI 2004/2243
s.21, see *Gil Insurance Ltd v Customs and Excise Commissioners (C308/01)* [2004] All E.R. (EC) 954 (ECJ), Judge Timmermans (President)
s.39, repealed (in part): 2002 c.23 Sch.40 Part 2
s.47, see *Marks & Spencer Plc v Customs and Excise Commissioners (C62/00)* [2003] Q.B. 866 (ECJ), P Jann (President)
s.51, enabling: SI 2002/761
s.52, amended: 2002 asp 17 Sch.3 para.26
s.52, enabling: SSI 2002/560
s.54, repealed (in part): 2004 c.12 Sch.42 Part 2
s.62, repealed: 2003 c.1 Sch.8 Part 1
s.63, repealed: 2003 c.1 Sch.8 Part 1

CAP.

1997–cont.

16. Finance Act 1997*–cont.*

s.67, repealed (in part): 2004 c.12 Sch.42 Part 2

s.83, repealed (in part): 2004 c.12 Sch.42 Part 2

s.110, amended: 2002 c.21 Sch.5 para.13, 2002 c.22 Sch.7 para.50

s.110, repealed (in part): 2002 c.21 Sch.6

Sch.2 Part II para.6, repealed: 2002 c.40 Sch.26

Sch.12 Part I para.1, amended: 2002 c.23 s.103, Sch.40 Part 3

Sch.12 Part I para.3, amended: 2002 c.23 s.103

Sch.12 Part I para.4, amended: 2002 c.23 s.103, Sch.40 Part 3

Sch.12 Part I para.6, amended: 2002 c.23 s.103

Sch.12 Part II para.15, amended: 2002 c.23 s.103, Sch.40 Part 3

Sch.12 Part IV para.22, amended: 2002 c.23 s.103

Sch.12 Part IV para.28, amended: 2002 c.23 s.103

Sch.12 Part IV para.28, repealed (in part): 2002 c.23 Sch.40 Part 3

Sch.12 Part IV para.30, amended: 2002 c.23 s.103

Sch.18 Part VI para.3, repealed (in part): 2003 c.1 Sch.8 Part 1

20. British Nationality (Hong Kong) Act 1997

applied: SI 2003/3157 Reg.6, Sch.1

s.1, amended: 2002 c.8 s.2

s.1, applied: SI 2003/3157 Sch.1

s.2, amended: 2002 c.8 s.2, SI 2003/1016 Sch.1 para.9

Sch.1 para.1, amended: 2002 c.8 s.2

Sch.1 para.2, amended: 2002 c.8 s.2

21. Knives Act 1997

s.6, applied: SI 2003/336 Sch.1 Part 2

s.7, applied: SI 2003/336 Sch.1 Part 2

22. Architects Act 1997

s.4, amended: SI 2002/2842 Art.3

s.6, amended: SI 2002/2842 Art.4

s.22A, added: SI 2002/2842 Art.5

s.25, amended: SI 2002/2842 Art.6

Sch.1 Part II para.13, substituted: SI 2004/655 Art.3

Sch.1 Part II para.15, amended: SI 2004/655 Art.4

Sch.1 Part IV para.24, enabling: SI 2004/655

24. Nurses, Midwives and Health Visitors Act 1997

applied: SI 2002/253 Art.6, Sch.1 para.3, Sch.2 para.3, Sch.2 para.11, Sch.2 para.12, Sch.2 para.16, SI 2003/3148 Reg.3, SI 2004/1762 Art.13

varied: SI 2002/253 Sch.2 para.16, SI 2004/1762 Art.1

s.2, applied: SI 2002/253 Sch.2 para.13

CAP.

1997–cont.

24. Nurses, Midwives and Health Visitors Act 1997*–cont.*

s.3, applied: SI 2002/253 Sch.2 para.13

s.4, applied: SI 2002/253 Sch.2 para.13

s.5, applied: SI 2002/253 Sch.2 para.13

s.6, applied: SI 2002/253 Sch.2 para.13

s.7, applied: SI 2002/253 Sch.2 para.3, Sch.2 para.10, SI 2002/2779 Sch.3 para.2, SI 2003/284 Sch.2 para.2, SI 2004/293 Sch.2 para.16, SI 2004/1267 Sch.2 para.4, SR 2002/386 Reg.2, Reg.4, SSI 2003/176 Art.7

s.8, applied: SI 2002/253 Sch.2 para.10

s.10, applied: SI 2004/1762 Art.2, Art.3, Art.4, Art.5, Art.6, Art.9, SR 2002/117 Sch.1

s.12, applied: SI 2002/253 Sch.2 para.17

s.12, disapplied: SI 2004/1762 Art.5

s.14, applied: SI 2002/253 Sch.2 para.13, SI 2004/1762 Art.14, SR 2002/1 Reg.11

s.15, applied: SI 2002/253 Sch.2 para.13, Sch.2 para.18, SI 2004/1762 Art.14

s.15, referred to: SI 2002/253 Sch.2 para.18

s.18, applied: SI 2002/253 Sch.2 para.25, SI 2002/923 Art.4

s.18, varied: SI 2002/253 Sch.2 para.25

s.19, applied: SI 2002/82 Sch.1, SI 2002/1169 Sch.1, SR 2002/117 Sch.1, SSI 2002/142 Sch.1

s.19, enabling: SI 2002/82, SI 2002/708, SI 2002/1169, SR 2002/43, SR 2002/117, SSI 2002/59, SSI 2002/142

s.20, applied: SI 2002/253 Sch.2 para.13

s.21, applied: SI 2002/253 Sch.2 para.13

s.21, varied: SI 2003/3148 Reg.2

s.22, enabling: SR 2002/43, SR 2002/117

Sch.3, enabling: SR 2002/43, SR 2002/117

Sch.4 para.5, repealed: SI 2003/431 Sch.5

25. Justices of the Peace Act 1997

applied: 2003 c.39 Sch.2 para.1, Sch.2 para.10

referred to: SI 2002/808 Art.2, 2003 c.26 Sch.7 para.61

repealed: 2003 c.39 s.6, Sch.10

s.1, applied: SI 2002/1440

s.1, enabling: SI 2002/1440, SI 2003/640, SI 2003/641

s.5, applied: 2003 c.39 Sch.9 para.4

s.7, applied: 2003 c.39 Sch.9 para.5

s.10A, applied: 2003 c.39 Sch.9 para.8

s.22, applied: SI 2002/193 r.18, 2003 c.39 Sch.9 para.7

s.24, enabling: SI 2002/193, SI 2004/1514

s.25, applied: 2003 c.39 Sch.9 para.6

s.29, enabling: SI 2003/2252

s.30B, enabling: SI 2003/385, SI 2004/76

s.32A, applied: SI 2002/1440, SI 2003/640, SI 2003/641

s.32A, enabling: SI 2002/1440, SI 2003/641

s.50, enabling: SI 2002/2143

s.59B, applied: 2004 c.i s.23

CAP.

1997–cont.

25. Justices of the Peace Act 1997–*cont.*
s.60, applied: 2002 c.29 s.55
s.62, amended: SI 2003/3191 Sch.1 para.3
s.62, applied: 2003 c.39 Sch.9 para.14
s.62, varied: SI 2003/3191 Art.3
s.64, applied: SI 2002/193 r.16, r.17, r.18
s.64A, added: 2002 c.30 Sch.7 para.20
s.65, repealed: 2002 c.40 Sch.26
s.67, amended: 2003 c.26 Sch.7 para.62
s.72, amended: 2003 c.26 Sch.7 para.63
Sch.4 Part II para.17, amended: 2003 c.17 Sch.7
Sch.4 Part II para.20, referred to: 2003 c.39 Sch.9 para.11
Sch.5 para.9, repealed: 2003 c.41 Sch.4
Sch.5 para.23, repealed: 2002 c.29 Sch.12
Sch.5 para.36, repealed: 2002 c.29 Sch.12

27. Social Security (Recovery of Benefits) Act 1997
see *Newman v Folkes* [2002] P.I.Q.R. Q2 (QBD), Garland, J.
applied: 2003 c.43 s.161
s.8, see *Bruce v Genesis Fast Food Ltd* [2003] EWHC 788, [2004] P.I.Q.R. P9 (QBD), McKinnon, J.; see *Williams v Devon CC* [2003] EWCA Civ 365, [2003] P.I.Q.R. Q4 (CA), Latham, L.J.
s.11, enabling: SI 2002/1379, SI 2004/3368
s.29, enabling: SI 2004/1141
Sch.1 Part I para.8, enabling: SI 2004/1141
Sch.2, see *Williams v Devon CC* [2003] EWCA Civ 365, [2003] P.I.Q.R. Q4 (CA), Latham, L.J.
Sch.2 column 1, see *Lowther v Chatwin* [2003] EWCA Civ 729, [2003] P.I.Q.R. Q5 (CA), Wilson, J.

28. Merchant Shipping and Maritime Security Act 1997
s.2, repealed: 2003 c.16 Sch.3
s.3, repealed: 2003 c.16 Sch.3
s.4, repealed (in part): 2004 c.21 Sch.2
s.10, repealed: 2003 c.16 Sch.3
s.24, amended: 2002 c.8 s.2
s.24, enabling: SI 2003/2496
Sch.6 para.20, amended: 2002 c.8 s.2

29. Local Government and Rating Act 1997
s.2, repealed (in part): 2003 c.26 Sch.8 Part 1
s.5, amended: 2003 asp 1 s.28
s.8, amended: 2003 asp 1 s.28
s.8, applied: SSI 2003/188
s.8, enabling: SSI 2003/141, SSI 2003/188
Sch.2, applied: 2003 asp 1 s.28
Sch.2 para.1, enabling: SSI 2004/91
Sch.2 para.3, amended: 2003 asp 1 s.29
Sch.2 para.3, applied: SSI 2002/91 Reg.16, SSI 2003/160 Reg.17, SSI 2003/188 Art.3, SSI 2004/92 Reg.3
Sch.2 para.3, enabling: SSI 2003/141, SSI 2003/188
Sch.2 para.3A, added: 2003 asp 1 s.28

CAP.

1997–cont.

29. Local Government and Rating Act 1997–*cont.*
Sch.2 para.3A, applied: SSI 2003/142 Art.2, SSI 2003/160 Reg.17, SSI 2004/92 Reg.3
Sch.2 para.3A, enabling: SSI 2003/142
Sch.2 para.4, amended: 2003 asp 1 s.28
Sch.2 para.4, applied: SSI 2002/91 Reg.18, SSI 2003/143 Art.3, SSI 2003/160 Reg.19, SSI 2004/92 Reg.5
Sch.2 para.4, enabling: SSI 2003/143

33. Confiscation of Alcohol (Young Persons) Act 1997
s.1, amended: 2003 c.17 s.155, Sch.6 para.115, Sch.7
s.1, applied: SI 2004/915 Sch.1 para.5
s.1, varied: 2002 c.30 Sch.4 para.6, Sch.5 para.5

34. Contract (Scotland) Act 1997
see *Bolton v Aberdeen City Council* 2002 Hous. L.R. 40 (Lands Tr (Scot)), JN Wright Q.C.

35. Scottish Legal Services Ombudsman and Commissioner for Local Administration in Scotland Act 1997
s.7, repealed: 2002 asp 11 Sch.6 para.20
s.8, repealed: 2002 asp 11 Sch.6 para.20

39. Sexual Offences (Protected Material) Act 1997
Commencement Orders: 2003 c.42 Sch.7
s.9, amended: 2003 c.44 Sch.36 para.39
s.9, repealed (in part): 2003 c.44 Sch.37 Part 4, Sch.3 para.67
Sch.1 para.1, repealed: 2003 c.42 Sch.7
Sch.1 para.2, repealed: 2003 c.42 Sch.7
Sch.1 para.3, repealed: 2003 c.42 Sch.7
Sch.1 para.4, repealed: 2003 c.42 Sch.7
Sch.1 para.5A, added: 2003 c.42 Sch.6 para.36
Sch.1 para.6, amended: 2003 c.42 Sch.6 para.36

40. Protection from Harassment Act 1997
see *Daiichi Pharmaceuticals UK Ltd v Stop Huntingdon Animal Cruelty* [2003] EWHC 2337, [2004] 1 W.L.R. 1503 (QBD), Owen, J.; see *Lomas v Parle* [2003] EWCA Civ 1804, [2004] 1 W.L.R. 1642 (CA), Thorpe, L.J.; see *Wong v Parkside Health NHS Trust* [2001] EWCA Civ 1721, [2003] 3 All E.R. 932 (CA), Hale, L.J.
applied: SI 2003/1593 Sch.1 Part I
s.1, see *Thomas v News Group Newspapers Ltd* [2001] EWCA Civ 1233, [2002] E.M.L.R. 4 (CA), Lord Phillips of Worth Matravers, M.R.
s.2, see *DPP v Dziurzynski* [2002] EWHC 1380, (2002) 166 J.P. 545 (QBD (Admin Ct)), Rose, L.J.; see *Kelly v DPP* [2002] EWHC 1428, (2002) 166 J.P. 621 (QBD (Admin Ct)), Burton, J.; see *R. v Goble (Francis George)* [2003] EWCA Crim

CAP.

1997–cont.

40. Protection from Harassment Act 1997–cont.

s.2–cont.

3171, [2004] 2 Cr. App. R. (S.) 4 (CA (Crim Div)), Mitting, J.

s.2, applied: SI 2003/1376 Sch.1

s.2, repealed (in part): 2002 c.30 Sch.8

s.4, see *Caurti v DPP* [2001] EWHC Admin 867, [2002] Crim. L.R. 131 (QBD (Admin Ct)), Cresswell, J.; see *DPP v Dziurzynski* [2002] EWHC 1380, (2002) 166 J.P. 545 (QBD (Admin Ct)), Rose, L.J.; see *Kelly v DPP* [2002] EWHC 1428, (2002) 166 J.P. 621 (QBD (Admin Ct)), Burton, J.; see *R. v Kennedy (Michael Edward)* [2003] EWCA Crim 3380, [2004] 2 Cr. App. R. (S.) 20 (CA (Crim Div)), Pitchford, J.; see *R. v Preston (Amanda Louise)* [2002] 1 Cr. App. R. (S.) 96 (CA (Crim Div)), Judge Beaumont Q.C.; see *R. v Tully (Joseph Arthur)* [2002] EWCA Crim 1660, [2003] 1 Cr. App. R. (S.) 56 (CA (Crim Div)), Davis, J.

s.4, applied: 2003 c.42 Sch.5 para.57, 2003 c.44 Sch.15 para.57, SI 2003/1376 Sch.1, SI 2004/1910 Sch.2

s.5, see *DPP v Dziurzynski* [2002] EWHC 1380, (2002) 166 J.P. 545 (QBD (Admin Ct)), Rose, L.J.; see *R. v Goble (Francis George)* [2003] EWCA Crim 3171, [2004] 2 Cr. App. R. (S.) 4 (CA (Crim Div)), Mitting, J.; see *R. v Kasoar (Jayesing)* [2002] EWCA Crim 12, [2002] 2 Cr. App. R. (S.) 60 (CA (Crim Div)), Judge Fawcus

s.5, amended: 2004 c.28 s.12, Sch.10 para.43, Sch.11

s.5A, added: 2004 c.28 s.12

s.7, amended: 2004 c.28 Sch.10 para.44

s.8, see *McCann v McGurran* 2002 S.L.T. 592 (Ex Div), Lord Caplan, Lord Cameron of Lochbroom, Lord Kingarth; see *McGuire v Kidston* 2002 S.L.T. (Sh Ct) 66 (Sh Pr), CGB Nicholson Q.C., Sheriff Principal

s.9, amended: 2003 asp 7 s.49

42. Police (Health and Safety) Act 1997

s.5, repealed: 2002 c.30 s.95, Sch.8

43. Crime (Sentences) Act 1997

see *R. (on the application of Noorkoiv) v Secretary of State for the Home Department (No.2)* [2002] EWCA Civ 770, [2002] 1 W.L.R. 3284 (CA), Buxton, L.J.

Part II c.II, applied: 2003 c.44 s.225, s.226, s.239, Sch.19 para.1

s.2, see *R. (on the application of Cawser) v Secretary of State for the Home Department* [2003] EWCA Civ 1522, [2004] U.K.H.R.R. 101 (CA), Arden, L.J.; see *R. v Close (Craig)* [2001] EWCA Crim 1066, [2002] 1 Cr. App. R. (S.) 16 (CA (Crim Div)), Leveson, J.; see *R. v Craig (Robert)* [2001] EWCA Crim 1641, [2002]

CAP.

1997–cont.

43. Crime (Sentences) Act 1997–cont.

s.2–cont.

1 Cr. App. R. (S.) 74 (CA (Crim Div)), Bell, J.; see *R. v Drew (Anthony James)* [2003] UKHL 25, [2003] 1 W.L.R. 1213 (HL), Lord Bingham of Cornhill; see *R. v Jackson (Mark Samuel)* [2003] EWCA Crim 3251, [2004] 2 Cr. App. R. (S.) 8 (CA (Crim Div)), Potter, L.J.; see *R. v Kelly (Edward) (No.2)* [2001] EWCA Crim 1751, [2002] 1 Cr. App. R. (S.) 85 (CA (Crim Div)), Buxton, L.J.; see *R. v Murphy (Brendan William)* [2002] EWCA Crim 1624, [2003] 1 Cr. App. R. (S.) 39 (CA (Crim Div)), Hunt, J.; see *R. v Noorkoiv (Leo Robert)* [2002] EWCA Crim 530, [2002] 2 Cr. App. R. (S.) 91 (CA (Crim Div)), Gibbs, J.; see *R. v Smith (Ruben)* [2001] EWCA Crim 1700, [2002] 1 Cr. App. R. (S.) 82 (CA (Crim Div)), Holman, J.; see *R. v Stark (Barry John)* [2002] EWCA Crim 542, [2002] 2 Cr. App. R. (S.) 104 (CA (Crim Div)), Keene, L.J.; see *R. v Tonks (William)* [2004] EWCA Crim 1392, (2004) 148 S.J.L.B. 789 (CA (Crim Div)), Scott Baker, L.J.; see *R. v Townsend (Tony)* [2003] EWCA Crim 2210, [2004] 1 Cr. App. R. (S.) 47 (CA (Crim Div)), Buxton, L.J.; see *R. v Watkins (Terrence George)* [2002] EWCA Crim 1014, [2003] 1 Cr. App. R. (S.) 16 (CA (Crim Div)), Waller, L.J.

s.3, see *R. v Hickson (Jeffrey)* [2001] EWCA Crim 1595, [2002] 1 Cr. App. R. (S.) 71 (CA (Crim Div)), Waller, L.J.

s.28, see *R. (on the application of Brooks) v Parole Board* [2004] EWCA Civ 80, (2004) 148 S.J.L.B. 233 (CA), Kennedy, L.J.; see *R. (on the application of Smith) v Secretary of State for the Home Department* [2003] EWHC 692, [2003] 1 W.L.R. 2176 (QBD (Admin Ct)), Kennedy, L.J.; see *R. v Flamson (Lee Andrew)* [2001] EWCA Crim 3030, [2002] 2 Cr. App. R. (S.) 48 (CA (Crim Div)), Mance, L.J.; see *R. v Mason (Kenneth)* [2002] EWCA Crim 699, [2002] 2 Cr. App. R. 32 (CA (Crim Div)), Clarke, L.J.; see *R. v McBean (Isa)* [2001] EWCA Crim 1891, [2002] 1 Cr. App. R. (S.) 98 (CA (Crim Div)), Bell, J.; see *R. v Royal (Carl Christopher)* [2003] EWCA Crim 1152, [2004] 1 Cr. App. R. (S.) 2 (CA (Crim Div)), Laws, L.J.

s.28, amended: 2003 c.44 s.275

s.28, applied: 2003 c.44 s.269

s.28, referred to: 2003 c.44 s.303

s.28, varied: 2003 c.44 Sch.22 para.16

s.29, see *R. (on the application of Anderson) v Secretary of State for the Home Department* [2002] UKHL 46, [2003] 1 A.C. 837 (HL), Lord Bingham of Cornhill; see *R. (on the application of Richards) v Secretary of State for the Home Department* [2004] EWHC 93, (2004) 154 N.L.J. 176 (QBD (Admin Ct)), Silber, J.

CAP.

1997–cont.

43. Crime (Sentences) Act 1997–*cont.*

s.29, repealed: 2003 c.44 Sch.37 Part 8

s.31, amended: 2003 c.44 Sch.18 para.1, Sch.32 para.83

s.31, repealed (in part): 2003 c.44 Sch.37 Part 8

s.31A, added: 2003 c.44 Sch.18 para.2

s.32, see *R. (on the application of Waite) v Hammersmith and Fulham LBC* [2002] EWCA Civ 482, [2003] H.L.R. 3 (CA), Laws, L.J.

s.32, amended: 2003 c.44 Sch.32 para.84

s.33, applied: 2003 c.44 Sch.22 para.17, Sch.22 para.18

s.33, repealed: 2003 c.44 Sch.37 Part 8

s.34, amended: 2003 c.44 s.273, Sch.18 para.3, Sch.37 Part 8

s.34, varied: 2003 c.44 Sch.22 para.17

s.35, amended: 2002 c.29 Sch.11 para.32

s.35, repealed: 2003 c.44 s.303, Sch.37 Part 7

s.36, repealed: 2003 c.44 Sch.37 Part 7

s.37, repealed: 2003 c.44 Sch.37 Part 7

s.38, repealed: 2003 c.44 Sch.37 Part 7

s.39, repealed: 2003 c.44 Sch.37 Part 7

s.40, amended: 2002 c.29 Sch.11 para.32

s.40, repealed: 2003 c.44 s.303, Sch.37 Part 7

s.47, see *R. (on the application of South West Yorkshire Mental Health NHS Trust) v Bradford Crown Court* [2003] EWCA Civ 1857, [2004] 1 W.L.R. 1664 (CA), Pill, L.J.; see *R. (on the application of South West Yorkshire Mental Health NHS Trust) v Bradford Crown Court* [2003] EWHC 640, [2003] A.C.D. 68 (QBD (Admin Ct)), Newman, J.

s.47, amended: 2004 c.28 Sch.10 para.45

s.47, repealed (in part): 2004 c.28 Sch.10 para.45, Sch.11

s.52, repealed: 2003 c.42 Sch.7

Sch.1 Part I para.1, amended: 2004 c.4 s.13

Sch.1 Part I para.1, applied: 2003 c.44 Sch.11 para.2, Sch.11 para.3, Sch.11 para.9, Sch.11 para.10, Sch.11 para.22

Sch.1 Part I para.4, applied: 2003 c.44 Sch.11 para.2, Sch.11 para.3, Sch.11 para.9, Sch.11 para.10, Sch.11 para.22

Sch.1 Part I para.5, amended: 2004 c.4 s.13

Sch.1 Part I para.5A, added: 2004 c.4 s.13

Sch.1 Part II para.6, amended: 2003 c.44 Sch.32 para.85, 2004 c.4 s.13

Sch.1 Part II para.7, applied: 2003 c.44 Sch.11 para.22

Sch.1 Part II para.8, amended: 2003 c.44 Sch.32 para.85, 2004 c.28 Sch.10 para.46

Sch.1 Part II para.9, amended: 2003 c.44 Sch.32 para.85, 2004 c.28 Sch.10 para.46

Sch.1 Part II para.12, amended: 2004 c.4 s.13

Sch.1 Part II para.13, amended: 2004 c.4 s.13

CAP.

1997–cont.

43. Crime (Sentences) Act 1997–*cont.*

Sch.1 Part II para.15, repealed (in part): 2003 c.44 Sch.32 para.85, Sch.37 Part 7

Sch.2 para.2, repealed: 2003 c.44 Sch.37 Part 7

Sch.2 para.3, repealed: 2003 c.44 Sch.37 Part 7

Sch.2 para.7, amended: 2003 asp 7 s.33

Sch.3 Part II para.6, repealed: 2003 asp 13 Sch.5 Part 1

Sch.3 Part II para.7, repealed: 2003 asp 13 Sch.5 Part 1

Sch.3 Part II para.8, repealed: 2003 asp 13 Sch.5 Part 1

Sch.3 Part II para.9, repealed: 2003 asp 13 Sch.5 Part 1

Sch.3 Part II para.10, repealed: 2003 asp 13 Sch.5 Part 1

Sch.4 para.4, repealed: 2003 c.44 Sch.37 Part 5

Sch.4 para.6, repealed (in part): 2003 c.44 Sch.37 Part 7

Sch.4 para.7, repealed: 2003 c.44 Sch.37 Part 7

Sch.4 para.10, repealed (in part): 2003 c.44 Sch.37 Part 7

Sch.4 para.12, repealed (in part): 2003 c.44 Sch.37 Part 7

Sch.4 para.13, repealed: 2003 c.44 Sch.37 Part 7

Sch.4 para.15, repealed (in part): 2003 c.44 Sch.37 Part 7

Sch.4 para.17, see *R. v Hickson (Jeffrey)* [2001] EWCA Crim 1595, [2002] 1 Cr. App. R. (S.) 71 (CA (Crim Div)), Waller, L.J.

44. Education Act 1997

Part V, applied: 2002 c.32 s.189

s.9, repealed: 2004 c.31 Sch.5 Part 1

s.15, repealed (in part): 2002 c.32 s.204, Sch.22 Part 3

s.16, applied: SI 2002/928 Sch.3

s.16, repealed (in part): 2002 c.32 s.204, Sch.22 Part 3

s.17, repealed (in part): 2002 c.32 s.204, Sch.22 Part 3

s.18, applied: SI 2002/928 Sch.3

s.18, repealed (in part): 2002 c.32 s.204, Sch.22 Part 3

s.19, enabling: SI 2002/840, SI 2002/895, SI 2002/2105, SI 2003/1970, SI 2004/2858, SI 2004/3323

s.23, amended: 2002 c.32 Sch.17 para.1

s.23, repealed (in part): 2002 c.32 Sch.22 Part 1

s.24, amended: 2002 c.32 Sch.17 para.2

s.24, applied: 2002 c.32 Sch.17 para.6

s.26, amended: 2002 c.32 Sch.17 para.3, Sch.21 para.69, Sch.22 Part 1

s.26A, added: 2002 c.32 Sch.17 para.4

s.29, amended: 2002 c.32 Sch.17 para.5

CAP.

1997–cont.

44. Education Act 1997–*cont.*

s.29, repealed (in part): 2002 c.32 Sch.17 para.5, Sch.22 Part 2

s.30, applied: 2002 c.32 Sch.17 para.6

s.32, amended: 2002 c.32 Sch.17 para.7, Sch.21 para.70, Sch.22 Part 2

s.32A, added: 2002 c.32 Sch.17 para.8

s.33, repealed: 2004 c.14 Sch.1 Part 7

s.34, repealed: 2004 c.14 Sch.1 Part 7

s.36, enabling: SI 2002/435, SI 2002/1331

s.37, repealed: 2004 c.14 Sch.1 Part 7

s.38, amended: 2004 c.31 s.51

s.39, applied: SI 2002/928 Sch.3

s.40, substituted: 2002 c.32 s.180

s.41, amended: 2004 c.23 Sch.2 para.18

s.41A, added: 2004 c.23 Sch.2 para.19

s.43, amended: 2002 c.32 Sch.7 para.8

s.43, applied: SI 2002/928 Sch.3

s.43, varied: SI 2003/2645 Reg.2

s.46, enabling: SI 2003/2645

s.49, repealed (in part): 2002 c.32 Sch.22 Part 3

s.53A, added: SI 2003/2867 Sch.1 para.26

s.54, enabling: SI 2002/435, SI 2002/840, SI 2002/895, SI 2002/1331, SI 2002/2105, SI 2003/1970, SI 2003/2645, SI 2004/2858, SI 2004/3323

s.58, amended: 2002 c.32 Sch.17 para.9

Sch.7 para.8, repealed (in part): 2002 c.32 Sch.22 Part 3

Sch.7 para.9, repealed (in part): 2002 c.32 Sch.22 Part 3

Sch.7 para.14, repealed (in part): 2002 c.32 Sch.22 Part 3

Sch.7 para.27, repealed (in part): 2002 c.32 Sch.22 Part 3

Sch.7 para.28, repealed (in part): 2002 c.32 Sch.22 Part 3

Sch.7 para.36, repealed (in part): 2002 c.32 Sch.22 Part 3

46. National Health Service (Primary Care) Act 1997

Commencement Orders: SI 2002/1616 Art.2, 2003 asp 4 Sch.4 para.14, 2003 c.43 Sch.14 Part 4, 2004 asp 1 Sch.1 para.2; SI 2004/287 Art.2, Art.3

applied: 2002 asp 13 Sch.1 para.35, SI 2002/325 Reg.3, SI 2002/327 Reg.21, SI 2002/2375 Reg.3, SI 2003/993 Reg.17, SI 2003/1587 Reg.18

referred to: 2003 c.43 Sch.11 para.26

Part I, applied: 2002 asp 11 Sch.2 para.5, SI 2002/2375 Reg.9, Reg.10, Reg.11, SI 2003/2124 Reg.3, SI 2003/2382 Reg.6, SSI 2003/376 Reg.5, SSI 2003/460 Reg.5

Part I, referred to: SI 2004/865 Art.58

s.1, amended: 2004 asp 1 Sch.1 para.2

s.1, applied: SI 2003/1250 Art.10, Sch.8 para.22, SI 2004/1768 Reg.2

CAP.

1997–cont.

46. National Health Service (Primary Care) Act 1997–*cont.*

s.1, repealed (in part): 2003 c.43 s.178, Sch.14 Part 4, 2004 asp 1 Sch.1 para.2, 2004 asp 7 Sch.2

s.1, varied: 2004 asp 1 s.3, SI 2004/288 Art.8, SI 2004/480 Art.7

s.2, amended: SI 2003/1250 Sch.9 para.6

s.2, applied: SI 2002/2548 Sch.1 para.7, SI 2003/2644 Reg.21

s.2, referred to: SI 2004/865 Art.60

s.2, repealed (in part): 2003 c.43 s.178, Sch.14 Part 4, 2004 asp 1 Sch.1 para.2

s.2, varied: 2004 asp 1 s.3, SSI 2004/163 Art.51

s.3, repealed (in part): 2003 c.43 s.178, Sch.14 Part 4, 2004 asp 7 Sch.2

s.3, varied: 2004 asp 1 s.3

s.4, applied: SI 2002/2375 Reg.4, SI 2002/3048 Reg.4

s.4, repealed (in part): 2003 c.43 s.178, Sch.14 Part 4

s.4, varied: 2004 asp 1 s.3, SSI 2004/163 Art.51

s.5, applied: SI 2002/2375 Reg.4

s.5, referred to: SI 2002/2375 Sch.3

s.5, repealed (in part): 2003 asp 4 Sch.4 para.14, 2003 c.43 s.178, Sch.14 Part 4, 2004 asp 1 Sch.1 para.2

s.5, varied: 2004 asp 1 s.3

s.6, applied: SI 2002/2375 Reg.4

s.6, referred to: SI 2002/2375 Sch.3

s.6, repealed (in part): 2003 c.43 s.178, Sch.14 Part 4

s.6, varied: 2004 asp 1 s.3

s.7, repealed (in part): 2003 c.43 s.178, Sch.14 Part 4

s.7, varied: 2004 asp 1 s.3

s.8, applied: SI 2002/2375 Reg.4

s.8, referred to: SI 2002/2375 Sch.3, SI 2004/865 Art.60

s.8, repealed (in part): 2003 c.43 s.178, Sch.14 Part 4

s.8, varied: 2004 asp 1 s.3, SSI 2004/163 Art.51

s.8A, repealed (in part): 2003 c.43 s.178, Sch.14 Part 4

s.8A, varied: 2004 asp 1 s.3

s.8A, amended: 2002 c.17 Sch.3 para.4

s.8A, repealed (in part): 2003 c.43 s.178, Sch.14 Part 4

s.8A, varied: 2004 asp 1 s.3

s.8ZA, amended: 2002 c.17 Sch.3 para.3

s.8ZA, applied: SI 2003/1250 Art.10, Sch.8 para.22, SI 2003/2644 Reg.8

s.8ZA, repealed (in part): 2003 c.43 s.178, Sch.14 Part 4

s.8ZA, varied: 2004 asp 1 s.3

s.8ZA, enabling: SI 2003/2644

s.9, amended: 2002 c.17 s.4

1997–cont.

46. National Health Service (Primary Care) Act 1997–*cont.*

s.9, repealed (in part): 2003 c.43 s.178, Sch.14 Part 4

s.9, varied: 2004 asp 1 s.3

s.9, enabling: SI 2003/2644

s.10, repealed (in part): 2003 c.43 s.178, Sch.14 Part 4

s.10, varied: 2004 asp 1 s.3

s.11, repealed (in part): 2003 c.43 s.178, Sch.14 Part 4, SI 2003/1250 Sch.9 para.6, 2004 asp 1 Sch.1 para.2

s.11, varied: 2004 asp 1 s.3

s.11, enabling: SI 2002/543

s.12, amended: 2002 c.17 Sch.3 para.5

s.12, repealed (in part): 2003 c.43 s.178, Sch.14 Part 4, 2004 asp 1 Sch.1 para.2

s.12, varied: 2004 asp 1 s.3

s.13, amended: 2002 c.17 Sch.3 para.6

s.13, applied: SI 2002/2375 Reg.4

s.13, repealed (in part): 2003 c.43 s.178, Sch.14 Part 4, 2004 asp 1 Sch.1 para.2

s.13, varied: 2004 asp 1 s.3

s.14, repealed (in part): 2003 c.43 s.178, Sch.14 Part 4

s.14, varied: 2004 asp 1 s.3

s.15, repealed (in part): 2003 c.43 s.178, Sch.14 Part 4, 2004 asp 1 Sch.1 para.2

s.15, varied: 2004 asp 1 s.3

s.16, applied: SI 2002/2375 Reg.4

s.16, repealed (in part): 2003 c.43 s.178, Sch.14 Part 4

s.16, varied: 2004 asp 1 s.3

s.17, repealed (in part): 2003 c.43 s.178, Sch.14 Part 4

s.17, varied: 2004 asp 1 s.3

s.17, enabling: SI 2002/2353

s.18, applied: SI 2002/2375 Reg.4

s.18, repealed (in part): 2003 c.43 s.178, Sch.14 Part 4

s.18, varied: 2004 asp 1 s.3

s.19, repealed (in part): 2003 c.43 s.178, Sch.14 Part 4

s.19, varied: 2004 asp 1 s.3

s.20, applied: SSI 2003/158 Reg.3, Reg.4, Reg.5, SSI 2003/376 Reg.3, Reg.5, SSI 2003/460 Reg.3, Reg.5

s.20, repealed (in part): 2003 c.43 s.178, Sch.14 Part 4

s.20, varied: 2004 asp 1 s.3

s.20, enabling: SI 2002/2353, SSI 2003/158

s.21, amended: 2002 c.17 Sch.3 para.7

s.22, amended: 2002 c.17 Sch.3 para.8, SI 2003/1250 Sch.9 para.6

s.23, repealed (in part): 2003 c.43 Sch.14 Part 4, 2004 asp 1 Sch.1 para.2

s.24, repealed (in part): 2003 c.43 Sch.14 Part 4

s.25, repealed (in part): 2003 c.43 Sch.14 Part 4

1997–cont.

46. National Health Service (Primary Care) Act 1997–*cont.*

s.32, repealed (in part): 2003 c.43 Sch.14 Part 4

s.33, repealed (in part): 2003 asp 4 Sch.4 para.14, SI 2003/1250 Sch.9 para.6, 2004 asp 1 Sch.1 para.2

s.39, enabling: SI 2002/2861, SI 2003/2644, SSI 2003/158, SSI 2004/38

s.40, amended: 2002 c.17 Sch.3 para.9, 2004 asp 1 Sch.1 para.2

s.40, repealed (in part): 2003 c.43 Sch.14 Part 4

s.40, enabling: SSI 2003/158, SSI 2004/38

s.41, enabling: SI 2002/1616, SI 2004/287

Sch.1, applied: SI 2002/2375 Reg.4, SSI 2004/38 Reg.30

Sch.1 para.1, amended: 2002 c.17 Sch.3 para.10

Sch.1 para.1, applied: SI 2004/865 Art.106, SI 2004/1016 Art.82, SSI 2004/163 Art.93

Sch.1 para.1, repealed (in part): 2003 c.43 Sch.14 Part 4, 2004 asp 1 Sch.1 para.2

Sch.1 para.2, repealed (in part): 2003 c.43 Sch.14 Part 4, 2004 asp 1 Sch.1 para.2

Sch.1 para.3, amended: 2002 asp 5 s.19

Sch.1 para.3, applied: SI 2002/2469 Sch.12 para.31, SI 2004/865 Art.106, SSI 2004/38 Reg.6, SSI 2004/163 Art.93

Sch.1 para.3, referred to: SSI 2004/34 Art.3

Sch.1 para.3, repealed (in part): 2003 c.43 Sch.14 Part 4, 2004 asp 1 Sch.1 para.2

Sch.1 para.3, enabling: SSI 2004/38

Sch.1 para.4, amended: 2002 asp 5 s.19

Sch.1 para.4, applied: SI 2002/2469 Sch.12 para.33, Sch.12 para.35, SSI 2004/38 Reg.21, Reg.25, Reg.28, SSI 2004/163 Art.93

Sch.1 para.4, referred to: SSI 2004/34 Art.3

Sch.1 para.4, repealed (in part): 2003 c.43 Sch.14 Part 4, 2004 asp 1 Sch.1 para.2

Sch.1 para.5, applied: SI 2002/2469 Sch.12 para.33, SSI 2004/38 Reg.25, Reg.28, SSI 2004/163 Art.93

Sch.1 para.5, repealed (in part): 2003 c.43 Sch.14 Part 4, 2004 asp 1 Sch.1 para.2

Sch.1 para.6, applied: SSI 2004/38 Reg.28

Sch.1 para.6, repealed (in part): 2003 c.43 Sch.14 Part 4, 2004 asp 1 Sch.1 para.2

Sch.1 para.7, repealed (in part): 2003 c.43 Sch.14 Part 4, 2004 asp 1 Sch.1 para.2

Sch.1 para.7, enabling: SSI 2004/38

Sch.1 para.8, repealed (in part): 2003 c.43 Sch.14 Part 4, 2004 asp 1 Sch.1 para.2

Sch.1 para.9, amended: 2002 c.17 Sch.3 para.10

Sch.1 para.9, repealed (in part): 2003 c.43 Sch.14 Part 4, 2004 asp 1 Sch.1 para.2

Sch.2 Part I para.6, repealed (in part): 2003 c.43 Sch.14 Part 4

1997–cont.

46. National Health Service (Primary Care) Act 1997–*cont.*

Sch.2 Part I para.8, repealed (in part): 2003 c.43 Sch.14 Part 4

Sch.2 Part I para.9, repealed (in part): 2003 c.43 Sch.14 Part 4

Sch.2 Part I para.10, repealed (in part): 2003 c.43 Sch.14 Part 4

Sch.2 Part I para.11, repealed (in part): 2003 c.43 Sch.14 Part 4

Sch.2 Part I para.12, repealed (in part): 2003 c.43 Sch.14 Part 4

Sch.2 Part I para.16, repealed (in part): 2003 c.43 Sch.14 Part 4

Sch.2 Part I para.17, repealed (in part): 2003 c.43 Sch.14 Part 4

Sch.2 Part I para.18, repealed (in part): 2003 c.43 Sch.14 Part 4

Sch.2 Part I para.19, repealed (in part): 2003 c.43 Sch.14 Part 4

Sch.2 Part I para.24, repealed (in part): 2003 c.43 Sch.14 Part 4

Sch.2 Part I para.25, repealed (in part): 2003 c.43 Sch.14 Part 4

Sch.2 Part I para.33, repealed: 2003 asp 4 Sch.4 para.14

Sch.2 Part I para.37, repealed: 2004 asp 1 Sch.1 para.2

Sch.2 Part I para.39, repealed: 2004 asp 1 Sch.1 para.2

Sch.2 Part I para.40, repealed: 2004 asp 1 Sch.1 para.2

Sch.2 Part I para.41, repealed: 2004 asp 1 Sch.1 para.2

Sch.2 Part I para.42, repealed: 2003 asp 4 Sch.4 para.14

Sch.2 Part I para.57, amended: 2004 asp 1 Sch.1 para.2

Sch.2 Part I para.57, repealed: 2002 asp 5 Sch.2 para.3

Sch.2 Part II para.71, repealed (in part): 2002 c.17 Sch.8 para.24, Sch.9 Part 3, 2003 c.43 Sch.14 Part 4

Sch.2 Part II para.72, repealed (in part): 2003 c.43 Sch.14 Part 4

Sch.2 Part II para.73, repealed (in part): 2002 c.17 Sch.8 para.24, Sch.9 Part 3, 2003 c.43 Sch.14 Part 4

Sch.2 Part II para.75, repealed (in part): 2002 c.17 Sch.8 para.24, Sch.9 Part 3

Sch.2 Part II para.80, repealed (in part): 2003 c.43 Sch.14 Part 4

Sch.2 Part II para.81, repealed (in part): 2003 c.43 Sch.14 Part 4

Sch.3 Part I, amended: 2003 asp 4 Sch.4 para.14

47. Social Security Administration (Fraud) Act 1997

Commencement Orders: SI 2004/564 Art.2

s.25, enabling: SI 2004/564

1997–cont.

47. Social Security Administration (Fraud) Act 1997–*cont.*

Sch.1 para.7, repealed (in part): 2003 c.26 Sch.8 Part 1

Sch.1 para.12, repealed (in part): 2002 c.22 Sch.8 Part 1

48. Crime and Punishment (Scotland) Act 1997

Commencement Orders: SSI 2004/176 Art.2

s.1, repealed: 2003 asp 7 s.19

s.7, repealed: 2003 asp 13 Sch.5 Part 1

s.8, repealed: 2003 asp 13 Sch.5 Part 1

s.15, referred to: SSI 2003/210 Art.7

s.15, repealed (in part): 2002 c.29 Sch.12

s.16, repealed (in part): 2003 asp 7 Sch.5

s.65, enabling: SSI 2004/176

Sch.1 para.9, repealed: 2003 asp 13 Sch.5 Part 1

Sch.1 para.10, repealed (in part): 2003 c.44 Sch.37 Part 8

Sch.1 para.20, referred to: SSI 2003/210 Art.7

Sch.1 para.20, repealed: 2002 c.29 Sch.12

Sch.1 para.21, amended: 2003 asp 7 Sch.4 para.4

49. Public Entertainments Licences (Drug Misuse) Act 1997

repealed: 2003 c.17 Sch.7

50. Police Act 1997

Commencement Orders: SI 2002/413 Art.2; SSI 2002/124 Art.3, Art.4, Art.5

see *R. v E* [2004] EWCA Crim 1243, [2004] 1 W.L.R. 3279 (CA (Crim Div)), Rose, L.J.

applied: 2002 c.17 s.42, SI 2002/324 Reg.7, Reg.9, Reg.19, Sch.2 para.2, Sch.2 para.7, SI 2002/325 Reg.9, Reg.11, Reg.18, Sch.2 para.2, SI 2002/327 Reg.6, Reg.8, Reg.26, Sch.2 para.2, SI 2002/812 Sch.2 para.2, SI 2002/919 Sch.2 para.4, Sch.2 para.10, Sch.3 para.12, Sch.3 para.13, Sch.8 para.4, SI 2003/237 Sch.1 para.2, SI 2003/710 Sch.3 para.2, SI 2003/2527 Sch.2 para.9, Sch.3 para.5

referred to: SI 2002/57 Reg.5, Reg.7, SI 2002/812 Reg.4, Reg.16, SI 2002/919 Reg.4, Reg.8, Sch.1 para.1, Sch.3 para.8, Sch.7 para.1, SI 2004/1941 Sch.1 para.9

Part III, applied: 2002 c.30 s.19

Part IV, referred to: 2002 c.30 s.99

Part V, applied: SI 2002/233 Reg.11, SSI 2002/143 Reg.9, 2004 c.35 Sch.3, Sch.8

Part V, referred to: 2003 c.44, s.328

s.6, amended: 2002 c.30 s.85

s.6, repealed (in part): 2002 c.30 s.85, Sch.8

s.6, varied: 2003 c.20 Sch.5 para.4

s.9, amended: 2002 c.30 s.86, Sch.8

s.9, applied: 2002 c.29 s.313, SI 2004/643 Reg.29

s.9, referred to: 2002 c.30 s.90

s.9, varied: 2003 c.20 Sch.5 para.4

s.9A, amended: 2002 c.30 s.90

1997–cont.

50. Police Act 1997–cont.

s.9A, repealed (in part): 2002 c.30 s.90, Sch.8

s.26, applied: SI 2002/778

s.26, enabling: SI 2002/778

s.28A, added: 2002 c.30 Sch.1 para.2

s.30, substituted: 2002 c.30 Sch.1 para.3

s.31A, added: 2002 c.30 Sch.1 para.4

s.31B, added: 2002 c.30 Sch.1 para.5

s.31C, added: 2002 c.30 Sch.1 para.5

s.34A, added: 2002 c.30 s.88

s.34A, applied: 2002 c.30 s.82

s.37, amended: 2002 c.30 s.88

s.38, amended: 2002 c.30 s.88

s.39, amended: 2002 c.30 s.25

s.39, applied: 2002 c.30 s.10

s.39, repealed (in part): 2002 c.30 s.25, Sch.8

s.39, enabling: SI 2004/643

s.42, amended: 2002 c.30 s.102, s.103, 2003 c.32 s.85

s.42, applied: SI 2004/1127 Art.2

s.42, repealed (in part): 2002 c.30 s.102, Sch.8

s.42, enabling: SI 2004/1127

s.45, amended: 2002 c.30 Sch.1 para.5

s.46, amended: 2002 c.30 Sch.7 para.21, 2003 c.20 Sch.5 para.4

s.46, varied: 2003 c.20 Sch.5 para.4

s.52, amended: 2002 c.30 Sch.7 para.21

s.54, applied: SI 2004/645 Reg.43

s.55, amended: 2002 c.30 s.87, Sch.8

s.55, applied: 2002 c.29 s.313, SI 2004/643 Reg.29

s.55, referred to: 2002 c.30 s.91

s.55, varied: 2003 c.20 Sch.5 para.4

s.55A, amended: 2002 c.30 s.91

s.55A, repealed (in part): 2002 c.30 Sch.8

s.61, applied: SI 2004/645 Reg.39

s.71, applied: SI 2002/779

s.71, enabling: SI 2002/779

s.73A, added: 2002 c.30 Sch.1 para.2

s.75, substituted: 2002 c.30 Sch.1 para.3

s.76A, added: 2002 c.30 Sch.1 para.4

s.76B, added: 2002 c.30 Sch.1 para.5

s.79A, added: 2002 c.30 s.89

s.79A, applied: 2002 c.30 s.82

s.79A, enabling: SI 2003/2594, SI 2003/2595, SI 2003/2600

s.80, substituted: 2002 c.30 Sch.1 para.6

s.80A, added: 2002 c.30 Sch.1 para.7

s.81, amended: 2002 c.30 s.89

s.81, enabling: SI 2003/2596, SI 2003/2599, SI 2004/645

s.82, amended: 2002 c.30 s.89

s.82, applied: SI 2004/645 Reg.34

s.82, enabling: SI 2003/2598

s.83, amended: 2002 c.30 s.25

s.83, applied: 2002 c.30 s.10, SI 2003/2601 Reg.4, Sch.1 para.3

1997–cont.

50. Police Act 1997–cont.

s.83, enabling: SI 2003/2601, SI 2003/2602, SI 2004/643

s.86, amended: 2002 c.30 s.102, s.103

s.86, applied: SI 2004/1127 Art.2

s.86, enabling: SI 2004/1127

s.90, amended: 2002 c.30 Sch.7 para.21

s.90, varied: 2003 c.20 Sch.5 para.4

s.91, amended: SI 2004/1941 Sch.1 para.10

s.93, amended: 2002 c.40 s.200

s.93, varied: 2003 c.20 Sch.5 para.4, SI 2004/815 Art.2

s.94, amended: 2002 c.40 s.200

s.94, varied: 2003 c.20 Sch.5 para.4, SI 2004/815 Art.2

s.95, varied: SI 2004/815 Art.2

s.105, varied: SI 2004/815 Art.2

s.107, varied: SI 2004/815 Art.2

s.112, amended: 2003 c.44 Sch.35 para.2

s.112, applied: SSI 2002/143 Reg.3, Reg.5, Reg.7

s.112, enabling: SSI 2002/143

s.113, amended: 2002 c.32 Sch.12 para.14, Sch.13 para.7, Sch.21 para.72, Sch.22 Part 3, 2002 c.38 s.135, SI 2002/2953 Reg.3, 2003 asp 5 s.12, 2003 c.44 Sch.35 para.3, SI 2003/417 Art.17, Art.47

s.113, applied: SI 2002/57 Sch.1 para.2, SI 2002/233 Reg.3, Reg.5, Reg.6, Reg.7, Reg.8, Reg.9, SI 2002/324 Sch.2 para.2, SI 2002/325 Sch.2 para.2, SI 2002/327 Sch.2 para.2, SI 2002/812 Sch.2 para.2, SI 2002/919 Sch.2 para.4, Sch.2 para.10, Sch.3 para.12, Sch.8 para.9A, Sch.8 para.4, Sch.8 para.10, SI 2002/3212 Reg.12, Sch.2 para.2, Sch.3 para.13, SI 2002/3213 Sch.2 para.2, SI 2002/3214 Reg.12, Sch.2 para.2, Sch.3 para.13, SI 2003/117, SI 2003/117 Reg.2, SI 2003/137 Reg.3, SI 2003/348 Sch.6 para.11, SI 2003/367 Sch.2 para.2, SI 2003/370 Sch.3 para.2, SI 2003/710 Sch.3 para.2, SI 2003/781 Sch.2 para.2, SI 2003/1558 Sch.2 para.10, SI 2003/2527 Sch.2 para.2, Sch.3 para.4, SI 2004/219 Sch.2 para.3, Sch.3 para.4, SI 2004/1007 Art.2, SI 2004/1756 Sch.3 para.2, SI 2004/2071 Sch.2 para.2, Sch.3 para.2, SI 2004/2880 Art.2, SSI 2002/23 Reg.3, Reg.4, SSI 2002/143 Reg.3, Reg.6, Reg.7

s.113, disapplied: SI 2002/919 Sch.2 para.10

s.113, referred to: SI 2002/57 Sch.1 para.2, SI 2002/233 Sch.1, SI 2002/324 Sch.2 para.8, SI 2002/325 Sch.2 para.9, SI 2002/327 Sch.2 para.8, SI 2002/812 Sch.2 para.8, SI 2002/919 Sch.2 para.4, Sch.2 para.10, Sch.3 para.12, Sch.8 para.4, Sch.8 para.10, SI 2002/3212 Reg.12, Sch.2 para.2, SI 2002/3213 Sch.2 para.2, SI 2002/3214 Reg.12, Sch.2 para.2, SI 2003/367 Sch.2 para.2, SI 2003/370 Sch.3 para.2, SI 2003/710 Sch.3 para.2,

1997–cont.

50. Police Act 1997–*cont.*

s.113, referred to:–*cont.*
SI 2003/2527 Sch.2 para.2, Sch.2 para.10, Sch.3 para.4, Sch.3 para.14, SI 2004/219 Sch.2 para.11, Sch.3 para.13

s.113, repealed (in part): 2002 c.32 Sch.21 para.72, Sch.22 Part 3

s.113, varied: SI 2002/3184 Reg.8

s.113, enabling: SI 2002/233, SI 2003/117, SI 2003/137, SI 2003/520, SI 2003/1418, SI 2004/367, SI 2004/1759, SSI 2002/143, SSI 2004/526

s.114, applied: SI 2002/233 Reg.3, Reg.5, Reg.9, SI 2003/117, SI 2003/117 Reg.2, SI 2003/137 Reg.3, SI 2004/1007 Art.2, SSI 2002/143 Reg.3, Reg.6, Reg.7

s.114, referred to: SI 2002/233 Sch.1

s.114, enabling: SI 2002/233, SI 2003/117, SI 2003/137, SI 2003/1418, SI 2004/367, SSI 2002/143

s.115, see *R. (on the application of X) v Chief Constable of West Midlands* [2004] EWHC 61, [2004] 1 W.L.R. 1518 (QBD (Admin Ct)), Wall, J.h.2 para.64, 2002 c.32 Sch.12 para.15, Sch.21 para.73, 2002 c.38 s.135, Sch.3 para.93, 2003 asp 5 s.12, 2003 asp 7 s.70, 2003 c.17 Sch.6 para.116, 2003 c.44 Sch.35 para.4, SI 2003/417 Art.17, Art.47, SSI 2004/167 Sch.1 para.4

s.115, applied: SI 2002/57 Sch.1 para.2, Sch.3 para.13, SI 2002/233 Reg.3, Reg.5, Reg.6, Reg.7, Reg.8, Reg.9, Reg.12, SI 2002/324 Sch.2 para.2, SI 2002/325 Sch.2 para.2, SI 2002/327 Sch.2 para.2, SI 2002/446 Reg.3, SI 2002/812 Sch.2 para.2, SI 2002/919 Sch.2 para.10, Sch.3 para.13, Sch.8 para.4, Sch.8 para.10, SI 2002/3212 Reg.12, Sch.2 para.2, Sch.3 para.13, SI 2002/3213 Sch.2 para.2, SI 2002/3214 Reg.12, Sch.2 para.2, Sch.3 para.13, SI 2003/117, SI 2003/117 Reg.2, SI 2003/118 Reg.6, SI 2003/137 Reg.3, SI 2003/237 Sch.1 para.2, Sch.3 para.13, SI 2003/250 Reg.9, SI 2003/367 Sch.2 para.2, SI 2003/370 Sch.3 para.2, SI 2003/710 Sch.3 para.2, SI 2003/781 Sch.2 para.2, SI 2003/2527 Sch.2 para.2, Sch.3 para.4, SI 2003/2644 Reg.9, SI 2004/219 Sch.2 para.3, Sch.3 para.4, SI 2004/585 Reg.4, Reg.9, Sch.1 para.13, SI 2004/1007 Art.2, SI 2004/1020 Reg.4, Reg.9, Sch.1 para.13, SI 2004/1756 Sch.3 para.2, SI 2004/2071 Sch.2 para.2, Sch.3 para.2, SI 2004/2880 Art.2, SSI 2002/23 Reg.3, Reg.4, SSI 2002/143 Reg.3, Reg.6, Reg.7, Reg.10, SSI 2002/217 Reg.3

s.115, referred to: SI 2002/57 Sch.1 para.2, Sch.3 para.13, SI 2002/233 Sch.1, SI 2002/324 Sch.2 para.8, SI 2002/325 Sch.2 para.9, SI 2002/327 Sch.2 para.8, SI 2002/812 Sch.2 para.8, SI 2002/919 Sch.2 para.4, Sch.2 para.10, Sch.3 para.13, Sch.8 para.4, Sch.8 para.10, SI 2002/3212

1997–cont.

50. Police Act 1997–*cont.*

s.115, referred to:–*cont.*
Reg.12, Sch.2 para.2, SI 2002/3213 Sch.2 para.2, SI 2002/3214 Reg.12, Sch.2 para.2, SI 2003/118 Reg.6, SI 2003/367 Sch.2 para.2, SI 2003/370 Sch.3 para.2, SI 2003/710 Sch.3 para.2, SI 2003/2527 Sch.2 para.2, Sch.2 para.10, Sch.3 para.4, Sch.3 para.14, SI 2004/219 Sch.2 para.11, Sch.3 para.13

s.115, repealed (in part): 2002 c.32 Sch.21 para.73, Sch.22 Part 3, 2003 c.44 Sch.35 para.4, Sch.37 Part 11, SSI 2004/167 Sch.1 para.4

s.115, varied: SI 2004/865 Art.116, SI 2004/1016 Art.92

s.115, enabling: SI 2002/233, SI 2002/446, SI 2003/117, SI 2003/137, SI 2003/520, SI 2003/1418, SI 2004/367, SI 2004/1759, SSI 2002/143, SSI 2002/217, SSI 2004/526

s.116, amended: 2003 c.44 Sch.35 para.5

s.116, applied: SI 2002/233 Reg.3, Reg.5, Reg.9, Reg.12, SI 2003/117, SI 2003/117 Reg.2, SI 2003/137 Reg.3, SI 2004/1007 Art.2, SSI 2002/143 Reg.3, Reg.6, Reg.7, Reg.10

s.116, referred to: SI 2002/233 Sch.1

s.116, enabling: SI 2002/233, SI 2003/117, SI 2003/137, SI 2003/1418, SI 2004/367, SSI 2002/143

s.118, referred to: SI 2002/233 Sch.1

s.118, enabling: SI 2002/233, SSI 2002/143

s.119, amended: 2003 asp 7 s.70, SI 2003/417 Art.17, Art.47

s.119, applied: SI 2004/2592

s.119, referred to: SI 2002/233 Sch.1, SI 2004/367

s.119, enabling: SSI 2002/143

s.119A, added: 2003 asp 7 s.70

s.120, amended: 2003 asp 7 s.70, 2003 c.44 Sch.35 para.6, SI 2003/417 Art.17

s.120, repealed (in part): 2003 c.44 Sch.37 Part 11

s.120, enabling: SSI 2002/23

s.120A, added: 2003 asp 7 s.70

s.120A, amended: 2003 c.44 Sch.35 para.8, SI 2003/417 Art.47

s.120A, applied: SI 2002/233 Reg.12

s.120AA, added: 2003 c.44 Sch.35 para.9

s.120AB, added: 2003 c.44 Sch.35 para.9

s.120ZA, added: 2003 c.44 Sch.35 para.7

s.122, amended: 2003 asp 7 s.70

s.122A, added: 2003 c.44 Sch.35 para.10

s.124A, added: 2003 asp 7 s.70, 2003 c.44 Sch.35 para.11

s.124B, added: 2003 asp 7 s.70

s.125, amended: 2003 c.44 Sch.35 para.12, Sch.37 Part 11

s.125, applied: SI 2003/137

s.125, referred to: SI 2003/520

CAP.

CAP.

1997–cont.

50. Police Act 1997–*cont.*

s.125, repealed (in part): 2003 c.44 Sch.35 para.12, Sch.37 Part 11

s.125, enabling: SI 2002/233, SI 2004/1759, SI 2004/2592, SSI 2002/143, SSI 2004/526

s.126, referred to: SI 2004/1759

s.133, applied: SI 2002/441 Art.1

s.135, enabling: SI 2002/413, SSI 2002/124

Sch.2, referred to: SI 2003/117 Reg.2

Sch.2 para.3, amended: SI 2004/1941 Sch.1 para.11

Sch.2A para.4, amended: 2002 c.30 s.93

Sch.8 para.7, amended: 2002 c.30 s.102

Sch.9 para.2, repealed: 2004 c.36 Sch.3

Sch.9 para.17, repealed: 2004 c.36 Sch.3

Sch.9 para.27, repealed: 2003 c.44 Sch.37 Part 10

Sch.9 para.90, repealed (in part): SI 2002/1860 Sch.6

Sch.9 para.92, repealed: 2003 c.39 Sch.10

51. Sex Offenders Act 1997

see *C (Sexual Abuse: Disclosure to Landlords), Re* [2002] EWHC 234, [2002] 2 F.L.R. 375 (Fam Div), Bodey, J.; see *R. (on the application of U) v Commissioner of Police of the Metropolis* [2002] EWHC 2486, [2003] 1 W.L.R. 897 (QBD (Admin Ct)), Latham, L.J.; see *R. v H (Fitness to Plead)* [2003] UKHL 1, [2003] 1 W.L.R. 411 (HL), Lord Bingham of Cornhill; see *Secretary of State for Transport, Local Government and the Regions v Snowdon* [2002] EWHC 2394, [2003] R.T.R. 15 (QBD (Admin Ct)), Nigel Pleming Q.C.

repealed: 2003 c.42 Sch.7

Part I, applied: SI 2002/1882 Reg.6, Reg.11, SI 2003/250 Reg.6, Reg.11, SI 2003/2644 Reg.6, Reg.11, SI 2004/585 Reg.6, Reg.11, SI 2004/1020 Reg.6, Reg.11

Part I, referred to: 2003 c.42 Sch.4 para.7

s.2, applied: 2003 c.42 s.83, s.84, s.94, SI 2004/1220 Reg.3, SSI 2004/205 Reg.3

s.4, amended: 2002 c.26 Sch.12 para.60

s.5, see *HM Advocate v Stopper (Thomas) (Sentencing)* 2002 S.L.T. 885 (HCJ), Lord Hamilton, Lord Kingarth, Lord Drummond Young

s.5A, see *R. v Halloren (Barry Philip)* [2004] EWCA Crim 233, [2004] 2 Cr. App. R. (S.) 57 (CA (Crim Div)), David Clarke, J.; see *R. v Yates (David Christopher)* [2003] EWCA Crim 1917, [2004] 1 Cr. App. R. (S.) 44 (CA (Crim Div)), Tugendhat, J

s.5A, applied: 2003 c.42 s.81, s.108, s.113

s.7, applied: SI 2002/635 Sch.1 para.4, SI 2002/896 Sch.1 para.81, SI 2004/2695 Sch.1 para.19

s.8, referred to: 2003 c.42 s.142

Sch.1 para.2, amended: 2003 asp 13 s.314

1997–cont.

51. Sex Offenders Act 1997–*cont.*

Sch.1 para.3, amended: SI 2003/1247 Sch.1 para.20

Sch.2 para.2, amended: SI 2003/1247 Sch.1 para.21, Sch.2

52. Police and Firemen's Pensions Act 1997

s.1, applied: SI 2004/2306 Sch.1

s.1, repealed (in part): 2004 c.21 Sch.2

s.1, varied: SI 2004/2918 Sch.1

s.3, repealed (in part): 2004 c.21 Sch.2

56. National Health Service (Private Finance) Act 1997

s.1, amended: 2004 asp 7 Sch.1 para.2

s.1, applied: 2003 c.43 s.11

s.1, varied: 2002 c.17 s.6

58. Finance (No.2) Act 1997

s.24, repealed (in part): 2003 c.14 Sch.43 Part 3

s.48, amended: 2002 c.23 s.100

s.48, applied: 2002 c.23 s.99, s.101, 2004 c.12 s.123

s.48, referred to: 2002 c.23 s.101

s.49, amended: 2003 c.14 Sch.20 para.3

Sch.3 para.1, repealed: 2004 c.12 Sch.42 Part 2

Sch.6 para.2, repealed: 2004 c.12 Sch.42 Part 2

59. Education (Schools) Act 1997

see *Mackay-Ludgate v Lord Advocate* 2002 S.C.L.R. 109 (OH), Lord Philip

s.2, applied: SI 2002/1879, SI 2002/1979, SI 2003/1705, SI 2003/1854, SI 2004/1812, SI 2004/1965

s.3, applied: SI 2002/1879, SI 2002/1979, SI 2003/1705, SI 2003/1854, SI 2004/1812, SI 2004/1965

s.3, enabling: SI 2002/1879, SI 2002/1880, SI 2002/1979, SI 2002/1984, SI 2003/1705, SI 2003/1707, SI 2003/1779, SI 2003/1854, SI 2004/1807, SI 2004/1812, SI 2004/1965, SI 2004/1970

60. Law Officers Act 1997

s.2, amended: 2002 c.26 s.27

63. Local Government Finance (Supplementary Credit Approvals) Act 1997

repealed (in part): 2003 c.26 Sch.8 Part 1

65. Local Government (Contracts) Act 1997

s.1, amended: 2003 c.26 Sch.7 para.64

s.8, amended: 2004 c.23 Sch.2 para.20

s.10, repealed: 2003 c.39 Sch.10

s.12, repealed (in part): 2003 c.39 Sch.10

66. Plant Varieties Act 1997

applied: SI 2002/247 Reg.27, SI 2002/2843 Art.8

Part II, applied: SI 2002/247 Reg.19

s.6, applied: SI 2002/2843 Art.8

s.7, applied: 2002 c.23 Sch.29 para.2

s.9, applied: SI 2002/2843 Art.8

s.11, applied: SI 2002/2843 Art.8

1997–cont.

66. Plant Varieties Act 1997–*cont.*
s.14, applied: SI 2002/2843 Art.8
s.15, applied: SI 2002/2843 Art.8
s.17, applied: SI 2002/247 Reg.17, Reg.23, Reg.25, Reg.27, SI 2002/2843 Art.8
s.17, disapplied: SI 2002/247 Reg.27
s.22, applied: SI 2002/2843 Art.8
s.23, disapplied: SI 2002/247 Reg.27
s.24, applied: SI 2002/247 Reg.21, Reg.23, SI 2002/2843 Art.8
s.26, applied: SI 2002/247 Reg.21, Reg.23, SI 2002/2843 Art.8
s.26, referred to: SI 2002/247 Reg.17
s.28, applied: SI 2002/247 Reg.21, Reg.23, SI 2002/2843 Art.8
s.29, applied: SI 2002/247 Reg.21, Reg.23, Reg.25, SI 2002/2843 Art.8
s.29, enabling: SI 2002/1677
s.42, enabling: SI 2002/3198
s.44, applied: SI 2002/247 Reg.21, Reg.23, SI 2002/2843 Art.8
s.45, applied: SI 2002/247 Reg.17
s.45, varied: SI 2002/3026 Reg.32, SR 2002/404 Reg.32
s.48, applied: SI 2002/247 Reg.21, Reg.23, Reg.25, SI 2002/2843 Art.8
s.48, enabling: SI 2002/1677
Sch.2, applied: SI 2002/2843 Art.8
Sch.3 para.1, varied: SI 2002/247 Reg.19, SI 2002/3026 Reg.32, SR 2002/404 Reg.32
Sch.3 para.2, varied: SI 2002/3026 Reg.32, SR 2002/404 Reg.32
Sch.3 para.3, varied: SI 2002/3026 Reg.32, SR 2002/404 Reg.32
Sch.3 para.4, varied: SI 2002/3026 Reg.32, SR 2002/404 Reg.32
Sch.3 para.5, varied: SI 2002/3026 Reg.32, SR 2002/404 Reg.32
Sch.3 para.6, varied: SI 2002/3026 Reg.32, SR 2002/404 Reg.32
Sch.3 para.7, varied: SI 2002/3026 Reg.32, SR 2002/404 Reg.32
Sch.3 para.8, varied: SI 2002/247 Reg.19, SI 2002/3026 Reg.32, SR 2002/404 Reg.32
Sch.3 para.9, varied: SI 2002/3026 Reg.32, SR 2002/404 Reg.32
Sch.3 para.10, varied: SI 2002/3026 Reg.32, SR 2002/404 Reg.32
Sch.3 para.11, varied: SI 2002/3026 Reg.32, SR 2002/404 Reg.32
Sch.3 para.12, varied: SI 2002/3026 Reg.32, SR 2002/404 Reg.32
Sch.3 para.13, applied: SI 2002/2843 Art.8
Sch.3 para.13, varied: SI 2002/3026 Reg.32, SR 2002/404 Reg.32
Sch.3 para.13, enabling: SI 2002/3198
Sch.3 para.14, varied: SI 2002/3026 Reg.32, SR 2002/404 Reg.32
Sch.3 para.15, varied: SI 2002/3026 Reg.32, SR 2002/404 Reg.32

1997–cont.

66. Plant Varieties Act 1997–*cont.*
Sch.3 para.16, varied: SI 2002/3026 Reg.32, SR 2002/404 Reg.32

68. Special Immigration Appeals Commission Act 1997
applied: 2002 c.41 s.21, s.109, Sch.3 para.17, SI 2003/1034 r.7, r.8
referred to: SI 2003/754 Sch.2 para.5
s.2, applied: 2002 c.41 s.72, s.96, SI 2003/658 Reg.3, SI 2003/1034 r.6, r.8, r.12
s.2, substituted: 2002 c.41 Sch.7 para.20
s.2A, repealed: 2002 c.41 Sch.9
s.2B, added: 2002 c.41 s.4
s.2B, amended: 2004 c.19 Sch.2 para.11
s.2B, applied: SI 2003/1034 r.2, r.6, r.56
s.3, amended: SI 2003/1016 Sch.1 para.10
s.4, repealed: 2002 c.41 Sch.9
s.5, amended: 2002 c.41 s.4, Sch.7 para.23, Sch.9
s.5, applied: SI 2003/1034
s.5, enabling: SI 2003/1034
s.6, referred to: SI 2003/1034 r.33
s.7, see *G v Secretary of State for the Home Department* [2004] EWCA Civ 265, [2004] 1 W.L.R. 1349 (CA), Lord Phillips of Worth Matravers, M.R.
s.7A, amended: 2002 c.41 Sch.9
s.7A, applied: SI 2003/754 Sch.2 para.5
s.8, applied: SI 2003/1034
s.8, enabling: SI 2003/1034
Sch.1 para.5, amended: 2002 c.41 Sch.7 para.25, 2004 c.19 Sch.2 para.12
Sch.1 para.5, applied: SI 2003/1034 r.5, 2004 c.19 Sch.2 para.12
Sch.2 para.1, repealed: 2002 c.41 Sch.9
Sch.2 para.2, repealed: 2002 c.41 Sch.9
Sch.2 para.3, repealed: 2002 c.41 Sch.9
Sch.2 para.3A, repealed: 2002 c.41 Sch.9
Sch.2 para.3B, repealed: 2002 c.41 Sch.9
Sch.2 para.3C, repealed: 2002 c.41 Sch.9
Sch.2 para.3D, repealed: 2002 c.41 Sch.9
Sch.2 para.3E, repealed: 2002 c.41 Sch.9
Sch.2 para.3F, repealed: 2002 c.41 Sch.9
Sch.2 para.3G, repealed: 2002 c.41 Sch.9
Sch.2 para.4, repealed: 2002 c.41 Sch.9
Sch.2 para.5, repealed: 2002 c.41 Sch.9
Sch.2 para.6, repealed: 2002 c.41 Sch.9
Sch.2 para.7, repealed: 2002 c.41 Sch.9
Sch.3 para.1, amended: 2004 c.19 Sch.2 para.13
Sch.3 para.2, amended: 2004 c.19 Sch.2 para.13
Sch.3 para.6, amended: 2004 c.19 Sch.2 para.13
Sch.3 para.7, amended: 2004 c.19 Sch.2 para.13

69. Supreme Court (Offices) Act 1997
repealed: 2004 c.14 Sch.1 Part 1

CAP.

1998

Databases Act (France) 1998

see *Societe Tigest Sarl v Societe Reed Expositions France (formerly Groupe Miller Freeman)* [2002] E.C.C. 29 (C d'A (Paris)), Marais (President)

Income and Corporation Taxes Act 1998

s.145, see *Toronto Dominion Bank v Oberoi* [2002] EWHC 3216, [2004] S.T.C. 1197 (Ch D), Nicholas Warren Q.C.

Rating Valuations Act 1998

see *Rodney DC v Attorney General of New Zealand* [2002] UKPC 47, [2003] R.A. 180 (PC (NZ)), Lord Hope of Craighead

2. Public Processions (Northern Ireland) Act 1998

s.6, applied: SI 2004/416 Reg.2

s.6, enabling: SI 2004/416

s.7, applied: SI 2004/416 Reg.2

s.7, enabling: SI 2004/416

6. Wireless Telegraphy Act 1998

applied: 2002 c.11 s.6, 2003 c.21 s.164, s.192, s.401, Sch.1 para.1

referred to: 2003 c.21 s.393

s.1, amended: 2003 c.21 s.161, Sch.17 para.145, Sch.17 para.146, Sch.19

s.1, applied: SI 2002/1700 Reg.4, Reg.5, Reg.6, 2003 c.21 Sch.8 para.33

s.1, referred to: 2003 c.21 s.156

s.1, repealed (in part): 2003 c.21 Sch.19

s.1, enabling: SI 2002/1700, SI 2003/2983, SI 2003/2984

s.2, amended: 2003 c.21 Sch.17 para.145, Sch.17 para.147

s.2, applied: SI 2002/1700

s.2, disapplied: 2003 c.21 s.154

s.2, referred to: 2003 c.21 s.156

s.2, substituted: 2003 c.21 Sch.17 para.147

s.2, enabling: SI 2003/2983

s.3, amended: 2003 c.21 s.167, Sch.17 para.145, Sch.19

s.3, applied: 2003 c.21 Sch.8 para.34, SI 2003/1902 Sch.2 para.2

s.3, referred to: 2003 c.21 s.156, SI 2003/3195 Art.3

s.3, repealed (in part): 2003 c.21 Sch.19

s.3, varied: 2003 c.21 Sch.18 para.21, SI 2003/3198 Art.3

s.3, enabling: SI 2002/1911, SI 2003/397

s.3A, added: 2003 c.21 s.161

s.3A, amended: 2003 c.21 Sch.17 para.145

s.3A, applied: 2003 c.21 Sch.8 para.35

s.3A, referred to: 2003 c.21 s.156

s.4, amended: 2003 c.21 Sch.17 para.145, Sch.17 para.148

s.4A, added: 2003 c.21 Sch.17 para.149

s.4A, applied: 2003 c.21 Sch.8 para.36

s.5, repealed: 2003 c.21 Sch.19

s.6, amended: 2003 c.21 Sch.17 para.150

s.6, applied: SI 2002/1700, SI 2002/1911, SI 2003/397, SI 2003/2983

s.6, substituted: 2003 c.21 Sch.17 para.150

CAP.

1998–cont.

6. Wireless Telegraphy Act 1998–*cont.*

s.6, enabling: SI 2002/1911, SI 2003/397

s.8, amended: 2003 c.21 Sch.17 para.151

s.9, applied: SI 2003/3195, SI 2003/3198, SI 2004/307, SI 2004/308, SI 2004/309

s.9, enabling: SI 2003/3195, SI 2003/3197, SI 2003/3198

Sch.1 para.1, repealed: 2003 c.21 Sch.19

Sch.1 para.2, repealed: 2003 c.21 Sch.19

Sch.1 para.3, repealed: 2003 c.21 Sch.19

Sch.1 para.4, repealed: 2003 c.21 Sch.19

7. Nuclear Explosions (Prohibition and Inspections) Act 1998

s.2, amended: 2002 c.8 s.2

8. Employment Rights (Dispute Resolution) Act 1998

s.13, repealed: 2002 c.22 Sch.8 Part 1

s.17, repealed (in part): 2004 c.14 Sch.1 Part 8

Sch.1 para.19, repealed: 2002 c.22 Sch.8 Part 1

Sch.1 para.20, repealed: 2002 c.22 Sch.8 Part 1

Sch.1 para.21, repealed: 2002 c.22 Sch.8 Part 1

Sch.1 para.23, repealed: 2002 c.22 Sch.8 Part 1

Sch.1 para.26, repealed: 2002 c.22 Sch.8 Part 1

11. Bank of England Act 1998

s.13, applied: SI 2003/409 Sch.1 Part I

s.17, amended: SI 2004/1862 Reg.14

s.17, varied: SI 2003/1633 Sch.2 para.8

s.19, applied: SI 2002/1792 Sch.2 para.9

s.40, applied: SI 2004/1270

s.40, enabling: SI 2004/1270

Sch.2 para.4, applied: SI 2004/1270 Art.3

Sch.2 para.5, enabling: SI 2004/1270

Sch.5 Part IV para.62, repealed: 2004 c.27 Sch.8

Sch.5 Part IV para.71, repealed: 2004 c.35 Sch.13 Part 1

Sch.7 para.3, amended: 2004 c.35 Sch.12 para.70

12. Northern Ireland (Elections) Act 1998

s.2, applied: SI 2003/2697 Art.2

14. Social Security Act 1998

applied: SI 2002/684 Reg.2, SI 2002/3237 Reg.19, SI 2003/601 Reg.2, SI 2003/916 Reg.26, SI 2003/1325 Art.2, 2004 c.6 s.24, SI 2004/291 Sch.4, SI 2004/478 Sch.4, SI 2004/583 Reg.2, SI 2004/627 Sch.2, SSI 2004/115 Sch.3

Part I c.I, applied: 2003 c.43 s.158, SI 2003/409 Sch.1 Part I, SI 2003/437 Sch.1 Part 2

Part I c.II, applied: 2002 c.21 s.50, SI 2003/962 Art.3, 2004 c.6 s.2, 2004 c.10 s.5

s.2, amended: 2002 c.16 Sch.1 para.5, Sch.3

s.3, amended: 2002 c.22 Sch.6 para.1, 2004 c.35 Sch.10 para.1

s.3, referred to: 2002 c.22 s.55

s.3, repealed (in part): 2002 c.22 Sch.6 para.4

1998–cont.

14. Social Security Act 1998–*cont.*

s.5, applied: SI 2003/409 Sch.1 Part I, SI 2003/437 Sch.1 Part 2

s.6, applied: SI 2002/1379, SI 2002/3196 Reg.9, Reg.10, SI 2003/409 Sch.1 Part I, SI 2003/437 Sch.1 Part 2

s.6, enabling: SI 2002/1379

s.7, applied: SI 2002/3196 Reg.19

s.7, enabling: SI 2002/3196, SI 2004/3368

s.8, amended: 2002 c.16 Sch.1 para.6

s.8, applied: 2002 c.16 s.6, SI 2003/916 Reg.5, Reg.8, Reg.9, Reg.10, Reg.11, Reg.12, Reg.27, SI 2004/960 Reg.2

s.8, repealed (in part): 2002 c.21 Sch.6

s.8, varied: 2002 c.21 Sch.4 para.15

s.9, applied: 2002 c.16 s.6, s.7, SI 2002/79 Reg.3, SI 2002/1703 Reg.15, SI 2002/3019 Reg.38, SI 2003/492 Reg.12, Reg.23, Reg.36, Reg.38, SI 2003/493 Reg.38, SI 2003/916 Reg.8, Reg.12, Reg.14, Reg.15, Reg.18, Reg.19, Reg.27, Reg.28, SI 2003/1886 Reg.14, SI 2003/2439 Reg.12, SI 2004/2244 Reg.9

s.9, referred to: SI 2003/916 Reg.7

s.9, varied: 2002 c.21 Sch.4 para.15

s.9, enabling: SI 2002/79, SI 2002/428, SI 2002/490, SI 2002/1379, SI 2003/492, SI 2003/916, SI 2003/1050, SI 2003/1189, SI 2003/2190, SI 2004/2283

s.10, applied: 2002 c.16 s.6, s.7, s.8, SI 2002/1703 Reg.15, SI 2002/1792 Reg.12, Reg.17, Sch.2 para.9, SI 2003/492 Reg.23, Reg.36, Reg.38, SI 2003/493 Reg.38, SI 2003/916 Reg.5, Reg.8, Reg.9, Reg.10, Reg.11, Reg.12, Reg.13, Reg.14, Reg.18, Reg.19, Reg.27, SI 2003/1886 Reg.14, SI 2003/2439 Reg.12, SI 2004/959 Reg.15, SI 2004/2244 Reg.9

s.10, referred to: SI 2003/916 Reg.7

s.10, varied: 2002 c.21 Sch.4 para.15

s.10, enabling: SI 2002/398, SI 2002/428, SI 2002/490, SI 2002/3019, SI 2002/3197, SI 2003/916, SI 2003/1050, SI 2003/1189, SI 2003/1731, SI 2003/2190, SI 2003/2274, SI 2004/647, SI 2004/2327

s.10A, varied: 2002 c.21 Sch.4 para.15

s.10A, enabling: SI 2002/1379

s.11, amended: 2002 c.16 Sch.1 para.7, Sch.3

s.11, varied: 2002 c.21 Sch.4 para.15

s.12, applied: SI 2002/1703 Reg.15, SI 2002/3196 Reg.3, SI 2003/916 Reg.24, Reg.25, Reg.31, SI 2003/1886 Reg.14, SI 2003/2439 Reg.12, SI 2004/959 Reg.15, SI 2004/2244 Reg.9

s.12, varied: 2002 c.21 Sch.4 para.15, SI 2002/2926 Reg.4

s.12, enabling: SI 2002/1379, SI 2002/3196, SI 2003/916, SI 2004/3368, SI 2004/3377

s.13, varied: 2002 c.21 Sch.4 para.15, SI 2002/2926 Reg.5

s.13, enabling: SI 2003/1864

1998–cont.

14. Social Security Act 1998–*cont.*

s.14, applied: SI 2002/3237 Reg.15, Reg.23, 2003 c.43 s.159

s.14, varied: 2002 c.21 Sch.4 para.15, SI 2002/2926 Reg.6, Reg.7

s.14, enabling: SI 2002/1379, SI 2002/3196, SI 2002/3237

s.15, applied: SI 2002/2926 Reg.8, SI 2002/3237 Reg.27

s.15, varied: 2002 c.21 Sch.4 para.15

s.15, enabling: SI 2002/3237

s.16, varied: 2002 c.21 Sch.4 para.15, SI 2002/2926 Reg.9

s.16, enabling: SI 2002/1379, SI 2002/3196, SI 2002/3237, SI 2003/916, SI 2004/3368

s.17, varied: 2002 c.21 Sch.4 para.15, SI 2002/2926 Reg.10

s.18, varied: 2002 c.21 Sch.4 para.15

s.18, enabling: SI 2002/3019

s.19, varied: 2002 c.21 Sch.4 para.15

s.20, varied: 2002 c.21 Sch.4 para.15

s.21, applied: SI 2003/916 Reg.18

s.21, varied: 2002 c.21 Sch.4 para.15

s.21, enabling: SI 2003/916

s.22, amended: 2002 c.16 Sch.1 para.8

s.22, varied: 2002 c.21 Sch.4 para.15

s.22, enabling: SI 2003/916

s.23, varied: 2002 c.21 Sch.4 para.15

s.23, enabling: SI 2003/916

s.24, varied: 2002 c.21 Sch.4 para.15

s.24A, varied: 2002 c.21 Sch.4 para.15

s.24A, enabling: SI 2002/1379

s.25, applied: SI 2003/916 Reg.22, Sch.2 para.4

s.25, referred to: SI 2003/916 Reg.22

s.25, varied: 2002 c.21 Sch.4 para.15

s.25, enabling: SI 2003/916

s.26, applied: SI 2003/916 Reg.13, Reg.23, Sch.2 para.4

s.26, referred to: SI 2003/916 Reg.16

s.26, varied: 2002 c.21 Sch.4 para.15

s.26, enabling: SI 2003/916

s.27, amended: 2002 c.16 Sch.1 para.9

s.27, applied: SI 2003/916 Reg.16

s.27, varied: 2002 c.21 Sch.4 para.15

s.28, amended: 2002 c.16 Sch.1 para.10, Sch.3

s.28, varied: 2002 c.21 Sch.4 para.15, SI 2002/2926 Reg.11

s.28, enabling: SI 2002/1379, SI 2002/3196, SI 2002/3237

s.29, varied: 2002 c.21 Sch.4 para.15

s.30, varied: 2002 c.21 Sch.4 para.15

s.31, varied: 2002 c.21 Sch.4 para.15

s.32, varied: 2002 c.21 Sch.4 para.15

s.33, varied: 2002 c.21 Sch.4 para.15

s.34, amended: 2002 c.16 Sch.2 para.41

s.34, applied: SI 2002/1888 Art.3, SI 2003/325 Sch.1

CAP.

1998–cont.

14. Social Security Act 1998–*cont.*

s.34, varied: 2002 c.21 Sch.4 para.15

s.34, enabling: SI 2003/325, SI 2003/1338, SI 2003/2275, SI 2004/14

s.35, varied: 2002 c.21 Sch.4 para.15

s.36, varied: 2002 c.21 Sch.4 para.15

s.37, varied: 2002 c.21 Sch.4 para.15

s.38, varied: 2002 c.21 Sch.4 para.15

s.39, varied: 2002 c.21 Sch.4 para.15, SI 2002/2926 Reg.12

s.39, enabling: SI 2002/3196, SI 2002/3237

s.72, amended: 2004 c.33 Sch.24 para.138

s.72, applied: 2002 c.21 s.49

s.74, referred to: SI 2003/325 Sch.1

s.79, amended: 2002 c.21 Sch.4 para.13

s.79, applied: SI 2003/325 Sch.1

s.79, enabling: SI 2002/490, SI 2002/1379, SI 2002/3019, SI 2002/3196, SI 2002/3197, SI 2002/3237, SI 2003/325, SI 2003/916, SI 2003/1189, SI 2003/1338, SI 2003/1581, SI 2003/2190, SI 2003/2274, SI 2003/2275, SI 2004/14, SI 2004/647, SI 2004/2283, SI 2004/2327, SI 2004/3368

s.80, amended: 2002 c.21 Sch.4 para.14

s.80, applied: SI 2002/1379, SI 2002/3196, SI 2002/3237, SI 2003/916, SI 2003/1581

s.80, enabling: SI 2004/3377

s.84, enabling: SI 2002/398, SI 2002/428, SI 2002/490, SI 2002/1379, SI 2002/3196, SI 2002/3197, SI 2002/3237, SI 2003/492, SI 2003/916, SI 2003/1050, SI 2003/1189, SI 2003/1338, SI 2003/1581, SI 2003/2274, SI 2003/2275, SI 2004/14, SI 2004/647, SI 2004/2283, SI 2004/2327, SI 2004/3368

Sch.1 para.11, enabling: SI 2002/3196

Sch.1 para.12, enabling: SI 2002/1379, SI 2002/3196

Sch.2, referred to: SI 2003/916 Reg.9, Reg.13

Sch.2 para.3, amended: SI 2002/1457 Sch.1 para.3

Sch.2 para.5A, amended: 2002 c.22 Sch.7 para.51

Sch.2 para.6, amended: 2002 c.16 Sch.1 para.11, Sch.3

Sch.2 para.9, enabling: SI 2002/1379, SI 2003/1581

Sch.3 Part I, added: 2002 c.16 Sch.1 para.12

Sch.4, enabling: SI 2002/3237

Sch.4 para.1, varied: SI 2002/2926 Reg.7

Sch.4 para.2, varied: SI 2002/2926 Reg.7

Sch.4 para.3, amended: 2004 c.32 s.7

Sch.4 para.3, varied: SI 2002/2926 Reg.7

Sch.4 para.4, varied: SI 2002/2926 Reg.7

Sch.4 para.5, varied: SI 2002/2926 Reg.7

Sch.4 para.6, varied: SI 2002/2926 Reg.7

Sch.4 para.7, varied: SI 2002/2926 Reg.7

Sch.4 para.8, applied: SI 2002/3237

Sch.4 para.8, varied: SI 2002/2926 Reg.7

CAP.

1998–cont.

14. Social Security Act 1998–*cont.*

Sch.5, enabling: SI 2002/3196, SI 2002/3237

Sch.5 para.1, varied: SI 2002/2926 Reg.9

Sch.5 para.1, enabling: SI 2002/1379, SI 2003/916, SI 2004/3368

Sch.5 para.2, varied: SI 2002/2926 Reg.9

Sch.5 para.2, enabling: SI 2002/1379, SI 2003/916, SI 2004/3368

Sch.5 para.3, varied: SI 2002/2926 Reg.9

Sch.5 para.3, enabling: SI 2002/1379, SI 2003/916, SI 2004/3368

Sch.5 para.4, varied: SI 2002/2926 Reg.9

Sch.5 para.4, enabling: SI 2002/1379, SI 2003/916, SI 2004/3368

Sch.5 para.5, varied: SI 2002/2926 Reg.9

Sch.5 para.6, varied: SI 2002/2926 Reg.9

Sch.5 para.6, enabling: SI 2002/1379, SI 2003/916

Sch.5 para.7, varied: SI 2002/2926 Reg.9

Sch.5 para.7, enabling: SI 2002/1379

Sch.5 para.8, varied: SI 2002/2926 Reg.9

Sch.5 para.9, varied: SI 2002/2926 Reg.9

Sch.7 para.71, repealed (in part): 2002 c.19 Sch.2

Sch.7 para.79, referred to: SI 2003/325 Sch.1

Sch.7 para.109, applied: SI 2003/2275 Sch.1

Sch.7 para.109, referred to: SI 2003/325 Sch.1

Sch.8, applied: SI 2003/2275 Sch.1

16. Tax Credits (Initial Expenditure) Act 1998

repealed: 2002 c.21 Sch.6

17. Petroleum Act 1998

applied: 2004 c.20 s.188, s.189, SI 2004/352 Sch.1 para.2, Sch.2 para.2, Sch.3 para.2, Sch.3 para.25, Sch.3 para.26, Sch.4 para.2, Sch.4 para.23, Sch.4 para.24

referred to: 2004 c.20 s.189

Part III, applied: SI 2002/1355 Reg.7

Part IV, applied: SI 2002/1355 Reg.7

s.4, applied: SI 2004/352 Reg.3

s.4, enabling: SI 2004/352

s.10, amended: 2004 c.20 s.103

s.11, applied: 2003 c.21 s.410

s.17, amended: 2004 c.20 s.151

s.17A, repealed: 2004 c.20 s.151, Sch.23 Part 1

s.17B, repealed: 2004 c.20 s.151, Sch.23 Part 1

s.17C, amended: SI 2004/2043 Sch.3 para.1

s.17H, amended: 2004 c.20 Sch.23 Part 1, SI 2004/2043 Sch.3 para.2

s.27, amended: 2004 c.20 Sch.23 Part 1

s.28, amended: 2004 c.20 Sch.23 Part 1, SI 2004/2043 Sch.3 para.3

s.47A, added: 2004 c.20 s.103

Sch.4 para.2, amended: 2003 c.21 Sch.19

Sch.4 para.19, repealed: 2003 c.21 Sch.19

18. Audit Commission Act 1998

applied: 2003 c.26 s.21, 2004 c.23 s.17

1998–cont.

18. Audit Commission Act 1998–*cont.*
Part II, applied: 2004 c.23 s.69, s.70
Part III, applied: 2004 c.23 s.69
s.3, applied: SI 2002/438 Reg.6, SI 2002/679 Reg.5, SI 2002/1857 Reg.6, 2004 c.23 s.69
s.3, referred to: 2003 c.43 Sch.1 para.23
s.4, amended: 2003 c.43 Sch.9 para.12
s.4, applied: 2004 c.23 s.17
s.7, amended: 2003 c.43 Sch.9 para.12
s.8, applied: SI 2003/533 Reg.17
s.9, applied: SI 2003/533 Reg.11, Reg.12
s.11, amended: 2003 c.26 s.107
s.11A, amended: 2003 c.26 s.107
s.13A, added: 2003 c.26 s.108
s.14, referred to: SI 2003/533 Reg.18
s.15, see *R. (on the application of HTV Ltd) v Bristol City Council* [2004] EWHC 1219, [2004] 1 W.L.R. 2717 (QBD (Admin Ct)), Elias, J.
s.15, applied: SI 2003/533 Reg.13
s.15, referred to: SI 2003/533 Reg.14, Reg.16
s.16, applied: SI 2003/533 Reg.13, Reg.17
s.16, referred to: SI 2003/533 Reg.16
s.17, applied: SI 2004/1742 Reg.5
s.17, disapplied: SI 2004/1778 Art.14
s.17, varied: SI 2004/1777 Art.14
s.18, see *Westminster City Council v Porter (No.1)* [2002] EWHC 1589, [2003] Ch. 436 (Ch D), Hart, J.
s.18, applied: SI 2003/533 Reg.17, SI 2004/1742 Reg.5
s.18, disapplied: SI 2004/1778 Art.14
s.18, varied: SI 2004/1777 Art.14
s.19A, applied: SI 2003/533 Reg.11, Reg.12
s.25, applied: SI 2003/533 Reg.21
s.26, applied: SI 2003/533 Reg.2
s.27, applied: SI 2003/533, SI 2004/556
s.27, enabling: SI 2003/533, SI 2004/556
s.29, amended: 2004 c.23 Sch.2 para.22
s.33, amended: 2002 c.17 s.12, 2003 c.43 Sch.9 para.12, 2004 c.23 Sch.2 para.23, Sch.4
s.33, applied: 2003 c.43 s.83, s.95, 2004 c.23 s.57, s.70
s.34, amended: 2003 c.43 Sch.9 para.12, 2004 c.23 Sch.2 para.24, Sch.4
s.34, applied: 2003 c.43 s.83, s.95, 2004 c.23 s.57
s.35, amended: 2003 c.43 Sch.9 para.12
s.35, applied: 2004 c.23 s.70
s.36, amended: 2004 c.23 Sch.2 para.25, Sch.4
s.37, substituted: 2003 c.43 Sch.9 para.12
s.38, amended: 2004 c.23 Sch.2 para.26
s.40, amended: 2004 c.23 Sch.2 para.27
s.40, repealed (in part): 2004 c.23 Sch.2 para.27, Sch.4
s.41, amended: 2004 c.23 Sch.2 para.28
s.41A, added: 2003 c.26 s.109

1998–cont.

18. Audit Commission Act 1998–*cont.*
s.41A, amended: 2004 c.23 Sch.2 para.29
s.41B, added: 2003 c.26 s.109
s.41B, amended: 2004 c.23 Sch.2 para.30, Sch.4
s.41B, repealed (in part): 2004 c.23 Sch.2 para.30, Sch.4
s.43, amended: 2004 c.23 Sch.2 para.31
s.47, amended: 2004 c.23 Sch.2 para.32, Sch.4
s.49, amended: 2003 c.43 Sch.9 para.12, 2004 c.23 Sch.2 para.33
s.49, referred to: 2004 c.23 s.54
s.51A, added: 2004 c.23 Sch.2 para.34
s.51B, added: 2004 c.23 Sch.2 para.34
s.52, amended: 2003 c.26 s.109, 2004 c.23 Sch.2 para.35, Sch.4
s.53, amended: 2004 c.23 Sch.2 para.36
Sch.1 para.4, applied: SI 2003/3279 Reg.4
Sch.1 para.7, applied: SI 2003/409 Sch.1 Part I
Sch.1 para.8, amended: 2003 c.26 s.109
Sch.1 para.8A, added: 2003 c.26 s.109
Sch.1 para.8A, amended: 2004 c.23 Sch.2 para.37
Sch.1 para.9, amended: 2003 c.26 Sch.7 para.65
Sch.1 para.9, enabling: SI 2002/743
Sch.1 para.11, amended: 2003 c.26 s.110, Sch.7 para.65
Sch.1 para.11, varied: 2003 c.26 s.110
Sch.1 para.11A, added: 2003 c.26 s.111
Sch.2 para.1, amended: 2004 c.21 Sch.1 para.88, 2004 c.23 Sch.2 para.38
Sch.2 para.1A, added: SI 2003/1324 Sch.2 para.2
Sch.2 para.1A, substituted: SI 2004/1714 Sch.2 para.2
Sch.2 para.1B, added: 2004 c.23 Sch.2 para.38
Sch.2 para.2, referred to: SI 2003/533 Reg.7
Sch.3 para.6, repealed: 2004 c.14 Sch.1 Part 10
Sch.3 para.8, repealed: 2004 c.14 Sch.1 Part 10
Sch.3 para.11, repealed: 2004 c.14 Sch.1 Part 10
Sch.3 para.16, repealed: 2004 c.14 Sch.1 Part 5
Sch.3 para.17, repealed: 2004 c.14 Sch.1 Part 5

19. Community Care (Residential Accommodation) Act 1998
see *B (A Child) v Todd* [2002] P.I.Q.R. P11 (QBD), Stanley Burnton, J.

20. Late Payment of Commercial Debts (Interest) Act 1998
Commencement Orders: SI 2002/1673 Art.2; SSI 2002/337 Art.2
applied: SI 2002/1674 Reg.3, SI 2002/1675 Art.4, SSI 2002/335 Reg.3, SSI 2002/336 Art.4

1998–cont.

20. Late Payment of Commercial Debts (Interest) Act 1998–*cont.*

s.2, repealed (in part): SSI 2002/335 Reg.2

s.2A, added: SSI 2002/335 Reg.2

s.3, repealed (in part): SI 2002/1674 Reg.2, SSI 2002/335 Reg.2

s.5A, added: SI 2002/1674 Reg.2, SSI 2002/335 Reg.2

s.6, enabling: SI 2002/1675, SSI 2002/336

s.17, enabling: SI 2002/1673, SSI 2002/337

22. National Lottery Act 1998

s.8, enabling: SI 2002/280

s.19, applied: SI 2003/235

s.19, enabling: SI 2003/235

23. Public Interest Disclosure Act 1998

see *Edgar v Meteorological Office* [2002] I.C.R. 149 (EAT), Judge Peter Clark; see *Miklaszewicz v Stolt Offshore Ltd* 2002 S.C. 232 (Ex Div), Lord Nimmo Smith, Lord Marnoch, Lord Weir

s.13, repealed: 2002 c.30 Sch.8

29. Data Protection Act 1998

see *Campbell v Mirror Group Newspapers Ltd* [2004] UKHL 22, [2004] 2 A.C. 457 (HL), Lord Nicholls of Birkenhead; see *Douglas v Hello! Ltd (No.8)* [2003] EWHC 2629, [2004] E.M.L.R. 2 (Ch D), Lindsay, J.; see *Douglas v Hello! Ltd (No.9)* [2004] EWHC 63, [2004] 2 Costs L.R. 304 (Ch D), Lindsay, J.; see *Igroup Ltd v Ocwen* [2003] EWHC 2431, [2004] 1 W.L.R. 451 (Ch D (Companies Court)), Lightman, J.; see *MG v United Kingdom (39393/98)* [2002] 3 F.C.R. 289 (ECHR), Judge Costa (President); see *R. (on the application of Mohtasham) v Visitor of King's College London* [2003] EWHC 2372, [2004] E.L.R. 29 (QBD), Richards, J.; see *R. (on the application of X) v Chief Constable of West Midlands* [2004] EWHC 61, [2004] 1 W.L.R. 1518 (QBD (Admin Ct)), Wall, J.; see *Totalise Plc v Motley Fool Ltd* [2001] EWCA Civ 1897, [2002] 1 W.L.R. 1233 (CA), Aldous, L.J.

applied: 2002 asp 11 Sch.5, 2002 c.29 s.436, s.438, s.439, s.441, 2002 c.40 s.237, 2002 c.iii s.7, 2002 c.iv s.8, SI 2003/1887 Sch.1, SI 2003/2426 Reg.4, 2004 c.17 s.7, 2004 c.31 s.12, s.29, SI 2004/1031 Sch.1 para.15, Sch.1 para.16, SI 2004/1768 Reg.7, Reg.15, SSI 2004/468 Sch.5 para.2

disapplied: SI 2003/2818 Art.8

referred to: 2003 c.32 Sch.5 para.68, 2003 c.42 s.94, 2003 c.43 Sch.4 para.106, 2004 c.17 s.4, 2004 c.28 s.54

varied: SI 2003/2818 Art.11

Part IV, applied: 2002 asp 13 s.38

s.1, see *Durant v Financial Services Authority (Disclosure of Information)* [2003] EWCA Civ 1746, [2004] F.S.R. 28 (CA), Auld, L.J.

s.1, applied: 2002 asp 13 s.38

s.2, applied: SSI 2003/581 Reg.6

1998–cont.

29. Data Protection Act 1998–*cont.*

s.3, see *Campbell v Mirror Group Newspapers Ltd* [2002] EWHC 499, [2002] E.M.L.R. 30 (QBD), Morland, J.

s.5, see *Douglas v Hello! Ltd (No.2)* [2003] EWCA Civ 139, [2003] E.M.L.R. 28 (CA), Rix, L.J.

s.6, amended: SI 2003/1887 Sch.2 para.9

s.6, disapplied: SI 2003/1887 Sch.1

s.7, see *Durant v Financial Services Authority (Disclosure of Information)* [2003] EWCA Civ 1746, [2004] F.S.R. 28 (CA), Auld, L.J.; see *P v Wozencroft* [2002] EWHC 1724, [2002] 2 F.L.R. 1118 (Fam Div), Wilson, J.

s.7, amended: SI 2003/1887 Sch.2 para.9

s.7, disapplied: 2002 asp 13 s.38

s.8, amended: SI 2003/1887 Sch.2 para.9

s.9, amended: SI 2003/1887 Sch.2 para.9

s.9A, amended: SI 2003/1887 Sch.2 para.9

s.9A, enabling: SI 2004/3244

s.10, amended: SI 2003/1887 Sch.2 para.9

s.10, applied: 2002 asp 13 s.38

s.11, see *R. (on the application of Robertson) v Wakefield MDC* [2001] EWHC Admin 915, [2002] Q.B. 1052 (QBD (Admin Ct)), Maurice Kay, J.

s.12, amended: SI 2003/1887 Sch.2 para.9

s.13, see *Campbell v Mirror Group Newspapers Ltd* [2002] EWHC 499, [2002] E.M.L.R. 30 (QBD), Morland, J.; see *Douglas v Hello! Ltd (No.6)* [2003] EWHC 786, [2003] 3 All E.R. 996 (Ch D), Lindsay, J.

s.14, see *P v Wozencroft* [2002] EWHC 1724, [2002] 2 F.L.R. 1118 (Fam Div), Wilson, J.

s.16, amended: SI 2003/1887 Sch.2 para.9

s.17, amended: SI 2003/1887 Sch.2 para.9

s.18, applied: SI 2004/400 Reg.5

s.22, amended: SI 2003/1887 Sch.2 para.9

s.23, amended: SI 2003/1887 Sch.2 para.9

s.25, amended: SI 2003/1887 Sch.2 para.9

s.25, varied: SI 2003/2818 Art.12

s.26, amended: SI 2003/1887 Sch.2 para.9

s.28, amended: 2003 c.32 Sch.5 para.69

s.28, applied: SI 2003/2426 Reg.28

s.28, disapplied: SI 2003/1887 Sch.1

s.30, amended: SI 2003/1887 Sch.2 para.9

s.30, applied: SI 2004/1026 Reg.5, SSI 2003/581 Reg.6

s.31, amended: 2002 c.40 Sch.25 para.37, 2003 c.43 s.119, 2004 c.27 s.59, SI 2004/1823 Art.19

s.31, applied: SI 2004/454 Art.11

s.32, see *Campbell v Mirror Group Newspapers Ltd* [2002] EWCA Civ 1373, [2003] Q.B. 633 (CA), Lord Phillips of Worth Matravers, M.R.

s.32, amended: SI 2003/1887 Sch.2 para.9

s.33, applied: 2003 asp 13 s.279

s.33A, disapplied: 2002 asp 13 s.38

s.38, amended: SI 2003/1887 Sch.2 para.9

1998–cont.

29. Data Protection Act 1998–*cont.*

s.38, applied: SSI 2003/581 Reg.6

s.40, varied: SI 2003/2426 Reg.31, Sch.1 para.1

s.41, varied: SI 2003/2426 Reg.31, Sch.1 para.2

s.42, varied: SI 2003/2426 Reg.31, Sch.1 para.3

s.43, varied: SI 2003/2426 Reg.31, Sch.1 para.4

s.44, varied: SI 2003/2426 Reg.31, Sch.1 para.5

s.45, varied: SI 2003/2426 Reg.31, Sch.1 para.5

s.46, varied: SI 2003/2426 Reg.31, Sch.1 para.5

s.47, varied: SI 2003/2426 Reg.31, Sch.1 para.6

s.48, varied: SI 2003/2426 Reg.31, Sch.1 para.7

s.49, varied: SI 2003/2426 Reg.31, Sch.1 para.8

s.50, varied: SI 2003/2426 Reg.31

s.51, amended: SI 2003/1887 Sch.2 para.9

s.52, amended: SI 2003/1887 Sch.2 para.9

s.54, amended: SI 2003/1887 Sch.2 para.9

s.54A, added: 2003 c.32 s.81

s.56, amended: SI 2003/1887 Sch.2 para.9

s.58, varied: SI 2003/2426 Reg.28

s.60, amended: 2003 c.32 Sch.5 para.70

s.63, amended: 2003 c.32 Sch.5 para.71

s.64, amended: SI 2003/1887 Sch.2 para.9

s.67, amended: SI 2003/1887 Sch.2 para.9

s.67, applied: SI 2002/2905, SI 2003/2426 Reg.28

s.67, enabling: SI 2002/2722, SI 2002/2905, SI 2004/3244

s.69, amended: 2002 c.17 Sch.5 para.41, SI 2002/253 Sch.5 para.14, SI 2002/254 Sch.4 para.7, SI 2002/2469 Sch.1 para.24, 2003 c.43 Sch.4 para.107, SI 2003/1590 Sch.1 para.1

s.69, referred to: SI 2002/1438 Reg.7

s.69, repealed (in part): SI 2003/1590 Sch.1 para.1

s.75, amended: SI 2003/1887 Sch.2 para.9

Sch.1 Part I para.1, amended: SI 2003/1887 Sch.2 para.9

Sch.1 Part I para.2, amended: SI 2003/1887 Sch.2 para.9

Sch.1 Part I para.3, amended: SI 2003/1887 Sch.2 para.9

Sch.1 Part I para.4, amended: SI 2003/1887 Sch.2 para.9

Sch.1 Part I para.5, amended: SI 2003/1887 Sch.2 para.9

Sch.1 Part I para.6, amended: SI 2003/1887 Sch.2 para.9

Sch.1 Part I para.7, amended: SI 2003/1887 Sch.2 para.9

1998–cont.

29. Data Protection Act 1998–*cont.*

Sch.1 Part I para.8, amended: SI 2003/1887 Sch.2 para.9

Sch.1 Part II para.1, amended: SI 2003/1887 Sch.2 para.9

Sch.1 Part II para.2, amended: SI 2003/1887 Sch.2 para.9

Sch.1 Part II para.3, amended: SI 2003/1887 Sch.2 para.9

Sch.1 Part II para.4, amended: SI 2003/1887 Sch.2 para.9

Sch.1 Part II para.5, amended: SI 2003/1887 Sch.2 para.9

Sch.1 Part II para.6, amended: SI 2003/1887 Sch.2 para.9

Sch.1 Part II para.7, amended: SI 2003/1887 Sch.2 para.9

Sch.1 Part II para.8, amended: SI 2003/1887 Sch.2 para.9

Sch.1 Part II para.9, amended: SI 2003/1887 Sch.2 para.9

Sch.1 Part II para.10, amended: SI 2003/1887 Sch.2 para.9

Sch.1 Part II para.11, amended: SI 2003/1887 Sch.2 para.9

Sch.1 Part II para.12, amended: SI 2003/1887 Sch.2 para.9

Sch.1 Part II para.13, amended: SI 2003/1887 Sch.2 para.9

Sch.1 Part II para.14, amended: SI 2003/1887 Sch.2 para.9

Sch.1 Part II para.15, amended: SI 2003/1887 Sch.2 para.9

Sch.2 para.1, amended: SI 2003/1887 Sch.2 para.9

Sch.2 para.2, amended: SI 2003/1887 Sch.2 para.9

Sch.2 para.3, amended: SI 2003/1887 Sch.2 para.9

Sch.2 para.4, amended: SI 2003/1887 Sch.2 para.9

Sch.2 para.5, amended: SI 2003/1887 Sch.2 para.9

Sch.2 para.6, amended: SI 2003/1887 Sch.2 para.9

Sch.3 para.1, amended: SI 2003/1887 Sch.2 para.9

Sch.3 para.2, amended: SI 2003/1887 Sch.2 para.9

Sch.3 para.3, amended: SI 2003/1887 Sch.2 para.9

Sch.3 para.4, amended: SI 2003/1887 Sch.2 para.9

Sch.3 para.5, amended: SI 2003/1887 Sch.2 para.9

Sch.3 para.6, amended: SI 2003/1887 Sch.2 para.9

Sch.3 para.7, amended: SI 2003/1887 Sch.2 para.9

Sch.3 para.8, amended: SI 2003/1887 Sch.2 para.9

1998–cont.

29. Data Protection Act 1998–*cont.*

Sch.3 para.9, amended: SI 2003/1887 Sch.2 para.9

Sch.3 para.10, amended: SI 2003/1887 Sch.2 para.9

Sch.3 para.10, applied: SI 2002/2905 Art.2

Sch.3 para.10, enabling: SI 2002/2905

Sch.4 para.1, amended: SI 2003/1887 Sch.2 para.9

Sch.4 para.2, amended: SI 2003/1887 Sch.2 para.9

Sch.4 para.3, amended: SI 2003/1887 Sch.2 para.9

Sch.4 para.4, amended: SI 2003/1887 Sch.2 para.9

Sch.4 para.5, amended: SI 2003/1887 Sch.2 para.9

Sch.4 para.6, amended: SI 2003/1887 Sch.2 para.9

Sch.4 para.7, amended: SI 2003/1887 Sch.2 para.9

Sch.4 para.8, amended: SI 2003/1887 Sch.2 para.9

Sch.4 para.9, amended: SI 2003/1887 Sch.2 para.9

Sch.5 Part I para.1, amended: SI 2003/1887 Sch.2 para.9

Sch.5 Part I para.2, amended: SI 2003/1887 Sch.2 para.9

Sch.5 Part I para.3, amended: SI 2003/1887 Sch.2 para.9

Sch.5 Part I para.4, amended: SI 2003/1887 Sch.2 para.9

Sch.5 Part I para.5, amended: SI 2003/1887 Sch.2 para.9

Sch.5 Part I para.6, amended: SI 2003/1887 Sch.2 para.9

Sch.5 Part I para.7, amended: SI 2003/1887 Sch.2 para.9

Sch.5 Part I para.8, amended: SI 2003/1887 Sch.2 para.9

Sch.5 Part I para.9, amended: SI 2003/1887 Sch.2 para.9

Sch.5 Part I para.10, amended: SI 2003/1887 Sch.2 para.9

Sch.5 Part I para.11, amended: SI 2003/1887 Sch.2 para.9

Sch.5 Part II para.12, amended: SI 2003/1887 Sch.2 para.9

Sch.5 Part II para.12, disapplied: SI 2003/1887 Sch.1

Sch.5 Part II para.13, amended: SI 2003/1887 Sch.2 para.9

Sch.5 Part II para.14, amended: SI 2003/1887 Sch.2 para.9

Sch.5 Part II para.15, amended: SI 2003/1887 Sch.2 para.9

Sch.6, applied: SI 2003/2426 Reg.28

Sch.6 para.1, varied: SI 2003/2426 Reg.31

Sch.6 para.2, disapplied: SI 2003/1887 Sch.1

Sch.6 para.2, varied: SI 2003/2426 Reg.31

1998–cont.

29. Data Protection Act 1998–*cont.*

Sch.6 para.3, disapplied: SI 2003/1887 Sch.1

Sch.6 para.3, varied: SI 2003/2426 Reg.31

Sch.6 para.4, varied: SI 2003/2426 Reg.31, Sch.1 para.9

Sch.6 para.5, varied: SI 2003/2426 Reg.31

Sch.6 para.6, varied: SI 2003/2426 Reg.31

Sch.6 para.7, amended: SI 2003/1887 Sch.2 para.9

Sch.6 para.7, varied: SI 2003/2426 Reg.31

Sch.6 para.7, enabling: SI 2002/2722

Sch.6 para.8, varied: SI 2003/2426 Reg.31

Sch.7 para.1, amended: SI 2003/1887 Sch.2 para.9

Sch.7 para.2, amended: SI 2003/1887 Sch.2 para.9

Sch.7 para.3, amended: SI 2003/1887 Sch.2 para.9

Sch.7 para.4, amended: SI 2003/1887 Sch.2 para.9

Sch.7 para.5, amended: SI 2003/1887 Sch.2 para.9

Sch.7 para.6, amended: SI 2002/1555 Art.25, SI 2003/1887 Sch.2 para.9

Sch.7 para.7, amended: SI 2003/1887 Sch.2 para.9

Sch.7 para.8, amended: SI 2003/1887 Sch.2 para.9

Sch.7 para.9, amended: SI 2003/1887 Sch.2 para.9

Sch.7 para.10, amended: SI 2003/1887 Sch.2 para.9

Sch.7 para.11, amended: SI 2003/1887 Sch.2 para.9

Sch.8 Part III, disapplied: 2002 asp 13 s.38

Sch.9 para.1, amended: 2003 c.39 Sch.4 para.8

Sch.9 para.1, varied: SI 2003/2426 Reg.31, Sch.1 para.10

Sch.9 para.2, varied: SI 2003/2426 Reg.31

Sch.9 para.3, varied: SI 2003/2426 Reg.31

Sch.9 para.4, varied: SI 2003/2426 Reg.31

Sch.9 para.5, varied: SI 2003/2426 Reg.31

Sch.9 para.6, varied: SI 2003/2426 Reg.31

Sch.9 para.7, varied: SI 2003/2426 Reg.31

Sch.9 para.8, varied: SI 2003/2426 Reg.31

Sch.9 para.9, varied: SI 2003/2426 Reg.31, Sch.1 para.11

Sch.9 para.10, varied: SI 2003/2426 Reg.31

Sch.9 para.11, varied: SI 2003/2426 Reg.31

Sch.9 para.12, disapplied: 2002 asp 11 Sch.5

Sch.9 para.12, varied: SI 2003/2426 Reg.31

Sch.9 para.13, varied: SI 2003/2426 Reg.31

Sch.9 para.14, varied: SI 2003/2426 Reg.31

Sch.9 para.15, varied: SI 2003/2426 Reg.31

30. Teaching and Higher Education Act 1998

Commencement Orders: 2002 c.32 Sch.21 para.84

CAP.

1998–cont.

30. Teaching and Higher Education Act 1998–*cont.*

applied: SI 2002/3200 Reg.20, Reg.22, Reg.26, Reg.31, Reg.37, Sch.3 para.1, SI 2003/1663 Sch.3 para.2

referred to: SI 2002/808 Art.2, 2004 c.8 s.42

s.1, repealed (in part): 2002 c.32 Sch.22 Part 3

s.1, enabling: SI 2003/389, SI 2004/1935

s.2, amended: 2002 c.32 Sch.12 para.2, Sch.21 para.75

s.3, amended: 2002 c.32 Sch.12 para.3, Sch.21 para.76, Sch.22 Part 3

s.3, applied: 2002 c.32 s.134, SI 2003/1663 Reg.7, SI 2004/1744 Reg.7

s.3, repealed (in part): 2002 c.32 Sch.22 Part 3

s.3, enabling: SI 2004/1741

s.4, amended: 2002 c.32 Sch.12 para.4, Sch.21 para.77

s.4, applied: SI 2002/377 Sch.1 para.27, SI 2002/3199 Sch.1 para.21, SI 2003/1663 Sch.3 para.2, SI 2003/3118 Sch.1 para.19, SI 2003/3170 Sch.1 para.21

s.4, enabling: SI 2004/1741

s.4A, added: 2002 c.32 Sch.12 para.5

s.5, enabling: SI 2003/1186

s.6, enabling: SI 2003/1186

s.6A, added: 2002 c.32 Sch.12 para.6

s.7, amended: 2002 c.32 Sch.21 para.78

s.7, applied: SI 2004/1886

s.7, enabling: SI 2004/1886

s.8, enabling: SI 2002/2940

s.9, amended: 2002 c.32 Sch.12 para.7

s.9, applied: SI 2003/3118 Sch.1 para.19

s.10, repealed: 2002 c.32 Sch.21 para.79, Sch.22 Part 3

s.10, enabling: SI 2003/140

s.11, repealed (in part): 2002 c.32 Sch.21 para.80, Sch.22 Part 3, Sch.22 Part 3

s.12, amended: 2002 c.32 Sch.12 para.8, Sch.21 para.81

s.12, applied: SI 2002/377 Sch.1 para.27, SI 2003/3118 Sch.1 para.19, SI 2003/3170 Sch.1 para.21

s.12, varied: SI 2002/3184 Reg.7

s.12, enabling: SI 2002/326, SI 2003/985

s.13, repealed (in part): 2002 c.32 Sch.21 para.82, Sch.22 Part 3

s.14, enabling: SI 2004/1741

s.15, substituted: 2002 c.32 Sch.21 para.83

s.15, enabling: SI 2003/542, SI 2003/1184, SI 2003/1186

s.15A, substituted: 2002 c.32 Sch.21 para.83

s.15A, enabling: SI 2003/542, SI 2003/1184, SI 2003/1186

s.18, repealed (in part): 2002 c.32 Sch.21 para.84, Sch.22 Part 3

s.19, amended: 2002 c.32 Sch.21 para.85

CAP.

1998–cont.

30. Teaching and Higher Education Act 1998–*cont.*

s.19, applied: SI 2002/377 Sch.1 para.30, SI 2002/3199 Sch.1 para.27, Sch.1 para.28, SI 2003/1963 Reg.3, SI 2003/3118 Sch.1 para.24, Sch.1 para.25, SI 2003/3170 Sch.1 para.27, Sch.1 para.28

s.19, enabling: SI 2002/2063, SI 2003/106, SI 2003/543, SI 2003/2148, SI 2004/872

s.22, amended: 2003 c.14 s.147, 2003 c.1 Sch.6 para.236, 2004 c.8 s.42, s.43, Sch.7

s.22, applied: 2002 c.32 s.186, SI 2002/195 Reg.5, Reg.29, Reg.39, SI 2002/535 Sch.1, SI 2002/2086 Reg.3, Reg.7, SI 2002/2820 Reg.4, SI 2002/3199 Sch.1 para.13, SI 2002/3200 Reg.5, Reg.28, Reg.38, SI 2003/1917 Reg.3, Reg.7, SI 2003/3118 Sch.1 para.13, SI 2003/3170 Sch.1 para.13, SR 2002/379 Reg.4, 2004 c.8 s.44

s.22, disapplied: 2004 c.31 s.18

s.22, referred to: 2004 c.8 s.44, s.52

s.22, repealed (in part): 2004 c.8 s.43, Sch.7

s.22, varied: 2004 c.8 s.44

s.22, enabling: SI 2002/174, SI 2002/195, SI 2002/1318, SI 2002/2087, SI 2002/2088, SI 2002/2104, SI 2002/2859, SI 2002/3059, SI 2002/3200, SI 2003/1065, SI 2003/1588, SI 2003/3280, SI 2004/161, SI 2004/1175, SI 2004/1602, SI 2004/1658, SI 2004/2041, SI 2004/2598, SI 2004/2752

s.23, amended: SI 2002/808 Art.33

s.23, applied: SI 2002/195 Reg.6, Reg.21, Reg.32, SI 2002/3200 Reg.6, Reg.20, Reg.31, 2004 c.8 s.44

s.23, varied: 2004 c.8 s.44

s.26, repealed: 2004 c.8 Sch.6 para.7, Sch.7

s.28, amended: 2004 c.8 Sch.6 para.8, Sch.7

s.28, applied: SI 2002/195 Reg.10, SI 2002/3200 Reg.10

s.42, amended: 2002 c.32 Sch.12 para.9, 2004 c.8 Sch.6 para.9

s.42, applied: SI 2002/326, SI 2003/503, SI 2003/542, SI 2003/985, SI 2003/1186, SI 2004/1741, SI 2004/1935

s.42, enabling: SI 2002/174, SI 2002/195, SI 2002/326, SI 2002/1318, SI 2002/2063, SI 2002/2087, SI 2002/2088, SI 2002/2104, SI 2002/2859, SI 2002/3059, SI 2002/3200, SI 2003/106, SI 2003/503, SI 2003/542, SI 2003/543, SI 2003/985, SI 2003/1065, SI 2003/1184, SI 2003/1186, SI 2003/1588, SI 2003/2148, SI 2003/3280, SI 2004/161, SI 2004/872, SI 2004/1175, SI 2004/1602, SI 2004/1658, SI 2004/1741, SI 2004/1935, SI 2004/2041, SI 2004/2598, SI 2004/2752

s.43, amended: 2002 c.32 Sch.12 para.10

s.43, enabling: SI 2002/174, SI 2002/195, SI 2002/1318, SI 2002/2088, SI 2002/2104, SI 2002/3059, SI 2002/3200, SI 2003/

1998–cont.

30. Teaching and Higher Education Act 1998–*cont.*

s.43, enabling:–*cont.*

1065, SI 2003/1588, SI 2003/3280, SI 2004/161, SI 2004/1602, SI 2004/1658, SI 2004/2041, SI 2004/2598

s.44, applied: SI 2002/1330 Reg.7

s.44, referred to: SI 2003/1994 Reg.7

s.46, amended: 2004 c.8 s.42

s.46, applied: 2004 c.8 s.42

Sch.1 para.3, enabling: SI 2003/389, SI 2004/1935

Sch.1 para.9, enabling: SI 2003/503, SI 2003/1186

Sch.1 para.18, added: 2002 c.32 Sch.12 para.11

Sch.2, enabling: SI 2003/542, SI 2003/1186

Sch.2 para.1, amended: 2002 c.32 Sch.21 para.86

Sch.2 para.1, repealed (in part): 2002 c.32 Sch.21 para.86, Sch.22 Part 3

Sch.2 para.1, enabling: SI 2003/503

Sch.2 para.4, substituted: 2002 c.32 Sch.12 para.12

Sch.2 para.4, enabling: SI 2003/503

Sch.2 para.8, amended: 2002 c.32 Sch.12 para.12

Sch.3 para.5, repealed: 2002 c.32 Sch.22 Part 3

Sch.4, applied: SI 2002/1330 Reg.7

Sch.4, referred to: SI 2003/1994 Reg.7

31. School Standards and Framework Act 1998

see *Green v Victoria Road Primary School Governing Body* [2003] I.C.R. 713 (EAT), Judge Ansell; see *R. (on the application of A (A Child)) v Kingsmead School Governors* [2002] EWCA Civ 1822, [2003] B.L.G.R. 371 (CA), Simon Brown, L.J.

applied: 2002 c.32 s.212, SI 2002/377 Reg.20, Reg.24, Reg.26, Sch.2 para.15, Sch.2 para.24, SI 2002/2550 Reg.9, SI 2003/287 Reg.9, SI 2003/1021 Reg.34, SI 2003/1200 Sch.2 para.24, Sch.2 para.40, SI 2003/1558 Reg.53, SI 2003/3247 Reg.20, Reg.23, Reg.25, Sch.1 para.15, Sch.1 para.24, SI 2004/1576 Reg.10, SI 2004/2506 Reg.12, Sch.1 para.17

varied: SI 2003/2045 Reg.6

Part I c.III, applied: 2002 c.32 s.128

Part I c.IV, referred to: 2002 c.32 s.25

Part I c.IV, added: 2002 c.32 s.59

Part II, applied: 2002 c.32 s.12

Part II, referred to: 2002 c.32 s.40

Part II c.II, applied: SI 2002/377 Sch.1 para.19, Sch.2 para.15, SI 2002/3199 Sch.1 para.11, SI 2003/453 Sch.1 para.15, SI 2003/3118 Sch.1 para.11, SI 2003/3170 Sch.1 para.11, SI 2003/3247 Sch.1 para.15, SI 2004/2506 Reg.17, Sch.1 para.17

1998–cont.

31. School Standards and Framework Act 1998–*cont.*

Part II c.II, referred to: 2002 c.32 s.24

Part II c.IV, applied: SI 2002/377 Sch.1 para.27, SI 2002/1394 Reg.17, Reg.31, SI 2002/3199 Sch.1 para.21, SI 2003/1965 Reg.28, SI 2003/3118 Sch.1 para.19, SI 2003/3170 Sch.1 para.21, SI 2004/2042 Reg.33

Part II c.IV, added: 2002 c.32 s.43

Part II c.IV, amended: 2002 c.32 Sch.3 para.4

Part III, referred to: 2002 c.32 s.24

Part III c.I, added: 2002 c.32 s.46

s.1, amended: 2002 c.32 Sch.21 para.87

s.1, applied: 2002 c.41 s.37, SI 2003/453 Reg.12, SI 2003/1041 Sch.1 para.1, SI 2003/3247 Reg.12, SI 2004/2506 Sch.1 para.35

s.1, varied: SI 2003/1041 Sch.1 para.2, Sch.1 para.3, Sch.1 para.4, Sch.1 para.5

s.2, repealed: 2004 c.31 Sch.5 Part 1

s.3, applied: SI 2003/453 Reg.12

s.3, repealed (in part): 2002 c.32 s.18, Sch.22 Part 3

s.4, amended: 2002 c.32 Sch.21 para.88

s.6, applied: SI 2002/377 Sch.1 para.18, SI 2002/3199 Sch.1 para.10, SI 2003/3118 Sch.1 para.10, SI 2003/3170 Sch.1 para.10

s.6, repealed: 2004 c.31 Sch.5 Part 1

s.6, varied: SI 2002/928 Sch.2

s.6, enabling: SI 2002/423, SI 2002/1187

s.7, applied: SI 2002/377 Sch.1 para.18, SI 2002/1187 Reg.26, Reg.32, SI 2002/3199 Sch.1 para.10, SI 2003/3118 Sch.1 para.10, SI 2003/3170 Sch.1 para.10

s.7, repealed (in part): 2002 c.32 Sch.21 para.89, Sch.22 Part 3, 2004 c.31 Sch.5 Part 1

s.7, enabling: SI 2002/423, SI 2002/1187

s.10, amended: 2002 c.32 Sch.15 para.2

s.10, applied: 2002 c.32 Sch.15 para.8

s.10, referred to: 2002 c.32 s.4

s.10, repealed (in part): 2002 c.32 Sch.15 para.2, Sch.22 Part 3

s.10, varied: 2002 c.32 Sch.15 para.8

s.10, enabling: SI 2002/2123, SI 2002/2124, SI 2002/2764, SI 2002/2765, SI 2002/2766, SI 2002/2767, SI 2002/2768, SI 2002/2769, SI 2002/2770, SI 2002/2771, SI 2002/2772, SI 2002/2773, SI 2002/2774, SI 2002/2775, SI 2002/3085, SI 2002/3086, SI 2002/3087, SI 2002/3088, SI 2002/3089, SI 2002/3090, SI 2002/3091, SI 2002/3092, SI 2002/3093, SI 2002/3094, SI 2002/3095, SI 2002/3096, SI 2002/3097, SI 2002/3098, SI 2002/3099, SI 2002/3100, SI 2002/3101, SI 2002/3102, SI 2002/3103, SI 2002/3104, SI 2002/3105, SI 2002/3106, SI 2002/3107, SI 2002/3108, SI 2002/3109, SI 2003/554,

1998–cont.

**31. School Standards and Framework Act
1998**–*cont.*

s.10, enabling:–*cont.*
SI 2003/555, SI 2003/556, SI 2003/557,
SI 2003/558, SI 2003/560, SI 2003/561

s.11, amended: 2002 c.32 Sch.22 Part 3

s.11, repealed (in part): 2002 c.32 Sch.22 Part
3

s.11A, added: 2002 c.32 Sch.15 para.4

s.11A, applied: 2002 c.32 Sch.15 para.8

s.11B, added: 2002 c.32 Sch.15 para.5

s.11C, added: 2002 c.32 Sch.15 para.5

s.11D, added: 2002 c.32 Sch.15 para.6

s.12, amended: 2002 c.32 Sch.15 para.7,
Sch.21 para.90

s.13, repealed: 2002 c.32 Sch.21 para.91,
Sch.22 Part 1

s.14, amended: 2002 c.32 s.57, Sch.5 para.1,
Sch.21 para.92

s.14, applied: SI 2002/928 Sch.2, SI 2002/
3199 Sch.1 para.10, SI 2003/3118 Sch.1
para.10, SI 2003/3170 Sch.1 para.10

s.14, referred to: SI 2002/2113 Reg.4

s.14, varied: SI 2002/3184 Reg.3

s.15, amended: 2002 c.32 s.55

s.15, applied: 2002 c.32 s.63, SI 2002/928
Sch.2, SI 2002/3199 Sch.1 para.10, SI
2003/543 Reg.6, SI 2003/3118 Sch.1
para.10, SI 2003/3170 Sch.1 para.10

s.15, varied: SI 2002/2113 Reg.4, SI 2002/
3184 Reg.3

s.16, amended: 2002 c.32 Sch.5 para.2,
Sch.21 para.93

s.16, applied: SI 2002/928 Sch.2, SI 2002/
3199 Sch.1 para.10, SI 2003/348 Reg.21,
SI 2003/3118 Sch.1 para.10, SI 2003/3170
Sch.1 para.10

s.16, referred to: SI 2002/2113 Reg.4

s.16, repealed (in part): 2002 c.32 Sch.5
para.2, Sch.22 Part 3

s.16, varied: SI 2002/3184 Reg.3

s.16A, added: 2002 c.32 s.57

s.16A, applied: SI 2002/928 Sch.2, SI 2002/
3199 Sch.1 para.10, SI 2003/348 Reg.21, SI
2003/3118 Sch.1 para.10, SI 2003/3170
Sch.1 para.10, SI 2004/530 Reg.5

s.16A, referred to: SI 2002/2113 Reg.4

s.17, amended: 2002 c.32 Sch.5 para.3

s.17, applied: 2002 c.32 s.35, s.37, SI 2002/
928 Sch.2, SI 2002/2978 Reg.13, SI 2002/
3199 Sch.1 para.10, SI 2003/3118 Sch.1
para.10, SI 2003/3170 Sch.1 para.10

s.17, referred to: SI 2002/2113 Reg.4

s.17, varied: SI 2002/3184 Reg.3

s.18, amended: 2002 c.32 s.56, Sch.21
para.94

s.18, applied: SI 2003/348 Reg.21, SI 2003/
1377 Reg.5, Reg.7

s.18, referred to: SI 2002/2113 Reg.4

s.18, varied: SI 2002/3184 Reg.3

s.18A, added: 2002 c.32 s.58

1998–cont.

**31. School Standards and Framework Act
1998**–*cont.*

s.18A, applied: SI 2003/348 Reg.21, SI
2004/530 Reg.5

s.18A, referred to: SI 2002/2113 Reg.4

s.19, amended: 2002 c.32 s.56

s.19, referred to: SI 2002/2113 Reg.4

s.19, varied: SI 2002/3184 Reg.3

s.19A, referred to: SI 2002/2113 Reg.4

s.20, amended: 2002 c.32 Sch.21 para.95

s.20, referred to: 2002 c.32 s.25, SI 2002/
2113 Reg.3, SI 2002/2316 Reg.3, SI
2002/2953 Reg.5, SI 2003/1717 Reg.3

s.21, applied: SI 2003/1200 Sch.2 para.24,
Sch.2 para.40

s.21, enabling: SI 2004/3264

s.22, amended: 2002 c.32 Sch.21 para.96,
Sch.22 Part 3, SI 2002/906 Art.3

s.24, enabling: SI 2004/3052

s.26, applied: SI 2002/377 Sch.1 para.19, SI
2002/928 Sch.2, SI 2002/3199 Sch.1
para.11, SI 2003/1732 Reg.4, SI 2003/
3118 Sch.1 para.11, SI 2003/3170 Sch.1
para.11

s.26, repealed: 2004 c.31 Sch.5 Part 1

s.26, enabling: SI 2003/1201, SI 2003/1732

s.26A, repealed: 2004 c.31 Sch.5 Part 1

s.26B, repealed: 2004 c.31 Sch.5 Part 1

s.27, amended: 2004 c.31 Sch.5 Part 1

s.28, amended: 2002 c.32 s.73, s.154, Sch.21
para.97

s.28, applied: 2002 c.32 s.71, s.74, s.129, SI
2002/432 Reg.8, SI 2002/928 Sch.2, SI
2002/3199 Reg.1, SI 2003/453 Reg.1, SI
2003/507 Reg.19, Reg.20, Reg.23, SI
2003/1041 Reg.2, Reg.4, Reg.6, Reg.7,
Reg.8, SI 2003/1377 Reg.17, SI 2004/
1576 Reg.16

s.28, referred to: 2002 c.32 s.74

s.28, enabling: SI 2003/1229, SI 2004/908,
SI 2004/3052

s.29, applied: 2002 c.32 s.71, SI 2003/507
Reg.20, Reg.23, SI 2003/1377 Reg.17

s.30, applied: SI 2003/1377 Reg.11, Reg.12,
Reg.17

s.31, applied: 2002 c.32 s.71, s.74, s.129, SI
2002/432 Reg.8, SI 2002/3199 Reg.1, SI
2003/453 Reg.1, SI 2003/507 Reg.19,
Reg.20, Reg.23, SI 2003/1377 Reg.17, SI
2004/1576 Reg.16

s.31, referred to: 2002 c.32 s.74

s.33, amended: 2002 c.32 Sch.21 para.98,
Sch.22 Part 3

s.33, enabling: SI 2003/1229

s.36, applied: SI 2002/2113 Reg.3, SI 2002/
2316 Reg.3

s.36, repealed (in part): 2002 c.32 Sch.22
Part 3

s.37, repealed (in part): 2002 c.32 Sch.22
Part 3

s.38, referred to: SI 2002/2113 Reg.3

1998–cont.

31. School Standards and Framework Act 1998–*cont.*

s.38, repealed (in part): 2002 c.32 Sch.22 Part 3

s.38, enabling: SI 2002/1396

s.39, repealed (in part): 2002 c.32 Sch.22 Part 3

s.40, repealed: 2002 c.32 Sch.22 Part 3

s.41, applied: SI 2002/928 Sch.2

s.41, repealed (in part): 2002 c.32 Sch.22 Part 3

s.42, applied: SI 2002/928 Sch.2

s.42, repealed (in part): 2002 c.32 Sch.22 Part 3

s.42, enabling: SI 2002/1171, SI 2002/1401, SI 2004/1735

s.43, repealed (in part): 2002 c.32 Sch.22 Part 3

s.44, amended: SI 2002/2113 Reg.7

s.44, applied: SI 2002/928 Sch.2, SI 2004/2507 Reg.2

s.44, repealed (in part): 2002 c.32 Sch.22 Part 3

s.44, substituted: SI 2002/2113 Reg.7

s.44, enabling: SI 2002/2113

s.45, amended: 2002 c.32 s.41, Sch.21 para.99, SI 2002/2316 Reg.2

s.45, applied: SI 2003/3118 Sch.2 para.24

s.45, varied: SI 2004/657 Art.3

s.45A, added: 2002 c.32 s.41

s.45A, amended: 2003 c.26 Sch.7 para.66

s.45A, applied: SI 2002/3199 Reg.2, Reg.3, SI 2003/3118 Reg.4, Reg.5, SI 2003/3170 Reg.2, Reg.3

s.45A, enabling: SI 2002/3199, SI 2003/3118, SI 2003/3170, SI 2004/659, SI 2004/804, SI 2004/3131

s.45B, added: 2002 c.32 s.42

s.45B, amended: 2003 c.26 Sch.7 para.66

s.45C, added: 2002 c.32 s.42

s.46, applied: SI 2002/377 Reg.3

s.46, repealed (in part): 2002 c.32 Sch.22 Part 3

s.46, enabling: SI 2002/136, SI 2002/377, SI 2003/538

s.47, applied: SI 2002/536 Reg.2, SI 2002/2114 Reg.7, SI 2002/3199 Reg.1, SI 2003/2909 Reg.8, SI 2003/3118 Reg.2

s.47, enabling: SI 2002/377, SI 2002/2114, SI 2002/2763, SI 2002/2868, SI 2003/453, SI 2003/3247, SI 2004/659, SI 2004/2506

s.47A, applied: SI 2002/3199 Sch.2 para.29, SI 2003/3118 Sch.1 para.28, SI 2003/3170 Sch.3 para.30

s.47A, enabling: SI 2002/2114, SI 2003/2909, SI 2004/447

s.48, amended: 2002 c.32 Sch.3 para.2

s.48, applied: 2002 c.32 s.19, s.28, Sch.1 para.3, SI 2002/377 Reg.33, SI 2002/535 Reg.2, SI 2002/928 Sch.2, SI 2003/

1998–cont.

31. School Standards and Framework Act 1998–*cont.*

s.48, applied:–*cont.*
453 Reg.29, SI 2003/1377 Reg.17, SI 2003/1558 Reg.49, SI 2003/1965 Reg.33, Reg.38, SI 2003/3118 Reg.5, SI 2003/3170 Reg.3, SI 2003/3247 Reg.29, SI 2004/2042 Reg.38, Reg.43, SI 2004/2507 Reg.4

s.48, referred to: SI 2002/3199 Reg.3

s.48, enabling: SI 2002/377, SI 2002/2062, SI 2003/453, SI 2003/3247, SI 2004/2507

s.49, amended: 2002 c.32 Sch.21 para.100, SI 2002/906 Art.4

s.49, applied: SI 2002/377 Sch.4 para.10, SI 2002/2978 Reg.12, SI 2002/3177 Reg.6

s.49, referred to: 2002 c.32 s.25, SI 2003/453 Sch.3 para.10, SI 2003/3247 Sch.3 para.10, SI 2004/2507 Sch.1 para.9

s.50, amended: 2002 c.32 Sch.3 para.3, Sch.21 para.101

s.50, applied: SI 2002/377 Sch.4 para.14, SI 2002/928 Sch.2, SI 2003/1965 Reg.33, Reg.38, SI 2004/2042 Reg.38, Reg.43, SI 2004/2507 Sch.1 para.13

s.50, referred to: 2002 c.32 s.25, SI 2003/453 Sch.3 para.14, SI 2003/3247 Sch.3 para.14

s.50, varied: SI 2003/1965 Reg.29, SI 2004/2042 Reg.34

s.50, enabling: SI 2002/378, SI 2004/444

s.51, applied: SI 2002/928 Sch.2

s.51, referred to: 2002 c.32 s.25

s.51A, added: 2002 c.32 Sch.3 para.4

s.51A, applied: SI 2002/3199 Reg.4, SI 2003/3118 Reg.2, SI 2003/3170 Reg.4

s.52, amended: 2002 c.32 s.45, Sch.22 Part 3

s.52, applied: SI 2002/122 Reg.5, SI 2002/535 Reg.3, Reg.4, SI 2002/536 Reg.4, Reg.5, SI 2002/928 Sch.2, SI 2003/475 Reg.3, Reg.4, SI 2003/1153 Reg.5, SI 2004/417 Reg.3, Reg.4, SI 2004/1279 Reg.5

s.52, enabling: SI 2002/122, SI 2002/535, SI 2002/536, SI 2003/475, SI 2003/873, SI 2003/1153, SI 2004/417, SI 2004/1279

s.53, amended: 2004 c.23 Sch.2 para.40

s.53A, added: 2004 c.23 Sch.2 para.41

s.54, applied: SI 2002/928 Sch.2

s.54, repealed (in part): 2002 c.32 Sch.22 Part 3

s.55, applied: SI 2002/928 Sch.2

s.55, repealed (in part): 2002 c.32 Sch.22 Part 3

s.56, repealed (in part): 2002 c.32 Sch.22 Part 3

s.57, applied: SI 2002/377 Sch.1 para.29

s.57, repealed (in part): 2002 c.32 Sch.22 Part 3

1998–cont.

31. **School Standards and Framework Act 1998**–*cont.*

s.58, amended: 2002 c.32 Sch.3 para.6

s.58, applied: 2002 c.32 s.35, s.36, Sch.2 para.4, Sch.2 para.10

s.58, referred to: SI 2003/1660 Reg.39

s.59, amended: 2002 c.32 Sch.3 para.7

s.59, referred to: SI 2003/1660 Reg.39

s.60, amended: 2002 c.32 Sch.3 para.8

s.60, referred to: SI 2003/1660 Reg.39

s.61, amended: 2002 c.32 Sch.21 para.102

s.61, applied: SI 2003/1377 Reg.17, SI 2003/1558 Reg.49

s.61, varied: SI 2003/1558 Reg.31, SI 2004/657 Art.3

s.62, amended: 2002 c.32 Sch.21 para.103

s.62, applied: SI 2002/928 Sch.2

s.62, varied: SI 2004/657 Art.3

s.63, amended: 2002 c.32 s.53, Sch.22 Part 3

s.64, see *R. (on the application of A (A Child)) v P School Head Teacher* [2001] EWHC Admin 721, [2002] E.L.R. 244 (QBD (Admin Ct)), Hooper, J.; see *R. (on the application of Begum (Shabina)) v Denbigh High School Governors* [2004] EWHC 1389, [2004] E.L.R. 374 (QBD (Admin Ct)), Bennett, J.; see *R. (on the application of S) v YP School Governing Body* [2003] EWCA Civ 1306, [2004] E.L.R. 37 (CA), Simon Brown, L.J.

s.64, applied: SI 2002/2952 Sch.1 para.4, SI 2002/3178 Reg.9, SI 2003/3227 Reg.11

s.64, referred to: SI 2002/2952 Sch.1 para.4

s.64, repealed (in part): 2002 c.32 Sch.22 Part 3

s.65, see *R. (on the application of Begum (Shabina)) v Denbigh High School Governors* [2004] EWHC 1389, [2004] E.L.R. 374 (QBD (Admin Ct)), Bennett, J.

s.65, applied: SI 2002/2952 Sch.1 para.4, SI 2002/3178 Reg.9, SI 2003/3227 Reg.11

s.65, referred to: SI 2002/2952 Sch.1 para.4

s.65, repealed (in part): 2002 c.32 Sch.22 Part 3

s.66, see *R. (on the application of Begum (Shabina)) v Denbigh High School Governors* [2004] EWHC 1389, [2004] E.L.R. 374 (QBD (Admin Ct)), Bennett, J.

s.66, applied: SI 2002/2952 Sch.1 para.4, SI 2002/3178 Reg.9, SI 2003/3227 Reg.11

s.66, referred to: SI 2002/2952 Sch.1 para.4

s.66, repealed (in part): 2002 c.32 Sch.22 Part 3

s.67, see *R. (on the application of Begum (Shabina)) v Denbigh High School Governors* [2004] EWHC 1389, [2004] E.L.R. 374 (QBD (Admin Ct)), Bennett, J.; see *R. (on the application of L (A Child)) v J School Governors* [2003] UKHL 9, [2003] 2 A.C. 633 (HL), Lord Bingham of Cornhill

1998–cont.

31. **School Standards and Framework Act 1998**–*cont.*

s.67, applied: SI 2002/2952 Sch.1 para.4, SI 2002/3178 Reg.9, SI 2003/3227 Reg.11

s.67, referred to: SI 2002/2952 Sch.1 para.4

s.67, repealed (in part): 2002 c.32 Sch.22 Part 3

s.68, see *R. (on the application of Begum (Shabina)) v Denbigh High School Governors* [2004] EWHC 1389, [2004] E.L.R. 374 (QBD (Admin Ct)), Bennett, J.; see *R. (on the application of S (A Child)) v Brent LBC* [2001] EWHC Admin 384, [2002] E.L.R. 57 (QBD (Admin Ct)), Scott Baker, J.; see *R. (on the application of S (A Child)) v Brent LBC* [2002] EWCA Civ 693, [2002] E.L.R. 556 (CA), Schiemann, L.J.

s.68, applied: SI 2002/2952 Sch.1 para.4, SI 2002/3178 Reg.9, SI 2003/3227 Reg.11

s.68, referred to: SI 2002/2952 Sch.1 para.4

s.68, repealed (in part): 2002 c.32 Sch.22 Part 3

s.69, amended: 2002 c.32 Sch.21 para.104

s.69, applied: SI 2002/928 Sch.2, SI 2003/348 Reg.30, Reg.32, SI 2003/2314 Reg.3, Reg.4, Reg.6, SI 2003/3233 Reg.3, Reg.4, Reg.6, SI 2004/2042 Reg.8

s.69, enabling: SI 2003/800, SI 2003/2314, SI 2003/2552, SI 2003/2749, SI 2003/3108, SI 2003/3233, SI 2003/3259, SI 2003/3262, SI 2003/3284, SI 2003/3328, SI 2004/72, SI 2004/146, SI 2004/150, SI 2004/354, SI 2004/577, SI 2004/764, SI 2004/1160, SI 2004/1169, SI 2004/1378, SI 2004/1513, SI 2004/1725, SI 2004/1734, SI 2004/1971, SI 2004/2089, SI 2004/2262, SI 2004/2474, SI 2004/2476, SI 2004/2477, SI 2004/2478, SI 2004/2564, SI 2004/2565, SI 2004/2698, SI 2004/2892, SI 2004/2986, SI 2004/3353

s.70, applied: SI 2002/438 Sch.1 para.1, SI 2002/928 Sch.2

s.71, amended: 2002 c.32 Sch.21 para.105

s.71, applied: 2002 c.32 s.80, s.101, SI 2002/928 Sch.2, SI 2002/2897 Sch.3 para.8

s.71, substituted: 2002 c.32 Sch.21 para.105

s.72, amended: 2002 c.32 Sch.21 para.106

s.72, applied: SI 2003/2909 Reg.1, SI 2004/2506 Reg.2

s.72, enabling: SI 2003/1041, SI 2003/1558, SI 2003/1963

s.79A, added: SI 2003/2867 Sch.1 para.28

s.80, applied: SI 2002/928 Sch.2

s.81, amended: 2002 c.32 Sch.21 para.107

s.81, enabling: SI 2003/1964, SI 2004/2325

s.82, amended: 2002 c.32 Sch.21 para.108

s.83, see *R. (on the application of M) v B LBC* [2002] EWHC 2483, [2003] E.L.R. 144 (QBD (Admin Ct)), Jack Beatson, Q.C.

1998–cont.

31. School Standards and Framework Act 1998–*cont.*

s.84, amended: 2002 c.32 Sch.4 para.2, Sch.22 Part 3

s.84, applied: SI 2002/2897 Reg.8, SI 2002/2952 Sch.1 para.3, SI 2003/1041 Sch.1 para.1

s.84, varied: SI 2003/1041 Sch.1 para.2, Sch.1 para.3, Sch.1 para.4, Sch.1 para.5

s.85, enabling: SI 2003/163

s.85A, applied: SI 2002/2900 Reg.13, SI 2002/2903 Reg.4, SI 2002/2904 Reg.4, SI 2002/3199 Sch.2 para.14, SI 2003/1041 Sch.1 para.1, SI 2003/3118 Sch.1 para.11, SI 2003/3170 Sch.3 para.14

s.85A, varied: SI 2003/1041 Sch.1 para.2, Sch.1 para.3, Sch.1 para.4, Sch.1 para.5

s.85A, enabling: SI 2002/2900, SI 2003/2962

s.85B, added: 2002 c.32 s.66

s.85B, enabling: SI 2002/2900

s.86, see *R. (on the application of K) v Newham LBC* [2002] EWHC 405, [2002] E.L.R. 390 (QBD (Admin Ct)), Collins, J.

s.86, amended: 2002 c.32 s.47, Sch.4 para.3

s.86, applied: SI 2002/928 Sch.2, SI 2002/2897 Reg.3, Sch.2 para.3, Sch.2 para.6, Sch.3 para.5, SI 2002/2899 Reg.6, Sch.2 para.1, SI 2002/2900 Reg.3, SI 2002/3185 Art.7, SI 2003/1041 Sch.1 para.1, SI 2003/2962 Reg.3

s.86, disapplied: 2002 c.41 s.36

s.86, referred to: SI 2002/2899 Reg.6

s.86, repealed (in part): 2002 c.32 Sch.4 para.3, Sch.22 Part 3

s.86, varied: SI 2003/1041 Sch.1 para.2, Sch.1 para.3, Sch.1 para.4, Sch.1 para.5

s.87, amended: 2002 c.32 Sch.4 para.4

s.87, applied: SI 2002/928 Sch.2, SI 2002/2952 Sch.1 para.3, SI 2003/1041 Sch.1 para.1, SI 2003/3170 Sch.1 para.24

s.87, varied: SI 2003/1041 Sch.1 para.2, Sch.1 para.3, Sch.1 para.4, Sch.1 para.5

s.88, applied: SI 2002/377 Sch.1 para.19, SI 2002/928 Sch.2, SI 2002/3199 Sch.2 para.13, SI 2003/1377 Reg.17, SI 2003/1558 Reg.49, SI 2003/3170 Sch.3 para.13

s.89, amended: 2002 c.32 Sch.4 para.5

s.89, applied: SI 2002/377 Sch.1 para.19, SI 2002/2898 Reg.3, Reg.4, SI 2002/3199 Sch.2 para.13, SI 2003/1377 Reg.17, SI 2003/1558 Reg.49, SI 2003/3118 Sch.1 para.11, SI 2003/3170 Sch.3 para.13

s.89, enabling: SI 2002/2896, SI 2002/2898

s.89A, added: 2002 c.32 s.47

s.89A, applied: SI 2003/1377 Reg.17, SI 2003/1558 Reg.49

s.89A, enabling: SI 2002/2896

s.89B, added: 2002 c.32 s.48

s.89B, applied: SI 2002/928 Sch.2, SI 2002/2897 Sch.2 para.3, Sch.3 para.3, Sch.3 para.5, SI 2002/2899 Sch.2 para.1, SI

1998–cont.

31. School Standards and Framework Act 1998–*cont.*

s.89B, applied:–*cont.*

2002/2903 Reg.4, Reg.7, SI 2002/2904 Reg.4, Reg.7, SI 2003/1041 Sch.1 para.1

s.89B, varied: SI 2003/1041 Sch.1 para.2, Sch.1 para.3, Sch.1 para.4, Sch.1 para.5

s.89B, enabling: SI 2002/2903, SI 2002/2904, SI 2003/2751, SI 2004/1515, SI 2004/1516

s.89C, added: 2002 c.32 s.48

s.89C, applied: SI 2002/2899 Sch.2 para.1, SI 2002/2903 Reg.3, Reg.6, SI 2002/2904 Reg.3, Reg.6, SI 2003/1041 Sch.1 para.1

s.89C, varied: SI 2003/1041 Sch.1 para.2, Sch.1 para.3, Sch.1 para.4, Sch.1 para.5

s.89C, enabling: SI 2002/2903, SI 2002/2904, SI 2003/2751, SI 2004/1515, SI 2004/1516

s.90, amended: 2002 c.32 Sch.4 para.6

s.90, applied: SI 2003/1377 Reg.17, SI 2003/1558 Reg.49

s.90, enabling: SI 2002/2901

s.90, see *R. (on the application of Watford Grammar School for Girls) v Adjudicator for Schools* [2003] EWHC 2480, [2004] E.L.R. 40 (QBD (Admin Ct)), Collins, J.

s.91, applied: SI 2002/3185 Art.7, SI 2003/1558 Reg.49

s.91, repealed (in part): 2002 c.32 s.49, Sch.22 Part 3

s.92, applied: SI 2002/928 Sch.2, SI 2002/2899 Reg.6, SI 2003/1041 Sch.1 para.1

s.92, referred to: SI 2002/2899 Reg.6

s.92, substituted: 2002 c.32 Sch.4 para.7

s.92, varied: SI 2003/1041 Sch.1 para.2, Sch.1 para.3, Sch.1 para.4, Sch.1 para.5

s.92, enabling: SI 2002/1172, SI 2002/2897

s.93, repealed (in part): 2002 c.32 Sch.22 Part 3

s.94, amended: 2002 c.32 s.50, Sch.4 para.8

s.94, applied: SI 2002/2897 Sch.2 para.3, Sch.3 para.3, SI 2002/2899 Reg.3, Sch.2 para.1, SI 2002/2952 Sch.1 para.3, SI 2003/1041 Sch.1 para.1, SI 2003/1377 Reg.17, SI 2003/1558 Reg.49

s.94, disapplied: 2002 c.41 s.36

s.94, varied: SI 2003/1041 Sch.1 para.2, Sch.1 para.3, Sch.1 para.4, Sch.1 para.5

s.94, enabling: SI 2002/2899

s.95, amended: 2002 c.32 Sch.4 para.9

s.95, applied: SI 2002/2899 Reg.3, Sch.1 para.5, Sch.2 para.2, SI 2002/2952 Sch.1 para.3, SI 2003/1041 Sch.1 para.1

s.95, referred to: SI 2002/2952 Sch.1 para.3

s.95, varied: SI 2003/1041 Sch.1 para.2, Sch.1 para.3, Sch.1 para.4, Sch.1 para.5

s.95, enabling: SI 2002/2899

s.96, amended: 2002 c.32 Sch.4 para.10

1998–cont.

31. School Standards and Framework Act 1998–*cont.*

s.96, applied: SI 2002/928 Sch.2, SI 2003/1041 Sch.1 para.1

s.96, varied: SI 2003/1041 Sch.1 para.2, Sch.1 para.3, Sch.1 para.4, Sch.1 para.5

s.97, amended: 2002 c.32 Sch.4 para.11

s.97, applied: SI 2002/928 Sch.2, SI 2003/1041 Sch.1 para.1

s.97, varied: SI 2003/1041 Sch.1 para.2, Sch.1 para.3, Sch.1 para.4, Sch.1 para.5

s.98, amended: 2002 c.32 Sch.4 para.12, SI 2002/2953 Reg.4

s.98, applied: SI 2003/1041 Sch.1 para.1

s.98, referred to: SI 2002/2952 Sch.1 para.2

s.98, varied: SI 2003/1041 Sch.1 para.2, Sch.1 para.3, Sch.1 para.4, Sch.1 para.5

s.99, applied: SI 2003/1041 Sch.1 para.1

s.99, disapplied: SI 2003/1041 Sch.1 para.6

s.99, varied: SI 2003/1041 Sch.1 para.2, Sch.1 para.3, Sch.1 para.4, Sch.1 para.5, Sch.1 para.6

s.101, amended: 2002 c.32 Sch.21 para.109

s.101, applied: SI 2003/1041 Sch.1 para.1, SI 2003/1200 Sch.2 para.10

s.101, referred to: SI 2003/1200 Sch.2 para.33

s.101, varied: SI 2003/1041 Sch.1 para.2, Sch.1 para.3, Sch.1 para.4, Sch.1 para.5, Sch.1 para.7

s.102, applied: SI 2003/1041 Sch.1 para.1

s.102, varied: SI 2003/1041 Sch.1 para.2, Sch.1 para.3, Sch.1 para.5

s.103, applied: SI 2003/1041 Sch.1 para.1

s.103, varied: SI 2003/1041 Sch.1 para.2, Sch.1 para.3, Sch.1 para.4, Sch.1 para.5, Sch.1 para.8

s.104, applied: SI 2003/1041 Sch.1 para.6

s.105, applied: SI 2002/928 Sch.2

s.110, amended: 2002 c.32 Sch.7 para.9

s.114, amended: 2002 c.32 s.201

s.115, repealed (in part): 2002 c.32 Sch.22 Part 3

s.117, amended: 2002 c.32 s.150

s.118, amended: 2002 c.32 s.150

s.118, applied: 2002 c.32 s.98, s.153, SI 2003/893 Reg.4

s.118, enabling: SI 2003/893, SI 2003/2939

s.118A, added: 2002 c.32 s.149

s.118A, amended: 2002 c.32 s.150

s.118A, applied: SI 2002/928 Sch.2, SI 2003/893 Reg.7

s.119, amended: 2002 c.32 s.150, Sch.22 Part 3

s.119, applied: SI 2002/3199 Sch.1 para.21, SI 2003/3118 Sch.1 para.19, SI 2003/3170 Sch.1 para.21

s.119, repealed (in part): 2004 c.31 Sch.5 Part 1

s.120, amended: 2002 c.32 s.150, Sch.22 Part 3

s.120, applied: SI 2002/377 Sch.1 para.27, SI 2002/510 Sch.1 para.3, SI 2002/3199 Sch.1 para.21, SI 2003/3118 Sch.1 para.19, SI 2003/3170 Sch.1 para.21

s.120, repealed: 2004 c.31 Sch.5 Part 1

s.120, varied: SI 2002/928 Sch.2

s.120, enabling: SI 2002/2466, SI 2003/893, SI 2003/2939

s.121, amended: 2002 c.32 s.150, Sch.22 Part 3

s.121, applied: SI 2002/377 Sch.1 para.27, SI 2002/3199 Sch.1 para.21, SI 2003/893 Reg.5, Reg.6, Reg.7, SI 2003/3118 Sch.1 para.19, SI 2003/3170 Sch.1 para.21

s.121, repealed: 2004 c.31 Sch.5 Part 1

s.121, enabling: SI 2002/2466, SI 2003/893, SI 2003/2939

s.122, amended: 2002 c.32 s.150

s.122, repealed (in part): 2004 c.14 Sch.1 Part 7

s.123, amended: 2002 c.32 s.150

s.124, amended: 2002 c.32 s.150

s.124A, amended: 2002 c.32 s.150

s.124A, added: SI 2003/2037 Reg.3

s.124A, referred to: SI 2003/1660 Reg.39

s.124B, amended: 2002 c.32 s.150

s.124B, enabling: SI 2004/72, SI 2004/354

s.124B, added: SI 2003/2037 Reg.3

s.124B, enabling: SI 2003/3108, SI 2003/3284, SI 2003/3328, SI 2004/72, SI 2004/354, SI 2004/577, SI 2004/1378, SI 2004/2089, SI 2004/2986

s.127, amended: 2002 c.32 Sch.21 para.110, SI 2003/2045 Reg.4, SI 2004/1743 Reg.4

s.127, repealed (in part): 2002 c.32 Sch.21 para.110, Sch.22 Part 3

s.131, see *R. (on the application of Williamson) v Secretary of State for Education and Employment* [2001] EWHC Admin 960, [2002] 1 F.L.R. 493 (QBD (Admin Ct)), Elias, J.; see *R. (on the application of Williamson) v Secretary of State for Education and Employment* [2002] EWCA Civ 1926, [2003] Q.B. 1300 (CA), Buxton, L.J.

s.131, repealed (in part): 2004 c.14 Sch.1 Part 7

s.132, repealed (in part): 2004 c.14 Sch.1 Part 7

s.133, repealed: 2004 c.14 Sch.1 Part 7

s.134, repealed (in part): 2004 c.14 Sch.1 Part 7

s.138, amended: 2002 c.32 Sch.21 para.111, Sch.22 Part 3

s.138, repealed (in part): 2002 c.32 Sch.22 Part 3

s.138, enabling: SI 2002/122, SI 2002/136, SI 2002/377, SI 2002/423, SI 2002/432, SI 2002/535, SI 2002/536, SI 2002/1171, SI

1998–cont.

**31. School Standards and Framework Act
1998**–*cont.*

s.138, enabling:–*cont.*

2002/1172, SI 2002/1187, SI 2002/1396,
SI 2002/1401, SI 2002/1720, SI 2002/
2301, SI 2002/2466, SI 2002/2896, SI
2002/2897, SI 2002/2898, SI 2002/
2899, SI 2002/2900, SI 2002/2901, SI
2002/2903, SI 2002/2904, SI 2002/
3199, SI 2003/453, SI 2003/475, SI
2003/507, SI 2003/538, SI 2003/873, SI
2003/893, SI 2003/1041, SI 2003/1153,
SI 2003/1201, SI 2003/1229, SI 2003/
1558, SI 2003/1732, SI 2003/1963, SI
2003/1964, SI 2003/2136, SI 2003/
2314, SI 2003/2552, SI 2003/2749, SI
2003/2939, SI 2003/2962, SI 2003/
3118, SI 2003/3170, SI 2003/3233, SI
2003/3247, SI 2004/417, SI 2004/659,
SI 2004/804, SI 2004/908, SI 2004/
1279, SI 2004/1513, SI 2004/1515, SI
2004/1516, SI 2004/1576, SI 2004/1734,
SI 2004/1735, SI 2004/2506, SI 2004/
2507, SI 2004/3052, SI 2004/3131, SI
2004/3264

s.142, amended: 2002 c.32 Sch.21 para.112,
SI 2003/2037 Reg.4

s.142, referred to: SI 2003/1041 Reg.5

s.142, enabling: SI 2003/873

s.143, amended: 2002 c.32 Sch.21 para.113,
Sch.22 Part 3, SI 2003/2037 Reg.5

s.144, enabling: SI 2002/536, SI 2003/507,
SI 2003/1229, SI 2003/2136, SI 2003/
2694, SI 2004/1515, SI 2004/1516

Sch.1A, applied: SI 2002/2113 Reg.6, SI
2004/530 Reg.4

Sch.1 para.4, enabling: SI 2002/2301

Sch.1A para.1, added: 2002 c.32 Sch.6

Sch.1A para.1, amended: SI 2002/2113 Reg.5

Sch.1A para.2, added: 2002 c.32 Sch.6

Sch.1A para.2, amended: SI 2002/2113 Reg.5

Sch.1A para.3, added: 2002 c.32 Sch.6

Sch.1A para.4, added: 2002 c.32 Sch.6

Sch.1A para.5, added: 2002 c.32 Sch.6

Sch.1A para.6, added: 2002 c.32 Sch.6

Sch.1A para.7, added: 2002 c.32 Sch.6

Sch.1A para.8, added: 2002 c.32 Sch.6

Sch.1A para.9, added: 2002 c.32 Sch.6

Sch.1A para.10, added: 2002 c.32 Sch.6

Sch.1A para.11, added: 2002 c.32 Sch.6

Sch.1A para.12, added: 2002 c.32 Sch.6

Sch.1A para.13, added: 2002 c.32 Sch.6

Sch.1A para.13, amended: SI 2002/2113
Reg.5

Sch.1A para.13, applied: SI 2002/2113 Reg.6

Sch.1A para.14, added: 2002 c.32 Sch.6

Sch.1A para.15, added: 2002 c.32 Sch.6

Sch.1A para.16, added: 2002 c.32 Sch.6

Sch.1A para.17, added: 2002 c.32 Sch.6

Sch.1A para.17, applied: SI 2004/530 Reg.5

Sch.1A para.18, added: 2002 c.32 Sch.6

1998–cont.

**31. School Standards and Framework Act
1998**–*cont.*

Sch.1A para.18, applied: SI 2004/530 Reg.16

Sch.1A para.19, added: 2002 c.32 Sch.6

Sch.1A para.19, enabling: SI 2004/530

Sch.3, applied: SI 2002/906 Art.13, Art.14, SI
2003/1200 Sch.2 para.23

Sch.3 Part II, amended: SI 2002/906 Art.9

Sch.3 Part II para.3, applied: SI 2002/906
Art.15

Sch.3 Part II para.3, referred to: SI 2002/906
Art.15

Sch.3 Part II para.3, substituted: SI 2002/906
Art.5

Sch.3 Part II para.4, amended: 2002 c.32
Sch.21 para.114, SI 2002/906 Art.6

Sch.3 Part II para.5, applied: SI 2002/906
Art.15, SI 2003/1200 Sch.2 para.23

Sch.3 Part II para.5, varied: SI 2002/906
Art.14

Sch.3 Part II para.5, enabling: SI 2002/1720,
SI 2003/507

Sch.3 Part II para.6, applied: SI 2003/1200
Sch.2 para.23

Sch.3 Part II para.6, varied: SI 2002/906
Art.14

Sch.4 para.5, repealed (in part): 2002 c.32
Sch.22 Part 3

Sch.4 para.5, enabling: SI 2003/507, SI
2004/3052

Sch.5 para.5, enabling: SI 2003/507, SI
2003/1229, SI 2004/3052

Sch.5 para.9, amended: SI 2002/1397 Sch.1
para.14

Sch.6, applied: SI 2003/1041 Reg.7

Sch.6, referred to: 2002 c.32 s.74

Sch.6 Part I para.2, amended: 2002 c.32
Sch.10 para.2

Sch.6 Part I para.2, enabling: SI 2003/1229

Sch.6 Part I para.3, amended: 2002 c.32
Sch.10 para.3, Sch.21 para.115, Sch.22
Part 3

Sch.6 Part I para.3, applied: SI 2002/2898
Reg.4, SI 2003/507 Reg.11, Reg.20, SI
2003/1041 Reg.6, Reg.8

Sch.6 Part I para.3, referred to: SI 2003/507
Reg.11

Sch.6 Part I para.3, repealed (in part): 2004
c.31 Sch.5 Part 1

Sch.6 Part I para.3, enabling: SI 2003/507, SI
2003/1229, SI 2004/3052

Sch.6 Part I para.4, amended: 2002 c.32
Sch.10 para.4, Sch.21 para.115, Sch.22
Part 3

Sch.6 Part I para.4, applied: SI 2003/1041
Reg.8

Sch.6 Part I para.4, enabling: SI 2003/1229

Sch.6 Part I para.5, amended: 2002 c.32
Sch.10 para.5

1998–cont.

31. School Standards and Framework Act 1998–cont.

Sch.6 Part I para.5, applied: SI 2002/928 Sch.2, SI 2002/2898 Reg.4, SI 2003/507 Reg.20, SI 2003/1041 Reg.6, Reg.8, SI 2003/1377 Reg.17

Sch.6 Part I para.5, referred to: SI 2003/507 Reg.20

Sch.6 Part I para.5, enabling: SI 2003/1229

Sch.6 Part II, applied: 2002 c.32 s.186, s.192

Sch.6 Part II para.7, enabling: SI 2004/908

Sch.6 Part II para.8, repealed (in part): 2004 c.31 Sch.5 Part 1

Sch.6 Part II para.8, enabling: SI 2004/908

Sch.6 Part II para.10, amended: 2002 c.32 Sch.10 para.6, Sch.22 Part 3

Sch.6 Part II para.10, enabling: SI 2004/908

Sch.6 Part III, applied: 2002 c.32 s.193

Sch.6 Part III para.12, amended: 2002 c.32 Sch.21 para.115

Sch.6 Part IV para.16, applied: 2002 c.32 Sch.8 para.7

Sch.6 Part IV para.17, applied: 2002 c.32 Sch.8 para.8

Sch.6 Part IV para.19, applied: 2002 c.32 Sch.8 para.8

Sch.7, referred to: 2002 c.32 s.74

Sch.7 Part II para.2, applied: 2002 c.32 s.71

Sch.7 Part II para.3, applied: 2002 c.32 s.71

Sch.7 Part II para.4, applied: 2002 c.32 s.71

Sch.7 Part III para.5, applied: 2002 c.32 s.71, s.74, SI 2002/3199 Reg.1, SI 2003/453 Reg.1

Sch.7 Part III para.5, enabling: SI 2004/908

Sch.7 Part IV para.7, amended: 2002 c.32 Sch.10 para.8

Sch.7 Part IV para.7, applied: 2002 c.32 s.71

Sch.7 Part IV para.7, enabling: SI 2003/1229

Sch.7 Part IV para.8, amended: 2002 c.32 Sch.10 para.9, Sch.21 para.116

Sch.7 Part IV para.8, applied: 2002 c.32 s.71

Sch.7 Part IV para.8, enabling: SI 2003/1229, SI 2004/3052

Sch.7 Part IV para.9, amended: 2002 c.32 Sch.10 para.10

Sch.7 Part IV para.9, applied: 2002 c.32 s.71

Sch.7 Part IV para.9, enabling: SI 2004/3052

Sch.7 Part IV para.10, applied: 2002 c.32 s.71

Sch.7 Part V, applied: 2002 c.32 s.193

Sch.7 Part V para.12, enabling: SI 2004/908

Sch.7 Part VI para.16, applied: 2002 c.32 s.71

Sch.7 Part VI para.17, applied: 2002 c.32 s.193

Sch.8, applied: SI 2002/432 Reg.11, SI 2003/507 Reg.28, SI 2003/1377 Reg.17, SI 2004/1576 Reg.19

Sch.8 para.2, enabling: SI 2003/2136

Sch.8 para.5, enabling: SI 2002/432, SI 2003/507, SI 2003/2136, SI 2004/1576

Sch.9 Part I para.1, repealed (in part): 2002 c.32 Sch.22 Part 3

1998–cont.

31. School Standards and Framework Act 1998–cont.

Sch.9 Part I para.2, repealed (in part): 2002 c.32 Sch.22 Part 3

Sch.9 Part I para.3, repealed (in part): 2002 c.32 Sch.22 Part 3

Sch.9 Part I para.4, repealed (in part): 2002 c.32 Sch.22 Part 3

Sch.9 Part I para.5, repealed (in part): 2002 c.32 Sch.22 Part 3

Sch.9 Part I para.6, repealed (in part): 2002 c.32 Sch.22 Part 3

Sch.9 Part I para.7, repealed (in part): 2002 c.32 Sch.22 Part 3

Sch.9 Part I para.8, repealed (in part): 2002 c.32 Sch.22 Part 3

Sch.9 Part II para.9, repealed (in part): 2002 c.32 Sch.22 Part 3

Sch.9 Part II para.10, amended: 2002 c.17 Sch.2 para.65

Sch.9 Part II para.10, repealed (in part): 2002 c.32 Sch.22 Part 3

Sch.9 Part II para.11, repealed (in part): 2002 c.32 Sch.22 Part 3

Sch.9 Part II para.12, repealed (in part): 2002 c.32 Sch.22 Part 3

Sch.9 Part II para.13, repealed (in part): 2002 c.32 Sch.22 Part 3

Sch.9 Part II para.14, repealed (in part): 2002 c.32 Sch.22 Part 3

Sch.9 Part II para.15, repealed (in part): 2002 c.32 Sch.22 Part 3

Sch.9 Part II para.16, repealed (in part): 2002 c.32 Sch.22 Part 3

Sch.9 Part II para.17, repealed (in part): 2002 c.32 Sch.22 Part 3

Sch.10 para.1, repealed (in part): 2002 c.32 Sch.22 Part 3

Sch.10 para.2, repealed (in part): 2002 c.32 Sch.22 Part 3

Sch.10 para.3, repealed (in part): 2002 c.32 Sch.22 Part 3

Sch.10 para.4, repealed (in part): 2002 c.32 Sch.22 Part 3

Sch.11 Part I para.1, repealed (in part): 2002 c.32 Sch.22 Part 3

Sch.11 Part I para.2, repealed (in part): 2002 c.32 Sch.22 Part 3

Sch.11 Part I para.3, repealed (in part): 2002 c.32 Sch.22 Part 3

Sch.11 Part I para.4, repealed (in part): 2002 c.32 Sch.22 Part 3

Sch.11 Part I para.5, repealed (in part): 2002 c.32 Sch.22 Part 3

Sch.11 Part II para.6, repealed (in part): 2002 c.32 Sch.22 Part 3

Sch.11 Part II para.7, applied: SI 2003/3118 Sch.2 para.33

Sch.11 Part II para.7, repealed (in part): 2002 c.32 Sch.22 Part 3

1998–cont.

31. **School Standards and Framework Act
1998**–*cont.*

Sch.11 Part III para.8, repealed (in part): 2002 c.32 Sch.22 Part 3

Sch.12 para.1, repealed (in part): 2002 c.32 Sch.22 Part 3

Sch.12 para.2, repealed (in part): 2002 c.32 Sch.22 Part 3

Sch.12 para.3, repealed (in part): 2002 c.32 Sch.22 Part 3

Sch.12 para.4, repealed (in part): 2002 c.32 Sch.22 Part 3

Sch.12 para.5, repealed (in part): 2002 c.32 Sch.22 Part 3

Sch.12 para.6, repealed (in part): 2002 c.32 Sch.22 Part 3

Sch.13 para.1, repealed (in part): 2002 c.32 Sch.22 Part 3

Sch.13 para.2, repealed (in part): 2002 c.32 Sch.22 Part 3

Sch.13 para.3, repealed (in part): 2002 c.32 Sch.22 Part 3

Sch.13 para.4, repealed (in part): 2002 c.32 Sch.22 Part 3

Sch.13 para.5, repealed (in part): 2002 c.32 Sch.22 Part 3

Sch.13 para.6, repealed (in part): 2002 c.32 Sch.22 Part 3

Sch.13 para.7, repealed (in part): 2002 c.32 Sch.22 Part 3

Sch.13 para.8, repealed (in part): 2002 c.32 Sch.22 Part 3

Sch.13 para.9, repealed (in part): 2002 c.32 Sch.22 Part 3

Sch.14 para.1, applied: SI 2002/377 Reg.34, Reg.35, SI 2002/928 Sch.2, SI 2003/453 Reg.30, Reg.31, SI 2003/3247 Reg.30, Reg.31, SI 2004/2507 Reg.5, Reg.6

Sch.14 para.1, enabling: SI 2002/377, SI 2003/453, SI 2004/2507

Sch.15, applied: 2002 c.32 s.35, s.37, SI 2002/928 Sch.2

Sch.15, referred to: 2002 c.32 s.25

Sch.16 para.1, repealed (in part): 2002 c.32 Sch.22 Part 3

Sch.16 para.2, repealed (in part): 2002 c.32 Sch.22 Part 3

Sch.16 para.3, repealed (in part): 2002 c.32 Sch.22 Part 3

Sch.16 para.4, repealed (in part): 2002 c.32 Sch.22 Part 3

Sch.16 para.5, repealed (in part): 2002 c.32 Sch.22 Part 3

Sch.16 para.6, repealed (in part): 2002 c.32 Sch.22 Part 3

Sch.16 para.7, repealed (in part): 2002 c.32 Sch.22 Part 3

Sch.16 para.8, repealed (in part): 2002 c.32 Sch.22 Part 3

Sch.16 para.9, repealed (in part): 2002 c.32 Sch.22 Part 3

1998–cont.

31. **School Standards and Framework Act
1998**–*cont.*

Sch.16 para.10, repealed (in part): 2002 c.32 Sch.22 Part 3

Sch.16 para.11, repealed (in part): 2002 c.32 Sch.22 Part 3

Sch.16 para.12, repealed (in part): 2002 c.32 Sch.22 Part 3

Sch.16 para.13, repealed (in part): 2002 c.32 Sch.22 Part 3

Sch.16 para.14, repealed (in part): 2002 c.32 Sch.22 Part 3

Sch.16 para.15, repealed (in part): 2002 c.32 Sch.22 Part 3

Sch.16 para.16, repealed (in part): 2002 c.32 Sch.22 Part 3

Sch.16 para.17, repealed (in part): 2002 c.32 Sch.22 Part 3

Sch.16 para.18, repealed (in part): 2002 c.32 Sch.22 Part 3

Sch.16 para.19, repealed (in part): 2002 c.32 Sch.22 Part 3

Sch.16 para.20, repealed (in part): 2002 c.32 Sch.22 Part 3

Sch.16 para.21, repealed (in part): 2002 c.32 Sch.22 Part 3

Sch.16 para.22, repealed (in part): 2002 c.32 Sch.22 Part 3

Sch.16 para.23, applied: SI 2002/1394 Reg.17

Sch.16 para.23, repealed (in part): 2002 c.32 Sch.22 Part 3

Sch.16 para.24, repealed (in part): 2002 c.32 Sch.22 Part 3

Sch.16 para.25, repealed (in part): 2002 c.32 Sch.22 Part 3

Sch.16 para.26, repealed (in part): 2002 c.32 Sch.22 Part 3

Sch.16 para.27, repealed (in part): 2002 c.32 Sch.22 Part 3

Sch.16 para.28, repealed (in part): 2002 c.32 Sch.22 Part 3

Sch.16 para.29, repealed (in part): 2002 c.32 Sch.22 Part 3

Sch.16 para.30, repealed (in part): 2002 c.32 Sch.22 Part 3

Sch.16 para.31, repealed (in part): 2002 c.32 Sch.22 Part 3

Sch.17 para.1, repealed (in part): 2002 c.32 Sch.22 Part 3

Sch.17 para.2, repealed (in part): 2002 c.32 Sch.22 Part 3

Sch.17 para.3, repealed (in part): 2002 c.32 Sch.22 Part 3

Sch.17 para.4, repealed (in part): 2002 c.32 Sch.22 Part 3

Sch.17 para.5, repealed (in part): 2002 c.32 Sch.22 Part 3

Sch.17 para.6, repealed (in part): 2002 c.32 Sch.22 Part 3

1998–cont.

31. School Standards and Framework Act 1998–cont.

Sch.17 para.7, repealed (in part): 2002 c.32 Sch.22 Part 3

Sch.17 para.8, repealed (in part): 2002 c.32 Sch.22 Part 3

Sch.17 para.9, repealed (in part): 2002 c.32 Sch.22 Part 3

Sch.17 para.10, repealed (in part): 2002 c.32 Sch.22 Part 3

Sch.17 para.11, repealed (in part): 2002 c.32 Sch.22 Part 3

Sch.17 para.12, repealed (in part): 2002 c.32 Sch.22 Part 3

Sch.17 para.13, repealed (in part): 2002 c.32 Sch.22 Part 3

Sch.17 para.14, repealed (in part): 2002 c.32 Sch.22 Part 3

Sch.17 para.15, repealed (in part): 2002 c.32 Sch.22 Part 3

Sch.17 para.16, repealed (in part): 2002 c.32 Sch.22 Part 3

Sch.17 para.17, repealed (in part): 2002 c.32 Sch.22 Part 3

Sch.17 para.18, repealed (in part): 2002 c.32 Sch.22 Part 3

Sch.17 para.19, repealed (in part): 2002 c.32 Sch.22 Part 3

Sch.17 para.20, repealed (in part): 2002 c.32 Sch.22 Part 3

Sch.17 para.21, repealed (in part): 2002 c.32 Sch.22 Part 3

Sch.17 para.22, applied: SI 2002/1394 Reg.17

Sch.17 para.22, repealed (in part): 2002 c.32 Sch.22 Part 3

Sch.17 para.23, repealed (in part): 2002 c.32 Sch.22 Part 3

Sch.17 para.24, repealed (in part): 2002 c.32 Sch.22 Part 3

Sch.17 para.25, repealed (in part): 2002 c.32 Sch.22 Part 3

Sch.17 para.26, repealed (in part): 2002 c.32 Sch.22 Part 3

Sch.17 para.27, repealed (in part): 2002 c.32 Sch.22 Part 3

Sch.17 para.28, repealed (in part): 2002 c.32 Sch.22 Part 3

Sch.17 para.29, repealed (in part): 2002 c.32 Sch.22 Part 3

Sch.17 para.30, repealed (in part): 2002 c.32 Sch.22 Part 3

Sch.18, applied: SI 2002/2952 Sch.1 para.4, SI 2002/3178 Reg.9, SI 2003/3227 Reg.11

Sch.18, referred to: SI 2002/2952 Sch.1 para.4

Sch.18 para.1, disapplied: SI 2002/2550 Reg.6, SI 2003/287 Reg.6

Sch.18 para.1, repealed (in part): 2002 c.32 Sch.22 Part 3

1998–cont.

31. School Standards and Framework Act 1998–cont.

Sch.18 para.1, varied: SI 2002/2550 Sch.1 para.1, Sch.1 para.2, Sch.1 para.3, SI 2003/287 Sch.1 para.1, Sch.1 para.2, Sch.1 para.3

Sch.18 para.2, repealed (in part): 2002 c.32 Sch.22 Part 3

Sch.18 para.2, varied: SI 2002/2550 Sch.1 para.1, Sch.1 para.4, SI 2003/287 Sch.1 para.1, Sch.1 para.4

Sch.18 para.3, repealed (in part): 2002 c.32 Sch.22 Part 3

Sch.18 para.4, repealed (in part): 2002 c.32 Sch.22 Part 3

Sch.18 para.4, varied: SI 2002/2550 Sch.1 para.1, SI 2003/287 Sch.1 para.1

Sch.18 para.5, repealed (in part): 2002 c.32 Sch.22 Part 3

Sch.18 para.5, varied: SI 2002/2550 Sch.1 para.1, SI 2003/287 Sch.1 para.1

Sch.18 para.6, repealed (in part): 2002 c.32 Sch.22 Part 3

Sch.18 para.6, varied: SI 2002/2550 Sch.1 para.1, SI 2003/287 Sch.1 para.1

Sch.18 para.7, repealed (in part): 2002 c.32 Sch.22 Part 3

Sch.18 para.8, repealed (in part): 2002 c.32 Sch.22 Part 3

Sch.18 para.9, repealed (in part): 2002 c.32 Sch.22 Part 3

Sch.18 para.10, repealed (in part): 2002 c.32 Sch.22 Part 3

Sch.18 para.10, varied: SI 2002/2550 Sch.1 para.5, SI 2003/287 Sch.1 para.5

Sch.18 para.11, repealed (in part): 2002 c.32 Sch.22 Part 3

Sch.18 para.12, repealed (in part): 2002 c.32 Sch.22 Part 3

Sch.18 para.13, repealed (in part): 2002 c.32 Sch.22 Part 3

Sch.18 para.14, repealed (in part): 2002 c.32 Sch.22 Part 3

Sch.18 para.14, varied: SI 2002/2550 Sch.1 para.6, SI 2003/287 Sch.1 para.6

Sch.18 para.15, repealed (in part): 2002 c.32 Sch.22 Part 3

Sch.18 para.16, amended: SI 2002/2550 Sch.1 para.2

Sch.18 para.16, repealed (in part): 2002 c.32 Sch.22 Part 3

Sch.18 para.16, varied: SI 2003/287 Sch.1 para.2

Sch.18 para.17, repealed (in part): 2002 c.32 Sch.22 Part 3

Sch.18 para.18, repealed (in part): 2002 c.32 Sch.22 Part 3

Sch.19, applied: 2002 c.32 s.80, s.101, SI 2003/800 Art.2, SI 2003/3259 Art.2, SI 2003/3262 Art.2, SI 2004/146 Art.2, SI 2004/150 Art.2, SI 2004/764 Art.2, SI 2004/1160 Art.2, SI 2004/1169 Art.2, SI 2004/1725 Art.2, SI 2004/1971 Art.2, SI

1998–cont.

31. School Standards and Framework Act 1998–*cont.*
Sch.19, applied:–*cont.*
2004/2474 Art.2, SI 2004/2476 Art.2, SI 2004/2477 Art.2, SI 2004/2478 Art.2, SI 2004/2564 Art.2, SI 2004/2565 Art.2, SI 2004/2698 Art.2, SI 2004/2892 Art.2
Sch.19 para.1, amended: 2002 c.32 Sch.21 para.117
Sch.19 para.4, amended: 2002 c.32 Sch.21 para.117
Sch.20, applied: SI 2002/928 Sch.2
Sch.22, applied: SI 2002/906 Art.13
Sch.22 Part I para.1, amended: 2002 c.32 Sch.21 para.118
Sch.22 Part I para.2, amended: 2002 c.32 Sch.21 para.118
Sch.22 Part I para.3, amended: 2002 c.32 Sch.21 para.118
Sch.22 Part II para.5, amended: 2002 c.32 Sch.21 para.118
Sch.22 Part II para.7, amended: 2002 c.32 Sch.21 para.118
Sch.22 Part III para.9, amended: 2002 c.9 Sch.11 para.37
Sch.22 Part IV para.11, added: SI 2002/906 Art.12
Sch.23 Part I para.1, repealed (in part): 2002 c.32 Sch.22 Part 3
Sch.23 Part I para.2, repealed (in part): 2002 c.32 Sch.22 Part 3
Sch.23 Part I para.2, varied: SI 2004/1743 Reg.5
Sch.23 Part II para.3, repealed (in part): 2002 c.32 Sch.22 Part 3
Sch.23 Part II para.4, repealed (in part): 2002 c.32 Sch.22 Part 3
Sch.23 Part II para.5, repealed (in part): 2002 c.32 Sch.22 Part 3
Sch.23 Part II para.5, enabling: SI 2003/1229
Sch.23 Part II para.6, repealed (in part): 2002 c.32 Sch.22 Part 3
Sch.23 Part III para.7, repealed (in part): 2002 c.32 Sch.22 Part 3
Sch.23 Part III para.8, repealed (in part): 2002 c.32 Sch.22 Part 3
Sch.23 Part III para.9, repealed (in part): 2002 c.32 Sch.22 Part 3
Sch.23 Part III para.10, repealed (in part): 2002 c.32 Sch.22 Part 3
Sch.23 Part IV para.11, repealed (in part): 2002 c.32 Sch.22 Part 3
Sch.24, applied: SI 2002/2952 Sch.1 para.3
Sch.24, referred to: SI 2002/2952 Sch.1 para.3
Sch.24 Part I para.1, applied: SI 2002/1895 Reg.17
Sch.24 Part I para.1, repealed (in part): 2002 c.32 Sch.22 Part 3
Sch.24 Part I para.2, applied: SI 2002/1895 Reg.17

1998–cont.

31. School Standards and Framework Act 1998–*cont.*
Sch.24 Part I para.2, repealed (in part): 2002 c.32 Sch.22 Part 3
Sch.24 Part I para.3, repealed (in part): 2002 c.32 Sch.22 Part 3
Sch.24 Part I para.4, repealed (in part): 2002 c.32 Sch.22 Part 3
Sch.24 Part I para.5, repealed (in part): 2002 c.32 Sch.22 Part 3
Sch.24 Part I para.6, repealed (in part): 2002 c.32 Sch.22 Part 3
Sch.24 Part I para.7, repealed (in part): 2002 c.32 Sch.22 Part 3
Sch.24 Part II para.8, repealed (in part): 2002 c.32 Sch.22 Part 3
Sch.24 Part II para.9, repealed (in part): 2002 c.32 Sch.22 Part 3
Sch.24 Part II para.10, repealed (in part): 2002 c.32 Sch.22 Part 3
Sch.24 Part II para.11, repealed (in part): 2002 c.32 Sch.22 Part 3
Sch.24 Part II para.12, repealed (in part): 2002 c.32 Sch.22 Part 3
Sch.24 Part II para.13, repealed (in part): 2002 c.32 Sch.22 Part 3
Sch.24 Part II para.14, repealed (in part): 2002 c.32 Sch.22 Part 3
Sch.24 Part II para.15, repealed (in part): 2002 c.32 Sch.22 Part 3
Sch.24 Part II para.16, repealed (in part): 2002 c.32 Sch.22 Part 3
Sch.24 Part II para.17, repealed (in part): 2002 c.32 Sch.22 Part 3
Sch.24 para.12, see *R. (on the application of Hounslow LBC) v School Admissions Appeal Panel for Hounslow LBC* [2002] EWCA Civ 900, [2002] 1 W.L.R. 3147 (CA), May, L.J.; see *R. (on the application of Khundakji) v Admissions Appeal Panel of Cardiff CC* [2003] EWHC 436, [2003] E.L.R. 495 (QBD (Admin Ct)), Richards, J.
Sch.25, applied: SI 2002/2952 Sch.1 para.3
Sch.25, disapplied: SI 2002/2952 Sch.1 para.3
Sch.25 para.1, repealed (in part): 2002 c.32 Sch.22 Part 3
Sch.25 para.2, repealed (in part): 2002 c.32 Sch.22 Part 3
Sch.25 para.3, repealed (in part): 2002 c.32 Sch.22 Part 3
Sch.25 para.4, repealed (in part): 2002 c.32 Sch.22 Part 3
Sch.25 para.5, repealed (in part): 2002 c.32 Sch.22 Part 3
Sch.25 para.6, repealed (in part): 2002 c.32 Sch.22 Part 3
Sch.25 para.7, repealed (in part): 2002 c.32 Sch.22 Part 3
Sch.25 para.8, repealed (in part): 2002 c.32 Sch.22 Part 3

1998–cont.

31. School Standards and Framework Act 1998–*cont.*

Sch.25 para.9, repealed (in part): 2002 c.32 Sch.22 Part 3

Sch.25 para.10, repealed (in part): 2002 c.32 Sch.22 Part 3

Sch.25 para.11, repealed (in part): 2002 c.32 Sch.22 Part 3

Sch.25 para.12, repealed (in part): 2002 c.32 Sch.22 Part 3

Sch.25 para.13, repealed (in part): 2002 c.32 Sch.22 Part 3

Sch.25 para.14, repealed (in part): 2002 c.32 Sch.22 Part 3

Sch.26 para.1, repealed (in part): 2002 c.32 Sch.22 Part 3

Sch.26 para.6, amended: 2002 c.32 Sch.14 para.1

Sch.26 para.6, repealed (in part): 2002 c.32 Sch.22 Part 3

Sch.26 para.8, amended: 2002 c.32 Sch.14 para.2

Sch.26 para.8, repealed (in part): 2002 c.32 Sch.14 para.2, Sch.22 Part 3

Sch.26 para.10, amended: 2002 c.32 Sch.14 para.5

Sch.26 para.10, applied: 2002 c.32 Sch.14 para.7, SI 2002/816 Reg.4, Sch.8 para.1, SI 2002/2953 Reg.6

Sch.26 para.15, repealed (in part): 2002 c.32 Sch.22 Part 3

Sch.28 Part I para.4, repealed (in part): 2002 c.32 Sch.22 Part 3

Sch.28 Part II para.6, repealed (in part): 2002 c.32 Sch.22 Part 3

Sch.28 Part II para.7, repealed (in part): 2002 c.32 Sch.22 Part 3

Sch.28 Part II para.8, repealed (in part): 2002 c.32 Sch.22 Part 3

Sch.30 para.3, repealed (in part): 2002 c.32 Sch.22 Part 3

Sch.30 para.13, referred to: 2003 c.26 s.128

Sch.30 para.13, repealed: 2003 c.26 Sch.8 Part 1

Sch.30 para.14, repealed (in part): 2002 c.32 Sch.22 Part 3

Sch.30 para.17, repealed (in part): 2002 c.32 Sch.22 Part 3

Sch.30 para.24, repealed: 2002 c.32 Sch.22 Part 1

Sch.30 para.25, repealed: 2002 c.32 Sch.22 Part 1

Sch.30 para.26, repealed: 2002 c.32 Sch.22 Part 1

Sch.30 para.27, repealed: 2002 c.32 Sch.22 Part 1

Sch.30 para.28, repealed: 2002 c.32 Sch.22 Part 1

Sch.30 para.44, repealed: 2002 c.32 Sch.22 Part 1

1998–cont.

31. School Standards and Framework Act 1998–*cont.*

Sch.30 para.47, repealed (in part): 2002 c.32 Sch.22 Part 3

Sch.30 para.56, repealed (in part): 2002 c.32 Sch.22 Part 3

Sch.30 para.74, repealed (in part): 2002 c.32 Sch.22 Part 3

Sch.30 para.85, repealed (in part): 2002 c.32 Sch.22 Part 3

Sch.30 para.86, repealed (in part): 2002 c.32 Sch.22 Part 3

Sch.30 para.87, repealed (in part): 2002 c.32 Sch.22 Part 3

Sch.30 para.88, repealed (in part): 2002 c.32 Sch.22 Part 3

Sch.30 para.89, repealed (in part): 2002 c.32 Sch.22 Part 3

Sch.30 para.90, repealed (in part): 2002 c.32 Sch.22 Part 3

Sch.30 para.133, repealed (in part): 2002 c.32 Sch.22 Part 3

Sch.30 para.144, repealed: 2004 c.31 Sch.5 Part 1

Sch.30 para.194, repealed (in part): 2002 c.32 Sch.22 Part 3

Sch.30 para.204, repealed (in part): 2002 c.32 Sch.22 Part 3

Sch.30 para.214, repealed (in part): 2002 c.32 Sch.22 Part 1

Sch.30 para.215, repealed: 2002 c.32 Sch.22 Part 2

Sch.32 Part II para.7, repealed: 2002 c.32 Sch.22 Part 1

32. Police (Northern Ireland) Act 1998

Part VII, referred to: 2003 c.6 s.34

s.19, see *Shields Application for Judicial Review, Re* [2003] UKHL 3, [2003] N.I. 161 (HL (NI)), Lord Bingham of Cornhill

s.22, see *Shields Application for Judicial Review, Re* [2003] UKHL 3, [2003] N.I. 161 (HL (NI)), Lord Bingham of Cornhill

s.25, see *Shields Application for Judicial Review, Re* [2003] UKHL 3, [2003] N.I. 161 (HL (NI)), Lord Bingham of Cornhill

s.25, amended: 2003 c.6 s.24

s.25, applied: SR 2002/95, SR 2002/100, SR 2003/68SI-BEGIN, SR 2003/60, SR 2003/184

s.25, enabling: SR 2002/385, SR 2003/184

s.26, applied: SR 2002/96, SR 2002/101, SR 2003/68SI-BEGIN, SR 2003/60

s.26, enabling: SR 2002/96, SR 2002/385

s.27, amended: 2002 c.1 Sch.3 para.12, Sch.4, 2002 c.29 Sch.11 para.34, 2003 c.6 s.20, s.25

s.29, applied: SI 2004/1127 Art.2

s.29, enabling: SI 2004/1127

s.35, referred to: 2004 c.20 s.64, s.65

1998–cont.

32. Police (Northern Ireland) Act 1998–*cont.*

s.36, see *Shields Application for Judicial Review, Re* [2003] UKHL 3, [2003] N.I. 161 (HL (NI)), Lord Bingham of Cornhill

s.41, applied: 2002 c.26 Sch.8 para.8

s.42, amended: 2002 c.26 Sch.12 para.61

s.50, amended: 2002 c.26 s.34

s.52, amended: 2002 c.26 s.34

s.55, amended: 2002 c.26 s.34, 2004 c.4 s.6, Sch.4

s.58, amended: 2002 c.26 Sch.13

s.58, repealed (in part): 2002 c.26 Sch.13

s.60A, added: 2003 c.6 s.13

s.61A, repealed: 2003 c.6 s.13, Sch.4

s.63, amended: SR 2002/414 Art.3, 2003 c.6 s.13

s.64, amended: 2004 c.4 s.6

s.66, amended: 2003 c.6 s.38

s.66, applied: 2003 c.44 Sch.17 para.56, SI 2004/702 Sch.4 para.8, SI 2004/1127 Art.2

s.66, varied: 2003 c.32 s.84

s.66, enabling: SI 2004/1127

s.67, amended: 2003 c.6 s.39

s.72, applied: SR 2003/60

Sch.4 para.15, repealed: SI 2004/702 Sch.8

33. Landmines Act 1998

s.3, amended: 2002 c.8 s.2

34. Private Hire Vehicles (London) Act 1998

Commencement Orders: SI 2003/580 Art.2; SI 2004/241 Art.2

applied: SI 2004/242 Reg.4, Reg.5

s.5, varied: SI 2003/655 Reg.8

s.6, varied: SI 2003/655 Reg.8

s.7, applied: SI 2004/242 Reg.4

s.12, varied: SI 2003/655 Reg.8

s.13, varied: SI 2003/655 Reg.7

s.14, disapplied: SI 2003/655 Reg.5

s.15, applied: SI 2003/655 Reg.5

s.16, applied: SI 2003/655 Reg.5

s.17, applied: SI 2003/655 Reg.6, SI 2004/242 Reg.6

s.20, applied: SI 2003/655 Reg.5, SI 2004/242 Reg.6

s.23, applied: SI 2004/242 Reg.3

s.36, varied: SI 2003/655 Reg.8

s.37, applied: SI 2003/655, SI 2003/3028

s.37, enabling: SI 2003/655, SI 2003/3028, SI 2004/242

s.40, enabling: SI 2003/580, SI 2004/241

35. Northern Ireland (Sentences) Act 1998

s.3, enabling: SI 2004/3009

Sch.2 para.7, amended: 2002 c.26 Sch.7 para.20

36. Finance Act 1998

referred to: 2004 c.12 Sch.5 para.9

1998–cont.

36. Finance Act 1998–*cont.*

s.9, repealed (in part): 2002 c.23 Sch.40 Part 1

s.30, applied: SI 2003/282 Reg.2

s.32, applied: 2004 c.20 s.44

s.32, enabling: SI 2003/1861

s.36, applied: SI 2003/282 Reg.2

s.42, amended: 2002 c.23 s.103

s.42, disapplied: 2002 c.23 s.65

s.43, referred to: 2002 c.23 Sch.22 para.11

s.44, repealed: 2002 c.23 Sch.40 Part 3

s.44, varied: 2002 c.23 s.64

s.45, repealed: 2002 c.23 Sch.40 Part 3

s.49, repealed: 2003 c.1 Sch.8 Part 1

s.50, repealed: 2003 c.1 Sch.8 Part 1

s.51, repealed: 2003 c.1 Sch.8 Part 1

s.52, repealed: 2003 c.1 Sch.8 Part 1

s.53, repealed: 2003 c.1 Sch.8 Part 1

s.55, repealed (in part): 2003 c.1 Sch.8 Part 1, 2004 c.12 Sch.42 Part 2

s.56, amended: 2004 c.12 Sch.12 para.15

s.57, repealed: 2004 c.12 Sch.42 Part 2

s.58, repealed: 2003 c.1 Sch.8 Part 1.8 Part 1

s.61, repealed: 2003 c.1 Sch.8 Part 1

s.63, repealed: 2003 c.1 Sch.8 Part 1

s.64, repealed: 2003 c.1 Sch.8 Part 1

s.65, repealed: 2003 c.1 Sch.8 Part 1

s.66, repealed: 2003 c.1 Sch.8 Part 1

s.67, repealed: 2003 c.1 Sch.8 Part 1

s.68, repealed: 2003 c.1 Sch.8 Part 1

s.69, repealed: 2003 c.1 Sch.8 Part 1

s.73, amended: 2004 c.12 Sch.42 Part 2

s.73, repealed (in part): 2004 c.12 Sch.42 Part 2

s.75, enabling: SI 2002/1974, SI 2002/3158, SI 2003/2747, SI 2004/1677, SI 2004/2996

s.82, repealed (in part): 2002 c.23 Sch.40 Part 3

s.92, repealed: 2004 c.12 Sch.42 Part 3

s.93, repealed: 2003 c.1 Sch.8 Part 1

s.94, repealed: 2004 c.12 Sch.42 Part 3

s.95, repealed: 2004 c.12 Sch.42 Part 3

s.96, repealed: 2004 c.12 Sch.42 Part 3

s.97, repealed: 2004 c.12 Sch.42 Part 3

s.98, repealed (in part): 2004 c.12 Sch.42 Part 3

s.99, repealed (in part): 2002 c.23 Sch.40 Part 3

s.108, repealed (in part): 2002 c.23 Sch.40 Part 3

s.109, repealed (in part): 2002 c.23 Sch.40 Part 3

s.110, repealed (in part): 2002 c.23 Sch.40 Part 3

s.118, amended: 2003 c.21 Sch.17 para.152

s.137, repealed (in part): 2003 c.14 Sch.43 Part 3

s.162, repealed (in part): 2003 c.14 Sch.43 Part 5

1998–cont.

36. Finance Act 1998–*cont.*

s.163, repealed (in part): 2002 c.23 Sch.40 Part 3

s.163, enabling: SI 2002/1971

Sch.3 para.9, repealed: 2004 c.12 Sch.42 Part 2

Sch.4 para.7, repealed: 2002 c.23 Sch.40 Part 3

Sch.6 para.1, repealed: 2002 c.23 Sch.40 Part 3

Sch.6 para.1, varied: 2002 c.23 s.64

Sch.6 para.2, repealed: 2002 c.23 Sch.40 Part 3

Sch.6 para.2, varied: 2002 c.23 s.64

Sch.6 para.3, repealed: 2002 c.23 Sch.40 Part 3

Sch.6 para.3, varied: 2002 c.23 s.64

Sch.6 para.4, repealed: 2002 c.23 Sch.40 Part 3

Sch.6 para.4, varied: 2002 c.23 s.64

Sch.6 para.5, repealed: 2002 c.23 Sch.40 Part 3

Sch.6 para.5, varied: 2002 c.23 s.64

Sch.6 para.6, repealed: 2002 c.23 Sch.40 Part 3

Sch.6 para.6, varied: 2002 c.23 s.64

Sch.6 para.7, repealed: 2002 c.23 Sch.40 Part 3

Sch.6 para.7, varied: 2002 c.23 s.64

Sch.6 para.8, repealed: 2002 c.23 Sch.40 Part 3

Sch.6 para.8, varied: 2002 c.23 s.64

Sch.6 para.16, repealed: 2002 c.23 Sch.40 Part 3

Sch.6 para.16, varied: 2002 c.23 s.64

Sch.7 para.1, amended: 2002 c.23 Sch.40 Part 3, 2004 c.12 Sch.42 Part 2

Sch.7 para.8, amended: 2002 c.23 Sch.40 Part 3

Sch.8 para.1, repealed: 2004 c.12 Sch.42 Part 2

Sch.8 para.2, repealed (in part): 2002 c.23 Sch.40 Part 3, 2004 c.12 Sch.42 Part 2

Sch.8 para.3, repealed: 2004 c.12 Sch.42 Part 2

Sch.8 para.4, repealed: 2004 c.12 Sch.42 Part 2

Sch.8 para.5, repealed: 2004 c.12 Sch.42 Part 2

Sch.8 para.6, repealed: 2004 c.12 Sch.42 Part 2

Sch.8 para.7, repealed: 2004 c.12 Sch.42 Part 2

Sch.9 Part I, repealed: 2003 c.1 Sch.8 Part 1

Sch.9 Part II para.1, repealed: 2003 c.1 Sch.8 Part 1

Sch.9 Part II para.2, repealed: 2003 c.1 Sch.8 Part 1

Sch.9 Part II para.3, repealed: 2003 c.1 Sch.8 Part 1

1998–cont.

36. Finance Act 1998–*cont.*

Sch.9 Part II para.4, repealed: 2003 c.1 Sch.8 Part 1

Sch.9 Part II para.5, repealed: 2003 c.1 Sch.8 Part 1

Sch.10, repealed: 2003 c.1 Sch.8 Part 1

Sch.13 Part I para.1, repealed (in part): 2004 c.12 Sch.42 Part 2

Sch.13 Part I para.21, repealed: 2004 c.12 Sch.42 Part 2

Sch.14 para.7, varied: 2003 c.14 Sch.34 para.12

Sch.15 para.1, repealed: 2004 c.12 Sch.42 Part 3

Sch.15 para.2, repealed: 2004 c.12 Sch.42 Part 3

Sch.15 para.3, repealed: 2004 c.12 Sch.42 Part 3

Sch.15 para.4, repealed: 2004 c.12 Sch.42 Part 3

Sch.15 para.5, repealed: 2004 c.12 Sch.42 Part 3

Sch.15 para.6, repealed: 2004 c.12 Sch.42 Part 3

Sch.15 para.7, repealed: 2004 c.12 Sch.42 Part 3

Sch.17 para.24, repealed: 2004 c.12 Sch.42 Part 2

Sch.18, applied: SI 2003/282 Reg.2

Sch.18 Part I para.1, amended: 2002 c.23 s.92

Sch.18 Part II para.3, applied: SI 2004/1864 Reg.8

Sch.18 Part II para.3, varied: 2004 c.12 s.101

Sch.18 Part II para.8, amended: 2002 c.23 s.92, Sch.17 para.5

Sch.18 Part II para.10, amended: 2002 c.23 Sch.14 para.2

Sch.18 Part II para.14, amended: 2002 c.23 Sch.40 Part 3

Sch.18 Part II para.20, applied: 2004 c.12 s.33, s.313

Sch.18 Part II para.20, varied: 2004 c.12 s.101

Sch.18 Part III para.22, amended: 2004 c.12 Sch.12 para.16

Sch.18 Part III para.23, applied: 2004 c.12 s.33

Sch.18 Part III para.23, disapplied: 2004 c.12 s.33

Sch.18 Part IV para.25, amended: 2004 c.12 Sch.5 para.10

Sch.18 Part IV para.32, referred to: 2002 c.23 Sch.13 para.18

Sch.18 Part V para.36, applied: 2002 c.23 Sch.29 para.70

Sch.18 Part V para.37, applied: 2002 c.23 Sch.29 para.70

Sch.18 Part V para.40, referred to: 2002 c.23 Sch.29 para.70

Sch.18 Part V para.41, referred to: 2002 c.23 Sch.29 para.70

1998–cont.

36. Finance Act 1998–*cont.*

Sch.18 Part VI para.52, amended: 2002 c.23 Sch.14 para.3

Sch.18 para.17, see *Lessex Ltd v Spence (Inspector of Taxes)* [2004] S.T.C. (S.C.D.) 79 (Sp Comm), David Williams

Sch.18 para.24, see *Hallamshire Estates Ltd v Walford (Inspector of Taxes)* [2004] S.T.C. (S.C.D.) 330 (Sp Comm), John F Avery Jones; see *Spring Salmon & Seafood Ltd v Advocate General for Scotland* [2004] S.T.C. 444 (OH), Lady Smith

Sch.18 para.25, see *Hallamshire Estates Ltd v Walford (Inspector of Taxes)* [2004] S.T.C. (S.C.D.) 330 (Sp Comm), John F Avery Jones

Sch.18 para.27, see *Alan Porter Ltd v Kingston (Inspector of Taxes)* [2004] S.T.C. (S.C.D.) 147 (Sp Comm), John F Avery Jones; see *Meditor Capital Management Ltd v Feighan (Inspector of Taxes)* [2004] S.T.C. (S.C.D.) 273 (Sp Comm), Julian Ghosh

Sch.18 Part IXC para.83M, added: 2002 c.23 Sch.14 para.4

Sch.18 Part IXC para.83N, added: 2002 c.23 Sch.14 para.4

Sch.18 Part IXC para.83O, added: 2002 c.23 Sch.14 para.4

Sch.18 Part IXC para.83P, added: 2002 c.23 Sch.14 para.4

Sch.18 Part IXC para.83Q, added: 2002 c.23 Sch.14 para.4

Sch.18 Part IXC para.83R, added: 2002 c.23 Sch.14 para.4

Sch.21 para.6, repealed (in part): 2002 c.23 Sch.40 Part 3

37. Crime and Disorder Act 1998

see *R. v Haye (Conrad)* [2002] EWCA Crim 2476, [2003] Crim. L.R. 287 (CA (Crim Div)), Potter, L.J.

disapplied: 2004 c.34 s.270

referred to: SI 2002/2782 r.2, SI 2002/2784 r.2, 2003 c.13 Sch.2 Part 13, 2004 c.9 Sch.2 Part 12

Part I c.I, referred to: 2003 c.44

s.1, see *Nottingham City Council v Thames* [2002] EWCA Civ 1098, [2003] H.L.R. 14 (CA), Ward, L.J.; see *R. (on the application of Chief Constable of West Midlands) v Birmingham Magistrates Court* [2002] EWHC 1087, Times, June 5, 2002 (QBD (Admin Ct)), Sedley, L.J.; see *R. (on the application of M (A Child)) v Sheffield Magistrates Court* [2004] EWHC 1830, [2004] 3 F.C.R. 281 (QBD (Admin Ct)), Newman, J.; see *R. (on the application of McCann) v Manchester Crown Court* [2002] UKHL 39, [2003] 1 A.C. 787 (HL), Lord Steyn; see *R. (on the application of Walkling) v DPP* [2003] EWHC 3139, (2004) 168 J.P. 65 (QBD (Admin Ct)), Stanley Burnton, J.

1998–cont.

37. Crime and Disorder Act 1998–*cont.*

s.1, amended: 2002 c.30 s.61, Sch.8, 2003 c.20 Sch.5 para.4, 2003 c.38 s.85, Sch.3, SI 2004/1573 Art.12

s.1, applied: 2002 c.30 s.50, s.61, Sch.4 para.3, Sch.4 para.4, Sch.5 para.3, SI 2002/2784 r.4, r.5, r.6, SI 2004/915 Sch.1 para.3

s.1, repealed (in part): 2002 c.30 s.61, Sch.8

s.1, varied: 2003 c.20 Sch.5 para.4

s.1A, added: 2002 c.30 s.62

s.1AA, added: 2003 c.44 s.322

s.1AB, added: 2003 c.44 s.322

s.1B, added: 2002 c.30 s.63

s.1B, amended: 2003 c.38 s.85

s.1C, see *C v Sunderland Youth Court* [2003] EWHC 2385, [2004] 1 Cr.App.R.(S.) 76 (QBD (Admin Ct)), Sullivan, J.

s.1C, added: 2002 c.30 s.64

s.1C, amended: 2003 c.38 s.86

s.1C, applied: SI 2002/2784 r.4, r.6

s.1D, added: 2002 c.30 s.65

s.1D, amended: 2002 c.30 s.65

s.1D, applied: SI 2002/2784 r.4, r.5, r.6

s.1E, added: 2002 c.30 s.66

s.1E, amended: 2002 c.30 s.66, 2003 c.38 s.85

s.1E, applied: SI 2002/2784 r.7

s.2, see *Hopson v Chief Constable of North Wales* [2002] EWHC 2430, Times, November 1, 2002 (QBD (Admin Ct)), Davis, J.

s.2, amended: 2002 c.30 s.67

s.2, applied: 2002 c.30 s.67, SI 2002/2782 r.5, 2003 c.42 s.81, s.88, s.108, s.113

s.2, referred to: SI 2002/2782 r.4

s.2, repealed: 2003 c.42 Sch.7

s.2A, added: 2002 c.30 s.68

s.2A, applied: SI 2002/2782 r.5, 2003 c.42 s.81, s.88, s.109, s.113

s.2A, repealed: 2003 c.42 Sch.7

s.2B, added: 2002 c.30 s.69

s.2B, repealed: 2003 c.42 Sch.7

s.3, see *Hopson v Chief Constable of North Wales* [2002] EWHC 2430, Times, November 1, 2002 (QBD (Admin Ct)), Davis, J.

s.3, repealed: 2003 c.42 Sch.7

s.4, amended: 2002 c.30 s.65, s.68, 2003 c.42 Sch.7, 2003 c.44 s.323

s.5, amended: 2002 c.30 s.97, Sch.8, 2004 c.21 Sch.1 para.89

s.5, applied: 2002 c.30 s.97, SI 2004/118 Art.2, Art.3

s.5, enabling: SI 2004/118

s.6, amended: 2002 c.30 s.97

s.6A, added: 2002 c.30 s.98

s.8, see *R. (on the application of M) v Inner London Crown Court* [2003] EWHC 301, [2003] 1 F.L.R. 994 (QBD (Admin Ct)), Henriques, J.

1998–cont.

37. Crime and Disorder Act 1998–*cont.*

s.8, amended: 2003 c.38 s.18, 2003 c.44 Sch.34 para.1, Sch.37 Part 12, 2004 c.31 s.60, Sch.2 para.5

s.8, applied: SI 2004/247 r.7

s.9, amended: 2003 c.38 s.85, 2003 c.44 Sch.34 para.2

s.9, varied: 2003 c.38 s.21, s.27

s.10, varied: 2003 c.38 s.22, s.28

s.11, amended: 2004 c.31 s.60

s.12, repealed (in part): 2004 c.31 Sch.5 Part 6

s.15, applied: 2002 c.30 Sch.4 para.4B

s.15, varied: 2002 c.30 Sch.4 para.4B

s.16, amended: 2002 c.30 s.75, 2003 c.20 Sch.5 para.4, SI 2004/1573 Art.12

s.16, varied: 2003 c.20 Sch.5 para.4

s.17, amended: 2002 c.30 s.97, 2004 c.21 Sch.1 para.89

s.18, amended: 2003 c.44 s.323, Sch.32 para.88

s.18, repealed (in part): 2003 c.44 Sch.32 para.88, Sch.37 Part 7

s.19, see *Moray Council v Hamilton* 2003 Hous. L.R. 83 (Sh Ct (Grampian, Highland and Islands)), PP Davies

s.19, amended: 2003 asp 7 s.44, s.45

s.19, applied: SSI 2002/321 Art.5

s.19, referred to: SSI 2004/455 r.2

s.19, repealed: 2004 asp 8 Sch.5

s.20, see *Chief Constable of Grampian v Beech* 2002 S.L.T. (Sh Ct) 106 (Sh Ct (Grampian, Highland and Islands)), DJ Cusine

s.20, amended: 2002 c.30 s.70

s.20, applied: 2002 c.30 s.70, 2003 c.42 s.81, s.88, s.108, s.109, s.113

s.20, repealed: 2003 c.42 Sch.7

s.21, amended: 2002 c.30 s.70, 2003 asp 7 s.44, s.45, 2003 c.42 Sch.6 para.38, Sch.7

s.21, repealed (in part): 2003 c.42 Sch.7, 2004 asp 8 Sch.5

s.21A, added: 2002 c.30 s.71

s.21A, repealed: 2003 c.42 Sch.7

s.22, amended: 2003 asp 7 s.44

s.22, repealed (in part): 2003 c.42 Sch.7, 2004 asp 8 Sch.5

s.22A, added: 2003 asp 7 s.83

s.22A, repealed: 2004 asp 8 Sch.5

s.23, see *Edinburgh City Council v Watson* 2002 Hous. L.R. 2 (Sh Ct (Lothian and Border)), AM Bell

s.28, see *DPP v M (A Minor)* [2004] EWHC 1453, [2004] 1 W.L.R. 2758 (QBD (Admin Ct)), Auld, L.J.; see *G v DPP* [2004] EWHC 183, (2004) 168 J.P. 313 (QBD (Admin Ct)), May, L.J.

s.28, applied: 2003 c.44 s.145, Sch.21 para.2

s.29, applied: 2003 c.42 Sch.5 para.58, 2003 c.44 s.145, Sch.15 para.58, Sch.21 para.2, SI 2003/2267 Art.2, SI 2004/1910 Sch.2

s.29, disapplied: 2003 c.44 s.145

1998–cont.

37. Crime and Disorder Act 1998–*cont.*

s.30, applied: 2003 c.38 s.43, 2003 c.44 s.145, Sch.21 para.2, SI 2003/2267 Art.2

s.30, disapplied: 2003 c.44 s.145

s.31, applied: 2003 c.42 Sch.5 para.59, 2003 c.44 s.145, Sch.15 para.59, Sch.21 para.2, SI 2003/2267 Art.2, SI 2004/1910 Sch.2

s.31, disapplied: 2003 c.44 s.145

s.32, applied: 2003 c.44 s.145, Sch.21 para.2, SI 2003/2267 Art.2

s.32, disapplied: 2003 c.44 s.145

s.32, repealed (in part): 2002 c.30 Sch.8, 2004 c.28 Sch.10 para.48, Sch.11

s.37, see *R. v Poulton (Sarah Jane)* [2002] EWCA Crim 2487, [2003] 4 All E.R. 869 (CA (Crim Div)), Rose, L.J.

s.38, amended: SI 2002/2469 Sch.1 para.25, 2003 c.38 s.29, 2003 c.44 s.323, Sch.32 para.89, Sch.37 Part 7

s.39, amended: SI 2002/2469 Sch.1 para.25, 2004 c.31 Sch.2 para.5

s.41, amended: SI 2002/2469 Sch.1 para.25

s.42, amended: SI 2002/2469 Sch.1 para.25

s.47, repealed (in part): 2003 c.44 Sch.37 Part 4

s.49, amended: SI 2004/2035 Sch.1 para.36

s.50, amended: 2003 c.44 Sch.37 Part 4, Sch.3 para.16

s.50A, added: 2003 c.44 Sch.3 para.17

s.51, see *Fehily v Governor of Wandsworth Prison* [2002] EWHC 1295, [2003] 1 Cr. App. R. 10 (QBD (Admin Ct)), Rose, L.J.; see *R. (on the application of CPS) v Bolton Magistrates Court* [2003] EWHC 2697, [2004] 1 W.L.R. 835 (QBD (Admin Ct)), Kennedy, L.J.; see *R. (on the application of Salubi) v Bow Street Magistrates Court* [2002] EWHC 919, [2002] 1 W.L.R. 3073 (QBD (Admin Ct)), Auld, L.J.; see *R. v Hoare (Jamie Matthew)* [2004] EWCA Crim 191, [2004] 2 Cr. App. R. (S.) 50 (CA (Crim Div)), Mantell, L.J.; see *R. v Webster (Christopher)* [2003] EWCA Crim 3597, [2004] 2 Cr. App. R. (S.) 25 (CA (Crim Div)), Pitchford, J.

s.51, applied: SI 2002/1688 r.2

s.51, substituted: 2003 c.44 Sch.3 para.18

s.51A, applied: 2004 c.28 s.6

s.51B, applied: 2003 c.44 s.43

s.52, see *Fehily v Governor of Wandsworth Prison* [2002] EWHC 1295, [2003] 1 Cr. App. R. 10 (QBD (Admin Ct)), Rose, L.J.

s.52, amended: 2003 c.44 Sch.3 para.69

s.52, applied: 2003 c.44 s.16

s.52A, added: 2003 c.44 Sch.3 para.19

s.52B, added: 2003 c.44 Sch.3 para.19

s.59, repealed: 2003 c.44 Sch.37 Part 7

s.60, repealed: 2003 c.44 Sch.37 Part 7

s.65, see *R. (on the application of F) v Crown Prosecution Service* [2003] EWHC 3266, (2004) 168 J.P. 93 (QBD (Admin Ct)),

1998–cont.

37. Crime and Disorder Act 1998–*cont.*

s.65–*cont.*

Jackson, J.; see *R. (on the application of U) v Commissioner of Police of the Metropolis* [2002] EWHC 2486, [2003] 1 W.L.R. 897 (QBD (Admin Ct)), Latham, L.J.

s.66, see *R. (on the application of F) v Crown Prosecution Service* [2003] EWHC 3266, (2004) 168 J.P. 93 (QBD (Admin Ct)), Jackson, J.; see *R. (on the application of U) v Commissioner of Police of the Metropolis* [2002] EWHC 2486, [2003] 1 W.L.R. 897 (QBD (Admin Ct)), Latham, L.J.

s.80, repealed: 2003 c.44 s.303, Sch.37 Part 7

s.81, repealed: 2003 c.44 s.303, Sch.37 Part 7

s.83, repealed: 2002 c.29 Sch.12

s.84, repealed (in part): 2002 c.30 Sch.8

s.96, applied: SSI 2003/441 Sch.1 para.20, SSI 2004/411 Sch.1 para.28

s.98, see *R. (on the application of SR) v Nottingham Magistrates Court* [2001] EWHC Admin 802, (2002) 166 J.P. 132 (QBD (Admin Ct)), Brooke, L.J.

s.98, amended: 2003 c.41 s.201

s.99, repealed: 2003 c.44 Sch.37 Part 7

s.100, repealed: 2003 c.44 Sch.37 Part 7

s.101, repealed (in part): 2003 c.44 Sch.37 Part 7

s.103, repealed: 2003 c.44 Sch.37 Part 7

s.104, repealed: 2003 c.44 Sch.37 Part 7

s.105, repealed: 2003 c.44 Sch.37 Part 7

s.114, amended: 2002 c.30 s.62, s.97

s.115, amended: 2002 c.30 s.97, SI 2002/2469 Sch.1 para.25, 2004 c.34 s.219

s.121, amended: 2003 c.44 Sch.37 Part 7, Sch.3 para.19, Sch.3 para.70

Sch.1, repealed: 2002 c.29 Sch.12

Sch.3 para.1, amended: 2003 c.44 Sch.3 para.20

Sch.3 para.2, see *Fehily v Governor of Wandsworth Prison* [2002] EWHC 1295, [2003] 1 Cr. App. R. 10 (QBD (Admin Ct)), Rose, L.J.

Sch.3 para.2, amended: 2003 c.44 Sch.36 para.73, Sch.3 para.20, SI 2004/2035 Sch.1 para.37

Sch.3 para.2, applied: 2004 c.28 s.6

Sch.3 para.2, repealed (in part): 2003 c.44 Sch.37 Part 4, Sch.3 para.20

Sch.3 para.3, amended: 2003 c.44 Sch.3 para.71

Sch.3 para.4, see *R. (on the application of CPS) v Bolton Magistrates Court* [2003] EWHC 2697, [2004] 1 W.L.R. 835 (QBD (Admin Ct)), Kennedy, L.J.

Sch.3 para.4, amended: 2003 c.44 Sch.3 para.20, Sch.3 para.72, SI 2004/2035 Sch.1 para.37

1998–cont.

37. Crime and Disorder Act 1998–*cont.*

Sch.3 para.5, amended: 2003 c.44 Sch.3 para.20

Sch.3 para.5, disapplied: 2003 c.44 s.84

Sch.3 para.5, repealed (in part): 2003 c.44 s.130, Sch.37 Part 6

Sch.3 para.6, see *R. v Nembhard (Shaun George)* [2002] EWCA Crim 134, (2002) 166 J.P. 363 (CA (Crim Div)), Keith, J.

Sch.3 para.6, amended: 2003 c.44 Sch.3 para.20

Sch.3 para.7, amended: 2003 c.44 Sch.3 para.20

Sch.3 para.8, amended: 2003 c.44 Sch.3 para.20

Sch.3 para.9, amended: 2003 c.44 Sch.3 para.20

Sch.3 para.10, amended: 2003 c.44 Sch.3 para.20

Sch.3 para.11, amended: 2003 c.44 Sch.3 para.20

Sch.3 para.12, repealed: 2003 c.44 Sch.37 Part 4, Sch.3 para.20

Sch.3 para.13, amended: 2003 c.44 Sch.37 Part 4, Sch.3 para.20

Sch.3 para.15, amended: 2003 c.44 Sch.3 para.20

Sch.7 para.50, repealed: 2003 c.44 Sch.37 Part 7

Sch.8 para.8, repealed: 2003 c.44 Sch.37 Part 4

Sch.8 para.11, repealed: 2003 c.44 Sch.37 Part 7

Sch.8 para.13, repealed (in part): 2003 c.44 Sch.37 Part 7

Sch.8 para.36, repealed: 2003 c.42 Sch.7

Sch.8 para.37, repealed: 2003 c.44 Sch.37 Part 4

Sch.8 para.40, repealed: 2003 c.44 Sch.37 Part 4

Sch.8 para.55, repealed: 2003 asp 13 Sch.5 Part 1

Sch.8 para.56, repealed: 2003 c.44 Sch.37 Part 7

Sch.8 para.57, repealed: 2003 c.44 Sch.37 Part 8

Sch.8 para.58, repealed: 2003 c.44 Sch.37 Part 7

Sch.8 para.59, repealed: 2003 c.44 Sch.37 Part 7

Sch.8 para.60, repealed: 2003 c.44 Sch.37 Part 8

Sch.8 para.65, repealed: 2003 c.44 Sch.37 Part 4

Sch.8 para.79, repealed: 2003 c.44 Sch.37 Part 7

Sch.8 para.80, repealed: 2003 c.44 Sch.37 Part 7

Sch.8 para.81, repealed: 2003 c.44 Sch.37 Part 7

1998–cont.

37. Crime and Disorder Act 1998–*cont.*

Sch.8 para.82, repealed: 2003 c.44 Sch.37 Part 7

Sch.8 para.83, repealed: 2003 c.44 Sch.37 Part 7

Sch.8 para.84, repealed: 2003 c.44 Sch.37 Part 7

Sch.8 para.86, repealed: 2003 c.44 Sch.37 Part 7

Sch.8 para.87, repealed: 2003 c.44 Sch.37 Part 7

Sch.8 para.88, repealed: 2003 c.44 Sch.37 Part 7

Sch.8 para.89, repealed: 2003 c.44 Sch.37 Part 7

Sch.8 para.90, repealed: 2003 c.44 Sch.37 Part 7

Sch.8 para.91, repealed: 2003 c.44 Sch.37 Part 7

Sch.8 para.93, repealed: 2003 c.44 Sch.37 Part 4

Sch.8 para.94, repealed: 2003 c.44 Sch.37 Part 7

Sch.8 para.97, repealed: 2003 c.44 Sch.37 Part 7

Sch.8 para.114, repealed: 2002 c.29 Sch.12

Sch.8 para.115, repealed: 2002 c.29 Sch.11 para.35

Sch.8 para.116, repealed: 2002 c.29 Sch.11 para.35

Sch.8 para.132, repealed: 2003 c.44 Sch.37 Part 7

Sch.8 para.135, repealed (in part): 2003 c.44 Sch.37 Part 7

Sch.8 para.144, repealed: 2003 c.42 Sch.7

Sch.9 para.8, repealed: 2002 c.29 Sch.12

38. Government of Wales Act 1998

applied: 2002 asp 11 s.21, SI 2002/1895, 2004 c.8 s.44

s.1, applied: SI 2002/1897 Art.3, Art.4, SI 2002/2143 Art.2

s.1, disapplied: SI 2002/1897 Art.3

s.2, applied: SI 2002/2905 Sch.1 para.2

s.4, applied: SI 2003/284 Art.3, Sch.5 para.22

s.5, applied: SI 2003/284 Sch.5 para.7, Sch.5 para.22, Sch.5 para.58

s.5, referred to: SI 2003/284 Sch.5 para.13, Sch.5 para.14, Sch.5 para.60

s.6, applied: SI 2003/284 Art.94, Sch.5 para.22, Sch.5 para.57, Sch.5 para.58

s.7, applied: SI 2003/284 Art.94, Sch.5 para.22, Sch.5 para.58

s.7, referred to: SI 2003/284 Sch.5 para.58

s.8, applied: SI 2003/284 Sch.5 para.66, Sch.5 para.68

s.9, applied: SI 2003/284 Art.86, Art.87, Art.88, Art.93, Art.95, Art.96, Art.107, Art.109, Sch.5 para.67, Sch.5 para.68

s.11, amended: 2002 c.24 Sch.3 para.6

s.11, referred to: SI 2002/834

1998–cont.

38. Government of Wales Act 1998–*cont.*

s.11, enabling: SI 2002/834, SI 2003/284

s.12, referred to: SI 2003/284 Sch.5 para.9, SI 2003/437

s.12, enabling: SI 2003/437

s.13, referred to: SI 2003/284 Sch.5 para.9

s.14, referred to: SI 2003/284 Sch.5 para.9

s.15, referred to: SI 2003/284 Sch.5 para.9

s.16, applied: 2003 c.1 s.293, s.294

s.18, applied: 2003 c.1 s.291

s.22, applied: 2002 c.32 s.208, s.211, 2004 c.5 s.55, SI 2004/1769 Reg.6

s.22, referred to: 2002 c.38 s.145

s.22, enabling: SI 2004/3044

s.24, enabling: SI 2004/3044

s.25, enabling: SI 2004/3137

s.27, amended: 2002 c.17 Sch.8 para.26, 2003 c.43 s.192

s.27, applied: SI 2003/150 Reg.3

s.27, repealed (in part): 2003 c.4 Sch.4

s.27, enabling: SI 2003/813, SI 2003/814

s.28, applied: SI 2004/803

s.28, referred to: SI 2002/784, SI 2004/803

s.28, enabling: SI 2002/784, SI 2004/803

s.29, applied: 2004 c.33 s.260

s.29, enabling: SI 2002/248, SI 2002/1080, SI 2002/3183, SI 2003/1246, SI 2003/1848, SI 2003/2901, SI 2004/706

s.35, applied: 2003 c.43 s.144

s.41A, added: 2004 c.23 Sch.2 para.43

s.44, applied: 2002 c.38 s.145

s.63, applied: SI 2002/920 Sch.1 para.4

s.63, referred to: SI 2002/920 Sch.1 para.2

s.66, applied: SI 2002/8, SI 2002/120, SI 2002/129, SI 2002/130, SI 2002/324, SI 2002/325, SI 2002/327, SI 2002/432, SI 2002/438, SI 2002/442, SI 2002/520, SI 2002/675, SI 2002/677, SI 2002/678, SI 2002/758, SI 2002/784, SI 2002/785, SI 2002/802, SI 2002/803, SI 2002/808, SI 2002/810, SI 2002/813, SI 2002/837, SI 2002/1038, SI 2002/1039, SI 2002/1090, SI 2002/1174, SI 2002/1350, SI 2002/1385, SI 2002/1387, SI 2002/1554, SI 2002/1661, SI 2002/1730, SI 2002/1735, SI 2002/1772, SI 2002/1796, SI 2002/1797, SI 2002/1806, SI 2002/1856, SI 2002/1857, SI 2002/1870, SI 2002/1875, SI 2002/1879, SI 2002/1880, SI 2002/1881, SI 2002/1885, SI 2002/1886, SI 2002/2023, SI 2002/2118, SI 2002/2127, SI 2002/2939

s.75, amended: 2003 c.44 Sch.26 para.50

s.81, amended: 2003 c.26 Sch.7 para.67, Sch.8 Part 1

s.86, amended: SI 2004/533 Art.6

s.90, amended: 2004 c.23 s.8

s.92, amended: 2004 c.23 s.9, Sch.4

s.92, repealed (in part): 2004 c.23 s.9, Sch.4

s.93, amended: 2004 c.23 s.6

s.93, repealed (in part): 2004 c.23 Sch.4

1998–cont.

38. Government of Wales Act 1998–cont.

s.93A, added: 2004 c.23 s.7

s.94A, added: 2004 c.23 s.10

s.95, substituted: 2004 c.23 s.11

s.96A, added: 2004 c.23 s.2

s.96B, added: 2004 c.23 s.2

s.96C, added: 2004 c.23 s.2

s.100, repealed (in part): 2004 c.23 Sch.2 para.44, Sch.4

s.101, amended: 2004 c.23 Sch.2 para.45

s.107, amended: 2002 c.26 Sch.7 para.6

s.110, amended: 2002 c.26 Sch.7 para.9

s.118, amended: 2003 c.4 Sch.3 para.10

s.119, applied: SI 2003/284 Art.136

s.144, amended: 2003 c.4 Sch.3 para.11, 2004 c.23 s.65, Sch.2 para.46, Sch.4

s.144, enabling: SI 2003/749

s.145, amended: 2004 c.23 Sch.2 para.47

s.145, applied: 2004 c.23 s.64

s.145, repealed (in part): 2004 c.23 Sch.2 para.47, Sch.4

s.145A, added: 2004 c.23 s.3

s.145A, applied: 2004 c.23 s.64

s.145B, added: 2004 c.23 s.4

s.145C, added: 2004 c.23 s.5

s.145C, applied: 2004 c.23 s.54

s.146A, added: 2004 c.23 s.1

s.148, repealed: 2002 c.17 Sch.9 Part 3

s.154, enabling: SI 2003/813, SI 2003/814

s.155, applied: 2004 c.36 s.31

s.155, referred to: SI 2002/676 Art.1, SI 2002/1897 Art.1

Sch.3 Part I para.1, enabling: SI 2004/3044

Sch.3 Part I para.3, enabling: SI 2004/3044

Sch.3 Part II para.6, applied: 2003 c.37 s.10

Sch.3 Part II para.9, enabling: SI 2004/3044

Sch.4 Part I, referred to: SI 2002/784, SI 2004/803

Sch.4 Part I, enabling: SI 2002/784, SI 2004/803

Sch.4 Part III para.17, repealed: SI 2002/253 Sch.5 para.15

Sch.5 para.11, amended: SI 2002/797 Art.2

Sch.5 para.12A, substituted: 2003 c.43 Sch.9 para.13

Sch.5 para.13, amended: 2003 c.4 Sch.4

Sch.5 para.20, amended: 2002 c.17 Sch.9 Part 1

Sch.5 para.20A, added: 2004 c.17 Sch.3 para.14

Sch.5 para.25A, added: 2002 c.17 Sch.5 para.42

Sch.5 para.35, repealed: 2004 c.17 Sch.4

Sch.5 para.39, repealed: 2003 c.43 Sch.13 para.9, Sch.14 Part 7

Sch.5 para.46, added: 2003 c.4 Sch.3 para.12

Sch.6 para.8, repealed (in part): 2004 c.23 Sch.2 para.48, Sch.4

Sch.7 para.8, repealed (in part): 2004 c.23 Sch.2 para.49, Sch.4

1998–cont.

38. Government of Wales Act 1998–cont.

Sch.8, applied: SI 2003/435 Sch.2 para.2

Sch.8 Part I para.1, applied: SI 2004/1861 Sch.1 para.56

Sch.8 Part I para.1, referred to: SI 2004/753 Sch.1 para.14

Sch.8 Part IV para.23, amended: 2002 c.26 Sch.7 para.3

Sch.8 Part IV para.24, amended: 2002 c.26 Sch.7 para.3

Sch.8 Part V para.30, amended: 2002 c.26 Sch.7 para.3

Sch.8 Part V para.34, enabling: SI 2003/1880

Sch.8 Part V para.36, enabling: SI 2004/1861, SI 2004/2351

Sch.9, applied: SI 2002/3146 Art.2

Sch.9 Part I para.12, repealed (in part): 2004 c.23 Sch.2 para.50, Sch.4

Sch.9 Part II para.14, amended: SI 2002/3146 Art.2, 2003 c.4 Sch.3 para.13

Sch.9 Part II para.14, enabling: SI 2002/3146

Sch.9 Part II para.15, amended: SI 2002/3146 Art.2

Sch.9 Part II para.15, enabling: SI 2002/3146

Sch.9 Part II para.26, amended: SI 2004/2359 Art.4

Sch.9 Part II para.27, amended: 2004 c.34 Sch.15 para.45, Sch.16, SI 2004/1823 Art.20

Sch.12 para.18, repealed: 2003 c.44 Sch.37 Part 10

Sch.15 para.16, repealed: SI 2002/1860 Sch.6

Sch.16 para.58, repealed: 2004 c.12 Sch.42 Part 2

Sch.16 para.99, repealed (in part): 2004 c.23 Sch.4

Sch.17 Part I para.1, amended: 2004 c.23 s.65, Sch.4

Sch.17 Part II para.12, amended: 2002 c.17 Sch.9 Part 1

Sch.17 Part II para.12A, added: 2002 c.17 Sch.5 para.42

Sch.17 Part II para.14A, added: 2004 c.23 Sch.2 para.51

39. National Minimum Wage Act 1998

see *Inland Revenue Commissioners v Post Office Ltd* [2003] I.C.R. 546 (EAT), Burton, J.

s.1, see *Inland Revenue Commissioners v Bebb Travel Plc* [2003] EWCA Civ 563, [2003] 3 All E.R. 546 (CA), Ward, L.J.

s.1, enabling: SI 2002/1999, SI 2003/1923, SI 2004/1930

s.2, enabling: SI 2002/1999, SI 2003/1923, SI 2004/1161, SI 2004/1930

s.3, enabling: SI 2002/1999, SI 2003/1923, SI 2004/1930

s.8, applied: SI 2003/409 Sch.1 Part I

s.8, repealed (in part): 2004 c.14 Sch.1 Part 8

s.14, amended: 2004 c.33 Sch.27 para.155

CAP.

1998–cont.

39. National Minimum Wage Act 1998–cont.

s.15, amended: 2004 c.24 Sch.1 para.40

s.16, amended: 2004 c.24 Sch.1 para.41

s.16A, added: 2004 c.24 s.44

s.19, see *Inland Revenue Commissioners v Bebb Travel Plc* [2002] 4 All E.R. 534 (EAT), Judge Reid Q.C.; see *Inland Revenue Commissioners v Bebb Travel Plc* [2003] EWCA Civ 563, [2003] 3 All E.R. 546 (CA), Ward, L.J.

s.19, amended: 2003 c.8 s.1, 2004 c.24 s.45, s.46

s.19, applied: SI 2004/1861 Reg.14

s.19, disapplied: 2004 c.24 s.45, s.46

s.19, referred to: 2003 c.8 s.2

s.20, applied: SI 2004/1861 Reg.14

s.22, amended: 2004 c.24 s.46

s.22, applied: SI 2004/1861 Reg.14

s.22, disapplied: 2004 c.24 s.46

s.22A, added: 2004 c.24 s.46

s.22B, added: 2004 c.24 s.46

s.22C, added: 2004 c.24 s.46

s.22D, added: 2004 c.24 s.46

s.22E, added: 2004 c.24 s.46

s.22F, added: 2004 c.24 s.46

s.24, applied: 2002 c.22 Sch.3, Sch.4, Sch.5, SI 2003/2902 Sch.2, Sch.3, Sch.4

s.45, added: 2003 c.39 Sch.8 para.382

s.45A, added: 2003 c.39 Sch.8 para.382

s.47, enabling: SSI 2003/283

s.49, applied: SI 2004/754 Art.2, Art.3

s.49, enabling: SI 2004/754, SI 2004/2515

s.51, applied: SI 2002/1999, SI 2003/1923, SI 2004/1161

s.51, enabling: SI 2002/1999, SI 2003/1923, SI 2004/1161, SI 2004/1930

Sch.2 Part I para.4, repealed (in part): 2004 c.14 Sch.1 Part 8

Sch.2 Part I para.5, repealed (in part): SI 2004/2178 Sch.1 Part I

Sch.2 Part I para.6, repealed: 2004 c.14 Sch.1 Part 8

Sch.2 Part I para.7, repealed (in part): 2004 c.14 Sch.1 Part 8

Sch.2 Part II para.15, repealed (in part): SSI 2004/384 Sch.1

41. Competition Act 1998

Commencement Orders: SI 2004/1261 Reg.6, Sch.1 para.51

see *Aberdeen Journals Ltd v Director General of Fair Trading* [2002] CAT 4, [2002] Comp. A.R. 167 (Competition Commission Appeal Tribunal), Sir Christopher Bellamy Q.C. (President); see *Argos Ltd v Director General of Fair Trading (Witness Statements: Admissibility)* [2003] CAT 10, [2003] Comp. A.R. 329 (Competition Appeal Tribunal), Sir Christopher Bellamy (President); see *Argos Ltd v Office of Fair Trading (Case Management: Witness*

CAP.

1998–cont.

41. Competition Act 1998–cont.

see–cont.

Statements) [2003] CAT 16, [2004] Comp. A.R. 80 (Competition Appeal Tribunal), Sir Christopher Bellamy (President); see *BetterCare Group Ltd v Director General of Fair Trading* [2002] CAT 7, [2002] Comp. A.R. 299 (Competition Commission Appeal Tribunal), Sir Christopher Bellamy Q.C. (President); see *Leeds City Council v Watkins* [2003] EWHC 598, [2003] U.K.C.L.R. 467 (Ch D), Peter Smith, J.; see *Napp Pharmaceutical Holdings Ltd v Director General of Fair Trading (No.4)* [2002] CAT 1, [2002] Comp. A.R. 13 (CCAT), Sir Christopher Bellamy Q.C. (President)

applied: 2002 c.40 s.209, Sch.14, Sch.15, 2003 c.21 s.94, s.317, s.371, s.392, SI 2003/419 Art.42, Art.45, Art.63, SI 2004/352 Sch.6 para.2, SI 2004/2751 Sch.1 para.2

referred to: 2002 c.40 s.209, 2003 c.21 s.392, s.393

varied: 2003 c.21 Sch.18 para.57

see *Aberdeen Journals Ltd v Director General of Fair Trading* [2002] CAT 4, [2002] Comp. A.R. 167 (Competition Commission Appeal Tribunal), Sir Christopher Bellamy Q.C. (President); see *Argos Ltd v Director General of Fair Trading (Witness Statements: Admissibility)* [2003] CAT 10, [2003] Comp. A.R. 329 (Competition Appeal Tribunal), Sir Christopher Bellamy (President); see *Argos Ltd v Office of Fair Trading (Case Management: Witness Statements)* [2003] CAT 16, [2004] Comp. A.R. 80 (Competition Appeal Tribunal), Sir Christopher Bellamy (President); see *BetterCare Group Ltd v Director General of Fair Trading* [2002] CAT 7, [2002] Comp. A.R. 299 (Competition Commission Appeal Tribunal), Sir Christopher Bellamy Q.C. (President); see *Leeds City Council v Watkins* [2003] EWHC 598, [2003] U.K.C.L.R. 467 (Ch D), Peter Smith, J.; see *Napp Pharmaceutical Holdings Ltd v Director General of Fair Trading (No.4)* [2002] CAT 1, [2002] Comp. A.R. 13 (CCAT), Sir Christopher Bellamy Q.C. (President)

amended: SI 2004/1261 Sch.1 para.1

Part I, applied: 2002 c.40 s.209, 2003 c.21 s.369, s.371, s.393, Sch.11 para.6, SI 2003/419 Art.63, SI 2003/1372 r.56, SI 2004/1261 Reg.7, Reg.9, SI 2004/2751

Part I c.V, added: 2002 c.40 s.20

Part II, see *Aberdeen Journals Ltd v Director General of Fair Trading (Preliminary Hearing: Jurisdiction)* [2002] Comp. A.R. 1 (Competition Commission Appeal Tribunal), Sir Christopher Bellamy Q.C. (President)

1998—cont.

41. Competition Act 1998—*cont.*

Part II, applied: SI 2004/2751

Part IIA, applied: SI 2004/2751

Chapter I., see *Claymore Dairies Ltd v Office of Fair Trading (Stay of Proceedings)* [2003] CAT 18, [2004] Comp. A.R. 177 (Competition Appeal Tribunal), Sir Christopher Bellamy (President); see *Hasbro UK Ltd v Director General of Fair Trading (Application for Time Extension)* [2003] CAT 1, [2003] Comp. A.R. 47 (Competition Commission Appeal Tribunal), Sir Christopher Bellamy (President); see *Umbro Holdings Ltd v Office of Fair Trading (Permission to Intervene)* [2003] CAT 25, [2004] Comp. A.R. 214 (Competition Appeal Tribunal), Sir Christopher Bellamy (President)

Chapter II., see *Aberdeen Journals Ltd v Office of Fair Trading (Costs)* [2003] CAT 21, [2004] Comp. A.R. 189 (Competition Appeal Tribunal), Sir Christopher Bellamy (President); see *Aquavitae (UK) Ltd v Director General of Water Services (Admissibility of Appeal)* [2003] CAT 17, [2004] Comp. A.R. 117 (Competition Appeal Tribunal), Sir Christopher Bellamy (President); see *Freeserve.com Plc v Director General of Telecommunications (Application for Further Time Extension)* [2003] CAT 22, [2004] Comp. A.R. 199 (Competition Appeal Tribunal), Sir Christopher Bellamy (President); see *Pernod-Ricard SA v Office of Fair Trading (Admissibility: Initial Consideration)* [2003] CAT 19, [2004] Comp. A.R. 181 (Competition Appeal Tribunal), Sir Christopher Bellamy (President)

s.2, see *3 Com Europe Ltd v Medea Vertriebs GmbH* [2004] U.K.C.L.R. 356 (QBD), Master Yoxall; see *Intel Corp v VIA Technologies Inc* [2002] EWHC 1159, [2002] U.K.C.L.R. 576 (Ch D), Lawrence Collins J.; see *Vendo Plc v Adams* [2002] N.I. 95 (Ch D (NI)), Girvan, J.

s.2, applied: SI 2004/1261 Reg.6, Reg.7

s.2, disapplied: SI 2004/1260 Art.4

s.2, referred to: 2003 c.21 s.371

s.3, amended: 2002 c.40 Sch.25 para.38

s.3, applied: 2002 c.40 Sch.24 para.20

s.3, repealed (in part): 2002 c.40 Sch.26

s.4, amended: 2002 c.40 Sch.25 para.38

s.4, applied: SI 2004/1261 Reg.6

s.4, referred to: SI 2004/1261 Reg.8

s.4, repealed: SI 2004/1261 Sch.1 para.2

s.5, amended: 2002 c.40 Sch.25 para.38

s.5, applied: SI 2004/1261 Reg.8, Reg.10, SI 2004/2751 Sch.1 para.11

s.5, referred to: SI 2004/1261 Reg.6, Reg.8

s.5, repealed: SI 2004/1261 Sch.1 para.3

s.5, varied: SI 2004/1261 Reg.6

1998—cont.

41. Competition Act 1998—*cont.*

s.6, amended: 2002 c.40 Sch.25 para.38, SI 2004/1261 Sch.1 para.4

s.7, amended: 2002 c.40 Sch.25 para.38

s.7, repealed: SI 2004/1261 Sch.1 para.5

s.8, amended: 2002 c.40 Sch.25 para.38

s.9, amended: SI 2004/1261 Sch.1 para.6

s.9, applied: 2003 c.21 Sch.11 para.6, SI 2004/2751 Sch.1 para.7, Sch.1 para.12

s.9, referred to: SI 2004/2751 Sch.1 para.12, Sch.1 para.16

s.9, substituted: SI 2004/1261 Sch.1 para.6

s.10, amended: 2002 c.40 Sch.25 para.38, SI 2004/1261 Sch.1 para.7

s.10, applied: SI 2004/1261 Reg.7, SI 2004/2751 Sch.1 para.12

s.10, referred to: SI 2004/2751 Sch.1 para.12

s.11, amended: SI 2004/1261 Sch.1 para.8

s.12, amended: 2002 c.40 Sch.25 para.38

s.12, repealed: SI 2004/1261 Sch.1 para.9

s.12, enabling: SI 2004/1078

s.13, amended: 2002 c.40 Sch.25 para.38

s.13, applied: SI 2004/1261 Reg.9

s.13, repealed: SI 2004/1261 Sch.1 para.9

s.14, amended: 2002 c.40 Sch.25 para.38

s.14, applied: SI 2004/1261 Reg.9

s.14, repealed: SI 2004/1261 Sch.1 para.9

s.15, amended: 2002 c.40 Sch.25 para.38

s.15, repealed: SI 2004/1261 Sch.1 para.9

s.16, amended: 2002 c.40 Sch.25 para.38

s.16, repealed: SI 2004/1261 Sch.1 para.9

s.18, see *Aberdeen Journals Ltd v Director General of Fair Trading* [2003] CAT 11, [2003] Comp. A.R. 67 (Competition Commission Appeal Tribunal), Sir Christopher Bellamy (President); see *BetterCare Group Ltd v Director General of Fair Trading (Preliminary Hearing: Jurisdiction)* [2002] Comp. A.R. 9 (CCAT), Sir Christopher Bellamy Q.C. (President); see *Freeserve.com Plc v Director General of Telecommunications* [2003] CAT 5, [2003] Comp. A.R. 202 (Competition Appeal Tribunal), Sir Christopher Bellamy (President); see *Getmapping Plc v Ordnance Survey* [2002] EWHC 1089, [2002] U.K.C.L.R. 410 (Pat Ct), Laddie, J.; see *Intel Corp v VIA Technologies Inc* [2002] EWHC 1159, [2002] U.K.C.L.R. 576 (Ch D), Lawrence Collins, J.; see *Napp Pharmaceutical Holdings Ltd v Director General of Fair Trading (No.5)* [2002] EWCA Civ 796, [2002] 4 All E.R. 376 (CA), Buxton, L.J.; see *Suretrack Rail Services Ltd v Infraco JNP Ltd* [2002] EWHC 1316, [2003] U.K.C.L.R. 3 (Ch D), Laddie, J.

s.18, referred to: 2003 c.21 s.371

s.20, amended: 2002 c.40 Sch.25 para.38

s.20, repealed: SI 2004/1261 Sch.1 para.9

s.21, amended: 2002 c.40 Sch.25 para.38

1998–cont.

41. Competition Act 1998–*cont.*
s.21, repealed: SI 2004/1261 Sch.1 para.9
s.22, amended: 2002 c.40 Sch.25 para.38
s.22, repealed: SI 2004/1261 Sch.1 para.9
s.23, amended: 2002 c.40 Sch.25 para.38
s.23, repealed: SI 2004/1261 Sch.1 para.9
s.24, amended: 2002 c.40 Sch.25 para.38
s.24, repealed: SI 2004/1261 Sch.1 para.9
s.25, amended: 2002 c.40 Sch.25 para.38
s.25, substituted: SI 2004/1261 Sch.1 para.10
s.26, see *Pernod-Ricard SA v Office of Fair Trading (Admissibility: Initial Consideration)* [2003] CAT 19, [2004] Comp. A.R. 181 (Competition Appeal Tribunal), Sir Christopher Bellamy (President)
s.26, amended: 2002 c.40 Sch.25 para.38, SI 2004/1261 Sch.1 para.11
s.26, applied: SI 2004/2751 Sch.1 para.3
s.27, amended: 2002 c.40 Sch.25 para.38, SI 2004/1261 Sch.1 para.12
s.27, applied: SI 2004/1077 Reg.8
s.28, see *Office of Fair Trading v D* [2003] EWHC 1042, [2003] 2 All E.R. (Comm) 183 (QBD (Comm Ct)), Morison, J.
s.28, amended: 2002 c.40 s.203, Sch.25 para.38, SI 2004/1261 Sch.1 para.13
s.28, applied: SI 2004/1077 Reg.8
s.28A, added: SI 2004/1261 Sch.1 para.14
s.28A, applied: SI 2004/1077 Reg.8
s.29, amended: SI 2004/1261 Sch.1 para.15
s.29, applied: SI 2004/1077 Reg.8
s.30A, added: 2002 c.40 s.198
s.30A, amended: SI 2004/1261 Sch.1 para.16
s.31, amended: 2002 c.40 Sch.25 para.38
s.31, substituted: SI 2004/1261 Sch.1 para.17
s.31A, added: SI 2004/1261 Sch.1 para.18
s.31B, added: SI 2004/1261 Sch.1 para.18
s.31C, added: SI 2004/1261 Sch.1 para.18
s.31D, added: SI 2004/1261 Sch.1 para.18
s.31D, disapplied: 2003 c.21 s.371
s.31E, added: SI 2004/1261 Sch.1 para.18
s.32, amended: 2002 c.40 Sch.25 para.38, SI 2004/1261 Sch.1 para.19
s.32, applied: SI 2004/2751 Sch.1 para.8
s.32, repealed (in part): SI 2004/1261 Sch.1 para.19
s.33, amended: 2002 c.40 Sch.25 para.38, SI 2004/1261 Sch.1 para.20
s.33, applied: SI 2004/2751 Sch.1 para.8
s.33, repealed (in part): SI 2004/1261 Sch.1 para.20
s.34, amended: 2002 c.40 Sch.25 para.38
s.35, amended: 2002 c.40 Sch.25 para.38, SI 2004/1261 Sch.1 para.21
s.35, applied: 2002 c.40 Sch.4 para.22, SI 2004/2751 Sch.1 para.9
s.36, see *Aberdeen Journals Ltd v Director General of Fair Trading (Penalty: Calculation of Interest)* [2003] CAT 13, [2004] Comp. A.R. 69 (Competition

1998–cont.

41. Competition Act 1998–*cont.*
s.36–*cont.*
  Commission Appeal Tribunal), Sir Christopher Bellamy (President)
s.36, amended: 2002 c.40 Sch.25 para.38, SI 2004/1261 Sch.1 para.22
s.36, applied: SI 2003/1372 r.56, SI 2004/2751 Sch.1 para.8
s.36, enabling: SI 2004/1259
s.37, amended: 2002 c.40 Sch.25 para.38
s.38, amended: 2002 c.40 Sch.25 para.38, SI 2004/1261 Sch.1 para.23
s.38, disapplied: 2003 c.21 s.371
s.39, amended: 2002 c.40 Sch.25 para.38, SI 2004/1261 Sch.1 para.24
s.40, amended: 2002 c.40 Sch.25 para.38, SI 2004/1261 Sch.1 para.25
s.41, amended: 2002 c.40 Sch.25 para.38
s.41, repealed: SI 2004/1261 Sch.1 para.26
s.42, amended: SI 2004/1261 Sch.1 para.27
s.43, amended: SI 2004/1261 Sch.1 para.28
s.44, amended: 2002 c.40 Sch.25 para.38
s.45, amended: 2002 c.40 s.187, Sch.25 para.38
s.46, see *Aquavitae (UK) Ltd v Director General of the Office of Water Services* [2003] CAT 4, [2003] Comp. A.R. 197 (Competition Appeal Tribunal), Sir Christopher Bellamy (President); see *Aquavitae (UK) Ltd v Director General of Water Services (Costs)* [2003] CAT 23, [2004] Comp. A.R. 203 (Competition Appeal Tribunal), Sir Christopher Bellamy (President); see *BetterCare Group Ltd v Director General of Fair Trading (Preliminary Hearing: Jurisdiction)* [2002] Comp. A.R. 9 (CCAT), Sir Christopher Bellamy Q.C. (President); see *Claymore Dairies Ltd v Office of Fair Trading (Stay of Proceedings)* [2003] CAT 18, [2004] Comp. A.R. 177 (Competition Appeal Tribunal), Sir Christopher Bellamy (President)
s.46, amended: 2002 c.40 Sch.5 para.2, Sch.25 para.38, SI 2004/1261 Sch.1 para.29
s.46, applied: 2002 c.40 Sch.4 para.22, SI 2003/1372 r.61, SI 2004/1078 Reg.2, SI 2004/1261 Reg.8
s.46, repealed (in part): 2002 c.40 Sch.5 para.2, Sch.26
s.46, enabling: SI 2004/1078
s.47, see *BetterCare Group Ltd v Director General of Fair Trading (Admissibility of Appeal)* [2002] CAT 6, [2002] Comp. A.R. 226 (CCAT), Sir Christopher Bellamy Q.C. (President); see *BetterCare Group Ltd v Director General of Fair Trading (Preliminary Hearing: Jurisdiction)* [2002] Comp. A.R. 9 (CCAT), Sir Christopher Bellamy Q.C. (President); see *Freeserve.com Plc v Director General of*

1998–cont.

41. Competition Act 1998–*cont.*

s.47–*cont.*

Telecommunications (Admissibility of Appeal) [2002] CAT 8, [2003] Comp. A.R. 1 (Competition Commission Appeal Tribunal), Sir Christopher Bellamy (President); see *Pernod-Ricard SA v Office of Fair Trading (Admissibility: Initial Consideration)* [2003] CAT 19, [2004] Comp. A.R. 181 (Competition Appeal Tribunal), Sir Christopher Bellamy (President)

s.47, amended: SI 2003/767 Art.4, SI 2004/1261 Sch.1 para.30

s.47, applied: 2002 c.40 Sch.4 para.22, SI 2003/1372 r.61, SI 2004/1078 Reg.2, SI 2004/1261 Reg.8, SI 2004/2751 Sch.1 para.19

s.47, substituted: 2002 c.40 s.17

s.47, enabling: SI 2004/1078

s.47A, added: 2002 c.40 s.18

s.47A, applied: 2002 c.40 s.16, Sch.4 para.6, Sch.4 para.8, Sch.4 para.11, Sch.4 para.13, Sch.4 para.17, Sch.4 para.25, SI 2003/1372 r.18, r.30, r.32, r.33, r.49

s.47A, disapplied: 2002 c.40 Sch.4 para.12, Sch.4 para.17

s.47A, referred to: SI 2003/1372 r.31

s.47B, added: 2002 c.40 s.19

s.47B, applied: 2002 c.40 Sch.4 para.4, Sch.4 para.5, Sch.4 para.6, Sch.4 para.7, Sch.4 para.8, Sch.4 para.11, Sch.4 para.13, Sch.4 para.17, Sch.4 para.21, Sch.4 para.23, SI 2003/1372 r.18, r.30, r.33, r.45, r.47, r.48

s.47B, disapplied: 2002 c.40 Sch.4 para.6, Sch.4 para.12, Sch.4 para.17

s.48, applied: 2002 c.40 Sch.24 para.12

s.48, repealed: 2002 c.40 Sch.26

s.49, see *Napp Pharmaceutical Holdings Ltd v Director General of Fair Trading (No.5)* [2002] CAT 5, [2002] Comp. A.R. 259 (CCAT), Sir Christopher Bellamy, Q.C. (President)

s.49, amended: 2002 c.40 Sch.5 para.4

s.49, substituted: 2002 c.40 Sch.5 para.4

s.50, amended: 2002 c.40 Sch.25 para.38

s.50, applied: SI 2004/2751 Sch.1 para.14

s.50, enabling: SI 2004/1260

s.51, amended: 2002 c.40 Sch.25 para.38

s.51, applied: SI 2004/2751

s.51, disapplied: 2003 c.21 s.371

s.51, enabling: SI 2004/2751

s.52, amended: 2002 c.40 Sch.25 para.38, SI 2004/1261 Sch.1 para.31

s.53, amended: 2002 c.40 Sch.25 para.38

s.53, repealed: SI 2004/1261 Sch.1 para.32

s.54, amended: 2002 c.40 Sch.25 para.38, 2003 c.20 Sch.2 para.19, 2003 c.21 s.371, 2003 c.37 Sch.7 para.32, SI 2004/1261 Sch.1 para.33

s.54, referred to: SI 2004/1261 Reg.3, SI 2004/2751

1998–cont.

41. Competition Act 1998–*cont.*

s.54, varied: 2003 c.21 Sch.18 para.58

s.54, enabling: SI 2004/1077

s.55, referred to: 2003 c.20 s.115

s.55, repealed: 2002 c.40 Sch.26

s.56, repealed: 2002 c.40 Sch.26

s.57, amended: 2002 c.40 Sch.25 para.38

s.58, amended: 2002 c.40 Sch.5 para.5, Sch.25 para.38, SI 2004/1261 Sch.1 para.34

s.59, amended: 2002 c.40 s.20, Sch.5 para.6, Sch.25 para.38, Sch.26, 2003 c.21 s.371, SI 2004/1261 Sch.1 para.35

s.59, applied: SI 2004/2751 Sch.1 para.1

s.59, enabling: SI 2004/1078

s.60, amended: 2002 c.40 Sch.25 para.38

s.61, amended: 2002 c.40 Sch.25 para.38, Sch.26, SI 2004/1261 Sch.1 para.36

s.61, substituted: SI 2004/1261 Sch.1 para.36

s.62, amended: 2002 c.40 s.203, Sch.25 para.38, SI 2004/1261 Sch.1 para.36, Sch.1 para.37

s.62, repealed (in part): SI 2004/1261 Sch.1 para.37

s.62A, added: SI 2004/1261 Sch.1 para.38

s.62A, amended: SI 2004/1261 Sch.1 para.36

s.62B, added: SI 2004/1261 Sch.1 para.39

s.62B, amended: SI 2004/1261 Sch.1 para.36

s.63, amended: 2002 c.40 s.203, Sch.25 para.38, SI 2004/1261 Sch.1 para.36, Sch.1 para.40

s.64, amended: SI 2004/1261 Sch.1 para.36, Sch.1 para.41

s.65, amended: SI 2004/1261 Sch.1 para.36, Sch.1 para.42

s.65A, added: SI 2004/1261 Sch.1 para.43

s.65A, amended: SI 2004/1261 Sch.1 para.36

s.65B, added: SI 2004/1261 Sch.1 para.43

s.65B, amended: SI 2004/1261 Sch.1 para.36

s.65C, added: SI 2004/1261 Sch.1 para.44

s.65D, added: SI 2004/1261 Sch.1 para.44

s.65E, added: SI 2004/1261 Sch.1 para.44

s.65E, applied: SI 2004/2751 Sch.1 para.3

s.65F, added: SI 2004/1261 Sch.1 para.44

s.65G, added: SI 2004/1261 Sch.1 para.44

s.65H, added: SI 2004/1261 Sch.1 para.44

s.65I, added: SI 2004/1261 Sch.1 para.44

s.65J, added: SI 2004/1261 Sch.1 para.44

s.65K, added: SI 2004/1261 Sch.1 para.44

s.65L, added: SI 2004/1261 Sch.1 para.44

s.65M, added: SI 2004/1261 Sch.1 para.44

s.65N, added: SI 2004/1261 Sch.1 para.44

s.66, repealed: 2002 c.40 Sch.26

s.67, repealed: 2002 c.40 Sch.26

s.71, amended: 2002 c.40 Sch.25 para.38

s.71, applied: SI 2004/2751

s.71, enabling: SI 2004/1077, SI 2004/1078, SI 2004/1259, SI 2004/1260, SI 2004/2751

s.72, amended: SI 2004/1261 Sch.1 para.45

1998–cont.

41. Competition Act 1998–*cont.*

s.73, amended: SI 2004/1261 Sch.1 para.46

s.73, repealed (in part): SI 2004/1261 Sch.1 para.46

s.75A, added: SI 2004/1261 Sch.1 para.47

s.75A, applied: SI 2004/2751

s.75A, enabling: SI 2004/2751

Sch.1 Part I para.1, amended: 2002 c.40 Sch.25 para.38

Sch.1 Part I para.1, applied: SI 2004/1260 Art.6, SI 2004/2751 Sch.1 para.14

Sch.1 Part I para.2, amended: 2002 c.40 Sch.25 para.38

Sch.1 Part I para.3, repealed: 2003 c.21 Sch.19

Sch.1 Part I para.4, amended: 2002 c.40 Sch.25 para.38, SI 2004/1261 Sch.1 para.48

Sch.1 Part I para.4, applied: SI 2004/1260 Art.6, SI 2004/2751 Sch.1 para.14

Sch.1 Part I para.4, disapplied: SI 2004/1260 Art.6

Sch.1 Part I para.4, repealed (in part): SI 2004/1261 Sch.1 para.48

Sch.1 Part I para.5, amended: 2002 c.40 Sch.25 para.38

Sch.1 Part I para.5, varied: SI 2003/1397 Art.3, SI 2003/1592 Sch.4 para.15, SI 2004/3233 Art.5

Sch.1 Part II para.6, amended: SI 2004/1079 Sch.1 para.1

Sch.2 Part II para.2, repealed (in part): SI 2004/1261 Sch.1 para.49

Sch.2 Part II para.3, repealed (in part): 2004 c.27 Sch.8, SI 2004/1261 Sch.1 para.49

Sch.2 Part III para.5, amended: 2003 c.21 s.291, s.371

Sch.2 Part IV para.6, repealed: SI 2004/1261 Sch.1 para.49

Sch.3 para.2, amended: 2002 c.40 Sch.25 para.38

Sch.3 para.2, applied: SI 2004/2751 Sch.1 para.14

Sch.3 para.2, repealed: SI 2004/1261 Sch.1 para.50

Sch.3 para.9, amended: 2002 c.40 Sch.25 para.38, SI 2004/1261 Sch.1 para.50

Sch.3 para.9, applied: SI 2004/2751 Sch.1 para.14

Sch.4, applied: 2002 c.40 Sch.24 para.20

Sch.4 Part I para.1, referred to: SI 2003/1372 r.50, r.53

Sch.4 Part I para.1, repealed: 2002 c.40 Sch.26

Sch.4 Part I para.2, repealed: 2002 c.40 Sch.26

Sch.4 Part I para.3, repealed: 2002 c.40 Sch.26

Sch.4 Part I para.4, repealed: 2002 c.40 Sch.26

Sch.4 Part I para.5, repealed: 2002 c.40 Sch.26

1998–cont.

41. Competition Act 1998–*cont.*

Sch.4 Part I para.6, repealed: 2002 c.40 Sch.26

Sch.4 Part I para.7, repealed: 2002 c.40 Sch.26

Sch.4 Part II para.8, repealed: 2002 c.40 Sch.26

Sch.4 Part II para.9, repealed: 2002 c.40 Sch.26

Sch.4 Part II para.10, repealed: 2002 c.40 Sch.26

Sch.4 Part II para.11, repealed: 2002 c.40 Sch.26

Sch.4 Part II para.12, repealed: 2002 c.40 Sch.26

Sch.4 Part II para.13, repealed: 2002 c.40 Sch.26

Sch.4 Part II para.14, repealed: 2002 c.40 Sch.26

Sch.4 Part II para.15, repealed: 2002 c.40 Sch.26

Sch.4 Part II para.16, repealed: 2002 c.40 Sch.26

Sch.4 Part II para.17, repealed: 2002 c.40 Sch.26

Sch.4 Part II para.18, repealed: 2002 c.40 Sch.26

Sch.4 Part II para.19, repealed: 2002 c.40 Sch.26

Sch.4 Part II para.20, repealed: 2002 c.40 Sch.26

Sch.4 Part II para.21, repealed: 2002 c.40 Sch.26

Sch.4 Part II para.22, repealed: 2002 c.40 Sch.26

Sch.4 Part II para.23, repealed: 2002 c.40 Sch.26

Sch.4 Part II para.24, repealed: 2002 c.40 Sch.26

Sch.4 Part II para.25, repealed: 2002 c.40 Sch.26

Sch.4 Part II para.26, repealed: 2002 c.40 Sch.26

Sch.5, amended: 2002 c.40 Sch.25 para.38

Sch.5 para.1, amended: 2002 c.40 Sch.25 para.38

Sch.5 para.1, repealed: SI 2004/1261 Sch.1 para.51

Sch.5 para.2, amended: 2002 c.40 Sch.25 para.38

Sch.5 para.2, repealed: SI 2004/1261 Sch.1 para.51

Sch.5 para.3, amended: 2002 c.40 Sch.25 para.38

Sch.5 para.3, repealed: SI 2004/1261 Sch.1 para.51

Sch.5 para.4, amended: 2002 c.40 Sch.25 para.38

Sch.5 para.4, repealed: SI 2004/1261 Sch.1 para.51

1998–cont.

41. Competition Act 1998–*cont.*

Sch.5 para.5, amended: 2002 c.40 Sch.25 para.38, Sch.26

Sch.5 para.5, repealed: SI 2004/1261 Sch.1 para.51

Sch.5 para.6, amended: 2002 c.40 Sch.25 para.38

Sch.5 para.6, repealed: SI 2004/1261 Sch.1 para.51

Sch.5 para.7, amended: 2002 c.40 Sch.25 para.38

Sch.5 para.7, repealed: SI 2004/1261 Sch.1 para.51

Sch.6, amended: 2002 c.40 Sch.25 para.38

Sch.6 para.1, amended: 2002 c.40 Sch.25 para.38

Sch.6 para.1, repealed: SI 2004/1261 Sch.1 para.51

Sch.6 para.2, amended: 2002 c.40 Sch.25 para.38

Sch.6 para.2, repealed: SI 2004/1261 Sch.1 para.51

Sch.6 para.3, amended: 2002 c.40 Sch.25 para.38

Sch.6 para.3, repealed: SI 2004/1261 Sch.1 para.51

Sch.6 para.4, amended: 2002 c.40 Sch.25 para.38

Sch.6 para.4, repealed: SI 2004/1261 Sch.1 para.51

Sch.6 para.5, amended: 2002 c.40 Sch.25 para.38, Sch.26

Sch.6 para.5, repealed: SI 2004/1261 Sch.1 para.51

Sch.6 para.6, amended: 2002 c.40 Sch.25 para.38

Sch.6 para.6, repealed: SI 2004/1261 Sch.1 para.51

Sch.6 para.7, amended: 2002 c.40 Sch.25 para.38

Sch.6 para.7, repealed: SI 2004/1261 Sch.1 para.51

Sch.6A Part I para.1, added: SI 2004/1261 Sch.1 para.52

Sch.6A Part I para.2, added: SI 2004/1261 Sch.1 para.52

Sch.6A Part I para.3, added: SI 2004/1261 Sch.1 para.52

Sch.6A Part I para.4, added: SI 2004/1261 Sch.1 para.52

Sch.6A Part I para.5, added: SI 2004/1261 Sch.1 para.52

Sch.6A Part I para.6, added: SI 2004/1261 Sch.1 para.52

Sch.6A Part I para.7, added: SI 2004/1261 Sch.1 para.52

Sch.6A Part I para.8, added: SI 2004/1261 Sch.1 para.52

Sch.6A Part II para.10, added: SI 2004/1261 Sch.1 para.52

1998–cont.

41. Competition Act 1998–*cont.*

Sch.6A Part II para.11, added: SI 2004/1261 Sch.1 para.52

Sch.6A Part II para.12, added: SI 2004/1261 Sch.1 para.52

Sch.6A Part II para.13, added: SI 2004/1261 Sch.1 para.52

Sch.6A Part II para.14, added: SI 2004/1261 Sch.1 para.52

Sch.7, applied: 2002 c.40 s.185

Sch.7 Part I para.1, amended: 2002 c.40 Sch.11 para.2, Sch.26, 2003 c.21 s.388

Sch.7 Part I para.1, repealed (in part): 2002 c.40 Sch.26

Sch.7 Part I para.1, varied: SI 2003/1592 Sch.4 para.15

Sch.7 Part I para.2, amended: 2002 c.40 Sch.11 para.3, 2003 c.21 Sch.17 para.153

Sch.7 Part I para.2, repealed (in part): 2002 c.40 Sch.26, 2003 c.21 Sch.19, 2003 c.37 Sch.9 Part 3

Sch.7 Part I para.4, repealed: 2002 c.40 Sch.26

Sch.7 Part I para.4, varied: 2002 c.40 Sch.24 para.7

Sch.7 Part I para.5, amended: 2002 c.40 Sch.11 para.4, Sch.26

Sch.7 Part I para.5, repealed (in part): 2002 c.40 Sch.26

Sch.7 Part I para.6, amended: 2002 c.40 Sch.11 para.5

Sch.7 Part I para.6, repealed (in part): 2002 c.40 Sch.26

Sch.7 Part I para.7, repealed (in part): 2002 c.40 Sch.26

Sch.7 Part I para.7A, added: 2002 c.40 Sch.11 para.7

Sch.7 Part I para.9, amended: 2002 c.40 Sch.11 para.8, Sch.26

Sch.7 Part I para.9, repealed (in part): 2002 c.40 Sch.26

Sch.7 Part I para.10, repealed: 2002 c.40 Sch.26

Sch.7 Part I para.12A, added: 2002 c.40 s.186

Sch.7 Part I para.12A, disapplied: SI 2003/419 Art.6

Sch.7 Part II, applied: 2004 c.20 s.174

Sch.7 Part II para.15, amended: 2002 c.40 Sch.11 para.10

Sch.7 Part II para.15, applied: 2002 c.40 s.119, SI 2003/419 Sch.2 para.6

Sch.7 Part II para.15, referred to: 2002 c.40 s.178

Sch.7 Part II para.15, repealed (in part): 2002 c.40 Sch.26

Sch.7 Part II para.15, varied: SI 2003/1592 Sch.4 para.15

Sch.7 Part II para.19, amended: 2002 c.40 s.187

Sch.7 Part II para.19A, added: 2002 c.40 s.187

1998–cont.

41. Competition Act 1998–*cont.*

Sch.7 Part II para.19A, amended: 2003 c.21 Sch.17 para.153, Sch.19, 2003 c.37 Sch.8 para.54

Sch.7 Part II para.19A, repealed (in part): 2003 c.21 Sch.19

Sch.7 Part II para.19A, varied: SI 2003/1592 Sch.4 para.15

Sch.7 Part II para.20, amended: 2002 c.40 Sch.11 para.11

Sch.7 Part II para.20, varied: SI 2003/1592 Sch.4 para.15

Sch.7 Part II para.22, amended: 2002 c.40 Sch.11 para.12

Sch.7 Part III para.23, repealed: 2002 c.40 Sch.26

Sch.7 Part III para.24, repealed: 2002 c.40 Sch.26

Sch.7 Part III para.25, repealed: 2002 c.40 Sch.26

Sch.7 Part III para.26, applied: 2002 c.40 Sch.24 para.10

Sch.7 Part III para.26, repealed: 2002 c.40 Sch.26

Sch.7 Part III para.27, applied: SI 2003/766 Art.3

Sch.7 Part III para.27, repealed: 2002 c.40 Sch.26

Sch.7A para.1, added: 2002 c.40 Sch.12

Sch.7A para.1, amended: 2003 c.21 Sch.17 para.154, Sch.19

Sch.7A para.1, varied: SI 2003/1592 Sch.4 para.15

Sch.7A para.2, added: 2002 c.40 Sch.12

Sch.7A para.3, added: 2002 c.40 Sch.12

Sch.7A para.4, added: 2002 c.40 Sch.12

Sch.7A para.5, added: 2002 c.40 Sch.12

Sch.7A para.6, added: 2002 c.40 Sch.12

Sch.7A para.7, added: 2002 c.40 Sch.12

Sch.8, applied: SI 2004/1261 Reg.8

Sch.8 Part I para.1, amended: 2002 c.40 Sch.25 para.38

Sch.8 Part I para.1, repealed: 2002 c.40 Sch.26

Sch.8 Part I para.2, amended: 2002 c.40 Sch.5 para.8, Sch.25 para.38

Sch.8 Part I para.3, amended: 2002 c.40 Sch.5 para.8, Sch.25 para.38, SI 2004/1261 Sch.1 para.53

Sch.8 Part I para.3, applied: SI 2004/1261 Reg.8

Sch.8 Part I para.3, repealed (in part): SI 2004/1261 Sch.1 para.53

Sch.8 Part I para.3A, added: SI 2004/1261 Sch.1 para.53

Sch.8 Part I para.3A, amended: 2002 c.40 Sch.25 para.38

Sch.8 Part I para.4, amended: 2002 c.40 Sch.25 para.38

Sch.8 Part I para.4, repealed: 2002 c.40 Sch.26

1998–cont.

41. Competition Act 1998–*cont.*

Sch.8 Part II para.5, amended: 2002 c.40 Sch.25 para.38

Sch.8 Part II para.5, repealed: 2002 c.40 Sch.26

Sch.8 Part II para.5, varied: 2002 c.40 Sch.24 para.8

Sch.8 Part II para.6, amended: 2002 c.40 Sch.25 para.38

Sch.8 Part II para.6, repealed: 2002 c.40 Sch.26

Sch.8 Part II para.7, amended: 2002 c.40 Sch.25 para.38

Sch.8 Part II para.7, repealed: 2002 c.40 Sch.26

Sch.8 Part II para.8, amended: 2002 c.40 Sch.25 para.38

Sch.8 Part II para.8, repealed: 2002 c.40 Sch.26

Sch.8 Part II para.9, amended: 2002 c.40 Sch.25 para.38

Sch.8 Part II para.9, repealed: 2002 c.40 Sch.26

Sch.8 Part II para.10, amended: 2002 c.40 Sch.25 para.38

Sch.8 Part II para.10, repealed: 2002 c.40 Sch.26

Sch.8 Part II para.11, amended: 2002 c.40 Sch.25 para.38

Sch.8 Part II para.11, repealed: 2002 c.40 Sch.26

Sch.8 Part II para.12, amended: 2002 c.40 Sch.25 para.38

Sch.8 Part II para.12, repealed: 2002 c.40 Sch.26

Sch.8 Part II para.13, amended: 2002 c.40 Sch.25 para.38

Sch.8 Part II para.13, repealed: 2002 c.40 Sch.26

Sch.8 Part II para.14, amended: 2002 c.40 Sch.25 para.38

Sch.8 Part II para.14, repealed: 2002 c.40 Sch.26

Sch.8 para.3, see *Freeserve.com Plc v Director General of Telecommunications (Application for Further Time Extension)* [2003] CAT 22, [2004] Comp. A.R. 199 (Competition Appeal Tribunal), Sir Christopher Bellamy (President)

Sch.9, enabling: SI 2004/2751

Sch.9 para.1, amended: 2002 c.40 Sch.25 para.38

Sch.9 para.1, substituted: SI 2004/1261 Sch.1 para.54

Sch.9 para.2, amended: 2002 c.40 Sch.25 para.38

Sch.9 para.2, repealed: SI 2004/1261 Sch.1 para.54

Sch.9 para.3, amended: 2002 c.40 Sch.25 para.38

1998–cont.

41. Competition Act 1998–*cont.*

Sch.9 para.3, repealed: SI 2004/1261 Sch.1 para.54

Sch.9 para.4, amended: 2002 c.40 Sch.25 para.38

Sch.9 para.4, repealed: SI 2004/1261 Sch.1 para.54

Sch.9 para.5, amended: 2002 c.40 Sch.25 para.38, SI 2004/1261 Sch.1 para.54

Sch.9 para.6, amended: 2002 c.40 Sch.25 para.38

Sch.9 para.6, applied: SI 2004/1261 Reg.10

Sch.9 para.6, repealed: SI 2004/1261 Sch.1 para.54

Sch.9 para.7, amended: 2002 c.40 Sch.25 para.38

Sch.9 para.7, repealed: SI 2004/1261 Sch.1 para.54

Sch.9 para.8, amended: 2002 c.40 Sch.25 para.38

Sch.9 para.8, substituted: SI 2004/1261 Sch.1 para.54

Sch.9 para.9, amended: 2002 c.40 Sch.25 para.38

Sch.9 para.10, amended: 2002 c.40 Sch.25 para.38

Sch.9 para.11, amended: 2002 c.40 Sch.25 para.38, SI 2004/1261 Sch.1 para.54

Sch.9 para.12, amended: 2002 c.40 Sch.25 para.38

Sch.9 para.13, amended: 2002 c.40 Sch.25 para.38

Sch.9 para.14, amended: 2002 c.40 Sch.25 para.38, SI 2004/1261 Sch.1 para.54

Sch.10 Part I para.1, amended: 2003 c.20 Sch.2 para.19

Sch.10 Part I para.1, repealed: 2002 c.40 Sch.26

Sch.10 Part II para.2, repealed (in part): 2002 c.40 Sch.26, 2003 c.21 Sch.19

Sch.10 Part II para.3, repealed (in part): 2002 c.40 Sch.26

Sch.10 Part II para.4, repealed (in part): 2002 c.40 Sch.26

Sch.10 Part II para.5, repealed (in part): 2002 c.40 Sch.26, 2003 c.37 Sch.7 para.32, Sch.9 Part 3

Sch.10 Part II para.6, repealed (in part): 2002 c.40 Sch.26

Sch.10 Part III para.7, repealed (in part): 2002 c.40 Sch.26, SI 2003/419 Sch.5

Sch.10 Part III para.8, repealed (in part): 2002 c.40 Sch.26, SI 2003/419 Sch.5

Sch.10 Part IV para.9, repealed (in part): 2002 c.40 Sch.26, 2003 c.21 Sch.19

Sch.10 Part IV para.10, repealed (in part): 2002 c.40 Sch.26, SI 2003/1398 Sch.1 para.32

Sch.10 Part IV para.12, repealed (in part): 2002 c.40 Sch.26

1998–cont.

41. Competition Act 1998–*cont.*

Sch.10 Part IV para.13, repealed (in part): 2002 c.40 Sch.26, 2003 c.37 Sch.9 Part 3

Sch.10 Part IV para.15, repealed (in part): 2002 c.40 Sch.26, SI 2003/1398 Sch.1 para.32

Sch.10 Part V para.17, repealed (in part): 2002 c.40 Sch.26, SI 2003/419 Sch.5

Sch.10 Part V para.18, repealed (in part): SI 2003/419 Sch.5, SI 2003/1398 Sch.1 para.32

Sch.11 para.1, amended: SI 2002/1555 Art.24, 2003 c.20 Sch.2 para.19

Sch.11 para.1, repealed: 2002 c.40 Sch.26

Sch.11 para.2, amended: SI 2002/1555 Art.24, 2003 c.20 Sch.2 para.19

Sch.11 para.2, repealed: 2002 c.40 Sch.26

Sch.12 para.1, repealed (in part): 2002 c.40 Sch.26, SI 2003/1398 Sch.1 para.32, SI 2003/3180 Sch.1 para.6

Sch.12 para.3, repealed: 2002 c.40 Sch.26

Sch.12 para.4, repealed (in part): 2002 c.40 Sch.26

Sch.12 para.7, repealed: SI 2003/1398 Sch.1 para.32

Sch.12 para.10, repealed: 2002 c.40 Sch.26

Sch.12 para.11, repealed: SI 2003/1398 Sch.1 para.32

Sch.12 para.14, repealed (in part): 2003 c.21 Sch.19, SI 2003/1398 Sch.1 para.32

Sch.12 para.16, repealed: SI 2003/1398 Sch.1 para.32

Sch.12 para.17, repealed: SI 2003/1398 Sch.1 para.32

Sch.12 para.20, repealed: SI 2003/1398 Sch.1 para.32

Sch.13 Part I para.3, applied: 2003 c.21 s.371

Sch.13 Part II para.7, applied: 2003 c.21 s.371

Sch.13 Part IV, applied: 2003 c.21 s.371

Sch.13 Part IV para.19, applied: 2003 c.21 s.371

Sch.13 Part IV para.19, enabling: SI 2004/1078

Sch.13 Part IV para.35, amended: 2003 c.37 Sch.7 para.32

Sch.13 Part IV para.35, repealed (in part): 2003 c.21 Sch.19

Sch.13 Part IV para.36, applied: 2003 c.21 s.371, SI 2004/2751 Sch.1 para.16

Sch.13 Part IV para.37, applied: SI 2004/2751 Sch.1 para.15

Sch.13 Part IV para.38, applied: SI 2004/2751 Sch.1 para.15

Sch.13 Part V para.42, applied: 2002 c.40 Sch.24 para.21

42. Human Rights Act 1998

see *A v B Plc* [2002] EWCA Civ 337, [2003] Q.B.195 (CA), LordWoolf of Barnes, L.C.J.; see *Advocate General for Scotland v MacDonald* [2003] UKHL 34, [2004] 1 All E.R. 339 (HL), Lord Nicholls of

1998–cont.

42. Human Rights Act 1998–*cont.*

see–*cont.*

Birkenhead; see *Appleby v United Kingdom (44306/98)* (2003) 37 E.H.R.R. 38 (ECHR), Judge Pellonpaa (President); see *Barry D Trentham Ltd v Lawfield Investments Ltd* 2002 S.C. 401 (OH), Lord Drummond Young; see *CA Webber (Transport) Ltd v Railtrack Plc* [2003] EWCA Civ 1167, [2004] 1 W.L.R. 320 (CA), Peter Gibson, L.J.; see *Chief Constable of Greater Manchester v McNally* [2002] EWCA Civ 14, [2002] 2 Cr. App. R. 37 (CA), Auld, L.J.; see *Chief Constable of West Yorkshire v A* [2002] EWCA Civ 1584, [2003] 1 All E.R. 255 (CA), Kennedy, L.J.; see *Davoodipanah v Secretary of State for the Home Department* [2004] EWCA Civ 106, [2004] I.N.L.R. 341 (CA), Kennedy, L.J.; see *E v United Kingdom (33218/96)* [2003] 1 F.L.R. 348 (ECHR), Judge Costa (President); see *Edwards v United Kingdom (46477/99)* (2002) 35 E.H.R.R. 19 (ECHR), Judge Cabral Barreto (President); see *Haston (Daryll Hugh) v HM Advocate* 2003 S.C.C.R. 740 (HCJ), Lord Kirkwood, Lord Maclean, Lord Osborne; see *HM Advocate v Hannigan (Michael James)* 2003 S.C.C.R. 594 (HCJ), Lord Johnston; see *Hooper v Secretary of State for Work and Pensions* [2002] EWHC 191, [2002] U.K.H.R.R. 785 (QBD (Admin Ct)), Moses, J.; see *L Teaching Hospitals NHS Trust v A (Preliminary Hearing)* [2003] 1 F.L.R. 412 (QBD), Dame Elizabeth Butler-Sloss (President); see *McKenna v British Aluminium Ltd* [2002] Env. L.R. 30 (Ch D), Neuberger, J.; see *Merton LBC v Williams* [2002] EWCA Civ 980, [2003] H.L.R. 20 (CA), Mance, L.J.; see *MH (A Child) (Care Proceedings: Children's Guardian), Re* [2002] 1 W.L.R. 189 (Fam Div), Wall, J.; see *MK (A Child) v Oldham NHS Trust* [2003] Lloyd's Rep. Med.1 (QBD), Simon, J.; see *Practice Statement (Admin Ct: Administration of Justice)* [2002] 1 W.L.R. 810 (QBD (Admin Ct)), Scott Baker, J.; see *R v Secretary of State for the Home Department* [2001] EWCA Civ 1365, [2002] Imm. A.R. 240 (CA), RP020190Sedley, L.J.; see *R. (on the application of Abbasi) v Secretary of State for Foreign and Commonwealth Affairs* [2002] EWCA Civ 1598, [2003] U.K.H.R.R. 76 (CA), Lord Phillips of Worth Matravers, M.R.; see *R. (on the application of Ford) v Press Complaints Commission* [2001] EWHC Admin 683, [2002] E.M.L.R. 5 (QBD (Admin Ct)), Silber, J.; see *R. (on the application of Hounslow LBC) v School Admissions Appeal Panel for Hounslow LBC* [2002] EWHC 313, [2002] E.L.R. 402 (QBD (Admin Ct)), Maurice Kay, J.; see *R. (on the application*

1998–cont.

42. Human Rights Act 1998–*cont.*

see–*cont.*

of Kariharan) v Secretary of State for the Home Department [2001] EWHC Admin 1004, [2002] Imm. A.R. 281 (QBD (Admin Ct)), Stanley Burnton, J.; see *R. (on the application of McGowan) v Brent Justices* [2001] EWHC Admin 814, (2002) 166 J.P. 29 (QBD (Admin Ct)), Tuckey, L.J.; see *R. (on the application of Quintavalle) v Secretary of State for Health* [2002] EWCA Civ 29, [2002] Q.B. 628 (CA), Lord Phillips of Worth Matravers, M.R.; see *R. (on the application of S (A Child)) v Brent LBC* [2002] EWCA Civ 693, [2002] E.L.R. 556 (CA), Schiemann, L.J.; see *R. (on the application of SR) v Nottingham Magistrates Court* [2001] EWHC Admin 802, (2002) 166 J.P. 132 (QBD (Admin Ct)), Brooke, L.J.; see *R. (on the application of Williamson) v Secretary of State for Education and Employment* [2001] EWHC Admin 960, [2002] 1 F.L.R. 493 (QBD (Admin Ct)), Elias, J.; see *R. v Allen (Brian Roger)* [2001] UKHL 45, [2002] 1 A.C. 509 (HL), Lord Hutton; see *R. v Clarke (Thomas George)* [2002] EWCA Crim 753, [2002] J.P.L. 1372 (CA (Crim Div)), Cooke, J.; see *R. v Lambert (Steven)* [2002] Q.B. 1112 (CA (Crim Div)), Lord Woolf of Barnes, L.C.J.; see *R. v Lyons (Isidore Jack) (No.3)* [2001] EWCA Crim 2860, [2002] 2 Cr. App. R. 15 (CA (Crim Div)), Rose, L.J.; see *R. v Qureshi (Sajid)* [2001] EWCA Crim 1807, [2002] 1 W.L.R. 518 (CA (Crim Div)), Kennedy, L.J.; see *Wainwright v Home Office* [2003] UKHL 53, [2004] 2 A.C. 406 (HL), Lord Bingham of Cornhill; see *Woodhouse v Consignia Plc* [2002] EWCA Civ 275, [2002] 1 W.L.R. 2558 (CA), Brooke, L.J.; see *Zenovics v Secretary of State for the Home Department* [2002] EWCA Civ 273, [2002] I.N.L.R. 219 (CA), Schiemann, L.J.

applied: 2002 c.29 s.266, 2002 c.41 s.55, 2003 c.32 s.21, 2003 c.38 s.9, 2003 c.41 s.21, s.87, SI 2003/694 Sch.1 para.13, Sch.1 para.89, SI 2003/1887 Sch.1, 2004 c.36 s.23, s.30, SI 2004/753 Sch.1 para.106, SI 2004/2333 Sch.1 para.109S, Sch.1 para.152S

referred to: SI 2003/694 Sch.1 para.4, SI 2004/753 Sch.1 para.111S, Sch.1 para.201S, Sch.1 para.4, SI 2004/2333 Sch.1 para.4, Sch.1 para.104, SR 2002/120 Sch.1

Part I Sch.1 Art.10, see *Chase v News Group Newspapers Ltd* [2002] EWCA Civ 1772, [2003] E.M.L.R. 11 (CA), Brooke, L.J.

Part I Sch.1 Art.6, see *R. (on the application of Lester) v London Rent Assessment Committee* [2002] EWHC 2790, [2003]

1998–cont.
42. Human Rights Act 1998–*cont.*

Part I Sch.1 Art.6–*cont.*

H.L.R. 29 (QBD (Admin Ct)), Sir Richard Tucker

Protocol 1 Art.1, see *Keelwalk Properties Ltd v Waller* [2002] EWCA Civ 1076, [2002] 3 E.G.L.R. 79 (CA), Jonathan Parker, L.J.; see *Rowe v Sanders* [2002] EWCA Civ 242, [2002] 2 All E.R. 800 (Note) (CA), Jonathan Parker, L.J.

s.1, amended: SI 2003/1887 Sch.2 para.10, SI 2004/1574 Art.2

s.1, applied: 2004 c.36 s.20

s.1, enabling: SI 2004/1574

s.2, see *O'Brien v Harwood (Valuation Officer) (Preliminary Issues)* [2003] R.V.R. 116 (Lands Tr), PH Clarke, FRICS

s.2, amended: SI 2003/1887 Sch.2 para.10

s.3, see *Advocate General for Scotland v MacDonald* 2003 S.C. 1 (Court of Session (Inner House, Extra Division)), Lord Prosser, Lord Caplan, Lord Kirkwood; see *Ashdown v Telegraph Group Ltd* [2001] EWCA Civ 1142, [2002] Ch. 149 (CA), Lord Phillips of Worth Matravers, M.R.; see *Aston Cantlow and Wilmcote with Billesley Parochial Church Council v Wallbank* [2003] UKHL 37, [2004] 1 A.C. 546 (HL), Lord Hobhouse of Woodborough; see *Barnfather v Islington Education Authority* [2003] EWHC 418, [2003] 1 W.L.R. 2318 (QBD (Admin Ct)), Maurice Kay, J.; see *Cannell v Scottish Ministers* 2003 S.C. 404 (Court of Session (Inner House, Extra Division)), Lord Macfadyen, Lord Marnoch, Lady Smith; see *Cream Holdings Ltd v Banerjee* [2003] EWCA Civ 103, [2003] Ch. 650 (CA), Simon Brown, L.J.; see *Deep Vein Thrombosis and Air Travel Group Litigation, Re* [2002] EWHC 2825, [2003] 1 All E.R. 935 (QBD), Nelson, J.; see *Ghaidan v Godin-Mendoza* [2004] UKHL 30, [2004] 2 A.C. 557 (HL), Lord Nicholls of Birkenhead; see *Goode v Martin* [2001] EWCA Civ 1899, [2002] 1 W.L.R. 1828 (CA), Brooke, L.J.; see *Hooper v Secretary of State for Work and Pensions* [2003] EWCA Civ 813, [2003] 1 W.L.R. 2623 (CA), Lord Phillips of Worth Matravers, M.R.; see *Karl Construction Ltd v Palisade Properties Plc* 2002 S.C. 270 (OH), Lord Drummond Young; see *M v Secretary of State for Work and Pensions* [2004] EWCA Civ 1343, [2004] 3 F.C.R. 507 (CA (Civ Div)), Kennedy, L.J.; see *Manchester City Council v Romano* [2004] EWCA Civ 834, [2004] 4 All E.R. 21 (CA), Brooke, L.J.; see *Matthews v Ministry of Defence* [2002] EWCA Civ 773, [2002] 1 W.L.R. 2621 (CA), Lord Phillips of Worth Matravers, M.R.; see *Mountney v Treharne* [2002] 2 F.L.R. 406

1998–cont.
42. Human Rights Act 1998–*cont.*

s.3–*cont.*

(Ch D), Stanley Burnton, J.; see *MP v Nottinghamshire Healthcare NHS Trust* [2003] EWHC 1782, [2003] A.C.D. 99 (QBD (Admin Ct)), Silber, J.; see *O'Brien v Harwood (Valuation Officer) (Preliminary Issues)* [2003] R.V.R. 116 (Lands Tr), PH Clarke, FRICS; see *Pearce v Mayfield Secondary School Governing Body* [2001] EWCA Civ 1347, [2002] I.C.R.198 (CA), Hale, L.J.; see *Pennycook v Shaws (EAL) Ltd* [2004] EWCA Civ 100, [2004] Ch. 296 (CA), Thorpe, L.J.; see *R. (on the application of A) v Secretary of State for the Home Department* [2002] EWHC 1618, [2003] 1 W.L.R. 330 (QBD (Admin Ct)), Crane, J.; see *R. (on the application of Barber) v Secretary of State for Work and Pensions* [2002] EWHC 1915, [2002] 2 F.L.R. 1181 (QBD (Admin Ct)), Sir Richard Tucker; see *R. (on the application of Khan) v Oxfordshire CC* [2004] EWCA Civ 309, [2004] H.L.R. 41 (CA), Ward, L.J.; see *R. (on the application of Mudie) v Dover Magistrates Court* [2003] EWCA Civ 237, [2003] Q.B. 1238 (CA), Laws, L.J.; see *R. (on the application of S) v Waltham Forest Youth Court* [2004] EWHC 715, [2004] 2 Cr. App. R. 21 (QBD (Admin Ct)), Laws, L.J.; see *R. (on the application of Sacker) v HM Coroner for West Yorkshire* [2004] UKHL 11, [2004] 1 W.L.R. 796 (HL), Lord Bingham of Cornhill; see *R. (on the application of Sim) v Parole Board* [2003] EWCA Civ 1845, [2004] Q.B. 1288 (CA), Ward, L.J.; see *R. v Greenaway (Stephen)* [2003] N.I. 5 (Crown Ct (Northern Ireland)), Kerr, J.; see *R. v JT* [2003] EWCA Crim 1011, [2003] 4 All E.R. 877 (CA (Crim Div)), Fulford, J.; see *R. v Kansal (Yash Pal) (Change of Law)* [2001] UKHL 62, [2002] 2 A.C. 69 (HL), Lord Hope of Craighead; see *R. v Matthews (Mark Anthony)* [2003] EWCA Crim 813, [2004] Q.B. 690 (CA (Crim Div)), Field, J.; see *R. v S (Trademark Defence)* [2002] EWCA Crim 2558, [2003] 1 Cr. App. R. 35 (CA (Crim Div)), Rose, L.J.; see *R. v White (Andre Barrington)* [2004] EWCA Crim 946, (2004) 148 S.J.L.B. 300 (CA (Crim Div)), Laws, L.J.; see *S (Children) (Care Order: Implementation of Care Plan), Re* [2002] UKHL 10, [2002] 2 A.C. 291 (HL), Lord Nicholls of Birkenhead; see *Sheldrake v DPP* [2003] EWHC 273, [2004] Q.B. 487 (QBD (Admin Ct)), Clarke, L.J.; see *Sheldrake v DPP* [2004] UKHL 43, [2004] 3 W.L.R. 976 (HL), Lord Bingham of Cornhill; see *Strathclyde Joint Police Board v Elderslie Estates Ltd* 2002 S.L.T. (Lands Tr) 2 (Lands Tr (Scot)), Lord McGhie; see *Wainwright v Home Office* [2001] EWCA Civ 2081, [2002] Q.B. 1334 (CA), Lord Woolf of

1998–cont.

42. Human Rights Act 1998–*cont.*

s.3–*cont.*

Barnes, L.C.J.; see *Wilson v First County Trust Ltd (No.2)* [2003] UKHL 40, [2004] 1 A.C. 816 (HL), Lord Nicholls of Birkenhead; see *X v Y (Employment: Sex Offender)* [2004] EWCA Civ 662, [2004] I.R.L.R. 625 (CA), Brooke, L.J.

s.3 Sch.1 Part I Art.6, see *Attorney General's Reference (No.1 of 2004), Re* [2004] EWCA Crim 1025, [2004] 1 W.L.R. 2111 (CA (Crim Div)), Lord Woolf of Barnes, L.C.J.

s.4, see *Family Housing Association v Donnellan* [2002] 1 P. & C.R. 34 (Ch D), Park, J.; see *McR's Application for Judicial Review, Re* [2003] N.I. 1 (QBD (NI)), Kerr, J.; see *R. (on the application of Anderson) v Secretary of State for the Home Department* [2002] UKHL 46, [2003] 1 A.C. 837 (HL), Lord Bingham of Cornhill; see *R. (on the application of H) v Secretary of State for the Home Department* [2001] EWHC Admin 1037, (2002) 5 C.C.L. Rep. 62 (QBD (Admin Ct)), Bell, J.; see *R. (on the application of J) v Enfield LBC* [2002] EWHC 432, [2002] 2 F.L.R. 1 (QBD (Admin Ct)), Elias, J.; see *R. (on the application of M) v Secretary of State for Health* [2003] EWHC 1094, [2003] U.K.H.R.R. 746 (QBD (Admin Ct)), Maurice Kay, J.; see *R. (on the application of Rusbridger) v Attorney General* [2003] UKHL 38, [2004] 1 A.C. 357 (HL), Lord Steyn; see *R. (on the application of Wilkinson) v Inland Revenue Commissioners* [2003] EWCA Civ 814, [2003] 1 W.L.R. 2683 (CA), Lord Phillips of Worth Matravers; see *R. v Parchment (Jamal Sky)* [2003] EWCA Crim 2428, (2003) 147 S.J.L.B. 1088 (CA (Crim Div)), Mantell, L.J.; see *Stevens (Andrew) v HM Advocate* 2002 S.L.T. 1249 (HCJ), Lady Paton; see *Whittaker v P&D Watson (t/a P&M Watson Haulage)* [2002] I.C.R. 1244 (EAT), Lindsay, J. (President)

s.5, see *Advocate General for Scotland v MacDonald* 2002 S.C. 1 (Court of Session (Inner House, Extra Division)), Lord Prosser, Lord Caplan, Lord Kirkwood

s.5, disapplied: SI 2003/1887 Sch.1

s.6, see *Anufrijeva v Southwark LBC* [2002] EWHC 3163, (2003) 6 C.C.L. Rep. 25 (QBD), Newman, J.; see *Aston Cantlow and Wilmcote with Billesley Parochial Church Council v Wallbank* [2001] EWCA Civ 713, [2002] Ch. 51 (CA), Sir Andrew Morritt V.C.; see *Aston Cantlow and Wilmcote with Billesley Parochial Church Council v Wallbank* [2003] UKHL 37, [2004] 1 A.C. 546 (HL), Lord Hobhouse of Woodborough; see *C v Bury MBC* Times, July 25, 2002 (Fam Div), Dame

1998–cont.

42. Human Rights Act 1998–*cont.*

s.6–*cont.*

Elizabeth Butler-Sloss (President); see *Conwy BC v Jones* [2002] EWHC 2393, [2003] A.C.D. 28 (QBD (Admin Ct)), Kennedy, L.J.; see *Davidson v Scottish Ministers (No.1)* 2002 S.C. 205 (Ex Div), Lord Marnoch, Lord Hardie, Lord Weir; see *Fab Tek Engineering Ltd v Carillion Construction Ltd* 2002 S.L.T. (Sh Ct) 113 (Sh Ct (Tayside, Central and Fife)), JS Forbes; see *HM Advocate v R* 2002 S.L.T. 834 (HCJ Appeal), Lord Coulsfield, Lord Cameron of Lochbroom, Lord Caplan; see *Hooper v Secretary of State for Work and Pensions* [2003] EWCA Civ 813, [2003] 1 W.L.R. 2623 (CA), Lord Phillips of Worth Matravers, M.R.; see *Malcolm v Mackenzie* [2004] EWHC 339, [2004] 1 W.L.R. 1803 (Ch D), Lloyd, J.; see *Marcic v Thames Water Utilities Ltd (Damages)* [2002] Q.B. 1003 (QBD (T&CC)), Judge Richard Havery Q.C.; see *Martin v McGuiness* 2003 S.L.T. 1424 (OH), Lord Bonomy; see *McFarland's Application for Judicial Review, Re* [2004] UKHL 17, [2004] 1 W.L.R. 1289 (HL (NI)), Lord Bingham of Cornhill; see *McKerr's Application for Judicial Review, Re* [2004] UKHL 12, [2004] 1 W.L.R. 807 (HL (NI)), Lord Nicholls of Birkenhead; see *MP v Nottinghamshire Healthcare NHS Trust* [2003] EWHC 1782, [2003] A.C.D. 99 (QBD (Admin Ct)), Silber, J.; see *O'Brien v Harwood (Valuation Officer) (Preliminary Issues)* [2003] R.V.R. 116 (Lands Tr), PH Clarke, FRICS; see *Pardeepan v Secretary of State for the Home Department* [2002] Imm. A.R. 249 (IAT), Collins, J.; see *R. (on the application of A) v Secretary of State for the Home Department* [2002] EWHC 1618, [2003] 1 W.L.R. 330 (QBD (Admin Ct)), Crane, J.; see *R. (on the application of Beer (t/a Hammer Trout Farm)) v Hampshire Farmers Markets Ltd* [2003] EWCA Civ 1056, [2004] 1 W.L.R. 233 (CA), Dyson, L.J.; see *R. (on the application of Bono) v Harlow DC* [2002] EWHC 423, [2002] 1 W.L.R. 2475 (QBD (Admin Ct)), Richards, J.; see *R. (on the application of Friends Provident Life Office) v Secretary of State for the Environment, Transport and the Regions* [2001] EWHC Admin 820, [2002] 1 W.L.R. 1450 (QBD (Admin Ct)), Forbes, J.; see *R. (on the application of Heather) v Leonard Cheshire Foundation* [2002] EWCA Civ 366, [2002] 2 All E.R. 936 (CA), Lord Woolf of Barnes, L.C.J.; see *R. (on the application of Kershaw) v Rochdale MBC* [2002] EWHC 2385, [2003] H.L.R. 34 (QBD (Admin Ct)), Roderick Evans, J.; see *R. (on the application of Quark Fishing Ltd) v Secretary of State for Foreign and Commonwealth Affairs (No.2)* [2004]

CAP.

CAP.

1998–cont.
42. **Human Rights Act 1998**–*cont.*
s.6–*cont.*

EWCA Civ 527, [2004] 3 W.L.R. 1 (CA), Pill, L.J.; see *R. (on the application of Richards) v Secretary of State for the Home Department* [2004] EWHC 93, (2004) 154 N.L.J. 176 (QBD (Admin Ct)), Silber, J.; see *R. (on the application of Rose) v Secretary of State for Health* [2002] EWHC 1593, [2002] 2 F.L.R. 962 (QBD (Admin Ct)), Scott Baker, J.; see *R. (on the application of W) v Doncaster MBC* [2003] EWHC 192, (2003) 6 C.C.L. Rep. 301 (QBD (Admin Ct)), Stanley Burnton, J.; see *R. (on the application of West) v Lloyd's of London* [2004] EWCA Civ 506, [2004] 3 All E.R. 251 (CA), Brooke, L.J.; see *R. (on the application of Wilkinson) v Inland Revenue Commissioners* [2002] EWHC 182, [2002] S.T.C. 347 (QBD (Admin Ct)), Moses, J.; see *R. (on the application of Wilkinson) v Inland Revenue Commissioners* [2003] EWCA Civ 814, [2003] 1 W.L.R. 2683 (CA), Lord Phillips of Worth Matravers; see *R. v H (Assault of Child: Reasonable Chastisement)* [2001] EWCA Crim 1024, [2002] 1 Cr. App. R. 7 (CA (Crim Div)), Rose, L.J.; see *R. v Kansal (Yash Pal) (Change of Law)* [2001] UKHL 62, [2002] 2 A.C. 69 (HL), Lord Hope of Craighead; see *R. v Lambert (Steven)* [2001] UKHL 37, [2002] 2 A.C. 545 (HL), Lord Slynn of Hadley; see *R. v Muhamad (Mithum)* [2002] EWCA Crim 1856, [2003] Q.B.1031 (CA (Crim Div)), Dyson, L.J.; see *R. v Stobie (William)* [2002] N.I. 20 (Crown Ct (Northern Ireland)), Carswell, L.C.J.; see *Ratcliffe v Sandwell MBC* [2002] EWCA Civ 6, [2002] 1 W.L.R.1488 (CA), Chadwick, L.J.; see *S (A Child) v Knowsley BC* [2004] EWHC 491, [2004] 2 F.L.R. 716 (Fam Div), Charles, J.; see *Wilson v First County Trust Ltd (No.2)* [2003] UKHL 40, [2004] 1 A.C. 816 (HL), Lord Nicholls of Birkenhead; see *X v Y (Employment: Sex Offender)* [2004] EWCA Civ 662, [2004] I.R.L.R. 625 (CA), Brooke, L.J.; see *XXX v YYY* [2004] I.R.L.R. 137 (EAT), Mitting, J.

s.6, applied: 2002 c.40 s.238, 2002 c.41 s.84, 2003 c.17 s.170, 2003 c.38 s.52, SI 2003/658 Reg.5, 2004 c.4 s.8, 2004 c.19 Sch.3 para.5, 2004 c.27 s.18, 2004 c.35 s.32, s.83, s.201, Sch.1 para.35, Sch.5 para.29

s.6, referred to: 2004 c.35 s.87

s.7, see *Advocate General for Scotland v MacDonald* 2002 S.C. 1 (Court of Session (Inner House, Extra Division)), Lord Prosser, Lord Caplan, Lord Kirkwood; see *C v Bury MBC* Times, July 25, 2002 (Fam Div), Dame Elizabeth Butler-Sloss (President); see *Director General of Fair Trading v Proprietary Association of Great*

1998–cont.
42. **Human Rights Act 1998**–*cont.*
s.7–*cont.*

Britain (Costs) [2001] EWCA Civ 1217, [2002] 1 W.L.R. 269 (CA), Brooke, L.J.; see *G (Care: Challenge to Local Authority's Decision), Re* [2003] EWHC 551, [2003] 2 F.L.R. 42 (Fam Div), Munby, J.; see *L (Care Proceedings: Human Rights Claims), Re* [2003] EWHC 665, [2003] 2 F.L.R. 160 (Fam Div), Munby, J.; see *Matthews v Secretary of State for the Environment, Transport and the Regions* [2001] EWHC Admin 815, [2002] 2 P. & C.R. 34 (QBD (Admin Ct)), Sullivan, J.; see *R. (on the application of Kehoe) v Secretary of State for Work and Pensions* [2003] EWHC 1021, [2003] 2 F.L.R. 578 (QBD (Admin Ct)), Wall, J.; see *R. (on the application of Kehoe) v Secretary of State for Work and Pensions* [2004] EWCA Civ 225, [2004] Q.B. 1378 (CA), Ward, L.J.; see *R. (on the application of Langton) v Department for the Environment, Food and Rural Affairs* [2001] EWHC Admin 1047, [2002] Env. L.R. 20 (QBD (Admin Ct)), Nigel Pleming Q.C.; see *R. (on the application of Quark Fishing Ltd) v Secretary of State for Foreign and Commonwealth Affairs (No.2)* [2003] EWHC 1743, [2003] A.C.D. 96 (QBD (Admin Ct)), Collins, J.; see *R. (on the application of Quark Fishing Ltd) v Secretary of State for Foreign and Commonwealth Affairs (No.2)* [2004] EWCA Civ 527, [2004] 3 W.L.R. 1 (CA), Pill, L.J.; see *R. (on the application of Westminster City Council) v Mayor of London* [2002] EWHC 2440, [2003] B.L.G.R. 611 (QBD (Admin Ct)), Maurice Kay, J.; see *R. (on the application of Wilkinson) v Broadmoor Hospital* [2001] EWCA Civ 1545, [2002] 1 W.L.R. 419 (CA), Simon Brown, L.J.; see *R. v Kansal (Yash Pal) (Change of Law)* [2001] UKHL 62, [2002] 2 A.C. 69 (HL), Lord Hope of Craighead; see *S (A Child) v Knowsley BC* [2004] EWHC 491, [2004] 2 F.L.R. 716 (Fam Div), Charles, J.; see *S (Children) (Care Order: Implementation of Care Plan), Re* [2002] UKHL 10, [2002] 2 A.C. 291 (HL), Lord Nicholls of Birkenhead

s.7, amended: SI 2003/1887 Sch.2 para.10

s.7, applied: SI 2002/1843 r.3, 2003 c.41 s.195, SI 2004/2187 Reg.3

s.8, see *Dennis v Ministry of Defence* [2003] EWHC 793, [2003] Env. L.R. 34 (QBD), Buckley, J.; see *Hooper v Secretary of State for Work and Pensions* [2003] EWCA Civ 813, [2003] 1 W.L.R. 2623 (CA), Lord Phillips of Worth Matravers, M.R.; see *Marcic v Thames Water Utilities Ltd (Damages)* [2002] Q.B. 1003 (QBD (T&CC)), Judge Richard Havery Q.C.; see *R. (on the application of Bernard) v Enfield LBC* [2002] EWHC 2282, [2003] H.R.L.R.

CAP.

1998–cont.

42. Human Rights Act 1998–*cont.*
s.8–*cont.*

4 (QBD (Admin Ct)), Sullivan, J.; see *R. (on the application of N) v Secretary of State for the Home Department* [2003] EWHC 207, [2003] H.R.L.R. 20 (QBD (Admin Ct)), Silber, J.; see *R. (on the application of Quark Fishing Ltd) v Secretary of State for Foreign and Commonwealth Affairs (No.2)* [2004] EWCA Civ 527, [2004] 3 W.L.R. 1 (CA), Pill, L.J.; see *R. (on the application of W) v Doncaster MBC* [2003] EWHC 192, (2003) 6 C.C.L. Rep. 301 (QBD (Admin Ct)), Stanley Burnton, J.; see *S (Children) (Care Order: Implementation of Care Plan), Re* [2002] UKHL 10, [2002] 2 A.C. 291 (HL), Lord Nicholls of Birkenhead

s.9, amended: 2002 c.26 Sch.4 para.39

s.10, applied: SI 2004/66

s.10, disapplied: SI 2003/1887 Sch.1

s.10, enabling: SI 2004/66

s.12, see *Attorney General v Parry* [2002] EWHC 3201, [2004] E.M.L.R. 13 (Ch D), Lewison, J.; see *Campbell v Frisbee* [2002] EWCA Civ 1374, [2003] I.C.R. 141 (CA), Lord Phillips of Worth Matravers, M.R.; see *Campbell v Frisbee* [2002] EWHC 328, [2002] E.M.L.R. 31 (Ch D), Lightman, J.; see *Cream Holdings Ltd v Banerjee* [2003] EWCA Civ 103, [2003] Ch. 650 (CA), Simon Brown, L.J.; see *Dickson Minto WS v Bonnier Media Ltd* 2002 S.L.T. 776 (OH), Lord Carloway; see *Douglas v Hello! Ltd (No.6)* [2003] EWHC 786, [2003] 3 All E.R. 996 (Ch D), Lindsay, J.; see *Theakston v MGN Ltd* [2002] EWHC 137, [2002] E.M.L.R. 22 (QBD), Ouseley, J.; see *Westminster City Council v Haw* [2002] EWHC 2073, (2002) 146 S.J.L.B. 221 (QBD), Gray, J.

s.14, amended: SI 2003/1887 Sch.2 para.10

s.15, amended: SI 2003/1887 Sch.2 para.10

s.16, amended: SI 2003/1887 Sch.2 para.10

s.18, disapplied: SI 2003/1887 Sch.1

s.19, disapplied: SI 2003/1887 Sch.1

s.20, amended: SI 2003/1887 Sch.2 para.10

s.21, amended: SI 2004/1574 Art.2

s.22, see *Hooper v Secretary of State for Work and Pensions* [2003] EWCA Civ 813, [2003] 1 W.L.R. 2623 (CA), Lord Phillips of Worth Matravers, M.R.; see *R. (on the application of Rogers) v Secretary of State for the Home Department* [2002] EWHC 2078, [2003] A.C.D. 9 (QBD (Admin Ct)), Jackson, J.; see *R. v Kansal (Yash Pal) (Change of Law)* [2001] UKHL 62, [2002] 2 A.C. 69 (HL), Lord Hope of Craighead

s.65, see *Kumarakuraparan v Secretary of State for the Home Department* [2002] EWHC 112, [2002] Imm. A.R. 498 (QBD (Admin Ct)), Newman, J.

CAP.

1998–cont.

42. Human Rights Act 1998–*cont.*

Sch.Part I Art.8, see *Ghaidan v Godin-Mendoza* [2002] EWCA Civ 1533, [2003] Ch. 380 (CA), Buxton, L.J.

Sch.Part I Art.14, see *Ghaidan v Godin-Mendoza* [2002] EWCA Civ 1533, [2003] Ch. 380 (CA), Buxton, L.J.

Sch.1 Part I, see *G v Secretary of State for the Home Department* [2004] EWCA Civ 265, [2004] 1 W.L.R. 1349 (CA), Lord Phillips of Worth Matravers, M.R.; see *O'Brien v Harwood (Valuation Officer) (Preliminary Issues)* [2003] R.V.R. 116 (Lands Tr), PH Clarke, FRICS

Sch.1 Part I Art.1, see *HM Advocate v McIntosh (Robert) (No.1)* [2001] UKPC D1, [2003] 1 A.C. 1078 (PC), Lord Bingham of Cornhill, L.C.J.; see *R. (on the application of Razgar) v Secretary of State for the Home Department (No.2)* [2003] EWCA Civ 840, [2003] Imm. A.R. 529 (CA), Dyson, L.J.; see *R. (on the application of Royden) v Wirral MBC* [2002] EWHC 2484, [2003] B.L.G.R. 290 (QBD (Admin Ct)), Sir Christopher Bellamy, Q.C.

Sch.1 Part I Art.2, see *A v Secretary of State for the Home Department* [2003] EWCA Civ 175, [2003] I.N.L.R. 249 (CA), Keene, L.J.; see *Jordan's Application for Judicial Review, Re* [2002] N.I. 151 (QBD (NI)), Kerr, J.; see *Jordan's Application for Judicial Review, Re* [2004] N.I. 198 (CA (NI)), Nicholson, L.J.; see *Koci v Secretary of State for the Home Department* [2003] EWCA Civ 1507, (2003) 147 S.J.L.B. 1397 (CA), Keene, L.J.; see *McKerr's Application for Judicial Review, Re* [2003] N.I. 117 (CA (NI)), Carswell, L.C.J.; see *McKerr's Application for Judicial Review, Re* [2004] UKHL 12, [2004] 1 W.L.R. 807 (HL (NI)), Lord Nicholls of Birkenhead; see *R. (on the application of A) v HM Coroner for Inner South London* [2004] EWHC 1592, (2004) 168 J.P. 511 (QBD (Admin Ct)), Mitting, J.; see *R. (on the application of A) v Lord Saville of Newdigate (Bloody Sunday Inquiry)* [2001] EWCA Civ 2048, [2002] 1 W.L.R. 1249 (CA), Lord Phillips of Worth Matravers, M.R.; see *R. (on the application of Amin (Imtiaz)) v Secretary of State for the Home Department* [2002] EWCA Civ 390, [2003] Q.B. 581 (CA), Lord Woolf of Barnes, L.C.J.; see *R. (on the application of Amin (Imtiaz)) v Secretary of State for the Home Department* [2003] UKHL 51, [2004] 1 A.C. 653 (HL), Lord Bingham of Cornhill; see *R. (on the application of Bloggs 61) v Secretary of State for the Home Department* [2003] EWCA Civ 686, [2003] 1 W.L.R. 2724 (CA), Auld, L.J.; see *R. (on the application of Bonyama) v Secretary of*

1998–cont.

42. Human Rights Act 1998–*cont.*

Sch.1 Part I Art.2–*cont.*

State for the Home Department [2001] EWCA Civ 1353, [2002] Imm. A.R. 234 (CA), Judge, L.J.; see *R. (on the application of Burke) v General Medical Council* [2004] EWHC 1879, [2004] 2 F.L.R. 1121 (QBD (Admin Ct)), Munby, J.; see *R. (on the application of Davies) v HM Deputy Coroner for Birmingham* [2003] EWCA Civ 1739, [2004] H.R.L.R. 13 (CA), Brooke, L.J.; see *R. (on the application of Green) v Police Complaints Authority* [2001] EWHC Admin 1160, [2002] U.K.H.R.R. 293 (QBD (Admin Ct)), Moses, J.; see *R. (on the application of Green) v Police Complaints Authority* [2002] EWCA Civ 389, [2002] U.K.H.R.R. 985 (CA), Simon Brown, L.J.; see *R. (on the application of Green) v Police Complaints Authority* [2004] UKHL 6, [2004] 1 W.L.R. 725 (HL), Lord Bingham of Cornhill; see *R. (on the application of H) v Ashworth Hospital Authority* [2001] EWHC Admin 872, [2002] 1 F.C.R. 206 (QBD (Admin Ct)), Sir Christopher Bellamy, Q.C.; see *R. (on the application of Haggerty) v St Helens BC* [2003] EWHC 803, [2003] H.L.R. 69 (QBD (Admin Ct)), Silber, J.; see *R. (on the application of Hurst) v HM Coroner for Northern District London* [2003] EWHC 1721, [2004] U.K.H.R.R. 139 (QBD (Admin Ct)), Henriques, J.; see *R. (on the application of Khan (Mohammed Farooq)) v Secretary of State for Health* [2003] EWCA Civ 1129, [2004] 1 W.L.R. 971 (CA), Brooke, L.J.; see *R. (on the application of Middleton) v HM Coroner for Western Somerset* [2001] EWHC Admin 1043, (2002) 166 J.P. 193 (QBD (Admin Ct)), Stanley Burnton, J.; see *R. (on the application of Middleton) v HM Coroner for Western Somerset* [2004] UKHL 10, [2004] 2 A.C. 182 (HL), Lord Bingham of Cornhill; see *R. (on the application of Pretty) v DPP* [2001] UKHL 61, [2002] 1 A.C. 800 (HL), Lord Bingham of Cornhill; see *R. (on the application of Quintavalle) v Human Fertilisation and Embryology Authority* [2002] EWHC 2785, [2003] 2 All E.R. 105 (QBD (Admin Ct)), Maurice Kay, J.; see *R. (on the application of Sacker) v HM Coroner for West Yorkshire* [2003] EWCA Civ 217, [2003] 2 All E.R. 278 (CA), Pill, L.J.; see *R. (on the application of Sacker) v HM Coroner for West Yorkshire* [2004] UKHL 11, [2004] 1 W.L.R. 796 (HL), Lord Bingham of Cornhill; see *R. (on the application of Wright) v Secretary of State for the Home Department* [2001] EWHC Admin 520, [2002] H.R.L.R. 1 (QBD (Admin Ct)), Jackson, J.; see *X (A Woman formerly known as Mary Bell) v SO* [2003] EWHC

1998–cont.

42. Human Rights Act 1998–*cont.*

Sch.1 Part I Art.2–*cont.*

1101, [2003] E.M.L.R. 37 (QBD), Dame Elizabeth Butler-Sloss (President)

Sch.1 Part.1 Art.3, see *A v Secretary of State for the Home Department* [2004 EWCA Civ 1165, [2004] I.N.L.R. 453 (CA), Mummery, L.J.

Sch.1 Part 1 Art.3, see *R. (on the application of Kurtolli) v Secretary of State for the Home Department* [2003] EWHC 2744, [2004] I.N.L.R. 198 (QBD (Admin Ct)), Silber, J.

Sch.1 Part I Art.3, see *A v Secretary of State for the Home Department* [2003] EWCA Civ 175, [2003] I.N.L.R. 249 (CA), Keene, L.J.; see *Ameen v Secretary of State for the Home Department* [2002] UKIAT 7246, [2003] I.N.L.R. 595 (IAT), AR Mackey (Chairman); see *B v H Bauer Publishing Ltd* [2002] E.M.L.R. 8 (QBD), Eady, J.; see *Batayav v Secretary of State for the Home Department* [2003] EWCA Civ 1489, [2004] I.N.L.R. 126 (CA), Munby, J.; see *Britton v Secretary of State for the Home Department* [2003] EWCA Civ 227, (2003) 100(13) L.S.G. 28 (CA), Tuckey, L.J.; see *Davidson v Scottish Ministers (No.1)* 2002 S.C.L.R. 166 (OH), Lord Johnston; see *Davidson v Scottish Ministers (No.2)* 2003 S.C. 103 (2 Div), Lord Gill L.J.C., Lord Kirkwood, Lord Philip; see *Devaseelan v Secretary of State for the Home Department* [2002] UKIAT 702, [2003] Imm. A.R. 1 (IAT), CMG Ockleton; see *Djali v Immigration Appeal Tribunal* [2003] EWCA Civ 1371, [2004] 1 F.C.R. 42 (CA), Simon Brown, L.J.; see *HM Advocate v AS* 2003 S.C.C.R. 551 (HCJ), Lady Smith; see *Koci v Secretary of State for the Home Department* [2003] EWCA Civ 1507, (2003) 147 S.J.L.B. 1397 (CA), Keene, L.J.; see *Kopel v Safeway Stores Plc* [2003] I.R.L.R. 753 (EAT), Mitting, J.; see *M v Chief Constable of Strathclyde* 2003 S.L.T. 1007 (OH), Lord McCluskey; see *McPherson v Secretary of State for the Home Department* [2001] EWCA Civ 1955, [2002] I.N.L.R. 139 (CA), Sedley, L.J.; see *N v Secretary of State for the Home Department* [2003] EWCA Civ 1369, [2004] 1 W.L.R. 1182 (CA), Laws, L.J.; see *Napier v Scottish Ministers* [2002] U.K.H.R.R. 308 (OH), Lord Macfadyen; see *R. (on the application of Bagdanavicius) v Secretary of State for the Home Department* [2003] EWCA Civ 1605, [2004] 1 W.L.R. 1207 (CA), Lord Woolf of Barnes, L.C.J.; see *R. (on the application of Bernard) v Enfield LBC* [2002] EWHC 2282, [2003] H.R.L.R. 4 (QBD (Admin Ct)), Sullivan, J.; see *R. (on the application of Borak) v Secretary of State for the Home Department* [2004]

1998–cont.

42. Human Rights Act 1998–*cont.*
Sch.1 Part I Art.3–*cont.*

EWHC 1861, [2004] 1 W.L.R. 3129 (QBD (Admin Ct)), Harrison, J.; see *R. (on the application of Burke) v General Medical Council* [2004] EWHC 1879, [2004] 2 F.L.R. 1121 (QBD (Admin Ct)), Munby, J.; see *R. (on the application of Dhima) v Immigration Appeal Tribunal* [2002] EWHC 80, [2002] Imm. A.R. 394 (QBD (Admin Ct)), Auld, L.J.; see *R. (on the application of Fuller) v Chief Constable of Dorset* [2001] EWHC Admin 1057, [2003] Q.B. 480 (QBD (Admin Ct)), Stanley Burnton, J.; see *R. (on the application of Gezer) v Secretary of State for the Home Department* [2003] EWHC 860, [2003] H.L.R. 64 (QBD (Admin Ct)), Moses, J.; see *R. (on the application of Green) v Police Complaints Authority* [2001] EWHC Admin 1160, [2002] U.K.H.R.R. 293 (QBD (Admin Ct)), Moses, J.; see *R. (on the application of Green) v Police Complaints Authority* [2002] EWCA Civ 389, [2002] U.K.H.R.R. 985 (CA), Simon Brown, L.J.; see *R. (on the application of Green) v Police Complaints Authority* [2004] UKHL 6, [2004] 1 W.L.R. 725 (HL), Lord Bingham of Cornhill; see *R. (on the application of Haggerty) v St Helens BC* [2003] EWHC 803, [2003] H.L.R. 69 (QBD (Admin Ct)), Silber, J.; see *R. (on the application of Kimani) v Lambeth LBC* [2003] EWCA Civ 1150, [2004] 1 W.L.R. 272 (CA), Lord Phillips of Worth Matravers, M.R.; see *R. (on the application of Kimani) v Lambeth LBC* [2003] EWHC 871, [2003] 2 F.L.R. 439 (QBD (Admin Ct)), Silber, J.; see *R. (on the application of L) v Secretary of State for the Home Department* [2003] EWCA Civ 25, [2003] 1 W.L.R. 1230 (CA), Lord Phillips of Worth Matravers, M.R.; see *R. (on the application of Limbuela) v Secretary of State for the Home Department* [2004] EWCA Civ 540, [2004] Q.B. 1440 (CA), Laws, L.J.; see *R. (on the application of Mohamad) v Immigration Adjudicator* [2002] EWHC 2496, Times, December 12, 2002 (QBD (Admin Ct)), Munby, J.; see *R. (on the application of Munjaz) v Mersey Care NHS Trust* [2003] EWCA Civ 1036, [2004] Q.B. 395 (CA), Lord Phillips of Worth Matravers, M.R.; see *R. (on the application of N) v M* [2002] EWHC 1911, [2003] A.C.D. 17 (QBD (Admin Ct)), Silber, J.; see *R. (on the application of N) v Secretary of State for the Home Department* [2003] EWHC 207, [2003] H.R.L.R. 20 (QBD (Admin Ct)), Silber, J.; see *R. (on the application of Pretty) v DPP* [2001] UKHL 61, [2002] 1 A.C. 800 (HL), Lord Bingham of Cornhill; see *R. (on the application of Q) v Secretary of State for the Home Department* [2003]

1998–cont.

42. Human Rights Act 1998–*cont.*
Sch.1 Part I Art.3–*cont.*

EWCA Civ 364, [2004] Q.B. 36 (CA), Lord Phillips of Worth Matravers, M.R.; see *R. (on the application of Razgar) v Secretary of State for the Home Department (No.2)* [2002] EWHC 2554, [2003] Imm. A.R. 269 (QBD (Admin Ct)), Richards, J.; see *R. (on the application of Razgar) v Secretary of State for the Home Department (No.2)* [2004] UKHL 27, [2004] 2 A.C. 368 (HL), Lord Bingham of Cornhill; see *R. (on the application of S) v Airedale NHS Trust* [2002] EWHC 1780, [2003] Lloyd's Rep. Med. 21 (QBD (Admin Ct)), Stanley Burnton, J.; see *R. (on the application of S) v Secretary of State for the Home Department* [2003] EWCA Civ 1285, [2003] U.K.H.R.R. 1321 (CA), Kennedy, L.J.; see *R. (on the application of S) v Secretary of State for the Home Department* [2003] EWHC 1941, [2004] H.L.R. 16 (QBD (Admin Ct)), Maurice Kay, J.; see *R. (on the application of Tataw) v Immigration Appeal Tribunal* [2003] EWCA Civ 925, [2003] I.N.L.R. 585 (CA), May, L.J.; see *R. (on the application of Ullah) v Special Adjudicator* [2002] EWCA Civ 1856, [2003] 1 W.L.R. 770 (CA), Lord Phillips of Worth Matravers, M.R.; see *R. (on the application of Ullah) v Special Adjudicator* [2004] UKHL 26, [2004] 2 A.C. 323 (HL), Lord Bingham of Cornhill; see *R. (on the application of Watts) v Bedford Primary Care Trust* [2003] EWHC 2228, [2003] 3 C.M.L.R. 23 (QBD (Admin Ct)), Munby, J.; see *R. (on the application of Wright) v Secretary of State for the Home Department* [2001] EWHC Admin 520, [2002] H.R.L.R. 1 (QBD (Admin Ct)), Jackson, J.; see *R. (on the application of Yogathas) v Secretary of State for the Home Department* [2002] UKHL 36, [2003] 1 A.C. 920 (HL), Lord Hope of Craighead; see *R. v Drew (Anthony James)* [2001] EWCA Crim 2861, [2002] 2 Cr. App. R. (S.) 45 (CA (Crim Div)), Kennedy, L.J.; see *R. v Drew (Anthony James)* [2003] UKHL 25, [2003] 1 W.L.R. 1213 (HL), Lord Bingham of Cornhill; see *R. v H (Assault of Child: Reasonable Chastisement)* [2001] EWCA Crim 1024, [2002] 1 Cr. App. R. 7 (CA (Crim Div)), Rose, L.J.; see *R. v Lichniak (Daniella Helen)* [2001] EWHC Admin 294, [2002] Q.B. 296 (QBD (Admin Ct)), Kennedy, L.J.; see *R. v Lichniak (Daniella Helen)* [2002] UKHL 47, [2003] 1 A.C. 903 (HL), Lord Bingham of Cornhill; see *R. v Parchment (Jamal Sky)* [2003] EWCA Crim 2428, (2003) 147 S.J.L.B. 1088 (CA (Crim Div)), Mantell, L.J.; see *R. v Stobie (William)* [2002] N.I. 20 (Crown Ct (Northern Ireland)), Carswell, L.C.J.; see *SS v Secretary of State for*

1998–cont.

42. Human Rights Act 1998–*cont.*

Sch.1 Part I Art.3–*cont.*

the Home Department [2004] UKIAT 39, [2004] Imm. A.R. 95 (IAT), Ouseley, J.; see *Tuncer v Secretary of State for the Home Department* 2003 S.C.L.R. 456 (OH), Lord Brodie; see *William Sinclair Holdings Ltd v English Nature* [2001] EWHC Admin 408, [2002] Env. L.R. 4 (QBD (Admin Ct)),Turner, J.

Sch.1 Part I Art.5, see *R. (on the application of Clift) v Secretary of State for the Home Department* [2004] EWCA Civ 514, [2004] 1 W.L.R. 2223 (CA), Lord Woolf of Barnes, L.C.J.; see *Taylor v Chief Constable of Thames Valley* [2004] EWCA Civ 858, [2004] 1 W.L.R. 3155 (CA), Sir Andrew Morritt V.C.

Sch.1 Part I Art.5, see *Anderson v Scottish Ministers* [2001] UKPC D5, [2003] 2 A.C. 602 (PC (Sc)), Lord Hope of Craighead; see *Chief Constable of Cleveland v McGrogan* [2002] EWCA Civ 86, [2002] 1 F.L.R. 707 (CA), Wall, J.; see *Donaldson's Application for Bail, Re* [2003] N.I. 93 (QBD (NI)), Sheil, J.; see *Flynn (Patrick Anthony) v HM Advocate* 2003 J.C. 153 (HCJ), Lord Cullen L.J.G., Lord Hamilton, Lord Osborne; see *King v Secretary of State for the Home Department* [2003] EWHC 2831, [2004] H.R.L.R. 9 (QBD (Admin Ct)), Beatson, J.; see *Lodhi v Governor of Brixton Prison (No.2)* [2002] EWHC 2029, (2002) 146 S.J.L.B. 230 (QBD (Admin Ct)), Brooke, L.J.; see *McDonald v Dickson* 2003 S.L.T. 467 (HCJ), Lord Macfadyen, Lord Caplan, Lord Marnoch; see *MP v Nottinghamshire Healthcare NHS Trust* [2003] EWHC 1782, [2003] A.C.D. 99 (QBD (Admin Ct)), Silber, J.; see *R. (on the application of A) v Secretary of State for the Home Department* [2002] EWHC 1618, [2003] 1 W.L.R. 330 (QBD (Admin Ct)), Crane, J.; see *R. (on the application of Anderson) v Secretary of State for the Home Department* [2001] EWCA Civ 1698, [2002] 2 W.L.R. 1143 (CA), Lord Woolf of Barnes, L.C.J.; see *R. (on the application of C) v Mental Health Review Tribunal* [2001] EWCA Civ 1110, [2002] 1 W.L.R. 176 (CA), Lord Phillips of Worth Matravers, M.R.; see *R. (on the application of Cawser) v Secretary of State for the Home Department* [2003] EWCA Civ 1522, [2004] U.K.H.R.R. 101 (CA), Arden, L.J.; see *R. (on the application of D) v Secretary of State for the Home Department* [2002] EWHC 2805, [2003] 1 W.L.R. 1315 (QBD (Admin Ct)), Stanley Burnton, J.; see *R. (on the application of DR) v Mersey Care NHS Trust* Times, October 11, 2002 (QBD (Admin Ct)),

1998–cont.

42. Human Rights Act 1998–*cont.*

Sch.1 Part I Art.5–*cont.*

Wilson, J.; see *R. (on the application of Giles) v Parole Board* [2001] EWHC Admin 834, [2002] 1 W.L.R. 654 (QBD (Admin Ct)), Elias, J.; see *R. (on the application of Giles) v Parole Board* [2002] EWCA Civ 951, [2003] 2 W.L.R. 196 (CA), Kennedy, L.J.; see *R. (on the application of Giles) v Parole Board* [2003] UKHL 42, [2004] 1 A.C. 1 (HL), Lord Bingham of Cornhill; see *R. (on the application of Gillan) v Commissioner of Police of the Metropolis* [2004] EWCA Civ 1067, [2004] 3 W.L.R. 1144 (CA (Civ Div)), Lord Woolf of Barnes, L.C.J.; see *R. (on the application of H) v Mental Health Review Tribunal for North and East London Region* [2001] EWCA Civ 415, [2002] Q.B. 1 (CA), Lord Phillips of Worth Matravers, M.R.; see *R. (on the application of H) v Secretary of State for the Home Department* [2001] EWHC Admin 1037, (2002) 5 C.C.L. Rep. 62 (QBD (Admin Ct)), Bell, J.; see *R. (on the application of H) v Secretary of State for the Home Department* [2002] EWCA Civ 646, [2003] Q.B. 320 (CA), Lord Phillips of Worth Matravers, M.R.; see *R. (on the application of H) v Secretary of State for the Home Department* [2003] UKHL 59, [2004] 2 A.C. 253 (HL), Lord Bingham of Cornhill; see *R. (on the application of K) v Camden and Islington HA* [2001] EWCA Civ 240, [2002] Q.B. 198 (CA), Lord Phillips of Worth Matravers, M.R.; see *R. (on the application of Kashamu) v Governor of Brixton Prison (No.2)* [2001] EWHC Admin 980, [2002] Q.B. 887 (QBD (Admin Ct)), Rose, L.J.; see *R. (on the application of KB) v Mental Health Review Tribunal (Damages)* [2003] EWHC 193, [2004] Q.B. 936 (QBD (Admin Ct)), Stanley Burnton, J.; see *R. (on the application of KB) v Mental Health Review Tribunal* [2002] EWHC 639, (2002) 5 C.C.L. Rep. 458 (QBD (Admin Ct)), Stanley Burnton, J.; see *R. (on the application of Laporte) v Chief Constable of Gloucestershire* [2004] EWHC 253, [2004] 2 All E.R. 874 (QBD (Admin Ct)), May, L.J.; see *R. (on the application of Middleton) v Secretary of State for the Home Department* [2003] EWHC 315, [2003] A.C.D. 44 (QBD (Admin Ct)), Pitchford, J.; see *R. (on the application of Munjaz) v Mersey Care NHS Trust* [2003] EWCA Civ 1036, [2004] Q.B. 395 (CA), Lord Phillips of Worth Matravers, M.R.; see *R. (on the application of Nadarajah) v Secretary of State for the Home Department* [2003] EWCA Civ 1768, [2004] I.N.L.R. 139 (CA), Lord Phillips of Worth Matravers, M.R.; see *R. (on the application of Noorkoiv) v Secretary of State for the Home Department (No.2)*

1998–cont.

42. Human Rights Act 1998–cont.
Sch.1 Part I Art.5–cont.

[2002] EWCA Civ 770, [2002] 1 W.L.R. 3284 (CA), Buxton, L.J.; see *R. (on the application of O) v Harrow Crown Court* [2003] EWHC 868, [2003] 1 W.L.R. 2756 (QBD (Admin Ct)), Kennedy, L.J.; see *R. (on the application of Roberts) v Parole Board* [2003] EWHC 3120, [2004] 2 All E.R. 776 (QBD (Admin Ct)), Maurice Kay, J.; see *R. (on the application of Roberts) v Parole Board* [2004] EWCA Civ 1031, [2004] 4 All E.R.1136 (CA (Civ Div)), Tuckey, L.J.; see *R. (on the application of S) v Airedale NHS Trust* [2002] EWHC 1780, [2003] Lloyd's Rep. Med. 21 (QBD (Admin Ct)), Stanley Burnton, J.; see *R. (on the application of S) v Mental Health Review Tribunal* [2002] EWHC 2522, Times, December 6, 2002 (QBD (Admin Ct)), Stanley Burnton, J.; see *R. (on the application of Saadi) v Secretary of State for the Home Department* [2001] EWCA Civ 1512, [2002] 1 W.L.R. 356 (CA), Lord Phillips of Worth Matravers, M.R.; see *R. (on the application of Saadi) v Secretary of State for the Home Department* [2002] UKHL 41, [2002] 1 W.L.R. 3131 (HL), Lord Slynn of Hadley; see *R. (on the application of Secretary of State for the Home Department) v Mental Health Review Tribunal* [2002] EWCA Civ 1868, (2003) 6 C.C.L. Rep. 319 (CA), Keene, L.J.; see *R. (on the application of Sezek) v Secretary of State for the Home Department (Bail Application)* [2001] EWCA Civ 795, [2002] 1 W.L.R. 348 (CA), Peter Gibson, L.J.; see *R. (on the application of Sim) v Parole Board* [2003] EWCA Civ 1845, [2004] Q.B. 1288 (CA), Ward, L.J.; see *R. (on the application of Sim) v Parole Board* [2003] EWHC 152, [2003] 2 W.L.R. 1374 (QBD (Admin Ct)), Elias, J.; see *R. (on the application of Smith) v Parole Board (Permission to Appeal)* [2003] EWCA Civ 1014, [2003] 1 W.L.R. 2548 (CA), Auld, L.J.; see *R. (on the application of Spence) v Secretary of State for the Home Department* [2003] EWCA Civ 732, (2003) 147 S.J.L.B. 660 (CA), Brooke, L.J.; see *R. (on the application of T) v Central and North West London Mental Health NHS Trust* [2002] EWHC 2803, Times, December 13, 2002 (QBD (Admin Ct)), Forbes, J.; see *R. (on the application of Vickers) v West London Magistrates Court* [2003] EWHC 1809, (2003) 167 J.P. 473 (QBD (Admin Ct)), Gage, J.; see *R. (on the application of von Brandenburg) v East London and the City Mental Health NHS Trust* [2001] EWCA Civ 239, [2002] Q.B. 235 (CA), Lord Phillips of Worth Matravers, M.R.; see *R. (on the application of W) v Doncaster MBC* [2003] EWHC 192, (2003) 6 C.C.L. Rep. 301

1998–cont.

42. Human Rights Act 1998–cont.
Sch.1 Part I Art.5–cont.

(QBD (Admin Ct)), Stanley Burnton, J.; see *R. (on the application of W) v Doncaster MBC* [2004] EWCA Civ 378, [2004] B.L.G.R. 743 (CA), Judge, L.J.; see *R. (on the application of Wardle) v Leeds Crown Court* [2001] UKHL 12, [2002] 1 A.C. 754 (HL), Lord Slynn of Hadley; see *R. v Drew (Anthony James)* [2001] EWCA Crim 2861, [2002] 2 Cr. App. R. (S.) 45 (CA (Crim Div)), Kennedy, L.J.; see *R. v Lichniak (Daniella Helen)* [2001] EWHC Admin 294, [2002] Q.B. 296 (QBD (Admin Ct)), Kennedy, L.J.; see *R. v Lichniak (Daniella Helen)* [2002] UKHL 47, [2003] 1 A.C. 903 (HL), Lord Bingham of Cornhill; see *R. v Parchment (Jamal Sky)* [2003] EWCA Crim 2428, (2003) 147 S.J.L.B. 1088 (CA (Crim Div)), Mantell, L.J.; see *R. v Tagg (Heather Susan)* [2001] EWCA Crim 1230, [2002] 1 Cr. App. R. 2 (CA (Crim Div)), Rose, L.J.; see *Scriven, Re* [2004] EWCA Civ 543, (2004) 148 S.J.L.B. 511 (CA), Tuckey, L.J.; see *Shaw's Application for Judicial Review, Re* [2004] N.I. 149 (QBD (NI)), Kerr, J.

Sch.1 Part 1 Art.6, see *D (A Child) (Intractable Contact Dispute: Publicity), Re* [2004] EWHC 727, [2004] 1 F.L.R. 1226 (Fam Div), Munby, J.

Sch.1 Part I Art.6, see *Jordan's Application for Judicial Review, Re* [2004] N.I. 198 (CA (NI)), Nicholson, L.J.

Sch.1 Part I Art.7, see *Flynn (Patrick Anthony) v HM Advocate* 2003 J.C. 153 (HCJ), Lord Cullen L.J.G., Lord Hamilton, Lord Osborne; see *Gough v Chief Constable of Derbyshire* [2001] EWHC Admin 554, [2002] Q.B. 459 (QBD (Admin Ct)), Laws, L.J.; see *Gough v Chief Constable of Derbyshire* [2002] EWCA Civ 351, [2002] Q.B. 1213 (CA), Lord Phillips of Worth Matravers, M.R.; see *HM Advocate v PH* 2002 S.C.C.R. 927 (HCJ), Lord MacLean; see *Phillips v DPP* [2002] EWHC 2093, [2003] R.T.R. 8 (QBD (Admin Ct)), McCombe, J.; see *R. (on the application of McFetrich) v Secretary of State for the Home Department* [2003] EWHC 1542, [2003] 4 All E.R. 1093 (QBD (Admin Ct)), Scott Baker, L.J.; see *R. (on the application of Uttley) v Secretary of State for the Home Department* [2003] EWCA Civ 1130, [2003] 1 W.L.R. 2590 (CA), Pill, L.J.; see *R. (on the application of Uttley) v Secretary of State for the Home Department* [2004] UKHL 38, [2004] 1 W.L.R. 2278 (HL), Lord Steyn; see *R. v C (Barry)* [2004] EWCA Crim 292, [2004] 1 W.L.R. 2098 (CA (Crim Div)), Judge, L.J.; see *R. v Cotter (Christopher James)* [2002]

1998–cont.
42. Human Rights Act 1998–*cont.*
Sch.1 Part I Art.7–*cont.*

EWCA Crim 1033, [2003] Q.B. 951 (CA (Crim Div)), Latham, L.J.; see *R. v Field (Brian John)* [2002] EWCA Crim 2913, [2003] 1 W.L.R. 882 (CA (Crim Div)), Kay, L.J.; see *R. v Ghafoor (Imran Hussain)* [2002] EWCA Crim 1857, [2003] 1 Cr. App. R. (S.) 84 (CA (Crim Div)), Dyson, L.J.; see *R. v Goldstein (Harry Chaim)* [2003] EWCA Crim 3450, [2004] 1 W.L.R. 2878 (CA (Crim Div)), Latham, L.J.; see *R. v H (Assault of Child: Reasonable Chastisement)* [2001] EWCA Crim 1024, [2002] 1 Cr. App. R. 7 (CA (Crim Div)), Rose, L.J.; see *R. v JT* [2003] EWCA Crim 1011, [2003] 4 All E.R. 877 (CA (Crim Div)), Fulford, J.; see *R. v Muhamad (Mithum)* [2002] EWCA Crim 1856, [2003] Q.B. 1031 (CA (Crim Div)), Dyson, L.J.; see *R. v R (Sentencing: Extended Licences)* [2003] EWCA Crim 2199, [2004] 1 W.L.R. 490 (CA (Crim Div)), Pitchers, J.; see *Webster v Dominick* 2003 S.L.T. 975 (HCJ), Lord Gill L.J.C., Lady Cosgrove, Lord Macfadyen, Lord Marnoch, Lord Sutherland

Sch.1 Part 1 Art.8, see *D (A Child) (Intractable Contact Dispute: Publicity), Re* [2004] EWHC 727, [2004] 1 F.L.R. 1226 (Fam Div), Munby, J.; see *Hooper v Secretary of State for Work and Pensions* [2002] EWHC 191, [2002] U.K.H.R.R. 785 (QBD (Admin Ct)), Moses, J.; see *R. (on the application of Ali) v Birmingham City Council* [2002] EWHC 1511, [2002] H.L.R. 51 (QBD (Admin Ct)), Moses, J.; see *R. (on the application of Bernard) v Enfield LBC* [2002] EWHC 2282, [2003] H.R.L.R. 4 (QBD (Admin Ct)), Sullivan, J.; see *R. (on the application of Kurtolli) v Secretary of State for the Home Department* [2003] EWHC 2744, [2004] I.N.L.R. 198 (QBD (Admin Ct)), Silber, J.

Sch.1 Part 1 s.8, see *R. (on the application of M) v Secretary of State for the Home Department* [2003] EWHC 319, (2003) 100(18) L.S.G. 35 (QBD (Admin Ct)), Richards, J.

Sch.1 Part I Art.9, see *A v Leeds Teaching Hospital NHS Trust* [2004] EWHC 644, [2004] 2 F.L.R. 365 (QBD), Gage, J.; see *Campbell v South Northamptonshire DC* [2004] EWCA Civ 409, [2004] 3 All E.R. 387 (CA), Peter Gibson, L.J.; see *Hammond v DPP* [2004] EWHC 69, (2004) 168 J.P. 601 (QBD (Admin Ct)), May, L.J.; see *Parsons Application for Judicial Review, Re* [2004] N.I. 38 (CA (NI)), Lord Carswell L.C.J.; see *R. (on the application of Begum (Shabina)) v Denbigh High School Governors* [2004] EWHC 1389, [2004] E.L.R. 374 (QBD (Admin Ct)), Bennett, J.; see *R. (on the*

1998–cont.
42. Human Rights Act 1998–*cont.*
Sch.1 Part I Art.9–*cont.*

application of Ullah) v Special Adjudicator [2002] EWCA Civ 1856, [2003] 1 W.L.R. 770 (CA), Lord Phillips of Worth Matravers, M.R.; see *R. (on the application of Ullah) v Special Adjudicator* [2002] EWHC 1584, [2002] Imm. A.R. 601 (QBD (Admin Ct)), Harrison, J.; see *R. (on the application of Ullah) v Special Adjudicator* [2004] UKHL 26, [2004] 2 A.C. 323 (HL), Lord Bingham of Cornhill; see *R. (on the application of Williamson) v Secretary of State for Education and Employment* [2002] EWCA Civ 1926, [2003] Q.B. 1300 (CA), Buxton, L.J.; see *R. v Taylor (Paul Simon)* [2001] EWCA Crim 2263, [2002] 1 Cr. App. R. 37 (CA (Crim Div)), Rose, L.J.

Sch.1 Part I Art.10, see *A Local Authority (Inquiry: Restraint on Publication), Re* [2003] EWHC 2746, [2004] Fam. 96 (Fam Div), Dame Elizabeth Butler-Sloss (President); see *Ashdown v Telegraph Group Ltd* [2001] EWCA Civ 1142, [2002] Ch. 149 (CA), Lord Phillips of Worth Matravers, M.R.; see *Ashworth Hospital Authority v MGN Ltd* [2002] UKHL 29, [2002] 1 W.L.R. 2033 (HL), Lord Woolf of Barnes, L.C.J.; see *Attorney General's Reference (No.4 of 2002), Re* [2003] EWCA Crim 762, [2003] 3 W.L.R. 1153 (CA (Crim Div)), Latham, L.J.; see *Briffett v DPP* [2001] EWHC Admin 841, (2002) 166 J.P. 66 (QBD (Admin Ct)), Laws, L.J.; see *Campbell v Mirror Group Newspapers Ltd* [2002] EWCA Civ 1373, [2003] Q.B. 633 (CA), Lord Phillips of Worth Matravers, M.R.; see *Campbell v Mirror Group Newspapers Ltd* [2004] UKHL 22, [2004] 2 A.C. 457 (HL), Lord Nicholls of Birkenhead; see *Daiichi Pharmaceuticals UK Ltd v Stop Huntingdon Animal Cruelty* [2003] EWHC 2337, [2004] 1 W.L.R. 1503 (QBD), Owen, J.; see *Douglas v Hello! Ltd (No.6)* [2003] EWHC 786, [2003] 3 All E.R. 996 (Ch D), Lindsay, J.; see *Hammond v DPP* [2004] EWHC 69, (2004) 168 J.P. 601 (QBD (Admin Ct)), May, L.J.; see *Interbrew SA v Financial Times Ltd* [2002] EWCA Civ 274, [2002] 2 Lloyd's Rep. 229 (CA), Sedley, L.J.; see *Jameel v Wall Street Journal Europe SPRL (No.2)* [2003] EWHC 2945, [2004] 2 All E.R. 92 (QBD), Eady, J.; see *Kearns v General Council of the Bar* [2002] EWHC 1681, [2002] 4 All E.R. 1075 (QBD), Eady, J.; see *Kent CC v B (A Child)* [2004] EWHC 411, [2004] 2 F.L.R. 142 (Fam Div), Munby, J.; see *Lady Archer v Williams* [2003] EWHC 1670, [2003] E.M.L.R. 38 (QBD), Jackson, J.; see *Levi Strauss & Co v Tesco Stores Ltd* [2002] EWHC 1625, [2002] 3

1998–cont.
42. Human Rights Act 1998–*cont.*
　Sch.1 Part I Art.10–*cont.*

C.M.L.R.11 (Ch D), Pumfrey, J.; see *Mersey Care NHS Trust v Ackroyd* [2003] EWCA Civ 663, [2003] E.M.L.R. 36 (CA), May, L.J.; see *O'Driscoll v Secretary of State for the Home Department* [2002] EWHC 2477, [2003] A.C.D. 35 (QBD), Kennedy, L.J.; see *Pay v Lancashire Probation Service* [2004] I.C.R. 187 (EAT), Judge McMullen Q.C.; see *Pelling v Bruce-Williams* [2003] EWHC 1541, [2004] Fam. 22 (Fam Div), Bennett, J.; see *Pelling v Bruce-Williams* [2004] EWCA Civ 845, [2004] Fam. 155 (CA), Thorpe, L.J.; see *Percy v DPP* [2001] EWHC Admin 1125, (2002) 166 J.P. 93 (QBD (Admin Ct)), Hallett, J.; see *R. (on the application of A) v Secretary of State for the Home Department* [2003] EWHC 2846, [2004] H.R.L.R. 12 (QBD (Admin Ct)), Kennedy, L.J.; see *R. (on the application of Farrakhan) v Secretary of State for the Home Department* [2001] EWHC Admin 634, [2001] EWHC Admin 781, [2002] A.C.D. 5 (QBD (Admin Ct)), Turner, J.; see *R. (on the application of Farrakhan) v Secretary of State for the Home Department* [2002] EWCA Civ 606, [2002] Q.B. 1391 (CA), Lord Phillips of Worth Matravers, M.R.; see *R. (on the application of Gillan) v Commissioner of Police of the Metropolis* [2004] EWCA Civ 1067, [2004] 3 W.L.R. 1144 (CA (Civ Div)), Lord Woolf of Barnes, L.C.J.; see *R. (on the application of Hirst) v Secretary of State for the Home Department (Contact with Media)* [2002] EWHC 602, [2002] 1 W.L.R. 2929 (QBD (Admin Ct)), Elias, J.; see *R. (on the application of Howard) v Secretary of State for Health* [2002] EWHC 396, [2003] Q.B. 830 (QBD (Admin Ct)), Scott Baker, J.; see *R. (on the application of Laporte) v Chief Constable of Gloucestershire* [2004] EWHC 253, [2004] 2 All E.R. 874 (QBD (Admin Ct)), May, L.J.; see *R. (on the application of Nilsen) v Full Sutton Prison Governor* [2003] EWHC 3160, [2004] E.M.L.R. 9 (QBD (Admin Ct)), Maurice Kay, J.; see *R. (on the application of Persey) v Secretary of State for the Environment, Food and Rural Affairs* [2002] EWHC 371, [2003] Q.B. 794 (QBD (Admin Ct)), Simon Brown, L.J.; see *R. (on the application of ProLife Alliance) v BBC* [2003] UKHL 23, [2004] 1 A.C. 185 (HL), Lord Nicholls of Birkenhead; see *R. (on the application of Rusbridger) v Attorney General* [2003] UKHL 38, [2004] 1 A.C. 357 (HL), Lord Steyn; see *R. v Shayler (David Michael)* [2002] UKHL 11, [2003] 1 A.C. 247 (HL), Lord Bingham of Cornhill; see *R. v Smethurst (John Russell)* [2001] EWCA Crim 772, [2002] 1 Cr. App. R. 6 (CA (Crim Div)), Lord

1998–cont.
42. Human Rights Act 1998–*cont.*
　Sch.1 Part I Art.10–*cont.*

Woolf of Barnes, L.C.J.; see *S (A Child) (Identification: Restrictions on Publication), Re* [2003] EWCA Civ 963, [2004] Fam. 43 (CA), Hale, L.J.; see *S (A Child) (Identification: Restrictions on Publication), Re* [2004] UKHL 47, [2004] 3 W.L.R. 1129 (HL), Lord Bingham of Cornhill; see *Theakston v MGN Ltd* [2002] EWHC 137, [2002] E.M.L.R. 22 (QBD), Ouseley, J.; see *Westminster City Council v Haw* [2002] EWHC 2073, (2002) 146 S.J.L.B. 221 (QBD), Gray, J.; see *X (A Woman formerly known as Mary Bell) v SO* [2003] EWHC 1101, [2003] E.M.L.R. 37 (QBD), Dame Elizabeth Butler-Sloss (President)

Sch.1 Part I Art.11, see *Aberdeen Bon Accord Loyal Orange Lodge 701 v Aberdeen City Council* 2002 S.L.T. (Sh Ct) 52 (Sh Ct (Grampian, Highland and Islands)), AM Cowan; see *Daiichi Pharmaceuticals UK Ltd v Stop Huntingdon Animal Cruelty* [2003] EWHC 2337, [2004] 1 W.L.R. 1503 (QBD), Owen, J.; see *O'Driscoll v Secretary of State for the Home Department* [2002] EWHC 2477, [2003] A.C.D. 35 (QBD), Kennedy, L.J.; see *R. (on the application of Gillan) v Commissioner of Police of the Metropolis* [2004] EWCA Civ 1067, [2004] 3 W.L.R. 1144 (CA (Civ Div)), Lord Woolf of Barnes, L.C.J.; see *R. (on the application of Laporte) v Chief Constable of Gloucestershire* [2004] EWHC 253, [2004] 2 All E.R. 874 (QBD (Admin Ct)), May, L.J.; see *RSPCA v Attorney General* [2002] 1 W.L.R. 448 (Ch D), Lightman, J.

Sch.1 Part I Art.12, see *Bellinger v Bellinger* [2003] UKHL 21, [2003] 2 A.C. 467 (HL), Lord Nicholls of Birkenhead; see *R. (on the application of CPS) v Registrar General of Births, Deaths and Marriages* [2002] EWCA Civ 1661, [2003] Q.B. 1222 (CA), Waller, L.J.; see *R. (on the application of Mellor) v Secretary of State for the Home Department* [2001] EWCA Civ 472, [2002] Q.B. 13 (CA), Lord Phillips of Worth Matravers, M.R.

Sch.1 Part 1 Art.14, see *R. (on the application of Ali) v Birmingham City Council* [2002] EWHC 1511, [2002] H.L.R. 51 (QBD (Admin Ct)), Moses, J.; see *R. (on the application of Clift) v Secretary of State for the Home Department* [2004] EWCA Civ 514, [2004] 1 W.L.R. 2223 (CA), Lord Woolf of Barnes, L.C.J.

Sch.1 Part I Art.14, see *A v Lord Grey School Governors* [2003] EWHC 1533, [2003] 4 All E.R. 1317 (QBD), Stanley Burnton, J.; see *Adams v Scottish Ministers* 2003 S.C. 171 (OH), Lord Nimmo Smith; see *Akbar (t/a Mumtaz Paan House) v Customs and*

1998–cont.
42. Human Rights Act 1998–*cont.*
  Sch.1 Part I Art.14–*cont.*

Excise Commissioners (Human Rights) [2002] B.P.I.R. 62 (Ch D), Judge Behrens Q.C.; see *Aston Cantlow and Wilmcote with Billesley Parochial Church Council v Wallbank* [2001] EWCA Civ 713, [2002] Ch. 51 (CA), Sir Andrew Morritt V.C.; see *Aston Cantlow and Wilmcote with Billesley Parochial Church Council v Wallbank* [2003] UKHL 37, [2004] 1 A.C. 546 (HL), Lord Hobhouse of Woodborough; see *Campbell v South Northamptonshire DC* [2004] EWCA Civ 409, [2004] 3 All E.R. 387 (CA), Peter Gibson, L.J.; see *Carney v Nathan (Inspector of Taxes)* [2003] S.T.C (S.C.D.) 28 (Sp Comm), John F Avery Jones; see *Evans v Amicus Healthcare Ltd* [2004] EWCA Civ 727, [2004] 3 W.L.R. 681 (CA), Thorpe, L.J.; see *Fielding v United Kingdom (36940/97)* Times, February 25, 2002 (ECHR), J-P Costa (President); see *Flynn (Patrick Anthony) v HM Advocate* 2003 J.C. 153 (HCJ), Lord Cullen L.J.G., Lord Hamilton, Lord Osborne; see *Ghaidan v Godin-Mendoza* [2004] UKHL 30, [2004] 2 A.C. 557 (HL), Lord Nicholls of Birkenhead; see *Haas v Netherlands (36983/97)* [2004] 1 F.L.R. 673 (ECHR), Judge Costa (President); see *Holland v Inland Revenue Commissioners* [2003] S.T.C. (S.C.D.) 43 (Sp Comm), Stephen Oliver Q.C.; see *Hooper v Secretary of State for Work and Pensions* [2003] EWCA Civ 813, [2003] 1 W.L.R. 2623 (CA), Lord Phillips of Worth Matravers, M.R.; see *Kensington and Chelsea RLBC v O'Sullivan* [2003] EWCA Civ 371, [2003] 2 F.L.R. 459 (CA), Arden, L.J.; see *M v Secretary of State for Work and Pensions* [2004] EWCA Civ 1343, [2004] 3 F.C.R. 507 (CA (Civ Div)), Kennedy, L.J.; see *Malcolm v Mackenzie* [2004] EWHC 339, [2004] 1 W.L.R. 1803 (Ch D), Lloyd, J.; see *Matthews v United Kingdom (40302/98)* Times, July 30, 2002 (ECHR), J-P Costa (President); see *Nasser v United Bank of Kuwait (Security for Costs)* [2001] EWCA Civ 556, [2002] 1 W.L.R. 1868 (CA), Mance, L.J.; see *Pearce v Mayfield Secondary School Governing Body* [2001] EWCA Civ 1347, [2002] I.C.R. 198 (CA), Hale, L.J.; see *Phillips v DPP* [2002] EWHC 2093, [2003] R.T.R. 8 (QBD (Admin Ct)), McCombe, J.; see *R. (on the application of Amicus) v Secretary of State for Trade and Industry* [2004] EWHC 860, [2004] I.R.L.R. 430 (QBD (Admin Ct)), Richards, J.; see *R. (on the application of Barber) v Secretary of State for Work and Pensions* [2002] EWHC 1915, [2002] 2 F.L.R. 1181 (QBD (Admin Ct)), Sir Richard Tucker; see *R. (on the application of Borak) v Secretary of*

1998–cont.
42. Human Rights Act 1998–*cont.*
  Sch.1 Part I Art.14–*cont.*

State for the Home Department [2004] EWHC 1861, [2004] 1 W.L.R. 3129 (QBD (Admin Ct)), Harrison, J.; see *R. (on the application of Burke) v General Medical Council* [2004] EWHC 1879, [2004] 2 F.L.R. 1121 (QBD (Admin Ct)), Munby, J.; see *R. (on the application of Carson) v Secretary of State for Work and Pensions* [2002] EWHC 978, [2002] 3 All E.R. 994 (QBD (Admin Ct)), Stanley Burnton, J.; see *R. (on the application of Carson) v Secretary of State for Work and Pensions* [2003] EWCA Civ 797, [2003] 3 All E.R. 577 (CA), Laws, L.J.; see *R. (on the application of Douglas) v North Tyneside MBC* [2003] EWCA Civ 1847, [2004] 1 W.L.R. 2363 (CA), Thorpe, L.J.; see *R. (on the application of Erskine) v Lambeth LBC* [2003] EWHC 2479, [2003] N.P.C. 118 (QBD (Admin Ct)), Mitting, J.; see *R. (on the application of G) v Immigration Appeal Tribunal* [2004] EWHC 588, [2004] 1 W.L.R. 2953 (QBD (Admin Ct)), Collins, J.; see *R. (on the application of Gangera) v Hounslow LBC* [2003] EWHC 794, [2003] H.L.R. 68 (QBD (Admin Ct)), Moses, J.; see *R. (on the application of Khundakji) v Admissions Appeal Panel of Cardiff CC* [2003] EWHC 436, [2003] E.L.R. 495 (QBD (Admin Ct)), Richards, J.; see *R. (on the application of L (A Child)) v Manchester City Council* [2001] EWHC Admin 707, [2002] 1 F.L.R. 43 (QBD (Admin Ct)), Munby, J.; see *R. (on the application of McLellan) v Bracknell Forest BC* [2001] EWCA Civ 1510, [2002] Q.B. 1129 (CA), Waller, L.J.; see *R. (on the application of Painter) v Carmarthenshire CC Housing Benefit Review Board* [2001] EWHC Admin 308, [2002] H.L.R. 23 (QBD (Admin Ct)), Lightman, J.; see *R. (on the application of Purja) v Ministry of Defence* [2003] EWCA Civ 1345, [2004] 1 W.L.R. 289 (CA), Simon Brown, L.J.; see *R. (on the application of Roberts) v Parole Board* [2003] EWHC 3120, [2004] 2 All E.R. 776 (QBD (Admin Ct)), Maurice Kay, J.; see *R. (on the application of S) v Chief Constable of South Yorkshire* [2002] EWCA Civ 1275, [2002] 1 W.L.R. 3223 (CA), Lord Woolf of Barnes, L.C.J.; see *R. (on the application of S) v Chief Constable of South Yorkshire* [2004] UKHL 39, [2004] 1 W.L.R. 2196 (HL), Lord Steyn; see *R. (on the application of Smith) v Barking and Dagenham LBC* [2002] EWHC 2400, [2002] 48 E.G.C.S. 141 (QBD (Admin Ct)), Burton, J.; see *R. (on the application of Smith) v Secretary of State for Defence* [2004] EWHC 1797, [2004] Pens. L.R. 323 (QBD (Admin Ct)), Wilson, J.; see *R. (on the application of Tucker) v Secretary of State for Social Security* [2001] EWCA

CAP.

1998-cont.
42. Human Rights Act 1998-*cont.*
Sch.1 Part I Art.14-*cont.*

Civ 1646, [2002] H.L.R. 27 (CA), Waller L.J.; see *R. (on the application of Wilkinson) v Inland Revenue Commissioners* [2002] EWHC 182, [2002] S.T.C. 347 (QBD (Admin Ct)), Moses, J.; see *R. v Kirk (Craig)* [2002] EWCA Crim 1580, Times, June 26, 2002 (CA (Crim Div)), Judge, L.J.; see *Shaw (Inspector of Taxes) v Vicky Construction Ltd* [2002] EWHC 2659, [2002] S.T.C. 1544 (Ch D), Ferris, J.; see *Shaw's Application for Judicial Review, Re* [2004] N.I. 149 (QBD (NI)), Kerr, J.; see *Somerset CC v Isaacs* [2002] EWHC 1014, [2002] E.H.L.R. 18 (QBD (Admin Ct)), Stanley Burnton, J.; see *St Brice v Southwark LBC* [2001] EWCA Civ 1138, [2002] 1 W.L.R. 1537 (CA), Kennedy, L.J.; see *Wandsworth LBC v Michalak* [2002] EWCA Civ 271, [2003] 1 W.L.R. 617 (CA), Brooke, L.J.; see *Whittaker v P&D Watson (t/a P&M Watson Haulage)* [2002] I.C.R. 1244 (EAT), Lindsay, J. (President); see *X v Y (Employment: Sex Offender)* [2003] I.C.R. 1138 (EAT), Judge Peter Clark; see *X v Y (Employment: Sex Offender)* [2004] EWCA Civ 662, [2004] I.R.L.R. 625 (CA), Brooke, L.J.

Sch.1 Part I Art.17, see *Flynn (Patrick Anthony) v HM Advocate* 2003 J.C. 153 (HCJ), Lord Cullen L.J.G., Lord Hamilton, Lord Osborne

Sch.1 Part I Art.34, see *McKerr's Application for Judicial Review, Re* [2003] N.I. 117 (CA (NI)), Carswell, L.C.J.

Sch.1 Part I Art.41, see *McKerr's Application for Judicial Review, Re* [2003] N.I. 117 (CA (NI)), Carswell, L.C.J.

Sch.1 Part II Art.1, see *Adams v Scottish Ministers* 2003 S.C. 171 (OH), Lord Nimmo Smith; see *Adams v South Lanarkshire Council* 2003 S.L.T. 145 (OH), Lord Wheatley; see *Ainsdale Investments Ltd v First Secretary of State* [2004] EWHC 1010, [2004] H.L.R. 50 (QBD (Admin Ct)), Owen, J.; see *Al-Fayed v Advocate General for Scotland* [2004] S.T.C. 1703 (1 Div), Lord Cullen L.P., Lord Kirkwood, Lord MacLean; see *Aston Cantlow and Wilmcote with Billesley Parochial Church Council v Wallbank* [2001] EWCA Civ 713, [2002] Ch. 51 (CA), Sir Andrew Morritt V.C.; see *Aston Cantlow and Wilmcote with Billesley Parochial Church Council v Wallbank* [2003] UKHL 37, [2004] 1 A.C. 546 (HL), Lord Hobhouse of Woodborough; see *Campbell v South Northamptonshire DC* [2004] EWCA Civ 409, [2004] 3 All E.R. 387 (CA), Peter Gibson, L.J.; see *Crompton (t/a David Crompton Haulage) v Department of Transport North Western Area* [2003] EWCA Civ 64, [2003] R.T.R.

CAP.

1998-cont.
42. Human Rights Act 1998-*cont.*
Sch.1 Part II Art.1-*cont.*

34 (CA), Kennedy, L.J.; see *Customs and Excise Commissioners v Newbury* [2003] EWHC 702, [2003] 1 W.L.R. 2131 (QBD (Admin Ct)), Hale, L.J.; see *Dennis v Ministry of Defence* [2003] EWHC 793, [2003] Env. L.R. 34 (QBD), Buckley, J.; see *Di Ciacca v Scottish Ministers* 2003 S.L.T. 1031 (OH), Lord Reed; see *Duggan v Full Sutton Prison Governor* [2003] EWHC 361, [2003] 2 All E.R. 678 (Ch D), Hart, J.; see *Duggan v Full Sutton Prison Governor* [2004] EWCA Civ 78, [2004] 1 W.L.R. 1010 (CA), Peter Gibson, L.J.; see *Fab Tek Engineering Ltd v Carillion Construction Ltd* 2002 S.L.T. (Sh Ct) 113 (Sh Ct (Tayside, Central and Fife)), JS Forbes; see *Family Housing Association v Donnellan* [2002] 1 P. & C.R. 34 (Ch D), Park, J.; see *Fielding v United Kingdom (36940/97)* Times, February 25, 2002 (ECHR), J-P Costa (President); see *Fox v Customs and Excise Commissioners* [2002] EWHC 1244, [2003] 1 W.L.R. 1331 (QBD (Admin Ct)), Lightman, J.; see *Gascoyne v Customs and Excise Commissioners* [2003] EWHC 257, [2003] Ch. 292 (Ch D), Neuberger, J.; see *Gladders v Prior (Inspector of Taxes)* [2003] S.T.C. (S.C.D.) 245 (Sp Comm), John F Avery Jones; see *Gora v Customs and Excise Commissioners* [2003] EWCA Civ 525, [2004] Q.B. 93 (CA), Pill, L.J.; see *Halliday v Secretary of State for Transport, Local Government and the Regions* [2003] R.V.R. 12 (LandsTr), George Bartlett Q.C. (President); see *Holder v Law Society* [2002] EWHC 1559, Times, September 9, 2002 (Ch D), Peter Smith, J.; see *Holder v Law Society* [2003] EWCA Civ 39, [2003] 1 W.L.R. 1059 (CA), Carnwath, L.J.; see *Hooper v Secretary of State for Work and Pensions* [2003] EWCA Civ 813, [2003] 1 W.L.R. 2623 (CA), Lord Phillips of Worth Matravers, M.R.; see *Hughes v Customs and Excise Commissioners* [2002] EWCA Civ 734, [2003] 1 W.L.R. 177 (CA), Simon Brown, L.J.; see *International Ferry Traders Ltd v Adur DC* [2004] EWCA Civ 288, [2004] 2 E.G.L.R. 89 (CA), Pill, L.J.; see *International Transport Roth GmbH v Secretary of State for the Home Department* [2002] EWCA Civ 158, [2003] Q.B. 728 (CA), Simon Brown, L.J.; see *Irving's Curator Bonis v Skillen* 2002 S.L.T. (Sh Ct) 119 (Sh Ct (Glasgow and Strathkelvin)), WH Holligan; see *Irving's Curator Bonis v Skillen* 2003 S.L.T. (Sh Ct) 27 (Sh Pr), EF Bowen Q.C., Sheriff Principal; see *Karl Construction Ltd v Palisade Properties Plc* 2002 S.C. 270 (OH), Lord Drummond Young; see *Legal & General Assurance Co Ltd v Kirk* [2001] EWCA Civ 1803, [2002] I.R.L.R.

1998–cont.
42. Human Rights Act 1998–*cont.*
Sch.1 Part II Art.1–*cont.*

124 (CA), Jonathan Parker, L.J.; see *Levi Strauss & Co v Tesco Stores Ltd* [2002] EWHC 1625, [2002] 3 C.M.L.R. 11 (Ch D), Pumfrey, J.; see *Local Authorities Mutual Investment Trust v Customs and Excise Commissioners* [2003] EWHC 2766, [2004] S.T.C. 246 (Ch D), Lawrence Collins, J.; see *Lough v First Secretary of State* [2004] EWCA Civ 905, [2004] 1 W.L.R. 2557 (CA), Pill, L.J.; see *MacPherson v Bevan Ashford (A Firm)* [2003] EWHC 636, [2003] 3 Costs L.R. 389 (Ch D), Patten, J.; see *Marcic v Thames Water Utilities Ltd* [2002] EWCA Civ 64, [2002] Q.B. 929 (CA), Lord Phillips of Worth Matravers, M.R.; see *Marcic v Thames Water Utilities Ltd* [2003] UKHL 66, [2004] 2 A.C. 42 (HL), Lord Nicholls of Birkenhead; see *Matthews v United Kingdom (40302/98)* Times, July 30, 2002 (ECHR), J-P Costa (President); see *Pennycook v Shaws (EAL) Ltd* [2004] EWCA Civ 100, [2004] Ch. 296 (CA), Thorpe, L.J.; see *Phillips v DPP* [2002] EWHC 2093, [2003] R.T.R. 8 (QBD (Admin Ct)), McCombe, J.; see *Prosser (Jempson's Personal Representative) v Inland Revenue Commissioners* [2003] S.T.C. (S.C.D.) 250 (Sp Comm), John F Avery Jones; see *R. (on the application of Association of British Civilian Internees (Far East Region)) v Secretary of State for Defence* [2002] EWHC 2119, Independent, October 31, 2002 (QBD (Admin Ct)), Scott Baker, J.; see *R. (on the application of Baker) v First Secretary of State* [2003] EWHC 2511, [2004] R.V.R. 13 (QBD (Admin Ct)), Nicholas Blake Q.C.; see *R. (on the application of Boyd) v English Nature* [2003] EWHC 1105, [2004] Env. L.R. D4 (QBD (Admin Ct)), Rabinder Singh Q.C.; see *R. (on the application of Brennon) v Bromsgrove DC* [2003] EWHC 752, [2003] 2 P. & C.R. 33 (QBD (Admin Ct)), Richards, J.; see *R. (on the application of Carson) v Secretary of State for Work and Pensions* [2002] EWHC 978, [2002] 3 All E.R. 994 (QBD (Admin Ct)), Stanley Burnton, J.; see *R. (on the application of Carson) v Secretary of State for Work and Pensions* [2003] EWCA Civ 797, [2003] 3 All E.R. 577 (CA), Laws, L.J.; see *R. (on the application of Carvill) v Inland Revenue Commissioners* [2003] EWHC 1852, [2003] S.T.C. 1539 (QBD (Admin Ct)), McCombe, J.; see *R. (on the application of Clays Lane Housing Cooperative Ltd) v Housing Corp* [2004] EWHC 1084, [2004] H.L.R. 51 (QBD (Admin Ct)), Keith, J.; see *R. (on the application of Denson) v Child Support Agency* [2002] EWHC 154, [2002] 1 F.L.R. 938 (QBD (Admin Ct)), Munby, J.; see *R. (on the applica-*

1998–cont.
42. Human Rights Act 1998–*cont.*
Sch.1 Part II Art.1–*cont.*

tion of Fisher) v English Nature [2003] EWHC 1599, [2004] 1 W.L.R. 503 (QBD (Admin Ct)), Lightman, J.; see *R. (on the application of Fuller) v Chief Constable of Dorset* [2001] EWHC Admin 1057, [2003] Q.B. 480 (QBD (Admin Ct)), Stanley Burnton, J.; see *R. (on the application of Hamilton) v United Kingdom Central Council for Nursing, Midwifery and Health Visiting* [2003] EWCA Civ 1600, (2004) 79 B.M.L.R. 30 (CA), Sedley, L.J.; see *R. (on the application of Langton) v Department for the Environment, Food and Rural Affairs* [2001] EWHC Admin 1047, [2002] Env. L.R. 20 (QBD (Admin Ct)), Nigel Pleming Q.C.; see *R. (on the application of London & Continental Stations & Property Ltd) v Rail Regulator* [2003] EWHC 2607, [2004] A.C.D. 13 (QBD (Admin Ct)), Moses, J.; see *R. (on the application of MWH&H Ward Estates Ltd) v Monmouthshire CC* [2002] EWHC 229, [2002] E.H.L.R. 14 (QBD (Admin Ct)), Richards, J.; see *R. (on the application of POW Trust) v Chief Executive and Registrar of Companies* [2002] EWHC 2783, [2004] B.C.C. 268 (QBD (Admin Ct)), Lightman, J.; see *R. (on the application of Quark Fishing Ltd) v Secretary of State for Foreign and Commonwealth Affairs (No.2)* [2003] EWHC 1743, [2003] A.C.D. 96 (QBD (Admin Ct)), Collins, J.; see *R. (on the application of Smith) v Secretary of State for Defence* [2004] EWHC 1797, [2004] Pens. L.R. 323 (QBD (Admin Ct)), Wilson, J.; see *R. (on the application of Thompson) v Law Society* [2004] EWCA Civ 167, [2004] 1 W.L.R. 2522 (CA), Kennedy, L.J.; see *R. (on the application of Trailer & Marina (Leven) Ltd) v Secretary of State for the Environment, Food and Rural Affairs* [2004] EWHC 153, [2004] Env. L.R. 40 (QBD (Admin Ct)), Ouseley, J.; see *R. (on the application of Westminster City Council) v Mayor of London* [2002] EWHC 2440, [2003] B.L.G.R. 611 (QBD (Admin Ct)), Maurice Kay, J.; see *R. (on the application of Wilkinson) v Inland Revenue Commissioners* [2002] EWHC 182, [2002] S.T.C. 347 (QBD (Admin Ct)), Moses, J.; see *R. v Rezvi (Syed)* [2002] UKHL 1, [2003] 1 A.C. 1099 (HL), Lord Steyn; see *Rowland v Environment Agency* [2002] EWHC 2785, [2003] Ch. 581 (Ch D), Lightman, J.; see *Rowland v Environment Agency* [2003] EWCA Civ 1885, [2004] 3 W.L.R. 249 (CA), Mance, L.J.; see *Shaw (Inspector of Taxes) v Vicky Construction Ltd* [2002] EWHC 2659, [2002] S.T.C. 1544 (Ch D), Ferris, J.; see *Soteriou v Ultrachem Ltd* [2004] EWHC 983, [2004] I.R.L.R. 870 (QBD), Judge

1998–cont.

42. Human Rights Act 1998–cont.

Sch.1 Part II Art.1–cont.

Altman; see *Stewart's Application for Judicial Review, Re* [2003] N.I. 149 (CA (NI)), Carswell, L.C.J.; see *Upton v National Westminster Bank Plc* [2004] EWHC 1962, [2004] W.T.L.R. 1339 (Ch D), Judge Behrens; see *Wilson v First County Trust Ltd (No.2)* [2003] UKHL 40, [2004] 1 A.C. 816 (HL), Lord Nicholls of Birkenhead

Sch.1 Part II Art.2, see *A v Lord Grey School Governors* [2003] EWHC 1533, [2003] 4 All E.R. 1317 (QBD), Stanley Burnton, J.; see *A v Lord Grey School Governors* [2004] EWCA Civ 382, [2004] Q.B. 1231 (CA), Dame Elizabeth Butler-Sloss (President); see *Dove v Scottish Ministers* 2002 S.L.T. 1296 (Ex Div), Lord Cameron of Lochbroom, Lord Macfadyen, Lord Sutherland; see *R. (on the application of B (A Child)) v Alperton Community School Head Teacher and Governing Body* [2001] EWHC Admin 229, [2002] B.L.G.R. 132 (QBD (Admin Ct)), Newman, J.; see *R. (on the application of Begum (Shabina)) v Denbigh High School Governors* [2004] EWHC 1389, [2004] E.L.R. 374 (QBD (Admin Ct)), Bennett, J.; see *R. (on the application of Douglas) v North Tyneside MBC* [2003] EWCA Civ 1847, [2004] 1 W.L.R. 2363 (CA), Thorpe, L.J.; see *R. (on the application of K) v Newham LBC* [2002] EWHC 405, [2002] E.L.R. 390 (QBD (Admin Ct)), Collins, J.; see *R. (on the application of Williamson) v Secretary of State for Education and Employment* [2002] EWCA Civ 1926, [2003] Q.B. 1300 (CA), Buxton, L.J.; see *Ram v Ram (No.1)* [2004] EWCA Civ 1452, [2004] 3 F.C.R. 425 (CA (Civ Div)), Potter, L.J.; see *T v Special Educational Needs Tribunal* [2002] EWHC 1474, [2002] E.L.R. 704 (QBD (Admin Ct)), Richards, J.

Sch.1 Part III, substituted: SI 2004/1574 Art.2

Sch.1 Part III Art.1, see *R. (on the application of St John) v Governor of Brixton Prison* [2001] EWHC Admin 543, [2002] Q.B. 613 (QBD (Admin Ct)), Harrison, J.

Sch.2 para.1, enabling: SI 2004/66

Sch.2 Part I Art.1, see *R. (on the application of MWH&H Ward Estates Ltd) v Monmouthshire CC* [2002] EWCA Civ 1915, [2003] E.H.L.R. 10 (CA), Laws, L.J.

Sch.4, disapplied: SI 2003/1887 Sch.1

Sch1 Part I Art.6, see *Pan Atlantic Insurance Co Ltd, Re* [2003] EWHC 1696, [2003] B.C.C. 847 (Ch D (Companies Ct)), Lloyd, J.

43. Statute Law (Repeals) Act 1998

Sch.2 para.3, repealed: 2003 c.39 Sch.10

1998–cont.

45. Regional Development Agencies Act 1998

s.7, applied: SI 2004/2203 Reg.10, SI 2004/2204 Reg.15

s.8, applied: 2003 c.10 s.25

s.39A, added: SI 2003/2867 Sch.1 para.27

Sch.1, applied: 2003 c.10 s.28

Sch.1, referred to: 2004 c.5 s.12

Sch.5 Part I para.1, repealed: 2004 c.5 Sch.9

Sch.6 para.1, amended: 2003 c.21 Sch.17 para.155

Sch.6 para.2, amended: 2003 c.21 Sch.17 para.155

Sch.6 para.8, amended: 2003 c.21 Sch.17 para.155

Sch.6 para.9, amended: 2003 c.21 Sch.17 para.155

Sch.6 para.11, amended: 2003 c.21 Sch.17 para.155

Sch.6 para.16, repealed (in part): 2003 c.21 Sch.19

46. Scotland Act 1998

applied: 2002 c.40 Sch.25 para.2, Sch.25 para.10, SI 2002/528 Reg.2, 2003 c.26 s.129, 2003 c.42 s.142, SI 2003/409 Sch.1 Part I, 2004 c.17 s.2, s.6, Sch.1 para.6, Sch.1 para.25

s.2, applied: SI 2002/2779 Art.85

s.2, referred to: SI 2002/2779 Art.91

s.5, referred to: SI 2002/2779 Sch.2 para.10

s.7, applied: SI 2002/2779 Sch.2 para.25, Sch.2 para.63, Sch.2 para.71, SI 2003/122 Art.4

s.8, amended: SI 2002/2779 Sch.2 para.64

s.8, applied: SI 2002/2779 Sch.2 para.25, Sch.2 para.63, Sch.2 para.66, SI 2003/122 Art.4

s.9, applied: SI 2002/2779 Art.82, Sch.2 para.2, Sch.2 para.72

s.9, referred to: SI 2002/2779 Sch.2 para.10

s.10, amended: SI 2002/2779 Art.84

s.10, applied: SI 2002/2779 Art.83, Sch.2 para.72

s.12, amended: 2002 c.24 Sch.3 para.7

s.12, enabling: SI 2002/2779

s.15, applied: SI 2002/2779 Sch.2 para.10

s.15, referred to: SI 2002/2779 Sch.2 para.10

s.15, enabling: SI 2003/409

s.16, referred to: SI 2002/2779 Sch.2 para.10

s.17, referred to: SI 2002/2779 Sch.2 para.10

s.18, referred to: SI 2002/2779 Sch.2 para.10

s.23, applied: 2002 asp 16 s.13, 2002 c.17 Sch.7 para.2, 2003 asp 17 s.9, Sch.2 para.2, 2004 c.17 Sch.1 para.6, 2004 c.20 Sch.1 para.17

s.30, enabling: SI 2002/1629, SI 2003/2617, SI 2004/2030, SI 2004/3324, SI 2004/3329

s.44, applied: SSI 2002/62 Sch.2 Part III

1998–cont.

46. Scotland Act 1998–*cont.*

s.57, see *Davidson v Scottish Ministers (No.1)* 2002 S.C. 205 (Ex Div), Lord Marnoch, Lord Hardie, Lord Weir; see *HM Advocate v R* [2002] UKPC D3, [2004] 1 A.C. 462 (Privy Council (Scotland)), Lord Hope of Craighead; see *HM Advocate v R* 2002 S.L.T. 834 (HCJ Appeal), Lord Coulsfield, Lord Cameron of Lochbroom, Lord Caplan; see *HM Advocate v Vervuren* 2002 S.L.T. 555 (HCJ), Lady Paton; see *Millar v Dickson* [2001] UKPC D4, [2002] 1 W.L.R. 1615 (PC (Sc)), Lord Bingham of Cornhill; see *Montgomery v HM Advocate* [2003] 1 A.C. 641 (Privy Council (Scotland)), Lord Hope of Craighead; see *Stevens (Andrew) v HM Advocate* 2002 S.L.T. 1249 (HCJ), Lady Paton

s.57, enabling: SI 2002/528

s.63, applied: SI 2003/2617 Art.2, Sch.1 para.2, 2004 c.20 s.93, SI 2004/2030 Art.2

s.63, enabling: SI 2002/1630, SI 2003/415, SI 2003/2617, SI 2004/2030

s.64, applied: SI 2004/953 Art.2

s.64, enabling: SI 2004/953

s.65, applied: 2002 asp 7 s.4, s.6, 2003 asp 6 s.4, s.6, 2004 asp 2 s.4, s.6

s.65, referred to: 2002 asp 7 s.4

s.70, applied: 2002 c.17 Sch.7 para.2, 2004 c.17 Sch.1 para.6, 2004 c.20 Sch.1 para.17

s.79, amended: 2003 c.1 Sch.6 para.237

s.81, applied: 2003 c.1 s.291, s.293, s.294

s.85, repealed (in part): 2003 c.44 Sch.37 Part 10

s.88, applied: SI 2002/302, SI 2002/303, SI 2003/285, SI 2003/286, SI 2004/368

s.88, referred to: SI 2004/369

s.88, enabling: SI 2002/302, SI 2002/303, SI 2003/285, SI 2003/286, SI 2004/368, SI 2004/369, SI 2004/1309

s.89, enabling: SI 2002/2636

s.91, applied: 2004 c.20 Sch.1 para.17

s.93, applied: 2002 asp 11 s.7, s.23, SI 2002/261 Art.2, SI 2002/800 Art.2, SI 2003/407 Art.2

s.93, enabling: SI 2002/261, SI 2002/800, SI 2003/407

s.100, see *Adams v Scottish Ministers* 2003 S.C. 171 (OH), Lord Nimmo Smith

s.100, amended: 2002 c.26 Sch.7 para.7

s.102, amended: 2002 c.26 Sch.7 para.10

s.103, enabling: SI 2003/1880

s.104, enabling: SI 2002/653, SI 2002/1264, SI 2002/2264, SI 2002/2367, SI 2003/2250, SI 2003/2278, SI 2004/956, SI 2004/957, SI 2004/1822, SI 2004/1823, SI 2004/2261, SI 2004/3089

s.106, enabling: SI 2004/2980

s.112, enabling: SI 2002/653, SI 2002/1264, SI 2002/2264, SI 2002/2367, SI 2003/2250, SI 2003/2278, SI 2004/956, SI

1998–cont.

46. Scotland Act 1998–*cont.*

s.112, enabling:–*cont.*
2004/957, SI 2004/1822, SI 2004/1823, SI 2004/2261, SI 2004/2980, SI 2004/3089

s.113, amended: 2003 c.44 Sch.27 para.7

s.113, enabling: SI 2002/261, SI 2002/800, SI 2002/1264, SI 2002/1630, SI 2002/2264, SI 2002/2636, SI 2002/2779, SI 2003/407, SI 2003/415, SI 2003/2250, SI 2003/2278, SI 2003/2617, SI 2004/956, SI 2004/957, SI 2004/1822, SI 2004/1823, SI 2004/2030, SI 2004/2261, SI 2004/3089

s.115, applied: SI 2004/956, SI 2004/957, SI 2004/1822, SI 2004/1823

s.115, enabling: SI 2004/953

s.117, applied: SI 2003/2617 Art.5, SI 2004/2030 Art.6

s.117, varied: SI 2002/1630 Art.3, SI 2003/415 Art.4

s.118, applied: SI 2004/2030 Art.6

s.118, varied: SI 2003/415 Art.4

s.119, applied: SI 2003/2617 Art.5, SI 2004/2030 Art.6

s.119, varied: SI 2002/1630 Art.3, SI 2003/415 Art.4

s.120, varied: SI 2003/415 Art.4

s.121, varied: SI 2002/1630 Art.3

s.124, enabling: SI 2002/1630, SI 2003/415, SI 2003/2617, SI 2004/2030

s.126, applied: SI 2002/801 Art.2, SSI 2002/62 Sch.3, 2004 c.36 s.31

s.126, enabling: SI 2002/653, SI 2002/801

Sch.1 para.1, substituted: 2004 c.13 Sch.1

Sch.1 para.1, varied: 2004 c.13 Sch.2 para.1

Sch.1 para.2, substituted: 2004 c.13 Sch.1

Sch.1 para.2, varied: 2004 c.13 Sch.2 para.1

Sch.1 para.3, applied: 2004 c.13 Sch.3 para.2

Sch.1 para.3, substituted: 2004 c.13 Sch.1

Sch.1 para.3, varied: 2004 c.13 Sch.2 para.1

Sch.1 para.4, substituted: 2004 c.13 Sch.1

Sch.1 para.4, varied: 2004 c.13 Sch.2 para.1

Sch.1 para.4A, substituted: 2004 c.13 Sch.1

Sch.1 para.4A, varied: 2004 c.13 Sch.2 para.1

Sch.1 para.5, substituted: 2004 c.13 Sch.1

Sch.1 para.5, varied: 2004 c.13 Sch.2 para.1, Sch.2 para.2

Sch.1 para.6, substituted: 2004 c.13 Sch.1

Sch.1 para.6, varied: 2004 c.13 Sch.2 para.1

Sch.1 para.7, substituted: 2004 c.13 Sch.1

Sch.1 para.7, varied: 2004 c.13 Sch.2 para.1, Sch.2 para.3

Sch.1 para.8, substituted: 2004 c.13 Sch.1

Sch.1 para.8, varied: 2004 c.13 Sch.2 para.1, Sch.2 para.4

Sch.1 para.9, substituted: 2004 c.13 Sch.1

Sch.1 para.9, varied: 2004 c.13 Sch.2 para.12004 c.13 Sch.1

Sch.1 para.10, varied: 2004 c.13 Sch.2 para.1

Sch.1 para.11, substituted: 2004 c.13 Sch.1

CAP.

1998–cont.

46. Scotland Act 1998–cont.

Sch.1 para.11, varied: 2004 c.13 Sch.2 para.1

Sch.1 para.12, substituted: 2004 c.13 Sch.1

Sch.1 para.12, varied: 2004 c.13 Sch.2 para.1

Sch.1 para.13, substituted: 2004 c.13 Sch.1

Sch.1 para.13, varied: 2004 c.13 Sch.2 para.1

Sch.1 para.14, substituted: 2004 c.13 Sch.1

Sch.1 para.14, varied: 2004 c.13 Sch.2 para.1

Sch.5 Part II paraE.2, amended: SI 2002/1629 Art.2

Sch.5 Part II paraL.2, applied: 2003 asp 4 s.2

Sch.5 Part II paraL.2, referred to: SI 2003/3006 Art.4

Sch.5 Part II paraB.3, amended: 2002 c.24 Sch.3 para.7

Sch.5 Part III para.1, applied: 2002 asp 13 s.4

Sch.5 Part III para.2, applied: 2002 asp 13 s.4

Sch.6, see *HM Advocate v PH* 2002 S.C.C.R. 927 (HCJ), Lord MacLean

Sch.6, applied: SI 2003/435 Sch.2 para.2

Sch.6 Part I para.1, applied: SI 2004/1861 Sch.1 para.56

Sch.6 Part I para.1, referred to: SI 2004/753 Sch.1 para.14

Sch.6 Part II para.10, applied: SSI 2002/494 Reg.4

Sch.6 Part II para.12, applied: SSI 2002/494 Reg.4

Sch.6 Part II para.13, applied: SSI 2002/494 Reg.4

Sch.6 Part IV para.25, amended: 2002 c.26 Sch.7 para.4

Sch.6 Part IV para.26, amended: 2002 c.26 Sch.7 para.4

Sch.6 Part V para.33, amended: 2002 c.26 Sch.7 para.4

Sch.6 Part V para.34, amended: 2002 c.26 Sch.7 para.4

Sch.6 Part V para.37, enabling: SI 2004/1861, SI 2004/2351

Sch.6 para.9, see *Webster v Dominick* 2003 S.L.T. 975 (HCJ), Lord Gill L.J.C., Lady Cosgrove, Lord Macfadyen, Lord Marnoch, Lord Sutherland

Sch.6 para.33, see *Clark v Kelly* [2003] UKPC D1, [2004] 1 A.C. 681 (Privy Council (Scotland)), Lord Hope of Craighead

Sch.7, enabling: SI 2004/953

Sch.7 para.1, applied: SI 2004/956, SI 2004/957, SI 2004/1822, SI 2004/1823

Sch.7 para.2, applied: SI 2004/956, SI 2004/957, SI 2004/1822, SI 2004/1823

Sch.7 para.3, applied: SI 2004/956, SI 2004/957, SI 2004/1822, SI 2004/1823

Sch.8 para.15, applied: 2004 c.33 s.260

47. Northern Ireland Act 1998

applied: 2002 c.18 Sch.2 Part 2, Sch.2 Part 39, SI 2002/2843, 2003 c.13 Sch.2 Part 1, Sch.2 Part 2, Sch.2 Part 43, SI 2003/435 Sch.2 para.2

CAP.

1998–cont.

47. Northern Ireland Act 1998–cont.

referred to: SI 2002/265, 2003 c.25 s.11, 2004 c.9 Sch.2 Part 2, Sch.2 Part 39

s.1, repealed: 2003 c.25 s.12

s.2, repealed: 2003 c.25 s.12

s.3, repealed: 2003 c.25 s.12

s.4, applied: 2004 c.17 s.2, s.6, Sch.1 para.26

s.4, referred to: 2002 c.17 Sch.7 para.16

s.6, applied: SI 2002/790, SI 2002/790 Sch.1 para.3, Sch.2 para.2, Sch.2 para.3, Sch.3 para.1, Sch.3 para.3, Sch.3 para.4, Sch.3 para.7

s.6, enabling: SI 2002/790

s.7, amended: 2002 c.26 s.84, Sch.13

s.11, amended: 2002 c.26 Sch.7 para.1

s.11, repealed: 2003 c.25 s.12

s.12, amended: 2002 c.26 Sch.7 para.1

s.14, amended: 2002 c.26 Sch.7 para.1

s.16, see *Robinson v Secretary of State for Northern Ireland* [2002] UKHL 32, [2002] N.I. 390 (HL (NI)), Lord Bingham of Cornhill

s.18, amended: 2003 c.25 s.5, s.10

s.30, amended: 2003 c.25 s.4, s.5

s.30A, added: 2003 c.25 s.5

s.30A, repealed: 2003 c.25 s.12

s.30B, added: 2003 c.25 s.6

s.31, amended: 2003 c.3 s.1, 2003 c.12 s.1

s.31, applied: 2003 c.12 s.1

s.31, enabling: SI 2003/2697

s.32, see *Robinson v Secretary of State for Northern Ireland* [2002] UKHL 32, [2002] N.I. 390 (HL (NI)), Lord Bingham of Cornhill

s.32, applied: 2003 c.3 s.1

s.34, enabling: SI 2002/1964, SI 2003/2989

s.43, applied: 2002 c.26 s.25

s.47, applied: 2003 c.12 s.4, 2003 c.1 s.293, s.294, SI 2003/3039 Art.2

s.47, referred to: 2003 c.12 s.4

s.47, varied: 2003 c.12 s.4, SI 2003/3039 Art.2

s.47A, added: 2003 c.25 s.7

s.47B, added: 2003 c.25 s.7

s.47B, repealed: 2003 c.25 s.12

s.47B, varied: SI 2004/1164 Art.2

s.47C, added: 2003 c.25 s.7

s.48, amended: 2003 c.25 s.7

s.48, applied: 2002 c.26 s.23, 2003 c.1 s.291

s.51A, added: 2003 c.25 s.8

s.51B, added: 2003 c.25 s.8

s.51B, repealed: 2003 c.25 s.12

s.51B, varied: SI 2004/1164 Art.3

s.51C, added: 2003 c.25 s.8

s.51D, added: 2003 c.25 s.9

s.68, see *R. (on the application of Northern Ireland Human Rights Commission) v Greater Belfast Coroner* [2002] UKHL 25, [2002] N.I. 236 (HL (NI)), Lord Slynn of Hadley

1998–cont.

47. Northern Ireland Act 1998–*cont.*

s.69, see *R. (on the application of Northern Ireland Human Rights Commission) v Greater Belfast Coroner* [2002] UKHL 25, [2002] N.I. 236 (HL (NI)), Lord Slynn of Hadley

s.71, amended: 2002 c.26 Sch.7 para.5

s.75, amended: 2002 c.26 s.38, Sch.12 para.63

s.75, applied: SI 2003/55 Art.2, Art.3, SI 2004/1957 Art.2, Art.3

s.75, enabling: SI 2003/55, SI 2004/1957

s.76, amended: 2002 c.26 s.38, Sch.12 para.64

s.81, amended: 2002 c.26 Sch.7 para.8

s.82, enabling: SI 2003/1880

s.84, enabling: SI 2002/2835, SI 2003/1245

s.85, enabling: SI 2002/796

s.86, applied: SI 2002/790, SI 2002/790 Sch.1 para.3, Sch.2 para.2, Sch.2 para.3, Sch.3 para.1, Sch.3 para.3, Sch.3 para.4, Sch.3 para.7

s.86, enabling: SI 2002/790, SI 2002/2843

s.87, amended: 2002 c.21 s.64, SI 2002/265 Art.2, SI 2003/1890 Art.2

s.87, applied: SI 2002/265, SI 2003/418 Art.4

s.87, enabling: SI 2002/265, SI 2002/771, SI 2003/1890, SR 2002/121

s.91, amended: 2002 c.26 Sch.7 para.19

s.91, applied: 2002 c.26 Sch.1, Sch.6

s.95A, added: 2003 c.25 s.10

s.96, amended: 2003 c.12 s.1

s.96, repealed (in part): 2003 c.12 s.1

s.98, applied: SI 2002/791, SI 2002/791 Art.2, Art.3, 2004 c.36 s.31

s.98, referred to: SR 2002/352 Reg.4

s.98, enabling: SI 2002/791

Sch.2 para.9A, added: 2004 c.6 s.25

Sch.2 para.10A, added: 2002 c.21 s.64

Sch.2 para.10B, added: 2002 c.21 s.64

Sch.2 para.11, amended: 2002 c.26 s.9, s.82, Sch.13

Sch.2 para.21A, added: 2002 c.26 s.27

Sch.3 para.1, amended: 2002 c.26 Sch.12 para.65

Sch.3 para.9, amended: 2002 c.26 s.83, Sch.12 para.65

Sch.3 para.9A, added: 2002 c.26 s.83

Sch.3 para.15A, added: 2002 c.26 s.83

Sch.3 para.25, amended: SI 2003/3075 Sch.2 para.2

Sch.3 para.35A, added: 2004 c.8 s.7

Sch.3 para.39, amended: SI 2002/3153 Sch.6 Part I

Sch.9, applied: SI 2003/435 Art.22

Sch.10, applied: SI 2003/435 Sch.2 para.2

Sch.10 Part II para.4, amended: 2002 c.26 Sch.7 para.2

Sch.10 Part II para.5, amended: 2002 c.26 Sch.7 para.2

1998–cont.

47. Northern Ireland Act 1998–*cont.*

Sch.10 Part II para.6, amended: 2002 c.26 Sch.13

Sch.10 Part III para.12, amended: 2002 c.26 Sch.13

Sch.10 Part III para.13, amended: 2002 c.26 Sch.7 para.2

Sch.10 Part III para.14, amended: 2002 c.26 Sch.13

Sch.10 Part IV para.22, amended: 2002 c.26 Sch.13

Sch.10 Part IV para.23, amended: 2002 c.26 Sch.7 para.2

Sch.10 Part IV para.24, amended: 2002 c.26 Sch.13

Sch.10 Part V para.33, amended: 2002 c.26 Sch.7 para.2

Sch.10 Part V para.34, amended: 2002 c.26 Sch.7 para.2

Sch.10 Part V para.35, amended: 2002 c.26 Sch.7 para.2

Sch.10 Part V para.36, repealed: 2002 c.26 Sch.13

Sch.10 Part V para.39, amended: SI 2003/435 Sch.4 para.14

Sch.10 Part V para.39, repealed (in part): SI 2003/435 Sch.5

Sch.11 para.2, amended: 2002 c.26 Sch.3 para.38

Sch.11 para.3, amended: 2002 c.26 Sch.3 para.38

Sch.11 para.4, amended: 2002 c.26 Sch.3 para.38

Sch.12 para.11, enabling: SR 2002/185, SR 2003/489

Sch.12A para.1, added: 2003 c.25 s.10

Sch.12A para.2, added: 2003 c.25 s.10

Sch.12A para.3, added: 2003 c.25 s.10

Sch.12A para.4, added: 2003 c.25 s.10

Sch.12A para.5, added: 2003 c.25 s.10

Sch.12A para.6, added: 2003 c.25 s.10

Sch.12A para.7, added: 2003 c.25 s.10

Sch.12A para.8, added: 2003 c.25 s.10

Sch.12A para.9, added: 2003 c.25 s.10

Sch.12A para.10, added: 2003 c.25 s.10

48. Registration of Political Parties Act 1998

Sch.3 para.1, consolidated: 2002 c.24 s.2

1999

i. City of Westminster Act 1999

s.2, amended: 2004 c.i Sch.5

s.2, varied: 2004 c.i s.20

s.24, applied: 2004 c.i Sch.2

s.27, applied: 2004 c.i Sch.2

Welfare Reform and Pension Act 1999

s.85, see *H v H (Pension Sharing: Rescission of Decree Nisi)* [2002] EWHC 767, [2002] 2 F.L.R. 116 (Fam Div), Bodey, J.

CAP.

1999–cont.

1. Cathedrals Measure 1999

Sch.1 para.1, consolidated: 2002 c.24 Sch.1 para.3

Sch.1 para.2, consolidated: 2002 c.24 Sch.1 para.3

Sch.1 para.3, consolidated: 2002 c.24 Sch.1 para.3

Sch.1 para.4, consolidated: 2002 c.24 Sch.1 para.3

Sch.1 para.5, consolidated: 2002 c.24 Sch.1 para.3

Sch.1 para.6, consolidated: 2002 c.24 Sch.1 para.3

1. European Parliamentary Elections Act 1999

repealed: 2002 c.24 Sch.4

s.1, consolidated: 2002 c.24 s.1, s.2, s.3, s.4, s.8, s.13

s.4, consolidated: 2002 c.24 s.6

Sch.1, consolidated: 2002 c.24 s.13, Sch.1 para.1, Sch.1 para.2, Sch.1 para.4

Sch.2 para.5, consolidated: 2002 c.24 s.7

Sch.2 para.6, consolidated: 2002 c.24 s.2, s.7

Sch.2 para.8, consolidated: 2002 c.24 s.13

Sch.2 para.9, consolidated: 2002 c.24 s.6

Sch.2 para.10, consolidated: 2002 c.24 s.10

Sch.2 para.11, consolidated: 2002 c.24 s.11, s.13

Sch.3, consolidated: 2002 c.24 s.9

Sch.3 para.2, consolidated: 2002 c.24 Sch.3 para.4

2. Care of Places of Worship Measure 1999

s.1, referred to: SI 2002/1892 Sch.1 Part TABLE proviso.001, SI 2003/1933 Sch.1 Part I proviso.001

s.3, applied: SI 2002/1892 Sch.1 Part TABLE, SI 2003/1933 Sch.1 Part I, SI 2004/1888 Sch.1 Part TABLE

s.3, referred to: SI 2002/1892 Sch.1 Part TABLE proviso.001, SI 2003/1933 Sch.1 Part I proviso.001, SI 2004/1888 Sch.1 Part TABLE proviso.001

2. Social Security Contributions (Transfer of Functions, etc.) Act 1999

s.4, amended: 2004 c.3 Sch.1 para.5, Sch.2 Part 1

s.4, repealed (in part): 2004 c.3 Sch.2 Part 1

s.8, amended: 2002 c.22 s.9

s.8, enabling: SI 2002/2366, SI 2002/2820, SI 2003/1192

s.8, see *Taylor Gordon & Co Ltd (t/a Plan Personnel) v Timmons* [2004] I.R.L.R. 180 (EAT), Recorder Luba Q.C.; see *Tilbury Consulting Ltd v Gittins (Inspector of Taxes) (No.2)* [2004] S.T.C. (S.C.D.) 72 (Sp Comm), Stephen Oliver Q.C.

s.9, enabling: SI 2002/3120

s.11, amended: 2002 c.22 s.9

s.11, enabling: SI 2002/3120

s.13, enabling: SI 2002/2976, SI 2002/3120

CAP.

1999–cont.

2. Social Security Contributions (Transfer of Functions, etc.) Act 1999–*cont.*

s.14, amended: 2002 c.22 s.9

s.24, enabling: SI 2002/3120

s.25, enabling: SI 2002/2366, SI 2002/2820, SI 2002/3120, SI 2003/1192

Sch.1 para.3, repealed: 2004 c.12 Sch.42 Part 3

Sch.1 para.4, repealed: 2004 c.12 Sch.42 Part 3

Sch.1 para.13, repealed: 2002 c.22 Sch.8 Part 1

Sch.1 para.67, repealed: 2004 c.35 Sch.13 Part 1

Sch.1 para.68, repealed: 2004 c.35 Sch.13 Part 1

Sch.3 para.16, repealed: 2002 c.19 Sch.2

Sch.3 para.29, applied: SI 2003/2275 Sch.1

Sch.3 para.52, repealed (in part): 2002 c.19 Sch.2, 2004 c.3 Sch.2 Part 1

Sch.5 para.1, repealed: 2004 c.3 Sch.2 Part 1

Sch.5 para.3, repealed: 2004 c.3 Sch.2 Part 1

3. Road Traffic (NHS Charges) Act 1999

repealed: 2003 c.43 s.169, Sch.14 Part 3

s.1, amended: 2002 asp 5 s.20

s.3, enabling: SI 2002/237, SI 2002/2995, SI 2004/560, SSI 2002/56, SSI 2002/528, SSI 2004/76

s.16, enabling: SI 2002/237, SI 2002/2995, SI 2004/560, SSI 2002/56, SSI 2002/528, SSI 2004/76

s.17, enabling: SI 2002/237, SI 2002/2995, SI 2004/560, SSI 2002/56

6. Rating (Valuation) Act 1999

s.1, see *Archer Ltd v Robinson (Valuation Officer) (Application for Permission to Appeal)* [2003 EWCA Civ 642, [2003] R.V.R. 447 (CA (Court of Appeal)), Pill, L.J.

8. Health Act 1999

Commencement Orders: 2003 c.43 Sch.14 Part 4; SSI 2004/167 Sch.1 para.5; SI 2004/289 Art.2; SI 2002/1167 Art.2; SI 2003/1689 Art.2; SI 2004/1859 Art.6; SSI 2004/32 Art.2; SI 2004/1859 Art.3, Art.4, Art.5

applied: SI 2002/2375 Reg.9, Reg.10, Reg.11

referred to: 2003 c.43 Sch.4 para.108

s.6, amended: 2002 c.17 Sch.3 para.14

s.6, repealed (in part): 2002 c.17 Sch.9 Part 1, 2003 c.43 Sch.14 Part 4

s.9, repealed (in part): 2003 c.43 Sch.14 Part 4

s.10, amended: 2002 c.17 Sch.2 para.68, 2003 c.43 Sch.14 Part 4

s.11, amended: 2003 c.43 Sch.14 Part 4

s.18, amended: 2002 c.17 s.11, Sch.8 para.29

s.18, applied: SI 2003/1587 Reg.2

s.18, referred to: SI 2002/2375 Sch.3

s.18, repealed: 2003 c.43 Sch.14 Part 2

s.19, repealed: 2003 c.43 Sch.14 Part 2

1999–cont.

8. Health Act 1999–*cont.*

s.20, amended: 2002 c.17 s.12, s.13, Sch.1 para.49, Sch.5 para.44, Sch.9 Part 1, SI 2002/2861 Reg.27

s.20, applied: SI 2003/993 Reg.1, Reg.4, Reg.10, Reg.19, SI 2003/1587, SI 2003/1587 Reg.1, Reg.2, Reg.5, Reg.11, Reg.17, Reg.20

s.20, repealed: 2003 c.43 Sch.14 Part 2

s.20, enabling: SI 2003/993, SI 2003/1587

s.21, amended: 2002 c.17 Sch.1 para.50, Sch.8 para.30

s.21, applied: SI 2003/993 Reg.20, SI 2003/1587 Reg.21

s.21, repealed: 2003 c.43 Sch.14 Part 2

s.23, amended: 2002 c.17 s.13, Sch.9 Part 1

s.23, repealed: 2003 c.43 Sch.14 Part 2

s.23, enabling: SI 2003/993, SI 2003/1587

s.24, repealed: 2003 c.43 Sch.14 Part 2

s.25, repealed: 2004 c.14 Sch.1 Part 5

s.26, amended: 2002 c.17 Sch.1 para.51, 2003 c.43 s.29

s.28, amended: 2002 c.17 Sch.1 para.52, Sch.2 para.69, SI 2003/154 Sch.1 para.6, Sch.1 para.7, Sch.1 para.8, Sch.1 para.9, Sch.1 para.10, Sch.1 para.11, Sch.1 para.12, Sch.1 para.13, Sch.1 para.14, Sch.1 para.15, Sch.1 para.16, Sch.1 para.17, Sch.1 para.18, Sch.1 para.19

s.28, applied: SI 2003/154 Reg.7

s.28, referred to: SI 2003/154 Sch.1 para.5

s.31, amended: 2002 c.17 Sch.1 para.53, Sch.5 para.45, 2003 c.43 Sch.4 para.109

s.31, applied: SI 2002/377 Sch.1 para.16, SI 2002/3199 Sch.1 para.8, 2003 c.43 s.113, s.114, s.122, SI 2003/993 Reg.17, SI 2003/3118 Sch.1 para.8, SI 2003/3170 Sch.1 para.8, 2004 c.17 s.4, 2004 c.31 s.18

s.31, enabling: SI 2003/629, SI 2004/1390

s.39, repealed (in part): 2003 c.43 Sch.14 Part 4

s.46, repealed: 2004 asp 7 Sch.2

s.47, repealed: 2004 asp 7 Sch.2

s.48, repealed: 2004 asp 7 Sch.2

s.49, repealed: 2004 asp 7 Sch.2

s.53, repealed: 2004 asp 7 Sch.2

s.54, repealed: 2004 asp 7 Sch.2

s.55, repealed: 2004 asp 7 Sch.2

s.56, repealed (in part): SSI 2004/167 Sch.1 para.5

s.60, amended: 2002 c.17 s.26, SI 2002/253 Sch.5 para.16, SI 2002/254 Sch.4 para.8

s.60, applied: 2002 c.17 s.25, s.26, s.29, SI 2002/254 Art.3, SI 2002/603 Reg.3, SI 2003/3148 Reg.2

s.60, referred to: SI 2003/2461 Art.2, SI 2003/2462 Art.2

s.60, enabling: SI 2002/253, SI 2002/254, SI 2002/3135, SI 2003/1250, SI 2004/2033

1999–cont.

8. Health Act 1999–*cont.*

s.61, amended: 2002 c.17 Sch.1 para.54, SI 2002/2469 Sch.1 para.26, 2003 c.43 Sch.14 Part 4

s.62, amended: 2003 c.43 Sch.14 Part 2

s.62, applied: SI 2002/253, SI 2002/254, SI 2002/3135, SI 2004/2033

s.62, referred to: SI 2003/1250

s.62, enabling: SI 2002/253, SI 2002/254, SI 2002/3135, SI 2003/1250, SI 2004/2033

s.63, enabling: SI 2002/880, SI 2002/881, SI 2003/1590, SI 2004/1771, SI 2004/1860, SSI 2004/31

s.64, amended: 2003 c.43 Sch.14 Part 2

s.66, repealed (in part): 2003 c.43 Sch.14 Part 2

s.67, enabling: SI 2002/1167, SI 2003/1689, SI 2004/289, SI 2004/1859, SSI 2004/32

Sch.2 para.1, repealed: 2003 c.43 Sch.14 Part 2

Sch.2 para.2, repealed: 2003 c.43 Sch.14 Part 2

Sch.2 para.3, repealed: 2003 c.43 Sch.14 Part 2

Sch.2 para.4, repealed: 2003 c.43 Sch.14 Part 2

Sch.2 para.5, repealed: 2003 c.43 Sch.14 Part 2

Sch.2 para.5A, added: 2002 c.17 s.14

Sch.2 para.5A, repealed: 2003 c.43 Sch.14 Part 2

Sch.2 para.6, repealed: 2003 c.43 Sch.14 Part 2

Sch.2 para.7, amended: 2002 c.17 Sch.9 Part 1

Sch.2 para.7, repealed (in part): 2002 c.17 Sch.9 Part 1, 2003 c.43 Sch.14 Part 2

Sch.2 para.8, amended: 2002 c.17 s.14

Sch.2 para.8, repealed: 2003 c.43 Sch.14 Part 2

Sch.2 para.9, repealed: 2003 c.43 Sch.14 Part 2

Sch.2 para.10, repealed: 2003 c.43 Sch.14 Part 2

Sch.2 para.11, repealed: 2003 c.43 Sch.14 Part 2

Sch.2 para.12, amended: 2002 c.17 s.14

Sch.2 para.12, repealed: 2003 c.43 Sch.14 Part 2

Sch.2 para.13, repealed: 2003 c.43 Sch.14 Part 2

Sch.2 para.14, repealed: 2003 c.43 Sch.14 Part 2

Sch.2 para.15, repealed: 2003 c.43 Sch.14 Part 2

Sch.2 para.16, repealed: 2003 c.43 Sch.14 Part 2

Sch.2 para.17, repealed: 2003 c.43 Sch.14 Part 2

Sch.2 para.18, repealed: 2003 c.43 Sch.14 Part 2

1999–cont.

8. Health Act 1999–*cont.*

Sch.2 para.19, repealed: 2003 c.43 Sch.14 Part 2

Sch.3, applied: 2002 c.17 s.25

Sch.3 para.2, amended: 2002 c.17 s.35

Sch.3 para.7, amended: 2002 c.17 s.26

Sch.3 para.8, amended: SI 2002/253 Sch.5 para.16

Sch.3 para.8, repealed (in part): SI 2002/254 Sch.4 para.8

Sch.3 para.9, applied: SI 2002/3135, SI 2003/1250, SI 2004/2033

Sch.3 para.9, referred to: SI 2002/3135, SI 2003/1250, SI 2004/2033

Sch.3 para.11, amended: 2003 c.43 Sch.11 para.67

Sch.3 para.11, applied: 2002 c.17 s.25

Sch.3 para.11, repealed (in part): 2003 c.43 Sch.14 Part 4

Sch.4 para.2, amended: 2003 c.43 Sch.14 Part 4

Sch.4 para.2, repealed (in part): SI 2004/957 Sch.1 para.9

Sch.4 para.5, repealed: 2002 c.17 Sch.9 Part 3

Sch.4 para.17, repealed (in part): 2003 c.43 Sch.14 Part 4

Sch.4 para.31, repealed (in part): 2002 c.17 Sch.9 Part 3

Sch.4 para.35, repealed: 2002 c.17 Sch.9 Part 3

Sch.4 para.40, repealed (in part): 2003 c.4 Sch.4

Sch.4 para.44, repealed: 2004 asp 7 Sch.2

Sch.4 para.45, repealed: 2004 asp 7 Sch.2

Sch.4 para.48, repealed (in part): SSI 2004/167 Sch.1 para.5

Sch.4 para.52, repealed (in part): 2002 asp 5 Sch.2 para.4

Sch.4 para.62, repealed: 2004 asp 7 Sch.2

Sch.4 para.63, repealed: 2004 asp 7 Sch.2

Sch.4 para.70, repealed: 2003 asp 13 Sch.5 Part 1

Sch.4 para.71, repealed: 2003 c.43 Sch.14 Part 2

Sch.4 para.88, repealed: 2003 c.43 Sch.14 Part 4

9. Water Industry Act 1999

s.12, repealed (in part): 2002 asp 3 Sch.7 para.26

s.13, repealed: 2002 asp 3 Sch.7 para.26

Sch.2, repealed: 2002 asp 3 Sch.7 para.26

Sch.3 Part II para.7, repealed: 2002 asp 3 Sch.7 para.26

Sch.3 Part II para.8, repealed: 2002 asp 3 Sch.7 para.26

Sch.3 Part II para.9, repealed: 2002 asp 3 Sch.7 para.26

Sch.3 Part II para.10, repealed: 2002 asp 3 Sch.7 para.26

1999–cont.

9. Water Industry Act 1999–*cont.*

Sch.3 Part II para.11, repealed: 2002 asp 3 Sch.7 para.26

Sch.3 Part II para.12, repealed: 2002 asp 3 Sch.7 para.26

Sch.3 Part II para.13, repealed: 2002 asp 3 Sch.7 para.26

Sch.3 Part II para.14, repealed: 2002 asp 3 Sch.7 para.26

Sch.3 Part II para.15, repealed: 2002 asp 3 Sch.7 para.26

10. Tax Credits Act 1999

applied: SI 2003/962 Art.5

referred to: 2003 c.1 Sch.6 para.239

repealed: 2002 c.21 Sch.6

s.1, applied: SI 2002/1339 Reg.2

s.2, enabling: SI 2002/14, SI 2002/524, SI 2002/525, SI 2002/829, SI 2002/1333, SI 2002/1334, SI 2002/1339, SI 2002/1340, SI 2002/1378, SI 2002/1696, SI 2002/1697, SI 2003/44, SI 2003/45

s.6, amended: 2003 c.1 Sch.6 para.240

s.15, enabling: SI 2002/1417

s.18, amended: 2002 c.22 Sch.7 para.52

s.21, applied: SI 2003/962 Art.3

s.23, applied: SI 2003/962 Art.3

Sch.1 para.6, repealed (in part): 2003 c.1 Sch.8 Part 1, 2003 c.39 Sch.10

Sch.2 Part I para.1, enabling: SI 2002/14, SI 2002/525, SI 2002/1333, SI 2002/1334, SI 2002/1696, SI 2003/44

Sch.2 Part I para.2, enabling: SI 2002/829

Sch.2 Part I para.3, enabling: SI 2002/524, SI 2002/1339, SI 2002/1340, SI 2002/1697, SI 2003/45

Sch.2 Part I para.4, enabling: SI 2002/829

Sch.2 Part III para.7, enabling: SI 2002/1696, SI 2003/44, SI 2003/45

Sch.2 Part III para.8, enabling: SI 2002/1378

Sch.2 Part III para.9, enabling: SI 2002/1378

Sch.2 Part IV para.10, amended: 2003 c.1 Sch.6 para.241

Sch.2 Part V para.20, enabling: SI 2002/14, SI 2002/525, SI 2002/829, SI 2002/1333, SI 2002/1334, SI 2002/1696, SI 2003/44

Sch.2 Part V para.22, enabling: SI 2002/524, SI 2002/1339, SI 2002/1340, SI 2002/1378, SI 2002/1697, SI 2003/45

Sch.2 Part V para.24, amended: SI 2002/1397 Sch.1 para.15

Sch.2 Part V para.31, applied: SI 2002/829

Sch.2 Part V para.33, applied: SI 2002/829

Sch.2 Part V para.36, enabling: SI 2002/1378

Sch.2 Part V para.37, applied: SI 2002/1378

Sch.3, applied: 2002 c.22 Sch.3, Sch.4, Sch.5

Sch.5 para.2, amended: 2002 c.22 Sch.6 para.9

Sch.5 para.3, amended: 2002 c.22 Sch.6 para.10

1999–cont.

11. Breeding and Sale of Dogs (Welfare) Act 1999

s.8, disapplied: 2003 c.44 Sch.25 para.104

s.9, amended: 2003 c.39 Sch.8 para.383, 2003 c.44 Sch.37 Part 9

s.9, disapplied: 2003 c.44 Sch.25 para.104

12. Road Traffic (Vehicle Testing) Act 1999

Commencement Orders: SI 2003/1095 Art.2

s.6, repealed: 2004 c.14 Sch.1 Part 14

s.9, enabling: SI 2003/1095

14. Protection of Children Act 1999

Commencement Orders: SI 2002/1436 Art.2

see R. (on the application of M) v Bromley LBC [2002] EWCA Civ 1113, [2002] 2 F.L.R. 802 (CA), Buxton, L.J.

applied: SI 2002/816 Sch.4 para.2

referred to: 2003 c.43 s.189

varied: 2004 c.31 s.39

s.1, applied: 2002 c.32 s.142, SI 2002/233 Reg.6, SI 2002/324 Reg.7, Reg.9, SI 2002/325 Reg.9, Reg.11, SI 2002/327 Reg.6, Reg.8, SI 2002/812 Reg.4B, Reg.4, SI 2002/816 Reg.4, SI 2002/896 Sch.1 para.1, SI 2002/919 Sch.2 para.9A, Sch.3 para.13A, Sch.8 para.9, Sch.8 para.9A, 2003 asp 5 s.17, SI 2003/348 Sch.6 para.9, SI 2003/781 Reg.5, Reg.7, SI 2003/1184 Reg.8, Reg.11, SI 2003/ 1558 Sch.2 para.8, SI 2003/3190 Reg.4, SI 2003/3279 Reg.4, SI 2004/2695 Sch.1 para.32, SR 2002/386 Reg.4

s.2, applied: SI 2002/816 Reg.8, Sch.4 para.4, SI 2002/3213 Sch.5, SI 2003/237 Sch.8, 2004 c.31 s.39

s.2A, amended: 2003 c.43 Sch.9 para.14

s.2A, applied: SI 2002/816 Reg.8, Sch.4 para.4, SI 2004/664 Art.13

s.2A, varied: SI 2004/664 Art.11, Art.12, Art.13, Art.14

s.2B, amended: 2002 c.38 Sch.3 para.94

s.2B, applied: SI 2002/816 Reg.8, Sch.4 para.4

s.2C, applied: SI 2002/816 Reg.8

s.2D, applied: SI 2002/816 Reg.8, Sch.4 para.4

s.3, see Secretary of State for Health v C [2003] EWCA Civ 10, [2003] 2 F.C.R. 274 (CA), Latham, L.J.

s.4, applied: SI 2002/816 Reg.4, Sch.4 para.1, Sch.4 para.2

s.4C, amended: 2004 c.31 Sch.2 para.6

s.5, repealed (in part): 2002 c.32 Sch.22 Part 3

s.7, amended: 2002 c.32 Sch.21 para.121, 2003 c.43 s.189

s.7, applied: SI 2002/233 Reg.6

s.7, referred to: 2004 c.31 s.39

s.7, repealed (in part): 2002 c.32 Sch.21 para.121

s.7, varied: 2003 c.43 s.189

1999–cont.

14. Protection of Children Act 1999–cont.

s.9, amended: 2002 c.32 Sch.14 para.6, Sch.21 para.122, Sch.22 Part 3

s.9, applied: 2002 c.32 s.144, s.166, s.167, SI 2002/816 Reg.16, SI 2002/2953 Reg.6, SI 2003/437 Sch.1 Part 2, SI 2003/626, SI 2004/2073

s.9, enabling: SI 2002/816, SI 2003/626, SI 2003/1060, SI 2003/2043, SI 2004/ 2073, SI 2004/3354

s.12, amended: 2002 c.32 Sch.21 para.123

s.12, applied: SI 2002/233 Reg.6

s.12, repealed (in part): 2002 c.32 Sch.21 para.123, Sch.22 Part 3

s.14, enabling: SI 2002/1436

Sch.1 para.2, enabling: SI 2002/816, SI 2003/1060

16. Finance Act 1999

s.30, repealed: 2002 c.21 Sch.6

s.31, repealed (in part): 2002 c.21 Sch.6

s.42, repealed: 2003 c.1 Sch.8 Part 1

s.43, repealed: 2003 c.1 Sch.8 Part 1

s.44, repealed: 2003 c.1 Sch.8 Part 1

s.45, repealed: 2003 c.1 Sch.8 Part 1

s.48, repealed: 2003 c.1 Sch.8 Part 1

s.49, repealed: 2003 c.1 Sch.8 Part 1

s.50, repealed: 2003 c.1 Sch.8 Part 1

s.51, repealed: 2003 c.1 Sch.8 Part 1

s.52, repealed: 2004 c.12 Sch.42 Part 3

s.53, repealed: 2004 c.12 Sch.42 Part 2

s.65, repealed (in part): 2004 c.12 Sch.42 Part 2

s.81, amended: 2002 c.23 s.67

s.85, varied: 2003 c.14 s.153

s.98, amended: 2004 c.12 Sch.37 para.12

s.98, applied: 2004 c.12 s.285

s.122, amended: 2003 c.14 Sch.20 para.3

s.123, amended: 2003 c.14 Sch.20 para.3

s.126, disapplied: SI 2004/674 Sch.2 para.2

s.126, varied: SI 2004/674 Sch.2 para.2

s.132, amended: 2003 c.21 Sch.17 para.156

s.132, applied: 2002 c.21 s.54, SI 2002/2014 Reg.3, SI 2002/3047 Reg.1, SI 2003/282 Reg.1, SI 2003/492 Sch.2 para.2, SI 2003/ 493 Reg.39, SI 2003/916 Reg.4, SI 2003/ 2718 Reg.1, SI 2004/1864 Reg.10

s.132, varied: 2002 c.22 Sch.7 para.53

s.132, enabling: SI 2002/680, SI 2002/761, SI 2002/3047, SI 2003/282, SI 2003/ 492, SI 2003/493, SI 2003/916, SI 2003/2718, SI 2003/3143, SI 2004/1864

s.133, varied: 2002 c.22 Sch.7 para.53

s.133, enabling: SI 2002/443, SI 2002/3006, SI 2002/3047, SI 2003/282, SI 2003/492, SI 2003/916, SI 2004/1675

s.135, applied: SI 2004/1864 Reg.10

Sch.3, repealed: 2002 c.21 Sch.6

Sch.5 para.1, repealed: 2003 c.1 Sch.8 Part 1

Sch.5 para.2, repealed: 2003 c.1 Sch.8 Part 1

Sch.5 para.3, repealed: 2003 c.1 Sch.8 Part 1

1999–cont.

16. Finance Act 1999–*cont.*

Sch.5 para.4, repealed: 2004 c.12 Sch.42 Part 3

Sch.5 para.5, repealed: 2004 c.12 Sch.42 Part 3

Sch.5 para.6, amended: 2004 c.12 Sch.42 Part 3

Sch.6 para.3, repealed (in part): 2002 c.23 Sch.40 Part 3

Sch.6 para.4, amended: SI 2004/2310 Sch.1 para.51

Sch.10 para.1, repealed: 2004 c.12 Sch.42 Part 3

Sch.10 para.2, repealed: 2004 c.12 Sch.42 Part 3

Sch.10 para.3, repealed: 2004 c.12 Sch.42 Part 3

Sch.10 para.4, repealed: 2003 c.1 Sch.8 Part 1, 2004 c.12 Sch.42 Part 3

Sch.10 para.5, repealed: 2003 c.1 Sch.8 Part 1, 2004 c.12 Sch.42 Part 3

Sch.10 para.6, repealed: 2003 c.1 Sch.8 Part 1, 2004 c.12 Sch.42 Part 3

Sch.10 para.7, repealed: 2004 c.12 Sch.42 Part 3

Sch.10 para.8, repealed: 2003 c.1 Sch.8 Part 1, 2004 c.12 Sch.42 Part 3

Sch.10 para.9, repealed: 2004 c.12 Sch.42 Part 3

Sch.10 para.10, repealed: 2004 c.12 Sch.42 Part 3

Sch.10 para.12, repealed: 2004 c.12 Sch.42 Part 3

Sch.10 para.13, repealed: 2004 c.12 Sch.42 Part 3

Sch.10 para.14, repealed: 2004 c.12 Sch.42 Part 3

Sch.10 para.15, repealed: 2004 c.12 Sch.42 Part 3

Sch.10 para.16, repealed: 2004 c.12 Sch.42 Part 3

Sch.10 para.17, repealed: 2004 c.12 Sch.42 Part 3

Sch.10 para.18, applied: SR 2002/352 Reg.21

Sch.10 para.18, repealed: 2004 c.12 Sch.42 Part 3

Sch.13, applied: 2003 c.14 s.125

Sch.13 Part I, applied: 2003 c.14 Sch.20 para.1, SI 2003/1056 Reg.5

Sch.13 Part I para.1, amended: 2003 c.14 Sch.20 para.3, Sch.20 para.6, Sch.40 para.5

Sch.13 Part I para.2, amended: 2003 c.14 Sch.20 para.3

Sch.13 Part I para.3, amended: 2003 c.14 Sch.20 para.3

Sch.13 Part I para.4, amended: 2003 c.14 Sch.20 para.3

Sch.13 Part I para.5, amended: 2003 c.14 Sch.20 para.3

1999–cont.

16. Finance Act 1999–*cont.*

Sch.13 Part I para.6, amended: 2003 c.14 Sch.20 para.3

Sch.13 Part I para.6, applied: 2002 c.23 Sch.37 para.3

Sch.13 Part I para.6, referred to: 2002 c.23 Sch.37 para.3

Sch.13 Part I para.7, amended: 2003 c.14 Sch.20 para.3

Sch.13 Part I para.7, referred to: 2003 c.14 Sch.19 para.7A, Sch.19 para.6

Sch.13 Part I para.8, amended: 2003 c.14 Sch.20 para.3

Sch.13 Part I para.9, amended: 2003 c.14 Sch.20 para.3

Sch.13 Part II, applied: 2003 c.14 s.128, SI 2003/1056 Reg.5

Sch.13 Part III, amended: 2003 c.14 Sch.20 para.3

Sch.13 Part III para.16, amended: 2003 c.14 Sch.20 para.3

Sch.13 Part III para.17, amended: 2003 c.14 Sch.20 para.3

Sch.13 Part III para.22, amended: 2003 c.14 Sch.20 para.3

Sch.13 Part III para.23, amended: 2003 c.14 Sch.20 para.3

Sch.14 para.3, amended: 2003 c.14 Sch.20 para.3

Sch.14 para.4, amended: 2003 c.14 Sch.20 para.3

Sch.14 para.5, amended: 2003 c.14 Sch.20 para.3

Sch.14 para.6, amended: 2003 c.14 Sch.20 para.3

Sch.14 para.8, amended: 2003 c.14 Sch.20 para.3

Sch.14 para.9, amended: 2003 c.14 Sch.20 para.3

Sch.14 para.10, amended: 2003 c.14 Sch.20 para.3

Sch.14 para.11, amended: 2003 c.14 Sch.20 para.3

Sch.14 para.12, amended: 2003 c.14 Sch.20 para.3

Sch.14 para.13, amended: 2003 c.14 Sch.20 para.3

Sch.14 para.14, amended: 2003 c.14 Sch.20 para.3

Sch.14 para.15, amended: 2003 c.14 Sch.20 para.3

Sch.14 para.16, amended: 2003 c.14 Sch.20 para.3

Sch.14 para.17, amended: 2003 c.14 Sch.20 para.3

Sch.14 para.21, amended: 2003 c.14 Sch.20 para.3

Sch.14 para.23, amended: 2003 c.14 Sch.20 para.3

Sch.14 para.26, amended: 2003 c.14 Sch.20 para.3

1999–cont.

16. Finance Act 1999–*cont.*

Sch.14 para.28, amended: 2003 c.14 Sch.20 para.3

Sch.14 para.29, amended: 2003 c.14 Sch.20 para.3

Sch.14 para.30, amended: 2003 c.14 Sch.20 para.3

Sch.14 para.31, amended: 2003 c.14 Sch.20 para.3

Sch.15 Part I para.2, amended: 2003 c.14 Sch.20 para.3

Sch.18 Part I, amended: 2003 c.14 s.206

Sch.18 Part I para.3, amended: 2003 c.14 s.206

Sch.19 Part I para.1, amended: 2003 c.14 Sch.20 para.3

Sch.19 Part II para.6A, amended: 2004 c.12 Sch.35 para.46

Sch.20 Part V, amended: 2003 c.14 Sch.20 para.3

17. Disability Rights Commission Act 1999

s.1, repealed (in part): 2004 c.14 Sch.1 Part 5

s.2, amended: SI 2003/1673 Reg.30

s.4, amended: SI 2003/1673 Reg.30

s.5, amended: SI 2003/1673 Reg.30

s.6, amended: SI 2003/1673 Reg.30

s.7, amended: SI 2003/1673 Reg.30

Sch.3 Part I para.3, amended: SI 2003/1673 Reg.30

Sch.3 Part II para.10, applied: SI 2004/1861 Reg.16

18. Adoption (Intercountry Aspects) Act 1999

Commencement Orders: SI 2003/189 Art.2; SI 2003/362 Art.2; SSI 2002/562 Art.2; SSI 2003/121 Art.2

applied: 2002 c.38 s.137

referred to: SI 2003/365 Art.3

s.1, applied: 2002 c.38 s.14, s.137

s.1, enabling: SI 2003/118, SSI 2003/19

s.2, amended: 2002 c.38 Sch.3 para.97, Sch.3 para.98, Sch.3 para.99, Sch.5

s.2, applied: 2002 c.38 s.14

s.2, referred to: 2002 c.38 Sch.3 para.96

s.3, repealed (in part): 2002 c.38 Sch.3 para.95

s.6, repealed (in part): 2002 c.38 Sch.3 para.95

s.7, repealed (in part): 2002 c.38 Sch.5

s.8, repealed (in part): 2002 c.38 Sch.3 para.95

s.9, repealed (in part): 2002 c.38 Sch.3 para.95

s.11, repealed (in part): 2002 c.38 Sch.3 para.95

s.12, repealed (in part): 2002 c.38 Sch.3 para.95

s.13, repealed (in part): 2002 c.38 Sch.3 para.95

s.14, repealed: 2002 c.38 Sch.3 para.100, Sch.5

1999–cont.

18. Adoption (Intercountry Aspects) Act 1999–*cont.*

s.16, amended: 2002 c.38 Sch.3 para.101, Sch.5

s.18, enabling: SI 2003/189, SI 2003/362, SSI 2002/562, SSI 2003/121

Sch.2 para.3, repealed: 2002 c.38 Sch.5

20. Commonwealth Development Corporation Act 1999

s.20, enabling: SI 2003/1282

Sch.3 para.1, enabling: SI 2003/1282

21. Football (Offences and Disorder) Act 1999

s.1, repealed (in part): 2002 c.30 Sch.8

s.8, repealed (in part): 2002 c.30 Sch.8

22. Access to Justice Act 1999

Commencement Orders: SI 2003/207 Art.2, Art.3; SI 2003/1241 Art.2; SI 2003/2571 Art.2

Part I, applied: 2003 c.21 s.119, SI 2003/1887 Sch.1

Part II, applied: SI 2003/1887 Sch.1

Part III, applied: SI 2003/1887 Sch.1

Part VII, applied: SI 2003/1887 Sch.1

s.1, amended: SI 2003/1887 Sch.2 para.11

s.2, amended: SI 2003/1887 Sch.2 para.11

s.3, amended: SI 2003/1887 Sch.2 para.11

s.4, amended: SI 2003/1887 Sch.2 para.11

s.5, amended: SI 2003/1887 Sch.2 para.11

s.6, see *R. (on the application of G) v Legal Services Commission* [2004] EWHC 276, [2004] P.I.Q.R. P26 (QBD (Admin Ct)), Pitchford, J.

s.6, amended: SI 2003/1887 Sch.2 para.11

s.6, enabling: SI 2003/651, SI 2003/851, SI 2003/2590, SI 2004/597, SI 2004/1055, SI 2004/2900

s.7, enabling: SI 2002/709, SI 2002/1766, SI 2003/650, SI 2003/2838, SI 2004/2899

s.8, amended: SI 2003/1887 Sch.2 para.11

s.9, amended: SI 2003/1887 Sch.2 para.11

s.10, applied: 2003 c.21 s.119

s.10, enabling: SI 2002/709, SI 2003/649, SI 2003/650, SI 2003/2838, SI 2004/2899

s.11, see *Hill v Bailey* [2003] EWHC 2835, [2004] 1 All E.R. 1210 (Ch D), Lightman, J.; see *Jones v Congregational and General Insurance Plc* [2003] EWHC 1027, [2003] 1 W.L.R. 3001 (QBD (Merc Ct)), Judge Chambers Q.C.

s.11, applied: SI 2003/421 r.53

s.11, enabling: SI 2003/649

s.12, amended: 2003 c.41 s.182, SI 2003/1887 Sch.2 para.11

s.12, enabling: SI 2002/712, SI 2002/2785, SI 2004/1196

s.13, amended: SI 2003/1887 Sch.2 para.11

s.13, enabling: SI 2002/712, SI 2002/2785, SI 2003/644, SI 2003/2378, SI 2004/1196

1999–cont.

22. Access to Justice Act 1999–*cont.*

s.14, see *R. v Conroy (Costs)* [2004] 1 Costs L.R. 182 (Crown Ct (Bristol)), Judge Crowther Q.C.

s.14, amended: SI 2003/1887 Sch.2 para.11

s.14, enabling: SI 2002/714, SI 2002/1620, SI 2003/651, SI 2004/2045

s.15, enabling: SI 2002/712, SI 2004/598, SI 2004/1196, SI 2004/2046, SI 2004/3345

s.16, amended: SI 2003/1887 Sch.2 para.11

s.17, enabling: SI 2002/713, SI 2003/643, SI 2004/1195

s.18, amended: SI 2003/1887 Sch.2 para.11

s.19, amended: SI 2003/1887 Sch.2 para.11

s.19, enabling: SI 2004/2900

s.20, amended: SI 2003/1887 Sch.2 para.11

s.21, amended: 2003 c.44 Sch.26 para.51

s.22, enabling: SI 2004/1196

s.23, amended: SI 2003/1887 Sch.2 para.11

s.25, amended: SI 2003/1887 Sch.2 para.11

s.25, referred to: SI 2002/714, SI 2003/651, SI 2003/851, SI 2003/2590, SI 2004/597, SI 2004/2045, SI 2004/2900

s.26, amended: SI 2003/1887 Sch.2 para.11

s.28, amended: SI 2003/1887 Sch.2 para.11

s.29, see *Claims Direct Test Cases (Case Management), Re* [2002] EWCA Civ 428, [2002] P.I.Q.R. Q11 (CA), Lord Phillips of Worth Matravers, M.R.; see *Claims Direct Test Cases, Re* [2003] EWCA Civ 136, [2003] 4 All E.R. 508 (CA), Brooke, L.J.; see *Claims Direct Test Cases, Re* [2003] Lloyd's Rep. I.R. 69 (Sup Ct Costs Office), Chief Master Hurst; see *Inline Logistics Ltd v UCI Logistics Ltd (Costs: Recovery of Insurance Premium)* [2002] EWHC 519, [2002] 2 Costs L.R. 304 (Ch D), Ferris, J.; see *Sharratt v London Central Bus Co Ltd (No.2)* [2004] EWCA Civ 575, [2004] 3 All E.R. 325 (CA), Kennedy, L.J.

s.30, see *Thornley v Lang* [2003] EWCA Civ 1484, [2004] 1 W.L.R. 378 (CA), Lord Phillips of Worth Matravers, M.R.

s.30, amended: SI 2003/1887 Sch.2 para.11

s.33, repealed: 2002 c.21 Sch.6

s.35, repealed (in part): 2004 c.14 Sch.1 Part 1

s.45, amended: SI 2003/1887 Sch.2 para.11

s.45, enabling: SI 2002/2037

s.46, amended: SI 2003/1887 Sch.2 para.11

s.47, amended: SI 2003/1887 Sch.2 para.11

s.47, applied: SI 2002/3235

s.47, enabling: SI 2002/3235

s.50, amended: SI 2003/1887 Sch.2 para.11

s.51, amended: SI 2003/1887 Sch.2 para.11

s.52, amended: SI 2003/1887 Sch.2 para.11

s.52, applied: SI 2004/2758, SI 2004/2758 Art.2

s.52, enabling: SI 2004/2758

s.54, see *Girls Day School Trust (1872) v Dadak* [2001] EWCA Civ 380, [2002] 1 P. & C.R. 4 (CA), Robert Walker, L.J.; see

1999–cont.

22. Access to Justice Act 1999–*cont.*

s.54–*cont.*

Gregory v Turner [2003] EWCA Civ 183, [2003] 1 W.L.R. 1149 (CA), Brooke, L.J.; see *James v Baily Gibson & Co* [2002] EWCA Civ 1690, (2002) 99(46) L.S.G. 33 (CA), May, L.J.; see *Plymouth City Council v Hoskin* [2002] EWCA Civ 684, [2002] C.P. Rep. 55 (CA), Pill, L.J.; see *Sierra Leone v Davenport (No.2)* [2002] EWCA Civ 230, [2002] C.P.L.R. 236 (CA), Jonathan Parker, L.J.; see *Slot v Isaac* [2002] EWCA Civ 481, [2002] C.P. Rep. 57 (CA), Brooke, L.J.; see *Westminster City Council v O'Reilly (Leave to Appeal: Jurisdiction)* [2003] EWCA Civ 1007, [2004] 1 W.L.R. 195 (CA), Auld, L.J.

s.55, see *Cooke v Secretary of State for Social Security* [2001] EWCA Civ 734, [2002] 3 All E.R. 279 (CA), Hale, L.J.; see *Cordle v Cordle* [2001] EWCA Civ 1791, [2002] 1 W.L.R. 1441 (CA), Thorpe, L.J.; see *Westminster City Council v O'Reilly (Leave to Appeal: Jurisdiction)* [2003] EWCA Civ 1007, [2004] 1 W.L.R. 195 (CA), Auld, L.J.

s.56, applied: 2002 c.40 s.268

s.57, see *Barnet LBC v Hurst* [2002] EWCA Civ 1009, [2003] 1 W.L.R. 722 (CA), Brooke, L.J.; see *Claims Direct Test Cases (Case Management), Re* [2002] EWCA Civ 428, [2002] P.I.Q.R. Q11 (CA), Lord Phillips of Worth Matravers, M.R.

s.58, repealed (in part): 2003 c.44 Sch.37 Part 7

s.67, repealed (in part): 2003 c.44 Sch.37 Part 4

s.70, repealed: 2004 c.14 Sch.1 Part 1

s.74, repealed: 2003 c.39 Sch.10

s.75, repealed: 2003 c.39 Sch.10

s.77, repealed: 2003 c.39 Sch.10

s.78, repealed (in part): 2003 c.39 Sch.10

s.79, repealed: 2004 c.14 Sch.1 Part 1

s.80, repealed (in part): 2003 c.39 Sch.10

s.81, repealed: 2003 c.39 Sch.10

s.82, repealed: 2003 c.39 Sch.10

s.83, repealed: 2003 c.39 Sch.10

s.84, repealed: 2003 c.39 Sch.10

s.85, repealed: 2003 c.39 Sch.10

s.86, repealed: 2003 c.39 Sch.10

s.87, repealed: 2003 c.39 Sch.10

s.88, repealed: 2003 c.39 Sch.10

s.89, repealed: 2003 c.39 Sch.10

s.90, repealed (in part): 2003 c.39 Sch.10

s.91, repealed: 2003 c.39 Sch.10

s.93, repealed (in part): 2003 c.39 Sch.10

s.98, repealed (in part): 2002 c.26 Sch.13, 2003 c.39 Sch.10

s.99, repealed: 2003 c.39 Sch.10

s.100, repealed: 2003 c.39 Sch.10

s.101, referred to: SI 2003/415 Sch.1

s.102, referred to: SI 2003/415 Art.1, Sch.1

1999–cont.

22. Access to Justice Act 1999–*cont.*

s.103, referred to: SI 2003/415 Art.1, Sch.1

s.105, enabling: SI 2002/714

s.108, amended: SI 2003/1887 Sch.2 para.11

s.108, varied: SI 2003/415 Sch.1

s.108, enabling: SI 2003/1241, SI 2003/2571, SSI 2003/207

Sch.1 para.1, amended: SI 2003/1887 Sch.2 para.11

Sch.1 para.2, amended: SI 2003/1887 Sch.2 para.11

Sch.1 para.3, amended: SI 2003/1887 Sch.2 para.11

Sch.1 para.4, amended: SI 2003/1887 Sch.2 para.11

Sch.1 para.5, amended: SI 2003/1887 Sch.2 para.11

Sch.1 para.6, amended: SI 2003/1887 Sch.2 para.11

Sch.1 para.7, amended: SI 2003/1887 Sch.2 para.11

Sch.1 para.8, amended: SI 2003/1887 Sch.2 para.11

Sch.1 para.9, amended: SI 2003/1887 Sch.2 para.11

Sch.1 para.10, amended: SI 2003/1887 Sch.2 para.11

Sch.1 para.11, amended: SI 2003/1887 Sch.2 para.11

Sch.1 para.12, amended: SI 2003/1887 Sch.2 para.11

Sch.1 para.13, amended: SI 2003/1887 Sch.2 para.11

Sch.1 para.14, amended: SI 2003/1887 Sch.2 para.11

Sch.1 para.15, amended: SI 2003/1887 Sch.2 para.11

Sch.1 para.16, amended: SI 2003/1887 Sch.2 para.11

Sch.1 para.17, amended: SI 2003/1887 Sch.2 para.11

Sch.2, see *R. (on the application of G) v Legal Services Commission* [2004] EWHC 276, [2004] P.I.Q.R. P26 (QBD (Admin Ct)), Pitchford, J.

Sch.2 para.1, amended: SI 2004/1055 Reg.2

Sch.2 para.2, amended: 2002 c.29 Sch.11 para.36, Sch.12, 2002 c.38 Sch.3 para.102, 2002 c.41 s.116, 2004 c.19 Sch.2 para.14, 2004 c.33 Sch.27 para.156

Sch.2 para.3, added: 2002 c.29 Sch.11 para.36

Sch.3, see *R. v Conroy (Costs)* [2004] 1 Costs L.R. 182 (Crown Ct (Bristol)), Judge Crowther Q.C.

Sch.3, enabling: SI 2002/712

Sch.3 para.1, amended: SI 2003/1887 Sch.2 para.11

Sch.3 para.2, amended: SI 2003/1887 Sch.2 para.11

1999–cont.

22. Access to Justice Act 1999–*cont.*

Sch.3 para.2, repealed (in part): SI 2004/2035 Sch.1 para.38

Sch.3 para.3, amended: SI 2003/1887 Sch.2 para.11

Sch.3 para.4, amended: SI 2003/1887 Sch.2 para.11

Sch.3 para.4, enabling: SI 2002/1620

Sch.3 para.5, amended: SI 2003/1887 Sch.2 para.11

Sch.4 para.16, repealed: 2003 c.44 Sch.37 Part 4

Sch.4 para.20, repealed: 2003 c.39 Sch.10

Sch.4 para.26, repealed: 2003 c.21 Sch.19

Sch.4 para.39, repealed: 2003 c.44 Sch.37 Part 4

Sch.4 para.47, repealed: 2003 c.44 Sch.37 Part 4

Sch.8 para.1, amended: SI 2003/1887 Sch.2 para.11

Sch.8 para.2, amended: SI 2003/1887 Sch.2 para.11

Sch.8 para.3, amended: SI 2003/1887 Sch.2 para.11

Sch.8 para.4, amended: SI 2003/1887 Sch.2 para.11

Sch.8 para.5, amended: SI 2003/1887 Sch.2 para.11

Sch.8 para.6, amended: SI 2003/1887 Sch.2 para.11

Sch.8 para.7, amended: SI 2003/1887 Sch.2 para.11

Sch.8 para.8, amended: SI 2003/1887 Sch.2 para.11

Sch.8 para.9, amended: SI 2003/1887 Sch.2 para.11

Sch.8 para.10, amended: SI 2003/1887 Sch.2 para.11

Sch.10 para.1, repealed: 2003 c.39 Sch.10, 2004 c.14 Sch.1 Part 6

Sch.10 para.2, repealed: 2003 c.39 Sch.10

Sch.10 para.3, repealed: 2003 c.39 Sch.10

Sch.10 para.4, repealed: 2003 c.39 Sch.10

Sch.10 para.5, repealed: 2003 c.39 Sch.10

Sch.10 para.6, repealed: 2003 c.39 Sch.10

Sch.10 para.7, repealed: 2003 c.39 Sch.10

Sch.10 para.9, repealed: 2003 c.39 Sch.10

Sch.10 para.10, repealed: 2003 c.39 Sch.10

Sch.10 para.10, varied: 2003 c.39 Sch.8 para.53

Sch.10 para.11, repealed: 2003 c.39 Sch.10

Sch.10 para.12, repealed: 2003 c.39 Sch.10

Sch.10 para.14, repealed: 2003 c.39 Sch.10

Sch.10 para.15, repealed: 2003 c.39 Sch.10

Sch.10 para.16, repealed: 2003 c.39 Sch.10

Sch.10 para.18, repealed: 2003 c.39 Sch.10

Sch.10 para.19, repealed: 2003 c.39 Sch.10

Sch.10 para.20, repealed: 2003 c.39 Sch.10

Sch.10 para.21, repealed (in part): 2003 c.39 Sch.10

Sch.10 para.23, repealed: 2003 c.17 Sch.7

1999–cont.

22. Access to Justice Act 1999–cont.

Sch.10 para.24, repealed: 2003 c.17 Sch.7

Sch.10 para.25, repealed: 2003 c.17 Sch.7

Sch.10 para.26, repealed: 2003 c.17 Sch.7

Sch.10 para.27, repealed: 2003 c.17 Sch.7

Sch.10 para.28, repealed: 2003 c.17 Sch.7

Sch.10 para.29, repealed: 2003 c.17 Sch.7

Sch.10 para.30, repealed (in part): 2003 c.39 Sch.10

Sch.10 para.31, repealed: 2003 c.17 Sch.7

Sch.10 para.32, repealed: 2003 c.39 Sch.10

Sch.10 para.35, repealed: 2003 c.39 Sch.10

Sch.10 para.36, repealed: 2003 c.39 Sch.10

Sch.10 para.39, repealed: 2003 c.39 Sch.10

Sch.10 para.47, repealed: 2003 c.39 Sch.10

Sch.10 para.48, repealed: 2003 c.39 Sch.10

Sch.10 para.49, repealed: 2003 c.39 Sch.10

Sch.10 para.50, repealed: 2003 c.39 Sch.10

Sch.10 para.51, repealed: 2003 c.39 Sch.10

Sch.10 para.52, repealed: 2003 c.39 Sch.10

Sch.10 para.53, repealed: 2003 c.39 Sch.10

Sch.11 para.3, repealed: 2003 c.39 Sch.10

Sch.11 para.6, repealed (in part): 2003 c.39 Sch.10

Sch.11 para.12, repealed: 2003 c.39 Sch.10

Sch.11 para.17, repealed: 2003 c.17 Sch.7

Sch.11 para.18, repealed: 2003 c.39 Sch.10, 2003 c.41 Sch.4

Sch.11 para.22, repealed: 2003 c.44 Sch.37 Part 10

Sch.11 para.28, repealed: 2003 c.39 Sch.10

Sch.11 para.29, repealed: 2003 c.39 Sch.10

Sch.11 para.30, repealed: 2003 c.39 Sch.10

Sch.11 para.31, repealed: 2003 c.41 Sch.4

Sch.11 para.32, repealed: 2003 c.39 Sch.10, 2003 c.41 Sch.4

Sch.11 para.33, repealed: 2003 c.41 Sch.4

Sch.11 para.34, repealed: 2003 c.41 Sch.4

Sch.11 para.35, repealed: 2003 c.41 Sch.4

Sch.11 para.36, repealed (in part): 2003 c.39 Sch.10, 2003 c.41 Sch.4

Sch.11 para.43, repealed: 2003 c.39 Sch.10

Sch.11 para.44, repealed: 2003 c.39 Sch.10

Sch.11 para.45, repealed: 2003 c.39 Sch.10

Sch.11 para.46, repealed: 2003 c.39 Sch.10

Sch.11 para.47, repealed: 2003 c.39 Sch.10

Sch.11 para.48, repealed: 2003 c.39 Sch.10

Sch.11 para.49, repealed: 2003 c.39 Sch.10

Sch.11 para.50, repealed: 2003 c.39 Sch.10

Sch.12 para.1, repealed: 2003 c.39 Sch.10

Sch.12 para.2, repealed: 2003 c.39 Sch.10

Sch.12 para.3, repealed: 2003 c.39 Sch.10

Sch.12 para.4, repealed: 2003 c.39 Sch.10

Sch.12 para.5, repealed (in part): 2003 c.26 Sch.8 Part 1, 2003 c.39 Sch.10

Sch.12 para.6, repealed: 2003 c.39 Sch.10

Sch.12 para.7, repealed: 2003 c.39 Sch.10

Sch.12 para.8, repealed: 2003 c.39 Sch.10

Sch.12 para.9, repealed: 2003 c.39 Sch.10

Sch.12 para.10, repealed: 2003 c.39 Sch.10

1999–cont.

22. Access to Justice Act 1999–cont.

Sch.12 para.11, repealed: 2003 c.39 Sch.10

Sch.12 para.12, repealed: 2003 c.39 Sch.10

Sch.12 para.13, repealed: 2003 c.39 Sch.10

Sch.12 para.14, repealed: 2003 c.39 Sch.10

Sch.12 para.15, repealed: 2003 c.39 Sch.10

Sch.12 para.16, repealed: 2003 c.39 Sch.10

Sch.12 para.17, repealed: 2003 c.39 Sch.10

Sch.12 para.18, repealed: 2003 c.39 Sch.10

Sch.12 para.19, repealed: 2003 c.39 Sch.10

Sch.13 para.1, repealed: 2003 c.39 Sch.10

Sch.13 para.5, repealed: 2003 c.39 Sch.10

Sch.13 para.5, varied: 2003 c.39 Sch.8 para.53

Sch.13 para.6, repealed: 2003 c.39 Sch.10

Sch.13 para.7, repealed: 2003 c.39 Sch.10

Sch.13 para.10, repealed: 2003 c.39 Sch.10

Sch.13 para.11, repealed: 2003 c.39 Sch.10

Sch.13 para.13, repealed (in part): 2003 c.39 Sch.10

Sch.13 para.14, repealed: 2003 c.39 Sch.10

Sch.13 para.15, repealed: 2003 c.39 Sch.10

Sch.13 para.25, repealed: 2003 c.39 Sch.10

Sch.13 para.26, repealed: 2003 c.39 Sch.10

Sch.13 para.27, repealed: 2003 c.39 Sch.10

Sch.13 para.28, repealed: 2003 c.39 Sch.10

Sch.13 para.29, repealed: 2003 c.39 Sch.10

Sch.13 para.30, repealed: 2003 c.39 Sch.10

Sch.13 para.31, repealed: 2003 c.39 Sch.10

Sch.13 para.36, repealed: 2003 c.17 Sch.7

Sch.13 para.37, repealed: 2003 c.17 Sch.7

Sch.13 para.38, repealed: 2003 c.17 Sch.7

Sch.13 para.39, repealed: 2003 c.17 Sch.7

Sch.13 para.40, repealed: 2003 c.17 Sch.7

Sch.13 para.41, repealed: 2003 c.17 Sch.7

Sch.13 para.42, repealed: 2003 c.17 Sch.7

Sch.13 para.43, repealed: 2003 c.17 Sch.7

Sch.13 para.44, repealed: 2003 c.17 Sch.7

Sch.13 para.45, repealed: 2003 c.17 Sch.7

Sch.13 para.46, repealed: 2003 c.17 Sch.7

Sch.13 para.47, repealed: 2003 c.17 Sch.7

Sch.13 para.48, repealed: 2003 c.17 Sch.7

Sch.13 para.49, repealed: 2003 c.17 Sch.7

Sch.13 para.50, repealed: 2003 c.17 Sch.7

Sch.13 para.51, repealed: 2003 c.17 Sch.7

Sch.13 para.52, repealed: 2003 c.17 Sch.7

Sch.13 para.53, repealed: 2003 c.17 Sch.7

Sch.13 para.54, repealed: 2003 c.17 Sch.7

Sch.13 para.55, repealed: 2003 c.17 Sch.7

Sch.13 para.56, repealed: 2003 c.17 Sch.7

Sch.13 para.59, repealed (in part): 2003 c.39 Sch.10

Sch.13 para.60, repealed: 2003 c.39 Sch.10

Sch.13 para.61, repealed: 2003 c.17 Sch.7

Sch.13 para.62, repealed: 2003 c.17 Sch.7

Sch.13 para.65, repealed: 2003 c.39 Sch.10

Sch.13 para.66, repealed: 2003 c.39 Sch.10

Sch.13 para.68, repealed: 2003 c.39 Sch.10

Sch.13 para.69, repealed: 2003 c.39 Sch.10

Sch.13 para.72, repealed: 2003 c.39 Sch.10

1999–cont.

22. Access to Justice Act 1999–*cont.*

Sch.13 para.73, repealed (in part): 2003 c.39 Sch.10

Sch.13 para.74, repealed: 2003 c.39 Sch.10

Sch.13 para.77, repealed: 2003 c.39 Sch.10

Sch.13 para.78, repealed: 2003 c.39 Sch.10

Sch.13 para.81, repealed: 2003 c.39 Sch.10

Sch.13 para.82, repealed: 2003 c.39 Sch.10

Sch.13 para.87, repealed: 2003 c.17 Sch.7

Sch.13 para.88, repealed: 2002 c.38 Sch.5

Sch.13 para.89, repealed: 2003 c.39 Sch.10

Sch.13 para.90, repealed: 2003 c.39 Sch.10

Sch.13 para.91, repealed: 2003 c.39 Sch.10

Sch.13 para.92, repealed: 2003 c.39 Sch.10

Sch.13 para.93, repealed: 2003 c.39 Sch.10

Sch.13 para.96, repealed: 2003 c.39 Sch.10, 2003 c.44 Sch.37 Part 4

Sch.13 para.97, repealed: 2003 c.39 Sch.10

Sch.13 para.98, repealed: 2003 c.39 Sch.10

Sch.13 para.99, repealed: 2003 c.39 Sch.10

Sch.13 para.100, repealed: 2003 c.39 Sch.10

Sch.13 para.101, repealed: 2003 c.39 Sch.10

Sch.13 para.102, repealed: 2003 c.39 Sch.10

Sch.13 para.103, repealed: 2003 c.39 Sch.10

Sch.13 para.104, repealed: 2003 c.39 Sch.10

Sch.13 para.105, repealed: 2003 c.39 Sch.10

Sch.13 para.106, repealed: 2003 c.39 Sch.10

Sch.13 para.107, repealed: 2003 c.39 Sch.10

Sch.13 para.108, repealed: 2003 c.39 Sch.10

Sch.13 para.109, repealed: 2003 c.39 Sch.10

Sch.13 para.110, repealed: 2003 c.39 Sch.10

Sch.13 para.111, repealed: 2003 c.39 Sch.10, 2003 c.44 Sch.37 Part 4

Sch.13 para.112, repealed: 2003 c.39 Sch.10

Sch.13 para.114, repealed: 2003 c.39 Sch.10

Sch.13 para.115, repealed: 2003 c.39 Sch.10

Sch.13 para.116, repealed: 2003 c.39 Sch.10

Sch.13 para.117, repealed: 2003 c.39 Sch.10

Sch.13 para.118, repealed: 2003 c.39 Sch.10

Sch.13 para.122, repealed (in part): 2003 c.39 Sch.10

Sch.13 para.124, repealed: 2003 c.17 Sch.7

Sch.13 para.126, repealed: 2003 c.39 Sch.10

Sch.13 para.127, repealed: 2003 c.39 Sch.10

Sch.13 para.129, repealed: 2003 c.39 Sch.10

Sch.13 para.130, repealed: 2003 c.39 Sch.10

Sch.13 para.131, repealed: 2003 c.39 Sch.10

Sch.13 para.132, repealed: 2003 c.17 Sch.7

Sch.13 para.135, repealed: 2003 c.39 Sch.10

Sch.13 para.136, repealed: 2003 c.39 Sch.10

Sch.13 para.137, repealed: 2003 c.39 Sch.10, 2003 c.44 Sch.37 Part 4

Sch.13 para.138, repealed: 2003 c.39 Sch.10

Sch.13 para.139, repealed: 2002 c.29 Sch.12

Sch.13 para.147, repealed: 2003 c.39 Sch.10

Sch.13 para.148, repealed: 2003 c.39 Sch.10

Sch.13 para.149, repealed: 2003 c.39 Sch.10

Sch.13 para.150, repealed (in part): 2003 c.39 Sch.10

1999–cont.

22. Access to Justice Act 1999–*cont.*

Sch.13 para.153, repealed (in part): 2003 c.39 Sch.10

Sch.13 para.154, repealed: 2003 c.39 Sch.10

Sch.13 para.155, repealed: 2003 c.39 Sch.10

Sch.13 para.156, repealed: 2003 c.39 Sch.10

Sch.13 para.159, repealed: 2003 c.39 Sch.10

Sch.13 para.160, repealed: 2003 c.39 Sch.10

Sch.13 para.161, repealed: 2003 c.39 Sch.10

Sch.13 para.162, repealed: 2003 c.39 Sch.10

Sch.13 para.163, repealed: 2004 c.28 Sch.11

Sch.13 para.165, repealed: 2003 c.39 Sch.10

Sch.13 para.167, repealed: 2003 c.39 Sch.10

Sch.13 para.168, repealed: 2003 c.39 Sch.10

Sch.13 para.169, repealed: 2003 c.39 Sch.10

Sch.13 para.171, repealed: 2003 c.39 Sch.10

Sch.13 para.172, repealed: 2002 c.29 Sch.12

Sch.14 Part I para.1, amended: SI 2003/1887 Sch.2 para.11

Sch.14 Part I para.1, varied: SI 2003/415 Sch.1

Sch.14 Part I para.1, enabling: SI 2003/651, SSI 2003/207

Sch.14 Part II para.9, enabling: SI 2002/714, SI 2003/642

Sch.14 Part V para.34A, added: SI 2003/2867 Sch.1 para.29

Sch.14 Part V para.35, applied: 2003 c.39 Sch.2 para.16

Sch.14 Part V para.36, enabling: SI 2002/2143

23. Youth Justice and Criminal Evidence Act 1999

Commencement Orders: SI 2002/1739 Art.2; SI 2003/707 Art.2; SI 2004/299 Art.2; SI 2004/2428 Art.2; SSI 2004/408 Art.3

s.16, see *R. (on the application of S) v Waltham Forest Youth Court* [2004] EWHC 715, [2004] 2 Cr. App. R. 21 (QBD (Admin Ct)), Laws, L.J.

s.16, applied: SI 2002/1687 r.2, SI 2002/1688 r.2

s.17, applied: SI 2002/1687 r.2, SI 2002/1688 r.2

s.19, see *R. v Mullen (James Arthur)* [2004] EWCA Crim 602, [2004] 2 Cr. App. R. 18 (CA (Crim Div)), Potter, L.J.

s.19, applied: SI 2002/1687 r.2, SI 2002/1688 r.2, 2003 c.44 s.116

s.20, amended: 2003 c.39 Sch.8 para.384

s.20, applied: SI 2002/1687 r.5, SI 2002/1688 r.5

s.20, enabling: SI 2002/1687, SI 2002/1688, SI 2004/184, SI 2004/185

s.21, applied: SI 2002/1687 r.7, SI 2002/1688 r.7

s.24, repealed (in part): 2003 c.39 Sch.8 para.385, Sch.10

s.27, see *R. (on the application of CPS) v Brentford Youth Court* [2003] EWHC 2409, (2003) 167 J.P. 614 (QBD (Admin Ct)), Mitting, J.; see *R. v Mullen (James*

CAP.

1999–cont.

23. Youth Justice and Criminal Evidence Act 1999–*cont.*

s.27–*cont.*

Arthur) [2004] EWCA Crim 602, [2004] 2 Cr. App. R. 18 (CA (Crim Div)), Potter, L.J.

s.27, amended: 2003 c.39 Sch.8 para.384

s.27, applied: SI 2002/1687 r.8, SI 2002/1688 r.8

s.27, repealed (in part): 2003 c.44 Sch.37 Part 4, Sch.3 para.73

s.28, amended: 2003 c.39 Sch.8 para.384

s.29, amended: 2003 c.39 Sch.8 para.384

s.29, applied: SI 2002/1687 r.9A, SI 2002/1688 r.9A

s.29, enabling: SI 2004/184, SI 2004/185

s.30, applied: SI 2002/1687 r.8, SI 2002/1688 r.8

s.32, amended: 2003 c.44 Sch.36 para.75

s.35, amended: 2003 c.42 Sch.6 para.41

s.35, repealed (in part): 2003 c.42 Sch.7

s.37, amended: 2003 c.39 Sch.8 para.384

s.37, enabling: SI 2002/1688

s.38, amended: 2003 c.39 Sch.8 para.384

s.38, applied: 2003 c.44 s.106

s.39, amended: 2003 c.44 Sch.36 para.76

s.41, see *R. v A (Complainant's Sexual History)* [2001] UKHL 25, [2002] 1 A.C. 45 (HL), Lord Steyn; see *R. v Martin (Durwayne Nathan)* [2004] EWCA Crim 916, [2004] 2 Cr. App. R. 22 (CA (Crim Div)), Rose, L.J.; see *R. v Mokrecovas (Andrius)* [2001] EWCA Crim 1644, [2002] 1 Cr. App. R. 20 (CA (Crim Div)), Lord Woolf of Barnes, L.C.J.; see *R. v T (Abdul)* [2004] EWCA Crim 1220, [2004] 2 Cr. App. R. 32 (CA (Crim Div)), Waller, L.J.; see *R. v T (Complainant's Sexual History)* [2001] EWCA Crim 1877, [2002] 1 W.L.R. 632 (CA (Crim Div)), Keene, L.J.; see *R. v White (Andre Barrington)* [2004] EWCA Crim 946, (2004) 148 S.J.L.B. 300 (CA (Crim Div)), Laws, L.J.

s.41, applied: 2003 c.44 s.112

s.42, amended: 2003 c.44 Sch.3 para.73

s.42, repealed (in part): 2003 c.44 Sch.37 Part 4, Sch.3 para.73

s.43, amended: 2003 c.39 Sch.8 para.384

s.44, amended: 2003 c.39 Sch.8 para.386, SI 2003/1247 Sch.1 para.23

s.46, applied: SI 2004/2419 r.3, r.4, SI 2004/2420 r.3, r.4

s.53, see *R. v D (Video Testimony)* [2002] EWCA Crim 990, [2003] Q.B. 90 (CA (Crim Div)), Waller, L.J.; see *R. v Sed (Ali Dahir)* [2004] EWCA Crim 1294, [2004] 1 W.L.R. 3218 (CA (Crim Div)), Auld, L.J.

s.59, see *R. v Lyons (Isidore Jack) (No.3)* [2002] UKHL 44, [2003] 1 A.C. 976 (HL), Lord Bingham of Cornhill

s.62, amended: 2003 c.42 Sch.6 para.41

s.64, enabling: SI 2002/1739, SI 2004/299, SI 2004/2428

CAP.

1999–cont.

23. Youth Justice and Criminal Evidence Act 1999–*cont.*

s.65, amended: 2003 c.39 Sch.8 para.384

s.65, repealed (in part): 2003 c.39 Sch.10

s.65, enabling: SI 2002/1687, SI 2002/1688, SI 2004/184, SI 2004/185

s.68, enabling: SI 2002/1739, SI 2003/707, SI 2004/299, SI 2004/2428, SSI 2004/408

Sch.3, see *R. v Lyons (Isidore Jack) (No.3)* [2002] UKHL 44, [2003] 1 A.C. 976 (HL), Lord Bingham of Cornhill

Sch.3 para.1, applied: SI 2002/1688 r.2

Sch.3 para.6, repealed: 2004 c.27 Sch.8

Sch.3 para.22, repealed: SI 2002/3150 Sch.4

Sch.4 para.1, repealed (in part): 2003 c.44 Sch.37 Part 5

Sch.4 para.16, repealed: 2003 c.44 Sch.37 Part 6

Sch.4 para.18, repealed: SI 2002/3150 Sch.4

Sch.4 para.26, repealed: 2003 c.44 Sch.37 Part 12

Sch.4 para.27, repealed: 2003 c.44 Sch.37 Part 12

24. Pollution Prevention and Control Act 1999

applied: 2004 c.20 s.188

s.2, applied: SI 2002/275, SI 2002/1355, SI 2002/1559, SI 2002/1702, SI 2002/2688, SI 2002/2980, SI 2003/1699, SI 2003/3296, SI 2004/107, SI 2004/434, SI 2004/1375, SSI 2002/493, SSI 2003/146, SSI 2003/170, SSI 2003/221, SSI 2003/235, SSI 2003/343, SSI 2004/26, SSI 2004/110, SSI 2004/112

s.2, enabling: SI 2002/275, SI 2002/1355, SI 2002/1559, SI 2002/1702, SI 2002/2688, SI 2002/2980, SI 2003/1699, SI 2003/3296, SI 2004/107, SI 2004/434, SI 2004/1375, SSI 2002/493, SSI 2003/146, SSI 2003/170, SSI 2003/221, SSI 2003/235, SSI 2003/343, SSI 2004/26, SSI 2004/110, SSI 2004/112

s.3, applied: SI 2002/1861

s.3, enabling: SI 2002/1861

s.7, enabling: SI 2002/1355, SI 2002/1861

Sch.1, enabling: SSI 2003/146, SSI 2003/170, SSI 2003/221, SSI 2004/110, SSI 2004/112

Sch.1 Part I para.20, applied: SI 2002/2528 Art.2, SI 2003/948 Art.2, SSI 2002/488 Art.2, SSI 2003/185 Art.2, SSI 2003/204 Art.2, SSI 2003/235, SSI 2003/343, SSI 2003/600 Art.2

Sch.1 Part I para.20, enabling: SI 2002/2528, SI 2003/948, SSI 2002/488, SSI 2002/493, SSI 2003/185, SSI 2003/204, SSI 2003/600

Sch.1 Part II, added: 2003 c.33 s.38

Sch.1 Part II para.25, amended: 2004 asp 8 Sch.2 para.5

1999–cont.

26. **Employment Relations Act 1999**

Commencement Orders: SI 2003/3357 Art.3, Art.4

see *P v National Association of School Masters Union of Women Teachers (NASUWT)* [2003] UKHL 8, [2003] 2 A.C. 663 (HL), Lord Bingham of Cornhill

s.10, see *London Underground Ltd v Ferenc-Batchelor* [2003] I.C.R. 656 (EAT), Judge Altman

s.10, amended: 2004 c.24 s.37

s.10, applied: 2002 c.22 Sch.2 para.14, SI 2004/752 Reg.13

s.11, amended: 2004 c.24 s.37

s.11, applied: SI 2002/2927 Art.4

s.11, repealed (in part): 2002 c.22 Sch.8 Part 1

s.12, amended: 2004 c.24 s.37

s.13, see *London Underground Ltd v Ferenc-Batchelor* [2003] I.C.R. 656 (EAT), Judge Altman

s.13, applied: 2002 c.22 Sch.2 para.14

s.17, repealed: 2004 c.24 Sch.2

s.18, repealed (in part): 2002 c.21 Sch.6

s.19, enabling: SI 2002/2035

s.23, amended: 2002 c.22 s.41, Sch.7 para.54, 2004 c.24 s.39, Sch.2

s.28, repealed (in part): 2004 c.14 Sch.1 Part 8

s.32, see *Lawson v Serco Ltd* [2004] EWCA Civ 12, [2004] 2 All E.R. 200 (CA), Pill, L.J.

s.33, amended: 2004 c.14 Sch.1 Part 8

s.33, repealed (in part): 2004 c.14 Sch.1 Part 8

s.34, amended: 2004 c.24 Sch.1 para.42

s.34, enabling: SI 2002/10, SI 2002/2927, SI 2003/3038, SI 2004/2989

s.37, repealed (in part): 2004 c.14 Sch.1 Part 8

s.38, enabling: SI 2003/2715

s.40, repealed (in part): 2002 c.32 Sch.22 Part 3

s.42, applied: SI 2002/2035

s.45, enabling: SI 2003/3357

Sch.4 Part III para.6, repealed: 2004 c.14 Sch.1 Part 8

Sch.4 Part III para.7, repealed: 2004 c.14 Sch.1 Part 8

Sch.4 Part III para.13, repealed: 2004 c.14 Sch.1 Part 8

Sch.4 Part III para.14, repealed: 2004 c.14 Sch.1 Part 8

Sch.4 Part III para.15, repealed (in part): 2004 c.14 Sch.1 Part 8

Sch.4 Part III para.17, repealed: 2004 c.14 Sch.1 Part 8

Sch.4 Part III para.18, repealed: 2004 c.14 Sch.1 Part 8

Sch.4 Part III para.19, repealed: 2004 c.14 Sch.1 Part 8

Sch.4 Part III para.20, repealed: 2004 c.14 Sch.1 Part 8

Sch.4 Part III para.21, repealed: 2004 c.14 Sch.1 Part 8

1999–cont.

26. **Employment Relations Act 1999**–*cont.*

Sch.4 Part III para.22, repealed: 2004 c.14 Sch.1 Part 8

Sch.4 Part III para.23, repealed: 2004 c.14 Sch.1 Part 8

Sch.4 Part III para.24, repealed: 2004 c.14 Sch.1 Part 8

Sch.4 Part III para.25, repealed: 2004 c.14 Sch.1 Part 8

Sch.4 Part III para.26, repealed: 2004 c.14 Sch.1 Part 8

Sch.4 Part III para.27, repealed: 2004 c.14 Sch.1 Part 8

Sch.4 Part III para.28, repealed: 2004 c.14 Sch.1 Part 8

Sch.4 Part III para.29, repealed: 2004 c.14 Sch.1 Part 8

Sch.4 Part III para.30, repealed: 2004 c.14 Sch.1 Part 8

Sch.4 Part III para.31, repealed (in part): 2002 c.21 Sch.6

Sch.4 Part III para.37, repealed: 2004 c.14 Sch.1 Part 8

Sch.4 Part III para.40, repealed: 2004 c.14 Sch.1 Part 8

Sch.4 Part III para.41, repealed: 2004 c.14 Sch.1 Part 8

Sch.6 para.2, repealed: 2004 c.14 Sch.1 Part 8

Sch.6 para.3, repealed: 2004 c.14 Sch.1 Part 8

Sch.6 para.5, repealed (in part): 2004 c.14 Sch.1 Part 8

Sch.6 para.7, repealed (in part): 2004 c.14 Sch.1 Part 8

Sch.6 para.9, repealed: 2004 c.14 Sch.1 Part 8

Sch.6 para.10, repealed (in part): 2004 c.14 Sch.1 Part 8

Sch.6 para.11, repealed (in part): 2004 c.14 Sch.1 Part 8

Sch.6 para.14, repealed: 2004 c.14 Sch.1 Part 8

Sch.6 para.15, repealed (in part): 2004 c.14 Sch.1 Part 8

Sch.6 para.16, repealed (in part): 2004 c.14 Sch.1 Part 8

Sch.8 para.2, repealed: 2004 c.14 Sch.1 Part 8

Sch.8 para.4, repealed: 2004 c.14 Sch.1 Part 8

Sch.8 para.7, repealed: 2004 c.14 Sch.1 Part 8

27. **Local Government Act 1999**

referred to: 2003 c.26 Sch.3 para.4

Part I, applied: SI 2002/377 Sch.1 para.27, SI 2002/3199 Sch.1 para.21, 2003 c.26 s.34, s.35, s.101, SI 2003/3118 Sch.1 para.19, SI 2003/3170 Sch.1 para.21, 2004 c.23 s.54

Part I, referred to: 2004 c.23 s.50

s.1, amended: 2004 c.21 Sch.1 para.91, 2004 c.23 Sch.1 para.2

s.1, applied: SI 2002/523 Art.2, SI 2003/519, SI 2003/530 Art.2, SI 2003/662 Art.1, SI 2004/589 Art.2, SI 2004/1705 Art.1

s.1, disapplied: SI 2002/678 Art.1

1999–cont.

27. Local Government Act 1999–*cont.*

s.1, referred to: SI 2002/305 Art.2, SI 2002/886 Art.1, SI 2003/1265, SI 2004/644, SI 2004/1575 Art.1

s.2, enabling: SI 2003/3343

s.2A, added: 2004 c.23 Sch.1 para.3

s.3, applied: 2003 c.26 s.34, s.35, s.36

s.3, referred to: SI 2003/3343 Art.2

s.4, amended: 2003 c.26 Sch.3 para.5, 2004 c.23 Sch.1 para.4

s.4, applied: SI 2002/523, SI 2002/694, SI 2002/757, 2003 c.20 s.54, 2003 c.26 s.34, s.35, s.36, s.100, SI 2003/519, SI 2003/530, SI 2003/864, SI 2003/1265, SI 2004/589, SI 2004/644, SI 2004/1176

s.4, referred to: SI 2003/3343 Art.2

s.4, enabling: SI 2002/523, SI 2002/694, SI 2002/757, SI 2003/519, SI 2003/530, SI 2003/864, SI 2003/1265, SI 2004/589, SI 2004/644, SI 2004/1176

s.5, amended: 2003 c.26 Sch.3 para.6

s.5, applied: 2003 c.20 s.54, 2003 c.26 s.34, s.35, s.36, s.100

s.5, referred to: SI 2003/3343 Art.2

s.5, enabling: SI 2002/305, SI 2002/886, SI 2003/662

s.6, amended: 2003 c.26 Sch.3 para.7

s.6, applied: SI 2002/305 Art.6, 2003 c.26 s.34, s.35, s.36, s.100

s.6, referred to: SI 2003/3343 Art.2

s.6, enabling: SI 2002/305, SI 2002/886, SI 2003/662, SI 2004/1575

s.7, amended: 2004 c.23 Sch.1 para.5

s.7, applied: SI 2002/305 Art.7

s.7, referred to: SI 2002/886 Art.4

s.7, enabling: SI 2002/305, SI 2002/886

s.8, repealed (in part): 2004 c.23 Sch.1 para.6, Sch.4

s.8A, added: 2004 c.23 Sch.1 para.7

s.8B, added: 2004 c.23 Sch.1 para.7

s.10, amended: 2004 c.23 Sch.1 para.8

s.10, varied: 2004 c.21 s.24

s.10A, added: 2004 c.23 Sch.1 para.9

s.10A, varied: 2004 c.21 s.24

s.11, amended: 2004 c.23 Sch.1 para.10

s.11, varied: 2004 c.21 s.24

s.12, amended: 2004 c.23 Sch.1 para.11

s.12, varied: 2004 c.21 s.24

s.12A, added: 2004 c.23 Sch.1 para.12

s.12A, varied: 2004 c.21 s.24

s.13, varied: 2004 c.21 s.24

s.13A, added: 2004 c.23 Sch.1 para.13

s.16, amended: 2003 c.26 Sch.3 para.8

s.16, applied: 2003 c.26 s.100

s.17, amended: 2003 c.26 Sch.3 para.9

s.17, applied: 2003 c.26 s.100

s.18, applied: 2003 c.26 s.100

s.19, amended: 2003 c.26 Sch.3 para.10

s.19, applied: 2003 c.26 s.100

s.19, enabling: SI 2002/678

1999–cont.

27. Local Government Act 1999–*cont.*

s.22, repealed (in part): 2003 c.26 Sch.8 Part 1, 2004 c.23 Sch.4

s.23, amended: 2004 c.23 Sch.1 para.14

s.24, repealed (in part): 2002 c.30 Sch.8

s.25, amended: 2003 c.43 Sch.9 para.15, 2004 c.23 Sch.1 para.15

s.26, amended: 2004 c.23 Sch.1 para.16

s.28, enabling: SI 2002/523, SI 2003/530, SI 2004/589, SI 2004/1176

s.29, repealed (in part): 2004 c.21 Sch.2

s.29, enabling: SI 2002/678, SI 2002/757, SI 2002/886, SI 2004/1575

s.31, referred to: 2003 c.26 s.128

s.31, repealed: 2003 c.26 Sch.8 Part 1

s.33, amended: 2004 c.23 Sch.1 para.17

28. Food Standards Act 1999

s.29, amended: SI 2002/794 Sch.1 para.38, Sch.2

s.29, applied: SI 2002/794 Art.3

s.30, repealed (in part): SI 2002/794 Sch.2 Sch.5 para.1, repealed: SI 2004/1109 Sch.1

29. Greater London Authority Act 1999

Commencement Orders: SI 2003/1920 Art.2

applied: 2002 c.18 Sch.2 Part 2, SI 2002/1043, 2003 c.26 s.23, s.29, s.103, SI 2003/1615 Sch.1 para.2

referred to: SI 2003/1615 Art.3

Part IV, applied: 2004 c.18 s.29

s.3, disapplied: SI 2004/222 Art.2

s.17A, enabling: SI 2003/1907

s.28, enabling: SI 2002/1044

s.34, disapplied: 2003 c.26 s.93

s.38, disapplied: 2003 c.26 s.3

s.52, amended: 2003 c.26 Sch.7 para.69

s.52, repealed (in part): 2003 c.26 Sch.8 Part 1

s.64, amended: 2003 c.44 Sch.26 para.52

s.85, amended: 2003 c.26 Sch.7 para.70

s.85, applied: 2003 c.26 s.25, s.26, s.27, s.29, 2003 c.iii Sch.2 para.1, Sch.2 para.7, SI 2003/2613 Sch.3 para.2, Sch.3 para.3, Sch.3 para.4

s.85, varied: SI 2002/155 Reg.6, SI 2003/195 Reg.6, SI 2004/243 Reg.6

s.86, enabling: SI 2002/155, SI 2003/195, SI 2004/243

s.88, applied: SI 2002/267 Reg.2, SI 2003/225 Reg.2, SI 2003/2613 Sch.1 para.6, SI 2004/300 Reg.2

s.88, varied: SI 2002/155 Reg.7, SI 2003/195 Reg.7, SI 2004/243 Reg.7

s.88, enabling: SI 2002/155, SI 2002/267, SI 2003/195, SI 2003/225, SI 2003/3012, SI 2004/243, SI 2004/300

s.89, applied: SI 2002/267 Reg.2, SI 2003/225 Reg.2, SI 2003/2613 Sch.1 para.6, SI 2004/300 Reg.2

s.89, varied: SI 2002/155 Reg.8, SI 2003/195 Reg.8, SI 2004/243 Reg.8

CAP.

1999–cont.

29. Greater London Authority Act 1999– *cont.*

s.89, enabling: SI 2002/155, SI 2002/267, SI 2003/195, SI 2003/225, SI 2003/3012, SI 2004/243, SI 2004/300

s.99, varied: SI 2002/155 Reg.9, SI 2003/195 Reg.9, SI 2004/243 Reg.9

s.102, varied: SI 2002/155 Reg.10, SI 2003/195 Reg.10, SI 2004/243 Reg.10

s.108, repealed (in part): 2003 c.26 Sch.8 Part 1

s.111, repealed: 2003 c.26 Sch.8 Part 1

s.112, repealed: 2003 c.26 Sch.7 para.71, Sch.8 Part 1

s.113, repealed: 2003 c.26 Sch.8 Part 1

s.114, repealed: 2003 c.26 Sch.7 para.71, Sch.8 Part 1

s.115, repealed (in part): 2003 c.26 Sch.7 para.71, Sch.8 Part 1

s.116, repealed: 2003 c.26 Sch.7 para.71, Sch.8 Part 1

s.117, repealed: 2003 c.26 Sch.7 para.71, Sch.8 Part 1

s.118, repealed: 2003 c.26 Sch.7 para.71, Sch.8 Part 1

s.119, amended: 2003 c.26 Sch.7 para.72, Sch.8 Part 1

s.120, amended: 2003 c.26 Sch.7 para.73

s.121, amended: 2003 c.26 Sch.7 para.74

s.122, amended: 2003 c.26 Sch.7 para.75, Sch.8 Part 1

s.123, amended: 2003 c.26 Sch.7 para.76

s.124, amended: 2003 c.26 Sch.7 para.77, Sch.8 Part 1

s.126, amended: 2003 c.26 Sch.7 para.78

s.127, applied: 2003 c.26 s.25

s.134, applied: SI 2003/533 Reg.8

s.134, enabling: SI 2003/533

s.136, referred to: 2003 c.26 s.128

s.136, repealed (in part): 2003 c.26 Sch.8 Part 1

s.141, see *R. (on the application of Westminster City Council) v Mayor of London* [2002] EWHC 2440, [2003] B.L.G.R. 611 (QBD (Admin Ct)), Maurice Kay, J.

s.163, disapplied: SI 2002/1066 Art.41, SI 2004/757 Art.48

s.163, enabling: SI 2004/257, SI 2004/965, SI 2004/1651

s.167, applied: 2003 c.iii

s.189, enabling: SI 2002/614

s.199, substituted: 2003 c.20 Sch.2 para.19

s.200, amended: 2003 c.20 Sch.2 para.19

s.207, disapplied: SI 2003/1613 Art.3, SI 2004/757 Art.48

s.207, repealed (in part): SI 2003/1613 Art.4

s.207, enabling: SI 2003/1613

s.210, applied: 2002 c.40 s.249

s.217, varied: 2003 c.20 s.114

s.219, repealed: 2002 c.9 Sch.13

s.221, varied: 2003 c.20 s.114

CAP.

1999–cont.

29. Greater London Authority Act 1999– *cont.*

s.222, varied: 2003 c.20 s.114

s.225, applied: 2003 c.20 s.115

s.228, amended: 2003 c.20 Sch.2 para.19, Sch.2 para.23

s.235, amended: 2002 c.40 Sch.25 para.39, 2003 c.20 Sch.2 para.19, 2003 c.21 Sch.17 para.157

s.240, amended: 2002 c.4 s.1

s.240, applied: 2002 c.4 s.2

s.283, repealed (in part): 2004 c.18 Sch.12 Part 1

s.284, repealed: 2004 c.18 Sch.12 Part 1

s.286, repealed: 2004 c.18 Sch.12 Part 1

s.302, enabling: SI 2003/1913

s.330, repealed: 2004 c.36 Sch.3

s.334, referred to: 2004 c.5 s.113

s.335, referred to: 2004 c.5 s.113

s.336, referred to: 2004 c.5 s.113

s.337, amended: 2004 c.5 Sch.7 para.22

s.337, applied: 2004 c.5 Sch.8 para.1

s.337, referred to: 2004 c.5 s.113

s.337, repealed (in part): 2004 c.5 Sch.7 para.22

s.338, referred to: 2004 c.5 s.113

s.339, referred to: 2004 c.5 s.113

s.340, referred to: 2004 c.5 s.113

s.341, referred to: 2004 c.5 s.113

s.342, amended: 2004 c.5 Sch.7 para.22

s.342, referred to: 2004 c.5 s.113

s.343, referred to: 2004 c.5 s.113

s.346, amended: 2004 c.5 Sch.7 para.22

s.353, amended: 2003 c.33 s.17, s.32

s.353, repealed (in part): 2003 c.33 s.35

s.354, amended: 2003 c.33 s.17

s.361, repealed: 2003 c.33 s.35

s.405, enabling: SI 2003/527, SI 2003/1614, SI 2003/1615

s.406, enabling: SI 2003/1614, SI 2003/1615

s.409, applied: 2003 c.20 s.114

s.411, enabling: SI 2002/1043, SI 2002/2468

s.412, disapplied: 2003 c.20 s.114

s.412, referred to: 2003 c.20 s.114

s.420, enabling: SI 2002/155, SI 2002/1043, SI 2002/1044, SI 2003/108, SI 2003/109, SI 2003/110, SI 2003/195, SI 2003/1614, SI 2003/1615, SI 2004/243

s.425, repealed (in part): 2003 c.20 Sch.8

s.425, enabling: SI 2003/1920

Sch.8 para.1, enabling: SI 2003/241

Sch.8 para.3, enabling: SI 2003/241

Sch.11 para.26, applied: SI 2003/1615 Art.3

Sch.12 para.1, applied: 2003 c.20 s.114

Sch.12 para.2, disapplied: 2003 c.20 s.114

Sch.12 para.2, referred to: 2003 c.20 s.114

Sch.13, applied: 2003 c.iii

Sch.14 Part I para.1, varied: 2003 c.20 s.114

Sch.14 Part I para.2, varied: 2003 c.20 s.114

Sch.14 Part I para.3, varied: 2003 c.20 s.114

CAP.

1999–cont.

29. Greater London Authority Act 1999– cont.

Sch.14 Part I para.4, varied: 2003 c.20 s.114
Sch.14 Part I para.5, varied: 2003 c.20 s.114
Sch.14 Part I para.6, varied: 2003 c.20 s.114
Sch.14 Part I para.7, varied: 2003 c.20 s.114
Sch.14 Part I para.8, varied: 2003 c.20 s.114
Sch.14 Part I para.9, varied: 2003 c.20 s.114
Sch.14 Part I para.10, varied: 2003 c.20 s.114
Sch.14 Part I para.11, varied: 2003 c.20 s.114
Sch.14 Part II para.12, varied: 2003 c.20 s.114
Sch.14 Part II para.13, varied: 2003 c.20 s.114
Sch.14 Part II para.14, varied: 2003 c.20 s.114
Sch.14 Part II para.15, varied: 2003 c.20 s.114
Sch.14 Part II para.16, varied: 2003 c.20 s.114
Sch.14 Part II para.17, varied: 2003 c.20 s.114
Sch.14 Part II para.18, varied: 2003 c.20 s.114
Sch.14 Part II para.19, varied: 2003 c.20 s.114
Sch.14 Part III para.20, varied: 2003 c.20 s.114
Sch.14 Part III para.21, varied: 2003 c.20 s.114
Sch.15 para.1, varied: 2003 c.20 s.114
Sch.15 para.2, varied: 2003 c.20 s.114
Sch.15 para.3, varied: 2003 c.20 s.114
Sch.15 para.4, varied: 2003 c.20 s.114
Sch.15 para.5, varied: 2003 c.20 s.114
Sch.15 para.6, varied: 2003 c.20 s.114
Sch.15 para.7, varied: 2003 c.20 s.114
Sch.17 para.1, varied: SI 2003/1614 Sch.1 para.1
Sch.17 para.2, varied: SI 2003/1614 Sch.1 para.2
Sch.17 para.3, varied: SI 2003/1614 Sch.1 para.3
Sch.17 para.4, varied: SI 2003/1614 Sch.1 para.4
Sch.17 para.5, varied: SI 2003/1614 Sch.1 para.5
Sch.17 para.6, varied: SI 2003/1614 Sch.1 para.6
Sch.17 para.7, varied: SI 2003/1614 Sch.1 para.7
Sch.17 para.8, varied: SI 2003/1614 Sch.1 para.8
Sch.17 para.9, applied: SI 2003/1614 Art.2
Sch.17 para.10, varied: SI 2003/1614 Sch.1 para.9
Sch.18 para.15, amended: 2003 c.20 Sch.2 para.19
Sch.20 Part I para.4, repealed: 2004 c.14 Sch.1 Part 14
Sch.20 Part II para.13, repealed: 2004 c.14 Sch.1 Part 14
Sch.23, applied: SI 2003/110 Reg.2
Sch.23 para.1, enabling: SI 2003/110
Sch.23 para.12, enabling: SI 2003/108, SI 2003/109
Sch.23 para.16, applied: SI 2003/110 Reg.2
Sch.23 para.27, enabling: SI 2003/109
Sch.23 para.28, enabling: SI 2003/108
Sch.24, applied: SI 2003/110 Reg.2

CAP.

1999–cont.

29. Greater London Authority Act 1999– cont.

Sch.24 para.1, enabling: SI 2003/110
Sch.24 para.22, applied: SI 2003/110 Reg.2
Sch.27 para.38, repealed: 2004 c.14 Sch.1 Part 10
Sch.27 para.43, repealed: 2004 c.14 Sch.1 Part 10
Sch.27 para.51, referred to: 2002 c.30 s.108
Sch.27 para.51, repealed: 2002 c.30 Sch.8
Sch.27 para.59, referred to: 2002 c.30 s.108
Sch.27 para.59, repealed: 2002 c.30 Sch.8
Sch.27 para.90, repealed: 2002 c.30 Sch.8
Sch.27 para.97, repealed: 2002 c.30 Sch.8
Sch.27 para.98, repealed: 2002 c.30 Sch.8
Sch.27 para.99, repealed: 2002 c.30 Sch.8
Sch.27 para.108, repealed: 2003 c.39 Sch.10
Sch.29 Part I para.6, repealed: 2003 c.17 Sch.7
Sch.29 Part I para.47, repealed: 2004 c.14 Sch.1 Part 10
Sch.29 Part I para.62, repealed: 2003 c.39 Sch.10
Sch.29 Part II para.67, repealed: 2003 c.17 Sch.7
Sch.29 Part II para.70, repealed: 2003 c.17 Sch.7
Sch.29 Part II para.71, repealed: 2003 c.17 Sch.7

30. Welfare Reform and Pensions Act 1999

Commencement Orders: SI 2002/153 Art.2; SI 2002/381 Art.2; SI 2002/818 Art.2, Art.3; SI 2003/936 Art.2

see *Fielding v United Kingdom (36940/97)* Times, February 25, 2002 (ECHR), J-P Costa (President); see *Hooper v Secretary of State for Work and Pensions* [2002] EWHC 191, [2002] U.K.H.R.R. 785 (QBD (Admin Ct)), Moses, J.; see *Hooper v Secretary of State for Work and Pensions* [2003] EWCA Civ 813, [2003] 1 W.L.R. 2623 (CA), Lord Phillips of Worth Matravers, M.R.

applied: SI 2003/1325 Art.2, 2004 c.35 s.7, s.87, s.201

Part I, applied: 2004 c.35 s.321
Part I, referred to: 2004 c.35 s.322
Part II, applied: 2004 c.35 s.321
Part II, referred to: 2004 c.35 s.322
Part III, applied: 2002 c.29 s.275, 2004 c.35 s.321
Part IV, applied: 2004 c.35 s.321
Part IV, referred to: 2004 c.35 s.322
Part IV c.I, applied: 2004 c.33 Sch.5 para.16, Sch.15 para.11, 2004 c.35 s.133, s.135, s.220
Part IV c.II, applied: 2004 c.33 Sch.5 para.16, Sch.15 para.11
Part V c.I, referred to: 2004 c.35 s.73

1999–cont.

30. Welfare Reform and Pensions Act 1999–cont.

s.1, amended: 2004 c.35 s.285, Sch.12 para.72

s.1, referred to: 2004 c.35 s.73

s.1, enabling: SI 2002/1480, SI 2002/2098

s.2, amended: 2004 c.35 s.285, Sch.12 para.73

s.2, applied: 2004 c.35 s.80, s.101, Sch.1 para.20, Sch.2 para.20

s.2, referred to: 2004 c.35 s.73

s.2, repealed (in part): 2004 c.35 Sch.13 Part 1

s.3, applied: 2004 c.35 s.74

s.4, repealed: 2004 c.35 Sch.13 Part 1

s.5, repealed: 2004 c.35 Sch.13 Part 1

s.8, amended: 2004 c.35 s.7, Sch.12 para.74

s.8, enabling: SI 2002/1480, SI 2002/2098

s.11, applied: SI 2002/427 Reg.2, Reg.3, Reg.5, Reg.6, Reg.11, Reg.12, Reg.14, Reg.15, SI 2002/836 Reg.2, Reg.3, Reg.5, Reg.6, Reg.11, Reg.12, Reg.14, Reg.15

s.11, referred to: SI 2002/836 Reg.3

s.11, enabling: SI 2002/427, SI 2002/836

s.12, applied: SI 2002/427 Reg.3, Reg.12, SI 2002/836 Reg.3, Reg.12

s.12, enabling: SI 2002/427, SI 2002/836

s.17, repealed: 2004 c.35 Sch.13 Part 1

s.23, amended: 2004 c.33 Sch.27 para.157, Sch.30

s.23, enabling: SI 2003/1727

s.24, amended: 2004 c.33 Sch.27 para.158, Sch.30

s.26, applied: 2004 c.33 Sch.5 para.29

s.28, amended: 2004 c.33 Sch.27 para.159, Sch.30

s.29, applied: 2002 c.29 s.275, SI 2002/3202 Reg.4, 2004 c.12 s.220, Sch.36 para.18, 2004 c.35 Sch.7 para.3, Sch.7 para.4, Sch.7 para.5, Sch.7 para.6

s.30, applied: 2004 c.33 Sch.5 para.28

s.30, enabling: SI 2003/1727

s.31, applied: 2004 c.35 s.150, s.318

s.33, amended: 2004 c.35 s.7

s.33, referred to: 2004 c.35 s.73

s.34, amended: 2004 c.33 Sch.27 para.160, Sch.30

s.38, amended: 2004 c.35 Sch.12 para.75

s.38, repealed (in part): 2004 c.35 Sch.13 Part 1

s.40, amended: 2004 c.35 s.280

s.41, applied: 2004 c.33 Sch.5 para.17, Sch.15 para.12

s.45, referred to: 2004 c.35 s.73

s.45, enabling: SI 2003/1727

s.46, amended: 2004 c.35 Sch.13 Part 1

s.48, amended: 2004 c.33 Sch.27 para.161, Sch.30

s.49, applied: 2004 c.33 Sch.5 para.28

s.50, referred to: 2004 c.35 s.322

1999–cont.

30. Welfare Reform and Pensions Act 1999–cont.

s.50, repealed (in part): 2004 c.35 Sch.13 Part 1

s.51, referred to: 2004 c.35 s.73

s.52, amended: 2004 c.35 Sch.11 para.25

s.53, repealed (in part): 2002 c.22 Sch.8 Part 1

s.60, applied: SI 2002/2005 Reg.4, SI 2004/959 Reg.17

s.60, enabling: SI 2003/2438, SI 2004/934, SI 2004/959, SI 2004/1043

s.62, referred to: 2004 c.35 s.73

s.63, referred to: 2004 c.35 s.73

s.64, referred to: 2004 c.35 s.73

s.65, referred to: 2004 c.35 s.73

s.72, amended: 2002 c.22 Sch.7 para.55

s.72, referred to: SI 2002/1703 Reg.2

s.72, enabling: SI 2002/2497

s.75, see *R. (on the application of Professional Contractors Group Ltd) v Inland Revenue Commissioners* [2001] EWCA Civ 1945, [2002] S.T.C. 165 (CA), Robert Walker, L.J.

s.76, see *R. (on the application of Professional Contractors Group Ltd) v Inland Revenue Commissioners* [2001] EWCA Civ 1945, [2002] S.T.C. 165 (CA), Robert Walker, L.J.

s.79, applied: 2003 c.1 s.677

s.83, see *W v W (Divorce Proceedings: Withdrawal of Consent before Perfection of Order)* [2002] EWHC 1826, [2002] 2 F.L.R. 1225 (Fam Div), Bodey, J.

s.83, enabling: SI 2002/427, SI 2002/836, SI 2002/1480, SI 2002/2098, SI 2002/2497, SI 2003/1727, SI 2003/2438, SI 2004/934, SI 2004/959, SI 2004/1043

s.85, see *S v S (Rescission of Decree Nisi: Pension Sharing Provision)* [2002] 1 F.L.R. 457 (Fam Div), Singer, J.

s.85, enabling: SI 2002/491

s.89, enabling: SI 2002/153, SI 2002/381, SI 2002/818, SI 2003/936

Sch.1 para.1, amended: 2004 c.35 Sch.12 para.76, Sch.13 Part 1

Sch.1 para.1, applied: 2004 c.35 s.78

Sch.1 para.1, repealed (in part): 2004 c.35 Sch.13 Part 1

Sch.1 para.2, repealed: 2004 c.35 Sch.13 Part 1

Sch.1 para.3, repealed: 2004 c.35 Sch.13 Part 1

Sch.2 para.3, repealed (in part): 2004 c.35 Sch.13 Part 1

Sch.2 para.9, repealed: 2004 c.35 Sch.13 Part 1

Sch.2 para.13, repealed: 2004 c.35 Sch.13 Part 1

Sch.2 para.14, repealed: 2004 c.35 Sch.13 Part 1

Sch.2 para.15, repealed: 2004 c.35 Sch.13 Part 1

CAP.

1999–cont.

30. Welfare Reform and Pensions Act 1999–cont.

Sch.2 para.16, repealed: 2004 c.35 Sch.13 Part 1

Sch.5 para.8, amended: 2004 c.35 Sch.12 para.77

Sch.5 para.8, enabling: SI 2003/1727

Sch.5 para.13A, added: 2004 c.35 Sch.12 para.77

Sch.8 Part I para.1, repealed (in part): 2003 c.1 Sch.8 Part 1

Sch.8 Part I para.11, repealed: 2002 c.21 Sch.6

Sch.8 Part I para.14, repealed: 2002 c.21 Sch.6

Sch.9 Part I para.4, repealed: 2002 c.19 Sch.2

Sch.10 Part I para.4, repealed: 2002 c.19 Sch.2

Sch.11 para.31, repealed (in part): 2004 c.3 Sch.2 Part 1

Sch.12 Part I para.13, repealed: 2004 c.12 Sch.42 Part 3

Sch.12 Part I para.39, repealed (in part): 2004 c.35 Sch.13 Part 1

Sch.12 Part I para.44, repealed: 2004 c.35 Sch.13 Part 1

Sch.12 Part I para.45, repealed: 2004 c.35 Sch.13 Part 1

Sch.12 Part I para.46, repealed: 2004 c.35 Sch.13 Part 1

Sch.12 Part I para.47, repealed: 2004 c.35 Sch.13 Part 1

Sch.12 Part I para.48, repealed: 2004 c.35 Sch.13 Part 1

Sch.12 Part I para.49, repealed: 2004 c.35 Sch.13 Part 1

Sch.12 Part I para.53, repealed: 2004 c.35 Sch.13 Part 1

Sch.12 Part I para.55, repealed: 2004 c.35 Sch.13 Part 1

Sch.12 Part I para.60, repealed: 2004 c.35 Sch.13 Part 1

Sch.12 Part II para.75, repealed: 2003 c.1 Sch.8 Part 1

31. Contracts (Rights of Third Parties) Act 1999

s.1, see *Nisshin Shipping Co Ltd v Cleaves & Co Ltd* [2003] EWHC 2602, [2004] 1 All E.R. (Comm) 481 (QBD (Comm Ct)), Colman, J.

s.8, see *Nisshin Shipping Co Ltd v Cleaves & Co Ltd* [2003] EWHC 2602, [2004] 1 All E.R. (Comm) 481 (QBD (Comm Ct)), Colman, J.

32. Mental Health (Amendment) (Scotland) Act 1999

repealed: 2003 asp 13 Sch.5 Part 1

33. Immigration and Asylum Act 1999

Commencement Orders: 2002 c.41 Sch.9; SI 2002/2815 Art.2, Sch.1; SI 2003/2 Art.2, Sch.1; SI 2003/758 Art.2; SI 2003/1469

CAP.

1999–cont.

33. Immigration and Asylum Act 1999–cont.

–cont.

Art.2, Sch.1; SI 2003/1862 Art.2; SI 2004/2997 Art.2

see *Kumarakuraparan v Secretary of State for the Home Department* [2002] EWHC 112, [2002] Imm. A.R. 498 (QBD (Admin Ct)), Newman, J.; see *Murua v Croydon LBC* (2002) 5 C.C.L. Rep. 51 (QBD (Admin Ct)), Rafferty, J.; see *R. (on the application of Mohamad) v Immigration Adjudicator* [2002] EWHC 2496, Times, December 12, 2002 (QBD (Admin Ct)), Munby, J.; see *R. v Woop (Michael Thomas)* [2002] EWCA Crim 58, [2002] 2 Cr. App. R. (S.) 65 (CA (Crim Div)), Mitchell, J.; see *Tehrani v Secretary of State for the Home Department* 2003 S.L.T. 808 (OH), Lord Philip

applied: 2002 c.41 s.67, s.77, s.78, Sch.3 para.1, Sch.6 para.4

referred to: 2002 c.41 Sch.6 para.5, SI 2002/2811 Art.4, SI 2003/754 Sch.2 para.6, SI 2003/1252 Art.2, SI 2003/2900 Art.2

Part II, see *International Transport Roth GmbH v Secretary of State for the Home Department* [2002] EWCA Civ 158, [2003] Q.B. 728 (CA), Simon Brown, L.J.

Part II, referred to: SI 2003/2900 Sch.1

Part IV, applied: 2002 c.41 s.115, SI 2003/1016 Sch.1 para.7

Part VI, applied: SI 2002/2367 Art.3, SI 2003/381 Reg.4, SI 2003/860 Reg.3, SI 2003/2382 Reg.5, SSI 2003/376 Reg.4, SSI 2003/460 Reg.4

s.1, varied: SI 2003/1252 Sch.1, SI 2003/2900 Sch.1

s.2, varied: SI 2003/1252 Sch.1, SI 2003/2900 Sch.1

s.3, applied: SI 2003/754 Sch.2 para.6

s.3, varied: SI 2003/2900 Sch.1

s.4, amended: 2002 c.41 s.49, 2004 c.19 s.10

s.4, applied: 2002 c.41 s.23, s.26, s.51, s.55

s.4, disapplied: 2004 c.19 s.10

s.4, substituted: 2002 c.41 s.49

s.5, amended: 2004 c.19 s.43

s.5, applied: SI 2003/754 Sch.2 para.6, SI 2003/1711 Reg.3, 2004 c.19 s.42

s.5, varied: SI 2003/1252 Sch.1, SI 2003/2900 Sch.1

s.5, enabling: SI 2003/1711, SI 2004/580, SI 2004/3105

s.6, varied: SI 2003/1252 Sch.1, SI 2003/2900 Sch.1

s.7, varied: SI 2003/1252 Sch.1, SI 2003/2900 Sch.1

s.8, varied: SI 2003/1252 Sch.1, SI 2003/2900 Sch.1

s.9, applied: SI 2003/754 Sch.2 para.2, Sch.2 para.3, Sch.2 para.6

1999–cont.

33. Immigration and Asylum Act 1999–
cont.

s.10, amended: 2002 c.41 s.73, s.74, s.75, s.76, Sch.9

s.10, applied: 2002 c.41 s.62, SI 2002/313 Sch.1, 2003 c.44 s.259, s.260, SI 2003/754 Sch.2 para.6, SI 2004/1219 Reg.6

s.10, varied: SI 2003/1252 Sch.1, SI 2003/2900 Sch.1

s.11, see *Ali v Secretary of State for the Home Department* 2003 S.L.T. 674 (OH), Lady Cosgrove; see *Ibrahim v Secretary of State for the Home Department* 2002 S.L.T. 1150 (OH), Lord Carloway; see *Khairandish v Secretary of State for the Home Department* 2003 S.L.T. 1358 (OH), Lord Drummond Young; see *R. (on the application of Benda) v Secretary of State for the Home Department (No.1)* [2002] EWHC 127, [2002] Imm. A.R. 314 (QBD (Admin Ct)), Maurice Kay, J.; see *R. (on the application of Gashi (Agim)) v Secretary of State for the Home Department* [2001] EWHC Admin 622, [2002] Imm. A.R. 82 (QBD (Admin Ct)), Scott Baker, J.; see *R. (on the application of Gashi (Agim)) v Secretary of the Home Department (Application for Permission to Appeal)* [2001] EWCA Civ 1850, [2002] Imm. A.R. 351 (CA), Dame Elizabeth Butler-Sloss (President); see *R. (on the application of Nadarajah) v Secretary of State for the Home Department* [2002] EWHC 2595, [2003] Imm. A.R. 373 (QBD (Admin Ct)), Stanley Burnton, J.; see *R. (on the application of Samer) v Secretary of State for the Home Department* [2001] EWHC Admin 545, [2002] Imm. A.R. 190 (QBD (Admin Ct)), Collins, J.; see *R. (on the application of Yogathas) v Secretary of State for the Home Department* [2002] UKHL 36, [2003] 1 A.C. 920 (HL), Lord Hope of Craighead

s.11, amended: 2002 c.41 s.80

s.11, applied: 2002 c.41 s.93, SI 2003/754 Sch.2 para.6, 2004 c.19 s.35

s.11, referred to: SI 2002/2811 Art.3

s.11, repealed: 2004 c.19 Sch.4

s.12, amended: SI 2003/1016 Sch.1 para.11

s.12, applied: 2002 c.41 s.93, 2004 c.19 s.35

s.12, repealed (in part): SI 2003/1016 Sch.1 para.11, 2004 c.19 Sch.4

s.13, varied: SI 2003/1252 Sch.1, SI 2003/2900 Sch.1

s.14, varied: SI 2003/1252 Sch.1, SI 2003/2900 Sch.1

s.15, see *S (Children) (Child Abduction: Asylum Appeal), Re* [2002] EWCA Civ 843, [2002] 1 W.L.R. 2548 (CA), Laws, L.J.; see *S (Children) (Child Abduction:*

1999–cont.

33. Immigration and Asylum Act 1999–
cont.

s.15–*cont.*
Asylum Appeal), Re [2002] EWHC 816, [2002] 2 F.L.R. 437 (Fam Div), Bennett, J.

s.15, repealed: 2002 c.41 Sch.9

s.15, varied: SI 2003/1252 Sch.1, SI 2003/2900 Sch.1

s.18, varied: SI 2003/1252 Sch.1, SI 2003/2900 Sch.1

s.19, varied: SI 2003/1252 Sch.1, SI 2003/2900 Sch.1

s.20, amended: 2002 c.41 s.132

s.20, applied: 2002 c.41 s.131

s.21, applied: SI 2003/1875 Reg.6

s.23, amended: 2002 c.41 Sch.7 para.27

s.24A, added: 2004 c.33 Sch.27 para.162

s.25, applied: SI 2003/612 Art.3

s.25, varied: SI 2003/2900 Sch.1

s.25, enabling: SI 2003/612

s.26, applied: SI 2003/1502 Reg.3

s.26, varied: SI 2003/1252 Sch.1, SI 2003/2900 Sch.1

s.26, enabling: SI 2003/1502

s.27, enabling: SI 2002/2155, SI 2004/579

s.28, varied: SI 2003/1252 Sch.1, SI 2003/2900 Sch.1

s.29, see *R. v Hobbs (Stephen Paul)* [2002] EWCA Crim 387, [2002] 2 Cr. App. R. 22 (CA (Crim Div)), Pill, L.J.

s.29, repealed: 2002 c.41 Sch.9

s.29, varied: SI 2003/1252 Sch.1, SI 2003/2900 Sch.1

s.30, varied: SI 2003/1252 Sch.1, SI 2003/2900 Sch.1

s.31, see *R. (on the application of Pepushi) v CPS* [2004] EWHC 798, [2004] I.N.L.R. 638 (QBD (Admin Ct)), Thomas, L.J.

s.31, varied: SI 2003/1252 Sch.1, SI 2003/2900 Sch.1

s.32, amended: 2002 c.41 Sch.8 para.2

s.32, applied: SI 2002/2816, SI 2002/2816 Art.2, SI 2002/2817 Reg.3, Reg.4, Reg.5, Reg.9, SI 2004/251, SI 2004/251 Art.2

s.32, varied: SI 2003/1252 Sch.1, SI 2003/2900 Sch.1

s.32, enabling: SI 2002/2817, SI 2004/244

s.32A, added: 2002 c.41 Sch.8 para.3

s.32A, applied: SI 2002/2816, SI 2004/251

s.32A, enabling: SI 2002/2816, SI 2004/251

s.33, amended: 2002 c.41 Sch.8 para.4, Sch.9

s.33, applied: 2002 c.41 Sch.8 para.17, SI 2004/250

s.33, referred to: SI 2004/250

s.33, repealed (in part): 2002 c.41 Sch.9

s.33, substituted: 2002 c.41 Sch.8 para.4

s.33, varied: SI 2003/1252 Sch.1, SI 2003/2900 Sch.1

s.33, enabling: SI 2004/250

1999–cont.

33. Immigration and Asylum Act 1999–
cont.

s.34, see *InternationalTransport Roth GmbH v Secretary of State for the Home Department* [2002] EWCA Civ 158, [2003] Q.B. 728 (CA), Simon Brown, L.J.

s.34, amended: 2002 c.41 Sch.8 para.6, Sch.9

s.34, repealed (in part): 2002 c.41 Sch.8 para.6, Sch.9

s.34, substituted: 2002 c.41 Sch.8 para.6

s.34, varied: SI 2003/1252 Sch.1, SI 2003/ 2900 Sch.1

s.35, amended: 2002 c.41 Sch.8 para.7

s.35, applied: SI 2002/2811 Art.4, SI 2002/ 2817 Reg.4, Reg.6, Reg.7, Reg.8, Reg.14

s.35, varied: SI 2003/1252 Sch.1, SI 2003/ 2900 Sch.1

s.35, enabling: SI 2002/2817

s.35A, added: 2002 c.41 Sch.8 para.8

s.36, amended: 2002 c.41 Sch.8 para.9, Sch.9

s.36, applied: SI 2002/2817 Reg.4, Reg.9

s.36, repealed (in part): 2002 c.41 Sch.8 para.9

s.36, varied: SI 2003/1252 Sch.1, SI 2003/ 2900 Sch.1

s.36, enabling: SI 2002/2817

s.36A, added: 2002 c.41 Sch.8 para.10

s.36A, applied: SI 2002/2817 Reg.9, Reg.12

s.37, amended: 2002 c.41 Sch.8 para.11, Sch.9

s.37, applied: SI 2002/2817 Reg.11, Reg.12, Reg.13

s.37, varied: SI 2003/1252 Sch.1, SI 2003/ 2900 Sch.1

s.37, enabling: SI 2002/2817

s.38, repealed (in part): 2002 c.41 Sch.9

s.38, varied: SI 2003/1252 Sch.1, SI 2003/ 2900 Sch.1

s.39, applied: 2002 c.41 Sch.8 para.17

s.39, repealed (in part): 2002 c.41 Sch.9

s.40, applied: SI 2003/2818 Art.8

s.40, referred to: 2002 c.41 s.124

s.40, substituted: 2002 c.41 Sch.8 para.13

s.40, varied: SI 2003/1252 Sch.1, SI 2003/ 2900 Sch.1

s.40A, applied: SI 2002/2817 Reg.6, Reg.7

s.40A, referred to: 2002 c.41 s.124

s.40A, enabling: SI 2002/2817

s.40B, referred to: 2002 c.41 s.124

s.41, referred to: 2002 c.41 s.124

s.41, enabling: SI 2003/1185, SI 2003/1598, SI 2003/2628, SI 2004/1304

s.42, referred to: 2002 c.41 s.124

s.42, repealed: 2002 c.41 Sch.9

s.42, varied: SI 2003/1252 Sch.1, SI 2003/ 2900 Sch.1

s.43, amended: 2002 c.41 Sch.8 para.15

s.43, referred to: 2002 c.41 s.124

s.43, repealed (in part): 2002 c.41 Sch.9

1999–cont.

33. Immigration and Asylum Act 1999–
cont.

s.43, substituted: 2002 c.41 Sch.8 para.15

s.43, varied: SI 2003/1252 Sch.1, SI 2003/ 2900 Sch.1

s.44, repealed: 2002 c.41 Sch.9

s.44, varied: SI 2003/2900 Sch.1

s.45, repealed: 2002 c.41 Sch.9

s.46, repealed: 2002 c.41 Sch.9

s.46, varied: SI 2003/2900 Sch.1

s.47, repealed: 2002 c.41 Sch.9

s.47, varied: SI 2003/2900 Sch.1

s.48, repealed: 2002 c.41 Sch.9

s.48, varied: SI 2003/2900 Sch.1

s.49, repealed: 2002 c.41 Sch.9

s.49, varied: SI 2003/2900 Sch.1

s.50, repealed: 2002 c.41 Sch.9

s.50, varied: SI 2003/2900 Sch.1

s.51, repealed: 2002 c.41 Sch.9

s.52, repealed: 2002 c.41 Sch.9

s.53, amended: 2002 c.41 s.62, Sch.7 para.28

s.53, repealed (in part): 2002 c.41 Sch.9

s.54, varied: SI 2003/2900 Sch.1

s.55, repealed: 2002 c.41 Sch.9

s.56, repealed: 2002 c.41 s.114, Sch.9

s.57, applied: 2002 c.41 Sch.6 para.2, SI 2003/409 Sch.1 Part I

s.57, repealed: 2002 c.41 s.114, Sch.9

s.58, see *Kanyenkiko v Secretary of State for the Home Department* [2003] EWCA Civ 542, [2003] I.N.L.R. 296 (CA), Laws, L.J.; see *Shirazi v Secretary of State for the Home Department* [2003] EWCA Civ 1562, [2004] 2 All E.R. 602 (CA), Sedley, L.J.

s.58, repealed: 2002 c.41 s.114, Sch.9

s.59, see *SS v Secretary of State for the Home Department* [2004] UKIAT 91, [2004] Imm. A.R. 153 (IAT), Ouseley, J.

s.59, applied: SI 2002/1147 Reg.3, SI 2003/ 754 Sch.2 para.6

s.59, repealed: 2002 c.41 s.114, Sch.9

s.60, applied: SI 2003/754 Sch.2 para.6

s.60, repealed: 2002 c.41 s.114, Sch.9

s.60, enabling: SI 2002/1147

s.61, applied: SI 2003/754 Sch.2 para.6

s.61, repealed: 2002 c.41 s.114, Sch.9

s.62, applied: SI 2003/754 Sch.2 para.6

s.62, repealed: 2002 c.41 s.114, Sch.9

s.63, applied: SI 2003/754 Sch.2 para.6, SI 2004/1219 Reg.6

s.63, repealed: 2002 c.41 s.114, Sch.9

s.64, applied: SI 2003/754 Sch.2 para.6

s.64, repealed: 2002 c.41 s.114, Sch.9

s.65, see *A v Secretary of State for the Home Department* [2003] EWCA Civ 175, [2003] I.N.L.R. 249 (CA), Keene, L.J.; see *AC v Immigration Appeal Tribunal* [2003] EWHC 389, [2003] I.N.L.R. 507 (QBD (Admin Ct)), Jack, J.; see *Ali v Secretary of State for the Home Department* 2003

1999–cont.
33. Immigration and Asylum Act 1999– *cont.*
s.65–*cont.*

S.L.T. 674 (OH), Lady Cosgrove; see *Edore v Secretary of State for the Home Department* [2003] EWCA Civ 716, [2003] 1 W.L.R. 2979 (CA), Simon Brown, L.J.; see *Kacaj v Secretary of State for the Home Department* [2002] Imm. A.R. 213 (IAT), Collins, J. (President); see *Pardeepan v Secretary of State for the Home Department* [2002] Imm. A.R. 249 (IAT), Collins, J.; see *R. (on the application of Borak) v Secretary of State for the Home Department* [2004] EWHC 1861, [2004] 1 W.L.R. 3129 (QBD (Admin Ct)), Harrison, J.; see *R. (on the application of Ekinci) v Secretary of State for the Home Department* [2003] EWCA Civ 765, [2004] Imm. A.R. 15 (CA), Simon Brown, L.J.; see *R. (on the application of Kariharan) v Secretary of State for the Home Department* [2001] EWHC Admin 1004, [2002] Imm. A.R. 281 (QBD (Admin Ct)), Stanley Burnton, J.; see *R. (on the application of Kariharan) v Secretary of State for the Home Department* [2002] EWCA Civ 1102, [2003] Q.B. 933 (CA), Auld, L.J.; see *R. (on the application of Yogathas) v Secretary of State for the Home Department* [2002] UKHL 36, [2003] 1 A.C. 920 (HL), Lord Hope of Craighead; see *Tuncer v Secretary of State for the Home Department* 2003 S.C.L.R. 456 (OH), Lord Brodie

s.65, applied: 2002 c.41 s.115, SI 2003/754 Sch.2 para.6

s.65, disapplied: 2002 c.41 s.115

s.65, repealed: 2002 c.41 s.114, Sch.9

s.66, see *R. (on the application of Ahmed (Khaled)) v Immigration Appeal Tribunal* [2002] EWHC 624, [2002] Imm. A.R. 427 (QBD (Admin Ct)), Sullivan, J.; see *Zeqaj v Secretary of State for the Home Department* [2002] EWCA Civ 1919, [2003] Imm. A.R. 298 (CA), Latham, L.J.

s.66, applied: SI 2003/754 Sch.2 para.6

s.66, repealed: 2002 c.41 s.114, Sch.9

s.67, applied: SI 2003/754 Sch.2 para.6

s.67, repealed: 2002 c.41 s.114, Sch.9

s.68, see *Kanyenkiko v Secretary of State for the Home Department* [2003] EWCA Civ 542, [2003] I.N.L.R. 296 (CA), Laws, L.J.

s.68, applied: SI 2003/754 Sch.2 para.6

s.68, repealed: 2002 c.41 s.114, Sch.9

s.69, see *Andrabi v Secretary of State for the Home Department* [2002] UKIAT 2884, [2002] Imm. A.R. 621 (IAT), HJE Latter (Chairman); see *Kanyenkiko v Secretary of State for the Home Department* [2003] EWCA Civ 542, [2003] I.N.L.R. 296 (CA), Laws, L.J.; see *R. (on the application of Ahmed (Khaled)) v Immigration Appeal Tribunal* [2002]

1999–cont.
33. Immigration and Asylum Act 1999– *cont.*
s.69–*cont.*

EWHC 624, [2002] Imm. A.R. 427 (QBD (Admin Ct)), Sullivan, J.; see *R. (on the application of Secretary of State for the Home Department) v Immigration Appeal Tribunal* [2001] EWHC Admin 1067, [2002] Imm. A.R. 491 (QBD (Admin Ct)), Schiemann, L.J.; see *Saad v Secretary of State for the Home Department* [2001] EWCA Civ 2008, [2002] Imm. A.R. 471 (CA), Lord Phillips of Worth Matravers, M.R.; see *Tuncer v Secretary of State for the Home Department* 2003 S.C.L.R. 456 (OH), Lord Brodie

s.69, applied: 2002 c.41 s.115, SI 2003/754 Sch.2 para.6

s.69, disapplied: 2002 c.41 s.115

s.69, repealed: 2002 c.41 s.114, Sch.9

s.70, applied: SI 2003/754 Sch.2 para.6

s.70, repealed: 2002 c.41 s.114, Sch.9

s.71, applied: SI 2003/754 Sch.2 para.6

s.71, repealed: 2002 c.41 s.114, Sch.9

s.72, see *R. (on the application of Ahmadi) v Secretary of State for the Home Department* [2002] EWHC 1897, [2003] A.C.D. 14 (QBD (Admin Ct)), Scott Baker, J.; see *R. (on the application of Ekinci) v Secretary of State for the Home Department* [2003] EWCA Civ 765, [2004] Imm. A.R. 15 (CA), Simon Brown, L.J.; see *R. (on the application of Nadarajah) v Secretary of State for the Home Department* [2002] EWHC 2595, [2003] Imm. A.R. 373 (QBD (Admin Ct)), Stanley Burnton, J.; see *R. (on the application of Nadarajah) v Secretary of State for the Home Department* [2003] EWCA Civ 1768, [2004] I.N.L.R. 139 (CA), Lord Phillips of Worth Matravers, M.R.; see *R. (on the application of Razgar) v Secretary of State for the Home Department (No.2)* [2003] EWCA Civ 840, [2003] Imm. A.R. 529 (CA), Dyson, L.J.; see *R. (on the application of Yogathas) v Secretary of State for the Home Department* [2002] UKHL 36, [2003] 1 A.C. 920 (HL), Lord Hope of Craighead

s.72, amended: 2004 c.19 Sch.4

s.72, applied: SI 2003/754 Sch.2 para.6

s.72, repealed: 2002 c.41 s.114, Sch.9

s.73, see *R. (on the application of Balamurali) v Secretary of State for the Home Department* [2003] EWCA Civ 1806, [2004] Imm. A.R. 190 (CA), Kennedy, L.J.; see *R. (on the application of Ngamguem) v Secretary of State for the Home Department* [2002] EWHC 1550, [2003] Imm. A.R. 69 (QBD (Admin Ct)), Ouseley, J.; see *R. (on the application of Vemenac) v Secretary of State for the Home Department* [2002]

1999–cont.

33. Immigration and Asylum Act 1999–
cont.

s.73–cont.
EWHC 1636, [2002] Imm. A.R. 613 (QBD (Admin Ct)), Burton, J.
s.73, applied: SI 2003/754 Sch.2 para.6
s.73, repealed: 2002 c.41 s.114, Sch.9
s.74, applied: SI 2003/754 Sch.2 para.6
s.74, repealed: 2002 c.41 s.114, Sch.9
s.75, applied: SI 2003/754 Sch.2 para.6
s.75, repealed: 2002 c.41 s.114, Sch.9
s.75, enabling: SI 2002/2731
s.76, applied: SI 2003/754 Sch.2 para.6
s.76, repealed: 2002 c.41 s.114, Sch.9
s.77, applied: 2002 c.41 s.115, SI 2003/754 Sch.2 para.6
s.77, disapplied: 2002 c.41 s.115
s.77, repealed: 2002 c.41 s.114, Sch.9
s.78, applied: SI 2003/754 Sch.2 para.6
s.78, repealed: 2002 c.41 s.114, Sch.9
s.79, repealed: 2002 c.41 s.114, Sch.9
s.80, repealed: 2002 c.41 s.114, Sch.9
s.81, repealed: 2002 c.41 s.114, Sch.9
s.82, amended: 2002 c.41 s.123
s.83, applied: SI 2003/409 Sch.1 Part I
s.84, amended: 2004 c.19 s.37
s.84, applied: SI 2003/1034 r.33, SI 2003/3214 Art.3
s.84, disapplied: SI 2002/9 Art.3, SI 2002/3025 Art.3
s.84, referred to: SI 2003/652 r.46
s.84, enabling: SI 2002/9, SI 2002/3025, SI 2003/3214
s.85, amended: 2004 c.19 Sch.4
s.86, amended: 2004 c.19 s.41
s.86, enabling: SI 2003/460, SI 2004/801
s.87, amended: 2002 c.41 s.140
s.87, repealed (in part): 2004 c.19 Sch.4
s.89, amended: 2004 c.19 s.37
s.90, amended: 2004 c.19 s.37
s.92A, added: 2004 c.19 s.38
s.92B, added: 2004 c.19 s.39
s.94, see *Dogan v Secretary of State for the Home Department* [2003] EWCA Civ 1673, [2004] H.L.R. 25 (CA), Laws, L.J.; see *R. (on the application of Arbab) v Secretary of State for the Home Department* [2002] EWHC 1249, [2002] Imm. A.R. 536 (QBD (Admin Ct)), Jackson, J.
s.94, amended: 2002 c.41 s.44, s.60
s.94, repealed (in part): 2002 c.41 s.44, Sch.9
s.94, enabling: SI 2002/471, SI 2002/472
s.95, see *Al-Ameri v Kensington and Chelsea RLBC* [2004] UKHL 4, [2004] 2 A.C. 159 (HL), Lord Bingham of Cornhill; see *Dogan v Secretary of State for the Home Department* [2003] EWCA Civ 1673, [2004] H.L.R. 25 (CA); see *R. (on the application of A) v National Asylum Support Service* [2003] EWCA Civ 1473,

1999–cont.

33. Immigration and Asylum Act 1999–
cont.

s.95–cont.
[2004] 1 W.L.R. 752 (CA), Waller, L.J.; see *R. (on the application of Erdogan) v Secretary of State for the Home Department (Application to Appeal Out of Time)* [2004] EWCA Civ 1087, [2004] I.N.L.R. 503 (CA (Civ Div)), Tuckey, L.J.; see *R. (on the application of Limbuela) v Secretary of State for the Home Department* [2004] EWCA Civ 540, [2004] Q.B. 1440 (CA), Laws, L.J.; see *R. (on the application of Mani) v Lambeth LBC* [2003] EWCA Civ 836, [2004] H.L.R. 5 (CA), Simon Brown, L.J.; see *R. (on the application of O) v Haringey LBC* [2003] EWHC 2798, [2004] A.C.D. 10 (QBD (Admin Ct)), Ouseley, J.; see *R. (on the application of O) v Haringey LBC* [2004] EWCA Civ 535, [2004] 2 F.L.R. 476 (CA), Lord Woolf of Barnes, L.C.J.; see *R. (on the application of Secretary of State for the Home Department) v Chief Asylum Support Adjudicator* [2002] EWHC 2218, Times, November 29, 2002 (QBD (Admin Ct)), Silber, J.; see *R. (on the application of Westminster City Council) v National Asylum Support Service* [2002] UKHL 38, [2002] 1 W.L.R. 2956 (HL), Lord Hoffmann
s.95, amended: 2002 c.41 s.44, s.50
s.95, applied: 2002 c.41 s.22, s.24, s.26, s.51, s.55, SI 2003/653 Reg.3, 2004 c.19 s.11
s.95, enabling: SI 2002/3110
s.96, see *R. (on the application of T) v Secretary of State for Health* [2002] EWHC 1887, (2003) 6 C.C.L. Rep. 277 (QBD (Admin Ct)), Sir Edwin Jowitt
s.96, amended: 2002 c.41 s.45
s.96, applied: 2002 c.41 s.43
s.96, repealed (in part): 2002 c.41 s.61, Sch.9, SI 2002/782 Art.2
s.96, enabling: SI 2002/782
s.97, see *Al-Ameri v Kensington and Chelsea RLBC* [2004] UKHL 4, [2004] 2 A.C. 159 (HL), Lord Bingham of Cornhill; see *R. (on the application of Hetoja) v Secretary of State for the Home Department* [2002] EWHC 2146, Times, November 11, 2002 (QBD (Admin Ct)), Lightman, J.
s.97, amended: 2002 c.41 s.45
s.98, applied: 2002 c.41 s.24, s.26, s.51, s.55, SI 2003/653 Reg.3
s.99, amended: 2002 c.41 s.56
s.99, applied: 2002 c.41 s.24
s.103, see *Dogan v Secretary of State for the Home Department* [2003] EWCA Civ 1673, [2004] H.L.R. 25 (CA), Laws, L.J.; see *R. (on the application of Secretary of State for the Home Department) v Chief Asylum Support Adjudicator* [2002] EWHC 2218,

1999–cont.

33. Immigration and Asylum Act 1999– cont.

s.103–*cont.*
Times, November 29, 2002 (QBD (Admin Ct)), Silber, J.
s.103, amended: 2004 c.19 s.10
s.103, applied: 2002 c.41 s.55, 2004 c.19 s.9
s.103, referred to: 2002 c.41 s.26
s.103, substituted: 2002 c.41 s.53
s.103A, amended: 2004 c.19 s.10
s.104, enabling: SI 2003/1735
s.105, amended: 2003 c.44 Sch.26 para.53
s.105, applied: 2002 c.41 s.35, s.134, s.135
s.106, applied: 2002 c.41 s.35, s.134, s.135
s.107, applied: 2002 c.41 s.35
s.108, amended: 2003 c.44 Sch.26 para.53
s.108, applied: 2002 c.41 s.35
s.109, applied: 2002 c.41 s.35
s.110, amended: 2002 c.41 s.60
s.110, varied: 2002 c.41 s.48
s.111, varied: 2002 c.41 s.48
s.112, applied: 2002 c.41 s.35
s.112, varied: 2002 c.41 s.35
s.113, applied: 2002 c.41 s.35
s.113, varied: 2002 c.41 s.35
s.115, see *Kaya v Haringey LBC* [2001] EWCA Civ 677, [2002] H.L.R.1 (CA), Buxton, L.J.; see *R. (on the application of Khan) v Oxfordshire CC* [2002] EWHC 2211, [2003] H.L.R. 23 (QBD (Admin Ct)), Moses, J.
s.115, amended: 2002 c.14 (NI) s.4, 2002 c.16 s.4, 2002 c.21 Sch.4 para.21, SI 2002/1457 Sch.1 para.3
s.115, applied: SI 2002/1792 Reg.2, Reg.5, SI 2004/1987 Art.6, SR 2003/28 Reg.2, Reg.5, 2004 c.10 s.4
s.115, repealed (in part): 2002 c.21 Sch.6
s.115, enabling: SI 2002/2497, SI 2003/2274, SR 2002/323
s.117, repealed (in part): 2002 c.7 Sch.2
s.120, repealed (in part): 2003 asp 13 Sch.5 Part 1
s.122, see *R. (on the application of A) v National Asylum Support Service* [2003] EWCA Civ 1473, [2004] 1 W.L.R. 752 (CA), Waller, L.J.; see *R. (on the application of O) v Haringey LBC* [2003] EWHC 2798, [2004] A.C.D. 10 (QBD (Admin Ct)), Ouseley, J.; see *R. (on the application of O) v Haringey LBC* [2004] EWCA Civ 535, [2004] 2 F.L.R. 476 (CA), Lord Woolf of Barnes, L.C.J.; see *R. (on the application of Ouji) v Secretary of State for the Home Department* [2002] EWHC 1839, [2003] Imm. A.R. 88 (QBD (Admin Ct)), Collins, J.; see *R. (on the application of W) v Lambeth LBC* [2002] EWCA Civ 613, [2002] 2 All E.R. 901 (CA), Brooke, L.J.
s.122, applied: 2002 c.41 s.55

1999–cont.

33. Immigration and Asylum Act 1999– cont.

s.122, substituted: 2002 c.41 s.47
s.123, amended: 2002 c.16 Sch.2 para.42, 2002 c.21 Sch.4 para.22, 2002 c.41 s.52
s.123, repealed: 2004 c.19 s.12, Sch.4
s.124, applied: 2002 c.41 s.35
s.127, applied: 2002 c.41 s.35
s.128, varied: SI 2003/1252 Sch.1, SI 2003/2900 Sch.1
s.129, varied: SI 2003/1252 Sch.1, SI 2003/2900 Sch.1
s.130, varied: SI 2003/1252 Sch.1, SI 2003/2900 Sch.1
s.131, varied: SI 2003/1252 Sch.1, SI 2003/2900 Sch.1
s.132, varied: SI 2003/1252 Sch.1, SI 2003/2900 Sch.1
s.133, varied: SI 2003/2900 Sch.1
s.134, varied: SI 2003/1252 Sch.1, SI 2003/2900 Sch.1
s.135, varied: SI 2003/1252 Sch.1, SI 2003/2900 Sch.1
s.136, varied: SI 2003/1252 Sch.1, SI 2003/2900 Sch.1
s.137, varied: SI 2003/1252 Sch.1, SI 2003/2900 Sch.1
s.138, varied: SI 2003/1252 Sch.1, SI 2003/2900 Sch.1
s.139, varied: SI 2003/1252 Sch.1, SI 2003/2900 Sch.1
s.140, varied: SI 2003/1252 Sch.1, SI 2003/2900 Sch.1
s.141, amended: 2002 c.41 s.66, 2004 c.19 s.15
s.141, applied: 2002 c.41 s.126
s.141, referred to: 2002 c.41 s.126
s.141, varied: SI 2003/1252 Sch.1, SI 2003/2900 Sch.1
s.142, varied: SI 2003/1252 Sch.1, SI 2003/2900 Sch.1
s.143, referred to: 2002 c.41 s.126
s.143, varied: SI 2003/1252 Sch.1, SI 2003/2900 Sch.1
s.144, substituted: 2002 c.41 s.128
s.144, varied: SI 2003/1252 Sch.1, SI 2003/2900 Sch.1
s.145, amended: 2002 c.41 s.128
s.146, amended: 2002 c.41 s.153
s.146, varied: SI 2003/1252 Sch.1, SI 2003/2900 Sch.1
s.147, amended: 2002 c.41 s.62, s.66, Sch.9
s.147, varied: 2002 c.41 s.66
s.148, amended: 2002 c.41 s.66
s.148, varied: 2002 c.41 s.66
s.149, amended: 2002 c.41 s.66, 2003 asp 11 Sch.1 para.52
s.149, varied: 2002 c.41 s.66, SI 2002/2538 Reg.2
s.150, amended: 2002 c.41 s.66
s.150, varied: 2002 c.41 s.66

1999–cont.

33. Immigration and Asylum Act 1999–
cont.

s.151, amended: 2002 c.41 s.66
s.151, varied: 2002 c.41 s.66
s.152, amended: 2002 c.41 s.66
s.152, varied: 2002 c.41 s.66
s.153, amended: 2002 c.41 s.66
s.153, varied: 2002 c.41 s.66
s.154, amended: 2002 c.41 s.65
s.154, varied: 2002 c.41 s.66
s.155, amended: 2002 c.41 s.66
s.155, varied: 2002 c.41 s.66
s.156, amended: 2004 c.19 Sch.2 para.15
s.156, varied: 2002 c.41 s.66
s.157, amended: 2002 c.41 s.66
s.157, varied: 2002 c.41 s.66
s.157, enabling: SI 2002/2538
s.158, amended: 2002 c.41 s.66
s.158, varied: 2002 c.41 s.66
s.159, amended: 2002 c.41 s.66
s.159, referred to: 2002 c.41 s.62
s.159, varied: 2002 c.41 s.66
s.161, repealed (in part): SI 2003/413 Sch.1
s.162, repealed (in part): SI 2003/413 Sch.1
s.163, repealed (in part): SI 2003/413 Sch.1
s.166, amended: 2004 c.19 s.10, s.41, 2004 c.33 Sch.27 para.163
s.166, repealed (in part): 2002 c.41 s.61, Sch.9
s.166, varied: SI 2003/1252 Sch.1
s.166, enabling: SI 2002/9, SI 2002/471, SI 2002/472, SI 2002/1147, SI 2002/2011, SI 2002/2155, SI 2002/2619, SI 2002/2731, SI 2002/2815, SI 2002/2817, SI 2002/3025, SI 2003/2, SI 2003/755, SI 2003/1711, SI 2003/1735, SI 2003/3214, SI 2004/244, SI 2004/579, SI 2004/580, SI 2004/763, SI 2004/802, SI 2004/1313, SI 2004/3105
s.167, amended: 2002 c.41 s.158, 2004 c.19 s.44
s.167, applied: SI 2002/2731, SI 2003/1711, SI 2004/580
s.167, referred to: SI 2002/471, SI 2002/472, SI 2002/2817, SI 2003/1502, SI 2004/566
s.167, varied: SI 2003/1252 Sch.1, SI 2003/2900 Sch.1
s.169, varied: SI 2003/1252 Sch.1, SI 2003/2900 Sch.1
s.170, varied: SI 2003/1252 Sch.1, SI 2003/2900 Sch.1
s.170, enabling: SI 2002/2815, SI 2003/2, SI 2003/758, SI 2003/1252, SI 2003/1469, SI 2003/1862, SI 2003/2900, SI 2004/2997
Sch.1, applied: SI 2002/2817 Reg.9, Reg.11
Sch.1, referred to: 2002 c.41 s.124
Sch.1 para.1, amended: 2002 c.41 Sch.8 para.16, Sch.9
Sch.1 para.1, varied: SI 2003/1252 Sch.1, SI 2003/2900 Sch.1

1999–cont.

33. Immigration and Asylum Act 1999–
cont.

Sch.1 para.2, varied: SI 2003/1252 Sch.1, SI 2003/2900 Sch.1
Sch.1 para.2, enabling: SI 2002/2817
Sch.1 para.2A, added: 2002 c.41 Sch.8 para.16
Sch.1 para.2A, varied: SI 2003/2900 Sch.1
Sch.1 para.3, varied: SI 2003/1252 Sch.1, SI 2003/2900 Sch.1
Sch.1 para.4, varied: SI 2003/1252 Sch.1, SI 2003/2900 Sch.1
Sch.1 para.5, amended: 2002 c.41 Sch.8 para.16, Sch.9
Sch.1 para.5, repealed (in part): 2002 c.41 Sch.8 para.16
Sch.1 para.5, varied: SI 2003/1252 Sch.1, SI 2003/2900 Sch.1
Sch.1 para.5, enabling: SI 2002/2817
Sch.2, applied: SI 2003/754 Sch.2 para.6
Sch.2 para.1, repealed: 2002 c.41 Sch.9
Sch.2 para.2, repealed: 2002 c.41 Sch.9
Sch.2 para.3, repealed: 2002 c.41 Sch.9
Sch.2 para.4, repealed: 2002 c.41 Sch.9
Sch.2 para.5, repealed: 2002 c.41 Sch.9
Sch.2 para.6, repealed: 2002 c.41 Sch.9
Sch.2 para.7, repealed: 2002 c.41 Sch.9
Sch.3, applied: SI 2003/754 Sch.2 para.6
Sch.3 para.1, repealed: 2002 c.41 Sch.9
Sch.3 para.2, repealed: 2002 c.41 Sch.9
Sch.3 para.3, repealed: 2002 c.41 Sch.9
Sch.3 para.4, repealed: 2002 c.41 Sch.9
Sch.3 para.5, repealed: 2002 c.41 Sch.9
Sch.3 para.6, repealed: 2002 c.41 Sch.9
Sch.3 para.7, repealed: 2002 c.41 Sch.9
Sch.4, see *Oleed v Secretary of State for the Home Department* [2002] EWCA Civ 1906, [2003] Imm. A.R. 499 (CA), Schiemann, L.J.
Sch.4, applied: SI 2003/754 Sch.2 para.6
Sch.4 Part I para.1, repealed: 2002 c.41 Sch.9
Sch.4 Part I para.2, repealed: 2002 c.41 Sch.9
Sch.4 Part I para.3, repealed: 2002 c.41 Sch.9
Sch.4 Part I para.4, repealed: 2002 c.41 Sch.9
Sch.4 Part I para.5, repealed: 2002 c.41 Sch.9
Sch.4 Part I para.6, repealed: 2002 c.41 Sch.9
Sch.4 Part I para.7, disapplied: SI 2003/754 Sch.2 para.1
Sch.4 Part I para.7, repealed: 2002 c.41 Sch.9
Sch.4 Part I para.8, repealed: 2002 c.41 Sch.9
Sch.4 Part I para.9, see *Zenovics v Secretary of State for the Home Department* [2002] EWCA Civ 273, [2002] I.N.L.R. 219 (CA), Schiemann, L.J.
Sch.4 Part I para.9, amended: 2002 c.41 Sch.9
Sch.4 Part I para.9, repealed (in part): 2002 c.41 Sch.9, Sch.9
Sch.4 Part I para.9A, repealed: 2002 c.41 Sch.9

1999–cont.

33. Immigration and Asylum Act 1999– *cont.*

Sch.4 Part II para.10, repealed: 2002 c.41 Sch.9

Sch.4 Part II para.11, repealed: 2002 c.41 Sch.9

Sch.4 Part II para.12, repealed: 2002 c.41 Sch.9

Sch.4 Part II para.13, repealed: 2002 c.41 Sch.9

Sch.4 Part II para.14, repealed: 2002 c.41 Sch.9

Sch.4 Part II para.15, repealed: 2002 c.41 Sch.9

Sch.4 Part II para.16, repealed: 2002 c.41 Sch.9

Sch.4 Part II para.17, repealed: 2002 c.41 Sch.9

Sch.4 Part II para.18, repealed: 2002 c.41 Sch.9

Sch.4 Part II para.19, repealed: 2002 c.41 Sch.9

Sch.4 Part II para.20, repealed: 2002 c.41 Sch.9

Sch.4 Part III para.21, repealed: 2002 c.41 Sch.9

Sch.4 Part III para.22, disapplied: SI 2003/ 754 Sch.2 para.1

Sch.4 Part III para.22, referred to: SI 2003/ 754 Sch.2 para.4

Sch.4 Part III para.22, repealed: 2002 c.41 Sch.9

Sch.4 Part III para.23, disapplied: SI 2003/ 754 Sch.2 para.1

Sch.4 Part III para.23, referred to: SI 2003/ 754 Sch.2 para.4

Sch.4 Part III para.23, repealed: 2002 c.41 Sch.9

Sch.4 Part III para.24, repealed: 2002 c.41 Sch.9

Sch.4 para.22, see *Subesh v Secretary of State for the Home Department* [2004] EWCA Civ 56, [2004] Imm. A.R. 112 (CA), Judge, L.J.

Sch.4 para.23, see *Gardi v Secretary of State for the Home Department (No.2)* [2002] EWCA Civ 1560, [2002] 1 W.L.R. 3282 (CA), Ward, L.J., Keene, L.J.; see *Subesh v Secretary of State for the Home Department* [2004] EWCA Civ 56, [2004] Imm. A.R. 112 (CA), Judge, L.J.

Sch.5 Part I para.1, amended: 2004 c.19 s.37

Sch.5 Part I para.3, amended: 2004 c.19 s.37

Sch.5 Part I para.4, amended: 2004 c.19 s.37

Sch.5 Part I para.5, amended: 2004 c.19 s.37

Sch.5 Part I para.5, applied: SI 2002/2811 Art.5

Sch.5 Part I para.6, amended: 2004 c.19 s.37

Sch.5 Part I para.7, amended: 2002 c.41 s.140, 2004 c.19 s.38

Sch.5 Part I para.9, amended: 2004 c.19 s.37

1999–cont.

33. Immigration and Asylum Act 1999– *cont.*

Sch.5 Part II para.16, applied: SI 2003/409 Sch.1 Part I

Sch.5 Part II para.21, amended: 2004 c.19 s.41

Sch.6 para.1, amended: 2004 c.19 Sch.4

Sch.6 para.3, amended: 2004 c.19 s.37

Sch.6 para.3A, added: 2002 c.41 s.140

Sch.6 para.5, enabling: SI 2002/2011, SI 2004/802

Sch.7 para.7, enabling: SI 2002/1716

Sch.8 para.1, enabling: SI 2003/241, SI 2003/ 755, SI 2004/763, SI 2004/1313

Sch.8 para.2, repealed: 2002 c.41 s.45, Sch.9

Sch.8 para.3, applied: SI 2003/653 Reg.3

Sch.8 para.3, enabling: SI 2002/472, SI 2002/2619, SI 2003/241, SI 2003/755, SI 2004/763, SI 2004/1313

Sch.8 para.4, enabling: SI 2002/472, SI 2004/1313

Sch.8 para.6, repealed: 2002 c.41 s.45, Sch.9

Sch.8 para.12, amended: 2002 c.41 s.57

Sch.8 para.12, enabling: SI 2002/3110, SI 2004/1313

Sch.9, applied: SI 2003/653 Reg.3

Sch.9 para.3, amended: 2002 c.41 s.45

Sch.9 para.5, enabling: SI 2002/471

Sch.9 para.6, enabling: SI 2002/471

Sch.9 para.6A, added: 2002 c.41 s.50

Sch.9 para.15, enabling: SI 2002/471, SI 2004/566

Sch.10 para.1, applied: SI 2003/409 Sch.1 Part I

Sch.11 para.1, amended: 2002 c.41 s.66

Sch.11 para.2, amended: 2002 c.41 s.66

Sch.11 para.2, varied: SI 2003/2818 Art.11

Sch.11 para.3, amended: 2002 c.41 s.66

Sch.11 para.3, varied: SI 2003/2818 Art.11

Sch.11 para.4, amended: 2002 c.41 s.66

Sch.11 para.4, applied: SI 2004/702 Sch.4 para.9

Sch.11 para.4, varied: SI 2003/2818 Art.12

Sch.11 para.5, amended: 2002 c.41 s.66

Sch.11 para.5, varied: SI 2003/2818 Art.12

Sch.11 para.6, amended: 2002 c.41 s.66

Sch.11 para.7, amended: 2002 c.41 s.66

Sch.11 para.8, added: 2002 c.41 s.65

Sch.11 para.8, amended: 2002 c.41 s.66

Sch.12 para.1, amended: 2002 c.41 s.66

Sch.12 para.2, amended: 2002 c.41 s.66

Sch.12 para.3, amended: 2002 c.41 s.66

Sch.12 para.4, amended: 2002 c.41 s.66

Sch.12 para.5, amended: 2002 c.41 s.66

Sch.12 para.6, amended: 2002 c.41 s.66

Sch.12 para.7, amended: 2002 c.41 s.66

Sch.12 para.8, amended: 2002 c.41 s.66

Sch.12 para.9, added: 2002 c.41 s.65

Sch.12 para.9, amended: 2002 c.41 s.66

Sch.13 para.1, amended: 2002 c.41 s.66

CAP.

1999–cont.

33. Immigration and Asylum Act 1999– *cont.*

Sch.13 para.2, amended: 2002 c.41 s.66

Sch.13 para.2, varied: SI 2003/2818 Art.11

Sch.13 para.3, amended: 2002 c.41 s.66

Sch.14 para.1, repealed: SI 2003/413 Sch.1

Sch.14 para.2, repealed: SI 2003/413 Sch.1

Sch.14 para.43, varied: SI 2003/2900 Sch.1

Sch.14 para.44, varied: SI 2003/1252 Sch.1, SI 2003/2900 Sch.1

Sch.14 para.45, varied: SI 2003/2900 Sch.1

Sch.14 para.46, repealed (in part): 2002 c.41 Sch.9

Sch.14 para.46, varied: SI 2003/2900 Sch.1

Sch.14 para.50, varied: SI 2003/2900 Sch.1

Sch.14 para.51, repealed: 2002 c.41 Sch.9

Sch.14 para.51, varied: SI 2003/2900 Sch.1

Sch.14 para.52, varied: SI 2003/2900 Sch.1

Sch.14 para.53, repealed: 2002 c.41 Sch.9

Sch.14 para.54, varied: SI 2003/1252 Sch.1, SI 2003/2900 Sch.1

Sch.14 para.56, varied: SI 2003/1252 Sch.1, SI 2003/2900 Sch.1

Sch.14 para.57, varied: SI 2003/1252 Sch.1, SI 2003/2900 Sch.1

Sch.14 para.58, varied: SI 2003/2900 Sch.1

Sch.14 para.59, varied: SI 2003/1252 Sch.1, SI 2003/2900 Sch.1

Sch.14 para.60, varied: SI 2003/2900 Sch.1

Sch.14 para.61, varied: SI 2003/2900 Sch.1

Sch.14 para.62, varied: SI 2003/1252 Sch.1, SI 2003/2900 Sch.1

Sch.14 para.64, varied: SI 2003/1252 Sch.1, SI 2003/2900 Sch.1

Sch.14 para.66, applied: SI 2003/754 Sch.2 para.2

Sch.14 para.66, repealed: 2002 c.41 Sch.9

Sch.14 para.68, varied: SI 2003/2900 Sch.1

Sch.14 para.69, applied: SI 2003/754 Sch.2 para.2

Sch.14 para.83, varied: SI 2003/2900 Sch.1

Sch.14 para.85, varied: SI 2003/2900 Sch.1

Sch.14 para.86, varied: SI 2003/2900 Sch.1

Sch.14 para.96, repealed: 2002 c.41 Sch.9

Sch.14 para.98, repealed (in part): 2002 c.41 Sch.9

Sch.14 para.105, applied: SI 2003/754 Sch.2 para.4

Sch.14 para.106, applied: SI 2003/754 Sch.2 para.4

Sch.14 para.108, varied: SI 2003/2900 Sch.1

Sch.14 para.109, varied: SI 2003/2900 Sch.1

Sch.14 para.114, varied: SI 2003/1252 Sch.1, SI 2003/2900 Sch.1

Sch.14 para.117, repealed (in part): 2002 c.32 Sch.22 Part 3

Sch.14 para.120, repealed: 2002 c.41 Sch.9

Sch.14 para.121, repealed: 2002 c.41 Sch.9

Sch.14 para.126, repealed: 2002 c.41 Sch.9

Sch.14 para.127, repealed: 2002 c.41 Sch.9

Sch.14 para.128, repealed: 2002 c.41 Sch.9

CAP.

1999–cont.

33. Immigration and Asylum Act 1999– *cont.*

Sch.14 para.129, repealed: 2002 c.41 Sch.9

Sch.15 para.1, varied: SI 2003/1252 Sch.1, SI 2003/2900 Sch.1

Sch.15 para.10, repealed: 2003 asp 13 Sch.5 Part 1

Sch.15 para.12, applied: SI 2003/658 Reg.3

Sch.16, varied: SI 2003/1252 Sch.1, SI 2003/2900 Sch.1

34. House of Lords Act 1999

see *Lord Gray's Motion, Re* [2002] 1 A.C. 124 (HL), Lord Slynn of Hadley; see *Lord Mayhew of Twysden's Motion, Re* [2002] 1 A.C. 109 (HL), Lord Slynn of Hadley

2000

viii. City of Newcastle upon Tyne Act 2000

s.15, amended: SI 2004/916 Art.2, SI 2004/1268 Art.2

s.15, repealed (in part): SI 2004/1268 Art.4

Criminal Courts (Sentencing) Act 2000

s.80, see *R. v Jowett-Hall (Michael Daniel)* [2002] EWCA Crim 1389, [2003] 1 Cr. App. R. (S.) 30 (CA (Crim Div)), Judge Colston Q.C.

Criminal Justice and Court Service Act 2000

s.28, see *R. v Wiles (Alan Ralph)* [2004] EWCA Crim 836, [2004] 2 Cr. App. R. (S.) 88 (CA (Crim Div)), Rose, L.J.

vii. London Local Authorities Act 2000

varied: 2004 c.i s.27

s.2, amended: 2004 c.i s.27, Sch.5

s.3, amended: 2004 c.18 Sch.12 Part 1

s.4, repealed (in part): 2004 c.18 Sch.12 Part 1, 2004 c.i s.27

s.5, repealed: 2004 c.18 Sch.12 Part 1

s.6, amended: 2004 c.21 Sch.1 para.93

s.6, repealed: 2004 c.18 Sch.12 Part 1

s.7, repealed: 2004 c.18 Sch.12 Part 1

s.8, repealed: 2004 c.18 Sch.12 Part 1

s.9, repealed: 2004 c.18 Sch.12 Part 1

s.10, repealed: 2004 c.18 Sch.12 Part 1

s.11, repealed: 2004 c.18 Sch.12 Part 1

s.12, repealed: 2004 c.18 Sch.12 Part 1

s.13, repealed: 2004 c.18 Sch.12 Part 1

s.14, repealed: 2004 c.18 Sch.12 Part 1

s.22, repealed: 2003 c.17 Sch.7

s.23, repealed: 2003 c.17 Sch.7

s.24, repealed: 2003 c.17 Sch.7

s.25, repealed: 2003 c.17 Sch.7

s.26, repealed: 2003 c.17 Sch.7

s.32, amended: 2003 c.17 Sch.6 para.117

s.45, amended: 2004 c.i s.10, s.27

Sch.1, repealed: 2003 c.17 Sch.7

2000–cont.

Power of Criminal Courts (Sentencing) Act 2000

s.111, see *R. v Gibson (Karl Mark)* [2004] EWCA Crim 593, [2004] 2 Cr. App. R. (S.) 84 (CA (Crim Div)), Laws, L.J.

1. Northern Ireland Act 2000

applied: 2002 c.18 Sch.2 Part 2, Sch.2 Part 39, 2003 c.13 Sch.2 Part 2, Sch.2 Part 43

referred to: 2004 c.9 Sch.2 Part 2, Sch.2 Part 39

s.1, amended: 2002 c.26 Sch.12 para.77

s.1, applied: 2003 c.6 s.44, 2003 c.12 s.4

s.1, referred to: SI 2003/410 Art.2, SI 2003/3039, SI 2004/1164 Art.2, Art.3

s.1, varied: SI 2003/2592 Art.2

s.2, enabling: SI 2002/2574

s.3, amended: 2002 c.26 Sch.12 para.78, SI 2004/1164 Art.4

s.5A, added: 2002 c.26 Sch.12 para.79

s.6, enabling: SI 2002/2587, SI 2003/3039, SI 2004/1164

Sch.1 para.1, applied: 2003 c.32 s.92, 2004 c.24 s.58, SI 2004/1105 Art.2

Sch.1 para.1, varied: SI 2003/1155 Art.2, SI 2004/1105 Art.2

Sch.1 para.1, enabling: SI 2002/2836, SI 2002/3149, SI 2002/3150, SI 2002/3151, SI 2002/3152, SI 2002/3153, SI 2002/3154, SI 2002/3155, SI 2003/410, SI 2003/412, SI 2003/413, SI 2003/417, SI 2003/418, SI 2003/419, SI 2003/420, SI 2003/424, SI 2003/430, SI 2003/431, SI 2003/435, SI 2003/439, SI 2003/1155, SI 2003/1247, SI 2003/1885, SI 2003/2592, SI 2003/2902, SI 2003/2903, SI 2003/2904, SI 2003/3194, SI 2003/3202, SI 2004/310, SI 2004/311, SI 2004/702, SI 2004/703, SI 2004/704, SI 2004/707, SI 2004/1105, SI 2004/1109, SI 2004/1272, SI 2004/1500, SI 2004/1501, SI 2004/1987, SI 2004/1988, SI 2004/1989, SI 2004/1990, SI 2004/1991, SI 2004/1993, SI 2004/1994, SI 2004/1996, SI 2004/2505, SI 2004/3078, SI 2004/3079, SI 2004/3080

Sch.1 para.2, disapplied: 2003 c.32 s.92, 2004 c.24 s.58

Sch.1 para.4, amended: 2002 c.26 Sch.7 para.11

Sch.1 para.4, enabling: SR 2003/489

Sch.1 para.7, amended: 2003 c.12 s.5

Sch.1 para.7, applied: SR 2002/394, SR 2002/395

Sch.1 para.8, amended: SI 2002/2587 Art.2

Sch.1 para.9, amended: SI 2002/2587 Art.2

Sch.1 para.9, applied: 2003 c.12 s.4

Sch.1 para.11, amended: 2003 c.12 s.5

Sch.1 para.11A, added: 2003 c.12 s.5

Sch.1 para.12, applied: SI 2002/3126 Art.2

Sch.1 para.12, enabling: SI 2002/3126, SI 2004/2556

Sch.1 para.13, amended: 2003 c.12 s.5

2000–cont.

1. Northern Ireland Act 2000–*cont.*

Sch.1 para.14, added: 2003 c.12 s.5

2. Representation of the People Act 2000

applied: SI 2004/870 Reg.10

referred to: SI 2002/834 Art.4

s.10, applied: 2004 c.2 s.5

s.10, disapplied: 2004 c.2 s.3

s.10, varied: SI 2004/870 Sch.3

s.11, varied: 2004 c.2 s.5, SI 2004/870 Sch.3

s.12, varied: SI 2004/870 Sch.3, SI 2004/1962 Sch.2 Part 1

Sch.1 para.9, applied: SI 2002/834 Art.23

Sch.4, applied: SI 2002/2626 Sch.1, SI 2003/1887 Sch.1

Sch.4 para.1, varied: SI 2002/185 Sch.2, SI 2004/870 Sch.3, SI 2004/1962 Sch.2 Part 1

Sch.4 para.2, varied: SI 2004/870 Sch.3, SI 2004/1962 Sch.2 Part 1

Sch.4 para.3, amended: 2004 c.33 Sch.27 para.164

Sch.4 para.3, applied: SSI 2002/561 Reg.8

Sch.4 para.3, varied: SI 2004/870 Sch.3, SI 2004/1962 Sch.2 Part 1

Sch.4 para.4, varied: SI 2004/870 Sch.3, SI 2004/1962 Sch.2 Part 1

Sch.4 para.5, varied: SI 2004/870 Sch.3, SI 2004/1962 Sch.2 Part 1

Sch.4 para.6, amended: 2004 c.33 Sch.27 para.164

Sch.4 para.6, varied: SI 2004/870 Sch.3, SI 2004/1962 Sch.2 Part 1

Sch.4 para.7, applied: SI 2004/1962 Sch.1, SSI 2002/561 Reg.8

Sch.4 para.7, varied: SI 2004/870 Sch.3, SI 2004/1962 Sch.2 Part 1

Sch.4 para.8, varied: SI 2004/1962 Sch.2 Part 1

Sch.6 para.2, consolidated: 2002 c.24 Sch.1 para.4

Sch.6 para.2, repealed: 2002 c.24 Sch.4

3. Consolidated Fund Act 2000

repealed: 2002 c.18 Sch.3

5. Nuclear Safeguards Act 2000

Commencement Orders: SI 2004/1242 Art.2, Art.3

referred to: SI 2004/1289 Art.2

varied: SI 2004/1290 Sch.2 para.2

s.1, varied: SI 2004/1288 Sch.2 para.1, SI 2004/1289 Sch.2 para.1, SI 2004/1290 Sch.2 para.1

s.2, varied: SI 2004/1288 Sch.2 para.2, SI 2004/1289 Sch.2 para.2, SI 2004/1290 Sch.2 para.3

s.3, varied: SI 2004/1288 Sch.2 para.3, SI 2004/1289 Sch.2 para.3, SI 2004/1290 Sch.2 para.4

s.3, enabling: SI 2004/1255

s.4, varied: SI 2004/1288 Sch.2 para.4, SI 2004/1289 Sch.2 para.4, SI 2004/1290 Sch.2 para.5

2000–cont.

5. Nuclear Safeguards Act 2000–*cont.*
s.5, varied: SI 2004/1288 Sch.2 para.5, SI 2004/1289 Sch.2 para.6, Sch.2 para.7, SI 2004/1290 Sch.2 para.6

s.6, varied: SI 2004/1288 Sch.2 para.6, SI 2004/1289 Sch.2 para.8, SI 2004/1290 Sch.2 para.7

s.7, varied: SI 2004/1288 Sch.2 para.7, SI 2004/1289 Sch.2 para.9, SI 2004/1290 Sch.2 para.8

s.8, varied: SI 2004/1288 Sch.2 para.8, SI 2004/1289 Sch.2 para.10, SI 2004/1290 Sch.2 para.9

s.9, varied: SI 2004/1288 Sch.2 para.9, SI 2004/1289 Sch.2 para.11, SI 2004/1290 Sch.2 para.10

s.10, applied: SI 2004/1255 Reg.5, Reg.6

s.10, varied: SI 2004/1288 Sch.2 para.10, SI 2004/1289 Sch.2 para.12, SI 2004/1290 Sch.2 para.11

s.11, varied: SI 2004/1288 Sch.2 para.11, SI 2004/1289 Sch.2 para.13, SI 2004/1290 Sch.2 para.12

s.12, varied: SI 2004/1288 Sch.2 para.12, SI 2004/1289 Sch.2 para.14, SI 2004/1290 Sch.2 para.13

s.12, enabling: SI 2004/1242, SI 2004/1288, SI 2004/1289, SI 2004/1290

6. Powers of Criminal Courts (Sentencing) Act 2000
applied: 2002 c.29 s.88, 2003 c.38 s.88
referred to: SI 2002/808 Art.2, 2003 c.32 Sch.5 para.72
Part V c.V, repealed: 2003 c.44 Sch.37 Part 7
s.1, substituted: 2003 c.44 Sch.23 para.1
s.1A, substituted: 2003 c.44 Sch.23 para.1
s.1B, substituted: 2003 c.44 Sch.23 para.1
s.1C, substituted: 2003 c.44 Sch.23 para.1
s.1D, substituted: 2003 c.44 Sch.23 para.1
s.2, substituted: 2003 c.44 Sch.23 para.1
s.3, see *R. v Chute (Patrick Joseph)* [2003] EWCA Crim 177, [2003] 2 Cr. App. R. (S.) 74 (CA (Crim Div)), Mackay, J.; see *R. v Sallis (Anne Elizabeth)* [2003] EWCA Crim 233, [2003] 2 Cr. App. R. (S.) 67 (CA (Crim Div)), Holland, J.; see *R. v Webster (Christopher)* [2003] EWCA Crim 3597, [2004] 2 Cr. App. R. (S.) 25 (CA (Crim Div)), Pitchford, J.
s.3, applied: 2002 c.29 s.6, s.27, s.70
s.3, substituted: 2003 c.44 Sch.3 para.22
s.3A, added: 2003 c.44 Sch.3 para.23
s.3A, applied: 2002 c.29 s.6, s.27
s.3B, added: 2003 c.44 Sch.3 para.23
s.3B, applied: 2002 c.29 s.6, s.27
s.3C, added: 2003 c.44 Sch.3 para.23
s.3C, applied: 2002 c.29 s.6, s.27
s.4, see *R. v Chute (Patrick Joseph)* [2003] EWCA Crim 177, [2003] 2 Cr. App. R. (S.) 74 (CA (Crim Div)), Mackay, J.; see *R. v Sallis (Anne Elizabeth)* [2003] EWCA

2000–cont.

6. Powers of Criminal Courts (Sentencing) Act 2000–*cont.*
s.4–*cont.*
Crim 233, [2003] 2 Cr. App. R. (S.) 67 (CA (Crim Div)), Holland, J.
s.4, amended: 2003 c.44 Sch.3 para.24
s.4, applied: 2002 c.29 s.6, s.27
s.4A, added: 2003 c.44 Sch.3 para.25
s.5, see *R. v Sallis (Anne Elizabeth)* [2003] EWCA Crim 233, [2003] 2 Cr. App. R. (S.) 67 (CA (Crim Div)), Holland, J.
s.5, substituted: 2003 c.44 Sch.3 para.26
s.5A, added: 2003 c.44 Sch.3 para.27
s.6, see *R. v Chute (Patrick Joseph)* [2003] EWCA Crim 177, [2003] 2 Cr. App. R. (S.) 74 (CA (Crim Div)), Mackay, J.
s.6, amended: 2003 c.44 Sch.32 para.91, Sch.3 para.28
s.6, applied: 2002 c.29 s.6, s.27
s.6, repealed (in part): 2003 c.44 Sch.37 Part 7, Sch.37 Part 9
s.7, amended: 2003 c.44 Sch.32 para.92
s.8, amended: 2003 c.44 Sch.3 para.74
s.8, applied: 2004 c.28 s.6
s.9, see *R. (on the application of Denny) v Acton Youth Court* [2004] EWHC 948, [2004] 1 W.L.R. 3051 (QBD (Admin Ct)), Maurice Kay, L.J.
s.11, applied: 2003 c.44 s.16
s.12, amended: 2003 c.44 Sch.32 para.93
s.12, applied: 2003 c.41 s.153
s.12, repealed (in part): 2003 c.44 Sch.32 para.93, Sch.37 Part 7
s.14, see *R. v Webster (Christopher)* [2003] EWCA Crim 3597, [2004] 2 Cr. App. R. (S.) 25 (CA (Crim Div)), Pitchford, J.
s.14, applied: 2003 c.42 s.134
s.17, amended: SI 2003/1605 Reg.2
s.17, enabling: SI 2003/1605
s.19, repealed (in part): 2003 c.44 Sch.34 para.3, Sch.37 Part 12
s.22, amended: 2003 c.44 Sch.34 para.4
s.28, amended: 2003 c.44 Sch.34 para.5
s.28A, see *R. v McStay (Paul David)* [2002] EWCA Crim 1449, [2003] 1 Cr. App. R. (S.) 38 (CA (Crim Div)), Judge Wakerley Q.C.
s.30, applied: SI 2003/1605
s.30, enabling: SI 2003/1605
s.31, amended: SI 2004/2035 Sch.1 para.40
s.31, repealed (in part): SI 2004/2035 Sch.1 para.40
s.33, amended: 2003 c.44 Sch.32 para.94
s.33, substituted: 2003 c.44 Sch.32 para.95
s.34, amended: 2003 c.44 Sch.32 para.94
s.34, repealed: 2003 c.44 Sch.37 Part 7
s.35, amended: 2003 c.44 Sch.32 para.94
s.35, repealed: 2003 c.44 Sch.37 Part 7
s.36, amended: 2003 c.44 Sch.32 para.94
s.36, repealed: 2003 c.44 Sch.37 Part 7
s.36A, amended: 2003 c.44 Sch.32 para.94
s.36A, repealed: 2003 c.44 Sch.37 Part 7

2000–cont.

6. Powers of Criminal Courts (Sentencing) Act 2000–*cont.*

s.36B, amended: 2003 c.44 Sch.32 para.94, Sch.32 para.96, Sch.37 Part 7

s.36B, repealed (in part): 2003 c.44 Sch.37 Part 7

s.37, amended: 2003 c.38 Sch.2 para.2, 2003 c.44 Sch.32 para.94, Sch.32 para.97, Sch.37 Part 7

s.37, repealed (in part): 2003 c.38 Sch.3, 2003 c.44 Sch.32 para.97, Sch.37 Part 7

s.38, amended: 2003 c.44 Sch.32 para.94

s.39, amended: 2003 c.44 Sch.32 para.94, Sch.32 para.98

s.40, amended: 2003 c.44 Sch.32 para.94, Sch.32 para.99

s.40A, amended: 2003 c.44 Sch.32 para.94, Sch.32 para.100, Sch.37 Part 7

s.40A, applied: SI 2004/2172 Art.2

s.40A, repealed (in part): 2003 c.44 Sch.32 para.100, Sch.37 Part 7

s.40A, enabling: SI 2004/2172

s.40B, amended: 2003 c.44 Sch.32 para.94, Sch.32 para.101

s.40C, amended: 2003 c.44 Sch.32 para.94

s.41, amended: 2003 c.44 Sch.32 para.94

s.41, applied: SI 2003/762 Reg.2, SI 2004/1748 Sch.1, SSI 2003/243 Reg.2

s.41, repealed: 2003 c.44 s.303, Sch.37 Part 7

s.42, see *Attorney General's Reference (No.105 of 2002), Re* [2003] EWCA Crim 182, [2003] 2 Cr. App. R. (S.) 50 (CA (Crim Div)), Rose, L.J.

s.42, amended: 2003 c.44 Sch.32 para.94

s.42, repealed: 2003 c.44 s.303, Sch.37 Part 7

s.43, amended: 2003 c.44 Sch.32 para.94

s.43, repealed: 2003 c.44 s.303, Sch.37 Part 7

s.44, amended: 2003 c.44 Sch.32 para.94

s.44, repealed (in part): 2003 c.44 s.303, Sch.37 Part 7

s.45, amended: 2003 c.44 Sch.32 para.94

s.45, repealed: 2003 c.44 s.303, Sch.37 Part 7

s.46, amended: 2003 c.44 Sch.32 para.94

s.46, repealed: 2003 c.44 s.303, Sch.37 Part 7

s.47, amended: 2003 c.44 Sch.32 para.94

s.47, repealed: 2003 c.44 s.303, Sch.37 Part 7

s.48, amended: 2003 c.44 Sch.32 para.94

s.48, repealed: 2003 c.44 s.303, Sch.37 Part 7

s.49, amended: 2003 c.44 Sch.32 para.94

s.49, repealed (in part): 2003 c.44 s.303, Sch.37 Part 7

s.50, amended: 2003 c.44 Sch.32 para.94

s.50, repealed: 2003 c.44 s.303, Sch.37 Part 7

2000–cont.

6. Powers of Criminal Courts (Sentencing) Act 2000–*cont.*

s.51, amended: 2003 c.44 Sch.32 para.94

s.51, applied: SI 2003/762 Reg.2, SI 2004/1748 Sch.1, SSI 2003/243 Reg.2

s.51, repealed (in part): 2003 c.44 s.303, Sch.37 Part 7

s.52, see *R. (on the application of Inner London Probation Service) v Tower Bridge Magistrates Court* [2001] EWHC Admin 401, [2002] 1 Cr. App. R. (S.) 43 (QBD (Admin Ct)), Bell, J.

s.52, amended: 2003 c.44 Sch.32 para.94

s.52, applied: SI 2003/762 Reg.2, SI 2004/1748 Sch.1, SSI 2003/243 Reg.2

s.52, repealed: 2003 c.44 s.303, Sch.37 Part 7

s.52, varied: 2003 c.44 Sch.38 para.4

s.53, amended: 2003 c.44 Sch.32 para.94

s.53, repealed: 2003 c.44 s.303, Sch.37 Part 7

s.54, amended: 2003 c.44 Sch.32 para.94

s.54, repealed: 2003 c.44 s.303, Sch.37 Part 7

s.55, amended: 2003 c.44 Sch.32 para.94

s.55, repealed: 2003 c.44 s.303, Sch.37 Part 7

s.56, amended: 2003 c.44 Sch.32 para.94

s.56, repealed: 2003 c.44 s.303, Sch.37 Part 7

s.57, amended: 2003 c.44 Sch.32 para.94

s.57, repealed: 2003 c.44 s.303, Sch.37 Part 7

s.58, amended: 2003 c.44 Sch.32 para.94

s.58, repealed: 2003 c.44 s.303, Sch.37 Part 7

s.58A, amended: 2003 c.44 Sch.32 para.94

s.58A, repealed: 2003 c.44 s.303, Sch.37 Part 7

s.58B, amended: 2003 c.44 Sch.32 para.94

s.58B, repealed: 2003 c.44 s.303, Sch.37 Part 7

s.59, amended: 2003 c.44 Sch.32 para.94

s.59, repealed: 2003 c.44 s.303, Sch.37 Part 7

s.60, amended: 2003 c.44 Sch.32 para.94, Sch.32 para.102

s.60, applied: 2003 c.44 s.221

s.60, repealed (in part): 2003 c.44 Sch.37 Part 7

s.61, amended: 2003 c.44 Sch.32 para.94

s.62, amended: 2003 c.44 Sch.32 para.94

s.62, repealed: 2003 c.44 Sch.37 Part 7

s.63, amended: 2003 c.44 Sch.32 para.94, Sch.32 para.103, SI 2004/2035 Sch.1 para.41

s.64, amended: 2003 c.44 Sch.32 para.94

s.64A, added: 2003 c.38 Sch.2 para.3

s.64A, amended: 2003 c.44 Sch.32 para.94

s.65, amended: 2003 c.44 Sch.32 para.94

s.66, amended: 2003 c.44 Sch.32 para.94

2000–cont.

6. Powers of Criminal Courts (Sentencing) Act 2000–cont.

s.67, amended: 2003 c.44 Sch.32 para.94

s.68, amended: 2003 c.44 Sch.32 para.94

s.69, amended: 2003 c.44 Sch.32 para.94, Sch.32 para.104

s.69, repealed (in part): 2003 c.44 Sch.32 para.104, Sch.37 Part 7

s.70, amended: 2003 c.44 Sch.24 para.1, Sch.32 para.94, Sch.32 para.105

s.71, amended: 2003 c.44 Sch.32 para.94

s.72, amended: 2003 c.44 Sch.32 para.94

s.73, amended: 2003 c.44 Sch.32 para.94, Sch.32 para.106

s.73, repealed (in part): 2003 c.44 Sch.32 para.106, Sch.37 Part 7

s.74, amended: 2003 c.44 Sch.32 para.94, Sch.32 para.107

s.75, amended: 2003 c.44 Sch.32 para.94

s.76, amended: 2003 c.44 Sch.32 para.108

s.76, applied: SI 2002/2051 Art.5, SI 2003/495 Reg.7

s.78, applied: 2003 c.20 s.11

s.78, referred to: SI 2003/3283

s.78, repealed: 2003 c.44 Sch.37 Part 7

s.79, see *Attorney General's Reference (No.70 of 2003), Re* [2004] EWCA Crim 163, [2004] 2 Cr. App. R. (S.) 49 (CA (Crim Div)), Latham, L.J.

s.79, repealed: 2003 c.44 Sch.37 Part 7

s.80, see *Attorney General's Reference (No.110 of 2002), Re* [2003] EWCA Crim 540, [2003] 2 Cr. App. R. (S.) 78 (CA (Crim Div)), Kennedy, L.J.; see *Attorney General's Reference (No.113 of 2001), Re* [2002] EWCA Crim 143, [2002] 2 Cr. App. R. (S.) 62 (CA (Crim Div)), Rose, L.J.; see *R. (on the application of Giles) v Parole Board* [2001] EWHC Admin 834, [2002] 1 W.L.R. 654 (QBD (Admin Ct)), Elias, J.; see *R. (on the application of Giles) v Parole Board* [2002] EWCA Civ 951, [2003] 2 W.L.R. 196 (CA), Kennedy, L.J.; see *R. (on the application of Giles) v Parole Board* [2003] UKHL 42, [2004] 1 A.C. 1 (HL), Lord Bingham of Cornhill; see *R. v Briggs (Paul)* [2003] EWCA Crim 1050, [2003] 2 Cr. App. R. (S.) 103 (CA (Crim Div)), Rix, L.J.; see *R. v Firth (John)* [2001] EWCA Crim 1570, [2002] 1 Cr. App. R. (S.) 73 (CA (Crim Div)), Jack, J.; see *R. v Fletcher (Andrew David)* [2002] EWCA Crim 834, [2002] 2 Cr. App. R. (S.) 127 (CA (Crim Div)), Rix, L.J.; see *R. v Gwillim-Jones (John)* [2001] EWCA Crim 904, [2002] 1 Cr. App. R. (S.) 6 (CA (Crim Div)), Holman, J.; see *R. v Jones (Donan Langford)* [2001] EWCA Crim 1524, [2002] 1 Cr. App. R. (S.) 52 (CA (Crim Div)), Sir Richard Tucker; see *R. v Lovett (Nicholas Eric)* [2002] EWCA Crim 1793, [2003] 1 Cr. App. R. (S.) 66 (CA

2000–cont.

6. Powers of Criminal Courts (Sentencing) Act 2000–cont.

s.80–cont.

(Crim Div)), Grigson, J.; see *R. v Nelson (Patrick Alan)* [2001] EWCA Crim 2264, [2002] 1 Cr. App. R. (S.) 134 (CA (Crim Div)), Rose, L.J.; see *R. v Odewale (Ayodele)* [2004] EWCA Crim 145, [2004] 2 Cr. App. R. (S.) 47 (CA (Crim Div)), Scott Baker, L.J.

s.80, repealed: 2003 c.44 Sch.37 Part 7

s.81, repealed: 2003 c.44 Sch.37 Part 7

s.82, repealed: 2003 c.44 Sch.37 Part 7

s.82A, see *R. (on the application of Smith) v Secretary of State for the Home Department* [2003] EWHC 692, [2003] 1 W.L.R. 2176 (QBD (Admin Ct)), Kennedy, L.J.; see *R. (on the application of Smith) v Secretary of State for the Home Department* [2004] EWCA Civ 99, [2004] Q.B. 1341 (CA), Lord Phillips of Worth Matravers, M.R.; see *R. v Anselmo (Robert Martin) (aka Tate)* [2004] EWCA Crim 207, [2004] 2 Cr. App. R. (S.) 56 (CA (Crim Div)), David Clarke, J.; see *R. v Burgess (Marcus McAllister)* [2002] EWCA Crim 1804, [2003] 1 Cr. App. R. (S.) 73 (CA), Tuckey, L.J.; see *R. v Jennings (Daniel Joseph)* [2003] EWCA Crim 2316, [2004] 1 Cr. App. R. (S.) 46 (CA (Crim Div)), Leveson, J.; see *R. v M (Keston)* [2003] EWCA Crim 2401, [2004] 1 Cr. App. R. (S.) 55 (CA (Crim Div)), Astill, J.; see *R. v Mason (Kenneth)* [2002] EWCA Crim 699, [2002] 2 Cr. App. R. 32 (CA (Crim Div)), Clarke, L.J.; see *R. v McBean (Isa)* [2001] EWCA Crim 1891, [2002] 1 Cr. App. R. (S.) 98 (CA (Crim Div)), Bell, J.; see *R. v Royal (Carl Christopher)* [2003] EWCA Crim 1152, [2004] 1 Cr. App. R. (S.) 2 (CA (Crim Div)), Laws, L.J.

s.82A, amended: 2003 c.44 Sch.18 para.4, Sch.32 para.109, Sch.37 Part 8

s.82A, repealed (in part): 2003 c.44 Sch.37 Part 8

s.84, repealed: 2003 c.44 Sch.37 Part 7

s.85, see *Attorney General's Reference (No.192 of 2003), Re* [2004] EWCA Crim 558, [2004] 2 Cr. App. R. (S.) 73 (CA (Crim Div)), Judge, L.J.; see *Attorney General's Reference (No.92 of 2002), Re* [2002] EWCA Crim 2904, [2003] 2 Cr. App. R. (S.) 16 (CA (Crim Div)), Rose, L.J.; see *R. (on the application of Sim) v Parole Board* [2003] EWCA Civ 1845, [2004] Q.B. 1288 (CA), Ward, L.J.; see *R. (on the application of Sim) v Parole Board* [2003] EWHC 152, [2003] 2 W.L.R. 1374 (QBD (Admin Ct)), Elias, J.; see *R. v Briggs (Paul)* [2003] EWCA Crim 1050, [2003] 2 Cr. App. R. (S.) 103 (CA (Crim Div)), Rix, L.J.; see *R. v Cornelius (Alan)* [2002] EWCA Crim 138, [2002] 2 Cr. App. R. (S.)

CAP.

CAP.

2000–cont.

6. Powers of Criminal Courts (Sentencing) Act 2000–*cont.*

s.85–*cont.*

69 (CA (Crim Div)), Mackay, J.; see *R. v Dillon (James Miller)* [2001] EWCA Crim 1342, [2002] 1 Cr. App. R. (S.) 41 (CA (Crim Div)), Penry-Davey, J.; see *R. v Figg (Joseph Albert)* [2003] EWCA Crim 2751, [2004] 1 Cr. App. R. (S.) 68 (CA (Crim Div)), Leveson, J.; see *R. v Horrobin (Terrence Roy)* [2002] EWCA Crim 808, [2002] 2 Cr. App. R. (S.) 126 (CA (Crim Div)), Douglas Brown, J.; see *R. v Hubbard (Gerald Leslie)* [2002] EWCA Crim 494, [2002] 2 Cr. App. R. (S.) 101 (CA (Crim Div)), Judge Sir Rhys Davies Q.C.; see *R. v Massie (Raymond)* [2002] EWCA Crim 1871, [2003] 1 Cr. App. R. (S.) 80 (CA (Crim Div)), Wright, J.; see *R. v Wadsworth (David Stephen)* [2003] EWCA Crim 1324, [2004] 1 Cr. App. R. (S.) 14 (CA (Crim Div)), Judge Mettyear; see *R. v Wiles (Alan Ralph)* [2004] EWCA Crim 836, [2004] 2 Cr. App. R. (S.) 88 (CA (Crim Div)), Rose, L.J.

s.85, repealed: 2003 c.44 s.303, Sch.37 Part 7

s.86, see *Attorney General's Reference (No.110 of 2002), Re* [2003] EWCA Crim 540, [2003] 2 Cr. App. R. (S.) 78 (CA (Crim Div)), Kennedy, L.J.; see *R. v JT* [2003] EWCA Crim 1011, [2003] 4 All E.R. 877 (CA (Crim Div)), Fulford, J.; see *R. v R (Sentencing: Extended Licences)* [2003] EWCA Crim 2199, [2004] 1 W.L.R. 490 (CA (Crim Div)), Pitchers, J.

s.87, repealed: 2003 c.44 s.303, Sch.37 Part 7

s.88, applied: SI 2002/2051 Art.5

s.88, repealed: 2003 c.44 s.303, Sch.37 Part 7

s.89, amended: 2003 c.44 Sch.37 Part 4, Sch.3 para.74

s.89, applied: 2003 c.44 s.300

s.89, referred to: 2003 c.44 s.301

s.90, see *R. v Hahn (Rudi)* [2003] EWCA Crim 825, [2003] 2 Cr. App. R. (S.) 106 (CA (Crim Div)), Simon, J.

s.90, applied: 2002 c.18 Sch.2 Part 2, Sch.2 Part 9, 2003 c.13 Sch.2 Part 2, Sch.2 Part 13, 2003 c.42 s.131, 2004 c.9 Sch.2 Part 2, Sch.2 Part 12

s.91, see *Attorney General's Reference (Nos.31 and 32 of 2002), Re* [2002] EWCA Crim 1606, (2002) 166 J.P. 557, (2002) 166 J.P.N. 611 (CA (Crim Div)), Kennedy, L.J.; see *R. (on the application of C) v Balham Youth Court* [2003] EWHC 1332, [2004] 1 Cr. App. R. (S.) 22 (QBD (Admin Ct)), Scott Baker, L.J.; see *R. (on the application of D) v Manchester City Youth Court* [2001] EWHC Admin 860,

2000–cont.

6. Powers of Criminal Courts (Sentencing) Act 2000–*cont.*

s.91–*cont.*

[2002] 1 Cr. App. R. (S.) 135 (QBD (Admin Ct)), Gage, J.; see *R. (on the application of D) v Sheffield Youth Court* [2003] EWHC 35, (2003) 167 J.P. 159 (QBD (Admin Ct)), Stanley Burnton, J.; see *R. (on the application of W) v Thetford Youth Court* [2002] EWHC 1252, (2002) 166 J.P. 453 (QBD (Admin Ct)), Gage, J.; see *R. v Akhtar (Waheed)* [2003] EWCA Crim 2984, [2004] 1 Cr.App.R.(S.) 78 (CA (Crim Div)), Stanley Burnton, J.; see *R. v Bevan (Matthew)* [2003] EWCA Crim 24, [2003] 2 Cr. App. R. (S.) 48 (CA (Crim Div)), Stanley Burnton, J.; see *R. v Coudjoe (Simon Phillip)* [2001] EWCA Crim 3015, [2002] 2 Cr. App R. (S.) 47 (CA (Crim Div)), Judge Maddison; see *R. v Gallagher (Patrick Timothy)* [2002] EWCA Crim 653, [2002] 2 Cr. App. R. (S.) 114 (CA (Crim Div)), Judge David Clarke Q.C.; see *R. v H (Anthony)* [2002] EWCA Crim 2938, (2003) 167 J.P. 30 (CA (Crim Div)), Mance, L.J.; see *R. v Hahn (Rudi)* [2003] EWCA Crim 825, [2003] 2 Cr. App. R. (S.) 106 (CA (Crim Div)), Simon, J.; see *R. v Islam (Fokrul)* [2001] EWCA Crim 2950, [2002] 2 Cr. App. R. (S.) 33 (CA (Crim Div)), Sir John Blofeld; see *R. v JM (Grievous Bodily Harm: Sentencing)* [2002] EWCA Crim 1636, [2003] 1 Cr. App. R. (S.) 51 (CA (Crim Div)), Davis, J.; see *R. v LM* [2002] EWCA Crim 3047, [2003] 2 Cr. App. R. (S.) 26 (CA (Crim Div)), Judge Gordon; see *R. v Michael (S)* [2003] EWCA Crim 1485, [2004] 1 Cr. App. R. (S.) 10 (CA (Crim Div)), Gray, J.; see *R. v P (Christopher) (A Juvenile)* [2001] EWCA Crim 1295, [2002] 1 Cr. App. R. (S.) 46 (CA (Crim Div)), Butterfield, J.; see *R. v Rooney (Tyler Arron)* [2003] EWCA Crim 3663, [2004] 2 Cr. App. R. (S.) 26 (CA (Crim Div)), Leveson, J.; see *R. v Sahadeo (Curtis Adrian)* [2002] EWCA Crim 784, [2002] 2 Cr. App. R. (S.) 125 (CA (Crim Div)), Pitchers, J; see *R. v Tabu (James)* [2002] EWCA Crim 626, [2002] 2 Cr. App. R. (S.) 107 (CA (Crim Div)), Sir Richard Tucker; see *R. v W (Darren James) (A Juvenile)* [2002] EWCA Crim 689, [2002] 2 Cr. App. R. (S.) 116 (CA (Crim Div)), Forbes, J.; see *R. v Wadsworth (David Stephen)* [2003] EWCA Crim 1324, [2004] 1 Cr. App. R. (S.) 14 (CA (Crim Div)), Judge Mettyear

s.91, amended: 2003 c.42 Sch.6 para.43, 2003 c.44 s.289, Sch.32 para.110

s.91, applied: 2002 c.18 Sch.2 Part 2, Sch.2 Part 9, 2003 c.13 Sch.2 Part 2, Sch.2 Part 13, 2003 c.42 s.131, 2003 c.44 s.238, s.240, s.264, s.291, s.327, 2004 c.9 Sch.2 Part 2, Sch.2 Part 12

2000–cont.

6. Powers of Criminal Courts (Sentencing) Act 2000–cont.

s.91, repealed (in part): 2003 c.44 Sch.37 Part 7

s.92, see *R. (on the application of W) v Thetford Youth Court* [2002] EWHC 1252, (2002) 166 J.P. 453 (QBD (Admin Ct)), Gage, J.

s.93, see *R. v Hahn (Rudi)* [2003] EWCA Crim 825, [2003] 2 Cr. App. R. (S.) 106 (CA (Crim Div)), Simon, J.

s.93, applied: 2003 c.42 s.131

s.94, applied: 2003 c.42 s.131

s.99, substituted: 2003 c.44 s.236

s.100, see *A v DPP* [2002] EWHC 403, [2002] 2 Cr. App. R. (S.) 88 (DC), Goldring, J.; see *R. (on the application of W) v Thetford Youth Court* [2002] EWHC 1252, (2002) 166 J.P. 453 (QBD (Admin Ct)), Gage, J.; see *R. v H (Anthony)* [2002] EWCA Crim 2938, (2003) 167 J.P. 30 (CA (Crim Div)), Mance, L.J.; see *R. v Hahn (Rudi)* [2003] EWCA Crim 825, [2003] 2 Cr. App. R. (S.) 106 (CA (Crim Div)), Simon, J.

s.100, amended: 2003 c.44 Sch.32 para.111

s.100, repealed (in part): 2003 c.44 Sch.32 para.111, Sch.37 Part 7

s.101, see *C (A Child) v DPP* [2001] EWHC Admin 453, [2002] 1 Cr. App. R. (S.) 45 (QBD (Admin Ct)), Bell, J.; see *R. v Jones (Martin Nigel)* [2003] EWCA Crim 1609, (2003) 167 J.P. 536 (CA (Crim Div)), Royce, J.; see *R. v March (Wayne Robin)* [2002] EWCA Crim 551, [2002] 2 Cr. App. R. (S.) 98 (CA (Crim Div)), Gross, J.; see *S v Doncaster Youth Offending Team* [2003] EWHC 1128, (2003) 167 J.P. 381 (QBD (Admin Ct)), Scott Baker, L.J.

s.101, amended: 2003 c.44 s.298

s.103, see *S v Doncaster Youth Offending Team* [2003] EWHC 1128, (2003) 167 J.P. 381 (QBD (Admin Ct)), Scott Baker, L.J.

s.104, see *S v Doncaster Youth Offending Team* [2003] EWHC 1128, (2003) 167 J.P. 381 (QBD (Admin Ct)), Scott Baker, L.J.

s.104, amended: 2004 c.28 Sch.5 para.2

s.106, repealed (in part): 2003 c.44 Sch.32 para.112, Sch.37 Part 7

s.106A, added: 2003 c.44 Sch.32 para.113

s.108, applied: 2002 c.29 s.38

s.109, see *Attorney General's Reference (No.62 of 2003). Re* [2004] EWCA Crim 277, [2004] 2 Cr. App. R. (S.) 60 (CA (Crim Div)), Rose, L.J.; see *R. v Benfield (Anthony John)* [2003] EWCA Crim 2223, [2004] 1 Cr. App. R. 8 (CA (Crim Div)), Lord Woolf of Barnes, L.C.J.; see *R. v Drew (Anthony James)* [2001] EWCA Crim 2861, [2002] 2 Cr. App. R. (S.) 45 (CA (Crim Div)), Kennedy, L.J.; see *R. v Drew (Anthony James)* [2003] UKHL 25,

2000–cont.

6. Powers of Criminal Courts (Sentencing) Act 2000–cont.

s.109–cont.

[2003] 1 W.L.R. 1213 (HL), Lord Bingham of Cornhill; see *R. v Faulkner (Lee)* [2001] EWCA Crim 2436, [2002] 1 Cr. App. R. (S.) 133 (CA (Crim Div)), Burton, J.; see *R. v Jackson (Mark Samuel)* [2003] EWCA Crim 3251, [2004] 2 Cr. App. R. (S.) 8 (CA (Crim Div)), Potter, L.J.; see *R. v Kelly (Edward) (No.2)* [2001] EWCA Crim 1751, [2002] 1 Cr. App. R. (S.) 85 (CA (Crim Div)), Buxton, L.J.; see *R. v Mason (Kenneth)* [2002] EWCA Crim 699, [2002] 2 Cr. App. R. 32 (CA (Crim Div)), Clarke, L.J.; see *R. v Millberry (William Christopher)* [2002] EWCA Crim 2891, [2003] 1 W.L.R. 546 (CA (Crim Div)), Lord Woolf of Barnes, L.C.J.; see *R. v Richards (Darrell) (No.1)* [2001] EWCA Crim 2712, [2002] 2 Cr. App. R. (S.) 26 (CA (Crim Div)), Keith, J.; see *R. v Richards (Scott)* [2001] EWCA Crim 1244, [2002] 1 Cr. App. R. (S.) 36 (CA (Crim Div)), Steel, J.; see *R. v Stark (Barry John)* [2002] EWCA Crim 542, [2002] 2 Cr. App. R. (S.) 104 (CA (Crim Div)), Keene, L.J.; see *R. v Watkins (Terrence George)* [2002] EWCA Crim 1014, [2003] 1 Cr. App. R. (S.) 16 (CA (Crim Div)), Waller, L.J.

s.109, amended: 2003 c.42 Sch.6 para.43

s.109, repealed: 2003 c.44 s.303, Sch.37 Part 7

s.110, see *R. v Hickson (Jeffrey)* [2001] EWCA Crim 1595, [2002] 1 Cr. App. R. (S.) 71 (CA (Crim Div)), Waller, L.J.; see *R. v Willoughby (Anthony Stanley)* [2003] EWCA Crim 208, [2003] 2 Cr. App. R. (S.) 60 (CA (Crim Div)), Davis, J.

s.110, amended: 2002 c.29 Sch.11 para.37

s.110, applied: 2003 c.44 s.142, s.144, s.150, s.152, s.153, s.163, s.174, s.305

s.110, repealed (in part): 2003 c.44 Sch.32 para.114, Sch.37 Part 7

s.111, see *R. v Hoare (Jamie Matthew)* [2004] EWCA Crim 191, [2004] 2 Cr. App. R. (S.) 50 (CA (Crim Div)), Mantell, L.J.; see *R. v Maguire (Gareth)* [2002] EWCA Crim 2689, [2003] 2 Cr. App. R. (S.) 10 (CA (Crim Div)), Longmore, L.J.; see *R. v McInerney (William Patrick)* [2002] EWCA Crim 3003, [2003] 1 All E.R. 1089 (CA (Crim Div)), Lord Woolf of Barnes, L.C.J.; see *R. v Webster (Christopher)* [2003] EWCA Crim 3597, [2004] 2 Cr. App. R. (S.) 25 (CA (Crim Div)), Pitchford, J.

s.111, applied: 2003 c.44 s.142, s.144, s.150, s.152, s.153, s.163, s.174, s.305

s.111, repealed (in part): 2003 c.44 Sch.32 para.115, Sch.37 Part 7

s.112, amended: 2003 c.44 Sch.37 Part 7

2000–cont.

6. Powers of Criminal Courts (Sentencing) Act 2000–*cont.*

s.113, amended: 2003 c.44 Sch.37 Part 7

s.114, amended: 2003 c.44 Sch.37 Part 7

s.115, amended: 2003 c.44 Sch.37 Part 7

s.116, see *Attorney General's Reference (No.32 of 2001), Re* [2001] EWCA Crim 2120, [2002] 1 Cr. App. R. (S.) 121 (CA (Crim Div)), Rose, L.J.; see *R. v Kennedy (Michael Edward)* [2003] EWCA Crim 3380, [2004] 2 Cr. App. R. (S.) 20 (CA (Crim Div)), Pitchford, J.; see *R. v Martin (Carl Francis)* [2002] EWCA Crim 775, [2002] 2 Cr. App. R. (S.) 112 (CA (Crim Div)), Forbes, J.; see *R. v Matthews (Jonathan Edward)* [2002] EWCA Crim 677, [2002] 1 W.L.R. 2578 (CA (Crim Div)), Johnson, J.; see *R. v Stocker (David Paul)* [2003] EWCA Crim 121, [2003] 2 Cr. App. R.(S.) 54 (CA (Crim Div)), Judge Fawcus; see *R. v Teasdale (Steven Mark) (Appeal against Sentence)* [2003] EWCA Crim 1641, [2004] 1 Cr. App. R. (S.) 6 (CA (Crim Div)), Moses, J.

s.116, repealed: 2003 c.44 Sch.32 para.116, Sch.37 Part 7

s.117, repealed: 2003 c.44 Sch.32 para.116, Sch.37 Part 7

s.118, see *R. v Elkington (Wayne)* [2003] EWCA Crim 888, [2003] 2 Cr. App. R. (S.) 112 (CA (Crim Div)), Wright, J.; see *R. v Stevens (Eileen)* [2002] EWCA Crim 1332, [2003] 1 Cr. App. R. (S.) 8 (CA (Crim Div)), McKinnon, J.

s.118, applied: 2002 c.29 s.38

s.118, repealed: 2003 c.44 s.303

s.119, see *R. v Elkington (Wayne)* [2003] EWCA Crim 888, [2003] 2 Cr. App. R. (S.) 112 (CA (Crim Div)), Wright, J.

s.119, repealed: 2003 c.44 s.303

s.120, repealed: 2003 c.44 s.303

s.121, repealed (in part): 2003 c.44 s.303

s.122, repealed: 2003 c.44 s.303

s.123, amended: 2004 c.28 Sch.5 para.3

s.123, repealed: 2003 c.44 s.303

s.124, repealed: 2003 c.44 s.303

s.125, repealed: 2003 c.44 s.303

s.126, repealed: 2003 c.44 Sch.37 Part 7

s.127, repealed: 2003 c.44 Sch.37 Part 7

s.128, amended: 2003 c.39 s.95

s.128, repealed: 2003 c.44 Sch.37 Part 7

s.129, repealed: 2003 c.44 Sch.37 Part 7

s.130, amended: 2003 c.44 Sch.32 para.117

s.130, applied: 2002 c.29 s.13, s.14, s.15, s.19, s.20, s.21, s.22, s.32, s.33, s.308, 2003 c.43 Sch.10 para.1

s.130, disapplied: 2002 c.29 s.13

s.132, amended: 2004 c.28 Sch.10 para.49, SI 2004/2035 Sch.1 para.42

s.133, amended: 2002 c.29 Sch.11 para.37

2000–cont.

6. Powers of Criminal Courts (Sentencing) Act 2000–*cont.*

s.136, amended: 2003 c.44 Sch.32 para.118, 2004 c.28 Sch.10 para.50

s.137, see *R. (on the application of M) v Inner London Crown Court* [2003] EWHC 301, [2003] 1 F.L.R. 994 (QBD (Admin Ct)), Henriques, J.; see *R. v JJB* [2004] EWCA Crim 14, [2004] 2 Cr. App. R. (S.) 41 (CA (Crim Div)), Auld, L.J.

s.137, amended: SI 2002/808 Art.34, 2004 c.28 Sch.10 para.51

s.138, amended: 2003 c.44 Sch.32 para.119, 2004 c.28 Sch.10 para.52

s.139, applied: 2002 c.29 s.37, s.38, s.39, 2003 c.44 s.165

s.139, varied: 2002 c.29 s.35, s.36

s.140, amended: 2003 c.44 Sch.37 Part 4, Sch.3 para.74

s.140, varied: 2002 c.29 s.35

s.142, amended: 2004 c.28 Sch.10 para.53

s.143, see *R. v Ball (Joseph Raphael)* [2002] EWCA Crim 2777, [2003] 2 Cr. App. R. (S.) 18 (CA (Crim Div)), Curtis, J.; see *R. v Haynes (Rodney)* [2003] EWCA Crim 3247, [2004] 2 Cr. App. R. (S.) 9 (CA (Crim Div)), Judge Jeremy Roberts Q.C.; see *R. v Robinson (Paula)* [2002] EWCA Crim 2812, [2003] 2 Cr. App. R. (S.) 13 (CA (Crim Div)), Gibbs, J.

s.143, amended: 2002 c.30 s.56

s.143, applied: 2002 c.29 s.13, s.82, s.148, s.230, SI 2003/336 Sch.1 Part 2

s.144, applied: SI 2003/336 Sch.1 Part 2

s.146, amended: 2003 c.32 Sch.5 para.73, Sch.6, 2003 c.44 Sch.32 para.120

s.147, amended: 2003 c.32 Sch.5 para.74, Sch.6

s.148, amended: 2003 c.44 Sch.3 para.74

s.148, applied: 2002 c.29 s.308

s.151, see *R. v Halloren (Barry Philip)* [2004] EWCA Crim 233, [2004] 2 Cr. App. R. (S.) 57 (CA (Crim Div)), David Clarke, J.

s.151, repealed: 2003 c.44 Sch.37 Part 7

s.152, see *R. v Hickson (Jeffrey)* [2001] EWCA Crim 1595, [2002] 1 Cr. App. R. (S.) 71 (CA (Crim Div)), Waller, L.J.; see *R. v Hussain (Altaf)* [2002] EWCA Crim 67, [2002] 2 Cr. App. R. (S.) 59 (CA (Crim Div)), Davis, J.

s.152, repealed: 2003 c.44 Sch.37 Part 7

s.153, see *G v DPP* [2004] EWHC 183, (2004) 168 J.P. 313 (QBD (Admin Ct)), May, L.J.

s.153, repealed: 2003 c.44 Sch.37 Part 7

s.154, see *R. v Salmon (Ishuba)* [2002] EWCA Crim 2088, [2003] 1 Cr. App. R. (S.) 85 (CA (Crim Div)), Rix, L.J.; see *R. v Whitfield (Lee David)* [2001] EWCA Crim 3043, [2002] 2 Cr. App. R. (S.) 44 (CA (Crim Div)), Gross, J.

s.154, amended: 2003 c.44 Sch.32 para.121

2000–cont.

6. Powers of Criminal Courts (Sentencing) Act 2000–cont.

s.155, see *R. v Jones (Timothy Dale)* [2003] EWCA Crim 1631, [2004] 1 Cr. App. R. (S.) 23 (CA (Crim Div)), Judge Hyam; see *R. v Whitfield (Lee David)* [2001] EWCA Crim 3043, [2002] 2 Cr. App. R. (S.) 44 (CA (Crim Div)), Gross, J.; see *R. v Woop (Michael Thomas)* [2002] EWCA Crim 58, [2002] 2 Cr. App. R. (S.) 65 (CA (Crim Div)), Mitchell, J.

s.155, amended: SI 2004/2035 Sch.1 para.43

s.156, repealed: 2003 c.44 Sch.37 Part 7

s.157, repealed: 2003 c.44 Sch.37 Part 7

s.158, repealed: 2003 c.44 Sch.37 Part 7

s.159, amended: 2003 c.44 Sch.23 para.2, Sch.32 para.122, Sch.36 para.98, Sch.37 Part 7

s.160, amended: 2003 c.44 Sch.37 Part 7

s.160, repealed (in part): 2003 c.44 Sch.37 Part 7

s.160, enabling: SI 2004/2172

s.161, see *Attorney General's Reference (No.113 of 2001), Re* [2002] EWCA Crim 143, [2002] 2 Cr. App. R. (S.) 62 (CA (Crim Div)), Rose, L.J.; see *R. v Barker (Shaun David)* [2002] EWCA Crim 1508, [2003] 1 Cr. App. R. (S.) 45 (CA (Crim Div)), Field, J.; see *R. v Szczerba (Ian Michael)* [2002] EWCA Crim 440, [2002] 2 Cr. App. R. (S.) 86 (CA (Crim Div)), Rose, L.J.

s.161, amended: 2003 c.42 Sch.6 para.43

s.161, applied: 2003 c.17 Sch.4 para.18, Sch.4 para.19

s.161, repealed (in part): 2003 c.42 Sch.7, 2003 c.44 Sch.37 Part 7

s.162, repealed: 2003 c.44 Sch.37 Part 7

s.163, amended: 2003 c.44 Sch.32 para.123, Sch.37 Part 7, SI 2004/2035 Sch.1 para.44

s.163, repealed (in part): 2003 c.44 Sch.37 Part 7

s.164, amended: 2003 c.44 Sch.32 para.124

s.168, amended: 2003 c.44 Sch.37 Part 7

s.168, repealed (in part): 2003 c.44 Sch.37 Part 7

Sch.1 Part 1A para.9A, added: 2003 c.44 Sch.34 para.6

Sch.1 Part 1A para.9B, added: 2003 c.44 Sch.34 para.6

Sch.1 Part 1A para.9C, added: 2003 c.44 Sch.34 para.6

Sch.1 Part 1A para.9D, added: 2003 c.44 Sch.34 para.6

Sch.1 Part 1A para.9D, applied: SI 2004/247 r.8, r.9

Sch.1 Part 1A para.9E, added: 2003 c.44 Sch.34 para.6

Sch.1 Part 1A para.9F, added: 2003 c.44 Sch.34 para.6

Sch.2 para.1, repealed: 2003 c.44 Sch.37 Part 7

2000–cont.

6. Powers of Criminal Courts (Sentencing) Act 2000–cont.

Sch.2 para.2, repealed: 2003 c.44 Sch.37 Part 7

Sch.2 para.3, repealed: 2003 c.44 Sch.37 Part 7

Sch.2 para.4, repealed: 2003 c.44 Sch.37 Part 7

Sch.2 para.5, repealed: 2003 c.44 Sch.37 Part 7

Sch.2 para.6, repealed: 2003 c.44 Sch.37 Part 7

Sch.2 para.7, repealed: 2003 c.44 Sch.37 Part 7

Sch.2 para.8, repealed: 2003 c.44 Sch.37 Part 7

Sch.3 Part II para.3, amended: 2004 c.28 Sch.5 para.4, Sch.5 para.5

Sch.3 Part II para.4, amended: 2004 c.28 Sch.5 para.4, Sch.5 para.5

Sch.3 Part II para.5, see *R. v Dale (Andrew Peter)* [2004] EWCA Crim 231, [2004] 2 Cr. App. R. (S.) 58 (CA (Crim Div)), Kay, L.J.

Sch.3 para.4, see *R. v Chute (Patrick Joseph)* [2003] EWCA Crim 177, [2003] 2 Cr. App. R. (S.) 74 (CA (Crim Div)), Mackay, J.

Sch.4 para.1, repealed: 2003 c.44 Sch.37 Part 7

Sch.4 para.2, repealed: 2003 c.44 Sch.37 Part 7

Sch.4 para.3, repealed: 2003 c.44 Sch.37 Part 7

Sch.4 para.4, repealed: 2003 c.44 Sch.37 Part 7

Sch.4 para.5, repealed: 2003 c.44 Sch.37 Part 7

Sch.4 para.6, repealed: 2003 c.44 Sch.37 Part 7

Sch.5 para.1, amended: 2003 c.44 Sch.32 para.126, 2004 c.28 Sch.5 para.6

Sch.5 para.2, amended: 2003 c.44 Sch.32 para.126, 2004 c.28 Sch.5 para.6

Sch.5 para.3, amended: 2003 c.44 Sch.32 para.126

Sch.6 para.1, amended: 2003 c.44 Sch.24 para.2

Sch.6 para.2, amended: 2003 c.38 Sch.2 para.4, 2003 c.44 Sch.32 para.127

Sch.6 para.3, amended: 2003 c.38 Sch.2 para.4, Sch.3, 2003 c.44 Sch.32 para.127

Sch.6 para.3, repealed (in part): 2003 c.38 Sch.3

Sch.6 para.4, repealed: 2003 c.38 Sch.3

Sch.6 para.5, applied: SI 2002/635 Reg.2, SI 2002/896 Sch.1 para.2, SI 2004/2695 Sch.1 para.22

Sch.6 para.5A, added: 2003 c.38 Sch.2 para.4

Sch.6 para.6A, added: 2003 c.44 Sch.24 para.2

2000–cont.

6. Powers of Criminal Courts (Sentencing) Act 2000–cont.

Sch.7 para.2, amended: 2003 c.38 Sch.2 para.6, 2003 c.44 Sch.24 para.3

Sch.7 para.3, amended: 2003 c.44 Sch.32 para.128

Sch.7 para.3, repealed (in part): 2003 c.44 Sch.32 para.128, Sch.37 Part 7

Sch.7 para.4, amended: 2003 c.44 Sch.32 para.128

Sch.7 para.5, amended: 2003 c.38 Sch.2 para.6

Sch.7 para.5, repealed (in part): 2003 c.38 Sch.3

Sch.8 para.3, amended: 2003 c.44 Sch.32 para.129

Sch.8 para.3, repealed (in part): 2003 c.44 Sch.32 para.129, Sch.37 Part 7

Sch.8 para.4, amended: 2003 c.44 Sch.32 para.129

Sch.9 para.7, repealed: 2003 c.44 Sch.37 Part 7

Sch.9 para.23, repealed: 2003 c.44 Sch.37 Part 5

Sch.9 para.24, repealed (in part): 2003 c.44 Sch.37 Part 7

Sch.9 para.26, repealed (in part): 2003 c.44 Sch.37 Part 7

Sch.9 para.28, repealed: 2003 c.44 Sch.37 Part 7

Sch.9 para.29, repealed: 2003 c.44 Sch.37 Part 7

Sch.9 para.52, repealed: 2003 c.44 Sch.37 Part 7

Sch.9 para.54, repealed (in part): 2003 c.44 Sch.37 Part 7

Sch.9 para.55, repealed: 2003 c.44 Sch.37 Part 7

Sch.9 para.61, repealed: 2003 c.44 Sch.37 Part 7

Sch.9 para.62, repealed: 2003 c.44 Sch.37 Part 4

Sch.9 para.63, repealed: 2003 c.44 Sch.37 Part 4

Sch.9 para.64, repealed (in part): 2003 c.44 Sch.37 Part 4

Sch.9 para.65, repealed: 2003 c.44 Sch.37 Part 4

Sch.9 para.76, repealed: 2003 c.44 Sch.37 Part 7

Sch.9 para.81, repealed: 2003 c.44 Sch.37 Part 7

Sch.9 para.82, repealed: 2003 c.44 Sch.37 Part 7

Sch.9 para.87, repealed (in part): 2003 c.44 Sch.37 Part 2

Sch.9 para.89, repealed (in part): 2003 c.44 Sch.37 Part 7

Sch.9 para.90, repealed (in part): 2003 c.44 Sch.37 Part 7

2000–cont.

6. Powers of Criminal Courts (Sentencing) Act 2000–cont.

Sch.9 para.91, repealed: 2003 c.44 Sch.37 Part 4

Sch.9 para.94, repealed: 2003 c.44 Sch.37 Part 7

Sch.9 para.102, repealed: 2003 c.44 Sch.37 Part 7

Sch.9 para.105, repealed: 2002 c.29 Sch.12

Sch.9 para.106, repealed: 2002 c.29 Sch.12

Sch.9 para.107, repealed: 2002 c.29 Sch.12

Sch.9 para.108, repealed: 2002 c.29 Sch.12

Sch.9 para.109, repealed: 2002 c.29 Sch.12

Sch.9 para.110, repealed: 2002 c.29 Sch.12

Sch.9 para.111, repealed: 2002 c.29 Sch.12

Sch.9 para.112, repealed: 2002 c.29 Sch.12

Sch.9 para.113, repealed: 2002 c.29 Sch.12

Sch.9 para.124, repealed: 2003 c.41 Sch.4

Sch.9 para.133, repealed: 2004 c.28 Sch.11

Sch.9 para.137, repealed: 2003 c.44 Sch.37 Part 7

Sch.9 para.138, repealed: 2003 c.44 Sch.37 Part 7

Sch.9 para.139, repealed: 2003 c.44 Sch.37 Part 7

Sch.9 para.140, repealed: 2003 c.44 Sch.37 Part 7

Sch.9 para.141, repealed: 2003 c.44 Sch.37 Part 7

Sch.9 para.142, repealed: 2003 c.44 Sch.37 Part 7

Sch.9 para.143, repealed: 2003 c.44 Sch.37 Part 7

Sch.9 para.144, repealed: 2003 c.44 Sch.37 Part 7

Sch.9 para.145, repealed: 2003 c.44 Sch.37 Part 7

Sch.9 para.147, repealed (in part): 2003 c.44 Sch.37 Part 7

Sch.9 para.151, repealed: 2003 c.44 Sch.37 Part 7

Sch.9 para.163, repealed: 2002 c.29 Sch.12

Sch.9 para.164, repealed: 2002 c.29 Sch.12

Sch.9 para.165, repealed: 2002 c.29 Sch.12

Sch.9 para.166, repealed: 2002 c.29 Sch.12

Sch.9 para.167, repealed: 2002 c.29 Sch.12

Sch.9 para.168, repealed: 2002 c.29 Sch.12

Sch.9 para.169, repealed: 2002 c.29 Sch.12

Sch.9 para.170, repealed: 2002 c.29 Sch.12

Sch.9 para.171, repealed: 2002 c.29 Sch.12

Sch.9 para.172, repealed: 2002 c.29 Sch.12

Sch.9 para.173, repealed: 2002 c.29 Sch.12

Sch.9 para.174, repealed: 2003 c.44 Sch.37 Part 7

Sch.9 para.176, repealed (in part): 2003 c.44 Sch.37 Part 7

Sch.9 para.177, repealed (in part): 2003 c.44 Sch.37 Part 7

Sch.9 para.184, repealed: 2003 c.44 Sch.37 Part 7

2000–cont.

6. Powers of Criminal Courts (Sentencing) Act 2000–cont.

Sch.9 para.185, repealed: 2003 c.44 Sch.37 Part 7

Sch.9 para.186, repealed (in part): 2003 c.44 Sch.37 Part 7

Sch.9 para.187, repealed (in part): 2003 c.44 Sch.37 Part 7

Sch.9 para.189, repealed: 2003 c.42 Sch.6 para.43, Sch.7

Sch.9 para.190, repealed: 2003 c.42 Sch.6 para.43, Sch.7

Sch.9 para.193, repealed: 2003 c.42 Sch.6 para.43, Sch.7

Sch.9 para.194, repealed: 2003 c.44 Sch.37 Part 12

Sch.9 para.195, repealed: 2003 c.44 Sch.37 Part 12

Sch.9 para.196, repealed: 2003 c.44 Sch.37 Part 7

Sch.9 para.201, repealed: 2003 c.44 Sch.37 Part 4

Sch.9 para.202, repealed: 2003 c.44 Sch.37 Part 7

Sch.11 Part II para.9, repealed: 2003 c.44 Sch.37 Part 4, Sch.3 para.74

7. Electronic Communications Act 2000

applied: SI 2002/2127 Reg.2, SI 2002/3171 Reg.2, SI 2002/3173 Reg.2, SI 2003/2004 Reg.5, SSI 2002/143 Reg.9, SSI 2002/292 Reg.2, SSI 2003/411 Reg.2

referred to: SI 2004/2885 Reg.6, SSI 2002/6 Reg.2, SSI 2002/223 Art.2, SSI 2002/255 Reg.3, 2003 asp 7 s.82, SSI 2003/52 Art.2, SSI 2003/129 Reg.2, SSI 2003/168 Reg.2, SSI 2003/229 Art.2, SSI 2003/273 Reg.1, SSI 2003/292 Reg.2, SSI 2003/576 Reg.2, SSI 2003/579 Reg.2, SSI 2003/608 Reg.2, SSI 2004/70 Reg.2, SSI 2004/111 Reg.2, SSI 2004/280 Reg.12, SSI 2004/453 Reg.5, SSI 2004/488 Art.2

s.7, applied: 2002 c.9 s.91, SI 2003/2004 Reg.5

s.8, applied: 2002 c.21 s.54, 2003 asp 7 s.82, SI 2003/492 Sch.2 para.1

s.8, referred to: 2002 c.21 s.54, 2003 asp 7 s.82

s.8, enabling: SI 2002/1789, SI 2003/404, SI 2003/512, SI 2003/956, SI 2003/2604, SI 2003/2800, SI 2003/3052, SI 2004/2521, SI 2004/3156, SI 2004/3157, SI 2004/3236, SSI 2004/332

s.9, applied: SI 2002/1789, 2003 asp 7 s.82, SSI 2004/332

s.9, enabling: SI 2002/1789, SI 2003/404, SI 2003/512, SI 2003/956, SI 2003/2800, SI 2004/2521, SI 2004/3156, SI 2004/3157, SI 2004/3236, SSI 2004/332

s.10, enabling: SI 2004/3156, SI 2004/3157

s.11, repealed: 2003 c.21 Sch.19

s.12, repealed: 2003 c.21 Sch.19

2000–cont.

7. Electronic Communications Act 2000–cont.

s.15, amended: 2003 c.21 Sch.17 para.158

8. Financial Services and Markets Act 2000

applied: 2002 c.13 (NI) s.1, 2002 c.23 Sch.29 para.75, 2002 c.29 Sch.9 para.4, 2002 c.40 Sch.15, Sch.17 para.53, SI 2002/682, SI 2002/1501 Art.9, SI 2002/1775 Reg.14, SI 2002/1968 Art.2, SI 2002/2848 Sch.1 Part I, SI 2002/3152 Art.2, SI 2003/335 Art.3, SI 2003/419 Art.63, SI 2003/1102 Reg.2, SI 2003/1475, SI 2003/3075 Reg.2, Reg.5, Reg.25, 2004 c.35 Sch.3, Sch.8, SI 2004/353 Reg.2, SI 2004/935 Art.3, SI 2004/2095 Reg.23, SI 2004/2615 Art.5, Sch.1 para.5, SR 2002/352 Sch.5 para.1, SSI 2003/93 Art.3

referred to: 2002 c.13 (NI) s.1, SI 2003/1397 Art.8, SI 2004/2737

Part I, applied: SI 2002/1775 Reg.7, SI 2003/1294 Reg.2

Part II, applied: SI 2003/1294 Reg.2

Part III, applied: SI 2003/1294 Reg.2

Part IV, applied: 2002 c.29 Sch.9 para.1, SI 2002/376 Reg.2, SI 2002/1501 Art.5, SI 2002/1998 Art.17, SI 2003/1294 Reg.2, SI 2003/1475 Art.27, SI 2004/1045 Reg.11, SI 2004/1450 Reg.12, SI 2004/2615 Art.2, Sch.1 para.2, SI 2004/2737 Art.4, SSI 2003/231 Sch.2 para.1, Sch.2 Part 2

Part IV, referred to: SI 2002/682 Art.9, SI 2002/1501 Art.5, Art.6

Part V, applied: SI 2003/1294 Reg.2, SI 2003/1475 Art.28, SI 2004/2615 Art.3, SSI 2003/231 Sch.2 Part 2

Part VI, applied: SI 2002/912 Sch.1, SI 2002/915 Sch.1, SSI 2003/231 Sch.2 para.3

Part VII, applied: SI 2003/1294 Reg.2

Part VIII, applied: SI 2003/1294 Reg.2

Part IX, applied: SI 2003/1294 Reg.2

Part X, applied: SI 2002/704 Art.5, SI 2003/1294 Reg.2

Part X c.III, applied: 2002 c.40 Sch.14

Part XI, applied: SI 2003/335 Sch.1, SI 2003/1294 Reg.2, SSI 2003/93 Sch.1

Part XII, applied: SI 2003/1294 Reg.2

Part XIII, applied: SI 2003/1294 Reg.2

Part XIII, amended: 2002 c.40 Sch.25 para.40

Part XIV, applied: SI 2003/1294 Reg.2

Part XV, applied: SI 2003/1294 Reg.2

Part XVI, applied: SI 2003/1294 Reg.2

Part XVII, applied: SI 2003/1294 Reg.2

Part XVII c.III, referred to: 2002 c.13 (NI) s.1

Part XVIII, applied: SI 2003/1294 Reg.2

Part XVIII c.II, applied: 2002 c.40 Sch.14

Part XIX, applied: SI 2003/1294 Reg.2

Part XX, applied: 2002 c.29 Sch.9 para.4, SI 2003/1294 Reg.2, SI 2003/3075 Reg.2

Part XXI, applied: SI 2003/1294 Reg.2

2000–cont.

8. **Financial Services and Markets Act 2000**–*cont.*

Part XXII, applied: SI 2003/1294 Reg.2

Part XXIII, applied: SI 2003/1294 Reg.2

Part XXIV, applied: SI 2003/1294 Reg.2

Part XXV, applied: SI 2003/1294 Reg.2, SI 2004/1862 Reg.5

Part XXVI, applied: SI 2003/1294 Reg.2

Part XXVII, applied: SI 2003/1294 Reg.2

Part XXVIII, applied: SI 2003/1294 Reg.2

Part XXIX, applied: SI 2003/1294 Reg.2

Part XXX, applied: SI 2003/1294 Reg.2

s.2, applied: SI 2002/1501 Art.9, Art.14, Art.15

s.5, applied: SI 2002/1501 Art.4, SI 2004/454 Art.10

s.10, applied: SI 2002/1501 Art.4, SI 2004/454 Art.10

s.14, applied: SI 2002/1501 Art.4, SI 2004/454 Art.10

s.20, applied: SI 2004/2615 Sch.1 para.2

s.21, applied: SI 2002/2157, SI 2003/1676, 2004 c.35 s.234, SI 2004/1484 Reg.10, SI 2004/2615 Sch.1 para.6

s.21, enabling: SI 2002/1310, SI 2002/1777, SI 2002/2157, SI 2003/1676

s.22, applied: 2002 c.29 Sch.9 para.1, Sch.9 para.3, 2003 c.43 Sch.10 para.4, SI 2003/1102 Reg.2, Reg.17, Reg.48, SI 2003/3075 Reg.2, SI 2004/347 Art.2, SI 2004/353 Reg.2, Reg.17, Reg.48, SR 2003/86 Reg.2, SSI 2003/231 Sch.2 Part 2

s.22, enabling: SI 2002/682, SI 2002/1310, SI 2002/1776, SI 2002/1777, SI 2003/1475, SI 2003/1476, SI 2003/2822, SI 2004/1610, SI 2004/2737

s.25, applied: SI 2004/2615 Sch.1 para.6

s.31, applied: SI 2002/376 Reg.2, SI 2004/1450 Reg.14, SSI 2003/231 Sch.2 Part 2

s.31, referred to: SI 2004/2615 Sch.1 para.4

s.38, applied: 2002 c.29 Sch.9 para.2, Sch.9 para.3, SI 2004/2615 Sch.1 para.3

s.38, varied: SI 2003/3075 Reg.2

s.38, enabling: SI 2002/1310, SI 2003/47, SI 2003/1675

s.39, applied: SI 2003/3075 Reg.6, SI 2004/2615 Sch.1 para.7, SR 2002/352 Sch.5 para.1

s.39, enabling: SI 2004/453

s.40, applied: SI 2002/682 Art.9, SI 2002/704 Art.3, SI 2004/2615 Sch.1 para.3

s.40, disapplied: SI 2002/704 Art.3

s.41, applied: SI 2004/1862 Reg.15

s.42, applied: SI 2002/682 Art.9, SI 2004/2615 Art.2, Sch.1 para.3, Sch.1 para.7

s.43, applied: SI 2002/682 Art.9, SI 2002/704 Art.5, SI 2004/1450 Reg.14, SI 2004/2615 Sch.1 para.3, SSI 2003/231 Sch.2 para.1

s.44, applied: SI 2004/1862 Reg.15, SI 2004/2615 Sch.1 para.3, SI 2004/2737 Art.4

2000–cont.

8. **Financial Services and Markets Act 2000**–*cont.*

s.44, varied: SI 2002/704 Art.7

s.45, applied: SI 2004/1045 Reg.11, SI 2004/1862 Reg.15, SI 2004/2737 Art.4

s.45, referred to: SI 2002/1775 Reg.6

s.45, varied: SI 2002/704 Art.7

s.48, applied: SI 2002/1775 Reg.6

s.49, amended: SI 2003/1476 Art.20

s.49, disapplied: SI 2004/1862 Reg.3

s.50, varied: SI 2002/704 Art.7

s.51, varied: SI 2002/704 Art.7

s.52, disapplied: SI 2003/1475 Art.27, SI 2003/1476 Art.23, Art.25

s.52, varied: SI 2002/704 Art.7

s.53, applied: SI 2004/2615 Art.2

s.53, varied: SI 2002/704 Art.7

s.54, varied: SI 2002/704 Art.7

s.55, varied: SI 2002/704 Art.7

s.56, see *R. (on the application of Davies) v Financial Services Authority* [2002] EWHC 2997, [2003] 1 W.L.R. 1284 (QBD (Admin Ct)), Lightman, J.; see *R. (on the application of Davies) v Financial Services Authority* [2003] EWCA Civ 1128, [2004] 1 W.L.R. 185 (CA), Mummery, L.J.

s.56, applied: SSI 2003/231 Sch.2 para.1

s.56, varied: SI 2002/704 Art.7

s.57, see *R. (on the application of Davies) v Financial Services Authority* [2002] EWHC 2997, [2003] 1 W.L.R. 1284 (QBD (Admin Ct)), Lightman, J.; see *R. (on the application of Davies) v Financial Services Authority* [2003] EWCA Civ 1128, [2004] 1 W.L.R. 185 (CA), Mummery, L.J.

s.59, applied: SI 2002/704 Art.6, Art.9, SI 2003/1475 Art.28, SI 2003/1476 Art.24, SI 2004/2615 Art.3, SSI 2003/231 Sch.2 para.1, Sch.2 Part 2

s.60, applied: SI 2004/2615 Art.3

s.60, varied: SI 2002/704 Art.7

s.61, applied: SI 2003/1475 Art.28

s.61, disapplied: SI 2003/1476 Art.24, Art.26

s.62, applied: SI 2004/2615 Art.3

s.65, disapplied: SI 2004/2615 Art.4

s.66, see *R. (on the application of Davies) v Financial Services Authority* [2002] EWHC 2997, [2003] 1 W.L.R. 1284 (QBD (Admin Ct)), Lightman, J.; see *R. (on the application of Davies) v Financial Services Authority* [2003] EWCA Civ 1128, [2004] 1 W.L.R. 185 (CA), Mummery, L.J.

s.74, applied: 2003 c.1 Sch.2 para.30, Sch.3 para.21, Sch.4 para.19, SSI 2003/231 Sch.2 Part 2

s.77, applied: SSI 2003/231 Sch.2 para.3

s.88, applied: SSI 2003/231 Sch.2 para.3, Sch.2 Part 2

s.95, applied: 2002 c.40 Sch.14

s.118, applied: 2002 c.23 s.117

2000–cont.

8. **Financial Services and Markets Act 2000**–*cont.*

s.122, see *WASA International (UK) Insurance Co Ltd v WASA International Insurance Co Ltd (Sweden)* [2002] EWHC 2698, [2003] 1 All E.R. (Comm) 696 (Ch D), Park, J.

s.132, varied: SI 2002/1775 Reg.12

s.133, varied: SI 2002/1775 Reg.12

s.138, applied: SI 2002/1775 Reg.3, SI 2002/2706 Reg.2

s.138, disapplied: SI 2002/1775 Reg.3

s.138, varied: SI 2002/1501 Art.4, SI 2002/1775 Reg.3, SI 2004/454 Art.10

s.140, amended: SI 2003/2066 Reg.5

s.140, disapplied: SI 2002/1775 Reg.5

s.141, disapplied: SI 2002/1775 Reg.5

s.148, applied: SI 2003/1476 Art.27, SI 2004/1862 Reg.4

s.148, referred to: SI 2004/1862 Reg.8, Reg.9, Reg.10

s.148, varied: SI 2002/1775 Reg.3, SI 2003/1475 Art.29, SI 2003/1476 Art.27

s.149, referred to: SI 2002/1501 Art.11

s.149, varied: SI 2002/1501 Art.11

s.150, applied: SI 2002/1501 Art.11, 2004 c.21 s.35

s.150, referred to: SI 2002/1501 Art.11

s.150, varied: SI 2002/1775 Reg.3

s.150, enabling: SI 2002/2706

s.154, disapplied: SI 2002/1501 Art.12

s.155, applied: SI 2002/1501 Art.15

s.155, disapplied: SI 2004/454 Art.12, SI 2004/2615 Art.4

s.155, referred to: SI 2002/682 Art.10

s.156, varied: SI 2002/1775 Reg.3

s.157, applied: SI 2002/1501 Art.14

s.157, disapplied: SI 2004/454 Art.12, SI 2004/2615 Art.4

s.159, amended: 2002 c.40 Sch.25 para.40

s.160, amended: 2002 c.40 Sch.25 para.40

s.161, amended: 2002 c.40 Sch.25 para.40

s.162, amended: 2002 c.40 Sch.25 para.40

s.162, applied: SI 2003/1397 Art.8

s.165, varied: SI 2002/704 Art.8, SI 2002/1775 Reg.12

s.166, applied: SI 2002/912 Sch.1, SI 2002/915 Sch.1

s.166, varied: SI 2002/1775 Reg.12

s.167, applied: SI 2002/912 Sch.1, SI 2002/915 Sch.1, SI 2003/3075 Reg.26, 2004 c.35 Sch.3, Sch.8

s.167, varied: SI 2002/1775 Reg.12

s.168, applied: SI 2002/912 Sch.1, SI 2002/915 Sch.1, SI 2003/3075 Reg.1, Reg.26, 2004 c.35 Sch.3, Sch.8

s.168, varied: SI 2002/1775 Reg.12

s.168, enabling: SI 2003/3075

s.169, applied: SI 2003/3075 Reg.26

s.176, varied: SI 2002/1775 Reg.12

s.177, amended: 2003 c.44 Sch.26 para.54

2000–cont.

8. **Financial Services and Markets Act 2000**–*cont.*

s.178, applied: SI 2003/1476 Art.21

s.178, referred to: SI 2003/1476 Art.21

s.183, enabling: SI 2003/2066, SI 2004/1862

s.185, applied: SI 2004/1862 Reg.8, Reg.9, Reg.10

s.186, applied: SI 2002/1501 Art.4, SI 2004/454 Art.10, SI 2004/1862 Reg.8, Reg.9, Reg.10

s.187, applied: SI 2004/1862 Reg.8, Reg.9, Reg.10

s.188, enabling: SI 2003/2066, SI 2004/1862

s.190, applied: SI 2003/1476 Art.21

s.190, referred to: SI 2003/1476 Art.21

s.192, enabling: SI 2003/1476

s.194, amended: 2002 c.40 Sch.25 para.40

s.203, amended: 2002 c.40 Sch.25 para.40

s.204, amended: 2002 c.40 Sch.25 para.40

s.205, applied: SI 2002/1775 Reg.12, SI 2004/1862 Reg.5

s.206, applied: SI 2002/1775 Reg.12, SI 2004/1862 Reg.5

s.207, applied: SI 2002/1775 Reg.12

s.208, applied: SI 2002/1775 Reg.12

s.209, applied: SI 2002/1775 Reg.12

s.212, applied: 2004 c.35 Sch.3, Sch.8

s.213, applied: 2004 c.35 Sch.3

s.213, disapplied: SI 2004/2615 Sch.1 para.8

s.213, referred to: SI 2002/1501 Art.5

s.213, enabling: SI 2003/2066

s.214, applied: SI 2002/1501 Art.5

s.214, enabling: SI 2003/2066

s.215, amended: 2002 c.40 Sch.17 para.54

s.224, referred to: SI 2002/1501 Art.5

s.224, enabling: SI 2003/2066

s.225, applied: SSI 2003/231 Sch.2 para.2, Sch.2 Part 2

s.226, applied: SI 2004/454 Art.2

s.226, referred to: SI 2004/454 Art.5

s.228, applied: SI 2004/454 Art.5

s.228, varied: SI 2004/454 Art.5

s.229, applied: SI 2004/454 Art.5

s.229, varied: SI 2004/454 Art.5

s.230, varied: SI 2004/454 Art.5

s.231, varied: SI 2004/454 Art.5, Art.11

s.232, varied: SI 2004/454 Art.5, Art.11

s.234, varied: SI 2004/454 Art.6

s.235, referred to: 2002 c.23 Sch.29 para.75

s.237, applied: SI 2004/266 Sch.2 para.4, SSI 2003/231 Sch.2 Part 2

s.238, enabling: SI 2002/1310, SI 2002/2157

s.243, applied: SSI 2003/231 Sch.2 para.1

s.251, applied: SSI 2003/231 Sch.2 para.1

s.257, applied: SSI 2003/231 Sch.2 para.1

s.262, applied: SI 2003/3075 Reg.26

s.264, applied: SI 2004/2095 Reg.4

s.264, enabling: SI 2003/2066

2000–cont.

8. **Financial Services and Markets Act 2000**–*cont.*

s.266, amended: SI 2003/2066 Reg.9

s.270, applied: SI 2003/1181 Art.2, Art.3, SSI 2003/231 Sch.2 para.1

s.270, referred to: SI 2003/1181

s.270, enabling: SI 2003/1181

s.272, applied: SSI 2003/231 Sch.2 para.1

s.284, applied: SI 2002/912 Sch.1, SI 2002/915 Sch.1, SI 2003/3075 Reg.26, 2004 c.35 Sch.3, Sch.8

s.285, applied: 2004 c.35 Sch.3, Sch.8

s.290, applied: SSI 2003/231 Sch.2 para.1

s.292, applied: SSI 2003/231 Sch.2 para.1

s.295, amended: 2002 c.40 Sch.25 para.40

s.296, applied: SSI 2003/231 Sch.2 para.1

s.303, amended: 2002 c.40 Sch.25 para.40

s.304, amended: 2002 c.40 Sch.25 para.40

s.305, amended: 2002 c.40 Sch.25 para.40

s.306, amended: 2002 c.40 Sch.25 para.40

s.306, applied: SI 2003/1397 Art.8

s.307, amended: 2002 c.40 Sch.25 para.40

s.310, amended: 2002 c.40 Sch.25 para.40

s.313, amended: 2002 c.40 Sch.25 para.40

s.316, referred to: SI 2003/1102 Reg.3, SI 2004/353 Reg.3

s.326, applied: 2004 c.35 Sch.3, Sch.8

s.327, applied: SSI 2003/231 Sch.2 Part 2

s.327, enabling: SI 2002/1777

s.328, amended: SI 2003/1473 Reg.9

s.329, applied: SSI 2003/231 Sch.2 para.1

s.340, applied: SI 2003/1294 Reg.2

s.342, referred to: SI 2003/1294 Reg.2

s.342, enabling: SI 2003/1294

s.343, referred to: SI 2003/1294 Reg.2

s.343, enabling: SI 2003/1294

s.347, disapplied: SI 2004/2615 Sch.1 para.9, Sch.1 para.10

s.348, applied: SI 2003/1102 Reg.16, Reg.50, SI 2004/353 Reg.16, Reg.50, SI 2004/1045 Reg.18, Reg.38

s.348, referred to: SI 2003/1102 Reg.50

s.348, varied: SI 2003/1102 Reg.50, SI 2004/353 Reg.50

s.349, applied: SI 2003/1102 Reg.16, Reg.50, SI 2004/353 Reg.16, Reg.50, SI 2004/1045 Reg.18, Reg.38

s.349, varied: SI 2003/1102 Reg.50

s.349, enabling: SI 2002/1775, SI 2003/693, SI 2003/1092, SI 2003/1473, SI 2003/2066, SI 2003/2174, SI 2003/2817

s.351, applied: 2002 c.40 s.243

s.351, repealed (in part): 2002 c.40 Sch.26

s.352, amended: 2003 c.44 Sch.26 para.54

s.352, applied: SI 2003/1102 Reg.16, Reg.50, SI 2004/353 Reg.16, Reg.50, SI 2004/1045 Reg.18, Reg.38

s.352, varied: SI 2003/1102 Reg.50

s.355, enabling: SI 2002/1242

s.359, substituted: 2002 c.40 Sch.17 para.55

2000–cont.

8. **Financial Services and Markets Act 2000**–*cont.*

s.360, enabling: SI 2002/1242, SI 2003/2134, SI 2004/952

s.361, substituted: 2002 c.40 Sch.17 para.56

s.362, amended: 2002 c.40 Sch.17 para.57

s.362A, added: 2002 c.40 Sch.17 para.58

s.376, applied: SI 2003/1102 Reg.21, SI 2004/353 Reg.21

s.377, applied: SI 2003/1102 Reg.9, Reg.34, Reg.36, SI 2004/353 Reg.9, Reg.34, Reg.36

s.377, disapplied: SI 2003/1102 Reg.4, SI 2004/353 Reg.4

s.380, applied: SI 2002/1775 Reg.12

s.381, referred to: SI 2004/1862 Reg.5

s.382, applied: 2002 c.29 s.308, SI 2002/1775 Reg.12

s.383, applied: 2002 c.29 s.308

s.383, referred to: SI 2004/1862 Reg.5

s.384, applied: 2002 c.29 s.308, SI 2002/1775 Reg.12

s.384, referred to: SI 2004/1862 Reg.5

s.391, applied: SI 2002/682 Art.9, SI 2002/1501 Art.4, SI 2002/1775 Reg.6, SI 2004/454 Art.10

s.397, enabling: SI 2002/1777, SI 2003/1474

s.398, applied: SI 2002/1775 Reg.12

s.399, amended: 2002 c.40 Sch.25 para.40

s.401, amended: 2002 c.40 Sch.25 para.40

s.402, applied: SI 2003/3075 Reg.1

s.402, enabling: SI 2003/3075

s.414, enabling: SI 2002/1775

s.416, enabling: SI 2002/1555

s.417, amended: SI 2002/1775 Reg.13

s.417, enabling: SI 2002/2706, SI 2003/693, SI 2003/1092, SI 2003/1473, SI 2003/2066, SI 2003/2174, SI 2003/2817, SI 2003/3075, SI 2004/453, SI 2004/1862

s.418, amended: SI 2002/1775 Reg.13

s.422, amended: 2004 c.33 Sch.27 para.165

s.422, varied: 2004 c.33 Sch.21 para.48

s.425, amended: SI 2003/1473 Reg.2, SI 2003/2066 Reg.2

s.426, enabling: SI 2002/704, SI 2002/1242, SI 2002/1409, SI 2002/1501, SI 2002/1555, SI 2003/1181, SI 2003/1475, SI 2003/1476, SI 2003/2134, SI 2004/355, SI 2004/454, SI 2004/952, SI 2004/1609, SI 2004/2615

s.427, amended: 2002 c.40 Sch.25 para.40

s.427, enabling: SI 2002/704, SI 2002/1501, SI 2002/1555, SI 2003/1475, SI 2003/1476, SI 2003/2134, SI 2004/454, SI 2004/952, SI 2004/1609, SI 2004/2615

s.427A, amended: 2002 c.40 Sch.17 para.59

s.427A, enabling: SI 2004/952, SI 2004/1609, SI 2004/2615

s.428, enabling: SI 2002/682, SI 2002/704, SI 2002/1242, SI 2002/1310, SI 2002/1501, SI 2002/1775, SI 2002/1776, SI

2000–cont.

8. Financial Services and Markets Act 2000–*cont.*

s.428, enabling:–*cont.*

2002/1777, SI 2002/2157, SI 2002/2707, SI 2003/47, SI 2003/693, SI 2003/1181, SI 2003/1294, SI 2003/1473, SI 2003/1475, SI 2003/1476, SI 2003/1675, SI 2003/1676, SI 2003/2066, SI 2003/2134, SI 2003/2822, SI 2003/3075, SI 2004/453, SI 2004/454, SI 2004/952, SI 2004/1609, SI 2004/1610, SI 2004/1862, SI 2004/2615, SI 2004/2737, SI 2004/2738

s.429, applied: SI 2003/1676

s.429, enabling: SI 2003/1675

Sch.1, applied: SI 2002/1501 Art.9, SI 2003/1294 Reg.2

Sch.1 Part I para.1, applied: SI 2004/2615 Art.4

Sch.1 Part I para.5, disapplied: SI 2004/2615 Art.4

Sch.1 Part I para.6, applied: SI 2002/1775 Reg.12

Sch.1 Part IV para.19A, added: 2002 c.29 Sch.11 para.38

Sch.2, applied: 2002 c.29 Sch.9 para.1, Sch.9 para.3, 2003 c.43 Sch.10 para.4, SI 2003/1102 Reg.2, Reg.17, Reg.48, SI 2003/1294 Reg.2, SI 2003/3075 Reg.2, SI 2004/353 Reg.2, Reg.17, Reg.48

Sch.2 Part II para.12, varied: SI 2003/1633 Sch.2 para.6, Sch.2 para.8

Sch.2 Part III para.25, enabling: SI 2002/682, SI 2002/1310, SI 2002/1777, SI 2003/1475, SI 2003/1476, SI 2003/2822, SI 2004/1610, SI 2004/2737

Sch.3, applied: SI 2002/682 Art.9, SI 2003/1294 Reg.2, SR 2003/86 Reg.2

Sch.3 Part I para.1, amended: SI 2003/1473 Reg.2, SI 2003/2066 Reg.2

Sch.3 Part I para.4A, added: SI 2003/1473 Reg.2

Sch.3 Part I para.4B, added: SI 2003/2066 Reg.2

Sch.3 Part I para.5, amended: SI 2003/1473 Reg.2, SI 2003/2066 Reg.2

Sch.3 Part I para.5, referred to: SI 2002/376 Reg.2, SI 2002/682 Art.9, SI 2002/1998 Art.17

Sch.3 Part I para.5A, added: SI 2003/1473 Reg.2

Sch.3 Part I para.6, substituted: SI 2003/1473 Reg.2

Sch.3 Part I para.7, amended: SI 2003/1473 Reg.2

Sch.3 Part I para.7A, added: SI 2003/1473 Reg.2

Sch.3 Part I para.10, amended: SI 2003/1473 Reg.2

Sch.3 Part I para.10A, added: SI 2003/1473 Reg.2

Sch.3 Part II para.12, applied: SI 2002/376 Reg.2, SI 2002/1998 Art.17

2000–cont.

8. Financial Services and Markets Act 2000–*cont.*

Sch.3 Part II para.13, amended: SI 2003/1473 Reg.3, SI 2003/2066 Reg.3

Sch.3 Part II para.13, applied: 2002 c.29 Sch.9 para.1, SI 2002/682 Art.9

Sch.3 Part II para.13, enabling: SI 2003/2066

Sch.3 Part II para.14, amended: SI 2003/1473 Reg.4, SI 2003/2066 Reg.3

Sch.3 Part II para.14, applied: 2002 c.29 Sch.9 para.1, SI 2002/682 Art.9

Sch.3 Part II para.14, enabling: SI 2003/1473, SI 2003/2066

Sch.3 Part II para.15, amended: 2002 c.40 Sch.25 para.40, SI 2003/2066 Reg.3

Sch.3 Part II para.15, applied: SI 2002/376 Reg.2, SI 2002/682 Art.9, SI 2002/1998 Art.17

Sch.3 Part II para.15A, added: SI 2003/2066 Reg.3

Sch.3 Part II para.17, enabling: SI 2003/1473, SI 2003/2066

Sch.3 Part III para.19, amended: SI 2003/1473 Reg.5, SI 2003/2066 Reg.4

Sch.3 Part III para.19, referred to: SI 2002/682 Art.9

Sch.3 Part III para.20, amended: SI 2003/1473 Reg.6, SI 2003/2066 Reg.4

Sch.3 Part III para.20, referred to: SI 2002/682 Art.9

Sch.3 Part III para.21, amended: SI 2003/1473 Reg.6

Sch.3 Part III para.22, enabling: SI 2003/2066

Sch.3 Part III para.23, amended: 2002 c.40 Sch.25 para.40

Sch.3 Part III para.25, added: SI 2003/1473 Reg.7

Sch.4, applied: SI 2002/376 Reg.2, SI 2003/1294 Reg.2

Sch.4 para.1, applied: SI 2002/1501 Art.4, SI 2004/454 Art.10

Sch.5, applied: SI 2003/1294 Reg.2, SI 2004/1450 Reg.14

Sch.5 para.1, amended: SI 2003/2066 Reg.10

Sch.5 para.1, applied: SI 2002/376 Reg.2

Sch.5 para.2, amended: SI 2003/2066 Reg.10

Sch.5 para.2, applied: SI 2002/376 Reg.2

Sch.6, applied: SI 2003/1294 Reg.2

Sch.6 Part I para.1, amended: SI 2002/682 Art.8

Sch.6 Part I para.2, amended: SI 2003/1476 Art.19

Sch.6 Part I para.2A, added: SI 2002/2707 Art.2

Sch.6 Part III para.9, enabling: SI 2002/2707

Sch.7, applied: SI 2003/1294 Reg.2

Sch.8, applied: SI 2003/1294 Reg.2

Sch.9, applied: SI 2003/1294 Reg.2

2000–cont.

8. **Financial Services and Markets Act 2000**–*cont.*

Sch.10, applied: SI 2003/1294 Reg.2

Sch.11, applied: SI 2003/1294 Reg.2

Sch.11 para.16, amended: 2004 c.33 Sch.27 para.166

Sch.11 para.16, varied: 2004 c.33 Sch.21 para.49

Sch.11 para.20, amended: SI 2002/765 Reg.4

Sch.11 para.23, varied: SI 2003/1633 Sch.2 para.8

Sch.12, applied: SI 2003/1294 Reg.2

Sch.13, applied: SI 2003/1294 Reg.2

Sch.14, applied: SI 2003/1294 Reg.2

Sch.14 para.2, amended: 2002 c.40 Sch.25 para.40

Sch.14 para.2A, added: 2002 c.40 Sch.25 para.40

Sch.14 para.2A, amended: 2003 c.21 Sch.16 para.5

Sch.14 para.2A, referred to: SI 2003/1371

Sch.14 para.2A, enabling: SI 2003/1371

Sch.14 para.2B, added: 2002 c.40 Sch.25 para.40

Sch.14 para.2C, added: 2002 c.40 Sch.25 para.40

Sch.14 para.3, repealed: 2002 c.40 Sch.26

Sch.15, applied: SI 2003/1294 Reg.2

Sch.15 Part I para.1, varied: SI 2002/704 Art.8

Sch.15 Part I para.2, varied: SI 2002/704 Art.8

Sch.15 Part I para.3, varied: SI 2002/704 Art.8

Sch.15 Part I para.4, varied: SI 2002/704 Art.8

Sch.15 Part I para.5, varied: SI 2002/704 Art.8

Sch.15 Part I para.6, varied: SI 2002/704 Art.8

Sch.15 Part I para.7, varied: SI 2002/704 Art.8

Sch.16, applied: SI 2003/1294 Reg.2

Sch.16 para.1, amended: 2002 c.40 Sch.25 para.40

Sch.16 para.2, amended: 2002 c.40 Sch.25 para.40

Sch.16 para.3, amended: 2002 c.40 Sch.25 para.40

Sch.16 para.4, amended: 2002 c.40 Sch.25 para.40

Sch.16 para.5, amended: 2002 c.40 Sch.25 para.40

Sch.17, applied: SI 2003/1294 Reg.2, SSI 2003/231 Sch.2 para.2, Sch.2 Part 2

Sch.17 Part II para.10, varied: SI 2004/454 Art.7

Sch.17 Part II para.11, varied: SI 2004/454 Art.8

Sch.17 Part III para.13, varied: SI 2004/454 Art.3

2000–cont.

8. **Financial Services and Markets Act 2000**–*cont.*

Sch.17 Part III para.14, applied: SI 2004/454 Art.4

Sch.17 Part III para.14, disapplied: SI 2004/454 Art.4, Art.12

Sch.17 Part III para.14, referred to: SI 2004/454 Art.4

Sch.17 Part III para.15, varied: SI 2004/454 Art.6

Sch.18, applied: SI 2003/1294 Reg.2

Sch.19, applied: SI 2003/1294 Reg.2

Sch.19 Part I para.1, amended: 2003 c.20 Sch.2 para.24

Sch.19 Part I para.1, repealed: 2002 c.40 Sch.26

Sch.19 Part II para.1, repealed: 2002 c.40 Sch.26

Sch.19 Part II para.2, repealed: 2002 c.40 Sch.26

Sch.19 Part II para.3, repealed: 2002 c.40 Sch.26

Sch.19 Part II para.4, repealed: 2002 c.40 Sch.26

Sch.19 Part II para.5, repealed: 2002 c.40 Sch.26

Sch.19 Part II para.6, repealed: 2002 c.40 Sch.26

Sch.19 Part II para.7, repealed: 2002 c.40 Sch.26

Sch.19 Part II para.8, repealed: 2002 c.40 Sch.26

Sch.19 Part II para.9, repealed: 2002 c.40 Sch.26

Sch.19 Part II para.10, repealed: 2002 c.40 Sch.26

Sch.19 Part II para.11, repealed: 2002 c.40 Sch.26

Sch.19 Part II para.12, repealed: 2002 c.40 Sch.26

Sch.19 Part II para.13, repealed: 2002 c.40 Sch.26

Sch.19 Part II para.14, repealed: 2002 c.40 Sch.26

Sch.19 Part II para.15, repealed: 2002 c.40 Sch.26

Sch.19 Part II para.16, repealed: 2002 c.40 Sch.26

Sch.19 Part II para.17, repealed: 2002 c.40 Sch.26

Sch.19 Part II para.18, repealed: 2002 c.40 Sch.26

Sch.19 Part II para.19, repealed: 2002 c.40 Sch.26

Sch.20, applied: SI 2003/1294 Reg.2

Sch.21, applied: SI 2003/1294 Reg.2

Sch.22, applied: SI 2003/1294 Reg.2

9. **Appropriation Act 2000**

repealed: 2002 c.18 Sch.3

2000–cont.

11. Terrorism Act 2000
referred to: 2003 c.32 Sch.4 para.1, Sch.5 para.75

Part VI, added: 2003 c.32 s.52

s.3, see *O'Driscoll v Secretary of State for the Home Department* [2002] EWHC 2477, [2003] A.C.D. 35 (QBD), Kennedy, L.J.

s.3, enabling: SI 2002/2724

s.5, applied: SI 2002/1843 r.3

s.11, see *Attorney General's Reference (No.4 of 2002), Re* [2003] EWCA Crim 762, [2003] 3 W.L.R. 1153 (CA (Crim Div)), Latham, L.J.; see *R. v Hundal (Avtar Singh)* [2004] EWCA Crim 389, [2004] 2 Cr. App. R. 19 (CA (Crim Div)), Lord Woolf of Barnes, L.C.J.; see *Sheldrake v DPP* [2004] UKHL 43, [2004] 3 W.L.R. 976 (HL), Lord Bingham of Cornhill

s.11, applied: SI 2004/1910 Sch.1

s.12, applied: SI 2004/1910 Sch.1

s.15, applied: SI 2004/1910 Sch.1

s.16, see *O'Driscoll v Secretary of State for the Home Department* [2002] EWHC 2477, [2003] A.C.D. 35 (QBD), Kennedy, L.J.

s.16, applied: SI 2004/1910 Sch.1

s.17, applied: SI 2004/1910 Sch.1

s.18, applied: 2002 c.29 s.364, s.398, SI 2003/3075 Reg.3, SI 2004/1910 Sch.1

s.19, applied: SI 2004/1910 Sch.1

s.21A, applied: SI 2003/3075 Reg.3

s.23, applied: 2002 c.29 s.13, s.82, s.97, s.148, s.163, s.230, SI 2003/336 Sch.1 Part 2

s.34, amended: SI 2004/1573 Art.12

s.34, varied: 2003 c.20 Sch.5 para.4

s.36, amended: 2003 c.44 Sch.26 para.55

s.36, applied: 2002 c.30 Sch.4 para.14

s.38B, applied: SI 2004/1910 Sch.1

s.39, amended: 2002 c.26 Sch.12 para.80

s.41, applied: SI 2003/705 Art.3, SI 2003/1100, SI 2003/1100 Art.2, SI 2004/81 Art.2, SR 2002/179 Art.2, SR 2003/232 Art.2

s.42, applied: 2003 c.6 Sch.2 para.1

s.42, varied: 2003 c.6 Sch.2 para.1

s.43, referred to: 2003 c.41 s.163

s.44, see *R. (on the application of Gillan) v Commissioner of Police of the Metropolis* [2004] EWCA Civ 1067, [2004] 3 W.L.R. 1144 (CA (Civ Div)), Lord Woolf of Barnes, L.C.J.

s.44, amended: 2004 c.20 s.57, Sch.23 Part 1, SI 2004/1573 Art.12

s.44, applied: 2002 c.30 Sch.4 para.15

s.44, varied: 2003 c.20 Sch.5 para.4

s.45, see *R. (on the application of Gillan) v Commissioner of Police of the Metropolis* [2004] EWCA Civ 1067, [2004] 3 W.L.R. 1144 (CA (Civ Div)), Lord Woolf of Barnes, L.C.J.

s.45, applied: 2002 c.30 Sch.4 para.15

2000–cont.

11. Terrorism Act 2000–*cont.*
s.45, varied: 2002 c.30 Sch.4 para.15

s.46, amended: 2004 c.20 s.57

s.51, amended: 2003 c.44 Sch.26 para.55

s.54, applied: SI 2004/1910 Sch.1

s.55, applied: 2003 c.44 Sch.4 para.30

s.56, applied: 2002 c.29 Sch.2 para.3, Sch.4 para.3, Sch.5 para.3, 2003 c.44 Sch.5 para.27, Sch.5 para.48, SI 2004/1500 Sch.2 para.22, SI 2004/1910 Sch.1

s.57, applied: SI 2004/1910 Sch.1

s.58, applied: SI 2004/1910 Sch.1

s.62, applied: SI 2002/1831

s.64, applied: SI 2002/1831

s.64, repealed: 2003 c.41 Sch.4

s.65, applied: SI 2003/1247 Art.11

s.65, repealed: SI 2004/431 Art.2

s.65, varied: SI 2002/365 Art.2, SI 2003/427 Art.2

s.66, repealed: SI 2004/431 Art.2

s.66, varied: SI 2002/365 Art.2, SI 2003/427 Art.2

s.67, see *Shaw's Application for Judicial Review, Re* [2004] N.I. 149 (QBD (NI)), Kerr, J.

s.67, applied: 2004 c.4 s.11, Sch.2 para.3, Sch.2 para.4

s.67, repealed: SI 2004/431 Art.2

s.67, varied: SI 2002/365 Art.2, SI 2003/427 Art.2

s.68, repealed: SI 2003/435 Sch.5, SI 2004/431 Art.2

s.68, varied: SI 2002/365 Art.2, SI 2003/427 Art.2

s.69, amended: SI 2003/1247 Sch.2

s.69, repealed: SI 2004/431 Art.2

s.69, varied: SI 2002/365 Art.2, SI 2003/427 Art.2

s.70, amended: 2002 c.26 Sch.11 para.23

s.70, repealed: SI 2004/431 Art.2

s.70, varied: SI 2002/365 Art.2, SI 2003/427 Art.2

s.71, repealed: SI 2004/431 Art.2

s.71, varied: SI 2002/365 Art.2, SI 2003/427 Art.2

s.72, see *Shaw's Application for Judicial Review, Re* [2004] N.I. 149 (QBD (NI)), Kerr, J.

s.72, amended: 2002 c.26 Sch.7 para.22, SI 2004/1500 Art.29

s.72, repealed: SI 2004/431 Art.2

s.72, varied: SI 2002/365 Art.2, SI 2003/427 Art.2

s.73, repealed: SI 2004/431 Art.2

s.73, varied: SI 2002/365 Art.2, SI 2003/427 Art.2

s.74, repealed: SI 2004/431 Art.2

s.74, varied: SI 2002/365 Art.2, SI 2003/427 Art.2

s.75, applied: 2004 c.28 s.21

s.75, repealed: SI 2004/431 Art.2

2000–cont.

11. Terrorism Act 2000–*cont.*

s.75, varied: SI 2002/365 Art.2, SI 2003/427 Art.2

s.76, repealed: SI 2002/2141 Art.2, SI 2004/431 Art.2

s.76, varied: SI 2002/365 Art.2, SI 2003/427 Art.2

s.77, see *R. v Shoukri* [2004] N.I. 181 (CA (Crim Div) (NI)), Lord Carswell L.C.J.

s.77, amended: SI 2004/702 Sch.7 para.23

s.77, repealed: SI 2004/431 Art.2

s.77, varied: SI 2002/365 Art.2, SI 2003/427 Art.2

s.78, amended: 2002 c.26 Sch.11 para.24

s.78, repealed: SI 2004/431 Art.2

s.78, varied: SI 2002/365 Art.2, SI 2003/427 Art.2

s.79, repealed: SI 2004/431 Art.2

s.79, varied: SI 2002/365 Art.2, SI 2003/427 Art.2

s.80, repealed: SI 2004/431 Art.2

s.80, varied: SI 2002/365 Art.2, SI 2003/427 Art.2

s.81, repealed: SI 2004/431 Art.2

s.81, varied: SI 2002/365 Art.2, SI 2003/427 Art.2

s.82, repealed: SI 2004/431 Art.2

s.82, varied: SI 2002/365 Art.2, SI 2003/427 Art.2

s.83, repealed: SI 2004/431 Art.2

s.83, varied: SI 2002/365 Art.2, SI 2003/427 Art.2

s.84, repealed: SI 2004/431 Art.2

s.84, varied: SI 2002/365 Art.2, SI 2003/427 Art.2

s.85, repealed: SI 2004/431 Art.2

s.85, varied: SI 2002/365 Art.2, SI 2003/427 Art.2

s.86, repealed: SI 2004/431 Art.2

s.86, varied: SI 2002/365 Art.2, SI 2003/427 Art.2

s.87, repealed: SI 2004/431 Art.2

s.87, varied: SI 2002/365 Art.2, SI 2003/427 Art.2

s.88, repealed: SI 2004/431 Art.2

s.88, varied: SI 2002/365 Art.2, SI 2003/427 Art.2

s.89, repealed: SI 2004/431 Art.2

s.89, varied: SI 2002/365 Art.2, SI 2003/427 Art.2

s.90, repealed: SI 2004/431 Art.2

s.90, varied: SI 2002/365 Art.2, SI 2003/427 Art.2

s.91, repealed: SI 2004/431 Art.2

s.91, varied: SI 2002/365 Art.2, SI 2003/427 Art.2

s.92, repealed: SI 2004/431 Art.2

s.92, varied: SI 2002/365 Art.2, SI 2003/427 Art.2

s.93, repealed: SI 2004/431 Art.2

2000–cont.

11. Terrorism Act 2000–*cont.*

s.93, varied: SI 2002/365 Art.2, SI 2003/427 Art.2

s.94, repealed: SI 2004/431 Art.2

s.94, varied: SI 2002/365 Art.2, SI 2003/427 Art.2

s.95, repealed: SI 2004/431 Art.2

s.95, varied: SI 2002/365 Art.2, SI 2003/427 Art.2

s.96, repealed: SI 2004/431 Art.2

s.96, varied: SI 2002/365 Art.2, SI 2003/427 Art.2

s.97, repealed (in part): SI 2003/427 Art.2, SI 2004/431 Art.2, Art.2

s.97, varied: SI 2002/365 Art.2, SI 2003/427 Art.2

s.98, repealed: SI 2004/431 Art.2

s.98, varied: SI 2002/365 Art.2, SI 2003/427 Art.2

s.99, repealed: SI 2004/431 Art.2

s.99, varied: SI 2002/365 Art.2, SI 2003/427 Art.2

s.100, repealed: SI 2004/431 Art.2

s.100, varied: SI 2002/365 Art.2, SI 2003/427 Art.2

s.101, amended: 2003 c.6 Sch.3 para.8

s.101, repealed: SI 2004/431 Art.2

s.101, varied: SI 2002/365 Art.2, SI 2003/427 Art.2

s.102, repealed: SI 2004/431 Art.2

s.102, varied: SI 2002/365 Art.2, SI 2003/427 Art.2

s.103, amended: 2004 c.4 s.14

s.103, repealed: SI 2004/431 Art.2

s.103, varied: SI 2002/365 Art.2, SI 2003/427 Art.2

s.104, repealed: SI 2004/431 Art.2

s.104, varied: SI 2002/365 Art.2, SI 2003/427 Art.2

s.105, repealed: SI 2004/431 Art.2

s.105, varied: SI 2002/365 Art.2, SI 2003/427 Art.2

s.106, repealed: SI 2004/431 Art.2

s.106, varied: SI 2002/365 Art.2, SI 2003/427 Art.2

s.107, repealed: SI 2004/431 Art.2

s.107, varied: SI 2002/365 Art.2, SI 2003/427 Art.2

s.108, repealed: SI 2004/431 Art.2

s.108, varied: SI 2002/365 Art.2, SI 2003/427 Art.2

s.109, repealed: SI 2004/431 Art.2

s.109, varied: SI 2002/365 Art.2, SI 2003/427 Art.2

s.110, repealed: SI 2004/431 Art.2

s.110, varied: SI 2002/365 Art.2, SI 2003/427 Art.2

s.111, applied: 2002 c.29 s.82, s.148, s.163, s.230

s.111, repealed: SI 2004/431 Art.2

2000–cont.

11. Terrorism Act 2000–*cont.*

s.111, varied: SI 2002/365 Art.2, SI 2003/427 Art.2

s.112, repealed: SI 2004/431 Art.2

s.112, varied: SI 2002/365 Art.2, SI 2003/427 Art.2

s.112, enabling: SI 2002/365, SI 2002/2141, SI 2003/427

s.113, repealed: SI 2004/431 Art.2

s.113, varied: SI 2002/365 Art.2, SI 2003/427 Art.2

s.117, amended: 2002 c.26 Sch.7 para.35

s.118, see *Attorney General's Reference (No.4 of 2002), Re* [2003] EWCA Crim 762, [2003] 3 W.L.R. 1153 (CA (Crim Div)), Latham, L.J.; see *R. v Shoukri* [2004] N.I. 181 (CA (Crim Div) (NI)), Lord Carswell L.C.J.

s.121, see *O'Driscoll v Secretary of State for the Home Department* [2002] EWHC 2477, [2003] A.C.D. 35 (QBD), Kennedy, L.J.

s.121, amended: 2003 c.20 Sch.5 para.4, 2003 c.32 Sch.5 para.76, SI 2004/1573 Art.12

s.121, varied: 2003 c.20 Sch.5 para.4

s.122, varied: 2003 c.20 Sch.5 para.4

s.123, amended: 2003 c.32 Sch.4 para.2, Sch.5 para.77

s.123, applied: SI 2003/427, SI 2003/1100

s.123, enabling: SI 2004/431

Sch.2, amended: SI 2002/2724 Art.2, Art.3

Sch.3 para.5, enabling: SI 2002/1843

Sch.3A Part I para.1, substituted: SI 2003/3076 Sch.1

Sch.3A Part I para.2, substituted: SI 2003/3076 Sch.1

Sch.3A Part I para.2, amended: SI 2003/3076 Sch.1

Sch.3A Part I para.2, substituted: SI 2003/3076 Sch.1

Sch.3A Part I para.3, amended: SI 2003/3076 Sch.1

Sch.3A Part I para.3, substituted: SI 2003/3076 Sch.1

Sch.3A Part II para.4, amended: 2002 c.40 Sch.25 para.41, SI 2003/3076 Art.3, 2004 c.35 Sch.12 para.78

Sch.3A Part III para.5, enabling: SI 2003/3076

Sch.4 Part I, added: 2003 c.32 Sch.4 para.3

Sch.4 Part I para.4, amended: 2003 c.39 Sch.8 para.388

Sch.4 Part I para.5, applied: SI 2003/1417 r.93

Sch.4 Part I para.8, amended: 2002 c.9 Sch.11 para.38

Sch.4 Part I para.8, repealed (in part): 2002 c.9 Sch.13

Sch.4 Part I para.11, amended: 2003 c.44 Sch.36 para.14

2000–cont.

11. Terrorism Act 2000–*cont.*

Sch.4 Part I para.11, substituted: 2003 c.44 Sch.36 para.14

Sch.4 Part I para.13, amended: 2003 c.39 Sch.8 para.388

Sch.4 Part I para.14, amended: 2003 c.32 Sch.4 para.4

Sch.4 Part II, added: 2003 c.32 Sch.4 para.5

Sch.4 Part II para.28, amended: 2003 c.32 Sch.4 para.6

Sch.4 Part III, added: 2003 c.32 Sch.4 para.7

Sch.4 Part III para.36, repealed: SI 2003/427 Art.2

Sch.4 Part III para.44, amended: 2003 c.32 Sch.4 para.8

Sch.4 Part IV para.45, amended: 2003 c.32 Sch.4 para.9

Sch.4 Part IV para.46, amended: 2003 c.39 Sch.8 para.388

Sch.5 Part I para.3, amended: 2003 c.44 Sch.26 para.55

Sch.5 Part I para.5, amended: 2003 c.39 Sch.4 para.9

Sch.5 Part I para.6, amended: 2003 c.39 Sch.4 para.9

Sch.5 Part I para.7, amended: 2003 c.39 Sch.4 para.9

Sch.5 Part I para.10, amended: 2003 c.39 Sch.4 para.9, Sch.8 para.389

Sch.5 Part I para.11, amended: 2003 c.39 Sch.4 para.9

Sch.5 Part I para.12, amended: 2003 c.39 Sch.4 para.9

Sch.5 Part I para.13, amended: 2003 c.39 Sch.4 para.9

Sch.5 Part I para.15, amended: 2003 c.44 Sch.26 para.55

Sch.5 Part I para.18, amended: 2003 c.39 Sch.8 para.389

Sch.5 Part I para.19, repealed: SI 2003/427 Art.2

Sch.5 Part I para.20, repealed: SI 2003/427 Art.2

Sch.5 Part I para.21, repealed: SI 2003/427 Art.2

Sch.6 para.3, amended: 2003 c.39 Sch.4 para.10

Sch.6 para.4, amended: 2003 c.39 Sch.8 para.390

Sch.6A para.2, amended: 2003 c.39 Sch.4 para.11

Sch.6A para.5, enabling: SR 2003/71

Sch.7, see *R. v Hundal (Avtar Singh)* [2004] EWCA Crim 389, [2004] 2 Cr. App. R. 19 (CA (Crim Div)), Lord Woolf of Barnes, L.C.J.

Sch.7, applied: SI 2003/705 Art.3, SI 2003/1100, SI 2003/1100 Art.2, SI 2003/2818 Art.11, SI 2004/81 Art.2

Sch.7 para.1, varied: SI 2003/2818 Sch.2 para.2

2000–cont.

11. Terrorism Act 2000–*cont.*

Sch.7 para.2, varied: SI 2003/2818 Sch.2 para.2

Sch.7 para.3, varied: SI 2003/2818 Sch.2 para.2

Sch.7 para.4, varied: SI 2003/2818 Sch.2 para.2

Sch.7 para.5, varied: SI 2003/2818 Sch.2 para.2

Sch.7 para.6, varied: SI 2003/2818 Sch.2 para.2

Sch.7 para.7, varied: SI 2003/2818 Sch.2 para.2

Sch.7 para.8, varied: SI 2003/2818 Sch.2 para.2

Sch.7 para.9, varied: SI 2003/2818 Sch.2 para.2

Sch.7 para.12, varied: SI 2003/2818 Sch.2 para.2

Sch.7 para.13, varied: SI 2003/2818 Sch.2 para.2

Sch.7 para.14, varied: SI 2003/2818 Sch.2 para.2

Sch.7 para.15, varied: SI 2003/2818 Sch.2 para.2

Sch.7 para.16, varied: SI 2003/2818 Sch.2 para.2

Sch.7 para.17, applied: SI 2002/1945, SI 2002/1945 Art.2

Sch.7 para.17, varied: SI 2003/2818 Sch.2 para.2

Sch.7 para.17, enabling: SI 2002/1945

Sch.7 para.18, amended: 2003 c.44 Sch.26 para.55

Sch.7 para.18, varied: SI 2003/2818 Art.12, Sch.2 para.2

Sch.8, applied: SI 2003/2818 Art.11

Sch.8 Part I para.1, applied: SI 2003/1100, SI 2003/1100 Art.2, SR 2002/179 Art.2, SR 2003/232 Art.2

Sch.8 Part I para.1, varied: SI 2003/2818 Sch.2 para.2

Sch.8 Part I para.2, applied: 2003 c.6 Sch.2 para.21

Sch.8 Part I para.2, varied: SI 2003/2818 Sch.2 para.2

Sch.8 Part I para.3, applied: SI 2003/1100

Sch.8 Part I para.3, varied: SI 2003/2818 Sch.2 para.2

Sch.8 Part I para.3, enabling: SI 2003/1100

Sch.8 Part I para.4, applied: SI 2003/1100

Sch.8 Part I para.4, varied: SI 2003/2818 Sch.2 para.2

Sch.8 Part I para.4, enabling: SI 2003/1100

Sch.8 Part I para.6, varied: SI 2003/2818 Sch.2 para.2

Sch.8 Part I para.7, varied: SI 2003/2818 Sch.2 para.2

Sch.8 Part I para.8, amended: 2002 c.29 Sch.11 para.39

2000–cont.

11. Terrorism Act 2000–*cont.*

Sch.8 Part I para.8, varied: SI 2003/2818 Sch.2 para.2

Sch.8 Part I para.9, varied: SI 2003/2818 Sch.2 para.2

Sch.8 Part I para.10, applied: 2003 c.6 Sch.2 para.15, Sch.2 para.18

Sch.8 Part I para.10, varied: SI 2003/2818 Sch.2 para.2

Sch.8 Part I para.11, varied: SI 2003/2818 Sch.2 para.2

Sch.8 Part I para.12, varied: SI 2003/2818 Sch.2 para.2

Sch.8 Part I para.13, varied: SI 2003/2818 Sch.2 para.2

Sch.8 Part I para.14, varied: SI 2003/2818 Sch.2 para.2

Sch.8 Part I para.15, varied: SI 2003/2818 Sch.2 para.2

Sch.8 Part I para.16, varied: SI 2003/2818 Sch.2 para.2

Sch.8 Part I para.17, amended: 2002 c.29 Sch.11 para.39

Sch.8 Part I para.17, varied: SI 2003/333 Art.10, SI 2003/2818 Sch.2 para.2

Sch.8 Part I para.18, varied: SI 2003/2818 Sch.2 para.2

Sch.8 Part I para.19, varied: SI 2003/2818 Sch.2 para.2

Sch.8 Part I para.20, varied: SI 2003/2818 Sch.2 para.2

Sch.8 Part II para.24, varied: SI 2003/2818 Sch.2 para.2

Sch.8 Part II para.25, varied: SI 2003/2818 Sch.2 para.2

Sch.8 Part II para.26, varied: SI 2003/2818 Sch.2 para.2

Sch.8 Part II para.27, varied: SI 2003/2818 Sch.2 para.2

Sch.8 Part II para.28, varied: SI 2003/2818 Sch.2 para.2

Sch.8 Part III, applied: SI 2004/81 Art.2

Sch.8 Part III para.29, amended: 2003 c.39 Sch.8 para.391, Sch.10, 2003 c.44 s.306

Sch.8 Part III para.29, applied: SI 2003/435 Art.25, SSI 2003/179 Reg.3, Reg.9

Sch.8 Part III para.34, amended: 2002 c.29 Sch.11 para.39

Sch.8 Part III para.36, amended: 2003 c.44 s.306

Sch.8 Part III para.36, applied: SI 2003/435 Art.25, SSI 2003/179 Reg.3, Reg.9

Sch.9 Part I para.1, amended: 2002 c.26 Sch.7 para.23

Sch.9 Part I para.2, amended: 2002 c.26 Sch.7 para.23

Sch.9 Part I para.16, substituted: SI 2004/702 Sch.7 para.24

Sch.9 Part I para.22A, added: 2004 c.4 Sch.2 para.1

2000–cont.

11. Terrorism Act 2000–*cont.*

Sch.9 Part III, amended: 2002 c.26 Sch.7 para.23

Sch.14, applied: SI 2003/2818 Art.11

Sch.14 para.1, varied: SI 2003/2818 Sch.2 para.2

Sch.14 para.2, varied: SI 2003/2818 Sch.2 para.2

Sch.14 para.3, varied: SI 2003/2818 Sch.2 para.2

Sch.15 para.4, repealed: SI 2003/435 Sch.5

Sch.15 para.6, repealed: 2002 c.29 Sch.12

Sch.15 para.10, repealed: 2002 c.29 Sch.12

Sch.15 para.11, referred to: SSI 2003/210 Art.7

Sch.15 para.11, repealed (in part): 2002 c.29 Sch.12

Sch.15 para.20, repealed: 2003 c.44 Sch.37 Part 7

12. Limited Liability Partnerships Act 2000

applied: 2002 c.29 s.364, s.398, SI 2002/915 Reg.8, Reg.11, Reg.14, SI 2003/1417 r.8, r.9, r.41, r.111, SI 2004/2620 Sch.3

s.2, amended: SI 2002/915 Sch.2 para.1

s.2, applied: SI 2002/915 Reg.8, Reg.11

s.3, applied: SI 2002/915 Reg.8, Reg.11

s.9, amended: SI 2002/915 Sch.2 para.3

s.9, applied: SI 2002/915 Reg.11

s.12, amended: 2003 c.14 Sch.20 para.3

s.15, enabling: SI 2002/913

s.16, enabling: SI 2002/913

s.17, applied: SI 2002/913

s.17, enabling: SI 2002/913

s.18, referred to: SI 2003/1375 Art.6

Sch.1 Part I para.4, applied: SI 2004/2620 Sch.3

Sch.1 Part I para.8, amended: 2004 c.27 Sch.6 para.10

13. Royal Parks (Trading) Act 2000

s.6, applied: SI 2003/336 Sch.1 Part 2

14. Care Standards Act 2000

Commencement Orders: SI 2002/629 Art.2; SI 2002/839 Art.2; SI 2002/920 Art.2, Art.3, Sch.1 para.2, para.4, para.5, para.7, para.8, para.9, Sch.2 para.2; SI 2002/1175 Art.2; SI 2002/1245 Art.2; SI 2002/1493 Art.3; SI 2003/152 Art.2; SI 2002/1493 Art.4; SI 2003/152 Art.3; SI 2003/365 Art.3, Sch.1 para.1, para.2, para.3, para.4, para.5, para.6, para.7; SI 2002/1790 Art.2, Art.3; SI 2004/484 Art.2; SI 2004/1015 Art.2; SI 2004/1730 Art.2; SI 2003/501 Art.2; SI 2003/933 Art.2; SI 2003/2528 Art.2; SI 2002/2001 Art.2; SI 2002/2215 Art.2; SI 2004/1757 Art.2

see *Kingscrest Associates Ltd (t/a Kingscrest Residential Care Homes) v Customs and Excise Commissioners* [2003] B.V.C. 2592 (V&DTr), Adrian Shipwright (Chairman)

2000–cont.

14. Care Standards Act 2000–*cont.*

applied: 2002 c.32 s.168, SI 2002/603 Reg.3, SI 2002/816 Reg.36, SI 2002/920 Sch.1 para.2, SI 2002/1250 Reg.3, SI 2002/3212 Reg.3, SI 2002/3213 Reg.3, 2003 c.43 s.128, s.145, 2003 c.44 s.207, SI 2003/781 Reg.3, SI 2003/3190 Reg.4, SI 2003/3279 Reg.4, SI 2004/219 Reg.3, SI 2004/293 Sch.2 para.16, SI 2004/615 Reg.3, SI 2004/1756 Reg.36, SI 2004/2071 Sch.10 para.2

referred to: 2002 c.38 Sch.3 para.103, SI 2002/919 Reg.3, 2003 c.43 s.189, Sch.4 para.110, Sch.9 para.16

see *Kingscrest Associates Ltd (t/a Kingscrest Residential Care Homes) v Customs and Excise Commissioners* [2003] B.V.C. 2592 (V&DTr), Adrian Shipwright (Chairman)

varied: SI 2004/664 Art.11, Art.12, Art.13, Art.14

see *Kingscrest Associates Ltd (t/a Kingscrest Residential Care Homes) v Customs and Excise Commissioners* [2003] B.V.C. 2592 (V&DTr), Adrian Shipwright (Chairman)

see *Kingscrest Associates Ltd (t/a Kingscrest Residential Care Homes) v Customs and Excise Commissioners* [2003] B.V.C. 2592 (V&DTr), Adrian Shipwright (Chairman)

see *Kingscrest Associates Ltd (t/a Kingscrest Residential Care Homes) v Customs and Excise Commissioners* [2003] B.V.C. 2592 (V&DTr), Adrian Shipwright (Chairman)

Part II, applied: 2002 c.38 s.2, s.6, s.7, s.63, SI 2002/57 Reg.3, Reg.50, Sch.1 para.2, SI 2002/324 Reg.4, Reg.22, Sch.2 para.2, SI 2002/325 Reg.5, Sch.2 para.2, SI 2002/327 Reg.4, Reg.15, Reg.16, Reg.27, SI 2002/603 Reg.3, SI 2002/816 Reg.3, Sch.1 para.1, SI 2002/920 Art.3, Sch.1 para.2, Sch.1 para.3, Sch.1 para.4, Sch.1 para.5, Sch.1 para.6, Sch.1 para.7, Sch.1 para.8, Sch.1 para.9, SI 2002/921 Reg.13i, Reg.5, Reg.6, Reg.7, Reg.8, SI 2002/3212 Reg.4, Sch.2 para.2, SI 2002/3213 Reg.4, Sch.2 para.2, SI 2002/3214 Reg.4, Sch.2 para.2, 2003 c.43 s.102, SI 2003/152 Art.3, SI 2003/237 Reg.3, Reg.52, SI 2003/365 Art.3, Sch.1 para.2, Sch.1 para.3, Sch.1 para.4, Sch.1 para.5, Sch.1 para.6, Sch.1 para.7, SI 2003/367 Reg.2, Reg.3, Sch.1 para.3, SI 2003/368 Reg.3, SI 2003/753 Reg.3, SI 2003/781 Reg.4, Reg.34, SI 2003/2527 Reg.4, Sch.2 para.2, Sch.5 para.1, Sch.5 para.2, Sch.5 para.3, Sch.5 para.4, SI 2003/3190 Reg.4, SI 2003/3279 Reg.4, SI 2004/219 Reg.7, SI 2004/661 Reg.3, SI 2004/662 Reg.3, SI 2004/692 Sch.4 para.5, SI 2004/1756 Reg.3, Reg.7, Sch.1 para.2, SI 2004/2071 Reg.4, Reg.7, Reg.40, Sch.2 para.2, Sch.10 para.2, Sch.10 para.3, Sch.10 para.4

Part II, referred to: SI 2004/1756 Reg.2, Sch.1 para.1

2000–cont.

14. Care Standards Act 2000–*cont.*

Part III, applied: 2003 c.43 s.102

Part IV, applied: SI 2002/816 Reg.4, Sch.6 para.1

s.1, enabling: SI 2002/327

s.2, amended: SI 2002/325 Reg.3, 2003 c.43 s.106

s.2, applied: SI 2002/325 Reg.3, Reg.32, SI 2002/919 Sch.6 para.1, SI 2004/692 Sch.4 para.5

s.2, enabling: SI 2002/325

s.3, applied: SI 2002/324 Reg.19, SI 2002/327 Reg.3, SI 2004/293 Sch.2 para.16, SI 2004/692 Sch.4 para.5

s.3, enabling: SI 2002/324, SI 2002/2935, SI 2003/1845, SI 2004/1756

s.4, amended: 2002 c.38 s.8, Sch.3 para.104, 2003 c.43 s.107, SI 2004/1771 Sch.1 para.2

s.4, applied: SI 2002/57 Reg.3, Reg.50, SI 2003/237 Reg.3, Reg.52

s.4, referred to: SI 2002/919 Reg.9, Sch.1 para.5, Sch.1 para.13, SI 2002/3214 Reg.3, SI 2003/3190 Reg.4

s.4, varied: SI 2002/3214 Reg.3, SI 2004/219 Reg.3

s.4, enabling: SI 2002/3212, SI 2002/3213, SI 2002/3214, SI 2003/781, SI 2003/2527, SI 2003/3054, SI 2004/219, SI 2004/1269

s.5, amended: 2002 c.38 Sch.3 para.105, 2003 c.43 Sch.9 para.17

s.5, applied: 2003 c.43 s.142, s.143, s.145

s.5, varied: SI 2004/664 Art.11, Art.12, Art.13, Art.14

s.5A, added: 2003 c.43 s.103

s.5A, varied: SI 2004/664 Art.11, Art.12, Art.13, Art.14

s.5B, added: 2003 c.43 s.104

s.5B, varied: SI 2004/664 Art.11, Art.12, Art.13, Art.14

s.6, repealed: 2003 c.43 Sch.14 Part 2

s.6, varied: SI 2004/664 Art.11, Art.12, Art.13, Art.14

s.7, repealed: 2003 c.43 Sch.14 Part 2

s.8, amended: 2003 c.43 s.109, Sch.9 para.18

s.8, applied: 2003 c.43 s.142, s.143, s.145

s.9, repealed: 2003 c.43 Sch.14 Part 2

s.9, varied: SI 2004/664 Art.11, Art.12, Art.13, Art.14

s.10, amended: 2003 c.43 Sch.9 para.19

s.10, repealed (in part): 2003 c.43 Sch.14 Part 2

s.11, amended: 2002 c.38 Sch.3 para.106, 2003 c.43 Sch.9 para.20

s.11, applied: SI 2002/635 Sch.1 para.1, SI 2002/896 Sch.1 para.50, SI 2002/920 Art.3, Sch.1 para.5, SI 2003/237 Reg.52, SI 2003/753 Reg.4, SI 2003/781 Reg.34, SI 2004/2071 Sch.10 para.2, SI 2004/2695 Sch.1 para.4

2000–cont.

14. Care Standards Act 2000–*cont.*

s.11, disapplied: SI 2002/920 Art.3, Sch.1 para.2, Sch.1 para.4, Sch.1 para.5, Sch.1 para.7, Sch.1 para.8, Sch.1 para.9, SI 2002/3210 Art.4, SI 2003/237 Reg.52, SI 2003/781 Reg.34

s.11, referred to: SI 2002/920 Sch.1 para.5

s.11, varied: SI 2004/2071 Sch.5 para.1

s.11, enabling: SI 2003/369, SI 2004/2071

s.12, amended: 2003 c.43 s.105

s.12, applied: SI 2002/603 Reg.3, SI 2002/1250 Reg.3, SI 2003/368 Reg.3, SI 2003/753 Reg.3, SI 2004/615 Reg.3, SI 2004/661 Reg.3, SI 2004/662 Reg.3

s.12, varied: SI 2004/2071 Sch.5 para.2

s.12, enabling: SI 2002/865, SI 2002/919, SI 2002/921, SI 2002/1505, SI 2002/2070, SI 2002/2622, SI 2002/2935, SI 2002/3211, SI 2003/368, SI 2003/369, SI 2003/710, SI 2003/753, SI 2003/1845, SI 2003/2323, SI 2004/219, SI 2004/661, SI 2004/662, SI 2004/2071

s.13, applied: SI 2002/635 Reg.2, SI 2004/2695 Sch.1 para.25

s.13, varied: SI 2004/2071 Sch.5 para.3

s.14, amended: 2002 c.38 Sch.3 para.107

s.14, applied: SI 2002/635 Reg.2, SI 2002/816 Sch.1 para.1, SI 2002/919 Reg.14, SI 2003/3190 Reg.4, SI 2003/3279 Reg.4, SI 2004/1972 Reg.2, SI 2004/2695 Sch.1 para.25

s.14, varied: SI 2004/1972 Reg.3, SI 2004/2071 Sch.5 para.4

s.14, enabling: SI 2002/919, SI 2004/219, SI 2004/2071

s.15, amended: 2003 c.43 s.105

s.15, applied: SI 2002/816 Sch.1 para.1, SI 2002/919 Reg.12, SI 2002/921 Reg.4, SI 2003/368 Reg.4, SI 2003/753 Reg.4, SI 2003/2527 Sch.5 para.4, SI 2003/3190 Reg.4, SI 2003/3279 Reg.4, SI 2004/661 Reg.4, SI 2004/662 Reg.4

s.15, enabling: SI 2002/919, SI 2002/921, SI 2003/368, SI 2003/710, SI 2003/753, SI 2004/219, SI 2004/661, SI 2004/662, SI 2004/2071

s.16, amended: 2002 c.38 Sch.3 para.108, Sch.5, 2003 c.43 s.105

s.16, applied: SI 2002/920 Sch.1 para.6, SI 2003/2527 Sch.5 para.1, SI 2004/1972 Reg.2

s.16, varied: SI 2004/1972 Reg.3

s.16, enabling: SI 2002/919, SI 2002/921, SI 2002/1505, SI 2002/2070, SI 2002/2622, SI 2002/2935, SI 2002/3211, SI 2003/237, SI 2003/367, SI 2003/368, SI 2003/369, SI 2003/710, SI 2003/753, SI 2003/781, SI 2003/896, SI 2003/2527, SI 2003/3054, SI 2004/219, SI 2004/661, SI 2004/662, SI 2004/2071

CAP.

2000–cont.

14. Care Standards Act 2000–*cont.*

s.17, applied: SI 2002/920 Sch.1 para.8, SI 2003/365 Sch.1 para.5, SI 2003/2527 Sch.5 para.4

s.17, varied: SI 2004/2071 Sch.5 para.5

s.18, applied: SI 2003/2527 Sch.5 para.4

s.18, varied: SI 2002/920 Sch.1 para.8

s.19, applied: SI 2002/816 Sch.1 para.3, SI 2002/920 Sch.1 para.3, Sch.1 para.6, Sch.1 para.9, SI 2003/365 Sch.1 para.2, SI 2003/2527 Sch.5 para.1, Sch.5 para.2

s.19, varied: SI 2004/2071 Sch.5 para.6

s.20, amended: 2002 c.17 Sch.2 para.70

s.20, applied: SI 2002/635 Reg.2, SI 2002/816 Reg.23, Sch.1 para.1, SI 2003/781 Reg.34, SI 2004/2695 Sch.1 para.25

s.20, referred to: SI 2002/920 Sch.1 para.5

s.20, varied: SI 2002/920 Sch.1 para.5, SI 2003/237 Reg.52, SI 2003/781 Reg.34, SI 2004/2071 Sch.5 para.7

s.21, applied: SI 2002/816 Reg.4, Sch.1 para.1, Sch.1 para.3, SI 2002/920 Sch.1 para.6, SI 2003/2527 Sch.5 para.1, SI 2003/3190 Reg.4, SI 2003/3279 Reg.4, SI 2004/2071 Sch.10 para.5

s.21, referred to: SI 2002/816 Sch.1 para.2, SI 2004/2071 Sch.10 para.5

s.21, varied: SI 2004/2071 Sch.5 para.8

s.22, amended: 2002 c.38 Sch.3 para.109, 2003 c.43 s.105, s.107

s.22, applied: SI 2002/2622, SI 2002/2935, SI 2004/1972 Reg.2, SI 2004/2414

s.22, repealed (in part): 2003 c.43 s.107, Sch.14 Part 2

s.22, varied: SI 2004/1756 Sch.1 para.4, SI 2004/1972 Reg.3

s.22, enabling: SI 2002/57, SI 2002/324, SI 2002/325, SI 2002/327, SI 2002/865, SI 2002/2622, SI 2002/2935, SI 2002/3212, SI 2002/3213, SI 2002/3214, SI 2003/237, SI 2003/534, SI 2003/710, SI 2003/781, SI 2003/896, SI 2003/947, SI 2003/1004, SI 2003/1703, SI 2003/1845, SI 2003/2323, SI 2003/2527, SI 2003/3054, SI 2004/219, SI 2004/1314, SI 2004/1756, SI 2004/1770, SI 2004/2071, SI 2004/2414

s.23, amended: 2002 c.38 Sch.3 para.110, 2003 c.43 Sch.9 para.21

s.23, applied: SI 2002/327 Reg.34, 2003 c.43 s.77, s.79, s.80

s.23, varied: SI 2004/2071 Sch.5 para.9

s.24, applied: SI 2002/635 Sch.1 para.1, SI 2002/896 Sch.1 para.50, SI 2004/2695 Sch.1 para.4

s.24, varied: SI 2004/2071 Sch.5 para.10

s.25, applied: SI 2002/635 Sch.1 para.1, SI 2002/896 Sch.1 para.50, SI 2004/1972 Reg.2, SI 2004/2695 Sch.1 para.4

s.25, enabling: SI 2002/57, SI 2002/324, SI 2002/325, SI 2002/327, SI 2002/865, SI 2002/919, SI 2002/3212, SI 2002/3213,

CAP.

2000–cont.

14. Care Standards Act 2000–*cont.*

s.25, enabling:–*cont.*
SI 2002/3214, SI 2003/237, SI 2003/781, SI 2003/896, SI 2003/1703, SI 2003/2527, SI 2003/3054, SI 2004/219, SI 2004/1756, SI 2004/2071

s.26, applied: SI 2002/635 Sch.1 para.1, SI 2002/896 Sch.1 para.50, SI 2004/2695 Sch.1 para.4

s.26, disapplied: SI 2002/3210 Art.4

s.26, varied: SI 2004/2071 Sch.5 para.11

s.27, applied: SI 2002/635 Sch.1 para.1, SI 2002/896 Sch.1 para.50, SI 2004/2695 Sch.1 para.4

s.28, varied: SI 2004/1756 Sch.1 para.5, SI 2004/2071 Sch.5 para.12

s.29, amended: 2003 c.43 Sch.9 para.22

s.29, applied: SI 2002/324 Reg.44, SI 2002/327 Reg.40

s.31, amended: 2002 c.38 Sch.3 para.111, 2003 c.43 s.108, Sch.9 para.23, Sch.14 Part 2

s.31, applied: SI 2002/327 Reg.15, SI 2002/921 Reg.4, SI 2004/1972 Reg.2

s.31, varied: SI 2002/920 Sch.1 para.6, SI 2004/1756 Sch.1 para.6, SI 2004/1972 Reg.3, SI 2004/2071 Sch.5 para.13

s.31, enabling: SI 2002/1505, SI 2002/2070, SI 2002/3211, SI 2003/368, SI 2003/753, SI 2004/661, SI 2004/662, SI 2004/2071

s.32, repealed (in part): 2003 c.43 Sch.14 Part 2

s.32, varied: SI 2002/920 Sch.1 para.6, SI 2004/2071 Sch.5 para.14

s.33, applied: SI 2004/1972 Reg.2

s.33, varied: SI 2004/1972 Reg.3

s.33, enabling: SI 2002/324, SI 2002/327, SI 2003/710, SI 2004/2071

s.34, applied: SI 2004/1972 Reg.2

s.34, varied: SI 2004/1972 Reg.3, SI 2004/2071 Sch.5 para.15

s.34, enabling: SI 2002/57, SI 2002/325, SI 2002/327, SI 2002/3212, SI 2002/3213, SI 2002/3214, SI 2003/237, SI 2003/367, SI 2003/710, SI 2003/781, SI 2003/896, SI 2003/2527, SI 2003/3054, SI 2004/1756, SI 2004/2071

s.35, applied: SI 2004/1972 Reg.2

s.35, varied: SI 2004/1972 Reg.3, SI 2004/2071 Sch.5 para.16

s.35, enabling: SI 2002/324, SI 2002/325, SI 2002/327, SI 2002/3212, SI 2002/3213, SI 2002/3214, SI 2003/237, SI 2003/710, SI 2003/781, SI 2003/896, SI 2003/2527, SI 2003/3054, SI 2004/219, SI 2004/2071

s.36, applied: SI 2004/1972 Reg.2

s.36, enabling: SI 2002/865

s.36A, added: 2002 c.38 s.16

s.36A, amended: 2002 c.38 Sch.4 para.4, 2003 c.43 Sch.9 para.24

2000–cont.

14. Care Standards Act 2000–*cont.*

s.36A, substituted: 2003 c.43 Sch.9 para.24

s.37, varied: SI 2004/1756 Sch.1 para.7, SI 2004/2071 Sch.5 para.17

s.42, amended: 2003 c.43 Sch.4 para.111, Sch.9 para.25

s.42, applied: SI 2004/1730 Art.2, SI 2004/1756 Reg.3, SI 2004/1972 Reg.2, SI 2004/2071 Reg.40

s.42, enabling: SI 2004/1756, SI 2004/1972, SI 2004/2071

s.43, amended: 2002 c.38 Sch.3 para.112

s.43, referred to: 2003 c.43 s.77, s.79, s.80, s.94

s.44, repealed: 2003 c.43 Sch.14 Part 2

s.45, amended: 2003 c.43 Sch.9 para.26

s.45, repealed (in part): 2003 c.43 Sch.14 Part 2

s.45, enabling: SI 2003/368, SI 2003/753, SI 2004/662

s.46, amended: 2002 c.38 Sch.3 para.113

s.46, repealed: 2003 c.43 Sch.14 Part 2

s.47, repealed: 2003 c.43 Sch.14 Part 2

s.48, amended: 2002 c.38 Sch.3 para.114

s.48, enabling: SI 2002/57, SI 2002/865, SI 2003/237, SI 2003/896

s.49, repealed (in part): 2003 c.43 Sch.14 Part 2

s.51, amended: 2003 c.43 Sch.9 para.27

s.51, repealed: 2003 c.43 Sch.14 Part 2

s.51, enabling: SI 2003/368, SI 2003/753, SI 2004/662

s.52, enabling: SI 2002/57

s.54, applied: SI 2002/797 Art.3, SI 2002/1176 Reg.3

s.55, amended: 2002 c.38 Sch.3 para.115, 2003 c.43 Sch.9 para.28

s.55, applied: SI 2004/561 Reg.2, SI 2004/2880 Art.2

s.55, referred to: SI 2002/1176 Reg.3

s.55, enabling: SI 2002/1176, SI 2004/561, SI 2004/711

s.56, applied: 2002 c.38 s.10, SI 2004/562 Art.2, SI 2004/709 Art.2, SI 2004/711 Reg.3, SI 2004/2880 Art.2

s.56, enabling: SI 2004/562, SI 2004/709, SI 2004/2880

s.58, applied: SI 2004/2253 Reg.3

s.62, applied: SI 2002/324 Reg.18

s.63, applied: SI 2004/561 Reg.2

s.64, amended: SI 2004/1947 Reg.20

s.68, applied: SI 2002/816 Reg.4, Sch.6 para.1

s.70, enabling: SI 2002/797

s.72B, applied: 2004 c.31 s.5

s.73, applied: 2004 c.31 s.5

s.74, applied: 2004 c.31 s.5

s.76, amended: 2004 c.31 s.61

s.79, referred to: SI 2002/819 Reg.4, SI 2002/920 Sch.2 para.2

s.80, amended: SI 2004/2070 Reg.2

2000–cont.

14. Care Standards Act 2000–*cont.*

s.81, applied: SI 2002/233 Reg.8, SI 2003/3190 Reg.4, SR 2002/386 Reg.4

s.82, applied: SI 2002/816 Reg.8, Sch.5 para.4

s.83, applied: SI 2002/816 Reg.8, Sch.5 para.4

s.84, applied: SI 2002/816 Reg.8, Sch.5 para.4

s.85, applied: SI 2002/816 Reg.8, Sch.5 para.4

s.86, applied: SI 2002/816 Reg.4, Sch.5 para.1, Sch.5 para.2

s.89, amended: 2003 c.43 s.189

s.92, applied: SI 2002/816 Reg.8

s.93, enabling: SI 2004/2070

s.95, varied: SI 2004/664 Art.11, Art.12, Art.13, Art.14

s.100, repealed (in part): 2002 c.32 Sch.22 Part 3

s.104, repealed (in part): 2003 c.44 Sch.37 Part 11

s.105, varied: SI 2004/664 Art.11, Art.12, Art.13, Art.14

s.113, amended: 2003 c.43 Sch.9 para.29, Sch.14 Part 2

s.113, applied: SI 2003/237 Sch.1 para.2

s.113A, added: 2003 c.43 s.105

s.115, applied: SI 2003/237 Sch.1 para.2, Sch.3 para.13

s.117, applied: SI 2002/920 Sch.1 para.4, Sch.1 para.9

s.117, referred to: SI 2002/920 Sch.1 para.4

s.117, varied: SI 2002/920 Sch.1 para.2, Sch.1 para.4

s.118, enabling: SI 2002/57, SI 2002/324, SI 2002/325, SI 2002/327, SI 2002/629, SI 2002/797, SI 2002/839, SI 2002/865, SI 2002/919, SI 2002/920, SI 2002/921, SI 2002/1175, SI 2002/1176, SI 2002/1245, SI 2002/1493, SI 2002/1505, SI 2002/1790, SI 2002/2001, SI 2002/2070, SI 2002/2215, SI 2002/2622, SI 2002/2935, SI 2002/3210, SI 2002/3211, SI 2002/3212, SI 2002/3213, SI 2002/3214, SI 2003/152, SI 2003/237, SI 2003/365, SI 2003/367, SI 2003/368, SI 2003/369, SI 2003/501, SI 2003/534, SI 2003/710, SI 2003/753, SI 2003/781, SI 2003/896, SI 2003/947, SI 2003/1004, SI 2003/1703, SI 2003/1845, SI 2003/2323, SI 2003/2527, SI 2003/2528, SI 2003/3054, SI 2004/219, SI 2004/561, SI 2004/562, SI 2004/661, SI 2004/662, SI 2004/711, SI 2004/1015, SI 2004/1269, SI 2004/1314, SI 2004/1730, SI 2004/1756, SI 2004/1757, SI 2004/1770, SI 2004/2070, SI 2004/2071, SI 2004/2414

s.119, enabling: SI 2002/546, SI 2002/920

2000–cont.

14. Care Standards Act 2000–cont.

s.121, amended: 2002 c.17 Sch.5 para.46, 2002 c.38 Sch.3 para.116, SI 2002/2469 Sch.1 para.27, 2003 c.43 Sch.4 para.112, Sch.9 para.30, Sch.14 Part 2

s.122, enabling: SI 2002/629, SI 2002/839, SI 2002/920, SI 2002/1175, SI 2002/1245, SI 2002/1493, SI 2002/1790, SI 2002/2001, SI 2002/2215, SI 2002/3210, SI 2003/152, SI 2003/365, SI 2003/501, SI 2003/933, SI 2003/2528, SI 2004/484, SI 2004/1015, SI 2004/1730, SI 2004/1757

Sch.1 para.1, amended: 2003 c.43 Sch.14 Part 2

Sch.1 para.9, repealed: 2003 c.43 Sch.14 Part 2

Sch.1 para.10, repealed: 2003 c.43 Sch.14 Part 2

Sch.1 para.10, enabling: SI 2002/1250

Sch.1 para.11, repealed: 2003 c.43 Sch.14 Part 2

Sch.1 para.11, enabling: SI 2002/603

Sch.1 para.15, repealed: 2003 c.43 Sch.14 Part 2

Sch.1 para.17, repealed: 2003 c.43 Sch.14 Part 2

Sch.1 para.22, varied: SI 2004/664 Art.11, Art.12, Art.13, Art.14

Sch.1 para.23, varied: SI 2004/664 Art.11, Art.12, Art.13, Art.14

Sch.1 para.24, varied: SI 2004/664 Art.11, Art.12, Art.13, Art.14

Sch.1 para.25, varied: SI 2004/664 Art.11, Art.12, Art.13, Art.14

Sch.1 para.27, repealed (in part): 2004 c.23 Sch.4

Sch.2A para.24, repealed: SI 2004/1771 Sch.1 para.2

Sch.4 para.2, repealed: 2003 c.42 Sch.7

Sch.4 para.5, repealed: 2002 c.38 Sch.5

Sch.4 para.7, repealed: 2003 c.39 Sch.10

Sch.4 para.13, repealed: 2003 c.1 Sch.8 Part 1

Sch.4 para.14, varied: SI 2004/664 Art.11, Art.12, Art.13, Art.14

Sch.4 para.16, repealed: 2004 c.28 Sch.11

Sch.4 para.24, repealed (in part): 2002 c.32 Sch.22 Part 3

Sch.4 para.25, repealed (in part): 2003 c.44 Sch.37 Part 11

Sch.4 para.27, repealed (in part): 2002 c.38 Sch.3 para.117, Sch.5

Sch.6, applied: SI 2002/920 Sch.1 para.4, Sch.1 para.9, SI 2002/1493 Art.4

Sch.6, referred to: SI 2002/920 Sch.3 para.3, Sch.3 para.4

15. Television Licences (Disclosure of Information) Act 2000

s.5, amended: 2003 c.21 Sch.17 para.159

2000–cont.

16. Carers and Disabled Children Act 2000

Commencement Orders: SI 2003/1183 Art.2

s.1, amended: 2004 c.15 s.2

s.1, applied: 2003 c.5 s.4

s.1, referred to: 2004 c.15 s.3

s.2, applied: 2003 c.5 s.4, s.15, SI 2003/762 Reg.4, SI 2004/1748 Reg.3

s.3, enabling: SI 2003/1216

s.6, see *R. (on the application of J) v Newham LBC* [2001] EWHC Admin 992, (2002) 5 C.C.L. Rep. 302 (QBD (Admin Ct)), Scott Baker, J.

s.6, amended: 2004 c.15 s.2

s.6, referred to: 2004 c.15 s.3

s.6A, added: 2004 c.15 s.1

s.12, enabling: SI 2003/1183

17. Finance Act 2000

applied: 2002 c.18 Sch.2 Part 2, Sch.2 Part 30, 2003 c.13 Sch.2 Part 34, 2004 c.9 Sch.2 Part 32

referred to: 2003 c.1 Sch.6 para.242

s.30, enabling: SI 2002/1152, SI 2003/560, SI 2003/604, SI 2003/665, SI 2003/861, SI 2003/2633

s.34, repealed: 2002 c.21 Sch.6

s.38, amended: 2003 c.14 s.146, 2003 c.1 Sch.6 para.243

s.38, applied: SI 2003/1745 Reg.1

s.38, repealed (in part): 2003 c.1 Sch.8 Part 1

s.38, enabling: SI 2003/1745

s.47, repealed: 2003 c.1 Sch.8 Part 1

s.49, applied: 2003 c.1 s.418

s.49, referred to: 2003 c.1 s.418

s.56, repealed: 2003 c.1 Sch.8 Part 1

s.57, repealed: 2003 c.1 Sch.8 Part 1

s.58, repealed: 2003 c.1 Sch.8 Part 1

s.59, repealed: 2003 c.1 Sch.8 Part 1

s.60, see *R. (on the application of Professional Contractors Group Ltd) v Inland Revenue Commissioners* [2001] EWCA Civ 1945, [2002] S.T.C. 165 (CA), Robert Walker, L.J.

s.60, repealed: 2003 c.1 Sch.8 Part 1

s.61, repealed: 2004 c.12 Sch.42 Part 3

s.62, repealed: 2003 c.1 Sch.8 Part 1

s.84, amended: 2002 c.21 Sch.6

s.84, referred to: 2003 c.1 s.655

s.85, referred to: 2003 c.1 s.655

s.106, repealed: 2002 c.23 Sch.40 Part 3

s.107, amended: 2003 c.14 s.153

s.107, enabling: SI 2003/2862

s.114, amended: 2003 c.14 Sch.20 para.3

s.118, amended: 2003 c.14 Sch.20 para.3

s.119, amended: 2003 c.14 Sch.20 para.3

s.120, amended: 2003 c.14 Sch.20 para.3

s.121, amended: 2003 c.14 Sch.20 para.3

s.122, amended: 2003 c.14 Sch.20 para.3

s.128, amended: 2002 c.9 Sch.11 para.39

s.131, amended: 2003 c.14 Sch.20 para.3

2000–cont.

17. Finance Act 2000–*cont.*

s.143, enabling: SI 2003/2495, SI 2004/1675

Sch.6 Part II para.5, amended: 2003 c.14 s.191

Sch.6 Part II para.6, amended: 2003 c.14 s.191

Sch.6 Part II para.13, amended: 2004 c.12 s.289

Sch.6 Part II para.13A, added: 2004 c.12 s.289

Sch.6 Part II para.14, amended: 2003 c.14 s.188

Sch.6 Part II para.15, amended: 2003 c.14 s.189

Sch.6 Part II para.15, repealed (in part): 2003 c.14 s.189, Sch.43 Part 4

Sch.6 Part II para.16, enabling: SI 2003/861

Sch.6 Part II para.18, enabling: SI 2003/560, SI 2003/665

Sch.6 Part II para.18A, added: 2003 c.14 s.188

Sch.6 Part II para.19, amended: 2002 c.23 s.126

Sch.6 Part II para.19, enabling: SI 2003/604, SI 2003/2633

Sch.6 Part II para.20, amended: 2002 c.23 s.125, 2003 c.14 s.193

Sch.6 Part II para.20, repealed (in part): 2002 c.23 s.125, Sch.40 Part 4

Sch.6 Part II para.20A, added: 2002 c.23 s.123

Sch.6 Part II para.20A, enabling: SI 2003/604

Sch.6 Part II para.20B, added: 2002 c.23 s.123

Sch.6 Part II para.20B, amended: 2003 c.14 s.193

Sch.6 Part II para.22, enabling: SI 2003/604

Sch.6 Part II para.24, amended: 2003 c.14 s.190

Sch.6 Part III para.34, amended: 2003 c.14 s.190

Sch.6 Part IV para.41, amended: 2003 c.14 s.192, Sch.43 Part 4

Sch.6 Part IV para.41, enabling: SI 2002/1152, SI 2003/604

Sch.6 Part V para.53, amended: 2003 c.14 s.192

Sch.6 Part VI para.62, amended: 2003 c.14 s.192

Sch.6 Part VI para.75, amended: SI 2003/2096 Sch.1 para.32

Sch.6 Part VII para.78, amended: 2003 c.14 s.192

Sch.6 Part VII para.91, amended: 2003 c.14 s.192

Sch.6 Part VIII para.93, amended: 2003 c.14 s.192

Sch.6 Part VIII para.100, amended: 2003 c.14 s.192, Sch.43 Part 4

2000–cont.

17. Finance Act 2000–*cont.*

Sch.6 Part VIII para.101, amended: 2002 c.23 s.127, 2003 c.14 s.188

Sch.6 Part X para.120, amended: SI 2003/2096 Sch.1 para.33

Sch.6 Part XII para.125, amended: 2003 c.14 s.192

Sch.6 Part XII para.125, enabling: SI 2003/604

Sch.6 Part XII para.126, repealed (in part): 2003 c.44 Sch.37 Part 6, SI 2004/1501 Sch.2

Sch.6 Part XII para.135, amended: 2003 c.14 s.192

Sch.6 Part XIII para.141A, added: 2002 c.23 s.128

Sch.6 Part XIII para.146, amended: 2003 c.14 s.188

Sch.6 Part XIII para.146, applied: SI 2003/665, SI 2003/861

Sch.6 Part XIII para.146, enabling: SI 2003/560, SI 2003/604, SI 2003/665, SI 2003/861, SI 2003/2633

Sch.6 Part XIV para.147, amended: 2003 c.14 s.188

Sch.6 Part XIV para.148, amended: 2003 c.14 s.189

Sch.6 Part XIV para.148, repealed (in part): 2003 c.14 s.189, Sch.43 Part 4

Sch.6 Part XIV para.149, amended: 2003 c.14 s.189, Sch.43 Part 4

Sch.6 Part XIV para.149A, added: 2002 c.23 s.124

Sch.6 Part XIV para.149A, enabling: SI 2003/604

Sch.7 para.2, repealed: 2002 c.40 Sch.26

Sch.7 para.3, repealed: 2002 c.40 Sch.26

Sch.8, applied: 2003 c.1 Sch.7 para.68

Sch.8 Part I para.1, repealed: 2003 c.1 Sch.8 Part 1

Sch.8 Part I para.2, repealed: 2003 c.1 Sch.8 Part 1

Sch.8 Part I para.3, repealed: 2003 c.1 Sch.8 Part 1

Sch.8 Part I para.4, repealed: 2003 c.1 Sch.8 Part 1

Sch.8 Part I para.5, repealed: 2003 c.1 Sch.8 Part 1

Sch.8 Part II para.6, repealed: 2003 c.1 Sch.8 Part 1

Sch.8 Part II para.7, repealed: 2003 c.1 Sch.8 Part 1

Sch.8 Part II para.8, repealed: 2003 c.1 Sch.8 Part 1

Sch.8 Part II para.9, repealed: 2003 c.1 Sch.8 Part 1

Sch.8 Part II para.10, repealed: 2003 c.1 Sch.8 Part 1

Sch.8 Part II para.11, repealed: 2003 c.1 Sch.8 Part 1

2000–cont.

17. Finance Act 2000–*cont.*

Sch.8 Part II para.12, repealed: 2003 c.1 Sch.8 Part 1

Sch.8 Part III para.13, repealed: 2003 c.1 Sch.8 Part 1

Sch.8 Part III para.14, repealed: 2003 c.1 Sch.8 Part 1

Sch.8 Part III para.15, repealed: 2003 c.1 Sch.8 Part 1

Sch.8 Part III para.16, repealed: 2003 c.1 Sch.8 Part 1

Sch.8 Part III para.17, repealed: 2003 c.1 Sch.8 Part 1

Sch.8 Part III para.18, repealed: 2003 c.1 Sch.8 Part 1

Sch.8 Part III para.19, repealed: 2003 c.1 Sch.8 Part 1

Sch.8 Part III para.20, repealed: 2003 c.1 Sch.8 Part 1

Sch.8 Part III para.21, repealed: 2003 c.1 Sch.8 Part 1

Sch.8 Part III para.22, repealed: 2003 c.1 Sch.8 Part 1

Sch.8 Part IV para.23, repealed: 2003 c.1 Sch.8 Part 1

Sch.8 Part IV para.24, repealed: 2003 c.1 Sch.8 Part 1

Sch.8 Part IV para.25, repealed: 2003 c.1 Sch.8 Part 1

Sch.8 Part IV para.26, repealed: 2003 c.1 Sch.8 Part 1

Sch.8 Part IV para.27, repealed: 2003 c.1 Sch.8 Part 1

Sch.8 Part IV para.28, repealed: 2003 c.1 Sch.8 Part 1

Sch.8 Part IV para.29, repealed: 2003 c.1 Sch.8 Part 1

Sch.8 Part IV para.30, repealed: 2003 c.1 Sch.8 Part 1

Sch.8 Part IV para.31, repealed: 2003 c.1 Sch.8 Part 1

Sch.8 Part IV para.32, repealed: 2003 c.1 Sch.8 Part 1

Sch.8 Part V para.33, repealed: 2003 c.1 Sch.8 Part 1

Sch.8 Part V para.34, repealed: 2003 c.1 Sch.8 Part 1

Sch.8 Part V para.35, repealed: 2003 c.1 Sch.8 Part 1

Sch.8 Part V para.36, repealed: 2003 c.1 Sch.8 Part 1

Sch.8 Part V para.37, repealed: 2003 c.1 Sch.8 Part 1

Sch.8 Part V para.38, repealed: 2003 c.1 Sch.8 Part 1

Sch.8 Part V para.39, repealed: 2003 c.1 Sch.8 Part 1

Sch.8 Part V para.40, repealed: 2003 c.1 Sch.8 Part 1

Sch.8 Part V para.41, repealed: 2003 c.1 Sch.8 Part 1

2000–cont.

17. Finance Act 2000–*cont.*

Sch.8 Part V para.42, repealed: 2003 c.1 Sch.8 Part 1

Sch.8 Part V para.43, repealed: 2003 c.1 Sch.8 Part 1

Sch.8 Part V para.44, repealed: 2003 c.1 Sch.8 Part 1

Sch.8 Part V para.45, repealed: 2003 c.1 Sch.8 Part 1

Sch.8 Part V para.46, repealed: 2003 c.1 Sch.8 Part 1

Sch.8 Part V para.47, repealed: 2003 c.1 Sch.8 Part 1

Sch.8 Part V para.48, repealed: 2003 c.1 Sch.8 Part 1

Sch.8 Part VI para.49, repealed: 2003 c.1 Sch.8 Part 1

Sch.8 Part VI para.50, repealed: 2003 c.1 Sch.8 Part 1

Sch.8 Part VI para.51, repealed: 2003 c.1 Sch.8 Part 1

Sch.8 Part VI para.52, repealed: 2003 c.1 Sch.8 Part 1

Sch.8 Part VII para.53, repealed: 2003 c.1 Sch.8 Part 1

Sch.8 Part VII para.54, repealed: 2003 c.1 Sch.8 Part 1

Sch.8 Part VII para.55, repealed: 2003 c.1 Sch.8 Part 1

Sch.8 Part VII para.56, repealed: 2003 c.1 Sch.8 Part 1

Sch.8 Part VII para.57, repealed: 2003 c.1 Sch.8 Part 1

Sch.8 Part VII para.58, repealed: 2003 c.1 Sch.8 Part 1

Sch.8 Part VIII para.59, repealed: 2003 c.1 Sch.8 Part 1

Sch.8 Part VIII para.60, repealed: 2003 c.1 Sch.8 Part 1

Sch.8 Part VIII para.61, repealed: 2003 c.1 Sch.8 Part 1

Sch.8 Part VIII para.62, repealed: 2003 c.1 Sch.8 Part 1

Sch.8 Part VIII para.63, repealed: 2003 c.1 Sch.8 Part 1

Sch.8 Part VIII para.64, repealed: 2003 c.1 Sch.8 Part 1

Sch.8 Part VIII para.65, repealed: 2003 c.1 Sch.8 Part 1

Sch.8 Part VIII para.66, repealed: 2003 c.1 Sch.8 Part 1

Sch.8 Part VIII para.67, repealed: 2003 c.1 Sch.8 Part 1

Sch.8 Part IX para.68, amended: 2002 c.34 s.1

Sch.8 Part IX para.68, repealed: 2003 c.1 Sch.8 Part 1

Sch.8 Part IX para.69, repealed: 2003 c.1 Sch.8 Part 1

Sch.8 Part IX para.70, repealed: 2003 c.1 Sch.8 Part 1

2000–cont.

17. Finance Act 2000–*cont.*

Sch.8 Part IX para.71, repealed: 2003 c.1 Sch.8 Part 1

Sch.8 Part IX para.72, repealed: 2003 c.1 Sch.8 Part 1

Sch.8 Part IX para.73, repealed: 2003 c.1 Sch.8 Part 1

Sch.8 Part IX para.74, repealed: 2003 c.1 Sch.8 Part 1

Sch.8 Part IX para.75, repealed: 2003 c.1 Sch.8 Part 1

Sch.8 Part IX para.76, repealed: 2003 c.1 Sch.8 Part 1

Sch.8 Part X para.77, repealed: 2003 c.1 Sch.8 Part 1

Sch.8 Part X para.78, repealed: 2003 c.1 Sch.8 Part 1

Sch.8 Part X para.79, repealed: 2003 c.1 Sch.8 Part 1

Sch.8 Part X para.80, repealed: 2003 c.1 Sch.8 Part 1

Sch.8 Part X para.81, repealed: 2003 c.1 Sch.8 Part 1

Sch.8 Part X para.82, repealed: 2003 c.1 Sch.8 Part 1

Sch.8 Part X para.83, repealed (in part): 2003 c.1 Sch.8 Part 1, 2004 c.12 Sch.42 Part 3

Sch.8 Part X para.84, repealed: 2003 c.1 Sch.8 Part 1

Sch.8 Part X para.85, repealed: 2003 c.1 Sch.8 Part 1

Sch.8 Part X para.86, repealed: 2003 c.1 Sch.8 Part 1

Sch.8 Part X para.87, repealed: 2003 c.1 Sch.8 Part 1

Sch.8 Part X para.88, amended: 2002 c.34 s.3

Sch.8 Part X para.88, repealed: 2003 c.1 Sch.8 Part 1

Sch.8 Part X para.89, repealed: 2003 c.1 Sch.8 Part 1

Sch.8 Part X para.90, repealed: 2003 c.1 Sch.8 Part 1

Sch.8 Part X para.91, repealed: 2003 c.1 Sch.8 Part 1

Sch.8 Part X para.92, repealed: 2003 c.1 Sch.8 Part 1

Sch.8 Part X para.93, repealed: 2003 c.1 Sch.8 Part 1

Sch.8 Part X para.94, amended: 2002 c.23 s.39

Sch.8 Part X para.94, repealed: 2003 c.1 Sch.8 Part 1

Sch.8 Part X para.95, amended: 2002 c.23 s.39

Sch.8 Part X para.95, repealed: 2003 c.1 Sch.8 Part 1

Sch.8 Part X para.96, amended: 2002 c.23 s.39

Sch.8 Part X para.96, repealed: 2003 c.1 Sch.8 Part 1

2000–cont.

17. Finance Act 2000–*cont.*

Sch.8 Part XI para.97, repealed: 2003 c.1 Sch.8 Part 1

Sch.8 Part XI para.98, amended: 2002 c.34 s.3

Sch.8 Part XI para.98, repealed: 2003 c.1 Sch.8 Part 1

Sch.8 Part XI para.99, repealed: 2003 c.1 Sch.8 Part 1

Sch.8 Part XI para.100, amended: 2002 c.34 s.3

Sch.8 Part XI para.100, repealed: 2003 c.1 Sch.8 Part 1

Sch.8 Part XI para.101, repealed: 2003 c.1 Sch.8 Part 1

Sch.8 Part XI para.102, repealed: 2003 c.1 Sch.8 Part 1

Sch.8 Part XI para.103, repealed: 2003 c.1 Sch.8 Part 1

Sch.8 Part XI para.104, repealed: 2003 c.1 Sch.8 Part 1

Sch.8 Part XII para.105, repealed: 2003 c.1 Sch.8 Part 1

Sch.8 Part XII para.106, repealed: 2003 c.1 Sch.8 Part 1

Sch.8 Part XII para.107, repealed: 2003 c.1 Sch.8 Part 1

Sch.8 Part XII para.108, amended: 2002 c.34 s.2

Sch.8 Part XII para.108, repealed: 2003 c.1 Sch.8 Part 1

Sch.8 Part XII para.109, repealed: 2003 c.1 Sch.8 Part 1

Sch.8 Part XII para.110, repealed: 2003 c.1 Sch.8 Part 1

Sch.8 Part XII para.111, repealed: 2003 c.1 Sch.8 Part 1

Sch.8 Part XII para.112, repealed: 2003 c.1 Sch.8 Part 1

Sch.8 Part XII para.112A, added: 2002 c.34 s.1

Sch.8 Part XII para.112A, repealed: 2003 c.1 Sch.8 Part 1

Sch.8 Part XII para.112B, added: 2002 c.34 s.1

Sch.8 Part XII para.112B, repealed: 2003 c.1 Sch.8 Part 1

Sch.8 Part XII para.113, amended: 2002 c.34 s.2

Sch.8 Part XII para.113, repealed: 2003 c.1 Sch.8 Part 1

Sch.8 Part XII para.114, repealed: 2003 c.1 Sch.8 Part 1

Sch.8 Part XIII para.115, repealed: 2003 c.1 Sch.8 Part 1

Sch.8 Part XIII para.116, repealed: 2003 c.1 Sch.8 Part 1

Sch.8 Part XIII para.116A, repealed: 2003 c.1 Sch.8 Part 1

Sch.8 Part XIII para.117, repealed: 2003 c.1 Sch.8 Part 1

2000–cont.

17. Finance Act 2000–*cont.*

Sch.8 Part XIII para.118, repealed: 2003 c.1
Sch.8 Part 1

Sch.8 Part XIII para.119, repealed: 2003 c.1
Sch.8 Part 1

Sch.8 Part XIII para.120, repealed: 2003 c.1
Sch.8 Part 1

Sch.8 Part XIII para.121, amended: 2002 c.34
s.2

Sch.8 Part XIII para.121, repealed: 2003 c.1
Sch.8 Part 1

Sch.8 Part XIII para.122, repealed: 2003 c.1
Sch.8 Part 1

Sch.8 Part XIII para.123, repealed: 2003 c.1
Sch.8 Part 1

Sch.8 Part XIII para.124, repealed: 2003 c.1
Sch.8 Part 1

Sch.8 Part XIII para.125, repealed: 2003 c.1
Sch.8 Part 1

Sch.8 Part XIII para.126, repealed: 2003 c.1
Sch.8 Part 1

Sch.8 Part XIII para.127, amended: 2002 c.23
s.39

Sch.8 Part XIII para.127, repealed: 2003 c.1
Sch.8 Part 1

Sch.8 Part XIII para.128, amended: 2002 c.23
s.39

Sch.8 Part XIII para.128, repealed: 2003 c.1
Sch.8 Part 1

Sch.8 Part XIII para.129, repealed: 2003 c.1
Sch.8 Part 1

Sch.8 Part XIII para.130, repealed: 2003 c.1
Sch.8 Part 1

Sch.10 para.1, repealed: 2003 c.1 Sch.8 Part 1
Sch.10 para.2, repealed: 2003 c.1 Sch.8 Part 1
Sch.10 para.3, repealed: 2003 c.1 Sch.8 Part 1
Sch.10 para.4, repealed: 2003 c.1 Sch.8 Part 1
Sch.10 para.5, repealed: 2003 c.1 Sch.8 Part 1
Sch.10 para.6, repealed: 2003 c.1 Sch.8 Part 1
Sch.11 para.1, repealed: 2003 c.1 Sch.8 Part 1
Sch.11 para.2, repealed: 2003 c.1 Sch.8 Part 1
Sch.12 para.1, see *Usetech Ltd v Young
(Inspector of Taxes)* [2004] EWHC 2248,
[2004] S.T.C. 1671 (Ch D), Park, J.

Sch.12 Part I para.1, repealed: 2003 c.1 Sch.8
Part 1

Sch.12 Part I para.2, repealed: 2003 c.1 Sch.8
Part 1

Sch.12 Part I para.3, repealed: 2003 c.1 Sch.8
Part 1

Sch.12 Part I para.4, repealed: 2003 c.1 Sch.8
Part 1

Sch.12 Part I para.5, repealed: 2003 c.1 Sch.8
Part 1

Sch.12 Part I para.6, repealed: 2003 c.1 Sch.8
Part 1

Sch.12 Part II para.7, repealed: 2003 c.1 Sch.8
Part 1

Sch.12 Part II para.7A, added: 2002 c.23 s.38
Sch.12 Part II para.7A, repealed: 2003 c.1
Sch.8 Part 1

2000–cont.

17. Finance Act 2000–*cont.*

Sch.12 Part II para.7B, added: 2002 c.23 s.38

Sch.12 Part II para.7B, repealed: 2003 c.1
Sch.8 Part 1

Sch.12 Part II para.8, repealed: 2003 c.1 Sch.8
Part 1

Sch.12 Part II para.9, repealed: 2003 c.1 Sch.8
Part 1

Sch.12 Part II para.10, repealed: 2003 c.1
Sch.8 Part 1

Sch.12 Part II para.11, repealed: 2003 c.1 Sch.8
Part 1

Sch.12 Part III para.12, amended: 2002 c.23
s.38

Sch.12 Part III para.12, repealed: 2003 c.1
Sch.8 Part 1

Sch.12 Part III para.13, repealed: 2003 c.1
Sch.8 Part 1

Sch.12 Part III para.14, repealed: 2003 c.1
Sch.8 Part 1

Sch.12 Part III para.15, repealed: 2003 c.1
Sch.8 Part 1

Sch.12 Part III para.16, repealed: 2003 c.1
Sch.8 Part 1

Sch.12 Part III para.17, amended: 2003 c.1
Sch.6 para.244

Sch.12 Part III para.18, amended: 2002 c.23
s.38, 2003 c.1 Sch.6 para.244

Sch.12 Part III para.19, repealed: 2003 c.1
Sch.8 Part 1

Sch.12 Part III para.20, repealed: 2003 c.1
Sch.8 Part 1

Sch.12 Part III para.21, repealed: 2003 c.1
Sch.8 Part 1

Sch.12 Part III para.22, repealed: 2003 c.1
Sch.8 Part 1

Sch.12 Part III para.23, repealed: 2003 c.1
Sch.8 Part 1

Sch.12 Part III para.24, repealed: 2003 c.1
Sch.8 Part 1

Sch.13 Part I para.1, repealed: 2004 c.12
Sch.42 Part 3

Sch.13 Part I para.2, repealed: 2004 c.12
Sch.42 Part 3

Sch.13 Part I para.3, repealed: 2004 c.12
Sch.42 Part 3

Sch.13 Part I para.4, repealed: 2004 c.12
Sch.42 Part 3

Sch.13 Part I para.5, repealed: 2004 c.12
Sch.42 Part 3

Sch.13 Part I para.6, repealed: 2004 c.12
Sch.42 Part 3

Sch.13 Part I para.7, repealed: 2004 c.12
Sch.42 Part 3

Sch.13 Part I para.8, repealed: 2004 c.12
Sch.42 Part 3

Sch.13 Part I para.9, repealed: 2004 c.12
Sch.42 Part 3

Sch.13 Part I para.10, repealed: 2004 c.12
Sch.42 Part 3

2000–cont.

17. Finance Act 2000–*cont.*

Sch.13 Part I para.11, repealed: 2004 c.12 Sch.42 Part 3

Sch.13 Part I para.12, repealed: 2004 c.12 Sch.42 Part 3

Sch.13 Part I para.13, repealed: 2004 c.12 Sch.42 Part 3

Sch.13 Part I para.14, repealed: 2004 c.12 Sch.42 Part 3

Sch.13 Part I para.15, repealed: 2004 c.12 Sch.42 Part 3

Sch.13 Part I para.16, repealed: 2004 c.12 Sch.42 Part 3

Sch.13 Part I para.17, repealed: 2004 c.12 Sch.42 Part 3

Sch.13 Part I para.18, repealed: 2004 c.12 Sch.42 Part 3

Sch.13 Part I para.19, repealed: 2004 c.12 Sch.42 Part 3

Sch.13 Part I para.20, repealed: 2004 c.12 Sch.42 Part 3

Sch.13 Part I para.21, repealed: 2004 c.12 Sch.42 Part 3

Sch.13 Part I para.22, repealed: 2004 c.12 Sch.42 Part 3

Sch.13 Part I para.23, repealed: 2004 c.12 Sch.42 Part 3

Sch.13 Part I para.24, repealed: 2004 c.12 Sch.42 Part 3

Sch.13 Part I para.25, repealed: 2004 c.12 Sch.42 Part 3

Sch.13 Part I para.26, repealed: 2004 c.12 Sch.42 Part 3

Sch.13 Part I para.27, repealed: 2004 c.12 Sch.42 Part 3

Sch.13 Part II para.28, repealed: 2004 c.12 Sch.42 Part 3

Sch.13 Part II para.29, repealed: 2004 c.12 Sch.42 Part 3

Sch.13 Part II para.30, repealed: 2004 c.12 Sch.42 Part 3

Sch.14, applied: 2003 c.1 Sch.7 para.77

Sch.14 Part I para.1, repealed: 2003 c.1 Sch.8 Part 1

Sch.14 Part I para.2, applied: 2003 c.1 Sch.7 para.67

Sch.14 Part I para.2, repealed: 2003 c.1 Sch.8 Part 1

Sch.14 Part I para.3, repealed: 2003 c.1 Sch.8 Part 1

Sch.14 Part I para.4, repealed: 2003 c.1 Sch.8 Part 1

Sch.14 Part I para.5, repealed: 2003 c.1 Sch.8 Part 1

Sch.14 Part I para.6, repealed: 2003 c.1 Sch.8 Part 1

Sch.14 Part I para.7, repealed: 2003 c.1 Sch.8 Part 1

Sch.14 Part II para.8, repealed: 2003 c.1 Sch.8 Part 1

2000–cont.

17. Finance Act 2000–*cont.*

Sch.14 Part II para.9, repealed: 2003 c.1 Sch.8 Part 1

Sch.14 Part II para.10, repealed: 2003 c.1 Sch.8 Part 1

Sch.14 Part II para.11, repealed: 2003 c.1 Sch.8 Part 1

Sch.14 Part III para.12, repealed: 2003 c.1 Sch.8 Part 1

Sch.14 Part III para.13, repealed: 2003 c.1 Sch.8 Part 1

Sch.14 Part III para.14, repealed: 2003 c.1 Sch.8 Part 1

Sch.14 Part III para.15, repealed: 2003 c.1 Sch.8 Part 1

Sch.14 Part III para.16, repealed: 2003 c.1 Sch.8 Part 1

Sch.14 Part III para.17, repealed: 2003 c.1 Sch.8 Part 1

Sch.14 Part III para.18, repealed: 2003 c.1 Sch.8 Part 1

Sch.14 Part III para.19, repealed: 2003 c.1 Sch.8 Part 1

Sch.14 Part III para.20, repealed: 2003 c.1 Sch.8 Part 1

Sch.14 Part III para.21, repealed: 2003 c.1 Sch.8 Part 1

Sch.14 Part III para.22, amended: 2002 c.23 s.103, Sch.40 Part 3

Sch.14 Part III para.22, repealed: 2003 c.1 Sch.8 Part 1

Sch.14 Part III para.23, repealed: 2003 c.1 Sch.8 Part 1

Sch.14 Part III para.24, repealed: 2003 c.1 Sch.8 Part 1

Sch.14 Part III para.25, repealed: 2003 c.1 Sch.8 Part 1

Sch.14 Part III para.26, repealed: 2003 c.1 Sch.8 Part 1

Sch.14 Part IV para.27, repealed: 2003 c.1 Sch.8 Part 1

Sch.14 Part IV para.28, repealed: 2003 c.1 Sch.8 Part 1

Sch.14 Part IV para.29, repealed: 2003 c.1 Sch.8 Part 1

Sch.14 Part IV para.30, repealed: 2003 c.1 Sch.8 Part 1

Sch.14 Part IV para.31, repealed: 2003 c.1 Sch.8 Part 1

Sch.14 Part IV para.32, repealed: 2003 c.1 Sch.8 Part 1

Sch.14 Part IV para.33, repealed: 2003 c.1 Sch.8 Part 1

Sch.14 Part IV para.34, repealed: 2003 c.1 Sch.8 Part 1

Sch.14 Part IV para.35, repealed: 2003 c.1 Sch.8 Part 1

Sch.14 Part IV para.36, repealed: 2003 c.1 Sch.8 Part 1

Sch.14 Part V para.37, repealed: 2003 c.1 Sch.8 Part 1

2000–cont.

17. Finance Act 2000–*cont.*

Sch.14 Part V para.38, repealed: 2003 c.1
Sch.8 Part 1

Sch.14 Part V para.39, repealed: 2003 c.1
Sch.8 Part 1

Sch.14 Part V para.40, repealed: 2003 c.1
Sch.8 Part 1

Sch.14 Part V para.41, repealed: 2003 c.1
Sch.8 Part 1

Sch.14 Part VI para.42, repealed: 2003 c.1
Sch.8 Part 1

Sch.14 Part VI para.43, repealed: 2003 c.1
Sch.8 Part 1

Sch.14 Part VI para.44, repealed: 2003 c.1
Sch.8 Part 1

Sch.14 Part VI para.45, repealed: 2003 c.1
Sch.8 Part 1

Sch.14 Part VI para.46, repealed: 2003 c.1
Sch.8 Part 1

Sch.14 Part VI para.47, repealed: 2003 c.1
Sch.8 Part 1

Sch.14 Part VI para.48, repealed: 2003 c.1
Sch.8 Part 1

Sch.14 Part VI para.49, repealed: 2003 c.1
Sch.8 Part 1

Sch.14 Part VI para.50, repealed: 2003 c.1
Sch.8 Part 1

Sch.14 Part VI para.51, repealed: 2003 c.1
Sch.8 Part 1

Sch.14 Part VI para.52, applied: 2003 c.1
Sch.7 para.78

Sch.14 Part VI para.52, repealed: 2003 c.1
Sch.8 Part 1

Sch.14 Part VI para.53, repealed: 2003 c.1
Sch.8 Part 1

Sch.14 Part VI para.54, repealed: 2003 c.1
Sch.8 Part 1

Sch.14 Part VI para.55, repealed: 2003 c.1
Sch.8 Part 1

Sch.14 Part VII para.56, repealed: 2003 c.1
Sch.8 Part 1

Sch.14 Part VII para.57, repealed: 2003 c.1
Sch.8 Part 1

Sch.14 Part VII para.58, repealed: 2003 c.1
Sch.8 Part 1

Sch.14 Part VIII para.59, repealed: 2003 c.1
Sch.8 Part 1

Sch.14 Part VIII para.60, repealed: 2003 c.1
Sch.8 Part 1

Sch.14 Part VIII para.61, repealed: 2003 c.1
Sch.8 Part 1

Sch.14 Part VIII para.62, repealed: 2003 c.1
Sch.8 Part 1

Sch.14 Part VIII para.63, repealed: 2003 c.1
Sch.8 Part 1

Sch.14 Part IX para.64, repealed: 2003 c.1
Sch.8 Part 1

Sch.14 Part IX para.65, repealed: 2003 c.1
Sch.8 Part 1

Sch.14 Part IX para.66, repealed: 2003 c.1
Sch.8 Part 1

2000–cont.

17. Finance Act 2000–*cont.*

Sch.14 Part IX para.67, repealed: 2003 c.1
Sch.8 Part 1

Sch.14 Part IX para.68, repealed: 2003 c.1
Sch.8 Part 1

Sch.14 Part IX para.69, repealed: 2003 c.1
Sch.8 Part 1

Sch.14 Part IX para.70, repealed: 2003 c.1
Sch.8 Part 1

Sch.14 Part IX para.71, repealed: 2003 c.1
Sch.8 Part 1

Sch.14 Part IX para.72, repealed: 2003 c.1
Sch.8 Part 1

Sch.15, referred to: SI 2004/712 Reg.1

Sch.15 Part I para.3, amended: 2004 c.12
Sch.20 para.2

Sch.15 Part III para.15, amended: 2004 c.12
Sch.20 para.3

Sch.15 Part III para.20, amended: 2004 c.12
Sch.20 para.4

Sch.15 Part III para.21, amended: SI 2003/
2096 Sch.1 para.34, 2004 c.12 Sch.20
para.5

Sch.15 Part III para.21, repealed (in part):
2004 c.12 Sch.42 Part 2

Sch.15 Part III para.21A, added: 2004 c.12
Sch.20 para.6

Sch.15 Part III para.23, amended: 2004 c.12
Sch.20 para.7, Sch.27 para.6

Sch.15 Part III para.24, amended: SI 2003/
2096 Sch.1 para.34, 2004 c.12 Sch.20
para.8, Sch.42 Part 2

Sch.15 Part III para.25, amended: 2004 c.12
Sch.20 para.9

Sch.15 Part III para.28, amended: 2004 c.12
Sch.27 para.6, Sch.42 Part 2

Sch.15 Part III para.29, amended: 2002 c.23
s.103, Sch.40 Part 3

Sch.15 Part IV para.35, amended: 2004 c.12
Sch.20 para.10

Sch.15 Part IV para.36, amended: 2004 c.12
Sch.20 para.11

Sch.15 Part V para.40, amended: SI 2003/
2096 Sch.1 para.34, 2004 c.12 Sch.20
para.12

Sch.15 Part VII para.71, amended: 2002 c.23
Sch.9 para.6

Sch.15 Part VIII para.79, amended: 2003 c.14
Sch.27 para.9

Sch.15 Part IX para.82, amended: 2002 c.23
Sch.9 para.6

Sch.15 Part IX para.84, amended: 2002 c.23
Sch.8 para.5

Sch.15 Part IX para.85, amended: 2002 c.23
Sch.8 para.5

Sch.15 Part XI para.93, amended: 2002 c.23
Sch.9 para.6

Sch.15 Part XI para.96, amended: 2002 c.23
Sch.9 para.6

2000–cont.

17. Finance Act 2000–*cont.*

Sch.15 Part XI para.102, amended: SI 2003/ 2096 Sch.1 para.34, 2004 c.12 Sch.20 para.13

Sch.15 Part XI para.103, amended: 2004 c.12 Sch.20 para.14

Sch.20, applied: 2002 c.23 Sch.12 para.10A, Sch.12 para.10B, Sch.12 para.7, Sch.13 para.1, Sch.13 para.14, Sch.13 para.15, Sch.13 para.17, 2004 c.12 s.53

Sch.20, referred to: 2002 c.23 s.56

Sch.20 Part I para.1, amended: 2002 c.23 Sch.15 para.2, 2003 c.14 Sch.31 para.2, Sch.31 para.3

Sch.20 Part I para.2, varied: 2002 c.23 Sch.13 para.5

Sch.20 Part I para.2, enabling: SI 2004/3267

Sch.20 Part I para.3, amended: 2003 c.14 Sch.31 para.4, 2004 c.12 s.141

Sch.20 Part I para.3, applied: 2002 c.23 Sch.12 para.10B

Sch.20 Part I para.4, varied: 2002 c.23 Sch.12 para.17

Sch.20 Part I para.5, amended: 2002 c.23 Sch.15 para.3, Sch.40 Part 3, 2003 c.14 Sch.31 para.5, Sch.43 Part 3, 2003 c.1 Sch.6 para.245, 2004 c.12 Sch.17 para.7

Sch.20 Part I para.5, applied: 2002 c.23 Sch.13 para.9, 2003 c.14 s.168

Sch.20 Part I para.5, repealed (in part): 2003 c.14 Sch.31 para.5, Sch.43 Part 3, 2004 c.12 Sch.42 Part 2

Sch.20 Part I para.5, varied: 2002 c.23 Sch.12 para.17, Sch.13 para.5, Sch.13 para.9

Sch.20 Part I para.6, amended: 2002 c.23 s.103

Sch.20 Part I para.6, substituted: 2004 c.12 s.141

Sch.20 Part I para.6, varied: 2002 c.23 Sch.12 para.17, Sch.13 para.5

Sch.20 Part I para.8, amended: 2002 c.23 Sch.15 para.4

Sch.20 Part I para.8, applied: 2002 c.23 Sch.12 para.10B

Sch.20 Part I para.8, varied: 2002 c.23 Sch.13 para.5, Sch.13 para.9

Sch.20 Part I para.8A, added: 2003 c.14 Sch.31 para.6

Sch.20 Part I para.8A, applied: 2002 c.23 Sch.12 para.17, Sch.13 para.5, Sch.13 para.9

Sch.20 Part I para.8B, added: 2003 c.14 Sch.31 para.6

Sch.20 Part I para.8B, applied: 2002 c.23 Sch.12 para.17, Sch.13 para.5, Sch.13 para.9

Sch.20 Part I para.8C, added: 2003 c.14 Sch.31 para.6

Sch.20 Part I para.8C, applied: 2002 c.23 Sch.12 para.17, Sch.13 para.5, Sch.13 para.9

Sch.20 Part I para.8D, added: 2003 c.14 Sch.31 para.6

Sch.20 Part I para.8D, applied: 2002 c.23 Sch.12 para.17, Sch.13 para.5, Sch.13 para.9

2000–cont.

17. Finance Act 2000–*cont.*

Sch.20 Part I para.8E, added: 2003 c.14 Sch.31 para.6

Sch.20 Part I para.8E, applied: 2002 c.23 Sch.12 para.17, Sch.13 para.5, Sch.13 para.9

Sch.20 Part I para.10, amended: 2002 c.23 s.103, 2003 c.14 Sch.31 para.7, 2004 c.12 s.141

Sch.20 Part I para.10, applied: 2002 c.23 Sch.12 para.10B

Sch.20 Part I para.12, amended: 2002 c.23 Sch.15 para.5, Sch.40 Part 3

Sch.20 Part II para.15, applied: 2002 c.23 Sch.13 para.16

Sch.20 Part II para.17, amended: 2002 c.21 Sch.3 para.59

Sch.20 Part II para.17, applied: 2002 c.23 Sch.13 para.17

Sch.20 Part III para.25, amended: 2002 c.23 s.103, Sch.40 Part 3

Sch.22, referred to: 2004 c.12 Sch.5 para.11

Sch.22 Part III para.20, repealed (in part): 2004 c.12 Sch.42 Part 2

Sch.22 Part IV para.24, enabling: SI 2003/ 2320

Sch.22 Part IV para.29, enabling: SI 2002/ 2265, SI 2003/2320, SI 2004/2255

Sch.22 Part IV para.31, enabling: SI 2002/ 2265, SI 2003/2320, SI 2004/2255

Sch.22 Part IV para.36, enabling: SI 2002/ 2265, SI 2003/2320, SI 2004/2255

Sch.22 Part V para.41, amended: 2003 c.14 Sch.32 para.2, Sch.43 Part 3

Sch.22 Part VI para.50, amended: 2002 c.23 Sch.23 para.23, Sch.27 para.23

Sch.22 Part VI para.50, repealed (in part): 2002 c.23 Sch.40 Part 3

Sch.22 Part VII para.58, amended: 2004 c.12 Sch.5 para.12

Sch.22 Part VII para.59, amended: 2004 c.12 Sch.5 para.13

Sch.22 Part VII para.63, amended: 2002 c.23 Sch.23 para.23, Sch.27 para.23

Sch.22 Part X para.89, amended: 2003 c.14 Sch.32 para.1, Sch.43 Part 3

Sch.22 Part X para.89A, added: 2003 c.14 Sch.32 para.1, Sch.32 para.4

Sch.22 Part X para.90, amended: 2003 c.14 Sch.43 Part 3

Sch.22 Part X para.92, amended: 2003 c.14 Sch.43 Part 3

Sch.22 Part X para.93, amended: 2003 c.14 Sch.32 para.4, Sch.43 Part 3

Sch.22 Part X para.94, amended: 2003 c.14 Sch.43 Part 3

Sch.22 Part X para.98, amended: 2003 c.14 Sch.43 Part 3

Sch.22 Part X para.99, amended: 2003 c.14 Sch.43 Part 3

Sch.22 Part XV para.147, amended: 2003 c.14 Sch.32 para.2, Sch.43 Part 3

2000–cont.

17. Finance Act 2000–*cont.*

Sch.23, applied: 2002 c.23 Sch.29 para.128

Sch.23 para.1, repealed (in part): 2002 c.23 Sch.29 para.128

Sch.23 para.2, amended: 2002 c.23 s.103

Sch.23 para.2, repealed (in part): 2002 c.23 Sch.29 para.128

Sch.23 para.3, amended: 2002 c.23 s.103

Sch.23 para.3, repealed (in part): 2002 c.23 Sch.29 para.128

Sch.23 para.4, repealed (in part): 2002 c.23 Sch.29 para.128

Sch.23 para.5, amended: 2002 c.23 s.103, Sch.40 Part 3

Sch.23 para.5, repealed (in part): 2002 c.23 Sch.29 para.128

Sch.23 para.6, repealed (in part): 2002 c.23 Sch.29 para.128

Sch.27 Part II para.7, repealed: 2004 c.12 Sch.42 Part 2

Sch.29 Part II para.20, repealed: 2002 c.23 Sch.40 Part 3

Sch.29 Part II para.21, repealed: 2002 c.23 Sch.40 Part 3

Sch.29 Part II para.41, repealed: 2002 c.23 Sch.40 Part 3

Sch.29 Part II para.42, repealed: 2002 c.23 Sch.40 Part 3

Sch.29 Part II para.43, repealed: 2002 c.23 Sch.40 Part 3

Sch.30 para.18, repealed (in part): 2003 c.14 Sch.43 Part 3

Sch.30 para.24, repealed (in part): 2002 c.23 Sch.40 Part 3

Sch.33 para.1, enabling: SI 2003/2760, SI 2003/2816

Sch.33 para.2, enabling: SI 2003/2760, SI 2003/2816

Sch.33 para.3, amended: 2003 c.14 Sch.20 para.3

Sch.33 para.3, enabling: SI 2003/2760, SI 2003/2816

Sch.33 para.7, enabling: SI 2003/2760, SI 2003/2816

Sch.33 para.8, enabling: SI 2003/2760, SI 2003/2816

Sch.33 para.9, enabling: SI 2003/2760, SI 2003/2816

Sch.34 para.2, amended: 2003 c.14 Sch.20 para.3

Sch.38, enabling: SI 2003/2495

Sch.38 para.1, enabling: SI 2004/1675

Sch.38 para.2, enabling: SI 2004/1675

Sch.38 para.3, enabling: SI 2004/1675

Sch.38 para.4, enabling: SI 2004/1675

Sch.38 para.5, enabling: SI 2004/1675

Sch.38 para.7, enabling: SI 2004/1675

Sch.38 para.8, amended: 2003 c.21 Sch.17 para.160

2000–cont.

19. Child Support, Pensions and Social Security Act 2000

Commencement Orders: SI 2002/437 Art.3; SI 2003/192 Art.2, Art.3, Art.4, Art.5, Art.6, Art.7, Sch.1, 2004 c.35 Sch.13 Part 1

applied: SI 2002/1204 Reg.1, SI 2002/1888 Art.3, SI 2003/1325 Art.2

referred to: SI 2003/129 Reg.1

Part II c.II, applied: 2004 c.35 s.321

Part II c.II, referred to: 2004 c.35 s.322

s.1, applied: SI 2004/2415 Reg.1

s.8, applied: SI 2004/2415 Reg.1

s.9, applied: SI 2004/2415 Reg.1

s.10, referred to: SI 2002/1915 Art.1, SSI 2003/96 Art.1

s.27, applied: SI 2002/1854

s.27, varied: SI 2002/1854 Reg.2

s.27, enabling: SI 2002/1854

s.29, enabling: SI 2003/231, SI 2003/328, SI 2003/347, SI 2003/2779, SI 2004/2415

s.42, amended: 2004 c.35 s.298, Sch.13 Part 1

s.42, applied: 2004 c.35 s.237

s.43, repealed: 2004 c.35 Sch.13 Part 1

s.44, repealed: 2004 c.35 Sch.13 Part 1

s.45, repealed: 2004 c.35 Sch.13 Part 1

s.46, repealed: 2004 c.35 Sch.13 Part 1

s.47, repealed (in part): 2004 c.35 Sch.13 Part 1

s.54, applied: 2004 c.35 s.276

s.54, referred to: 2004 c.35 s.276

s.54, repealed: 2004 c.35 s.276, Sch.13 Part 1

s.57, repealed (in part): 2004 c.14 Sch.1 Part 11, 2004 c.32 Sch.3

s.62, amended: 2003 c.44 Sch.32 para.131

s.62, repealed (in part): 2003 c.44 Sch.37 Part 7

s.62, enabling: SI 2002/490

s.64, amended: 2003 c.44 Sch.32 para.132

s.65, enabling: SI 2002/490

s.68, enabling: SI 2002/1379, SI 2002/1703, SI 2004/3368

s.69, applied: SI 2002/2006 Reg.7

s.69, enabling: SI 2002/490

s.70, amended: 2003 c.26 Sch.8 Part 1

s.70, enabling: SI 2004/2329

s.75, repealed (in part): 2004 c.3 Sch.2 Part 1

s.79, repealed (in part): 2004 c.3 Sch.2 Part 1

s.86, enabling: SI 2002/437, SI 2003/192, SI 2003/346

Sch.3 para.11, applied: SI 2004/2415 Reg.1

Sch.5 Part I para.3, repealed (in part): 2004 c.35 Sch.13 Part 1

Sch.5 Part I para.10, repealed: 2004 c.35 Sch.13 Part 1

Sch.5 Part I para.11, repealed: 2004 c.35 Sch.13 Part 1

Sch.5 Part I para.12, repealed (in part): 2004 c.35 Sch.13 Part 1

Sch.6 para.4, repealed (in part): 2004 c.3 Sch.2 Part 1

2000–cont.

19. Child Support, Pensions and Social Security Act 2000–*cont.*

Sch.7, referred to: SI 2003/325 Sch.1

Sch.7 para.3, applied: SI 2003/325 Reg.30

Sch.7 para.3, enabling: SI 2002/490, SI 2002/1379, SI 2002/1703, SI 2003/2275, SI 2003/2399, SI 2003/2526

Sch.7 para.4, applied: SI 2003/1338 Reg.4, Reg.21, SI 2004/14 Reg.27

Sch.7 para.4, enabling: SI 2002/490, SI 2002/1703, SI 2003/308, SI 2003/325, SI 2003/1050, SI 2003/1338, SI 2003/2275, SI 2003/2399, SI 2004/14, SI 2004/290, SI 2004/2327

Sch.7 para.6, see *Secretary of State for Work and Pensions v Chiltern DC* [2003] EWCA Civ 508, [2003] H.L.R. 67 (CA), Hale, L.J.

Sch.7 para.6, enabling: SI 2002/1379, SI 2002/1703, SI 2003/1581, SI 2004/3368

Sch.7 para.10, enabling: SI 2002/1379, SI 2003/1050, SI 2004/3368

Sch.7 para.12, enabling: SI 2003/325

Sch.7 para.19, enabling: SI 2002/1379

Sch.7 para.20, applied: SI 2003/1581

Sch.7 para.20, referred to: SI 2003/325 Sch.1

Sch.7 para.20, enabling: SI 2002/1379, SI 2002/1703, SI 2003/308, SI 2003/325, SI 2003/1581, SI 2003/2275, SI 2003/2399, SI 2003/2526, SI 2004/290, SI 2004/2327, SI 2004/3368

Sch.7 para.21, referred to: SI 2003/325 Sch.1

Sch.7 para.23, enabling: SI 2002/490, SI 2002/1379, SI 2002/1703, SI 2003/308, SI 2003/1050, SI 2003/1338, SI 2003/1581, SI 2003/2275, SI 2003/2399, SI 2003/2526, SI 2004/14, SI 2004/290, SI 2004/2327, SI 2004/3368

Sch.9 Part III, amended: 2004 c.35 Sch.13 Part 1

20. Government Resources and Accounts Act 2000

applied: 2002 c.40 Sch.15

s.1, repealed (in part): 2004 c.14 Sch.1 Part 9

s.2, applied: 2002 c.18 s.3, 2002 c.44 s.1, 2003 c.13 s.3, Sch.2 Part 1, Sch.2 Part 2, Sch.2 Part 3, Sch.2 Part 4, Sch.2 Part 5, Sch.2 Part 6, Sch.2 Part 7, Sch.2 Part 8, Sch.2 Part 9, Sch.2 Part 10, Sch.2 Part 11, Sch.2 Part 12, Sch.2 Part 13, Sch.2 Part 14, Sch.2 Part 15, Sch.2 Part 16, Sch.2 Part 17, Sch.2 Part 18, Sch.2 Part 19, Sch.2 Part 20, Sch.2 Part 21, Sch.2 Part 22, Sch.2 Part 23, Sch.2 Part 24, Sch.2 Part 25, Sch.2 Part 26, Sch.2 Part 27, Sch.2 Part 28, Sch.2 Part 29, Sch.2 Part 30, Sch.2 Part 31, Sch.2 Part 32, Sch.2 Part 33, Sch.2 Part 34, Sch.2 Part 35, Sch.2 Part 36, Sch.2 Part 37, Sch.2 Part 38, Sch.2 Part 39, Sch.2 Part 40, Sch.2 Part 41, Sch.2 Part 42, Sch.2 Part 43, Sch.2 Part 44, Sch.2 Part 45, Sch.2 Part 46, Sch.2 Part 47, Sch.2 Part 48, Sch.2 Part 49, Sch.2 Part 50, Sch.2 Part 51, Sch.2 Part 52, Sch.2 Part 53,

2000–cont.

20. Government Resources and Accounts Act 2000–*cont.*

s.2, applied:–*cont.*

　Sch.2 Part 54, Sch.2 Part 55, Sch.2 Part 56, Sch.2 Part 57, Sch.2 Part 58, Sch.2 Part 59, Sch.2 Part 60, Sch.2 Part 61, 2004 c.9 s.3, Sch.2 Part 1, Sch.2 Part 2, Sch.2 Part 3, Sch.2 Part 4, Sch.2 Part 5, Sch.2 Part 6, Sch.2 Part 7, Sch.2 Part 8, Sch.2 Part 9, Sch.2 Part 10, Sch.2 Part 11, Sch.2 Part 12, Sch.2 Part 13, Sch.2 Part 14, Sch.2 Part 15, Sch.2 Part 16, Sch.2 Part 17, Sch.2 Part 18, Sch.2 Part 19, Sch.2 Part 20, Sch.2 Part 21, Sch.2 Part 22, Sch.2 Part 23, Sch.2 Part 24, Sch.2 Part 25, Sch.2 Part 26, Sch.2 Part 27, Sch.2 Part 28, Sch.2 Part 29, Sch.2 Part 30, Sch.2 Part 31, Sch.2 Part 32, Sch.2 Part 33, Sch.2 Part 34, Sch.2 Part 35, Sch.2 Part 36, Sch.2 Part 37, Sch.2 Part 38, Sch.2 Part 39, Sch.2 Part 40, Sch.2 Part 41, Sch.2 Part 42, Sch.2 Part 43, Sch.2 Part 44, Sch.2 Part 45, Sch.2 Part 46, Sch.2 Part 47, Sch.2 Part 48, Sch.2 Part 49, Sch.2 Part 50, Sch.2 Part 51, Sch.2 Part 52, Sch.2 Part 53, Sch.2 Part 54, Sch.2 Part 55, Sch.2 Part 56, Sch.2 Part 57

s.2, repealed (in part): 2004 c.14 Sch.1 Part 9

s.3, repealed (in part): 2004 c.14 Sch.1 Part 9

s.5, applied: SI 2003/983, SI 2004/1416

s.5, repealed (in part): 2004 c.14 Sch.1 Part 9

s.5, varied: SI 2002/794 Art.6

s.5, enabling: SI 2003/983, SI 2004/1416

s.6, repealed (in part): 2004 c.14 Sch.1 Part 9

s.7, repealed (in part): 2004 c.14 Sch.1 Part 9

s.8, applied: SI 2003/1325 Art.2, Art.3, Art.4, Art.5, Art.6

s.8, repealed (in part): 2004 c.14 Sch.1 Part 9

s.9, applied: SI 2003/983

s.9, enabling: SI 2003/983

s.10, applied: SI 2002/454 Art.3, SI 2003/489 Art.2

s.10, enabling: SI 2002/454, SI 2003/489

s.14, enabling: SI 2003/983, SI 2004/1416

s.21, repealed (in part): 2004 c.14 Sch.1 Part 9

s.25, applied: SI 2003/1324, SI 2003/1325, SI 2003/1326, SI 2004/1714, SI 2004/1715

s.25, enabling: SI 2003/1324, SI 2003/1325, SI 2003/1326, SI 2004/1714, SI 2004/1715

s.26, repealed (in part): 2004 c.14 Sch.1 Part 9

Sch.1 para.9, repealed: 2004 c.14 Sch.1 Part 9

Sch.1 para.12, repealed: 2004 c.14 Sch.1 Part 9

Sch.1 para.13, repealed: 2004 c.14 Sch.1 Part 9

Sch.1 para.25, repealed: 2002 c.21 Sch.6

21. Learning and Skills Act 2000

Commencement Orders: SI 2002/279 Art.2, Art.3

applied: SI 2003/514 Sch.2 para.2, SI 2004/1576 Reg.10

referred to: SI 2002/2523 Sch.2 para.2

s.5, amended: 2002 c.32 s.178

2000–cont.

21. Learning and Skills Act 2000–*cont.*

s.7, amended: 2002 c.32 Sch.21 para.124

s.7, applied: SI 2002/377 Reg.11, Reg.17, SI 2003/453 Reg.15, SI 2003/3170 Sch.2 para.1, SI 2003/3247 Reg.16, Sch.2 para.1

s.13, applied: 2004 c.31 s.10

s.23, applied: SI 2002/928 Sch.3

s.23, disapplied: 2004 c.31 s.18

s.36, amended: 2002 c.32 Sch.21 para.125

s.36, applied: SI 2004/2506 Reg.8, Reg.14

s.65, amended: 2002 c.32 s.178

s.65, applied: SI 2002/928 Sch.3, SI 2002/3177 Reg.2

s.67, varied: SI 2002/928 Sch.3

s.77, enabling: SI 2004/783

s.80, enabling: SI 2004/783

s.83, amended: 2002 c.32 s.178

s.83, enabling: SI 2004/783

s.84, enabling: SI 2004/783

s.94A, added: SI 2003/2867 Sch.1 para.31

s.96, applied: SI 2002/2897 Sch.3 para.12, Sch.3 para.13, SI 2003/252 Reg.10

s.98, applied: SI 2002/2897 Sch.3 para.12, Sch.3 para.13, SI 2003/252 Reg.10

s.99, applied: SI 2004/549 Reg.3

s.104, applied: 2003 c.1 s.255, SSI 2004/83 Reg.9

s.105, applied: 2003 c.1 s.255, SI 2003/918 Reg.3

s.105, enabling: SI 2003/918

s.106, applied: 2003 c.1 s.255

s.108, enabling: SI 2003/918

s.113, applied: SI 2002/928 Sch.3

s.113A, added: 2002 c.32 s.72

s.113A, applied: 2002 c.32 s.74, SI 2002/3199 Reg.1, Sch.1 para.11, SI 2003/453 Reg.1, SI 2003/507 Reg.3, Reg.4, Reg.8, Reg.9, Reg.11, Reg.28, SI 2003/1041 Reg.6, Reg.7, SI 2003/3118 Sch.1 para.11, SI 2003/3170 Sch.1 para.11, SI 2004/1576 Reg.3, Reg.4, Reg.5, Reg.6, Reg.8, Reg.9, Reg.19, Sch.1 para.2, SI 2004/2506 Reg.17

s.113A, referred to: 2002 c.32 s.74, SI 2004/1576 Reg.2

s.114, applied: 2003 c.42 s.21, 2004 c.31 s.10, s.11, s.13

s.114, referred to: 2002 c.21 Sch.5 para.10

s.115, amended: SI 2002/2469 Sch.1 para.28

s.116, applied: SI 2002/3199 Sch.1 para.20, SI 2003/3170 Sch.1 para.20

s.117, amended: 2002 c.32 Sch.7 para.10

s.120, amended: SI 2002/2469 Sch.1 para.28

s.121, amended: SI 2002/2469 Sch.1 para.28

s.123, applied: SI 2003/3118 Sch.1 para.18, 2004 c.31 s.25, s.28, s.30

s.128, applied: SI 2004/679 Reg.2

s.128, enabling: SI 2004/679

s.130, repealed (in part): 2002 c.32 Sch.22 Part 3

s.131, repealed (in part): 2002 c.32 Sch.22 Part 3

2000–cont.

21. Learning and Skills Act 2000–*cont.*

s.132, repealed (in part): 2002 c.32 Sch.22 Part 3

s.138, amended: 2002 c.17 Sch.5 para.47

s.140, varied: 2002 c.41 s.36

s.146, repealed (in part): 2004 c.8 Sch.7

s.148, repealed (in part): 2002 c.32 Sch.22 Part 3

s.150, enabling: SI 2003/918

s.152, enabling: SI 2002/279, SI 2002/432, SI 2003/507, SI 2003/918, SI 2004/1576

s.154, enabling: SI 2002/279

Sch.2 para.4, substituted: 2002 c.32 s.209

Sch.7, applied: SI 2002/432 Reg.11, SI 2004/1576 Reg.18, Reg.19, Sch.3 para.8, Sch.3 para.18

Sch.7, referred to: SI 2004/1576 Reg.2

Sch.7A, applied: SI 2002/3199 Reg.1, Sch.1 para.11, SI 2003/453 Reg.1, SI 2003/3118 Sch.1 para.11, SI 2003/3170 Sch.1 para.11

Sch.7A, referred to: 2002 c.32 s.74, SI 2004/1576 Reg.2

Sch.7 Part I, applied: SI 2002/928 Sch.3

Sch.7 Part II, applied: SI 2002/432 Sch.2 para.7, Sch.2 para.14, SI 2003/507 Sch.3 para.7, Sch.3 para.14, Sch.5 para.1, SI 2004/1576 Sch.3 para.8, Sch.3 para.18

Sch.7 Part II para.16, applied: SI 2003/507 Reg.13, Reg.14, Reg.17, Reg.28

Sch.7 Part II para.16, enabling: SI 2003/507

Sch.7 Part II para.17, amended: 2002 c.32 Sch.21 para.126

Sch.7 Part II para.17, applied: SI 2003/507 Reg.15, Reg.16, Reg.23, Sch.4 para.5, Sch.4 para.6

Sch.7 Part II para.17, varied: SI 2003/507 Sch.5 para.2

Sch.7 Part II para.17, enabling: SI 2003/507

Sch.7 Part II para.20, applied: SI 2002/432 Reg.3, Reg.4, SI 2004/1576 Reg.11, Reg.12

Sch.7 Part II para.20, enabling: SI 2002/432, SI 2004/1576

Sch.7 Part II para.21, amended: 2002 c.32 Sch.21 para.126

Sch.7 Part II para.21, applied: SI 2002/432 Reg.5, Reg.6, Sch.3 para.5, Sch.3 para.6, SI 2004/1576 Reg.13, Reg.14, Sch.4 para.5, Sch.4 para.6

Sch.7 Part II para.21, enabling: SI 2002/432, SI 2004/1576

Sch.7 Part II para.22, enabling: SI 2002/432, SI 2004/1576

Sch.7 Part II para.24, applied: SI 2003/507 Reg.13, Reg.14, Reg.17, Reg.28

Sch.7 Part II para.24, enabling: SI 2003/507

Sch.7 Part II para.25, amended: 2002 c.32 Sch.21 para.126

Sch.7 Part II para.25, applied: SI 2003/507 Reg.15, Reg.16, Reg.23, Sch.4 para.5, Sch.4 para.6

2000–cont.

21. Learning and Skills Act 2000–*cont.*
Sch.7 Part II para.25, varied: SI 2003/507 Sch.5 para.2

Sch.7 Part II para.25, enabling: SI 2003/507

Sch.7 Part II para.28, applied: SI 2002/432 Reg.3, Reg.4, SI 2004/1576 Reg.11, Reg.12

Sch.7 Part II para.28, enabling: SI 2002/432, SI 2004/1576

Sch.7 Part II para.29, amended: 2002 c.32 Sch.21 para.126

Sch.7 Part II para.29, applied: SI 2002/432 Reg.5, Reg.6, Sch.3 para.5, Sch.3 para.6, SI 2004/1576 Reg.13, Reg.14, Sch.4 para.5, Sch.4 para.6

Sch.7 Part II para.29, enabling: SI 2002/432, SI 2004/1576

Sch.7 Part II para.30, enabling: SI 2002/432, SI 2004/1576

Sch.7 Part II para.31, enabling: SI 2003/507

Sch.7 Part III, applied: SI 2002/432 Sch.2 para.7, Sch.2 para.14, SI 2003/507 Sch.3 para.7, Sch.3 para.14, Sch.5 para.1, SI 2004/1576 Sch.3 para.8, Sch.3 para.18

Sch.7 Part III para.32, amended: 2002 c.32 Sch.21 para.126

Sch.7 Part III para.33, enabling: SI 2003/507

Sch.7 Part III para.34, amended: 2002 c.32 Sch.10 para.12

Sch.7 Part III para.34, applied: SI 2003/507 Reg.17, Reg.20

Sch.7 Part III para.34, referred to: SI 2003/507 Sch.2 para.10

Sch.7 Part III para.34, enabling: SI 2003/507

Sch.7 Part III para.35, amended: 2002 c.32 Sch.10 para.13, Sch.22 Part 3

Sch.7 Part III para.35, applied: SI 2003/507 Reg.18, Reg.19, Reg.20, Reg.21, Reg.23, Reg.24, Reg.25

Sch.7 Part III para.35, repealed (in part): 2004 c.31 Sch.5 Part 1

Sch.7 Part III para.35, varied: SI 2003/507 Sch.5 para.3

Sch.7 Part III para.35, enabling: SI 2003/507

Sch.7 Part III para.36, applied: SI 2003/507 Reg.20, Reg.22, Reg.23, Reg.24, Reg.26

Sch.7 Part III para.36, enabling: SI 2003/507

Sch.7 Part III para.37, amended: 2002 c.32 Sch.10 para.14

Sch.7 Part III para.37, applied: SI 2003/507 Reg.20, Reg.21, Reg.22, Reg.23, Reg.25

Sch.7 Part III para.37, enabling: SI 2003/507

Sch.7 Part III para.38, disapplied: SI 2003/507 Reg.28

Sch.7 Part III para.39, amended: 2002 c.32 Sch.21 para.126

Sch.7 Part III para.39, enabling: SI 2002/432, SI 2004/1576

Sch.7 Part III para.40, enabling: SI 2002/432, SI 2004/1576

Sch.7 Part III para.41, applied: SI 2002/432 Reg.7, Sch.1 para.9, SI 2004/1576 Reg.15

2000–cont.

21. Learning and Skills Act 2000–*cont.*
Sch.7 Part III para.41, referred to: SI 2004/1576 Sch.2 para.10

Sch.7 Part III para.41, enabling: SI 2002/432, SI 2004/1576

Sch.7 Part III para.42, amended: 2002 c.32 Sch.10 para.15

Sch.7 Part III para.42, applied: SI 2002/432 Reg.8, Reg.9, SI 2004/1576 Reg.16, Reg.17

Sch.7 Part III para.42, repealed (in part): 2004 c.31 Sch.5 Part 1

Sch.7 Part III para.42, enabling: SI 2002/432, SI 2004/1576

Sch.7 Part III para.43, applied: SI 2002/432 Reg.9, Reg.10, SI 2004/1576 Reg.17, Reg.18

Sch.7 Part III para.43, enabling: SI 2002/432, SI 2004/1576

Sch.7 Part III para.44, applied: SI 2002/432 Reg.11, SI 2004/1576 Reg.19

Sch.7 Part III para.45, enabling: SI 2003/507

Sch.7A para.1, added: 2002 c.32 Sch.9

Sch.7A para.1, applied: SI 2003/507 Reg.10, SI 2003/1041 Reg.6, SI 2004/1576 Reg.10

Sch.7A para.1, referred to: SI 2004/1576 Reg.10

Sch.7A para.1, enabling: SI 2003/507, SI 2004/1576

Sch.7A para.2, added: 2002 c.32 Sch.9

Sch.7A para.3, added: 2002 c.32 Sch.9

Sch.7A para.3, applied: SI 2004/1576 Reg.19

Sch.7A para.3, disapplied: SI 2003/507 Reg.28

Sch.7A para.4, added: 2002 c.32 Sch.9

Sch.7A para.4, applied: SI 2004/1576 Reg.19

Sch.7A para.4, disapplied: SI 2003/507 Reg.28

Sch.7A para.5, added: 2002 c.32 Sch.9

Sch.7A para.6, added: 2002 c.32 Sch.9

Sch.7A para.7, added: 2002 c.32 Sch.9

Sch.8 para.1, repealed (in part): 2002 c.32 Sch.22 Part 3

Sch.8 para.2, repealed (in part): 2002 c.32 Sch.22 Part 3

Sch.8 para.3, repealed (in part): 2002 c.32 Sch.22 Part 3

Sch.8 para.4, repealed (in part): 2002 c.32 Sch.22 Part 3

Sch.8 para.5, repealed (in part): 2002 c.32 Sch.22 Part 3

Sch.8 para.6, repealed (in part): 2002 c.32 Sch.22 Part 3

Sch.8 para.7, repealed (in part): 2002 c.32 Sch.22 Part 3

Sch.8 para.8, repealed (in part): 2002 c.32 Sch.22 Part 3

Sch.8 para.9, repealed (in part): 2002 c.32 Sch.22 Part 3

Sch.8 para.10, repealed (in part): 2002 c.32 Sch.22 Part 3

CAP.

CAP.

2000–cont.

21. Learning and Skills Act 2000–*cont.*

Sch.8 para.11, repealed (in part): 2002 c.32 Sch.22 Part 3

Sch.8 para.12, repealed (in part): 2002 c.32 Sch.22 Part 3

Sch.8 para.13, repealed (in part): 2002 c.32 Sch.22 Part 3

Sch.8 para.14, repealed (in part): 2002 c.32 Sch.22 Part 3

Sch.9 para.18, repealed: 2002 c.32 Sch.22 Part 3

Sch.9 para.26, repealed (in part): 2002 c.32 Sch.22 Part 3

Sch.9 para.30, repealed (in part): 2002 c.32 Sch.22 Part 3

Sch.9 para.35, repealed (in part): 2002 c.32 Sch.22 Part 3

Sch.9 para.58, repealed (in part): 2002 c.32 Sch.22 Part 3

Sch.9 para.59, repealed (in part): 2002 c.32 Sch.22 Part 3

Sch.9 para.74, repealed: 2004 c.8 Sch.7

Sch.9 para.75, repealed: 2004 c.8 Sch.7

Sch.9 para.80, repealed: 2004 c.31 Sch.5 Part 1

Sch.9 para.81, repealed: 2004 c.31 Sch.5 Part 1

Sch.9 para.91, repealed (in part): 2002 c.32 Sch.22 Part 3

22. Local Government Act 2000

Commencement Orders: SI 2002/1359 Art.2; SI 2002/1718 Art.2

applied: SI 2003/533 Reg.17

referred to: SI 2002/803 Art.2, 2003 c.26 Sch.3 para.11

Part II, applied: 2002 c.32 s.183, SI 2002/803 Art.7, 2003 c.10 s.7, 2003 c.39 s.41, SI 2003/1021 Reg.5, SI 2003/2123 Reg.4, 2004 c.2 Sch.1 para.3, SI 2004/870 Reg.14, Reg.17, SI 2004/1412 Art.2

Part II, referred to: SI 2004/1425 Art.2

Part III, applied: SI 2003/533 Reg.17, SI 2003/1021 Reg.4, Reg.5, Reg.8, Reg.9, Reg.10, Reg.25, Reg.26, SI 2003/1483 Reg.7, 2004 c.23 s.54, SI 2004/2555 Reg.7, Reg.8, Reg.10, Reg.13, Reg.15, Reg.16

s.2, see *R. (on the application of A) v East Sussex CC (No.1)* [2002] EWHC 2771, [2003] B.L.G.R. 529 (QBD (Admin Ct)), Munby, J.; see *R. (on the application of Grant) v Lambeth LBC* [2004] EWHC 1524, [2004] 3 F.C.R. 494 (QBD (Admin Ct)), Mitting, J.; see *R. (on the application of J) v Enfield LBC* [2002] EWHC 432, [2002] 2 F.L.R. 1 (QBD (Admin Ct)), Elias, J.; see *R. (on the application of Khan) v Oxfordshire CC* [2002] EWHC 2211, [2003] H.L.R. 23 (QBD (Admin Ct)), Moses, J.; see *R. (on the application of Khan) v Oxfordshire CC* [2004] EWCA Civ 309, [2004] H.L.R. 41 (CA), Ward,

2000–cont.

22. Local Government Act 2000–*cont.*

s.2–*cont.*

L.J.; see *R. (on the application of Theophilus) v Lewisham LBC* [2002] EWHC 1371, [2002] 3 All E.R. 851 (QBD (Admin Ct)), Silber, J.; see *R. (on the application of Umo) v Commissioner for Local Adminstration in England* [2003] EWHC 3202, [2004] E.L.R. 265 (QBD (Admin Ct)), Beatson, J.

s.2, applied: 2002 c.41 s.55, Sch.3 para.1, SI 2002/522 Art.2, 2003 c.26 s.116, SI 2003/1987 Reg.3, SI 2004/684 Reg.3

s.3, see *R. (on the application of Grant) v Lambeth LBC* [2004] EWHC 1524, [2004] 3 F.C.R. 494 (QBD (Admin Ct)), Mitting, J.; see *R. (on the application of Khan) v Oxfordshire CC* [2002] EWHC 2211, [2003] H.L.R. 23 (QBD (Admin Ct)), Moses, J.; see *R. (on the application of Khan) v Oxfordshire CC* [2004] EWCA Civ 309, [2004] H.L.R. 41 (CA), Ward, L.J.

s.3, amended: 2003 c.26 Sch.3 para.12

s.3, applied: 2003 c.26 s.100.93

s.4, applied: SI 2003/154 Reg.8, 2004 c.5 s.19, s.62

s.5, applied: 2003 c.26 s.100

s.6, applied: 2003 c.26 s.100

s.6, enabling: SI 2003/1716

s.7, repealed (in part): 2003 c.33 s.35

s.9, amended: 2003 c.26 Sch.3 para.13

s.9, applied: SI 2002/3048 Reg.7, SI 2003/1716(c)

s.10, applied: SI 2003/1115 Art.4

s.11, applied: SI 2002/808 Art.40, Art.41, SI 2002/2880 Reg.5

s.13, applied: 2002 c.32 s.183, SI 2003/2676

s.13, enabling: SI 2002/783, SI 2002/1916, SI 2003/153, SI 2004/870, SI 2004/1158, SI 2004/2211, SI 2004/2748, SI 2004/3093

s.14, applied: SI 2002/802 Reg.3, Reg.9

s.15, applied: SI 2002/802 Reg.4, Reg.9

s.16, applied: SI 2002/802 Reg.9

s.18, enabling: SI 2002/802, SI 2002/2941, SI 2003/147

s.19, enabling: SI 2002/802, SI 2002/2941, SI 2003/147

s.20, enabling: SI 2002/802, SI 2002/2941, SI 2003/147

s.21, amended: 2003 c.26 Sch.7 para.80

s.21, applied: SI 2002/3048 Reg.2, Reg.7, 2003 c.43 s.9, SI 2003/1021 Reg.9, SI 2004/1412 Art.2, SI 2004/1425 Art.2

s.21, varied: SI 2002/3048 Reg.7

s.22, enabling: SI 2002/716, SI 2002/1385

s.27, applied: 2003 c.10 s.7, SI 2004/870 Reg.17

s.29, applied: SI 2002/2880 Reg.2, Reg.7, SI 2004/870 Reg.16, Reg.17

s.29, varied: SI 2004/870 Reg.17

s.30, enabling: SI 2002/2880, SI 2004/3158

2000–cont.

22. Local Government Act 2000–*cont.*
s.31, enabling: SI 2002/810
s.32, applied: SI 2003/2676
s.32, enabling: SI 2002/810, SI 2003/155, SI 2004/3092
s.33, applied: SI 2002/2880 Reg.2, Reg.7, SI 2004/870 Reg.16, Reg.17
s.33, enabling: SI 2002/2880, SI 2004/3158
s.34, enabling: SI 2003/398
s.36, applied: SI 2004/870 Reg.4
s.38, applied: SI 2002/802 Reg.6, Reg.11, SI 2002/3048 Reg.2, SI 2004/870 Reg.4
s.39, applied: SI 2004/555 Reg.2, SI 2004/557 Reg.2
s.39, enabling: SI 2002/975, SI 2004/1815
s.42, applied: SI 2002/185 Sch.3 para.48
s.44, applied: SI 2002/185, SI 2002/185 Reg.6, SI 2003/284 Sch.4 para.2, SI 2004/225, SI 2004/293 Reg.11, Sch.2 para.14, Sch.2 para.27, SI 2004/294 Reg.4, Reg.5, Reg.6, Reg.7, Reg.8
s.44, enabling: SI 2002/185, SI 2004/225, SI 2004/294
s.45, applied: SI 2002/185 Sch.3 para.41, SI 2004/226, SI 2004/293 Reg.11, Sch.2 para.14, Sch.2 para.27, SI 2004/294 Reg.4, Reg.5, Reg.6, Reg.7, Reg.8
s.45, enabling: SI 2002/521, SI 2004/226, SI 2004/294, SI 2004/870
s.47, enabling: SI 2002/803, SI 2002/808, SI 2002/1057
s.49, amended: 2004 c.21 Sch.1 para.94, 2004 c.23 Sch.2 para.53
s.49, applied: SI 2004/163, SI 2004/1510, SI 2004/1777 Art.14, SI 2004/1778 Art.14
s.49, varied: SI 2004/1777 Art.14, SI 2004/1778 Art.14
s.50, applied: 2003 c.20 Sch.4 para.9, SI 2004/163, SI 2004/1508 Art.3, SI 2004/1510
s.50, varied: SI 2004/1777 Art.14, SI 2004/1778 Art.14
s.50, enabling: SI 2002/1044, SI 2002/1719, SI 2004/163, SI 2004/1510
s.51, applied: SI 2004/1508 Art.3, SI 2004/1777 Art.14, SI 2004/1778 Art.14
s.51, varied: SI 2004/1777 Art.14, SI 2004/1778 Art.14
s.52, applied: SI 2004/870 Reg.8
s.52, varied: SI 2004/1777 Art.14, SI 2004/1778 Art.14
s.52, enabling: SI 2004/1508
s.53, varied: SI 2004/1777 Art.14, SI 2004/1778 Art.14
s.53, enabling: SI 2002/339, SI 2003/1483, SI 2004/2617
s.54, applied: SI 2004/870 Reg.8
s.54, varied: SI 2004/1777 Art.14, SI 2004/1778 Art.14
s.54, enabling: SI 2003/1483, SI 2004/2617
s.54A, added: 2003 c.26 s.113

2000–cont.

22. Local Government Act 2000–*cont.*
s.54A, varied: SI 2004/1777 Art.14, SI 2004/1778 Art.14
s.55, varied: SI 2004/1777 Art.14, SI 2004/1778 Art.14
s.55, enabling: SI 2003/1483, SI 2004/2617
s.56, varied: SI 2004/1777 Art.14, SI 2004/1778 Art.14
s.57, applied: SI 2003/1483 Reg.5, Reg.6
s.57, varied: SI 2004/1777 Art.14, SI 2004/1778 Art.14
s.57, enabling: SI 2004/2618
s.58, varied: SI 2004/1777 Art.14, SI 2004/1778 Art.14
s.59, varied: SI 2004/1777 Art.14, SI 2004/1778 Art.14
s.60, applied: SI 2003/1483 Reg.5, SI 2004/2618 Art.3
s.60, varied: SI 2004/1777 Art.14, SI 2004/1778 Art.14
s.61, varied: SI 2004/1777 Art.14, SI 2004/1778 Art.14
s.62, varied: SI 2004/1777 Art.14, SI 2004/1778 Art.14
s.63, amended: 2004 c.23 Sch.2 para.54
s.63, varied: SI 2003/1483 Reg.4, SI 2004/1777 Art.14, SI 2004/1778 Art.14
s.64, applied: SI 2003/1483 Reg.5, Reg.6, SI 2004/2618 Art.3
s.64, varied: SI 2004/1777 Art.14, SI 2004/1778 Art.14
s.65, varied: SI 2004/1777 Art.14, SI 2004/1778 Art.14
s.66, varied: SI 2004/1777 Art.14, SI 2004/1778 Art.14
s.66, enabling: SI 2003/1483, SI 2004/2617
s.67, varied: SI 2004/1777 Art.14, SI 2004/1778 Art.14
s.68, varied: SI 2004/1777 Art.14, SI 2004/1778 Art.14
s.69, varied: SI 2004/1777 Art.14, SI 2004/1778 Art.14
s.70, applied: SI 2004/2618 Art.3
s.70, varied: SI 2004/1777 Art.14, SI 2004/1778 Art.14
s.71, applied: SI 2003/1483 Reg.5, Reg.6, SI 2004/2618 Art.3
s.71, varied: SI 2004/1777 Art.14, SI 2004/1778 Art.14
s.72, varied: SI 2004/1777 Art.14, SI 2004/1778 Art.14
s.73, varied: SI 2004/1777 Art.14, SI 2004/1778 Art.14
s.73, enabling: SI 2003/1483, SI 2004/2617
s.74, varied: SI 2004/1777 Art.14, SI 2004/1778 Art.14
s.75, varied: SI 2004/1777 Art.14, SI 2004/1778 Art.14
s.76, varied: SI 2004/1777 Art.14, SI 2004/1778 Art.14

CAP.

2000–cont.

22. Local Government Act 2000–*cont.*

s.77, varied: SI 2004/1777 Art.14, SI 2004/1778 Art.14

s.78, varied: SI 2004/1777 Art.14, SI 2004/1778 Art.14

s.79, applied: SI 2003/3190 Reg.4

s.79, varied: SI 2004/1777 Art.14, SI 2004/1778 Art.14

s.80, varied: SI 2004/1777 Art.14, SI 2004/1778 Art.14

s.81, applied: SI 2002/339 Reg.4

s.81, varied: SI 2004/1777 Art.14, SI 2004/1778 Art.14

s.81, enabling: SI 2002/339, SI 2004/163, SI 2004/1510

s.82, amended: 2004 c.23 Sch.2 para.55

s.82, varied: SI 2004/1777 Art.14, SI 2004/1778 Art.14

s.82A, added: 2003 c.26 s.113

s.82A, applied: SI 2003/1483 Reg.2

s.82A, varied: SI 2004/1777 Art.14, SI 2004/1778 Art.14

s.83, varied: SI 2004/1777 Art.14, SI 2004/1778 Art.14

s.86, applied: SI 2002/1962 Art.2, SI 2002/2954 Art.2

s.86, referred to: SI 2003/984 Art.2

s.86, enabling: SI 2002/1962, SI 2002/2954, SI 2003/984

s.87, applied: SI 2002/1962 Art.2

s.87, enabling: SI 2002/1670, SI 2002/1962, SI 2002/2876, SI 2003/984

s.93, amended: 2002 c.38 s.136

s.93, applied: SI 2002/1792 Sch.5 para.20, SI 2002/2006 Reg.19

s.94, amended: 2002 c.16 Sch.2 para.43

s.99, enabling: SI 2003/2437, SI 2004/928

s.100, applied: SI 2002/1895, SI 2002/1895 Reg.3, SI 2003/895 Reg.3, SI 2003/1021, SI 2003/1692, SI 2004/2555, SI 2004/2555 Reg.3, SI 2004/2596

s.100, enabling: SI 2003/895, SI 2003/1021, SI 2003/1692, SI 2004/2555, SI 2004/2596

s.101, applied: SI 2002/802 Reg.5, SI 2004/1815 Reg.2

s.101, enabling: SI 2004/3082

s.102, amended: 2004 c.31 s.55

s.102, repealed (in part): 2004 c.31 s.55

s.104, referred to: 2003 c.26 s.128

s.104, repealed: 2003 c.26 Sch.8 Part 1

s.105, amended: 2003 c.26 Sch.3 para.14

s.105, applied: SI 2002/185 Sch.3 para.41, SI 2002/1895, SI 2003/2676, SI 2004/293 Reg.11, Sch.2 para.14, Sch.2 para.27, SI 2004/294 Reg.4, Reg.5, Reg.6, Reg.7, Reg.8

s.105, enabling: SI 2002/185, SI 2002/339, SI 2002/521, SI 2002/716, SI 2002/783, SI 2002/802, SI 2002/803, SI 2002/808, SI 2002/975, SI 2002/1044, SI

CAP.

2000–cont.

22. Local Government Act 2000–*cont.*

s.105, enabling:–*cont.*

2002/1057, SI 2002/1385, SI 2002/1670, SI 2002/1718, SI 2002/1719, SI 2002/1916, SI 2002/1962, SI 2002/2876, SI 2002/2880, SI 2002/2941, SI 2002/2954, SI 2003/147, SI 2003/153, SI 2003/155, SI 2003/398, SI 2003/895, SI 2003/984, SI 2003/1021, SI 2003/1483, SI 2003/1692, SI 2003/1716, SI 2004/225, SI 2004/226, SI 2004/294, SI 2004/870, SI 2004/1158, SI 2004/1510, SI 2004/1815, SI 2004/2211, SI 2004/2555, SI 2004/2596, SI 2004/2617, SI 2004/2618, SI 2004/2748, SI 2004/3082, SI 2004/3092, SI 2004/3093, SI 2004/3158

s.106, applied: SI 2003/2676

s.106, enabling: SI 2002/783, SI 2002/802, SI 2002/803, SI 2002/808, SI 2002/810, SI 2002/1385, SI 2002/2880, SI 2002/2941, SI 2003/147, SI 2003/153, SI 2003/155, SI 2003/398, SI 2004/3092, SI 2004/3093, SI 2004/3158

s.108, enabling: SI 2002/1359, SI 2002/1718

Sch.1, applied: SI 2002/3048 Reg.7

Sch.1 para.6, enabling: SI 2002/975

Sch.1 para.12, added: 2003 c.26 s.115

Sch.1 para.13, added: 2003 c.26 s.115

Sch.1 para.14, added: 2003 c.26 s.115

Sch.2, applied: SI 2002/185 Sch.3 para.48

Sch.2 para.2, applied: SI 2002/185 Sch.3 para.45

Sch.2 para.3, applied: SI 2002/185 Sch.3 para.45, Sch.3 para.47

Sch.4 para.9A, added: 2003 c.26 s.112

Sch.4 para.13, amended: SI 2003/1326 Art.20

Sch.5 para.14, repealed (in part): 2004 c.21 Sch.2

Sch.5 para.16, repealed: 2002 c.38 Sch.5

Sch.5 para.29, repealed: 2003 c.43 Sch.14 Part 2

23. Regulation of Investigatory Powers Act 2000

Commencement Orders: SI 2003/3140 Art.2

applied: SI 2003/3172 Sch.2 Part I

referred to: 2003 c.32 Sch.5 para.78

Part I, applied: 2002 c.29 s.436, s.438, s.439, s.441

Part I c.I, applied: SI 2002/1693, SI 2002/1693 Art.2

Part II, applied: 2002 c.30 s.19, SI 2002/1932, SI 2002/1932 Art.2, SI 2002/1933, SI 2002/1933 Art.2

Part IV, applied: 2002 c.30 s.19

s.1, see *R. (on the application of NTL Group Ltd) v Ipswich Crown Court* [2002] EWHC 1585, [2003] Q.B. 131 (QBD (Admin Ct)), Lord Woolf of Barnes, L.C.J.; see *R. v E* [2004] EWCA Crim 1243, [2004] 1 W.L.R. 3279 (CA (Crim Div)), Rose, L.J.

2000–cont.

23. Regulation of Investigatory Powers Act 2000–*cont.*
s.1, applied: SI 2004/158 Art.2
s.1, enabling: SI 2004/158
s.2, see *R. v E* [2004] EWCA Crim 1243, [2004] 1 W.L.R. 3279 (CA (Crim Div)), Rose, L.J.; see *R. v Hardy (Brian)* [2002] EWCA Crim 3012, [2003] 1 Cr. App. R. 30 (CA (Crim Div)), Hughes, J.
s.4, enabling: SI 2004/157
s.5, applied: SI 2003/2617 Art.2, Sch.1 para.1, Sch.1 para.2
s.5, varied: SI 2003/2617 Sch.2
s.8, applied: SI 2003/2617 Sch.1 para.1
s.9, applied: SI 2003/2617 Art.2, Sch.1 para.2
s.9, varied: SI 2003/2617 Sch.2
s.10, applied: SI 2003/2617 Art.2, Sch.1 para.2
s.10, varied: SI 2003/2617 Sch.2
s.12, applied: SI 2002/1931
s.12, enabling: SI 2002/1931
s.15, applied: SI 2003/2617 Art.2, Sch.1 para.2
s.15, varied: SI 2003/2617 Sch.2
s.17, see *Attorney General's Reference (No.5 of 2002), Re* [2003] EWCA Crim 1632, [2003] 1 W.L.R. 2902 (CA (Crim Div)), Clarke, L.J.; see *Attorney General's Reference (No.5 of 2002), Re* [2004] UKHL 40, [2004] 3 W.L.R. 957 (HL), Lord Bingham of Cornhill; see *R. v E* [2004] EWCA Crim 1243, [2004] 1 W.L.R. 3279 (CA (Crim Div)), Rose, L.J.
s.18, see *Attorney General's Reference (No.5 of 2002), Re* [2004] UKHL 40, [2004] 3 W.L.R. 957 (HL), Lord Bingham of Cornhill
s.18, repealed (in part): 2003 c.21 Sch.19
s.21, applied: SI 2003/3172 Art.7, Art.8, Art.10
s.22, referred to: SI 2003/3172 Art.6, Art.7
s.25, applied: SI 2003/3172 Art.2, Art.3, Art.4, Art.5
s.25, enabling: SI 2003/3172
s.26, see *R. v Hardy (Brian)* [2002] EWCA Crim 3012, [2003] 1 Cr. App. R. 30 (CA (Crim Div)), Hughes, L.J.
s.26, amended: 2003 c.21 Sch.17 para.161
s.28, applied: SI 2003/3171 Art.4, Art.7, Art.8, Art.10, Sch.1 Part I, Sch.1 Part II, SI 2004/815 Art.4, SR 2002/292 Art.4
s.28, referred to: SI 2003/3171 Sch.1 Part I, Sch.1 Part II, SI 2004/815 Art.4
s.29, applied: SI 2003/3171 Art.4, Art.7, Art.8, Art.10, Sch.1 Part I, Sch.1 Part II, SI 2004/815 Art.4
s.29, referred to: SI 2003/3171 Sch.1 Part I, Sch.1 Part II, SI 2004/815 Art.4
s.30, applied: SI 2003/3171 Art.4, Art.5, Art.6, SI 2004/815 Art.4, Art.5, SR 2002/292 Art.2, Art.3

2000–cont.

23. Regulation of Investigatory Powers Act 2000–*cont.*
s.30, enabling: SI 2002/1298, SI 2003/3171, SR 2002/183, SR 2002/292
s.31, enabling: SR 2002/183, SR 2002/292
s.32, amended: 2002 c.40 s.199, Sch.26
s.32, varied: SI 2004/815 Art.3
s.33, amended: 2002 c.40 s.199
s.33, varied: SI 2004/815 Art.3
s.34, amended: 2002 c.40 s.199
s.34, varied: SI 2004/815 Art.3
s.35, amended: 2002 c.40 s.199, Sch.26
s.35, varied: SI 2004/815 Art.3
s.36, amended: 2002 c.40 s.199, Sch.26
s.36, varied: SI 2004/815 Art.3
s.37, amended: 2002 c.40 s.199, Sch.26
s.37, varied: SI 2004/815 Art.3
s.40, amended: 2002 c.40 s.199
s.40, varied: SI 2004/815 Art.3
s.41, applied: SI 2003/3174 Art.2
s.41, enabling: SI 2003/3174
s.45, varied: SI 2004/815 Art.3
s.46, amended: 2002 c.40 s.199, 2004 c.20 Sch.14 para.8
s.48, amended: 2002 c.40 s.199
s.65, amended: 2003 c.32 Sch.5 para.79
s.65, applied: SI 2003/409 Sch.1 Part I
s.65, varied: SI 2004/815 Art.3
s.68, varied: SI 2004/815 Art.3
s.71, applied: SI 2002/1693, SI 2002/1932, SI 2002/1933
s.71, referred to: SI 2002/1693, SI 2002/1932, SI 2002/1933
s.71, enabling: SI 2002/1693, SI 2002/1932, SI 2002/1933
s.76A, added: 2003 c.32 s.83
s.76A, applied: 2003 c.32 s.84, SI 2004/1128 Art.2
s.76A, enabling: SI 2004/1128
s.78, amended: 2003 c.32 Sch.5 para.80
s.78, enabling: SI 2002/1298, SI 2002/1931, SI 2003/3171
s.81, amended: 2002 c.26 Sch.4 para.40
s.83, enabling: SI 2003/3140
Sch.1 Part I, referred to: SI 2003/3171 Sch.1 Part I
Sch.1 Part I para.1A, added: SI 2003/3171 Art.2
Sch.1 Part I para.1A, substituted: 2004 c.20 Sch.14 para.8
Sch.1 Part I para.4A, varied: SI 2004/815 Art.3
Sch.1 Part I para.9, amended: SI 2002/794 Sch.2
Sch.1 Part I para.10i, amended: SI 2002/794 Sch.1 para.39
Sch.1 Part I para.13A, added: SI 2003/3171 Art.2
Sch.1 Part I para.14, amended: SI 2002/1397 Sch.1 para.16, SI 2002/2626 Sch.2 para.24

2000–cont.

23. Regulation of Investigatory Powers Act 2000–*cont.*

Sch.1 Part I para.15i, amended: SI 2002/2626
Sch.2 para.24

Sch.1 Part I para.15ii, amended: SI 2002/1397
Sch.1 para.16

Sch.1 Part I para.17, substituted: SI 2003/3171
Art.2

Sch.1 Part I para.17A, added: SI 2003/3171
Art.2

Sch.1 Part I para.17B, added: SI 2003/3171
Art.2

Sch.1 Part I para.20A, added: SI 2003/3171
Art.2

Sch.1 Part I para.20B, added: SI 2003/3171
Art.2

Sch.1 Part I para.20C, added: SI 2003/3171
Art.2

Sch.1 Part I para.20D, added: SI 2003/3171
Art.2

Sch.1 Part I para.22, repealed: SI 2002/1555
Art.26

Sch.1 Part I para.23A, added: 2003 c.21
Sch.17 para.161

Sch.1 Part I para.23A, added: SR 2002/183
Art.3

Sch.1 Part I para.23B, added: SR 2002/183
Art.3

Sch.1 Part I para.23C, added: SR 2002/183
Art.3

Sch.1 Part I para.23D, added: SR 2002/183
Art.3

Sch.1 Part II, referred to: SI 2003/3171 Sch.1
Part II

Sch.1 Part II para.27A, added: SI 2003/3171
Art.3

Sch.1 Part II para.27B, added: SI 2003/3171
Art.3

Sch.1 Part II para.27C, added: SI 2003/3171
Art.3

Sch.1 Part II para.27D, added: SI 2003/3171
Art.3

Sch.1 Part II para.29, added: SR 2002/183
Art.4

Sch.1 Part II para.30, added: SR 2002/183
Art.4

Sch.1 Part II para.31, added: SR 2002/183
Art.4

Sch.1 Part II para.32, added: SR 2002/183
Art.4

Sch.1 Part II para.33, added: SR 2002/183
Art.4

Sch.1 Part II para.34, added: SR 2002/183
Art.4

Sch.1 Part II para.35, added: SR 2002/183
Art.4

Sch.1 Part II para.36, added: SR 2002/183
Art.4

Sch.1 Part II para.37, added: SR 2002/183
Art.4

2000–cont.

23. Regulation of Investigatory Powers Act 2000–*cont.*

Sch.1 Part II para.38, added: SR 2002/183
Art.4

Sch.1 Part II para.39, added: SR 2002/183
Art.4

Sch.1 Part II para.40, added: SR 2002/183
Art.4

Sch.2 para.1, amended: 2003 c.39 Sch.4
para.12

Sch.4 para.3, repealed: 2003 c.21 Sch.19

25. Football (Disorder) Act 2000

see *Gough v Chief Constable of Derbyshire*
[2001] EWHC Admin 554, [2002] Q.B.
459 (QBD (Admin Ct)), Laws, L.J.; see
Gough v Chief Constable of Derbyshire
[2002] EWCA Civ 351, [2002] Q.B. 1213
(CA), Lord Phillips of Worth Matravers,
M.R.

s.3, amended: 2002 c.12 s.1

s.3, enabling: SI 2004/2409

s.5, amended: 2002 c.12 s.1

s.5, repealed (in part): 2002 c.12 s.1

26. Postal Services Act 2000

see *Consignia Plc v Hays Plc* Times, January
24, 2002 (Ch D), Jacob, J.

applied: 2002 c.18 Sch.2 Part 2, 2002 c.40
Sch.15, SI 2003/284 Art.135, SI 2003/
3171 Sch.1 Part I, SI 2003/3172 Sch.2 Part
III, SI 2004/293 Reg.122, SI 2004/1267
Reg.111

referred to: SI 2002/3113 Reg.4, SI 2004/
2443 Sch.2 para.10

Part II, applied: SI 2003/1907 Art.9, SI 2004/
2443 Sch.2 para.10

Part IV, applied: SI 2003/409 Sch.1 Part I, SI
2003/437 Sch.1 Part 2

s.4, referred to: SI 2002/2779 Art.28

s.6, amended: SI 2002/3050 Reg.2

s.7, amended: SI 2002/200 Art.2, SI 2002/
3050 Reg.3

s.7, applied: SI 2003/1907 Art.9, SI 2004/
2443 Sch.2 para.10

s.7, referred to: SI 2002/200

s.7A, added: SI 2002/3050 Reg.4

s.8, applied: SI 2002/200

s.8, enabling: SI 2002/200

s.12A, added: SI 2002/3050 Reg.5

s.12B, added: SI 2002/3050 Reg.6

s.12B, amended: SI 2002/3050 Reg.8

s.15, applied: SI 2003/1397 Art.8

s.15A, added: 2002 c.40 Sch.25 para.42

s.15B, added: 2002 c.40 Sch.25 para.42

s.15B, amended: 2003 c.21 Sch.16 para.6

s.15B, referred to: SI 2003/1371

s.15B, enabling: SI 2003/1371

s.16A, added: 2002 c.40 Sch.25 para.42

s.19A, added: 2002 c.40 Sch.25 para.42

s.19A, amended: 2003 c.21 Sch.16 para.6

s.19A, referred to: SI 2003/1371

s.19A, enabling: SI 2003/1371

2000–cont.

26. Postal Services Act 2000–*cont.*
s.20, repealed: 2002 c.40 Sch.26
s.21, amended: 2002 c.40 Sch.9 para.14
s.21, varied: SI 2003/1592 Sch.4 para.16
s.30, enabling: SI 2002/125
s.57, amended: 2002 c.40 Sch.25 para.42
s.74, varied: SI 2003/1633 Sch.2 para.8
s.89, applied: SI 2002/2779 Art.59, SI 2003/284 Art.64, SI 2004/293 Reg.124, SI 2004/1267 Reg.113
s.116, see *Royal Mail Group Plc (formerly Consignia Plc) v i-CD Publishing (UK) Ltd (Preliminary Issue)* [2004] EWHC 286, [2004] E.C.D.R. 18 (Ch D), Lloyd, J.
s.122, applied: SI 2002/125, SI 2002/200, SI 2003/2908
s.122, enabling: SI 2003/1542, SI 2003/2908
s.125, amended: SI 2002/3050 Reg.7, 2003 c.21 Sch.17 para.162
s.127, enabling: SI 2003/2908
s.128, enabling: SI 2003/1542
Sch.7 para.1, amended: 2003 c.20 Sch.2 para.19
Sch.7 para.2, amended: 2003 c.20 Sch.2 para.19
Sch.7 para.3, amended: 2002 c.40 Sch.25 para.42, 2003 c.20 Sch.2 para.19, 2003 c.21 Sch.17 para.162, 2003 c.37 Sch.7 para.33
Sch.7 para.3, repealed (in part): 2003 c.21 Sch.19
Sch.7 para.4, amended: 2003 c.20 Sch.2 para.19
Sch.7 para.5, amended: 2003 c.20 Sch.2 para.19
Sch.7 para.6, amended: 2003 c.20 Sch.2 para.19
Sch.8 Part I para.3, referred to: 2003 asp 2 s.98

27. Utilities Act 2000
applied: 2002 c.40 Sch.15, SI 2003/419 Art.63, SI 2004/2541 Reg.3, SI 2004/2542 Reg.3
referred to: 2003 c.30
s.5, amended: 2002 c.40 Sch.25 para.43
s.5A, added: 2003 c.30 s.6
s.17, amended: 2004 c.20 s.179
s.28, repealed (in part): 2004 c.20 Sch.23 Part 1
s.33, amended: 2004 c.20 Sch.19 para.20, Sch.23 Part 1
s.33, applied: SI 2004/2541 Reg.3
s.40, repealed (in part): 2002 c.40 Sch.26
s.53, repealed (in part): 2004 c.20 Sch.23 Part 1
s.67, enabling: SSI 2002/92, SSI 2002/93
s.81, amended: 2004 c.20 s.168
s.81, applied: SI 2004/2542 Reg.3
s.103, enabling: SI 2004/3392
s.104, amended: 2003 c.37 s.53, Sch.9 Part 2

2000–cont.

27. Utilities Act 2000–*cont.*
s.104, applied: 2003 c.37 s.53, 2004 c.20 s.176, Sch.22 para.5
s.104, repealed (in part): 2003 c.37 s.53
s.105, amended: 2002 c.40 Sch.25 para.43, SI 2002/1555 Art.27, 2003 c.20 Sch.2 para.19, 2003 c.21 Sch.17 para.163, 2003 c.37 Sch.7 para.34, 2004 c.20 s.186
s.105, disapplied: 2004 c.20 s.140
s.105, referred to: 2003 c.20 s.115
Sch.6 Part I para.9, repealed: 2002 c.40 Sch.26
Sch.6 Part II para.31, repealed (in part): 2004 c.20 Sch.23 Part 1

29. Trustee Act 2000
applied: 2004 c.iv s.12
s.41, applied: SI 2004/1194
s.41, enabling: SI 2004/1194
Sch.2 Part II para.26, repealed: 2002 c.9 Sch.13
Sch.2 Part II para.34, repealed: 2004 c.25 Sch.6

30. Licensing (Young Persons) Act 2000
see *Haringey LBC v Marks & Spencer Plc* [2004] EWHC 1141, [2004] 3 All E.R. 868 (QBD (Admin Ct)), Maurice Kay, L.J.
repealed: 2003 c.17 Sch.7

31. Warm Homes and Energy Conservation Act 2000
Commencement Orders: SI 2002/758 Art.2
s.2, referred to: 2003 c.30 s.4
s.4, enabling: SI 2002/758

32. Police (Northern Ireland) Act 2000
Commencement Orders: SR 2002/146 Sch.1, Art.2; SR 2003/66 Art.2, Art.3
applied: 2002 c.29 s.220, s.302, SI 2004/702 Art.78
referred to: 2003 c.6 s.40
Part VI, added: 2003 c.6 s.20
s.3, amended: 2003 c.6 s.20
s.4, applied: SR 2002/258 Reg.3, Reg.4, Reg.5, Reg.6, Reg.7, Reg.8
s.5A, added: 2003 c.6 s.5
s.8, repealed (in part): 2002 c.1 Sch.4
s.9, amended: 2003 c.6 s.6, s.12
s.9, applied: SR 2002/76 Reg.3
s.10, amended: 2003 c.6 s.6
s.10, applied: SR 2002/76 Reg.3
s.12, amended: 2003 c.6 s.7
s.15A, added: 2003 c.6 Sch.1 para.2
s.17, amended: 2003 c.6 Sch.1 para.3
s.18, amended: 2003 c.6 Sch.1 para.4
s.21, substituted: 2003 c.6 Sch.1 para.5
s.21A, added: 2003 c.6 Sch.1 para.6
s.21B, added: 2003 c.6 Sch.1 para.7
s.21C, added: 2003 c.6 Sch.1 para.8
s.21D, added: 2003 c.6 Sch.1 para.9
s.22, amended: 2003 c.6 Sch.1 para.10
s.24, amended: 2003 c.6 s.1
s.24, applied: SR 2002/76 Reg.3

CAP.

2000–cont.

32. Police (Northern Ireland) Act 2000– *cont.*

s.25, amended: 2003 c.6 s.3, Sch.4
s.25, applied: SR 2002/76 Reg.3
s.26, applied: SR 2002/76 Reg.3
s.26, enabling: SR 2002/76
s.27, amended: 2003 c.6 s.2, s.6
s.28, amended: 2003 c.6 s.8
s.28, applied: SR 2002/76 Reg.3
s.28, repealed (in part): 2003 c.6 s.8, Sch.4
s.29, amended: 2003 c.6 s.9
s.31, amended: 2003 c.6 s.9
s.32, repealed (in part): 2003 c.6 s.20, Sch.4
s.33, amended: 2003 c.6 s.21
s.33A, added: 2003 c.6 s.22
s.36, amended: 2003 c.6 s.23
s.36, repealed (in part): 2003 c.6 s.23
s.36A, added: 2003 c.6 s.24
s.37, applied: SR 2003/28 Sch.6 para.2
s.38, applied: 2002 c.26 Sch.4 para.1
s.41, enabling: SR 2002/385
s.43, enabling: SR 2002/258, SR 2002/385
s.44, enabling: SR 2002/258, SR 2002/385
s.46, see *Parsons Application for Judicial Review, Re* [2004] N.I. 38 (CA (NI)), Lord Carswell L.C.J.
s.46, applied: SR 2002/258 Reg.8
s.47A, added: 2003 c.6 s.23
s.47A, repealed: 2003 c.6 s.23
s.49, applied: SR 2003/60
s.51, applied: 2003 c.6 s.36
s.51, varied: 2003 c.6 s.36
s.52, amended: 2004 c.4 s.8
s.52, applied: 2003 c.6 s.37, SR 2003/68SI-BEGIN
s.52, referred to: SR 2003/68 Reg.2
s.54, enabling: SR 2002/23
s.57, amended: 2003 c.6 s.20
s.59, amended: 2003 c.6 s.10, s.27
s.59, applied: 2003 c.6 s.10, s.29
s.60, amended: 2003 c.6 s.11
s.60, applied: 2003 c.6 s.11, s.29
s.63, repealed (in part): 2003 c.6 Sch.4
s.66, amended: 2003 c.6 s.13
s.66, substituted: 2003 c.6 s.13
s.67, applied: SR 2003/237 Art.2
s.67, enabling: SR 2003/237
s.70, enabling: SR 2002/260
s.73, applied: SR 2002/179 Art.2, SR 2003/232 Art.2
s.73, enabling: SR 2002/179, SR 2003/232
s.74A, added: 2003 c.6 s.27
s.76A, added: 2003 c.6 s.29
s.77, amended: 2003 c.6 s.6, s.28, SR 2003/184 Reg.2
Sch.1 Part II para.3, amended: 2003 c.6 Sch.1 para.11, Sch.4
Sch.1 Part III para.10, amended: 2003 c.6 Sch.1 para.11, Sch.4
Sch.1 Part VI para.17, amended: 2003 c.6 s.23

CAP.

2000–cont.

32. Police (Northern Ireland) Act 2000– *cont.*

Sch.1 Part VI para.17A, added: 2003 c.6 s.23
Sch.1 Part VI para.17A, repealed: 2003 c.6 s.23
Sch.1 Part VI para.18, amended: 2003 c.6 s.12
Sch.1 Part VI para.18, applied: 2003 c.6 s.12
Sch.1 Part VI para.19, amended: 2003 c.6 s.4
Sch.1 Part VI para.19, repealed (in part): 2003 c.6 s.4, Sch.4
Sch.1 Part VI para.24, amended: 2003 c.6 s.28
Sch.3 para.1, amended: 2003 c.6 s.15
Sch.3 para.4, amended: 2003 c.6 s.14
Sch.3 para.5, amended: 2003 c.6 s.15
Sch.3 para.7, amended: 2003 c.6 s.15
Sch.3 para.8, amended: 2003 c.6 s.16, s.17
Sch.3 para.10A, added: 2003 c.6 s.18
Sch.3 para.10B, added: 2003 c.6 s.18
Sch.3 para.17, added: 2003 c.6 Sch.1 para.12
Sch.3 para.17, amended: 2003 c.6 Sch.1 para.16
Sch.3 para.17, repealed (in part): 2003 c.6 Sch.1 para.16
Sch.3A para.1, added: 2003 c.6 Sch.1 para.13
Sch.3A para.2, added: 2003 c.6 Sch.1 para.13
Sch.3A para.3, added: 2003 c.6 Sch.1 para.13
Sch.3A para.4, added: 2003 c.6 Sch.1 para.13
Sch.3A para.4, amended: 2003 c.6 Sch.1 para.16
Sch.3A para.4, repealed (in part): 2003 c.6 Sch.1 para.16
Sch.3A para.5, added: 2003 c.6 Sch.1 para.13
Sch.3A para.6, added: 2003 c.6 Sch.1 para.13
Sch.3A para.7, added: 2003 c.6 Sch.1 para.13
Sch.3A para.8, added: 2003 c.6 Sch.1 para.13
Sch.3A para.9, added: 2003 c.6 Sch.1 para.13
Sch.3A para.10, added: 2003 c.6 Sch.1 para.13
Sch.3A para.11, added: 2003 c.6 Sch.1 para.13
Sch.3A para.12, added: 2003 c.6 Sch.1 para.13
Sch.3A para.13, added: 2003 c.6 Sch.1 para.13
Sch.3A para.14, added: 2003 c.6 Sch.1 para.13
Sch.3A para.15, added: 2003 c.6 Sch.1 para.13
Sch.3A para.16, added: 2003 c.6 Sch.1 para.13
Sch.3A para.17, added: 2003 c.6 Sch.1 para.13

33. Fur Farming (Prohibition) Act 2000

s.1, applied: SI 2002/221 Art.3, Sch.1 para.1, Sch.1 para.3, Sch.5 para.11, Sch.5 para.17, SI 2004/1964 Art.3, Sch.2 para.1, Sch.2 para.3, Sch.6 para.10, Sch.6 para.16
s.5, amended: SI 2002/794 Sch.1 para.40
s.5, applied: SI 2002/221 Art.5, Art.8, Sch.2 para.9, Sch.2 para.10, Sch.4 para.11, Sch.4 para.12, SI 2004/1964 Art.5, Art.6, Sch.4 para.7, Sch.5 para.9

2000–cont.

33. Fur Farming (Prohibition) Act 2000–
cont.
s.5, referred to: SI 2002/221 Sch.4 para.12
s.5, enabling: SI 2002/221, SI 2004/1964
s.6, amended: SI 2002/794 Sch.1 para.41
s.7, amended: SI 2002/794 Sch.1 para.42

34. Race Relations (Amendment) Act 2000
see *Chief Constable of Bedfordshire v Liversidge* [2002] EWCA Civ 894, [2002] I.C.R. 1135 (CA), Peter Gibson, L.J.; see *Chief Constable of Bedfordshire v Liversidge* [2002] I.R.L.R. 15 (EAT), Lindsay, J. (President)
Sch.2 para.23, repealed: 2002 c.41 Sch.9
Sch.2 para.24, repealed: 2002 c.41 Sch.9
Sch.2 para.25, repealed: 2002 c.41 Sch.9
Sch.2 para.26, repealed: 2002 c.41 Sch.9
Sch.2 para.27, repealed: 2002 c.41 Sch.9
Sch.2 para.28, repealed: 2002 c.41 Sch.9
Sch.2 para.29, repealed: 2002 c.41 Sch.9
Sch.2 para.32, repealed: 2002 c.41 Sch.9
Sch.2 para.33, repealed: 2002 c.41 Sch.9
Sch.2 para.34, repealed: 2002 c.41 Sch.9
Sch.2 para.35, repealed: 2002 c.41 Sch.9
Sch.2 para.36, repealed: 2002 c.41 Sch.9
Sch.2 para.37, repealed: 2002 c.41 Sch.9
Sch.2 para.38, repealed: 2002 c.41 Sch.9
Sch.2 para.39, repealed: 2002 c.41 Sch.9
Sch.2 para.40, repealed: 2002 c.41 Sch.9

35. Children (Leaving Care) Act 2000
see *R. (on the application of Berhe) v Hillingdon LBC* [2003] EWHC 2075, [2004] 1 F.L.R. 439 (QBD (Admin Ct)), Sullivan, J.; see *R. (on the application of M) v Barking and Dagenham LBC* [2002] EWHC 2663, (2003) C.C.L. Rep. 87 (QBD (Admin Ct)), Crane, J.
s.6, applied: SI 2004/747, SI 2004/747 Reg.2, SSI 2003/608 Reg.13
s.6, enabling: SI 2004/565, SI 2004/747

36. Freedom of Information Act 2000
Commencement Orders: SI 2002/2812 Art.2, Art.3, Art.4, Art.5; SI 2003/2603 Art.2, Art.3, Art.4, Sch.1 Part 1, 2; SI 2004/1909 Art.2; SI 2004/3122 Art.2
applied: 2002 asp 13 s.3, s.35, SI 2003/1887 Sch.1, SI 2004/1768 Reg.7, Reg.15
referred to: 2003 c.43 Sch.4 para.113
Part IV, applied: 2002 asp 11 Sch.5
Part V, applied: 2002 asp 11 Sch.5
s.1, applied: SI 2004/1468 Sch.6 para.12
s.4, amended: SI 2003/1887 Sch.2 para.12
s.4, applied: SI 2002/2623, SI 2003/1882
s.4, enabling: SI 2002/2623, SI 2003/1882, SI 2003/1883, SI 2004/938, SI 2004/1641, SI 2004/1870
s.5, amended: SI 2003/1887 Sch.2 para.12
s.6, applied: SI 2003/2603 Art.3
s.7, amended: SI 2003/1887 Sch.2 para.12
s.7, enabling: SI 2002/2623, SI 2003/1882

2000–cont.

36. Freedom of Information Act 2000–
cont.
s.9, amended: SI 2003/1887 Sch.2 para.12
s.9, enabling: SI 2004/3244
s.10, amended: SI 2003/1887 Sch.2 para.12
s.10, enabling: SI 2004/3364
s.12, amended: SI 2003/1887 Sch.2 para.12
s.12, enabling: SI 2004/3244
s.13, amended: SI 2003/1887 Sch.2 para.12
s.13, enabling: SI 2004/3244
s.15, disapplied: SI 2003/1887 Sch.1
s.23, disapplied: SI 2003/1887 Sch.1
s.24, disapplied: SI 2003/1887 Sch.1
s.36, disapplied: SI 2003/1887 Sch.1
s.45, amended: SI 2003/1887 Sch.2 para.12
s.46, amended: SI 2003/1887 Sch.2 para.12
s.46, disapplied: SI 2003/1887 Sch.1
s.47, amended: SI 2003/1887 Sch.2 para.12
s.48, applied: 2002 asp 11 Sch.5
s.53, amended: SI 2003/1887 Sch.2 para.12
s.53, disapplied: SI 2003/1887 Sch.1
s.65, disapplied: SI 2003/1887 Sch.1
s.66, disapplied: SI 2003/1887 Sch.1
s.69, amended: SI 2003/1887 Sch.2 para.12
s.75, amended: SI 2003/1887 Sch.2 para.12
s.75, enabling: SI 2004/3363
s.76, amended: 2002 asp 11 Sch.6 para.23, 2004 c.34 Sch.15 para.46
s.76, applied: 2002 asp 11 s.19
s.77, applied: 2002 asp 11 Sch.5
s.82, amended: SI 2003/1887 Sch.2 para.12
s.82, enabling: SI 2004/3363, SI 2004/3364
s.83, amended: SI 2003/1887 Sch.2 para.12
s.83, applied: SI 2002/2832, SI 2002/2832 Art.2
s.83, enabling: SI 2002/2832
s.84, amended: SI 2003/1887 Sch.2 para.12
s.85, amended: SI 2003/1887 Sch.2 para.12
s.87, amended: SI 2003/1887 Sch.2 para.12
s.87, enabling: SI 2002/2812, SI 2003/2603, SI 2004/1909, SI 2004/3122
Sch.1 Part II para.14, substituted: 2004 c.21 Sch.1 para.95
Sch.1 Part II para.17, repealed: 2003 c.17 Sch.7
Sch.1 Part II para.19, amended: 2004 c.36 Sch.2 para.10
Sch.1 Part II para.34, repealed: 2003 c.39 Sch.8 para.392, Sch.10
Sch.1 Part II para.35A, added: SI 2004/938 Sch.1
Sch.1 Part III, referred to: SI 2003/2603 Art.2
Sch.1 Part III para.36A, added: SI 2002/2469 Sch.1 para.29
Sch.1 Part III para.39A, added: 2002 c.17 Sch.5 para.48
Sch.1 Part III para.40A, added: 2003 c.43 Sch.4 para.114
Sch.1 Part III para.41, amended: 2003 c.4 Sch.3 para.14
Sch.1 Part III para.41A, added: 2002 c.17 s.19

CAP.

CAP.

2000–cont.

36. Freedom of Information Act 2000–
cont.

Sch.1 Part III para.42, repealed: 2003 c.43
Sch.14 Part 4

Sch.1 Part III para.43, repealed: 2003 c.43
Sch.13 para.10, Sch.14 Part 7

Sch.1 Part III para.43A, added: 2003 c.43
Sch.11 para.68

Sch.1 Part III para.44, amended: 2003 c.43
Sch.14 Part 4

Sch.1 Part III para.45, repealed: 2003 c.43
Sch.14 Part 4

Sch.1 Part III para.45B, added: 2002 c.17
Sch.6 para.19

Sch.1 Part III para.51, amended: SI 2004/311
Sch.1 para.18

Sch.1 Part IV, referred to: SI 2003/2603 Art.3

Sch.1 Part IV para.52, referred to: SI 2003/
2603 Art.3

Sch.1 Part IV para.52, substituted: 2002 c.32
Sch.21 para.127

Sch.1 Part V para.63A, added: 2004 c.20
Sch.10 para.18

Sch.1 Part V para.63B, added: 2004 c.20
Sch.10 para.18

Sch.1 Part VI, amended: 2002 c.11 Sch.1
para.22, 2002 c.17 Sch.7 para.24, 2002
c.30 Sch.7 para.23, Sch.8, SI 2002/253
Sch.5 para.17, SI 2002/254 Sch.4 para.9,
SI 2002/797 Art.2, SI 2002/2623 Sch.1,
2003 c.43 Sch.9 para.31, Sch.14 Part 2,
2003 c.4 Sch.3 para.15, 2003 c.21 Sch.17
para.164, Sch.19, 2003 c.26 Sch.4
para.24, SI 2003/1882 Sch.1, SI 2003/
1883 Sch.1, 2004 c.8 Sch.6 para.10, 2004
c.11 Sch.1 para.6, 2004 c.17 Sch.3 para.15,
Sch.4, 2004 c.20 Sch.1 para.18, 2004
c.25 Sch.2 para.22, Sch.4 para.9, Sch.6,
2004 c.30 Sch.2 para.27, 2004 c.35
Sch.12 para.79, Sch.13 Part 1, SI 2004/
803 Art.3, SI 2004/938 Sch.2, SI 2004/
1641 Sch.1

Sch.1 Part VI, varied: SI 2004/664 Art.11,
Art.12, Art.13, Art.14

Sch.1 Part VII, amended: 2002 c.1 (NI) Sch.1
para.21, (NI) Sch.4, 2002 c.26 s.23, Sch.2
para.20, Sch.8 para.16, Sch.9 para.15,
Sch.13, SI 2002/2623 Sch.2, 2003 c.6
Sch.1 para.15, 2003 c.21 Sch.19, SI 2003/
410 Sch.1 para.23, SI 2003/435 Sch.4
para.15, SI 2003/439 Sch.2 para.15, SI
2003/1882 Sch.2, SI 2004/938 Sch.3, SI
2004/1641 Sch.2

Sch.3 para.1, amended: 2003 c.39 Sch.4
para.13

Sch.7 para.13, repealed: 2002 asp 11 Sch.6
para.23

**37. Countryside and Rights of Way Act
2000**

Commencement Orders: SI 2002/2615 Art.2;
SI 2002/2833 Art.2; SI 2003/272 Art.2; SI
2004/292 Art.2, Art.3; SI 2004/315 Art.2;

2000–cont.

**37. Countryside and Rights of Way Act
2000–**cont.

–*cont.*

SI 2004/1489 Art.2, Art.3; SI 2004/2173
Art.2; SI 2004/3088 Art.2

applied: 2002 c.i s.41, SI 2003/142 Reg.14

referred to: SI 2003/142 Reg.10

Part I, applied: SI 2003/135 Reg.3, Reg.5

s.1, referred to: 2002 c.i s.11

s.2, applied: SI 2002/1710 Reg.4, Reg.5, SI
2002/1796 Reg.4, Reg.8

s.2, referred to: 2002 c.i s.11, s.12, s.42

s.5, applied: SI 2002/1796 Reg.3, Reg.4, SI
2003/1591 Reg.3

s.6, applied: SI 2002/1710 Reg.2, Reg.16,
Reg.19, SI 2002/1794 Reg.4, Reg.5,
Reg.6, Reg.8, Reg.34, Reg.36, SI 2002/
1796 Reg.6, Reg.7, SI 2003/1591 Reg.4

s.6, referred to: SI 2002/1794 Reg.6

s.9, applied: SI 2002/1796 Reg.7, Reg.8, SI
2003/1591 Reg.4

s.11, enabling: SI 2002/1710, SI 2002/1794,
SI 2002/1796, SI 2003/32, SI 2003/142,
SI 2003/1591

s.13, applied: 2002 c.i s.42

s.15, applied: 2002 c.i s.41

s.16, applied: SI 2003/135 Reg.3, Reg.7, SI
2003/2004 Reg.3, Reg.4, Reg.5, Reg.6,
Reg.7

s.16, referred to: SI 2003/2004 Reg.7

s.16, varied: SI 2003/2004 Reg.7

s.16, enabling: SI 2003/135, SI 2003/2004

s.17, amended: 2003 c.21 Sch.17 para.165

s.20, applied: SI 2003/142 Reg.14

s.22, applied: SI 2003/142 Reg.5, Reg.14, SI
2003/2713 Reg.4, Reg.6, Reg.17

s.23, applied: SI 2003/142 Reg.4, Reg.14, SI
2003/2713 Reg.5, Reg.17

s.23, enabling: SI 2003/142, SI 2003/2713

s.24, applied: SI 2003/142 Reg.5, Reg.6,
Reg.10, Reg.12, Reg.14, SI 2003/2713
Reg.6, Reg.7, Reg.8, Reg.9, Reg.10,
Reg.11, Reg.13, Reg.14, Reg.15, Reg.17,
Reg.20, Reg.22, Reg.23, Reg.24, Reg.64

s.25, applied: SI 2003/142 Reg.5, Reg.6,
Reg.10, Reg.12, Reg.13, Reg.14, SI 2003/
2713 Reg.6, Reg.7, Reg.8, Reg.9, Reg.10,
Reg.11, Reg.13, Reg.14, Reg.15, Reg.17,
Reg.20, Reg.22, Reg.23, Reg.24, Reg.56,
Reg.64

s.26, applied: SI 2003/142 Reg.6, Reg.9,
Reg.10, Reg.12, Reg.13, Reg.14, SI 2003/
2713 Reg.7, Reg.9, Reg.11, Reg.13, Reg.14,
Reg.15, Reg.17

s.27, applied: SI 2003/142 Reg.7, Reg.10,
Reg.12, SI 2003/2713 Reg.9, Reg.10,
Reg.11, Reg.13, Reg.14, Reg.15, Reg.20,
Reg.22, Reg.23, Reg.24

s.28, applied: SI 2003/142 Reg.10, SI 2003/
2713 Reg.7, Reg.9, Reg.12, Reg.14, Reg.16,
Reg.17

2000–cont.

37. Countryside and Rights of Way Act 2000–*cont.*

s.29, amended: SI 2002/794 Sch.1 para.43, Sch.2

s.29, applied: SI 2002/1794 Reg.6, Reg.12, Reg.22, Reg.36

s.29, repealed (in part): SI 2002/794 Sch.2

s.30, amended: SI 2002/794 Sch.1 para.44, Sch.2

s.30, applied: SI 2002/1794 Reg.6, Reg.12, Reg.22, Reg.36, SI 2003/2713 Reg.20

s.30, repealed (in part): SI 2002/794 Sch.2

s.32, enabling: SI 2002/1794, SI 2003/142, SI 2003/2713

s.38, enabling: SI 2002/1794, SI 2004/3305

s.44, enabling: SI 2002/1710, SI 2002/1794, SI 2002/1796, SI 2003/32, SI 2003/135, SI 2003/142, SI 2003/1591, SI 2003/2004, SI 2003/2713, SI 2004/3305

s.45, amended: 2003 c.21 Sch.19

s.45, enabling: SI 2002/1710, SI 2003/32, SI 2003/1591, SI 2003/2004, SI 2003/2713, SI 2004/3305

s.68, see *Massey v Boulden* [2002] EWCA Civ 1634, [2003] 1 W.L.R. 1792 (CA), Simon Brown, L.J.

s.68, applied: SI 2002/1711 Reg.3, Sch.1 para.2, SI 2004/248 Reg.3, Reg.4, Sch.1 para.2

s.68, referred to: SI 2002/1711 Reg.4

s.68, enabling: SI 2002/1711, SI 2004/248

s.75, see *R. (on the application of Trailer & Marina (Leven) Ltd) v Secretary of State for the Environment, Food and Rural Affairs* [2004] EWHC 153, [2004] Env. L.R. 40 (QBD (Admin Ct)), Ouseley, J.

s.81, repealed (in part): 2003 c.44 Sch.37 Part 9

s.82, applied: SI 2003/54 Art.2, Art.3

s.85, applied: SI 2004/1777 Art.27, SI 2004/1778 Art.27

s.86, amended: 2004 c.5 Sch.7 para.23, Sch.9

s.86, applied: SI 2004/1777, SI 2004/1778

s.86, enabling: SI 2004/1777, SI 2004/1778

s.87, referred to: SI 2004/1777, SI 2004/1778

s.87, enabling: SI 2004/1777, SI 2004/1778

s.88, enabling: SI 2004/1777, SI 2004/1778

s.94, applied: SI 2004/1778 Art.25

s.94, enabling: SI 2002/1836, SI 2003/2713

s.95, enabling: SI 2002/1836, SI 2003/2713

s.98, see *Oxfordshire CC v Oxford City Council* [2004] EWHC 12, [2004] Ch. 253 (Ch D), Lightman, J.; see *R. (on the application of Beresford) v Sunderland City Council* [2003] UKHL 60, [2004] 1 A.C. 889 (HL), Lord Bingham of Cornhill

s.103, enabling: SI 2002/2615, SI 2002/2833, SI 2003/272, SI 2004/292, SI 2004/315, SI 2004/1489, SI 2004/2173, SI 2004/3088

2000–cont.

37. Countryside and Rights of Way Act 2000–*cont.*

Sch.1 Part I para.8, amended: 2003 c.21 Sch.17 para.165

Sch.2, applied: SI 2003/2004 Reg.3, Reg.4, Reg.5, Reg.7

Sch.2, referred to: 2002 c.i s.42

Sch.2 para.1, referred to: 2002 c.i s.11, SI 2003/135 Reg.3, Reg.7

Sch.2 para.2, referred to: 2002 c.i s.11

Sch.2 para.4, referred to: SI 2003/135 Reg.3, Reg.7

Sch.2 para.5, referred to: SI 2003/135 Reg.3, Reg.7

Sch.3 para.2, applied: SI 2002/1710 Reg.59, SI 2003/2713 Reg.69

Sch.3 para.4, applied: SI 2002/1794 Reg.32

Sch.9, see *R. (on the application of Trailer & Marina (Leven) Ltd) v Secretary of State for the Environment, Food and Rural Affairs* [2004] EWHC 153, [2004] Env. L.R. 40 (QBD (Admin Ct)), Ouseley, J.

Sch.11 para.11, enabling: SI 2002/1772

Sch.11 para.17, enabling: SI 2002/1772

Sch.12 para.13, repealed: 2002 c.30 Sch.8

Sch.13, applied: SI 2004/1777 Art.9, SI 2004/1778 Art.9

Sch.13, enabling: SI 2004/1777, SI 2004/1778

Sch.13 para.4, applied: SI 2004/1777 Art.9, SI 2004/1778 Art.9

Sch.13 para.5, applied: SI 2004/1777 Art.9, SI 2004/1778 Art.9

Sch.13 para.7, applied: SI 2004/1777 Sch.3 para.5, SI 2004/1778 Sch.3 para.5

38. Transport Act 2000

Commencement Orders: SI 2002/658 Art.2, Art.3, Sch.1 Part 1, 2; SI 2002/846 Art.2; SI 2002/1014 Art.2, Art.3, Sch.1 Part 1; SI 2002/2024 Art.2; SI 2003/1694 Art.2

applied: 2002 c.40 Sch.15

Part I, applied: 2002 c.40 Sch.15, SI 2003/335 Sch.1, SSI 2003/93 Sch.1

Part I c.I, applied: SI 2002/2626 Art.6, SI 2003/409 Sch.1 Part I

s.4, applied: SSI 2003/231 Sch.3 para.7

s.5, applied: SSI 2003/231 Sch.3 para.7

s.12, applied: SI 2003/1397 Art.8

s.12, repealed (in part): 2002 c.40 Sch.26

s.12A, added: 2002 c.40 Sch.25 para.44

s.12B, added: 2002 c.40 Sch.25 para.44

s.12B, amended: 2003 c.21 Sch.16 para.7

s.12B, referred to: SI 2003/1371

s.12B, enabling: SI 2003/1371

s.13, amended: 2002 c.40 Sch.25 para.44

s.18, amended: 2003 c.21 Sch.16 para.7

s.18, referred to: SI 2003/1371

s.18, substituted: 2002 c.40 Sch.25 para.44

s.18, enabling: SI 2003/1371

s.19, amended: 2002 c.40 Sch.9 para.15

s.19, varied: SI 2003/1592 Sch.4 para.17

2000–cont.

38. Transport Act 2000–*cont.*

s.26, applied: 2002 c.40 s.249

s.82, amended: 2003 c.44 Sch.32 para.161

s.82, disapplied: 2003 c.44 Sch.25 para.105

s.82, repealed (in part): 2003 c.44 Sch.37 Part 9

s.85, amended: 2002 c.40 Sch.9 para.23, Sch.25 para.44, Sch.26

s.86, amended: 2002 c.40 Sch.9 para.24, Sch.25 para.44, SI 2004/1261 Sch.2 para.10

s.87, amended: 2002 c.40 Sch.9 para.25

s.88, amended: SI 2003/1398 Sch.1 para.37

s.89, amended: 2002 c.40 Sch.9 para.26, Sch.25 para.44

s.90, amended: 2002 c.40 Sch.25 para.44

s.90, repealed (in part): 2002 c.40 Sch.25 para.44, Sch.26

s.91, amended: 2002 c.40 Sch.25 para.44

s.91, repealed (in part): 2002 c.40 Sch.25 para.44, Sch.26

s.108, applied: SI 2004/2204 Reg.15

s.115, applied: SI 2002/3017 Reg.3, Reg.4

s.115, varied: SI 2002/3017 Reg.5

s.118, referred to: SI 2002/1014 Art.3

s.119, enabling: SI 2002/3017

s.129, referred to: SI 2002/1014 Art.3

s.138, referred to: SI 2002/1014 Art.3

s.140, referred to: SI 2002/1014 Art.3

s.144, applied: 2004 c.18 s.81, s.88, Sch.8 para.4, Sch.8 para.9

s.144, repealed: 2004 c.18 Sch.12 Part 1

s.145, applied: SI 2002/1015 Reg.3, SI 2002/2022 Reg.3

s.146, amended: 2002 c.4 s.1

s.146, applied: SI 2002/1016 Art.3, SI 2002/2023 Art.3

s.146, enabling: SI 2002/1016, SI 2002/2023

s.154, applied: SI 2002/1015 Reg.3, SI 2002/2022 Reg.3, SI 2002/2023 Art.3

s.154, enabling: SI 2002/1015, SI 2002/2022, SI 2003/943, SI 2003/1036, SI 2004/9, SI 2004/1827

s.155, applied: SI 2002/1014 Art.3

s.155, disapplied: SI 2002/1014 Art.3

s.160, enabling: SI 2003/1036

s.167, enabling: SI 2002/1040

s.168, enabling: SI 2002/1040

s.171, enabling: SI 2002/1040

s.172, enabling: SI 2002/1040

s.173, enabling: SI 2002/3029

s.197, enabling: SI 2002/3029, SI 2003/110, SI 2003/298

s.206, amended: 2003 c.20 Sch.2 para.19

s.216, amended: 2003 c.20 Sch.2 para.19

s.247, enabling: SI 2002/1166

s.251, repealed (in part): 2003 c.20 Sch.8

s.258, referred to: SI 2002/643 r.1

s.259, referred to: SI 2002/643 r.1

s.269, repealed: 2004 c.14 Sch.1 Part 14

2000–cont.

38. Transport Act 2000–*cont.*

s.272, varied: SI 2003/415 Art.3

s.275, repealed (in part): 2004 c.14 Sch.1 Part 14

s.275, enabling: SI 2002/658, SI 2002/846, SI 2002/1014, SI 2002/2024, SI 2003/1694

s.276, enabling: SI 2002/658, SI 2002/1014

s.277, applied: SI 2004/1755

s.277, enabling: SI 2004/1755

Sch.5 para.1, amended: 2004 c.34 Sch.16

Sch.5 para.3, repealed: 2004 c.36 Sch.3

Sch.8 Part IV para.11, repealed: 2002 c.40 Sch.26

Sch.8 Part IV para.12, repealed: 2002 c.40 Sch.26

Sch.8 Part IV para.14, repealed (in part): 2003 c.21 Sch.19

Sch.8 Part IV para.15, repealed: SI 2003/1400 Sch.5

Sch.9 para.3, amended: 2002 c.40 Sch.25 para.44, 2003 c.20 Sch.2 para.19, 2003 c.21 Sch.17 para.166, 2003 c.37 Sch.7 para.35

Sch.9 para.3, repealed (in part): 2003 c.21 Sch.19

Sch.9 para.5, amended: 2002 c.40 Sch.25 para.44, SI 2003/1400 Sch.6

Sch.10 para.1, amended: 2002 c.40 Sch.25 para.44

Sch.10 para.2, amended: 2002 c.40 Sch.25 para.44

Sch.10 para.3, amended: 2002 c.40 Sch.25 para.44

Sch.10 para.4, amended: 2002 c.40 Sch.25 para.44, Sch.26

Sch.10 para.5, amended: 2002 c.40 Sch.25 para.44

Sch.10 para.6, amended: 2002 c.40 Sch.25 para.44

Sch.10 para.7, amended: 2002 c.40 Sch.25 para.44

Sch.10 para.8, amended: 2002 c.40 Sch.25 para.44

Sch.10 para.9, amended: 2002 c.40 Sch.25 para.44

Sch.10 para.10, amended: 2002 c.40 Sch.25 para.44

Sch.10 para.11, amended: 2002 c.40 Sch.25 para.44

Sch.10 para.12, amended: 2002 c.40 Sch.25 para.44

Sch.10 para.13, amended: 2002 c.40 Sch.25 para.44, 2003 c.20 Sch.2 para.19

Sch.10 para.14, amended: 2002 c.40 Sch.25 para.44

Sch.10 para.15, amended: 2002 c.40 Sch.25 para.44

Sch.10 para.16, amended: 2002 c.40 Sch.25 para.44

2000–cont.

38. Transport Act 2000–*cont.*

Sch.10 para.22, amended: 2002 c.40 Sch.25 para.44

Sch.12 para.2, applied: SI 2003/110 Reg.2

Sch.12 para.2, enabling: SI 2003/110, SI 2003/298

Sch.12 para.5, enabling: SI 2003/298

Sch.12 para.8, applied: SI 2003/110 Reg.2

Sch.16 para.57, repealed: SI 2003/1400 Sch.5

Sch.17 Part III para.31, amended: 2003 c.20 Sch.2 para.19

Sch.17 Part III para.32, amended: 2003 c.20 Sch.2 para.19

Sch.17 Part III para.33, amended: 2003 c.20 Sch.2 para.19

Sch.17 Part III para.34, amended: 2003 c.20 Sch.2 para.19

Sch.17 Part III para.35, amended: 2003 c.20 Sch.2 para.19

Sch.17 Part III para.36, amended: 2003 c.20 Sch.2 para.19

Sch.17 Part III para.37, amended: 2003 c.20 Sch.2 para.19

Sch.17 Part III para.38, amended: 2003 c.20 Sch.2 para.19

Sch.17 Part III para.39, amended: 2003 c.20 Sch.2 para.19

Sch.17 Part III para.40, amended: 2003 c.20 Sch.2 para.19

Sch.17 Part III para.41, amended: 2003 c.20 Sch.2 para.19

Sch.17 Part III para.42, amended: 2003 c.20 Sch.2 para.19

Sch.17 Part III para.43, amended: 2003 c.20 Sch.2 para.19

Sch.17 Part III para.44, amended: 2003 c.20 Sch.2 para.19

Sch.18 Part I para.7, repealed: 2003 c.20 Sch.8

Sch.18 Part I para.8, repealed: 2003 c.20 Sch.8

Sch.18 Part I para.9, repealed: 2003 c.20 Sch.8

Sch.18 Part I para.10, repealed: 2003 c.20 Sch.8

Sch.26 Part II para.2, amended: 2003 c.20 Sch.2 para.19

Sch.26 Part II para.3, amended: 2003 c.20 Sch.2 para.19

Sch.26 Part II para.4, amended: 2003 c.20 Sch.2 para.19

Sch.26 Part II para.5, amended: 2003 c.20 Sch.2 para.19

Sch.26 Part II para.6, amended: 2003 c.20 Sch.2 para.19

Sch.26 Part II para.7, amended: 2003 c.20 Sch.2 para.19, 2004 c.12 Sch.10 para.46

Sch.26 Part VII para.40A, added: SI 2003/2867 Sch.1 para.32

Sch.27 para.45, repealed: 2003 c.20 Sch.8

2000–cont.

38. Transport Act 2000–*cont.*

Sch.29 para.12, referred to: SI 2002/643 r.1

39. Insolvency Act 2000

Commencement Orders: SI 2002/2711 Art.2, Art.3, Art.4, Art.5

s.3, disapplied: SI 2002/2711 Art.4

s.4, disapplied: SI 2002/2711 Art.5

s.6, see *Blackspur Group Plc (No.3), Re* [2001] EWCA Civ 1595, [2002] 2 B.C.L.C. 263 (CA), Chadwick, L.J.

s.7, enabling: SI 2004/1941

s.9, repealed: 2002 c.40 Sch.26

s.15, disapplied: SI 2002/2711 Art.3, Art.4

s.16, enabling: SI 2002/2711

Sch.1 para.4, amended: SI 2002/1555 Art.28, Art.29, Art.30

Sch.2 Part I, disapplied: SI 2002/2711 Art.3

Sch.2 Part II para.13, amended: SI 2002/1555 Art.31

Sch.3, disapplied: SI 2002/2711 Art.4

Sch.4 Part I para.13, repealed (in part): 2002 c.40 Sch.26

Sch.5, disapplied: SI 2002/2711 Art.3, Art.4

40. Protection of Animals (Amendment) Act 2000

s.1, amended: SI 2002/794 Sch.1 para.45

s.2, see *Cornwall CC v Baker* [2003] EWHC 374, [2003] 1 W.L.R. 1813 (QBD (Admin Ct)), Toulson, J.; see *Worcestershire CC v Tongue* [2004] EWCA Civ 140, [2004] Ch. 236 (CA), Peter Gibson, L.J.

s.3, see *Worcestershire CC v Tongue* [2004] EWCA Civ 140, [2004] Ch. 236 (CA), Peter Gibson, L.J.

41. Political Parties, Elections and Referendums Act 2000

applied: 2002 c.18 Sch.2 Part 58, 2003 c.13 Sch.2 Part 2, Sch.2 Part 61, SI 2003/284 Art.52, 2004 c.9 Sch.2 Part 57, SI 2004/293 Reg.33, SI 2004/870 Reg.10

referred to: 2003 c.10 s.12, SI 2004/366 Sch.1 para.1

Part II, applied: SI 2002/185 Sch.3 para.6, SI 2002/2779 Sch.2 para.7, SI 2003/284 Sch.5 para.7, Sch.5 para.69, SI 2004/293 Sch.1 para.5

Part III, applied: 2002 c.18 Sch.2 Part 58, 2003 c.13 Sch.2 Part 61

Part IV, applied: 2002 c.18 Sch.2 Part 58, 2003 c.13 Sch.2 Part 61

Part IV c.II, applied: SI 2002/2626 Sch.1

Part IV c.III, applied: SI 2002/2626 Sch.1

Part VI c.I, applied: SI 2002/2626 Sch.1

Part VI c.II, applied: SI 2002/2626 Sch.1

Part VII, applied: 2003 c.10 s.5

Part VII, referred to: 2003 c.10 s.12

Part VII c.I, applied: SI 2002/2626 Sch.1

Part VII c.II, applied: SI 2002/2626 Sch.1

Part VII c.II, referred to: 2003 c.10 s.2

Part VII c.II, applied: SI 2002/2626 Sch.1

s.1, applied: SI 2002/2626 Sch.1

2000–cont.

**41. Political Parties, Elections and Refer-
endums Act 2000**–*cont.*

s.2, amended: SI 2002/2626 Sch.2 para.25

s.2, applied: SI 2002/2626 Art.11, Sch.1

s.3, applied: SI 2002/2626 Sch.1

s.4, applied: SI 2002/2626 Sch.1

s.5, applied: SI 2002/2626 Sch.1, 2004 c.2
s.4

s.5, varied: SI 2004/1962 Sch.3 Part 1

s.6, applied: SI 2002/2626 Sch.1

s.7, amended: 2002 c.24 Sch.3 para.8

s.7, applied: SI 2002/1871 (b), SI 2002/1872,
SI 2002/1964, SI 2002/2626 Sch.1, SI
2002/2835, SI 2003/1156, SI 2003/
1245, SI 2003/1892, SI 2003/1899, SI
2003/1942, SI 2003/2989, SI 2003/
3362, SI 2004/223, SI 2004/224, SI
2004/227, SI 2004/293, SI 2004/294, SI
2004/1040, SI 2004/1041, SI 2004/1056,
SI 2004/1204, SI 2004/1267, SI 2004/
1848, SI 2004/1960

s.7, enabling: SI 2003/1245, SI 2004/293, SI
2004/294

s.8, amended: 2002 c.24 Sch.3 para.8

s.8, applied: SI 2002/834, SI 2002/2626
Sch.1, SI 2002/2779 Art.24, SI 2004/293

s.9, applied: SI 2002/2626 Sch.1

s.10, applied: SI 2002/2626 Sch.1

s.10, referred to: SI 2004/293 Sch.1 para.8

s.11, amended: 2003 c.21 Sch.17 para.167

s.11, applied: SI 2002/2626 Sch.1

s.11, repealed (in part): 2003 c.21 Sch.19

s.12, applied: SI 2002/224, SI 2002/224
Sch.1 para.3, SI 2002/2626 Sch.1

s.12, enabling: SI 2002/224

s.13, amended: SI 2004/366 Sch.1 para.2

s.13, applied: SI 2002/505 Art.2, SI 2002/
2626 Sch.1

s.13, enabling: SI 2002/505

s.14, applied: SI 2002/2626 Sch.1

s.15, applied: SI 2002/2626 Sch.1

s.16, applied: SI 2002/2626 Sch.1

s.17, applied: SI 2002/2626 Sch.1

s.18, applied: SI 2002/2626 Sch.1

s.18, enabling: SI 2002/1723

s.19, applied: SI 2002/2626 Sch.1

s.20, applied: SI 2002/2626 Sch.1

s.21, applied: SI 2002/2626 Sch.1

s.22, applied: SI 2002/2626 Sch.1

s.23, applied: SI 2002/2626 Sch.1

s.24, amended: SI 2004/366 Sch.1 para.3

s.24, applied: SI 2002/2626 Sch.1, SI 2004/
293 Reg.33

s.25, applied: SI 2002/2626 Sch.1

s.26, applied: SI 2002/414, SI 2002/2626
Sch.1

s.26, enabling: SI 2002/414

s.27, applied: SI 2002/2626 Sch.1

s.28, amended: SI 2004/366 Sch.1 para.4

s.28, applied: SI 2002/2626 Sch.1

s.29, applied: SI 2002/2626 Sch.1

2000–cont.

**41. Political Parties, Elections and Refer-
endums Act 2000**–*cont.*

s.30, amended: SI 2004/366 Sch.1 para.5

s.30, applied: SI 2002/2626 Sch.1

s.31, amended: SI 2004/366 Sch.1 para.6

s.31, applied: SI 2002/2626 Sch.1

s.32, applied: SI 2002/2626 Sch.1

s.33, applied: SI 2002/2626 Sch.1

s.34, applied: SI 2002/2626 Sch.1

s.35, applied: SI 2002/2626 Sch.1

s.36, applied: SI 2002/2626 Sch.1

s.37, amended: SI 2004/366 Sch.1 para.7

s.37, applied: SI 2002/2626 Sch.1, 2003 c.21
s.333, Sch.12 para.18

s.38, applied: SI 2002/2626 Sch.1

s.39, applied: SI 2002/2626 Sch.1

s.40, amended: SI 2004/366 Sch.1 para.8

s.40, applied: SI 2002/2626 Sch.1

s.41, applied: SI 2002/2626 Sch.1

s.42, applied: SI 2002/2626 Sch.1

s.43, applied: SI 2002/2626 Sch.1

s.44, amended: SI 2004/366 Sch.1 para.9

s.44, applied: SI 2002/2626 Sch.1

s.45, applied: SI 2002/2626 Sch.1

s.46, applied: SI 2002/2626 Sch.1

s.47, applied: SI 2002/2626 Sch.1

s.48, amended: SI 2004/366 Sch.1 para.10

s.48, applied: SI 2002/2626 Sch.1

s.49, applied: SI 2002/2626 Sch.1

s.50, applied: SI 2002/2626 Sch.1

s.51, applied: SI 2002/2626 Sch.1

s.52, amended: SI 2004/366 Sch.1 para.11

s.52, applied: SI 2002/2626 Sch.1

s.53, applied: SI 2002/2626 Sch.1

s.54, amended: SI 2004/366 Sch.1 para.12

s.54, applied: SI 2003/284 Sch.6 para.6, SI
2004/293 Sch.6 para.6, SI 2004/1267
Sch.4 para.6

s.54, referred to: SI 2004/293 Sch.6 para.6

s.55, amended: SI 2004/366 Sch.1 para.13

s.56, applied: SI 2003/284 Sch.6 para.4,
Sch.6 para.7, Sch.6 para.8, Sch.6 para.12,
SI 2004/293 Sch.6 para.4, Sch.6 para.7,
Sch.6 para.8, Sch.6 para.12, SI 2004/1267
Sch.4 para.4, Sch.4 para.7, Sch.4 para.8,
Sch.4 para.12

s.56, referred to: SI 2003/284 Sch.6 para.8,
Sch.6 para.12, SI 2004/293 Sch.6 para.7,
Sch.6 para.8, Sch.6 para.12, SI 2004/1267
Sch.4 para.8, Sch.4 para.12

s.56, varied: SI 2003/284 Sch.6 para.7, SI
2004/293 Sch.6 para.7, SI 2004/1267
Sch.4 para.7

s.57, applied: SI 2003/284 Sch.6 para.7, SI
2004/293 Sch.6 para.7, SI 2004/1267
Sch.4 para.7

s.57, referred to: SI 2004/293 Sch.6 para.7

s.57A, added: SI 2004/366 Sch.1 para.14

s.57A, applied: SI 2003/284 Sch.6 para.7, SI
2004/293 Sch.6 para.7, SI 2004/1267
Sch.4 para.7

2000–cont.

41. Political Parties, Elections and Referendums Act 2000–*cont.*

s.57A, referred to: SI 2004/293 Sch.6 para.7

s.58, amended: SI 2004/366 Sch.1 para.15

s.58, applied: SI 2003/284 Sch.6 para.7, SI 2004/293 Sch.6 para.7, SI 2004/1267 Sch.4 para.7

s.58, referred to: SI 2004/293 Sch.6 para.7

s.59, amended: SI 2004/366 Sch.1 para.16

s.59, applied: SI 2003/284 Sch.6 para.7, SI 2003/1646 r.2, SI 2004/293 Sch.6 para.7, SI 2004/1267 Sch.4 para.7

s.59, referred to: SI 2004/293 Sch.6 para.7

s.60, amended: SI 2004/366 Sch.1 para.17

s.60, applied: SI 2003/284 Sch.6 para.7, SI 2004/293 Sch.6 para.7, SI 2004/1267 Sch.4 para.7

s.60, referred to: SI 2004/293 Sch.6 para.7

s.60, enabling: SI 2003/1645, SI 2003/1646

s.61, varied: SI 2003/284 Sch.6 para.9, SI 2004/293 Sch.6 para.9, SI 2004/1267 Sch.4 para.9

s.65, applied: SI 2003/1645 r.1

s.69, applied: 2003 asp 1 s.42, 2003 c.26 s.114

s.70, applied: SI 2004/293 Sch.6 para.1

s.71, applied: SI 2002/2626 Sch.1

s.72, applied: SI 2002/2626 Sch.1

s.73, amended: SI 2004/366 Sch.1 para.18

s.73, applied: SI 2002/2626 Sch.1

s.74, amended: SI 2004/366 Sch.1 para.19

s.74, applied: SI 2002/2626 Sch.1

s.75, applied: SI 2002/2626 Sch.1

s.76, applied: SI 2002/2626 Sch.1

s.77, amended: SI 2004/366 Sch.1 para.20

s.77, applied: SI 2002/2626 Sch.1

s.78, applied: SI 2002/2626 Sch.1

s.79, applied: SI 2002/2626 Sch.1

s.80, applied: SI 2002/2626 Sch.1, SI 2003/284 Art.52

s.81, applied: SI 2002/2626 Sch.1

s.82, applied: SI 2002/2626 Sch.1

s.83, applied: SI 2002/2626 Sch.1

s.84, applied: SI 2002/2626 Sch.1

s.85, amended: SI 2004/366 Sch.1 para.21

s.87, amended: SI 2004/366 Sch.1 para.22

s.88, amended: SI 2004/366 Sch.1 para.23

s.90, amended: SI 2004/366 Sch.1 para.24

s.91, amended: SI 2004/366 Sch.1 para.25

s.92, amended: SI 2004/366 Sch.1 para.26

s.94, amended: SI 2004/366 Sch.1 para.27

s.101, varied: SI 2004/1962 Sch.3 Part 1

s.102, varied: SI 2004/1962 Sch.3 Part 1

s.105, applied: SI 2004/1961 Art.3, Art.4, Art.5

s.105, varied: SI 2004/1962 Sch.3 Part 1

s.106, varied: SI 2004/1962 Sch.3 Part 1

s.107, varied: SI 2004/1962 Sch.3 Part 1

s.108, applied: 2003 c.10 s.9, SI 2004/1961 Art.3, Art.4, Art.5

2000–cont.

41. Political Parties, Elections and Referendums Act 2000–*cont.*

s.108, disapplied: SI 2004/1961 Art.3, Art.4, Art.5

s.109, applied: 2003 c.10 s.9, SI 2004/1963 Art.6

s.109, varied: SI 2004/1963 Art.6

s.109, enabling: SI 2004/1963

s.110, applied: 2003 c.10 s.9

s.111, varied: SI 2004/1962 Sch.3 Part 2

s.112, varied: SI 2004/1962 Sch.3 Part 2

s.113, varied: SI 2004/1962 Sch.3 Part 2

s.114, varied: SI 2004/1962 Sch.3 Part 2

s.115, varied: SI 2004/1962 Sch.3 Part 2

s.116, varied: SI 2004/1962 Sch.3 Part 2

s.117, varied: SI 2004/1962 Sch.3 Part 2

s.118, varied: SI 2004/1962 Sch.3 Part 2

s.119, varied: SI 2004/1962 Sch.3 Part 2

s.120, varied: SI 2004/1962 Sch.3 Part 2

s.121, varied: SI 2004/1962 Sch.3 Part 2

s.122, varied: SI 2004/1962 Sch.3 Part 2

s.123, varied: SI 2004/1962 Sch.3 Part 2

s.124, varied: SI 2004/1962 Sch.3 Part 2

s.125, applied: SI 2002/2626 Sch.1

s.125, varied: SI 2004/1962 Sch.3 Part 1

s.126, applied: SI 2002/2626 Sch.1

s.126, disapplied: 2003 c.10 s.12

s.126, varied: SI 2004/1962 Sch.3 Part 1

s.127, applied: SI 2002/2626 Sch.1, 2003 c.21 s.333, Sch.12 para.18

s.127, varied: SI 2004/1962 Sch.3 Part 1

s.128, applied: SI 2002/2626 Sch.1, 2003 c.10 s.6, SI 2004/1962 Art.9, Sch.1

s.129, applied: SI 2002/2626 Sch.1, 2003 c.10 s.12, s.29, SI 2004/1962

s.129, enabling: SI 2004/1962

s.130, applied: SI 2002/2626 Sch.1

s.131, applied: SI 2002/2626 Sch.1

s.132, applied: SI 2002/2626 Sch.1

s.133, applied: SI 2002/2626 Sch.1

s.134, applied: SI 2002/2626 Sch.1

s.134, repealed (in part): 2004 asp 9 s.14

s.135, applied: SI 2002/2626 Sch.1

s.135, repealed (in part): 2004 asp 9 s.14

s.136, applied: SI 2002/2626 Sch.1

s.137, applied: SI 2002/2626 Sch.1

s.138, amended: 2004 asp 9 s.14

s.138, applied: SI 2002/2626 Sch.1

s.139, applied: SI 2002/2626 Sch.1

s.140, applied: SI 2002/2626 Sch.1

s.141, applied: SI 2002/2626 Sch.1

s.142, applied: SI 2002/2626 Sch.1

s.142, consolidated: 2002 c.24 s.10, s.11

s.142, repealed: 2002 c.24 Sch.4

s.143, applied: SI 2002/2626 Sch.1

s.144, applied: SI 2002/2626 Sch.1

s.145, applied: SI 2002/2626 Sch.1

s.146, applied: SI 2002/2626 Sch.1

s.147, applied: SI 2002/2626 Sch.1

s.148, applied: SI 2002/2626 Sch.1

2000–cont.

41. Political Parties, Elections and Referendums Act 2000–*cont.*

s.149, applied: SI 2002/2626 Sch.1

s.150, amended: SI 2004/366 Sch.1 para.28

s.150, applied: SI 2002/2626 Sch.1

s.151, amended: SI 2004/366 Sch.1 para.29

s.151, applied: SI 2002/2626 Sch.1

s.152, applied: SI 2002/2626 Sch.1

s.153, amended: SI 2004/366 Sch.1 para.30

s.153, applied: SI 2002/2626 Sch.1

s.154, applied: SI 2002/2626 Sch.1

s.155, applied: SI 2002/2626 Sch.1

s.156, applied: SI 2002/2626 Sch.1, SI 2004/366, SI 2004/1963

s.156, enabling: SI 2002/1723, SI 2004/1962

s.157, applied: SI 2002/2626 Sch.1

s.158, amended: 2004 asp 9 s.14

s.158, applied: SI 2002/2626 Sch.1

s.159, applied: SI 2002/2626 Sch.1

s.159A, added: SI 2002/2626 Sch.2 para.25

s.159A, applied: SI 2002/2626 Sch.1

s.160, amended: SI 2004/366 Sch.1 para.31

s.160, applied: SI 2002/2626 Sch.1

s.161, applied: SI 2002/2626 Sch.1

s.162, amended: SI 2004/366 Sch.1 para.32

s.162, applied: SI 2002/2626 Sch.1, SI 2003/284 Sch.6 para.6, SI 2004/293 Sch.6 para.6, SI 2004/1267 Sch.4 para.6

s.163, amended: SI 2004/366 Art.4

s.163, applied: SI 2002/2626 Sch.1

Sch.1, referred to: SI 2002/1872 Sch.1 Part I

Sch.1 para.14, applied: 2003 c.7 s.25, 2003 c.10 s.19, s.24

Sch.2 para.2, amended: SI 2002/2626 Sch.2 para.25

Sch.2A para.11, applied: SI 2002/2779 Art.44

Sch.2A para.12, applied: SI 2002/2779 Art.44

Sch.3 Part I para.1, applied: SI 2002/2626 Sch.1

Sch.3 Part I para.2, applied: SI 2002/2626 Sch.1

Sch.3 Part I para.3, applied: SI 2002/2626 Sch.1

Sch.3 Part I para.4, applied: SI 2002/2626 Sch.1

Sch.3 Part I para.5, applied: SI 2002/2626 Sch.1

Sch.3 Part I para.6, applied: SI 2002/2626 Sch.1

Sch.3 Part I para.7, applied: SI 2002/2626 Sch.1

Sch.3 Part II, applied: SI 2002/2626 Sch.1

Sch.3 Part II para.17, repealed: 2004 c.13 s.1

Sch.3 Part II para.18, repealed: 2004 c.13 s.1

Sch.3 Part II para.19, repealed: 2004 c.13 s.1

Sch.3 Part II para.20, repealed: 2004 c.13 s.1

Sch.3 Part II para.21, repealed: 2004 c.13 s.1

Sch.3 Part II para.22, repealed: 2004 c.13 s.1

2000–cont.

41. Political Parties, Elections and Referendums Act 2000–*cont.*

Sch.3 Part II para.23, repealed: 2004 c.13 s.1

Sch.3 Part II para.24, repealed: 2004 c.13 s.1

Sch.4 Part I para.1, applied: SI 2002/2626 Sch.1

Sch.4 Part I para.2, applied: SI 2002/2626 Sch.1

Sch.4 Part I para.3, applied: SI 2002/2626 Sch.1

Sch.4 Part I para.4, applied: SI 2002/2626 Sch.1

Sch.4 Part I para.5, applied: SI 2002/2626 Sch.1

Sch.4 Part I para.6, applied: SI 2002/2626 Sch.1

Sch.4 Part I para.7, applied: SI 2002/2626 Sch.1

Sch.4 Part II para.8, applied: SI 2002/2626 Sch.1

Sch.4 Part II para.9, applied: SI 2002/2626 Sch.1

Sch.4 Part II para.10, applied: SI 2002/2626 Sch.1

Sch.4 Part III para.11, applied: SI 2002/2626 Sch.1

Sch.4 Part III para.12, applied: SI 2002/2626 Sch.1

Sch.4 Part III para.13, applied: SI 2002/2626 Sch.1

Sch.4 Part IV para.14, applied: SI 2002/2626 Sch.1

Sch.6 para.2, amended: SI 2004/366 Sch.1 para.33

Sch.6 para.2, applied: SI 2003/284 Sch.6 para.11, SI 2004/293 Sch.6 para.11, SI 2004/1267 Sch.4 para.11

Sch.6 para.6, amended: SI 2004/366 Sch.1 para.33

Sch.7 Part I para.1, amended: SI 2004/366 Sch.1 para.34

Sch.7 Part I para.1, applied: SI 2002/2626 Sch.1

Sch.7 Part I para.2, applied: SI 2002/2626 Sch.1

Sch.7 Part I para.3, applied: SI 2002/2626 Sch.1

Sch.7 Part I para.4, amended: 2003 asp 1 s.42, 2003 c.26 s.114

Sch.7 Part I para.4, applied: SI 2002/2626 Sch.1

Sch.7 Part I para.5, applied: SI 2002/2626 Sch.1

Sch.7 Part II para.6, applied: SI 2002/2626 Sch.1

Sch.7 Part II para.7, amended: SI 2004/366 Sch.1 para.34

Sch.7 Part II para.7, applied: SI 2002/2626 Sch.1

Sch.7 Part II para.8, applied: SI 2002/2626 Sch.1, SI 2003/1645 r.1

2000–cont.

41. Political Parties, Elections and Referendums Act 2000–*cont.*

Sch.7 Part II para.9, applied: SI 2002/2626 Sch.1

Sch.7 Part III para.10, applied: SI 2002/2626 Sch.1

Sch.7 Part III para.11, applied: SI 2002/2626 Sch.1

Sch.7 Part III para.12, applied: SI 2002/2626 Sch.1, SI 2003/1645 r.1

Sch.7 Part III para.13, applied: SI 2002/2626 Sch.1

Sch.7 Part IV para.14, applied: SI 2002/2626 Sch.1

Sch.7 Part V para.15, applied: SI 2002/2626 Sch.1

Sch.7 Part VI para.16, applied: SI 2002/2626 Sch.1

Sch.8 Part I para.1, applied: SI 2002/2626 Sch.1

Sch.8 Part I para.2, applied: SI 2002/2626 Sch.1

Sch.8 Part I para.2, substituted: SI 2004/366 Art.7

Sch.8 Part II para.3, applied: SI 2002/2626 Sch.1

Sch.8 Part II para.4, applied: SI 2002/2626 Sch.1, SI 2004/366

Sch.9 Part I para.1, applied: SI 2002/2626 Sch.1

Sch.9 Part I para.2, amended: SI 2004/366 Sch.1 para.35

Sch.9 Part I para.2, applied: SI 2002/2626 Sch.1

Sch.9 Part II para.3, applied: SI 2002/2626 Sch.1

Sch.9 Part II para.4, amended: SI 2004/366 Sch.1 para.35

Sch.9 Part II para.4, applied: SI 2002/2626 Sch.1

Sch.9 Part II para.5, applied: SI 2002/2626 Sch.1

Sch.9 Part II para.6, applied: SI 2002/2626 Sch.1

Sch.9 Part II para.7, applied: SI 2002/2626 Sch.1

Sch.9 Part II para.7, varied: 2003 c.3 s.1, 2003 c.12 s.1

Sch.9 Part III para.8, applied: SI 2002/2626 Sch.1

Sch.9 Part III para.9, applied: SI 2002/2626 Sch.1

Sch.9 Part III para.10, applied: SI 2002/2626 Sch.1

Sch.9 Part III para.11, applied: SI 2002/2626 Sch.1

Sch.10 Part I para.1, amended: SI 2004/366 Sch.1 para.36

Sch.10 Part I para.1, applied: SI 2002/2626 Sch.1

2000–cont.

41. Political Parties, Elections and Referendums Act 2000–*cont.*

Sch.10 Part I para.2, amended: SI 2004/366 Sch.1 para.36

Sch.10 Part I para.2, applied: SI 2002/2626 Sch.1

Sch.10 Part II para.3, applied: SI 2002/2626 Sch.1

Sch.10 Part II para.4, amended: SI 2004/366 Sch.1 para.36

Sch.10 Part II para.4, applied: SI 2002/2626 Sch.1

Sch.10 Part II para.5, applied: SI 2002/2626 Sch.1

Sch.10 Part II para.6, applied: SI 2002/2626 Sch.1

Sch.10 Part II para.7, applied: SI 2002/2626 Sch.1

Sch.10 Part II para.7, varied: 2003 c.12 s.1

Sch.10 Part III para.8, applied: SI 2002/2626 Sch.1

Sch.10 Part III para.9, applied: SI 2002/2626 Sch.1

Sch.10 Part III para.10, applied: SI 2002/2626 Sch.1

Sch.10 Part III para.11, applied: SI 2002/2626 Sch.1

Sch.11 Part I para.1, applied: SI 2002/2626 Sch.1

Sch.11 Part I para.2, applied: SI 2002/2626 Sch.1

Sch.11 Part I para.3, applied: SI 2002/2626 Sch.1

Sch.11 Part I para.4, applied: SI 2002/2626 Sch.1

Sch.11 Part I para.5, applied: SI 2002/2626 Sch.1

Sch.11 Part II para.6, amended: SI 2004/366 Sch.1 para.37

Sch.11 Part II para.6, applied: SI 2002/2626 Sch.1

Sch.11 Part II para.7, applied: SI 2002/2626 Sch.1, SI 2003/1645 r.1

Sch.11 Part II para.8, applied: SI 2002/2626 Sch.1

Sch.11 Part III para.9, applied: SI 2002/2626 Sch.1

Sch.11 Part III para.10, applied: SI 2002/2626 Sch.1

Sch.11 Part III para.11, applied: SI 2002/2626 Sch.1

Sch.12 para.4, amended: 2003 c.21 Sch.17 para.167, Sch.19

Sch.12 para.4, repealed (in part): 2003 c.21 Sch.19

Sch.13 Part I para.1, applied: SI 2002/2626 Sch.1

Sch.13 Part I para.1, varied: SI 2004/1962 Sch.3 Part 2

Sch.13 Part I para.2, applied: SI 2002/2626 Sch.1

2000–cont.

41. Political Parties, Elections and Referendums Act 2000–*cont.*

Sch.13 Part I para.2, varied: SI 2004/1962 Sch.3 Part 2

Sch.13 Part II para.3, applied: SI 2002/2626 Sch.1

Sch.13 Part II para.3, varied: SI 2004/1962 Sch.3 Part 2

Sch.13 Part II para.4, applied: SI 2002/2626 Sch.1

Sch.13 Part II para.4, varied: SI 2004/1962 Sch.3 Part 2

Sch.14 para.2, applied: SI 2004/1961

Sch.14 para.2, varied: SI 2004/1962 Sch.3 Part 2

Sch.14 para.2, enabling: SI 2004/1961

Sch.15 Part I para.1, applied: SI 2002/2626 Sch.1

Sch.15 Part I para.1, varied: SI 2004/1962 Sch.3 Part 2

Sch.15 Part I para.2, applied: SI 2002/2626 Sch.1

Sch.15 Part I para.2, varied: SI 2004/1962 Sch.3 Part 2

Sch.15 Part I para.3, applied: SI 2002/2626 Sch.1

Sch.15 Part I para.3, varied: SI 2004/1962 Sch.3 Part 2

Sch.15 Part I para.4, applied: SI 2002/2626 Sch.1

Sch.15 Part I para.4, varied: SI 2004/1962 Sch.3 Part 2

Sch.15 Part I para.5, applied: SI 2002/2626 Sch.1

Sch.15 Part I para.5, varied: SI 2004/1962 Sch.3 Part 2

Sch.15 Part II para.6, applied: SI 2002/2626 Sch.1

Sch.15 Part II para.6, varied: SI 2004/1962 Sch.3 Part 2

Sch.15 Part II para.7, applied: SI 2002/2626 Sch.1, SI 2003/1645 r.1

Sch.15 Part II para.7, varied: SI 2004/1962 Sch.3 Part 2

Sch.15 Part II para.8, applied: SI 2002/2626 Sch.1

Sch.15 Part II para.8, varied: SI 2004/1962 Sch.3 Part 2

Sch.15 Part III para.9, applied: SI 2002/2626 Sch.1

Sch.15 Part III para.9, varied: SI 2004/1962 Sch.3 Part 2

Sch.15 Part III para.10, applied: SI 2002/2626 Sch.1

Sch.15 Part III para.10, varied: SI 2004/1962 Sch.3 Part 2

Sch.15 Part III para.11, applied: SI 2002/2626 Sch.1

Sch.15 Part III para.11, varied: SI 2004/1962 Sch.3 Part 2

Sch.17 para.1, applied: SI 2002/2626 Sch.1

2000–cont.

41. Political Parties, Elections and Referendums Act 2000–*cont.*

Sch.17 para.2, applied: SI 2002/2626 Sch.1

Sch.17 para.3, applied: SI 2002/2626 Sch.1

Sch.17 para.4, applied: SI 2002/2626 Sch.1

Sch.17 para.5, applied: SI 2002/2626 Sch.1

Sch.17 para.6, applied: SI 2002/2626 Sch.1

Sch.17 para.7, applied: SI 2002/2626 Sch.1

Sch.17 para.8, applied: SI 2002/2626 Sch.1

Sch.17 para.9, applied: SI 2002/2626 Sch.1

Sch.17 para.10, applied: SI 2002/2626 Sch.1

Sch.18 para.1, applied: SI 2002/2626 Sch.1

Sch.18 para.2, applied: SI 2002/2626 Sch.1

Sch.18 para.3, applied: SI 2002/2626 Sch.1

Sch.18 para.4, applied: SI 2002/2626 Sch.1

Sch.18 para.5, applied: SI 2002/2626 Sch.1

Sch.18 para.6, applied: SI 2002/2626 Sch.1

Sch.18 para.7, applied: SI 2002/2626 Sch.1

Sch.18 para.8, applied: SI 2002/2626 Sch.1

Sch.18 para.9, applied: SI 2002/2626 Sch.1

Sch.18 para.10, applied: SI 2002/2626 Sch.1

Sch.18 para.11, applied: SI 2002/2626 Sch.1

Sch.18 para.12, applied: SI 2002/2626 Sch.1

Sch.18 para.13, applied: SI 2002/2626 Sch.1

Sch.18 para.14, applied: SI 2002/2626 Sch.1

Sch.18 para.15, applied: SI 2002/2626 Sch.1

Sch.18 para.16, applied: SI 2002/2626 Sch.1

Sch.18 para.17, applied: SI 2002/2626 Sch.1

Sch.18 para.18, applied: SI 2002/2626 Sch.1

Sch.18 para.19, applied: SI 2002/2626 Sch.1

Sch.21 para.1, applied: SI 2002/2626 Sch.1

Sch.21 para.2, applied: SI 2002/2626 Sch.1

Sch.21 para.3, applied: SI 2002/2626 Sch.1

Sch.21 para.4, applied: SI 2002/2626 Sch.1

Sch.21 para.5, applied: SI 2002/2626 Sch.1

Sch.21 para.5, consolidated: 2002 c.24 s.2, s.7

Sch.21 para.5, repealed: 2002 c.24 Sch.4

Sch.21 para.6, applied: SI 2002/2626 Sch.1

Sch.21 para.7, applied: SI 2002/2626 Sch.1

Sch.21 para.8, applied: SI 2002/2626 Sch.1

Sch.21 para.8, repealed: 2003 c.21 Sch.19

Sch.21 para.9, applied: SI 2002/2626 Sch.1

Sch.21 para.10, applied: SI 2002/2626 Sch.1

Sch.21 para.11, applied: SI 2002/2626 Sch.1

Sch.21 para.12, applied: SI 2002/2626 Sch.1

Sch.21 para.13, applied: SI 2002/2626 Sch.1

Sch.21 para.14, applied: SI 2002/2626 Sch.1

Sch.21 para.15, applied: SI 2002/2626 Sch.1

Sch.21 para.16, applied: SI 2002/2626 Sch.1

Sch.21 para.17, applied: SI 2002/2626 Sch.1

Sch.21 para.18, applied: SI 2002/2626 Sch.1

Sch.23 Part I para.1, applied: SI 2002/2626 Sch.1

Sch.23 Part I para.2, applied: SI 2002/2626 Sch.1

Sch.23 Part I para.3, applied: SI 2002/2626 Sch.1

Sch.23 Part I para.4, applied: SI 2002/2626 Sch.1

2000–cont.

41. Political Parties, Elections and Referendums Act 2000–cont.

Sch.23 Part I para.5, applied: SI 2002/2626 Sch.1

Sch.23 Part I para.6, applied: SI 2002/2626 Sch.1

Sch.23 Part I para.7, applied: SI 2002/2626 Sch.1

Sch.23 Part II para.8, applied: SI 2002/2626 Sch.1

Sch.23 Part II para.9, applied: SI 2002/2626 Sch.1

Sch.23 Part II para.10, applied: SI 2002/2626 Sch.1

Sch.23 Part II para.11, applied: SI 2002/2626 Sch.1

Sch.23 Part II para.12, applied: SI 2002/2626 Sch.1

Sch.23 Part II para.13, applied: SI 2002/2626 Sch.1

43. Criminal Justice and Court Services Act 2000

Commencement Orders: SI 2004/780 Art.2; SI 2003/709 Art.2; SI 2002/1149 Art.2; SI 2002/1862 Art.2; SI 2004/2171 Art.2

Part I, applied: 2004 c.31 s.41

Part II, applied: SI 2002/233 Reg.5, SI 2002/325 Reg.13, SI 2002/327 Reg.10, SI 2002/812 Reg.6, 2003 asp 5 s.17, 2004 c.28 s.45

s.1, amended: 2003 c.44 s.26, Sch.32 para.134

s.4, applied: 2004 c.28 s.9, s.54

s.9, applied: 2003 c.44 s.253

s.11, applied: 2004 c.31 s.41

s.12, see *MH (A Child) (Care Proceedings: Children's Guardian), Re* [2002] 1 W.L.R. 189 (Fam Div), Wall, J.; see *R. (on the application of R) v Children and Family Court Advisory and Support Service* [2003] EWHC 235, [2003] 1 F.L.R. 953 (QBD (Admin Ct)), Charles, J.

s.12, amended: 2004 c.31 Sch.3 para.13

s.12, applied: SI 2004/2187 Reg.3

s.12, repealed (in part): 2002 c.38 Sch.5

s.12, varied: SI 2003/3191 Art.3

s.17, repealed: 2003 c.39 Sch.10

s.19, amended: SI 2003/2867 Sch.1 para.30, SI 2003/3191 Sch.1 para.4

s.19, varied: SI 2003/3191 Art.3

s.20, amended: SI 2003/3191 Sch.1 para.4

s.20, varied: SI 2003/3191 Art.3

s.23, amended: SI 2003/3191 Sch.1 para.4

s.23, varied: SI 2003/3191 Art.3

s.25, amended: SI 2003/3191 Sch.1 para.4

s.26, applied: SI 2002/635 Reg.2, SI 2004/2695 Sch.1 para.1

s.28, see *Attorney General's Reference (Nos. 37, 38, 44, 54, 51, 53, 35, 40, 43, 45, 41 and 42 of 2003), Re* [2003] EWCA Crim 2973, [2004] 1 Cr. App. R. (S.) 84 (CA (Crim Div)), Kay, L.J.; see *R. v Clayton*

2000–cont.

43. Criminal Justice and Court Services Act 2000–cont.

s.28–cont.

(Daniel) [2003] EWCA Crim 2161, [2004] 1 Cr. App. R. (S.) 30 (CA (Crim Div)), Mance, L.J.; see *R. v Field (Brian John)* [2002] EWCA Crim 2913, [2003] 1 W.L.R. 882 (CA (Crim Div)), Kay, L.J.; see *R. v G (Mark John)* [2001] EWCA Crim 2308, [2002] 2 Cr. App. R. (S.) 1 (CA (Crim Div)), Judge David Clarke Q.C.; see *R. v Yates (David Christopher)* [2003] EWCA Crim 1917, [2004] 1 Cr. App. R. (S.) 44 (CA (Crim Div)), Tugendhat, J

s.28, applied: 2002 c.32 s.169, SI 2003/348 Sch.6 para.9, SI 2003/1558 Sch.2 para.8

s.29, applied: 2002 c.32 s.169, 2003 c.44 s.327, SI 2003/348 Sch.6 para.9, SI 2003/1558 Sch.2 para.8

s.29A, added: 2003 c.44 Sch.30 para.2

s.29A, applied: 2003 c.44 s.327

s.29B, added: 2003 c.44 Sch.30 para.2

s.30, amended: 2003 c.44 Sch.30 para.3

s.31, amended: 2003 c.44 Sch.30 para.4

s.31, applied: SI 2004/2695 Sch.1 para.1, Sch.1 para.2

s.32, applied: SI 2004/2695 Sch.1 para.1, Sch.1 para.2

s.33, amended: 2003 c.44 Sch.30 para.5

s.34, amended: 2004 c.31 Sch.2 para.7

s.34, applied: SI 2004/2695 Sch.1 para.1, Sch.1 para.2

s.35, amended: 2002 c.32 Sch.21 para.128

s.35, applied: SI 2002/233 Reg.6, Reg.7, Reg.8

s.35, repealed (in part): 2002 c.32 Sch.21 para.128, Sch.22 Part 3

s.36, amended: SI 2003/439 Sch.2 para.16, 2004 c.31 Sch.1 para.11, Sch.2 para.7

s.39, repealed: 2003 c.42 Sch.7

s.41, see *R. v Oliver (Mark David)* [2002] EWCA Crim 2766, [2003] 1 Cr. App. R. 28 (CA (Crim Div)), Rose, L.J.

s.42, amended: 2003 c.44 Sch.32 para.135

s.47, repealed: 2003 c.44 Sch.37 Part 7

s.48, repealed: 2003 c.44 Sch.37 Part 7

s.49, repealed: 2003 c.44 Sch.37 Part 7

s.50, repealed: 2003 c.44 Sch.37 Part 7

s.51, repealed: 2003 c.44 Sch.37 Part 7

s.53, repealed: 2003 c.44 Sch.37 Part 7

s.54, repealed: 2003 c.44 Sch.37 Part 7

s.55, repealed: 2003 c.44 Sch.37 Part 7

s.56, see *R. (on the application of U) v Commissioner of Police of the Metropolis* [2002] EWHC 2486, [2003] 1 W.L.R. 897 (QBD (Admin Ct)), Latham, L.J.

s.60, see *R. (on the application of Smith) v Secretary of State for the Home Department* [2004] EWCA Civ 99, [2004] Q.B. 1341 (CA), Lord Phillips of Worth Matravers, M.R.

2000–cont.

43. Criminal Justice and Court Services Act 2000–*cont.*

s.62, amended: 2003 c.44 Sch.32 para.136

s.62, applied: 2003 c.44 s.250, s.251

s.63, repealed: 2003 c.44 Sch.37 Part 7

s.64, amended: 2003 c.44 s.266

s.64, applied: 2003 c.44 s.250, s.251

s.64, repealed (in part): 2003 c.44 Sch.37 Part 7

s.66, repealed: 2003 c.42 Sch.7

s.67, repealed: 2003 c.44 Sch.37 Part 12

s.68, amended: 2003 c.42 Sch.6 para.44

s.68, repealed: 2003 c.44 Sch.37 Part 12

s.69, amended: 2003 c.42 Sch.6 para.44, 2003 c.44 Sch.32 para.137

s.69, repealed: 2004 c.28 Sch.10 para.55, Sch.11

s.70, amended: 2003 c.44 Sch.32 para.138

s.70, referred to: SI 2004/1892 Art.2

s.70, enabling: SI 2004/1892

s.77, enabling: SI 2002/3220

s.78, amended: 2003 c.44 Sch.37 Part 7

s.80, enabling: SI 2002/1149, SI 2002/1862, SI 2003/709, SI 2004/780, SI 2004/2171

Sch.1 para.2, amended: 2003 c.39 Sch.8 para.393

Sch.2 para.1, amended: SI 2003/3191 Sch.1 para.4, 2004 c.31 Sch.3 para.14

Sch.2 para.1, varied: SI 2003/3191 Art.3

Sch.2 para.2, amended: SI 2003/3191 Sch.1 para.4

Sch.2 para.2, varied: SI 2003/3191 Art.3

Sch.2 para.3, amended: SI 2003/3191 Sch.1 para.4

Sch.2 para.3, varied: SI 2003/3191 Art.3

Sch.2 para.4, amended: SI 2003/3191 Sch.1 para.4

Sch.2 para.4, varied: SI 2003/3191 Art.3

Sch.2 para.5, amended: SI 2003/3191 Sch.1 para.4

Sch.2 para.5, varied: SI 2003/3191 Art.3

Sch.2 para.6, amended: SI 2003/3191 Sch.1 para.4

Sch.2 para.6, varied: SI 2003/3191 Art.3

Sch.2 para.7, amended: SI 2003/3191 Sch.1 para.4

Sch.2 para.7, varied: SI 2003/3191 Art.3

Sch.2 para.8, amended: SI 2003/3191 Sch.1 para.4

Sch.2 para.8, varied: SI 2003/3191 Art.3

Sch.2 para.9, amended: SI 2003/3191 Sch.1 para.4

Sch.2 para.9, varied: SI 2003/3191 Art.3

Sch.2 para.10, amended: SI 2003/3191 Sch.1 para.4

Sch.2 para.10, varied: SI 2003/3191 Art.3

Sch.2 para.11, amended: SI 2003/3191 Sch.1 para.4

Sch.2 para.11, varied: SI 2003/3191 Art.3

Sch.2 para.12, amended: SI 2003/3191 Sch.1 para.4

2000–cont.

43. Criminal Justice and Court Services Act 2000–*cont.*

Sch.2 para.12, varied: SI 2003/3191 Art.3

Sch.2 para.13, amended: SI 2003/3191 Sch.1 para.4

Sch.2 para.13, varied: SI 2003/3191 Art.3

Sch.2 para.14, amended: SI 2003/3191 Sch.1 para.4

Sch.2 para.14, varied: SI 2003/3191 Art.3

Sch.2 para.15, amended: SI 2003/3191 Sch.1 para.4

Sch.2 para.15, varied: SI 2003/3191 Art.3

Sch.2 para.16, amended: SI 2003/3191 Sch.1 para.4

Sch.2 para.16, varied: SI 2003/3191 Art.3

Sch.2 para.17, amended: SI 2003/3191 Sch.1 para.4

Sch.2 para.17, varied: SI 2003/3191 Art.3

Sch.2 para.18, amended: SI 2003/3191 Sch.1 para.4

Sch.2 para.18, varied: SI 2003/3191 Art.3

Sch.2 para.19, amended: SI 2003/3191 Sch.1 para.4

Sch.2 para.19, varied: SI 2003/3191 Art.3

Sch.3 para.1, varied: SI 2003/3191 Art.3

Sch.3 para.2, varied: SI 2003/3191 Art.3

Sch.3 para.3, varied: SI 2003/3191 Art.3

Sch.3 para.4, varied: SI 2003/3191 Art.3

Sch.3 para.5, amended: SI 2003/3191 Sch.1 para.4

Sch.3 para.5, varied: SI 2003/3191 Art.3

Sch.4 para.1, amended: 2003 c.42 Sch.6 para.44

Sch.4 para.1, repealed (in part): 2003 c.42 Sch.7

Sch.4 para.2, amended: 2002 c.41 s.146, 2003 c.42 Sch.6 para.44, 2004 c.19 s.5

Sch.4 para.2, referred to: SI 2004/2695 Sch.1 para.2

Sch.4 para.2, repealed (in part): 2003 c.42 Sch.7

Sch.4 para.3, amended: 2003 c.42 Sch.6 para.44, 2004 c.28 Sch.10 para.56

Sch.4 para.3, repealed (in part): 2003 c.42 Sch.7

Sch.5 para.1, repealed: 2003 c.42 Sch.7

Sch.5 para.2, repealed: 2003 c.42 Sch.7

Sch.5 para.3, repealed: 2003 c.42 Sch.7

Sch.5 para.4, repealed: 2003 c.42 Sch.7

Sch.5 para.5, repealed: 2003 c.42 Sch.7

Sch.5 para.6, repealed: 2003 c.42 Sch.7

Sch.5 para.7, repealed: 2003 c.42 Sch.7

Sch.5 para.8, repealed: 2003 c.42 Sch.7

Sch.5 para.9, repealed: 2003 c.42 Sch.7

Sch.5 para.10, repealed: 2003 c.42 Sch.7

Sch.6 para.1, amended: SI 2004/1892 Art.2

Sch.6 para.3, added: SI 2004/1892 Art.2

Sch.6 para.4, added: SI 2004/1892 Art.2

Sch.7 Part I para.1, repealed: 2003 c.44 Sch.37 Part 7

2000–cont.

43. Criminal Justice and Court Services Act 2000–*cont.*

Sch.7 Part I para.2, repealed: 2003 c.44 Sch.37 Part 7

Sch.7 Part I para.3, repealed: 2003 c.44 Sch.37 Part 7

Sch.7 Part II para.47, repealed: 2003 c.44 Sch.37 Part 10

Sch.7 Part II para.51, repealed: 2002 c.38 Sch.5

Sch.7 Part II para.52, repealed: 2002 c.38 Sch.5

Sch.7 Part II para.53, repealed: 2002 c.38 Sch.5

Sch.7 Part II para.83, repealed (in part): 2002 c.32 Sch.22 Part 3

Sch.7 Part II para.84, repealed: 2003 c.39 Sch.10

Sch.7 Part II para.85, repealed: 2003 c.39 Sch.10

Sch.7 Part II para.86, repealed: 2003 c.39 Sch.10

Sch.7 Part II para.99, repealed: 2004 c.28 Sch.11

Sch.7 Part II para.100, repealed: 2004 c.28 Sch.11

Sch.7 Part II para.101, repealed: 2004 c.28 Sch.11

Sch.7 Part II para.102, repealed: 2004 c.28 Sch.11

Sch.7 Part II para.104, repealed: 2003 c.44 Sch.37 Part 7

Sch.7 Part II para.105, repealed: 2003 c.44 Sch.37 Part 7

Sch.7 Part II para.106, repealed: 2003 c.44 Sch.37 Part 7

Sch.7 Part II para.107, repealed: 2003 c.44 Sch.37 Part 7

Sch.7 Part II para.111, repealed (in part): 2003 c.44 Sch.37 Part 7

Sch.7 Part II para.123, repealed (in part): 2003 c.44 Sch.37 Part 7

Sch.7 Part II para.124, repealed (in part): 2003 c.44 Sch.37 Part 7

Sch.7 Part II para.133, repealed: 2003 c.44 Sch.37 Part 7

Sch.7 Part II para.139, repealed: 2003 c.44 Sch.37 Part 7

Sch.7 Part II para.140, repealed: 2003 c.44 Sch.37 Part 7

Sch.7 Part II para.151, amended: 2002 c.30 Sch.8

Sch.7 Part II para.161, repealed: 2003 c.44 Sch.37 Part 7

Sch.7 Part II para.162, repealed: 2003 c.44 Sch.37 Part 7

Sch.7 Part II para.165, repealed: 2003 c.44 Sch.37 Part 7

Sch.7 Part II para.166, repealed: 2003 c.44 Sch.37 Part 7

2000–cont.

43. Criminal Justice and Court Services Act 2000–*cont.*

Sch.7 Part II para.167, repealed: 2003 c.44 Sch.37 Part 7

Sch.7 Part II para.168, repealed: 2003 c.44 Sch.37 Part 7

Sch.7 Part II para.169, repealed: 2003 c.44 Sch.37 Part 7

Sch.7 Part II para.170, repealed: 2003 c.44 Sch.37 Part 7

Sch.7 Part II para.171, repealed: 2003 c.44 Sch.37 Part 7

Sch.7 Part II para.172, repealed: 2003 c.44 Sch.37 Part 7

Sch.7 Part II para.177, repealed: 2003 c.44 Sch.37 Part 7

Sch.7 Part II para.179, repealed: 2003 c.44 Sch.37 Part 7

Sch.7 Part II para.189, repealed: 2003 c.44 Sch.37 Part 7

Sch.7 Part II para.196, repealed (in part): 2003 c.44 Sch.37 Part 7

Sch.7 Part II para.197, repealed (in part): 2003 c.44 Sch.37 Part 7

Sch.7 Part II para.198, repealed: 2003 c.44 Sch.37 Part 7

Sch.7 Part II para.199, repealed: 2003 c.44 Sch.37 Part 7

Sch.7 Part II para.200, repealed: 2003 c.44 Sch.37 Part 7

Sch.7 Part II para.206, repealed (in part): 2003 c.44 Sch.37 Part 7

44. Sexual Offences (Amendment) Act 2000

Commencement Orders: SI 2003/1935 Art.2; SSI 2003/378 Art.2

see *B v United Kingdom (53760/00)* (2004) 39 E.H.R.R. 30 (ECHR), Judge Pellonpaa (President)

s.1, repealed (in part): 2003 c.42 Sch.7

s.2, repealed (in part): 2003 c.42 Sch.7

s.3, see *R. v Hubbard (Gerald Leslie)* [2002] EWCA Crim 494, [2002] 2 Cr. App. R. (S.) 101 (CA (Crim Div)), Judge Sir Rhys Davies Q.C.; see *R. v MacNicol (Andrew Brian)* [2003] EWCA Crim 3093, [2004] 2 Cr. App. R. (S.) 2 (CA (Crim Div)), Cresswell, J.

s.3, amended: 2004 c.33 Sch.28 para.62

s.3, applied: SI 2002/57 Sch.4 para.5, Sch.4 para.11, SI 2002/635 Sch.1 para.2, Sch.1 para.3, SI 2002/896 Sch.1 para.49, Sch.1 para.65, Sch.1 para.79, 2003 c.42 Sch.3 para.16, Sch.3 para.57, Sch.3 para.83, 2003 c.44 Sch.16 para.20, SI 2003/237 Sch.4 para.5, Sch.4 para.11, SI 2004/1910 Sch.3, SI 2004/2695 Sch.1 para.9, SSI 2003/441 Sch.1 para.16, SSI 2004/411 Sch.1 para.20

s.3, repealed (in part): 2003 c.42 Sch.7

s.4, repealed (in part): 2003 c.42 Sch.7

s.5, repealed: 2003 c.42 Sch.7

s.6, repealed (in part): 2003 c.42 Sch.7

2000–cont.

44. Sexual Offences (Amendment) Act 2000–*cont.*
s.7, enabling: SI 2003/1935, SSI 2003/378
45. Consolidated Fund (No.2) Act 2000
repealed: 2002 c.18 Sch.3

2001

International Criminal Courts Act 2001
see *R. v Jones (Margaret)* [2004] EWCA Crim 1981, [2004] 3 W.L.R. 1362 (CA (Crim Div)), Latham, L.J.
1. Consolidated Fund Act 2001
repealed: 2003 c.13 Sch.3
2. Capital Allowances Act 2001
see *Barclays Mercantile Business Finance Ltd v Mawson (Inspector of Taxes)* [2002] EWHC 1527, [2002] S.T.C. 1068 (Ch D), Park, J.
applied: 2002 c.23 Sch.22 para.11, Sch.29 para.122, Sch.29 para.125, 2003 c.14 Sch.36 para.18, 2004 c.20 Sch.9 para.7, Sch.9 para.8
referred to: 2002 c.23 Sch.29 para.83, 2003 c.1 Sch.6 para.246
varied: 2003 c.14 Sch.36 para.16, Sch.36 para.17
Part 2, applied: 2002 c.23 s.63, Sch.29 para.73A, 2004 c.20 Sch.4 para.4, Sch.9 para.9, Sch.9 para.21
Part 2 c.17, applied: 2004 c.20 Sch.4 para.4
Part 2 c.17, added: 2004 c.12 s.134
Part 3, applied: 2002 c.29 Sch.10 para.18, 2004 c.20 Sch.4 para.5
Part 3 c.8, applied: 2004 c.20 Sch.4 para.6
Part 4A, applied: 2002 c.29 Sch.10 para.22
Part 12 c.5, added: 2003 c.14 s.164
s.4, amended: 2003 c.1 Sch.6 para.247, 2004 c.12 Sch.35 para.48
s.11, varied: 2002 c.29 Sch.10 para.12, 2004 c.20 Sch.9 para.10, Sch.9 para.22
s.12, varied: 2002 c.29 Sch.10 para.12, 2004 c.20 Sch.9 para.10, Sch.9 para.22
s.13, varied: 2002 c.29 Sch.10 para.12, 2003 c.14 Sch.36 para.17, Sch.36 para.19, 2004 c.20 Sch.9 para.10, Sch.9 para.22
s.14, varied: 2002 c.29 Sch.10 para.12, 2004 c.20 Sch.9 para.10, Sch.9 para.22
s.15, amended: SI 2004/2310 Sch.1 para.52
s.15, varied: 2002 c.29 Sch.10 para.12, 2004 c.20 Sch.9 para.10, Sch.9 para.22
s.16, varied: 2002 c.29 Sch.10 para.12, 2004 c.20 Sch.9 para.10, Sch.9 para.22
s.17, varied: 2002 c.29 Sch.10 para.12, 2004 c.20 Sch.9 para.10, Sch.9 para.22
s.18, substituted: SI 2004/2310 Sch.1 para.53
s.18, varied: 2002 c.29 Sch.10 para.12, 2004 c.20 Sch.9 para.10, Sch.9 para.22
s.19, varied: 2002 c.29 Sch.10 para.12, 2004 c.20 Sch.9 para.10, Sch.9 para.22
s.20, amended: 2003 c.1 Sch.6 para.248

2001–cont.

2. Capital Allowances Act 2001–*cont.*
s.20, varied: 2002 c.29 Sch.10 para.12, 2004 c.20 Sch.9 para.10, Sch.9 para.22
s.21, varied: 2002 c.29 Sch.10 para.12, 2004 c.20 Sch.9 para.10, Sch.9 para.22
s.22, varied: 2002 c.29 Sch.10 para.12, 2004 c.20 Sch.9 para.10, Sch.9 para.22
s.23, varied: 2002 c.29 Sch.10 para.12, 2004 c.20 Sch.9 para.10, Sch.9 para.22
s.24, varied: 2002 c.29 Sch.10 para.12, 2004 c.20 Sch.9 para.10, Sch.9 para.22
s.25, varied: 2002 c.29 Sch.10 para.12, 2004 c.20 Sch.9 para.10, Sch.9 para.22
s.26, varied: 2002 c.29 Sch.10 para.12, 2004 c.20 Sch.9 para.10, Sch.9 para.22
s.27, varied: 2002 c.29 Sch.10 para.12, 2004 c.20 Sch.9 para.10, Sch.9 para.22
s.28, varied: 2002 c.29 Sch.10 para.12, 2004 c.20 Sch.9 para.10, Sch.9 para.22
s.29, amended: 2004 c.21 Sch.1 para.96
s.29, varied: 2002 c.29 Sch.10 para.12, 2004 c.20 Sch.9 para.10, Sch.9 para.22
s.30, varied: 2002 c.29 Sch.10 para.12, 2004 c.20 Sch.9 para.10, Sch.9 para.22
s.31, varied: 2002 c.29 Sch.10 para.12, 2004 c.20 Sch.9 para.10, Sch.9 para.22
s.32, varied: 2002 c.29 Sch.10 para.12, 2004 c.20 Sch.9 para.10, Sch.9 para.22
s.33, varied: 2002 c.29 Sch.10 para.12, 2004 c.20 Sch.9 para.10, Sch.9 para.22
s.34, varied: 2002 c.29 Sch.10 para.12, 2004 c.20 Sch.9 para.10, Sch.9 para.22
s.35, varied: 2002 c.29 Sch.10 para.12, 2004 c.20 Sch.9 para.10, Sch.9 para.22
s.36, varied: 2002 c.29 Sch.10 para.12, 2004 c.20 Sch.9 para.10, Sch.9 para.22
s.37, varied: 2002 c.29 Sch.10 para.12, 2004 c.20 Sch.9 para.10, Sch.9 para.22
s.38, varied: 2002 c.29 Sch.10 para.12, 2004 c.20 Sch.9 para.10, Sch.9 para.22
s.39, amended: 2002 c.23 Sch.19 para.2, Sch.20 para.2, Sch.21 para.2, Sch.40 Part 3, 2003 c.14 Sch.30 para.2, Sch.43 Part 3
s.39, varied: 2002 c.29 Sch.10 para.12, 2004 c.20 Sch.9 para.10, Sch.9 para.22
s.40, varied: 2002 c.29 Sch.10 para.12, 2004 c.20 Sch.9 para.10, Sch.9 para.22
s.41, varied: 2002 c.29 Sch.10 para.12, 2004 c.20 Sch.9 para.10, Sch.9 para.22
s.42, varied: 2002 c.29 Sch.10 para.12, 2004 c.20 Sch.9 para.10, Sch.9 para.22
s.43, varied: 2002 c.29 Sch.10 para.12, 2004 c.20 Sch.9 para.10, Sch.9 para.22
s.44, applied: 2004 c.12 s.142
s.44, varied: 2002 c.29 Sch.10 para.12, 2004 c.20 Sch.9 para.10, Sch.9 para.22
s.45, amended: 2003 c.14 s.165, s.166
s.45, varied: 2002 c.29 Sch.10 para.12, 2004 c.20 Sch.9 para.10, Sch.9 para.22
s.45A, varied: 2002 c.29 Sch.10 para.12, 2004 c.20 Sch.9 para.10, Sch.9 para.22

2001–cont.

2. **Capital Allowances Act 2001**–*cont.*

s.45A, enabling: SI 2002/1818, SI 2003/1744, SI 2004/2093

s.45B, varied: 2002 c.29 Sch.10 para.12, 2004 c.20 Sch.9 para.10, Sch.9 para.22

s.45B, enabling: SI 2003/1744

s.45C, varied: 2002 c.29 Sch.10 para.12, 2004 c.20 Sch.9 para.10, Sch.9 para.22

s.45C, enabling: SI 2002/1818

s.45D, added: 2002 c.23 Sch.19 para.3

s.45D, varied: 2002 c.29 Sch.10 para.12, 2004 c.20 Sch.9 para.10, Sch.9 para.22

s.45E, added: 2002 c.23 Sch.20 para.3

s.45E, varied: 2002 c.29 Sch.10 para.12, 2004 c.20 Sch.9 para.10, Sch.9 para.22

s.45F, added: 2002 c.23 Sch.21 para.3

s.45F, varied: 2002 c.29 Sch.10 para.12, 2004 c.20 Sch.9 para.10, Sch.9 para.22

s.45G, added: 2002 c.23 Sch.21 para.4

s.45G, varied: 2002 c.29 Sch.10 para.12, 2004 c.20 Sch.9 para.10, Sch.9 para.22

s.45H, added: 2003 c.14 Sch.30 para.3

s.45H, applied: SI 2003/2076 Art.3

s.45H, varied: 2002 c.29 Sch.10 para.12, 2004 c.20 Sch.9 para.10, Sch.9 para.22

s.45H, enabling: SI 2003/2076, SI 2004/2094

s.45I, added: 2003 c.14 Sch.30 para.3

s.45I, varied: 2002 c.29 Sch.10 para.12, 2004 c.20 Sch.9 para.10, Sch.9 para.22

s.45J, added: 2003 c.14 Sch.30 para.3

s.45J, applied: SI 2003/2076 Art.4

s.45J, varied: 2002 c.29 Sch.10 para.12, 2004 c.20 Sch.9 para.10, Sch.9 para.22

s.45J, enabling: SI 2003/2076

s.46, amended: 2002 c.23 s.62, Sch.19 para.4, Sch.20 para.4, Sch.21 para.5, Sch.40 Part 3, 2003 c.14 Sch.30 para.4, Sch.43 Part 3

s.46, varied: 2002 c.29 Sch.10 para.12, 2004 c.20 Sch.9 para.10, Sch.9 para.22

s.47, varied: 2002 c.29 Sch.10 para.12, 2004 c.20 Sch.9 para.10, Sch.9 para.22

s.48, varied: 2002 c.29 Sch.10 para.12, 2004 c.20 Sch.9 para.10, Sch.9 para.22

s.49, varied: 2002 c.29 Sch.10 para.12, 2004 c.20 Sch.9 para.10, Sch.9 para.22

s.50, varied: 2002 c.29 Sch.10 para.12, 2004 c.20 Sch.9 para.10, Sch.9 para.22

s.51, varied: 2002 c.29 Sch.10 para.12, 2004 c.20 Sch.9 para.10, Sch.9 para.22

s.52, amended: 2002 c.23 Sch.19 para.5, Sch.20 para.5, Sch.21 para.6, 2003 c.14 Sch.30 para.5, 2004 c.12 s.142

s.52, varied: 2002 c.29 Sch.10 para.12, 2004 c.12 s.142, 2004 c.20 Sch.9 para.10, Sch.9 para.22

s.53, varied: 2002 c.29 Sch.10 para.12, 2004 c.20 Sch.9 para.10, Sch.9 para.22

s.54, varied: 2002 c.29 Sch.10 para.12, 2004 c.20 Sch.9 para.10, Sch.9 para.22

2001–cont.

2. **Capital Allowances Act 2001**–*cont.*

s.55, varied: 2002 c.29 Sch.10 para.12, 2004 c.20 Sch.9 para.10, Sch.9 para.22

s.56, varied: 2002 c.29 Sch.10 para.12, 2004 c.20 Sch.9 para.10, Sch.9 para.22

s.57, varied: 2002 c.29 Sch.10 para.12, 2004 c.20 Sch.9 para.10, Sch.9 para.22

s.58, varied: 2002 c.29 Sch.10 para.12, 2004 c.20 Sch.9 para.10, Sch.9 para.22

s.59, applied: 2003 c.14 Sch.36 para.17

s.59, varied: 2002 c.29 Sch.10 para.12, 2004 c.20 Sch.9 para.10, Sch.9 para.22

s.60, varied: 2002 c.29 Sch.10 para.12, 2004 c.20 Sch.9 para.10, Sch.9 para.22

s.61, amended: 2003 c.1 Sch.6 para.249

s.61, applied: 2004 c.20 Sch.9 para.9, Sch.9 para.21

s.61, varied: 2002 c.29 Sch.10 para.12, Sch.10 para.17, 2004 c.20 Sch.9 para.10, Sch.9 para.22

s.62, varied: 2002 c.29 Sch.10 para.12, 2004 c.20 Sch.9 para.10, Sch.9 para.22

s.63, amended: 2003 c.1 Sch.6 para.250

s.63, varied: 2002 c.23 Sch.18 para.9, 2002 c.29 Sch.10 para.12, 2004 c.20 Sch.9 para.10, Sch.9 para.22

s.64, varied: 2002 c.29 Sch.10 para.12, 2004 c.20 Sch.9 para.10, Sch.9 para.22

s.65, varied: 2002 c.29 Sch.10 para.12, 2004 c.20 Sch.9 para.10, Sch.9 para.22

s.66, varied: 2002 c.29 Sch.10 para.12, 2004 c.20 Sch.9 para.10, Sch.9 para.22

s.67, applied: SI 2002/1970 Reg.2

s.67, referred to: SI 2002/1970 Reg.2

s.67, varied: 2002 c.29 Sch.10 para.12, 2004 c.20 Sch.9 para.10, Sch.9 para.22

s.68, varied: 2002 c.29 Sch.10 para.12, 2004 c.20 Sch.9 para.10, Sch.9 para.22

s.69, varied: 2002 c.29 Sch.10 para.12, 2004 c.20 Sch.9 para.10, Sch.9 para.22

s.70, varied: 2002 c.29 Sch.10 para.12, 2004 c.20 Sch.9 para.10, Sch.9 para.22

s.71, varied: 2002 c.29 Sch.10 para.12, 2004 c.20 Sch.9 para.10, Sch.9 para.22

s.72, amended: 2003 c.1 Sch.6 para.251

s.72, applied: 2002 c.23 Sch.29 para.83

s.72, varied: 2002 c.29 Sch.10 para.12, 2004 c.20 Sch.9 para.10, Sch.9 para.22

s.73, varied: 2002 c.29 Sch.10 para.12, 2004 c.20 Sch.9 para.10, Sch.9 para.22

s.74, amended: 2002 c.23 Sch.19 para.6, Sch.40 Part 3

s.74, varied: 2002 c.29 Sch.10 para.12, 2004 c.20 Sch.9 para.10, Sch.9 para.22

s.75, varied: 2002 c.29 Sch.10 para.12, 2004 c.20 Sch.9 para.10, Sch.9 para.22

s.76, varied: 2002 c.29 Sch.10 para.12, 2004 c.20 Sch.9 para.10, Sch.9 para.22

s.77, varied: 2002 c.29 Sch.10 para.12, 2004 c.20 Sch.9 para.10, Sch.9 para.22

2001–cont.

2. Capital Allowances Act 2001–cont.

s.78, varied: 2002 c.29 Sch.10 para.12, 2004 c.20 Sch.9 para.10, Sch.9 para.22

s.79, varied: 2002 c.29 Sch.10 para.12, 2004 c.20 Sch.9 para.10, Sch.9 para.22

s.80, varied: 2002 c.29 Sch.10 para.12, 2004 c.20 Sch.9 para.10, Sch.9 para.22

s.81, varied: 2002 c.29 Sch.10 para.12, 2004 c.20 Sch.9 para.10, Sch.9 para.22

s.82, varied: 2002 c.29 Sch.10 para.12, 2004 c.20 Sch.9 para.10, Sch.9 para.22

s.83, varied: 2002 c.29 Sch.10 para.12, 2004 c.20 Sch.9 para.10, Sch.9 para.22

s.84, varied: 2002 c.29 Sch.10 para.12, 2004 c.20 Sch.9 para.10, Sch.9 para.22

s.85, varied: 2002 c.29 Sch.10 para.12, 2004 c.20 Sch.9 para.10, Sch.9 para.22

s.86, varied: 2002 c.29 Sch.10 para.12, 2004 c.20 Sch.9 para.10, Sch.9 para.22

s.87, varied: 2002 c.29 Sch.10 para.12, 2004 c.20 Sch.9 para.10, Sch.9 para.22

s.88, amended: 2003 c.1 Sch.6 para.252

s.88, varied: 2002 c.29 Sch.10 para.12, 2004 c.20 Sch.9 para.10, Sch.9 para.22

s.89, varied: 2002 c.29 Sch.10 para.12, 2004 c.20 Sch.9 para.10, Sch.9 para.22

s.90, varied: 2002 c.29 Sch.10 para.12, 2004 c.20 Sch.9 para.10, Sch.9 para.22

s.91, varied: 2002 c.29 Sch.10 para.12, 2004 c.20 Sch.9 para.10, Sch.9 para.22

s.92, varied: 2002 c.29 Sch.10 para.12, 2004 c.20 Sch.9 para.10, Sch.9 para.22

s.93, varied: 2002 c.29 Sch.10 para.12, 2004 c.20 Sch.9 para.10, Sch.9 para.22

s.94, repealed (in part): 2004 c.12 Sch.42 Part 2

s.94, varied: 2002 c.29 Sch.10 para.12, 2004 c.20 Sch.9 para.10, Sch.9 para.22

s.95, varied: 2002 c.29 Sch.10 para.12, 2004 c.20 Sch.9 para.10, Sch.9 para.22

s.96, varied: 2002 c.29 Sch.10 para.12, 2004 c.20 Sch.9 para.10, Sch.9 para.22

s.97, varied: 2002 c.29 Sch.10 para.12, 2004 c.20 Sch.9 para.10, Sch.9 para.22

s.98, varied: 2002 c.29 Sch.10 para.12, 2004 c.20 Sch.9 para.10, Sch.9 para.22

s.99, varied: 2002 c.29 Sch.10 para.12, 2004 c.20 Sch.9 para.10, Sch.9 para.22

s.100, varied: 2002 c.29 Sch.10 para.12, 2004 c.20 Sch.9 para.10, Sch.9 para.22

s.101, varied: 2002 c.29 Sch.10 para.12, 2004 c.20 Sch.9 para.10, Sch.9 para.22

s.102, varied: 2002 c.29 Sch.10 para.12, 2004 c.20 Sch.9 para.10, Sch.9 para.22

s.103, varied: 2002 c.29 Sch.10 para.12, 2004 c.20 Sch.9 para.10, Sch.9 para.22

s.104, varied: 2002 c.29 Sch.10 para.12, 2004 c.20 Sch.9 para.10, Sch.9 para.22

s.105, varied: 2002 c.29 Sch.10 para.12, 2004 c.20 Sch.9 para.10, Sch.9 para.22

2001–cont.

2. Capital Allowances Act 2001–cont.

s.106, varied: 2002 c.29 Sch.10 para.12, 2004 c.20 Sch.9 para.10, Sch.9 para.22

s.107, varied: 2002 c.29 Sch.10 para.12, 2004 c.20 Sch.9 para.10, Sch.9 para.22

s.108, varied: 2002 c.29 Sch.10 para.12, 2004 c.20 Sch.9 para.10, Sch.9 para.22

s.109, varied: 2002 c.29 Sch.10 para.12, 2004 c.20 Sch.9 para.10, Sch.9 para.22

s.110, varied: 2002 c.29 Sch.10 para.12, 2004 c.20 Sch.9 para.10, Sch.9 para.22

s.111, applied: 2002 c.23 Sch.22 para.13

s.111, disapplied: 2002 c.23 Sch.22 para.13

s.111, varied: 2002 c.29 Sch.10 para.12, 2004 c.20 Sch.9 para.10, Sch.9 para.22

s.112, varied: 2002 c.29 Sch.10 para.12, 2004 c.20 Sch.9 para.10, Sch.9 para.22

s.113, varied: 2002 c.29 Sch.10 para.12, 2004 c.20 Sch.9 para.10, Sch.9 para.22

s.114, varied: 2002 c.29 Sch.10 para.12, 2004 c.20 Sch.9 para.10, Sch.9 para.22

s.115, varied: 2002 c.29 Sch.10 para.12, 2004 c.20 Sch.9 para.10, Sch.9 para.22

s.116, varied: 2002 c.29 Sch.10 para.12, 2004 c.20 Sch.9 para.10, Sch.9 para.22

s.117, varied: 2002 c.29 Sch.10 para.12, 2004 c.20 Sch.9 para.10, Sch.9 para.22

s.118, varied: 2002 c.29 Sch.10 para.12, 2004 c.20 Sch.9 para.10, Sch.9 para.22

s.119, varied: 2002 c.29 Sch.10 para.12, 2004 c.20 Sch.9 para.10, Sch.9 para.22

s.120, varied: 2002 c.29 Sch.10 para.12, 2004 c.20 Sch.9 para.10, Sch.9 para.22

s.121, varied: 2002 c.29 Sch.10 para.12, 2004 c.20 Sch.9 para.10, Sch.9 para.22

s.122, varied: 2002 c.29 Sch.10 para.12, 2004 c.20 Sch.9 para.10, Sch.9 para.22

s.123, varied: 2002 c.29 Sch.10 para.12, 2004 c.20 Sch.9 para.10, Sch.9 para.22

s.124, varied: 2002 c.29 Sch.10 para.12, 2004 c.20 Sch.9 para.10, Sch.9 para.22

s.125, varied: 2002 c.29 Sch.10 para.12, 2004 c.20 Sch.9 para.10, Sch.9 para.22

s.126, varied: 2002 c.29 Sch.10 para.12, 2004 c.20 Sch.9 para.10, Sch.9 para.22

s.127, varied: 2002 c.29 Sch.10 para.12, 2004 c.20 Sch.9 para.10, Sch.9 para.22

s.128, varied: 2002 c.29 Sch.10 para.12, 2004 c.20 Sch.9 para.10, Sch.9 para.22

s.129, varied: 2002 c.29 Sch.10 para.12, 2004 c.20 Sch.9 para.10, Sch.9 para.22

s.130, varied: 2002 c.29 Sch.10 para.12, 2004 c.20 Sch.9 para.10, Sch.9 para.22

s.131, varied: 2002 c.29 Sch.10 para.12, 2004 c.20 Sch.9 para.10, Sch.9 para.22

s.132, varied: 2002 c.29 Sch.10 para.12, 2004 c.20 Sch.9 para.10, Sch.9 para.22

s.133, varied: 2002 c.29 Sch.10 para.12, 2004 c.20 Sch.9 para.10, Sch.9 para.22

s.134, varied: 2002 c.29 Sch.10 para.12, 2004 c.20 Sch.9 para.10, Sch.9 para.22

2001–cont.

2. Capital Allowances Act 2001–*cont.*

s.135, varied: 2002 c.29 Sch.10 para.12, 2004 c.20 Sch.9 para.10, Sch.9 para.22

s.136, varied: 2002 c.29 Sch.10 para.12, 2004 c.20 Sch.9 para.10, Sch.9 para.22

s.137, varied: 2002 c.29 Sch.10 para.12, 2004 c.20 Sch.9 para.10, Sch.9 para.22

s.138, varied: 2002 c.29 Sch.10 para.12, 2004 c.20 Sch.9 para.10, Sch.9 para.22

s.139, varied: 2002 c.29 Sch.10 para.12, 2004 c.20 Sch.9 para.10, Sch.9 para.22

s.140, varied: 2002 c.29 Sch.10 para.12, 2004 c.20 Sch.9 para.10, Sch.9 para.22

s.141, varied: 2002 c.29 Sch.10 para.12, 2004 c.20 Sch.9 para.10, Sch.9 para.22

s.142, varied: 2002 c.29 Sch.10 para.12, 2004 c.20 Sch.9 para.10, Sch.9 para.22

s.143, varied: 2002 c.29 Sch.10 para.12, 2004 c.20 Sch.9 para.10, Sch.9 para.22

s.144, varied: 2002 c.29 Sch.10 para.12, 2004 c.20 Sch.9 para.10, Sch.9 para.22

s.145, varied: 2002 c.29 Sch.10 para.12, 2004 c.20 Sch.9 para.10, Sch.9 para.22

s.146, varied: 2002 c.29 Sch.10 para.12, 2004 c.20 Sch.9 para.10, Sch.9 para.22

s.147, varied: 2002 c.29 Sch.10 para.12, 2004 c.20 Sch.9 para.10, Sch.9 para.22

s.148, varied: 2002 c.29 Sch.10 para.12, 2004 c.20 Sch.9 para.10, Sch.9 para.22

s.149, varied: 2002 c.29 Sch.10 para.12, 2004 c.20 Sch.9 para.10, Sch.9 para.22

s.150, varied: 2002 c.29 Sch.10 para.12, 2004 c.20 Sch.9 para.10, Sch.9 para.22

s.151, varied: 2002 c.29 Sch.10 para.12, 2004 c.20 Sch.9 para.10, Sch.9 para.22

s.152, varied: 2002 c.29 Sch.10 para.12, 2004 c.20 Sch.9 para.10, Sch.9 para.22

s.153, amended: 2004 c.12 Sch.27 para.9

s.153, repealed (in part): 2004 c.12 Sch.42 Part 2

s.153, varied: 2002 c.29 Sch.10 para.12, 2004 c.20 Sch.9 para.10, Sch.9 para.22

s.154, varied: 2002 c.29 Sch.10 para.12, 2004 c.20 Sch.9 para.10, Sch.9 para.22

s.155, varied: 2002 c.29 Sch.10 para.12, 2004 c.20 Sch.9 para.10, Sch.9 para.22

s.156, varied: 2002 c.29 Sch.10 para.12, 2004 c.20 Sch.9 para.10, Sch.9 para.22

s.157, varied: 2002 c.29 Sch.10 para.12, 2004 c.20 Sch.9 para.10, Sch.9 para.22

s.158, varied: 2002 c.29 Sch.10 para.12, 2004 c.20 Sch.9 para.10, Sch.9 para.22

s.159, varied: 2002 c.29 Sch.10 para.12, 2004 c.20 Sch.9 para.10, Sch.9 para.22

s.160, varied: 2002 c.29 Sch.10 para.12, 2004 c.20 Sch.9 para.10, Sch.9 para.22

s.161, varied: 2002 c.29 Sch.10 para.12, 2004 c.20 Sch.9 para.10, Sch.9 para.22

s.161A, varied: 2002 c.29 Sch.10 para.12, 2004 c.20 Sch.9 para.10, Sch.9 para.22

2001–cont.

2. Capital Allowances Act 2001–*cont.*

s.161B, varied: 2002 c.29 Sch.10 para.12, 2004 c.20 Sch.9 para.10, Sch.9 para.22

s.161C, varied: 2002 c.29 Sch.10 para.12, 2004 c.20 Sch.9 para.10, Sch.9 para.22

s.161D, varied: 2002 c.29 Sch.10 para.12, 2004 c.20 Sch.9 para.10, Sch.9 para.22

s.162, varied: 2002 c.29 Sch.10 para.12, 2004 c.20 Sch.9 para.10, Sch.9 para.22

s.163, varied: 2002 c.29 Sch.10 para.12, 2004 c.20 Sch.9 para.10, Sch.9 para.22

s.164, varied: 2002 c.29 Sch.10 para.12, 2004 c.20 Sch.9 para.10, Sch.9 para.22

s.165, varied: 2002 c.29 Sch.10 para.12, 2004 c.20 Sch.9 para.10, Sch.9 para.22

s.166, varied: 2002 c.29 Sch.10 para.12, 2004 c.20 Sch.9 para.10, Sch.9 para.22

s.167, varied: 2002 c.29 Sch.10 para.12, 2004 c.20 Sch.9 para.10, Sch.9 para.22

s.168, varied: 2002 c.29 Sch.10 para.12, 2004 c.20 Sch.9 para.10, Sch.9 para.22

s.169, varied: 2002 c.29 Sch.10 para.12, 2004 c.20 Sch.9 para.10, Sch.9 para.22

s.170, varied: 2002 c.29 Sch.10 para.12, 2004 c.20 Sch.9 para.10, Sch.9 para.22

s.171, varied: 2002 c.29 Sch.10 para.12, 2004 c.20 Sch.9 para.10, Sch.9 para.22

s.172, varied: 2002 c.29 Sch.10 para.12, 2004 c.20 Sch.9 para.10, Sch.9 para.22

s.173, varied: 2002 c.29 Sch.10 para.12, 2004 c.20 Sch.9 para.10, Sch.9 para.22

s.174, varied: 2002 c.29 Sch.10 para.12, 2004 c.20 Sch.9 para.10, Sch.9 para.22

s.175, varied: 2002 c.29 Sch.10 para.12, 2004 c.20 Sch.9 para.10, Sch.9 para.22

s.175A, varied: 2002 c.29 Sch.10 para.12, 2004 c.20 Sch.9 para.10, Sch.9 para.22

s.176, varied: 2002 c.29 Sch.10 para.12, 2004 c.20 Sch.9 para.10, Sch.9 para.22

s.177, varied: 2002 c.29 Sch.10 para.12, 2004 c.20 Sch.9 para.10, Sch.9 para.22

s.178, varied: 2002 c.29 Sch.10 para.12, 2004 c.20 Sch.9 para.10, Sch.9 para.22

s.179, amended: 2002 c.23 s.103

s.179, repealed (in part): 2002 c.23 Sch.40 Part 3

s.179, varied: 2002 c.29 Sch.10 para.12, 2004 c.20 Sch.9 para.10, Sch.9 para.22

s.180, varied: 2002 c.29 Sch.10 para.12, 2004 c.20 Sch.9 para.10, Sch.9 para.22

s.180A, varied: 2002 c.29 Sch.10 para.12, 2004 c.20 Sch.9 para.10, Sch.9 para.22

s.181, varied: 2002 c.29 Sch.10 para.12, 2004 c.20 Sch.9 para.10, Sch.9 para.22

s.182, varied: 2002 c.29 Sch.10 para.12, 2004 c.20 Sch.9 para.10, Sch.9 para.22

s.182A, varied: 2002 c.29 Sch.10 para.12, 2004 c.20 Sch.9 para.10, Sch.9 para.22

s.183, varied: 2002 c.29 Sch.10 para.12, 2004 c.20 Sch.9 para.10, Sch.9 para.22

2001-cont.

2. **Capital Allowances Act 2001**-cont.

s.184, varied: 2002 c.29 Sch.10 para.12, 2004 c.20 Sch.9 para.10, Sch.9 para.22

s.185, varied: 2002 c.29 Sch.10 para.12, 2004 c.20 Sch.9 para.10, Sch.9 para.22

s.186, varied: 2002 c.29 Sch.10 para.12, 2004 c.20 Sch.9 para.10, Sch.9 para.22

s.187, varied: 2002 c.29 Sch.10 para.12, 2004 c.20 Sch.9 para.10, Sch.9 para.22

s.188, varied: 2002 c.29 Sch.10 para.12, 2004 c.20 Sch.9 para.10, Sch.9 para.22

s.189, varied: 2002 c.29 Sch.10 para.12, 2004 c.20 Sch.9 para.10, Sch.9 para.22

s.190, varied: 2002 c.29 Sch.10 para.12, 2004 c.20 Sch.9 para.10, Sch.9 para.22

s.191, varied: 2002 c.29 Sch.10 para.12, 2004 c.20 Sch.9 para.10, Sch.9 para.22

s.192, varied: 2002 c.29 Sch.10 para.12, 2004 c.20 Sch.9 para.10, Sch.9 para.22

s.192A, varied: 2002 c.29 Sch.10 para.12, 2004 c.20 Sch.9 para.10, Sch.9 para.22

s.193, varied: 2002 c.29 Sch.10 para.12, 2004 c.20 Sch.9 para.10, Sch.9 para.22

s.194, varied: 2002 c.29 Sch.10 para.12, 2004 c.20 Sch.9 para.10, Sch.9 para.22

s.195, varied: 2002 c.29 Sch.10 para.12, 2004 c.20 Sch.9 para.10, Sch.9 para.22

s.195A, varied: 2002 c.29 Sch.10 para.12, 2004 c.20 Sch.9 para.10, Sch.9 para.22

s.195B, varied: 2002 c.29 Sch.10 para.12, 2004 c.20 Sch.9 para.10, Sch.9 para.22

s.196, varied: 2002 c.29 Sch.10 para.12, 2004 c.20 Sch.9 para.10, Sch.9 para.22

s.197, varied: 2002 c.29 Sch.10 para.12, 2004 c.20 Sch.9 para.10, Sch.9 para.22

s.198, varied: 2002 c.29 Sch.10 para.12, 2004 c.20 Sch.9 para.10, Sch.9 para.22

s.199, varied: 2002 c.29 Sch.10 para.12, 2004 c.20 Sch.9 para.10, Sch.9 para.22

s.200, varied: 2002 c.29 Sch.10 para.12, 2004 c.20 Sch.9 para.10, Sch.9 para.22

s.201, varied: 2002 c.29 Sch.10 para.12, 2004 c.20 Sch.9 para.10, Sch.9 para.22

s.202, varied: 2002 c.29 Sch.10 para.12, 2004 c.20 Sch.9 para.10, Sch.9 para.22

s.203, varied: 2002 c.29 Sch.10 para.12, 2004 c.20 Sch.9 para.10, Sch.9 para.22

s.204, varied: 2002 c.29 Sch.10 para.12, 2004 c.20 Sch.9 para.10, Sch.9 para.22

s.205, varied: 2002 c.29 Sch.10 para.12, 2004 c.20 Sch.9 para.10, Sch.9 para.22

s.206, varied: 2002 c.29 Sch.10 para.12, 2004 c.20 Sch.9 para.10, Sch.9 para.22

s.207, varied: 2002 c.29 Sch.10 para.12, 2004 c.20 Sch.9 para.10, Sch.9 para.22

s.208, varied: 2002 c.29 Sch.10 para.12, 2004 c.20 Sch.9 para.10, Sch.9 para.22

s.209, varied: 2002 c.29 Sch.10 para.12, 2004 c.20 Sch.9 para.10, Sch.9 para.22

s.210, varied: 2002 c.29 Sch.10 para.12, 2004 c.20 Sch.9 para.10, Sch.9 para.22

2001-cont.

2. **Capital Allowances Act 2001**-cont.

s.211, varied: 2002 c.29 Sch.10 para.12, 2004 c.20 Sch.9 para.10, Sch.9 para.22

s.212, varied: 2002 c.29 Sch.10 para.12, 2004 c.20 Sch.9 para.10, Sch.9 para.22

s.213, varied: 2002 c.29 Sch.10 para.12, 2004 c.20 Sch.9 para.10, Sch.9 para.22

s.214, varied: 2002 c.29 Sch.10 para.12, 2004 c.20 Sch.9 para.10, Sch.9 para.22

s.215, varied: 2002 c.29 Sch.10 para.12, 2004 c.20 Sch.9 para.10, Sch.9 para.22

s.216, varied: 2002 c.29 Sch.10 para.12, 2004 c.20 Sch.9 para.10, Sch.9 para.22

s.217, varied: 2002 c.29 Sch.10 para.12, 2004 c.20 Sch.9 para.10, Sch.9 para.22

s.218, varied: 2002 c.29 Sch.10 para.12, 2004 c.20 Sch.9 para.10, Sch.9 para.22

s.219, amended: 2002 c.23 s.103

s.219, repealed (in part): 2002 c.23 Sch.40 Part 3

s.219, varied: 2002 c.29 Sch.10 para.12, 2004 c.20 Sch.9 para.10, Sch.9 para.22

s.220, varied: 2002 c.29 Sch.10 para.12, 2004 c.20 Sch.9 para.10, Sch.9 para.22

s.221, varied: 2002 c.29 Sch.10 para.12, 2004 c.20 Sch.9 para.10, Sch.9 para.22

s.222, varied: 2002 c.29 Sch.10 para.12, 2004 c.20 Sch.9 para.10, Sch.9 para.22

s.223, varied: 2002 c.29 Sch.10 para.12, 2004 c.20 Sch.9 para.10, Sch.9 para.22

s.224, varied: 2002 c.29 Sch.10 para.12, 2004 c.20 Sch.9 para.10, Sch.9 para.22

s.225, varied: 2002 c.29 Sch.10 para.12, 2004 c.20 Sch.9 para.10, Sch.9 para.22

s.226, applied: 2004 c.12 Sch.23 para.6

s.226, referred to: 2004 c.12 Sch.23 para.6

s.226, varied: 2002 c.29 Sch.10 para.12, 2004 c.20 Sch.9 para.10, Sch.9 para.22

s.227, varied: 2002 c.29 Sch.10 para.12, 2004 c.20 Sch.9 para.10, Sch.9 para.22

s.228, varied: 2002 c.29 Sch.10 para.12, 2004 c.20 Sch.9 para.10, Sch.9 para.22

s.228A, varied: 2002 c.29 Sch.10 para.12, 2004 c.12 s.134, 2004 c.20 Sch.9 para.10, Sch.9 para.22

s.228B, applied: 2004 c.12 Sch.23 para.2

s.228B, disapplied: 2004 c.12 Sch.23 para.2

s.228B, referred to: 2004 c.12 Sch.23 para.1, Sch.23 para.2

s.228B, varied: 2002 c.29 Sch.10 para.12, 2004 c.12 s.134, 2004 c.20 Sch.9 para.10, Sch.9 para.22

s.228C, applied: 2004 c.12 Sch.23 para.5, Sch.23 para.6

s.228C, disapplied: 2004 c.12 Sch.23 para.4, Sch.23 para.6

s.228C, referred to: 2004 c.12 Sch.23 para.1

s.228C, varied: 2002 c.29 Sch.10 para.12, 2004 c.12 s.134, 2004 c.20 Sch.9 para.10, Sch.9 para.22

s.228D, applied: 2004 c.12 Sch.23 para.7

2001–cont.

2. **Capital Allowances Act 2001**–*cont.*
s.228D, disapplied: 2004 c.12 Sch.23 para.7
s.228D, referred to: 2004 c.12 Sch.23 para.1,
Sch.23 para.7
s.228D, varied: 2002 c.29 Sch.10 para.12,
2004 c.12 s.134, 2004 c.20 Sch.9 para.10,
Sch.9 para.22
s.228E, disapplied: 2004 c.12 Sch.23 para.9
s.228E, referred to: 2004 c.12 Sch.23 para.1
s.228E, varied: 2002 c.29 Sch.10 para.12,
2004 c.12 s.134, 2004 c.20 Sch.9 para.10,
Sch.9 para.22
s.228F, varied: 2002 c.29 Sch.10 para.12,
2004 c.12 s.134, 2004 c.20 Sch.9 para.10,
Sch.9 para.22
s.228G, varied: 2002 c.29 Sch.10 para.12,
2004 c.12 s.134, 2004 c.20 Sch.9 para.10,
Sch.9 para.22
s.228H, applied: 2004 c.12 Sch.23 para.10
s.228H, varied: 2002 c.29 Sch.10 para.12,
2004 c.12 s.134, 2004 c.20 Sch.9 para.10,
Sch.9 para.22
s.228J, varied: 2002 c.29 Sch.10 para.12,
2004 c.12 s.134, 2004 c.20 Sch.9 para.10,
Sch.9 para.22
s.229, varied: 2002 c.29 Sch.10 para.12,
2004 c.20 Sch.9 para.10, Sch.9 para.22
s.230, varied: 2002 c.29 Sch.10 para.12,
2004 c.20 Sch.9 para.10, Sch.9 para.22
s.231, varied: 2002 c.29 Sch.10 para.12, 2004
c.20 Sch.9 para.10, Sch.9 para.22
s.232, varied: 2002 c.29 Sch.10 para.12,
2004 c.20 Sch.9 para.10, Sch.9 para.22
s.233, varied: 2002 c.29 Sch.10 para.12,
2004 c.20 Sch.9 para.10, Sch.9 para.22
s.234, varied: 2002 c.29 Sch.10 para.12,
2004 c.20 Sch.9 para.10, Sch.9 para.22
s.235, varied: 2002 c.29 Sch.10 para.12,
2004 c.20 Sch.9 para.10, Sch.9 para.22
s.236, varied: 2002 c.29 Sch.10 para.12,
2004 c.20 Sch.9 para.10, Sch.9 para.22
s.237, varied: 2002 c.29 Sch.10 para.12,
2004 c.20 Sch.9 para.10, Sch.9 para.22
s.238, varied: 2002 c.29 Sch.10 para.12,
2004 c.20 Sch.9 para.10, Sch.9 para.22
s.239, varied: 2002 c.29 Sch.10 para.12,
2004 c.20 Sch.9 para.10, Sch.9 para.22
s.240, varied: 2002 c.29 Sch.10 para.12,
2004 c.20 Sch.9 para.10, Sch.9 para.22
s.241, varied: 2002 c.29 Sch.10 para.12, 2004
c.20 Sch.9 para.10, Sch.9 para.22
s.242, varied: 2002 c.29 Sch.10 para.12,
2004 c.20 Sch.9 para.10, Sch.9 para.22
s.243, varied: 2002 c.29 Sch.10 para.12,
2004 c.20 Sch.9 para.10, Sch.9 para.22
s.244, varied: 2002 c.29 Sch.10 para.12,
2004 c.20 Sch.9 para.10, Sch.9 para.22
s.245, varied: 2002 c.29 Sch.10 para.12,
2004 c.20 Sch.9 para.10, Sch.9 para.22
s.246, varied: 2002 c.29 Sch.10 para.12,
2004 c.20 Sch.9 para.10, Sch.9 para.22

2001–cont.

2. **Capital Allowances Act 2001**–*cont.*
s.247, varied: 2002 c.29 Sch.10 para.12, 2004
c.20 Sch.9 para.10, Sch.9 para.22
s.248, varied: 2002 c.29 Sch.10 para.12,
2004 c.20 Sch.9 para.10, Sch.9 para.22
s.249, varied: 2002 c.29 Sch.10 para.12,
2004 c.20 Sch.9 para.10, Sch.9 para.22
s.250, varied: 2002 c.29 Sch.10 para.12,
2004 c.20 Sch.9 para.10, Sch.9 para.22
s.251, varied: 2002 c.29 Sch.10 para.12, 2004
c.20 Sch.9 para.10, Sch.9 para.22
s.252, varied: 2002 c.29 Sch.10 para.12,
2004 c.20 Sch.9 para.10, Sch.9 para.22
s.253, amended: SI 2004/2310 Sch.1 para.54
s.253, varied: 2002 c.29 Sch.10 para.12,
2004 c.20 Sch.9 para.10, Sch.9 para.22
s.254, varied: 2002 c.29 Sch.10 para.12,
2004 c.20 Sch.9 para.10, Sch.9 para.22
s.255, amended: SI 2004/2200 Reg.10
s.255, varied: 2002 c.29 Sch.10 para.12,
2004 c.20 Sch.9 para.10, Sch.9 para.22
s.256, amended: SI 2004/2310 Sch.1 para.55
s.256, varied: 2002 c.29 Sch.10 para.12,
2004 c.20 Sch.9 para.10, Sch.9 para.22,
SI 2004/2680 Reg.21
s.257, amended: SI 2004/2310 Sch.1 para.56
s.257, varied: 2002 c.29 Sch.10 para.12, 2004
c.20 Sch.9 para.10, Sch.9 para.22
s.258, varied: 2002 c.29 Sch.10 para.12,
2004 c.20 Sch.9 para.10, Sch.9 para.22
s.259, varied: 2002 c.29 Sch.10 para.12,
2004 c.20 Sch.9 para.10, Sch.9 para.22
s.260, referred to: 2004 c.20 s.44
s.260, varied: 2002 c.29 Sch.10 para.12,
2004 c.20 Sch.9 para.10, Sch.9 para.22
s.261, varied: 2002 c.29 Sch.10 para.12, 2004
c.20 Sch.9 para.10, Sch.9 para.22
s.262, amended: 2003 c.1 Sch.6 para.253
s.262, applied: 2003 c.1 s.23, s.54, s.315,
s.327, s.381
s.262, varied: 2002 c.29 Sch.10 para.12,
2004 c.20 Sch.9 para.10, Sch.9 para.22
s.263, varied: 2002 c.29 Sch.10 para.12,
2004 c.20 Sch.9 para.10, Sch.9 para.22
s.264, varied: 2002 c.29 Sch.10 para.12,
2004 c.20 Sch.9 para.10, Sch.9 para.22
s.265, varied: 2002 c.29 Sch.10 para.12,
2004 c.20 Sch.9 para.10, Sch.9 para.22
s.266, varied: 2002 c.29 Sch.10 para.12,
2004 c.20 Sch.9 para.10, Sch.9 para.22
s.267, varied: 2002 c.29 Sch.10 para.12, 2004
c.20 Sch.9 para.10, Sch.9 para.22
s.268, varied: 2002 c.29 Sch.10 para.12,
2004 c.20 Sch.9 para.10, Sch.9 para.22
s.269, varied: 2002 c.29 Sch.10 para.12,
2004 c.20 Sch.9 para.10, Sch.9 para.22
s.270, varied: 2002 c.29 Sch.10 para.12,
2004 c.20 Sch.9 para.10, Sch.9 para.22
s.271, varied: 2002 c.29 Sch.10 para.18,
Sch.10 para.21

2001–cont.

2. **Capital Allowances Act 2001**–*cont.*
s.272, varied: 2002 c.29 Sch.10 para.18, Sch.10 para.21

s.273, varied: 2002 c.29 Sch.10 para.18, Sch.10 para.21

s.274, varied: 2002 c.29 Sch.10 para.18, Sch.10 para.21

s.275, varied: 2002 c.29 Sch.10 para.18, Sch.10 para.21

s.276, varied: 2002 c.29 Sch.10 para.18, Sch.10 para.21

s.277, varied: 2002 c.29 Sch.10 para.18, Sch.10 para.21

s.278, varied: 2002 c.29 Sch.10 para.18, Sch.10 para.21

s.279, varied: 2002 c.29 Sch.10 para.18, Sch.10 para.21

s.280, varied: 2002 c.29 Sch.10 para.18, Sch.10 para.21

s.281, varied: 2002 c.29 Sch.10 para.18, Sch.10 para.21

s.282, varied: 2002 c.29 Sch.10 para.18, Sch.10 para.21

s.283, varied: 2002 c.29 Sch.10 para.18, Sch.10 para.21

s.284, varied: 2002 c.29 Sch.10 para.18, Sch.10 para.21

s.285, varied: 2002 c.29 Sch.10 para.18, Sch.10 para.21

s.286, varied: 2002 c.29 Sch.10 para.18, Sch.10 para.21

s.287, varied: 2002 c.29 Sch.10 para.18, Sch.10 para.21

s.288, varied: 2002 c.29 Sch.10 para.18, Sch.10 para.21

s.289, varied: 2002 c.29 Sch.10 para.18, Sch.10 para.21

s.290, varied: 2002 c.29 Sch.10 para.18, Sch.10 para.21

s.291, varied: 2002 c.29 Sch.10 para.18, Sch.10 para.21

s.292, varied: 2002 c.29 Sch.10 para.18, Sch.10 para.21

s.293, varied: 2002 c.29 Sch.10 para.18, Sch.10 para.21

s.294, varied: 2002 c.29 Sch.10 para.18, Sch.10 para.21

s.295, varied: 2002 c.29 Sch.10 para.18, Sch.10 para.21

s.296, varied: 2002 c.29 Sch.10 para.18, Sch.10 para.21

s.297, varied: 2002 c.29 Sch.10 para.18, Sch.10 para.21

s.298, varied: 2002 c.29 Sch.10 para.18, Sch.10 para.21

s.299, varied: 2002 c.29 Sch.10 para.18, Sch.10 para.21

s.300, varied: 2002 c.29 Sch.10 para.18, Sch.10 para.21

s.301, varied: 2002 c.29 Sch.10 para.18, Sch.10 para.21

2001–cont.

2. **Capital Allowances Act 2001**–*cont.*
s.302, varied: 2002 c.29 Sch.10 para.18, Sch.10 para.21

s.303, varied: 2002 c.29 Sch.10 para.18, Sch.10 para.21

s.304, varied: 2002 c.29 Sch.10 para.18, Sch.10 para.21

s.305, varied: 2002 c.29 Sch.10 para.18, Sch.10 para.21

s.306, varied: 2002 c.29 Sch.10 para.18, Sch.10 para.21

s.307, varied: 2002 c.29 Sch.10 para.18, Sch.10 para.21

s.308, varied: 2002 c.29 Sch.10 para.18, Sch.10 para.21

s.309, varied: 2002 c.29 Sch.10 para.18, Sch.10 para.21

s.310, varied: 2002 c.29 Sch.10 para.18, Sch.10 para.21

s.311, varied: 2002 c.29 Sch.10 para.18, Sch.10 para.21

s.312, varied: 2002 c.29 Sch.10 para.18, Sch.10 para.21

s.313, applied: 2004 c.20 Sch.4 para.6

s.313, varied: 2002 c.29 Sch.10 para.18, Sch.10 para.21

s.314, varied: 2002 c.29 Sch.10 para.18, Sch.10 para.21

s.315, applied: 2002 c.29 Sch.10 para.18

s.315, varied: 2002 c.29 Sch.10 para.18, Sch.10 para.21

s.316, varied: 2002 c.29 Sch.10 para.18, Sch.10 para.21

s.317, varied: 2002 c.29 Sch.10 para.18, Sch.10 para.21

s.318, varied: 2002 c.29 Sch.10 para.18, Sch.10 para.21

s.319, applied: 2002 c.29 Sch.10 para.19

s.319, varied: 2002 c.29 Sch.10 para.18, Sch.10 para.21

s.320, varied: 2002 c.29 Sch.10 para.18, Sch.10 para.21

s.321, varied: 2002 c.29 Sch.10 para.18, Sch.10 para.21

s.322, varied: 2002 c.29 Sch.10 para.18, Sch.10 para.21

s.323, varied: 2002 c.29 Sch.10 para.18, Sch.10 para.21

s.324, varied: 2002 c.29 Sch.10 para.18, Sch.10 para.21

s.325, varied: 2002 c.29 Sch.10 para.18, Sch.10 para.21

s.326, varied: 2002 c.29 Sch.10 para.18, Sch.10 para.21

s.327, varied: 2002 c.29 Sch.10 para.18, Sch.10 para.21

s.328, varied: 2002 c.29 Sch.10 para.18, Sch.10 para.21

s.329, varied: 2002 c.29 Sch.10 para.18, Sch.10 para.21

2001–cont.
2. Capital Allowances Act 2001–*cont.*

s.330, varied: 2002 c.29 Sch.10 para.18, Sch.10 para.21

s.331, varied: 2002 c.29 Sch.10 para.18, Sch.10 para.21

s.332, varied: 2002 c.29 Sch.10 para.18, Sch.10 para.21

s.333, varied: 2002 c.29 Sch.10 para.18, Sch.10 para.21

s.334, varied: 2002 c.29 Sch.10 para.18, Sch.10 para.21

s.335, varied: 2002 c.29 Sch.10 para.18, Sch.10 para.21

s.336, varied: 2002 c.29 Sch.10 para.18, Sch.10 para.21

s.337, varied: 2002 c.29 Sch.10 para.18, Sch.10 para.21

s.338, varied: 2002 c.29 Sch.10 para.18, Sch.10 para.21

s.339, varied: 2002 c.29 Sch.10 para.18, Sch.10 para.21

s.340, varied: 2002 c.29 Sch.10 para.18, Sch.10 para.21

s.341, varied: 2002 c.29 Sch.10 para.18, Sch.10 para.21

s.342, varied: 2002 c.29 Sch.10 para.18, Sch.10 para.21

s.343, varied: 2002 c.29 Sch.10 para.18, Sch.10 para.21

s.344, varied: 2002 c.29 Sch.10 para.18, Sch.10 para.21

s.345, varied: 2002 c.29 Sch.10 para.18, Sch.10 para.21

s.346, varied: 2002 c.29 Sch.10 para.18, Sch.10 para.21

s.347, varied: 2002 c.29 Sch.10 para.18, Sch.10 para.21

s.348, varied: 2002 c.29 Sch.10 para.18, Sch.10 para.21

s.349, varied: 2002 c.29 Sch.10 para.18, Sch.10 para.21

s.350, varied: 2002 c.29 Sch.10 para.18, Sch.10 para.21

s.351, varied: 2002 c.29 Sch.10 para.18, Sch.10 para.21

s.352, varied: 2002 c.29 Sch.10 para.18, Sch.10 para.21

s.353, varied: 2002 c.29 Sch.10 para.18, Sch.10 para.21

s.354, varied: 2002 c.29 Sch.10 para.18, Sch.10 para.21

s.355, varied: 2002 c.29 Sch.10 para.18, Sch.10 para.21

s.356, varied: 2002 c.29 Sch.10 para.18, Sch.10 para.21

s.357, varied: 2002 c.29 Sch.10 para.18, Sch.10 para.21

s.358, varied: 2002 c.29 Sch.10 para.18, Sch.10 para.21

s.359, varied: 2002 c.29 Sch.10 para.18, Sch.10 para.21

2001–cont.
2. Capital Allowances Act 2001–*cont.*

s.360, varied: 2002 c.29 Sch.10 para.18, Sch.10 para.21

s.393, applied: 2002 c.29 Sch.10 para.22

s.393A, varied: 2002 c.29 Sch.10 para.22, Sch.10 para.25

s.393B, varied: 2002 c.29 Sch.10 para.22, Sch.10 para.25

s.393C, varied: 2002 c.29 Sch.10 para.22, Sch.10 para.25

s.393D, varied: 2002 c.29 Sch.10 para.22, Sch.10 para.25

s.393E, varied: 2002 c.29 Sch.10 para.22, Sch.10 para.25

s.393F, varied: 2002 c.29 Sch.10 para.22, Sch.10 para.25

s.393G, varied: 2002 c.29 Sch.10 para.22, Sch.10 para.25

s.393H, varied: 2002 c.29 Sch.10 para.22, Sch.10 para.25

s.393I, varied: 2002 c.29 Sch.10 para.22, Sch.10 para.25

s.393J, varied: 2002 c.29 Sch.10 para.22, Sch.10 para.25

s.393K, varied: 2002 c.29 Sch.10 para.22, Sch.10 para.25

s.393L, varied: 2002 c.29 Sch.10 para.22, Sch.10 para.25

s.393M, varied: 2002 c.29 Sch.10 para.22, Sch.10 para.25

s.393N, varied: 2002 c.29 Sch.10 para.22, Sch.10 para.25

s.393O, varied: 2002 c.29 Sch.10 para.22, Sch.10 para.25

s.393P, varied: 2002 c.29 Sch.10 para.22, Sch.10 para.25

s.393Q, varied: 2002 c.29 Sch.10 para.22, Sch.10 para.25

s.393R, varied: 2002 c.29 Sch.10 para.22, Sch.10 para.25

s.393S, varied: 2002 c.29 Sch.10 para.22, Sch.10 para.25

s.393T, varied: 2002 c.29 Sch.10 para.22, Sch.10 para.25

s.393U, varied: 2002 c.29 Sch.10 para.22, Sch.10 para.25

s.393V, varied: 2002 c.29 Sch.10 para.22, Sch.10 para.25

s.393W, varied: 2002 c.29 Sch.10 para.22, Sch.10 para.25

s.416A, added: 2002 c.23 Sch.21 para.9

s.416B, added: 2002 c.23 Sch.21 para.9

s.416C, added: 2002 c.23 Sch.21 para.9

s.416D, added: 2002 c.23 Sch.21 para.10

s.416E, added: 2002 c.23 Sch.21 para.11

s.418, amended: 2002 c.23 Sch.21 para.12

s.419, amended: 2002 c.23 Sch.21 para.13

s.423, amended: 2003 c.1 Sch.6 para.254

s.437, amended: 2002 c.23 s.103

s.437, varied: 2002 c.29 Sch.10 para.29

s.438, varied: 2002 c.29 Sch.10 para.29

2001–cont.

2. Capital Allowances Act 2001–*cont.*
s.439, varied: 2002 c.29 Sch.10 para.29
s.440, varied: 2002 c.29 Sch.10 para.29
s.441, varied: 2002 c.29 Sch.10 para.29
s.442, varied: 2002 c.29 Sch.10 para.29
s.443, applied: 2002 c.29 Sch.10 para.26
s.443, disapplied: 2002 c.29 Sch.10 para.26
s.443, varied: 2002 c.29 Sch.10 para.29
s.444, varied: 2002 c.29 Sch.10 para.29
s.445, varied: 2002 c.29 Sch.10 para.29
s.446, varied: 2002 c.29 Sch.10 para.29
s.447, varied: 2002 c.29 Sch.10 para.29
s.448, varied: 2002 c.29 Sch.10 para.29
s.449, varied: 2002 c.29 Sch.10 para.29
s.450, varied: 2002 c.29 Sch.10 para.29
s.451, varied: 2002 c.29 Sch.10 para.29
s.544, amended: SI 2004/2310 Sch.1 para.57
s.560, amended: 2003 c.14 s.153
s.561, amended: 2003 c.14 s.153
Sch.1 Part 1, amended: 2003 c.1 Sch.6 para.255, 2004 c.12 Sch.35 para.49
Sch.1 Part 2, amended: 2003 c.14 Sch.43 Part 3, 2003 c.1 Sch.6 para.256, 2004 c.12 Sch.27 para.10
Sch.2 para.15, repealed: 2004 c.12 Sch.42 Part 2
Sch.2 para.24, repealed: 2003 c.1 Sch.8 Part 1
Sch.2 para.25, repealed: 2003 c.1 Sch.8 Part 1
Sch.2 para.51, repealed (in part): 2003 c.1 Sch.8 Part 1
Sch.2 para.53, repealed: 2004 c.12 Sch.42 Part 3
Sch.2 para.54, repealed: 2004 c.12 Sch.42 Part 3
Sch.2 para.70, repealed: 2004 c.12 Sch.42 Part 2
Sch.2 para.88, repealed: 2004 c.12 Sch.42 Part 2
Sch.2 para.89, repealed: 2004 c.12 Sch.42 Part 2
Sch.2 para.102, repealed: 2002 c.23 Sch.40 Part 3
Sch.2 para.107, repealed: 2003 c.1 Sch.8 Part 1

3. Vehicles (Crime) Act 2001
Commencement Orders: SI 2002/1914 Art.2; SI 2002/2377 Art.2; SI 2002/2957 Art.2, Art.3, Art.4
applied: SI 2002/2977 Reg.6, 2003 c.ii s.7
Part 1, applied: SI 2002/1916 Reg.4
Part 2, applied: SI 2002/2977 Reg.4
s.1, referred to: SI 2002/1916 Reg.3, Reg.4
s.2, applied: SI 2002/1916 Reg.3
s.2, enabling: SI 2002/1916
s.3, applied: SI 2002/1916 Reg.4, SI 2002/1917 Art.2
s.3, enabling: SI 2002/1916, SI 2002/1917
s.7, applied: SI 2002/1916 Reg.5
s.7, referred to: SI 2002/1916 Reg.5
s.7, enabling: SI 2002/1916

2001–cont.

3. Vehicles (Crime) Act 2001–*cont.*
s.16, amended: 2003 c.21 Sch.17 para.168
s.16, applied: SI 2002/1870, SI 2002/1916
s.17, enabling: SI 2002/2977
s.18, applied: SI 2002/2977 Reg.4, Reg.7
s.18, enabling: SI 2002/2977
s.19, applied: SI 2002/2977 Reg.5
s.19, enabling: SI 2002/2977 Reg.7
s.24, enabling: SI 2002/2977, SI 2003/228
s.25, applied: SI 2002/2977 Reg.6
s.25, enabling: SI 2002/2977
s.31, amended: 2003 c.21 Sch.17 para.168
s.38, amended: 2003 c.39 Sch.8 para.394
s.38, repealed (in part): 2003 c.39 Sch.8 para.394, Sch.10
s.40, amended: 2003 c.21 Sch.17 para.168
s.41, enabling: SI 2002/1916, SI 2002/2977
s.44, enabling: SI 2002/1914, SI 2002/2377, SI 2002/2957
Sch.para.7, repealed: 2003 c.39 Sch.10
Sch.para.8, repealed: 2003 c.39 Sch.10
Sch.para.9, repealed: 2003 c.39 Sch.10
Sch.para.10, repealed: 2003 c.39 Sch.10

5. Election Publications Act 2001
applied: SI 2002/2626 Sch.1, SI 2003/1887 Sch.1
s.2, amended: SI 2002/2626 Sch.2 para.26, SI 2003/1887 Sch.2 para.13

6. Regulatory Reform Act 2001
applied: 2004 c.19 s.20
s.1, applied: 2002 c.32 s.2, SI 2002/1860, 2003 c.26 s.100, 2003 c.43 s.189, 2004 c.7 Sch.3 para.11, 2004 c.33 s.35
s.1, referred to: 2002 c.32 s.2, 2003 c.43 s.189
s.1, varied: 2003 c.24 s.2
s.1, enabling: SI 2002/906, SI 2002/1062, SI 2002/1457, SI 2002/1592, SI 2002/1860, SI 2002/3203, SI 2002/3205, SI 2003/256, SI 2003/259, SI 2003/940, SI 2003/986, SI 2003/1281, SI 2003/1545, SI 2003/3096, SI 2003/3275, SI 2004/470, SI 2004/1939, SI 2004/2357, SI 2004/2359
s.3, amended: 2003 c.44 Sch.27 para.8
s.4, applied: SI 2002/1592 Art.4, SI 2003/3096 Art.28
s.4, enabling: SI 2002/1592, SI 2003/3096
s.5, amended: 2002 c.26 Sch.12 para.81
s.6, applied: SI 2002/1457(d), SI 2002/1592(d), SI 2002/3203(d), SI 2002/3205(c), SI 2003/259(c), SI 2003/256(c), SI 2003/940(c), SI 2003/986(c), SI 2003/1281(c), SI 2003/1545(c), SI 2003/3096(d), SI 2003/3275(d), SI 2003/1885 Art.3, Art.5, SI 2004/2357(c), SI 2004/2359(c), SI 2004/470(c), SI 2004/1939(c)
s.6, referred to: SI 2002/906(e), SI 2002/1062(e), SI 2002/1860(d)

2001–cont.

6. Regulatory Reform Act 2001–*cont.*

s.8, applied: SI 2002/1062(e), SI 2002/1457(d), SI 2002/1592(d), SI 2002/1860(e), SI 2002/3203(d), SI 2002/3205(c), SI 2003/259(c), SI 2003/256(c), SI 2003/940(c), SI 2003/986(c), SI 2003/1545(c), SI 2003/3275(d), SI 2003/1885 Art.6, SI 2004/1939(c), SI 2004/2357(c), SI 2004/2359(c), SI 2004/470(c)

s.8, referred to: SI 2002/1860(g), SI 2003/1545(e), SI 2003/1281(f)

s.15, enabling: SI 2002/1592

8. Appropriation Act 2001

repealed: 2003 c.13 Sch.3

9. Finance Act 2001

see *R. (on the application of British Aggregates Associates) v Customs and Excise Commissioners* [2002] EWHC 926, [2002] 2 C.M.L.R. 51 (QBD (Admin Ct)), Moses, J.

referred to: 2003 c.1 s.515

s.16, amended: 2002 c.23 Sch.38 para.2

s.16, varied: SI 2002/809 Art.2

s.16, enabling: SI 2002/809

s.17, see *East Midlands Aggregates Ltd v Customs and Excise Commissioners* [2004] EWHC 856, [2004] S.T.C. 1582 (Ch D), Rimer, J.

s.17, amended: 2002 c.23 s.129, s.130, Sch.38 para.3, Sch.40 Part 4

s.17, applied: SI 2002/761 Reg.13, SI 2002/1927 Reg.3, SI 2004/1959 Reg.3

s.17, repealed (in part): 2002 c.23 Sch.40 Part 4

s.17, enabling: SI 2002/761, SI 2002/1927, SI 2004/1959

s.18, amended: 2002 c.23 s.131, Sch.38 para.4

s.18, repealed (in part): 2002 c.23 Sch.40 Part 4

s.19, amended: 2002 c.23 Sch.38 para.5

s.19, applied: SI 2002/761 Reg.12

s.19, referred to: SI 2002/761 Reg.3

s.20, amended: 2002 c.23 Sch.40 Part 4

s.20, repealed (in part): 2002 c.23 Sch.40 Part 4

s.21, repealed (in part): 2002 c.23 Sch.40 Part 4

s.22, amended: 2002 c.23 Sch.38 para.6

s.23, enabling: SI 2002/761

s.24, amended: 2002 c.23 Sch.38 para.7

s.24, applied: SI 2002/761 Reg.34, Reg.35, Reg.37

s.24, repealed (in part): 2002 c.23 Sch.40 Part 4

s.24, enabling: SI 2003/465

s.25, enabling: SI 2002/761

s.30, applied: SI 2004/1959 Reg.8

s.30, referred to: SI 2002/761 Reg.15, Reg.16

s.30, enabling: SI 2002/761, SI 2003/466

2001–cont.

9. Finance Act 2001–*cont.*

s.30A, added: 2002 c.23 s.129

s.30A, amended: 2004 c.12 s.290

s.30A, substituted: 2004 c.12 s.291

s.30A, enabling: SI 2002/1927, SI 2004/1959

s.31, applied: SI 2002/761 Reg.19

s.31, enabling: SI 2002/761

s.32, applied: SI 2002/761 Reg.15, Reg.16, Reg.21

s.37, amended: SI 2003/2096 Sch.1 para.36

s.37, referred to: SI 2002/761 Reg.35, Reg.36

s.37, repealed (in part): 2002 c.23 Sch.40 Part 4

s.37, enabling: SI 2002/761

s.38, enabling: SI 2002/761

s.39, enabling: SI 2002/761

s.45, enabling: SI 2002/761, SI 2002/1927, SI 2004/1959

s.48, amended: 2004 c.12 s.291

s.52, repealed: 2002 c.21 Sch.6

s.53, repealed: 2002 c.21 Sch.6

s.57, repealed (in part): 2003 c.1 Sch.8 Part 1

s.58, repealed: 2003 c.1 Sch.8 Part 1

s.60, repealed: 2003 c.1 Sch.8 Part 1

s.61, repealed: 2003 c.1 Sch.8 Part 1

s.62, repealed: 2003 c.1 Sch.8 Part 1

s.74, repealed: 2004 c.12 Sch.42 Part 3

s.92, amended: 2002 c.23 s.110, 2003 c.14 Sch.20 para.3

s.92, applied: 2003 c.14 Sch.6 para.2, SI 2003/1056 Reg.3, Reg.4, Reg.5

s.92, disapplied: 2002 c.23 s.110, SI 2003/1056 Reg.3, Reg.4, Reg.6

s.92, referred to: SI 2003/1056 Reg.5

s.92A, added: 2002 c.23 s.110

s.92A, applied: 2002 c.23 s.110

s.92A, enabling: SI 2003/1056

s.92B, added: 2002 c.23 s.110

s.92B, referred to: SI 2003/1056 Reg.5

s.92B, enabling: SI 2003/1056

s.95, referred to: 2003 c.1 s.515

s.95, substituted: 2003 c.1 Sch.6 para.257

Sch.1 para.1, repealed: 2002 c.23 Sch.40 Part 1

Sch.4, applied: SI 2002/761 Reg.34, Reg.35, Reg.37

Sch.4 para.1, amended: 2002 c.23 Sch.38 para.9

Sch.4 para.1A, enabling: SI 2003/465

Sch.4 para.4, applied: SI 2002/761 Reg.16

Sch.4 para.5, enabling: SI 2003/465

Sch.4 para.6, enabling: SI 2002/1929, SI 2003/465

Sch.5 para.2, referred to: SI 2002/761 Reg.28

Sch.5 para.3, referred to: SI 2002/761 Reg.28

Sch.5 para.4, referred to: SI 2002/761 Reg.28

Sch.5 para.17, repealed (in part): 2002 c.40 Sch.26

Sch.5 para.18, repealed: 2002 c.40 Sch.26

CAP.

2001–cont.

9. Finance Act 2001–*cont.*

Sch.6 Part 2 para.7, amended: 2002 c.23 s.133, Sch.40 Part 4

Sch.6 Part 2 para.7, repealed (in part): 2002 c.23 Sch.40 Part 4

Sch.6 Part 2 para.9, applied: SI 2002/761 Reg.27, Reg.29

Sch.6 Part 2 para.9, enabling: SI 2002/761

Sch.6 Part 2 para.9A, added: 2002 c.23 s.133

Sch.7 para.2, enabling: SI 2002/761, SI 2002/1927, SI 2004/1959

Sch.7 para.3, repealed (in part): 2003 c.44 Sch.37 Part 6, SI 2004/1501 Sch.2

Sch.8 para.1, enabling: SI 2002/761

Sch.8 para.3, applied: SI 2002/761 Reg.18

Sch.8 para.5, applied: SI 2002/761 Reg.28

Sch.8 para.9, enabling: SI 2002/761

Sch.8 para.10, enabling: SI 2002/761

Sch.8 para.11, amended: SI 2003/2096 Sch.1 para.37

Sch.8 para.11, referred to: SI 2002/761 Reg.32

Sch.8 para.11, repealed (in part): 2002 c.23 Sch.40 Part 4

Sch.8 para.11, enabling: SI 2002/761

Sch.11 para.1, repealed: 2002 c.21 Sch.6

Sch.11 para.2, repealed: 2002 c.21 Sch.6

Sch.11 para.3, repealed: 2002 c.21 Sch.6

Sch.11 para.4, repealed: 2002 c.21 Sch.6

Sch.11 para.5, repealed: 2002 c.21 Sch.6

Sch.11 para.6, repealed: 2002 c.21 Sch.6

Sch.12 Part 1, repealed: 2003 c.1 Sch.8 Part 1

Sch.12 Part 2 para.1, repealed: 2003 c.1 Sch.8 Part 1

Sch.12 Part 2 para.2, repealed: 2003 c.1 Sch.8 Part 1

Sch.12 Part 2 para.3, repealed: 2003 c.1 Sch.8 Part 1

Sch.12 Part 2 para.4, repealed: 2003 c.1 Sch.8 Part 1

Sch.12 Part 2 para.5, repealed: 2003 c.1 Sch.8 Part 1

Sch.12 Part 2 para.6, repealed: 2003 c.1 Sch.8 Part 1

Sch.12 Part 2 para.7, repealed: 2003 c.1 Sch.8 Part 1

Sch.12 Part 2 para.8, repealed: 2003 c.1 Sch.8 Part 1

Sch.12 Part 2 para.9, repealed: 2003 c.1 Sch.8 Part 1

Sch.12 Part 2 para.10, repealed: 2003 c.1 Sch.8 Part 1

Sch.12 Part 2 para.12, repealed: 2003 c.1 Sch.8 Part 1

Sch.12 Part 2 para.13, repealed: 2003 c.1 Sch.8 Part 1

Sch.12 Part 2 para.14, repealed: 2003 c.1 Sch.8 Part 1

Sch.12 Part 2 para.15, repealed: 2003 c.1 Sch.8 Part 1

CAP.

2001–cont.

9. Finance Act 2001–*cont.*

Sch.12 Part 2 para.16, repealed: 2003 c.1 Sch.8 Part 1

Sch.13 para.1, repealed: 2003 c.1 Sch.8 Part 1

Sch.13 para.2, repealed: 2003 c.1 Sch.8 Part 1

Sch.13 para.3, repealed: 2003 c.1 Sch.8 Part 1

Sch.13 para.4, repealed: 2003 c.1 Sch.8 Part 1

Sch.13 para.5, repealed: 2003 c.1 Sch.8 Part 1

Sch.13 para.6, repealed: 2003 c.1 Sch.8 Part 1

Sch.13 para.7, repealed: 2003 c.1 Sch.8 Part 1

Sch.13 para.8, repealed: 2003 c.1 Sch.8 Part 1

Sch.14 para.1, repealed: 2003 c.1 Sch.8 Part 1

Sch.14 para.2, repealed: 2003 c.1 Sch.8 Part 1

Sch.14 para.3, repealed: 2003 c.1 Sch.8 Part 1

Sch.14 para.4, repealed: 2003 c.1 Sch.8 Part 1

Sch.14 para.5, repealed: 2003 c.1 Sch.8 Part 1

Sch.14 para.6, repealed: 2003 c.1 Sch.8 Part 1

Sch.14 para.7, repealed: 2003 c.1 Sch.8 Part 1

Sch.14 para.8, repealed: 2003 c.1 Sch.8 Part 1

Sch.14 para.9, repealed: 2003 c.1 Sch.8 Part 1

Sch.14 para.10, repealed: 2003 c.1 Sch.8 Part 1

Sch.14 para.11, repealed: 2003 c.1 Sch.8 Part 1

Sch.14 para.12, repealed: 2003 c.1 Sch.8 Part 1

Sch.14 para.13, repealed: 2003 c.1 Sch.8 Part 1

Sch.22 Part 1 para.5, amended: 2003 c.1 Sch.6 para.258, 2004 c.12 Sch.17 para.7

Sch.22 Part 1 para.5, repealed (in part): 2004 c.12 Sch.42 Part 2

Sch.22 Part 1 para.10, amended: 2002 c.23 s.103

Sch.22 Part 3 para.14, amended: SI 2004/2310 Sch.1 para.58

Sch.22 Part 3 para.16, amended: 2003 c.1 Sch.8 Part 1

Sch.22 Part 3 para.17, amended: SI 2004/2310 Sch.1 para.59

Sch.22 Part 4 para.22, amended: SI 2004/2310 Sch.1 para.60

Sch.22 Part 4 para.23, amended: SI 2004/2310 Sch.1 para.61

Sch.22 Part 4 para.24, amended: SI 2004/2310 Sch.1 para.62

Sch.22 Part 4 para.27, amended: SI 2004/2310 Sch.1 para.63

Sch.23 para.2, repealed: 2004 c.12 Sch.42 Part 2

Sch.28 Part 1 para.13, repealed: 2004 c.12 Sch.42 Part 2

Sch.30, applied: SI 2003/1056 Reg.3, Reg.4, Reg.5

Sch.30, disapplied: SI 2003/1056 Reg.3, Reg.4

Sch.30, referred to: SI 2003/1056 Reg.5

Sch.30 para.1, amended: 2002 c.23 s.110, 2003 c.14 Sch.20 para.3

Sch.30 para.1, disapplied: 2002 c.23 s.110, SI 2003/1056 Reg.6

2001–cont.

9. Finance Act 2001–*cont.*

Sch.30 para.1, referred to: SI 2003/1056 Reg.5

Sch.30 para.3, amended: 2002 c.23 s.110

Sch.30 para.3, disapplied: SI 2003/1056 Reg.6

Sch.30 para.3, referred to: SI 2003/1056 Reg.5

10. Special Educational Needs and Disability Act 2001

Commencement Orders: SI 2002/74 Art.4, Art.5, Sch.1 Part I, II; SI 2002/1647 Art.3; SI 2002/1721 Art.3, Art.4, Sch.1 Part II; SI 2002/2217 Art.3, Art.4, Art.5, Art.6, Sch.1 Part 1, 2; SI 2003/2532 Art.2, Sch.1

see *Practice Direction (SENT: Notification of Right to Appeal: Time Limits)* [2002] E.L.R. 341 (SENT), Trevor Aldridge Q.C. (President)

s.28I, applied: 2002 c.32 Sch.18 para.17

s.42, repealed (in part): 2002 c.32 Sch.18 para.16, Sch.22 Part 2

s.43, enabling: SI 2002/74, SI 2002/1647, SI 2002/1721, SI 2002/2217, SI 2003/2532

Sch.8 Part 1 para.2, repealed: 2002 c.32 Sch.22 Part 2

11. Social Security Fraud Act 2001

Commencement Orders: SI 2002/117 Art.2; SI 2002/403 Art.2; SI 2002/1222 Art.2; SI 2003/273 Art.2

s.4, varied: SI 2004/1822 Sch.1 para.19

s.7, amended: 2002 c.16 Sch.2 para.45

s.7, applied: SI 2002/486

s.7, repealed (in part): 2002 c.21 Sch.6

s.7, enabling: SI 2002/486, SI 2002/1792

s.8, applied: SI 2002/486

s.9, amended: 2002 c.16 Sch.2 para.46

s.9, applied: SI 2002/486

s.9, enabling: SI 2002/1792

s.10, amended: 2002 c.16 Sch.2 para.47, Sch.3

s.10, applied: SI 2002/486

s.11, amended: 2002 c.16 Sch.2 para.48

s.11, applied: SI 2002/486, SI 2002/1792

s.11, enabling: SI 2002/486, SI 2002/1792

s.12, applied: SI 2002/486

s.13, amended: 2002 c.16 Sch.2 para.49

s.13, applied: SI 2002/486

s.20, enabling: SI 2002/117, SI 2002/403, SI 2002/1222, SI 2003/273

12. Private Security Industry Act 2001

Commencement Orders: SI 2002/3125 Art.2, Art.3; SI 2003/2710 Art.2; SI 2004/1431 Art.2, Art.3, Art.4; SI 2004/2191 Art.2, Art.3; SI 2004/2591 Art.2, Art.3; SI 2004/3141 Art.2, Art.3; SI 2003/2710 Art.3; SI 2002/3125 Art.4; SI 2004/3141 Art.3, Art.4; SI 2004/3230 Art.2

applied: 2003 c.1 s.343

referred to: 2003 c.13 Sch.2 Part 13, 2004 c.9 Sch.2 Part 12

2001–cont.

12. Private Security Industry Act 2001–*cont.*

s.3, applied: 2003 c.17 Sch.4 para.20, SI 2004/255 Reg.3, Reg.4, SI 2004/917 Art.2

s.3, enabling: SI 2004/917

s.7, applied: SI 2004/255 Reg.4

s.8, applied: SI 2004/255 Reg.2, Reg.3

s.8, enabling: SI 2004/255

s.9, enabling: SI 2004/255

s.11, amended: 2003 c.39 Sch.8 para.395, Sch.10

s.11, repealed (in part): 2003 c.39 Sch.8 para.395, Sch.10

s.13, applied: SI 2004/916, SI 2004/1268

s.13, enabling: SI 2004/916, SI 2004/1268, SI 2004/3145

s.18, amended: 2003 c.39 Sch.8 para.396, Sch.10

s.18, repealed (in part): 2003 c.39 Sch.8 para.396, Sch.10

s.21, repealed (in part): 2003 c.44 Sch.37 Part 11

s.24, applied: SI 2004/255, SI 2004/916, SI 2004/917, SI 2004/1268, SI 2004/1431, SI 2004/2191, SI 2004/2591

s.24, referred to: SI 2004/3230

s.24, enabling: SI 2004/255

s.26, repealed (in part): 2003 c.44 Sch.37 Part 11

s.26, enabling: SI 2002/3125, SI 2003/2710, SI 2004/1431, SI 2004/2191, SI 2004/2591, SI 2004/3141, SI 2004/3230

Sch.2 Part 1 para.2, applied: SI 2004/917 Art.2

Sch.2 Part 2 para.8, amended: 2003 c.17 Sch.6 para.118

Sch.2 Part 2 para.8, applied: SI 2004/255 Reg.3, Reg.4, SI 2004/917 Art.2

13. House of Commons (Removal of Clergy Disqualification) Act 2001

Sch.1 para.2, consolidated: 2002 c.24 s.10

Sch.1 para.2, repealed: 2002 c.24 Sch.4

14. Rating (Former Agricultural Premises and Rural Shops) Act 2001

s.1, repealed (in part): 2003 c.26 Sch.8 Part 1

15. Health and Social Care Act 2001

Commencement Orders: SI 2002/1095 Art.2, Sch.1; SI 2002/1170 Art.2; SI 2002/1312 Art.2, Art.3; SI 2002/1475 Art.2, Sch.1 Part 1, 2; SI 2002/1919 Art.2, Sch.1 Part II, I; SI 2002/2363 Art.2; SI 2003/53 Art.2; SI 2002/2363 Art.3; SI 2003/53 Art.3, Art.4; SI 2003/713 Art.2; SI 2003/850 Art.2, Art.3; SI 2003/939 Art.2; SI 2004/103 Art.2, Art.3; SI 2003/939 Sch.1; SI 2004/103 Art.4; SI 2003/2245 Art.2; SI 2004/1754 Art.2; SSI 2002/75 Art.2

applied: SI 2002/2375 Reg.9, Reg.10, Reg.11

referred to: SI 2002/2469 Reg.16, 2003 c.43 Sch.4 para.115, Sch.11 para.69

2001–cont.

15. Health and Social Care Act 2001–*cont.*

s.1, repealed (in part): 2002 c.17 Sch.9 Part 3

s.1, varied: SI 2003/49 Art.2

s.2, varied: SI 2003/49 Art.2

s.3, repealed (in part): 2002 c.17 Sch.9 Part 3

s.3, varied: SI 2003/49 Art.2

s.4, varied: SI 2003/49 Art.2

s.5, varied: SI 2003/49 Art.2

s.6, varied: SI 2003/49 Art.2

s.7, amended: 2002 c.17 s.21, Sch.1 para.55, Sch.5 para.50, 2003 c.43 Sch.4 para.116

s.7, varied: SI 2004/1425 Art.2

s.7, enabling: SI 2002/3048, SI 2003/1617, SI 2004/1427

s.8, varied: SI 2004/1425 Art.2

s.8, enabling: SI 2002/3048, SI 2004/1427

s.11, amended: 2002 c.17 Sch.8 para.35, 2003 c.43 s.30, Sch.14 Part 1

s.11, applied: 2002 c.17 s.16, SI 2003/2124 Reg.7

s.11, varied: SI 2003/49 Art.2

s.12, added: 2002 c.17 s.16

s.12, varied: SI 2003/49 Art.2

s.13, varied: SI 2003/49 Art.2

s.14, varied: SI 2003/49 Art.2

s.15, repealed (in part): 2003 c.43 Sch.14 Part 4

s.15, varied: SI 2003/49 Art.2

s.16, varied: SI 2003/49 Art.2

s.17, repealed (in part): 2003 c.43 Sch.14 Part 4

s.17, varied: SI 2003/49 Art.2

s.18, amended: 2002 c.17 Sch.2 para.72

s.18, repealed (in part): 2003 c.43 Sch.14 Part 4

s.18, varied: SI 2003/49 Art.2

s.18, enabling: SI 2002/2548, SI 2003/26

s.19, repealed: 2003 c.44 Sch.37 Part 11

s.19, varied: SI 2003/49 Art.2

s.20, amended: SI 2002/2469 Sch.1 para.30

s.20, repealed (in part): 2003 c.43 Sch.14 Part 4

s.20, varied: SI 2003/49 Art.2

s.21, varied: SI 2003/49 Art.2

s.22, repealed: 2003 c.43 Sch.14 Part 4

s.22, varied: SI 2003/49 Art.2

s.23, repealed (in part): 2003 c.43 Sch.14 Part 4

s.23, varied: SI 2003/49 Art.2

s.24, varied: SI 2003/49 Art.2

s.25, varied: SI 2003/49 Art.2

s.26, amended: 2002 c.17 Sch.3 para.16

s.26, repealed: 2003 c.43 Sch.14 Part 4

s.26, varied: SI 2003/49 Art.2

s.27, repealed (in part): 2003 c.43 Sch.14 Part 4

s.27, substituted: SI 2002/1919 Sch.1 Part III

s.27, varied: SI 2003/49 Art.2

2001–cont.

15. Health and Social Care Act 2001–*cont.*

s.28, amended: 2002 c.17 Sch.2 para.73, Sch.9 Part 1, 2003 c.43 Sch.4 para.117, Sch.11 para.71

s.28, applied: 2002 c.17 s.17, SI 2003/2124 Reg.3, SI 2004/905 Reg.20, SI 2004/1768 Reg.2

s.28, varied: SI 2003/49 Art.2, SI 2004/288 Art.8, SI 2004/480 Art.7

s.28, enabling: SI 2002/888

s.29, varied: SI 2003/49 Art.2

s.30, amended: 2002 c.17 Sch.2 para.74

s.30, applied: SI 2002/888 Reg.3, Reg.6

s.30, varied: SI 2003/49 Art.2

s.30, enabling: SI 2002/888

s.31, amended: 2002 c.17 Sch.2 para.75

s.31, varied: SI 2003/49 Art.2

s.32, amended: 2002 c.17 Sch.2 para.76

s.32, applied: SI 2002/2016 Reg.3

s.32, varied: SI 2003/49 Art.2

s.33, amended: 2003 c.43 Sch.4 para.118

s.33, varied: SI 2003/49 Art.2

s.33, enabling: SI 2002/2016

s.34, amended: 2002 c.17 Sch.2 para.77

s.34, applied: SI 2002/888 Reg.8

s.34, varied: SI 2003/49 Art.2

s.34, enabling: SI 2002/888

s.35, varied: SI 2003/49 Art.2

s.35, enabling: SI 2002/2352, SI 2003/1084

s.36, amended: 2002 c.17 s.4

s.36, varied: SI 2003/49 Art.2

s.37, varied: SI 2003/49 Art.2

s.37, enabling: SI 2002/2016

s.38, varied: SI 2003/49 Art.2

s.38, enabling: SI 2002/2861, SI 2003/1084

s.39, varied: SI 2003/49 Art.2

s.40, amended: 2002 c.17 Sch.2 para.78

s.40, varied: SI 2003/49 Art.2

s.41, amended: 2003 c.43 Sch.14 Part 4

s.41, repealed (in part): 2003 c.43 Sch.14 Part 4

s.41, varied: SI 2003/49 Art.2

s.41, enabling: SI 2002/2016, SI 2002/2861

s.42, varied: SI 2003/49 Art.2

s.43, repealed (in part): 2002 c.17 Sch.9 Part 3

s.43, varied: SI 2003/49 Art.2

s.45, applied: SI 2002/2233 Art.2

s.45, varied: SI 2003/49 Art.2

s.45, enabling: SI 2002/557, SI 2002/1122, SI 2002/1251, SI 2002/1322, SI 2002/1494, SI 2002/2233, SI 2003/760, SI 2003/844, SI 2003/2168

s.46, amended: 2002 c.17 Sch.1 para.55, Sch.5 para.51

s.46, varied: SI 2003/49 Art.2

s.47, varied: SI 2003/49 Art.2

s.48, varied: SI 2003/49 Art.2

s.49, varied: SI 2003/761 Art.2

2001–cont.

15. Health and Social Care Act 2001–*cont.*

s.50, applied: SSI 2002/76 Reg.2, Reg.3, Reg.4

s.50, disapplied: SSI 2002/76 Reg.2

s.50, enabling: SSI 2002/76

s.54, varied: SI 2003/761 Art.2

s.54, enabling: SI 2003/931

s.55, applied: SI 2003/931 Reg.6, SI 2003/969 Reg.2

s.55, varied: SI 2003/761 Art.2

s.55, enabling: SI 2003/931

s.56, varied: SI 2003/761 Art.2

s.57, applied: SI 2002/2006 Reg.19, SI 2003/762 Reg.2, Reg.4, Reg.5, SI 2004/1748 Reg.3

s.57, disapplied: SI 2002/2006 Reg.19, SI 2003/762 Reg.5, SI 2004/1748 Reg.6

s.57, referred to: SI 2003/762 Reg.5, Reg.10, SI 2004/1748 Reg.3, Reg.6, Reg.11

s.57, varied: SI 2003/761 Art.2

s.57, enabling: SI 2003/762, SI 2004/1748

s.58, varied: SI 2003/761 Art.2

s.59, varied: SI 2003/761 Art.2

s.60, applied: SI 2002/1438, SI 2002/1438 Reg.3

s.60, enabling: SI 2002/1438

s.61, applied: SI 2002/1438

s.64, applied: SI 2002/1438

s.64, enabling: SI 2002/1095, SI 2002/1170, SI 2002/1438, SI 2002/1475, SI 2002/1919, SI 2002/2363, SI 2002/2548, SI 2002/2861, SI 2002/3048, SI 2003/26, SI 2003/49, SI 2003/53, SI 2003/713, SI 2003/761, SI 2003/762, SI 2003/850, SI 2003/931, SI 2003/939, SI 2003/2245, SI 2004/103, SI 2004/1425, SI 2004/1427, SI 2004/1748, SI 2004/1754

s.65, enabling: SI 2002/554, SI 2002/888, SI 2002/916, SI 2002/1881, SI 2002/1882, SI 2002/1920, SI 2002/2016, SI 2002/2802, SI 2002/2861, SI 2003/250, SI 2003/2644

s.66, enabling: SI 2002/1475

s.67, varied: SI 2003/761 Art.2

s.70, enabling: SI 2002/1095, SI 2002/1170, SI 2002/1312, SI 2002/1475, SI 2002/1919, SI 2002/2363, SI 2003/49, SI 2003/53, SI 2003/713, SI 2003/761, SI 2003/850, SI 2003/939, SI 2003/2245, SI 2004/103, SI 2004/1425, SI 2004/1754, SSI 2002/75

Sch.1 Part 1 para.10, amended: 2002 c.17 Sch.2 para.79

Sch.1 Part 1 para.11, amended: 2002 c.17 Sch.3 para.17

Sch.1 Part 1 para.11, substituted: 2003 c.43 Sch.11 para.72

Sch.1 Part 1 para.11, varied: SI 2004/288 Art.7, SI 2004/480 Art.6, SI 2004/865 Art.109, SI 2004/1016 Art.85

2001–cont.

15. Health and Social Care Act 2001–*cont.*

Sch.1 Part 1 para.12, substituted: 2003 c.43 Sch.11 para.72

Sch.1 Part 1 para.12, varied: SI 2004/288 Art.7, SI 2004/480 Art.6

Sch.1 Part 1 para.13, amended: 2003 c.43 Sch.11 para.72

Sch.1 Part 1 para.13, varied: SI 2004/288 Art.7, SI 2004/480 Art.6

Sch.2, applied: SI 2004/1768 Reg.2

Sch.2 para.1, amended: 2002 c.17 Sch.2 para.80

Sch.2 para.1, enabling: SI 2002/888

Sch.2 para.2, amended: 2002 c.17 Sch.2 para.80

Sch.2 para.2, applied: SI 2002/888 Reg.7A, Reg.7

Sch.2 para.3, amended: 2002 c.17 Sch.2 para.80

Sch.2 para.3, applied: SI 2002/888 Reg.1, SI 2002/2016 Reg.4

Sch.2 para.4, amended: 2002 c.17 Sch.2 para.80

Sch.2 para.4, applied: SI 2002/888 Reg.1

Sch.2 para.5, amended: 2002 c.17 Sch.2 para.80, 2003 c.43 Sch.11 para.73

Sch.2 para.6, amended: 2002 c.17 Sch.2 para.80

Sch.2 para.7, amended: 2002 c.17 Sch.2 para.80

Sch.2 para.7, applied: SI 2002/888 Reg.1, Reg.8

Sch.2 para.13, amended: 2002 c.17 Sch.2 para.80

Sch.3, amended: 2002 c.17 Sch.2 para.81, Sch.9 Part 1

Sch.5 Part 1 para.1, varied: SI 2003/49 Art.2

Sch.5 Part 1 para.2, varied: SI 2003/49 Art.2

Sch.5 Part 1 para.3, varied: SI 2003/49 Art.2

Sch.5 Part 1 para.4, varied: SI 2003/49 Art.2

Sch.5 Part 1 para.5, amended: SI 2002/1919 Sch.1 Part III

Sch.5 Part 1 para.5, repealed (in part): 2002 c.17 Sch.9 Part 3, 2003 c.43 Sch.14 Part 4

Sch.5 Part 1 para.5, varied: SI 2003/49 Art.2

Sch.5 Part 1 para.6, varied: SI 2003/49 Art.2

Sch.5 Part 1 para.7, varied: SI 2003/49 Art.2

Sch.5 Part 1 para.8, varied: SI 2003/49 Art.2

Sch.5 Part 1 para.9, amended: 2002 c.17 Sch.2 para.82

Sch.5 Part 1 para.9, varied: SI 2003/49 Art.2

Sch.5 Part 1 para.10, amended: SI 2002/1919 Sch.1 Part III

Sch.5 Part 1 para.10, substituted: SI 2002/1919 Sch.1 Part III

Sch.5 Part 1 para.10, varied: SI 2003/49 Art.2

Sch.5 Part 1 para.11, repealed (in part): 2003 c.43 Sch.14 Part 4

Sch.5 Part 1 para.11, varied: SI 2003/49 Art.2

Sch.5 Part 1 para.12, repealed (in part): 2003 c.43 Sch.14 Part 4

2001–cont.

15. Health and Social Care Act 2001–*cont.*
Sch.5 Part 1 para.12, varied: SI 2003/49 Art.2
Sch.5 Part 1 para.13, varied: SI 2003/49 Art.2
Sch.5 Part 1 para.14, varied: SI 2003/49 Art.2
Sch.5 Part 2 para.15, varied: SI 2003/761 Art.2
Sch.5 Part 2 para.16, varied: SI 2003/761 Art.2
Sch.6 Part 1, varied: SI 2003/49 Art.2
Sch.6 Part 2, varied: SI 2003/49 Art.2
Sch.6 Part 3, varied: SI 2003/761 Art.2

16. Criminal Justice and Police Act 2001
Commencement Orders: 2002 c.29 Sch.12; SI 2002/344 Art.2, Art.3; SI 2002/533 Art.2, Art.3; SI 2002/1097 Art.2, Sch.1; SI 2002/2050 Art.2, Art.3; SI 2002/3032 Art.2; SI 2003/708 Art.2; SI 2004/1376 Art.2, Art.3
Part 1 c.1, applied: 2002 c.30 s.43, Sch.4 para.1, Sch.5 para.1, SI 2004/915 Sch.1 para.1, Sch.1 para.11
Part 2, applied: 2003 c.6 Sch.2 para.10
s.1, amended: SI 2002/1934 Art.2, 2003 c.17 Sch.6 para.120, Sch.7, 2003 c.21 Sch.17 para.169, Sch.19, 2003 c.22 Sch.1, 2004 c.21 Sch.1 para.97, Sch.2, SI 2004/2540 Art.2
s.1, applied: 2002 c.30 Sch.4 para.15A
s.1, referred to: 2002 c.30 Sch.5 para.9A
s.1, enabling: SI 2002/1934, SI 2004/2540
s.2, amended: 2003 c.38 s.87
s.2, enabling: SI 2004/3166
s.3, amended: 2003 c.38 s.87, 2003 c.39 Sch.8 para.397, 2004 c.28 s.15, SI 2004/2540 Art.3
s.3, applied: SI 2002/1838, SI 2002/1838 Reg.2
s.3, enabling: SI 2002/1837, SI 2002/1838, SI 2004/316, SI 2004/2468, SI 2004/3167, SI 2004/3169, SI 2004/3371
s.7, amended: 2003 c.39 Sch.8 para.398
s.8, amended: 2003 c.39 Sch.8 para.399
s.9, amended: 2003 c.39 Sch.8 para.400
s.9, applied: 2003 c.39 Sch.5 para.3
s.12, amended: 2003 c.17 Sch.6 para.121, Sch.7
s.12, applied: SI 2002/1837 Sch.1 Part II, SI 2004/915 Sch.1 para.4
s.12, repealed (in part): 2002 c.30 Sch.8
s.12, varied: 2002 c.30 Sch.4 para.5, Sch.5 para.4
s.13, amended: 2003 c.17 Sch.6 para.122
s.14, amended: 2003 c.17 Sch.6 para.123
s.14, repealed (in part): 2003 c.17 Sch.6 para.123, Sch.7
s.15, amended: 2003 c.17 Sch.6 para.124
s.16, amended: 2003 c.17 Sch.6 para.125
s.16, repealed (in part): 2003 c.17 Sch.7
s.17, repealed: 2003 c.17 Sch.7
s.18, repealed: 2003 c.17 Sch.7
s.19, amended: 2003 c.17 Sch.6 para.126
s.20, amended: 2003 c.17 Sch.6 para.126

2001–cont.

16. Criminal Justice and Police Act 2001– *cont.*
s.21, amended: 2003 c.17 Sch.6 para.126, 2003 c.39 Sch.8 para.401
s.22, amended: 2003 c.39 Sch.8 para.402
s.25, amended: 2003 c.44 Sch.26 para.56
s.27, amended: 2003 c.17 Sch.6 para.126
s.28, amended: 2003 c.17 Sch.6 para.127, Sch.7
s.30, repealed: 2003 c.17 Sch.7
s.31, repealed: 2003 c.17 Sch.7
s.32, repealed: 2003 c.17 Sch.7
s.33, see *R. v Mee (Jason David)* [2004] EWCA Crim 629, [2004] 2 Cr. App. R. (S.) 81 (CA (Crim Div)), Laws, L.J.
s.37, applied: SI 2002/313 Art.2
s.37, enabling: SI 2002/313
s.42, amended: 2003 c.44 Sch.26 para.56
s.46, repealed (in part): 2002 c.30 Sch.8
s.50, applied: 2003 c.32 s.26, 2003 c.41 s.172
s.50, varied: 2002 c.30 Sch.4 para.24
s.51, applied: 2003 c.41 s.172
s.51, varied: 2002 c.30 Sch.4 para.24
s.52, varied: 2002 c.30 Sch.4 para.24
s.53, applied: 2003 c.32 s.26
s.53, varied: 2002 c.30 Sch.4 para.24
s.54, varied: 2002 c.30 Sch.4 para.24
s.55, amended: 2002 c.29 Sch.11 para.40, Sch.12
s.55, repealed (in part): 2002 c.29 Sch.12
s.55, varied: 2002 c.30 Sch.4 para.24
s.56, amended: 2003 c.44 Sch.1 para.14
s.56, varied: 2002 c.30 Sch.4 para.24, 2003 c.6 Sch.2 para.10
s.57, amended: 2004 c.30 Sch.6 para.5
s.57, varied: 2002 c.30 Sch.4 para.24
s.58, varied: 2002 c.30 Sch.4 para.24
s.59, varied: 2002 c.30 Sch.4 para.24
s.60, amended: 2002 c.29 Sch.11 para.40, Sch.12
s.60, repealed (in part): 2002 c.29 Sch.12
s.60, varied: 2002 c.30 Sch.4 para.24
s.60A, varied: 2002 c.30 Sch.4 para.24
s.61, referred to: 2003 c.32 s.26
s.61, varied: 2002 c.30 Sch.4 para.24
s.62, varied: 2002 c.30 Sch.4 para.24
s.63, varied: 2002 c.30 Sch.4 para.24
s.64, amended: 2002 c.29 Sch.11 para.40, Sch.12
s.64, varied: 2002 c.30 Sch.4 para.24
s.65, amended: 2002 c.29 Sch.11 para.40
s.65, varied: 2002 c.30 Sch.4 para.24
s.66, amended: 2004 c.30 Sch.6 para.5
s.66, varied: 2002 c.30 Sch.4 para.24
s.67, varied: 2002 c.30 Sch.4 para.24
s.68, varied: 2002 c.30 Sch.4 para.24
s.69, applied: SI 2003/934
s.69, varied: 2002 c.30 Sch.4 para.24
s.69, enabling: SI 2003/934
s.70, varied: 2002 c.30 Sch.4 para.24

CAP.

2001–cont.

16. Criminal Justice and Police Act 2001– cont.

s.71, repealed: 2002 c.30 Sch.8

s.80, repealed (in part): 2002 c.30 Sch.8

s.82, see *R. (on the application of S) v Chief Constable of South Yorkshire* [2002] EWCA Civ 1275, [2002] 1 W.L.R. 3223 (CA), Lord Woolf of Barnes, L.C.J.; see *R. (on the application of S) v Chief Constable of South Yorkshire* [2002] EWHC 478, Times, April 4, 2002 (QBD (Admin Ct)), Leveson, J.; see *R. (on the application of S) v Chief Constable of South Yorkshire* [2004] UKHL 39, [2004] 1 W.L.R. 2196 (HL), Lord Steyn

s.88, amended: 2002 c.30 Sch.7 para.24, 2004 c.20 Sch.14 para.9

s.88, repealed (in part): 2004 c.20 Sch.14 para.9, Sch.23 Part 1

s.103, enabling: SI 2002/534

s.109, enabling: SI 2002/344

s.116, enabling: SI 2002/344

s.119, enabling: SI 2002/344

s.122, repealed (in part): 2002 c.30 Sch.8

s.123, repealed (in part): 2002 c.30 Sch.8

s.125, repealed (in part): 2002 c.30 Sch.8

s.134, repealed (in part): 2003 c.44 Sch.37 Part 11

s.138, enabling: SI 2002/344, SI 2002/533, SI 2002/1097, SI 2002/2050, SI 2002/3032, SI 2002/3072, SI 2003/708, SI 2004/1376

Sch.1 Part 1, added: SI 2003/934 Art.2

Sch.1 Part 1, added: 2002 c.40 s.194

Sch.1 Part 1, added: 2003 c.32 s.26

Sch.1 Part 1, added: 2003 c.41 s.165

Sch.1 Part 1 para.7, repealed: 2003 c.17 Sch.7

Sch.1 Part 1 para.30, substituted: SI 2004/702 Sch.7 para.25

Sch.1 Part 1 para.47, repealed: 2002 c.29 Sch.12

Sch.1 Part 1 para.48, substituted: SI 2003/934 Art.2

Sch.1 Part 1 para.49, repealed: 2003 c.32 Sch.6

Sch.1 Part 1 para.58A, added: SI 2003/934 Art.2

Sch.1 Part 1 para.73A, added: 2002 c.29 Sch.11 para.40

Sch.1 Part 1 para.73E, added: 2004 c.30 Sch.6 para.5

Sch.1 Part 1 para.74, added: 2003 c.17 Sch.6 para.128

Sch.1 Part 2, added: 2003 c.41 s.165

Sch.1 Part 2 para.80, substituted: SI 2004/702 Sch.7 para.25

Sch.1 Part 3 para.90, repealed: 2003 c.17 Sch.7

Sch.1 Part 3 para.102, substituted: SI 2004/702 Sch.7 para.25

Sch.1 Part 3 para.105, repealed: 2002 c.29 Sch.12

CAP.

2001–cont.

16. Criminal Justice and Police Act 2001– cont.

Sch.1 Part 3 para.106, substituted: SI 2003/934 Art.3

Sch.1 Part 3 para.107A, added: SI 2003/934 Art.3

Sch.1 Part 3 para.110, added: 2002 c.29 Sch.11 para.40, 2003 c.17 Sch.6 para.128

Sch.2 Part 2 para.17, amended: 2004 c.27 Sch.2 para.30

Sch.3 para.14, amended: 2002 c.30 s.102

Sch.6 Part 2 para.53, repealed (in part): 2003 c.26 Sch.8 Part 1

Sch.6 Part 3 para.74, referred to: 2002 c.30 s.108

Sch.6 Part 3 para.74, repealed: 2002 c.30 Sch.8

Sch.6 Part 3 para.80, repealed: SI 2002/1860 Sch.6

17. International Criminal Court Act 2001

s.5, applied: SI 2002/313 Sch.1

s.6, enabling: SR 2003/28

s.7, amended: 2003 c.39 Sch.8 para.403

s.7, applied: SI 2002/313 Sch.1

s.8, enabling: SR 2003/28

s.10, enabling: SR 2003/28

s.13, amended: 2003 c.39 Sch.8 para.403

s.15, applied: SI 2002/313 Sch.1

s.23, varied: SI 2004/714 Art.2

s.26, repealed (in part): 2003 c.39 Sch.8 para.404, Sch.10

s.32, amended: SI 2003/1016 Sch.1 para.13

s.32, applied: SI 2002/313 Sch.1

s.42, varied: SI 2004/714 Art.2

s.43, applied: SI 2002/313 Sch.1

s.44, varied: SI 2004/714 Art.2, Sch.1 para.1

s.45, varied: SI 2004/714 Art.2, Sch.1 para.2

s.47, applied: 2003 c.42 Sch.5 para.62

s.48, applied: 2003 c.42 Sch.5 para.63

s.49, applied: 2003 c.42 Sch.5 para.63

s.49, enabling: SI 2002/822

s.50, applied: 2003 c.42 Sch.5 para.63

s.50, referred to: SI 2004/1080 Reg.2

s.50, enabling: SI 2004/1080, SI 2004/3239

s.51, applied: 2003 c.41 s.64, s.65, s.137, s.138, s.196, 2003 c.42 Sch.5 para.61, Sch.5 para.63, Sch.5 para.107, Sch.5 para.169, 2003 c.44 Sch.4 para.28, Sch.5 para.25, Sch.5 para.46, Sch.15 para.60, Sch.17 para.57, SI 2004/1500 Sch.2 para.20, SI 2004/1910 Sch.6

s.52, applied: 2003 c.41 s.64, s.65, s.137, s.138, s.196, 2003 c.42 Sch.5 para.61, Sch.5 para.63, Sch.5 para.107, Sch.5 para.169, 2003 c.44 Sch.4 para.28, Sch.5 para.25, Sch.5 para.46, Sch.15 para.60, Sch.17 para.57, SI 2004/1500 Sch.2 para.20

s.53, applied: 2003 c.42 Sch.5 para.63

s.55, applied: 2003 c.41 s.137, s.196

s.55, referred to: 2003 c.41 s.64, s.65, s.138

CAP.

2001–cont.

17. International Criminal Court Act 2001– cont.

s.57, applied: 2003 c.42 Sch.5 para.63

s.58, applied: 2003 c.41 s.64, s.65, s.137, s.138, s.196, 2003 c.42 Sch.5 para.63, SI 2004/1910 Sch.6

s.59, applied: 2003 c.41 s.64, s.65, s.137, s.138, s.196, 2003 c.42 Sch.5 para.63

s.62, applied: 2003 c.41 s.137, s.196

s.62, referred to: 2003 c.41 s.64, s.65, s.138

s.67, amended: 2002 c.8 s.2

s.70, varied: SI 2004/714 Art.2, Sch.1 para.3

s.71, repealed: 2003 c.41 Sch.4

s.72, repealed: 2003 c.41 Sch.4

s.73, repealed: 2003 c.41 Sch.4

s.79, enabling: SI 2004/714

s.83, varied: SI 2004/714 Art.2

Sch.1 para.1, enabling: SI 2002/793

Sch.1 para.4, applied: SI 2002/793

Sch.2 Part 2 para.7, substituted: 2003 c.41 Sch.3 para.13

Sch.2 Part 2 para.8, amended: 2003 c.41 Sch.3 para.13

Sch.2 Part 2 para.9, amended: 2003 c.41 Sch.3 para.13

Sch.2 Part 2 para.10, amended: 2003 c.41 Sch.3 para.13, Sch.4

Sch.5 Part 1 para.1, amended: 2003 c.39 Sch.4 para.14

Sch.5 Part 1 para.5, amended: 2003 c.39 Sch.8 para.405

Sch.5 Part 2 para.8, amended: 2003 c.39 Sch.4 para.14

Sch.6, applied: SI 2003/1417 r.93

Sch.6 para.7, amended: 2002 c.9 Sch.11 para.40

Sch.6 para.7, repealed (in part): 2002 c.9 Sch.13

Sch.7 para.2, amended: 2003 c.44 Sch.32 para.139

Sch.7 para.3, amended: 2003 c.44 Sch.32 para.139

Sch.10, varied: SI 2004/714 Art.2

19. Armed Forces Act 2001

Commencement Orders: SI 2002/345 Art.2, Art.3; SI 2003/2268 Art.2, Art.4; SI 2004/1938 Art.2

referred to: 2003 c.44 s.337

Part 2, enabling: SI 2003/2315

s.1, enabling: SI 2002/1820, SI 2003/1869, SI 2004/1496

s.2, amended: 2003 c.44 Sch.1 para.15, Sch.37 Part 1

s.2, applied: SI 2003/2273 Art.3, Art.4

s.2, referred to: SI 2003/2273 Art.3, Art.5

s.3, enabling: SI 2003/2273

s.5, applied: SI 2003/2272 Art.4, SI 2003/2273 Art.6, Art.7, Art.8, Art.15, Sch.1 para.2

s.5, referred to: SI 2003/2272 Art.4

s.5, enabling: SI 2003/2273

s.6, amended: 2003 c.39 Sch.4 para.15

CAP.

2001–cont.

19. Armed Forces Act 2001–cont.

s.6, enabling: SI 2003/2273

s.7, applied: SI 2003/2272 Art.4, SI 2003/2273 Art.15

s.7, referred to: SI 2003/2272 Art.4

s.8, enabling: SI 2003/2272

s.10, applied: SI 2003/2273 Art.17

s.10, enabling: SI 2003/2273

s.11, enabling: SI 2003/2273

s.15, applied: SI 2003/2272 Art.2, SI 2003/2273 Art.2, Art.12

s.20, enabling: SI 2004/1937

s.30, amended: 2003 c.44 Sch.32 para.140

s.31, amended: 2003 c.32 Sch.5 para.81

s.31, applied: 2003 c.44 s.94

s.32, amended: 2003 c.20 Sch.7 para.13

s.35, applied: SI 2003/2272

s.35, enabling: SI 2003/2272, SI 2003/2273, SI 2004/1937

s.39, enabling: SI 2002/345, SI 2003/2268, SI 2004/1938

Sch.6 Part 1 para.2, repealed: 2003 c.42 Sch.7

Sch.6 Part 6 para.59, repealed: 2003 c.42 Sch.7

20. Social Security Contributions (Share Options) Act 2001

disapplied: 2003 c.1 s.482

referred to: 2003 c.1 Sch.6 para.259

s.1, applied: 2003 c.1 s.482

s.2, amended: 2003 c.14 Sch.22 para.56, 2003 c.1 Sch.6 para.260

s.2, applied: 2003 c.1 s.481, s.482

s.3, amended: 2003 c.14 Sch.22 para.57, 2003 c.1 Sch.6 para.261

s.4, repealed: 2003 c.1 Sch.8 Part 1

s.5, amended: 2003 c.14 Sch.22 para.58, 2003 c.1 Sch.6 para.262

21. Appropriation (No.2) Act 2001

repealed: 2003 c.13 Sch.3

24. Anti-terrorism, Crime and Security Act 2001

Commencement Orders: SI 2002/228 Art.2; SI 2002/1279 Art.2; SI 2002/1558 Art.2; SI 2004/751 Art.2; SI 2003/691 Art.2

see *A v Secretary of State for the Home Department* [2002] H.R.L.R. 45 (Sp Imm App Comm), Collins, J. (Chairman)

applied: SI 2003/1034 r.7, r.8, r.14, r.27

referred to: 2003 c.43 Sch.4 para.119

s.2, repealed (in part): SI 2003/435 Sch.5

s.9, amended: 2002 c.8 s.2

s.17, applied: 2003 c.21 s.393, 2004 c.35 s.83, s.87

s.17, referred to: 2003 c.21 s.393, 2004 c.35 s.83

s.17, varied: SI 2003/419 Art.63

s.18, applied: 2002 c.29 s.442, 2003 c.21 s.393, 2004 c.35 s.83, s.87, s.201

s.18, varied: 2002 c.29 s.442, SI 2003/419 Art.63

CAP.

2001–cont.

24. Anti-terrorism, Crime and Security Act 2001–*cont.*

s.19, applied: 2004 c.35 s.88, s.202

s.20, disapplied: 2002 c.29 s.442

s.21, see *G v Secretary of State for the Home Department* [2004] EWCA Civ 265, [2004] 1 W.L.R. 1349 (CA), Lord Phillips of Worth Matravers, M.R.; see *R. (on the application of A) v Secretary of State for the Home Department* [2003] EWHC 2846, [2004] H.R.L.R. 12 (QBD (Admin Ct)), Kennedy, L.J.; see *Secretary of State for the Home Department v M* [2004] EWCA Civ 324, [2004] 2 All E.R. 863 (CA), Lord Woolf of Barnes, L.C.J.

s.21, repealed: SI 2004/751 Art.2

s.22, amended: SI 2003/1016 Sch.1 para.15

s.22, repealed: SI 2004/751 Art.2

s.23, see *A v Secretary of State for the Home Department* [2002] EWCA Civ 1502, [2004] Q.B. 335 (CA), Lord Woolf of Barnes, L.C.J.

s.23, amended: 2002 c.41 s.62

s.23, repealed: SI 2004/751 Art.2

s.24, see *G v Secretary of State for the Home Department* [2004] EWCA Civ 265, [2004] 1 W.L.R. 1349 (CA), Lord Phillips of Worth Matravers, M.R.

s.24, amended: 2002 c.41 s.62, 2004 c.19 s.32

s.24, applied: SI 2003/1034 r.28

s.24, enabling: SI 2003/1034

s.25, applied: SI 2003/1034 r.13

s.26, applied: SI 2003/1034 r.21, r.22

s.27, amended: 2002 c.41 Sch.7 para.30, 2004 c.19 s.32

s.27, applied: SI 2003/1034 r.46

s.27, enabling: SI 2003/1034

s.29, applied: SI 2003/691 Art.2

s.29, enabling: SI 2003/691, SI 2004/751

s.33, amended: SI 2003/1016 Sch.1 para.16

s.34, applied: 2002 c.41 s.72

s.39, repealed (in part): 2003 c.44 Sch.37 Part 7

s.44, amended: 2002 c.8 s.2

s.47, applied: 2002 c.26 Sch.7 para.36, SI 2004/1910 Sch.1

s.50, applied: 2002 c.26 Sch.7 para.36

s.55, amended: 2002 c.26 Sch.7 para.36

s.56, amended: 2002 c.8 s.2

s.58, disapplied: SI 2002/1281 Reg.2, Reg.3

s.58, enabling: SI 2002/1281

s.64, applied: SI 2002/1845 r.6

s.70, applied: SI 2002/1844 r.3

s.74, referred to: SI 2002/1281

s.76, applied: SI 2003/403 Reg.3, 2004 c.20 s.56, s.71

s.76, disapplied: SI 2002/1151 Art.2

s.76, referred to: SI 2003/403 Reg.3

s.76, repealed: 2004 c.20 Sch.23 Part 1

s.76, enabling: SI 2002/1151, SI 2003/403

CAP.

2001–cont.

24. Anti-terrorism, Crime and Security Act 2001–*cont.*

s.77, amended: 2004 c.20 s.77, Sch.14 para.10

s.77, applied: SI 2003/403, 2004 c.20 Sch.23 para.1

s.77, referred to: SI 2003/403 Reg.11, Reg.21

s.77, enabling: SI 2003/403

s.78, repealed (in part): 2004 c.20 Sch.23 Part 1

s.79, amended: 2004 c.20 Sch.14 para.10

s.79, applied: 2002 c.26 Sch.7 para.36

s.80, applied: 2002 c.26 Sch.7 para.36, SI 2004/1818, SI 2004/1818 Reg.7

s.80, referred to: SI 2004/1818 Reg.3

s.80, enabling: SI 2004/1818

s.81, amended: 2002 c.8 s.2, 2002 c.26 Sch.7 para.36

s.82, amended: 2003 c.19 s.1

s.82, repealed (in part): 2002 c.30 Sch.8

s.91, repealed (in part): SI 2004/1500 Sch.3

s.94, repealed (in part): 2002 c.30 Sch.8

s.98, repealed (in part): 2004 c.20 Sch.23 Part 1

s.100, amended: 2003 c.20 Sch.5 para.4, 2004 c.20 Sch.14 para.10, Sch.23 Part 1

s.100, varied: 2003 c.20 Sch.5 para.4

s.102, applied: SI 2003/3175

s.102, enabling: SI 2003/3175

s.103, applied: SI 2003/3175

s.103, enabling: SI 2003/3175

s.105, varied: SI 2003/3173 Art.2

s.105, enabling: SI 2003/3173

s.108, referred to: 2003 asp 7 s.68

s.109, amended: 2002 c.8 s.2

s.111, applied: SI 2002/419, SI 2002/1662

s.111, enabling: SI 2002/419, SI 2002/1662

s.112, applied: SI 2002/419, SI 2002/1662

s.113, applied: SI 2004/1910 Sch.1

s.113A, added: 2003 c.32 s.53

s.113B, added: 2003 c.32 s.53

s.114, applied: SI 2004/1910 Sch.1

s.127, enabling: SI 2002/228, SI 2002/1279, SI 2002/1558

Sch.1 Part 2 para.3, applied: SI 2003/435 Sch.2 para.2

Sch.1 Part 2 para.5, applied: SI 2003/435 Sch.2 para.2

Sch.1 Part 3 para.6, applied: SI 2003/336 Sch.1 Part 2, SI 2003/435 Sch.2 para.2

Sch.1 Part 6 para.19, amended: 2003 c.44 Sch.36 para.77

Sch.4, applied: SI 2003/419 Art.63

Sch.4 Part 1 para.5, repealed: 2002 c.40 Sch.26

Sch.4 Part 1 para.9, repealed: 2002 c.40 Sch.26

Sch.4 Part 1 para.10, repealed: 2002 c.40 Sch.26

Sch.4 Part 1 para.11, repealed: 2002 c.40 Sch.26

CAP.

2001–cont.

24. Anti-terrorism, Crime and Security Act 2001–*cont.*

Sch.4 Part 1 para.17, repealed: 2002 c.40 Sch.26

Sch.4 Part 1 para.24, amended: 2004 c.27 Sch.2 para.31

Sch.4 Part 1 para.27, repealed: 2002 c.40 Sch.26

Sch.4 Part 1 para.29, repealed: 2003 c.21 Sch.19

Sch.4 Part 1 para.30, repealed: 2002 c.40 Sch.26

Sch.4 Part 1 para.33, repealed: 2002 c.40 Sch.26

Sch.4 Part 1 para.37, repealed: 2004 c.35 Sch.13 Part 1

Sch.4 Part 1 para.53A, added: 2003 c.43 Sch.4 para.120

Sch.4 Part 2 para.57, amended: SI 2003/435 Sch.4 para.18

Sch.5, referred to: SI 2002/1281 Reg.3

Sch.6 para.4, applied: SI 2002/1845 r.4

Sch.6 para.5, enabling: SI 2002/1844, SI 2002/1845

Sch.6 para.6, referred to: SI 2002/1845 r.17

Sch.7 para.6, repealed: 2003 c.20 Sch.8

Sch.7 para.25, repealed: 2003 c.20 Sch.8

Sch.7 para.26, repealed: 2004 c.20 Sch.23 Part 1

25. Consolidated Fund (No.2) Act 2001

applied: 2002 c.18 Sch.1

repealed: 2003 c.13 Sch.3

2002

iv. Barclays Group Reorganisation Act 2002

vi. City of London (Ward Elections) Act 2002

applied: 1983 c.2 Sch.6 para.5

referred to: 1983 c.2 s.191, Sch.6 para.1

i. Greenham and Crookham Commons Act 2002

iii. HSBC Investment Banking Act 2002

ii. Land at Palace Avenue, Kensington (Acquisition of Freehold) Act 2002

1. International Development Act 2002

Commencement Orders: SI 2002/1408 Art.2

applied: 1971 c.56 Sch.2 para.15, 1973 c.21 s.2, 1976 c.35 s.7, s.11, 1979 c.3 s.13B, 2002 c.18 Sch.2 Part 22, 2003 c.13 Sch.2 Part 2, Sch.2 Part 26, 2004 c.9 Sch.2 Part 2, Sch.2 Part 25

referred to: 2003 c.43 Sch.4 para.121

Part 1, applied: 1967 c.13 Sch.3 para.10

s.11, applied: SI 2002/2404, SI 2002/2405, SI 2003/700, SI 2003/2157

s.11, referred to: SI 2002/2404, SI 2002/2405, SI 2003/700, SI 2003/2157

CAP.

2002–cont.

1. International Development Act 2002–*cont.*

s.11, enabling: SI 2002/2404, SI 2002/2405, SI 2003/700, SI 2003/1739, SI 2003/2157, SI 2004/3170

s.20, enabling: SI 2002/1408

Sch.1, amended: SI 2002/2469 Sch.1 para.31, 2003 c.43 Sch.4 para.122, Sch.13 para.11, Sch.14 Part 7, 2004 c.17 Sch.3 para.16

Sch.3 para.10, repealed: 2003 c.1 Sch.8 Part 1

2. Sex Discrimination (Election Candidates) Act 2002

3. European Communities (Amendment) Act 2002

4. Travel Concessions (Eligibility) Act 2002

see *Matthews v United Kingdom (40302/98)* Times, July 30, 2002 (ECHR), J-P Costa (President)

s.2, enabling: SI 2002/673, SI 2002/3014

5. Civil Defence (Grant) Act 2002

repealed: 2004 c.36 Sch.3

6. Northern Ireland Arms Decommissioning (Amendment) Act 2002

7. Homelessness Act 2002

Commencement Orders: SI 2002/1736 Art.2, Sch.1 Part 1, 2; SI 2002/1799 Art.2, Art.3; SI 2002/2324 Art.3; SI 2002/3114 Art.2, Art.3

see *R. (on the application of Maali) v Lambeth LBC* [2003] EWHC 2231, [2004] H.L.R.12 (QBD (Admin Ct)), Crane, J.

see *R. (on the application of Maali) v Lambeth LBC* [2003] EWHC 2231, [2004] H.L.R.12 (QBD (Admin Ct)), Crane, J.

see *R. (on the application of Maali) v Lambeth LBC* [2003] EWHC 2231, [2004] H.L.R.12 (QBD (Admin Ct)), Crane, J.

see *R. (on the application of Maali) v Lambeth LBC* [2003] EWHC 2231, [2004] H.L.R.12 (QBD (Admin Ct)), Crane, J.

s.3, amended: 2003 c.26 Sch.7 para.81

s.20, enabling: SI 2002/1736, SI 2002/1799, SI 2002/2324, SI 2002/3114

Sch.1, see *Van Aken v Camden LBC* [2002] EWCA Civ 1724, [2003] 1 W.L.R. 684 (CA), Jonathan Parker, L.J.

8. British Overseas Territories Act 2002

Commencement Orders: SI 2002/1252 Art.2

applied: 1981 c.61 s.37

s.8, enabling: SI 2002/1252

9. Land Registration Act 2002

Commencement Orders: SI 2003/935 Art.2; SI 2003/1028 Art.2; SI 2003/1612 Art.2; SI 2003/1725 Art.2

see *Overseas & Commercial Developments Ltd v Cox* [2002] EWCA Civ 635, [2002] B.P.I.R. 1150 (CA), Dyson, L.J.

applied: 1925 c.20 s.115, 1925 c.23 s.43, 1945 c.43 s.37, 1965 c.36 s.12, s.13, 1967 c.88 s.5, Sch.4 para.1, 1969 c.59 s.24, 1972

2002–cont.

9. Land Registration Act 2002–*cont.*

applied: 1925 c.20 s.115–*cont.*

c.61 s.14, 1974 c.39 s.177, 1974 c.47 s.22, s.56, 1975 c.76 s.10, 1977 c.42 s.136, 1979 c.53 s.3, 1985 c.68 s.154, Sch.9A para.9, Sch.17 para.2, Sch.20 para.17, 1986 c.53 Sch.2A para.1, SI 1986/1925 r.6.237A, r.6.237D, 1987 c.31 s.24, s.28, s.30, s.34, 1988 c.33 s.77, s.79, 1988 c.50 s.81, s.90, s.133, 1989 c.42 s.173, 1991 c.57 s.158, 1992 c.13 Sch.5 para.6, 1992 c.23 s.4, s.5, 1993 c.10 s.37, s.39, 1993 c.28 s.34, s.57, s.97, SI 1993/938 Sch.1 para.1, 1994 c.36 s.6, s.17, 1994 c.37 s.26, s.28, 1995 c.30 s.3, s.15, s.20, 1996 c.27 s.31, Sch.4 para.4, 1996 c.52 s.13, 1998 c.31 Sch.22 para.9, 2000 c.11 Sch.4 para.8, 2000 c.17 s.128, 2001 c.17 Sch.6 para.7, 2002 c.15 s.65, s.66, s.69, 2002 c.29 s.248, SI 2003/1417 r.20, r.186, r.221, SI 2004/595 Sch.4

referred to: 2002 c.29 s.47, SI 2003/2092 Sch.4

varied: SI 2003/1417 r.38, SI 2003/1953 Art.9

Part 2 c.1, applied: SI 2003/1417 r.178

Part 2 c.2, applied: SI 2003/1417 r.52

s.1, enabling: SI 2003/1417

s.3, applied: SI 2003/1417 r.27

s.4, applied: 1925 c.20 s.44, 1993 c.10 s.39, SI 2003/1417 r.21, r.22, r.180

s.4, referred to: 1988 c.50 s.133, 1989 c.42 s.173

s.6, applied: 1972 c.61 s.14, SI 2003/1417 r.27, r.38, SI 2003/1953 Art.23

s.6, enabling: SI 2003/1417

s.7, applied: 1972 c.61 s.14, SI 2003/1953 Art.22

s.13, enabling: SI 2003/1417

s.14, enabling: SI 2003/1417

s.16, applied: SI 2003/1417 r.53

s.16, enabling: SI 2003/1417

s.18, applied: SI 2003/1417 r.44, r.45, r.46, r.47, r.53

s.18, referred to: SI 2003/1417 r.46

s.18, enabling: SI 2003/1417

s.19, enabling: SI 2003/1417

s.20, applied: SI 2003/1417 r.48

s.20, enabling: SI 2003/1417

s.21, applied: SI 2003/1417 r.49, r.50, r.51

s.21, enabling: SI 2003/1417

s.22, referred to: SI 2003/1417 r.52

s.22, enabling: SI 2003/1417

s.23, disapplied: 1925 c.20 s.87

s.25, enabling: SI 2003/1417

s.27, applied: SI 2003/1953 Art.16, SI 2003/2092 Art.4

s.27, enabling: SI 2003/1417

s.28, applied: 1991 c.57 s.158

s.29, applied: 1985 c.68 Sch.9A para.6, 1991 c.57 s.158

s.30, applied: 1991 c.57 s.158

2002–cont.

9. Land Registration Act 2002–*cont.*

s.32, applied: SI 2003/1417 r.84

s.33, applied: SI 2003/1417 r.28, r.35, r.57

s.34, applied: 2003 c.14 s.79, SI 2003/1417 r.172

s.34, referred to: SI 2003/1417 r.81

s.34, enabling: SI 2003/1417

s.35, applied: SI 2003/1417 r.85

s.35, enabling: SI 2003/1417

s.36, applied: SI 2003/1417 r.86

s.36, enabling: SI 2003/1417

s.37, applied: SI 2003/1417 r.89

s.37, enabling: SI 2003/1417

s.39, enabling: SI 2003/1417

s.40, applied: SI 2003/1417 r.8, r.9

s.41, applied: SI 2003/1417 r.96, SI 2003/2092 Sch.3 Part 1, Sch.4, SI 2004/595 Sch.4

s.42, applied: SI 2003/1417 r.98

s.43, applied: SI 2003/1417 r.91, r.93, r.172, Sch.7 para.3, Sch.7 para.7

s.43, enabling: SI 2003/1417

s.44, applied: SI 2003/1417 r.95

s.44, enabling: SI 2003/1417

s.45, applied: SI 2003/1417 r.92

s.45, enabling: SI 2003/1417

s.46, applied: SI 2003/1417 r.92, r.98, r.100

s.46, enabling: SI 2003/1417

s.47, enabling: SI 2003/1417

s.48, applied: SI 2003/1417 r.101

s.48, enabling: SI 2003/1417

s.49, applied: SI 2003/1417 r.107, r.108, r.109, SI 2003/1953 Art.25

s.49, enabling: SI 2003/1417

s.50, applied: SI 2003/1417 r.105, r.106

s.50, enabling: SI 2003/1417

s.57, enabling: SI 2003/1417

s.60, applied: SI 2003/1417 r.120, r.122

s.60, enabling: SI 2003/1417

s.61, enabling: SI 2003/1417

s.62, applied: SI 2003/1417 r.124, SI 2003/1953 Art.15

s.64, applied: SI 2003/1417 r.125, SI 2003/2092 Sch.3 Part 1

s.64, enabling: SI 2003/1417

s.66, applied: SI 2003/1417 r.133, r.140

s.66, enabling: SI 2003/1417

s.67, referred to: SI 2003/1953 Art.29

s.67, enabling: SI 2003/1417

s.68, applied: SI 2003/1417 r.10

s.68, enabling: SI 2003/1417

s.69, enabling: SI 2003/1417

s.70, enabling: SI 2003/1417

s.71, enabling: SI 2003/1417

s.72, applied: SI 2003/1417 r.151, r.152, SI 2003/1953 Art.28

s.72, varied: SI 2003/1953 Art.28

s.72, enabling: SI 2003/1417

s.73, applied: SI 2003/1417 r.19, r.52, r.55, r.198, r.221, SI 2003/2114 r.3, r.5

CAP.

2002–cont.

9. Land Registration Act 2002–*cont.*
s.73, referred to: SI 2003/1417 r.52
s.73, enabling: SI 2003/1417, SI 2003/2114
s.74, applied: SI 2003/1417 r.20
s.75, applied: SI 2003/1417 r.201
s.75, enabling: SI 2003/1417
s.76, enabling: SI 2003/1417
s.79, applied: SI 2003/1417 r.23
s.81, enabling: SI 2003/1417
s.82, enabling: SI 2003/1417
s.86, applied: SI 2003/1417 r.8, r.9
s.86, enabling: SI 2003/1417
s.87, enabling: SI 2003/1417
s.89, referred to: SI 2003/1417 Sch.7 para.16
s.89, enabling: SI 2003/1417
s.90, applied: SI 2003/1417 r.28, r.35, r.57
s.91, amended: 2003 c.15 s.5
s.95, enabling: SI 2003/1417
s.97, applied: SI 2003/1417 r.224
s.98, enabling: SI 2003/1417
s.99, applied: SI 2003/1953 Art.2
s.100, applied: SI 2003/1417 r.15, r.19, r.208
s.100, enabling: SI 2003/2040, SI 2003/2281
s.102, applied: 2002 c.15 s.65, SI 2003/1417 r.207
s.102, enabling: SI 2003/2092, SI 2004/595, SI 2004/1833
s.106, applied: SI 2003/1417 r.105
s.107, applied: SI 2003/2342 Reg.3
s.109, enabling: SI 2003/2171
s.110, applied: SI 2003/2171 r.6, r.7, r.8, r.9, r.10, r.11, r.55
s.110, enabling: SI 2003/2171
s.114, enabling: SI 2003/2171
s.117, applied: SI 2003/2092 Sch.3 Part 1, SI 2004/595 Sch.3 Part 1
s.125, amended: 2004 c.33 Sch.27 para.167
s.127, applied: SI 2003/1417, SI 2003/2092, SI 2003/2114, SI 2004/595, SI 2004/1830, SI 2004/1833
s.127, enabling: SI 2003/1417, SI 2003/2114, SI 2004/1830, SI 2004/1833
s.128, enabling: SI 2003/2171
s.134, enabling: SI 2003/1953, SI 2003/2431
s.136, enabling: SI 2003/935, SI 2003/1028, SI 2003/1612, SI 2003/1725
Sch.1, applied: 1967 c.88 s.5, SI 2003/1417 r.28
Sch.1 para.1, applied: SI 2003/1417 r.28
Sch.1 para.2, applied: 1992 c.23 s.5, 1996 c.27 s.31
Sch.1 para.2, referred to: 1995 c.30 s.20
Sch.1 para.16, added: SI 2003/2431 Art.2
Sch.1 para.16, repealed: SI 2003/2431 Art.2
Sch.2 Part 1 para.2, enabling: SI 2003/1417
Sch.2 Part 1 para.5, applied: SI 2003/1417 r.90
Sch.2 Part 1 para.7, applied: SI 2003/1417 r.90

CAP.

2002–cont.

9. Land Registration Act 2002–*cont.*
Sch.2 Part 1 para.7, enabling: SI 2003/1417
Sch.3, applied: 1967 c.88 s.5, 1985 c.68 Sch.9A para.6, SI 2003/1417 r.57
Sch.3 para.1, applied: SI 2003/1417 r.57
Sch.3 para.2, applied: 1992 c.23 s.5, 1996 c.27 s.31
Sch.3 para.2, referred to: 1995 c.30 s.20
Sch.3 para.16, added: SI 2003/2431 Art.2
Sch.3 para.16, repealed: SI 2003/2431 Art.2
Sch.4, applied: 2002 c.15 s.6
Sch.4 para.2, applied: SI 2003/1417 r.126
Sch.4 para.4, enabling: SI 2003/1417
Sch.4 para.7, enabling: SI 2003/1417
Sch.6, applied: SI 2003/1417 r.192, r.193, r.194
Sch.6, referred to: SI 2003/1417 r.187
Sch.6 para.1, applied: SI 2003/1417 r.188
Sch.6 para.1, disapplied: SI 2003/1417 r.188
Sch.6 para.1, varied: SI 2003/1417 Sch.8
Sch.6 para.2, applied: SI 2003/1417 r.188, r.194
Sch.6 para.2, varied: SI 2003/1417 Sch.8
Sch.6 para.2, enabling: SI 2003/1417
Sch.6 para.3, applied: SI 2003/1417 r.189, r.190, r.198
Sch.6 para.3, varied: SI 2003/1417 Sch.8
Sch.6 para.3, enabling: SI 2003/1417
Sch.6 para.4, varied: SI 2003/1417 Sch.8
Sch.6 para.5, applied: SI 2003/1417 r.188
Sch.6 para.5, referred to: SI 2003/1417 r.188
Sch.6 para.5, varied: SI 2003/1417 Sch.8
Sch.6 para.6, applied: SI 2003/1417 r.188
Sch.6 para.6, disapplied: SI 2003/1417 r.188
Sch.6 para.6, varied: SI 2003/1417 Sch.8
Sch.6 para.7, varied: SI 2003/1417 Sch.8
Sch.6 para.8, disapplied: SI 2003/1417 r.188
Sch.6 para.8, varied: SI 2003/1417 Sch.8
Sch.6 para.9, varied: SI 2003/1417 Sch.8
Sch.6 para.10, varied: SI 2003/1417 Sch.8
Sch.6 para.11, varied: SI 2003/1417 Sch.8
Sch.6 para.12, varied: SI 2003/1417 Sch.8
Sch.6 para.13, applied: SI 2003/1417 r.188
Sch.6 para.13, varied: SI 2003/1417 Sch.8
Sch.6 para.14, varied: SI 2003/1417 Sch.8
Sch.6 para.14, enabling: SI 2003/1417
Sch.6 para.15, varied: SI 2003/1417 Sch.8
Sch.6 para.15, enabling: SI 2003/1417
Sch.8, applied: 1985 c.68 s.165, 2002 c.15 s.6, SI 2003/1417 r.195
Sch.8 para.1, applied: SI 2003/1417 r.195
Sch.8 para.2, disapplied: SI 2003/1417 r.70
Sch.8 para.3, applied: SI 2003/1417 r.195
Sch.8 para.9, enabling: SI 2003/1417
Sch.9 para.5, enabling: SI 2003/2342
Sch.10 Part 1 para.1, enabling: SI 2003/1417
Sch.10 Part 1 para.3, enabling: SI 2003/1417
Sch.10 Part 2 para.5, enabling: SI 2003/1417
Sch.10 Part 2 para.6, enabling: SI 2003/1417
Sch.10 Part 2 para.7, enabling: SI 2003/1417

2002–cont.

9. Land Registration Act 2002–*cont.*
Sch.10 Part 2 para.8, enabling: SI 2003/1417
Sch.11 para.22, repealed: 2002 c.29 Sch.12
Sch.11 para.32, repealed: 2002 c.29 Sch.12
Sch.12, applied: SI 2003/1953 Art.5
Sch.12 para.2, varied: SI 2003/1953 Art.17
Sch.12 para.2, enabling: SI 2003/1417
Sch.12 para.3, referred to: SI 2003/1953 Art.24
Sch.12 para.5, applied: SI 2003/1953 Art.3, Art.7
Sch.12 para.5, disapplied: SI 2003/1953 Art.24
Sch.12 para.6, applied: SI 2003/1953 Art.3
Sch.12 para.18, enabling: SI 2003/1417
Sch.12 para.20, applied: SI 2003/1417 r.8, r.66
Sch.12 para.20, varied: SI 2003/1417 r.60

10. Consolidated Fund Act 2002
applied: 2002 c.18 Sch.1
repealed: 2004 c.9 Sch.3

11. Office of Communications Act 2002
Commencement Orders: SI 2002/1483 Art.2; SI 2002/2955 Art.2; SI 2003/3142 Art.3
applied: 2003 c.21 s.390, s.393, s.394, SI 2003/3104 Reg.3
s.1, amended: SI 2002/2956 Art.2
s.1, varied: SI 2003/3195 Art.5, Sch.1 para.1, SI 2003/3197 Art.5, Sch.1 para.1, SI 2003/3198 Art.5, Sch.1 para.1
s.1, enabling: SI 2002/2956
s.2, repealed: 2003 c.21 Sch.19
s.4, repealed: 2003 c.21 Sch.19
s.5, repealed: 2003 c.21 Sch.19
s.6, repealed: 2003 c.21 Sch.19
s.6, varied: SI 2003/3195 Art.5, Sch.1 para.2
s.7, varied: SI 2003/3195 Art.5, Sch.1 para.3, SI 2003/3197 Art.5, Sch.1 para.2, SI 2003/3198 Art.5, Sch.1 para.2
s.7, enabling: SI 2002/1483, SI 2002/2955, SI 2003/3142, SI 2003/3195, SI 2003/3197, SI 2003/3198
Sch.1 para.1, repealed (in part): 2003 c.21 Sch.19
Sch.1 para.1, varied: SI 2003/3195 Art.5, Sch.1 para.4, SI 2003/3197 Art.5, Sch.1 para.3, SI 2003/3198 Art.5, Sch.1 para.3
Sch.1 para.2, varied: SI 2003/3195 Art.5, Sch.1 para.4, SI 2003/3197 Art.5, Sch.1 para.3, SI 2003/3198 Art.5, Sch.1 para.3
Sch.1 para.3, varied: SI 2003/3195 Art.5, Sch.1 para.4, SI 2003/3197 Art.5, Sch.1 para.3, SI 2003/3198 Art.5, Sch.1 para.3
Sch.1 para.4, varied: SI 2003/3195 Art.5, Sch.1 para.4, SI 2003/3197 Art.5, Sch.1 para.3, SI 2003/3198 Art.5, Sch.1 para.3
Sch.1 para.5, varied: SI 2003/3195 Art.5, Sch.1 para.4, SI 2003/3197 Art.5, Sch.1 para.3, SI 2003/3198 Art.5, Sch.1 para.3

2002–cont.

11. Office of Communications Act 2002–*cont.*
Sch.1 para.6, varied: SI 2003/3195 Art.5, Sch.1 para.4, SI 2003/3197 Art.5, Sch.1 para.3, SI 2003/3198 Art.5, Sch.1 para.3
Sch.1 para.7, varied: SI 2003/3195 Art.5, Sch.1 para.4, SI 2003/3197 Art.5, Sch.1 para.3, SI 2003/3198 Art.5, Sch.1 para.3
Sch.1 para.8, amended: 2003 c.21 Sch.17 para.172
Sch.1 para.8, repealed (in part): 2003 c.21 Sch.19
Sch.1 para.8, varied: SI 2003/3195 Art.5, Sch.1 para.4, SI 2003/3197 Art.5, Sch.1 para.3, SI 2003/3198 Art.5, Sch.1 para.3
Sch.1 para.9, varied: SI 2003/3195 Art.5, Sch.1 para.4, SI 2003/3197 Art.5, Sch.1 para.3, SI 2003/3198 Art.5, Sch.1 para.3
Sch.1 para.10, varied: SI 2003/3195 Art.5, Sch.1 para.4, SI 2003/3197 Art.5, Sch.1 para.3, SI 2003/3198 Art.5, Sch.1 para.3
Sch.1 para.11, varied: SI 2003/3195 Art.5, Sch.1 para.4, SI 2003/3197 Art.5, Sch.1 para.3, SI 2003/3198 Art.5, Sch.1 para.3
Sch.1 para.12, applied: 2003 c.21 s.3, s.7, s.8
Sch.1 para.12, varied: SI 2003/3195 Art.5, SI 2003/3197 Art.5, SI 2003/3198 Art.5
Sch.1 para.13, varied: SI 2003/3195 Art.5, SI 2003/3197 Art.5, SI 2003/3198 Art.5
Sch.1 para.14, amended: 2003 c.21 Sch.17 para.172
Sch.1 para.14, applied: 2003 c.21 s.12, s.13, s.20, s.21
Sch.1 para.14, varied: SI 2003/3195 Art.5, SI 2003/3197 Art.5, SI 2003/3198 Art.5
Sch.1 para.15, varied: SI 2003/3195 Art.5, SI 2003/3197 Art.5, SI 2003/3198 Art.5
Sch.1 para.16, varied: SI 2003/3195 Art.5, SI 2003/3197 Art.5, SI 2003/3198 Art.5
Sch.1 para.17, repealed (in part): 2003 c.21 Sch.19
Sch.1 para.17, varied: SI 2003/3195 Art.5, SI 2003/3197 Art.5, SI 2003/3198 Art.5
Sch.1 para.18, varied: SI 2003/3195 Art.5, SI 2003/3197 Art.5, SI 2003/3198 Art.5
Sch.1 para.19, varied: SI 2003/3195 Art.5, SI 2003/3197 Art.5, SI 2003/3198 Art.5
Sch.1 para.20, repealed: 2003 c.21 Sch.19
Sch.1 para.20, varied: SI 2003/3195 Art.5, SI 2003/3197 Art.5, SI 2003/3198 Art.5
Sch.1 para.21, varied: SI 2003/3195 Art.5, Sch.1 para.4, SI 2003/3197 Art.5, Sch.1 para.3, SI 2003/3198 Art.5, Sch.1 para.3
Sch.1 para.22, varied: SI 2003/3195 Art.5, Sch.1 para.4, SI 2003/3197 Art.5, Sch.1 para.3, SI 2003/3198 Art.5, Sch.1 para.3
Sch.1 para.23, varied: SI 2003/3195 Art.5, Sch.1 para.4, SI 2003/3197 Art.5, Sch.1 para.3, SI 2003/3198 Art.5, Sch.1 para.3
Sch.1 para.24, varied: SI 2003/3195 Art.5, Sch.1 para.4, SI 2003/3197 Art.5, Sch.1 para.3, SI 2003/3198 Art.5, Sch.1 para.3

2002–cont.

12. Football (Disorder) (Amendment) Act 2002

Commencement Orders: SI 2002/2200 Art.2

s.1, applied: 2000 c.25 s.5

s.3, enabling: SI 2002/2200

13. Electoral Fraud (Northern Ireland) Act 2002

Commencement Orders: SI 2002/1648 Art.2, Art.3, Art.4

s.8, enabling: SI 2002/1648

15. Commonhold and Leasehold Reform Act 2002

Commencement Orders: SI 2002/1912 Art.2, Sch.1 Part 1; SI 2003/1986 Art.2, Art.3, Sch.1 Part 1, 2, Sch.2 para.1, para.2, para.3, para.4, para.5, para.6, para.7, para.8, para.9, para.10, para.11; SI 2004/669 Art.2, Sch.2 para.8, para.9, para.10, para.13; SI 2004/3056 Art.2; SI 2004/3056art4(2); SI 2002/1912 Sch.1 Part 2, 3; SI 2002/3012 Art.2, Sch.1 Part 1, 2; SI 2003/1986 Sch.2 para.12, para.13; SI 2002/3012 Sch.1 Part 3; SI 2004/669 Art.2, Sch.1 Part 1, 2; SI 2004/1832 Art.2; SI 2003/1986 Sch.2 para.13; SI 2004/3056 Art.3; SI 2003/2377 Art.2

see *Earl Cadogan v Search Guarantees Plc* [2004] EWCA Civ 969, [2004] 1 W.L.R. 2768 (CA), Jonathan Parker, L.J.

applied: 1985 c.68 s.118, SI 1998/3132 r.56.4, SI 2004/675 Sch.1 para.3, Sch.1 para.4, Sch.1 para.5, SI 2004/1829 Reg.3, Reg.11, SI 2004/1830 r.3, r.4, r.12, Sch.2

referred to: SI 2004/595 Sch.3 Part 1, SI 2004/1830 r.4, r.27, SI 2004/3056 Art.1

Part 1, applied: 1993 c.28 s.4A, SI 2004/1829 Reg.17

Part 2 c.1, applied: 1925 c.21 s.111A, s.49, s.64, SI 2003/2099 Sch.2 para.4, SI 2004/681 Sch.2 para.4

s.2, applied: SI 2004/1829 Reg.3, Reg.4, Reg.5, Reg.6, Reg.7, Reg.15, SI 2004/1830 r.10, r.28, r.29

s.3, applied: SI 2004/1829 Reg.4, SI 2004/1830 r.6, r.7, r.9, r.10, r.11

s.3, enabling: SI 2004/1829

s.7, applied: SI 2004/1829 Reg.3, Reg.11, SI 2004/1830 r.11, r.29

s.8, applied: SI 2004/1829 Reg.4

s.9, applied: SI 2004/595 Sch.3 Part 1, SI 2004/1829 Reg.3, Reg.6, Reg.11, SI 2004/1830 r.5, r.10, r.28

s.9, enabling: SI 2004/1829

s.11, referred to: SI 2004/1829 Reg.7

s.11, varied: SI 2004/1829 Reg.7

s.11, enabling: SI 2004/1829

s.13, amended: SI 2004/1829 Reg.2

s.13, repealed (in part): SI 2004/1829 Reg.2

s.13, enabling: SI 2004/1829

s.17, applied: 1922 c.16 Sch.15 para.5, 1925 c.20 s.149

s.17, enabling: SI 2004/1829

2002–cont.

15. Commonhold and Leasehold Reform Act 2002–*cont.*

s.18, applied: 1922 c.16 Sch.15 para.5, 1925 c.20 s.149

s.19, enabling: SI 2004/1829

s.21, applied: 1925 c.20 s.101, 1996 c.47 s.7

s.21, enabling: SI 2004/1829

s.22, applied: 1996 c.47 s.7, SI 2004/1830 r.6

s.24, applied: SI 2004/1829 Reg.10, SI 2004/1830 r.31

s.24, enabling: SI 2004/1829

s.28, applied: SI 2004/1830 r.32

s.29, applied: SI 2004/1830 Sch.2

s.30, applied: SI 2004/1830 r.18

s.31, enabling: SI 2004/1829

s.32, enabling: SI 2004/1829

s.33, applied: SI 2004/1829 Reg.15

s.37, applied: 1980 c.58 s.19A

s.37, enabling: SI 2004/1829

s.41, applied: SI 2004/1830 r.7, r.20

s.43, applied: 1986 c.45 s.84

s.45, applied: SI 2004/1829 Reg.19

s.45, enabling: SI 2004/1829

s.51, applied: SI 2004/1829 Reg.19

s.51, enabling: SI 2004/1829

s.52, applied: SI 2004/1830 r.23

s.54, applied: SI 2004/1830 r.22

s.57, enabling: SI 2004/1829

s.58, applied: SI 2004/595 Sch.3 Part 1, SI 2004/1830 r.24

s.58, enabling: SI 2004/1829

s.61, amended: 2004 c.33 Sch.9 para.24

s.65, enabling: SI 2004/1830

s.73, amended: 2003 c.14 Sch.20 para.3

s.74, enabling: SI 2003/2120, SI 2004/675

s.75, referred to: SI 2004/675 Sch.1 para.5

s.76, amended: 2004 c.33 Sch.8 para.64

s.77, amended: 2004 c.33 Sch.8 para.65

s.78, applied: SI 2003/2099 Sch.2 para.4, SI 2004/681 Sch.2 para.4

s.78, referred to: SI 2003/1988 Reg.3, SI 2004/678 Reg.3

s.78, enabling: SI 2003/1988, SI 2004/678

s.79, applied: SI 2003/2099 Sch.2 para.4, SI 2004/681 Sch.2 para.4

s.80, applied: SI 2003/1988 Reg.4, SI 2004/678 Reg.4

s.80, enabling: SI 2003/1988, SI 2004/678

s.84, applied: SI 2003/2099 Sch.1 para.4, Sch.2 para.4, SI 2004/681 Sch.1 para.4, Sch.2 para.4

s.84, referred to: SI 2003/1988 Reg.5, SI 2004/678 Reg.5

s.84, enabling: SI 2003/1988, SI 2004/678

s.85, applied: SI 2003/2099 Sch.1 para.4, Sch.2 para.4, SI 2004/681 Sch.1 para.4, Sch.2 para.4

s.86, applied: SI 2004/675 Sch.1 para.12

s.87, amended: SI 2003/2096 Sch.1 para.39

s.87, applied: SI 2004/675 Sch.1 para.12

2002–cont.

15. Commonhold and Leasehold Reform Act 2002–*cont.*

s.88, applied: SI 2003/2099 Sch.1 para.4, SI 2004/681 Sch.1 para.4

s.90, applied: SI 2004/675 Sch.1 para.12

s.92, applied: SI 2003/1988 Reg.4, SI 2004/678 Reg.4

s.92, referred to: SI 2003/1988 Reg.6, Reg.7, SI 2004/678 Reg.6, Reg.7

s.92, enabling: SI 2003/1988, SI 2004/678

s.94, applied: SI 2003/2099 Sch.1 para.4, Sch.2 para.4, SI 2004/681 Sch.1 para.4, Sch.2 para.4

s.96, applied: SI 2004/675 Sch.1 para.4

s.97, applied: SI 2004/675 Sch.1 para.4

s.98, applied: SI 2004/675 Sch.1 para.4

s.99, applied: SI 2003/2099 Sch.1 para.4, Sch.2 para.4, SI 2004/675 Sch.1 para.4, SI 2004/681 Sch.1 para.4, Sch.2 para.4

s.100, applied: SI 2004/675 Sch.1 para.4

s.101, applied: SI 2004/675 Sch.1 para.4

s.105, amended: SI 2003/2096 Sch.1 para.40

s.117, applied: 1993 c.28 s.69

s.121, referred to: SI 2004/3056 art4(1)

s.122, referred to: SI 2004/3056 art4(1)

s.123, referred to: SI 2004/3056 art4(1)

s.124, referred to: SI 2004/3056 art4(1)

s.141, applied: 1967 c.88 s.1AA

s.152, referred to: 1985 c.70 s.21

s.159, applied: SI 2003/2099 Sch.1 para.2, SI 2004/681 Sch.1 para.2

s.164, enabling: SI 2004/3097

s.166, enabling: SI 2004/3096

s.167, enabling: SI 2004/3086

s.168, referred to: SI 2004/3056 art4(2)

s.170, referred to: SI 2004/3056 art4(3)

s.175, applied: SI 1996/1022 r.5A, r.28, r.52

s.178, enabling: SI 2003/1988, SI 2003/2120, SI 2004/675, SI 2004/678

s.181, enabling: SI 2002/1912, SI 2002/3012, SI 2003/1986, SI 2003/2377, SI 2004/669, SI 2004/1832, SI 2004/3056

Sch.3 Part 1 para.2, applied: SI 2004/1829 Reg.13, Reg.14

Sch.3 Part 1 para.2, enabling: SI 2004/1829

Sch.3 Part 3 para.16, enabling: SI 2004/1829

Sch.4 para.3, referred to: SI 2004/1829 Reg.18

Sch.6 para.1, applied: SI 2004/675 Sch.1 para.39

Sch.6 para.3, amended: 2004 c.33 Sch.8 para.66

Sch.6 para.3, varied: 2004 c.33 Sch.21 para.52

Sch.6 para.5, applied: SI 2003/2099 Sch.1 para.4, Sch.2 para.4, SI 2004/681 Sch.1 para.4, Sch.2 para.4

Sch.7, referred to: SI 2003/1988 Reg.3, SI 2004/678 Reg.3

2002–cont.

15. Commonhold and Leasehold Reform Act 2002–*cont.*

Sch.11 Part 1 para.3, applied: SI 2003/2098 Reg.3, SI 2003/2099 Sch.1 para.2, Sch.2 para.2, SI 2004/681 Sch.1 para.2, Sch.2 para.2, SI 2004/683 Reg.3

Sch.11 Part 1 para.5, applied: SI 2003/2098 Reg.3, SI 2003/2099 Sch.1 para.2, SI 2004/681 Sch.1 para.2, SI 2004/683 Reg.3

Sch.12, applied: 1987 c.31 s.35

Sch.12, enabling: SI 2003/2099, SI 2004/681, SI 2004/3098

Sch.12 para.1, enabling: SI 2003/2098, SI 2004/683

Sch.12 para.4, applied: SI 2003/2099 Reg.22, SI 2004/681 Reg.22

Sch.12 para.9, enabling: SI 2003/2098, SI 2004/683

16. State Pension Credit Act 2002

Commencement Orders: SI 2002/1691 Art.2; SI 2003/83 Art.2; SI 2003/966 Art.2, Sch.1; SI 2003/1766 Art.2; SI 2002/2248 Art.2

applied: 1988 c.1 s.617, 1992 c.5 s.124, s.125, s.150, s.169, s.179, s.180, SI 1992/1814 Reg.17, 1995 c.26 Sch.4 para.1, SI 1996/2447 Sch.2 para.5, SI 1996/2890 Reg.10, Sch.2 para.12, Sch.3 para.4, Sch.4 para.6, 1998 c.47 s.87, 1999 c.33 s.115, SI 1999/687 Art.5, SI 1999/689 Art.5, SI 1999/3441 Reg.2, SI 2000/636 Reg.2, 2001 c.11 s.10, SI 2002/2005 Reg.18, SI 2002/2008 Reg.4, SI 2003/2098 Reg.8, SI 2004/683 Reg.8, SI 2004/3114 Art.3, SI 2004/3121 Art.4

referred to: SI 2003/325 Sch.1

s.1, applied: 1980 c.43 Sch.6 Part I, 1982 c.49 s.70, SI 1987/1968 Sch.9A para.2A, 1989 c.41 s.29, SI 2000/516 Reg.4, SI 2001/1437 Reg.5, SI 2002/3197, 2003 c.1 s.677, SSI 2004/83 Reg.3

s.1, enabling: SI 2002/1792, SI 2002/3019, SI 2003/2274, SI 2004/1232

s.2, amended: 2004 c.33 Sch.24 para.140, Sch.24 para.141

s.2, applied: 1992 c.5 s.150, SI 2002/1792 Sch.3 para.2, SI 2002/3019 Reg.36, SI 2002/3197

s.2, referred to: SI 2003/650 Reg.1

s.2, varied: SI 2002/1792 Sch.3 para.2

s.2, enabling: SI 2002/1792, SI 2002/3019, SI 2002/3197, SI 2003/1195, SI 2003/2274, SI 2004/2327, SI 2004/2825

s.3, amended: SI 2002/1792 Sch.3 para.1, 2004 c.33 Sch.24 para.140

s.3, applied: SI 1987/1968 Sch.9A para.2A, 1992 c.5 s.150, SI 2002/1792 Reg.9, SI 2002/3197

s.3, varied: SI 2002/1792 Sch.3 para.2

s.3, enabling: SI 2002/1792, SI 2002/3019

2002–cont.

16. State Pension Credit Act 2002–*cont.*

s.4, amended: SI 2002/1792 Sch.3 para.1, 2004 c.33 Sch.24 para.140

s.4, applied: SI 2002/3197

s.4, enabling: SI 2002/1792

s.5, amended: 2004 c.33 Sch.24 para.140

s.5, applied: 1992 c.4 s.136A, SI 2002/3197

s.5, substituted: SI 2002/1792 Sch.3 para.1

s.5, enabling: SI 2002/1792

s.6, amended: 2004 c.33 Sch.24 para.140

s.6, applied: SI 1987/1968 Reg.7, SI 1987/1971 Reg.23, 1992 c.4 s.136A, SI 1992/1814 Reg.15, 1998 c.14 Sch.3 para.8A, SI 1999/991 Reg.6, SI 2002/1792 Reg.10, SI 2002/3197

s.6, enabling: SI 2002/1792

s.7, applied: SI 2002/1792 Reg.10, SI 2002/3197

s.7, enabling: SI 2002/1792, SI 2002/3019, SI 2004/647

s.8, applied: SI 2002/3197

s.9, amended: 2004 c.33 Sch.24 para.140

s.9, applied: SI 1987/1971 Reg.23, SI 1992/1814 Reg.15, 1998 c.14 Sch.3 para.8C, SI 1999/991 Sch.3B para.1, SI 2002/3197

s.9, enabling: SI 2002/1792

s.10, applied: SI 2002/3197

s.11, applied: SI 2002/3197

s.12, applied: SI 1987/1968 Sch.9A para.2A, 1992 c.4 s.136A, SI 2001/4022 Reg.3A, SI 2002/1792 Sch.3 para.1, SI 2002/3197

s.12, referred to: SI 2002/1792 Sch.3 para.1

s.12, enabling: SI 2002/1792, SI 2002/3019, SI 2002/3197, SI 2003/2274

s.13, applied: SI 2002/3197

s.13, enabling: SI 2002/3019, SI 2002/3197, SI 2003/325, SI 2003/1195, SI 2003/2274

s.14, applied: SI 2002/3197

s.14, referred to: SI 2003/325

s.15, applied: 1992 c.4 s.136A, SI 2002/1792 Reg.15, SI 2002/3197

s.15, enabling: SI 2002/1792, SI 2002/3019, SI 2002/3197, SI 2003/2274, SI 2004/647, SI 2004/1141, SI 2004/2327

s.16, amended: SI 2002/1792 Reg.16

s.16, applied: SI 2002/1792 Reg.18, SI 2002/3197

s.16, enabling: SI 2002/1792, SI 2002/3197, SI 2004/2327

s.17, amended: 2003 c.1 Sch.6 para.263, 2004 c.33 Sch.24 para.142, Sch.24 para.143, Sch.30

s.17, applied: SI 2002/3197

s.17, enabling: SI 2002/1792, SI 2002/3019, SI 2002/3197, SI 2003/1195, SI 2003/2274, SI 2004/647, SI 2004/1141, SI 2004/1232, SI 2004/2327, SI 2004/2825

s.19, applied: SI 2002/1792

s.19, referred to: SI 2003/325 Sch.1

s.19, enabling: SI 2003/1195, SI 2004/2825

s.20, applied: 1992 c.5 s.165

2002–cont.

16. State Pension Credit Act 2002–*cont.*

s.22, enabling: SI 2002/1691, SI 2002/2248, SI 2003/83, SI 2003/966, SI 2003/1766

Sch.1 Part 3 para.13, enabling: SI 2002/3019

Sch.2 Part 1 para.3, applied: SI 2003/2275 Sch.1

Sch.2 Part 1 para.3, referred to: SI 2003/325 Sch.1

Sch.2 Part 3 para.25, repealed: 2003 c.39 Sch.10

Sch.2 Part 3 para.28, repealed: 2003 c.1 Sch.8 Part 1

Sch.2 Part 3 para.42, repealed: 2004 c.19 Sch.4

17. National Health Service Reform and Health Care Professions Act 2002

Commencement Orders: SI 2002/2202 Art.2, Art.3; SI 2002/2478 Art.3, Art.5; SI 2002/2532 Art.2, Sch.1; SI 2002/3190 Art.2, 2003 c.43 Sch.14 Part 2; SI 2003/833 Art.2, Art.3, Art.4; SI 2003/1580 Art.2, Art.3; SI 2003/2246 Art.2; SI 2003/3083 Art.2

see *Practice Direction (Administrative Court: Annual Statement)* [2004] 1 All E.R. 322 (QBD (Admin Ct)), Maurice Kay, J.

applied: SI 2002/2375 Reg.9, Reg.10, Reg.11

referred to: 2003 c.43 Sch.4 para.123

see *Practice Direction (Administrative Court: Annual Statement)* [2004] 1 All E.R. 322 (QBD (Admin Ct)), Maurice Kay, J.

varied: SI 2004/664 Art.11, Art.12, Art.13, Art.14

Part 2, applied: 1986 c.47 Sch.2 para.5

Part 3, applied: 1986 c.47 Sch.2 para.5

s.1, varied: SI 2003/50 Art.2

s.2, varied: SI 2003/50 Art.2

s.3, repealed (in part): 2003 c.4 Sch.4

s.3, varied: SI 2003/50 Art.2

s.4, repealed (in part): 2003 c.43 Sch.14 Part 4

s.4, varied: SI 2003/50 Art.2

s.5, repealed (in part): 2003 c.43 Sch.14 Part 4

s.5, varied: SI 2003/50 Art.2

s.6, applied: 2000 c.23 Sch.1 para.27A, SI 2003/3171 Sch.1 Part II

s.7, varied: SI 2003/50 Art.2

s.8, varied: SI 2003/50 Art.2

s.10, varied: SI 2003/50 Art.2

s.11, repealed: 2003 c.43 Sch.14 Part 2

s.11, varied: SI 2003/50 Art.2

s.12, repealed: 2003 c.43 Sch.14 Part 2

s.12, varied: SI 2003/50 Art.2

s.13, repealed: 2003 c.43 Sch.14 Part 2

s.13, varied: SI 2003/50 Art.2

s.14, repealed: 2003 c.43 Sch.14 Part 2

s.14, varied: SI 2003/50 Art.2

s.15, amended: 2003 c.43 s.31, Sch.14 Part 1

2002–cont.

17. National Health Service Reform and Health Care Professions Act 2002– *cont.*

s.15, applied: 2000 c.36 Sch.1 para.41A, SI 2002/3048 Reg.2, SI 2003/2123 Reg.4, Reg.10, SI 2003/2124 Reg.8

s.15, varied: SI 2003/50 Art.2

s.15, enabling: SI 2003/2124

s.16, varied: SI 2003/50 Art.2

s.17, amended: 2003 c.43 s.31, Sch.11 para.74, Sch.14 Part 4

s.17, applied: 1987 c.18 s.9

s.17, varied: SI 2003/50 Art.2, SI 2004/288 Art.7

s.17, enabling: SI 2003/2124, SI 2004/540

s.18, amended: 2003 c.43 s.31

s.18, varied: SI 2003/50 Art.2

s.19, amended: 2003 c.43 s.31

s.19, varied: SI 2003/50 Art.2

s.19, enabling: SI 2003/2123, SI 2003/2124, SI 2004/540

s.20, amended: 2003 c.43 s.32

s.20, applied: 1987 c.18 s.9, SI 2002/3007 Reg.2, Reg.3, Reg.4, Reg.5, Reg.7, Reg.8, 2003 c.43 s.9

s.20, referred to: SI 2002/3007 Reg.2, Reg.6

s.20, varied: SI 2003/50 Art.2

s.20, enabling: SI 2002/3007, SI 2003/497, SI 2003/2044, SI 2004/540

s.21, varied: SI 2003/50 Art.2

s.22, applied: 1987 c.18 s.9

s.22, referred to: SI 2002/2469 Reg.17, SI 2003/2660 Art.2

s.22, repealed (in part): 2003 c.4 Sch.4

s.22, varied: SI 2003/50 Art.2

s.23, amended: 2003 c.43 Sch.4 para.124

s.23, varied: SI 2003/50 Art.2

s.24, applied: 1987 c.18 s.9, SI 2003/154 Reg.4, Reg.5

s.24, enabling: SI 2003/154

s.25, referred to: SI 2002/2376 Reg.4

s.25, varied: SI 2003/50 Art.2

s.26, varied: SI 2003/50 Art.2

s.27, varied: SI 2003/50 Art.2

s.28, varied: SI 2003/50 Art.2

s.29, see *Council for the Regulation of Health Care Professionals v General Medical Council* [2004] EWHC 527, [2004] 1 W.L.R. 2068 (QBD (Admin Ct)), Leveson, J.; see *Council for the Regulation of Health Care Professionals v General Medical Council* [2004] EWHC 944, [2004] 1 W.L.R. 2432 (QBD (Admin Ct)), Leveson, J.

s.29, amended: SI 2002/3135 Sch.1 para.13, SI 2004/1771 Sch.1 para.1

s.29, varied: SI 2003/50 Art.2

s.30, varied: SI 2003/50 Art.2

s.31, varied: SI 2003/50 Art.2

s.32, varied: SI 2003/50 Art.2

s.33, varied: SI 2003/50 Art.2

2002–cont.

17. National Health Service Reform and Health Care Professions Act 2002– *cont.*

s.34, varied: SI 2003/50 Art.2

s.35, varied: SI 2003/50 Art.2

s.38, enabling: SI 2002/2202, SI 2002/2376, SI 2002/2469, SI 2002/2478, SI 2002/2532, SI 2002/2861, SI 2002/3007, SI 2002/3038, SI 2003/50, SI 2003/154, SI 2003/497, SI 2003/833, SI 2003/1580, SI 2003/1937, SI 2003/2044, SI 2003/2123, SI 2003/2124, SI 2003/2246, SI 2004/540

s.39, enabling: SI 2002/2469, SI 2002/2861, SI 2003/154, SI 2003/1937

s.42, repealed (in part): 2003 c.44 Sch.37 Part 11

s.42, enabling: SI 2002/2202, SI 2002/2478, SI 2002/2532, SI 2002/3190, SI 2003/50, SI 2003/833, SI 2003/1580, SI 2003/2246, SI 2003/3083

Sch.1 Part 1 para.1, varied: SI 2003/50 Art.2

Sch.1 Part 1 para.2, varied: SI 2003/50 Art.2

Sch.1 Part 1 para.3, varied: SI 2003/50 Art.2

Sch.1 Part 1 para.4, varied: SI 2003/50 Art.2

Sch.1 Part 1 para.5, varied: SI 2003/50 Art.2

Sch.1 Part 1 para.6, varied: SI 2003/50 Art.2

Sch.1 Part 1 para.7, varied: SI 2003/50 Art.2

Sch.1 Part 1 para.8, varied: SI 2003/50 Art.2

Sch.1 Part 1 para.9, varied: SI 2003/50 Art.2

Sch.1 Part 1 para.10, varied: SI 2003/50 Art.2

Sch.1 Part 1 para.11, varied: SI 2003/50 Art.2

Sch.1 Part 1 para.12, varied: SI 2003/50 Art.2

Sch.1 Part 1 para.13, varied: SI 2003/50 Art.2

Sch.1 Part 1 para.14, varied: SI 2003/50 Art.2

Sch.1 Part 1 para.15, varied: SI 2003/50 Art.2

Sch.1 Part 1 para.16, varied: SI 2003/50 Art.2

Sch.1 Part 1 para.17, repealed: 2003 c.43 Sch.14 Part 4

Sch.1 Part 1 para.17, varied: SI 2003/50 Art.2

Sch.1 Part 1 para.18, varied: SI 2003/50 Art.2

Sch.1 Part 1 para.19, varied: SI 2003/50 Art.2

Sch.1 Part 1 para.20, varied: SI 2003/50 Art.2

Sch.1 Part 1 para.21, varied: SI 2003/50 Art.2

Sch.1 Part 1 para.22, varied: SI 2003/50 Art.2

Sch.1 Part 1 para.23, varied: SI 2003/50 Art.2

Sch.1 Part 1 para.24, varied: SI 2003/50 Art.2

Sch.1 Part 1 para.25, varied: SI 2003/50 Art.2

Sch.1 Part 1 para.26, varied: SI 2003/50 Art.2

Sch.1 Part 1 para.27, varied: SI 2003/50 Art.2

Sch.1 Part 1 para.28, varied: SI 2003/50 Art.2

Sch.1 Part 1 para.29, varied: SI 2003/50 Art.2

Sch.1 Part 1 para.30, varied: SI 2003/50 Art.2

Sch.1 Part 1 para.31, varied: SI 2003/50 Art.2

Sch.1 Part 1 para.32, varied: SI 2003/50 Art.2

Sch.1 Part 1 para.33, varied: SI 2003/50 Art.2

Sch.1 Part 1 para.34, varied: SI 2003/50 Art.2

Sch.1 Part 1 para.35, varied: SI 2003/50 Art.2

Sch.1 Part 2, varied: SI 2003/50 Art.2

Sch.1 Part 2 para.37, repealed: 2003 c.43 Sch.14 Part 2

CAP.

2002–cont.

17. National Health Service Reform and Health Care Professions Act 2002– cont.

Sch.1 Part 2 para.49, repealed: 2003 c.43 Sch.14 Part 2

Sch.1 Part 2 para.50, repealed: 2003 c.43 Sch.14 Part 2

Sch.2 Part 1 para.1, varied: SI 2003/50 Art.2

Sch.2 Part 1 para.2, varied: SI 2003/50 Art.2

Sch.2 Part 1 para.3, repealed (in part): 2003 c.43 Sch.14 Part 4

Sch.2 Part 1 para.3, varied: SI 2003/50 Art.2

Sch.2 Part 1 para.4, repealed (in part): 2003 c.43 Sch.14 Part 4

Sch.2 Part 1 para.4, varied: SI 2003/50 Art.2

Sch.2 Part 1 para.5, repealed (in part): 2003 c.43 Sch.14 Part 4

Sch.2 Part 1 para.5, varied: SI 2003/50 Art.2

Sch.2 Part 1 para.6, repealed (in part): 2003 c.43 Sch.14 Part 4

Sch.2 Part 1 para.6, varied: SI 2003/50 Art.2

Sch.2 Part 1 para.7, repealed (in part): 2003 c.43 Sch.14 Part 4

Sch.2 Part 1 para.7, varied: SI 2003/50 Art.2

Sch.2 Part 1 para.8, repealed (in part): 2003 c.43 Sch.14 Part 4

Sch.2 Part 1 para.8, varied: SI 2003/50 Art.2

Sch.2 Part 1 para.9, repealed: 2003 c.43 Sch.14 Part 4

Sch.2 Part 1 para.9, varied: SI 2003/50 Art.2

Sch.2 Part 1 para.10, repealed: 2003 c.43 Sch.14 Part 4

Sch.2 Part 1 para.10, varied: SI 2003/50 Art.2

Sch.2 Part 1 para.11, varied: SI 2003/50 Art.2

Sch.2 Part 1 para.12, varied: SI 2003/50 Art.2

Sch.2 Part 1 para.13, varied: SI 2003/50 Art.2

Sch.2 Part 1 para.14, varied: SI 2003/50 Art.2

Sch.2 Part 1 para.15, varied: SI 2003/50 Art.2

Sch.2 Part 1 para.16, varied: SI 2003/50 Art.2

Sch.2 Part 1 para.17, varied: SI 2003/50 Art.2

Sch.2 Part 1 para.18, varied: SI 2003/50 Art.2

Sch.2 Part 1 para.19, varied: SI 2003/50 Art.2

Sch.2 Part 1 para.20, varied: SI 2003/50 Art.2

Sch.2 Part 1 para.21, varied: SI 2003/50 Art.2

Sch.2 Part 1 para.22, varied: SI 2003/50 Art.2

Sch.2 Part 1 para.23, varied: SI 2003/50 Art.2

Sch.2 Part 1 para.24, varied: SI 2003/50 Art.2

Sch.2 Part 1 para.25, varied: SI 2003/50 Art.2

Sch.2 Part 1 para.26, varied: SI 2003/50 Art.2

Sch.2 Part 1 para.27, varied: SI 2003/50 Art.2

Sch.2 Part 1 para.28, varied: SI 2003/50 Art.2

Sch.2 Part 1 para.29, varied: SI 2003/50 Art.2

Sch.2 Part 1 para.30, varied: SI 2003/50 Art.2

Sch.2 Part 1 para.31, varied: SI 2003/50 Art.2

Sch.2 Part 1 para.32, varied: SI 2003/50 Art.2

Sch.2 Part 1 para.33, varied: SI 2003/50 Art.2

Sch.2 Part 1 para.34, varied: SI 2003/50 Art.2

Sch.2 Part 1 para.35, varied: SI 2003/50 Art.2

Sch.2 Part 1 para.36, varied: SI 2003/50 Art.2

Sch.2 Part 1 para.37, varied: SI 2003/50 Art.2

CAP.

2002–cont.

17. National Health Service Reform and Health Care Professions Act 2002– cont.

Sch.2 Part 2, varied: SI 2003/50 Art.2

Sch.2 Part 2 para.64, repealed (in part): 2003 c.44 Sch.37 Part 11

Sch.2 Part 2 para.72, repealed (in part): 2003 c.43 Sch.14 Part 4

Sch.3 Part 1 para.2, repealed: 2003 c.43 Sch.14 Part 4

Sch.3 Part 1 para.3, repealed: 2003 c.43 Sch.14 Part 4

Sch.3 Part 1 para.4, repealed: 2003 c.43 Sch.14 Part 4

Sch.3 Part 1 para.5, repealed (in part): 2003 c.43 Sch.14 Part 4

Sch.3 Part 1 para.6, repealed (in part): 2003 c.43 Sch.14 Part 4

Sch.3 Part 1 para.10, repealed (in part): 2003 c.43 Sch.14 Part 4

Sch.3 Part 2 para.15, repealed: 2003 c.43 Sch.14 Part 4

Sch.3 Part 2 para.16, repealed: 2003 c.43 Sch.14 Part 4

Sch.3 Part 2 para.17, repealed: 2003 c.43 Sch.14 Part 4

Sch.5 para.24, repealed (in part): 2003 c.4 Sch.4

Sch.5 para.44, repealed: 2003 c.43 Sch.14 Part 2

Sch.6 para.1, varied: SI 2003/50 Art.2

Sch.6 para.2, varied: SI 2003/50 Art.2

Sch.6 para.3, varied: SI 2003/50 Art.2

Sch.6 para.4, varied: SI 2003/50 Art.2

Sch.6 para.4, enabling: SI 2002/3038, SI 2004/540

Sch.6 para.5, varied: SI 2003/50 Art.2

Sch.6 para.5, enabling: SI 2002/3038

Sch.6 para.6, varied: SI 2003/50 Art.2

Sch.6 para.7, applied: SI 2002/3038 Reg.10

Sch.6 para.7, varied: SI 2003/50 Art.2

Sch.6 para.8, varied: SI 2003/50 Art.2

Sch.6 para.9, varied: SI 2003/50 Art.2

Sch.6 para.10, varied: SI 2003/50 Art.2

Sch.6 para.11, varied: SI 2003/50 Art.2

Sch.6 para.12, varied: SI 2003/50 Art.2

Sch.6 para.12, enabling: SI 2003/2124

Sch.6 para.13, varied: SI 2003/50 Art.2

Sch.6 para.14, varied: SI 2003/50 Art.2

Sch.6 para.15, varied: SI 2003/50 Art.2

Sch.6 para.16, varied: SI 2003/50 Art.2

Sch.6 para.17, varied: SI 2003/50 Art.2

Sch.6 para.18, varied: SI 2003/50 Art.2

Sch.6 para.19, varied: SI 2003/50 Art.2

Sch.7 para.1, varied: SI 2003/50 Art.2

Sch.7 para.2, varied: SI 2003/50 Art.2

Sch.7 para.3, varied: SI 2003/50 Art.2

Sch.7 para.4, applied: SI 2002/2376 Reg.4, Reg.10

Sch.7 para.4, varied: SI 2003/50 Art.2

Sch.7 para.5, varied: SI 2003/50 Art.2

2002–cont.

17. National Health Service Reform and Health Care Professions Act 2002– *cont.*

Sch.7 para.6, varied: SI 2003/50 Art.2

Sch.7 para.6, enabling: SI 2002/2376

Sch.7 para.7, varied: SI 2003/50 Art.2

Sch.7 para.8, varied: SI 2003/50 Art.2

Sch.7 para.9, varied: SI 2003/50 Art.2

Sch.7 para.10, varied: SI 2003/50 Art.2

Sch.7 para.11, varied: SI 2003/50 Art.2

Sch.7 para.12, varied: SI 2003/50 Art.2

Sch.7 para.13, varied: SI 2003/50 Art.2

Sch.7 para.14, varied: SI 2003/50 Art.2

Sch.7 para.15, varied: SI 2003/50 Art.2

Sch.7 para.16, varied: SI 2003/50 Art.2

Sch.7 para.17, varied: SI 2003/50 Art.2

Sch.7 para.18, varied: SI 2003/50 Art.2

Sch.7 para.19, varied: SI 2003/50 Art.2

Sch.7 para.20, varied: SI 2003/50 Art.2

Sch.7 para.21, varied: SI 2003/50 Art.2

Sch.7 para.22, varied: SI 2003/50 Art.2

Sch.7 para.23, varied: SI 2003/50 Art.2

Sch.7 para.24, varied: SI 2003/50 Art.2

Sch.8 para.1, varied: SI 2003/50 Art.2

Sch.8 para.2, repealed (in part): 2003 c.43 Sch.14 Part 4

Sch.8 para.2, varied: SI 2003/50 Art.2

Sch.8 para.3, varied: SI 2003/50 Art.2

Sch.8 para.4, varied: SI 2003/50 Art.2

Sch.8 para.5, varied: SI 2003/50 Art.2

Sch.8 para.6, varied: SI 2003/50 Art.2

Sch.8 para.7, varied: SI 2003/50 Art.2

Sch.8 para.8, varied: SI 2003/50 Art.2

Sch.8 para.9, varied: SI 2003/50 Art.2

Sch.8 para.10, varied: SI 2003/50 Art.2

Sch.8 para.11, repealed (in part): 2003 c.4 Sch.4

Sch.8 para.11, varied: SI 2003/50 Art.2

Sch.8 para.12, varied: SI 2003/50 Art.2

Sch.8 para.13, varied: SI 2003/50 Art.2

Sch.8 para.14, varied: SI 2003/50 Art.2

Sch.8 para.15, varied: SI 2003/50 Art.2

Sch.8 para.16, varied: SI 2003/50 Art.2

Sch.8 para.17, varied: SI 2003/50 Art.2

Sch.8 para.18, varied: SI 2003/50 Art.2

Sch.8 para.19, varied: SI 2003/50 Art.2

Sch.8 para.20, varied: SI 2003/50 Art.2

Sch.8 para.21, varied: SI 2003/50 Art.2

Sch.8 para.22, varied: SI 2003/50 Art.2

Sch.8 para.23, varied: SI 2003/50 Art.2

Sch.8 para.24, varied: SI 2003/50 Art.2

Sch.8 para.25, varied: SI 2003/50 Art.2

Sch.8 para.26, varied: SI 2003/50 Art.2

Sch.8 para.27, varied: SI 2003/50 Art.2

Sch.8 para.28, repealed: 2003 c.43 Sch.14 Part 2

Sch.8 para.28, varied: SI 2003/50 Art.2

Sch.8 para.29, repealed: 2003 c.43 Sch.14 Part 2

Sch.8 para.29, varied: SI 2003/50 Art.2

2002–cont.

17. National Health Service Reform and Health Care Professions Act 2002– *cont.*

Sch.8 para.30, repealed: 2003 c.43 Sch.14 Part 2

Sch.8 para.30, varied: SI 2003/50 Art.2

Sch.8 para.31, repealed: 2003 c.43 Sch.14 Part 2

Sch.8 para.31, varied: SI 2003/50 Art.2

Sch.8 para.32, varied: SI 2003/50 Art.2

Sch.8 para.33, varied: SI 2003/50 Art.2

Sch.8 para.34, varied: SI 2003/50 Art.2

Sch.8 para.35, varied: SI 2003/50 Art.2

Sch.8 para.36, varied: SI 2003/50 Art.2

Sch.8 para.37, varied: SI 2003/50 Art.2

Sch.9 Part 1, varied: SI 2003/50 Art.2

Sch.9 Part 2, varied: SI 2003/50 Art.2

Sch.9 Part 3, varied: SI 2003/50 Art.2

18. Appropriation Act 2002

repealed: 2004 c.9 Sch.3

21. Tax Credits Act 2002

Commencement Orders: SI 2002/1727 Art.2, 2003 c.1 Sch.8 Part 1; SI 2003/392 Art.2, Art.3; SI 2003/938 Art.2; SI 2003/962 Art.2, Art.3, Art.5, Sch.1, Sch.2

applied: 1971 c.32 s.24, 1987 c.18 s.73, SI 1987/1971 Reg.25, Reg.68, SI 1992/1814 Reg.17, Reg.24, Reg.59, 1996 c.56 s.512ZB, s.457, SI 1996/2447 Sch.2 para.5, SI 1999/991 Sch.3B para.3, SSI 2001/222 Reg.18, SSI 2001/223 Sch.1 para.17, 2002 c.32 s.151, SI 2002/2006 Reg.7, SI 2002/2926 Reg.1, SI 2002/3196 Reg.24, Reg.25, SI 2003/493 Reg.10, SI 2003/653 Reg.3

referred to: 2003 c.1 Sch.6 para.264, SI 2003/692 Reg.2, SR 2003/213 Reg.1

Part 1, applied: 1992 c.4 s.30C, s.42, SI 1997/790 Reg.4, 1998 c.47 Sch.2 para.10A, SI 1999/3441 Reg.2, SI 2002/195 Reg.15, Sch.3 para.1, SI 2002/1330 Sch.3 para.1, SI 2002/3200 Reg.15, Reg.16, Sch.3 para.1, 2003 c.1 s.677, SI 2003/653 Reg.4, SI 2003/654 Reg.3, SI 2003/1994 Sch.2 para.14, SI 2003/2098 Reg.8, SI 2004/683 Reg.8

Part 3, applied: SI 1997/790 Reg.4

s.1, applied: SI 2002/2402, SR 2003/1

s.1, referred to: SI 2003/653 Reg.3, Reg.5, SI 2003/654 Reg.7

s.3, amended: 2004 c.33 Sch.24 para.144

s.3, applied: SI 2002/2014 Reg.21

s.3, referred to: SI 1999/687 Art.5, SI 1999/689 Art.5, SI 1999/690 Art.4, SI 2004/3114 Art.3, SI 2004/3121 Art.4

s.3, varied: SI 2003/742 Reg.4

s.3, enabling: SI 2003/654, SI 2003/742, SI 2004/1243

s.4, amended: 2004 c.33 Sch.24 para.145, Sch.24 para.146

s.4, varied: SI 2003/742 Reg.5

2002–cont.

21. Tax Credits Act 2002–*cont.*

s.4, enabling: SI 2002/2014, SI 2003/723, SI 2003/742, SI 2003/2815, SI 2003/3240, SI 2004/762

s.5, applied: SI 2002/2014 Reg.27

s.6, enabling: SI 2002/2014, SI 2003/723, SI 2003/742, SI 2003/2815, SI 2003/3240, SI 2004/762, SI 2004/1241

s.7, applied: SI 2002/1727 Art.3, SI 2002/2006, SI 2002/2008 Reg.3, Reg.4, Reg.5, Reg.6, SI 2002/2173 Reg.12A, SI 2003/381 Reg.3, SI 2003/383 Art.3, SI 2003/860 Reg.4, SI 2003/879 Art.3, SSI 2001/222 Reg.18, SSI 2001/223 Sch.1 para.17, SSI 2003/350 Reg.3

s.7, varied: SI 2002/1727 Art.3, SI 2003/742 Reg.6

s.7, enabling: SI 2002/2006, SI 2003/732, SI 2003/742, SI 2003/2815, SI 2004/762, SI 2004/941, SI 2004/2663

s.8, varied: SI 2003/742 Reg.7

s.8, enabling: SI 2002/2007, SI 2002/2008, SI 2003/738, SI 2003/742, SI 2003/2815, SI 2004/762

s.9, applied: SI 1992/1813 Reg.35A, SI 2001/157 Reg.10, SI 2002/2007, SI 2002/2007 Reg.8, SI 2002/2008 Reg.8, SSI 2004/83 Reg.3

s.9, varied: SI 2003/742 Reg.8

s.9, enabling: SI 2002/2007, SI 2003/2815, SI 2004/941

s.10, applied: SI 1992/1989 Reg.8, SI 2001/156 Reg.7

s.10, varied: SI 2003/742 Reg.9

s.10, enabling: SI 2002/2005, SI 2003/701, SI 2003/742, SI 2003/2815, SI 2004/762

s.11, amended: 2004 c.33 Sch.24 para.145

s.11, applied: SI 2002/2005

s.11, varied: SI 2003/742 Reg.10

s.11, enabling: SI 2002/2005, SI 2003/701, SI 2003/742, SI 2003/2815, SI 2004/941

s.12, applied: SI 2002/2005, SI 2002/2005 Reg.14, SI 2002/3196 Reg.27, SI 2003/463, SI 2003/469

s.12, varied: SI 2003/742 Reg.11

s.12, enabling: SI 2002/2005, SI 2003/463, SI 2003/701, SI 2003/742, SI 2003/2815, SI 2004/762, SI 2004/1276, SI 2004/2663

s.13, applied: SI 2002/3196 Reg.27

s.13, enabling: SI 2002/2008, SI 2004/941

s.14, applied: SI 1986/975 Reg.13, SI 1988/551 Reg.4, SI 1996/1434 Reg.3, Reg.4, Reg.5, Reg.6, Reg.7, Sch.2A para.3, SI 1998/642 Reg.8, SI 2002/2014 Reg.26A, Reg.5, Reg.8, Reg.14, Reg.15, Reg.30, Reg.31, Reg.32, SI 2002/2173 Reg.7, Reg.12, SI 2002/3196 Reg.27, SI 2003/692 Reg.3, SI 2003/2382 Reg.5, SSI 2003/376 Reg.4, SSI 2003/460 Reg.4

s.14, varied: SI 2003/653 Reg.4, SI 2003/742 Reg.12

2002–cont.

21. Tax Credits Act 2002–*cont.*

s.14, enabling: SI 2002/2014

s.15, applied: SI 2002/2014 Reg.26A, Reg.26, Reg.30, Reg.31, Reg.32, SI 2002/2173 Reg.12, SI 2003/692 Reg.3

s.15, varied: SI 2003/653 Reg.4

s.15, enabling: SI 2002/2014

s.16, applied: SI 2002/2014 Reg.20, Reg.30, Reg.31, Reg.32, SI 2002/2173 Reg.11, Reg.12, SI 2003/692 Reg.3

s.16, varied: SI 2003/653 Reg.4, SI 2003/742 Reg.13

s.16, enabling: SI 2002/2014

s.17, amended: 2004 c.33 Sch.24 para.145, Sch.24 para.146

s.17, applied: SI 2002/2014 Reg.11, Reg.12, Reg.13, Reg.29, Reg.33, Reg.34, Reg.35, Reg.36, SI 2002/2173 Reg.7, SI 2002/3237 Reg.19, SR 2003/18 Reg.19

s.17, varied: SI 2003/653 Reg.4, SI 2003/742 Reg.14

s.17, enabling: SI 2002/2014, SI 2004/762

s.18, applied: SI 2002/2014 Reg.15, Reg.32, SI 2002/2173 Reg.7, SI 2003/692 Reg.3, 2004 c.6 s.9, SI 2004/1450 Reg.22

s.18, varied: SI 2003/653 Reg.4, SI 2003/742 Reg.15

s.19, applied: SI 2002/2014 Reg.30, Reg.31, Reg.32, SI 2002/3196 Reg.3, SI 2002/3237 Reg.19, SI 2003/692 Reg.3, SR 2002/403 Reg.3, SR 2003/18 Reg.19, 2004 c.6 s.9, SI 2004/1450 Reg.22

s.19, varied: SI 2003/653 Reg.4, SI 2003/742 Reg.16

s.19, enabling: SI 2002/2014

s.20, applied: SI 2003/692 Reg.3, 2004 c.6 s.9, SI 2004/1450 Reg.22

s.20, varied: SI 2003/742 Reg.17

s.21, applied: 2004 c.6 s.9, SI 2004/1450 Reg.22

s.21, enabling: SI 2003/692

s.22, enabling: SI 2002/2014, SI 2003/2815, SI 2004/762, SI 2004/1241

s.23, applied: SI 2002/2014 Reg.20

s.24, amended: 2004 c.33 Sch.24 para.145

s.24, applied: SI 2002/2173 Reg.3, Reg.4, Reg.5, Reg.6, Reg.7, Reg.12

s.24, varied: SI 2003/742 Reg.18

s.24, enabling: SI 2002/2173, SI 2003/723, SI 2003/742, SI 2004/1241

s.25, amended: 2003 c.1 Sch.6 para.265

s.25, applied: 1996 c.18 s.47D, s.104B, s.49, SI 2002/2014 Reg.30, SI 2002/2172 Reg.2

s.25, repealed (in part): 2003 c.1 Sch.8 Part 1

s.25, enabling: SI 2002/2172, SI 2003/715, SI 2004/762

s.29, amended: 2003 c.1 Sch.6 para.266

s.29, applied: SI 2002/2173 Reg.12A

s.29, varied: SI 2003/742 Reg.19

s.29, enabling: SI 2004/762

2002–cont.

21. Tax Credits Act 2002–*cont.*
s.31, applied: SI 2003/123 Reg.3
s.31, varied: SI 2003/742 Reg.20
s.32, amended: 2004 c.33 Sch.24 para.145
s.32, applied: SI 2003/123 Reg.3
s.33, applied: SI 2003/123 Reg.3
s.37, applied: SI 2003/123 Reg.3
s.37, varied: SI 2003/742 Reg.21
s.37, enabling: SI 2003/123
s.38, applied: SI 2003/1382 Reg.3
s.39, applied: SI 2002/3119 Reg.2, SI 2002/
3196 Reg.5, Reg.16, SR 2002/403 Reg.5
s.39, referred to: SI 2002/3196 Reg.4, Reg.5,
SR 2002/403 Reg.4, Reg.5, Reg.16
s.39, enabling: SI 2002/3119, SI 2003/1382
s.41, referred to: SI 2004/941
s.42, enabling: SI 2003/653, SI 2003/742
s.43, enabling: SI 2003/742, SI 2004/762
s.48, amended: 2004 c.33 Sch.30
s.48, substituted: 2004 c.33 Sch.24 para.147
s.49, enabling: SI 2003/493
s.50, referred to: SI 2003/916 Reg.1
s.50, enabling: SI 2003/492, SI 2003/916, SI
2003/1945, SI 2003/2106, SI 2003/2107
s.52, enabling: SI 2003/457
s.54, enabling: SI 2003/492, SI 2003/493, SI
2003/495, SI 2003/916
s.58, enabling: SI 2002/3036, SI 2003/494
s.60, applied: SI 2002/2402
s.61, enabling: SI 2002/1727, SI 2003/392, SI
2003/938, SI 2003/962
s.62, enabling: SI 2002/1727, SI 2002/2158,
SI 2003/392, SI 2003/938, SI 2003/962,
SI 2003/2170, SR 2003/212
s.63, applied: SI 2002/3196 Reg.1, SR 2002/
403 Reg.1, SR 2003/18 Reg.1
s.63, enabling: SI 2002/2926, SI 2004/372
s.65, enabling: SI 2002/2005, SI 2002/
2006, SI 2002/2007, SI 2002/2008, SI
2002/2014, SI 2002/2172, SI 2002/2173,
SI 2002/2926, SI 2002/3036, SI 2002/
3119, SI 2003/123, SI 2003/463, SI
2003/494, SI 2003/653, SI 2003/654,
SI 2003/692, SI 2003/701, SI 2003/715,
SI 2003/723, SI 2003/731, SI 2003/732,
SI 2003/738, SI 2003/742, SI 2003/1382,
SI 2003/1650, SI 2003/2041, SI 2003/
2815, SI 2003/3240, SI 2003/3308, SI
2004/372, SI 2004/762, SI 2004/941, SI
2004/1241, SI 2004/1243, SI 2004/1276,
SI 2004/1414, SI 2004/1895, SI 2004/
2663
s.66, applied: SI 2004/941
s.67, enabling: SI 2002/2005, SI 2002/
2006, SI 2002/2007, SI 2002/2008, SI
2002/2014, SI 2002/2172, SI 2002/2173,
SI 2002/3119, SI 2003/123, SI 2003/701,
SI 2003/715, SI 2003/723, SI 2003/731,
SI 2003/732, SI 2003/1382, SI 2003/
1650, SI 2003/2041, SI 2003/2815, SI
2003/3308, SI 2004/762, SI 2004/1241,

2002–cont.

21. Tax Credits Act 2002–*cont.*
s.67, enabling:–*cont.*
SI 2004/1243, SI 2004/1414, SI 2004/
1895, SI 2004/2663
Sch.2, applied: SI 2002/2926 Reg.5, Reg.6,
Reg.7
Sch.2 para.3, applied: SI 2002/3196 Reg.20,
SR 2002/403 Reg.20
Sch.2 para.4, applied: SI 1994/1443 Sch.2
para.41.25
Sch.3 para.2, repealed: 2003 c.39 Sch.10
Sch.3 para.4, repealed: SI 2003/435 Sch.5
Sch.3 para.5, repealed: SI 2003/435 Sch.5
Sch.3 para.6, repealed: SI 2003/435 Sch.5
Sch.3 para.7, repealed: SI 2003/435 Sch.5
Sch.3 para.14, repealed: 2003 c.1 Sch.8 Part 1
Sch.4 para.15, enabling: SI 2003/916
Sch.4 para.19, enabling: SI 2003/916
Sch.4 para.22, repealed: 2004 c.19 Sch.4
Sch.5 para.4, applied: 1992 c.5 s.122, SI
2003/3308 Reg.2, SI 2004/1414 Reg.2
Sch.5 para.4, enabling: SI 2003/3308, SI
2004/1414
Sch.5 para.5, applied: SI 2003/2041 Reg.2
Sch.5 para.5, enabling: SI 2003/2041
Sch.5 para.6, applied: 1997 c.16 s.110
Sch.5 para.9, applied: SI 2003/731 Reg.3, SI
2003/1650 Reg.2, SI 2004/1895 Reg.2
Sch.5 para.9, enabling: SI 2003/731, SI
2003/1650, SI 2004/1895
Sch.5 para.10A, added: 2004 c.31 s.63
Sch.5 para.10A, varied: 2004 c.31 s.63
Sch.6, applied: SI 2002/2402, SI 2003/2275
Sch.1, SR 2003/1

22. Employment Act 2002
Commencement Orders: SI 2002/1989 Art.2;
SI 2002/2256 Art.2, Sch.1; SI 2002/2866
Art.2, Sch.1 Part 1; SI 2003/1190 Art.2; SI
2003/1666 Art.2; SI 2004/2822 Art.2 (a),
2004/2822 Art.2 (b); SI 2004/1717 Art.2,
Art.3; SI 2002/2866 Sch.1 Part 2; SI
2004/2185 Art.2; SI 2002/2866 Sch.1
Part 3, Sch.2 Part 1, 2, 3
applied: 1999 c.26 s.23, SI 2003/659
referred to: SI 2004/752 Reg.2
enabling: SI 2002/2034, SI 2003/659
Part 3, applied: 1992 c.52 s.145E
s.2, applied: SI 2002/2006 Reg.4, SI 2002/
2818, SI 2002/2819, SI 2002/2821, SI
2002/2822, SI 2003/499, SI 2003/500,
SI 2003/1193, SI 2003/1194
s.4, applied: SI 2002/2818, SI 2002/2819, SI
2002/2821, SI 2002/2822, SI 2003/499,
SI 2003/500, SI 2003/1193, SI 2003/1194
s.7, applied: 1999 c.2 s.8, SI 2002/2820
Reg.3, Reg.5, SI 2002/3047 Reg.5
s.7, enabling: SI 2002/2820, SI 2003/1192
s.8, applied: SI 2002/3047 Reg.5
s.8, enabling: SI 2002/2820, SI 2003/1192
s.10, enabling: SI 2002/2820, SI 2003/1192
s.14, applied: 1997 c.16 s.110

2002–cont.

22. Employment Act 2002–*cont.*

s.29, referred to: SI 2003/1963 Sch.1 para.2

s.30, applied: 1996 c.57 s.17

s.31, applied: 1996 c.18 s.98A, s.124A

s.31, enabling: SI 2004/752

s.32, applied: SI 2004/752 Reg.15, SI 2004/1861 Sch.1 para.1, Sch.1 para.3

s.32, referred to: SI 2004/752 Reg.15, SI 2004/1861 Sch.1 para.1, Sch.1 para.3

s.32, enabling: SI 2004/752

s.33, enabling: SI 2004/752

s.38, applied: 1996 c.18 s.124A

s.41, repealed: 2004 c.24 Sch.2

s.45, enabling: SI 2002/2034

s.51, applied: SI 2002/2034, SI 2004/752

s.51, enabling: SI 2002/2034, SI 2002/2820, SI 2003/1192, SI 2004/752

s.53, applied: SI 2002/2818, SI 2002/2822, SI 2003/500, SI 2003/1194

s.55, enabling: SI 2002/1989, SI 2002/2256, SI 2002/2866, SI 2003/1190, SI 2003/1666, SI 2004/1717, SI 2004/2185, SI 2004/2822

Sch.1 para.8, referred to: 1989 c.26 s.178

Sch.2, applied: SI 1996/3147 Reg.2, SI 2004/752 Reg.8

Sch.2, referred to: SI 2004/752 Reg.2

Sch.2 Part 1, applied: 1996 c.18 s.98A

Sch.2 Part 1 para.1, applied: SI 2004/752 Reg.5, Reg.11

Sch.2 Part 1 para.2, applied: SI 2004/752 Reg.5

Sch.2 Part 1 para.3, applied: SI 2004/752 Reg.5

Sch.2 Part 1 para.3, referred to: SI 2004/752 Reg.7

Sch.2 Part 1 para.4, applied: SI 2004/752 Reg.5, Reg.11

Sch.2 Part 1 para.4, referred to: SI 2004/752 Reg.3

Sch.2 Part 1 para.5, applied: SI 2004/752 Reg.5

Sch.2 Part 1 para.5, referred to: SI 2004/752 Reg.7

Sch.2 Part 2 para.6, applied: SI 2004/752 Reg.6, Reg.8, Reg.11, Reg.14, Reg.15

Sch.2 Part 2 para.7, applied: SI 2004/752 Reg.8

Sch.2 Part 2 para.8, applied: SI 2004/752 Reg.8

Sch.2 Part 2 para.9, applied: SI 2004/752 Reg.6, Reg.11, Reg.14, Reg.15

Sch.2 Part 3, applied: SI 2004/752 Reg.12

Sch.3, amended: 2002 c.21 Sch.6, SI 2003/1660 Sch.5 para.4, SI 2003/1661 Sch.5 para.4, SI 2003/1673 Reg.31, 2004 c.24 Sch.1 para.43

Sch.3, referred to: SI 2004/752 Reg.6, Reg.15

2002–cont.

22. Employment Act 2002–*cont.*

Sch.4, amended: 2002 c.21 Sch.6, SI 2003/1660 Sch.5 para.4, SI 2003/1661 Sch.5 para.4, SI 2003/1673 Reg.31, 2004 c.24 Sch.1 para.43

Sch.4, referred to: SI 2004/752 Reg.6, Reg.15

Sch.5, amended: 2002 c.21 Sch.6, SI 2003/1660 Sch.5 para.4, SI 2003/1661 Sch.5 para.4, SI 2003/1673 Reg.31, 2004 c.24 Sch.1 para.43

Sch.6 para.1, repealed (in part): 2004 c.35 Sch.13 Part 1

Sch.6 para.9, repealed: 2002 c.21 Sch.6

Sch.6 para.10, repealed: 2002 c.21 Sch.6

Sch.7 para.8, applied: SI 2002/2818, SI 2002/2822, SI 2003/500, SI 2003/1194

Sch.7 para.11, applied: SI 2002/2818, SI 2002/2822, SI 2003/500, SI 2003/1194

Sch.7 para.52, repealed: 2002 c.21 Sch.6

23. Finance Act 2002

Commencement Orders: SI 2002/1926 Art.2; SI 2002/3028 Art.2; SI 2002/3056 Art.2; SI 2003/88 Art.2, Art.3; SI 2003/3043 Art.2; SI 2003/3086 Art.2; SI 2004/689 Art.2

applied: 1981 c.63 s.7D, s.7E, s.7F

referred to: 2004 c.12 Sch.5 para.14

varied: SI 2002/1975 Reg.2

s.5, enabling: SI 2002/1926

s.6, enabling: SI 2002/3056

s.19, enabling: SI 2003/3086

s.22, enabling: SI 2002/3028

s.24, enabling: SI 2003/3043

s.33, repealed: 2003 c.1 Sch.8 Part 1

s.34, repealed: 2003 c.1 Sch.8 Part 1

s.35, repealed: 2003 c.1 Sch.8 Part 1

s.36, repealed: 2003 c.1 Sch.8 Part 1

s.37, repealed: 2003 c.1 Sch.8 Part 1

s.38, repealed (in part): 2003 c.1 Sch.8 Part 1

s.39, repealed: 2003 c.1 Sch.8 Part 1

s.40, amended: 2004 c.12 Sch.42 Part 2

s.40, repealed (in part): 2004 c.12 Sch.42 Part 2

s.41, repealed: 2003 c.1 Sch.8 Part 1

s.57, enabling: SI 2003/88

s.66, amended: SI 2004/2200 Reg.11

s.66, applied: 1988 c.1 s.473

s.66, varied: SI 1997/473 Reg.53E

s.72, repealed: 2004 c.12 Sch.42 Part 2

s.73, repealed: 2004 c.12 Sch.42 Part 2

s.74, repealed: 2004 c.12 Sch.42 Part 2

s.75, repealed: 2004 c.12 Sch.42 Part 2

s.76, repealed: 2004 c.12 Sch.42 Part 2

s.77, repealed: 2004 c.12 Sch.42 Part 2

s.79, applied: 2003 c.14 s.177

s.79, referred to: SI 2002/1969 Part 2, Reg.2, Reg.12, Reg.18, Reg.28

s.80, applied: 2003 c.14 s.177

s.80, referred to: 2003 c.14 s.177

s.81, applied: 2003 c.14 s.177

2002–cont.

23. Finance Act 2002–*cont.*

s.81, enabling: SI 2002/1969

s.83, applied: 2003 c.14 s.177

s.96, repealed (in part): 2003 c.14 Sch.43 Part 5

s.98, applied: 1990 c.29 s.25

s.98, disapplied: 2004 c.12 s.83

s.103, amended: 2003 c.1 Sch.8 Part 1, 2004 c.12 Sch.42 Part 2

s.104, repealed (in part): 2003 c.14 Sch.43 Part 3

s.108, repealed (in part): 2004 c.12 Sch.42 Part 2

s.110, enabling: SI 2003/1056

s.111, amended: 2003 c.14 s.126

s.111, varied: 2003 c.14 Sch.19 para.6

s.113, amended: 2003 c.14 s.127

s.113, varied: 2003 c.14 Sch.19 para.6

s.115, amended: 2003 c.14 Sch.20 para.3

s.117, referred to: SI 2004/2421 Reg.2

s.117, enabling: SI 2002/1975, SI 2004/2421

s.123, applied: SI 2003/603 Art.2

s.123, enabling: SI 2003/603

s.126, applied: SI 2003/2622 Art.2

s.126, enabling: SI 2003/2622

s.134, referred to: 2004 c.12 s.322

s.134, varied: 2004 c.12 s.322

s.135, applied: SI 1993/744 Reg.46ZC, SI 2001/1004 Reg.90A, SI 2003/2682 Reg.205

s.135, enabling: SI 2004/1864

s.136, enabling: SI 2003/2494

s.137, amended: 2004 c.12 s.292

s.139, enabling: SI 2002/2521

s.140, applied: SI 2004/1486 Art.1, Art.3

s.140, referred to: SI 2004/1662 Art.2

s.140, enabling: SI 2004/689, SI 2004/1486, SI 2004/1662, SI 2004/2744

s.141, referred to: SI 2002/1969 Part 2, Reg.2, Reg.12, Reg.18, Reg.28

Sch.6 para.1, repealed: 2003 c.1 Sch.8 Part 1

Sch.6 para.2, repealed: 2003 c.1 Sch.8 Part 1

Sch.6 para.3, repealed: 2003 c.1 Sch.8 Part 1

Sch.6 para.4, repealed: 2003 c.1 Sch.8 Part 1

Sch.6 para.5, repealed: 2003 c.1 Sch.8 Part 1

Sch.6 para.6, repealed: 2003 c.1 Sch.8 Part 1

Sch.8 Part 1 para.1, amended: 2003 c.14 Sch.20 para.3

Sch.12, applied: 2000 c.17 Sch.20 para.8, 2003 c.14 s.168, 2004 c.12 s.53

Sch.12 Part 1 para.1, amended: 2003 c.14 Sch.31 para.9

Sch.12 Part 1 para.4, amended: 2003 c.14 Sch.31 para.10, 2004 c.12 s.141

Sch.12 Part 2 para.7, amended: 2003 c.14 Sch.31 para.12, Sch.31 para.13, Sch.43 Part 3

Sch.12 Part 2 para.8, applied: 2000 c.17 Sch.20 para.1

Sch.12 Part 2 para.9, amended: 2003 c.14 Sch.31 para.14, 2004 c.12 s.141

2002–cont.

23. Finance Act 2002–*cont.*

Sch.12 Part 2A para.10A, added: 2003 c.14 Sch.31 para.15

Sch.12 Part 2A para.10B, added: 2003 c.14 Sch.31 para.15

Sch.12 Part 2A para.10B, referred to: 2000 c.17 Sch.20 para.1

Sch.12 Part 3 para.11, amended: 2003 c.14 Sch.31 para.17, Sch.43 Part 3

Sch.12 Part 4 para.13, amended: SI 2004/2310 Sch.1 para.64

Sch.12 Part 4 para.13, applied: 1988 c.1 s.76

Sch.12 Part 5 para.15, amended: 2003 c.14 Sch.31 para.18, Sch.43 Part 3

Sch.12 Part 6 para.17, amended: 2003 c.14 Sch.31 para.19, Sch.43 Part 3, 2004 c.12 s.141

Sch.12 Part 6 para.17, applied: 2003 c.14 s.168

Sch.13, applied: 1988 c.1 s.826, 1998 c.36 Sch.18 para.83M, Sch.18 para.83R, Sch.18 para.52, 2000 c.17 Sch.20 para.8, SI 2003/1472, 2004 c.12 s.53

Sch.13 Part 1 para.1, amended: 2003 c.14 Sch.31 para.21

Sch.13 Part 1 para.3, amended: 2003 c.14 Sch.31 para.22, 2004 c.12 s.141

Sch.13 Part 1 para.5, amended: 2003 c.14 Sch.31 para.23, Sch.43 Part 3, 2004 c.12 s.141

Sch.13 Part 1 para.9, amended: 2003 c.14 Sch.31 para.24, 2004 c.12 s.141

Sch.13 Part 4 para.23, amended: SI 2004/2310 Sch.1 para.65

Sch.13 Part 4 para.23, applied: 1988 c.1 s.76

Sch.13 Part 5 para.27, amended: 2003 c.1 Sch.8 Part 1

Sch.13 Part 5 para.28, enabling: SI 2003/1472

Sch.14, applied: SI 2003/1472

Sch.16 Part 2 para.4, applied: SI 2003/96 Reg.3

Sch.16 Part 2 para.4, enabling: SI 2003/96

Sch.16 Part 2 para.5, enabling: SI 2003/96

Sch.16 Part 5, applied: 1998 c.36 Sch.18 para.8

Sch.16 Part 5 para.19, applied: 1988 c.1 s.289A, Sch.15B para.1

Sch.16 Part 5 para.19, referred to: 1990 c.29 s.25

Sch.18, applied: 1988 c.41 s.43, s.45, s.46, s.48, s.67, SI 1999/3379 Reg.10, Reg.13, Sch.2 para.4, Sch.2 para.5, Sch.2 para.6, SI 2002/1966 Art.2

Sch.18 Part 2 para.4, amended: 2004 c.12 s.56

Sch.18 Part 2 para.6, amended: 2004 c.12 s.56

Sch.18 Part 6 para.14, enabling: SI 2002/1966

Sch.22, applied: 1999 c.16 s.81

Sch.22 Part 2 para.4, amended: 2004 c.12 Sch.35 para.51

2002–cont.

23. Finance Act 2002–*cont.*

Sch.22 Part 3 para.10, amended: 2003 c.14 s.153, SI 2004/2200 Reg.11

Sch.22 Part 3 para.10, varied: SI 1997/473 Reg.53F

Sch.23 Part 1 para.4, repealed: 2004 c.12 Sch.42 Part 2

Sch.23 Part 1 para.5, repealed: 2004 c.12 Sch.42 Part 2

Sch.23 Part 1 para.8, repealed: 2004 c.12 Sch.42 Part 2

Sch.23 Part 3 para.26, enabling: SI 2002/1970, SI 2004/3259

Sch.24, applied: 2003 c.14 s.177

Sch.24, referred to: 2003 c.14 s.177

Sch.24 para.1, repealed: 2004 c.12 Sch.42 Part 2

Sch.24 para.2, repealed: 2004 c.12 Sch.42 Part 2

Sch.24 para.3, repealed: 2004 c.12 Sch.42 Part 2

Sch.24 para.4, repealed: 2004 c.12 Sch.42 Part 2

Sch.24 para.5, repealed: 2004 c.12 Sch.42 Part 2

Sch.24 para.6, repealed: 2004 c.12 Sch.42 Part 2

Sch.25 Part 1 para.4, repealed: 2004 c.12 Sch.42 Part 2

Sch.25 Part 1 para.5, repealed: 2004 c.12 Sch.42 Part 2

Sch.25 Part 1 para.6, repealed: 2004 c.12 Sch.42 Part 2led: 2004 c.12 Sch.42 Part 2

Sch.25 Part 1 para.12, repealed: 2004 c.12 Sch.42 Part 2

Sch.25 Part 2 para.46, repealed: 2003 c.14 Sch.43 Part 3

Sch.25 Part 2 para.58, repealed (in part): SI 2004/2310 Sch.1 para.66

Sch.25 Part 3 para.61A, added: 2003 c.14 Sch.37 para.6

Sch.26, applied: 1988 c.1 s.730A, s.440, Sch.28AA para.8, Sch.27 para.5, 1994 c.9 s.226, 1996 c.8 s.94A, s.86, 2000 c.17 Sch.22 para.50, Sch.22 para.63, 2003 c.14 s.177, 2004 c.12 Sch.10 para.12, 2004 c.20 s.27, Sch.9 para.33, SI 2004/1863 Sch.1 para.7

Sch.26, disapplied: 1996 c.8 s.101

Sch.26, referred to: 1988 c.1 s.501A, s.15, 2004 c.12 Sch.9 para.1

Sch.26 Part 1 para.1, varied: 2004 c.20 Sch.9 para.12, Sch.9 para.24

Sch.26 Part 2 para.2, amended: SI 2004/2201 Art.3, SI 2004/3270 Art.3

Sch.26 Part 2 para.2, varied: 2004 c.20 Sch.9 para.12, Sch.9 para.24

Sch.26 Part 2 para.3, amended: SI 2004/2201 Art.4

Sch.26 Part 2 para.3, repealed (in part): SI 2004/2201 Art.4

2002–cont.

23. Finance Act 2002–*cont.*

Sch.26 Part 2 para.3, varied: 2004 c.20 Sch.9 para.12, Sch.9 para.24

Sch.26 Part 2 para.4, amended: SI 2004/2201 Art.5

Sch.26 Part 2 para.4, disapplied: SI 2004/1863 Sch.1 para.7

Sch.26 Part 2 para.4, repealed (in part): SI 2004/2201 Art.5

Sch.26 Part 2 para.4, varied: 2004 c.20 Sch.9 para.12, Sch.9 para.24

Sch.26 Part 2 para.5, amended: SI 2004/2201 Art.6

Sch.26 Part 2 para.5, repealed (in part): SI 2004/2201 Art.6

Sch.26 Part 2 para.5, varied: 2004 c.20 Sch.9 para.12, Sch.9 para.24

Sch.26 Part 2 para.5A, added: SI 2004/2201 Art.7

Sch.26 Part 2 para.5A, amended: SI 2004/3270 Art.4

Sch.26 Part 2 para.5A, repealed (in part): SI 2004/3270 Art.4

Sch.26 Part 2 para.5A, varied: 2004 c.20 Sch.9 para.12, Sch.9 para.24

Sch.26 Part 2 para.6, amended: SI 2004/2201 Art.8

Sch.26 Part 2 para.6, applied: 1996 c.8 s.93A

Sch.26 Part 2 para.6, referred to: 1996 c.8 s.93A

Sch.26 Part 2 para.6, repealed (in part): SI 2004/2201 Art.8

Sch.26 Part 2 para.6, varied: 2004 c.20 Sch.9 para.12, Sch.9 para.24

Sch.26 Part 2 para.7, amended: SI 2004/2201 Art.9

Sch.26 Part 2 para.7, repealed (in part): SI 2004/2201 Art.9

Sch.26 Part 2 para.7, varied: 2004 c.20 Sch.9 para.12, Sch.9 para.24

Sch.26 Part 2 para.8, amended: SI 2004/2201 Art.10

Sch.26 Part 2 para.8, repealed (in part): SI 2004/2201 Art.10

Sch.26 Part 2 para.8, varied: 2004 c.20 Sch.9 para.12, Sch.9 para.24

Sch.26 Part 2 para.9, amended: SI 2004/2201 Art.11

Sch.26 Part 2 para.9, repealed (in part): SI 2004/2201 Art.11

Sch.26 Part 2 para.9, varied: 2004 c.20 Sch.9 para.12, Sch.9 para.24

Sch.26 Part 2 para.10, varied: 2004 c.20 Sch.9 para.12, Sch.9 para.24

Sch.26 Part 2 para.11, amended: SI 2004/2201 Art.12

Sch.26 Part 2 para.11, applied: 1996 c.8 s.93A

Sch.26 Part 2 para.11, varied: 2004 c.20 Sch.9 para.12, Sch.9 para.24

Sch.26 Part 2 para.12, amended: SI 2004/2201 Art.13

2002–cont.

23. Finance Act 2002–*cont.*

Sch.26 Part 2 para.12, varied: 2004 c.20 Sch.9 para.12, Sch.9 para.24

Sch.26 Part 2 para.13, amended: 2004 c.12 Sch.9 para.2

Sch.26 Part 2 para.13, varied: 2004 c.20 Sch.9 para.12, Sch.9 para.24

Sch.26 Part 2 para.13, enabling: SI 2004/2201, SI 2004/3270

Sch.26 Part 3 para.14, applied: 1988 c.1 s.768C, s.768, s.768B

Sch.26 Part 3 para.14, varied: 2004 c.20 Sch.9 para.12, Sch.9 para.24

Sch.26 Part 3 para.15, amended: 2004 c.12 Sch.10 para.47, Sch.42 Part 2

Sch.26 Part 3 para.15, repealed (in part): 2004 c.12 Sch.42 Part 2

Sch.26 Part 3 para.15, varied: 2004 c.20 Sch.9 para.12, Sch.9 para.24

Sch.26 Part 3 para.16, amended: 2004 c.12 Sch.10 para.48

Sch.26 Part 3 para.16, applied: SI 2002/1970 Reg.3, Reg.7

Sch.26 Part 3 para.16, referred to: SI 2002/1970 Reg.3, Reg.7

Sch.26 Part 3 para.16, repealed (in part): 2004 c.12 Sch.42 Part 2

Sch.26 Part 3 para.16, varied: 2004 c.20 Sch.9 para.12, Sch.9 para.24

Sch.26 Part 3 para.16, enabling: SI 2002/1970, SI 2004/3256, SI 2004/3259

Sch.26 Part 4 para.17, amended: 2004 c.12 Sch.10 para.49

Sch.26 Part 4 para.17, substituted: 2004 c.12 Sch.10 para.50

Sch.26 Part 4 para.17, varied: 2004 c.20 Sch.9 para.12, Sch.9 para.24

Sch.26 Part 4 para.17A, amended: 2004 c.12 Sch.10 para.49

Sch.26 Part 4 para.17A, substituted: 2004 c.12 Sch.10 para.50

Sch.26 Part 4 para.17A, varied: 2004 c.20 Sch.9 para.12, Sch.9 para.24

Sch.26 Part 4 para.17B, amended: 2004 c.12 Sch.10 para.49

Sch.26 Part 4 para.17B, substituted: 2004 c.12 Sch.10 para.50

Sch.26 Part 4 para.17B, varied: 2004 c.20 Sch.9 para.12, Sch.9 para.24

Sch.26 Part 4 para.17C, amended: 2004 c.12 Sch.10 para.49

Sch.26 Part 4 para.17C, substituted: 2004 c.12 Sch.10 para.50

Sch.26 Part 4 para.17C, varied: 2004 c.20 Sch.9 para.12, Sch.9 para.24

Sch.26 Part 4 para.17C, enabling: SI 2004/3256, SI 2004/3271

Sch.26 Part 4 para.18, amended: 2004 c.12 Sch.10 para.49

Sch.26 Part 4 para.18, substituted: 2004 c.12 Sch.10 para.50

2002–cont.

23. Finance Act 2002–*cont.*

Sch.26 Part 4 para.18, varied: 2004 c.20 Sch.9 para.12, Sch.9 para.24

Sch.26 Part 4 para.19, amended: 2004 c.12 Sch.10 para.49

Sch.26 Part 4 para.19, applied: 1996 c.8 s.86

Sch.26 Part 4 para.19, disapplied: 1996 c.8 s.86

Sch.26 Part 4 para.19, substituted: 2004 c.12 Sch.10 para.50

Sch.26 Part 4 para.19, varied: 2004 c.20 Sch.9 para.12, Sch.9 para.24

Sch.26 Part 4 para.20, amended: 2004 c.12 Sch.10 para.49

Sch.26 Part 4 para.20, substituted: 2004 c.12 Sch.10 para.50

Sch.26 Part 4 para.20, varied: 2004 c.20 Sch.9 para.12, Sch.9 para.24

Sch.26 Part 4 para.21, amended: 2004 c.12 Sch.10 para.49, Sch.10 para.51

Sch.26 Part 4 para.21, varied: 2004 c.20 Sch.9 para.12, Sch.9 para.24

Sch.26 Part 5 para.22, amended: 2004 c.12 Sch.10 para.52, Sch.10 para.53

Sch.26 Part 5 para.22, repealed (in part): 2004 c.12 Sch.42 Part 2

Sch.26 Part 5 para.22, varied: 2004 c.20 Sch.9 para.12, Sch.9 para.24

Sch.26 Part 6 para.22A, added: 2004 c.12 Sch.9 para.3

Sch.26 Part 6 para.22A, repealed (in part): 2004 c.12 Sch.42 Part 2

Sch.26 Part 6 para.22A, varied: 2004 c.20 Sch.9 para.12, Sch.9 para.24

Sch.26 Part 6 para.23, amended: 2004 c.12 Sch.9 para.4, Sch.42 Part 2

Sch.26 Part 6 para.23, varied: 2004 c.20 Sch.9 para.12, Sch.9 para.24

Sch.26 Part 6 para.24, varied: 2004 c.20 Sch.9 para.12, Sch.9 para.24

Sch.26 Part 6 para.25, amended: 2004 c.12 Sch.10 para.56, Sch.42 Part 2

Sch.26 Part 6 para.25, varied: 2004 c.20 Sch.9 para.12, Sch.9 para.24

Sch.26 Part 6 para.26, varied: 2004 c.20 Sch.9 para.12, Sch.9 para.24

Sch.26 Part 6 para.27, referred to: 1988 c.1 Sch.28AA para.8

Sch.26 Part 6 para.27, varied: 2004 c.20 Sch.9 para.12, Sch.9 para.24

Sch.26 Part 6 para.28, amended: 2003 c.14 s.179, 2004 c.12 Sch.5 para.15, SI 2004/2200 Reg.11

Sch.26 Part 6 para.28, varied: SI 1997/473 Reg.53G, 2004 c.20 Sch.9 para.12, Sch.9 para.24

Sch.26 Part 6 para.29, varied: 2004 c.20 Sch.9 para.12, Sch.9 para.24

Sch.26 Part 6 para.30, amended: 2004 c.12 Sch.10 para.57

2002–cont.

23. Finance Act 2002–*cont.*

Sch.26 Part 6 para.30, substituted: 2003 c.14 s.179

Sch.26 Part 6 para.30, varied: 2004 c.20 Sch.9 para.12, Sch.9 para.24

Sch.26 Part 6 para.31, varied: 2003 c.14 s.153, 2004 c.20 Sch.9 para.12, Sch.9 para.24

Sch.26 Part 6 para.31A, added: 2004 c.12 Sch.5 para.15

Sch.26 Part 6 para.31A, amended: 2004 c.12 Sch.42 Part 2

Sch.26 Part 6 para.31A, varied: 2004 c.20 Sch.9 para.12, Sch.9 para.24

Sch.26 Part 7 para.32, amended: 2004 c.12 Sch.10 para.59, Sch.42 Part 2

Sch.26 Part 7 para.32, varied: 2004 c.20 Sch.9 para.12, Sch.9 para.24

Sch.26 Part 7 para.33, amended: 2004 c.12 Sch.10 para.60, Sch.42 Part 2

Sch.26 Part 7 para.33, varied: 2004 c.20 Sch.9 para.12, Sch.9 para.24

Sch.26 Part 7 para.34, amended: 2004 c.12 Sch.10 para.61

Sch.26 Part 7 para.34, varied: 2004 c.20 Sch.9 para.12, Sch.9 para.24

Sch.26 Part 7 para.35, repealed: 2004 c.12 Sch.42 Part 2

Sch.26 Part 7 para.35, varied: 2004 c.20 Sch.9 para.12, Sch.9 para.24, SI 2004/ 2572 Reg.6, Reg.7

Sch.26 Part 7 para.36, amended: 2004 c.12 Sch.10 para.62

Sch.26 Part 7 para.36, varied: 2004 c.20 Sch.9 para.12, Sch.9 para.24

Sch.26 Part 7 para.37, varied: 2004 c.20 Sch.9 para.12, Sch.9 para.24

Sch.26 Part 7 para.38, substituted: 2004 c.12 Sch.10 para.63

Sch.26 Part 7 para.38, varied: 2004 c.20 Sch.9 para.12, Sch.9 para.24

Sch.26 Part 7 para.38A, varied: 2004 c.20 Sch.9 para.12, Sch.9 para.24

Sch.26 Part 7 para.39, varied: 2004 c.20 Sch.9 para.12, Sch.9 para.24

Sch.26 Part 7 para.40, varied: 2004 c.20 Sch.9 para.12, Sch.9 para.24

Sch.26 Part 8 para.41, varied: 2004 c.20 Sch.9 para.12, Sch.9 para.24

Sch.26 Part 8 para.42, amended: SI 2004/ 2201 Art.18

Sch.26 Part 8 para.42, varied: 2004 c.20 Sch.9 para.12, Sch.9 para.24

Sch.26 Part 8 para.43, varied: 2004 c.20 Sch.9 para.12, Sch.9 para.24

Sch.26 Part 9 para.44, varied: 2004 c.20 Sch.9 para.12, Sch.9 para.24

Sch.26 Part 9 para.45, varied: 2004 c.20 Sch.9 para.12, Sch.9 para.24

Sch.26 Part 9 para.45A, added: SI 2004/ 2201 Art.15

2002–cont.

23. Finance Act 2002–*cont.*

Sch.26 Part 9 para.45A, varied: 2004 c.20 Sch.9 para.12, Sch.9 para.24

Sch.26 Part 9 para.45B, added: SI 2004/ 2201 Art.15

Sch.26 Part 9 para.45B, varied: 2004 c.20 Sch.9 para.12, Sch.9 para.24

Sch.26 Part 9 para.45C, added: SI 2004/ 2201 Art.15

Sch.26 Part 9 para.45C, varied: 2004 c.20 Sch.9 para.12, Sch.9 para.24

Sch.26 Part 9 para.45D, added: SI 2004/ 2201 Art.15

Sch.26 Part 9 para.45D, amended: SI 2004/ 3270 Art.6

Sch.26 Part 9 para.45D, varied: 2004 c.20 Sch.9 para.12, Sch.9 para.24

Sch.26 Part 9 para.45E, added: SI 2004/ 2201 Art.15

Sch.26 Part 9 para.45E, varied: 2004 c.20 Sch.9 para.12, Sch.9 para.24

Sch.26 Part 9 para.45F, added: SI 2004/ 2201 Art.15

Sch.26 Part 9 para.45F, amended: SI 2004/ 3270 Art.7

Sch.26 Part 9 para.45F, varied: 2004 c.20 Sch.9 para.12, Sch.9 para.24

Sch.26 Part 9 para.45G, added: SI 2004/ 2201 Art.15

Sch.26 Part 9 para.45G, amended: SI 2004/ 3270 Art.8

Sch.26 Part 9 para.45G, varied: 2004 c.20 Sch.9 para.12, Sch.9 para.24

Sch.26 Part 9 para.45H, added: SI 2004/ 2201 Art.15

Sch.26 Part 9 para.45H, repealed: SI 2004/ 3270 Art.9

Sch.26 Part 9 para.45H, varied: 2004 c.20 Sch.9 para.12, Sch.9 para.24

Sch.26 Part 9 para.45I, added: SI 2004/2201 Art.15

Sch.26 Part 9 para.45I, varied: 2004 c.20 Sch.9 para.12, Sch.9 para.24

Sch.26 Part 9 para.46, amended: SI 2004/ 2201 Art.16

Sch.26 Part 9 para.46, varied: 2004 c.20 Sch.9 para.12, Sch.9 para.24

Sch.26 Part 9 para.47, repealed: SI 2004/ 2201 Art.17

Sch.26 Part 9 para.47, varied: 2004 c.20 Sch.9 para.12, Sch.9 para.24

Sch.26 Part 9 para.48, amended: 2004 c.12 Sch.10 para.64

Sch.26 Part 9 para.48, varied: 2004 c.20 Sch.9 para.12, Sch.9 para.24

Sch.26 Part 9 para.49, amended: 2004 c.12 Sch.10 para.65

Sch.26 Part 9 para.49, varied: 2004 c.20 Sch.9 para.12, Sch.9 para.24

Sch.26 Part 9 para.50, substituted: 2004 c.12 Sch.10 para.66

2002–cont.

23. Finance Act 2002–*cont.*

Sch.26 Part 9 para.50, varied: 2004 c.20 Sch.9 para.12, Sch.9 para.24

Sch.26 Part 9 para.50A, added: 2004 c.12 Sch.10 para.67

Sch.26 Part 9 para.50A, varied: 2004 c.20 Sch.9 para.12, Sch.9 para.24

Sch.26 Part 9 para.51, varied: 2004 c.20 Sch.9 para.12, Sch.9 para.24

Sch.26 Part 10 para.52, repealed: 2004 c.12 Sch.42 Part 2

Sch.26 Part 10 para.52, varied: 2004 c.20 Sch.9 para.12, Sch.9 para.24

Sch.26 Part 10 para.53, varied: 2004 c.20 Sch.9 para.12, Sch.9 para.24

Sch.26 Part 10 para.54, amended: 2004 c.12 Sch.10 para.69, Sch.42 Part 2, SI 2004/2201 Art.19

Sch.26 Part 10 para.54, referred to: 1988 c.1 Sch.28AA para.8

Sch.26 Part 10 para.54, varied: 2004 c.20 Sch.9 para.12, Sch.9 para.24

Sch.27, applied: 2003 c.14 s.177

Sch.27 para.18, repealed: 2004 c.12 Sch.42 Part 2

Sch.28, applied: 2003 c.14 s.177

Sch.28 para.1, varied: 2003 c.14 s.177

Sch.28 para.2, varied: 2003 c.14 s.177

Sch.28 para.3, varied: 2003 c.14 s.177

Sch.28 para.4, varied: 2003 c.14 s.177

Sch.28 para.5, varied: 2003 c.14 s.177

Sch.28 para.6, varied: 2003 c.14 s.177

Sch.28 para.7, varied: 2003 c.14 s.177

Sch.29, applied: 1988 c.1 s.338B, s.797B, s.505, 1996 c.8 Sch.9 para.14, SI 2002/1967 Reg.3, 2004 c.20 Sch.9 para.13, Sch.9 para.25

Sch.29, disapplied: SI 2002/1967 Reg.6

Sch.29, referred to: 1988 c.1 s.337A, SI 2002/1967 Reg.6, 2004 c.20 Sch.9 para.28

Sch.29 Part 1 para.1, disapplied: 1988 c.1 s.795, s.811

Sch.29 Part 1 para.1, varied: 1988 c.1 s.768C, SI 2002/1967 Reg.4, Reg.6, 2004 c.20 Sch.9 para.14

Sch.29 Part 1 para.2, varied: 1988 c.1 s.768C, SI 2002/1967 Reg.4, Reg.6, 2004 c.20 Sch.9 para.14

Sch.29 Part 1 para.3, varied: 1988 c.1 s.768C, SI 2002/1967 Reg.4, Reg.6, 2004 c.20 Sch.9 para.14

Sch.29 Part 1 para.4, varied: 1988 c.1 s.768C, SI 2002/1967 Reg.4, Reg.6, 2004 c.20 Sch.9 para.14

Sch.29 Part 1 para.5, varied: 1988 c.1 s.768C, SI 2002/1967 Reg.4, Reg.6, 2004 c.20 Sch.9 para.14

Sch.29 Part 1 para.6, varied: 1988 c.1 s.768C, SI 2002/1967 Reg.4, Reg.6, 2004 c.20 Sch.9 para.14

2002–cont.

23. Finance Act 2002–*cont.*

Sch.29 Part 2 para.7, varied: 1988 c.1 s.768C, SI 2002/1967 Reg.4, Reg.6, 2004 c.20 Sch.9 para.14

Sch.29 Part 2 para.8, varied: 1988 c.1 s.768C, SI 2002/1967 Reg.4, Reg.6, 2004 c.20 Sch.9 para.14

Sch.29 Part 2 para.9, varied: 1988 c.1 s.768C, SI 2002/1967 Reg.4, Reg.6, 2004 c.20 Sch.9 para.14

Sch.29 Part 2 para.10, varied: 1988 c.1 s.768C, SI 2002/1967 Reg.4, Reg.6, 2004 c.20 Sch.9 para.14

Sch.29 Part 2 para.11, varied: 1988 c.1 s.768C, SI 2002/1967 Reg.4, Reg.6, 2004 c.20 Sch.9 para.14

Sch.29 Part 2 para.12, varied: 1988 c.1 s.768C, SI 2002/1967 Reg.4, Reg.6, 2004 c.20 Sch.9 para.14

Sch.29 Part 3 para.13, varied: 1988 c.1 s.768C, SI 2002/1967 Reg.4, Reg.6, 2004 c.20 Sch.9 para.14

Sch.29 Part 3 para.14, varied: 1988 c.1 s.768C, SI 2002/1967 Reg.4, Reg.6, 2004 c.20 Sch.9 para.14

Sch.29 Part 3 para.15, amended: 2004 c.12 Sch.10 para.74

Sch.29 Part 3 para.15, varied: 1988 c.1 s.768C, SI 2002/1967 Reg.4, Reg.6, 2004 c.20 Sch.9 para.14

Sch.29 Part 3 para.16, varied: 1988 c.1 s.768C, SI 2002/1967 Reg.4, Reg.6, 2004 c.20 Sch.9 para.14

Sch.29 Part 3 para.17, varied: 1988 c.1 s.768C, SI 2002/1967 Reg.4, Reg.6, 2004 c.20 Sch.9 para.14

Sch.29 Part 4, applied: SI 2002/1967 Reg.5

Sch.29 Part 4 para.18, varied: 1988 c.1 s.768C, SI 2002/1967 Reg.4, Reg.6, 2004 c.20 Sch.9 para.14

Sch.29 Part 4 para.19, varied: 1988 c.1 s.768C, SI 2002/1967 Reg.4, Reg.6, 2004 c.20 Sch.9 para.14

Sch.29 Part 4 para.20, amended: 2004 c.12 Sch.10 para.75

Sch.29 Part 4 para.20, varied: 1988 c.1 s.768C, SI 2002/1967 Reg.4, Reg.6, 2004 c.20 Sch.9 para.14

Sch.29 Part 4 para.21, varied: 1988 c.1 s.768C, SI 2002/1967 Reg.4, Reg.6, 2004 c.20 Sch.9 para.14

Sch.29 Part 4 para.22, applied: SI 2002/1967 Reg.5

Sch.29 Part 4 para.22, varied: 1988 c.1 s.768C, SI 2002/1967 Reg.4, Reg.6, 2004 c.20 Sch.9 para.14

Sch.29 Part 4 para.23, varied: 1988 c.1 s.768C, SI 2002/1967 Reg.4, Reg.6, 2004 c.20 Sch.9 para.14

Sch.29 Part 4 para.24, varied: 1988 c.1 s.768C, SI 2002/1967 Reg.4, Reg.6, 2004 c.20 Sch.9 para.14

2002–cont.

23. Finance Act 2002–*cont.*

Sch.29 Part 4 para.25, varied: 1988 c.1 s.768C, SI 2002/1967 Reg.4, Reg.6, 2004 c.20 Sch.9 para.14

Sch.29 Part 4 para.26, varied: 1988 c.1 s.768C, SI 2002/1967 Reg.4, Reg.6, 2004 c.20 Sch.9 para.14

Sch.29 Part 5 para.27, amended: 2004 c.12 Sch.10 para.76

Sch.29 Part 5 para.27, varied: 1988 c.1 s.768C, SI 2002/1967 Reg.4, Reg.6, 2004 c.20 Sch.9 para.14

Sch.29 Part 5 para.28, varied: 1988 c.1 s.768C, SI 2002/1967 Reg.4, Reg.6, 2004 c.20 Sch.9 para.14

Sch.29 Part 5 para.29, varied: 1988 c.1 s.768C, SI 2002/1967 Reg.4, Reg.6, 2004 c.20 Sch.9 para.14

Sch.29 Part 6 para.30, varied: 1988 c.1 s.768C, SI 2002/1967 Reg.4, Reg.6, 2004 c.20 Sch.9 para.14

Sch.29 Part 6 para.31, varied: 1988 c.1 s.768C, SI 2002/1967 Reg.4, Reg.6, 2004 c.20 Sch.9 para.14

Sch.29 Part 6 para.32, varied: 1988 c.1 s.768C, SI 2002/1967 Reg.4, Reg.6, 2004 c.20 Sch.9 para.14

Sch.29 Part 6 para.33, varied: 1988 c.1 s.768C, SI 2002/1967 Reg.4, Reg.6, 2004 c.20 Sch.9 para.14

Sch.29 Part 6 para.34, applied: 1988 c.1 Sch.28A para.6, Sch.28A para.13

Sch.29 Part 6 para.34, varied: 1988 c.1 s.768C, SI 2002/1967 Reg.4, Reg.6, 2004 c.20 Sch.9 para.14

Sch.29 Part 6 para.35, applied: 1988 c.1 s.768E, s.797B, Sch.28A para.6, Sch.28A para.13, SI 2001/1757 Reg.3

Sch.29 Part 6 para.35, referred to: 2004 c.20 s.44

Sch.29 Part 6 para.35, varied: 1988 c.1 s.768C, SI 2002/1967 Reg.4, Reg.6, 2004 c.20 Sch.9 para.14

Sch.29 Part 6 para.36, amended: SI 2004/2310 Sch.1 para.67

Sch.29 Part 6 para.36, applied: 1988 c.1 s.76

Sch.29 Part 6 para.36, varied: 1988 c.1 s.768C, SI 1997/473 Reg.53H, SI 2002/1967 Reg.4, Reg.6, 2004 c.20 Sch.9 para.14

Sch.29 Part 7 para.37, varied: 1988 c.1 s.768C, SI 2002/1967 Reg.4, Reg.6, 2004 c.20 Sch.9 para.14

Sch.29 Part 7 para.38, varied: 1988 c.1 s.768C, SI 2002/1967 Reg.4, Reg.6, 2004 c.20 Sch.9 para.14

Sch.29 Part 7 para.39, varied: 1988 c.1 s.768C, SI 2002/1967 Reg.4, Reg.6, 2004 c.20 Sch.9 para.14

Sch.29 Part 7 para.40, varied: 1988 c.1 s.768C, SI 2002/1967 Reg.4, Reg.6, 2004 c.20 Sch.9 para.14

2002–cont.

23. Finance Act 2002–*cont.*

Sch.29 Part 7 para.41, varied: 1988 c.1 s.768C, SI 2002/1967 Reg.4, Reg.6, 2004 c.20 Sch.9 para.14

Sch.29 Part 7 para.42, varied: 1988 c.1 s.768C, SI 2002/1967 Reg.4, Reg.6, 2004 c.20 Sch.9 para.14

Sch.29 Part 7 para.43, varied: 1988 c.1 s.768C, SI 2002/1967 Reg.4, Reg.6, 2004 c.20 Sch.9 para.14

Sch.29 Part 7 para.44, varied: 1988 c.1 s.768C, SI 2002/1967 Reg.4, Reg.6, 2004 c.20 Sch.9 para.14

Sch.29 Part 7 para.45, varied: 1988 c.1 s.768C, SI 2002/1967 Reg.4, Reg.6, 2004 c.20 Sch.9 para.14

Sch.29 Part 8, applied: 2004 c.20 Sch.9 para.28, Sch.9 para.35

Sch.29 Part 8 para.46, varied: 1988 c.1 s.768C, SI 2002/1967 Reg.4, Reg.6, 2004 c.20 Sch.9 para.14

Sch.29 Part 8 para.47, varied: 1988 c.1 s.768C, SI 2002/1967 Reg.4, Reg.6, 2004 c.20 Sch.9 para.14

Sch.29 Part 8 para.48, varied: 1988 c.1 s.768C, SI 2002/1967 Reg.4, Reg.6, 2004 c.20 Sch.9 para.14

Sch.29 Part 8 para.49, varied: 1988 c.1 s.768C, SI 2002/1967 Reg.4, Reg.6, 2004 c.20 Sch.9 para.14

Sch.29 Part 8 para.50, varied: 1988 c.1 s.768C, SI 2002/1967 Reg.4, Reg.6, 2004 c.20 Sch.9 para.14

Sch.29 Part 8 para.51, varied: 1988 c.1 s.768C, SI 2002/1967 Reg.4, Reg.6, 2004 c.20 Sch.9 para.14

Sch.29 Part 8 para.52, varied: 1988 c.1 s.768C, SI 2002/1967 Reg.4, Reg.6, 2004 c.20 Sch.9 para.14

Sch.29 Part 8 para.53, varied: 1988 c.1 s.768C, SI 2002/1967 Reg.4, Reg.6, 2004 c.20 Sch.9 para.14

Sch.29 Part 8 para.54, varied: 1988 c.1 s.768C, SI 2002/1967 Reg.4, Reg.6, 2004 c.20 Sch.9 para.14

Sch.29 Part 9 para.55, amended: 2004 c.12 Sch.5 para.16

Sch.29 Part 9 para.55, varied: 1988 c.1 s.768C, SI 2002/1967 Reg.4, Reg.6, 2004 c.20 Sch.9 para.14

Sch.29 Part 9 para.56, varied: 1988 c.1 s.768C, SI 2002/1967 Reg.4, Reg.6, 2004 c.20 Sch.9 para.14

Sch.29 Part 9 para.57, varied: 1988 c.1 s.768C, SI 2002/1967 Reg.4, Reg.6, 2004 c.20 Sch.9 para.14

Sch.29 Part 9 para.58, disapplied: 2004 c.20 Sch.9 para.14, Sch.9 para.26

Sch.29 Part 9 para.58, varied: 1988 c.1 s.768C, SI 2002/1967 Reg.4, Reg.6, 2004 c.20 Sch.9 para.14, Sch.9 para.26

2002–cont.

23. **Finance Act 2002**–*cont.*

Sch.29 Part 9 para.59, varied: 1988 c.1 s.768C, SI 2002/1967 Reg.4, Reg.6, 2004 c.20 Sch.9 para.14

Sch.29 Part 9 para.60, varied: 1988 c.1 s.768C, SI 2002/1967 Reg.4, Reg.6, 2004 c.20 Sch.9 para.14

Sch.29 Part 9 para.61, varied: 1988 c.1 s.768C, SI 2002/1967 Reg.4, Reg.6, 2004 c.20 Sch.9 para.14

Sch.29 Part 9 para.62, varied: 1988 c.1 s.768C, SI 2002/1967 Reg.4, Reg.6, 2004 c.20 Sch.9 para.14

Sch.29 Part 9 para.63, varied: 1988 c.1 s.768C, SI 2002/1967 Reg.4, Reg.6, 2004 c.20 Sch.9 para.14

Sch.29 Part 9 para.64, varied: 1988 c.1 s.768C, SI 2002/1967 Reg.4, Reg.6, 2004 c.20 Sch.9 para.14

Sch.29 Part 9 para.65, varied: 1988 c.1 s.768C, SI 2002/1967 Reg.4, Reg.6, 2004 c.20 Sch.9 para.14

Sch.29 Part 9 para.66, amended: 2003 c.14 s.153

Sch.29 Part 9 para.66, varied: 1988 c.1 s.768C, SI 2002/1967 Reg.4, Reg.6, 2004 c.20 Sch.9 para.14

Sch.29 Part 9 para.67, varied: 1988 c.1 s.768C, SI 2002/1967 Reg.4, Reg.6, 2004 c.20 Sch.9 para.14

Sch.29 Part 9 para.68, amended: 2003 c.14 s.153

Sch.29 Part 9 para.68, varied: 1988 c.1 s.768C, SI 2002/1967 Reg.4, Reg.6, 2004 c.20 Sch.9 para.14

Sch.29 Part 9 para.69, applied: 1970 c.9 s.87A

Sch.29 Part 9 para.69, varied: 1988 c.1 s.768C, SI 2002/1967 Reg.4, Reg.6, 2004 c.20 Sch.9 para.14

Sch.29 Part 9 para.70, varied: 1988 c.1 s.768C, SI 2002/1967 Reg.4, Reg.6, 2004 c.20 Sch.9 para.14

Sch.29 Part 9 para.71, varied: 1988 c.1 s.768C, SI 2002/1967 Reg.4, Reg.6, 2004 c.20 Sch.9 para.14

Sch.29 Part 10 para.72, varied: 1988 c.1 s.768C, SI 2002/1967 Reg.4, Reg.6, 2004 c.20 Sch.9 para.14

Sch.29 Part 10 para.73, varied: 1988 c.1 s.768C, SI 2002/1967 Reg.4, Reg.6, 2004 c.20 Sch.9 para.14

Sch.29 Part 10 para.73A, added: 2004 c.12 Sch.10 para.71

Sch.29 Part 10 para.73A, varied: 1988 c.1 s.768C, SI 2002/1967 Reg.4, Reg.6, 2004 c.20 Sch.9 para.14

Sch.29 Part 10 para.74, varied: 1988 c.1 s.768C, SI 2002/1967 Reg.4, Reg.6, 2004 c.20 Sch.9 para.14

2002–cont.

23. **Finance Act 2002**–*cont.*

Sch.29 Part 10 para.75, varied: 1988 c.1 s.768C, SI 2002/1967 Reg.4, Reg.6, 2004 c.20 Sch.9 para.14

Sch.29 Part 10 para.76, varied: 1988 c.1 s.768C, SI 2002/1967 Reg.4, Reg.6, 2004 c.20 Sch.9 para.14

Sch.29 Part 10 para.77, varied: 1988 c.1 s.768C, SI 2002/1967 Reg.4, Reg.6, 2004 c.20 Sch.9 para.14

Sch.29 Part 10 para.78, varied: 1988 c.1 s.768C, SI 2002/1967 Reg.4, Reg.6, 2004 c.20 Sch.9 para.14

Sch.29 Part 10 para.79, varied: 1988 c.1 s.768C, SI 2002/1967 Reg.4, Reg.6, 2004 c.20 Sch.9 para.14

Sch.29 Part 10 para.80, varied: 1988 c.1 s.768C, SI 2002/1967 Reg.4, Reg.6, 2004 c.20 Sch.9 para.14

Sch.29 Part 10 para.81, varied: 1988 c.1 s.768C, SI 2002/1967 Reg.4, Reg.6, 2004 c.20 Sch.9 para.14

Sch.29 Part 10 para.82, varied: 1988 c.1 s.768C, SI 2002/1967 Reg.4, Reg.6, 2004 c.20 Sch.9 para.14

Sch.29 Part 10 para.83, varied: 1988 c.1 s.768C, SI 2002/1967 Reg.4, Reg.6, 2004 c.20 Sch.9 para.14

Sch.29 Part 11 para.84, varied: 1988 c.1 s.768C, SI 2002/1967 Reg.4, Reg.6, 2004 c.20 Sch.9 para.14

Sch.29 Part 11 para.85, varied: 1988 c.1 s.768C, SI 2002/1967 Reg.4, Reg.6, 2004 c.20 Sch.9 para.14

Sch.29 Part 11 para.86, amended: 2003 c.14 s.153

Sch.29 Part 11 para.86, varied: 1988 c.1 s.768C, SI 2002/1967 Reg.4, Reg.6, 2004 c.20 Sch.9 para.14

Sch.29 Part 11 para.87, amended: 2003 c.14 s.153

Sch.29 Part 11 para.87, varied: 1988 c.1 s.768C, SI 2002/1967 Reg.4, Reg.6, 2004 c.20 Sch.9 para.14

Sch.29 Part 11 para.88, varied: 1988 c.1 s.768C, SI 2002/1967 Reg.4, Reg.6, 2004 c.20 Sch.9 para.14

Sch.29 Part 11 para.89, amended: SI 2004/2200 Reg.11

Sch.29 Part 11 para.89, varied: 1988 c.1 s.768C, SI 1997/473 Reg.53J, SI 2002/1967 Reg.4, Reg.6, 2004 c.20 Sch.9 para.14

Sch.29 Part 11 para.90, varied: 1988 c.1 s.768C, SI 2002/1967 Reg.4, Reg.6, 2004 c.20 Sch.9 para.14

Sch.29 Part 11 para.91, varied: 1988 c.1 s.768C, SI 2002/1967 Reg.4, Reg.6, 2004 c.20 Sch.9 para.14

Sch.29 Part 12 para.92, amended: 2004 c.12 Sch.5 para.16

2002–cont.

23. Finance Act 2002–*cont.*

Sch.29 Part 12 para.92, repealed (in part): 2004 c.12 Sch.42 Part 2

Sch.29 Part 12 para.92, varied: 1988 c.1 s.768C, SI 2002/1967 Reg.4, Reg.6, 2004 c.20 Sch.9 para.14

Sch.29 Part 12 para.93, varied: 1988 c.1 s.768C, SI 2002/1967 Reg.4, Reg.6, 2004 c.20 Sch.9 para.14

Sch.29 Part 12 para.94, varied: 1988 c.1 s.768C, SI 2002/1967 Reg.4, Reg.6, 2004 c.20 Sch.9 para.14

Sch.29 Part 12 para.95, amended: 2003 c.14 s.184

Sch.29 Part 12 para.95, varied: 1988 c.1 s.768C, SI 2002/1967 Reg.4, Reg.6, 2004 c.20 Sch.9 para.14

Sch.29 Part 12 para.96, applied: SI 2002/1967 Reg.6

Sch.29 Part 12 para.96, varied: 1988 c.1 s.768C, SI 2002/1967 Reg.4, Reg.6, 2004 c.20 Sch.9 para.14

Sch.29 Part 12 para.97, applied: SI 2002/1967 Reg.6

Sch.29 Part 12 para.97, varied: 1988 c.1 s.768C, SI 2002/1967 Reg.4, Reg.6, 2004 c.20 Sch.9 para.14

Sch.29 Part 12 para.98, applied: SI 2002/1967 Reg.6

Sch.29 Part 12 para.98, varied: 1988 c.1 s.768C, SI 2002/1967 Reg.4, Reg.6, 2004 c.20 Sch.9 para.14

Sch.29 Part 12 para.99, applied: SI 2002/1967 Reg.6

Sch.29 Part 12 para.99, varied: 1988 c.1 s.768C, SI 2002/1967 Reg.4, Reg.6, 2004 c.20 Sch.9 para.14

Sch.29 Part 12 para.100, applied: SI 2002/1967 Reg.6

Sch.29 Part 12 para.100, varied: 1988 c.1 s.768C, SI 2002/1967 Reg.4, Reg.6, 2004 c.20 Sch.9 para.14

Sch.29 Part 12 para.101, applied: SI 2002/1967 Reg.6

Sch.29 Part 12 para.101, varied: 1988 c.1 s.768C, SI 2002/1967 Reg.4, Reg.6, 2004 c.20 Sch.9 para.14

Sch.29 Part 13 para.102, varied: 1988 c.1 s.768C, SI 2002/1967 Reg.4, Reg.6, 2004 c.20 Sch.9 para.14

Sch.29 Part 13 para.103, varied: 1988 c.1 s.768C, SI 2002/1967 Reg.4, Reg.6, 2004 c.20 Sch.9 para.14

Sch.29 Part 13 para.104, varied: 1988 c.1 s.768C, SI 2002/1967 Reg.4, Reg.6, 2004 c.20 Sch.9 para.14

Sch.29 Part 13 para.104, enabling: SI 2002/1967

Sch.29 Part 13 para.105, varied: 1988 c.1 s.768C, SI 2002/1967 Reg.4, Reg.6, 2004 c.20 Sch.9 para.14

2002–cont.

23. Finance Act 2002–*cont.*

Sch.29 Part 13 para.106, varied: 1988 c.1 s.768C, SI 2002/1967 Reg.4, Reg.6, 2004 c.20 Sch.9 para.14

Sch.29 Part 13 para.107, varied: 1988 c.1 s.768C, SI 2002/1967 Reg.4, Reg.6, 2004 c.20 Sch.9 para.14

Sch.29 Part 13 para.108, varied: 1988 c.1 s.768C, SI 2002/1967 Reg.4, Reg.6, 2004 c.20 Sch.9 para.14

Sch.29 Part 13 para.109, amended: 2003 c.14 s.153

Sch.29 Part 13 para.109, varied: 1988 c.1 s.768C, SI 2002/1967 Reg.4, Reg.6, 2004 c.20 Sch.9 para.14

Sch.29 Part 13 para.110, amended: 2003 c.14 s.153

Sch.29 Part 13 para.110, varied: 1988 c.1 s.768C, SI 2002/1967 Reg.4, Reg.6, 2004 c.20 Sch.9 para.14

Sch.29 Part 13 para.111, amended: 2003 c.14 s.184

Sch.29 Part 13 para.111, varied: 1988 c.1 s.768C, SI 2002/1967 Reg.4, Reg.6, 2004 c.20 Sch.9 para.14

Sch.29 Part 13 para.112, amended: 2004 c.12 Sch.35 para.52

Sch.29 Part 13 para.112, varied: 1988 c.1 s.768C, SI 2002/1967 Reg.4, Reg.6, 2004 c.20 Sch.9 para.14

Sch.29 Part 13 para.113, amended: 2003 c.14 Sch.43 Part 3, 2004 c.12 Sch.17 para.8

Sch.29 Part 13 para.113, varied: 1988 c.1 s.768C, SI 2002/1967 Reg.4, Reg.6, 2004 c.20 Sch.9 para.14

Sch.29 Part 13 para.114, amended: 2004 c.12 Sch.35 para.53

Sch.29 Part 13 para.114, varied: 1988 c.1 s.768C, SI 2002/1967 Reg.4, Reg.6, 2004 c.20 Sch.9 para.14

Sch.29 Part 13 para.115, varied: 1988 c.1 s.768C, SI 2002/1967 Reg.4, Reg.6, 2004 c.20 Sch.9 para.14

Sch.29 Part 13 para.116, varied: 1988 c.1 s.768C, SI 2002/1967 Reg.4, Reg.6, 2004 c.20 Sch.9 para.14

Sch.29 Part 13 para.116A, added: 2004 c.12 Sch.10 para.72

Sch.29 Part 13 para.116A, varied: 1988 c.1 s.768C, SI 2002/1967 Reg.4, Reg.6, 2004 c.20 Sch.9 para.14

Sch.29 Part 14, applied: SI 1997/473 Reg.53H

Sch.29 Part 14 para.117, varied: 1988 c.1 s.768C, SI 2002/1967 Reg.4, Reg.6, 2004 c.20 Sch.9 para.14

Sch.29 Part 14 para.118, applied: SI 2002/1967 Reg.6

Sch.29 Part 14 para.118, disapplied: SI 2002/1967 Reg.6

Sch.29 Part 14 para.118, varied: 1988 c.1 s.768C, SI 2002/1967 Reg.4, Reg.6, 2004 c.20 Sch.9 para.14

2002–cont.

23. Finance Act 2002–*cont.*

Sch.29 Part 14 para.119, varied: 1988 c.1 s.768C, SI 2002/1967 Reg.4, Reg.6, 2004 c.20 Sch.9 para.14

Sch.29 Part 14 para.120, varied: 1988 c.1 s.768C, SI 2002/1967 Reg.4, Reg.6, 2004 c.20 Sch.9 para.14

Sch.29 Part 14 para.121, varied: 1988 c.1 s.768C, SI 2002/1967 Reg.4, Reg.6, 2004 c.20 Sch.9 para.14

Sch.29 Part 14 para.122, varied: 1988 c.1 s.768C, SI 2002/1967 Reg.4, Reg.6, 2004 c.20 Sch.9 para.14

Sch.29 Part 14 para.123, varied: 1988 c.1 s.768C, SI 2002/1967 Reg.4, Reg.6, 2004 c.20 Sch.9 para.14

Sch.29 Part 14 para.124, varied: 1988 c.1 s.768C, SI 2002/1967 Reg.4, Reg.6, 2004 c.20 Sch.9 para.14

Sch.29 Part 14 para.125, varied: 1988 c.1 s.768C, SI 2002/1967 Reg.4, Reg.6, 2004 c.20 Sch.9 para.14

Sch.29 Part 14 para.126, varied: 1988 c.1 s.768C, SI 2002/1967 Reg.4, Reg.6, 2004 c.20 Sch.9 para.14

Sch.29 Part 14 para.127, varied: 1988 c.1 s.768C, SI 2002/1967 Reg.4, Reg.6, 2004 c.20 Sch.9 para.14

Sch.29 Part 14 para.128, varied: 1988 c.1 s.768C, SI 2002/1967 Reg.4, Reg.6, 2004 c.20 Sch.9 para.14

Sch.29 Part 14 para.129, varied: 1988 c.1 s.768C, SI 2002/1967 Reg.4, Reg.6, 2004 c.20 Sch.9 para.14

Sch.29 Part 14 para.130, varied: 1988 c.1 s.768C, SI 2002/1967 Reg.4, Reg.6, 2004 c.20 Sch.9 para.14

Sch.29 Part 14 para.131, varied: 1988 c.1 s.768C, SI 2002/1967 Reg.4, Reg.6, 2004 c.20 Sch.9 para.14

Sch.29 Part 14 para.132, varied: 1988 c.1 s.768C, SI 2002/1967 Reg.4, Reg.6, 2004 c.20 Sch.9 para.14

Sch.29 Part 15 para.133, varied: 1988 c.1 s.768C, SI 2002/1967 Reg.4, Reg.6, 2004 c.20 Sch.9 para.14

Sch.29 Part 15 para.134, amended: 2004 c.12 Sch.10 para.73

Sch.29 Part 15 para.134, varied: 1988 c.1 s.768C, SI 2002/1967 Reg.4, Reg.6, 2004 c.20 Sch.9 para.14

Sch.29 Part 15 para.135, varied: 1988 c.1 s.768C, SI 2002/1967 Reg.4, Reg.6, 2004 c.20 Sch.9 para.14

Sch.29 Part 15 para.136, varied: 1988 c.1 s.768C, SI 2002/1967 Reg.4, Reg.6, 2004 c.20 Sch.9 para.14

Sch.29 Part 15 para.137, varied: 1988 c.1 s.768C, SI 2002/1967 Reg.4, Reg.6, 2004 c.20 Sch.9 para.14

2002–cont.

23. Finance Act 2002–*cont.*

Sch.29 Part 15 para.138, varied: 1988 c.1 s.768C, SI 2002/1967 Reg.4, Reg.6, 2004 c.20 Sch.9 para.14

Sch.29 Part 15 para.139, varied: 1988 c.1 s.768C, SI 2002/1967 Reg.4, Reg.6, 2004 c.20 Sch.9 para.14

Sch.29 Part 15 para.140, varied: 1988 c.1 s.768C, SI 2002/1967 Reg.4, Reg.6, 2004 c.20 Sch.9 para.14

Sch.29 Part 15 para.141, varied: 1988 c.1 s.768C, SI 2002/1967 Reg.4, Reg.6, 2004 c.20 Sch.9 para.14

Sch.29 Part 15 para.142, varied: 1988 c.1 s.768C, SI 2002/1967 Reg.4, Reg.6, 2004 c.20 Sch.9 para.14

Sch.29 Part 15 para.143, varied: 1988 c.1 s.768C, SI 2002/1967 Reg.4, Reg.6, 2004 c.20 Sch.9 para.14

Sch.33, applied: 1970 c.9 s.98

Sch.33 Part 1, applied: SI 2004/2199 Reg.2

Sch.33 Part 1 para.2, enabling: SI 2004/2199

Sch.33 Part 1 para.3, enabling: SI 2004/2199

Sch.33 Part 1 para.4, enabling: SI 2004/2199

Sch.33 Part 1 para.5, enabling: SI 2004/2199

Sch.33 Part 1 para.7, applied: SI 2004/2199 Reg.2

Sch.33 Part 1 para.7, enabling: SI 2004/2199

Sch.33 Part 2 para.8, enabling: SI 2004/2199

Sch.33 Part 2 para.9, enabling: SI 2004/2199

Sch.33 Part 2 para.10, referred to: SI 2004/ 2199 Reg.9

Sch.33 Part 3 para.11, applied: 1988 c.1 s.842AA

Sch.33 Part 3 para.11, enabling: SI 2004/2199

Sch.33 Part 4 para.16, enabling: SI 2004/ 2199

Sch.34 para.4, amended: 2003 c.14 s.126

Sch.34 para.4, varied: 2003 c.14 Sch.19 para.6

Sch.35 para.3, amended: 2003 c.14 s.127

Sch.35 para.3, varied: 2003 c.14 Sch.19 para.6

Sch.35 para.4, amended: 2003 c.14 s.127

Sch.35 para.4, varied: 2003 c.14 Sch.19 para.6

Sch.36 Part 2 para.4, amended: 2003 c.14 Sch.20 para.3

Sch.36 Part 2 para.5, amended: 2003 c.14 Sch.20 para.3

Sch.36 Part 2 para.6, amended: 2003 c.14 Sch.20 para.3

Sch.37 para.1, amended: 2003 c.14 Sch.20 para.3

Sch.39, applied: SI 2004/674 Reg.3

Sch.39 para.1, varied: 2004 c.12 s.322

Sch.39 para.2, varied: 2004 c.12 s.322

Sch.39 para.2, enabling: SI 2004/674

Sch.39 para.3, referred to: 2004 c.12 s.322

Sch.39 para.3, varied: 2004 c.12 s.322

Sch.39 para.3, enabling: SI 2004/674

CAP.

CAP.

2002–cont.

2002–cont.

23. Finance Act 2002–*cont.*

Sch.39 para.4, applied: SI 2004/674 Reg.6, Reg.9

Sch.40 Part 3, referred to: SI 2002/1969 Part 2, Reg.2, Reg.12, Reg.18, Reg.28

24. European Parliamentary Elections Act 2002

applied: SI 2002/2626 Sch.1, 2003 c.7 s.24, SI 2003/1887 Sch.1, 2004 c.2 s.9, SI 2004/293 Sch.2 para.2, Sch.2 para.7

s.1, amended: SI 2004/366 Art.3, SI 2004/1245 Art.2

s.1, referred to: 2003 c.7 s.5, s.6

s.1, substituted: 2003 c.7 s.1

s.1A, added: 2003 c.7 s.7

s.1A, referred to: SI 2004/320 Art.2

s.2, amended: SI 2004/366 Art.3

s.2, applied: SI 2004/293 Sch.1 para.20, Sch.1 para.54, Sch.1 para.55, Sch.1 para.56

s.2, varied: SI 2004/293 Sch.1 para.54

s.4, applied: SI 2004/1267 Sch.1 para.66

s.4, enabling: SI 2004/217

s.5, enabling: SI 2004/293, SI 2004/1267

s.6, amended: 2003 c.7 s.20

s.6, applied: 2004 c.2 s.2, SI 2004/293 Reg.6, SI 2004/294 Reg.7, SI 2004/1299 Sch.1 para.1

s.6, disapplied: SI 2004/294 Reg.7

s.6, enabling: SI 2003/3362, SI 2004/293, SI 2004/1056, SI 2004/1267

s.7, amended: 2003 c.7 s.22

s.7, applied: 1996 c.55 Sch.10 para.30, 2003 c.7 s.23, s.25, SI 2004/294 Reg.5, Reg.6, SI 2004/1373

s.7, enabling: SI 2004/293, SI 2004/1267

s.8, amended: 2003 c.7 s.15

s.8, referred to: SI 2004/320 Art.2

s.9, amended: SI 2004/366 Art.3, SI 2004/1374 Reg.2

s.10, amended: 2003 c.7 s.21, SI 2004/1374 Reg.2

s.10, applied: SI 2004/293 Sch.1 para.13, Sch.1 para.17, SI 2004/1246, SI 2004/1267 Sch.1 para.7, Sch.1 para.12, Sch.1 para.15

s.10, enabling: SI 2004/1246

s.11, amended: 2003 c.7 s.21, SI 2004/366 Art.3

s.11, applied: SI 2004/293 Reg.88, SI 2004/1267 Reg.79

s.12, applied: 2003 c.35 s.1

s.13, amended: 2003 c.7 s.21

s.13, repealed (in part): 2003 c.7 s.8

s.16A, added: SI 2002/2626 Sch.2 para.27

s.16A, repealed: SI 2003/1887 Sch.2 para.14

s.17, amended: 2003 c.7 s.20

Sch.1A, referred to: SI 2004/320 Art.2

Sch.1 para.1, amended: SI 2004/366 Art.3

Sch.1 para.1, substituted: 2003 c.7 s.8

Sch.1 para.2, amended: 2003 c.7 s.8, SI 2004/366 Art.3

24. European Parliamentary Elections Act 2002–*cont.*

Sch.1 para.3, amended: SI 2004/366 Art.3

Sch.1 para.3, repealed: 2003 c.7 s.8

Sch.1 para.4, amended: SI 2004/366 Art.3

Sch.1 para.4, repealed: 2003 c.7 s.8

Sch.1A para.1, added: 2003 c.7 Sch.1

Sch.1A para.2, added: 2003 c.7 Sch.1

Sch.1A para.3, added: 2003 c.7 Sch.1

Sch.1A para.4, added: 2003 c.7 Sch.1

Sch.1A para.5, added: 2003 c.7 Sch.1

Sch.1A para.6, added: 2003 c.7 Sch.1

Sch.1A para.6, amended: SI 2004/1374 Reg.2

Sch.3 para.2, repealed: 2003 c.44 Sch.37 Part 10

25. Copyright, etc and Trade Marks (Offences and Enforcement) Act 2002

Commencement Orders: SI 2002/2749 Art.2

s.2, repealed (in part): SI 2003/2498 Sch.2

s.7, enabling: SI 2002/2749

26. Justice (Northern Ireland) Act 2002

Commencement Orders: SR 2002/319 Art.2, Sch.1

s.2, amended: 2004 c.4 Sch.1 para.1

s.3, amended: 2004 c.4 s.2, Sch.1 para.2

s.5, amended: 2004 c.4 s.3, Sch.1 para.3

s.5, referred to: SI 2003/431 Sch.2 para.7

s.7, amended: 2004 c.4 s.5

s.9, applied: 2003 c.21 s.366

s.10, applied: 2003 c.21 s.366

s.18, amended: 2003 c.39 Sch.10

s.22, applied: SI 2003/435 Art.47

s.27, referred to: 2000 c.11 s.63E

s.31, applied: SI 2004/1988 Art.6

s.32A, added: 2004 c.4 s.7

s.34, repealed (in part): 2004 c.4 Sch.4

s.37, amended: 2004 c.4 s.8

s.37, applied: 2004 c.4 s.8

s.41, referred to: SI 2003/431 Art.29

s.46, amended: SR 2002/414 Art.2, 2004 c.4 s.9, Sch.4

s.46, enabling: SR 2002/414

s.61, repealed: SI 2003/435 Sch.5

s.68, applied: SR 2003/293 Art.5

s.68, enabling: SR 2003/293

s.76, repealed: SI 2003/435 Sch.5

s.77, repealed: SI 2003/435 Sch.5

s.79, repealed: 2004 c.4 Sch.4

s.80, repealed: 2004 c.4 Sch.4

s.81, repealed: 2004 c.4 Sch.4

s.87, enabling: SR 2002/405, SR 2003/265, SR 2003/416, SR 2003/488

s.89, enabling: SR 2003/416

s.90, amended: 2004 c.4 Sch.1 para.4

s.90, repealed (in part): 2004 c.4 Sch.1 para.4, Sch.4

Sch.2 para.1, amended: 2004 c.4 s.2, Sch.1 para.5

2002–cont.

26. Justice (Northern Ireland) Act 2002–cont.

Sch.2 para.2, amended: 2004 c.4 Sch.1 para.5

Sch.2 para.3, amended: 2004 c.4 Sch.1 para.5

Sch.2 para.4, amended: 2004 c.4 Sch.1 para.5

Sch.2 para.5, amended: 2004 c.4 Sch.1 para.5

Sch.2 para.6, amended: 2004 c.4 Sch.1 para.5

Sch.2 para.7, amended: 2004 c.4 Sch.1 para.5

Sch.3 para.26, repealed: SI 2003/431 Sch.5

Sch.3 para.27, repealed: SI 2003/431 Sch.5

Sch.3 para.28, repealed: SI 2003/431 Sch.5

Sch.6, amended: SI 2003/431 Sch.4

Sch.7 para.7A, added: 2004 c.4 s.8

Sch.12 para.16, repealed: SI 2003/435 Sch.5

Sch.12 para.17, repealed: SI 2003/435 Sch.5

Sch.12 para.18, repealed: SI 2003/435 Sch.5

Sch.12 para.19, repealed: SI 2003/435 Sch.5

Sch.12 para.20, repealed: SI 2003/435 Sch.5

Sch.12 para.21, repealed: SI 2003/435 Sch.5

Sch.12 para.22, repealed: SI 2003/435 Sch.5

Sch.12 para.23, repealed: SI 2003/435 Sch.5

Sch.12 para.24, repealed: SI 2003/435 Sch.5

Sch.12 para.25, repealed: SI 2003/435 Sch.5

Sch.12 para.26, repealed: SI 2003/435 Sch.5

Sch.12 para.27, repealed: SI 2003/435 Sch.5

Sch.12 para.28, repealed: SI 2003/435 Sch.5

Sch.12 para.75, repealed: 2004 c.4 Sch.4

27. Divorce (Religious Marriages) Act 2002

Commencement Orders: SI 2003/186 Art.2

s.2, enabling: SI 2003/186

28. Export Control Act 2002

Commencement Orders: SI 2003/2629 Art.2, Art.3

applied: SI 2003/2759 Art.8, SI 2003/2764 Art.22, SI 2003/2765 Art.4, Art.13, SI 2004/318 Art.3, Art.12, SI 2004/1818 Reg.3

s.1, enabling: SI 2003/2759, SI 2003/2764, SI 2004/1050, SI 2004/2561, SI 2004/2741

s.2, enabling: SI 2003/2764

s.3, enabling: SI 2003/2764

s.4, enabling: SI 2003/2765, SI 2004/318, SI 2004/1049, SI 2004/2741

s.5, enabling: SI 2003/2759, SI 2003/2764, SI 2003/2765, SI 2004/318, SI 2004/1049, SI 2004/1050, SI 2004/2561, SI 2004/2741

s.7, enabling: SI 2003/2759, SI 2003/2764, SI 2003/2765, SI 2004/318, SI 2004/1049, SI 2004/1050, SI 2004/2561, SI 2004/2741

s.8, referred to: SI 2003/2764, SI 2004/1050

s.11, referred to: SI 2003/2765 Art.1

s.15, referred to: SI 2003/2629 Art.3

2002–cont.

28. Export Control Act 2002–cont.

s.16, enabling: SI 2003/2629, SI 2004/3102, SI 2004/3103

29. Proceeds of Crime Act 2002

Commencement Orders: SI 2002/3015 Art.2, Sch.1; SI 2003/120 Art.2, Art.3, Art.4, Art.5, Art.6, Art.7, Sch.1; SI 2003/333 Art.2, Art.3, Art.4, Art.5, Art.6, Art.7, Art.8, Art.9, Sch.1, Sch.1; SSI 2003/210 Art.2, Art.4, Art.6, Art.5, Art.7, Art.3, Sch.1; SI 2002/3015 Sch.1; SI 2002/3055 Art.2; SI 2002/3145 Art.2; SSI 2003/210 Art.2

applied: SI 1982/1109 r.25B, r.25C, SI 2000/627 Art.5, SI 2001/2188 Reg.12BI, Reg.12C, Sch.2, SI 2003/421 r.53, SI 2003/435 Sch.2 para.2

referred to: 2003 c.32 Sch.5 para.82, SI 2003/172 Art.2

Part 1, applied: 1999 c.22 Sch.2 para.3

Part 2, applied: 1968 c.19 s.50, 1974 c.53 s.1, 1982 c.27 s.18, 1984 c.60 s.22, s.56, s.58, 1985 c.66 s.31C, s.55, 1986 c.45 s.306C, s.281, SI 1986/1925 r.12.3, r.6.223, 1990 c.5 s.13, 2000 c.11 Sch.8 para.8, Sch.8 para.34, SI 2001/2188 Reg.4, Sch.1 Part 1, SI 2002/3133 Art.9, Art.11, Art.14, Art.16, SI 2003/82 Art.3, Art.5, Art.6, Art.7, Art.8, Art.10, SI 2003/421 r.2, r.3, r.4, r.55, r.56, SI 2003/428 r.13, r.14, r.16, r.17, r.20, r.21, r.22, 2004 c.35 Sch.3, Sch.8

Part 2, referred to: 2000 c.11 Sch.8 para.17

Part 3, applied: 1974 c.53 s.1, 1982 c.27 s.18, 1985 c.66 s.31C, s.55, 1986 c.45 s.306C, s.281, SI 1986/1925 r.12.3, r.6.223, 1990 c.5 s.13, SI 1994/1443 Sch.2 para.76A.1, SI 1999/929 r.3.19.1, 2000 c.11 Sch.8 para.17, Sch.8 para.34, SI 2001/2188 Reg.4, Sch.1 Part 1, SI 2002/3133 Art.4, Art.6, Art.14, Art.16, SSI 2003/120 r.1, 2004 c.35 Sch.3, Sch.8

Part 4, applied: 1982 c.27 s.18, 1985 c.66 s.31C, s.55, 1986 c.45 s.306C, s.281, SI 1986/1925 r.12.3, r.6.223, 1990 c.5 s.13, SI 2001/2188 Reg.4, Sch.1 Part 1, SI 2002/3133 Art.4, Art.6, Art.9, Art.11, SI 2003/435 Sch.2 para.3, SI 2003/458 Art.3, Art.4, Art.5, Art.6, Art.7, Art.8, Art.9, 2004 c.35 Sch.3, Sch.8

Part 5, see *Practice Direction (Administrative Court: Annual Statement)* [2004] 1 All E.R. 322 (QBD (Admin Ct)), Maurice Kay, J.

Part 5, applied: 1967 c.77 s.38A, 1980 c.58 s.27A, SI 1994/1443 Sch.2 para.76A.1, SI 1998/3132 r.34.13A, SI 1999/929 r.3.19.1

Part 5, referred to: 1973 c.52 s.19B

Part 5 c.2, applied: 1973 c.52 s.19B, 1980 c.58 s.27A

Part 5 c.3, applied: SI 2002/2998 r.10, r.11, SR 2003/17 r.13

Part 7, applied: SI 2003/173 Reg.3, SI 2003/3075 Reg.3

CAP.

2002–cont.

29. Proceeds of Crime Act 2002–*cont.*

Part 8, see *Practice Direction (Administrative Court: Annual Statement)* [2004] 1 All E.R. 322 (QBD (Admin Ct)), Maurice Kay, J.

Part 8, applied: 1967 c.77 s.38A, 1984 c.60 s.15, s.16, s.21, s.22, 1989 c.33 s.22, Sch.1 para.15, SI 1994/1443 Sch.2 para.76A.1, 1999 c.22 Sch.2 para.3, SI 1999/929 r.3.19.1, 2001 c.16 s.64, SI 2003/425 Art.33, SI 2003/435 Sch.2 para.3

Part 8 c.2, applied: SI 2003/334

Part 8 c.3, applied: SSI 2003/94, SSI 2003/120 r.1

s.3, applied: SI 1982/1109 r.25E

s.5, applied: SI 2003/82 Art.13

s.6, amended: 2003 c.44 Sch.3 para.75

s.6, applied: 1985 c.66 s.31B, s.31C, 1986 c.45 s.306B, s.306C, 1997 c.43 s.35, s.40, 2003 c.44 s.300, s.301, SI 2003/421 r.5, r.11

s.6, referred to: SI 2003/333 Art.3

s.14, applied: SI 2003/421 r.6

s.16, applied: SI 2003/421 r.5

s.17, applied: SI 2003/421 r.5

s.18, applied: SI 2003/421 r.5

s.19, applied: SI 2003/421 r.7

s.20, applied: SI 2003/421 r.7

s.21, applied: 1968 c.19 s.50, SI 2003/421 r.7

s.22, applied: 1968 c.19 s.50, SI 2003/421 r.8

s.23, applied: SI 2003/421 r.9

s.24, amended: 2003 c.39 Sch.8 para.406

s.24, applied: SI 2003/421 r.10

s.25, amended: 2003 c.39 Sch.8 para.406

s.25, applied: SI 2003/421 r.10

s.27, amended: 2003 c.44 Sch.3 para.75

s.27, referred to: SI 2003/333 Art.3

s.28, applied: SI 2003/421 r.11, r.12, r.15

s.29, applied: 1968 c.19 s.50, 1999 c.22 Sch.2 para.3, SI 2003/421 r.11, r.15

s.30, applied: 1986 c.45 s.306C, SI 2003/421 r.12, r.15

s.31, applied: SI 2003/82 Art.3, SI 2003/428 r.3, r.5, r.20

s.33, applied: SI 2003/82 Art.11, Art.12, Art.13, Art.14

s.34, applied: SI 2003/421 r.8, r.9, r.11, r.12, r.13, r.15

s.38, amended: 2003 c.44 Sch.32 para.141

s.39, applied: SI 2003/421 r.13

s.41, applied: 1999 c.22 Sch.2 para.3, SI 2002/3133 Art.7, Art.12, Art.17, SI 2003/421 r.16, r.17, r.18, r.19, r.20, SI 2003/1417 r.93

s.42, applied: 1999 c.22 Sch.2 para.3, SI 2003/421 r.16, r.18, r.19, r.20, r.45, r.46

s.42, varied: SI 2003/172 Sch.1

s.43, applied: SI 2003/82 Art.3, SI 2003/428 r.6, r.7, r.8, r.9, r.10, r.11, r.12

s.44, applied: SI 2003/82 Art.11, Art.12, Art.13, Art.14

s.47, applied: SI 2002/3133 Art.7

CAP.

2002–cont.

29. Proceeds of Crime Act 2002–*cont.*

s.48, applied: 1999 c.22 Sch.2 para.3, SI 2003/421 r.21, r.25, r.26, r.27, r.28

s.49, applied: 1985 c.66 s.31A, s.31C, 1986 c.45 s.306A, 1999 c.22 Sch.2 para.3, SI 2003/421 r.22, r.26

s.49, disapplied: SI 2002/3133 Art.12

s.50, applied: 1985 c.66 s.31A, 1986 c.45 s.306A, 1999 c.22 Sch.2 para.3, SI 2003/421 r.8, r.9, r.10, r.21, r.25, r.26, r.27, r.28

s.51, applied: 1999 c.22 Sch.2 para.3, SI 2003/421 r.22

s.51, disapplied: SI 2002/3133 Art.12

s.52, applied: 1985 c.66 s.31A, 1986 c.45 s.306A, 1999 c.22 Sch.2 para.3, SI 2003/421 r.8, r.9, r.25, r.26, r.27, r.28

s.53, applied: 1999 c.22 Sch.2 para.3, SI 2003/421 r.22

s.53, disapplied: SI 2002/3133 Art.12

s.54, amended: 2003 c.39 Sch.8 para.407

s.54, applied: 1999 c.22 Sch.2 para.3

s.55, amended: 2003 c.39 Sch.8 para.408

s.55, applied: SI 2003/421 r.26

s.56, applied: 1999 c.22 Sch.2 para.3

s.57, applied: SI 2003/421 r.26

s.58, applied: SI 2003/421 r.29

s.59, applied: SI 2003/421 r.29

s.60, applied: SI 2003/421 r.29

s.62, applied: 1999 c.22 Sch.2 para.3, SI 2003/421 r.23

s.63, applied: 1999 c.22 Sch.2 para.3, SI 2003/421 r.23

s.65, applied: SI 2003/82 Art.3, SI 2003/428 r.6, r.7, r.8, r.9, r.10, r.11, r.12

s.66, applied: SI 2003/82 Art.11, Art.12, Art.13, Art.14

s.67, amended: 2003 c.39 Sch.8 para.409

s.67, applied: SI 1981/552 r.57A

s.68, applied: SI 2003/421 r.16, r.19, r.21, r.22

s.68, varied: SI 2003/172 Sch.1

s.70, amended: 2003 c.44 Sch.3 para.75

s.72, applied: 1999 c.22 Sch.2 para.3, SI 2003/421 r.14

s.73, applied: 1999 c.22 Sch.2 para.3, SI 2003/421 r.15

s.76, applied: SI 2003/333 Art.9

s.85, amended: 2003 c.44 Sch.36 para.15

s.85, applied: SI 2003/428 r.5

s.85, substituted: 2003 c.44 Sch.36 para.15

s.89, amended: 2003 c.39 s.94

s.89, enabling: SI 2003/82

s.90, enabling: SI 2003/82

s.91, amended: 2003 c.39 s.94, Sch.8 para.410

s.91, enabling: SI 2003/421

s.92, applied: 1985 c.66 s.31B, s.31C, 1986 c.45 s.306B, 1995 c.46 s.108, s.175, SI 1996/513 Sch.2 para.37AA.2, SSI 2003/179 Reg.5, SSI 2003/210 Art.5

s.98, applied: SI 1996/513 Sch.2 para.37AA.3

2002–cont.

29. Proceeds of Crime Act 2002–*cont.*

s.99, applied: SI 1996/513 Sch.2 para.37AA.4

s.101, applied: SI 1996/513 Sch.2 para.37AA.5

s.102, applied: SI 1996/513 Sch.2 para.37AA.5

s.104, applied: SI 1996/513 Sch.2 para.37AA.6

s.105, applied: SI 1996/513 Sch.2 para.37AA.6

s.106, applied: SI 1996/513 Sch.2 para.37AA.6

s.107, applied: SI 1996/513 Sch.2 para.37AA.6

s.108, applied: SI 1996/513 Sch.2 para.37AA.7

s.109, applied: SI 1996/513 Sch.2 para.37AA.7

s.110, applied: SI 1996/513 Sch.2 para.37AA.5

s.111, applied: SI 1996/513 Sch.2 para.37AA.2

s.112, applied: SI 1996/513 Sch.2 para.37AA.2

s.113, applied: SI 1996/513 Sch.2 para.37AA.7

s.114, applied: 1985 c.66 s.31C, 1986 c.45 s.306C, SI 1996/513 Sch.2 para.37AA.7

s.116, applied: SI 1996/513 Sch.2 para.37AA.8

s.118, applied: 1995 c.46 s.219

s.120, applied: SI 2002/3133 Art.7, Art.12, Art.17

s.121, applied: SI 1994/1443 Sch.2 para.76A.2, SI 1999/929 r.3.19.6, r.3.19.7, r.3.19.9

s.123, applied: SI 1994/1443 Sch.2 para.76A.2, SI 2002/3133 Art.12

s.124, applied: SI 1994/1443 Sch.2 para.76A.2, SI 1999/929 r.3.19.9, SI 2002/3133 Art.12

s.125, applied: SI 1994/1443 Sch.2 para.76A.1, Sch.2 para.76A.2, SI 1999/929 r.3.19.10

s.128, applied: 1985 c.66 s.31A, 1986 c.45 s.306A, SI 1994/1443 Sch.2 para.76A.2, SI 1999/929 r.3.19.10

s.134, applied: SI 1994/1443 Sch.2 para.76A.2

s.135, applied: SI 1994/1443 Sch.2 para.76A.2

s.140, applied: SI 1994/1443 Sch.2 para.76A.2

s.142, applied: SSI 2003/210 Art.5

s.142, referred to: SSI 2003/210 Art.5

s.142, enabling: SSI 2003/594

s.155, enabling: SSI 2003/98, SSI 2003/222

s.156, applied: 1985 c.66 s.31B, s.31C, 1986 c.45 s.306B, s.306C

s.156, referred to: SI 2003/333 Art.4

2002–cont.

29. Proceeds of Crime Act 2002–*cont.*

s.177, referred to: SI 2003/333 Art.4

s.179, applied: SI 2003/435 Sch.2 para.3

s.180, applied: 1985 c.66 s.31C, 1986 c.45 s.306C

s.181, applied: SI 2003/458 Art.3

s.183, applied: SI 2003/458 Art.10, Art.11, Art.12, Art.13

s.190, applied: SI 2002/3133 Art.7, Art.12, Art.17

s.190, referred to: SR 2003/54 r.1

s.191, varied: SI 2003/172 Sch.1

s.192, applied: SI 2003/458 Art.3

s.193, applied: SI 2003/458 Art.10, Art.11, Art.12, Art.13

s.195, applied: SI 2002/3133 Art.17

s.196, applied: SI 2003/435 Sch.2 para.3

s.197, applied: 1985 c.66 s.31A, s.31C, 1986 c.45 s.306A, s.306C, SI 2003/435 Sch.2 para.3

s.197, disapplied: SI 2002/3133 Art.12

s.198, applied: 1985 c.66 s.31A, 1986 c.45 s.306A, SI 2003/435 Sch.2 para.3

s.199, applied: SI 2003/435 Sch.2 para.3

s.199, disapplied: SI 2002/3133 Art.12

s.200, applied: 1985 c.66 s.31A, 1986 c.45 s.306A, SI 2003/435 Sch.2 para.3

s.201, applied: SI 2003/435 Sch.2 para.3

s.201, disapplied: SI 2002/3133 Art.12

s.202, applied: SI 2003/435 Sch.2 para.3

s.204, applied: SI 2003/435 Sch.2 para.3

s.210, applied: SI 2003/435 Sch.2 para.3

s.211, applied: SI 2003/435 Sch.2 para.3

s.213, applied: SI 2003/458 Art.3

s.214, applied: SI 2003/458 Art.10, Art.11, Art.12, Art.13

s.215, applied: SR 2003/122 r.3

s.216, varied: SI 2003/172 Sch.1

s.218, applied: SR 2003/122 r.5

s.220, applied: SI 2003/435 Sch.2 para.3

s.221, applied: SI 2003/435 Sch.2 para.3

s.224, applied: SI 2003/333 Art.9

s.237, enabling: SI 2003/458

s.238, enabling: SI 2003/458

s.239, enabling: SR 2003/71

s.244, applied: SI 1994/1443 Sch.2 para.76A.10

s.246, applied: SI 2003/1417 r.93

s.256, applied: SI 1994/1443 Sch.2 para.76A.10

s.258, applied: SI 1994/1443 Sch.2 para.76A.10

s.260, applied: SI 1994/1443 Sch.2 para.76A.10

s.265, applied: SI 1994/1443 Sch.2 para.76A.10

s.273, enabling: SI 2003/291

s.275, enabling: SI 2003/291

s.281, applied: 1980 c.58 s.27A

2002–cont.

29. Proceeds of Crime Act 2002–*cont.*
s.283, applied: SI 1994/1443 Sch.2 para.76A.10
s.285, amended: 2002 asp 17 Sch.3 para.29
s.287, applied: SI 2003/175 Art.2
s.287, enabling: SI 2003/175
s.289, applied: SI 2002/2998 r.3, SI 2002/3115, SR 2003/17 r.3, SSI 2002/569
s.289, varied: SI 2004/420 Art.2
s.289, enabling: SI 2002/3115, SSI 2002/569
s.290, applied: SI 2002/2998 r.3, SR 2003/17 r.3
s.290, varied: SI 2004/420 Art.2
s.291, varied: SI 2004/420 Art.2
s.292, applied: SI 2002/3115
s.292, varied: SI 2004/420 Art.2
s.292, enabling: SI 2002/3115
s.293, applied: SSI 2002/569
s.293, referred to: SSI 2002/569
s.293, varied: SI 2004/420 Art.2
s.293, enabling: SSI 2002/569
s.294, applied: SI 2002/2998 r.4, SR 2003/17 r.4
s.294, varied: SI 2004/420 Art.2
s.295, applied: SI 1982/1109 r.8., 1999 c.22 Sch.2 para.2, SI 1999/929 r.3.19.2, r.3.19.3, r.3.19.4, r.3.19.5, SI 2002/2998 r.4, r.5, r.6, r.7, r.8, SI 2003/435 Sch.2 para.2, SR 2003/17 r.4, r.5, r.6, r.7, r.8, r.11
s.295, varied: SI 2004/420 Art.2
s.296, varied: SI 2004/420 Art.2
s.297, applied: 1999 c.22 Sch.2 para.2, SI 1999/929 r.3.19.3, SI 2002/2998 r.6, SI 2003/435 Sch.2 para.2, SR 2003/17 r.7
s.297, varied: SI 2004/420 Art.2
s.298, applied: 1999 c.22 Sch.2 para.2, Sch.2 para.3, SI 1999/929 r.3.19.4, SI 2002/2998 r.6, r.7, SI 2003/435 Sch.2 para.2, SR 2003/17 r.8, r.9
s.298, varied: SI 2004/420 Art.2
s.299, applied: SI 1982/1109 r.8., SI 1994/1443 Sch.2 para.41.43A, SR 2003/17 r.10
s.299, varied: SI 2004/420 Art.2
s.300, varied: SI 2004/420 Art.2
s.301, applied: SI 1982/1109 r.8., 1999 c.22 Sch.2 para.2, SI 1999/929 r.3.19.3, SI 2002/2998 r.6, SI 2003/435 Sch.2 para.2, SR 2003/17 r.7, r.10
s.301, varied: SI 2004/420 Art.2
s.302, applied: 1999 c.22 Sch.2 para.2, SI 1999/929 r.3.19.5, SI 2002/2998 r.8, SI 2003/435 Sch.2 para.2, SR 2003/17 r.11
s.302, varied: SI 2004/420 Art.2
s.303, applied: SI 2002/3016 Art.2
s.303, varied: SI 2004/420 Art.2
s.303, enabling: SI 2002/3016, SI 2004/420
s.309, enabling: SI 2003/336
s.316, amended: 2003 c.44 Sch.36 para.78
s.317, applied: 1967 c.13 Sch.2 paraA.1
s.320, applied: SI 1994/1811 Reg.12A, Reg.15

2002–cont.

29. Proceeds of Crime Act 2002–*cont.*
s.320, enabling: SI 2003/968
s.321, applied: 1967 c.13 Sch.2 paraA.1
s.322, applied: 1967 c.13 Sch.2 paraA.1
s.327, applied: 1984 c.60 s.116, SI 2004/1910 Sch.1
s.328, applied: 1984 c.60 s.116, SI 2004/1910 Sch.1
s.329, applied: 1984 c.60 s.116, SI 2004/1910 Sch.1
s.330, applied: SI 2003/171 Art.2
s.330, enabling: SI 2003/171
s.332, applied: SI 2004/1910 Sch.1
s.333, see *P v P (Ancillary Relief: Proceeds of Crime)* [2003] EWHC 2260, [2004] Fam.1 (Fam Div), Dame Elizabeth Butler-Sloss (President)
s.333, applied: SI 2004/1910 Sch.1
s.335, see *P v P (Ancillary Relief: Proceeds of Crime)* [2003] EWHC 2260, [2004] Fam.1 (Fam Div), Dame Elizabeth Butler-Sloss (President)
s.338, see *P v P (Ancillary Relief: Proceeds of Crime)* [2003] EWHC 2260, [2004] Fam.1 (Fam Div), Dame Elizabeth Butler-Sloss (President)
s.342, see *P v P (Ancillary Relief: Proceeds of Crime)* [2003] EWHC 2260, [2004] Fam.1 (Fam Div), Dame Elizabeth Butler-Sloss (President)
s.342, applied: SI 2003/173 Reg.3
s.342, disapplied: SI 2003/120 Art.5
s.345, applied: SI 1982/1109 r.25B, r.25E, SI 2003/425 Art.3, Art.13, Art.23, Art.24
s.345, varied: SI 2003/425 Art.3, Art.13, Art.23, Art.24
s.347, applied: SI 2003/425 Art.3, Art.13, Art.23, Art.24
s.347, varied: SI 2003/425 Art.3, Art.13, Art.23, Art.24
s.348, disapplied: SI 2003/425 Art.23, Art.24
s.348, varied: SI 2003/425 Art.3, Art.4, Art.13, Art.14, Art.23, Art.24
s.349, varied: SI 2003/425 Art.3, Art.13, Art.23, Art.24
s.350, disapplied: SI 2003/425 Art.23, Art.24
s.350, varied: SI 2003/425 Art.3, Art.4, Art.13, Art.14
s.351, applied: 1999 c.22 Sch.2 para.3, SI 2003/435 Sch.2 para.3
s.351, enabling: SI 2003/422, SR 2003/71
s.352, applied: 1984 c.60 s.15, s.16, s.21, s.22, 2001 c.16 s.55, s.60, s.64, s.65, Sch.1 para.73A, Sch.1 para.110
s.352, referred to: 1984 c.60 s.15, s.16
s.352, varied: SI 2003/425 Art.5, Art.15, Art.25, Art.26
s.354, applied: 2001 c.16 s.65

2002–cont.

29. Proceeds of Crime Act 2002–*cont.*

s.354, disapplied: SI 2003/425 Art.25, Art.26

s.354, varied: SI 2003/425 Art.5, Art.6, Art.15, Art.16

s.355, enabling: SI 2003/174

s.357, applied: SI 1982/1109 r.25E

s.359, applied: SI 2003/425 Art.7, Art.8, Art.17, Art.18

s.359, disapplied: SI 2003/425 Art.27, Art.28

s.359, varied: SI 2003/425 Art.8, Art.18, Art.27, Art.28

s.360, applied: SI 2003/425 Art.7, Art.17

s.360, referred to: SI 2003/425 Art.27, Art.28

s.360, varied: SI 2003/425 Art.27, Art.28

s.361, disapplied: SI 2003/425 Art.8, Art.18, Art.27, Art.28

s.361, varied: SI 2003/425 Art.7, Art.8, Art.17, Art.18

s.362, applied: 1999 c.22 Sch.2 para.3, SI 2003/435 Sch.2 para.3

s.362, enabling: SI 2003/422, SR 2003/71

s.363, applied: SI 1982/1109 r.25E

s.364, varied: 2003 c.32 s.32

s.366, applied: SI 2003/425 Art.9, Art.19

s.366, varied: SI 2003/425 Art.10, Art.20, Art.29, Art.30

s.367, applied: SI 2003/425 Art.9, Art.19

s.367, varied: SI 2003/425 Art.29, Art.30

s.368, varied: SI 2003/425 Art.9, Art.10, Art.19, Art.20

s.369, applied: SI 1982/1109 r.25D, 1999 c.22 Sch.2 para.3, SI 2003/435 Sch.2 para.3

s.369, enabling: SI 2003/422, SR 2003/71

s.370, applied: SI 1982/1109 r.25E

s.370, varied: SI 2003/425 Art.11, Art.21, Art.31, Art.32

s.372, applied: SI 2003/425 Art.11, Art.21, Art.31, Art.32

s.374, varied: SI 2003/425 Art.11, Art.12, Art.21, Art.22

s.375, applied: SI 1982/1109 r.25C, 1999 c.22 Sch.2 para.3, SI 2003/435 Sch.2 para.3

s.375, enabling: SI 2003/422, SR 2003/71

s.376, amended: 2003 c.32 Sch.5 para.83

s.376, repealed (in part): 2003 c.32 Sch.5 para.83, Sch.6

s.377, applied: SI 2003/334, SI 2003/425 Art.33

s.377, enabling: SI 2003/334

s.378, varied: SI 2003/172 Sch.1

s.380, applied: SI 1996/513 Sch.2 para.37AA.10, SI 2003/425 Art.4, Art.14

s.380, varied: SI 2003/425 Art.4, Art.14

s.382, applied: SI 1996/513 Sch.2 para.37AA.10, SI 1999/929 r.3.19.21, SI 2003/425 Art.4, Art.14

s.382, varied: SI 2003/425 Art.4, Art.14

s.383, disapplied: SI 2003/425 Art.4, Art.14

2002–cont.

29. Proceeds of Crime Act 2002–*cont.*

s.383, varied: SI 2003/425 Art.4, Art.14, Art.23, Art.24

s.384, varied: SI 2003/425 Art.4, Art.14

s.385, applied: SI 1999/929 r.3.19.21

s.385, disapplied: SI 2003/425 Art.4, Art.14

s.385, varied: SI 2003/425 Art.23, Art.24

s.386, applied: SI 1996/513 Sch.2 para.37AA.10, SI 1999/929 r.3.19.21

s.386, enabling: SSI 2003/98, SSI 2003/120

s.387, applied: SI 1996/513 Sch.2 para.37AA.10, SI 1999/929 r.3.19.22

s.387, varied: SI 2003/425 Art.6, Art.16

s.389, disapplied: SI 2003/425 Art.6, Art.16

s.389, varied: SI 2003/425 Art.25, Art.26

s.390, applied: SI 2003/425 Art.25, Art.26

s.390, disapplied: SI 2003/425 Art.6, Art.16, Art.25, Art.26

s.390, varied: SI 2003/425 Art.6, Art.16

s.391, applied: SI 1994/1443 Sch.2 para.76A.11, SI 1996/513 Sch.2 para.37AA.10

s.393, applied: SI 2003/425 Art.27, Art.28

s.393, disapplied: SI 2003/425 Art.8, Art.18

s.393, varied: SI 2003/425 Art.8, Art.18, Art.27, Art.28

s.394, referred to: SI 2003/425 Art.8, Art.18

s.394, varied: SI 2003/425 Art.8, Art.18

s.395, disapplied: SI 2003/425 Art.8, Art.18, Art.27, Art.28

s.395, varied: SI 2003/425 Art.27, Art.28

s.396, applied: SI 1994/1443 Sch.2 para.76A.11, SI 1996/513 Sch.2 para.37AA.10

s.396, enabling: SSI 2003/98, SSI 2003/120, SSI 2003/222

s.397, applied: SI 1996/513 Sch.2 para.37AA.10

s.398, varied: 2003 c.32 s.37

s.400, applied: SI 2003/425 Art.10

s.400, varied: SI 2003/425 Art.20, Art.29, Art.30

s.401, varied: SI 2003/425 Art.10, Art.20

s.402, varied: SI 2003/425 Art.29, Art.30

s.403, applied: SI 1996/513 Sch.2 para.37AA.10, SI 1999/929 r.3.19.23

s.403, enabling: SSI 2003/98, SSI 2003/120

s.404, applied: SI 1996/513 Sch.2 para.37AA.10

s.404, varied: SI 2003/425 Art.12, Art.22

s.406, applied: SI 2003/425 Art.12, Art.22

s.407, varied: SI 2003/425 Art.31, Art.32

s.408, applied: SI 1996/513 Sch.2 para.37AA.10, SI 1999/929 r.3.19.24

s.408, enabling: SSI 2003/120

s.409, varied: 2003 c.32 s.22, s.38, s.41

s.410, applied: SI 2003/425 Art.33, SSI 2003/94

s.410, referred to: SSI 2003/94

s.410, enabling: SSI 2003/94

2002–cont.

29. Proceeds of Crime Act 2002–*cont.*

s.412, applied: 1994 c.33 s.139, 2001 c.16 s.65

s.415, applied: 1989 c.33 s.22, Sch.1 para.15

s.417, applied: 1986 c.45 s.306A, s.306C, s.306B

s.420, applied: 1985 c.66 s.31A, s.31C, s.31B

s.436, applied: SI 2003/335 Art.2

s.436, enabling: SI 2003/335

s.438, applied: SI 2003/335 Art.3

s.438, enabling: SI 2003/335

s.439, applied: SSI 2003/93 Art.2

s.439, enabling: SSI 2003/93

s.441, applied: SSI 2003/93 Art.3

s.441, enabling: SSI 2003/93

s.443, enabling: SI 2002/3133, SI 2003/425

s.446, applied: SI 2003/425 Art.3, Art.4, Art.11, Art.12, Art.13, Art.14, Art.21, Art.22, Art.23, Art.24, Art.31, Art.32

s.446, enabling: SI 2003/421, SSI 2003/222

s.449, applied: SI 1982/1109 r.25E

s.452, enabling: SI 2003/173

s.453, enabling: SI 2003/172, SI 2004/8, SI 2004/3339

s.458, enabling: SI 2002/3015, SI 2002/3055, SI 2002/3145, SI 2003/120, SI 2003/333, SI 2003/531, SSI 2003/210

s.459, applied: SI 2002/3115, SI 2003/334, SI 2003/335, SI 2003/336, SSI 2002/569, SSI 2003/93, SSI 2003/94

s.459, enabling: SI 2002/3015, SI 2003/82, SI 2003/120, SI 2003/172, SI 2003/291, SI 2003/333, SI 2003/425, SI 2003/458, SI 2003/531, SI 2003/3074, SI 2004/8, SI 2004/3339, SSI 2003/210

Sch.2 para.1, applied: 1984 c.60 s.116, 1989 c.33 s.22

Sch.2 para.1, referred to: 1971 c.38 s.27

Sch.2 para.2, applied: 1989 c.33 Sch.1 para.15

Sch.2 para.4, amended: 2003 c.42 Sch.6 para.46, 2004 c.19 s.5

Sch.2 para.4, substituted: 2002 c.41 Sch.7 para.31

Sch.2 para.8, substituted: 2003 c.42 Sch.6 para.46

Sch.2 para.9A, added: 2004 c.11 s.14

Sch.2 para.10, applied: 1989 c.33 s.22, Sch.1 para.15

Sch.2 para.10, referred to: 1971 c.38 s.27

Sch.3 para.7, amended: 2002 asp 17 Sch.3 para.29

Sch.3 para.9, applied: SI 1994/1443 Sch.2 para.76A.9, SI 1999/929 r.3.19.20

Sch.4 para.2, applied: 1989 c.33 s.22, Sch.1 para.15

Sch.4 para.4, amended: 2002 c.41 Sch.7 para.32, 2004 c.19 s.5

Sch.4 para.8A, added: SSI 2003/594 Art.3

Sch.4 para.9A, added: 2004 c.11 s.14

Sch.4 para.10, applied: 1989 c.33 s.22, Sch.1 para.15

2002–cont.

29. Proceeds of Crime Act 2002–*cont.*

Sch.5 para.1, applied: 1989 c.33 s.22, Sch.1 para.15

Sch.5 para.4, amended: 2003 c.42 Sch.6 para.46, 2004 c.19 s.5

Sch.5 para.4, substituted: 2002 c.41 Sch.7 para.33

Sch.5 para.5, amended: SI 2004/702 Sch.7 para.26

Sch.5 para.8, amended: 2003 c.42 Sch.6 para.46

Sch.5 para.8, repealed (in part): 2003 c.42 Sch.7

Sch.5 para.9A, added: 2004 c.11 s.14

Sch.5 para.10, applied: 1989 c.33 s.22, Sch.1 para.15

Sch.9 Part 1 para.1, substituted: SI 2003/3074 Sch.1

Sch.9 Part 1 para.2, substituted: SI 2003/3074 Sch.1

Sch.9 Part 1 para.2, amended: SI 2003/3074 Sch.1

Sch.9 Part 1 para.2, substituted: SI 2003/3074 Sch.1

Sch.9 Part 1 para.3, amended: SI 2003/3074 Sch.1

Sch.9 Part 1 para.3, substituted: SI 2003/3074 Sch.1

Sch.9 Part 2 para.4, amended: SI 2003/3074 Art.3, 2004 c.35 Sch.12 para.80

Sch.9 Part 3 para.5, enabling: SI 2003/3074

Sch.11 para.10, repealed: SI 2003/435 Sch.5

Sch.11 para.18, disapplied: SI 2003/120 Art.7

Sch.11 para.18, repealed: 2003 c.41 Sch.4

Sch.11 para.32, repealed: 2003 c.44 Sch.37 Part 7

30. Police Reform Act 2002

Commencement Orders: SI 2002/2306 Art.2, Art.3, Art.4, Art.5; SI 2002/2750 Art.2; SI 2003/525 Art.2; SI 2002/2750 Art.3; SI 2003/808 Art.2; SI 2003/2593 Art.2; SI 2004/119 Art.2; SI 2004/636 Art.2; SI 2004/913 Art.2, Art.3; SI 2004/1319 Art.2; SI 2004/3338 Art.2; SI 2002/2750 Art.4, Art.5; SI 2004/3338 Art.3; SSI 2002/420 Art.2

Part 2, applied: 1997 c.50 s.83, SI 2004/643 Reg.7, Reg.15, Reg.16, Reg.17, Reg.20, Reg.21, Reg.22, Reg.24, Reg.25, Reg.26, Reg.28, Reg.29, SI 2004/645 Reg.29, SI 2004/672 Art.2, Art.3

Part 2, disapplied: SI 2004/643 Reg.15, Reg.17, SI 2004/671 Art.2, Art.3

Part 2, referred to: SI 2004/643 Reg.28

s.2, applied: 2004 c.34 s.217

s.9, varied: SI 2004/643 Reg.29

s.10, varied: SI 2004/643 Reg.29

s.11, varied: SI 2004/643 Reg.29

s.12, applied: SI 2004/671 Art.3

s.12, varied: SI 2004/643 Reg.29

s.13, varied: SI 2004/643 Reg.29

2002–cont.

30. Police Reform Act 2002–*cont.*
s.13, enabling: SI 2004/643
s.14, varied: SI 2004/643 Reg.29
s.15, varied: SI 2004/643 Reg.29
s.16, varied: SI 2004/643 Reg.29
s.17, varied: SI 2004/643 Reg.29
s.18, varied: SI 2004/643 Reg.29
s.19, varied: SI 2004/643 Reg.29
s.19, enabling: SI 2004/815
s.20, applied: SI 2004/643 Reg.11
s.20, referred to: SI 2004/643 Reg.12
s.20, varied: SI 2004/643 Reg.29
s.20, enabling: SI 2004/643
s.21, applied: SI 2004/643 Reg.11, Reg.13, Reg.23, SI 2004/645 Reg.25, Reg.29
s.21, referred to: SI 2004/643 Reg.12
s.21, varied: SI 2004/643 Reg.29
s.21, enabling: SI 2004/643
s.22, varied: SI 2004/643 Reg.29
s.23, varied: SI 2004/643 Reg.29
s.23, enabling: SI 2004/643
s.24, applied: SI 2004/643, SI 2004/660
s.24, varied: SI 2004/643 Reg.29
s.25, varied: SI 2004/643 Reg.29
s.26, applied: 1990 c.31 s.22, SI 2004/672
s.26, varied: 2003 c.20 Sch.5 para.4, SI 2004/643 Reg.29
s.26, enabling: SI 2004/672
s.27, applied: SI 2004/660
s.27, varied: SI 2004/643 Reg.29
s.27, enabling: SI 2004/660
s.28, varied: SI 2004/643 Reg.29
s.28, enabling: SI 2004/671, SI 2004/1092
s.29, applied: SI 2004/645 Reg.11
s.29, varied: SI 2004/643 Reg.29
s.29, enabling: SI 2004/643
s.38, applied: 1984 c.60 s.67
s.38, varied: 2003 c.20 s.28
s.39, applied: 1984 c.60 s.67, SI 2004/643, SI 2004/643 Reg.28, SI 2004/671 Art.3
s.39, varied: 2003 c.20 s.28
s.39, enabling: SI 2004/643
s.41, applied: 1984 c.60 s.67
s.42, varied: 2003 c.20 s.28
s.43, amended: SI 2004/1573 Art.12
s.43, applied: SI 2004/915
s.43, varied: 2003 c.20 Sch.5 para.4
s.43, enabling: SI 2004/915
s.45, varied: 2003 c.20 s.28
s.46, amended: 2003 c.44 Sch.26 para.57
s.46, varied: 2003 c.20 s.28
s.47, varied: 2003 c.20 s.28
s.50, applied: SI 2004/915 Sch.1 para.3
s.57, see *Russell (Superintendent of the Royal Ulster Constabulary) v Devine* [2003] UKHL 24, [2003] 1 W.L.R. 1187 (HL (NI)), Lord Bingham of Cornhill
s.59, applied: SI 2002/3049 Reg.5
s.60, enabling: SI 2002/3049
s.67, repealed: 2003 c.42 Sch.7

2002–cont.

30. Police Reform Act 2002–*cont.*
s.68, repealed: 2003 c.42 Sch.7
s.69, repealed: 2003 c.42 Sch.7
s.70, repealed: 2003 c.42 Sch.7
s.71, repealed: 2003 c.42 Sch.7
s.72, repealed: 2003 c.42 Sch.7
s.73, repealed: 2003 c.42 Sch.7
s.74, repealed: 2003 c.42 Sch.7
s.81, repealed (in part): SI 2004/702 Sch.8
s.82, amended: 2004 c.20 Sch.14 para.11, Sch.23 Part 1
s.82, varied: 2003 c.20 Sch.5 para.4
s.82, enabling: SSI 2003/21, SSI 2004/257
s.105, amended: 2003 c.38 s.89
s.105, enabling: SI 2002/3049, SI 2004/643, SI 2004/660, SI 2004/671, SI 2004/672, SI 2004/915
s.106, amended: 2003 c.20 Sch.5 para.4
s.106, varied: 2003 c.20 Sch.5 para.4
s.108, enabling: SI 2002/2306, SI 2002/2750, SI 2003/525, SI 2003/808, SI 2003/2593, SI 2004/119, SI 2004/636, SI 2004/913, SI 2004/1319, SI 2004/3338, SSI 2002/420
Sch.2 para.6, applied: 1967 c.77 s.38A
Sch.3, applied: SI 2004/643 Reg.3
Sch.3 Part 1 para.2, applied: SI 2004/643 Reg.15, SI 2004/671 Art.4
Sch.3 Part 1 para.3, applied: SI 2004/643 Reg.8, Reg.15
Sch.3 Part 1 para.3, referred to: SI 2004/643 Reg.8
Sch.3 Part 1 para.3, enabling: SI 2004/643
Sch.3 Part 1 para.4, applied: SI 2004/643 Reg.2, Reg.15
Sch.3 Part 1 para.4, disapplied: SI 2004/643 Reg.2
Sch.3 Part 1 para.4, enabling: SI 2004/643
Sch.3 Part 1 para.5, applied: SI 2004/643 Reg.15
Sch.3 Part 1 para.7, applied: SI 2004/643 Reg.3
Sch.3 Part 1 para.7, enabling: SI 2004/643
Sch.3 Part 1 para.8, applied: SI 2004/643 Reg.3
Sch.3 Part 1 para.8, enabling: SI 2004/643
Sch.3 Part 1 para.9, applied: SI 2004/643 Reg.9, Reg.15
Sch.3 Part 1 para.9, enabling: SI 2004/643
Sch.3 Part 2, applied: SI 2004/643 Reg.15
Sch.3 Part 2, disapplied: SI 2004/643 Reg.15
Sch.3 Part 2 para.10, applied: SI 2004/643 Reg.24, SI 2004/671 Art.4
Sch.3 Part 2 para.11, applied: SI 2004/643 Reg.5, SI 2004/671 Art.4
Sch.3 Part 2 para.11, enabling: SI 2004/643
Sch.3 Part 2 para.13, applied: SI 2004/643 Reg.5
Sch.3 Part 2 para.13, enabling: SI 2004/643
Sch.3 Part 3 para.16, applied: SI 2004/643 Reg.18, SI 2004/645 Reg.8

2002–cont.

30. Police Reform Act 2002–*cont.*

Sch.3 Part 3 para.17, applied: SI 2004/643 Reg.6, Reg.18, SI 2004/645 Reg.7, Reg.8, Reg.19, Reg.30, SI 2004/653 Reg.7

Sch.3 Part 3 para.18, applied: SI 2004/643 Reg.18, SI 2004/645 Reg.7, Reg.8, Reg.19, Reg.30, SI 2004/653 Reg.7

Sch.3 Part 3 para.19, applied: SI 2004/643 Reg.7, SI 2004/645 Reg.7, Reg.8, Reg.19, Reg.30

Sch.3 Part 3 para.21, applied: SI 2004/643 Reg.7

Sch.3 Part 3 para.22, applied: SI 2004/643 Reg.7, Reg.11

Sch.3 Part 3 para.23, applied: 1985 c.23 s.3, SI 2004/643 Reg.3, Reg.11, Reg.23

Sch.3 Part 3 para.23, referred to: SI 2004/643 Reg.12, Reg.23

Sch.3 Part 3 para.23, enabling: SI 2004/643

Sch.3 Part 3 para.24, applied: 1985 c.23 s.3, SI 2004/643 Reg.3, Reg.10, Reg.11

Sch.3 Part 3 para.24, referred to: SI 2004/643 Reg.12

Sch.3 Part 3 para.24, enabling: SI 2004/643

Sch.3 Part 3 para.25, applied: SI 2004/643 Reg.10, Reg.15, Reg.23

Sch.3 Part 3 para.25, referred to: SI 2004/643 Reg.23

Sch.3 Part 3 para.25, enabling: SI 2004/643

Sch.3 Part 3 para.27, applied: SI 2004/645 Reg.11, Reg.12, Reg.25, Reg.42

Sch.4 Part 1 para.1, amended: 2003 c.38 s.23, s.46, Sch.3

Sch.4 Part 1 para.1, varied: 2003 c.20 s.28, SI 2004/2540 Art.4

Sch.4 Part 1 para.2, amended: 2003 c.38 s.23, s.33

Sch.4 Part 1 para.2, varied: 2003 c.20 s.28

Sch.4 Part 1 para.3, varied: 2003 c.20 s.28

Sch.4 Part 1 para.4, varied: 2003 c.20 s.28

Sch.4 Part 1 para.4A, added: 2003 c.38 s.33

Sch.4 Part 1 para.4A, varied: 2003 c.20 s.28

Sch.4 Part 1 para.4B, added: 2003 c.38 s.33

Sch.4 Part 1 para.4B, varied: 2003 c.20 s.28

Sch.4 Part 1 para.5, varied: 2003 c.20 s.28

Sch.4 Part 1 para.6, varied: 2003 c.20 s.28

Sch.4 Part 1 para.7, varied: 2003 c.20 s.28

Sch.4 Part 1 para.8, varied: 2003 c.20 s.28

Sch.4 Part 1 para.9, varied: 2003 c.20 s.28

Sch.4 Part 1 para.10, varied: 2003 c.20 s.28

Sch.4 Part 1 para.11, varied: 2003 c.20 s.28

Sch.4 Part 1 para.11A, added: 2003 c.38 s.89

Sch.4 Part 1 para.11A, varied: 2003 c.20 s.28

Sch.4 Part 1 para.12, varied: 2003 c.20 s.28

Sch.4 Part 1 para.13, varied: 2003 c.20 s.28

Sch.4 Part 1 para.14, varied: 2003 c.20 s.28

Sch.4 Part 1 para.15, varied: 2003 c.20 s.28

Sch.4 Part 1 para.15A, added: 2003 c.38 s.89

Sch.4 Part 1 para.15A, varied: 2003 c.20 s.28

Sch.4 Part 1 para.15A, enabling: SI 2004/2540

2002–cont.

30. Police Reform Act 2002–*cont.*

Sch.4 Part 2 para.16, varied: 2003 c.20 s.28

Sch.4 Part 2 para.17, amended: 2003 c.44 Sch.1 para.17

Sch.4 Part 2 para.17, varied: 2003 c.20 s.28

Sch.4 Part 2 para.18, varied: 2003 c.20 s.28

Sch.4 Part 2 para.19, varied: 2003 c.20 s.28

Sch.4 Part 2 para.20, amended: 2003 c.44 Sch.1 para.18

Sch.4 Part 2 para.20, varied: 2003 c.20 s.28

Sch.4 Part 2 para.21, varied: 2003 c.20 s.28

Sch.4 Part 2 para.22, applied: 1984 c.60 s.118

Sch.4 Part 2 para.22, varied: 2003 c.20 s.28

Sch.4 Part 2 para.23, varied: 2003 c.20 s.28

Sch.4 Part 2 para.24, varied: 2003 c.20 s.28

Sch.4 Part 2 para.24A, added: 2003 c.44 Sch.1 para.19

Sch.4 Part 2 para.24A, varied: 2003 c.20 s.28

Sch.4 Part 3 para.25, varied: 2003 c.20 s.28

Sch.4 Part 3 para.26, varied: 2003 c.20 s.28

Sch.4 Part 3 para.27, varied: 2003 c.20 s.28

Sch.4 Part 3 para.28, varied: 2003 c.20 s.28

Sch.4 Part 3 para.29, varied: 2003 c.20 s.28

Sch.4 Part 3 para.30, varied: 2003 c.20 s.28

Sch.4 Part 3 para.31, varied: 2003 c.20 s.28

Sch.4 Part 3 para.32, varied: 2003 c.20 s.28

Sch.4 Part 3 para.33, varied: 2003 c.20 s.28

Sch.4 Part 4 para.34, amended: 2003 c.44 Sch.1 para.20

Sch.4 Part 4 para.34, applied: 1984 c.60 s.118

Sch.4 Part 4 para.34, varied: 2003 c.20 s.28

Sch.4 Part 4 para.35, applied: 1984 c.60 s.118

Sch.4 Part 4 para.35, varied: 2003 c.20 s.28

Sch.4 Part 5 para.36, varied: 2003 c.20 s.28

Sch.5 para.1, amended: 2003 c.38 s.23, s.46, s.89, Sch.3

Sch.5 para.1, varied: SI 2004/2540 Art.5

Sch.5 para.2, amended: 2003 c.38 s.23

Sch.5 para.8A, added: 2003 c.38 s.89

Sch.5 para.9A, added: 2003 c.38 s.89

Sch.5 para.9A, enabling: SI 2004/2540

Sch.7 para.9, repealed (in part): 2003 c.44 Sch.37 Part 1

Sch.7 para.20, repealed: 2003 c.39 Sch.10

31. Mobile Telephones (Re-programming) Act 2002

Commencement Orders: SI 2002/2294 Art.2 s.3, enabling: SI 2002/2294

32. Education Act 2002

Commencement Orders: SI 2002/2002 Art.2, Art.3, Art.4; SI 2002/2018 Art.3; SI 2002/2439 Art.2, Art.3, Sch.1 para.1; SI 2002/2952 Art.2; SI 2002/3185 Art.4, Art.5, Art.6, Sch.1 Part II, III; SI 2003/124 Art.2, Art.3, Art.4, Art.5; SI 2003/1115 Art.2, Art.3, Art.4, Art.5; SI 2003/1667 Art.2, Art.3, Art.4, Art.5, Art.6, Sch.1 para.1, para.4; SI 2002/3185 Sch.1 Part 1; SI 2003/1667 Sch.1 para.6; SI 2003/1718 Art.4, Art.5, Art.6, Sch.1 Part II, III; SI 2003/2071 Art.2; SI 2003/2959 Reg.8;

2002–cont.

32. Education Act 2002–*cont.*

–*cont.*

SI 2003/2961 Art.4, Art.5, Art.6; SI 2004/912 Art.4, Art.5, Sch.1 Part 1; SI 2003/2961 Art.7, Sch.1 Part IV; SI 2004/912 Sch.1 Part 2; SI 2004/1318 Art.2; SI 2004/1728 Art.4, Art.5, Sch.1 Part 1, 2; SI 2003/2961 Sch.1 Part III

applied: 1996 c.56 s.408, 1998 c.31 s.82, SI 2003/287 Reg.9, SI 2003/1021 Reg.34, SI 2003/1558 Reg.53, SI 2003/1963 Reg.6

referred to: 1996 c.56 s.409

varied: SI 2003/2045 Reg.6

Part 6, applied: 1996 c.56 s.408, SI 2003/1558 Reg.34

Part 6, referred to: 1996 c.56 s.408

Part 7, applied: 1996 c.56 s.408

Part 10, applied: SI 2003/1910 Reg.5, SI 2003/3234 Reg.3

s.1, applied: SI 2004/108, SI 2004/657, SI 2004/1712, SI 2004/2683, SI 2004/2685

s.1, referred to: SI 2002/3063, SI 2003/716, SI 2003/1671, SI 2004/592, SI 2004/1191, SI 2004/2810

s.2, applied: SI 2004/1191

s.2, enabling: SI 2002/3063, SI 2003/716, SI 2003/1671, SI 2004/108, SI 2004/592, SI 2004/657, SI 2004/1191, SI 2004/1712, SI 2004/2683, SI 2004/2685, SI 2004/2810

s.4, applied: SI 2002/3063, SI 2003/716, SI 2003/1671, SI 2004/108, SI 2004/592, SI 2004/657, SI 2004/1191, SI 2004/1712, SI 2004/2683, SI 2004/2685, SI 2004/2810

s.11, applied: SI 2002/2978 Reg.4, Reg.15, SI 2002/3177 Reg.4, Reg.7

s.12, applied: SI 2002/3199 Sch.1 para.21, SI 2003/3118 Sch.1 para.19, SI 2003/3170 Sch.1 para.21

s.12, enabling: SI 2002/2978, SI 2002/3177, SI 2003/2049, SI 2004/3264

s.14, amended: 2004 c.31 s.59

s.14, applied: SI 1987/1971 Sch.4 para.10, Sch.5 para.60, SI 1992/1814 Sch.4 para.10, Sch.5 para.60, SI 1992/1815 Sch.2 para.36A, SI 2002/3199 Sch.2 para.1, SI 2003/453 Reg.7, SI 2003/2564 Sch.1 para.1, SI 2003/3118 Sch.2 para.1, SI 2003/3170 Sch.2 para.1, Sch.3 para.1, SI 2003/3247 Sch.2 para.1, SI 2004/2506 Sch.1 para.36

s.15, amended: 2004 c.31 s.59

s.15, applied: SI 2003/2564 Sch.1 para.1

s.16, amended: 2004 c.31 s.59

s.16, applied: SI 2003/2564 Sch.1 para.1

s.17, amended: 2004 c.31 s.59

s.17, applied: SI 2003/2564 Sch.1 para.1

s.18, amended: 2004 c.31 s.59

s.19, applied: 1992 c.13 s.21, 1998 c.31 s.16, s.18, s.50, s.127, Sch.1A para.2, Sch.1A para.13, Sch.1A para.19

s.19, disapplied: SI 2004/657 Art.2

2002–cont.

32. Education Act 2002–*cont.*

s.19, referred to: SI 2002/2113 Reg.5, SI 2002/2316 Reg.3

s.19, varied: SI 2004/530 Reg.3

s.19, enabling: SI 2003/348, SI 2003/523, SI 2003/1377, SI 2003/1916, SI 2003/1962, SI 2003/1963, SI 2003/1965, SI 2003/2133, SI 2003/2136, SI 2004/450, SI 2004/530, SI 2004/2042, SI 2004/3264

s.20, applied: 1998 c.31 Sch.1A para.19

s.20, disapplied: SI 2004/657 Art.2

s.20, enabling: SI 2003/348, SI 2003/1965, SI 2003/2136, SI 2004/2042

s.21, referred to: SI 2002/2113 Reg.3

s.21, varied: SI 2004/657 Art.3, SI 2004/1743 Reg.3

s.22, applied: SI 2003/3118 Sch.2 para.33

s.23, applied: 1998 c.31 Sch.1A para.19

s.23, varied: SI 2004/530 Reg.3

s.23, enabling: SI 2003/1377, SI 2003/1962, SI 2003/1965

s.24, applied: SI 1999/2213 Reg.9, Sch.2 para.9A, SI 2003/1200 Sch.2 para.19, Sch.2 para.37, SI 2003/1965 Reg.4, SI 2004/2042 Reg.4

s.24, enabling: SI 2003/1965, SI 2003/2133, SI 2004/2042

s.25, enabling: SI 2003/1965, SI 2004/2042

s.26, enabling: SI 2003/1962, SI 2003/1963

s.27, applied: 1996 c.56 s.3, 1998 c.31 s.51A, s.48, s.50, Sch.15 para.1, SI 2002/378 Reg.3, SI 2003/348 Sch.1 para.8, SI 2003/453 Sch.3 para.28, SI 2003/1558 Reg.10, SI 2003/1963 Reg.3, SI 2003/3170 Sch.1 para.21, SI 2003/3247 Sch.3 para.28, SI 2004/2042 Sch.2 para.9, SI 2004/2507 Sch.1 para.27

s.27, referred to: SI 2002/377 Sch.4 para.28

s.27, varied: SI 2002/2113 Reg.3, SI 2002/2316 Reg.3, SI 2003/1558 Reg.31, SI 2003/1717 Reg.3

s.28, applied: SI 2002/3199 Sch.1 para.21, SI 2003/3118 Sch.1 para.19

s.28, varied: SI 2002/2113 Reg.3, SI 2003/1558 Reg.31, SI 2003/1717 Reg.3

s.29, varied: SI 2003/1717 Reg.3

s.30, applied: 1996 c.57 s.17, 1998 c.31 s.127, SI 2004/2683, SI 2004/2810

s.30, disapplied: SI 2004/2683 Art.2, SI 2004/2810 Art.2

s.30, varied: SI 2002/2316 Reg.3, SI 2004/1743 Reg.3

s.30, enabling: SI 2002/2214, SI 2004/1076

s.32, varied: SI 2004/657 Art.3

s.33, applied: SI 2003/1921 Reg.4, Reg.5, Reg.6, Reg.7

s.33, enabling: SI 2003/1921

s.34, applied: 1998 c.31 s.72, SI 2003/507 Reg.10, SI 2004/2507 Reg.2

2002–cont.

32. Education Act 2002–*cont.*

s.34, enabling: SI 2003/1558, SI 2003/1963, SI 2003/1965, SI 2004/450, SI 2004/2042, SI 2004/3264

s.35, applied: 1998 c.31 s.12, s.81

s.35, enabling: SI 2003/1963, SI 2003/1965, SI 2003/2725, SI 2004/2042

s.36, applied: 1998 c.31 s.12, s.81

s.36, enabling: SI 2003/1963, SI 2003/2725, SI 2004/2042

s.37, applied: SI 1997/3001 Reg.3, 1998 c.31 s.12, s.81

s.37, varied: SI 2002/2316 Reg.3

s.39, applied: SI 2003/1377 Reg.3, SI 2003/1558 Reg.6, SI 2003/1921 Reg.3

s.39, referred to: SI 2002/2113 Reg.3, SI 2002/2316 Reg.3, SI 2003/1717 Reg.3

s.41, referred to: 2003 c.26 Sch.7 para.66

s.41, varied: SI 2002/3184 Reg.4

s.42, referred to: 2003 c.26 Sch.7 para.66

s.44, applied: SI 2002/928 Sch.3, SI 2003/373 Reg.2, SI 2003/3118 Sch.1 para.19, SI 2003/3170 Sch.1 para.21

s.44, enabling: SI 2003/373, SI 2004/393

s.49, disapplied: SI 2002/3185 Art.7

s.50, disapplied: SI 2002/2952 Sch.1 para.3

s.52, see *R. (on the application of Begum (Shabina)) v Denbigh High School Governors* [2004] EWHC 1389, [2004] E.L.R. 374 (QBD (Admin Ct)), Bennett, J.

s.52, applied: 1972 c.70 s.177, 1974 c.7 s.25, 1992 c.53 Sch.1 Part I, SI 1995/2089 Reg.9, 1998 c.31 s.87, SI 1999/495 Reg.4, SI 2001/3446 Sch.9 para.6, SI 2002/2550 Reg.3, SI 2002/3178 Reg.7A, Reg.3, Reg.7, SI 2002/3179 Reg.8A, Reg.3, Reg.4, Reg.7, Reg.8, SI 2003/287 Reg.3, SI 2003/1377 Reg.17, SI 2003/1558 Reg.49, SI 2003/3227 Reg.8A, Reg.3, Reg.8, SI 2003/3246 Reg.9A, Reg.3, Reg.4, Reg.8, Reg.9, SI 2004/182 Reg.4

s.52, disapplied: SI 2002/2952 Sch.1 para.4, SI 2003/2959 Reg.7

s.52, varied: SI 2002/2953 Reg.5, SI 2003/2959 Reg.6, SI 2004/657 Art.3

s.52, enabling: SI 2002/2550, SI 2002/3178, SI 2002/3179, SI 2003/287, SI 2003/1377, SI 2003/3227, SI 2003/3246, SI 2004/402, SI 2004/1805

s.55, referred to: SI 2002/2113 Reg.4

s.63, applied: SI 2002/3199 Sch.1 para.10, SI 2003/3118 Sch.1 para.10, SI 2003/3170 Sch.1 para.10

s.67, applied: SI 1997/1612 Sch.2

s.70, applied: 1996 c.56 s.530, Sch.35A para.1, 1998 c.31 s.28, SI 2002/3199 Reg.1, Sch.1 para.11, SI 2003/453 Reg.1, SI 2003/1041 Reg.6, Reg.7, SI 2003/1200 Reg.3, Reg.4, Reg.5, Reg.6, Reg.7, Reg.15, SI 2003/3170 Sch.1 para.11

s.70, referred to: SI 2003/1200 Reg.2, Reg.3, Sch.1 para.8

2002–cont.

32. Education Act 2002–*cont.*

s.70, enabling: SI 2003/1200

s.71, applied: 1998 c.31 Sch.6 para.4, SI 1999/2213 Reg.2, Reg.4, Reg.5

s.71, enabling: SI 2003/1229

s.74, applied: SI 1999/2213 Sch.2 para.9A, SI 2003/1200 Sch.2 para.19, Sch.2 para.37

s.77, applied: SI 2003/1327 Art.1

s.78, applied: 1997 c.44 s.26, SI 2003/1200 Sch.2 para.21, Sch.2 para.38

s.78, referred to: 1996 c.56 s.482, Sch.1 para.6

s.79, amended: SI 2002/2316 Reg.4

s.80, applied: 1998 c.31 s.69, s.71, Sch.19 para.1, Sch.19 para.4, SI 2003/1200 Sch.2 para.21, Sch.2 para.38

s.82, applied: SI 2001/3446 Reg.2, SI 2002/2897 Reg.3, SI 2003/1038 Art.3, SI 2003/1039 Art.3, SI 2004/2783 Art.3

s.82, referred to: SI 2003/1037 Art.3, SI 2003/1038 Art.3, SI 2003/1039 Art.3

s.83, referred to: SI 2003/391 Art.2

s.84, applied: SI 2004/260 Art.3

s.84, enabling: SI 2004/260

s.85, applied: SI 2003/2946 Art.3

s.85, substituted: SI 2003/2946 Art.2

s.86, enabling: SI 2003/2946

s.87, applied: SI 2002/3199 Sch.1 para.24, SI 2003/1037 Art.10, SI 2004/2783 Art.9

s.87, referred to: SI 2003/1037 Art.4, SI 2003/1038 Art.11, SI 2003/1039 Art.12

s.87, enabling: SI 2003/391, SI 2003/1037, SI 2003/1038, SI 2003/1039, SI 2003/1327, SI 2004/256, SI 2004/261, SI 2004/622, SI 2004/1217, SI 2004/1793, SI 2004/1794, SI 2004/1800, SI 2004/2783

s.88, applied: 1996 c.56 s.451

s.89, amended: SI 2002/2316 Reg.4

s.90, amended: SI 2002/2316 Reg.4

s.90, applied: SI 2004/1076 Reg.3

s.90, varied: SI 2004/657 Art.3

s.91, enabling: SI 2003/252, SI 2004/264

s.92, applied: SI 2001/3446 Sch.1 para.1, Sch.2 para.2, SI 2002/2897 Sch.3 para.9, Sch.3 para.10, Sch.3 para.11

s.93, applied: SI 2001/3446 Sch.1 para.1, Sch.2 para.2, SI 2002/2897 Sch.3 para.9, Sch.3 para.10, Sch.3 para.11

s.94, amended: SI 2002/2316 Reg.4

s.95, amended: SI 2002/2316 Reg.4

s.95, varied: SI 2004/657 Art.3

s.96, applied: SI 2003/252, SI 2003/391, SI 2004/256, SI 2004/261, SI 2004/264, SI 2004/1217, SI 2004/1793, SI 2004/1794, SI 2004/1800

s.96, enabling: SI 2003/252, SI 2003/391, SI 2004/264

s.97, applied: 1996 c.56 s.408

s.98, applied: 1996 c.56 s.408

2002–cont.

32. Education Act 2002–*cont.*

s.99, applied: 1996 c.56 s.408, 1997 c.44 s.32

s.99, referred to: 1996 c.56 Sch.1 para.6

s.99, varied: SI 2002/3184 Reg.5

s.100, applied: 1996 c.56 s.408

s.100, varied: SI 2002/3184 Reg.5

s.101, amended: SI 2003/932 Art.2

s.101, applied: 1996 c.56 s.408, 1996 c.57 s.23, 1998 c.31 s.69, s.71, Sch.19 para.1, Sch.19 para.4

s.101, varied: SI 2002/3184 Reg.5

s.101, enabling: SI 2003/932

s.102, applied: 1996 c.56 s.408

s.102, referred to: SI 2002/3184 Reg.5

s.103, applied: 1996 c.56 s.408, SI 2004/1025 Reg.2, SI 2004/2915 Art.3

s.104, applied: 1996 c.56 s.408

s.104, referred to: SI 2002/3184 Reg.5

s.105, applied: 1996 c.56 s.408, SI 2003/543 Reg.6

s.106, applied: 1996 c.56 s.408, SI 2003/543 Reg.6

s.107, applied: 1996 c.56 s.408

s.108, applied: 1996 c.56 s.408, SI 2003/3118 Sch.1 para.21, SI 2004/2915 Art.4

s.108, referred to: SI 2002/3184 Reg.5, SI 2004/2915 Art.8

s.108, varied: SI 2002/3184 Reg.5

s.108, enabling: SI 2004/2915

s.109, applied: 1996 c.56 s.408, s.451

s.110, applied: 1996 c.56 s.408

s.111, applied: 1996 c.56 s.408

s.111, varied: SI 2002/3184 Reg.5

s.112, applied: 1996 c.56 s.408

s.113, applied: 1996 c.56 s.408, SI 2004/1025 Sch.1 para.2, Sch.3 para.1, Sch.3 para.2, Sch.3 para.3, Sch.3 para.4

s.114, applied: 1996 c.56 s.408, SI 2004/1025 Sch.1 para.2, Sch.3 para.1, Sch.3 para.2, Sch.3 para.3, Sch.3 para.4

s.114, varied: SI 2002/3184 Reg.5

s.115, applied: 1996 c.56 s.408

s.115, varied: SI 2002/3184 Reg.5

s.116, applied: 1996 c.56 s.408

s.117, applied: 1996 c.56 s.408

s.122, applied: 1992 c.13 s.43, SI 1997/3001 Reg.1, SI 2001/2897 Sch.2 para.5, SI 2003/543 Sch.1 para.5, SI 2003/1709 Art.4, Art.5, Art.6, Art.7, SI 2003/2169 Art.2, SI 2004/658 Art.1, SI 2004/2142 Art.3, SI 2004/2506 Sch.1 para.21, Sch.1 para.22

s.122, disapplied: SI 2002/3184 Reg.6

s.122, referred to: SI 2002/3184 Reg.6, SI 2003/1558 Reg.6

s.122, enabling: SI 2003/1709, SI 2003/2169, SI 2003/2640, SI 2004/658, SI 2004/2142

s.123, enabling: SI 2003/2169, SI 2003/2640, SI 2004/658, SI 2004/2142

2002–cont.

32. Education Act 2002–*cont.*

s.124, enabling: SI 2003/2169, SI 2003/2640, SI 2004/658, SI 2004/2142

s.125, enabling: SI 2003/2640, SI 2004/658

s.126, applied: SI 2003/1709, SI 2003/2169, SI 2003/2640, SI 2004/658, SI 2004/2142

s.131, disapplied: 1998 c.30 s.19

s.132, applied: 1998 c.30 s.7, SI 2003/1662, SI 2003/1662 Sch.2 para.3, SI 2003/1917 Reg.5, SI 2003/1963 Reg.3, SI 2003/1994 Reg.12, SI 2004/1729 Sch.2 para.3

s.132, varied: SI 2002/3184 Reg.6

s.132, enabling: SI 2003/1662, SI 2004/1729

s.133, applied: SI 2000/1979 Sch.1 para.19, Sch.2 para.11, SI 2002/3184 Reg.6, SI 2003/1963 Reg.3

s.133, enabling: SI 2003/1663, SI 2004/1744

s.134, applied: 1998 c.30 s.12, SI 2001/3993 Reg.3, Reg.6, SI 2002/326 Reg.3, Reg.4, SI 2003/1963 Reg.3

s.134, varied: SI 2002/3184 Reg.7

s.134, enabling: SI 2003/1663, SI 2004/1744

s.135, applied: SI 2003/1963 Reg.3

s.135, enabling: SI 2003/3111

s.141, applied: SI 2003/1963 Reg.3, SI 2003/3139 Reg.5, SI 2004/2733 Reg.5

s.141, enabling: SI 2003/3139, SI 2004/2733

s.142, applied: 1989 c.41 Sch.9A para.4, 1997 c.50 s.113, s.115, SI 1997/3001 Reg.3, 1998 c.30 s.2, s.3, s.4, Sch.2 para.1, 1999 c.14 s.7, s.12, SI 1999/1726 Reg.5, Reg.10, 2000 c.43 s.35, SI 2000/1979 Sch.1 para.21, Sch.2 para.12, SI 2001/1268 Reg.9, SI 2001/1424 Reg.9, SI 2002/233 Reg.7, SI 2002/2978 Sch.1 para.8, SI 2002/3177 Sch.1 para.8, 2003 asp 5 s.11, s.17, SI 2003/348 Sch.6 para.9, SI 2003/1184 Reg.3, Reg.4, Reg.5, Reg.6, Reg.7, Reg.8, Reg.9, Reg.10, Reg.11, Reg.12, Sch.1 para.7, SI 2003/1558 Sch.2 para.8, SI 2003/1910 Sch.1 para.4, SI 2003/1934 Reg.8, Sch.1 para.20, SI 2003/1963 Reg.3, SI 2003/3230 Reg.1, Reg.6, SI 2003/3234 Sch.1 para.4

s.142, referred to: 1998 c.30 s.15, s.15A, 2003 asp 5 s.17

s.142, varied: 1998 c.30 s.15

s.142, enabling: SI 2003/1184, SI 2004/1493

s.144, applied: 1999 c.14 s.9

s.144, enabling: SI 2003/1184

s.145, enabling: SI 2003/1662, SI 2003/1663, SI 2003/3111, SI 2004/1729, SI 2004/1744

s.150, amended: 2004 c.31 Sch.5 Part 1

s.150, repealed (in part): 2004 c.31 Sch.5 Part 1

s.151, enabling: SI 2003/469

s.157, enabling: SI 2003/1910, SI 2003/3234, SI 2004/3374

s.160, applied: SI 2003/1926 Reg.3

CAP.

2002–cont.

32. Education Act 2002–*cont.*

s.160, enabling: SI 2003/1934, SI 2003/3230, SI 2004/3373

s.161, applied: SI 1997/3001 Reg.3

s.162, applied: SI 2002/816 Sch.9 para.1, SI 2003/3230 Reg.9

s.162, varied: SI 2003/1934 Reg.11

s.163, applied: SI 2003/1910 Sch.1 para.6, Sch.1 para.7, SI 2003/1926 Reg.3, Reg.8, SI 2003/3232 Reg.4, SI 2003/3234 Sch.1 para.6, Sch.1 para.7

s.163, enabling: SI 2003/1926, SI 2003/3232

s.164, enabling: SI 2003/1926

s.165, applied: SI 2002/816 Sch.9 para.1

s.166, applied: 1999 c.14 s.9, SI 2002/816 Reg.6A, Reg.6, Reg.7, Reg.9, Reg.23, Reg.25, Reg.26, Sch.9 para.1, Sch.9 para.7

s.166, referred to: SI 2002/816 Sch.9 para.2

s.168, enabling: SI 2003/1934, SI 2003/3230, SI 2004/3373

s.175, applied: SI 2002/3199 Sch.1 para.7, SI 2003/3118 Sch.1 para.7, SI 2003/3170 Sch.1 para.7, 2004 c.31 s.11, s.12, s.29

s.175, disapplied: 2004 c.31 s.28

s.181, applied: SI 1987/1971 Sch.4 para.10, Sch.5 para.60, SI 1992/1814 Sch.4 para.10, Sch.5 para.60, SI 2003/3118 Sch.1 para.16

s.186, applied: SI 2001/1004 Sch.3 para.16

s.186, enabling: SI 2002/2086, SI 2002/2087, SI 2003/1917

s.197, applied: SI 2003/3118 Sch.1 para.10

s.203, applied: SI 2004/571

s.203, enabling: SI 2004/571

s.207, applied: SI 2002/3199 Sch.2 para.12, SI 2003/3118 Sch.2 para.10

s.207, varied: 1996 c.56 s.493

s.210, applied: SI 2003/2946

s.210, enabling: SI 2002/2086, SI 2002/2087, SI 2002/2550, SI 2002/2978, SI 2002/3177, SI 2002/3178, SI 2002/3179, SI 2003/252, SI 2003/287, SI 2003/348, SI 2003/523, SI 2003/1037, SI 2003/1038, SI 2003/1039, SI 2003/1184, SI 2003/1200, SI 2003/1229, SI 2003/1327, SI 2003/1377, SI 2003/1558, SI 2003/1662, SI 2003/1663, SI 2003/1709, SI 2003/1910, SI 2003/1916, SI 2003/1917, SI 2003/1921, SI 2003/1926, SI 2003/1934, SI 2003/1962, SI 2003/1963, SI 2003/1965, SI 2003/2049, SI 2003/2136, SI 2003/2169, SI 2003/2640, SI 2003/2725, SI 2003/2946, SI 2003/3111, SI 2003/3139, SI 2003/3227, SI 2003/3230, SI 2003/3232, SI 2003/3234, SI 2003/3246, SI 2004/256, SI 2004/261, SI 2004/264, SI 2004/402, SI 2004/450, SI 2004/571, SI 2004/592, SI 2004/622, SI 2004/658, SI 2004/1076, SI 2004/1217, SI 2004/1493, SI 2004/1729, SI 2004/1744, SI 2004/1793, SI 2004/

CAP.

2002–cont.

32. Education Act 2002–*cont.*

s.210, enabling:–*cont.*
1794, SI 2004/1800, SI 2004/1805, SI 2004/2042, SI 2004/2142, SI 2004/2733, SI 2004/2783, SI 2004/2915, SI 2004/3264, SI 2004/3373, SI 2004/3374

s.214, enabling: SI 2002/2113, SI 2002/2316, SI 2002/2904, SI 2002/2953, SI 2002/3178, SI 2002/3179, SI 2002/3184, SI 2003/348, SI 2003/537, SI 2003/689, SI 2003/1184, SI 2003/1558, SI 2003/1708, SI 2003/1717, SI 2003/1934, SI 2003/1965, SI 2003/2039, SI 2003/2045, SI 2003/2136, SI 2003/2694, SI 2003/2751, SI 2003/2959, SI 2003/3227, SI 2003/3246, SI 2003/3247, SI 2004/571, SI 2004/1493, SI 2004/1743, SI 2004/1745, SI 2004/2042, SI 2004/2914

s.216, enabling: SI 2002/2002, SI 2002/2018, SI 2002/2439, SI 2002/2952, SI 2002/3185, SI 2003/124, SI 2003/606, SI 2003/1115, SI 2003/1667, SI 2003/1718, SI 2003/2071, SI 2003/2961, SI 2003/2992, SI 2004/912, SI 2004/1318, SI 2004/1728

Sch.1, applied: 1998 c.31 Sch.1A para.19

Sch.1 para.1, referred to: SI 2002/2113 Reg.3, SI 2003/1717 Reg.3

Sch.1 para.1, varied: SI 2002/2316 Reg.3, SI 2003/1558 Reg.32

Sch.1 para.2, varied: SI 2002/2316 Reg.3, SI 2003/1558 Reg.31, Reg.32

Sch.1 para.3, varied: SI 2002/2113 Reg.3, SI 2002/2316 Reg.3, SI 2003/1558 Reg.32, SI 2003/1717 Reg.3

Sch.1 para.4, varied: SI 2002/2316 Reg.3, SI 2003/1558 Reg.32

Sch.1 para.5, applied: 1998 c.31 Sch.22 para.7

Sch.1 para.5, varied: SI 2002/2316 Reg.3, SI 2003/1558 Reg.32

Sch.1 para.26, varied: SI 2002/2316 Reg.3, SI 2003/1558 Reg.32

Sch.2, applied: 1998 c.31 s.12

Sch.2 Part 1, applied: SI 2003/1963 Reg.36

Sch.2 Part 1 para.1, varied: SI 2003/1963 Reg.33

Sch.2 Part 1 para.2, varied: SI 2003/1963 Reg.33

Sch.2 Part 1 para.3, varied: SI 2003/1963 Reg.33

Sch.2 Part 1 para.4, varied: SI 2003/1963 Reg.33

Sch.2 Part 2, applied: SI 2003/1963 Reg.37

Sch.2 Part 2 para.5, varied: SI 2003/1963 Reg.33

Sch.2 Part 2 para.6, varied: SI 2003/1963 Reg.33

Sch.2 Part 2 para.7, applied: 1996 c.18 s.134

Sch.2 Part 2 para.7, varied: SI 2003/1963 Reg.33

Sch.2 Part 2 para.8, varied: SI 2003/1963 Reg.33

CAP.

2002–cont.

32. Education Act 2002–*cont.*

Sch.2 Part 2 para.9, varied: SI 2003/1963 Reg.33

Sch.2 Part 2 para.10, varied: SI 2003/1963 Reg.33

Sch.4 para.2, disapplied: SI 2002/2952 Sch.1 para.3

Sch.4 para.3, referred to: SI 2002/2439 Sch.1 para.4

Sch.4 para.8, disapplied: SI 2002/2952 Sch.1 para.3

Sch.4 para.9, disapplied: SI 2002/2952 Sch.1 para.3

Sch.4 para.12, disapplied: SI 2002/2952 Sch.1 para.2

Sch.8, applied: SI 2003/1041 Reg.7

Sch.8, referred to: SI 2003/1200 Reg.2

Sch.8 para.2, enabling: SI 2003/1200, SI 2003/1421

Sch.8 para.3, applied: SI 2003/1041 Reg.6, SI 2003/1200 Reg.16, Reg.17

Sch.8 para.3, enabling: SI 2003/1200

Sch.8 para.5, applied: SI 2003/1041 Reg.6, SI 2003/1200 Reg.16, Reg.17

Sch.8 para.5, enabling: SI 2003/1200

Sch.8 para.7, referred to: SI 2003/1200 Sch.1 para.2

Sch.8 para.8, applied: 1998 c.31 s.49, Sch.22 para.2, Sch.22 para.3

Sch.8 para.8, referred to: SI 2003/1200 Sch.1 para.2

Sch.12 Part 2 para.15, repealed (in part): 2003 c.44 Sch.37 Part 11

Sch.13 para.8, repealed (in part): 2003 c.44 Sch.37 Part 11

Sch.14 para.5, referred to: SI 2002/2953 Reg.6

Sch.21 para.6, repealed: 2004 c.22 Sch.1

Sch.21 para.121, referred to: 2003 c.43 s.189

Sch.22, referred to: SI 2002/2113 Reg.7

Sch.22 Part 3, applied: SI 2003/1184 Reg.3

33. Copyright (Visually Impaired Persons) Act 2002

Commencement Orders: SI 2003/2499 Art.2

referred to: SI 2003/115 Sch.1 para.1, SI 2003/2500 Sch.1 Part 1

s.1, amended: SI 2003/2498 Sch.1 para.22

s.2, amended: SI 2003/2498 Sch.1 para.22

s.7, amended: SI 2003/2498 Sch.1 para.22

s.8, enabling: SI 2003/2499

34. Employee Share Schemes Act 2002

repealed: 2003 c.1 Sch.8 Part 1

35. Public Trustee (Liability and Fees) Act 2002

36. Tobacco Advertising and Promotion Act 2002

Commencement Orders: SI 2002/2865 Art.2; SI 2003/77 Reg.3; SI 2004/3138 Art.2; SI 2003/258 Art.2; SI 2003/396 Art.2; SI 2002/2865 Art.2, Art.3; SSI 2004/546 Art.2; SSI 2002/512 Art.2; SSI

CAP.

2002–cont.

36. Tobacco Advertising and Promotion Act 2002–*cont.*

–*cont.*

2003/34 Reg.3; SSI 2003/80 Art.2; SSI 2002/512 Art.2; SSI 2003/113 Art.2; SSI 2002/512 Art.3

applied: SI 2003/1376 Sch.1, SI 2003/1593 Sch.1 Part I

referred to: SI 2003/115 Sch.1 para.2

s.2, applied: SI 2004/765 Reg.4, Reg.5, Reg.6, SI 2004/1824 Reg.6, SSI 2004/144 Reg.4, Reg.5, Reg.6

s.3, applied: SI 2004/1824 Reg.6

s.4, enabling: SI 2004/765, SSI 2004/144

s.6, applied: SI 2004/1277 Reg.2, SSI 2004/211 Reg.2

s.6, enabling: SI 2004/1277, SSI 2004/211

s.9, applied: SI 2004/1824 Reg.6

s.10, applied: SI 2004/1824 Reg.6

s.10, disapplied: SI 2003/77 Reg.3, SSI 2003/34 Reg.3

s.11, applied: SI 2004/1824 Reg.6

s.11, enabling: SI 2004/1824

s.12, amended: 2003 c.21 Sch.17 para.173

s.12, repealed (in part): 2003 c.21 Sch.19

s.19, applied: SI 2004/1824

s.19, enabling: SI 2003/77, SI 2003/1415, SI 2004/765, SI 2004/1277, SI 2004/1824, SSI 2003/34, SSI 2003/265, SSI 2004/144, SSI 2004/211

s.20, enabling: SI 2003/77, SI 2003/1415, SSI 2003/34, SSI 2003/265

s.22, enabling: SI 2002/2865, SI 2003/258, SI 2003/396, SI 2004/3138, SSI 2002/512, SSI 2003/80, SSI 2003/113, SSI 2004/546

37. Private Hire Vehicles (Carriage of Guide Dogs etc.) Act 2002

Commencement Orders: SI 2003/3123 Art.2; SSI 2004/57 Art.2

s.6, enabling: SI 2003/3123, SSI 2004/57

38. Adoption and Children Act 2002

Commencement Orders: SI 2003/181 Art.2; SI 2003/288 Art.2; SI 2004/252 Art.2; SI 2004/1403 Art.2; SI 2003/366 Art.2; SI 2004/3203 Art.2; SI 2003/3079 Art.2

applied: 1988 c.1 s.327A, SI 2003/288

referred to: 2003 c.43 Sch.4 para.125

varied: SI 2004/664 Art.11, Art.12, Art.13, Art.14

Part 1 c.2, applied: 2000 c.14 s.36A

s.1, applied: SI 2004/1011 Reg.3

s.1, referred to: SI 2003/1348 Reg.2

s.2, applied: SI 2003/1348 Reg.2, SI 2004/1011 Reg.3, SI 2004/3203

s.2, referred to: 1988 c.1 s.327A

s.2, enabling: SI 2003/1348, SI 2004/1011

s.3, applied: SI 2004/3203

s.4, applied: SI 2004/3203

s.4, referred to: 1988 c.1 s.327A

s.4, enabling: SI 2003/1348, SI 2004/1011

CAP.

2002–cont.

38. Adoption and Children Act 2002–*cont.*
s.5, repealed: 2004 c.31 Sch.5 Part 1

s.8, amended: 2003 c.43 Sch.4 para.126

s.8, applied: SI 2004/3203

s.9, applied: SI 2004/3203

s.10, applied: SI 2004/3203

s.11, applied: SI 2004/3203

s.12, amended: 2004 c.31 s.57

s.12, applied: SI 2004/3203

s.13, amended: 2003 c.39 Sch.8 para.411

s.19, applied: 2004 c.33 Sch.2 para.1

s.21, amended: 2004 c.33 s.79

s.25, applied: 2004 c.33 Sch.2 para.1

s.27, applied: SI 2004/3203

s.29, applied: 1989 c.41 s.14A, s.14C

s.47, amended: 2004 c.33 s.79

s.51, amended: 2003 c.24 Sch.1 para.18, 2004 c.33 s.79

s.53, applied: SI 2004/3203

s.55, amended: 2003 c.39 Sch.8 para.412

s.56, applied: SI 2004/3203

s.57, applied: SI 2004/3203

s.58, applied: SI 2004/3203

s.59, applied: SI 2004/3203

s.60, applied: SI 2004/3203

s.61, applied: SI 2004/3203

s.62, applied: SI 2004/3203

s.63, applied: SI 2004/3203

s.64, amended: 2004 c.33 s.79

s.64, applied: SI 2004/3203

s.65, applied: SI 2004/3203

s.74, amended: 2003 c.42 Sch.6 para.47, 2004 c.33 s.79

s.79, amended: 2004 c.33 s.79

s.81, amended: 2004 c.33 s.79

s.98, amended: 2004 c.33 s.79

s.98, applied: SI 2004/3203

s.99, amended: 2003 c.43 Sch.9 para.32

s.99, substituted: 2003 c.43 Sch.9 para.32

s.99, varied: SI 2004/664 Art.11, Art.12, Art.13, Art.14

s.102, amended: 2004 c.31 Sch.3 para.16

s.103, amended: 2004 c.31 Sch.3 para.17

s.139, enabling: SI 2003/1348, SI 2004/1011

s.140, enabling: SI 2003/1348, SI 2003/3079, SI 2004/3203

s.141, amended: 2003 c.39 Sch.8 para.413, 2004 c.31 s.62

s.141, repealed (in part): 2003 c.39 Sch.8 para.413, Sch.10

s.142, applied: 2004 c.35 s.265

s.142, enabling: SI 2003/1348, SI 2004/1011

s.144, amended: 2003 c.39 Sch.8 para.414, 2004 c.33 s.79

s.148, enabling: SI 2003/181, SI 2003/288, SI 2003/366, SI 2003/3079, SI 2004/252, SI 2004/1403, SI 2004/3203

Sch.3 para.44, repealed: 2003 c.39 Sch.10

CAP.

2002–cont.

38. Adoption and Children Act 2002–*cont.*
Sch.4 para.3, applied: SI 1987/1967 Sch.9 para.25, Sch.10 para.68, SI 1987/1971 Sch.4 para.23, Sch.5 para.70, 1988 c.1 s.327A, SI 1992/1814 Sch.4 para.24, Sch.5 para.70, SI 1992/2977 Sch.3 para.17, Sch.4 para.24, Sch.4 para.25, SI 1996/207 Sch.7 para.26, Sch.8 para.61, SI 2004/1011 Reg.3

Sch.4 para.3, enabling: SI 2003/1348, SI 2004/1011

40. Enterprise Act 2002
Commencement Orders: SI 2003/765 Art.2, Sch.1; SI 2003/766 Art.2, Art.3, Sch.1; SI 2003/1397 Art.2, Art.3, Art.4, Art.5, Art.6, Art.8, Art.12, Sch.1; SI 2003/2093 Art.2, Art.3, Art.4, Art.5, Art.6, Art.7, Art.8, Sch.1, Sch.2; SI 2003/3340 Art.2, Art.3; SI 2004/1866 Art.2; SI 2004/3233 Art.2, Sch.1

see *Exeter City AFC Ltd v Football Conference Ltd* [2004] EWHC 831, [2004] 1 W.L.R. 2910 (Ch D), Judge Weeks Q.C.; see *Transbus International Ltd (In Liquidation), Re* [2004] EWHC 932, [2004] 1 W.L.R. 2654 (Ch D), Lawrence Collins, J.

applied: 1958 c.47 s.47, 1973 c.41 s.93B, 1986 c.31 s.56, SI 1988/1334 Art.2, SI 1989/2009 Art.2, 1990 c.42 s.197, Sch.4 para.8C, 1991 c.22 s.10, s.33, 1991 c.56 s.12, 1995 c.46 s.235, 1998 c.41 s.3, SI 1999/2450 Sch.1 para.31.2, SI 2003/419 Art.63, 2004 c.35 s.121

referred to: 1984 c.12 s.101, s.103, 1991 c.56 Sch.15 Part II, 1991 c.57 Sch.24 Part II, 1993 c.43 s.145, 2000 c.26 Sch.7 para.3, 2000 c.38 s.19, Sch.9 para.3, 2003 c.21 s.393

varied: 2003 c.21 Sch.18 para.56

Part 3, applied: 1977 c.37 s.50A, s.53, 1980 c.21 s.11C, 1984 c.12 s.13B, 1986 c.31 s.54, 1986 c.44 s.24B, 1989 c.29 s.12B, s.56CB, s.14A, s.15, 1991 c.56 s.17, 1993 c.43 s.13B, s.15C, s.66, Sch.4A para.10A, 1998 c.41 Sch.1 para.1, Sch.1 para.2, Sch.7 para.20, 2000 c.8 Sch.14 para.2A, 2003 c.21 s.193, Sch.18 para.62, SI 2003/419 Sch.2 para.5, SI 2003/1592 Sch.3 para.1, SI 2003/1594 Art.2

Part 3, referred to: 1949 c.88 s.11AB, 1986 c.44 s.27, 2000 c.38 s.19, 2003 c.21 s.391

Part 4, applied: 1958 c.47 s.19A, 1977 c.37 s.50A, s.53, 1984 c.12 s.50, 1986 c.31 s.54, 1986 c.44 s.36A, 1989 c.29 s.15, s.43, 1991 c.56 s.17, s.31, 1993 c.43 s.67, 1996 c.61 s.22, 1998 c.41 Sch.7 para.5, Sch.7 para.20, SI 2000/2956 Reg.5, 2003 c.21 s.369, s.370, SI 2003/1372 r.27, SI 2003/1594 Art.2

Part 4, referred to: 1949 c.88 s.11AB, 1986 c.44 s.27, 2000 c.38 s.19, 2003 c.21 s.370

2002–cont.

40. Enterprise Act 2002–*cont.*

Part 8, applied: SI 1989/2009 Art.3, SI 2003/1399 Art.3, Art.4, Art.6, SI 2003/1594 Art.2, SI 2004/935 Art.3

Part 9, applied: 1984 c.12 s.101, 1991 c.56 s.206, 1993 c.43 s.145, 2000 c.27 s.105, 2000 c.38 Sch.9 para.5, 2003 c.21 s.393, SI 2003/419 Art.63

Part 9, referred to: SI 2003/419 Sch.4 para.18

s.2, referred to: SI 2003/419 Sch.4 para.17

s.6, applied: 1984 c.12 s.48, 1989 c.29 s.48, 1991 c.56 s.201, 1993 c.43 s.71, 2000 c.38 s.90, SI 2003/419 Art.7

s.11, applied: SI 2004/1517, SI 2004/1517 Art.2

s.11, disapplied: SI 2003/1368 Art.2

s.11, varied: SI 2003/1368 Art.2

s.11, enabling: SI 2004/1517, SI 2004/3366

s.12, applied: 1967 c.13 Sch.4, 1992 c.53 Sch.1 Part I, SI 2003/1372 r.4

s.14, applied: 1998 c.41 Sch.8 para.2, SI 2001/2916 Reg.27, Sch.2 para.1, SI 2003/766 Art.3

s.15, applied: 1998 c.41 Sch.8 para.2, SI 2001/2916 Reg.2, SI 2003/1372, 2004 c.20 Sch.18 para.19, Sch.18 para.20

s.15, enabling: SI 2003/1372, SI 2004/2068

s.16, enabling: SSI 2004/350

s.17, disapplied: SI 2003/1397 Art.5

s.22, amended: 2003 c.21 Sch.19, SI 2004/1079 Sch.1 para.2

s.22, applied: 1998 c.41 Sch.1 para.5, SI 2003/1370 Art.3, Art.10, SI 2003/1592 Art.4

s.22, referred to: SI 2003/1592 Sch.2 para.8

s.22, varied: 1986 c.44 s.26A, s.41EB, 1990 c.42 Sch.4 para.4A, 2000 c.38 s.12B, s.18

s.23, applied: SI 2003/1592 Art.2, Art.4

s.23, disapplied: SI 2003/1592 Art.7

s.23, referred to: SI 2003/1592 Art.7

s.23, varied: 1986 c.44 s.26A, s.41EB, 1990 c.42 Sch.4 para.4A, 2000 c.38 s.12B, s.18, SI 2003/1592 Sch.1

s.24, applied: SI 2003/1592 Art.2

s.24, varied: 1986 c.44 s.26A, s.41EB, 1990 c.42 Sch.4 para.4A, 2000 c.38 s.12B, s.18, SI 2003/1592 Sch.1

s.25, amended: SI 2004/1079 Sch.1 para.2

s.25, applied: SI 2003/1592 Art.2

s.25, varied: 1986 c.44 s.26A, s.41EB, 1990 c.42 Sch.4 para.4A, 2000 c.38 s.12B, s.18, SI 2003/1592 Sch.1

s.26, applied: 1998 c.41 Sch.1 para.1, Sch.1 para.2, Sch.1 para.5, SI 2003/1370 Sch.1 para.7, SI 2003/1592 Art.2

s.26, disapplied: 1998 c.41 Sch.1 para.5

s.26, referred to: SI 2003/1370 Art.4

s.26, varied: 1986 c.44 s.26A, s.41EB, 1990 c.42 Sch.4 para.4A, 1998 c.41 Sch.1 para.1, 2000 c.38 s.12B, s.18, SI 2003/1592 Sch.1

2002–cont.

40. Enterprise Act 2002–*cont.*

s.27, applied: SI 2003/1397 Art.4, SI 2003/1592 Art.2, SI 2003/1595 Art.3, Art.4, SI 2004/3233 Art.3

s.27, varied: 1986 c.44 s.26A, s.41EB, 1990 c.42 Sch.4 para.4A, 2000 c.38 s.12B, s.18, SI 2003/1592 Sch.1, SI 2003/1595 Art.3

s.28, applied: SI 2003/1592 Art.2

s.28, referred to: SI 2003/1370 Art.11

s.28, varied: 1986 c.44 s.26A, s.41EB, 1990 c.42 Sch.4 para.4A, 2000 c.38 s.12B, s.18, SI 2003/1592 Sch.1

s.28, enabling: SI 2003/1370, SI 2004/3204

s.29, applied: SI 2003/1397 Art.4, SI 2003/1592 Art.2, SI 2003/1595 Art.3, Art.4, SI 2004/3233 Art.3

s.29, varied: 1986 c.44 s.26A, s.41EB, 1990 c.42 Sch.4 para.4A, 2000 c.38 s.12B, s.18, SI 2003/1592 Sch.1, SI 2003/1595 Art.3

s.30, applied: SI 2003/1592 Art.2

s.30, varied: 1986 c.44 s.26A, s.41EB, 1990 c.42 Sch.4 para.4A, 2000 c.38 s.12B, s.18, SI 2003/1592 Sch.1

s.31, applied: SI 2003/1592 Art.2

s.31, varied: 1986 c.44 s.26A, s.41EB, 1990 c.42 Sch.4 para.4A, 2000 c.38 s.12B, s.18, SI 2003/1592 Sch.1

s.32, applied: SI 2003/1592 Art.2

s.32, varied: 1986 c.44 s.26A, s.41EB, 1990 c.42 Sch.4 para.4A, 2000 c.38 s.12B, s.18, SI 2003/1592 Sch.1

s.33, see *IBA Health Ltd v Office of Fair Trading (Application for Leave to Appeal)* [2003] CAT 28, [2004] Comp. A.R. 294 (Competition Appeal Tribunal), Sir Christopher Bellamy (President); see *IBA Health Ltd v Office of Fair Trading* [2004] EWCA Civ 142, [2004] 4 All E.R. 1103 (CA), Sir Andrew Morritt V.C.

s.33, amended: 2003 c.21 Sch.19, SI 2004/1079 Sch.1 para.2

s.33, applied: 1998 c.41 Sch.1 para.5, SI 2003/1370 Art.3, Art.4, Art.10

s.33, referred to: SI 2003/1592 Sch.2 para.8

s.33, varied: 1986 c.44 s.26A, s.41EB, 1990 c.42 Sch.4 para.4A, 2000 c.38 s.12B, s.18

s.34, referred to: SI 2003/1592 Art.2

s.34, varied: 1986 c.44 s.26A, s.41EB, 1990 c.42 Sch.4 para.4A, 2000 c.38 s.12B, s.18

s.34, enabling: SI 2003/1595

s.34A, added: SI 2004/1079 Sch.1 para.2

s.34A, varied: 1986 c.44 s.26A, s.41EB, 1990 c.42 Sch.4 para.4A, 2000 c.38 s.12B, s.18

s.34B, added: SI 2004/1079 Sch.1 para.2

s.34B, varied: 1986 c.44 s.26A, s.41EB, 1990 c.42 Sch.4 para.4A, 2000 c.38 s.12B, s.18

s.35, applied: 1949 c.88 s.11AB, 1998 c.41 Sch.7 para.20

s.35, varied: 1977 c.37 s.50A, 1986 c.44 s.26A, s.41EB, 1990 c.42 Sch.4 para.4A, 2000 c.38 s.12B, s.18

2002–cont.

40. Enterprise Act 2002–*cont.*

s.36, applied: 1949 c.88 s.11AB, 1998 c.41 Sch.7 para.20

s.36, varied: 1977 c.37 s.50A, 1986 c.44 s.26A, s.41EB, 1990 c.42 Sch.4 para.4A, 2000 c.38 s.12B, s.18, SI 2003/1595 Art.4

s.37, applied: 1998 c.41 Sch.7 para.15

s.37, varied: 1986 c.44 s.26A, s.41EB, 1990 c.42 Sch.4 para.4A, 2000 c.38 s.12B, s.18

s.38, varied: 1986 c.44 s.26A, s.41EB, 1990 c.42 Sch.4 para.4A, 2000 c.38 s.12B, s.18

s.39, repealed (in part): SI 2004/1079 Sch.1 para.2

s.39, varied: 1986 c.44 s.26A, s.41EB, 1990 c.42 Sch.4 para.4A, 2000 c.38 s.12B, s.18

s.40, amended: SI 2004/1079 Sch.1 para.2

s.40, repealed (in part): SI 2004/1079 Sch.1 para.2

s.40, varied: 1986 c.44 s.26A, s.41EB, 1990 c.42 Sch.4 para.4A, 2000 c.38 s.12B, s.18

s.41, applied: 1949 c.88 s.11AB, 1977 c.37 s.50A, 1988 c.48 s.144, s.238, Sch.2A para.17, SI 1997/3032 Sch.2 para.15

s.41, varied: 1986 c.44 s.26A, s.41EB, 1990 c.42 Sch.4 para.4A, 2000 c.38 s.12B, s.18

s.42, varied: 1986 c.44 s.26A, s.41EB, 1990 c.42 Sch.4 para.4A, 2000 c.38 s.12B, s.18

s.43, amended: 2003 c.21 Sch.16 para.8

s.43, varied: 1986 c.44 s.26A, s.41EB, 1990 c.42 Sch.4 para.4A, 2000 c.38 s.12B, s.18

s.44, amended: 2003 c.21 s.376

s.44, applied: 2003 c.21 s.391

s.44, varied: 1986 c.44 s.26A, s.41EB, 1990 c.42 Sch.4 para.4A, 2000 c.38 s.12B, s.18

s.44A, added: 2003 c.21 s.377

s.44A, varied: 1986 c.44 s.26A, s.41EB, 1990 c.42 Sch.4 para.4A, 2000 c.38 s.12B, s.18

s.45, amended: 2003 c.21 Sch.16 para.9

s.45, applied: 1998 c.41 Sch.1 para.5, SI 2003/1370 Art.3

s.45, varied: 1986 c.44 s.26A, s.41EB, 1990 c.42 Sch.4 para.4A, 2000 c.38 s.12B, s.18

s.46, amended: 2003 c.21 Sch.19, SI 2004/1079 Sch.1 para.2

s.46, varied: 1986 c.44 s.26A, s.41EB, 1990 c.42 Sch.4 para.4A, 2000 c.38 s.12B, s.18

s.46A, added: SI 2004/1079 Sch.1 para.2

s.46A, varied: 1986 c.44 s.26A, s.41EB, 1990 c.42 Sch.4 para.4A, 2000 c.38 s.12B, s.18

s.46B, added: SI 2004/1079 Sch.1 para.2

s.46B, varied: 1986 c.44 s.26A, s.41EB, 1990 c.42 Sch.4 para.4A, 2000 c.38 s.12B, s.18

s.46C, added: SI 2004/1079 Sch.1 para.2

s.46C, varied: 1986 c.44 s.26A, s.41EB, 1990 c.42 Sch.4 para.4A, 2000 c.38 s.12B, s.18

s.47, applied: 1949 c.88 s.11AB, 1998 c.41 Sch.7 para.20

s.47, varied: 1977 c.37 s.50A, 1986 c.44 s.26A, s.41EB, 1990 c.42 Sch.4 para.4A, 2000 c.38 s.12B, s.18

s.48, applied: 1998 c.41 Sch.7 para.15

2002–cont.

40. Enterprise Act 2002–*cont.*

s.48, varied: 1986 c.44 s.26A, s.41EB, 1990 c.42 Sch.4 para.4A, 2000 c.38 s.12B, s.18

s.49, varied: 1986 c.44 s.26A, s.41EB, 1990 c.42 Sch.4 para.4A, 2000 c.38 s.12B, s.18

s.50, amended: 2003 c.21 Sch.16 para.10

s.50, varied: 1986 c.44 s.26A, s.41EB, 1990 c.42 Sch.4 para.4A, 2000 c.38 s.12B, s.18

s.51, repealed (in part): SI 2004/1079 Sch.1 para.2

s.51, varied: 1986 c.44 s.26A, s.41EB, 1990 c.42 Sch.4 para.4A, 2000 c.38 s.12B, s.18

s.52, amended: SI 2004/1079 Sch.1 para.2

s.52, applied: SI 2003/1592 Art.10

s.52, repealed (in part): SI 2004/1079 Sch.1 para.2

s.52, varied: 1986 c.44 s.26A, s.41EB, 1990 c.42 Sch.4 para.4A, 2000 c.38 s.12B, s.18

s.53, amended: SI 2004/1079 Sch.1 para.2

s.53, repealed (in part): SI 2004/1079 Sch.1 para.2

s.53, varied: 1986 c.44 s.26A, s.41EB, 1990 c.42 Sch.4 para.4A, 2000 c.38 s.12B, s.18

s.54, varied: 1986 c.44 s.26A, s.41EB, 1990 c.42 Sch.4 para.4A, 2000 c.38 s.12B, s.18

s.55, applied: 1949 c.88 s.11AB, 1977 c.37 s.50A, 1988 c.48 s.144, s.238, Sch.2A para.17, SI 1997/3032 Sch.2 para.15

s.55, varied: 1986 c.44 s.26A, s.41EB, 1990 c.42 Sch.4 para.4A, 2000 c.38 s.12B, s.18

s.56, varied: 1986 c.44 s.26A, s.41EB, 1990 c.42 Sch.4 para.4A, 2000 c.38 s.12B, s.18

s.57, amended: 2003 c.21 Sch.16 para.11

s.57, varied: 1986 c.44 s.26A, s.41EB, 1990 c.42 Sch.4 para.4A, 2000 c.38 s.12B, s.18

s.58, amended: 2003 c.21 s.375, Sch.16 para.12, SI 2004/1079 Sch.1 para.2

s.58, applied: 2003 c.21 s.391

s.58, varied: 1986 c.44 s.26A, s.41EB, 1990 c.42 Sch.4 para.4A, 2000 c.38 s.12B, s.18

s.58A, added: 2003 c.21 s.375

s.58A, varied: 1986 c.44 s.26A, s.41EB, 1990 c.42 Sch.4 para.4A, 2000 c.38 s.12B, s.18

s.59, amended: 2003 c.21 s.378

s.59, applied: 2003 c.21 s.391

s.59, varied: 1986 c.44 s.26A, s.41EB, 1990 c.42 Sch.4 para.4A, 2000 c.38 s.12B, s.18

s.59A, added: 2003 c.21 s.378

s.59A, varied: 1986 c.44 s.26A, s.41EB, 1990 c.42 Sch.4 para.4A, 2000 c.38 s.12B, s.18

s.60, amended: 2003 c.21 Sch.16 para.13

s.60, varied: 1986 c.44 s.26A, s.41EB, 1990 c.42 Sch.4 para.4A, 2000 c.38 s.12B, s.18

s.61, amended: 2003 c.21 s.379

s.61, varied: 1986 c.44 s.26A, s.41EB, 1990 c.42 Sch.4 para.4A, 2000 c.38 s.12B, s.18

s.61A, added: 2003 c.21 s.380

s.61A, varied: 1986 c.44 s.26A, s.41EB, 1990 c.42 Sch.4 para.4A, 2000 c.38 s.12B, s.18

s.62, amended: 2003 c.21 Sch.16 para.14, Sch.19

2002–cont.

40. Enterprise Act 2002–*cont.*

s.62, applied: 1998 c.41 Sch.1 para.5

s.62, varied: 1986 c.44 s.26A, s.41EB, 1990 c.42 Sch.4 para.4A, 2000 c.38 s.12B, s.18

s.63, applied: 1949 c.88 s.11AB, 1998 c.41 Sch.7 para.20

s.63, varied: 1977 c.37 s.50A, 1986 c.44 s.26A, s.41EB, 1990 c.42 Sch.4 para.4A, 2000 c.38 s.12B, s.18

s.64, applied: 1998 c.41 Sch.7 para.15

s.64, varied: 1986 c.44 s.26A, s.41EB, 1990 c.42 Sch.4 para.4A, 2000 c.38 s.12B, s.18

s.65, amended: 2003 c.21 Sch.16 para.15

s.65, varied: 1986 c.44 s.26A, s.41EB, 1990 c.42 Sch.4 para.4A, 2000 c.38 s.12B, s.18

s.66, applied: 1949 c.88 s.11AB, 1977 c.37 s.50A, 1988 c.48 s.144, s.238, Sch.2A para.17, SI 1997/3032 Sch.2 para.15

s.66, varied: 1986 c.44 s.26A, s.41EB, 1990 c.42 Sch.4 para.4A, 2000 c.38 s.12B, s.18

s.67, amended: 2003 c.21 Sch.16 para.16, Sch.19, SI 2004/1079 Sch.1 para.2

s.67, applied: SI 2003/1592 Art.4A, Art.3, Art.4

s.67, varied: 1986 c.44 s.26A, s.41EB, 1990 c.42 Sch.4 para.4A, 2000 c.38 s.12B, s.18

s.68, amended: 2003 c.21 Sch.16 para.17, Sch.19, SI 2004/1079 Sch.1 para.2

s.68, applied: SI 2003/1592 Art.2

s.68, varied: 1986 c.44 s.26A, s.41EB, 1990 c.42 Sch.4 para.4A, 2000 c.38 s.12B, s.18

s.68, enabling: SI 2003/1592

s.69, applied: SI 2003/1592 Art.5, Sch.3 para.1

s.69, repealed: 2003 c.21 Sch.19

s.69, varied: 1986 c.44 s.26A, s.41EB, 1990 c.42 Sch.4 para.4A, 2000 c.38 s.12B, s.18, SI 2003/1592 Sch.3 para.1

s.70, applied: SI 2003/1397 Art.3

s.70, varied: 1986 c.44 s.26A, s.41EB, 1990 c.42 Sch.4 para.4A, 2000 c.38 s.12B, s.18

s.71, varied: 1986 c.44 s.26A, s.41EB, 1990 c.42 Sch.4 para.4A, 2000 c.38 s.12B, s.18

s.72, varied: 1986 c.44 s.26A, s.41EB, 1990 c.42 Sch.4 para.4A, 2000 c.38 s.12B, s.18

s.73, varied: 1986 c.44 s.26A, s.41EB, 1990 c.42 Sch.4 para.4A, 2000 c.38 s.12B, s.18

s.74, varied: 1986 c.44 s.26A, s.41EB, 1990 c.42 Sch.4 para.4A, 2000 c.38 s.12B, s.18

s.75, applied: 1949 c.88 s.11AB, 1977 c.37 s.50A, 1988 c.48 s.144, s.238, Sch.2A para.17, SI 1997/3032 Sch.2 para.15

s.75, referred to: 1988 c.48 s.144

s.75, varied: 1986 c.44 s.26A, s.41EB, 1990 c.42 Sch.4 para.4A, 2000 c.38 s.12B, s.18

s.76, varied: 1986 c.44 s.26A, s.41EB, 1990 c.42 Sch.4 para.4A, 2000 c.38 s.12B, s.18

s.77, applied: SI 2003/1592 Sch.2 para.8

s.77, varied: 1986 c.44 s.26A, s.41EB, 1990 c.42 Sch.4 para.4A, 2000 c.38 s.12B, s.18

s.78, applied: SI 2003/1592 Sch.2 para.8

2002–cont.

40. Enterprise Act 2002–*cont.*

s.78, varied: 1986 c.44 s.26A, s.41EB, 1990 c.42 Sch.4 para.4A, 2000 c.38 s.12B, s.18

s.79, applied: SI 2003/1592 Sch.2 para.8

s.79, varied: 1986 c.44 s.26A, s.41EB, 1990 c.42 Sch.4 para.4A, 2000 c.38 s.12B, s.18, SI 2003/1592 Sch.2 para.8

s.80, varied: 1986 c.44 s.26A, s.41EB, 1990 c.42 Sch.4 para.4A, 2000 c.38 s.12B, s.18

s.81, varied: 1986 c.44 s.26A, s.41EB, 1990 c.42 Sch.4 para.4A, 2000 c.38 s.12B, s.18

s.82, varied: 1986 c.44 s.26A, s.41EB, 1990 c.42 Sch.4 para.4A, 2000 c.38 s.12B, s.18

s.83, applied: 1949 c.88 s.11AB, 1977 c.37 s.50A, 1988 c.48 s.144, s.238, Sch.2A para.17, SI 1997/3032 Sch.2 para.15

s.83, referred to: 1988 c.48 s.144

s.83, varied: 1986 c.44 s.26A, s.41EB, 1990 c.42 Sch.4 para.4A, 2000 c.38 s.12B, s.18

s.84, applied: 1988 c.48 Sch.2A para.17, SI 1997/3032 Sch.2 para.15

s.84, referred to: 1988 c.48 s.144

s.84, varied: 1986 c.44 s.26A, s.41EB, 1990 c.42 Sch.4 para.4A, 2000 c.38 s.12B, s.18

s.85, varied: 1986 c.44 s.26A, s.41EB, 1990 c.42 Sch.4 para.4A, 2000 c.38 s.12B, s.18

s.86, applied: 1980 c.21 s.11D, s.12, 1994 c.17 s.33, SI 2003/1592 Sch.3 para.1

s.86, varied: 1986 c.44 s.26A, s.41EB, 1990 c.42 Sch.4 para.4A, 2000 c.38 s.12B, s.18, SI 2003/1592 Sch.3 para.1

s.87, applied: 1980 c.21 s.11D, s.12, SI 2003/1592 Sch.3 para.1

s.87, varied: 1986 c.44 s.26A, s.41EB, 1990 c.42 Sch.4 para.4A, 2000 c.38 s.12B, s.18

s.88, applied: 1980 c.21 s.12, SI 2003/1592 Sch.3 para.1

s.88, varied: 1986 c.44 s.26A, s.41EB, 1990 c.42 Sch.4 para.4A, 2000 c.38 s.12B, s.18, SI 2003/1592 Sch.3 para.1

s.89, applied: 1988 c.48 Sch.2A para.17, SI 1997/3032 Sch.2 para.15, SI 2003/1592 Sch.3 para.1

s.89, referred to: 1988 c.48 s.144

s.89, varied: 1986 c.44 s.26A, s.41EB, 1990 c.42 Sch.4 para.4A, 2000 c.38 s.12B, s.18, SI 2003/1592 Sch.3 para.1

s.90, varied: 1986 c.44 s.26A, s.41EB, 1990 c.42 Sch.4 para.4A, 2000 c.38 s.12B, s.18, 2003 c.21 Sch.18 para.62

s.91, applied: 1949 c.88 s.11AB, 1977 c.37 s.50A, 2003 c.21 Sch.18 para.62, SI 2003/1592 Sch.3 para.1

s.91, varied: 1986 c.44 s.26A, s.41EB, 1990 c.42 Sch.4 para.4A, 2000 c.38 s.12B, s.18, 2003 c.21 Sch.18 para.62, SI 2003/1592 Sch.3 para.1

s.91, enabling: SI 2003/1373

s.92, applied: 1949 c.88 s.11AB, 1977 c.37 s.50A, SI 2003/1592 Sch.3 para.1

2002–cont.

40. Enterprise Act 2002–*cont.*

s.92, varied: 1986 c.44 s.26A, s.41EB, 1990 c.42 Sch.4 para.4A, 2000 c.38 s.12B, s.18, 2003 c.21 Sch.18 para.62, SI 2003/1592 Sch.3 para.1

s.93, applied: SI 2003/1592 Sch.3 para.1

s.93, varied: 1986 c.44 s.26A, s.41EB, 1990 c.42 Sch.4 para.4A, 2000 c.38 s.12B, s.18, 2003 c.21 Sch.18 para.62, SI 2003/1592 Sch.3 para.1

s.94, applied: 1980 c.21 s.11D, s.12, SI 2003/1592 Sch.3 para.1

s.94, varied: 1986 c.44 s.26A, s.41EB, 1990 c.42 Sch.4 para.4A, 2000 c.38 s.12B, s.18, 2003 c.21 Sch.18 para.62, SI 2003/1592 Sch.3 para.1

s.95, applied: SI 2003/1592 Sch.3 para.1

s.95, varied: 1986 c.44 s.26A, s.41EB, 1990 c.42 Sch.4 para.4A, 2000 c.38 s.12B, s.18, SI 2003/1592 Sch.3 para.1

s.96, applied: SI 2003/1369 Reg.3, Reg.5, SI 2003/1370 Art.3

s.96, varied: 1986 c.44 s.26A, s.41EB, 1990 c.42 Sch.4 para.4A, 2000 c.38 s.12B, s.18

s.97, amended: SI 2004/1079 Sch.1 para.2

s.97, applied: SI 2003/1369 Reg.8, Reg.10, Reg.11, Reg.12

s.97, varied: 1986 c.44 s.26A, s.41EB, 1990 c.42 Sch.4 para.4A, 2000 c.38 s.12B, s.18

s.98, varied: 1986 c.44 s.26A, s.41EB, 1990 c.42 Sch.4 para.4A, 2000 c.38 s.12B, s.18

s.99, amended: SI 2004/1079 Sch.1 para.2

s.99, applied: SI 2003/1369 Reg.6, Reg.8

s.99, referred to: SI 2003/1370 Art.10

s.99, varied: 1986 c.44 s.26A, s.41EB, 1990 c.42 Sch.4 para.4A, 2000 c.38 s.12B, s.18

s.100, applied: SI 2003/1369 Reg.4

s.100, varied: 1986 c.44 s.26A, s.41EB, 1990 c.42 Sch.4 para.4A, 2000 c.38 s.12B, s.18

s.101, varied: 1986 c.44 s.26A, s.41EB, 1990 c.42 Sch.4 para.4A, 2000 c.38 s.12B, s.18

s.101, enabling: SI 2003/1369

s.102, varied: 1986 c.44 s.26A, s.41EB, 1990 c.42 Sch.4 para.4A, 2000 c.38 s.12B, s.18

s.103, applied: SI 2003/1592 Sch.3 para.1

s.103, varied: 1986 c.44 s.26A, s.41EB, 1990 c.42 Sch.4 para.4A, 2000 c.38 s.12B, s.18, SI 2003/1592 Sch.3 para.1

s.104, applied: SI 2003/1592 Sch.3 para.1

s.104, varied: 1986 c.44 s.26A, s.41EB, 1990 c.42 Sch.4 para.4A, 2000 c.38 s.12B, s.18, SI 2003/1592 Sch.3 para.1

s.104A, added: 2003 c.21 s.381

s.104A, varied: 1986 c.44 s.26A, s.41EB, 1990 c.42 Sch.4 para.4A, 2000 c.38 s.12B, s.18, SI 2003/1592 Sch.3 para.1

s.105, amended: 2003 c.21 s.382

s.105, applied: SI 2003/1592 Sch.3 para.1

s.105, varied: 1986 c.44 s.26A, s.41EB, 1990 c.42 Sch.4 para.4A, 2000 c.38 s.12B, s.18, SI 2003/1592 Sch.3 para.1

2002–cont.

40. Enterprise Act 2002–*cont.*

s.106, applied: 1998 c.41 Sch.7 para.5

s.106, varied: 1986 c.44 s.26A, s.41EB, 1990 c.42 Sch.4 para.4A, 2000 c.38 s.12B, s.18

s.106A, added: 2003 c.21 s.383

s.106A, varied: 1986 c.44 s.26A, s.41EB, 1990 c.42 Sch.4 para.4A, 2000 c.38 s.12B, s.18

s.106B, added: 2003 c.21 s.384

s.106B, varied: 1986 c.44 s.26A, s.41EB, 1990 c.42 Sch.4 para.4A, 2000 c.38 s.12B, s.18, SI 2003/1592 Sch.3 para.1

s.107, amended: 2003 c.21 Sch.16 para.18

s.107, varied: 1986 c.44 s.26A, s.41EB, 1990 c.42 Sch.4 para.4A, 2000 c.38 s.12B, s.18

s.108, amended: 2003 c.21 Sch.16 para.19

s.108, applied: SI 2003/1592 Sch.3 para.1

s.108, varied: 1986 c.44 s.26A, s.41EB, 1990 c.42 Sch.4 para.4A, 2000 c.38 s.12B, s.18, SI 2003/1592 Sch.3 para.1

s.109, applied: 1984 c.12 s.13B, 1989 c.29 s.12B, 1993 c.43 s.13B, Sch.4A para.10A, 2000 c.8 Sch.14 para.2A, SI 2003/419 Sch.2 para.5, SI 2003/1592 Art.9, Sch.3 para.1

s.109, varied: 1980 c.21 s.11B, 1984 c.12 s.13B, 1986 c.31 s.44A, 1986 c.44 s.26A, s.24B, s.41EB, 1989 c.29 s.14A, s.12B, s.56CB, 1990 c.42 Sch.4 para.4A, 1991 c.56 s.14B, s.16B, 1993 c.43 s.15C, s.13B, Sch.4A para.10A, SI 1999/3088 Reg.8, 2000 c.26 s.19A, s.15B, 2000 c.38 s.12B, s.18, SI 2003/1592 Sch.3 para.1

s.110, applied: 1984 c.12 s.13B, 1989 c.29 s.12B, 1993 c.43 s.13B, Sch.4A para.10A, 2000 c.8 Sch.14 para.2A, SI 2003/419 Sch.2 para.5, SI 2003/1592 Sch.3 para.1, SI 2004/2528 Sch.1 para.5

s.110, referred to: SI 2004/2528 Sch.1 para.5

s.110, varied: 1980 c.21 s.11B, 1984 c.12 s.13B, 1986 c.31 s.44A, 1986 c.44 s.26A, s.24B, s.41EB, 1989 c.29 s.14A, s.12B, s.56CB, 1990 c.42 Sch.4 para.4A, 1991 c.56 s.14B, s.16B, 1993 c.43 s.15C, s.13B, Sch.4A para.10A, Sch.4A para.15, SI 1999/3088 Reg.8, 2000 c.8 Sch.14 para.2A, 2000 c.26 s.19A, s.15B, 2000 c.38 s.12B, s.18, SI 2003/419 Sch.2 para.5, SI 2003/1592 Sch.3 para.1

s.111, applied: 1980 c.21 s.31, 1984 c.12 s.13B, 1989 c.29 s.12B, 1993 c.43 s.13B, Sch.4A para.10A, 2000 c.8 Sch.14 para.2A, SI 2003/419 Sch.2 para.5, SI 2003/1371 Art.2, SI 2003/1592 Sch.3 para.1, SI 2004/2528 Sch.1 para.5

s.111, referred to: SI 2003/1371

s.111, varied: 1980 c.21 s.11B, 1984 c.12 s.13B, 1986 c.31 s.44A, 1986 c.44 s.26A, s.24B, s.41EB, 1989 c.29 s.14A, s.12B, s.56CB, 1990 c.42 Sch.4 para.4A, 1991 c.56 s.14B, s.16B, 1993 c.43 s.15C, s.13B, Sch.4A para.10A, Sch.4A para.15, SI 1999/3088

2002–cont.

40. Enterprise Act 2002–*cont.*

s.111, varied:–*cont.*

Reg.8, 2000 c.8 Sch.14 para.2A, 2000 c.26 s.19A, s.15B, 2000 c.38 s.12B, s.18, SI 2003/419 Sch.2 para.5, SI 2003/1592 Sch.3 para.1

s.111, enabling: SI 2003/1371

s.112, applied: 1984 c.12 s.13B, 1989 c.29 s.12B, 1993 c.43 s.13B, Sch.4A para.10A, 2000 c.8 Sch.14 para.2A, SI 2003/419 Sch.2 para.5, SI 2003/1372 r.29, SI 2003/1592 Sch.3 para.1, SI 2004/2528 Sch.1 para.5

s.112, varied: 1980 c.21 s.11B, 1984 c.12 s.13B, 1986 c.31 s.44A, 1986 c.44 s.26A, s.24B, s.41EB, 1989 c.29 s.14A, s.12B, s.56CB, 1990 c.42 Sch.4 para.4A, 1991 c.56 s.14B, s.16B, 1993 c.43 s.15C, s.13B, Sch.4A para.10A, SI 1999/3088 Reg.8, 2000 c.26 s.19A, s.15B, 2000 c.38 s.12B, s.18

s.113, applied: 1984 c.12 s.13B, 1989 c.29 s.12B, 1993 c.43 s.13B, Sch.4A para.10A, 2000 c.8 Sch.14 para.2A, SI 2003/419 Sch.2 para.5, SI 2003/1592 Sch.3 para.1, SI 2004/2528 Sch.1 para.5

s.113, varied: 1980 c.21 s.11B, 1984 c.12 s.13B, 1986 c.31 s.44A, 1986 c.44 s.26A, s.24B, s.41EB, 1989 c.29 s.14A, s.12B, s.56CB, 1990 c.42 Sch.4 para.4A, 1991 c.56 s.14B, s.16B, 1993 c.43 s.15C, s.13B, Sch.4A para.10A, SI 1999/3088 Reg.8, 2000 c.26 s.19A, s.15B, 2000 c.38 s.12B, s.18

s.114, applied: 1980 c.21 s.31, 1984 c.12 s.13B, 1989 c.29 s.12B, 1993 c.43 s.13B, Sch.4A para.10A, 2000 c.8 Sch.14 para.2A, SI 2003/419 Sch.2 para.5, SI 2003/1372 r.25, r.29, SI 2003/1592 Sch.3 para.1, SI 2004/2528 Sch.1 para.5

s.114, varied: 1980 c.21 s.11B, 1984 c.12 s.13B, 1986 c.31 s.44A, 1986 c.44 s.26A, s.24B, s.41EB, 1989 c.29 s.14A, s.12B, s.56CB, 1990 c.42 Sch.4 para.4A, 1991 c.56 s.14B, s.16B, 1993 c.43 s.15C, s.13B, Sch.4A para.10A, SI 1999/3088 Reg.8, 2000 c.26 s.19A, s.15B, 2000 c.38 s.12B, s.18

s.115, applied: 1984 c.12 s.13B, 1989 c.29 s.12B, 1993 c.43 s.13B, Sch.4A para.10A, 2000 c.8 Sch.14 para.2A, SI 2003/419 Sch.2 para.5, SI 2003/1592 Sch.3 para.1, SI 2004/2528 Sch.1 para.5

s.115, varied: 1980 c.21 s.11B, 1984 c.12 s.13B, 1986 c.31 s.44A, 1986 c.44 s.26A, s.24B, s.41EB, 1989 c.29 s.14A, s.12B, s.56CB, 1990 c.42 Sch.4 para.4A, 1991 c.56 s.14B, s.16B, 1993 c.43 s.15C, s.13B, Sch.4A para.10A, SI 1999/3088 Reg.8, 2000 c.26 s.19A, s.15B, 2000 c.38 s.12B, s.18

s.116, applied: 1984 c.12 s.13B, 1989 c.29 s.12B, 1993 c.43 s.13B, Sch.4A para.10A, 1998 c.41 Sch.7 para.5, 2000 c.8 Sch.14 para.2A, SI 2003/419 Sch.2 para.5, SI 2003/1592 Sch.3 para.1

2002–cont.

40. Enterprise Act 2002–*cont.*

s.116, varied: 1980 c.21 s.11B, 1984 c.12 s.13B, 1986 c.31 s.44A, 1986 c.44 s.26A, s.24B, s.41EB, 1989 c.29 s.14A, s.12B, s.56CB, 1990 c.42 Sch.4 para.4A, 1991 c.56 s.14B, s.16B, 1993 c.43 s.15C, s.13B, Sch.4A para.10A, SI 1999/3088 Reg.8, 2000 c.26 s.19A, s.15B, 2000 c.38 s.12B, s.18

s.117, amended: 2003 c.21 Sch.16 para.20

s.117, applied: 1993 c.43 s.13B, Sch.4A para.10A, 2000 c.8 Sch.14 para.2A, 2003 c.21 s.193, s.370, SI 2003/419 Sch.2 para.5, SI 2003/1592 Sch.3 para.1

s.117, varied: 1980 c.21 s.11C, 1984 c.12 s.50, 1986 c.44 s.26A, s.36A, s.41EB, 1989 c.29 s.56CB, s.43, 1990 c.42 Sch.4 para.4A, SI 1990/1715 Reg.5, 1991 c.56 s.31, 1993 c.43 s.13B, s.15C, s.67, Sch.4A para.10A, 2000 c.8 Sch.14 para.2A, 2000 c.38 s.12B, s.18, 2003 c.21 s.370, SI 2003/419 Sch.2 para.5, SI 2003/1592 Sch.3 para.1

s.118, amended: 2003 c.21 Sch.16 para.21

s.118, applied: SI 2003/1592 Sch.3 para.1

s.118, varied: 1986 c.44 s.26A, s.41EB, 1990 c.42 Sch.4 para.4A, 2000 c.38 s.12B, s.18, SI 2003/1592 Sch.3 para.1

s.119, applied: 2003 c.21 s.3, SI 2003/1592 Sch.3 para.1

s.119, varied: 1986 c.44 s.26A, s.41EB, 1990 c.42 Sch.4 para.4A, 2000 c.38 s.12B, s.18, SI 2003/1592 Sch.3 para.1

s.119A, added: 2003 c.21 s.385

s.119A, varied: 1986 c.44 s.26A, s.41EB, 1990 c.42 Sch.4 para.4A, 2000 c.38 s.12B, s.18

s.119B, added: 2003 c.21 s.386

s.119B, varied: 1986 c.44 s.26A, s.41EB, 1990 c.42 Sch.4 para.4A, 2000 c.38 s.12B, s.18

s.120, see *IBA Health Ltd v Office of Fair Trading* [2004] EWCA Civ 142, [2004] 4 All E.R. 1103 (CA), Sir Andrew Morritt V.C.

s.120, amended: 2003 c.21 Sch.16 para.22

s.120, applied: SI 2003/1372 r.25, r.26, r.28, SI 2003/1592 Sch.3 para.1, 2004 c.20 Sch.18 para.15

s.120, varied: 1986 c.44 s.26A, s.41EB, 1990 c.42 Sch.4 para.4A, 2000 c.38 s.12B, s.18, SI 2003/1592 Sch.3 para.1

s.121, amended: 2003 c.21 Sch.16 para.23, Sch.19

s.121, repealed (in part): 2003 c.21 Sch.19

s.121, varied: 1986 c.44 s.26A, s.41EB, 1990 c.42 Sch.4 para.4A, 2000 c.38 s.12B, s.18, SI 2003/1397 Art.3, SI 2004/3233 Art.5

s.121, enabling: SI 2003/1370, SI 2004/3204

s.122, amended: SI 2004/1079 Sch.1 para.2

s.122, varied: 1986 c.44 s.26A, s.41EB, 1990 c.42 Sch.4 para.4A, 2000 c.38 s.12B, s.18

s.123, varied: 1986 c.44 s.26A, s.41EB, 1990 c.42 Sch.4 para.4A, 2000 c.38 s.12B, s.18

s.124, amended: 2003 c.21 Sch.16 para.24

s.124, applied: SI 2003/1592 Sch.3 para.1

2002–cont.

40. Enterprise Act 2002–*cont.*

s.124, varied: 1986 c.44 s.26A, s.41EB, 1990 c.42 Sch.4 para.4A, 2000 c.38 s.12B, s.18, SI 2003/1592 Sch.3 para.1

s.124, enabling: SI 2003/1369, SI 2003/1370, SI 2003/1592, SI 2003/1594, SI 2003/1595, SI 2004/3204

s.125, applied: 1980 c.21 s.11C, SI 2003/1592 Sch.3 para.1

s.125, varied: 1986 c.44 s.26A, s.41EB, 1990 c.42 Sch.4 para.4A, 2000 c.38 s.12B, s.18, SI 2003/1592 Sch.3 para.1

s.126, amended: 2003 c.21 Sch.17 para.174

s.126, applied: SI 2003/1592 Sch.3 para.1

s.126, varied: 1986 c.44 s.26A, s.41EB, 1990 c.42 Sch.4 para.4A, 2000 c.38 s.12B, s.18, SI 2003/1592 Sch.3 para.1

s.127, amended: 2003 c.21 s.375, 2004 c.33 Sch.27 para.168

s.127, applied: SI 2003/1370 Sch.1 para.7, SI 2003/1592 Sch.3 para.1

s.127, referred to: SI 2003/1370 Art.6

s.127, varied: 1986 c.44 s.26A, s.41EB, 1990 c.42 Sch.4 para.4A, 2000 c.38 s.12B, s.18, SI 2003/1592 Sch.3 para.1, 2004 c.33 Sch.21 para.53

s.128, amended: 2003 c.21 Sch.17 para.174

s.128, applied: SI 2003/1592 Sch.3 para.1

s.128, varied: 1986 c.44 s.26A, s.41EB, 1990 c.42 Sch.4 para.4A, 2000 c.38 s.12B, s.18, SI 2003/1592 Sch.3 para.1

s.128, enabling: SI 2003/1594

s.129, amended: SI 2004/1079 Sch.1 para.2

s.129, applied: SI 2003/1592 Sch.3 para.1

s.129, varied: 1986 c.44 s.26A, s.41EB, 1990 c.42 Sch.4 para.4A, 2000 c.38 s.12B, s.18, SI 2003/1592 Sch.3 para.1

s.130, amended: 2003 c.21 Sch.16 para.25, SI 2004/1079 Sch.1 para.2

s.130, varied: 1986 c.44 s.26A, s.41EB, 1990 c.42 Sch.4 para.4A, 2000 c.38 s.12B, s.18

s.131, applied: 1989 c.29 s.43, 2000 c.38 s.86

s.131, varied: 1984 c.12 s.50, 1986 c.44 s.36A, 1993 c.43 s.67

s.132, applied: 1989 c.29 s.43, 2000 c.38 s.86

s.132, varied: 1984 c.12 s.50, 1986 c.44 s.36A, 1993 c.43 s.67

s.133, applied: 1989 c.29 s.43, 2000 c.38 s.86

s.133, varied: 1984 c.12 s.50, 1986 c.44 s.36A, 1993 c.43 s.67

s.134, applied: 1949 c.88 s.11AB, 1989 c.29 s.43, 1998 c.41 Sch.7 para.20, 2000 c.38 s.86

s.134, varied: 1977 c.37 s.50A, 1984 c.12 s.50, 1986 c.44 s.36A, 1993 c.43 s.67

s.135, applied: 1989 c.29 s.43, 2000 c.38 s.86

s.135, varied: 1984 c.12 s.50, 1986 c.44 s.36A, 1993 c.43 s.67

2002–cont.

40. Enterprise Act 2002–*cont.*

s.136, amended: 2003 c.20 Sch.2 para.19, 2003 c.21 Sch.17 para.174, Sch.19, 2003 c.37 Sch.7 para.36

s.136, applied: 1989 c.29 s.43, 1993 c.43 s.67, 2000 c.38 s.86

s.136, repealed (in part): 2003 c.21 Sch.19

s.136, varied: 1984 c.12 s.50, 1986 c.44 s.36A, 1993 c.43 s.67

s.137, applied: 1989 c.29 s.43, 2000 c.38 s.86

s.137, varied: 1984 c.12 s.50, 1986 c.44 s.36A, 1993 c.43 s.67

s.138, applied: 1949 c.88 s.11AB, 1958 c.47 s.19A, 1977 c.37 s.50A, 1988 c.48 s.144, s.238, Sch.2A para.17, SI 1997/3032 Sch.2 para.15

s.138, varied: 1984 c.12 s.50, 1986 c.44 s.36A, 1993 c.43 s.67

s.139, applied: 1989 c.29 s.43, 2000 c.38 s.86

s.139, varied: 1984 c.12 s.50, 1986 c.44 s.36A, 1993 c.43 s.67

s.140, applied: 1989 c.29 s.43, 2000 c.38 s.86

s.140, varied: 1984 c.12 s.50, 1986 c.44 s.36A, 1993 c.43 s.67

s.141, applied: 1949 c.88 s.11AB, 1989 c.29 s.43, 1998 c.41 Sch.7 para.20, 2000 c.38 s.86

s.141, varied: 1977 c.37 s.50A, 1984 c.12 s.50, 1986 c.44 s.36A, 1993 c.43 s.67

s.142, applied: 1989 c.29 s.43, 1993 c.43 s.67, 2000 c.38 s.86

s.142, varied: 1984 c.12 s.50, 1986 c.44 s.36A, 1993 c.43 s.67

s.143, applied: 1989 c.29 s.43, 2000 c.38 s.86

s.143, varied: 1984 c.12 s.50, 1986 c.44 s.36A, 1993 c.43 s.67

s.144, applied: 1989 c.29 s.43, 2000 c.38 s.86

s.144, varied: 1984 c.12 s.50, 1986 c.44 s.36A, 1993 c.43 s.67

s.145, applied: 1989 c.29 s.43, 2000 c.38 s.86

s.145, varied: 1984 c.12 s.50, 1986 c.44 s.36A, 1993 c.43 s.67

s.146, applied: 1989 c.29 s.43, 2000 c.38 s.86

s.146, varied: 1984 c.12 s.50, 1986 c.44 s.36A, 1993 c.43 s.67

s.147, applied: 1949 c.88 s.11AB, 1958 c.47 s.19A, 1977 c.37 s.50A, 1988 c.48 s.144, s.238, Sch.2A para.17, 1989 c.29 s.43, SI 1997/3032 Sch.2 para.15, 2000 c.38 s.86

s.147, varied: 1984 c.12 s.50, 1986 c.44 s.36A, 1993 c.43 s.67

s.148, applied: 1989 c.29 s.43, 2000 c.38 s.86

s.148, varied: 1984 c.12 s.50, 1986 c.44 s.36A, 1993 c.43 s.67

2002–cont.

40. Enterprise Act 2002–*cont.*

s.149, applied: 1989 c.29 s.43, 2000 c.38 s.86

s.149, varied: 1984 c.12 s.50, 1986 c.44 s.36A, 1993 c.43 s.67

s.150, applied: 1989 c.29 s.43, 2000 c.38 s.86

s.150, varied: 1984 c.12 s.50, 1986 c.44 s.36A, 1993 c.43 s.67

s.151, applied: 1989 c.29 s.43, 2000 c.38 s.86

s.151, varied: 1984 c.12 s.50, 1986 c.44 s.36A, 1993 c.43 s.67

s.152, applied: 1989 c.29 s.43, 2000 c.38 s.86

s.152, varied: 1984 c.12 s.50, 1986 c.44 s.36A, 1993 c.43 s.67

s.153, amended: SI 2004/1079 Sch.1 para.2

s.153, applied: 1989 c.29 s.43, 2000 c.38 s.86

s.153, varied: 1984 c.12 s.50, 1986 c.44 s.36A, 1993 c.43 s.67

s.154, applied: 1989 c.29 s.43, 2000 c.38 s.86

s.154, varied: 1984 c.12 s.50, 1986 c.44 s.36A, 1993 c.43 s.67

s.155, applied: 1989 c.29 s.43, 2000 c.38 s.86

s.155, varied: 1984 c.12 s.50, 1986 c.44 s.36A, 1993 c.43 s.67

s.156, applied: 1989 c.29 s.43, 2000 c.38 s.86

s.156, varied: 1984 c.12 s.50, 1986 c.44 s.36A, 1993 c.43 s.67

s.157, applied: 1989 c.29 s.43, 2000 c.38 s.86

s.157, varied: 1984 c.12 s.50, 1986 c.44 s.36A, 1993 c.43 s.67

s.158, applied: 1989 c.29 s.43, 2000 c.38 s.86

s.158, varied: 1984 c.12 s.50, 1986 c.44 s.36A, 1993 c.43 s.67

s.159, applied: 1989 c.29 s.43, 2000 c.38 s.86

s.159, varied: 1984 c.12 s.50, 1986 c.44 s.36A, 1993 c.43 s.67

s.160, applied: 1949 c.88 s.11AB, 1977 c.37 s.50A, 1988 c.48 s.144, s.238, Sch.2A para.17, 1989 c.29 s.43, 1990 c.42 s.193, SI 1997/3032 Sch.2 para.15, 2000 c.38 s.86

s.160, referred to: 1988 c.48 s.144, 1994 c.17 s.33

s.160, varied: 1984 c.12 s.50, 1986 c.44 s.36A, 1993 c.43 s.67

s.161, applied: 1988 c.48 Sch.2A para.17, 1989 c.29 s.43, 1990 c.42 s.193, SI 1997/3032 Sch.2 para.15, 2000 c.38 s.86

s.161, referred to: 1988 c.48 s.144, 1994 c.17 s.33

s.161, varied: 1984 c.12 s.50, 1986 c.44 s.36A, 1993 c.43 s.67

2002–cont.

40. Enterprise Act 2002–*cont.*

s.162, applied: 1949 c.88 s.11AB, 1958 c.47 s.19A, 1977 c.37 s.50A, 1989 c.29 s.43, 2000 c.38 s.86

s.162, varied: 1984 c.12 s.50, 1986 c.44 s.36A, 1993 c.43 s.67

s.163, applied: 1989 c.29 s.43, 2000 c.38 s.86

s.163, varied: 1984 c.12 s.50, 1986 c.44 s.36A, 1993 c.43 s.67

s.164, applied: 1988 c.48 Sch.2A para.17, 1989 c.29 s.43, 1994 c.17 s.33, SI 1997/3032 Sch.2 para.15, 2000 c.38 s.86

s.164, referred to: 1988 c.48 s.144, 1994 c.17 s.33

s.164, varied: 1984 c.12 s.50, 1986 c.44 s.36A, 1993 c.43 s.67

s.165, applied: 1989 c.29 s.43, 2000 c.38 s.86

s.165, varied: 1984 c.12 s.50, 1986 c.44 s.36A, 1993 c.43 s.67

s.166, applied: 1949 c.88 s.11AB, 1958 c.47 s.19A, 1977 c.37 s.50A

s.166, disapplied: 1984 c.12 s.50, 1991 c.56 s.31, 1993 c.43 s.67, 2003 c.21 s.370

s.166, referred to: 1986 c.44 s.36A

s.166, varied: 1984 c.12 s.50, 1986 c.44 s.36A, 1993 c.43 s.67

s.166, enabling: SI 2003/1373

s.167, applied: 1989 c.29 s.43, 2000 c.38 s.86

s.167, varied: 1984 c.12 s.50, 1986 c.44 s.36A, 1993 c.43 s.67

s.168, amended: 2003 c.20 Sch.2 para.19, 2003 c.21 Sch.17 para.174, 2003 c.37 Sch.7 para.36, Sch.8 para.55

s.168, applied: 1989 c.29 s.43, 2000 c.38 s.86

s.168, repealed (in part): 2003 c.21 Sch.19

s.168, varied: 1984 c.12 s.50, 1986 c.44 s.36A, 1993 c.43 s.67

s.169, applied: 1989 c.29 s.43, 2000 c.38 s.86

s.169, varied: 1984 c.12 s.50, 1986 c.44 s.36A, 1993 c.43 s.67

s.170, applied: 1989 c.29 s.43, 2000 c.38 s.86

s.170, varied: 1984 c.12 s.50, 1986 c.44 s.36A, 1993 c.43 s.67

s.171, applied: 1998 c.41 Sch.7 para.5

s.171, disapplied: 1984 c.12 s.50, 1991 c.56 s.31, 1993 c.43 s.67, 2003 c.21 s.370

s.171, referred to: 1986 c.44 s.36A

s.171, varied: 1984 c.12 s.50, 1986 c.44 s.36A, 1993 c.43 s.67

s.172, applied: 1989 c.29 s.43, 2000 c.38 s.86

s.172, varied: 1984 c.12 s.50, 1986 c.44 s.36A, 1993 c.43 s.67

s.173, applied: 1989 c.29 s.43, 2000 c.38 s.86

2002–cont.

40. Enterprise Act 2002–*cont.*

s.173, varied: 1984 c.12 s.50, 1986 c.44 s.36A, 1993 c.43 s.67

s.174, applied: 1989 c.29 s.43, 2000 c.38 s.86

s.174, varied:1984 c.12 s.50,1986 c.44 s.36A, 1993 c.43 s.67

s.175, applied: 1989 c.29 s.43, 2000 c.38 s.86

s.175, varied: 1984 c.12 s.50, 1986 c.44 s.36A, 1993 c.43 s.67

s.176, applied: 1989 c.29 s.43, 2000 c.38 s.86, SI 2003/1372 r.25, r.29

s.176, referred to: 1998 c.41 Sch.7 para.5, SI 2003/1371

s.176, varied: 1984 c.12 s.50, 1986 c.44 s.36A, 1993 c.43 s.67

s.176, enabling: SI 2003/1371

s.177, applied: 1989 c.29 s.43, 2000 c.38 s.86

s.177, varied:1984 c.12 s.50,1986 c.44 s.36A, 1993 c.43 s.67

s.178, applied: 1989 c.29 s.43, 2000 c.38 s.86

s.178, varied: 1984 c.12 s.50, 1986 c.44 s.36A, 1993 c.43 s.67

s.179, applied: 1989 c.29 s.43, 2000 c.38 s.86, SI 2003/1372 r.25, r.27, r.28

s.179, varied: 1984 c.12 s.50, 1986 c.44 s.36A, 1993 c.43 s.67

s.180, amended: 2003 c.21 Sch.16 para.26

s.180, applied:1989 c.29 s.43,1991 c.56 s.31, 2000 c.38 s.86

s.180, referred to: 1986 c.44 s.36A, 2003 c.21 s.370

s.180, varied: 1984 c.12 s.50, 1986 c.44 s.36A, 1993 c.43 s.67

s.181, applied:1989 c.29 s.43, 2000 c.38 s.86

s.181, varied:1984 c.12 s.50,1986 c.44 s.36A, 1993 c.43 s.67

s.181, enabling: SI 2003/1594

s.182, applied: 1989 c.29 s.43, 2000 c.38 s.86

s.182, varied: 1984 c.12 s.50, 1986 c.44 s.36A, 1993 c.43 s.67

s.183, applied: 1989 c.29 s.43, 2000 c.38 s.86, SI 2003/1594

s.183, varied: 1984 c.12 s.50, 1986 c.44 s.36A, 1993 c.43 s.67

s.184, applied: 1989 c.29 s.43, 2000 c.38 s.86

s.184, varied: 1984 c.12 s.50, 1986 c.44 s.36A, 1993 c.43 s.67

s.186, referred to: SI 2003/419 Sch.4 para.18

s.188, applied: 1997 c.50 s.93, 1998 c.41 s.30A, s.65B, s.65K, 2000 c.23 s.32, s.33

s.191, repealed: 2003 c.41 Sch.4

s.192, applied: 2001 c.16 Sch.1 para.73B

s.194, applied: 2001 c.16 Sch.1 para.73B

s.205, enabling: SI 2003/1368

s.209, enabling: SI 2004/1261

s.210, enabling: SI 2003/1374

2002–cont.

40. Enterprise Act 2002–*cont.*

s.211, applied: SI 2003/1593 Art.2

s.211, enabling: SI 2003/1593

s.212, applied: SI 2003/1374 Art.3

s.212, enabling: SI 2003/1374

s.213, applied: SI 2003/1399 Art.3, Art.5, SI 2004/935 Art.2

s.213, enabling: SI 2003/1399, SI 2004/935

s.214, applied: SI 2003/1375 Art.3

s.214, enabling: SI 2003/1375

s.222, amended: 2004 c.33 Sch.27 para.169

s.230, applied: SI 2003/1376 Art.2

s.230, enabling: SI 2003/1376

s.234, amended: 2003 c.21 Sch.17 para.174

s.234, enabling: SI 2003/1594

s.237, see *Umbro Holdings Ltd v Office of Fair Trading (Application for Leniency: Confidentiality)* [2003] CAT 26, [2004] Comp. A.R. 217 (Competition Appeal Tribunal), Sir Christopher Bellamy (President)

s.237, referred to: 2003 c.20 s.115

s.237, varied: SI 1990/1715 Reg.5

s.238, applied: SI 2003/1400 Art.5, SI 2004/693 Art.2

s.238, varied: SI 1990/1715 Reg.5

s.238, enabling: SI 2003/1400, SI 2003/2580, SI 2004/693

s.239, see *Umbro Holdings Ltd v Office of Fair Trading (Application for Leniency: Confidentiality)* [2003] CAT 26, [2004] Comp. A.R. 217 (Competition Appeal Tribunal), Sir Christopher Bellamy (President)

s.239, varied: SI 1990/1715 Reg.5

s.240, varied: SI 1990/1715 Reg.5

s.241, applied: SI 2003/1400 Art.6, SI 2004/693 Art.2

s.241, varied: SI 1990/1715 Reg.5

s.241, enabling: SI 2003/1400, SI 2004/693

s.242, varied: SI 1990/1715 Reg.5

s.243, disapplied: SI 2003/1592 Sch.3 para.3

s.243, varied: SI 1990/1715 Reg.5, 2004 c.27 s.59

s.244, see *Aberdeen Journals Ltd v Director General of Fair Trading (Confidentiality of Judgment)* [2003] CAT 14, [2004] Comp. A.R. 71 (Competition Commission Appeal Tribunal), Sir Christopher Bellamy (President); see *Umbro Holdings Ltd v Office of Fair Trading (Application for Leniency: Confidentiality)* [2003] CAT 26, [2004] Comp. A.R. 217 (Competition Appeal Tribunal), Sir Christopher Bellamy (President)

s.244, referred to: 1980 c.21 s.17

s.244, varied: SI 1990/1715 Reg.5

s.245, varied: SI 1990/1715 Reg.5

s.246, varied: SI 1990/1715 Reg.5

s.247, varied: SI 1990/1715 Reg.5

s.248, applied: 2004 c.20 s.170

2002–cont.

40. Enterprise Act 2002–*cont.*

s.248, enabling: SI 2003/2096

s.249, amended: 2003 c.37 Sch.8 para.55

s.253, applied: SI 2003/1102 Reg.4, SI 2004/353 Reg.4

s.254, applied: 2004 c.20 s.170, SI 2004/1045 Reg.3

s.261, applied: SI 1986/1925 r.6.237A, r.6.237B

s.265, repealed: 2003 c.39 Sch.10

s.268, applied: 2003 c.26 Sch.4 para.25

s.268, varied: 2003 c.26 Sch.4 para.2, Sch.4 para.25, 2004 c.30 Sch.6 para.6

s.276, applied: 2003 c.21 s.389

s.276, enabling: SI 2003/766, SI 2003/1397, SI 2003/1399, SI 2003/2093, SI 2003/2332, SI 2004/3233

s.277, applied: 2003 c.21 s.389, 2004 c.20 s.170

s.277, enabling: SI 2003/767, SI 2003/1376, SI 2003/1398, SI 2003/1400, SI 2003/2096, SI 2003/2108, SI 2003/3180, SI 2004/693, SI 2004/935, SI 2004/2312

s.279, enabling: SI 2003/765, SI 2003/766, SI 2003/1397, SI 2003/2093, SI 2003/3340, SI 2004/1866, SI 2004/3233

Sch.4, see *Aberdeen Journals Ltd v Director General of Fair Trading (Confidentiality of Judgment)* [2003] CAT 14, [2004] Comp. A.R. 71 (Competition Commission Appeal Tribunal), Sir Christopher Bellamy (President)

Sch.4, applied: SI 2003/1372 r.66

Sch.4 para.1, see *Umbro Holdings Ltd v Office of Fair Trading (Application for Leniency: Confidentiality)* [2003] CAT 26, [2004] Comp. A.R. 217 (Competition Appeal Tribunal), Sir Christopher Bellamy (President)

Sch.4 Part 1 para.1, referred to: SI 2003/1372 r.16, r.57

Sch.4 Part 1 para.1, varied: 2003 c.21 s.195, Sch.11 para.10

Sch.4 Part 2, enabling: SI 2003/1372, SI 2004/2068

Sch.4 Part 2 para.17, referred to: SI 2001/2916 Sch.2 para.5

Sch.6, applied: SI 2003/1397 Art.3

Sch.7 para.5, applied: 1949 c.88 s.11AB, 1977 c.37 s.50A, 1988 c.48 s.144, s.238, Sch.2A para.17, SI 1997/3032 Sch.2 para.15

Sch.7 para.5, referred to: 1988 c.48 s.144

Sch.7 para.7, applied: 1980 c.21 s.11D

Sch.7 para.10, applied: 1949 c.88 s.11AB, 1977 c.37 s.50A, 1988 c.48 s.144, s.238, Sch.2A para.17, SI 1997/3032 Sch.2 para.15, 2003 c.21 Sch.18 para.62

Sch.7 para.10, referred to: 1988 c.48 s.144

Sch.7 para.10, varied: 2003 c.21 Sch.18 para.62

2002–cont.

40. Enterprise Act 2002–*cont.*

Sch.7 para.11, applied: 1980 c.21 s.12, 1988 c.48 Sch.2A para.17, SI 1997/3032 Sch.2 para.15

Sch.7 para.11, referred to: 1988 c.48 s.144

Sch.8, applied: 1988 c.48 s.144, 1993 c.21 s.33, 1994 c.17 s.33, SI 1997/3032 Sch.2 para.15, SI 2003/1592 Sch.2 para.5, Sch.2 para.11, Sch.3 para.2

Sch.8, referred to: 1994 c.17 s.33

Sch.8 para.1, applied: 1980 c.21 s.12

Sch.8 para.1, varied: SI 2003/1592 Sch.3 para.2

Sch.8 para.2, applied: 1980 c.21 s.12

Sch.8 para.3, applied: 1980 c.21 s.12

Sch.8 para.4, applied: 1980 c.21 s.12

Sch.8 para.5, applied: 1980 c.21 s.12

Sch.8 para.6, applied: 1980 c.21 s.12

Sch.8 para.7, applied: 1980 c.21 s.12

Sch.8 para.9, applied: 1980 c.21 s.12

Sch.8 para.10, applied: 1980 c.21 s.12

Sch.8 para.11, applied: 1980 c.21 s.12

Sch.8 para.12, applied: 1980 c.21 s.12

Sch.8 para.14, varied: SI 2003/1592 Sch.3 para.2

Sch.8 para.15, applied: 1980 c.21 s.12

Sch.8 para.16, applied: 1980 c.21 s.12

Sch.8 para.17, applied: 1980 c.21 s.12

Sch.8 para.18, applied: 1980 c.21 s.12

Sch.8 para.19, applied: 1980 c.21 s.11D, s.12, SI 2003/1592 Sch.2 para.6

Sch.8 para.20, applied: 1980 c.21 s.12

Sch.8 para.20A, added: 2003 c.21 s.387

Sch.8 para.20A, applied: 1980 c.21 s.12

Sch.8 para.21, applied: 1980 c.21 s.12

Sch.8 para.22, applied: 1980 c.21 s.12

Sch.8 para.23, applied: 1980 c.21 s.12

Sch.8 para.24, applied: 1980 c.21 s.12

Sch.8 para.24, varied: SI 2003/1592 Sch.3 para.2

Sch.9 Part 1 para.1, repealed: 2003 c.21 Sch.19

Sch.9 Part 2 para.16, repealed: 2003 c.21 Sch.19

Sch.10, applied: 1980 c.21 s.12, SI 2003/1592 Sch.3 para.2

Sch.10 para.1, varied: 2003 c.21 Sch.18 para.62, SI 2003/1592 Sch.3 para.2

Sch.10 para.2, varied: 2003 c.21 Sch.18 para.62, SI 2003/1592 Sch.3 para.2

Sch.10 para.3, varied: 2003 c.21 Sch.18 para.62

Sch.10 para.4, varied: 2003 c.21 Sch.18 para.62

Sch.10 para.5, varied: 2003 c.21 Sch.18 para.62

Sch.10 para.6, varied: 2003 c.21 Sch.18 para.62, SI 2003/1592 Sch.3 para.2

Sch.10 para.7, varied: 2003 c.21 Sch.18 para.62

CAP.

2002–cont.

40. **Enterprise Act 2002**–*cont.*

Sch.10 para.8, varied: 2003 c.21 Sch.18 para.62

Sch.10 para.9, varied: 2003 c.21 Sch.18 para.62

Sch.13 Part 1 para.9A, added: SI 2004/2095 Reg.26

Sch.13 Part 2 para.11, amended: SI 2003/1374 Art.2

Sch.14, amended: 2003 c.22 s.12, SI 2003/ 1400 Sch.1 para.2, Sch.1 para.3, Sch.1 para.4, Sch.1 para.5, Sch.1 para.6, SI 2003/2580 Sch.1 para.2, Sch.1 para.3

Sch.14, referred to: SI 2003/1400 Art.3, Sch.1 para.1

Sch.15, amended: 2003 c.21 Sch.17 para.174, 2003 c.22 s.12, 2003 c.37 Sch.7 para.36, SI 2003/1400 Sch.2 para.2, Sch.2 para.3, Sch.2 para.4, Sch.2 para.5, Sch.2 para.6, Sch.2 para.7, Sch.2 para.8, Sch.2 para.9, Sch.2 para.10, Sch.2 para.11, Sch.2 para.12, Sch.2 para.13, Sch.2 para.14, Sch.2 para.15, Sch.2 para.16, Sch.2 para.17, Sch.2 para.18

Sch.15, referred to: SI 2003/1400 Art.4, Sch.2 para.1

Sch.16, added: SI 2003/2096 Art.2

Sch.16, amended: SI 2003/2096 Art.2

Sch.19 para.4, amended: SI 2003/2096 Art.3

Sch.19 para.4, applied: SI 2003/2093 Art.8

Sch.24, applied: SI 2003/3180 Art.3

Sch.24 para.5, referred to: SI 2003/1397 Art.9

Sch.24 para.13, applied: SI 2003/1397 Art.2

Sch.24 para.13, disapplied: SI 2003/1397 Art.3, Art.4, SI 2004/3233 Art.5

Sch.24 para.13, referred to: SI 2003/1397 Art.4

Sch.24 para.14, applied: SI 2003/1397 Art.2, SI 2003/3180 Art.3

Sch.24 para.15, applied: SI 2003/1397 Art.2, Art.4, SI 2004/2181 Art.3, SI 2004/3233 Art.3, Art.4

Sch.24 para.15, enabling: SI 2004/2181

Sch.24 para.16, applied: SI 2003/1397 Art.2, Art.4, SI 2004/2181 Art.3, SI 2004/3233 Art.3, Art.4

Sch.24 para.16, enabling: SI 2004/2181

Sch.24 para.17, applied: SI 2003/1397 Art.2, Art.4, SI 2004/2181 Art.3, SI 2004/3233 Art.3, Art.4

Sch.24 para.17, enabling: SI 2004/2181

Sch.24 para.18, applied: SI 2003/1397 Art.2, Art.4, SI 2004/3233 Art.3, Art.4

Sch.24 para.19, enabling: SI 2003/1397

Sch.25 para.5, repealed (in part): SI 2003/ 3180 Sch.1 para.7

Sch.25 para.13, repealed (in part): 2003 c.21 Sch.19

Sch.25 para.22, repealed: 2004 c.27 Sch.8

CAP.

2002–cont.

40. **Enterprise Act 2002**–*cont.*

Sch.25 para.24, repealed (in part): 2003 c.21 Sch.19

Sch.25 para.34, repealed: 2003 c.21 Sch.19

41. **Nationality, Immigration and Asylum Act 2002**

Commencement Orders: SI 2002/2811 Art.2, Sch.1; SI 2003/1 Art.2, Sch.1; SI 2003/249 Art.2, Sch.1; SI 2003/754 Art.2, Art.3, Sch.1, Sch.2 para.1, para.6; SI 2003/1339 Art.3; SI 2003/1747 Art.2; SI 2003/2993 Art.3; SI 2003/3156 Art.2, Art.3; SI 2004/1201 Art.2; SI 2004/1707 Art.2, Art.3; SI 2004/2998 Art.2

applied: 1971 c.77 Sch.2 para.4, 1997 c.68 s.3, 1999 c.33 s.54, 2001 c.17 s.32, SI 2003/ 754 Sch.2 para.1

referred to: 2003 c.13 Sch.2 Part 2, Sch.2 Part 13, 2003 c.43 Sch.4 para.127, SI 2003/754 Sch.2 para.5, 2004 c.9 Sch.2 Part 2, Sch.2 Part 12, 2004 c.19 s.9

Part 5, applied: 1971 c.77 Sch.2 para.29, Sch.2 para.2A, 1975 c.24 Sch.1 Part III, 1976 c.74 s.57A, s.53, s.62, s.66, 1990 c.41 Sch.11, 1993 c.8 Sch.1 Part II, Sch.5, 1993 c.23 s.9A, SI 2003/435 Sch.2 para.2, SI 2003/658 Reg.5, SI 2003/ 1034 r.8, 2004 c.19 s.9

Part 5, referred to: SI 2002/2811 Art.3

Part 5, applied: 2001 c.24 s.27

s.10, applied: 2004 c.19 s.42

s.22, applied: 2004 c.19 s.11

s.52, repealed: 2004 c.19 Sch.4

s.54, see *R. (on the application of Grant) v Lambeth LBC* [2004] EWHC 1524, [2004] 3 F.C.R. 494 (QBD (Admin Ct)), Mitting, J.; see *R. (on the application of Kimani) v Lambeth LBC* [2003] EWCA Civ 1150, [2004] 1 W.L.R. 272 (CA), Lord Phillips of Worth Matravers, M.R.; see *R. (on the application of Kimani) v Lambeth LBC* [2003] EWHC 871, [2003] 2 F.L.R. 439 (QBD (Admin Ct)), Silber, J.

s.54, enabling: SI 2002/3078

s.55, see *R. (on the application of Limbuela) v Secretary of State for the Home Department* [2004] EWCA Civ 540, [2004] Q.B. 1440 (CA), Laws, L.J.; see *R. (on the application of Q) v Secretary of State for the Home Department* [2003] EWCA Civ 364, [2004] Q.B. 36 (CA), Lord Phillips of Worth Matravers, M.R.; see *R. (on the application of S) v Secretary of State for the Home Department* [2003] EWCA Civ 1285, [2003] U.K.H.R.R. 1321 (CA), Kennedy, L.J.; see *R. (on the application of S) v Secretary of State for the Home Department* [2003] EWHC 1941, [2004] H.L.R. 16 (QBD (Admin Ct)), Maurice Kay, J.

s.62, applied: 1983 c.20 s.48, 1984 c.36 s.71, s.74, 1999 c.33 s.53, 2001 c.24 s.23, s.24

2002–cont.

41. Nationality, Immigration and Asylum Act 2002–cont.

s.67, see *R. (on the application of Khadir) v Secretary of State for the Home Department* [2003] EWCA Civ 475, [2003] I.N.L.R. 426 (CA), Kennedy, L.J.

s.68, referred to: 1971 c.77 s.11

s.72, amended: 2004 c.19 Sch.2 para.17

s.72, applied: SI 2004/1910 Art.2

s.72, enabling: SI 2004/1910

s.76, applied: 1999 c.33 s.10

s.77, applied: 1999 c.33 s.11, 2001 c.24 s.33

s.77, disapplied: 1999 c.33 s.12, 2004 c.19 Sch.3 para.4, Sch.3 para.9, Sch.3 para.14, Sch.3 para.18

s.77, varied: SI 2003/754 Sch.2 para.1

s.78, applied: 1997 c.68 s.2

s.78, varied: SI 2003/754 Sch.2 para.1

s.79, applied: 1997 c.68 s.2

s.79, varied: SI 2003/754 Sch.2 para.1

s.80, applied: SI 2002/2811 Art.3, SI 2003/754 Sch.2 para.6

s.80, repealed: 2004 c.19 Sch.4

s.81, applied: 1981 c.61 s.40A, 1992 c.53 Sch.1 Part I, 1997 c.68 Sch.1 para.5, SI 2000/627 Art.5, 2004 c.19 s.48, Sch.2 para.27, Sch.2 para.29

s.81, substituted: 2004 c.19 s.26

s.82, see *R. (on the application of Erdogan) v Secretary of State for the Home Department (Application to Appeal Out of Time)* [2004] EWCA Civ 1087, [2004] I.N.L.R. 503 (CA (Civ Div)), Tuckey, L.J.

s.82, amended: 2004 c.19 s.26, s.31

s.82, applied: 1971 c.77 s.3C, Sch.3 para.3, 1997 c.68 s.2, 1999 c.33 s.11, s.12, SI 2000/2326 Reg.29, Reg.32, Reg.33, Sch.2, SI 2003/652 r.9, SI 2003/754 Sch.2 para.1, SI 2004/1219 Reg.6

s.82, referred to: 1971 c.77 Sch.3 para.3, SI 2003/658 Reg.5

s.83, amended: 2004 c.19 s.26

s.83, applied: 1997 c.68 s.2, SI 2000/2326 Reg.33, SI 2003/652 r.7, SI 2003/658 Reg.4

s.84, applied: 1997 c.68 s.2, SI 2000/2326 Reg.33

s.84, referred to: SI 2000/2326 Reg.33, SI 2003/658 Reg.5

s.84, varied: SI 2000/2326 Sch.2

s.85, amended: 2004 c.19 Sch.2 para.18

s.85, applied: 1997 c.68 s.2, SI 2003/652 r.11, r.48, SI 2003/1034 r.11

s.85, varied: SI 2000/2326 Sch.2

s.86, amended: 2004 c.19 Sch.2 para.18

s.86, applied: 1997 c.68 s.2

s.86, varied: SI 2000/2326 Sch.2

s.87, see *R. (on the application of Erdogan) v Secretary of State for the Home Department (Application to Appeal Out of Time)* [2004]

2002–cont.

41. Nationality, Immigration and Asylum Act 2002–cont.

s.87–cont.
EWCA Civ 1087, [2004] I.N.L.R. 503 (CA (Civ Div)), Tuckey, L.J.

s.87, amended: 2004 c.19 Sch.2 para.18, Sch.2 para.19

s.87, applied: 1997 c.68 s.2

s.87, repealed (in part): 2004 c.19 Sch.4

s.87, varied: SI 2000/2326 Sch.2

s.88, applied: SI 2003/658 Reg.5

s.88A, added: 2004 c.19 s.29

s.89, applied: SI 2003/658 Reg.5

s.90, applied: 1999 c.33 s.23, SI 2003/518 Reg.2, SI 2003/658 Reg.5

s.90, enabling: SI 2003/518

s.91, applied: 1999 c.33 s.23, SI 2003/658 Reg.5

s.92, amended: 2004 c.19 s.28

s.92, applied: 2004 c.19 Sch.3 para.5

s.92, disapplied: 2004 c.19 Sch.3 para.5, Sch.3 para.10, Sch.3 para.15, Sch.3 para.19

s.93, applied: 1999 c.33 s.11, s.12

s.93, repealed: 2004 c.19 Sch.4

s.94, amended: SI 2003/970 Art.3, SI 2003/1919 Art.2, 2004 c.19 s.27

s.94, repealed (in part): 2004 c.19 Sch.4

s.94, enabling: SI 2003/970, SI 2003/1919

s.96, see *Djebbar v Secretary of State for the Home Department* [2004] EWCA Civ 804, [2004] Imm. A.R. 497 (CA), Judge, L.J.; see *R. (on the application of Borak) v Secretary of State for the Home Department* [2004] EWHC 1861, [2004] 1 W.L.R. 3129 (QBD (Admin Ct)), Harrison, J.

s.96, amended: 2004 c.19 s.30

s.96, applied: 1997 c.68 s.2, SI 2000/2326 Reg.33, SI 2003/652 r.41

s.97, applied: 1997 c.68 s.2, SI 2003/652 r.41, SI 2003/1034 r.8

s.98, applied: SI 2003/652 r.41, SI 2003/658 Reg.5

s.99, applied: 1997 c.68 s.2, SI 2003/652 r.12, r.23, r.41

s.100, applied: 1992 c.53 Sch.1 Part I

s.100, repealed: 2004 c.19 s.26, Sch.4

s.101, see *A v Secretary of State for the Home Department* [2004 EWCA Civ 1165, [2004] I.N.L.R. 453 (CA), Mummery, L.J.; see *Practice Direction (Administrative Court: Annual Statement)* [2004] 1 All E.R. 322 (QBD (Admin Ct)), Maurice Kay, J.; see *R. (on the application of G) v Immigration Appeal Tribunal* [2004] EWHC 588, [2004] 1 W.L.R. 2953 (QBD (Admin Ct)), Collins, J.

s.101, applied: SI 1994/1443 Sch.2 para.41.46, Sch.2 para.41.47, SI 1998/3132 r.54.21, r.54.22, r.54.26, SI 2003/652 r.25, 2004 c.19 s.48

2002–cont.

41. Nationality, Immigration and Asylum Act 2002–*cont.*

s.101, repealed: 2004 c.19 s.26, Sch.4

s.101, varied: SI 2000/2326 Sch.2, SI 2003/754 Sch.2 para.1

s.102, applied: SI 2003/652 r.48

s.102, repealed: 2004 c.19 s.26, Sch.4

s.102, varied: SI 2000/2326 Sch.2, SI 2003/754 Sch.2 para.1

s.103, applied: SI 1994/1443 Sch.2 para.41.20, 2004 c.19 s.48

s.103, repealed: 2004 c.19 s.26, Sch.4

s.103, varied: SI 2000/2326 Sch.2, SI 2003/754 Sch.2 para.1

s.103A, added: 2004 c.19 s.26

s.103A, applied: 2004 c.19 Sch.2 para.30

s.103A, referred to: 2004 c.19 s.26

s.103A, varied: 2004 c.19 Sch.2 para.30

s.103B, added: 2004 c.19 s.26

s.103C, added: 2004 c.19 s.26

s.103C, applied: 2004 c.19 Sch.2 para.30

s.103D, added: 2004 c.19 s.26

s.103E, added: 2004 c.19 s.26

s.104, see *R. (on the application of Erdogan) v Secretary of State for the Home Department (Application to Appeal Out of Time)* [2004] EWCA Civ 1087, [2004] I.N.L.R. 503 (CA (Civ Div)), Tuckey, L.J.

s.104, amended: 2004 c.19 Sch.2 para.20

s.104, applied: 1971 c.77 s.33, s.3C, 1997 c.68 s.2, 1999 c.33 s.11, s.12, SI 2003/652 r.12, r.23, r.43, SI 2003/1034 r.12

s.104, referred to: SI 2003/652 r.43

s.104, repealed (in part): 2004 c.19 Sch.2 para.20, Sch.4

s.105, applied: 1971 c.77 s.3C, Sch.3 para.2, 1997 c.68 s.2, 1999 c.33 s.131, 2001 c.24 s.22, 2004 c.19 s.8

s.105, varied: SI 2000/2326 Sch.2

s.105, enabling: SI 2003/658

s.106, amended: 2004 c.19 Sch.2 para.21, Sch.4

s.106, applied: 1971 c.77 Sch.2 para.25, 1981 c.61 s.40A, SI 1994/1443 Sch.2 para.41.48, 1997 c.68 s.5, SI 1998/3132 r.54.23, SI 2003/652 r.3, 2004 c.19 Sch.2 para.30

s.106, repealed (in part): 2004 c.19 Sch.2 para.21, Sch.4

s.106, varied: SI 2000/2326 Sch.2

s.106, enabling: SI 2003/652, SI 2003/801, SI 2004/1891

s.107, amended: 2004 c.19 Sch.2 para.22

s.107, applied: 1981 c.61 s.40A

s.107, repealed (in part): 2004 c.19 Sch.2 para.22, Sch.4

s.107, varied: 2004 c.19 Sch.2 para.22

s.108, amended: 2004 c.19 Sch.2 para.23

s.108, applied: SI 2003/652 r.48

s.108, referred to: SI 2003/652 r.50

s.109, enabling: SI 2003/549, SI 2003/3188, SI 2004/1236

2002–cont.

41. Nationality, Immigration and Asylum Act 2002–*cont.*

s.110, applied: 1997 c.68 s.2, 2001 c.24 s.27, SI 2003/1034 r.33

s.112, amended: 2004 c.19 s.27, s.29, Sch.2 para.24

s.112, enabling: SI 2003/518, SI 2003/652, SI 2003/658, SI 2003/801, SI 2004/1891

s.113, applied: 1999 c.33 s.11, s.12, 2001 c.24 s.33

s.115, see *R. (on the application of Bagdanavicius) v Secretary of State for the Home Department* [2003] EWCA Civ 1605, [2004] 1 W.L.R. 1207 (CA), Lord Woolf of Barnes, L.C.J.; see *R. (on the application of L) v Secretary of State for the Home Department* [2003] EWCA Civ 25, [2003] 1 W.L.R. 1230 (CA), Lord Phillips of Worth Matravers, M.R.

s.115, amended: SI 2003/970 Art.4

s.115, applied: SI 2003/754 Sch.2 para.1

s.115, enabling: SI 2003/970

s.117, repealed: SI 2003/435 Sch.5

s.118, referred to: SI 2003/754 Sch.2 para.2

s.120, applied: SI 2000/2326 Reg.26A

s.122, applied: 2004 c.19 s.42

s.122, enabling: SI 2003/541, SI 2003/1277, SI 2003/2447, SI 2003/2626, SI 2004/1044, SI 2004/1485

s.126, enabling: SI 2003/1875, SI 2004/474, SI 2004/1834

s.133, amended: 2003 c.43 Sch.4 para.128, Sch.13 para.12, 2004 c.17 Sch.3 para.17, Sch.4

s.133, repealed (in part): 2003 c.43 Sch.13 para.12, Sch.14 Part 7

s.134, applied: 1971 c.77 s.28FB

s.134, referred to: SI 2002/2811 Art.6

s.137, amended: 2003 c.44 Sch.26 para.58

s.137, applied: 1971 c.77 s.28FB

s.140, disapplied: SI 2002/2811 Art.5

s.141, enabling: SI 2003/2818

s.145, applied: 1971 c.77 s.25B, 2000 c.43 Sch.4 para.2, 2002 c.29 Sch.2 para.4, Sch.5 para.4, SI 2004/1910 Sch.6

s.145, repealed: 2003 c.42 Sch.7

s.146, repealed: 2003 c.42 Sch.7

s.154, applied: SI 2002/2811 Art.6

s.157, applied: SI 2003/1016

s.157, enabling: SI 2003/1016

s.158, amended: 2004 c.19 s.44

s.158, applied: 2001 c.17 s.32

s.162, enabling: SI 2002/2811, SI 2003/1, SI 2003/249, SI 2003/754, SI 2003/1040, SI 2003/1339, SI 2003/1747, SI 2003/2993, SI 2003/3156, SI 2004/1201, SI 2004/1707, SI 2004/2998

Sch.3, see *R. (on the application of Grant) v Lambeth LBC* [2004] EWHC 1524, [2004] 3 F.C.R. 494 (QBD (Admin Ct)), Mitting, J.; see *R. (on the application of*

2002–cont.

41. Nationality, Immigration and Asylum Act 2002–cont.

Sch.3–cont.

Kimani) v Lambeth LBC [2003] EWCA Civ 1150, [2004] 1 W.L.R. 272 (CA), Lord Phillips of Worth Matravers, M.R.

Sch.3, applied: SI 2002/3078 Reg.2, 2004 c.19 s.9

Sch.3 para.1, see *R. (on the application of Kimani) v Lambeth LBC* [2003] EWHC 871, [2003] 2 F.L.R. 439 (QBD (Admin Ct)), Silber, J.

Sch.3 para.2, see *R. (on the application of M) v Islington LBC* [2004] EWCA Civ 235, [2004] 4 All E.R. 709 (CA), Waller, L.J.

Sch.3 para.7, see *R. (on the application of M) v Islington LBC* [2004] EWCA Civ 235, [2004] 4 All E.R. 709 (CA), Waller, L.J.

Sch.3 para.7A, added: 2004 c.19 s.9

Sch.3 para.7A, applied: 2004 c.19 s.9

Sch.3 para.7A, disapplied: 2004 c.19 s.9

Sch.3 para.8, enabling: SI 2002/3078

Sch.3 para.9, enabling: SI 2002/3078

Sch.3 para.10, enabling: SI 2002/3078

Sch.3 para.11, enabling: SI 2002/3078

Sch.3 para.12, enabling: SI 2002/3078

Sch.3 para.14, amended: 2004 c.19 s.9

Sch.3 para.16, enabling: SI 2002/3078

Sch.3 para.17, enabling: SI 2002/3078

Sch.4 para.1, applied: 2004 c.19 Sch.2 para.27, Sch.2 para.28

Sch.4 para.1, substituted: 2004 c.19 Sch.1

Sch.4 para.2, substituted: 2004 c.19 Sch.1

Sch.4 para.3, substituted: 2004 c.19 Sch.1

Sch.4 para.4, substituted: 2004 c.19 Sch.1

Sch.4 para.5, substituted: 2004 c.19 Sch.1

Sch.4 para.6, substituted: 2004 c.19 Sch.1

Sch.4 para.7, substituted: 2004 c.19 Sch.1

Sch.4 para.8, applied: 2004 c.19 Sch.2 para.30

Sch.4 para.8, substituted: 2004 c.19 Sch.1

Sch.4 para.9, applied: 2004 c.19 Sch.2 para.29

Sch.4 para.9, substituted: 2004 c.19 Sch.1

Sch.4 para.10, substituted: 2004 c.19 Sch.1

Sch.4 para.11, substituted: 2004 c.19 Sch.1

Sch.5, applied: 2004 c.19 Sch.2 para.28

Sch.5 para.1, repealed: 2004 c.19 s.26, Sch.4

Sch.5 para.2, repealed: 2004 c.19 s.26, Sch.4

Sch.5 para.3, repealed: 2004 c.19 s.26, Sch.4

Sch.5 para.4, repealed: 2004 c.19 s.26, Sch.4

Sch.5 para.5, repealed: 2004 c.19 s.26, Sch.4

Sch.5 para.6, repealed: 2004 c.19 s.26, Sch.4

Sch.5 para.7, applied: SI 2003/652 r.3

Sch.5 para.7, repealed: 2004 c.19 s.26, Sch.4

Sch.5 para.8, repealed: 2004 c.19 s.26, Sch.4

Sch.5 para.9, repealed: 2004 c.19 s.26, Sch.4

Sch.5 para.10, repealed: 2004 c.19 s.26, Sch.4

Sch.5 para.11, referred to: 1997 c.68 Sch.1 para.5

2002–cont.

41. Nationality, Immigration and Asylum Act 2002–cont.

Sch.5 para.11, repealed: 2004 c.19 s.26, Sch.4

Sch.8 para.1, disapplied: SI 2002/2811 Art.4

Sch.8 para.2, disapplied: SI 2002/2811 Art.4

Sch.8 para.3, disapplied: SI 2002/2811 Art.4

Sch.8 para.4, disapplied: SI 2002/2811 Art.4

Sch.8 para.5, disapplied: SI 2002/2811 Art.4

Sch.8 para.6, disapplied: SI 2002/2811 Art.4

Sch.8 para.7, disapplied: SI 2002/2811 Art.4

Sch.8 para.8, disapplied: SI 2002/2811 Art.4

Sch.8 para.9, disapplied: SI 2002/2811 Art.4

Sch.8 para.10, disapplied: SI 2002/2811 Art.4

Sch.8 para.11, disapplied: SI 2002/2811 Art.4

Sch.8 para.12, disapplied: SI 2002/2811 Art.4

Sch.8 para.15, disapplied: SI 2002/2811 Art.4

Sch.8 para.16, disapplied: SI 2002/2811 Art.4

Sch.8 para.17, disapplied: SI 2002/2811 Art.4

42. Animal Health Act 2002

Commencement Orders: SI 2002/3044 Art.2

referred to: 1981 c.22 s.14A, s.32B, s.6A

s.1, referred to: 1981 c.22 s.32A

s.19, enabling: SI 2002/3044

43. Consolidated Fund (No.2) Act 2002

applied: 2003 c.13 Sch.1

repealed: 2004 c.9 Sch.3

44. Appropriation (No.2) Act 2002

repealed: 2004 c.9 Sch.3

2003

iii. London Local Authorities and Transport for London Act 2003

s.4, applied: 2004 c.i s.7

s.4, repealed: 2004 c.18 Sch.12 Part 1

s.5, applied: 2004 c.i s.7

s.5, repealed: 2004 c.18 Sch.12 Part 1

s.6, repealed: 2004 c.18 Sch.12 Part 1

s.7, repealed: 2004 c.18 Sch.12 Part 1

s.11, amended: 2004 c.18 s.64

s.12, repealed: 2004 c.18 Sch.12 Part 2

s.14, repealed: 2004 c.18 Sch.12 Part 1

s.15, repealed: 2004 c.18 Sch.12 Part 1

s.20, amended: 2004 c.18 Sch.11 para.7

Sch.1 para.1, repealed: 2004 c.18 Sch.12 Part 1

Sch.1 para.2, repealed: 2004 c.18 Sch.12 Part 1

Sch.1 para.3, repealed: 2004 c.18 Sch.12 Part 1

Sch.1 para.4, repealed: 2004 c.18 Sch.12 Part 1

Sch.1 para.5, repealed: 2004 c.18 Sch.12 Part 1

Sch.1 para.6, repealed: 2004 c.18 Sch.12 Part 1

Sch.1 para.7, repealed: 2004 c.18 Sch.12 Part 1

Sch.1 para.8, repealed: 2004 c.18 Sch.12 Part 1

Sch.1 para.9, repealed: 2004 c.18 Sch.12 Part 1

CAP.

2003–cont.

iii. London Local Authorities and Transport for London Act 2003–cont.

Sch.1 para.10, repealed: 2004 c.18 Sch.12 Part 1

Sch.1 para.11, repealed: 2004 c.18 Sch.12 Part 1

Sch.2, applied: 2004 c.18 s.88

Sch.2 para.1, amended: 2004 c.18 Sch.12 Part 1

Sch.2 para.1, repealed (in part): 2004 c.18 Sch.12 Part 1

Sch.2 para.2, amended: 2004 c.18 Sch.12 Part 1

Sch.2 para.3, amended: 2004 c.18 Sch.12 Part 1

Sch.2 para.4, amended: 2004 c.18 Sch.12 Part 1

Sch.2 para.5, amended: 2004 c.18 Sch.12 Part 1

Sch.2 para.5, repealed: 2004 c.18 Sch.12 Part 1

Sch.2 para.6, amended: 2004 c.18 Sch.12 Part 1

Sch.2 para.6, repealed: 2004 c.18 Sch.12 Part 1

Sch.2 para.7, amended: 2004 c.18 Sch.12 Part 1

Sch.2 para.8, amended: 2004 c.18 Sch.12 Part 1

Sch.2 para.9, amended: 2004 c.18 Sch.12 Part 1

Sch.3 para.1, repealed: 2004 c.18 Sch.12 Part 1

Sch.3 para.2, repealed: 2004 c.18 Sch.12 Part 1

Sch.3 para.3, repealed: 2004 c.18 Sch.12 Part 1

Sch.3 para.4, repealed: 2004 c.18 Sch.12 Part 1

1. Income Tax (Earnings and Pensions) Act 2003

applied: 1970 c.9 s.119, 1973 c.51 Sch.15 para.5, 1988 c.1 s.18, 1992 c.12 s.119A, s.149B, SI 2000/727 Reg.5, Reg.7, 2001 c.2 s.61, s.63, s.72, s.88, s.423, SI 2001/1004 Reg.22, Sch.3 para.4D, Sch.3 para.5, Sch.4 para.16, 2003 c.14 Sch.23 para.7, Sch.23 para.14, Sch.24 para.5, 2004 c.35 Sch.3, Sch.8

referred to: 1992 c.12 s.120, 2000 c.17 Sch.12 para.18, SI 2003/2682 Sch.1 para.6, Sch.1 para.7, 2004 c.12 s.78, s.80

Part 2, applied: 1970 c.9 s.15, 1988 c.1 s.1, s.9, s.314, s.376, SI 2003/2682 Reg.85

Part 2 c.4, applied: 1988 c.1 s.68A, s.251A, s.336, 2003 c.14 Sch.24 para.2

Part 2 c.5, applied: 1988 c.1 s.68A, s.251A, s.336

Part 2 c.7, applied: 1988 c.1 s.559, 2000 c.17 Sch.20 para.8C, 2004 c.12 s.60

Part 2 c.8, applied: 2000 c.17 Sch.12 para.17

CAP.

2003–cont.

1. Income Tax (Earnings and Pensions) Act 2003–cont.

Part 3, applied: 1988 c.1 s.418, 2004 c.12 Sch.15 para.19

Part 3, referred to: 1988 c.1 s.580A, SI 2003/2682 Reg.88

Part 3 c.1, applied: 1992 c.12 s.149AA, 2003 c.14 Sch.23 para.22C, Sch.23 para.20, Sch.23 para.21

Part 3 c.10, applied: 1970 c.9 s.15, 1988 c.1 s.418, SI 2002/205 Reg.3, Reg.4, SI 2002/2006 Reg.4

Part 3 c.10, referred to: 1988 c.1 s.418, SI 2003/2682 Reg.87

Part 3 c.11, applied: SI 2002/2006 Reg.4

Part 3 c.2, referred to: 1992 c.4 s.10, SI 2001/1004 Reg.36

Part 3 c.4, applied: 1970 c.9 s.15, SI 2001/1004 Sch.3 para.3, SI 2002/2006 Reg.4

Part 3 c.5, applied: 1970 c.9 s.15, 2003 c.14 Sch.4 para.12

Part 3 c.6, applied: 1970 c.9 s.15, 1988 c.1 s.418

Part 3 c.6, referred to: 1988 c.1 s.418, SI 2003/2682 Reg.87

Part 3 c.7, applied: 1970 c.9 s.15, 1988 c.1 s.418, 1989 c.26 s.178, SI 2004/1863 Sch.1 para.5

Part 3 c.7, referred to: 1988 c.1 s.418, SI 2003/2682 Reg.87

Part 3 c.8, applied: 1970 c.9 s.15, 1988 c.1 s.418, 1992 c.12 s.120

Part 3 c.8, referred to: 1988 c.1 s.418, SI 2003/2682 Reg.87

Part 3 c.9, applied: 1970 c.9 s.15, 1988 c.1 s.418

Part 3 c.9, referred to: 1988 c.1 s.418, SI 2003/2682 Reg.87

Part 4, referred to: 1988 c.1 s.580A

Part 4 c.4, applied: SI 2002/2006 Reg.4

Part 4 c.5, applied: SI 2002/2006 Reg.4

Part 4 c.6, applied: SI 2002/2006 Reg.4

Part 4 c.7, applied: SI 2002/2006 Reg.4

Part 5, applied: 1988 c.1 s.646

Part 5, referred to: 1988 c.1 s.580A

Part 5 c.2, applied: 2004 c.12 Sch.33 para.1, Sch.36 para.51

Part 5 c.6, applied: SI 2003/2682 Reg.15

Part 6, referred to: 1988 c.1 s.580A

Part 6 c.2, applied: 1988 c.1 s.606

Part 6 c.3, applied: 1988 c.1 s.644, s.833, SI 2002/2006 Reg.4, SI 2003/2682 Reg.91

Part 7, applied: SI 2001/1004 Sch.4 para.7, SI 2002/2006 Reg.4

Part 7, referred to: 1988 c.1 s.580A

Part 7 c.1, applied: SI 2001/1004 Sch.2 para.7

Part 7 c.2, applied: 1992 c.12 s.149B, s.120, SI 2001/1004 Reg.22, Sch.2 para.7, 2003 c.14 Sch.23 para.19

Part 7 c.3, applied: 1992 c.12 s.120, SI 2001/1004 Sch.2 para.7

CAP.

CAP.

2003–cont.

2003–cont.

1. **Income Tax (Earnings and Pensions) Act 2003**–*cont.*

Part 7 c.3A, applied: 1992 c.4 Sch.1 para.3A, Sch.1 para.3B, 1992 c.12 s.120, SI 2001/1004 Sch.2 para.7

Part 7 c.3B, applied: 1992 c.12 s.120, SI 2001/1004 Sch.2 para.7, 2004 c.12 s.88, s.89

Part 7 c.3C, applied: 1992 c.12 s.120, SI 2001/1004 Sch.2 para.7

Part 7 c.3D, applied: 1992 c.12 s.120, SI 2001/1004 Sch.2 para.7

Part 7 c.4, applied: 1992 c.12 s.120, SI 2001/1004 Reg.22, Sch.2 para.7

Part 7 c.5, applied: 1992 c.12 s.120, 2001 c.20 s.3, SI 2001/1004 Sch.2 para.7

Part 7 c.5, referred to: 1992 c.12 s.288

Part 7 c.9, referred to: SI 2004/712 Reg.1

Part 9, applied: 1988 c.1 s.659B, s.1, s.9, s.336, s.348, s.392, s.545, 1995 c.4 s.128

Part 9, referred to: 1988 c.1 s.580A

Part 9 c.5A, applied: 2004 c.12 Sch.36 para.44, Sch.36 para.45

Part 9 c.5A, disapplied: 2004 c.12 Sch.36 para.43

Part 9 c.7, applied: 2004 c.12 Sch.36 para.44, Sch.36 para.45

Part 9 c.9, applied: 2004 c.12 Sch.36 para.43

Part 10, applied: 1988 c.1 s.1, s.9, s.336

s.3, amended: 2003 c.14 Sch.22 para.16

s.7, amended: 2003 c.14 Sch.22 para.17

s.7, applied: 1973 c.51 Sch.15 para.2, 1984 c.51 s.14, 2004 c.12 s.280

s.10, applied: 1970 c.9 s.62, s.64, SI 2000/727 Reg.7, 2004 c.12 Sch.34 para.10, Sch.34 para.11

s.10, referred to: 1986 c.45 Sch.6 para.1, 1992 c.4 s.126, 1995 c.18 s.15, 2001 c.2 s.20

s.14, referred to: 1988 c.1 s.251A

s.15, applied: 1988 c.1 s.624

s.18, applied: 1989 c.26 s.43, s.44, SI 2000/727 Reg.7, 2002 c.23 Sch.29 para.113, 2003 c.14 Sch.24 para.2

s.19, amended: 2003 c.14 Sch.43 Part 3

s.19, applied: 1989 c.26 s.43, s.44, SI 2000/727 Reg.7, 2002 c.23 Sch.29 para.113

s.20, referred to: 1988 c.1 s.251A

s.22, applied: 2001 c.2 s.20

s.23, amended: 2004 c.12 Sch.35 para.55

s.23, applied: 1988 c.1 s.391

s.26, applied: 2001 c.2 s.20

s.28, applied: 1990 c.29 s.25

s.31, applied: 1989 c.26 s.43, s.44, 2002 c.23 Sch.29 para.113

s.32, amended: 2003 c.14 Sch.43 Part 3

s.32, applied: 1989 c.26 s.43, s.44, 2002 c.23 Sch.29 para.113

s.40, amended: 2004 c.12 Sch.27 para.12

s.41, applied: 1970 c.9 s.46B

s.42, applied: 1988 c.1 s.645, 1989 c.26 s.76, 1992 c.12 s.9

s.42, referred to: 1988 c.1 s.645, 1992 c.12 s.9

1. **Income Tax (Earnings and Pensions) Act 2003**–*cont.*

s.43, applied: 1988 c.1 s.645, 1989 c.26 s.76, 1992 c.12 s.9

s.44, applied: 1970 c.9 s.16A

s.45, applied: 1970 c.9 s.16A

s.49, amended: 2003 c.14 s.136

s.49, repealed (in part): 2003 c.14 Sch.43 Part 3

s.54, amended: 2004 c.12 Sch.12 para.17, Sch.35 para.56

s.56, amended: 2003 c.14 s.136, 2004 c.12 Sch.35 para.57

s.56, repealed (in part): 2003 c.14 Sch.43 Part 3, 2004 c.12 Sch.42 Part 3

s.62, applied: SI 2002/2006 Reg.4

s.63, amended: 2003 c.14 Sch.43 Part 3

s.63, referred to: 1970 c.9 s.15

s.63, varied: 1992 c.12 s.222

s.64, referred to: SI 2002/2006 Reg.4

s.64, repealed (in part): 2003 c.14 Sch.43 Part 3

s.64, varied: 1992 c.12 s.222

s.65, varied: 1992 c.12 s.222

s.66, applied: 1988 c.1 s.376

s.66, referred to: SI 2003/2682 Reg.85

s.66, varied: 1992 c.12 s.222

s.67, applied: 1988 c.1 s.565, 2004 c.12 Sch.11 para.11

s.67, varied: 1992 c.12 s.222

s.68, varied: 1992 c.12 s.222

s.69, varied: 1992 c.12 s.222

s.72, applied: SI 2002/2006 Reg.4

s.81, applied: SI 2002/2006 Reg.4

s.84, amended: 2004 c.12 Sch.13 para.2

s.86, applied: 1994 c.9 Sch.24 para.27, SI 2001/1004 Sch.3 para.2

s.86, referred to: 1994 c.9 Sch.24 para.27

s.87, amended: 2004 c.12 Sch.13 para.2

s.87, applied: SI 2002/2006 Reg.4

s.87, referred to: SI 2003/2682 Reg.86

s.89, applied: SI 2002/2006 Reg.4

s.94, applied: SI 2002/2006 Reg.4

s.94, referred to: SI 2003/2682 Reg.86

s.95, amended: 2004 c.12 Sch.13 para.2

s.99, applied: SI 2001/1004 Sch.3 para.10, Sch.3 para.11

s.99, referred to: 2003 c.14 Sch.4 para.12

s.100, applied: SI 2001/1004 Sch.3 para.10, Sch.3 para.11

s.102, referred to: SI 2003/2682 Reg.86

s.105, applied: 2003 c.14 Sch.4 para.12

s.106, applied: 2003 c.14 Sch.4 para.12

s.114, amended: 2004 c.12 Sch.14 para.2, Sch.42 Part 2

s.116, amended: 2004 c.12 Sch.14 para.3

s.119, amended: 2004 c.12 Sch.14 para.4

s.120, applied: SI 2002/2006 Reg.4, SI 2003/2682 Reg.90

s.121, referred to: SI 2003/2682 Reg.90

CAP.

2003–cont.

1. Income Tax (Earnings and Pensions) Act 2003–*cont.*

s.139, amended: 2003 c.14 s.138, Sch.43 Part 3

s.149, applied: SI 2001/1004 Reg.22, Sch.3 para.7D, SI 2002/2006 Reg.4

s.155, substituted: 2004 c.12 Sch.14 para.5

s.156, substituted: 2004 c.12 Sch.14 para.5

s.157, substituted: 2004 c.12 Sch.14 para.5

s.158, substituted: 2004 c.12 Sch.14 para.5

s.159, substituted: 2004 c.12 Sch.14 para.5

s.160, substituted: 2004 c.12 Sch.14 para.5

s.161, substituted: 2004 c.12 Sch.14 para.5

s.162, substituted: 2004 c.12 Sch.14 para.5

s.163, substituted: 2004 c.12 Sch.14 para.5

s.164, substituted: 2004 c.12 Sch.14 para.5

s.165, substituted: 2004 c.12 Sch.14 para.5

s.166, substituted: 2004 c.12 Sch.14 para.5

s.169A, added: 2004 c.12 Sch.14 para.6

s.170, amended: 2003 c.14 s.138, 2004 c.12 Sch.14 para.7

s.171, amended: 2004 c.12 Sch.42 Part 2

s.192, repealed: 2003 c.14 Sch.43 Part 3

s.193, repealed: 2003 c.14 Sch.43 Part 3

s.194, repealed: 2003 c.14 Sch.43 Part 3

s.195, applied: 1992 c.12 s.120

s.195, repealed: 2003 c.14 Sch.43 Part 3

s.196, repealed: 2003 c.14 Sch.43 Part 3

s.197, repealed: 2003 c.14 Sch.43 Part 3

s.198, repealed: 2003 c.14 Sch.43 Part 3

s.199, repealed: 2003 c.14 Sch.43 Part 3

s.200, repealed: 2003 c.14 Sch.43 Part 3

s.207, applied: 2004 c.12 Sch.34 para.13

s.210, enabling: SI 2003/1434, SI 2004/3087

s.211, disapplied: SI 2002/2006 Reg.4

s.212, disapplied: SI 2002/2006 Reg.4

s.213, disapplied: SI 2002/2006 Reg.4

s.214, disapplied: SI 2002/2006 Reg.4

s.215, disapplied: SI 2002/2006 Reg.4

s.216, amended: 2003 c.14 Sch.43 Part 3

s.216, applied: 1988 c.1 s.418

s.216, referred to: SI 2003/2682 Reg.85

s.217, applied: SI 2001/1004 Sch.3 para.2

s.218, amended: 2004 c.12 Sch.35 para.58

s.222, amended: 2003 c.14 s.144

s.222, applied: 1970 c.9 s.15, SI 2001/1004 Reg.22

s.222, referred to: SI 2003/2682 Reg.86

s.223, applied: 1970 c.9 s.15

s.223, referred to: 1988 c.1 s.418, SI 2003/2682 Reg.87

s.224, repealed: 2004 c.12 Sch.42 Part 3

s.225, applied: 1988 c.39 s.73, 1992 c.4 s.4, SI 2002/2006 Reg.4

s.226, applied: 1992 c.4 s.4

s.227, amended: 2003 c.14 Sch.22 para.25

s.227, repealed (in part): 2003 c.14 Sch.43 Part 3

s.229, applied: SI 2001/1004 Reg.22A

CAP.

2003–cont.

1. Income Tax (Earnings and Pensions) Act 2003–*cont.*

s.230, applied: SI 2001/1004 Reg.22A, Sch.3 para.7B

s.231, applied: SI 2000/727 Reg.7, SI 2002/2006 Reg.4

s.232, applied: 1988 c.1 s.646, SI 2002/2006 Reg.4

s.233, applied: SI 2000/727 Reg.7, SI 2001/1004 Sch.3 para.7C

s.234, applied: SI 2001/1004 Sch.3 para.7C

s.236, amended: 2004 c.12 s.81

s.237, amended: 2004 c.12 Sch.14 para.8

s.237, applied: SI 2001/1004 Sch.3 para.8

s.239, applied: SI 2001/1004 Sch.3 para.7, SI 2002/2006 Reg.4

s.240, applied: SI 2001/1004 Sch.3 para.4, SI 2002/2006 Reg.4

s.241, applied: SI 2001/1004 Sch.3 para.4

s.242, applied: SI 2001/1004 Sch.3 para.5A

s.243, applied: SI 2001/1004 Sch.3 para.5A

s.244, applied: SI 2001/1004 Sch.3 para.5A

s.245, applied: SI 2001/1004 Sch.3 para.5B, Sch.3 para.8, SI 2002/2006 Reg.4

s.246, applied: SI 2001/1004 Sch.3 para.5, Sch.3 para.8, SI 2002/2006 Reg.4

s.246, referred to: SI 2002/2006 Reg.4

s.247, applied: SI 2001/1004 Sch.3 para.5, SI 2002/2006 Reg.4

s.248, applied: SI 2001/1004 Sch.3 para.5, Sch.3 para.8, SI 2002/2006 Reg.4

s.248A, added: 2004 c.12 s.81

s.250, applied: SI 2001/1004 Sch.3 para.2

s.251, applied: SI 2001/1004 Sch.3 para.2

s.251, referred to: SI 2002/2006 Reg.4

s.252, applied: SI 2001/1004 Sch.3 para.2

s.253, applied: SI 2001/1004 Sch.3 para.2

s.254, applied: SI 2001/1004 Sch.3 para.2

s.255, applied: SI 2001/1004 Sch.3 para.3

s.256, referred to: SI 2002/2006 Reg.4

s.261, applied: SI 2001/1004 Sch.3 para.5B

s.263, enabling: SI 2004/3087

s.264, amended: SI 2003/1361 Art.2

s.264, applied: SI 2001/1004 Sch.3 para.5B

s.266, applied: SI 2001/1004 Sch.3 para.5A, Sch.3 para.5B, Sch.3 para.3, Sch.3 para.5

s.269, applied: SI 2001/1004 Sch.3 para.3

s.270, applied: SI 2001/1004 Sch.3 para.6, SI 2002/2006 Reg.4

s.270A, added: 2004 c.12 Sch.13 para.3

s.271, applied: SI 2001/1004 Reg.40, Sch.3 para.2, SI 2003/2682 Reg.86, Reg.87

s.271, varied: SI 2001/1004 Sch.3 para.2

s.272, varied: SI 2001/1004 Sch.3 para.2

s.273, varied: SI 2001/1004 Sch.3 para.2

s.274, varied: SI 2001/1004 Sch.3 para.2

s.275, varied: SI 2001/1004 Sch.3 para.2

s.276, varied: SI 2001/1004 Sch.3 para.2

s.277, amended: 2003 c.14 Sch.18 para.6

s.277, varied: SI 2001/1004 Sch.3 para.2

CAP.

2003–cont.

1. Income Tax (Earnings and Pensions) Act 2003–*cont.*

s.278, varied: SI 2001/1004 Sch.3 para.2
s.279, varied: SI 2001/1004 Sch.3 para.2
s.280, varied: SI 2001/1004 Sch.3 para.2
s.281, varied: SI 2001/1004 Sch.3 para.2
s.282, varied: SI 2001/1004 Sch.3 para.2
s.283, varied: SI 2001/1004 Sch.3 para.2
s.284, varied: SI 2001/1004 Sch.3 para.2
s.285, varied: SI 2001/1004 Sch.3 para.2
s.286, amended: 2004 c.12 Sch.17 para.9
s.286, varied: SI 2001/1004 Sch.3 para.2
s.287, applied: SI 2003/2682 Reg.86
s.287, varied: SI 2001/1004 Sch.3 para.2
s.288, applied: SI 2004/1863 Sch.1 para.5
s.288, varied: SI 2001/1004 Sch.3 para.2
s.289, applied: SI 2004/1863 Sch.1 para.5
s.289, varied: SI 2001/1004 Sch.3 para.2
s.294, amended: 2004 c.12 s.82
s.296, applied: SI 2001/1004 Sch.3 para.5B
s.297, applied: SI 2002/2006 Reg.4
s.297, referred to: SI 2001/1004 Reg.143
s.298, applied: SI 2002/2006 Reg.4
s.298, referred to: SI 2001/1004 Reg.143
s.299, applied: SI 2000/727 Reg.7, SI 2001/1004 Sch.3 para.12, SI 2002/2006 Reg.4
s.303, applied: 1988 c.1 s.323, 1992 c.12 s.11
s.304, applied: SI 2001/1004 Sch.3 para.15, SI 2002/2006 Reg.4
s.305, amended: 2004 c.12 Sch.42 Part 2
s.305, applied: SI 2001/1004 Sch.3 para.6, SI 2002/2006 Reg.4
s.305, referred to: SI 2002/2006 Reg.4
s.306, applied: SI 2002/2006 Reg.4
s.307, amended: 2004 c.12 s.201, s.248
s.307, applied: 2004 c.12 Sch.34 para.1, Sch.34 para.8
s.308, applied: SI 2001/1004 Sch.3 para.2
s.308, substituted: 2004 c.12 s.201
s.308A, added: 2004 c.12 Sch.33 para.3
s.311, applied: 1988 c.1 s.588, SI 2002/2006 Reg.4
s.312, referred to: 1988 c.1 s.588
s.315, amended: 2004 c.12 Sch.35 para.59
s.316A, added: 2003 c.14 s.137
s.316A, applied: SI 2002/2006 Reg.4
s.317, amended: 2004 c.12 Sch.17 para.1
s.317, applied: SI 2001/1004 Sch.3 para.5B, SI 2002/2006 Reg.4
s.318, substituted: 2004 c.12 Sch.13 para.1
s.319, amended: 2003 c.21 Sch.17 para.175
s.320, amended: 2003 c.21 Sch.17 para.175, 2004 c.12 s.79
s.320, applied: SI 2002/2006 Reg.4
s.320, repealed (in part): 2003 c.21 Sch.19, 2004 c.12 Sch.42 Part 2
s.321, applied: SI 2001/1004 Sch.3 para.6, Sch.3 para.8, SI 2002/2006 Reg.4
s.322, applied: SI 2002/2006 Reg.4
s.323, amended: SI 2003/1361 Art.3

2003–cont.

1. Income Tax (Earnings and Pensions) Act 2003–*cont.*

s.323, applied: SI 2001/1004 Sch.3 para.2, Sch.3 para.6, SI 2002/2006 Reg.4
s.324, amended: SI 2003/1361 Art.4
s.324, applied: SI 2001/1004 Sch.3 para.6, SI 2002/2006 Reg.4
s.326, applied: SI 2002/2006 Reg.4
s.326, referred to: SI 2002/2006 Reg.4
s.327, amended: 2004 c.12 Sch.35 para.60, Sch.42 Part 3
s.327, applied: SI 2000/727 Reg.7
s.328, applied: 1970 c.9 s.15
s.336, applied: 1988 c.1 s.617, s.646, s.779, s.781, SI 2002/2006 Reg.4
s.337, applied: SI 2002/2006 Reg.4
s.338, applied: SI 2001/1004 Sch.3 para.3, SI 2002/2006 Reg.4
s.339, applied: SI 2001/1004 Sch.3 para.3, SI 2002/2006 Reg.4
s.340, applied: SI 2002/2006 Reg.4
s.341, applied: SI 2001/1004 Sch.3 para.4, SI 2002/2006 Reg.4
s.342, applied: SI 2001/1004 Sch.3 para.4A, SI 2002/2006 Reg.4
s.343, amended: SI 2003/1652 Art.2, SI 2004/1360 Art.2
s.343, applied: 1988 c.1 s.646, SI 2001/1004 Sch.3 para.11, SI 2002/2006 Reg.4
s.343, enabling: SI 2003/1652, SI 2004/1360
s.344, applied: 1988 c.1 s.646, SI 2001/1004 Sch.3 para.11, SI 2002/2006 Reg.4
s.346, applied: SI 2001/1004 Sch.3 para.10, SI 2002/2006 Reg.4
s.347, applied: SI 2002/2006 Reg.4
s.351, applied: 1988 c.1 s.617, s.646, SI 2002/2006 Reg.4
s.352, applied: SI 2002/2006 Reg.4
s.355, applied: 1988 c.1 s.347A, 2004 c.12 Sch.33 para.1, Sch.36 para.51
s.355, disapplied: 1988 c.39 s.38
s.357, amended: SI 2004/2310 Sch.1 para.68
s.362, applied: 1970 c.9 s.15, SI 2002/2006 Reg.4
s.363, applied: 1970 c.9 s.15, SI 2002/2006 Reg.4
s.364, applied: 1970 c.9 s.15
s.365, applied: 1970 c.9 s.15
s.367, applied: SI 2002/2006 Reg.4
s.368, applied: SI 2002/2006 Reg.4
s.370, applied: SI 2001/1004 Sch.3 para.4B, SI 2002/2006 Reg.4
s.371, applied: SI 2001/1004 Sch.3 para.4C, SI 2002/2006 Reg.4
s.373, applied: SI 2001/1004 Sch.3 para.5, SI 2002/2006 Reg.4
s.374, applied: SI 2001/1004 Sch.3 para.5, SI 2002/2006 Reg.4
s.376, applied: SI 2001/1004 Sch.3 para.4D, SI 2002/2006 Reg.4

CAP.

2003–cont.

1. Income Tax (Earnings and Pensions) Act 2003–cont.

s.377, applied: SI 2002/2006 Reg.4

s.381, amended: 2004 c.12 Sch.35 para.61

s.385, substituted: 2004 c.12 Sch.27 para.14

s.386, applied: 1988 c.1 Sch.14 para.5, 1989 c.26 s.76, 2004 c.12 Sch.36 para.52, Sch.36 para.53

s.386, disapplied: SI 2001/1004 Reg.40, Sch.3 para.3

s.386, referred to: 1988 c.1 s.266A

s.386, repealed: 2004 c.12 s.247, Sch.42 Part 3

s.387, applied: SI 2001/1004 Reg.40, Sch.3 para.3

s.387, referred to: 1988 c.1 s.645, s.657

s.387, repealed: 2004 c.12 s.247, Sch.42 Part 3

s.388, applied: 1988 c.1 s.266A

s.388, repealed: 2004 c.12 s.247, Sch.42 Part 3

s.389, referred to: 1988 c.1 s.266A

s.389, repealed: 2004 c.12 s.247, Sch.42 Part 3

s.389, substituted: 2004 c.12 Sch.17 para.2

s.390, applied: SI 2001/1004 Reg.40, Sch.3 para.3, SI 2004/1863 Sch.1 para.4

s.390, referred to: 1988 c.1 s.266A

s.390, repealed: 2004 c.12 s.247, Sch.42 Part 3

s.391, repealed: 2004 c.12 s.247, Sch.42 Part 3

s.392, applied: 2004 c.12 Sch.36 para.52

s.392, repealed: 2004 c.12 s.247, Sch.42 Part 3

s.393, amended: 2004 c.12 s.249

s.393, substituted: 2004 c.12 s.249

s.393A, amended: 2004 c.12 s.249

s.393B, amended: 2004 c.12 s.249

s.394, amended: 2004 c.12 s.249

s.394, applied: 1970 c.9 s.9, 2004 c.12 s.255, Sch.36 para.53

s.394, disapplied: 2004 c.12 Sch.36 para.54, Sch.36 para.55

s.395, amended: 2004 c.12 s.249

s.395, applied: 2004 c.12 Sch.36 para.54

s.395, referred to: 2004 c.12 Sch.36 para.55

s.395, substituted: 2004 c.12 s.249

s.396, amended: 2004 c.12 s.249

s.396, substituted: 2004 c.12 s.249

s.397, amended: 2004 c.12 s.249

s.397, substituted: 2004 c.12 s.249

s.398, amended: 2004 c.12 s.249

s.398, applied: SI 2000/727 Reg.4

s.399, amended: 2004 c.12 s.249

s.399A, amended: 2004 c.12 s.249

s.400, amended: 2004 c.12 s.249

s.400, substituted: 2004 c.12 s.249

s.403, applied: 1988 c.1 s.550

s.404, referred to: SI 2003/2682 Reg.91

2003–cont.

1. Income Tax (Earnings and Pensions) Act 2003–cont.

s.407, amended: 2004 c.12 Sch.35 para.62

s.407, repealed (in part): 2004 c.12 Sch.35 para.62, Sch.42 Part 3

s.408, amended: 2004 c.12 Sch.35 para.63

s.408, repealed (in part): 2004 c.12 Sch.35 para.63, Sch.42 Part 3

s.415, applied: SI 2003/2682 Reg.91

s.417, substituted: 2003 c.14 Sch.22 para.2

s.418, substituted: 2003 c.14 Sch.22 para.2

s.419, substituted: 2003 c.14 Sch.22 para.2

s.420, substituted: 2003 c.14 Sch.22 para.2

s.421, substituted: 2003 c.14 Sch.22 para.2

s.421A, substituted: 2003 c.14 Sch.22 para.2

s.421B, applied: 1992 c.12 s.119A, SI 2001/1004 Reg.22

s.421B, substituted: 2003 c.14 Sch.22 para.2

s.421C, amended: 2004 c.12 s.90

s.421C, substituted: 2003 c.14 Sch.22 para.2

s.421D, substituted: 2003 c.14 Sch.22 para.2

s.421E, substituted: 2003 c.14 Sch.22 para.2

s.421F, amended: 2004 c.12 s.89

s.421F, substituted: 2003 c.14 Sch.22 para.2

s.421G, repealed: 2004 c.12 Sch.42 Part 2

s.421G, substituted: 2003 c.14 Sch.22 para.2

s.421H, substituted: 2003 c.14 Sch.22 para.2

s.421I, substituted: 2003 c.14 Sch.22 para.2

s.421J, applied: 1970 c.9 s.98

s.421J, substituted: 2003 c.14 Sch.22 para.2

s.421K, substituted: 2003 c.14 Sch.22 para.2

s.421L, substituted: 2003 c.14 Sch.22 para.2

s.422, substituted: 2003 c.14 Sch.22 para.3

s.423, referred to: 2003 c.14 Sch.23 para.19

s.423, substituted: 2003 c.14 Sch.22 para.3

s.424, referred to: 2003 c.14 Sch.23 para.19

s.424, substituted: 2003 c.14 Sch.22 para.3

s.425, substituted: 2003 c.14 Sch.22 para.3

s.425, applied: SI 2001/1004 Sch.3 para.9

s.425, substituted: 2003 c.14 Sch.22 para.3

s.426, applied: 1992 c.12 s.119A, 2003 c.14 Sch.23 para.20, Sch.23 para.21

s.426, substituted: 2003 c.14 Sch.22 para.3

s.426, amended: 2004 c.12 Sch.16 para.1

s.426, applied: SI 2001/1004 Sch.5 para.1

s.426, substituted: 2003 c.14 Sch.22 para.3

s.427, applied: 2003 c.14 Sch.22 para.3, Sch.23 para.20, Sch.23 para.21

s.427, substituted: 2003 c.14 Sch.22 para.3

s.428, applied: SI 2001/1004 Reg.22

s.428, disapplied: 2003 c.14 Sch.23 para.21

s.428, substituted: 2003 c.14 Sch.22 para.3

s.428A, added: 2004 c.12 Sch.16 para.1

s.428A, applied: SI 2001/1004 Sch.2 para.7, 2003 c.14 Sch.23 para.21

s.428A, substituted: 2003 c.14 Sch.22 para.3

s.429, amended: 2004 c.12 s.86

s.429, repealed (in part): 2004 c.12 Sch.42 Part 2

s.429, substituted: 2003 c.14 Sch.22 para.3

2003–cont.

1. Income Tax (Earnings and Pensions) Act 2003–*cont.*

s.430, substituted: 2003 c.14 Sch.22 para.3
s.431, amended: 2003 c.14 Sch.22 para.3
s.431, applied: 2004 c.12 s.88
s.431, substituted: 2003 c.14 Sch.22 para.3
s.431A, added: 2004 c.12 s.88
s.431A, substituted: 2003 c.14 Sch.22 para.3
s.432, applied: 1970 c.9 s.98
s.432, substituted: 2003 c.14 Sch.22 para.3
s.433, applied: 1970 c.9 s.98
s.433, substituted: 2003 c.14 Sch.22 para.3
s.434, substituted: 2003 c.14 Sch.22 para.3
s.435, substituted: 2003 c.14 Sch.22 para.4
s.436, substituted: 2003 c.14 Sch.22 para.4
s.437, applied: 2003 c.14 Sch.23 para.22C
s.437, substituted: 2003 c.14 Sch.22 para.4
s.438, applied: 1992 c.12 s.119A
s.438, substituted: 2003 c.14 Sch.22 para.4
s.438, amended: 2004 c.12 Sch.16 para.2
s.438, applied: SI 2001/1004 Sch.5 para.1
s.438, substituted: 2003 c.14 Sch.22 para.4
s.439, applied: 1992 c.12 s.119A
s.439, substituted: 2003 c.14 Sch.22 para.4
s.440, substituted: 2003 c.14 Sch.22 para.4
s.441, substituted: 2003 c.14 Sch.22 para.4
s.442, substituted: 2003 c.14 Sch.22 para.4
s.442A, added: 2004 c.12 Sch.16 para.2
s.442A, applied: SI 2001/1004 Sch.2 para.7, 2003 c.14 Sch.23 para.22C
s.442A, substituted: 2003 c.14 Sch.22 para.4
s.443, amended: 2004 c.12 s.86
s.443, repealed (in part): 2004 c.12 Sch.42 Part 2
s.443, substituted: 2003 c.14 Sch.22 para.4
s.444, substituted: 2003 c.14 Sch.22 para.4
s.445, applied: 1970 c.9 s.98
s.445, substituted: 2003 c.14 Sch.22 para.4
s.446, substituted: 2003 c.14 Sch.22 para.4
s.446A, added: 2003 c.14 Sch.22 para.5
s.446B, added: 2003 c.14 Sch.22 para.5
s.446C, added: 2003 c.14 Sch.22 para.5
s.446D, added: 2003 c.14 Sch.22 para.5
s.446E, added: 2003 c.14 Sch.22 para.5
s.446E, amended: 2004 c.12 s.87
s.446E, disapplied: 2003 c.14 Sch.23 para.21, 2004 c.12 s.87
s.446F, added: 2003 c.14 Sch.22 para.5
s.446G, added: 2003 c.14 Sch.22 para.5
s.446G, disapplied: 2003 c.14 Sch.23 para.22C
s.446H, added: 2003 c.14 Sch.22 para.5
s.446H, disapplied: 2003 c.14 Sch.23 para.22C
s.446I, added: 2003 c.14 Sch.22 para.5
s.446IA, added: 2003 c.14 Sch.22 para.5, 2004 c.12 s.86
s.446J, added: 2003 c.14 Sch.22 para.5
s.446K, added: 2003 c.14 Sch.22 para.6
s.446L, added: 2003 c.14 Sch.22 para.6

2003–cont.

1. Income Tax (Earnings and Pensions) Act 2003–*cont.*

s.446M, added: 2003 c.14 Sch.22 para.6
s.446N, added: 2003 c.14 Sch.22 para.6
s.446NA, added: 2003 c.14 Sch.22 para.6, 2004 c.12 s.86
s.446O, added: 2003 c.14 Sch.22 para.6
s.446O, varied: 2004 c.12 s.88, s.89
s.446P, added: 2003 c.14 Sch.22 para.6
s.446Q, added: 2003 c.14 Sch.22 para.7
s.446R, added: 2003 c.14 Sch.22 para.7
s.446R, amended: 2004 c.12 s.86
s.446R, repealed (in part): 2004 c.12 Sch.42 Part 2
s.446S, added: 2003 c.14 Sch.22 para.7
s.446T, added: 2003 c.14 Sch.22 para.7
s.446U, added: 2003 c.14 Sch.22 para.7
s.446U, applied: 1992 c.12 s.119A
s.446V, added: 2003 c.14 Sch.22 para.7
s.446W, added: 2003 c.14 Sch.22 para.7
s.446X, added: 2003 c.14 Sch.22 para.8
s.446Y, added: 2003 c.14 Sch.22 para.8
s.446Z, added: 2003 c.14 Sch.22 para.8
s.447, applied: 1992 c.12 s.120
s.447, substituted: 2003 c.14 Sch.22 para.9
s.448, substituted: 2003 c.14 Sch.22 para.9
s.449, applied: 2003 c.14 Sch.22 para.3
s.449, substituted: 2003 c.14 Sch.22 para.9
s.449, amended: 2004 c.12 s.86
s.449, repealed (in part): 2004 c.12 Sch.42 Part 2
s.449, substituted: 2003 c.14 Sch.22 para.9
s.450, substituted: 2003 c.14 Sch.22 para.9
s.451, substituted: 2003 c.14 Sch.22 para.9
s.452, substituted: 2003 c.14 Sch.22 para.9
s.453, substituted: 2003 c.14 Sch.22 para.9
s.454, substituted: 2003 c.14 Sch.22 para.9
s.455, substituted: 2003 c.14 Sch.22 para.9
s.456, substituted: 2003 c.14 Sch.22 para.9
s.457, substituted: 2003 c.14 Sch.22 para.9
s.458, substituted: 2003 c.14 Sch.22 para.9
s.459, substituted: 2003 c.14 Sch.22 para.9
s.460, substituted: 2003 c.14 Sch.22 para.9
s.461, substituted: 2003 c.14 Sch.22 para.9
s.462, substituted: 2003 c.14 Sch.22 para.9
s.463, substituted: 2003 c.14 Sch.22 para.9
s.464, substituted: 2003 c.14 Sch.22 para.9
s.465, applied: 1970 c.9 s.98
s.465, substituted: 2003 c.14 Sch.22 para.9
s.466, applied: 1970 c.9 s.98
s.466, substituted: 2003 c.14 Sch.22 para.9
s.467, substituted: 2003 c.14 Sch.22 para.9
s.468, substituted: 2003 c.14 Sch.22 para.9
s.469, substituted: 2003 c.14 Sch.22 para.9
s.470, substituted: 2003 c.14 Sch.22 para.9
s.471, substituted: 2003 c.14 Sch.22 para.10
s.471, varied: 2001 c.20 s.3
s.472, amended: 2004 c.12 s.90
s.472, substituted: 2003 c.14 Sch.22 para.10
s.472, varied: 2001 c.20 s.3

2003–cont.

1. Income Tax (Earnings and Pensions) Act 2003–*cont.*

s.473, substituted: 2003 c.14 Sch.22 para.10

s.473, varied: 2001 c.20 s.3

s.474, substituted: 2003 c.14 Sch.22 para.10

s.474, varied: 2001 c.20 s.3

s.474, substituted: 2003 c.14 Sch.22 para.10

s.474, varied: 2001 c.20 s.3

s.475, substituted: 2003 c.14 Sch.22 para.10

s.475, varied: 2001 c.20 s.3

s.476, amended: 2004 c.12 Sch.16 para.3

s.476, applied: 1992 c.4 s.4, 1992 c.12 s.119A, s.120, SI 2001/1004 Sch.3 para.16, Sch.5 para.1, 2003 c.14 Sch.23 para.22C, Sch.23 para.14, Sch.23 para.21

s.476, substituted: 2003 c.14 Sch.22 para.10

s.476, varied: 2001 c.20 s.3

s.477, amended: 2004 c.12 s.90

s.477, applied: 1992 c.4 s.4, 1992 c.12 s.119A, s.120, SI 2001/1004 Sch.3 para.16, 2003 c.14 Sch.23 para.14

s.477, substituted: 2003 c.14 Sch.22 para.10

s.477, varied: 2001 c.20 s.3, s.5

s.478, substituted: 2003 c.14 Sch.22 para.10

s.478, varied: 2001 c.20 s.3

s.479, applied: 1992 c.4 s.4, 2001 c.20 s.2, s.3

s.479, substituted: 2003 c.14 Sch.22 para.10

s.479, varied: 2001 c.20 s.3

s.480, applied: 1992 c.4 s.4, 1992 c.12 s.119A, 2001 c.20 s.2, s.3

s.480, repealed (in part): 2004 c.12 Sch.16 para.3, Sch.42 Part 2

s.480, substituted: 2003 c.14 Sch.22 para.10

s.480, varied: 2001 c.20 s.3

s.481, amended: 2004 c.12 Sch.16 para.3

s.481, applied: 1992 c.12 s.119A, 2003 c.14 Sch.23 para.22C, Sch.23 para.21

s.481, substituted: 2003 c.14 Sch.22 para.10

s.481, varied: 2001 c.20 s.3

s.482, amended: 2004 c.12 Sch.16 para.3

s.482, applied: 1992 c.12 s.119A, 2003 c.14 Sch.23 para.22C, Sch.23 para.21

s.482, substituted: 2003 c.14 Sch.22 para.10

s.482, varied: 2001 c.20 s.3

s.483, applied: 2001 c.20 s.3

s.483, disapplied: 2001 c.20 s.3

s.483, substituted: 2003 c.14 Sch.22 para.10

s.483, varied: 2001 c.20 s.3, s.5

s.484, amended: 2004 c.12 Sch.16 para.7, Sch.42 Part 2

s.484, substituted: 2003 c.14 Sch.22 para.10

s.484, varied: 2001 c.20 s.3

s.485, applied: SI 2001/1004 Sch.3 para.16

s.485, disapplied: 2001 c.20 s.3

s.485, substituted: 2003 c.14 Sch.22 para.10

s.485, varied: 2001 c.20 s.3

s.486, applied: 1970 c.9 s.98

s.486, substituted: 2003 c.14 Sch.22 para.10

s.486, varied: 2001 c.20 s.3

s.487, substituted: 2003 c.14 Sch.22 para.10

2003–cont.

1. Income Tax (Earnings and Pensions) Act 2003–*cont.*

s.487, varied: 2001 c.20 s.3

s.488, referred to: 1988 c.1 s.686C, s.68C, s.251D, Sch.4AA para.1, 1992 c.12 s.238A, Sch.7D para.1, 2001 c.9 s.95

s.491, repealed: 2003 c.14 Sch.43 Part 3

s.492, repealed (in part): 2004 c.12 Sch.42 Part 3

s.494, repealed: 2003 c.14 Sch.43 Part 3

s.495, repealed: 2003 c.14 Sch.43 Part 3

s.498, applied: 1988 c.1 s.68B, s.251C

s.500, applied: SI 2001/1004 Reg.22

s.501, applied: 1988 c.1 s.68B, s.251C, SI 2001/1004 Reg.22

s.502, applied: SI 2001/1004 Reg.22

s.503, applied: SI 2001/1004 Reg.22

s.504, applied: SI 2001/1004 Reg.22

s.505, amended: 2004 c.12 s.88

s.505, applied: SI 2001/1004 Reg.22

s.506, amended: 2004 c.12 s.88

s.506, applied: SI 2001/1004 Reg.22

s.507, applied: SI 2001/1004 Reg.22

s.508, applied: SI 2001/1004 Reg.22

s.509, amended: 2003 c.14 Sch.22 para.11

s.516, applied: 1989 c.26 s.69, Sch.5 para.15

s.516, referred to: 1992 c.12 s.238A, Sch.7D para.9

s.518, repealed: 2003 c.14 Sch.22 para.29, Sch.43 Part 3

s.519, amended: 2004 c.12 s.88, Sch.42 Part 2

s.519, referred to: 1992 c.12 Sch.7D para.10

s.519, repealed (in part): 2003 c.14 Sch.22 para.30, Sch.43 Part 3

s.520, repealed: 2003 c.14 Sch.43 Part 3

s.521, referred to: 1992 c.12 s.238A, Sch.7D para.11

s.523, repealed: 2003 c.14 Sch.22 para.32, Sch.43 Part 3

s.524, amended: 2003 c.14 Sch.21 para.14, 2004 c.12 s.88

s.524, applied: 1992 c.12 Sch.7D para.13

s.524, repealed (in part): 2003 c.14 Sch.22 para.33, Sch.43 Part 3, 2004 c.12 Sch.42 Part 2

s.525, amended: 2003 c.14 Sch.21 para.14

s.525, repealed: 2003 c.14 Sch.43 Part 3

s.526, amended: 2003 c.14 Sch.22 para.35

s.526, applied: 1992 c.12 Sch.7D para.12

s.527, referred to: 1992 c.12 s.238A, Sch.7D para.14

s.528, repealed: 2003 c.14 Sch.22 para.36, Sch.43 Part 3

s.531, amended: 2003 c.14 Sch.22 para.37

s.532, amended: 2003 c.14 Sch.22 para.38

s.538, amended: 2003 c.14 Sch.22 para.39

s.540, amended: 2003 c.14 Sch.22 para.40

s.541, amended: 2003 c.14 Sch.22 para.41

s.542, applied: 1992 c.12 s.149C, SI 2001/1004 Sch.3 para.5

2003–cont.

1. **Income Tax (Earnings and Pensions) Act 2003**–*cont.*

s.544, applied: 1992 c.12 s.149C

s.554, amended: 2004 c.12 Sch.17 para.9

s.555, applied: 1988 c.1 s.391, 1992 c.12 s.263ZA

s.563, amended: 2004 c.12 Sch.35 para.64

s.565, amended: 2004 c.12 Sch.31 para.2

s.566, amended: 2004 c.12 Sch.31 para.3, Sch.42 Part 3

s.567, amended: 2004 c.12 Sch.31 para.4

s.567, applied: SI 2002/2006 Reg.12

s.568, amended: 2004 c.12 Sch.31 para.5

s.573, applied: 1988 c.1 s.336

s.577, amended: 2004 c.12 Sch.17 para.9

s.577, referred to: 1995 c.4 s.128

s.577, repealed (in part): 2004 c.12 Sch.42 Part 2

s.579A, added: 2004 c.12 Sch.31 para.6

s.579B, added: 2004 c.12 Sch.31 para.6

s.579C, added: 2004 c.12 Sch.31 para.6

s.579D, added: 2004 c.12 Sch.31 para.6

s.580, applied: 1988 c.1 s.659B

s.580, repealed: 2004 c.12 Sch.31 para.7, Sch.42 Part 3

s.581, repealed: 2004 c.12 Sch.31 para.7, Sch.42 Part 3

s.582, repealed: 2004 c.12 Sch.31 para.7, Sch.42 Part 3

s.583, applied: 1988 c.1 s.336, s.392

s.583, referred to: 1988 c.1 s.336

s.583, repealed: 2004 c.12 Sch.31 para.7, Sch.42 Part 3

s.584, repealed: 2004 c.12 Sch.31 para.7, Sch.42 Part 3

s.585, repealed: 2004 c.12 Sch.31 para.7, Sch.42 Part 3

s.586, repealed: 2004 c.12 Sch.31 para.7, Sch.42 Part 3

s.587, referred to: 1988 c.1 s.336, s.392

s.587, repealed: 2004 c.12 Sch.31 para.7, Sch.42 Part 3

s.588, repealed: 2004 c.12 Sch.31 para.7, Sch.42 Part 3

s.589, applied: 1970 c.9 s.98, 1988 c.1 s.659B

s.589, repealed: 2004 c.12 Sch.31 para.7, Sch.42 Part 3

s.590, applied: SI 2001/1004 Sch.3 para.3

s.590, repealed: 2004 c.12 Sch.31 para.7, Sch.42 Part 3

s.591, applied: SI 2001/1004 Sch.3 para.3

s.591, repealed: 2004 c.12 Sch.31 para.7, Sch.42 Part 3

s.592, repealed: 2004 c.12 Sch.31 para.7, Sch.42 Part 3

s.593, repealed: 2004 c.12 Sch.31 para.7, Sch.42 Part 3

s.594, repealed: 2004 c.12 Sch.31 para.7, Sch.42 Part 3

s.595, applied: 1988 c.1 s.659B

2003–cont.

1. **Income Tax (Earnings and Pensions) Act 2003**–*cont.*

s.595, repealed: 2004 c.12 Sch.31 para.7, Sch.42 Part 3

s.596, applied: 2004 c.12 Sch.36 para.44, Sch.36 para.45

s.596, repealed: 2004 c.12 Sch.31 para.7, Sch.42 Part 3

s.597, repealed: 2004 c.12 Sch.31 para.7, Sch.42 Part 3

s.598, repealed: 2004 c.12 Sch.31 para.7, Sch.42 Part 3

s.599, repealed: 2004 c.12 Sch.31 para.7, Sch.42 Part 3

s.600, repealed: 2004 c.12 Sch.31 para.7, Sch.42 Part 3

s.601, repealed: 2004 c.12 Sch.31 para.7, Sch.42 Part 3

s.602, repealed: 2004 c.12 Sch.31 para.7, Sch.42 Part 3

s.603, repealed: 2004 c.12 Sch.31 para.7, Sch.42 Part 3

s.604, repealed: 2004 c.12 Sch.31 para.7, Sch.42 Part 3

s.605, applied: 1988 c.1 s.336, s.348

s.605, referred to: 1995 c.4 s.128

s.605, repealed: 2004 c.12 Sch.31 para.7, Sch.42 Part 3

s.606, repealed: 2004 c.12 Sch.31 para.7, Sch.42 Part 3

s.607, repealed: 2004 c.12 Sch.31 para.7, Sch.42 Part 3

s.608, repealed: 2004 c.12 Sch.31 para.7, Sch.42 Part 3

s.609, applied: 1988 c.1 s.336, s.348, s.545

s.609, referred to: 1995 c.4 s.128

s.610, amended: 2004 c.12 Sch.31 para.8

s.610, applied: 1988 c.1 s.336, s.348, s.545

s.610, referred to: 1995 c.4 s.128

s.611, amended: 2004 c.12 Sch.31 para.9

s.611, applied: 1988 c.1 s.336, s.348, s.545

s.611, referred to: 1995 c.4 s.128

s.612, applied: 2004 c.12 Sch.36 para.46

s.615, applied: 1988 c.1 s.391

s.617, applied: SI 2002/2006 Reg.12

s.623, applied: 1988 c.1 s.336, s.392

s.623, repealed: 2004 c.12 Sch.31 para.10, Sch.42 Part 3

s.624, repealed: 2004 c.12 Sch.31 para.10, Sch.42 Part 3

s.625, repealed: 2004 c.12 Sch.31 para.10, Sch.42 Part 3

s.626, applied: 1970 c.9 s.59B, s.9

s.626, repealed: 2004 c.12 Sch.31 para.10, Sch.42 Part 3

s.627, repealed: 2004 c.12 Sch.31 para.10, Sch.42 Part 3

s.628, repealed: 2004 c.12 Sch.31 para.10, Sch.42 Part 3

s.629, applied: 1988 c.1 s.336

s.636A, added: 2004 c.12 Sch.31 para.11

2003–cont.

1. Income Tax (Earnings and Pensions) Act 2003–*cont.*

s.636B, added: 2004 c.12 Sch.31 para.11

s.636B, varied: 2004 c.12 Sch.36 para.35

s.636C, added: 2004 c.12 Sch.31 para.11

s.637, applied: SI 2002/2006 Reg.5

s.637, repealed: 2004 c.12 Sch.31 para.12, Sch.42 Part 3

s.638, referred to: SI 2002/2006 Reg.5

s.639, applied: SI 2002/2006 Reg.5

s.639, referred to: SI 2002/2006 Reg.5

s.640, referred to: SI 2002/2006 Reg.5

s.641, applied: SI 2002/2006 Reg.5

s.644, amended: 2004 c.12 Sch.31 para.13

s.644, applied: SI 2002/2006 Reg.5

s.646, applied: SI 2002/2006 Reg.5

s.648, referred to: 1988 c.1 s.614, 1992 c.12 s.271

s.649, referred to: 1988 c.1 s.614, 1992 c.12 s.271

s.650, referred to: 1988 c.1 s.614, 1992 c.12 s.271

s.651, referred to: 1988 c.1 s.614, 1992 c.12 s.271

s.653, referred to: 1992 c.12 s.271

s.660, applied: SI 2002/2006 Reg.4

s.660, referred to: 1995 c.4 s.128

s.677, amended: 2004 c.12 Sch.42 Part 2

s.677, applied: 1995 c.34 s.10

s.677, referred to: 1995 c.18 s.26

s.678, applied: 1988 c.1 s.336

s.681, applied: SI 2002/2006 Reg.12

s.683, amended: 2004 c.12 Sch.31 para.14

s.683, applied: 2004 c.12 Sch.36 para.43, Sch.36 para.46

s.683, repealed (in part): 2004 c.12 Sch.31 para.14, Sch.42 Part 3

s.684, amended: 2003 c.14 s.145

s.684, applied: 1988 c.1 Sch.10 para.7, SI 2001/1004 Reg.67, Sch.4 para.16

s.684, enabling: SI 2003/2494, SI 2004/851

s.685, amended: 2003 c.14 s.145

s.691, applied: SI 2001/1004 Sch.4 para.3

s.696, applied: SI 2001/1004 Sch.3 para.2

s.697, applied: SI 2001/1004 Sch.3 para.2

s.698, amended: 2004 c.12 Sch.16 para.4

s.698, applied: SI 2001/1004 Reg.22

s.698, substituted: 2003 c.14 Sch.22 para.12

s.699, substituted: 2003 c.14 Sch.22 para.12

s.700, amended: 2004 c.12 Sch.16 para.4

s.700, substituted: 2003 c.14 Sch.22 para.13

s.701, amended: 2003 c.14 Sch.21 para.18, Sch.22 para.14, Sch.43 Part 3, 2004 c.12 s.88

s.701, applied: 1992 c.12 Sch.7D para.2

s.701, repealed (in part): 2004 c.12 Sch.42 Part 2

s.702, amended: 2003 c.14 Sch.22 para.15

s.702, applied: 1992 c.12 Sch.7D para.2, SI 2001/1004 Sch.3 para.1

2003–cont.

1. Income Tax (Earnings and Pensions) Act 2003–*cont.*

s.707, amended: 2003 c.14 s.145

s.710, amended: 2003 c.14 s.145

s.710, applied: SI 2001/1004 Sch.3 para.17, SI 2003/2682 Sch.1 para.10

s.713, applied: 1990 c.29 s.25, SI 2002/2006 Reg.4, Reg.5, Reg.7

s.714, applied: 2000 c.17 s.38

s.715, applied: 1970 c.9 s.98

s.716, enabling: SI 2003/1361

s.717, applied: 1988 c.1 s.828

s.721, amended: 2004 c.12 Sch.16 para.7

s.721, applied: 1992 c.4 s.10ZA, SI 2000/727 Reg.2, 2004 c.12 s.173

Sch.1 Part 1, amended: 2004 c.12 Sch.35 para.65

Sch.1 Part 2, amended: 2003 c.14 Sch.22 para.42, Sch.43 Part 3, 2004 c.12 s.249, Sch.16 para.7, Sch.27 para.15, Sch.31 para.15, Sch.35 para.65, Sch.42 Part 2, Sch.42 Part 3

Sch.2, applied: 1984 c.51 s.13, s.72, s.86, 1988 c.1 s.251D, s.686C, 1989 c.26 s.69, 1992 c.12 Sch.7C para.2, SI 2001/1004 Sch.3 para.7, SI 2004/1863 Sch.1 para.3, Sch.1 para.4

Sch.2, referred to: 1988 c.1 s.68C, 1992 c.12 Sch.7D para.1, 2001 c.9 s.95

Sch.2 Part 3 para.13, amended: 2003 c.14 Sch.21 para.3

Sch.2 Part 3 para.14, amended: 2003 c.14 Sch.21 para.4

Sch.2 Part 3 para.18, repealed (in part): 2003 c.14 Sch.43 Part 3

Sch.2 Part 3 para.18A, added: 2003 c.14 Sch.21 para.2

Sch.2 Part 4, applied: 1988 c.1 s.686B, 1992 c.12 Sch.7D para.2

Sch.2 Part 4 para.27, disapplied: 1992 c.12 Sch.7C para.2

Sch.2 Part 5 para.35, amended: 2003 c.14 Sch.22 para.43

Sch.2 Part 6 para.46, amended: 2003 c.14 Sch.21 para.7

Sch.2 Part 6 para.47, amended: 2003 c.14 Sch.21 para.8

Sch.2 Part 6 para.47, repealed (in part): 2003 c.14 Sch.43 Part 3

Sch.2 Part 8 para.68, applied: 1988 c.1 s.68B, s.251B

Sch.2 Part 9 para.71, applied: SI 2004/1863 Sch.1 para.3

Sch.2 Part 9 para.71A, added: 2003 c.14 Sch.21 para.6

Sch.2 Part 9 para.77, applied: 1992 c.12 Sch.7D para.8

Sch.2 Part 9 para.78, amended: 2003 c.14 s.142

Sch.2 Part 9 para.78, applied: 1992 c.12 Sch.7D para.2, Sch.7D para.4

CAP.

2003–cont.

1. Income Tax (Earnings and Pensions) Act 2003–cont.

Sch.2 Part 11 para.89, applied: 1988 c.1 Sch.4AA para.12

Sch.2 Part 11 para.92, applied: 1992 c.12 Sch.7D para.1

Sch.2 Part 11 para.93, applied: 1970 c.9 s.98

Sch.2 Part 11 para.97, applied: 1992 c.12 Sch.7C para.2

Sch.3, applied: 1989 c.26 s.69, Sch.5 para.10, SI 2004/1863 Sch.1 para.3, Sch.1 para.4

Sch.3, referred to: 1992 c.12 Sch.7D para.9

Sch.3 Part 5 para.25, amended: 2003 c.14 Sch.21 para.10

Sch.3 Part 6 para.32, applied: 1992 c.12 Sch.7D para.10

Sch.3 Part 6 para.34, amended: 2003 c.14 Sch.21 para.11, Sch.43 Part 3

Sch.3 Part 8 para.42, amended: 2003 c.14 Sch.21 para.12, Sch.22 para.44

Sch.3 Part 8 para.42, applied: 1992 c.12 Sch.7D para.10

Sch.3 Part 8 para.43, substituted: 2003 c.14 Sch.21 para.12

Sch.3 Part 8 para.44, amended: 2003 c.14 Sch.21 para.12

Sch.3 Part 9 para.45, applied: 1970 c.9 s.98

Sch.4 Part 3 para.10, amended: 2003 c.14 Sch.21 para.16

Sch.4 Part 3 para.11, amended: 2003 c.14 Sch.21 para.16

Sch.4 Part 3 para.13, amended: 2003 c.14 Sch.21 para.16

Sch.4 Part 5 para.25, applied: 1992 c.12 Sch.7D para.13

Sch.4 Part 7 para.30, amended: 2003 c.14 Sch.21 para.17

Sch.4 Part 7 para.31, substituted: 2003 c.14 Sch.21 para.17

Sch.4 Part 7 para.32, amended: 2003 c.14 Sch.21 para.17

Sch.4 Part 8 para.33, applied: 1970 c.9 s.98

Sch.4 Part 8 para.35A, added: 2003 c.14 Sch.21 para.15

Sch.5, referred to: 1992 c.12 Sch.7D para.14, SI 2004/1863 Sch.1 para.3

Sch.5 Part 2 para.5, amended: 2003 c.14 Sch.22 para.45

Sch.5 Part 3 para.8, amended: 2004 c.12 s.96

Sch.5 Part 3 para.10, amended: 2004 c.12 s.96

Sch.5 Part 3 para.11, amended: 2004 c.12 s.96

Sch.5 Part 3 para.11, repealed (in part): 2004 c.12 s.96

Sch.5 Part 3 para.11A, added: 2004 c.12 s.96

Sch.5 Part 3 para.11B, added: 2004 c.12 s.96

Sch.5 Part 3 para.18, amended: 2004 c.12 Sch.27 para.17, Sch.42 Part 2

Sch.5 Part 5 para.35, applied: 1992 c.12 Sch.7D para.14

CAP.

2003–cont.

1. Income Tax (Earnings and Pensions) Act 2003–cont.

Sch.5 Part 5 para.37, amended: 2003 c.14 Sch.22 para.45

Sch.5 Part 7, applied: SI 2004/1863 Sch.1 para.3

Sch.5 Part 8 para.51, applied: 1970 c.9 s.98

Sch.5 Part 8 para.52, applied: 1970 c.9 s.98

Sch.5 Part 8 para.59, amended: 2004 c.12 Sch.27 para.17

Sch.6 Part 1 para.58, repealed: 2004 c.12 Sch.42 Part 2

Sch.6 Part 1 para.59, repealed: 2004 c.12 Sch.42 Part 2

Sch.6 Part 1 para.60, repealed: 2004 c.12 Sch.42 Part 2

Sch.6 Part 1 para.61, repealed: 2004 c.12 Sch.42 Part 2

Sch.6 Part 1 para.72, repealed: 2004 c.12 Sch.42 Part 3

Sch.6 Part 1 para.73, repealed: 2004 c.12 Sch.42 Part 3

Sch.6 Part 1 para.79, repealed: 2004 c.12 Sch.42 Part 3

Sch.6 Part 1 para.80, repealed (in part): 2004 c.12 Sch.42 Part 3

Sch.6 Part 1 para.82, repealed: 2004 c.12 Sch.42 Part 3

Sch.6 Part 1 para.89, repealed: 2004 c.12 Sch.42 Part 3

Sch.6 Part 1 para.90, repealed: 2004 c.12 Sch.42 Part 3

Sch.6 Part 1 para.92, repealed: 2004 c.12 Sch.42 Part 3

Sch.6 Part 1 para.93, repealed: 2004 c.12 Sch.42 Part 3

Sch.6 Part 1 para.94, repealed: 2004 c.12 Sch.42 Part 3

Sch.6 Part 1 para.95, repealed: 2004 c.12 Sch.42 Part 3

Sch.6 Part 1 para.97, repealed: 2004 c.12 Sch.42 Part 3

Sch.6 Part 1 para.98, repealed: 2004 c.12 Sch.42 Part 3

Sch.6 Part 1 para.99, repealed: 2004 c.12 Sch.42 Part 3

Sch.6 Part 2 para.125, repealed (in part): 2004 c.12 Sch.42 Part 3

Sch.6 Part 2 para.161, repealed: 2004 c.12 Sch.42 Part 3

Sch.6 Part 2 para.166, repealed (in part): 2004 c.12 Sch.42 Part 2

Sch.6 Part 2 para.245, repealed: 2004 c.12 Sch.42 Part 2

Sch.7 Part 3 para.24, repealed: 2004 c.12 Sch.42 Part 2

Sch.7 Part 3 para.30, repealed: 2003 c.14 Sch.43 Part 3

Sch.7 Part 3 para.31, repealed: 2003 c.14 Sch.43 Part 3

2003–cont.

1. **Income Tax (Earnings and Pensions) Act 2003**–*cont.*

Sch.7 Part 6 para.41, amended: 2003 c.14 Sch.22 para.46

Sch.7 Part 6 para.41, repealed: 2004 c.12 Sch.42 Part 3

Sch.7 Part 6 para.42, amended: 2003 c.14 Sch.22 para.46

Sch.7 Part 6 para.43, amended: 2003 c.14 Sch.22 para.46

Sch.7 Part 7 para.43A, added: 2003 c.14 Sch.22 para.46

Sch.7 Part 7 para.43A, amended: 2003 c.14 Sch.22 para.46

Sch.7 Part 7 para.44, amended: 2003 c.14 Sch.22 para.46

Sch.7 Part 7 para.45, amended: 2003 c.14 Sch.22 para.46

Sch.7 Part 7 para.46, amended: 2003 c.14 Sch.22 para.46

Sch.7 Part 7 para.47, amended: 2003 c.14 Sch.22 para.46

Sch.7 Part 7 para.47, repealed: 2003 c.14 Sch.43 Part 3

Sch.7 Part 7 para.48, amended: 2003 c.14 Sch.22 para.46

Sch.7 Part 7 para.48, repealed: 2003 c.14 Sch.43 Part 3

Sch.7 Part 7 para.49, amended: 2003 c.14 Sch.22 para.46

Sch.7 Part 7 para.50, amended: 2003 c.14 Sch.22 para.46

Sch.7 Part 7 para.50, repealed: 2003 c.14 Sch.22 para.46, Sch.43 Part 3

Sch.7 Part 7 para.51, amended: 2003 c.14 Sch.22 para.46

Sch.7 Part 7 para.51, repealed: 2003 c.14 Sch.22 para.46, Sch.43 Part 3

Sch.7 Part 7 para.52, amended: 2003 c.14 Sch.22 para.46

Sch.7 Part 7 para.52, repealed: 2003 c.14 Sch.22 para.46, Sch.43 Part 3

Sch.7 Part 7 para.53, amended: 2003 c.14 Sch.22 para.46

Sch.7 Part 7 para.53, repealed: 2003 c.14 Sch.43 Part 3

Sch.7 Part 7 para.54, amended: 2003 c.14 Sch.22 para.46

Sch.7 Part 7 para.55, amended: 2003 c.14 Sch.22 para.46

Sch.7 Part 7 para.55, repealed (in part): 2003 c.14 Sch.43 Part 3

Sch.7 Part 7 para.56, amended: 2003 c.14 Sch.22 para.46

Sch.7 Part 7 para.57, amended: 2003 c.14 Sch.22 para.46

Sch.7 Part 7 para.58, amended: 2003 c.14 Sch.22 para.46

Sch.7 Part 7 para.59, amended: 2003 c.14 Sch.22 para.46

2003–cont.

1. **Income Tax (Earnings and Pensions) Act 2003**–*cont.*

Sch.7 Part 7 para.59, repealed: 2003 c.14 Sch.43 Part 3

Sch.7 Part 7 para.60, amended: 2003 c.14 Sch.22 para.46

Sch.7 Part 7 para.60, repealed: 2003 c.14 Sch.43 Part 3

Sch.7 Part 7 para.61, amended: 2003 c.14 Sch.22 para.46

Sch.7 Part 7 para.61, repealed: 2003 c.14 Sch.43 Part 3

Sch.7 Part 7 para.61A, added: 2003 c.14 Sch.22 para.46

Sch.7 Part 7 para.61A, amended: 2003 c.14 Sch.22 para.46

Sch.7 Part 7 para.62, amended: 2003 c.14 Sch.22 para.46

Sch.7 Part 7 para.62, repealed: 2003 c.14 Sch.22 para.46, Sch.43 Part 3

Sch.7 Part 7 para.63, amended: 2003 c.14 Sch.22 para.46

Sch.7 Part 7 para.63, substituted: 2003 c.14 Sch.22 para.46

Sch.7 Part 7 para.64, amended: 2003 c.14 Sch.22 para.46

Sch.7 Part 7 para.65, amended: 2003 c.14 Sch.22 para.46

Sch.7 Part 7 para.66, amended: 2003 c.14 Sch.22 para.46

Sch.7 Part 7 para.66, repealed: 2003 c.14 Sch.22 para.46, Sch.43 Part 3

Sch.7 Part 7 para.67, amended: 2003 c.14 Sch.22 para.46

Sch.7 Part 7 para.67, repealed: 2003 c.14 Sch.43 Part 3

Sch.7 Part 7 para.68, amended: 2003 c.14 Sch.22 para.46

Sch.7 Part 7 para.69, amended: 2003 c.14 Sch.22 para.46

Sch.7 Part 7 para.70, amended: 2003 c.14 Sch.22 para.46

Sch.7 Part 7 para.71, amended: 2003 c.14 Sch.22 para.46

Sch.7 Part 7 para.72, amended: 2003 c.14 Sch.22 para.46

Sch.7 Part 7 para.73, amended: 2003 c.14 Sch.22 para.46

Sch.7 Part 7 para.74, amended: 2003 c.14 Sch.22 para.46

Sch.7 Part 7 para.75, amended: 2003 c.14 Sch.22 para.46

Sch.7 Part 7 para.76, amended: 2003 c.14 Sch.22 para.46

Sch.7 Part 7 para.77, amended: 2003 c.14 Sch.22 para.46

Sch.7 Part 7 para.78, amended: 2003 c.14 Sch.22 para.46

Sch.7 Part 7 para.79, amended: 2003 c.14 Sch.22 para.46

2003–cont.

1. Income Tax (Earnings and Pensions) Act 2003–cont.

Sch.7 Part 7 para.80, amended: 2003 c.14 Sch.22 para.46

Sch.7 Part 7 para.81, amended: 2003 c.14 Sch.22 para.46

Sch.7 Part 7 para.82, amended: 2003 c.14 Sch.22 para.46

Sch.7 Part 7 para.83, amended: 2003 c.14 Sch.22 para.46

Sch.7 Part 7 para.84, amended: 2003 c.14 Sch.22 para.46

2. Consolidated Fund Act 2003

applied: 2003 c.13 Sch.1

3. Northern Ireland Assembly Elections Act 2003

s.1, applied: 2003 c.12 s.3

s.1, repealed (in part): 2003 c.12 s.1

4. Health (Wales) Act 2003

Commencement Orders: SI 2003/2660 Art.2, Art.3, Art.4; SI 2003/3064 Art.2

s.4, enabling: SI 2004/551

s.5, enabling: SI 2004/550, SI 2004/551

s.8, enabling: SI 2003/2660, SI 2003/3064, SI 2004/550, SI 2004/551, SI 2004/1742

s.10, enabling: SI 2003/2660, SI 2003/3064

Sch.2 para.10, enabling: SI 2004/1742

Sch.2 para.25, repealed (in part): 2004 c.23 Sch.2 para.56, Sch.4

5. Community Care (Delayed Discharges etc.) Act 2003

Commencement Orders: SI 2003/2280 Art.2

referred to: 2003 c.43 Sch.4 para.129

Part 1, applied: SI 2003/2277 Reg.12, Reg.14

s.1, amended: 2003 c.43 Sch.4 para.130

s.1, referred to: SI 2003/2277 Reg.3

s.1, enabling: SI 2003/2277

s.2, applied: SI 2003/2277 Reg.4, Reg.10, Reg.18

s.2, referred to: SI 2003/2277 Reg.4

s.3, enabling: SI 2003/2277

s.4, applied: SI 2003/2277 Reg.4, Reg.5, Reg.8, Reg.11, Reg.18

s.5, applied: SI 2003/2277 Reg.5, Reg.6, Reg.10

s.5, enabling: SI 2003/2277

s.6, applied: SI 2003/2277 Reg.7, Reg.18

s.6, enabling: SI 2003/2277

s.7, referred to: SI 2003/2277

s.7, enabling: SI 2003/2277

s.8, applied: SI 2003/2277 Reg.18

s.9, enabling: SI 2003/2277

s.10, enabling: SI 2003/2277

s.12, applied: SI 2003/2276 Art.2

s.12, enabling: SI 2003/2276

s.15, applied: 1948 c.29 s.22, s.26, 1983 c.41 s.17, SI 2003/1196 Reg.3

s.15, enabling: SI 2003/1196

s.20, enabling: SI 2003/2280

2003–cont.

6. Police (Northern Ireland) Act 2003

Sch.2 Part 3 para.22, amended: SI 2004/1500 Sch.1 para.6

Sch.3 para.2, repealed: SI 2004/1500 Sch.3

7. European Parliament (Representation) Act 2003

Commencement Orders: SI 2003/1401 Art.2; SI 2003/1402 Art.2; SI 2004/24 Art.2; SI 2004/320 Art.2; SI 2004/700 Art.2; SI 2004/1035 Art.2

applied: SI 2003/1887 Sch.1, SI 2004/293 Reg.13, Sch.2 para.2, Sch.2 para.7

s.3, amended: SI 2003/1887 Sch.2 para.15

s.5, amended: SI 2003/1887 Sch.2 para.15

s.5, enabling: SI 2004/1245

s.6, amended: SI 2003/1887 Sch.2 para.15

s.10, amended: SI 2003/1887 Sch.2 para.15

s.11, amended: SI 2003/1887 Sch.2 para.15

s.11, enabling: SI 2004/366

s.12, amended: 2003 c.21 Sch.19, SI 2003/1887 Sch.2 para.15

s.12, enabling: SI 2004/366

s.13, amended: SI 2003/1887 Sch.2 para.15

s.13, enabling: SI 2004/366

s.15, disapplied: SI 2004/293 Sch.4 para.5

s.16, applied: SI 2004/293 Sch.4 para.8, Sch.4 para.9, Sch.4 para.10, Sch.4 para.11, Sch.4 para.13, Sch.4 para.14, Sch.4 para.19

s.16, disapplied: SI 2004/293 Sch.4 para.5

s.16, varied: SI 2004/293 Sch.5 para.2

s.17, amended: SI 2003/1887 Sch.2 para.15

s.17, applied: SI 2004/293

s.17, enabling: SI 2004/293

s.18, amended: SI 2003/1887 Sch.2 para.15

s.18, enabling: SI 2004/293

s.21, amended: SI 2003/1887 Sch.2 para.15

s.23, enabling: SI 2004/293, SI 2004/366

s.25, enabling: SI 2004/293, SI 2004/366

s.26, repealed: SI 2003/1887 Sch.2 para.15

s.26, enabling: SI 2004/366

s.27, varied: SI 2004/293 Sch.5 para.3

s.28, amended: SI 2003/1887 Sch.2 para.15

s.28, enabling: SI 2003/1401, SI 2003/1402, SI 2004/24, SI 2004/320, SI 2004/700, SI 2004/1035

8. National Minimum Wage (Enforcement Notices) Act 2003

s.2, disapplied: 1949 c.30 s.3A

10. Regional Assemblies (Preparations) Act 2003

applied: 2004 c.9 Sch.2 Part 57

Part 1, applied: SI 2004/1962 Sch.1

s.1, applied: SI 2004/1962 Art.1, Art.3

s.1, enabling: SI 2004/1963

s.2, applied: SI 2004/1961, SI 2004/1962 Art.1, Art.3, Sch.1

s.2, enabling: SI 2004/1961, SI 2004/1962, SI 2004/1963

s.3, applied: SI 2004/1963

s.3, referred to: SI 2004/1962 Sch.1, SI 2004/1963 Art.7, Art.8

2003–cont.

10. Regional Assemblies (Preparations) Act 2003–*cont.*

s.3, enabling: SI 2004/1963

s.5, enabling: SI 2004/1963

s.7, applied: SI 2004/2105 Art.3, Art.4

s.7, enabling: SI 2004/1962

s.9, applied: SI 2004/1962 Sch.1, SI 2004/1963 Art.6

s.10, enabling: SI 2004/2105

s.12, applied: SI 2004/1961, SI 2004/1962, SI 2004/2105

s.13, applied: SI 2004/1963

s.17, applied: 1947 c.41 s.6, s.10, 1988 c.13 s.1, 1988 c.41 s.74, s.89, s.91, 1989 c.42 s.39, 2004 c.21 s.2, s.4

Sch.1 para.1, repealed (in part): 2004 c.21 Sch.2

12. Northern Ireland Assembly (Elections and Periods of Suspension) Act 2003

s.1, applied: SI 2003/2696, SI 2003/2752

s.4, applied: SI 2003/2696

s.6, enabling: SI 2003/2696, SI 2003/2752

13. Appropriation Act 2003

Sch.2 Part 16, referred to: 2004 c.9 Sch.2 Part 2

Sch.2 Part 17, referred to: 2004 c.9 Sch.2 Part 2

Sch.2 Part 29, referred to: 2004 c.9 Sch.2 Part 2

14. Finance Act 2003

Commencement Orders: SI 2003/2497 Art.2; SI 2003/2985 Art.2; SI 2003/3077 Art.2

applied: 1971 c.29 s.9A, SI 2003/2837 Reg.2

referred to: 2003 c.1 Sch.7 para.54

Part 4, applied: 1986 c.41 s.99, 1988 c.1 s.827, SI 2003/2837 Reg.28, SI 2003/2899 Art.2, 2004 c.12 s.301, s.302

Part 4, referred to: SI 2003/2837 Reg.18, SI 2003/2867 Reg.2

s.24, enabling: SI 2003/2985

s.25, applied: 1988 c.1 s.827

s.26, applied: 1988 c.1 s.827, SI 2003/3113 Reg.3

s.26, enabling: SI 2003/3113

s.28, applied: SI 1986/590 r.19

s.30, referred to: SI 1986/590 r.8A

s.33, applied: SI 1986/590 r.20

s.35, applied: SI 1986/590 r.4

s.41, enabling: SI 2003/2985, SI 2003/3113

s.43, amended: 2004 c.12 s.297, Sch.39 para.2, Sch.42 Part 4

s.44, amended: SI 2003/2760 Sch.1 para.1, SI 2003/2816 Sch.1 para.1, 2004 c.12 Sch.39 para.3, Sch.39 para.15

s.44A, added: 2004 c.12 Sch.39 para.4

s.45, amended: 2004 c.12 Sch.39 para.5, Sch.42 Part 4

s.45A, added: 2004 c.12 Sch.39 para.5

2003–cont.

14. Finance Act 2003–*cont.*

s.47, amended: SI 2003/2760 Sch.1 para.3, SI 2003/2816 Sch.1 para.3, 2004 c.12 Sch.42 Part 4, SI 2004/1069 Reg.3

s.48, amended: 2004 c.12 s.297, Sch.39 para.4

s.50, enabling: SI 2003/3293, SI 2004/1069, SI 2004/1206

s.51, amended: SI 2003/2760 Sch.1 para.8, SI 2003/2816 Sch.1 para.8, 2004 c.12 Sch.39 para.22

s.51, referred to: SI 2003/2837 Reg.18

s.53, amended: 2004 c.12 s.297

s.57A, added: SI 2003/2760 Sch.1 para.2, SI 2003/2816 Sch.1 para.2, 2004 c.12 Sch.39 para.16

s.57A, amended: 2004 c.12 Sch.39 para.6

s.57A, repealed (in part): 2004 c.12 Sch.39 para.6

s.58, substituted: SI 2003/2760 Sch.1 para.3, SI 2003/2816 Sch.1 para.3

s.58A, substituted: SI 2003/2760 Sch.1 para.3, SI 2003/2816 Sch.1 para.3, 2004 c.12 Sch.39 para.17

s.59, substituted: SI 2003/2760 Sch.1 para.3, SI 2003/2816 Sch.1 para.3

s.64A, added: SI 2003/2760 Sch.1 para.4, SI 2003/2816 Sch.1 para.4, 2004 c.12 Sch.39 para.18

s.66, applied: 1980 c.33 s.2A

s.76, applied: SI 2003/2837 Reg.4

s.77, amended: SI 2003/2760 Sch.1 para.8, SI 2003/2816 Sch.1 para.8, 2004 c.12 s.298, Sch.39 para.4, Sch.42 Part 4

s.78, enabling: SI 2004/3208

s.79, amended: 2004 c.12 s.297, s.298, Sch.39 para.7

s.79, enabling: SI 2003/2837

s.80, amended: SI 2003/2760 Sch.1 para.5, Sch.1 para.8, SI 2003/2816 Sch.1 para.5, Sch.1 para.8, 2004 c.12 s.299, Sch.39 para.22, Sch.42 Part 4

s.80, disapplied: SI 2003/2837 Reg.26

s.81, amended: SI 2003/2760 Sch.1 para.3, Sch.1 para.5, SI 2003/2816 Sch.1 para.3, Sch.1 para.5, 2004 c.12 s.302, Sch.39 para.17, Sch.39 para.19

s.81A, added: SI 2003/2760 Sch.1 para.5, SI 2003/2816 Sch.1 para.5, 2004 c.12 Sch.39 para.19

s.81B, added: SI 2003/2760 Sch.1 para.6, SI 2003/2816 Sch.1 para.6, 2004 c.12 Sch.39 para.20

s.82A, added: 2004 c.12 s.299

s.87, amended: SI 2003/2760 Sch.1 para.3, Sch.1 para.5, Sch.1 para.8, SI 2003/2816 Sch.1 para.3, Sch.1 para.5, Sch.1 para.8, 2004 c.12 s.302, Sch.39 para.17, Sch.39 para.19, Sch.39 para.22

s.87, referred to: 1989 c.26 s.178

s.88, referred to: 1989 c.26 s.178

CAP.

2003–cont.

14. Finance Act 2003–*cont.*

s.89, referred to: 1989 c.26 s.178

s.90, amended: SI 2003/2760 Sch.1 para.8, SI 2003/2816 Sch.1 para.8, 2004 c.12 Sch.39 para.22

s.90, referred to: SI 2003/2837 Reg.17, Reg.26

s.90, enabling: SI 2003/2837

s.99, amended: 2004 c.12 s.298

s.104, amended: 2004 c.12 Sch.41 para.2

s.107, amended: SI 2003/2760 Sch.1 para.7, SI 2003/2816 Sch.1 para.7, 2004 c.12 Sch.39 para.21

s.107, enabling: SI 2003/2862

s.109, applied: 2004 c.12 Sch.39 para.14

s.109, enabling: SI 2003/2760, SI 2003/2816

s.111, amended: 2004 c.12 s.299

s.112, applied: SI 2003/2914

s.112, enabling: SI 2003/2914

s.113, amended: 2004 c.12 s.299

s.113, enabling: SI 2003/2837

s.115, enabling: SI 2004/1363

s.119, amended: 2004 c.12 Sch.39 para.8, Sch.42 Part 4

s.119, applied: SI 2003/2837 Reg.5

s.120, added: SI 2003/2816 Sch.1 para.8

s.120, amended: 2004 c.12 Sch.39 para.22

s.120, substituted: SI 2003/2760 Sch.1 para.8

s.122, amended: SI 2003/2760 Sch.1 para.8, Sch.1 para.11, SI 2003/2816 Sch.1 para.8, Sch.1 para.11, 2004 c.12 Sch.39 para.5, Sch.39 para.22, Sch.39 para.25

s.123, enabling: SI 2003/2867, SI 2003/2868

s.125, amended: SI 2003/2760 Sch.1 para.9, SI 2003/2816 Sch.1 para.9, 2004 c.12 Sch.39 para.23, Sch.41 para.2

s.125, applied: 1986 c.41 s.92

s.142, applied: 2003 c.1 Sch.2 para.78

s.147, repealed (in part): 2004 c.12 Sch.42 Part 2

s.149, enabling: SI 2003/2714

s.150, applied: 1988 c.1 s.606

s.151, applied: 1988 c.1 Sch.28AA para.5

s.153, amended: 2004 c.12 Sch.42 Part 3

s.156, enabling: SI 2004/2200

s.168, enabling: SI 2003/2497

s.174, repealed: 2004 c.12 Sch.42 Part 3

s.195, applied: 1988 c.1 Sch.15B para.1

s.195, enabling: SI 2003/3077

s.197, amended: SI 2003/3092 Art.3

s.197, enabling: SI 2003/3092, SI 2004/3207

s.199, applied: 1970 c.9 s.98

s.199, enabling: SI 2003/3297

s.205, enabling: SI 2003/2494, SI 2004/1075

s.212, enabling: SI 2004/2823

Sch.3 para.3A, added: 2004 c.12 s.300

Sch.3 para.4, amended: 2004 c.12 s.301

CAP.

2003–cont.

14. Finance Act 2003–*cont.*

Sch.4 para.5, amended: SI 2003/2760 Sch.1 para.3, SI 2003/2816 Sch.1 para.3, SI 2003/3293 Reg.2, 2004 c.12 Sch.42 Part 4, SI 2004/1069 Reg.4

Sch.4 para.8, amended: 2004 c.12 s.301

Sch.4 para.8A, added: 2004 c.12 s.301

Sch.4 para.10, amended: SI 2003/3293 Reg.2, 2004 c.12 Sch.39 para.9

Sch.4 para.11, substituted: SI 2003/3293 Reg.2

Sch.4 para.13, repealed: SI 2003/2760 Sch.1 para.8, SI 2003/2816 Sch.1 para.8, 2004 c.12 Sch.42 Part 4

Sch.4 para.14, repealed: SI 2003/2760 Sch.1 para.8, SI 2003/2816 Sch.1 para.8, 2004 c.12 Sch.42 Part 4

Sch.4 para.15, repealed: SI 2003/2760 Sch.1 para.8, SI 2003/2816 Sch.1 para.8, 2004 c.12 Sch.42 Part 4

Sch.4 para.17, added: SI 2003/3293 Reg.2

Sch.4 para.17, amended: 2004 c.12 Sch.39 para.9, SI 2004/1069 Reg.4, SI 2004/1206 Reg.3

Sch.5, referred to: SI 2003/2914 Reg.2

Sch.5 para.1A, added: 2004 c.12 Sch.39 para.10

Sch.5 para.2, amended: SI 2003/2914 Sch.1 para.1

Sch.5 para.3, amended: SI 2003/2760 Sch.1 para.8, SI 2003/2816 Sch.1 para.8, 2004 c.12 Sch.42 Part 4

Sch.5 para.4, repealed: SI 2003/2760 Sch.1 para.8, SI 2003/2816 Sch.1 para.8, 2004 c.12 Sch.42 Part 4

Sch.5 para.5, repealed: SI 2003/2760 Sch.1 para.8, SI 2003/2816 Sch.1 para.8, 2004 c.12 Sch.42 Part 4

Sch.5 para.6, repealed: SI 2003/2760 Sch.1 para.8, SI 2003/2816 Sch.1 para.8, 2004 c.12 Sch.42 Part 4

Sch.5 para.7, repealed: SI 2003/2760 Sch.1 para.8, SI 2003/2816 Sch.1 para.8, 2004 c.12 Sch.42 Part 4

Sch.5 para.9, amended: SI 2003/2914 Sch.1 para.2

Sch.5 para.10, repealed: SI 2003/2760 Sch.1 para.8, SI 2003/2816 Sch.1 para.8, 2004 c.12 Sch.42 Part 4

Sch.5 para.11, repealed: SI 2003/2760 Sch.1 para.8, SI 2003/2816 Sch.1 para.8, 2004 c.12 Sch.42 Part 4

Sch.6 Part 4 para.11, amended: 2004 c.12 s.298

Sch.6 Part 4 para.12, amended: 2004 c.12 s.298

Sch.6 Part 4 para.13, added: 2004 c.12 s.298

Sch.6 Part 4 para.13, amended: 2004 c.12 s.298

Sch.6A para.1, added: SI 2003/2760 Sch.1 para.3, SI 2003/2816 Sch.1 para.3, 2004 c.12 Sch.39 para.17

2003–cont.

14. Finance Act 2003–*cont.*

Sch.6A para.2, added: SI 2003/2760 Sch.1 para.3, SI 2003/2816 Sch.1 para.3, 2004 c.12 Sch.39 para.17

Sch.6A para.3, added: SI 2003/2760 Sch.1 para.3, SI 2003/2816 Sch.1 para.3, 2004 c.12 Sch.39 para.17

Sch.6A para.4, added: SI 2003/2760 Sch.1 para.3, SI 2003/2816 Sch.1 para.3, 2004 c.12 Sch.39 para.17

Sch.6A para.5, added: SI 2003/2760 Sch.1 para.3, SI 2003/2816 Sch.1 para.3, 2004 c.12 Sch.39 para.17

Sch.6A para.6, added: SI 2003/2760 Sch.1 para.3, SI 2003/2816 Sch.1 para.3, 2004 c.12 Sch.39 para.17

Sch.6A para.7, added: SI 2003/2760 Sch.1 para.3, SI 2003/2816 Sch.1 para.3, 2004 c.12 Sch.39 para.17

Sch.6A para.8, added: SI 2003/2760 Sch.1 para.3, SI 2003/2816 Sch.1 para.3, 2004 c.12 Sch.39 para.17

Sch.6A para.9, added: SI 2003/2760 Sch.1 para.3, SI 2003/2816 Sch.1 para.3, 2004 c.12 Sch.39 para.17

Sch.6A para.10, added: SI 2003/2760 Sch.1 para.3, SI 2003/2816 Sch.1 para.3, 2004 c.12 Sch.39 para.17

Sch.6A para.11, added: SI 2003/2760 Sch.1 para.3, SI 2003/2816 Sch.1 para.3, 2004 c.12 Sch.39 para.17

Sch.7 Part 1 para.2, applied: 2004 c.25 s.4

Sch.8 para.1, amended: 2004 c.12 s.302

Sch.8 para.2, amended: 2004 c.12 s.302

Sch.8 para.3, added: 2004 c.12 s.302

Sch.8 para.4, added: 2004 c.12 s.302

Sch.9 para.4A, added: 2004 c.12 s.303

Sch.9 para.5, amended: 2004 c.12 s.303

Sch.10 Part 1 para.1, applied: SI 2003/2837 Reg.4

Sch.10 Part 1 para.1, enabling: SI 2003/2837

Sch.10 Part 1 para.8, applied: 2004 c.12 s.313

Sch.10 Part 6 para.33, amended: 2004 c.12 s.299

Sch.10 Part 6 para.33, repealed (in part): 2004 c.12 Sch.42 Part 4

Sch.10 Part 6 para.34, amended: 2004 c.12 s.299, Sch.42 Part 4

Sch.10 Part 6 para.34, repealed (in part): 2004 c.12 Sch.42 Part 4

Sch.11 Part 1 para.2, enabling: SI 2003/2837

Sch.11A para.1, added: 2004 c.12 Sch.40

Sch.11A para.2, added: 2004 c.12 Sch.40

Sch.11A para.3, added: 2004 c.12 Sch.40

Sch.11A para.4, added: 2004 c.12 Sch.40

Sch.11A para.5, added: 2004 c.12 Sch.40

Sch.11A para.6, added: 2004 c.12 Sch.40

Sch.11A para.7, added: 2004 c.12 Sch.40

Sch.11A para.8, added: 2004 c.12 Sch.40

Sch.11A para.9, added: 2004 c.12 Sch.40

Sch.11A para.10, added: 2004 c.12 Sch.40

2003–cont.

14. Finance Act 2003–*cont.*

Sch.11A para.11, added: 2004 c.12 Sch.40

Sch.11A para.12, added: 2004 c.12 Sch.40

Sch.11A para.13, added: 2004 c.12 Sch.40

Sch.11A para.14, added: 2004 c.12 Sch.40

Sch.11A para.15, added: 2004 c.12 Sch.40

Sch.12 Part 1 para.2, applied: SI 2003/2837 Reg.30

Sch.12 Part 1 para.2, enabling: SI 2003/2837

Sch.13 Part 6 para.32, applied: SI 2003/2837 Reg.37

Sch.13 Part 6 para.33, enabling: SI 2003/2837

Sch.13 Part 6 para.36, enabling: SI 2003/2837

Sch.13 Part 6 para.37, enabling: SI 2003/2837

Sch.13 Part 6 para.41, enabling: SI 2003/2837

Sch.13 Part 6 para.42, enabling: SI 2003/2837

Sch.15 Part 2 para.5, amended: 2004 c.12 Sch.41 para.2

Sch.15 Part 2 para.7, amended: 2004 c.12 s.305

Sch.15 Part 3 para.9, substituted: 2004 c.12 Sch.41 para.1

Sch.15 Part 3 para.10, substituted: 2004 c.12 Sch.41 para.1

Sch.15 Part 3 para.11, substituted: 2004 c.12 Sch.41 para.1

Sch.15 Part 3 para.12, substituted: 2004 c.12 Sch.41 para.1

Sch.15 Part 3 para.13, substituted: 2004 c.12 Sch.41 para.1

Sch.15 Part 3 para.14, substituted: 2004 c.12 Sch.41 para.1

Sch.15 Part 3 para.15, substituted: 2004 c.12 Sch.41 para.1

Sch.15 Part 3 para.16, substituted: 2004 c.12 Sch.41 para.1

Sch.15 Part 3 para.17, substituted: 2004 c.12 Sch.41 para.1

Sch.15 Part 3 para.18, substituted: 2004 c.12 Sch.41 para.1

Sch.15 Part 3 para.19, substituted: 2004 c.12 Sch.41 para.1

Sch.15 Part 3 para.20, substituted: 2004 c.12 Sch.41 para.1

Sch.15 Part 3 para.21, substituted: 2004 c.12 Sch.41 para.1

Sch.15 Part 3 para.22, substituted: 2004 c.12 Sch.41 para.1

Sch.15 Part 3 para.23, substituted: 2004 c.12 Sch.41 para.1

Sch.15 Part 3 para.24, substituted: 2004 c.12 Sch.41 para.1

Sch.15 Part 3 para.25, substituted: 2004 c.12 Sch.41 para.1

Sch.15 Part 3 para.26, substituted: 2004 c.12 Sch.41 para.1

2003–cont.

14. Finance Act 2003–*cont.*

Sch.15 Part 3 para.27, substituted: 2004 c.12 Sch.41 para.1

Sch.15 Part 3 para.28, substituted: 2004 c.12 Sch.41 para.1

Sch.15 Part 3 para.29, substituted: 2004 c.12 Sch.41 para.1

Sch.15 Part 3 para.30, substituted: 2004 c.12 Sch.41 para.1

Sch.15 Part 3 para.31, substituted: 2004 c.12 Sch.41 para.1

Sch.15 Part 3 para.32, substituted: 2004 c.12 Sch.41 para.1

Sch.15 Part 3 para.33, substituted: 2004 c.12 Sch.41 para.1

Sch.15 Part 3 para.34, substituted: 2004 c.12 Sch.41 para.1

Sch.15 Part 3 para.35, substituted: 2004 c.12 Sch.41 para.1

Sch.15 Part 3 para.36, substituted: 2004 c.12 Sch.41 para.1

Sch.15 Part 3 para.37, substituted: 2004 c.12 Sch.41 para.1

Sch.15 Part 3 para.38, substituted: 2004 c.12 Sch.41 para.1

Sch.15 Part 3 para.39, substituted: 2004 c.12 Sch.41 para.1

Sch.15 Part 3 para.40, substituted: 2004 c.12 Sch.41 para.1

Sch.17 para.2, enabling: SI 2004/1363

Sch.17 para.3, enabling: SI 2004/1363

Sch.17 para.5, enabling: SI 2004/1363

Sch.17 para.6, enabling: SI 2004/1363

Sch.17 para.7, enabling: SI 2004/1363

Sch.17 para.9, enabling: SI 2004/1363

Sch.17 para.11, enabling: SI 2004/1363

Sch.17A para.1, added: SI 2003/2760 Sch.1 para.8, SI 2003/2816 Sch.1 para.8, 2004 c.12 Sch.39 para.22

Sch.17A para.2, added: SI 2003/2760 Sch.1 para.8, SI 2003/2816 Sch.1 para.8, 2004 c.12 Sch.39 para.22

Sch.17A para.3, added: SI 2003/2760 Sch.1 para.8, SI 2003/2816 Sch.1 para.8, 2004 c.12 Sch.39 para.22

Sch.17A para.4, added: SI 2003/2760 Sch.1 para.8, SI 2003/2816 Sch.1 para.8, 2004 c.12 Sch.39 para.22

Sch.17A para.5, added: SI 2003/2760 Sch.1 para.8, SI 2003/2816 Sch.1 para.8, 2004 c.12 Sch.39 para.22

Sch.17A para.6, added: SI 2003/2760 Sch.1 para.8, SI 2003/2816 Sch.1 para.8, 2004 c.12 Sch.39 para.22

Sch.17A para.7, added: SI 2003/2760 Sch.1 para.8, SI 2003/2816 Sch.1 para.8, 2004 c.12 Sch.39 para.22

Sch.17A para.7A, added: SI 2003/2760 Sch.1 para.8, SI 2003/2816 Sch.1 para.8, 2004 c.12 Sch.39 para.11, Sch.39 para.22

2003–cont.

14. Finance Act 2003–*cont.*

Sch.17A para.8, added: SI 2003/2760 Sch.1 para.8, SI 2003/2816 Sch.1 para.8, 2004 c.12 Sch.39 para.22

Sch.17A para.9, added: SI 2003/2760 Sch.1 para.8, SI 2003/2816 Sch.1 para.8, 2004 c.12 Sch.39 para.22

Sch.17A para.9, amended: 2004 c.12 Sch.39 para.11

Sch.17A para.10, added: SI 2003/2760 Sch.1 para.8, SI 2003/2816 Sch.1 para.8, 2004 c.12 Sch.39 para.22

Sch.17A para.11, added: SI 2003/2760 Sch.1 para.8, SI 2003/2816 Sch.1 para.8, 2004 c.12 Sch.39 para.22

Sch.17A para.12, added: SI 2003/2760 Sch.1 para.8, SI 2003/2816 Sch.1 para.8, 2004 c.12 Sch.39 para.22

Sch.17A para.12A, added: SI 2003/2760 Sch.1 para.8, SI 2003/2816 Sch.1 para.8, 2004 c.12 Sch.39 para.11, Sch.39 para.22

Sch.17A para.12B, added: SI 2003/2760 Sch.1 para.8, SI 2003/2816 Sch.1 para.8, 2004 c.12 Sch.39 para.11, Sch.39 para.22

Sch.17A para.13, added: SI 2003/2760 Sch.1 para.8, SI 2003/2816 Sch.1 para.8, 2004 c.12 Sch.39 para.22

Sch.17A para.14, added: SI 2003/2760 Sch.1 para.8, SI 2003/2816 Sch.1 para.8, 2004 c.12 Sch.39 para.22

Sch.17A para.15, added: SI 2003/2760 Sch.1 para.8, SI 2003/2816 Sch.1 para.8, 2004 c.12 Sch.39 para.22

Sch.17A para.15A, added: SI 2003/2760 Sch.1 para.8, SI 2003/2816 Sch.1 para.8, 2004 c.12 Sch.39 para.22

Sch.17A para.16, added: SI 2003/2760 Sch.1 para.8, SI 2003/2816 Sch.1 para.8, 2004 c.12 Sch.39 para.22

Sch.17A para.16, amended: 2004 c.12 Sch.39 para.11

Sch.17A para.17, added: SI 2003/2760 Sch.1 para.8, SI 2003/2816 Sch.1 para.8, 2004 c.12 Sch.39 para.22

Sch.17A para.18, added: SI 2003/2760 Sch.1 para.8, SI 2003/2816 Sch.1 para.8, 2004 c.12 Sch.39 para.22

Sch.17A para.19, added: SI 2003/2760 Sch.1 para.8, SI 2003/2816 Sch.1 para.8, 2004 c.12 Sch.39 para.22

Sch.17A para.19, amended: 2004 c.12 Sch.39 para.11

Sch.19, applied: SI 2003/2899 Art.2

Sch.19 para.1, applied: 1931 c.28 s.28, 1994 c.9 s.245

Sch.19 para.2, enabling: SI 2003/2899

Sch.19 para.3, amended: 2004 c.12 Sch.39 para.12

Sch.19 para.4A, added: SI 2003/2760 Sch.1 para.10, SI 2003/2816 Sch.1 para.10, 2004 c.12 Sch.39 para.24

CAP.

2003–cont.

14. Finance Act 2003–*cont.*

Sch.19 para.4B, added: SI 2003/2760 Sch.1 para.10, SI 2003/2816 Sch.1 para.10, 2004 c.12 Sch.39 para.24

Sch.19 para.6, repealed (in part): SI 2003/2760 Sch.1 para.11, SI 2003/2816 Sch.1 para.11, 2004 c.12 Sch.42 Part 4

Sch.19 para.7, amended: SI 2003/2760 Sch.1 para.8, SI 2003/2816 Sch.1 para.8, 2004 c.12 s.303, Sch.39 para.22

Sch.19 para.7A, added: SI 2003/2760 Sch.1 para.11, SI 2003/2816 Sch.1 para.11, 2004 c.12 Sch.39 para.25

Sch.19 para.8, amended: SI 2003/2760 Sch.1 para.11, SI 2003/2816 Sch.1 para.11, 2004 c.12 Sch.39 para.25

Sch.20 Part 2 para.7, enabling: SI 2003/2868

Sch.21 Part 3 para.18, repealed (in part): 2004 c.12 Sch.42 Part 2

Sch.22, referred to: 1992 c.12 s.119A, SI 2001/1004 Reg.22, Sch.2 para.7

Sch.22 para.3, applied: 1992 c.12 s.149AA, s.149B, 2003 c.1 s.431

Sch.22 para.3, referred to: 2003 c.1 s.431

Sch.22 para.3, enabling: SI 2003/1997

Sch.23, applied: 2003 c.1 s.702

Sch.23 Part 2 para.9, amended: SI 2004/2310 Sch.1 para.69

Sch.23 Part 3 para.16, amended: SI 2004/2310 Sch.1 para.70

Sch.23 Part 4A para.22C, amended: 2004 c.12 Sch.16 para.5, Sch.42 Part 2

Sch.23 Part 4 para.21, amended: 2004 c.12 Sch.16 para.5, Sch.42 Part 2

Sch.24, applied: SI 2004/1863 Sch.1 para.4

Sch.24 para.1, amended: 2004 c.12 s.245

Sch.24 para.2, amended: 2004 c.12 s.245, Sch.42 Part 3

Sch.24 para.7, substituted: SI 2004/2310 Sch.1 para.71

Sch.24 para.8, amended: 2004 c.12 s.245

Sch.24 para.9, amended: 2004 c.12 s.245

Sch.26 para.3, applied: SI 2003/2173 Reg.2

Sch.26 para.3, referred to: SI 2003/2173 Reg.2

Sch.26 para.3, enabling: SI 2003/2173

Sch.27 para.1, repealed (in part): 2004 c.12 Sch.42 Part 3

Sch.27 para.3, repealed: 2004 c.12 Sch.42 Part 2

Sch.33 para.6, repealed (in part): 2004 c.12 Sch.42 Part 2

Sch.33 para.8, repealed (in part): 2004 c.12 Sch.42 Part 2

Sch.33 para.12, repealed (in part): 2004 c.12 Sch.42 Part 2

Sch.33 para.13, repealed (in part): 2004 c.12 Sch.42 Part 2

Sch.34 Part 2 para.12, applied: 1988 c.1 s.547

CAP.

2003–cont.

15. Co-operatives and Community Benefit Societies Act 2003

Commencement Orders: SI 2003/2678 Art.2; SI 2004/3257 Art.2

s.7, enabling: SI 2003/2678, SI 2004/3257

16. Marine Safety Act 2003

s.2, repealed (in part): 2004 c.21 Sch.2

17. Licensing Act 2003

Commencement Orders: SI 2003/1911 Art.2; SI 2003/2100 Art.2; SI 2003/3222 Art.2, Sch.1; SI 2004/1738 Art.2; SI 2004/2360 Art.2, Sch.1

Part 3, applied: 2004 c.i s.22

s.5, amended: 2004 c.21 Sch.1 para.98

s.5, applied: SI 2004/2362 Art.2

s.5, enabling: SI 2004/2362

s.13, amended: 2004 c.21 Sch.1 para.98

s.69, amended: 2004 c.21 Sch.1 para.98

s.101, amended: 2004 c.33 Sch.27 para.170

s.177, amended: 2004 c.21 Sch.1 para.98

s.201, enabling: SI 2003/1911, SI 2003/2100, SI 2003/3222, SI 2004/1738, SI 2004/2360

Sch.1 Part 1 para.2, applied: 2004 c.i s.22

Sch.1 Part 1 para.3, applied: 2004 c.i s.22

Sch.6 para.116, repealed: 2003 c.44 Sch.37 Part 11

Sch.8 Part 1 para.1, enabling: SI 2004/1739

Sch.8 Part 2 para.13, enabling: SI 2004/1739

Sch.8 Part 3 para.23, enabling: SI 2004/1739

18. Sunday Working (Scotland) Act 2003

Commencement Orders: SI 2004/958 Art.2

s.3, enabling: SI 2004/958

20. Railways and Transport Safety Act 2003

Commencement Orders: SI 2003/2681 Art.2; SI 2004/827 Art.2, Art.3, Art.4; SI 2004/1572 Art.2, Art.3, Art.4; SI 2004/2759 Art.2

s.21, applied: SI 2004/1573 Art.5

s.22, applied: SI 2004/1573 Art.5

s.23, applied: SI 2004/1573 Art.5

s.24, referred to: 1996 c.16 s.24

s.31, applied: 1998 c.37 s.1

s.31, referred to: 1994 c.33 s.60, 1998 c.37 s.16, 2000 c.11 s.34, 2002 c.30 s.43

s.33, applied: SI 2004/1573 Art.10

s.34, applied: SI 2004/1522

s.34, enabling: SI 2004/1522

s.36, applied: SI 2004/1573 Art.11

s.37, applied: SI 2004/1573 Art.11

s.39, applied: SI 2004/1573 Art.11

s.39, referred to: 2004 c.20 s.64, s.65

s.40, applied: SI 2004/1573 Art.11

s.50, applied: SI 2004/1573 Art.4

s.52, applied: SI 2004/915 Reg.5, SI 2004/1573 Art.4

s.55, applied: SI 2004/1573 Art.4

s.73, enabling: SI 2004/1573

s.74, enabling: SI 2004/1522, SI 2004/1573

2003–cont.

20. Railways and Transport Safety Act 2003–*cont.*

s.120, enabling: SI 2003/2681, SI 2004/827, SI 2004/1572, SI 2004/2759

Sch.4 Part 3 para.19, applied: SI 2004/1573 Art.4

Sch.4 Part 3 para.20, referred to: SI 2004/1573 Art.4

Sch.4 Part 3 para.24, applied: SI 2004/1573

Sch.4 Part 3 para.24, enabling: SI 2004/1573

21. Communications Act 2003

Commencement Orders: SI 2003/1900 Art.2, Art.3, Art.4, Art.5, Art.6, Sch.1, Sch.2; SI 2003/3142 Art.2, Art.3, Art.4, Art.9, Sch.1, Sch.2; SI 2004/545 Art.2; SI 2004/697 Art.2; SI 2004/3309 Art.2, Art.3

applied: 1972 c.70 s.142, 1985 c.66 s.70, 1988 c.48 s.69, Sch.2 para.17, 1990 c.42 s.4, s.51, s.87, s.117, 1996 c.55 s.4, s.43, 2000 c.27 s.105, 2000 c.38 Sch.9 para.3, 2002 c.40 Sch.15, SI 2003/1902 Sch.4 para.2, Sch.5 para.1, Sch.6 para.1, SI 2004/1975 Art.2, Art.8, Art.9

referred to: 1991 c.56 Sch.15 Part II, 1991 c.57 Sch.24 Part II, 1993 c.43 s.145, 1999 c.29 s.235, 2000 c.26 Sch.7 para.3, SI 2003/1368 Sch.1, SI 2003/2760 Reg.2

Part 2 c.1, applied: 1989 c.22 s.9, 1990 c.42 s.86, 1996 c.55 s.3, s.42, SI 1999/2093 Reg.30, SI 2003/2426 Reg.9

Part 2 c.1, disapplied: SI 2003/3281 Art.2

Part 2 c.1, referred to: SI 2003/2426 Sch.2 para.5

Part 2 c.2, applied: 1949 c.54 s.19

Part 3, applied: 1990 c.42 s.41, s.42, s.49, s.202, 1996 c.55 s.10, 1998 c.41 Sch.2 para.5, 2002 c.36 s.12

Part 3 c.4, applied: 1990 c.42 s.15, s.16, s.17, s.184, 1996 c.55 s.119

Part 4, applied: 1949 c.54 s.1, 2000 c.23 s.26

s.1, applied: SI 2004/1975

s.1, varied: SI 2003/3195 Art.6, Sch.2 para.3, SI 2003/3197 Art.6, Sch.2 para.2, SI 2003/3198 Art.6, Sch.2 para.1

s.1A, varied: SI 2003/3195 Art.6, Sch.2 para.4, SI 2003/3197 Art.6, Sch.2 para.3, SI 2003/3198 Art.6, Sch.2 para.2

s.2, varied: SI 2003/3195 Art.6, SI 2003/3197 Art.6, SI 2003/3198 Art.6

s.3, disapplied: 2002 c.40 s.119A

s.3, varied: SI 2003/3195 Art.6, Sch.2 para.5, SI 2003/3197 Art.6, Sch.2 para.4, SI 2003/3198 Art.6, Sch.2 para.3

s.5, varied: SI 2003/3195 Art.6, Sch.2 para.6, SI 2003/3197 Art.6, Sch.2 para.5, SI 2003/3198 Art.6, Sch.2 para.4

s.6, varied: SI 2003/3195 Art.6, SI 2003/3197 Art.6, SI 2003/3198 Art.6

s.7, varied: SI 2003/3195 Art.6, Sch.2 para.7, SI 2003/3197 Art.6, Sch.2 para.6, SI 2003/3198 Art.6, Sch.2 para.5

2003–cont.

21. Communications Act 2003–*cont.*

s.8, varied: SI 2003/3195 Art.6, SI 2003/3197 Art.6, SI 2003/3198 Art.6

s.9, varied: SI 2003/3195 Art.6, SI 2003/3197 Art.6, SI 2003/3198 Art.6

s.11, varied: SI 2003/3195 Art.6, SI 2003/3197 Art.6

s.12, varied: SI 2003/3195 Art.6, Sch.2 para.8, SI 2003/3197 Art.6, Sch.2 para.7, SI 2003/3198 Art.6

s.13, applied: 2002 c.11 Sch.1 para.14

s.13, varied: SI 2003/3195 Art.6, Sch.2 para.9, SI 2003/3197 Art.6, Sch.2 para.8, SI 2003/3198 Art.6, Sch.2 para.6

s.14, varied: SI 2003/3198 Art.6, Sch.2 para.7

s.15, varied: SI 2003/3198 Art.6, Sch.2 para.8

s.16, applied: 2000 c.36 Sch.1 Part VI

s.21, varied: SI 2003/3197 Art.6

s.22, applied: SI 2003/3195 Art.4, SI 2003/3197 Art.4, SI 2003/3198 Art.4

s.22, referred to: SI 2003/3195 Art.4, SI 2003/3197 Art.4, SI 2003/3198 Art.4

s.22, varied: SI 2003/3195 Art.6, SI 2003/3197 Art.6, SI 2003/3198 Art.6

s.23, varied: SI 2003/3195 Sch.2 para.10, SI 2003/3197 Art.6, Sch.2 para.9

s.24, varied: SI 2003/3195 Sch.2 para.11, SI 2003/3197 Art.6, Sch.2 para.10, SI 2003/3198 Art.6

s.25, varied: SI 2003/3197 Art.6, SI 2003/3198 Art.6

s.26, varied: SI 2003/3195 Art.6, SI 2003/3197 Art.6, SI 2003/3198 Art.6

s.28, varied: SI 2003/3195 Art.6, SI 2003/3197 Art.6, SI 2003/3198 Art.6

s.29, applied: SI 2003/3195 Sch.2 para.2, SI 2003/3197 Sch.2 para.1

s.29, varied: SI 2003/3195 Sch.2 para.2, SI 2003/3197 Art.6, Sch.2 para.1

s.30, applied: 1988 c.48 s.69, Sch.2 para.17

s.30, varied: SI 2003/3195 Art.6, SI 2003/3197 Art.6, SI 2003/3198 Art.6

s.31, varied: SI 2003/3195 Art.6, Sch.2 para.12, SI 2003/3197 Art.6, Sch.2 para.11, SI 2003/3198 Art.6, Sch.2 para.9

s.32, applied: SI 2003/1901 Reg.4, 2004 c.21 s.48, 2004 c.36 Sch.1 para.22, Sch.1 para.33

s.32, varied: SI 2003/3195 Art.6, SI 2003/3197 Art.6, SI 2003/3198 Art.6

s.45, applied: 1949 c.54 s.1, SI 2003/1901 Reg.4

s.56, enabling: SI 2003/3281

s.65, applied: SI 2003/1904, SI 2003/1904 Art.3

s.65, disapplied: SI 2003/2426 Reg.35

s.65, enabling: SI 2003/1904

s.94, varied: SI 2000/730 Reg.18

s.95, varied: SI 2000/730 Reg.18

s.96, varied: SI 2000/730 Reg.18

CAP.

2003–cont.

21. Communications Act 2003–*cont.*

s.97, applied: SI 2003/2712, SI 2003/2712 Art.3

s.97, varied: SI 2000/730 Reg.18

s.97, enabling: SI 2003/2712

s.98, varied: SI 2000/730 Reg.18

s.106, applied: 1984 c.12 Sch.2 para.26, Sch.2 para.29

s.106, referred to: SI 2003/2553 Reg.18

s.107, referred to: SI 2003/2553 Reg.18

s.108, referred to: SI 2003/2553 Reg.18

s.109, applied: SI 2003/1900 Art.3, SI 2003/2553

s.109, referred to: SI 2003/2553 Reg.18

s.109, enabling: SI 2003/2553

s.110, referred to: SI 2003/2553 Reg.18

s.110, varied: SI 2003/1900 Art.3

s.111, referred to: SI 2003/2553 Reg.18

s.112, referred to: SI 2003/2553 Reg.18

s.113, referred to: SI 2003/2553 Reg.18

s.113, varied: SI 2003/1900 Art.3

s.114, referred to: SI 2003/2553 Reg.18

s.115, referred to: SI 2003/2553 Reg.18

s.116, referred to: SI 2003/2553 Reg.18

s.117, referred to: SI 2003/2553 Reg.18

s.117, varied: 2002 c.40 s.180, SI 2003/1900 Art.3

s.118, referred to: SI 2003/2553 Reg.18

s.119, referred to: SI 2003/2553 Reg.18

s.125, amended: SI 2003/2498 Sch.2

s.127, applied: SI 2002/1837 Sch.1 Part I

s.138, varied: SI 2003/3195 Art.6, SI 2003/3197 Art.6, SI 2003/3198 Art.6

s.139, applied: SI 2003/3195 Sch.2 para.2, SI 2003/3197 Sch.2 para.1

s.139, varied: SI 2003/3195 Art.6, Sch.2 para.2, Sch.2 para.13, SI 2003/3197 Art.6, Sch.2 para.1, Sch.2 para.12, SI 2003/3198 Art.6

s.140, varied: SI 2003/3195 Art.6, SI 2003/3197 Art.6, SI 2003/3198 Art.6

s.141, varied: SI 2003/3195 Art.6, SI 2003/3197 Art.6, SI 2003/3198 Art.6

s.142, varied: SI 2003/3195 Art.6, SI 2003/3197 Art.6, SI 2003/3198 Art.6

s.143, varied: SI 2003/3195 Art.6, Sch.2 para.14, SI 2003/3197 Art.6, Sch.2 para.13, SI 2003/3198 Art.6

s.144, varied: SI 2003/3195 Art.6, Sch.2 para.15, SI 2003/3197 Art.6, Sch.2 para.14, SI 2003/3198 Art.6

s.152, applied: SI 2003/3195 Art.4, SI 2003/3197 Art.4, SI 2003/3198 Art.4

s.152, referred to: SI 2003/3195 Art.4, SI 2003/3197 Art.4

s.152, varied: SI 2003/3195 Art.6, Sch.2 para.16, SI 2003/3197 Art.6, Sch.2 para.15, SI 2003/3198 Art.6, Sch.2 para.10

s.153, applied: SI 2000/730 Reg.19

s.153, varied: SI 2003/3198 Art.6, Sch.2 para.11

CAP.

2003–cont.

21. Communications Act 2003–*cont.*

s.154, applied: 1998 c.6 s.2

s.154, referred to: SI 2003/2983

s.154, varied: SI 2003/3195 Art.6, SI 2003/3197 Art.6, SI 2003/3198 Art.6

s.155, varied: SI 2003/3195 Art.6, SI 2003/3197 Art.6, SI 2003/3198 Art.6

s.156, varied: SI 2003/3195 Art.6, Sch.2 para.17, SI 2003/3197 Art.6, Sch.2 para.16, SI 2003/3198 Art.6, Sch.2 para.12

s.157, varied: SI 2003/3195 Art.6, Sch.2 para.18, SI 2003/3197 Art.6, Sch.2 para.17, SI 2003/3198 Art.6, Sch.2 para.13

s.158, varied: SI 2003/3195 Art.6, SI 2003/3197 Art.6, SI 2003/3198 Art.6

s.159, applied: 1998 c.6 s.1

s.159, varied: SI 2003/3195 Art.6, Sch.2 para.19, SI 2003/3197 Art.6, Sch.2 para.18, SI 2003/3198 Art.6, Sch.2 para.14

s.160, varied: SI 2003/3195 Art.6, Sch.2 para.20, SI 2003/3197 Art.6, SI 2003/3198 Art.6

s.161, varied: SI 2003/3195 Art.6, SI 2003/3197 Art.6, SI 2003/3198 Art.6

s.162, varied: SI 2003/3195 Art.6, SI 2003/3197 Art.6, SI 2003/3198 Art.6

s.163, varied: SI 2003/3195 Art.6, SI 2003/3197 Art.6, SI 2003/3198 Art.6

s.164, varied: SI 2003/3195 Art.6, SI 2003/3197 Art.6, SI 2003/3198 Art.6

s.164, enabling: SI 2003/1902

s.165, varied: SI 2003/3195 Art.6, SI 2003/3197 Art.6, SI 2003/3198 Art.6

s.166, varied: SI 2003/3195 Art.6, SI 2003/3197 Art.6, SI 2003/3198 Art.6

s.167, varied: SI 2003/3195 Art.6, SI 2003/3197 Art.6, SI 2003/3198 Art.6

s.168, varied: SI 2003/3195 Art.6

s.168, enabling: SI 2004/3154

s.169, varied: SI 2003/3195 Art.6, SI 2003/3197 Art.6, Sch.2 para.19, SI 2003/3198 Art.6, Sch.2 para.15

s.170, varied: SI 2003/3195 Art.6, SI 2003/3197 Art.6, SI 2003/3198 Art.6

s.170, enabling: SI 2004/3155

s.171, varied: SI 2003/3195 Art.6, Sch.2 para.21, SI 2003/3197 Art.6, Sch.2 para.20, SI 2003/3198 Art.6

s.172, varied: SI 2003/3195 Art.6, SI 2003/3197 Art.6, SI 2003/3198 Art.6

s.173, varied: SI 2003/3195 Art.6, SI 2003/3197 Art.6, SI 2003/3198 Art.6

s.174, varied: SI 2003/3195 Art.6, Sch.2 para.22, SI 2003/3197 Art.6, Sch.2 para.21, SI 2003/3198 Art.6, Sch.2 para.16

s.175, varied: SI 2003/3195 Art.6, SI 2003/3197 Art.6, SI 2003/3198 Art.6

s.176, applied: SI 2003/3195 Sch.2 para.2, SI 2003/3197 Sch.2 para.1

2003–cont.

21. Communications Act 2003–*cont.*

s.176, varied: SI 2003/3195 Art.6, Sch.2 para.2, Sch.2 para.23, SI 2003/3197 Art.6, Sch.2 para.1, Sch.2 para.22, SI 2003/3198 Art.6

s.177, varied: SI 2003/3195 Art.6, SI 2003/3197 Art.6, SI 2003/3198 Art.6

s.178, varied: SI 2003/3195 Art.6, Sch.2 para.24, SI 2003/3197 Art.6, Sch.2 para.23, SI 2003/3198 Art.6, Sch.2 para.17

s.179, varied: SI 2003/3195 Art.6, Sch.2 para.25, SI 2003/3197 Art.6, Sch.2 para.24, SI 2003/3198 Art.6, Sch.2 para.18

s.183, varied: SI 2003/3195 Art.6, SI 2003/3197 Art.6, SI 2003/3198 Art.6

s.184, varied: SI 2003/3195 Art.6, Sch.2 para.26, SI 2003/3197 Art.6, Sch.2 para.25, SI 2003/3198 Art.6

s.185, varied: SI 2003/3195 Sch.2 para.27, SI 2003/3197 Art.6, Sch.2 para.26, SI 2003/3198 Art.6, Sch.2 para.19

s.186, varied: SI 2003/3197 Art.6, SI 2003/3198 Art.6

s.187, varied: SI 2003/3195 Sch.2 para.28, SI 2003/3197 Art.6, Sch.2 para.27, SI 2003/3198 Art.6, Sch.2 para.20

s.188, varied: SI 2003/3197 Art.6, SI 2003/3198 Art.6

s.189, varied: SI 2003/3197 Art.6, SI 2003/3198 Art.6

s.190, varied: SI 2003/3195 Sch.2 para.29, SI 2003/3197 Art.6, Sch.2 para.28, SI 2003/3198 Art.6, Sch.2 para.21

s.191, applied: SI 2003/3195 Art.6, SI 2003/3197 Art.6

s.191, varied: SI 2003/3197 Art.6, SI 2003/3198 Art.6

s.192, varied: SI 2003/3195 Art.6, Sch.2 para.30, SI 2003/3197 Art.6, Sch.2 para.29, SI 2003/3198 Art.6, Sch.2 para.22

s.192, enabling: SI 2004/2068

s.193, applied: SI 2004/2068 r.3

s.193, enabling: SI 2004/2068

s.194, applied: 1998 c.41 Sch.7 para.2

s.195, varied: SI 2003/3195 Art.6, Sch.2 para.31, SI 2003/3197 Art.6, Sch.2 para.30, SI 2003/3198 Art.6, Sch.2 para.23

s.196, varied: SI 2003/3195 Art.6, Sch.2 para.32, SI 2003/3197 Art.6, Sch.2 para.31, SI 2003/3198 Art.6, Sch.2 para.24

s.197, varied: SI 2003/3195 Art.6, Sch.2 para.33, SI 2003/3197 Art.6, Sch.2 para.32, SI 2003/3198 Art.6, Sch.2 para.25

s.198, applied: SI 2003/3195 Sch.2 para.2, SI 2003/3197 Sch.2 para.1

s.198, varied: SI 2003/3195 Art.6, Sch.2 para.2, Sch.2 para.34, SI 2003/3197 Art.6, Sch.2 para.1, SI 2003/3198 Art.6

2003–cont.

21. Communications Act 2003–*cont.*

s.199, varied: SI 2003/3142 Art.7, SI 2003/3195 Art.6, SI 2003/3197 Art.6, SI 2003/3198 Art.6

s.200, varied: SI 2003/3195 Art.6, SI 2003/3197 Art.6, SI 2003/3198 Art.6

s.201, varied: SI 2003/3195 Art.6, SI 2003/3197 Art.6, SI 2003/3198 Art.6

s.202, varied: SI 2003/3195 Art.6, SI 2003/3197 Art.6, Sch.2 para.33, SI 2003/3198 Art.6

s.202, enabling: SI 2003/3176

s.204, applied: 1990 c.42 Sch.6 para.1

s.207, applied: 1990 c.42 s.61A, s.61, SI 2003/1900 Art.4

s.211, applied: 2002 c.36 s.12

s.211, varied: SI 2003/3195 Art.6, Sch.2 para.35, SI 2003/3197 Art.6, Sch.2 para.34, SI 2003/3198 Art.6, Sch.2 para.26

s.212, varied: SI 2003/3195 Art.6, Sch.2 para.36, SI 2003/3197 Art.6, Sch.2 para.35, SI 2003/3198 Art.6

s.214, varied: SI 2003/3195 Art.6, Sch.2 para.37, SI 2003/3197 Art.6, Sch.2 para.36, SI 2003/3198 Art.6, Sch.2 para.27

s.215, varied: SI 2003/3195 Art.6, SI 2003/3197 Art.6, SI 2003/3198 Art.6

s.216, varied: SI 2003/3195 Art.6, SI 2003/3197 Art.6, SI 2003/3198 Art.6

s.217, varied: SI 2003/3195 Art.6, SI 2003/3197 Art.6, SI 2003/3198 Art.6

s.218, varied: SI 2003/3195 Art.6, Sch.2 para.38, SI 2003/3197 Art.6, Sch.2 para.37, SI 2003/3198 Art.6, Sch.2 para.28

s.219, applied: SI 2003/1900 Art.6

s.219, disapplied: SI 2003/3142 Art.8

s.219, varied: SI 2003/3195 Art.6, Sch.2 para.39, SI 2003/3197 Art.6, Sch.2 para.38, SI 2003/3198 Art.6, Sch.2 para.29

s.220, disapplied: SI 2003/3142 Art.8

s.220, varied: SI 2003/3195 Art.6, SI 2003/3197 Art.6, SI 2003/3198 Art.6

s.221, referred to: SI 2003/3142 Art.8

s.221, varied: SI 2003/3195 Art.6, SI 2003/3197 Art.6, SI 2003/3198 Art.6

s.222, varied: SI 2003/3195 Art.6, SI 2003/3197 Art.6, SI 2003/3198 Art.6

s.223, varied: SI 2003/3195 Art.6, SI 2003/3197 Art.6, SI 2003/3198 Art.6

s.224, applied: SI 2003/3195 Sch.2 para.2, SI 2003/3197 Sch.2 para.1

s.224, varied: SI 2003/3195 Art.6, Sch.2 para.2, SI 2003/3197 Art.6, Sch.2 para.1, SI 2003/3198 Art.6

s.225, varied: SI 2003/3195 Art.6, SI 2003/3197 Art.6, SI 2003/3198 Art.6

s.226, varied: SI 2003/3195 Art.6, SI 2003/3197 Art.6, SI 2003/3198 Art.6

CAP.

2003–cont.

21. Communications Act 2003–*cont.*

s.227, varied: SI 2003/3195 Art.6, SI 2003/3197 Art.6, SI 2003/3198 Art.6

s.228, varied: SI 2003/3195 Art.6, SI 2003/3197 Art.6, SI 2003/3198 Art.6

s.229, varied: SI 2003/3195 Art.6, SI 2003/3197 Art.6, SI 2003/3198 Art.6, Sch.2 para.30

s.230, varied: SI 2003/3195 Art.6, SI 2003/3197 Art.6, Sch.2 para.39, SI 2003/3198 Art.6

s.231, varied: SI 2003/3195 Art.6, Sch.2 para.40, SI 2003/3197 Art.6, Sch.2 para.40, SI 2003/3198 Art.6, Sch.2 para.31

s.232, applied: 1990 c.42 s.201

s.232, varied: SI 2003/3195 Art.6

s.233, applied: 1990 c.42 s.201

s.233, varied: SI 2003/3195 Art.6

s.234, varied: SI 2003/3195 Art.6

s.235, applied: 1990 c.42 s.3

s.235, varied: SI 2003/3195 Art.6

s.236, applied: SI 2004/1975 Sch.1 para.2

s.236, varied: SI 2003/3195 Art.6

s.237, applied: 1990 c.42 s.4, SI 2003/3195 Sch.2 para.2, SI 2003/3197 Sch.2 para.1

s.237, varied: SI 2003/3195 Art.6, Sch.2 para.2, Sch.2 para.41, SI 2003/3197 Sch.2 para.1, Sch.2 para.41

s.238, applied: 1990 c.42 s.4

s.238, varied: SI 2003/3195 Art.6

s.239, varied: SI 2003/3195 Art.6

s.240, varied: SI 2003/3195 Art.6, Sch.2 para.42, SI 2003/3197 Sch.2 para.42

s.241, referred to: SI 2003/1900 Art.6

s.241, varied: SI 2003/3195 Art.6, Sch.2 para.43, SI 2003/3197 Sch.2 para.43, SI 2003/3198 Art.6

s.242, varied: SI 2003/3195 Art.6, SI 2003/3198 Art.6

s.243, varied: SI 2003/3195 Art.6, Sch.2 para.44, SI 2003/3197 Sch.2 para.44, SI 2003/3198 Art.6

s.244, varied: SI 2003/3195 Art.6, Sch.2 para.45, SI 2003/3197 Sch.2 para.45

s.245, applied: 2002 c.36 s.12

s.245, varied: SI 2003/3195 Art.6, Sch.2 para.46, SI 2003/3197 Art.6, Sch.2 para.46, SI 2003/3198 Art.6, Sch.2 para.32, SI 2004/1944 Sch.1 para.10

s.246, varied: SI 2003/3195 Art.6, SI 2003/3197 Art.6, SI 2003/3198 Art.6

s.247, varied: SI 2003/3195 Art.6, Sch.2 para.2, SI 2003/3197 Art.6, Sch.2 para.1

s.248, applied: 1990 c.42 s.201

s.248, varied: SI 2003/3195 Art.6, Sch.2 para.2, SI 2003/3197 Art.6, Sch.2 para.1

s.249, applied: SI 2003/3195 Sch.2 para.2, SI 2003/3197 Sch.2 para.1

s.249, varied: SI 2003/3195 Art.6, Sch.2 para.47, SI 2003/3197 Art.6, Sch.2 para.47

CAP.

2003–cont.

21. Communications Act 2003–*cont.*

s.250, varied: SI 2003/3195 Art.6, Sch.2 para.48, SI 2003/3197 Art.6

s.251, varied: SI 2003/3195 Art.6, SI 2003/3197 Art.6

s.252, varied: SI 2003/3195 Art.6, Sch.2 para.49, SI 2003/3197 Art.6

s.253, applied: 1990 c.42 s.104A, s.103A

s.253, varied: SI 2003/3195 Art.6, SI 2003/3197 Art.6, SI 2003/3198 Art.6, Sch.2 para.33

s.256, varied: SI 2003/3195 Art.6, SI 2003/3197 Art.6, SI 2003/3198 Art.6

s.257, varied: SI 2003/3195 Art.6, SI 2003/3197 Art.6, SI 2003/3198 Art.6

s.258, referred to: SI 2003/1900 Art.6

s.258, varied: SI 2003/3195 Art.6, SI 2003/3197 Art.6, SI 2003/3198 Art.6

s.259, varied: SI 2003/3195 Art.6, SI 2003/3197 Art.6, SI 2003/3198 Art.6

s.260, varied: SI 2003/3195 Art.6, SI 2003/3197 Art.6, SI 2003/3198 Art.6

s.261, varied: SI 2003/3195 Art.6, SI 2003/3197 Art.6, SI 2003/3198 Art.6

s.262, applied: SI 2004/1944

s.262, varied: SI 2003/3195 Art.6, Sch.2 para.50, SI 2003/3197 Art.6

s.262, enabling: SI 2004/1944

s.263, applied: 1990 c.42 s.111B, s.184, 1996 c.55 s.119

s.263, varied: SI 2003/3195 Art.6, Sch.2 para.51, SI 2003/3197 Art.6, Sch.2 para.48, SI 2003/3198 Art.6

s.264, varied: SI 2003/3195 Art.6, Sch.2 para.52, SI 2003/3197 Art.6, Sch.2 para.49, SI 2003/3198 Art.6, Sch.2 para.34

s.266, applied: SI 2003/1900 Art.4

s.268, applied: SI 2003/1900 Art.4

s.271, varied: SI 2003/3195 Art.6, Sch.2 para.53, SI 2003/3197 Art.6, Sch.2 para.50, SI 2003/3198 Art.6, Sch.2 para.35

s.275, varied: SI 2003/3195 Art.6, Sch.2 para.54, SI 2003/3197 Art.6, Sch.2 para.51, SI 2003/3198 Art.6

s.276, disapplied: SI 2003/3142 Art.8

s.276, varied: SI 2003/3195 Art.6, SI 2003/3197 Art.6, SI 2003/3198 Art.6

s.277, applied: SI 2003/3195 Sch.2 para.2, SI 2003/3197 Sch.2 para.1

s.277, varied: SI 2003/3195 Art.6, Sch.2 para.2, Sch.2 para.55, SI 2003/3197 Art.6, Sch.2 para.1, Sch.2 para.52, SI 2003/3198 Art.6

s.278, applied: SI 2003/3195 Sch.2 para.2, SI 2003/3197 Sch.2 para.1, SI 2004/1652

s.278, referred to: SI 2004/1652 Art.3

2003–cont.

21. Communications Act 2003–*cont.*

s.278, varied: SI 2003/3195 Art.6, Sch.2 para.2, Sch.2 para.56, SI 2003/3197 Art.6, Sch.2 para.1, Sch.2 para.53, SI 2003/3198 Art.6

s.278, enabling: SI 2004/1652

s.279, varied: SI 2003/3195 Art.6, SI 2003/3197 Art.6, SI 2003/3198 Art.6

s.280, applied: 1990 c.42 s.194A

s.280, referred to: 1994 c.23 s.33

s.280, varied: SI 2003/3195 Art.6, Sch.2 para.57, SI 2003/3197 Art.6, Sch.2 para.54, SI 2003/3198 Art.6, Sch.2 para.36

s.281, amended: SI 2003/3299 Art.13

s.281, varied: SI 2003/3195 Art.6, SI 2003/3197 Art.6, SI 2003/3198 Art.6

s.282, applied: SI 2003/3299

s.282, varied: SI 2003/3195 Art.6, Sch.2 para.58, SI 2003/3197 Art.6, Sch.2 para.55, SI 2003/3198 Art.6

s.282, enabling: SI 2003/3299

s.283, varied: SI 2003/3195 Art.6, Sch.2 para.59, SI 2003/3197 Art.6, Sch.2 para.56, SI 2003/3198 Art.6

s.284, varied: SI 2003/3195 Art.6, SI 2003/3197 Art.6, SI 2003/3198 Art.6

s.285, varied: SI 2003/3195 Art.6, Sch.2 para.60, SI 2003/3197 Art.6, Sch.2 para.57, SI 2003/3198 Art.6

s.286, varied: SI 2003/3195 Art.6, Sch.2 para.61, SI 2003/3197 Art.6, Sch.2 para.58, SI 2003/3198 Art.6, Sch.2 para.37

s.287, varied: SI 2003/3195 Art.6, Sch.2 para.62, SI 2003/3197 Art.6, Sch.2 para.59, SI 2003/3198 Art.6, Sch.2 para.38

s.288, varied: SI 2003/3195 Art.6, SI 2003/3197 Art.6, SI 2003/3198 Art.6, Sch.2 para.39

s.289, varied: SI 2003/3195 Art.6, SI 2003/3197 Art.6, SI 2003/3198 Art.6, Sch.2 para.40

s.290, varied: SI 2003/3195 Art.6, Sch.2 para.63, SI 2003/3197 Art.6, Sch.2 para.60, SI 2003/3198 Art.6, Sch.2 para.41

s.291, applied: 1998 c.41 Sch.2 para.5

s.291, varied: SI 2003/3195 Art.6, Sch.2 para.64, SI 2003/3197 Art.6, Sch.2 para.61, SI 2003/3198 Art.6, Sch.2 para.42

s.292, varied: SI 2003/3195 Art.6, SI 2003/3197 Art.6, SI 2003/3198 Art.6

s.293, varied: SI 2003/3195 Art.6, SI 2003/3197 Art.6, SI 2003/3198 Art.6

s.294, varied: SI 2003/3195 Art.6, SI 2003/3197 Art.6, SI 2003/3198 Art.6

s.295, varied: SI 2003/3195 Art.6, SI 2003/3197 Art.6, SI 2003/3198 Art.6

s.296, varied: SI 2003/3195 Art.6, SI 2003/3197 Art.6, SI 2003/3198 Art.6, Sch.2 para.43

2003–cont.

21. Communications Act 2003–*cont.*

s.297, varied: SI 2003/3195 Art.6, SI 2003/3197 Art.6, SI 2003/3198 Art.6

s.298, disapplied: SI 2003/3142 Art.8

s.298, varied: SI 2003/3195 Art.6, SI 2003/3197 Art.6, SI 2003/3198 Art.6

s.299, varied: SI 2003/3195 Art.6, SI 2003/3197 Art.6, SI 2003/3198 Art.6

s.300, varied: SI 2003/3195 Art.6, Sch.2 para.65, SI 2003/3197 Art.6, Sch.2 para.62, SI 2003/3198 Art.6

s.301, varied: SI 2003/3195 Art.6, SI 2003/3197 Art.6, SI 2003/3198 Art.6

s.302, varied: SI 2003/3195 Art.6, SI 2003/3197 Art.6, SI 2003/3198 Art.6

s.303, applied: 1990 c.42 s.48

s.303, varied: SI 2003/3195 Art.6, Sch.2 para.66, SI 2003/3197 Art.6, Sch.2 para.63, SI 2003/3198 Art.6, Sch.2 para.44

s.304, varied: SI 2003/3195 Art.6, SI 2003/3197 Art.6, SI 2003/3198 Art.6

s.305, varied: SI 2003/3195 Art.6, Sch.2 para.67, SI 2003/3197 Art.6, Sch.2 para.64, SI 2003/3198 Art.6

s.306, varied: SI 2003/3195 Art.6, Sch.2 para.68, SI 2003/3197 Art.6, Sch.2 para.65, SI 2003/3198 Art.6

s.307, varied: SI 2003/3195 Art.6, SI 2003/3197 Art.6, SI 2003/3198 Art.6

s.308, disapplied: SI 2003/3142 Art.8

s.308, varied: SI 2003/3195 Art.6, SI 2003/3197 Art.6, SI 2003/3198 Art.6

s.309, applied: SI 2003/3195 Sch.2 para.2, SI 2003/3197 Sch.2 para.1

s.309, varied: SI 2003/3195 Art.6, Sch.2 para.2, Sch.2 para.69, SI 2003/3197 Art.6, Sch.2 para.1, Sch.2 para.66

s.310, varied: SI 2003/3195 Art.6, Sch.2 para.70, SI 2003/3197 Art.6, Sch.2 para.67, SI 2003/3198 Art.6, Sch.2 para.45

s.311, varied: SI 2003/3195 Art.6, SI 2003/3197 Art.6, SI 2003/3198 Art.6

s.312, varied: SI 2003/3195 Art.6, SI 2003/3197 Art.6, SI 2003/3198 Art.6, Sch.2 para.46

s.313, varied: SI 2003/3195 Art.6, SI 2003/3197 Art.6

s.314, varied: SI 2003/3195 Art.6, SI 2003/3197 Art.6, SI 2004/1944 Sch.1 para.11

s.315, varied: SI 2003/3195 Art.6, SI 2003/3197 Art.6, SI 2003/3198 Art.6, Sch.2 para.47

s.319, applied: 2002 c.40 s.58, SI 2004/1975 Sch.1 para.1

s.319, referred to: 1990 c.42 s.111B, SI 2004/1975 Art.5

s.319, varied: SI 2003/3195 Art.6, Sch.2 para.2, Sch.2 para.71, SI 2003/3197 Art.6, Sch.2 para.1, Sch.2 para.68, SI 2003/3198 Art.6

2003–cont.

21. Communications Act 2003–*cont.*

s.320, varied: SI 2003/3195 Art.6, SI 2003/3197 Art.6, SI 2003/3198 Art.6, Sch.2 para.48

s.321, applied: SI 2004/1975 Art.5

s.321, varied: SI 2003/3195 Art.6, Sch.2 para.72, SI 2003/3197 Art.6, Sch.2 para.69, SI 2003/3198 Art.6, Sch.2 para.49

s.322, applied: SI 2004/1975 Art.5

s.322, varied: SI 2003/3195 Art.6, Sch.2 para.73, SI 2003/3197 Art.6, Sch.2 para.70, Sch.2 para.71, SI 2003/3198 Art.6

s.323, applied: SI 2003/3195 Sch.2 para.2, SI 2003/3197 Sch.2 para.1

s.323, varied: SI 2003/3195 Art.6, Sch.2 para.74, SI 2003/3197 Art.6, SI 2003/3198 Art.6

s.324, varied: SI 2003/3195 Art.6, Sch.2 para.75, SI 2003/3197 Art.6, Sch.2 para.72, SI 2003/3198 Art.6

s.325, applied: SI 1988/915 Reg.9, SI 1994/1933 Reg.11, SI 2003/3142 Art.11, SI 2004/1975 Art.5, Sch.1 para.1

s.325, varied: SI 2003/3195 Art.6, SI 2003/3197 Art.6, SI 2003/3198 Art.6

s.326, varied: SI 2003/3195 Art.6, SI 2003/3197 Art.6, SI 2003/3198 Art.6

s.327, varied: SI 2003/3195 Art.6, SI 2003/3197 Art.6, SI 2003/3198 Art.6

s.328, varied: SI 2003/3195 Art.6, SI 2003/3197 Art.6, SI 2003/3198 Art.6

s.329, varied: SI 2003/3195 Art.6, Sch.2 para.76, SI 2003/3197 Art.6, Sch.2 para.73, SI 2003/3198 Art.6

s.330, varied: SI 2003/3195 Art.6, Sch.2 para.77, SI 2003/3197 Art.6, Sch.2 para.74, SI 2003/3198 Art.6

s.331, varied: SI 2003/3195 Art.6, Sch.2 para.78, SI 2003/3197 Art.6, Sch.2 para.75, SI 2003/3198 Art.6

s.332, varied: SI 2003/3195 Art.6, Sch.2 para.79, SI 2003/3197 Art.6, Sch.2 para.76, SI 2003/3198 Art.6

s.334, applied: 1988 c.48 s.69, Sch.2 para.17

s.334, referred to: SI 2004/1975 Art.9

s.334, varied: SI 2003/3195 Art.6, SI 2003/3197 Art.6, SI 2003/3198 Art.6

s.335, varied: SI 2003/3195 Art.6, Sch.2 para.80, SI 2003/3197 Art.6, Sch.2 para.77

s.336, varied: SI 2003/3195 Art.6, Sch.2 para.81, SI 2003/3197 Art.6, Sch.2 para.78

s.338, varied: SI 2003/3195 Art.6, Sch.2 para.82, SI 2003/3197 Art.6, Sch.2 para.79

s.341, applied: SI 2004/1975 Sch.1 para.5

s.343, varied: SI 2004/1975 Art.10

s.344, varied: SI 2003/3195 Art.6, SI 2003/3197 Art.6, SI 2003/3198 Art.6

s.345, varied: SI 2003/3195 Art.6, SI 2003/3197 Art.6, SI 2003/3198 Art.6

s.346, varied: SI 2003/3195 Art.6, SI 2003/3197 Art.6, SI 2003/3198 Art.6

2003–cont.

21. Communications Act 2003–*cont.*

s.347, varied: SI 2003/3195 Art.6, Sch.2 para.83, SI 2003/3197 Art.6, Sch.2 para.80, SI 2003/3198 Art.6

s.348, applied: SI 2003/3195 Sch.2 para.2, SI 2003/3197 Sch.2 para.1

s.348, varied: SI 2003/3195 Art.6, Sch.2 para.2, Sch.2 para.84, SI 2003/3197 Art.6, Sch.2 para.1, Sch.2 para.81, SI 2003/3198 Art.6

s.350, referred to: SI 2003/1900 Art.5

s.350, varied: SI 2003/3195 Art.6, SI 2003/3197 Art.6, SI 2003/3198 Art.6

s.351, varied: SI 2003/3195 Art.6, Sch.2 para.85, SI 2003/3197 Art.6, Sch.2 para.82, SI 2003/3198 Art.6, Sch.2 para.50

s.352, varied: SI 2003/3195 Art.6, SI 2003/3197 Art.6, SI 2003/3198 Art.6

s.353, varied: SI 2003/3195 Art.6, SI 2003/3197 Art.6, SI 2003/3198 Art.6, Sch.2 para.51

s.354, varied: SI 2003/3195 Art.6, SI 2003/3197 Art.6, SI 2003/3198 Art.6

s.355, varied: SI 2003/3195 Art.6, SI 2003/3197 Art.6, SI 2004/1944 Sch.1 para.11

s.356, varied: SI 2003/3195 Art.6, SI 2003/3197 Art.6, SI 2004/1944 Sch.1 para.11

s.357, varied: SI 2003/3195 Art.6, SI 2003/3197 Art.6, SI 2003/3198 Art.6

s.358, varied: SI 2003/3195 Art.6, Sch.2 para.86, SI 2003/3197 Art.6, Sch.2 para.83, SI 2003/3198 Art.6, Sch.2 para.52

s.359, varied: SI 2003/3195 Art.6, Sch.2 para.87, SI 2003/3197 Art.6, Sch.2 para.84

s.360, varied: SI 2003/3195 Art.6, SI 2003/3197 Art.6, SI 2003/3198 Art.6

s.361, applied: 1990 c.42 s.66, 1996 c.55 s.63

s.361, varied: SI 2003/3195 Art.6, Sch.2 para.88, SI 2003/3197 Art.6, Sch.2 para.85, SI 2003/3198 Art.6

s.362, applied: 1990 c.42 s.202

s.362, varied: SI 2003/3195 Art.6, Sch.2 para.89, SI 2003/3197 Art.6, Sch.2 para.86, SI 2003/3198 Art.6, Sch.2 para.53

s.363, applied: 1996 c.55 s.98

s.363, varied: SI 2004/307 Sch.1 para.1, SI 2004/308 Sch.1 para.1

s.364, applied: 1995 c.46 Sch.9

s.364, varied: SI 2004/307 Sch.1 para.2, SI 2004/308 Sch.1 para.2

s.365, referred to: SI 2004/692

s.365, varied: SI 2004/307 Sch.1 para.3, SI 2004/308 Sch.1 para.3

s.365, enabling: SI 2004/692

s.366, varied: SI 2003/3198 Sch.2 para.54, SI 2004/307 Sch.1 para.4, SI 2004/308 Sch.1 para.4

s.368, varied: SI 2003/3198 Art.6

2003–cont.

21. Communications Act 2003–*cont.*

s.368, enabling: SI 2004/692

s.371, amended: SI 2004/1261 Sch.2 para.11

s.371, applied: 1998 c.41 s.54

s.389, applied: SI 2003/3180

s.390, varied: SI 2003/3195 Art.6, SI 2003/3197 Art.6

s.391, varied: SI 2003/3195 Art.6, Sch.2 para.90, SI 2003/3197 Art.6, Sch.2 para.87

s.392, varied: SI 2003/3195 Art.6, Sch.2 para.91, SI 2003/3197 Art.6, Sch.2 para.88, SI 2003/3198 Art.6

s.393, applied: SI 2004/1975, SI 2004/1975 Art.11

s.393, varied: SI 2003/3195 Art.6, Sch.2 para.92, SI 2003/3197 Art.6, Sch.2 para.89, SI 2003/3198 Art.6, SI 2004/1975 Art.11

s.393, enabling: SI 2004/1975

s.394, applied: 1984 c.12 Sch.2 para.24

s.394, varied: SI 2003/3195 Art.6, Sch.2 para.93, SI 2003/3197 Art.6, Sch.2 para.90, SI 2003/3198 Art.6, Sch.2 para.55

s.395, varied: SI 2003/3195 Art.6, SI 2003/3197 Art.6

s.396, varied: SI 2003/3195 Art.6, SI 2003/3197 Art.6

s.398, varied: SI 2003/3198 Art.6, Sch.2 para.56

s.400, varied: SI 2003/3195 Art.6, Sch.2 para.94, SI 2003/3197 Art.6, Sch.2 para.91, SI 2003/3198 Art.6, Sch.2 para.57

s.402, applied: SI 2004/307, SI 2004/309

s.402, varied: SI 2003/3195 Art.6, SI 2003/3197 Art.6, SI 2003/3198 Art.6

s.402, enabling: SI 2003/2155, SI 2003/2553, SI 2003/2712, SI 2003/3195, SI 2003/3197, SI 2003/3198, SI 2003/3299, SI 2004/692, SI 2004/715, SI 2004/716, SI 2004/718, SI 2004/1114, SI 2004/1115, SI 2004/1116, SI 2004/1944

s.403, applied: 1949 c.54 s.16, 1996 c.55 s.104ZA, 1998 c.6 s.6, SI 2003/1902

s.403, disapplied: 1998 c.6 s.6

s.403, referred to: 1998 c.6 s.6, SI 2003/2983

s.403, varied: SI 2003/3195 Art.6, Sch.2 para.95, SI 2003/3197 Art.6, Sch.2 para.92, SI 2003/3198 Art.6, Sch.2 para.58

s.403, enabling: SI 2004/3154, SI 2004/3155

s.404, varied: SI 2003/3195 Art.6, Sch.2 para.96, SI 2003/3197 Art.6, Sch.2 para.93, SI 2003/3198 Art.6, Sch.2 para.59

s.405, varied: SI 2003/3195 Art.6, Sch.2 para.97, SI 2003/3197 Art.6, Sch.2 para.94, SI 2003/3198 Art.6, Sch.2 para.60

2003–cont.

21. Communications Act 2003–*cont.*

s.406, varied: SI 2003/3195 Art.6, Sch.2 para.98, SI 2003/3197 Art.6, Sch.2 para.95, SI 2003/3198 Art.6, Sch.2 para.61

s.406, enabling: SI 2003/1900, SI 2003/2155, SI 2003/3093, SI 2003/3182, SI 2004/945

s.408, applied: SI 2003/1901 Reg.2, SI 2003/1902, SI 2003/2155 Sch.1 para.45, SI 2003/2983

s.408, varied: SI 2003/3198 Sch.2 para.62

s.408, enabling: SI 2003/3142

s.410, amended: 2004 c.20 s.87

s.410, varied: SI 2003/3195 Art.6, Sch.2 para.99, SI 2003/3197 Art.6, Sch.2 para.96, SI 2003/3198 Art.6, Sch.2 para.63

s.411, applied: SI 2003/2426 Sch.2 para.5, SI 2003/2553 Reg.18, SI 2004/307, SI 2004/309

s.411, varied: SI 2003/3195 Art.6, Sch.2 para.100, SI 2003/3197 Art.6, Sch.2 para.97, SI 2003/3198 Art.6, Sch.2 para.64

s.411, enabling: SI 2003/1900, SI 2003/3142, SI 2003/3195, SI 2003/3197, SI 2003/3198, SI 2004/545, SI 2004/697, SI 2004/715, SI 2004/716, SI 2004/718, SI 2004/1114, SI 2004/1115, SI 2004/1116, SI 2004/1492, SI 2004/3309

Sch.1 para.1, varied: SI 2003/3195 Art.6, Sch.2 para.101, SI 2003/3197 Art.6, Sch.2 para.98, SI 2003/3198 Art.6, Sch.2 para.65

Sch.1 para.2, varied: SI 2003/3195 Art.6, SI 2003/3197 Art.6, SI 2003/3198 Art.6

Sch.1 para.3, varied: SI 2003/3195 Art.6, SI 2003/3197 Art.6, Sch.2 para.98, SI 2003/3198 Art.6

Sch.1 para.4, varied: SI 2003/3195 Art.6, SI 2003/3197 Art.6, Sch.2 para.98, SI 2003/3198 Art.6

Sch.1 para.5, varied: SI 2003/3195 Art.6, SI 2003/3197 Art.6, Sch.2 para.98, SI 2003/3198 Art.6

Sch.1 para.6, varied: SI 2003/3195 Art.6, SI 2003/3197 Art.6, Sch.2 para.98, SI 2003/3198 Art.6, Sch.2 para.65

Sch.1 para.7, varied: SI 2003/3195 Art.6, SI 2003/3197 Art.6, Sch.2 para.98, SI 2003/3198 Art.6, Sch.2 para.65

Sch.1 para.8, varied: SI 2003/3195 Art.6, SI 2003/3197 Art.6, Sch.2 para.98, SI 2003/3198 Art.6

Sch.1 para.9, varied: SI 2003/3195 Art.6, SI 2003/3197 Art.6, Sch.2 para.98, SI 2003/3198 Art.6

Sch.1 para.10, varied: SI 2003/3195 Art.6, SI 2003/3197 Art.6, Sch.2 para.98, SI 2003/3198 Art.6

2003–cont.

21. Communications Act 2003–*cont.*

Sch.1 para.11, varied: SI 2003/3195 Art.6, SI 2003/3197 Art.6, Sch.2 para.98, SI 2003/3198 Art.6

Sch.1 para.12, varied: SI 2003/3195 Art.6, SI 2003/3197 Art.6, Sch.2 para.98, SI 2003/3198 Art.6

Sch.1 para.13, varied: SI 2003/3195 Art.6, SI 2003/3197 Art.6, Sch.2 para.98, SI 2003/3198 Art.6

Sch.1 para.14, varied: SI 2003/3195 Art.6, SI 2003/3197 Art.6, Sch.2 para.98, SI 2003/3198 Art.6

Sch.2 para.1, varied: SI 2003/3197 Art.6, SI 2003/3198 Art.6

Sch.2 para.2, varied: SI 2003/3197 Art.6, SI 2003/3198 Art.6

Sch.2 para.3, varied: SI 2003/3197 Art.6, SI 2003/3198 Art.6

Sch.2 para.4, varied: SI 2003/3197 Art.6, SI 2003/3198 Art.6, Sch.2 para.66

Sch.2 para.5, varied: SI 2003/3195 Sch.2 para.102, SI 2003/3197 Art.6, Sch.2 para.99, SI 2003/3198 Art.6, Sch.2 para.66

Sch.2 para.5A, added: SI 2003/2867 Sch.1 para.33

Sch.2 para.5A, varied: SI 2003/3197 Art.6, SI 2003/3198 Art.6

Sch.2 para.6, varied: SI 2003/3197 Art.6, SI 2003/3198 Art.6

Sch.4 para.3, applied: 1981 c.67 s.28

Sch.5 para.1, varied: SI 2003/3195 Art.6, SI 2003/3197 Art.6, SI 2003/3198 Art.6

Sch.5 para.2, varied: SI 2003/3195 Art.6, SI 2003/3197 Art.6, SI 2003/3198 Art.6

Sch.5 para.3, varied: SI 2003/3195 Art.6, SI 2003/3197 Art.6, SI 2003/3198 Art.6

Sch.5 para.4, varied: SI 2003/3195 Art.6, SI 2003/3197 Art.6, SI 2003/3198 Art.6

Sch.5 para.5, varied: SI 2003/3195 Art.6, SI 2003/3197 Art.6, SI 2003/3198 Art.6

Sch.5 para.6, varied: SI 2003/3195 Art.6, Sch.2 para.103, SI 2003/3197 Art.6, Sch.2 para.100, SI 2003/3198 Art.6

Sch.5 para.7, varied: SI 2003/3195 Art.6, Sch.2 para.103, SI 2003/3197 Art.6, Sch.2 para.100, SI 2003/3198 Art.6

Sch.5 para.8, varied: SI 2003/3195 Art.6, SI 2003/3197 Art.6, SI 2003/3198 Art.6

Sch.7, applied: 1984 c.12 s.79, s.83, s.91

Sch.8 para.1, varied: SI 2003/3195 Art.6, SI 2003/3197 Art.6, SI 2003/3198 Art.6

Sch.8 para.2, varied: SI 2003/3195 Art.6, SI 2003/3197 Art.6, SI 2003/3198 Art.6

Sch.8 para.3, varied: SI 2003/3195 Art.6, Sch.2 para.104, SI 2003/3197 Art.6, Sch.2 para.101, SI 2003/3198 Art.6, Sch.2 para.67

2003–cont.

21. Communications Act 2003–*cont.*

Sch.8 para.4, varied: SI 2003/3195 Art.6, Sch.2 para.104, SI 2003/3197 Art.6, Sch.2 para.101, SI 2003/3198 Art.6, Sch.2 para.67

Sch.8 para.5, varied: SI 2003/3195 Art.6, Sch.2 para.104, SI 2003/3197 Art.6, Sch.2 para.101, SI 2003/3198 Art.6, Sch.2 para.67

Sch.8 para.6, varied: SI 2003/3195 Art.6, Sch.2 para.104, SI 2003/3197 Art.6, Sch.2 para.101, SI 2003/3198 Art.6, Sch.2 para.67

Sch.8 para.7, varied: SI 2003/3195 Art.6, Sch.2 para.104, SI 2003/3197 Art.6, Sch.2 para.101, SI 2003/3198 Art.6, Sch.2 para.67

Sch.8 para.8, varied: SI 2003/3195 Art.6, Sch.2 para.104, SI 2003/3197 Art.6, Sch.2 para.101, SI 2003/3198 Art.6, Sch.2 para.67

Sch.8 para.9, varied: SI 2003/3195 Art.6, Sch.2 para.104, SI 2003/3197 Art.6, Sch.2 para.101, SI 2003/3198 Art.6, Sch.2 para.67

Sch.8 para.10, varied: SI 2003/3195 Art.6, Sch.2 para.104, SI 2003/3197 Art.6, Sch.2 para.101, SI 2003/3198 Art.6, Sch.2 para.67

Sch.8 para.11, varied: SI 2003/3195 Art.6, Sch.2 para.104, SI 2003/3197 Art.6, Sch.2 para.101, SI 2003/3198 Art.6, Sch.2 para.67

Sch.8 para.12, varied: SI 2003/3195 Art.6, Sch.2 para.104, SI 2003/3197 Art.6, Sch.2 para.101, SI 2003/3198 Art.6, Sch.2 para.67

Sch.8 para.13, varied: SI 2003/3195 Art.6, Sch.2 para.104, SI 2003/3197 Art.6, Sch.2 para.101, SI 2003/3198 Art.6

Sch.8 para.14, varied: SI 2003/3195 Art.6, SI 2003/3197 Art.6, SI 2003/3198 Art.6

Sch.8 para.15, varied: SI 2003/3195 Art.6, SI 2003/3197 Art.6, SI 2003/3198 Art.6

Sch.8 para.16, varied: SI 2003/3195 Art.6, Sch.2 para.104, SI 2003/3197 Art.6, Sch.2 para.101, SI 2003/3198 Art.6

Sch.8 para.17, varied: SI 2003/3195 Art.6, SI 2003/3197 Art.6, SI 2003/3198 Art.6, Sch.2 para.67

Sch.8 para.18, varied: SI 2003/3195 Art.6, SI 2003/3197 Art.6, SI 2003/3198 Art.6, Sch.2 para.67

Sch.8 para.19, varied: SI 2003/3195 Art.6, SI 2003/3197 Art.6, SI 2003/3198 Art.6, Sch.2 para.67

Sch.8 para.20, varied: SI 2003/3195 Art.6, SI 2003/3197 Art.6, SI 2003/3198 Art.6, Sch.2 para.67

Sch.8 para.21, varied: SI 2003/3195 Art.6, SI 2003/3197 Art.6, SI 2003/3198 Art.6

2003–cont.

21. Communications Act 2003–cont.

Sch.8 para.22, varied: SI 2003/3195 Art.6, Sch.2 para.104, SI 2003/3197 Art.6, Sch.2 para.101, SI 2003/3198 Art.6

Sch.8 para.23, varied: SI 2003/3195 Art.6, Sch.2 para.104, SI 2003/3197 Art.6, Sch.2 para.101, SI 2003/3198 Art.6

Sch.8 para.24, varied: SI 2003/3195 Art.6, SI 2003/3197 Art.6, SI 2003/3198 Art.6, Sch.2 para.67

Sch.8 para.25, varied: SI 2003/3195 Art.6, Sch.2 para.104, SI 2003/3197 Art.6, Sch.2 para.101, SI 2003/3198 Art.6, Sch.2 para.67

Sch.8 para.26, varied: SI 2003/3195 Art.6, Sch.2 para.104, SI 2003/3197 Art.6, Sch.2 para.101, SI 2003/3198 Art.6

Sch.8 para.27, varied: SI 2003/3195 Art.6, SI 2003/3197 Art.6, SI 2003/3198 Art.6

Sch.8 para.28, varied: SI 2003/3195 Art.6, SI 2003/3197 Art.6, SI 2003/3198 Art.6

Sch.8 para.29, varied: SI 2003/3195 Art.6, SI 2003/3197 Art.6, SI 2003/3198 Art.6

Sch.8 para.30, varied: SI 2003/3195 Art.6, SI 2003/3197 Art.6, SI 2003/3198 Art.6

Sch.8 para.31, varied: SI 2003/3195 Art.6, SI 2003/3197 Art.6, SI 2003/3198 Art.6, Sch.2 para.67

Sch.8 para.32, varied: SI 2003/3195 Art.6, SI 2003/3197 Art.6, SI 2003/3198 Art.6

Sch.8 para.33, varied: SI 2003/3195 Art.6, SI 2003/3197 Art.6, SI 2003/3198 Art.6

Sch.8 para.34, varied: SI 2003/3195 Art.6, SI 2003/3197 Art.6, SI 2003/3198 Art.6

Sch.8 para.35, varied: SI 2003/3195 Art.6, SI 2003/3197 Art.6, SI 2003/3198 Art.6, Sch.2 para.67

Sch.8 para.36, varied: SI 2003/3195 Art.6, SI 2003/3197 Art.6, SI 2003/3198 Art.6, Sch.2 para.67

Sch.9 para.1, varied: SI 2003/3195 Art.6, SI 2003/3197 Art.6, SI 2003/3198 Art.6

Sch.9 para.2, varied: SI 2003/3195 Art.6, SI 2003/3197 Art.6, SI 2003/3198 Art.6

Sch.9 para.3, varied: SI 2003/3195 Art.6, SI 2003/3197 Art.6, SI 2003/3198 Art.6

Sch.9 para.4, varied: SI 2003/3195 Art.6, SI 2003/3197 Art.6, SI 2003/3198 Art.6

Sch.9 para.5, varied: SI 2003/3195 Art.6, SI 2003/3197 Art.6, SI 2003/3198 Art.6

Sch.9 para.6, varied: SI 2003/3195 Art.6, SI 2003/3197 Art.6, SI 2003/3198 Art.6

Sch.9 para.7, varied: SI 2003/3195 Art.6, Sch.2 para.105, SI 2003/3197 Art.6, Sch.2 para.102, SI 2003/3198 Art.6

Sch.9 para.8, varied: SI 2003/3195 Art.6, SI 2003/3197 Art.6, SI 2003/3198 Art.6

Sch.9 para.9, varied: SI 2003/3195 Art.6, SI 2003/3197 Art.6, SI 2003/3198 Art.6

Sch.9 para.10, varied: SI 2003/3195 Art.6, SI 2003/3197 Art.6, SI 2003/3198 Art.6

Sch.10, disapplied: SI 2003/3142 Art.8

2003–cont.

21. Communications Act 2003–cont.

Sch.10 Part 1 para.1, varied: SI 2003/3195 Art.6, SI 2003/3197 Art.6, SI 2003/3198 Art.6

Sch.10 Part 1 para.2, varied: SI 2003/3195 Art.6, SI 2003/3197 Art.6, SI 2003/3198 Art.6

Sch.10 Part 1 para.3, varied: SI 2003/3195 Art.6, SI 2003/3197 Art.6, SI 2003/3198 Art.6, Sch.2 para.68

Sch.10 Part 1 para.4, varied: SI 2003/3195 Art.6, SI 2003/3197 Art.6, SI 2003/3198 Art.6

Sch.10 Part 1 para.5, varied: SI 2003/3195 Art.6, SI 2003/3197 Art.6, SI 2003/3198 Art.6

Sch.10 Part 1 para.6, varied: SI 2003/3195 Art.6, SI 2003/3197 Art.6, SI 2003/3198 Art.6

Sch.10 Part 2 para.7, varied: SI 2003/3195 Art.6, SI 2003/3197 Art.6, SI 2003/3198 Art.6

Sch.10 Part 2 para.8, varied: SI 2003/3195 Art.6, SI 2003/3197 Art.6, SI 2003/3198 Art.6

Sch.10 Part 2 para.9, varied: SI 2003/3195 Art.6, SI 2003/3197 Art.6, SI 2003/3198 Art.6

Sch.10 Part 2 para.10, varied: SI 2003/3195 Art.6, SI 2003/3197 Art.6, SI 2003/3198 Art.6

Sch.10 Part 2 para.11, varied: SI 2003/3195 Art.6, SI 2003/3197 Art.6, SI 2003/3198 Art.6

Sch.10 Part 2 para.12, varied: SI 2003/3195 Art.6, Sch.2 para.2, SI 2003/3197 Art.6, Sch.2 para.1, SI 2003/3198 Art.6

Sch.10 Part 2 para.13, applied: SI 2003/3195 Sch.2 para.2, SI 2003/3197 Sch.2 para.1

Sch.10 Part 2 para.13, varied: SI 2003/3195 Art.6, Sch.2 para.106, SI 2003/3197 Art.6, Sch.2 para.103, SI 2003/3198 Art.6

Sch.10 Part 3 para.14, varied: SI 2003/3195 Art.6, SI 2003/3197 Art.6, SI 2003/3198 Art.6

Sch.10 Part 3 para.15, varied: SI 2003/3195 Art.6, SI 2003/3197 Art.6, SI 2003/3198 Art.6

Sch.11 para.1, varied: SI 2003/3195 Art.6, SI 2003/3197 Art.6

Sch.11 para.2, varied: SI 2003/3195 Art.6, SI 2003/3197 Art.6

Sch.11 para.3, varied: SI 2003/3195 Art.6, SI 2003/3197 Art.6

Sch.11 para.4, varied: SI 2003/3195 Art.6, SI 2003/3197 Art.6

Sch.11 para.5, varied: SI 2003/3195 Art.6, Sch.2 para.107, SI 2003/3197 Art.6, Sch.2 para.104

Sch.11 para.6, varied: SI 2003/3195 Art.6, Sch.2 para.107, SI 2003/3197 Art.6, Sch.2 para.104

2003–cont.

21. Communications Act 2003–*cont.*

Sch.11 para.7, varied: SI 2003/3195 Art.6, SI 2003/3197 Art.6

Sch.11 para.8, varied: SI 2003/3195 Art.6, SI 2003/3197 Art.6

Sch.11 para.9, varied: SI 2003/3195 Art.6, SI 2003/3197 Art.6, Sch.2 para.104

Sch.11 para.10, varied: SI 2003/3195 Art.6, Sch.2 para.107, SI 2003/3197 Art.6, Sch.2 para.104

Sch.11 para.11, varied: SI 2003/3195 Art.6, Sch.2 para.107, SI 2003/3197 Art.6, Sch.2 para.104

Sch.11 para.12, varied: SI 2003/3195 Art.6, SI 2003/3197 Art.6

Sch.11 para.13, varied: SI 2003/3195 Art.6, Sch.2 para.107, SI 2003/3197 Art.6, Sch.2 para.104

Sch.11 para.14, varied: SI 2003/3195 Art.6, SI 2003/3197 Art.6

Sch.11 para.15, varied: SI 2003/3195 Art.6, Sch.2 para.107, SI 2003/3197 Art.6, Sch.2 para.104

Sch.12 Part 1 para.1, varied: SI 2003/3195 Art.6, Sch.2 para.108, SI 2003/3197 Art.6, Sch.2 para.105

Sch.12 Part 1 para.2, varied: SI 2003/3195 Art.6, SI 2003/3197 Art.6

Sch.12 Part 2, applied: 1990 c.42 s.176, 1996 c.55 s.33, s.107

Sch.12 Part 2 para.3, applied: 1990 c.42 s.58

Sch.12 Part 2 para.3, referred to: 1990 c.42 s.58

Sch.12 Part 2 para.3, varied: SI 2003/3195 Art.6, Sch.2 para.108, SI 2003/3197 Art.6, Sch.2 para.105

Sch.12 Part 2 para.4, varied: SI 2003/3195 Art.6, Sch.2 para.108, SI 2003/3197 Art.6, Sch.2 para.105

Sch.12 Part 2 para.5, varied: SI 2003/3195 Art.6, Sch.2 para.108, SI 2003/3197 Art.6, Sch.2 para.105

Sch.12 Part 2 para.6, varied: SI 2003/3195 Art.6, Sch.2 para.108, SI 2003/3197 Art.6, Sch.2 para.105

Sch.12 Part 2 para.7, varied: SI 2003/3195 Art.6, Sch.2 para.108, SI 2003/3197 Art.6, Sch.2 para.105

Sch.12 Part 2 para.8, applied: SI 2004/1652

Sch.12 Part 2 para.8, referred to: SI 2004/1652 Art.4

Sch.12 Part 2 para.8, varied: SI 2003/3195 Art.6, Sch.2 para.108, SI 2003/3197 Art.6, Sch.2 para.105

Sch.12 Part 2 para.8, enabling: SI 2004/1652

Sch.12 Part 2 para.9, varied: SI 2003/3195 Art.6, Sch.2 para.108, SI 2003/3197 Art.6, Sch.2 para.105

Sch.12 Part 2 para.10, varied: SI 2003/3195 Art.6, Sch.2 para.108, SI 2003/3197 Art.6, Sch.2 para.105

2003–cont.

21. Communications Act 2003–*cont.*

Sch.12 Part 2 para.11, varied: SI 2003/3195 Art.6, Sch.2 para.108, SI 2003/3197 Art.6, Sch.2 para.105

Sch.12 Part 2 para.12, varied: SI 2003/3195 Art.6, Sch.2 para.108, SI 2003/3197 Art.6, Sch.2 para.105

Sch.12 Part 2 para.13, varied: SI 2003/3195 Art.6, Sch.2 para.108, SI 2003/3197 Art.6, Sch.2 para.105

Sch.12 Part 2 para.14, applied: SI 1988/915 Reg.11, SI 1994/1933 Reg.11, SI 2004/1975 Sch.1 para.1

Sch.12 Part 2 para.14, varied: SI 2003/3195 Art.6, Sch.2 para.108, SI 2003/3197 Art.6, Sch.2 para.105

Sch.12 Part 2 para.15, applied: SI 2004/1975 Sch.1 para.2

Sch.12 Part 2 para.15, varied: SI 2003/3195 Art.6, Sch.2 para.108, SI 2003/3197 Art.6, Sch.2 para.105

Sch.12 Part 2 para.16, applied: SI 2004/1975 Art.5

Sch.12 Part 2 para.16, varied: SI 2003/3195 Art.6, Sch.2 para.108, SI 2003/3197 Art.6, Sch.2 para.105

Sch.12 Part 2 para.17, varied: SI 2003/3195 Art.6, Sch.2 para.108, SI 2003/3197 Art.6, Sch.2 para.105

Sch.12 Part 2 para.18, varied: SI 2003/3195 Art.6, Sch.2 para.108, SI 2003/3197 Art.6, Sch.2 para.105

Sch.12 Part 2 para.19, varied: SI 2003/3195 Art.6, Sch.2 para.108, SI 2003/3197 Art.6, Sch.2 para.105

Sch.12 Part 2 para.20, applied: 1988 c.48 s.69, Sch.2 para.17

Sch.12 Part 2 para.20, varied: SI 2003/3195 Art.6, Sch.2 para.108, SI 2003/3197 Art.6, Sch.2 para.105

Sch.12 Part 2 para.21, varied: SI 2003/3195 Art.6, Sch.2 para.108, SI 2003/3197 Art.6, Sch.2 para.105

Sch.12 Part 2 para.22, varied: SI 2003/3195 Art.6, Sch.2 para.108, SI 2003/3197 Art.6, Sch.2 para.105

Sch.12 Part 2 para.23, varied: SI 2003/3195 Art.6, Sch.2 para.108, SI 2003/3197 Art.6, Sch.2 para.105

Sch.12 Part 2 para.24, varied: SI 2003/3195 Art.6, Sch.2 para.108, SI 2003/3197 Art.6, Sch.2 para.105

Sch.13 Part 1 para.1, varied: SI 2003/3195 Art.6, SI 2003/3197 Art.6, SI 2003/3198 Art.6

Sch.13 Part 1 para.2, varied: SI 2003/3195 Art.6, Sch.2 para.109, SI 2003/3197 Art.6, Sch.2 para.106, SI 2003/3198 Art.6

Sch.13 Part 1 para.3, varied: SI 2003/3195 Art.6, Sch.2 para.109, SI 2003/3197 Art.6, Sch.2 para.106, SI 2003/3198 Art.6

2003–cont.

21. Communications Act 2003–*cont.*

Sch.13 Part 1 para.4, varied: SI 2003/3195
Art.6, Sch.2 para.109, SI 2003/3197
Art.6, Sch.2 para.106, SI 2003/3198
Art.6, Sch.2 para.69

Sch.13 Part 1 para.5, varied: SI 2003/3195
Art.6, Sch.2 para.109, SI 2003/3197
Art.6, Sch.2 para.106, SI 2003/3198 Art.6

Sch.13 Part 1 para.6, varied: SI 2003/3195
Art.6, Sch.2 para.109, SI 2003/3197
Art.6, Sch.2 para.106, SI 2003/3198 Art.6

Sch.13 Part 1 para.7, varied: SI 2003/3195
Art.6, Sch.2 para.109, SI 2003/3197
Art.6, Sch.2 para.106, SI 2003/3198 Art.6

Sch.13 Part 1 para.8, varied: SI 2003/3195
Art.6, Sch.2 para.109, SI 2003/3197
Art.6, Sch.2 para.106, SI 2003/3198 Art.6

Sch.13 Part 1 para.9, varied: SI 2003/3195
Art.6, Sch.2 para.109, SI 2003/3197
Art.6, Sch.2 para.106, SI 2003/3198 Art.6

Sch.13 Part 2 para.10, varied: SI 2003/3195
Art.6, SI 2003/3197 Art.6, SI 2003/3198
Art.6

Sch.13 Part 2 para.11, varied: SI 2003/3195
Art.6, Sch.2 para.109, SI 2003/3197
Art.6, Sch.2 para.106, SI 2003/3198 Art.6

Sch.13 Part 2 para.12, varied: SI 2003/3195
Art.6, SI 2003/3197 Art.6, SI 2003/3198
Art.6

Sch.13 Part 2 para.13, varied: SI 2003/3195
Art.6, Sch.2 para.109, SI 2003/3197
Art.6, Sch.2 para.106, SI 2003/3198 Art.6

Sch.13 Part 2 para.14, varied: SI 2003/3195
Art.6, Sch.2 para.109, SI 2003/3197
Art.6, Sch.2 para.106, SI 2003/3198 Art.6

Sch.13 Part 2 para.15, varied: SI 2003/3195
Art.6, Sch.2 para.109, SI 2003/3197
Art.6, Sch.2 para.106, SI 2003/3198 Art.6

Sch.13 Part 2 para.16, referred to: SI 2003/
3197 Sch.2 para.106

Sch.13 Part 2 para.16, varied: SI 2003/3195
Art.6, Sch.2 para.109, SI 2003/3197
Art.6, Sch.2 para.106, SI 2003/3198 Art.6

Sch.13 Part 2 para.17, varied: SI 2003/3195
Art.6, Sch.2 para.109, SI 2003/3197
Art.6, Sch.2 para.106, SI 2003/3198 Art.6

Sch.13 Part 2 para.18, varied: SI 2003/3195
Art.6, SI 2003/3197 Art.6, SI 2003/3198
Art.6

Sch.13 Part 2 para.19, varied: SI 2003/3195
Art.6, Sch.2 para.109, SI 2003/3197
Art.6, Sch.2 para.106, SI 2003/3198 Art.6

Sch.13 Part 2 para.20, varied: SI 2003/3195
Art.6, Sch.2 para.109, SI 2003/3197 Art.6,
Sch.2 para.106, SI 2003/3198 Art.6

Sch.13 Part 2 para.21, varied: SI 2003/3195
Art.6, Sch.2 para.109, SI 2003/3197
Art.6, Sch.2 para.106, SI 2003/3198 Art.6

Sch.13 Part 2 para.22, referred to: SI 2003/
3197 Sch.2 para.106

2003–cont.

21. Communications Act 2003–*cont.*

Sch.13 Part 2 para.22, varied: SI 2003/3195
Art.6, Sch.2 para.109, SI 2003/3197 Art.6,
Sch.2 para.106, SI 2003/3198 Art.6

Sch.14, applied: 1990 c.42 s.5, s.88, s.115,
1996 c.55 s.5, s.44, SI 2004/1944

Sch.14 Part 1, applied: 1990 c.42 s.5, s.88,
1996 c.55 s.5, s.44

Sch.14 Part 1 para.1, varied: SI 2003/3195
Art.6, SI 2003/3197 Art.6, SI 2003/3198
Art.6

Sch.14 Part 1 para.2, varied: SI 2003/3195
Art.6, SI 2003/3197 Art.6, SI 2003/3198
Art.6

Sch.14 Part 1 para.3, applied: SI 2003/3299
Art.4

Sch.14 Part 1 para.3, varied: SI 2003/3195
Art.6, Sch.2 para.110, SI 2003/3197 Art.6,
Sch.2 para.107, SI 2003/3198 Art.6, Sch.2
para.70

Sch.14 Part 1 para.4, applied: SI 2003/3299
Art.4

Sch.14 Part 1 para.4, varied: SI 2003/3195
Art.6, SI 2003/3197 Art.6, SI 2003/3198
Art.6

Sch.14 Part 1 para.5, varied: SI 2003/3195
Art.6, SI 2003/3197 Art.6, SI 2003/3198
Art.6, Sch.2 para.70

Sch.14 Part 1 para.6, varied: SI 2003/3195
Art.6, Sch.2 para.110, SI 2003/3197 Art.6,
Sch.2 para.107, SI 2003/3198 Art.6

Sch.14 Part 2 para.7, varied: SI 2003/3195
Art.6, SI 2003/3197 Art.6, SI 2003/3198
Art.6

Sch.14 Part 2 para.8, amended: SI 2003/
3299 Art.14

Sch.14 Part 2 para.8, repealed (in part): SI
2003/3299 Art.14

Sch.14 Part 2 para.8, varied: SI 2003/3195
Art.6, SI 2003/3197 Art.6, SI 2003/3198
Art.6, Sch.2 para.70

Sch.14 Part 2 para.9, varied: SI 2003/3195
Art.6, SI 2003/3197 Art.6, SI 2003/3198
Art.6

Sch.14 Part 2 para.10, varied: SI 2003/3195
Art.6, Sch.2 para.110, SI 2003/3197 Art.6,
Sch.2 para.107, SI 2003/3198 Art.6

Sch.14 Part 2 para.10, enabling: SI 2003/
3299

Sch.14 Part 3 para.11, varied: SI 2003/3195
Art.6, Sch.2 para.110, SI 2003/3197 Art.6,
Sch.2 para.107, SI 2003/3198 Art.6, Sch.2
para.70

Sch.14 Part 3 para.11, enabling: SI 2003/
3299, SI 2004/1944

Sch.14 Part 3 para.12, varied: SI 2003/3195
Art.6, Sch.2 para.110, SI 2003/3197 Art.6,
Sch.2 para.107, SI 2003/3198 Art.6, Sch.2
para.70

Sch.14 Part 3 para.12, enabling: SI 2003/
3299

2003–cont.

21. Communications Act 2003–*cont.*

Sch.14 Part 3 para.13, varied: SI 2003/3195 Art.6, SI 2003/3197 Art.6, SI 2003/3198 Art.6, Sch.2 para.70

Sch.14 Part 3 para.13, enabling: SI 2003/3299, SI 2004/1944

Sch.14 Part 3 para.14, varied: SI 2003/3195 Art.6, SI 2003/3197 Art.6, SI 2003/3198 Art.6, Sch.2 para.70

Sch.14 Part 4, applied: SI 2003/1900 Art.5

Sch.14 Part 4 para.15, varied: SI 2003/3195 Art.6, SI 2003/3197 Art.6, SI 2003/3198 Art.6

Sch.14 Part 4 para.16, varied: SI 2003/3195 Art.6, Sch.2 para.110, SI 2003/3197 Art.6, Sch.2 para.107, SI 2003/3198 Art.6

Sch.14 Part 5 para.17, applied: SI 2003/3299, SI 2004/1944

Sch.14 Part 5 para.17, varied: SI 2003/3195 Art.6, Sch.2 para.110, SI 2003/3197 Art.6, Sch.2 para.107, SI 2003/3198 Art.6

Sch.14 Part 5 para.18, varied: SI 2003/3195 Art.6, SI 2003/3197 Art.6, SI 2003/3198 Art.6

Sch.15 Part 1 para.1, varied: SI 2003/3195 Art.6, SI 2003/3197 Art.6, SI 2003/3198 Art.6, Sch.2 para.71

Sch.15 Part 1 para.2, varied: SI 2003/3195 Art.6, SI 2003/3197 Art.6, SI 2003/3198 Art.6

Sch.15 Part 1 para.3, varied: SI 2003/3195 Art.6, SI 2003/3197 Art.6, SI 2003/3198 Art.6

Sch.15 Part 1 para.4, varied: SI 2003/3195 Art.6, SI 2003/3197 Art.6, SI 2003/3198 Art.6

Sch.15 Part 1 para.5, varied: SI 2003/3195 Art.6, SI 2003/3197 Art.6, SI 2003/3198 Art.6, Sch.2 para.71

Sch.15 Part 1 para.6, varied: SI 2003/3195 Art.6, SI 2003/3197 Art.6, SI 2003/3198 Art.6

Sch.15 Part 1 para.7, varied: SI 2003/3195 Art.6, SI 2003/3197 Art.6, SI 2003/3198 Art.6

Sch.15 Part 1 para.8, varied: SI 2003/3195 Art.6, SI 2003/3197 Art.6, SI 2003/3198 Art.6

Sch.15 Part 1 para.9, varied: SI 2003/3195 Art.6, SI 2003/3197 Art.6, SI 2003/3198 Art.6

Sch.15 Part 1 para.10, varied: SI 2003/3195 Art.6, SI 2003/3197 Art.6, SI 2003/3198 Art.6

Sch.15 Part 1 para.11, varied: SI 2003/3195 Art.6, SI 2003/3197 Art.6, SI 2003/3198 Art.6

Sch.15 Part 1 para.12, varied: SI 2003/3195 Art.6, SI 2003/3197 Art.6, SI 2003/3198 Art.6

2003–cont.

21. Communications Act 2003–*cont.*

Sch.15 Part 1 para.13, varied: SI 2003/3195 Art.6, SI 2003/3197 Art.6, SI 2003/3198 Art.6

Sch.15 Part 1 para.14, varied: SI 2003/3195 Art.6, SI 2003/3197 Art.6, SI 2003/3198 Art.6

Sch.15 Part 1 para.15, varied: SI 2003/3195 Art.6, SI 2003/3197 Art.6, SI 2003/3198 Art.6

Sch.15 Part 1 para.16, varied: SI 2003/3195 Art.6, SI 2003/3197 Art.6, SI 2003/3198 Art.6

Sch.15 Part 1 para.17, varied: SI 2003/3195 Art.6, SI 2003/3197 Art.6, SI 2003/3198 Art.6

Sch.15 Part 1 para.18, varied: SI 2003/3195 Art.6, SI 2003/3197 Art.6, SI 2003/3198 Art.6, Sch.2 para.71

Sch.15 Part 1 para.19, varied: SI 2003/3195 Art.6, SI 2003/3197 Art.6, SI 2003/3198 Art.6, Sch.2 para.71

Sch.15 Part 1 para.20, varied: SI 2003/3195 Art.6, Sch.2 para.111, SI 2003/3197 Art.6, Sch.2 para.108, SI 2003/3198 Art.6

Sch.15 Part 1 para.21, disapplied: SI 2003/3142 Art.8

Sch.15 Part 1 para.21, varied: SI 2003/3195 Art.6, SI 2003/3197 Art.6, SI 2003/3198 Art.6

Sch.15 Part 1 para.22, varied: SI 2003/3195 Art.6, SI 2003/3197 Art.6, SI 2003/3198 Art.6

Sch.15 Part 1 para.23, varied: SI 2003/3195 Art.6, SI 2003/3197 Art.6, SI 2003/3198 Art.6

Sch.15 Part 1 para.24, varied: SI 2003/3195 Art.6, SI 2003/3197 Art.6, SI 2003/3198 Art.6

Sch.15 Part 1 para.25, varied: SI 2003/3195 Art.6, SI 2003/3197 Art.6, SI 2003/3198 Art.6

Sch.15 Part 1 para.26, varied: SI 2003/3195 Art.6, SI 2003/3197 Art.6, SI 2003/3198 Art.6

Sch.15 Part 1 para.27, varied: SI 2003/3195 Art.6, SI 2003/3197 Art.6, SI 2003/3198 Art.6, Sch.2 para.71

Sch.15 Part 1 para.28, varied: SI 2003/3195 Art.6, Sch.2 para.111, SI 2003/3197 Art.6, Sch.2 para.108, SI 2003/3198 Art.6, Sch.2 para.71

Sch.15 Part 1 para.29, varied: SI 2003/3195 Art.6, SI 2003/3197 Art.6, SI 2003/3198 Art.6

Sch.15 Part 1 para.30, varied: SI 2003/3195 Art.6, SI 2003/3197 Art.6, SI 2003/3198 Art.6

Sch.15 Part 1 para.31, varied: SI 2003/3195 Art.6, Sch.2 para.111, SI 2003/3197 Art.6, Sch.2 para.108, SI 2003/3198 Art.6, Sch.2 para.71

2003–cont.

21. Communications Act 2003–*cont.*

Sch.15 Part 1 para.32, varied: SI 2003/3195 Art.6, Sch.2 para.111, SI 2003/3197 Art.6, Sch.2 para.108, SI 2003/3198 Art.6

Sch.15 Part 1 para.33, varied: SI 2003/3195 Art.6, SI 2003/3197 Art.6, SI 2003/3198 Art.6

Sch.15 Part 1 para.34, varied: SI 2003/3195 Art.6, SI 2003/3197 Art.6, SI 2003/3198 Art.6

Sch.15 Part 1 para.35, varied: SI 2003/3195 Art.6, SI 2003/3197 Art.6, SI 2003/3198 Art.6

Sch.15 Part 1 para.36, varied: SI 2003/3195 Art.6, SI 2003/3197 Art.6, SI 2003/3198 Art.6, Sch.2 para.71

Sch.15 Part 1 para.37, varied: SI 2003/3195 Art.6, SI 2003/3197 Art.6, SI 2003/3198 Art.6, Sch.2 para.71

Sch.15 Part 1 para.38, varied: SI 2003/3195 Art.6, SI 2003/3197 Art.6, SI 2003/3198 Art.6

Sch.15 Part 1 para.39, varied: SI 2003/3195 Art.6, SI 2003/3197 Art.6, SI 2003/3198 Art.6

Sch.15 Part 1 para.40, varied: SI 2003/3195 Art.6, SI 2003/3197 Art.6, SI 2003/3198 Art.6

Sch.15 Part 1 para.41, varied: SI 2003/3195 Art.6, SI 2003/3197 Art.6, SI 2003/3198 Art.6

Sch.15 Part 1 para.42, varied: SI 2003/3195 Art.6, SI 2003/3197 Art.6, SI 2003/3198 Art.6

Sch.15 Part 1 para.43, varied: SI 2003/3195 Art.6, SI 2003/3197 Art.6, SI 2003/3198 Art.6

Sch.15 Part 1 para.44, varied: SI 2003/3195 Art.6, SI 2003/3197 Art.6, SI 2003/3198 Art.6

Sch.15 Part 1 para.45, varied: SI 2003/3195 Art.6, SI 2003/3197 Art.6, SI 2003/3198 Art.6, Sch.2 para.71

Sch.15 Part 1 para.46, varied: SI 2003/3195 Art.6, SI 2003/3197 Art.6, SI 2003/3198 Art.6, Sch.2 para.71

Sch.15 Part 1 para.47, varied: SI 2003/3195 Art.6, SI 2003/3197 Art.6, SI 2003/3198 Art.6, Sch.2 para.71

Sch.15 Part 1 para.48, varied: SI 2003/3195 Art.6, SI 2003/3197 Art.6, SI 2003/3198 Art.6, Sch.2 para.71

Sch.15 Part 1 para.49, varied: SI 2003/3195 Art.6, SI 2003/3197 Art.6, SI 2003/3198 Art.6

Sch.15 Part 1 para.50, varied: SI 2003/3195 Art.6, SI 2003/3197 Art.6, SI 2003/3198 Art.6

Sch.15 Part 1 para.51, varied: SI 2003/3195 Art.6, SI 2003/3197 Art.6, SI 2003/3198 Art.6, Sch.2 para.71

2003–cont.

21. Communications Act 2003–*cont.*

Sch.15 Part 1 para.52, varied: SI 2003/3195 Art.6, SI 2003/3197 Art.6, SI 2003/3198 Art.6

Sch.15 Part 1 para.53, varied: SI 2003/3195 Art.6, SI 2003/3197 Art.6, SI 2003/3198 Art.6

Sch.15 Part 1 para.54, varied: SI 2003/3195 Art.6, SI 2003/3197 Art.6, SI 2003/3198 Art.6

Sch.15 Part 1 para.55, varied: SI 2003/3195 Art.6, SI 2003/3197 Art.6, SI 2003/3198 Art.6

Sch.15 Part 1 para.56, varied: SI 2003/3195 Art.6, SI 2003/3197 Art.6, SI 2003/3198 Art.6

Sch.15 Part 1 para.57, varied: SI 2003/3195 Art.6, SI 2003/3197 Art.6, SI 2003/3198 Art.6

Sch.15 Part 1 para.58, varied: SI 2003/3195 Art.6, SI 2003/3197 Art.6, SI 2003/3198 Art.6

Sch.15 Part 1 para.59, varied: SI 2003/3195 Art.6, SI 2003/3197 Art.6, SI 2003/3198 Art.6

Sch.15 Part 1 para.60, varied: SI 2003/3195 Art.6, Sch.2 para.111, SI 2003/3197 Art.6, Sch.2 para.108, SI 2003/3198 Art.6

Sch.15 Part 1 para.61, varied: SI 2003/3195 Art.6, SI 2003/3197 Art.6, SI 2003/3198 Art.6, Sch.2 para.71

Sch.15 Part 1 para.62, varied: SI 2003/3195 Art.6, Sch.2 para.111, SI 2003/3197 Art.6, Sch.2 para.108, SI 2003/3198 Art.6, Sch.2 para.71

Sch.15 Part 1 para.63, varied: SI 2003/3195 Art.6, Sch.2 para.111, SI 2003/3197 Art.6, Sch.2 para.108, SI 2003/3198 Art.6, Sch.2 para.71

Sch.15 Part 1 para.64, varied: SI 2003/3195 Art.6, Sch.2 para.111, SI 2003/3197 Art.6, SI 2003/3198 Art.6

Sch.15 Part 1 para.65, varied: SI 2003/3195 Art.6, SI 2003/3197 Art.6, SI 2003/3198 Art.6, Sch.2 para.71

Sch.15 Part 1 para.66, varied: SI 2003/3195 Art.6, SI 2003/3197 Art.6, Sch.2 para.108, SI 2003/3198 Art.6

Sch.15 Part 1 para.67, varied: SI 2003/3195 Art.6, SI 2003/3197 Art.6, SI 2003/3198 Art.6

Sch.15 Part 1 para.68, varied: SI 2003/3195 Art.6, SI 2003/3197 Art.6, SI 2003/3198 Art.6

Sch.15 Part 1 para.69, varied: SI 2003/3195 Art.6, SI 2003/3197 Art.6, SI 2003/3198 Art.6

Sch.15 Part 1 para.70, varied: SI 2003/3195 Art.6, SI 2003/3197 Art.6, SI 2003/3198 Art.6

2003–cont.

21. Communications Act 2003–*cont.*
Sch.15 Part 1 para.71, varied: SI 2003/3195
Art.6, Sch.2 para.111, SI 2003/3197 Art.6,
Sch.2 para.108, SI 2003/3198 Art.6,
Sch.2 para.71
Sch.15 Part 1 para.72, varied: SI 2003/3195
Art.6, SI 2003/3197 Art.6, SI 2003/3198
Art.6
Sch.15 Part 1 para.73, varied: SI 2003/3195
Art.6, Sch.2 para.111, SI 2003/3197 Art.6,
Sch.2 para.108, SI 2003/3198 Art.6,
Sch.2 para.71
Sch.15 Part 2 para.74, varied: SI 2003/3195
Art.6, Sch.2 para.111, SI 2003/3197 Art.6,
Sch.2 para.108, SI 2003/3198 Art.6,
Sch.2 para.71
Sch.15 Part 2 para.75, varied: SI 2003/3195
Art.6, Sch.2 para.111, SI 2003/3197 Art.6,
Sch.2 para.108, SI 2003/3198 Art.6,
Sch.2 para.71
Sch.15 Part 2 para.76, varied: SI 2003/3195
Art.6, SI 2003/3197 Art.6, SI 2003/3198
Art.6, Sch.2 para.71
Sch.15 Part 2 para.77, varied: SI 2003/3195
Art.6, SI 2003/3197 Art.6, SI 2003/3198
Art.6
Sch.15 Part 2 para.78, varied: SI 2003/3195
Art.6, SI 2003/3197 Art.6, SI 2003/3198
Art.6
Sch.15 Part 2 para.79, varied: SI 2003/3195
Art.6, SI 2003/3197 Art.6, SI 2003/3198
Art.6
Sch.15 Part 2 para.80, varied: SI 2003/3195
Art.6, SI 2003/3197 Art.6, SI 2003/3198
Art.6
Sch.15 Part 2 para.81, varied: SI 2003/3195
Art.6, SI 2003/3197 Art.6, SI 2003/3198
Art.6
Sch.15 Part 2 para.82, varied: SI 2003/3195
Art.6, SI 2003/3197 Art.6, SI 2003/3198
Art.6
Sch.15 Part 2 para.83, varied: SI 2003/3195
Art.6, SI 2003/3197 Art.6, SI 2003/3198
Art.6
Sch.15 Part 2 para.84, varied: SI 2003/3195
Art.6, SI 2003/3197 Art.6, SI 2003/3198
Art.6
Sch.15 Part 2 para.85, varied: SI 2003/3195
Art.6, SI 2003/3197 Art.6, SI 2003/3198
Art.6
Sch.15 Part 2 para.86, varied: SI 2003/3195
Art.6, SI 2003/3197 Art.6, SI 2003/3198
Art.6
Sch.15 Part 2 para.87, varied: SI 2003/3195
Art.6, SI 2003/3197 Art.6, SI 2003/3198
Art.6
Sch.15 Part 2 para.88, varied: SI 2003/3195
Art.6, SI 2003/3197 Art.6, SI 2003/3198
Art.6
Sch.15 Part 2 para.89, varied: SI 2003/3195
Art.6, SI 2003/3197 Art.6, SI 2003/3198
Art.6

2003–cont.

21. Communications Act 2003–*cont.*
Sch.15 Part 2 para.90, varied: SI 2003/3195
Art.6, SI 2003/3197 Art.6, SI 2003/3198
Art.6
Sch.15 Part 2 para.91, varied: SI 2003/3195
Art.6, SI 2003/3197 Art.6, SI 2003/3198
Art.6
Sch.15 Part 2 para.92, varied: SI 2003/3195
Art.6, SI 2003/3197 Art.6, SI 2003/3198
Art.6
Sch.15 Part 2 para.93, varied: SI 2003/3195
Art.6, Sch.2 para.111, SI 2003/3197 Art.6,
Sch.2 para.108, SI 2003/3198 Art.6,
Sch.2 para.71
Sch.15 Part 2 para.94, varied: SI 2003/3195
Art.6, SI 2003/3197 Art.6, SI 2003/3198
Art.6, Sch.2 para.71
Sch.15 Part 2 para.95, varied: SI 2003/3195
Art.6, SI 2003/3197 Art.6, SI 2003/3198
Art.6
Sch.15 Part 2 para.96, varied: SI 2003/3195
Art.6, SI 2003/3197 Art.6, SI 2003/3198
Art.6
Sch.15 Part 2 para.97, varied: SI 2003/3195
Art.6, Sch.2 para.111, SI 2003/3197 Art.6,
Sch.2 para.108, SI 2003/3198 Art.6,
Sch.2 para.71
Sch.15 Part 2 para.98, varied: SI 2003/3195
Art.6, Sch.2 para.111, SI 2003/3197 Art.6,
Sch.2 para.108, SI 2003/3198 Art.6,
Sch.2 para.71
Sch.15 Part 2 para.99, varied: SI 2003/3195
Art.6, SI 2003/3197 Art.6, SI 2003/3198
Art.6
Sch.15 Part 2 para.100, varied: SI 2003/3195
Art.6, Sch.2 para.111, SI 2003/3197 Art.6,
Sch.2 para.108, SI 2003/3198 Art.6,
Sch.2 para.71
Sch.15 Part 2 para.101, varied: SI 2003/3195
Art.6, SI 2003/3197 Art.6, SI 2003/3198
Art.6
Sch.15 Part 2 para.102, varied: SI 2003/3195
Art.6, SI 2003/3197 Art.6, SI 2003/3198
Art.6, Sch.2 para.71
Sch.15 Part 2 para.103, varied: SI 2003/3195
Art.6, SI 2003/3197 Art.6, SI 2003/3198
Art.6
Sch.15 Part 2 para.104, varied: SI 2003/3195
Art.6, SI 2003/3197 Art.6, SI 2003/3198
Art.6
Sch.15 Part 2 para.105, varied: SI 2003/3195
Art.6, SI 2003/3197 Art.6, SI 2003/3198
Art.6
Sch.15 Part 2 para.106, varied: SI 2003/3195
Art.6, SI 2003/3197 Art.6, SI 2003/3198
Art.6
Sch.15 Part 2 para.107, varied: SI 2003/3195
Art.6, SI 2003/3197 Art.6, SI 2003/3198
Art.6
Sch.15 Part 2 para.108, varied: SI 2003/3195
Art.6, SI 2003/3197 Art.6, Sch.2 para.108,
SI 2003/3198 Art.6, Sch.2 para.71

2003–cont.

21. Communications Act 2003–*cont.*

Sch.15 Part 2 para.109, varied: SI 2003/3195 Art.6, SI 2003/3197 Art.6, SI 2003/3198 Art.6, Sch.2 para.71

Sch.15 Part 2 para.110, varied: SI 2003/3195 Art.6, SI 2003/3197 Art.6, SI 2003/3198 Art.6, Sch.2 para.71

Sch.15 Part 2 para.111, varied: SI 2003/3195 Art.6, SI 2003/3197 Art.6, SI 2003/3198 Art.6, Sch.2 para.71

Sch.15 Part 2 para.112, varied: SI 2003/3195 Art.6, SI 2003/3197 Art.6, SI 2003/3198 Art.6

Sch.15 Part 2 para.113, varied: SI 2003/3195 Art.6, SI 2003/3197 Art.6, SI 2003/3198 Art.6

Sch.15 Part 2 para.114, varied: SI 2003/3195 Art.6, SI 2003/3197 Art.6, SI 2003/3198 Art.6

Sch.15 Part 2 para.115, varied: SI 2003/3195 Art.6, SI 2003/3197 Art.6, SI 2003/3198 Art.6

Sch.15 Part 2 para.116, varied: SI 2003/3195 Art.6, SI 2003/3197 Art.6, SI 2003/3198 Art.6

Sch.15 Part 2 para.117, varied: SI 2003/3195 Art.6, SI 2003/3197 Art.6, SI 2003/3198 Art.6, Sch.2 para.71

Sch.15 Part 2 para.118, varied: SI 2003/3195 Art.6, SI 2003/3197 Art.6, SI 2003/3198 Art.6

Sch.15 Part 2 para.119, varied: SI 2003/3195 Art.6, SI 2003/3197 Art.6, SI 2003/3198 Art.6

Sch.15 Part 2 para.120, varied: SI 2003/3195 Art.6, SI 2003/3197 Art.6, SI 2003/3198 Art.6

Sch.15 Part 2 para.121, varied: SI 2003/3195 Art.6, SI 2003/3197 Art.6, SI 2003/3198 Art.6

Sch.15 Part 2 para.121A, varied: SI 2003/3195 Art.6, SI 2003/3197 Art.6, SI 2003/3198 Art.6, Sch.2 para.71

Sch.15 Part 2 para.122, varied: SI 2003/3195 Art.6, SI 2003/3197 Art.6, SI 2003/3198 Art.6

Sch.15 Part 2 para.123, varied: SI 2003/3195 Art.6, SI 2003/3197 Art.6, SI 2003/3198 Art.6

Sch.15 Part 2 para.124, varied: SI 2003/3195 Art.6, SI 2003/3197 Art.6, SI 2003/3198 Art.6

Sch.15 Part 2 para.125, varied: SI 2003/3195 Art.6, SI 2003/3197 Art.6, SI 2003/3198 Art.6

Sch.15 Part 2 para.125A, varied: SI 2003/3195 Art.6, SI 2003/3197 Art.6, SI 2003/3198 Art.6, Sch.2 para.71

Sch.15 Part 2 para.126, varied: SI 2003/3195 Art.6, SI 2003/3197 Art.6, SI 2003/3198 Art.6

2003–cont.

21. Communications Act 2003–*cont.*

Sch.15 Part 2 para.127, varied: SI 2003/3195 Art.6, Sch.2 para.111, SI 2003/3197 Art.6, Sch.2 para.108, SI 2003/3198 Art.6

Sch.15 Part 2 para.128, varied: SI 2003/3195 Art.6, SI 2003/3197 Art.6, SI 2003/3198 Art.6

Sch.15 Part 2 para.129, varied: SI 2003/3195 Art.6, SI 2003/3197 Art.6, SI 2003/3198 Art.6

Sch.15 Part 2 para.130, varied: SI 2003/3195 Art.6, SI 2003/3197 Art.6, SI 2003/3198 Art.6

Sch.15 Part 2 para.131, varied: SI 2003/3195 Art.6, SI 2003/3197 Art.6, SI 2003/3198 Art.6

Sch.15 Part 2 para.132, varied: SI 2003/3195 Art.6, SI 2003/3197 Art.6, SI 2003/3198 Art.6

Sch.15 Part 2 para.133, varied: SI 2003/3195 Art.6, Sch.2 para.111, SI 2003/3197 Art.6, Sch.2 para.108, SI 2003/3198 Art.6, Sch.2 para.71

Sch.15 Part 2 para.134, varied: SI 2003/3195 Art.6, SI 2003/3197 Art.6, SI 2003/3198 Art.6

Sch.15 Part 2 para.135, varied: SI 2003/3195 Art.6, SI 2003/3197 Art.6, SI 2003/3198 Art.6

Sch.15 Part 2 para.136, varied: SI 2003/3195 Art.6, SI 2003/3197 Art.6, SI 2003/3198 Art.6

Sch.15 Part 2 para.137, varied: SI 2003/3195 Art.6, SI 2003/3197 Art.6, SI 2003/3198 Art.6

Sch.15 Part 2 para.138, varied: SI 2003/3195 Art.6, SI 2003/3197 Art.6, SI 2003/3198 Art.6

Sch.15 Part 2 para.139, varied: SI 2003/3195 Art.6, SI 2003/3197 Art.6, SI 2003/3198 Art.6

Sch.15 Part 2 para.140, varied: SI 2003/3195 Art.6, SI 2003/3197 Art.6, SI 2003/3198 Art.6

Sch.15 Part 2 para.141, varied: SI 2003/3195 Art.6, SI 2003/3197 Art.6, SI 2003/3198 Art.6

Sch.15 Part 2 para.142, varied: SI 2003/3195 Art.6, SI 2003/3197 Art.6, SI 2003/3198 Art.6

Sch.17 para.1, varied: SI 2003/3195 Art.6, SI 2003/3197 Art.6, SI 2003/3198 Art.6, Sch.2 para.72

Sch.17 para.2, varied: SI 2003/3195 Art.6, Sch.2 para.112, SI 2003/3197 Art.6, Sch.2 para.109, SI 2003/3198 Art.6, Sch.2 para.72

Sch.17 para.3, varied: SI 2003/3195 Art.6, Sch.2 para.112, SI 2003/3197 Art.6, Sch.2 para.109, SI 2003/3198 Art.6, Sch.2 para.72

2003–cont.

21. Communications Act 2003–*cont.*

Sch.17 para.4, varied: SI 2003/3195 Art.6, Sch.2 para.112, SI 2003/3197 Art.6, Sch.2 para.109, SI 2003/3198 Art.6, Sch.2 para.72

Sch.17 para.5, varied: SI 2003/3195 Art.6, Sch.2 para.112, SI 2003/3197 Art.6, Sch.2 para.109, SI 2003/3198 Art.6, Sch.2 para.72

Sch.17 para.6, varied: SI 2003/3195 Art.6, SI 2003/3197 Art.6, SI 2003/3198 Art.6

Sch.17 para.7, varied: SI 2003/3195 Art.6, SI 2003/3197 Art.6, SI 2003/3198 Art.6, Sch.2 para.72

Sch.17 para.8, varied: SI 2003/3195 Art.6, Sch.2 para.112, SI 2003/3197 Art.6, Sch.2 para.109, SI 2003/3198 Art.6, Sch.2 para.72

Sch.17 para.9, varied: SI 2003/3195 Art.6, Sch.2 para.112, SI 2003/3197 Art.6, SI 2003/3198 Art.6

Sch.17 para.10, varied: SI 2003/3195 Art.6, SI 2003/3197 Art.6, SI 2003/3198 Art.6

Sch.17 para.11, varied: SI 2003/3195 Art.6, SI 2003/3197 Art.6, SI 2003/3198 Art.6

Sch.17 para.12, varied: SI 2003/3195 Art.6, SI 2003/3197 Art.6, SI 2003/3198 Art.6

Sch.17 para.13, varied: SI 2003/3195 Art.6, SI 2003/3197 Art.6, SI 2003/3198 Art.6

Sch.17 para.14, varied: SI 2003/3195 Art.6, Sch.2 para.112, SI 2003/3197 Art.6, Sch.2 para.109, SI 2003/3198 Art.6, Sch.2 para.72

Sch.17 para.15, varied: SI 2003/3195 Art.6, Sch.2 para.112, SI 2003/3197 Art.6, Sch.2 para.109, SI 2003/3198 Art.6

Sch.17 para.16, varied: SI 2003/3195 Art.6, Sch.2 para.112, SI 2003/3197 Art.6, Sch.2 para.109, SI 2003/3198 Art.6

Sch.17 para.17, varied: SI 2003/3195 Art.6, SI 2003/3197 Art.6, SI 2003/3198 Art.6

Sch.17 para.18, varied: SI 2003/3195 Art.6, SI 2003/3197 Art.6, SI 2003/3198 Art.6

Sch.17 para.19, varied: SI 2003/3195 Art.6, Sch.2 para.112, SI 2003/3197 Art.6, Sch.2 para.109, SI 2003/3198 Art.6, Sch.2 para.72

Sch.17 para.20, varied: SI 2003/3195 Art.6, Sch.2 para.112, SI 2003/3197 Art.6, Sch.2 para.109, SI 2003/3198 Art.6, Sch.2 para.72

Sch.17 para.21, varied: SI 2003/3195 Art.6, Sch.2 para.112, SI 2003/3197 Art.6, Sch.2 para.109, SI 2003/3198 Art.6, Sch.2 para.72

Sch.17 para.22, varied: SI 2003/3195 Art.6, Sch.2 para.112, SI 2003/3197 Art.6, Sch.2 para.109, SI 2003/3198 Art.6, Sch.2 para.72

Sch.17 para.23, varied: SI 2003/3195 Art.6, SI 2003/3197 Art.6, Sch.2 para.109, SI 2003/3198 Art.6, Sch.2 para.72

2003–cont.

21. Communications Act 2003–*cont.*

Sch.17 para.24, varied: SI 2003/3195 Art.6, SI 2003/3197 Art.6, Sch.2 para.109, SI 2003/3198 Art.6, Sch.2 para.72

Sch.17 para.25, varied: SI 2003/3195 Art.6, Sch.2 para.112, SI 2003/3197 Art.6, Sch.2 para.109, SI 2003/3198 Art.6, Sch.2 para.72

Sch.17 para.26, varied: SI 2003/3195 Art.6, Sch.2 para.112, SI 2003/3197 Art.6, Sch.2 para.109, SI 2003/3198 Art.6, Sch.2 para.72

Sch.17 para.27, varied: SI 2003/3195 Art.6, Sch.2 para.112, SI 2003/3197 Art.6, Sch.2 para.109, SI 2003/3198 Art.6, Sch.2 para.72

Sch.17 para.28, varied: SI 2003/3195 Art.6, Sch.2 para.112, SI 2003/3197 Art.6, Sch.2 para.109, SI 2003/3198 Art.6, Sch.2 para.72

Sch.17 para.29, varied: SI 2003/3195 Art.6, Sch.2 para.112, SI 2003/3197 Art.6, Sch.2 para.109, SI 2003/3198 Art.6, Sch.2 para.72

Sch.17 para.30, varied: SI 2003/3195 Art.6, Sch.2 para.112, SI 2003/3197 Art.6, Sch.2 para.109, SI 2003/3198 Art.6, Sch.2 para.72

Sch.17 para.31, varied: SI 2003/3195 Art.6, Sch.2 para.112, SI 2003/3197 Art.6, Sch.2 para.109, SI 2003/3198 Art.6, Sch.2 para.72

Sch.17 para.32, varied: SI 2003/3195 Art.6, SI 2003/3197 Art.6, Sch.2 para.109, SI 2003/3198 Art.6, Sch.2 para.72

Sch.17 para.33, varied: SI 2003/3195 Art.6, SI 2003/3197 Art.6, Sch.2 para.109, SI 2003/3198 Art.6

Sch.17 para.34, varied: SI 2003/3195 Art.6, SI 2003/3197 Art.6, SI 2003/3198 Art.6

Sch.17 para.35, varied: SI 2003/3195 Art.6, SI 2003/3197 Art.6, SI 2003/3198 Art.6

Sch.17 para.36, varied: SI 2003/3195 Art.6, SI 2003/3197 Art.6, SI 2003/3198 Art.6

Sch.17 para.37, varied: SI 2003/3195 Art.6, SI 2003/3197 Art.6, Sch.2 para.109, SI 2003/3198 Art.6

Sch.17 para.38, varied: SI 2003/3195 Art.6, SI 2003/3197 Art.6, Sch.2 para.109, SI 2003/3198 Art.6

Sch.17 para.39, varied: SI 2003/3195 Art.6, SI 2003/3197 Art.6, Sch.2 para.109, SI 2003/3198 Art.6

Sch.17 para.40, varied: SI 2003/3195 Art.6, Sch.2 para.112, SI 2003/3197 Art.6, Sch.2 para.109, SI 2003/3198 Art.6, Sch.2 para.72

Sch.17 para.41, varied: SI 2003/3195 Art.6, Sch.2 para.112, SI 2003/3197 Art.6, Sch.2 para.109, SI 2003/3198 Art.6, Sch.2 para.72

2003–cont.

21. Communications Act 2003–*cont.*

Sch.17 para.42, varied: SI 2003/3195 Art.6, Sch.2 para.112, SI 2003/3197 Art.6, Sch.2 para.109, SI 2003/3198 Art.6, Sch.2 para.72

Sch.17 para.43, varied: SI 2003/3195 Art.6, Sch.2 para.112, SI 2003/3197 Art.6, Sch.2 para.109, SI 2003/3198 Art.6, Sch.2 para.72

Sch.17 para.44, varied: SI 2003/3195 Art.6, Sch.2 para.112, SI 2003/3197 Art.6, Sch.2 para.109, SI 2003/3198 Art.6, Sch.2 para.72

Sch.17 para.45, varied: SI 2003/3195 Art.6, Sch.2 para.112, SI 2003/3197 Art.6, Sch.2 para.109, SI 2003/3198 Art.6, Sch.2 para.72

Sch.17 para.46, varied: SI 2003/3195 Art.6, Sch.2 para.112, SI 2003/3197 Art.6, Sch.2 para.109, SI 2003/3198 Art.6, Sch.2 para.72

Sch.17 para.47, varied: SI 2003/3195 Art.6, Sch.2 para.112, SI 2003/3197 Art.6, Sch.2 para.109, SI 2003/3198 Art.6, Sch.2 para.72

Sch.17 para.48, varied: SI 2003/3195 Art.6, Sch.2 para.112, SI 2003/3197 Art.6, Sch.2 para.109, SI 2003/3198 Art.6, Sch.2 para.72

Sch.17 para.49, varied: SI 2003/3195 Art.6, Sch.2 para.112, SI 2003/3197 Art.6, Sch.2 para.109, SI 2003/3198 Art.6, Sch.2 para.72

Sch.17 para.50, varied: SI 2003/3195 Art.6, Sch.2 para.112, SI 2003/3197 Art.6, Sch.2 para.109, SI 2003/3198 Art.6, Sch.2 para.72

Sch.17 para.51, varied: SI 2003/3195 Art.6, Sch.2 para.112, SI 2003/3197 Art.6, Sch.2 para.109, SI 2003/3198 Art.6, Sch.2 para.72

Sch.17 para.52, varied: SI 2003/3195 Art.6, Sch.2 para.112, SI 2003/3197 Art.6, Sch.2 para.109, SI 2003/3198 Art.6, Sch.2 para.72

Sch.17 para.53, varied: SI 2003/3195 Art.6, Sch.2 para.112, SI 2003/3197 Art.6, Sch.2 para.109, SI 2003/3198 Art.6, Sch.2 para.72

Sch.17 para.54, varied: SI 2003/3195 Art.6, Sch.2 para.112, SI 2003/3197 Art.6, Sch.2 para.109, SI 2003/3198 Art.6, Sch.2 para.72

Sch.17 para.55, varied: SI 2003/3195 Art.6, Sch.2 para.112, SI 2003/3197 Art.6, Sch.2 para.109, SI 2003/3198 Art.6, Sch.2 para.72

Sch.17 para.56, varied: SI 2003/3195 Art.6, Sch.2 para.112, SI 2003/3197 Art.6, Sch.2 para.109, SI 2003/3198 Art.6, Sch.2 para.72

2003–cont.

21. Communications Act 2003–*cont.*

Sch.17 para.57, varied: SI 2003/3195 Art.6, Sch.2 para.112, SI 2003/3197 Art.6, Sch.2 para.109, SI 2003/3198 Art.6, Sch.2 para.72

Sch.17 para.58, varied: SI 2003/3195 Art.6, Sch.2 para.112, SI 2003/3197 Art.6, Sch.2 para.109, SI 2003/3198 Art.6, Sch.2 para.72

Sch.17 para.59, varied: SI 2003/3195 Art.6, Sch.2 para.112, SI 2003/3197 Art.6, Sch.2 para.109, SI 2003/3198 Art.6, Sch.2 para.72

Sch.17 para.60, varied: SI 2003/3195 Art.6, Sch.2 para.112, SI 2003/3197 Art.6, Sch.2 para.109, SI 2003/3198 Art.6, Sch.2 para.72

Sch.17 para.61, varied: SI 2003/3195 Art.6, Sch.2 para.112, SI 2003/3197 Art.6, Sch.2 para.109, SI 2003/3198 Art.6, Sch.2 para.72

Sch.17 para.62, varied: SI 2003/3195 Art.6, Sch.2 para.112, SI 2003/3197 Art.6, Sch.2 para.109, SI 2003/3198 Art.6, Sch.2 para.72

Sch.17 para.63, varied: SI 2003/3195 Art.6, Sch.2 para.112, SI 2003/3197 Art.6, Sch.2 para.109, SI 2003/3198 Art.6, Sch.2 para.72

Sch.17 para.64, varied: SI 2003/3195 Art.6, Sch.2 para.112, SI 2003/3197 Art.6, Sch.2 para.109, SI 2003/3198 Art.6, Sch.2 para.72

Sch.17 para.65, varied: SI 2003/3195 Art.6, Sch.2 para.112, SI 2003/3197 Art.6, Sch.2 para.109, SI 2003/3198 Art.6, Sch.2 para.72

Sch.17 para.66, varied: SI 2003/3195 Art.6, Sch.2 para.112, SI 2003/3197 Art.6, Sch.2 para.109, SI 2003/3198 Art.6, Sch.2 para.72

Sch.17 para.67, varied: SI 2003/3195 Art.6, SI 2003/3197 Art.6, Sch.2 para.109, SI 2003/3198 Art.6, Sch.2 para.72

Sch.17 para.68, varied: SI 2003/3195 Art.6, SI 2003/3197 Art.6, Sch.2 para.109, SI 2003/3198 Art.6, Sch.2 para.72

Sch.17 para.69, varied: SI 2003/3195 Art.6, Sch.2 para.112, SI 2003/3197 Art.6, Sch.2 para.109, SI 2003/3198 Art.6, Sch.2 para.72

Sch.17 para.70, varied: SI 2003/3195 Art.6, Sch.2 para.112, SI 2003/3197 Art.6, Sch.2 para.109, SI 2003/3198 Art.6, Sch.2 para.72

Sch.17 para.71, varied: SI 2003/3195 Art.6, Sch.2 para.112, SI 2003/3197 Art.6, Sch.2 para.109, SI 2003/3198 Art.6, Sch.2 para.72

CAP.

CAP.

2003–cont.

21. Communications Act 2003–*cont.*

Sch.17 para.72, varied: SI 2003/3195 Art.6, Sch.2 para.112, SI 2003/3197 Art.6, Sch.2 para.109, SI 2003/3198 Art.6, Sch.2 para.72

Sch.17 para.73, varied: SI 2003/3195 Art.6, Sch.2 para.112, SI 2003/3197 Art.6, Sch.2 para.109, SI 2003/3198 Art.6, Sch.2 para.72

Sch.17 para.74, varied: SI 2003/3195 Art.6, Sch.2 para.112, SI 2003/3197 Art.6, Sch.2 para.109, SI 2003/3198 Art.6, Sch.2 para.72

Sch.17 para.75, varied: SI 2003/3195 Art.6, Sch.2 para.112, SI 2003/3197 Art.6, Sch.2 para.109, SI 2003/3198 Art.6, Sch.2 para.72

Sch.17 para.76, varied: SI 2003/3195 Art.6, Sch.2 para.112, SI 2003/3197 Art.6, Sch.2 para.109, SI 2003/3198 Art.6, Sch.2 para.72

Sch.17 para.77, varied: SI 2003/3195 Art.6, Sch.2 para.112, SI 2003/3197 Art.6, Sch.2 para.109, SI 2003/3198 Art.6, Sch.2 para.72

Sch.17 para.78, varied: SI 2003/3195 Art.6, Sch.2 para.112, SI 2003/3197 Art.6, Sch.2 para.109, SI 2003/3198 Art.6, Sch.2 para.72

Sch.17 para.79, varied: SI 2003/3195 Art.6, Sch.2 para.112, SI 2003/3197 Art.6, Sch.2 para.109, SI 2003/3198 Art.6, Sch.2 para.72

Sch.17 para.80, varied: SI 2003/3195 Art.6, Sch.2 para.112, SI 2003/3197 Art.6, Sch.2 para.109, SI 2003/3198 Art.6, Sch.2 para.72

Sch.17 para.81, varied: SI 2003/3195 Art.6, Sch.2 para.112, SI 2003/3197 Art.6, Sch.2 para.109, SI 2003/3198 Art.6, Sch.2 para.72

Sch.17 para.82, varied: SI 2003/3195 Art.6, Sch.2 para.112, SI 2003/3197 Art.6, Sch.2 para.109, SI 2003/3198 Art.6, Sch.2 para.72

Sch.17 para.83, varied: SI 2003/3195 Art.6, Sch.2 para.112, SI 2003/3197 Art.6, Sch.2 para.109, SI 2003/3198 Art.6, Sch.2 para.72

Sch.17 para.84, varied: SI 2003/3195 Art.6, Sch.2 para.112, SI 2003/3197 Art.6, Sch.2 para.109, SI 2003/3198 Art.6, Sch.2 para.72

Sch.17 para.85, varied: SI 2003/3195 Art.6, Sch.2 para.112, SI 2003/3197 Art.6, Sch.2 para.109, SI 2003/3198 Art.6, Sch.2 para.72

Sch.17 para.86, varied: SI 2003/3195 Art.6, Sch.2 para.112, SI 2003/3197 Art.6, Sch.2 para.109, SI 2003/3198 Art.6, Sch.2 para.72

2003–cont.

21. Communications Act 2003–*cont.*

Sch.17 para.87, varied: SI 2003/3195 Art.6, Sch.2 para.112, SI 2003/3197 Art.6, Sch.2 para.109, SI 2003/3198 Art.6, Sch.2 para.72

Sch.17 para.88, varied: SI 2003/3195 Art.6, Sch.2 para.112, SI 2003/3197 Art.6, Sch.2 para.109, SI 2003/3198 Art.6, Sch.2 para.72

Sch.17 para.89, varied: SI 2003/3195 Art.6, Sch.2 para.112, SI 2003/3197 Art.6, Sch.2 para.109, SI 2003/3198 Art.6, Sch.2 para.72

Sch.17 para.90, varied: SI 2003/3195 Art.6, Sch.2 para.112, SI 2003/3197 Art.6, Sch.2 para.109, SI 2003/3198 Art.6, Sch.2 para.72

Sch.17 para.91, varied: SI 2003/3195 Art.6, Sch.2 para.112, SI 2003/3197 Art.6, Sch.2 para.109, SI 2003/3198 Art.6, Sch.2 para.72

Sch.17 para.92, amended: SI 2003/2498 Sch.1 para.23

Sch.17 para.92, varied: SI 2003/3195 Art.6, Sch.2 para.112, SI 2003/3197 Art.6, Sch.2 para.109, SI 2003/3198 Art.6, Sch.2 para.72

Sch.17 para.93, varied: SI 2003/3195 Art.6, Sch.2 para.112, SI 2003/3197 Art.6, Sch.2 para.109, SI 2003/3198 Art.6, Sch.2 para.72

Sch.17 para.94, varied: SI 2003/3195 Art.6, Sch.2 para.112, SI 2003/3197 Art.6, Sch.2 para.109, SI 2003/3198 Art.6, Sch.2 para.72

Sch.17 para.95, varied: SI 2003/3195 Art.6, Sch.2 para.112, SI 2003/3197 Art.6, Sch.2 para.109, SI 2003/3198 Art.6, Sch.2 para.72

Sch.17 para.96, varied: SI 2003/3195 Art.6, Sch.2 para.112, SI 2003/3197 Art.6, Sch.2 para.109, SI 2003/3198 Art.6, Sch.2 para.72

Sch.17 para.97, varied: SI 2003/3195 Art.6, Sch.2 para.112, SI 2003/3197 Art.6, Sch.2 para.109, SI 2003/3198 Art.6, Sch.2 para.72

Sch.17 para.98, varied: SI 2003/3195 Art.6, Sch.2 para.112, SI 2003/3197 Art.6, Sch.2 para.109, SI 2003/3198 Art.6, Sch.2 para.72

Sch.17 para.99, varied: SI 2003/3195 Art.6, Sch.2 para.112, SI 2003/3197 Art.6, Sch.2 para.109, SI 2003/3198 Art.6, Sch.2 para.72

Sch.17 para.100, varied: SI 2003/3195 Art.6, Sch.2 para.112, SI 2003/3197 Art.6, Sch.2 para.109, SI 2003/3198 Art.6, Sch.2 para.72

2003–cont.

21. Communications Act 2003–*cont.*

Sch.17 para.101, varied: SI 2003/3195 Art.6, Sch.2 para.112, SI 2003/3197 Art.6, Sch.2 para.109, SI 2003/3198 Art.6, Sch.2 para.72

Sch.17 para.102, varied: SI 2003/3195 Art.6, Sch.2 para.112, SI 2003/3197 Art.6, Sch.2 para.109, SI 2003/3198 Art.6, Sch.2 para.72

Sch.17 para.103, varied: SI 2003/3195 Art.6, Sch.2 para.112, SI 2003/3197 Art.6, Sch.2 para.109, SI 2003/3198 Art.6, Sch.2 para.72

Sch.17 para.104, varied: SI 2003/3195 Art.6, Sch.2 para.112, SI 2003/3197 Art.6, Sch.2 para.109, SI 2003/3198 Art.6, Sch.2 para.72

Sch.17 para.105, varied: SI 2003/3195 Art.6, Sch.2 para.112, SI 2003/3197 Art.6, Sch.2 para.109, SI 2003/3198 Art.6, Sch.2 para.72

Sch.17 para.106, varied: SI 2003/3195 Art.6, Sch.2 para.112, SI 2003/3197 Art.6, Sch.2 para.109, SI 2003/3198 Art.6, Sch.2 para.72

Sch.17 para.107, varied: SI 2003/3195 Art.6, Sch.2 para.112, SI 2003/3197 Art.6, Sch.2 para.109, SI 2003/3198 Art.6, Sch.2 para.72

Sch.17 para.108, varied: SI 2003/3195 Art.6, Sch.2 para.112, SI 2003/3197 Art.6, Sch.2 para.109, SI 2003/3198 Art.6, Sch.2 para.72

Sch.17 para.109, varied: SI 2003/3195 Art.6, Sch.2 para.112, SI 2003/3197 Art.6, Sch.2 para.109, SI 2003/3198 Art.6, Sch.2 para.72

Sch.17 para.110, varied: SI 2003/3195 Art.6, Sch.2 para.112, SI 2003/3197 Art.6, Sch.2 para.109, SI 2003/3198 Art.6, Sch.2 para.72

Sch.17 para.111, varied: SI 2003/3195 Art.6, Sch.2 para.112, SI 2003/3197 Art.6, Sch.2 para.109, SI 2003/3198 Art.6, Sch.2 para.72

Sch.17 para.112, varied: SI 2003/3195 Art.6, Sch.2 para.112, SI 2003/3197 Art.6, Sch.2 para.109, SI 2003/3198 Art.6, Sch.2 para.72

Sch.17 para.113, varied: SI 2003/3195 Art.6, Sch.2 para.112, SI 2003/3197 Art.6, Sch.2 para.109, SI 2003/3198 Art.6, Sch.2 para.72

Sch.17 para.114, varied: SI 2003/3195 Art.6, Sch.2 para.112, SI 2003/3197 Art.6, Sch.2 para.109, SI 2003/3198 Art.6, Sch.2 para.72

Sch.17 para.115, varied: SI 2003/3195 Art.6, Sch.2 para.112, SI 2003/3197 Art.6, Sch.2 para.109, SI 2003/3198 Art.6, Sch.2 para.72

2003–cont.

21. Communications Act 2003–*cont.*

Sch.17 para.116, varied: SI 2003/3195 Art.6, Sch.2 para.112, SI 2003/3197 Art.6, Sch.2 para.109, SI 2003/3198 Art.6, Sch.2 para.72

Sch.17 para.117, varied: SI 2003/3195 Art.6, Sch.2 para.112, SI 2003/3197 Art.6, Sch.2 para.109, SI 2003/3198 Art.6, Sch.2 para.72

Sch.17 para.118, varied: SI 2003/3195 Art.6, Sch.2 para.112, SI 2003/3197 Art.6, Sch.2 para.109, SI 2003/3198 Art.6, Sch.2 para.72

Sch.17 para.119, varied: SI 2003/3195 Art.6, Sch.2 para.112, SI 2003/3197 Art.6, Sch.2 para.109, SI 2003/3198 Art.6, Sch.2 para.72

Sch.17 para.120, varied: SI 2003/3195 Art.6, Sch.2 para.112, SI 2003/3197 Art.6, Sch.2 para.109, SI 2003/3198 Art.6, Sch.2 para.72

Sch.17 para.121, varied: SI 2003/3195 Art.6, Sch.2 para.112, SI 2003/3197 Art.6, Sch.2 para.109, SI 2003/3198 Art.6, Sch.2 para.72

Sch.17 para.122, varied: SI 2003/3195 Art.6, Sch.2 para.112, SI 2003/3197 Art.6, Sch.2 para.109, SI 2003/3198 Art.6, Sch.2 para.72

Sch.17 para.123, varied: SI 2003/3195 Art.6, Sch.2 para.112, SI 2003/3197 Art.6, Sch.2 para.109, SI 2003/3198 Art.6, Sch.2 para.72

Sch.17 para.124, varied: SI 2003/3195 Art.6, Sch.2 para.112, SI 2003/3197 Art.6, Sch.2 para.109, SI 2003/3198 Art.6, Sch.2 para.72

Sch.17 para.125, varied: SI 2003/3195 Art.6, Sch.2 para.112, SI 2003/3197 Art.6, Sch.2 para.109, SI 2003/3198 Art.6, Sch.2 para.72

Sch.17 para.126, varied: SI 2003/3195 Art.6, Sch.2 para.112, SI 2003/3197 Art.6, Sch.2 para.109, SI 2003/3198 Art.6, Sch.2 para.72

Sch.17 para.127, varied: SI 2003/3195 Art.6, Sch.2 para.112, SI 2003/3197 Art.6, Sch.2 para.109, SI 2003/3198 Art.6, Sch.2 para.72

Sch.17 para.128, varied: SI 2003/3195 Art.6, Sch.2 para.112, SI 2003/3197 Art.6, Sch.2 para.109, SI 2003/3198 Art.6, Sch.2 para.72

Sch.17 para.129, varied: SI 2003/3195 Art.6, Sch.2 para.112, SI 2003/3197 Art.6, Sch.2 para.109, SI 2003/3198 Art.6, Sch.2 para.72

Sch.17 para.130, varied: SI 2003/3195 Art.6, Sch.2 para.112, SI 2003/3197 Art.6, Sch.2 para.109, SI 2003/3198 Art.6, Sch.2 para.72

2003–cont.

21. Communications Act 2003–*cont.*

Sch.17 para.131, varied: SI 2003/3195 Art.6, Sch.2 para.112, SI 2003/3197 Art.6, Sch.2 para.109, SI 2003/3198 Art.6, Sch.2 para.72

Sch.17 para.132, varied: SI 2003/3195 Art.6, Sch.2 para.112, SI 2003/3197 Art.6, Sch.2 para.109, SI 2003/3198 Art.6, Sch.2 para.72

Sch.17 para.133, varied: SI 2003/3195 Art.6, Sch.2 para.112, SI 2003/3197 Art.6, Sch.2 para.109, SI 2003/3198 Art.6, Sch.2 para.72

Sch.17 para.134, varied: SI 2003/3195 Art.6, Sch.2 para.112, SI 2003/3197 Art.6, Sch.2 para.109, SI 2003/3198 Art.6, Sch.2 para.72

Sch.17 para.135, varied: SI 2003/3195 Art.6, Sch.2 para.112, SI 2003/3197 Art.6, Sch.2 para.109, SI 2003/3198 Art.6, Sch.2 para.72

Sch.17 para.136, varied: SI 2003/3195 Art.6, Sch.2 para.112, SI 2003/3197 Art.6, Sch.2 para.109, SI 2003/3198 Art.6, Sch.2 para.72

Sch.17 para.137, varied: SI 2003/3195 Art.6, Sch.2 para.112, SI 2003/3197 Art.6, Sch.2 para.109, SI 2003/3198 Art.6, Sch.2 para.72

Sch.17 para.138, varied: SI 2003/3195 Art.6, Sch.2 para.112, SI 2003/3197 Art.6, Sch.2 para.109, SI 2003/3198 Art.6, Sch.2 para.72

Sch.17 para.139, varied: SI 2003/3195 Art.6, Sch.2 para.112, SI 2003/3197 Art.6, Sch.2 para.109, SI 2003/3198 Art.6, Sch.2 para.72

Sch.17 para.140, varied: SI 2003/3195 Art.6, Sch.2 para.112, SI 2003/3197 Art.6, Sch.2 para.109, SI 2003/3198 Art.6, Sch.2 para.72

Sch.17 para.141, varied: SI 2003/3195 Art.6, Sch.2 para.112, SI 2003/3197 Art.6, Sch.2 para.109, SI 2003/3198 Art.6, Sch.2 para.72

Sch.17 para.142, varied: SI 2003/3195 Art.6, Sch.2 para.112, SI 2003/3197 Art.6, Sch.2 para.109, SI 2003/3198 Art.6, Sch.2 para.72

Sch.17 para.143, varied: SI 2003/3195 Art.6, Sch.2 para.112, SI 2003/3197 Art.6, Sch.2 para.109, SI 2003/3198 Art.6, Sch.2 para.72

Sch.17 para.144, varied: SI 2003/3195 Art.6, Sch.2 para.112, SI 2003/3197 Art.6, Sch.2 para.109, SI 2003/3198 Art.6, Sch.2 para.72

Sch.17 para.145, varied: SI 2003/3195 Art.6, SI 2003/3197 Art.6, SI 2003/3198 Art.6

Sch.17 para.146, varied: SI 2003/3195 Art.6, SI 2003/3197 Art.6, SI 2003/3198 Art.6

2003–cont.

21. Communications Act 2003–*cont.*

Sch.17 para.147, varied: SI 2003/3195 Art.6, SI 2003/3197 Art.6, SI 2003/3198 Art.6

Sch.17 para.147A, varied: SI 2003/3195 Art.6, SI 2003/3197 Art.6, SI 2003/3198 Art.6, Sch.2 para.72

Sch.17 para.148, varied: SI 2003/3195 Art.6, SI 2003/3197 Art.6, SI 2003/3198 Art.6

Sch.17 para.149, varied: SI 2003/3195 Art.6, SI 2003/3197 Art.6, SI 2003/3198 Art.6

Sch.17 para.150, varied: SI 2003/3195 Art.6, Sch.2 para.112, SI 2003/3197 Art.6, Sch.2 para.109, SI 2003/3198 Art.6

Sch.17 para.151, varied: SI 2003/3195 Art.6, SI 2003/3197 Art.6, SI 2003/3198 Art.6

Sch.17 para.152, varied: SI 2003/3195 Art.6, Sch.2 para.112, SI 2003/3197 Art.6, Sch.2 para.109, SI 2003/3198 Art.6, Sch.2 para.72

Sch.17 para.153, varied: SI 2003/3195 Art.6, Sch.2 para.112, SI 2003/3197 Art.6, Sch.2 para.109, SI 2003/3198 Art.6, Sch.2 para.72

Sch.17 para.154, varied: SI 2003/3195 Art.6, Sch.2 para.112, SI 2003/3197 Art.6, Sch.2 para.109, SI 2003/3198 Art.6, Sch.2 para.72

Sch.17 para.155, varied: SI 2003/3195 Art.6, Sch.2 para.112, SI 2003/3197 Art.6, Sch.2 para.109, SI 2003/3198 Art.6, Sch.2 para.72

Sch.17 para.156, varied: SI 2003/3195 Art.6, Sch.2 para.112, SI 2003/3197 Art.6, Sch.2 para.109, SI 2003/3198 Art.6, Sch.2 para.72

Sch.17 para.157, varied: SI 2003/3195 Art.6, Sch.2 para.112, SI 2003/3197 Art.6, Sch.2 para.109, SI 2003/3198 Art.6, Sch.2 para.72

Sch.17 para.158, varied: SI 2003/3195 Art.6, Sch.2 para.112, SI 2003/3197 Art.6, Sch.2 para.109, SI 2003/3198 Art.6, Sch.2 para.72

Sch.17 para.159, varied: SI 2003/3195 Art.6, Sch.2 para.112, SI 2003/3197 Art.6, Sch.2 para.109, SI 2003/3198 Art.6, Sch.2 para.72

Sch.17 para.160, varied: SI 2003/3195 Art.6, Sch.2 para.112, SI 2003/3197 Art.6, Sch.2 para.109, SI 2003/3198 Art.6, Sch.2 para.72

Sch.17 para.161, varied: SI 2003/3195 Art.6, Sch.2 para.112, SI 2003/3197 Art.6, Sch.2 para.109, SI 2003/3198 Art.6, Sch.2 para.72

Sch.17 para.162, varied: SI 2003/3195 Art.6, Sch.2 para.112, SI 2003/3197 Art.6, Sch.2 para.109, SI 2003/3198 Art.6, Sch.2 para.72

2003–cont.

21. **Communications Act 2003**–*cont.*

Sch.17 para.163, varied: SI 2003/3195 Art.6, Sch.2 para.112, SI 2003/3197 Art.6, Sch.2 para.109, SI 2003/3198 Art.6, Sch.2 para.72

Sch.17 para.164, varied: SI 2003/3195 Art.6, Sch.2 para.112, SI 2003/3197 Art.6, Sch.2 para.109, SI 2003/3198 Art.6, Sch.2 para.72

Sch.17 para.165, varied: SI 2003/3195 Art.6, Sch.2 para.112, SI 2003/3197 Art.6, Sch.2 para.109, SI 2003/3198 Art.6, Sch.2 para.72

Sch.17 para.166, varied: SI 2003/3195 Art.6, Sch.2 para.112, SI 2003/3197 Art.6, Sch.2 para.109, SI 2003/3198 Art.6, Sch.2 para.72

Sch.17 para.167, varied: SI 2003/3195 Art.6, Sch.2 para.112, SI 2003/3197 Art.6, Sch.2 para.109, SI 2003/3198 Art.6, Sch.2 para.72

Sch.17 para.168, varied: SI 2003/3195 Art.6, Sch.2 para.112, SI 2003/3197 Art.6, Sch.2 para.109, SI 2003/3198 Art.6, Sch.2 para.72

Sch.17 para.169, varied: SI 2003/3195 Art.6, Sch.2 para.112, SI 2003/3197 Art.6, Sch.2 para.109, SI 2003/3198 Art.6, Sch.2 para.72

Sch.17 para.170, varied: SI 2003/3195 Art.6, Sch.2 para.112, SI 2003/3197 Art.6, Sch.2 para.109, SI 2003/3198 Art.6, Sch.2 para.72

Sch.17 para.171, varied: SI 2003/3195 Art.6, SI 2003/3197 Art.6, Sch.2 para.109, SI 2003/3198 Art.6

Sch.17 para.172, varied: SI 2003/3195 Art.6, Sch.2 para.112, SI 2003/3197 Art.6, Sch.2 para.109, SI 2003/3198 Art.6

Sch.17 para.173, varied: SI 2003/3195 Art.6, Sch.2 para.112, SI 2003/3197 Art.6, Sch.2 para.109, SI 2003/3198 Art.6, Sch.2 para.72

Sch.17 para.174, varied: SI 2003/3195 Art.6, Sch.2 para.112, SI 2003/3197 Art.6, Sch.2 para.109, SI 2003/3198 Art.6, Sch.2 para.72

Sch.17 para.175, varied: SI 2003/3195 Art.6, Sch.2 para.112, SI 2003/3197 Art.6, Sch.2 para.109, SI 2003/3198 Art.6, Sch.2 para.72

Sch.18 para.1, varied: SI 2003/3195 Art.6, SI 2003/3197 Art.6, SI 2003/3198 Art.6

Sch.18 para.2, varied: SI 2003/3195 Art.6, Sch.2 para.113, SI 2003/3197 Art.6, Sch.2 para.110, SI 2003/3198 Art.6

Sch.18 para.3, varied: SI 2003/3195 Art.6, Sch.2 para.113, SI 2003/3197 Art.6, Sch.2 para.110, SI 2003/3198 Art.6, Sch.2 para.73

2003–cont.

21. **Communications Act 2003**–*cont.*

Sch.18 para.4, varied: SI 2003/3195 Art.6, Sch.2 para.113, SI 2003/3197 Art.6, Sch.2 para.110, SI 2003/3198 Art.6, Sch.2 para.73

Sch.18 para.5, varied: SI 2003/3195 Art.6, SI 2003/3197 Art.6, SI 2003/3198 Art.6

Sch.18 para.6, varied: SI 2003/3195 Art.6, Sch.2 para.113, SI 2003/3197 Art.6, Sch.2 para.110, SI 2003/3198 Art.6

Sch.18 para.7, varied: SI 2003/3195 Art.6, Sch.2 para.113, SI 2003/3197 Art.6, Sch.2 para.110, SI 2003/3198 Art.6, Sch.2 para.73

Sch.18 para.8, varied: SI 2003/3195 Art.6, Sch.2 para.113, SI 2003/3197 Art.6, Sch.2 para.110, SI 2003/3198 Art.6, Sch.2 para.73

Sch.18 para.9, varied: SI 2003/3195 Art.6, Sch.2 para.113, SI 2003/3197 Art.6, Sch.2 para.110, SI 2003/3198 Art.6, Sch.2 para.73

Sch.18 para.10, varied: SI 2003/3195 Art.6, Sch.2 para.113, SI 2003/3197 Art.6, Sch.2 para.110, SI 2003/3198 Art.6, Sch.2 para.73

Sch.18 para.11, varied: SI 2003/3195 Art.6, Sch.2 para.113, SI 2003/3197 Art.6, Sch.2 para.110, SI 2003/3198 Art.6, Sch.2 para.73

Sch.18 para.12, varied: SI 2003/3195 Art.6, Sch.2 para.113, SI 2003/3197 Art.6, Sch.2 para.110, SI 2003/3198 Art.6, Sch.2 para.73

Sch.18 para.13, varied: SI 2003/3195 Art.6, Sch.2 para.113, SI 2003/3197 Art.6, Sch.2 para.110, SI 2003/3198 Art.6, Sch.2 para.73

Sch.18 para.14, varied: SI 2003/3195 Art.6, Sch.2 para.113, SI 2003/3197 Art.6, Sch.2 para.110, SI 2003/3198 Art.6, Sch.2 para.73

Sch.18 para.15, varied: SI 2003/3195 Art.6, Sch.2 para.113, SI 2003/3197 Art.6, Sch.2 para.110, SI 2003/3198 Art.6, Sch.2 para.73

Sch.18 para.16, varied: SI 2003/3195 Art.6, Sch.2 para.113, SI 2003/3197 Art.6, Sch.2 para.110, SI 2003/3198 Art.6, Sch.2 para.73

Sch.18 para.17, applied: SI 2003/1900 Art.3

Sch.18 para.17, varied: SI 2003/3195 Art.6, Sch.2 para.113, SI 2003/3197 Art.6, Sch.2 para.110, SI 2003/3198 Art.6, Sch.2 para.73

Sch.18 para.18, varied: SI 2003/3195 Art.6, Sch.2 para.113, SI 2003/3197 Art.6, Sch.2 para.110, SI 2003/3198 Art.6, Sch.2 para.73

2003–cont.

21. Communications Act 2003–*cont.*

Sch.18 para.19, varied: SI 2003/3195 Art.6, Sch.2 para.113, SI 2003/3197 Art.6, Sch.2 para.110, SI 2003/3198 Art.6, Sch.2 para.73

Sch.18 para.20, varied: SI 2003/3195 Art.6, Sch.2 para.113, SI 2003/3197 Art.6, Sch.2 para.110, SI 2003/3198 Art.6, Sch.2 para.73

Sch.18 para.21, varied: SI 2003/3195 Art.6, SI 2003/3197 Art.6, SI 2003/3198 Art.6

Sch.18 para.22, varied: SI 2003/3195 Art.6, Sch.2 para.113, SI 2003/3197 Art.6, Sch.2 para.110, SI 2003/3198 Art.6, Sch.2 para.73

Sch.18 para.23, applied: SI 2004/2068 r.6

Sch.18 para.23, varied: SI 2003/3195 Art.6, Sch.2 para.113, SI 2003/3197 Art.6, Sch.2 para.110, SI 2003/3198 Art.6, Sch.2 para.73

Sch.18 para.23, enabling: SI 2004/2068

Sch.18 para.24, varied: SI 2003/3195 Art.6, Sch.2 para.113, SI 2003/3197 Art.6, Sch.2 para.110, SI 2003/3198 Art.6, Sch.2 para.73

Sch.18 para.25, varied: SI 2003/3195 Art.6, Sch.2 para.113, SI 2003/3197 Art.6, Sch.2 para.110, SI 2003/3198 Art.6, Sch.2 para.73

Sch.18 para.26, varied: SI 2003/3195 Art.6, Sch.2 para.113, SI 2003/3197 Art.6, Sch.2 para.110, SI 2003/3198 Art.6, Sch.2 para.73

Sch.18 para.27, varied: SI 2003/3195 Art.6, Sch.2 para.113, SI 2003/3197 Art.6, Sch.2 para.110, SI 2003/3198 Art.6, Sch.2 para.73

Sch.18 para.28, varied: SI 2003/3195 Art.6, Sch.2 para.113, SI 2003/3197 Art.6, Sch.2 para.110, SI 2003/3198 Art.6, Sch.2 para.73

Sch.18 para.29, varied: SI 2003/3195 Art.6, Sch.2 para.113, SI 2003/3197 Art.6, Sch.2 para.110, SI 2003/3198 Art.6, Sch.2 para.73

Sch.18 para.30, varied: SI 2003/3195 Art.6, SI 2003/3197 Art.6, SI 2003/3198 Art.6

Sch.18 para.31, varied: SI 2003/3195 Art.6, SI 2003/3197 Art.6, SI 2003/3198 Art.6

Sch.18 para.32, varied: SI 2003/3195 Art.6, SI 2003/3197 Art.6, SI 2003/3198 Art.6

Sch.18 para.33, varied: SI 2003/3195 Art.6, SI 2003/3197 Art.6, SI 2003/3198 Art.6

Sch.18 para.34, varied: SI 2003/3195 Art.6, SI 2003/3197 Art.6, SI 2003/3198 Art.6

Sch.18 para.35, varied: SI 2003/3195 Art.6, SI 2003/3197 Art.6, SI 2003/3198 Art.6

Sch.18 para.36, varied: SI 2003/3195 Art.6, SI 2003/3197 Art.6, SI 2003/3198 Art.6

Sch.18 para.37, varied: SI 2003/3195 Art.6, SI 2003/3197 Art.6, SI 2003/3198 Art.6

2003–cont.

21. Communications Act 2003–*cont.*

Sch.18 para.38, varied: SI 2003/3195 Art.6, Sch.2 para.113, SI 2003/3197 Art.6, Sch.2 para.110, SI 2003/3198 Art.6, Sch.2 para.73

Sch.18 para.39, varied: SI 2003/3195 Art.6, SI 2003/3197 Art.6, SI 2003/3198 Art.6, Sch.2 para.73

Sch.18 para.40, varied: SI 2003/3195 Art.6, SI 2003/3197 Art.6, SI 2003/3198 Art.6, Sch.2 para.73

Sch.18 para.41, varied: SI 2003/3195 Art.6, SI 2003/3197 Art.6, SI 2003/3198 Art.6

Sch.18 para.42, varied: SI 2003/3195 Art.6, SI 2003/3197 Art.6, SI 2003/3198 Art.6

Sch.18 para.43, varied: SI 2003/3195 Art.6, Sch.2 para.113, SI 2003/3197 Art.6, Sch.2 para.110, SI 2003/3198 Art.6, Sch.2 para.73

Sch.18 para.44, varied: SI 2003/3195 Art.6, SI 2003/3197 Art.6, SI 2003/3198 Art.6, Sch.2 para.73

Sch.18 para.45, varied: SI 2003/3195 Art.6, SI 2003/3197 Art.6, Sch.2 para.110, SI 2003/3198 Art.6, Sch.2 para.73

Sch.18 para.46, varied: SI 2003/3195 Art.6, SI 2003/3197 Art.6, SI 2003/3198 Art.6

Sch.18 para.47, varied: SI 2003/3195 Art.6, SI 2003/3197 Art.6, SI 2003/3198 Art.6

Sch.18 para.48, varied: SI 2003/3195 Art.6, SI 2003/3197 Art.6, SI 2003/3198 Art.6

Sch.18 para.49, varied: SI 2003/3195 Art.6, SI 2003/3197 Art.6, SI 2003/3198 Art.6

Sch.18 para.50, varied: SI 2003/3195 Art.6, Sch.2 para.113, SI 2003/3197 Art.6, SI 2003/3198 Art.6, Sch.2 para.73

Sch.18 para.51, varied: SI 2003/3195 Art.6, Sch.2 para.113, SI 2003/3197 Art.6, SI 2003/3198 Art.6

Sch.18 para.52, varied: SI 2003/3195 Art.6, SI 2003/3197 Art.6, SI 2003/3198 Art.6

Sch.18 para.53, varied: SI 2003/3195 Art.6, SI 2003/3197 Art.6, SI 2003/3198 Art.6

Sch.18 para.54, varied: SI 2003/3195 Art.6, SI 2003/3197 Art.6, SI 2003/3198 Art.6

Sch.18 para.55, varied: SI 2003/3195 Art.6, Sch.2 para.113, SI 2003/3197 Art.6, SI 2003/3198 Art.6

Sch.18 para.56, varied: SI 2003/3195 Art.6, Sch.2 para.113, SI 2003/3197 Art.6, Sch.2 para.110, SI 2003/3198 Art.6, Sch.2 para.73

Sch.18 para.57, varied: SI 2003/3195 Art.6, Sch.2 para.113, SI 2003/3197 Art.6, Sch.2 para.110, SI 2003/3198 Art.6, Sch.2 para.73

Sch.18 para.58, varied: SI 2003/3195 Art.6, Sch.2 para.113, SI 2003/3197 Art.6, Sch.2 para.110, SI 2003/3198 Art.6, Sch.2 para.73

2003–cont.

21. Communications Act 2003–cont.

Sch.18 para.59, varied: SI 2003/3195 Art.6, Sch.2 para.113, SI 2003/3197 Art.6, Sch.2 para.110, SI 2003/3198 Art.6, Sch.2 para.73

Sch.18 para.60, varied: SI 2003/3195 Art.6, Sch.2 para.113, SI 2003/3197 Art.6, Sch.2 para.110, SI 2003/3198 Art.6, Sch.2 para.73

Sch.18 para.61, varied: SI 2003/3195 Art.6, Sch.2 para.113, SI 2003/3197 Art.6, Sch.2 para.110, SI 2003/3198 Art.6, Sch.2 para.73

Sch.18 para.62, varied: SI 2003/3195 Art.6, Sch.2 para.113, SI 2003/3197 Art.6, Sch.2 para.110, SI 2003/3198 Art.6, Sch.2 para.73

Sch.18 para.63, varied: SI 2003/3195 Art.6, Sch.2 para.113, SI 2003/3197 Art.6, Sch.2 para.110, SI 2003/3198 Art.6, Sch.2 para.73

Sch.18 para.64, varied: SI 2003/3195 Art.6, Sch.2 para.113, SI 2003/3197 Art.6, Sch.2 para.110, SI 2003/3198 Art.6, Sch.2 para.73

Sch.19, varied: SI 2003/3195 Art.6, Sch.2 para.114, SI 2003/3197 Art.6, Sch.2 para.111, SI 2003/3198 Art.6, Sch.2 para.74

22. Fireworks Act 2003

Commencement Orders: SI 2003/3084 Sch.1; SI 2004/1831 Art.2, Sch.1

applied: 2002 c.40 Sch.14, Sch.15

s.2, applied: SI 2003/3085, SI 2004/1836, SI 2004/2030 Sch.1, SSI 2004/393

s.2, referred to: SSI 2004/393 Reg.4

s.2, enabling: SI 2003/3085, SI 2004/1836, SI 2004/3262, SSI 2004/393

s.3, enabling: SI 2003/3085, SI 2004/1836

s.4, applied: SI 2004/2030 Sch.1

s.4, enabling: SI 2004/1836, SI 2004/3262, SSI 2004/393

s.5, enabling: SI 2003/3085, SI 2004/1836

s.6, applied: SI 2004/2030 Sch.1

s.7, enabling: SI 2004/1836, SI 2004/3262

s.8, enabling: SI 2004/1836, SI 2004/3262

s.9, enabling: SI 2004/1836

s.11, applied: SI 2002/1837 Sch.1 Part I, SI 2003/3085, SI 2003/3085 Reg.7, SI 2004/1836, SI 2004/1836 Reg.9, Reg.13, SI 2004/2030 Sch.1, SSI 2004/393 Reg.6

s.11, referred to: 2001 c.16 s.1, SI 2004/2468 Art.1

s.11, enabling: SSI 2004/393

s.12, applied: SI 2003/3085, SI 2003/3085 Reg.6, SI 2004/1836, SI 2004/2030 Sch.1

s.12, enabling: SSI 2004/393

s.18, enabling: SI 2003/3084, SI 2004/1831

24. Human Fertilisation and Embryology (Deceased Fathers) Act 2003

Commencement Orders: SI 2003/3095 Art.2

s.4, enabling: SI 2003/3095

2003–cont.

25. Northern Ireland (Monitoring Commission etc.) Act 2003

Commencement Orders: SI 2003/2646 Art.2; SI 2004/83 Art.2

s.1, enabling: SI 2003/3126

s.2, applied: SI 2003/3126 Art.4

s.12, enabling: SI 2003/2646, SI 2004/83

26. Local Government Act 2003

Commencement Orders: SI 2003/2938 Art.2, Art.3, Art.4, Art.5, Art.6, Art.7, Art.8, Sch.1 para.15, para.16, para.19, para.20, para.21; SI 2003/3034 Art.2, Sch.1 Part I; SI 2004/3132 Art.2, Art.3; SI 2003/3034 Sch.1 Part II, Sch.2 para.4

applied: SI 2004/533 Art.3

Part 1, applied: SI 2003/3146 Reg.34, SI 2003/3239 Reg.27

Part 1 c.1, applied: 1993 c.28 s.136, 1997 c.65 s.1, 1999 c.29 s.85, SI 2003/2938 Sch.1 para.17, Sch.1 para.18, SI 2003/3034 Sch.2 para.3, SI 2003/3146 Reg.5, Reg.7, Reg.8, Reg.9, Reg.10, Reg.11, Reg.22, Reg.24, Reg.25, Reg.26, SI 2003/3239 Reg.5A, Reg.9A, Reg.6, Reg.7, Reg.8, Reg.9, Reg.15, Reg.19, Reg.20, SI 2004/533 Art.7

Part 4, applied: 1997 c.25 s.67

s.1, applied: 1965 c.63 s.2, 1967 c.61 s.2

s.3, applied: SI 2003/3146 Reg.2, SI 2003/3239 Reg.2

s.3, enabling: SI 2003/3146, SI 2003/3239, SI 2004/1010

s.7, applied: SI 2003/2938 Sch.1 para.17, SI 2003/3034 Sch.2 para.3, SI 2003/3146 Reg.3, Reg.4, SI 2003/3239 Reg.3, Reg.4

s.7, enabling: SI 2003/3146, SI 2003/3239, SI 2004/1010

s.8, applied: 1999 c.29 s.122, SI 2003/3146 Reg.6, SI 2003/3239 Reg.5

s.8, enabling: SI 2003/3146, SI 2003/3239, SI 2004/1010

s.9, applied: SI 2003/2938 Sch.1 para.18, SI 2003/3034 Sch.2 para.3, SI 2003/3146 Reg.10, Reg.22, SI 2003/3239 Reg.9, Reg.15

s.9, enabling: SI 2003/3146, SI 2003/3239, SI 2004/1010, SI 2004/3055

s.10, applied: 1993 c.28 s.136

s.10, enabling: SI 2003/3146, SI 2003/3239, SI 2004/1010, SI 2004/3055

s.11, enabling: SI 2003/3146, SI 2003/3239, SI 2004/534, SI 2004/1010, SI 2004/3055

s.12, applied: SI 1996/1883 Art.4, SI 2003/3239 Reg.20

s.13, disapplied: SI 2004/533 Art.7

s.15, enabling: SI 2003/3146, SI 2003/3239, SI 2004/1010

s.16, applied: SI 2003/533 Reg.7, SI 2003/3146 Reg.25, SI 2003/3239 Reg.20

2003–cont.

26. Local Government Act 2003–*cont.*

s.16, enabling: SI 2003/3146, SI 2003/3239, SI 2004/534, SI 2004/1010, SI 2004/3055

s.19, enabling: SI 2004/1010

s.21, applied: 1989 c.42 s.88, SI 2003/3146 Reg.31

s.21, enabling: SI 2003/3146, SI 2003/3239, SI 2004/1010, SI 2004/3055

s.23, amended: 2004 c.21 Sch.1 para.100, 2004 c.36 Sch.2 para.10

s.23, applied: SI 2003/3146 Reg.32, SI 2003/3239 Reg.26

s.23, enabling: SI 2003/3146, SI 2003/3239, SI 2004/1010

s.24, enabling: SI 2003/3239, SI 2004/1010

s.31, applied: 1999 c.29 s.124, 2003 c.13 Sch.2 Part 11, SI 2003/3170 Sch.3 para.3, 2004 c.9 Sch.2 Part 2, Sch.2 Part 10

s.32, applied: 1999 c.29 s.124

s.33, amended: 2004 c.21 Sch.1 para.101, 2004 c.36 Sch.2 para.10

s.43, applied: SI 2004/2443 Sch.3 para.1

s.44, varied: SI 2004/2443 Reg.16, Reg.17

s.45, varied: SI 2004/2443 Reg.16, Reg.17

s.46, applied: SI 2004/2443 Sch.4 para.12, Sch.4 para.13

s.46, varied: SI 2004/2443 Reg.16, Reg.17

s.47, varied: SI 2004/2443 Reg.16, Reg.17

s.47, enabling: SI 2004/2443

s.48, applied: 1994 c.40 s.71

s.48, enabling: SI 2004/2443

s.49, enabling: SI 2004/2443

s.51, applied: SI 2004/2443 Reg.12, Reg.13

s.51, enabling: SI 2004/2443

s.52, applied: SI 2004/2443 Reg.13

s.52, enabling: SI 2004/2443

s.54, enabling: SI 2004/2443

s.55, enabling: SI 2004/2443

s.56, enabling: SI 2004/2443

s.87, amended: 2004 c.34 Sch.15 para.47

s.87, applied: 2004 c.34 s.225

s.95, enabling: SI 2004/1705, SI 2004/2307, SI 2004/2573

s.96, enabling: SI 2004/1705, SI 2004/2307, SI 2004/2573

s.99, amended: 2004 c.21 Sch.1 para.102, Sch.2

s.99, applied: 1990 c.9 s.93, SI 2004/1704, SI 2004/1705 Art.1

s.99, referred to: SI 2004/1705 Art.4

s.99, enabling: SI 2004/1704, SI 2004/3211

s.100, amended: 2004 c.18 s.95

s.100, referred to: 1990 c.9 s.93

s.100, varied: 2004 c.31 s.17

s.101, repealed (in part): 2004 c.21 Sch.2

s.103, enabling: SI 2004/222

s.104, applied: SI 2004/218

s.104, enabling: SI 2004/218

s.105, applied: SI 2004/558 Reg.3

2003–cont.

26. Local Government Act 2003–*cont.*

s.109, repealed (in part): 2004 c.23 Sch.4

s.118, applied: 1972 c.70 Sch.12B para.2

s.121, repealed (in part): 2004 c.21 Sch.2

s.123, enabling: SI 2003/3146, SI 2003/3239, SI 2004/218, SI 2004/222, SI 2004/482, SI 2004/533, SI 2004/534, SI 2004/1010, SI 2004/1705, SI 2004/2044, SI 2004/2307, SI 2004/2443, SI 2004/2573, SI 2004/3055

s.124, enabling: SI 2003/3239, SI 2004/1010

s.127, enabling: SI 2004/482, SI 2004/533, SI 2004/2044

s.128, enabling: SI 2003/2938, SI 2003/3034, SI 2004/533, SI 2004/3132

Sch.1, applied: SI 2003/3146 Reg.34, SI 2003/3239 Reg.27

Sch.1 para.2, applied: 1965 c.63 s.2, 1967 c.61 s.2, SI 2004/533 Art.7

Sch.1 para.4, applied: SI 2003/3146 Reg.34, SI 2003/3239 Reg.27

Sch.1 para.4, enabling: SI 2003/3146, SI 2003/3239, SI 2004/1010

Sch.4 para.2, amended: 2004 c.33 Sch.27 para.171

Sch.7 para.1, repealed (in part): 2004 c.21 Sch.2

28. Legal Deposit Libraries Act 2003

Commencement Orders: SI 2004/130 Art.2

s.1, applied: 1925 c.73 s.5

s.5, applied: 1925 c.73 s.5

s.7, applied: 1988 c.48 s.44A, SI 1997/3032 Reg.20A

s.10, applied: 1988 c.48 s.44A, SI 1997/3032 Reg.20A

s.16, enabling: SI 2004/130

30. Sustainable Energy Act 2003

Commencement Orders: SI 2003/2986 Art.2; SI 2004/1203 Art.2

s.1, amended: 2004 c.20 s.81

s.5, applied: SI 2003/2987 Art.2, Art.3

s.5, enabling: SI 2003/2987

s.9, enabling: SI 2003/2986, SI 2004/1203

31. Female Genital Mutilation Act 2003

Commencement Orders: SI 2004/286 Art.2

applied: 1952 c.67 Sch.1 para.1

s.1, applied: 2003 c.44 Sch.15 para.61, Sch.17 para.58, SI 2004/1910 Sch.6

s.2, applied: 2003 c.44 Sch.15 para.62, Sch.17 para.59

s.3, applied: 2003 c.44 Sch.15 para.63, Sch.17 para.60

s.8, enabling: SI 2004/286

32. Crime (International Co-operation) Act 2003

Commencement Orders: SI 2004/786 Art.3; SI 2004/1897 Art.2; SI 2004/2624 Art.2; SSI 2004/175 Art.2

Part 3 c.2, applied: SI 2003/2903

s.3, applied: SI 1982/1109 r.30, SI 2004/1048 r.3

2003–cont.

32. Crime (International Co-operation) Act 2003–*cont.*

s.4, applied: SI 1982/1109 r.31, SI 2004/1048 r.4

s.4A, added: 2003 c.44 Sch.36 para.16

s.4B, added: 2003 c.44 Sch.36 para.16

s.5, applied: SI 1996/513 Sch.2 para.36

s.6, applied: SI 1996/513 Sch.2 para.36a, Sch.2 para.36

s.7, applied: SI 1982/1109 r.32, 1988 c.33 s.24, s.26, Sch.13 para.6, SI 1996/513 Sch.2 para.36c, Sch.2 para.36d, Sch.2 para.36e, 2003 c.44 s.117, SI 2004/1034 Art.2, SI 2004/1048 r.5, SI 2004/1501 Art.21

s.7, enabling: SI 2004/1034, SI 2004/1747

s.8, applied: SI 1982/1109 r.32, SI 1996/513 Sch.2 para.36f, SI 2004/1048 r.5

s.9, amended: 2003 c.44 Sch.37 Part 6, SI 2004/1501 Sch.2

s.13, applied: SI 1996/513 Sch.2 para.36h

s.13, referred to: 1987 c.38 s.2

s.15, applied: SI 1982/1109 r.32A, r.32B, 1987 c.38 s.2, 1995 c.39 s.27, SI 1996/513 Sch.2 para.36j, SI 2004/1048 r.6, r.7

s.17, applied: 2001 c.16 Sch.1 para.73C

s.22, applied: 2001 c.16 Sch.1 para.73C

s.30, applied: SI 1982/1109 r.32C, r.32D, SI 1996/513 Sch.2 para.36i, Sch.2 para.36j, SI 2004/1048 r.8, r.9

s.30, referred to: SI 2004/1048 r.8

s.31, applied: SI 1982/1109 r.32C, r.32E, SI 1996/513 Sch.2 para.36i, Sch.2 para.36j, SI 2004/1048 r.8, r.10

s.31, referred to: SI 2004/1048 r.8

s.47, applied: 1995 c.46 s.210

s.49, enabling: SI 2004/1047, SI 2004/1048

s.86, repealed: SI 2004/1897 Art.2

s.87, repealed: SI 2004/1897 Art.2

s.92, referred to: SI 2003/2903

s.93, applied: SI 2004/787

s.93, enabling: SI 2004/787

s.94, enabling: SI 2004/786, SI 2004/2624, SSI 2004/175

Sch.1, applied: SI 1982/1109 r.32A, r.32B, 2004/1048 r.6, r.7

Sch.1 para.6, applied: SI 1982/1109 r.32B, SI 1996/513 Sch.2 para.36j, SI 2004/1048 r.7

Sch.2 Part 1, applied: SI 1982/1109 r.32C, r.32D, SI 2004/1048 r.8, r.9

Sch.2 Part 2, applied: SI 1982/1109 r.32E, SI 2004/1048 r.8, r.10

33. Waste and Emissions Trading Act 2003

Commencement Orders: SI 2004/1163 Art.2; SI 2004/1488 Art.2; SI 2004/1874 Art.2; SI 2004/3181 Art.2; SI 2004/3192 Art.2; SI 2004/3319 Art.2; SI 2004/3320 Art.2

applied: SI 2004/1490 Reg.15

Part 1 c.1, applied: SI 2004/1490 Reg.11

s.1, applied: SI 2004/1936

s.1, enabling: SI 2004/1936

2003–cont.

33. Waste and Emissions Trading Act 2003–*cont.*

s.2, applied: SI 2004/1936

s.2, enabling: SI 2004/1936, SI 2004/3027

s.4, applied: SI 2004/1490 Reg.10

s.5, applied: SI 2004/1490 Reg.10

s.6, enabling: SI 2004/3212

s.7, enabling: SI 2004/3212

s.9, applied: SI 2004/1490 Reg.13

s.10, enabling: SI 2004/1490, SI 2004/3212

s.11, enabling: SI 2004/1490, SI 2004/3212

s.12, applied: SI 2004/1490 Reg.14

s.12, enabling: SI 2004/1490, SI 2004/3212

s.13, enabling: SI 2004/1490, SI 2004/3212

s.15, enabling: SI 2004/1490, SI 2004/3212

s.16, enabling: SI 2004/1490, SI 2004/3212

s.17, applied: 1999 c.29 s.353, s.354

s.23, amended: SI 2004/1936 Reg.2

s.23, applied: SI 2004/1936

s.23, enabling: SI 2004/1936

s.26, applied: SI 2004/1490 Reg.11

s.26, enabling: SI 2004/1490, SI 2004/3212

s.28, applied: SI 2004/1936

s.33, enabling: SI 2004/3242

s.36, enabling: SI 2004/1490, SI 2004/1936

s.40, enabling: SI 2004/1163, SI 2004/1488, SI 2004/1874, SI 2004/3181, SI 2004/3192, SI 2004/3319, SI 2004/3320, SI 2004/3321

35. European Union (Accessions) Act 2003

s.2, enabling: SI 2004/1219

36. Fire Services Act 2003

s.1, amended: 2004 c.21 Sch.1 para.105, Sch.2

s.1, repealed (in part): 2004 c.21 Sch.1 para.105, Sch.2

s.1, substituted: 2004 c.21 Sch.2

s.3, amended: 2004 c.21 Sch.1 para.106, Sch.2

s.3, repealed (in part): 2004 c.21 Sch.1 para.106, Sch.2

s.3, substituted: 2004 c.21 Sch.2

37. Water Act 2003

Commencement Orders: SI 2004/641 Art.2, Art.3, Art.4, Art.5, Sch.1, Sch.2, Sch.3 para.7; SI 2004/910 Art.2; SI 2004/2528 Art.2, Art.3, Sch.1 para.5, para.8; SI 2004/2916 Art.2

applied: 1991 c.56 s.206, 1991 c.57 s.204, 2002 c.40 Sch.15

referred to: 1984 c.12 s.101, 1986 c.31 s.74, 2000 c.26 Sch.7 para.3, 2000 c.27 s.105

varied: SI 2004/641 Sch.3 para.7

s.35, applied: SI 2004/2528 Sch.1 para.3

s.55, applied: 1991 c.56 s.16A

s.67, referred to: SI 2004/910

s.100, applied: SI 2004/2528 Sch.1 para.7

s.104, enabling: SI 2004/641, SI 2004/2528

s.105, enabling: SI 2004/641, SI 2004/910, SI 2004/2528, SI 2004/2916

2003–cont.

38. Anti-social Behaviour Act 2003

Commencement Orders: SI 2003/3300 Art.2, Art.3, Art.4, Art.5; SI 2004/690 Art.2, Art.3, Art.4; SI 2004/999 Art.2; SI 2004/1502 Art.2, Art.3, Sch.1 para.3; SI 2004/2168 Art.2, Art.3, Art.4, Art.5; SI 2004/2557 Art.2, Sch.1 para.1, para.2, para.3; SI 2004/3238 Art.2

Part 2, applied: SI 2003/3300 Art.5

s.2, applied: SI 2001/1437 Reg.3

s.5, applied: SI 2001/1437 Reg.3

s.6, applied: SI 2001/1437 Reg.3

s.12, applied: 1996 c.52 s.218A

s.20, applied: SI 2004/182, SI 2004/182 Reg.3, SI 2004/247 r.3, r.4, r.9

s.20, enabling: SI 2004/182

s.21, applied: SI 2004/182

s.21, enabling: SI 2004/182

s.25, applied: 1998 c.37 s.38

s.26, applied: 1998 c.37 s.38, SI 2004/247 r.5, r.6, r.9

s.27, applied: 1998 c.37 s.38

s.30, applied: 2002 c.30 Sch.4 para.4A

s.40, amended: 2003 c.44 Sch.26 para.59

s.43, applied: 2002 c.30 Sch.5 para.1, SI 2004/915 Sch.1 para.1

s.68, enabling: SI 2004/3241

s.72, enabling: SI 2004/3240

s.91, applied: SI 1998/3132 r.65.1, r.65.8, r.65.9, r.65.10

s.91, disapplied: SI 2004/1502 Sch.1 para.3

s.93, enabling: SI 2003/3300, SI 2004/690, SI 2004/999, SI 2004/1502, SI 2004/2168, SI 2004/2557, SI 2004/3238

s.94, applied: SI 2004/182

s.94, enabling: SI 2004/182, SI 2004/1502, SI 2004/2168, SI 2004/2557

39. Courts Act 2003

Commencement Orders: SI 2003/3345 Art.2; SI 2004/174 Art.2, Art.3, Art.4; SI 2004/175 Sch.1 Part I, II; SI 2004/401 Art.2, Art.3; SI 2004/798 Art.2; SI 2004/1104 Art.3; SI 2004/2066 Art.2; SI 2004/2195 Art.2; SI 2004/3123 Art.2

applied: SI 1998/3132 Sch.1 para.1, Sch.2 para.7

s.2, referred to: SI 2004/1193 Reg.4

s.4, enabling: SI 2004/1192, SI 2004/1303

s.8, referred to: 2004 c.28 Sch.12 para.9

s.37, referred to: 2004 c.28 Sch.12 para.9, SI 2004/2408 Reg.2

s.69, applied: SI 2004/2066 Art.3

s.76, amended: 2004 c.31 s.62, 2004 c.33 Sch.27 para.172

s.92, applied: SI 2004/3114, SI 2004/3121

s.92, enabling: SI 2004/3114, SI 2004/3120, SI 2004/3121

s.97, applied: SI 2004/176 Reg.2

s.97, enabling: SI 2004/175, SI 2004/176, SI 2004/1406, SI 2004/1407, SI 2004/2198

s.98, applied: SI 2003/3184 Reg.2, Reg.8

2003–cont.

39. Courts Act 2003–*cont.*

s.98, enabling: SI 2003/3184

s.100, referred to: SI 2004/3129 r.1

s.108, applied: SI 2004/1192

s.108, enabling: SI 2003/3184, SI 2004/175, SI 2004/176, SI 2004/400, SI 2004/401, SI 2004/1406, SI 2004/1407, SI 2004/2066, SI 2004/3114, SI 2004/3120, SI 2004/3121, SI 2004/3123

s.109, varied: 2004 c.28 Sch.5 para.10

s.109, enabling: SI 2004/175, SI 2004/176, SI 2004/1406, SI 2004/2035, SI 2004/3123

s.110, enabling: SI 2003/3345, SI 2004/174, SI 2004/401, SI 2004/798, SI 2004/1104, SI 2004/2066, SI 2004/2195, SI 2004/3123

Sch.1 para.2, referred to: SI 2004/1193 Reg.5

Sch.1 para.3, enabling: SI 2004/1193

Sch.1 para.4, enabling: SI 2004/1193

Sch.1 para.5, enabling: SI 2004/1193

Sch.1 para.7, enabling: SI 2004/1193

Sch.2 Part 2 para.13, referred to: SI 2004/1193 Reg.4

Sch.5, applied: SI 2003/3184 Reg.4, SI 2004/176 Reg.2, Reg.4, Reg.5, Reg.6, Reg.12, Reg.20, SI 2004/1407 Reg.1

Sch.5, disapplied: 2004 c.28 s.14

Sch.5, referred to: SI 2003/3184 Reg.1, Reg.4, 2004 c.28 s.14, SI 2004/176 Reg.1

Sch.5 Part 1 para.1, amended: 2004 c.28 s.14

Sch.5 Part 1 para.1, varied: SI 2004/176 Reg.10

Sch.5 Part 1 para.2, varied: SI 2004/176 Reg.10

Sch.5 Part 1 para.3, varied: SI 2004/175 Art.2, SI 2004/176 Reg.10

Sch.5 Part 2 para.4, varied: SI 2004/175 Art.2, Sch.1 para.1, SI 2004/176 Reg.10

Sch.5 Part 2 para.5, varied: SI 2004/175 Art.2, Sch.1 para.1, SI 2004/176 Reg.10

Sch.5 Part 2 para.6, varied: SI 2004/175 Art.2, Sch.1 para.1, SI 2004/176 Reg.10

Sch.5 Part 3 para.7, varied: SI 2004/176 Reg.10

Sch.5 Part 3 para.8, varied: SI 2004/176 Reg.10

Sch.5 Part 3 para.9, varied: SI 2004/176 Reg.10

Sch.5 Part 3 para.10, varied: SI 2004/176 Reg.10

Sch.5 Part 4 para.11, varied: SI 2004/175 Art.2, SI 2004/176 Reg.10

Sch.5 Part 4 para.12, varied: SI 2004/175 Art.2, SI 2004/176 Reg.10

Sch.5 Part 4 para.13, varied: SI 2004/175 Art.2, SI 2004/176 Reg.10

Sch.5 Part 4 para.14, varied: SI 2004/175 Art.2, SI 2004/176 Reg.10

Sch.5 Part 4 para.15, varied: SI 2004/175 Art.2, SI 2004/176 Reg.10

2003–cont.

39. Courts Act 2003–*cont.*

Sch.5 Part 4 para.16, varied: SI 2004/175 Art.2, SI 2004/176 Reg.10

Sch.5 Part 4 para.17, varied: SI 2004/175 Art.2, SI 2004/176 Reg.10

Sch.5 Part 5 para.18, varied: SI 2004/175 Art.2, Sch.1 para.1, SI 2004/176 Reg.10

Sch.5 Part 5 para.19, varied: SI 2004/175 Art.2, Sch.1 para.1, SI 2004/176 Reg.10

Sch.5 Part 5 para.20, varied: SI 2004/175 Art.2, Sch.1 para.1, SI 2004/176 Reg.10

Sch.5 Part 6 para.21, varied: SI 2004/175 Art.2, SI 2004/176 Reg.10

Sch.5 Part 6 para.22, varied: SI 2004/175 Art.2, SI 2004/176 Reg.10

Sch.5 Part 6 para.23, varied: SI 2004/175 Art.2, SI 2004/176 Reg.10

Sch.5 Part 6 para.24, varied: SI 2004/175 Art.2, SI 2004/176 Reg.10

Sch.5 Part 7 para.25, varied: SI 2004/175 Art.2, SI 2004/176 Reg.10

Sch.5 Part 7 para.26, varied: SI 2004/175 Art.2, SI 2004/176 Reg.10

Sch.5 Part 7 para.27, applied: SI 2004/176 Reg.7

Sch.5 Part 7 para.27, varied: SI 2004/175 Art.2, Sch.1 para.2, SI 2004/176 Reg.10

Sch.5 Part 7 para.27, enabling: SI 2004/176

Sch.5 Part 7 para.28, applied: SI 2004/176 Reg.8

Sch.5 Part 7 para.28, varied: SI 2004/175 Art.2, Sch.1 para.2, SI 2004/176 Reg.10

Sch.5 Part 8 para.29, varied: SI 2004/175 Art.2, SI 2004/176 Reg.10

Sch.5 Part 8 para.30, varied: SI 2004/175 Art.2, SI 2004/176 Reg.10

Sch.5 Part 8 para.31, varied: SI 2004/175 Art.2, Sch.1 para.3, SI 2004/176 Reg.10

Sch.5 Part 8 para.32, varied: SI 2004/175 Art.2, SI 2004/176 Reg.10

Sch.5 Part 8 para.33, applied: SI 2004/176 Reg.7

Sch.5 Part 8 para.33, varied: SI 2004/175 Art.2, Sch.1 para.3, SI 2004/176 Reg.10

Sch.5 Part 8 para.33, enabling: SI 2004/176

Sch.5 Part 8 para.34, varied: SI 2004/175 Art.2, Sch.1 para.3, SI 2004/176 Reg.10

Sch.5 Part 9 para.35, applied: SI 2004/176 Reg.11

Sch.5 Part 9 para.35, varied: SI 2004/175 Art.2, Sch.1 para.3, SI 2004/176 Reg.10

Sch.5 Part 9 para.36, varied: SI 2004/175 Art.2, Sch.1 para.3, SI 2004/176 Reg.10

Sch.5 Part 9 para.37, applied: SI 2004/176 Reg.8, Reg.11

Sch.5 Part 9 para.37, varied: SI 2004/175 Art.2, Sch.1 para.3, SI 2004/176 Reg.10

Sch.5 Part 9 para.38, referred to: SI 2004/176 Reg.9

2003–cont.

39. Courts Act 2003–*cont.*

Sch.5 Part 9 para.38, varied: SI 2004/175 Art.2, Sch.1 para.4, Sch.1 para.5, Sch.1 para.6, SI 2004/176 Reg.10

Sch.5 Part 9 para.38, enabling: SI 2004/176 Reg.13

Sch.5 Part 9 para.39, applied: SI 2004/176 Reg.13

Sch.5 Part 9 para.39, varied: SI 2004/175 Art.2, Sch.1 para.3, SI 2004/176 Reg.10

Sch.5 Part 9 para.40, applied: SI 2004/176 Reg.13

Sch.5 Part 9 para.40, varied: SI 2004/175 Art.2, SI 2004/176 Reg.10

Sch.5 Part 9 para.41, applied: SI 2004/176 Reg.18, Reg.23, Reg.24

Sch.5 Part 9 para.41, varied: SI 2004/175 Art.2, Sch.1 para.7, SI 2004/176 Reg.10

Sch.5 Part 9 para.41, enabling: SI 2004/176

Sch.5 Part 9 para.42, applied: SI 2004/176 Reg.11, Reg.22, Reg.24

Sch.5 Part 9 para.42, varied: SI 2004/175 Art.2, SI 2004/176 Reg.10

Sch.5 Part 9 para.42, enabling: SI 2004/176

Sch.5 Part 10 para.43, varied: SI 2004/176 Reg.10

Sch.5 Part 10 para.43, enabling: SI 2004/176, SI 2004/1407

Sch.5 Part 10 para.44, varied: SI 2004/176 Reg.10

Sch.5 Part 10 para.44, enabling: SI 2004/176, SI 2004/1407

Sch.5 Part 10 para.45, varied: SI 2004/176 Reg.10

Sch.5 Part 10 para.45, enabling: SI 2004/176, SI 2004/1407

Sch.5 Part 10 para.46, varied: SI 2004/176 Reg.10

Sch.5 Part 10 para.46, enabling: SI 2004/176

Sch.5 Part 10 para.47, varied: SI 2004/175 Art.2, SI 2004/176 Reg.10

Sch.5 Part 10 para.47, enabling: SI 2004/176

Sch.5 Part 10 para.48, varied: SI 2004/176 Reg.10

Sch.5 Part 10 para.49, applied: SI 2004/176 Reg.19

Sch.5 Part 10 para.49, varied: SI 2004/175 Art.2, Sch.1 para.7, SI 2004/176 Reg.10

Sch.5 Part 10 para.50, varied: SI 2004/176 Reg.10

Sch.5 Part 10 para.50, enabling: SI 2004/176

Sch.5 Part 10 para.51, varied: SI 2004/176 Reg.10

Sch.5 Part 10 para.52, varied: SI 2004/176 Reg.10

Sch.5 Part 10 para.53, varied: SI 2004/176 Reg.10

Sch.6, disapplied: 2004 c.28 s.14

Sch.6, referred to: 2004 c.28 s.14

Sch.6 para.1, applied: SI 2004/2197

Sch.6 para.1, varied: SI 2004/2196 Reg.2, SI 2004/2198 Art.2

2003–cont.

39. Courts Act 2003–*cont.*
Sch.6 para.1, enabling: SI 2004/2196
Sch.6 para.2, varied: SI 2004/2198 Art.2
Sch.6 para.3, varied: SI 2004/2198 Art.2
Sch.6 para.4, varied: SI 2004/2198 Art.2
Sch.6 para.5, varied: SI 2004/2198 Art.2
Sch.6 para.6, varied: SI 2004/2198 Art.2
Sch.6 para.7, varied: SI 2004/2198 Art.2
Sch.6 para.8, applied: SI 2004/2197 Reg.2
Sch.6 para.8, varied: SI 2004/2198 Art.2
Sch.6 para.8, enabling: SI 2004/2197
Sch.6 para.9, varied: SI 2004/2198 Art.2
Sch.6 para.10, varied: SI 2004/2198 Art.2
Sch.6 para.11, varied: SI 2004/2198 Art.2
Sch.6 para.12, varied: SI 2004/2198 Art.2
Sch.6 para.13, varied: SI 2004/2198 Art.2
Sch.7, applied: SI 2004/400 Reg.2, Reg.3
Sch.7 para.4, varied: SI 2004/401 Art.3
Sch.7 para.7, varied: SI 2004/401 Art.3
Sch.7 para.8, varied: SI 2004/401 Art.3
Sch.7 para.9, varied: SI 2004/401 Art.3
Sch.7 para.10, applied: SI 1998/3132 Sch.1 para.6
Sch.7 para.10, varied: SI 2004/401 Art.3
Sch.7 para.11, varied: SI 2004/401 Art.3
Sch.7 para.12, applied: SI 2004/673
Sch.7 para.12, enabling: SI 2004/400, SI 2004/673
Sch.9 para.15, enabling: SI 2004/175, SI 2004/176, SI 2004/1406

41. Extradition Act 2003
Commencement Orders: SI 2003/3103 Art.2, Art.3, Art.4, Art.5; SI 2003/3258 Art.2
applied: 1967 c.13 Sch.3 para.4,1978 c.26 s.5, 2001 c.17 Sch.2 para.10
referred to: SI 2003/3150 Art.2
varied: SI 2003/3150 Sch.1 para.1
Part 1, applied: 1985 c.23 s.3, SI 1996/513 Sch.2 para.34c, SI 2003/3109 Art.2
Part 2, applied: 1985 c.23 s.3, SI 2003/3334 Art.2
Part 3, applied: SI 1996/513 Sch.2 para.34g
Part 4, applied: SI 2003/3336
s.1, applied: SI 2003/3333 Art.2
s.1, enabling: SI 2003/3333, SI 2004/1898
s.2, applied: 2002 c.41 s.94
s.2, enabling: SI 2003/3109
s.5, applied: SI 1996/513 Sch.2 para.34c, 2002 c.41 s.94
s.10, varied: SI 2003/3150 Sch.1 para.2
s.11, varied: SI 2003/3150 Sch.1 para.3
s.20, varied: SI 2003/3150 Sch.1 para.4
s.21, varied: SI 2003/3150 Sch.1 para.5
s.26, applied: SI 1996/513 Sch.2 para.34b, Sch.2 para.34c
s.26, varied: SI 2003/3150 Sch.1 para.6
s.27, varied: SI 2003/3150 Sch.1 para.7
s.28, applied: SI 1996/513 Sch.2 para.34b, Sch.2 para.34c
s.28, varied: SI 2003/3150 Sch.1 para.8

2003–cont.

41. Extradition Act 2003–*cont.*
s.29, varied: SI 2003/3150 Sch.1 para.9
s.30, varied: SI 2003/3150 Sch.1 para.10
s.31, applied: SI 1996/513 Sch.2 para.34c, Sch.2 para.34d
s.32, varied: SI 2003/3150 Sch.1 para.11
s.33, varied: SI 2003/3150 Sch.1 para.12
s.35, varied: SI 2003/3150 Sch.1 para.13
s.36, varied: SI 2003/3150 Sch.1 para.14
s.41, varied: SI 2003/3150 Sch.1 para.15
s.42, varied: SI 2003/3150 Sch.1 para.16
s.43, varied: SI 2003/3150 Sch.1 para.17
s.45, varied: SI 2003/3150 Sch.1 para.18
s.47, varied: SI 2003/3150 Sch.1 para.19
s.49, varied: SI 2003/3150 Sch.1 para.20
s.54, applied: SI 1996/513 Sch.2 para.34f
s.56, applied: SI 1996/513 Sch.2 para.34f
s.69, enabling: SI 2003/3334, SI 2004/1898
s.70, applied: 2002 c.41 s.94
s.71, applied: SI 2003/3334 Art.3
s.71, varied: SI 2003/3150 Sch.1 para.21
s.71, enabling: SI 2003/3334, SI 2004/1898
s.73, applied: 2002 c.41 s.94, SI 2003/3334 Art.3
s.73, varied: SI 2003/3150 Sch.1 para.22
s.73, enabling: SI 2003/3334, SI 2004/1898
s.74, applied: SI 1996/513 Sch.2 para.34a, SI 2003/3334 Art.4
s.74, enabling: SI 2003/3334, SI 2004/1898
s.78, varied: SI 2003/3150 Sch.1 para.23
s.79, varied: SI 2003/3150 Sch.1 para.24
s.84, applied: SI 2003/3334 Art.3
s.84, varied: SI 2003/3150 Sch.1 para.25
s.84, enabling: SI 2003/3334, SI 2004/1898
s.85, varied: SI 2003/3150 Sch.1 para.26
s.86, applied: SI 2003/3334 Art.3
s.86, varied: SI 2003/3150 Sch.1 para.27
s.86, enabling: SI 2003/3334, SI 2004/1898
s.87, varied: SI 2003/3150 Sch.1 para.28
s.92, varied: SI 2003/3150 Sch.1 para.29
s.93, varied: SI 2003/3150 Sch.1 para.30
s.94, varied: SI 2003/3150 Sch.1 para.31
s.95, varied: SI 2003/3150 Sch.1 para.32
s.100, varied: SI 2003/3150 Sch.1 para.33
s.103, applied: SI 1996/513 Sch.2 para.34b, Sch.2 para.34c
s.103, varied: SI 2003/3150 Sch.1 para.34
s.104, varied: SI 2003/3150 Sch.1 para.35
s.105, applied: SI 1996/513 Sch.2 para.34b, Sch.2 para.34c
s.105, varied: SI 2003/3150 Sch.1 para.36
s.106, varied: SI 2003/3150 Sch.1 para.37
s.107, varied: SI 2003/3150 Sch.1 para.38
s.108, applied: SI 1996/513 Sch.2 para.34b, Sch.2 para.34c
s.108, varied: SI 2003/3150 Sch.1 para.39
s.109, varied: SI 2003/3150 Sch.1 para.40
s.110, applied: SI 1996/513 Sch.2 para.34b, Sch.2 para.34c
s.110, varied: SI 2003/3150 Sch.1 para.41

CAP.

41. Extradition Act 2003–*cont.*

s.111, varied: SI 2003/3150 Sch.1 para.42

s.112, varied: SI 2003/3150 Sch.1 para.43

s.113, applied: SI 1996/513 Sch.2 para.34c, Sch.2 para.34d

s.114, varied: SI 2003/3150 Sch.1 para.44

s.115, varied: SI 2003/3150 Sch.1 para.45

s.117, varied: SI 2003/3150 Sch.1 para.46

s.118, varied: SI 2003/3150 Sch.1 para.47

s.122, varied: SI 2003/3150 Sch.1 para.48

s.123, varied: SI 2003/3150 Sch.1 para.49

s.124, varied: SI 2003/3150 Sch.1 para.50

s.125, varied: SI 2003/3150 Sch.1 para.51

s.127, varied: SI 2003/3150 Sch.1 para.52

s.128, varied: SI 2003/3150 Sch.1 para.53

s.142, applied: SI 1996/513 Sch.2 para.34g, SI 2003/3335 Art.2

s.142, enabling: SI 2003/3335

s.156, applied: 2001 c.16 Sch.1 para.73D

s.160, applied: 2001 c.16 Sch.1 para.73D

s.161, applied: 2001 c.16 Sch.1 para.73D

s.162, applied: 2001 c.16 Sch.1 para.73D

s.163, applied: 2001 c.16 Sch.1 para.83A

s.164, applied: 2001 c.16 Sch.1 para.73D

s.171, referred to: SI 2003/3107 Art.2

s.171, enabling: SI 2003/3106, SI 2003/3107

s.173, applied: SI 2003/3336

s.173, enabling: SI 2003/3336

s.207, enabling: SI 2003/3150

s.208, varied: SI 2003/3150 Sch.1 para.54

s.210, enabling: SSI 2004/346

s.219, enabling: SI 2004/1897

s.221, enabling: SI 2003/3103, SI 2003/3258, SI 2003/3312

s.223, applied: SI 2003/3336

s.223, enabling: SI 2003/3103, SI 2003/3150, SI 2003/3258, SI 2003/3312

42. Sexual Offences Act 2003

Commencement Orders: SI 2004/874 Art.2; SSI 2004/138 Art.2

applied: SI 2004/1178 Reg.2, SI 2004/2695 Sch.1 para.3

Part 1, applied: 1952 c.67 Sch.1 para.1, 1980 c.43 s.103, 1988 c.33 s.32, 1992 c.34 s.2, 1997 c.39 Sch.1 para.5A, 1999 c.23 s.35

Part 2, applied: 1974 c.53 s.7, 1991 c.53 s.46A, s.34A, SI 1996/513 Sch.2 para.46, 2000 c.43 s.69, 2003 c.44 s.246, s.260, s.327, SI 2004/1220 Reg.10, SSI 2004/205 Reg.10

Part 2, referred to: 1991 c.53 s.46A, 2004 c.28 s.45

s.1, applied: 1933 c.12 Sch.1, 1955 c.18 s.70, 1955 c.19 s.70, 1957 c.53 s.48, 1968 c.27 Sch.1 para.6, 1978 c.17 s.1, 1978 c.26 Sch.1 para.9, 1994 c.33 s.25, 1996 c.29 Sch.1 para.1, 2000 c.6 s.109, s.161, 2000 c.43 Sch.4 para.2, 2003 c.44 Sch.4 para.7, Sch.4 para.8, Sch.5 para.6, Sch.5 para.7, Sch.15 para.102, SI 2003/1184 Sch.2 para.14B, SI 2004/1910 Sch.2

CAP.

42. Sexual Offences Act 2003–*cont.*

s.1, referred to: 1984 c.60 Sch.5 para.18

s.2, applied: 1933 c.12 Sch.1, 1968 c.27 Sch.1 para.6, 1978 c.17 s.1, 1978 c.26 Sch.1 para.9, 1994 c.33 s.25, 1996 c.29 Sch.1 para.1, 2000 c.6 s.109, s.161, 2000 c.43 Sch.4 para.2, 2003 c.44 Sch.4 para.11, Sch.5 para.10, Sch.15 para.103, SI 2003/1184 Sch.2 para.14C, SI 2004/1910 Sch.2

s.2, referred to: 1984 c.60 Sch.5 para.19

s.3, applied: 1933 c.12 Sch.1, 1996 c.29 Sch.1 para.1, 2000 c.6 s.91, s.161, 2000 c.43 Sch.4 para.2, 2003 c.44 Sch.15 para.104, SI 2003/1184 Sch.2 para.14D, SI 2004/1910 Sch.2

s.4, applied: 1933 c.12 Sch.1, 1968 c.27 Sch.1 para.6, 1978 c.17 s.1, 1978 c.26 Sch.1 para.9, 1994 c.33 s.25, 1996 c.29 Sch.1 para.1, 2000 c.6 s.109, s.161, 2000 c.43 Sch.4 para.2, 2003 c.44 Sch.4 para.12, Sch.5 para.11, Sch.15 para.105, SI 2003/1184 Sch.2 para.14E, SI 2004/1910 Sch.2

s.4, referred to: 1984 c.60 Sch.5 para.20

s.5, applied: 1933 c.12 Sch.1, 1968 c.27 Sch.1 para.6, 1978 c.17 s.1, 1978 c.26 Sch.1 para.9, 1994 c.33 s.25, 1996 c.29 Sch.1 para.1, 2000 c.6 s.109, s.161, 2000 c.43 Sch.4 para.1, 2003 c.44 Sch.4 para.13, Sch.4 para.14, Sch.5 para.12, Sch.5 para.13, Sch.15 para.106, SI 2003/1184 Sch.2 para.14F, SI 2004/1910 Sch.2

s.5, referred to: 1984 c.60 Sch.5 para.21

s.6, applied: 1933 c.12 Sch.1, 1968 c.27 Sch.1 para.6, 1978 c.17 s.1, 1978 c.26 Sch.1 para.9, 1994 c.33 s.25, 1996 c.29 Sch.1 para.1, 2000 c.6 s.109, s.161, 2000 c.43 Sch.4 para.1, 2003 c.44 Sch.4 para.15, Sch.5 para.14, Sch.15 para.107, SI 2003/1184 Sch.2 para.14G, SI 2004/1910 Sch.2

s.6, referred to: 1984 c.60 Sch.5 para.22

s.7, applied: 1933 c.12 Sch.1, 1996 c.29 Sch.1 para.1, 2000 c.6 s.161, 2000 c.43 Sch.4 para.1, 2003 c.44 Sch.15 para.108, SI 2003/1184 Sch.2 para.14H, SI 2004/1910 Sch.2

s.8, applied: 1933 c.12 Sch.1, 1968 c.27 Sch.1 para.6, 1978 c.17 s.1, 1978 c.26 Sch.1 para.9, 1994 c.33 s.25, 1996 c.29 Sch.1 para.1, 2000 c.6 s.109, s.161, 2000 c.43 Sch.4 para.1, 2003 c.44 Sch.4 para.16, Sch.5 para.15, Sch.15 para.109, SI 2003/1184 Sch.2 para.14I, SI 2004/1910 Sch.2

s.8, referred to: 1984 c.60 Sch.5 para.23

s.9, applied: 1933 c.12 Sch.1, 1996 c.29 Sch.1 para.1, 2000 c.6 s.161, 2000 c.43 Sch.4 para.1, 2003 c.44 Sch.15 para.110, SI 2003/1184 Sch.2 para.14J, SI 2004/1910 Sch.2

s.10, applied: 1933 c.12 Sch.1, 1996 c.29 Sch.1 para.1, 2000 c.6 s.161, 2000 c.43 Sch.4 para.1, 2003 c.44 Sch.15 para.111, SI

2003–cont.

42. Sexual Offences Act 2003–*cont.*

s.10, applied:–*cont.*

2003/1184 Sch.2 para.14K, SI 2004/1910 Sch.2

s.11, applied: 1933 c.12 Sch.1, 1996 c.29 Sch.1 para.1, 2000 c.6 s.161, 2000 c.43 Sch.4 para.1, 2003 c.44 Sch.15 para.112, SI 2003/1184 Sch.2 para.14L, SI 2004/1910 Sch.2

s.12, applied: 1933 c.12 Sch.1, 1996 c.29 Sch.1 para.1, 2000 c.6 s.161, 2000 c.43 Sch.4 para.1, 2003 c.44 Sch.15 para.113, SI 2003/1184 Sch.2 para.14M, SI 2004/1910 Sch.2

s.13, applied: 1933 c.12 Sch.1, 2000 c.6 s.91, s.161, 2000 c.43 Sch.4 para.1, 2003 c.44 Sch.15 para.114, SI 2004/1910 Sch.2

s.14, applied: 1933 c.12 Sch.1, 1996 c.29 Sch.1 para.1, 2000 c.6 s.161, 2000 c.43 Sch.4 para.1, 2003 c.44 Sch.15 para.115, SI 2003/1184 Sch.2 para.14N, SI 2004/1910 Sch.2

s.15, applied: 1933 c.12 Sch.1, 1992 c.34 s.2, 1996 c.29 Sch.1 para.1, 2000 c.6 s.161, 2000 c.43 Sch.4 para.1, 2003 c.44 Sch.15 para.116, Sch.17 para.90, SI 2003/1184 Sch.2 para.14O, SI 2004/1910 Sch.6

s.16, applied: 1933 c.12 Sch.1, 1992 c.34 s.2, 1996 c.29 Sch.1 para.1, 2000 c.6 s.161, 2000 c.43 Sch.4 para.1, 2003 c.44 Sch.15 para.117, Sch.17 para.91, SI 2003/1184 Sch.2 para.14P, SI 2004/1910 Sch.6

s.17, applied: 1933 c.12 Sch.1, 1992 c.34 s.2, 1996 c.29 Sch.1 para.1, 2000 c.6 s.161, 2000 c.43 Sch.4 para.1, 2003 c.44 Sch.15 para.118, Sch.17 para.92, SI 2003/1184 Sch.2 para.14Q, SI 2004/1910 Sch.6

s.18, applied: 1933 c.12 Sch.1, 1992 c.34 s.2, 1996 c.29 Sch.1 para.1, 2000 c.6 s.161, 2000 c.43 Sch.4 para.1, 2003 c.44 Sch.15 para.119, Sch.17 para.93, SI 2003/1184 Sch.2 para.14R

s.19, applied: 1933 c.12 Sch.1, 1992 c.34 s.2, 1996 c.29 Sch.1 para.1, 2000 c.6 s.161, 2000 c.43 Sch.4 para.1, 2003 c.44 Sch.15 para.120, Sch.17 para.94, SI 2003/1184 Sch.2 para.14S

s.20, applied: 1933 c.12 Sch.1, 1992 c.34 s.2, 1996 c.29 Sch.1 para.1, 2000 c.6 s.161, 2000 c.43 Sch.4 para.1

s.21, amended: 2004 c.31 Sch.3 para.18

s.21, applied: 1933 c.12 Sch.1, 1992 c.34 s.2, 1996 c.29 Sch.1 para.1, 2000 c.6 s.161, 2000 c.43 Sch.4 para.1

s.22, applied: 1933 c.12 Sch.1, 1996 c.29 Sch.1 para.1, 2000 c.6 s.161, 2000 c.43 Sch.4 para.1

s.23, amended: 2004 c.33 Sch.27 para.173

s.23, applied: 1933 c.12 Sch.1, 1996 c.29 Sch.1 para.1, 2000 c.6 s.161, 2000 c.43 Sch.4 para.1

2003–cont.

42. Sexual Offences Act 2003–*cont.*

s.24, applied: 1933 c.12 Sch.1, 1996 c.29 Sch.1 para.1, 2000 c.6 s.161, 2000 c.43 Sch.4 para.1

s.25, applied: 1933 c.12 Sch.1, 1996 c.29 Sch.1 para.1, 2000 c.6 s.91, s.161, 2000 c.43 Sch.4 para.1, 2003 c.44 Sch.15 para.121, SI 2003/1184 Sch.2 para.14T, SI 2004/1910 Sch.2

s.26, applied: 1933 c.12 Sch.1, 1996 c.29 Sch.1 para.1, 2000 c.6 s.91, s.161, 2000 c.43 Sch.4 para.1, 2003 c.44 Sch.15 para.122, SI 2003/1184 Sch.2 para.14U, SI 2004/1910 Sch.2

s.27, applied: 1933 c.12 Sch.1, 2000 c.6 s.161

s.28, amended: 2004 c.33 Sch.27 para.174

s.28, applied: 1933 c.12 Sch.1, 2000 c.6 s.161

s.29, applied: 1933 c.12 Sch.1, 2000 c.6 s.161

s.30, applied: 1933 c.12 Sch.1, 1968 c.27 Sch.1 para.6, 1978 c.17 s.1, 1978 c.26 Sch.1 para.9, 1994 c.33 s.25, 1995 c.53 s.11, 2000 c.6 s.109, s.161, 2000 c.43 Sch.4 para.2, 2003 c.44 Sch.4 para.17, Sch.5 para.16, Sch.15 para.123, SI 2004/1910 Sch.2

s.30, referred to: 1984 c.60 Sch.5 para.24

s.31, applied: 1933 c.12 Sch.1, 1968 c.27 Sch.1 para.6, 1978 c.17 s.1, 1978 c.26 Sch.1 para.9, 1994 c.33 s.25, 2000 c.6 s.109, s.161, 2000 c.43 Sch.4 para.2, 2003 c.44 Sch.4 para.18, Sch.5 para.17, Sch.15 para.124, SI 2004/1910 Sch.2

s.31, referred to: 1984 c.60 Sch.5 para.25

s.32, applied: 1933 c.12 Sch.1, 2000 c.6 s.161, 2000 c.43 Sch.4 para.2, 2003 c.44 Sch.15 para.125, SI 2004/1910 Sch.2

s.33, applied: 1933 c.12 Sch.1, 2000 c.6 s.161, 2000 c.43 Sch.4 para.2, 2003 c.44 Sch.15 para.126, SI 2004/1910 Sch.2

s.34, applied: 1933 c.12 Sch.1, 2000 c.6 s.161, 2000 c.43 Sch.4 para.2, 2003 c.44 Sch.15 para.127, SI 2004/1910 Sch.2

s.35, applied: 1933 c.12 Sch.1, 2000 c.6 s.161, 2000 c.43 Sch.4 para.2, 2003 c.44 Sch.15 para.128, SI 2004/1910 Sch.2

s.36, applied: 1933 c.12 Sch.1, 2000 c.6 s.161, 2000 c.43 Sch.4 para.2, 2003 c.44 Sch.15 para.129, SI 2004/1910 Sch.2

s.37, applied: 1933 c.12 Sch.1, 2000 c.6 s.161, 2000 c.43 Sch.4 para.2, 2003 c.44 Sch.15 para.130, SI 2004/1910 Sch.2

s.38, applied: 1933 c.12 Sch.1, 2000 c.6 s.161, 2000 c.43 Sch.4 para.2, 2003 c.44 Sch.15 para.131, SI 2004/1910 Sch.2

s.39, applied: 1933 c.12 Sch.1, 2000 c.6 s.161, 2000 c.43 Sch.4 para.2, 2003 c.44 Sch.15 para.132, SI 2004/1910 Sch.2

s.40, applied: 1933 c.12 Sch.1, 2000 c.6 s.161, 2000 c.43 Sch.4 para.2, 2003 c.44 Sch.15 para.133

s.41, applied: 1933 c.12 Sch.1, 2000 c.6 s.161, 2000 c.43 Sch.4 para.2, 2003 c.44 Sch.15 para.134

2003–cont.

42. Sexual Offences Act 2003–cont.

s.42, applied: 2000 c.6 s.161

s.43, amended: 2004 c.33 Sch.27 para.175

s.43, applied: 2000 c.6 s.161

s.44, applied: 2000 c.6 s.161

s.45, applied: 2000 c.6 s.161

s.46, applied: 2000 c.6 s.161

s.47, applied: 1933 c.12 Sch.1, 1992 c.34 s.2, 2000 c.6 s.161, 2000 c.43 Sch.4 para.1, 2003 c.44 Sch.15 para.135, Sch.17 para.95, SI 2003/1184 Sch.2 para.14V, SI 2004/1910 Sch.6

s.48, applied: 1933 c.12 Sch.1, 1992 c.34 s.2, 2000 c.6 s.161, 2000 c.43 Sch.4 para.1, 2002 c.29 Sch.5 para.8, 2003 c.44 Sch.15 para.136, Sch.17 para.96, SI 2003/1184 Sch.2 para.14W, SI 2004/1910 Sch.6

s.49, applied: 1933 c.12 Sch.1, 1992 c.34 s.2, 2000 c.6 s.161, 2000 c.43 Sch.4 para.1, 2002 c.29 Sch.5 para.8, 2003 c.44 Sch.15 para.137, Sch.17 para.97, SI 2003/1184 Sch.2 para.14X, SI 2004/1910 Sch.6

s.50, applied: 1933 c.12 Sch.1, 1992 c.34 s.2, 2000 c.6 s.161, 2000 c.43 Sch.4 para.1, 2002 c.29 Sch.5 para.8, 2003 c.44 Sch.15 para.138, Sch.17 para.98, SI 2003/1184 Sch.2 para.14Y, SI 2004/1910 Sch.6

s.51, applied: 1933 c.12 Sch.1, 1992 c.34 s.2, 2000 c.6 s.161

s.52, applied: 1933 c.12 Sch.1, 1992 c.34 s.2, 2000 c.43 Sch.4 para.2, 2002 c.29 Sch.5 para.8, 2003 c.44 Sch.15 para.139, Sch.17 para.99

s.53, applied: 1933 c.12 Sch.1, 1992 c.34 s.2, 2000 c.43 Sch.4 para.2, 2002 c.29 Sch.5 para.8, 2003 c.44 Sch.15 para.140, Sch.17 para.100

s.54, applied: 2000 c.6 s.161

s.55, applied: 2000 c.6 s.161

s.56, applied: 2000 c.6 s.161

s.57, applied: 1933 c.12 Sch.1, 1992 c.34 s.2, 2000 c.6 s.161, 2000 c.43 Sch.4 para.2, 2002 c.29 Sch.2 para.4, Sch.5 para.4, 2003 c.44 Sch.15 para.141, Sch.17 para.101, SI 2003/1184 Sch.2 para.14Z, 2004 c.19 s.14, SI 2004/1910 Sch.6

s.58, applied: 1933 c.12 Sch.1, 1992 c.34 s.2, 2000 c.6 s.161, 2000 c.43 Sch.4 para.2, 2002 c.29 Sch.2 para.4, Sch.5 para.4, 2003 c.44 Sch.15 para.142, Sch.17 para.102, SI 2003/1184 Sch.2 para.14AA, 2004 c.19 s.14, SI 2004/1910 Sch.6

s.59, applied: 1933 c.12 Sch.1, 1992 c.34 s.2, 2000 c.6 s.161, 2000 c.43 Sch.4 para.2, 2002 c.29 Sch.2 para.4, Sch.5 para.4, 2003 c.44 Sch.15 para.143, Sch.17 para.103, SI 2003/1184 Sch.2 para.14BB, 2004 c.19 s.14

s.60, applied: 1933 c.12 Sch.1, 2000 c.6 s.161, 2000 c.43 Sch.4 para.2

2003–cont.

42. Sexual Offences Act 2003–cont.

s.61, applied: 1933 c.12 Sch.1, 2000 c.6 s.161, 2000 c.43 Sch.4 para.2, 2003 c.44 Sch.15 para.144, SI 2004/1910 Sch.2

s.62, applied: 1933 c.12 Sch.1, 2000 c.6 s.161, 2000 c.43 Sch.4 para.3, 2003 c.44 Sch.15 para.145, SI 2004/1910 Sch.2

s.63, applied: 1933 c.12 Sch.1, 2000 c.6 s.161, 2000 c.43 Sch.4 para.3, 2003 c.44 Sch.15 para.146, SI 2004/1910 Sch.2

s.64, applied: 2000 c.6 s.161, 2003 c.44 Sch.15 para.147

s.64, disapplied: 1992 c.34 s.2, 1997 c.39 Sch.1 para.5A

s.65, applied: 2000 c.6 s.161, 2003 c.44 Sch.15 para.148

s.65, disapplied: 1992 c.34 s.2, 1997 c.39 Sch.1 para.5A

s.66, applied: 1933 c.12 Sch.1, 1984 c.60 Sch.1A para.27, 1992 c.34 s.2, 2000 c.6 s.161, 2000 c.43 Sch.4 para.2, 2003 c.44 Sch.15 para.149, Sch.17 para.104

s.67, applied: 1933 c.12 Sch.1, 1984 c.60 Sch.1A para.27, 1992 c.34 s.2, 2000 c.6 s.161, 2000 c.43 Sch.4 para.2, 2003 c.44 Sch.15 para.150, Sch.17 para.105

s.68, applied: 2000 c.6 s.161

s.69, applied: 1984 c.60 Sch.1A para.27, 2000 c.6 s.161, 2003 c.44 Sch.15 para.151, Sch.17 para.106

s.69, disapplied: 1992 c.34 s.2, 1997 c.39 Sch.1 para.5A

s.70, applied: 1984 c.60 Sch.1A para.27, 1992 c.34 s.2, 2000 c.6 s.161, 2003 c.44 Sch.15 para.152, Sch.17 para.107

s.71, applied: 1984 c.60 Sch.1A para.27

s.71, disapplied: 1992 c.34 s.2, 1997 c.39 Sch.1 para.5A

s.72, applied: 1992 c.34 s.2, 2000 c.6 s.161

s.73, applied: 2000 c.6 s.161

s.74, applied: 2000 c.6 s.161

s.75, applied: 2000 c.6 s.161

s.76, applied: 2000 c.6 s.161

s.77, applied: 2000 c.6 s.161

s.78, applied: 2000 c.6 s.161

s.79, applied: 2000 c.6 s.161

s.80, referred to: 1991 c.53 s.46A

s.83, applied: SI 2004/1220 Reg.10, SSI 2004/205 Reg.10

s.84, applied: SI 2004/1220 Reg.10, SSI 2004/205 Reg.10

s.85, applied: SI 2004/1220 Reg.10, SSI 2004/205 Reg.10

s.86, applied: SI 2004/1220 Reg.4, Reg.5, Reg.6, Reg.7, Reg.8, Reg.9, Reg.10, SSI 2004/205 Reg.4, Reg.5, Reg.6, Reg.7, Reg.8, Reg.9, Reg.10

s.86, referred to: SSI 2004/205 Reg.5, Reg.6, Reg.7

s.86, enabling: SI 2004/1220, SSI 2004/205

2003–cont.

42. Sexual Offences Act 2003–*cont.*

s.87, applied: SI 2004/875 Reg.2, SI 2004/1220 Reg.10, SSI 2004/137 Reg.2, SSI 2004/205 Reg.10

s.87, enabling: SI 2004/875, SSI 2004/137, SSI 2004/370

s.88, applied: SI 2004/1220 Reg.10, SSI 2004/205 Reg.10

s.89, applied: SI 1996/513 Sch.2 para.46

s.90, applied: SI 1996/513 Sch.2 para.46a

s.92, applied: SI 1996/513 Sch.2 para.20ba

s.97, applied: SI 2004/1052 r.3

s.99, applied: SI 1999/929 r.3.25.2, SI 2004/1052 r.4

s.99, enabling: SSI 2004/222

s.100, applied: SI 2004/1052 r.3

s.104, applied: SI 2004/1054 r.4

s.106, applied: SI 1999/929 r.3.25.3, SI 2004/1054 r.5

s.106, enabling: SSI 2004/222

s.108, applied: SI 1999/929 r.3.25.5, r.3.25.6

s.108, referred to: SI 1999/929 r.3.25.5, r.3.25.6

s.109, applied: SI 2004/1054 r.4

s.114, applied: SI 2004/1051 r.3

s.116, applied: SI 1999/929 r.3.25.4, SI 2004/1051 r.4

s.116, enabling: SSI 2004/222

s.123, applied: SI 2004/1053 r.3

s.126, applied: SI 2004/1053 r.3

s.131, amended: 2003 c.44 Sch.32 para.143

s.133, amended: 2003 c.44 Sch.32 para.144, 2004 c.28 Sch.10 para.57

s.135, repealed (in part): 2004 c.28 Sch.10 para.58, Sch.11

s.138, applied: SSI 2004/205

s.141, enabling: SI 2004/874, SSI 2004/138 Art.2

Sch.3, applied: SI 1996/513 Sch.2 para.20ba, 2004 c.34 s.66

Sch.3, referred to: 2004 c.34 s.89

Sch.5 para.63A, added: 2004 c.28 Sch.10 para.59

Sch.5 para.145, amended: SI 2004/702 Sch.7 para.27

Sch.5 para.146, amended: SI 2004/702 Sch.7 para.28

Sch.5 para.147, amended: SI 2004/702 Sch.7 para.29

Sch.5 para.148, amended: SI 2004/702 Sch.7 para.30

Sch.5 para.149, amended: SI 2004/702 Sch.7 para.31

Sch.5 para.171A, added: 2004 c.28 Sch.10 para.59

Sch.5 para.172, amended: 2004 c.28 Sch.10 para.59

2003–cont.

43. Health and Social Care (Community Health and Standards) Act 2003

Commencement Orders: SI 2003/3346 Art.2, Art.3, Art.4, Art.5; SI 2004/288 Art.2, Art.3, Art.4, Art.5, Art.6; SI 2004/480 Art.2, Art.3, Art.4, Art.5; SI 2004/759 Art.2, Art.3, Art.4, Art.5, Art.6, Art.7, Art.8, Art.9, Art.10, Art.11, Art.12, Art.13; SI 2004/873 Art.2; SI 2004/1019 Art.2; SI 2004/2626 Art.2

applied: SI 2002/2375 Reg.10, Reg.11, SI 2004/1768 Reg.16

varied: SI 2004/567 Art.2

varied: SI 2004/664 Art.11, Art.12, Art.13, Art.14

Part 1, applied: 1977 c.49 s.28, s.84, s.122

Part 1, referred to: 1986 c.46 s.22C

Part 2, applied: 1998 c.18 s.33, s.34

Part 2 c.10, applied: 2004 c.17 s.10

Part 2 c.2, applied: 2004 c.17 s.10

Part 2 c.3, applied: 1998 c.18 s.37, s.49, 2004 c.17 s.10, SI 2004/557 Reg.2

Part 2 c.4, applied: 1998 c.18 s.49

Part 2 c.5, applied: 1998 c.18 s.37, s.49, SI 2004/555 Reg.2

s.1, applied: SI 1980/1923 Sch.1, SI 1991/1325 Art.2, SI 1992/2645 Reg.7A, SI 1993/3167 Sch.1 para.2ZA, SI 1999/641 Sch.1, SI 1999/2864 Reg.9, SI 2000/415 Sch.1 para.1, SI 2001/1403 Sch.3 para.1, 2004 c.36 Sch.1 para.6, SI 2004/118 Art.2

s.1, referred to: SI 1992/1703 Sch.1

s.9, applied: SI 2002/3048 Reg.4A

s.14, applied: 1988 c.1 s.519A

s.22, referred to: 1977 c.49 s.96A, SI 2004/2517 Art.2

s.22, enabling: SI 2004/2517

s.28, applied: 1990 c.19 Sch.2 para.32

s.44, varied: SI 2004/664 Art.11, Art.12, Art.13, Art.14

s.45, applied: 2004 c.17 s.10, SI 2004/557 Reg.3

s.52, applied: SI 2004/557 Reg.3

s.52, enabling: SI 2004/557

s.53, applied: 2004 c.17 s.10

s.57, disapplied: 2004 c.17 s.10

s.60, amended: 2004 c.23 Sch.2 para.58

s.66, applied: SI 2004/291 Sch.6 para.91, SI 2004/478 Sch.6 para.89, SI 2004/557 Reg.2, SI 2004/627 Sch.5 para.85

s.67, applied: SI 2004/557 Reg.2

s.68, applied: SI 2004/557 Reg.2

s.69, enabling: SI 2004/557

s.69A, added: 2004 c.23 Sch.2 para.59

s.70, amended: 2004 c.23 Sch.2 para.60

s.73, applied: SI 2004/478 Sch.6 para.89

s.79, amended: 2004 c.31 s.24

s.80, applied: 2000 c.14 s.45, s.51

s.81, amended: 2004 c.31 s.24

s.81, applied: SI 2004/615 Reg.3

2003–cont.

43. Health and Social Care (Community Health and Standards) Act 2003–*cont.*

s.88, applied: 2000 c.14 s.55, SI 2004/555 Reg.2

s.89, applied: SI 2004/555 Reg.2

s.90, applied: SI 2004/555 Reg.2

s.91, enabling: SI 2004/555

s.92, varied: 2004 c.31 s.30

s.93, varied: 2004 c.31 s.30

s.94, applied: 2004 c.23 s.41

s.94, varied: 2004 c.31 s.30

s.95, applied: 2004 c.23 s.41, s.42

s.95, varied: 2004 c.31 s.30

s.96, varied: 2004 c.31 s.30

s.97, varied: 2004 c.31 s.30

s.98, applied: 2000 c.14 s.55

s.98, varied: 2004 c.31 s.30

s.99, varied: 2004 c.31 s.30

s.100, varied: 2004 c.31 s.30

s.101, varied: 2004 c.31 s.30

s.102, applied: SI 2004/664 Art.11

s.102, varied: SI 2004/664 Art.11, Art.12, Art.13, Art.14

s.113, applied: 1993 c.46 s.3, s.4, 1998 c.29 s.31, SI 2004/291 Sch.6 para.92, SI 2004/478 Sch.6 para.90, SI 2004/627 Sch.5 para.86

s.113, enabling: SI 2004/1768

s.114, applied: 1998 c.29 s.31

s.115, enabling: SI 2004/1768

s.120, applied: SI 2004/555 Reg.3, SI 2004/557 Reg.4

s.120, enabling: SI 2004/555, SI 2004/557

s.136, applied: 2004 c.23 s.64

s.145A, added: 2004 c.23 Sch.2 para.61

s.172, referred to: SI 2004/288 Art.7, SI 2004/480 Art.6

s.176, applied: SI 1996/623 Reg.1A, SI 2004/291 Reg.3, SI 2004/433 Art.2, Art.13, SI 2004/477 Art.2, Art.13, SI 2004/478 Reg.3, SI 2004/865 Art.108, Art.109, Art.115, SI 2004/1016 Art.84

s.176, enabling: SI 2004/433, SI 2004/477, SI 2004/865, SI 2004/1016

s.178, applied: SI 2004/865 Art.58

s.178, referred to: SI 2004/288 Art.8, SI 2004/480 Art.7

s.185, applied: SI 2003/3202

s.185, enabling: SI 2004/557

s.186, applied: SI 2003/3202

s.187, applied: 1954 c.61 s.15, Sch.1 para.3A, 1983 c.54 Sch.1 para.4ZA, 1984 c.24 Sch.1 para.2A, 1989 c.44 Sch.1 para.2A, 1993 c.21 Sch.1 para.11A, 1994 c.17 Sch.1 para.11A, SI 2002/253 Sch.1 para.15A, SI 2002/254 Sch.1 para.16A

s.195, enabling: SI 2003/3190, SI 2003/3279, SI 2004/288, SI 2004/433, SI 2004/477, SI 2004/480, SI 2004/539, SI 2004/555, SI 2004/557, SI 2004/615, SI 2004/865, SI 2004/866, SI 2004/1009,

2003–cont.

43. Health and Social Care (Community Health and Standards) Act 2003–*cont.*

s.195, enabling:–*cont.*
SI 2004/1016, SI 2004/1019, SI 2004/1768

s.198, enabling: SI 2004/567

s.199, applied: SI 2004/759

s.199, enabling: SI 2003/3346, SI 2004/288, SI 2004/480, SI 2004/759, SI 2004/866, SI 2004/873, SI 2004/1009, SI 2004/1019, SI 2004/2626

s.200, enabling: SI 2004/433, SI 2004/477, SI 2004/664, SI 2004/865, SI 2004/1016, SI 2004/1772, SI 2004/1825

s.201, enabling: SI 2004/433, SI 2004/477, SI 2004/664, SI 2004/696, SI 2004/865, SI 2004/1016, SI 2004/2627, SI 2004/2987

Sch.1 para.22, enabling: SI 2004/539

Sch.5 para.8, referred to: 2001 c.24 Sch.4 para.53A

Sch.6 para.3, applied: SI 2003/3279 Reg.1

Sch.6 para.3, referred to: SI 2000/89 Reg.5, SI 2003/3279 Reg.7

Sch.6 para.3, enabling: SI 2003/3279

Sch.7 para.3, referred to: SI 2003/3190 Reg.7

Sch.7 para.3, enabling: SI 2003/3190

Sch.7 para.5, enabling: SI 2004/615

Sch.8 para.1, varied: SI 2004/664 Art.11, Art.12, Art.13, Art.14

Sch.9 para.10, varied: SI 2004/664 Art.11, Art.12, Art.13, Art.14

Sch.9 para.32, varied: SI 2004/664 Art.11, Art.12, Art.13, Art.14

Sch.11 para.47, disapplied: SI 2004/865 Art.111

Sch.11 para.48, disapplied: SI 2004/865 Art.111

Sch.11 para.49, disapplied: SI 2004/865 Art.111

Sch.11 para.59, disapplied: SI 2004/865 Art.112

Sch.11 para.62, disapplied: SI 2004/865 Art.113

Sch.11 para.63, disapplied: SI 2004/865 Art.113

Sch.14 Part 2, varied: SI 2004/664 Art.11, Art.12, Art.13, Art.14

44. Criminal Justice Act 2003

Commencement Orders: SI 2003/3282 Art.2, Sch.1; SI 2004/81 Art.2, Art.3, Art.4, Art.5; SI 2004/829 Art.2, Art.3, Art.4; SI 2004/1629 Art.2, Art.3; SI 2004/1867 Art.2; SI 2004/3033 Art.2, Art.3, Art.4

referred to: SI 2004/1500

Part 7, applied: SI 2004/2167 Art.3

Part 12 c.1, added: 2004 c.28 s.14

s.3, applied: SI 2003/3194

s.16, applied: SI 1982/1109 Sch.3 Part III

s.20, varied: SI 2004/829 Art.2

2003–cont.

44. Criminal Justice Act 2003–*cont.*

s.25, applied: SI 2004/1683

s.25, enabling: SI 2004/1683

s.30, amended: SI 2004/2035 Sch.1 para.46

s.30, repealed (in part): SI 2004/2035 Sch.1 para.46

s.48, amended: 2004 c.28 Sch.10 para.60

s.50, amended: 2004 c.28 Sch.10 para.61

s.55, amended: SI 2004/2035 Sch.1 para.47

s.56, amended: SI 2004/2035 Sch.1 para.48

s.58, amended: 2004 c.28 s.30

s.74, amended: 2004 c.28 Sch.10 para.62

s.80, applied: SI 2004/1500 Art.10

s.101, applied: 1898 c.36 s.1

s.103, enabling: SI 2004/3346

s.111, amended: SI 2004/2035 Sch.1 para.49

s.111, enabling: SI 2004/2991, SI 2004/2992, SI 2004/2993

s.118, referred to: 2004 c.33 s.84

s.127, amended: SI 2004/2035 Sch.1 para.50

s.132, amended: SI 2004/2035 Sch.1 para.51

s.151, amended: 2004 c.28 Sch.10 para.63

s.154, referred to: 2004 c.11 s.12, 2004 c.19 s.2, s.5, s.35, 2004 c.21 s.34, 2004 c.27 s.25, Sch.7 para.5, 2004 c.28 Sch.12 para.1

s.161, applied: 1976 c.63 Sch.1 para.6B

s.164, amended: 2004 c.28 s.14

s.168, enabling: SI 2004/246

s.174, applied: 1998 c.37 s.1AB

s.177, applied: 1974 c.23 Sch.1 para.7

s.183, amended: SI 2003/3283 Art.2

s.183, applied: 1952 c.52 s.49, 1961 c.39 s.23, 1968 c.27 s.21, 1980 c.43 s.131, 1989 c.37 s.14E, s.18, 1995 c.16 s.1

s.183, referred to: SI 2003/3283

s.202, enabling: SI 2004/117

s.215, applied: SI 2004/117 Art.3

s.215, enabling: SI 2004/117

s.227, applied: 1974 c.23 Sch.1 para.6

s.228, applied: 1974 c.23 Sch.1 para.6

s.241, amended: SI 2003/3283 Art.3

s.243, repealed (in part): SI 2004/1897 Art.3

s.244, amended: 2004 c.28 Sch.6 para.2

s.244, applied: 2000 c.6 s.82A

s.246, amended: 2004 c.28 Sch.6 para.3, Sch.11

s.249, amended: 2004 c.28 Sch.6 para.4

s.250, amended: 2004 c.28 Sch.6 para.5

s.250, applied: SI 2003/3337 Art.2, Art.3, Art.4

s.250, referred to: SI 2003/3337

s.250, enabling: SI 2003/3337

s.264, amended: 2004 c.28 Sch.6 para.6, Sch.11

s.264A, added: 2004 c.28 Sch.6 para.7

s.267, see *Practice Direction (Sup Ct: Crime: Mandatory Life Sentences) (No.2)* [2004] 1 W.L.R. 2551 (Sup Ct), Lord Woolf of Barnes, L.C.J.

2003–cont.

44. Criminal Justice Act 2003–*cont.*

s.269, see *Practice Direction (Sup Ct: Crime: Mandatory Life Sentences) (No.2)* [2004] 1 W.L.R. 2551 (Sup Ct), Lord Woolf of Barnes, L.C.J.

s.269, applied: 1968 c.19 s.9, 1968 c.20 s.8, 1988 c.33 s.36, 1993 c.9 s.10

s.269, disapplied: 1993 c.9 s.10

s.277, referred to: 1968 c.19 s.9, 1968 c.20 s.8

s.281, applied: 2004 c.18 s.10, 2004 c.25 s.10

s.281, referred to: 1997 c.50 s.124A, 2004 c.11 s.13, s.18, 2004 c.21 s.49, 2004 c.31 s.45

s.282, applied: 2004 c.25 s.10

s.292, repealed: SI 2004/702 Sch.8

s.305, amended: 2004 c.28 Sch.10 para.64

s.322, amended: 2004 c.31 Sch.2 para.8

s.327, varied: SI 2004/829 Art.2

s.330, applied: SI 2004/1683

s.330, enabling: SI 2004/81, SI 2004/117, SI 2004/829, SI 2004/1629, SI 2004/3033

s.333, enabling: SI 2003/3283

s.334, applied: SI 2003/3194

s.336, enabling: SI 2003/3282, SI 2004/81, SI 2004/829, SI 2004/1629, SI 2004/1867, SI 2004/3033

s.337, amended: SI 2004/702 Sch.8

Sch.3 Part 2 para.51, referred to: 2004 c.28 Sch.12 para.3

Sch.6 para.5, amended: SI 2004/2035 Sch.1 para.52

Sch.7 para.2, amended: SI 2004/2035 Sch.1 para.53

Sch.8 Part 2 para.7, amended: 2004 c.28 Sch.5 para.7

Sch.8 Part 2 para.9, amended: 2004 c.28 Sch.5 para.7

Sch.8 Part 6 para.27, amended: 2004 c.28 Sch.5 para.7

Sch.12 Part 2 para.6, amended: 2004 c.28 Sch.5 para.8

Sch.12 Part 2 para.8, amended: 2004 c.28 Sch.5 para.8

Sch.12 Part 3 para.22, amended: 2004 c.28 Sch.5 para.8

Sch.13 Part 3 para.12, amended: 2004 c.28 Sch.5 para.9

Sch.15, referred to: 2004 c.28 s.45

Sch.15 Part 1 para.63A, added: 2004 c.28 Sch.10 para.65

Sch.17 Part 1 para.33, amended: SI 2004/702 Sch.7 para.32

Sch.17 Part 1 para.34, amended: SI 2004/702 Sch.7 para.33

Sch.17 Part 1 para.35, amended: SI 2004/702 Sch.7 para.34

Sch.17 Part 1 para.36, amended: SI 2004/702 Sch.7 para.35

Sch.17 Part 1 para.37, amended: SI 2004/702 Sch.7 para.36

CAP.

44. Criminal Justice Act 2003–*cont.*
Sch.17 Part 1 para.60A, added: 2004 c.28 Sch.10 para.66
Sch.21, see *Practice Direction (Sup Ct: Crime: Mandatory Life Sentences) (No.2)* [2004] 1 W.L.R. 2551 (Sup Ct), Lord Woolf of Barnes, L.C.J.
Sch.22, see *Practice Direction (Sup Ct: Crime: Mandatory Life Sentences) (No.2)* [2004] 1 W.L.R. 2551 (Sup Ct), Lord Woolf of Barnes, L.C.J.
Sch.22 para.3, applied: 1993 c.9 s.10
Sch.22 para.3, disapplied: 1993 c.9 s.10
Sch.29 para.1, repealed: SI 2004/702 Sch.8
Sch.29 para.2, repealed: SI 2004/702 Sch.8
Sch.29 para.3, repealed: SI 2004/702 Sch.8
Sch.29 para.4, repealed: SI 2004/702 Sch.8
Sch.29 para.5, repealed: SI 2004/702 Sch.8
Sch.29 para.6, repealed: SI 2004/702 Sch.8
Sch.35 para.4, applied: SI 2004/865 Art.116
Sch.38 para.6, enabling: SI 2003/3283

45. Consolidated Fund (No.2) Act 2003
applied: 2004 c.9 Sch.1

2004

1. Consolidated Fund Act 2004
Royal Assent, March 22, 2004

2. European Parliamentary and Local Elections (Pilots) Act 2004
Royal Assent, April 1, 2004

3. National Insurance Contributions and Statutory Payments Act 2004
Commencement Orders: SI 2004/1943 Art.2, Art.3, Art.4, Art.5, Art.6
Royal Assent, May 13, 2004
s.13, enabling: SI 2004/1943

4. Justice (Northern Ireland) Act 2004
Royal Assent, May 13, 2004

5. Planning and Compulsory Purchase Act 2004
Commencement Orders: SI 2004/1813 Art.2; SI 2004/1814 Art.2, Art.3; SI 2004/2097 Art.2; SI 2004/2202 Art.2, Art.3, Sch.1 Part 1, 2; SI 2004/2593 Art.2, Art.2
Royal Assent, May 13, 2004
applied: 1990 c.8 s.303A, SI 2004/2203 Reg.4
Part1, applied: 1990 c.8 s.296, Sch.1 para.7, SI 2004/2203 Reg.3, Reg.22, SI 2004/2208
Part 2, applied: 1969 c.32 s.58, 1980 c.66 s.232, 1990 c.8 s.61A, s.296, s.324, Sch.13 para.1A, 1999 c.29 s.346, 2000 c.37 s.86, SI 2004/2204 Reg.45, Reg.51, SI 2004/2205 Reg.6
Part 2, referred to: SI 2004/2204 Reg.10
Part 6, applied: 1969 c.32 s.58, 1980 c.66 s.232, 1990 c.8 s.61A, s.296, s.324, 2000 c.37 s.86
s.1, enabling: SI 2004/2206
s.2, applied: SI 2004/2203 Reg.4

CAP.

5. Planning and Compulsory Purchase Act 2004–*cont.*
s.2, enabling: SI 2004/2203
s.3, applied: SI 2004/2203 Reg.5
s.3, enabling: SI 2004/2203
s.4, applied: SI 2004/2203 Reg.11
s.4, referred to: SI 2004/2203 Reg.8
s.5, applied: 1990 c.8 Sch.1 para.7, SI 2004/2203 Reg.6, Reg.8, Reg.10, Reg.11, Reg.12, Reg.13, Reg.18, SI 2004/2208 Sch.1
s.5, referred to: SI 2004/2203 Reg.10
s.5, enabling: SI 2004/2203
s.6, applied: SI 2004/2203 Reg.6
s.7, applied: SI 2004/2203 Reg.15, SI 2004/2208 Sch.1
s.8, applied: SI 2004/2203 Reg.14, SI 2004/2208 Sch.1, SI 2004/2209 Reg.2
s.9, applied: SI 2004/2203 Reg.16, Reg.17, Reg.18, SI 2004/2208 Sch.1
s.10, applied: SI 2004/2203 Reg.19, Reg.23
s.10, enabling: SI 2004/2208
s.11, enabling: SI 2004/2203, SI 2004/2209
s.12, enabling: SI 2004/2207
s.13, applied: 1990 c.8 s.306
s.13, enabling: SI 2004/2204
s.14, applied: 1990 c.8 s.306, SI 2004/2204 Reg.5
s.14, enabling: SI 2004/2204
s.15, applied: SI 2004/2204 Reg.10, Reg.11
s.15, referred to: SI 2004/2204 Reg.8
s.15, enabling: SI 2004/2204
s.16, applied: SI 2004/2204 Reg.3
s.16, referred to: SI 2004/2204 Reg.12
s.17, applied: SI 2004/2204 Reg.6
s.17, enabling: SI 2004/2204
s.19, applied: SI 2004/2204 Reg.15, SI 2004/2205 Reg.6
s.19, referred to: SI 2004/2204 Reg.15
s.19, enabling: SI 2004/2204
s.20, applied: 1990 c.8 s.303A, Sch.1 para.7, Sch.13 para.1A, SI 2004/2204 Reg.8, Reg.28, Reg.29, Reg.33, Reg.34, Reg.35, Reg.38, Reg.41
s.20, referred to: SI 2000/2853 Sch.1
s.20, enabling: SI 2004/2204
s.21, applied: 1990 c.8 Sch.13 para.1A, SI 2004/2204 Reg.22, Reg.23, Reg.35, Reg.38, Reg.39, Reg.40, Reg.41, Reg.42, Reg.43, Reg.44
s.21, referred to: SI 2000/2853 Sch.1
s.22, applied: 1990 c.8 Sch.13 para.1A, SI 2004/2204 Reg.37
s.22, referred to: SI 2000/2853 Sch.1
s.23, applied: 1990 c.8 Sch.1 para.7
s.23, referred to: SI 2000/2853 Sch.1
s.24, applied: SI 2004/2204 Reg.17, Reg.30
s.24, referred to: SI 2004/2204 Reg.29
s.24, enabling: SI 2004/2204
s.25, applied: 1990 c.8 Sch.4A para.2
s.25, referred to: SI 2000/2853 Sch.1

CAP.

2004–cont.

5. Planning and Compulsory Purchase Act 2004–*cont.*

s.26, applied: 1990 c.8 Sch.4A para.2, Sch.13 para.1A

s.26, referred to: SI 2000/2853 Sch.1

s.27, applied: 1990 c.8 Sch.13 para.1A, SI 2004/2204 Reg.45

s.28, applied: SI 2004/2204 Reg.46

s.28, referred to: SI 2004/2204 Reg.46

s.28, enabling: SI 2004/2204

s.29, applied: SI 2004/2204 Reg.47

s.31, applied: SI 2004/2204 Reg.47

s.31, enabling: SI 2004/2204

s.35, applied: 1990 c.8 Sch.4A para.1, Sch.4A para.4, SI 2004/2204 Reg.48

s.35, enabling: SI 2004/2204

s.36, enabling: SI 2004/2204

s.61, applied: 1990 c.8 s.306

s.64, applied: 1990 c.8 s.303A

s.68, applied: 1990 c.8 Sch.4A para.2

s.70, applied: 1990 c.8 Sch.4A para.2

s.76, applied: 1990 c.8 Sch.4A para.1, Sch.4A para.5

s.79, applied: 1990 c.10 s.30B

s.113, applied: SI 2004/2203 Reg.20, SI 2004/2204 Reg.49

s.121, enabling: SI 2004/1813, SI 2004/1814, SI 2004/2097, SI 2004/2202, SI 2004/2593

s.122, enabling: SI 2004/1814, SI 2004/2202

Sch.8 para.1, applied: 1990 c.8 Sch.1 para.7, SI 2004/2204 Reg.13, Reg.48

Sch.8 para.1, referred to: SI 2004/2204 Reg.13

Sch.8 para.2, applied: SI 2004/2205 Reg.3

Sch.8 para.4, applied: SI 1999/3280 Reg.26, SI 2004/2204 Reg.8, SI 2004/2205 Reg.4

Sch.8 para.5, applied: SI 1999/3280 Reg.24A, Reg.26, SI 2004/2204 Reg.8, SI 2004/2205 Reg.4

Sch.8 para.9, applied: SI 1999/3280 Reg.26, SI 2004/2204 Reg.8, SI 2004/2205 Reg.5

Sch.8 para.10, applied: SI 1999/3280 Reg.24A, Reg.26, SI 2004/2204 Reg.8, SI 2004/2205 Reg.5

Sch.8 para.17, enabling: SI 2004/2205

Sch.8 para.18, enabling: SI 2004/2205

6. Child Trust Funds Act 2004

Commencement Orders: SI 2004/2422 Art.1, Art.2; SI 2004/3369 Art.2

Royal Assent, May 13, 2004

applied: SI 2004/1450 Reg.16

s.2, applied: SI 2004/1450 Reg.3, Reg.7

s.3, applied: SI 2004/1450 Reg.10, Reg.13

s.3, enabling: SI 2004/1450, SI 2004/2676, SI 2004/3382

s.5, applied: SI 2004/1450 Reg.3

s.5, enabling: SI 2004/1450, SI 2004/2676

s.6, applied: SI 2004/1450 Reg.6

s.6, enabling: SI 2004/1450

s.7, enabling: SI 2004/1450, SI 2004/2676

CAP.

2004–cont.

6. Child Trust Funds Act 2004–*cont.*

s.8, applied: SI 2004/1450 Reg.7, SI 2004/2676 Reg.1, SI 2004/2680 Reg.1

s.8, enabling: SI 2004/1450, SI 2004/2676

s.9, applied: SI 2004/1450 Reg.7, Reg.22, Reg.30, SI 2004/2676 Reg.1, SI 2004/2680 Reg.1

s.9, enabling: SI 2004/1450

s.11, enabling: SI 2004/1450

s.12, enabling: SI 2004/1450

s.13, enabling: SI 2004/1450, SI 2004/2676

s.14, applied: SI 2004/2680

s.15, enabling: SI 2004/1450

s.16, enabling: SI 2004/1450, SI 2004/2676, SI 2004/3382

s.20, applied: SI 2004/1450 Reg.23

s.23, enabling: SI 2004/1450

s.27, applied: SI 2004/2676 Reg.1, SI 2004/2680 Reg.1

s.27, enabling: SI 2004/2422, SI 2004/3369

s.28, enabling: SI 2004/1450, SI 2004/2676, SI 2004/3382

7. Gender Recognition Act 2004

Royal Assent, July 01, 2004

applied: 2004 c.33 s.50, s.86, s.117, s.216

s.3, amended: 2004 c.33 s.250

s.4, amended: 2004 c.33 s.250

s.5, amended: 2004 c.33 s.250

s.5, applied: 2004 c.33 s.96, Sch.3 para.1

s.5A, added: 2004 c.33 s.250

s.7, amended: 2004 c.33 s.250

s.8, amended: 2004 c.33 s.250

s.21, amended: 2004 c.33 s.250

s.22, amended: 2004 c.33 s.250

s.25, amended: 2004 c.33 s.250

Sch.1 para.5, amended: 2004 c.33 s.250

Sch.3 Part 1 para.9, amended: 2004 c.33 s.250

Sch.3 Part 2 para.19, amended: 2004 c.33 s.250

Sch.3 Part 3 para.29, amended: 2004 c.33 s.250

Sch.4 Part 1 para.2, repealed: 2004 c.33 Sch.30

8. Higher Education Act 2004

Commencement Orders: SI 2004/2781 Art.2, Art.3, Art.4, Art.5; SI 2004/3144 Art.4, Art.5, Art.6, Sch.1 Part 1, 2; SI 2004/3255 Art.2

Royal Assent, July 01, 2004

s.20, disapplied: SI 2004/2781 Art.5

s.24, applied: SI 2004/1932 Reg.4, Reg.5, SI 2004/2473 Reg.9, Reg.10

s.24, enabling: SI 2004/1932

s.26, applied: SI 2004/1932

s.33, enabling: SI 2004/2473

s.34, applied: SI 2004/2473 Reg.9

s.34, enabling: SI 2004/2473

s.35, enabling: SI 2004/2473

s.36, enabling: SI 2004/2473

CAP.

CAP.

2004–cont.

2004–cont.

8. Higher Education Act 2004–*cont.*
s.37, applied: SI 2004/2473 Reg.9, Reg.10, Reg.12, Reg.13, Reg.14
s.37, enabling: SI 2004/2473
s.39, enabling: SI 2004/2473
s.46, disapplied: SI 2004/2781 Art.5
s.47, enabling: SI 2004/1932, SI 2004/2473, SI 2004/2781, SI 2004/3144
s.52, enabling: SI 2004/2781, SI 2004/3144, SI 2004/3255

9. Appropriation Act 2004
Royal Assent, July 8, 2004

10. Age-Related Payments Act 2004
Royal Assent, July 08, 2004
s.2, applied: SI 1992/2977 Sch.4 para.24, Sch.4 para.25
s.3, applied: SI 1992/2977 Sch.4 para.24, Sch.4 para.25

11. Gangmasters (Licensing) Act 2004
Commencement Orders: SI 2004/2857 Art.2
Royal Assent, July 08, 2004
s.29, enabling: SI 2004/2857

12. Finance Act 2004
Commencement Orders: SI 2004/1945 Art.2; SI 2004/2571 Art.2; SI 2004/3268 Art.2
Royal Assent, July 22, 2004
Part 3 c.3, applied: 1988 c.1 s.829
Part 3 c.6, applied: 1988 c.1 s.18, s.349
Part 4, disapplied: 1988 c.1 s.828
Part 7, applied: 1970 c.9 s.98C, SI 2004/1863 Reg.2
s.19, applied: SI 2004/1934 Art.2
s.19, enabling: SI 2004/1934, SI 2004/1942 Art.2
s.22, enabling: SI 2004/3104
s.43, applied: SI 2004/2310 Art.1
s.43, referred to: SI 2004/2310 Sch.1 para.13, Sch.1 para.14
s.44, applied: SI 2004/2310 Art.1
s.46, enabling: SI 2004/2310, SI 2004/3269
s.53, enabling: SI 2004/3268
s.55, applied: 1970 c.9 s.98, SI 2004/2502 Reg.2
s.55, referred to: SI 2004/2502 Reg.2
s.55, enabling: SI 2004/2502
s.58, applied: 1970 c.9 s.12B, 1998 c.36 Sch.18 para.22
s.59, applied: 1988 c.1 s.582A
s.61, applied: 1970 c.9 s.12B, s.59DA, s.62, s.63, s.64, 1988 c.1 s.829, 1988 c.39 s.130, 1998 c.36 Sch.18 para.22, 2003 c.1 s.54
s.62, applied: 1970 c.9 s.59D
s.65, applied: 1970 c.9 s.98
s.69, applied: 1970 c.9 s.98
s.70, applied: 1970 c.9 s.98A, s.12B, s.98, 1992 c.4 Sch.1 para.7, 1998 c.36 Sch.18 para.22
s.71, applied: 1970 c.9 s.98A, s.98, 1992 c.4 Sch.1 para.7
s.83, applied: 1990 c.29 s.25

12. Finance Act 2004–*cont.*
s.85, enabling: SI 2004/1945
s.98, applied: SI 2004/2622 Reg.4, Reg.6, Reg.7, Reg.8, Reg.9
s.99, applied: SI 2004/2622 Reg.4
s.100, enabling: SI 2004/2622
s.103, applied: SI 2004/2622 Reg.5
s.104, applied: SI 2004/2622 Reg.7
s.104, disapplied: SI 2004/2622 Reg.4, Reg.9
s.111, applied: 1988 c.1 s.811, 1992 c.12 s.281
s.142, applied: 2001 c.2 s.52
s.145, enabling: SI 2004/2572
s.282, referred to: 1988 c.1 s.828
s.291, enabling: SI 2004/1942
s.294, enabling: SI 2004/2571
s.306, enabling: SI 2004/1863, SI 2004/2429
s.307, applied: SI 2004/1865 Reg.4, Reg.5
s.307, disapplied: SI 2004/1865 Reg.4, Reg.5
s.307, referred to: SI 2004/1865 Reg.2
s.307, enabling: SI 2004/1865, SI 2004/2613
s.308, applied: 1970 c.9 s.98C, SI 2004/1864 Reg.1, Reg.3, Reg.4, Reg.5, Reg.6, SI 2004/1865 Reg.2, Reg.4
s.308, referred to: SI 2004/1864 Reg.5, SI 2004/1865 Reg.2
s.308, enabling: SI 2004/1864
s.309, applied: 1970 c.9 s.98C, SI 2004/1864 Reg.1, Reg.3, Reg.4, Reg.6
s.309, enabling: SI 2004/1864
s.310, applied: 1970 c.9 s.98C, SI 2004/1864 Reg.1, Reg.3, Reg.4, Reg.6, SI 2004/2613 Reg.1
s.310, enabling: SI 2004/1864, SI 2004/2613
s.311, applied: SI 2004/1864 Reg.8
s.312, applied: 1970 c.9 s.98C, SI 2004/1864 Reg.7, Reg.8
s.312, enabling: SI 2004/1864
s.313, applied: 1970 c.9 s.98C, SI 2004/1864 Reg.4, Reg.8, Reg.9
s.313, enabling: SI 2004/1864
s.314, applied: SI 2004/1865 Reg.6
s.317, enabling: SI 2004/1864, SI 2004/2613
s.318, enabling: SI 2004/1864, SI 2004/1865, SI 2004/2613
Sch.10, applied: 1996 c.8 Sch.9 para.9
Sch.26 para.1, applied: SI 2004/2572 Reg.6, Reg.7
Sch.26 para.1, varied: SI 2004/2572 Reg.6, Reg.7
Sch.26 para.2, applied: SI 2004/2572 Reg.6, Reg.7
Sch.26 para.2, varied: SI 2004/2572 Reg.6, Reg.7
Sch.37 Part 2, applied: 1983 c.56 s.6A

CAP.

2004–cont.

13. Scottish Parliament (Constituencies) Act 2004 c. 13
Royal Assent, July 22, 2004

14. Statute Law (Repeals) Act 2004 c.14
Royal Assent, July 22, 2004

15. Carers (Equal Opportunities) Act 2004 c. 15
Royal Assent, July 22, 2004

16. Patents Act 2004
Commencement Orders: SI 2004/2177 Art.2, Art.6, Art.7, Art.8; SI 2004/3205 Art.2
Royal Assent, July 22, 2004
s.17, enabling: SI 2004/2177, SI 2004/3205

17. Health Protection Agency Act 2004
Royal Assent, July 22, 2004
s.1, applied: 2004 c.36 Sch.1 para.9
s.1, referred to: 2004 c.36 Sch.1 para.9

18. Traffic Management Act 2004
Commencement Orders: SI 2004/2380 Art.2, Art.3; SI 2004/3110 Art.2
Royal Assent, July 22, 2004
s.99, enabling: SI 2004/2380, SI 2004/3110

19. Asylum and Immigration (Treatment of Claimants, etc.) Act 2004
Commencement Orders: SI 2004/2523 Art.2, Sch.1; SI 2004/2999 Art.2, Art.4, Sch.1; SI 2004/3398 Art.3; SSI 2004/494 Art.2; SI 2004/3398 Art.2
Royal Assent, July 22, 2004
s.4, amended: 2004 c.30 Sch.6 para.7
s.4, applied: 1971 c.77 s.25C, 2000 c.43 Sch.4 para.2, 2002 c.29 Sch.2 para.4, Sch.4 para.4, Sch.5 para.4
s.8, enabling: SI 2004/3263
s.9, varied: SI 2004/2999 Art.3
s.9, enabling: SI 2004/2999
s.14, referred to: 1976 c.74 s.19D
s.19, applied: 2004 c.33 Sch.23 para.2
s.21, applied: 2004 c.33 Sch.23 para.2
s.23, applied: 2004 c.33 Sch.23 para.2
s.25, applied: 2004 c.33 Sch.23 para.2
s.44, applied: 1976 c.74 s.19D, 1981 c.45 s.5
s.48, enabling: SI 2004/2523, SI 2004/2999, SI 2004/3398, SSI 2004/494

20. Energy Act 2004
Commencement Orders: SI 2004/1973 Art.2; SI 2004/2184 Art.2, Sch.1, Sch.2; SI 2004/2575 Art.2, Sch.1, Sch.2
Royal Assent, July 22, 2004
applied: 2000 c.27 s.33, s.81, SI 2004/2541 Reg.3
Part 2, applied: 1989 c.29 s.3A
Part 3, applied: 1989 c.29 s.3A
s.21, applied: 1989 c.29 Sch.12 para.3A
s.44, amended: SI 2004/2310 Sch.1 para.72
s.84, applied: SI 2004/2668 Art.1
s.84, enabling: SI 2004/2668
s.137, applied: 1989 c.29 s.8A, SI 2004/2541 Reg.3
s.141, enabling: SI 2004/2242

CAP.

2004–cont.

20. Energy Act 2004–*cont.*
s.147, applied: SI 2004/2542 Reg.3
s.184, applied: 2000 c.27 s.105
s.185, applied: 2000 c.27 s.105
s.198, enabling: SI 2004/1973, SI 2004/2184, SI 2004/2575
Sch.9 Part 1 para.3, applied: 1992 c.12 s.35
Sch.9 Part 2 para.18, applied: 1992 c.12 s.35
Sch.9 Part 3 para.29, applied: 1992 c.12 s.35
Sch.9 Part 4 para.32, applied: 1992 c.12 s.35
Sch.18, applied: SI 2004/2242 Art.2
Sch.18 para.21, enabling: SI 2004/2242

21. Fire and Rescue Services Act 2004
Commencement Orders: SI 2004/2304 Art.2; SI 2004/2917 Art.2
Royal Assent, July 22, 2004
applied: 1951 c.65 s.46, 1961 c.64 s.75, 1968 c.65 s.43, 1981 c.37 s.3, 1988 c.20 s.19
referred to: SI 2004/2918 Art.3
s.1, applied: 2004 c.36 Sch.1 para.4
s.2, applied: 1959 c.53 Sch.4 para.9., 1965 c.63 s.2, 1972 c.70 s.100J, 1974 c.7 s.25, 1976 c.74 Sch.1A para.21, 1980 c.65 s.2, 1988 c.9 Sch.2 Part 1, 1988 c.41 s.144, 1989 c.42 s.21, s.67, s.152, s.155, 1992 c.14 s.39, 1992 c.19 s.18, 1993 c.25 s.1, 1993 c.38 s.6, 1998 c.18 Sch.2 para.1, 1999 c.27 s.1, 2000 c.22 s.49, 2000 c.36 Sch.1 para.14, 2003 c.26 s.33, 2004 c.23 s.46
s.4, applied: 1959 c.53 Sch.4 para.9., 1965 c.63 s.2, 1972 c.70 s.100J, 1974 c.7 s.25, 1976 c.74 Sch.1A para.21, 1980 c.65 s.2, 1988 c.9 Sch.2 Part 1, 1988 c.41 s.144, 1989 c.42 s.21, s.67, s.152, s.155, 1992 c.14 s.39, 1993 c.25 s.1, 1993 c.38 s.6, 1998 c.18 Sch.2 para.1, 1999 c.27 s.1, 2000 c.22 s.49, 2000 c.36 Sch.1 para.14, 2003 c.26 s.33, 2004 c.23 s.46
s.5, applied: 1993 c.25 s.1
s.6, applied: SI 2004/1705 Sch.1
s.19, enabling: SI 2004/2305
s.21, enabling: SI 2004/2305, SI 2004/3217
s.34, applied: 1951 c.65 s.61, 1971 c.56 Sch.2 para.16, Sch.2 para.16A, Sch.2 para.44
s.36, enabling: SI 2004/2306, SI 2004/2918
s.38, disapplied: 1991 c.56 s.147
s.49, applied: SI 2002/1837 Sch.1 Part I
s.49, referred to: 2001 c.16 s.1
s.53, enabling: SI 2004/3168
s.60, enabling: SI 2004/2304, SI 2004/2305, SI 2004/2306, SI 2004/2917, SI 2004/2918, SI 2004/3168
s.61, enabling: SI 2004/2304, SI 2004/2917
s.62, enabling: SI 2004/2917, SI 2004/2918

24. Employment Relations Act 2004
Commencement Orders: SI 2004/2566 Art.3; SI 2004/3342 Art.4
Royal Assent, September 16, 2004
s.59, enabling: SI 2004/2566, SI 2004/3342

2004–cont.

25. Horserace Betting and Olympic Lottery Act 2004
Commencement Orders: SI 2004/3283 Art.3, Art.4
Royal Assent, October 28, 2004
s.40, enabling: SI 2004/3283

26. Christmas Day (Trading) Act 2004
Royal Assent, October 28, 2004
s.1, referred to: 1994 c.20 Sch.1 para.2
s.2, referred to: 1994 c.20 Sch.3 para.10
s.6, enabling: SI 2004/3235

27. Companies (Audit, Investigations and Community Enterprise) Act 2004
Commencement Orders: SI 2004/3322 Art.2, Sch.1, Sch.2, Sch.3, Sch.4
Royal Assent, October 28, 2004
s.65, enabling: SI 2004/3322

2004–cont.

31. Children Act 2004
Royal Assent, November 15, 2004
Part 1, applied: 2000 c.43 s.36

35. Pensions Act 2004
Commencement Orders: SI 2004/3350 Art.2, Sch.1
Royal Assent, November 18, 2004
Part 2 c.3, applied: 2004 c.33 Sch.5 para.37
s.315, enabling: SI 2004/3350
s.322, enabling: SI 2004/3350

36. Civil Contingencies Act 2004
Commencement Orders: SI 2004/3281 Art.2
Royal Assent, November 18, 2004
s.34, enabling: SI 2004/3281

STATUTORY INSTRUMENT CITATOR 2002-04

The Statutory Instrument Citator covers the period 2002-04 and is up to date to **January 1, 2005** (orders and Acts received). It comprises in a single table:

   (i)   Statutory Instruments amended, repealed, modified, etc. by statute passed or Statutory Instrument issued during this period;

   (ii) Statutory Instruments judicially considered during this period;

   (iii) Statutory Instruments consolidated during this period;

   (iv) Statutory Instruments made under the powers of any Statutory Instrument issued during this period.

The material is arranged in numerical order under the relevant year.

Definitions of legislative effects:

"added"	: new provisions are inserted by subsequent legislation
"amended"	: text of legislation is modified by subsequent legislation
"applied"	: brought to bear, or exercised by subsequent legislation
"consolidated"	: used where previous Acts in the same subject area are brought together in subsequent legislation, with or without amendments
"disapplied"	: an exception made to the application of an earlier enactment
"enabling"	: giving power for the relevant SI to be made
"referred to"	: direction from other legislation without specific effect or application
"repealed"	: rescinded by subsequent legislation
"restored"	: reinstated by subsequent legislation (where previously repealed/ revoked)
"substituted"	: text of provision is completely replaced by subsequent legislation
"varied"	: provisions modified in relation to their application to specified areas or circumstances, however the text itself remains unchanged

STATUTORY INSTRUMENTS ISSUED BY THE SCOTTISH PARLIAMENT

NO.

1999

1. Environmental Impact Assessment (Scotland) Regulations 1999

applied: SSI 2002/6 Reg.3

Reg.2, amended: SSI 2002/324 Reg.2, SSI 2003/331 Sch.1 para.11, SSI 2004/332 Sch.11 para.1

Reg.2A, added: SSI 2004/332 Sch.11 para.2

Reg.2B, added: SSI 2004/332 Sch.11 para.2

Reg.2C, added: SSI 2004/332 Sch.11 para.2

Reg.13, amended: SSI 2004/332 Sch.11 para.3

Reg.21, amended: SSI 2004/332 Sch.11 para.4

Reg.28A, added: SSI 2002/324 Reg.2

Reg.38, amended: SSI 2004/332 Sch.11 para.5

Reg.42, substituted: SSI 2004/332 Sch.11 para.6

1999–cont.

1. Environmental Impact Assessment (Scotland) Regulations 1999–*cont.*

Sch.2 para.2, amended: SSI 2002/324 Reg.2, SSI 2003/341 Reg.4

43. Environmental Impact Assessment (Forestry) (Scotland) Regulations 1999

Reg.3, referred to: SSI 2002/6 Reg.3

53. National Health Service (Service Committees and Tribunal) (Scotland) Amendment Regulations 1999

Reg.2, amended: SSI 2004/38 Sch.3

Reg.12, revoked: SSI 2004/38 Sch.3

Reg.13, revoked: SSI 2004/38 Sch.3

Reg.14, revoked: SSI 2004/38 Sch.3

Reg.19, revoked: SSI 2004/38 Sch.3

NO.

1999–cont.

54. National Health Service (General Medical Services) (Scotland) Amendment (No.4) Regulations 1999
revoked: SSI 2004/114 Sch.2

59. Road Traffic (Permitted Parking Area and Special Parking Area) (City of Glasgow) Designation Order 1999
Sch.2 para.1, amended: SSI 2002/187 Art.2

63. National Health Service (Travelling Expenses and Remission of Charges) (Scotland) Amendment Regulations 1999
revoked: SSI 2003/376 Sch.3 para.15

77. Argyll and Clyde Acute Hospitals National Health Service Trust (Establishment) Amendment (No.2) Order 1999
revoked: SSI 2003/325 Sch.2

78. Lanarkshire Acute Hospitals National Health Service Trust (Establishment) Amendment Order 1999
revoked: SSI 2004/107 Sch.2

79. Forth Valley Acute Hospitals National Health Service Trust (Establishment) Amendment Order 1999
revoked: SSI 2004/107 Sch.2

80. Highland Acute Hospitals National Health Service Trust (Establishment) Amendment Order 1999
revoked: SSI 2004/107 Sch.2

81. Lothian University Hospitals National Health Service Trust (Establishment) Amendment (No.2) Order 1999
revoked: SSI 2003/597 Sch.1

82. Grampian University Hospitals National Health Service Trust (Establishment) Amendment Order 1999
revoked: SSI 2004/107 Sch.2

83. Tayside Primary Care National Health Service Trust (Establishment) Amendment (No.2) Order 1999
revoked: SSI 2004/107 Sch.2

84. Tayside University Hospitals National Health Service Trust (Establishment) Amendment Order 1999
revoked: SSI 2004/107 Sch.2

85. South Glasgow University Hospitals National Health Service Trust (Establishment) Amendment Order 1999
revoked: SSI 2004/107 Sch.2

86. North Glasgow University Hospitals National Health Service Trust (Establishment) Amendment Order 1999
revoked: SSI 2004/107 Sch.2

87. Greater Glasgow Primary Care National Health Service Trust (Establishment) Amendment Order 1999
revoked: SSI 2004/107 Sch.2

NO.

1999–cont.

89. Lanarkshire Primary Care National Health Service Trust (Establishment) Amendment Order 1999
revoked: SSI 2004/107 Sch.2

91. West Lothian Healthcare National Health Service Trust (Establishment) Amendment Order 1999
revoked: SSI 2004/107 Sch.2

92. Borders Primary Care National Health Service Trust (Establishment) Amendment Order 1999
revoked: SSI 2003/189 Sch.2

93. Highland Primary Care National Health Service Trust (Establishment) Amendment (No.2) Order 1999
revoked: SSI 2004/107 Sch.2

94. Fife Primary Care National Health Service Trust (Establishment) Amendment Order 1999
revoked: SSI 2003/448 Sch.2

95. Lothian Primary Care National Health Service Trust (Establishment) Amendment Order 1999
revoked: SSI 2004/107 Sch.2

96. Dumfries and Galloway Primary Care National Health Service Trust (Establishment) Amendment Order 1999
revoked: SSI 2003/189 Sch.2

97. Renfrewshire and Inverclyde Primary Care National Health Service Trust (Establishment) Amendment Order 1999
revoked: SSI 2003/325 Sch.2

98. Grampian Primary Care National Health Service Trust (Establishment) Amendment Order 1999
revoked: SSI 2004/107 Sch.2

99. Lomond and Argyll Primary Care National Health Service Trust (Establishment) Amendment Order 1999
revoked: SSI 2003/325 Sch.2

100. Ayrshire and Arran Acute Hospitals National Health Service Trust (Establishment) Amendment Order 1999
revoked: SSI 2004/107 Sch.2

150. Act of Sederunt (Fees of Sheriff Officers) 1999
revoked: SSI 2002/567 Sch.2

151. Act of Sederunt (Fees of Messengers-at-Arms) 1999
revoked: SSI 2002/566 Sch.2

164. Forth Valley Primary Care National Health Service Trust (Establishment) Amendment (No.2) Order 1999
revoked: SSI 2004/107 Sch.2

165. Ayrshire and Arran Primary Care National Health Service Trust (Establishment) Amendment (No.2) Order 1999
revoked: SSI 2004/107 Sch.2

NO.

1999–cont.

171. Contaminants in Food Amendment (Scotland) Regulations 1999
revoked: SSI 2002/267 Sch.1

185. Hill Livestock (Compensatory Allowances) (Scotland) Regulations 1999
applied: SSI 2004/70 Reg.4

187. Hill Livestock (Compensatory Allowances) (Scotland) Regulations 1999
applied: SSI 2003/129 Reg.4, Reg.13
Reg.12, applied: SSI 2004/381 Reg.4
Reg.17, applied: SSI 2004/381 Reg.4
Reg.18, applied: SSI 2004/381 Reg.4

194. Shetland Islands Regulated Fishery (Scotland) Order 1999
referred to: SSI 2004/1
Art.2, amended: SSI 2004/1 Art.2
Art.6, amended: SSI 2004/1 Art.2

197. Ayrshire and Arran Acute Hospitals National Health Service Trust (Establishment) Amendment (No.2) Order 1999
revoked: SSI 2004/107 Sch.2

198. Fife Acute Hospitals National Health Service Trust (Establishment) Amendment (No.2) Order 1999
revoked: SSI 2003/448 Sch.2

200. Montrose Harbour Revision Order 1999
Art.4, revoked (in part): SSI 2003/258 Sch.3

2000

1. Seeds (Fees) (Scotland) Regulations 2000
revoked: SSI 2002/526 Reg.6

7. Sea Fishing (Enforcement of Community Control Measures) (Scotland) Order 2000
Art.2, amended: SSI 2003/56 Art.7, SSI 2003/300 Art.3, SSI 2003/623 Art.3, SSI 2004/44 Art.8, SSI 2004/209 Art.16
Sch.1, amended: SSI 2003/56 Art.7, SSI 2004/44 Art.8

20. Sea Fishing (Enforcement of Community Satellite Monitoring Measures) (Scotland) Order 2000
revoked: SSI 2004/392 Art.17

22. Pesticides (Maximum Residue Levels in Crops, Food and Feeding Stuffs) (Scotland) Regulations 2000
Reg.2, amended: SSI 2002/271 Reg.2
Reg.6, amended: SSI 2002/489 Reg.2
Sch.1, amended: SSI 2002/271 Reg.2, SSI 2002/489 Reg.2, SSI 2003/118 Reg.2, SSI 2003/445 Reg.2, SSI 2004/104 Reg.2, SSI 2004/220 Reg.2, SSI 2004/ 399 Reg.2
Sch.2 Part 1, amended: SSI 2002/489 Reg.2, SSI 2003/118 Reg.2, SSI 2003/445 Reg.2, SSI 2004/104 Reg.2, SSI 2004/399 Reg.2

NO.

2000–cont.

22. Pesticides (Maximum Residue Levels in Crops, Food and Feeding Stuffs) (Scotland) Regulations 2000–*cont.*
Sch.2 Part 2, amended: SSI 2002/271 Reg.2, Sch.2, SSI 2002/489 Sch.1, SSI 2003/118 Sch.1, SSI 2004/104 Reg.2, Sch.1, SSI 2004/220 Reg.2, Sch.1
Sch.2 Part 2, varied: SSI 2003/445 Reg.2, Sch.1, SSI 2004/399 Reg.2, Sch.1
Sch.5, added: SSI 2002/271 Sch.1
Sch.5, substituted: SSI 2002/489 Sch.2, SSI 2003/118 Sch.2, SSI 2003/445 Sch.2, SSI 2004/104 Sch.2, SSI 2004/220 Sch.2, SSI 2004/399 Sch.2

23. National Health Service (Vocational Training for General Medical Practice) (Scotland) Amendment Regulations 2000
revoked: SI 2003/1250 Sch.10 Part 2

28. National Health Service (General Medical Services) (Scotland) Amendment Regulations 2000
revoked: SSI 2004/114 Sch.2

35. Food (Peanuts from Egypt) (Emergency Control) (Scotland) Order 2000
revoked: SSI 2003/418 Reg.7

44. National Health Service (Dental Charges) (Scotland) Amendment Regulations 2000
revoked: SSI 2003/158 Sch.4

47. Health Technology Board for Scotland Order 2000
revoked: SSI 2002/534 Art.7
Art.5, applied: SSI 2002/535
Sch.1 Part I, applied: SSI 2002/535

52. Dairy Produce Quotas Amendment (Scotland) Regulations 2000
revoked: SSI 2002/110 Reg.34

53. Sea Fishing (Enforcement of Community Conservation Measures) (Scotland) Order 2000
Art.2, amended: SSI 2002/81 Art.2
Sch.1, added: SSI 2002/81 Sch.1
Sch.1, amended: SSI 2002/81 Art.3

54. National Health Service (Clinical Negligence and Other Risks Indemnity Scheme) (Scotland) Regulations 2000
Reg.3, amended: SSI 2002/239 Reg.2

59. Disabled Persons (Badges for Motor Vehicles) (Scotland) Regulations 2000
Reg.2, amended: SSI 2002/451 Reg.2
Reg.12, applied: SSI 2002/450 Reg.3

60. Local Authorities Traffic Orders (Exemptions for Disabled Persons) (Scotland) Regulations 2000
revoked: SSI 2002/450 Reg.1

NO.

2000–cont.

62. Food Standards Act 1999 (Transitional and Consequential Provisions and Savings) (Scotland) Regulations 2000

Reg.6, revoked (in part): SSI 2002/255 Sch.9 Part I

Reg.7, disapplied: SSI 2002/445 Sch.7

Sch.4 Part X para.1, revoked: SSI 2002/255 Sch.9 Part I

Sch.4 Part X para.2, revoked: SSI 2002/255 Sch.9 Part I

Sch.4 Part X para.3, revoked: SSI 2002/255 Sch.9 Part I

Sch.4 Part X para.4, revoked: SSI 2002/255 Sch.9 Part I

Sch.4 Part X para.5, revoked: SSI 2002/255 Sch.9 Part I

79. National Health Service (Travelling Expenses and Remission of Charges) (Scotland) Amendment Regulations 2000

revoked: SSI 2003/376 Sch.3 para.16

83. Genetically Modified and Novel Foods (Labelling) (Scotland) Regulations 2000

revoked: SSI 2004/432 Reg.7

86. Electricity Generators (Rateable Values) (Scotland) Order 2000

Art.2, amended: SSI 2002/158 Art.17

88. Electricity Lands (Rateable Values) (Scotland) Order 2000

Art.2, amended: SSI 2002/158 Art.3

Art.4, amended: SSI 2002/158 Art.4

Art.5, amended: SSI 2002/158 Art.5

Art.6, amended: SSI 2002/158 Art.6

Art.7, amended: SSI 2002/158 Art.7

Art.8, amended: SSI 2002/158 Art.8

Art.9, amended: SSI 2002/158 Art.9

Art.10, amended: SSI 2002/158 Art.10

Art.11, amended: SSI 2002/158 Art.11

Art.12, amended: SSI 2002/158 Art.12

Art.15, revoked (in part): SSI 2002/158 Art.13

Sch.1, amended: SSI 2002/158 Art.14

Sch.2, amended: SSI 2002/158 Art.15

Sch.3, amended: SSI 2002/158 Art.16

90. Water Undertakings (Rateable Values) (Scotland) Order 2000

referred to: SSI 2003/187 Art.9

revoked: SSI 2003/187 Art.9

Sch.2, amended: SSI 2002/159 Art.2

97. Air Quality (Scotland) Regulations 2000

Reg.3, amended: SSI 2002/297 Reg.2

Sch.1, amended: SSI 2002/297 Reg.2

109. Advice and Assistance (Assistance by Way of Representation) (Scotland) Amendment Regulations 2000

revoked: SSI 2003/179 Sch.1

112. Divorce etc (Pensions) (Scotland) Regulations 2000

Reg.3, applied: SI 2002/427 Reg.16

NO.

2000–cont.

112. Divorce etc (Pensions) (Scotland) Regulations 2000–*cont.*

Reg.3, disapplied: SI 2002/427 Reg.16

Reg.3, varied: SI 2002/836 Reg.16, SI 2003/291 Reg.2

120. Right to Purchase (Application Form) (Scotland) Order 2000

revoked: SSI 2002/322 Art.1

121. European Communities (Lawyer's Practice) (Scotland) Regulations 2000

Reg.1, varied: SSI 2004/302 Reg.2

Reg.2, amended: SSI 2004/302 Reg.3

Reg.12, amended: SSI 2004/302 Reg.4

Reg.13, amended: SSI 2004/302 Reg.5

Reg.21, applied: SSI 2004/302 Reg.2

Reg.22, applied: SSI 2004/302 Reg.2

130. Foods for Special Medical Purposes (Scotland) Regulations 2000

Reg.2, amended: SSI 2004/395 Reg.6

150. Town and Country Planning (Fees for Applications and Deemed Applications) (Scotland) Amendment Regulations 2000

revoked: SSI 2004/219 Reg.15

177. Civic Government (Scotland) Act 1982 (Licensing of Houses in Multiple Occupation) Order 2000

Art.2, amended: SSI 2002/161 Art.3, Art.4, Art.5, SSI 2003/463 Art.3, Art.4

Art.2, revoked (in part): SSI 2002/161 Art.4

Art.5, substituted: SSI 2003/463 Art.5

Sch.1 para.3A, added: SSI 2003/463 Art.6

Sch.1 para.7A, added: SSI 2003/463 Art.6

182. Civil Legal Aid (Scotland) Amendment Regulations 2000

revoked: SSI 2002/494 Sch.1

183. Community Care (Direct Payments) (Scotland) Amendment Regulations 2000

revoked: SSI 2003/243 Sch.1

184. Bovines and Bovine Products (Trade) Amendment (Scotland) Regulations 2000

Reg.2, revoked (in part): SSI 2002/449 Reg.3

190. National Health Service (General Medical Services) (Scotland) Amendment (No.2) Regulations 2000

revoked: SSI 2004/114 Sch.2

191. National Health Service (Choice of Medical Practitioner) (Scotland) Amendment Regulations 2000

revoked: SSI 2004/163 Art.102

200. Education (Student Loans) (Scotland) Regulations 2000

Reg.2, amended: SSI 2004/469 Reg.6

Sch.1 para.4, amended: SSI 2004/469 Reg.6

Sch.1 para.6, amended: SSI 2004/469 Reg.6

Sch.1 para.7, amended: SSI 2004/469 Reg.6

NO.

2000–cont.

201. Seed Potatoes (Scotland) Regulations 2000

applied: SSI 2004/250 Reg.2

214. Processed Cereal-based Foods and Baby Foods for Infants and Young Children Amendment (Scotland) Regulations 2000

revoked: SSI 2004/8 Reg.14

216. Animals and Animal Products (Import and Export) (Scotland) Regulations 2000

applied: SSI 2003/202 Art.3

Reg.12, amended: SSI 2002/125 Reg.2

Sch.3 Part 1 para.9, amended: SSI 2002/125 Reg.2, SSI 2002/196 Reg.2

Sch.3 Part 1 para.16, added: SSI 2002/196 Reg.2

227. Sea Fish (Specified Sea Areas) (Regulation of Nets and Other Fishing Gear) (Scotland) Order 2000

Art.5, amended: SSI 2003/167 Art.2

233. Comhairle nan Eilean Siar (Ardveenish) Harbour Revision Order 2000

revoked: SSI 2002/410 Sch.2 Part II

249. Oil and Fibre Plant Seeds (Amendment) (Scotland) Regulations 2000

revoked: SSI 2004/317 Sch.8

284. Electricity Lands and Water Undertakings (Rateable Values) (Scotland) Amendment Order 2000

Art.3, revoked: SSI 2003/187 Art.9

292. Education and Training (Scotland) Regulations 2000

revoked (in part): SSI 2004/83 Reg.15

293. Education (Listed Bodies) Order 2000

revoked: SSI 2002/406 Art.3

303. Food Protection (Emergency Prohibitions) (Amnesic Shellfish Poisoning) (West Coast) (No.3) (Scotland) Order 2000

revoked: SSI 2002/218 Art.2

308. General Medical Council (Legal Assessors) Amendment (Scotland) Rules 2000

revoked: SI 2004/2625 r.6

323. Pollution Prevention and Control (Scotland) Regulations 2000

applied: SI 2002/843 Reg.64, Reg.68, SI 2002/1416 Reg.64, Reg.68, SSI 2002/255 Reg.63, Reg.67, SSI 2003/170 Reg.4

referred to: SSI 2003/146 Reg.2

Reg.2, amended: SSI 2002/493 Reg.3, SSI 2003/146 Reg.3, SSI 2003/170 Reg.6, SSI 2003/235 Sch.6 para.3, SSI 2004/26 Reg.10, SSI 2004/112 Reg.3

Reg.2, applied: SSI 2004/26 Reg.2

Reg.4, amended: SSI 2003/235 Sch.6 para.3

Reg.4, applied: SSI 2003/235 Reg.10, Reg.13

Reg.6, amended: SSI 2003/146 Reg.4, SSI 2003/221 Reg.2, SSI 2004/26 Reg.12

NO.

2000–cont.

323. Pollution Prevention and Control (Scotland) Regulations 2000–cont.

Reg.7, amended: SSI 2003/146 Reg.5, SSI 2003/235 Sch.6 para.3, SSI 2004/26 Reg.13

Reg.7, applied: SSI 2003/170 Reg.3, SSI 2003/235 Sch.5 para.1, SSI 2004/26 Reg.3, Reg.6

Reg.8, disapplied: SSI 2003/235 Reg.8

Reg.9, amended: SI 2003/3311 Sch.5 para.2, SSI 2003/146 Reg.6, SSI 2003/235 Sch.6 para.3, SSI 2004/26 Reg.14

Reg.9, disapplied: SSI 2003/235 Reg.8

Reg.9C, added: SSI 2004/26 Reg.15

Reg.10, amended: SSI 2004/26 Reg.16

Reg.13, amended: SSI 2003/235 Sch.6 para.3, SSI 2004/26 Reg.17

Reg.13, applied: SSI 2002/493 Reg.4, Reg.5, SSI 2003/170 Reg.3, SSI 2003/235 Sch.5 para.1, SSI 2004/26 Reg.3

Reg.13, varied: SSI 2004/26 Reg.4

Reg.14, amended: SSI 2003/146 Reg.7

Reg.15, amended: SSI 2003/170 Reg.7

Reg.15, disapplied: SSI 2003/235 Reg.17

Reg.16, amended: SSI 2003/170 Reg.8

Reg.16, disapplied: SSI 2003/235 Reg.17

Reg.17, disapplied: SSI 2003/235 Reg.17

Reg.19, applied: SSI 2004/26 Reg.3, Reg.8

Reg.22, amended: SSI 2003/146 Reg.8, SSI 2003/235 Sch.6 para.3

Reg.23, amended: SSI 2003/235 Sch.6 para.3, SSI 2004/26 Reg.11

Reg.24, amended: SSI 2003/146 Reg.9, SSI 2003/235 Sch.6 para.3

Reg.26, amended: SSI 2003/146 Reg.10, SSI 2003/235 Sch.6 para.3

Reg.26, applied: SSI 2004/26 Reg.8

Reg.27, amended: SSI 2003/146 Reg.11

Reg.28, amended: SSI 2003/146 Reg.12

Reg.29, amended: SSI 2003/146 Reg.13

Reg.30, amended: SSI 2003/235 Sch.6 para.3, 2004 asp 8 Sch.2 para.7

Reg.34, amended: SSI 2003/235 Sch.6 para.3

Reg.35, amended: SSI 2003/146 Reg.14, SSI 2003/235 Sch.6 para.3

Sch.1 Part I, amended: SSI 2003/146 Reg.15, Reg.16

Sch.1 Part I, added: SSI 2003/146 Reg.19, SSI 2004/26 Sch.1

Sch.1 Part I, amended: SSI 2003/146 Reg.16, Reg.17, Reg.18, Reg.19, Reg.20, SSI 2003/170 Reg.10, SSI 2003/411 Sch.5 para.2, SSI 2004/110 Reg.2

Sch.1 Part I, applied: SSI 2003/235 Reg.8, Reg.10, Sch.5 para.1, Sch.5 para.2, Sch.5 para.4

Sch.1 Part I, referred to: SSI 2003/170 Reg.3

Sch.1 Part I, revoked (in part): SSI 2004/110 Reg.2

2000–cont.

323. Pollution Prevention and Control (Scotland) Regulations 2000–*cont.*

Sch.1 Part I, substituted: SSI 2003/146 Reg.19, SSI 2003/170 Reg.9, SSI 2003/235 Reg.8

Sch.1 Part 2 para.2, amended: SSI 2004/26 Reg.18

Sch.1 Part 2 para.3, amended: SSI 2004/26 Reg.18

Sch.1 Part 2 para.4, amended: SSI 2004/26 Reg.18

Sch.1 Part 2 para.5, amended: SSI 2004/26 Reg.18

Sch.1 Part 2 para.6, amended: SSI 2004/26 Reg.18

Sch.1 Part 2 para.7, amended: SSI 2004/26 Reg.18

Sch.1 Part 2 para.7A, added: SSI 2004/26 Reg.18

Sch.1 Part 2 para.9, amended: SSI 2004/26 Reg.18

Sch.1 Part 2 para.10, amended: SSI 2004/26 Reg.18, SSI 2004/110 Reg.2

Sch.1 Part 3 para.18, amended: SSI 2004/26 Reg.18

Sch.2 para.1, amended: SSI 2004/26 Reg.11

Sch.3, applied: SSI 2003/235 Sch.5 para.2, SSI 2004/26 Reg.2

Sch.3 Part 1, applied: SSI 2003/170 Reg.4, SSI 2003/235 Sch.5 para.1

Sch.3 Part 1 para.1, amended: SSI 2003/146 Reg.21

Sch.3 Part 1 para.1, varied: SSI 2003/235 Sch.5 para.4

Sch.3 Part 1 para.1A, added: SSI 2003/146 Reg.21

Sch.3 Part 1 para.2, amended: SSI 2003/146 Reg.21, SSI 2003/170 Reg.11, SSI 2003/235 Sch.6 para.3, SSI 2004/112 Reg.3

Sch.3 Part 1 para.4, varied: SSI 2003/170 Reg.4

Sch.3 Part 1 para.5, amended: SSI 2004/26 Reg.19

Sch.3 Part 1 para.6, amended: SSI 2003/146 Reg.21

Sch.3 Part 1 para.6, varied: SSI 2003/170 Reg.4

Sch.3 Part 2 para.9, amended: SSI 2004/26 Reg.19

Sch.3 Part 2 para.9, applied: SSI 2004/26 Reg.7

Sch.3 Part 3, applied: SSI 2004/26 Reg.8

Sch.3 Part 3 para.12, added: SSI 2004/26 Sch.2

Sch.3 Part 3 para.12, varied: SSI 2004/26 Reg.4

Sch.3 Part 3 para.13, added: SSI 2004/26 Sch.2

Sch.3 Part 3 para.13, varied: SSI 2004/26 Reg.4

2000–cont.

323. Pollution Prevention and Control (Scotland) Regulations 2000–*cont.*

Sch.3 Part 3 para.14, added: SSI 2004/26 Sch.2

Sch.3 Part 3 para.14, varied: SSI 2004/26 Reg.4

Sch.3 Part 3 para.15, added: SSI 2004/26 Sch.2

Sch.3 Part 3 para.15, varied: SSI 2004/26 Reg.4

Sch.3 Part 3 para.16, added: SSI 2004/26 Sch.2

Sch.3 Part 3 para.16, varied: SSI 2004/26 Reg.4

Sch.3 Part 3 para.17, added: SSI 2004/26 Sch.2

Sch.3 Part 3 para.17, varied: SSI 2004/26 Reg.4

Sch.3 Part 4 para.18, added: SSI 2004/26 Sch.2

Sch.3 Part 4 para.18, applied: SSI 2004/26 Reg.4, Reg.5, Reg.6

Sch.3 Part 4 para.19, added: SSI 2004/26 Sch.2

Sch.4, applied: SSI 2004/26 Reg.6

Sch.4 Part 1, referred to: SSI 2004/26 Reg.3

Sch.4 Part 1 para.1, amended: SSI 2003/146 Reg.22, SSI 2003/170 Reg.12, SSI 2004/26 Reg.20

Sch.4 Part 1 para.1A, added: SSI 2003/235 Sch.6 para.3

Sch.4 Part 1 para.1B, added: SSI 2003/170 Reg.12

Sch.4 Part 1 para.1B, referred to: SSI 2003/170 Reg.3

Sch.4 Part 1 para.1C, added: SSI 2004/26 Reg.20

Sch.4 Part 1 para.1C, varied: SSI 2004/26 Reg.3

Sch.4 Part 1 para.2, amended: SSI 2003/146 Reg.22

Sch.4 Part 1 para.3A, added: SSI 2004/26 Reg.20

Sch.4 Part 1 para.5, disapplied: SSI 2003/235 Reg.8

Sch.4 Part 1 para.8, substituted: SSI 2004/26 Reg.20

Sch.4 Part 2 para.9, amended: SSI 2003/146 Reg.23, SSI 2003/331 Sch.1 para.12

Sch.4 Part 2 para.10, substituted: SSI 2004/26 Reg.20

Sch.4 Part 2 para.13, substituted: SSI 2003/146 Reg.23

Sch.4 Part 2 para.17, amended: SSI 2004/26 Reg.11

Sch.4 Part 3 para.21, amended: SSI 2003/146 Reg.24

Sch.4 Part 3 para.22, amended: SSI 2003/146 Reg.24

Sch.6 para.7, amended: SSI 2003/146 Reg.25

NO.

2000—cont.

323. Pollution Prevention and Control (Scotland) Regulations 2000—*cont.*

Sch.7 Part 1 para.1, amended: SSI 2003/170 Reg.13, SSI 2004/26 Reg.21

Sch.7 Part 1 para.1, varied: SSI 2004/26 Reg.4

Sch.7 Part 1 para.2, amended: SSI 2004/26 Reg.21

Sch.7 Part 1 para.2, varied: SSI 2004/26 Reg.4

Sch.7 Part 1 para.3, varied: SSI 2004/26 Reg.4

Sch.7 Part 2 para.4, amended: SSI 2004/26 Reg.21

Sch.7 Part 2 para.4, disapplied: SSI 2003/235 Reg.8

Sch.7 Part 2 para.4, varied: SSI 2004/26 Reg.4

Sch.7 Part 2 para.5, varied: SSI 2004/26 Reg.4

Sch.7 Part 2 para.6, varied: SSI 2004/26 Reg.4

Sch.7 Part 2 para.7, varied: SSI 2004/26 Reg.4

Sch.7 Part 2 para.8, varied: SSI 2004/26 Reg.4

Sch.7 Part 2 para.9, amended: SSI 2004/26 Reg.11

Sch.7 Part 2 para.9, varied: SSI 2004/26 Reg.4

Sch.7 Part 2 para.10, varied: SSI 2004/26 Reg.4

Sch.7 Part 2 para.11, varied: SSI 2004/26 Reg.4

Sch.7 Part 2 para.12, varied: SSI 2004/26 Reg.4

Sch.7 Part 3 para.13, varied: SSI 2004/26 Reg.4

Sch.7 Part 3 para.14, amended: SSI 2003/146 Reg.26

Sch.7 Part 3 para.14, varied: SSI 2004/26 Reg.4

Sch.7 Part 3 para.15, varied: SSI 2004/26 Reg.4

Sch.8 para.4, amended: SSI 2003/146 Reg.27

Sch.8 para.6, amended: SSI 2003/146 Reg.27

Sch.9 para.1, amended: SSI 2003/170 Reg.14, SSI 2003/235 Sch.6 para.3

342. Education and Training (Scotland) Amendment Regulations 2000

revoked: SSI 2004/83 Reg.15

343. Regulation of Investigatory Powers (Prescription of Offices, Ranks and Positions) (Scotland) Order 2000

Sch.1, amended: SSI 2003/50 Art.3

344. Specified Risk Material Order Amendment (Scotland) Regulations 2000

Reg.2, revoked (in part): SSI 2002/255 Sch.9 Part I

NO.

2000—cont.

345. Specified Risk Material Amendment (Scotland) Regulations 2000

revoked: SSI 2002/255 Sch.9 Part I

347. Agricultural Subsidies (Appeals) (Scotland) Regulations 2000

applied: SSI 2002/139 Reg.22, SSI 2003/129 Reg.24, SSI 2004/70 Reg.23, SSI 2004/143 Reg.25

referred to: SSI 2004/70 Reg.26

revoked: SSI 2004/381 Sch.1

Reg.3, amended: SSI 2002/139 Reg.25, SSI 2003/129 Reg.27, SSI 2004/70 Reg.26

Reg.4, amended: SSI 2002/139 Reg.25, SSI 2002/228 Reg.3, SSI 2003/129 Reg.27, SSI 2003/302 Reg.2, SSI 2004/70 Reg.26, SSI 2004/143 Reg.25

353. Borders General Hospital National Health Service Trust (Establishment) Amendment Order 2000

revoked: SSI 2003/189 Sch.2

354. Dumfries and Galloway Acute and Maternity Hospitals National Health Service Trust (Establishment) Amendment Order 2000

revoked: SSI 2003/189 Sch.2

355. Yorkhill National Health Service Trust (Establishment) Amendment Order 2000

revoked: SSI 2004/107 Sch.2

391. Dairy Produce Quotas Amendment (No.2) (Scotland) Regulations 2000

revoked: SSI 2002/110 Reg.34

405. Prohibition of Fishing with Multiple Trawls (No.2) (Scotland) Order 2000

Art.3, amended: SSI 2003/166 Art.2

418. Sheep and Goats Identification (Scotland) Regulations 2000

applied: SSI 2002/34 Art.4

Reg.2, amended: SSI 2002/39 Reg.2

Reg.4, amended: SSI 2002/39 Reg.2

Reg.4, referred to: SSI 2002/38 Art.3

Reg.6, amended: SSI 2002/39 Reg.2, SSI 2002/531 Reg.2

Reg.6, referred to: SSI 2002/38 Art.3

Reg.6A, added: SSI 2002/39 Reg.2

Reg.7, amended: SSI 2002/39 Reg.2

Reg.7, applied: SSI 2002/38 Art.3

Reg.7A, added: SSI 2002/39 Reg.2

Reg.8, amended: SSI 2002/39 Reg.2

Reg.12, amended: SSI 2002/39 Reg.2

Reg.12, revoked (in part): SSI 2002/39 Reg.2

Reg.13, amended: SSI 2002/39 Reg.2, SSI 2002/531 Reg.2

Reg.13, applied: SSI 2002/38 Art.3

Reg.14, applied: SSI 2002/38 Art.3

Reg.15, amended: SSI 2002/39 Reg.2

Reg.16, amended: SSI 2002/39 Reg.2

419. Act of Sederunt (Fees of Sheriff Officers) 2000

revoked: SSI 2002/567 Sch.2

NO.

2000–cont.

421. Act of Sederunt (Fees of Messengers-At-Arms) 2000
revoked: SSI 2002/566 Sch.2

429. Common Agricultural Policy Support Schemes (Modulation) (Scotland) Regulations 2000
Reg.3, amended: SSI 2004/398 Reg.2
Reg.5, amended: SSI 2004/398 Reg.2

442. Welfare of Farmed Animals (Scotland) Regulations 2000
Reg.2, amended: SSI 2002/334 Reg.2, SSI 2003/488 Reg.2
Reg.4, revoked: SSI 2002/334 Reg.2
Reg.5, substituted: SSI 2002/334 Reg.2
Reg.5A, added: SSI 2002/334 Reg.2
Reg.8A, added: SSI 2003/488 Reg.2
Reg.12, amended: SSI 2002/334 Reg.2
Sch.1 para.2, amended: SSI 2002/334 Reg.2
Sch.2 para.1, revoked: SSI 2002/334 Reg.2
Sch.2 para.2, revoked: SSI 2002/334 Reg.2
Sch.2 para.3, revoked: SSI 2002/334 Reg.2
Sch.2 para.4, revoked: SSI 2002/334 Reg.2
Sch.2 para.5, revoked: SSI 2002/334 Reg.2
Sch.2 para.6, revoked: SSI 2002/334 Reg.2
Sch.2 para.7, revoked: SSI 2002/334 Reg.2
Sch.2 para.8, revoked: SSI 2002/334 Reg.2
Sch.2 para.9, revoked: SSI 2002/334 Reg.2
Sch.2 para.10, revoked: SSI 2002/334 Reg.2
Sch.3, substituted: SSI 2002/334 Reg.2
Sch.3A para.1, added: SSI 2002/334 Sch.1
Sch.3A para.2, added: SSI 2002/334 Sch.1
Sch.3A para.3, added: SSI 2002/334 Sch.1
Sch.3A para.4, added: SSI 2002/334 Sch.1
Sch.3A para.5, added: SSI 2002/334 Sch.1
Sch.3A para.6, added: SSI 2002/334 Sch.1
Sch.3A para.7, added: SSI 2002/334 Sch.1
Sch.3A para.8, added: SSI 2002/334 Sch.1
Sch.3B para.1, added: SSI 2002/334 Sch.1
Sch.3B para.2, added: SSI 2002/334 Sch.1
Sch.3B para.3, added: SSI 2002/334 Sch.1
Sch.3C para.1, added: SSI 2002/334 Sch.1
Sch.3C para.2, added: SSI 2002/334 Sch.1
Sch.3C para.3, added: SSI 2002/334 Sch.1
Sch.3C para.4, added: SSI 2002/334 Sch.1
Sch.3C para.5, added: SSI 2002/334 Sch.1
Sch.3C para.6, added: SSI 2002/334 Sch.1
Sch.3D para.1, added: SSI 2002/334 Sch.1
Sch.3D para.2, added: SSI 2002/334 Sch.1
Sch.3D para.3, added: SSI 2002/334 Sch.1
Sch.3D para.4, added: SSI 2002/334 Sch.1
Sch.3D para.5, added: SSI 2002/334 Sch.1
Sch.3D para.6, added: SSI 2002/334 Sch.1
Sch.3D para.7, added: SSI 2002/334 Sch.1
Sch.3D para.8, added: SSI 2002/334 Sch.1
Sch.3D para.9, added: SSI 2002/334 Sch.1
Sch.6, referred to: SSI 2003/488 Reg.2
Sch.6 Part I para.1, substituted: SSI 2003/488 Sch.1
Sch.6 Part II para.2, substituted: SSI 2003/488 Sch.1

NO.

2000–cont.

442. Welfare of Farmed Animals (Scotland) Regulations 2000–cont.
Sch.6 Part II para.3, substituted: SSI 2003/488 Sch.1
Sch.6 Part II para.4, substituted: SSI 2003/488 Sch.1
Sch.6 Part II para.5, substituted: SSI 2003/488 Sch.1
Sch.6 Part II para.6, substituted: SSI 2003/488 Sch.1
Sch.6 Part II para.7, substituted: SSI 2003/488 Sch.1
Sch.6 Part II para.8, substituted: SSI 2003/488 Sch.1
Sch.6 Part II para.9, substituted: SSI 2003/488 Sch.1
Sch.6 Part II para.10, substituted: SSI 2003/488 Sch.1
Sch.6 Part II para.11, substituted: SSI 2003/488 Sch.1
Sch.6 Part II para.12, substituted: SSI 2003/488 Sch.1
Sch.6 Part II para.13, referred to: SSI 2003/488 Reg.2
Sch.6 Part II para.13, substituted: SSI 2003/488 Sch.1
Sch.6 Part II para.14, substituted: SSI 2003/488 Sch.1
Sch.6 Part II para.15, substituted: SSI 2003/488 Sch.1
Sch.6 Part II para.16, substituted: SSI 2003/488 Sch.1
Sch.6 Part II para.17, substituted: SSI 2003/488 Sch.1
Sch.6 Part II para.18, substituted: SSI 2003/488 Sch.1
Sch.6 Part II para.19, substituted: SSI 2003/488 Sch.1
Sch.6 Part II para.20, substituted: SSI 2003/488 Sch.1
Sch.6 Part II para.21, substituted: SSI 2003/488 Sch.1
Sch.6 Part II para.22, substituted: SSI 2003/488 Sch.1
Sch.6 Part II para.23, substituted: SSI 2003/488 Sch.1
Sch.6 Part II para.24, substituted: SSI 2003/488 Sch.1
Sch.6 Part II para.25, substituted: SSI 2003/488 Sch.1
Sch.6 Part II para.26, substituted: SSI 2003/488 Sch.1
Sch.6 Part III para.17, substituted: SSI 2003/488 Sch.1
Sch.6 Part III para.18, substituted: SSI 2003/488 Sch.1
Sch.6 Part III para.19, substituted: SSI 2003/488 Sch.1
Sch.6 Part III para.27, substituted: SSI 2003/488 Sch.1

NO.

2000–cont.

442. Welfare of Farmed Animals (Scotland) Regulations 2000–*cont.*

Sch.6 Part III para.28, substituted: SSI 2003/488 Sch.1

Sch.6 Part III para.29, referred to: SSI 2003/488 Reg.2

Sch.6 Part III para.29, substituted: SSI 2003/488 Sch.1

Sch.6 Part IV para.20, substituted: SSI 2003/488 Sch.1

Sch.6 Part IV para.21, substituted: SSI 2003/488 Sch.1

Sch.6 Part IV para.22, substituted: SSI 2003/488 Sch.1

Sch.6 Part IV para.23, substituted: SSI 2003/488 Sch.1

Sch.6 Part IV para.24, substituted: SSI 2003/488 Sch.1

Sch.6 Part IV para.30, substituted: SSI 2003/488 Sch.1

Sch.6 Part IV para.31, substituted: SSI 2003/488 Sch.1

Sch.6 Part IV para.32, substituted: SSI 2003/488 Sch.1

Sch.6 Part IV para.33, substituted: SSI 2003/488 Sch.1

Sch.6 Part IV para.34, substituted: SSI 2003/488 Sch.1

Sch.6 Part IV para.35, substituted: SSI 2003/488 Sch.1

Sch.6 Part IV para.36, substituted: SSI 2003/488 Sch.1

Sch.6 Part IV para.37, referred to: SSI 2003/488 Reg.2

Sch.6 Part IV para.37, substituted: SSI 2003/488 Sch.1

Sch.6 Part IV para.38, referred to: SSI 2003/488 Reg.2

Sch.6 Part IV para.38, substituted: SSI 2003/488 Sch.1

Sch.6 Part IV para.39, referred to: SSI 2003/488 Reg.2

Sch.6 Part IV para.39, substituted: SSI 2003/488 Sch.1

Sch.6 Part IV para.40, substituted: SSI 2003/488 Sch.1

Sch.6 Part IV para.41, substituted: SSI 2003/488 Sch.1

Sch.6 Part IV para.42, substituted: SSI 2003/488 Sch.1

Sch.6 Part V para.25, substituted: SSI 2003/488 Sch.1

Sch.6 Part V para.26, substituted: SSI 2003/488 Sch.1

Sch.6 Part V para.27, substituted: SSI 2003/488 Sch.1

Sch.6 Part V para.28, substituted: SSI 2003/488 Sch.1

Sch.6 Part V para.29, substituted: SSI 2003/488 Sch.1

NO.

2000–cont.

442. Welfare of Farmed Animals (Scotland) Regulations 2000–*cont.*

Sch.6 Part V para.43, substituted: SSI 2003/488 Sch.1

Sch.6 Part V para.44, substituted: SSI 2003/488 Sch.1

Sch.6 Part V para.45, substituted: SSI 2003/488 Sch.1

Sch.6 Part V para.46, substituted: SSI 2003/488 Sch.1

Sch.6 Part V para.47, substituted: SSI 2003/488 Sch.1

Sch.6 Part VI para.30, substituted: SSI 2003/488 Sch.1

Sch.6 Part VI para.31, substituted: SSI 2003/488 Sch.1

Sch.6 Part VI para.48, substituted: SSI 2003/488 Sch.1

Sch.6 Part VI para.49, substituted: SSI 2003/488 Sch.1

Sch.6 Part VI para.50, substituted: SSI 2003/488 Sch.1

Sch.6 Part VI para.51, substituted: SSI 2003/488 Sch.1

Sch.6 Part VI para.52, substituted: SSI 2003/488 Sch.1

448. Agricultural Business Development Scheme (Scotland) Regulations 2000

Reg.2, amended: SSI 2004/267 Reg.2

453. Feeding Stuffs (Scotland) Regulations 2000

referred to: SSI 2003/101 Reg.2

Reg.2, amended: SSI 2002/255 Sch.8 Part V, SSI 2002/285 Reg.3, SSI 2003/101 Reg.3, SSI 2003/312 Reg.3

Reg.14, amended: SSI 2003/101 Reg.4, SSI 2004/458 Reg.2

Reg.14, substituted: SSI 2003/312 Reg.4

Reg.15, substituted: SSI 2004/458 Reg.2

Reg.19, amended: SSI 2002/285 Reg.4

Reg.19A, added: SSI 2003/312 Reg.5

Reg.25, amended: SSI 2002/285 Reg.5, SSI 2003/312 Reg.6

Reg.27, revoked (in part): SSI 2002/285 Reg.6

Sch.3 para.11, amended: SSI 2002/285 Sch.1, SSI 2003/312 Sch.1, SSI 2003/474 Sch.1, Sch.2, SSI 2004/208 Reg.3, Sch.1, SSI 2004/458 Reg.2

Sch.3 para.11, substituted: SSI 2003/101 Reg.5, Sch.1

Sch.4 Part 1 para.14, revoked (in part): SSI 2003/312 Reg.8

Sch.4 Part 1 para.15, amended: SSI 2003/312 Reg.8

Sch.4 Part 1 para.19, substituted: SSI 2003/312 Reg.8

Sch.4 Part 1 para.22, amended: SSI 2002/285 Reg.8

NO.

2000–cont.

453. Feeding Stuffs (Scotland) Regulations 2000–*cont.*

Sch.7 Part I, amended: SSI 2002/285 Sch.2, SSI 2003/312 Reg.9, SSI 2004/208 Sch.2, SSI 2004/458 Sch.1

Sch.7 Part II, amended: SSI 2002/285 Sch.2

Sch.7 Part II, revoked: SSI 2003/312 Reg.9

Sch.8, amended: SSI 2002/285 Reg.10, SSI 2004/208 Sch.3

Sch.9 Part A, amended: SSI 2002/285 Sch.3

Sch.10 Part II, revoked: SSI 2003/312 Reg.10

2001

1. Cattle (Identification of Older Animals) (Scotland) Regulations 2001

Reg.2, amended: SSI 2002/1 Reg.4

Reg.7, amended: SSI 2002/22 Reg.3

Reg.9, amended: SSI 2002/255 Sch.8 Part VI

2. Advice and Assistance (Assistance by Way of Representation) (Scotland) Amendment Regulations 2001

revoked: SSI 2003/179 Sch.1

3. Specified Risk Material Amendment (Scotland) Regulations 2001

revoked: SSI 2002/255 Sch.9 Part I

38. Coffee Extracts and Chicory Extracts (Scotland) Regulations 2001

Reg.5, amended: SSI 2003/527 Sch.2

43. Advice and Assistance (Assistance by Way of Representation) (Scotland) Amendment (No.2) Regulations 2001

revoked: SSI 2003/179 Sch.1

45. Diseases of Animals (Approved Disinfectants) Amendment (Scotland) Order 2001

Art.2, revoked (in part): SSI 2003/334 Art.3

50. Less Favoured Area Support Scheme (Scotland) Regulations 2001

applied: SSI 2003/129 Reg.4, Reg.13, SSI 2004/70 Reg.4

revoked (in part): SSI 2002/139 Reg.26

Reg.10, applied: SSI 2002/139 Reg.11

Reg.10, disapplied: SSI 2002/139 Reg.10

Reg.10, referred to: SSI 2003/129 Reg.13

Reg.13, applied: SSI 2004/381 Reg.4

Reg.20, amended: SSI 2004/381 Reg.14

Reg.20, revoked (in part): SSI 2004/381 Sch.1

Sch.5 Part I, applied: SSI 2002/139 Reg.4

Sch.5 Part II, applied: SSI 2002/139 Reg.4

51. Diseases of Animals (Approved Disinfectants) Amendment (No.2) (Scotland) Order 2001

revoked: SSI 2003/334 Art.3

54. Nurses, Midwives and Health Visitors (Professional Conduct) (Amendment) Rules 2001 Approval (Scotland) Order 2001

varied: SI 2004/1762 Art.1

NO.

2001–cont.

66. Foot-and-Mouth Disease (Scotland) (Declaratory and Controlled Area) Amendment Order 2001

revoked: SSI 2002/54 Sch.1

69. National Health Service (Dental Charges) (Scotland) Amendment Regulations 2001

revoked: SSI 2003/158 Sch.4

71. Non-Domestic Rates (Levying) (Scotland) Regulations 2001

revoked: SSI 2002/91 Reg.19

Part III, applied: SSI 2002/91 Reg.6, Reg.11

Reg.7, applied: SSI 2002/91 Reg.6, Reg.11

72. National Health Service (Personal Medical Services) (Scotland) Regulations 2001

revoked: SSI 2004/116 Reg.27

Reg.7, amended: SI 2002/3135 Sch.1 para.46

73. Restriction on Pithing (Scotland) Regulations 2001

revoked: SSI 2002/255 Sch.9 Part I

75. Adults with Incapacity (Public Guardian's Fees) (Scotland) Regulations 2001

Sch., amended: SSI 2002/131 Reg.2, Sch.1

78. Adults with Incapacity (Countersignatories of Applications for Authority to Intromit) (Scotland) Regulations 2001

applied: SSI 2002/113 Sch.1 para.22

81. Adults with Incapacity (Scotland) Act 2000 (Commencement No 1) Order 2001

Sch.2, amended: SSI 2002/172 Art.2

82. Civil Legal Aid (Scotland) Amendment Regulations 2001

revoked: SSI 2002/494 Sch.1

83. Gaming Act (Variation of Fees) (Scotland) Order 2001

revoked: SSI 2002/281 Art.3

84. Pesticides (Maximum Residue Levels in Crops, Food and Feeding Stuffs) (Scotland) Amendment Regulations 2001

Reg.2, revoked (in part): SSI 2002/489 Reg.3

Sch.1, amended: SSI 2002/489 Reg.3

85. National Health Service (Choice of Medical Practitioner) (Scotland) Amendment Regulations 2001

revoked: SSI 2004/163 Art.102

86. Specified Risk Material Amendment (No.2) (Scotland) Regulations 2001

revoked: SSI 2002/255 Sch.9 Part I

90. Foot-and-Mouth Disease (Scotland) (Declaratory and Controlled Area) Amendment (No.2) Order 2001

revoked: SSI 2002/54 Sch.1

100. National Assistance (Sums for Personal Requirements) (Scotland) Regulations 2001

revoked: SSI 2002/85 Reg.3

NO.

2001-cont.

111. Foot-and-Mouth Disease Declaratory (Controlled Area) (Scotland) (No.3) Order 2001

referred to: SSI 2002/34 Art.12

revoked: SSI 2002/54 Sch.1

Art.4, amended: SSI 2002/54 Art.2

114. Domestic Water and Sewerage Charges (Reduction) (Scotland) Regulations 2001

revoked: 2002 asp 3 Sch.7 para.23

117. Sea Fishing (Enforcement of Community Quota and Third Country Fishing Measures) (Scotland) Order 2001

revoked: SSI 2002/51 Art.14

119. National Health Service (General Medical Services) (Scotland) Amendment Regulations 2001

revoked: SSI 2004/114 Sch.2

123. Civil Legal Aid (Financial Conditions) (Scotland) Regulations 2001

revoked: SSI 2002/145 Reg.5

124. Advice and Assistance (Financial Conditions) (Scotland) Regulations 2001

revoked: SSI 2002/144 Reg.6

125. Liquor Licensing (Fees) (Scotland) Order 2001

revoked: SSI 2004/157 Art.3

137. NHS 24 (Scotland) Order 2001

Sch.Part II, amended: SSI 2003/242 Art.8

Sch.Part III, amended: SI 2003/1590 Sch.1 para.19

138. National Assistance (Assessment of Resources) Amendment (No.3) (Scotland) Regulations 2001

Reg.3, revoked: SSI 2004/103 Reg.5

Reg.4, revoked: SSI 2004/103 Reg.5

146. Foot-and-Mouth Disease (Scotland) (Declaratory and Controlled Area) Amendment (No.3) Order 2001

revoked: SSI 2002/54 Sch.1

150. Foot-and-Mouth Disease Declaratory (Controlled Area) (Scotland) (No.3) Amendment (No.2) Order 2001

revoked: SSI 2002/54 Sch.1

159. Foot-and-Mouth Disease (Scotland) (Declaratory and Controlled Area) Amendment (No.4) Order 2001

revoked: SSI 2002/54 Sch.1

160. Foot-and-Mouth Disease (Marking of Meat and Meat Products) (Scotland) Regulations 2001

Reg.2, revoked (in part): SSI 2002/35 Reg.6

161. Plant Protection Products Amendment (Scotland) Regulations 2001

revoked: SSI 2003/579 Sch.5

170. Foot-and-Mouth Disease Declaratory (Controlled Area) (Scotland) (No.3) Amendment (No.3) Order 2001

revoked: SSI 2002/54 Sch.1

NO.

2001-cont.

171. Animal By-Products Amendment (Scotland) Order 2001

revoked: SSI 2003/411 Sch.6

174. Inshore Fishing (Prohibition of Fishing and Fishing Methods) (Scotland) Amendment Order 2001

revoked: SSI 2004/276 Sch.4

187. Foot-and-Mouth Disease (Scotland) (Declaratory and Controlled Area) Amendment (No.5) Order 2001

revoked: SSI 2002/54 Sch.1

188. Sex Offenders (Notice Requirements) (Foreign Travel) (Scotland) Regulations 2001

applied: SSI 2004/205 Reg.3

revoked: SSI 2004/205 Reg.3

varied: SSI 2004/205 Reg.3

189. Rendering (Fluid Treatment) (Scotland) Order 2001

Art.2, amended: SSI 2002/255 Sch.8 PartVII, SSI 2003/411 Sch.5 para.3

190. Sex Offenders (Notification Requirements) (Prescribed Police Stations) (Scotland) (No.2) Regulations 2001

revoked: SSI 2004/137 Reg.3

204. Foot-and-Mouth Disease (Scotland) (Declaratory and Controlled Area) Amendment (No.6) Order 2001

revoked: SSI 2002/54 Sch.1

206. Control of Pollution (Silage, Slurry and Agricultural Fuel Oil) (Scotland) Regulations 2001

applied: SSI 2003/129 Sch.2 para.2, SSI 2003/531 Reg.5

referred to: SSI 2004/70 Sch.2 para.2

revoked: SSI 2003/531 Reg.12

207. Water Supply (Water Quality) (Scotland) Regulations 2001

Reg.2, amended: SSI 2003/331 Sch.1 para.13

Sch.1, referred to: 2003 asp 8 Sch.1 para.5

209. Sports Grounds and Sporting Events (Designation) (Scotland) Amendment Order 2001

revoked: SSI 2004/356 Sch.3

219. Public Service Vehicles (Registration of Local Services) (Scotland) Regulations 2001

Reg.13, amended: SSI 2002/548 Reg.2, SSI 2004/415 Reg.2

221. Pesticides (Maximum Residue Levels in Crops, Food and Feeding Stuffs) (Scotland) Amendment (No.2) Regulations 2001

Reg.2, amended: SSI 2002/271 Reg.3

Reg.2, revoked (in part): SSI 2002/489 Reg.3

222. Education (Assisted Places) (Scotland) Regulations 2001

Reg.9, amended: SSI 2002/249 Reg.2, SSI 2003/281 Reg.2, SSI 2004/239 Reg.2

Reg.13, amended: SSI 2002/249 Reg.2, SSI 2003/281 Reg.2, SSI 2004/239 Reg.2

NO.

NO.

2001–cont.

222. Education (Assisted Places) (Scotland) Regulations 2001–*cont.*

Reg.15, amended: SSI 2002/249 Reg.2, SSI 2003/281 Reg.2, SSI 2004/239 Reg.2

Reg.16, amended: SSI 2002/249 Reg.2, SSI 2003/281 Reg.2, SSI 2004/239 Reg.2

Reg.17, amended: SSI 2002/249 Reg.2, SSI 2003/281 Reg.2, SSI 2004/239 Reg.2

Reg.18, substituted: SSI 2003/281 Reg.2

Sch.2, substituted: SSI 2002/249 Reg.2, SSI 2003/281 Reg.2, SSI 2004/239 Reg.2

223. St Mary's Music School (Aided Places) (Scotland) Regulations 2001

Sch.1 Part III para.10, amended: SSI 2002/248 Reg.2, SSI 2003/280 Reg.2, SSI 2004/238 Reg.2

Sch.1 Part III para.13, amended: SSI 2002/248 Reg.2, SSI 2003/280 Reg.2, SSI 2004/238 Reg.2

Sch.1 Part III para.14, amended: SSI 2002/248 Reg.2, SSI 2003/280 Reg.2, SSI 2004/238 Reg.2

Sch.1 Part IV para.17, substituted: SSI 2003/280 Reg.2

Sch.1 Part IV para.18, amended: SSI 2002/248 Reg.2, SSI 2003/280 Reg.2, SSI 2004/238 Reg.2

Sch.1 Part IV para.24, amended: SSI 2002/248 Reg.2, SSI 2003/280 Reg.2, SSI 2004/238 Reg.2

224. Air Quality Limit Values (Scotland) Regulations 2001

revoked: SSI 2003/428 Reg.16

Reg.2, amended: SSI 2002/556 Reg.2

Reg.2A, added: SSI 2002/556 Reg.2

Reg.4, referred to: SI 2002/800 Sch.1

Reg.5, amended: SSI 2002/556 Reg.2

Reg.7, amended: SSI 2002/556 Reg.2

Reg.7, referred to: SI 2002/800 Sch.1

Reg.11, amended: SSI 2002/556 Reg.2

Reg.11, referred to: SI 2002/800 Sch.1

Reg.12, amended: SSI 2002/556 Reg.2

Sch.1 Part I para.1, amended: SSI 2002/556 Reg.2

Sch.1 Part II para.2, amended: SSI 2002/556 Reg.2

Sch.1 Part III, amended: SSI 2002/556 Reg.2

Sch.1 Part IV, amended: SSI 2002/556 Reg.2

Sch.1 Part V, added: SSI 2002/556 Reg.2

Sch.1 Part VI, added: SSI 2002/556 Reg.2

Sch.2 Part I, amended: SSI 2002/556 Reg.2

Sch.2 Part II, amended: SSI 2002/556 Reg.2

Sch.3 Part II, amended: SSI 2002/556 Reg.2

Sch.4 Part I, amended: SSI 2002/556 Reg.2

Sch.5 Part I, amended: SSI 2002/556 Reg.2

Sch.6 Part V, added: SSI 2002/556 Reg.2

Sch.6 Part VI, added: SSI 2002/556 Reg.2

225. Suckler Cow Premium (Scotland) Regulations 2001

Reg.5, applied: SSI 2002/278 Reg.8

Reg.6, applied: SSI 2002/278 Reg.8

2001–cont.

226. Agricultural Subsidies (Appeals) (Scotland) Amendment Regulations 2001

Reg.1, revoked (in part): SSI 2004/381 Sch.1

Reg.2, revoked: SSI 2004/381 Sch.1

Reg.3, revoked: SSI 2004/381 Sch.1

Reg.5, revoked: SSI 2004/381 Sch.1

230. Gaming Act (Variation of Fees) (No.2) (Scotland) Order 2001

revoked: SSI 2002/281 Art.3

231. BSE Monitoring (Scotland) Regulations 2001

applied: SSI 2002/255 Reg.102, Sch.9 para.1, Sch.9 para.2

Reg.2, amended: SSI 2002/1 Reg.2

Reg.2, revoked (in part): SSI 2002/1 Reg.2, SSI 2002/255 Sch.9 Part I

Reg.3, applied: SSI 2002/255 Sch.9 para.3

Reg.3, revoked: SSI 2002/255 Sch.9 Part I

Reg.4, amended: SSI 2002/1 Reg.2

Reg.4, revoked: SSI 2002/255 Sch.9 Part I

Reg.5, revoked: SSI 2002/255 Sch.9 Part I

Reg.6, revoked: SSI 2002/255 Sch.9 Part I

Reg.7, revoked: SSI 2002/255 Sch.9 Part I

Reg.8, revoked: SSI 2002/255 Sch.9 Part I

Reg.9, revoked: SSI 2002/255 Sch.9 Part I

236. Adoption of Children from Overseas (Scotland) Regulations 2001

Reg.3, varied: SSI 2003/19 Sch.6

246. Foot-and-Mouth Disease (Scotland) (Declaratory and Controlled Area) Amendment (No.7) Order 2001

revoked: SSI 2002/54 Sch.1

249. Plant Health (Great Britain) Amendment (Scotland) Order 2001

Art.3, revoked (in part): SSI 2002/164 Art.9

Art.8, revoked: SSI 2002/164 Art.9

Art.9, revoked: SSI 2002/164 Art.9

Art.11, revoked (in part): SSI 2002/164 Art.9

Art.13, revoked: SSI 2002/164 Art.9

255. Food Protection (Emergency Prohibitions) (Paralytic Shellfish Poisoning) (Orkney) (No.3) (Scotland) Order 2001

revoked: SSI 2002/82 Art.2

257. Products of Animal Origin (Import and Export) Amendment (Scotland) Regulations 2001

Reg.2, disapplied: SSI 2002/445 Sch.7

259. Farm Business Development (Scotland) Scheme 2001

Art.2, amended: SSI 2004/236 Art.2

260. Local Government Finance (Scotland) (No.2) Order 2001

Art.3, revoked: SSI 2002/70 Art.5

Sch.2, amended: SSI 2002/70 Art.5

262. Comhairle nan Eilean Siar (Aird Mhor, Barra) Harbour Empowerment Order 2001

Art.3, revoked: SSI 2002/410 Sch.2 Part II

Art.4, revoked: SSI 2002/410 Sch.2 Part II

2001–cont.

262. Comhairle nan Eilean Siar (Aird Mhor, Barra) Harbour Empowerment Order 2001–cont.

Art.19, revoked: SSI 2002/410 Sch.2 Part II
Art.20, revoked: SSI 2002/410 Sch.2 Part II
Art.21, revoked: SSI 2002/410 Sch.2 Part II
Art.22, revoked: SSI 2002/410 Sch.2 Part II
Art.23, revoked: SSI 2002/410 Sch.2 Part II
Art.24, revoked: SSI 2002/410 Sch.2 Part II
Art.25, revoked: SSI 2002/410 Sch.2 Part II
Art.26, revoked: SSI 2002/410 Sch.2 Part II
Art.27, revoked: SSI 2002/410 Sch.2 Part II
Art.28, revoked: SSI 2002/410 Sch.2 Part II
Art.29, revoked: SSI 2002/410 Sch.2 Part II
Art.30, revoked: SSI 2002/410 Sch.2 Part II
Art.31, revoked: SSI 2002/410 Sch.2 Part II
Art.32, revoked: SSI 2002/410 Sch.2 Part II
Art.33, revoked: SSI 2002/410 Sch.2 Part II
Art.34, revoked: SSI 2002/410 Sch.2 Part II
Art.35, revoked: SSI 2002/410 Sch.2 Part II
Art.36, revoked: SSI 2002/410 Sch.2 Part II
Art.37, revoked: SSI 2002/410 Sch.2 Part II
Art.38, revoked: SSI 2002/410 Sch.2 Part II
Art.39, revoked: SSI 2002/410 Sch.2 Part II
Sch.1, revoked: SSI 2002/410 Sch.2 Part II

276. Processed Animal Protein (Scotland) Regulations 2001

applied: SSI 2002/255 Reg.3, Reg.102, Sch.9 para.7, Sch.9 para.8
varied: SSI 2002/255 Reg.3
Reg.4, revoked: SSI 2002/255 Sch.9 Part I
Reg.5, applied: SSI 2002/255 Sch.9 para.1
Reg.5, revoked: SSI 2002/255 Sch.9 Part I
Reg.6, applied: SSI 2002/255 Sch.9 para.2
Reg.6, revoked: SSI 2002/255 Sch.9 Part I
Reg.7, applied: SSI 2002/255 Sch.9 para.3
Reg.7, revoked: SSI 2002/255 Sch.9 Part I
Reg.8, revoked: SSI 2002/255 Sch.9 Part I
Reg.9, revoked: SSI 2002/255 Sch.9 Part I
Reg.12, revoked: SSI 2002/255 Sch.9 Part I
Reg.13, applied: SSI 2002/255 Sch.9 para.4
Reg.13, revoked: SSI 2002/255 Sch.9 Part I
Reg.14, applied: SSI 2002/255 Sch.9 para.5
Reg.14, revoked: SSI 2002/255 Sch.9 Part I
Reg.15, applied: SSI 2002/255 Sch.9 para.6
Reg.15, revoked: SSI 2002/255 Sch.9 Part I
Reg.16, revoked: SSI 2002/255 Sch.9 Part I
Reg.26, revoked: SSI 2002/255 Sch.9 Part I
Sch.1 para.1, revoked: SSI 2002/255 Sch.9 Part I
Sch.1 para.2, revoked: SSI 2002/255 Sch.9 Part I
Sch.1 para.3, revoked: SSI 2002/255 Sch.9 Part I
Sch.1 para.4, revoked: SSI 2002/255 Sch.9 Part I
Sch.1 para.5, revoked: SSI 2002/255 Sch.9 Part I
Sch.2 para.1, revoked: SSI 2002/255 Sch.9 Part I

2001–cont.

276. Processed Animal Protein (Scotland) Regulations 2001–cont.

Sch.2 para.2, revoked: SSI 2002/255 Sch.9 Part I
Sch.2 para.3, revoked: SSI 2002/255 Sch.9 Part I
Sch.3 para.1, revoked: SSI 2002/255 Sch.9 Part I
Sch.3 para.2, revoked: SSI 2002/255 Sch.9 Part I

280. Graduate Endowment (Scotland) Regulations 2001

Sch.1 para.1, amended: SSI 2004/469 Reg.7
Sch.1 para.3, amended: SSI 2004/469 Reg.7
Sch.1 para.4, amended: SSI 2004/469 Reg.7
Sch.1 para.5, amended: SSI 2004/469 Reg.7
Sch.1 para.7, amended: SSI 2004/469 Reg.7
Sch.2 para.2, amended: SSI 2004/469 Reg.7

281. Food Protection (Emergency Prohibitions) (Amnesic Shellfish Poisoning) (West Coast) (No.2) (Scotland) Order 2001

revoked: SSI 2002/182 Art.2
varied: SSI 2002/67 Art.3

282. Food Protection (Emergency Prohibitions) (Amnesic, Paralytic and Diarrhetic Shellfish Poisoning) (Orkney) (Scotland) Order 2001

revoked: SSI 2002/197 Art.2

288. Specified Risk Material Amendment (No.3) (Scotland) Regulations 2001

revoked: SSI 2002/255 Sch.9 Part I

289. Food Protection (Emergency Prohibitions) (Amnesic Shellfish Poisoning) (West Coast) (No.4) (Scotland) Order 2001

revoked (in part): SSI 2002/19 Art.3, SSI 2002/160 Art.2

290. Foot-and-Mouth Disease Declaratory (Controlled Area) (Scotland) (No.3) Amendment (No.5) Order 2001

revoked: SSI 2002/54 Sch.1

295. Food Protection (Emergency Prohibitions) (Amnesic Shellfish Poisoning) (West Coast) (No.5) (Scotland) Order 2001

revoked: SSI 2002/126 Art.2

300. Rural Stewardship Scheme (Scotland) Regulations 2001

applied: SSI 2004/381 Reg.4
Reg.2, amended: SSI 2003/177 Reg.2
Reg.9, amended: SSI 2003/177 Reg.2
Reg.14, amended: SSI 2003/177 Reg.2
Reg.18, amended: SSI 2004/381 Reg.14
Reg.18, revoked (in part): SSI 2004/381 Sch.1
Sch.2, amended: SSI 2003/177 Reg.2, SSI 2004/109 Reg.2
Sch.3, amended: SSI 2003/177 Reg.2, SSI 2004/109 Reg.2

NO.

2001–cont.

300. Rural Stewardship Scheme (Scotland) Regulations 2001–*cont.*

Sch.4 Part I, amended: SSI 2003/177 Reg.2, SSI 2003/303 Reg.2, SSI 2004/109 Reg.2

Sch.4 Part II, amended: SSI 2003/177 Reg.2, SSI 2004/109 Reg.2

Sch.4 Part III, amended: SSI 2004/109 Reg.2

301. National Health Service Trusts (Membership and Procedure) (Scotland) Regulations 2001

Reg.6, amended: SI 2004/1771 Sch.1 para.33

302. Health Boards (Membership and Procedure) (Scotland) Regulations 2001

applied: SSI 2002/103 Sch.1 Part III, SSI 2002/305 Sch.1 Part III

disapplied: SSI 2004/386 Reg.11

varied: SSI 2002/534 Sch.1 Part III

Reg.6, amended: SSI 2004/212 Sch.1 para.9

303. Scottish Social Services Council (Appointments, Procedure and Access to the Register) Regulations 2001

Reg.4, amended: SI 2003/1590 Sch.1 para.18

Reg.11, amended: SSI 2002/60 Reg.2

320. Building Standards (Scotland) Amendment Regulations 2001

Reg.4, added: SSI 2002/40 Reg.2

322. Food Protection (Emergency Prohibitions) (Amnesic Shellfish Poisoning) (West Coast) (No.7) (Scotland) Order 2001

revoked: SSI 2002/20 Art.2

329. Education and Training (Scotland) Amendment Regulations 2001

revoked: SSI 2004/83 Reg.15

338. Argyll and Clyde Acute Hospitals National Health Service Trust (Establishment) Amendment Order 2001

revoked: SSI 2003/325 Sch.2

339. Ayrshire and Arran Primary Care National Health Service Trust (Establishment) Amendment Order 2001

revoked: SSI 2004/107 Sch.2

340. Ayrshire and Arran Acute Hospitals National Health Service Trust (Establishment) Amendment Order 2001

revoked: SSI 2004/107 Sch.2

341. Borders General Hospital National Health Service Trust (Establishment) Amendment Order 2001

revoked: SSI 2003/189 Sch.2

342. Fife Acute Hospitals National Health Service Trust (Establishment) Amendment Order 2001

revoked: SSI 2003/448 Sch.2

343. Dumfries and Galloway Primary Care National Health Service Trust (Establishment) Amendment Order 2001

revoked: SSI 2003/189 Sch.2

NO.

2001–cont.

344. Borders Primary Care National Health Service Trust (Establishment) Amendment Order 2001

revoked: SSI 2003/189 Sch.2

345. Dumfries and Galloway Acute and Maternity Hospitals National Health Service Trust (Establishment) Amendment Order 2001

revoked: SSI 2003/189 Sch.2

346. Grampian Primary Care National Health Service Trust (Establishment) Amendment Order 2001

revoked: SSI 2004/107 Sch.2

347. Forth Valley Primary Care National Health Service Trust (Establishment) Amendment Order 2001

revoked: SSI 2004/107 Sch.2

348. Forth Valley Acute Hospitals National Health Service Trust (Establishment) Amendment Order 2001

revoked: SSI 2004/107 Sch.2

349. Fife Primary Care National Health Service Trust (Establishment) Amendment Order 2001

revoked: SSI 2003/448 Sch.2

350. Grampian University Hospitals National Health Service Trust (Establishment) Amendment Order 2001

revoked: SSI 2004/107 Sch.2

351. Greater Glasgow Primary Care National Health Service Trust (Establishment) Amendment Order 2001

revoked: SSI 2004/107 Sch.2

352. Highland Acute Hospitals National Health Service Trust (Establishment) Amendment Order 2001

revoked: SSI 2004/107 Sch.2

353. Highland Primary Care National Health Service Trust (Establishment) Amendment Order 2001

revoked: SSI 2004/107 Sch.2

354. Lomond and Argyll Primary Care National Health Service Trust (Establishment) Amendment Order 2001

revoked: SSI 2003/325 Sch.2

355. Lothian Primary Care National Health Service Trust (Establishment) Amendment Order 2001

revoked: SSI 2004/107 Sch.2

356. Lanarkshire Primary Care National Health Service Trust (Establishment) Amendment Order 2001

revoked: SSI 2004/107 Sch.2

357. Lanarkshire Acute Hospitals National Health Service Trust (Establishment) Amendment Order 2001

revoked: SSI 2004/107 Sch.2

NO.

2001–cont.

358. Foot-and-Mouth Disease (Marking of Meat, Meat Products, Minced Meat and Meat Preparations) (Scotland) Regulations 2001
revoked: SSI 2002/35 Reg.6

359. Lothian University Hospitals National Health Service Trust (Establishment) Amendment Order 2001
revoked: SSI 2003/597 Sch.1

360. North Glasgow University Hospitals National Health Service Trust (Establishment) Amendment Order 2001
revoked: SSI 2004/107 Sch.2

361. Renfrewshire and Inverclyde Primary Care National Health Service Trust (Establishment) Amendment Order 2001
revoked: SSI 2003/325 Sch.2

362. South Glasgow University Hospitals National Health Service Trust (Establishment) Amendment Order 2001
revoked: SSI 2004/107 Sch.2

363. Tayside Primary Care National Health Service Trust (Establishment) Amendment Order 2001
revoked: SSI 2004/107 Sch.2

364. Tayside University Hospitals National Health Service Trust (Establishment) Amendment Order 2001
revoked: SSI 2004/107 Sch.2

365. West Lothian Healthcare National Health Service Trust (Establishment) Amendment Order 2001
revoked: SSI 2004/107 Sch.2

366. Yorkhill National Health Service Trust (Establishment) Amendment Order 2001
revoked: SSI 2004/107 Sch.2

374. Food Protection (Emergency Prohibitions) (Amnesic Shellfish Poisoning) (West Coast) (No.8) (Scotland) Order 2001
revoked: SSI 2002/127 Art.2

382. Advice and Assistance (Assistance by Way of Representation) (Scotland) Amendment (No.3) Regulations 2001
revoked: SSI 2003/179 Sch.1

383. Processed Animal Protein (Scotland) Amendment Regulations 2001
Reg.2, revoked (in part): SSI 2002/255 Sch.9 Part I

388. Food Protection (Emergency Prohibitions) (Amnesic Shellfish Poisoning) (West Coast) (No.9) (Scotland) Order 2001
revoked: SSI 2002/9 Art.2

390. Abolition of the Intervention Board for Agricultural Produce (Consequential Provisions) (Scotland) Regulations 2001
Reg.3, revoked (in part): SSI 2002/110 Reg.34

NO.

2001–cont.

391. Food Protection (Emergency Prohibitions) (Diarrhetic Shellfish Poisoning) (Orkney) (Scotland) Order 2001
revoked: SSI 2002/57 Art.2

394. Import and Export Restrictions (Foot-and-Mouth Disease) (Scotland) (No.2) Amendment (No.4) Regulations 2001
Reg.4, revoked: SSI 2002/35 Reg.6
Reg.5, revoked: SSI 2002/35 Reg.6
Reg.6, revoked (in part): SSI 2002/35 Reg.6
Reg.7, revoked: SSI 2002/35 Reg.6

421. Potatoes Originating in Egypt (Scotland) Regulations 2001
revoked: SSI 2004/111 Reg.8
Sch.1, amended: SSI 2002/518 Reg.2

423. Food Protection (Emergency Prohibitions) (Amnesic Shellfish Poisoning) (West Coast) (No.12) (Scotland) Order 2001
revoked: SSI 2002/198 Art.2
varied: SSI 2002/66 Art.3

424. Scottish Social Services Council (Consultation on Codes of Practice) Order 2001
Art.2, amended: SI 2003/1590 Sch.1 para.17

429. Import and Export Restrictions (Foot-and-Mouth Disease) (Scotland) (No.3) Regulations 2001
revoked: SSI 2002/109 Sch.1
Reg.1, amended: SSI 2002/35 Reg.2
Reg.2, amended: SSI 2002/35 Reg.2
Reg.4, amended: SSI 2002/35 Reg.2
Reg.5, amended: SSI 2002/35 Reg.2
Reg.6, amended: SSI 2002/35 Reg.2
Reg.6, revoked (in part): SSI 2002/21 Reg.2
Reg.7, amended: SSI 2002/35 Reg.2
Reg.7, revoked (in part): SSI 2002/35 Reg.2
Reg.8, revoked: SSI 2002/35 Reg.2
Reg.9, revoked: SSI 2002/35 Reg.2
Reg.10, amended: SSI 2002/35 Reg.2
Reg.10, revoked (in part): SSI 2002/35 Reg.2
Reg.11, revoked: SSI 2002/35 Reg.2
Reg.12, revoked: SSI 2002/35 Reg.2
Reg.13, revoked: SSI 2002/35 Reg.2
Reg.16, revoked: SSI 2002/35 Reg.2
Reg.27, revoked: SSI 2002/35 Reg.2
Reg.28, revoked: SSI 2002/35 Reg.2
Reg.29, revoked: SSI 2002/35 Reg.2
Sch.1, revoked: SSI 2002/35 Reg.2
Sch.3, amended: SSI 2002/35 Reg.2

430. National Health Service (Charges for Drugs and Appliances) (Scotland) Regulations 2001
applied: SSI 2003/64 Sch.1 para.11
Reg.2, amended: SI 2004/1771 Sch.1 para.31, SSI 2002/100 Reg.2, SSI 2003/295 Reg.2, SSI 2004/212 Sch.1 para.10
Reg.2, revoked (in part): SSI 2003/295 Reg.2

NO.

2001–cont.

430. National Health Service (Charges for Drugs and Appliances) (Scotland) Regulations 2001–cont.

Reg.3, amended: SSI 2002/100 Reg.2, SSI 2003/130 Reg.2, SSI 2004/66 Reg.2

Reg.3, referred to: SSI 2003/460 Reg.4

Reg.4, amended: SSI 2004/212 Sch.1 para.10

Reg.5, referred to: SSI 2003/376 Reg.11, SSI 2003/460 Reg.11

Reg.7, applied: SSI 2003/64 Sch.1 para.8, SSI 2004/114 Sch.1 para.3, SSI 2004/115 Sch.5 para.44, SSI 2004/116 Sch.1 para.15

Reg.8, amended: SSI 2002/100 Reg.2, SSI 2003/130 Reg.2, SSI 2004/66 Reg.2

Sch.1, substituted: SSI 2002/100 Sch.1, SSI 2003/130 Sch.1, SSI 2004/66 Sch.1

Sch.2, substituted: SSI 2002/100 Sch.1, SSI 2003/130 Sch.1, SSI 2004/66 Sch.1

Sch.3, substituted: SSI 2002/100 Sch.1, SSI 2003/130 Sch.1, SSI 2004/66 Sch.1

433. Smoke Control Areas (Authorised Fuels) (Scotland) Regulations 2001

Sch.1 para.3, amended: SSI 2002/527 Reg.2

Sch.1 para.11A, added: SSI 2002/527 Reg.2

Sch.1 para.11B, added: SSI 2002/527 Reg.2

Sch.1 para.15, amended: SSI 2002/527 Reg.2

Sch.1 para.15, applied: SSI 2002/527 Reg.3

Sch.1 para.28, amended: SSI 2002/527 Reg.2

Sch.1 para.28, applied: SSI 2002/527 Reg.3

Sch.1 para.29, amended: SSI 2002/527 Reg.2

Sch.1 para.29, applied: SSI 2002/527 Reg.3

Sch.1 para.31, amended: SSI 2002/527 Reg.2

Sch.1 para.31, applied: SSI 2002/527 Reg.3

434. Food Protection (Emergency Prohibitions) (Amnesic Shellfish Poisoning) (West Coast) (No.2) (Scotland) Partial Revocation Order 2001

revoked: SSI 2002/182 Art.2

435. Pesticides (Maximum Residue Levels in Crops, Food and Feeding Stuffs) (Scotland) Amendment (No.3) Regulations 2001

Reg.2, revoked (in part): SSI 2002/271 Reg.4, SSI 2002/489 Reg.3

Sch.1, revoked: SSI 2002/271 Reg.4

Sch.2, revoked: SSI 2002/489 Reg.3

437. National Health Service (Superannuation Scheme, Injury Benefits and Compensation for Premature Retirement) (Scotland) Amendment Regulations 2001

Reg.1, amended: SSI 2003/344 Sch.2

Reg.19, revoked: SSI 2003/344 Sch.2

439. Act of Sederunt (Fees of Sheriff Officers) 2001

revoked: SSI 2002/567 Sch.2

NO.

2001–cont.

440. Act of Sederunt (Fees of Messengers-At-Arms) 2001

revoked: SSI 2002/566 Sch.2

445. Beef Special Premium (Scotland) Regulations 2001

Reg.15, applied: SSI 2002/278 Reg.8

Reg.16, applied: SSI 2002/278 Reg.8

447. Community Care (Direct Payments) (Scotland) Amendment Regulations 2001

revoked: SSI 2003/243 Sch.1

448. Sea Fishing (Enforcement of Community Satellite Monitoring Measures) (Scotland) Order 2000 Amendment Regulations 2001

revoked: SSI 2004/391 Reg.2

451. Food Protection (Emergency Prohibitions) (Amnesic Shellfish Poisoning) (West Coast) (No.14) (Scotland) Order 2001

revoked: SSI 2002/48 Art.2

454. Plant Protection Products Amendment (No.3) (Scotland) Regulations 2001

revoked: SSI 2003/579 Sch.5

Reg.6, amended: SSI 2002/279 Reg.3

455. Import and Export Restrictions (Foot-and-Mouth Disease) (Scotland) (No.3) Amendment Regulations 2001

referred to: SSI 2002/109 Sch.1

revoked: SSI 2002/109 Sch.1

Reg.1, amended: SSI 2002/35 Reg.6

Reg.2, revoked (in part): SSI 2002/35 Reg.6

458. Sheep and Goats Spongiform Encephalopathy (Compensation) Amendment (Scotland) Order 2001

revoked: SSI 2002/255 Sch.9 Part I

463. Food Protection (Emergency Prohibitions) (Amnesic, Paralytic and Diarrhetic Shellfish Poisoning) (Orkney) (Scotland) Partial Revocation Order 2001

revoked: SSI 2002/197 Art.2

469. Food Protection (Emergency Prohibitions) (Amnesic Shellfish Poisoning) (West Coast) (No.9) (Scotland) Partial Revocation Order 2001

revoked: SSI 2002/9 Art.2

473. Food Protection (Emergency Prohibitions) (Amnesic Shellfish Poisoning) (West Coast) (No.4) (Scotland) Partial Revocation Order 2001

revoked: SSI 2002/160 Art.2

476. Panels of Persons to Safeguard the Interests of Children (Scotland) Regulations 2001

applied: SSI 2002/63 r.5

NO.

2001–cont.

477. Curators ad Litem and Reporting Officers (Panels) (Scotland) Regulations 2001
applied: SSI 2002/63 r.5

478. Children's Hearings (Legal Representation) (Scotland) Rules 2001
revoked: SSI 2002/63 r.6
r.5, amended: SSI 2002/30 r.2

481. Foot-and-Mouth Disease Declaratory (Controlled Area) (Scotland) (No.3) Amendment (No.6) Order 2001
revoked: SSI 2002/54 Sch.1

483. Import and Export Restrictions (Foot-and-Mouth Disease) (Scotland) (No.3) Amendment (No.2) Regulations 2001
referred to: SSI 2002/109 Sch.1
revoked: SSI 2002/109 Sch.1
Reg.1, amended: SSI 2002/35 Reg.6
Reg.2, revoked (in part): SSI 2002/35 Reg.6
Reg.3, revoked (in part): SSI 2002/35 Reg.6

2002

1. BSE Monitoring (Scotland) Amendment Regulations 2002
Reg.2, revoked: SSI 2002/255 Sch.9 Part I

6. Environmental Impact Assessment (Uncultivated Land and Semi-Natural Areas) (Scotland) Regulations 2002
applied: SSI 2004/70 Sch.3 para.6

13. Road Works (Inspection Fees) (Scotland) Amendment Regulations 2002
revoked: SSI 2003/415 Reg.4

15. Local Authorities Etc (Allowances) (Scotland) Amendment Regulations 2002
revoked: SSI 2004/146 Reg.6

19. Food Protection (Emergency Prohibitions) (Amnesic Shellfish Poisoning) (West Coast) (No.4) (Scotland) Partial Revocation (No.2) Order 2002
revoked: SSI 2002/160 Art.2

21. Import and Export Restrictions (Foot-and-Mouth Disease) (Scotland) (No.3) Amendment Regulations 2002
revoked: SSI 2002/35 Reg.6

30. Children's Hearings (Legal Representation) (Scotland) Amendment Rules 2002
revoked: SSI 2002/63 r.6

33. Water Services Charges (Billing and Collection) (Scotland) Order 2002
applied: SSI 2002/47 Reg.3, SSI 2003/65 Reg.3, SSI 2004/68 Reg.3
revoked: 2002 asp 3 Sch.7 para.23
Art.1, amended: SSI 2002/166 Art.6
Art.2, amended: SSI 2002/166 Art.6
Art.3, amended: SSI 2002/166 Art.6
Art.4, revoked: SSI 2002/166 Art.6
Art.5, revoked: SSI 2002/166 Art.6

NO.

2002–cont.

33. Water Services Charges (Billing and Collection) (Scotland) Order 2002–cont.
Art.6, amended: SSI 2002/166 Art.6
Art.7, amended: SSI 2002/166 Art.6
Art.8, amended: SSI 2002/166 Art.6
Art.11, applied: SI 1992/1332 Reg.30
Art.13, amended: SSI 2002/166 Art.6
Art.13, revoked (in part): SSI 2002/166 Art.6

34. Disease Control (Interim Measures) (Scotland) Order 2002
Art.2, amended: SSI 2002/369 Art.2
Art.3, amended: SSI 2002/221 Art.2, SSI 2002/369 Art.2, SSI 2003/228 Art.2
Art.4, amended: SSI 2002/221 Art.2, SSI 2002/369 Art.2, SSI 2002/530 Art.2, SSI 2003/228 Art.2
Art.4, applied: SSI 2000/418 Reg.4, Reg.6, Reg.13
Art.4, revoked (in part): SSI 2002/369 Art.2
Art.4A, added: SSI 2002/369 Art.2
Art.5, amended: SSI 2003/228 Art.2
Art.6A, added: SSI 2002/221 Art.2
Art.11, revoked (in part): SSI 2002/221 Art.2
Sch.2 para.2, amended: SSI 2002/221 Art.2
Sch.2 para.3, amended: SSI 2002/369 Art.2
Sch.2 para.3, substituted: SSI 2002/221 Art.2
Sch.2 para.5, amended: SSI 2002/369 Art.2

35. Import and Export Restrictions (Foot-and-Mouth Disease) (Scotland) (No.3) Amendment (No.2) Regulations 2002
Reg.1, revoked (in part): SSI 2002/169 Reg.2
Reg.2, revoked: SSI 2002/109 Sch.1
Reg.6, revoked (in part): SSI 2002/109 Sch.1

36. Food and Animal Feedingstuffs (Products of Animal Origin from China) (Control) (Scotland) Regulations 2002
revoked: SSI 2002/300 Reg.6

37. Advice and Assistance (Assistance by Way of Representation) (Scotland) Amendment Regulations 2002
revoked: SSI 2003/179 Sch.1

38. Sheep and Goats Movement (Interim Measures) (Scotland) Order 2002
applied: SSI 2000/418 Reg.16
Art.3, applied: SSI 2000/418 Reg.12, Reg.13
Art.3, referred to: SSI 2000/418 Reg.4, Reg.6
Art.4, substituted: SSI 2002/221 Art.4

47. Domestic Water and Sewerage Charges (Reduction) (Scotland) Regulations 2002
applied: SSI 2002/33 Art.9
revoked: 2002 asp 3 Sch.7 para.23
Reg.2, amended: SSI 2002/166 Art.7
Reg.3, amended: SSI 2002/166 Art.7
Reg.4, amended: SSI 2002/166 Art.7

NO.

2002–cont.

49. Food Protection (Emergency Prohibitions) (Amnesic Shellfish Poisoning) (West Coast) (Scotland) Order 2002
revoked: SSI 2002/152 Art.2

51. Sea Fishing (Enforcement of Community Quota and Third Country Fishing Measures) (Scotland) Order 2002
revoked: SSI 2003/88 Art.14

58. Sea Fish (Prohibited Methods of Fishing) (Firth of Clyde) Order 2002
revoked: SSI 2003/79 Art.5

59. Nurses, Midwives and Health Visitors (Professional Conduct) (Amendment) Rules 2002 Approval (Scotland) Order 2002
revoked: 1999 c.8 Sch.5
varied: SI 2004/1762 Art.1

62. Race Relations Act 1976 (Statutory Duties) (Scotland) Order 2002
Art.2, varied: SSI 2003/566 Art.5
Art.5, amended: SSI 2003/566 Art.3
Art.5A, added: SSI 2003/566 Art.4
Sch.1, amended: SSI 2003/331 Sch.1 para.14, SSI 2003/566 Art.5
Sch.3, amended: SSI 2003/566 Art.6

64. Food (Star Anise from Third Countries) (Emergency Control) (Scotland) Order 2002
revoked: SSI 2003/437 Art.2

65. Food Protection (Emergency Prohibitions) (Amnesic Shellfish Poisoning) (West Coast) (No.2) (Scotland) Order 2002
revoked: SSI 2002/183 Art.2

66. Food Protection (Emergency Prohibitions) (Amnesic Shellfish Poisoning) (West Coast) (No.12) (Scotland) Partial Revocation Order 2002
revoked: SSI 2002/198 Art.2

67. Food Protection (Emergency Prohibitions) (Amnesic Shellfish Poisoning) (West Coast) (No.2) (Scotland) Partial Revocation Order 2002
revoked: SSI 2002/182 Art.2

70. Local Government Finance (Scotland) Order 2002
Art.1, revoked: SSI 2002/230 Art.5
Art.2, revoked: SSI 2002/230 Art.5
Art.3, revoked: SSI 2002/230 Art.5
Art.4, revoked: SSI 2002/230 Art.5

77. Public Finance and Accountability (Scotland) Act 2000 (Economy, efficiency and effectiveness examinations) (Specified bodies etc.) Order 2002
revoked: SSI 2004/482 Art.3

78. Public Finance and Accountability (Scotland) Act 2000 (Access to Documents and Information) (Relevant Persons) Order 2002
revoked: SSI 2003/530 Art.4

NO.

2002–cont.

85. National Assistance (Sums for Personal Requirements) (Scotland) Regulations 2002
revoked: SSI 2003/86 Reg.3

88. Civil Legal Aid (Scotland) Amendment Regulations 2002
revoked: SSI 2002/494 Sch.1

91. Non-Domestic Rates (Levying) (Scotland) Regulations 2002
revoked: SSI 2003/160 Reg.20
Part III, applied: SSI 2003/160 Reg.6, Reg.11
Reg.7, applied: SSI 2003/160 Reg.6, Reg.11
Reg.8, applied: SSI 2003/160 Reg.7

99. National Health Service (General Dental Services and Dental Charges) (Scotland) Amendment Regulations 2002
Reg.3, revoked: SSI 2003/158 Sch.4

103. NHS Education for Scotland Order 2002
Art.6, applied: SSI 2002/105
Sch.1 Part I, applied: SSI 2002/105
Sch.1 Part II, amended: SSI 2003/242 Art.9
Sch.1 Part III, amended: SI 2003/1590 Sch.1 para.13

106. Scottish Commission for the Regulation of Care (Appointments and Procedure) Regulations 2002
Reg.4, amended: SI 2003/1590 Sch.1 para.12

110. Dairy Produce Quotas (Scotland) Regulations 2002
Reg.1, amended: SSI 2002/228 Reg.2
Reg.2, amended: SSI 2004/118 Reg.4
Reg.4, substituted: SSI 2004/118 Reg.5
Reg.5, amended: SSI 2004/118 Reg.6
Reg.7, amended: SSI 2002/228 Reg.2, SSI 2004/118 Reg.7
Reg.7, applied: SSI 2000/347 Reg.4
Reg.8, amended: SSI 2002/228 Reg.2, SSI 2004/118 Reg.8
Reg.12, applied: SSI 2000/347 Reg.4
Reg.12, substituted: SSI 2004/118 Reg.9
Reg.13, amended: SSI 2004/118 Reg.10
Reg.14, amended: SSI 2002/228 Reg.2, SSI 2004/118 Reg.11
Reg.14, applied: SSI 2000/347 Reg.4
Reg.16, amended: SSI 2004/118 Reg.12
Reg.16, applied: SSI 2000/347 Reg.4
Reg.18, amended: SSI 2004/118 Reg.13
Reg.20, amended: SSI 2002/228 Reg.2, SSI 2004/118 Reg.14
Reg.22, amended: SSI 2004/118 Reg.15
Reg.24, applied: SSI 2000/347 Reg.4
Reg.25, amended: SSI 2004/118 Reg.16
Reg.27, amended: SSI 2004/118 Reg.17
Reg.28, amended: SSI 2002/228 Reg.2
Reg.30, amended: SSI 2002/228 Reg.2, SSI 2004/118 Reg.18
Reg.30, applied: SSI 2000/347 Reg.4
Reg.32, amended: SSI 2002/228 Reg.2
Reg.32, substituted: SSI 2004/118 Reg.19

2002–cont.

110. Dairy Produce Quotas (Scotland) Regulations 2002–*cont.*

Reg.33, amended: SSI 2002/228 Reg.2

Reg.33A, added: SSI 2002/228 Reg.2

Sch.1, amended: SSI 2004/118 Reg.20

Sch.2 Part II para.3, amended: SSI 2004/118 Reg.21

Sch.3 para.8, applied: SSI 2000/347 Reg.4

Sch.3 para.9, amended: SSI 2004/118 Reg.22

Sch.3 para.10, applied: SSI 2000/347 Reg.4

Sch.3 para.11, amended: SSI 2002/228 Reg.2

Sch.3 para.11, applied: SSI 2000/347 Reg.4

Sch.3 para.13, amended: SSI 2002/228 Reg.2

Sch.3 para.14, amended: SSI 2002/228 Reg.2

Sch.3 para.15, amended: SSI 2002/228 Reg.2

Sch.3 para.17, amended: SSI 2004/118 Reg.22

Sch.3 para.19, amended: SSI 2004/118 Reg.22

Sch.3 para.19, applied: SSI 2000/347 Reg.4

Sch.3 para.20, applied: SSI 2000/347 Reg.4

111. National Health Service (General Medical Services and Pharmaceutical Services) (Scotland) Amendment Regulations 2002

Reg.2, amended: SSI 2002/153 Reg.2

Reg.3, amended: SSI 2002/153 Reg.2

Reg.3, revoked: SSI 2004/114 Sch.2

112. Regulation of Care (Fees) (Scotland) Order 2002

revoked: SSI 2003/152 Art.4

113. Regulation of Care (Applications and Provision of Advice) (Scotland) Order 2002

Art.1, amended: SSI 2003/151 Art.2, SSI 2003/570 Art.2

Art.2, amended: SSI 2003/570 Art.2, SSI 2004/95 Art.2

Art.2, substituted: SSI 2003/151 Art.2

Art.3A, added: SSI 2004/95 Art.2

Art.4, amended: SSI 2003/151 Art.2, SSI 2004/95 Art.2

Art.5, amended: SSI 2003/151 Art.2

Sch.1 para.4, amended: SSI 2003/151 Art.2

Sch.1 para.8, amended: SSI 2003/151 Art.2

Sch.1 para.13, amended: SSI 2003/151 Art.2

Sch.1 para.17, amended: SSI 2003/151 Art.2

Sch.1 para.20, amended: SSI 2003/151 Art.2

Sch.1 para.21, amended: SSI 2003/151 Art.2

Sch.1 para.23, amended: SSI 2003/151 Art.2

Sch.1 para.26, amended: SSI 2003/151 Art.2

Sch.1 para.27, amended: SSI 2003/151 Art.2

Sch.1 para.31, amended: SSI 2003/570 Art.2

2002–cont.

114. Regulation of Care (Requirements as to Care Services) (Scotland) Regulations 2002

Reg.1, amended: SI 2003/1590 Sch.1 para.11, SSI 2003/149 Reg.2, SSI 2003/572 Reg.2

Reg.4, amended: SSI 2003/149 Reg.2, SSI 2004/94 Reg.2

Reg.5, amended: SSI 2003/149 Reg.2, SSI 2004/94 Reg.2

Reg.6, amended: SSI 2003/572 Reg.2

Reg.7, amended: SSI 2003/572 Reg.2

Reg.8, amended: SSI 2003/572 Reg.2

Reg.9, amended: SSI 2003/572 Reg.2

Reg.10, amended: SSI 2003/572 Reg.2

Reg.10, applied: SSI 2002/162 Art.5

Reg.11, amended: SSI 2003/572 Reg.2

Reg.19, amended: SSI 2003/149 Reg.2, SSI 2003/572 Reg.2, SSI 2004/94 Reg.2

115. Regulation of Care (Registration and Registers) (Scotland) Regulations 2002

Reg.1, amended: SSI 2003/148 Reg.2

Reg.2, amended: SSI 2003/148 Reg.2

Reg.3, amended: SSI 2003/148 Reg.2

Sch.1 para.2, amended: SSI 2003/148 Reg.2

Sch.1 para.3, amended: SSI 2003/148 Reg.2

Sch.1 para.4, amended: SSI 2003/148 Reg.2

Sch.1 para.6, amended: SSI 2003/148 Reg.2

Sch.1 para.7, amended: SSI 2003/148 Reg.2

Sch.1 para.12, added: SSI 2004/96 Reg.2

117. Plant Protection Products Amendment (Scotland) Regulations 2002

revoked: SSI 2003/579 Sch.5

Reg.3, amended: SSI 2002/279 Reg.4

120. Regulation of Care (Excepted Services) (Scotland) Regulations 2002

Reg.2, revoked (in part): SSI 2003/571 Reg.2

122. Town and Country Planning (Fees for Applications and Deemed Applications) (Scotland) Amendment Regulations 2002

revoked: SSI 2004/219 Reg.15

132. Act of Sederunt (Summary Cause Rules) 2002

Sch.1 Appendix, added: SSI 2003/601 r.5

Sch.1 Appendix, amended: SSI 2003/26 r.4, SSI 2003/601 r.5, Sch.1

Sch.1 Part 4 para.4.4, amended: SSI 2004/197 r.4

Sch.1 Part 5 para.5.7, amended: SSI 2004/197 r.4

Sch.1 Part 10 para.10.1, amended: SSI 2004/197 r.4

Sch.1 Part 11 para.11.3, amended: SSI 2004/197 r.4

Sch.1 Part 18 para.18.7, amended: SSI 2003/601 r.5

Sch.1 Part 18 para.18.7A, added: SSI 2003/601 r.5

NO.

2002–cont.

132. Act of Sederunt (Summary Cause Rules) 2002–*cont.*

Sch.1 Part 23 para.23.2, amended: SSI 2002/516 r.2

Sch.1 Part 23 para.23.3, amended: SSI 2002/516 r.2

Sch.1 Part 23 para.23.3A, added: SSI 2002/516 r.2

Sch.1 Part 23 para.23.3B, added: SSI 2002/516 r.2

Sch.1 Part 27 para.27.5, amended: SSI 2003/26 r.4

133. Act of Sederunt (Small Claim Rules) 2002

Sch.1 Appendix1, amended: SSI 2003/26 r.5

Sch.1 Part 4 para.4.4, amended: SSI 2004/197 r.5

Sch.1 Part 6 para.6.5, amended: SSI 2004/197 r.5

Sch.1 Part 11 para.11.1, amended: SSI 2004/197 r.5

139. Less Favoured Area Support Scheme (Scotland) Regulations 2002

applied: SSI 2003/129 Reg.4, SSI 2004/70 Reg.4

revoked (in part): SSI 2003/129 Reg.28

Reg.6, applied: SSI 2003/129 Reg.9

Reg.15, applied: SSI 2000/347 Reg.4, SSI 2004/381 Reg.4

Reg.22, amended: SSI 2004/381 Reg.14

Reg.25, revoked: SSI 2004/381 Sch.1

142. Nurses, Midwives and Health Visitors (Professional Conduct) (Amendment) (No.2) Rules 2002 Approval (Scotland) Order 2002

revoked: 1999 c.8 Sch.5

varied: SI 2004/1762 Art.1

144. Advice and Assistance (Financial Conditions) (Scotland) Regulations 2002

revoked: SSI 2003/180 Reg.7

145. Civil Legal Aid (Financial Conditions) (Scotland) Regulations 2002

revoked: SSI 2003/182 Reg.7

148. Food (Figs, Hazelnuts and Pistachios from Turkey) (Emergency Control) (Scotland) Regulations 2002

revoked: SSI 2002/424 Reg.7

149. Food (Peanuts from China) (Emergency Control) (Scotland) Regulations 2002

revoked: SSI 2002/425 Reg.7

153. National Health Service (General Medical Services and Pharmaceutical Services) (Scotland) Amendment (No.2) Regulations 2002

Reg.2, revoked (in part): SSI 2004/114 Sch.2

159. Water Undertakings (Rateable Values) (Scotland) Variation Order 2002

revoked: SSI 2003/187 Art.9

NO.

2002–cont.

163. Renewables Obligation (Scotland) Order 2002

applied: SSI 2004/170 Art.14

revoked: SSI 2004/170 Art.14

Art.3, referred to: SSI 2004/170 Art.14

Art.4, referred to: SI 2003/2562 Sch.2 para.2

Art.6, referred to: SSI 2004/170 Art.14

Art.7, referred to: SSI 2004/170 Art.14

Art.12, referred to: SSI 2004/170 Art.14

Sch.1, applied: SSI 2004/170 Art.14

167. Water and Sewerage Charges (Exemption) (Scotland) Regulations 2002

applied: SSI 2002/166 Art.4

177. Home Zones (Scotland) Regulations 2002

revoked: SSI 2002/292 Reg.17

185. Loch Ewe, Isle of Ewe, Wester Ross, Scallops Several Fishery (Variation) Order 2002

referred to: SI 1997/830 Art.2

190. Adults with Incapacity (Ethics Committee) (Scotland) Regulations 2002

Reg.3, amended: SI 2003/1590 Sch.1 para.10, SSI 2004/212 Sch.1 para.11

193. Registration of Fish Farming and Shellfish Farming Businesses Amendment (Scotland) Order 2002

Art.2, amended: SSI 2002/220 Art.2

221. Disease Control and Animal Movements (Interim Measures) (Scotland) Amendment Order 2002

Art.2, revoked (in part): SSI 2003/228 Art.3

223. Plant Health (Phytophthora ramorum) (Scotland) Order 2002

revoked: SSI 2002/483 Art.15

Art.2, referred to: SSI 2002/483 Art.15

Art.3, applied: SSI 2002/483 Art.15

Art.3, revoked: SSI 2004/488 Art.16

228. Dairy Produce Quotas (Scotland) Amendment Regulations 2002

Reg.3, revoked: SSI 2004/381 Sch.1

230. Local Government Finance (Scotland) (No.2) Order 2002

Art.3, revoked: SSI 2003/42 Art.5

Sch.2, revoked: SSI 2003/42 Art.5

231. Food Protection (Emergency Prohibitions) (Amnesic Shellfish Poisoning) (West Coast) (No.4) (Scotland) Order 2002

revoked: SSI 2002/550 Art.2

254. Civil Legal Aid (Scotland) Amendment (No.2) Regulations 2002

revoked: SSI 2002/494 Sch.1

255. TSE (Scotland) Regulations 2002

applied: SSI 2004/6 Reg.6

referred to: SI 1995/731 Reg.3A, SI 1999/646 Art.3, Art.7, Art.8

Reg.3, amended: SSI 2003/198 Reg.2, SSI 2003/411 Sch.5 para.2

NO.

2002–cont.

255. TSE (Scotland) Regulations 2002– cont.

Reg.10, applied: SSI 2001/1 Reg.9

Reg.13, amended: SSI 2003/198 Reg.2, SSI 2003/411 Sch.5 para.3

Reg.16, amended: SSI 2003/411 Sch.5 para.4

Reg.17, amended: SSI 2003/411 Sch.5 para.4

Reg.20, amended: SSI 2003/411 Sch.5 para.4

Reg.33, revoked (in part): SSI 2003/411 Sch.6

Reg.34, revoked (in part): SSI 2003/411 Sch.6

Reg.34A, added: SSI 2003/411 Sch.5 para.5

Reg.39, amended: SSI 2003/198 Reg.2

Reg.40, substituted: SSI 2003/411 Sch.5 para.6

Reg.44, amended: SSI 2003/198 Reg.2

Reg.48, amended: SSI 2003/198 Reg.2

Reg.50, revoked: SSI 2003/411 Sch.6

Reg.52, revoked: SSI 2003/411 Sch.6

Reg.55, applied: SI 1997/2964 Art.6

Reg.55, revoked (in part): SSI 2003/411 Sch.6

Reg.61, amended: SSI 2003/198 Reg.2

Reg.62, revoked: SSI 2003/411 Sch.6

Reg.63, amended: SSI 2003/198 Reg.2

Reg.63, revoked: SSI 2003/411 Sch.6

Reg.64, revoked: SSI 2003/411 Sch.6

Reg.65, revoked: SSI 2003/411 Sch.6

Reg.66, revoked: SSI 2003/411 Sch.6

Reg.67, revoked: SSI 2003/411 Sch.6

Reg.68, revoked (in part): SSI 2003/411 Sch.6

Reg.69, amended: SSI 2003/198 Reg.2

Reg.70, amended: SSI 2003/198 Reg.2

Reg.84A, added: SSI 2004/277 Reg.2

Sch.5, amended: SSI 2003/198 Reg.2

Sch.5, substituted: SSI 2003/411 Sch.5 para.7

Sch.6 Part I para.1, revoked: SSI 2003/411 Sch.6

Sch.6 Part I para.2, revoked: SSI 2003/411 Sch.6

Sch.6 Part I para.3, revoked: SSI 2003/411 Sch.6

Sch.6 Part I para.4, revoked: SSI 2003/411 Sch.6

Sch.6 Part I para.5, revoked: SSI 2003/411 Sch.6

Sch.6 Part I para.6, revoked: SSI 2003/411 Sch.6

Sch.6 Part I para.7, revoked: SSI 2003/411 Sch.6

Sch.6 Part I para.8, revoked: SSI 2003/411 Sch.6

Sch.6 Part II para.1, revoked: SSI 2003/411 Sch.6

Sch.6 Part II para.2, revoked: SSI 2003/411 Sch.6

NO.

2002–cont.

255. TSE (Scotland) Regulations 2002– cont.

Sch.6 Part II para.3, revoked: SSI 2003/411 Sch.6

Sch.6 Part II para.4, revoked: SSI 2003/411 Sch.6

Sch.6 Part II para.5, revoked: SSI 2003/411 Sch.6

Sch.6 Part II para.6, revoked: SSI 2003/411 Sch.6

Sch.6 Part II para.7, revoked: SSI 2003/411 Sch.6

Sch.6A Part I para.1, added: SSI 2004/277 Sch.1

Sch.6A Part I para.2, added: SSI 2004/277 Sch.1

Sch.6A Part I para.3, added: SSI 2004/277 Sch.1

Sch.6A Part I para.4, added: SSI 2004/277 Sch.1

Sch.6A Part I para.5, added: SSI 2004/277 Sch.1

Sch.6A Part I para.6, added: SSI 2004/277 Sch.1

Sch.6A Part I para.7, added: SSI 2004/277 Sch.1

Sch.6A Part I para.8, added: SSI 2004/277 Sch.1

Sch.6A Part IA para.9, added: SSI 2004/277 Sch.1

Sch.6A Part IA para.10, added: SSI 2004/277 Sch.1

Sch.6A Part IA para.11, added: SSI 2004/277 Sch.1

Sch.6A Part IA para.12, added: SSI 2004/277 Sch.1

Sch.6A Part IA para.13, added: SSI 2004/277 Sch.1

Sch.6A Part IA para.14, added: SSI 2004/277 Sch.1

Sch.6A Part II para.15, added: SSI 2004/277 Sch.1

Sch.6A Part II para.16, added: SSI 2004/277 Sch.1

Sch.6A Part III para.17, added: SSI 2004/277 Sch.1

Sch.8 Part IV para.1, revoked: SSI 2003/411 Sch.6

Sch.8 Part IV para.2, revoked: SSI 2003/411 Sch.6

Sch.8 Part IV para.3, revoked: SSI 2003/411 Sch.6

264. Community Care (Disregard of Resources) (Scotland) Order 2002

Art.2, referred to: SSI 2002/266 Reg.3

267. Contaminants in Food (Scotland) Regulations 2002

revoked: SSI 2003/289 Reg.12

Reg.2, amended: SSI 2002/349 Reg.3

Reg.8, amended: SSI 2002/349 Reg.4

Reg.9, amended: SSI 2002/349 Reg.5

NO.

2002–cont.

271. Pesticides (Maximum Residue Levels in Crops, Food and Feeding Stuffs) (Scotland) Amendment Regulations 2002
Reg.2, revoked (in part): SSI 2002/489 Reg.3
Sch.1, revoked: SSI 2002/489 Reg.3
Sch.2, revoked: SSI 2002/489 Reg.3

274. Act of Sederunt (Fees of Solicitors in the Sheriff Court) (Amendment No 2) 2002
Sch.1, substituted: SSI 2002/328 Sch.1

275. Adults with Incapacity (Specified Medical Treatments) (Scotland) Regulations 2002
Sch.1 Part 1 para.1, revoked: SSI 2002/302 Reg.2

279. Plant Protection Products Amendment (No.2) (Scotland) Regulations 2002
revoked: SSI 2003/579 Sch.5

281. Gaming Act (Variation of Fees) (Scotland) Order 2002
applied: SSI 2003/403 Art.2
revoked: SSI 2003/403 Art.3

300. Food and Animal Feedingstuffs (Products of Animal Origin from China) (Emergency Control) (Scotland) Regulations 2002
revoked: SSI 2003/165 Reg.3
Reg.2, amended: SSI 2002/356 Reg.2

305. National Waiting Times Centre Board (Scotland) Order 2002
Sch.1 Part II, amended: SSI 2003/242 Art.10
Sch.1 Part III, amended: SI 2003/1590 Sch.1 para.9

306. Food Protection (Emergency Prohibitions) (Amnesic Shellfish Poisoning) (West Coast) (No.5) (Scotland) Order 2002
revoked: SSI 2002/431 Art.2
Sch.1, varied: SSI 2002/383 Art.3, SSI 2002/409 Art.3

307. Food Protection (Emergency Prohibitions) (Amnesic Shellfish Poisoning) (West Coast) (No.6) (Scotland) Order 2002
revoked: SSI 2003/17 Art.2
Sch.1, revoked: SSI 2002/551 Art.3

314. Scottish Secure Tenancies (Exceptions) Regulations 2002
Reg.2, amended: SSI 2002/434 Reg.2

318. Housing (Scotland) Act 2001 (Scottish Secure Tenancy etc.) Order 2002
Art.3, amended: SSI 2002/415 Art.2
Art.4, amended: SSI 2002/415 Art.2
Sch.1, amended: SSI 2003/331 Sch.1 para.15
Sch.1, substituted: SSI 2002/415 Art.2

321. Housing (Scotland) Act 2001 (Commencement No 5, Transitional Provisions and Savings) Order 2002
Sch.1, amended: SSI 2002/433 Art.3

NO.

2002–cont.

325. Common Agricultural Policy (Wine) (Scotland) Regulations 2002
referred to: SSI 2003/164 Reg.2, SSI 2004/272 Reg.2
Reg.2, amended: SSI 2003/164 Reg.3, SSI 2004/272 Reg.3
Reg.6A, added: SSI 2003/164 Reg.4
Reg.6B, added: SSI 2003/164 Reg.4
Reg.8, amended: SSI 2003/164 Reg.5, SSI 2004/272 Reg.4
Reg.11, amended: SSI 2003/164 Reg.6
Sch.1, revoked: SSI 2004/272 Reg.5
Sch.3, revoked: SSI 2004/272 Reg.6
Sch.6, referred to: SSI 2003/164 Reg.7
Sch.6, substituted: SSI 2003/164 Sch.1, SSI 2004/272 Sch.1
Sch.9 Part I, amended: SSI 2003/164 Reg.8
Sch.9 Part II, amended: SSI 2004/272 Sch.2
Sch.9 Part III, amended: SSI 2003/164 Reg.8
Sch.9 Part IV, amended: SSI 2003/164 Reg.8

329. Advice and Assistance (Financial Conditions) (Scotland) (No.2) Regulations 2002
revoked: SSI 2003/180 Reg.7

330. Civil Legal Aid (Financial Conditions) (Scotland) (No.2) Regulations 2002
revoked: SSI 2003/182 Reg.7

332. Food Protection (Emergency Prohibitions) (Amnesic Shellfish Poisoning) (West Coast) (No.7) (Scotland) Order 2002
revoked: SSI 2002/422 Art.2

333. Food Protection (Emergency Prohibitions) (Amnesic Shellfish Poisoning) (West Coast) (No.8) (Scotland) Order 2002
revoked: SSI 2002/384 Art.2

334. Welfare of Farmed Animals (Scotland) Amendment Regulations 2002
referred to: SSI 2000/442 Sch.3A para.8

345. Food Protection (Emergency Prohibitions) (Amnesic Shellfish Poisoning) (Orkney) (Scotland) Order 2002
revoked: SSI 2002/402 Art.2

349. Contaminants in Food (Scotland) Amendment Regulations 2002
revoked: SSI 2003/289 Reg.12

350. Food Protection (Emergency Prohibitions) (Amnesic Shellfish Poisoning) (West Coast) (No.9) (Scotland) Order 2002
revoked: SSI 2002/401 Art.2

353. Food Protection (Emergency Prohibitions) (Amnesic Shellfish Poisoning) (Orkney) (No.2) (Scotland) Order 2002
revoked: SSI 2002/403 Art.2

2002–cont.

356. Food and Animal Feedingstuffs (Products of Animal Origin from China) (Emergency Control) (Scotland) Amendment Regulations 2002
revoked: SSI 2003/165 Reg.3

357. Food Protection (Emergency Prohibitions) (Amnesic Shellfish Poisoning) (West Coast) (No.10) (Scotland) Order 2002
revoked: SSI 2002/510 Art.2
Sch.1 para.3, varied: SSI 2002/421 Art.3

382. Sports Grounds and Sporting Events (Designation) (Scotland) Amendment Order 2002
revoked: SSI 2004/356 Sch.3

383. Food Protection (Emergency Prohibitions) (Amnesic Shellfish Poisoning) (West Coast) (No.5) (Scotland) Partial Revocation Order 2002
revoked: SSI 2002/431 Art.2

388. Food Protection (Emergency Prohibitions) (Amnesic Shellfish Poisoning) (West Coast) (No.11) (Scotland) Order 2002
revoked: SSI 2003/81 Art.2
Sch.1, amended: SSI 2002/545 Art.3

391. Education (Disability Strategies) (Scotland) Regulations 2002
Reg.3, revoked (in part): SSI 2003/10 Reg.2

397. Food for Particular Nutritional Uses (Addition of Substances for Specific Nutritional Purposes) (Scotland) Regulations 2002
Reg.2, amended: SSI 2004/90 Reg.3
Reg.3, amended: SSI 2004/90 Reg.4
Sch.1, amended: SSI 2004/90 Reg.5
Sch.2, substituted: SSI 2004/90 Sch.1
Sch.3, added: SSI 2004/90 Sch.2

398. Road Traffic (Permitted Parking Area and Special Parking Area) (Perth and Kinross Council) Designation Order 2002
applied: SSI 2002/400 Reg.2

408. Food Protection (Emergency Prohibitions) (Amnesic Shellfish Poisoning) (Orkney) (No.3) (Scotland) Order 2002
revoked: SSI 2003/197 Art.2

409. Food Protection (Emergency Prohibitions) (Amnesic Shellfish Poisoning) (West Coast) (No.5) (Scotland) Partial Revocation (No.2) Order 2002
revoked: SSI 2002/431 Art.2

421. Food Protection (Emergency Prohibitions) (Amnesic Shellfish Poisoning) (West Coast) (No.10) (Scotland) Partial Revocation Order 2002
revoked: SSI 2002/510 Art.2

2002–cont.

424. Food (Figs, Hazelnuts and Pistachios from Turkey) (Emergency Control) (Scotland) (No.2) Regulations 2002
Reg.2, amended: SSI 2003/413 Reg.2, SSI 2004/210 Reg.3
Reg.4, amended: SSI 2003/413 Reg.2

425. Food (Peanuts from China) (Emergency Control) (Scotland) (No.2) Regulations 2002
referred to: SSI 2003/419
Reg.2, amended: SSI 2003/419 Reg.2, SSI 2004/210 Reg.2
Reg.4, amended: SSI 2003/419 Reg.2

430. Food Protection (Emergency Prohibitions) (Amnesic Shellfish Poisoning) (West Coast) (No.12) (Scotland) Order 2002
revoked: SSI 2003/23 Art.3
Sch.1, revoked: SSI 2002/552 Art.3

438. National Health Service (General Medical Services) (Scotland) Amendment Regulations 2002
revoked: SSI 2004/114 Sch.2

445. Products of Animal Origin (Third Country Imports) (Scotland) Regulations 2002
Reg.2, amended: SSI 2003/165 Reg.2, SSI 2003/225 Reg.2, SSI 2003/411 Sch.5 para.4
Reg.3, substituted: SSI 2002/565 Reg.2
Reg.3A, amended: SSI 2003/165 Reg.2
Reg.4, amended: SSI 2003/165 Reg.2, SSI 2003/225 Reg.2
Reg.12A, added: SSI 2003/225 Reg.2
Reg.13, amended: SSI 2003/225 Reg.2
Reg.16, substituted: SSI 2003/225 Reg.2
Reg.21, amended: SSI 2003/411 Sch.5 para.4
Reg.24, amended: SSI 2003/411 Sch.5 para.4
Reg.28, amended: SSI 2003/225 Reg.2
Reg.29, amended: SSI 2003/411 Sch.5 para.4
Reg.33, amended: SSI 2003/165 Reg.2
Reg.34, applied: SI 1995/614 Reg.5
Reg.39, amended: SSI 2003/411 Sch.5 para.4
Reg.63, amended: SSI 2002/565 Reg.2
Sch.2 Part I, amended: SSI 2003/165 Reg.2
Sch.2 Part V, added: SSI 2003/165 Reg.2
Sch.2 Part VIII para.1, amended: SSI 2003/333 Reg.2
Sch.2 Part IX para.2, revoked: SSI 2003/165 Reg.2
Sch.2 Part IX para.5, revoked: SSI 2003/165 Reg.2
Sch.2 Part IX para.7, revoked: SSI 2003/165 Reg.2
Sch.6 Part I, amended: SSI 2003/225 Reg.2

450. Local Authorities Traffic Orders (Exemptions for Disabled Persons) (Scotland) Regulations 2002
Reg.6, amended: SSI 2002/547 Reg.2

NO.

NO.

2002–cont.

2002–cont.

450. Local Authorities Traffic Orders (Exemptions for Disabled Persons) (Scotland) Regulations 2002–*cont.*

Reg.7, amended: SSI 2002/547 Reg.2

457. Scottish Local Government Elections Rules 2002

Appendix 1., amended: SSI 2002/522 Sch.1

Appendix 1., varied: SI 2002/2779 Sch.5 para.40, Sch.5 para.41, Sch.5 para.42

Sch.1, amended: SSI 2002/522 r.3

Sch.2, applied: SI 2002/2779 Sch.5 para.22

Sch.2 Part I para.1, varied: SI 2002/2779 Sch.5 para.23

Sch.2 Part III para.13, varied: SI 2002/2779 Sch.5 para.24

Sch.2 Part III para.17, varied: SI 2002/2779 Sch.5 para.25

Sch.2 Part III para.18, applied: SSI 2002/561 Reg.11

Sch.2 Part III para.20, applied: SSI 2002/561 Reg.13

Sch.2 Part III para.21, varied: SI 2002/2779 Sch.5 para.26

Sch.2 Part III para.22, varied: SI 2002/2779 Sch.5 para.27

Sch.2 Part III para.23, varied: SI 2002/2779 Sch.5 para.28

Sch.2 Part III para.28, varied: SI 2002/2779 Sch.5 para.29

Sch.2 Part III para.30, varied: SI 2002/2779 Sch.5 para.30

Sch.2 Part III para.31, amended: SSI 2002/522 r.3

Sch.2 Part III para.31, varied: SI 2002/2779 Sch.5 para.31

Sch.2 Part III para.32, varied: SI 2002/2779 Sch.5 para.32

Sch.2 Part III para.33, varied: SI 2002/2779 Sch.5 para.33

Sch.2 Part III para.35, varied: SI 2002/2779 Sch.5 para.34

Sch.2 Part III para.36, applied: SSI 2002/561 Reg.25

Sch.2 Part III para.36, referred to: SSI 2002/561 Reg.16

Sch.2 Part III para.36, varied: SI 2002/2779 Sch.5 para.35

Sch.2 Part III para.37, varied: SI 2002/2779 Sch.5 para.36

Sch.2 Part III para.38, amended: SSI 2002/522 r.3

Sch.2 Part III para.38, applied: SSI 2002/561 Reg.16, Reg.20

Sch.2 Part III para.38, varied: SI 2002/2779 Sch.5 para.37

Sch.2 Part IV para.45, referred to: SSI 2002/561 Reg.28

Sch.2 Part IV para.45, varied: SI 2002/2779 Sch.5 para.38

Sch.2 Part IV para.46, applied: SSI 2002/561 Reg.28

457. Scottish Local Government Elections Rules 2002–*cont.*

Sch.2 Part IV para.47, applied: SSI 2002/561 Reg.28

Sch.2 Part V para.48, varied: SI 2002/2779 Sch.5 para.39

Sch.3 para.4, amended: SSI 2002/522 r.3

Sch.3 para.17, amended: SSI 2002/522 r.3

465. Food Protection (Emergency Prohibitions) (Amnesic Shellfish Poisoning) (West Coast) (No.13) (Scotland) Order 2002

revoked: SSI 2003/115 Art.3

varied: SSI 2003/90 Art.2

Sch.1, revoked: SSI 2003/22 Art.3

482. Food Protection (Emergency Prohibitions) (Amnesic Shellfish Poisoning) (West Coast) (No.14) (Scotland) Order 2002

revoked: SSI 2003/24 Art.3

Sch.1, revoked: SSI 2002/553 Art.3

483. Plant Health (Phytophthora ramorum) (Scotland) (No.2) Order 2002

revoked: SSI 2004/488 Art.16

489. Pesticides (Maximum Residue Levels in Crops, Food and Feeding Stuffs) (Scotland) Amendment (No.2) Regulations 2002

Reg.2, revoked (in part): SSI 2003/118 Reg.3

Sch.1, revoked: SSI 2003/118 Reg.3

Sch.2, revoked: SSI 2003/118 Reg.3

494. Civil Legal Aid (Scotland) Regulations 2002

referred to: SSI 2003/49 Reg.3

Reg.9, amended: SSI 2004/491 Reg.3

Reg.11, amended: SSI 2003/49 Reg.4

Reg.18, applied: SI 1989/1490 Sch.7

Reg.23, amended: SSI 2003/486 Reg.3, Reg.4

Reg.23A, added: SSI 2004/491 Reg.4

Reg.26, substituted: SSI 2003/486 Reg.5

Reg.29, amended: SSI 2004/491 Reg.4

Reg.31, amended: SSI 2004/491 Reg.4

Reg.31A, added: SSI 2004/491 Reg.4

Reg.33, amended: 2002 asp 17 Sch.3 para.38, SSI 2003/49 Reg.5, SSI 2004/50 Reg.3

Reg.35, amended: SSI 2003/49 Reg.6

Reg.48, added: SSI 2004/491 Reg.5

500. Taxi Drivers Licences (Carrying of Guide Dogs and Hearing Dogs) (Scotland) Regulations 2002

revoked: SSI 2003/73 Reg.9

Reg.1, revoked (in part): SSI 2002/521 Reg.2

Reg.2, amended: SSI 2002/521 Reg.2

511. Food Protection (Emergency Prohibitions) (Amnesic Shellfish Poisoning) (West Coast) (No.15) (Scotland) Order 2002

revoked: SSI 2003/18 Art.2

NO.

2002–cont.

512. Tobacco Advertising and Promotion Act 2002 (Commencement) (Scotland) Order 2002
Art.2, amended: SSI 2003/80 Art.2
Art.3, added: SSI 2003/80 Art.2

513. Act of Sederunt (Fees of Messengers-At-Arms) 2002
revoked: SSI 2002/566 Sch.2

515. Act of Sederunt (Fees of Sheriff Officers) 2002
revoked: SSI 2002/567 Sch.2

518. Potatoes Originating in Egypt (Scotland) Amendment Regulations 2002
revoked: SSI 2004/111 Reg.8

520. Seeds (Miscellaneous Amendments) (Scotland) Regulations 2002
revoked: SSI 2002/564 Reg.2

521. Taxi Drivers Licences (Carrying of Guide Dogs and Hearing Dogs) (Scotland) Amendment Regulations 2002
revoked: SSI 2003/73 Reg.9

523. Kava-kava in Food (Scotland) Regulations 2002
Reg.2, amended: SSI 2004/244 Reg.2
Reg.3, amended: SSI 2004/244 Reg.2

524. Food Labelling Amendment (Scotland) Regulations 2002
Reg.3, referred to: SI 1996/1499 Reg.50
Reg.5, referred to: SI 1996/1499 Reg.50

526. Seeds (Fees) (Scotland) Regulations 2002
Sch.3, amended: SSI 2004/317 Reg.26

529. Poultry Breeding Flocks, Hatcheries and Animal By-Products (Fees) (Scotland) Order 2002
Art.2, substituted: SSI 2003/411 Sch.5 para.5
Art.3, amended: SSI 2003/411 Sch.5 para.5
Sch.1, amended: SSI 2003/411 Sch.5 para.5

534. NHS Quality Improvement Scotland Order 2002
Art.5, applied: SSI 2002/535
Sch.1 Part I, applied: SSI 2002/535
Sch.1 Part III, amended: SI 2003/1590 Sch.1 para.8

537. Plant Protection Products Amendment (No.3) (Scotland) Regulations 2002
revoked: SSI 2003/579 Sch.5

541. Genetically Modified Organisms (Deliberate Release) (Scotland) Regulations 2002
Reg.2, amended: SSI 2004/439 Reg.3
Reg.15, amended: SSI 2004/439 Reg.4
Reg.17A, added: SSI 2004/439 Reg.5
Reg.21, amended: SSI 2004/439 Reg.6

544. Food Protection (Emergency Prohibitions) (Amnesic Shellfish Poisoning) (West Coast) (No.16) (Scotland) Order 2002
revoked: SSI 2003/195 Art.2

NO.

2002–cont.

545. Food Protection (Emergency Prohibitions) (Amnesic Shellfish Poisoning) (West Coast) (No.11) (Scotland) Partial Revocation Order 2002
revoked: SSI 2003/81 Art.2

551. Food Protection (Emergency Prohibitions) (Amnesic Shellfish Poisoning) (West Coast) (No.6) (Scotland) Partial Revocation Order 2002
revoked: SSI 2003/17 Art.2

552. Food Protection (Emergency Prohibitions) (Amnesic Shellfish Poisoning) (West Coast) (No.12) (Scotland) Partial Revocation Order 2002
revoked: SSI 2003/23 Art.3

553. Food Protection (Emergency Prohibitions) (Amnesic Shellfish Poisoning) (West Coast) (No.14) (Scotland) Partial Revocation Order 2002
revoked: SSI 2003/24 Art.3

556. Air Quality Limit Values (Scotland) Amendment Regulations 2002
revoked: SSI 2003/428 Reg.16

558. Food Protection (Emergency Prohibitions) (Amnesic Shellfish Poisoning) (Orkney) (No.3) (Scotland) Partial Revocation Order 2002
revoked: SSI 2003/197 Art.2

560. Act of Sederunt (Debt Arrangement and Attachment (Scotland) Act 2002) 2002
Sch.1 Appendix, amended: SSI 2004/505 Sch.1
Sch.1 Part CHAPTERc para.37, added: SSI 2004/505 Art.2
Sch.1 Part CHAPTERc para.38, added: SSI 2004/505 Art.2
Sch.1 Part CHAPTERc para.39, added: SSI 2004/505 Art.2
Sch.1 Part CHAPTERc para.40, added: SSI 2004/505 Art.2
Sch.1 Part CHAPTERc para.41, added: SSI 2004/505 Art.2

566. Act of Sederunt (Fees of Messengers-at-Arms) (No.2) 2002
Sch.1 para.15, amended: SSI 2003/536 Sch.1

567. Act of Sederunt (Fees of Sheriff Officers) (No.2) 2002
Sch.1 para.17, amended: SSI 2003/538 Sch.1

2003

1. Cairngorms National Park Designation, Transitional and Consequential Provisions (Scotland) Order 2003
Art.7, applied: SI 1992/224 Art.14

9. Plastic Materials and Articles in Contact with Food (Amendment) (Scotland) Regulations 2003
referred to: SI 1998/1376 Reg.10
Reg.4, referred to: SI 1998/1376 Reg.10
Reg.6, referred to: SI 1998/1376 Reg.10

2003–cont.

11. **National Health Service (General Medical Services) (Scotland) Amendment Regulations 2003**
revoked: SSI 2004/114 Sch.2
20. **Regulations of Investigatory Powers (Prescription of Offices, Ranks and Positions) (Scotland) Amendment Order 2003**
revoked: SSI 2003/50 Art.2
21. **Police and Police (Special Constables) (Scotland) Amendment Regulations 2003**
revoked: SSI 2004/257 Sch.4
22. **Food Protection (Emergency Prohibitions) (Amnesic Shellfish Poisoning) (West Coast) (No.13) (Scotland) Order 2002 Partial Revocation Order 2003**
revoked: SSI 2003/115 Art.3
34. **Tobacco Advertising and Promotion (Sponsorship Transitional Provisions) (Scotland) Regulations 2003**
Reg.3, amended: SSI 2003/265 Reg.2
42. **Local Government Finance (Scotland) Order 2003**
Art.2, revoked: SSI 2004/14 Art.6
Art.4, revoked: SSI 2004/14 Art.6
Sch.1, amended: SSI 2004/14 Art.6
Sch.2, revoked: SSI 2004/14 Art.6
51. **Action Programme for Nitrate Vulnerable Zones (Scotland) Regulations 2003**
amended: SSI 2003/169 Reg.2
applied: SSI 2003/129 Sch.2 para.6
referred to: SSI 2004/70 Sch.2 para.6
Reg.2, amended: SSI 2003/169 Reg.2
Reg.4, amended: SSI 2003/169 Reg.2
Reg.5, amended: SSI 2003/169 Reg.2
Sch.1 para.5, amended: SSI 2003/169 Reg.2
Sch.1 para.10, amended: SSI 2003/169 Reg.2
Sch.1 para.11, amended: SSI 2003/169 Reg.2
52. **Nitrate Vulnerable Zones (Grants) (Scotland) Scheme 2003**
Art.5, amended: SSI 2003/518 Art.2
Art.5, revoked (in part): SSI 2003/518 Art.2
Art.6, amended: SSI 2003/518 Art.2
56. **Sea Fishing (Restriction on Days at Sea) (Scotland) Order 2003**
revoked: SSI 2004/44 Art.24
Art.2, amended: SSI 2003/300 Art.2, SSI 2003/623 Art.2
Art.3, amended: SSI 2003/66 Art.2, SSI 2003/300 Art.2, SSI 2003/623 Art.2
Art.4, substituted: SSI 2003/623 Art.2
Art.6, amended: SSI 2003/66 Art.2, SSI 2003/300 Art.2
Art.6A, added: SSI 2003/66 Art.2
Art.6A, amended: SSI 2003/300 Art.2
Art.8, amended: SSI 2003/66 Art.2, SSI 2003/300 Art.2
Art.9, amended: SSI 2003/300 Art.2

2003–cont.

56. **Sea Fishing (Restriction on Days at Sea) (Scotland) Order 2003**–cont.
Art.10, amended: SSI 2003/300 Art.2
Art.12, amended: SSI 2003/66 Art.2
Art.13, amended: SSI 2003/66 Art.2
Art.14, amended: SSI 2003/300 Art.2
Art.15, amended: SSI 2003/300 Art.2
62. **Community Care and Health (Scotland) Act 2002 (Commencement No 2) Order 2003**
varied: SSI 2003/63 Art.2
64. **National Health Service (General Medical Services Supplementary Lists) (Scotland) Regulations 2003**
revoked: SSI 2004/114 Sch.2
Reg.2, amended: SSI 2003/298 Reg.2, SSI 2004/40 Reg.2
Reg.5, amended: SSI 2003/298 Reg.3, SSI 2004/40 Reg.2
Reg.6, amended: SSI 2003/298 Reg.4
Reg.8, amended: SSI 2003/298 Reg.5
Reg.9, amended: SSI 2003/298 Reg.6, SSI 2004/40 Reg.2
Reg.11, amended: SSI 2003/298 Reg.7
Reg.13A, added: SSI 2004/40 Reg.2
Sch.2 para.1, amended: SSI 2004/40 Reg.2
Sch.2 para.2, amended: SSI 2004/40 Reg.2
66. **Sea Fishing (Restriction on Days at Sea) (Scotland) Amendment Order 2003**
revoked: SSI 2004/44 Art.24
79. **Sea Fish (Prohibited Methods of Fishing) (Firth of Clyde) Order 2003**
revoked: SSI 2004/55 Art.5
Art.2, amended: SSI 2003/100 Art.2
Art.4, amended: SSI 2003/100 Art.2
86. **National Assistance (Sums for Personal Requirements) (Scotland) Regulations 2003**
revoked: SSI 2004/106 Reg.3
87. **Fishing Vessels (Decommissioning) (Scotland) Scheme 2003**
Art.11, substituted: SSI 2003/116 Art.13
88. **Sea Fishing (Enforcement of Community Quota and Third Country Fishing Measures) (Scotland) Order 2003**
applied: SSI 2004/209 Art.15
revoked: SSI 2004/209 Art.15
Art.11, applied: SSI 2004/209 Art.15
90. **Food Protection (Emergency Prohibitions) (Amnesic Shellfish Poisoning) (West Coast) (No.13) (Scotland) Order 2002 Partial Revocation (No.2) Order 2003**
revoked: SSI 2003/115 Art.3
92. **Sea Fishing (Transitional Support) (Scotland) Scheme 2003**
revoked: SSI 2003/116 Art.14

2003-cont.

100. **Sea Fish (Prohibited Methods of Fishing) (Firth of Clyde) Amendment Order 2003**
revoked: SSI 2004/55 Art.5

118. **Pesticides (Maximum Residue Levels in Crops, Food and Feeding Stuffs) (Scotland) Amendment Regulations 2003**
Reg.2, revoked (in part): SSI 2003/445 Reg.3
Sch.2, revoked: SSI 2003/445 Reg.3

129. **Less Favoured Area Support Scheme (Scotland) Regulations 2003**
applied: SSI 2004/70 Reg.4
revoked (in part): SSI 2004/70 Reg.27
Reg.9, applied: SSI 2000/347 Reg.4, SSI 2004/381 Reg.4
Reg.10, applied: SSI 2000/347 Reg.4, SSI 2004/381 Reg.4
Reg.11, applied: SSI 2000/347 Reg.4, SSI 2004/381 Reg.4
Reg.13, applied: SSI 2000/347 Reg.4, SSI 2004/381 Reg.4
Reg.17, applied: SSI 2000/347 Reg.4, SSI 2004/381 Reg.4
Reg.24, amended: SSI 2004/381 Reg.14
Reg.27, revoked: SSI 2004/381 Sch.1

135. **Ethical Standards in Public Life etc (Scotland) Act 2000 (Register of Interests) Regulations 2003**
Reg.2, amended: SSI 2003/203 Reg.2
Reg.4, amended: SSI 2003/203 Reg.2

136. **Adults with Incapacity (Scotland) Act 2000 (Commencement No 3) Order 2003**
Art.2, revoked (in part): SSI 2003/227 Art.2

140. **Housing (Scotland) Act 2001 (Payments out of Grants for Housing Support Services) Order 2003**
Sch.1 Part I para.3, amended: SSI 2004/348 Art.2
Sch.1 Part I para.3, substituted: SSI 2004/108 Art.2

152. **Regulation of Care (Fees) (Scotland) Order 2003**
referred to: SSI 2004/93 Art.1
revoked: SSI 2004/93 Art.4
Art.1, amended: SSI 2003/573 Art.2
Sch.1, amended: SSI 2003/573 Art.2

158. **National Health Service (Dental Charges) (Scotland) Regulations 2003**
Reg.1, amended: SSI 2004/101 Reg.2
Reg.4, amended: SSI 2004/101 Reg.2
Reg.4, applied: SSI 2004/101 Reg.3
Reg.5, amended: SSI 2004/101 Reg.2
Reg.6, amended: SSI 2004/101 Reg.2
Reg.8, amended: SSI 2004/101 Reg.2
Sch.3 para.2, amended: SSI 2004/101 Reg.2
Sch.3 para.3, amended: SSI 2004/101 Reg.2

2003-cont.

160. **Non-Domestic Rates (Levying) (Scotland) Regulations 2003**
revoked: SSI 2004/92 Reg.6

171. **Waste Management Licensing Amendment (Scotland) Regulations 2003**
applied: SI 1994/1056 Reg.4

176. **Council Tax (Discounts) (Scotland) Consolidation and Amendment Order 2003**
Art.7, amended: SI 2004/1771 Sch.1 para.18

178. **Civil Legal Aid (Scotland) (Fees) Amendment Regulations 2003**
applied: SSI 2004/281 Reg.3

179. **Advice and Assistance (Assistance by Way of Representation) (Scotland) Regulations 2003**
referred to: SSI 2003/500 Reg.2
Reg.6, amended: SSI 2003/500 Reg.3, SSI 2004/307 Reg.3
Reg.7, amended: SSI 2003/500 Reg.4, SSI 2004/307 Reg.4

180. **Advice and Assistance (Financial Conditions) (Scotland) Regulations 2003**
revoked: SSI 2004/140 Reg.7

182. **Civil Legal Aid (Financial Conditions) (Scotland) Regulations 2003**
revoked: SSI 2004/141 Reg.7

198. **TSE (Scotland) Amendment Regulations 2003**
Reg.2, revoked (in part): SSI 2003/411 Sch.6

200. **National Health Service (Optical Charges and Payments) (Scotland) Amendment Regulations 2003**
revoked: SSI 2003/218 Reg.2

209. **SFGS Farmland Premium Scheme 2003**
applied: SSI 2004/381 Reg.4
referred to: SI 1997/829 Art.7A
Art.14, applied: SSI 2000/347 Reg.4, SSI 2004/381 Reg.4

220. **Police (Scotland) Amendment (No.2) Regulations 2003**
revoked: SSI 2004/257 Sch.4

229. **Pet Travel Scheme (Scotland) Order 2003**
applied: SI 1974/2211 Art.4C, Art.5C, Art.6
Sch.1, referred to: SI 1974/2211 Art.5C
Sch.5, referred to: SI 1974/2211 Art.5C

231. **Rehabilitation of Offenders Act 1974 (Exclusions and Exceptions) (Scotland) Order 2003**
Sch.4 Part1 para.6, substituted: SI 2004/1771 Sch.1 para.17
Sch.4 Part 1 para.10, substituted: SI 2003/1590 Sch.1 para.7

235. **Landfill (Scotland) Regulations 2003**
applied: SSI 2000/323 Reg.23, Reg.24, Reg.26, Reg.30, Reg.35, Sch.1 Part I, Sch.9 para.1
referred to: SSI 2000/323 Reg.34

NO.

NO.

2003–cont.

235. Landfill (Scotland) Regulations 2003–
cont.

Reg.2, amended: SSI 2003/343 Reg.3

Reg.6, disapplied: SSI 2000/323 Sch.4 para.1A

Reg.10, applied: SSI 2000/323 Reg.7, Reg.9, Reg.13, Reg.22

Reg.17, applied: SI 1994/1056 Reg.10, SSI 2000/323 Reg.22, Sch.9 para.1

Reg.18, applied: SSI 2000/323 Reg.22, Reg.30

Reg.19, amended: SSI 2003/343 Reg.4, 2004 asp 8 Sch.2 para.8

Reg.19, applied: SI 1994/1056 Reg.3, Reg.10, SSI 2000/323 Reg.34, Sch.9 para.1

Sch.5 para.1, applied: SI 1994/1056 Reg.10, SSI 2000/323 Reg.22, Sch.3 para.2, Sch.9 para.1

Sch.5 para.1, referred to: SI 1994/1056 Reg.10, SSI 2000/323 Sch.9 para.1

Sch.6 para.3, amended: SSI 2003/343 Reg.5

244. Food Protection (Emergency Prohibitions) (Amnesic Shellfish Poisoning) (West Coast) (Scotland) Order 2003

revoked: SSI 2004/179 Art.2

varied: SSI 2003/315 Art.2

245. Food Protection (Emergency Prohibitions) (Amnesic Shellfish Poisoning) (West Coast) (No.2) (Scotland) Order 2003

revoked: SSI 2004/22 Art.2

259. Lanarkshire Primary Care National Health Service Trust (Establishment) Amendment Order 2003

revoked: SSI 2004/107 Sch.2

260. Food Protection (Emergency Prohibitions) (Amnesic Shellfish Poisoning) (Orkney) (Scotland) Order 2003

revoked: SSI 2003/605 Art.2

298. National Health Service (General Medical Services Supplementary Lists) (Scotland) Amendment Regulations 2003

revoked: SSI 2004/114 Sch.2

299. Collagen and Gelatine (Intra-Community Trade) (Scotland) Regulations 2003

revoked: SSI 2003/466 Reg.2

Reg.1, amended: SSI 2003/328 Reg.2

Reg.2, amended: SSI 2003/405 Reg.2

Reg.5, amended: SSI 2003/405 Reg.2

300. Sea Fishing (Restriction on Days at Sea) (Scotland) Amendment (No.2) Order 2003

referred to: SSI 2003/56 Art.3

revoked: SSI 2004/44 Art.24

302. Agricultural Subsidies (Appeals) (Scotland) Amendment Regulations 2003

revoked: SSI 2004/381 Sch.1

2003–cont.

304. Oil and Fibre Plant Seeds Amendment (Scotland) Regulations 2003

revoked: SSI 2004/317 Sch.8

310. National Health Service (General Medical Services) (Scotland) Amendment (No.2) Regulations 2003

revoked: SSI 2004/114 Sch.2

311. Condensed Milk and Dried Milk (Scotland) Regulations 2003

Reg.8, amended: SSI 2004/395 Reg.7

Sch.1, amended: SSI 2003/492 Reg.2

315. Food Protection (Emergency Prohibitions) (Amnesic Shellfish Poisoning) (West Coast) (Scotland) Partial Revocation Order 2003

revoked: SSI 2004/179 Art.2

321. Food Protection (Emergency Prohibitions) (Amnesic Shellfish Poisoning) (Orkney) (No.2) (Scotland) Order 2003

revoked: SSI 2004/130 Art.2

328. Collagen and Gelatine (Intra-Community Trade) (Scotland) Amendment Regulations 2003

revoked: SSI 2003/466 Reg.2

354. Diseases of Poultry (Scotland) Order 2003

Art.3, amended: SSI 2004/453 Reg.8

365. Food Protection (Emergency Prohibitions) (Amnesic Shellfish Poisoning) (West Coast) (No.3) (Scotland) Order 2003

revoked: SSI 2004/79 Art.2

366. Food Protection (Emergency Prohibitions) (Amnesic Shellfish Poisoning) (East Coast) (Scotland) Order 2003

revoked: SSI 2003/589 Art.2

369. Food Protection (Emergency Prohibitions) (Amnesic Shellfish Poisoning) (East Coast) (No.2) (Scotland) Order 2003

revoked: SSI 2003/494 Art.2

374. Food Protection (Emergency Prohibitions) (Amnesic Shellfish Poisoning) (West Coast) (No.4) (Scotland) Order 2003

revoked: SSI 2004/124 Art.2

Sch.1, revoked: SSI 2004/42 Art.2, SSI 2004/65 Art.2, SSI 2004/69 Art.2

376. National Health Service (Travelling Expenses and Remission of Charges) (Scotland) Regulations 2003

revoked: SSI 2003/460 Reg.14

380. Food Protection (Emergency Prohibitions) (Amnesic Shellfish Poisoning) (East Coast) (No.3) (Scotland) Order 2003

revoked: SSI 2003/590 Art.2

NO.

2003–cont.

381. **Food Protection (Emergency Prohibitions) (Amnesic Shellfish Poisoning) (West Coast) (No.5) (Scotland) Order 2003**
revoked: SSI 2004/131 Art.2
Sch.1, revoked: SSI 2003/606 Art.2, SSI 2004/61 Art.2

382. **Food (Hot Chilli and Hot Chilli Products) (Emergency Control) (Scotland) Regulations 2003**
revoked: SSI 2004/56 Reg.9
Reg.3, amended: SSI 2003/493 Reg.2
Reg.4, amended: SSI 2003/493 Reg.2
Reg.5, amended: SSI 2003/493 Reg.2
Reg.6, amended: SSI 2003/493 Reg.2
Reg.7, amended: SSI 2003/493 Reg.2
Reg.7, revoked (in part): SSI 2003/493 Reg.2
Reg.8, added: SSI 2003/493 Reg.2

392. **Food Protection (Emergency Prohibitions) (Amnesic Shellfish Poisoning) (West Coast) (No.6) (Scotland) Order 2003**
revoked: SSI 2004/177 Art.2
Sch.1, revoked: SSI 2004/125 Art.2

393. **Food Protection (Emergency Prohibitions) (Amnesic Shellfish Poisoning) (East Coast) (No.4) (Scotland) Order 2003**
revoked: SSI 2004/19 Art.2
Sch.1, revoked: SSI 2003/592 Art.3

394. **Food Protection (Emergency Prohibitions) (Amnesic Shellfish Poisoning) (East Coast) (No.5) (Scotland) Order 2003**
revoked: SSI 2003/495 Art.2

396. **Food (Brazil Nuts) (Emergency Control) (Scotland) Regulations 2003**
Reg.2, amended: SSI 2003/558 Reg.2, SSI 2004/210 Reg.4
Reg.3, amended: SSI 2003/558 Reg.2
Reg.4, amended: SSI 2003/558 Reg.2
Reg.5, amended: SSI 2003/558 Reg.2
Reg.6, substituted: SSI 2003/558 Reg.2
Reg.7, substituted: SSI 2003/558 Reg.2
Reg.8, substituted: SSI 2003/558 Reg.2
Reg.9, amended: SSI 2003/558 Reg.2
Reg.9, revoked (in part): SSI 2003/558 Reg.2

397. **Food Protection (Emergency Prohibitions) (Amnesic Shellfish Poisoning) (West Coast) (No.7) (Scotland) Order 2003**
revoked: SSI 2003/598 Art.2

402. **Food Protection (Emergency Prohibitions) (Amnesic Shellfish Poisoning) (West Coast) (No.8) (Scotland) Order 2003**
revoked: SSI 2004/135 Art.2

NO.

2003–cont.

404. **Inshore Fishing (Prohibition of Fishing and Fishing Methods) (Scotland) Amendment Order 2003**
revoked: SSI 2004/276 Sch.4
Art.2, revoked (in part): SSI 2003/514 Art.3
Sch.1, revoked: SSI 2003/514 Art.3

405. **Collagen and Gelatine (Intra-Community Trade) (Scotland) Amendment (No.2) Regulations 2003**
revoked: SSI 2003/466 Reg.2

409. **Food Protection (Emergency Prohibitions) (Amnesic Shellfish Poisoning) (West Coast) (No.9) (Scotland) Order 2003**
revoked: SSI 2004/178 Art.2

410. **Food Protection (Emergency Prohibitions) (Amnesic Shellfish Poisoning) (West Coast) (No.10) (Scotland) Order 2003**
revoked: SSI 2004/129 Art.2

411. **Animal By-Products (Scotland) Regulations 2003**
applied: SSI 2002/255 Reg.13, Reg.40
Reg.14, applied: SSI 2002/445 Reg.29
Reg.30, applied: SSI 2002/445 Reg.29

414. **Food (Pistachios from Iran) (Emergency Control) (Scotland) Regulations 2003**
Reg.2, amended: SSI 2004/210 Reg.5

415. **Road Works (Inspection Fees) (Scotland) Regulations 2003**
Reg.3, amended: SSI 2004/84 Reg.2

418. **Food (Peanuts from Egypt) (Emergency Control) (Scotland) Regulations 2003**
Reg.2, amended: SSI 2004/210 Reg.6

428. **Air Quality Limit Values (Scotland) Regulations 2003**
Sch.2 Part II, amended: SSI 2003/547 Reg.2
Sch.5 Part I para.1.1, amended: SSI 2003/547 Reg.2

429. **Food Protection (Emergency Prohibitions) (Amnesic Shellfish Poisoning) (Orkney) (No.3) (Scotland) Order 2003**
revoked: SSI 2003/557 Art.2

438. **Criminal Justice (Scotland) Act 2003 (Transitional Provisions) Order 2003**
Art.2, applied: SSI 2003/475 Art.3

439. **Criminal Justice (Scotland) Act 2003 (Commencement No 2) Order 2003**
revoked: SSI 2003/475 Art.4

441. **Victim Statements (Prescribed Offences) (Scotland) Order 2003**
Sch.1 para.4A, added: SSI 2003/519 Art.2
Sch.1 para.15, amended: SSI 2004/287 Art.3
Sch.1 para.21, amended: SSI 2004/287 Art.3

443. **National Health Service (General Medical Services) (Scotland) Amendment (No.3) Regulations 2003**
revoked: SSI 2004/114 Sch.2

2003–cont.

445. Pesticides (Maximum Residue Levels in Crops, Food and Feeding Stuffs) (Scotland) Amendment (No.2) Regulations 2003

Reg.2, revoked (in part): SSI 2004/104 Reg.3, SSI 2004/220 Reg.3

Sch.2, revoked: SSI 2004/104 Reg.3, SSI 2004/220 Reg.3

453. Title Conditions (Scotland) Act 2003 (Conservation Bodies) Order 2003

Sch.1 Part II, amended: SSI 2003/621 Art.2, SSI 2004/400 Sch.1

460. National Health Service (Travelling Expenses and Remission of Charges) (Scotland) (No.2) Regulations 2003

applied: SSI 2004/114 Sch.1 para.3, SSI 2004/115 Sch.5 para.44, SSI 2004/116 Sch.1 para.15

Reg.2, amended: SSI 2004/102 Reg.2, SSI 2004/166 Reg.2

Reg.3, amended: SSI 2004/102 Reg.2

Reg.3, revoked (in part): SSI 2004/102 Reg.2

Reg.4, amended: SSI 2004/102 Reg.2, SSI 2004/166 Reg.2

Reg.6, substituted: SSI 2004/166 Reg.2

Reg.7, amended: SSI 2004/102 Reg.2, SSI 2004/166 Reg.2

Reg.8, amended: SSI 2004/102 Reg.2

Reg.9, amended: SSI 2004/102 Reg.2

Reg.10, amended: SSI 2004/166 Reg.2

Reg.11, amended: SSI 2004/166 Reg.2

Reg.12, amended: SSI 2004/166 Reg.2

Sch.1 Part II para.4, amended: SSI 2004/102 Reg.2

461. Housing Grants (Assessment of Contributions) (Scotland) Regulations 2003

Reg.2, amended: SSI 2004/456 Reg.3

Reg.13, amended: SSI 2004/456 Reg.4

Reg.14, amended: SSI 2004/456 Reg.5

Reg.15, amended: SSI 2004/456 Reg.6

Reg.18, amended: SSI 2004/456 Reg.7

Reg.19, amended: SSI 2004/456 Reg.8

Reg.20, amended: SSI 2004/456 Reg.8

Reg.21, amended: SSI 2004/456 Reg.8

Reg.22, amended: SSI 2004/456 Reg.9

Reg.23, amended: SSI 2004/456 Reg.8

Reg.23, revoked (in part): SSI 2004/456 Reg.10

Reg.23A, added: SSI 2004/456 Reg.11

Reg.25, amended: SSI 2004/456 Reg.12

Reg.28, amended: SSI 2004/456 Reg.13

493. Food (Hot Chilli and Hot Chilli Products) (Emergency Control) (Scotland) Amendment Regulations 2003

revoked: SSI 2004/56 Reg.9

2003–cont.

501. Food Protection (Emergency Prohibitions) (Amnesic Shellfish Poisoning) (Orkney) (No.4) (Scotland) Order 2003

revoked: SSI 2003/591 Art.2

502. Horticultural Produce (Community Grading Rules) (Scotland) Regulations 2003

revoked: SSI 2004/245 Reg.2

514. Inshore Fishing (Prohibition of Fishing and Fishing Methods) (Scotland) Amendment (No.2) Order 2003

revoked: SSI 2004/276 Sch.4

527. Specified Sugar Products (Scotland) Regulations 2003

applied: SSI 2001/38 Reg.5

561. Food Protection (Emergency Prohibitions) (Amnesic Shellfish Poisoning) (West Coast) (No.11) (Scotland) Order 2003

revoked: SSI 2004/181 Art.2

Sch.1, revoked: SSI 2004/139 Art.2

565. Pig Carcase (Grading) Amendment (Scotland) Regulations 2003

revoked: SSI 2004/279 Reg.3

573. Regulation of Care (Fees) (Scotland) Amendment Order 2003

revoked: SSI 2004/93 Art.4

574. Regulation of Care (Scotland) Act 2001 (Transitional Provisions) Order 2003

revoked: SSI 2003/587 Art.3

576. Registration of Establishments Keeping Laying Hens (Scotland) Regulations 2003

Reg.2, amended: SSI 2004/27 Reg.2

Reg.4, amended: SSI 2004/27 Reg.2

Reg.5, amended: SSI 2004/27 Reg.2

Reg.7, amended: SSI 2004/27 Reg.2

Reg.8, amended: SSI 2004/27 Reg.2

Reg.12, amended: SSI 2004/27 Reg.2

578. Food Labelling Amendment (Scotland) Regulations 2003

Reg.5, referred to: SI 1996/1499 Reg.50

Reg.6, referred to: SI 1996/1499 Reg.50

579. Plant Protection Products (Scotland) Regulations 2003

applied: SI 2003/660 Reg.2, SSI 2004/70 Sch.2 para.8

Reg.4, applied: SI 2003/660 Reg.2

Reg.5, applied: SI 2003/660 Sch.1

Reg.7, applied: SI 2003/660 Sch.1

Reg.8, applied: SI 2003/660 Sch.1

Reg.9, applied: SI 2003/660 Sch.1

Reg.10, applied: SI 2003/660 Reg.2, Sch.1

Reg.11, applied: SI 2003/660 Sch.1

Reg.13, applied: SI 2003/660 Reg.2, Sch.1

Reg.28, amended: SSI 2004/368 Reg.2

Reg.28, revoked (in part): SSI 2004/368 Reg.2

Sch.1, substituted: SSI 2004/368 Sch.1

NO.

2003–cont.

586. **African Swine Fever (Scotland) Order 2003**

applied: SI 1980/146 Art.2

587. **Regulation of Care (Scotland) Act 2001 (Transitional Provisions and Revocation) Order 2003**

Art.2, amended: SSI 2004/293 Art.2

592. **Food Protection (Emergency Prohibitions) (Amnesic Shellfish Poisoning) (East Coast) (No.4) (Scotland) Partial Revocation Order 2003**

revoked: SSI 2004/19 Art.2

593. **End-of-Life Vehicles (Storage and Treatment) (Scotland) Regulations 2003**

Reg.4, applied: SI 1994/1056 Sch.3 para.45

Reg.6, applied: SI 1994/1056 Sch.3 para.45

Sch.1 Part 1 para.1, referred to: SI 1994/1056 Sch.3 para.41

Sch.1 Part 2 para.1, referred to: SI 1994/1056 Sch.3 para.41

602. **Public Appointments and Public Bodies etc (Scotland) Act 2003 (Commencement No 4) Order 2003**

Art.1, amended: SSI 2004/45 Art.2

Art.2, amended: SSI 2004/45 Art.2

Art.2, referred to: SSI 2004/46 Reg.2

606. **Food Protection (Emergency Prohibitions) (Amnesic Shellfish Poisoning) (West Coast) (No.5) (Scotland) Partial Revocation Order 2003**

revoked: SSI 2004/131 Art.2

623. **Sea Fishing (Restriction on Days at Sea) (Scotland) Amendment (No.3) Order 2003**

revoked: SSI 2004/44 Art.24

2004

5. **Ura Firth, Shetland Scallops Several Fishery Order 2004**

Sch.1, applied: SSI 1999/194 Art.2

6. **Meat Products (Scotland) Regulations 2004**

applied: SI 1996/1499 Sch.4A para.1

15. **National Health Service (Transfer of Property between Health Boards) (Scotland) Regulations 2004**

revoked: SSI 2004/285 Reg.3

16. **National Health Service (Borrowing and Loans from Endowments) (Scotland) Regulations 2004**

revoked: SSI 2004/284 Reg.4

21. **Food Protection (Emergency Prohibitions) (Amnesic Shellfish Poisoning) (West Coast) (Scotland) Order 2004**

revoked: SSI 2004/159 Art.2

26. **Solvent Emissions (Scotland) Regulations 2004**

Reg.3, applied: SSI 2000/323 Sch.3 para.5

NO.

2004–cont.

38. **National Health Service (Tribunal) (Scotland) Regulations 2004**

Reg.2, amended: SSI 2004/122 Reg.2

Reg.3A, added: SSI 2004/122 Reg.2

Reg.6, amended: SSI 2004/122 Reg.2, SSI 2004/271 Reg.2

Reg.6, revoked (in part): SSI 2004/122 Reg.2

Reg.8, amended: SSI 2004/122 Reg.2

Reg.9, amended: SSI 2004/122 Reg.2

Reg.11, amended: SSI 2004/122 Reg.2

Reg.12, amended: SSI 2004/122 Reg.2

Reg.15, amended: SSI 2004/122 Reg.2

Reg.18, amended: SSI 2004/122 Reg.2

Reg.20, amended: SSI 2004/122 Reg.2

Reg.21, amended: SSI 2004/122 Reg.2

Reg.21, revoked (in part): SSI 2004/122 Reg.2

Reg.22, amended: SSI 2004/122 Reg.2

Reg.23, amended: SSI 2004/122 Reg.2

Reg.24, amended: SSI 2004/122 Reg.2

Reg.25, amended: SSI 2004/122 Reg.2

Reg.25, revoked (in part): SSI 2004/122 Reg.2

Reg.26, amended: SSI 2004/122 Reg.2

Reg.26, applied: SI 1995/416 Reg.4, SI 1996/177 Reg.4, SSI 2003/64 Reg.9, SSI 2004/114 Reg.7

Reg.26, revoked (in part): SSI 2004/122 Reg.2

Reg.28, revoked (in part): SSI 2004/122 Reg.2

Reg.29, amended: SSI 2004/122 Reg.2, SSI 2004/271 Reg.2

Reg.30, revoked: SSI 2004/122 Reg.2

Reg.31, amended: SSI 2004/122 Reg.2

Sch.1 para.8, amended: SSI 2004/122 Reg.2

Sch.2, amended: SSI 2004/122 Reg.2

40. **National Health Service (General Medical Services Supplementary Lists) (Scotland) Amendment Regulations 2004**

revoked: SSI 2004/114 Sch.2

41. **National Health Service (General Medical Services) (Scotland) Amendment Regulations 2004**

revoked: SSI 2004/114 Sch.2

42. **Food Protection (Emergency Prohibitions) (Amnesic Shellfish Poisoning) (West Coast) (No.4) (Scotland) Partial Revocation Order 2004**

revoked: SSI 2004/124 Art.2

43. **Food Protection (Emergency Prohibitions) (Amnesic Shellfish Poisoning) (West Coast) (No.2) (Scotland) Order 2004**

revoked: SSI 2004/192 Art.2

44. **Sea Fishing (Restriction on Days at Sea) (Scotland) Order 2004**

Art.6, amended: SSI 2004/81 Art.2

Art.13, substituted: SSI 2004/81 Art.2

Art.14, amended: SSI 2004/81 Art.2

NO.

2004–cont.

44. Sea Fishing (Restriction on Days at Sea) (Scotland) Order 2004–*cont.*
Art.17, amended: SSI 2004/81 Art.2
Art.18, amended: SSI 2004/81 Art.2
Art.23, amended: SSI 2004/81 Art.2

61. Food Protection (Emergency Prohibitions) (Amnesic Shellfish Poisoning) (West Coast) (No.5) (Scotland) Order 2003 Partial Revocation Order 2004
revoked: SSI 2004/131 Art.2

65. Food Protection (Emergency Prohibitions) (Amnesic Shellfish Poisoning) (West Coast) (No.4) (Scotland) Partial Revocation (No.2) Order 2004
revoked: SSI 2004/124 Art.2

69. Food Protection (Emergency Prohibitions) (Amnesic Shellfish Poisoning) (West Coast) (No.4) (Scotland) Partial Revocation (No.3) Order 2004
revoked: SSI 2004/124 Art.2

70. Less Favoured Area Support Scheme (Scotland) Regulations 2004
Reg.7, applied: SSI 2000/347 Reg.4, SSI 2004/381 Reg.4
Reg.9, applied: SSI 2000/347 Reg.4, SSI 2004/381 Reg.4
Reg.10, applied: SSI 2000/347 Reg.4, SSI 2004/381 Reg.4
Reg.11, applied: SSI 2004/381 Reg.4
Reg.14, amended: SSI 2004/128 Reg.2
Reg.16, applied: SSI 2000/347 Reg.4, SSI 2004/381 Reg.4
Reg.18, substituted: SSI 2004/128 Reg.2
Reg.23, amended: SSI 2004/381 Reg.14
Reg.26, revoked: SSI 2004/381 Sch.1
Sch.2 Part I para.8, substituted: SSI 2004/128 Reg.2
Sch.9, substituted: SSI 2004/128 Sch.1

83. Individual Learning Account (Scotland) Regulations 2004
Reg.1, amended: SSI 2004/469 Reg.8
Reg.3, amended: SSI 2004/270 Reg.3, Reg.4, SSI 2004/469 Reg.8

87. Road Traffic (Permitted Parking Area and Special Parking Area) (Dundee City Council) Designation Order 2004
referred to: SSI 2004/86 Reg.2

100. Regulation of Care (Scotland) Act 2001 (Commencement No 5 and Transitional Provisions) Order 2004
Art.3, amended: SSI 2004/377 Art.2
Art.4, amended: SSI 2004/377 Art.2

104. Pesticides (Maximum Residue Levels in Crops, Food and Feeding Stuffs) (Scotland) Amendment Regulations 2004
Reg.2, revoked (in part): SSI 2004/220 Reg.3
Reg.3, revoked: SSI 2004/220 Reg.3
Sch.2, revoked: SSI 2004/220 Reg.3

NO.

2004–cont.

112. Special Waste Amendment (Scotland) Regulations 2004
Reg.2, amended: SSI 2004/204 Reg.2

114. National Health Service (Primary Medical Services Performers Lists) (Scotland) Regulations 2004
Reg.3, disapplied: SSI 2004/163 Art.88
Reg.6, applied: SSI 2004/38 Reg.6
Reg.7, amended: SSI 2004/216 Reg.2
Reg.7, applied: SSI 2004/38 Reg.6
Reg.10, amended: SSI 2004/216 Reg.2
Reg.11, amended: SSI 2004/216 Reg.2
Reg.14, amended: SSI 2004/216 Reg.2
Sch.1 para.2, amended: SSI 2004/216 Reg.2
Sch.1 para.3, amended: SSI 2004/216 Reg.2

115. National Health Service (General Medical Services Contracts) (Scotland) Regulations 2004
applied: SSI 2004/116 Reg.24
Reg.2, amended: SSI 2004/215 Reg.2
Reg.4, applied: SSI 2004/116 Reg.24
Reg.4, referred to: SSI 2004/116 Reg.24
Reg.5, applied: SSI 2004/116 Reg.3, Reg.24
Reg.5, referred to: SSI 2004/116 Reg.24
Reg.9, applied: SSI 2004/116 Reg.24, SSI 2004/142 Art.5, Art.6, Art.7, Art.8, Art.10, Art.11, Art.13, Art.14
Reg.10, amended: SSI 2004/215 Reg.2
Reg.15, amended: SSI 2004/215 Reg.2
Reg.15, applied: SSI 2004/163 Art.38
Reg.17, amended: SSI 2004/215 Reg.2
Reg.17, applied: SSI 2004/142 Art.17
Reg.18, applied: SSI 2004/142 Art.26
Reg.24, applied: SSI 2004/163 Art.43
Reg.27, applied: SSI 2004/163 Art.26
Reg.29, applied: SSI 2004/142 Art.24
Reg.30, applied: SSI 2004/142 Art.19, Art.20, SSI 2004/163 Art.75
Sch.1 para.2, applied: SSI 2004/163 Art.70
Sch.2, referred to: SSI 2004/142 Art.24
Sch.2 para.3, amended: SSI 2004/215 Reg.2
Sch.2 para.4, amended: SSI 2004/215 Reg.2
Sch.2 para.4, applied: SSI 2004/142 Art.20, SSI 2004/163 Art.74
Sch.2 para.5, applied: SSI 2004/142 Art.20, SSI 2004/163 Art.74
Sch.2 para.6, applied: SSI 2004/163 Art.74
Sch.2 para.6, referred to: SSI 2004/142 Art.24
Sch.3, referred to: SSI 2004/116 Reg.19
Sch.4 para.1, referred to: SSI 2004/116 Reg.22
Sch.4 para.1, varied: SSI 2004/116 Reg.22
Sch.5 Part 1 para.4, applied: SSI 2004/163 Art.14, Art.36
Sch.5 Part 1 para.5, applied: SSI 2004/163 Art.27
Sch.5 Part 1 para.6, applied: SSI 2004/163 Art.28
Sch.5 Part 1 para.11, applied: SSI 2004/163 Art.74

2004–cont.

115. National Health Service (General Medical Services Contracts) (Scotland) Regulations 2004–*cont.*

Sch.5 Part 2 para.14, applied: SSI 2004/116 Reg.24

Sch.5 Part 2 para.15, applied: SSI 2004/163 Art.4

Sch.5 Part 2 para.15, referred to: SSI 2004/ 142 Art.32, SSI 2004/163 Art.3

Sch.5 Part 2 para.16, applied: SSI 2004/163 Art.10, Art.11, Art.37

Sch.5 Part 2 para.17, applied: SSI 2004/163 Art.10

Sch.5 Part 2 para.18, applied: SSI 2004/163 Art.35

Sch.5 Part 2 para.19, applied: SSI 2004/163 Art.5, Art.39

Sch.5 Part 2 para.20, applied: SSI 2004/163 Art.6, Art.35

Sch.5 Part 2 para.23, applied: SSI 2004/163 Art.39

Sch.5 Part 2 para.24, applied: SSI 2004/163 Art.8, Art.39

Sch.5 Part 2 para.24, referred to: SSI 2004/ 163 Art.8

Sch.5 Part 2 para.25, applied: SSI 2004/163 Art.8

Sch.5 Part 2 para.28, referred to: SSI 2004/ 142 Art.24

Sch.5 Part 2 para.29, referred to: SSI 2004/ 142 Art.32

Sch.5 Part 3 para.41, amended: SSI 2004/215 Reg.2

Sch.5 Part 3 para.44, applied: SSI 2001/430 Reg.4, SSI 2004/163 Art.40

Sch.5 Part 4 para.50, applied: SSI 2004/163 Art.16, Art.35

Sch.5 Part 4 para.51, applied: SSI 2004/163 Art.16, Art.35

Sch.5 Part 4 para.52, applied: SSI 2004/163 Art.16, Art.35

Sch.5 Part 4 para.53, applied: SSI 2004/163 Art.35

Sch.5 Part 4 para.57, applied: SSI 2004/163 Art.29

Sch.5 Part 4 para.58, applied: SSI 2004/163 Art.17

Sch.5 Part 4 para.62, amended: SSI 2004/ 162 Reg.4

Sch.5 Part 4 para.62, applied: SSI 2004/163 Art.35

Sch.5 Part 4 para.62, disapplied: SSI 2004/ 163 Art.41

Sch.5 Part 4 para.63, applied: SSI 2004/163 Art.73, Art.74

Sch.5 Part 4 para.63, varied: SSI 2004/142 Art.21, Art.22

Sch.5 Part 4 para.64, applied: SSI 2004/163 Art.74

Sch.5 Part 4 para.65, applied: SSI 2004/163 Art.74

2004–cont.

115. National Health Service (General Medical Services Contracts) (Scotland) Regulations 2004–*cont.*

Sch.5 Part 5 para.66, applied: SSI 2004/163 Art.18, Art.35

Sch.5 Part 5 para.72, applied: SSI 2004/163 Art.23

Sch.5 Part 5 para.73, disapplied: SSI 2004/ 163 Art.44

Sch.5 Part 5 para.74, amended: SSI 2004/ 215 Reg.2

Sch.5 Part 5 para.74, applied: SSI 2004/163 Art.15

Sch.5 Part 5 para.78, applied: SSI 2004/163 Art.35

Sch.5 Part 5 para.79, applied: SSI 2004/163 Art.35

Sch.5 Part 5 para.81, applied: SSI 2004/163 Art.19

Sch.5 Part 6 para.82, applied: SSI 2004/163 Art.22, Art.42

Sch.5 Part 6 para.83, applied: SSI 2004/163 Art.42

Sch.5 Part 6 para.84, applied: SSI 2004/163 Art.42

Sch.5 Part 6 para.85, applied: SSI 2004/163 Art.42

Sch.5 Part 6 para.86, applied: SSI 2004/163 Art.42

Sch.5 Part 6 para.88, applied: SSI 2004/163 Art.42

Sch.5 Part 7 para.91, varied: SSI 2004/142 Art.5, Art.11, Art.13, Art.33

Sch.5 Part 7 para.92, varied: SSI 2004/142 Art.5, Art.11, Art.13, Art.33

Sch.5 Part 8 para.94, applied: SSI 2004/116 Sch.4 para.9

Sch.5 Part 8 para.94, referred to: SSI 2004/ 142 Art.23

Sch.5 Part 8 para.101, amended: SSI 2004/ 215 Reg.2

Sch.5 Part 8 para.101, applied: SSI 2004/116 Sch.1 para.66, SSI 2004/142 Art.12, SSI 2004/163 Art.46

Sch.5 Part 8 para.101, varied: SSI 2004/142 Art.34

Sch.5 Part 8 para.102A, added: SSI 2004/ 162 Reg.4

Sch.5 Part 8 para.103, applied: SSI 2004/163 Art.24, Art.79, Art.80, Art.81

Sch.5 Part 8 para.107, amended: SSI 2004/ 215 Reg.2

Sch.5 Part 9 para.114, amended: SSI 2004/ 215 Reg.2

Sch.5 Part 9 para.114, applied: SSI 2004/114 Sch.1 para.3

Sch.6, applied: SSI 2004/163 Art.74

Sch.6, referred to: SSI 2004/142 Art.23

Sch.6 para.1, varied: SSI 2004/142 Art.21, Art.22

NO.

NO.

2004–cont.

115. National Health Service (General Medical Services Contracts) (Scotland) Regulations 2004–*cont.*

Sch.6 para.2, applied: SSI 2004/163 Art.64, Art.65, Art.66, Art.67, Art.68, Art.69, Art.71, Art.72, Art.73

Sch.6 para.4, applied: SSI 2004/163 Art.67, Art.68, Art.69, Art.71, Art.72

Sch.6 para.4, referred to: SSI 2004/163 Art.67

Sch.6 para.5, applied: SSI 2004/163 Art.70, Art.71, Art.72

Sch.6 para.5, varied: SSI 2004/142 Art.21, Art.22

Sch.8, applied: SSI 2004/163 Art.25

Sch.8 para.18, amended: SSI 2004/215 Reg.2

116. National Health Service (Primary Medical Services Section 17C Agreements) (Scotland) Regulations 2004

applied: SSI 2004/163 Art.50

Reg.2, amended: SSI 2004/217 Reg.2

Reg.8, applied: SSI 2004/163 Art.58

Reg.11, amended: SSI 2004/217 Reg.2

Reg.12, amended: SSI 2004/217 Reg.2

Reg.21, amended: SSI 2004/217 Reg.2

Reg.22, amended: SSI 2004/217 Reg.2

Sch.1 Part 2 para.8, amended: SSI 2004/217 Reg.2

Sch.1 Part 3 para.15, applied: SSI 2001/430 Reg.4

Sch.1 Part 4 para.25, amended: SSI 2004/217 Reg.2

Sch.1 Part 4 para.32, amended: SSI 2004/162 Reg.5

Sch.1 Part 5 para.40, amended: SSI 2004/217 Reg.2

Sch.1 Part 5 para.42, amended: SSI 2004/217 Reg.2

Sch.1 Part 7 para.56, amended: SSI 2004/217 Reg.2

Sch.1 Part 7 para.57, amended: SSI 2004/217 Reg.2

Sch.1 Part 8 para.59, amended: SSI 2004/217 Reg.2

Sch.1 Part 8 para.66, amended: SSI 2004/217 Reg.2

Sch.1 Part 8 para.66, applied: SSI 2004/163 Art.51, Art.57

Sch.1 Part 8 para.66, referred to: SSI 2004/163 Art.51, Art.57

Sch.1 Part 8 para.67A, added: SSI 2004/162 Reg.5

Sch.1 Part 9 para.78, amended: SSI 2004/217 Reg.2

Sch.1 Part 9 para.78, applied: SSI 2004/114 Sch.1 para.3

Sch.2 Part 1 para.1, amended: SSI 2004/217 Reg.2

Sch.2 Part 1 para.4, amended: SSI 2004/217 Reg.2

2004–cont.

116. National Health Service (Primary Medical Services Section 17C Agreements) (Scotland) Regulations 2004–*cont.*

Sch.2 Part 2 para.13, amended: SSI 2004/217 Reg.2

Sch.2 Part 2 para.13, applied: SSI 2004/163 Art.55

Sch.2 Part 2 para.14, applied: SSI 2004/163 Art.55

Sch.2 Part 2 para.23, amended: SSI 2004/217 Reg.2

Sch.2 Part 2 para.28, amended: SSI 2004/217 Reg.2

Sch.2 Part 3 para.31, amended: SSI 2004/217 Reg.2

Sch.5, amended: SSI 2004/217 Reg.2

Sch.6 para.18, amended: SSI 2004/217 Reg.2

Sch.6 para.24, amended: SSI 2004/217 Reg.2

121. Police (Scotland) Amendment Regulations 2004

revoked: SSI 2004/257 Sch.4

125. Food Protection (Emergency Prohibitions) (Amnesic Shellfish Poisoning) (West Coast) (No.6) (Scotland) Order 2003 Partial Revocation Order 2004

revoked: SSI 2004/177 Art.2

137. Sexual Offences Act 2003 (Prescribed Police Stations) (Scotland) Regulations 2004

Sch.1, amended: SSI 2004/370 Reg.2

139. Food Protection (Emergency Prohibitions) (Amnesic Shellfish Poisoning) (West Coast) (No.11) (Scotland) Order 2003 Partial Revocation Order 2004

revoked: SSI 2004/181 Art.2

142. General Medical Services (Transitional and Other Ancillary Provisions) (Scotland) Order 2004

Part 2, applied: SSI 2004/163 Art.75

Art.3, amended: SSI 2004/223 Art.2

Art.3, applied: SSI 2004/163 Art.2

Art.4, amended: SSI 2004/223 Art.2

Art.4, applied: SSI 2004/163 Art.2

Art.5, amended: SSI 2004/223 Art.2

Art.13, applied: SSI 2004/163 Art.2, Art.95, Art.96

Art.15, applied: SSI 2004/163 Art.64, Art.65, Art.66, Art.70

Art.20, amended: SSI 2004/223 Art.2

Art.24, applied: SSI 2004/163 Art.74

Art.25, applied: SSI 2004/163 Art.74

143. Organic Aid (Scotland) Regulations 2004

applied: SSI 2004/381 Reg.4

Reg.4, amended: SSI 2004/174 Reg.2

Reg.20, applied: SSI 2000/347 Reg.4, SSI 2004/381 Reg.4

NO.

NO.

2004–cont.

143. **Organic Aid (Scotland) Regulations 2004**–*cont.*

Reg.25, amended: SSI 2004/381 Reg.14

152. **Act of Sederunt (Fees of Solicitors and Witnesses in the Sheriff Court) (Amendment) 2004**

Art.2, amended: SSI 2004/196 Art.2

163. **General Medical Services and Section 17C Agreements (Transitional and other Ancillary Provisions) (Scotland) Order 2004**

Art.2, amended: SSI 2004/223 Art.3

Art.4, amended: SSI 2004/223 Art.3

Art.6, amended: SSI 2004/223 Art.3

Art.17, amended: SSI 2004/223 Art.3

Art.18, amended: SSI 2004/223 Art.3

Art.20, amended: SSI 2004/223 Art.3

Art.24, amended: SSI 2004/223 Art.3

Art.51, amended: SSI 2004/223 Art.3

Art.52, amended: SSI 2004/223 Art.3

Art.65, amended: SSI 2004/223 Art.3

Art.70, amended: SSI 2004/223 Art.3

Art.101, amended: SSI 2004/372 Art.2

220. **Pesticides (Maximum Residue Levels in Crops, Food and Feeding Stuffs) (Scotland) Amendment (No.2) Regulations 2004**

Reg.2, revoked (in part): SSI 2004/399 Reg.3

Sch.2, revoked: SSI 2004/399 Reg.3

221. **Food Protection (Emergency Prohibitions) (Amnesic Shellfish Poisoning) (Orkney) (Scotland) Order 2004**

revoked: SSI 2004/315 Art.2

246. **Victim Statements (Prescribed Offences) (Scotland) Amendment Order 2004**

revoked: SSI 2004/287 Art.2

257. **Police (Scotland) Regulations 2004**

applied: SI 1996/1642 Reg.22

Reg.8, applied: SI 1996/1642 Sch.1 para.8, SI 1999/1074 Sch.1 para.8

Sch.1, applied: SI 1996/1642 Sch.1 para.8, SI 1999/1074 Sch.1 para.8

262. **Advice and Assistance (Scotland) Amendment (No.2) Regulations 2004**

Reg.2, substituted: SSI 2004/305 Reg.2

273. **Education Maintenance Allowances (Scotland) Regulations 2004**

Reg.2, amended: SSI 2004/469 Reg.9

Sch.1 para.2, amended: SSI 2004/469 Reg.9

Sch.1 para.3, amended: SSI 2004/469 Reg.9

Sch.1 para.4, amended: SSI 2004/469 Reg.9

Sch.1 para.6, amended: SSI 2004/301 Reg.2

Sch.2 para.2, amended: SSI 2004/469 Reg.9

280. **Beef Carcase (Classification) (Scotland) Regulations 2004**

Reg.9, applied: 1967 c.22 Sch.1 para.10A

2004–cont.

289. **Environmental Protection (Restriction on Use of Lead Shot) (Scotland) Regulations 2004**

revoked: SSI 2004/358 Reg.7

292. **National Health Service (Vocational Training for General Dental Practice) (Scotland) Regulations 2004**

Reg.3, applied: SI 1996/177 Reg.5

298. **Food Protection (Emergency Prohibitions) (Diarrhetic Shellfish Poisoning) (East Coast) (Scotland) Order 2004**

revoked: SSI 2004/349 Art.2

319. **Food Protection (Emergency Prohibitions) (Amnesic Shellfish Poisoning) (West Coast) (No.4) (Scotland) Order 2004**

revoked: SSI 2004/345 Art.2

340. **Food Protection (Emergency Prohibitions) (Amnesic Shellfish Poisoning) (Irish Sea) (Scotland) Order 2004**

revoked: SSI 2004/446 Art.2

360. **International Criminal Court (Enforcement of Fines, Forfeiture and Reparation Orders) (Scotland) Regulations 2004**

revoked: SSI 2004/437 Reg.2

378. **Food Protection (Emergency Prohibitions) (Diarrhetic Shellfish Poisoning) (East Coast) (No.2) (Scotland) Order 2004**

revoked: SSI 2004/463 Art.2

381. **Agricultural Subsidies (Appeals) (Scotland) Regulations 2004**

applied: SSI 2001/50 Reg.20, SSI 2001/300 Reg.18, SSI 2003/129 Reg.24

Reg.4, amended: SSI 2004/143 Reg.25

387. **Mental Health (Advance Statements) (Prescribed Class of Persons) (Scotland) Regulations 2004**

revoked: SSI 2004/429 Reg.3

388. **Mental Health (Patient Representation) (Prescribed Persons) (Scotland) Regulations 2004**

revoked: SSI 2004/430 Reg.3

396. **Scottish Network 1 Tourist Board Scheme Order 2004**

Sch.1 Part IV para.11, amended: SSI 2004/464 Art.2

397. **Scottish Network 2 Tourist Board Scheme Order 2004**

Art.3, amended: SSI 2004/465 Art.2

Sch.1 Part II para.3, amended: SSI 2004/465 Art.2

Sch.1 Part IV para.11, amended: SSI 2004/465 Art.2

401. **Debt Arrangement and Attachment (Scotland) Act 2002 (Commencement) Order 2004**

revoked: SSI 2004/416 Art.3

NO.

2004–cont.

413. Miscellaneous Food Additives Amendment (Scotland) Regulations 2004

Reg.3, referred to: SI 1995/3187 Reg.11

468. Debt Arrangement Scheme (Scotland) Regulations 2004

Reg.2, applied: 1985 c.66 s.14, s.15

NO.

2004–cont.

472. Food Labelling Amendment (No.2) (Scotland) Regulations 2004

applied: SI 1996/1499 Reg.50

NORTHERN IRELAND LEGISLATION PASSED BY ORDER IN COUNCIL OR STATUTORY RULE

NO.

1921

1825. Celluloid, etc Factories, and Workshops Regulations 1921

revoked: SR 2003/152 Sch.8 Part I

1928

82. Manufacture of Cinematograph Film Regulations 1928

revoked: SR 2003/152 Sch.8 Part I

1930

11. Petroleum-spirit (Motor Vehicles, c.) Regulations 1930

Reg.2, substituted: SR 2003/152 Sch.7 para.3

Reg.7, amended: SR 2003/152 Sch.7 para.3

Reg.15A, amended: SR 2003/152 Sch.7 para.3

20. Petroleum (Carbide of Clacium) Order (Northern Ireland) 1930

revoked: SR 2003/152 Sch.8 Part I

1949

79. Petroleum (Carbide of Calcium) Order (Northern Ireland) 1949

revoked: SR 2003/152 Sch.8 Part I

1950

117. Dry Cleaning Special Regulations (Northern Ireland) 1950

revoked: SR 2003/152 Sch.8 Part I

1960

181. National Insurance (Non-Participation Assurance of Equivalent Pension Benefits) Regulations (Northern Ireland) 1960

Reg.2, applied: SR 2002/353 Reg.15

NO.

1963

79. Motor Vehicles (International Circulation) (Registration and Licensing) Regulations Northern Ireland 1963

Reg.5, referred to: SR 2003/303 Reg.6

199. Coroners (Practice and Procedure) Rules (Northern Ireland) 1963

r.9, substituted: SR 2002/37 r.2

1965

246. Contracts of Employment and Redundancy Payments (Pensions) Regulations (Northern Ireland) 1965

applied: SR 2003/61 Reg.12

1969

11. Weights and Measures (Prescribed Stamp) Regulations (Northern Ireland) 1969

Reg.2, amended: SR 2002/36 Reg.2

Sch.1, amended: SR 2002/36 Reg.2

Sch.2, amended: SR 2002/36 Reg.2

201. Livestock Marketing Commission (Levy) Regulations (Northern Ireland) 1969

revoked: SR 2003/21 Reg.7, SR 2003/104 Reg.7

337. Asbestos Regulations (Northern Ireland) 1969

Reg.13, applied: SR 2003/33 Reg.16

1971

136. Warrenpoint Harbour Authority Order (Northern Ireland) 1971

referred to: SR 2002/42 Art.1

Art.3, amended: SR 2002/42 Art.9

Art.3, revoked (in part): SR 2002/42 Sch.2

Art.7, revoked (in part): SR 2002/42 Sch.2

Art.9, revoked (in part): SR 2002/42 Sch.2

Sch.1, substituted: SR 2002/42 Sch.1

372. Shipbuilding and Ship-repairing Regulations (Northern Ireland) 1971

referred to: SI 2003/2002 Reg.12

NO.

1971–cont.

372. Shipbuilding and Ship-repairing Regulations (Northern Ireland) 1971–cont.

Reg.47, revoked: SR 2003/152 Sch.8 Part I
Reg.48, revoked: SR 2003/152 Sch.8 Part I
Reg.49, revoked: SR 2003/152 Sch.8 Part I
Reg.50, revoked: SR 2003/152 Sch.8 Part I
Reg.51, revoked: SR 2003/152 Sch.8 Part I
Reg.53, revoked: SR 2003/152 Sch.8 Part I
Reg.54, revoked: SR 2003/152 Sch.8 Part I
Reg.55, revoked: SR 2003/152 Sch.8 Part I
Reg.56, revoked: SR 2003/152 Sch.8 Part I
Reg.57, revoked: SR 2003/152 Sch.8 Part I
Reg.58, revoked: SR 2003/152 Sch.8 Part I
Reg.59, revoked: SR 2003/152 Sch.8 Part I
Reg.60, revoked: SR 2003/152 Sch.8 Part I
Reg.61, revoked: SR 2003/152 Sch.8 Part I
Reg.62, revoked: SR 2003/152 Sch.8 Part I
Reg.63, revoked: SR 2003/152 Sch.8 Part I
Reg.64, revoked: SR 2003/152 Sch.8 Part I
Reg.65, revoked: SR 2003/152 Sch.8 Part I

1972

351. European Communities (Agriculture) Order (Northern Ireland) 1972

Art.4, revoked: SI 2004/1109 Art.7

1973

4. Warrenpoint Harbour Authority Order (Northern Ireland) 1973

referred to: SR 2002/42 Art.1

208. Forest Reproductive Material Regulations (Northern Ireland) 1973

applied: SR 2002/404 Reg.7, Reg.9
referred to: SR 2002/404 Reg.7
Reg.5, applied: SR 2002/404 Reg.7

313. Local Government (Modification and Repeal of Transferred Provisions relating to Harbours) Order (Northern Ireland) 1973

Art.5, revoked (in part): SR 2002/395 Sch.2 Part II
Sch.3, applied: SR 2003/73 Art.3

366. Local Government (Travelling and Subsistence Allowances to Councillors) (No.2) Regulations (Northern Ireland) 1973

Reg.7, substituted: SR 2003/125 Reg.4
Sch.1, substituted: SR 2003/125 Reg.2
Sch.2, substituted: SR 2003/125 Sch.1

490. Road Vehicles (Registration and Licensing) Regulations (Northern Ireland) 1973

Reg.18, applied: SR 2003/303 Sch.2 para.1, Sch.2 para.2, Sch.2 para.3, Sch.2 para.4, Sch.2 para.5, Sch.2 para.6, Sch.2 para.7
Reg.19, applied: SR 2003/303 Sch.2 para.1, Sch.2 para.2, Sch.2 para.3, Sch.2 para.4, Sch.2 para.5, Sch.2 para.6, Sch.2 para.7

NO.

1973–cont.

490. Road Vehicles (Registration and Licensing) Regulations (Northern Ireland) 1973–cont.

Reg.20, applied: SR 2003/303 Sch.2 para.1, Sch.2 para.2, Sch.2 para.3, Sch.2 para.4, Sch.2 para.5, Sch.2 para.6, Sch.2 para.7
Reg.21, applied: SR 2003/303 Sch.2 para.1, Sch.2 para.2, Sch.2 para.3, Sch.2 para.4, Sch.2 para.5, Sch.2 para.6, Sch.2 para.7

528. Petroleum (Liquid Methane) Order (Northern Ireland) 1973

Sch.1, amended: SR 2003/152 Sch.7 para.4

1974

215. Warrenpoint Harbour Authority Order (Northern Ireland) 1974

referred to: SR 2002/42 Art.1

1975

48. National Insurance (Non-Participation Transitional Provisions) (Nothern Ireland) Regulations 1975

Reg.2, applied: SR 2002/353 Reg.15
Reg.10, applied: SR 2002/353 Reg.15

98. Social Security (Guardian's Allowances) Regulations (Northern Ireland) 1975

revoked: SI 2003/495 Sch.1 Part 2
Reg.5, amended: SR 2002/87 Reg.2

109. Social Security (Hospital In-Patients) Regulations (Northern Ireland) 1975

applied: SR 2003/28 Reg.15, Sch.3 para.2
Reg.2, amended: SR 2002/106 Reg.2, SR 2003/261 Reg.2
Reg.2, applied: SI 2004/1987 Art.6
Reg.4, substituted: SR 2003/261 Reg.2
Reg.4A, amended: SR 2003/261 Reg.2
Reg.5, amended: SR 2002/106 Reg.2
Reg.5, revoked: SR 2003/261 Reg.2
Reg.6, amended: SR 2003/261 Reg.2
Reg.9, amended: SR 2003/261 Reg.2
Reg.11, amended: SR 2003/261 Reg.2
Reg.17, amended: SR 2003/261 Reg.2
Reg.17, revoked (in part): SR 2003/261 Reg.2

113. Social Security (Credits) Regulations (Northern Ireland) 1975

Reg.2, amended: SR 2002/80 Reg.2, SR 2003/195 Sch.4 para.1
Reg.7A, amended: SR 2002/80 Reg.2, SR 2002/323 Sch.1 para.1
Reg.7B, amended: SR 2003/195 Sch.4 para.1
Reg.7C, amended: SR 2003/195 Sch.4 para.1
Reg.7C, revoked (in part): SR 2003/195 Sch.4 para.1
Reg.8A, amended: SR 2002/80 Reg.2
Reg.8B, amended: SR 2003/151 Reg.2
Reg.9C, substituted: SR 2003/151 Reg.2

NO.

1975–cont.

**256. Highly Flammable Liquids and Lique-
fied Petroleum Gases Regulations
(Northern Ireland)1975**
Reg.6, applied: SR 2002/301 Reg.8

1976

**99. Social Security (Invalid Care Allow-
ance) Regulations (Northern Ireland)
1976**
Reg.2A(a), revoked (in part): SR 2003/213
Reg.2

**165. Specified Sugar Products Regulations
(Northern Ireland) 1976**
applied: SR 2003/301 Reg.11
revoked: SR 2003/301 Reg.10

**183. Cocoa and Chocolate Products Regu-
lations (Northern Ireland) 1976**
referred to: SR 2003/313 Reg.11, Reg.12
revoked: SR 2003/313 Reg.11

**184. Livestock Marketing Commission
(Maximum Levy) Regulations (Northern Ireland) 1976**
revoked: SR 2003/20 Reg.3

**223. Child Benefit and Social Security
(Fixing and Adjustment of Rates)
Regulations (Northern Ireland) 1976**
Reg.2, amended: SI 2004/943 Art.3, SR
2002/99 Art.13, SR 2003/155 Art.14
Reg.2, applied: SR 2002/99 Art.13, SR
2003/155 Art.14

**389. Londonderry Port and Harbour
Commissioners Acts (Amendment)
Order (Northern Ireland) 1976**
Sch.1, substituted: SR 2002/41 Sch.1

1977

**73. Social Security (Child Benefit Conse-
quential) Regulations (Northern
Ireland) 1977**
Reg.9, revoked: SI 2003/495 Sch.1 Part 2

**74. Social Security Benefit (Dependency)
Regulations (Northern Ireland) 1977**
Reg.1, amended: SR 2002/323 Sch.1 para.1
Reg.3, amended: SR 2003/213 Reg.2
Reg.4A, amended: SR 2003/213 Reg.2
Reg.4B, revoked (in part): SR 2003/213
Reg.2
Reg.12, amended: SR 2002/323 Sch.1 para.1
Sch.2, amended: SR 2002/108 Reg.4, SR
2002/323 Sch.1 para.1, SR 2003/156
Reg.4

**194. Forest Reproductive Material Regula-
tions (Northern Ireland) 1977**
applied: SR 2002/404 Reg.7, Reg.9, Reg.31
referred to: SR 2002/404 Reg.7
revoked: SR 2002/404 Reg.34

**196. Condensed Milk and Dried Milk Regu-
lations (Northern Ireland) 1977**
applied: SR 2003/300 Reg.11
revoked: SR 2003/300 Reg.10

NO.

1977–cont.

**316. Social Security (Hospital In-Patients)
(Amendment) Regulations (Northern
Ireland) 1977**
Reg.5, revoked (in part): SR 2003/261 Sch.1

**327. Road Transport (Qualifications of
Operators) Regulations (Northern
Ireland) 1977**
Reg.5, revoked: SR 2003/217 Reg.8

1978

**105. Social Security (Graduated Retire-
ment Benefit) (No.2) Regulations
(Northern Ireland) 1978**
Sch.2, varied: SR 2002/99 Art.11, SR 2003/
155 Art.12

**114. Social Security Benefit (Persons
Abroad) Regulations (Northern
Ireland) 1978**
Reg.5, applied: SI 2004/960 Reg.3, SR
2002/108 Reg.3, SR 2003/156 Reg.3
Reg.12, amended: SR 2002/323 Sch.1 para.1

**349. Control of Noise (Code of Practice
for Construction Sites) Order (Northern Ireland) 1978**
revoked: SR 2002/303 Art.3

**376. Magistrates Courts (Blood Tests)
Rules (Northern Ireland) 1978**
r.2, amended: SR 2002/163 r.4, r.5
r.3, revoked: SR 2002/163 r.6
r.9, amended: SR 2002/163 r.7
r.11, amended: SR 2002/163 r.8
r.12, amended: SR 2002/163 r.9
Sch.1, amended: SR 2002/163 r.11, r.12
Sch.1, revoked: SR 2002/163 r.10

**378. County Court (Blood Tests) Rules
(Northern Ireland) 1978**
amended: SR 2002/240 r.2
Sch.1, amended: SR 2002/240 r.3

**379. Blood Tests (Evidence of Paternity)
Regulations (Northern Ireland) 1978**
Reg.2, amended: SR 2002/150 Reg.4, Reg.5
Reg.6, amended: SR 2002/150 Reg.6
Reg.7, amended: SR 2002/150 Reg.7
Reg.7, revoked (in part): SR 2002/150 Reg.7
Reg.8, amended: SR 2002/150 Reg.8
Reg.9, amended: SR 2002/150 Reg.9
Reg.9A, added: SR 2002/150 Reg.10
Reg.10, amended: SR 2002/150 Reg.11
Sch.1, added: SR 2002/150 Reg.13
Sch.1, amended: SR 2002/150 Reg.12,
Reg.13, Reg.14

**401. Social Security (Categorisation of
Earners) Regulations (Northern
Ireland) 1978**
applied: SR 2002/378 Reg.32
Reg.1, amended: SI 2003/2421 Reg.3
Reg.2, amended: SI 2004/770 Reg.34
Reg.5, substituted: SI 2003/2421 Reg.4
Sch.1, amended: SI 2003/733 Reg.3, SI
2004/770 Reg.34

NO.

1978–cont.

401. Social Security (Categorisation of Earners) Regulations (Northern Ireland) 1978–*cont.*
Sch.3, amended: SI 2003/733 Reg.4, SI 2003/2421 Reg.5, SI 2004/770 Reg.34

1979

5. Child Benefit (General) Regulations (Northern Ireland) 1979
revoked: SI 2003/493 Sch.2 Part 2

32. Belfast Harbour Acts (Amendment) Order (Northern Ireland) 1979
Sch.1, substituted: SR 2002/40 Sch.1

90. Crown Court Rules (Northern Ireland) 1979
Part XI, added: SR 2003/71 Sch.1
r.34, amended: SR 2003/71 r.3
r.36, substituted: SR 2003/71 r.3
r.36A, added: SR 2003/71 r.3

167. Fire Services (Appointments and Promotion) Regulations (Northern Ireland) 1979
Reg.4, amended: SR 2002/283 Reg.2, SR 2003/207 Reg.2

193. Social Security (Earnings Factor) Regulations (Northern Ireland) 1979
Sch.1, amended: SR 2003/161 Reg.2

195. Rehabilitation of Offenders (Exceptions) Order (Northern Ireland) 1979
Art.2, amended: SR 2003/355 Art.3
Sch.1, added: SR 2003/355 Art.4
Sch.1, amended: SR 2003/355 Art.4
Sch.3, added: SR 2003/355 Art.5

196. Dunrod Circuit (Admission Charges) Regulations (Northern Ireland) 1979
revoked: SR 2002/167 Reg.3

242. Social Security (Overlapping Benefirs) Regulations (Northern Ireland) 1979
applied: SR 2003/28 Reg.15
Reg.2, amended: SR 2003/213 Reg.2
Reg.4, amended: SR 2002/323 Sch.1 para.1
Reg.8, amended: SR 2003/44 Reg.2
Reg.8, revoked (in part): SR 2003/44 Reg.2
Reg.12, amended: SR 2002/323 Sch.1 para.1
Sch.1, amended: SR 2002/323 Sch.1 para.1

243. Social Security (Widow's Benefit and Retirement Pensions) Regulations (Northern Ireland) 1979
Reg.1A, revoked (in part): SR 2003/213 Reg.2
Reg.6, amended: SR 2003/213 Reg.2
Reg.6, revoked (in part): SR 2003/213 Reg.2
Reg.17, amended: SR 2002/323 Sch.1 para.1

261. Child Benefit (General) (Amendment) Regulations (Northern Ireland) 1979
revoked: SI 2003/493 Sch.2 Part 2

361. Child Benefit (General) (Amendment) Regulations (Northern Ireland) 1979
revoked: SI 2003/493 Sch.2 Part 2

NO.

1979–cont.

407. Lead in Food Regulations (Northern Ireland) 1979
revoked: SR 2002/219 Sch.1

1980

346. Rules of the Supreme Court (Northern Ireland) 1980
applied: SR 2003/358 r.2
referred to: SR 2002/15 r.1
Sch.1, added: SR 2002/15 r.4, SR 2003/54 Sch.1, Sch.2
Sch.1, amended: SR 2002/15 r.3, r.4, SR 2002/202 r.4, r.5, r.7, Sch.2, SR 2003/54 Sch.3
Sch.1, applied: SR 2003/28 Sch.5 para.16
Sch.1, revoked (in part): SR 2002/15 r.3, SR 2002/202 r.6, r.6, SR 2003/263 r.2
Sch.1, substituted: SR 2002/15 r.3, SR 2002/202 r.4, Sch.1
Sch.1, varied: SR 2003/358 r.10

427. Child Benefit (General) (Amendment No 2) Regulations (Northern Ireland) 1980
revoked: SI 2003/493 Sch.2 Part 2

1981

2. Road Transport (Qualifications of Operators) (Amendment) Regulations (Northern Ireland) 1981
Reg.3, revoked (in part): SR 2003/217 Reg.8
Reg.4, amended: SR 2003/217 Reg.7

96. Local Government (Superannuation) Regulations (Northern Ireland) 1981
applied: SR 2003/61 Reg.2

179. Legal Aid (Remuneration of Solicitors and Counsel in County Court Proceedings) Order (Northern Ireland) 1981
Art.2, amended: SR 2003/43 Art.3, Art.4

189. Legal Aid (Assessment of Resources) Regulations (Northern Ireland) 1981
Reg.1, referred to: SR 2002/60 Reg.2, SR 2003/88 Reg.2

225. County Court Rules (Northern Ireland) 1981
amended: SR 2002/255 r.3
applied: SR 2002/255 r.14, Sch.2
referred to: SR 2002/412 r.1, SR 2003/272 r.1
Part 1, amended: SR 2002/255 r.4
Part 3, applied: SR 2003/28 Sch.5 para.16
Part 6A, amended: SR 2002/255 r.5
Part 25, revoked (in part): SR 2002/255 r.6
Part 26, added: SR 2002/255 Sch.2
Part 26, amended: SR 2002/255 Sch.2
Part 26, substituted: SR 2002/255 Sch.1, SR 2003/272 r.2
Part 32, amended: SR 2003/272 r.3
Part 33, amended: SR 2002/255 r.8
Part 44, applied: SR 2003/28 Sch.5 para.16
Part 50, amended: SR 2003/272 r.4

NO.

1981–cont.

225. County Court Rules (Northern Ireland) 1981–cont.

Part 53, amended: SR 2002/255 r.9

Part 53, revoked (in part): SR 2002/255 r.9, r.9

Part 55, added: SR 2002/412 r.2

Part 55, amended: SR 2002/412 r.2

Part 55, revoked (in part): SR 2002/412 r.2

Part 55, substituted: SR 2002/255 r.10

Part 58, added: SR 2002/255 r.11

Part 58, amended: SR 2002/255 r.11

Part 58, substituted: SR 2002/255 r.11

Appendix 2., substituted: SR 2002/412 Sch.1, SR 2003/272 r.5

231. Pensions Appeals Tribunals (Northern Ireland) Rules 1981

r.4, amended: SR 2003/316 r.2

r.24, amended: SR 2003/316 r.3

366. Legal Advice and Assistance Regulations (Northern Ireland) 1981

Reg.3, amended: SR 2003/94 Reg.3

Reg.5, amended: SR 2003/94 Reg.3

Reg.6, amended: SR 2003/94 Reg.3

Reg.7, amended: SR 2003/94 Reg.3

Reg.17, amended: SR 2002/212 Reg.2

Sch.2, amended: SR 2002/62 Reg.3

Sch.2, substituted: SR 2003/90 Reg.3

Sch.4, amended: SR 2003/94 Reg.4

1982

114. Child Benefit (General) (Amendment) Regulations (Northern Ireland) 1982

revoked: SI 2003/493 Sch.2 Part 2

263. Statutory Sick Pay (General) Regulations (Northern Ireland) 1982

Reg.3, amended: SR 2002/354 Reg.4

Reg.17, amended: SR 2002/359 Reg.4

311. Specified Sugar Products Regulations (Northern Ireland) 1982

revoked: SR 2003/301 Reg.10

349. Cocoa and Chocolate Products (Amendment) Regulations (Northern Ireland) 1982

referred to: SR 2003/313 Reg.11

revoked: SR 2003/313 Reg.11

350. Legal Aid (Remuneration of Solicitors and Counsel in County Court Proceedings) (Amendment) Order (Northern Ireland) 1982

revoked: SR 2003/43 Art.2

1983

2. M1-M2 Link (Belfast) Order (Northern Ireland) 1983

Art.6, amended: SR 2003/149 Art.7

4. Child Benefit (General) (Amendment) Regulations (Northern Ireland) 1983

revoked: SI 2003/493 Sch.2 Part 2

NO.

1983–cont.

26. Condensed Milk and Dried Milk (Amendment) Regulations (Northern Ireland) 1983

revoked: SR 2003/300 Reg.10

43. Petroleum Spirit (Plastic Containers) Regulations (Northern Ireland) 1983

Reg.7, amended: SR 2003/152 Sch.7 para.5

101. Workmen's Compensation (Supplementation) Regulations (Northern Ireland) 1983

applied: SR 2003/164 Reg.6

referred to: SR 2003/164 Reg.5

Reg.5, amended: SR 2002/114 Reg.2, SR 2003/164 Reg.2

Reg.5, applied: SR 2003/164 Reg.3

Reg.7, applied: SR 2002/114 Reg.4, SR 2003/164 Reg.4

Sch.1, referred to: SR 2002/114 Reg.5, SR 2003/164 Reg.3, Reg.5

Sch.1, substituted: SR 2002/114 Sch.1, SR 2003/164 Sch.1

150. Quarries (Northern Ireland) Order 1983

Art.2, applied: SR 2003/152 Reg.3

Sch.1, revoked: SI 2004/703 Sch.4

1984

78. Child Benefit (General) (Amendment) Regulations (Northern Ireland) 1984

revoked: SI 2003/493 Sch.2 Part 2

92. Social Security (General Benefit) Regulations (Northern Ireland) 1984

Reg.14, amended: SR 2002/276 Reg.2

117. Measuring Equipment (Liquid Fuel by Road Tanker) Regulations (Northern Ireland) 1984

Reg.11A, amended: SR 2002/71 Sch.1 para.1

Reg.16A, amended: SR 2002/71 Sch.1 para.1

Reg.65, referred to: SR 2002/308 Sch.1 Part 1

Reg.66, referred to: SR 2002/308 Sch.1 Part 1

188. Measuring Equipment (Intoxicating Liquor) Regulations (Northern Ireland) 1984

Reg.7A, amended: SR 2002/71 Sch.1 para.2

205. Asbestos (Licensing) Regulations (Northern Ireland) 1984

applied: SR 2003/33 Reg.8

Reg.5, amended: SR 2003/33 Reg.27

225. Magistrates Courts Rules (Northern Ireland) 1984

applied: SR 2002/158 r.4, SR 2003/17 r.14, SR 2003/122 r.6

referred to: SR 2002/12 r.16

r.11, applied: SR 2002/158 r.16

r.13, applied: SR 2002/158 r.16

244. Child Benefit (General) (Amendment No 2) Regulations (Northern Ireland) 1984

revoked: SI 2003/493 Sch.2 Part 2

NO.

1984–cont.

317. Social Security (Severe Disablement Allowance) Regulations (Northern Ireland) 1984

Reg.2A, revoked (in part): SR 2003/213
Reg.2

Sch.2, amended: SI 2003/493 Sch.2 Part 2

1985

123. Public Service Vehicles Regulations (Northern Ireland) 1985

Reg.6, amended: SR 2003/40 Reg.2

Sch.7, substituted: SR 2002/49 Reg.2, SR 2003/99 Reg.2

124. Child Benefit (Claims and Payments) Regulations (Northern Ireland) 1985

Reg.7, referred to: SI 2003/492 Reg.35

161. Landing of Carcases and Animal Products Order (Northern Ireland) 1985

disapplied: SR 2002/340 Reg.61

163. Lead in Food (Amendment) Regulations (Northern Ireland) 1985

revoked: SR 2002/219 Sch.1

227. Social Security (Guardian's Allowances) (Amendment) Regulations (Northern Ireland) 1985

revoked: SI 2003/495 Sch.1 Part 2

319. Weighing Equipment (Beltweighers) Regulations (Northern Ireland) 1985

Reg.13A, amended: SR 2002/71 Sch.1 para.3

1986

7. Business Names (Northern Ireland) Order 1986

applied: SI 2003/1593 Sch.1 Part II

52. Misuse of Drugs (Northern Ireland) Regulations 1986

revoked: SR 2002/1 Sch.7

Reg.15, applied: SR 2002/1 Reg.28

Reg.23, applied: SR 2002/1 Reg.28

Reg.24, applied: SR 2002/1 Reg.28

163. Health and Personal Social Service (General Ophthalmic Services) Regulations (Northern Ireland) 1986

Reg.2, amended: SR 2003/176 Reg.8

Reg.15, amended: SR 2002/85 Reg.6, SR 2003/176 Reg.9

Reg.15, applied: SR 2003/176 Reg.10

Reg.15, referred to: SR 2003/176 Reg.10

Reg.15, revoked (in part): SR 2003/176 Reg.9

Sch.1, amended: SR 2003/74 Reg.2

179. Social Security (Industrial Injuries) (Prescribed Diseases) Regulations (Northern Ireland) 1986

Reg.4, amended: SR 2003/63 Reg.2

Reg.7, amended: SR 2003/63 Reg.2

Reg.7, applied: SR 2003/63 Reg.3

Reg.8, amended: SR 2003/63 Reg.2

Reg.18, amended: SR 2002/237 Reg.2

Reg.18A, added: SR 2002/237 Reg.2

NO.

1986–cont.

179. Social Security (Industrial Injuries) (Prescribed Diseases) Regulations (Northern Ireland) 1986–*cont.*

Sch.1, amended: SR 2003/63 Reg.2

264. Companies (Tables A to F) Regulations (Northern Ireland) 1986

referred to: SR 2003/3 Art.29

Sch.1, amended: SR 2003/3 Sch.1 para.1, Sch.1 para.2, Sch.1 para.3, Sch.1 para.4, Sch.1 para.5, Sch.1 para.7, Sch.1 para.8

Sch.1, substituted: SR 2003/3 Sch.1 para.6

308. Measuring Equipment (Measures of Length) Regulations (Northern Ireland) 1986

Reg.17A, amended: SR 2002/71 Sch.1 para.4

311. Weighing Equipment (Filling and Discontinuous Totalising Automatic Weighing Machines) Regulations (Northern Ireland) 1986

Reg.12A, amended: SR 2002/71 Sch.1 para.5

359. Magistrates Courts (Civil Jurisdiction and Judgments Act 1982) Rules (Northern Ireland) 1986

r.3, amended: SR 2002/159 r.3

r.4, amended: SR 2002/159 r.4

r.5, amended: SR 2002/159 r.5

r.7, amended: SR 2002/159 r.6

r.8, amended: SR 2002/159 r.7

r.9, amended: SR 2002/159 r.7

r.10, amended: SR 2002/159 r.8

r.11, amended: SR 2002/159 r.9

r.12, amended: SR 2002/159 r.10

r.13, amended: SR 2002/159 r.11

r.14, amended: SR 2002/159 r.12

1987

8. Gaming (Bingo) Regulations (Northern Ireland) 1987

revoked: SR 2003/233 Reg.4

30. Statutory Maternity Pay (General) Regulations (Northern Ireland) 1987

Reg.2, amended: SR 2002/354 Reg.2

Reg.2, revoked (in part): SR 2002/354 Reg.2

Reg.6, amended: SR 2002/99 Art.10

Reg.6, applied: SR 2003/155 Art.10

Reg.6, substituted: SR 2002/354 Reg.2

Reg.11, amended: SR 2002/359 Reg.2

Reg.20, amended: SR 2002/359 Reg.2

Reg.21A, revoked: SR 2002/359 Reg.6

Reg.23, amended: SR 2002/354 Reg.2

Reg.25A, amended: SR 2002/354 Reg.2

Reg.28, amended: SR 2002/354 Reg.2

33. Dry Cleaning (Metrication) Regulations (Northern Ireland) 1987

revoked: SR 2003/152 Sch.8 Part I

NO.

38. **Food (Revision of Penalties and Mode of Trial) Regulations (Northern Ireland) 1987**
Sch.1, amended: SR 2002/219 Sch.1, SR 2003/300 Reg.10, SR 2003/301 Reg.10, SR 2003/313 Reg.11

65. **Condensed Milk and Dried Milk (Amendment) Regulations (Northern Ireland) 1987**
revoked: SR 2003/300 Reg.10

68. **Misuse of Drugs (Amendment) Regulations (Northern Ireland) 1987**
revoked: SR 2002/1 Sch.7

130. **Child Benefit (General) (Amendment) Regulations 1987**
revoked: SI 2003/493 Sch.2 Part 2

150. **Social Fund (Maternity and Funeral Expenses) (General) Regulations (Northern Ireland) 1987**
referred to: SR 2002/14 Reg.3
Reg.2, amended: SR 2003/195 Sch.4 para.2
Reg.3, referred to: SR 2002/14 Reg.3
Reg.4, amended: SR 2002/14 Reg.2, SR 2003/191 Reg.25, SR 2003/195 Sch.4 para.2
Reg.4, varied: SR 2002/14 Reg.3
Reg.5, amended: SR 2003/195 Sch.4 para.2
Reg.6, amended: SR 2002/284 Reg.3, SR 2003/191 Reg.25, SR 2003/195 Sch.4 para.2
Reg.6A, amended: SR 2003/117 Reg.2, SR 2003/264 Reg.2, SR 2003/308 Reg.2

170. **Social Security (Maternity Allowance) Regulations (Northern Ireland) 1987**
Reg.3, amended: SR 2002/354 Reg.5
Reg.3, revoked (in part): SR 2002/354 Reg.5

286. **Pension Schemes (Voluntary Contributions Requirements and Voluntary and Compulsory Membership) Regulations (Northern Ireland) 1987**
Reg.2, referred to: SR 2002/352 Reg.62

288. **Personal Pension Schemes (Disclosure of Information) Regulations (Northern Ireland) 1987**
Reg.1, amended: SR 2002/410 Reg.2, SR 2003/256 Reg.2
Reg.5, amended: SR 2002/410 Reg.2
Reg.6, amended: SR 2003/256 Reg.2
Sch.1, amended: SR 2003/256 Reg.2
Sch.1, substituted: SR 2003/256 Reg.2
Sch.2, added: SR 2002/410 Reg.2
Sch.3, amended: SR 2003/256 Reg.2

391. **Social Security (Hospital In-Patients) (Amendment) Regulations (Northern Ireland) 1987**
Reg.2, revoked (in part): SR 2003/261 Sch.1

414. **Control of Pesticides Regulations (Northern Ireland) 1987**
applied: SR 2002/301 Reg.3, Reg.9, Reg.16
Reg.5, applied: SR 2003/105 Reg.3

NO.

454. **Social Security (Industrial Injuries) (Prescribed Diseases) (Amendment No 2) Regulations (Northern Ireland) 1987**
Reg.3, revoked (in part): SR 2003/63 Reg.4

459. **Income Support (General) Regulations (Northern Ireland) 1987**
applied: SR 2002/56 Reg.4, SR 2003/191 Reg.34
referred to: SR 2003/1 Reg.2, SR 2003/155 Art.17, SR 2003/195 Reg.2
Reg.2, amended: SR 2002/80 Reg.3, SR 2002/128 Reg.2, SR 2002/132 Sch.1 para.1, SR 2002/203 Reg.2, SR 2002/275 Reg.3, SR 2002/363 Reg.2, SR 2003/1 Sch.1 para.1, SR 2003/261 Reg.3
Reg.2A, revoked (in part): SR 2003/195 Sch.1 para.1
Reg.5, amended: SR 2002/363 Reg.2, SR 2003/195 Sch.1 para.15
Reg.6, amended: SR 2002/132 Sch.1 para.2
Reg.6, referred to: SR 2003/191 Reg.34
Reg.10, referred to: SR 2003/191 Reg.35
Reg.14, amended: SR 2003/1 Sch.1 para.2
Reg.15, amended: SR 2003/1 Sch.1 para.3
Reg.17, amended: SR 2002/132 Sch.1 para.3, SR 2003/195 Sch.1 para.2
Reg.17, applied: SR 2003/155 Art.17, SR 2003/191 Reg.34, SR 2003/195 Reg.6
Reg.17, referred to: SR 2002/99 Art.16
Reg.17, revoked (in part): SR 2003/195 Sch.1 para.2
Reg.18, amended: SR 2002/132 Sch.1 para.4, SR 2003/195 Sch.1 para.3
Reg.18, applied: SR 2003/155 Art.17, SR 2003/195 Reg.6
Reg.18, referred to: SR 2002/99 Art.16
Reg.18, revoked (in part): SR 2003/195 Sch.1 para.3
Reg.19, applied: SR 2002/136 Reg.2
Reg.19, revoked: SR 2002/132 Sch.1 para.5
Reg.21, amended: SR 2002/132 Sch.1 para.6, SR 2003/195 Sch.1 para.4
Reg.21, applied: SI 2003/654 Reg.7, SR 2003/155 Art.17
Reg.21, referred to: SR 2002/99 Art.16
Reg.21A, amended: SR 2003/195 Sch.1 para.5
Reg.21A, revoked: 2004 c.19 s.12
Reg.22A, applied: SR 2002/79 Reg.3
Reg.22A, referred to: SR 2002/99 Sch.5, SR 2003/155 Sch.5
Reg.22A, revoked (in part): SR 2002/132 Sch.1 para.7
Reg.23, amended: SR 2003/195 Sch.1 para.6
Reg.25, amended: SR 2003/195 Sch.1 para.7
Reg.31, amended: SR 2003/1 Sch.1 para.4
Reg.35, amended: SR 2002/363 Reg.2
Reg.40, amended: SR 2002/222 Reg.7, SR 2003/195 Sch.1 para.8
Reg.41, amended: SR 2002/299 Reg.2

NO.

1987–cont.

459. Income Support (General) Regulations (Northern Ireland) 1987–*cont.*

Reg.41, revoked (in part): SR 2003/195 Sch.1 para.9

Reg.42, amended: SR 2002/128 Reg.2, SR 2003/191 Reg.24, SR 2003/195 Sch.1 para.10

Reg.42, revoked (in part): SR 2003/195 Sch.1 para.10

Reg.44, revoked: SR 2003/195 Sch.1 para.11

Reg.47, revoked: SR 2003/195 Sch.1 para.11

Reg.48, amended: SR 2003/195 Sch.1 para.12

Reg.48, revoked (in part): SR 2003/195 Sch.1 para.12

Reg.51, amended: SR 2002/128 Reg.2, SR 2002/132 Sch.1 para.8, SR 2003/195 Sch.1 para.13

Reg.53, amended: SR 2003/191 Reg.24

Reg.54, revoked (in part): SR 2003/195 Sch.1 para.14

Reg.57, amended: SR 2002/323 Sch.1 para.1, SR 2003/195 Sch.1 para.15

Reg.57, revoked (in part): SR 2003/195 Sch.1 para.15

Reg.61, amended: SR 2002/222 Reg.2

Reg.62, amended: SR 2002/222 Reg.3, Reg.4, Reg.7, SR 2002/270 Reg.2, SR 2003/195 Sch.1 para.16, SR 2003/351 Reg.2

Reg.66A, amended: SR 2002/222 Reg.3, Reg.5, SR 2003/351 Reg.2

Reg.66B, amended: SR 2002/132 Sch.1 para.9, SR 2003/195 Sch.1 para.17

Reg.68, amended: SR 2002/132 Sch.1 para.10, SR 2003/195 Sch.1 para.17

Reg.71, amended: SR 2002/132 Sch.1 para.11, SR 2003/195 Sch.1 para.18

Reg.71, applied: SR 2003/155 Art.17

Reg.71, referred to: SR 2002/99 Art.16, Sch.5, SR 2003/155 Sch.5

Reg.71, revoked (in part): SR 2002/132 Sch.1 para.11, SR 2003/195 Sch.1 para.18

Reg.73, amended: SR 2002/132 Sch.1 para.12

Reg.73, revoked (in part): SR 2002/132 Sch.1 para.12

Sch.1B, added: SR 2002/363 Reg.2

Sch.1B, amended: SR 2002/80 Reg.3, SR 2002/323 Sch.1 para.1, SR 2002/332 Reg.2, SR 2003/195 Sch.1 para.19

Sch.1B, revoked: SR 2003/191 Reg.24, 2004 c.19 s.12

Sch.2, amended: SR 2002/80 Reg.3, SR 2002/99 Art.16, SR 2002/128 Reg.5, SR 2002/132 Sch.1 para.13, SR 2002/267 Reg.2, SR 2002/322 Reg.2, SR 2002/323 Sch.1 para.1, SR 2003/155 Art.17, Sch.2, Sch.3, SR 2003/191 Reg.24, SR 2003/195 Sch.1 para.20, SR 2003/261 Reg.3

NO.

1987–cont.

459. Income Support (General) Regulations (Northern Ireland) 1987–*cont.*

Sch.2, applied: SR 2002/79 Reg.3, SR 2002/99 Art.16, SR 2003/155 Art.17

Sch.2, referred to: SR 2002/99 Art.16

Sch.2, revoked (in part): SR 2002/132 Sch.1 para.13, SR 2003/195 Sch.1 para.20, Sch.1 para.20

Sch.2, substituted: SR 2002/99 Sch.2, Sch.3, SR 2003/191 Reg.24

Sch.3, amended: SR 2002/16 Reg.2, SR 2002/58 Reg.2, SR 2002/99 Art.16, SR 2002/128 Reg.5, SR 2003/155 Art.17, SR 2003/191 Reg.24, SR 2003/261 Reg.3

Sch.3, applied: SR 2002/99 Art.16, SR 2003/155 Art.17

Sch.3, referred to: SR 2002/99 Sch.5, SR 2003/155 Sch.5

Sch.4, revoked: SR 2002/132 Sch.1 para.14

Sch.7, amended: SR 2002/132 Sch.1 para.15, SR 2003/155 Sch.4 Part I, SR 2003/195 Sch.1 para.21, SR 2003/261 Reg.3

Sch.7, applied: SR 2002/99 Art.16, SR 2003/191 Reg.34

Sch.7, referred to: SR 2003/155 Art.17, Sch.4 Part II, SR 2003/191 Reg.34

Sch.7, revoked (in part): SR 2002/132 Sch.1 para.15, SR 2003/261 Reg.3

Sch.7, substituted: SR 2002/99 Sch.4

Sch.8, added: SR 2003/191 Reg.24

Sch.8, amended: SR 2002/132 Sch.1 para.16, SR 2002/323 Sch.1 para.1, SR 2003/191 Reg.24, SR 2003/195 Sch.1 para.22

Sch.8, revoked (in part): SR 2003/191 Reg.24, SR 2003/195 Sch.1 para.22

Sch.9, added: SR 2002/275 Reg.3, SR 2003/1 Sch.1 para.5, SR 2003/154 Reg.2, SR 2003/195 Sch.1 para.23

Sch.9, amended: SR 2002/99 Art.16, SR 2002/128 Reg.2, SR 2002/132 Sch.1 para.17, SR 2002/299 Reg.3, SR 2002/363 Reg.2, SR 2003/155 Art.17, SR 2003/195 Sch.1 para.23

Sch.9, revoked (in part): SR 2002/132 Sch.1 para.17, SR 2003/195 Sch.1 para.23, 2004 c.19 s.12

Sch.10, added: SR 2002/275 Reg.3, SR 2003/154 Reg.2

Sch.10, amended: SR 2002/132 Sch.1 para.18, SR 2002/295 Reg.2, SR 2003/154 Reg.2, SR 2003/195 Sch.1 para.24

460. Income Support (Transitional) Regulations (Northern Ireland) 1987

Part III, applied: SR 2002/224 Sch.3 para.1, SR 2003/28 Sch.1 para.6

Reg.15, varied: SR 2002/99 Art.17, SR 2003/155 Art.18

461. Housing Benefit (General) Regulations (Northern Ireland) 1987

applied: SR 2002/56 Reg.4

referred to: SR 2003/1 Reg.3, SR 2003/155 Art.20, SR 2003/195 Reg.4

NO.

NO.

1987–cont.

461. Housing Benefit (General) Regulations (Northern Ireland) 1987–*cont.*

Reg.2, amended: SR 2002/80 Reg.4, SR 2002/128 Reg.3, SR 2002/363 Reg.4, SR 2003/1 Sch.2 para.1, SR 2003/80 Reg.2

Reg.2, applied: SR 2003/28 Reg.22

Reg.4, amended: SR 2002/363 Reg.4

Reg.7B, revoked: 2004 c.19 s.12

Reg.12, amended: SR 2003/108 Reg.2

Reg.13, amended: SR 2003/1 Sch.2 para.2

Reg.14, amended: SR 2003/1 Sch.2 para.3

Reg.16, amended: SR 2003/261 Reg.4

Reg.16, applied: SR 2003/155 Art.20

Reg.16, referred to: SR 2002/99 Art.19

Reg.17, applied: SR 2003/155 Art.20

Reg.17, referred to: SR 2002/99 Art.19

Reg.18, amended: SR 2002/99 Art.19, SR 2003/155 Art.20, SR 2003/261 Reg.4

Reg.21, amended: SR 2003/195 Sch.3 para.1

Reg.21A, amended: SR 2002/363 Reg.4, SR 2003/195 Sch.3 para.2

Reg.26, amended: SR 2003/1 Sch.2 para.4

Reg.28, amended: SR 2002/363 Reg.4

Reg.29, amended: SR 2002/363 Reg.6

Reg.33, amended: SR 2002/222 Reg.7, SR 2003/1 Sch.2 para.5

Reg.34, amended: SR 2002/299 Reg.2

Reg.35, amended: SR 2003/1 Sch.2 para.6

Reg.40, amended: SR 2003/1 Sch.2 para.7

Reg.43, amended: SR 2003/1 Sch.2 para.8

Reg.43A, revoked (in part): SR 2003/195 Sch.3 para.3

Reg.46, amended: SR 2002/222 Reg.2

Reg.48A, amended: SR 2002/243 Reg.2

Reg.51, revoked: SR 2002/222 Reg.6

Reg.52, amended: SR 2002/222 Reg.6

Reg.53, amended: SR 2002/222 Reg.3, Reg.4, Reg.7, SR 2002/270 Reg.2, SR 2003/351 Reg.2

Reg.57A, amended: SR 2002/222 Reg.3, Reg.5, SR 2003/351 Reg.2

Reg.58, revoked (in part): SR 2002/222 Reg.6

Reg.63, amended: SR 2002/99 Art.19, SR 2003/155 Art.20, SR 2003/261 Reg.4

Reg.63, applied: SR 2002/99 Art.19, SR 2003/155 Art.20

Reg.68, amended: SR 2003/189 Reg.2

Reg.72, amended: SR 2003/80 Reg.3

Reg.105, amended: SR 2003/195 Sch.3 para.4

Sch.A1, revoked: 2004 c.19 s.12

Sch.1, amended: SR 2002/99 Art.19, SR 2003/108 Reg.3, SR 2003/155 Art.20

Sch.1, applied: SR 2003/28 Sch.2 para.13

Sch.1, referred to: SR 2003/28 Sch.2 para.13

Sch.1A, revoked (in part): SR 2003/187 Reg.2

Sch.1B, amended: SR 2002/280 Reg.2

1987–cont.

461. Housing Benefit (General) Regulations (Northern Ireland) 1987–*cont.*

Sch.2, amended: SR 2002/80 Reg.4, SR 2002/99 Art.19, Sch.7, SR 2002/267 Reg.2, SR 2002/322 Reg.2, SR 2002/323 Sch.1 para.1, SR 2003/1 Sch.2 para.9, SR 2003/155 Art.20, SR 2003/195 Sch.3 para.5, SR 2003/261 Reg.4

Sch.2, applied: SR 2002/79 Reg.17, SR 2002/99 Art.19, SR 2003/155 Art.20

Sch.2, referred to: SR 2002/99 Art.19, SR 2003/155 Art.20

Sch.2, substituted: SR 2002/99 Sch.6, SR 2003/155 Sch.6, Sch.7

Sch.3, substituted: SR 2003/1 Sch.2 para.10

Sch.4, added: SR 2002/275 Reg.4, SR 2003/154 Reg.4

Sch.4, amended: SR 2002/99 Art.19, SR 2002/128 Reg.3, SR 2002/299 Reg.3, SR 2003/1 Sch.2 para.11, SR 2003/155 Art.20

Sch.4, revoked: SR 2003/1 Sch.2 para.11, 2004 c.19 s.12

Sch.5, added: SR 2002/275 Reg.4, SR 2003/154 Reg.4

Sch.5, amended: SR 2002/295 Reg.3, SR 2003/1 Sch.2 para.12

Sch.5, revoked: 2004 c.19 s.12

Sch.5, substituted: SR 2002/295 Reg.3

463. Family Credit (General) Regulations (Northern Ireland) 1987

Part VI, applied: SI 2002/1339 Reg.2

Reg.2, amended: SI 2003/45 Reg.8

Reg.4, amended: SI 2003/45 Reg.9

Reg.19, amended: SI 2003/45 Reg.10

Reg.38, amended: SI 2002/1340 Reg.3, Reg.4

Reg.42A, amended: SI 2002/1340 Reg.3, Reg.4

Reg.46, amended: SI 2002/1340 Reg.5

Reg.46A, amended: SI 2003/45 Reg.11

Reg.47, amended: SI 2002/829 Art.3

Sch.2, added: SI 2003/45 Reg.12

Sch.2, amended: SI 2002/524 Reg.4, Reg.5, Reg.6

Sch.4, amended: SI 2002/1340 Reg.6

Sch.4, substituted: SI 2002/829 Sch.1

465. Social Security (Claims and Payments) Regulations (Northern Ireland) 1987

applied: SR 2003/63 Reg.3

revoked: SI 2003/492 Sch.3 Part 2

Part IV, referred to: SR 2003/28 Sch.2 para.5

Reg.2, amended: SR 2002/323 Sch.1 para.1, SR 2003/191 Reg.3

Reg.4, amended: SR 2003/191 Reg.4

Reg.4, revoked (in part): 2004 c.19 s.12

Reg.4A, amended: SR 2002/323 Sch.1 para.1

Reg.4B, amended: SR 2003/191 Reg.4

Reg.4C, added: SR 2003/191 Reg.4

Reg.4D, added: SR 2003/191 Reg.4

NO.

1987–cont.

465. Social Security (Claims and Payments) Regulations (Northern Ireland) 1987–cont.

Reg.4E, added: SR 2003/191 Reg.4

Reg.6, amended: SR 2002/67 Reg.2, SR 2002/323 Sch.1 para.2, SR 2003/195 Sch.4 para.3

Reg.6, revoked (in part): 2004 c.19 s.12

Reg.7, amended: SR 2003/191 Reg.5

Reg.13, amended: SR 2003/191 Reg.6

Reg.13D, added: SR 2003/191 Reg.6

Reg.16, amended: SR 2003/191 Reg.7

Reg.16A, added: SR 2003/191 Reg.7

Reg.17, amended: SR 2003/191 Reg.8

Reg.19, amended: SI 2002/527 Reg.3, SR 2002/67 Reg.2, SR 2002/323 Sch.1 para.2, SR 2002/327 Reg.2, SR 2003/ 191 Reg.8

Reg.19, revoked (in part): 2004 c.19 s.12

Reg.21, amended: SR 2002/297 Reg.2

Reg.21, applied: SR 2003/191 Reg.34

Reg.21, revoked (in part): SR 2002/297 Reg.2

Reg.22, amended: SR 2002/297 Reg.2

Reg.23, amended: SR 2002/297 Reg.2

Reg.24, amended: SR 2002/297 Reg.2

Reg.26B, added: SR 2003/191 Reg.9

Reg.26B, disapplied: SR 2003/191 Reg.34

Reg.28, amended: SR 2002/254 Reg.2

Reg.28, substituted: SR 2002/254 Reg.2

Reg.29, amended: SR 2002/297 Reg.2

Reg.30, amended: SR 2002/297 Reg.2, SR 2003/191 Reg.10

Reg.32, amended: SR 2003/191 Reg.11

Reg.32, substituted: SR 2003/224 Reg.2

Reg.33, amended: SR 2002/297 Reg.2

Reg.33, applied: SI 2002/2014 Reg.18, Reg.29, Reg.36, SR 2002/403 Reg.3

Reg.34A, amended: SR 2002/297 Reg.2

Reg.34A, applied: SR 2003/191 Reg.34

Reg.34B, amended: SR 2003/191 Reg.13

Reg.34ZA, amended: SR 2003/191 Reg.12

Reg.34ZA, applied: SR 2003/191 Reg.34

Reg.34ZB, added: SR 2003/191 Reg.12

Reg.35, amended: SR 2002/327 Reg.2

Reg.35, substituted: SR 2002/327 Reg.2

Sch.1, amended: SR 2002/323 Sch.1 para.1

Sch.2, applied: SR 2003/28 Sch.1 para.6

Sch.3, applied: SR 2003/28 Sch.2 para.5

Sch.3, referred to: SR 2003/28 Sch.2 para.9

Sch.6, amended: SR 2002/297 Reg.2, SR 2002/323 Sch.1 para.1

Sch.7, applied: SR 2003/28 Sch.1 para.6

Sch.8A, amended: SR 2002/132 Reg.3, SR 2003/191 Reg.14

Sch.8A, revoked (in part): SR 2002/132 Reg.3

Sch.8B, added: SR 2003/191 Reg.14

Sch.8B, amended: SR 2002/59 Reg.2, SR 2003/118 Reg.2, SR 2003/191 Reg.14

NO.

1987–cont.

465. Social Security (Claims and Payments) Regulations (Northern Ireland) 1987–cont.

Sch.8B, applied: SR 2003/191 Reg.34

Sch.8C, amended: SR 2002/254 Reg.2, SR 2003/191 Reg.14

Sch.8C, applied: SR 2003/191 Reg.34

1988

18. Malicious Communications (Northern Ireland) Order 1988

applied: SI 2003/1593 Sch.1 Part II

21. Social Fund (Recovery by Deductions from Benefits) Regulations (Northern Ireland) 1988

Reg.2, amended: SR 2002/323 Sch.1 para.1, SR 2003/191 Reg.25

Reg.2, revoked (in part): SR 2003/213 Reg.2

67. Social Security (Claims and Payments) (Amendment) Regulations (Northern Ireland) 1988

revoked: SI 2003/492 Sch.3 Part 2

74. Control of Asbestos at Work Regulations (Northern Ireland) 1988

revoked: SR 2003/33 Reg.27

128. Statutory Maternity Pay (General) (Amendment) Regulations (Northern Ireland) 1988

Reg.3, revoked: SR 2002/359 Reg.6

130. Social Fund (Applications) Regulations (Northern Ireland) 1988

Reg.2, amended: SR 2002/284 Reg.2

Reg.2A, added: SR 2002/284 Reg.2

Reg.3, amended: SR 2002/284 Reg.2

137. Welfare Foods Regulations (Northern Ireland) 1988

applied: SR 2003/253 Art.3

Reg.1, amended: SR 2003/202 Reg.2

Reg.2, amended: SR 2003/202 Reg.3

Reg.4, amended: SR 2002/83 Reg.2, SR 2003/202 Reg.4

Reg.9, amended: SR 2003/202 Reg.5

Reg.14, amended: SR 2003/202 Reg.6

Sch.1, amended: SR 2003/202 Reg.7

141. Social Security (Claims and Payments) (Amendment No 2) Regulations (Northern Ireland) 1988

revoked: SI 2003/492 Sch.3 Part 2

142. Social Security (Payments on account, Overpayments and Recovery) Regulations (Northern Ireland) 1988

revoked: SI 2003/492 Sch.3 Part 2

Reg.1, amended: SR 2003/191 Reg.26

Reg.5, amended: SR 2003/191 Reg.26

Reg.7, amended: SR 2003/191 Reg.26

Reg.8, amended: SR 2003/191 Reg.26

Reg.10, amended: SR 2003/256 Reg.3

Reg.13, amended: SR 2003/191 Reg.26

Reg.14, amended: SR 2003/191 Reg.26

NO.

1988–cont.

142. **Social Security (Payments on account, Overpayments and Recovery) Regulations (Northern Ireland) 1988**–cont.

Reg.15, amended: SR 2003/191 Reg.26

Reg.16, amended: SR 2003/191 Reg.26

Reg.17, amended: SR 2003/191 Reg.26

206. **Misuse of Drugs (Amendment) Regulations (Northern Ireland) 1988**

revoked: SR 2002/1 Sch.7

242. **Pneumoconiosis, etc., (Workers Compensation) (Payment of Claims) Regulations (Northern Ireland) 1988**

Reg.5, amended: SR 2002/133 Reg.2

Reg.6, amended: SR 2002/133 Reg.2

Sch.1, substituted: SR 2002/133 Sch.1

273. **Child Benefit (General) (Amendment) Regulations (Northern Ireland) 1988**

revoked: SI 2003/493 Sch.2 Part 2

286. **River Bann Navigation Act 1879 (Amendment) Order (Northern Ireland) 1988**

revoked: SR 2002/395 Sch.2 Part II

343. **Livestock Marketing Commission (Levy) (Amendment) Regulations (Northern Ireland) 1988**

revoked: SR 2003/104 Reg.7

368. **Social Fund (Cold Weather Payments) (General) Regulations (Northern Ireland) 1988**

Reg.1A, amended: SR 2003/191 Reg.25

Sch.1, amended: SR 2002/315 Reg.2

369. **Social Security (Common Provisions) (Miscellaneous Amendments) Regulations (Northern Ireland) 1988**

Reg.3, revoked: SI 2003/492 Sch.3 Part 2

Reg.4, revoked: SI 2003/492 Sch.3 Part 2

374. **Royal Ulster Constabulary Pensions Regulations 1988**

applied: SR 2003/60 Reg.4, Reg.8

Reg.A13A, added: SR 2002/100 Reg.3

Reg.B2, referred to: SR 2003/60 Reg.13

Reg.B2, varied: SR 2003/60 Reg.13

Reg.B3, applied: SR 2003/60reg12(1), SR 2003/60reg12(2)

Reg.B4, applied: SR 2003/60 Reg.11

Reg.B5, applied: SR 2003/60reg12(1), SR 2003/60reg12(2)

Reg.B7, applied: SR 2003/60 Reg.13

Reg.F1, amended: SR 2002/100 Reg.4

Reg.F1, varied: SR 2002/100 Reg.5

Reg.F2, amended: SR 2002/100 Reg.4

Reg.G1, amended: SR 2002/100 Reg.4

Reg.G2, applied: SR 2003/60 Reg.6

Sch.A, amended: SR 2002/100 Reg.4

Sch.B, applied: SR 2003/60 Reg.11

386. **Working Time Regulations (Northern Ireland) 1988**

referred to: SI 2003/2002 Reg.12

NO.

1988–cont.

449. **Personal Pension Schemes (Compensation) Regulations (Northern Ireland) 1988**

Reg.1, amended: SR 2003/256 Reg.4

Reg.2, amended: SR 2003/256 Reg.4

Reg.2, revoked (in part): SR 2003/256 Reg.4

Reg.3, amended: SR 2003/256 Reg.4

1989

40. **Social Security (Claims and Payments) (Amendments) Regulations (Northern Ireland) 1989**

revoked: SI 2003/492 Sch.3 Part 2

102. **Child Benefit (General) (Amendment) Regulations (Northern Ireland) 1989**

revoked: SI 2003/493 Sch.2 Part 2

111. **Dental Charges Regulations (Northern Ireland) 1989**

Reg.1, amended: SR 2003/48 Reg.4

Reg.4, amended: SR 2002/84 Reg.2, SR 2003/134 Reg.2

Reg.8A, added: SR 2003/48 Reg.5

Sch.2, amended: SR 2003/48 Reg.6

253. **Adoption Agencies Regulations (Northern Ireland) 1989**

applied: SI 2003/493 Reg.16

referred to: SR 2003/16 Reg.33

Reg.7, referred to: SR 2003/16 Reg.23

Reg.7, varied: SR 2003/16 Sch.4

Reg.8, applied: SR 2002/144 Reg.4

Reg.8, varied: SR 2003/16 Sch.4

Reg.9, varied: SR 2003/16 Sch.4

Reg.10, applied: SR 2002/144 Reg.4

Reg.10, varied: SR 2003/16 Sch.4

Reg.11, see *J (Freeing for Adoption: Adoption Agencies: Procedural Requirements), Re* [2004] N.I.10 (Fam Div (NI)), Gillen, J.

Reg.11, applied: SR 2002/144 Reg.4, SR 2002/377 Reg.2, SR 2002/378 Reg.2, SR 2002/379 Reg.11, SR 2002/382 Reg.1

Reg.11, varied: SR 2003/16 Sch.4

Reg.12, applied: SR 2002/377 Reg.15

Reg.12, varied: SR 2003/16 Sch.4

Reg.14, varied: SR 2003/16 Sch.4

Sch.1, referred to: SR 2003/16 Reg.6

320. **Docks Regulations (Northern Ireland) 1989**

referred to: SI 2003/2002 Reg.12

346. **Misuse of Drugs (Amendment) Regulations (Northern Ireland) 1989**

revoked: SR 2002/1 Sch.7

347. **Diseases of Animals (Animal Protein) (No.2) Order (Northern Ireland) 1989**

revoked: SR 2002/209 Art.33

Art.3, applied: SR 2002/209 Art.32

348. **Travelling Expenses and Remission of Charges Regulations (Northern Ireland) 1989**

Reg.2, amended: SR 2003/48 Reg.2, SR 2003/170 Reg.2

NO.

1989–cont.

348. Travelling Expenses and Remission of Charges Regulations (Northern Ireland) 1989–cont.

Reg.4, amended: SR 2002/46 Reg.2, SR 2003/170 Reg.3

Reg.4, revoked (in part): SR 2003/170 Reg.3

Reg.7ZA, added: SR 2003/170 Reg.4

Sch.1, amended: SR 2002/46 Reg.3, SR 2002/172 Reg.2, SR 2003/48 Reg.3, SR 2003/170 Reg.5

Sch.1A, amended: SR 2002/46 Reg.4

373. Social Security (Abolition of Earnings Rule) (Consequential) Regulations (Northern Ireland) 1989

Reg.12, revoked: SI 2003/492 Sch.3 Part 2

398. Social Security (Claims and Payments) (Amendment No 2) Regulations (Northern Ireland) 1989

revoked: SI 2003/492 Sch.3 Part 2

430. Condensed Milk and Dried Milk (Amendment) Regulations (Northern Ireland) 1989

revoked: SR 2003/300 Reg.10

440. Road Service Licensing Regulations (Northern Ireland) 1989

Reg.7, referred to: SR 2002/116 Reg.10

Reg.10, amended: SR 2003/14 Reg.2

444. Fair Employment Tribunal Regulations (Northern Ireland) 1989

Reg.2, amended: 2002 c.26 Sch.3 para.31

Reg.4, amended: 2002 c.26 Sch.3 para.32

445. Fair Employment Tribunal (Rules of Procedure) Regulations (Northern Ireland) 1989

Reg.2, amended: 2002 c.26 Sch.3 para.33

1990

112. Statutory Maternity Pay (General) (Amendment) Regulations (Northern Ireland) 1990

Reg.5, revoked: SR 2002/359 Reg.6

131. Income Support (General) (Amendment) Regulations (Northern Ireland) 1990

Reg.19, revoked (in part): SR 2003/261 Reg.10

137. Income-Related Benefits (Miscellaneous Amendments) Regulations (Northern Ireland) 1990

Reg.2, revoked: SI 2003/492 Sch.3 Part 2

145. Air Quality Standards Regulations (Northern Ireland) 1990

Reg.3, revoked (in part): SR 2002/94 Reg.12

Reg.4, revoked: SR 2002/94 Reg.12

Reg.5, revoked: SR 2002/94 Reg.12

Reg.6, revoked: SR 2002/94 Reg.12

Reg.7, revoked: SR 2002/94 Reg.12

Reg.8, revoked: SR 2002/94 Reg.12

NO.

1990–cont.

181. Harbour Works (Assessment of Environmental Effects) Regulations (Northern Ireland) 1990

referred to: SR 2003/136 Reg.1

245. Sludge (Use in Agriculture) Regulations (Northern Ireland) 1990

applied: SR 2002/248 Reg.8

329. Tryptophan in Food Regulations (Northern Ireland) 1990

Reg.2, amended: SR 2002/264 Reg.10

375. Income Support (Liable Relatives) Regulations (Northern Ireland) 1990

Reg.2, amended: SR 2002/323 Sch.1 para.1

389. Code of Practice (Disciplinary Practice and Procedures) Order (Northern Ireland) 1990

applied: SR 2002/347 Art.3

398. Social Security (Miscellaneous Provisions) (Amendment) Regulations (Northern Ireland) 1990

Reg.7, revoked: SI 2003/492 Sch.3 Part 2

1991

1. Misuse of Drugs (Amendment) Regulations (Northern Ireland) 1991

revoked: SR 2002/1 Sch.7

25. Children and Young Persons (Protection from Tobacco) (Northern Ireland) Order 1991

Art.5, applied: SI 2003/1593 Sch.1 Part II

132. Teachers (Compensation for Redundancy and Premature Retirement) Regulations (Northern Ireland) 1991

Reg.2, amended: SR 2002/393 Reg.3

Reg.3, amended: SR 2002/393 Reg.3

Reg.4, amended: SR 2002/393 Reg.3

Reg.5, amended: SR 2002/393 Reg.3

Reg.6, amended: SR 2002/393 Reg.3

Reg.17, amended: SR 2002/393 Reg.3

Sch.1, added: SR 2002/393 Reg.3

Sch.1, substituted: SR 2002/393 Reg.3

198. Food Safety (Sampling and Qualifications) Regulations (Northern Ireland) 1991

Reg.6, referred to: SR 2002/141 Reg.4

Reg.8, referred to: SR 2002/141 Reg.4

203. Food Safety (Northern Ireland) Order 1991 (Consequential Modifications) Order (Northern Ireland) 1991

revoked: SR 2003/300 Reg.10

Sch.1, amended: SR 2002/219 Sch.1, SR 2003/300 Reg.10, SR 2003/301 Reg.10, SR 2003/313 Reg.11

Sch.2, amended: SR 2002/219 Sch.1, SR 2003/300 Reg.10, SR 2003/301 Reg.10, SR 2003/313 Reg.11

Sch.3, amended: SR 2003/300 Reg.10, SR 2003/301 Reg.10, SR 2003/313 Reg.11

Sch.4, amended: SR 2002/219 Sch.1

NO.

NO.

1991–cont.

203. Food Safety (Northern Ireland) Order 1991 (Consequential Modifications) Order (Northern Ireland) 1991–*cont.*

Sch.5, amended: SR 2003/300 Reg.10, SR 2003/301 Reg.10, SR 2003/313 Reg.11

Sch.6, amended: SR 2002/219 Sch.1

257. Road Transport (Qualifications of Operators) (Amendment) Regulations (Northern Ireland) 1991

Reg.5, revoked: SR 2003/217 Reg.8

Reg.6, revoked: SR 2003/217 Reg.8

261. Londonderry Harbour Order (Northern Ireland) 1991

Art.5, revoked (in part): SR 2002/41 Sch.2

266. Weighing Equipment (Non-automatic Weighing Machines) Regulations (Northern Ireland) 1991

Reg.17A, amended: SR 2002/71 Sch.1 para.6

344. Food Safety (Exports) Regulations (Northern Ireland) 1991

Sch.1, amended: SR 2002/219 Sch.1, SR 2003/300 Reg.10, SR 2003/301 Reg.10, SR 2003/313 Reg.11

364. Insolvency Rules (Northern Ireland) 1991

added: SR 2002/261 r.5

added: SR 2002/261 r.6

added: SR 2002/261 r.7

added: SR 2002/261 r.8

added: SR 2002/261 r.9

added: SR 2002/261 r.10

applied: SI 2003/1400 Sch.4

referred to: SR 2002/261 r.3

r.0.1, amended: SR 2002/261 r.4

r.1.01, amended: SR 2002/261 r.5

r.1.03, amended: SR 2002/261 r.5

r.1.24, amended: SR 2002/261 r.5

r.2.03, amended: SR 2002/261 r.6

r.2.06, amended: SR 2002/261 r.6

r.2.10, amended: SR 2002/261 r.6

r.2.19, amended: SR 2002/261 r.6

r.2.25, amended: SR 2002/261 r.6

r.2.34, amended: SR 2002/261 r.6

r.2.57, amended: SR 2002/261 r.6

r.4.007, amended: SR 2002/261 r.7

r.4.010, amended: SR 2002/261 r.7

r.4.019, amended: SR 2002/261 r.7

r.4.025, amended: SR 2002/261 r.7

r.4.027, amended: SR 2002/261 r.7

r.4.073, amended: SR 2002/261 r.7

r.4.080, applied: SI 2003/1102 Reg.12, Reg.13, SI 2004/353 Reg.12, Reg.13, SI 2004/1045 Reg.14, Reg.15

r.4.081, amended: SR 2002/261 r.7

r.4.097, disapplied: SI 2003/3226 Reg.14

r.4.102, amended: SR 2002/261 r.7

r.4.228, applied: SI 2003/1102 Reg.30, SI 2004/353 Reg.30

r.5.04, amended: SR 2002/261 r.8

r.5.25, amended: SR 2002/261 r.8

1991–cont.

364. Insolvency Rules (Northern Ireland) 1991–*cont.*

r.6.007, amended: SR 2002/261 r.9

r.6.013, amended: SR 2002/261 r.9

r.6.027, amended: SR 2002/261 r.9

r.6.049, amended: SR 2002/261 r.9

r.6.090, amended: SR 2002/261 r.9

r.6.096, amended: SR 2002/261 r.9

r.6.113, amended: SR 2002/261 r.9

r.6.195, amended: SR 2002/261 r.9

r.7.56, applied: SI 2003/1102 Reg.7

r.7.56, varied: SI 2003/1102 Reg.7, SI 2004/353 Reg.7, SI 2004/1045 Reg.6

r.11.01, amended: SR 2002/261 r.11

r.11.02, amended: SR 2002/261 r.11

r.11.03, amended: SR 2002/261 r.11

r.11.06, amended: SR 2002/261 r.11

r.12.13, amended: SR 2002/261 r.11

r.12.19, amended: SR 2002/261 r.11

Sch.2, amended: SR 2002/261 Sch.1 Part 1, Sch.1 Part 2

365. Administration of Insolvent Estates of Deceased Persons Order (Northern Ireland) 1991

referred to: SR 2003/103 Art.2

Sch.1, amended: SR 2003/103 Art.3

Sch.1, substituted: SR 2003/103 Art.3

Sch.3, amended: SR 2003/103 Sch.1

367. Insolvent Companies (Disqualification of Unfit Directors) Proceedings Rules (Northern Ireland) 1991

applied: SR 2003/358 r.12

revoked: SR 2003/358 r.12

373. Motor Cars (Driving Instruction) Regulations (Northern Ireland) 1991

Reg.2, amended: SR 2003/65 Reg.3

Reg.9, substituted: SR 2003/65 Reg.4

Reg.10, substituted: SR 2003/65 Reg.5

Reg.11, amended: SR 2003/65 Reg.6

Reg.16, amended: SR 2003/65 Reg.7

Reg.24, amended: SR 2003/65 Reg.8

399. Companies (Forms) (Amendment No 2 and Company's Type and Principle Business Activities) Regulations (Northern Ireland) 1991

Reg.2, amended: SR 2003/4 Reg.2

Reg.5, amended: SR 2003/4 Reg.2

Reg.5, applied: SR 2003/4 Reg.3

Sch.3, amended: SR 2003/4 Sch.1

446. Fire Certificates (Special Premises) Regulations (Northern Ireland) 1991

Sch.1, amended: SR 2003/152 Sch.7 para.8

471. Pressure Systems and Transportable Gas Containers Regulations (Northern Ireland) 1991

Sch.2, revoked: SR 2002/34 Sch.1

475. Imported Food Regulations (Northern Ireland) 1991

disapplied: SR 2002/340 Sch.7

NO.

1991–cont.

488. Social Security (Miscellaneous Provisions) (Amendment) Regulations (Northern Ireland) 1991

Reg.6, revoked: SI 2003/492 Sch.3 Part 2

509. Dangerous Substances in Harbour Areas Regulations (Northern Ireland) 1991

Reg.29, amended: SR 2003/152 Sch.7 para.6

Reg.29, revoked (in part): SR 2003/152 Sch.8 Part I

516. Classification and Labelling of Explosives Regulations (Northern Ireland) 1991

applied: SR 2002/147 Reg.9, SR 2003/152 Sch.5

1992

6. Disability Living Allowance and Disability Working Allowance (Consequential Provisions) Regulations (Northern Ireland) 1992

Reg.14, revoked: SI 2003/492 Sch.3 Part 2

7. Social Security (Claims and Payments) (Amendment) Regulations (Northern Ireland) 1992

revoked: SI 2003/492 Sch.3 Part 2

Reg.12, revoked: SR 2002/297 Sch.1

17. Statutory Maternity Pay (Health and Social Services Employees) Regulations (Northern Ireland) 1992

Reg.2, amended: SR 2002/354 Reg.3

20. Social Security (Attendance Allowance) Regulations (Northern Ireland) 1992

Reg.7, amended: SR 2002/31 Reg.2, SR 2002/132 Reg.4

Reg.7, revoked (in part): SR 2002/132 Reg.4

Reg.7A, revoked: SR 2002/132 Reg.4

Reg.8, amended: SR 2003/191 Reg.28

Sch.2, revoked: SR 2002/132 Reg.4

32. Social Security (Disability Living Allowance) Regulations (Northern Ireland 1992

Reg.4, amended: SR 2002/99 Art.12, SR 2003/155 Art.13

Reg.9, amended: SR 2002/31 Reg.3, SR 2002/132 Reg.5

Reg.9, revoked (in part): SR 2002/132 Reg.5

Reg.9A, revoked: SR 2002/132 Reg.5

Reg.10, amended: SR 2003/191 Reg.29

Reg.12, amended: SR 2002/97 Reg.2

Sch.2A, revoked: SR 2002/132 Reg.5

62. Diseases of Animals (Animal Protein) (No.2) (Amendment) Order (Northern Ireland) 1992

revoked: SR 2002/209 Art.33

78. Disability Working Allowance (General) Regulations (Northern Ireland) 1992

PartVII, applied: SI 2002/1339 Reg.2

1992–cont.

78. Disability Working Allowance (General) Regulations (Northern Ireland) 1992–*cont.*

Reg.2, amended: SI 2003/45 Reg.3

Reg.6, amended: SI 2003/45 Reg.4

Reg.21, amended: SI 2003/45 Reg.5

Reg.42, amended: SI 2002/1340 Reg.3, Reg.4

Reg.47, amended: SI 2002/1340 Reg.3, Reg.4

Reg.51, amended: SI 2002/829 Art.4, SI 2002/1340 Reg.5

Reg.51A, amended: SI 2003/45 Reg.6

Sch.3, added: SI 2003/45 Reg.7

Sch.3, amended: SI 2002/524 Reg.4, Reg.5, Reg.6

Sch.5, amended: SI 2002/1340 Reg.6

Sch.5, substituted: SI 2002/829 Sch.2

83. Social Security (Miscellaneous Provisions) (Amendment) Regulations (Northern Ireland) 1992

Reg.7, revoked (in part): SI 2003/492 Sch.3 Part 2, SR 2002/297 Sch.1

178. Electricity (Applications for Consent) (Fees) Regulations (Northern Ireland) 1992

Reg.2, amended: SR 2002/364 Reg.2

241. Trade Union Elections and Ballots (Independent Scrutineer Qualifications) Order (Northern Ireland) 1992

Art.9, substituted: SR 2003/331 Art.2

254. Waste Collection and Disposal Regulations (Northern Ireland) 1992

Reg.3, revoked: SR 2002/248 Reg.11

Reg.7, revoked: SR 2002/248 Reg.11

Reg.9, applied: SR 2002/248 Reg.10

Sch.1, revoked: SR 2002/248 Reg.11

Sch.4, revoked: SR 2002/248 Reg.11

271. Social Security (Claims and Payments) (Amendment No 2) Regulations (Northern Ireland) 1992

revoked: SI 2003/492 Sch.3 Part 2

304. Occupational and Personal Pension Schemes (Miscellaneous Amendments) Regulations (Northern Ireland) 1992

Reg.22, revoked (in part): SR 2003/256 Reg.19

314. Legal Aid in Criminal Proceedings (Costs) (Amendment) Rules (Northern Ireland) 1992

r.6, amended: SR 2002/376 Reg.2

r.9, amended: SR 2002/376 Reg.2

339. Child Support (Information, Evidence and Disclosure) Regulations (Northern Ireland) 1992

Reg.2, amended: SR 2002/164 Reg.2

340. Child Support (Maintenance Assessments Procedure) Regulations (Northern Ireland) 1992

Reg.19, amended: SR 2003/224 Reg.5

NO.

1992–cont.

**340. Child Support (Maintenance Asses-
ments Procedure) Regulations
(Northern Ireland) 1992**–*cont.*
Reg.22, amended: SR 2003/224 Reg.5
Reg.31A, amended: SR 2002/164 Reg.3
Reg.34A, amended: SR 2003/84 Reg.2

**341. Child Support (Maintenance Assess-
ments and Special Cases) Regula-
tions (Northern Ireland) 1992**
Reg.1, amended: SR 2003/84 Reg.3
Reg.9, amended: SR 2002/164 Reg.4, SR
2002/323 Sch.1 para.1
Reg.10A, amended: SR 2003/84 Reg.3
Reg.11, amended: SR 2003/84 Reg.3
Sch.1, added: SR 2003/84 Reg.3
Sch.1, amended: SR 2003/84 Reg.3
Sch.1, revoked (in part): SR 2003/84 Reg.3
Sch.2, added: SR 2003/84 Reg.3
Sch.2, amended: SR 2003/84 Reg.3
Sch.4, amended: SR 2002/323 Sch.1 para.1,
SR 2003/84 Reg.3

**342. Child Support (Arrears, Interest and
Adjustment of Maintenance Asses-
ments) Regulations (Northern
Ireland) 1992**
Reg.1, amended: SR 2003/191 Reg.27
Reg.6, amended: SR 2003/84 Reg.4
Reg.10A, amended: SR 2003/191 Reg.27
Reg.10B, amended: SR 2003/191 Reg.27

**390. Child Support (Collection and Enfor-
cement) Regulations (Northern
Ireland) 1992**
Reg.8, amended: SR 2003/84 Reg.5

**416. Flavourings in Food (Northern
Ireland) 1992**
Reg.10, revoked: SR 2002/219 Sch.1

**453. Social Security (Miscellaneous Provi-
sions) (Amendment No 3) Regula-
tions 1992**
Reg.6, revoked (in part): SI 2003/492 Sch.3
Part 2, SR 2003/224 Reg.6

**464. Food (Forces Exemptions) (Revoca-
tions) Regulations (Northern Ireland)
1992**
Sch.1, amended: SR 2003/300 Reg.10, SR
2003/301 Reg.10, SR 2003/313 Reg.11

**476. Sheep Annual Premium Regulations
(Northern Ireland) 1992**
Reg.2, amended: SR 2002/368 Reg.3
Reg.3, amended: SR 2002/368 Reg.3

**483. Weights and Measures (Testing and
Adjustment Fees) Regulations
(Northern Ireland) 1992**
revoked: SR 2002/308 Reg.2

**501. Motor Vehicles (Driving Licences)
(Designation of Relevant External
Law) Order (Northern Ireland) 1992**
revoked: SR 2003/83 Art.3

**547. Local Government (Superannuation)
Regulations (Northern Ireland) 1992**
applied: SR 2003/61 Reg.2

NO.

1992–cont.

**547. Local Government (Superannuation)
Regulations (Northern Ireland) 1992**–
cont.
Reg.C1, referred to: SR 2002/352 Reg.88
Reg.C2, referred to: SR 2002/352 Reg.88
Reg.C3, referred to: SR 2002/352 Reg.88
Reg.C6, referred to: SR 2002/352 Reg.88
Reg.C7, referred to: SR 2002/352 Reg.88
Reg.C9, applied: SR 2002/353 Reg.8
Reg.C9, referred to: SR 2002/352 Reg.88
Reg.E12, applied: SR 2002/353 Reg.8
Reg.F6, applied: SR 2002/352 Sch.3

1993

**20. Personal Protective Equipment at
Work Regulations (Northern Ireland)
1993**
referred to: SI 2003/2002 Reg.12

**26. Control of Asbestos at Work (Amend-
ment) Regulations (Northern Ireland)
1993**
revoked: SR 2003/33 Reg.27

**37. Workplace (Health, Safety and
Welfare) Regulations (Northern
Ireland) 1993**
Reg.6, revoked (in part): SR 2003/152 Sch.8
Part I

**54. Radioactive Substances (Hospitals)
Exemption Order (Northern Ireland)
1993**
Art.2, amended: SR 2003/46 Sch.11 para.4

**67. Companies (1990 Order) (Eligibility for
Appointment as Company Auditor)
(Consequential Amendments) Regu-
lations (Northern Ireland) 1993**
Sch.1, revoked: SI 2003/435 Sch.5

**76. Registered Homes Tribunal Rules
(Northern Ireland) 1993**
revoked: SR 2003/138 r.15

**104. Child Support Appeals (Jurisdiction
of Courts) Order (Northern Ireland)
1993**
revoked: SR 2002/391 Art.2
Art.2, applied: SI 2003/435 Sch.2 para.2

**117. Child Support (Great Britain Recipro-
cal Arrangements) Regulations
(Northern Ireland) 1993**
Reg.2, amended: SR 2002/121 Reg.2
Reg.2, revoked (in part): SR 2002/121 Reg.2
Sch.1B, added: SR 2002/121 Sch.1
Sch.2, amended: SR 2002/121 Reg.2
Sch.3, added: SR 2002/121 Sch.2

**127. Health and Personal Social Service
(Assessment of Resources) Regula-
tions (Northern Ireland) 1993**
Reg.20, amended: SR 2002/113 Reg.2
Reg.28, amended: SR 2002/113 Reg.3
Sch.4, added: SR 2002/113 Reg.4

NO.

1993–cont.

142. Health and Personal Social Services (Fund-holding Practices) Regulations (Northern Ireland) 1993
Reg.21, applied: SR 2002/66 Reg.13
Reg.21, varied: SR 2002/66 Reg.13
Reg.22, varied: SR 2002/66 Reg.14

146. Social Security (Claims and Payments) (Amendment) Regulations 1993
revoked: SI 2003/492 Sch.3 Part 2

148. Social Security (Industrial Diseases) (Prescribed Diseases) (Amendment) Regulations (Northern Ireland) 1993
Reg.6, revoked (in part): SR 2003/63 Reg.4

149. Social Security Benefits (Amendments Consequential Upon the Introduction of Community Care) Regulations 1993
Reg.1, amended: SI 2003/492 Sch.3 Part 2
Sch.1, revoked: SI 2003/492 Sch.3 Part 2
Sch.2, revoked: SI 2003/492 Sch.3 Part 2

175. Social Security (Payments on Account, Overpayments and Recovery) (Amendment) Regulations (Northern Ireland) 1993
revoked: SI 2003/492 Sch.3 Part 2

192. Animal By-Products Regulations (Northern Ireland) 1993
revoked: SR 2002/210 Reg.2
Reg.5, applied: SR 2002/209 Art.32
Reg.7, applied: SR 2002/209 Art.32
Reg.9, applied: SR 2002/209 Art.32

193. Diseases of Animals (Animal Protein) (No.2) (Amendment) Order (Northern Ireland) 1993
revoked: SR 2002/209 Art.33

197. Forest Reproductive Material (Amendment) Regulations 1993
revoked: SR 2002/404 Reg.34

217. Social Security (Claims and Payments) (Amendment No 2) Regulations (Northern Ireland) 1993
revoked: SI 2003/492 Sch.3 Part 2

249. Royal Ulster Constabulary Pensions (Additional Voluntary Contributions) Regulations 1993
Reg.2, amended: SR 2002/100 Reg.3

256. Plant Health Order (Northern Ireland) 1993
applied: SR 2003/193 Art.8
referred to: SR 2002/7 Art.2
Art.3, amended: SR 2002/273 Art.3
Art.12, varied: SR 2003/193 Art.9
Art.13, applied: SR 2003/193 Art.10
Art.13, varied: SR 2003/193 Art.10
Art.14, applied: SR 2003/193 Art.10
Art.15, applied: SR 2003/193 Art.9
Art.15, varied: SR 2003/193 Art.9
Art.17, applied: SR 2003/193 Art.8
Art.18, applied: SR 2003/193 Art.8
Art.22, applied: SR 2002/7 Art.4

NO.

1993–cont.

256. Plant Health Order (Northern Ireland) 1993–cont.
Art.23, applied: SR 2002/7 Art.4
Art.25, applied: SR 2002/7 Art.4, SR 2002/269 Art.6
Art.25, varied: SR 2003/193 Art.13
Art.30A, applied: SR 2003/193 Art.12
Art.30A, varied: SR 2003/193 Art.12
Art.47, applied: SR 2002/269 Art.6
Sch.1, amended: SR 2002/273 Art.4
Sch.2, amended: SR 2002/273 Art.5
Sch.3, amended: SR 2002/273 Art.6
Sch.4, amended: SR 2002/273 Art.7
Sch.8, amended: SR 2002/273 Art.8, Art.9
Sch.13, amended: SR 2003/235 Art.2

278. Planning (General Development) Order (Northern Ireland) 1993
Sch.1, applied: SR 2002/195 Art.3
Sch.1, referred to: SR 2003/98 Art.2
Sch.1, substituted: SR 2002/195 Art.2, SR 2003/98 Sch.1

313. Nurses, Midwives and Health Visitors (Professional Conduct) Rules 1993
Sch.1, amended: SR 2002/117 Sch.1
Sch.1, substituted: SR 2002/43 Sch.1, SR 2002/117 Sch.1

326. Health and Personal Social Services General Dental Services Regulations (Northern Ireland) 1993
Reg.2, amended: SR 2002/2 Reg.2
Reg.4, amended: SR 2002/2 Reg.2
Reg.4, revoked (in part): SR 2002/2 Reg.2
Reg.5F, revoked: SR 2002/2 Reg.2
Reg.5G, amended: SR 2002/2 Reg.2
Reg.5G, revoked: SR 2002/2 Reg.2
Reg.5G, substituted: SR 2002/2 Reg.2
Reg.9, amended: SR 2003/135 Reg.2
Reg.9, revoked (in part): SR 2003/135 Reg.2
Reg.19, amended: SR 2003/325 Reg.2
Sch.2, amended: SR 2002/2 Reg.2
Sch.2, revoked: SR 2002/2 Reg.2
Sch.2, substituted: SR 2002/2 Reg.2
Sch.5, amended: SR 2002/171 Reg.2, SR 2003/325 Reg.2

375. Social Security (Claims and Payments) (Amendment No 3) Regulations (Northern Ireland) 1993
Reg.3, revoked: SI 2003/492 Sch.3 Part 2

441. Capacity Serving Measures (Intoxicating Liquor) Regulations (Northern Ireland) 1993
Reg.10, amended: SR 2002/71 Sch.1 para.7

460. Plant Health (Wood and Bark) Order (Northern Ireland) 1993
applied: SR 2003/175 Art.8
referred to: SR 2003/175 Art.9
Art.2, amended: SR 2002/285 Art.2
Art.12, referred to: SR 2003/175 Art.6
Art.12, varied: SR 2003/175 Art.6
Art.13, varied: SR 2003/175 Art.6

NO.

NO.

1993–cont.

460. Plant Health (Wood and Bark) Order (Northern Ireland) 1993*–cont.*
Art.23, varied: SR 2003/175 Art.9
Art.25, applied: SR 2003/175 Art.9
Art.26, amended: SR 2002/285 Art.2
Art.26A, varied: SR 2003/175 Art.8
Sch.2, amended: SR 2002/285 Art.2
Sch.2, revoked: SR 2002/285 Art.2
Sch.4, referred to: SR 2003/175 Sch.1
Sch.4, revoked: SR 2002/285 Art.2
Sch.5, revoked: SR 2002/285 Art.2
Sch.8, revoked: SR 2002/285 Art.2

470. Measuring Instruments (EEC Requirements) (Verification Fees) Regulations (Northern Ireland) 1993
revoked: SR 2002/309 Reg.2

1994

6. Notification of New Substances Regulations (Northern Ireland) 1994
Reg.4, applied: SR 2002/301 Reg.4
Reg.6, applied: SR 2002/301 Reg.3, Reg.4, Sch.5 para.7
Reg.18, applied: SR 2002/301 Sch.5 para.3
Sch.2, added: SR 2003/36 Reg.3
Sch.3, substituted: SR 2003/36 Reg.3

43. Motor Vehicles (Driving Licences) (Designation of Relevant External Law) Order (Northern Ireland) 1994
revoked: SR 2003/83 Art.3

46. Motor Vehicles (Third-Party Risks) Regulations (Northern Ireland) 1994
Reg.2, amended: SR 2002/154 Reg.2
Reg.8, amended: SR 2002/154 Reg.3

64. Health and Social Services Trusts (Exercise of Functions) Regulations (Northern Ireland) 1994
Sch.1, amended: SR 2003/200 Reg.2

65. Health and Social Services Trusts (Consequential Amendments) Regulations (Northern Ireland) 1994
Sch.15, revoked: SI 2003/492 Sch.3 Part 2

144. Genetically Modified Organisms (Deliberate Release) Regulations (Northern Ireland) 1994
applied: SR 2003/167 Reg.13, Reg.17
revoked: SR 2003/167 Sch.5
Reg.16, applied: SR 2003/167 Reg.17

191. Social Security Maternity Benefits, Statutory Maternity Pay and Statutory Sick Pay (Amendment) Regulations (Northern Ireland) 1994
Reg.2, revoked (in part): SR 2002/354 Reg.8

197. Royal Ulster Constabulary Reserve (Full-time) Pensions Regulations 1994
added: SR 2002/101 Reg.3
applied: SR 2003/60 Reg.4, Reg.8
Reg.B2, referred to: SR 2003/60 Reg.13
Reg.B2, varied: SR 2003/60 Reg.13

1994–cont.

197. Royal Ulster Constabulary Reserve (Full-time) Pensions Regulations 1994*–cont.*
Reg.B3, applied: SR 2003/60reg12(1), SR 2003/60reg12(2)
Reg.B4, applied: SR 2003/60 Reg.11
Reg.B5, applied: SR 2003/60reg12(1), SR 2003/60reg12(2)
Reg.B7, applied: SR 2003/60 Reg.13
Reg.F1, amended: SR 2002/101 Reg.3
Reg.F1, varied: SR 2002/101 Reg.4
Reg.F2, amended: SR 2002/101 Reg.3
Reg.G2, applied: SR 2003/60 Reg.6, Reg.11
Reg.2, amended: SR 2002/101 Reg.3, Reg.5
Sch.B, applied: SR 2003/60 Reg.11

202. Pharmaceutical Society of Northern Ireland (General) Regulations (Northern Ireland) 1994
Reg.2, amended: SR 2002/206 Reg.2
Reg.3, amended: SR 2003/356 Reg.2
Reg.4, amended: SR 2002/206 Reg.3, SR 2003/356 Reg.3
Reg.5, amended: SR 2002/206 Reg.4

237. Private Water Supplies Regulations (Northern Ireland) 1994
Reg.21, revoked: SR 2002/331 Reg.38

250. Vegetable Seeds Regulations (Northern Ireland) 1994
applied: SR 2002/257 Sch.5, SR 2002/407 Sch.5

251. Beet Seeds Regulations (Northern Ireland) 1994
applied: SR 2002/257 Sch.4, SR 2002/407 Sch.4

252. Fodder Plant Seeds Regulations (Northern Ireland) 1994
applied: SR 2002/257 Sch.2, SR 2002/407 Sch.2
Reg.3, amended: SR 2003/42 Reg.3
Reg.8, amended: SR 2003/42 Reg.3
Reg.9, amended: SR 2003/42 Reg.3
Reg.9B, added: SR 2003/42 Reg.3
Reg.9C, added: SR 2003/42 Reg.3
Sch.5, added: SR 2003/42 Reg.3

253. Seeds (Registration, Licensing and Enforcement) regulations (Northern Ireland) 1994
applied: SR 2002/257 Sch.6, SR 2002/407 Sch.6

254. Cereal Seeds Regulations (Northern Ireland) 1994
applied: SR 2002/257 Sch.1, SR 2002/407 Sch.1
Reg.3, amended: SR 2003/42 Reg.2
Reg.8, amended: SR 2003/42 Reg.2
Reg.9, amended: SR 2003/42 Reg.2
Reg.9B, added: SR 2003/42 Reg.2
Reg.9C, added: SR 2003/42 Reg.2
Sch.5, added: SR 2003/42 Reg.2

1994–cont.

255. Oil and Plant Fibre Plant Seeds Regulations (Northern Ireland) 1994
applied: SR 2002/257 Sch.3, SR 2002/407 Sch.3

271. Statutory Maternity Pay (Compensation of Employers) and Miscellaneous Amendment Regulations (Northern Ireland) 1994
Reg.2, amended: SI 2004/698

300. Occupational and Personal Pension Schemes (Consequential Amendments) Regulations (Northern Ireland) 1994
Sch.2, revoked (in part): SR 2003/256 Reg.19

306. Domestic Energy Efficiency Grants Regulations (Northern Ireland) 1994
revoked: SR 2002/56 Reg.8

308. Industrial Tribunals Extension of Jurisdiction Order (Northern Ireland) 1994
applied: SI 2003/2902 Sch.2, Sch.4

345. Social Security (Claims and Payments) (Amendment) Regulations (Northern Ireland) 1994
revoked: SI 2003/492 Sch.3 Part 2
Reg.2, revoked (in part): SR 2002/297 Sch.1

364. Motor Vehicles (Exchangeable Licences) Order (Northern Ireland) 1994
Art.2, amended: SR 2002/328 Reg.3

370. Social Security (Severe Disablement Allowance and Invalid Care Allowance) (Amendment) Regulations (Northern Ireland) 1994
Reg.5, revoked (in part): SR 2002/323 Reg.4

399. Warrenpoint Harbour Authority (Amendment) Order (Northern Ireland) 1994
referred to: SR 2002/42 Art.1

424. Land Registration Rules (Northern Ireland) 1994
Part VIIA, added: SR 2002/229 Sch.1 para.4
r.2, amended: SR 2002/229 Sch.1 para.1
r.116, amended: SR 2002/229 Sch.1 para.2
r.116A, added: SR 2002/229 Sch.1 para.3
Sch.2, amended: SR 2002/229 Sch.1 para.5

456. Social Security (Claims and Payments) (Amendment No 2) Regulations (Northern Ireland) 1994
revoked: SI 2003/492 Sch.3 Part 2

461. Social Security (Incapacity Benefit) Regulations (Northern Ireland) 1994
Reg.1A, revoked (in part): SR 2003/213 Reg.2
Reg.1B, amended: SR 2002/323 Sch.1 para.1, SR 2003/195 Sch.4 para.4
Reg.6A, added: SR 2002/359 Reg.3
Reg.6B, added: SR 2002/359 Reg.3
Reg.6C, added: SR 2003/231 Reg.2
Reg.7, amended: SR 2002/276 Reg.3

1994–cont.

461. Social Security (Incapacity Benefit) Regulations (Northern Ireland) 1994–cont.
Reg.9, amended: SR 2002/99 Art.14, SR 2003/155 Art.15
Reg.17, amended: SR 2002/276 Reg.3
Reg.17, revoked (in part): SR 2002/276 Reg.3
Reg.18, amended: SR 2002/86 Reg.3

484. Social Security (Claims and Payments) (Amendment No 4) Regulations (Northern Ireland) 1994
revoked: SI 2003/492 Sch.3 Part 2
Reg.2, revoked (in part): SR 2002/297 Sch.1

485. Social Security (Incapacity Benefit Increases for Dependants) Regulations (Northern Ireland) 1994
Part II, revoked: SR 2003/213 Reg.2
Reg.3, substituted: SR 2003/213 Reg.2
Reg.9, amended: SR 2003/213 Reg.2
Reg.9, revoked (in part): SR 2003/213 Reg.2

1995

12. Urban Waste Water Treatment Regulations (Northern Ireland) 1995
Reg.3, revoked (in part): SR 2003/278 Reg.2
Reg.3A, added: SR 2003/278 Reg.2
Reg.3B, added: SR 2003/278 Reg.2
Reg.12, revoked (in part): SR 2003/278 Reg.2

25. Milk Marketing Board (Residuary Functions) Regulations (Northern Ireland) 1995
Reg.20, amended: SR 2002/151 Reg.3
Reg.26, amended: SR 2002/151 Reg.4
Reg.26A, added: SR 2002/151 Reg.5

32. Pesticides (Maximum Residue Levels in Crops, Food and Feeding Stuffs) (National Limits) Regulations (Northern Ireland) 1995
revoked: SR 2002/20 Sch.4

33. Pesticides (Maximum Residue Levels in Crops, Food and Feeding Stuffs) (EEC Limits) Regulations (Northern Ireland) 1995
revoked: SR 2002/20 Sch.4

35. Social Security (Incapacity Benefit) (Transitional) Regulations (Northern Ireland) 1995
Reg.7, revoked: SR 2002/86 Reg.5
Reg.7, varied: SR 2002/86 Reg.4
Reg.18, amended: SR 2002/99 Art.15, SR 2003/155 Art.16

41. Social Security (Incapacity for Work) (General) Regulations (Northern Ireland) 1995
Reg.10A, amended: SR 2002/86 Reg.2
Reg.17, amended: SR 2002/86 Reg.2, SR 2002/276 Reg.4
Reg.17, referred to: SR 2002/86 Reg.4
Reg.17, varied: SR 2002/86 Reg.4

NO.

1995–cont.

60. **Chemicals (Hazard Information and Packaging for Supply) Regulations (Northern Ireland) 1995**
applied: SR 2002/301 Reg.16, SR 2003/152 Sch.5
revoked: SR 2002/301 Sch.8

78. **Planning (Fees) Regulations (Northern Ireland) 1995**
Reg.2, amended: SR 2003/41 Reg.2
Reg.9, amended: SR 2003/41 Reg.2
Reg.11, amended: SR 2003/41 Reg.2
Reg.13, amended: SR 2003/41 Reg.2
Reg.16, amended: SR 2003/41 Reg.2
Reg.18, amended: SR 2003/41 Reg.2
Reg.19, amended: SR 2003/41 Reg.2
Sch.1, amended: SR 2003/41 Reg.2
Sch.1, substituted: SR 2003/41 Sch.1
Sch.2, amended: SR 2003/41 Reg.2

95. **Health and Personal Social Services (Superannuation) Regulations (Northern Ireland) 1995**
Reg.2, amended: SR 2002/69 Reg.3
Reg.14, amended: SR 2002/69 Reg.4
Reg.22, amended: SR 2002/69 Reg.5
Reg.49, amended: SR 2002/69 Reg.6
Reg.78, amended: SR 2002/69 Reg.7
Reg.84, amended: SR 2002/69 Reg.8
Reg.85, amended: SR 2002/69 Reg.9

122. **Batteries and Accumulators (Containing Dangerous Substances) Regulations (Northern Ireland) 1995**
Reg.2, amended: SR 2002/300 Reg.3
Reg.2A, added: SR 2002/300 Reg.3
Reg.3, substituted: SR 2002/300 Reg.3
Reg.7, amended: SR 2002/300 Reg.3

150. **Social Security (Incapacity Benefit) (Consequential and Transitional Amendments and Savings) Regulations (Northern Ireland) 1995**
Reg.21, revoked: SI 2003/492 Sch.3 Part 2

201. **Dairy Products (Hygiene) Regulations (Northern Ireland) 1995**
referred to: SR 2003/300 Sch.1
Reg.2, amended: SR 2002/340 Sch.8 para.1
Reg.22, referred to: SR 2002/340 Reg.15
Reg.22, substituted: SR 2002/340 Sch.8 para.1

225. **Insolvent Partnerships Order (Northern Ireland) 1995**
varied: SR 2003/144 Art.2
Art.7, amended: SR 2003/144 Art.3
Art.8, amended: SR 2003/144 Art.4
Sch.3, amended: SR 2003/144 Art.5
Sch.3, applied: SI 2003/2553 Reg.16
Sch.4, amended: SR 2003/144 Art.5
Sch.5, amended: SR 2003/144 Art.5
Sch.6, amended: SR 2003/144 Art.5
Sch.9, amended: SR 2003/144 Art.6

NO.

1995–cont.

301. **Social Security (Income Support and Claims and Payments) (Amendment) Regulations (Northern Ireland) 1995**
Reg.1, amended: SI 2003/492 Sch.3 Part 2
Reg.3, revoked: SI 2003/492 Sch.3 Part 2
Sch.2, revoked: SI 2003/492 Sch.3 Part 2

305. **Misuse of Drugs (Amendment) Regulations (Northern Ireland) 1995**
revoked: SR 2002/1 Sch.7

367. **Income-Related Benefits and Social Security (Claims and Payments) (Miscellaneous Amendments) Regulations 1995**
Reg.5, revoked: SI 2003/492 Sch.3 Part 2

371. **Plant Protection Products Regulations (Northern Ireland) 1995**
applied: SR 2002/301 Reg.3, Reg.9, Reg.16
Reg.2, amended: SR 2002/21 Reg.2, SR 2002/125 Reg.2, SR 2002/289 Reg.2, SR 2003/79 Reg.2
Reg.5, applied: SR 2002/21 Reg.3, SR 2002/289 Reg.3
Reg.7, amended: SR 2003/79 Reg.2
Reg.7, applied: SR 2002/21 Reg.3
Reg.7, varied: SR 2002/21 Reg.3, SR 2002/125 Reg.3
Reg.13, applied: SR 2002/289 Reg.3
Reg.27, revoked (in part): SR 2003/79 Reg.2
Sch.AA1, added: SR 2003/79 Sch.1
Sch.A1, added: SR 2003/79 Sch.1
Sch.1, amended: SR 2003/79 Reg.2
Sch.2, amended: SR 2003/79 Reg.2
Sch.2, referred to: SR 2002/301 Reg.8

380. **Conservation (Nature Habitats, etc.) Regulations (Northern Ireland) 1995**
s.63A, added: SR 2003/46 Sch.11 para.5

396. **Poultry Meat, Farmed Game Bird Meat and Rabbit Meat (Hygiene and Inspection) Regulations (Northern Ireland) 1995**
applied: SR 2002/225 Reg.56, SR 2002/340 Reg.4
Reg.8, amended: SR 2002/217 Reg.4
Reg.17, amended: SR 2002/217 Reg.4

413. **Genetically Modified Organisms (Deliberate Release) (Amendment) Regulations (Northern Ireland) 1995**
revoked: SR 2003/167 Sch.5

447. **Public Service Vehicles (Conditions of Fitness, Equipment and Use) Regulations 1995**
Reg.2, amended: SR 2003/38 Reg.2
Reg.4, amended: SR 2003/38 Reg.3
Reg.13, amended: SR 2003/38 Reg.4
Reg.14, amended: SR 2003/38 Reg.5
Reg.15, amended: SR 2003/38 Reg.6
Reg.16, amended: SR 2003/38 Reg.7
Reg.19, amended: SR 2003/38 Reg.8
Reg.19, revoked (in part): SR 2003/38 Reg.8
Reg.21, amended: SR 2003/38 Reg.9
Reg.21, revoked (in part): SR 2003/38 Reg.9

NO.

1995–cont.

447. Public Service Vehicles (Conditions of Fitness, Equipment and Use) Regulations 1995–cont.

Reg.22, amended: SR 2003/38 Reg.10

Reg.38, substituted: SR 2002/384 Reg.2

Reg.60A, added: SR 2003/38 Reg.11

Sch.1, amended: SR 2003/38 Reg.12

448. Motor Vehicle Testing Regulations (Northern Ireland) 1995

revoked: SR 2003/303 Sch.4

Sch.1, substituted: SR 2002/47 Reg.2, SR 2003/101 Reg.2

450. Goods Vehicles (Testing) Regulations (Northern Ireland) 1995

Sch.1, substituted: SR 2002/48 Reg.2, SR 2003/102 Reg.2

460. Pesticides (Maximum Residue Levels in Crops, Food and Feeding Stuffs) (National Limits) (Amendment) Regulations (Northern Ireland) 1995

revoked: SR 2002/20 Sch.4

461. Pesticides (Maximum Residue Levels in Crops, Food and Feeding Stuffs) (EEC Limits) (Amendment) Regulations (Northern Ireland) 1995

revoked: SR 2002/20 Sch.4

480. Misuse of Drugs (Amendment) (No.2) Regulations (Northern Ireland) 1995

revoked: SR 2002/1 Sch.7

491. Borehole Sites and Operations (Northern Ireland) 1995

Reg.2, applied: SR 2003/152 Reg.3

1996

11. Social Security (Persons from Abroad) (Miscellaneous Amendments) Regulations (Northern Ireland) 1996

Reg.7, revoked: SI 2003/492 Sch.3 Part 2

16. Disease of Fish (Control) Regulations (Northern Ireland) 1996

Reg.2, substituted: SR 2002/53 Sch.1 para.1

Reg.7, substituted: SR 2002/53 Sch.1 para.1

Reg.8, revoked: SR 2002/53 Sch.1 para.2

Reg.9, amended: SR 2002/53 Sch.1 para.3

Reg.10, amended: SR 2002/53 Sch.1 para.4

Reg.11, amended: SR 2002/53 Sch.1 para.5

Reg.12, substituted: SR 2002/53 Sch.1 para.6

Reg.14, amended: SR 2002/53 Sch.1 para.7

Sch.1, revoked: SR 2002/53 Sch.1 para.8

Sch.4, amended: SR 2002/53 Sch.1 para.9

Sch.5, revoked: SR 2002/53 Sch.1 para.8

48. Sweetners in Food Regulations (Northern Ireland) 1996

Reg.2, amended: SR 2002/39 Reg.3, SR 2003/257 Reg.2

Reg.3, amended: SR 2003/257 Reg.2

Sch.1, amended: SR 2002/39 Sch.1

NO.

1996–cont.

49. Colours in Food Regulations (Northern Ireland) 1996

Reg.12, revoked (in part): SR 2003/301 Reg.10

Sch.2, amended: SR 2003/300 Reg.10, SR 2003/313 Reg.11

Sch.6, amended: SR 2002/219 Sch.1

50. Micellaneous Food Additives Regulations (Northern Ireland) 1996

Reg.2, amended: SR 2003/158 Reg.2

Reg.10, revoked (in part): SR 2003/300 Reg.10, SR 2003/301 Reg.10

Sch.2, amended: SR 2003/301 Reg.10

Sch.3, amended: SR 2003/313 Reg.11

Sch.7, amended: SR 2003/300 Reg.10, SR 2003/313 Reg.11

Sch.9, amended: SR 2003/300 Reg.10, SR 2003/301 Reg.10, SR 2003/313 Reg.11

53. Food (Miscellaneous Revocations and Amendments) Regulations (Northern Ireland) 1996

Sch.1, revoked: SR 2002/219 Sch.1

57. Social Security (Industrial Diseases) (Prescribed Diseases) (Amendment) Regulations (Northern Ireland) 1996

Reg.3, revoked (in part): SR 2003/63 Reg.4

65. Child Support (Maintenance Assessments and Special Cases) and Social Security (Claims and Payments) (Amendment) Regulations (Northern Ireland) 1996

Reg.4, revoked: SI 2003/492 Sch.3 Part 2

73. Social Security Up-rating Order (Northern Ireland) 1996

Art.18, revoked: SR 2002/99 Art.23

85. Social Security (Claims and Payments Etc.) (Amendment) Regulations (Northern Ireland) 1996

Reg.2, revoked (in part): SI 2003/492 Sch.3 Part 2, SR 2002/297 Sch.1

94. Occupational Pension Schemes (Discharge of Protected Rights on Winding Up) Regulations (Northern Ireland) 1996

Reg.3, substituted: SR 2003/256 Reg.5

100. Supreme Court Fees Order (Northern Ireland) 1996

Art.2, substituted: SR 2002/341 Art.3

Art.7, amended: SR 2002/341 Art.4

Sch.1, substituted: SR 2002/341 Sch.1

102. Magistrate's Courts Fees Order (Northern Ireland) 1996

Art.2, amended: SR 2002/343 Art.3

Art.5, amended: SR 2002/343 Art.4

Sch.1, substituted: SR 2002/343 Sch.1

103. County Court Fees Order (Northern Ireland) 1996

Art.2, amended: SR 2002/342 Art.3

Art.5, amended: SR 2002/342 Art.4

Sch.1, substituted: SR 2002/342 Sch.1

NO.

1996–cont.

111. Housing Benefit (General) (Amendment No 2) Regulations (Northern Ireland) 1996
Reg.16, amended: SR 2003/108 Reg.4

119. Health and Safety (Safety Signs and Signals) Regulations (Northern Ireland) 1996
applied: SR 2003/152 Sch.5
referred to: SR 2003/34 Sch.7, SR 2003/35 Sch.2

140. Motor Vehicle Testing (Amendment) Regulations (Northern Ireland) 1996
revoked: SR 2003/303 Sch.4

143. Public Service Vehicles (License Fees) (Amendment) Regulations (Northern Ireland) 1996
revoked: SR 2002/49 Reg.3

145. Passenger and Goods Vehicles (Recording Equipment) Regulations (Northern Ireland) 1996
Reg.9, amended: SR 2002/50 Reg.2

173. Industrial Tribunals (Constitution and Rules of Procedure) Regulations (Northern Ireland) 1996
applied: SR 2002/245 Art.6

179. Companies (Summary Financial Statement) Regulations (Northern Ireland) 1996
referred to: SR 2003/3 Art.29, Sch.2 para.1
Part I, amended: SR 2003/3 Sch.2 para.2
Part II, amended: SR 2003/3 Sch.2 para.3, Sch.2 para.4, Sch.2 para.5
Part III, amended: SR 2003/3 Sch.2 para.6

190. Students Awards Regulations (Northern Ireland) 1996
Reg.2, varied: SR 2002/265 Reg.18
Sch.6, varied: SR 2002/265 Reg.18

192. Equipment and Protective Systems Intended for Use in Potentially Explosive Atmospheres Regulations 1996
referred to: SR 2003/152 Sch.3 para.1

196. Agricultural Processing and Marketing Grant Regulations (Northern Ireland) 1996
revoked: SR 2002/30 Reg.17
Reg.2, referred to: SR 2002/30 Reg.17
Reg.4, referred to: SR 2002/30 Reg.17
Reg.5, referred to: SR 2002/30 Reg.17
Reg.8, referred to: SR 2002/30 Reg.17

198. Jobseeker's Allowance Regulations (Northern Ireland) 1996
referred to: SR 2003/1 Reg.4, SR 2003/155 Art.22, SR 2003/195 Reg.3
Reg.1, amended: SR 2002/80 Reg.5, SR 2002/128 Reg.4, SR 2002/132 Sch.1 para.1, SR 2002/203 Reg.2, SR 2002/222 Reg.2, SR 2002/275 Reg.2, SR 2002/363 Reg.3, SR 2003/1 Sch.3 para.1, SR 2003/261 Reg.5
Reg.2A, revoked (in part): SR 2003/195 Sch.2 para.1

NO.

1996–cont.

198. Jobseeker's Allowance Regulations (Northern Ireland) 1996–cont.
Reg.3E, amended: SR 2002/332 Reg.3
Reg.5, amended: SR 2002/388 Reg.2
Reg.12, substituted: SR 2002/388 Reg.2
Reg.15, amended: SR 2002/388 Reg.2
Reg.19, applied: SI 2002/2006 Reg.17
Reg.30, amended: SR 2002/388 Reg.2
Reg.46, amended: SR 2002/323 Sch.1 para.1
Reg.47, amended: SR 2002/80 Reg.5
Reg.48, amended: SR 2002/275 Reg.2, SR 2002/323 Sch.1 para.1
Reg.48A, amended: SR 2002/243 Reg.2
Reg.51, amended: SR 2002/323 Sch.1 para.1
Reg.52, amended: SR 2002/363 Reg.3
Reg.53, amended: SR 2002/132 Sch.1 para.2
Reg.75, amended: SR 2002/275 Reg.2
Reg.75, applied: SI 2002/2006 Reg.17
Reg.75, referred to: SR 2003/28 Sch.2 para.5
Reg.76, amended: SR 2003/1 Sch.3 para.2
Reg.77, amended: SR 2003/1 Sch.3 para.3
Reg.79, amended: SR 2002/99 Art.20, SR 2003/155 Art.21
Reg.82, amended: SR 2002/132 Sch.1 para.3
Reg.83, amended: SR 2002/132 Sch.1 para.4, SR 2003/195 Sch.2 para.2
Reg.83, applied: SR 2003/155 Art.22, SR 2003/195 Reg.7
Reg.83, referred to: SR 2002/99 Art.21
Reg.83, revoked (in part): SR 2003/195 Sch.2 para.2
Reg.84, amended: SR 2002/132 Sch.1 para.5, SR 2003/195 Sch.2 para.3
Reg.84, applied: SR 2003/155 Art.22, SR 2003/195 Reg.7
Reg.84, referred to: SR 2002/99 Art.21
Reg.84, revoked (in part): SR 2003/195 Sch.2 para.3
Reg.85, amended: SR 2002/132 Sch.1 para.6, SR 2003/195 Sch.2 para.4
Reg.85, applied: SI 2003/654 Reg.7, SR 2003/155 Art.22
Reg.85, referred to: SR 2002/99 Art.21
Reg.86, revoked: SR 2002/132 Sch.1 para.7
Reg.86A, amended: SR 2002/132 Sch.1 para.8
Reg.86B, amended: SR 2002/132 Sch.1 para.8, SR 2003/195 Sch.2 para.5
Reg.86C, amended: SR 2002/132 Sch.1 para.9
Reg.86D, revoked: SR 2002/132 Sch.1 para.10
Reg.87, applied: SR 2003/28 Sch.1 para.6
Reg.88, amended: SR 2003/195 Sch.2 para.6
Reg.89, amended: SR 2003/195 Sch.2 para.7
Reg.96, amended: SR 2003/1 Sch.3 para.4
Reg.98, amended: SR 2002/363 Reg.3
Reg.103, amended: SR 2002/222 Reg.7, SR 2003/195 Sch.2 para.8

NO.

1996–cont.

198. Jobseeker's Allowance Regulations (Northern Ireland) 1996–cont.

Reg.104, amended: SR 2002/299 Reg.2

Reg.104, revoked (in part): SR 2003/195 Sch.2 para.9

Reg.105, amended: SR 2002/128 Reg.4, SR 2003/195 Sch.2 para.10

Reg.105, revoked (in part): SR 2003/195 Sch.2 para.10

Reg.106, revoked: SR 2003/195 Sch.2 para.11

Reg.109, revoked: SR 2003/195 Sch.2 para.11

Reg.110, revoked (in part): SR 2003/195 Sch.2 para.12

Reg.113, amended: SR 2002/128 Reg.4, SR 2002/132 Sch.1 para.11, SR 2003/195 Sch.2 para.13

Reg.117, revoked (in part): SR 2003/195 Sch.2 para.14

Reg.121, amended: SR 2002/323 Sch.1 para.1, SR 2003/195 Sch.2 para.15

Reg.121, revoked (in part): SR 2003/195 Sch.2 para.15

Reg.130, amended: SR 2002/222 Reg.2

Reg.131, amended: SR 2002/222 Reg.3, Reg.4, Reg.7, SR 2002/270 Reg.2, SR 2003/195 Sch.2 para.16, SR 2003/351 Reg.2

Reg.136, amended: SR 2002/222 Reg.3, Reg.5, SR 2003/351 Reg.2

Reg.136A, amended: SR 2002/132 Sch.1 para.12, SR 2003/195 Sch.2 para.17

Reg.138, amended: SR 2002/132 Sch.1 para.13, SR 2003/195 Sch.2 para.17

Reg.140, amended: SR 2003/195 Sch.2 para.18

Reg.145, referred to: SR 2002/99 Sch.13, SR 2003/155 Sch.13

Reg.146G, referred to: SR 2002/99 Sch.13, SR 2003/155 Sch.13

Reg.148, amended: SR 2002/132 Sch.1 para.14, SR 2003/195 Sch.2 para.19

Reg.148, applied: SR 2003/155 Art.22

Reg.148, referred to: SR 2002/99 Art.21, Sch.13, SR 2003/155 Sch.13

Reg.148, revoked (in part): SR 2002/132 Sch.1 para.14, SR 2003/195 Sch.2 para.19

Reg.148A, amended: SR 2002/132 Sch.1 para.15

Reg.148A, referred to: SR 2002/99 Sch.13, SR 2003/155 Sch.13

Reg.148A, revoked (in part): SR 2002/132 Sch.1 para.15

Reg.150, amended: SR 2002/323 Sch.1 para.1

Reg.151, revoked: SR 2002/132 Sch.1 para.16

Reg.153, amended: SR 2002/323 Sch.1 para.1

Reg.170, amended: SR 2002/99 Art.22, SR 2003/155 Art.23

NO.

1996–cont.

198. Jobseeker's Allowance Regulations (Northern Ireland) 1996–cont.

Sch.A1, amended: SR 2002/323 Sch.1 para.1

Sch.A1, applied: SR 2002/79 Reg.12, Reg.13

Sch.1, added: SR 2002/80 Reg.5

Sch.1, amended: SR 2002/80 Reg.5, SR 2002/99 Art.21, Sch.8, SR 2002/132 Sch.1 para.17, SR 2002/267 Reg.2, SR 2002/322 Reg.3, SR 2002/323 Sch.1 para.1, SR 2003/155 Art.22, SR 2003/195 Sch.2 para.20, SR 2003/261 Reg.5

Sch.1, applied: SR 2002/79 Reg.4, Reg.5, Reg.10, Reg.11, Reg.16, SR 2002/99 Art.21, SR 2003/28 Sch.1 para.6, SR 2003/155 Art.22

Sch.1, referred to: SR 2002/99 Art.21, SR 2003/155 Art.22

Sch.1, revoked (in part): SR 2002/132 Sch.1 para.17, SR 2003/195 Sch.2 para.20, Sch.2 para.20

Sch.1, substituted: SR 2002/99 Sch.8, Sch.9, Sch.10, SR 2003/155 Sch.8, Sch.9, Sch.10

Sch.2, amended: SR 2002/99 Art.21, SR 2003/155 Art.22, SR 2003/191 Reg.32, SR 2003/261 Reg.5

Sch.2, applied: SR 2002/99 Art.21, SR 2003/155 Art.22

Sch.2, referred to: SR 2002/99 Sch.13, SR 2003/155 Sch.13

Sch.3, revoked: SR 2002/132 Sch.1 para.18

Sch.3A, revoked: SR 2002/132 Sch.1 para.18

Sch.4, amended: SR 2002/99 Sch.11, 2002/132 Sch.1 para.19, SR 2003/155 Sch.11 Part I, SR 2003/195 Sch.2 para.21, SR 2003/261 Reg.5

Sch.4, applied: SR 2002/99 Art.21

Sch.4, referred to: SR 2003/155 Art.22, Sch.11 Part II

Sch.4, revoked (in part): SR 2002/132 Sch.1 para.19, SR 2003/261 Reg.5

Sch.4A, amended: SR 2002/99 Sch.12, SR 2002/132 Sch.1 para.20, SR 2003/261 Reg.5

Sch.4A, applied: SR 2002/99 Art.21

Sch.4A, referred to: SR 2003/155 Art.22

Sch.4A, revoked: SR 2002/132 Sch.1 para.20

Sch.4A, substituted: SR 2003/155 Sch.12

Sch.5, amended: SR 2002/132 Sch.1 para.21, SR 2002/323 Sch.1 para.1, SR 2003/195 Sch.2 para.22

Sch.5, applied: SR 2003/28 Sch.1 para.6

Sch.5, revoked: SR 2003/195 Sch.2 para.22

Sch.5A, amended: SR 2002/132 Sch.1 para.22, SR 2003/154 Reg.3

Sch.6, added: SR 2002/275 Reg.2, SR 2003/1 Sch.3 para.5, SR 2003/154 Reg.3, SR 2003/195 Sch.2 para.23

Sch.6, amended: SR 2002/99 Art.21, SR 2002/128 Reg.4, SR 2002/132 Sch.1 para.23, SR 2002/299 Reg.3, SR 2002/363 Reg.3, SR 2003/155 Art.22, SR 2003/195 Sch.2 para.23

NO.

NO.

1996–cont.

198. **Jobseeker's Allowance Regulations (Northern Ireland) 1996**–*cont.*
Sch.6, revoked (in part): SR 2002/132 Sch.1 para.23, Sch.1 para.23, SR 2003/195 Sch.2 para.23
Sch.7, added: SR 2002/275 Reg.2, SR 2003/154 Reg.3
Sch.7, amended: SR 2002/132 Sch.1 para.24, SR 2002/295 Reg.4, SR 2003/154 Reg.3, SR 2003/195 Sch.2 para.24

225. **Social Security (Disability Living Allowance and Claims and Payments) (Amendment) Regulations 1996**
Reg.2, revoked: SI 2003/492 Sch.3 Part 2

252. **Financial Markets and Insolvency Regulations (Northern Ireland) 1996**
applied: 2002 c.29 s.282

260. **Teachers Superannuation (Additional Voluntary Contributions) Regulations (Northern Ireland) 1996**
Reg.2, amended: SR 2003/86 Reg.2
Reg.5, amended: SR 2003/86 Reg.2
Reg.10, amended: SR 2003/86 Reg.2
Reg.12, amended: SR 2003/86 Reg.2
Sch.1, added: SR 2003/86 Reg.2
Sch.1, amended: SR 2003/86 Reg.2

288. **Child Benefit, Child Support and Social Security (Miscellaneous Amendments) Regulations (Northern Ireland) 1996**
Reg.3, revoked: SI 2003/493 Sch.2 Part 2
Reg.6, revoked: SI 2003/492 Sch.3 Part 2

289. **Social Security and Child Support (Jobseeker's Allowance) (Consequential Amendments) Regulations (Northern Ireland) 1996**
Reg.10, revoked: SI 2003/493 Sch.2 Part 2
Reg.15, revoked: SI 2003/492 Sch.3 Part 2

300. **Children (Allocation of Proceedings) Order (Northern Ireland) 1996**
Sch.1, amended: SR 2002/350 Art.2

322. **Family Proceedings Rules (Northern Ireland) 1996**
Part IVA, added: SR 2003/75 Sch.1
Part IVB, added: SR 2003/75 Sch.1
Part IVC, added: SR 2003/75 Sch.1
r.1.3, amended: SR 2002/137 r.4, SR 2003/75 r.3
r.2.29A, added: SR 2002/137 r.5
r.2.73, amended: SR 2002/137 r.6
r.3.24, added: SR 2002/137 r.7
r.3.38, added: SR 2002/137 r.7
r.8.33, added: SR 2002/137 r.8
r.8.43, added: SR 2002/137 r.8
Sch.1, amended: SR 2002/137 r.9, r.10, r.12, Sch.1
Sch.2, amended: SR 2003/75 Sch.2
Sch.3, added: SR 2003/75 Sch.3

353. **Misuse of Drugs (Amendment) Regulations (Northern Ireland) 1996**
revoked: SR 2002/1 Sch.7

1996–cont.

354. **Social Security (Claims and Payments) (Jobseeker's Allowance Consequential Amendments) Regulations (Northern Ireland) 1996**
revoked: SI 2003/492 Sch.3 Part 2
Reg.2, revoked (in part): SR 2003/224 Reg.6

369. **Harbour Works (Assessment of Environmental Effects) (Amendment) Regulations (Northern Ireland) 1996**
revoked: SR 2003/136 Reg.1

376. **Chemicals (Hazard Information and Packaging for Supply) (Amendment) Regulations (Northern Ireland) 1996**
revoked: SR 2002/301 Sch.8

383. **Food Labelling Regulations (Northern Ireland) 1996**
applied: SR 2003/313 Reg.6, Reg.7
referred to: SR 2003/159 Reg.2
Part II, referred to: SR 2003/300 Reg.5, SR 2003/301 Reg.5, SR 2003/313 Reg.6
Reg.4, revoked (in part): SR 2003/300 Reg.10, SR 2003/301 Reg.10, SR 2003/313 Reg.11
Reg.6, applied: SR 2003/160 Reg.4
Reg.7, applied: SR 2003/160 Reg.4
Reg.8, applied: SR 2003/160 Reg.4
Reg.14, amended: SR 2003/159 Reg.3
Reg.35, varied: SR 2003/300 Reg.6, SR 2003/301 Reg.6, SR 2003/313 Reg.7
Reg.36, varied: SR 2003/300 Reg.6, SR 2003/301 Reg.6, SR 2003/313 Reg.7
Reg.38, varied: SR 2003/300 Reg.6, SR 2003/313 Reg.7
Reg.49, amended: SR 2003/313 Reg.11
Reg.49, revoked (in part): SR 2003/300 Reg.10, SR 2003/301 Reg.10
Reg.50, amended: SR 2003/159 Reg.4
Sch.1, revoked: SR 2003/160 Reg.11
Sch.3, added: SR 2003/159 Reg.5
Sch.3, amended: SR 2003/159 Reg.5, SR 2003/301 Reg.10
Sch.3, substituted: SR 2003/159 Reg.5
Sch.9, amended: SR 2003/313 Reg.11

404. **Fresh Meat (Beef Controls) Regulations (Northern Ireland) 1996**
Reg.3, applied: SR 2002/225 Reg.33

417. **Domestic Energy Efficiency Grants (Amendment) Regulations (Northern Ireland) 1996**
revoked: SR 2002/56 Reg.8

422. **Child Benefit (General) (Amendment) Regulations (Northern Ireland) 1996**
revoked: SI 2003/493 Sch.2 Part 2

426. **Driving Licences (Community Driving Licence) Regulations (Northern Ireland) 1996**
Sch.1, revoked (in part): SR 2002/374 Reg.4, Reg.4

NO.

1996–cont.

431. Occupational Pension Schemes (Member-nominated Trustees and Directors) Regulations (Northern Ireland) 1996

referred to: SR 2002/279 Reg.1

Reg.2, amended: SR 2003/256 Reg.6

Reg.9, amended: SR 2002/279 Reg.2

Reg.15, amended: SR 2002/279 Reg.3

Reg.20, amended: SR 2002/279 Reg.4

Sch.3, amended: SR 2002/279 Reg.5

432. Social Security (Claims and Payments and Adjudication) (Amendment) Regulations (Northern Ireland) 1996

Reg.2, revoked: SI 2003/492 Sch.3 Part 2

449. Income Support and Social Security (Claims and Payments) (Miscellaneous Amendments) Regulations (Northern Ireland) 1996

Reg.3, revoked: SI 2003/492 Sch.3 Part 2

453. Arrangements for Placement of Children (General) Regulations (Northern Ireland) 1996

applied: SI 2003/493 Reg.16

464. Social Security (Jobseeker's Allowance and Payments on Account) (Miscellaneous Amendments) Regulations (Northern Ireland) 1996

Reg.3, revoked: SI 2003/492 Sch.3 Part 2

467. Foster Placement (Children) Regulations (Northern Ireland) 1996

applied: SI 2002/2005 Reg.14, SI 2003/493 Reg.16, Reg.36

469. Child Benefit (General) (Amendment No 2) Regulations (Northern Ireland) 1996

revoked: SI 2003/493 Sch.2 Part 2

470. Child Benefit (General) (Amendment No 3) Regulations (Northern Ireland) 1996

revoked: SI 2003/493 Sch.2 Part 2

473. Royal Ulster Constabulary Regulations 1996

Reg.1, revoked (in part): SR 2002/95 Reg.10

Reg.2, amended: SR 2002/95 Reg.3, Reg.21

Reg.2, varied: SR 2002/95 Reg.2

Reg.4, amended: SR 2003/184 Reg.3

Reg.5, amended: SR 2002/95 Reg.4

Reg.7, amended: SR 2002/95 Reg.5

Reg.9, added: SR 2003/184 Reg.4

Reg.12, amended: SR 2002/95 Reg.6

Reg.13, amended: SR 2002/95 Reg.21

Reg.15, amended: SR 2002/95 Reg.7

Reg.17, amended: SR 2002/95 Reg.8

Reg.20, amended: SR 2002/95 Reg.21

Reg.20, varied: SR 2002/95 Reg.21

Reg.22, amended: SR 2002/95 Reg.9

Reg.27, amended: SR 2003/184 Reg.3

Reg.36, amended: SR 2002/95 Reg.10

Reg.36, revoked (in part): SR 2002/95 Reg.10

NO.

1996–cont.

473. Royal Ulster Constabulary Regulations 1996–*cont.*

Reg.37, amended: SR 2002/95 Reg.11, SR 2003/184 Reg.3

Reg.37A, added: SR 2002/95 Reg.12

Reg.37B, added: SR 2002/95 Reg.13

Reg.37C, added: SR 2002/95 Reg.14

Reg.39, amended: SR 2002/95 Reg.15

Reg.42, amended: SR 2002/95 Reg.16

Reg.43, amended: SR 2002/95 Reg.17

Reg.49, amended: SR 2002/95 Reg.18, SR 2003/184 Reg.3

Reg.52, amended: SR 2003/184 Reg.3

Reg.54, amended: SR 2003/184 Reg.3

Sch.1, amended: SR 2002/95 Reg.6, Reg.21

Sch.1, varied: SR 2002/95 Reg.21

Sch.4, added: SR 2002/95 Reg.22

Sch.4, amended: SR 2003/184 Reg.3

Sch.5, amended: SR 2002/95 Reg.23

Sch.6, revoked: SR 2002/95 Reg.10

Sch.8, amended: SR 2003/184 Reg.3

Sch.10, amended: SR 2002/95 Reg.24

Sch.10, substituted: SR 2002/95 Reg.24

Sch.13, amended: SR 2002/95 Reg.25

Sch.14, added: SR 2003/184 Reg.5

493. Occupational Pension Schemes (Contracting-out) Regulations (Northern Ireland) 1996

Reg.1, referred to: SR 2002/352 Reg.121

Reg.3, amended: SR 2002/109 Reg.2

Reg.3, revoked (in part): SR 2002/109 Reg.2

Reg.6, revoked (in part): SR 2002/109 Reg.2

Reg.9, amended: SR 2002/109 Reg.2

Reg.16, amended: SR 2002/109 Reg.2

Reg.18, amended: SR 2002/109 Reg.2

Reg.19, substituted: SR 2002/109 Reg.2

Reg.20, substituted: SR 2002/109 Reg.2

Reg.20A, added: SR 2002/109 Reg.2

Reg.23, amended: SR 2002/109 Reg.2

Reg.31, amended: SR 2002/109 Reg.2

Reg.51, amended: SI 2002/681 Reg.7

Reg.52, amended: SI 2002/681 Reg.7

Reg.54, applied: SR 2002/352 Reg.93

Reg.60, amended: SR 2002/109 Reg.2

Reg.61, amended: SR 2002/109 Reg.2

Reg.62, amended: SR 2002/109 Reg.2

Reg.63, amended: SR 2002/109 Reg.2

Reg.72, amended: SR 2002/109 Reg.2

495. Family Proceedings Fees (Amendment) Fees 1996

Art.2, amended: SR 2002/344 Art.3

Art.5, amended: SR 2002/344 Art.4

Sch.1, substituted: SR 2002/344 Sch.1

509. Protected Rights (Transfer Payment) Regulations (Northern Ireland) 1996

Reg.4A, added: SR 2002/109 Reg.3

Reg.5, amended: SR 2002/109 Reg.3

NO.

1996–cont.

518. Jobseeker's Allowance (Transitional Provisions) (No.2) Regulations (Northern Ireland) 1996

Reg.3, amended: SR 2002/323 Sch.1 para.2

519. Social Security (Back to Work Bonus) (No.2) Regulations (Northern Ireland) 1996

Reg.3, amended: SR 2002/80 Reg.6

Reg.4, amended: SR 2002/323 Sch.1 para.1

Reg.17, amended: SR 2003/191 Reg.30

520. Social Security Benefit (Computation of Earnings) Regulations (Northern Ireland) 1996

Reg.2, amended: SI 2002/2925 Reg.2

Reg.2, applied: SR 2002/99 Art.6

Reg.7, amended: SI 2002/2925 Reg.2, SR 2002/323 Sch.1 para.1

Reg.7, applied: SR 2002/99 Art.6, SR 2003/155 Art.6

Reg.9, amended: SI 2002/2925 Reg.2

Reg.10, amended: SI 2002/2925 Reg.2, SR 2002/323 Sch.1 para.1

Reg.11, varied: SR 2003/28 Reg.17B

Reg.12, varied: SR 2003/28 Reg.17B

Reg.13, amended: SI 2002/2925 Reg.2, SR 2002/323 Sch.1 para.1

Reg.13, varied: SR 2003/28 Reg.17B

Reg.14, varied: SR 2003/28 Reg.17B

Sch.3, amended: SI 2002/2925 Reg.2, SR 2002/323 Sch.1 para.1

521. Social Security (Invalid Care Allowance) (Amendment) Regulations (Northern Ireland) 1996

Reg.2, revoked (in part): SR 2002/323 Reg.4

Reg.3, amended: SR 2002/323 Sch.1 para.1

525. Health and Safety at Work Order (Application to Environmentally Hazardous Substances) Regulations (Northern Ireland) 1996

revoked: SR 2003/52 Reg.4

526. Pesticides (Maximum Residue Levels in Crops, Food, and Feeding Stuffs) (National Limits) (Amendment) Regulations (Northern Ireland) 1996

revoked: SR 2002/20 Sch.4

527. Pesticides (Maximum Residue Levels in Crops, Food and Feeding Stuffs) (EEC Limits) (Amendment) Regulations (Northern Ireland) 1996

revoked: SR 2002/20 Sch.4

541. Child Support Departure Direction and Consequential Amendments Regulations (Northern Ireland) 1996

Reg.9, amended: SR 2003/84 Reg.6

Reg.12, amended: SR 2003/84 Reg.6

Reg.23, amended: SR 2002/164 Reg.5

542. Motor Vehicles (Driving Licenses) Regulations (Northern Ireland) 1996

referred to: SR 2002/383 Reg.2

Reg.2, amended: SR 2002/383 Reg.3

NO.

1996–cont.

542. Motor Vehicles (Driving Licenses) Regulations (Northern Ireland) 1996– cont.

Reg.24, amended: SR 2002/51 Reg.2, SR 2002/383 Reg.4

Reg.29, amended: SR 2002/383 Reg.5

Reg.31, revoked (in part): SR 2003/64 Reg.2

Reg.32, amended: SR 2003/64 Reg.3

Reg.50, amended: SR 2003/64 Reg.4

Reg.51, amended: SR 2003/64 Reg.5

Sch.4, substituted: SR 2002/51 Reg.2, SR 2003/100 Reg.2

Sch.6, substituted: SR 2003/183 Sch.1 Part 1, Sch.1 Part 2

Sch.7, added: SR 2003/64 Reg.6

Sch.7, substituted: SR 2003/64 Reg.6

558. Welfare of Animals (Slaughter or Killing) Regulations (Northern Ireland) 1996

Sch.7, amended: SR 2002/304 Reg.2

564. Royal Ulster Constabulary Reserve (Full-time) (Appointment and Conditions of Service) Regulations 1996

Reg.1, revoked (in part): SR 2002/96 Reg.3

Reg.2, varied: SR 2002/96 Reg.2, Reg.4

Reg.4A, amended: SR 2002/96 Reg.4

Reg.11, varied: SR 2002/96 Reg.4

Reg.18, varied: SR 2002/96 Reg.4

Reg.20, amended: SR 2002/96 Reg.4

Reg.20, varied: SR 2002/96 Reg.4

Reg.21, varied: SR 2002/96 Reg.4

Reg.22, varied: SR 2002/96 Reg.4

Reg.23, varied: SR 2002/96 Reg.4

Reg.25, varied: SR 2002/96 Reg.4

Reg.30, amended: SR 2002/96 Reg.5

Reg.30, revoked (in part): SR 2002/96 Reg.4

Reg.30, varied: SR 2002/96 Reg.4

Reg.38, amended: SR 2002/96 Reg.6

Reg.38, varied: SR 2002/96 Reg.4

Sch.4, revoked: SR 2002/96 Reg.7

Sch.7, varied: SR 2002/96 Reg.4

Sch.8, amended: SR 2002/96 Reg.8

Sch.8, substituted: SR 2002/96 Reg.8

Sch.11, amended: SR 2002/96 Reg.9

570. Occupational Pension Schemes (Minimum Funding Requirement and Actuarial Valuations) Regulations (Northern Ireland) 1996

Reg.2, amended: SR 2002/64 Reg.2, SR 2003/256 Reg.7

Reg.7, amended: SR 2002/64 Reg.2

Reg.12, amended: SR 2002/64 Reg.2

Reg.16, amended: SR 2002/64 Reg.2

Reg.17, amended: SR 2002/64 Reg.2

Reg.18, amended: SR 2002/64 Reg.2

Reg.20, amended: SR 2002/64 Reg.2

Reg.20, revoked (in part): SR 2002/64 Reg.2

Reg.21, amended: SR 2002/64 Reg.2

Sch.2, amended: SR 2002/64 Reg.2

Sch.2, substituted: SR 2002/64 Reg.2

NO.

1996–cont.

570. Occupational Pension Schemes (Minimum Funding Requirement and Actuarial Valuations) Regulations (Northern Ireland) 1996–*cont.*

Sch.3, substituted: SR 2002/64 Reg.2

Sch.4, amended: SR 2002/64 Reg.2, SR 2003/256 Reg.7

584. Occupational Pension Schemes (Investment) Regulations (Northern Ireland) 1996

Reg.1, amended: SR 2003/256 Reg.8

Reg.2, amended: SR 2002/109 Reg.4

Reg.5, amended: SR 2003/256 Reg.8

Reg.6, amended: SR 2003/256 Reg.8

Reg.6, revoked (in part): SR 2003/256 Reg.8

Reg.8, amended: SR 2003/256 Reg.8

Reg.10, amended: SR 2003/256 Reg.8

585. Occupational Pension Schemes (Deficiency on Winding Up, etc.) Regulations (Northern Ireland) 1996

Reg.3, amended: SR 2002/64 Reg.3

Reg.3A, added: SR 2002/64 Reg.3

Sch.1, amended: SR 2002/64 Reg.3

603. Surface Waters (Abstraction for Drinking Water) (Classification) Regulations (Northern Ireland) 1996

referred to: SR 2002/331 Reg.26

Reg.8, revoked (in part): SR 2002/331 Reg.38

619. Occupational Pension Schemes (Transfer Values) Regulations (Northern Ireland) 1996

Reg.2, disapplied: SR 2002/352 Reg.119

Reg.3, referred to: SR 2002/352 Reg.119

Reg.4, referred to: SR 2002/352 Reg.119

Reg.5, applied: SR 2002/352 Reg.119

Reg.10, disapplied: SR 2002/352 Reg.119

Reg.18, applied: SR 2002/352 Reg.119

621. Occupational Pension Schemes (Winding Up) Regulations (Northern Ireland) 1996

applied: SR 2002/74 Reg.11

Reg.4, amended: SR 2002/64 Reg.4

Reg.4A, added: SR 2002/64 Reg.4

Reg.13, amended: SR 2002/64 Reg.4

622. Social Security (Child Maintenance Bonus) Regulations (Northern Ireland) 1996

Reg.4, amended: SR 2002/323 Sch.1 para.1

Reg.8, amended: SR 2003/191 Reg.31

Reg.16, revoked (in part): SI 2003/492 Sch.3 Part 2

1997

39. Personal and Occupational Pension Schemes (Pensions Ombudsman) Regulations (Northern Ireland) 1997

Reg.1, amended: SR 2003/256 Reg.9

Reg.4, amended: SR 2003/256 Reg.9

Reg.6, amended: SR 2003/256 Reg.9

NO.

1997–cont.

50. Rates (Making and Levying of Different Rates) (No.2) Regulations (Northern Ireland) 1997

revoked: SR 2002/409 Reg.4

56. Personal and Occupational Pension Schemes (Protected Rights) Regulations (Northern Ireland) 1997

Reg.4, amended: SR 2002/109 Reg.5

Reg.5, substituted: SR 2002/109 Reg.5

Reg.7, amended: SR 2002/109 Reg.5

Reg.9, amended: SR 2002/109 Reg.5

Reg.11, amended: SR 2003/256 Reg.10

Reg.12, amended: SR 2002/109 Reg.5

Reg.12, revoked (in part): SR 2002/109 Reg.5

Reg.13, amended: SR 2002/109 Reg.5

Reg.13, revoked (in part): SR 2002/109 Reg.5

80. Rates (Industrial Hereditaments) Order (Northern Ireland) 1997

revoked: SI 2004/703 Art.9

81. Valuation for Rating (Decapitalisation Rate) Regulations (Northern Ireland) 1997

revoked: SR 2003/30 Reg.5

82. Valuation (Telecommunications) Regulations (Northern Ireland) 1997

revoked: SR 2003/93 Reg.6

83. Valuation for Rating (Docks) Order (Northern Ireland) 1997

revoked: SR 2003/129 Art.3

84. Valuation for Rating (Plant and Machinery) Order (Northern Ireland) 1997

revoked: SR 2003/31 Art.3

94. Occupational Pension Schemes (Scheme Administration) Regulations (Northern Ireland) 1997

Reg.1, amended: SR 2003/256 Reg.11

Reg.3, amended: SR 2003/256 Reg.11

Reg.5, amended: SR 2003/256 Reg.11

Reg.11, amended: SR 2003/256 Reg.11

Reg.15, amended: SR 2003/256 Reg.11

97. Occupational Pension Schemes (Modification of Schemes) Regulations (Northern Ireland) 1997

referred to: SR 2002/109 Sch.1

Reg.6, amended: SR 2002/109 Reg.6

98. Occupational Pension Schemes (Disclosure of Information) Regulations (Northern Ireland) 1997

Reg.1, amended: SR 2002/410 Reg.3

Reg.5, amended: SR 2002/74 Reg.14, SR 2002/410 Reg.3

Sch.2, added: SR 2002/410 Reg.3

106. Railways (Rateable Value) Order (Northern Ireland) 1997

revoked: SR 2003/76 Art.10

107. Rates (Transitional Relief) Order (Northern Ireland) 1997

revoked: SR 2003/143 Art.8

NO.

1997–cont.

118. Valuation (Electricity) Order (Northern Ireland) 1997
revoked: SR 2003/77 Art.10

137. Local Government (Superannuation) (Milk Marketing Board for Northern Ireland) Regulations (Northern Ireland)1997
applied: SR 2002/353 Sch.2 para.2
disapplied: SR 2002/353 Sch.2 para.5
Reg.1, amended: SR 2002/353 Sch.4 para.2
Reg.2, amended: SR 2002/353 Sch.4 para.3

139. Personal Pension Schemes (Appropriate Schemes) Regulations (Northern Ireland) 1997
Reg.1, amended: SR 2003/256 Reg.12
Reg.2, amended: SR 2003/256 Reg.12
Reg.3, amended: SR 2003/256 Reg.12
Reg.3, revoked (in part): SR 2003/256 Reg.12
Reg.6A, added: SR 2002/109 Reg.7
Sch.1, amended: SR 2003/256 Reg.12

141. Occupational Pension Schemes (Pensions Compensation Provisions) Regulations (Northern Ireland) 1997
Reg.1, amended: SR 2003/256 Reg.13

153. Occupational Pension Schemes (Assignment, Forfeiture, Bankruptcy etc.) Regulations (Northern Ireland) 1997
referred to: SR 2002/109 Sch.1
Reg.2, amended: SR 2002/109 Reg.8

155. Social Security (Social Fund and Claims and Payments) (Miscellaneous Amendments) Regulations (Northern Ireland) 1997
Reg.3, revoked: SI 2003/492 Sch.3 Part 2

156. Social Security (Miscellaneous Amendments No 2) Regulations (Northern Ireland) 1997
Reg.3, revoked: SI 2003/492 Sch.3 Part 2

159. Occupational Pension Schemes (Discharge of Liability) Regulations (Northern Ireland) 1997
Reg.2, amended: SR 2003/256 Reg.14

165. Social Security (Income Support, Jobseeker's Allowance and Claims and Payments) (Miscellaneous Amendments) Regulations (Northern Ireland) 1997
Reg.4, revoked: SI 2003/492 Sch.3 Part 2

170. Housing Benefit (General) (Amendment No 4) Regulations (Northern Ireland) 1997
Reg.5, applied: SR 2003/108 Reg.2

191. Health and Personal Social Services (Optical Charges and Payments) Regulations (Northern Ireland) 1997
Part IV, applied: SR 2003/176 Reg.10
Part V, applied: SR 2003/176 Reg.10
Reg.1, amended: SR 2002/5 Reg.2, SR 2002/221 Reg.2, SR 2003/176 Reg.2

NO.

1997–cont.

191. Health and Personal Social Services (Optical Charges and Payments) Regulations (Northern Ireland) 1997–cont.
Reg.2, amended: SR 2002/85 Reg.2
Reg.8, amended: SR 2002/85 Reg.3, SR 2003/176 Reg.3
Reg.8, applied: SR 2003/176 Reg.10
Reg.8, referred to: SR 2003/176 Reg.10
Reg.8, revoked (in part): SR 2003/176 Reg.3
Reg.12, applied: SR 2003/176 Reg.7
Reg.12A, added: SR 2003/176 Reg.4
Reg.17, applied: SR 2003/176 Reg.7
Reg.19, amended: SR 2002/85 Reg.4, SR 2003/176 Reg.5
Sch.1, amended: SR 2002/85 Reg.5, SR 2003/176 Reg.6
Sch.2, amended: SR 2002/85 Reg.5, SR 2003/176 Reg.6
Sch.3, substituted: SR 2002/85 Sch.1, SR 2003/176 Sch.1

194. Gas Safety (Installation and Use) Regulations (Northern Ireland) 1997
applied: SR 2003/152 Reg.3

218. Fresh Meat (Import Conditions) Regulations (Northern Ireland) 1997
Reg.2, amended: SR 2002/340 Sch.8 para.2
Reg.16, disapplied: SR 2002/340 Sch.7

243. Pesticides (Maximum Residue Levels in Crops, Food and Feeding Stuffs) (National Limits) (Amendment) Regulations (Northern Ireland) 1997
revoked: SR 2002/20 Sch.4

244. Pesticides (Maximum Residue Levels in Crops, Food and Feeding Stuffs) (EEC Limits) (Amendment) Regulations (Northern Ireland) 1997
revoked: SR 2002/20 Sch.4

247. Carriage of Dangerous Goods (Classification, Packaging and Labelling) and Use of Transportable Pressure Receptacles Regulations (Northern Ireland) 1997
applied: SR 2002/301 Reg.7, SR 2003/33 Reg.23, Sch.2 para.1, SR 2003/152 Sch.5
referred to: SR 2003/34 Sch.7, SR 2003/35 Sch.2
Reg.2, amended: SR 2002/34 Sch.2 para.1, SR 2002/301 Reg.18
Reg.3, amended: SR 2002/34 Sch.2 para.2
Reg.4, amended: SR 2002/34 Sch.2 para.3
Reg.8, amended: SR 2002/34 Sch.2 para.4
Reg.9, applied: SR 2002/301 Reg.8, Reg.9
Reg.9, substituted: SR 2002/301 Reg.18
Reg.10, applied: SR 2002/301 Reg.8, Reg.9
Reg.10, substituted: SR 2002/301 Reg.18
Reg.11, amended: SR 2002/301 Reg.18
Reg.18, amended: SR 2002/34 Sch.2 para.5
Reg.24, revoked (in part): SR 2003/152 Sch.8 Part I
Sch.1, amended: SR 2002/34 Sch.2 para.6

NO.

1997–cont.

247. Carriage of Dangerous Goods (Classi-fication, Packaging and Labelling) and Use of Transportable Pressure Receptacles Regulations (Northern Ireland) 1997–*cont.*

Sch.3, amended: SR 2002/34 Sch.2 para.7

Sch.9, amended: SR 2002/34 Sch.2 para.8

248. Carriage of Dangerous Goods by Road Regulations (Northern Ireland) 1997

applied: SR 2003/33 Reg.23, SR 2003/152 Sch.5

referred to: SR 2003/34 Sch.7, SR 2003/35 Sch.2

Reg.2, amended: SR 2002/34 Sch.3 para.1

Reg.5, amended: SR 2002/34 Sch.3 para.2

Reg.8, amended: SR 2002/34 Sch.3 para.3

Reg.9, amended: SR 2002/34 Sch.3 para.4

Reg.10, amended: SR 2002/34 Sch.3 para.5

Reg.12, amended: SR 2002/34 Sch.3 para.6

Reg.13, amended: SR 2002/34 Sch.3 para.7

Reg.14, amended: SR 2002/34 Sch.3 para.8

Reg.17, amended: SR 2002/34 Sch.3 para.9

Reg.20, substituted: SR 2003/152 Sch.7 para.9

Reg.23, amended: SR 2002/34 Sch.3 para.10

Reg.24, amended: SR 2002/34 Sch.3 para.11

Reg.25, amended: SR 2002/34 Sch.3 para.12

Reg.25A, added: SR 2002/34 Sch.3 para.13

Reg.27, amended: SR 2002/34 Sch.3 para.14

Sch.2, added: SR 2002/34 Sch.3 para.15

Sch.2, amended: SR 2002/34 Sch.3 para.15

Sch.4, added: SR 2002/34 Sch.3 para.16

Sch.4, amended: SR 2002/34 Sch.3 para.16

Sch.5, added: SR 2002/34 Sch.3 para.17

Sch.5, amended: SR 2002/34 Sch.3 para.17

Sch.5, revoked (in part): SR 2002/34 Sch.3 para.17, Sch.3 para.17

Sch.5, substituted: SR 2002/34 Sch.3 para.17

Sch.6, amended: SR 2002/34 Sch.3 para.18, Sch.3 para.19

Sch.6, revoked (in part): SR 2002/34 Sch.3 para.18, Sch.3 para.18

Sch.6, substituted: SR 2002/34 Sch.3 para.18

Sch.7, added: SR 2002/34 Sch.3 para.19

Sch.7, amended: SR 2002/34 Sch.3 para.19

Sch.7, revoked: SR 2002/34 Sch.3 para.19

Sch.9A, added: SR 2002/34 Sch.3 para.20

Sch.10, added: SR 2002/34 Sch.3 para.21

Sch.10, amended: SR 2002/34 Sch.3 para.21

Sch.11, amended: SR 2002/34 Sch.3 para.22

Sch.12, revoked: SR 2003/152 Sch.8 Part I

249. Carriage of Dangerous Goods by Road (Driver Training) Regulations (Northern Ireland) 1997

Reg.1, amended: SR 2002/34 Sch.4 para.1

Reg.2, amended: SR 2002/34 Sch.4 para.2

Reg.4, amended: SR 2002/34 Sch.4 para.3

NO.

1997–cont.

249. Carriage of Dangerous Goods by Road (Driver Training) Regulations (Northern Ireland) 1997–*cont.*

Reg.9, amended: SR 2002/34 Sch.4 para.4

Sch.1, amended: SR 2002/34 Sch.4 para.5

Sch.3, amended: SR 2002/34 Sch.4 para.6

Sch.3, substituted: SR 2002/34 Sch.4 para.6

Sch.4, revoked: SR 2002/34 Sch.4 para.7

251. Open-Ended Investment Companies (Companies with Variable Capital) Regulations (Northern Ireland) 1997

applied: SI 2003/1400 Sch.4

referred to: 2002 c.13 (NI) s.1

Reg.22, applied: SI 2002/912 Sch.1, SI 2002/915 Sch.1

338. Contaminants in Food Regulations (Northern Ireland) 1997

revoked: SR 2002/219 Sch.1

352. Specified Diseases (Notification and Movement Restrictions) Order (Northern Ireland) 1997

Sch.1, amended: SR 2003/55 Art.14

380. General Medical Services Regula-tions (Northern Ireland) 1997

Reg.37, applied: SR 2002/66 Reg.8

Sch.2, added: SR 2003/133 Reg.2

Sch.2, amended: SR 2002/92 Reg.7

Sch.2, applied: SR 2002/66 Reg.12

Sch.3, amended: SR 2002/213 Reg.2

Sch.10, amended: SR 2002/266 Reg.2, SR 2003/6 Reg.2

Sch.11, amended: SR 2003/6 Reg.3, SR 2003/205 Reg.2

381. Pharmaceutical Services Regulations (Northern Ireland) 1997

Reg.2, amended: SR 2002/92 Reg.2, SR 2002/397 Reg.2

Reg.7, amended: SR 2002/92 Reg.3

Reg.7, revoked (in part): SR 2002/92 Reg.3

Reg.9, amended: SR 2002/92 Reg.4

Reg.11, amended: SR 2002/92 Reg.5

Sch.2, amended: SR 2002/92 Reg.6, SR 2002/397 Reg.3

382. Charges for Drugs and Appliances Regulations (Northern Ireland) 1997

varied: SR 2003/153 Reg.7

Reg.2, amended: SR 2002/397 Reg.4

Reg.3, amended: SR 2002/91 Reg.2, SR 2003/153 Reg.2

Reg.4, amended: SR 2002/91 Reg.3, SR 2003/153 Reg.3

Reg.5, amended: SR 2002/91 Reg.4, SR 2003/153 Reg.4

Reg.9, amended: SR 2002/91 Reg.5, SR 2003/153 Reg.5

Reg.9, applied: SR 2002/91 Reg.7, SR 2003/153 Reg.7

Sch.1, referred to: SR 2003/153 Reg.7

Sch.1, substituted: SR 2002/91 Reg.6, SR 2003/153 Reg.6

NO.

1997–cont.

386. Traffic Signs Regulations (Northern Ireland) 1997

Reg.2, amended: SR 2002/143 Reg.2

Reg.11, amended: SR 2002/143 Reg.2, SR 2003/214 .2

Reg.21, amended: SR 2002/143 Reg.2, SR 2003/214 Reg.2

Reg.44, amended: SR 2002/143 Reg.2

Sch.1, added: SR 2003/214 Reg.2

Sch.2, amended: SR 2002/143 Reg.2

Sch.2, revoked: SR 2003/214 .2

Sch.3, substituted: SR 2003/214 Reg.2

Sch.4, added: SR 2003/214 Reg.2

Sch.5, amended: SR 2002/143 Reg.2

Sch.5, substituted: SR 2003/214 Reg.2

Sch.6, amended: SR 2002/143 Reg.2

Sch.12, added: SR 2003/214 Reg.2

Sch.12, amended: SR 2002/143 Reg.2

Sch.15, amended: SR 2003/214 Reg.2

Sch.16, amended: SR 2002/143 Reg.2, SR 2003/214 Reg.2

Sch.17, amended: SR 2002/143 Reg.2, SR 2003/214 .2, Reg.2

398. Chemicals (Hazard Information and Packaging for Supply) (Amendment) Regulations (Northern Ireland) 1997

revoked: SR 2002/301 Sch.8

416. Social Security (Claims and Payments and Adjudication) (Amendment) (Regulations (Northern Ireland) 1997

Reg.2, revoked: SI 2003/492 Sch.3 Part 2

421. Food (Pistachios from Iran) (Emergency Control) Order (Northern Ireland) 1997

revoked: SR 2003/360 Reg.7

425. Fisheries Byelaws (Northern Ireland) 1997

referred to: SR 2002/371 Art.2, SR 2003/271 Art.2

Part XIX, added: SR 2002/11 Byelaw.4

Art.2, amended: SR 2002/11 Byelaw.3, SR 2002/371 Art.3, SR 2003/271 Art.3

Art.6, amended: SR 2002/371 Art.4

Art.7, substituted: SR 2002/371 Art.5

Art.8, amended: SR 2002/274 Art.3

Art.10A, added: SR 2002/274 Art.4

Art.16, substituted: SR 2002/274 Art.5

Art.24, amended: SR 2002/274 Art.6

Art.24, substituted: SR 2002/274 Art.6

Art.29A, added: SR 2002/274 Art.7

Art.86, substituted: SR 2002/371 Art.6

Art.88, substituted: SR 2003/271 Art.4

Sch.1, substituted: SR 2002/371 Art.7

Sch.4, amended: SR 2002/371 Art.8

435. Social Security (Miscellaneous Amendments No 4) Regulations (Northern Ireland) 1997

Reg.3, revoked: SI 2003/492 Sch.3 Part 2

NO.

1997–cont.

456. Housing Renovation etc Grants (Reduction of Grant) Regulations (Northern Ireland) 1997

referred to: SR 2003/282 Reg.2

Reg.2, amended: SR 2003/234 Reg.3, SR 2003/282 Reg.3

Reg.6, amended: SR 2003/234 Reg.4

Reg.8, amended: SR 2003/234 Reg.5

Reg.9, amended: SR 2003/234 Reg.6

Reg.11, amended: SR 2003/234 Reg.7

Reg.13, amended: SR 2003/234 Reg.8

Reg.17, amended: SR 2003/234 Reg.9, SR 2003/282 Reg.4

Reg.18, amended: SR 2003/234 Reg.10, SR 2003/282 Reg.5

Reg.30, amended: SR 2003/234 Reg.11

Reg.30, revoked (in part): SR 2003/234 Reg.11

Reg.37, amended: SR 2003/234 Reg.12

Reg.37, revoked (in part): SR 2003/234 Reg.12

Reg.40, amended: SR 2003/234 Reg.13

Reg.42, amended: SR 2003/234 Reg.14

Reg.45, amended: SR 2003/234 Reg.15

Sch.1, added: SR 2003/234 Reg.16

Sch.1, amended: SR 2003/234 Reg.16, SR 2003/282 Reg.6

Sch.2, substituted: SR 2003/282 Reg.7

Sch.3, added: SR 2003/234 Reg.17

Sch.3, amended: SR 2003/234 Reg.17, SR 2003/282 Reg.8

Sch.3, revoked: SR 2003/282 Reg.8

Sch.3, substituted: SR 2003/234 Reg.17

Sch.4, added: SR 2003/234 Reg.18

Sch.4, amended: SR 2003/234 Reg.18, SR 2003/282 Reg.9

Sch.4, substituted: SR 2003/234 Reg.18

474. Carriage of Explosives by Road Regulations (Northern Ireland) 1997

applied: SR 2003/152 Sch.5

referred to: SR 2003/34 Sch.7, SR 2003/35 Sch.2

488. Surface Waters (Fishlife) (Classification) Regulations (Northern Ireland) 1997

Reg.7, amended: SR 2003/194 Reg.2

493. Fresh Meat (Hygiene and Inspection) Regulations (Northern Ireland) 1997

applied: SR 2002/225 Reg.46, Reg.56, Reg.81, Reg.82, Reg.90, Reg.91, SR 2002/340 Reg.4, SR 2003/21 Reg.4, SR 2003/104 Reg.4

Reg.7, amended: SR 2002/217 Reg.3

Reg.19, amended: SR 2002/217 Reg.3

Sch.17A, added: SR 2002/217 Reg.3

Sch.17C, added: SR 2002/217 Reg.3

494. Meat Products (Hygiene) Regulations (Northern Ireland) 1997

applied: SR 2002/225 Reg.56, SR 2002/340 Reg.4

NO.

1997–cont.

495. Minced Meat and Meat Preparations (Hygiene) Regulations (Northern Ireland) 1997

applied: SR 2002/225 Reg.56, SR 2002/340 Reg.4

496. Wild Game Meat (Hygiene and Inspection) Regulations (Northern Ireland) 1997

applied: SR 2002/225 Reg.56, SR 2002/340 Reg.4

499. Imported Food Regulations (Northern Ireland) 1997

Sch.1, added: SR 2002/340 Sch.8 para.3

534. Genetically Modified Organisms (Deliberate Release and Risk Assessment) (Amendment) Regulations (Northern Ireland) 1997

Reg.2, revoked: SR 2003/167 Sch.5

544. Personal and Occupational Pension Schemes (Miscellaneous Amendments No 2) Regulations (Northern Ireland) 1997

Reg.5, revoked (in part): SR 2003/256 Reg.19

Reg.7, revoked: SR 2003/256 Reg.19

551. Specified Risk Material Order (Northern Ireland) 1997

referred to: SR 2002/209 Art.7, Art.8

Art.3, amended: SR 2002/225 Sch.7 para.1

Art.4, amended: SR 2002/225 Sch.7 para.2

Art.5, revoked: SR 2002/225 Sch.8 Part I

Art.6, amended: SR 2002/225 Sch.7 para.3

Art.7, revoked: SR 2002/225 Sch.8 Part I

Art.8, applied: SR 2002/225 Sch.8 para.1

Art.10, applied: SR 2002/225 Sch.8 para.2

Art.12, applied: SR 2002/225 Sch.8 para.3

Art.13, revoked: SR 2002/225 Sch.8 Part I

Sch.2, amended: SR 2002/225 Sch.7 para.4

552. Specified Risk Material Regulations (Northern Ireland) 1997

referred to: SR 2002/209 Art.7, Art.8, SR 2003/46 Sch.11 para.7

Reg.3, amended: SR 2002/225 Sch.7 para.1

Reg.4, amended: SR 2002/225 Sch.7 para.2

Reg.5, applied: SR 2002/225 Sch.8 para.1, Sch.8 para.2

Reg.5, revoked: SR 2002/225 Sch.8 Part I

Reg.10, revoked: SR 2002/225 Sch.8 Part I

Reg.12, revoked: SR 2002/225 Sch.8 Part I

Reg.15A, applied: SR 2002/225 Sch.8 para.3

Reg.16A, applied: SR 2002/225 Reg.33, Reg.47

Reg.24, amended: SR 2003/46 Sch.11 para.8, Sch.11 para.9

Reg.28, applied: SR 2002/225 Sch.8 para.4

Reg.28, revoked: SR 2002/225 Sch.8 Part I

Sch.2, amended: SR 2003/46 Sch.11 para.10

NO.

1998

13. Vocational Training Regulations (Northern Ireland) 1998

applied: SI 2003/1250 Sch.8 para.4, Sch.8 para.5, Sch.8 para.6, SI 2004/1947 Reg.4

revoked: SI 2003/1250 Sch.10 Part 2

varied: SI 2004/1947 Reg.6

Reg.5, applied: SI 2003/1250 Art.10, Art.11, Sch.8 para.22

Reg.5, referred to: SI 2003/1250 Sch.8 para.22

Reg.6, applied: SI 2003/1250 Art.11, Sch.8 para.2

Reg.6, referred to: SI 2003/1250 Sch.8 para.22, SI 2004/585 Reg.23

Reg.7, applied: SI 2003/1250 Art.11, Sch.8 para.3

Reg.7, referred to: SI 2003/1250 Sch.8 para.4, Sch.8 para.22

Reg.8, applied: SI 2003/1250 Art.11, Sch.8 para.2

Reg.8, referred to: SI 2003/1250 Sch.8 para.22

Reg.10, applied: SI 2004/585 Reg.23

Reg.11, applied: SI 2004/585 Reg.23

Reg.12, applied: SI 2003/1250 Art.8

Reg.12A, applied: SI 2003/1250 Sch.8 para.6

Reg.12A, referred to: SI 2003/1250 Sch.8 para.5

Reg.13, applied: SI 2003/1250 Sch.8 para.6

Reg.13, referred to: SI 2003/1250 Sch.8 para.6

28. Industrial Pollution Control (Prescribed Processes and Substances) Regulations (Northern Ireland) 1998

referred to: SR 2003/96 Reg.3

Reg.3, applied: SR 2003/96 Sch.1 para.2, Sch.1 para.3

Reg.3, disapplied: SR 2003/96 Sch.1 para.1

Reg.3A, added: SR 2003/46 Sch.11 para.13

Sch.1, amended: SR 2003/96 Reg.4, Reg.5

Sch.1, applied: SR 2003/96 Sch.1 para.1, Sch.1 para.2, Sch.1 para.3

Sch.1, referred to: SR 2003/96 Sch.1 para.2

45. Products of Animal Origin (Import and Export) Regulations (Northern Ireland) 1998

Reg.3, disapplied: SR 2002/340 Sch.7

Reg.4, disapplied: SR 2002/340 Sch.7

Reg.5, disapplied: SR 2002/340 Sch.7

Reg.6, disapplied: SR 2002/340 Sch.7

Reg.7, disapplied: SR 2002/340 Sch.7

Reg.18, disapplied: SR 2002/340 Sch.7

Reg.19, disapplied: SR 2002/340 Sch.7

Reg.20, disapplied: SR 2002/340 Sch.7

Reg.21, disapplied: SR 2002/340 Sch.7

Reg.22, disapplied: SR 2002/340 Sch.7

Reg.23, disapplied: SR 2002/340 Sch.7

Reg.24, disapplied: SR 2002/340 Sch.7

Reg.25, disapplied: SR 2002/340 Sch.7

Reg.26, disapplied: SR 2002/340 Sch.7

1998–cont.

45. Products of Animal Origin (Import and Export) Regulations (Northern Ireland) 1998–*cont.*

Reg.27, disapplied: SR 2002/340 Sch.7
Reg.28, disapplied: SR 2002/340 Sch.7
Reg.29, disapplied: SR 2002/340 Sch.7
Reg.30, disapplied: SR 2002/340 Sch.7
Reg.31, disapplied: SR 2002/340 Sch.7
Reg.32, disapplied: SR 2002/340 Sch.7
Reg.33, disapplied: SR 2002/340 Sch.7
Reg.34, disapplied: SR 2002/340 Sch.7
Reg.35, disapplied: SR 2002/340 Sch.7
Reg.36, disapplied: SR 2002/340 Sch.7
Reg.37, disapplied: SR 2002/340 Sch.7
Reg.38, disapplied: SR 2002/340 Sch.7
Reg.39, disapplied: SR 2002/340 Sch.7
Sch.4, disapplied: SR 2002/340 Sch.7
Sch.8, disapplied: SR 2002/340 Sch.7

48. Measuring Equipment (Capacity Measures) Regulations (Northern Ireland) 1998

Reg.16, amended: SR 2002/71 Sch.1 para.8

58. Education (Student Loans) Regulations (Northern Ireland) 1998

applied: SR 2003/253 Art.3
Reg.3, amended: SR 2002/241 Reg.2
Reg.6, amended: SR 2002/241 Reg.2, SR 2003/340 Reg.2

74. Motor Vehicle Testing (Amendment) Regulations (Northern Ireland) 1998

revoked: SR 2003/303 Sch.4

81. Social Security (Miscellaneous Amendments No 2) Regulations (Northern Ireland) 1998

Reg.11, revoked (in part): SI 2003/493 Sch.2 Part 2

107. Potatoes Originating in Egypt Regulations (Northern Ireland) 1998

Reg.5, substituted: SR 2002/246 Reg.2
Reg.5A, amended: SR 2002/246 Reg.2
Sch.1, amended: SR 2002/246 Reg.2, SR 2003/70 Reg.2

108. Animal By-Products (Amendment) Regulations (Northern Ireland) 1998

revoked: SR 2002/210 Reg.2

113. Measuring Equipment (Liquid Fuel and Lubricants) Regulations (Northern Ireland) 1998

Reg.6, amended: SR 2002/71 Sch.1 para.9

125. Health and Safety (Fees) Regulations (Northern Ireland) 1998

Reg.11B, added: SR 2002/34 Sch.5 para.1
Sch.8B, added: SR 2002/34 Sch.5 para.2

128. Misuse of Drugs (Amendment) Regulations (Northern Ireland) 1998

revoked: SR 2002/1 Sch.7

131. Carriage of Dangerous Goods by Rail Regulation (Northern Ireland) 1998

applied: SR 2003/152 Sch.5
referred to: SR 2003/34 Sch.7, SR 2003/35 Sch.2

1998–cont.

131. Carriage of Dangerous Goods by Rail Regulation (Northern Ireland) 1998–*cont.*

Reg.1, amended: SR 2002/34 Sch.6 para.1
Reg.2, amended: SR 2002/34 Sch.6 para.2
Reg.3, amended: SR 2002/34 Sch.6 para.3
Reg.5, amended: SR 2002/34 Sch.6 para.4
Reg.7, amended: SR 2002/34 Sch.6 para.5, Sch.6 para.6
Reg.8, amended: SR 2002/34 Sch.6 para.7
Reg.9, amended: SR 2002/34 Sch.6 para.8
Reg.11, amended: SR 2002/34 Sch.6 para.9
Reg.12, amended: SR 2002/34 Sch.6 para.10
Reg.18, amended: SR 2002/34 Sch.6 para.11
Reg.24A, added: SR 2002/34 Sch.6 para.12
Reg.25, amended: SR 2002/34 Sch.6 para.13
Reg.27, amended: SR 2002/34 Sch.6 para.14
Sch.1, amended: SR 2002/34 Sch.6 para.15
Sch.2, amended: SR 2002/34 Sch.6 para.16
Sch.2, substituted: SR 2002/34 Sch.6 para.16
Sch.3, amended: SR 2002/34 Sch.6 para.17
Sch.3, revoked (in part): SR 2002/34 Sch.6 para.17
Sch.3A, added: SR 2002/34 Sch.6 para.18
Sch.5, added: SR 2002/34 Sch.6 para.19
Sch.5, amended: SR 2002/34 Sch.6 para.19
Sch.5, substituted: SR 2002/34 Sch.6 para.19
Sch.6, substituted: SR 2002/34 Sch.6 para.20
Sch.7, substituted: SR 2002/34 Sch.6 para.21

132. Packaging, Labelling and Carriage of Radioactive Material by Rail Regulations (Northern Ireland) 1998

applied: SR 2003/152 Sch.5
referred to: SR 2003/34 Sch.7, SR 2003/35 Sch.2
Reg.1, amended: SR 2002/34 Sch.7 para.1
Reg.2, amended: SR 2002/34 Sch.7 para.2
Reg.3, amended: SR 2002/34 Sch.7 para.3
Reg.18, amended: SR 2002/34 Sch.7 para.4
Reg.21, amended: SR 2002/34 Sch.7 para.5
Reg.24, amended: SR 2002/34 Sch.7 para.6
Reg.27, amended: SR 2002/34 Sch.7 para.7
Reg.38, amended: SR 2002/34 Sch.7 para.8
Reg.41, amended: SR 2002/34 Sch.7 para.9
Reg.43, amended: SR 2002/34 Sch.7 para.10
Sch.10A, added: SR 2002/34 Sch.7 para.11
Sch.13, added: SR 2002/34 Sch.7 para.12
Sch.13, amended: SR 2002/34 Sch.7 para.12
Sch.13, substituted: SR 2002/34 Sch.7 para.12, Sch.7 para.15
Sch.14, amended: SR 2002/34 Sch.7 para.16

187. Fertilisers (Mammalian Meat and Bone Meal) Regulations (Northern Ireland) 1998

referred to: SR 2002/225 Reg.13
revoked: SR 2002/225 Sch.8 Part I

NO.

1998–cont.

188. Fertilisers (Mammalian Meat and Bone Meal) (Conditions of Manufacture) Regulations (Northern Ireland) 1998

revoked: SR 2002/225 Sch.8 Part I

233. Occupational Pension Schemes (Bank of England Act) (Consequential Amendments) Regulations (Northern Ireland) 1998

Reg.3, revoked: SR 2003/256 Reg.19

263. Social Security (Guardian's Allowance) (Amendment) Regulations (Northern Ireland) 1998

revoked: SI 2003/495 Sch.1 Part 2

264. Plastic Materials and Articles in Contact with Food Regulations (Northern Ireland) 1998

referred to: SR 2002/316 Reg.2, SR 2003/2 Reg.2

Reg.1A, added: SR 2002/316 Reg.3

Reg.2, amended: SR 2002/316 Reg.4

Reg.3, amended: SR 2002/316 Reg.5

Reg.3, substituted: SR 2002/316 Reg.5

Reg.4, amended: SR 2002/316 Reg.6

Reg.4, substituted: SR 2002/316 Reg.6

Reg.4A, added: SR 2002/316 Reg.7

Reg.5, amended: SR 2002/316 Reg.8

Reg.5, substituted: SR 2002/316 Reg.8

Reg.6, amended: SR 2002/316 Reg.9

Reg.6, substituted: SR 2002/316 Reg.9

Reg.7A, substituted: SR 2002/316 Reg.10

Reg.8A, added: SR 2002/316 Reg.11

Reg.8B, added: SR 2002/316 Reg.11

Reg.10, amended: SR 2002/316 Reg.12, SR 2003/2 Reg.3

Reg.11, amended: SR 2002/316 Reg.13

Reg.12, amended: SR 2002/316 Reg.14

Sch.1, amended: SR 2002/316, SR 2003/2 Reg.4

Sch.1, substituted: SR 2002/316, SR 2002/316 Reg.15

Sch.2, added: SR 2002/316 Reg.16

Sch.2, amended: SR 2002/316 Reg.16, Sch.2 Part I, Sch.2 Part II, Sch.2 Part II, SR 2003/2 Reg.5

Sch.2, substituted: SR 2002/316 Reg.16, Sch.2 Part III, Sch.2 Part IV

Sch.2B, amended: SR 2002/316 Sch.3, SR 2003/2 Reg.6

Sch.3, amended: SR 2002/316 Reg.18

268. Industrial Pollution Control (Prescribed Processes and Substances) (Amendment) Regulations (Northern Ireland) 1998

Sch.1, applied: SR 2003/96 Sch.1 para.3

281. Control of Lead at Work Regulations (Northern Ireland) 1998

revoked: SR 2003/35 Reg.15

NO.

1998–cont.

287. Code of Practice (Redundancy Consultation and Procedures) (Appointed Day) Order (Northern Ireland) 1998

applied: SR 2002/346 Art.3

289. Special Waste Regulations (Northern Ireland) 1998

applied: SR 2002/301 Reg.3

referred to: SR 2002/271 Reg.2

Reg.16, amended: SR 2003/46 Sch.11 para.14

298. Education (Student Support) Regulations (Northern Ireland) 1998

applied: SR 2002/224 Reg.3

disapplied: SR 2002/224 Reg.3

306. Education (Student Support) (Northern Ireland) Order 1998 (Commencement and Transitional Provisions) Order (Northern Ireland) 1998

Art.3, applied: SR 2002/265 Reg.5

Art.4, applied: SR 2002/265 Reg.5

330. Births, Deaths and Marriages (Fees) Order (Northern Ireland) 1998

revoked: SR 2002/242 Art.4

333. Teachers Superannuation Regulations (Northern Ireland) 1998

Reg.G3, revoked (in part): SR 2003/147 Reg.2

365. Diseases of Animals (Modification) Order (Northern Ireland) 1998

revoked: SR 2002/225 Sch.8 Part I

366. Sheep and Goats (Spongiform Encephalopathy) Order (Northern Ireland) 1998

revoked: SR 2002/225 Sch.8 Part I

Art.5, applied: SR 2002/225 Sch.8 para.1, Sch.8 para.2

Art.6, applied: SR 2002/225 Sch.8 para.1, Sch.8 para.2

Art.7, applied: SR 2002/225 Sch.8 para.3

367. Sheep and Goats (Spongiform Encephalopathy) Regulations (Northern Ireland) 1998

applied: SR 2002/225 Sch.8 para.4

revoked: SR 2002/225 Sch.8 Part I

386. Working Time Regulations (Northern Ireland) 1998

referred to: SR 2003/119 Reg.3

Reg.2, amended: SR 2003/119 Reg.4

Reg.3, amended: SR 2003/119 Reg.5

Reg.3, substituted: SR 2003/119 Reg.5

Reg.4, amended: SR 2003/119 Reg.6

Reg.5A, added: SR 2003/119 Reg.7

Reg.6, revoked (in part): SR 2003/119 Reg.8

Reg.6A, added: SR 2003/119 Reg.9

Reg.7, amended: SR 2003/119 Reg.10

Reg.9, amended: SR 2003/119 Reg.11

Reg.10, amended: SR 2003/119 Reg.12

Reg.11, amended: SR 2003/119 Reg.13

Reg.12, amended: SR 2003/119 Reg.14

Reg.13, amended: SR 2002/93 Reg.3

Reg.13, revoked (in part): SR 2002/93 Reg.3

NO.

1998–cont.

386. Working Time Regulations (Northern Ireland) 1998–*cont.*
Reg.14, amended: SR 2002/93 Reg.4
Reg.15, amended: SR 2002/93 Reg.4
Reg.15A, added: SR 2002/93 Reg.5
Reg.18, amended: SI 2003/3049 Sch.2 para.7, SI 2004/1713 Sch.2 para.6
Reg.19, amended: SR 2003/119 Reg.15
Reg.25, amended: SR 2003/119 Reg.16
Reg.26, amended: SR 2003/119 Reg.17
Reg.27, amended: SR 2003/119 Reg.18
Reg.27A, added: SR 2003/119 Reg.19
Reg.28, amended: SR 2003/119 Reg.20
Reg.30, amended: SR 2002/93 Reg.4, SR 2003/119 Reg.21
Reg.30, applied: SI 2003/2902 Sch.2, Sch.3, Sch.4
Sch.1, applied: SR 2002/120 Sch.1

401. Groundwater Regulations (Northern Ireland) 1998
referred to: SR 2003/46 Sch.11 para.15
Reg.2, amended: SR 2003/46 Sch.11 para.16
Reg.4, amended: SR 2003/46 Sch.11 para.17

425. Street Works (Reinstatement) Regulations (Northern Ireland) 1998
applied: SR 2002/10 Reg.3

442. Diseases of Animals (Modification) (No.2) Order (Northern Ireland) 1998
revoked: SR 2002/225 Sch.8 Part I

459. Chemicals (Hazard Information and Packaging for Supply) (Amendment) Regulations (Northern Ireland) 1998
revoked: SR 2002/301 Sch.8

1999

4. Gaming (Variation of Monetary Limits) Order (Northern Ireland) 1999
Art.5, revoked: SR 2003/15 Art.4

13. Confined Spaces Regulations (Northern Ireland) 1999
referred to: SI 2003/2002 Reg.12

59. Marketing and Use of Dangerous Substances Regulations (Northern Ireland) 1999
revoked: SR 2003/106 Reg.6

78. Motor Vehicle Testing (Amendment) (Fees) Regulations (Northern Ireland) 1999
revoked: SR 2003/303 Sch.4

90. Health and Safety (Enforcing Authority) Regulations (Northern Ireland) 1999
Reg.4, disapplied: SR 2002/301 Reg.14
Sch.2, added: SR 2003/33 Reg.27

114. Pesticides (Maximum Residue Levels in Crops, Food and Feeding Stuffs) (EEC Limits) (Amendment) Regulations (Northern Ireland) 1999
revoked: SR 2002/20 Sch.4

NO.

1999–cont.

115. Producer Responsibility Obligations (Packaging Waste) (Amendment) Regulations (Northern Ireland) 1999
Sch.2, amended: SR 2002/239 Reg.2

148. Fair Employment (Monitoring) Regulations (Northern Ireland) 1999
applied: SR 2002/258 Reg.3

162. Social Security and Child Support (Decisions and Appeals) Regulations (Northern Ireland) 1999
Reg.1, amended: SI 2002/1378 Reg.3, SR 2002/80 Reg.7, SR 2002/189 Reg.2, SR 2003/191 Reg.16, SR 2003/224 Reg.3
Reg.3, amended: SI 2002/527 Reg.4, SR 2002/67 Reg.3, SR 2002/80 Reg.7, SR 2002/189 Reg.2, SR 2003/224 Reg.3
Reg.3A, amended: SR 2002/164 Reg.6
Reg.6, amended: SI 2002/527 Reg.4, SR 2002/67 Reg.3, SR 2002/80 Reg.7, SR 2003/191 Reg.17, SR 2003/224 Reg.3
Reg.6A, amended: SR 2003/224 Reg.3
Reg.6B, amended: SR 2002/164 Reg.6
Reg.7, amended: SI 2002/527 Reg.4, SR 2002/67 Reg.3, SR 2002/80 Reg.7, SR 2003/191 Reg.18, SR 2003/224 Reg.3
Reg.7B, amended: SR 2002/164 Reg.6, 2003/84 Reg.7, SR 2003/224 Reg.3
Reg.7B, revoked (in part): SR 2002/164 Reg.6
Reg.9A, added: SI 2002/1378 Reg.5, SR 2002/189 Reg.2
Reg.11A, amended: SR 2002/189 Reg.2
Reg.13, amended: SR 2003/191 Reg.19
Reg.14, amended: SR 2003/191 Reg.20
Reg.14A, added: SR 2002/189 Reg.2
Reg.25, amended: SI 2002/1378 Reg.6, SR 2002/189 Reg.2
Reg.31, amended: SI 2002/1378 Reg.7, SR 2002/164 Reg.6, SR 2002/189 Reg.2
Reg.31, varied: SR 2002/391 Art.5
Reg.32, amended: SR 2002/189 Reg.2
Reg.32, varied: SR 2002/391 Art.5
Reg.33, amended: SR 2002/189 Reg.2
Reg.38A, amended: SR 2002/189 Reg.2
Reg.47, amended: SI 2002/1378 Reg.10
Reg.47, substituted: SR 2002/189 Reg.2
Reg.49, amended: SR 2002/189 Reg.2
Reg.51, revoked (in part): SI 2002/1378 Reg.12, SR 2002/189 Reg.2
Reg.53, amended: SI 2002/1378 Reg.13, SR 2002/189 Reg.2
Reg.54, amended: SR 2002/189 Reg.2
Reg.57, amended: SR 2002/189 Reg.2
Reg.57A, added: SI 2002/1378 Reg.16
Reg.57A, amended: SR 2002/189 Reg.2
Reg.58, amended: SR 2002/189 Reg.2
Reg.58, revoked (in part): SR 2002/189 Reg.2
Sch.1, added: SR 2002/79 Reg.21, SR 2003/191 Reg.21
Sch.1, amended: SR 2003/312 Reg.2

NO.

1999–cont.

162. Social Security and Child Support (Decisions and Appeals) Regulations (Northern Ireland) 1999–*cont.*

Sch.1, substituted: SI 2002/1378 Reg.18, SR 2002/189 Reg.2

Sch.2A, amended: SR 2002/132 Reg.6, SR 2002/189 Reg.2

Sch.2A, applied: SR 2002/16 Reg.1, SR 2002/58 Reg.1

Sch.2B, added: SR 2003/191 Reg.22

189. Miscellaneous Products of Animal Origin (Import Conditions) Regulations (Northern Ireland) 1999

Reg.4, disapplied: SR 2002/340 Sch.7

224. Magistrates Courts (Sex Offender Orders) Rules (Northern Ireland) 1999

r.3A, added: SR 2003/32 r.2

r.4, amended: SR 2003/32 r.2

Sch.1, amended: SR 2003/32 Sch.1

244. Miscellaneous Food Additives (Amendment) Regulations (Northern Ireland) 1999

Reg.14, amended: SR 2003/300 Reg.10, SR 2003/301 Reg.10, SR 2003/313 Reg.11

246. Social Security Act 1998 (Commencement No 6 and Consequential and Transitional Provisions) Order (Northern Ireland) 1999

Art.5, revoked: SI 2003/492 Sch.3 Part 2

251. Misuse of Drugs (Amendment) Regulations (Northern Ireland) 1999

revoked: SR 2002/1 Sch.7

258. Motor Vehicles (Authorised Weight) Regulations (Northern Ireland) 1999

Reg.2, amended: SR 2002/8 Reg.2

Reg.3, substituted: SR 2002/8 Reg.3

Reg.4, amended: SR 2002/8 Reg.4

Reg.5, substituted: SR 2002/8 Reg.5

Sch.2, amended: SR 2002/8 Reg.6

Sch.3, added: SR 2002/8 Reg.7

Sch.3, amended: SR 2002/8 Reg.7

289. Smoke Control Areas (Exempted Fireplaces) (Amendment) Regulations (Northern Ireland) 1999

Sch.1, amended: SR 2003/343 Sch.1

294. Health and Personal Social Services (Superannuation) (Additional Voluntary Contributions) Regulations (Northern Ireland) 1999

Reg.2, amended: SR 2002/129 Reg.3

Reg.3, amended: SR 2002/129 Reg.4

Reg.4, amended: SR 2002/129 Reg.5

Reg.5, amended: SR 2002/129 Reg.6

Reg.6, amended: SR 2002/129 Reg.7

Reg.9, amended: SR 2002/129 Reg.8

Reg.11, amended: SR 2002/129 Reg.9

Reg.15, amended: SR 2002/129 Reg.10

Sch.1, added: SR 2002/129 Reg.11

Sch.1, amended: SR 2002/129 Reg.11

NO.

1999–cont.

296. Feeding Stuffs (Sampling and Analysis) Regulations (Northern Ireland) 1999

Reg.1, amended: SR 2003/287 Reg.3

Reg.3, substituted: SR 2003/287 Reg.4

Reg.5, amended: SR 2003/287 Reg.5

Reg.5A, added: SR 2003/287 Reg.6

Sch.1, amended: SR 2002/263 Reg.11

Sch.2, amended: SR 2002/263 Reg.11, SR 2003/287 Reg.7

Sch.3, amended: SR 2002/263 Reg.11

301. Natural Mineral Water, Spring Water and Bottled Drinking Water Regulations (Northern Ireland) 1999

referred to: SR 2003/182 Reg.2

Reg.2, amended: SR 2003/182 Reg.3

Reg.3, amended: SR 2003/182 Reg.4

Reg.4, amended: SR 2003/182 Reg.5

Reg.5, amended: SR 2003/182 Reg.6

Reg.10, amended: SR 2003/182 Reg.7

Reg.11, substituted: SR 2003/182 Reg.8

Reg.12, amended: SR 2003/182 Reg.9

Reg.13, amended: SR 2003/182 Reg.10

Reg.16, substituted: SR 2003/182 Reg.11

Reg.17, amended: SR 2003/182 Reg.12

Reg.18, amended: SR 2003/182 Reg.13

Reg.19, amended: SR 2003/182 Reg.14

Sch.1, amended: SR 2003/182 Reg.15

Sch.2, amended: SR 2003/182 Reg.16

Sch.3, amended: SR 2003/182 Reg.17

Sch.3, substituted: SR 2003/182 Reg.18, Reg.19, Reg.20, Reg.21

302. Contaminants in Food (Amendment) Regulations (Northern Ireland) 1999

revoked: SR 2002/219 Sch.1

303. Chemicals (Hazard Information and Packaging for Supply) (Amendment) Regulations (Northern Ireland) 1999

revoked: SR 2002/301 Sch.8

304. Lifting Operations and Lifting Equipment Regulations (Northern Ireland) 1999

referred to: SI 2003/2002 Reg.12

305. Provision and Use of Work Equipment Regulations (Northern Ireland) 1999

applied: SR 2003/152 Reg.5

referred to: SI 2003/2002 Reg.12

Sch.2, amended: SI 2004/129 Reg.32

308. Bovines and Bovine Products (Trade) Regulations (Northern Ireland) 1999

Reg.2, amended: SR 2002/278 Reg.3

Reg.2, revoked (in part): SR 2002/278 Reg.3

Reg.3, amended: SR 2002/278 Reg.3

Reg.5A, added: SR 2002/278 Reg.3

Reg.10, amended: SR 2002/278 Reg.3

Reg.12, amended: SR 2002/278 Reg.3

Reg.12, revoked (in part): SR 2002/278 Reg.3

Reg.13, amended: SR 2002/278 Reg.3

NO.

308. Bovines and Bovine Products (Trade) Regulations (Northern Ireland) 1999– cont.

Reg.13, revoked (in part): SR 2002/278 Reg.3

Reg.17, amended: SR 2002/278 Reg.3

Sch.1, substituted: SR 2002/278 Sch.1

Sch.2, substituted: SR 2002/278 Sch.2

Sch.3, substituted: SR 2002/278 Sch.3

310. Social Security (1998 Order) (Commencement No 7 and Savings, Consequential and Transitional Provisions) Order (Northern Ireland) 1999

Art.5, revoked: SI 2003/495 Sch.1 Part 2

Art.7, revoked: SI 2003/493 Sch.2 Part 2

320. Pesticides (Maximum Residue Levels in Crops, Food and Feeding Stuffs) (National Limits) (Amendment) Regulations (Northern Ireland) 1999

revoked: SR 2002/20 Sch.4

321. Pesticides (Maximum Residue Levels in Crops, Food and Feeding Stuffs) (EEC Limits) (Amendment No 2) Regulations (Northern Ireland) 1999

revoked: SR 2002/20 Sch.4

322. Bovine Spongiform Encephalopathy Order (Northern Ireland) 1999

applied: SR 2002/225 Sch.8 para.1, Sch.8 para.2

revoked: SR 2002/225 Sch.8 Part I

Art.9, applied: SR 2002/225 Sch.8 para.3

Art.10, applied: SR 2002/225 Sch.8 para.4

Art.11, applied: SR 2002/225 Sch.8 para.5

323. Bovine Spongiform Encephalopathy (Feedingstuffs and Surveillance) Regulations (Northern Ireland) 1999

applied: SR 2002/225 Sch.8 Part VI

revoked: SR 2002/225 Sch.8 Part I

338. Planning Applications (Exemption from Publication) Order (Northern Ireland) 1999

revoked: SR 2003/283 Art.2

362. Controlled Waste (Registration of Carriers and Seizure of Vehicles) Regulations (Northern Ireland) 1999

Sch.1, amended: SR 2003/46 Sch.11 para.18

365. Social Security (Claims and Payments) (Amendment) Regulations (Northern Ireland) 1999

revoked: SI 2003/492 Sch.3 Part 2

379. Seeds (Fees) Regulations (Northern Ireland) 1999

revoked: SR 2002/257 Reg.3

381. Social Security (Miscellaneous Amendments No 2) Regulations (Northern Ireland) 1999

Reg.5, revoked: SI 2003/492 Sch.3 Part 2

NO.

385. Social Security and Child Support (Tax Credits Consequential Amendments) Regulations (Northern Ireland) 1999

Reg.4, revoked: SI 2003/492 Sch.3 Part 2

Sch.2, amended: SR 2003/84 Reg.12

392. Explosives (Fireworks) Regulations (Northern Ireland) 1999

revoked: SR 2002/147 Reg.14

Reg.11, applied: SI 2003/1593 Sch.1 Part II

408. Social Security and Child Support (Decisions and Appeals) and Jobseeker's Allowance (Amendment) Regulations (Northern Ireland) 1999

Reg.3, revoked (in part): SR 2002/189 Reg.4

415. Environmental Impact Assessment (Fish Farming in Marine Waters) Regulations (Northern Ireland) 1999

Reg.3, applied: SR 2003/136 Reg.3

416. Housing Benefit (General) (Amendment No 3) Regulations (Northern Ireland) 1999

Reg.12, amended: SR 2003/108 Reg.5

418. Animal By-Products (Identification) Regulations (Northern Ireland) 1999

Reg.2, amended: SR 2002/238 Reg.2, SR 2003/9 Reg.2

Reg.2, revoked (in part): SR 2003/9 Reg.2

Reg.3, amended: SR 2003/9 Reg.2

Reg.4, amended: SR 2002/238 Reg.2, SR 2003/9 Reg.2

Reg.5, amended: SR 2002/238 Reg.2, SR 2003/9 Reg.2

Reg.6, amended: SR 2003/9 Reg.2

Reg.6, revoked (in part): SR 2003/9 Reg.2

Reg.6, substituted: SR 2002/238 Reg.2

Reg.7, amended: SR 2003/9 Reg.2

Reg.8, amended: SR 2003/9 Reg.2

Reg.8, substituted: SR 2002/238 Reg.2

Reg.9, amended: SR 2003/9 Reg.2

Reg.9, substituted: SR 2002/238 Reg.2

Reg.10, amended: SR 2003/9 Reg.2

Reg.10, substituted: SR 2002/238 Reg.2

428. Social Security Act 1998 (Commencement No 10, and Savings and Consequential and Transitional Provisions) Order (Northern Ireland) 1999

Art.5, revoked: SI 2003/492 Sch.3 Part 2

434. Specified Animal Pathogens Order (Northern Ireland) 1999

Art.4, applied: SR 2003/55 Art.3

454. Motor Vehicles (Construction and Use) Regulations (Northern Ireland) 1999

Reg.2, amended: SR 2002/375 Reg.2

Reg.2, applied: SR 2003/303 Reg.2

Reg.6, amended: SR 2002/375 Reg.3

Reg.6, applied: SR 2003/303 Sch.2 para.3, Sch.2 para.4, Sch.2 para.5, Sch.2 para.6, Sch.2 para.7

NO.

1999–cont.

454. Motor Vehicles (Construction and Use) Regulations (Northern Ireland) 1999–*cont.*

Reg.7, applied: SR 2003/303 Sch.2 para.3, Sch.2 para.4, Sch.2 para.5, Sch.2 para.6, Sch.2 para.7

Reg.8, applied: SR 2003/303 Sch.2 para.3, Sch.2 para.4, Sch.2 para.5, Sch.2 para.6, Sch.2 para.7

Reg.9, applied: SR 2003/303 Sch.2 para.3, Sch.2 para.4, Sch.2 para.5, Sch.2 para.6, Sch.2 para.7

Reg.13, applied: SR 2003/303 Sch.2 para.3, Sch.2 para.4, Sch.2 para.5, Sch.2 para.6, Sch.2 para.7

Reg.14, applied: SR 2003/303 Sch.2 para.3, Sch.2 para.4, Sch.2 para.5, Sch.2 para.6, Sch.2 para.7

Reg.16, substituted: SR 2002/375 Reg.4

Reg.20, amended: SR 2002/375 Reg.5

Reg.20, applied: SR 2003/303 Sch.2 para.1, Sch.2 para.2, Sch.2 para.3, Sch.2 para.4, Sch.2 para.5, Sch.2 para.6, Sch.2 para.7

Reg.21, applied: SR 2003/303 Sch.2 para.1, Sch.2 para.2, Sch.2 para.3, Sch.2 para.4, Sch.2 para.5, Sch.2 para.6, Sch.2 para.7

Reg.22, applied: SR 2003/303 Sch.2 para.4, Sch.2 para.5, Sch.2 para.6, Sch.2 para.7

Reg.24, applied: SR 2003/303 Sch.2 para.1, Sch.2 para.2, Sch.2 para.3, Sch.2 para.4, Sch.2 para.5, Sch.2 para.6, Sch.2 para.7

Reg.27, applied: SR 2003/303 Sch.2 para.2, Sch.2 para.3, Sch.2 para.4, Sch.2 para.5, Sch.2 para.6, Sch.2 para.7

Reg.29, applied: SR 2003/303 Sch.2 para.1, Sch.2 para.2, Sch.2 para.3, Sch.2 para.4, Sch.2 para.5, Sch.2 para.6, Sch.2 para.7

Reg.30, applied: SR 2003/303 Sch.2 para.1, Sch.2 para.2, Sch.2 para.3, Sch.2 para.4, Sch.2 para.5, Sch.2 para.6, Sch.2 para.7

Reg.31, applied: SR 2003/303 Sch.2 para.1, Sch.2 para.2, Sch.2 para.3, Sch.2 para.4, Sch.2 para.5, Sch.2 para.6, Sch.2 para.7

Reg.32, applied: SR 2003/303 Sch.2 para.1, Sch.2 para.2, Sch.2 para.3, Sch.2 para.4, Sch.2 para.5, Sch.2 para.6, Sch.2 para.7

Reg.34, applied: SR 2003/303 Sch.2 para.1, Sch.2 para.2, Sch.2 para.3, Sch.2 para.4, Sch.2 para.5, Sch.2 para.6, Sch.2 para.7

Reg.35, applied: SR 2003/303 Sch.2 para.2, Sch.2 para.3, Sch.2 para.4, Sch.2 para.5, Sch.2 para.6, Sch.2 para.7

Reg.36, applied: SR 2003/303 Sch.2 para.2, Sch.2 para.3, Sch.2 para.4, Sch.2 para.5, Sch.2 para.6, Sch.2 para.7

Reg.37, applied: SR 2003/303 Sch.2 para.2, Sch.2 para.3, Sch.2 para.4, Sch.2 para.5, Sch.2 para.6, Sch.2 para.7

Reg.38, applied: SR 2003/303 Sch.2 para.2, Sch.2 para.3, Sch.2 para.4, Sch.2 para.5, Sch.2 para.6, Sch.2 para.7

NO.

1999–cont.

454. Motor Vehicles (Construction and Use) Regulations (Northern Ireland) 1999–*cont.*

Reg.39, applied: SR 2003/303 Sch.2 para.2, Sch.2 para.3, Sch.2 para.4, Sch.2 para.5, Sch.2 para.6, Sch.2 para.7

Reg.40, applied: SR 2003/303 Sch.2 para.1, Sch.2 para.2, Sch.2 para.3, Sch.2 para.4, Sch.2 para.5, Sch.2 para.6, Sch.2 para.7

Reg.41, applied: SR 2003/303 Sch.2 para.1, Sch.2 para.2, Sch.2 para.3, Sch.2 para.4, Sch.2 para.5, Sch.2 para.6, Sch.2 para.7

Reg.42, applied: SR 2003/303 Sch.2 para.3, Sch.2 para.4, Sch.2 para.5, Sch.2 para.6, Sch.2 para.7

Reg.43, amended: SR 2002/375 Reg.6

Reg.44, amended: SR 2002/375 Reg.7, SR 2003/39 Reg.2

Reg.44, applied: SR 2003/303 Sch.2 para.1, Sch.2 para.2, Sch.2 para.3, Sch.2 para.4, Sch.2 para.5, Sch.2 para.6, Sch.2 para.7

Reg.45, applied: SR 2003/303 Sch.2 para.1

Reg.46, applied: SR 2003/303 Sch.2 para.1, Sch.2 para.2, Sch.2 para.3, Sch.2 para.4, Sch.2 para.5, Sch.2 para.6, Sch.2 para.7

Reg.50, referred to: SR 2003/303 Sch.2 para.6

Reg.54, applied: SR 2003/303 Sch.2 para.2, Sch.2 para.3, Sch.2 para.4, Sch.2 para.5, Sch.2 para.6, Sch.2 para.7

Reg.54, substituted: SR 2002/197 Sch.1, SR 2002/256 Sch.1

Reg.55, amended: SR 2002/197 Reg.3, SR 2002/256 Reg.3, SR 2002/294 Reg.4

Reg.55, applied: SR 2003/303 Sch.2 para.2, Sch.2 para.3, Sch.2 para.4, Sch.2 para.5, Sch.2 para.6, Sch.2 para.7

Reg.56, amended: SR 2002/197 Reg.4, SR 2002/256 Reg.4

Reg.56, applied: SR 2003/303 Sch.2 para.2, Sch.2 para.3, Sch.2 para.4, Sch.2 para.5, Sch.2 para.6, Sch.2 para.7

Reg.57, amended: SR 2002/197 Reg.5, SR 2002/256 Reg.5

Reg.58, applied: SR 2003/303 Sch.2 para.3

Reg.59, applied: SR 2003/303 Sch.2 para.3

Reg.60, amended: SR 2002/375 Reg.8

Reg.60, applied: SR 2003/303 Sch.2 para.3

Reg.61, applied: SR 2003/303 Sch.2 para.3

Reg.62, applied: SR 2003/303 Sch.2 para.2, Sch.2 para.3, Sch.2 para.4, Sch.2 para.5, Sch.2 para.6, Sch.2 para.7

Reg.65, applied: SR 2003/303 Sch.2 para.1, Sch.2 para.2, Sch.2 para.3, Sch.2 para.4, Sch.2 para.5, Sch.2 para.6, Sch.2 para.7

Reg.73, amended: SR 2003/145 Reg.2

Reg.74, added: SR 2002/375 Reg.9

Reg.74, amended: SR 2002/375 Reg.9

Reg.74, applied: SR 2003/303 Sch.2 para.3, Sch.2 para.4, Sch.2 para.5, Sch.2 para.6, Sch.2 para.7

NO.

1999–cont.

454. Motor Vehicles (Construction and Use) Regulations (Northern Ireland) 1999–*cont.*

Reg.74A, added: SR 2002/375 Reg.10

Reg.79, amended: SR 2002/294 Reg.2, SR 2002/375 Reg.11

Reg.79, applied: SR 2003/303 Sch.2 para.2, Sch.2 para.3, Sch.2 para.4, Sch.2 para.5, Sch.2 para.6, Sch.2 para.7

Reg.80, applied: SR 2003/303 Sch.2 para.1, Sch.2 para.2, Sch.2 para.3, Sch.2 para.4, Sch.2 para.5, Sch.2 para.6, Sch.2 para.7

Reg.82, applied: SR 2003/303 Sch.2 para.1

Reg.83, applied: SR 2003/303 Sch.2 para.3, Sch.2 para.4, Sch.2 para.5, Sch.2 para.6, Sch.2 para.7

Reg.88, amended: SR 2002/375 Reg.12

Reg.114, amended: SR 2003/39 Reg.3

Reg.115, applied: SR 2003/303 Sch.2 para.2, Sch.2 para.3, Sch.2 para.4, Sch.2 para.5, Sch.2 para.6, Sch.2 para.7

Sch.1, amended: SR 2002/197 Reg.6, SR 2002/256 Reg.6, SR 2002/375 Reg.13, SR 2003/145 Reg.3

Sch.1A, added: SR 2002/375 Reg.14

Sch.1A, amended: SR 2002/375 Reg.14

Sch.6, referred to: SR 2003/303 Sch.2 para.6, Sch.2 para.7

Sch.7, referred to: SR 2003/303 Sch.2 para.6, Sch.2 para.7

Sch.8, amended: SR 2002/375 Reg.15

Sch.10, added: SR 2002/294 Reg.3

Sch.10, amended: SR 2002/294 Reg.3

Sch.10, substituted: SR 2002/197 Reg.7, SR 2002/256 Reg.7

471. Maternity and Parental Leave etc Regulations (Northern Ireland) 1999

referred to: SR 2002/355 Reg.3

Reg.2, amended: SR 2002/355 Reg.4

Reg.4, amended: SR 2002/355 Reg.5

Reg.5, amended: SR 2002/355 Reg.6

Reg.6, amended: SR 2002/355 Reg.7

Reg.7, amended: SR 2002/355 Reg.8

Reg.9, substituted: SR 2002/355 Reg.9

Reg.11, amended: SR 2002/355 Reg.10

Reg.12, revoked: SR 2002/355 Reg.11

Reg.13, amended: SR 2002/110 Reg.4, SR 2002/135 Reg.5

Reg.13, revoked (in part): SR 2002/110 Reg.4, SR 2002/135 Reg.5

Reg.14, amended: SR 2002/110 Reg.5, SR 2002/135 Reg.6

Reg.15, substituted: SR 2002/110 Reg.6, SR 2002/135 Reg.7

Reg.18, substituted: SR 2002/355 Reg.12

Reg.19, amended: SR 2002/355 Reg.13

Reg.20, amended: SR 2002/355 Reg.14

Sch.2, added: SR 2002/110 Reg.7, SR 2002/135 Reg.8

Sch.2, amended: SR 2002/110 Reg.7, SR 2002/135 Reg.8

NO.

1999–cont.

472. Social Security Act 1998(Commencement No 11 and Consequential and Transitional Provisions) Order (Northern Ireland) 1999

Art.11, revoked: SI 2003/492 Sch.3 Part 2

2000

71. Social Security (Immigration and Asylum) Consequential Amendments Regulations (Northern Ireland) 2000

Reg.1, amended: SI 2003/492 Sch.3 Part 2

Reg.2, amended: SR 2002/323 Sch.1 para.1

Reg.7, revoked: SI 2003/492 Sch.3 Part 2

Reg.11, amended: SR 2002/323 Sch.1 para.1

Reg.11, revoked (in part): 2004 c.19 s.12

Sch.1, amended: SR 2002/323 Sch.1 para.1

78. Food Standards Act 1999 (Transitional and Consequential Provisions and Savings) Regulations (Northern Ireland) 2000

Reg.14, applied: SR 2002/263, SR 2003/287

83. Dairy Produce Quotas (Amendment) Regulations (Northern Ireland) 2000

revoked: SR 2002/88 Sch.4

84. Environmental Impact Assessment (Forestry) Regulations (Northern Ireland) 2000

Reg.3, amended: SR 2002/249 Reg.3

Reg.21, amended: SR 2002/249 Reg.3

86. Health and Safety at Work Order (Application to Environmentally Hazardous Substances) (Amendment) Regulations 2000

revoked: SR 2003/52 Reg.4

91. Social Fund Winter Fuel Payment Regulations (Northern Ireland) 2000

applied: SI 2004/1987 Art.5

Reg.2, amended: SR 2002/327 Reg.3

Reg.2, substituted: SR 2003/349 Reg.2

93. Control of Major Accident Hazards Regulations (Northern Ireland) 2000

Reg.5, applied: SR 2003/46 Sch.4 para.9

98. Control of Asbestos at Work (Amendment) Regulations (Northern Ireland) 2000

revoked: SR 2003/33 Reg.27

104. Social Security (Maternity Allowance) (Earnings) Regulations (Northern Ireland) 2000

Reg.2, amended: SR 2002/359 Reg.5

Reg.3, amended: SR 2002/354 Reg.6

Reg.4, amended: SR 2002/354 Reg.6

Reg.4, revoked (in part): SR 2002/354 Reg.6

Reg.5, substituted: SR 2002/354 Reg.6, SR 2003/168 Reg.2

Reg.6, amended: SR 2002/354 Reg.6, SR 2003/168 Reg.2

2000–cont.

120. Control of Substances Hazardous to Health Regulations (Northern Ireland) 2000
revoked: SR 2003/34 Reg.18

121. Education (Student Loans) (Repayment) Regulations (Northern Ireland) 2000
applied: 2002 c.29 s.323
Reg.36, amended: SR 2003/166 Reg.3
Reg.36, referred to: SR 2003/166 Reg.2

135. Social Security (National Insurance Number Information Exemption) Regulations (Northern Ireland) 2000
Reg.2, revoked: SI 2003/493 Sch.2 Part 2

142. Pensions on Divorce etc (Provision of Information) Regulations (Northern Ireland) 2000
Reg.3, varied: SI 2003/291 Reg.2, SR 2002/127 Reg.7

145. Pension Sharing (Implementation and Discharge of Liability) Regulations (Northern Ireland) 2000
Reg.1, amended: SR 2003/256 Reg.15
Reg.10, applied: SR 2002/352 Reg.133
Reg.11, amended: SR 2003/256 Reg.15

146. Pension Sharing (Pension Credit Benefit) Regulations (Northern Ireland) 2000
Reg.1, amended: SR 2003/256 Reg.16
Reg.5, amended: SR 2003/256 Reg.16
Reg.24, applied: SI 2003/291 Reg.3
Reg.24, varied: SR 2002/127 Reg.9

147. Pension Sharing (Safeguarded Rights) Regulations (Northern Ireland) 2000
Reg.8, amended: SR 2003/256 Reg.17

151. Motor Vehicle Testing (Amendment) Regulations (Northern Ireland) 2000
revoked: SR 2003/303 Sch.4

169. Road Vehicles Lighting Regulations (Northern Ireland) 2000
Reg.21, applied: SR 2003/303 Sch.2 para.1, Sch.2 para.2, Sch.2 para.3, Sch.2 para.4, Sch.2 para.5, Sch.2 para.6, Sch.2 para.7
Reg.26, applied: SR 2003/303 Sch.2 para.1, Sch.2 para.2, Sch.2 para.3, Sch.2 para.4, Sch.2 para.5, Sch.2 para.6, Sch.2 para.7
Sch.19, referred to: SR 2003/19 Reg.2
Sch.19, substituted: SR 2003/19 Sch.1

177. Local Government Pension Scheme Regulations (Northern Ireland) 2000
applied: SR 2002/352 Reg.113, Reg.114, Reg.118, SR 2003/61 Reg.2, Reg.32
disapplied: SR 2002/352 Reg.120
referred to: SR 2003/61 Reg.2
Part D, applied: SR 2002/352 Reg.60
Reg.B6, amended: SR 2002/115 Reg.3
Reg.B13, applied: SR 2002/353 Reg.7, Reg.9
Reg.C3, referred to: SR 2002/352 Reg.88
Reg.C5, applied: SR 2002/353 Reg.9
Reg.C5, referred to: SR 2002/352 Reg.88
Reg.C6, applied: SR 2002/353 Reg.9

2000–cont.

177. Local Government Pension Scheme Regulations (Northern Ireland) 2000–cont.
Reg.C6, referred to: SR 2002/352 Reg.88
Reg.C7, applied: SR 2002/353 Reg.9
Reg.C7, referred to: SR 2002/352 Reg.88, SR 2002/353 Reg.9
Reg.C9, applied: SR 2002/353 Reg.9
Reg.C13, applied: SR 2002/353 Reg.8
Reg.C13, referred to: SR 2002/352 Reg.88
Reg.C14, referred to: SR 2002/352 Reg.88
Reg.C21, applied: SR 2002/352 Reg.118
Reg.C24, applied: SR 2002/353 Reg.12
Reg.D7, applied: SR 2002/352 Reg.60
Reg.D8, applied: SR 2002/352 Reg.89
Reg.D12, applied: SR 2002/352 Reg.34, Reg.119, Sch.3
Reg.J10, amended: SR 2002/115 Reg.5
Reg.K7, referred to: SR 2002/352 Reg.119
Reg.L2, substituted: SR 2002/115 Reg.6
Sch.A2, substituted: SR 2002/115 Reg.4
Sch.C3, applied: SR 2002/352 Sch.4 para.7
Sch.C5, applied: SR 2002/353 Reg.10
Sch.L1, substituted: SR 2002/115 Reg.7
Sch.L2, added: SR 2002/115 Reg.8

178. Local Government Pension Scheme (Management and Investment of Funds) Regulations (Northern Ireland) 2000
applied: SR 2002/352 Sch.6 para.11, SR 2002/353 Reg.3, Sch.2 para.2, Sch.2 para.9
disapplied: SR 2002/353 Sch.2 para.5
referred to: SR 2002/352 Sch.6 para.16, SR 2002/353 Sch.5 para.2
Part J, revoked: SR 2002/353 Reg.23
Part K, applied: SR 2002/353 Reg.18
Part K, revoked: SR 2002/353 Reg.23
Part N, revoked: SR 2002/353 Reg.23
Part L, revoked: SR 2002/353 Reg.23
Reg.B11, applied: SR 2002/353 Reg.2, Reg.3
Reg.B13, amended: SR 2002/353 Sch.3 para.2
Reg.B13, applied: SR 2002/353 Reg.2
Reg.C6, substituted: SR 2002/353 Sch.3 para.3
Reg.C7, applied: SR 2002/353 Reg.2
Reg.C9, applied: SR 2002/353 Sch.2 para.9
Reg.C13, applied: SR 2002/353 Sch.2 para.9
Reg.C21, revoked: SR 2002/353 Reg.23
Reg.C26A, revoked: SR 2002/353 Reg.23
Reg.D8, amended: SR 2002/353 Sch.4 para.5
Reg.D11, applied: SR 2002/353 Sch.2 para.6
Reg.D12, amended: SR 2002/353 Sch.4 para.6
Reg.D12, applied: SR 2002/353 Sch.2 para.6, Sch.2 para.7
Reg.D15, amended: SR 2002/353 Sch.4 para.7

NO.

2000–cont.

178. Local Government Pension Scheme (Management and Investment of Funds) Regulations (Northern Ireland) 2000–cont.

Reg.D16, amended: SR 2002/353 Sch.4 para.8

Reg.D20, amended: SR 2002/353 Sch.4 para.9

Reg.E4, amended: SR 2002/353 Sch.4 para.10

Reg.E6, amended: SR 2002/353 Sch.4 para.11

Reg.F1, amended: SR 2002/353 Sch.4 para.12

Reg.F2, amended: SR 2002/353 Sch.4 para.13

Reg.F4, amended: SR 2002/353 Sch.4 para.14

Reg.F5, amended: SR 2002/353 Sch.4 para.15

Reg.F9, amended: SR 2002/353 Sch.4 para.16

Reg.F10, amended: SR 2002/353 Sch.4 para.17

Reg.G3, amended: SR 2002/353 Sch.4 para.18

Reg.G6, amended: SR 2002/353 Sch.4 para.19

Reg.G7, amended: SR 2002/353 Sch.4 para.19

Reg.G12, amended: SR 2002/353 Sch.4 para.20

Reg.H1, revoked: SR 2002/353 Reg.23

Reg.H3, revoked: SR 2002/353 Reg.23

Reg.H4, revoked: SR 2002/353 Reg.23

Reg.H5, revoked: SR 2002/353 Reg.23

Reg.H6, revoked: SR 2002/353 Reg.23

Reg.H7, revoked: SR 2002/353 Reg.23

Reg.K13, referred to: SR 2002/353 Reg.18

Reg.L6, applied: SR 2002/353 Reg.14, Reg.17

Reg.L6, disapplied: SR 2002/353 Reg.17

Reg.M2, revoked: SR 2002/353 Reg.23

Reg.M3, revoked: SR 2002/353 Reg.23

Reg.M4, revoked: SR 2002/353 Reg.23

Sch.A1, amended: SR 2002/353 Sch.3 para.4, Sch.4 para.21

Sch.B1, amended: SR 2002/353 Sch.4 para.22

Sch.C4, applied: SR 2002/353 Sch.2 para.8

Sch.C5, applied: SR 2002/353 Reg.13

Sch.D5, applied: SR 2002/353 Sch.2 para.3, Sch.2 para.4, Sch.2 para.5

Sch.D5, disapplied: SR 2002/353 Sch.2 para.3, Sch.2 para.4, Sch.2 para.5

Sch.K1, revoked: SR 2002/353 Reg.23

Sch.K2, revoked: SR 2002/353 Reg.23

Sch.L1, revoked: SR 2002/353 Reg.23

Sch.L2, revoked: SR 2002/353 Reg.23

Sch.M2, applied: SR 2002/353 Sch.5 para.2

NO.

2000–cont.

181. Social Security (Claims and Payments) (Amendment) Regulations (Northern Ireland) 2000

revoked: SI 2003/492 Sch.3 Part 2, SR 2002/59 Reg.3

215. Social Security and Child Support (Miscellaneous Amendments) Regulations (Northern Ireland) 2000

Reg.3, revoked: SI 2003/492 Sch.3 Part 2

Reg.6, revoked (in part): SR 2002/67 Reg.4, SR 2002/189 Reg.4, SR 2003/224 Reg.6

219. Part-time Workers (Prevention of Less Favourable Treatment) Regulations (Northern Ireland) 2000

Reg.2, amended: SR 2002/286 Reg.2

Reg.8, amended: SR 2002/286 Reg.2

Reg.8, revoked (in part): SR 2002/286 Reg.2

253. Animals and Animal Products (Import and Export) Regulations (Northern Ireland) 2000

Reg.12, amended: SR 2002/296 Reg.3

Reg.12, applied: SR 2003/21 Reg.5, SR 2003/104 Reg.5

Sch.2, added: SR 2002/296 Reg.3

Sch.2, revoked: SR 2002/296 Reg.3

262. Stakeholder Pension Schemes Regulations (Northern Ireland) 2000

referred to: SR 2002/268 Reg.1

Reg.1, amended: SR 2002/216 Reg.2, SR 2002/268 Reg.2, SR 2002/410 Reg.4, SR 2003/256 Reg.18

Reg.1, revoked (in part): SR 2002/216 Reg.2

Reg.8, amended: SR 2003/256 Reg.18

Reg.10, amended: SR 2003/256 Reg.18

Reg.11, amended: SR 2002/268 Reg.3

Reg.12, amended: SR 2002/216 Reg.2

Reg.12, substituted: SR 2002/268 Reg.4

Reg.15, amended: SR 2002/268 Reg.5, SR 2003/256 Reg.18

Reg.18, amended: SR 2002/410 Reg.4

266. Social Security (Payments on Account, Overpayments and Recovery) (Amendment) Regulations (Northern Ireland) 2000

revoked: SI 2003/492 Sch.3 Part 2

270. Welfare of Farmed Animals Regulations (Northern Ireland) 2000

Reg.2, amended: SR 2002/259 Reg.3, SR 2003/244 Reg.3

Reg.4, revoked: SR 2002/259 Reg.4

Reg.5, substituted: SR 2002/259 Reg.5

Reg.5A, added: SR 2002/259 Reg.6

Reg.8A, added: SR 2003/244 Reg.4

Reg.14, amended: SR 2002/259 Reg.7

Sch.1, amended: SR 2002/259 Reg.8

Sch.2, revoked: SR 2002/259 Reg.4

Sch.3, substituted: SR 2002/259 Reg.9

Sch.3A, added: SR 2002/259 Sch.1

Sch.3B, added: SR 2002/259 Sch.1

Sch.3C, added: SR 2002/259 Sch.1

Sch.3D, added: SR 2002/259 Sch.1

NO.

2000–cont.

270. Welfare of Farmed Animals Regulations (Northern Ireland) 2000–*cont.*
Sch.6, added: SR 2003/244 Reg.5

315. Royal Ulster Constabulary (Conduct) Regulations 2000
amended: SR 2003/68 Reg.5
Reg.4, amended: SR 2003/68 Reg.3
Reg.8, revoked (in part): SR 2003/68 Reg.5
Reg.9, amended: SR 2003/68 Reg.3
Reg.11, amended: SR 2003/68 Reg.5
Reg.12, amended: SR 2003/68 Reg.5
Reg.17, amended: SR 2003/68 Reg.3
Reg.31, amended: SR 2003/68 Reg.5
Sch.2, amended: SR 2003/68 Reg.3
Sch.3, amended: SR 2003/68 Reg.3, Reg.5
Sch.4, substituted: SR 2003/68 Sch.1

316. Royal Ulster Constabulary (Unsatisfactory Performance) Regulations 2000
amended: SR 2003/68 Reg.4

317. Royal Ulster Constabulary (Appeals) Regulations 2000
amended: SR 2003/68 Reg.7

320. Royal Ulster Constabulary (Conduct) (Senior Officer) Regulations 2000
amended: SR 2003/68 Reg.6
Reg.4, amended: SR 2003/68 Reg.3, Reg.6
Reg.7, revoked (in part): SR 2003/68 Reg.6
Reg.8, amended: SR 2003/68 Reg.3
Reg.9, amended: SR 2003/68 Reg.3
Reg.11, amended: SR 2003/68 Reg.3
Reg.25, amended: SR 2003/68 Reg.6
Sch.1, amended: SR 2003/68 Reg.3
Sch.2, amended: SR 2003/68 Reg.3

324. Statutory Maternity Pay (General) (Modification and Amendment) Regulations (Northern Ireland) 2000
Reg.3, revoked: SR 2002/354 Reg.8

335. Pension Sharing (Consequential and Miscellaneous Amendments) Regulations (Northern Ireland) 2000
revoked: SR 2002/410 Reg.5
Reg.11, revoked (in part): SR 2003/256 Reg.19
Reg.12, revoked (in part): SR 2003/256 Reg.19

347. Flags Regulations (Northern Ireland) 2000
varied: 2002 c.26 s.67

361. Child Benefit (General) (Amendment) Regulations (Northern Ireland) 2000
revoked: SI 2003/493 Sch.2 Part 2

365. Social Security (Joint Claims Consequential Amendments) Regulations (Northern Ireland) 2000
Reg.2, revoked: SI 2003/492 Sch.3 Part 2

371. Fair Employment (Specification of Public Authorities) (No.2) Order (Northern Ireland) 2000
Sch.1, substituted: SR 2002/367 Sch.1

NO.

2000–cont.

388. Management of Health and Safety at Work Regulations (Northern Ireland) 2000
referred to: SR 2003/33 Reg.14, SR 2003/34 Reg.13, SR 2003/35 Reg.12
Reg.21, applied: SR 2003/33 Reg.28, SR 2003/34 Reg.21

404. Social Security (Incapacity Benefit) (Miscellaneous Amendments) Regulations (Northern Ireland) 2000
Reg.4, revoked: SI 2003/492 Sch.3 Part 2
Reg.5, revoked: SI 2003/492 Sch.3 Part 2

2001

5. Organic Farming (Northern Ireland) Regulations 2001
applied: SI 2003/2261 Sch.3 Part I

12. Child Support (Temporary Compensation Payment Scheme) Regulations (Northern Ireland) 2001
Reg.3, amended: SR 2002/247 Reg.3

15. Child Support (Collection and Enforcement and Miscellaneous Amendments) Regulations (Northern Ireland) 2001
Reg.5, amended: SR 2003/91 Reg.2

16. Child Support (Information, Evidence and Disclosure and Maintenance Arrangements and Jurisdiction) (Amendment) Regulations (Northern Ireland) 2001
Reg.4, amended: SR 2003/91 Reg.2

17. Child Support (Maintenance Calculation Procedure) Regulations (Northern Ireland) 2001
Reg.1, amended: SR 2002/164 Reg.7
Reg.5, amended: SR 2003/84 Reg.8
Reg.9A, added: SR 2002/164 Reg.7
Reg.10, amended: SR 2003/84 Reg.8
Reg.24, amended: SR 2003/84 Reg.8
Reg.25, amended: SR 2002/164 Reg.7
Reg.26, amended: SR 2002/164 Reg.7
Reg.27, amended: SR 2002/164 Reg.7
Reg.28, amended: SR 2002/164 Reg.7, SR 2003/84 Reg.8
Reg.29, amended: SR 2003/84 Reg.8, SR 2003/91 Reg.2
Reg.30, amended: SR 2002/164 Reg.7, SR 2003/84 Reg.8
Sch.3, added: SR 2003/84 Sch.1

18. Child Support (Maintenance Calculations and Special Cases) Regulations (Northern Ireland) 2001
Reg.1, amended: SR 2003/84 Reg.9, SR 2003/191 Reg.33
Reg.4, amended: SR 2002/323 Sch.1 para.1, SR 2003/191 Reg.33
Reg.5, amended: SR 2003/191 Reg.33, SR 2003/261 Reg.6
Reg.8, amended: SR 2003/84 Reg.9
Reg.15, amended: SR 2003/91 Reg.2

NO.

2001—cont.

18. Child Support (Maintenance Calculations and Special Cases) Regulations (Northern Ireland) 2001—*cont.*

Sch.1, added: SR 2003/84 Reg.9

Sch.1, amended: SR 2002/164 Reg.8, SR 2003/84 Reg.9

Sch.1, revoked (in part): SR 2003/84 Reg.9, Reg.9

Sch.1, substituted: SR 2002/164 Reg.8

19. Child Support (Transitional Provisions) Regulations (Northern Ireland) 2001

Reg.2, amended: SR 2003/84 Reg.10

Reg.3, amended: SR 2003/84 Reg.10

Reg.4, substituted: SR 2002/164 Reg.9

Reg.9, amended: SR 2002/164 Reg.9

Reg.10, amended: SR 2002/164 Reg.9, SR 2003/84 Reg.10

Reg.11, amended: SR 2003/84 Reg.10

Reg.12, amended: SR 2002/164 Reg.9

Reg.12, revoked (in part): SR 2002/164 Reg.9

Reg.13, amended: SR 2002/164 Reg.9

Reg.13, substituted: SR 2002/164 Reg.9

Reg.15, amended: SR 2002/164 Reg.9, SR 2003/84 Reg.10

Reg.16, amended: SR 2003/84 Reg.10, SR 2003/91 Reg.3

Reg.17, amended: SR 2002/164 Reg.9

Reg.21, amended: SR 2002/164 Reg.9

Reg.22, amended: SR 2002/164 Reg.9, SR 2003/84 Reg.10

Reg.23, amended: SR 2002/164 Reg.9

Reg.23A, added: SR 2002/164 Reg.9

Reg.24, amended: SR 2002/164 Reg.9, SR 2003/84 Reg.10

Reg.25, amended: SR 2003/84 Reg.10

Reg.27, amended: SR 2002/164 Reg.9, SR 2003/84 Reg.10

Reg.28, amended: SR 2002/164 Reg.9, SR 2003/84 Reg.10

Reg.33, amended: SR 2003/84 Reg.10

20. Child Support (Variations) Regulations (Northern Ireland) 2001

Reg.7, amended: SR 2002/164 Reg.10, SR 2003/84 Reg.11

Reg.16, amended: SR 2002/164 Reg.10

Reg.18, amended: SR 2002/164 Reg.10

Reg.19, amended: SR 2002/164 Reg.10

Reg.33, amended: SR 2003/91 Reg.2

22. Social Security (Claims and Payments) (Amendment) Regulations (Northern Ireland) 2001

revoked: SI 2003/492 Sch.3 Part 2

23. Social Security and Child Support (Decisions and Appeals) (Amendment) Regulations (Northern Ireland) 2001

Reg.3, amended: SR 2003/91 Reg.2

Reg.4, amended: SR 2003/91 Reg.2

NO.

2001—cont.

25. Social Security (Child Maintenance Premium and Miscellaneous Amendments) Regulations (Northern Ireland) 2001

Reg.4, substituted: SR 2003/57 Reg.2

27. Dairy Produce Quotas (Amendment) Regulations (Northern Ireland) 2001

revoked: SR 2002/88 Sch.4

29. Child Support (Consequential Amendments and Transitional Provisions) Regulations (Northern Ireland) 2001

Reg.1, amended: SI 2003/495 Sch.1 Part 2

Reg.2, revoked: SI 2003/495 Sch.1 Part 2

Reg.9, amended: SR 2003/91 Reg.2

Reg.9, revoked (in part): SI 2003/495 Sch.1 Part 2

41. Social Security Benefits Up-rating Order (Northern Ireland) 2001

revoked: SR 2002/99 Art.23

46. Miscellaneous Food Additives (Amendment) Regulations (Northern Ireland) 2001

Reg.6, amended: SR 2003/300 Reg.10, SR 2003/301 Reg.10, SR 2003/313 Reg.11

47. Feeding Stuffs Regulations (Northern Ireland) 2001

referred to: SR 2003/219 r.2

Reg.2, amended: SR 2002/263 Reg.3, SR 2003/219 r.3

Reg.12, amended: SR 2003/219 r.4

Reg.17, amended: SR 2002/263 Reg.4

Reg.23, amended: SR 2002/263 Reg.5, SR 2003/219 r.5

Reg.25, revoked (in part): SR 2002/263 Reg.6

Sch.3, amended: SR 2003/219 r.6

Sch.3, substituted: SR 2002/263 Sch.1, SR 2003/219Sch

Sch.7, amended: SR 2002/263 Sch.2

Sch.8, amended: SR 2002/263 Reg.9

Sch.9, amended: SR 2002/263 Sch.3

54. Employment Rights (Increase of Limits) Order (Northern Ireland) 2001

revoked: SR 2002/24 Art.2

65. Magistrates Courts (Terrorism Act 2000) Rules (Northern Ireland) 2001

revoked: SR 2002/12 r.2

78. Social Security (Miscellaneous Amendments) Regulations (Northern Ireland) 2001

Reg.11, revoked: SI 2003/492 Sch.3 Part 2

102. Social Security (Crediting and Treatment of Contributions, and National Insurance Numbers) Regulations (Northern Ireland) 2001

Reg.5, amended: SI 2002/2366 Reg.20

Reg.6, amended: SI 2002/2366 Reg.20

106. Social Security Benefits Up-rating Regulations (Northern Ireland) 2001

Reg.2, revoked: SR 2002/108 Reg.5

NO.

2001–cont.

106. Social Security Benefits Up-rating Regulations (Northern Ireland) 2001–cont.
Reg.3, revoked: SR 2002/108 Reg.5
Reg.4, revoked (in part): SR 2002/108 Reg.5
Reg.8, revoked: SR 2002/108 Reg.5

107. Social Security (Industrial Injuries) (Dependency) (Permitted Earnings Limits) Order (Northern Ireland) 2001
Art.2, revoked (in part): SR 2002/107 Art.3

108. Social Security (Benefits for Widows and Widowers) (Consequential Amendments) Regulations (Northern Ireland) 2001
Reg.10, revoked: SI 2003/492 Sch.3 Part 2
Reg.11, revoked: SI 2003/492 Sch.3 Part 2

111. Legal Aid (Financial Conditions) Regulations (Northern Ireland) 2001
revoked: SR 2002/60 Reg.2

112. Legal Advice and Assistance (Financial Conditions) Regulations (Northern Ireland) 2001
revoked: SR 2002/61 Reg.2

113. Legal Advice and Assistance (Amendment No 2) Regulations (Northern Ireland) 2001
revoked: SR 2002/62 Reg.2

115. Social Security (Hospital In-Patients) (Amendment) Regulations (Northern Ireland) 2001
revoked: SR 2002/106 Reg.3

116. Workmen's Compensation (Supplementation) (Amendment) Regulations (Northern Ireland) 2001
revoked: SR 2002/114 Reg.7

119. Stakeholder Pension Schemes (Amendment No 2) Regulations (Northern Ireland) 2001
Reg.5, revoked: SR 2003/256 Reg.19
Reg.8, revoked: SR 2002/268 Reg.6

120. Social Security Amendment (Joint Claim Amendments) Regulations (Northern Ireland) 2001
Reg.5, revoked: SI 2003/492 Sch.3 Part 2

124. Dental Charges (Amendment) Regulations (Northern Ireland) 2001
Reg.2, revoked: SR 2002/84 Reg.3

125. Road Traffic (Health Service Charges) Regulations (Northern Ireland) 2001
Reg.4, amended: SR 2002/373 Reg.2
Reg.4, referred to: SR 2002/52 Reg.3
Reg.4, substituted: SR 2002/52 Reg.2
Reg.10, amended: SR 2002/52 Reg.4
Reg.18, amended: SR 2002/52 Reg.5

140. Police (Recruitment) (Northern Ireland) Regulations 2001
Part III, applied: SR 2002/258 Reg.7
Reg.2, amended: SR 2002/385 Reg.2
Reg.3A, added: SR 2002/385 Reg.3
Reg.5, amended: SR 2002/385 Reg.4

NO.

2001–cont.

140. Police (Recruitment) (Northern Ireland) Regulations 2001–cont.
Reg.6, amended: SR 2002/385 Reg.5
Reg.10, amended: SR 2002/385 Reg.6
Reg.10, applied: SR 2002/258 Reg.9
Reg.12, amended: SR 2002/385 Reg.7
Reg.12, applied: SR 2002/258 Reg.7
Reg.13, applied: SR 2002/258 Reg.7
Reg.14, varied: SR 2002/258 Reg.7
Reg.15, varied: SR 2002/258 Reg.7

152. Social Security (Work-focused Interviews for Lone Parents) Regulations (Northern Ireland) 2001
Reg.1, amended: SR 2002/105 Reg.2, SR 2003/107 Reg.2
Reg.2, amended: SR 2002/105 Reg.2
Reg.4, amended: SR 2002/105 Reg.2
Reg.4, revoked (in part): SR 2003/107 Reg.2

168. Chemicals (Hazard Information and Packaging for Supply) (Amendment) Regulations (Northern Ireland) 2001
revoked: SR 2002/301 Sch.8

172. Motor Vehicles (Approval) Regulations (Northern Ireland) 2001
Reg.2, amended: SR 2003/124 Reg.2
Reg.3A, added: SR 2003/124 Reg.3
Reg.4, amended: SR 2003/124 Reg.4
Sch.2, added: SR 2003/124 Sch.1
Sch.2, amended: SR 2003/124 Reg.5
Sch.3, amended: SR 2003/124 Sch.2
Sch.4, amended: SR 2003/124 Reg.7

175. Social Security (Claims and Information) Regulations (Northern Ireland) 2001
Reg.3, revoked: SI 2003/492 Sch.3 Part 2
Reg.13, amended: SR 2002/323 Sch.1 para.1
Sch.2, revoked: SI 2003/492 Sch.3 Part 2

176. Social Security (Work-focused Interviews) Regulations (Northern Ireland) 2001
Reg.1, amended: SI 2003/492 Sch.3 Part 2
Reg.5, amended: SR 2002/323 Sch.1 para.1
Reg.15, revoked (in part): SI 2003/492 Sch.3 Part 2
Sch.3, revoked: SI 2003/492 Sch.3 Part 2

186. Restriction on Pithing Regulations (Northern Ireland) 2001
Reg.2, revoked: SR 2002/225 Sch.8 Part I
Reg.5, revoked: SR 2002/225 Sch.8 Part I
Reg.8, revoked: SR 2002/225 Sch.8 Part I

188. Seed Potatoes Regulations (Northern Ireland) 2001
Reg.8, applied: SR 2002/169

199. Slaughter Premium Regulations (Northern Ireland) 2001
Reg.2, amended: SR 2003/192 Reg.3
Reg.2, revoked (in part): SR 2003/192 Reg.3
Reg.8, amended: SR 2003/192 Reg.3
Reg.9, amended: SR 2003/192 Reg.3

NO.

2001–cont.

213. Housing Benefit (Decisions and Appeals) Regulations (Northern Ireland) 2001

Reg.1, amended: SR 2002/80 Reg.8, SR 2002/189 Reg.3

Reg.1, revoked (in part): SR 2002/189 Reg.3

Reg.4, amended: SR 2002/80 Reg.8, SR 2002/189 Reg.3

Reg.7, amended: SR 2002/80 Reg.8, SR 2003/224 Reg.4

Reg.8, amended: SR 2002/80 Reg.8, SR 2003/224 Reg.4

Reg.10A, added: SR 2002/189 Reg.3

Reg.18, amended: SR 2002/189 Reg.3

Reg.19, amended: SR 2002/189 Reg.3

Reg.23, amended: SR 2002/189 Reg.3

Sch.1, added: SR 2003/312 Reg.3

216. Discretionary Financial Assistance Regulations (Northern Ireland) 2001

Reg.3, amended: SR 2002/80 Reg.9

Reg.4, substituted: SR 2003/154 Reg.5

244. Public Service Vehicles (License Fees) (Amendment) Regulations (Northern Ireland) 2001

revoked: SR 2002/49 Reg.3

245. Motor Vehicles (Driving Licenses) (Amendment) (Test Fees) Regulations (Northern Ireland) 2001

revoked: SR 2002/51 Reg.3

246. Motor Vehicle Testing (Amendment) (Fees) Regulations (Northern Ireland) 2001

revoked: SR 2003/303 Sch.4

247. Goods Vehicles (Testing) (Fees) (Amendment) Regulations (Northern Ireland) 2001

revoked: SR 2002/48 Reg.3

249. Child Support, Pensions and Social Security (2000 Act) (Commencement No 6) Order (Northern Ireland) 2001

Art.2, revoked (in part): SR 2002/68 Art.3

277. Education (Student Support) Regulations (Northern Ireland) 2001

revoked: SR 2002/224 Reg.3

Part IX, applied: SR 2002/224 Reg.3

Reg.16, amended: SR 2002/111 Reg.3

Reg.30, amended: SR 2002/111 Reg.4

279. Local Government (Discretionary Payments) Regulations (Northern Ireland) 2001

Part II, revoked: SR 2003/61 Reg.34

Part III, applied: SR 2002/352 Reg.130

Part III, revoked: SR 2003/61 Reg.34

Part IV, revoked: SR 2003/61 Reg.34

Reg.2, amended: SR 2002/353 Sch.4 para.24

Reg.4, amended: SR 2002/353 Sch.4 para.25

Reg.5, amended: SR 2002/353 Sch.4 para.26

NO.

2001–cont.

279. Local Government (Discretionary Payments) Regulations (Northern Ireland) 2001–cont.

Reg.6, amended: SR 2002/353 Sch.4 para.27

Reg.7, amended: SR 2002/353 Sch.4 para.28

Reg.7, applied: SR 2003/61 Reg.34

Reg.8, amended: SR 2002/353 Sch.4 para.29

Reg.9, amended: SR 2002/353 Sch.4 para.29

Reg.10, amended: SR 2002/353 Sch.4 para.30

Reg.15, amended: SR 2002/353 Sch.4 para.31

Reg.16, amended: SR 2002/353 Sch.4 para.32

Reg.16, applied: SR 2003/61 Reg.34

Reg.17, amended: SR 2002/353 Sch.4 para.33

Reg.17, applied: SR 2003/61 Reg.34

Reg.18, amended: SR 2002/353 Sch.4 para.34

Reg.19, amended: SR 2002/353 Sch.4 para.35

Reg.20, amended: SR 2002/353 Sch.4 para.36

Reg.21, amended: SR 2002/353 Sch.4 para.37

Reg.23, amended: SR 2002/353 Sch.4 para.38

Reg.24, amended: SR 2002/353 Sch.4 para.39

Reg.25, amended: SR 2002/353 Sch.4 para.40

Reg.28, amended: SR 2002/353 Sch.4 para.41

Reg.31, amended: SR 2002/353 Sch.4 para.41

Reg.31, applied: SR 2002/352 Reg.54

Reg.35, amended: SR 2002/353 Sch.4 para.42

Sch.1, revoked: SR 2003/61 Reg.34

Sch.2, revoked: SR 2003/61 Reg.34

Sch.3, amended: SR 2002/353 Sch.4 para.43

280. Plant Protection Products (Amendment) Regulations (Northern Ireland) 2001

revoked: SR 2002/21 Reg.4

284. Control of Pollution (Applications and Registers) Regulations (Northern Ireland) 2001

Reg.7, amended: SR 2003/7 Reg.5

Reg.8, amended: SR 2003/7 Reg.5

285. Education (Grants for Disabled Postgraduate Students) Regulations (Northern Ireland) 2001

applied: SR 2003/253 Art.3

Reg.2, referred to: SR 2002/272 Reg.3

NO.

2001–cont.

285. Education (Grants for Disabled Post-
graduate Students) Regulations
(Northern Ireland) 2001–*cont.*
Reg.9, amended: SR 2002/272 Reg.2

286. Catering Waste (Feeding to Livestock) Order (Northern Ireland) 2001
revoked: SR 2002/209 Art.33

291. Fisheries (Tagging and Logbook)
Byelaws (Northern Ireland) 2001
referred to: SR 2002/372 Art.2
Art.2, amended: SR 2002/372 Art.3
Art.7, substituted: SR 2002/372 Art.4
Sch.1, substituted: SR 2002/372 Art.5

292. Bovine Spongiform Encephalopathy
Monitoring Regulations (Northern
Ireland) 2001
applied: SR 2002/225 Sch.8 para.1, Sch.8
para.2
revoked: SR 2002/225 Sch.8 Part I

293. Lands Tribunal (Salaries) Order
(Northern Ireland) 2001
revoked: SR 2003/227 Art.2

295. Genetically Modified Organisms
(Contained Use) Regulations (North-
ern Ireland) 2001
applied: SR 2003/34 Sch.3 para.5
Reg.16, applied: SR 2003/167 Reg.12
Reg.31, revoked (in part): SR 2003/167 Sch.5

298. Students Awards Regulations (Northern Ireland) 2001
applied: SR 2002/265 Reg.18
revoked: SR 2002/265 Reg.18
Sch.6, amended: SR 2002/112 Reg.3

302. Salaries (Assembly Ombudsman and
Commissioner for Complaints) Order
(Northern Ireland) 2001
revoked: SR 2002/320 Reg.2

310. Motor Vehicles (Driving Licenses)
(Amendment No.2) (Test Fees) Regulations (Northern Ireland) 2001
revoked: SR 2002/51 Reg.3

313. Northern Ireland Health and Social
Care Council (Appointments and
Procedure) Regulations (Northern
Ireland) 2001
Reg.3, amended: SR 2002/349 Reg.2
Reg.4, amended: SR 2002/349 Reg.3
Reg.5, amended: SR 2002/349 Reg.4
Reg.6, amended: SR 2002/349 Reg.5
Reg.10, amended: SR 2002/349 Reg.6

316. Social Security (Incapacity Benefit)
(Miscellaneous Amendments) Regu-
lations (Northern Ireland) 2001
Reg.2, revoked: SR 2002/276 Reg.5
Reg.3, revoked (in part): SR 2002/276 Reg.5
Reg.4, revoked: SR 2002/276 Reg.5
Reg.5, revoked: SR 2002/276 Reg.5

348. Fire Precautions (Workplace) Regulations (Northern Ireland) 2001
Reg.9, amended: SR 2003/152 Sch.7 para.7

NO.

2001–cont.

363. Beef Special Premium Regulations
(Northern Ireland) 2001
referred to: SR 2002/335 Reg.3
Reg.2, amended: SR 2002/335 Reg.4
Reg.5, amended: SR 2002/335 Reg.5

364. Motor Vehicle Testing (Amendment)
Regulations (Northern Ireland) 2001
revoked: SR 2003/303 Sch.4

387. Carriage of Explosives by Rail Regulations (Northern Ireland) 2001
referred to: SR 2003/35 Sch.2

391. Farm Subsidies (Review of Decisions)
Regulations (Northern Ireland) 2001
Reg.4, amended: SR 2002/72 Reg.16, SR
2003/162 Reg.16

397. Foyle Area and Carlingford Area
(Licensing of Fishing Engines) Regu-
lations 2001
referred to: SR 2003/114 Reg.2
Reg.2, amended: SR 2003/114 Reg.3
Reg.3, amended: SR 2003/114 Reg.4
Sch.1, substituted: SR 2003/114 Reg.5

405. Processed Animal Protein Regula-
tions (Northern Ireland) 2001
applied: SR 2002/225 Sch.8 para.7, Sch.8
para.8
Reg.4, revoked: SR 2002/225 Sch.8 Part I
Reg.5, applied: SR 2002/225 Sch.8 para.1
Reg.6, applied: SR 2002/225 Sch.8 para.2
Reg.7, applied: SR 2002/225 Sch.8 para.3
Reg.9, revoked: SR 2002/225 Sch.8 Part I
Reg.12, revoked: SR 2002/225 Sch.8 Part I
Reg.13, applied: SR 2002/225 Sch.8 para.4
Reg.14, applied: SR 2002/225 Sch.8 para.5
Reg.15, applied: SR 2002/225 Sch.8 para.6
Reg.17, revoked: SR 2002/225 Sch.8 Part I
Sch.1, revoked: SR 2002/225 Sch.8 Part I
Sch.3, revoked: SR 2002/225 Sch.8 Part I

410. Income Support (General) (Standard
Interest Rate Amendment No.3)
Regulations (Northern Ireland) 2001
revoked: SR 2002/16 Reg.3

414. Gaming (Variation of Monetary
Limits) Order (Northern Ireland)
2001
Art.4, revoked (in part): SR 2003/15 Art.4

415. Gaming (Bingo) (Amendment) Regulations (Northern Ireland) 2001
revoked: SR 2003/233 Reg.4

420. Social Security (Notification of
Change of Circumstances) Regula-
tions (Northern Ireland) 2001
Reg.5, revoked: SI 2003/492 Sch.3 Part 2

422. Biocidal Products Regulations
(Northern Ireland) 2001
applied: SR 2002/301 Reg.16
Reg.2, amended: SI 2003/429 Reg.4
Reg.8, amended: SR 2002/302 Reg.2
Reg.39A, added: SI 2003/429 Reg.4
Sch.10, amended: SR 2002/302 Reg.2
Sch.11A, added: SI 2003/429 Sch.2

NO.

2001–cont.

424. Foot-and-Mouth Disease (Controlled Area) (No.6) Order (Northern Ireland) 2001
revoked: SR 2002/44 Art.4

434. Road Traffic (Health Services Charges) (Amendment) Regulations (Northern Ireland) 2001
revoked: SR 2002/52 Reg.6

438. Welfare Reform and Pensions (1999 Order) (Commencement No 9) Order (Northern Ireland) 2001
Art.2, revoked (in part): SR 2002/25 Art.3

2002

1. Misuse of Drugs Regulations (Northern Ireland) 2002
Reg.2, amended: SR 2003/324 Reg.3
Reg.6, amended: SR 2003/324 Reg.3
Reg.6A, added: SR 2003/324 Reg.3
Sch.2, amended: SR 2003/314 Reg.3
Sch.4, amended: SR 2003/314 Reg.3

10. Street Works (Register, Notices, Directions and Designations) Regulations (Northern Ireland) 2002
Reg.3, applied: SR 2003/236 Reg.3

14. Social Fund (Maternity and Funeral Expenses) (General) (Amendment) Regulations (Northern Ireland) 2002
Reg.3, amended: SR 2002/90 Reg.2

16. Income Support (General) (Standard Interest Rate Amendment) Regulations (Northern Ireland) 2002
revoked: SR 2002/58 Reg.3

20. Pesticides (Maximum Residue Levels in Crops, Food and Feeding Stuffs) Regulations (Northern Ireland) 2002
Reg.2, amended: SR 2002/27 Reg.2, SR 2002/250 Reg.2, SR 2003/123 Reg.2
Reg.6, amended: SR 2003/123 Reg.2
Sch.1, amended: SR 2002/27 Reg.2, SR 2002/250 Reg.2, SR 2003/123 Reg.2
Sch.2, added: SR 2003/123 Reg.2
Sch.2, amended: SR 2002/27 Reg.2, Sch.1, SR 2002/250 Reg.2, Sch.1, SR 2003/123 Reg.2, Sch.1
Sch.2, applied: SR 2002/27, SR 2002/250

21. Plant Protection Products (Amendment) Regulations (Northern Ireland) 2002
revoked: SR 2002/125 Reg.4

24. Employment Rights (Increase of Limits) Order (Northern Ireland) 2002
revoked: SR 2003/241 Art.2

25. Welfare Reform and Pensions (1999 Order) (Commencement No 10) Order (Northern Ireland) 2002
Art.2, revoked (in part): SR 2002/126 Art.3

NO.

2002–cont.

33. Food and Animal Feedingstuffs (Products of Animal Origin from China) (Control) Regulations (Northern Ireland) 2002
revoked: SR 2002/226 Reg.6

47. Motor Vehicle Testing (Amendment) (Fees) Regulations (Northern Ireland) 2002
revoked: SR 2003/303 Sch.4

49. Public Service Vehicles (License Fees) (Amendment) Regulations (Northern Ireland) 2002
revoked: SR 2003/99 Reg.3

51. Motor Vehicles (Driving Licenses) (Amendment) (Test Fees) Regulations (Northern Ireland) 2002
revoked: SR 2003/100 Reg.3

59. Social Security (Claims and Payments) (Amendment) Regulations (Northern Ireland) 2002
revoked: SI 2003/492 Sch.3 Part 2, SR 2003/118 Reg.3

60. Legal Aid (Financial Conditions) Regulations (Northern Ireland) 2002
revoked: SR 2003/88 Reg.2

61. Legal Advice and Assistance (Financial Conditions) Regulations (Northern Ireland) 2002
revoked: SR 2003/89 Reg.2

62. Legal Advice and Assistance (Amendment) Regulations (Northern Ireland) 2002
revoked: SR 2003/90 Reg.2

67. Social Security (Claims and Payments and Miscellaneous Amendments) Regulations (Northern Ireland) 2002
Reg.2, revoked: SI 2003/492 Sch.3 Part 2

79. Social Security (Loss of Benefit) Regulations (Northern Ireland) 2002
Reg.2, amended: SR 2003/28 Reg.25
Reg.3A, added: SR 2003/28 Reg.25

84. Dental Charges (Amendment) Regulations (Northern Ireland) 2002
Reg.2, revoked: SR 2003/134 Reg.3

87. Social Security (Guardian's Allowances) (Amendment) Regulations (Northern Ireland) 2002
revoked: SI 2003/495 Sch.1 Part 2

94. Air Quality Limit Values Regulations (Northern Ireland) 2002
Reg.2, amended: SR 2002/357 Reg.3
Reg.7, amended: SR 2002/357 Reg.3
Reg.9, applied: SR 2003/240 Reg.8
Reg.11, amended: SR 2002/357 Reg.3
Sch.1, added: SR 2002/357 Reg.3
Sch.2, amended: SR 2002/357 Reg.3
Sch.3, amended: SR 2002/357 Reg.3
Sch.3, substituted: SR 2002/357 Reg.3
Sch.4, amended: SR 2002/357 Reg.3
Sch.5, amended: SR 2002/357 Reg.3
Sch.6, added: SR 2002/357 Reg.3

NO.

2002-cont.

94. Air Quality Limit Values Regulations (Northern Ireland) 2002-*cont.*
Sch.6, referred to: SR 2003/240 Sch.4
Sch.6, substituted: SR 2002/357 Reg.3
Sch.7, referred to: SR 2003/240 Reg.8

99. Social Security Benefits Up-rating Order (Northern Ireland) 2002
revoked: SR 2003/155 Art.25

106. Social Security (Work-focused Interviews for Lone Parents Amendment) Regulations (Northern Ireland) 2002
revoked: SR 2003/261 Sch.1

107. Social Security (Industrial Injuries) (Dependency) (Permitted Earnings Limits) Order (Northern Ireland) 2002
revoked: SR 2003/157 Art.3

108. Social Security Benefits Up-rating Regulations (Northern Ireland) 2002
revoked: SR 2003/156 Reg.5

110. Maternity and Parental Leave etc (Amendment) Regulations (Northern Ireland) 2002
revoked: SR 2002/135 Reg.3

111. Education (Student Support) (Amendment) Regulations (Northern Ireland) 2002
revoked: SR 2002/224 Reg.3

114. Workmen's Compensation (Supplementation) (Amendment) Regulations (Northern Ireland) 2002
revoked: SR 2003/164 Reg.7

125. Plant Protection Products (Amendment) (No.2) Regulations (Northern Ireland) 2002
revoked: SR 2002/289 Reg.4
Reg.7, varied: SR 2002/289 Reg.3

132. Social Security (Amendment) (Residential Care and Nursing Homes) Regulations (Northern Ireland) 2002
Reg.3, revoked: SI 2003/492 Sch.3 Part 2

140. Food (Figs, Hazelnuts and Pistachios from Turkey) (Emergency Control) Regulations (Northern Ireland) 2002
revoked: SR 2002/307 Reg.7

147. Explosives (Fireworks) Regulations (Northern Ireland) 2002
Sch.1, applied: SI 2003/1593 Sch.1 Part I

164. Social Security and Child Support (Miscellaneous Amendments) Regulations (Northern Ireland) 2002
Reg.8, revoked (in part): SR 2003/84 Reg.12

179. Police (Northern Ireland) Act 2000 (Designated Places of Detention) Order 2002
revoked: SR 2003/232 Art.3

197. Motor Vehicles (Construction and Use) (Amendment) Regulations (Northern Ireland) 2002
revoked: SR 2002/256 Reg.8

NO.

2002-cont.

209. Animal By-Products Order (Northern Ireland) 2002
applied: SR 2002/340 Reg.24, Reg.39
Art.5, referred to: SR 2002/340 Reg.22, Reg.29

216. Stakeholder Pension Schemes (Amendment) Regulations (Northern Ireland) 2002
Reg.2, revoked (in part): SR 2002/268 Reg.6

219. Contaminants in Food Regulations (Northern Ireland) 2002
Reg.2, amended: SR 2002/262 Reg.2

224. Education (Student Support) Regulations (Northern Ireland) 2002
applied: SR 2003/253 Art.3
referred to: SR 2003/121 Reg.2
Part IV, amended: SR 2003/121 Reg.3
Part V, amended: SR 2003/121 Reg.4

226. Food and Animal Feedingstuffs (Products of Animal Origin from China) (Emergency Control) Regulations (Northern Ireland) 2002
revoked: SR 2002/340 Reg.62

248. Controlled Waste Regulations (Northern Ireland) 2002
Reg.3, amended: SR 2002/271 Reg.5
Reg.4, amended: SR 2002/271 Reg.5
Reg.6, amended: SR 2002/271 Reg.5
Reg.8, amended: SR 2002/271 Reg.5
Sch.3, amended: SR 2002/271 Reg.5

254. Social Security (Claims and Payments) (Amendment No.2) Regulations (Northern Ireland) 2002
revoked: SI 2003/492 Sch.3 Part 2

257. Seeds (Fees) Regulations (Northern Ireland) 2002
revoked: SR 2002/407 Reg.4

265. Student Awards Regulations (Northern Ireland) 2002
applied: SR 2003/253 Art.3

269. Plant Health (Phytophthora ramorum) Order (Northern Ireland) 2002
revoked: SR 2003/193 Art.15
Art.3, applied: SR 2003/193 Art.15

271. Controlled Waste (Duty of Care) Regulations (Northern Ireland) 2002
Reg.2, amended: SR 2003/46 Sch.11 para.19

283. Fire Services (Appointments and Promotion) (Amendment) Regulations (Northern Ireland) 2002
revoked: SR 2003/207 Reg.3

289. Plant Protection Products (Amendment) (No.3) Regulations (Northern Ireland) 2002
revoked: SR 2003/79 Reg.4

293. Food (Peanuts from China) (Emergency Control) Regulations (Northern Ireland) 2002
Reg.2, amended: SR 2003/361 Reg.2
Reg.4, amended: SR 2003/361 Reg.2

NO.

2002–cont.

297. Social Security (Claims and Payments) (Amendment No 3) Regulations (Northern Ireland) 2002
revoked: SI 2003/492 Sch.3 Part 2

301. Chemicals (Hazard Information and Packaging for Supply) Regulations (Northern Ireland) 2002
applied: SR 2003/33 Sch.2 para.1
referred to: SR 2003/34 Sch.7, SR 2003/35 Sch.2

327. Social Security (Claims and Payments and Miscellaneous Amendments No 2) Regulations (Northern Ireland) 2002
Reg.2, revoked: SI 2003/492 Sch.3 Part 2

339. Food Protection (Emergency Prohibitions) Order (Northern Ireland) 2002
revoked: SR 2002/370 Reg.2

340. Products of Animal Origin (Third Country Imports) Regulations (Northern Ireland) 2002
Reg.3, substituted: SR 2003/215 Reg.2
Reg.61, amended: SR 2003/215 Reg.2
Sch.2, substituted: SR 2003/215 Sch.1

352. Local Government Pension Scheme Regulations (Northern Ireland) 2002
applied: SR 2002/353 Reg.10, Reg.11, Reg.12, Sch.5 para.2, SR 2003/61 Reg.2, Reg.9, Reg.16, Reg.18, Reg.19, Reg.20, Reg.28, Reg.30
disapplied: SR 2002/353 Sch.2 para.5
referred to: SR 2002/353 Reg.2, Reg.11, Reg.15, Sch.5 para.2, SR 2003/61 Reg.2
Part II, disapplied: SR 2002/353 Reg.4, Sch.2 para.2
Part III, disapplied: SR 2002/353 Reg.4, Sch.2 para.2
Reg.8, applied: SR 2002/353 Sch.2 para.6
Reg.8, referred to: SR 2002/353 Reg.6, Reg.7, Reg.8, Reg.9, Reg.10, Reg.11
Reg.15, referred to: SR 2002/353 Reg.14
Reg.19, applied: SR 2002/353 Reg.15
Reg.19, referred to: SR 2002/353 Reg.11
Reg.26, applied: SR 2002/353 Reg.15
Reg.28, applied: SR 2002/353 Reg.15, SR 2003/61 Reg.9, Reg.10, Reg.11
Reg.29, applied: SR 2002/353 Reg.8, Reg.15
Reg.31, applied: SR 2002/353 Reg.15, Sch.2 para.4, Sch.2 para.5, Sch.2 para.6, Sch.2 para.8
Reg.33, applied: SR 2002/353 Reg.15
Reg.34, applied: SR 2002/353 Sch.2 para.6, Sch.2 para.7, Sch.2 para.8, Sch.2 para.9
Reg.34, referred to: SR 2002/353 Sch.2 para.6
Reg.36, applied: SR 2003/61 Reg.19
Reg.36, disapplied: SR 2003/61 Reg.19
Reg.37, applied: SR 2002/353 Reg.15
Reg.41, applied: SR 2002/353 Reg.15
Reg.42, applied: SR 2003/61 Reg.20
Reg.43, applied: SR 2003/61 Reg.20

2002–cont.

352. Local Government Pension Scheme Regulations (Northern Ireland) 2002–cont.
Reg.44, applied: SR 2002/353 Reg.15, SR 2003/61 Reg.20
Reg.45, applied: SR 2003/61 Reg.20
Reg.47, applied: SR 2002/353 Reg.15, SR 2003/61 Reg.22
Reg.48, applied: SR 2002/353 Reg.15, SR 2003/61 Reg.23
Reg.49, applied: SR 2003/61 Reg.24
Reg.50, applied: SR 2002/353 Sch.2 para.5
Reg.51, applied: SR 2002/353 Reg.4, Sch.2 para.2
Reg.52, applied: SR 2002/353 Reg.4, Sch.2 para.2
Reg.54, amended: SR 2003/61 Reg.33
Reg.54, applied: SR 2003/61 Reg.5, Reg.6
Reg.57, applied: SR 2002/353 Reg.13, Sch.2 para.9
Reg.57, disapplied: SR 2002/353 Reg.13
Reg.57, referred to: SR 2002/353 Reg.13
Reg.88, applied: SR 2002/353 Reg.15
Reg.112, applied: SR 2002/353 Sch.2 para.3
Reg.113, applied: SR 2002/353 Sch.2 para.3
Reg.122, referred to: SR 2002/353 Reg.11
Reg.127, referred to: SR 2002/353 Reg.15
Reg.130, amended: SR 2003/61 Reg.33
Sch.4, applied: SR 2002/353 Reg.11, Sch.2 para.8

353. Local Government Pension Scheme (Amendment No 2 and Transitional Provisions) Regulations (Northern Ireland) 2002
applied: SR 2002/352 Reg.8, Reg.131
disapplied: SR 2002/352 Reg.120
Reg.11, applied: SR 2003/61 Reg.6, Reg.7

354. Social Security, Statutory Maternity Pay and Statutory Sick Pay (Miscellaneous Amendments) Regulations (Northern Ireland) 2002
Reg.2, referred to: SR 2003/155 Art.1
Reg.6, revoked (in part): SR 2003/168 Reg.3

359. Social Security, Statutory Maternity Pay and Statutory Sick Pay (Miscellaneous Amendments No 2) Regulations (Northern Ireland) 2002
Reg.6, enabled: SR 1995/150 Reg.18

377. Paternity and Adoption Leave Regulations (Northern Ireland) 2002
Reg.2, amended: SR 2003/222 Reg.4
Reg.3, amended: SR 2003/222 Reg.5
Reg.4, applied: SR 2002/378 Reg.4
Reg.4, revoked: SR 2003/222 Reg.6
Reg.5, revoked: SR 2003/222 Reg.6
Reg.6, revoked: SR 2003/222 Reg.6
Reg.7, revoked: SR 2003/222 Reg.6
Reg.8, substituted: SR 2003/222 Reg.7
Reg.9, substituted: SR 2003/222 Reg.7
Reg.10, substituted: SR 2003/222 Reg.7
Reg.11, amended: SR 2003/222 Reg.8

NO.

2002–cont.

377. Paternity and Adoption Leave Regulations (Northern Ireland) 2002–*cont.*
Reg.15, substituted: SR 2003/222 Reg.9
Reg.16, substituted: SR 2003/222 Reg.9
Reg.17, substituted: SR 2003/222 Reg.9
Reg.18, amended: SR 2003/222 Reg.10
Reg.20, amended: SR 2003/222 Reg.11
Reg.22, amended: SR 2003/222 Reg.12

378. Statutory Paternity Pay and Statutory Adoption Pay (General) Regulations (Northern Ireland) 2002
Reg.17, applied: SR 2003/223 Reg.4
Reg.17, varied: SR 2003/223 Reg.3
Reg.18, applied: SR 2003/223 Reg.4
Reg.18, varied: SR 2003/223 Reg.3
Reg.19, applied: SR 2003/223 Reg.4
Reg.19, varied: SR 2003/223 Reg.3
Reg.26, applied: SR 2003/223 Reg.4
Reg.26, varied: SR 2003/223 Reg.3
Reg.27, applied: SR 2003/223 Reg.4
Reg.27, varied: SR 2003/223 Reg.3
Reg.28, applied: SR 2003/223 Reg.4
Reg.28, varied: SR 2003/223 Reg.3
Reg.31, applied: SR 2003/223 Reg.4
Reg.31, varied: SR 2003/223 Reg.3
Reg.32, applied: SR 2002/382 Reg.2, Reg.3, SR 2003/223 Reg.4
Reg.32, varied: SR 2003/223 Reg.3
Reg.33, applied: SR 2003/223 Reg.4
Reg.33, varied: SR 2003/223 Reg.3
Reg.34, applied: SR 2003/223 Reg.4
Reg.34, varied: SR 2003/223 Reg.3
Reg.35, applied: SR 2003/223 Reg.4
Reg.35, varied: SR 2003/223 Reg.3
Reg.36, applied: SR 2003/223 Reg.4
Reg.36, varied: SR 2003/223 Reg.3
Reg.37, applied: SR 2003/223 Reg.4
Reg.37, varied: SR 2003/223 Reg.3
Reg.38, applied: SR 2003/223 Reg.4
Reg.38, varied: SR 2003/223 Reg.3
Reg.39, applied: SR 2002/380 Reg.2, Reg.3, SR 2003/223 Reg.4
Reg.39, varied: SR 2003/223 Reg.3
Reg.40, applied: SR 2002/380 Reg.2, Reg.3, SR 2003/223 Reg.4
Reg.40, varied: SR 2003/223 Reg.3
Reg.41, applied: SR 2003/223 Reg.4
Reg.41, varied: SR 2003/223 Reg.3
Reg.42, applied: SR 2003/223 Reg.4
Reg.42, varied: SR 2003/223 Reg.3
Reg.43, applied: SR 2003/223 Reg.4
Reg.43, varied: SR 2003/223 Reg.3
Reg.44, applied: SR 2003/223 Reg.4
Reg.44, varied: SR 2003/223 Reg.3
Reg.45, applied: SR 2003/223 Reg.4
Reg.45, varied: SR 2003/223 Reg.3
Reg.46, applied: SR 2003/223 Reg.4
Reg.46, varied: SR 2003/223 Reg.3
Reg.47, applied: SR 2003/223 Reg.4
Reg.47, varied: SR 2003/223 Reg.3

NO.

2002–cont.

379. Statutory Paternity Pay and Statutory Adoption Pay (Administration) Regulations (Northern Ireland) 2002
Reg.2, varied: SR 2003/276 Reg.2
Reg.11, varied: SR 2003/276 Reg.2

380. Statutory Paternity Pay and Statutory Adoption Pay (Weekly Rates) Regulations (Northern Ireland) 2002
Reg.2, applied: SR 2003/155 Art.11
Reg.3, applied: SR 2003/155 Art.11

382. Statutory Paternity Pay and Statutory Adoption Pay (Persons Abroad and Mariners) Regulations (Northern Ireland) 2002
Reg.1, varied: SR 2003/277 Reg.3
Reg.5, varied: SR 2003/277 Reg.3
Reg.6, varied: SR 2003/277 Reg.3

2003

1. Income-Related Benefits and Jobseeker's Allowance (Working Tax Credit and Child Tax Credit Amendment) Regulations (Northern Ireland) 2003
Sch.1, revoked: SR 2003/195 Sch.4 para.5
Sch.2, amended: SR 2003/196 Reg.2
Sch.2, referred to: SR 2003/195 Reg.1
Sch.2, revoked: SR 2003/195 Sch.4 para.6
Sch.3, revoked: SR 2003/195 Sch.4 para.5

21. Livestock and Meat Commission (Levy) Regulations (Northern Ireland) 2003
revoked: SR 2003/104 Reg.7

28. State Pension Credit Regulations (Northern Ireland) 2003
referred to: SR 2003/155 Art.24
Reg.1, amended: SI 2003/2175 Reg.4, SR 2003/191 Reg.23
Reg.6, applied: SR 2003/155 Art.24
Reg.6, referred to: SR 2003/155 Sch.14
Reg.7, applied: SR 2003/155 Art.24
Reg.7, referred to: SR 2003/155 Sch.14
Reg.13A, added: SR 2003/191 Reg.23
Reg.13B, added: SR 2003/191 Reg.23
Reg.17, amended: SR 2003/191 Reg.23
Reg.17A, added: SI 2003/2175 Reg.5
Reg.17B, added: SI 2003/2175 Reg.5
Reg.24A, added: SR 2003/191 Reg.23
Sch.1, amended: SR 2003/191 Reg.23
Sch.2, amended: SR 2003/191 Reg.23, SR 2003/261 Reg.7
Sch.2, applied: SR 2003/155 Art.24
Sch.2, referred to: SR 2003/155 Sch.14
Sch.3, amended: SR 2003/261 Reg.7
Sch.3, applied: SR 2003/155 Art.24
Sch.3, revoked (in part): SR 2003/261 Reg.7
Sch.3, varied: SR 2003/191 Reg.34
Sch.4, added: SR 2003/191 Reg.23
Sch.4, amended: SR 2003/191 Reg.23
Sch.5, added: SR 2003/191 Reg.23
Sch.6, added: SR 2003/191 Reg.23

2003–cont.

33. Control of Asbestos at Work Regulations (Northern Ireland) 2003
applied: SR 2003/34 Reg.5

34. Control of Substances Hazardous to Health Regulations (Northern Ireland) 2003
Reg.2, amended: SR 2003/288 Reg.2
Reg.7, amended: SR 2003/288 Reg.2
Reg.13, amended: SR 2003/288 Reg.2
Sch.1, amended: SR 2003/288 Reg.2

35. Control of Lead at Work Regulations (Northern Ireland) 2003
applied: SR 2003/34 Reg.5

46. Pollution Prevention and Control Regulations (Northern Ireland) 2003
Reg.8, applied: SI 2003/3311 Reg.6
Reg.10, applied: SR 2003/210 Reg.3
Reg.12, amended: SI 2003/3311 Sch.5 para.4
Reg.27, amended: SI 2003/3311 Sch.5 para.4
Reg.27, applied: SI 2003/3311 Reg.3

53. Child Support, Pensions and Social Security (2000 Act) (Commencement No 9) Order (Northern Ireland) 2003
Art.6, substituted: SR 2003/92 Art.2

80. Housing Benefit (General) (Amendment) Regulations (Northern Ireland) 2003
Reg.3, amended: SR 2003/189 Reg.3

87. Infected Waters (Infectious Pancreatic Necrosis) Order Northern Ireland 2003
revoked: SR 2003/242 Art.2
Sch.1, referred to: SR 2003/242

101. Motor Vehicle Testing (Amendment) (Fees) Regulations (Northern Ireland) 2003
revoked: SR 2003/303 Sch.4

124. Motor Vehicles (Approval) (Amendment) Regulations (Northern Ireland) 2003
revoked: SR 2003/275 Reg.2

152. Dangerous Substances and Explosive Atmospheres Regulations (Northern Ireland) 2003
referred to: SI 2003/2002 Reg.12

155. Social Security Benefits Up-rating Order (Northern Ireland) 2003
applied: SR 2003/156 Reg.2, Reg.3

167. Genetically Modified Organisms (Deliberate Release) Regulations (Northern Ireland) 2003
Reg.37, revoked: SR 2003/206 Reg.3

2003–cont.

173. Flexible Working (Procedural Requirements) Regulations (Northern Ireland) 2003
referred to: SR 2003/174 Reg.6
Reg.3, applied: SR 2003/174 Reg.6
Reg.4, applied: SR 2003/174 Reg.6
Reg.8, applied: SR 2003/174 Reg.6
Reg.9, applied: SR 2003/174 Reg.6

191. State Pension Credit (Consequential, Transitional and Miscellaneous Provisions) Regulations (Northern Ireland) 2003
Reg.34, revoked (in part): SR 2003/261 Reg.8

197. Housing Benefit (State Pension Credit) Regulations (Northern Ireland) 2003
Reg.22, revoked: SR 2003/261 Reg.9

212. Tax Credits Act 2002 (Transitional Provisions and Savings) Order (Northern Ireland) 2003
Art.2, applied: SR 2003/213 Reg.1

221. Social Security Contributions and Benefits (Northern Ireland) Act 1992 (Application of Parts XIIZA and XIIZB to Adoptions from Overseas) Regulations (Northern Ireland) 2003
referred to: SR 2003/223 Reg.2

261. Social Security (Hospital In-Patients and Miscellaneous Amendments) Regulations (Northern Ireland) 2003
varied: 1992 c.8 s.165

278. Urban Waste Water Treatment (Amendment) Regulations (Northern Ireland) 2003
varied: 1972 c.68 s.2

298. Education (Student Support) Regulations (Northern Ireland) 2003
Reg.20, amended: SR 2003/339 Reg.2

329. Social Security (Students and Income-Related Benefits Amendment) Regulations (Northern Ireland) 2003
Reg.2, revoked (in part): SR 2003/351 Reg.3

346. Company Directors Disqualification (2002 Order) (Transitional Provisions) Order (Northern Ireland) 2003
Art.3, applied: SR 2003/345 Art.3
Art.6, applied: SR 2003/345 Art.3

STATUTORY INSTRUMENTS ISSUED BY THE UK PARLIAMENT

1912

348. Public Trustee Rules 1912
r.30, amended: SI 2002/2469 Sch.1 para.32

1919

1961. Land Settlement (Annuities) Regulations 1919
Reg.8, varied: SI 2003/1633 Sch.2 para.14

1921

1825. Celluloid, etc Factories, and Workshops Regulations 1921
revoked: SI 2002/2776 Sch.7 Part 1

1925

1093. LAND REGISTRATION RULES, 1925, DATED NOVEMBER 3, 1925, MADE BY THE LORD CHANCELLOR UNDER SECTION 144 OF THE LAND REGISTRATION ACT, 1925 (15 &amp 16 GEO 5 C. 1925
Part I r.8, applied: SI 2003/1953 Art.21
Part I r.10, applied: SI 2003/1953 Art.21
Part I r.10, disapplied: SI 2003/1953 Art.21
Part I r.10, referred to: SI 2003/1953 Art.21
Part II r.20, amended: SI 2002/2539 Sch.1 para.1
Part III r.82A, substituted: SI 2002/2539 Sch.1 para.2
Part III r.82B, substituted: SI 2002/2539 Sch.1 para.3
Part III r.83A, applied: SI 2003/1953 Art.19
Part III r.83A, referred to: SI 2003/1953 Art.19
Part III r.90, substituted: SI 2002/2539 Sch.1 para.4
Part III r.145, amended: SI 2002/2539 Sch.1 para.5
Part III r.185, amended: SI 2003/2096 Sch.1 para.41
Part III r.185A, added: SI 2002/2539 Sch.1 para.6
Part IV r.215, amended: SI 2002/2539 Sch.1 para.7, Sch.1 para.8
Part IV r.215, applied: SI 2003/1953 Art.6, Art.15, Art.19
Part IV r.218, applied: SI 2003/1953 Art.6
Part IV r.219, applied: SI 2003/1953 Art.6
Part IV r.234, amended: SI 2002/2539 Sch.1 para.9
Part IV r.239, applied: 2002 c.9 Sch.12 para.3
Part V r.259, amended: SI 2002/2539 Sch.1 para.10
Part V r.271, applied: SI 2003/165 Sch.3 Part I
Part V r.277, applied: SI 2003/165 Art.14
Part V r.298, applied: SI 2003/1953 Art.6, Art.8

1925–cont.

1093. LAND REGISTRATION RULES, 1925, DATED NOVEMBER 3, 1925, MADE BY THE LORD CHANCELLOR UNDER SECTION 144 OF THE LAND REGISTRATION–cont.
Part V r.299, applied: SI 2003/1953 Art.6, Art.8
Part V r.299, referred to: SI 2003/1953 Art.6
Part V r.300, applied: SI 2003/1953 Art.8
Sch.2, added: SI 2002/2539 Sch.2 para.5, Sch.2 para.6
Sch.2, amended: SI 2002/2539 Sch.2 para.2, Sch.2 para.3, Sch.2 para.4
Sch.2, revoked: SI 2002/2539 Sch.2 para.1
1349. Markets, Sales and Lairs Order 1925
disapplied: SI 2002/202 Art.6, SI 2002/283 Art.6, SI 2003/253 Art.8, Art.9, SI 2003/481 Art.9, SSI 2002/34 Art.6
revoked (in part): SI 2003/1723 Art.11, SI 2003/1967 Art.11

1926

546. Markets and Fairs (Amendment) Order 1926
revoked (in part): SI 2003/1723 Art.11, SI 2003/1967 Art.11

1927

290. Animals (Miscellaneous Provisions) Order 1927
Art.9, disapplied: SI 2002/2154 Art.15, SI 2002/2303 Art.15
343. Coroners (Orders as to Districts) Rules 1927
applied: SI 2002/1588, SI 2002/2257, SI 2003/2753, SI 2003/3224, SI 2004/535, SI 2004/2192
referred to: SI 2002/3084
982. Markets, Sales and Lairs (Amendment) Order 1927
revoked (in part): SI 2003/1723 Art.11, SI 2003/1967 Art.11

1928

82. Manufacture of Cinematograph Film Regulations 1928
revoked: SI 2002/2776 Sch.7 Part 1

1929

952. Petroleum-spirit (Motor Vehicles etc.) Regulations 1929
Reg.2, substituted: SI 2002/2776 Sch.6 para.3
Reg.7, amended: SI 2002/2776 Sch.6 para.3

NO.

NO.

1929–cont.

952. Petroleum-spirit (Motor Vehicles etc.) Regulations 1929–*cont.*
Reg.15A, amended: SI 2002/2776 Sch.6 para.3

992. Petroleum (Carbide of Calcium) Order 1929
revoked: SI 2002/2776 Sch.7 Part 1

1930

34. Petroleum (Compressed Gases) Order 1930
revoked: SI 2002/2776 Sch.7 Part 1

1933

53. Merchant Shipping Load Line Convention (Jersey) Order 1933
revoked: SI 2004/1284 Sch.1

1935

247. Cremation (Scotland) Regulations 1935
amended: SSI 2003/301 Reg.2
Reg.7, amended: SSI 2003/301 Reg.2
Reg.15A, added: SSI 2003/301 Reg.2
Reg.18, amended: SSI 2003/301 Reg.2
Sch.1, amended: SSI 2003/301 Reg.2

560. Merchant Shipping Safety Convention (Jersey) (No.1) Order 1935
revoked: SI 2004/1284 Sch.1

561. Merchant Shipping Safety Convention (Jersey) (No.2) Order 1935
revoked: SI 2004/1284 Sch.1

837. Merchant Shipping (Helm Orders) Order 1935
revoked: SI 2004/1284 Sch.1

1939

571. Cinematograph Film Stripping Regulations 1939
revoked: SI 2002/2776 Sch.7 Part 1

1946

2197. Magnesium (Grinding of Castings and other Articles) Special Regulations 1946
revoked: SI 2002/2776 Sch.7 Part 2

1947

1442. Petroleum (Carbide of Calcium) Order 1947
revoked: SI 2002/2776 Sch.7 Part 1

1949

1516. Lochmaddy Pier Order 1949
revoked: SSI 2002/410 Sch.2 Part II
s.1, referred to: SSI 2002/410 Sch.2 Part II

1949–cont.

1516. Lochmaddy Pier Order 1949–*cont.*
s.3, referred to: SSI 2002/410 Sch.2 Part II
s.5, referred to: SSI 2002/410 Sch.2 Part II
s.7, referred to: SSI 2002/410 Sch.2 Part II
s.11, referred to: SSI 2002/410 Sch.2 Part II
s.14, referred to: SSI 2002/410 Sch.2 Part II
s.18, referred to: SSI 2002/410 Sch.2 Part II

1885. Agricultural Wages Committees Regulations, 1949
Reg.16, revoked (in part): SI 2004/2178 Sch.1 Part II

2224. Dry Cleaning Special Regulations, 1949
revoked: SI 2002/2776 Sch.7 Part 2

1950

65. Pottery (Health and Welfare) Special Regulations, 1950
Reg.2, amended: SI 2002/3135 Sch.1 para.14

124. Coast Protection (Notices) Regulations, 1950
revoked (in part): SI 2002/1278 Reg.5, SI 2003/1847 Reg.7

430. Registered Designs Appeal Tribunal Rules 1950
see *Practice Direction (PO: 1/2003 (Revised))* [2003] R.P.C. 46 (PO), Not specified

1326. British Wool Marketing Scheme (Approval) Order, 1950
applied: SI 2002/2843 Art.9

1951

1866. Portnaguiran Pier Order 1951
revoked: SSI 2002/410 Sch.2 Part II
s.1, referred to: SSI 2002/410 Sch.2 Part II
s.4, referred to: SSI 2002/410 Sch.2 Part II
s.11, referred to: SSI 2002/410 Sch.2 Part II
s.16, referred to: SSI 2002/410 Sch.2 Part II
s.20, referred to: SSI 2002/410 Sch.2 Part II
s.21, referred to: SSI 2002/410 Sch.2 Part II

1952

1689. Factories (Testing of Aircraft Engines and Accessories) Special Regulations, 1952
revoked: SI 2002/2776 Sch.7 Part 2

1899. Wireless Telegraphy (Isle of Man) Order, 1952
applied: SI 2003/663

1900. Wireless Telegraphy (Channel Islands) Order, 1952
applied: SI 2003/663

1953

197. Reserve and Auxiliary Forces (Protection of Civil Interests) (Northern Ireland) Order 1953
Part V, applied: SR 2002/352 Reg.90

NO.

1955

554. Transfer of Functions (Ministry of Food) Order, 1955
Art.3, applied: SI 2002/794 Art.5

1125. Cinematograph (Safety) (Scotland) Regulations 1955
Reg.4, amended: SSI 2003/144 Reg.2
Reg.26, amended: SSI 2003/144 Reg.2
Reg.31, amended: SSI 2003/144 Reg.2
Reg.38, amended: SSI 2003/144 Reg.2

1129. Cinematograph (Safety) Regulations, 1955
Reg.4, amended: SI 2002/1903 Reg.2
Reg.5, amended: SI 2004/3168 Art.2
Reg.26, amended: SI 2002/1903 Reg.2
Reg.31, amended: SI 2002/1903 Reg.2
Reg.38, amended: SI 2002/1903 Reg.2

1956

894. Schools (Scotland) Code 1956
Reg.5, revoked (in part): SSI 2003/75 Reg.2
Reg.6, revoked (in part): SSI 2003/75 Reg.2
Reg.8, revoked: SSI 2003/75 Reg.2
Reg.14, revoked: SSI 2003/75 Reg.2
Reg.15, revoked: SSI 2003/75 Reg.2
Reg.23, revoked (in part): SSI 2003/75 Reg.2
Reg.24, revoked: SSI 2003/75 Reg.2
Reg.29, revoked: SSI 2003/75 Reg.2
Reg.30, revoked: SSI 2003/75 Reg.2

1750. Swine Fever (Infected Areas Restrictions) Order, 1956
revoked (in part): SI 2003/2329 Art.19, SI 2003/2456 Art.19, SSI 2003/426 Art.19

1957

448. Watford and South of St Albans-Redbourn-Kidney Wood, Luton, Special Road Scheme 1957
revoked: SI 2003/3339 Art.2

859. Petroleum (Liquid Methane) Order, 1957
Sch.1, amended: SI 2002/2776 Sch.6 para.4

1958

1284. Swine Fever (Infected Areas Restrictions) Amendment Order, 1958
revoked (in part): SSI 2003/426 Art.19

1959

364. Schools Regulations 1959
Reg.15, applied: SI 2003/1662 Sch.1 para.2
Reg.20, referred to: SI 2003/1662 Sch.1 para.1
Sch.2, applied: SI 2003/1663 Sch.1 para.1, SI 2004/1744 Sch.1 para.1

377. Maintenance Orders (Facilities for Enforcement) Order 1959
Sch.1, amended: SI 2002/789 Art.2

NO.

1959–cont.

406. Service Departments Registers Order 1959
Art.5, amended: SI 2002/3122 Art.2

477. Further Education (Scotland) Regulations 1959
Reg.8, applied: SSI 2002/314 Reg.2

1960

543. Election Petition Rules 1960
varied: SI 2003/284 Art.133, Sch.9 para.1, SI 2004/870 Reg.15
r.2, see *Ahmed v Kennedy* [2002] EWHC 2061, [2002] EWHC 2060, [2002] 4 All E.R. 764 (QBD), Hooper, J.
r.2, varied: SI 2003/284 Sch.9 para.2, Sch.9 para.3, SI 2004/870 Sch.6
r.4, varied: SI 2003/284 Sch.9 para.4, SI 2004/870 Sch.6
r.6, see *Ahmed v Kennedy* [2002] EWCA Civ 1793, [2003] 1 W.L.R. 1820 (CA), Simon Brown, L.J.
r.9, varied: SI 2003/284 Sch.9 para.5
r.10, varied: SI 2003/284 Sch.9 para.6, Sch.9 para.7, SI 2004/870 Sch.6
r.12, varied: SI 2003/284 Sch.9 para.7, SI 2004/870 Sch.6
r.14, varied: SI 2003/284 Sch.9 para.7, SI 2004/870 Sch.6
r.16, varied: SI 2003/284 Sch.9 para.7, SI 2004/870 Sch.6
r.18, varied: SI 2004/870 Sch.6
r.19, amended: SI 2003/972 r.2
Sch.1, varied: SI 2003/284 Sch.9 para.8, SI 2004/870 Sch.6

1932. Shipbuliding and Ship-Repairing Regulations 1960
Reg.48, revoked: SI 2002/2776 Sch.7 Part 2
Reg.52, revoked: SI 2002/2776 Sch.7 Part 2
Reg.54, revoked: SI 2002/2776 Sch.7 Part 2
Reg.55, revoked: SI 2002/2776 Sch.7 Part 2
Reg.66, revoked: SI 2002/2776 Sch.7 Part 2

1962

209. Foot-and-Mouth Disease Order (Northern Ireland) 1962
Art.29, applied: SR 2002/44 Art.2
Art.29, enabled: SR 2002/44
Art.32, disapplied: SR 2002/44 Sch.1 para.1
Art.34, disapplied: SR 2002/44 Sch.1 para.1
Sch.5, amended: SR 2002/44 Sch.1 para.2

1550. Jamaica (Constitution) Order in Council 1962
s.4, see *DPP of Jamaica v Mollison* [2003] UKPC 6, [2003] 2 A.C. 411 (PC (Jam)), Lord Bingham of Cornhill
Sch.2 Ch.III s.15, see *DPP of Jamaica v Mollison* [2003] UKPC 6, [2003] 2 A.C. 411 (PC (Jam)), Lord Bingham of Cornhill

NO.

1962–cont.

1550. Jamaica (Constitution) Order in Council 1962–cont.

Sch.2 Ch.III s.20, see *DPP of Jamaica v Mollison* [2003] UKPC 6, [2003] 2 A.C. 411 (PC (Jam)), Lord Bingham of Cornhill

Sch.2 Ch.III s.26, see *DPP of Jamaica v Mollison* [2003] UKPC 6, [2003] 2 A.C. 411 (PC (Jam)), Lord Bingham of Cornhill

1562. Exchange of Securities (Consolidation) Rules 1962

Reg.3, amended: SI 2002/2521 Sch.2 Part II

1642. Copyright (Bermuda) Order 1962

revoked: SI 2003/1517 Art.3

2167. Exchange of Securities Rules (No.5) 1962

r.1, amended: SI 2002/2521 Sch.2 Part II
r.2, amended: SI 2002/2521 Sch.2 Part II

2545. Professions Supplementary to Medicine (Registration (Appeals) Rules) Order of Council 1962

r.6, referred to: SI 2003/1700 Art.6

2557. Veterinary Surgery (Exemptions) Order 1962

varied: SI 2002/1646 Reg.3
Art.4, revoked (in part): SR 2002/259 Reg.11

1963

199. Coroners (Practice and Procedure) Rules (Northern Ireland) 1963

see *Jordan's Application for Judicial Review, Re* [2002] N.I. 151 (QBD (NI)), Kerr, J.

286. Swine Fever Order 1963

revoked (in part): SI 2003/2329 Art.19, SI 2003/2456 Art.19, SSI 2003/426 Art.19

1172. Various Trunk Roads (Prohibition of Waiting)(Clearways) Order 1963

Art.5, amended: SI 2004/3168 Art.3

1710. Weights and Measures Regulations 1963

applied: SI 2003/2454 Reg.4
Reg.1, amended: SI 2003/2454 Reg.1, SI 2003/2761 Reg.17

1964

209. Mines (Medical Examinations) Regulations 1964

Reg.5, amended: SI 2002/3135 Sch.1 para.15

388. Prison Rules 1964

see *Ezeh v United Kingdom (39665/98)* (2004) 39 E.H.R.R. 1 (ECHR (Grand Chamber)), Judge Wildhaber (President)

928. Merchant Shipping (Liability of Ship Owners and Others) Act 1958 (Jersey) Order 1964

revoked: SI 2004/1284 Sch.1

939. National Assistance (Professions Supplementary to Medicine) Regulations 1964

Reg.2, amended: SI 2002/880 Sch.1 para.1, SI 2003/1590 Sch.1 para.31

NO.

1964–cont.

939. National Assistance (Professions Supplementary to Medicine) Regulations 1964–cont.

Reg.3, amended: SI 2003/1590 Sch.1 para.31
Reg.3A, added: SI 2003/1590 Sch.1 para.31
Reg.4, substituted: SI 2003/1590 Sch.1 para.31

1001. Judicial Committee (Professions Supplementary to Medicine Rules) Order 1964

Sch.1, amended: SI 2003/1590 Sch.1 para.30

1003. Special Roads (Notice of Opening) (Scotland) Regulations 1964

applied: SSI 2004/53 Reg.1, SSI 2004/54 Reg.1

1143. Act of Sederunt (Confirmation of Executors) 1964

applied: SSI 2003/179 Reg.3

1203. Professions Supplementary to Medicine (Disciplinary Committees) (Procedure) Rules 1964

r.10, see *Collier v Council for Professions Supplementary to Medicine* [2003] UKPC 72, (2004) 78 B.M.L.R. 156 (Privy Council (United Kingdom)), Lord Steyn

1203. Professions Supplementary to Medicine (Disciplinary Committees) (Procedure) Rules Order of Council 1964

applied: SI 2003/1700 Art.11
varied: SI 2003/1700 Art.1
Sch.1, applied: SI 2003/1700 Art.5, Art.8, Art.9, Art.11
Sch.1, referred to: SI 2003/1700 Art.8

1456. British Transport Police Force Scheme 1963 (Approval) Order 1964

revoked: SI 2004/1573 Art.12
Sch.1, amended: SI 2003/1615 Sch.1 para.37
Sch.1, applied: SI 2002/412 Art.31, SI 2004/915 Reg.6
Sch.1, referred to: SI 2004/1573 Art.4, Art.5

1755. Ecclesiastical Jurisdiction (Discipline) Rules 1964

applied: SI 2003/1936 para.4
r.49., applied: SI 2002/1893 para.4, SI 2003/1936 para.4
r.55., referred to: SI 2003/1936 para.4

2007. Pensions (Polish Forces) Scheme 1964

Art.14, varied: SI 2002/671 Art.2

1965

r.8. Rules of the Supreme Court 1965

see *Hashtroodi v Hancock* [2004] EWCA Civ 652, [2004] 1 W.L.R. 3206 (CA), Thorpe, L.J.

321. Act of Sederunt (Rules of Court, consolidation and amendment) 1965

Part II r.131., applied: SI 2002/1792 Reg.21, Sch.5 para.16

NO.

1965–cont.

536. Special Constables Regulations 1965
varied: SI 2004/1573 Art.11
Reg.1, substituted: SI 2002/3180 Reg.2
Reg.2, revoked: SI 2004/645 Reg.2
Reg.5A, substituted: SI 2002/3180 Reg.2
Sch.2 para.1, revoked: SI 2002/3180 Reg.2
Sch.2 para.2, revoked: SI 2002/3180 Reg.2
Sch.2 para.3, revoked: SI 2002/3180 Reg.2

1420. Government Stock Regulations 1965
applied: SI 2004/1611 Reg.32, Reg.35
revoked: SI 2004/1611 Reg.34
Reg.1, amended: SI 2002/2521 Sch.2 Part II
Reg.2, applied: SI 2002/2521 Art.7
Reg.3, revoked (in part): SI 2002/2521 Sch.2
Part II
Reg.6, amended: SI 2002/2521 Sch.2 Part II
Reg.8, revoked (in part): SI 2002/2521 Sch.2
Part II
Reg.12, amended: SI 2002/2521 Sch.2 Part II
Reg.17, revoked: SI 2002/2521 Sch.2 Part II
Reg.18, amended: SI 2002/2521 Sch.2 Part II
Reg.18, revoked (in part): SI 2002/2521
Sch.2 Part II
Reg.19, amended: SI 2002/2521 Sch.2 Part II
Reg.20, amended: SI 2002/2521 Sch.2 Part II
Reg.23, amended: SI 2002/2521 Sch.1
para.6, Sch.2 Part II

1776. Rules of the Supreme Court 1965
see *St Brice v Southwark LBC* [2001] EWCA
Civ 1138, [2002] 1 W.L.R. 1537 (CA),
Kennedy, L.J.
Ord.18 r.9, see *Taylor v Midland Bank Trust Co
Ltd (No.2)* [2002] W.T.L.R. 95 (CA),
Rattee, J.
Ord.45 r.8, see *Halifax Plc v Halifax
Repossessions Ltd* [2004] EWCA Civ 331,
[2004] B.C.C. 281 (CA), Latham, L.J.
Ord.52 r.7, see *Leicester City Council v
Saracen Dyers Ltd* [2002] EWHC 2068,
[2003] Env. L.R.18 (QBD), Pitchford, J.
Ord.53, see *R. (on the application of G) v
Ealing LBC (No.2)* [2002] EWHC 250,
Times, March 18, 2002 (QBD (Admin
Ct)), Munby, J.
Ord.80, see *Masterman-Lister v Jewell*
[2002] EWCA Civ 1889, [2003] 1 W.L.R.
1511 (CA), Kennedy, L.J.

1776. Rules of the Supreme Court (Revision) 1965
Ord.48, see *Mubarak v Mubarak (No.2)*
[2002] EWHC 2171, [2003] 2 F.L.R. 553
(Fam Div), Hughes, J.
Sch.1 Part 10, applied: SI 2002/1792 Reg.21,
Sch.5 para.16

**2040. Hares (Control of Importation) Order
1965**
disapplied: SI 2004/853 Sch.6

NO.

1966

**97. Police (Special Constables) (Scotland)
Regulations 1966**
varied: SI 2004/1573 Art.11
Reg.4, amended: SSI 2003/21 Reg.3

**199. Alexandra Park and Palace Order
1966**
referred to: SI 2004/160

283. Manchester (Ullswater and Windermere) Water Order 1966
Sch.1, varied: SI 2003/3341 Art.3

**395. Oil in Navigable Waters (Jersey) Order
1966**
revoked: SI 2004/1284 Sch.1

**987. National Insurance (Industrial Injuries)
(Prescribed Diseases) Amendment
Regulations 1966**
see *Cape Plc v IronTrades Employers Insurance
Association Ltd* [2004] Lloyd's Rep. I.R. 75
(QBD (Comm Ct)), Rix, J.

1073. Mineral Hydrocarbons in Food Regulations 1966
applied: SI 2004/554 Reg.3
referred to: SI 2003/1008 Reg.3
varied: SI 2002/329 Reg.9, SI 2003/945
Reg.3, SI 2003/3295 Reg.3

1455. Barbados Independence Order 1966
Art.4, see *Boyce (Lennox Ricardo) v Queen,
The* [2004] UKPC 32, [2004] 3 W.L.R.
786 (PC (Bar)), Lord Hoffmann

**1471. Commons Registration (General)
Regulations 1966**
Sch.1, amended: SI 2003/994 Reg.3, SI
2003/2260 Reg.2
Sch.3, amended: SI 2003/994 Reg.2, SI
2003/2260 Reg.2

1967

**480. Carriage by Air Acts (Application of
Provisions) Order 1967**
revoked: SI 2004/1899 Sch.4
see *Disley v Levine (t/a Airtrak Levine
Paragliding)* [2001] EWCA Civ 1087,
[2002] 1 W.L.R. 785 (CA), Henry, L.J.

**659. Veterinary Surgeons and Veterinary
Practitioners (Disciplinary Committee) (Procedure and Evidence) Rules
Order of Council 1967**
revoked: SI 2004/1680 Art.3
r.8 para.2, see *Kirk v Royal College of
Veterinary Surgeons* 51 of 2002 (PC
(UK)), Lord Hoffmann

1021. Police (Discipline) (Scotland) Regulations 1967
applied: SSI 2004/257 Reg.15

**1199. School Premises (General Requirements and Standards) (Scotland)
Regulations 1967**
applied: SSI 2003/75 Reg.3

NO.

1967–cont.

1485. Ammonium Nitrate Mixtures Exemption Order 1967
applied: SI 2002/655 Sch.9 Part VI, SI 2003/547 Sch.9 Part VI, SI 2004/456 Sch.8 Part VI
Art.3, applied: SI 2002/655 Sch.9 Part V, SI 2003/547 Sch.9 Part V, SI 2004/456 Sch.8 Part V

1879. Leasehold Reform (Enfranchisement and Extension) Regulations 1967
Sch.1 Part I para.2, amended: SI 2003/1989 Reg.3, SI 2004/699 Reg.3
Sch.1 Part I para.2A, added: SI 2003/1989 Reg.3, SI 2004/699 Reg.3
Sch.1 Part 2 para.1, amended: SI 2003/1989 Reg.3, SI 2004/699 Reg.3
Sch.1 Part 2 para.1A, added: SI 2003/1989 Reg.3, SI 2004/699 Reg.3

1905. Fugitive Offenders (Bermuda) Order 1967
revoked: SI 2002/1823 Sch.5

1909. Fugitive Offenders (Gibraltar) Order 1967
revoked: SI 2002/1823 Sch.5

1913. Fugitive Offenders (Montserrat) Order 1967
revoked: SI 2002/1823 Sch.5

1915. Fugitive Offenders (Virgin Islands) Order 1967
revoked: SI 2002/1823 Sch.5

1916. Fugitive Offenders (Sovereign Base Areas of Akrotiri and Dhekelia) Order 1967
revoked: SI 2002/1823 Sch.5

1968

112. Fugitive Offenders (Cayman Islands) Order 1968
revoked: SI 2002/1823 Sch.5

113. Fugitive Offenders (Falkland Islands and Dependencies) Order 1968
revoked: SI 2002/1823 Sch.5

182. Bermuda Constitution Order 1968
applied: SI 2003/456 Art.1
Sch.2, added: SI 2003/456 Sch.1
Sch.2, amended: SI 2003/456 Art.3, Art.5, Art.6, Art.7, Art.8
Sch.2, substituted: SI 2003/456 Art.4

183. Fugitive Offenders (British Indian Ocean Territory) Order 1968
revoked: SI 2002/1823 Sch.5

184. Fugitive Offenders (St Helena) Order 1968
revoked: SI 2002/1823 Sch.5

185. Fugitive Offenders (Turks and Caicos Islands) Order 1968
revoked: SI 2002/1823 Sch.5

292. Fugitive Offenders (Overseas Territories) Order 1968
revoked: SI 2002/1823 Sch.5

NO.

1968–cont.

414. Treasury Bills Regulations 1968
Reg.1, varied: SI 2003/1633 Sch.1 para.7
Reg.2, varied: SI 2003/1633 Sch.1 para.8
Reg.3, varied: SI 2003/1633 Sch.1 para.9
Reg.4, varied: SI 2003/1633 Sch.1 para.10
Reg.6, varied: SI 2003/1633 Sch.1 para.11
Reg.7, varied: SI 2003/1633 Sch.1 para.12
Reg.8, varied: SI 2003/1633 Sch.1 para.12
Reg.9, varied: SI 2003/1633 Sch.1 para.13

532. Lancaster Port Commission Revision Order 1968
Art.5, revoked: SI 2003/2724 Sch.3
Art.14, revoked: SI 2003/2724 Sch.3
Art.24, referred to: SI 2003/2724 Art.14
Art.27, referred to: SI 2003/2724 Art.14
Art.34, revoked: SI 2003/2724 Sch.3
Sch.1, revoked: SI 2003/2724 Sch.3
Sch.2, revoked: SI 2003/2724 Sch.3
Sch.3, revoked (in part): SI 2003/2724 Sch.3, Sch.3

884. Fugitive Offenders (Pitcairn) Order 1968
revoked: SI 2002/1823 Sch.5

1262. Criminal Appeal Rules 1968
r.3, applied: SI 2003/428 r.14
r.5, referred to: SI 2003/428 r.18, r.22
r.8, applied: SI 2003/428 r.16
r.9, applied: SI 2003/428 r.15
r.9, referred to: SI 2003/428 r.15
r.11, applied: SI 2003/428 r.18, r.22
r.11, substituted: SI 2004/1293 r.2
r.12, applied: SI 2003/428 r.19, r.22
r.12, referred to: SI 2003/428 r.19, r.22
r.12, substituted: SI 2004/1293 r.2
r.18, applied: SI 2003/428 r.21
r.19, applied: SI 2003/428 r.21
r.20, applied: SI 2003/428 r.21

1375. Fugitive Offenders (Overseas Territories) (No.2) Order 1968
revoked: SI 2002/1823 Sch.5

1862. Inter-Governmental Maritime Consultative Organisation (Immunities and Privileges) Order 1968
revoked: SI 2002/1826 Sch.1

2042. Shoreham Port Authority Revision Order 1968
applied: SI 2004/1506 Art.4, Art.7
Art.5, revoked (in part): SI 2004/1506 Sch.3
Sch.1, amended: SI 2004/1506 Art.12, Sch.3
Sch.1, applied: SI 2004/1506 Art.4, Art.5
Sch.1, revoked (in part): SI 2004/1506 Sch.3, Sch.3

1969

17. Town and Country Planning (Tree Preservation Order) Regulations 1969
Sch.1, applied: SI 2002/1327 Art.14
Sch.1, referred to: SI 2002/412 Art.14, SI 2004/757 Art.20

NO.

1969–cont.

17. Town and Country Planning (Tree Preservation Order) Regulations 1969–*cont.*
Sch.1, varied: SI 2002/1066 Art.17

388. Transfer of Functions (Wales) Order 1969
applied: SI 2002/794 Art.1

418. Motor Vehicles (Production of Test Certificates) Regulations 1969
revoked: SI 2004/1896 Reg.1

468. Charities (Sir John Soane's Museum) Order 1969
Appendix 1., amended: SI 2003/1326 Art.7

592. Civil Aviation Act 1949 (Overseas Territories) Order 1969
applied: SI 2003/433, SI 2004/2038

690. Asbestos Regulations 1969
Reg.13, applied: SI 2002/2675 Reg.16

741. Merchant Shipping Act 1965 (Jersey) Order 1969
revoked: SI 2004/1284 Sch.1

1083. Carriage by Air Acts (Application of Provisions) (Amendment) Order 1969
revoked: SI 2004/1899 Sch.4

1110. Gaming Clubs (Licensing) Regulations 1969
Reg.6, revoked: SI 2002/1910 Reg.2
Sch.1, amended: SI 2003/1513 Sch.1
Sch.2, amended: SI 2003/1513 Sch.1, SI 2004/3168 Art.4
Sch.2, referred to: SI 2003/1513 Reg.2
Sch.3, referred to: SI 2003/1513 Reg.3

1115. Gaming Clubs (Licensing) (Scotland) Regulations 1969
see *North Rotunda Casino Ltd v Glasgow City Licensing Board* 2002 S.L.T. 974 (OH), Lord Emslie

1787. Police Federation Regulations 1969
Reg.2, revoked (in part): SI 2004/2660 Reg.3
Reg.5, amended: SI 2004/2660 Reg.4
Reg.6, substituted: SI 2004/2660 Reg.5
Reg.7, amended: SI 2004/2660 Reg.6
Reg.8, amended: SI 2004/2660 Reg.7
Reg.9, amended: SI 2004/2660 Reg.8
Reg.10, amended: SI 2004/2660 Reg.9
Reg.12, amended: SI 2004/2660 Reg.10
Reg.13, amended: SI 2004/2660 Reg.11
Reg.13, revoked (in part): SI 2004/2660 Reg.11
Reg.16, amended: SI 2004/2660 Reg.12
Reg.18, amended: SI 2004/2660 Reg.13
Reg.20, amended: SI 2004/2660 Reg.14
Sch.2 para.1, amended: SI 2004/2660 Reg.15
Sch.4 Part I para.2, amended: SI 2004/2660 Reg.16
Sch.6 para.1, substituted: SI 2004/2660 Sch.1
Sch.6 para.2, substituted: SI 2004/2660 Sch.1

NO.

1969–cont.

1787. Police Federation Regulations 1969–*cont.*
Sch.6 para.3, substituted: SI 2004/2660 Sch.1
Sch.6 para.4, substituted: SI 2004/2660 Sch.1
Sch.6 para.5, substituted: SI 2004/2660 Sch.1
Sch.6 para.6, substituted: SI 2004/2660 Sch.1
Sch.6 para.7, substituted: SI 2004/2660 Sch.1

1843. Commons Registration (New Land) Regulations 1969
see *Oxfordshire CC v Oxford City Council* [2004] EWHC 12, [2004] Ch. 253 (Ch D), Lightman, J.

1970

145. Drivers Hours (Passenger Vehicles) (Exemptions) Regulations 1970
Reg.2, amended: SI 2003/2155 Sch.1 para.25

1434. Pitcairn Order 1970
.5(2A)., amended: SI 2002/2638 Art.2

1681. Secretary of State for the Environment Order 1970
Sch.2, referred to: SI 2002/2626 Art.17

1958. Functions of Traffic Wardens Order 1970
Art.3, amended: SI 2002/2975 Art.2
Sch.1 para.5A, added: SI 2002/2975 Art.3
Sch.1 para.5B, added: SI 2002/2975 Art.3
Sch.1 para.6, revoked (in part): SI 2002/2975 Art.3

1997. Vehicle and Driving Licences Records (Evidence) Regulations 1970
Reg.2, amended: SI 2002/2742 Sch.1 Part II
Reg.3, revoked (in part): SI 2002/2742 Sch.1 Part II

1971

218. Lands Tribunal for Scotland Rules 1971
Part I, revoked: SSI 2003/452 Sch.3
Part III, revoked: SSI 2003/452 Sch.3
Part VB, amended: SSI 2003/452 Sch.3
Part VI, revoked (in part): SSI 2003/452 Sch.3
Part VC, amended: SSI 2003/452 Sch.3
Sch.1, amended: SSI 2003/452 Sch.3
Sch.2, amended: SSI 2003/521 Sch.1, SSI 2004/480 r.2

450. Road Vehicles (Registration and Licensing) Regulations 1971
applied: SSI 2002/410 Art.28
revoked: SI 2002/2742 Sch.1 Part I
Reg.8, amended: SI 2002/2382 Reg.3
Reg.8A, added: SI 2002/2382 Reg.4
Reg.12, amended: SI 2002/2382 Reg.5
Reg.12B, added: SI 2002/2382 Reg.5

NO.

1971-cont.

729. Farm and Garden Chemicals Regulations 1971

disapplied: SI 2003/3241 Reg.27, SSI 2003/579 Reg.28

Reg.3, applied: SI 2002/1689 Reg.8

Reg.4, applied: SI 2002/1689 Reg.8

809. Magistrates Courts (Attachment of Earnings) Rules 1971

r.2, revoked (in part): SI 2003/1236 r.3

r.5, revoked: SI 2003/1236 r.4

r.14, revoked (in part): SI 2003/1236 r.5

r.15, varied: SI 2004/176 Reg.4A

r.23, amended: SI 2003/1236 r.6

r.23, revoked (in part): SI 2003/1236 r.6

r.24, revoked: SI 2003/1236 r.7

Sch.1, revoked: SI 2003/1236 r.8

972. Medicines (Standard Provisions for Licences and Certificates) Regulations 1971

revoked (in part): SI 2004/1031 Sch.11

Reg.2, amended: SI 2002/236 Reg.3, SI 2003/2321 Reg.3, SI 2004/1031 Sch.10 para.1, SI 2004/1678 Reg.2

Reg.3, revoked (in part): SI 2003/3309 Reg.3, SI 2004/1031 Sch.10 para.1

Sch.1 Part I para.16, amended: SI 2002/236 Reg.3, SI 2003/2321 Reg.3

Sch.1 Part II para.1, revoked: SI 2004/1031 Sch.10 para.1

Sch.1 Part II para.2, revoked: SI 2004/1031 Sch.10 para.1

Sch.1 Part II para.3, revoked: SI 2004/1031 Sch.10 para.1

Sch.1 Part II para.4, revoked: SI 2004/1031 Sch.10 para.1

Sch.1 Part II para.5, revoked: SI 2004/1031 Sch.10 para.1

Sch.1 Part II para.6, revoked: SI 2004/1031 Sch.10 para.1

Sch.1 Part III para.1, revoked: SI 2003/3309 Reg.3

Sch.1 Part III para.2, revoked: SI 2003/3309 Reg.3

Sch.1 Part III para.3, revoked: SI 2003/3309 Reg.3

Sch.1 Part III para.4, revoked: SI 2003/3309 Reg.3

Sch.1 Part III para.5, revoked: SI 2003/3309 Reg.3

Sch.1 Part III para.6, revoked: SI 2003/3309 Reg.3

Sch.1 Part III para.7, revoked: SI 2003/3309 Reg.3

Sch.1 Part III para.8, revoked: SI 2003/3309 Reg.3

Sch.1 Part III para.9, revoked: SI 2003/3309 Reg.3

Sch.1 Part III para.10, revoked: SI 2003/3309 Reg.3

Sch.2 para.16, amended: SI 2002/236 Reg.3

NO.

1971-cont.

972. Medicines (Standard Provisions for Licences and Certificates) Regulations 1971-*cont.*

Sch.3 para.4A, amended: SI 2002/236 Reg.3

Sch.3 para.4B, amended: SI 2002/236 Reg.3

Sch.3 para.7A, amended: SI 2002/236 Reg.3

Sch.3 para.7B, amended: SI 2002/236 Reg.3

Sch.3 para.7C, amended: SI 2002/236 Reg.3

Sch.3 para.8, amended: SI 2002/236 Reg.3

Sch.5 Part I para.3A, amended: SI 2002/236 Reg.3

973. Medicines (Applications for Product Licences and Clinical Trial and Animal Test Certificates) Regulations 1971

revoked (in part): SI 2004/1031 Sch.11

974. Medicines (Applications for Manufacturer's and Wholesale Dealer's Licences) Regulations 1971

Reg.2, amended: SI 2002/236 Reg.4

Sch.2 para.8A, amended: SI 2002/236 Reg.4

Sch.2 para.8B, amended: SI 2002/236 Reg.4

Sch.2 para.8C, amended: SI 2002/236 Reg.4

1039. Reciprocal Enforcement of Foreign Judgments (Israel) Order 1971

Art.3, amended: SI 2003/2618 Art.3

Art.4, amended: SI 2003/2618 Art.4

Art.5, amended: SI 2003/2618 Art.4

Art.6, amended: SI 2003/2618 Art.4

Art.7, amended: SI 2003/2618 Art.4

1117. Employers Liability (Compulsory Insurance) General Regulations 1971

see *T&N Ltd (In Administration) v Royal & Sun Alliance Plc* [2003] EWHC 1016, [2003] 2 All E.R. (Comm.) 939 (Ch D), Lawrence Collins, J.

1267. Medicines (Surgical Materials) Order 1971

Art.3, amended: SI 2004/1031 Sch.10 para.2

1450. Medicines (Exemption from Licences) (Special and Transitional Cases) Order 1971

Art.2, referred to: SI 2004/2750 Sch.1 para.4, Sch.2 para.2

1861. Blood Tests (Evidence of Paternity) Regulations 1971

Reg.2, amended: SI 2004/2033 Art.5

Reg.12, substituted: SI 2004/596 Reg.4

Sch.2, revoked: SI 2004/596 Reg.5

Sch.2 Part I, revoked: SI 2004/596 Reg.5

Sch.2 Part II, revoked: SI 2004/596 Reg.5

1959. M62 Motorway (Rawcliffe to Balkholme Section) Connecting Roads Scheme 1971

Sch.1, substituted: SI 2003/913 Art.2

1991. Magistrates Courts (Blood Tests) Rules 1971

r.2., amended: SI 2004/2033 Art.6

NO.

1972

118. Inter-Governmental Maritime Consultative Organization (Immunities and Privileges) (Amendment) Order 1972
revoked: SI 2002/1826 Sch.1

275. Aberdeen Harbour Revision Order 1972
revoked: SSI 2002/310 Sch.3

538. Prosecution of Offences (Northern Ireland) Order 1972
applied: 2002 c.26 s.89
revoked: 2002 c.26 Sch.13
Art.5, applied: SI 2004/1988 Art.6
Art.9, referred to: 2002 c.26 Sch.12 para.2, Sch.12 para.6
Art.10, referred to: 2002 c.26 Sch.12 para.1

674. Hovercraft (General) Order 1972
Art.7A, amended: SI 2004/302 Sch.1 para.17
Art.35, enabled: SI 2004/1976

730. Explosives (Northern Ireland) Order 1972
applied: SR 2002/301 Reg.3

764. National Savings Bank Regulations 1972
Reg.2A, added: SI 2003/2895 Reg.3
Reg.2B, added: SI 2003/2895 Reg.3
Reg.11, amended: SI 2003/2895 Reg.4
Reg.38A, amended: SI 2004/1662 Sch.1 para.21
Reg.41, amended: SI 2004/1662 Sch.1 para.21

765. Premium Savings Bonds Regulations 1972
referred to: SI 2004/2353 Reg.3
Reg.3A, added: SI 2004/2353 Reg.4
Reg.3B, added: SI 2004/2353 Reg.4
Reg.5, amended: SI 2003/1085 Reg.2
Reg.8, amended: SI 2004/2353 Reg.5
Reg.8, revoked (in part): SI 2004/2353 Reg.5

917. Highly Flammable Liquids and Liquefied Petroleum Gases Regulations 1972
revoked (in part): SI 2002/2776 Sch.7 Part 2, SR 2003/152 Sch.8 Part I
Reg.6, applied: SI 2002/1689 Reg.8

985. Land Registration (Souvenir Land) Rules 1972
r.3, applied: SI 2003/1953 Art.10
r.5, amended: SI 2002/2539 Sch.4 para.1

1073. Superannuation (Northern Ireland) Order 1972
Art.2, referred to: SR 2002/352 Reg.3
Art.3, applied: 2002 c.26 Sch.2 para.4, SI 2003/439 Sch.2 para.5
Art.3, enabled: SR 2002/211
Art.9, applied: SR 2002/352 Reg.5, Reg.111
Art.9, enabled: SR 2002/115, SR 2002/352, SR 2002/353, SR 2003/61
Art.11, applied: SR 2003/86, SR 2003/147
Art.11, enabled: SR 2003/86, SR 2003/147
Art.12, enabled: SR 2002/69, SR 2002/129
Art.12, referred to: SR 2002/129

NO.

1972–cont.

1073. Superannuation (Northern Ireland) Order 1972–cont.
Art.14, applied: SR 2003/60
Art.14, enabled: SR 2002/69, SR 2002/115, SR 2002/129, SR 2002/353, SR 2003/86, SR 2003/147
Art.15, applied: SR 2003/60
Art.19, applied: SR 2003/61 Reg.5
Art.19, enabled: SR 2002/393, SR 2003/61
Sch.1, amended: 2002 c.9 (NI) Sch.1 para.18, 2002 c.26 Sch.2 para.4, SI 2003/431 Sch.4, SI 2003/439 Sch.2 para.5, SR 2002/211 Art.2
Sch.3, enabled: SR 2002/69, SR 2002/115, SR 2002/129, SR 2002/352, SR 2002/353, SR 2002/393, SR 2003/86, SR 2003/147

1101. Cayman Islands (Constitution) Order 1972
referred to: SI 2004/2673 Art.1
s.5A, added: SI 2003/1515 Art.3
s.24A, added: SI 2003/1515 Art.4
s.28A, added: SI 2003/1515 Art.2
s.28B, added: SI 2003/1515 Art.2
s.47, disapplied: SI 2004/2673 Art.3
Sch.2, amended: SI 2004/2029 Art.2, SI 2004/2673 Art.2

1200. Medicines (Exemption from Licences) (Special Cases and Miscellaneous Provisions) Order 1972
Art.2, applied: SI 2004/1031 Sch.12 para.6
Art.2, referred to: SI 2004/1031 Sch.12 para.6
Art.4, amended: SI 2004/1031 Sch.10 para.3
Art.4, revoked (in part): SI 2004/1031 Sch.10 para.3

1264. Electoral Law (Northern Ireland) Order 1972
Art.9, applied: SR 2002/352 Reg.129

1265. Health and Personal Social Services (Northern Ireland) Order 1972
applied: 2002 c.5 (NI) s.5, 2002 c.6 (NI) s.1, (NI) s.2, (NI) s.7, (NI) s.8, SI 2004/1022 Sch.2, SI 2004/1031 Reg.28, SR 2002/1 Reg.9, Reg.17
referred to: SI 2003/431 Art.2
Part VI, applied: SI 2003/439 Sch.1 para.1
Art.2, amended: SI 2004/311 Sch.1 para.2, Sch.2
Art.2, applied: 2002 c.9 (NI) s.3
Art.5, amended: SI 2004/311 Sch.1 para.3
Art.5, applied: SR 2003/28 Reg.4
Art.6, amended: SI 2004/311 Sch.1 para.4
Art.7, amended: 2002 c.41 s.46
Art.7, applied: SR 2003/28 Reg.4
Art.8, applied: SR 2003/28 Reg.4
Art.11, amended: SI 2004/311 Sch.1 para.5
Art.14A, applied: SR 2003/28 Reg.4
Art.15, amended: 2002 c.41 s.46
Art.15, applied: SI 2004/1267 Sch.2 para.4, SR 2002/136 Reg.3, SR 2003/28 Reg.15
Art.15, revoked (in part): 2002 c.5 (NI) Sch.1

NO.

1972–cont.

1265. Health and Personal Social Services (Northern Ireland) Order 1972–*cont.*

Art.15A, applied: SI 2002/2006 Reg.19

Art.15A, revoked: 2002 c.6 (NI) Sch.1

Art.15B, amended: SI 2004/311 Art.6

Art.15B, applied: SI 2003/439 Sch.1 para.1, SI 2003/1250 Art.10, Sch.8 para.22

Art.15B, substituted: SI 2004/311 Art.6

Art.15C, amended: SI 2004/311 Art.6, Sch.2

Art.15D, amended: SI 2004/311 Art.6, Sch.2

Art.15D, revoked (in part): SI 2004/311 Art.6, Sch.2

Art.15E, revoked: SI 2004/311 Art.6, Sch.2

Art.16, applied: SR 2002/224 Reg.12, SR 2002/292 Sch.1 Part II, SR 2003/28 Sch.1 para.1, Sch.1 para.2, Sch.2 para.14, Sch.6 para.4

Art.17, applied: 2002 c.6 (NI) s.1

Art.36, amended: 2002 c.9 (NI) s.1, SI 2003/431 Art.45

Art.36, applied: SI 2002/2006 Reg.19, SR 2002/136 Reg.3

Art.36, enabled: SR 2002/113

Art.36, referred to: SR 2002/136 Reg.3

Art.36, revoked (in part): 2002 c.5 (NI) Sch.1

Art.36A, applied: 2002 c.5 (NI) s.1

Art.36A, revoked: 2002 c.5 (NI) s.1, (NI) Sch.1

Art.44, applied: SI 2003/1994 Reg.12, Reg.23, SR 2002/224 Reg.4, Reg.10, Reg.12, Reg.29, Sch.3 para.1, SR 2003/253 Art.3

Art.45, enabled: SR 2002/46, SR 2002/172, SR 2003/48, SR 2003/170

Art.50, amended: SI 2003/431 Sch.4

Art.51, amended: SI 2004/311 Sch.1 para.6

Art.55, amended: SI 2004/311 Sch.1 para.7, Sch.2

Art.55, revoked (in part): SI 2004/311 Sch.1 para.7, Sch.2

Art.55A, amended: SI 2004/311 Sch.1 para.8, Sch.2

Art.55A, revoked (in part): SI 2004/311 Sch.1 para.8, Sch.2

Art.55B, added: SI 2004/311 Sch.1 para.9

Art.56, applied: SI 2003/1250 Art.10, Sch.8 para.22, SI 2004/311 Art.5, SR 2002/92, SR 2002/213, SR 2002/266, SR 2003/6, SR 2003/133, SR 2003/205

Art.56, enabled: SR 2002/92, SR 2002/213, SR 2002/266, SR 2003/6, SR 2003/133, SR 2003/205

Art.56, substituted: SI 2004/311 Art.3

Art.57, substituted: SI 2004/311 Art.4

Art.57A, substituted: SI 2004/311 Art.4

Art.57G, added: SI 2004/311 Art.8

Art.57H, added: SI 2004/311 Art.9

Art.59, amended: SI 2004/311 Sch.1 para.10

Art.61, applied: SR 2002/171, SR 2003/135, SR 2003/325

NO.

1972–cont.

1265. Health and Personal Social Services (Northern Ireland) Order 1972–*cont.*

Art.61, enabled: SR 2002/2, SR 2002/171, SR 2003/135, SR 2003/325

Art.61, referred to: SR 2002/2

Art.62, applied: SR 2002/85, SR 2002/221, SR 2003/74, SR 2003/176

Art.62, enabled: SR 2002/5, SR 2002/8, SR 2002/221, SR 2003/74, SR 2003/176

Art.62, referred to: SR 2002/5

Art.63, amended: SI 2003/431 Art.47

Art.63, applied: SR 2002/92, SR 2002/397

Art.63, enabled: SR 2002/92, SR 2002/397

Art.64, amended: SI 2004/311 Sch.1 para.10

Art.64, enabled: SR 2002/92, SR 2002/397

Art.90, applied: SI 2002/3126 Art.2, SI 2003/418 Art.8, SR 2002/66 Reg.9

Art.90, substituted: SI 2003/418 Art.6

Art.90, varied: SR 2002/66 Reg.9

Art.91, applied: SI 2003/418 Art.8

Art.91, substituted: SI 2003/418 Art.6

Art.92, revoked: SI 2003/418 Art.6

Art.92A, revoked: SI 2003/418 Art.6

Art.92A, varied: SR 2002/66 Reg.10

Art.92B, amended: SI 2003/418 Sch.2 para.2

Art.98, enabled: SR 2002/5, SR 2002/8, SR 2002/46, SR 2002/84, SR 2002/91, SR 2002/172, SR 2002/181, SR 2002/221, SR 2002/397, SR 2003/48, SR 2003/134, SR 2003/153, SR 2003/170, SR 2003/176

Art.99, amended: 2002 c.9 (NI) s.1

Art.99, enabled: SR 2002/113

Art.101, applied: SI 2003/435 Sch.2 para.2

Art.106, enabled: SR 2002/2, SR 2002/5, SR 2002/8, SR 2002/46, SR 2002/84, SR 2002/91, SR 2002/92, SR 2002/171, SR 2002/172, SR 2002/181, SR 2002/213, SR 2002/221, SR 2002/266, SR 2002/397, SR 2003/6, SR 2003/48, SR 2003/74, SR 2003/133, SR 2003/134, SR 2003/135, SR 2003/153, SR 2003/170, SR 2003/176, SR 2003/205, SR 2003/325

Art.107, enabled: SR 2002/2, SR 2002/5, SR 2002/8, SR 2002/46, SR 2002/92, SR 2002/171, SR 2002/172, SR 2002/181, SR 2002/213, SR 2002/221, SR 2002/266, SR 2002/397, SR 2003/6, SR 2003/48, SR 2003/74, SR 2003/133, SR 2003/135, SR 2003/170, SR 2003/176, SR 2003/205, SR 2003/325

Sch.6, amended: SI 2004/311 Sch.1 para.10

Sch.8, applied: 2003 c.21 Sch.4 para.5, SR 2003/136 Reg.10

Sch.8, varied: 2003 c.21 Sch.4 para.5, 2004 c.31 s.7, SI 2004/1769 Reg.17

Sch.9, amended: SI 2004/311 Sch.1 para.10

Sch.10, amended: SI 2004/311 Sch.1 para.11

Sch.11, amended: SI 2004/311 Art.8, Sch.1 para.12

NO.

1972–cont.

1265. Health and Personal Social Services (Northern Ireland) Order 1972–*cont.*
Sch.15, enabled: SR 2002/5, SR 2002/8, SR 2002/46, SR 2002/84, SR 2002/91, SR 2002/172, SR 2002/181, SR 2002/221, SR 2002/397, SR 2003/48, SR 2003/134, SR 2003/153, SR 2003/170, SR 2003/176
Sch.15, referred to: SR 2002/181 Reg.2, Reg.3

1542. Offshore Installations (Logbooks and Registration of Death) Regulations 1972
applied: SR 2002/1 Reg.21

1590. European Communities (Enforcement of Community Judgments) Order 1972
Art.2, amended: SI 2003/3204 Art.2

1610. Immigration (Control of Entry through Republic of Ireland) Order 1972
Art.3, applied: SI 2002/1832 Art.2

1634. Planning (Northern Ireland) Order 1972
applied: SR 2003/136 Reg.3
Art.66, amended: SI 2003/430 Art.26
Art.67, amended: SI 2003/430 Art.11, Sch.1 para.1, Sch.2
Art.67A, added: SI 2003/430 Art.25

1704. Aberdeen Harbour Revision Order 1972
revoked: SSI 2002/310 Sch.3

1705. Railway Bridges (Load-Bearing Standards) (England and Wales) Order 1972
Art.2, amended: SI 2003/1615 Sch.1 para.38

1814. Telecommunication Services (Jersey) Order 1972
revoked: SI 2002/799 Art.3

1815. Telecommunication Services (Guernsey) Order 1972
revoked: SI 2002/799 Art.3

1816. Telecommunication Services (Channel Islands Consequential Provisions) Order 1972
revoked: SI 2002/799 Art.3

1865. Road Vehicles (Registration and Licensing) (Amendment) Regulations 1972
revoked: SI 2002/2742 Sch.1 Part I

1931. Bristol Port and Harbour Revision Order 1972
Art.3, applied: SI 2002/3268 Art.11
Sch.1, applied: SI 2002/3268 Art.11

1999. Local Government c (Northern Ireland) Order 1972
Art.2, revoked (in part): SI 2002/3149 Sch.1
Art.3, revoked: SI 2002/3149 Sch.1
Art.4, revoked: SI 2002/3149 Sch.1
Art.5, revoked: SI 2002/3149 Sch.1
Art.6, revoked: SI 2002/3149 Sch.1

NO.

1972–cont.

1999. Local Government c (Northern Ireland) Order 1972–*cont.*
Sch.1, applied: SR 2002/182 Art.2
Sch.1, enabled: SR 2002/182
Sch.1, revoked: SI 2002/3149 Sch.1

1973

19. Adoption (Designation of Overseas Adoptions) Order 1973
Art.4, applied: SI 2003/1255 Reg.5

22. Grading of Horticultural Produce (Amendment) Regulations 1973
applied: SI 2003/1846 Reg.2, SSI 2003/502 Reg.2
see *Department for Environment, Food and Rural Affairs v ASDA Stores Ltd* [2002] EWHC 1335, [2002] 2 C.M.L.R. 66 (QBD (Admin Ct)), Rose, L.J.; see *Department for Environment, Food and Rural Affairs v ASDA Stores Ltd* [2003] UKHL 71, [2004] 1 W.L.R. 105 (HL), Lord Nicholls of Birkenhead
Reg.2, applied: SI 2003/1846 Reg.2, SSI 2003/502 Reg.2

56. Aycliffe School Instrument of Management Order 1973
referred to: SI 2003/1649
Art.9, amended: SI 2003/1649 Art.2

69. Drainage (Northern Ireland) Order 1973
Sch.9, amended: 2003 c.21 Sch.17 para.45

70. Water and Sewerage Services (Northern Ireland) Order 1973
applied: SI 2003/419 Art.63
Art.2, applied: SR 2003/46 Reg.2
Art.3A, applied: SR 2002/331 Reg.15
Art.3A, referred to: SR 2002/331 Reg.29
Art.3B, enabled: SR 2002/331
Art.3C, enabled: SR 2002/331
Art.57A, amended: 2003 c.21 Sch.17 para.46
Art.58, amended: 2003 c.21 Sch.17 para.46

490. Road Vehicles (Registration and Licensing) Regulations (Northern Ireland) 1973
Reg.9, amended: SI 2002/2381 Reg.3
Reg.9A, added: SI 2002/2381 Reg.4
Reg.13, amended: SI 2002/2381 Reg.5
Reg.13A, added: SI 2002/2381 Reg.5

600. Births, Deaths and Marriages Registration (Northern Ireland) Order 1973
revoked: SI 2003/413 Sch.1

870. Road Vehicles (Registration and Licensing) (Amendment) Regulations 1973
revoked: SI 2002/2742 Sch.1 Part I

944. Forest Reproductive Material Regulations 1973
applied: SI 2002/3026 Reg.7, Reg.9
referred to: SI 2002/3026 Reg.7
Reg.5, applied: SI 2002/3026 Reg.7

NO.

NO.

1973–cont.

1114. Criminal Appeal (Reference of Points of Law) Rules 1973
r.6, see *B v H Bauer Publishing Ltd* [2002] E.M.L.R. 8 (QBD), Eady, J.

1228. Enterprise Ulster (Northern Ireland) Order 1973
Art.9, substituted: SI 2003/418 Sch.1 para.2
Art.10, amended: SI 2003/418 Sch.3

1311. Hydrocarbon Oil Regulations 1973
Reg.2, amended: SI 2002/1471 Reg.11, SI 2002/1773 Reg.18
Reg.5, amended: SI 2002/1471 Reg.11
Reg.12, amended: SI 2002/1773 Reg.18
Reg.17, revoked: SI 2002/1773 Reg.18
Reg.30A, revoked: SI 2002/1773 Reg.18
Reg.37, revoked: SI 2002/1471 Reg.11
Reg.42, revoked: SI 2002/1471 Reg.11

1315. Merchant Shipping (Safety Convention) (Bermuda) Order 1973
revoked: SI 2002/3147 Art.2

1316. Merchant Shipping (Safety Convention) (Bermuda) (No.2) Order 1973
revoked: SI 2002/3147 Art.2

1822. Medicines (Pharmacies) (Applications for Registration and Fees) Regulations 1973
Reg.3, amended: SI 2002/3024 Reg.2, SI 2003/3141 Reg.2

1865. Church Representation Rules (Amendment) Resolution 1973
referred to: SI 2004/1889

1896. Land Acquisition and Compensation (Northern Ireland) Order 1973
applied: SR 2003/7 Sch.1 para.4
Art.30, amended: SI 2003/430 Art.36

1952. Crystal Glass (Descriptions) Regulations 1973
applied: SI 2003/1400 Sch.3, Sch.4

2163. Northern Ireland (Modification of Enactments-;No 1) Order 1973
Sch.2, amended: 2002 c.26 Sch.13
Sch.5 para.50, revoked (in part): 2002 c.26 Sch.13

1974

29. National Health Service (Venereal Diseases) Regulations 1974
Reg.2, amended: SI 2002/2469 Sch.1 para.33, SI 2004/696 Art.3

176. Charter Trustees Order 1974
Art.13, revoked: SI 2004/533 Art.7

191. National Health Service (Family Practitioner Committees-Supply of Goods) Regulations 1974
Reg.3, amended: SI 2002/2469 Sch.10

267. National Health Service (Constitution of Health Boards) (Scotland) Order 1974
Art.5, revoked: SSI 2003/217 Art.2
Sch.1, substituted: SSI 2003/217 Sch.1

1974–cont.

284. National Health Service (Charges for Appliances) Regulations 1974
Reg.2, amended: SI 2003/1937 Sch.1 para.2
Reg.5, amended: SI 2004/696 Art.3
Reg.6, amended: SI 2004/696 Art.3

355. Lancashire (Coroners Districts) Order 1974
referred to: SI 2002/2257 Art.2
revoked: SI 2002/2257 Art.4

366. Cornwall (Coroners Districts) Order 1974
revoked: SI 2003/3224 Art.4

367. Cumbria (Coroners&apos Districts) Order 1974
revoked: SI 2004/535 Art.4

371. Lincolnshire (Coroners Districts) Order 1974
applied: SI 2002/1588 Art.2
revoked: SI 2002/1588 Art.4

374. Hertfordshire (Coroners Districts) Order 1974
referred to: SI 2002/3084 Art.2
revoked: SI 2002/3084 Art.4

467. National Health Service (Functions of Common Services Agency) (Scotland) Order 1974
Art.3, amended: SSI 2003/306 Art.2
Art.3, applied: SI 2003/335 Sch.1, SSI 2003/93 Sch.1
Art.3, revoked (in part): SSI 2003/159 Art.2

468. National Health Service (Financial Provisions) (Scotland) Regulations 1974
applied: SSI 2002/103 Sch.1 Part III
varied: SSI 2002/305 Sch.1 Part III, SSI 2002/534 Sch.1 Part III

482. Local Authorities etc (Miscellaneous Provision) Order 1974
see *Leeds City Council v Watkins* [2003] EWHC 598, [2003] U.K.C.L.R. 467 (Ch D), Peter Smith, J.

494. National Health Service (Professions Supplementary to Medicine) Regulations 1974
Reg.2, amended: SI 2002/880 Sch.1 para.2, SI 2003/1590 Sch.1 para.27
Reg.3, amended: SI 2003/1590 Sch.1 para.27, SI 2004/2033 Art.7

495. National Health Service (Speech Therapists) Regulations 1974
Reg.3, amended: SI 2003/1590 Sch.1 para.29
Reg.4, amended: SI 2002/2469 Sch.1 para.34

498. Medicines (Exemption from Licences) (Clinical Trials) Order 1974
applied: SI 2004/1031 Sch.12 para.5
revoked: SI 2004/1031 Sch.11

NO.

1974–cont.

514. Agricultural Wages Committees (Transitional Provisions) Order 1974

Art.6, revoked (in part): SI 2004/2178 Sch.1 Part II

549. National Health Service (Professions Supplementary to Medicine) (Scotland) Regulations 1974

applied: SSI 2002/103 Sch.1 Part III, SSI 2002/305 Sch.1 Part III, SSI 2002/534 Sch.1 Part III

Reg.2, amended: SI 2003/1590 Sch.1 para.28

Reg.3, amended: SI 2003/1590 Sch.1 para.28, SI 2004/2033 Art.8

583. West Midlands (Coroners Districts) Order 1974

revoked: SI 2004/1799 Art.6

668. Magistrates Courts (Reciprocal Enforcement of Maintenance Orders) Rules 1974

Sch.1, amended: SI 2002/1734 r.2

832. Medicines (Renewal Application for Licences and Certificates) Regulations 1974

revoked (in part): SI 2004/1031 Sch.11

968. Local Authorities etc (Miscellaneous Provision) (No.3) Order 1974

Art.6, amended: SI 2004/3168 Art.5

1136. Plant Varieties and Seeds Tribunal Rules 1974

Part 1 r.2, amended: SI 2002/3198 r.2

Part 3 r.17, amended: SI 2002/3198 r.2

Part 3 r.18, amended: SI 2002/3198 r.2

Sch.1, amended: SI 2002/3198 r.2

Sch.2, amended: SI 2002/3198 r.2

1260. Specialized Agencies of the United Nations (Immunities and Privileges) Order 1974

Art.13A, added: SI 2002/1827 Art.2

Art.16A, amended: 2002 c.8 s.2

1261. United Nations and International Court of Justice (Immunities and Privileges) Order 1974

Part II, applied: SI 2003/1516 Art.9, SI 2003/1519 Art.9, SI 2003/1521 Art.9, SI 2003/1522 Art.9

Art.8A, added: SI 2002/1828 Art.2

1267. Pensions (Increase) (Northern Ireland) Order 1974

applied: SR 2002/352 Reg.126, Reg.139

1587. Abstract of Special Regulations (Highly Flammable Liquids and Liquefied Petroleum Gases) Order 1974

revoked: SI 2002/2776 Sch.7 Part 2

1982. Housing (Forms) (Scotland) Regulations 1974

Sch.1, added: SSI 2003/503 Sch.1 para.16

Sch.1, amended: SSI 2003/503 Sch.1 para.16

NO.

1974–cont.

2034. Agriculture (Tractor Cabs) Regulations 1974

applied: SI 2002/655 Reg.4, SI 2003/547 Reg.4, SI 2004/456 Reg.3

2040. Health and Safety Licensing Appeals (Hearings Procedure) Rules 1974

applied: SI 2004/1309 Reg.15

2068. Health and Safety Licensing Appeals (Hearings Procedure) (Scotland) Rules 1974

applied: SI 2004/1309 Reg.15

2211. Rabies (Importation of Dogs, Cats and Other Mammals) Order 1974

applied: SI 2004/853 Sch.6, SI 2004/2363 Reg.10, SSI 2003/229 Art.8, Sch.5 para.7

disapplied: SI 2004/853 Sch.6, SI 2004/2363 Reg.4, SSI 2003/229 Art.3

Art.2, amended: SI 2002/3135 Sch.1 para.17

Art.4, amended: SI 2004/2364 Art.2

Art.4, revoked (in part): SI 2004/2364 Art.2

Art.4A, substituted: SI 2004/2364 Art.2

Art.4B, substituted: SI 2004/2364 Art.2

Art.4C, added: SSI 2003/229 Art.11

Art.5, amended: SI 2004/2364 Art.2

Art.5A, revoked (in part): SI 2004/828 Art.3

Art.5A, substituted: SI 2004/2364 Art.2

Art.5B, added: SI 2002/882 Art.2

Art.5C, added: SSI 2003/229 Art.11

Art.6, amended: SI 2004/2364 Art.2, SSI 2003/229 Art.11

Art.7, amended: SI 2004/2364 Art.2

Sch.1, applied: SI 2004/853 Sch.3 para.10

Sch.1, referred to: SI 2004/853 Reg.17

Sch.2 Part II, amended: SI 2004/2364 Art.2

1975

116. Merchant Shipping (Diving Operations) Regulations 1975

revoked: SI 2002/1587 Reg.21

Reg.10, applied: SI 2002/1587 Reg.21

Reg.11, applied: SI 2002/1587 Reg.21

148. Town and Country Planning (Tree Preservation Order) (Amendment) and (Trees in Conservation Areas) (Exempted Cases) Regulations 1975

Reg.3, applied: SI 2002/1066 Art.17, SI 2002/1327 Art.14, SI 2004/757 Art.20

Reg.3, referred to: SI 2002/412 Art.14

330. Fishing Vessels (Safety Provisions) Rules 1975

applied: SI 2003/2669 Art.3, SSI 2003/116 Art.3

referred to: SI 2002/2201 Reg.2, Reg.4, Reg.14

Part I r.1, amended: SI 2002/2201 Sch.1 para.3, Sch.1 para.4

Part I r.1, revoked (in part): SI 2002/2201 Sch.1 para.3

Part I r.1B, added: SI 2002/2201 Sch.1 para.5

1975–cont.

330. Fishing Vessels (Safety Provisions) Rules 1975–*cont.*

Part II r.2, amended: SI 2002/2201 Sch.1 para.2

Part II r.3, amended: SI 2002/2201 Sch.1 para.2

Part II r.4, amended: SI 2002/2201 Sch.1 para.2

Part II r.5, amended: SI 2002/2201 Sch.1 para.2, Sch.1 para.6

Part II r.5, revoked (in part): SI 2002/2201 Sch.1 para.6

Part II r.6, amended: SI 2002/2201 Sch.1 para.2

Part II r.7, amended: SI 2002/2201 Sch.1 para.2

Part II r.8, amended: SI 2002/2201 Sch.1 para.2, Sch.1 para.7

Part II r.9, amended: SI 2002/2201 Sch.1 para.2

Part II r.10, amended: SI 2002/2201 Sch.1 para.2

Part II r.11, amended: SI 2002/2201 Sch.1 para.2

Part II r.12, amended: SI 2002/2201 Sch.1 para.2

Part II r.13, amended: SI 2002/2201 Sch.1 para.2

Part II r.14, amended: SI 2002/2201 Sch.1 para.2

Part II r.15, amended: SI 2002/2201 Sch.1 para.2

Part II r.16, amended: SI 2002/2201 Sch.1 para.2

Part II r.16A, amended: SI 2002/2201 Sch.1 para.2, Sch.1 para.8

Part II r.17, amended: SI 2002/2201 Sch.1 para.2

Part II r.18, amended: SI 2002/2201 Sch.1 para.2

Part II r.19, amended: SI 2002/2201 Sch.1 para.2

Part II r.20, amended: SI 2002/2201 Sch.1 para.2

Part II r.20A, amended: SI 2002/2201 Sch.1 para.2, Sch.1 para.9

Part II r.21, amended: SI 2002/2201 Sch.1 para.2

Part II r.22, amended: SI 2002/2201 Sch.1 para.2

Part II r.23, amended: SI 2002/2201 Sch.1 para.2

Part II r.24, amended: SI 2002/2201 Sch.1 para.2

Part II r.25, amended: SI 2002/2201 Sch.1 para.10

Part II r.26, revoked: SI 2002/2201 Sch.1 para.11

Part II r.27, amended: SI 2002/2201 Sch.1 para.10

1975–cont.

330. Fishing Vessels (Safety Provisions) Rules 1975–*cont.*

Part II r.28, revoked: SI 2002/2201 Sch.1 para.11

Part II r.29, amended: SI 2002/2201 Sch.1 para.2

Part II r.30, amended: SI 2002/2201 Sch.1 para.10

Part II r.31, revoked: SI 2002/2201 Sch.1 para.11

Part II r.32, amended: SI 2002/2201 Sch.1 para.2

Part II r.33, amended: SI 2002/2201 Sch.1 para.2

Part II r.34, amended: SI 2002/2201 Sch.1 para.2, Sch.1 para.12

Part II r.34, revoked (in part): SI 2002/2201 Sch.1 para.12

Part II r.35, amended: SI 2002/2201 Sch.1 para.2

Part II r.36, amended: SI 2002/2201 Sch.1 para.13

Part II r.37, revoked: SI 2002/2201 Sch.1 para.11

Part II r.38, amended: SI 2002/2201 Sch.1 para.2

Part II r.39, amended: SI 2002/2201 Sch.1 para.2

Part II r.40, amended: SI 2002/2201 Sch.1 para.2

Part II r.41, amended: SI 2002/2201 Sch.1 para.14

Part II r.41A, amended: SI 2002/2201 Sch.1 para.15

Part II r.42, revoked: SI 2002/2201 Sch.1 para.11

Part II r.42A, revoked: SI 2002/2201 Sch.1 para.11

Part II r.43, amended: SI 2002/2201 Sch.1 para.2

Part II r.43, revoked (in part): SI 2002/2201 Sch.1 para.11

Part II r.44, amended: SI 2002/2201 Sch.1 para.2

Part II r.45, amended: SI 2002/2201 Sch.1 para.16

Part II r.46, revoked: SI 2002/2201 Sch.1 para.11

Part II r.47, amended: SI 2002/2201 Sch.1 para.2

Part II r.48, amended: SI 2002/2201 Sch.1 para.2

Part II r.49, amended: SI 2002/2201 Sch.1 para.17

Part II r.50, amended: SI 2002/2201 Sch.1 para.2

Part II r.51, amended: SI 2002/2201 Sch.1 para.2, Sch.1 para.18

Part II r.52, amended: SI 2002/2201 Sch.1 para.2

NO.

1975–cont.

330. Fishing Vessels (Safety Provisions) Rules 1975–*cont.*

Part II r.53, amended: SI 2002/2201 Sch.1 para.2

Part II r.54, amended: SI 2002/2201 Sch.1 para.2

Part II r.54A, amended: SI 2002/2201 Sch.1 para.2, Sch.1 para.19

Part II r.54B, amended: SI 2002/2201 Sch.1 para.2

Part II r.54B, revoked: SI 2002/2201 Sch.1 para.11

Part II r.55, amended: SI 2002/2201 Sch.1 para.2

Part II r.56, amended: SI 2002/2201 Sch.1 para.20

Part II r.57, amended: SI 2002/2201 Sch.1 para.2, Sch.1 para.21

Part II r.58, amended: SI 2002/2201 Sch.1 para.2, Sch.1 para.21

Part II r.59, amended: SI 2002/2201 Sch.1 para.2

Part II r.60, amended: SI 2002/2201 Sch.1 para.22

Part II r.60, revoked (in part): SI 2002/2201 Sch.1 para.22

Part II r.60A, amended: SI 2002/2201 Sch.1 para.23

Part II r.61, amended: SI 2002/2201 Sch.1 para.2

Part II r.62, amended: SI 2002/2201 Sch.1 para.2, Sch.1 para.24

Part II r.63, amended: SI 2002/2201 Sch.1 para.2

Part II r.63A, amended: SI 2002/2201 Sch.1 para.2, Sch.1 para.25

Part II r.64, amended: SI 2002/2201 Sch.1 para.2

Part II r.65A, amended: SI 2002/2201 Sch.1 para.26

Part II r.65B, amended: SI 2002/2201 Sch.1 para.27

Part II r.67, revoked: SI 2002/2201 Sch.1 para.11

Part II r.68, amended: SI 2002/2201 Sch.1 para.2

Part II r.69, revoked: SI 2002/2201 Sch.1 para.11

Part II r.71, revoked: SI 2002/2201 Sch.1 para.11

Part II r.72A, amended: SI 2002/2201 Sch.1 para.28

Part III r.78, amended: SI 2002/2201 Sch.1 para.29

Part III r.79, revoked: SI 2002/2201 Sch.1 para.11

Part III r.80, revoked: SI 2002/2201 Sch.1 para.11

Part III r.87, amended: SI 2002/2201 Sch.1 para.30

NO.

1975–cont.

330. Fishing Vessels (Safety Provisions) Rules 1975–*cont.*

Part III r.87, revoked (in part): SI 2002/2201 Sch.1 para.30

Part III r.103, amended: SI 2002/2201 Sch.1 para.29

Part III r.104, revoked: SI 2002/2201 Sch.1 para.11

Part III r.105, revoked: SI 2002/2201 Sch.1 para.11

Part III r.106A, amended: SI 2002/2201 Sch.1 para.31

Part III r.111, amended: SI 2002/2201 Sch.1 para.32

Part III r.120, revoked: SI 2002/2201 Sch.1 para.11

Part III r.121, amended: SI 2002/2201 Sch.1 para.2, Sch.1 para.33

Part III r.121, revoked (in part): SI 2002/2201 Sch.1 para.33

Part V r.123, amended: SI 2002/2201 Sch.1 para.2

Part V r.124, amended: SI 2002/2201 Sch.1 para.34

Part V r.125A, amended: SI 2002/2201 Sch.1 para.35

Part V r.126B, amended: SI 2002/2201 Sch.1 para.36

r.16, see *Todd v Adams (t/a Trelawney Fishing Co) (The Maragetha Maria)* [2002] EWCA Civ 509, [2002] 2 All E.R. (Comm) 97 (CA), Neuberger, J.

r.95, see *Ziemniak v ETPM Deep Sea Ltd* [2003] EWCA Civ 636, [2003] 2 All E.R. (Comm) 283 (CA), Kay, L.J.

Sch.15, see *Ziemniak v ETPM Deep Sea Ltd* [2003] EWCA Civ 636, [2003] 2 All E.R. (Comm) 283 (CA), Kay, L.J.

412. Merchant Shipping (Load Lines) (Bermuda) Order 1975

revoked: SI 2002/3147 Art.2

423. Recovery Abroad of Maintenance (Convention Countries) Order 1975

Sch.1, amended: SI 2002/2839 Art.2

434. Industrial Training (Transfer of the Activities of Establishments) Order 1975

referred to: SI 2004/368 Sch.1

467. Social Security (Employed Earners Employments for Industrial Injuries Purposes) Regulations 1975

Sch.1 Part I para.2, amended: SI 2004/3168 Art.6

Sch.3, amended: SI 2004/3168 Art.6

492. Social Security (Contributions) Regulations 1975

applied: SI 2003/964 Reg.9

501. Royal Mint Trading Fund Order 1975

applied: SI 2002/831

NO.

NO.

1975–cont.

515. Social Security (Guardian's Allowances) Regulations 1975
revoked: SI 2003/495 Sch.1 Part 1
Reg.5, amended: SI 2002/492 Reg.2
Reg.6B, added: SI 2002/1789 Art.7

529. Social Security (Mariners Benefits) Regulations 1975
applied: SSI 2003/461 Reg.13

533. Medicines (Dental Filling Substances) Order 1975
Art.2, amended: SI 2004/1031 Sch.10 para.4

555. Social Security (Hospital In-Patients) Regulations 1975
applied: SI 2002/1792 Reg.15, Sch.3 para.2
Reg.2, amended: SI 2002/685 Reg.2, SI 2003/1195 Reg.2, SI 2004/101 Reg.2
Reg.2, applied: 2004 c.10 s.4
Reg.4, substituted: SI 2003/1195 Reg.2
Reg.4A, amended: SI 2003/1195 Reg.2
Reg.5, amended: SI 2002/685 Reg.2
Reg.5, revoked: SI 2003/1195 Reg.2
Reg.6, amended: SI 2003/1195 Reg.2, SI 2004/101 Reg.2
Reg.9, amended: SI 2003/1195 Reg.2
Reg.11, amended: SI 2003/1195 Reg.2
Reg.17, amended: SI 2003/1195 Reg.2
Reg.17, revoked (in part): SI 2003/1195 Reg.2

556. Social Security (Credits) Regulations 1975
applied: SI 2002/2005 Reg.18
Reg.2, amended: SI 2003/455 Sch.4 para.1
Reg.7A, amended: SI 2002/490 Reg.3
Reg.7B, amended: SI 2003/455 Sch.4 para.1
Reg.7C, amended: SI 2003/455 Sch.4 para.1
Reg.7C, revoked (in part): SI 2003/455 Sch.4 para.1
Reg.8A, amended: SI 2002/490 Reg.3
Reg.8B, amended: SI 2003/521 Reg.2
Reg.8B, applied: SI 2002/2005 Reg.6
Reg.9C, substituted: SI 2003/521 Reg.2

563. Social Security Benefit (Persons Abroad) Regulations 1975
Reg.5, applied: SI 2002/684 Reg.3, SI 2003/601 Reg.3, SI 2004/960 Reg.3
Reg.5, varied: SI 2004/583 Reg.3
Reg.10B, amended: SI 2002/2497 Sch.2 para.1

1023. Rehabilitation of Offenders Act 1974 (Exceptions) Order 1975
applied: SI 2002/57 Sch.1 para.7, Sch.3 para.13, SI 2002/324 Reg.19, Sch.2 para.7, SI 2002/325 Reg.18, Sch.2 para.8, SI 2002/327 Reg.26, Sch.2 para.7, SI 2002/812 Reg.16, Sch.2 para.7, SI 2002/919 Reg.5, Sch.1 para.1, Sch.1 para.16, Sch.2 para.9A, Sch.3 para.13A, Sch.3 para.8, Sch.7 para.1, Sch.7 para.13, Sch.8 para.9, Sch.8 para.9A, SI 2002/3212 Sch.3 para.4, SI 2002/3214 Sch.3 para.4, SI 2003/781 Sch.2 para.7, SI 2003/2527 Sch.2 para.9, Sch.3 para.5

1975–cont.

1023. Rehabilitation of Offenders Act 1974 (Exceptions) Order 1975–*cont.*
referred to: SI 2003/965 Art.2
revoked (in part): SSI 2003/231 Art.6
Art.2, amended: SI 2003/965 Art.3
Art.3, amended: SI 2002/441 Art.3, SI 2003/965 Art.4, Art.5
Art.4, amended: SI 2002/441 Art.4, SI 2003/965 Art.6, Art.7
Sch.1 Part I para.1, varied: SSI 2004/383 Reg.15
Sch.1 Part I para.2, varied: SSI 2004/383 Reg.15
Sch.1 Part I para.3, varied: SSI 2004/383 Reg.15
Sch.1 Part I para.4, varied: SSI 2004/383 Reg.15
Sch.1 Part I para.5, varied: SSI 2004/383 Reg.15
Sch.1 Part I para.6, varied: SSI 2004/383 Reg.15
Sch.1 Part I para.7, varied: SSI 2004/383 Reg.15
Sch.1 Part I para.8, varied: SSI 2004/383 Reg.15
Sch.1 Part I para.9, varied: SSI 2004/383 Reg.15
Sch.1 Part I para.10, amended: SI 2003/1590 Sch.1 para.26
Sch.1 Part I para.10, varied: SSI 2004/383 Reg.15
Sch.1 Part I para.11, varied: SSI 2004/383 Reg.15
Sch.1 Part I para.12, varied: SSI 2004/383 Reg.15
Sch.1 Part I para.13, added: SI 2002/441 Art.5
Sch.1 Part I para.13, varied: SSI 2004/383 Reg.15
Sch.1 Part I para.14, added: SI 2002/441 Art.5
Sch.1 Part I para.14, varied: SSI 2004/383 Reg.15
Sch.1 Part I para.15, added: SI 2002/441 Art.5
Sch.1 Part I para.15, varied: SSI 2004/383 Reg.15
Sch.1 Part I para.16, added: SI 2002/441 Art.5
Sch.1 Part I para.16, varied: SSI 2004/383 Reg.15
Sch.1 Part I para.17, added: SI 2002/441 Art.5
Sch.1 Part I para.17, varied: SSI 2004/383 Reg.15
Sch.1 Part II para.2, substituted: SI 2002/441 Art.5
Sch.1 Part II para.12, substituted: SI 2002/441 Art.5
Sch.1 Part II para.15, added: SI 2002/441 Art.5
Sch.1 Part II para.16, added: SI 2002/441 Art.5
Sch.1 Part II para.17, added: SI 2002/441 Art.5
Sch.1 Part II para.18, added: SI 2002/441 Art.5
Sch.1 Part II para.19, added: SI 2002/441 Art.5

NO.

1975–cont.

1023. Rehabilitation of Offenders Act 1974 (Exceptions) Order 1975–*cont.*

Sch.1 Part II para.20, added: SI 2003/965 Art.8

Sch.1 Part II para.21, added: SI 2003/965 Art.8

Sch.1 Part III para.9, added: SI 2002/441 Art.5

Sch.1 Part III para.9, revoked (in part): SI 2003/965 Art.9

Sch.1 Part IV, amended: SI 2003/965 Art.10

Sch.1 Part IV, substituted: SI 2002/441 Art.5

Sch.2 para.4, added: SI 2003/965 Art.11

Sch.2 para.5, added: SI 2003/965 Art.11

Sch.3 para.16, added: SI 2002/441 Art.6

Sch.3 para.16, amended: SI 2003/965 Art.12

Sch.3 para.17, added: SI 2002/441 Art.6

Sch.3 para.18, added: SI 2003/965 Art.13

Sch.3 para.19, added: SI 2003/965 Art.13

1038. Agriculture (Miscellaneous Provisions) (Northern Ireland) Order 1975

Art.3, revoked: SI 2004/1109 Sch.1

1135. Schools General (Scotland) Regulations 1975

Reg.10, amended: SSI 2003/581 Reg.11

Reg.10, revoked (in part): SSI 2003/581 Reg.11

1157. Industrial Training (Transfer of the Activities of Establishments) (No.2) Order 1975

referred to: SI 2004/368 Sch.1

1208. Motor Vehicles (International Circulation) Order 1975

Art.1, amended: SI 2004/1992 Art.3

Art.2, amended: SI 2004/1992 Art.4

Art.2, revoked (in part): SI 2004/1992 Art.4

1209. International Organisations (Immunities and Privileges) Miscellaneous Provisions Order 1975

Sch.1, amended: SI 2002/1826 Sch.1

1342. Road Vehicles (Registration and Licensing) (Amendment) (No.2) Regulations 1975

revoked: SI 2002/2742 Sch.1 Part I

1379. Tribunals and Inquiries (Discretionary Inquiries) Order 1975

Sch.1 Part I para.19A, added: SI 2004/3168 Art.7

1433. Coal Mines (Respirable Dust) Regulations 1975

applied: SI 2002/2677 Reg.5

1483. Social Security (Credits) Regulations 1975

Reg.7A, amended: SI 2002/2497 Sch.2 para.1

1503. Social Security Pensions (Northern Ireland) Order 1975

Art.23, applied: SR 2002/352 Reg.40

Art.69, applied: SR 2002/102 Art.6, SR 2003/169 Art.6

Art.69, enabled: SR 2002/102, SR 2003/169

NO.

1975–cont.

1503. Social Security Pensions (Northern Ireland) Order 1975–*cont.*

Art.69A, applied: SR 2002/102 Art.5, SR 2003/169 Art.5

1918. Borough of Luton (Electoral Arrangements) Order 1975

revoked: SI 2002/1787 Art.6

1990. District of Chiltern (Electoral Arrangements) Order 1975

revoked: SI 2002/1784 Art.10

1991. District of South Cambridgeshire (Electoral Arrangements) Order 1975

revoked (in part): SI 2002/2374 Art.9

Art.5, referred to: SI 2002/2374 Art.9

Art.6, referred to: SI 2002/2374 Art.9

2000. Medicines (Child Safety) Regulations 1975

revoked: SI 2003/2317 Reg.7

2048. Sex Discrimination (Questions and Replies) Order 1975

Art.5, amended: SI 2004/752 Reg.17

2062. Merchant Shipping (Diving Operations) (Amendment) Regulations 1975

revoked: SI 2002/1587 Reg.21

2083. District of Aylesbury Vale (Electoral Arrangements) Order 1975

revoked: SI 2002/1788 Art.11

2088. District of Fenland (Electoral Arrangements) Order 1975

revoked: SI 2002/2595 Art.10

Art.8, referred to: SI 2002/2595 Art.10

2103. Borough of Hartlepool (Electoral Arrangements) Order 1975

revoked: SI 2003/1088 Art.8

Art.8, referred to: SI 2003/1088 Art.8

Art.9, referred to: SI 2003/1088 Art.8

2143. City of Cambridge (Electoral Arrangements) Order 1975

revoked (in part): SI 2002/2369 Art.7

Art.8, referred to: SI 2002/2369 Art.7

Art.9, referred to: SI 2002/2369 Art.7

2220. Merchant Shipping (Crew Accommodation) (Fishing Vessels) Regulations 1975

Reg.1, amended: SI 2002/2201 Sch.1 para.38

Reg.2, amended: SI 2002/2201 Sch.1 para.39, Sch.1 para.40

Reg.2, revoked (in part): SI 2002/2201 Sch.1 para.40

Reg.3, amended: SI 2002/2201 Sch.1 para.41

Reg.6, amended: SI 2002/2201 Sch.1 para.42, Sch.1 para.43

Reg.7, amended: SI 2002/2201 Sch.1 para.44

Reg.10A, amended: SI 2002/2201 Sch.1 para.44

Reg.11, amended: SI 2002/2201 Sch.1 para.44

Reg.14A, amended: SI 2002/2201 Sch.1 para.43

NO.

1975–cont.

2220. Merchant Shipping (Crew Accommodation) (Fishing Vessels) Regulations 1975–*cont.*

Reg.15A, amended: SI 2002/2201 Sch.1 para.44

Reg.16A, amended: SI 2002/2201 Sch.1 para.42

Reg.25A, amended: SI 2002/2201 Sch.1 para.42

Reg.25B, amended: SI 2002/2201 Sch.1 para.45

Reg.27A, amended: SI 2002/2201 Sch.1 para.42

Reg.29A, amended: SI 2002/2201 Sch.1 para.44

Reg.36, amended: SI 2002/2201 Sch.1 para.46

1976

(NI.15). Sex Discrimination (Northern Ireland) Order 1976

Art.3, see *Shamoon v Chief Constable of the Royal Ulster Constabulary* [2003] UKHL 11, [2003] 2 All E.R. 26 (HL (NI)), Lord Nicholls of Birkenhead

Art.7, see *Shamoon v Chief Constable of the Royal Ulster Constabulary* [2003] UKHL 11, [2003] 2 All E.R. 26 (HL (NI)), Lord Nicholls of Birkenhead

57. Unsolicited Goods and Services (Northern Ireland) Order 1976

applied: 2002 c.40 Sch.15

99. Social Security (Invalid Care Allowance) Regulations (Northern Ireland) 1976

Reg.2A, amended: SR 2002/323 Sch.1 para.1

Reg.3, amended: SR 2002/323 Sch.1 para.1

Reg.6, amended: SR 2002/323 Sch.1 para.1

Reg.7, amended: SR 2002/323 Sch.1 para.1

Reg.8, amended: SR 2002/323 Sch.1 para.1

Reg.9, amended: SR 2002/323 Sch.1 para.1

Reg.10, revoked: SR 2002/323 Reg.4

Reg.10A, amended: SR 2002/323 Reg.2, Sch.1 para.1

Reg.11, revoked: SR 2002/323 Reg.4

Reg.11A, amended: SR 2002/323 Sch.1 para.1

Reg.11B, amended: SR 2002/323 Sch.1 para.1

Sch.1, amended: SR 2002/323 Sch.1 para.1

142. Occupational Pension Schemes (Equal Access to Membership) Regulations 1976

Reg.12, see *Preston v Wolverhampton Healthcare NHS Trust (No.3)* [2004] I.C.R. 993 (EAT), Judge J McMullen Q.C.

226. Treatment of Offenders (Northern Ireland) Order 1976

Art.5, applied: 2002 c.26 s.10

NO.

1976–cont.

246. Local Government Area Changes Regulations 1976

Reg.3, amended: SI 2002/2469 Sch.1 para.35, Sch.8

Reg.28, amended: SI 2002/2469 Sch.1 para.35

Reg.41, applied: SI 2002/1129 Art.6

Sch.2 para.1, amended: SI 2002/2469 Sch.1 para.35

Sch.2 para.2, amended: SI 2002/2469 Sch.1 para.35

Sch.2 para.3, amended: SI 2002/2469 Sch.1 para.35

Sch.2 para.4, amended: SI 2002/2469 Sch.1 para.35

Sch.2 para.5, amended: SI 2002/2469 Sch.1 para.35

Sch.2 para.6, amended: SI 2002/2469 Sch.1 para.35

Sch.2 para.7, amended: SI 2002/2469 Sch.1 para.35

Sch.2 para.8, amended: SI 2002/2469 Sch.1 para.35

Sch.2 para.10, amended: SI 2002/2469 Sch.1 para.35

396. Industrial Training (Transfer of the Activities of Establishments) Order 1976

referred to: SI 2004/368 Sch.1

401. District of Huntingdon (Electoral Arrangements) Order 1976

revoked: SI 2002/2984 Art.13

409. Social Security (Invalid Care Allowance) Regulations 1976

Reg.2A, amended: SI 2002/2497 Sch.2 para.1

Reg.2A, revoked (in part): SI 2003/937 Reg.2

Reg.3, amended: SI 2002/2497 Sch.2 para.1

Reg.5, see *Flemming v Secretary of State for Work and Pensions* [2002] EWCA Civ 641, [2002] 1 W.L.R. 2322 (CA), Pill, L.J.

Reg.6, amended: SI 2002/2497 Sch.2 para.1

Reg.7, amended: SI 2002/2497 Sch.2 para.1

Reg.8, amended: SI 2002/2497 Sch.2 para.1

Reg.9, amended: SI 2002/2497 Sch.2 para.1

Reg.10, revoked: SI 2002/2497 Reg.2

Reg.10A, amended: SI 2002/2497 Reg.2, Sch.2 para.1

Reg.11, revoked: SI 2002/2497 Reg.2

Reg.11A, amended: SI 2002/2497 Sch.2 para.1

Reg.14, amended: SI 2002/2497 Sch.2 para.1

Sch.1, amended: SI 2002/2497 Sch.2 para.1

476. Act of Sederunt (Summary Cause Rules) 1976

r.18, see *Edinburgh City Council v Forbes* 2002 Hous. L.R. 61 (Sh Pr), Nicholson Q.C., Sheriff Principal

NO.

1976–cont.

476. Act of Sederunt (Summary Cause Rules, Sheriff Court) 1976

revoked: SSI 2002/132 Sch.2

r.17, see *Ross & Liddell Ltd v Haggerty* 2003 S.C.L.R. 491 (Sh Ct (Glasgow and Strathkelvin)), Sheriff Brian Kearney

509. Specified Sugar Products Regulations 1976

applied: SI 2003/1563 Reg.11

referred to: SI 2003/1008 Reg.3, SI 2003/3047 Reg.11

revoked (in part): SI 2003/1563 Reg.10, SI 2003/3047 Reg.10

varied: SI 2002/329 Reg.9, SI 2003/945 Reg.3

541. Cocoa and Chocolate Products Regulations 1976

applied: SI 2003/3037 Reg.12

referred to: SI 2003/1008 Reg.3

revoked (in part): SI 2003/1659 Reg.11, SI 2003/3037 Reg.11

varied: SI 2002/329 Reg.9, SI 2003/945 Reg.3

555. Goods Vehicles (Ascertainment of Maximum Gross Weights) Regulations 1976

Sch.1, see *Pritchard v Crown Prosecution Service* [2003] EWHC 1851, [2004] R.T.R. 22 (QBD (Admin Ct)), McCombe, J.

582. Solicitors (Northern Ireland) Order 1976

Art.3, amended: SI 2003/435 Sch.4 para.2

Art.44, amended: SI 2003/435 Sch.4 para.2

Art.51, amended: SI 2003/435 Sch.4 para.2

Art.51B, amended: SI 2003/435 Sch.4 para.2

Art.51B, applied: SI 2003/435 Art.35

Art.51B, revoked (in part): SI 2003/435 Sch.5

Art.71A, applied: SI 2003/435 Art.38

Sch.1A, amended: SI 2003/435 Sch.4 para.2

Sch.1A, revoked (in part): SI 2003/435 Sch.5

615. Social Security (Medical Evidence) Regulations 1976

Reg.1, amended: SI 2002/881 Sch.1 para.1, SI 2002/2469 Sch.8

Reg.2, applied: SI 2004/291 Reg.21, SI 2004/478 Reg.21, SI 2004/627 Reg.12, SSI 2004/115 Reg.21, SSI 2004/116 Reg.19

Sch.1 Part I para.3, substituted: SI 2004/865 Sch.1 para.1, SI 2004/1016 Sch.1 para.1

Sch.2 Part I para.4, amended: SI 2004/1771 Sch.1 para.56

Sch.2 Part II, amended: SI 2002/2469 Sch.5, SI 2004/865 Sch.1 para.1, SI 2004/1016 Sch.1 para.1, SI 2004/1771 Sch.1 para.56

Sch.2 Part II, applied: SI 2004/1016 Art.83, SSI 2004/163 Art.94

Sch.2 Part II, referred to: SI 2002/2469 Reg.18, SI 2004/865 Art.107

NO.

1976–cont.

714. Employment Agencies Act 1973 (Charging Fees to Workers) Regulations 1976

applied: SI 2003/3319 Sch.1 para.3

revoked: SI 2003/3319 Reg.4

715. Conduct of Employment Agencies and Employment Businesses Regulations 1976

revoked: SI 2003/3319 Reg.4

Reg.2, applied: SI 2003/3319 Sch.1 para.3

Reg.3, applied: SI 2003/3319 Sch.1 para.6

Reg.4, applied: SI 2003/3319 Sch.1 para.3

Reg.5, applied: SI 2003/3319 Sch.1 para.6

Reg.6, applied: SI 2003/3319 Sch.1 para.6

Reg.7, applied: SI 2003/3319 Sch.1 para.5, Sch.1 para.6

Reg.8, applied: SI 2003/3319 Sch.1 para.6

Reg.9, applied: SI 2003/3319 Sch.1 para.3, Sch.1 para.4, Sch.1 para.6

Reg.10, applied: SI 2003/3319 Sch.1 para.6

Reg.11, applied: SI 2003/3319 Sch.1 para.6

Reg.12, applied: SI 2003/3319 Sch.1 para.6

Sch.2, applied: SI 2003/3319 Sch.1 para.5

730. Hallmarking (International Convention) Order 1976

revoked: SI 2002/506 Art.1

766. Employment Protection (Offshore Employment) Order 1976

applied: SI 2002/302 Art.2, SI 2003/285 Art.2, SI 2004/369 Art.2

817. Aberdeen Harbour Revision Order 1976

revoked: SSI 2002/310 Sch.3

820. Compulsory Purchase of Land (Scotland) Regulations 1976

revoked: SSI 2003/446 Reg.6

914. Cocoa and Chocolate Products (Scotland) Regulations 1976

revoked: SSI 2003/291 Reg.12

919. Diseases of Animals (Local Authorities) (Miscellaneous Provisions) Order 1976

Art.4, revoked (in part): SSI 2003/426 Art.19

946. Specified Sugar Products (Scotland) Regulations 1976

applied: SSI 2003/527 Reg.10

revoked: SSI 2003/527 Reg.11

963. Child Benefit (Residence and Persons Abroad) Regulations 1976

applied: SI 2003/392 Art.3

965. Child Benefit (General) Regulations 1976

revoked: SI 2003/493 Sch.2 Part 1

Reg.2A, added: SI 2002/1789 Art.6

Reg.3, applied: SI 2002/2007 Reg.3

968. Medicines (Specified Articles and Substances) Order 1976

Art.2, amended: SI 2004/1031 Sch.10 para.5

NO.

1976–cont.

1019. Offshore installations (Operational safety, Health and Welfare) Regulations 1976

see *Simpson v Transocean Offshore (UK) Inc* 2003 S.L.T. (Sh Ct) 119 (Sh Pr), Sir SST Young, Sheriff Principal

1041. Births and Deaths Registration (Northern Ireland) Order 1976

applied: 2004 c.7 Sch.3 para.30
Art.14, amended: 2003 c.24 Sch.1 para.8
Art.14A, added: 2003 c.24 Sch.1 para.9
Art.14A, varied: 2003 c.24 s.3
Art.18, amended: 2003 c.24 Sch.1 para.10
Art.18, varied: 2004 c.7 Sch.3 para.27
Art.19, varied: 2004 c.7 Sch.3 para.27
Art.19A, varied: 2004 c.7 Sch.3 para.27
Art.34, amended: SR 2002/242 Sch.1
Art.34, applied: 2004 c.7 Sch.3 para.30
Art.37, amended: SR 2002/242 Sch.1
Art.38, amended: SR 2002/242 Sch.1
Art.40, amended: SR 2002/242 Sch.1
Art.40, applied: 2004 c.7 Sch.3 para.26
Art.42, amended: SR 2002/242 Sch.1
Art.42, applied: 2004 c.7 Sch.3 para.31
Art.47, applied: SR 2002/242, 2004 c.7 Sch.3 para.32

1042. Sex Discrimination (Northern Ireland) Order 1976

referred to: SR 2002/120 Sch.1
Art.10A, amended: 2004 c.7 Sch.6 para.7
Art.10B, amended: 2004 c.7 Sch.6 para.8
Art.12, see *Jones v Friends Provident Life Office* [2004] N.I. 125 (CA (NI)), Lord Carswell L.C.J.
Art.12, amended: 2004 c.7 Sch.6 para.9
Art.14, amended: 2004 c.7 Sch.6 para.10
Art.43A, added: 2002 c.2 s.2
Art.45, referred to: 2004 c.7 s.19
Art.63, applied: SI 2003/2902 Sch.2, Sch.3, Sch.4
Art.75, amended: SI 2003/435 Sch.4 para.3

1053. Borough of Stockton-on-Tees (Electoral Arrangements) Order 1976

revoked (in part): SI 2003/2506 Art.11

1073. Police (Scotland) Regulations 1976

applied: SSI 2004/257 Sch.3 para.6, Sch.3 para.7
revoked: SSI 2004/257 Sch.4
Reg.2A, revoked (in part): SSI 2003/220 Reg.2
Reg.6, amended: SSI 2003/21 Reg.2
Reg.21A, amended: SSI 2003/220 Reg.3
Reg.22, amended: SSI 2003/220 Reg.4
Reg.23, amended: SSI 2003/220 Reg.5
Reg.36, amended: 2002 c.8 s.1
Reg.42A, applied: SSI 2004/257 Sch.3 para.7
Reg.47, amended: SSI 2003/220 Reg.6
Reg.47, revoked (in part): SSI 2003/220 Reg.6

NO.

1976–cont.

1073. Police (Scotland) Regulations 1976–cont.

Reg.50, revoked: SSI 2004/121 Reg.2
Reg.52, amended: SSI 2003/220 Reg.7
Reg.53, revoked: SSI 2003/220 Sch.1
Reg.63, revoked: SSI 2003/220 Sch.1
Sch.1A para.2, amended: SSI 2003/220 Reg.8
Sch.1A para.8, substituted: SSI 2003/220 Reg.8
Sch.1A para.9, revoked: SSI 2003/220 Reg.8
Sch.1B para.4, revoked: SSI 2003/220 Reg.9
Sch.1B para.5, amended: SSI 2003/220 Reg.9
Sch.1B para.5, revoked (in part): SSI 2003/220 Reg.9
Sch.1B para.6, amended: SSI 2003/220 Reg.9
Sch.1B para.16, revoked: SSI 2003/220 Reg.9
Sch.1B para.17, revoked: SSI 2004/121 Reg.2
Sch.1B para.19, substituted: SSI 2003/220 Reg.9
Sch.4 para.1, revoked: SSI 2003/220 Sch.1
Sch.4 para.2, revoked: SSI 2003/220 Sch.1
Sch.4 para.3, revoked: SSI 2003/220 Sch.1
Sch.4 para.4, revoked: SSI 2003/220 Sch.1
Sch.4 para.5, revoked: SSI 2003/220 Sch.1
Sch.4 para.6, revoked: SSI 2003/220 Sch.1

1131. Borough of Middlesbrough (Electoral Arrangements) Order 1976

revoked (in part): SI 2003/159 Art.6
Art.8, referred to: SI 2003/159 Art.6

1212. Financial Provisions (Northern Ireland) Order 1976

Art.15, applied: SR 2002/242

1213. Pharmacy (Northern Ireland) Order 1976

applied: SI 2002/2376 Reg.4
Art.2, referred to: SSI 2002/190 Reg.3
Art.5, enabled: SR 2002/206, SR 2003/356

1267. Child Benefit and Social Security (Fixing and Adjustment of Rates) Regulations 1976

Reg.2, amended: SI 2002/668 Art.13, SI 2003/526 Art.14, SI 2004/942 Art.3
Reg.2, applied: SI 2003/526 Art.14, SI 2004/942 Art.3

1433. Police (Scotland) Amendment (No.3) Regulations 1976

revoked: SSI 2004/257 Sch.4

1635. Industrial Training (Transfer of the Activities of Establishments) (No.2) Order 1976

referred to: SI 2004/368 Sch.1

1643. Medicines (Child Safety) Amendment Regulations 1976

revoked: SI 2003/2317 Reg.7

NO.

1976–cont.

1680. Road Vehicles (Registration and Licensing) (Amendment) Regulations 1976
revoked: SI 2002/2742 Sch.1 Part I

1726. Medicines (Labelling) Regulations 1976
Reg.1, amended: SI 2004/1031 Sch.10 para.6
Reg.2, amended: SI 2004/1031 Sch.10 para.6
Reg.3, amended: SI 2002/236 Reg.5
Reg.4A, amended: SI 2002/236 Reg.5
Reg.4B, amended: SI 2002/236 Reg.5
Reg.4F, amended: SI 2002/236 Reg.5
Reg.6, revoked: SI 2004/1031 Sch.10 para.6
Reg.10, amended: SI 2004/1031 Sch.10 para.6
Reg.16, amended: SI 2004/1031 Sch.10 para.6
Sch.2 para.1, revoked: SI 2004/1031 Sch.10 para.6
Sch.2 para.2, revoked: SI 2004/1031 Sch.10 para.6
Sch.2 para.3, revoked: SI 2004/1031 Sch.10 para.6
Sch.2 para.4, revoked: SI 2004/1031 Sch.10 para.6
Sch.2 para.5, revoked: SI 2004/1031 Sch.10 para.6

1757. District of Malvern Hills (Electoral Arrangements) Order 1976
revoked: SI 2002/187 Art.11

1758. Child Benefit (Miscellaneous Minor Amendments) Regulations 1976
Reg.3, revoked: SI 2003/493 Sch.2 Part 1

1813. Consumer Transactions (Restrictions on Statements) Order 1976
applied: SI 2003/1593 Sch.1 Part I
Art.3, referred to: SI 2003/1374 Sch.1
Art.4, referred to: SI 2003/1374 Sch.1
Art.5, referred to: SI 2003/1374 Sch.1

1818. Honey (Scotland) Regulations 1976
applied: SSI 2003/569 Reg.11
revoked: SSI 2003/569 Reg.12

1832. Honey Regulations 1976
applied: SI 2003/2243 Reg.11, SI 2003/3044 Reg.11
revoked (in part): SI 2003/2243 Reg.10, SI 2003/3044 Reg.10

2003. Fire Certificates (Special Premises) Regulations 1976
Sch.1 Part III para.25, amended: SI 2002/2776 Sch.6 para.9

2012. National Savings Stock Register Regulations 1976
Reg.14, amended: SI 2004/1662 Sch.1 para.22
Reg.39A, amended: SI 2004/1662 Sch.1 para.22
Reg.41, amended: SI 2004/1662 Sch.1 para.22
Reg.42, amended: SI 2004/1662 Sch.1 para.22

NO.

1976–cont.

2019. Motor Vehicles (Competitions and Trials) (Scotland) Regulations 1976
Reg.7, amended: SSI 2002/14 Reg.2

2089. Road Vehicles (Registration and Licensing) (Amendment) (No.2) Regulations 1976
revoked: SI 2002/2742 Sch.1 Part I

2110. Industrial Training (Transfer of the Activities of Establishments) (No.3) Order 1976
referred to: SI 2004/368 Sch.1

2144. United States of America (Extradition) Order 1976
Sch.1, see *Warda v Governor of Brixton Prison* [2002] EWHC 194, Times, March 18, 2002 (QBD (Admin Ct)), Keene, L.J.

2151. Double Taxation Relief (Taxes on Income) (Republic of Ireland) Order 1976
referred to: SI 2002/427 Reg.2
Sch.1, applied: SI 2002/836 Reg.2, SR 2002/127 Reg.2

1977

8. Local Government Area Changes (Scotland) Regulations 1977
applied: SSI 2002/154 Art.3, SSI 2002/155 Art.3, SSI 2002/156 Art.3, SSI 2002/157 Art.3

176. General Optical Council (Registration and Enrolment Rules) Order of Council 1977
Sch.1, amended: SI 2002/775 Sch.1, SI 2003/1080 Sch.1, SI 2004/258 Sch.1

204. Local Authorities Cemeteries Order 1977
Art.16, see *Keynsham Cemetery, Re* [2003] 1 W.L.R. 66 (Cons Ct (Bath & Wells)), Timothy Briden (Chancellor)

230. Road Vehicles (Registration and Licensing) (Amendment) Regulations 1977
revoked: SI 2002/2742 Sch.1 Part I

237. District of South Norfolk (Electoral Arrangements) Order 1977
revoked: SI 2002/3218 Art.11

339. Land Drainage (Compensation) Regulations 1977
Reg.2, amended: SI 2002/2469 Sch.1 para.36

342. Social Security (Child Benefit Consequential) Regulations 1977
Reg.9, revoked: SI 2003/495 Sch.1 Part 1

343. Social Security Benefit (Dependency) Regulations 1977
Reg.1, amended: SI 2002/2497 Sch.2 para.1
Reg.3, amended: SI 2003/937 Reg.2
Reg.4A, amended: SI 2003/937 Reg.2
Reg.4B, revoked (in part): SI 2003/937 Reg.2

NO.

NO.

1977–cont.

1977–cont.

343. Social Security Benefit (Dependency) Regulations 1977–*cont.*

Reg.12, amended: SI 2002/2497 Sch.2 para.1

Sch.2 Part I para.1, amended: SI 2002/2497 Sch.2 para.1

Sch.2 Part I para.2, amended: SI 2002/2497 Sch.2 para.1

Sch.2 Part I para.2A, amended: SI 2002/2497 Sch.2 para.1

Sch.2 Part I para.2B, amended: SI 2002/684 Reg.4, SI 2002/2497 Sch.2 para.1, SI 2003/601 Reg.4, SI 2004/583 Reg.4

Sch.2 Part I para.2BB, amended: SI 2002/2497 Sch.2 para.1

Sch.2 Part I para.2C, amended: SI 2002/2497 Sch.2 para.1

Sch.2 Part I para.3, amended: SI 2002/2497 Sch.2 para.1

Sch.2 Part I para.4, amended: SI 2002/2497 Sch.2 para.1

Sch.2 Part I para.5, amended: SI 2002/2497 Sch.2 para.1

Sch.2 Part II para.6, amended: SI 2002/2497 Sch.2 para.1

Sch.2 Part II para.7, amended: SI 2002/2497 Sch.2 para.1

Sch.2 Part II para.8, amended: SI 2002/2497 Sch.2 para.1

Sch.2 Part II para.9, amended: SI 2002/2497 Sch.2 para.1

372. National Savings Stock Register (Registrar's Fees) Warrant 1977

r.3, amended: SI 2004/1662 Sch.1 para.23

413. City of Hereford (Electoral Arrangements) Order 1977

revoked: SI 2002/187 Art.11

414. City of Worcester (Electoral Arrangements) Order 1977

revoked: SI 2002/3225 Art.9

426. Criminal Damage (Northern Ireland) Order 1977

Art.3, applied: 2003 c.44 Sch.17 para.31, Sch.17 para.32, SI 2004/702 Sch.4 para.4, SI 2004/1500 Sch.2 para.17

Art.4, applied: SI 2004/702 Sch.4 para.4

438. District of South Herefordshire (Electoral Arrangements) Order 1977

revoked: SI 2002/187 Art.11

500. Safety Representatives and Safety Committees Regulations 1977

applied: SI 2002/377 Sch.1 para.36, SI 2002/3199 Sch.2 para.20, SI 2003/3118 Sch.2 para.20, SI 2003/3170 Sch.3 para.20

Reg.4, see *Duthie v Bath and North East Somerset Council* [2003] I.C.R. 1405 (EAT), Judge Ansell

534. Child Benefit (General) Amendment Regulations 1977

revoked: SI 2003/493 Sch.2 Part 1

607. Lymington Harbour Revision Order 1977

referred to: SI 2002/2586 Art.1

681. District of West Oxfordshire (Electoral Arrangements) Order 1977

revoked: SI 2002/48 Art.7

723. Borough of Oadby and Wigston (Electoral Arrangements) Order 1977

revoked: SI 2002/2889 Art.6

731. Borough of Melton (Electoral Arrangements) Order 1977

revoked: SI 2002/2599 Art.7

Art.8, referred to: SI 2002/2599 Art.7

842. Race Relations (Questions and Replies) Order 1977

Art.5, amended: SI 2004/752 Reg.17

865. District of Chichester (Electoral Arrangements) Order 1977

revoked: SI 2002/2883 Art.8

Art.5, referred to: SI 2002/2883 Art.8

874. National Health Service (Association of Community Health Councils) Regulations 1977

applied: SI 2003/2660 Art.2

revoked (in part): SI 2004/905 Reg.31

891. Forest Reproductive Material Regulations 1977

applied: SI 2002/3026 Reg.7, Reg.9, Reg.31

referred to: SI 2002/3026 Reg.7, Reg.31

revoked: SI 2002/3026 Reg.35

927. Fruit Juices and Fruit Nectars Regulations 1977

applied: SI 2003/1564 Reg.11, SI 2003/3041 Reg.11

referred to: SI 2003/1008 Reg.3

revoked (in part): SI 2003/1564 Reg.10, SI 2003/3041 Reg.10

varied: SI 2002/329 Reg.9, SI 2003/945 Reg.3

928. Condensed Milk and Dried Milk Regulations 1977

applied: SI 2003/1596 Reg.11, SI 2003/3053 Reg.11

referred to: SI 2003/1008 Reg.3

revoked (in part): SI 2003/1596 Reg.10, SI 2003/3053 Reg.10

varied: SI 2002/329 Reg.9, SI 2003/945 Reg.3

932. Measuring Container Bottles (EEC Requirements) Regulations 1977

applied: SI 2003/1400 Sch.4

944. Importation of Animals Order 1977

Art.3, applied: SI 2004/853 Sch.6

Art.3, disapplied: SI 2004/853 Sch.6

Art.4, disapplied: SI 2004/853 Sch.6

Art.5, disapplied: SI 2004/853 Sch.6

Art.7, disapplied: SI 2004/853 Sch.6

Art.8, disapplied: SI 2004/853 Sch.6

Art.9, disapplied: SI 2004/853 Sch.6

Art.10, disapplied: SI 2004/853 Sch.6

Art.11, disapplied: SI 2004/853 Sch.6

NO.

1977–cont.

944. Importation of Animals Order 1977– *cont.*
Art.12, disapplied: SI 2004/853 Sch.6
Art.13, disapplied: SI 2004/853 Sch.6
Art.14, disapplied: SI 2004/853 Sch.6
Art.16, disapplied: SI 2004/853 Sch.6
Art.17, disapplied: SI 2004/853 Sch.6
Art.18, disapplied: SI 2004/853 Sch.6
Art.19, disapplied: SI 2004/853 Sch.6
Art.20, disapplied: SI 2004/853 Sch.6
Art.21, disapplied: SI 2004/853 Sch.6
Art.23, disapplied: SI 2004/853 Sch.6
Art.24, disapplied: SI 2004/853 Sch.6
Art.25, disapplied: SI 2004/853 Sch.6
Sch.1 para.4, revoked (in part): SSI 2003/426 Art.19

985. Local Land Charges Rules 1977
Sch.3, substituted: SI 2003/2502 Sch.1

1016. Police (Scotland) Amendment Regulations 1977
revoked: SSI 2004/257 Sch.4

1026. Fruit Juices and Fruit Nectars (Scotland) Regulations 1977
applied: SSI 2003/293 Reg.9
revoked: SSI 2003/293 Reg.11

1027. Condensed Milk and Dried Milk (Scotland) Regulations 1977
applied: SSI 2003/311 Reg.9
revoked: SSI 2003/311 Reg.11

1210. National Savings Bank (Investment Deposits) (Limits) Order 1977
Art.3ZA, added: SI 2003/2895 Reg.6

1245. Agriculture (Miscellaneous Provisions) (Northern Ireland) Order 1977
Art.4, revoked: SI 2004/1109 Sch.1
Sch.2, amended: SI 2004/1109 Sch.1

1250. Family Law Reform (Northern Ireland) Order 1977
Art.10, enabled: SR 2002/150

1251. Fatal Accidents (Northern Ireland) Order 1977
Art.3A, amended: SI 2002/645 Art.2
Art.3A, enabled: SI 2002/645

1264. Forest Reproductive Material (Amendment) Regulations 1977
revoked: SI 2002/3026 Reg.35

1273. District of Bracknell (Electoral Arrangements) Order 1977
revoked (in part): SI 2002/2371 Art.11

1274. City of Norwich (Electoral Arrangements) Order 1977
revoked: SI 2002/3222 Art.7

1277. District of Bromsgrove (Electoral Arrangements) Order 1977
revoked: SI 2003/158 Art.12
Art.8, referred to: SI 2003/158 Art.12

1390. District of Broadland (Electoral Arrangements) Order 1977
revoked: SI 2003/157 Art.13
Art.5, referred to: SI 2003/157 Art.13

NO.

1977–cont.

1390. District of Broadland (Electoral Arrangements) Order 1977–*cont.*
Art.6, referred to: SI 2003/157 Art.13

1433. Borough of Crawley (Electoral Arrangements) Order 1977
revoked: SI 2002/2990 Art.7

1753. Alcoholometers and Alcohol Hydrometers (EEC Requirements) Regulations 1977
Reg.5, applied: SI 2004/1300 Reg.5
Reg.7, applied: SI 2004/1300 Reg.4

1865. District of Rutland (Electoral Arrangements) Order 1977
revoked: SI 2003/322 Art.7

1883. Fruit Juices and Fruit Nectars (Scotland) Amendment Regulations 1977
revoked: SSI 2003/293 Reg.11

1918. Business Advertisements (Disclosure) Order 1977
applied: SI 2003/1593 Sch.1 Part I

1951. Industrial Training (Transfer of the Activities of Establishments) Order 1977
referred to: SI 2004/368 Sch.1

1979. Tobacco Products (Cigarettes and Cigars) Order 1977
revoked: SI 2003/1471 Art.3

2008. Police (Scotland) Amendment (No.2) Regulations 1977
revoked: SSI 2004/257 Sch.4

2151. Agricultural Wages (Regulation) (Northern Ireland) Order 1977
Art.8A, amended: 2004 c.24 s.46

2157. Rates (Northern Ireland) Order 1977
applied: SI 2002/3149 Art.5
Art.2, amended: SI 2004/703 Sch.3 para.1
Art.2, enabled: SR 2002/26, SR 2003/73, SR 2003/76, SR 2003/77, SR 2003/78, SR 2003/129, SR 2003/143
Art.4, applied: SR 2003/28 Sch.2 para.6
Art.6, enabled: SR 2002/409
Art.7, applied: SR 2003/78
Art.7, enabled: SR 2002/26, SR 2003/78
Art.7, referred to: SR 2002/26
Art.13, amended: SI 2004/703 Sch.3 para.2
Art.13, varied: SR 2003/73 Sch.1
Art.15, amended: SI 2004/703 Sch.3 para.3
Art.19, amended: SI 2004/703 Sch.3 para.4
Art.20, varied: SR 2003/73 Sch.1
Art.25A, added: SI 2004/703 Art.4
Art.25B, added: SI 2004/703 Art.5
Art.26, amended: SI 2004/703 Art.6
Art.26A, added: SI 2004/703 Art.7
Art.27, applied: SR 2002/26 Art.3, SR 2003/78 Art.3
Art.27, enabled: SR 2002/26, SR 2003/78
Art.31, see *Queens University of Belfast v Commissioner of Valuation (No.2)* [2002] R.A. 189 (LandsTr (NI)), Coghlin, J.
Art.31B, referred to: SI 2002/3149 Art.5
Art.33, amended: SI 2004/703 Sch.3 para.5

NO.

1977–cont.

2157. Rates (Northern Ireland) Order 1977– cont.

Art.33A, enabled: SR 2003/143

Art.33B, added: SI 2004/703 Art.8

Art.37, enabled: SR 2003/72, SR 2003/93, SR 2003/185, SR 2003/186

Art.37A, amended: SI 2004/703 Sch.3 para.6

Art.39, enabled: SR 2003/31, SR 2003/76, SR 2003/129

Art.39C, enabled: SR 2003/77

Art.42, amended: SI 2004/703 Sch.3 para.7

Art.42, referred to: SI 2002/3149 Art.5

Art.42, revoked (in part): SI 2004/703 Sch.3 para.7, Sch.4

Art.45, enabled: SR 2003/73

Art.56, amended: SI 2004/703 Sch.3 para.8

Art.60, amended: SI 2004/703 Sch.3 para.9

Sch.2, revoked: SI 2004/703 Sch.4

Sch.4, varied: SR 2003/73 Sch.1

Sch.5, applied: SR 2003/28 Sch.2 para.6

Sch.7, amended: SI 2004/703 Art.3, Sch.4

Sch.7, referred to: SI 2002/3149 Art.5

Sch.7, revoked (in part): SI 2004/703 Art.3, Sch.4, Sch.4

Sch.8A, added: SI 2004/703 Sch.1

Sch.8B, added: SI 2004/703 Sch.2

Sch.12, added: SI 2004/703 Art.5

Sch.12, amended: SI 2004/703 Sch.3 para.10

Sch.12, applied: SR 2003/76 Art.4, Art.5, Art.6, Art.7, Art.8

Sch.12, disapplied: SR 2003/76 Art.3, Art.5

Sch.12, enabled: SR 2003/30, SR 2003/31, SR 2003/76, SR 2003/129

Sch.12, referred to: SR 2003/31 Art.2, SR 2003/76 Art.2, Art.3

Sch.12, substituted: SR 2003/31 Sch.1, SR 2003/129 Sch.1

Sch.12, varied: SR 2003/30 Reg.4

Sch.14, revoked (in part): SI 2004/703 Sch.4, Sch.4

Sch.14, varied: SR 2003/73 Sch.1

Sch.15, revoked: SI 2002/3149 Sch.1

Sch.16, amended: SI 2004/703 Sch.3 para.11

2157. The Rates Order (Northern Ireland) 1977

Art.54, see *A-Wear Ltd v Commissioner of Valuation for Northern Ireland* [2003] R.A. 217 (LandsTr (NI)), MR Curry, FRICS

1978

20. Pharmaceutical Society (Statutory Committee) Order of Council 1978

Part IV para.31, amended: SI 2002/3135 Sch.1 para.18

NO.

1978–cont.

27. Rehabilitation of Offenders (Northern Ireland) Order 1978

see *R. (on the application of McParland) v Department of the Environment in Northern Ireland* [2002] N.I. 292 (CA (NI)), Carswell, L.C.J.

32. Diseases of Animals (Approved Disinfectants) Order 1978

applied: SI 2003/255 Sch.2 para.4, SI 2003/482 Sch.2 para.4, SI 2003/1470 Sch.2 para.4, SI 2003/1968 Sch.2 para.4, SI 2003/2329 Art.12, SI 2003/2456 Art.12, SI 2003/2913 Art.12, SI 2003/3273 Art.12, SSI 2003/426 Art.12, SSI 2003/586 Art.12

Art.2, amended: SSI 2003/354 Art.19

Art.3, amended: SSI 2003/334 Art.2

Art.4, amended: SSI 2003/334 Art.2

Art.5, amended: SSI 2003/334 Art.2

Art.6, added: SSI 2003/334 Art.2

Art.6, amended: SI 2003/1428 Art.2

Sch.1, substituted: SI 2003/1428 Sch.1, SSI 2003/334 Sch.1

Sch.2, added: SSI 2003/334 Sch.2

Sch.2, substituted: SI 2003/1428 Sch.2

40. Medicines (Fluted Bottles) Regulations 1978

Reg.3, amended: SI 2004/1031 Sch.10 para.7

41. Medicines (Labelling and Advertising to the Public) Regulations 1978

Reg.1, amended: SI 2004/1771 Sch.1 para.55

Reg.5, amended: SI 2002/880 Sch.1 para.3, SI 2003/1590 Sch.1 para.25, SI 2004/1771 Sch.1 para.55

49. District of Wychavon (Electoral Arrangements) Order 1978

revoked: SI 2002/2987 Art.9

Art.5, referred to: SI 2002/2987 Art.9

112. Act of Sederunt (Summary Cause Rules, Sheriff Court) (Amendment) 1978

revoked: SSI 2002/132 Sch.2

272. Transfer of Functions (Wales) (No.1) Order 1978

applied: SI 2002/794 Art.1

393. Social Security (Graduated Retirement Benefit) (No.2) Regulations 1978

Sch.2, applied: SI 2002/668 Art.11

Sch.2 para.1, varied: SI 2002/668 Art.11, SI 2003/526 Art.12, SI 2004/552 Art.12

Sch.2 para.2, varied: SI 2002/668 Art.11, SI 2003/526 Art.12, SI 2004/552 Art.12

Sch.2 para.3, varied: SI 2002/668 Art.11, SI 2003/526 Art.12, SI 2004/552 Art.12

Sch.2 para.4, varied: SI 2002/668 Art.11, SI 2003/526 Art.12, SI 2004/552 Art.12

436. Fire Services (Appointments and Promotion) Regulations 1978

revoked: SI 2004/481 Sch.2

NO.

448. Industrial Training (Transfer of the Activities of Establishments) Order 1978

referred to: SI 2004/368 Sch.1

460. Sexual Offences (Northern Ireland) Order 1978

Art.2, revoked (in part): SI 2003/1247 Sch.2

Art.3, revoked: SI 2003/1247 Sch.2

528. Police (Scotland) Amendment Regulations 1978

revoked: SSI 2004/257 Sch.4

540. Child Benefit (Miscellaneous Amendments) Regulations 1978

revoked: SI 2003/493 Sch.2 Part 1

610. Borough of Sandwell (Electoral Arrangements) Order 1978

revoked (in part): SI 2003/2510 Art.7

621. Patents Act 1977 (Isle of Man) Order 1978

revoked: SI 2003/1249 Art.4

647. Shoreham Port Authority Revision Order 1978

Art.4, revoked: SI 2004/1506 Sch.3

1039. Health and Safety at Work (Northern Ireland) Order 1978

applied: 2002 c.40 Sch.15, SI 2003/403 Reg.27, SI 2003/750 Sch.5 para.12, SI 2003/751 Sch.6 para.12, SI 2004/129 Reg.25, Reg.27, SR 2002/1 Reg.8, SR 2002/301 Reg.14

referred to: SI 2004/1468 Sch.6 para.12

Art.2, enabled: SR 2003/34, SR 2003/288

Art.3, varied: 2002 c.8 (NI) s.1, SR 2003/34 Reg.19, SR 2003/52 Reg.3

Art.4, varied: 2002 c.8 (NI) s.1, SR 2003/34 Reg.19

Art.5, varied: 2002 c.8 (NI) s.1, SR 2003/34 Reg.19, Reg.20

Art.6, varied: 2002 c.8 (NI) s.1, SR 2003/34 Reg.19

Art.7, varied: 2002 c.8 (NI) s.1, SR 2003/34 Reg.19

Art.8, varied: 2002 c.8 (NI) s.1, SR 2003/34 Reg.19

Art.9, varied: 2002 c.8 (NI) s.1, SR 2003/34 Reg.19

Art.10, varied: 2002 c.8 (NI) s.1, SR 2003/34 Reg.19

Art.11, varied: 2002 c.8 (NI) s.1, SR 2003/34 Reg.19

Art.12, varied: 2002 c.8 (NI) s.1, SR 2003/34 Reg.19

Art.13, applied: SR 2002/34, SR 2002/301, SR 2002/302, SR 2003/33, SR 2003/34, SR 2003/35, SR 2003/36, SR 2003/152, SR 2003/288

Art.13, varied: 2002 c.8 (NI) s.1, SR 2003/34 Reg.19

Art.14, varied: 2002 c.8 (NI) s.1, SR 2003/34 Reg.19

NO.

1039. Health and Safety at Work (Northern Ireland) Order 1978–*cont.*

Art.15, varied: 2002 c.8 (NI) s.1, SR 2003/34 Reg.19

Art.16, varied: 2002 c.8 (NI) s.1, SR 2003/34 Reg.19

Art.17, applied: SR 2003/52 Reg.3

Art.17, enabled: SR 2002/34, SR 2002/301, SR 2002/302, SR 2003/33, SR 2003/34, SR 2003/35, SR 2003/36, SR 2003/152, SR 2003/288

Art.17, referred to: 2002 c.8 (NI) s.1

Art.17, varied: 2002 c.8 (NI) s.1, SR 2003/34 Reg.19

Art.18, amended: 2004 c.17 Sch.3 para.10

Art.18, applied: SR 2002/301 Reg.14

Art.18, varied: 2002 c.8 (NI) s.1, SR 2003/34 Reg.19

Art.19, applied: SR 2002/301 Reg.14

Art.19, varied: 2002 c.8 (NI) s.1, SR 2003/34 Reg.19

Art.20, applied: SI 2002/1166 Reg.32, SR 2002/301 Reg.14

Art.20, varied: 2002 c.8 (NI) s.1, SR 2003/34 Reg.19

Art.21, applied: SI 2002/1166 Reg.32, SI 2003/403 Reg.24, SR 2002/301 Reg.14, SR 2003/34 Sch.9 para.1, Sch.9 para.2

Art.21, varied: 2002 c.8 (NI) s.1, SI 2003/403 Reg.24, SI 2004/129 Reg.24, SR 2003/34 Reg.19

Art.22, applied: SI 2002/1166 Reg.32, SI 2003/403 Reg.24, SR 2002/301 Reg.14

Art.22, varied: 2002 c.8 (NI) s.1, SI 2003/403 Reg.24, SI 2004/129 Reg.24, SR 2003/34 Reg.19

Art.23, applied: SI 2002/1166 Reg.32, SR 2002/301 Reg.14

Art.23, varied: 2002 c.8 (NI) s.1, SI 2004/129 Reg.24, SR 2003/34 Reg.19

Art.24, applied: SI 2002/1166 Reg.32, SR 2002/301 Reg.14

Art.24, varied: 2002 c.8 (NI) s.1, SI 2004/129 Reg.24, SR 2003/34 Reg.19

Art.25, applied: SI 2002/1166 Reg.32, SR 2002/301 Reg.14

Art.25, varied: 2002 c.8 (NI) s.1, SI 2004/129 Reg.24, SR 2003/34 Reg.19

Art.26, applied: SI 2002/1166 Reg.32, SR 2002/301 Reg.14

Art.26, varied: 2002 c.8 (NI) s.1, SI 2004/129 Reg.24, SR 2003/34 Reg.19

Art.27, applied: SR 2002/301 Reg.14

Art.27, varied: 2002 c.8 (NI) s.1, SR 2003/34 Reg.19

Art.27A, varied: 2002 c.8 (NI) s.1, SI 2004/129 Reg.24, SR 2003/34 Reg.19

Art.28, applied: SI 2002/1166 Reg.32, SI 2003/403 Reg.24, SR 2002/301 Reg.14

NO.

NO.

1978–cont.

1039. Health and Safety at Work (Northern Ireland) Order 1978–*cont.*

Art.28, varied: 2002 c.8 (NI) s.1, SI 2003/403 Reg.24, SI 2004/129 Reg.24, SR 2003/34 Reg.19

Art.29, applied: SI 2003/403 Reg.24

Art.29, varied: 2002 c.8 (NI) s.1, SI 2003/403 Reg.24, SI 2004/129 Reg.24, SR 2003/34 Reg.19

Art.29A, varied: 2002 c.8 (NI) s.1, SI 2004/129 Reg.24, SR 2003/34 Reg.19

Art.30, applied: SI 2003/403 Reg.24

Art.30, varied: 2002 c.8 (NI) s.1, SI 2003/403 Reg.24, SR 2003/34 Reg.19

Art.31, applied: SI 2002/1166 Reg.32, SI 2003/403 Reg.24, Reg.25, SR 2002/301 Reg.14

Art.31, disapplied: SI 2004/129 Reg.24

Art.31, referred to: SI 2003/403 Reg.28

Art.31, varied: 2002 c.8 (NI) s.1, SI 2003/403 Reg.24, SI 2004/129 Reg.24, SR 2003/34 Reg.19

Art.32, applied: SI 2002/1166 Reg.32, SR 2002/301 Reg.14

Art.32, varied: 2002 c.8 (NI) s.1, SI 2004/129 Reg.24, SR 2003/34 Reg.19

Art.33, applied: SI 2002/1166 Reg.32, SI 2003/403 Reg.24, SR 2002/301 Reg.14

Art.33, varied: 2002 c.8 (NI) s.1, SI 2003/403 Reg.24, SI 2004/129 Reg.24, SR 2003/34 Reg.19

Art.34, applied: SI 2002/1166 Reg.32, SI 2003/403 Reg.24, SR 2002/301 Reg.14

Art.34, varied: 2002 c.8 (NI) s.1, SI 2003/403 Reg.24, SI 2004/129 Reg.24, SR 2003/34 Reg.19

Art.34A, applied: SI 2002/1166 Reg.32, SI 2003/403 Reg.24

Art.34A, varied: 2002 c.8 (NI) s.1, SI 2003/403 Reg.24, SR 2003/34 Reg.19

Art.35, applied: SI 2002/1166 Reg.32, SI 2003/403 Reg.24, SR 2002/301 Reg.14

Art.35, varied: 2002 c.8 (NI) s.1, SI 2003/403 Reg.24, SI 2004/129 Reg.24, SR 2003/34 Reg.19

Art.36, applied: SI 2002/1166 Reg.32, SR 2002/301 Reg.14

Art.36, varied: 2002 c.8 (NI) s.1, SI 2004/129 Reg.24, SR 2003/34 Reg.19

Art.37, applied: SI 2002/1166 Reg.32, SR 2002/301 Reg.14

Art.37, varied: 2002 c.8 (NI) s.1, SI 2004/129 Reg.24, SR 2003/34 Reg.19

Art.38, applied: SI 2002/1166 Reg.32, SR 2002/301 Reg.14

Art.38, varied: 2002 c.8 (NI) s.1, SI 2004/129 Reg.24, SR 2003/34 Reg.19

Art.39, applied: SI 2002/1166 Reg.32, SI 2003/403 Reg.24, SR 2002/301 Reg.14

Art.39, varied: 2002 c.8 (NI) s.1, SI 2003/403 Reg.24, SI 2004/129 Reg.24, SR 2003/34 Reg.19

1978–cont.

1039. Health and Safety at Work (Northern Ireland) Order 1978–*cont.*

Art.40, enabled: SR 2002/34, SR 2002/302

Art.40, varied: 2002 c.8 (NI) s.1, SR 2003/34 Reg.19

Art.41, varied: 2002 c.8 (NI) s.1, SR 2003/34 Reg.19

Art.42, varied: 2002 c.8 (NI) s.1, SR 2003/34 Reg.19

Art.43, applied: SR 2002/301 Reg.14

Art.43, varied: 2002 c.8 (NI) s.1, SR 2003/34 Reg.19

Art.44, applied: SI 2002/1166 Reg.32

Art.44, varied: 2002 c.8 (NI) s.1, SI 2004/129 Reg.24, SR 2003/34 Reg.19

Art.45, enabled: SR 2003/152

Art.45, varied: 2002 c.8 (NI) s.1, SR 2003/34 Reg.19

Art.46, amended: 2004 c.17 Sch.3 para.10

Art.46, applied: SR 2002/34, SR 2002/301, SR 2002/302, SR 2003/33, SR 2003/34, SR 2003/35, SR 2003/36, SR 2003/152, SR 2003/288

Art.46, varied: 2002 c.8 (NI) s.1, SR 2003/34 Reg.19

Art.47, varied: 2002 c.8 (NI) s.1, SR 2003/34 Reg.19

Art.47A, varied: 2002 c.8 (NI) s.1, SR 2003/34 Reg.19

Art.52, revoked: 2004 c.17 Sch.4

Art.54, enabled: SR 2003/152

Art.55, enabled: SR 2002/34, SR 2002/301, SR 2002/302, SR 2003/33, SR 2003/34, SR 2003/35, SR 2003/36, SR 2003/152, SR 2003/288

Sch.1, referred to: 2002 c.8 (NI) s.1

Sch.2 para.17A, amended: SI 2003/418 Sch.1 para.7

Sch.2 para.18, substituted: SI 2003/418 Sch.1 para.7

Sch.2 para.19, revoked: SI 2003/418 Sch.1 para.7

Sch.3 para.1, enabled: SR 2002/34, SR 2002/301, SR 2002/302, SR 2003/33, SR 2003/34, SR 2003/35, SR 2003/36, SR 2003/152, SR 2003/288

Sch.3 para.2, enabled: SR 2002/34, SR 2002/301, SR 2003/33, SR 2003/34, SR 2003/35, SR 2003/288

Sch.3 para.3, enabled: SR 2002/302

Sch.3 para.5, enabled: SR 2002/34, SR 2003/33, SR 2003/34, SR 2003/35, SR 2003/152, SR 2003/288

Sch.3 para.6, enabled: SR 2002/34, SR 2003/35

Sch.3 para.7, enabled: SR 2003/33, SR 2003/34, SR 2003/35, SR 2003/288

Sch.3 para.8, enabled: SR 2003/33, SR 2003/34, SR 2003/35, SR 2003/152, SR 2003/288

NO.

1978–cont.

1039. Health and Safety at Work (Northern Ireland) Order 1978–*cont.*
Sch.3 para.9, enabled: SR 2003/33, SR 2003/35
Sch.3 para.10, enabled: SR 2003/33, SR 2003/34, SR 2003/35, SR 2003/152, SR 2003/288
Sch.3 para.11, enabled: SR 2002/34
Sch.3 para.12, enabled: SR 2002/302, SR 2003/33, SR 2003/34, SR 2003/35, SR 2003/288
Sch.3 para.13, enabled: SR 2002/34, SR 2003/33, SR 2003/34, SR 2003/35, SR 2003/152, SR 2003/288
Sch.3 para.14, enabled: SR 2002/301, SR 2002/302, SR 2003/33, SR 2003/34, SR 2003/35, SR 2003/36, SR 2003/288
Sch.3 para.15, enabled: SR 2002/34, SR 2002/301, SR 2002/302, SR 2003/33, SR 2003/34, SR 2003/35, SR 2003/36, SR 2003/152, SR 2003/288
Sch.3 para.17, enabled: SR 2003/152
Sch.3 para.18, enabled: SR 2003/152
Sch.3 para.19, enabled: SR 2003/33, SR 2003/34, SR 2003/152, SR 2003/288

1045. Matrimonial Causes (Northern Ireland) Order 1978
Art.3, see *Dooris v Dooris* [2002] N.I.121 (CA (NI)), Higgins, J.

1045. Matrimonial Causes (Northern Ireland) Order 1978
Art.14, amended: 2004 c.7 Sch.2 para.9, Sch.4 para.10
Art.16, amended: 2004 c.7 Sch.2 para.10, Sch.4 para.11
Art.26, applied: SI 2003/412 Art.14, Art.15, Art.16, Art.85
• Sch.3, amended: 2004 c.7 Sch.2 para.11

1047. Protection of Children (Northern Ireland) Order 1978
Art.3, amended: SI 2003/1247 Sch.1 para.8
Art.3, applied: SI 2002/635 Sch.1 para.3, SI 2002/896 Sch.1 para.70, 2003 c.44 Sch.17 para.82, SI 2003/237 Sch.4 para.8, SI 2003/1184 Reg.8, Sch.2 para.42, SSI 2003/19 Sch.5 para.14
Art.5, applied: 2002 c.26 Sch.4 para.3

1049. Pollution Control and Local Government (Northern Ireland) Order 1978
Art.2, amended: SI 2002/3153 Sch.6 Part I
Art.5, referred to: SI 2002/3153 Art.6
Art.7, applied: SI 2002/3153 Art.6, SR 2002/225 Reg.64, Reg.68, SR 2002/248 Reg.10
Art.7, referred to: SR 2002/271 Reg.2
Art.9, applied: SI 2002/3153 Art.6
Art.10, applied: SR 2003/46 Reg.19
Art.11, applied: SI 2002/3153 Art.6
Art.13, applied: SR 2002/248 Reg.10
Art.30, applied: SR 2003/303 Reg.6
Art.38, amended: SR 2003/46 Sch.11 para.1
Art.40, referred to: SR 2002/303 Art.2

NO.

1978–cont.

1049. Pollution Control and Local Government (Northern Ireland) Order 1978–*cont.*
Art.51, enabled: SR 2002/303
Art.55, amended: SI 2002/3153 Sch.5 para.3, Sch.6 Part I
Art.56, amended: SI 2002/3153 Sch.5 para.3, Sch.6 Part I
Art.57, amended: SI 2002/3153 Sch.5 para.3, Sch.6 Part I
Art.58, amended: SI 2002/3153 Sch.5 para.3
Art.58, revoked (in part): SI 2002/3153 Sch.6 Part I
Art.84, amended: 2002 c.26 Sch.4 para.19
Art.86, enabled: SR 2002/303

1050. Rent (Northern Ireland) Order 1978
Part V, amended: SR 2002/54 Art.2
Part V, varied: SR 2003/62 Art.2
Art.25, amended: SI 2003/412 Sch.1 para.1
Art.25, applied: SI 2003/412 Art.121
Art.25A, substituted: SI 2003/412 Sch.1 para.2
Art.25B, amended: SI 2003/412 Sch.1 para.2
Art.26, amended: SI 2003/412 Sch.1 para.3
Art.27, amended: SI 2003/412 Sch.1 para.3
Art.30, amended: SI 2003/412 Sch.1 para.3
Art.33, amended: SI 2003/412 Sch.1 para.4
Art.33, applied: SR 2003/62
Art.33, enabled: SR 2002/54, SR 2003/62
Art.33, referred to: SR 2002/54
Art.34, amended: SI 2003/412 Sch.1 para.5
Art.38, applied: SI 2003/412 Art.122
Art.39, amended: SI 2003/412 Art.122
Art.46, applied: SI 2003/412 Art.142
Art.48, amended: SI 2003/412 Sch.1 para.6, Sch.4 para.2
Art.72, amended: SI 2003/412 Sch.1 para.7
Sch.6, amended: SI 2003/412 Sch.1 para.8

1096. State Awards Regulations 1978
Reg.4, applied: SI 2003/1994 Reg.3
Reg.7, referred to: SI 2002/1330 Reg.12, SI 2003/1994 Reg.12

1170. Police (Scotland) Amendment (No.2) Regulations 1978
revoked: SSI 2003/220 Sch.1, SSI 2004/257 Sch.4

1225. Industrial Training (Transfer of the Activities of Establishments) (No.2) Order 1978
referred to: SI 2004/368 Sch.1

1275. Child Benefit (General) Amendment Regulations 1978
revoked: SI 2003/493 Sch.2 Part 1

1356. District of Kerrier (Electoral Arrangements) Order 1978
revoked: SI 2002/2604 Art.12
Art.8, referred to: SI 2002/2604 Art.12

1370. District of Carrick (Electoral Arrangements) Order 1978
revoked: SI 2002/2594 Art.12
Art.5, referred to: SI 2002/2594 Art.12

NO.

1978–cont.

1407. Theft (Northern Ireland) Order 1978
Art.3, applied: 2004 c.19 s.14
Art.4, applied: 2004 c.19 s.14

1434. District of Adur (Electoral Arrangements) Order 1978
revoked: SI 2002/2991 Art.10

1438. District of North Norfolk (Electoral Arrangements) Order 1978
revoked: SI 2003/160 Art.10
Art.5, referred to: SI 2003/160 Art.10

1483. Brucellosis and Tuberculosis (England and Wales) Compensation Order 1978
applied: SI 2002/843 Sch.7 para.5, SI 2002/1416 Sch.7 para.4

1485. Brucellosis and Tuberculosis Compensation (Scotland) Order 1978
applied: SSI 2002/255 Sch.7 para.4

1495. District of Wyre Forest (Electoral Arrangements) Order 1978
revoked: SI 2002/2985 Art.10

1505. District of Penwith (Electoral Arrangements) Order 1978
revoked: SI 2002/2593 Art.12
Art.8, referred to: SI 2002/2593 Art.12
Art.9, referred to: SI 2002/2593 Art.12

1510. Police (Scotland) Amendment (No.3) Regulations 1978
revoked: SSI 2004/257 Sch.4

1536. Road Vehicles (Registration and Licensing) (Amendment) Regulations 1978
revoked: SI 2002/2742 Sch.1 Part I

1605. Borough of Oldham (Electoral Arrangements) Order 1978
revoked (in part): SI 2004/124 Art.8

1606. Borough of Solihull (Electoral Arrangements) Order 1978
revoked: SI 2003/2508 Art.11

1612. District of Breckland (Electoral Arrangements) Order 1978
revoked: SI 2002/3221 Art.9

1639. Borough of Barnsley (Electoral Arrangements) Order 1978
revoked (in part): SI 2003/3090 Art.9

1640. District of Wokingham (Electoral Arrangements) Order 1978
revoked: SI 2002/2989 Art.15
Art.5, referred to: SI 2002/2989 Art.15
Art.6, referred to: SI 2002/2989 Art.15

1643. Industrial Training (Transfer of the Activities of Establishments) (No.3) Order 1978
referred to: SI 2004/368 Sch.1

1684. Public Service Vehicles (Lost Property) Regulations 1978
Reg.4, amended: SI 2003/1615 Sch.1 para.39

1689. Social Security (Categorisation of Earners) Regulations 1978
applied: SI 2002/2822 Reg.32
Reg.1, amended: SI 2003/2420 Reg.3

NO.

1978–cont.

1689. Social Security (Categorisation of Earners) Regulations 1978–*cont.*
Reg.2, amended: SI 2004/770 Reg.34
Reg.5, substituted: SI 2003/2420 Reg.4
Sch.1 Part I, amended: SI 2003/736 Reg.3, SI 2004/770 Reg.34
Sch.3, amended: SI 2003/736 Reg.4, SI 2003/2420 Reg.5, SI 2004/770 Reg.34

1694. Borough of Weymouth and Portland (Electoral Arrangements) Order 1978
revoked (in part): SI 2002/2368 Art.9

1722. Borough of Bury (Electoral Arrangements) Order 1978
Art.1, revoked: SI 2004/357 Art.7
Art.2, revoked: SI 2004/357 Art.7
Art.3, revoked: SI 2004/357 Art.7
Art.4, revoked: SI 2004/357 Art.7
Art.5, revoked: SI 2004/357 Art.7
Art.6, revoked: SI 2004/357 Art.7
Art.7, revoked: SI 2004/357 Art.7
Art.9, revoked (in part): SI 2004/357 Art.7

1723. Compressed Acetylene (Importation) Regulations 1978
applied: SI 2003/547 Sch.9 Part 1
referred to: SI 2002/655 Sch.9 Part I, SI 2004/456 Sch.8 Part 1
Reg.1A, substituted: SI 2004/568 Sch.13 para.2

1793. City of Plymouth (Electoral Arrangements) Order 1978
revoked: SI 2002/2236 Art.6, SI 2002/2954 Art.5
Art.7, revoked: SI 2002/2236 Art.6
Art.8, referred to: SI 2002/2236 Art.6

1805. Act of Sederunt (Summary Cause Rules, Sheriff Court) (Amendment No 2) 1978
revoked: SSI 2002/132 Sch.2

1806. District of North Cornwall (Electoral Arrangements) Order 1978
revoked: SI 2002/2603 Art.8
Art.5, referred to: SI 2002/2603 Art.8

1813. Borough of Bournemouth (Electoral Arrangements) Order 1978
revoked: SI 2002/1783 Art.6

1841. Borough of Christchurch (Electoral Arrangements) Order 1978
revoked: SI 2002/2241 Art.6
Art.7, revoked: SI 2002/2241 Art.6
Art.8, referred to: SI 2002/2241 Art.6

1843. District of Leominster (Electoral Arrangements) Order 1978
revoked: SI 2002/187 Art.11

1861. District of Horsham (Electoral Arrangements) Order 1978
revoked: SI 2002/2890 Art.8
Art.8, referred to: SI 2002/2890 Art.8

1893. International Lead and Zinc Study Group (Immunities and Privileges) Order 1978
Art.14, amended: 2002 c.8 s.2

1978–cont.

1901. Saint Lucia Constitution Order 1978

Sch.2 para.10, see *Queen, The v Hughes (Peter)* [2002] UKPC 12, [2002] 2 A.C. 259 (PC (StL)), Lord Rodger of Earlsferry

1907. Health and Personal Social Services (Northern Ireland) Order 1978

Part III, revoked: SI 2003/1250 Sch.9 para.4

Art.3, applied: SI 2003/1593 Sch.1 Part II

Art.4, applied: SI 2003/1593 Sch.1 Part II

Art.8, applied: SI 2003/1250 Sch.6 para.1

1908. Rehabilitation of Offenders (Northern Ireland) Order 1978

Art.3, amended: 2002 c.29 Sch.11 para.8

Art.5, enabled: SR 2003/355

Art.6, amended: 2002 c.26 Sch.11 para.3, Sch.12 para.14

Art.6, revoked (in part): 2002 c.26 Sch.13

Art.8, applied: SI 2003/417 Art.33

Art.8, enabled: SR 2003/355

1910. European Communities (Services of Lawyers) Order 1978

amended: SI 2004/1117 Art.2

Art.2, amended: SI 2004/1117 Art.2, Art.3, SSI 2004/186 Art.3, Art.4

Art.4, amended: SI 2004/1117 Art.2, SSI 2004/186 Art.3

Art.5, amended: SI 2004/1117 Art.2, SSI 2004/186 Art.3

Art.6, amended: SI 2004/1117 Art.2, SSI 2004/186 Art.3

Art.7, amended: SI 2004/1117 Art.2, SSI 2004/186 Art.3

Art.8, amended: SI 2004/1117 Art.2, SSI 2004/186 Art.3

Art.9, amended: SI 2004/1117 Art.2, SSI 2004/186 Art.3

Art.10, amended: SI 2004/1117 Art.2, SSI 2004/186 Art.3

Art.10, applied: SI 2003/435 Art.2

Art.11, amended: SI 2004/1117 Art.2, Art.4, SSI 2004/186 Art.3, Art.5

Art.12, amended: SI 2004/1117 Art.2, SSI 2004/186 Art.3

Art.13, amended: SI 2004/1117 Art.2, SSI 2004/186 Art.3

Art.15, amended: SI 2004/1117 Art.2, SSI 2004/186 Art.3

Art.16, amended: SI 2004/1117 Art.2, SSI 2004/186 Art.3

Art.17, amended: SI 2004/1117 Art.2, SSI 2004/186 Art.3

Art.18, amended: SI 2004/1117 Art.2, SSI 2004/186 Art.3, Art.6

Sch.1 Part 1, amended: SI 2003/435 Sch.4 para.4, SI 2004/1117 Art.5, SSI 2004/186 Art.7

Sch.1 Part 2, amended: SI 2004/1117 Art.5, SSI 2004/186 Art.7

Sch.1 Part 3, amended: SI 2004/1117 Art.5, SSI 2004/186 Art.7

1979

Sale of Goods Act 1979

s.10, see *Alpha Chauffeurs Ltd v Citygate Dealership Ltd (t/a HR Owen)* [2002] EWCA Civ 207, (2003) 100(15) L.S.G. 25 (CA), Chadwick, L.J.

29. General Medical Council (Review Board for Overseas Qualified Practitioners Rules) Order of Council 1979

applied: SI 2002/3135 Sch.2 para.3

Appendix 1 para.10., substituted: SI 2002/3135 Sch.1 para.20, SI 2003/1343 Sch.1

Appendix 1 para.11., amended: SI 2002/3135 Sch.1 para.20, SI 2003/1343 Sch.1

Appendix 1 para.11., revoked (in part): SI 2002/3135 Sch.1 para.20, SI 2003/1343 Sch.1

Appendix 1 para.13., revoked (in part): SI 2003/1343 Sch.1

Appendix 1 para.2., amended: SI 2003/1343 Sch.1

Appendix 1 para.5., substituted: SI 2003/1343 Sch.1

Appendix 1 para.6., revoked: SI 2003/1343 Sch.1

Appendix 1 para.7., substituted: SI 2003/1343 Sch.1

90. Crown Court Rules (Northern Ireland) 1979

r.21, see *R. v Drake (Anthony Patrick)* [2002] N.I. 144 (CA (Crim Div) (NI)), Carswell, L.C.J.

112. General Medical Council (Constitution) Order 1979

revoked: SI 2002/3136 Art.9

361. Price Marking (Food and Drink on Premises) Order 1979

revoked: SI 2003/2253 Art.2

427. Petroleum (Consolidation) Act 1928 (Enforcement) Regulations 1979

Reg.1, amended: SI 2002/2776 Sch.6 para.5

Reg.2, amended: SI 2002/2776 Sch.6 para.5

Reg.2, revoked (in part): SI 2002/2776 Sch.6 para.5

521. European Assembly Election Petition Rules 1979

r.1, substituted: SI 2004/1415 Sch.1 para.1

r.2, amended: SI 2004/1415 Sch.1 para.2

r.4, amended: SI 2004/1415 Sch.1 para.3

r.4, revoked (in part): SI 2004/1415 Sch.1 para.3

r.5, amended: SI 2004/1415 Sch.1 para.4

r.6, amended: SI 2004/1415 Sch.1 para.5

r.7, amended: SI 2004/1415 Sch.1 para.6

r.8, revoked: SI 2004/1415 Sch.1 para.7

r.10, amended: SI 2004/1415 Sch.1 para.8

r.11, amended: SI 2004/1415 Sch.1 para.9

r.12, amended: SI 2004/1415 Sch.1 para.10

r.13, amended: SI 2004/1415 Sch.1 para.11

r.14, amended: SI 2004/1415 Sch.1 para.12

r.16, revoked: SI 2004/1415 Sch.1 para.13

NO.

1979–cont.

521. European Assembly Election Petition Rules 1979–*cont.*

r.18, amended: SI 2003/971 r.2, SI 2004/1415 Sch.1 para.14

r.20, amended: SI 2004/1415 Sch.1 para.15

Sch.1, amended: SI 2004/1415 Sch.1 para.16

591. Social Security (Contributions) Regulations 1979

Reg.3, see *RCI (Europe) Ltd v Woods (Inspector of Taxes)* [2003] S.T.C. (S.C.D.) 128 (Sp Comm), John F Avery Jones

Reg.4, see *RCI (Europe) Ltd v Woods (Inspector of Taxes)* [2003] S.T.C. (S.C.D.) 128 (Sp Comm), John F Avery Jones

Reg.6A, see *RCI (Europe) Ltd v Woods (Inspector of Taxes)* [2003] S.T.C. (S.C.D.) 128 (Sp Comm), John F Avery Jones

Reg.19, see *Ableway Ltd v Inland Revenue Commissioners* [2002] S.T.C. (S.C.D.) 1 (Sp Comm), N Brice; see *Channel 5 TV Group Ltd v Morehead (Inspector of Taxes)* [2003] S.T.C. (S.C.D.) 327 (Sp Comm), Nuala Brice; see *Frost Skip Hire (Newcastle) Ltd v Wood (Inspector of Taxes)* [2004] S.T.C. (S.C.D.) 387 (Sp Comm), MS Johnson (Chairman)

597. Social Security (Overlapping Benefits) Regulations 1979

applied: SI 2002/1792 Reg.15

Reg.2, amended: SI 2003/937 Reg.2

Reg.4, amended: SI 2002/2497 Sch.2 para.1

Reg.8, amended: SI 2003/136 Reg.2, SI 2004/565 Reg.8

Reg.8, revoked (in part): SI 2003/136 Reg.2

Reg.12, amended: SI 2002/2497 Sch.2 para.1

Sch.1, amended: SI 2002/2497 Sch.2 para.1

Sch.1 para.1, amended: SI 2002/2497 Sch.2 para.1

Sch.1 para.2, amended: SI 2002/2497 Sch.2 para.1

Sch.1 para.3, amended: SI 2002/2497 Sch.2 para.1

Sch.1 para.4, amended: SI 2002/2497 Sch.2 para.1

Sch.1 para.7, amended: SI 2002/2497 Sch.2 para.1

642. Social Security (Widow's Benefit and Retirement Pensions) Regulations 1979

Reg.1A, revoked (in part): SI 2003/937 Reg.2

Reg.6, amended: SI 2003/937 Reg.2

Reg.6, revoked (in part): SI 2003/937 Reg.2

Reg.17, amended: SI 2002/2497 Sch.2 para.1

676. Social Security (Earnings Factor) Regulations 1979

Sch.1 Part I para.1, amended: SI 2003/608 Reg.2

710. Borough of Great Yarmouth (Electoral Arrangements) Order 1979

revoked: SI 2002/3228 Art.12

NO.

1979–cont.

767. Police (Scotland) Amendment Regulations 1979

revoked: SSI 2004/257 Sch.4

791. Forestry (Felling of Trees) Regulations 1979

Reg.3, amended: SI 2003/2155 Sch.1 para.26

Reg.4, substituted: SI 2002/226 Reg.2

Sch.2, substituted: SI 2002/226 Reg.2

Sch.2 para.1, substituted: SI 2002/226 Reg.2

Sch.2 para.2, substituted: SI 2002/226 Reg.2

Sch.2 para.3, substituted: SI 2002/226 Reg.2

Sch.2 para.4, substituted: SI 2002/226 Reg.2

Sch.2 para.5, substituted: SI 2002/226 Reg.2

Sch.2 para.6, substituted: SI 2002/226 Reg.2

Sch.2 para.7, substituted: SI 2002/226 Reg.2

Sch.2 para.8, substituted: SI 2002/226 Reg.2

Sch.2 para.9, substituted: SI 2002/226 Reg.2

793. Industrial Training (Transfer of the Activities of Establishments) Order 1979

referred to: SI 2004/368 Sch.1

844. General Medical Council (Registration Regulations) Order of Council 1979

revoked: SI 2003/1342 Art.2

Sch.1 Part III para.9, applied: SI 2003/1342 Sch.1

Sch.1 Part III para.9, referred to: SI 2003/1342 Sch.1

911. INTELSAT (Immunities and Privileges) Order 1979

Art.14, amended: 2002 c.8 s.2

924. Inheritance (Provision for Family and Dependants) (Northern Ireland) Order 1979

Art.4, applied: SI 2003/412 Art.85

925. Pneumoconiosis, etc., (Workers Compensation) (Northern Ireland) Order 1979

applied: SR 2003/28 Reg.15

Art.3, enabled: SR 2002/133

Art.4, enabled: SR 2002/133

Art.11, enabled: SR 2002/133

931. Carriage by Air Acts (Application of Provisions) (Second Amendment) Order 1979

revoked: SI 2004/1899 Sch.4

1027. Borough of Doncaster (Electoral Arrangements) Order 1979

revoked (in part): SI 2004/121 Art.14

1028. Borough of Trafford (Electoral Arrangements) Order 1979

revoked (in part): SI 2004/720 Art.7

NO.

1979–cont.

1112. District of Harborough (Electoral Arrangements) Order 1979
revoked: SI 2002/2597 Art.8
Art.8, referred to: SI 2002/2597 Art.8

1198. Motor Vehicles (Authorisation of Special Types) General Order 1979
revoked: SI 2003/1998 Art.2
Art.18, applied: SI 2003/1998 Sch.1 para.37
Art.26, amended: SI 2003/1615 Sch.1 para.40

1254. Lead in Food Regulations 1979
revoked (in part): SI 2002/890 Sch.1, SI 2002/1886 Sch.1

1263. Police (Scotland) Amendment (No.2) Regulations 1979
revoked: SSI 2004/257 Sch.4

1266. Borough of Worthing (Electoral Arrangements) Orde 1979
revoked: SI 2002/2884 Art.7
Art.8, referred to: SI 2002/2884 Art.7
Art.9, referred to: SI 2002/2884 Art.7

1295. District of West Norfolk (Electoral Arrangements) Order 1979
revoked: SI 2002/3227 Art.8

1320. Borough of Calderdale (Electoral Arrangements) Order 1979
revoked (in part): SI 2003/3088 Art.8

1321. Borough of Bolton (Electoral Arrangements) Order 1979
Art.1, revoked: SI 2004/356 Art.9
Art.2, revoked: SI 2004/356 Art.9
Art.3, revoked: SI 2004/356 Art.9
Art.4, revoked: SI 2004/356 Art.9
Art.5, revoked: SI 2004/356 Art.9
Art.6, revoked: SI 2004/356 Art.9
Art.7, revoked: SI 2004/356 Art.9
Art.9, revoked (in part): SI 2004/356 Art.9

1322. City of Coventry (Electoral Arrangements) Order 1979
revoked (in part): SI 2003/2507 Art.7

1323. Borough of Rotherham (Electoral Arrangements) Order 1979
revoked (in part): SI 2004/123 Art.14

1324. Borough of Stockport (Electoral Arrangements) Order 1979
Art.1, revoked: SI 2004/360 Art.7, SI 2004/361 Art.8
Art.2, revoked: SI 2004/360 Art.7, SI 2004/361 Art.8
Art.3, revoked: SI 2004/360 Art.7, SI 2004/361 Art.8
Art.4, revoked: SI 2004/360 Art.7, SI 2004/361 Art.8
Art.5, revoked: SI 2004/360 Art.7, SI 2004/361 Art.8
Art.6, revoked: SI 2004/360 Art.7, SI 2004/361 Art.8
Art.7, revoked: SI 2004/360 Art.7, SI 2004/361 Art.8
Art.9, revoked (in part): SI 2004/360 Art.7, SI 2004/361 Art.8

NO.

1979–cont.

1341. Borough of Rochdale (Electoral Arrangements) Order 1979
revoked (in part): SI 2004/125 Art.7

1346. Borough of Reading (Electoral Arrangements) Order 1979
revoked: SI 2002/2892 Art.7
Art.8, referred to: SI 2002/2892 Art.7
Art.9, referred to: SI 2002/2892 Art.7

1347. Borough of Poole (Electoral Arrangements) Order 1979
revoked: SI 2002/2887 Art.6
Art.8, referred to: SI 2002/2887 Art.6

1348. Borough of St Helens (Electoral Arrangements) Order 1979
revoked (in part): SI 2003/1979 Art.11

1368. Borough of Tameside (Electoral Arrangements) Order 1979
Art.1, revoked: SI 2004/127 Art.7
Art.7, revoked: SI 2004/127 Art.7
Art.9, revoked (in part): SI 2004/127 Art.7

1379. Taximeters (EEC Requirements) Regulations 1979
Reg.6, applied: SI 2004/1300 Reg.5

1411. City of Liverpool (Electoral Arrangements) Order 1979
revoked (in part): SI 2003/2505 Art.7

1472. Borough of Walsall (Electoral Arrangements) Order 1979
revoked (in part): SI 2003/2511 Art.7

1474. City of Leicester (Electoral Arrangements) Order 1979
revoked: SI 2002/2988 Art.6

1496. Borough of Torbay (Electoral Arrangements) Order 1979
revoked: SI 2002/1786 Art.6

1523. Borough of Wirral (Electoral Arrangements) Order 1979
revoked (in part): SI 2003/1980 Art.7

1524. Borough of Wigan (Electoral Arrangements) Order 1979
Art.1, revoked: SI 2004/365 Art.7
Art.2, revoked: SI 2004/365 Art.7
Art.3, revoked: SI 2004/365 Art.7
Art.4, revoked: SI 2004/365 Art.7
Art.5, revoked: SI 2004/365 Art.7
Art.6, revoked: SI 2004/365 Art.7
Art.7, revoked: SI 2004/365 Art.7
Art.9, revoked (in part): SI 2004/365 Art.7

1573. Statutory Rules (Northern Ireland) Order 1979
applied: 2002 c.17 Part 3, 2002 c.21 s.65, 2002 c.22 s.46, 2002 c.26 s.90, SI 2002/790 Sch.1 para.4, Sch.2 para.2, Sch.2 para.3, Sch.3 para.3, Sch.3 para.4, Sch.3 para.7, SI 2002/2843 Art.8, 2003 c.6 s.44, 2003 c.32 s.73, 2003 c.33 s.36, s.40, SI 2003/431 Sch.1 para.16, Sch.1 para.17, 2004 c.4 s.21, 2004 c.7 s.24, 2004 c.17 s.2, s.12
disapplied: 2002 c.1 (NI) Sch.2 para.5, SI 2003/410 Art.27, SI 2003/418 Art.8

NO.

1979–cont.

1573. Statutory Rules (Northern Ireland) Order 1979–*cont.*
Sch.1, amended: SI 2003/419 Sch.1 para.10

1585. Medicines (Contact Lens Fluids and Other Substances) (Exemption from Licences) Order 1979
Art.1, amended: SI 2002/3135 Sch.1 para.21

1615. City of Sheffield (Electoral Arrangements) Order 1979
revoked (in part): SI 2004/120 Art.10

1616. City of Leeds (Electoral Arrangements) Order 1979
revoked (in part): SI 2003/3089 Art.9

1634. City of Bradford (Electoral Arrangements) Orde 1979
revoked (in part): SI 2004/122 Art.9

1641. Lead in Food (Scotland) Regulations 1979
revoked: SSI 2002/267 Sch.1

1644. National Health Service (Vocational Training) Regulations 1979
Reg.8, applied: SI 2003/1250 Sch.6 para.1

1670. Borough of Restormel (Electoral Arrangements) Order 1979
revoked: SI 2002/2601 Art.11
Art.8, referred to: SI 2002/2601 Art.11

1678. Exchange of Securities (General) Rules 1979
disapplied: SI 2004/1611 Reg.29
r.3, amended: SI 2002/2521 Sch.2 Part II, SI 2004/1662 Sch.1 para.24
r.5, amended: SI 2004/1662 Sch.1 para.24
r.6, amended: SI 2004/1662 Sch.1 para.24
r.7, amended: SI 2004/1662 Sch.1 para.24
r.12, substituted: SI 2004/1662 Sch.1 para.24

1702. Importation of Birds, Poultry and Hatching Eggs Order 1979
Art.4, applied: SI 2004/853 Sch.6
Art.4, disapplied: SI 2004/853 Sch.6
Art.5, disapplied: SI 2004/853 Sch.6
Art.6, disapplied: SI 2004/853 Sch.6
Art.7, disapplied: SI 2004/853 Sch.6
Art.9, disapplied: SI 2004/853 Sch.6
Art.10, disapplied: SI 2004/853 Sch.6
Art.11, disapplied: SI 2004/853 Sch.6
Art.12, disapplied: SI 2004/853 Sch.6

1709. Building Regulations (Northern Ireland) Order 1979
Sch.1, amended: 2003 c.21 Sch.17 para.51

1714. Perjury (Northern Ireland) Order 1979
Art.3, applied: 2003 c.32 s.30, s.31
Art.8, applied: 2004 c.19 s.14
Art.8, referred to: 2004 c.19 s.14
Art.9, applied: 2004 c.19 s.14
Art.9, referred to: 2004 c.19 s.14
Art.10, applied: 2002 c.29 s.360, Sch.6 para.2, SI 2002/3150 Art.23
Art.12, applied: 2004 c.19 s.14

NO.

1980

12. Importation of Embryos, Ova and Semen Order 1980
disapplied: SI 2004/853 Sch.6, SI 2004/1214 Reg.67, SI 2004/1740 Reg.67, SI 2004/2640 Reg.67
Art.4, applied: SI 2004/853 Sch.6

14. Importation of Animal Products and Poultry Products Order 1980
disapplied: SI 2002/1227 Reg.63, SI 2002/1387 Reg.63, SI 2003/3177 Reg.67, SI 2004/1214 Reg.67, SI 2004/1430 Reg.67, SI 2004/1740 Reg.67, SI 2004/2640 Reg.67, SSI 2002/445 Reg.63

30. National Health Service (Vocational Training) (Scotland) Regulations 1980
Reg.8, applied: SI 2003/1250 Sch.6 para.1

51. Consumer Credit (Total Charge for Credit) Regulations 1980
applied: SI 2002/195 Reg.39, SI 2002/3200 Reg.38, SR 2002/224 Reg.40
Part IV, referred to: SI 2004/1484 Sch.1 para.1
Reg.7, applied: SI 2004/1484 Sch.1 para.3, Sch.1 para.4
Reg.11, applied: SI 2004/1483 Reg.1
Reg.11, disapplied: SI 2004/1483 Reg.1

63. City of Salford (Electoral Arrangements) Order 1980
revoked (in part): SI 2004/126 Art.7
Art.1, revoked: SI 2004/359 Art.7
Art.2, revoked: SI 2004/359 Art.7
Art.3, revoked: SI 2004/359 Art.7
Art.4, revoked: SI 2004/359 Art.7
Art.5, revoked: SI 2004/359 Art.7
Art.6, revoked: SI 2004/359 Art.7
Art.7, revoked: SI 2004/359 Art.7
Art.9, revoked (in part): SI 2004/359 Art.7

85. Borough of Wolverhampton (Electoral Arrangements) Order 1980
revoked: SI 2003/2509 Art.7

138. Borough of Hinckley and Bosworth (Electoral Arrangements) Order 1980
revoked: SI 2002/2888 Art.9

145. African Swine Fever Order 1980
revoked (in part): SI 2003/2913 Art.19, SI 2003/3273 Art.19, SSI 2003/586 Art.19
Sch.1, revoked (in part): SI 2003/2913 Art.19, SSI 2003/586 Art.19

146. African Swine Fever (Compensation) Order 1980
Art.2, amended: SSI 2003/586 Art.19

178. Church Representation Rules (Amendment) Resolution 1980
referred to: SI 2004/1889

231. District of Redditch (Electoral Arrangements) Order 1980
revoked: SI 2002/2986 Art.7
Art.8, referred to: SI 2002/2986 Art.7
Art.9, referred to: SI 2002/2986 Art.7

NO.

1980–cont.

346. Rules of the Supreme Court (Northern Ireland) 1980

Ord.11 r.1, see *ICS Computing Ltd v Capital One Services Inc* [2002] N.I. 76 (QBD (NI)), Weatherup, J.

Ord.62 r.3, see *O'Neill v J Donal Murphy (A Firm) (t/a Murphy Kerr & Co Solicitors)* [2004] N.I. 1 (QBD (NI)), Weatherup, J.

362. National Health Service (Superannuation) Regulations 1980

see *Quirk v Burton Hospitals NHS Trust* [2002] EWCA Civ 149, [2002] 1 C.M.L.R. 47 (CA), Mummery, L.J.

Reg.44, applied: SI 2002/1311 Reg.6

Reg.49, applied: SI 2002/1311 Reg.5

Reg.50, applied: SI 2002/1311 Reg.5

397. County Courts (Northern Ireland) Order 1980

Art.2, amended: 2002 c.26 Sch.13

Art.3, applied: 2002 c.26 s.9

Art.4, amended: 2002 c.26 Sch.5 para.13

Art.5, amended: 2002 c.26 Sch.5 para.14

Art.6, amended: 2002 c.26 Sch.5 para.15

Art.7, amended: 2002 c.26 Sch.5 para.16

Art.12, varied: SR 2003/73 Sch.1

Art.13, varied: SR 2003/73 Sch.1

Art.14, varied: SR 2003/73 Sch.1

Art.16, varied: SR 2003/73 Sch.1

Art.21, applied: SR 2003/28 Sch.5 para.16

Art.30, amended: 2002 c.26 s.74

Art.46, amended: 2002 c.26 s.73, Sch.5 para.17

Art.46, applied: SR 2002/240, SR 2002/255, SR 2003/272

Art.47, enabled: SR 2002/240, SR 2002/255, SR 2002/412, SR 2003/272

Art.55, applied: 2002 c.26 s.80, 2004 c.4 Sch.3 para.3

Art.56, amended: 2002 c.26 Sch.5 para.18

Art.56, applied: 2002 c.26 Sch.4 para.2

Art.58, amended: 2002 c.26 Sch.5 para.19

Art.61, amended: 2002 c.26 s.75

Art.64, see *Motor Insurers Bureau v Monaghan* [2002] N.I. 162 (QBD (NI)), Kerr, J.

408. City of Wakefield (Electoral Arrangements) Order 1980

revoked (in part): SI 2003/3087 Art.9

428. District of Beaconsfield (Electoral Arrangements) Order 1980

revoked: SI 2002/1785 Art.12

429. Borough of Slough (Electoral Arrangements) Order 1980

revoked: SI 2002/2600 Art.7

Art.8, referred to: SI 2002/2600 Art.7

Art.9, referred to: SI 2002/2600 Art.7

Art.10, revoked: SI 2002/2600 Art.7

430. Borough of South Tyneside (Electoral Arrangements) Order 1980

Art.1, revoked: SI 2004/358 Art.7

Art.2, revoked: SI 2004/358 Art.7

NO.

1980–cont.

430. Borough of South Tyneside (Electoral Arrangements) Order 1980–*cont.*

Art.3, revoked: SI 2004/358 Art.7

Art.4, revoked: SI 2004/358 Art.7

Art.5, revoked: SI 2004/358 Art.7

Art.6, revoked: SI 2004/358 Art.7

Art.7, revoked: SI 2004/358 Art.7

Art.9, revoked (in part): SI 2004/358 Art.7

447. Borough of Dudley (Electoral Arrangements) Order 1980

Art.1, revoked: SI 2003/2767 Art.7

Art.2, revoked: SI 2003/2767 Art.7

Art.3, revoked: SI 2003/2767 Art.7

Art.4, revoked: SI 2003/2767 Art.7

Art.5, revoked: SI 2003/2767 Art.7

Art.6, revoked: SI 2003/2767 Art.7

Art.7, revoked: SI 2003/2767 Art.7

Art.9, revoked (in part): SI 2003/2767 Art.7

455. Act of Sederunt (Summary Cause Rules Sheriff Court) (Amendment) Order 1980

revoked: SSI 2002/132 Sch.2

538. Merchant Shipping (Life-Saving Appliances) Regulations 1980

s.43, see *Ziemniak v ETPM Deep Sea Ltd* [2003] EWCA Civ 636, [2003] 2 All E.R. (Comm) 283 (CA), Kay, L.J.

Sch.16 Part II, see *Ziemniak v ETPM Deep Sea Ltd* [2003] EWCA Civ 636, [2003] 2 All E.R. (Comm) 283 (CA), Kay, L.J.

563. Domestic Proceedings (Northern Ireland) Order 1980

applied: SI 2003/435 Sch.2 para.2

570. Merchant Shipping Act 1979 (Jersey) Order 1980

revoked: SI 2004/1284 Sch.1

594. City of Birmingham (Electoral Arrangements) Order 1980

Art.1, revoked: SI 2003/2769 Art.7

Art.2, revoked: SI 2003/2769 Art.7

Art.3, revoked: SI 2003/2769 Art.7

Art.4, revoked: SI 2003/2769 Art.7

Art.5, revoked: SI 2003/2769 Art.7

Art.6, revoked: SI 2003/2769 Art.7

Art.7, revoked: SI 2003/2769 Art.7

Art.9, revoked (in part): SI 2003/2769 Art.7

643. District of West Dorset (Electoral Arrangements) Order 1980

revoked: SI 2002/2370 Art.10

645. Protection of Wrecks (Designation No 1) Order 1980

revoked: SI 2004/2395 Sch.2 para.1

652. District of Arun (Electoral Arrangements) Order 1980

revoked: SI 2002/2885 Art.12

653. District of Mid Sussex (Electoral Arrangements) Order 1980

revoked: SI 2002/2891 Art.12

NO.

NO.

1980–cont.

704. Criminal Justice (Northern Ireland) Order 1980

Art.9, applied: SI 2002/896 Sch.1 para.72, 2003 c.44 Sch.17 para.84, SI 2003/1184 Sch.2 para.43, SSI 2003/19 Sch.5 para.15

Art.9, referred to: SI 2003/237 Sch.4 para.9

Sch.1, revoked: 2002 c.26 Sch.13

709. Double Taxation Relief (Taxes on Income) (Canada) Order 1980

Sch.1, varied: SI 2003/2619 Sch.1 Part I

733. Royal Borough of Windsor and Maidenhead (Electoral Arrangements) Order 1980

revoked (in part): SI 2002/2372 Art.11

Art.8, referred to: SI 2002/2372 Art.11

756. Borough of Sunderland (Electoral Arrangements) Order 1980

Art.1, revoked: SI 2004/362 Art.7

Art.2, revoked: SI 2004/362 Art.7

Art.3, revoked: SI 2004/362 Art.7

Art.4, revoked: SI 2004/362 Art.7

Art.5, revoked: SI 2004/362 Art.7

Art.6, revoked: SI 2004/362 Art.7

Art.7, revoked: SI 2004/362 Art.7

Art.9, revoked (in part): SI 2004/362 Art.7

757. District of Caradon (Electoral Arrangements) Order 1980

revoked: SI 2002/2602 Art.10

Art.4, referred to: SI 2002/2602 Art.10

777. Borough of Charnwood (Electoral Arrangements) Order 1980

revoked: SI 2002/2886 Art.11

Art.8, referred to: SI 2002/2886 Art.11

778. District of North West Leicestershire (Electoral Arrangements) Order 1980

revoked: SI 2002/2598 Art.9

Art.8, referred to: SI 2002/2598 Art.9

842. District of Wycombe (Electoral Arrangements) Order1 1980

revoked: SI 2002/1781 Art.9

Art.8, referred to: SI 2002/1781 Art.9

918. Education (Middle Schools) Regulations 1980

revoked (in part): SI 2002/1983 Reg.7

941. General Medical Council (Legal Assessors) Rules 1980

revoked: SI 2004/2625 r.6

r.4, see *Walker v General Medical Council* [2002] UKPC 57, (2003) 71 B.M.L.R. 53 (PC (UK)), Gault, J.

1045. Child Benefit (General) Amendment Regulations 1980

revoked: SI 2003/493 Sch.2 Part 1

1050. Police (Scotland) Amendment Regulations 1980

revoked: SSI 2004/257 Sch.4

1054. City of Newcastle upon Tyne (Electoral Arrangements) Order 1980

Art.1, revoked: SI 2004/363 Art.11, SI 2004/364 Art.7

1980–cont.

1054. City of Newcastle upon Tyne (Electoral Arrangements) Order 1980– cont.

Art.2, revoked: SI 2004/363 Art.11, SI 2004/364 Art.7

Art.3, revoked: SI 2004/363 Art.11, SI 2004/364 Art.7

Art.4, revoked: SI 2004/363 Art.11, SI 2004/364 Art.7

Art.5, revoked: SI 2004/363 Art.11, SI 2004/364 Art.7

Art.6, revoked: SI 2004/363 Art.11, SI 2004/364 Art.7

Art.7, revoked: SI 2004/363 Art.11, SI 2004/364 Art.7

Art.9, revoked (in part): SI 2004/364 Art.7

1120. Pensions Appeal Tribunals (England and Wales) Rules 1980

r.5, see *Secretary of State for Defence v Pensions Appeal Tribunals (England and Wales)* [2004] EWHC 141, [2004] 2 All E.R. 159 (QBD (Admin Ct)), Newman, J.

r.12, amended: SI 2002/3135 Sch.1 para.22

r.37, see *Secretary of State for Defence v Pensions Appeal Tribunals (England and Wales)* [2004] EWHC 141, [2004] 2 All E.R. 159 (QBD (Admin Ct)), Newman, J.

1128. District of Wimborne (Electoral Arrangements) Order 1980

revoked: SI 2002/2238 Art.15

Art.3, revoked: SI 2002/2238 Art.15

Art.4, referred to: SI 2002/2238 Art.15

1177. National Health Service (Superannuation) (Scotland) Regulations 1980

Reg.27, see *Secretary of State for Scotland v Turner* 2003 S.C. 525 (1 Div), Lord Cullen L.P., Lord Osborne, Lord Weir

Reg.46, applied: SSI 2003/344 Reg.6

Reg.51, applied: SSI 2003/344 Reg.6

Reg.52, applied: SSI 2003/344 Reg.6

1297. County of Shropshire (Electoral Arrangements) Order 1980

revoked: SI 2004/2817 Art.6

1306. Protection of Wrecks (Designation No 1 Order 1980) (Amendment) Order 1980

revoked: SI 2004/2395 Sch.2 para.2

1340. District of East Cambridgeshire (Electoral Arrangements) Order 1980

revoked: SI 2002/2596 Art.10

Art.4, referred to: SI 2002/2596 Art.10

1341. District of Blaby (Electoral Arrangements) Order 1980

Art.4, referred to: SI 2002/2882 Art.13

Art.4, revoked: SI 2002/2882 Art.13

1343. District of South Oxfordshire (Electoral Arrangements) Order 1980

revoked: SI 2002/49 Art.8

1344. County of Nottinghamshire (Electoral Arrangements) Order 1980

revoked: SI 2004/2816 Art.6

NO.

1980–cont.

1375. Housing (Right to Buy) (Designated Rural Areas and Designated Regions) (Wales) Order 1980
revoked: SI 2003/54 Art.5

1402. Borough of Knowsley (Electoral Arrangements) Order 1980
revoked (in part): SI 2003/2156 Art.12

1413. Land Registration (Scotland) Rules 1980
Part I r.2, amended: SSI 2004/476 r.3
Part II r.4, amended: SSI 2004/476 r.4
Part II r.7, amended: SSI 2004/476 r.5
Part II r.7, revoked (in part): SSI 2004/476 r.5
Part III r.9, amended: SSI 2004/476 r.6
Sch.1, amended: SSI 2004/476 Sch.1

1463. Borough of Kirklees (Electoral Arrangements) Order 1980
revoked (in part): SI 2003/3091 Art.9

1487. District of North Dorset (Electoral Arrangements) Order 1980
revoked: SI 2002/2239 Art.9
Art.3, revoked: SI 2002/2239 Art.9
Art.4, referred to: SI 2002/2239 Art.9

1510. Merchant Shipping Act 1979 (Bermuda) Order 1980
revoked: SI 2002/3147 Art.2

1520. Prevention of Oil Pollution Act 1971 (Bermuda) Order 1980
revoked: SI 2002/3147 Art.2

1521. Prevention of Oil Pollution (Enforcement of Convention) (Bermuda) Order 1980
revoked: SI 2002/3147 Art.2

1522. Prevention of Oil Pollution (Shipping Casualties) (Bermuda) Order 1980
revoked: SI 2002/3147 Art.2

1528. Double Taxation Relief (Taxes on Income) (Canada) (No.2) Order 1980
Sch.1, referred to: SI 2003/2619 Art.2

1647. Housing (Forms) (Scotland) Regulations 1980
Sch.1, amended: SSI 2003/335 Reg.1, SSI 2003/336 Reg.1, SSI 2003/337 Reg.1, SSI 2003/338 Reg.1, SSI 2003/420 Reg.1

1702. County of Staffordshire (Electoral Arrangements) Order 1980
revoked: SI 2004/2818 Art.7

1753. Industrial Training (Transfer of the Activities of Establishments) (No.2) Order 1980
referred to: SI 2004/368 Sch.1

1830. County of Surrey (Electoral Arrangements) Order (1980) 1980
revoked: SI 2004/2819 Art.8

1923. Medicines (Sale or Supply) (Miscellaneous Provisions) Regulations 1980
Reg.1, amended: SI 2002/2469 Sch.1 para.37, SI 2003/698 Reg.2, SI 2004/1771 Sch.1 para.54
Reg.5, amended: SI 2003/698 Reg.3
Reg.5, revoked (in part): SI 2003/698 Reg.3

NO.

1980–cont.

1923. Medicines (Sale or Supply) (Miscellaneous Provisions) Regulations 1980–*cont.*
Reg.6, amended: SI 2003/698 Reg.4
Sch.1, amended: SI 2003/698 Reg.5, SI 2004/696 Art.3
Sch.2 para.1, amended: SI 2003/698 Reg.6
Sch.2 para.3, amended: SI 2003/698 Reg.6
Sch.2 para.4, amended: SI 2003/698 Reg.6

1924. Medicines (Pharmacy and General Sale Exemption) Order 1980
Art.1, amended: SI 2002/880 Sch.1 para.4, SI 2002/2469 Sch.1 para.38, SI 2003/697 Art.2, SI 2003/1590 Sch.1 para.24, SI 2004/1 Art.2, SI 2004/696 Art.3, SI 2004/1190 Art.2, SI 2004/1771 Sch.1 para.53
Art.4A, amended: SI 2004/696 Sch.1 para.1
Art.4AA, added: SI 2004/1 Art.3
Art.4B, amended: SI 2004/865 Sch.1 para.2, SI 2004/1016 Sch.1 para.2, SI 2004/2261 Sch.1 para.1, SSI 2004/212 Sch.1 para.1
Art.4B, revoked (in part): SI 2004/1016 Sch.1 para.2
Art.4C, added: SI 2003/697 Art.3
Art.4D, added: SI 2003/697 Art.3
Sch.1 Part II, amended: SI 2002/2469 Sch.5, SI 2004/1771 Sch.1 para.53
Sch.3 Part II, amended: SI 2004/696 Art.3
Sch.3 Part IIA, added: SI 2003/697 Art.4
Sch.3 Part III, amended: SI 2002/880 Sch.1 para.5, SI 2003/1590 Sch.1 para.24, SI 2004/1190 Art.3

1951. Veterinary Surgeons Qualifications (EEC Recognition) Order 1980
revoked: SI 2003/2919 Art.13

1961. Double Taxation Relief (Taxes on Income) (Netherlands) Order 1980
Art.10, see *Oce van der Grinten NV v Inland Revenue Commissioners (C58/01)* [2003] S.T.C. 1248 (ECJ), Judge Wathelet (President)

1985. County of Derbyshire (Electoral Arrangements) Order 1980
revoked (in part): SI 2004/2811 Art.5

2010. Town and Country Planning (Prescription of County Matters) Regulations 1980
applied: SI 2003/1033 Reg.3
revoked (in part): SI 2003/1033 Reg.3

1981

67. Police (Scotland) Amendment Regulations 1981
revoked: SSI 2004/257 Sch.4

85. County of Kent (Electoral Arrangements) Order 1981
revoked: SI 2004/2815 Art.6

118. County of Warwickshire (Electoral Arrangements) Order 1981
revoked: SI 2004/2820 Art.7

NO.

NO.

1981–cont.

141. County of Essex (Electoral Arrangements) Order 1981
revoked: SI 2004/2813 Art.6

154. Road Traffic (Northern Ireland) Order 1981
referred to: 2003 c.32 Sch.5 para.5
Part II, applied: 2003 c.32 s.69, s.82, SI 2004/1267 Sch.1 para.37, SR 2003/83 Art.2
Art.4, amended: 2003 c.32 Sch.5 para.6, SI 2003/2903 Sch.1 para.2, SR 2002/374 Sch.1 para.1
Art.5, enabled: SR 2002/51, SR 2002/383, SR 2003/64, SR 2003/83, SR 2003/100, SR 2003/183
Art.9, amended: SI 2003/2903 Sch.1 para.3, SR 2002/374 Sch.1 para.2
Art.9, enabled: SR 2003/64
Art.10, amended: SI 2003/2903 Art.6, SR 2002/374 Sch.1 para.3
Art.13, amended: SI 2003/2903 Art.5, Sch.1 para.4, SR 2002/374 Sch.1 para.4
Art.13, applied: 2003 c.32 s.69
Art.14, amended: SR 2002/374 Sch.1 para.5
Art.15, amended: SI 2003/2903 Art.5, SR 2002/374 Sch.1 para.6
Art.15A, amended: SR 2002/374 Sch.1 para.7
Art.15A, applied: 2003 c.32 s.65
Art.16, amended: SI 2003/2903 Sch.1 para.5
Art.18, amended: SI 2003/2903 Art.5
Art.18A, added: SI 2003/2903 Art.3
Art.19C, amended: SI 2003/2903 Sch.1 para.6, SR 2002/374 Sch.1 para.8
Art.19C, applied: SR 2002/51, SR 2002/383, SR 2003/100
Art.19C, enabled: SR 2002/383, SR 2003/64, SR 2003/183
Art.19D, amended: SI 2003/2903 Sch.1 para.7, Sch.2, SR 2002/374 Sch.1 para.9
Art.19D, applied: SR 2002/328 Reg.2
Art.19D, enabled: SR 2002/328
Art.19E, amended: SI 2003/2903 Sch.1 para.8
Art.19E, revoked (in part): SI 2003/2903 Sch.1 para.8, Sch.2
Art.19F, added: SI 2003/2903 Art.4
Art.19G, added: SI 2003/2903 Art.6
Art.19H, added: SI 2003/2903 Art.6
Art.31A, amended: SI 2003/1099 Reg.4
Art.31A, applied: SI 2003/1959 Reg.13
Art.31A, enabled: SR 2003/124, SR 2003/275
Art.31D, enabled: SR 2003/124, SR 2003/275
Art.61, enabled: SR 2002/49, SR 2002/384, SR 2003/40, SR 2003/99
Art.65, enabled: SR 2003/350
Art.66, enabled: SR 2002/49, SR 2003/40, SR 2003/99
Art.74A, amended: SR 2002/374 Sch.1 para.10

1981–cont.

154. Road Traffic (Northern Ireland) Order 1981–*cont.*
Art.75, amended: SR 2002/374 Sch.1 para.11
Art.84, applied: SR 2003/8 Reg.2
Art.92, applied: SI 2002/3061 Reg.2
Art.92ZA, added: SI 2003/2903 Art.4
Art.92ZB, added: SI 2003/2903 Art.4
Art.103, enabled: SR 2002/154
Art.132, enabled: SR 2003/65
Art.167, applied: 2003 c.32 Sch.3 para.5
Art.172, applied: SI 2004/702 Sch.4 para.5
Art.174, amended: SI 2003/2903 Sch.1 para.9
Art.175, applied: 2003 c.32 Sch.3 para.6
Art.180, amended: SI 2003/2903 Sch.1 para.10
Art.218, enabled: SR 2002/49, SR 2002/51, SR 2002/154, SR 2002/383, SR 2002/384, SR 2003/40, SR 2003/64, SR 2003/65, SR 2003/99, SR 2003/100, SR 2003/124, SR 2003/183, SR 2003/275
Sch.1, amended: SR 2002/116 Reg.11
Sch.2, amended: SR 2002/116 Reg.11

155. Firearms (Northern Ireland) Order 1981
applied: SI 2003/2764 Art.11
revoked: SI 2004/702 Sch.8
Art.3, see *R. v Shoukri* [2004] N.I. 181 (CA (Crim Div) (NI)), Lord Carswell L.C.J.
Art.17, applied: 2003 c.44 Sch.17 para.33
Art.17A, applied: 2003 c.44 Sch.17 para.34
Art.18, applied: 2003 c.44 Sch.17 para.35, Sch.17 para.36
Art.19, applied: 2003 c.44 Sch.17 para.37
Art.23, see *R. v Greenaway (Stephen)* [2003] N.I. 5 (Crown Ct (Northern Ireland)), Kerr, J.; see *R. v Shoukri* [2004] N.I. 181 (CA (Crim Div) (NI)), Lord Carswell L.C.J.

156. Housing (Northern Ireland) Order 1981
referred to: SI 2003/412 Art.1
Part IV, revoked: SI 2003/412 Art.127, Sch.5
Art.2, revoked (in part): SI 2003/412 Art.123, Sch.5
Art.2A, added: SI 2003/412 Art.123
Art.13, applied: SI 2003/412 Art.114
Art.21, amended: SI 2003/418 Sch.1 para.13
Art.22, amended: SI 2003/412 Art.124
Art.22A, added: SI 2003/412 Art.124
Art.28A, added: SI 2003/412 Art.125
Art.28A, applied: SI 2003/412 Sch.2 para.3
Art.31, applied: SI 2003/412 Art.28
Art.31B, added: SI 2003/412 Art.126
Art.35, applied: SI 2003/412 Art.113, Art.116, Art.117
Art.38, applied: SI 2003/412 Art.113, Art.116, Art.117
Art.41, applied: SI 2003/412 Art.30, Art.43, Art.48, Art.58, Art.60, Art.113, Art.116, Art.117, Art.120
Art.41A, amended: SI 2003/412 Sch.4 para.3

1981–cont.

156. Housing (Northern Ireland) Order 1981–*cont.*

Art.46, applied: SI 2003/412 Art.30, Art.48, Art.55, Art.112

Art.46, referred to: SI 2003/412 Art.49

Art.46A, applied: SI 2003/412 Art.30, Art.113, Art.114, Art.115

Art.58, amended: SI 2003/412 Sch.4 para.4, Sch.5

Art.88C, amended: SI 2003/412 Art.128

Art.88C, revoked (in part): SI 2003/412 Art.128, Sch.5

Art.159A, amended: 2003 c.21 Sch.17 para.59

Art.160, amended: SI 2003/412 Art.129

Art.160, applied: SI 2003/412 Art.114

Art.162, amended: SI 2003/412 Sch.4 para.5

Sch.1, amended: SI 2003/412 Art.130

Sch.1, substituted: SI 2003/412 Art.130

Sch.2, amended: SI 2003/412 Art.130

158. Clean Air (Northern Ireland) Order 1981

Art.17, enabled: SR 2003/343

Art.24A, revoked: SI 2002/3153 Sch.6 Part I

Art.24B, added: SR 2003/46 Sch.11 para.2

226. Judgments Enforcement (Northern Ireland) Order 1981

Art.3, amended: 2002 c.21 Sch.3 para.3

227. Fisheries Amendment (Northern Ireland) Order 1981

Sch.4, amended: SI 2002/790 Sch.4

228. Legal Aid, Advice and Assistance (Northern Ireland) Order 1981

applied: 2003 c.21 s.119, SI 2003/435 Sch.3 para.2, Sch.3 para.3, Sch.3 para.4, Sch.3 para.9, Sch.4 para.16, SI 2004/1500 Art.30

referred to: SI 2003/435 Sch.4 para.2

revoked: SI 2003/435 Sch.5

Part II, applied: SI 2003/435 Sch.3 para.2, Sch.3 para.4, Sch.3 para.7

Part II, referred to: SI 2003/435 Sch.3 para.4

Part II, varied: SI 2003/435 Sch.3 para.4

Part III, applied: SI 2003/435 Sch.3 para.5

Art.1, amended: 2002 c.26 Sch.12 para.17

Art.3, amended: 2002 c.21 Sch.3 para.5, SR 2002/61 Reg.3, SR 2003/89 Reg.3

Art.3, enabled: SR 2002/61, SR 2003/89

Art.4, amended: 2002 c.26 Sch.12 para.18, Sch.13

Art.5, enabled: SR 2002/212

Art.7, amended: 2002 c.21 Sch.3 para.6, SR 2002/61 Reg.4, SR 2003/89 Reg.4

Art.7, enabled: SR 2002/61, SR 2002/62, SR 2003/89, SR 2003/90

Art.9, amended: SR 2002/60 Reg.3, SR 2003/88 Reg.3

Art.9, applied: 2002 c.26 s.77

Art.9, enabled: SR 2002/60, SR 2003/88

Art.10, applied: 2002 c.29 Sch.11 para.10, 2002 c.41 s.117

Art.10, revoked (in part): 2002 c.26 Sch.13

1981–cont.

228. Legal Aid, Advice and Assistance (Northern Ireland) Order 1981–*cont.*

Art.10A, added: 2002 c.26 s.76

Art.12, amended: SR 2002/60 Reg.4, SR 2003/88 Reg.4

Art.12, enabled: SR 2002/60, SR 2003/88

Art.13, amended: 2002 c.26 Sch.12 para.19

Art.13, enabled: SR 2003/43

Art.14, amended: 2002 c.21 Sch.3 para.7

Art.15, amended: SI 2003/435 Sch.4 para.6

Art.15, revoked (in part): SI 2003/435 Sch.4 para.6

Art.15A, added: 2002 c.26 Sch.12 para.20

Art.18, applied: SI 2003/435 Sch.3 para.3

Art.19, applied: SI 2003/435 Sch.3 para.3

Art.19, referred to: SI 2003/435 Sch.3 para.3

Art.20, applied: SI 2003/435 Sch.3 para.3

Art.21, applied: SI 2003/435 Sch.3 para.10, Sch.3 para.12

Art.22, enabled: SR 2002/60, SR 2002/61, SR 2002/62, SR 2002/212, SR 2003/88, SR 2003/89, SR 2003/90, SR 2003/94

Art.23, disapplied: SI 2003/435 Sch.3 para.4

Art.24, disapplied: SI 2003/435 Sch.3 para.4

Art.24, varied: SI 2003/435 Sch.3 para.4

Art.26, amended: 2002 c.26 Sch.12 para.21

Art.27, amended: 2002 c.26 Sch.12 para.22

Art.27, enabled: SR 2002/60, SR 2002/61, SR 2002/62, SR 2003/88, SR 2003/89, SR 2003/90, SR 2003/94

Art.28, amended: 2002 c.26 Sch.12 para.23, Sch.12 para.24

Art.28A, added: 2002 c.26 s.61

Art.32, amended: 2002 c.26 Sch.12 para.25

Art.34, amended: 2002 c.26 Sch.13

Art.35A, added: 2002 c.26 s.61

Art.36, amended: 2002 c.26 Sch.12 para.26

Art.36, applied: SI 2003/435 Sch.3 para.5

Art.36, enabled: SR 2002/376

Art.37, amended: SI 2003/435 Sch.4 para.6

Art.39, amended: 2002 c.26 Sch.12 para.27, Sch.12 para.28

Sch.1, added: 2002 c.29 Sch.11 para.10

Sch.1, amended: 2002 c.29 Sch.11 para.10, SI 2004/1988 Art.5

Sch.1, referred to: 2002 c.26 Sch.12 para.17

Sch.1, revoked: 2002 c.26 s.77, Sch.13

Sch.1, substituted: 2004 c.19 Sch.2 para.5

Sch.2, amended: SI 2003/435 Sch.4 para.6

Sch.2, enabled: SR 2003/43

231. Weights and Measures (Northern Ireland) Order 1981

applied: 2002 c.40 Sch.15

referred to: SI 2003/750 Sch.5 para.12, SI 2003/751 Sch.6 para.12, SI 2004/1468 Sch.6 para.12

Art.6, amended: SR 2002/70 Reg.3

Art.9, enabled: SR 2002/36, SR 2002/308

Art.9, referred to: SR 2002/308 Reg.4

NO.

231. Weights and Measures (Northern Ireland) Order 1981–*cont.*

Art.9B, referred to: SR 2002/308 Reg.4, Sch.1 Part 2

Art.19, applied: SI 2003/1593 Sch.1 Part II

Art.20, applied: SI 2003/1593 Sch.1 Part II

Art.22, applied: SI 2003/1593 Sch.1 Part II

Art.25, applied: SI 2003/1593 Sch.1 Part II

Art.32, applied: SI 2003/1593 Sch.1 Part II

Art.43, applied: SR 2002/308 Reg.4

Art.43, enabled: SR 2002/308

234. Judgements Enforcement (Northern Ireland) Order 1981

Part VI, applied: SI 2002/3150 Art.16

Art.86, amended: SI 2002/3150 Sch.3 para.1

Art.86, applied: SI 2002/3150 Art.16

Art.127, applied: SI 2003/419 Art.48

257. Public Service Vehicles (Conditions of Fitness, Equipment, Use and Certification) Regulations 1981

Reg.3, amended: SI 2002/335 Reg.3

Reg.6, amended: SI 2002/335 Reg.4

Reg.6, referred to: SI 2003/1998 Sch.12 para.12

Reg.20, amended: SI 2002/335 Reg.5

Reg.21, amended: SI 2002/335 Reg.6

Reg.22, amended: SI 2002/335 Reg.7

Reg.23, amended: SI 2002/335 Reg.8

Reg.26, amended: SI 2002/335 Reg.9

Reg.26, revoked (in part): SI 2002/335 Reg.9

Reg.28, amended: SI 2002/335 Reg.10

Reg.28, revoked (in part): SI 2002/335 Reg.10

Reg.28A, amended: SI 2002/335 Reg.10

Reg.45B, added: SI 2002/335 Reg.11

Reg.46, amended: SI 2002/489 Reg.2, SI 2003/1817 Reg.2, SI 2004/1880 Reg.2

Reg.50, amended: SI 2002/489 Reg.2, SI 2003/1817 Reg.2, SI 2004/1880 Reg.2

Reg.53, amended: SI 2002/489 Reg.2, SI 2003/1817 Reg.2, SI 2004/1880 Reg.2

Reg.57, amended: SI 2002/489 Reg.2, SI 2004/1880 Reg.2

Sch.2 para.11, amended: SI 2002/335 Reg.9

Sch.2 para.13, amended: SI 2002/335 Reg.10

Sch.6, amended: SI 2002/335 Sch.1

Sch.8, amended: SI 2002/335 Sch.2

Sch.9, amended: SI 2002/335 Sch.3

366. Road Vehicles (Registration and Licensing) (Amendment) Regulations 1981

revoked: SI 2002/2742 Sch.1 Part I

440. Carriage by Air Acts (Application of Provisions) (Third Amendment) Order 1981

revoked: SI 2004/1899 Sch.4

552. Magistrates Courts Rules 1981

amended: SI 2003/1236 r.24

r.2., amended: SI 2003/1236 r.11

r.10., amended: SI 2003/1236 r.12

NO.

552. Magistrates Courts Rules 1981–*cont.*

r.11., amended: SI 2003/1236 r.13

r.11., revoked (in part): SI 2003/1236 r.13

r.11A., amended: SI 2003/1236 r.14

r.11A., revoked (in part): SI 2003/1236 r.14

r.15., amended: SI 2003/1236 r.15

r.16., amended: SI 2003/1236 r.16

r.16., revoked (in part): SI 2003/1236 r.16

r.17., amended: SI 2003/1236 r.17

r.17., revoked (in part): SI 2003/1236 r.17

r.18., amended: SI 2003/1236 r.18

r.19., amended: SI 2003/1236 r.19

r.19., revoked (in part): SI 2003/1236 r.19

r.20., amended: SI 2003/1236 r.20

r.24., amended: SI 2003/1236 r.21

r.25., amended: SI 2003/1236 r.22

r.25., revoked (in part): SI 2003/1236 r.22

r.27., amended: SI 2003/1236 r.23

r.28., substituted: SI 2003/1236 r.25

r.29., amended: SI 2003/1236 r.26

r.30., amended: SI 2003/1236 r.27

r.40., revoked: SI 2003/1236 r.28

r.46., amended: SI 2003/1236 r.29

r.57., amended: SI 2003/1236 r.30

r.57A, added: SI 2003/423 r.2

r.65., amended: SI 2003/1236 r.31

r.66., amended: SI 2003/1236 r.32

r.66., revoked (in part): SI 2003/1236 r.32

r.67., amended: SI 2003/1236 r.33

r.68., amended: SI 2003/1236 r.34

r.72A, added: SI 2004/2993 r.2

r.86., amended: SI 2003/1236 r.35

r.87., amended: SI 2003/1236 r.36

r.90., amended: SI 2003/1236 r.37

r.93A., amended: SI 2003/1236 r.38

r.93B., amended: SI 2003/1236 r.39

r.96., revoked (in part): SI 2003/1236 r.40

r.97., revoked (in part): SI 2003/1236 r.41

r.98., amended: SI 2003/1236 r.42

r.99, see *R. (on the application of Durham CC) v North Durham Justices* [2004] EWHC 1073, (2004) 168 J.P. 269 (QBD (Admin Ct)), Moses, J.

r.102., revoked: SI 2003/1236 r.43

r.104., amended: SI 2003/1236 r.44

r.109., amended: SI 2003/1236 r.45

r.113., revoked: SI 2003/1236 r.46

553. Magistrates Courts (Forms) Rules 1981

Sch.2 Part 1, added: SI 2004/2993 Sch.1

Sch.2 Part 1, amended: SI 2003/423 r.3, SI 2003/1236 r.48

Sch.2 Part 2, amended: SI 2003/1236 r.48

Sch.2 Part 3, amended: SI 2003/1236 r.48

Sch.2 Part 4, amended: SI 2003/1236 r.48

Sch.2 Part 5, amended: SI 2003/1236 r.48

Sch.2 Part 6, amended: SI 2003/1236 r.48

Sch.2 Part 7, amended: SI 2003/1236 r.48

NO.

1981–cont.

569. Merchant Shipping (Official Log Books) Regulations 1981

Reg.1, amended: SI 2002/1473 Sch.1 para.3, Sch.2 para.2

Sch.1 Part I, amended: SI 2002/1473 Sch.2 para.2

570. Merchant Shipping (Official Log Books) (Fishing Vessels) Regulations 1981

Reg.1, amended: SI 2002/1473 Sch.1 para.4, Sch.2 para.3

Sch.1, amended: SI 2002/1473 Sch.2 para.3

571. Merchant Shipping (Automatic Pilot and Testing of Steering Gear) Regulations 1981

revoked: SI 2002/1473 Sch.1 para.2

608. Planning Blight (Compensation) (Northern Ireland) Order 1981

applied: SI 2003/410 Sch.2 para.1, Sch.2 para.3

Art.3, referred to: SI 2003/410 Sch.2 para.1, Sch.2 para.3

Art.4, varied: SR 2003/73 Sch.1

740. Merchant Shipping (Fishing Boats Registry) Order 1981

revoked: SI 2004/1284 Sch.1

829. Town and Country Planning (Development by Planning Authorities) (Scotland) Regulations 1981

Reg.2, amended: SSI 2004/332 Sch.1 para.1

Reg.2A, added: SSI 2004/332 Sch.1 para.2

Reg.10A, added: SSI 2004/332 Sch.1 para.3

833. European Communities (Designation) (No.2) Order 1981

Sch.1, amended: SI 2003/2901 Sch.4

839. Employment (Miscellaneous Provisions) (Northern Ireland) Order 1981

Art.11, revoked (in part): SI 2003/431 Sch.5

880. Capital Transfer Tax (Delivery of Accounts) Regulations 1981

revoked: SI 2002/1733 Sch.1

881. Capital Transfer Tax (Delivery of Accounts) (Scotland) Regulations 1981. 1981

revoked: SI 2002/1733 Sch.1

917. Health and Safety (First-Aid) Regulations 1981

Reg.3, amended: SI 2002/2174 Reg.2

Reg.3, applied: SI 2002/655 Reg.23, Reg.25, SI 2003/547 Reg.23, Reg.25, SI 2004/456 Reg.22, Reg.24

931. Road Vehicles (Excise) (Prescribed Particulars) Regulations 1981

revoked: SI 2002/2742 Sch.1 Part I

959. Church Representation Rules (Amendment) Resolution 1981

referred to: SI 2004/1889

1041. Industrial Training (Transfer of the Activities of Establishments) Order 1981

referred to: SI 2004/368 Sch.1

NO.

1981–cont.

1063. Jam and Similar Products Regulations 1981

applied: SI 2003/3120 Reg.11, SI 2004/553 Reg.11

referred to: SI 2003/1008 Reg.3

revoked (in part): SI 2003/3120 Reg.10, SI 2004/553 Reg.10

varied: SI 2002/329 Reg.9, SI 2003/945 Reg.3

Reg.2, referred to: SI 2002/330 Reg.3

Reg.2, varied: SI 2002/379 Reg.5, SI 2003/1182 Reg.3, SI 2003/1713 Reg.3

1089. Dangerous Substances (Conveyance by Road in Road Tankers and Tank-containers) Regulations 1981

Reg.7, applied: SI 2004/568 Sch.1 para.4

1096. Brightlingsea Harbour Revision Order 1981

revoked: SI 2002/2476 Art.12

1115. Diseases of Animals (Northern Ireland) Order 1981

applied: SI 2002/3153 Art.48, SI 2004/1604 Reg.13, SR 2002/88 Reg.15

Art.2, enabled: SR 2002/209

Art.5, enabled: SR 2002/44, SR 2002/209, SR 2003/55

Art.10, enabled: SR 2002/44, SR 2003/55

Art.12, applied: SR 2002/88 Reg.12

Art.12, enabled: SR 2002/44, SR 2003/55

Art.14, enabled: SR 2002/44, SR 2003/55

Art.18, applied: SR 2002/225 Reg.102

Art.19, enabled: SR 2002/44, SR 2002/209, SR 2003/55

Art.20, enabled: SR 2002/44, SR 2003/55

Art.29, enabled: SR 2002/209

Art.44, enabled: SR 2002/209, SR 2003/55

Art.46, enabled: SR 2002/209, SR 2003/55

Art.60, enabled: SR 2002/44, SR 2002/209, SR 2003/55

Sch.1, varied: SR 2002/209 Art.3

Sch.2, revoked: SR 2002/225 Sch.8 Part I

1117. Road Traffic (Car-Sharing Arrangements) (Northern Ireland) Order 1981

Art.2, applied: SR 2003/303 Reg.2

1121. Double Taxation Relief (Taxes on Income) (Mauritius) Order 1981

Sch.1, varied: SI 2003/2620 Sch.1

1259. Aircraft (Customs and Excise) Regulations 1981

Reg.4, applied: SI 2003/3113 Sch.1

1260. Ship's Report, Importation and Exportation by Sea Regulations 1981

Reg.3, applied: SI 2003/3113 Sch.1

Reg.4, applied: SI 2003/3113 Sch.1

Reg.5, applied: SI 2003/3113 Sch.1

1263. National Health Service (Compensation for Premature Retirement) Regulations 1981

Reg.1, revoked: SI 2002/1311 Sch.2

Reg.2, revoked: SI 2002/1311 Sch.2

Reg.3, revoked: SI 2002/1311 Sch.2

1981–cont.

1263. National Health Service (Compensation for Premature Retirement) Regulations 1981–cont.

Reg.4, revoked: SI 2002/1311 Sch.2

Reg.5, revoked (in part): SI 2002/1311 Sch.2

Reg.6, revoked: SI 2002/1311 Sch.2

Reg.7, revoked: SI 2002/1311 Sch.2

Reg.8, revoked: SI 2002/1311 Sch.2

Reg.9, revoked: SI 2002/1311 Sch.2

Reg.10, revoked: SI 2002/1311 Sch.2

Reg.11, revoked: SI 2002/1311 Sch.2

Reg.12, revoked: SI 2002/1311 Sch.2

Reg.13, revoked: SI 2002/1311 Sch.2

Reg.14, revoked: SI 2002/1311 Sch.2

Sch.1 para.1, revoked: SI 2002/1311 Sch.2

Sch.1 para.2, revoked: SI 2002/1311 Sch.2

Sch.1 para.3, revoked: SI 2002/1311 Sch.2

Sch.1 para.4, revoked: SI 2002/1311 Sch.2

1320. Jam and Similar Products (Scotland) Regulations 1981

applied: SSI 2004/133 Reg.9

revoked: SSI 2004/133 Reg.11

Reg.11, amended: SSI 2003/293 Reg.11

Reg.12, amended: SSI 2003/293 Reg.11

Sch.4, amended: SSI 2003/527 Sch.2

1440. Capital Transfer Tax (Delivery of Accounts) (No.2) Regulations 1981

revoked: SI 2002/1731 Reg.8

1481. Employment Agencies Act 1973 (Charging Fees to Au Pairs) Regulations 1981

revoked: SI 2003/3319 Reg.4

1518. Estate Agents (Appeals) Regulations 1981

Reg.22, revoked: SI 2003/1400 Sch.5

1536. European Communities (Designation) (No.3) Order 1981

Sch.1, amended: SI 2002/2840 Sch.3

1675. Magistrates Court (Northern Ireland) Order 1981

Art.146, see *Wallace v Quinn* [2004] N.I. 164 (CA (NI)), Lord Carswell L.C.J.

1675. Magistrates Courts (Northern Ireland) Order 1981

applied: 2002 c.29 s.215, SI 2004/1267 Reg.104

Part VI, applied: SI 2003/435 Sch.2 para.2

Part VII, applied: SR 2002/293 Reg.6, SR 2002/307 Reg.6, SR 2002/340 Reg.21, SR 2003/115 Reg.23, SR 2003/353 Reg.6, SR 2003/360 Reg.6

Art.2, amended: 2002 c.26 Sch.4 para.21, Sch.13

Art.3, amended: 2002 c.26 Sch.4 para.22

Art.4, amended: 2002 c.26 Sch.4 para.23

Art.5, amended: 2002 c.26 Sch.4 para.24

Art.6, amended: 2002 c.26 Sch.4 para.24

Art.6A, amended: 2002 c.26 Sch.4 para.25

Art.7, amended: 2002 c.26 Sch.4 para.26

Art.10, amended: 2002 c.26 Sch.4 para.27

Art.12, amended: 2002 c.26 Sch.5 para.21

1981–cont.

1675. Magistrates Courts (Northern Ireland) Order 1981–cont.

Art.13, amended: 2002 c.26 Sch.5 para.22

Art.13, applied: SI 2004/1501 Art.31

Art.13, enabled: SR 2002/12, SR 2002/158, SR 2002/159, SR 2002/163, SR 2003/17, SR 2003/32, SR 2003/122

Art.15, amended: 2002 c.26 Sch.5 para.23

Art.18, amended: 2002 c.26 Sch.4 para.28, Sch.13

Art.19, applied: SI 2003/1519 Art.20

Art.19, disapplied: SI 2002/111 Art.20, SI 2002/2628 Art.16, 2003 c.21 s.174, SI 2003/413 Art.38, SI 2003/1247 Art.16, SI 2004/348 Art.15, SI 2004/702 Art.69

Art.20, amended: SI 2003/1247 Art.25

Art.20, applied: 2002 c.26 s.44

Art.24, amended: SI 2003/1247 Art.26, Sch.2

Art.29, amended: SI 2003/1247 Art.29, 2004 c.4 s.12, Sch.2 para.1, SI 2004/702 Sch.7 para.6

Art.32, see *Shaw's Application for Judicial Review, Re* [2004] N.I. 149 (QBD (NI)), Kerr, J.

Art.34, amended: 2002 c.26 Sch.13

Art.42, amended: 2002 c.26 Sch.4 para.29

Art.44, revoked (in part): 2002 c.26 Sch.13

Art.45, amended: 2002 c.26 Sch.11 para.4

Art.47, amended: 2002 c.26 Sch.12 para.30, SI 2003/1247 Art.27, Sch.2

Art.47, revoked (in part): SI 2003/1247 Art.27, Sch.2

Art.51, applied: SI 2003/1247 Art.3

Art.58, disapplied: SI 2003/1901 Sch.1 para.8

Art.62, disapplied: SI 2003/435 Sch.2 para.2

Art.90, revoked (in part): 2002 c.26 Sch.13

Art.95, applied: SI 2002/272 Art.5, SI 2004/1237 Art.6, SR 2003/59 Art.13, SSI 2002/51 Art.6, SSI 2003/56 Art.13, SSI 2003/88 Art.6, SSI 2004/392 Art.11

Art.100, amended: 2002 c.21 Sch.3 para.8

Art.114, amended: 2002 c.26 Sch.4 para.30

Art.114, applied: SR 2003/59 Art.13

Art.114, referred to: SI 2002/272 Art.5, SR 2003/59 Art.13

Art.114, varied: SI 2002/272 Art.5

Art.126, amended: 2002 c.26 Sch.4 para.31

Art.127, applied: SI 2003/435 Art.25

Art.132A, added: SI 2003/1247 Art.9

Art.133A, added: SI 2003/1247 Art.10

Art.138, amended: SI 2003/1247 Art.24

Art.140, amended: 2002 c.26 Sch.12 para.31

Art.146, see *Foyle Carlingford and Irish Lights Commission v McGillion* [2002] N.I. 86 (CA (NI)), Carswell, L.C.J.

Art.146, applied: 2002 c.29 s.164, 2003 c.32 s.62, SI 2003/750 Sch.5 para.9, SI 2003/751 Sch.6 para.9, SI 2003/1901 Sch.1 para.7, SI 2004/1468 Sch.6 para.9

Art.152, amended: 2002 c.26 Sch.13

1981–cont.

1675. Magistrates Courts (Northern Ireland) Order 1981–cont.

Art.152, applied: 2002 c.26 Sch.4 para.3

Art.154, applied: SR 2003/59 Art.13

Art.154, referred to: SI 2002/272 Art.5, SR 2003/59 Art.13

Art.154, varied: SI 2002/272 Art.5

Art.156, amended: 2002 c.26 Sch.4 para.32

Art.158, amended: 2002 c.26 Sch.4 para.33

Art.158A, amended: 2002 c.26 Sch.13

Art.160, amended: 2002 c.26 Sch.4 para.34

Art.160, applied: 2002 c.26 s.80, 2004 c.4 Sch.3 para.3

Art.168, revoked: 2002 c.26 Sch.13

Sch.1, amended: 2002 c.26 Sch.4 para.35, Sch.13

Sch.1, revoked: 2002 c.26 Sch.13

Sch.2, added: SI 2003/1247 Sch.1 para.9

Sch.4, applied: 2004 c.11 s.21, s.22

Sch.6, revoked: SI 2003/435 Sch.5, SI 2004/702 Sch.8, SI 2004/1501 Sch.2

1679. Police (Scotland) Amendment (No.2) Regulations 1981

revoked: SSI 2004/257 Sch.4

1685. Company and Business Names Regulations 1981

Sch.1, amended: SI 2002/1397 Sch.1 para.17, SI 2004/1771 Sch.1 para.52

1687. County Court Rules 1981

see *St Brice v Southwark LBC* [2001] EWCA Civ 1138, [2002] 1 W.L.R. 1537 (CA), Kennedy, L.J.

Part 10, applied: SI 2002/1792 Reg.21, Sch.5 para.16

Part 45 r.1, varied: SI 2003/284 Art.22

Part 45 r.2, varied: SI 2003/284 Art.5

Ord.11 r.1, see *Scriven, Re* [2004] EWCA Civ 683, [2004] B.P.I.R. 972 (CA), Clarke, L.J.

Ord.17 r.11, see *Hawkins v Keppe Shaw Solicitors* [2001] EWCA Civ 1160, [2002] P.I.Q.R. P9 (CA), Latham, L.J.

Ord.29, see *Medina Housing Association Ltd v Connolly* [2002] EWCA Civ 1263, [2003] C.P. Rep. 4 (CA), Peter Gibson, L.J.

1694. Motor Vehicles (Tests) Regulations 1981

referred to: SI 2003/1698 Reg.2, SI 2003/1815 Reg.2

Part III, applied: SI 2003/1113 Reg.1

Part IV, applied: SI 2003/1113 Reg.1

Reg.3, amended: SI 2003/1113 Reg.3, SI 2003/1698 Reg.3

Reg.5, applied: SI 2003/1113 Reg.24

Reg.6, amended: SI 2003/1113 Reg.4

Reg.7, substituted: SI 2003/1113 Sch.1

Reg.7A, substituted: SI 2003/1113 Sch.1

Reg.8, substituted: SI 2003/1113 Sch.1

Reg.8A, referred to: SI 2003/1113 Reg.25

Reg.8A, substituted: SI 2003/1113 Sch.1

Reg.8B, referred to: SI 2003/1113 Reg.25

Reg.8B, substituted: SI 2003/1113 Sch.1

1981–cont.

1694. Motor Vehicles (Tests) Regulations 1981–cont.

Reg.8C, substituted: SI 2003/1113 Sch.1

Reg.8D, referred to: SI 2003/1113 Reg.25

Reg.8D, substituted: SI 2003/1113 Sch.1

Reg.8E, referred to: SI 2003/1113 Reg.25

Reg.8E, substituted: SI 2003/1113 Sch.1

Reg.8F, substituted: SI 2003/1113 Sch.1

Reg.9, referred to: SI 2003/1113 Reg.25

Reg.9, substituted: SI 2003/1113 Sch.1

Reg.10, substituted: SI 2003/1113 Sch.1

Reg.11, substituted: SI 2003/1113 Sch.1

Reg.12, amended: SI 2003/1113 Reg.6, SI 2003/1698 Reg.4

Reg.13, amended: SI 2003/1113 Reg.7

Reg.13, revoked (in part): SI 2003/1113 Reg.7

Reg.13, substituted: SI 2003/1698 Reg.5

Reg.14, amended: SI 2003/1113 Reg.8

Reg.15, substituted: SI 2003/1113 Reg.9

Reg.16, amended: SI 2003/1113 Reg.10

Reg.16, revoked (in part): SI 2003/1113 Reg.10

Reg.17, amended: SI 2003/1113 Reg.11

Reg.18, amended: SI 2003/1113 Reg.12

Reg.19, amended: SI 2003/1113 Reg.13

Reg.20, amended: SI 2002/488 Reg.3, SI 2002/1698 Reg.3, SI 2003/1113 Reg.14, SI 2003/1698 Reg.6, SI 2003/1815 Reg.3, SI 2004/1632 Reg.2, SI 2004/1879 Reg.2

Reg.20, revoked (in part): SI 2002/488 Reg.3

Reg.21, amended: SI 2003/1113 Reg.15

Reg.22, substituted: SI 2003/1113 Reg.16

Reg.23, substituted: SI 2003/1113 Reg.17

Reg.23A, added: SI 2003/1113 Reg.18

Reg.24, amended: SI 2003/1113 Reg.19

Reg.24, revoked (in part): SI 2003/1113 Reg.19

Reg.24A, added: SI 2003/1113 Reg.20

Reg.24, amended: SI 2003/1698 Reg.7

Reg.25, referred to: SI 2003/1113 Reg.24

Reg.25, substituted: SI 2003/1113 Reg.21

Reg.25, varied: SI 2003/1698 Reg.7

Reg.25A, amended: SI 2003/1698 Reg.8

Reg.29, added: SI 2003/1113 Reg.22

Reg.30, added: SI 2003/1113 Reg.22

Sch.1 Part I, revoked: SI 2003/1113 Reg.26

Sch.2 para.1, amended: SI 2003/1698 Reg.9

Sch.2 para.2, amended: SI 2003/1698 Reg.9

Sch.2 para.5, amended: SI 2002/488 Reg.4

Sch.3, added: SI 2003/1113 Reg.23

Sch.3, amended: SI 2003/1698 Reg.10

Sch.3 Part I para.1, added: SI 2003/1113 Reg.23

Sch.3 Part I para.2, added: SI 2003/1113 Reg.23

Sch.3 Part II para.3, added: SI 2003/1113 Reg.23

Sch.3 Part III para.4, added: SI 2003/1113 Reg.23

NO.

1981—cont.

1694. Motor Vehicles (Tests) Regulations 1981—*cont.*

Sch.3 Part IV para.6, added: SI 2003/1113 Reg.23

Sch.3 Part IV para.7, added: SI 2003/1113 Reg.23

Sch.3 Part V para.8, added: SI 2003/1113 Reg.23

Sch.3 Part VI para.9, added: SI 2003/1113 Reg.23

Sch.3 Part VII para.10, added: SI 2003/1113 Reg.23

Sch.3 Part VIII para.11, added: SI 2003/1113 Reg.23

Sch.3 Part IX para.12, added: SI 2003/1113 Reg.23

Sch.3 Part X para.13, added: SI 2003/1113 Reg.23

Sch.3 Part XI para.15, added: SI 2003/1113 Reg.23

Sch.3 Part XII, added: SI 2003/1113 Reg.23

1748. County of Devon (Electoral Arrangements) Order 1981

revoked: SI 2004/2812 Art.7

1785. National Health Service (Compensation for Premature Retirement) (Scotland) Regulations 1981

revoked: SSI 2003/344 Sch.2

Reg.1, revoked: SSI 2003/344 Sch.2

Reg.4, revoked: SSI 2003/344 Sch.2

Reg.5, applied: SSI 2003/344 Reg.5

Reg.5, revoked (in part): SSI 2003/344 Sch.2

Reg.6, revoked: SSI 2003/344 Sch.2

Reg.14, revoked: SSI 2003/344 Sch.2

1794. Transfer of Undertakings (Protection of Employment) Regulations 1981

applied: 2002 asp 3 s.23, 2002 c.32 s.129, SI 2002/534 Art.2, 2003 c.39 Sch.2 para.11, Sch.2 para.12, SI 2003/973 Art.8, SI 2003/2715 Reg.2, 2004 c.20 Sch.5 para.10, 2004 c.25 s.3, 2004 c.35 s.301, 2004 c.iv s.8, SI 2004/1777 Sch.4 para.2, SI 2004/1778 Sch.4 para.2, SSI 2002/178 Art.4, 2003 asp 1 s.7, 2003 c.1 s.498, Sch.2 para.32

referred to: 2002 c.iv s.9, 2004 c.25 s.32, Sch.3 para.12

see *Alderson v Secretary of State for Trade and Industry* [2003] EWCA Civ 1767, [2004] 1 All E.R. 1148 (CA), Lord Phillips of Worth Matravers, M.R.; see *Beckmann v Dynamco Whicheloe Macfarlane Ltd (C164/00)* [2002] All E.R. (EC) 865 (ECJ), GC Rodriguez Iglesias (President); see *Fairhurst Ward Abbotts Ltd v Botes Building Ltd* [2004] EWCA Civ 83, [2004] I.C.R. 919 (CA), Pill, L.J.; see *Hagen v ICI Chemicals & Polymers Ltd* [2002] I.R.L.R. 31 (QBD), Elias, J.; see *Lowe v Dudley Bower Building Services Ltd* [2003] I.C.R. 843 (EAT), Nelson, J.; see *Ministry of Defence v Rentokil* [2002]

NO.

1981—cont.

1794. Transfer of Undertakings (Protection of Employment) Regulations 1981—*cont.*

see—*cont.*

Emp. L.R. 536 (EAT), Charles, J.; see *Nelson v Carillion Services Ltd* [2003] EWCA Civ 544, [2003] I.C.R. 1256 (CA), Simon Brown, L.J.; see *P&O Trans European Ltd v Initial Transport Services Ltd* [2003] I.R.L.R. 128 (EAT), Nelson, J.; see *Perth and Kinross Council v Donaldson* [2004] I.C.R. 667 (EAT), Lord Johnston; see *Preston v Wolverhampton Healthcare NHS Trust (No.3)* [2002] O.P.L.R. 323 (ET), JK Macmillan; see *RCO Support Services Ltd v UNISON* [2002] EWCA Civ 464, [2002] 2 C.M.L.R. 34 (CA), Mummery, L.J.; see *Thorpe v Dul* [2003] I.C.R. 1556 (EAT), Wall, J.; see *Wynnwith Engineering Co Ltd v Bennett* [2002] I.R.L.R. 170 (EAT), Judge D Pugsley

Reg.2, see *Dowling v Ilic (t/a ME Ilic Haulage)* [2004] I.C.R. 1176 (EAT), Burton, J.

Reg.3, see *CPL Distribution Ltd v Todd* [2002] EWCA Civ 1481, [2003] I.R.L.R. 28 (CA), Pill, L.J.

Reg.5, see *Alamo Group (Europe) Ltd v Tucker* [2003] I.C.R. 829 (EAT), Judge Altman; see *French v MITIE Management Services Ltd* [2002] I.C.R. 1395 (EAT), Maurice Kay, J.; see *Matthews (t/a Anton Motors) v Smith* [2002] EWCA Civ 1722, [2003] I.C.R. 460 (CA), Mummery, L.J.; see *Powerhouse Retail Ltd v Burroughs* [2004] EWCA Civ 1281, [2004] I.R.L.R. 979 (CA (Civ Div)), Pill, L.J.; see *Rossiter v Pendragon Plc* [2002] EWCA Civ 745, [2002] 2 C.M.L.R. 43 (CA), Peter Gibson, L.J.

Reg.5, applied: SI 2003/973 Art.3

Reg.5, varied: 2003 c.39 Sch.2 para.12

Reg.7, see *Martin v South Bank University (C4/01)* [2003] Pens. L.R. 199 (AGO), Advocate General Alber; see *Powerhouse Retail Ltd v Burroughs* [2004] EWCA Civ 1281, [2004] I.R.L.R. 979 (CA (Civ Div)), Pill, L.J.

Reg.7, disapplied: 2004 c.35 s.301

Reg.9, see *Powerhouse Retail Ltd v Burroughs* [2004] EWCA Civ 1281, [2004] I.R.L.R. 979 (CA (Civ Div)), Pill, L.J.

Reg.10, applied: SI 2002/377 Sch.1 para.36, SI 2002/3199 Sch.2 para.20, SI 2003/3170 Sch.3 para.20, SI 2004/753 Sch.1 para.147, SR 2002/120 Sch.1

Reg.10, referred to: SI 2003/3118 Sch.2 para.20

Reg.10, see *Alamo Group (Europe) Ltd v Tucker* [2003] I.C.R. 829 (EAT), Judge Altman

Reg.10A, applied: SI 2002/377 Sch.1 para.36

NO.

1981–cont.

1794. Transfer of Undertakings (Protection of Employment) Regulations 1981– cont.

Reg.11, applied: SI 2002/377 Sch.1 para.36, SI 2002/3199 Sch.2 para.20, SI 2003/ 3170 Sch.3 para.20, SI 2004/753 Sch.1 para.147, SI 2004/1861 Sch.1 para.22, SR 2002/120 Sch.1

Reg.11, referred to: SI 2003/3118 Sch.2 para.20

Reg.11, see *Ashford School v Nixon* [2002] Emp. L.R. 556 (EAT), Wall, J.

Reg.11A, applied: SI 2002/377 Sch.1 para.36

Reg.11A, referred to: SI 2002/3199 Sch.2 para.20, SI 2003/3118 Sch.2 para.20, SI 2003/3170 Sch.3 para.20

Reg.12, see *Solectron Scotland Ltd v Roper* [2004] I.R.L.R. 4 (EAT), Elias, J.

1950. Church Representation Rules (Amendment) Resolution 1981

referred to: SI 2004/1889

1982

17. Cocoa and Chocolate Products (Amendment) Regulations 1982

revoked (in part): SI 2003/1659 Reg.11, SI 2003/3037 Reg.11

92. Oil Taxation (Gas Banking Schemes) Regulations 1982

Reg.5, applied: SI 2003/2718 Sch.1 para.13

Reg.6, applied: SI 2003/2718 Sch.1 para.14

Reg.6, varied: SI 2003/2718 Sch.1 para.14

106. Education (Teachers) Regulations 1982

applied: SI 2004/1729 Sch.2 para.14

Reg.15, referred to: SI 2003/1662 Sch.1 para.1

Reg.16, referred to: SI 2003/1662 Sch.1 para.2

Reg.18, applied: SI 2003/1662 Sch.1 para.3

Sch.4, applied: SI 2003/1663 Sch.2 para.2, SI 2003/1709 Art.5, SI 2004/1744 Sch.2 para.2

Sch.6, applied: SI 2003/1663 Sch.1 para.1, SI 2004/1744 Sch.1 para.1

108. Cocoa and Chocolate Products (Scotland) (Amendment) Regulations 1982

revoked: SSI 2003/291 Reg.12

159. Transfer of Functions (Legal Aid and Maintenance Orders) (Northern Ireland) Order 1982

Sch.1 para.1, revoked: SI 2003/435 Sch.5

Sch.1 para.2, revoked: SI 2003/435 Sch.5

Sch.1 para.3, revoked: SI 2003/435 Sch.5

Sch.1 para.5, revoked: SI 2003/435 Sch.5

255. Specified Sugar Products (Amendment) Regulations 1982

revoked (in part): SI 2003/1563 Reg.10, SI 2003/3047 Reg.10

1982–cont.

286. National Health Service (Notification of Births and Deaths) Regulations 1982

Reg.3, amended: SI 2002/2469 Sch.1 para.39, Sch.7, Sch.11

Reg.4, amended: SI 2002/2469 Sch.1 para.39, Sch.7, Sch.11

334. Anguilla Constitution Order 1982

Sch.1, amended: 2002 c.8 s.2

336. Merchant Shipping (Liability of Ship Owners and Others) (Jersey) Order 1982

revoked: SI 2004/1284 Sch.1

410. Specified Sugar Products (Scotland) Amendment Regulations 1982

revoked: SSI 2003/527 Reg.11

470. Child Benefit (General) Amendment Regulations 1982

revoked: SI 2003/493 Sch.2 Part 1

630. Petroleum-Spirit (Plastic Containers) Regulations 1982

Reg.8, amended: SI 2002/2776 Sch.6 para.6

681. Police (Scotland) Amendment Regulations 1982

revoked: SSI 2004/257 Sch.4

709. Inter-Governmental Maritime Consultative Organisation (Immunities and Privileges) (Amendment) Order 1982

revoked: SI 2002/1826 Sch.1

712. Land Compensation (Northern Ireland) Order 1982

Art.4, applied: SI 2002/3153 Sch.3 para.5, SR 2003/46 Sch.8 para.5

Art.4, varied: SR 2003/7 Sch.1 para.6, SR 2003/46 Sch.6 para.7

Art.5, applied: SI 2002/3153 Sch.3 para.5, SR 2003/46 Sch.8 para.5

Art.5, varied: SR 2003/7 Sch.1 para.6, SR 2003/46 Sch.6 para.7

Art.6, applied: SR 2003/46 Sch.6 para.6

Art.6, referred to: SR 2003/7 Sch.1 para.5

713. Probation Board (Northern Ireland) Order 1982

Art.14, revoked: 2002 c.26 Sch.13

Art.15, revoked (in part): 2002 c.26 Sch.13

719. Public Lending Right Scheme 1982 (Commencement) Order 1982

referred to: SI 2002/3123

Part III para.14A, amended: SI 2002/3135 Sch.1 para.23

Part V para.46, amended: SI 2002/3123 Art.2, SI 2003/3045 Art.2

Appendix 1., applied: SI 2002/1792 Reg.15, Reg.17, SI 2004/1258

Sch.1 Part I para.5, amended: SI 2002/3135 Sch.1 para.23

817. Town and Country Planning (Telecommunication Networks) (Railway Operational Land) Special Development Order 1982

Art.2, amended: SI 2003/2155 Sch.1 para.25

NO.

1982–cont.

846. Departments (Northern Ireland) Order 1982

Sch.3, amended: SI 2003/413 Sch.1

894. Statutory Sick Pay (General) Regulations 1982

Reg.3, amended: SI 2002/2690 Reg.13

Reg.9B, amended: SI 2003/2096 Sch.1 para.42

Reg.17, amended: SI 2002/2690 Reg.14

986. British Nationality (General) Regulations 1982

revoked: SI 2003/548 Reg.15

Reg.4, amended: 2002 c.8 s.1, s.2

Reg.9, amended: 2002 c.8 s.1

Sch.2 para.7, amended: 2002 c.8 s.2

Sch.2 para.9, amended: 2002 c.8 s.2

Sch.2 para.11, amended: 2002 c.8 s.2

Sch.2 para.31, amended: 2002 c.8 s.2

Sch.2 para.38, amended: 2002 c.8 s.2

Sch.3, amended: 2002 c.8 s.1

987. British Nationality (Dependent Territories) Regulations 1982

referred to: SI 2003/539 Reg.2

amended: 2002 c.8 s.2

Reg.2, amended: 2002 c.8 s.1

Reg.3, amended: 2002 c.8 s.2

Reg.4, amended: 2002 c.8 s.1

Reg.6, amended: SI 2003/3159 Reg.3

Reg.8, amended: 2002 c.8 s.2

Reg.9, amended: 2002 c.8 s.1

Reg.10, amended: 2002 c.8 s.2

Reg.10, revoked: SI 2003/539 Reg.3

Reg.11, amended: 2002 c.8 s.1

Reg.11, revoked: SI 2003/539 Reg.3

Reg.12, amended: 2002 c.8 s.2

Reg.12, revoked: SI 2003/539 Reg.3

Reg.13, amended: 2002 c.8 s.2

Reg.13, revoked: SI 2003/539 Reg.3

Reg.15, amended: 2002 c.8 s.2

Sch.2 para.1, amended: 2002 c.8 s.1, s.2

Sch.2 para.3, amended: 2002 c.8 s.1

Sch.2 para.4, amended: 2002 c.8 s.2

Sch.2 para.6, amended: 2002 c.8 s.2

Sch.2 para.9, amended: 2002 c.8 s.2

Sch.2 para.11, amended: 2002 c.8 s.1

Sch.2 para.12, revoked: SI 2003/539 Reg.3

Sch.2 para.13, revoked: SI 2003/539 Reg.3

Sch.2 para.14, amended: 2002 c.8 s.2

Sch.2 para.14, revoked: SI 2003/539 Reg.3

Sch.2 para.15, amended: 2002 c.8 s.2

Sch.2 para.15, revoked: SI 2003/539 Reg.3

Sch.2 para.16, amended: 2002 c.8 s.2

Sch.2 para.16, revoked: SI 2003/539 Reg.3

Sch.2 para.17, amended: 2002 c.8 s.2

Sch.2 para.17, revoked: SI 2003/539 Reg.3

Sch.2 para.18, amended: 2002 c.8 s.1, SI 2003/539 Reg.4

Sch.2 para.19, amended: 2002 c.8 s.1, SI 2003/539 Reg.5

Sch.2 para.20, amended: 2002 c.8 s.2

NO.

1982–cont.

987. British Nationality (Dependent Territories) Regulations 1982–*cont.*

Sch.2 para.21, amended: 2002 c.8 s.2

Sch.2 para.22, amended: 2002 c.8 s.2

Sch.2 para.24, amended: 2002 c.8 s.2

Sch.2 para.26, amended: 2002 c.8 s.2

Sch.3, amended: 2002 c.8 s.1, SI 2003/3159 Reg.4

Sch.4, amended: 2002 c.8 s.2

Sch.5 para.2, amended: 2002 c.8 s.2

989. British Dependent Territories Citizenship (Deprivation) Rules 1982

amended: 2002 c.8 s.2

r.1, amended: 2002 c.8 s.2

r.2, amended: 2002 c.8 s.2

r.5, amended: 2002 c.8 s.1

1009. Local Government (Compensation for Premature Retirement) Regulations 1982

Reg.14, see *Tameside MBC v Pensions Ombudsman* [2002] EWHC 17, [2002] O.P.L.R. 145 (Ch D), Rimer, J.

1066. Condensed Milk and Dried Milk (Amendment) Regulations 1982

revoked (in part): SI 2003/1596 Reg.10, SI 2003/3053 Reg.10

1070. British Protectorates, Protected States and Protected Persons Order 1982

Art.2, amended: 2002 c.8 s.1

Art.7, amended: 2002 c.8 s.1

Art.8, amended: 2002 c.8 s.1

Art.10, amended: 2002 c.8 s.2

Art.11, amended: 2002 c.8 s.2

1076. Medical, Nursing, Dental and Veterinary Qualifications (EEC Recognition) Order 1982

revoked: SI 2003/2919 Art.13

1080. Agricultural Marketing (Northern Ireland) Order 1982

Art.7, revoked (in part): SI 2004/1109 Sch.1

Sch.8, amended: SI 2003/1398 Sch.1 para.3

1083. Industrial Development (Northern Ireland) Order 1982

varied: 2002 c.1 (NI) s.5

Part II, revoked: 2002 c.1 (NI) Sch.3 para.3, (NI) Sch.4

Part V, revoked: 2002 c.1 (NI) Sch.4

Art.2, amended: 2002 c.1 (NI) Sch.3 para.1, (NI) Sch.4

Art.2, revoked (in part): 2002 c.1 (NI) Sch.3 para.2, (NI) Sch.4

Art.7, amended: 2002 c.1 (NI) s.5, (NI) Sch.3 para.4, (NI) Sch.3 para.5, (NI) Sch.4

Art.7, applied: 2002 c.1 (NI) s.2, (NI) s.6

Art.7, revoked (in part): 2002 c.1 (NI) s.5, (NI) Sch.4

Art.8, amended: 2002 c.1 (NI) Sch.3 para.6, (NI) Sch.4

Art.9, amended: 2002 c.1 (NI) Sch.3 para.6, (NI) Sch.4

NO.

NO.

1982–cont.

1083. Industrial Development (Northern Ireland) Order 1982–*cont.*

Art.9, applied: 2002 c.1 (NI) s.6

Art.10, amended: 2002 c.1 (NI) Sch.3 para.7, (NI) Sch.4

Art.10, revoked (in part): 2002 c.1 (NI) Sch.3 para.7, (NI) Sch.4

Art.11, amended: 2002 c.1 (NI) Sch.3 para.4

Art.11, applied: 2002 c.1 (NI) s.2

Art.13, amended: 2002 c.1 (NI) Sch.3 para.4, (NI) Sch.3 para.8, (NI) Sch.4

Art.13, applied: 2002 c.1 (NI) s.2

Art.14, amended: 2002 c.1 (NI) Sch.3 para.9, (NI) Sch.3 para.10

Art.30, amended: 2002 c.1 (NI) Sch.4

Art.30, revoked (in part): 2002 c.1 (NI) Sch.3 para.11, (NI) Sch.4

Art.32, revoked: 2002 c.1 (NI) Sch.4

Art.33, revoked: 2002 c.1 (NI) Sch.3 para.12, (NI) Sch.4

Art.34, amended: 2002 c.1 (NI) Sch.3 para.13

Art.34, revoked (in part): 2002 c.1 (NI) Sch.3 para.13, (NI) Sch.4

Art.35, revoked: 2002 c.1 (NI) Sch.4

Sch.1, revoked: 2002 c.1 (NI) Sch.3 para.14, (NI) Sch.4

Sch.2, substituted: 2002 c.1 (NI) Sch.3 para.15

Sch.3, revoked: 2002 c.1 (NI) Sch.4

Sch.5, revoked: 2002 c.1 (NI) Sch.4

1109. Crown Court Rules 1982

referred to: SI 2002/2997 r.2, SI 2003/422 r.2

Part III r.7., amended: SI 2003/1646 r.2

Part III r.7., revoked (in part): SI 2003/1646 r.2

Part III r.8., amended: SI 2002/2997 r.3

Part IV r.12., applied: SI 2003/421 r.50

Part IV r.14., applied: SI 2003/421 r.51, r.52

Part IV r.15., varied: SI 2003/421 r.26

Part IV r.16., varied: SI 2003/421 r.26

Part IV r.17., varied: SI 2003/421 r.26

Part IV r.18., varied: SI 2003/421 r.26

Part V r.23., applied: SI 2003/421 r.38

Part V r.23A, revoked: SI 2002/1688 r.11

Part V r.23C, revoked: SI 2002/1688 r.11

Part V r.23E, added: SI 2004/2991 r.3

Part V r.24A, applied: SI 2004/2420 r.9

Part V r.24B, amended: SI 2002/1688 r.10

Part V r.24C, amended: SI 2002/1688 r.10

Part V r.24D, amended: SI 2002/1688 r.10

Part V r.24E, added: SI 2002/1688 r.10

Part V r.25B, amended: SI 2003/422 r.3

Part V r.25C, amended: SI 2003/422 r.4

Part V r.25C, substituted: SI 2003/422 r.4

Part V r.25D, added: SI 2003/422 r.5

Part V r.25E, added: SI 2003/422 r.5

Part V r.27., amended: SI 2003/639 r.2, SI 2003/1664 r.2, SI 2004/1292 r.2

Part V r.28., disapplied: SI 2003/421 r.58

Part V r.29., disapplied: SI 2003/421 r.58

1982–cont.

1109. Crown Court Rules 1982–*cont.*

Part V r.30, disapplied: SI 2003/421 r.58

Part V r.30, substituted: SI 2004/1047 Sch.1

Part V r.31, substituted: SI 2004/1047 Sch.1

Part V r.32, substituted: SI 2004/1047 Sch.1

Part V r.37, substituted: SI 2003/1664 r.2

Part V r.38, added: SI 2002/2783 r.2

Part V r.38I, added: SI 2003/639 r.3

Part V r.38I, substituted: SI 2003/1664 r.2

Part V r.39, amended: SI 2003/1664 r.2

r.3, see *R. (on the application of Chief Constable of Lancashire) v Preston Crown Court* [2001] EWHC Admin 928, [2002] 1 W.L.R. 1332 (QBD (Admin Ct)), Laws, L.J.

r.11, see *Hayes v Chelmsford Crown Court* [2003] EWHC 73, (2003) 167 J.P. 65 (QBD (Admin Ct)), Henriques, J.

r.35, see *R. v Phillips (Richard William)* [2001] EWCA Crim 2790, [2002] 2 Cr. App. R. (S.) 16 (CA (Crim Div)), Wright, J.

Sch.3 Part III, amended: SI 2002/2997 r.4, SI 2004/1047 r.3

Sch.5, revoked: SI 2002/1688 r.11

Sch.7, revoked: SI 2002/1688 r.11

Sch.11, substituted: SI 2003/1664 Sch.1

Sch.11 Part I, substituted: SI 2003/1664 Sch.1

Sch.11 Part II, substituted: SI 2003/1664 Sch.1

Sch.12, revoked: SI 2003/1664 r.2

Sch.13, added: SI 2002/2783 Sch.1

Sch.14, added: SI 2004/2991 Sch.1

1113. Police (Scotland) Amendment (No.2) Regulations 1982

revoked: SSI 2004/257 Sch.4

1123. Registration of Overseas Births and Deaths Regulations 1982

Reg.5, amended: 2002 c.8 s.2

Reg.7, amended: 2002 c.8 s.2

Reg.8, amended: 2002 c.8 s.2

1163. Motorways Traffic (England and Wales) Regulations 1982

Reg.5, varied: SI 2003/2186 Sch.1

Reg.7, amended: SI 2003/2186 Sch.1

Reg.15, varied: SI 2003/2186 Sch.1

Reg.16, amended: SI 2004/3168 Art.8

Reg.16, varied: SI 2003/2186 Sch.1

1209. Condensed Milk and Dried Milk (Scotland) (Amendment) Regulations 1982

revoked: SSI 2003/311 Reg.11

1221. Wildlife and Countryside (Registration and Ringing of Certain Captive Birds) Regulations 1982

applied: SI 2003/3235 Reg.6

revoked (in part): SI 2003/3235 Reg.6

Reg.1, amended: SI 2004/640 Reg.2

Reg.3, amended: SI 2004/640 Reg.2

Reg.4, amended: SI 2004/640 Reg.2

Reg.4, revoked (in part): SI 2004/640 Reg.2

Reg.5, amended: SI 2004/640 Reg.2

NO.

NO.

1982–cont.

1271. Motor Vehicles (Type Approval for Goods Vehicles) (Great Britain) Regulations 1982
varied: SI 2003/1866 Reg.3
Reg.2, amended: SI 2003/1866 Reg.2
Reg.3, amended: SI 2003/1866 Reg.2
Reg.4, amended: SI 2003/582 Reg.2, SI 2003/1866 Reg.2
Reg.4, revoked (in part): SI 2003/1866 Reg.2
Sch.1A Part I para.1, revoked: SI 2003/1866 Reg.2
Sch.1A Part I para.2, revoked: SI 2003/1866 Reg.2
Sch.1A Part I para.3, revoked: SI 2003/1866 Reg.2
Sch.1A Part I para.4, revoked: SI 2003/1866 Reg.2
Sch.1A Part II, revoked: SI 2003/1866 Reg.2
Sch.1B Part I para.1, revoked: SI 2003/1866 Reg.2
Sch.1B Part I para.1A, revoked: SI 2003/1866 Reg.2
Sch.1B Part I para.2, revoked: SI 2003/1866 Reg.2
Sch.1B Part I para.3, revoked: SI 2003/1866 Reg.2
Sch.1B Part II, revoked: SI 2003/1866 Reg.2
Sch.1B Part III para.1, revoked: SI 2003/1866 Reg.2
Sch.1B Part III para.2, revoked: SI 2003/1866 Reg.2
Sch.1B Part IV para.1, revoked: SI 2003/1866 Reg.2
Sch.1B Part IV para.2, revoked: SI 2003/1866 Reg.2
Sch.1C Part I para.1, amended: SI 2003/1866 Reg.2
Sch.1i Part I, substituted: SI 2003/1866 Sch.1
Sch.1i Part II para.1, substituted: SI 2003/1866 Sch.1
Sch.1i Part II para.2, substituted: SI 2003/1866 Sch.1
Sch.1i Part II para.3, substituted: SI 2003/1866 Sch.1

1311. Fruit Juices and Fruit Nectars (Amendment) Regulations 1982
revoked (in part): SI 2003/1564 Reg.10, SI 2003/3041 Reg.10

1357. Notification of Installations Handling Hazardous Substances Regulations 1982
referred to: SI 2002/2979 Reg.2
Reg.3, amended: SI 2002/2979 Reg.3
Reg.7, amended: SI 2002/2979 Reg.4
Reg.9, added: SI 2002/2979 Reg.5
Sch.1 Part I, amended: SI 2002/2979 Reg.6

1408. Social Security (General Benefit) Regulations 1982
Reg.16, amended: SI 2003/2262 Reg.2, SI 2004/2301 Reg.2
Reg.16, substituted: SI 2002/2311 Reg.2

1982–cont.

1489. Workmen's Compensation (Supplementation) Scheme 1982
Art.5, amended: SI 2002/718 Art.2, SI 2003/656 Art.2, SI 2004/582 Art.2
Art.7, applied: SI 2002/718 Art.4
Art.7, referred to: SI 2003/656 Art.4
Sch.1 Part I, substituted: SI 2002/718 Art.3, SI 2003/656 Art.3, SI 2004/582 Art.3
Sch.1 Part II, referred to: SI 2002/718 Art.5, SI 2003/656 Art.4
Sch.1 Part II, substituted: SI 2002/718 Art.3, SI 2003/656 Art.3, SI 2004/582 Art.3

1496. Notification of New Substances Regulations 1982
Reg.4, applied: SI 2003/547 Sch.15, SI 2004/456 Sch.14

1536. Homosexual Offences (Northern Ireland) Order 1982
Art.2, amended: SI 2003/1247 Sch.2
Art.6, revoked: SI 2003/1247 Sch.2
Art.7, applied: 2003 c.44 Sch.17 para.85
Art.8, applied: 2002 c.29 Sch.5 para.8, 2003 c.44 Sch.17 para.86
Art.11, amended: SI 2003/1247 Sch.1 para.10
Sch.1, revoked: SI 2003/1247 Sch.2

1619. Fruit Juices and Fruit Nectars (Scotland) (Amendment) Regulations 1982
revoked: SSI 2003/293 Reg.11

1628. Police (Scotland) Amendment (No.3) Regulations 1982
revoked: SSI 2004/257 Sch.4

1647. Registration of Overseas Births and Deaths (Amendment) Regulations 1982
Reg.3, amended: 2002 c.8 s.2

1662. Carriage of Goods by Sea (Bermuda) Order 1982
revoked: SI 2002/3147 Art.2

1667. Merchant Shipping (Tonnage) (Bermuda) Order 1982
revoked: SI 2002/3147 Art.2

1675. European Communities (Designation) (No.3) Order 1982
Sch.1, amended: SI 2003/2901 Sch.4

1676. Judicial Committee (General Appellate Jurisdiction) Rules Order 1982
Sch.B Part II, amended: SI 2003/1879 Sch.1
Sch.II Part 1 para.4, amended: SI 2003/1879 Art.2
Sch.II Part 1 para.8, amended: SI 2003/1879 Art.2
Sch.II Part 1 para.44, amended: SI 2003/1879 Art.2
Sch.II Part 1 para.47, amended: SI 2003/1879 Art.2
Sch.II Part 1 para.77, amended: SI 2003/1879 Art.2

1710. British Dependent Territories Citizenship (Designated Service) Order 1982
amended: 2002 c.8 s.1
Art.2, amended: 2002 c.8 s.2

NO.

1982–cont.

1710. British Dependent Territories Citizenship (Designated Service) Order 1982–cont.

Sch.1 para.1, amended: 2002 c.8 s.1

1727. Food (Revision of Penalties) Regulations 1982

Sch.1, amended: SI 2002/890 Sch.1, SI 2002/1886 Sch.1, SI 2003/1563 Reg.10, SI 2003/1564 Reg.10, SI 2003/1596 Reg.10, SI 2003/1659 Reg.11, SI 2003/2243 Reg.10, SI 2003/3037 Reg.11, SI 2003/3041 Reg.10, SI 2003/3044 Reg.10, SI 2003/3047 Reg.10, SI 2003/3053 Reg.10, SI 2003/3120 Reg.10, SI 2004/553 Reg.10

1802. Road Vehicles (Registration and Licensing) (Amendment) Regulations 1982

revoked: SI 2002/2742 Sch.1 Part I

1983

3. Child Benefit (General) Amendment Regulations 1983

revoked: SI 2003/493 Sch.2 Part 1

67. Offshore Installations (Safety Zones) (No.2) Order 1983

revoked: SI 2003/845 Art.4

133. Landlord and Tenant Act 1954, Part II (Notices) Regulations 1983

revoked: SI 2004/1005 Reg.4

142. African Development Bank (Immunities and Privileges) Order 1983

Art.14, amended: 2002 c.8 s.2

143. Commonwealth Foundation (Immunities and Privileges) Order 1983

Art.12, amended: 2002 c.8 s.2
Art.13, amended: 2002 c.8 s.2
Art.14, amended: 2002 c.8 s.2

144. Commonwealth Telecommunications Organisation (Immunities and Privileges) Order 1983

Art.13, amended: 2002 c.8 s.2
Art.14, amended: 2002 c.8 s.2

270. Food and Drugs (Scotland) Act 1956 (Transfer of Enforcement Functions) Regulations 1983

Sch.1, amended: SSI 2003/291 Reg.12, SSI 2003/293 Reg.11, SSI 2003/311 Reg.11, SSI 2003/527 Reg.11, SSI 2003/569 Reg.12
Sch.2, amended: SSI 2002/349 Sch.1, SSI 2004/133 Reg.11

316. Peterhead Bay Harbour Trust and Transfer Order 1983

referred to: SSI 2002/294 Art.1
Art.2, amended: SSI 2002/294 Art.13, Sch.3
Art.3, revoked (in part): SSI 2002/294 Sch.3
Sch.1, revoked: SSI 2002/294 Sch.3
Sch.2, amended: SSI 2002/294 Art.13
Sch.2, referred to: SSI 2002/294 Art.13
Sch.3, amended: SSI 2002/294 Art.14

NO.

1983–cont.

316. Peterhead Bay Harbour Trust and Transfer Order 1983–cont.

Sch.3, revoked: SSI 2002/294 Sch.3
Sch.6, revoked: SSI 2002/294 Art.13, Sch.3

317. Police (Scotland) Amendment Regulations 1983

revoked: SSI 2004/257 Sch.4

370. Judicial Trustee Rules 1983

r.8, see *Practice Direction (Judicial Trustees: Remuneration)* [2003] 1 W.L.R. 1653 (Ch D), Chief Chancery Master Winegarten
r.11, see *Practice Direction (Judicial Trustees: Remuneration)* [2003] 1 W.L.R. 1653 (Ch D), Chief Chancery Master Winegarten

479. British Nationality (Falkland Islands) Regulations 1983

Sch.2 para.1, amended: 2002 c.8 s.2
Sch.2 para.2, amended: 2002 c.8 s.2

605. Parliamentary Writs Order 1983

referred to: SI 2002/1057 Art.2

686. Personal Injuries (Civilians) Scheme 1983

referred to: SI 2004/717 Art.2
Art.2, revoked (in part): SI 2002/672 Sch.1 para.1
Art.14, applied: SR 2002/56 Reg.4, SSI 2003/176 Art.4
Art.15, applied: SR 2002/56 Reg.4
Art.16, applied: SR 2002/56 Reg.4
Art.18, amended: SI 2002/672 Sch.1 para.2
Art.18, applied: SSI 2003/176 Art.4
Art.19, amended: SI 2002/672 Sch.1 para.3
Art.25A, applied: SI 2002/1792 Sch.4 para.3, Sch.6 para.4, SR 2002/56 Reg.4, SR 2003/28 Sch.4 para.3, Sch.6 para.4
Art.26A, amended: SI 2004/717 Sch.1 para.1
Art.27, amended: SI 2002/672 Sch.1 para.4, Sch.1 para.5
Art.27, applied: SI 2002/1792 Sch.4 para.5, SR 2003/28 Sch.4 para.5
Art.31, amended: SI 2002/672 Sch.1 para.4, Sch.1 para.6
Art.32, revoked: SI 2002/672 Sch.1 para.1
Art.33, amended: SI 2002/672 Sch.1 para.7
Art.34, amended: SI 2002/672 Sch.1 para.8
Art.35, amended: SI 2002/672 Sch.1 para.9
Art.36, amended: SI 2002/672 Sch.1 para.10
Art.38, amended: SI 2002/672 Sch.1 para.11
Art.39, amended: SI 2002/672 Sch.1 para.12
Art.43, applied: SR 2002/56 Reg.4
Art.44, applied: SR 2002/56 Reg.4
Art.48A, applied: SR 2002/56 Reg.4
Art.49, amended: SI 2002/672 Sch.1 para.4, Sch.1 para.13
Art.49, revoked (in part): SI 2002/672 Sch.1 para.13
Art.51, amended: SI 2002/672 Sch.1 para.4
Art.54, amended: SI 2002/672 Sch.1 para.14
Art.60, amended: SI 2002/672 Sch.1 para.4
Art.64, applied: SI 2004/717 Sch.1 para.2
Art.71, amended: SI 2002/672 Sch.1 para.15

NO.

1983–cont.

686. Personal Injuries (Civilians) Scheme 1983–*cont.*

Sch.3, referred to: SI 2004/717 Sch.1 para.2

Sch.3, substituted: SI 2002/672 Sch.2, SI 2003/637 Sch.2, SI 2004/717 Sch.2

Sch.4, referred to: SI 2002/1792 Sch.4 para.5, SI 2004/717 Sch.1 para.2, SR 2003/28 Sch.4 para.5

Sch.4, substituted: SI 2002/672 Sch.2, SI 2003/637 Sch.2, SI 2004/717 Sch.2

Sch.7, referred to: SI 2004/717 Sch.1 para.2

Sch.7, substituted: SI 2002/672 Sch.3, SI 2003/637 Sch.3, SI 2004/717 Sch.3

747. Act of Sederunt (Ordinary Cause Rules, Sheriff Court) 1983

r.4, revoked: SSI 2002/132 Sch.2

808. Merchant Shipping (Medical Examination) Regulations 1983

revoked: SI 2002/2055 Reg.1

829. County of Gloucestershire (Electoral Arrangements) Order 1983

revoked: SI 2004/2814 Art.6

873. Nurses, Midwives and Health Visitors Rules Approval Order 1983

Sch.1, added: SI 2002/1169 Sch.1

Sch.1, amended: SI 2002/1169 Sch.1

Sch.1, revoked: SI 2002/1169 Sch.1

Sch.1, varied: SI 2003/3148 Reg.3

881. St Christopher and Nevis Constitution Order 1983

s.7, see *Fox (Berthill) v Queen, The (Appeal against Sentence)* [2002] UKPC 13, [2002] 2 A.C. 284 (PC (StC)), Lord Rodger of Earlsferry

883. Naval, Military and Air Forces Etc (Disablement and Death) Service Pensions Order 1983

applied: SI 2002/1792 Sch.4 para.1, SR 2003/28 Sch.4 para.1

referred to: SI 2002/792, SI 2003/434, SI 2004/708

see *Matthews v Ministry of Defence* [2003] UKHL 4, [2003] 1 A.C. 1163 (HL), Lord Bingham of Cornhill

Part IV, applied: SI 2002/1792 Sch.4 para.12, SR 2003/28 Sch.4 para.12

Art.3A, amended: SI 2002/792 Sch.1 para.1

Art.3A, revoked (in part): SI 2002/792 Sch.1 para.1

Art.3B, amended: SI 2002/792 Sch.1 para.2

Art.3B, revoked (in part): SI 2002/792 Sch.1 para.2

Art.9, amended: SI 2004/708 Sch.1 para.1

Art.10, applied: SR 2002/56 Reg.4

Art.14, applied: SSI 2003/176 Art.4

Art.18, amended: SI 2002/792 Sch.1 para.3

Art.18, applied: SSI 2003/176 Art.4

Art.18, referred to: SI 2002/792 Art.2

Art.19, amended: SI 2002/792 Sch.1 para.4

Art.19, referred to: SI 2002/792 Art.2

NO.

1983–cont.

883. Naval, Military and Air Forces Etc (Disablement and Death) Service Pensions Order 1983–*cont.*

Art.26A, applied: SI 2002/1792 Sch.4 para.3, Sch.6 para.4, SR 2002/56 Reg.4, SR 2003/28 Sch.4 para.3, Sch.6 para.4

Art.27, amended: SI 2002/792 Sch.1 para.5

Art.27, referred to: SI 2002/792 Art.2

Art.29, amended: SI 2002/792 Sch.1 para.6, SI 2003/434 Sch.1 para.1, SI 2004/708 Sch.1 para.2

Art.29, applied: SI 2002/1792 Sch.4 para.4, SR 2003/28 Sch.4 para.4

Art.29, referred to: SI 2002/1792 Sch.4 para.6, SR 2003/28 Sch.4 para.6

Art.31, amended: SI 2002/792 Sch.1 para.7

Art.32, amended: SI 2002/792 Sch.1 para.8

Art.33, amended: SI 2002/792 Sch.1 para.9

Art.33, referred to: SI 2002/792 Art.2

Art.34, revoked: SI 2002/792 Sch.1 para.10

Art.35, amended: SI 2002/792 Sch.1 para.11

Art.36, amended: SI 2002/792 Sch.1 para.12

Art.37, amended: SI 2002/792 Sch.1 para.13

Art.37, applied: SI 2002/1792 Reg.15, SR 2003/28 Reg.15

Art.38, amended: SI 2002/792 Sch.1 para.14

Art.40, amended: SI 2002/792 Sch.1 para.15

Art.41, amended: SI 2002/792 Sch.1 para.16

Art.42A, amended: SI 2004/708 Sch.1 para.3

Sch.1 Part II, amended: SI 2002/792 Sch.2, SI 2003/434 Sch.2, SI 2004/708 Sch.2

Sch.1 Part II, referred to: SI 2003/434 Sch.1 para.2

Sch.1 Part III, amended: SI 2002/792 Sch.3, Sch.4, SI 2003/434 Sch.3, Sch.4, SI 2004/708 Sch.3, Sch.4

Sch.1 Part III, referred to: SI 2003/434 Sch.1 para.2

Sch.1 Part IV, referred to: SI 2003/434 Sch.1 para.2

Sch.1 Part IV, substituted: SI 2002/792 Sch.5, SI 2003/434 Sch.5, SI 2004/708 Sch.5 Part IV

Sch.1 Part VI, added: SI 2004/708 Sch.6 Part VI

Sch.2 Part II, amended: SI 2002/792 Sch.6, SI 2003/434 Sch.6, SI 2004/708 Sch.7

Sch.2 Part II, referred to: SI 2003/434 Sch.1 para.3

Sch.2 Part III, referred to: SI 2003/434 Sch.1 para.3

Sch.2 Part III, substituted: SI 2002/792 Sch.7, SI 2003/434 Sch.7, SI 2004/708 Sch.8 Part III

Sch.4 Part II, amended: SI 2002/792 Sch.1 para.19, SI 2003/434 Sch.1 para.4

Sch.7, amended: SI 2003/434 Sch.8, SI 2004/708 Sch.9

Sch.7, referred to: SI 2003/434 Sch.1 para.5

Sch.7, substituted: SI 2002/792 Sch.8

NO.

1983–cont.

893. Mental Health (Hospital, Guardianship and Consent to Treatment) Regulations 1983
applied: SI 2002/325 Reg.46
Reg.7, amended: SI 2002/2469 Sch.1 para.40, Sch.5

894. Mental Health Act Commission Regulations 1983
Reg.9, amended: SI 2004/696 Sch.1 para.2

934. Offshore Installations (Safety Zones) (No.21) Order 1983
revoked: SI 2003/845 Art.4

942. Mental Health Review Tribunal Rules 1983
Part I r.2, amended: SI 2002/2469 Sch.5, SI 2004/696 Art.3
Part II r.7, amended: SI 2002/2469 Sch.6, SI 2004/696 Art.3
Part II r.8, amended: SI 2002/2469 Sch.6, SI 2004/696 Art.3
r.8, see *R. (on the application of PD) v West Midlands and North West Mental Health Review Tribunal* [2004] EWCA Civ 311, (2004) 148 S.J.L.B. 384 (CA), Lord Phillips of Worth Matravers, M.R.
r.16, see *R. (on the application of Secretary of State for the Home Department) v Mental Health Review Tribunal* (2002) 63 B.M.L.R.181 (QBD (Admin Ct)), Collins, J.
r.21, see *R. (on the application of T) v Mental Health Review Tribunal* [2002] EWHC 247, [2002] Lloyd's Rep. Med. 354 (QBD (Admin Ct)), Scott Baker, J.
Sch.1 Part A para.4, amended: SI 2002/2469 Sch.1 para.41, Sch.5

977. Dry Cleaning (Metrication) Regulations 1983
revoked: SI 2002/2776 Sch.7 Part 2

979. Factories (Testing of Aircraft Engines and Accessories) (Metrication) Regulations 1983
revoked: SI 2002/2776 Sch.7 Part 2

1039. Capital Transfer Tax (Delivery of Accounts) (No.3) Regulations 1983
revoked: SI 2002/1733 Sch.1

1040. Capital Transfer Tax (Delivery of Accounts) (Scoltand) (No.2) Regulations 1983
revoked: SI 2002/1733 Sch.1

1106. Merchant Shipping (Prevention of Oil Pollution) Order 1983
Art.3, enabled: SI 2004/303

1118. Housing (Northern Ireland) Order 1983
referred to: SI 2003/412 Art.1
Part II, applied: SI 2003/412 Art.5
Art.3A, added: SI 2003/412 Art.131
Art.24, amended: SI 2003/412 Sch.4 para.6
Art.24, referred to: SI 2003/412 Art.5
Art.26, amended: SI 2003/412 Sch.4 para.7
Art.28, substituted: SI 2003/412 Art.25

NO.

1983–cont.

1118. Housing (Northern Ireland) Order 1983–*cont.*
Art.29, amended: SI 2003/412 Art.25, Sch.5
Art.34A, added: SI 2003/412 Art.132
Art.35, amended: SI 2003/412 Art.132
Art.38, amended: SI 2003/412 Sch.4 para.8
Art.38A, applied: SI 2003/412 Art.17
Art.38A, substituted: SI 2003/412 Art.133
Art.92, amended: SI 2003/412 Sch.1 para.9
Sch.2, added: SI 2003/412 Art.134, Sch.4 para.9
Sch.2, amended: SI 2003/412 Art.134
Sch.2, substituted: SI 2003/412 Art.134, Sch.4 para.9
Sch.3, added: SI 2003/412 Art.23
Sch.3, amended: SI 2003/412 Art.24, Art.25
Sch.3, substituted: SI 2003/412 Art.22

1120. Criminal Attempts and Conspiracy (Northern Ireland) Order 1983
Art.3, applied: SI 2004/1500 Sch.2 para.2
Art.5, revoked (in part): SI 2003/1247 Sch.2
Art.9, applied: SI 2004/1500 Sch.2 para.31

1140. Classification and Labelling of Explosives Regulations 1983
applied: SI 2002/655 Sch.9 PartV, Sch.9 Part VI, SI 2003/547 Sch.9 PartV, Sch.9 PartVI, SI 2004/456 Sch.8 PartV, Sch.8 PartVI
referred to: SI 2002/2776 Sch.5
Reg.2, amended: SI 2004/568 Sch.12 para.2
Reg.3, amended: SI 2004/568 Sch.12 para.3
Reg.6, substituted: SI 2004/568 Sch.12 para.4
Reg.7, revoked: SI 2004/568 Sch.12 para.5
Reg.9, revoked: SI 2004/568 Sch.12 para.5
Reg.10, amended: SI 2004/568 Sch.12 para.6
Reg.12A, amended: SI 2004/568 Sch.12 para.7
Sch.1, revoked: SI 2004/568 Sch.12 para.8
Sch.2, revoked: SI 2004/568 Sch.12 para.8
Sch.3, amended: SI 2004/568 Sch.12 para.9
Sch.3 para.1, revoked: SI 2004/568 Sch.12 para.9
Sch.3 para.2, revoked: SI 2004/568 Sch.12 para.9
Sch.3 para.3, revoked: SI 2004/568 Sch.12 para.9
Sch.3 para.4, revoked: SI 2004/568 Sch.12 para.9
Sch.3 para.5, revoked: SI 2004/568 Sch.12 para.9
Sch.3 para.6, revoked: SI 2004/568 Sch.12 para.9
Sch.3 para.7, revoked: SI 2004/568 Sch.12 para.9
Sch.3 para.8, revoked: SI 2004/568 Sch.12 para.9
Sch.3 para.9, revoked: SI 2004/568 Sch.12 para.9
Sch.3 para.10, revoked: SI 2004/568 Sch.12 para.9

NO.

1983–cont.

1140. Classification and Labelling of Explosives Regulations 1983–*cont.*

Sch.3 para.11, revoked: SI 2004/568 Sch.12 para.9

Sch.3 para.12, amended: SI 2004/568 Sch.12 para.9

Sch.3 para.12, revoked (in part): SI 2004/568 Sch.12 para.9

Sch.3 para.13, amended: SI 2004/568 Sch.12 para.9

Sch.3 para.13, revoked (in part): SI 2004/568 Sch.12 para.9

Sch.3 para.16, revoked: SI 2004/568 Sch.12 para.9

Sch.3 para.17, revoked: SI 2004/568 Sch.12 para.9

1168. Electrically Assisted Pedal Cycles Regulations 1983

Reg.4, see *Winter v DPP* [2002] EWHC 1524, [2003] R.T.R. 14 (QBD (Admin Ct)), Michael Supperstone Q.C.

Reg.4, referred to: SI 2002/2742 Reg.4

1248. Road Vehicles (Registration and Licensing) (Amendment) Regulations 1983

revoked: SI 2002/2742 Sch.1 Part I

1354. Police (Scotland) Amendment (No.2) Regulations 1983

revoked: SSI 2004/257 Sch.4

1390. Measuring Equipment (Liquid Fuel delivered from Road Tankers) Regulations 1983

Reg.55A, amended: SI 2003/214 Sch.1 para.1

1553. Consumer Credit (Agreements) Regulations 1983

Reg.1, amended: SI 2004/1482 Reg.3

Reg.2, applied: SI 2004/1481 Reg.3

Reg.2, substituted: SI 2004/1482 Reg.4

Reg.3, amended: SI 2004/1482 Reg.5

Reg.3, applied: SI 2004/1481 Reg.3

Reg.4, amended: SI 2004/1482 Reg.6

Reg.5, amended: SI 2004/1482 Reg.7

Reg.6, amended: SI 2004/1482 Reg.8

Reg.7, amended: SI 2004/1482 Reg.9

Reg.7, applied: SI 2004/1481 Reg.3

Sch.1, amended: SI 2004/1482 Reg.10

Sch.2 Part I, substituted: SI 2004/1482 Reg.11

Sch.2 Part II, substituted: SI 2004/1482 Reg.11

Sch.3, amended: SI 2004/1482 Reg.12

Sch.4, substituted: SI 2004/1482 Reg.13

Sch.5 Part III, added: SI 2004/1482 Reg.14

Sch.6, see *Broadwick Financial Services Ltd v Spencer* [2002] EWCA Civ 35, [2002] 1 All E.R. (Comm) 446 (CA), Dyson, L.J.

Sch.7 para.1, substituted: SI 2004/1482 Reg.15

Sch.8 Part I, amended: SI 2004/1482 Reg.16

Sch.8 Part II, amended: SI 2004/1482 Reg.17

NO.

1983–cont.

1557. Consumer Credit (Cancellation Notices and Copies of Documents) Regulations 1983

Reg.5, amended: SI 2004/2619 Reg.5

Sch.1 Part II, substituted: SI 2004/2619 Reg.5

Sch.1 Part III, substituted: SI 2004/2619 Reg.5

Sch.1 Part VI, substituted: SI 2004/2619 Reg.5

1562. Consumer Credit (Rebate on Early Settlement) Regulations 1983

revoked: SI 2004/1483 Reg.8

1564. Consumer Credit (Settlement Information) Regulations 1983

Reg.3, amended: SI 2004/1483 Reg.9

Reg.3, revoked (in part): SI 2004/1483 Reg.9

Reg.4, amended: SI 2004/1483 Reg.9

Sch.1 para.7, amended: SI 2004/1483 Reg.9

1590. Town and Country Planning (Structure and Local Plans) (Scotland) Regulations 1983

referred to: SSI 2003/1 Art.7

Reg.2, amended: SSI 2004/332 Sch.2 para.1

Reg.2A, added: SSI 2004/332 Sch.2 para.2

Reg.4, amended: SSI 2002/201 Art.7, SSI 2003/1 Art.7

Reg.12, amended: SSI 2003/1 Art.7

Reg.19A, added: SSI 2004/332 Sch.2 para.3

Reg.41A, added: SSI 2004/332 Sch.2 para.4

Reg.45A, added: SSI 2004/332 Sch.2 para.5

1649. Asbestos (Licensing) Regulations 1983

applied: SI 2002/655 Reg.6, SI 2002/2675 Reg.8, SI 2003/547 Reg.6, SI 2004/456 Reg.5

1702. Merchant Shipping Act 1983 (Jersey) Order 1983

revoked: SI 2004/1284 Sch.1

1850. Police (Scotland) Amendment (No.3) Regulations 1983

revoked: SSI 2004/257 Sch.4

1899. Firearms (Northern Ireland) Order 1983

revoked: SI 2004/702 Sch.8

1950. Foot-and-Mouth Disease Order 1983

applied: SI 2002/2 Reg.4, SI 2002/8 Reg.4, Reg.5, SI 2002/76 Reg.4, SI 2002/119 Reg.4, SI 2002/130 Reg.4, Reg.5, SI 2002/242 Art.3, SI 2002/280 Art.3, Art.6, SI 2002/2152 Art.3, SI 2002/2304 Art.3, SI 2003/254 Art.3, SI 2003/1279 Art.3, SI 2003/1414 Art.3, SI 2003/1729 Art.3, SSI 2002/34 Art.12, SSI 2002/139 Reg.6, Reg.9, SSI 2003/129 Reg.10, Reg.11, SSI 2004/70 Reg.10, Reg.11

disapplied: SI 2003/483 Art.3, SI 2003/1966 Art.3

Art.8, applied: SI 2002/240 Art.10, SI 2002/274 Reg.10, SI 2002/1357 Art.10, SI 2002/2153 Art.10, SI 2002/2302 Art.10

Art.30, enabled: SSI 2002/54

NO.

1983–cont.

1950. Foot-and-Mouth Disease Order 1983–*cont.*

Art.31, applied: SI 2002/2 Reg.5, SI 2002/8 Reg.5, SI 2002/76 Reg.5, Reg.6, SI 2002/240 Art.10, SI 2002/242 Art.3, SI 2002/274 Reg.10, SI 2002/280 Art.3, SI 2002/1357 Art.10, SI 2002/2153 Art.10, SI 2002/2302 Art.10

Art.36, applied: SI 2002/242 Art.7, SI 2002/280 Art.7, SI 2002/2152 Art.5, SI 2002/2304 Art.5

Art.37C, applied: SI 2002/242 Art.5, SI 2002/280 Art.5

Art.37CC, applied: SI 2002/242 Art.5, SI 2002/280 Art.6

1964. Adoption Agencies Regulations 1983

applied: SI 2003/118 Reg.35, SI 2003/367 Reg.10, Reg.13, SI 2003/493 Reg.16, SI 2003/1021 Reg.5, SI 2003/1173 Reg.4

referred to: SI 2002/808 Art.2

Reg.1, amended: SI 2003/367 Reg.25, SI 2004/190 Reg.13

Reg.2, revoked: SI 2003/367 Reg.25

Reg.3, applied: SI 2003/365 Sch.1 para.3

Reg.3, revoked: SI 2003/367 Reg.25

Reg.5, added: SI 2002/808 Art.35

Reg.5A, amended: SI 2003/2555 Reg.2, SI 2003/3223 Reg.2

Reg.6, amended: SI 2003/367 Reg.25

Reg.6, revoked (in part): SI 2003/367 Reg.25

Reg.7, applied: SI 2003/118 Reg.25, SI 2003/1348 Reg.5, SI 2004/1011 Reg.5

Reg.7, varied: SI 2003/118 Sch.4

Reg.8, varied: SI 2003/118 Sch.4

Reg.8A, amended: SI 2003/710 Reg.21

Reg.8A, varied: SI 2003/118 Sch.4

Reg.9, applied: SI 2003/1348 Reg.5, SI 2004/1011 Reg.5

Reg.9, varied: SI 2003/118 Sch.4

Reg.10, applied: SI 2004/190 Reg.1, SI 2004/1011 Reg.5, Reg.11

Reg.10, referred to: SI 2003/1348 Reg.7

Reg.10, varied: SI 2003/118 Sch.4

Reg.11, applied: SI 2002/2788 Reg.2, SI 2002/2820 Reg.11, SI 2002/2822 Reg.2, SI 2003/118 Reg.25, SI 2003/1348 Reg.7, SI 2004/1011 Reg.5, Reg.10, Reg.11, SR 2002/377 Reg.2, SR 2002/378 Reg.2, SR 2002/379 Reg.11, SR 2002/382 Reg.1

Reg.11, varied: SI 2003/118 Sch.4

Reg.11A, amended: SI 2004/190 Reg.13, SI 2004/1081 Reg.2

Reg.11A, applied: SI 2004/190 Reg.2, Reg.3

Reg.11A, varied: SI 2003/118 Sch.4

Reg.12, see *A v Essex CC* [2002] EWHC 2707, [2003] 1 F.L.R. 615 (QBD), Buckley, J.

Reg.12, amended: SI 2002/2469 Sch.11

Reg.12, applied: SI 2003/1348 Reg.5, SI 2004/1011 Reg.5, SR 2002/377 Reg.15

Reg.12, varied: SI 2003/118 Sch.4

NO.

1983–cont.

1964. Adoption Agencies Regulations 1983–*cont.*

Reg.14, applied: SI 2003/365 Sch.1 para.3

Reg.14, varied: SI 2003/118 Sch.4

Reg.15, see *Gunn-Russo v Nugent Care Society* [2001] EWHC Admin 566, [2002] 1 F.L.R. 1 (QBD (Admin Ct)), Scott Baker, J.

Reg.15, amended: SI 2002/3220 Art.2, SI 2003/367 Reg.25

Reg.15, applied: SI 2003/365 Sch.1 para.3, SI 2004/1011 Reg.15

Reg.16, amended: SI 2003/367 Reg.25

Reg.16, applied: SI 2003/365 Sch.1 para.3

Sch.1 Part VII, referred to: SI 2003/118 Reg.8

Sch.2, referred to: SI 2003/118 Reg.6

1984

145. Pedal Bicycles (Safety) Regulations 1984

revoked: SI 2003/1101 Reg.2

248. Gaming Clubs (Hours and Charges) Regulations 1984

Reg.5, amended: SI 2002/1902 Reg.2

265. Adoption Rules 1984

Part I r.2., amended: SI 2003/183 r.3

Part I r.3., amended: SI 2003/183 r.4

Part II r.6., applied: 2003 c.42 s.21

Part III r.18., amended: SI 2003/183 r.5

Part III r.18., applied: 2003 c.42 s.21

Part IV r.27., amended: SI 2003/183 r.6

Part IV r.27., revoked (in part): SI 2003/183 r.6

Part IV r.29., revoked (in part): SI 2003/183 r.7

Part IV r.30., substituted: SI 2003/183 r.8

Part IV r.31., revoked (in part): SI 2003/183 r.9

Part IV r.32., revoked (in part): SI 2003/183 r.9

Part IV r.33., revoked (in part): SI 2003/183 r.9

Part IV r.34., amended: SI 2003/183 r.10

Part IV r.35., amended: SI 2003/183 r.10

Part IV r.36., revoked (in part): SI 2003/183 r.11

Part IV r.37A, added: SI 2003/183 r.12

Part IV r.37B, added: SI 2003/183 r.12

Part IV r.39., amended: SI 2003/183 r.13

Part IV r.40., amended: SI 2003/183 r.14

Part IV r.41., amended: SI 2003/183 r.15

Part IV r.41., revoked (in part): SI 2003/183 r.15

Part IV r.42., revoked (in part): SI 2003/183 r.16

Part IV r.43., revoked (in part): SI 2003/183 r.16

Part V r.47A, added: SI 2003/183 r.17

Part V r.47B, added: SI 2003/183 r.17

Part V r.51., amended: SI 2003/183 r.18

Part V r.52., amended: SI 2003/183 r.19

r.14, see *X (Children) (Adoption: Confidential Procedure), Re* [2002] EWCA Civ 828, [2002] 2 F.L.R. 476 (CA), Hale, L.J.

Sch.1, added: SI 2003/183 r.20, r.21, Sch.1

1984–cont.

265. Adoption Rules 1984–*cont.*
Sch.1, amended: SI 2003/183 r.20, r.21, r.22, r.23, r.24, r.25
Sch.2 para.1, amended: SI 2003/183 r.27
Sch.2 para.6A, added: SI 2003/183 r.27
Sch.4, amended: SI 2003/183 r.28

337. Child Benefit (General) Amendment Regulations 1984
revoked: SI 2003/493 Sch.2 Part 1

340. Supreme Court (Review of Taxation in Criminal Cases) Fees Order 1984
Art.2, substituted: SI 2003/647 Art.2
Sch.1, amended: SI 2003/647 Art.2

365. Double Taxation Relief (Taxes on Income) (New Zealand) Order 1984
Sch.1, added: SI 2004/1274 Sch.1 Part I
Sch.1, substituted: SI 2004/1274 Sch.1 Part I

455. Diseases of Fish Regulations 1984
Reg.2, disapplied: SI 2004/853 Sch.6
Reg.5, disapplied: SI 2004/853 Sch.6

467. Town and Country Planning (Control of Advertisements) (Scotland) Regulations 1984
applied: SI 2002/2779 Art.86, SSI 2004/219 Reg.2, SSI 2004/406 Sch.3 para.16
Reg.2, amended: SSI 2004/332 Sch.3 para.1
Reg.2A, added: SSI 2004/332 Sch.3 para.2
Reg.6, amended: SSI 2003/503 Sch.1 para.17
Reg.11, applied: SSI 2004/219 Reg.14
Reg.15, applied: SSI 2004/219 Reg.14
Reg.20, amended: SSI 2004/332 Sch.3 para.3
Reg.32A, added: SSI 2004/332 Sch.3 para.4
Sch.4, amended: SSI 2003/503 Sch.1 para.17

470. Gaming Clubs (Hours and Charges) (Scotland) Regulations 1984
Reg.5, amended: SI 2002/1902 Reg.2

488. Car Tax (Vehicles for the Handicapped) Order 1984
revoked: 2004 c.14 Sch.1 Part 9

510. Explosives Act 1875 etc (Metrication and Miscellaneous Amendment) Regulations 1984
Sch.1, amended: 2003 c.22 Sch.1

552. Coroners Rules 1984
see *R. (on the application of Middleton) v HM Coroner for Western Somerset* [2004] UKHL 10, [2004] 2 A.C. 182 (HL), Lord Bingham of Cornhill
see *R. (on the application of Middleton) v HM Coroner for Western Somerset* [2004] UKHL 10, [2004] 2 A.C. 182 (HL), Lord Bingham of Cornhill
Part VII r.46, amended: SI 2004/921 r.2
Part VII r.51, referred to: SI 2004/921 r.1
Part VII r.51, substituted: SI 2004/921 r.3
r.17, see *R. (on the application of Middleton) v HM Coroner for Western Somerset* [2001] EWHC Admin 1043, (2002) 166 J.P. 193 (QBD (Admin Ct)), Stanley Burnton, J.

1984–cont.

552. Coroners Rules 1984–*cont.*
r.36, see *R. (on the application of Sacker) v HM Coroner for West Yorkshire* [2004] UKHL 11, [2004] 1 W.L.R. 796 (HL), Lord Bingham of Cornhill
r.37, see *R. (on the application of Mulholland) v HM Coroner for St Pancras* [2003] EWHC 2612, (2004) 78 B.M.L.R. 75 (QBD (Admin Ct)), Kennedy, L.J.
r.43, see *R. (on the application of Sacker) v HM Coroner for West Yorkshire* [2003] EWCA Civ 217, [2003] 2 All E.R. 278 (CA), Pill, L.J.; see *R. (on the application of Sacker) v HM Coroner for West Yorkshire* [2004] UKHL 11, [2004] 1 W.L.R. 796 (HL), Lord Bingham of Cornhill
Sch.4, amended: SI 2004/921 r.4

672. Driving Licences (Exchangeable Licences) Order 1984
Art.2, amended: SI 2002/1593 Art.3

746. Value Added Tax (Imported Goods) Relief Order 1984
applied: SI 2002/1935 Art.2, Art.3

748. Road Transport (International Passenger Services) Regulations 1984
Reg.2, amended: SI 2004/1882 Reg.2
Reg.14, amended: SI 2003/1118 Reg.2, SI 2004/1882 Reg.2

769. Medicines (Products Other Than Veterinary Drugs) (General Sale List) Order 1984
Art.1, amended: SI 2002/933 Art.2
Art.2, substituted: SI 2002/933 Art.2

779. Savings Certificates (Yearly Plan) Regulations 1984
Reg.17, amended: SI 2004/1662 Sch.1 para.25

880. Bankruptcy Fees Order 1984
Sch.1, amended: SI 2004/593 Sch.1

942. Mental Health Review Tribunal Rules 1984
r.11, see *R. (on the application of S) v Mental Health Review Tribunal* [2002] EWHC 2522, Times, December 6, 2002 (QBD (Admin Ct)), Stanley Burnton, J.

988. Adoption Agencies (Scotland) Regulations 1984
applied: SI 2003/493 Reg.16

998. Bridlington Harbour Revision Order 1984
Art.3, revoked: SI 2004/1426 Sch.3
Art.5, revoked: SI 2004/1426 Sch.3

1039. Church Representation Rules (Amendment) (No.1) Resolution 1984
referred to: SI 2004/1889

1040. Church Representation Rules (Amendment) (No.2) Resolution 1984
referred to: SI 2004/1889

1044. Offshore Installations (Safety Zones) (No.50) Order 1984
revoked: SI 2003/845 Art.4

NO.

1984–cont.

1047. Dairy Produce Quotas Regulations 1984

applied: SI 2003/409 Sch.1 Part I

1057. Pedal Bicycles (Safety) (Amendment) Regulations 1984

revoked: SI 2003/1101 Reg.2

1115. Fishing Vessels (Certification of Deck Officers and Engineer Officers) Regulations 1984

referred to: SI 2002/2934 Sch.1 Part 3

1159. Industrial Training (Northern Ireland) Order 1984

Art.16, applied: SI 2003/493 Reg.6, Reg.10

Art.21, amended: SI 2003/418 Sch.1 para.8, Sch.3

Art.23, applied: SR 2002/245

Art.23, enabled: SR 2002/245

Art.24, enabled: SR 2002/245

1303. Social Security (Severe Disablement Allowance) Regulations 1984

Reg.2A, revoked (in part): SI 2003/937 Reg.2

1325. Importation of Bovine Semen Regulations 1984

disapplied: SI 2004/853 Sch.6, SI 2004/1214 Reg.67, SI 2004/1740 Reg.67, SI 2004/2640 Reg.67

1345. Residential Care Homes Regulations 1984

revoked (in part): SI 2002/324 Reg.49

1494. Mental Health (Specified Treatments, Guardianship Duties etc.) (Scotland) Regulations 1984

Reg.4, revoked: SSI 2002/95 Reg.4

Reg.7, revoked: SSI 2002/95 Reg.4

1522. Undersized Scallops (West Coast) Order 1984

revoked (in part): SI 2004/12 Art.9

1566. Meat Products and Spreadable Fish Products Regulations 1984

applied: SI 2003/2075 Reg.10, SI 2004/554 Reg.3, SI 2004/1396 Reg.10

referred to: SI 2003/1008 Reg.3

revoked (in part): SI 2003/2075 Reg.11, SI 2004/1396 Reg.11

varied: SI 2002/329 Reg.9, SI 2003/945 Reg.3

Reg.2, referred to: SI 2002/330 Reg.3

Reg.2, varied: SI 2002/379 Reg.5, SI 2003/1182 Reg.3, SI 2003/1713 Reg.3

1578. Nursing Homes and Mental Nursing Homes Regulations 1984

revoked (in part): SI 2002/324 Reg.49

Reg.2, amended: SI 2002/3135 Sch.1 para.24

Reg.12, see *R. (on the application of A) v Partnerships in Care Ltd* [2002] EWHC 529, [2002] 1 W.L.R. 2610 (QBD (Admin Ct)), Keith, J.

NO.

1984–cont.

1651. Police (Scotland) Amendment Regulations 1984

revoked: SSI 2004/257 Sch.4

1714. Meat Products and Spreadable Fish Products (Scotland) Regulations 1984

applied: SSI 2004/6 Reg.8

revoked: SSI 2004/6 Reg.11

1795. Lincolnshire (Coroners Districts) (Amendment) Order 1984

revoked: SI 2002/1588 Art.4

1810. Motor Vehicles (Authorisation of Special Types) (Amendment) Order 1984

revoked: SI 2003/1998 Art.2

1821. Fire Services (Northern Ireland) Order 1984

applied: SR 2002/352 Reg.5, SR 2003/28 Sch.6 para.2

referred to: 2003 c.36 s.3

Art.9, enabled: SR 2002/283, SR 2003/207

Art.12, substituted: SI 2003/418 Sch.1 para.3

Art.52, enabled: SR 2002/283, SR 2003/207

1822. General Consumer Council (Northern Ireland) Order 1984

Sch.1, amended: SI 2003/418 Sch.1 para.5, SI 2003/419 Art.9

Sch.1, applied: SI 2003/419 Art.9

Sch.1, revoked (in part): SI 2003/418 Sch.3, SI 2003/419 Sch.5

1890. Freight Containers (Safety Convention) Regulations 1984

applied: SI 2002/655 Reg.5, SI 2003/547 Reg.5, SI 2004/456 Reg.4

1918. Imported Food Regulations 1984

disapplied: SI 2002/1227 Sch.7, SI 2002/1387 Sch.7, SI 2003/3177 Reg.67, SI 2004/1214 Reg.67, SI 2004/1430 Reg.67, SI 2004/1740 Reg.67, SI 2004/2640 Reg.67

1960. Child Benefit (Claims and Payments) Regulations 1984

Reg.7, referred to: SI 2003/492 Reg.35

1978. Consular Relations (Privileges and Immunities) (People's Republic of China) Order 1984

Art.4, amended: 2002 c.8 s.2

1981. Inter-American Development Bank (Immunities and Privileges) (Amendment) Order 1984

amended: 2002 c.8 s.2

Art.2, amended: 2002 c.8 s.2

1982. International Lead and Zinc Study Group (Immunities and Privileges) (Amendment) Order 1984

amended: 2002 c.8 s.2

1984. Family Law (Miscellaneous Provisions) (Northern Ireland) Order 1984

Art.18, amended: 2004 c.7 Sch.4 para.8

Art.18, applied: SI 2003/413 Art.6

NO.

1984-cont.

1992. Control of Noise (Codes of Practice for Construction and Open Sites) Order 1984

revoked (in part): SI 2002/461 Art.3, SI 2002/1795 Art.3

2010. General Dental Council Health Committee (Procedure) Rules Order of Council 1984

Sch.1, amended: SI 2002/2469 Sch.2, Sch.6

1985

67. Food (Revision of Penalties) Regulations 1985

Sch.1, amended: SI 2002/890 Sch.1, SI 2002/1886 Sch.1, SI 2003/1563 Reg.10, SI 2003/1564 Reg.10, SI 2003/1596 Reg.10, SI 2003/1659 Reg.11, SI 2003/2243 Reg.10, SI 2003/3041 Reg.10, SI 2003/3044 Reg.10, SI 2003/3047 Reg.10, SI 2003/3053 Reg.10, SI 2003/3120 Reg.10, SI 2004/553 Reg.10

111. Police (Scotland) Amendment Regulations 1985

revoked: SSI 2004/257 Sch.4

170. Nature Conservation and Amenity Lands (Northern Ireland) Order 1985

Part VI, revoked: SI 2002/3153 Sch.6 Part II

Art.9, applied: SI 2003/2261 Sch.3 Part I, Sch.4 para.3

Art.10, amended: SI 2002/3153 Sch.6 Part II

Art.16, amended: SI 2002/3153 Sch.5 para.9

Art.24, applied: SI 2002/3153 Sch.4 para.2, Sch.4 para.6

Art.25, applied: SI 2002/3153 Sch.4 para.3, Sch.4 para.5

Art.26, applied: SI 2002/3153 Sch.4 para.7

Art.26, referred to: SI 2002/3153 Sch.4 para.7

Art.30, amended: SI 2002/3153 Sch.6 Part II

Art.33, revoked (in part): SI 2002/3153 Sch.6 Part II

Sch.2, referred to: SI 2002/3153 Art.41

171. Wildlife (Northern Ireland) Order 1985

referred to: SR 2003/115 Reg.6

Art.2, amended: SI 2004/702 Sch.7 para.8

Reg.16, applied: SR 2002/1 Reg.6

Sch.11, amended: SI 2004/702 Sch.7 para.9

454. Local Elections (Northern Ireland) Order 1985

applied: SI 2003/1557 Reg.7

Art.2, amended: SI 2002/2835 Art.10

Sch.2, amended: SI 2002/2835 Art.11, Art.12, Art.14

Sch.2, revoked (in part): SI 2002/2835 Art.11, Art.13

Sch.2, substituted: SI 2002/2835 Sch.1

Sch.2, varied: SI 2003/1557 Sch.2 para.3

NO.

1985-cont.

512. Merchant Shipping (Medical Examination) (Amendment) Regulations 1985

revoked: SI 2002/2055 Reg.1

518. Police (Discipline) Regulations 1985

Reg.14.7, see *R. (on the application of Bennion) v Chief Constable of Merseyside* [2001] EWCA Civ 638, [2002] I.C.R. 136 (CA), Judge, L.J.

520. Police (Complaints) (General) Regulations 1985

Reg.2, amended: SI 2003/2602 Reg.2

Reg.4, amended: SI 2003/2602 Reg.3

Reg.5, amended: SI 2003/2602 Reg.4

Reg.7, amended: SI 2003/2602 Reg.5

Reg.8, amended: SI 2003/2602 Reg.6

Reg.8, revoked (in part): SI 2003/2602 Reg.6

Reg.10, amended: SI 2003/2602 Reg.7

Reg.11, amended: SI 2003/2602 Reg.8

Reg.11, referred to: SI 2003/2601 Reg.4

Reg.13, amended: SI 2003/2602 Reg.9

671. Police (Complaints) (Informal Resolution) Regulations 1985

applied: SI 2004/671 Art.4

672. Police (Anonymous, Repetitious Etc Complaints) Regulations 1985

Reg.3, applied: SI 2003/2601 Reg.4, SI 2004/671 Art.4

699. Protection of Wrecks (Designation No 1) Order 1985

revoked: SI 2004/2395 Sch.2 para.3

747. Six Pit and Upper Bank Junctions Light Railway Order 1985

Art.7, amended: SI 2003/2155 Sch.1 para.18, Sch.1 para.20, Sch.2

753. Specialized Agencies of the United Nations (Immunities and Privileges) (Amendment) (No.2) Order 1985

amended: 2002 c.8 s.2

Art.2, amended: 2002 c.8 s.2

810. Alton Station Light Railway Order 1985

Art.7, amended: SI 2003/2155 Sch.1 para.18

844. Lydney and Parkend Light Railway Order 1985

Art.7, amended: SI 2003/2155 Sch.1 para.18

854. Companies (Forms) Regulations 1985

see *Igroup Ltd v Ocwen* [2003] EWHC 2431, [2004] 1 W.L.R. 451 (Ch D (Companies Court)), Lightman, J.

913. Imported Food (Scotland) Regulations 1985

disapplied: SSI 2002/445 Sch.7

967. Social Security (Industrial Injuries) (Prescribed Diseases) Regulations 1985

Reg.4, amended: SI 2003/270 Reg.2

Reg.7, amended: SI 2003/270 Reg.3

Reg.8, amended: SI 2003/270 Reg.4

Reg.20, amended: SI 2002/1717 Reg.2

Reg.20A, added: SI 2002/1717 Reg.2

NO.

NO.

1985–cont.

967. Social Security (Industrial Injuries) (Prescribed Diseases) Regulations 1985–*cont.*

Reg.29, substituted: SI 2003/2190 Reg.2

Reg.30, revoked (in part): SI 2003/2190 Reg.2

Reg.31, revoked (in part): SI 2003/2190 Reg.2

Reg.32, revoked (in part): SI 2003/2190 Reg.2

Reg.33, revoked (in part): SI 2003/2190 Reg.2

Sch.1 Part I, see *R. (on the application of National Association of Colliery Overmen Deputies and Shotfirers) v Secretary of State for Work and Pensions* [2003] EWHC 607, [2004] A.C.D. 14 (QBD (Admin Ct)), Pitchford, J.

Sch.1 Part I, amended: SI 2003/270 Reg.5, SI 2003/2190 Reg.3

980. Seeds (Registration, Licensing and Enforcement) Regulations 1985

applied: SI 2002/3176 Reg.42

revoked (in part): SI 2002/3176 Reg.42

Reg.4, applied: SI 2002/3176 Reg.42, SSI 2004/317 Reg.16, Reg.24

Reg.9, applied: SI 2002/3176 Reg.42

Reg.10, applied: SI 2002/3176 Reg.42

Reg.13, applied: SSI 2004/317 Reg.24

981. Seeds (Fees) Regulations 1985

applied: SI 2002/3176 Reg.42

Reg.2, amended: SI 2002/1554 Reg.2

Sch.1, referred to: SI 2002/1563 Reg.2

Sch.1, revoked (in part): SI 2002/3173 Reg.32

Sch.1, substituted: SI 2002/1563 Sch.1, SI 2002/1870 Sch.1

Sch.2, referred to: SI 2002/1563 Reg.2

Sch.2, revoked (in part): SI 2002/3172 Reg.32

Sch.2, substituted: SI 2002/1563 Sch.1, SI 2002/1870 Sch.1

Sch.3, referred to: SI 2002/1563 Reg.2

Sch.3, revoked (in part): SI 2002/3174 Reg.32, SI 2004/2881 Reg.32

Sch.3, substituted: SI 2002/1563 Sch.1, SI 2002/1870 Sch.1

Sch.4, referred to: SI 2002/1563 Reg.2

Sch.4, revoked (in part): SI 2002/3171 Reg.29

Sch.4, substituted: SI 2002/1563 Sch.1, SI 2002/1870 Sch.1

Sch.5, referred to: SI 2002/1563 Reg.2

Sch.5, revoked (in part): SI 2002/3175 Reg.32

Sch.5, substituted: SI 2002/1563 Sch.1, SI 2002/1870 Sch.1

Sch.6, referred to: SI 2002/1563 Reg.2

Sch.6, revoked (in part): SI 2002/3176 Reg.42

Sch.6, substituted: SI 2002/1563 Sch.1, SI 2002/1870 Sch.1

1985–cont.

1033. Hydrocarbon Oil (Amendment) Regulations 1985

revoked: SI 2002/1773 Reg.20

1047. Radioactive Substances (Gaseous Tritium Light Devices) Exemption Order 1985

Art.3, amended: SI 2004/3168 Art.9

1068. Food (Revision of Penalties and Mode of Trial) (Scotland) Regulations 1985

Sch.1, amended: SSI 2002/349 Sch.1, SSI 2003/291 Reg.12, SSI 2003/293 Reg.11, SSI 2003/311 Reg.11, SSI 2003/527 Reg.11, SSI 2003/569 Reg.12, SSI 2004/6 Reg.11, SSI 2004/133 Reg.11

Sch.2, amended: SSI 2002/349 Sch.1, SSI 2003/293 Reg.11, SSI 2003/311 Reg.11, SSI 2003/569 Reg.12, SSI 2004/133 Reg.11

1071. International Carriage of Perishable Foodstuffs Regulations 1985

referred to: SI 2003/1693 Reg.2

Reg.25, amended: SI 2003/1693 Reg.3

Sch.1 Part I, amended: SI 2003/1693 Reg.4

Sch.1 Part II, amended: SI 2003/1693 Reg.4

Sch.1 Part III, amended: SI 2003/1693 Reg.4

1116. European Assembly (United Kingdom Representatives) Pensions (Amendment) Order 1985

applied: SI 2003/2922 Art.2

1204. Betting, Gaming, Lotteries and Amusements (Northern Ireland) Order 1985

applied: SI 2004/310 Art.10, Sch.3 para.1

varied: SI 2004/310 Sch.3 para.2

Art.3, amended: SI 2004/310 Art.3, Art.4, Sch.4

Art.8, amended: SI 2004/310 Art.9

Art.12, see *McLean v Kirkpatrick* [2003] N.I. 14 (CA (NI)), Carswell, L.C.J.

Art.12, amended: SI 2004/310 Art.9, Sch.2 para.1

Art.12, revoked (in part): SI 2004/310 Art.5, Sch.4

Art.12, varied: SR 2003/73 Sch.1

Art.13, amended: SI 2004/310 Sch.2 para.2

Art.14, amended: SI 2004/310 Sch.2 para.3

Art.15, amended: SI 2004/310 Sch.2 para.4

Art.17, amended: SI 2004/310 Art.9

Art.19, amended: SI 2004/310 Art.9

Art.23, amended: SI 2004/310 Art.9

Art.27, amended: SI 2004/310 Art.9

Art.28, amended: SI 2004/310 Art.9

Art.32, amended: SI 2004/310 Art.6

Art.32, revoked (in part): SI 2004/310 Art.6, Sch.4

Art.36, revoked (in part): SI 2004/310 Art.4, Sch.4

Art.44, amended: SI 2004/310 Art.3

Art.46, amended: SI 2004/310 Art.4

Art.48, amended: SI 2004/310 Art.4, Sch.4

NO.

1985–cont.

1204. Betting, Gaming, Lotteries and Amusements (Northern Ireland) Order 1985–*cont.*

Art.49, amended: SI 2004/310 Art.4
Art.53, amended: SI 2004/310 Art.9
Art.53A, added: SI 2004/310 Art.4
Art.53B, added: SI 2004/310 Art.4
Art.56, applied: SR 2003/233 Reg.2
Art.76, enabled: SR 2003/233
Art.77, amended: SR 2003/15 Art.2
Art.77, applied: SR 2003/233 Reg.1
Art.77, enabled: SR 2003/15
Art.86, amended: SI 2004/310 Art.12, Sch.4
Art.96, amended: SI 2004/310 Art.7
Art.107, amended: SI 2004/310 Art.8, Sch.4
Art.108, amended: SI 2004/310 Art.8, Art.10, SR 2003/15 Art.3
Art.108, applied: SI 2004/310 Art.10
Art.108, enabled: SR 2003/15
Art.111, amended: SI 2004/310 Art.10
Art.114, amended: SI 2004/310 Art.10
Art.115, amended: SI 2004/310 Art.10
Art.117, amended: SI 2004/310 Art.10
Art.130, amended: SI 2004/310 Art.11
Art.130, revoked (in part): SI 2004/310 Art.11, Sch.4
Art.131, applied: SI 2003/1593 Sch.1 Part II
Art.132, applied: SI 2003/1593 Sch.1 Part II
Art.133, applied: SI 2003/1593 Sch.1 Part II
Art.134, applied: SI 2003/1593 Sch.1 Part II
Art.135, applied: SI 2003/1593 Sch.1 Part II
Art.161, amended: SI 2004/310 Art.12
Art.168, applied: SI 2003/1593 Sch.1 Part II
Art.173, amended: SI 2004/310 Sch.2 para.5
Art.174, amended: SI 2004/310 Art.9, Sch.2 para.6, Sch.4
Art.177, amended: SI 2004/310 Sch.2 para.7
Art.178, amended: SI 2004/310 Sch.2 para.8, Sch.4
Art.179, amended: SI 2004/310 Sch.2 para.9
Art.179, applied: SI 2004/310 Sch.3 para.2
Art.182, amended: SI 2004/310 Art.9
Art.184, substituted: SI 2004/310 Sch.2 para.10
Art.186, amended: SI 2004/310 Sch.2 para.11, Sch.4
Art.187, amended: SI 2004/310 Sch.2 para.12
Sch.2, amended: SI 2004/310 Sch.2 para.13
Sch.2, referred to: SI 2004/310 Sch.3 para.1
Sch.2 para.4, see *McLean v Kirkpatrick* [2003] N.I. 14 (CA (NI)), Carswell, L.C.J.
Sch.8A, added: SI 2004/310 Sch.1
Sch.13, amended: SI 2004/310 Art.7

1208. Local Government (Miscellaneous Provisions) (Northern Ireland) Order 1985

Part IV, revoked: SI 2003/412 Sch.2 para.4, Sch.5
Art.41, revoked: SI 2002/3149 Sch.1
Sch.4, amended: SI 2003/418 Sch.3

NO.

1985–cont.

1251. Shoreham Port Authority Revision Order 1985

Art.3, amended: SI 2004/1506 Art.10
Art.3, referred to: SI 2004/1506 Art.11

1325. Police (Scotland) Amendment (No.2) Regulations 1985

revoked: SSI 2004/257 Sch.4

1327. Social Security (Guardian's Allowances) Amendment Regulations 1985

revoked: SI 2003/495 Sch.1 Part 1

1391. Registration of Fish Farming and Shellfish Farming Businesses Order 1985

Art.2, amended: SSI 2002/193 Art.2
Art.4A, added: SSI 2002/193 Art.2
Art.4B, added: SSI 2002/193 Art.2
Sch.3 Part I para.3, added: SSI 2002/193 Art.2
Sch.4, added: SSI 2002/193 Sch.1
Sch.5, added: SSI 2002/193 Sch.2

1438. Lead in Food (Scotland) Amendment Regulations 1985

revoked: SSI 2002/349 Sch.1

1504. Harbour Authorities (Constitution) Order 1985

Art.6, revoked: SI 2003/2724 Sch.3

1531. Police Federation (Scotland) Regulations 1985

Reg.7, referred to: SSI 2004/257 Reg.23

1604. Statutory Sick Pay (Medical Evidence) Regulations 1985

Sch.1 Part I para.3, substituted: SI 2004/865 Sch.1 para.3, SI 2004/1016 Sch.1 para.3

1638. Child Abduction (Northern Ireland) Order 1985

applied: SI 2004/702 Sch.4 para.6
Art.3, amended: 2002 c.26 Sch.12 para.33
Art.7, revoked (in part): SI 2004/702 Sch.8
Sch.1, amended: 2002 c.26 Sch.12 para.34

1659. National Health Service (Compensation for Premature Retirement) Amendment Regulations 1985

revoked: SI 2002/1311 Sch.2

1662. Industrial Training (Transfer of the Activities of Establishments) Order 1985

referred to: SI 2004/368 Sch.1

1699. Deposits in the Sea (Exemptions) Order 1985

Sch.1 para.14, amended: SI 2002/1355 Reg.20
Sch.1 para.15A, added: SI 2002/1355 Reg.20

1733. Police (Scotland) Amendment (No.3) Regulations 1985

revoked: SSI 2004/257 Sch.4

1765. Diseases of Animals (Ascertainment of Disease) Order 1985

revoked (in part): SI 2002/3229 Art.13, SI 2003/399 Art.13, SSI 2003/353 Art.13

NO.

1985–cont.

1773. European Communities (Immunities and Privileges of the North Atlantic Salmon Conservation Organization) Order 1985

Art.11, amended: 2002 c.8 s.2

Art.12, amended: 2002 c.8 s.2

1783. Bankruptcy Fees (Amendment) Order 1985

revoked: SI 2004/593 Sch.1

1784. Companies (Department of Trade and Industry) Fees Order 1985

Sch.1, amended: SI 2004/593 Sch.1

1799. Boarding-out and Fostering of Children (Scotland) Regulations 1985

Reg.9, applied: SI 2002/2006 Reg.19

1820. Royal Air Force Terms of Service Regulations 1985

Reg.15, amended: SI 2003/2305 Reg.2

1857. Artificial Insemination of Cattle (Animal Health) (Scotland) Regulations 1985

Reg.2, amended: SSI 2002/191 Reg.2

Reg.4, amended: SSI 2002/191 Reg.2

Reg.21, amended: SSI 2002/191 Reg.2

Reg.24, amended: SSI 2002/191 Reg.2

1861. Artificial Insemination of Cattle (Animal Health) (England and Wales) Regulations 1985

Reg.4, amended: SI 2002/824 Reg.2, SI 2002/1131 Reg.2

1903. Transport Act 1985 (Modifications in Schedule 4 to the Transport Act 1968) Order 1985

Sch.2, amended: 2003 c.14 Sch.20 para.3

1921. Service Subsidy Agreements (Tendering) Regulations 1985

revoked (in part): SI 2002/2090 Sch.2

Reg.3, substituted: SI 2002/520 Reg.2

1925. Bankruptcy (Scotland) Regulations 1985

referred to: SI 2003/2109 Reg.4

Reg.18, amended: SI 2003/2109 Reg.20

Sch.1, amended: SI 2003/2109 Sch.1

Sch.1, referred to: SI 2003/2109 Reg.21

1970. M11 London to Cambridge Motorway (Stansted Airport Spur Roads and Connecting Roads at Birchanger) Scheme 1985

revoked: SI 2004/446 Art.2

1996. Double Taxation Relief (Taxes on Income) (Canada) Order 1985

Sch.1, referred to: SI 2003/2619 Art.2

2036. National Health Service (Compensation for Premature Retirement) (Scotland) Amendment Regulations 1985

revoked: SSI 2003/344 Sch.2

NO.

1986

26. Textile Products (Indications of Fibre Content) Regulations 1986

applied: SI 2003/1400 Sch.3, Sch.4

149. General Medical Council (Registration (Fees) Regulations) Order of Council 1986

Sch.1, added: SI 2003/1074 Sch.1, SI 2003/1342 Sch.1

Sch.1, amended: SI 2003/1074 Sch.1, SI 2003/1342 Sch.1

Sch.1, applied: SI 2003/1341 Sch.1, SI 2003/1342 Sch.1, SI 2004/2609 Sch.1, SI 2004/2612 Sch.1

174. Bo'ness and Kinneil Light Railway Order 1986

Art.10, amended: SI 2003/2155 Sch.1 para.18

183. Removal and Disposal of Vehicles Regulations 1986

Reg.3, varied: SI 2003/2186 Sch.2

Reg.4, see *Clarke v Chief Constable of West Midlands* [2001] EWCA Civ 1169, [2002] R.T.R. 5 (CA), Longmore, L.J.

Reg.4, varied: SI 2003/2186 Sch.2

Reg.4A, amended: SI 2002/2777 Reg.3

Reg.10, amended: SI 2002/746 Reg.3, SSI 2002/538 Reg.3

Reg.14, amended: SI 2002/746 Reg.4, SSI 2002/538 Reg.4

260. Postal Packets (Customs and Excise) Regulations 1986

Reg.5A, applied: SI 2003/3113 Sch.1

Reg.9, applied: SI 2003/3113 Sch.1

Reg.11, applied: SI 2003/3113 Sch.1

Reg.12, applied: SI 2003/3113 Sch.1

Reg.14, applied: SI 2003/3113 Sch.1

Reg.17, applied: SI 2003/3113 Sch.1

275. Legal Advice and Assistance (Amendment) Regulations 1986

revoked: SI 2003/435 Sch.5

277. East Lancashire Light Railway Order 1986

Art.8, amended: SI 2003/2155 Sch.1 para.18, Sch.1 para.21, Sch.2

297. Mersey Tunnels Order 1986

applied: 2004 c.ii

313. Motor Vehicles (Authorisation of Special Types) (Amendment) Order 1986

revoked: SI 2003/1998 Art.2

343. Bluebell Extension Light Railway Order 1986

Art.8, amended: SI 2003/2155 Sch.1 para.18

416. Misuse of Drugs (Licence Fees) Regulations 1986

Reg.3, amended: SI 2003/611 Reg.2

428. Heather and Grass etc (Burning) Regulations 1986

Reg.2, amended: SI 2003/1615 Sch.1 para.41

Reg.4, amended: SI 2003/1615 Sch.1 para.41

Reg.5, amended: SI 2003/1615 Sch.1 para.41

Reg.7, amended: SI 2003/1615 Sch.1 para.41

NO.

1986–cont.

428. Heather and Grass etc (Burning) Regulations 1986–*cont.*

Reg.9, amended: SI 2003/1615 Sch.1 para.41

524. National Health Service (Transfer of Officers) (No.2) Regulations 1986

Reg.1, amended: SI 2002/2469 Sch.1 para.42

576. Police (Scotland) Amendment Regulations 1986

revoked: SSI 2004/257 Sch.4

590. Value Added Tax Tribunals Rules 1986

referred to: SI 2002/2851 r.2, SI 2003/2757 r.1, SI 2004/1032 r.1

r.2, amended: SI 2002/2851 r.3, SI 2003/2757 r.2, SI 2004/1032 r.2

r.4, amended: SI 2002/2851 r.4, SI 2003/2757 r.3, SI 2004/1032 r.3

r.6, see *J&W Waste Management Ltd v Customs and Excise Commissioners* [2003] V. & D.R. 350 (VAT and Duties Tribunal (London)), Paul Heim

r.7, amended: SI 2003/2757 r.4

r.8, amended: SI 2003/2757 r.5

r.8A, amended: SI 2003/2757 r.6, SI 2004/1032 r.4

r.16, amended: SI 2002/2851 r.5

r.19, see *Kett v Customs and Excise Commissioners* [2003] V. & D.R. 363 (VAT and Duties Tribunal (London)), Theodore Wallace (Chairman)

r.19, amended: SI 2002/2851 r.6, SI 2003/2757 r.7

r.20, amended: SI 2002/2851 r.7, SI 2003/2757 r.8, SI 2004/1032 r.5

r.21, see *Hossain v Customs and Excise Commissioners* [2004] EWHC 1898, [2004] S.T.C.1572 (Ch D), Hart, J.

r.26, see *Pasquet Online (t/a Balade Gourmande) v Customs and Excise Commissioners* [2002] V. & D.R. 494 (V&DTr), Theodore Wallace (Chairman)

r.27, see *Hossain v Customs and Excise Commissioners* [2004] EWHC 1898, [2004] S.T.C.1572 (Ch D), Hart, J.

r.29, see *Dave v Customs and Excise Commissioners (Costs)* [2002] EWHC 969, [2002] S.T.C. 900 (Ch D), Burton, J.

r.29, amended: SI 2003/2757 r.9

r.31, amended: SI 2003/2757 r.10, SI 2004/1032 r.6

r.32, amended: SI 2003/2757 r.11

594. Education and Libraries (Northern Ireland) Order 1986

applied: SI 2003/439 Sch.1 para.5, Sch.1 para.6, SR 2002/224 Reg.14

referred to: SR 2003/61 Sch.3

Part VII, applied: SI 2003/424 Art.11

Art.2, amended: SI 2003/424 Sch.2 para.1

Art.2, applied: SI 2003/424 Art.2, SR 2002/352 Reg.4, SSI 2003/176 Sch.3 para.8

Art.2, referred to: SR 2003/46 Sch.1 para.3, SR 2003/61 Sch.3

NO.

1986–cont.

594. Education and Libraries (Northern Ireland) Order 1986–*cont.*

Art.3, applied: SI 2003/417 Art.31, SI 2003/493 Reg.8

Art.14, amended: SI 2003/424 Art.24

Art.37, applied: SI 2003/424 Art.11

Art.46, applied: SR 2003/16 Reg.11

Art.49, amended: SI 2003/424 Art.25

Art.49A, revoked: SI 2003/424 Sch.3 Part I

Art.50, applied: SI 2003/424 Art.11, SR 2002/265 Reg.5, Reg.8, Reg.18, Sch.7 para.1, SR 2003/253 Art.3

Art.50, disapplied: SR 2002/265 Reg.18

Art.50, enabled: SR 2002/112, SR 2002/265

Art.51, applied: SR 2002/265 Sch.7 para.1, SR 2003/253 Art.3

Art.52, applied: SI 2003/424 Art.11

Art.58, applied: SR 2002/224 Reg.18, SR 2002/265 Sch.6 para.15

Art.59, applied: SR 2002/224 Reg.18, SR 2002/265 Sch.6 para.15

Art.60, applied: SI 2003/424 Art.11, SR 2003/253 Art.3

Art.70, amended: SI 2003/417 Art.15

Art.70, applied: SI 2003/417 Art.15, Art.16, Art.17, Art.30, Art.50

Art.70, referred to: SI 2003/417 Art.15, Art.16, Art.30

Art.79, amended: SI 2003/424 Art.29, Sch.3 Part I

Art.80, amended: SI 2003/424 Art.29

Art.83, substituted: SI 2003/424 Art.30

Art.88A, amended: SI 2003/417 Art.15

Art.88A, applied: SI 2003/417 Art.15, Art.16, Art.17, Art.30, Art.50

Art.88A, referred to: SI 2003/417 Art.15, Art.16, Art.30

Art.92, amended: SI 2003/424 Art.29, Sch.3 Part I

Art.101, applied: SI 2003/424 Art.17

Art.103, revoked: SI 2003/424 Sch.3 Part I

Art.112, amended: SI 2003/424 Sch.2 para.2

Art.113, referred to: SI 2003/424 Art.1

Art.113, revoked: SI 2003/424 Sch.3 Part I

Art.114, referred to: SI 2003/424 Art.1

Art.114, revoked: SI 2003/424 Sch.3 Part I

Art.119, referred to: SI 2003/424 Art.1

Art.119, revoked: SI 2003/424 Sch.3 Part I

Art.134, enabled: SR 2002/112, SR 2002/265

Sch.1, applied: SSI 2003/176 Sch.3 para.9

Sch.3, amended: SI 2003/424 Art.31, Sch.3 Part I

Sch.15, added: SI 2003/424 Sch.2 para.4

Sch.15, amended: SI 2003/424 Sch.2 para.3

Sch.15, revoked (in part): SI 2003/418 Sch.3

Sch.15, substituted: SI 2003/424 Sch.2 para.4

Sch.18, amended: SI 2003/435 Sch.5

NO.

1986–cont.

595. Mental Health (Northern Ireland) Order 1986

applied: SI 2003/417 Art.28, SI 2003/431 Art.2, Art.15

Art.2, amended: SI 2003/431 Sch.4

Art.15, applied: SI 2003/431 Art.2

Art.44, amended: 2002 c.26 Sch.12 para.36, SI 2004/702 Sch.7 para.10

Art.44, applied: SI 2003/495 Reg.7, SI 2003/1247 Art.13

Art.45, applied: SI 2003/495 Reg.7

Art.49A, applied: SI 2004/1501 Art.12, Art.29

Art.50A, amended: 2002 c.26 Sch.12 para.37

Art.50A, applied: SI 2003/495 Reg.7, SI 2003/1247 Art.3

Art.51, applied: SI 2003/495 Reg.7

Art.53, amended: 2002 c.26 Sch.12 para.38

Art.54, amended: 2002 c.41 s.62

Art.56, amended: 2002 c.26 Sch.12 para.39

Art.59, varied: 2002 c.41 s.62

Art.61, amended: 2002 c.26 Sch.12 para.40

Art.77, amended: SI 2004/1272 Art.3

Art.78, amended: SI 2004/1272 Art.4

Art.89, substituted: SI 2003/418 Sch.1 para.12

Art.90, referred to: SI 2003/431 Art.10, Art.11

Art.110, applied: SR 2003/28 Reg.5

Art.121, applied: 2003 c.44 Sch.17 para.44

Art.123, applied: 2003 c.44 Sch.17 para.88

s.122, applied: 2002 c.29 Sch.5 para.8, 2003 c.44 Sch.17 para.87

Sch.3, amended: 2002 c.26 Sch.3 para.39

Sch.5, amended: SI 2003/413 Sch.1, SI 2003/435 Sch.5

599. Air Navigation (Aircraft and Aircraft Engine Emissions) Order 1986

revoked: SI 2002/798 Sch.1

607. Road Vehicles (Registration and Licensing) (Amendment) Regulations 1986

revoked: SI 2002/2742 Sch.1 Part I

833. Gaming (Bingo) Act (Fees) Order 1986

Art.2, amended: SI 2002/640 Art.2

834. Gaming Clubs (Multiple Bingo) Regulations 1986

Reg.2, amended: SI 2002/1901 Reg.2

887. Dental Auxiliaries Regulations 1986

Reg.5, amended: SI 2002/3135 Sch.1 para.25

Reg.6, amended: SI 2003/3105 Reg.2

Reg.18, amended: SI 2002/3135 Sch.1 para.25

Reg.23, amended: SI 2002/1671 Reg.3

Reg.27, amended: SI 2002/1671 Reg.4

Reg.27, revoked (in part): SI 2002/1671 Reg.4

948. Hong Kong (British Nationality) Order 1986

amended: 2002 c.8 s.2

NO.

1986–cont.

948. Hong Kong (British Nationality) Order 1986–*cont.*

Art.2, amended: 2002 c.8 s.2

Art.3, amended: 2002 c.8 s.2

Art.4, amended: 2002 c.8 s.2

Art.6, amended: 2002 c.8 s.2

Art.7, amended: 2002 c.8 s.2

Sch.1 Part 1, amended: 2002 c.8 s.2

Sch.1 Part 2, amended: 2002 c.8 s.2

Sch.1 Part 3, amended: 2002 c.8 s.2

Sch.1 Part 4, amended: 2002 c.8 s.2

Sch.1 Part 5 para.1, amended: 2002 c.8 s.2

Sch.1 Part 5 para.2, amended: 2002 c.8 s.2

Sch.1 Part 6, amended: 2002 c.8 s.2

Sch.1 Part 7, amended: 2002 c.8 s.2

Sch.1 Part 8, amended: 2002 c.8 s.2

Sch.1 Part 9 para.1, amended: 2002 c.8 s.2

Sch.1 Part 9 para.2, amended: 2002 c.8 s.2

Sch.1 Part 10, amended: 2002 c.8 s.2

Sch.1 Part 11, amended: 2002 c.8 s.2

Sch.1 Part 12, amended: 2002 c.8 s.2

Sch.1 Part 13, amended: 2002 c.8 s.2

Sch.2, amended: 2002 c.8 s.2

965. National Health Service (General Ophthalmic Services) (Scotland) Regulations 1986

Reg.2, amended: SSI 2003/201 Reg.2, SSI 2003/432 Reg.2, SSI 2004/98 Reg.2, SSI 2004/169 Reg.2

Reg.6, amended: SSI 2004/36 Reg.2, SSI 2004/169 Reg.2

Reg.6, applied: SSI 2004/386 Reg.3

Reg.7, amended: SSI 2004/169 Reg.2

Reg.8, amended: SSI 2004/36 Reg.2, SSI 2004/169 Reg.2

Reg.9, amended: SSI 2004/169 Reg.2

Reg.10, amended: SSI 2004/169 Reg.2

Reg.12, amended: SSI 2004/169 Reg.2

Reg.13, amended: SSI 2004/169 Reg.2

Reg.13A, amended: SSI 2004/169 Reg.2

Reg.14, amended: SSI 2002/86 Reg.4, SSI 2003/201 Reg.2, SSI 2003/432 Reg.2, SSI 2004/98 Reg.2, SSI 2004/169 Reg.2

Reg.14, revoked (in part): SSI 2003/201 Reg.2

Reg.14A, amended: SSI 2004/169 Reg.2

Reg.14ZA, added: SSI 2003/201 Reg.2

Reg.16, amended: SSI 2004/169 Reg.2

Reg.17, amended: SSI 2004/169 Reg.2

Sch.1, amended: SSI 2004/36 Reg.2, SSI 2004/169 Reg.2

Sch.1, revoked: SSI 2004/212 Sch.1 para.2

975. National Health Service (General Ophthalmic Services) Regulations 1986

applied: SI 2002/553 Art.9, SI 2002/2469 Sch.12 para.5

referred to: SI 2002/2802 Reg.8

Reg.2, amended: SI 2002/1883 Reg.2, SI 2002/2469 Sch.5, Sch.7, SI 2003/657 Reg.8, SI 2003/955 Reg.8, SI 2003/

NO.

1986–cont.

975. National Health Service (General Ophthalmic Services) Regulations 1986–*cont.*

Reg.2, amended:–*cont.*

2381 Reg.3, SI 2004/642 Reg.2, SI 2004/865 Sch.1 para.4, SI 2004/1014 Reg.7, SI 2004/1016 Sch.1 para.4

Reg.6, amended: SI 2002/1883 Reg.2, SI 2002/2469 Sch.7

Reg.7, amended: SI 2002/601 Reg.14, SI 2002/1883 Reg.2, Reg.3, SI 2002/2469 Sch.7

Reg.7A, added: SI 2002/1883 Reg.4

Reg.7A, amended: SI 2002/601 Reg.14, SI 2002/2469 Sch.7

Reg.7B, added: SI 2002/1883 Reg.4

Reg.7B, amended: SI 2002/2469 Sch.7

Reg.7C, added: SI 2002/1883 Reg.4

Reg.7C, amended: SI 2002/2469 Sch.7

Reg.7D, added: SI 2002/1883 Reg.4

Reg.8, amended: SI 2002/1883 Reg.2, Reg.5, SI 2002/2469 Sch.7

Reg.9, amended: SI 2002/1883 Reg.2, SI 2002/2469 Sch.5, Sch.7

Reg.9A, added: SI 2002/1883 Reg.6

Reg.9B, added: SI 2002/1883 Reg.6

Reg.9B, amended: SI 2002/601 Reg.14, SI 2002/2469 Sch.7

Reg.9C, added: SI 2002/1883 Reg.6

Reg.9C, amended: SI 2002/2469 Sch.7

Reg.9D, added: SI 2002/1883 Reg.6

Reg.9D, amended: SI 2002/2469 Sch.7

Reg.9E, added: SI 2002/1883 Reg.6

Reg.9E, amended: SI 2002/2469 Sch.7

Reg.9F, added: SI 2002/1883 Reg.6

Reg.9F, amended: SI 2002/2469 Sch.7

Reg.9G, added: SI 2002/1883 Reg.6

Reg.9G, amended: SI 2002/2469 Sch.7

Reg.9H, added: SI 2002/1883 Reg.6

Reg.10, amended: SI 2002/1883 Reg.2, SI 2002/2469 Sch.7

Reg.11, amended: SI 2002/1883 Reg.2, SI 2002/2469 Sch.7

Reg.12, amended: SI 2002/1883 Reg.2, SI 2002/2469 Sch.7

Reg.12A, amended: SI 2002/601 Reg.11, SI 2002/2469 Sch.7

Reg.12A, substituted: SI 2002/1883 Reg.7

Reg.13, amended: SI 2003/657 Reg.9, SI 2003/955 Reg.9, SI 2003/2381 Reg.3, SI 2004/642 Reg.2, SI 2004/936 Reg.3, SI 2004/1014 Reg.8, SI 2004/1042 Reg.4, SI 2004/1138 Reg.3

Reg.13, applied: SI 2004/1042 Reg.5

Reg.13, revoked (in part): SI 2003/657 Reg.9, SI 2003/955 Reg.9

Reg.13A, amended: SI 2002/1883 Reg.2, SI 2002/2469 Sch.7

Reg.13B, amended: SI 2002/1883 Reg.2, SI 2002/2469 Sch.7

NO.

1986–cont.

975. National Health Service (General Ophthalmic Services) Regulations 1986–*cont.*

Reg.15, amended: SI 2002/1883 Reg.2, SI 2002/2469 Sch.7

Reg.16, amended: SI 2002/1883 Reg.2, SI 2002/2469 Sch.5, Sch.7

Sch.1 para.2, amended: SI 2003/2863 Reg.4

Sch.1 para.3A, amended: SI 2002/2469 Sch.5

Sch.1 para.4, amended: SI 2002/1883 Reg.2, SI 2002/2469 Sch.5, Sch.7

Sch.1 para.5, amended: SI 2002/2469 Sch.5

Sch.1 para.6, amended: SI 2002/1883 Reg.2, SI 2002/2469 Sch.5

Sch.1 para.6A, added: SI 2002/1883 Reg.8

Sch.1 para.6A, amended: SI 2002/2469 Sch.7

Sch.1 para.6B, added: SI 2002/1883 Reg.8

Sch.1 para.6B, amended: SI 2002/2469 Sch.7

Sch.1 para.7, amended: SI 2002/1883 Reg.2, SI 2002/2469 Sch.5, Sch.7

Sch.1 para.8, amended: SI 2002/1883 Reg.2, SI 2002/2469 Sch.5, Sch.7

Sch.1 para.8A, amended: SI 2003/837 Reg.2

Sch.1 para.8B, amended: SI 2002/2469 Sch.5

Sch.1 para.8C, amended: SI 2002/2469 Sch.5

Sch.1 para.8C, substituted: SI 2004/865 Sch.1 para.4, SI 2004/1016 Sch.1 para.4

Sch.1 para.9, amended: SI 2002/1883 Reg.2, SI 2002/2469 Sch.7

Sch.1A para.1, added: SI 2002/1883 Reg.9

Sch.1A para.2, added: SI 2002/1883 Reg.9

Sch.1A para.3, added: SI 2002/1883 Reg.9

Sch.1A para.4, added: SI 2002/1883 Reg.9

Sch.1A para.5, added: SI 2002/1883 Reg.9

Sch.1A para.6, added: SI 2002/1883 Reg.9

Sch.1A para.7, added: SI 2002/1883 Reg.9

Sch.1A para.7, amended: SI 2002/2469 Sch.7, SI 2002/2802 Reg.9

Sch.1A para.8, added: SI 2002/1883 Reg.9

Sch.1A para.9, added: SI 2002/1883 Reg.9

Sch.1A para.10, added: SI 2002/1883 Reg.9

Sch.1A para.10, amended: SI 2002/2469 Sch.7, SI 2004/865 Sch.1 para.4, SI 2004/1016 Sch.1 para.4

Sch.1A para.11, added: SI 2002/1883 Reg.9

Sch.1A para.11, amended: SI 2002/2469 Sch.7

Sch.1A para.12, added: SI 2002/1883 Reg.9

Sch.1A para.12, amended: SI 2002/2469 Sch.7

Sch.1A para.13, added: SI 2002/1883 Reg.9

Sch.1A para.13, amended: SI 2002/2469 Sch.7

Sch.1A para.14, added: SI 2002/1883 Reg.9

Sch.1A para.14, amended: SI 2002/2469 Sch.7

NO.

NO.

1986–cont.

975. National Health Service (General Ophthalmic Services) Regulations 1986–*cont.*

Sch.2i para.1, substituted: SI 2002/601 Reg.14

Sch.2i para.2, substituted: SI 2002/601 Reg.14

Sch.2i para.3, substituted: SI 2002/601 Reg.14

Sch.2i para.4, substituted: SI 2002/601 Reg.14

Sch.2i para.5, substituted: SI 2002/601 Reg.14

Sch.2i para.6, substituted: SI 2002/601 Reg.14

Sch.2i para.7, substituted: SI 2002/601 Reg.14

Sch.2i para.8, substituted: SI 2002/601 Reg.14

Sch.2i para.9, substituted: SI 2002/601 Reg.14

Sch.2i para.10, substituted: SI 2002/601 Reg.14

Sch.2i para.11, substituted: SI 2002/601 Reg.14

Sch.2i para.12, substituted: SI 2002/601 Reg.14

Sch.2i para.13, substituted: SI 2002/601 Reg.14

Sch.2i para.14, substituted: SI 2002/601 Reg.14

1000. Nene Valley Light Railway Order 1986

Art.8, amended: SI 2003/2155 Sch.1 para.18

1030. Public Service Vehicles (Traffic Regulation Conditions) Regulations 1986

disapplied: SI 2004/2682 Reg.2

1032. Companies (Northern Ireland) Order 1986

applied: 2002 c.23 Sch.29 para.46, 2002 c.29 s.364, s.398, 2002 c.40 Sch.15, SI 2002/2376 Reg.2, SI 2002/3038 Reg.5, SI 2002/3040 Reg.3, SI 2003/410 Art.5, SI 2003/506 Reg.3, SI 2003/1102 Reg.5, SI 2003/2773 Reg.3, SI 2003/3060 Reg.3, 2004 c.12 s.50, s.51, s.52, s.54, SI 2004/291 Reg.5, Sch.6 para.113, SI 2004/478 Reg.5, Sch.6 para.111, SSI 2004/116 Reg.3, Sch.1 para.66

referred to: SI 2002/3150 Art.25, Sch.1 para.6, Sch.1 para.7

Part I, applied: 2002 c.12 (NI) Reg.13, SI 2002/3150 Art.2

Part II, applied: 2002 c.12 (NI) Reg.13, SI 2003/3190 Reg.4

Part VI, applied: 2002 c.12 (NI) Reg.13

Part VIII, applied: 2002 c.12 (NI) Reg.13

Part XII, applied: 2002 c.12 (NI) Reg.13

Part XIII, applied: 2002 c.12 (NI) Reg.13

Part XIV, applied: 2002 c.12 (NI) Reg.13

1986–cont.

1032. Companies (Northern Ireland) Order 1986–*cont.*

Part XV, applied: SI 2002/912 Sch.1, SI 2002/915 Sch.1, 2004 c.35 Sch.3, Sch.8

Part XVII, applied: 2002 c.12 (NI) Reg.13

Part XVIII, applied: 2002 c.12 (NI) Reg.13

Part XX, applied: 2002 c.12 (NI) Reg.13

Part XXIV, applied: 2002 c.12 (NI) Reg.13

Part XXV, applied: 2002 c.12 (NI) Reg.13

Art.2, amended: SR 2003/3 Art.26

Art.2, referred to: SI 2002/3150 Art.2

Art.2A, amended: SI 2002/3150 Sch.3 para.3, SR 2003/3 Art.27, Art.28

Art.4, applied: SI 2003/410 Art.5, SI 2003/3311 Reg.8, SR 2003/46 Sch.4 para.1

Art.10, amended: SR 2003/3 Art.25

Art.13, amended: SR 2003/3 Art.2

Art.18, amended: SR 2003/3 Art.3

Art.23, amended: SR 2003/3 Art.4

Art.25, applied: 2004 c.12 Sch.11 para.12

Art.39, amended: SR 2003/3 Art.28

Art.39, applied: 2002 c.12 (NI) Sch.1 para.3

Art.40, amended: SR 2003/3 Art.5

Art.46, referred to: SR 2003/5 Reg.2

Art.46, varied: SR 2003/5 Reg.3, Reg.4

Art.46A, referred to: SR 2003/5 Reg.2

Art.46A, varied: SR 2003/5 Reg.3, Reg.5

Art.46B, referred to: SR 2003/5 Reg.2

Art.46B, varied: SR 2003/5 Reg.3

Art.53, amended: SR 2003/3 Art.6

Art.57, amended: SR 2003/3 Art.7

Art.59, amended: SR 2003/3 Art.8

Art.127, amended: SR 2003/3 Art.9

Art.205, disapplied: SI 2003/3226 Reg.11

Art.217, amended: SI 2002/765 Reg.3

Art.229, applied: SI 2002/3150 Sch.1 para.4

Art.230, applied: SI 2002/3150 Sch.1 para.4

Art.234, applied: 2004 c.12 Sch.11 para.12

Art.234, referred to: SI 2002/3150 Sch.1 para.5

Art.235, referred to: SI 2002/3150 Sch.1 para.5

Art.241, referred to: SI 2002/3150 Sch.1 para.5

Art.246, amended: SR 2003/3 Art.10

Art.247, amended: SR 2003/3 Art.11

Art.249, applied: 2004 c.12 Sch.11 para.12

Art.250, applied: SI 2002/3150 Art.6, 2004 c.12 Sch.11 para.12

Art.253B, applied: SI 2002/3150 Art.6

Art.253C, applied: 2004 c.27 s.15

Art.253D, added: 2004 c.27 s.11

Art.253D, applied: 2004 c.27 s.15

Art.253E, added: 2004 c.27 s.11

Art.253E, applied: 2004 c.27 s.15

Art.253E, varied: 2004 c.27 s.15

Art.259, amended: SR 2003/3 Art.12

Art.261, amended: SR 2003/3 Art.13

Art.270, amended: SI 2002/765 Reg.3, SR 2003/3 Art.14

NO.

NO.

1986–cont.

1032. Companies (Northern Ireland) Order 1986–*cont.*

Art.270A, amended: SR 2003/3 Art.14

Art.296, applied: SI 2002/3150 Sch.1 para.4, 2004 c.12 Sch.11 para.12

Art.309, applied: SI 2002/3150 Art.22

Art.356, applied: SI 2003/1593 Sch.1 Part II

Art.357, applied: SI 2003/1593 Sch.1 Part II

Art.359, applied: SI 2003/1593 Sch.1 Part II

Art.360, applied: SI 2002/3150 Sch.1 para.4

Art.361, applied: SI 2002/3150 Sch.1 para.4

Art.371, applied: SI 2002/3150 Sch.1 para.4, 2004 c.12 Sch.11 para.12

Art.372, applied: SR 2003/4 Reg.3, 2004 c.12 Sch.11 para.12

Art.372, enabled: SR 2003/4

Art.372, referred to: SR 2003/4 Reg.3

Art.372A, applied: 2004 c.12 Sch.11 para.12

Art.373, applied: 2004 c.12 Sch.11 para.12

Art.374A, amended: SR 2003/3 Art.15

Art.377, amended: SR 2003/3 Art.16

Art.380, amended: SR 2003/3 Art.17

Art.381, amended: SR 2003/3 Art.18

Art.387A, amended: SR 2003/3 Art.19

Art.398, amended: SR 2003/3 Art.28

Art.402, disapplied: SI 2003/3226 Reg.7

Art.403, applied: SI 2003/1417 r.111

Art.405, applied: SI 2002/3150 Sch.1 para.4

Art.409, applied: SI 2003/1417 r.111

Art.411, amended: SR 2003/3 Art.20

Art.418, applied: SI 2003/1102 Reg.5, SI 2004/353 Reg.5, SI 2004/1045 Reg.4

Art.424, applied: SI 2003/3075 Reg.26

Art.425, applied: SI 2003/3075 Reg.26

Art.434, amended: SI 2002/3150 Sch.3 para.4

Art.435, applied: SI 2003/3075 Reg.26

Art.439, applied: SI 2003/3075 Reg.26

Art.440, applied: SI 2002/912 Sch.1, SI 2002/915 Sch.1, SI 2003/3075 Reg.26, 2004 c.35 Sch.3, Sch.8

Art.442, amended: SI 2002/3150 Sch.3 para.5

Art.451, applied: SI 2002/3150 Art.7

Art.634, amended: SR 2003/3 Art.21

Art.635, amended: SR 2003/3 Art.22

Art.641, amended: SR 2003/3 Art.23

Art.641, applied: 2004 c.12 Sch.11 para.12

Art.642, applied: 2004 c.12 Sch.11 para.12

Art.643, applied: 2004 c.12 Sch.11 para.12

Art.649, applied: 2004 c.12 Sch.11 para.12

Art.652D, applied: SI 2002/3150 Sch.1 para.4

Art.655, amended: SR 2003/3 Art.28

Art.656, revoked: SR 2003/3 Art.28

Art.656B, added: SR 2003/3 Art.24

Art.660, amended: SR 2003/3 Art.28

Art.662, applied: SI 2002/3150 Art.6

Art.663, amended: 2002 c.12 (NI) Sch.1 para.1

1986–cont.

1032. Companies (Northern Ireland) Order 1986–*cont.*

Art.663, applied: 2002 c.12 (NI) Sch.1 para.3, (NI) Sch.1 para.4, (NI) Sch.1 para.5

Art.665, amended: 2002 c.13 (NI) s.3

Art.665, revoked: SI 2003/2904 Sch.1

Art.666, revoked: SI 2003/2904 Sch.1

Art.681, enabled: SR 2003/4

Sch.23, amended: SR 2003/3 Art.28

1035. Companies Consolidation (Consequential Provisions) (Northern Ireland) Order 1986

Sch.1, amended: SI 2003/435 Sch.5

1078. Road Vehicles (Construction and Use) Regulations 1986

applied: SI 2003/1998 Art.46, Art.49, Art.50, Art.51, Art.53, Sch.1 para.16, Sch.1 para.21, Sch.1 para.22, Sch.1 para.35, Sch.1 para.36, Sch.2 para.2, Sch.2 para.34, Sch.2 para.35, Sch.3 para.2, Sch.3 para.8, Sch.3 para.21, Sch.3 para.24, Sch.3 para.25, Sch.4 para.17, Sch.10 para.12, Sch.11 para.8

referred to: SI 2003/1998 Art.29, SI 2003/3145 Reg.2

Part II, varied: SI 2003/1998 Sch.11 para.10

Reg.3, amended: SI 2003/182 Reg.2, SI 2003/2155 Sch.1 para.27

Reg.3, applied: SI 2003/1959 Reg.2

Reg.4, amended: SI 2003/1946 Reg.3

Reg.7, amended: SI 2003/182 Reg.3

Reg.7, applied: SI 2003/1998 Art.38, Sch.10 para.8

Reg.7, disapplied: SI 2003/1998 Art.46, Sch.1 para.35, Sch.1 para.36, Sch.2 para.35, Sch.3 para.25, Sch.10 para.13

Reg.7, referred to: SI 2003/1998 Art.49

Reg.8, see *Bramhill v Edwards* [2004] EWCA Civ 403, [2004] 2 Lloyd's Rep. 653 (CA), Auld, L.J.

Reg.8, applied: SI 2003/1998 Sch.4 para.11

Reg.8, disapplied: SI 2003/1998 Art.46, Art.51, Sch.1 para.35, Sch.1 para.36, Sch.2 para.34, Sch.2 para.35, Sch.3 para.25, Sch.10 para.13

Reg.8, referred to: SI 2003/1998 Art.47, Art.49

Reg.10, varied: SI 2003/1998 Sch.11 para.10

Reg.10A, disapplied: SI 2003/1998 Sch.3 para.25

Reg.10B, amended: SI 2004/3168 Art.10

Reg.10B, disapplied: SI 2003/1998 Sch.3 para.25

Reg.10C, amended: SI 2004/3168 Art.10

Reg.10C, disapplied: SI 2003/1998 Sch.3 para.25

Reg.11, disapplied: SI 2003/1998 Art.46, Art.49, Sch.3 para.25

Reg.11, referred to: SI 2003/1998 Art.47, Art.49

Reg.12, disapplied: SI 2003/1998 Sch.3 para.25

NO.

1986–cont.

1078. Road Vehicles (Construction and Use) Regulations 1986–*cont.*

Reg.13, amended: SI 2003/182 Reg.4

Reg.13, disapplied: SI 2003/1998 Sch.3 para.25

Reg.13A, disapplied: SI 2003/1998 Sch.3 para.25

Reg.13B, disapplied: SI 2003/1998 Sch.3 para.25

Reg.13C, disapplied: SI 2003/1998 Sch.3 para.25

Reg.14, disapplied: SI 2003/1998 Sch.3 para.25

Reg.15, amended: SI 2002/1474 Reg.5

Reg.15, disapplied: SI 2003/1998 Sch.1 para.36, Sch.2 para.35, Sch.3 para.25

Reg.16, applied: SI 2003/1998 Sch.3 para.6, Sch.3 para.25

Reg.16, disapplied: SI 2003/1998 Art.46, Art.50, Sch.1 para.36, Sch.2 para.35, Sch.3 para.25, Sch.10 para.13

Reg.16, varied: SI 2003/1998 Sch.11 para.10

Reg.17, disapplied: SI 2003/1998 Sch.3 para.25

Reg.18, disapplied: SI 2003/1998 Art.46, Art.50, Sch.1 para.36, Sch.2 para.35, Sch.3 para.25, Sch.10 para.13

Reg.18, varied: SI 2003/1998 Sch.11 para.10

Reg.19, disapplied: SI 2003/1998 Sch.3 para.25

Reg.20, disapplied: SI 2003/1998 Sch.3 para.25

Reg.20, referred to: SI 2003/1998 Art.49

Reg.20, varied: SI 2003/1998 Sch.11 para.10

Reg.21, disapplied: SI 2003/1998 Sch.3 para.25

Reg.22, disapplied: SI 2003/1998 Art.46, Sch.3 para.25, Sch.10 para.13

Reg.22, referred to: SI 2003/1998 Art.47

Reg.23, disapplied: SI 2003/1998 Art.50, Sch.3 para.26

Reg.23, referred to: SI 2003/1998 Art.49

Reg.24, disapplied: SI 2003/1998 Sch.3 para.25

Reg.25, disapplied: SI 2003/1998 Sch.1 para.36, Sch.2 para.35, Sch.3 para.25

Reg.26, disapplied: SI 2003/1998 Sch.3 para.25

Reg.26, varied: SI 2003/1998 Sch.11 para.10

Reg.27, applied: SI 2003/1998 Art.52

Reg.27, disapplied: SI 2003/1998 Sch.3 para.26, Sch.3 para.27

Reg.27, varied: SI 2003/1998 Sch.11 para.10

Reg.28, disapplied: SI 2003/1998 Sch.3 para.28, Sch.3 para.29

Reg.29, varied: SI 2003/1998 Sch.11 para.10

Reg.31, disapplied: SI 2003/1998 Sch.3 para.28

Reg.32, amended: SI 2003/3145 Reg.3

Reg.34, disapplied: SI 2003/1998 Sch.3 para.28

NO.

1986–cont.

1078. Road Vehicles (Construction and Use) Regulations 1986–*cont.*

Reg.34, varied: SI 2003/1998 Sch.11 para.10

Reg.35, disapplied: SI 2003/1998 Sch.3 para.25

Reg.36, disapplied: SI 2003/1998 Sch.3 para.25

Reg.36A, amended: SI 2004/2102 Reg.3

Reg.36A, disapplied: SI 2003/1998 Sch.3 para.25, Sch.4 para.17

Reg.36A, revoked (in part): SI 2003/1946 Reg.4

Reg.36B, amended: SI 2003/1946 Reg.5, SI 2004/2102 Reg.4, SI 2004/3168 Art.10

Reg.36B, disapplied: SI 2003/1998 Sch.3 para.25, Sch.4 para.17

Reg.36B, revoked (in part): SI 2004/2102 Reg.4

Reg.36C, disapplied: SI 2003/1998 Sch.3 para.25, Sch.4 para.17

Reg.37, amended: SI 2004/3168 Art.10

Reg.37, varied: SI 2003/1998 Sch.11 para.10

Reg.39A, disapplied: SI 2003/1998 Sch.3 para.25

Reg.39B, disapplied: SI 2003/1998 Sch.3 para.25

Reg.40, amended: SI 2003/1690 Reg.3

Reg.49, disapplied: SI 2003/1998 Sch.2 para.35, Sch.3 para.25

Reg.50, disapplied: SI 2003/1998 Sch.3 para.25

Reg.51, disapplied: SI 2003/1998 Sch.2 para.35, Sch.3 para.25, Sch.4 para.17

Reg.52, disapplied: SI 2003/1998 Sch.3 para.25

Reg.53, disapplied: SI 2003/1998 Sch.3 para.25

Reg.53, varied: SI 2003/1998 Sch.11 para.10

Reg.53A, disapplied: SI 2003/1998 Sch.3 para.25

Reg.53B, disapplied: SI 2003/1998 Sch.3 para.25

Reg.54, varied: SI 2003/1998 Sch.11 para.10

Reg.60, amended: SI 2002/2126 Reg.2

Reg.61, amended: SI 2003/3145 Reg.4

Reg.61, applied: SI 2002/1808 Reg.19, SSI 2003/212 Reg.20

Reg.61, disapplied: SI 2003/1998 Art.50

Reg.61, referred to: SI 2003/300 Reg.19, SSI 2003/212 Reg.20

Reg.61, varied: SI 2003/1998 Sch.11 para.10

Reg.61A, amended: SI 2002/1474 Reg.2

Reg.61A, applied: SI 2002/1808 Reg.19, SSI 2003/212 Reg.20

Reg.61A, referred to: SI 2003/300 Reg.19, SSI 2003/212 Reg.20

Reg.62, disapplied: SI 2003/1998 Sch.3 para.25

Reg.62, varied: SI 2003/1998 Sch.11 para.10

Reg.63, disapplied: SI 2003/1998 Sch.3 para.25, Sch.10 para.13

NO.

NO.

1986–cont.

1078. Road Vehicles (Construction and Use) Regulations 1986–*cont.*

Reg.64, disapplied: SI 2003/1998 Sch.1 para.36, Sch.2 para.35, Sch.3 para.25

Reg.65, disapplied: SI 2003/1998 Sch.1 para.36, Sch.2 para.35, Sch.3 para.25

Reg.66, applied: SI 2003/1998 Sch.1 para.27, Sch.2 para.16, Sch.4 para.9, Sch.4 para.15

Reg.66, disapplied: SI 2003/1998 Art.46, Sch.3 para.25, Sch.10 para.13

Reg.67, disapplied: SI 2003/1998 Sch.3 para.25

Reg.68, disapplied: SI 2003/1998 Sch.3 para.25

Reg.69, disapplied: SI 2003/1998 Sch.3 para.25

Reg.70, disapplied: SI 2003/1998 Sch.3 para.25, Sch.4 para.17

Reg.70A, amended: SI 2004/2102 Reg.5

Reg.70A, disapplied: SI 2003/1998 Sch.3 para.25, Sch.4 para.17

Reg.70B, disapplied: SI 2003/1998 Sch.3 para.25, Sch.4 para.17

Reg.71, applied: SI 2003/1998 Sch.2 para.16

Reg.71, disapplied: SI 2003/1998 Sch.3 para.25

Reg.71A, disapplied: SI 2003/1998 Sch.3 para.25

Reg.72, disapplied: SI 2003/1998 Sch.3 para.25, Sch.4 para.17

Reg.73, disapplied: SI 2003/1998 Sch.3 para.25, Sch.4 para.17

Reg.74, disapplied: SI 2003/1998 Sch.3 para.25

Reg.75, applied: SI 2003/1998 Art.26, Art.40

Reg.75, disapplied: SI 2003/1998 Sch.1 para.36, Sch.2 para.35, Sch.3 para.25, Sch.4 para.17, Sch.10 para.13

Reg.75, referred to: SI 2003/1998 Art.35

Reg.76, applied: SI 2003/1998 Art.40

Reg.76, disapplied: SI 2003/1998 Sch.1 para.36, Sch.2 para.35, Sch.3 para.25, Sch.4 para.17, Sch.10 para.13

Reg.76, referred to: SI 2003/1998 Art.35

Reg.77, applied: SI 2003/1998 Art.40

Reg.77, disapplied: SI 2003/1998 Sch.1 para.36, Sch.2 para.35, Sch.3 para.25, Sch.4 para.17, Sch.10 para.13

Reg.77, referred to: SI 2003/1998 Art.35

Reg.78, applied: SI 2003/1998 Art.40

Reg.78, disapplied: SI 2003/1998 Sch.1 para.36, Sch.2 para.35, Sch.3 para.25, Sch.4 para.17, Sch.10 para.13

Reg.78, referred to: SI 2003/1998 Art.35

Reg.79, applied: SI 2003/1998 Art.40

Reg.79, disapplied: SI 2003/1998 Sch.1 para.36, Sch.2 para.35, Sch.3 para.25, Sch.4 para.17, Sch.10 para.13

Reg.79, referred to: SI 2003/1998 Art.35

1986–cont.

1078. Road Vehicles (Construction and Use) Regulations 1986–*cont.*

Reg.79A, disapplied: SI 2003/1998 Sch.1 para.36, Sch.2 para.35, Sch.3 para.25, Sch.4 para.17, Sch.10 para.13

Reg.79B, disapplied: SI 2003/1998 Sch.1 para.36, Sch.2 para.35, Sch.3 para.25, Sch.10 para.13

Reg.79C, disapplied: SI 2003/1998 Sch.1 para.36, Sch.2 para.35, Sch.3 para.25, Sch.10 para.13

Reg.80, disapplied: SI 2003/1998 Sch.1 para.35, Sch.1 para.36, Sch.2 para.34, Sch.2 para.35, Sch.3 para.25, Sch.10 para.13

Reg.81, varied: SI 2003/1998 Sch.11 para.10

Reg.82, amended: SI 2004/3168 Art.10

Reg.82, disapplied: SI 2003/1998 Art.51, Sch.1 para.35, Sch.1 para.36, Sch.2 para.35, Sch.3 para.25, Sch.4 para.17

Reg.82, referred to: SI 2003/1998 Art.29, Art.49

Reg.82, varied: SI 2003/1998 Sch.11 para.10

Reg.83, disapplied: SI 2003/1998 Sch.1 para.36, Sch.4 para.17

Reg.86, varied: SI 2003/1998 Sch.11 para.10

Reg.89, varied: SI 2003/1998 Sch.11 para.10

Reg.90, varied: SI 2003/1998 Sch.11 para.10

Reg.92, varied: SI 2003/1998 Sch.11 para.10

Reg.97, varied: SI 2003/1998 Sch.11 para.10

Reg.98, varied: SI 2003/1998 Sch.11 para.10

Reg.99, varied: SI 2003/1998 Sch.11 para.10

Reg.100, see *Reid v First Glasgow Ltd* 2003 Rep. L.R. 66 (Sh Pr), EF Bowen Q.C., Sheriff Principal

Reg.100, applied: SI 2003/1998 Art.52, Art.54, Art.55

Reg.100, referred to: SI 2003/1998 Art.42

Reg.100, varied: SI 2003/1998 Sch.11 para.10

Reg.101, amended: SI 2003/2155 Sch.1 para.27, SI 2004/3168 Art.10

Reg.101, varied: SI 2003/1998 Sch.11 para.10

Reg.102, varied: SI 2003/1998 Sch.11 para.10

Reg.103, varied: SI 2003/1998 Sch.11 para.10

Reg.104, varied: SI 2003/1998 Sch.11 para.10

Reg.105, varied: SI 2003/1998 Sch.11 para.10

Reg.106, varied: SI 2003/1998 Sch.11 para.10

Reg.107, amended: SI 2004/3168 Art.10

Reg.107, varied: SI 2003/1998 Sch.11 para.10

Reg.108, varied: SI 2003/1998 Sch.11 para.10

Reg.109, varied: SI 2003/1998 Sch.11 para.10

Reg.110, added: SI 2003/2695 Reg.2

Sch.2, amended: SI 2002/1474 Reg.3, SI 2002/2126 Reg.3, SI 2003/1690 Reg.4

Sch.3B Part I para.5, amended: SI 2003/2096 Sch.1 para.43

Sch.3B Part II para.6, amended: SI 2003/1946 Reg.6

Sch.3B Part II para.7, amended: SI 2003/1946 Reg.6

NO.

1986–cont.

1078. Road Vehicles (Construction and Use) Regulations 1986–*cont.*

Sch.3B Part II para.8, amended: SI 2003/1946 Reg.6

Sch.3B Part II para.10, amended: SI 2003/1946 Reg.6

Sch.5 para.1, amended: SI 2003/1690 Reg.5

Sch.5 para.4, amended: SI 2003/1690 Reg.5

Sch.5 para.8, amended: SI 2003/1690 Reg.5

Sch.7B Part I para.2, amended: SI 2002/227 Reg.2

Sch.7B Part I para.3, amended: SI 2002/227 Reg.2, SI 2003/3145 Reg.5

Sch.7B Part I para.3A, added: SI 2002/227 Reg.2

Sch.7B Part I para.3A, amended: SI 2003/3145 Reg.5

Sch.7B Part I para.7, amended: SI 2002/1474 Reg.4, SI 2003/1690 Reg.6, SI 2004/1706 Reg.2

Sch.7B Part II para.8, substituted: SI 2003/3145 Reg.5

Sch.8 Part I, applied: SI 2003/1998 Sch.1 para.13

Sch.8 Part II, applied: SI 2003/1998 Sch.1 para.13

1081. Representation of the People Regulations 1986

revoked: SI 2004/294 Reg.3

Part V, applied: SI 2003/284 Sch.4 para.2

Reg.29, applied: 2002 c.vi s.8

Reg.54, see *R. (on the application of Robertson) v Wakefield MDC* [2001] EWHC Admin 915, [2002] Q.B. 1052 (QBD (Admin Ct)), Maurice Kay, J.

Reg.97, varied: SI 2002/185 Sch.2

Reg.98, varied: SI 2002/185 Sch.2

Reg.100, varied: SI 2002/185 Sch.3 Part I

1110. Horticultural Development Council Order 1986

referred to: SI 2003/908 Art.2

Art.2, amended: SI 2002/1676 Art.4, Art.5, SI 2003/908 Art.3

Art.4, amended: SI 2003/908 Art.4

Art.6, amended: SI 2003/908 Art.5

Art.7, substituted: SI 2003/908 Art.6

Art.9, amended: SI 2002/1676 Art.6, SI 2003/908 Art.7

Art.12, amended: SI 2003/908 Art.8

Sch.1, amended: SI 2002/1676 Art.7

Sch.1, substituted: SI 2003/908 Sch.1

Sch.1 Part I, substituted: SI 2003/908 Sch.1

Sch.1 Part II, substituted: SI 2003/908 Sch.1

Sch.1 Part III, substituted: SI 2003/908 Sch.1

Sch.2 para.4, added: SI 2003/908 Art.10

Sch.2 para.5, added: SI 2003/908 Art.10

Sch.2 para.6, added: SI 2003/908 Art.10

Sch.2 para.7, added: SI 2003/908 Art.10

Sch.2 para.8, added: SI 2003/908 Art.10

NO.

1986–cont.

1111. Representation of the People (Scotland) Regulations 1986

Reg.76, applied: SSI 2002/457 Sch.3 para.21

1159. Child Abduction and Custody (Parties to Conventions) Order 1986

Sch.1, substituted: SI 2003/1518 Sch.1

Sch.2, substituted: SI 2003/1518 Sch.1

1177. Road Vehicles (Registration and Licensing) (Amendment) (No.2) Regulations 1986

revoked: SI 2002/2742 Sch.1 Part I

1245. Community Bus Regulations 1986

Reg.4, amended: SI 2002/2537 Reg.2, SI 2004/2252 Reg.2

1249. Rehabilitation of Offenders Act 1974 (Exceptions) (Amendment) Order 1986

revoked (in part): SSI 2003/231 Art.6

1288. Meat Products and Spreadable Fish Products (Scotland) (Amendment) Regulations 1986

revoked: SSI 2004/6 Reg.11

1301. Housing (Northern Ireland) Order 1986

referred to: SI 2003/412 Art.1

Part II, applied: SI 2003/412 Art.85

Art.6, amended: SI 2003/412 Sch.4 para.10

Art.39, revoked: SI 2003/412 Sch.5

Sch.2, applied: SI 2003/412 Art.85

Sch.4, referred to: SI 2003/412 Sch.4 para.9

1320. Weighing Equipment (Filling and Discontinuous Totalising Automatic Weighing Machines) Regulations 1986

Reg.23A, amended: SI 2003/214 Sch.1 para.2

Reg.32A, amended: SI 2003/214 Sch.1 para.2

1335. Costs in Criminal Cases (General) Regulations 1986

see *R. v Mashhour (Costs)* [2003] 2 Costs L.R. 318 (Supreme Court Costs Office), Master GN Pollard

Reg.3A, amended: SI 2004/2408 Reg.3

Reg.3B, amended: SI 2004/2408 Reg.4

Reg.3C, amended: SI 2004/2408 Reg.5

Reg.3D, amended: SI 2004/2408 Reg.6

Reg.3E, added: SI 2004/2408 Reg.7

Reg.3F, added: SI 2004/2408 Reg.7

Reg.3G, added: SI 2004/2408 Reg.7

Reg.3H, added: SI 2004/2408 Reg.7

Reg.3I, added: SI 2004/2408 Reg.7

Reg.26, amended: SI 2004/2408 Reg.8

1456. Community Drivers Hours and Recording Equipment (Exemptions and Supplementary Provisions) Regulations 1986

Sch.1 para.2, amended: SI 2002/2469 Sch.1 para.43, SI 2003/1615 Sch.1 para.42, SI 2004/696 Sch.1 para.3

NO.

1986–cont.

1467. Road Vehicles (Exemptions from Duty) Regulations 1986
revoked: SI 2002/2742 Sch.1 Part I

1492. Drivers Hours (Goods Vehicles) (Exemptions) Regulations 1986
Reg.2, amended: SI 2003/2155 Sch.1 para.25

1510. Control of Pesticides Regulations 1986
applied: SI 2002/1689 Reg.3, Reg.9, Reg.16, SI 2002/3173 Sch.4 para.10, SI 2003/660 Sch.1, SI 2003/2913 Art.12, SI 2003/3241 Sch.4 para.1, Sch.4 para.4, SI 2003/3273 Art.12, SSI 2003/129 Sch.2 para.7, SSI 2003/579 Sch.4 para.1, SSI 2003/586 Art.12
disapplied: SI 2003/3241 Reg.27, SSI 2003/579 Reg.28
referred to: SSI 2004/70 Sch.2 para.7
see *R. v Searby (Alan Edward)* [2003] EWCA Crim 1910, [2003] 3 C.M.L.R.15 (CA (Crim Div)), Buxton, L.J.
Reg.3, applied: SI 2003/3241 Sch.4 para.3
Reg.5, applied: SI 2003/3241 Sch.4 para.9, SSI 2003/579 Sch.4 para.4, Sch.4 para.9

1629. Public Service Vehicles (Traffic Commissioners Publication and Inquiries) Regulations 1986
Reg.9, disapplied: SI 2004/2682 Reg.2

1671. Public Service Vehicles (Registration of Local Services) Regulations 1986
referred to: SI 2004/10 Reg.2
added: SI 2004/10 Reg.12
Reg.2, amended: SI 2004/10 Reg.3
Reg.2, revoked (in part): SI 2004/10 Reg.3
Reg.3, amended: SI 2004/10 Reg.4
Reg.4, substituted: SI 2004/10 Reg.5
Reg.5, amended: SI 2002/182 Reg.2
Reg.5, substituted: SI 2004/10 Reg.6
Reg.7, amended: SI 2004/10 Reg.7
Reg.7, referred to: SI 2004/10 Reg.13
Reg.8, amended: SI 2004/10 Reg.8
Reg.8, referred to: SI 2004/10 Reg.13
Reg.9, revoked (in part): SI 2002/182 Reg.2, SI 2004/10 Reg.9
Reg.12, amended: SI 2002/2536 Reg.2, SI 2004/10 Reg.10, SI 2004/2250 Reg.2
Reg.13, substituted: SI 2004/10 Reg.11
Sch.1 para.1, substituted: SI 2004/10 Sch.1
Sch.1 Part 1 para.1, substituted: SI 2004/10 Sch.1
Sch.1 Part 1 para.2, substituted: SI 2004/10 Sch.1
Sch.1 Part 1 para.3, substituted: SI 2004/10 Sch.1
Sch.1 Part 1 para.4, substituted: SI 2004/10 Sch.1
Sch.1 Part 1 para.5, substituted: SI 2004/10 Sch.1
Sch.1 para.2, substituted: SI 2004/10 Sch.1

NO.

1986–cont.

1671. Public Service Vehicles (Registration of Local Services) Regulations 1986– cont.
Sch.1 Part 2 para.1, substituted: SI 2004/10 Sch.1
Sch.1 Part 2 para.2, substituted: SI 2004/10 Sch.1
Sch.1 Part 2 para.3, substituted: SI 2004/10 Sch.1
Sch.1 Part 2 para.4, substituted: SI 2004/10 Sch.1
Sch.1 Part 2 para.5, substituted: SI 2004/10 Sch.1
Sch.1 Part 2 para.6, substituted: SI 2004/10 Sch.1
Sch.1 para.3, substituted: SI 2004/10 Sch.1
Sch.1 Part 3 para.1, substituted: SI 2004/10 Sch.1
Sch.1 Part 3 para.2, substituted: SI 2004/10 Sch.1
Sch.1 Part 3 para.3, substituted: SI 2004/10 Sch.1
Sch.1 Part 3 para.4, substituted: SI 2004/10 Sch.1
Sch.1 Part 3 para.5, substituted: SI 2004/10 Sch.1
Sch.1 Part 3 para.6, substituted: SI 2004/10 Sch.1
Sch.1 Part 3 para.7, substituted: SI 2004/10 Sch.1
Sch.1 para.4, substituted: SI 2004/10 Sch.1
Sch.1 para.5, substituted: SI 2004/10 Sch.1
Sch.1 para.6, substituted: SI 2004/10 Sch.1
Sch.1 para.7, substituted: SI 2004/10 Sch.1
Sch.1 para.8, substituted: SI 2004/10 Sch.1
Sch.1 para.9, substituted: SI 2004/10 Sch.1
Sch.1 para.10, substituted: SI 2004/10 Sch.1
Sch.1 para.11, substituted: SI 2004/10 Sch.1
Sch.1 para.12, substituted: SI 2004/10 Sch.1

1682. Measuring Equipment (Measures of Length) Regulations 1986
Reg.23B, amended: SI 2003/214 Sch.1 para.3

1711. Stamp Duty Reserve Tax Regulations 1986
varied: 2002 c.23 Sch.34 para.7, Sch.35 para.8
Sch.1 Part II, amended: 2002 asp 17 Sch.3 para.30
Sch.1 Part II, substituted: 2002 asp 17 Sch.3 para.30

1801. Airports Act 1986 (Modifications in Schedule 4 to the Transport Act 1968) Order 1986
Sch.2, amended: 2003 c.14 Sch.20 para.3

1887. Road Races (Northern Ireland) Order 1986
Art.3, enabled: SR 2002/167

1986–cont.

1888. Social Security (Northern Ireland) Order 1986

Art.64, varied: SR 2002/99 Art.4, SR 2003/155 Art.4

Sch.9, revoked: SI 2003/413 Sch.1, SI 2003/435 Sch.5

1915. Insolvency (Scotland) Rules 1986

applied: SI 2003/2109 Reg.23

referred to: SI 2003/2109 Reg.23

see *Rankin, Noter* 2003 S.L.T.107 (OH), Lord Nimmo Smith

Part I, applied: SI 2002/2709 r.4

Part I, added: SI 2002/2709 Sch.1 para.16

Part I, added: SI 2003/2109 Reg.25

Part 001 r.0.2, amended: SI 2002/2709 r.3, SI 2003/2108 Art.3, SI 2003/2109 Reg.24

Part I r.1.1, amended: SI 2002/2709 Sch.1 para.1, SI 2003/2109 Reg.25, SI 2003/2111 Sch.2 para.1

Part I r.1.3, amended: SI 2002/2709 Sch.1 para.2, SI 2003/2108 Art.4, SI 2003/2109 Reg.25

Part I r.1.4, applied: SI 2002/2709 r.4, SI 2002/2710 Reg.2, SI 2002/2711 Art.3

Part I r.1.7, amended: SI 2002/2709 Sch.1 para.3

Part I r.1.8, substituted: SI 2002/2709 Sch.1 para.4

Part I r.1.10, amended: SI 2003/2108 Art.4, SI 2003/2111 Sch.2 para.2

Part I r.1.11, applied: SI 2002/2709 r.4, SI 2002/2710 Reg.2, SI 2002/2711 Art.3

Part I r.1.12, applied: SI 2002/2709 r.4, SI 2002/2710 Reg.2, SI 2002/2711 Art.3

Part I r.1.14, amended: SI 2002/2709 Sch.1 para.5

Part I r.1.14A, added: SI 2002/2709 Sch.1 para.6

Part I r.1.15A, added: SI 2002/2709 Sch.1 para.7

Part I r.1.15B, added: SI 2002/2709 Sch.1 para.7

Part I r.1.16, substituted: SI 2002/2709 Sch.1 para.8

Part I r.1.17, amended: SI 2002/2709 Sch.1 para.9, SI 2003/2109 Reg.25

Part I r.1.18, amended: SI 2002/2709 Sch.1 para.10

Part I r.1.18, revoked (in part): SI 2002/2709 Sch.1 para.10

Part I r.1.18A, added: SI 2002/2709 Sch.1 para.11

Part I r.1.19, amended: SI 2002/2709 Sch.1 para.12, SI 2003/2111 Sch.2 para.3

Part I r.1.22, amended: SI 2002/2709 Sch.1 para.13

Part I r.1.23, amended: SI 2003/2108 Art.4

Part I r.1.23, substituted: SI 2002/2709 Sch.1 para.14

Part I r.1.24, revoked: SI 2002/2709 Sch.1 para.15

1986–cont.

1915. Insolvency (Scotland) Rules 1986– cont.

Part 2, added: SI 2003/2109 Reg.26

Part 2 r.2.1, substituted: SI 2003/2111 Sch.1 Part 1

Part 2 r.2.2, substituted: SI 2003/2111 Sch.1 Part 1

Part 2 r.2.3, substituted: SI 2003/2111 Sch.1 Part 1

Part 2 r.2.4, substituted: SI 2003/2111 Sch.1 Part 1

Part 2 r.2.5, substituted: SI 2003/2111 Sch.1 Part 1

Part 2 r.2.6, substituted: SI 2003/2111 Sch.1 Part 1

Part 2 r.2.7, amended: SI 2003/2109 Reg.26

Part 2 r.2.7, substituted: SI 2003/2111 Sch.1 Part 1

Part 2 r.2.8, substituted: SI 2003/2111 Sch.1 Part 1

Part 2 r.2.9, substituted: SI 2003/2111 Sch.1 Part 1

Part 2 r.2.9A, added: SI 2003/2109 Reg.26

Part 2 r.2.9A, substituted: SI 2003/2111 Sch.1 Part 1

Part 2 r.2.9B, added: SI 2003/2109 Reg.26

Part 2 r.2.9B, substituted: SI 2003/2111 Sch.1 Part 1

Part 2 r.2.10, substituted: SI 2003/2111 Sch.1 Part 1

Part 2 r.2.11, substituted: SI 2003/2111 Sch.1 Part 1

Part 2 r.2.12, substituted: SI 2003/2111 Sch.1 Part 1

Part 2 r.2.13, substituted: SI 2003/2111 Sch.1 Part 1

Part 2 r.2.14, substituted: SI 2003/2111 Sch.1 Part 1

Part 2 r.2.15, substituted: SI 2003/2111 Sch.1 Part 1

Part 2 r.2.16, substituted: SI 2003/2111 Sch.1 Part 1

Part 2 r.2.17, substituted: SI 2003/2111 Sch.1 Part 1

Part 2 r.2.18, substituted: SI 2003/2111 Sch.1 Part 1

Part 2 r.2.18, amended: SI 2003/2109 Reg.26

Part 2 r.2.18, substituted: SI 2003/2111 Sch.1 Part 1

Part 2 r.2.19, substituted: SI 2003/2111 Sch.1 Part 1

Part 2 r.2.20, substituted: SI 2003/2111 Sch.1 Part 1

Part 2 r.2.21, substituted: SI 2003/2111 Sch.1 Part 1

Part 2 r.2.22, substituted: SI 2003/2111 Sch.1 Part 1

Part 2 r.2.23, substituted: SI 2003/2111 Sch.1 Part 1

Part 2 r.2.24, substituted: SI 2003/2111 Sch.1 Part 1

NO.

1986–cont.

1915. Insolvency (Scotland) Rules 1986– cont.

Part 2 r.2.25, substituted: SI 2003/2111 Sch.1 Part 1

Part 2 r.2.26, substituted: SI 2003/2111 Sch.1 Part 1

Part 2 r.2.27, substituted: SI 2003/2111 Sch.1 Part 1

Part 2 r.2.28, substituted: SI 2003/2111 Sch.1 Part 1

Part 2 r.2.29, substituted: SI 2003/2111 Sch.1 Part 1

Part 2 r.2.30, substituted: SI 2003/2111 Sch.1 Part 1

Part 2 r.2.31, substituted: SI 2003/2111 Sch.1 Part 1

Part 2 r.2.32, substituted: SI 2003/2111 Sch.1 Part 1

Part 2 r.2.33, substituted: SI 2003/2111 Sch.1 Part 1

Part 2 r.2.34, substituted: SI 2003/2111 Sch.1 Part 1

Part 2 r.2.35, substituted: SI 2003/2111 Sch.1 Part 1

Part 2 r.2.36, substituted: SI 2003/2111 Sch.1 Part 1

Part 2 r.2.37, substituted: SI 2003/2111 Sch.1 Part 1

Part 2 r.2.38, substituted: SI 2003/2111 Sch.1 Part 1

Part 2 r.2.39, substituted: SI 2003/2111 Sch.1 Part 1

Part 2 r.2.40, substituted: SI 2003/2111 Sch.1 Part 1

Part 2 r.2.41, substituted: SI 2003/2111 Sch.1 Part 1

Part 2 r.2.42, substituted: SI 2003/2111 Sch.1 Part 1

Part 2 r.2.43, substituted: SI 2003/2111 Sch.1 Part 1

Part 2 r.2.44, substituted: SI 2003/2111 Sch.1 Part 1

Part 2 r.2.45, substituted: SI 2003/2111 Sch.1 Part 1

Part 2 r.2.46, substituted: SI 2003/2111 Sch.1 Part 1

Part 2 r.2.47, substituted: SI 2003/2111 Sch.1 Part 1

Part 2 r.2.48, substituted: SI 2003/2111 Sch.1 Part 1

Part 2 r.2.49, substituted: SI 2003/2111 Sch.1 Part 1

Part 2 r.2.50, substituted: SI 2003/2111 Sch.1 Part 1

Part 2 r.2.51, substituted: SI 2003/2111 Sch.1 Part 1

Part 2 r.2.52, substituted: SI 2003/2111 Sch.1 Part 1

Part 2 r.2.53, substituted: SI 2003/2111 Sch.1 Part 1

NO.

1986–cont.

1915. Insolvency (Scotland) Rules 1986– cont.

Part 2 r.2.54, substituted: SI 2003/2111 Sch.1 Part 1

Part 2 r.2.55, substituted: SI 2003/2111 Sch.1 Part 1

Part 2 r.2.56, substituted: SI 2003/2111 Sch.1 Part 1

Part 2 r.2.57, substituted: SI 2003/2111 Sch.1 Part 1

Part 2 r.2.58, substituted: SI 2003/2111 Sch.1 Part 1

Part 2 r.2.59, substituted: SI 2003/2111 Sch.1 Part 1

Part 2 r.2.60, substituted: SI 2003/2111 Sch.1 Part 1

Part 3 r.3.8A, added: SI 2003/2108 Art.5

Part 4, added: SI 2003/2109 Reg.27

Part 4 r.4.5, applied: SI 2004/353 Reg.12

Part 4 r.4.10, amended: SI 2003/2108 Art.6, SI 2003/2111 Sch.2 para.4

Part 4 r.4.13, applied: SI 2003/1102 Reg.29

Part 4 r.4.13, referred to: SI 2003/1102 Reg.29, SI 2004/353 Reg.29

Part 4 r.4.15, amended: SI 2003/2109 Reg.27

Part 4 r.4.15, applied: SI 2003/1102 Reg.12, Reg.13, SI 2004/353 Reg.13, SI 2004/1045 Reg.14, Reg.15

Part 4 r.4.16, disapplied: SI 2003/3226 Reg.15

Part 4 r.4.16, referred to: SI 2003/3226 Reg.15

Part 4 r.4.17, disapplied: SI 2003/3226 Reg.15

Part 4 r.4.28, amended: SI 2003/2108 Art.6

Part 4 r.4.31, amended: SI 2003/2108 Art.6

Part 4 r.4.60, amended: SI 2003/2111 Sch.2 para.5

Part 4 r.4.61, amended: SI 2003/2111 Sch.2 para.6

Part 4 r.4.62, amended: SI 2003/2111 Sch.2 para.6

Part 4 r.4.63, amended: SI 2003/2111 Sch.2 para.6

Part 4 r.4.67, applied: SI 2003/1102 Reg.30, SI 2004/353 Reg.30

Part 4 r.4.68, amended: SI 2003/2109 Reg.27

Part 7, applied: SI 2002/2709 r.4

Part 7, added: SI 2003/2108 Art.7

Part 7 r.7.3, amended: SI 2003/2111 Sch.2 para.7

Part 7 r.7.6, amended: SI 2003/2111 Sch.2 para.8

Part 7 r.7.9, amended: SI 2003/2111 Sch.2 para.9

Part 7 r.7.10, revoked (in part): SI 2002/2709 Sch.1 para.17

Part 7 r.7.20A, added: SI 2003/2109 Reg.28

Part 7 r.7.26, amended: SI 2003/2109 Reg.28

Part 7 r.7.31, amended: SI 2003/2108 Art.8

NO.

NO.

1986–cont.

1915. Insolvency (Scotland) Rules 1986– cont.

Part 7 r.7.33, amended: SI 2003/2111 Sch.2 para.10

Sch.1 para.6, substituted: SI 2003/2108 Art.9

Sch.1 para.18, amended: SI 2003/2108 Art.9

Sch.4, amended: SI 2002/2709 r.5, SI 2003/ 2111 r.4, Sch.2 para.11

Sch.5, amended: SI 2002/2709 Sch.1 Part 3, SI 2003/2108 Sch.1 Part 1, Sch.1 Part 2, SI 2003/2109 Sch.2 Part I, Sch.2 Part II, SI 2003/2111 Sch.1 Part 2, Sch.2 Part 2

1917. Receivers (Scotland) Regulations 1986

Reg.7, substituted: SI 2003/2108 Art.11

1925. Insolvency Act 1986

Part 7 r.7.47, see *Casterbridge Properties Ltd (No.2), Re* [2003] EWCA Civ 1246, [2004] 1 W.L.R. 602 (CA), Chadwick, L.J.

s.271, see *Barnes v Whitehead* [2004] B.P.I.R. 693 (Ch D), Judge Maddocks

s.291, see *Kansal v United Kingdom (21413/ 02)* (2004) 39 E.H.R.R. 31 (ECHR), Judge Pellonpaa (President)

s.365, see *Barnes v Whitehead* [2004] B.P.I.R. 693 (Ch D), Judge Maddocks

1925. Insolvency Rules 1986

see *Oakhouse Property Holdings Ltd, Re* [2003] B.P.I.R. 469 (Ch D), Rimer, J.

applied: SI 2003/1400 Sch.4

referred to: SI 2004/584 r.3

see *Shalson v DF Keane Ltd* [2003] EWHC 599, [2003] B.P.I.R. 1045 (Ch D), Blackburne, J.

see *Miller v Bain* [2002] B.C.C. 899 (Ch D (Companies Ct)), Sir Andrew Morritt V.C.

Part 0 r.0.3, amended: SI 2003/1730 r.3

Part 1, revoked: SI 2002/2712 Sch.1 para.20

Part 1, added: SI 2002/1307 r.4

Part 1, added: SI 2002/2712 Sch.1 para.21

Part 1 r.1.1, amended: SI 2002/1307 r.4, SI 2002/2712 Sch.1 para.1, SI 2003/1730 Sch.1 para.1

Part 1 r.1.3, amended: SI 2002/1307 r.4, SI 2002/2712 Sch.1 para.2, SI 2003/1730 Sch.1 para.2

Part 1 r.1.4, applied: SI 2002/2708 Art.11, SI 2002/2710 Reg.2, SI 2002/2711 Art.3, SI 2002/2712 r.3

Part 1 r.1.7, amended: SI 2002/2712 Sch.1 para.3

Part 1 r.1.8, substituted: SI 2002/2712 Sch.1 para.4

Part 1 r.1.10, amended: SI 2003/1730 Sch.1 para.3

Part 1 r.1.11, applied: SI 2002/2708 Art.11, SI 2002/2710 Reg.2, SI 2002/2711 Art.3, SI 2002/2712 r.3

Part 1 r.1.12, amended: SI 2002/2712 Sch.1 para.5

1986–cont.

1925. Insolvency Rules 1986–*cont.*

Part 1 r.1.12, applied: SI 2002/2708 Art.11, SI 2002/2710 Reg.2, SI 2002/2711 Art.3, SI 2002/2712 r.3

Part 1 r.1.13, amended: SI 2002/2712 Sch.1 para.6

Part 1 r.1.13, substituted: SI 2003/1730 Sch.1 para.4

Part 1 r.1.14, amended: SI 2002/2712 Sch.1 para.7

Part 1 r.1.14, revoked (in part): SI 2002/2712 Sch.1 para.7

Part 1 r.1.17, amended: SI 2003/1730 Sch.1 para.5

Part 1 r.1.17, substituted: SI 2002/2712 Sch.1 para.8

Part 1 r.1.18, revoked (in part): SI 2002/2712 Sch.1 para.9

Part 1 r.1.19, amended: SI 2002/2712 Sch.1 para.10

Part 1 r.1.20, revoked (in part): SI 2002/2712 Sch.1 para.11

Part 1 r.1.21, substituted: SI 2002/2712 Sch.1 para.12

Part 1 r.1.22, amended: SI 2002/2712 Sch.1 para.13

Part 1 r.1.22, revoked (in part): SI 2002/2712 Sch.1 para.13

Part 1 r.1.22A, added: SI 2002/2712 Sch.1 para.14

Part 1 r.1.23, amended: SI 2002/2712 Sch.1 para.15, SI 2003/1730 Sch.1 para.6

Part 1 r.1.24, amended: SI 2002/1307 r.4, SI 2002/2712 Sch.1 para.16

Part 1 r.1.27, amended: SI 2002/2712 Sch.1 para.17

Part 1 r.1.28, amended: SI 2002/2712 Sch.1 para.18

Part 1 r.1.29, amended: SI 2003/1730 Sch.1 para.7

Part 1 r.1.29, substituted: SI 2002/2712 Sch.1 para.19

Part 1 r.1.52, amended: SI 2003/1730 Sch.1 para.8

Part 2, applied: SI 2003/1730 r.5

Part 2, added: SI 2002/1307 r.5

Part 2 r.1.120, substituted: SI 2003/1730 Sch.1 para.9

Part 2 r.1.121, substituted: SI 2003/1730 Sch.1 para.9

Part 2 r.1.122, substituted: SI 2003/1730 Sch.1 para.9

Part 2 r.1.123, substituted: SI 2003/1730 Sch.1 para.9

Part 2 r.1.124, substituted: SI 2003/1730 Sch.1 para.9

Part 2 r.1.125, substituted: SI 2003/1730 Sch.1 para.9

Part 2 r.1.126, substituted: SI 2003/1730 Sch.1 para.9

NO.

1986–cont.

1925. Insolvency Rules 1986–*cont.*

Part 2 r.1.127, substituted: SI 2003/1730 Sch.1 para.9

Part 2 r.1.128, substituted: SI 2003/1730 Sch.1 para.9

Part 2 r.1.129, substituted: SI 2003/1730 Sch.1 para.9

Part 2 r.2.1, substituted: SI 2003/1730 Sch.1 para.9

Part 2 r.2.2, see *Practice Statement (Ch D: Administration Orders: Reports)* [2002] 1 W.L.R. 1358 (Ch D), Sir Robert Andrew Morritt V.C.

Part 2 r.2.2, applied: SI 2004/353 Reg.12

Part 2 r.2.2, substituted: SI 2003/1730 Sch.1 para.9

Part 2 r.2.2, see *Practice Statement (Ch D: Administration Orders: Reports)* [2002] 1 W.L.R. 1358 (Ch D), Sir Robert Andrew Morritt V.C.

Part 2 r.2.3, amended: SI 2002/1307 r.5

Part 2 r.2.3, substituted: SI 2003/1730 Sch.1 para.9

Part 2 r.2.4, substituted: SI 2003/1730 Sch.1 para.9

Part 2 r.2.5, substituted: SI 2003/1730 Sch.1 para.9

Part 2 r.2.6, amended: SI 2002/1307 r.5

Part 2 r.2.6, substituted: SI 2003/1730 Sch.1 para.9

Part 2 r.2.6A, substituted: SI 2003/1730 Sch.1 para.9

Part 2 r.2.7, substituted: SI 2003/1730 Sch.1 para.9

Part 2 r.2.8, substituted: SI 2003/1730 Sch.1 para.9

Part 2 r.2.9, amended: SI 2002/1307 r.5

Part 2 r.2.9, substituted: SI 2003/1730 Sch.1 para.9

Part 2 r.2.9, varied: SI 2002/1242 Art.4

Part 2 r.2.9, substituted: SI 2003/1730 Sch.1 para.9

Part 2 r.2.10, substituted: SI 2003/1730 Sch.1 para.9

Part 2 r.2.11, substituted: SI 2003/1730 Sch.1 para.9

Part 2 r.2.12, substituted: SI 2003/1730 Sch.1 para.9

Part 2 r.2.12, varied: SI 2002/1242 Art.4

Part 2 r.2.12, substituted: SI 2003/1730 Sch.1 para.9

Part 2 r.2.13, substituted: SI 2003/1730 Sch.1 para.9

Part 2 r.2.14, substituted: SI 2003/1730 Sch.1 para.9

Part 2 r.2.15, substituted: SI 2003/1730 Sch.1 para.9

Part 2 r.2.16, amended: SI 2002/1307 r.5

Part 2 r.2.16, substituted: SI 2003/1730 Sch.1 para.9

NO.

1986–cont.

1925. Insolvency Rules 1986–*cont.*

Part 2 r.2.17, substituted: SI 2003/1730 Sch.1 para.9

Part 2 r.2.18, substituted: SI 2003/1730 Sch.1 para.9

Part 2 r.2.19, substituted: SI 2003/1730 Sch.1 para.9

Part 2 r.2.20, substituted: SI 2003/1730 Sch.1 para.9

Part 2 r.2.21, substituted: SI 2003/1730 Sch.1 para.9

Part 2 r.2.22, amended: SI 2002/1307 r.5

Part 2 r.2.22, substituted: SI 2003/1730 Sch.1 para.9

Part 2 r.2.23, substituted: SI 2003/1730 Sch.1 para.9

Part 2 r.2.24, substituted: SI 2003/1730 Sch.1 para.9

Part 2 r.2.25, substituted: SI 2003/1730 Sch.1 para.9

Part 2 r.2.26, substituted: SI 2003/1730 Sch.1 para.9

Part 2 r.2.27, substituted: SI 2003/1730 Sch.1 para.9

Part 2 r.2.28, substituted: SI 2003/1730 Sch.1 para.9

Part 2 r.2.29, substituted: SI 2003/1730 Sch.1 para.9

Part 2 r.2.30, substituted: SI 2003/1730 Sch.1 para.9

Part 2 r.2.31, amended: SI 2002/1307 r.5

Part 2 r.2.31, substituted: SI 2003/1730 Sch.1 para.9

Part 2 r.2.32, substituted: SI 2003/1730 Sch.1 para.9

Part 2 r.2.33, substituted: SI 2003/1730 Sch.1 para.9

Part 2 r.2.34, substituted: SI 2003/1730 Sch.1 para.9

Part 2 r.2.35, substituted: SI 2003/1730 Sch.1 para.9

Part 2 r.2.36, substituted: SI 2003/1730 Sch.1 para.9

Part 2 r.2.37, substituted: SI 2003/1730 Sch.1 para.9

Part 2 r.2.38, substituted: SI 2003/1730 Sch.1 para.9

Part 2 r.2.39, substituted: SI 2003/1730 Sch.1 para.9

Part 2 r.2.40, substituted: SI 2003/1730 Sch.1 para.9

Part 2 r.2.41, substituted: SI 2003/1730 Sch.1 para.9

Part 2 r.2.42, substituted: SI 2003/1730 Sch.1 para.9

Part 2 r.2.43, substituted: SI 2003/1730 Sch.1 para.9

Part 2 r.2.44, substituted: SI 2003/1730 Sch.1 para.9

Part 2 r.2.45, substituted: SI 2003/1730 Sch.1 para.9

1986–cont.

1925. Insolvency Rules 1986–*cont.*

Part 2 r.2.46, substituted: SI 2003/1730 Sch.1 para.9

Part 2 r.2.46A, substituted: SI 2003/1730 Sch.1 para.9

Part 2 r.2.47, substituted: SI 2003/1730 Sch.1 para.9

Part 2 r.2.48, substituted: SI 2003/1730 Sch.1 para.9

Part 2 r.2.49, substituted: SI 2003/1730 Sch.1 para.9

Part 2 r.2.50, substituted: SI 2003/1730 Sch.1 para.9

Part 2 r.2.51, substituted: SI 2003/1730 Sch.1 para.9

Part 2 r.2.52, substituted: SI 2003/1730 Sch.1 para.9

Part 2 r.2.53, amended: SI 2002/1307 r.5

Part 2 r.2.53, substituted: SI 2003/1730 Sch.1 para.9

Part 2 r.2.54, substituted: SI 2003/1730 Sch.1 para.9

Part 2 r.2.55, substituted: SI 2003/1730 Sch.1 para.9

Part 2 r.2.55, amended: SI 2004/584 r.4

Part 2 r.2.55, substituted: SI 2003/1730 Sch.1 para.9

Part 2 r.2.56, substituted: SI 2003/1730 Sch.1 para.9

Part 2 r.2.57, substituted: SI 2003/1730 Sch.1 para.9

Part 2 r.2.57, amended: SI 2004/584 r.5

Part 2 r.2.57, substituted: SI 2003/1730 Sch.1 para.9

Part 2 r.2.58, substituted: SI 2003/1730 Sch.1 para.9

Part 2 r.2.59, substituted: SI 2003/1730 Sch.1 para.9

Part 2 r.2.60, substituted: SI 2003/1730 Sch.1 para.9

Part 2 r.2.61, substituted: SI 2003/1730 Sch.1 para.9

Part 2 r.2.62, substituted: SI 2003/1730 Sch.1 para.9

Part 2 r.2.63, substituted: SI 2003/1730 Sch.1 para.9

Part 2 r.2.64, substituted: SI 2003/1730 Sch.1 para.9

Part 2 r.2.65, substituted: SI 2003/1730 Sch.1 para.9

Part 2 r.2.66, substituted: SI 2003/1730 Sch.1 para.9

Part 2 r.2.67, substituted: SI 2003/1730 Sch.1 para.9

Part 2 r.2.68, substituted: SI 2003/1730 Sch.1 para.9

Part 2 r.2.69, substituted: SI 2003/1730 Sch.1 para.9

Part 2 r.2.70, substituted: SI 2003/1730 Sch.1 para.9

1986–cont.

1925. Insolvency Rules 1986–*cont.*

Part 2 r.2.71, substituted: SI 2003/1730 Sch.1 para.9

Part 2 r.2.72, substituted: SI 2003/1730 Sch.1 para.9

Part 2 r.2.73, substituted: SI 2003/1730 Sch.1 para.9

Part 2 r.2.74, substituted: SI 2003/1730 Sch.1 para.9

Part 2 r.2.75, substituted: SI 2003/1730 Sch.1 para.9

Part 2 r.2.76, substituted: SI 2003/1730 Sch.1 para.9

Part 2 r.2.77, substituted: SI 2003/1730 Sch.1 para.9

Part 2 r.2.78, substituted: SI 2003/1730 Sch.1 para.9

Part 2 r.2.79, substituted: SI 2003/1730 Sch.1 para.9

Part 2 r.2.80, substituted: SI 2003/1730 Sch.1 para.9

Part 2 r.2.81, substituted: SI 2003/1730 Sch.1 para.9

Part 2 r.2.82, substituted: SI 2003/1730 Sch.1 para.9

Part 2 r.2.83, substituted: SI 2003/1730 Sch.1 para.9

Part 2 r.2.84, substituted: SI 2003/1730 Sch.1 para.9

Part 2 r.2.85, disapplied: SI 2003/3226 Reg.12

Part 2 r.2.85, substituted: SI 2003/1730 Sch.1 para.9

Part 2 r.2.86, disapplied: SI 2003/3226 Reg.14

Part 2 r.2.86, substituted: SI 2003/1730 Sch.1 para.9

Part 2 r.2.87, substituted: SI 2003/1730 Sch.1 para.9

Part 2 r.2.88, substituted: SI 2003/1730 Sch.1 para.9

Part 2 r.2.89, substituted: SI 2003/1730 Sch.1 para.9

Part 2 r.2.90, substituted: SI 2003/1730 Sch.1 para.9

Part 2 r.2.91, substituted: SI 2003/1730 Sch.1 para.9

Part 2 r.2.92, substituted: SI 2003/1730 Sch.1 para.9

Part 2 r.2.93, substituted: SI 2003/1730 Sch.1 para.9

Part 2 r.2.94, substituted: SI 2003/1730 Sch.1 para.9

Part 2 r.2.95, substituted: SI 2003/1730 Sch.1 para.9

Part 2 r.2.96, substituted: SI 2003/1730 Sch.1 para.9

Part 2 r.2.97, substituted: SI 2003/1730 Sch.1 para.9

Part 2 r.2.98, substituted: SI 2003/1730 Sch.1 para.9

1986–*cont.*

1925. Insolvency Rules 1986–*cont.*

Part 2 r.2.99, substituted: SI 2003/1730 Sch.1 para.9

Part 2 r.2.100, substituted: SI 2003/1730 Sch.1 para.9

Part 2 r.2.101, substituted: SI 2003/1730 Sch.1 para.9

Part 2 r.2.102, substituted: SI 2003/1730 Sch.1 para.9

Part 2 r.2.103, substituted: SI 2003/1730 Sch.1 para.9

Part 2 r.2.104, substituted: SI 2003/1730 Sch.1 para.9

Part 2 r.2.105, substituted: SI 2003/1730 Sch.1 para.9

Part 2 r.2.106, substituted: SI 2003/1730 Sch.1 para.9

Part 2 r.2.107, substituted: SI 2003/1730 Sch.1 para.9

Part 2 r.2.108, substituted: SI 2003/1730 Sch.1 para.9

Part 2 r.2.109, substituted: SI 2003/1730 Sch.1 para.9

Part 2 r.2.110, substituted: SI 2003/1730 Sch.1 para.9

Part 2 r.2.111, substituted: SI 2003/1730 Sch.1 para.9

Part 2 r.2.112, substituted: SI 2003/1730 Sch.1 para.9

Part 2 r.2.113, substituted: SI 2003/1730 Sch.1 para.9

Part 2 r.2.114, substituted: SI 2003/1730 Sch.1 para.9

Part 2 r.2.115, substituted: SI 2003/1730 Sch.1 para.9

Part 2 r.2.116, substituted: SI 2003/1730 Sch.1 para.9

Part 2 r.2.117, substituted: SI 2003/1730 Sch.1 para.9

Part 2 r.2.118, substituted: SI 2003/1730 Sch.1 para.9

Part 2 r.2.119, substituted: SI 2003/1730 Sch.1 para.9

Part 2 r.2.130, substituted: SI 2003/1730 Sch.1 para.9

Part 2 r.2.131, substituted: SI 2003/1730 Sch.1 para.9

Part 2 r.2.132, substituted: SI 2003/1730 Sch.1 para.9

Part 2 r.2.133, substituted: SI 2003/1730 Sch.1 para.9

Part 3, added: SI 2003/1730 Sch.1 para.11

Part 3 r.3.8, amended: SI 2003/1730 Sch.1 para.10

Part 3 r.3.21, amended: SI 2004/584 r.6

Part 3 r.3.23, amended: SI 2004/584 r.7

Part 4, added: SI 2002/1307 r.6

Part 4 r.4.1, amended: SI 2003/1730 Sch.1 para.12

Part 4 r.4.2, amended: SI 2002/2712 Sch.1 para.22

1986–*cont.*

1925. Insolvency Rules 1986–*cont.*

Part 4 r.4.7, amended: SI 2002/1307 r.6, SI 2003/1730 Sch.1 para.13, SI 2004/584 r.8

Part 4 r.4.10, amended: SI 2002/1307 r.6, SI 2003/1730 Sch.1 para.14

Part 4 r.4.19, amended: SI 2002/1307 r.6

Part 4 r.4.22, amended: SI 2002/1307 r.6

Part 4 r.4.25, amended: SI 2002/1307 r.6

Part 4 r.4.43, amended: SI 2003/1730 Sch.1 para.15

Part 4 r.4.49, substituted: SI 2003/1730 Sch.1 para.16

Part 4 r.4.49A, amended: SI 2003/1730 Sch.1 para.17

Part 4 r.4.67, amended: SI 2002/1307 r.6

Part 4 r.4.73, amended: SI 2003/1730 Sch.1 para.18

Part 4 r.4.74, applied: SI 2003/1102 Reg.12, Reg.13, SI 2004/353 Reg.12, Reg.13, SI 2004/1045 Reg.14, Reg.15

Part 4 r.4.74, substituted: SI 2004/584 r.9

Part 4 r.4.75, amended: SI 2002/1307 r.6, SI 2004/584 r.10

Part 4 r.4.83, see *Menastar Finance Ltd (In Liquidation), Re* [2002] EWHC 2610, [2003] B.C.C. 404 (Ch D), Etherton, J.

Part 4 r.4.90, see *Archer Structures Ltd v Griffiths* [2003] EWHC 957, [2004] B.C.C. 156 (Ch D), Judge Kirkham

Part 4 r.4.90, amended: SI 2003/1730 Sch.1 para.19

Part 4 r.4.90, applied: SI 2002/1242 Art.5

Part 4 r.4.90, disapplied: SI 2003/3226 Reg.12

Part 4 r.4.91, amended: SI 2003/1730 Sch.1 para.20

Part 4 r.4.91, disapplied: SI 2003/3226 Reg.14

Part 4 r.4.96, amended: SI 2002/1307 r.6

Part 4 r.4.105, amended: SI 2003/1730 Sch.1 para.21

Part 4 r.4.120, see *Quicksons (South & West) Ltd v Katz (No.1)* [2003] EWHC 1981, [2003] 4 All E.R. 864 (Ch D (Companies Ct)), Evans-Lombe, J.

Part 4 r.4.124, amended: SI 2003/1730 Sch.1 para.22, SI 2004/584 r.11

Part 4 r.4.125, amended: SI 2003/1730 Sch.1 para.23, SI 2004/584 r.12

Part 4 r.4.125A, added: SI 2004/584 r.13

Part 4 r.4.126, amended: SI 2003/1730 Sch.1 para.24

Part 4 r.4.127, amended: SI 2004/584 r.14

Part 4 r.4.127, applied: SI 2004/584 r.3

Part 4 r.4.127A, added: SI 2004/584 r.15

Part 4 r.4.127B, added: SI 2004/584 r.15

Part 4 r.4.128, applied: SI 2004/584 r.3

Part 4 r.4.128, revoked (in part): SI 2004/584 r.16

Part 4 r.4.138, revoked (in part): SI 2004/584 r.17

NO.

1986–cont.

1925. Insolvency Rules 1986–*cont.*

Part 4 r.4.148A, amended: SI 2004/584 r.18

Part 4 r.4.148A, applied: SI 2004/584 r.3

Part 4 r.4.148B, added: SI 2004/584 r.19

Part 4 r.4.159, amended: SI 2004/584 r.20

Part 4 r.4.161, amended: SI 2004/584 r.21

Part 4 r.4.173, amended: SI 2003/1730 Sch.1 para.25

Part 4 r.4.174, amended: SI 2003/1730 Sch.1 para.26

Part 4 r.4.175, amended: SI 2003/1730 Sch.1 para.27

Part 4 r.4.218, see *Demaglass Ltd (In Liquidation), Re* [2002] EWHC 3138, [2003] 1 B.C.L.C. 412 (Ch D), Anthony Mann Q.C.; see *Toshoku Finance UK Plc (In Liquidation), Re* [2002] UKHL 6, [2002] 1 W.L.R. 671 (HL), Lord Hoffmann

Part 4 r.4.218, amended: SI 2002/2712 Sch.1 para.23, SI 2004/584 r.22

Part 4 r.4.218, applied: SI 2003/1102 Reg.30, SI 2004/353 Reg.30

Part 4 r.4.218, revoked (in part): SI 2002/2712 Sch.1 para.23

Part 4 r.4.231, amended: SI 2004/584 r.23

Part 5, added: SI 2002/1307 r.7

Part 5, substituted: SI 2003/1730 Sch.1 para.31

Part 5 r.5.1, substituted: SI 2002/2712 Sch.1 para.24

Part 5 r.5.1, amended: SI 2003/1730 Sch.1 para.28

Part 5 r.5.1, substituted: SI 2002/2712 Sch.1 para.24

Part 5 r.5.2, substituted: SI 2002/2712 Sch.1 para.24

Part 5 r.5.3, amended: SI 2002/1307 r.7

Part 5 r.5.3, substituted: SI 2002/2712 Sch.1 para.24

Part 5 r.5.4, applied: SI 2002/2711 Art.4, SI 2002/2712 r.5

Part 5 r.5.4, substituted: SI 2002/2712 Sch.1 para.24

Part 5 r.5.5, substituted: SI 2002/2712 Sch.1 para.24

Part 5 r.5.5A, substituted: SI 2002/2712 Sch.1 para.24

Part 5 r.5.6, substituted: SI 2002/2712 Sch.1 para.24

Part 5 r.5.7, substituted: SI 2002/2712 Sch.1 para.24

Part 5 r.5.7, amended: SI 2003/1730 Sch.1 para.29

Part 5 r.5.7, substituted: SI 2002/2712 Sch.1 para.24

Part 5 r.5.8, substituted: SI 2002/2712 Sch.1 para.24

Part 5 r.5.9, substituted: SI 2002/2712 Sch.1 para.24

Part 5 r.5.10, substituted: SI 2002/2712 Sch.1 para.24

NO.

1986–cont.

1925. Insolvency Rules 1986–*cont.*

Part 5 r.5.11, substituted: SI 2002/2712 Sch.1 para.24

Part 5 r.5.12, substituted: SI 2002/2712 Sch.1 para.24

Part 5 r.5.13, substituted: SI 2002/2712 Sch.1 para.24

Part 5 r.5.14, substituted: SI 2002/2712 Sch.1 para.24

Part 5 r.5.15, substituted: SI 2002/2712 Sch.1 para.24

Part 5 r.5.16, substituted: SI 2002/2712 Sch.1 para.24

Part 5 r.5.17, substituted: SI 2002/2712 Sch.1 para.24

Part 5 r.5.18, substituted: SI 2002/2712 Sch.1 para.24

Part 5 r.5.19, substituted: SI 2002/2712 Sch.1 para.24

Part 5 r.5.20, substituted: SI 2002/2712 Sch.1 para.24

Part 5 r.5.21, substituted: SI 2002/2712 Sch.1 para.24

Part 5 r.5.22, see *Roberts v Pinnacle Entertainment Ltd* [2003] EWHC 2394, [2004] B.P.I.R. 208 (Ch D), Evans-Lombe, J.

Part 5 r.5.22, amended: SI 2002/1307 r.7

Part 5 r.5.22, substituted: SI 2002/2712 Sch.1 para.24

Part 5 r.5.22, see *Roberts v Pinnacle Entertainment Ltd* [2003] EWHC 2394, [2004] B.P.I.R. 208 (Ch D), Evans-Lombe, J.

Part 5 r.5.23, see *Roberts v Pinnacle Entertainment Ltd* [2003] EWHC 2394, [2004] B.P.I.R. 208 (Ch D), Evans-Lombe, J.

Part 5 r.5.23, substituted: SI 2002/2712 Sch.1 para.24

Part 5 r.5.23, see *Roberts v Pinnacle Entertainment Ltd* [2003] EWHC 2394, [2004] B.P.I.R. 208 (Ch D), Evans-Lombe, J.

Part 5 r.5.24, substituted: SI 2002/2712 Sch.1 para.24

Part 5 r.5.25, substituted: SI 2002/2712 Sch.1 para.24

Part 5 r.5.26, substituted: SI 2002/2712 Sch.1 para.24

Part 5 r.5.27, substituted: SI 2002/2712 Sch.1 para.24

Part 5 r.5.28, substituted: SI 2002/2712 Sch.1 para.24

Part 5 r.5.28, revoked: SI 2003/1730 Sch.1 para.30

Part 5 r.5.28, substituted: SI 2002/2712 Sch.1 para.24

Part 5 r.5.29, substituted: SI 2002/2712 Sch.1 para.24

Part 5 r.5.30, substituted: SI 2002/2712 Sch.1 para.24

NO.

1986–cont.

1925. Insolvency Rules 1986–cont.

Part 5 r.5.31, substituted: SI 2002/2712 Sch.1 para.24

Part 5 r.5.32, substituted: SI 2002/2712 Sch.1 para.24

Part 5 r.5.33, substituted: SI 2002/2712 Sch.1 para.24

Part 5 r.5.34, substituted: SI 2002/2712 Sch.1 para.24

Part 5 r.5.35, substituted: SI 2002/2712 Sch.1 para.24

Part 5 r.5.36, substituted: SI 2002/2712 Sch.1 para.24

Part 5 r.5.37, substituted: SI 2002/2712 Sch.1 para.24

Part 5 r.5.38, substituted: SI 2002/2712 Sch.1 para.24

Part 5 r.5.39, substituted: SI 2002/2712 Sch.1 para.24

Part 5 r.5.40, substituted: SI 2002/2712 Sch.1 para.24

Part 5 r.5.41, substituted: SI 2002/2712 Sch.1 para.24

Part 5 r.5.42, substituted: SI 2002/2712 Sch.1 para.24

Part 5 r.5.43, amended: SI 2004/584 r.24

Part 5 r.5.43, substituted: SI 2002/2712 Sch.1 para.24

Part 5 r.5.44, substituted: SI 2002/2712 Sch.1 para.24

Part 5 r.5.45, substituted: SI 2002/2712 Sch.1 para.24

Part 5 r.5.46, substituted: SI 2002/2712 Sch.1 para.24

Part 5 r.5.47, substituted: SI 2002/2712 Sch.1 para.24

Part 5 r.5.48, substituted: SI 2002/2712 Sch.1 para.24

Part 5 r.5.49, substituted: SI 2002/2712 Sch.1 para.24

Part 5 r.5.50, substituted: SI 2002/2712 Sch.1 para.24

Part 5 r.5.51, substituted: SI 2002/2712 Sch.1 para.24

Part 5 r.5.52, substituted: SI 2002/2712 Sch.1 para.24

Part 5 r.5.53, substituted: SI 2002/2712 Sch.1 para.24

Part 5 r.5.54, substituted: SI 2002/2712 Sch.1 para.24

Part 5 r.5.55, substituted: SI 2002/2712 Sch.1 para.24

Part 5 r.5.56, substituted: SI 2002/2712 Sch.1 para.24

Part 5 r.5.57, substituted: SI 2002/2712 Sch.1 para.24

Part 5 r.5.58, substituted: SI 2002/2712 Sch.1 para.24

Part 5 r.5.59, substituted: SI 2002/2712 Sch.1 para.24

Part 5 r.5.60, amended: SI 2004/584 r.25

NO.

1986–cont.

1925. Insolvency Rules 1986–cont.

Part 5 r.5.60, revoked (in part): SI 2004/584 r.25

Part 5 r.5.60, substituted: SI 2002/2712 Sch.1 para.24

Part 5 r.5.61, substituted: SI 2002/2712 Sch.1 para.24

Part 5 r.5.62, substituted: SI 2002/2712 Sch.1 para.24

Part 5 r.5.63, substituted: SI 2002/2712 Sch.1 para.24

Part 5 r.5.64, substituted: SI 2002/2712 Sch.1 para.24

Part 5 r.5.65, substituted: SI 2002/2712 Sch.1 para.24

Part 6, added: SI 2003/1730 Sch.1 para.39

Part 6, added: SI 2003/1730 Sch.1 para.46

Part 6, revoked: SI 2003/1730 Sch.1 para.50

Part 6, added: SI 2002/1307 r.8

Part 6, added: SI 2003/1730 Sch.1 para.52

Part 6 r.6.7, amended: SI 2002/1307 r.8

Part 6 r.6.9, amended: SI 2003/1730 Sch.1 para.32

Part 6 r.6.10, amended: SI 2004/584 r.26

Part 6 r.6.14, amended: SI 2002/1307 r.8

Part 6 r.6.30, amended: SI 2002/1307 r.8

Part 6 r.6.40, amended: SI 2003/1730 Sch.1 para.33

Part 6 r.6.48, revoked: SI 2003/1730 Sch.1 para.34

Part 6 r.6.49, revoked: SI 2003/1730 Sch.1 para.34

Part 6 r.6.50, applied: SI 2003/1730 r.9

Part 6 r.6.50, revoked: SI 2003/1730 Sch.1 para.34

Part 6 r.6.51, amended: SI 2002/1307 r.8

Part 6 r.6.83, amended: SI 2003/1730 Sch.1 para.35

Part 6 r.6.93, amended: SI 2002/1307 r.8

Part 6 r.6.97, revoked (in part): SI 2003/1730 Sch.1 para.36

Part 6 r.6.97, substituted: SI 2004/584 r.27

Part 6 r.6.98, amended: SI 2002/1307 r.8, SI 2004/584 r.28, SI 2004/1070 r.2

Part 6 r.6.99, amended: SI 2004/584 r.29

Part 6 r.6.111, amended: SI 2003/1730 Sch.1 para.37

Part 6 r.6.116, amended: SI 2002/1307 r.8

Part 6 r.6.121, amended: SI 2003/1730 Sch.1 para.38

Part 6 r.6.136, amended: SI 2004/584 r.30

Part 6 r.6.137, amended: SI 2004/584 r.31

Part 6 r.6.137A, added: SI 2004/584 r.32

Part 6 r.6.138, amended: SI 2004/584 r.33

Part 6 r.6.138, applied: SI 2004/584 r.3

Part 6 r.6.138A, added: SI 2004/584 r.34

Part 6 r.6.139, amended: SI 2004/584 r.35

Part 6 r.6.139, applied: SI 2004/584 r.3

Part 6 r.6.146, revoked (in part): SI 2004/584 r.36

Part 6 r.6.156, amended: SI 2004/584 r.37

NO.

1986–cont.

1925. Insolvency Rules 1986–*cont.*

Part 6 r.6.158, amended: SI 2004/584 r.38

Part 6 r.6.198, amended: SI 2002/1307 r.8

Part 6 r.6.202A, added: SI 2003/1730 Sch.1 para.40

Part 6 r.6.205, amended: SI 2003/1730 Sch.1 para.41

Part 6 r.6.206, amended: SI 2003/1730 Sch.1 para.42

Part 6 r.6.212A, applied: SI 2003/1730 r.9

Part 6 r.6.212A, revoked: SI 2003/1730 Sch.1 para.43

Part 6 r.6.213, amended: SI 2003/1730 Sch.1 para.44, SI 2004/584 r.39

Part 6 r.6.213, applied: SI 2003/1730 r.9

Part 6 r.6.214, amended: SI 2003/1730 Sch.1 para.45

Part 6 r.6.214, applied: SI 2003/1730 r.9

Part 6 r.6.214A, disapplied: SI 2003/1730 r.9

Part 6 r.6.214A, amended: SI 2004/584 r.40

Part 6 r.6.215, applied: SI 2003/1730 r.9

Part 6 r.6.215, substituted: SI 2003/1730 Sch.1 para.47

Part 6 r.6.216, applied: SI 2003/1730 r.9

Part 6 r.6.216, substituted: SI 2003/1730 Sch.1 para.48

Part 6 r.6.223, amended: SI 2003/1730 Sch.1 para.49

Part 6 r.6.224, amended: SI 2002/2712 Sch.1 para.25, SI 2004/584 r.41

Part 6 r.6.224, revoked (in part): SI 2002/2712 Sch.1 para.25

Part 6 r.6.237, substituted: SI 2003/1730 Sch.1 para.51

Part 6 r.6.237CA, added: SI 2004/584 r.42

Part 6 r.6.237D, amended: SI 2004/584 r.43

Part 6A r.6A.1, added: SI 2003/1730 Sch.1 para.53

Part 6A r.6A.2, added: SI 2003/1730 Sch.1 para.53

Part 6A r.6A.3, added: SI 2003/1730 Sch.1 para.53

Part 6A r.6A.4, added: SI 2003/1730 Sch.1 para.53

Part 6A r.6A.5, added: SI 2003/1730 Sch.1 para.53

Part 6A r.6A.5, amended: SI 2004/584 r.44

Part 6A r.6A.6, added: SI 2003/1730 Sch.1 para.53

Part 6A r.6A.6, amended: SI 2004/584 r.45

Part 6A r.6A.7, added: SI 2003/1730 Sch.1 para.53

Part 6A r.6A.8, added: SI 2003/1730 Sch.1 para.53

Part 7, added: SI 2002/1307 r.9

Part 7 r.7.1, amended: SI 2003/1730 Sch.1 para.54

Part 7 r.7.3A, added: SI 2003/1730 Sch.1 para.55

Part 7 r.7.4A, added: SI 2003/1730 Sch.1 para.56

NO.

1986–cont.

1925. Insolvency Rules 1986–*cont.*

Part 7 r.7.10, see *Gunningham, Re* [2002] B.P.I.R. 302 (Ch D), Neuberger, J.

Part 7 r.7.20, amended: SI 2003/1730 Sch.1 para.57

Part 7 r.7.31, see *Practice Statement (Ch D: Administration Orders: Reports)* [2002] 1 W.L.R. 1358 (Ch D), Sir Robert Andrew Morritt V.C.

Part 7 r.7.50, substituted: SI 2003/1730 Sch.1 para.58

Part 7 r.7.57, amended: SI 2003/1730 Sch.1 para.59

Part 7 r.7.62, amended: SI 2003/1730 Sch.1 para.60

Part 7 r.7.62, applied: SI 2003/1102 Reg.7

Part 7 r.7.62, varied: SI 2003/1102 Reg.7, SI 2004/353 Reg.7, SI 2004/1045 Reg.6

Part 8 r.8.8, added: SI 2002/1307 r.9

Part 9 r.9, see *Anglo American Insurance Co Ltd (Disclosure), Re* [2002] B.C.C. 715 (Ch D), Neuberger, J.

Part 11 r.11.1, amended: SI 2002/1307 r.10

Part 11 r.11.2, amended: SI 2002/1307 r.10

Part 11 r.11.3, amended: SI 2002/1307 r.10

Part 11 r.11.6, amended: SI 2002/1307 r.10

Part 12 r.12.1, enabled: SI 2004/472

Part 12 r.12.2, amended: SI 2003/1730 Sch.1 para.61

Part 12 r.12.2, substituted: SI 2003/1730 Sch.1 para.61

Part 12 r.12.3, see *Cartwright v Cartwright* [2002] 1 F.L.R. 919 (Ch D), Rimer, J.; see *Cartwright v Cartwright* [2002] EWCA Civ 931, [2002] 2 F.L.R. 610 (CA), Arden, L.J.

Part 12 r.12.3, amended: SI 2003/1730 Sch.1 para.62

Part 12 r.12.12, amended: SI 2002/1307 r.10

Part 12 r.12.17, amended: SI 2002/1307 r.10

Part 12 r.12.22, added: SI 2003/1730 Sch.1 para.63

Part 13 r.13.9, amended: SI 2002/2712 r.7

Part 13 r.13.11, amended: SI 2003/1730 Sch.1 para.64

Part 13 r.13.12, amended: SI 2003/1730 Sch.1 para.65

Part 13 r.13.13, amended: SI 2002/1307 r.10, SI 2003/1730 Sch.1 para.66

r.2.9, see *Farnborough Aircraft.com Ltd, Re* [2002] EWHC 1224, [2002] 2 B.C.L.C. 641 (Ch D (Companies Court)), Neuberger, J.

r.4.85, see *Globe Legal Services Ltd, Re* [2002] B.C.C. 858 (Ch D), Neuberger, J.

r.4.90, see *Company (No.1641 of 2003), Re* [2003] EWHC 2652, [2004] 1 B.C.L.C. 210 (Ch D), Judge Norris Q.C.; see *Isovel Contracts Ltd (In Administration) v ABB Building Technologies Ltd (formerly ABB Steward Ltd)* [2002] 1 B.C.L.C. 390 (Ch

NO.

NO.

1986–cont.

1925. Insolvency Rules 1986–*cont.*

r.4.90–*cont.*

D), Simon Berry Q.C.; see *Secretary of State for Trade and Industry v Frid* [2002] B.P.I.R. 1040 (Ch D (Bankruptcy Ct)), Registrar Jaques; see *Secretary of State for Trade and Industry v Frid* [2004] UKHL 24, [2004] 2 A.C. 506 (HL), Lord Nicholls of Birkenhead

r.5.17, see *Fender v Inland Revenue Commissioners* [2003] B.P.I.R. 1304 (Ch D), Judge Norris Q.C.

r.6.3, see *Anderson v KAS Bank NV* [2004] EWHC 532, [2004] B.P.I.R. 685 (Ch D), David Richards, J

r.6.5, see *Everard v Society of Lloyds* [2003] EWHC 1890, [2003] B.P.I.R. 1286 (Ch D), Laddie, J.; see *Popely v Popely* [2003] EWHC 2028, [2003] B.P.I.R. 1398 (Ch D), E Bartley Jones Q.C.; see *Popely v Popely* [2004] EWCA Civ 463, [2004] B.P.I.R. 778 (CA), Ward, L.J.; see *Sadrolashrafi v Marvel International Food Logistics Ltd* [2004] EWHC 777, [2004] B.P.I.R. 834 (Ch D), Bernard Livesey Q.C.; see *Society of Lloyd's v Bowman* [2003] EWCA Civ 1886, [2004] B.P.I.R. 324 (CA), Chadwick, L.J.; see *West Bromwich Building Society v Crammer* [2002] EWHC 2618, [2003] B.P.I.R. 783 (Ch D), Neuberger, J.

r.6.11, see *Balendran v Law Society (No.2)* [2004] EWHC 495, [2004] B.P.I.R. 859 (Ch D), Judge Weeks Q.C.

r.6.25, see *Barnes v Whitehead* [2004] B.P.I.R. 693 (Ch D), Judge Maddocks

r.6.35, see *Yee Fun Chu v Price (as Trustee in Bankruptcy)* [2003] EWCA Civ 1744, [2004] B.P.I.R. 603 (CA), Arden, L.J.

r.6.52, see *Rehman v Boardman (No.1)* [2004] B.P.I.R. 820 (Ch D), Lewison, J.

r.6.215, see *Bagnall v Official Receiver* [2003] EWCA Civ 1925, [2004] 1 W.L.R. 2832 (CA), Latham, L.J.; see *Bagnall v Official Receiver* [2003] EWHC 1398, [2003] 3 All E.R. 613 (Ch D), Evans-Lombe, J.

r.7.4, see *Bagnall v Official Receiver* [2003] EWCA Civ 1925, [2004] 1 W.L.R. 2832 (CA), Latham, L.J.; see *Bagnall v Official Receiver* [2003] EWHC 1398, [2003] 3 All E.R. 613 (Ch D), Evans-Lombe, J.

r.7.7, see *Highberry Ltd v Colt Telecom Group Plc (No.1)* [2002] EWHC 2503, [2003] 1 B.C.L.C. 290 (Ch D (Companies Court)), Lawrence Collins, J.

r.7.41, see *Scriven, Re* [2004] EWCA Civ 683, [2004] B.P.I.R. 972 (CA), Clarke, L.J.

r.7.55, see *McKay v Rogers* [2002] EWHC 2825, [2004] B.P.I.R. 1272 (Ch D), Hart, J.

r.7.60, see *Highberry Ltd v Colt Telecom Group Plc (No.1)* [2002] EWHC 2503, [2003] 1 B.C.L.C. 290 (Ch D (Companies Court)), Lawrence Collins, J.

1986–cont.

1925. Insolvency Rules 1986–*cont.*

r.12.3, see *Ram v Ram (No.1)* [2004] EWCA Civ 1452, [2004] 3 F.C.R. 425 (CA (Civ Div)), Potter, L.J.

Sch.4, added: SI 2002/2712 Sch.1 Part 6

Sch.4, amended: SI 2002/1307 r.11, Sch.1 Part 1, Sch.1 Part 2, SI 2002/2712 r.8, Sch.1 Part 6, SI 2003/1730 r.14, Sch.2 Part A, Sch.2 Part B, Sch.2 Part C, SI 2004/584 Sch.1

Sch.4, substituted: SI 2002/2712 Sch.1 Part 5

Sch.5, amended: SI 2002/2712 r.9, SI 2003/1730 r.15

Sch.5, applied: SI 2003/1730 r.15

Sch.6, added: SI 2004/584 r.47

1946. Act of Sederunt (Civil Jurisdiction of the Sheriff Court) 1986

r.3, revoked: SSI 2002/132 Sch.2

1960. Statutory Maternity Pay (General) Regulations 1986

Reg.2, amended: SI 2002/2690 Reg.2

Reg.2, revoked (in part): SI 2002/2690 Reg.2

Reg.6, amended: SI 2002/668 Art.10, SI 2004/552 Art.10

Reg.6, applied: SI 2003/526 Art.10

Reg.6, substituted: SI 2002/2690 Reg.3

Reg.7, amended: SI 2003/2096 Sch.1 para.44

Reg.11, amended: SI 2002/2690 Reg.4

Reg.20, amended: SI 2002/2690 Reg.5

Reg.21, see *Alabaster v Woolwich Plc (C147/02)* [2004] 2 C.M.L.R. 9 (ECJ), Judge Skouris (President)

Reg.21A, revoked: SI 2002/2690 Reg.6

Reg.23, amended: SI 2002/2690 Reg.7

Reg.25A, amended: SI 2002/2690 Reg.8

Reg.28, amended: SI 2002/2690 Reg.9

1962. Magistrates Courts (Civil Jurisdiction and Judgments Act 1982) Rules 1986

amended: SI 2002/194 r.3

Part II r.3, amended: SI 2002/194 r.4

Part II r.4, amended: SI 2002/194 r.5

Part II r.5, amended: SI 2002/194 r.6

Part II r.6, amended: SI 2002/194 r.7

Part II r.6A, amended: SI 2002/194 r.8

Part II r.7, amended: SI 2002/194 r.9

Part II r.8, amended: SI 2002/194 r.10

Part II r.9, amended: SI 2002/194 r.10

Part III r.10, amended: SI 2002/194 r.11, r.12

Part III r.11, amended: SI 2002/194 r.11, r.13

Part III r.12, amended: SI 2002/194 r.11, r.14

Part IV r.13, amended: SI 2002/194 r.15

Part IV r.14, amended: SI 2002/194 r.16

1966. Act of Sederunt (Miscellaneous Amendments) 1986

r.3, revoked: SSI 2002/132 Sch.2

1996. Insolvency Proceedings (Monetary Limits) Order 1986

Art.5, added: SI 2004/547 Art.3

Sch.1 Part II, amended: SI 2004/547 Sch.1

NO.

1986–cont.

1999. Administration of Insolvent Estates of Deceased Persons Order 1986
Sch.1 Part II para.1, amended: SI 2002/1309 Art.3
Sch.1 Part II para.2, amended: SI 2002/1309 Art.3
Sch.1 Part II para.25, substituted: SI 2002/1309 Art.3
Sch.3, substituted: SI 2002/1309 Sch.1

2000. Companies (Unfair Prejudice Applications) Proceedings Rules 1986
r.3, see *Smiths of Smithfield Ltd, Re* [2003] EWHC 568, [2003] B.C.C. 769 (Ch D), Leslie Kosmin Q.C.

2019. Suppression of Terrorism Act 1978 (Overseas Territories) Order 1986
Sch.1 Part I, amended: 2002 c.8 s.2

2030. Insolvency Fees Order 1986
revoked: SI 2004/593 Sch.1
varied: SI 2004/593 Sch.1

2067. Companies (Disqualification Orders) Regulations 1986
referred to: SI 2002/689 Reg.2
Sch.1, amended: SI 2002/689 Sch.1
Sch.1, referred to: SI 2002/689 Reg.3

2092. Local Government Reorganisation (Preservation of Right to Buy) Order 1986
Art.12, amended: 2003 c.14 Sch.20 para.3
Sch.1 Part I para.42, amended: SI 2004/3168 Art.11

2100. Road Vehicles (Excise) (Prescribed Particulars) (Amendment) Regulations 1986
revoked: SI 2002/2742 Sch.1 Part I

2101. Road Vehicles (Registration and Licensing) (Amendment) (No.3) Regulations 1986
revoked: SI 2002/2742 Sch.1 Part I

2128. Passenger and Goods Vehicles (Recording Equipment) (Approval of fitters and workshops) (Fees) Regulations 1986
Reg.3, amended: SI 2002/538 Reg.2, SI 2003/1812 Reg.2, SI 2004/1885 Reg.2

2150. Vickers Shipbuilding and Engineering Limited (Barrow-in-Furness) Light Railway Order 1986
Art.5, amended: SI 2003/2155 Sch.1 para.18

2175. British Nationality (Hong Kong) Regulations 1986
Reg.4, amended: 2002 c.8 s.1
Reg.7, amended: 2002 c.8 s.1
Reg.8, revoked: SI 2003/540 Reg.2
Reg.9, amended: 2002 c.8 s.1
Reg.9, revoked: SI 2003/540 Reg.2
Reg.10, revoked: SI 2003/540 Reg.2
Sch.1 Part I para.3, amended: 2002 c.8 s.2

2176. Status of British National (Overseas) (Deprivation) Rules 1986
r.5, amended: 2002 c.8 s.1

NO.

1986–cont.

2194. Housing (Right to Buy) (Prescribed Forms) Regulations 1986
Sch.1, amended: SI 2003/1615 Sch.1 para.43, SI 2004/696 Sch.1 para.4

2209. European Assembly Elections Regulations 1986
applied: SI 2003/284 Art.111, Art.124

2211. Charitable Deductions (Approved Schemes) Regulations 1986
Reg.2, amended: SI 2003/1745 Reg.3
Reg.4A, amended: SI 2003/1745 Reg.4
Reg.9, amended: SI 2003/1745 Reg.5
Reg.11, amended: SI 2003/1745 Reg.6
Reg.16, substituted: SI 2003/1745 Reg.7

2213. Scottish Local Elections Rules 1986
revoked: SSI 2002/457 Sch.1

2214. Local Elections (Principal Areas) Rules 1986
applied: SI 2004/870 Reg.10
r.4, amended: SI 2004/223 r.2
r.4A, see *R. (on the application of De Beer) v Balabanoff* [2002] EWHC 670, Times, April 25, 2002 (QBD (Admin Ct)), Scott Baker, J.
r.6, substituted: SI 2004/223 r.2
r.7, revoked: SI 2004/223 r.2
Sch.2, amended: SI 2004/223 r.2
Sch.2, varied: SI 2003/284 Sch.4 para.23, Sch.4 para.24, Sch.4 para.25, Sch.4 para.26, Sch.4 para.27, Sch.4 para.28, Sch.4 para.29, Sch.4 para.30, Sch.4 para.31, Sch.4 para.32, Sch.4 para.33, Sch.4 para.34, Sch.4 para.35, Sch.4 para.36, Sch.4 para.37, Sch.4 para.38, Sch.4 para.39, Sch.4 para.40, Sch.4 para.41, Sch.4 para.42, Sch.4 para.43, SI 2004/870 Sch.3, Sch.4
Sch.2 Part IV r.45, see *Gough v Local Sunday Newspapers (North) Ltd (No.2)* [2003] EWCA Civ 297, [2003] 1 W.L.R. 1836 (CA), Simon Brown, L.J.
Sch.2 Part IV r.46, see *Gough v Local Sunday Newspapers (North) Ltd (No.2)* [2003] EWCA Civ 297, [2003] 1 W.L.R. 1836 (CA), Simon Brown, L.J.
Sch.2 Part IV r.47, see *Gough v Local Sunday Newspapers (North) Ltd (No.2)* [2003] EWCA Civ 297, [2003] 1 W.L.R. 1836 (CA), Simon Brown, L.J.
Sch.2 r.19, see *Knight v Nicholls* [2004] EWCA Civ 68, [2004] 1 W.L.R. 1653 (CA), Tuckey, L.J.
Sch.3, amended: SI 2004/1041 r.2
Sch.3, applied: SI 2004/1234 Art.3, Art.4
Sch.3, substituted: SI 2004/223 Sch.1
Sch.3 para.1, substituted: SI 2004/223 Sch.1
Sch.3 para.2, substituted: SI 2004/223 Sch.1
Sch.3 para.3, substituted: SI 2004/223 Sch.1
Sch.3 para.4, substituted: SI 2004/223 Sch.1
Sch.3 para.5, substituted: SI 2004/223 Sch.1
Sch.3 para.6, substituted: SI 2004/223 Sch.1
Sch.3 para.7, substituted: SI 2004/223 Sch.1

NO.

1986–cont.

2214. Local Elections (Principal Areas) Rules 1986–*cont.*

Sch.3 para.8, substituted: SI 2004/223 Sch.1
Sch.3 para.9, substituted: SI 2004/223 Sch.1
Sch.3 para.10, substituted: SI 2004/223 Sch.1
Sch.3 para.11, substituted: SI 2004/223 Sch.1
Sch.3 para.12, substituted: SI 2004/223 Sch.1
Sch.3 para.13, substituted: SI 2004/223 Sch.1
Sch.3 para.14, substituted: SI 2004/223 Sch.1
Sch.3 para.15, substituted: SI 2004/223 Sch.1
Sch.3 para.16, substituted: SI 2004/223 Sch.1
Sch.3 para.17, substituted: SI 2004/223 Sch.1
Sch.3 para.18, substituted: SI 2004/223 Sch.1
Sch.3 para.19, substituted: SI 2004/223 Sch.1
Sch.3 para.20, substituted: SI 2004/223 Sch.1
Sch.3 para.21, substituted: SI 2004/223 Sch.1
Sch.4 para.1, revoked: SI 2004/223 r.2
Sch.4 para.2, revoked: SI 2004/223 r.2
Sch.4 para.3, revoked: SI 2004/223 r.2
Sch.4 para.4, revoked: SI 2004/223 r.2
Sch.4 para.5, revoked: SI 2004/223 r.2
Sch.4 para.6, revoked: SI 2004/223 r.2
Sch.4 para.6, varied: SI 2002/185 Sch.3 Part I
Sch.4 para.7, revoked: SI 2004/223 r.2
Sch.4 para.8, revoked: SI 2004/223 r.2
Sch.4 para.9, revoked: SI 2004/223 r.2
Sch.4 para.10, revoked: SI 2004/223 r.2
Sch.4 para.11, revoked: SI 2004/223 r.2
Sch.4 para.12, revoked: SI 2004/223 r.2
Sch.4 para.13, revoked: SI 2004/223 r.2
Sch.4 para.14, amended: SI 2002/185 Reg.8
Sch.4 para.14, revoked: SI 2004/223 r.2
Sch.4 para.14, varied: SI 2002/185 Sch.3 Part I
Sch.4 para.15, revoked: SI 2004/223 r.2
Sch.4 para.16, revoked: SI 2004/223 r.2
Sch.4 para.17, revoked: SI 2004/223 r.2
Sch.4 para.18, revoked: SI 2004/223 r.2
Sch.4 para.19, revoked: SI 2004/223 r.2
Sch.4 para.20, revoked: SI 2004/223 r.2
Sch.4 para.21, revoked: SI 2004/223 r.2
Sch.4 para.21, varied: SI 2002/185 Sch.3 Part I
Sch.4 para.22, revoked: SI 2004/223 r.2
Sch.4 para.23, revoked: SI 2004/223 r.2
Sch.4 para.24, revoked: SI 2004/223 r.2

2215. Local Elections (Parishes and Communities) Rules 1986

varied: SI 2002/3228 Art.9

NO.

1986–cont.

2215. Local Elections (Parishes and Communities) Rules 1986–*cont.*

r.4, amended: SI 2004/224 r.2
r.6, substituted: SI 2004/224 r.2
r.7, revoked: SI 2004/224 r.2
r.8, applied: SI 2002/2374 Art.6, SI 2003/157 Art.10
r.8, varied: SI 2002/48 Art.6, SI 2002/2368 Art.6, SI 2002/2593 Art.9, SI 2002/2991 Art.7, SI 2002/3225 Art.6, SI 2003/161 Art.9, SI 2004/218 Art.3
Sch.2, amended: SI 2004/224 r.2
Sch.2, varied: SI 2003/284 Sch.4 para.44, Sch.4 para.45, Sch.4 para.46, Sch.4 para.47, Sch.4 para.48, Sch.4 para.49, Sch.4 para.50, Sch.4 para.51, Sch.4 para.52, Sch.4 para.53, Sch.4 para.54, Sch.4 para.55, Sch.4 para.56, Sch.4 para.57, Sch.4 para.58, Sch.4 para.59, Sch.4 para.60, Sch.4 para.61, Sch.4 para.62, Sch.4 para.63, Sch.4 para.64
Sch.3, referred to: SI 2004/224 r.2
Sch.3, applied: SI 2004/1233 Art.3, Art.4
Sch.3, substituted: SI 2004/224 Sch.1
Sch.3 para.1, substituted: SI 2004/224 Sch.1
Sch.3 para.2, substituted: SI 2004/224 Sch.1
Sch.3 para.3, substituted: SI 2004/224 Sch.1
Sch.3 para.4, substituted: SI 2004/224 Sch.1
Sch.3 para.5, substituted: SI 2004/224 Sch.1
Sch.3 para.6, substituted: SI 2004/224 Sch.1
Sch.3 para.7, substituted: SI 2004/224 Sch.1
Sch.3 para.8, substituted: SI 2004/224 Sch.1
Sch.3 para.9, substituted: SI 2004/224 Sch.1
Sch.3 para.10, substituted: SI 2004/224 Sch.1
Sch.3 para.11, substituted: SI 2004/224 Sch.1
Sch.3 para.12, substituted: SI 2004/224 Sch.1
Sch.3 para.13, substituted: SI 2004/224 Sch.1
Sch.3 para.14, substituted: SI 2004/224 Sch.1
Sch.3 para.15, substituted: SI 2004/224 Sch.1
Sch.3 para.16, substituted: SI 2004/224 Sch.1
Sch.3 para.17, substituted: SI 2004/224 Sch.1
Sch.3 para.18, substituted: SI 2004/224 Sch.1
Sch.3 para.19, substituted: SI 2004/224 Sch.1
Sch.3 para.20, substituted: SI 2004/224 Sch.1
Sch.4 para.1, revoked: SI 2004/224 r.2
Sch.4 para.2, revoked: SI 2004/224 r.2
Sch.4 para.3, revoked: SI 2004/224 r.2
Sch.4 para.4, revoked: SI 2004/224 r.2
Sch.4 para.5, revoked: SI 2004/224 r.2
Sch.4 para.5, varied: SI 2002/185 Sch.3 Part I

NO.

1986–cont.

2215. Local Elections (Parishes and Communities) Rules 1986–*cont.*

Sch.4 para.6, revoked: SI 2004/224 r.2
Sch.4 para.7, revoked: SI 2004/224 r.2
Sch.4 para.8, revoked: SI 2004/224 r.2
Sch.4 para.9, revoked: SI 2004/224 r.2
Sch.4 para.10, revoked: SI 2004/224 r.2
Sch.4 para.11, revoked: SI 2004/224 r.2
Sch.4 para.12, revoked: SI 2004/224 r.2
Sch.4 para.13, revoked: SI 2004/224 r.2
Sch.4 para.14, revoked: SI 2004/224 r.2
Sch.4 para.15, revoked: SI 2004/224 r.2
Sch.4 para.16, revoked: SI 2004/224 r.2
Sch.4 para.17, revoked: SI 2004/224 r.2
Sch.4 para.18, revoked: SI 2004/224 r.2
Sch.4 para.19, revoked: SI 2004/224 r.2
Sch.4 para.20, revoked: SI 2004/224 r.2
Sch.4 para.20, varied: SI 2002/185 Sch.3 Part I
Sch.4 para.21, revoked: SI 2004/224 r.2
Sch.4 para.22, revoked: SI 2004/224 r.2

2222. Foreign Compensation (Union of Soviet Socialist Republics) (Registration and Determination of Claims) Order 1986

Art.3, amended: 2002 c.8 s.2

2226. Repatriation of Prisoners (Overseas Territories) Order 1986

Sch.1 para.1, amended: 2002 c.8 s.2

2232. Recreation and Youth Service (Northern Ireland) Order 1986

Art.3, applied: SR 2003/253 Art.3
Art.7, revoked (in part): SI 2003/418 Sch.3
Art.11, applied: SR 2003/253 Art.3

2250. European Parliamentary Elections (Northern Ireland) Regulations 1986

revoked: SI 2004/1267 Sch.7

2268. Rehabilitation of Offenders Act 1974 (Exceptions) (Amendment No 2) Order 1986

revoked (in part): SSI 2003/231 Art.6

2297. Act of Sederunt (Sheriff Court Company Insolvency Rules) 1986

referred to: SSI 2003/388 Sch.1 para.1
Part I r.4, amended: SSI 2003/388 Sch.1 para.2
Part I r.5, amended: SSI 2003/388 Sch.1 para.3
Part I r.6, amended: SSI 2003/388 Sch.1 para.4
Part I r.7, amended: SSI 2003/388 Sch.1 para.5
Part I r.8, amended: SSI 2003/388 Sch.1 para.6
Part I r.9, amended: SSI 2003/388 Sch.1 para.7
Part II r.10, amended: SSI 2003/388 r.2
Part II r.10, revoked (in part): SSI 2003/388 r.2
Part II r.11, amended: SSI 2003/388 r.2
Part II r.12, amended: SSI 2003/388 r.2
Part II r.12, substituted: SSI 2003/388 r.2

1986–cont.

2297. Act of Sederunt (Sheriff Court Company Insolvency Rules) 1986–*cont.*

Part II r.13, amended: SSI 2003/388 r.2
Part II r.14, amended: SSI 2003/388 r.2
Part II r.14, substituted: SSI 2003/388 r.2
Part II r.14A, amended: SSI 2003/388 r.2
Part III r.15, amended: SSI 2003/388 Sch.1 para.8
Part III r.16, amended: SSI 2003/388 Sch.1 para.9
Part IV r.19, amended: SSI 2003/388 Sch.1 para.10
Part IV r.23, amended: SSI 2003/388 Sch.1 para.11
Part V r.31A, added: SSI 2003/388 r.3

2299. Condensed Milk and Dried Milk (Amendment) Regulations 1986

revoked (in part): SI 2003/1596 Reg.10, SI 2003/3053 Reg.10

1987

2. National Health Service (Food Premises) (Scotland) Regulations 1987

applied: SSI 2002/103 Sch.1 Part III, SSI 2002/305 Sch.1 Part III, SSI 2002/534 Sch.1 Part III

26. Condensed Milk and Dried Milk (Scotland) (Amendment) Regulations 1987

revoked: SSI 2003/311 Reg.11

37. Dangerous Substances in Harbour Areas Regulations 1987

Part IX, applied: SI 2002/655 Reg.12, SI 2003/547 Reg.12, SI 2004/456 Reg.11
Reg.2, amended: SI 2004/568 Sch.13 para.3
Reg.3, amended: SI 2004/568 Sch.13 para.3
Reg.24, amended: SI 2003/1431 Reg.2
Reg.24, substituted: SI 2004/568 Sch.13 para.3
Reg.25, amended: SI 2004/568 Sch.13 para.3
Reg.29, amended: SI 2002/2776 Sch.6 para.7
Reg.29, revoked (in part): SI 2002/2776 Sch.7 Part 2
Reg.30, amended: SI 2004/3168 Art.12
Sch.1 Part I, amended: SI 2004/568 Sch.13 para.3
Sch.3, amended: SI 2004/568 Sch.13 para.3

75. Derwent Valley Railway (Transfer) Light Railway Order 1987

Art.5, amended: SI 2003/2155 Sch.1 para.18

116. Gas Cylinders (Pattern Approval) Regulations 1987

revoked: SI 2004/568 Sch.14

235. Statutory Maternity Pay (Medical Evidence) Regulations 1987

Reg.1, amended: SI 2002/881 Sch.1 para.2, SI 2002/2469 Sch.8

NO.

NO.

1987–cont.

235. Statutory Maternity Pay (Medical Evidence) Regulations 1987–*cont.*

Sch.1 Part I para.4, amended: SI 2002/881 Sch.1 para.3, SI 2004/1771 Sch.1 para.51

Sch.1 Part II, amended: SI 2002/2469 Sch.5, SI 2004/865 Sch.1 para.5, SI 2004/1016 Sch.1 para.5, SI 2004/1771 Sch.1 para.51

Sch.1 Part II, applied: SI 2004/1016 Art.83, SSI 2004/163 Art.94

Sch.1 Part II, referred to: SI 2004/865 Art.107

257. Police Pensions Regulations 1987

referred to: SI 2003/27 Reg.2, SI 2003/535 Reg.2

see *Cantwell v Criminal Injuries Compensation Board* [2001] UKHL 36, 2002 S.C. (H.L.) 1 (HL), Lord Hope of Craighead; see *Grubb v Jones* 2003 S.L.T. 1101 (OH), Lord Eassie

Reg.A11, see *R. (on the application of South Wales Police Authority) v Morgan* [2003] EWHC 2274, [2003] Pens. L.R. 355 (QBD (Admin Ct)), Stanley Burnton, J.

Reg.B4, see *Clinch v Dorset Police Authority* [2003] EWHC 161, [2003] Pens. L.R. 59 (QBD (Admin Ct)), McCombe, J.

Reg.H1, see *Clinch v Dorset Police Authority* [2003] EWHC 161, [2003] Pens. L.R. 59 (QBD (Admin Ct)), McCombe, J.

Reg.H2, see *Lothian and Borders Police Board v Ward* 2003 S.L.T. 1072 (OH), Lord Drummond Young

Reg.H5, see *Clinch v Dorset Police Authority* [2003] EWHC 161, [2003] Pens. L.R. 59 (QBD (Admin Ct)), McCombe, J.

Reg.1, amended: SI 2002/2529 Reg.3, SI 2003/27 Sch.1 para.2, SI 2004/2354 Reg.2, SSI 2003/406 Sch.1 para.4, SSI 2004/486 Sch.1 para.3

Reg.1, amended: SI 2003/27 Sch.1 para.3, SI 2004/1491 Sch.1 para.9, Sch.1 para.14, SSI 2003/406 Sch.1 para.5, SSI 2004/486 Sch.1 para.4, Sch.1 para.5

Reg.1, varied: SI 2004/1491 Reg.4, SSI 2004/486 Reg.4

Reg.1, amended: SI 2004/1491 Sch.1 para.11, SSI 2004/486 Sch.1 para.8

Reg.1, amended: SI 2003/535 Sch.1 para.3, SI 2004/1491 Sch.1 para.2, SSI 2003/406 Sch.1 para.7, SSI 2004/486 Sch.1 para.9

Reg.1, revoked (in part): SI 2004/1491 Sch.1 para.2, SSI 2004/486 Sch.1 para.9

Reg.1, amended: SI 2002/3202 Sch.1 para.10

Reg.1, added: SI 2002/3202 Sch.1 para.12

Reg.2, amended: SI 2004/2354 Reg.2

Reg.2, amended: SI 2003/535 Sch.1 para.4, SI 2004/1491 Sch.1 para.3, SSI 2003/406 Sch.1 para.8, Sch.1 para.9, Sch.1 para.10, SSI 2004/486 Sch.1 para.10

Reg.2, revoked (in part): SI 2004/1491 Sch.1 para.4, SSI 2004/486 Sch.1 para.10

Reg.2, added: SI 2002/3202 Sch.1 para.12

Reg.2, amended: SI 2003/535 Sch.1 para.8

1987–cont.

257. Police Pensions Regulations 1987–*cont.*

Reg.3, amended: SI 2004/2354 Reg.2

Reg.3, revoked (in part): SI 2003/2716 Sch.1 para.2

Reg.3, amended: SI 2003/535 Sch.1 para.5, SI 2004/1491 Sch.1 para.4, SSI 2003/406 Sch.1 para.9, Sch.1 para.11, SSI 2004/486 Sch.1 para.11

Reg.3, added: SI 2002/3202 Sch.1 para.12

Reg.3, added: SI 2003/535 Sch.1 para.9

Reg.3A, revoked (in part): SI 2003/2716 Sch.1 para.4

Reg.4, amended: SI 2004/2354 Reg.2

Reg.4, amended: SI 2004/1491 Sch.1 para.5, SSI 2003/406 Sch.1 para.9

Reg.4, amended: SI 2004/1491 Sch.1 para.13, SSI 2004/486 Sch.1 para.12

Reg.4, revoked (in part): SI 2003/2716 Sch.1 para.5

Reg.4, amended: SI 2002/3202 Sch.1 para.11

Reg.4, added: SI 2002/3202 Sch.1 para.12

Reg.5, amended: SI 2004/2354 Reg.2

Reg.5, amended: SI 2003/535 Sch.1 para.6, SSI 2003/406 Sch.1 para.12

Reg.5, amended: SI 2002/3202 Sch.1 para.9, SSI 2004/486 Sch.1 para.13

Reg.5, added: SI 2002/3202 Sch.1 para.12

Reg.6, added: SI 2002/3202 Sch.1 para.5

Reg.6, amended: SI 2004/1760 Reg.3, SSI 2004/486 Sch.1 para.6

Reg.6, amended: SI 2003/27 Sch.1 para.4, SSI 2003/406 Sch.1 para.6

Reg.6, amended: SI 2003/535 Sch.1 para.7, SSI 2003/406 Sch.1 para.13

Reg.6, added: SI 2002/3202 Sch.1 para.12

Reg.7, added: SI 2004/2354 Reg.2

Reg.7, added: SI 2002/3202 Sch.1 para.12

Reg.8, amended: SI 2002/3202 Sch.1 para.2

Reg.8, added: SI 2004/2354 Reg.2

Reg.8, added: SI 2002/3202 Sch.1 para.12

Reg.8A, amended: SI 2002/3202 Sch.1 para.7, SI 2003/2716 Sch.1 para.3

Reg.9, amended: SI 2003/27 Sch.1 para.1, SSI 2003/406 Sch.1 para.1

Reg.9, added: SI 2002/3202 Sch.1 para.12

Reg.10, amended: SI 2002/3202 Sch.1 para.1, SI 2004/1491 Sch.1 para.8, SSI 2004/486 Sch.1 para.1

Reg.10, added: SI 2002/3202 Sch.1 para.4

Reg.10, amended: SI 2004/1491 Sch.1 para.10, SSI 2004/486 Sch.1 para.7

Reg.10, added: SI 2002/3202 Sch.1 para.12

Reg.10A, added: SI 2002/3202 Sch.1 para.8

Reg.11, added: SI 2002/3202 Sch.1 para.6

Reg.11, added: SI 2002/3202 Sch.1 para.12

Reg.12, amended: SI 2003/535 Sch.1 para.1, SSI 2003/406 Sch.1 para.2

Reg.12, added: SI 2002/3202 Sch.1 para.3

Reg.12, added: SI 2002/3202 Sch.1 para.12

Reg.13, added: SI 2002/3202 Sch.1 para.12

NO.

1987–cont.

257. Police Pensions Regulations 1987–
cont.

Reg.14, added: SI 2002/3202 Sch.1 para.12

Reg.15, added: SI 2002/3202 Sch.1 para.12

Reg.16, added: SI 2002/3202 Sch.1 para.12

Reg.17, revoked (in part): SI 2003/2716 Sch.1 para.1

Reg.17, added: SI 2002/3202 Sch.1 para.12

Reg.18, amended: SSI 2004/486 Sch.1 para.2

Reg.18, added: SI 2002/3202 Sch.1 para.12

Reg.19, added: SI 2002/3202 Sch.1 para.12

Reg.20, amended: SI 2003/535 Sch.1 para.2, SI 2004/1491 Sch.1 para.1, SSI 2003/406 Sch.1 para.3

Sch.A, added: SSI 2004/486 Sch.1 para.14

Sch.A, amended: SI 2002/3202 Sch.1 para.13, SI 2003/535 Sch.1 para.10, SI 2003/2716 Sch.1 para.6, SI 2004/1491 Sch.1 para.6, Sch.1 para.12, SI 2004/2354 Reg.2, SSI 2003/406 Sch.1 para.14

Sch.A, substituted: SSI 2004/486 Sch.1 para.14

Sch.B Part I para.2, amended: SI 2002/3202 Sch.1 para.14

Sch.B Part I para.3, added: SI 2002/3202 Sch.1 para.14

Sch.B Part V para.3, amended: SI 2002/3202 Sch.1 para.15

Sch.F Part IV para.1, amended: SI 2004/1760 Reg.3, SSI 2004/486 Sch.1 para.15

Sch.F Part IV para.1A, added: SI 2004/1760 Reg.3, SSI 2004/486 Sch.1 para.15

Sch.F Part IV para.2, added: SI 2004/1760 Reg.3

Sch.F Part IV para.2, amended: SSI 2004/486 Sch.1 para.15

Sch.F Part IV para.5, added: SI 2002/3202 Sch.1 para.17

Sch.F Part II para.9A, added: SI 2002/3202 Sch.1 para.16

Sch.H para1, amended: SI 2004/1760 Reg.3

Sch.H para1, substituted: SI 2004/1491 Sch.1 para.7, SSI 2004/486 Sch.1 para.16

Sch.H para2, substituted: SI 2004/1491 Sch.1 para.7, SSI 2003/406 Sch.1 para.15, SSI 2004/486 Sch.1 para.16

Sch.H para3, amended: SSI 2004/486 Sch.1 para.16

Sch.H para3, revoked (in part): SSI 2004/486 Sch.1 para.16

Sch.H para3, substituted: SI 2004/1491 Sch.1 para.7, SSI 2003/406 Sch.1 para.15

Sch.H para4, substituted: SI 2004/1491 Sch.1 para.7, SSI 2003/406 Sch.1 para.15

Sch.H para5, substituted: SI 2004/1491 Sch.1 para.7, SSI 2004/486 Sch.1 para.16

Sch.H para6, substituted: SI 2004/1491 Sch.1 para.7, SSI 2003/406 Sch.1 para.15, SSI 2004/486 Sch.1 para.16

Sch.H para7, amended: SI 2004/1760 Reg.3

1987–cont.

257. Police Pensions Regulations 1987–
cont.

Sch.H para7, substituted: SI 2004/1491 Sch.1 para.7, SSI 2003/406 Sch.1 para.15

Sch.H para8, amended: SSI 2003/406 Sch.1 para.15

Sch.H para8, substituted: SI 2004/1491 Sch.1 para.7

298. Misuse of Drugs (Licence Fees) (Amendment) Regulations 1987

revoked: SI 2003/611 Sch.1

299. Prosecution of Offences (Custody Time Limits) Regulations 1987

Reg.4, see *R. (on the application of Wardle) v Leeds Crown Court* [2001] UKHL 12, [2002] 1 A.C. 754 (HL), Lord Slynn of Hadley

Reg.5, see *R. (on the application of Haque) v Central Criminal Court* [2003] EWHC 2457, [2004] Crim. L.R. 298 (QBD (Admin Ct)), Mitting, J.

357. Child Benefit (General) Amendment Regulations 1987

revoked: SI 2003/493 Sch.2 Part 1

408. Merchant Shipping (Seamen's Documents) Regulations 1987

Reg.1, amended: 2002 c.8 s.2

Reg.3, amended: 2002 c.8 s.2

416. Social Security (Maternity Allowance) Regulations 1987

Reg.3, amended: SI 2002/2690 Reg.15

Reg.3, revoked (in part): SI 2002/2690 Reg.15

423. Police (Scotland) Amendment Regulations 1987

revoked: SSI 2004/257 Sch.4

447. Veterinary Surgeons Qualifications (EEC Recognition) (Spanish and Portuguese Qualifications) Order 1987

revoked: SI 2003/2919 Art.13

451. Aviation Security (Anguilla) Order 1987

Sch.1 para.38, amended: 2002 c.8 s.2

452. Fugitive Offenders (Anguilla) Order 1987

revoked: SI 2002/1823 Sch.5

457. General Medical Council (Constitution) Amendment Order 1987

revoked: SI 2002/3136 Art.9

458. Agriculture (Environmental Areas) (Northern Ireland) Order 1987

Art.3, applied: SI 2003/2261 Sch.3 Part I

460. Audit (Northern Ireland) Order 1987

applied: SI 2003/419 Art.63

Part III, applied: SR 2002/265 Sch.7 para.1

Art.6, amended: SI 2003/418 Sch.2 para.3

Art.8, applied: SI 2003/418 Art.1, Art.3

Art.8, revoked (in part): SI 2003/418 Sch.3

Art.9, applied: SI 2003/418 Art.1, Art.3

Art.10, revoked: SI 2003/418 Sch.3

1987–cont.

460. Audit (Northern Ireland) Order 1987–cont.

Art.11, applied: SI 2002/3126 Art.2

Sch.1, amended: SI 2003/418 Sch.2 para.3

461. Education (Corporal Punishment) (Northern Ireland) Order 1987

revoked: SI 2003/424 Sch.3 Part I

463. Public Order (Northern Ireland) Order 1987

Art.18, amended: SI 2003/1247 Art.28, Sch.2

467. Double Taxation Relief (Taxes on Income) (Mauritius) Order 1987

Art.2, referred to: SI 2003/2620 Art.2

468. Reciprocal Enforcement of Foreign Judgments (Canada) Order 1987

see *Naghshineh v Chaffe* [2003] EWHC 2107, [2003] N.P.C. 146 (Ch D), Jonathan Crow

470. Merchant Shipping (Prevention and Control of Pollution) Order 1987

Art.3, enabled: SI 2004/930

481. Social Fund Maternity and Funeral Expenses (General) Regulations 1987

varied: SI 2002/79 Reg.3

Reg.3, amended: SI 2002/881 Sch.1 para.4, SI 2003/455 Sch.4 para.2, SI 2004/1771 Sch.1 para.50

Reg.4, referred to: SI 2002/79 Reg.3

Reg.5, amended: SI 2002/79 Reg.2, SI 2002/3019 Reg.31, SI 2003/455 Sch.4 para.2

Reg.5, varied: SI 2002/79 Reg.3

Reg.6, amended: SI 2003/455 Sch.4 para.2

Reg.6, revoked (in part): SI 2003/455 Sch.4 para.2

Reg.7, amended: SI 2002/2323 Reg.3, SI 2002/3019 Reg.31, SI 2003/455 Sch.4 para.2, SI 2004/2536 Reg.3

Reg.7A, amended: SI 2003/471 Reg.2, SI 2003/1570 Reg.2, SI 2004/2536 Reg.4

Reg.8, amended: SI 2004/1141 Reg.8

516. Stamp Duty (Exempt Instruments) Regulations 1987

Reg.2, amended: 2003 c.14 Sch.20 para.3

Sch.1, amended: 2003 c.14 Sch.20 para.3

Sch.1, referred to: 2002 c.23 Sch.35 para.2

530. Income Tax (Entertainers and Sportsmen) Regulations 1987

Reg.6, see *Agassi v Robinson (Inspector of Taxes)* [2003] S.T.C. (S.C.D.) 382 (Sp Comm), John Avery-Jones

671. Home-Grown Cereals Authority Levy Scheme (Approval) Order 1987

referred to: SI 2004/1445

701. Town and Country Planning (Appeals) (Written Representations Procedure) Regulations 1987

revoked (in part): SI 2003/390 Reg.13

1987–cont.

716. Crown Court (Advance Notice of Expert Evidence) Rules 1987

r.3, see *R. (on the application of Haque) v Central Criminal Court* [2003] EWHC 2457, [2004] Crim. L.R. 298 (QBD (Admin Ct)), Mitting, J.

752. Companies (Forms) (Amendment) Regulations 1987

Sch.2 Part I, referred to: SI 2003/2982 Reg.2

755. Secure Tenancies (Notices) Regulations 1987

Reg.3, added: SI 2004/1627 Reg.2

Sch.1 Part III, added: SI 2004/1627 Reg.2

764. Town and Country Planning (Use Classes) Order 1987

applied: SI 2004/932 Art.4

see *North Devon DC v First Secretary of State* [2003] EWHC 157, [2004] 1 P. & C.R. 38 (QBD (Admin Ct)), Collins, J.; see *Waltham Forest LBC v Secretary of State for Transport, Local Government and the Regions* [2002] EWCA Civ 330, Independent, March 22, 2002 (CA), Schiemann, L.J.

Art.3, amended: SI 2002/1875 Art.2

Art.3, see *R. (on the application of Bennett Fergusson Coal Ltd) v First Secretary of State* [2003] EWHC 1858, [2004] 1 P. & C.R. 30 (QBD (Admin Ct)), Blackburne, J.

Class C3, see *R. (on the application of Hossack) v Kettering BC* [2003] EWHC 1929, [2003] N.P.C. 105 (QBD (Admin Ct)), Richards, J.

Sch.1 Part 3 para.3, see *R. (on the application of Hossack) v Kettering BC* [2002] EWCA Civ 886, [2003] 2 P. & C.R. 34 (CA), Simon Brown, L.J.; see *Waltham Forest LBC v Secretary of State for the Environment, Transport and the Regions* [2001] EWHC Admin 817, [2002] J.P.L. 727 (QBD (Admin Ct)), Sullivan, J.

Sch.1 Part.3 para.3 Class C3, see *R. (on the application of Hossack) v Kettering BC* [2002] EWHC 493, Times, April 22, 2002 (QBD (Admin Ct)), Lightman, J.

Sch.1 Part 4 Class D2, see *Belmont Riding Centre v First Secretary of State* [2003] EWHC 1895, [2004] J.P.L. 593 (QBD (Admin Ct)), Richards, J.

Sch.1 Part 4 para.2, see *Rugby Football Union v Secretary of State for Transport, Local Government and the Regions* [2002] EWCA Civ 1169, Times, August 13, 2002 (CA), Schiemann, L.J.

773. Patronage (Benefices) Rules 1987

applied: SI 2003/1933 Sch.1 Part V

Part II r.10, applied: SI 2004/1888 Sch.1 Part TABLEe

Part II r.10, referred to: SI 2003/1933 Sch.1 Part V

821. Court Funds Rules 1987

applied: SI 2002/1711 Reg.14, SI 2004/248 Reg.14

NO.

1987–cont.

821. Court Funds Rules 1987–cont.
referred to: SI 2003/375 r.2
Part A r.2, amended: SI 2003/375 r.3
Part A r.2, revoked (in part): SI 2003/375 r.3
Part II, amended: SI 2003/375 r.7
Part II r.14, amended: SI 2003/375 r.4
Part II r.15, amended: SI 2003/375 r.5
Part II r.16, amended: SI 2003/375 r.6
Part II r.19, substituted: SI 2003/375 r.7
Part II r.21, revoked: SI 2003/375 r.8
Part II r.23, revoked: SI 2003/375 r.8
Part II r.24, amended: SI 2003/375 r.9
Part III r.25, amended: SI 2003/375 r.10
Part III r.25, revoked (in part): SI 2003/375 r.10
Part IV r.31, amended: SI 2003/375 r.11
Part IV r.31, revoked (in part): SI 2003/375 r.11
Part IV r.32, amended: SI 2003/375 r.12
Part V r.34, amended: SI 2003/720 r.2
Part VII r.50, revoked: SI 2003/375 r.13

851. Police Regulations 1987
Reg.49, applied: SI 2003/527 Sch.3 para.6
Reg.49A, disapplied: SI 2003/527 Sch.3 para.7
Reg.50, applied: SI 2003/527 Sch.3 para.6

874. Stansted Airport Aircraft Movement Limit Order 1987
revoked: SI 2004/1946 Art.2

877. Medicines (Child Safety) Amendment Regulations 1987
revoked: SI 2003/2317 Reg.7

950. North Norfolk (Extension and Amendment) Light Railway Order 1987
Art.6, amended: SI 2003/2155 Sch.1 para.18

1088. Yorkshire Dales Light Railway Order 1987
Art.9, amended: SI 2003/2155 Sch.1 para.18

1110. Personal Pension Schemes (Disclosure of Information) Regulations 1987
Reg.1, amended: SI 2002/1383 Reg.2
Reg.5, amended: SI 2002/1383 Reg.2
Reg.6, amended: SI 2002/1555 Art.32
Sch.2 para.2A, added: SI 2002/1383 Reg.2
Sch.3 para.4, amended: SI 2002/1555 Art.32

1127. Inheritance Tax (Delivery of Accounts) Regulations 1987
revoked: SI 2002/1733 Sch.1

1128. Inheritance Tax (Delivery of Accounts) (Scotland) Regulations 1987
revoked: SI 2002/1733 Sch.1

1131. Restriction on Agreements and Conduct (Tour Operators) Order 1987
applied: SI 2004/2181 Sch.2

1208. Heather and Grass etc (Burning) (Amendment) Regulations 1987
Reg.3, revoked: SI 2003/1615 Sch.1 para.44

NO.

1987–cont.

1208. Heather and Grass etc (Burning) (Amendment) Regulations 1987–cont.
Reg.4, revoked: SI 2003/1615 Sch.1 para.44

1230. Minibus and Other Section 19 Permit Buses Regulations 1987
Reg.4, amended: SI 2002/2534 Reg.2

1327. Motor Vehicles (Authorisation of Special Types) (Amendment) Order 1987
revoked: SI 2003/1998 Art.2

1338. Petroleum Revenue Tax (Nomination Scheme for Disposals and Appropriations) Regulations 1987
Reg.3, amended: SI 2003/2155 Sch.1 para.23

1443. Swanage Light Railway Order 1987
Art.7, amended: SI 2003/2155 Sch.1 para.18

1529. Town and Country Planning (Listed Building and Buildings in Conservation Areas) (Scotland) Regulations 1987
Reg.2, amended: SSI 2004/332 Sch.4 para.1
Reg.2A, added: SSI 2004/332 Sch.4 para.2
Reg.8A, added: SSI 2004/332 Sch.4 para.3

1730. Control of Noise (Code of Practice for Construction and Open Sites) Order 1987
revoked (in part): SI 2002/461 Art.3, SI 2002/1795 Art.3

1783. Olive Oil (Marketing Standards) Regulations 1987
applied: SI 2003/2577 Reg.17
revoked: SI 2003/2577 Reg.17
Reg.2, amended: SI 2002/2761 Reg.2

1806. Value Added Tax (Tour Operators) Order 1987
Art.7, see *Customs and Excise Commissioners v First Choice Holidays Plc* [2004] EWCA Civ 1044, [2004] S.T.C. 1407 (CA), Mummery, L.J.; see *Simply Travel Ltd v Customs and Excise Commissioners* [2002] S.T.C. 194 (Ch D), Lightman, J.

1828. Repatriation of Prisoners (Overseas Territories) (Amendment) Order 1987
Art.2, amended: 2002 c.8 s.2

1850. Local Government Superannuation (Scotland) Regulations 1987
applied: SSI 2002/178 Art.5
see *Bain, Petitioner* 2002 S.L.T. 1112 (Court of Session (Inner House, Extra Division)), Lord Cameron of Lochbroom, Lord Johnston, Lord Wheatley

1914. Police (Scotland) Amendment (No 2) Regulations 1987
revoked: SSI 2004/257 Sch.4

1941. Safety of Sports Grounds Regulations 1987
Reg.5, amended: SI 2004/3168 Art.13
Sch.1, amended: SI 2004/3168 Art.13

NO.

NO.

1987–cont.

1967. Income Support (General) Regulations 1987

see *R. (on the application of Anufrijeva) v Secretary of State for the Home Department* [2003] UKHL 36, [2004] 1 A.C. 604 (HL), Lord Bingham of Cornhill

applied: SI 2002/668 Art.16, SI 2002/2005 Reg.18, SI 2003/2382 Reg.16, Reg.17, SSI 2003/140 Sch.1 para.5

referred to: SI 2002/580 Reg.3, SI 2003/2382 Reg.16, Reg.17, SI 2004/552 Art.19

varied: SI 2003/2382 Reg.15, SSI 2003/376 Sch.1 para.2

Part IV, referred to: SI 2002/1792 Sch.2 para.5

Part V, applied: SSI 2003/376 Sch.1 para.1

Part V, referred to: SI 2003/2382 Reg.16

Part V, varied: SSI 2003/460 Sch.1 para.2

Reg.2, amended: SI 2002/841 Reg.2, SI 2002/1411 Reg.2, SI 2002/2314 Reg.3, SI 2002/2402 Sch.1 para.1, SI 2002/2689 Reg.2, SI 2003/1121 Sch.1 para.1, SI 2003/1195 Reg.3, SI 2003/2279 Reg.2, SI 2004/565 Reg.2, SI 2004/963 Reg.2, SI 2004/1141 Reg.2

Reg.2, referred to: SI 2002/338 Reg.1

Reg.2, varied: SSI 2003/376 Sch.1 para.2, SSI 2003/460 Sch.1 para.2

Reg.2A, revoked (in part): SI 2003/455 Sch.1 para.1

Reg.3, varied: SI 2003/2382 Sch.1, SSI 2003/376 Sch.1 para.4

Reg.4, amended: SI 2004/1869 Reg.2

Reg.5, amended: SI 2002/2689 Reg.2

Reg.6, amended: SI 2003/1589 Reg.2, SI 2004/963 Reg.3

Reg.6, applied: SI 2002/2008 Reg.4, SI 2003/962 Art.5

Reg.6, revoked (in part): SI 2003/1589 Reg.2

Reg.12, amended: SI 2004/2308 Reg.5

Reg.13, applied: SI 2003/455 Reg.7

Reg.13, referred to: SI 2004/747 Reg.2

Reg.14, amended: SI 2002/2402 Sch.1 para.2

Reg.15, amended: SI 2002/2402 Sch.1 para.3

Reg.17, amended: SI 2003/455 Sch.1 para.2

Reg.17, applied: SI 2002/3019 Reg.36, SI 2003/455 Reg.7, SI 2003/526 Art.17, SI 2004/552 Art.16

Reg.17, referred to: SSI 2003/376 Sch.1 para.3

Reg.17, revoked (in part): SI 2003/455 Sch.1 para.2, SI 2003/1121 Sch.1 para.2

Reg.17, varied: SI 2003/2382 Sch.1, SSI 2003/376 Sch.1 para.4, SSI 2003/460 Sch.1 para.4

Reg.18, amended: SI 2003/455 Sch.1 para.3

Reg.18, applied: SI 2003/455 Reg.7, SI 2003/526 Art.17, SI 2004/552 Art.16

Reg.18, referred to: SSI 2003/376 Sch.1 para.3

1987–cont.

1967. Income Support (General) Regulations 1987–*cont.*

Reg.18, revoked (in part): SI 2003/455 Sch.1 para.3, SI 2003/1121 Sch.1 para.3

Reg.18, varied: SI 2003/2382 Sch.1, SSI 2003/376 Sch.1 para.4, SSI 2003/460 Sch.1 para.4

Reg.19, applied: SSI 2002/76 Reg.2

Reg.21, see *Gingi v Secretary of State for Work and Pensions* [2001] EWCA Civ 1685, [2002] 1 C.M.L.R. 20 (CA), Buxton, L.J.

Reg.21, amended: SI 2003/455 Sch.1 para.4, SI 2003/1121 Sch.1 para.4, SI 2003/2325 Reg.3, SI 2004/1232 Reg.3

Reg.21, applied: SI 2003/526 Art.17, SI 2003/654 Reg.7, SI 2004/552 Art.16

Reg.21, referred to: SSI 2003/376 Sch.1 para.3

Reg.21, revoked (in part): SI 2003/2325 Reg.3

Reg.21, varied: SI 2003/2382 Sch.1, SSI 2003/376 Sch.1 para.4, SSI 2003/460 Sch.1 para.4

Reg.21A, varied: SI 2003/2382 Sch.1

Reg.21ZB, amended: SI 2003/455 Sch.1 para.5

Reg.21ZB, applied: SI 2003/653 Reg.3

Reg.21ZB, revoked: 2004 c.19 s.12

Reg.21ZB, varied: SI 2003/2382 Sch.1

Reg.22, varied: SI 2003/2382 Sch.1

Reg.22A, referred to: SI 2003/526 Sch.5, SI 2004/552 Sch.5

Reg.22A, varied: SI 2003/2382 Sch.1

Reg.23, amended: SI 2003/455 Sch.1 para.6

Reg.23, varied: SI 2003/2382 Sch.1, SSI 2003/376 Sch.1 para.2, SSI 2003/460 Sch.1 para.2

Reg.23A, varied: SSI 2003/460 Sch.1 para.2

Reg.24, varied: SSI 2003/460 Sch.1 para.2

Reg.25, amended: SI 2003/455 Sch.1 para.7

Reg.25, varied: SI 2003/2382 Sch.1, SSI 2003/376 Sch.1 para.2, SSI 2003/460 Sch.1 para.2

Reg.25A, varied: SI 2003/2382 Sch.1, SSI 2003/460 Sch.1 para.2

Reg.26, varied: SSI 2003/460 Sch.1 para.2

Reg.27, varied: SSI 2003/460 Sch.1 para.2

Reg.28, varied: SI 2003/2382 Sch.1, SSI 2003/376 Sch.1 para.2, SSI 2003/460 Sch.1 para.2

Reg.29, varied: SI 2003/2382 Sch.1, SSI 2003/376 Sch.1 para.2, SSI 2003/460 Sch.1 para.2

Reg.30, applied: SSI 2003/376 Sch.2

Reg.30, varied: SI 2003/2382 Sch.1, SSI 2003/376 Sch.1 para.2, SSI 2003/460 Sch.1 para.2

Reg.31, amended: SI 2002/2402 Sch.1 para.4, SI 2003/1731 Reg.2

1987–cont.

1967. Income Support (General) Regulations 1987–*cont.*

Reg.31, varied: SI 2003/2382 Sch.1, SSI 2003/376 Sch.1 para.2, SSI 2003/460 Sch.1 para.2

Reg.32, varied: SI 2003/2382 Sch.1, SSI 2003/376 Sch.1 para.2, SSI 2003/460 Sch.1 para.2

Reg.33, varied: SSI 2003/460 Sch.1 para.2

Reg.34, varied: SSI 2003/460 Sch.1 para.2

Reg.35, amended: SI 2002/2689 Reg.2

Reg.35, varied: SI 2003/2382 Sch.1, SSI 2003/376 Sch.1 para.2, SSI 2003/460 Sch.1 para.2

Reg.36, amended: SI 2003/1589 Reg.2

Reg.36, varied: SI 2003/2382 Sch.1, SSI 2003/376 Sch.1 para.2, SSI 2003/460 Sch.1 para.2

Reg.37, varied: SSI 2003/460 Sch.1 para.2

Reg.38, amended: SI 2003/1589 Reg.2

Reg.38, varied: SI 2003/2382 Sch.1, SSI 2003/376 Sch.1 para.2, SSI 2003/460 Sch.1 para.2

Reg.39, varied: SSI 2003/460 Sch.1 para.2

Reg.39A, varied: SI 2003/2382 Sch.1, SSI 2003/460 Sch.1 para.2

Reg.39B, varied: SI 2003/2382 Sch.1, SSI 2003/460 Sch.1 para.2

Reg.39C, varied: SI 2003/2382 Sch.1, SSI 2003/460 Sch.1 para.2

Reg.39D, varied: SI 2003/2382 Sch.1, SSI 2003/460 Sch.1 para.2

Reg.40, amended: SI 2003/455 Sch.1 para.8

Reg.40, varied: SI 2003/2382 Sch.1, SSI 2003/376 Sch.1 para.2, SSI 2003/460 Sch.1 para.2

Reg.41, amended: SI 2002/2442 Reg.2, SI 2004/1141 Reg.5

Reg.41, revoked (in part): SI 2003/455 Sch.1 para.9

Reg.41, varied: SI 2003/2382 Sch.1, SSI 2003/376 Sch.1 para.2, SSI 2003/460 Sch.1 para.2

Reg.42, amended: SI 2002/841 Reg.2, SI 2002/3019 Reg.29, SI 2003/455 Sch.1 para.10, SI 2004/2308 Reg.5

Reg.42, revoked (in part): SI 2003/455 Sch.1 para.10, SI 2004/2308 Reg.5

Reg.42, varied: SI 2003/2382 Sch.1, SSI 2003/376 Sch.1 para.2, SSI 2003/460 Sch.1 para.2

Reg.43, varied: SSI 2003/460 Sch.1 para.2

Reg.44, revoked: SI 2003/455 Sch.1 para.11

Reg.44, varied: SI 2003/2382 Sch.1, SSI 2003/376 Sch.1 para.2, SSI 2003/460 Sch.1 para.2

Reg.45, varied: SI 2003/2382 Sch.1, SSI 2003/376 Sch.1 para.2, SSI 2003/460 Sch.1 para.2

1987–cont.

1967. Income Support (General) Regulations 1987–*cont.*

Reg.46, varied: SI 2003/2382 Sch.1, SSI 2003/376 Sch.1 para.2, SSI 2003/460 Sch.1 para.2

Reg.47, revoked: SI 2003/455 Sch.1 para.11

Reg.47, varied: SSI 2003/460 Sch.1 para.2

Reg.48, amended: SI 2003/455 Sch.1 para.12

Reg.48, revoked (in part): SI 2003/455 Sch.1 para.12

Reg.48, varied: SI 2003/2382 Sch.1, SSI 2003/376 Sch.1 para.2, SSI 2003/460 Sch.1 para.2

Reg.49, varied: SI 2003/2382 Sch.1, SSI 2003/376 Sch.1 para.2, SSI 2003/460 Sch.1 para.2

Reg.50, varied: SSI 2003/460 Sch.1 para.2

Reg.51, amended: SI 2002/841 Reg.2, SI 2003/455 Sch.1 para.13, SI 2004/2308 Reg.3

Reg.51, varied: SI 2003/2382 Sch.1, SSI 2003/460 Sch.1 para.2

Reg.51A, varied: SI 2003/2382 Sch.1, SSI 2003/460 Sch.1 para.2

Reg.52, see *Secretary of State for Work and Pensions v Hourigan* [2002] EWCA Civ 1890, [2003] 1 W.L.R. 608 (CA), Brooke, L.J.

Reg.52, varied: SSI 2003/460 Sch.1 para.2

Reg.53, amended: SI 2002/3019 Reg.29

Reg.53, varied: SI 2003/2382 Sch.1, SSI 2003/376 Sch.1 para.2, SSI 2003/460 Sch.1 para.2

Reg.54, revoked (in part): SI 2003/455 Sch.1 para.14

Reg.54, varied: SI 2003/2382 Sch.1, SSI 2003/376 Sch.1 para.2, SSI 2003/460 Sch.1 para.2

Reg.55, varied: SI 2003/2382 Sch.1, SSI 2003/376 Sch.1 para.2, SSI 2003/460 Sch.1 para.2

Reg.55A, varied: SI 2003/2382 Sch.1, SSI 2003/376 Sch.1 para.2, SSI 2003/460 Sch.1 para.2

Reg.56, varied: SI 2003/2382 Sch.1, SSI 2003/376 Sch.1 para.2, SSI 2003/460 Sch.1 para.2

Reg.57, amended: SI 2002/2497 Sch.2 para.1, SI 2003/455 Sch.1 para.15

Reg.57, revoked (in part): SI 2003/455 Sch.1 para.15

Reg.57, varied: SI 2003/2382 Sch.1, SSI 2003/376 Sch.1 para.2, SSI 2003/460 Sch.1 para.2

Reg.58, varied: SI 2003/2382 Sch.1, SSI 2003/376 Sch.1 para.2, SSI 2003/460 Sch.1 para.2

Reg.59, varied: SI 2003/2382 Sch.1, SSI 2003/376 Sch.1 para.2, SSI 2003/460 Sch.1 para.2

NO.

NO.

1987–cont.

1967. Income Support (General) Regulations 1987–*cont.*

Reg.60, varied: SI 2003/2382 Sch.1, SSI 2003/376 Sch.1 para.2, SSI 2003/460 Sch.1 para.2

Reg.60A, varied: SI 2003/2382 Sch.1, SSI 2003/460 Sch.1 para.2

Reg.60B, varied: SI 2003/2382 Sch.1, SSI 2003/460 Sch.1 para.2

Reg.60C, varied: SI 2003/2382 Sch.1, SSI 2003/460 Sch.1 para.2

Reg.60D, varied: SI 2003/2382 Sch.1, SSI 2003/460 Sch.1 para.2

Reg.60E, varied: SI 2003/2382 Sch.1, SSI 2003/460 Sch.1 para.2

Reg.61, amended: SI 2002/1589 Reg.2, SI 2004/1708 Reg.5

Reg.61, varied: SI 2003/2382 Sch.1, SSI 2003/376 Sch.1 para.2, SSI 2003/460 Sch.1 para.2

Reg.62, amended: SI 2002/1589 Reg.3, Reg.4, SI 2002/2207 Reg.2, SI 2003/455 Sch.1 para.16, SI 2003/1701 Reg.2, Reg.3, SI 2003/1914 Reg.2, SI 2004/1708 Reg.2, Reg.3

Reg.62, varied: SI 2003/2382 Sch.1, SI 2004/1708 Reg.3, SSI 2003/376 Sch.1 para.2, SSI 2003/460 Sch.1 para.2

Reg.63, varied: SI 2003/2382 Sch.1, SSI 2003/376 Sch.1 para.2, SSI 2003/460 Sch.1 para.2

Reg.64, varied: SI 2003/2382 Sch.1, SSI 2003/376 Sch.1 para.2, SSI 2003/460 Sch.1 para.2

Reg.65, varied: SI 2003/2382 Sch.1, SSI 2003/376 Sch.1 para.2, SSI 2003/460 Sch.1 para.2

Reg.66, varied: SSI 2003/460 Sch.1 para.2

Reg.66A, amended: SI 2002/1589 Reg.3, Reg.5, SI 2003/1701 Reg.2, SI 2003/1914 Reg.2, SI 2004/1708 Reg.2

Reg.66A, varied: SI 2003/2382 Sch.1, SSI 2003/376 Sch.1 para.2, SSI 2003/460 Sch.1 para.2

Reg.66B, amended: SI 2003/455 Sch.1 para.17

Reg.66B, varied: SSI 2003/460 Sch.1 para.2

Reg.67, varied: SSI 2003/460 Sch.1 para.2

Reg.67A, varied: SSI 2003/460 Sch.1 para.2

Reg.68, amended: SI 2003/455 Sch.1 para.17

Reg.68, varied: SSI 2003/460 Sch.1 para.2

Reg.69, varied: SSI 2003/460 Sch.1 para.2

Reg.70, see *R. (on the application of Anufrijeva) v Secretary of State for the Home Department* [2002] EWCA Civ 399, Independent, April 18, 2002 (CA), Schiemann, L.J.; see *Shire v Secretary of State for Work and Pensions* [2003] EWCA Civ 1465, [2004] C.P. Rep. 11 (CA), LordWoolf of Barnes, L.C.J.

Reg.71, amended: SI 2003/455 Sch.1 para.18

1987–cont.

1967. Income Support (General) Regulations 1987–*cont.*

Reg.71, applied: SI 2003/526 Art.17, SI 2004/552 Art.16

Reg.71, referred to: SI 2003/526 Sch.5, SI 2004/552 Sch.5

Reg.71, revoked (in part): SI 2003/455 Sch.1 para.18, SI 2003/1121 Sch.1 para.5

Sch.1B para.1, amended: SI 2002/2497 Sch.2 para.1

Sch.1B para.1, referred to: SI 2004/747 Reg.2

Sch.1B para.2, amended: SI 2002/2497 Sch.2 para.1

Sch.1B para.2, referred to: SI 2004/747 Reg.2

Sch.1B para.3, amended: SI 2002/2497 Sch.2 para.1

Sch.1B para.4, amended: SI 2002/490 Reg.4, SI 2002/2497 Sch.2 para.1

Sch.1B para.5, amended: SI 2002/2497 Sch.2 para.1

Sch.1B para.6, amended: SI 2002/2497 Sch.2 para.1

Sch.1B para.7, amended: SI 2002/2497 Sch.2 para.1

Sch.1B para.7, applied: SI 2002/2005 Reg.6

Sch.1B para.7, referred to: SI 2004/747 Reg.2

Sch.1B para.8, amended: SI 2002/2497 Sch.2 para.1

Sch.1B para.8, referred to: SI 2004/747 Reg.2

Sch.1B para.9, amended: SI 2002/2497 Sch.2 para.1

Sch.1B para.9A, amended: SI 2002/2497 Sch.2 para.1

Sch.1B para.10, amended: SI 2002/2497 Sch.2 para.1

Sch.1B para.10, referred to: SI 2004/747 Reg.2

Sch.1B para.11, amended: SI 2002/2497 Sch.2 para.1

Sch.1B para.11, referred to: SI 2004/747 Reg.2

Sch.1B para.12, amended: SI 2002/2497 Sch.2 para.1

Sch.1B para.12, referred to: SI 2004/747 Reg.2

Sch.1B para.13, amended: SI 2002/2497 Sch.2 para.1

Sch.1B para.13, referred to: SI 2004/747 Reg.2

Sch.1B para.14, amended: SI 2002/2497 Sch.2 para.1, SI 2002/2689 Reg.2

Sch.1B para.14, applied: SI 2002/2005 Reg.6

Sch.1B para.14A, amended: SI 2002/2497 Sch.2 para.1, SI 2003/455 Sch.1 para.19, SI 2003/1731 Reg.2

Sch.1B para.14B, added: SI 2002/2689 Reg.2

Sch.1B para.14B, amended: SI 2002/2497 Sch.2 para.1, SI 2003/455 Sch.1 para.19, SI 2003/1731 Reg.2

1987–cont.

1967. Income Support (General) Regulations 1987–cont.

Sch.1B para.15, amended: SI 2002/2497 Sch.2 para.1

Sch.1B para.16, amended: SI 2002/2497 Sch.2 para.1

Sch.1B para.16A, amended: SI 2002/2497 Sch.2 para.1

Sch.1B para.17, amended: SI 2002/2497 Sch.2 para.1

Sch.1B para.17, revoked: SI 2002/3019 Reg.29

Sch.1B para.18, amended: SI 2002/2497 Sch.2 para.1

Sch.1B para.18A, amended: SI 2002/2497 Sch.2 para.1

Sch.1B para.18A, revoked: 2004 c.19 s.12

Sch.1B para.19, amended: SI 2002/2497 Sch.2 para.1

Sch.1B para.20, amended: SI 2002/2497 Sch.2 para.1

Sch.1B para.21, amended: SI 2002/2497 Sch.2 para.1

Sch.1B para.22, amended: SI 2002/2497 Sch.2 para.1

Sch.1B para.23, amended: SI 2002/2497 Sch.2 para.1

Sch.1B para.24, amended: SI 2002/2497 Sch.2 para.1

Sch.1B para.24, referred to: SI 2004/747 Reg.2

Sch.1B para.25, amended: SI 2002/2497 Sch.2 para.1

Sch.1B para.25, referred to: SI 2004/747 Reg.2

Sch.1B para.26, amended: SI 2002/2497 Sch.2 para.1

Sch.1B para.27, amended: SI 2002/2497 Sch.2 para.1

Sch.1B para.28, amended: SI 2002/2497 Sch.2 para.1

Sch.2, referred to: SSI 2003/376 Sch.1 para.3

Sch.2 Part I para.1, amended: SI 2002/668 Sch.2

Sch.2 Part I para.1, referred to: SSI 2002/494 Sch.2 para.13

Sch.2 Part I para.1, substituted: SI 2003/526 Sch.2, SI 2004/552 Sch.2

Sch.2 Part I para.1, varied: SI 2003/2382 Sch.1, SSI 2003/376 Sch.1 para.4, SSI 2003/460 Sch.1 para.4

Sch.2 Part I para.1A, varied: SI 2003/2382 Sch.1, SSI 2003/376 Sch.1 para.4, SSI 2003/460 Sch.1 para.4

Sch.2 Part I para.2, amended: SI 2002/668 Sch.2, SI 2002/2019 Reg.2

Sch.2 Part I para.2, applied: SI 2002/1792 Sch.1 para.6

Sch.2 Part I para.2, referred to: SSI 2002/494 Sch.2 para.13

1987–cont.

1967. Income Support (General) Regulations 1987–cont.

Sch.2 Part I para.2, revoked: SI 2003/455 Sch.1 para.20

Sch.2 Part I para.2, substituted: SI 2003/526 Sch.2, SI 2004/552 Sch.2

Sch.2 Part I para.2, varied: SI 2003/2382 Sch.1, SSI 2003/376 Sch.1 para.4, SSI 2003/460 Sch.1 para.4

Sch.2 Part I para.2A, amended: SI 2002/668 Sch.2

Sch.2 Part I para.2A, applied: SI 2002/1792 Sch.1 para.6

Sch.2 Part I para.2A, revoked: SI 2003/1121 Sch.1 para.6

Sch.2 Part I para.2A, substituted: SI 2003/526 Sch.2

Sch.2 Part I para.2A, varied: SI 2003/2382 Sch.1, SSI 2003/376 Sch.1 para.4, SSI 2003/460 Sch.1 para.4

Sch.2 Part II para.3, amended: SI 2002/668 Art.16, SI 2003/526 Art.17

Sch.2 Part II para.3, applied: SI 2002/1792 Sch.1 para.6, SI 2003/526 Art.17

Sch.2 Part II para.3, revoked: SI 2003/455 Sch.1 para.20

Sch.2 Part II para.3, varied: SI 2003/2382 Sch.1, SI 2004/552 Art.16, SSI 2003/376 Sch.1 para.4, SSI 2003/460 Sch.1 para.4

Sch.2 Part III para.4, amended: SI 2002/2497 Sch.2 para.1

Sch.2 Part III para.4, varied: SSI 2003/460 Sch.1 para.4

Sch.2 Part III para.5, amended: SI 2002/2497 Sch.2 para.1

Sch.2 Part III para.5, varied: SSI 2003/460 Sch.1 para.4

Sch.2 Part III para.6, amended: SI 2002/2497 Sch.2 para.1

Sch.2 Part III para.6, revoked (in part): SI 2003/455 Sch.1 para.20

Sch.2 Part III para.6, varied: SSI 2003/460 Sch.1 para.4

Sch.2 Part III para.7, amended: SI 2002/2497 Sch.2 para.1

Sch.2 Part III para.7, varied: SSI 2003/460 Sch.1 para.4

Sch.2 Part III para.8, amended: SI 2002/2497 Sch.2 para.1

Sch.2 Part III para.8, varied: SSI 2003/460 Sch.1 para.4

Sch.2 Part III para.8A, amended: SI 2002/2497 Sch.2 para.1

Sch.2 Part III para.8A, varied: SSI 2003/460 Sch.1 para.4

Sch.2 Part III para.9, amended: SI 2002/2497 Sch.2 para.1

Sch.2 Part III para.9, substituted: SI 2002/3019 Reg.29

Sch.2 Part III para.9, varied: SI 2003/2382 Sch.1, SSI 2003/376 Sch.1 para.4, SSI 2003/460 Sch.1 para.4

NO.

1987–cont.

1967. Income Support (General) Regulations 1987–*cont.*

Sch.2 Part III para.9A, amended: SI 2002/2497 Sch.2 para.1

Sch.2 Part III para.9A, substituted: SI 2002/3019 Reg.29

Sch.2 Part III para.9A, varied: SI 2003/2382 Sch.1, SSI 2003/376 Sch.1 para.4, SSI 2003/460 Sch.1 para.4

Sch.2 Part III para.10, amended: SI 2002/2497 Sch.2 para.1, SI 2002/3019 Reg.29, SI 2003/2379 Reg.2

Sch.2 Part III para.10, applied: SI 2002/2005 Reg.9, SSI 2003/376 Sch.2

Sch.2 Part III para.10, varied: SI 2003/2382 Sch.1, SSI 2003/376 Sch.1 para.4, SSI 2003/460 Sch.1 para.4

Sch.2 Part III para.11, amended: SI 2002/2497 Sch.2 para.1, SI 2002/3019 Reg.29, SI 2003/2379 Reg.2

Sch.2 Part III para.11, applied: SI 2002/2005 Reg.9, SSI 2003/376 Sch.2

Sch.2 Part III para.11, varied: SSI 2003/376 Sch.1 para.4, SSI 2003/460 Sch.1 para.4

Sch.2 Part III para.12, amended: SI 2002/2497 Sch.2 para.1, SI 2002/3019 Reg.29, SI 2003/455 Sch.1 para.20, SI 2003/2379 Reg.2, SI 2004/1141 Reg.6

Sch.2 Part III para.12, applied: SI 2002/2005 Reg.9, SSI 2003/176 Art.4

Sch.2 Part III para.12, revoked (in part): SI 2003/1589 Reg.2

Sch.2 Part III para.12, varied: SI 2003/2382 Sch.1, SSI 2003/376 Sch.1 para.4, SSI 2003/460 Sch.1 para.4

Sch.2 Part III para.13, amended: SI 2002/490 Reg.2, SI 2002/2497 Sch.2 para.1

Sch.2 Part III para.13, varied: SI 2003/2382 Sch.1, SSI 2003/376 Sch.1 para.4, SSI 2003/460 Sch.1 para.4

Sch.2 Part III para.13A, amended: SI 2002/2497 Sch.2 para.1, SI 2002/3019 Reg.29, SI 2003/455 Sch.1 para.20, SI 2003/1195 Reg.3

Sch.2 Part III para.13A, applied: SI 2002/1792 Sch.1 para.6, SI 2003/526 Art.17, SI 2004/552 Art.16

Sch.2 Part III para.13A, revoked (in part): SI 2003/455 Sch.1 para.20

Sch.2 Part III para.13A, varied: SSI 2003/460 Sch.1 para.4

Sch.2 Part III para.14, amended: SI 2002/2497 Sch.2 para.1

Sch.2 Part III para.14, applied: SI 2002/1792 Sch.1 para.6, SI 2004/552 Art.16

Sch.2 Part III para.14, revoked: SI 2003/455 Sch.1 para.20

Sch.2 Part III para.14, varied: SSI 2003/460 Sch.1 para.4

Sch.2 Part III para.14A, amended: SI 2002/2497 Sch.2 para.1

NO.

1987–cont.

1967. Income Support (General) Regulations 1987–*cont.*

Sch.2 Part III para.14A, applied: SI 2003/526 Art.17

Sch.2 Part III para.14A, varied: SSI 2003/460 Sch.1 para.4

Sch.2 Part III para.14B, amended: SI 2002/2497 Sch.2 para.1

Sch.2 Part III para.14B, varied: SSI 2003/460 Sch.1 para.4

Sch.2 Part III para.14ZA, amended: SI 2002/2020 Reg.2, SI 2002/2497 Sch.2 para.1, SI 2003/2279 Reg.2

Sch.2 Part III para.14ZA, revoked (in part): SI 2003/2279 Reg.2

Sch.2 Part III para.14ZA, varied: SSI 2003/460 Sch.1 para.4

Sch.2 Part IV para.15, amended: SI 2002/668 Sch.3, SI 2002/2497 Sch.2 para.1, SI 2002/3019 Reg.29, SI 2003/455 Sch.1 para.20

Sch.2 Part IV para.15, substituted: SI 2003/526 Sch.3, SI 2004/552 Sch.3

Sch.2 Part IV para.15, varied: SI 2003/2382 Sch.1, SSI 2003/376 Sch.1 para.4, SSI 2003/460 Sch.1 para.4

Sch.2 Part V para.16, varied: SSI 2003/460 Sch.1 para.4

Sch.3, applied: SI 2002/1792 Sch.2 para.7

Sch.3, referred to: SSI 2003/376 Sch.1 para.3

Sch.3C, revoked: SI 2003/1121 Sch.1 para.7

Sch.3 para.1, amended: SI 2004/2825 Reg.2

Sch.3 para.1, varied: SI 2003/2382 Sch.1, SSI 2003/376 Sch.1 para.4, SSI 2003/460 Sch.1 para.4

Sch.3 para.1A, varied: SI 2003/2382 Sch.1, SSI 2003/460 Sch.1 para.4

Sch.3 para.2, varied: SI 2003/2382 Sch.1, SSI 2003/376 Sch.1 para.4, SSI 2003/460 Sch.1 para.4

Sch.3 para.3, amended: SI 2004/2327 Reg.5

Sch.3 para.3, varied: SI 2003/2382 Sch.1, SSI 2003/376 Sch.1 para.4, SSI 2003/460 Sch.1 para.4

Sch.3 para.4, varied: SI 2003/2382 Sch.1, SSI 2003/376 Sch.1 para.4, SSI 2003/460 Sch.1 para.4

Sch.3 para.5, referred to: SI 2003/526 Sch.5, SI 2004/552 Sch.5

Sch.3 para.5, varied: SSI 2003/460 Sch.1 para.4

Sch.3 para.5A, applied: SI 2002/1792 Sch.2 para.5

Sch.3 para.5A, varied: SSI 2003/460 Sch.1 para.4

Sch.3 para.6, amended: SI 2002/3019 Reg.29

Sch.3 para.6, referred to: SI 2003/526 Sch.5, SI 2004/552 Sch.5

Sch.3 para.6, varied: SI 2003/2382 Sch.1, SSI 2003/376 Sch.1 para.4, SSI 2003/460 Sch.1 para.4

1987–cont.

1967. Income Support (General) Regulations 1987–*cont.*

Sch.3 para.7, applied: SI 2002/1792 Sch.1 para.6

Sch.3 para.7, referred to: SI 2003/526 Sch.5, SI 2004/552 Sch.5

Sch.3 para.7, varied: SI 2003/2382 Sch.1, SSI 2003/376 Sch.1 para.4, SSI 2003/460 Sch.1 para.4

Sch.3 para.7A, varied: SI 2003/2382 Sch.1, SSI 2003/376 Sch.1 para.4, SSI 2003/460 Sch.1 para.4

Sch.3 para.7B, varied: SI 2003/2382 Sch.1, SSI 2003/376 Sch.1 para.4, SSI 2003/460 Sch.1 para.4

Sch.3 para.8, amended: SI 2002/3019 Reg.29

Sch.3 para.8, referred to: SI 2003/526 Sch.5, SI 2004/552 Sch.5

Sch.3 para.8, varied: SI 2003/2382 Sch.1, SSI 2003/376 Sch.1 para.4, SSI 2003/460 Sch.1 para.4

Sch.3 para.9, amended: SI 2002/3019 Reg.29

Sch.3 para.9, varied: SI 2003/2382 Sch.1, SSI 2003/376 Sch.1 para.4, SSI 2003/460 Sch.1 para.4

Sch.3 para.10, amended: SI 2004/2825 Reg.2

Sch.3 para.10, referred to: SI 2003/526 Sch.5, SI 2004/552 Sch.5

Sch.3 para.10, varied: SI 2003/2382 Sch.1, SSI 2003/376 Sch.1 para.4, SSI 2003/460 Sch.1 para.4

Sch.3 para.11, referred to: SI 2003/526 Sch.5, SI 2004/552 Sch.5

Sch.3 para.11, varied: SI 2003/2382 Sch.1, SSI 2003/376 Sch.1 para.4, SSI 2003/460 Sch.1 para.4

Sch.3 para.12, amended: SI 2002/105 Reg.2, SI 2002/338 Reg.2, SI 2003/2693 Reg.2, SI 2004/440 Reg.2, SI 2004/1520 Reg.2, SI 2004/2174 Reg.2, SI 2004/2825 Reg.2

Sch.3 para.12, referred to: SI 2002/1792 Sch.2 para.9, SI 2003/526 Sch.5, SI 2004/552 Sch.5

Sch.3 para.12, varied: SI 2003/2382 Sch.1, SSI 2003/376 Sch.1 para.4, SSI 2003/460 Sch.1 para.4

Sch.3 para.13, varied: SI 2003/2382 Sch.1, SSI 2003/376 Sch.1 para.4, SSI 2003/460 Sch.1 para.4

Sch.3 para.14, amended: SI 2002/841 Reg.6, SI 2002/3019 Reg.29

Sch.3 para.14, varied: SI 2003/2382 Sch.1, SSI 2003/376 Sch.1 para.4, SSI 2003/460 Sch.1 para.4

Sch.3 para.15, applied: SI 2002/1792 Sch.2 para.7

Sch.3 para.15, varied: SI 2003/2382 Sch.1, SSI 2003/376 Sch.1 para.4, SSI 2003/460 Sch.1 para.4

1987–cont.

1967. Income Support (General) Regulations 1987–*cont.*

Sch.3 para.16, applied: SI 2002/1792 Sch.2 para.7

Sch.3 para.16, varied: SI 2003/2382 Sch.1, SSI 2003/376 Sch.1 para.4, SSI 2003/460 Sch.1 para.4

Sch.3 para.17, varied: SI 2003/2382 Sch.1, SSI 2003/376 Sch.1 para.4, SSI 2003/460 Sch.1 para.4

Sch.3 para.18, amended: SI 2002/668 Art.16, SI 2002/3019 Reg.29, SI 2003/526 Art.17, SI 2004/552 Art.16, SI 2004/2327 Reg.5

Sch.3 para.18, applied: SI 2003/526 Art.17, SI 2004/552 Art.16

Sch.3 para.18, varied: SI 2003/2382 Sch.1, SSI 2003/376 Sch.1 para.4, SSI 2003/460 Sch.1 para.4

Sch.3 para.19, varied: SSI 2003/460 Sch.1 para.4

Sch.4A para.1, varied: SI 2003/2382 Sch.1

Sch.4A para.2, varied: SI 2003/2382 Sch.1

Sch.7, amended: SI 2002/668 Sch.4 Part I, SI 2003/455 Sch.1 para.21, SI 2003/1121 Sch.1 para.8, SI 2003/1195 Reg.3, SI 2004/552 Sch.4 Part I

Sch.7, applied: SI 2002/3019 Reg.36, SI 2003/526 Sch.4 Part II

Sch.7, referred to: SI 2002/1792 Sch.1 para.6, SI 2004/552 Art.16, Sch.4 Part II, SSI 2003/376 Sch.1 para.3

Sch.7, substituted: SI 2003/455 Sch.1 para.21, SI 2003/526 Sch.4 Part I

Sch.7, varied: SI 2003/2382 Sch.1, SSI 2003/376 Sch.1 para.4, SSI 2003/460 Sch.1 para.4

Sch.8, applied: SSI 2003/376 Sch.1 para.1

Sch.8 para.1, amended: SI 2002/2497 Sch.2 para.1

Sch.8 para.1, revoked (in part): SI 2002/3019 Reg.29

Sch.8 para.1, varied: SSI 2003/460 Sch.1 para.2

Sch.8 para.1A, added: SI 2002/3019 Reg.29

Sch.8 para.1A, amended: SI 2002/2497 Sch.2 para.1

Sch.8 para.1A, varied: SSI 2003/460 Sch.1 para.2

Sch.8 para.2, amended: SI 2002/2497 Sch.2 para.1

Sch.8 para.2, varied: SSI 2003/460 Sch.1 para.2

Sch.8 para.3, amended: SI 2002/2497 Sch.2 para.1

Sch.8 para.3, varied: SSI 2003/460 Sch.1 para.2

Sch.8 para.4, amended: SI 2002/2497 Sch.2 para.1, SI 2002/3019 Reg.29

Sch.8 para.4, revoked (in part): SI 2002/3019 Reg.29

NO.

1967. Income Support (General) Regulations 1987–*cont.*

Sch.8 para.4, varied: SI 2003/2382 Sch.1, SSI 2003/376 Sch.1 para.2, SSI 2003/460 Sch.1 para.2

Sch.8 para.5, amended: SI 2002/2497 Sch.2 para.1

Sch.8 para.5, varied: SSI 2003/460 Sch.1 para.2

Sch.8 para.6, amended: SI 2002/2497 Sch.2 para.1

Sch.8 para.6, varied: SSI 2003/376 Sch.1 para.2, SSI 2003/460 Sch.1 para.2

Sch.8 para.6A, amended: SI 2002/2497 Sch.2 para.1

Sch.8 para.6A, varied: SI 2003/2382 Sch.1, SSI 2003/460 Sch.1 para.2

Sch.8 para.6B, amended: SI 2002/2497 Sch.2 para.1

Sch.8 para.6B, varied: SSI 2003/460 Sch.1 para.2

Sch.8 para.7, amended: SI 2002/2497 Sch.2 para.1, SI 2004/3168 Art.14

Sch.8 para.7, varied: SI 2003/2382 Sch.1, SSI 2003/376 Sch.1 para.2, SSI 2003/460 Sch.1 para.2

Sch.8 para.8, amended: SI 2002/2497 Sch.2 para.1

Sch.8 para.8, varied: SI 2003/2382 Sch.1, SSI 2003/376 Sch.1 para.2, SSI 2003/460 Sch.1 para.2

Sch.8 para.8A, amended: SI 2002/2497 Sch.2 para.1

Sch.8 para.8A, varied: SI 2003/2382 Sch.1, SSI 2003/376 Sch.1 para.2, SSI 2003/460 Sch.1 para.2

Sch.8 para.9, amended: SI 2002/2497 Sch.2 para.1

Sch.8 para.9, varied: SSI 2003/376 Sch.1 para.2, SSI 2003/460 Sch.1 para.2

Sch.8 para.10, amended: SI 2002/2497 Sch.2 para.1

Sch.8 para.10, varied: SSI 2003/376 Sch.1 para.2, SSI 2003/460 Sch.1 para.2

Sch.8 para.11, amended: SI 2002/2497 Sch.2 para.1

Sch.8 para.11, varied: SSI 2003/460 Sch.1 para.2

Sch.8 para.12, amended: SI 2002/2497 Sch.2 para.1

Sch.8 para.12, varied: SSI 2003/460 Sch.1 para.2

Sch.8 para.13, amended: SI 2002/2497 Sch.2 para.1

Sch.8 para.13, varied: SSI 2003/376 Sch.1 para.2, SSI 2003/460 Sch.1 para.2

Sch.8 para.14, amended: SI 2002/2497 Sch.2 para.1, SI 2003/455 Sch.1 para.22

Sch.8 para.14, varied: SSI 2003/460 Sch.1 para.2

Sch.8 para.15, amended: SI 2002/2497 Sch.2 para.1

NO.

1967. Income Support (General) Regulations 1987–*cont.*

Sch.8 para.15, revoked: SI 2003/455 Sch.1 para.22

Sch.8 para.15, varied: SSI 2003/460 Sch.1 para.2

Sch.8 para.15A, amended: SI 2002/2497 Sch.2 para.1

Sch.8 para.15A, varied: SSI 2003/460 Sch.1 para.2

Sch.8 para.15B, amended: SI 2002/2497 Sch.2 para.1

Sch.8 para.15B, revoked: SI 2003/1589 Reg.2

Sch.8 para.15B, varied: SSI 2003/460 Sch.1 para.2

Sch.8 para.15C, amended: SI 2002/2497 Sch.2 para.1

Sch.8 para.15C, varied: SSI 2003/460 Sch.1 para.2

Sch.8 para.16, amended: SI 2002/2497 Sch.2 para.1

Sch.8 para.16, varied: SSI 2003/376 Sch.1 para.2, SSI 2003/460 Sch.1 para.2

Sch.9, applied: SSI 2003/376 Sch.1 para.1

Sch.9 para.1, varied: SSI 2003/460 Sch.1 para.2

Sch.9 para.2, varied: SSI 2003/460 Sch.1 para.2

Sch.9 para.3, varied: SSI 2003/460 Sch.1 para.2

Sch.9 para.4, amended: SI 2002/2689 Reg.2

Sch.9 para.4, varied: SSI 2003/460 Sch.1 para.2

Sch.9 para.4A, varied: SSI 2003/460 Sch.1 para.2

Sch.9 para.5, varied: SSI 2003/460 Sch.1 para.2

Sch.9 para.5A, added: SI 2002/2402 Sch.1 para.5, SI 2003/455 Sch.1 para.23

Sch.9 para.5A, varied: SSI 2003/460 Sch.1 para.2

Sch.9 para.5B, added: SI 2003/455 Sch.1 para.23

Sch.9 para.5B, varied: SSI 2003/460 Sch.1 para.2

Sch.9 para.6, varied: SSI 2003/460 Sch.1 para.2

Sch.9 para.7, varied: SSI 2003/460 Sch.1 para.2

Sch.9 para.8, varied: SSI 2003/460 Sch.1 para.2

Sch.9 para.9, amended: SI 2003/1121 Sch.1 para.9

Sch.9 para.9, varied: SSI 2003/460 Sch.1 para.2

Sch.9 para.9A, varied: SSI 2003/460 Sch.1 para.2

Sch.9 para.10, varied: SSI 2003/460 Sch.1 para.2

1987–cont.

1967. Income Support (General) Regulations 1987–cont.

Sch.9 para.11, varied: SI 2004/1708 Reg.5, SSI 2003/460 Sch.1 para.2

Sch.9 para.11A, added: SI 2002/2380 Reg.2

Sch.9 para.11A, varied: SSI 2003/460 Sch.1 para.2

Sch.9 para.12, varied: SSI 2003/460 Sch.1 para.2

Sch.9 para.13, substituted: SI 2004/565 Reg.2

Sch.9 para.13, varied: SSI 2003/460 Sch.1 para.2

Sch.9 para.14, varied: SSI 2003/460 Sch.1 para.2

Sch.9 para.15, amended: SI 2002/2442 Reg.3, SI 2004/2308 Reg.2

Sch.9 para.15, varied: SI 2003/2382 Sch.1, SSI 2003/376 Sch.1 para.2, SSI 2003/460 Sch.1 para.2

Sch.9 para.15A, varied: SSI 2003/460 Sch.1 para.2

Sch.9 para.15B, revoked: SI 2003/1121 Sch.1 para.9

Sch.9 para.15B, varied: SSI 2003/460 Sch.1 para.2

Sch.9 para.16, amended: SI 2002/841 Reg.2

Sch.9 para.16, varied: SI 2003/2382 Sch.1, SSI 2003/376 Sch.1 para.2, SSI 2003/460 Sch.1 para.2

Sch.9 para.17, varied: SSI 2003/460 Sch.1 para.2

Sch.9 para.18, varied: SSI 2003/460 Sch.1 para.2

Sch.9 para.19, amended: SI 2002/668 Art.16, SI 2003/526 Art.17, SI 2004/552 Art.16

Sch.9 para.19, varied: SI 2003/2382 Sch.1, SSI 2003/460 Sch.1 para.2

Sch.9 para.20, varied: SSI 2003/460 Sch.1 para.2

Sch.9 para.21, varied: SI 2003/2382 Sch.1, SSI 2003/376 Sch.1 para.2, SSI 2003/460 Sch.1 para.2

Sch.9 para.22, varied: SSI 2003/460 Sch.1 para.2

Sch.9 para.23, varied: SSI 2003/460 Sch.1 para.2

Sch.9 para.24, varied: SSI 2003/460 Sch.1 para.2

Sch.9 para.25, amended: SI 2003/455 Sch.1 para.23, SI 2003/2279 Reg.2, SI 2004/2308 Reg.4

Sch.9 para.25, varied: SSI 2003/460 Sch.1 para.2

Sch.9 para.25A, added: SI 2003/455 Sch.1 para.23

Sch.9 para.25A, varied: SSI 2003/460 Sch.1 para.2

Sch.9 para.26, amended: SI 2004/1141 Reg.4

Sch.9 para.26, varied: SSI 2003/460 Sch.1 para.2

1987–cont.

1967. Income Support (General) Regulations 1987–cont.

Sch.9 para.27, varied: SSI 2003/460 Sch.1 para.2

Sch.9 para.28, amended: SI 2004/1141 Reg.4

Sch.9 para.28, varied: SI 2003/2382 Sch.1, SSI 2003/376 Sch.1 para.2, SSI 2003/460 Sch.1 para.2

Sch.9 para.29, varied: SI 2003/2382 Sch.1, SSI 2003/376 Sch.1 para.2, SSI 2003/460 Sch.1 para.2

Sch.9 para.30, varied: SI 2003/2382 Sch.1, SSI 2003/460 Sch.1 para.2

Sch.9 para.30A, varied: SSI 2003/460 Sch.1 para.2

Sch.9 para.30ZA, varied: SSI 2003/460 Sch.1 para.2

Sch.9 para.31, varied: SSI 2003/460 Sch.1 para.2

Sch.9 para.32, varied: SSI 2003/460 Sch.1 para.2

Sch.9 para.33, varied: SSI 2003/460 Sch.1 para.2

Sch.9 para.34, varied: SI 2003/2382 Sch.1, SSI 2003/460 Sch.1 para.2

Sch.9 para.35, varied: SSI 2003/460 Sch.1 para.2

Sch.9 para.36, varied: SSI 2003/460 Sch.1 para.2

Sch.9 para.37, varied: SI 2003/2382 Sch.1, SSI 2003/460 Sch.1 para.2

Sch.9 para.38, varied: SSI 2003/460 Sch.1 para.2

Sch.9 para.39, amended: SI 2004/2308 Reg.3

Sch.9 para.39, varied: SSI 2003/460 Sch.1 para.2

Sch.9 para.40, varied: SSI 2003/460 Sch.1 para.2

Sch.9 para.41, varied: SSI 2003/460 Sch.1 para.2

Sch.9 para.42, varied: SSI 2003/460 Sch.1 para.2

Sch.9 para.43, varied: SSI 2003/460 Sch.1 para.2

Sch.9 para.44, varied: SSI 2003/460 Sch.1 para.2

Sch.9 para.45, varied: SSI 2003/460 Sch.1 para.2

Sch.9 para.46, varied: SSI 2003/460 Sch.1 para.2

Sch.9 para.47, varied: SSI 2003/460 Sch.1 para.2

Sch.9 para.48, varied: SSI 2003/460 Sch.1 para.2

Sch.9 para.49, varied: SSI 2003/460 Sch.1 para.2

Sch.9 para.50, varied: SSI 2003/460 Sch.1 para.2

Sch.9 para.51, amended: SI 2004/565 Reg.2

NO.

1967. Income Support (General) Regulations 1987–*cont.*

Sch.9 para.51, varied: SSI 2003/460 Sch.1 para.2

Sch.9 para.52, varied: SSI 2003/460 Sch.1 para.2

Sch.9 para.53, varied: SSI 2003/460 Sch.1 para.2

Sch.9 para.54, amended: SI 2002/841 Reg.2

Sch.9 para.54, varied: SSI 2003/460 Sch.1 para.2

Sch.9 para.55, amended: SI 2002/841 Reg.2

Sch.9 para.55, varied: SSI 2003/460 Sch.1 para.2

Sch.9 para.56, amended: SI 2002/841 Reg.2

Sch.9 para.56, varied: SSI 2003/460 Sch.1 para.2

Sch.9 para.57, revoked: 2004 c.19 s.12

Sch.9 para.57, varied: SSI 2003/460 Sch.1 para.2

Sch.9 para.58, amended: SI 2003/762 Reg.11, SI 2004/1748 Sch.2 para.2

Sch.9 para.58, varied: SSI 2003/460 Sch.1 para.2

Sch.9 para.59, revoked: SI 2004/565 Reg.2

Sch.9 para.59, varied: SSI 2003/460 Sch.1 para.2

Sch.9 para.60, revoked: SI 2004/565 Reg.2

Sch.9 para.60, varied: SSI 2003/460 Sch.1 para.2

Sch.9 para.61, varied: SSI 2003/460 Sch.1 para.2

Sch.9 para.62, amended: SI 2002/2314 Reg.3

Sch.9 para.62, revoked: SI 2004/565 Reg.2

Sch.9 para.62, varied: SSI 2003/460 Sch.1 para.2

Sch.9 para.62A, added: SI 2002/2314 Reg.3

Sch.9 para.62A, revoked: SI 2004/565 Reg.2

Sch.9 para.62A, varied: SSI 2003/460 Sch.1 para.2

Sch.9 para.63, revoked: SI 2004/565 Reg.2

Sch.9 para.63, varied: SSI 2003/460 Sch.1 para.2

Sch.9 para.64, varied: SSI 2003/460 Sch.1 para.2

Sch.9 para.64i, varied: SSI 2003/460 Sch.1 para.2

Sch.9 para.65, revoked: SI 2004/565 Reg.2

Sch.9 para.65, varied: SSI 2003/460 Sch.1 para.2

Sch.9 para.66, varied: SSI 2003/460 Sch.1 para.2

Sch.9 para.67, varied: SSI 2003/460 Sch.1 para.2

Sch.9 para.68, varied: SSI 2003/460 Sch.1 para.2

Sch.9 para.69, varied: SSI 2003/460 Sch.1 para.2

NO.

1967. Income Support (General) Regulations 1987–*cont.*

Sch.9 para.70, amended: SI 2003/455 Sch.1 para.23, SI 2004/565 Reg.2

Sch.9 para.70, revoked: SI 2003/1589 Reg.2

Sch.9 para.70, varied: SSI 2003/460 Sch.1 para.2

Sch.9 para.71, varied: SSI 2003/460 Sch.1 para.2

Sch.9 para.72, varied: SSI 2003/460 Sch.1 para.2

Sch.9 para.73, substituted: SI 2004/98 Reg.2

Sch.9 para.73, varied: SSI 2003/460 Sch.1 para.2

Sch.9 para.74, varied: SSI 2003/460 Sch.1 para.2

Sch.9 para.75, varied: SSI 2003/460 Sch.1 para.2

Sch.9 para.76, added: SI 2003/511 Reg.2

Sch.9 para.76, amended: SI 2003/2279 Reg.2

Sch.9 para.76, varied: SSI 2003/460 Sch.1 para.2

Sch.9 para.77, added: SI 2003/2279 Reg.2

Sch.9 para.77, revoked: SI 2004/565 Reg.2

Sch.9 para.77, varied: SSI 2003/460 Sch.1 para.2

Sch.9 para.77A, varied: SI 2003/2382 Sch.1, SSI 2003/460 Sch.1 para.2

Sch.9 para.78, added: SI 2003/2439 Reg.13

Sch.9 para.78, revoked: SI 2004/565 Reg.2

Sch.9 para.78, varied: SSI 2003/460 Sch.1 para.2

Sch.10, applied: SSI 2003/376 Sch.1 para.1

Sch.10, referred to: SI 2003/2382 Reg.16

Sch.10 para.1, varied: SSI 2003/460 Sch.1 para.2

Sch.10 para.2, varied: SSI 2003/460 Sch.1 para.2

Sch.10 para.3, varied: SSI 2003/460 Sch.1 para.2

Sch.10 para.4, varied: SSI 2003/460 Sch.1 para.2

Sch.10 para.5, varied: SSI 2003/460 Sch.1 para.2

Sch.10 para.6, varied: SSI 2003/460 Sch.1 para.2

Sch.10 para.7, amended: SI 2003/455 Sch.1 para.24

Sch.10 para.7, applied: SI 2002/1792 Sch.5 para.20A

Sch.10 para.7, substituted: SI 2002/2380 Reg.2

Sch.10 para.7, varied: SSI 2003/460 Sch.1 para.2

Sch.10 para.8, varied: SSI 2003/460 Sch.1 para.2

Sch.10 para.9, varied: SSI 2003/460 Sch.1 para.2

1987–cont.

1967. Income Support (General) Regulations 1987–*cont.*

Sch.10 para.10, varied: SSI 2003/460 Sch.1 para.2

Sch.10 para.10A, varied: SSI 2003/460 Sch.1 para.2

Sch.10 para.11, varied: SSI 2003/460 Sch.1 para.2

Sch.10 para.12, varied: SSI 2003/460 Sch.1 para.2

Sch.10 para.13, varied: SSI 2003/460 Sch.1 para.2

Sch.10 para.14, varied: SSI 2003/460 Sch.1 para.2

Sch.10 para.15, varied: SSI 2003/460 Sch.1 para.2

Sch.10 para.16, varied: SSI 2003/460 Sch.1 para.2

Sch.10 para.17, amended: SI 2004/1141 Reg.3

Sch.10 para.17, varied: SI 2003/2382 Sch.1, SSI 2003/376 Sch.1 para.2, SSI 2003/460 Sch.1 para.2

Sch.10 para.18, varied: SSI 2003/460 Sch.1 para.2

Sch.10 para.19, varied: SSI 2003/460 Sch.1 para.2

Sch.10 para.20, amended: SI 2003/455 Sch.1 para.24

Sch.10 para.20, varied: SSI 2003/460 Sch.1 para.2

Sch.10 para.21, varied: SSI 2003/460 Sch.1 para.2

Sch.10 para.22, amended: SI 2004/1141 Reg.3

Sch.10 para.22, varied: SSI 2003/460 Sch.1 para.2

Sch.10 para.23, varied: SSI 2003/460 Sch.1 para.2

Sch.10 para.23A, varied: SSI 2003/460 Sch.1 para.2

Sch.10 para.24, varied: SSI 2003/460 Sch.1 para.2

Sch.10 para.25, amended: SI 2003/511 Reg.2

Sch.10 para.25, varied: SSI 2003/460 Sch.1 para.2

Sch.10 para.26, varied: SSI 2003/460 Sch.1 para.2

Sch.10 para.27, varied: SSI 2003/460 Sch.1 para.2

Sch.10 para.28, varied: SSI 2003/460 Sch.1 para.2

Sch.10 para.29, varied: SSI 2003/460 Sch.1 para.2

Sch.10 para.30, substituted: SI 2004/565 Reg.2

Sch.10 para.30, varied: SSI 2003/460 Sch.1 para.2

Sch.10 para.31, varied: SSI 2003/460 Sch.1 para.2

Sch.10 para.32, varied: SSI 2003/460 Sch.1 para.2

1987–cont.

1967. Income Support (General) Regulations 1987–*cont.*

Sch.10 para.33, varied: SSI 2003/460 Sch.1 para.2

Sch.10 para.34, varied: SSI 2003/460 Sch.1 para.2

Sch.10 para.35, varied: SSI 2003/460 Sch.1 para.2

Sch.10 para.36, varied: SSI 2003/460 Sch.1 para.2

Sch.10 para.37, varied: SSI 2003/460 Sch.1 para.2

Sch.10 para.38, varied: SSI 2003/460 Sch.1 para.2

Sch.10 para.39, varied: SSI 2003/460 Sch.1 para.2

Sch.10 para.40, varied: SSI 2003/460 Sch.1 para.2

Sch.10 para.41, varied: SSI 2003/460 Sch.1 para.2

Sch.10 para.42, amended: SI 2004/565 Reg.2

Sch.10 para.42, varied: SSI 2003/460 Sch.1 para.2

Sch.10 para.43, varied: SSI 2003/460 Sch.1 para.2

Sch.10 para.44, amended: SI 2003/2279 Reg.2

Sch.10 para.44, varied: SSI 2003/460 Sch.1 para.2

Sch.10 para.45, amended: SI 2003/2279 Reg.2

Sch.10 para.45, varied: SSI 2003/460 Sch.1 para.2

Sch.10 para.46, varied: SSI 2003/460 Sch.1 para.2

Sch.10 para.47, varied: SSI 2003/460 Sch.1 para.2

Sch.10 para.48, varied: SSI 2003/460 Sch.1 para.2

Sch.10 para.49, varied: SSI 2003/460 Sch.1 para.2

Sch.10 para.50, amended: SI 2002/2314 Reg.3

Sch.10 para.50, revoked: SI 2004/565 Reg.2

Sch.10 para.50, varied: SSI 2003/460 Sch.1 para.2

Sch.10 para.50A, added: SI 2002/2314 Reg.3

Sch.10 para.50A, revoked: SI 2004/565 Reg.2

Sch.10 para.50A, varied: SSI 2003/460 Sch.1 para.2

Sch.10 para.51, revoked: SI 2004/565 Reg.2

Sch.10 para.51, varied: SSI 2003/460 Sch.1 para.2

Sch.10 para.52, varied: SSI 2003/460 Sch.1 para.2

Sch.10 para.53, revoked: SI 2004/565 Reg.2

Sch.10 para.53, varied: SSI 2003/460 Sch.1 para.2

NO.

1987-cont.

1967. Income Support (General) Regulations 1987-*cont.*

Sch.10 para.54, varied: SSI 2003/460 Sch.1 para.2

Sch.10 para.55, varied: SSI 2003/460 Sch.1 para.2

Sch.10 para.56, varied: SSI 2003/460 Sch.1 para.2

Sch.10 para.57, revoked: SI 2003/1589 Reg.2

Sch.10 para.57, varied: SSI 2003/460 Sch.1 para.2

Sch.10 para.57i, varied: SSI 2003/460 Sch.1 para.2

Sch.10 para.58, varied: SSI 2003/460 Sch.1 para.2

Sch.10 para.58i, varied: SSI 2003/460 Sch.1 para.2

Sch.10 para.59, varied: SSI 2003/460 Sch.1 para.2

Sch.10 para.60, varied: SSI 2003/460 Sch.1 para.2

Sch.10 para.61, varied: SSI 2003/460 Sch.1 para.2

Sch.10 para.62, varied: SSI 2003/460 Sch.1 para.2

Sch.10 para.63, varied: SI 2004/1708 Reg.5, SSI 2003/460 Sch.1 para.2

Sch.10 para.64, varied: SSI 2003/460 Sch.1 para.2

Sch.10 para.65, varied: SSI 2003/460 Sch.1 para.2

Sch.10 para.66, added: SI 2003/511 Reg.2

Sch.10 para.66, amended: SI 2003/2279 Reg.2

Sch.10 para.66, varied: SSI 2003/460 Sch.1 para.2

Sch.10 para.67, added: SI 2003/2279 Reg.2

Sch.10 para.67, varied: SSI 2003/460 Sch.1 para.2

Sch.10 para.68, added: SI 2003/2279 Reg.2

Sch.10 para.68, varied: SSI 2003/460 Sch.1 para.2

Sch.10 para.68A, added: SI 2003/2279 Reg.2, SI 2004/2308 Reg.4

Sch.10 para.68A, varied: SSI 2003/460 Sch.1 para.2

Sch.10 para.69, added: SI 2003/2279 Reg.2

Sch.10 para.69, revoked: SI 2004/565 Reg.2

Sch.10 para.69, varied: SSI 2003/460 Sch.1 para.2

Sch.10 para.70, added: SI 2003/2439 Reg.13

Sch.10 para.70, revoked: SI 2004/565 Reg.2

Sch.10 para.70, varied: SSI 2003/460 Sch.1 para.2

1968. Social Security (Claims and Payments) Regulations 1987

applied: SI 2003/1050 Reg.6

referred to: SI 2002/2441 Reg.15

revoked (in part): SI 2003/492 Sch.3 Part 1

NO.

1987-cont.

1968. Social Security (Claims and Payments) Regulations 1987-*cont.*

Reg.2, amended: SI 2002/1397 Sch.1 para.18, SI 2002/1696 Reg.13, SI 2002/1789 Art.2, SI 2002/2497 Sch.2 para.1, SI 2002/3019 Reg.3, SI 2003/2800 Art.2

Reg.3, amended: SI 2003/1589 Reg.5

Reg.4, amended: SI 2002/3019 Reg.4, SI 2003/1632 Reg.2

Reg.4, revoked (in part): 2004 c.19 s.12

Reg.4A, amended: SI 2002/2497 Sch.2 para.1

Reg.4B, amended: SI 2002/3019 Reg.4

Reg.4C, added: SI 2002/1789 Art.3

Reg.4D, added: SI 2002/3019 Reg.4

Reg.4D, amended: SI 2003/1632 Reg.2

Reg.4E, added: SI 2002/3019 Reg.4

Reg.4F, added: SI 2002/3019 Reg.4

Reg.4F, amended: SI 2003/1632 Reg.2, SI 2004/2327 Reg.8

Reg.4ZC, added: SI 2003/2800 Art.2

Reg.6, amended: SI 2002/428 Reg.2, SI 2002/2497 Sch.2 para.3, SI 2003/455 Sch.4 para.3, SI 2003/1632 Reg.2, SI 2004/2283 Reg.2

Reg.6, applied: SI 2003/938 Art.3

Reg.6, revoked (in part): 2004 c.19 s.12

Reg.6A, amended: SI 2002/1703 Sch.2 para.1, SI 2004/959 Reg.22

Reg.7, amended: SI 2002/3019 Reg.5

Reg.13, amended: SI 2002/3019 Reg.6

Reg.13D, added: SI 2002/3019 Reg.6

Reg.16, amended: SI 2002/3019 Reg.7

Reg.16A, added: SI 2002/3019 Reg.7

Reg.17, amended: SI 2002/3019 Reg.8

Reg.19, see *Secretary of State for Work and Pensions v Nelligan* [2003] EWCA Civ 555, [2004] 1 W.L.R. 894 (CA), Scott Baker, L.J.

Reg.19, amended: SI 2002/428 Reg.3, SI 2002/1397 Sch.1 para.18, SI 2002/2497 Sch.2 para.3, SI 2002/2660 Reg.2, SI 2002/3019 Reg.8

Reg.19, revoked (in part): 2004 c.19 s.12, SI 2004/1821 Reg.2

Reg.21, amended: SI 2002/2441 Reg.2

Reg.21, revoked (in part): SI 2002/2441 Reg.2

Reg.22, amended: SI 2002/2441 Reg.3

Reg.22, applied: SI 2004/101 Reg.1

Reg.23, amended: SI 2002/2441 Reg.4

Reg.24, amended: SI 2002/2441 Reg.5

Reg.26A, amended: SI 2002/1397 Sch.1 para.18

Reg.26B, added: SI 2002/3019 Reg.9

Reg.26B, disapplied: SI 2002/3019 Reg.36

Reg.28, amended: SI 2002/1950 Reg.2

Reg.29, amended: SI 2002/2441 Reg.6

Reg.30, amended: SI 2002/2441 Reg.7, SI 2002/3019 Reg.10

NO.

NO.

1987–cont.

1968. Social Security (Claims and Payments) Regulations 1987–*cont.*

Reg.32, amended: SI 2002/3019 Reg.11, SI 2003/1050 Reg.2, SI 2003/1632 Reg.2, SI 2003/2274 Reg.4, SI 2003/3209 Reg.2

Reg.32, applied: SI 2002/1792 Reg.10

Reg.32A, added: SI 2002/1789 Art.4

Reg.32ZA, added: SI 2003/2800 Art.2

Reg.33, amended: SI 2002/2441 Reg.8

Reg.33, applied: SI 2002/2014 Reg.18, Reg.29, Reg.36, SI 2002/3196 Reg.3

Reg.34, see *R. (on the application of Barber) v Secretary of State for Work and Pensions* [2002] EWHC 1915, [2002] 2 F.L.R. 1181 (QBD (Admin Ct)), Sir Richard Tucker

Reg.34A, amended: SI 2002/3019 Reg.12, SI 2002/3197 Reg.5

Reg.34A, applied: SI 2002/3019 Reg.36

Reg.34B, added: SI 2002/3197 Reg.5

Reg.35, amended: SI 2002/2441 Reg.9

Reg.35, applied: SI 2002/3019 Reg.36

Reg.35A, amended: SI 2002/3019 Reg.13

Reg.36, substituted: SI 2002/2660 Reg.2

Reg.38, amended: SI 2002/2441 Reg.10

Reg.43, amended: SI 2002/2469 Sch.1 para.44, SI 2004/696 Art.3

Sch.1 Part I, amended: SI 2002/2497 Sch.2 para.1

Sch.4, amended: SI 2004/1821 Reg.2

Sch.6, applied: SI 2004/101 Reg.1

Sch.6 para.1, amended: SI 2002/2497 Sch.2 para.1

Sch.6 para.2, amended: SI 2002/2497 Sch.2 para.1

Sch.6 para.3, amended: SI 2002/2497 Sch.2 para.1

Sch.6 para.4, amended: SI 2002/2497 Sch.2 para.1

Sch.6 para.5, amended: SI 2002/2441 Reg.11, SI 2002/2497 Sch.2 para.1

Sch.6 para.6, amended: SI 2002/2441 Reg.11, SI 2002/2497 Sch.2 para.1

Sch.6 para.7, amended: SI 2002/2497 Sch.2 para.1

Sch.9A, applied: SI 2002/3019 Reg.36

Sch.9B, applied: SI 2002/3019 Reg.36

Sch.9 para.1, amended: SI 2002/398 Reg.2, SI 2002/2441 Reg.12, SI 2002/3019 Reg.14

Sch.9 para.1, revoked (in part): SI 2002/2441 Reg.12

Sch.9 para.3, amended: SI 2002/3019 Reg.14, SI 2002/3197 Reg.5

Sch.9 para.4, amended: SI 2002/398 Reg.2, SI 2003/2325 Reg.2, SI 2004/576 Reg.2

Sch.9 para.4, revoked (in part): SI 2002/398 Reg.2

Sch.9 para.5, amended: SI 2002/3019 Reg.14

Sch.9 para.6, amended: SI 2002/3019 Reg.14

1987–cont.

1968. Social Security (Claims and Payments) Regulations 1987–*cont.*

Sch.9 para.7, amended: SI 2002/3019 Reg.14

Sch.9 para.8, amended: SI 2002/3019 Reg.14

Sch.9A para.1, amended: SI 2002/2441 Reg.13, SI 2002/3019 Reg.14, SI 2002/3197 Reg.5

Sch.9A para.1, revoked (in part): SI 2002/2441 Reg.13

Sch.9A para.2, amended: SI 2002/3019 Reg.14, SI 2002/3197 Reg.5, SI 2004/2825 Reg.3

Sch.9A para.2A, added: SI 2002/3197 Reg.5

Sch.9A para.2A, amended: SI 2002/3197 Reg.5

Sch.9A para.3, amended: SI 2002/3019 Reg.14, SI 2002/3197 Reg.5

Sch.9A para.4, amended: SI 2002/3019 Reg.14, SI 2002/3197 Reg.5

Sch.9A para.5, amended: SI 2002/3197 Reg.5

Sch.9A para.6, amended: SI 2002/3197 Reg.5

Sch.9A para.7, amended: SI 2002/355 Reg.2, SI 2002/3197 Reg.5, SI 2003/470 Reg.2, SI 2004/576 Reg.3

Sch.9A para.8, amended: SI 2002/3197 Reg.5

Sch.9A para.9, amended: SI 2002/3197 Reg.5

Sch.9A para.10, amended: SI 2002/3019 Reg.14, SI 2002/3197 Reg.5

Sch.9A para.11, amended: SI 2002/3197 Reg.5, SI 2004/2825 Reg.3

Sch.9B para.1, amended: SI 2002/1950 Reg.3

Sch.9B para.2, amended: SI 2002/3019 Reg.14

Sch.9B para.3, amended: SI 2002/1950 Reg.3, SI 2002/3019 Reg.14

Sch.9B para.5, amended: SI 2002/3019 Reg.14

Sch.9B para.6, amended: SI 2002/3019 Reg.14

Sch.9C Part I para.1, added: SI 2002/1789 Sch.1

Sch.9C Part II para.2, added: SI 2002/1789 Sch.1

Sch.9C Part II para.3, added: SI 2002/1789 Sch.1

Sch.9C Part III para.4, added: SI 2002/1789 Sch.1

Sch.9C Part III para.5, added: SI 2002/1789 Sch.1

Sch.9C Part III para.6, added: SI 2002/1789 Sch.1

Sch.9C Part III para.7, added: SI 2002/1789 Sch.1

Sch.9ZC Part I para.1, added: SI 2003/2800 Sch.1

NO.

1987–cont.

1968. Social Security (Claims and Payments) Regulations 1987–*cont.*

Sch.9ZC Part II para.2, added: SI 2003/2800 Sch.1

Sch.9ZC Part II para.3, added: SI 2003/2800 Sch.1

Sch.9ZC Part III para.4, added: SI 2003/2800 Sch.1

Sch.9ZC Part III para.5, added: SI 2003/2800 Sch.1

Sch.9ZC Part III para.6, added: SI 2003/2800 Sch.1

Sch.9ZC Part III para.7, added: SI 2003/2800 Sch.1

1969. Income Support (Transitional) Regulations 1987

Part II, applied: SI 2002/1792 Sch.1 para.6

Reg.15, varied: SI 2003/526 Art.18, SI 2004/552 Art.17

1971. Housing Benefit (General) Regulations 1987

amended: SI 2002/1397 Sch.1 para.19

applied: SI 2003/325 Reg.2, Reg.21, SI 2003/1338 Reg.2

referred to: SI 2003/325 Reg.1, Reg.2, SI 2003/770 Reg.2, SI 2004/552 Art.19, Art.20

Reg.2, amended: SI 2002/490 Reg.5, SI 2002/841 Reg.5, SI 2002/1397 Sch.1 para.19, SI 2002/2402 Sch.4 para.1, SI 2002/2689 Reg.4, SI 2003/48 Reg.4, SI 2003/325 Reg.3, SI 2003/1338 Reg.8, SI 2003/2279 Reg.4, SI 2003/2399 Reg.2, SI 2004/14 Reg.2, Reg.36, SI 2004/319 Reg.2, SI 2004/565 Reg.3, Reg.9, SI 2004/963 Reg.2, SI 2004/1141 Reg.2, SI 2004/2303 Reg.2

Reg.2, applied: SI 2002/1792 Reg.22

Reg.4, amended: SI 2002/2689 Reg.4, SI 2003/325 Reg.3A, Reg.27, SI 2003/2275 Reg.3, SI 2004/2327 Reg.2

Reg.4, applied: SI 2002/1703 Reg.2

Reg.4, revoked (in part): SI 2004/2327 Reg.2

Reg.5, amended: SI 2003/325 Reg.4, SI 2004/2303 Reg.2, SI 2004/2327 Reg.2

Reg.7, see *Campbell v South Northamptonshire DC* [2004] EWCA Civ 409, [2004] 3 All E.R. 387 (CA), Peter Gibson, L.J.; see *M v Secretary of State for Work and Pensions* [2004] EWCA Civ 1343, [2004] 3 F.C.R. 507 (CA (Civ Div)), Kennedy, L.J.; see *R. (on the application of Kershaw) v Rochdale MBC* [2002] EWHC 2385, [2003] H.L.R. 34 (QBD (Admin Ct)), Roderick Evans, J.; see *R. (on the application of Painter) v Carmarthenshire CC Housing Benefit Review Board* [2001] EWHC Admin 308, [2002] H.L.R. 23 (QBD (Admin Ct)), Lightman, J.

Reg.7, amended: SI 2003/1338 Reg.9, SI 2004/14 Reg.3

NO.

1987–cont.

1971. Housing Benefit (General) Regulations 1987–*cont.*

Reg.7A, amended: SI 2003/325 Reg.5, SI 2004/1232 Reg.2

Reg.7B, revoked: 2004 c.19 s.12

Reg.8, amended: SI 2003/2399 Reg.3

Reg.8A, added: SI 2003/2399 Reg.4

Reg.10, see *R. (on the application of Laali) v Westminster Housing Benefit Review Board* [2002] H.L.R. 8 (QBD (Admin Ct)), Silber, J.; see *R. (on the application of Naghshbandi) v Camden LBC* [2002] EWCA Civ 1038, [2003] H.L.R. 21 (CA), Schiemann, L.J.

Reg.10, amended: SI 2003/2399 Reg.5, Reg.14, SI 2004/14 Reg.36

Reg.10, applied: SI 2003/907 Reg.3

Reg.10, varied: SI 2004/781 Reg.5

Reg.11, see *Shepherd v Dundee City Council* 2002 S.L.T. 1427 (OH), Lord Carloway

Reg.11, amended: SI 2003/1338 Reg.10, Reg.19, SI 2004/14 Reg.4, Reg.25, SI 2004/781 Reg.2

Reg.11A, added: SI 2003/2399 Reg.6

Reg.11A, amended: SI 2003/2399 Reg.14, SI 2004/14 Reg.36

Reg.11A, varied: SI 2004/781 Reg.5

Reg.11B, added: SI 2003/2399 Reg.6

Reg.12, amended: SI 2003/363 Reg.2

Reg.12A, amended: SI 2003/48 Reg.5, SI 2003/363 Reg.2, SI 2003/1338 Reg.11, SI 2003/2399 Reg.7, Reg.14, SI 2004/14 Reg.5, Reg.36, SI 2004/781 Reg.3

Reg.12A, applied: SI 2003/1338 Reg.21, SI 2004/14 Reg.27

Reg.12A, revoked (in part): SI 2003/363 Reg.2

Reg.12A, varied: SI 2004/781 Reg.5

Reg.12B, amended: SI 2003/2399 Reg.8

Reg.12C, amended: SI 2003/2399 Reg.9

Reg.12CA, amended: SI 2003/2399 Reg.10

Reg.12E, added: SI 2003/2399 Reg.11

Reg.13, amended: SI 2002/2402 Sch.4 para.2

Reg.14, amended: SI 2002/2402 Sch.4 para.3

Reg.16, amended: SI 2003/325 Reg.6, SI 2003/1195 Reg.4, SI 2004/2327 Reg.2

Reg.16, applied: SI 2003/526 Art.20, SI 2004/552 Art.19, Art.20

Reg.16, substituted: SI 2003/325 Reg.6

Reg.17, amended: SI 2004/2327 Reg.2

Reg.17, applied: SI 2003/526 Art.20, SI 2004/552 Art.19

Reg.17, substituted: SI 2003/325 Reg.6

Reg.18, amended: SI 2002/668 Art.19, SI 2003/526 Art.20, SI 2003/1195 Reg.4, SI 2004/552 Art.19

Reg.18, substituted: SI 2003/325 Reg.6

Reg.19, amended: SI 2003/325 Reg.7, SI 2004/2327 Reg.2

NO.

NO.

1987–cont.

1971. Housing Benefit (General) Regulations 1987–*cont.*

Reg.19, revoked (in part): SI 2004/2327 Reg.2

Reg.21, amended: SI 2003/455 Sch.3 para.1, SI 2004/14 Reg.6, SI 2004/552 Art.19

Reg.21, substituted: SI 2003/325 Reg.8

Reg.21A, amended: SI 2002/499 Reg.2, SI 2002/2689 Reg.4, SI 2003/455 Sch.3 para.2, SI 2004/14 Reg.7

Reg.21A, applied: SI 2002/2005 Reg.13

Reg.21A, substituted: SI 2003/325 Reg.8

Reg.22, amended: SI 2004/14 Reg.8

Reg.22, substituted: SI 2003/325 Reg.8

Reg.23, amended: SI 2004/14 Reg.9, SI 2004/2327 Reg.2

Reg.23, revoked (in part): SI 2003/325 Reg.8, SI 2004/2327 Reg.2

Reg.23, substituted: SI 2003/325 Reg.8

Reg.24, amended: SI 2004/14 Reg.10

Reg.24, substituted: SI 2003/325 Reg.8

Reg.25, amended: SI 2003/325 Reg.8, SI 2004/565 Reg.9, SI 2004/2327 Reg.2

Reg.25, substituted: SI 2003/325 Reg.8

Reg.26, amended: SI 2002/2402 Sch.4 para.4, SI 2004/552 Art.20

Reg.26, substituted: SI 2003/325 Reg.8

Reg.27, amended: SI 2003/325 Reg.8

Reg.27, substituted: SI 2003/325 Reg.8

Reg.28, substituted: SI 2003/325 Reg.8

Reg.28, amended: SI 2002/2689 Reg.4

Reg.28, substituted: SI 2003/325 Reg.8

Reg.29, substituted: SI 2003/325 Reg.8

Reg.29, amended: SI 2002/2689 Reg.4

Reg.29, substituted: SI 2003/325 Reg.8

Reg.30, amended: SI 2003/325 Reg.8

Reg.30, substituted: SI 2003/325 Reg.8

Reg.31, amended: SI 2003/325 Reg.8

Reg.31, substituted: SI 2003/325 Reg.8

Reg.32, substituted: SI 2003/325 Reg.8

Reg.33, substituted: SI 2003/325 Reg.8

Reg.33, amended: SI 2002/841 Reg.5, SI 2002/2402 Sch.4 para.5, SI 2004/565 Reg.9, SI 2004/2327 Reg.2

Reg.33, substituted: SI 2003/325 Reg.8

Reg.34, substituted: SI 2003/325 Reg.8

Reg.34, amended: SI 2002/2442 Reg.2

Reg.34, substituted: SI 2003/325 Reg.8

Reg.35, amended: SI 2003/325 Reg.8

Reg.35, substituted: SI 2003/325 Reg.8

Reg.35, amended: SI 2002/2402 Sch.4 para.6

Reg.35, substituted: SI 2003/325 Reg.8

Reg.36, amended: SI 2003/325 Reg.8

Reg.36, revoked: SI 2004/2327 Reg.2

Reg.36, substituted: SI 2003/325 Reg.8

Reg.37, substituted: SI 2003/325 Reg.8

Reg.38, substituted: SI 2003/325 Reg.8

Reg.39, substituted: SI 2003/325 Reg.8

1987–cont.

1971. Housing Benefit (General) Regulations 1987–*cont.*

Reg.40, amended: SI 2002/2402 Sch.4 para.7

Reg.40, substituted: SI 2003/325 Reg.8

Reg.41, substituted: SI 2003/325 Reg.8

Reg.42, amended: SI 2004/2327 Reg.2

Reg.42, substituted: SI 2003/325 Reg.8

Reg.43, amended: SI 2002/2402 Sch.4 para.8, SI 2004/2308 Reg.3

Reg.43, substituted: SI 2003/325 Reg.8

Reg.43A, revoked (in part): SI 2003/455 Sch.3 para.3

Reg.43A, substituted: SI 2003/325 Reg.8

Reg.44, substituted: SI 2003/325 Reg.8

Reg.45, substituted: SI 2003/325 Reg.8

Reg.46, amended: SI 2002/1589 Reg.2, SI 2004/1708 Reg.4

Reg.46, disapplied: SI 2003/325 Reg.9

Reg.47, disapplied: SI 2003/325 Reg.9

Reg.48, disapplied: SI 2003/325 Reg.9

Reg.48A, amended: SI 2002/1763 Reg.2

Reg.48A, disapplied: SI 2003/325 Reg.9

Reg.49, disapplied: SI 2003/325 Reg.9

Reg.50, amended: SI 2004/1708 Reg.7

Reg.50, disapplied: SI 2003/325 Reg.9

Reg.51, disapplied: SI 2003/325 Reg.9

Reg.51, revoked: SI 2002/1589 Reg.6

Reg.52, amended: SI 2002/1589 Reg.6

Reg.52, disapplied: SI 2003/325 Reg.9

Reg.53, amended: SI 2002/1589 Reg.3, Reg.4, SI 2002/2207 Reg.2, SI 2003/1701 Reg.2, Reg.3, SI 2003/1914 Reg.2, SI 2004/1708 Reg.2, Reg.3

Reg.53, disapplied: SI 2003/325 Reg.9

Reg.53, revoked (in part): SI 2004/1708 Reg.3

Reg.53ZB, disapplied: SI 2003/325 Reg.9

Reg.54, disapplied: SI 2003/325 Reg.9

Reg.55, disapplied: SI 2003/325 Reg.9

Reg.56, disapplied: SI 2003/325 Reg.9

Reg.56B, disapplied: SI 2003/325 Reg.9

Reg.57, disapplied: SI 2003/325 Reg.9

Reg.57A, amended: SI 2002/1589 Reg.3, Reg.5, SI 2003/1701 Reg.2, SI 2003/1914 Reg.2, SI 2004/1708 Reg.2

Reg.57A, disapplied: SI 2003/325 Reg.9

Reg.57B, disapplied: SI 2003/325 Reg.9

Reg.58, disapplied: SI 2003/325 Reg.9

Reg.58, revoked (in part): SI 2002/1589 Reg.6

Reg.58A, disapplied: SI 2003/325 Reg.9

Reg.59, disapplied: SI 2003/325 Reg.9

Reg.60, disapplied: SI 2003/325 Reg.9

Reg.62A, amended: SI 2003/1338 Reg.12, SI 2003/1589 Reg.3

Reg.62A, applied: SI 2004/14 Reg.28

Reg.62A, revoked (in part): SI 2003/1589 Reg.3

Reg.62A, substituted: SI 2004/14 Reg.11

1987–cont.

1971. Housing Benefit (General) Regulations 1987–*cont.*

Reg.62B, added: SI 2003/325 Reg.10

Reg.62B, amended: SI 2003/1338 Reg.3

Reg.62ZB, added: SI 2004/319 Reg.3

Reg.63, amended: SI 2002/668 Art.19, SI 2003/325 Reg.11, SI 2003/526 Art.20, SI 2003/1195 Reg.4, SI 2003/2275 Reg.3, SI 2004/552 Art.19, SI 2004/2327 Reg.2

Reg.63, applied: SI 2003/526 Art.20, SI 2004/552 Art.19

Reg.65, see *Secretary of State for Work and Pensions v Robinson* [2004] EWCA Civ 342, [2004] H.L.R. 39 (CA), Ward, L.J.

Reg.65, amended: SI 2003/1338 Reg.14, SI 2004/14 Reg.15, SI 2004/2303 Reg.2

Reg.65A, added: SI 2004/14 Reg.12

Reg.65B, added: SI 2004/319 Reg.4

Reg.66, disapplied: SI 2003/325 Reg.9

Reg.66, revoked: SI 2004/14 Reg.13

Reg.66, varied: SI 2003/1338 Reg.5

Reg.67, see *Secretary of State for Work and Pensions v Chiltern DC* [2003] EWCA Civ 508, [2003] H.L.R. 67 (CA), Hale, L.J.

Reg.67, disapplied: SI 2003/325 Reg.9

Reg.67, revoked: SI 2004/14 Reg.13

Reg.68, amended: SI 2003/308 Reg.2, SI 2003/325 Reg.22, SI 2003/1338 Reg.13, SI 2004/14 Reg.14, SI 2004/2327 Reg.2

Reg.68, substituted: SI 2004/2327 Reg.2

Reg.68B, added: SI 2003/325 Reg.22

Reg.68B, amended: SI 2004/290 Reg.3, SI 2004/2327 Reg.2

Reg.68B, substituted: SI 2003/325 Reg.22

Reg.69, amended: SI 2004/319 Reg.5, SI 2004/2303 Reg.2

Reg.70, amended: SI 2003/1338 Reg.19, SI 2004/14 Reg.16

Reg.71, amended: SI 2002/1703 Sch.2 para.2

Reg.72, amended: SI 2002/1703 Sch.2 para.2, SI 2003/48 Reg.6, SI 2003/325 Reg.23, SI 2003/1589 Reg.3, SI 2003/1632 Reg.3

Reg.72, disapplied: SI 2003/1338 Reg.4

Reg.72, revoked (in part): SI 2003/1338 Reg.14, SI 2004/14 Reg.15

Reg.72BA, added: SI 2004/2303 Reg.2

Reg.73, amended: SI 2004/2308 Reg.3

Reg.75, amended: SI 2003/325 Reg.24, SI 2003/1338 Reg.19, SI 2004/14 Reg.25

Reg.76, amended: SI 2003/1589 Reg.3, SI 2004/14 Reg.17

Reg.76, revoked (in part): SI 2003/1338 Reg.15, SI 2003/1589 Reg.3, SI 2004/14 Reg.17

Reg.81, see *R. (on the application of Bono) v Harlow DC* [2002] EWHC 423, [2002] 1 W.L.R. 2475 (QBD (Admin Ct)), Richards, J.

1987–cont.

1971. Housing Benefit (General) Regulations 1987–*cont.*

Reg.82, see *Godwin v Rossendale BC* [2002] EWCA Civ 726, [2003] H.L.R. 9 (CA), Peter Gibson, L.J.

Reg.93, amended: SI 2003/325 Reg.27, SI 2003/2399 Reg.12

Reg.94, amended: SI 2003/2399 Reg.12

Reg.99, amended: SI 2002/1397 Sch.1 para.19

Reg.101, see *Secretary of State for Work and Pensions v Chiltern DC* [2003] EWCA Civ 508, [2003] H.L.R. 67 (CA), Hale, L.J.

Reg.104, revoked (in part): SI 2003/1338 Reg.16, SI 2004/14 Reg.18

Reg.105, amended: SI 2003/325 Reg.26, SI 2003/455 Sch.3 para.4

Sch.A1 para.1, revoked: 2004 c.19 s.12

Sch.A1 para.2, revoked: 2004 c.19 s.12

Sch.A1 para.2A, revoked: 2004 c.19 s.12

Sch.A1 para.3, revoked: 2004 c.19 s.12

Sch.A1 para.4, revoked: 2004 c.19 s.12

Sch.A1 para.5, revoked: 2004 c.19 s.12

Sch.A1 para.6, revoked: 2004 c.19 s.12

Sch.A1 para.7, revoked: 2004 c.19 s.12

Sch.A1 para.8, revoked: 2004 c.19 s.12

Sch.A1 para.9, revoked: 2004 c.19 s.12

Sch.A1 para.10, revoked: 2004 c.19 s.12

Sch.1B, applied: SSI 2002/444 Reg.4

Sch.1B, referred to: SI 2003/907 Reg.3

Sch.1 Part I para.1, amended: SI 2003/363 Reg.3, SI 2003/2279 Reg.4

Sch.1 Part I para.1, applied: SI 2002/1792 Sch.2 para.13

Sch.1 Part I para.1A, amended: SI 2002/668 Art.19, SI 2003/526 Art.20, SI 2004/552 Art.19

Sch.1 Part II para.5, amended: SI 2002/668 Art.19, SI 2003/526 Art.20, SI 2004/552 Art.19

Sch.1 Part II para.5, referred to: SI 2002/1792 Sch.2 para.13

Sch.1 Part II para.7, amended: SI 2003/363 Reg.3, SI 2003/2279 Reg.4

Sch.1A para.2, amended: SI 2003/1338 Reg.17, SI 2004/14 Reg.20

Sch.1A para.2, revoked (in part): SI 2003/1338 Reg.17, SI 2004/14 Reg.20

Sch.1A para.4, revoked (in part): SI 2003/1338 Reg.17, SI 2004/14 Reg.20

Sch.1A para.11A, amended: SI 2002/2322 Reg.2, SI 2004/2984 Reg.2

Sch.2 Part I para.1, amended: SI 2002/668 Sch.6

Sch.2 Part I para.1, substituted: SI 2003/526 Sch.6, SI 2004/552 Sch.6

Sch.2 Part I para.2, amended: SI 2002/668 Sch.6, SI 2002/2019 Reg.2

Sch.2 Part I para.2, substituted: SI 2003/526 Sch.6, SI 2004/552 Sch.6

NO.

NO.

1987–cont.

1987–cont.

1971. Housing Benefit (General) Regulations 1987–*cont.*

Sch.2 Part II para.3, amended: SI 2002/668 Art.19, SI 2002/2402 Sch.4 para.9, SI 2003/526 Art.20, SI 2004/552 Art.19

Sch.2 Part II para.3, applied: SI 2003/526 Art.20

Sch.2 Part III para.4, amended: SI 2002/2497 Sch.2 para.1

Sch.2 Part III para.5, amended: SI 2002/2497 Sch.2 para.1

Sch.2 Part III para.6, amended: SI 2002/2497 Sch.2 para.1

Sch.2 Part III para.7, amended: SI 2002/2497 Sch.2 para.1

Sch.2 Part III para.8, amended: SI 2002/2497 Sch.2 para.1

Sch.2 Part III para.8A, amended: SI 2002/2497 Sch.2 para.1

Sch.2 Part III para.8A, revoked (in part): SI 2004/14 Reg.21

Sch.2 Part III para.9, amended: SI 2002/2497 Sch.2 para.1

Sch.2 Part III para.9A, amended: SI 2002/2497 Sch.2 para.1

Sch.2 Part III para.10, amended: SI 2002/2497 Sch.2 para.1

Sch.2 Part III para.10, applied: SI 2002/2005 Reg.9, Reg.13

Sch.2 Part III para.11, amended: SI 2002/2497 Sch.2 para.1

Sch.2 Part III para.11, applied: SI 2002/2005 Reg.9

Sch.2 Part III para.12, amended: SI 2002/2497 Sch.2 para.1, SI 2003/455 Sch.3 para.5

Sch.2 Part III para.12, applied: SI 2002/2005 Reg.9

Sch.2 Part III para.13, amended: SI 2002/490 Reg.2, SI 2002/2497 Sch.2 para.1

Sch.2 Part III para.13A, amended: SI 2002/2497 Sch.2 para.1, SI 2003/1195 Reg.4

Sch.2 Part III para.13A, applied: SI 2003/526 Art.20, SI 2004/552 Art.19

Sch.2 Part III para.14, amended: SI 2002/2497 Sch.2 para.1, SI 2003/1731 Reg.3

Sch.2 Part III para.14, applied: SI 2004/552 Art.19

Sch.2 Part III para.14, revoked (in part): SI 2004/2327 Reg.2

Sch.2 Part III para.14A, amended: SI 2002/2497 Sch.2 para.1

Sch.2 Part III para.14A, applied: SI 2003/526 Art.20

Sch.2 Part III para.14B, amended: SI 2002/2497 Sch.2 para.1

Sch.2 Part III para.14ZA, amended: SI 2002/2020 Reg.2, SI 2002/2497 Sch.2 para.1, SI 2003/2279 Reg.4

Sch.2 Part III para.14ZA, revoked (in part): SI 2003/2279 Reg.4

1971. Housing Benefit (General) Regulations 1987–*cont.*

Sch.2 Part IV para.15, amended: SI 2002/668 Sch.7, SI 2002/2497 Sch.2 para.1, SI 2003/526 Sch.7

Sch.2 Part IV para.15, substituted: SI 2004/552 Sch.7

Sch.2A Part I para.1, added: SI 2003/325 Reg.6

Sch.2A Part I para.1, amended: SI 2004/2327 Reg.2

Sch.2A Part I para.1, substituted: SI 2004/552 Sch.8

Sch.2A Part I para.2, added: SI 2003/325 Reg.6

Sch.2A Part I para.2, substituted: SI 2004/552 Sch.8

Sch.2A Part II para.3, added: SI 2003/325 Reg.6

Sch.2A Part II para.3, amended: SI 2004/552 Art.20

Sch.2A Part III para.4, added: SI 2003/325 Reg.6

Sch.2A Part III para.5, added: SI 2003/325 Reg.6

Sch.2A Part III para.6, added: SI 2003/325 Reg.6

Sch.2A Part III para.6, amended: SI 2003/325 Reg.6

Sch.2A Part III para.7, added: SI 2003/325 Reg.6

Sch.2A Part III para.8, added: SI 2003/325 Reg.6

Sch.2A Part III para.8, amended: SI 2003/325 Reg.6

Sch.2A Part III para.9, added: SI 2003/325 Reg.6

Sch.2A Part III para.10, added: SI 2003/325 Reg.6

Sch.2A Part III para.11, added: SI 2003/325 Reg.6

Sch.2A Part IV, added: SI 2003/325 Reg.6

Sch.2A Part IV, substituted: SI 2004/552 Sch.9

Sch.3 para.1, amended: SI 2002/2497 Sch.2 para.1

Sch.3 para.2, amended: SI 2002/2497 Sch.2 para.1

Sch.3 para.3, amended: SI 2002/2497 Sch.2 para.1

Sch.3 para.4, amended: SI 2002/2497 Sch.2 para.1

Sch.3 para.4A, amended: SI 2002/2497 Sch.2 para.1

Sch.3 para.4B, amended: SI 2002/2497 Sch.2 para.1

Sch.3 para.5, amended: SI 2002/2497 Sch.2 para.1

Sch.3 para.6, amended: SI 2002/2497 Sch.2 para.1, SI 2004/3168 Art.15

1987–cont.

1971. Housing Benefit (General) Regulations 1987–*cont.*

Sch.3 para.7, amended: SI 2002/2497 Sch.2 para.1

Sch.3 para.8, amended: SI 2002/2497 Sch.2 para.1

Sch.3 para.9, amended: SI 2002/2497 Sch.2 para.1

Sch.3 para.10, amended: SI 2002/2497 Sch.2 para.1

Sch.3 para.11, amended: SI 2002/2497 Sch.2 para.1

Sch.3 para.12, amended: SI 2002/2497 Sch.2 para.1

Sch.3 para.13, amended: SI 2002/2497 Sch.2 para.1, SI 2004/2327 Reg.2

Sch.3 para.14, amended: SI 2002/2497 Sch.2 para.1

Sch.3 para.14, revoked: SI 2004/2327 Reg.2

Sch.3 para.15, amended: SI 2002/2497 Sch.2 para.1

Sch.3 para.16, amended: SI 2002/2402 Sch.4 para.10, SI 2002/2497 Sch.2 para.1, SI 2003/2634 Reg.3, SI 2004/552 Art.19

Sch.3 para.16, revoked (in part): SI 2003/2634 Reg.3

Sch.3 para.16, substituted: SI 2002/2402 Sch.4 para.10

Sch.3A para.1, added: SI 2003/325 Sch.2 Part I

Sch.3A para.2, added: SI 2003/325 Sch.2 Part I

Sch.3A para.3, added: SI 2003/325 Sch.2 Part I

Sch.3A para.3, amended: SI 2003/325 Sch.2 Part I, SI 2004/3168 Art.15

Sch.3A para.4, added: SI 2003/325 Sch.2 Part I

Sch.3A para.4, amended: SI 2003/325 Sch.2 Part I

Sch.3A para.5, added: SI 2003/325 Sch.2 Part I

Sch.3A para.5, amended: SI 2003/325 Sch.2 Part I

Sch.3A para.6, added: SI 2003/325 Sch.2 Part I

Sch.3A para.7, added: SI 2003/325 Sch.2 Part I

Sch.3A para.8, added: SI 2003/325 Sch.2 Part I

Sch.3A para.9, added: SI 2003/325 Sch.2 Part I

Sch.3A para.9, amended: SI 2003/325 Sch.2 Part I, SI 2004/552 Art.20

Sch.3A para.9, substituted: SI 2003/325 Sch.2 Part I

Sch.3A para.10, added: SI 2003/325 Sch.2 Part I

Sch.4 para.10, substituted: SI 2004/1708 Reg.4

Sch.4 para.10A, added: SI 2002/2380 Reg.4

1987–cont.

1971. Housing Benefit (General) Regulations 1987–*cont.*

Sch.4 para.11, substituted: SI 2004/565 Reg.3

Sch.4 para.13, amended: SI 2002/2442 Reg.3, SI 2004/2308 Reg.2

Sch.4 para.14, amended: SI 2002/841 Reg.5

Sch.4 para.20, amended: SI 2002/668 Art.19, SI 2003/526 Art.20, SI 2004/552 Art.19

Sch.4 para.23, amended: SI 2003/2279 Reg.4, SI 2004/2308 Reg.4, SI 2004/2327 Reg.2

Sch.4 para.24, amended: SI 2004/1141 Reg.4

Sch.4 para.26, amended: SI 2004/1141 Reg.4

Sch.4 para.34, amended: SI 2004/2308 Reg.3

Sch.4 para.49, amended: SI 2004/565 Reg.3

Sch.4 para.53, amended: SI 2002/841 Reg.5

Sch.4 para.54, amended: SI 2002/841 Reg.5

Sch.4 para.55, amended: SI 2002/841 Reg.5

Sch.4 para.57, revoked: SI 2002/2402 Sch.4 para.11

Sch.4 para.58, amended: SI 2002/2402 Sch.4 para.11, SI 2003/2634 Reg.3, SI 2004/552 Art.19

Sch.4 para.61, revoked: 2004 c.19 s.12

Sch.4 para.62, revoked: 2004 c.19 s.12

Sch.4 para.63, revoked: SI 2004/565 Reg.3

Sch.4 para.64, revoked: SI 2004/565 Reg.3

Sch.4 para.64A, added: SI 2002/2314 Reg.4

Sch.4 para.64A, revoked: SI 2004/565 Reg.3

Sch.4 para.65, revoked: SI 2004/565 Reg.3

Sch.4 para.67, amended: SI 2003/762 Reg.11, SI 2004/1748 Sch.2 para.2

Sch.4 para.68, revoked: SI 2004/565 Reg.3

Sch.4 para.75, added: SI 2003/511 Reg.4

Sch.4 para.75, amended: SI 2003/2279 Reg.4

Sch.4 para.76, added: SI 2003/2279 Reg.4

Sch.4 para.76, revoked: SI 2004/565 Reg.3

Sch.4 para.77, added: SI 2003/2439 Reg.14

Sch.4 para.77, revoked: SI 2004/565 Reg.3

Sch.4A para.1, added: SI 2003/325 Sch.2 Part II

Sch.4A para.2, added: SI 2003/325 Sch.2 Part II

Sch.4A para.3, added: SI 2003/325 Sch.2 Part II

Sch.4A para.4, added: SI 2003/325 Sch.2 Part II

Sch.4A para.5, added: SI 2003/325 Sch.2 Part II

Sch.4A para.6, added: SI 2003/325 Sch.2 Part II

Sch.4A para.6, amended: SI 2003/325 Sch.2 Part II

Sch.4A para.7, added: SI 2003/325 Sch.2 Part II

1987–cont.

1971. Housing Benefit (General) Regulations 1987–*cont.*

Sch.4A para.8, added: SI 2003/325 Sch.2 Part II

Sch.4A para.9, added: SI 2003/325 Sch.2 Part II

Sch.4A para.10, added: SI 2003/325 Sch.2 Part II

Sch.4A para.11, added: SI 2003/325 Sch.2 Part II

Sch.4A para.12, added: SI 2003/325 Sch.2 Part II

Sch.4A para.13, added: SI 2003/325 Sch.2 Part II

Sch.4A para.14, added: SI 2003/325 Sch.2 Part II

Sch.4A para.15, added: SI 2003/325 Sch.2 Part II

Sch.4A para.16, added: SI 2003/325 Sch.2 Part II

Sch.4A para.17, added: SI 2003/325 Sch.2 Part II

Sch.4A para.18, added: SI 2003/325 Sch.2 Part II

Sch.4A para.19, added: SI 2003/325 Sch.2 Part II

Sch.4A para.20, added: SI 2003/325 Sch.2 Part II

Sch.4A para.21, added: SI 2003/325 Sch.2 Part II

Sch.4A para.21, amended: SI 2003/325 Sch.2 Part II, SI 2004/552 Art.20

Sch.4A para.22, added: SI 2003/325 Sch.2 Part II

Sch.4A para.23, added: SI 2003/325 Sch.2 Part II

Sch.5 para.8, amended: SI 2002/2380 Reg.4, SI 2002/2402 Sch.4 para.12, SI 2004/14 Reg.22

Sch.5 para.8, applied: SI 2002/1792 Sch.5 para.20A

Sch.5 para.18, amended: SI 2004/1141 Reg.3

Sch.5 para.21, amended: SI 2004/2327 Reg.2

Sch.5 para.23, amended: SI 2004/1141 Reg.3

Sch.5 para.33, substituted: SI 2004/565 Reg.3

Sch.5 para.43, amended: SI 2004/565 Reg.3

Sch.5 para.45, revoked: SI 2003/2279 Reg.4

Sch.5 para.46, amended: SI 2003/2279 Reg.4

Sch.5 para.47, amended: SI 2003/2279 Reg.4

Sch.5 para.49, revoked: SI 2003/1589 Reg.9

Sch.5 para.50, revoked: 2004 c.19 s.12

Sch.5 para.51, revoked: 2004 c.19 s.12

Sch.5 para.53, revoked: SI 2004/565 Reg.3

Sch.5 para.53A, added: SI 2002/2314 Reg.4

Sch.5 para.53A, revoked: SI 2004/565 Reg.3

Sch.5 para.54, revoked: SI 2004/565 Reg.3

1987–cont.

1971. Housing Benefit (General) Regulations 1987–*cont.*

Sch.5 para.56, revoked: SI 2004/565 Reg.3

Sch.5 para.60, substituted: SI 2004/1708 Reg.4

Sch.5 para.65, revoked: SI 2004/565 Reg.3

Sch.5 para.68, added: SI 2003/511 Reg.4

Sch.5 para.68, amended: SI 2003/2279 Reg.4

Sch.5 para.69, added: SI 2003/2279 Reg.4

Sch.5 para.70, added: SI 2003/2279 Reg.4

Sch.5 para.70A, added: SI 2003/2279 Reg.4, SI 2004/2308 Reg.4

Sch.5 para.71, added: SI 2003/2279 Reg.4

Sch.5 para.71, revoked: SI 2004/565 Reg.3

Sch.5 para.72, added: SI 2003/2439 Reg.14

Sch.5 para.72, revoked: SI 2004/565 Reg.3

Sch.5A Part I para.1, revoked: SI 2004/14 Reg.23

Sch.5A Part I para.1A, added: SI 2004/14 Reg.23

Sch.5A Part I para.2, amended: SI 2004/14 Reg.23

Sch.5A Part I para.2, revoked (in part): SI 2004/14 Reg.23

Sch.5A Part I para.3, amended: SI 2004/14 Reg.23

Sch.5A Part II para.4, amended: SI 2004/14 Reg.23

Sch.5A Part II para.6, amended: SI 2004/14 Reg.23

Sch.5A Part II para.8, amended: SI 2004/14 Reg.23

Sch.5A Part IV para.12, amended: SI 2003/1589 Reg.3, SI 2004/14 Reg.23, SI 2004/781 Reg.4

Sch.5B para.1, added: SI 2004/319 Sch.1

Sch.5B para.2, added: SI 2004/319 Sch.1

Sch.5B para.3, added: SI 2004/319 Sch.1

Sch.5B para.4, added: SI 2004/319 Sch.1

Sch.5B para.5, added: SI 2004/319 Sch.1

Sch.5B para.6, added: SI 2004/319 Sch.1

Sch.5B para.7, added: SI 2004/319 Sch.1

Sch.5B para.8, added: SI 2004/319 Sch.1

Sch.5B para.9, added: SI 2004/319 Sch.1

Sch.5B para.10, added: SI 2004/319 Sch.1

Sch.5ZA Part I para.1, added: SI 2003/325 Sch.2 Part III

Sch.5ZA Part I para.2, added: SI 2003/325 Sch.2 Part III

Sch.5ZA Part I para.3, added: SI 2003/325 Sch.2 Part III

Sch.5ZA Part I para.4, added: SI 2003/325 Sch.2 Part III

Sch.5ZA Part I para.4, amended: SI 2004/2327 Reg.2

Sch.5ZA Part I para.5, added: SI 2003/325 Sch.2 Part III

Sch.5ZA Part I para.6, added: SI 2003/325 Sch.2 Part III

NO.

NO.

1987–cont.

1971. Housing Benefit (General) Regulations 1987–*cont.*

Sch.5ZA Part I para.6, revoked (in part): SI 2003/325 Sch.2 Part III

Sch.5ZA Part I para.7, added: SI 2003/325 Sch.2 Part III

Sch.5ZA Part I para.8, added: SI 2003/325 Sch.2 Part III

Sch.5ZA Part I para.9, added: SI 2003/325 Sch.2 Part III

Sch.5ZA Part I para.10, added: SI 2003/325 Sch.2 Part III

Sch.5ZA Part I para.11, added: SI 2003/325 Sch.2 Part III

Sch.5ZA Part I para.12, added: SI 2003/325 Sch.2 Part III

Sch.5ZA Part I para.13, added: SI 2003/325 Sch.2 Part III

Sch.5ZA Part I para.14, added: SI 2003/325 Sch.2 Part III

Sch.5ZA Part I para.14, revoked (in part): SI 2003/325 Sch.2 Part III

Sch.5ZA Part I para.15, added: SI 2003/325 Sch.2 Part III

Sch.5ZA Part I para.16, added: SI 2003/325 Sch.2 Part III

Sch.5ZA Part I para.16, amended: SI 2004/1141 Reg.3

Sch.5ZA Part I para.17, added: SI 2003/325 Sch.2 Part III

Sch.5ZA Part I para.17, amended: SI 2003/325 Sch.2 Part III

Sch.5ZA Part I para.18, added: SI 2003/325 Sch.2 Part III

Sch.5ZA Part I para.19, added: SI 2003/325 Sch.2 Part III

Sch.5ZA Part I para.20, added: SI 2003/325 Sch.2 Part III

Sch.5ZA Part I para.21, added: SI 2003/325 Sch.2 Part III

Sch.5ZA Part I para.21, amended: SI 2003/325 Sch.2 Part III

Sch.5ZA Part I para.21, revoked (in part): SI 2003/325 Sch.2 Part III

Sch.5ZA Part I para.21A, added: SI 2003/325 Sch.2 Part III

Sch.5ZA Part I para.21A, applied: SI 2002/1792 Sch.5 para.20A

Sch.5ZA Part I para.22, added: SI 2003/325 Sch.2 Part III

Sch.5ZA Part I para.23, added: SI 2003/325 Sch.2 Part III

Sch.5ZA Part I para.24, added: SI 2003/325 Sch.2 Part III

Sch.5ZA Part I para.25, added: SI 2003/325 Sch.2 Part III

Sch.5ZA Part I para.25A, added: SI 2003/325 Sch.2 Part III

Sch.5ZA Part II para.26, added: SI 2003/325 Sch.2 Part III

1987–cont.

1971. Housing Benefit (General) Regulations 1987–*cont.*

Sch.5ZA Part II para.27, added: SI 2003/325 Sch.2 Part III

Sch.5ZA Part II para.28, added: SI 2003/325 Sch.2 Part III

Sch.5ZA Part II para.29, added: SI 2003/325 Sch.2 Part III

Sch.5ZA Part II para.29, revoked (in part): SI 2003/325 Sch.2 Part III

Sch.5ZA Part II para.30, added: SI 2003/325 Sch.2 Part III

Sch.6 Part II para.9, amended: SI 2003/325 Reg.25

Sch.6 Part II para.9, revoked (in part): SI 2003/1338 Reg.18, SI 2004/14 Reg.24

Sch.6 Part VII para.14, amended: SI 2004/14 Reg.24

Sch.6 para.14, see *Godwin v Rossendale BC* [2002] EWCA Civ 726, [2003] H.L.R. 9 (CA), Peter Gibson, L.J.

Sch.7, see *R. (on the application of Bono) v Harlow DC* [2002] EWHC 423, [2002] 1 W.L.R. 2475 (QBD (Admin Ct)), Richards, J.

Sch.8, added: SI 2003/2399 Sch.2

1973. Family Credit (General) Regulations 1987

Part VI, applied: SI 2002/1334 Reg.2

Reg.2, amended: SI 2002/1696 Reg.4, SI 2002/2469 Reg.11, SI 2003/44 Reg.8

Reg.2A, amended: SI 2002/1696 Reg.5

Reg.3, amended: SI 2002/1696 Reg.6

Reg.4, amended: SI 2003/44 Reg.9

Reg.14, amended: SI 2002/1696 Reg.7

Reg.19, amended: SI 2003/44 Reg.10

Reg.20, amended: SI 2002/1696 Reg.8

Reg.38, amended: SI 2002/1333 Reg.3, Reg.4

Reg.42A, amended: SI 2002/1333 Reg.3, Reg.4

Reg.46, amended: SI 2002/1333 Reg.5

Reg.46A, amended: SI 2002/14 Reg.3, SI 2002/525 Reg.3, SI 2002/1696 Reg.9, SI 2003/44 Reg.11

Reg.46A, revoked (in part): SI 2003/44 Reg.11

Reg.47, amended: SI 2002/829 Art.3

Sch.2 para.14, amended: SI 2002/525 Reg.5

Sch.2 para.24, amended: SI 2002/2469 Reg.8

Sch.2 para.25, amended: SI 2002/14 Reg.4

Sch.2 para.27A, added: SI 2003/44 Reg.12

Sch.2 para.52, amended: SI 2002/525 Reg.6

Sch.2 para.53, amended: SI 2002/525 Reg.6

Sch.2 para.54, amended: SI 2002/525 Reg.6, Reg.7

Sch.2 para.57, amended: SI 2003/762 Reg.11, SI 2004/1748 Sch.2 para.2

Sch.3 para.18, amended: SI 2002/14 Reg.5

Sch.4, amended: SI 2002/1333 Reg.6

NO.

1987–cont.

1973. Family Credit (General) Regulations 1987–*cont.*

Sch.4, substituted: SI 2002/829 Sch.1

1984. South Tynedale Railway (Light Railway) Order 1987

Art.7, amended: SI 2003/2155 Sch.1 para.18

2023. Insolvent Companies (Disqualification of Unfit Directors) Proceedings Rules 1987

r.1, amended: SI 2003/1367 Sch.1 para.1

r.4, amended: SI 2003/1367 Sch.1 para.2

2024. Non-Contentious Probate Rules 1987

r.2, amended: SI 2004/2985 r.2

r.60, substituted: SI 2003/185 r.5

r.61, see *CI v NS* [2004] EWHC 659, [2004] W.T.L.R. 1113 (Fam Div), Baron, J

r.65, amended: SI 2003/185 r.6

2045. Suppression of Terrorism Act 1978 (Hong Kong) Order 1987

Sch.1, amended: 2002 c.8 s.2

2049. Consumer Protection (Northern Ireland) Order 1987

applied: 2002 c.40 Sch.14, Sch.15, SI 2003/419 Art.63

referred to: 2003 c.21 s.393, SI 2003/750 Sch.5 para.12, SI 2003/751 Sch.6 para.12, SI 2004/1468 Sch.6 para.12

Part III, applied: SI 2003/1593 Sch.1 Part II

Art.29, amended: 2003 c.21 Sch.17 para.87

Art.29, revoked: SI 2003/1400 Sch.5

2085. Road Vehicles (Prescribed Regulations for the Purposes of Increased Penalties) Regulations 1987

revoked: SI 2002/2742 Sch.1 Part I

2088. Registration of Births and Deaths Regulations 1987

Reg.9, amended: SI 2003/3048 Reg.2

Reg.10, amended: SI 2003/3048 Reg.3

Reg.13, amended: SI 2003/3048 Reg.4

Reg.17, amended: SI 2003/3048 Reg.5

Reg.34A, amended: SI 2003/3048 Reg.6

2089. Registration of Births and Deaths (Welsh Language) Regulations 1987

Sch.3, amended: SI 2003/3048 Reg.7

2115. Control of Asbestos at Work Regulations 1987

applied: SI 2002/655 Reg.3, Reg.7

revoked: SI 2002/2675 Reg.27

2117. Consumer Protection (Cancellation of Contracts Concluded away from Business Premises) Regulations 1987

applied: SI 2003/1376 Sch.1, SI 2003/1400 Sch.3, Sch.4

referred to: SI 2003/1374 Sch.1

Reg.3, varied: SI 2003/1633 Sch.2 para.8

Reg.4G, revoked: SI 2003/1400 Sch.5

2122. Road Vehicles (Excise) (Prescribed Particulars) (Amendment) Regulations 1987

revoked: SI 2002/2742 Sch.1 Part I

NO.

1987–cont.

2123. Road Vehicles (Registration and Licensing) (Amendment) Regulations 1987

revoked: SI 2002/2742 Sch.1 Part I

2161. Motor Vehicles (Authorisation of Special Types) (Amendment) (No.2) Order 1987

revoked: SI 2003/1998 Art.2

2174. General Medical Council Health Committee (Procedure) Rules 1987

r.24, see *Brocklebank v General Medical Council* [2003] UKPC 57, (2004) 79 B.M.L.R. 122 (PC (UK)), Lord Hoffmann

2174. General Medical Council Health Committee (Procedure) Rules Order of Council 1987

applied: SI 2003/1340 Art.3

Appendix 1 r.24, see *Anjaneyulu v General Medical Council* [2001] UKPC 60, (2003) 69 B.M.L.R. 1 (PC (UK)), Sir Martin Nourse

Appendix 1., added: SI 2003/1343 Sch.1

Appendix 1., amended: SI 2002/2572 Sch.1 para.4, SI 2003/1343 Sch.1

Appendix 1., revoked: SI 2002/2572 Sch.1 para.4, SI 2003/1343 Sch.1

Appendix 1., substituted: SI 2002/2572 Sch.1 para.4, SI 2003/1343 Sch.1

Appendix 1., varied: SI 2003/1340 Art.3

2197. Civil Jurisdiction (Offshore Activities) Order 1987

Art.1, applied: SI 2002/655 Reg.22, SI 2003/547 Reg.22, SI 2004/352 Sch.1 para.21, SI 2004/456 Reg.21

Art.1, referred to: SI 2004/352 Sch.2 para.33, Sch.2 para.34, Sch.2 para.39, Sch.3 para.34, Sch.3 para.35, Sch.3 para.40, Sch.4 para.32, Sch.4 para.33, Sch.4 para.38

2201. Foreign Compensation (People's Republic of China) Order 1987

Art.14, amended: 2002 c.8 s.2

Art.21, amended: 2002 c.8 s.2

2203. Adoption (Northern Ireland) Order 1987

referred to: SI 2003/431 Sch.3 para.2, SR 2003/16 Reg.32

Art.2, amended: SI 2003/431 Sch.4, Sch.5

Art.3, amended: SI 2003/431 Sch.4

Art.4, applied: SI 2003/431 Sch.3 para.2

Art.4, revoked: SI 2003/431 Sch.5

Art.5, amended: SI 2003/431 Sch.4, Sch.5

Art.5, revoked (in part): SI 2003/431 Sch.5

Art.6, revoked: SI 2003/431 Sch.5

Art.7, revoked: SI 2003/431 Sch.5

Art.8, amended: SI 2003/431 Sch.4

Art.9, applied: SR 2003/16 Reg.24, Reg.27

Art.10, amended: SI 2003/431 Sch.4

Art.10, applied: SI 2003/431 Art.15, Art.40

Art.10, enabled: SR 2002/144, SR 2003/16

Art.11, amended: SI 2003/431 Sch.4

Art.12, varied: SR 2003/16 Sch.3

NO.

1987–cont.

2203. Adoption (Northern Ireland) Order 1987–*cont.*
Art.14, applied: SR 2003/16 Reg.26
Art.15, amended: 2003 c.24 Sch.1 para.12
Art.15, applied: SR 2003/16 Reg.4, Reg.26
Art.16, see *N, K, T and TM (Adoption: Requirement to Dispense with Parental Consent), Re* [2002] N.I. 108 (Fam Div (NI)), Gillen, J.
Art.16, varied: SR 2003/16 Sch.3
Art.16A, applied: SR 2003/16 Reg.19, Reg.30, Reg.35
Art.16A, enabled: SR 2003/16
Art.17, applied: SI 2003/118 Reg.25, Reg.27, Reg.32, SR 2003/16 Reg.23, Reg.25, Reg.30, SSI 2003/19 Reg.22, Reg.24, Reg.30
Art.18, see *J (Freeing for Adoption: Adoption Agencies: Procedural Requirements), Re* [2004] N.I. 10 (Fam Div (NI)), Gillen, J.; see *N, K, T and TM (Adoption: Requirement to Dispense with Parental Consent), Re* [2002] N.I. 108 (Fam Div (NI)), Gillen, J.
Art.18, applied: SI 2003/118 Reg.25, Reg.27, Reg.32, SR 2003/16 Reg.23, Reg.25, Reg.30, SSI 2003/19 Reg.22, Reg.24, Reg.30
Art.22, applied: SR 2002/144 Reg.3, SR 2003/16 Reg.13
Art.22, varied: SR 2003/16 Sch.3
Art.23, amended: SI 2003/431 Sch.4
Art.28, varied: SR 2003/16 Sch.3
Art.31, applied: SR 2002/377 Reg.22, SR 2002/378 Reg.22
Art.31, varied: SR 2003/16 Sch.3
Art.32, varied: SR 2003/16 Sch.3
Art.33, amended: SI 2003/431 Sch.4
Art.53, applied: SR 2003/255 Art.5
Art.53, enabled: SR 2003/255
Art.54, amended: SI 2003/431 Sch.4
Art.55A, applied: SR 2003/16 Reg.17, Reg.22
Art.58ZA, enabled: SR 2002/144
Art.59A, applied: SI 2002/2006 Reg.19, SR 2002/224 Reg.16, Sch.3 para.1, SR 2002/265 Sch.7 para.1
Art.63, applied: 2002 c.38 s.107
Sch.1, revoked: SI 2003/431 Sch.5

2215. Police Pensions (Purchase of Increased Benefits) Regulations 1987
Reg.3, amended: SI 2002/3202 Reg.3
Reg.8, amended: SI 2004/2354 Reg.3
Sch.1 Part I para.3, amended: SI 2004/2354 Reg.3

1988

1. Origin of Goods (Petroleum Products) Regulations 1988
revoked: SI 2002/2266 Reg.2

NO.

1988–cont.

24. Civil Procedure Rules 1988
see *Andrew Weir Shipping Ltd v Wartsila UK Ltd* [2004] EWHC 1284, [2004] 2 Lloyd's Rep. 377 (QBD (Comm Ct)), Cooke, J.

31. Fire Services (Appointments and Promotion) (Amendment) Regulations 1988
revoked: SI 2004/481 Sch.2

35. Social Fund (Recovery by Deductions from Benefits) Regulations 1988
Reg.3, amended: SI 2002/2497 Sch.2 para.1, SI 2002/3019 Reg.31, SI 2003/1589 Reg.6
Reg.3, revoked (in part): SI 2003/937 Reg.2

38. Fishing Vessels (Life-Saving Appliances) Regulations 1988
Reg.2, amended: SI 2002/2201 Sch.1 para.48
Reg.5, amended: SI 2002/2201 Sch.1 para.49
Reg.5A, revoked: SI 2002/2201 Sch.1 para.51
Reg.5B, amended: SI 2002/2201 Sch.1 para.50
Reg.5C, amended: SI 2002/2201 Sch.1 para.52

47. Wireless Telegraphy (Content of Transmission) Regulations 1988
Reg.2, amended: SI 2003/2155 Sch.2
Reg.4, amended: SI 2003/2155 Sch.1 para.28

93. Department of Trade and Industry (Fees) Order 1988
Art.7, referred to: SI 2004/2358

95. Insolvency Fees (Amendment) Order 1988
revoked (in part): SI 2004/593 Sch.1

120. Capacity Serving Measures (Intoxicating Liquor) Regulations 1988
Reg.17A, amended: SI 2003/214 Sch.1 para.4

186. Measuring Instruments (EEC Requirements) Regulations 1988
applied: SR 2002/309 Reg.5
Reg.3, applied: SR 2002/309 Reg.4
Reg.8, applied: SI 2004/1300 Reg.5
Reg.13, applied: SI 2004/1300 Reg.4, SR 2002/309 Reg.4
Reg.23, referred to: SR 2002/309 Sch.1
Reg.24, referred to: SR 2002/309 Sch.1
Sch.2, applied: SI 2004/1300 Reg.5
Sch.3, applied: SI 2004/1300 Reg.4

247. Turks and Caicos Islands Constitution Order 1988
referred to: SI 2002/2637 Art.1
Sch.2, amended: SI 2002/2637 Art.2
Sch.2, revoked (in part): SI 2002/2637 Art.3

311. Misuse of Drugs (Licence Fees) (Amendment) Regulations 1988
revoked: SI 2003/611 Sch.1

329. Magistrates Courts (Family Law Act 1986) Rules 1988
r.2, amended: 2002 c.8 s.1

NO.

1988–cont.

333. Bingo Duty Regulations 1988
revoked: SI 2003/2503 Reg.3

370. International Carriage of Dangerous Goods by Road (Fees) Regulations 1988
Reg.3, amended: SI 2002/537 Reg.2, SI 2003/1811 Reg.2, SI 2004/1884 Reg.2
Reg.4, amended: SI 2002/537 Reg.2, SI 2003/1811 Reg.2, SI 2004/1884 Reg.2
Reg.5, amended: SI 2002/537 Reg.2, SI 2003/1811 Reg.2, SI 2004/1884 Reg.2
Reg.6, amended: SI 2002/537 Reg.2
Reg.8, amended: SI 2002/537 Reg.2, SI 2003/1811 Reg.3

371. International Transport of Goods under Cover of TIR Carnets (Fees) Regulations 1988
Reg.3, amended: SI 2002/539 Reg.2, SI 2003/1813 Reg.2, SI 2004/1911 Reg.2
Reg.4, amended: SI 2002/539 Reg.2
Reg.5, amended: SI 2002/539 Reg.2, SI 2003/1813 Reg.2, SI 2004/1911 Reg.2

390. Salmon (Weekly Close Time) (Scotland) Regulations 1988
applied: SSI 2002/138 Sch.2 para.1, SSI 2003/615 Sch.2 para.1

522. Social Security (Claims and Payments) Amendment Regulations 1988
revoked (in part): SI 2003/492 Sch.3 Part 1

524. Social Fund (Applications) Regulations 1988
Reg.2, amended: SI 2002/2323 Reg.2
Reg.2A, added: SI 2002/2323 Reg.2
Reg.3, amended: SI 2002/2323 Reg.2

546. National Health Service (Travelling Expenses and Remission of Charges) (Scotland) Regulations 1988
applied: SSI 2003/64 Sch.1 para.8, SSI 2003/376 Reg.13
revoked: SSI 2003/376 Sch.3 para.1
Reg.3, applied: SI 2002/2006 Reg.19
Reg.5, applied: SI 2002/2006 Reg.19
Reg.8, applied: SI 2002/2006 Reg.19

551. National Health Service (Travelling Expenses and Remission of Charges) Regulations 1988
applied: SI 2003/2382 Reg.18
revoked (in part): SI 2003/2382 Sch.2
Reg.2, amended: SI 2002/2353 Reg.2, SI 2003/671 Reg.2, SI 2003/975 Reg.2, SI 2003/2561 Reg.2, SI 2004/871 Reg.2
Reg.3, amended: SI 2002/2353 Reg.3, SI 2003/975 Reg.3
Reg.3, applied: SI 2002/2006 Reg.19, SI 2003/671 Reg.6
Reg.3A, added: SI 2003/975 Reg.4
Reg.4, amended: SI 2003/671 Reg.3, SI 2003/975 Reg.5, SI 2003/2561 Reg.3, SI 2004/871 Reg.3, SI 2004/1042 Reg.2

NO.

1988–cont.

551. National Health Service (Travelling Expenses and Remission of Charges) Regulations 1988–cont.
Reg.4, applied: SI 2003/975 Reg.14, SI 2004/1042 Reg.5
Reg.4, referred to: SI 2003/671 Reg.6
Reg.4, revoked (in part): SI 2003/671 Reg.3, SI 2003/975 Reg.5
Reg.4, substituted: SI 2003/975 Reg.5
Reg.5, applied: SI 2002/2006 Reg.19
Reg.5A, amended: SI 2003/975 Reg.6
Reg.7, amended: SI 2003/975 Reg.7, SI 2003/2561 Reg.4
Reg.7, revoked (in part): SI 2003/2561 Reg.4
Reg.7A, added: SI 2003/975 Reg.8
Reg.7B, added: SI 2003/975 Reg.9
Reg.7ZA, added: SI 2003/671 Reg.4
Reg.7ZA, revoked (in part): SI 2003/2561 Reg.5
Reg.8, amended: SI 2002/2353 Reg.4, SI 2003/975 Reg.10
Reg.8, applied: SI 2002/2006 Reg.19
Reg.8A, amended: SI 2003/975 Reg.11
Reg.8A, revoked: SI 2002/2353 Reg.5
Reg.8A, substituted: SI 2002/2353 Reg.5
Sch.1A, amended: SI 2003/975 Reg.13
Sch.1A, revoked (in part): SI 2003/2561 Reg.8
Sch.1 Part I para.2, added: SI 2002/2353 Reg.6
Sch.1 Part I para.2, amended: SI 2002/580 Reg.3, SI 2003/671 Reg.5, SI 2003/975 Reg.12, SI 2003/2561 Reg.6, SI 2004/871 Reg.4
Sch.1 Part II para.4, amended: SI 2003/2561 Reg.7

590. Social Security (Sweden) Order 1988
Sch.1, amended: 2002 c.8 s.2

594. Social Security (Northern Ireland) Order 1988
Art.13, enabled: SR 2002/83, SR 2003/202
Art.13, substituted: SI 2003/3202 Art.3
Art.15A, amended: SI 2003/3202 Art.3

643. Department of Transport (Fees) Order 1988
applied: SI 2002/487, SI 2002/488, SI 2002/489, SI 2002/538, SI 2002/539, SI 2002/1698, SI 2003/1698, SI 2003/1815, SI 2003/1816, SI 2003/1817, SI 2004/1632, SI 2004/1873, SI 2004/1879, SI 2004/1880, SI 2004/1884, SI 2004/1885, SI 2004/1911
enabled: SI 2002/537, SI 2003/1811, SI 2003/1812, SI 2003/1813, SI 2003/1960, SI 2003/2258, SI 2004/2106
Sch.1, added: SI 2003/1094 Sch.1, Sch.2
Sch.1, amended: SI 2003/1094 Sch.1, SI 2003/2994 Art.4
Sch.1, substituted: SI 2003/1094 Sch.1

NO.

1988–cont.

662. **Housing Benefit (Supply of Information) Regulations 1988**
amended: SI 2002/1397 Sch.1 para.20
Reg.1, amended: SI 2002/1397 Sch.1 para.20
Reg.5, amended: SI 2004/14 Reg.29
Reg.5, revoked (in part): SI 2003/1589 Reg.7, SI 2004/14 Reg.29
Reg.6, added: SI 2004/574 Reg.3

664. **Social Security (Payments on account, Overpayments and Recovery) Regulations 1988**
revoked (in part): SI 2003/492 Sch.3 Part 1
Reg.1, amended: SI 2002/3019 Reg.24
Reg.5, amended: SI 2002/3019 Reg.24
Reg.7, amended: SI 2002/3019 Reg.24
Reg.8, amended: SI 2002/3019 Reg.24
Reg.13, amended: SI 2002/3019 Reg.24
Reg.14, amended: SI 2002/3019 Reg.24
Reg.15, amended: SI 2002/3019 Reg.24
Reg.16, amended: SI 2002/2441 Reg.14, SI 2002/3019 Reg.24
Reg.17, amended: SI 2002/3019 Reg.24

668. **Pneumoconiosis etc (Workers Compensation) (Payment of Claims) Regulations 1988**
Reg.5, amended: SI 2004/726 Reg.2
Reg.6, amended: SI 2004/726 Reg.2
Reg.8, amended: SI 2004/726 Reg.2
Sch.1, referred to: SI 2004/726 Reg.2
Sch.1 Part 1, substituted: SI 2004/726 Sch.1
Sch.1 Part 2, substituted: SI 2004/726 Sch.1

688. **Social Security (Payments on account, Overpayments and Recovery) Amendment Regulations 1988**
revoked (in part): SI 2003/492 Sch.3 Part 1

725. **Kinneil and Manuel Light Railway Order 1988**
Art.7, amended: SI 2003/2155 Sch.1 para.18

784. **Veterinary Surgeons (Agreement with the Republic of Ireland) Order 1988**
applied: SI 2003/3342 Sch.1

788. **Merchant Shipping (Prevention of Oil Pollution) (Bermuda) Order 1988**
revoked: SI 2002/3147 Art.2

795. **General Assistance Grants (Abolition)(Northern Ireland) Order 1988**
revoked: 2002 c.1 (NI) Sch.4

809. **Excise Warehousing (Etc.) Regulations 1988**
referred to: SI 2004/1003 Reg.7
Reg.10A, added: SI 2002/501 Reg.27
Reg.17, amended: SI 2002/501 Reg.27
Sch.2, amended: SI 2002/1265 Reg.3
Sch.4, amended: SI 2002/501 Sch.1, SI 2002/1265 Reg.3

835. **Stamp Duty Reserve Tax (Amendment) Regulations 1988**
varied: 2002 c.23 Sch.34 para.7, Sch.35 para.8

NO.

1988–cont.

847. **Road Vehicles (Excise) (Prescribed Particulars) (Amendment) Regulations 1988**
revoked: SI 2002/2742 Sch.1 Part I

865. **National Health Service (Payment of Remuneration Special Arrangement) Order 1988**
Art.2, amended: SI 2002/2469 Sch.1 para.45, SI 2002/2861 Reg.28

896. **Pressure Vessels (Verification) Regulations 1988**
revoked: SI 2004/568 Sch.14

915. **Control of Misleading Advertisements Regulations 1988**
applied: SI 2003/419 Art.63, SI 2003/1400 Sch.3, Sch.4, SI 2003/1593 Sch.1 Part I, SI 2004/1975 Art.6, Art.8
referred to: 2003 c.21 s.393, SI 2003/3183 Reg.2
Reg.1, referred to: SI 2003/1374 Sch.1
Reg.2, amended: SI 2003/3183 Sch.1 para.1
Reg.2, referred to: SI 2003/1374 Sch.1
Reg.3, referred to: SI 2003/1374 Sch.1
Reg.4, amended: SI 2003/3183 Sch.1 para.2
Reg.4, referred to: SI 2003/1374 Sch.1
Reg.5, referred to: SI 2003/1374 Sch.1
Reg.6, referred to: SI 2003/1374 Sch.1
Reg.7, referred to: SI 2003/1374 Sch.1
Reg.7, revoked (in part): 2002 c.40 Sch.26, SI 2003/1400 Sch.5
Reg.8, amended: SI 2003/3183 Sch.1 para.3
Reg.8, referred to: SI 2003/1374 Sch.1
Reg.8, revoked (in part): SI 2003/3183 Sch.1 para.3
Reg.9, amended: SI 2003/3183 Sch.1 para.4
Reg.9, referred to: SI 2003/1374 Sch.1
Reg.10, amended: SI 2003/3183 Sch.1 para.5
Reg.10, referred to: SI 2003/1374 Sch.1
Reg.10, revoked (in part): SI 2003/3183 Sch.1 para.5
Reg.11, amended: SI 2003/3183 Sch.1 para.6
Reg.11, referred to: SI 2003/1374 Sch.1

926. **European Committee for the Prevention of Torture and Inhuman or Degrading Treatment or Punishment (Immunities and Privileges) Order 1988**
Art.2, amended: 2002 c.8 s.2

997. **Measuring Equipment (Cold-water Meters) Regulations 1988**
Reg.7A, amended: SI 2003/214 Sch.1 para.5

1010. **Merchant Shipping Act 1988 (Commencement No 1) Order 1988**
Sch.1, amended: 2002 c.8 s.1

1040. **Gloucester Harbour Revision Order 1988**
Art.10, revoked: SI 2002/3268 Sch.3

1057. **Electricity Supply Regulations 1988**
applied: SI 2002/2665 Reg.2
revoked: SI 2002/2665 Sch.5

1988–cont.

1099. Ministry of Defence Police (Representation at Disciplinary Proceedings) Regulations 1988

revoked: SI 2004/653 Reg.1

1199. Town and Country Planning (Assessment of Environmental Effects) Regulations 1988

see *Gillespie v First Secretary of State* [2003] EWHC 8, [2003] 1 P. & C.R. 30 (QBD (Admin Ct)), Richards, J.; see *R. (on the application of Barker) v Bromley LBC* [2001] EWCA Civ 1766, [2002] Env. L.R. 25 (CA), Latham, L.J.; see *R. (on the application of Goodman) v Lewisham LBC* [2002] EWHC 1769, [2003] Env. L.R. 16 (QBD (Admin Ct)), Sir Richard Tucker

see *Gillespie v First Secretary of State* [2003] EWCA Civ 400, [2003] Env. L.R. 30 (CA), Pill, L.J.

Reg.2, see *R. (on the application of Jones) v Mansfield DC* [2003] EWHC 7, [2003] Env. L.R. 26 (QBD (Admin Ct)), Richards, J.

Reg.4, see *R. (on the application of Burkett) v Hammersmith and Fulham LBC (No.2)* [2003] EWHC 1031, [2004] Env. L.R. 3 (QBD (Admin Ct)), Newman, J.; see *R. (on the application of Elmbridge BC) v Secretary of State for the Environment, Transport and the Regions* [2002] Env. L.R. 1 (QBD (Admin Ct)), Richards, J.; see *R. (on the application of Jones) v Mansfield DC* [2003] EWCA Civ 1408, [2004] Env. L.R. 21 (CA), Laws, L.J.; see *R. (on the application of Jones) v Mansfield DC* [2003] EWHC 7, [2003] Env. L.R. 26 (QBD (Admin Ct)), Richards, J.; see *Smith v Secretary of State for the Environment, Transport and Regions* [2003] EWCA Civ 262, [2003] Env. L.R. 32 (CA), Waller, L.J.

Reg.25, see *R. (on the application of Elmbridge BC) v Secretary of State for the Environment, Transport and the Regions* [2002] Env. L.R. 1 (QBD (Admin Ct)), Richards, J.

Sch.3, see *R. (on the application of Burkett) v Hammersmith and Fulham LBC (No.2)* [2003] EWHC 1031, [2004] Env. L.R. 3 (QBD (Admin Ct)), Newman, J.

1227. Child Benefit (General) Amendment Regulations 1988

revoked: SI 2003/493 Sch.2 Part 1

1285. Service Charge (Estimates and Consultation) Order 1988

applied: SI 2004/669 Art.2

referred to: SI 2003/1986 Art.3

1291. Farm Woodland Scheme 1988

applied: SSI 2004/381 Reg.4

Art.14, applied: SSI 2004/381 Reg.4

1296. Antarctic Treaty (Agreed Measures) (No.2) Order 1988

Art.3, amended: 2002 c.8 s.2

1988–cont.

1298. EUMETSAT (Immunities and Privileges) Order 1988

Art.2, amended: 2002 c.8 s.2

1299. EUTELSAT (Immunities and Privileges) Order 1988

Art.2, amended: 2002 c.8 s.2

1334. Companies (Disclosure of Information) (Designated Authorities) Order 1988

Art.2, amended: SI 2003/1398 Sch.1 para.7

1362. Fire Services (Appointments and Promotion) (Amendment) (No.2) Regulations 1988

revoked: SI 2004/481 Sch.2

1395. Royal Marines Terms of Service Regulations 1988

Reg.4, amended: SI 2002/201 Reg.2

Reg.11, amended: SI 2002/201 Reg.2

1478. Goods Vehicles (Plating and Testing) Regulations 1988

referred to: SI 2003/1816 Reg.2

Reg.8, amended: SI 2003/1816 Reg.4

Reg.12, amended: SI 2002/487 Reg.3, SI 2003/1816 Reg.3, SI 2004/1873 Reg.3, Reg.5

Reg.16, amended: SI 2002/487 Reg.3, Reg.4, SI 2003/1816 Reg.3, Reg.5, SI 2004/1873 Reg.4, Reg.5

Reg.34, amended: SI 2002/487 Reg.3, SI 2003/1816 Reg.3, SI 2004/1873 Reg.5

Reg.37B, amended: SI 2002/487 Reg.3, SI 2003/1816 Reg.3, SI 2004/1873 Reg.5

Reg.39, amended: SI 2002/487 Reg.3, SI 2003/1816 Reg.6

Reg.41, amended: SI 2002/487 Reg.3

Sch.2 para.25, amended: SI 2002/487 Reg.5

Sch.2 para.31, amended: SI 2003/1816 Reg.7

Sch.3i Part II para.4, amended: SI 2004/1873 Reg.6

1496. Teignmouth (Pilotage) Harbour Revision Order 1988

referred to: SI 2003/2574 Art.1

1501. Police (Scotland) Amendment Regulations 1988

revoked: SSI 2004/257 Sch.4

1546. Public Health (Infectious Diseases) Regulations 1988

Reg.2, amended: SI 2002/2469 Sch.1 para.46, Sch.11

Reg.6, amended: SI 2002/2469 Sch.1 para.46

Reg.8, amended: SI 2002/2469 Sch.1 para.46

1567. Agricultural or Forestry Tractors and Tractor Components (Type Approval) Regulations 1988

Reg.6, amended: SI 2002/1890 Reg.2

1655. Docks Regulations 1988

referred to: SI 2003/2002 Reg.12

NO.

NO.

1988–cont.

1988–cont.

1657. Control of Substances Hazardous to Health Regulations 1988

Reg.7, see *Dugmore v Swansea NHS Trust* [2002] EWCA Civ 1689, [2003] 1 All E.R. 333 (CA), Hale, L.J.

1701. Magistrates Courts (Notices of Transfer) Rules 1988

r.2, substituted: SI 2003/1236 r.51

r.7, amended: SI 2003/1236 r.52

r.7, revoked (in part): SI 2003/1236 r.52

r.8, revoked: SI 2003/1236 r.53

Sch.1, revoked: SI 2003/1236 r.53

1724. Social Fund Cold Weather Payments (General) Regulations 1988

Reg.1A, amended: SI 2002/3019 Reg.31, SI 2003/1121 Reg.3, SI 2004/2600 Reg.2

Sch.1, amended: SI 2002/2524 Sch.1, SI 2003/3023 Reg.2

Sch.1, substituted: SI 2003/2605 Sch.1, SI 2004/2600 Sch.1

Sch.2, substituted: SI 2003/2605 Sch.2

Sch.2 para.1, substituted: SI 2003/2605 Sch.2

Sch.2 para.2, substituted: SI 2003/2605 Sch.2

1725. Social Security (Common Provisions) Miscellaneous Amendment Regulations 1988

Reg.1, amended: SI 2003/492 Sch.3 Part 1

Reg.3, revoked (in part): SI 2003/492 Sch.3 Part 1

Reg.4, revoked (in part): SI 2003/492 Sch.3 Part 1

Reg.4, varied: SI 2003/492 Sch.3 Part 1

1729. Mines (Safety of Exit) Regulations 1988

Reg.6, see *Young v Scottish Coal (Deep Mining) Co Ltd* 2002 S.L.T. 1215 (OH), Lord Mackay of Drumadoon

1807. Safety of Places of Sport Regulations 1988

Reg.4, amended: SI 2004/3168 Art.16

Sch.1, amended: SI 2004/3168 Art.16

1812. Town and Country Planning (Applications) Regulations 1988

referred to: SI 2003/956 Art.13

Reg.2, amended: SI 2003/956 Sch.5 para.1

Reg.3, amended: SI 2003/956 Sch.5 para.2

Reg.5, added: SI 2003/956 Sch.5 para.3

1845. Criminal Justice (Firearms) (Northern Ireland) Order 1988

revoked: SI 2004/702 Sch.8

1846. Criminal Justice (Serious Fraud) (Northern Ireland) Order 1988

Art.3, amended: SI 2003/435 Sch.4 para.9

Art.6, amended: 2003 c.44 Sch.36 para.57

Art.7, applied: SI 2003/1247 Art.13

Art.8, amended: 2003 c.44 Sch.36 para.58

Art.8, revoked (in part): 2003 c.44 Sch.36 para.19, Sch.37 Part 3

1846. Criminal Justice (Serious Fraud) (Northern Ireland) Order 1988–cont.

Art.9, amended: 2003 c.44 Sch.36 para.59, Sch.36 para.60

Art.10, amended: SI 2003/435 Sch.4 para.9

Sch.1, revoked (in part): SI 2003/435 Sch.5, Sch.5

1847. Criminal Justice (Evidence etc.) (Northern Ireland) Order 1988

referred to: 2003 c.32 Sch.5 para.38

Part II, revoked: SI 2004/1501 Art.38, Sch.2

Art.4, amended: 2003 c.32 Sch.5 para.39

Art.5, applied: 2003 c.32 s.9

Art.5, see *R. v Singleton (Geoffrey)* [2004] N.I. 71 (CA (Crim Div) (NI)), Lord Carswell L.C.J.

Art.6, amended: 2003 c.32 Sch.5 para.40

Art.6, see *R. v Singleton (Geoffrey)* [2004] N.I. 71 (CA (Crim Div) (NI)), Lord Carswell L.C.J.

Art.15, applied: SI 2002/635 Sch.1 para.3, SI 2002/896 Sch.1 para.73, 2003 c.44 Sch.17 para.89, SSI 2003/19 Sch.5 para.16

Art.15, referred to: SI 2003/237 Sch.4 para.10

Sch.1, revoked: SI 2004/1501 Art.38, Sch.2

Sch.2, revoked: SI 2004/1501 Sch.2

1976. Act of Sederunt (Small Claim Rules) 1988

applied: SSI 2002/132 r.4

revoked: SSI 2002/133 Sch.2

r.3, revoked: SSI 2002/132 Sch.2

1978. Act of Sederunt (Amendment of Sheriff Court Ordinary Cause, and Summary Cause, Rules) 1988

r.19, revoked: SSI 2002/132 Sch.2

r.35, revoked: SSI 2002/132 Sch.2

Sch.2, revoked: SSI 2002/132 Sch.2

1987. Criminal Evidence (Northern Ireland) Order 1988

Art.5, applied: 2003 c.6 Sch.2 para.7, Sch.2 para.9

Art.5, referred to: 2003 c.6 Sch.2 para.9

Art.6, applied: 2003 c.6 Sch.2 para.9

Art.6, referred to: 2003 c.6 Sch.2 para.9

1989. Education (Unrecognised Degrees) (Northern Ireland) Order 1988

applied: 2002 c.40 Sch.15

1990. Housing (Northern Ireland) Order 1988

referred to: SI 2003/412 Art.1

Part II, applied: SI 2003/412 Art.26

Art.3, amended: SI 2003/412 Art.135

Art.6, amended: SI 2003/412 Art.136

Art.7A, added: SI 2003/412 Art.137

Art.7B, added: SI 2003/412 Art.137

Art.29A, added: SI 2003/412 Art.138

1994. Air Navigation (Aeroplane and Aeroplane Engine Emission of Unburned Hydrocarbons) Order 1988

revoked: SI 2002/798 Sch.1

NO.

1988–cont.

2013. Act of Sederunt (Proceedings in the Sheriff Court under the Debtors (Scotland) Act 1987) 1988
Part III, revoked: SSI 2002/560 Sch.4
r.6, amended: SSI 2002/560 Sch.3 para.1
Sch., amended: SSI 2002/560 Sch.3 para.1
Sch.1, amended: SSI 2002/560 Sch.3 para.1, Sch.4

2019. Criminal Justice Act 1988 (Offensive Weapons) Order 1988
Sch.1 para.1, amended: SI 2002/1668 Art.3, SI 2004/1271 Art.3, SSI 2002/323 Art.2

2050. Distress for Rent Rules 1988
Appendix 1 para.1., amended: SI 2003/1858 r.2
Appendix 1 para.1., substituted: SI 2003/2141 r.2
Appendix 1 para.2., amended: SI 2003/1858 r.2
Appendix 1 para.3., amended: SI 2003/1858 r.2
Appendix 1 para.4., amended: SI 2003/1858 r.2
Appendix 1 para.5., amended: SI 2003/1858 r.2
Appendix 1 para.7., amended: SI 2003/1858 r.2
Appendix 2., amended: SI 2003/1858 r.3

2059. Act of Sederunt (Form of Charge for Payment) 1988
Sch.1, amended: SSI 2002/560 Sch.3 para.2

2075. Falmouth and Truro Port Health Authority Order 1988
Art.3, amended: SI 2002/2000 Art.2, Art.3
Art.9, amended: SI 2002/2000 Art.4

2235. Fire Services (Appointments and Promotion) (Amendment) (No.3) Regulations 1988
revoked: SI 2004/481 Sch.2

2238. Personal Pension Schemes (Compensation) Regulations 1988
Reg.2, amended: SI 2002/1555 Art.33
Reg.3, amended: SI 2002/1555 Art.33

2240. European Communities (Designation) (No.2) Order 1988
Sch.1, amended: SI 2002/2840 Sch.3

2249. Health and Medicines (Northern Ireland) Order 1988
Art.3, amended: 2002 c.9 (NI) Sch.1 para.19
Art.10, amended: SI 2004/311 Sch.1 para.13, Sch.2

2255. General Medical Council Preliminary Proceedings Committee and Professional Conduct Committee (Procedure) Rules Order of Council 1988
applied: SI 2003/1340 Art.2
applied: SI 2003/1341 Sch.1
Part I para.2, amended: SI 2002/2572 Sch.1 para.3, SI 2003/1343 Sch.1
Part I para.2, varied: SI 2003/1340 Art.2
Part II, applied: SI 2003/1344 Sch.1

NO.

1988–cont.

2255. General Medical Council Preliminary Proceedings Committee and Professional Conduct Committee (Procedure) Rules Order of Council 1988–cont.
Part II para.4, applied: SI 2003/1344 Sch.1
Part II para.4, varied: SI 2003/1340 Art.2
Part II para.5, amended: SI 2002/2572 Sch.1 para.3
Part II para.5, applied: SI 2003/1341 Sch.1, SI 2003/1344 Sch.1
Part II para.6, amended: SI 2002/2572 Sch.1 para.3
Part II para.6, applied: SI 2003/1341 Sch.1
Part II para.6, revoked (in part): SI 2002/2572 Sch.1 para.3
Part II para.6, varied: SI 2003/1340 Art.2
Part III para.11, amended: SI 2002/2572 Sch.1 para.3, SI 2003/1343 Sch.1
Part III para.13, amended: SI 2003/1343 Sch.1
Part III para.14, amended: SI 2002/2572 Sch.1 para.3
Part IV para.17, amended: SI 2002/2572 Sch.1 para.3
Part IV para.18, substituted: SI 2002/2572 Sch.1 para.3
Part IV para.19, amended: SI 2002/2572 Sch.1 para.3, SI 2003/1343 Sch.1
Part IV para.19A, added: SI 2003/1343 Sch.1
Part IV para.22, amended: SI 2002/2572 Sch.1 para.3
Part V para.24, applied: SI 2003/1341 Sch.1, SI 2004/2609 Sch.1
Part VI para.37, amended: SI 2002/2572 Sch.1 para.3
Part VI para.38, amended: SI 2002/2572 Sch.1 para.3
Part VIIA para.46A, amended: SI 2003/1343 Sch.1
Part VIIA para.46B, added: SI 2003/1343 Sch.1
Part VIIA para.46B, amended: SI 2003/1343 Sch.1
Part VIII para.51, amended: SI 2002/2572 Sch.1 para.3
Part VIII para.55, substituted: SI 2002/2572 Sch.1 para.3

2287. Police (Scotland) Amendment (No.2) Regulations 1988
revoked: SSI 2004/257 Sch.4

1989

76. Fire Precautions (Factories, Offices, Shops and Railway Premises) Order 1989
Art.5, amended: SI 2004/3168 Art.17
Art.6, amended: SI 2004/3168 Art.17

126. Fishing Vessels (Safety Training) Regulations 1989
Reg.1, amended: SI 2004/2169 Reg.3
Reg.2, substituted: SI 2004/2169 Reg.4

NO.

1989–cont.

136. Social Security (Claims and Payments and Payments on account, Overpayments and Recovery) Amendment Regulations 1989

revoked (in part): SI 2003/492 Sch.3 Part 1

193. Town and Country Planning (Fees for Applications and Deemed Applications) Regulations 1989

Reg.10, applied: SI 2002/2682 Reg.5, SI 2003/394 Reg.4

Reg.10A, amended: SI 2002/2258 Reg.2, SI 2004/2736 Reg.2

Reg.11A, amended: SI 2002/1876 Reg.2, SI 2002/2258 Reg.2, SI 2004/2736 Reg.2

Sch.1 Part I para.4, amended: SI 2002/768 Reg.2, SI 2002/2258 Reg.2, SI 2004/2736 Reg.2

Sch.1 Part I para.6, amended: SI 2002/768 Reg.2, SI 2002/2258 Reg.2, SI 2004/2736 Reg.2

Sch.1 Part I para.7, amended: SI 2002/768 Reg.2, SI 2002/2258 Reg.2, SI 2004/2736 Reg.2

Sch.1 Part I para.7A, amended: SI 2002/768 Reg.2, SI 2002/2258 Reg.2, SI 2004/2736 Reg.2

Sch.1 Part I para.7B, amended: SI 2002/768 Reg.2, SI 2002/2258 Reg.2, SI 2004/2736 Reg.2

Sch.1 Part I para.11, revoked (in part): SI 2004/2736 Reg.3

Sch.1 Part I para.15, amended: SI 2002/768 Reg.2, SI 2002/2258 Reg.2, SI 2004/2736 Reg.2

Sch.1 Part II, referred to: SI 2002/768 Reg.2, SI 2004/2736 Reg.2

Sch.1 Part II, substituted: SI 2002/768 Sch.1, SI 2002/2258 Sch.1, SI 2004/2736 Sch.1

Sch.2, referred to: SI 2002/768 Reg.2, SI 2004/2736 Reg.2

Sch.2, substituted: SI 2002/768 Sch.2, SI 2002/2258 Sch.2, SI 2004/2736 Sch.2

245. Misuse of Drugs (Licence Fees) (Amendment) Regulations 1989

revoked: SI 2003/611 Sch.1

306. National Health Service (Charges to Overseas Visitors) Regulations 1989

Reg.1, amended: SI 2004/614 Reg.2, SI 2004/696 Art.3, Sch.1 para.5, SI 2004/1433 Reg.2

Reg.2, amended: SI 2004/696 Art.3

Reg.3, amended: SI 2004/614 Reg.3

Reg.4, amended: SI 2004/614 Reg.4, SI 2004/696 Art.3, SI 2004/1433 Reg.3

Reg.4, substituted: SI 2004/1433 Reg.3

Reg.4A, added: SI 2004/614 Reg.5, SI 2004/1433 Reg.4

Reg.5, amended: SI 2004/614 Reg.6, SI 2004/1433 Reg.5

Reg.6A, added: SI 2004/614 Reg.7

Reg.6B, added: SI 2004/1433 Reg.6

NO.

1989–cont.

306. National Health Service (Charges to Overseas Visitors) Regulations 1989–cont.

Reg.8, amended: SI 2004/696 Art.3

Sch.1 Part IV, added: SI 2004/614 Reg.8, SI 2004/1433 Reg.7

Sch.2, amended: SI 2004/1433 Reg.8

317. Air Quality Standards Regulations 1989

Reg.2, revoked (in part): SI 2002/3183 Reg.13, SI 2003/2121 Sch.10, SSI 2003/428 Reg.16

Reg.4, revoked (in part): SI 2002/3183 Reg.13, SI 2003/2121 Sch.10, SSI 2003/428 Reg.16

Reg.6, revoked (in part): SI 2002/3183 Reg.13, SI 2003/2121 Sch.10, SSI 2003/428 Reg.16

338. Civil Legal Aid (Assessment of Resources) Regulations 1989

Sch.2 para.6, amended: SI 2003/762 Reg.11, SI 2004/1748 Sch.2 para.1

Sch.3 para.8, amended: SI 2003/762 Reg.11, SI 2004/1748 Sch.2 para.1

339. Civil Legal Aid (General) Regulations 1989

referred to: SI 2003/1312 Reg.1

see *Brawley v Marczynski (No.2)* [2002] EWCA Civ 1453, [2003] 1 W.L.R. 813 (CA), Longmore, L.J.; see *Howarth v Green* [2002] EWHC 2687, [2003] 2 Costs L.R. 160 (QBD), Cox, J.

Reg.51, amended: SI 2002/711 Reg.3

Reg.67, see *R. (on the application of Machi) v Legal Services Commission* [2001] EWCA Civ 2010, [2002] 1 W.L.R. 983 (CA), Sedley, L.J.

Reg.81, amended: SI 2002/711 Reg.4

Reg.81, see *R. (on the application of Machi) v Legal Services Commission* [2001] EWHC Admin 580, [2002] A.C.D. 8 (QBD (Admin Ct)), Ouseley, J.

Reg.102, amended: SI 2002/3033 Reg.3

Reg.102A, added: SI 2002/3033 Reg.4

Reg.102B, added: SI 2002/3033 Reg.4

Reg.104, amended: SI 2002/3033 Reg.5

Reg.105, amended: SI 2002/3033 Reg.6, SI 2003/1312 Reg.2

Reg.105, revoked (in part): SI 2002/3033 Reg.6

Reg.106A, amended: SI 2003/1312 Reg.3

Reg.109, see *Official Receiver v Dobson* [2002] 1 Costs. L.R. 71 (Ch D), Park, J.

Reg.113, revoked (in part): SI 2003/1312 Reg.4

Reg.124, see *Hill v Bailey* [2003] EWHC 2835, [2004] 1 All E.R. 1210 (Ch D), Lightman, J.

NO.

NO.

1989–cont.

340. Legal Advice and Assistance Regulations 1989

see *R. (on the application of Beale) v South East Wiltshire Magistrates* [2002] EWHC 2961, (2003) 167 J.P. 41 (QBD (Admin Ct)), Fulford, J.

Sch.2 para.9A, amended: SI 2003/762 Reg.11, SI 2004/1748 Sch.2 para.1

343. Legal Aid in Criminal and Care Proceedings Regulations 1989

Reg.15, see *Jackson v Lord Chancellor* [2003] EWHC 626, [2003] 3 Costs L.R. 395 (QBD), Leveson, J.

343. Legal Aid in Criminal and Care Proceedings (Costs) Regulations 1989

see *R. v Oldcorn (Costs)* [2003] 2 Costs L.R. 310 (Supreme Court Costs Office), Costs Judge PR Rogers

Reg.5, see *Ali v Lord Chancellor's Department* [2002] 2 Costs L.R. 258 (QBD), Butterfield, J.

Reg.8, see *R. v O'Brien (Costs)* [2003] 4 Costs L.R. 625 (Supreme Court Costs Office), Costs Judge Rogers

Reg.14, see *R. v O'Brien (Costs)* [2003] 4 Costs L.R. 625 (Supreme Court Costs Office), Costs Judge Rogers; see *R. v Walpole (John) (Costs)* [2002] 1 Costs L.R. 199 (Supreme Court Costs Office), Costs Judge Rogers

Reg.19, see *R. v Carlyle (Costs)* [2002] 1 Costs L.R. 192 (Supreme Court Costs Office), Costs Judge Rogers; see *R. v Singh (Hardev) (Costs)* [2002] 1 Costs L.R. 196 (Supreme Court Costs Office), Costs Judge Pollard

Reg.24, see *R. v Carlyle (Costs)* [2002] 1 Costs L.R. 192 (Supreme Court Costs Office), Costs Judge Rogers

Sch.3 Part I para.1, see *R. v Faulkner (Costs)* [2003] 1 Costs L.R. 148 (Supreme Court Costs Office), Costs Judge GN Pollard

Sch.3 Part I para.2, see *R. v Bell (Costs)* [2003] 1 Costs L.R. 144 (Supreme Court Costs Office), Costs Judge PR Rogers

Sch.3 Part II, see *Lord Chancellor v Singh* [2002] EWHC 1819, [2003] 1 Costs L.R. 62 (QBD), Hallett, J.

Sch.3 Part III, see *Lord Chancellor v Singh* [2002] EWHC 1819, [2003] 1 Costs L.R. 62 (QBD), Hallett, J.

Sch.3 Part V para.23, see *Lord Chancellor v Singh* [2002] EWHC 1819, [2003] 1 Costs L.R. 62 (QBD), Hallett, J.

Sch.3 para.9, see *R. v Chubb (Costs)* [2002] 2 Costs L.R. 333 (Supreme Court Costs Office), Master Pollard

1989–cont.

344. Legal Aid in Criminal and Care Proceedings (General) Regulations 1989

Sch.3 para.6, amended: SI 2003/762 Reg.11, SI 2004/1748 Sch.2 para.1

351. Education (Schools and Further and Higher Education) Regulations 1989

Reg.2, revoked (in part): SI 2004/571 Sch.1

Reg.4, revoked (in part): SI 2004/571 Sch.1

Reg.7, amended: SI 2004/571 Sch.1

Reg.10, revoked (in part): SI 2004/571 Sch.1

Reg.11, revoked (in part): SI 2004/571 Sch.1

Reg.12, revoked (in part): SI 2004/571 Sch.1

Reg.13, revoked (in part): SI 2004/571 Sch.1

Sch.1 para.1, revoked (in part): SI 2004/571 Sch.1

Sch.1 para.2, revoked (in part): SI 2004/571 Sch.1

Sch.2 para.1, revoked (in part): SI 2004/571 Sch.1

Sch.2 para.2, revoked (in part): SI 2004/571 Sch.1

363. National Health Service (Dental Charges) (Scotland) Regulations 1989

revoked: SSI 2003/158 Sch.4

Reg.3, amended: SSI 2002/99 Reg.3

Reg.4, amended: SSI 2002/99 Reg.3

Reg.4, applied: SSI 2002/99 Reg.4

Reg.4, referred to: SSI 2003/158 Reg.13

364. National Health Service (Charges to Overseas Visitors) (Scotland) Regulations 1989

Reg.1, amended: SSI 2004/369 Reg.2

Reg.4, substituted: SSI 2004/369 Reg.3

Reg.4A, added: SSI 2004/369 Reg.4

Reg.5, amended: SSI 2004/369 Reg.5

Reg.6A, added: SSI 2004/369 Reg.6

Sch.1, amended: SSI 2004/369 Reg.7

394. National Health Service (Dental Charges) Regulations 1989

Reg.1, amended: SI 2002/2353 Reg.7

Reg.2, amended: SI 2004/1091 Reg.3

Reg.3, amended: SI 2003/138 Reg.4, SI 2004/1091 Reg.3

Reg.4, amended: SI 2002/544 Reg.2, SI 2002/2353 Reg.8, SI 2003/586 Reg.2, SI 2004/696 Art.3, SI 2004/1091 Reg.2

Reg.4, applied: SI 2004/1091 Reg.5

Reg.5, amended: SI 2004/696 Art.3

Reg.6, amended: SI 2002/2353 Reg.9, SI 2004/696 Art.3

Reg.7, revoked (in part): SI 2003/2382 Sch.2

Reg.7A, added: SI 2002/2353 Reg.10

Reg.8, amended: SI 2004/696 Art.3

Reg.9, amended: SI 2002/2353 Reg.11

Reg.10, amended: SI 2002/2353 Reg.12

Reg.11, amended: SI 2002/2353 Reg.13, SI 2004/696 Art.3

Reg.11A, amended: SI 2002/2353 Reg.14

Sch.2, amended: SI 2002/2353 Reg.15

NO.

1989–cont.

394. National Health Service (Dental Charges) Regulations 1989–*cont.*

Sch.4 para.1, amended: SI 2002/2353 Reg.16

Sch.4 para.2, amended: SI 2002/2353 Reg.16

Sch.4 para.3, amended: SI 2002/2353 Reg.16

Sch.4 para.4, amended: SI 2002/2353 Reg.16

428. European Parliamentary Elections (Welsh Forms) Order 1989

revoked: SI 2004/1373 Art.3

436. Act of Sederunt (Amendment of Ordinary Cause and Summary Cause Rules) (Written Statements) 1989

r.3, revoked: SSI 2002/132 Sch.2

438. Community Charges (Administration and Enforcement) Regulations 1989

Reg.47, see *Sutton v Islington LBC* [2002] R.V.R. 128 (QBD), Brooke, L.J.

439. Valuation and Community Charge Tribunals Regulations 1989

Reg.2, amended: SI 2004/482 Art.2

Reg.9, substituted: SI 2004/482 Art.2

Reg.11, revoked: SI 2004/482 Art.2

Reg.12, revoked: SI 2004/482 Art.2

Reg.13, revoked: SI 2004/482 Art.2

Reg.14, revoked: SI 2004/482 Art.2

Reg.32, see *Smith v Head* [2002] R.V.R. 264 (QBD), Dyson, J.

464. Service Subsidy Agreements (Tendering) (Amendment) Regulations 1989

revoked (in part): SI 2002/2090 Sch.2

469. Personal Equity Plan Regulations 1989

referred to: SI 2004/1863 Sch.1 para.7

Reg.2, amended: SI 2003/2066 Reg.13, SI 2003/2748 Reg.3, SI 2004/1676 Reg.3

Reg.5, amended: SI 2003/2748 Reg.4

Reg.6, amended: SI 2003/2748 Reg.5, Reg.6

Reg.24A, amended: SI 2003/2748 Reg.7

480. CSCE Information Forum (Immunities and Privileges) Order 1989

Art.2, amended: 2002 c.8 s.2

490. Laganside Development (Northern Ireland) Order 1989

Sch.1, amended: SI 2003/418 Sch.3

Sch.1, revoked: SI 2003/418 Sch.1 para.10

Sch.1, substituted: SI 2003/418 Sch.1 para.10

492. Nature Conservation and Amenity Lands (Amendment) (Northern Ireland) 1989

Art.8, revoked (in part): SI 2002/3153 Sch.6 Part II

Art.9, revoked: SI 2002/3153 Sch.6 Part II

Art.10, revoked: SI 2002/3153 Sch.6 Part II

Art.11, revoked: SI 2002/3153 Sch.6 Part II

Art.12, revoked: SI 2002/3153 Sch.6 Part II

496. General Medical Council (Constitution) Amendment Order 1989

revoked: SI 2002/3136 Art.9

NO.

1989–cont.

502. European Parliamentary Elections (Northern Ireland) (Amendment) Regulations 1989

revoked: SI 2004/1267 Sch.7

507. Community Charges (Deductions from Income Support) (Scotland) Regulations 1989

Reg.1, amended: SI 2002/3019 Reg.34, SI 2002/3197 Reg.7

Reg.2, amended: SI 2002/3019 Reg.34

Reg.3, amended: SI 2002/3019 Reg.34

Reg.4, amended: SI 2002/3019 Reg.34

638. European Economic Interest Grouping Regulations 1989

Reg.9, applied: SI 2004/2643 Sch.2

Reg.11, applied: SI 2004/2643 Sch.2

Reg.12, applied: SI 2004/2643 Sch.2

Sch.4 para.4, applied: SI 2004/2643 Sch.2

662. Merchant Shipping (Merchant Navy Reserve) Regulations 1989

revoked: SI 2003/2861 Reg.2

677. Matrimonial and Family Proceedings (Northern Ireland) Order 1989

Art.21, applied: SI 2003/412 Art.14, Art.15, Art.16, Art.85

Art.31B, applied: SR 2002/119 Art.4, Art.5, Art.6, SR 2002/158 r.5, r.14, r.15, r.16

684. Medicines (Fixing of Fees Relating to Medicinal Products for Human Use) Order 1989

Sch.1 para.9B, added: SI 2004/1031 Sch.10 para.8

728. Low Voltage Electrical Equipment (Safety) Regulations 1989

referred to: SI 2004/1468 Sch.6 para.12

835. Bure Valley Railway Light Railway Order 1989

Art.2, amended: SI 2003/2155 Sch.2

Art.8, amended: SI 2003/2155 Sch.1 para.18

869. Consumer Credit (Exempt Agreements) Order 1989

see *Lagden v O'Connor* [2002] Lloyd's Rep. I.R. 138 (CC (Oxford)), Judge Charles Harris Q.C.

Art.3, see *Thew v Cole* [2003] EWCA Civ 1828, [2004] R.T.R. 25 (CA), Tuckey, L.J.

878. Tuberculosis (Deer) Order 1989

applied: SI 2002/242 Art.3, SI 2002/280 Art.3, SI 2002/2152 Art.3, SI 2002/2304 Art.3

954. Education (School Curriculum and Related Information) Regulations 1989

Reg.5, revoked: SI 2003/2694 Sch.1 Part 1

Reg.6, revoked: SI 2003/2694 Sch.1 Part 1

Reg.7, revoked: SI 2003/2694 Sch.1 Part 1

Reg.12, revoked: SI 2003/2694 Sch.1 Part 1

Reg.13, revoked: SI 2003/2694 Sch.1 Part 1

Reg.14, revoked: SI 2003/2694 Sch.1 Part 1

NO.

1989–cont.

1012. Copyright (Recordings of Folksongs for Archives) (Designated Bodies) Order 1989

referred to: SI 2003/2500 Sch.1 Part 1

Art.3, amended: SI 2003/2498 Sch.1 para.24

1058. Non-Domestic Rating (Collection and Enforcement) (Local Lists) Regulations 1989

referred to: SI 2003/2604 Art.5

Part II, applied: SI 2003/2613 Reg.4

Reg.1, amended: SI 2003/2604 Art.6, SI 2003/3052 Art.5

Reg.2, amended: SI 2003/2604 Art.7

Reg.10, varied: SI 2004/2443 Sch.4 para.9, Sch.4 para.13

Reg.11, applied: SI 2004/2443 Sch.4 para.13

Reg.11, varied: SI 2004/2443 Sch.4 para.9, Sch.4 para.13

Reg.12, see *Liverpool City Council v Plemora Distribution Ltd* [2002] EWHC 2467, [2003] R.A. 34 (QBD (Admin Ct)), Maurice Kay, J.; see *R. v Lewes and Crowborough Magistrates Court Ex p. Mackelden* [2002] R.V.R. 363 (QBD), Collins, J.

Reg.12, applied: SI 2004/2443 Sch.4 para.10, Sch.4 para.13

Reg.12, varied: SI 2004/2443 Sch.4 para.9, Sch.4 para.13

Reg.13, see *R. (on the application of Pilot Foods Ltd) v Horsferry Road Magistrates Court* [2003] EWHC 1447, [2003] R.V.R. 268 (QBD (Admin Ct)), Newman, J.

Reg.13, amended: SI 2003/1714 Reg.3, SI 2003/2210 Reg.3

Reg.13, referred to: SI 2004/2443 Sch.4 para.14

Reg.13, varied: SI 2004/2443 Sch.4 para.9, Sch.4 para.13

Reg.14, applied: SI 2004/2443 Sch.4 para.10, Sch.4 para.13

Reg.14, varied: SI 2004/2443 Sch.4 para.9, Sch.4 para.13

Reg.15, varied: SI 2004/2443 Sch.4 para.9, Sch.4 para.13

Reg.16, see *R. (on the application of Lee) v Dorset Magistrates Court* [2002] EWHC 603, [2003] R.V.R. 112 (QBD (Admin Ct)), Silber, J.

Reg.16, applied: SI 2004/2443 Sch.4 para.10, Sch.4 para.13, Sch.4 para.14

Reg.16, varied: SI 2004/2443 Sch.4 para.9, Sch.4 para.13

Reg.17, amended: SI 2003/1714 Reg.3, SI 2003/2210 Reg.3

Reg.17, varied: SI 2004/2443 Sch.4 para.9, Sch.4 para.13

Reg.18, varied: SI 2004/2443 Sch.4 para.9, Sch.4 para.13, Sch.4 para.14

Reg.19, varied: SI 2004/2443 Sch.4 para.9, Sch.4 para.13

Reg.20, applied: SI 2004/2443 Sch.4 para.10

NO.

1989–cont.

1058. Non-Domestic Rating (Collection and Enforcement) (Local Lists) Regulations 1989–*cont.*

Reg.20, varied: SI 2004/2443 Sch.4 para.9, Sch.4 para.13

Reg.21, varied: SI 2004/2443 Sch.4 para.9, Sch.4 para.13

Reg.22, varied: SI 2004/2443 Sch.4 para.9, Sch.4 para.13

Reg.23, applied: SI 2004/2443 Sch.4 para.10

Reg.23, varied: SI 2004/2443 Sch.4 para.9, Sch.4 para.13

Sch.2, revoked (in part): SI 2003/1714 Reg.3, SI 2003/2210 Reg.3

Sch.2, varied: SI 2004/2443 Sch.4 para.9, Sch.4 para.13

Sch.3, applied: SI 2004/2443 Sch.4 para.13

Sch.3 para.1, amended: SI 2003/2210 Reg.4

Sch.3 para.1, applied: SI 2004/2443 Sch.4 para.13

Sch.3 para.1, substituted: SI 2004/1013 Reg.3

Sch.3 para.1, varied: SI 2004/2443 Sch.4 para.9, Sch.4 para.13

Sch.3 para.2, amended: SI 2003/2210 Reg.4, SI 2004/1013 Reg.3

Sch.3 para.2, varied: SI 2004/2443 Sch.4 para.9, Sch.4 para.13

Sch.3 para.2A, varied: SI 2004/2443 Sch.4 para.9, Sch.4 para.13

Sch.3 para.3, varied: SI 2004/2443 Sch.4 para.9, Sch.4 para.13

Sch.4, varied: SI 2004/2443 Sch.4 para.9, Sch.4 para.13

1067. Copyright (Application of Provisions relating to Educational Establishments to Teachers) (No.2) Order 1989

referred to: SI 2003/2500 Sch.1 Part 1

Art.2, amended: SI 2003/2498 Sch.2

1078. Inheritance Tax (Delivery of Accounts) Regulations 1989

revoked: SI 2002/1733 Sch.1

1079. Inheritance Tax (Delivery of Accounts) (Scotland) Regulations 1989

revoked: SI 2002/1733 Sch.1

1111. Dock Work (Compensation Payments Scheme) Regulations 1989

Sch.1 para.9, amended: SI 2003/2096 Sch.1 para.45

1125. Consumer Credit (Advertisements) Regulations 1989

applied: SI 2004/1484 Reg.12

revoked: SI 2004/1484 Reg.11

1129. Copyright Tribunal Rules 1989

referred to: SI 2003/2500 Sch.1 Part 1

amended: SI 2003/2498 Sch.2

r.26A, amended: SI 2003/2498 Sch.2

Sch.3, amended: SI 2003/2498 Sch.1 para.25, Sch.2

NO.

1989–cont.

1147. Water Supply (Water Quality) Regulations 1989

Reg.30, amended: SI 2002/2469 Sch.1 para.47

1212. Copyright (Librarians and Archivists) (Copying of Copyright Material) Regulations 1989

referred to: SI 2003/2500 Sch.1 Part 1

Reg.4, amended: SI 2003/2498 Sch.1 para.26

Reg.5, amended: SI 2003/2498 Sch.1 para.26

Reg.6, amended: SI 2003/2498 Sch.1 para.26

Reg.7, amended: SI 2003/2498 Sch.1 para.26

Sch.2, amended: SI 2003/2498 Sch.1 para.26

1214. Lotteries (Variation of Monetary Limits) (Scotland) Order 1989

Sch.1, amended: SI 2002/1410 Art.5

1218. Lotteries (Variation of Monetary Limits) Order 1989

Sch.1, amended: SI 2002/1410 Art.5

1230. Sight Testing (Examination and Prescription) (No.2) Regulations 1989

Reg.2, amended: SI 2002/3135 Sch.1 para.26

1276. Banks (Administration Proceedings) Order 1989

Art.2, amended: SI 2002/1555 Art.34

Sch.1 para.2, amended: SI 2002/1555 Art.34

1301. Stamp Duty Reserve Tax (Amendment) Regulations 1989

varied: 2002 c.23 Sch.34 para.7, Sch.35 para.8

1319. Education (Teachers) Regulations 1989

applied: SI 2004/1729 Sch.2 para.14

Reg.14, applied: SI 2003/1663 Sch.1 para.1

Reg.14, varied: SI 2004/1744 Sch.1 para.1

Reg.15, applied: SI 2003/1662 Sch.1 para.1

Reg.16, applied: SI 2003/1662 Sch.1 para.2

Sch.3, applied: SI 2003/1663 Sch.2 para.3

Sch.6, applied: SI 2003/1663 Sch.1 para.1

Sch.6, varied: SI 2004/1744 Sch.1 para.1

1327. European Communities (Designation) Order 1989

revoked (in part): SI 2003/2901 Sch.4

varied: SI 2002/248 Sch.3

1338. Firearms (Amendment) (Northern Ireland) Order 1989

revoked: SI 2004/702 Sch.8

1339. Limitation (Northern Ireland) Order 1989

Art.11, see *McKillen v Russell* [2002] N.I. 35 (CA (NI)), Kerr, J.

Art.72A, added: 2002 c.29 s.288

NO.

1989–cont.

1341. Police and Criminal Evidence (Northern Ireland) Order 1989

applied: SI 2002/868 Reg.4, SI 2003/1519 Art.20, SI 2004/221 Reg.4, SI 2004/373 Reg.4, SI 2004/1315 Reg.4

referred to: 2003 c.6 Sch.2 para.24

see *Wallace v Quinn* [2004] N.I. 164 (CA (NI)), Lord Carswell L.C.J.

Part III, varied: 2003 c.32 s.16

Part V, applied: 2003 c.20 s.85, s.97, SI 2003/1247 Art.15

Art.2, amended: 2002 c.26 Sch.12 para.43, Sch.12 para.44, 2003 c.6 Sch.3 para.1

Art.3, amended: SI 2004/1500 Art.3, Sch.3

Art.10, applied: 2003 c.6 Sch.2 para.2, 2003 c.32 s.16

Art.10, varied: 2003 c.6 Sch.2 para.2

Art.11, applied: 2003 c.6 Sch.2 para.3

Art.17, amended: SI 2003/174 Art.6

Art.17, applied: 2002 c.29 s.355, 2003 c.6 Sch.2 para.1, Sch.2 para.2, Sch.2 para.3

Art.17, referred to: SI 2003/174 Art.10, Sch.2

Art.17, revoked (in part): SI 2003/174 Art.6

Art.18, amended: SI 2003/174 Art.7

Art.18, applied: 2002 c.29 s.355

Art.18, referred to: SI 2003/174 Art.10, Sch.2

Art.18, revoked (in part): SI 2003/174 Art.7

Art.18, varied: 2003 c.6 Sch.2 para.1, Sch.2 para.2, Sch.2 para.3

Art.19, amended: 2002 c.26 Sch.12 para.45

Art.20, amended: 2003 c.6 Sch.3 para.2, SI 2004/1500 Sch.1 para.1

Art.20, applied: 2003 c.6 Sch.2 para.4

Art.20, varied: 2003 c.6 Sch.2 para.4

Art.21, applied: 2002 c.29 s.215, 2003 c.6 Sch.2 para.2, Sch.2 para.3, Sch.2 para.4, Sch.2 para.5, SR 2003/122 r.3

Art.22, applied: 2003 c.6 Sch.2 para.2, Sch.2 para.3, Sch.2 para.4

Art.22, disapplied: SI 2003/425 Art.5, Art.26

Art.22, varied: SI 2003/425 Art.15, Art.16

Art.23, amended: SI 2003/174 Art.8

Art.23, applied: 2002 c.29 s.355, 2003 c.6 Sch.2 para.2, Sch.2 para.3, Sch.2 para.4, Sch.2 para.5, Sch.2 para.6

Art.23, referred to: SI 2003/174 Art.10, Sch.2

Art.23, varied: 2003 c.6 Sch.2 para.2, Sch.2 para.3, Sch.2 para.4, Sch.2 para.5, Sch.2 para.6, 2003 c.32 s.22

Art.24, amended: SI 2003/174 Art.9

Art.24, applied: 2002 c.29 s.355, 2003 c.6 Sch.2 para.2, Sch.2 para.3, Sch.2 para.4, Sch.2 para.5

Art.24, referred to: SI 2003/174 Art.10, Sch.2

Art.24, revoked (in part): SI 2003/174 Art.9

Art.26, amended: 2003 c.21 s.181, SI 2003/1247 Art.30, SI 2003/3194 Art.3, 2004 c.4 s.15

Art.26, applied: SI 2002/868 Reg.4, SI 2002/2628 Art.16, SI 2003/1519 Art.20

NO.

1989–cont.

1341. Police and Criminal Evidence (Northern Ireland) Order 1989–cont.

Art.26, varied: SI 2002/111 Art.20, SI 2004/221 Reg.4, SI 2004/348 Art.15, SI 2004/373 Reg.4, SI 2004/1315 Reg.4

Art.29, applied: 2003 c.6 Sch.2 para.11

Art.32, amended: SI 2004/1500 Art.4

Art.32A, added: SI 2004/1500 Art.4

Art.32D, added: SI 2004/1500 Art.4

Art.33, applied: 2003 c.6 Sch.2 para.7

Art.33, referred to: 2003 c.6 Sch.2 para.7

Art.35, amended: SI 2004/1500 Sch.1 para.2

Art.36, amended: SI 2004/1500 Sch.1 para.3

Art.37, amended: SI 2004/1500 Sch.1 para.4

Art.39, amended: 2002 c.26 Sch.12 para.46, SI 2003/1247 Art.7, Sch.2

Art.40, applied: 2003 c.6 Sch.2 para.23

Art.40, varied: 2003 c.6 Sch.2 para.8

Art.42, amended: SI 2004/1500 Sch.1 para.5

Art.43, amended: SI 2004/1500 Art.5

Art.44, applied: 2002 c.26 Sch.4 para.3, SI 2003/435 Art.25

Art.45, applied: 2002 c.26 Sch.4 para.3, SI 2003/435 Art.25

Art.48, amended: SI 2003/1247 Art.8, Sch.2

Art.48A, added: SI 2003/1247 Art.8

Art.53, amended: 2002 c.29 Sch.12, 2003 c.6 s.42

Art.53, substituted: 2003 c.6 s.42

Art.55, amended: SI 2004/1500 Art.6, Sch.3

Art.55, applied: 2003 c.6 Sch.2 para.12, Sch.2 para.23, SI 2003/3107 Art.2

Art.55, varied: SI 2003/3107 Art.2

Art.55A, amended: 2003 c.6 Sch.3 para.3

Art.55A, applied: 2003 c.6 Sch.2 para.13

Art.56, amended: 2003 c.6 s.41

Art.56, applied: SI 2003/3107 Art.2

Art.56, varied: SI 2003/3107 Art.2

Art.57, amended: 2002 c.29 Sch.11 para.19

Art.57, applied: SI 2003/3107 Art.2

Art.57, varied: SI 2003/3107 Art.2

Art.58, varied: SI 2003/3107 Art.2

Art.59, amended: 2002 c.29 Sch.11 para.19

Art.59, applied: SI 2003/3107 Art.2

Art.59, varied: SI 2003/3107 Art.2

Art.61, amended: 2003 c.6 Sch.3 para.4, SI 2004/1500 Art.7

Art.61, applied: 2003 c.6 Sch.2 para.14

Art.61, revoked (in part): SI 2004/1500 Art.7, Sch.3

Art.62, amended: 2003 c.6 s.42

Art.62, applied: 2003 c.6 Sch.2 para.16

Art.63, amended: 2003 c.6 Sch.3 para.5, SI 2004/1500 Art.8, Sch.3

Art.63, applied: 2003 c.6 Sch.2 para.17

Art.63A, applied: 2003 c.6 Sch.2 para.19

Art.64A, amended: 2003 c.6 Sch.3 para.6

Art.64A, applied: 2003 c.6 Sch.2 para.20

Art.66, amended: 2003 c.6 s.43, Sch.3 para.7

Art.66, applied: 2002 c.29 s.377

NO.

1989–cont.

1341. Police and Criminal Evidence (Northern Ireland) Order 1989–cont.

Art.72, amended: SI 2004/1501 Sch.1 para.3, Sch.2

Art.74, applied: SI 2004/1501 Art.32

Art.74A, added: SI 2004/1501 Art.32

Art.75, amended: 2003 c.44 Sch.36 para.61

Art.76, applied: SI 2004/1501 Art.30

Art.80, applied: SI 2004/1501 Art.31

Art.80A, added: SI 2003/1247 Art.31

Art.81, referred to: 2003 c.32 s.29

Art.87, amended: 2002 c.29 Sch.11 para.19

Art.89, amended: 2003 c.6 s.42

Sch.1, applied: 2003 c.6 Sch.2 para.3, 2003 c.32 s.16

Sch.1, varied: 2003 c.6 Sch.2 para.3

Sch.5, added: SI 2004/702 Sch.7 para.12

Sch.5, revoked: SI 2004/702 Sch.8

Sch.5, substituted: SI 2003/1247 Sch.1 para.11

1342. Social Security (Northern Ireland) Order 1989

Sch.5, applied: SR 2002/377 Reg.14, Reg.27

1343. Solicitors (Amendment) (Northern Ireland) Order 1989

Art.26, revoked: SI 2003/435 Sch.5

1344. Treatment of Offenders (Northern Ireland) Order 1989

Art.13, amended: 2002 c.26 Sch.11 para.5

1376. Recovery Vehicles (Prescribed Purposes) Regulations 1989

revoked: SI 2002/2742 Sch.1 Part I

1401. Fire Precautions (Sub-surface Railway Stations) Regulations 1989

Reg.2, amended: SI 2004/3168 Art.18

Reg.12, amended: SI 2004/3168 Art.18

1490. Civil Legal Aid (Scotland) (Fees) Regulations 1989

referred to: SSI 2002/496 Reg.2, SSI 2003/178 Reg.3

Reg.2, amended: SSI 2002/496 Reg.3

Reg.3, amended: SSI 2002/496 Reg.4

Reg.4, amended: SSI 2003/178 Reg.4

Reg.5, see *Caldwell v I* 2002 S.L.T. (Sh Ct) 28 (Sh Pr), JC McInnes Q.C., Sheriff Principal

Reg.5, amended: SSI 2002/496 Reg.5, SSI 2003/178 Reg.5, Reg.6, Reg.7, Reg.8, SSI 2004/281 Reg.3

Reg.6, amended: SSI 2003/178 Reg.9

Reg.10, amended: SSI 2002/496 Reg.6

Reg.11, amended: SSI 2003/178 Reg.10

Reg.11, revoked (in part): SSI 2003/178 Reg.10

Sch.5, added: SSI 2003/178 Sch.1

Sch.6 Part I, added: SSI 2003/178 Sch.1

Sch.6 Part II, added: SSI 2003/178 Sch.1

Sch.6 Part II para.1, added: SSI 2003/178 Sch.1

Sch.6 Part II para.2, added: SSI 2003/178 Sch.1

NO.

NO.

1989–cont.

1490. Civil Legal Aid (Scotland) (Fees) Regulations 1989–*cont.*

Sch.6 Part II para.3, added: SSI 2003/178 Sch.1

Sch.6 Part II para.4, added: SSI 2003/178 Sch.1

Sch.6 Part II para.5, added: SSI 2003/178 Sch.1

Sch.6 Part II para.6, added: SSI 2003/178 Sch.1

Sch.6 Part II para.7, added: SSI 2003/178 Sch.1

Sch.6 Part II para.8, added: SSI 2003/178 Sch.1

Sch.6 Part II para.9, added: SSI 2003/178 Sch.1

Sch.6 Part II para.10, added: SSI 2003/178 Sch.1

Sch.6 Part II para.11, added: SSI 2003/178 Sch.1

Sch.6 Part II para.12, added: SSI 2003/178 Sch.1

Sch.6 Part II para.13, added: SSI 2003/178 Sch.1

Sch.6 Part II para.14, added: SSI 2003/178 Sch.1

Sch.6 Part II para.15, added: SSI 2003/178 Sch.1

Sch.6 Part II para.16, added: SSI 2003/178 Sch.1

Sch.6 Part II para.17, added: SSI 2003/178 Sch.1

Sch.6 Part II para.18, added: SSI 2003/178 Sch.1

Sch.6 Part II para.19, added: SSI 2003/178 Sch.1

Sch.6 Part II para.20, added: SSI 2003/178 Sch.1

Sch.6 Part II para.21, added: SSI 2003/178 Sch.1

Sch.6 Part II para.22, added: SSI 2003/178 Sch.1

Sch.6 Part II para.23, added: SSI 2003/178 Sch.1

Sch.6 Part II para.24, added: SSI 2003/178 Sch.1

Sch.6 Part III, added: SSI 2003/178 Sch.1

Sch.6 Part III para.1, added: SSI 2003/178 Sch.1

Sch.6 Part III para.2, added: SSI 2003/178 Sch.1

Sch.6 Part III para.3, added: SSI 2003/178 Sch.1

Sch.6 Part III para.4, added: SSI 2003/178 Sch.1

Sch.6 Part III para.5, added: SSI 2003/178 Sch.1

Sch.6 Part III para.6, added: SSI 2003/178 Sch.1

Sch.7, added: SSI 2003/178 Sch.1

Sch.7, amended: SSI 2004/281 Reg.3

1989–cont.

1491. Criminal Legal Aid (Scotland) (Fees) Regulations 1989

Reg.2, amended: SSI 2002/440 Reg.2

Reg.6, amended: SSI 2003/249 Reg.2, SSI 2004/264 Reg.4, SSI 2004/316 Reg.2

Reg.7, amended: SSI 2004/264 Reg.5

Reg.8, amended: SSI 2002/246 Reg.3

Reg.9, substituted: SSI 2004/264 Reg.6

Sch.1, substituted: SSI 2004/264 Sch.1

Sch.1 para.1, substituted: SSI 2004/264 Sch.1

Sch.1 para.2, substituted: SSI 2004/264 Sch.1

Sch.1 para.3, substituted: SSI 2004/264 Sch.1

Sch.1 para.4, substituted: SSI 2004/264 Sch.1

Sch.1 para.5, substituted: SSI 2004/264 Sch.1

Sch.1 para.6, substituted: SSI 2004/264 Sch.1

1503. Education (School Government) Regulations 1989

Sch.1, see *R. (on the application of McNally) v Secretary of State for Education and Employment* [2001] EWCA Civ 332, [2002] I.C.R. 15 (CA), Kennedy, L.J.

1548. Landlord and Tenant Act 1954, Part II (Notices) (Amendment) Regulations 1989

revoked: SI 2004/1005 Reg.4

1597. Magistrates Courts (Extradition) Rules 1989

r.2, amended: SI 2002/1135 r.3

r.7, added: SI 2002/1135 r.4

Sch.1, amended: SI 2002/1135 r.5

1625. Bodmin Moor Railway Centre Light Railway Order 1989

Art.5, amended: SI 2003/2155 Sch.1 para.18

1642. Social Security (Abolition of Earnings Rule) (Consequential) Regulations 1989

Reg.2, revoked (in part): SI 2003/492 Sch.3 Part 1

1662. Motor Vehicles (Authorisation of Special Types) (Amendment) Order 1989

revoked: SI 2003/1998 Art.2

1671. Offshore Installations and Pipeline Works (First-Aid) Regulations 1989

Reg.2, varied: SI 2002/2175 Reg.3

Reg.5, applied: SI 2002/655 Reg.24, SI 2003/547 Reg.24, SI 2004/456 Reg.23

1686. Social Security (Medical Evidence, Claims and Payments) Amendment Regulations 1989

Reg.1, amended: SI 2003/492 Sch.3 Part 1

Reg.3, revoked (in part): SI 2003/492 Sch.3 Part 1

Reg.4, revoked (in part): SI 2003/492 Sch.3 Part 1

NO.

1989–cont.

1686. Social Security (Medical Evidence, Claims and Payments) Amendment Regulations 1989–*cont.*

Reg.5, revoked (in part): SI 2003/492 Sch.3 Part 1

Reg.6, revoked (in part): SI 2003/492 Sch.3 Part 1

Reg.7, revoked (in part): SI 2003/492 Sch.3 Part 1

Reg.8, revoked (in part): SI 2003/492 Sch.3 Part 1

Reg.9, revoked (in part): SI 2003/492 Sch.3 Part 1

1796. Road Vehicles Lighting Regulations 1989

applied: SI 2003/1998 Art.46, Art.50, Art.51, Art.52, Art.53, Sch.1 para.35, Sch.1 para.36, Sch.3 para.21, Sch.3 para.25, Sch.4 para.17, Sch.8 para.5, Sch.8 para.8, Sch.10 para.12, Sch.11 para.8

referred to: SI 2003/1998 Art.29, Art.42, Art.49

Reg.3, amended: SI 2004/3168 Art.19

Reg.7, applied: SI 2004/568 Reg.6

Reg.11, applied: SI 2003/1998 Sch.8 para.8

Reg.11, varied: SI 2003/1998 Sch.11 para.10

Reg.13, varied: SI 2003/1998 Sch.11 para.10

Reg.16, varied: SI 2003/1998 Sch.11 para.10

Reg.17, varied: SI 2003/1998 Sch.11 para.10

Reg.18, varied: SI 2003/1998 Sch.11 para.10

Reg.19, varied: SI 2003/1998 Sch.11 para.10

Reg.21, applied: SI 2003/1998 Sch.8 para.4

Reg.21, varied: SI 2003/1998 Sch.11 para.10

Reg.22, varied: SI 2003/1998 Sch.11 para.10

1833. Chosley and Wallingford Light Railway Order 1989

Art.6, amended: SI 2003/2155 Sch.1 para.18

1837. General Medical Council Professional Conduct Committee (EC Practitioners) (Procedure) Rules Order of Council 1989

revoked: SI 2004/2607 Art.2

Part I para.1, revoked: SI 2004/2607 Sch.1

Part I para.2, revoked: SI 2004/2607 Sch.1

Part II para.3, revoked: SI 2004/2607 Sch.1

Part II para.4, revoked: SI 2004/2607 Sch.1

Part II para.5, revoked: SI 2004/2607 Sch.1

Part III para.10, revoked: SI 2004/2607 Sch.1

Part III para.11, revoked: SI 2004/2607 Sch.1

Part III para.12, revoked: SI 2004/2607 Sch.1

Part III para.13, revoked: SI 2004/2607 Sch.1

Part III para.6, revoked: SI 2004/2607 Sch.1

Part III para.7, revoked: SI 2004/2607 Sch.1

Part III para.8, revoked: SI 2004/2607 Sch.1

Part III para.9, revoked: SI 2004/2607 Sch.1

Part IV para.14, revoked: SI 2004/2607 Sch.1

Appendix 1., revoked: SI 2004/2607 Sch.1

Sch.1, revoked: SI 2004/2607 Sch.1

NO.

1989–cont.

1959. Condensed Milk and Dried Milk (Amendment) Regulations 1989

revoked (in part): SI 2003/1596 Reg.10, SI 2003/3053 Reg.10

1975. Condensed Milk and Dried Milk (Scotland) Amendment Regulations 1989

revoked: SSI 2003/311 Reg.11

2009. Financial Services (Disclosure of Information) (Designated Authorities) (No.6) Order 1989

Art.2, amended: SI 2003/1398 Sch.1 para.11

Art.3, amended: SI 2003/1398 Sch.1 para.11

2057. Motor Cars (Driving Instruction) Regulations 1989

Reg.3, amended: SI 2002/2640 Reg.3, SI 2003/3027 Reg.3

Reg.4, amended: SI 2002/2640 Reg.4

Reg.5, amended: SI 2003/3027 Reg.4

Reg.5, substituted: SI 2002/2640 Reg.5

Reg.13, amended: SI 2004/2871 Reg.2

2089. Protection of Wrecks (Designation No 1) Order 1989

revoked: SI 2004/2395 Sch.2 para.4

2094. Church Representation Rules (Amendment) (No.1) Resolution 1989

referred to: SI 2004/1889

2095. Church Representation Rules (Amendment) (No.2) Resolution 1989

referred to: SI 2004/1889

2108. Human Organ Transplants (Supply of Information) Regulations 1989

Reg.1, amended: SI 2004/696 Art.3

Reg.2, amended: SI 2004/696 Art.3

Sch.1 Part I para.1, amended: SI 2004/696 Art.3

Sch.1 Part II para.1, amended: SI 2004/696 Art.3

2222. Police (Scotland) Amendment Regulations 1989

revoked: SSI 2004/257 Sch.4

2258. Supply of Beer (Loan Ties, Licensed Premises and Wholesale Prices) Order 1989

revoked: SI 2003/52 Art.2

Art.2, see *Scottish & Newcastle v Dixon* [2002] U.K.C.L.R. 484 (QBD), Judge McGonigal

2277. Apple and Pear Research Council Order 1989

revoked: SI 2003/909 Art.8

Art.8, varied: SI 2003/909 Art.3

Art.9, applied: SI 2003/909 Art.5

Art.9, varied: SI 2003/909 Art.5

Art.11, applied: SI 2003/909 Art.5

Art.11, varied: SI 2003/909 Art.5

2295. Protection of Wrecks (Designation No 3) Order 1989

revoked: SI 2004/2395 Sch.2 para.5

1989–cont.

2303. Non-Domestic Rating (Miscellaneous Provisions) (No.2) Regulations 1989

Reg.2, amended: SI 2004/1000 Reg.2, SI 2004/1494 Reg.2

Reg.5, see *Barratclough (Valuation Officer) v Tees and Hartlepool Port Authority* [2004] R.A. 1 (Lands Tr), George Bartlett Q.C. (President)

2307. Inshore Fishing (Prohibition of Fishing and Fishing Methods) (Scotland) Order 1989

referred to: SSI 2004/276 Art.12

revoked: SSI 2004/276 Sch.4

Art.2, amended: SSI 2003/404 Art.2

Art.5A, added: SSI 2003/404 Art.2

Art.8, added: SSI 2003/404 Art.2

Sch.2, amended: SSI 2003/404 Sch.1, SSI 2003/514 Sch.1

Sch.2, referred to: SSI 2003/404 Art.2

2361. Valuation (Stud Farms) (Scotland) Order 1989

revoked: SSI 2003/143 Art.4

2390. Supply of Beer (Tied Estate) Order 1989

revoked: SI 2002/3204 Art.2

see *Bavarian Lager Co Ltd v Secretary of State for Trade and Industry* [2002] U.K.C.L.R. 160 (QBD), Tomlinson, J.; see *Crehan v Inntrepreneur Pub Co (CPC)* [2003] EWHC 1510, [2003] U.K.C.L.R. 834 (Ch D), Park, J.

2393. European Communities (Designation) (No.2) Order 1989

Sch.1, amended: SI 2003/2901 Sch.4

2404. Companies (Northern Ireland) Order 1989

applied: 2002 c.40 Sch.15, 2003 c.20 Sch.4 para.7, SR 2003/346 Art.4

Part II, revoked: SI 2002/3150 Sch.4

Art.4, applied: SR 2003/346 Art.4

Art.10, applied: 2004 c.35 s.201

Art.11, applied: 2004 c.35 s.201

Art.20, varied: SR 2003/346 Art.4

Art.349, varied: SR 2003/346 Art.6

Sch.1, revoked: SI 2002/3150 Sch.4

Sch.2, revoked: SI 2002/3150 Sch.4

Sch.3, revoked: SI 2002/3150 Sch.4

2405. Insolvency (Northern Ireland) Order 1989

added: SI 2002/3152 Sch.3 para.7

applied: 2002 c.12 (NI) Reg.13, 2002 c.29 s.311, 2002 c.40 Sch.15, SI 2002/3150 Art.23, SI 2003/1102 Reg.2, 2004 c.35 s.201, Sch.3, Sch.8, SI 2004/353 Reg.2, Reg.5, SI 2004/1045 Reg.3, Reg.4

disapplied: 2002 c.29 s.424, s.428, s.430

referred to: 2002 c.29 s.424, s.425, s.428, s.432, SI 2002/3150 Art.25, SI 2002/3152 Sch.1 para.1, Sch.3 para.1, SR 2002/334 Reg.3

1989–cont.

2405. Insolvency (Northern Ireland) Order 1989–*cont.*

Part II, applied: 2002 c.12 (NI) Reg.10, 2002 c.29 s.311, SI 2002/3152 Art.3, Art.4

Part II, referred to: SI 2002/3150 Art.24

Part III, applied: 2002 c.12 (NI) Reg.10

Part III, referred to: SI 2002/3150 Art.24

Part IV, applied: 2002 c.12 (NI) Reg.10

Part IV, referred to: SI 2002/3150 Art.24

Part V, applied: 2002 c.12 (NI) Reg.10, SI 2003/1102 Reg.11, SI 2004/353 Reg.11, SI 2004/1045 Reg.12

Part VII, applied: 2002 c.12 (NI) Reg.10

Part VIII, applied: 2002 c.12 (NI) Reg.10, 2002 c.29 s.311, SI 2002/3152 Art.5, SR 2002/127 Reg.4, Reg.6

Part IX, applied: 2002 c.29 s.424

Part IX, varied: 2002 c.29 s.423

Part X, applied: SR 2002/127 Reg.4, Reg.6

Art.2, amended: SI 2002/3152 Sch.1 para.2, SR 2002/223 Reg.3

Art.2, applied: SR 2002/74 Reg.7

Art.2A, added: SR 2002/334 Reg.4

Art.3, applied: 2002 c.29 s.433, Sch.9 para.1, SI 2002/3150 Art.2, SI 2003/3075 Reg.2, SR 2002/74 Reg.7

Art.3, amended: SI 2002/3152 Art.6, SR 2002/334 Reg.5

Art.3, disapplied: 2002 c.29 s.433

Art.6, amended: SR 2002/334 Reg.6

Art.6, applied: SI 2002/3150 Art.2

Art.9, applied: SR 2002/127 Reg.4, Reg.6

Art.14, amended: SI 2002/3152 Sch.2 para.2, SR 2002/334 Reg.7

Art.14, applied: SI 2003/1102 Reg.33, SI 2004/353 Reg.33

Art.14A, added: SI 2002/3152 Sch.1 para.3

Art.15, amended: SI 2002/3152 Sch.1 para.4, Sch.2 para.3

Art.17, amended: SI 2002/3152 Sch.2 para.4

Art.17, applied: SI 2003/1102 Reg.4, SI 2004/353 Reg.4, SI 2004/1045 Reg.3

Art.17, varied: SI 2003/1102 Reg.33, SI 2004/353 Reg.33

Art.17A, added: SI 2002/3152 Sch.2 para.5

Art.17A, applied: SI 2004/353 Reg.11, Reg.34, Reg.36, SI 2004/1045 Reg.12, Reg.19, Reg.21

Art.18, amended: SI 2002/3152 Sch.2 para.6, Sch.4

Art.19, amended: SI 2002/3152 Sch.2 para.7

Art.19, applied: SI 2003/1102 Reg.11, SI 2004/353 Reg.11, SI 2004/1045 Reg.12

Art.19A, added: SI 2002/3152 Sch.2 para.8

Art.20, amended: SI 2002/3152 Sch.2 para.9

Art.20A, added: SI 2002/3152 Sch.2 para.10

Art.20A, applied: SI 2002/3152 Sch.2 para.13

Art.20B, added: SI 2002/3152 Sch.2 para.10

Art.21, amended: SR 2002/334 Reg.8

NO.

1989–cont.

2405. Insolvency (Northern Ireland) Order 1989–*cont.*

Art.21, applied: SI 2003/1102 Reg.34, Reg.36, SR 2002/74 Reg.7

Art.22, applied: SI 2003/1102 Reg.9, SI 2004/1045 Reg.9, SR 2002/74 Reg.7

Art.23, amended: SI 2002/3152 Art.7

Art.23, applied: SR 2002/74 Reg.7

Art.23, disapplied: SI 2003/3226 Reg.9

Art.24, amended: SI 2002/3152 Art.7

Art.24, applied: SR 2002/74 Reg.7

Art.24, disapplied: SI 2003/3226 Reg.9

Art.25, applied: SR 2002/74 Reg.7

Art.26, applied: SR 2002/74 Reg.7

Art.27, applied: SR 2002/74 Reg.7

Art.28, applied: SR 2002/74 Reg.7

Art.28, disapplied: SI 2003/3226 Reg.9

Art.29, applied: SR 2002/74 Reg.7

Art.34, applied: SI 2002/3150 Sch.1 para.12

Art.39, amended: SI 2002/3152 Sch.1 para.6

Art.39, applied: SI 2003/1102 Reg.11

Art.51, applied: SI 2002/3150 Art.6

Art.57, applied: SI 2002/3150 Sch.1 para.12

Art.70, applied: SI 2004/1045 Reg.8

Art.74, disapplied: SI 2003/3226 Reg.11

Art.81, applied: SI 2003/1102 Reg.9, SI 2004/353 Reg.9, SI 2004/1045 Reg.9

Art.84, applied: SI 2003/3226 Reg.12

Art.84, referred to: SI 2002/3150 Sch.1 para.11

Art.85, applied: SI 2002/3150 Sch.1 para.12

Art.86, applied: SI 2003/1102 Reg.14, Reg.34, Reg.36, SI 2004/353 Reg.14, Reg.34, Reg.36, SI 2004/1045 Reg.9, Reg.11, Reg.12, Reg.16, Reg.19, Reg.21

Art.86, referred to: SI 2003/1102 Reg.9, Reg.11, Reg.18, SI 2004/353 Reg.9, Reg.11, Reg.18

Art.98, applied: SI 2004/353 Reg.11, SI 2004/1045 Reg.12

Art.102, amended: SI 2002/3152 Sch.1 para.7

Art.104, amended: SI 2002/3152 Sch.1 para.8, SR 2002/334 Reg.9

Art.105, applied: SI 2003/1102 Reg.9, SI 2004/353 Reg.9, SI 2004/1045 Reg.9, Reg.11

Art.107, applied: SI 2002/3150 Sch.1 para.10

Art.107, disapplied: SI 2003/3226 Reg.11

Art.111, applied: SI 2002/3150 Sch.1 para.12

Art.115, applied: SI 2003/1102 Reg.9, SI 2004/353 Reg.9, Reg.11, SI 2004/1045 Reg.9, Reg.11, Reg.12

Art.143, applied: SI 2003/1102 Reg.29

Art.143, referred to: SI 2003/1102 Reg.29, SI 2004/353 Reg.29

Art.144, applied: SI 2002/3150 Art.6

Art.149, applied: SI 2003/1102 Reg.27, Reg.31, SI 2004/353 Reg.27, Reg.31

Art.149, disapplied: SI 2003/1102 Reg.20, SI 2004/353 Reg.20

Art.152, disapplied: SI 2003/3226 Reg.11

NO.

1989–cont.

2405. Insolvency (Northern Ireland) Order 1989–*cont.*

Art.165, amended: 2002 c.26 Sch.4 para.36

Art.176, applied: SI 2003/1102 Reg.31, SI 2004/353 Reg.31

Art.177, applied: SI 2002/3150 Art.14

Art.178, applied: SI 2002/3150 Art.14

Art.182, amended: SI 2002/3152 Art.8, Sch.4

Art.183, amended: SI 2002/3152 Art.8, Art.9

Art.185, amended: SR 2002/334 Reg.10

Art.185, applied: SI 2003/1102 Reg.4, SI 2004/353 Reg.4

Art.186, applied: SI 2003/2553 Reg.16

Art.186, varied: SI 2003/2553 Reg.16

Art.187, applied: SI 2003/2553 Reg.16

Art.188, applied: SI 2003/2553 Reg.16

Art.189, amended: SR 2002/334 Reg.11

Art.189, substituted: SR 2002/334 Reg.11

Art.197, amended: SI 2002/3152 Sch.1 para.9, 2003 c.21 Sch.17 para.101

Art.198, applied: SI 2002/3150 Sch.1 para.12

Art.199, applied: SI 2002/3150 Sch.1 para.12

Art.202, applied: 2002 c.29 s.429, SI 2002/3150 Sch.1 para.10, SR 2002/74 Reg.7

Art.203, applied: 2002 c.29 s.429, SI 2002/3150 Sch.1 para.10, SR 2002/74 Reg.7

Art.204, amended: SR 2002/334 Reg.12

Art.204, applied: SI 2002/3150 Sch.1 para.10

Art.205, applied: SI 2002/3150 Sch.1 para.10, SR 2002/74 Reg.7

Art.207, disapplied: SI 2003/3226 Reg.11

Art.226, amended: SI 2002/3152 Sch.3 para.2

Art.226, applied: SR 2002/74 Reg.7

Art.227, amended: SI 2002/3152 Sch.3 para.3

Art.228, amended: SI 2002/3152 Sch.3 para.4

Art.229, amended: SI 2002/3152 Sch.3 para.5, Sch.4

Art.230, amended: SI 2002/3152 Sch.3 para.6

Art.231, amended: SI 2002/3152 Sch.3 para.8

Art.232, amended: SI 2002/3152 Sch.3 para.9

Art.234, amended: SI 2002/3152 Sch.3 para.10

Art.236, amended: SI 2002/3152 Sch.3 para.11

Art.236A, added: SI 2002/3152 Sch.3 para.12

Art.236B, added: SI 2002/3152 Sch.3 para.12

Art.236C, added: SI 2002/3152 Sch.3 para.12

Art.237, amended: SI 2002/3152 Sch.3 para.13

Art.238, amended: SR 2002/334 Reg.13

Art.238, applied: SR 2002/74 Reg.7

NO.

NO.

1989–cont.

2405. Insolvency (Northern Ireland) Order 1989–*cont.*

Art.239, amended: SR 2002/334 Reg.14

Art.242, applied: SI 2003/2553 Reg.16, SR 2002/74 Reg.7

Art.252, applied: SR 2002/74 Reg.7

Art.254, applied: 2002 c.29 s.424, SR 2002/74 Reg.7

Art.255, amended: 2002 c.29 Sch.11 para.20

Art.255, applied: SR 2002/74 Reg.7

Art.259, applied: 2002 c.29 s.311, s.423, SR 2002/74 Reg.7

Art.260, applied: SR 2002/74 Reg.7

Art.274, applied: SR 2002/74 Reg.7

Art.279, applied: SR 2002/127 Reg.5, Reg.6

Art.279A, added: 2002 c.29 Sch.11 para.20

Art.279B, added: 2002 c.29 Sch.11 para.20

Art.279B, referred to: SI 2003/421 r.24

Art.279C, added: 2002 c.29 Sch.11 para.20

Art.280, applied: 2002 c.29 s.424, SR 2002/74 Reg.7, SR 2002/224 Reg.41

Art.281, applied: 2002 c.29 s.424, SR 2002/74 Reg.7

Art.283, applied: SR 2002/74 Reg.7, SR 2002/224 Reg.41, SR 2002/352 Reg.97

Art.288, applied: SR 2002/74 Reg.7

Art.303, amended: SR 2002/334 Reg.15

Art.312, applied: 2002 c.29 s.425, SR 2002/127 Reg.10

Art.313, applied: 2002 c.29 s.425, SR 2002/127 Reg.10

Art.315B, applied: SR 2002/127 Reg.7

Art.315C, applied: SR 2002/127 Reg.10

Art.315C, enabled: SR 2002/127

Art.315E, applied: SR 2002/127 Reg.9

Art.315F, applied: SR 2002/127 Reg.10

Art.315F, enabled: SR 2002/127

Art.343, amended: 2003 c.21 Sch.17 para.101, SI 2004/945 Art.2

Art.347, amended: SI 2002/3152 Sch.1 para.10, Sch.2 para.11, Sch.3 para.14, SR 2002/334 Reg.16

Art.348, amended: SI 2002/3152 Art.6

Art.348A, added: SI 2002/3152 Art.6

Art.349, amended: SI 2002/3150 Sch.3 para.6

Art.350, applied: SI 2003/419 Art.63, 2004 c.35 Sch.3, Sch.8

Art.359, amended: SR 2002/223 Reg.4

Art.359, applied: SI 2002/3150 Art.24

Art.359, enabled: SR 2002/261, SR 2003/358

Art.360, amended: 2002 c.26 Sch.5 para.24

Art.360, applied: SR 2002/261, SR 2003/358

Art.361, applied: SI 2002/3150 Art.24

Art.362, amended: SI 2002/3152 Sch.1 para.11

Art.362, applied: SI 2003/2553 Reg.16

Art.364, amended: SR 2002/223 Reg.4

Art.364, applied: SI 2002/3150 Art.24

1989–cont.

2405. Insolvency (Northern Ireland) Order 1989–*cont.*

Art.364, enabled: SR 2003/144

Art.364, referred to: 2002 c.29 s.311

Art.365, amended: SI 2002/3152 Art.10, SR 2002/223 Reg.4

Art.365, enabled: SR 2003/103

Art.365, referred to: 2002 c.29 s.311

Art.365A, added: SI 2002/3152 Art.10

Art.366, applied: SI 2002/3150 Art.24

Art.367, applied: 2002 c.29 s.425, s.429, SI 2002/3150 Sch.1 para.3

Art.368, applied: SI 2002/3150 Sch.1 para.3

Art.369, applied: SI 2002/3150 Sch.1 para.3

Art.378, applied: SI 2002/3150 Art.24

Sch.A1, added: SI 2002/3152 Sch.1 para.5

Sch.5, amended: SI 2002/3150 Sch.3 para.7

Sch.7, amended: SI 2002/3152 Sch.1 para.12, Sch.2 para.12, Sch.3 para.15

2406. Education Reform (Northern Ireland) Order 1989

Art.29, amended: SI 2003/424 Sch.2 para.5

Art.31, amended: SI 2003/424 Art.27

Art.33, amended: SI 2003/424 Art.26

Art.46, revoked: SI 2003/424 Sch.1 para.1, Sch.3 Part II

Art.47, revoked: SI 2003/424 Sch.1 para.1, Sch.3 Part II

Art.48, revoked: SI 2003/424 Sch.1 para.1, Sch.3 Part II

Art.49, revoked: SI 2003/424 Sch.1 para.1, Sch.3 Part II

Art.50, revoked: SI 2003/424 Sch.1 para.1, Sch.3 Part II

Art.51, revoked: SI 2003/424 Sch.1 para.1, Sch.3 Part II

Art.52, revoked: SI 2003/424 Sch.1 para.1, Sch.3 Part II

Art.53, revoked: SI 2003/424 Sch.1 para.1, Sch.3 Part II

Art.54, revoked: SI 2003/424 Sch.1 para.1, Sch.3 Part II

Art.55, revoked: SI 2003/424 Sch.1 para.1, Sch.3 Part II

Art.56, revoked: SI 2003/424 Sch.1 para.1, Sch.3 Part II

Art.57, revoked: SI 2003/424 Sch.1 para.1, Sch.3 Part II

Art.58, revoked: SI 2003/424 Sch.1 para.1, Sch.3 Part II

Art.59, revoked: SI 2003/424 Sch.1 para.1, Sch.3 Part II

Art.60, amended: SI 2003/424 Sch.1 para.2

Art.60, applied: SI 2003/424 Art.4

Art.60, revoked (in part): SI 2003/424 Sch.1 para.2, Sch.3 Part II

Art.61, amended: SI 2003/424 Sch.1 para.3

Art.61, revoked (in part): SI 2003/424 Sch.1 para.3, Sch.3 Part II

Art.62, revoked: SI 2003/424 Sch.1 para.4, Sch.3 Part II

NO.

1989–cont.

2406. Education Reform (Northern Ireland) Order 1989–*cont.*

Art.63, revoked: SI 2003/424 Sch.1 para.4, Sch.3 Part II

Art.65, referred to: SR 2003/61 Sch.3

Art.77, amended: SI 2003/424 Sch.1 para.5

Art.77, applied: SI 2003/424 Art.4

Art.77, revoked (in part): SI 2003/424 Sch.1 para.5, Sch.3 Part II

Art.78, amended: SI 2003/424 Sch.1 para.6

Art.78, revoked (in part): SI 2003/424 Sch.1 para.6, Sch.3 Part II

Art.127, amended: SI 2003/424 Art.22

Art.128, disapplied: SI 2003/424 Art.22

Art.129, disapplied: SI 2003/424 Art.22

Art.130, disapplied: SI 2003/424 Art.22

Art.131, amended: 2002 c.21 Sch.3 para.21, Sch.6

Art.131, disapplied: SI 2003/424 Art.22

Art.148, amended: SI 2003/424 Sch.2 para.6

Art.149, amended: SI 2003/424 Art.32, Sch.3 Part I

Art.149, revoked (in part): SI 2003/424 Art.32, Sch.3 Part I

Art.161, revoked: SI 2003/424 Sch.3 Part I

Sch.8, amended: SI 2003/424 Art.33, Sch.3 Part I

Sch.8, applied: SI 2003/424 Art.33

Sch.8, revoked (in part): SI 2003/424 Art.33

Sch.8, substituted: SI 2003/418 Sch.1 para.1

Sch.9, amended: SI 2003/424 Sch.3 Part I

2408. Human Organ Transplants (Northern Ireland) Order 1989

applied: 2004 c.19 s.4

revoked: 2004 c.30 Sch.7 Part 2

2413. Youth Service (Northern Ireland) Order 1989

Art.6, revoked (in part): SI 2003/418 Sch.3

Art.7, applied: SR 2003/253 Art.3

2423. Credit Unions (Increase in Limits of Shareholding, of Deposits by persons too young to be members and of Loans) Order 1989

revoked: SI 2002/1501 Art.3

3132. Civil Procedure Rules 1989

Part 7 r.7.2, see *Salford City Council v Garner* [2004] EWCA Civ 364, [2004] H.L.R. 35 (CA), Chadwick, L.J.

Part 20 r.20, see *Abbey National Bank Plc v Matthews & Son* [2003] EWHC 925, [2003] 1 W.L.R. 2042 (Ch D), Simon Berry Q.C.

3341. Criminal Defence Service (Funding) (Amendment No 3) Order 1989

see *R. v Bell (Costs)* [2003] 1 Costs L.R. 144 (Supreme Court Costs Office), Costs Judge PR Rogers

NO.

1990

44. Act of Sederunt (Fees in the Scottish Record Office) 1990

revoked: SSI 2003/234 Art.3

161. Household Appliances (Noise Emission) Regulations 1990

referred to: SI 2004/693 Sch.1

Reg.8, amended: SI 2004/693 Sch.2

Reg.8, revoked (in part): SI 2004/693 Sch.2

200. Official Secrets Act 1989 (Prescription) Order 1990

Sch.1, amended: SI 2003/1918 Sch.1

Sch.2, amended: SI 2004/1823 Art.11

Sch.3, amended: SI 2003/1918 Sch.2

223. General Drainage Charges (Anglian Region) Order 1990

revoked: SI 2004/388 Art.1

237. European Communities (Privileges of the European School) Order 1990

Art.7, amended: 2002 c.8 s.2

262. Scottish Local Elections Amendment Rules 1990

revoked: SSI 2002/457 Sch.1

304. Dangerous Substances (Notification and Marking of Sites) Regulations 1990

Reg.2, amended: SI 2004/568 Sch.13 para.4, SI 2004/3168 Art.20

Sch.1 para.1, amended: SI 2004/568 Sch.13 para.4

390. Electricity Supply (Amendment) Regulations 1990

revoked: SI 2002/2665 Sch.5

426. Local Authorities (Capital Finance) (Approved Investments) Regulations 1990

varied: SI 2003/1633 Sch.2 para.2, Sch.2 para.4

Reg.1, amended: SI 2002/1884 Reg.2

Reg.2, amended: SI 2002/1884 Reg.2

Reg.3, amended: SI 2002/1884 Reg.2

Reg.3, revoked (in part): SI 2002/1884 Reg.2

431. Local Government and Housing Act 1989 (Commencement No 5 and Transitional Provisions) Order 1990

Sch.1, revoked: SI 2004/533 Art.7

439. Insolvency Practitioners Regulations 1990

Reg.9, revoked: SI 2004/473 Reg.2

Reg.13, amended: SI 2002/2710 Reg.3

Reg.15A, amended: SI 2002/2710 Reg.4

Sch.2 Part II para.1, amended: SI 2002/2710 Reg.5

Sch.2 Part II para.2, amended: SI 2002/2710 Reg.5

469. Police (Scotland) Amendment Regulations 1990

revoked: SSI 2004/257 Sch.4

507. Town and Country Planning (Appeals) (Written Submissions Procedure) (Scotland) Regulations 1990

Reg.2, amended: SSI 2004/332 Sch.5 para.1

NO.

507. Town and Country Planning (Appeals) (Written Submissions Procedure) (Scotland) Regulations 1990–*cont.*

Reg.2A, added: SSI 2004/332 Sch.5 para.2

Reg.3, amended: SSI 2004/332 Sch.5 para.3

Reg.4, amended: SSI 2004/332 Sch.5 para.4

Reg.8A, added: SSI 2004/332 Sch.5 para.5

512. Compulsory Purchase by Non-Ministerial Acquiring Authorities (Inquiries Procedure) Rules 1990

referred to: SI 2004/2730 Sch.1

527. Electricity (Connection Charges) Regulations 1990

applied: SI 2002/93 Reg.5, Reg.6

revoked: SI 2002/93 Reg.9

545. Community Charges (Deductions from Income Support) (No.2) Regulations 1990

Reg.1, amended: SI 2002/3019 Reg.35

Reg.2, amended: SI 2002/3019 Reg.35

Reg.3, amended: SI 2002/3019 Reg.35

Reg.4, amended: SI 2002/3019 Reg.35

548. National Health Service (Travelling Expenses and Remission of Charges) Amendment Regulations 1990

revoked: SI 2003/2382 Sch.2

551. National Health Service (Travelling Expenses and Remission of Charges) (Scotland) Amendment Regulations 1990

revoked: SSI 2003/376 Sch.3 para.2

559. Bankruptcy and Companies (Department of Trade &amp Industry) Fees (Amendment) Order 1990

revoked: SI 2004/593 Sch.1

560. Insolvency Fees (Amendment) Order 1990

revoked: SI 2004/593 Sch.1

562. European Parliamentary Elections (Northern Ireland) (Amendment) Regulations 1990

revoked: SI 2004/1267 Sch.7

593. Companies (Northern Ireland) Order 1990

applied: 2002 c.40 Sch.15

Art.28, applied: 2002 c.29 Sch.9 para.1, SI 2002/253 Art.52, SI 2002/254 Art.46, SI 2003/1250 Art.29, SI 2003/3075 Reg.2

Art.49, revoked: 2004 c.27 Sch.2 para.4

Sch.10, revoked: SI 2002/3150 Sch.4

Sch.14, added: SI 2003/1398 Sch.1 para.15

Sch.14, revoked (in part): SI 2003/1398 Sch.1 para.15, Sch.1 para.15, 2004 c.27 Sch.2 para.4

595. Local Elections (Northern Ireland) (Amendment) Order 1990

Art.8, revoked: SI 2002/2835 Art.3

608. Non-Domestic Rating (Transitional Period) Regulations 1990

Reg.18, amended: SI 2003/2000 Reg.2

NO.

661. Act of Sederunt (Amendment of Sheriff Court Ordinary Cause, Summary Cause, and Small Claim, Rules) 1990

revoked (in part): SSI 2002/132 Sch.2, SSI 2002/133 Sch.2

673. Non-Domestic Rating (Caravan Sites) Regulations 1990

see *Oades v Eke (Valuation Officer)* [2004] R.A. 161 (Lands Tr), PR Francis FRICS

720. Passenger Transport Executives (Capital Finance) Order 1990

referred to: SI 2004/533 Art.8

revoked (in part): 2003 c.26 Sch.8 Part 1

725. Social Security (Claims and Payments) Amendment Regulations 1990

revoked (in part): SI 2003/492 Sch.3 Part 1

760. Movement of Animals (Restrictions) Order 1990

revoked (in part): SI 2002/3229 Art.13, SI 2003/399 Art.13, SSI 2003/353 Art.13

767. Local Authorities (Borrowing) Regulations 1990

Reg.2, varied: SI 2003/1633 Sch.1 para.24

Reg.3, varied: SI 2003/1633 Sch.1 para.25

Reg.4, varied: SI 2003/1633 Sch.1 para.26

Reg.5, varied: SI 2003/1633 Sch.1 para.27

Reg.6, varied: SI 2003/1633 Sch.1 para.28

Reg.7, varied: SI 2003/1633 Sch.1 para.29

Reg.8, varied: SI 2003/1633 Sch.1 para.30

Reg.9, varied: SI 2003/1633 Sch.1 para.31

Sch.1 para.1, varied: SI 2003/1633 Sch.1 para.32

Sch.1 para.5, varied: SI 2003/1633 Sch.1 para.32

Sch.2 para.1, varied: SI 2003/1633 Sch.1 para.33

Sch.2 para.2, varied: SI 2003/1633 Sch.1 para.33

879. Copyright (Certification of Licensing Scheme for Educational Recording of Broadcasts and Cable Programmes) (Educational Recording Agency Limited) Order 1990

applied: SI 2003/188

referred to: SI 2003/2500 Sch.1 Part 1

Art.2, amended: SI 2003/2498 Sch.2

Sch.1, referred to: SI 2003/188

Sch.1 para.4, amended: SI 2003/2498 Sch.2

Sch.1 para.10, substituted: SI 2003/188 Art.2

917. National Health Service (Travelling Expenses and Remission of Charges) (Modification of Time Limit) (Scotland) Regulations 1990

revoked: SSI 2003/376 Sch.3 para.3

928. Industrial Training (Transfer of the Activities of Establishment) Order 1990

referred to: SI 2004/368 Sch.1

NO.

1990–cont.

932. Local Elections (Principal Areas) (Declaration of Acceptance of Office) Order 1990

revoked (in part): SI 2004/1508 Art.4

956. Local Authorities (Councillors) (Declaration of Acceptance of Office) (Scotland) Order 1990

Sch.1, amended: SSI 2003/199 Sch.1

1020. Public Service Vehicles (Conduct of Drivers, Inspectors, Conductors and Passengers) Regulations 1990

Reg.3, amended: SI 2002/1724 Reg.3

Reg.5, amended: SI 2002/1724 Reg.4

Reg.6, amended: SI 2002/1724 Reg.5

Reg.6, revoked (in part): SI 2002/1724 Reg.5

Reg.11, added: SI 2002/1724 Reg.6

Reg.12, added: SI 2002/1724 Reg.6

Reg.13, added: SI 2002/1724 Reg.6

Reg.14, added: SI 2002/1724 Reg.6

Reg.15, added: SI 2002/1724 Reg.6

Reg.16, added: SI 2002/1724 Reg.6

Reg.17, added: SI 2002/1724 Reg.6

1110. Inheritance Tax (Delivery of Accounts) Regulations 1990

revoked: SI 2002/1733 Sch.1

1111. Inheritance Tax (Delivery of Accounts) (Scotland) Regulations 1990

revoked: SI 2002/1733 Sch.1

1312. Police (Scotland) Amendment (No.2) Regulations 1990

revoked: SSI 2004/257 Sch.4

1317. Home-Grown Cereals Authority Oilseeds Levy Scheme (Approval) Order 1990

referred to: SI 2004/1445

1330. Family Health Services Authorities (Membership and Procedure) Regulations 1990

Reg.1, amended: SI 2004/696 Art.3

Reg.2, amended: SI 2002/881 Sch.1 para.5

Reg.6, amended: SI 2004/696 Art.3

1331. Regional and District Health Authorities (Membership and Procedure) Regulations 1990

Reg.1, amended: SI 2004/696 Art.3, Sch.1 para.6

Reg.13, amended: SI 2004/696 Art.3, Sch.1 para.6

1338. Pilotage Act 1987 (Pilotage Commission Transfer of Property, Rights and Liabilities) Order 1990

Sch.1, varied: SI 2003/1633 Sch.2 para.2

Sch.1 para.1, varied: SI 2003/1633 Sch.2 para.2

Sch.1 para.2, varied: SI 2003/1633 Sch.2 para.2

Sch.1 para.3, varied: SI 2003/1633 Sch.2 para.2

Sch.1 para.4, varied: SI 2003/1633 Sch.2 para.2

NO.

1990–cont.

1504. Companies (No.2) (Northern Ireland) Order 1990

applied: 2002 c.40 Sch.15

Part II, applied: 2004 c.35 Sch.3, Sch.8

Art.1, applied: SI 2002/3150 Sch.1 para.4

Art.26, revoked: SI 2002/3150 Sch.4

Art.27, revoked: SI 2002/3152 Sch.4

Art.65, enabled: SR 2003/5

Art.74, referred to: SR 2003/4 Reg.3

Art.74, revoked (in part): SI 2002/3150 Sch.4

Sch.2, referred to: SI 2002/3150 Sch.1 para.4

Sch.2, revoked: SI 2002/3150 Sch.4

Sch.5, revoked: SI 2003/2904 Sch.1

1506. Education (Student Loans) (Northern Ireland) Order 1990

applied: SI 2002/2086 Reg.7, Reg.12, SR 2002/224 Reg.4

Art.3, enabled: SR 2002/241, SR 2003/340

Sch.2, enabled: SR 2002/241, SR 2003/340

1511. Social Security (Northern Ireland) Order 1990

Art.17, enabled: SR 2002/56

1514. Air Navigation (Noise Certification) Order 1990

revoked: SI 2002/798 Sch.1

1519. Planning (Listed Buildings and Conservation Areas) Regulations 1990

referred to: SI 2003/956 Art.15

Reg.2, amended: SI 2003/956 Sch.8 para.1

Reg.3, amended: SI 2003/2048 Reg.2

Reg.4, amended: SI 2003/2048 Reg.3

Reg.5, amended: SI 2004/2210 Reg.2

Reg.5A, added: SI 2004/2210 Reg.2

Reg.8, amended: SI 2003/2048 Reg.4

Reg.8A, added: SI 2003/956 Sch.8 para.2

Reg.8A, amended: SI 2004/2210 Reg.2

Reg.11, referred to: SI 2003/394 Reg.11

Sch.1 Part I, amended: SI 2003/2048 Reg.5

Sch.1 Part II, amended: SI 2003/2048 Reg.5

Sch.1 Part III, amended: SI 2003/2048 Reg.5

1541. Life Assurance (Apportionment of Receipts of Participating Funds) (Applicable Percentage) Order 1990

revoked: SI 2003/1860 Art.3

1551. School Pupil Records (Scotland) Regulations 1990

revoked: SSI 2003/581 Reg.12

1563. EEC Merger Control (Consequential Provisions) Regulations 1990

Reg.1, revoked: SI 2003/1398 Sch.1 para.16

Reg.2, revoked: 2002 c.40 Sch.26

Reg.3, revoked: SI 2003/1398 Sch.1 para.16

1640. Export of Goods (Control) (Iraq and Kuwait Sanctions) Order 1990

revoked: SI 2003/1555 Art.2

1651. Iraq and Kuwait (United Nations Sanctions) Order 1990

revoked: SI 2003/1519 Art.2

Art.4, amended: 2002 c.8 s.2

NO.

NO.

1990–cont.

1651. Iraq and Kuwait (United Nations Sanctions) Order 1990–*cont.*
Art.4A, amended: 2002 c.8 s.1
Art.5, amended: 2002 c.8 s.2
Art.8, amended: 2002 c.26 Sch.7 para.33

1652. Iraq and Kuwait (United Nations Sanctions) (Dependent Territories) Order 1990
revoked: SI 2003/1516 Art.2
Art.5, amended: 2002 c.8 s.2
Art.7, amended: 2002 c.8 s.2

1656. Secretary of State's Traffic Orders (Procedure) (England and Wales) Regulations 1990
Reg.2, amended: SI 2004/3168 Art.21
Reg.14, amended: SI 2004/3168 Art.21

1661. National Health Service (Travelling Expenses and Remission of Charges) Amendment No 2 Regulations 1990
revoked: SI 2003/2382 Sch.2

1665. National Health Service (Travelling Expenses and Remission of Charges) (Scotland) Amendment (No.2) Regulations 1990
revoked: SSI 2003/376 Sch.3 para.4

1715. EEC Merger Control (Distinct Market Investigations) Regulations 1990
Reg.1, amended: SI 2004/1079 Sch.1 para.3
Reg.2, amended: SI 2003/1398 Sch.1 para.17
Reg.3, substituted: SI 2003/1398 Sch.1 para.17
Reg.4, substituted: SI 2003/1398 Sch.1 para.17
Reg.5, added: SI 2003/1398 Sch.1 para.17

1718. Prescription Pricing Authority Constitution Order 1990
Art.2, amended: SI 2002/2469 Sch.1 para.48
Art.4, amended: SI 2002/2469 Sch.1 para.48, SI 2002/2861 Reg.29
Art.5, amended: SI 2002/881 Sch.1 para.6, SI 2002/2469 Sch.1 para.48, SI 2002/2861 Reg.29, SI 2004/865 Sch.1 para.6, SI 2004/1016 Sch.1 para.6, SI 2004/1771 Sch.1 para.49
Art.6, amended: SI 2002/2469 Sch.7

1728. Tryptophan in Food Regulations 1990
Reg.2, amended: SI 2002/1817 Reg.10, SI 2002/2939 Reg.10, SI 2003/3207 Reg.14

1730. Housing (Prescribed Forms) (No.2) Regulations 1990
Sch.1, amended: SI 2004/3168 Art.22

1766. Companies (Forms Amendment No 2 and Company's Type and Principal Business Activities) Regulations 1990
Reg.2, amended: SI 2002/3081 Reg.2
Reg.5, amended: SI 2002/3081 Reg.2
Sch.2, applied: SI 2002/691 Reg.3
Sch.3 Part II, amended: SI 2002/3081 Reg.2

1990–cont.

1771. Iraq and Kuwait (United Nations Sanctions) (Channel Islands) Order 1990
revoked: SI 2003/1521 Art.2
Art.5, amended: 2002 c.8 s.2
Art.6, amended: 2002 c.8 s.2
Art.8, amended: 2002 c.8 s.2

1772. National Health Service (General Dental Services) (Miscellaneous Amendments) (Scotland) Regulations 1990
Reg.17, revoked: SSI 2003/158 Sch.4

1777. Income Support (Liable Relatives) Regulations 1990
Reg.2, amended: SI 2002/2497 Sch.2 para.1

1792. Tryptophan in Food (Scotland) Regulations 1990
Reg.2, amended: SSI 2002/397 Reg.9, SSI 2004/8 Reg.13
Reg.3, amended: SSI 2002/397 Reg.9

1871. Social Security (Attendence Allowance and Claims and Payments) Amendment Regulations 1990
Reg.3, revoked (in part): SI 2003/492 Sch.3 Part 1

1985. Merchant Shipping (Medical Examination) (Amendment) Regulations 1990
revoked: SI 2002/2055 Reg.1

1987. Iraq and Kuwait (United Nations Sanctions) (No.2) Order 1990
revoked: SI 2003/1519 Art.2
Art.3, amended: 2002 c.8 s.2

1988. Iraq and Kuwait (United Nations Sanctions) (Dependent Territories) (No.2) Order 1990
revoked: SI 2003/1516 Art.2
Art.3, amended: 2002 c.8 s.2

2024. National Health Service Trusts (Membership and Procedure) Regulations 1990
Reg.1, amended: SI 2002/2469 Sch.1 para.49, SI 2002/2861 Reg.30, SI 2004/696 Art.3, Sch.1 para.7, SI 2004/865 Sch.1 para.7, SI 2004/1016 Sch.1 para.7
Reg.4, amended: SI 2002/881 Sch.1 para.7, SI 2004/1771 Sch.1 para.48
Reg.11, amended: SI 2004/19 Reg.2, SI 2004/696 Art.3, Sch.1 para.7, SI 2004/865 Sch.1 para.7, SI 2004/1016 Sch.1 para.7

2035. Overhead Lines (Exemption) Regulations 1990
Reg.3, amended: SI 2003/2155 Sch.1 para.29

2085. Jam and Similar Products (Amendment) Regulations 1990
revoked (in part): SI 2003/3120 Reg.10, SI 2004/553 Reg.10

NO.

NO.

1990–cont.

2101. Retirement Benefits Schemes (Continuation of Rights of Members of Approved Schemes) Regulations 1990
applied: SR 2002/352 Sch.4 para.7

2105. Act of Sederunt (Amendment of Sheriff Court Ordinary Cause, Summary Cause, and Small Claim, Rules) (No.2) 1990
r.3, revoked: SSI 2002/132 Sch.2
r.4, revoked: SSI 2002/133 Sch.2

2144. Iraq and Kuwait (United Nations Sanctions) (Second Amendment) Order 1990
referred to: 2002 c.26 Sch.7 para.33

2145. Civil Aviation Act 1982 (Jersey) Order 1990
referred to: SI 2002/1078

2158. Credit Cards (Merchant Acquisition) Order 1990
applied: SI 2004/2181 Sch.2

2159. Credit Cards (Price Discrimination) Order 1990
applied: SI 2004/2181 Sch.2

2179. Building Standards (Scotland) Regulations 1990
referred to: SSI 2003/461 Reg.33

2180. Jam and Similar Products (Scotland) Amendment Regulations 1990
revoked: SSI 2004/133 Reg.11

2185. Road Vehicles (Registration and Licensing) (Amendment) Regulations 1990
revoked: SI 2002/2742 Sch.1 Part I

2208. Social Security (Miscellaneous Provisions) Amendment Regulations 1990
Reg.1, amended: SI 2003/492 Sch.3 Part 1
Reg.7, revoked (in part): SI 2003/492 Sch.3 Part 1
Reg.8, revoked (in part): SI 2003/492 Sch.3 Part 1
Reg.9, revoked (in part): SI 2003/492 Sch.3 Part 1
Reg.10, revoked (in part): SI 2003/492 Sch.3 Part 1
Reg.11, revoked (in part): SI 2003/492 Sch.3 Part 1
Reg.12, revoked (in part): SI 2003/492 Sch.3 Part 1
Reg.13, revoked (in part): SI 2003/492 Sch.3 Part 1
Reg.14, revoked (in part): SI 2003/492 Sch.3 Part 1
Reg.15, revoked (in part): SI 2003/492 Sch.3 Part 1
Reg.16, revoked (in part): SI 2003/492 Sch.3 Part 1

2211. British Nationality (Hong Kong) (Registration of Citizens) Regulations 1990
Sch.1, amended: 2002 c.8 s.1

1990–cont.

2231. Income Tax (Building Societies) (Dividends and Interest) Regulations 1990
applied: SI 2003/3297 Reg.16
Reg.2, amended: SI 2003/2155 Sch.1 para.24
Reg.11, referred to: SI 2003/3297 Reg.16
Reg.15, referred to: SI 2003/3297 Reg.16

2232. Income Tax (Deposit-takers) (Interest Payments) Regulations 1990
applied: SI 2003/3297 Reg.16
Reg.2, amended: SI 2003/2155 Sch.1 para.24
Reg.12, referred to: SI 2003/3297 Reg.16

2244. Local Authority Social Services (Complaints Procedure) Order 1990
applied: SI 2003/710 Sch.1 para.8, Sch.2 para.3

2291. Protection of Trading Interests Act 1980 (Hong Kong) Order 1990
Sch.1 para.3, amended: 2002 c.8 s.2
Sch.1 para.6, amended: 2002 c.8 s.2

2292. British Nationality (Hong Kong) (Selection Scheme) Order 1990
Sch.1 Part I para.3, amended: 2002 c.8 s.2

2295. Patents Act 1977 (Isle of Man) (Variation) Order 1990
revoked: SI 2003/1249 Art.4

2350. Peak Rail Light Railway Order 1990
Art.6, amended: SI 2003/2155 Sch.1 para.18

2359. Aberdeen Harbour Revisions Order 1990
revoked: SSI 2002/310 Sch.3

2360. Public Lending Right Scheme 1982 (Commencement of Variations) Order 1990
Part I para.2, amended: SI 2004/1258
Part II para.5, amended: SI 2004/1258
Part V para.46, varied: SI 2003/3045 Art.2
Sch.5, revoked: SI 2004/1258

2361. Tax-exempt Special Savings Account Regulations 1990
Reg.11, amended: SI 2003/2096 Sch.1 para.46

2402. Bradford Hospitals N.H.S Trust (Establishment) Order 1990
Art.1, amended: SI 2003/834 Art.2
Art.2, amended: SI 2003/834 Art.2
Art.4, substituted: SI 2003/834 Art.4

2406. Chester and Halton Community National Health Service Trust (Establishment) Order 1990
revoked: SI 2002/1499 Art.2

2407. Christie Hospital Health Service Trust (Establishment) Order 1990
applied: SI 2003/3059 Sch.1

2410. Croydon Community National Health Service Trust (Establishment) Order 1990
revoked: SI 2002/1323 Sch.1

1990–cont.

2434. Nuffield Orthopaedic Centre N.H.S Trust (Establishment) Order 1990

applied: SI 2003/3059 Sch.1

2440. Royal National Orthopaedic Hospital National Health Service Trust (Establishment) Order 1990

applied: SI 2003/3059 Sch.1

2463. Food Safety (Sampling and Qualifications) Regulations 1990

varied: SI 2002/1090 Reg.4, SSI 2004/187 Reg.4

Reg.6, applied: SI 2002/1090 Reg.4, SSI 2002/300 Reg.4, SSI 2004/187 Reg.4

Reg.6, varied: SI 2002/931 Reg.4, SSI 2002/179 Reg.4

Reg.7, applied: SI 2002/1090 Reg.4, SSI 2002/300 Reg.4, SSI 2004/187 Reg.4

Reg.7, varied: SI 2002/931 Reg.4, SSI 2002/179 Reg.4

Reg.8, applied: SI 2002/1090 Reg.4, SSI 2002/300 Reg.4, SSI 2004/187 Reg.4

Reg.8, varied: SI 2002/931 Reg.4, SSI 2002/179 Reg.4

Reg.9, varied: SSI 2002/179 Reg.7, SSI 2002/300 Reg.5, SSI 2004/187 Reg.7

Sch.1, amended: SI 2002/890 Reg.10, SI 2002/1886 Reg.10, SI 2002/2364 Reg.19, SI 2002/2834 Reg.19, SI 2002/3008 Reg.7, SI 2003/302 Reg.7, SI 2003/666 Reg.22, SI 2003/1478 Reg.11, SI 2003/1721 Reg.11, SI 2003/3042 Reg.22, SI 2004/656 Reg.15, SI 2004/1509 Reg.15, SSI 2002/267 Reg.10, SSI 2003/289 Reg.11

2477. Local Elections (Parishes and Communities) (Declaration of Acceptance of Office) Order 1990

revoked (in part): SI 2004/1508 Art.4

2486. Food Safety Act 1990 (Consequential Modifications) (England and Wales) Order 1990

Art.19, revoked (in part): SI 2002/890 Sch.1, SI 2002/1886 Sch.1

Sch.1 Part I, amended: SI 2002/890 Sch.1, SI 2002/1886 Sch.1, SI 2003/1563 Reg.10, SI 2003/1564 Reg.10, SI 2003/1596 Reg.10, SI 2003/1659 Reg.11, SI 2003/2243 Reg.10, SI 2003/3037 Reg.11, SI 2003/3041 Reg.10, SI 2003/3044 Reg.10, SI 2003/3047 Reg.10, SI 2003/3053 Reg.10, SI 2003/3120 Reg.10, SI 2004/553 Reg.10

Sch.2, amended: SI 2002/890 Sch.1, SI 2002/1886 Sch.1, SI 2003/1563 Reg.10, SI 2003/1564 Reg.10, SI 2003/1596 Reg.10, SI 2003/1659 Reg.11, SI 2003/2243 Reg.10, SI 2003/3037 Reg.11, SI 2003/3041 Reg.10, SI 2003/3044 Reg.10, SI 2003/3047 Reg.10, SI 2003/3053 Reg.10

1990–cont.

2486. Food Safety Act 1990 (Consequential Modifications) (England and Wales) Order 1990–*cont.*

Sch.3 Part I, amended: SI 2002/890 Sch.1, SI 2002/1886 Sch.1, SI 2003/1563 Reg.10, SI 2003/1564 Reg.10, SI 2003/1596 Reg.10, SI 2003/1659 Reg.11, SI 2003/2243 Reg.10, SI 2003/3037 Reg.11, SI 2003/3041 Reg.10, SI 2003/3044 Reg.10, SI 2003/3047 Reg.10, SI 2003/3053 Reg.10, SI 2003/3120 Reg.10, SI 2004/553 Reg.10

Sch.5, amended: SI 2002/890 Sch.1, SI 2002/1886 Sch.1

Sch.6, amended: SI 2003/1563 Reg.10, SI 2003/1564 Reg.10, SI 2003/1596 Reg.10, SI 2003/1659 Reg.11, SI 2003/2243 Reg.10, SI 2003/3037 Reg.11, SI 2003/3041 Reg.10, SI 2003/3044 Reg.10, SI 2003/3047 Reg.10, SI 2003/3053 Reg.10, SI 2003/3120 Reg.10, SI 2004/553 Reg.10

Sch.7, amended: SI 2002/890 Sch.1, SI 2002/1886 Sch.1

Sch.12, amended: SI 2003/1563 Reg.10, SI 2003/1564 Reg.10, SI 2003/1596 Reg.10, SI 2003/1659 Reg.11, SI 2003/2243 Reg.10, SI 2003/3037 Reg.11, SI 2003/3041 Reg.10, SI 2003/3044 Reg.10, SI 2003/3047 Reg.10, SI 2003/3053 Reg.10

2490. Food (Control of Irradiation) Regulations 1990

Reg.2, amended: SI 2002/1922 Reg.2

Reg.6A, revoked (in part): SSI 2002/284 Reg.4

Reg.7, amended: SI 2002/1922 Reg.2

Sch.1 Part I para.1, amended: SI 2002/1922 Reg.2, SSI 2002/284 Reg.5

Sch.1 Part II para.9, substituted: SSI 2002/284 Reg.5

Sch.1 Part III para.1, amended: SI 2002/1922 Reg.2

Sch.1 Part VI para.2, amended: SI 2002/1922 Reg.2

Sch.2 Part I para.2, amended: SSI 2002/284 Reg.6

Sch.2 Part II para.3, amended: SI 2002/1922 Reg.2

Sch.3 para.2, substituted: SSI 2002/284 Reg.7

2536. Broadcasting Act 1990 (Independent Radio Services Exceptions) Order 1990

Art.2, amended: SI 2003/2155 Sch.1 para.30

2546. Life Assurance (Apportionment of Receipts of Participating Funds) (Applicable Percentage) (Amendment) Order 1990

revoked: SI 2003/1860 Art.3

2588. Criminal Justice (Confiscation) (Northern Ireland) Order 1990

applied: 2002 c.29 s.8, s.94, s.118, s.158

NO.

1990–cont.

2588. Criminal Justice (Confiscation) (Northern Ireland) Order 1990–*cont.*

Art.14, applied: 2002 c.29 s.41, s.49, s.51, s.53, s.79, s.120, s.125, s.128, s.145, s.190, s.197, s.199, s.201, s.227

Art.37, revoked (in part): 2002 c.29 Sch.12

2615. Quick-frozen Foodstuffs Regulations 1990

Reg.5, amended: SI 2004/2145 Reg.2, SI 2004/2731 Reg.2, SSI 2004/395 Reg.2

2621. Firearms (Removal to Northern Ireland) Order 1990

revoked: SI 2003/3228 Art.2

2625. Food Safety Act 1990 (Consequential Modifications) (Scotland) Order 1990

Sch.1 Part I, amended: SSI 2002/267 Sch.1, SSI 2003/291 Reg.12, SSI 2003/293 Reg.11, SSI 2003/311 Reg.11, SSI 2003/527 Reg.11, SSI 2003/569 Reg.12, SSI 2004/6 Reg.11, SSI 2004/133 Reg.11

Sch.2, amended: SSI 2002/267 Sch.1, SSI 2003/291 Reg.12, SSI 2003/311 Reg.11, SSI 2003/569 Reg.12

Sch.3 Part II, amended: SSI 2002/267 Sch.1, SSI 2003/291 Reg.12, SSI 2003/293 Reg.11, SSI 2003/311 Reg.11, SSI 2003/569 Reg.12, SSI 2004/6 Reg.11, SSI 2004/133 Reg.11

Sch.4, amended: SSI 2002/267 Sch.1

Sch.5, amended: SSI 2003/291 Reg.12, SSI 2003/293 Reg.11, SSI 2003/311 Reg.11, SSI 2003/569 Reg.12, SSI 2004/6 Reg.11, SSI 2004/133 Reg.11

Sch.6, amended: SSI 2002/267 Sch.1

Sch.8, amended: SSI 2002/267 Sch.1, SSI 2003/291 Reg.12, SSI 2003/293 Reg.11, SSI 2003/311 Reg.11, SSI 2003/569 Reg.12, SSI 2004/6 Reg.11, SSI 2004/133 Reg.11

2639. Health Education Board for Scotland Order 1990

Art.2, amended: SSI 2003/154 Art.3

Art.3, amended: SSI 2003/154 Art.4

Art.4, amended: SSI 2003/154 Art.5

Art.5, applied: SSI 2003/153

Sch.1 Part I, amended: SSI 2003/154 Art.6

Sch.1 Part I, applied: SSI 2003/153

Sch.1 Part III, amended: SI 2003/1590 Sch.1 para.23, SSI 2003/154 Art.7

1991

20. Food Protection (Emergency Prohibitions) (Radioactivity in Sheep) Order 1991

Sch.1 Part II para.2, amended: SSI 2003/375 Sch.2

Sch.1 Part II para.3, amended: SSI 2004/48 Sch.2

Sch.1 Part II para.3, revoked (in part): SSI 2003/375 Sch.1, SSI 2004/48 Art.2

NO.

1991–cont.

111. Litter (Fixed Penalty Notices) Order 1991

revoked (in part): SSI 2004/427 Art.3

122. Land Registration (Open Register) Rules 1991

applied: SI 2003/1953 Art.27

r.4A, applied: SI 2003/165 Sch.3 Part II

r.4B, applied: SI 2003/165 Sch.3 Part IV

r.13, applied: SI 2003/165 Sch.3 Part II

Sch.1, amended: SI 2002/2539 Sch.3 para.1

Sch.1, referred to: SI 2003/165 Art.10

Sch.2, amended: SI 2002/2539 Sch.3 para.2, Sch.3 para.3

134. Bitton Light Railway Order 1991

Art.7, amended: SI 2003/2155 Sch.1 para.18

167. Occupational Pension Schemes (Preservation of Benefit) Regulations 1991

Reg.12, see *Merchant Navy Ratings Pension Fund Trustees Ltd v Chambers* [2002] I.C.R. 359 (Ch D), Blackburne, J.

194. Health and Personal Social Services (Northern Ireland) Order 1991

Art.8, amended: 2004 c.17 Sch.3 para.12

Art.10, applied: SR 2002/224 Reg.12, SR 2002/292 Sch.1 Part II, SR 2002/381 Reg.2

Art.12, applied: SR 2002/381 Reg.2, Reg.5

Art.18, applied: SR 2002/66 Reg.1

Art.21, amended: SI 2004/311 Sch.1 para.14

Art.22, revoked: SI 2003/418 Sch.3

Art.26, revoked: 2002 c.5 (NI) Sch.1

Sch.1, amended: SI 2004/311 Sch.1 para.14

Sch.3, applied: 2002 c.6 (NI) s.1, SR 2003/28 Reg.4

Sch.5, amended: 2004 c.30 Sch.7 Part 2

238. Whitehaven Harbour Revision Order 1991

revoked: SI 2002/306 Sch.3

269. Hydrocarbon (Heavy) Oil Regulations 1991

Reg.12, see *Masterson v DPP* [2003] Eu. L.R. 25 (HC (Irl)), Roderick H Murphy, J.

330. European Communities (Recognition of Qualifications in Pharmacy) Regulations (Ireland) 1991

Reg.4, see *Sam McCauley Chemists (Blackpool) Ltd v Pharmaceutical Society of Ireland* [2003] Eu. L.R. 37 (HC (Irl)), McCracken, J.

339. Misuse of Drugs (Licence Fees) (Amendment) Regulations 1991

revoked: SI 2003/611 Sch.1

346. Control of Pollution (Silage, Slurry and Agricultural Fuel Oil) (Scotland) Regulations 1991

revoked: SSI 2003/531 Reg.12

351. Local Authorities (Members Allowances) Regulations 1991

applied: SI 2002/1895 Reg.20, SI 2003/1021 Reg.17, Reg.23

NO.

1991–cont.

351. Local Authorities (Members Allowances) Regulations 1991–*cont.*

revoked (in part): SI 2003/895 Reg.15, SI 2003/1021 Reg.33

364. Insolvency Rules (Northern Ireland) 1991

r.6.005, see *Moore (t/a James Moore Earth Moving) v Inland Revenue Commissioners* [2002] N.I. 26 (Ch D (NI)), Girvan, J.

369. Fire Services (Appointments and Promotion) (Amendment) Regulations 1991

revoked: SI 2004/481 Sch.2

387. Enterprise (Scotland) Consequential Amendments Order 1991

Art.14, revoked (in part): SI 2003/492 Sch.3 Part 1

407. United Kingdom Transplant Support Service Authority (Establishment and Constitution) Order 1991

referred to: SI 2004/1119 Sch.1

408. United Kingdom Transplant Support Service Authority Regulations 1991

Reg.8, amended: SI 2004/696 Sch.1 para.8

460. Abortion (Scotland) Regulations 1991

Reg.5, amended: SI 2002/3135 Sch.1 para.27

472. Environmental Protection (Prescribed Processes and Substances) Regulations 1991

Reg.5, amended: SSI 2004/26 Reg.22

Reg.6, amended: SSI 2004/26 Reg.22

Sch.1, applied: SSI 2004/26 Reg.3

Sch.1, referred to: SSI 2004/26 Reg.3

Sch.1 Part 1, referred to: SI 2004/107 Reg.3

481. National Health Service (Remuneration and Conditions of Service) Regulations 1991

Reg.1, amended: SI 2002/2469 Sch.2

494. Bankruptcy and Companies (Department of Trade and Industry) Fees (Amendment) Order 1991

revoked: SI 2004/593 Sch.1

496. Insolvency Fees (Amendment) Order 1991

revoked (in part): SI 2004/593 Sch.1

499. Abortion Regulations 1991

Reg.2, substituted: SI 2002/887 Reg.2, SI 2002/2879 Reg.2

Reg.3, amended: SI 2002/887 Reg.3, SI 2002/2879 Reg.3

Reg.4, amended: SI 2002/887 Reg.4, SI 2002/2879 Reg.4

Reg.5, amended: SI 2002/887 Reg.5, SI 2002/2879 Reg.5, SI 2002/3135 Sch.1 para.28

Sch.2, amended: SI 2002/887 Sch.1, SI 2002/2879 Sch.1

NO.

1991–cont.

507. Environmental Protection (Applications, Appeals and Registers) Regulations 1991

see *R. (on the application of Furness) v Environment Agency* [2001] EWHC Admin 1058, [2002] Env. L.R. 26 (QBD (Admin Ct)), Turner, J.

537. National Health Service (Remuneration and Conditions of Service) (Scotland) Regulations 1991

applied: SSI 2002/103 Sch.1 Part III, SSI 2002/305 Sch.1 Part III, SSI 2002/534 Sch.1 Part III

557. National Health Service (Travelling Expenses and Remission of Charges) Regulations 1991

revoked: SI 2003/2382 Sch.2

564. Common Services Agency (Membership and Procedure) Regulations 1991

Reg.4, amended: SSI 2004/212 Sch.1 para.3

569. National Health Service (Dental Services) (Miscellaneous Amendments) (Scotland) Regulations 1991

Reg.7, revoked: SSI 2003/158 Sch.4

575. National Health Service (Travelling Expenses and Remission of Charges) (Scotland) Amendment Regulations 1991

revoked: SSI 2003/376 Sch.3 para.5

580. National Health Service (Dentists Remuneration-Special Arrangement) Order 1991

Art.2, amended: SI 2002/2469 Sch.10

584. National Health Service Superannuation, Premature Retirement and Injury Benefits (Amendment) Regulations 1991

Reg.8, revoked: SI 2002/1311 Sch.2

Reg.9, revoked: SI 2002/1311 Sch.2

Reg.10, revoked: SI 2002/1311 Sch.2

589. Statutory Sick Pay (National Health Service Employees) Regulations 1991

Reg.1, amended: SI 2002/2469 Sch.1 para.50, SI 2004/696 Art.3

Reg.5, amended: SI 2002/2469 Sch.3

590. Statutory Maternity Pay (National Health Service Employees) Regulations 1991

Reg.1, amended: SI 2002/2469 Sch.1 para.51, SI 2004/696 Art.3

Reg.3, amended: SI 2002/2690 Reg.11

Reg.4, amended: SI 2002/2690 Reg.12

Reg.5, amended: SI 2002/2469 Sch.3

720. Borough of Langbaurgh (Electoral Arrangements) Order 1991

revoked: SI 2003/162 Art.10

757. European Bank for Reconstruction and Development (Immunities and Privileges) Order 1991

Art.13, amended: 2002 c.8 s.2

1991–cont.

762. Food Safety (Northern Ireland) Order 1991

applied: SR 2002/39, SR 2003/353 Reg.4, SR 2003/360 Reg.4

referred to: SR 2002/307 Reg.4

Art.2, applied: SI 2002/3170 Art.3, SR 2002/140 Reg.5, SR 2002/141 Reg.5, SR 2002/226 Reg.5, SR 2002/301 Reg.3

Art.2, varied: SR 2002/35 Reg.6, SR 2002/264 Reg.9, SR 2003/10 Reg.5, SR 2003/300 Reg.9, SR 2003/301 Reg.9, SR 2003/313 Reg.10

Art.3, applied: SR 2002/140 Reg.5, SR 2002/141 Reg.5

Art.3, varied: SR 2002/35 Reg.6, SR 2002/264 Reg.9, SR 2003/10 Reg.5, SR 2003/300 Reg.9, SR 2003/301 Reg.9, SR 2003/313 Reg.10

Art.4, applied: SR 2002/82 Art.5, SR 2003/160 Reg.10

Art.4, varied: SR 2002/35 Reg.6, SR 2002/219 Reg.7, SR 2002/264 Reg.9, SR 2003/10 Reg.5, SR 2003/300 Reg.9, SR 2003/301 Reg.9, SR 2003/313 Reg.10

Art.7, applied: SR 2002/35 Reg.6, SR 2002/219 Reg.7, SR 2002/264 Reg.9, SR 2003/10 Reg.5, SR 2003/160 Reg.10, SR 2003/301 Reg.9, SR 2003/313 Reg.10

Art.8, applied: 2002 c.26 Sch.4 para.1, SR 2002/82 Art.5, SR 2002/140 Reg.5, SR 2002/141 Reg.5, SR 2002/219 Reg.3, SR 2002/225 Reg.47, Reg.77

Art.8, referred to: SR 2002/141 Reg.5

Art.8, revoked (in part): 2002 c.26 Sch.13

Art.8, varied: SR 2002/82 Art.5, SR 2002/140 Reg.5, SR 2002/141 Reg.5, SR 2002/219 Reg.7, SR 2002/225 Reg.77, SR 2002/226 Reg.5, SR 2003/10 Reg.5

Art.9, varied: SR 2002/141 Reg.5

Art.12, applied: SR 2002/82 Art.4

Art.12, enabled: SR 2002/82

Art.13, applied: SR 2002/35 Reg.6, SR 2002/219 Reg.7, SR 2002/264 Reg.9, SR 2003/10 Reg.5, SR 2003/160 Reg.10, SR 2003/301 Reg.9, SR 2003/313 Reg.10

Art.14, applied: SR 2002/35 Reg.6, SR 2002/219 Reg.7, SR 2002/264 Reg.9, SR 2003/10 Reg.5, SR 2003/160 Reg.10, SR 2003/301 Reg.9, SR 2003/313 Reg.10

Art.15, enabled: SR 2002/39, SR 2002/217, SR 2002/219, SR 2002/238, SR 2002/262, SR 2002/264, SR 2002/316, SR 2003/2, SR 2003/9, SR 2003/10, SR 2003/158, SR 2003/159, SR 2003/160, SR 2003/182, SR 2003/257, SR 2003/300, SR 2003/301, SR 2003/313

Art.16, enabled: SR 2002/35, SR 2002/39, SR 2002/217, SR 2002/219, SR 2002/262, SR 2002/264, SR 2002/316, SR 2003/2, SR 2003/158, SR 2003/159, SR 2003/160, SR 2003/182, SR 2003/257,

1991–cont.

762. Food Safety (Northern Ireland) Order 1991–*cont.*

Art.16, enabled:–*cont.* SR 2003/300, SR 2003/301, SR 2003/313

Art.19, applied: SR 2002/82 Art.5, SR 2002/141 Reg.5, SR 2002/226 Reg.5, SR 2003/160 Reg.10

Art.19, varied: SR 2002/35 Reg.6, SR 2002/140 Reg.5, SR 2002/219 Reg.7, SR 2002/264 Reg.9, SR 2002/293 Reg.5, SR 2002/307 Reg.5, SR 2003/10 Reg.5, SR 2003/300 Reg.9, SR 2003/301 Reg.9, SR 2003/313 Reg.10, SR 2003/353 Reg.5, SR 2003/360 Reg.5

Art.20, applied: SR 2003/160 Reg.10

Art.20, varied: SR 2002/35 Reg.6, SR 2002/219 Reg.7, SR 2002/264 Reg.9, SR 2003/10 Reg.5, SR 2003/300 Reg.9, SR 2003/301 Reg.9, SR 2003/313 Reg.10

Art.21, varied: SR 2002/35 Reg.6, SR 2002/264 Reg.9, SR 2003/10 Reg.5, SR 2003/300 Reg.9, SR 2003/301 Reg.9, SR 2003/313 Reg.10

Art.25, enabled: SR 2002/35, SR 2002/39, SR 2002/219, SR 2002/238, SR 2002/262, SR 2002/264, SR 2002/316, SR 2003/2, SR 2003/9, SR 2003/10, SR 2003/158, SR 2003/159, SR 2003/160, SR 2003/182, SR 2003/257, SR 2003/300, SR 2003/301, SR 2003/313

Art.26, enabled: SR 2002/35, SR 2002/39, SR 2002/82, SR 2002/219, SR 2002/262, SR 2002/264, SR 2003/10, SR 2003/158, SR 2003/160, SR 2003/182, SR 2003/257, SR 2003/300, SR 2003/301, SR 2003/313

Art.27, applied: SR 2002/1 Reg.8, Reg.9

Art.29, applied: SR 2002/140 Reg.5, SR 2002/141 Reg.4, SR 2002/219 Reg.5, SR 2002/226 Reg.5, SR 2002/293 Reg.5, SR 2002/307 Reg.5, SR 2003/353 Reg.5, SR 2003/360 Reg.5

Art.29, varied: SR 2002/140 Reg.5, SR 2002/141 Reg.5, SR 2002/219 Reg.5, SR 2002/226 Reg.5, SR 2002/293 Reg.5, SR 2002/307 Reg.5, SR 2003/300 Reg.9, SR 2003/353 Reg.5, SR 2003/360 Reg.5

Art.30, applied: SI 2002/3170 Art.3, SR 2003/160 Reg.10

Art.30, varied: SR 2002/35 Reg.6, SR 2002/141 Reg.5, SR 2002/219 Reg.7, SR 2002/225 Reg.77, SR 2002/264 Reg.9, SR 2003/10 Reg.5, SR 2003/300 Reg.9, SR 2003/301 Reg.9, SR 2003/313 Reg.10

Art.31, applied: SI 2002/3170 Art.3

Art.32, enabled: SR 2002/316, SR 2003/2, SR 2003/182

Art.33, applied: SR 2002/141 Reg.4, SR 2002/293 Reg.4, SR 2002/307 Reg.4, SR 2003/160 Reg.10, SR 2003/360 Reg.4

NO.

1991–cont.

762. Food Safety (Northern Ireland) Order 1991–*cont.*

Art.33, referred to: SR 2002/140 Reg.4, SR 2002/226 Reg.4

Art.34, applied: SR 2002/82 Art.5, SR 2002/141 Reg.5, SR 2002/219 Reg.7, SR 2002/226 Reg.5, SR 2002/264 Reg.9, SR 2002/293 Reg.5, SR 2003/10 Reg.5, SR 2003/160 Reg.10, SR 2003/300 Reg.9, SR 2003/301 Reg.9, SR 2003/313 Reg.10, SR 2003/353 Reg.5, SR 2003/360 Reg.5

Art.34, referred to: SR 2002/35 Reg.6, SR 2002/141 Reg.5

Art.34, varied: SR 2002/35 Reg.6, SR 2002/140 Reg.5, SR 2002/219 Reg.7, SR 2002/264 Reg.9, SR 2002/293 Reg.5, SR 2002/307 Reg.5, SR 2003/10 Reg.5, SR 2003/300 Reg.9, SR 2003/301 Reg.9, SR 2003/313 Reg.10, SR 2003/353 Reg.5, SR 2003/360 Reg.5

Art.36, applied: SR 2002/82 Art.5, SR 2002/141 Reg.5, SR 2002/226 Reg.5, SR 2003/160 Reg.10

Art.36, varied: SR 2002/35 Reg.6, SR 2002/140 Reg.5, SR 2002/219 Reg.7, SR 2002/264 Reg.9, SR 2002/293 Reg.5, SR 2002/307 Reg.5, SR 2003/10 Reg.5, SR 2003/300 Reg.9, SR 2003/301 Reg.9, SR 2003/313 Reg.10, SR 2003/353 Reg.5, SR 2003/360 Reg.5

Art.43, applied: SR 2002/82 Art.5

Art.47, applied: SR 2002/35, SR 2002/82, SR 2002/217, SR 2002/219, SR 2002/238, SR 2002/262, SR 2002/264, SR 2002/316, SR 2003/9SI-BEGIN, SR 2003/2, SR 2003/10, SR 2003/158, SR 2003/159, SR 2003/160, SR 2003/182, SR 2003/257, SR 2003/300, SR 2003/301, SR 2003/313

Art.47, enabled: SR 2002/35, SR 2002/39, SR 2002/82, SR 2002/219, SR 2002/238, SR 2002/262, SR 2002/264, SR 2002/316, SR 2003/2, SR 2003/9, SR 2003/10, SR 2003/158, SR 2003/159, SR 2003/160, SR 2003/182, SR 2003/257, SR 2003/300, SR 2003/301, SR 2003/313

Art.47, referred to: SR 2002/35

Sch.1, enabled: SR 2002/39, SR 2002/238, SR 2003/9, SR 2003/158, SR 2003/182, SR 2003/257

773. Vehicle Inspectorate Trading Fund Order 1991

applied: SI 2003/942

Art.6, amended: SI 2003/942 Art.7

Sch.1 para.1, referred to: SI 2003/942 Art.4

Sch.1 para.1, substituted: SI 2003/942 Sch.2

Sch.1 para.2, referred to: SI 2003/942 Art.4

Sch.1 para.2, substituted: SI 2003/942 Sch.2

Sch.1 para.3, referred to: SI 2003/942 Art.4

Sch.1 para.3, substituted: SI 2003/942 Sch.2

Sch.1 para.4, referred to: SI 2003/942 Art.4

NO.

1991–cont.

773. Vehicle Inspectorate Trading Fund Order 1991–*cont.*

Sch.1 para.4, substituted: SI 2003/942 Sch.2

Sch.1 para.5, referred to: SI 2003/942 Art.4

Sch.1 para.5, substituted: SI 2003/942 Sch.2

Sch.2, referred to: SI 2003/942

789. Costs in Criminal Cases (General) (Amendment) Regulations 1991

Reg.7, see *R. v Martin (Costs)* [2004] 1 Costs L.R. 167 (Supreme Court Costs Office), Costs Judge Rogers

Reg.9, see *R. v Martin (Costs)* [2004] 1 Costs L.R. 167 (Supreme Court Costs Office), Costs Judge Rogers

816. District of South Herefordshire (Electoral Arrangements) Order 1991

revoked: SI 2002/187 Art.11

821. Act of Sederunt (Amendment of Summary Cause and Small Claim Rules) 1991

revoked: SSI 2002/132 Sch.2

r.3, revoked: SSI 2002/133 Sch.2

824. European Communities (Recognition of Professional Qualifications) Regulations 1991

amended: SI 2002/3051 Sch.1 para.2

applied: SI 2002/253 Art.9, SI 2002/254 Art.12, SI 2004/1886 Art.3

referred to: SI 2002/254 Art.9, SI 2002/3051 Sch.1 para.1

Reg.2, amended: SI 2002/3051 Sch.1 para.3

Reg.2, applied: SI 2003/835 Reg.9, SI 2004/2152 Reg.9

Reg.5, amended: SI 2002/3051 Sch.1 para.4

Reg.6, amended: SI 2002/3051 Sch.1 para.5

Reg.9, amended: SI 2002/3051 Sch.1 para.6

Sch.1 Part 1, amended: SI 2002/880 Sch.1 para.6, SI 2002/881 Sch.1 para.8, SI 2002/3051 Sch.1 para.7, SI 2004/1771 Sch.1 para.47, SI 2004/2033 Art.9

Sch.1 Part 2, amended: SI 2002/3051 Sch.1 para.7

Sch.1 Part 2, referred to: SI 2002/2934 Reg.24

875. Buying Agency Trading Fund Order 1991

Sch.1, amended: SI 2002/2469 Sch.2

880. Financial Markets and Insolvency Regulations 1991

Reg.14, amended: SI 2003/2096 Sch.1 para.48

Reg.15, amended: SI 2003/2096 Sch.1 para.49

Reg.19, amended: SI 2003/2096 Sch.1 para.50

890. Arrangements for Placement of Children (General) Regulations 1991

referred to: SI 2003/493 Reg.16

Reg.1, amended: SI 2002/2935 Reg.5

Reg.2, amended: SI 2002/2935 Reg.5

NO.

1991—cont.

890. Arrangements for Placement of Children (General) Regulations 1991—cont.

Reg.5, amended: SI 2002/2469 Sch.1 para.52, SI 2002/2935 Reg.5, SI 2002/3013 Reg.2

Reg.6, amended: SI 2002/546 Reg.2, SI 2002/2935 Reg.5

Reg.7, substituted: SI 2002/546 Reg.2, SI 2002/3013 Reg.2

Reg.10, amended: SI 2002/546 Reg.2, SI 2002/2935 Reg.5

Reg.11, amended: SI 2002/2935 Reg.5

Sch.2 para.1, amended: SI 2002/546 Reg.2, SI 2002/3013 Reg.2

Sch.2 para.2, amended: SI 2002/546 Reg.2, SI 2002/3013 Reg.2

Sch.2 para.6, amended: SI 2002/546 Reg.2, SI 2002/3013 Reg.2

Sch.3 para.4, amended: SI 2002/2935 Reg.5

Sch.4 para.5, amended: SI 2002/546 Reg.2, SI 2002/2935 Reg.5

892. Definition of Independent Visitors (Children) Regulations 1991

referred to: SI 2002/808 Art.2

Reg.2, amended: SI 2002/808 Art.36

893. Placement of Children with Parents etc Regulations 1991

Reg.1, amended: SI 2002/546 Reg.3, SI 2002/2935 Reg.6

Reg.8, amended: SI 2002/2469 Sch.1 para.53

Reg.8, substituted: SI 2002/546 Reg.3

Sch.1 para.1, amended: SI 2002/2935 Reg.6

894. Representations Procedure (Children) Regulations 1991

applied: SI 2002/57 Reg.18, SI 2002/327 Reg.24, SI 2003/237 Reg.18

referred to: SI 2002/327 Reg.15

Reg.2, amended: SI 2004/719 Reg.6, SI 2004/1448 Reg.6

Reg.4, amended: SI 2004/719 Reg.6, SI 2004/1448 Reg.6

Reg.7, amended: SI 2004/719 Reg.6, SI 2004/1448 Reg.6

Reg.8, added: SI 2004/1448 Reg.6

Reg.8, amended: SI 2004/719 Reg.6, SI 2004/1448 Reg.6

Reg.8, applied: SI 2004/719 Reg.7, SI 2004/1448 Reg.7

Reg.9, amended: SI 2004/719 Reg.6, SI 2004/1448 Reg.6

Reg.9, applied: SI 2004/719 Reg.7, SI 2004/1448 Reg.7

Reg.11, amended: SI 2002/546 Reg.5, SI 2002/2935 Reg.8

Reg.11A, amended: SI 2002/546 Reg.5, SI 2002/2935 Reg.8

1991—cont.

895. Review of Children's Cases Regulations 1991

applied: SI 2002/57 Sch.6 para.5, SI 2003/237 Sch.6 para.5

Reg.1, amended: SI 2002/2935 Reg.7

Reg.2A, added: SI 2004/1419 Reg.2, SI 2004/1449 Reg.2

Reg.2A, amended: SI 2004/2253 Reg.2

Reg.3, substituted: SI 2004/1419 Reg.2, SI 2004/1449 Reg.2

Reg.6, substituted: SI 2002/546 Reg.4, SI 2002/3013 Reg.3

Reg.8A, added: SI 2004/1419 Reg.2, SI 2004/1449 Reg.2

Reg.12, amended: SI 2002/546 Reg.4, SI 2002/2935 Reg.7

Reg.13, amended: SI 2002/546 Reg.4, SI 2002/2935 Reg.7

Sch.2 para.4, amended: SI 2002/546 Reg.4, SI 2002/2935 Reg.7

Sch.3 para.1, amended: SI 2002/546 Reg.4, SI 2002/3013 Reg.3

Sch.3 para.2, amended: SI 2002/546 Reg.4, SI 2002/3013 Reg.3

Sch.3 para.6, amended: SI 2002/546 Reg.4, SI 2002/3013 Reg.3

910. Foster Placement (Children) Regulations 1991

applied: SI 2003/493 Reg.36

referred to: SI 2003/493 Reg.16

revoked (in part): SI 2002/57 Reg.51, SI 2003/237 Reg.53

933. North Tyneside Steam Railway Light Railway Order 1991

Art.9, amended: SI 2003/2155 Sch.1 para.18

975. Inspection of Premises, Children and Records (Independent Schools) Regulations 1991

revoked (in part): SI 2002/552 Reg.7, SI 2002/3161 Reg.7

998. Broadcasting Act 1990 (Isle of Man) (No.2) Order 1991

referred to: SI 2003/3193 Art.3

Art.2, amended: SI 2003/3193 Sch.2 para.1, Sch.2 para.2

Sch.1 para.1, amended: SI 2003/3193 Sch.2 para.3

Sch.1 para.8, substituted: SI 2003/3193 Sch.2 para.3

Sch.1 para.10A, added: SI 2003/3193 Sch.2 para.3

Sch.1 para.14, revoked: SI 2003/3193 Sch.2 para.3

Sch.1 para.18A, added: SI 2003/3193 Sch.2 para.3

Sch.1 para.21, amended: SI 2003/3193 Sch.2 para.3

Sch.1 para.44, amended: SI 2003/3193 Sch.2 para.3

Sch.1 para.51, substituted: SI 2003/3193 Sch.2 para.3

NO.

NO.

1991–cont.

1030. Swine Fever (Amendment) Order 1991
revoked (in part): SSI 2003/426 Art.19

1031. Savings Certificates Regulations 1991
Reg.17, amended: SI 2004/1662 Sch.1 para.26

1043. Litter (Statutory Undertakers) (Designation and Relevant Land) Order 1991
Art.2, amended: SI 2003/1615 Sch.1 para.45

1111. Yorkshire Dales Light Railway Order 1991
Art.8, amended: SI 2003/2155 Sch.1 para.18

1136. Teachers (Entitlement to Registration) (Scotland) Regulations 1991
Reg.2, revoked (in part): SSI 2004/390 Reg.2

1162. Tanfield Railway (Causey Extension) Light Railway Order 1991
Art.8, amended: SI 2003/2155 Sch.1 para.18

1169. Local Elections (Declaration of Acceptance of Office) (Welsh Forms) Order 1991
revoked: SI 2004/1508 Art.4

1176. Broadcasting (Restrictions on the Holding of Licences) Order 1991
revoked: 2003 c.21 Sch.19
varied: 2003 c.21 Sch.18 para.26

1184. County Courts (Interest on Judgment Debts) Order 1991
see *Director General of Fair Trading v First National Bank Plc* [2001] UKHL 52, [2002] 1 A.C. 481 (HL), Lord Bingham of Cornhill

1206. Companies (Fees) Regulations 1991
revoked: SI 2004/2621 Sch.3
Reg.2, amended: SI 2002/2894 Reg.4
Sch.1, amended: SI 2002/317 Reg.2, SI 2002/2894 Reg.3

1209. Common Investment Scheme 1991
applied: SI 2003/778 Art.2, Art.3, Art.5
revoked: SI 2004/266 Art.7
Art.2, amended: SI 2003/778 Art.7
Art.3, amended: SI 2003/778 Art.7
Art.4, amended: SI 2003/778 Art.7
Art.5, amended: SI 2003/778 Art.7
Art.7, amended: SI 2003/778 Art.7
Art.8, amended: SI 2003/778 Art.7
Art.9, amended: SI 2003/778 Art.7
Sch.1 para.1, amended: SI 2003/778 Art.7
Sch.1 para.1, revoked (in part): SI 2003/778 Art.7
Sch.1 para.2, amended: SI 2003/778 Art.7
Sch.1 para.3, amended: SI 2003/778 Art.7
Sch.1 para.4, amended: SI 2003/778 Art.7
Sch.1 para.5, amended: SI 2003/778 Art.7
Sch.1 para.6, amended: SI 2003/778 Art.7
Sch.1 para.7, amended: SI 2003/778 Art.7
Sch.1 para.8, amended: SI 2003/778 Art.7
Sch.1 para.8A, amended: SI 2003/778 Art.7

1991–cont.

1209. Common Investment Scheme 1991– cont.
Sch.2, amended: SI 2003/778 Art.7
Sch.3 para.1, amended: SI 2003/778 Art.7
Sch.3 para.2, amended: SI 2003/778 Art.7
Sch.3 para.3, amended: SI 2003/778 Art.7
Sch.3 para.4, amended: SI 2003/778 Art.7

1218. Veterinary Surgeons Qualifications (EEC Recognition) (German Democratic Republic Qualifications) Order 1991
revoked: SI 2003/2919 Art.13

1220. Planning (Northern Ireland) Order 1991
applied: SI 2002/3153 Art.34, SI 2003/410 Art.25, SR 2003/46 Reg.10
Part III, applied: SI 2003/430 Art.28, Art.29
Part IV, applied: SI 2002/3153 Art.46
Art.2, amended: SI 2003/430 Art.24, Sch.1 para.2, Sch.2
Art.3, amended: SI 2003/430 Art.27
Art.3, disapplied: SI 2003/430 Art.29
Art.4, amended: SI 2003/430 Art.27, Art.30
Art.4, disapplied: SI 2003/430 Art.29
Art.5, applied: SI 2003/430 Art.28
Art.6, applied: SI 2003/430 Art.28
Art.8, applied: SI 2003/430 Art.28
Art.8, disapplied: SI 2003/430 Art.29
Art.8, referred to: SI 2003/430 Art.29
Art.11, amended: SI 2003/430 Art.18
Art.12, substituted: SI 2003/430 Art.19
Art.13, enabled: SR 2002/195, SR 2003/98, SR 2003/283
Art.18, amended: SI 2002/3153 Sch.5 para.10
Art.21, enabled: SR 2003/283
Art.22, amended: SI 2003/430 Art.17
Art.25A, added: SI 2003/430 Art.20
Art.25B, added: SI 2003/430 Art.21
Art.28A, added: SI 2003/430 Sch.1 para.3
Art.29, revoked: SI 2003/430 Sch.1 para.4, Sch.2
Art.32, amended: SI 2003/430 Art.22, Sch.1 para.5
Art.33, amended: SI 2003/430 Art.20
Art.34, amended: SI 2003/430 Sch.1 para.6
Art.39, amended: SI 2003/430 Sch.1 para.7
Art.40, substituted: SI 2003/430 Art.23
Art.40A, added: SI 2003/430 Art.23
Art.40B, added: SI 2003/430 Art.23
Art.41, revoked: SI 2003/430 Sch.1 para.8, Sch.2
Art.42A, added: SI 2003/430 Art.25
Art.42B, added: SI 2003/430 Art.25
Art.42C, added: SI 2003/430 Art.25
Art.44, amended: SI 2003/430 Art.14
Art.61, amended: SI 2003/430 Art.15
Art.65, amended: SI 2003/430 Art.26
Art.65A, added: SI 2003/430 Art.26
Art.65B, added: SI 2003/430 Art.26

NO.

1991–cont.

1220. Planning (Northern Ireland) Order 1991–*cont.*

Art.66, amended: SI 2003/430 Art.26, Sch.2

Art.66, revoked (in part): SI 2003/430 Art.26, Sch.2

Art.66A, added: SI 2003/430 Art.26

Art.66B, added: SI 2003/430 Art.26

Art.67A, added: SI 2003/430 Art.6

Art.67B, added: SI 2003/430 Art.6

Art.67C, added: SI 2003/430 Art.3

Art.67D, added: SI 2003/430 Art.3

Art.68, applied: SI 2003/430 Art.6

Art.68, substituted: SI 2003/430 Art.7

Art.68A, added: SI 2003/430 Art.7

Art.68B, added: SI 2003/430 Art.7

Art.69, amended: SI 2003/430 Sch.1 para.9

Art.69(3), amended: SI 2003/430 Art.8

Art.69(4), amended: SI 2003/430 Art.8

Art.70, amended: SI 2003/430 Sch.1 para.10

Art.71, substituted: SI 2003/430 Art.8

Art.72, substituted: SI 2003/430 Art.9

Art.73, amended: SI 2003/430 Art.11, Sch.1 para.11

Art.74, amended: SI 2003/430 Art.10

Art.75, substituted: SI 2003/430 Sch.1 para.12

Art.76, amended: SI 2003/430 Sch.1 para.13

Art.76A, added: SI 2003/430 Art.4

Art.76B, added: SI 2003/430 Art.5

Art.77, amended: SI 2003/430 Art.14, Sch.1 para.14, Sch.2

Art.78, amended: SI 2003/430 Art.14, Sch.1 para.15, Sch.2

Art.81, amended: SI 2003/430 Art.15

Art.81A, added: SI 2003/430 Art.15

Art.82, substituted: SI 2003/430 Art.16

Art.82A, added: SI 2003/430 Art.16

Art.82B, added: SI 2003/430 Art.16

Art.82C, added: SI 2003/430 Art.16

Art.83A, added: SI 2003/430 Art.12

Art.83B, added: SI 2003/430 Art.12

Art.83C, added: SI 2003/430 Art.12

Art.83D, added: SI 2003/430 Art.12

Art.83E, added: SI 2003/430 Art.12

Art.83F, added: SI 2003/430 Art.12

Art.84A, added: SI 2003/430 Art.13

Art.84B, added: SI 2003/430 Art.13

Art.84C, added: SI 2003/430 Art.13

Art.86, amended: SI 2003/430 Art.27

Art.91A, added: SI 2003/430 Art.31

Art.100, applied: SR 2002/10 Reg.13

Art.103, amended: 2003 c.21 Sch.17 para.117

Art.104, amended: 2003 c.21 Sch.17 para.117

Art.104, revoked (in part): 2003 c.21 Sch.19

Art.110, amended: SI 2003/430 Art.32

Art.111, amended: SI 2003/430 Art.32

Art.111, applied: SR 2003/46 Sch.9 para.4

Art.111, enabled: SR 2003/254

Art.112, amended: SI 2003/430 Sch.1 para.16

Art.113, amended: SI 2003/430 Sch.1 para.17

NO.

1991–cont.

1220. Planning (Northern Ireland) Order 1991–*cont.*

Art.114, amended: SI 2003/430 Sch.1 para.18

Art.115, amended: SI 2003/430 Art.26

Art.119, amended: SI 2003/430 Art.33

Art.120, amended: SI 2003/430 Art.34

Art.121, amended: SI 2003/430 Art.13, Art.25

Art.121, revoked (in part): SI 2003/430 Art.13, Sch.2

Art.122, amended: SI 2003/430 Art.17, Sch.1 para.19

Art.124, amended: SI 2003/430 Art.35

Art.125, amended: SI 2003/430 Art.17

Art.127, enabled: SR 2003/41

Art.128, amended: SI 2003/430 Sch.1 para.20

Art.129, enabled: SR 2003/41

1222. County Court Remedies Regulations 1991

Reg.3, amended: SI 2002/439 Art.10

1247. Family Proceedings Rules 1991

see *Pelling v Bruce-Williams* [2004] EWCA Civ 845, [2004] Fam. 155 (CA), Thorpe, L.J.

referred to: SI 2004/3114 Art.1

see *Clibbery v Allan* [2002] EWCA Civ 45, [2002] Fam. 261 (CA), Dame Elizabeth Butler-Sloss (President)

Part 2 r.2.2, see *C v FC (Brussels II: Freestanding Application for Parental Responsibility)* [2004] 1 F.L.R. 317 (Fam Div (Family Division)), RexTedd Q.C.

Part II r.2.45A, added: SI 2003/184 r.3

Part II r.2.45B, added: SI 2003/184 r.3

Part II r.2.49, amended: SI 2003/184 r.4

Part II r.2.61, amended: SI 2003/2839 r.3

Part II r.2.61D, amended: SI 2003/184 r.5

Part 2 r.2.69, see *C v C (Costs: Ancillary Relief)* [2003] EWHC 2321, [2004] 1 F.L.R. 291 (Fam Div), Charles, J.

Part II r.2.69A, revoked: SI 2003/184 r.6

Part II r.2.69C, revoked: SI 2003/184 r.7

Part II r.2.69D, amended: SI 2003/184 r.8

Part II r.2.69D, revoked (in part): SI 2003/184 r.8

Part II r.2.70, amended: SI 2003/184 r.9

Part III r.3.13, amended: SI 2003/184 r.10

Part IV r.4.1, amended: SI 2003/2839 r.4

Part VII r.7.4, amended: SI 2003/184 r.11

Part VII r.7.5, revoked (in part): SI 2003/184 r.12

Part VII r.7.6, amended: SI 2003/184 r.13

Part VIII r.8.1, amended: SI 2003/184 r.14, r.15

Part IX r.9.5, applied: 2003 c.42 s.21

Part X r.10.27, added: SI 2003/184 r.16

Appendix 1., amended: SI 2003/184 r.17, Sch.1, SI 2003/2839 r.5, r.7, Sch.1

Appendix 1A., amended: SI 2003/184 Sch.2

Appendix 3., amended: SI 2003/2839 r.8

NO.

1991–cont.

1247. Family Proceedings Rules 1991–*cont.*

r.2.39, see *Practice Direction (Fam Div: Conciliation)* [2004] 1 W.L.R. 1287 (Fam Div), Senior District Judge Waller

r.4.7, see *B (A Child) (Parentage: Knowledge of Proceedings), Re* [2003] EWCA Civ 1842, [2004] 1 F.L.R. 527 (CA), Thorpe, L.J.

r.4.8, see *B (A Child) (Parentage: Knowledge of Proceedings), Re* [2003] EWCA Civ 1842, [2004] 1 F.L.R. 527 (CA), Thorpe, L.J.

r.4.16, see *Pelling v Bruce-Williams* [2003] EWHC 1541, [2004] Fam. 22 (Fam Div), Bennett, J.

r.4.23, see *G (A Child) (Contempt: Committal Order), Re* [2003] EWCA Civ 489, [2003] 1 W.L.R. 2051 (CA), Dame Elizabeth Butler-Sloss (President); see *G (A Child) (Litigants In Person), Re* [2003] EWCA Civ 1055, [2003] 2 F.L.R. 963 (CA), Thorpe, L.J.; see *Kent CC v B (A Child)* [2004] EWHC 411, [2004] 2 F.L.R. 142 (Fam Div), Munby, J.; see *M (A Child) (Children and Family Reporter: Disclosure), Re* [2002] EWCA Civ 1199, [2003] Fam. 26 (CA), Thorpe, L.J.; see *Pelling v Bruce-Williams* [2003] EWHC 1541, [2004] Fam. 22 (Fam Div), Bennett, J.

r.7.4, see *Corbett v Corbett* [2003] EWCA Civ 559, [2003] 2 F.L.R. 385 (CA),Thorpe, L.J.

r.9.5, see *Practice Direction (CAFCASS: Representation of Children in Family Proceedings)* [2004] 1 F.L.R. 1190 (Court not applicable), Charles Prest; see *Practice Direction (Family Proceedings: Representation of Children)* [2004] 1 W.L.R. 1180 (Fam Div), Dame Elizabeth Butler-Sloss (President)

r.10.20, see *Pelling v Bruce-Williams* [2003] EWHC 1541, [2004] Fam. 22 (Fam Div), Bennett, J.

1248. Inheritance Tax (Delivery of Accounts) Regulations 1991

revoked: SI 2002/1733 Sch.1

1249. Inheritance Tax (Delivery of Accounts) (Scotland) Regulations 1991

revoked: SI 2002/1733 Sch.1

1251. Movement of Animals (Restrictions) (Amendment) Order 1991

Art.2, revoked (in part): SSI 2003/353 Art.13

1284. Fruit Juices and Fruit Nectars (England, Wales and Scotland) (Amendment) Regulations 1991

revoked (in part): SI 2003/1564 Reg.10, SI 2003/3041 Reg.10, SSI 2003/293 Reg.11

1304. Police Pensions (Additional Voluntary Contributions) Regulations 1991

referred to: SI 2003/535 Reg.3

NO.

1991–cont.

1304. Police Pensions (Additional Voluntary Contributions) Regulations 1991–*cont.*

Reg.2, amended: SI 2002/3202 Sch.2 para.1, SI 2003/27 Sch.2 para.1, SSI 2003/406 Sch.2 para.1

Reg.5, amended: SI 2003/27 Sch.2 para.2, SSI 2003/406 Sch.2 para.2

Reg.6, amended: SI 2003/27 Sch.2 para.2, SSI 2003/406 Sch.2 para.2

Reg.9, amended: SI 2003/27 Sch.2 para.3, SSI 2003/406 Sch.2 para.3

Reg.10, amended: SI 2002/3202 Sch.2 para.2, SI 2003/27 Sch.2 para.4, SSI 2003/406 Sch.2 para.4

Reg.10A, added: SI 2002/3202 Sch.2 para.3

Reg.10A, substituted: SI 2003/27 Sch.2 para.5, SI 2003/535 Sch.2, SSI 2003/406 Sch.2 para.5

Reg.11, amended: SI 2003/27 Sch.2 para.6, SSI 2003/406 Sch.2 para.6

Reg.12, amended: SI 2003/27 Sch.2 para.7, SSI 2003/406 Sch.2 para.7

Reg.15, amended: SI 2002/3202 Sch.2 para.4, SI 2003/27 Sch.2 para.8, SSI 2003/406 Sch.2 para.8

Reg.16, amended: SI 2002/3202 Sch.2 para.5

Reg.17, amended: SI 2003/2717 Reg.2

Sch.1A para.1, added: SI 2002/3202 Sch.2 para.6

Sch.1A para.2, added: SI 2002/3202 Sch.2 para.6

Sch.1A para.3, added: SI 2002/3202 Sch.2 para.6

Sch.1A para.4, added: SI 2002/3202 Sch.2 para.6

Sch.1A para.5, added: SI 2002/3202 Sch.2 para.6

Sch.1A para.6, added: SI 2002/3202 Sch.2 para.6

Sch.1A para.7, added: SI 2002/3202 Sch.2 para.6

Sch.1A para.8, added: SI 2002/3202 Sch.2 para.6

1325. Litter Control Areas Order 1991

Art.2, amended: SI 2004/696 Art.3

1395. Family Proceedings Courts (Children Act 1989) Rules 1991

r.21, see *Oxfordshire CC v S* [2003] EWHC 2174, [2004] 1 F.L.R. 426 (Fam Div), Munby, J.

Sch.1, amended: SI 2003/2840 r.2

Sch.2, amended: SI 2003/2840 r.3

1397. Act of Sederunt (Messengers-at-Arms and Sheriff Officers Rules) 1991

amended: SSI 2002/560 Sch.3 para.3

1405. Family Proceedings Courts (Constitution) Rules 1991

referred to: SI 2003/3367 r.2

NO.

1991-cont.

1405. Family Proceedings Courts (Constitution) Rules 1991–*cont.*

r.2, amended: SI 2003/3367 r.3

r.3, substituted: SI 2003/3367 r.4

1408. Broadcasting (Independent Productions) Order 1991

referred to: SI 2003/1672 Art.2

Art.1, amended: SI 2003/1672 Art.4, Art.6

Art.2, amended: SI 2003/1672 Art.5, Art.6

Art.2, revoked (in part): SI 2003/1672 Art.5

Art.3, amended: SI 2003/1672 Art.3

1426. Family Proceedings Courts (Constitution) (Metropolitan Area) Rules 1991

revoked: SI 2003/2960 r.3

1463. Criminal Justice (International Cooperation) Act 1990 (Enforcement of Overseas Forfeiture Orders) Order 1991

Sch.2, amended: SI 2002/255 Sch.1, SI 2002/2845 Sch.1

Sch.3, amended: SI 2002/255 Sch.2, SI 2002/2845 Sch.2

1464. Criminal Justice (International Cooperation) Act 1990 (Enforcement of Overseas Forfeiture Orders) (Northern Ireland) Order 1991

Sch.2, amended: SI 2002/255 Sch.1, SI 2002/2845 Sch.1

Sch.3, amended: SI 2002/255 Sch.2, SI 2002/2845 Sch.2

1467. Confiscation of the Proceeds of Drug Trafficking (Designated Countries and Territories) (Scotland) Order 1991

Sch.3, amended: 2002 asp 17 Sch.3 para.31

1476. Food Safety (Exports) Regulations 1991

Sch.1 Part I, amended: SI 2002/890 Sch.1, SI 2002/1886 Sch.1, SI 2003/1563 Reg.10, SI 2003/1564 Reg.10, SI 2003/1596 Reg.10, SI 2003/1659 Reg.11, SI 2003/2243 Reg.10, SI 2003/3037 Reg.11, SI 2003/3041 Reg.10, SI 2003/3044 Reg.10, SI 2003/3047 Reg.10, SI 2003/3053 Reg.10, SI 2003/3120 Reg.10, SI 2004/553 Reg.10

Sch.2, amended: SSI 2002/267 Sch.1, SSI 2003/291 Reg.12, SSI 2003/293 Reg.11, SSI 2003/311 Reg.11, SSI 2003/527 Reg.11, SSI 2003/569 Reg.12, SSI 2004/6 Reg.11, SSI 2004/133 Reg.11

1478. Parental Responsibility Agreement Regulations 1991

Reg.3, amended: SI 2004/3123 Sch.1 Part 3

1505. Children (Secure Accommodation) Regulations 1991

referred to: SI 2002/808 Art.2

Reg.2, amended: SI 2002/546 Reg.7, SI 2002/2935 Reg.10

Reg.5, amended: SI 2002/546 Reg.7, SI 2002/2935 Reg.10

NO.

1991-cont.

1505. Children (Secure Accommodation) Regulations 1991–*cont.*

Reg.7, amended: SI 2002/2935 Reg.10, SI 2004/696 Sch.1 para.9

Reg.8, amended: SI 2002/808 Art.37

1506. Children's Homes Regulations 1991

revoked (in part): SI 2002/327 Reg.43

1507. Refuges (Children's Homes and Foster Placements) Regulations 1991

Reg.2, amended: SI 2002/546 Reg.6, SI 2002/2935 Reg.9

Reg.4, amended: SI 2002/2935 Reg.9

1530. Tobacco Products Labelling (Safety) Regulations 1991

applied: SI 2002/3041 Reg.17

revoked: SI 2002/3041 Reg.16

Reg.10, applied: SI 2002/3041 Reg.17

Reg.10, referred to: SI 2002/3041 Reg.17

1531. Control of Explosives Regulations 1991

Reg.10, amended: SI 2004/568 Sch.13 para.5

Sch.1, referred to: SI 2004/568 Reg.46

1597. Bathing Waters (Classification) Regulations 1991

Reg.2, amended: SI 2003/1238 Reg.2

Reg.3, amended: SI 2003/1238 Reg.2

1614. Retirement Benefits Schemes (Restriction on Discretion to Approve) (Small Self-administered Schemes) Regulations 1991

Reg.6, amended: SI 2003/2096 Sch.1 para.51

1619. Isle of Wight Light Railway Order 1991

Art.8, amended: SI 2003/2155 Sch.1 para.18

1675. European Parliamentary Elections (Northern Ireland) (Amendment) Regulations 1991

revoked: SI 2004/1267 Sch.7

1677. Children (Allocation of Proceedings) Order 1991

Sch.2, amended: SI 2003/331 Art.2

1700. Extradition (Designated Commonwealth Countries) Order 1991

Sch.1, amended: SI 2003/1870 Art.2

1703. Merchant Shipping Act 1988 (Bermuda) Order 1991

revoked: SI 2002/3147 Art.2

1709. Broadcasting Act 1990 (Guernsey) (No.2) Order 1991

applied: SI 2003/3192 Sch.1 para.1

Sch.1, referred to: SI 2003/3192 Art.3

Sch.1 para.1, amended: SI 2003/3192 Sch.2

Sch.1 para.7, substituted: SI 2003/3192 Sch.2

Sch.1 para.10A, added: SI 2003/3192 Sch.2

Sch.1 para.12A, added: SI 2003/3192 Sch.2

Sch.1 para.13, substituted: SI 2003/3192 Sch.2

Sch.1 para.18A, added: SI 2003/3192 Sch.2

NO.

1991–cont.

1709. Broadcasting Act 1990 (Guernsey) (No.2) Order 1991–*cont.*

Sch.1 para.21, amended: SI 2003/3192 Sch.2
Sch.1 para.29AA, added: SI 2003/3192 Sch.2
Sch.1 para.51, amended: SI 2003/3192 Sch.2

1710. Broadcasting Act 1990 (Jersey) (No.2) Order 1991

Art.3, revoked (in part): SI 2003/3196 Art.4
Sch.1 para.1, amended: SI 2003/3203 Sch.2
Sch.1 para.7, substituted: SI 2003/3203 Sch.2
Sch.1 para.10A, added: SI 2003/3203 Sch.2
Sch.1 para.12A, added: SI 2003/3203 Sch.2
Sch.1 para.13, substituted: SI 2003/3203 Sch.2
Sch.1 para.18A, added: SI 2003/3203 Sch.2
Sch.1 para.21, amended: SI 2003/3203 Sch.2
Sch.1 para.29AA, added: SI 2003/3203 Sch.2
Sch.1 para.41, revoked: SI 2003/3196 Art.4
Sch.1 para.51, amended: SI 2003/3203 Sch.2

1711. Criminal Justice (Northern Ireland) Order 1991

Art.7, revoked (in part): 2002 c.26 Sch.13

1712. Disability Living Allowance and Disability Working Allowance (Northern Ireland) Order 1991

Sch.3, revoked: 2002 c.21 Sch.6

1714. Genetically Modified Organisms (Northern Ireland) Order 1991

applied: SR 2003/167 Reg.11, Reg.16, Reg.23
referred to: SR 2003/167 Reg.23, Reg.25
Art.3, amended: SR 2003/167 Reg.3
Art.3, applied: SR 2003/167 Reg.5
Art.3, enabled: SR 2003/167
Art.3, revoked (in part): SR 2003/167 Reg.3
Art.4, amended: SR 2003/167 Reg.4
Art.4, applied: SR 2003/167 Reg.5
Art.5, applied: SR 2003/167 Reg.15
Art.5, disapplied: SR 2003/167 Reg.15
Art.7, applied: SR 2003/167 Reg.32, Reg.34
Art.8, amended: SR 2003/167 Reg.19
Art.8, applied: SR 2003/167 Reg.8, Reg.9, Reg.14, Reg.15, Reg.16, Reg.18, Reg.19, Reg.21, Reg.22, Reg.23, Reg.28, Reg.31, Reg.32, Reg.34
Art.8, disapplied: SR 2003/167 Reg.9, Reg.15
Art.8, enabled: SR 2003/167
Art.9, amended: SR 2003/167 Reg.29
Art.9, applied: SR 2003/167 Reg.34
Art.9, revoked (in part): SR 2003/167 Reg.29
Art.15, applied: SR 2003/167 Reg.34
Art.16, amended: SR 2003/167 Reg.30
Art.17, applied: SR 2003/167 Reg.34
Art.19, enabled: SR 2003/167
Art.20, amended: SR 2003/167 Reg.33
Art.20, applied: SR 2003/167 Reg.33
Art.20, enabled: SR 2003/167

NO.

1991–cont.

1714. Genetically Modified Organisms (Northern Ireland) Order 1991–*cont.*

Art.20, revoked (in part): SR 2003/167 Reg.33
Art.22, applied: SR 2003/167, SR 2003/167 Reg.32
Art.22A, added: SR 2003/167 Reg.37, SR 2003/206 Reg.3

1715. Local Elections (Northern Ireland) (Amendment) Order 1991

Art.5, revoked: SI 2002/2835 Art.3
Art.6, revoked: SI 2002/2835 Art.3

1721. Statistics (Confidentiality) (Northern Ireland) Order 1991

Art.3, revoked (in part): SI 2004/1109 Sch.1

1723. Family Law Act 1986 (Dependent Territories) Order 1991

Sch.1, amended: 2002 c.8 s.1

1745. Montrose Harbour Revision Order 1991

Art.4, amended: SSI 2003/258 Sch.3
Art.4, revoked (in part): SSI 2003/258 Sch.3
Art.5, revoked: SSI 2003/258 Sch.3
Art.6, revoked: SSI 2003/258 Sch.3

1796. Patent Office Trading Fund Order 1991

Art.6, revoked: 2004 c.16 s.16

1874. School Teachers Pay and Conditions Act 1991 (Commencement No.1) Order 1991

revoked: 2002 c.32 Sch.22 Part 1

1965. Leicester North Station Light Railway Order 1991

Art.7, amended: SI 2003/2155 Sch.1 para.18

1991/1392. Medicines (Veterinary Drugs) (Prescription Only) Order 1991

Sch.1, see *Department for the Environment, Food and Rural Affairs v Atkinson* [2002] EWHC 2028, [2002] 3 C.M.L.R. 38 (QBD (Admin Ct)), Brooke, L.J.

1997. Companies Act 1989 (Eligibility for Appointment as Company Auditor) (Consequential Amendments) Regulations 1991

Sch.1 para.6, revoked: 2004 c.14 Sch.1 Part 2
Sch.1 para.43, revoked: 2004 c.14 Sch.1 Part 2

2001. National Health Service Supplies Authority (Establishment and Constitution) Order 1991

referred to: SI 2004/1119 Sch.1

2030. Adoption Allowance Regulations 1991

applied: SI 2003/1348 Reg.15, SI 2004/1011 Reg.9, Reg.16
Reg.1, amended: SI 2003/1348 Reg.15, SI 2004/1011 Reg.16

2034. Children (Secure Accommodation) (No.2) Regulations 1991

Reg.2, amended: SI 2002/2935 Reg.11, SI 2004/696 Art.3, Sch.1 para.10

1991–cont.

2038. Legal Aid in Family Proceedings (Remuneration) Regulations 1991

varied: SI 2002/710 Reg.2

Reg.3, amended: SI 2002/710 Reg.3

2050. Children (Private Arrangements for Fostering) Regulations 1991

Reg.2, amended: SI 2004/865 Sch.1 para.8, SI 2004/1016 Sch.1 para.8

2094. Disqualification for Caring for Children Regulations 1991

revoked (in part): SI 2002/635 Reg.3, SI 2002/896 Reg.5

Reg.3, applied: SI 2002/920 Sch.3 para.2, Sch.3 para.4, SI 2002/1493 Art.4

2097. Packaging of Explosives for Carriage Regulations 1991

revoked: SI 2004/568 Sch.14

2105. Child Benefit (General) Amendment Regulations 1991

revoked: SI 2003/493 Sch.2 Part 1

2194. Kirklees Light Railway Order 1991

Art.8, amended: SI 2003/2155 Sch.1 para.18

2206. Seed Potatoes Regulations 1991

applied: SI 2004/1316 Reg.2

Sch.1 Part II para.4, applied: SI 2004/1316 Sch.1

2210. Grimsby and Louth Light Railway Order 1991

Art.7, amended: SI 2003/2155 Sch.1 para.18

2242. Beef Carcase (Classification) Regulations 1991

revoked (in part): SI 2004/1317 Reg.16, SSI 2004/280 Reg.17

Reg.4, applied: SI 2004/1317 Reg.4, SSI 2004/280 Reg.4

Reg.6, applied: SSI 2004/280 Reg.16

Reg.8, applied: SSI 2004/280 Reg.16

Reg.9, applied: SSI 2004/280 Reg.16

Sch.2, referred to: SI 2004/1317 Reg.4

2284. Social Security (Miscellaneous Provisions) Amendment Regulations 1991

Reg.1, amended: SI 2003/492 Sch.3 Part 1

Reg.5, revoked (in part): SI 2003/492 Sch.3 Part 1

Reg.6, revoked (in part): SI 2003/492 Sch.3 Part 1

Reg.7, revoked (in part): SI 2003/492 Sch.3 Part 1

Reg.8, revoked (in part): SI 2003/492 Sch.3 Part 1

Reg.9, revoked (in part): SI 2003/492 Sch.3 Part 1

Reg.10, revoked (in part): SI 2003/492 Sch.3 Part 1

Reg.11, revoked (in part): SI 2003/492 Sch.3 Part 1

Reg.12, revoked (in part): SI 2003/492 Sch.3 Part 1

Reg.13, revoked (in part): SI 2003/492 Sch.3 Part 1

1991–cont.

2284. Social Security (Miscellaneous Provisions) Amendment Regulations 1991–cont.

Reg.14, revoked (in part): SI 2003/492 Sch.3 Part 1

Reg.15, revoked (in part): SI 2003/492 Sch.3 Part 1

Reg.16, revoked (in part): SI 2003/492 Sch.3 Part 1

Reg.17, revoked (in part): SI 2003/492 Sch.3 Part 1

Reg.18, revoked (in part): SI 2003/492 Sch.3 Part 1

Reg.19, revoked (in part): SI 2003/492 Sch.3 Part 1

Reg.20, revoked (in part): SI 2003/492 Sch.3 Part 1

2316. Aintree Hospitals National Health Service Trust (Establishment) Order 1991

Art.3, amended: SI 2004/2391 Art.2

Art.4, substituted: SI 2004/2391 Art.3

2320. Avon Ambulance Service National Health Service Trust (Establishment) Order 1991

referred to: SI 2004/569 Sch.1

2323. Barnsley Community and Priority Services National Health Service Trust (Establishment) Order 1991

revoked: SI 2002/1294 Art.2

2325. Basildon and Thurrock General Hospitals National Health Service Trust (Establishment) Order 1991

Art.1, amended: SI 2002/2617 Art.2

Art.2, amended: SI 2002/2617 Art.2

2329. Bedford Hospital National Health Service Trust (Establishment Order) 1991

referred to: SI 2004/569 Sch.2

2330. Bradford Community Health National Health Service Trust (Establishment) Order 1991

revoked: SI 2002/1322 Art.6

2331. Burnley Health Care National Health Service Trust (Establishment) Order 1991

revoked: SI 2002/2073 Art.8

2338. Doncaster Healthcare National Health Service Trust (Establishment) Order 1991

Art.3, substituted: SI 2002/1295 Art.2

Art.4, substituted: SI 2002/1295 Art.2

2344. Eastbourne Hospitals National Health Service Trust (Establishment) Order 1991

revoked: SI 2003/216 Art.6

2345. Essex Ambulance Service National Health Service Trust (Establishment) Order 1991

referred to: SI 2004/569 Sch.1

NO.

1991–cont.

2356. Hastings and Rother National Health Service Trust (Establishment) Order 1991
revoked: SI 2003/216 Art.6

2357. Heatherwood and Wexham Park Hospitals National Health Service Trust (Establishment) Order 1991
applied: SI 2003/3059 Sch.1

2369. Mersey Regional Ambulance Service National Health Service Trust (Establishment) Order 1991
Art.3, amended: SI 2004/2898 Art.2
Art.4, amended: SI 2004/2898 Art.3

2372. Milton Keynes General National Health Service Trust (Establishment) Order 1991
applied: SI 2003/3059 Sch.1

2376. North Mersey Community National Health Service Trust (Establishment) Order 1991
revoked: SI 2002/1497 Art.2

2378. Northallerton Health Services National Health Service Trust (Establishment) Order 1991
revoked: SI 2002/1342 Art.2

2380. Nottingham City Hospital National Health Service Trust (Establishment) Order 1991
applied: SI 2003/3059 Sch.1

2382. Oldham National Health Service Trust (Establishment) Order 1991
revoked (in part): SI 2002/308 Art.8

2384. Parkside National Health Service Trust (Establishment) Order 1991
revoked: SI 2002/1323 Sch.1

2391. Royal Cornwall Hospitals and West Cornwall Hospital National Health Service Trust (Establishment) Order 1991
Art.4, amended: SI 2003/2434 Art.2

2394. St Helens and Knowsley Community Health National Health Service Trust (Establishment) Order 1991
revoked: SI 2002/1489 Art.2

2395. St Mary's National Health Service Trust (Establishment) Order 1991
applied: SI 2003/3059 Sch.1, Sch.2

2399. Sheffield Children's Hospital National Health Service Trust (Establishment) Order 1991
referred to: SI 2004/569 Sch.1
Art.1, amended: SI 2002/1297 Art.2
Art.2, amended: SI 2002/1297 Art.2
Art.3, substituted: SI 2002/1297 Art.3

2402. South Tees Acute Hospitals National Health Service Trust (Establishment) Order 1991
applied: SI 2003/3059 Sch.1
Art.3, substituted: SI 2002/1491 Art.2
Art.4, substituted: SI 2002/1491 Art.2

NO.

1991–cont.

2404. South Yorkshire Metropolitan Ambulance and Paramedic Service National Health Service Trust (Establishment) Order 1991
Art.1, amended: SI 2002/1791 Art.2
Art.2, amended: SI 2002/1791 Art.2

2411. Walton Centre for Neurology and Neurosurgery National Health Service Trust (Establishment) Order 1991
applied: SI 2003/3059 Sch.1

2418. York Health Services National Health Service Trust (Establishment) Order 1991
Art.1, amended: SI 2003/1276 Art.2
Art.2, amended: SI 2003/1276 Art.2
Art.3, revoked (in part): SI 2003/1276 Art.4

2567. Education (National Curriculum) (Modern Foreign Languages) Order 1991
revoked (in part): SI 2004/260 Art.2

2628. Child Support (Northern Ireland) Order 1991 (N.I.23) 1991
Art.2, amended: 2002 c.21 Sch.6
Art.2, referred to: SI 2003/495 Reg.6
Art.7, applied: SR 2003/56 Reg.2
Art.7, enabled: SR 2003/56
Art.16, enabled: SR 2002/164
Art.18, enabled: SR 2002/164
Art.19, enabled: SR 2002/164, SR 2003/84, SR 2003/224
Art.22, applied: SI 2003/435 Sch.2 para.2, SR 2002/391 Art.4
Art.22, enabled: SR 2002/164
Art.22, varied: SR 2002/391 Art.3
Art.28, applied: SI 2003/435 Sch.2 para.2
Art.28B, enabled: SR 2002/164, SR 2003/84
Art.28E, enabled: SR 2002/164
Art.28G, enabled: SR 2002/164
Art.31, enabled: SR 2003/84
Art.38, enabled: SR 2003/84
Art.39, enabled: SR 2003/84
Art.40, enabled: SR 2002/254
Art.42, enabled: SR 2002/391
Art.43, enabled: SR 2002/164, SR 2003/84
Art.44, amended: 2002 c.21 Sch.3 para.23
Art.47, enabled: SR 2002/164, SR 2003/84
Art.48, enabled: SR 2002/164, SR 2003/84, SR 2003/261
Art.50, enabled: SR 2002/164
Sch.1, enabled: SR 2002/164, SR 2002/323, SR 2003/84, SR 2003/261
Sch.4B, enabled: SR 2002/164, SR 2003/84

2680. Public Works Contracts Regulations 1991
applied: SI 2004/669 Art.2
referred to: SI 2003/1986 Art.3
Reg.2, amended: SI 2003/46 Reg.3
Reg.9, amended: SI 2003/46 Reg.3
Reg.11, amended: SI 2003/46 Reg.3

1991–cont.

2680. Public Works Contracts Regulations 1991–*cont.*

Reg.12, amended: SI 2003/46 Reg.3

Reg.13, amended: SI 2003/46 Reg.3

Reg.21, amended: SI 2003/46 Reg.3

Reg.22, amended: SI 2003/46 Reg.3

Reg.25, amended: SI 2003/46 Reg.3

Reg.26, amended: SI 2003/46 Reg.3

Sch.2 Part A para.1, revoked: SI 2003/46 Reg.3

Sch.2 Part A para.2, revoked: SI 2003/46 Reg.3

Sch.2 Part A para.3, revoked: SI 2003/46 Reg.3

Sch.2 Part A para.4, revoked: SI 2003/46 Reg.3

Sch.2 Part A para.5, revoked: SI 2003/46 Reg.3

Sch.2 Part A para.6, revoked: SI 2003/46 Reg.3

Sch.2 Part A para.7, revoked: SI 2003/46 Reg.3

Sch.2 Part B para.1, revoked: SI 2003/46 Reg.3

Sch.2 Part B para.2, revoked: SI 2003/46 Reg.3

Sch.2 Part B para.3, revoked: SI 2003/46 Reg.3

Sch.2 Part B para.4, revoked: SI 2003/46 Reg.3

Sch.2 Part B para.5, revoked: SI 2003/46 Reg.3

Sch.2 Part B para.6, revoked: SI 2003/46 Reg.3

Sch.2 Part B para.7, revoked: SI 2003/46 Reg.3

Sch.2 Part B para.8, revoked: SI 2003/46 Reg.3

Sch.2 Part B para.9, revoked: SI 2003/46 Reg.3

Sch.2 Part B para.10, revoked: SI 2003/46 Reg.3

Sch.2 Part B para.11, revoked: SI 2003/46 Reg.3

Sch.2 Part B para.12, revoked: SI 2003/46 Reg.3

Sch.2 Part B para.13, revoked: SI 2003/46 Reg.3

Sch.2 Part B para.14, revoked: SI 2003/46 Reg.3

Sch.2 Part B para.15, revoked: SI 2003/46 Reg.3

Sch.2 Part B para.16, revoked: SI 2003/46 Reg.3

Sch.2 Part B para.17, revoked: SI 2003/46 Reg.3

Sch.2 Part B para.18, revoked: SI 2003/46 Reg.3

Sch.2 Part E para.1, revoked: SI 2003/46 Reg.3

1991–cont.

2680. Public Works Contracts Regulations 1991–*cont.*

Sch.2 Part E para.2, revoked: SI 2003/46 Reg.3

Sch.2 Part E para.3, revoked: SI 2003/46 Reg.3

Sch.2 Part E para.4, revoked: SI 2003/46 Reg.3

Sch.2 Part E para.5, revoked: SI 2003/46 Reg.3

Sch.2 Part E para.6, revoked: SI 2003/46 Reg.3

Sch.2 Part E para.7, revoked: SI 2003/46 Reg.3

Sch.2 Part E para.8, revoked: SI 2003/46 Reg.3

Sch.2 Part E para.9, revoked: SI 2003/46 Reg.3

Sch.2 Part E para.10, revoked: SI 2003/46 Reg.3

Sch.2 Part E para.11, revoked: SI 2003/46 Reg.3

Sch.2 Part E para.12, revoked: SI 2003/46 Reg.3

Sch.2 Part E para.13, revoked: SI 2003/46 Reg.3

Sch.2 Part F para.1, revoked: SI 2003/46 Reg.3

Sch.2 Part F para.2, revoked: SI 2003/46 Reg.3

Sch.2 Part F para.3, revoked: SI 2003/46 Reg.3

Sch.2 Part F para.4, revoked: SI 2003/46 Reg.3

Sch.2 Part F para.5, revoked: SI 2003/46 Reg.3

Sch.2 Part F para.6, revoked: SI 2003/46 Reg.3

Sch.2 Part F para.7, revoked: SI 2003/46 Reg.3

Sch.2 Part F para.8, revoked: SI 2003/46 Reg.3

Sch.2 Part G para.1, revoked: SI 2003/46 Reg.3

Sch.2 Part G para.2, revoked: SI 2003/46 Reg.3

Sch.2 Part G para.3, revoked: SI 2003/46 Reg.3

Sch.2 Part G para.4, revoked: SI 2003/46 Reg.3

Sch.2 Part G para.5, revoked: SI 2003/46 Reg.3

Sch.2 Part G para.6, revoked: SI 2003/46 Reg.3

Sch.2 Part G para.7, revoked: SI 2003/46 Reg.3

Sch.2 Part G para.8, revoked: SI 2003/46 Reg.3

Sch.2 Part G para.9, revoked: SI 2003/46 Reg.3

NO.

1991–cont.

2680. Public Works Contracts Regulations 1991–*cont.*

Sch.2 Part C para.1, revoked: SI 2003/46 Reg.3

Sch.2 Part C para.2, revoked: SI 2003/46 Reg.3

Sch.2 Part C para.3, revoked: SI 2003/46 Reg.3

Sch.2 Part C para.4, revoked: SI 2003/46 Reg.3

Sch.2 Part C para.5, revoked: SI 2003/46 Reg.3

Sch.2 Part C para.6, revoked: SI 2003/46 Reg.3

Sch.2 Part C para.7, revoked: SI 2003/46 Reg.3

Sch.2 Part C para.8, revoked: SI 2003/46 Reg.3

Sch.2 Part C para.9, revoked: SI 2003/46 Reg.3

Sch.2 Part C para.10, revoked: SI 2003/46 Reg.3

Sch.2 Part C para.11, revoked: SI 2003/46 Reg.3

Sch.2 Part C para.12, revoked: SI 2003/46 Reg.3

Sch.2 Part C para.13, revoked: SI 2003/46 Reg.3

Sch.2 Part C para.14, revoked: SI 2003/46 Reg.3

Sch.2 Part C para.15, revoked: SI 2003/46 Reg.3

Sch.2 Part C para.16, revoked: SI 2003/46 Reg.3

Sch.2 Part D para.1, revoked: SI 2003/46 Reg.3

Sch.2 Part D para.2, revoked: SI 2003/46 Reg.3

Sch.2 Part D para.3, revoked: SI 2003/46 Reg.3

Sch.2 Part D para.4, revoked: SI 2003/46 Reg.3

Sch.2 Part D para.5, revoked: SI 2003/46 Reg.3

Sch.2 Part D para.6, revoked: SI 2003/46 Reg.3

Sch.2 Part D para.7, revoked: SI 2003/46 Reg.3

Sch.2 Part D para.8, revoked: SI 2003/46 Reg.3

Sch.2 Part D para.9, revoked: SI 2003/46 Reg.3

Sch.2 Part D para.10, revoked: SI 2003/46 Reg.3

Sch.2 Part D para.11, revoked: SI 2003/46 Reg.3

Sch.2 Part D para.12, revoked: SI 2003/46 Reg.3

Sch.2 Part D para.13, revoked: SI 2003/46 Reg.3

NO.

1991–cont.

2680. Public Works Contracts Regulations 1991–*cont.*

Sch.2 Part D para.14, revoked: SI 2003/46 Reg.3

Sch.2 Part D para.15, revoked: SI 2003/46 Reg.3

Sch.2 Part D para.16, revoked: SI 2003/46 Reg.3

2682. Saundersfoot Steam Railway (Light Railway) Order 1991

Art.9, amended: SI 2003/2155 Sch.1 para.18

2684. Solicitors Incorporated Practices Order 1991

Sch.1, amended: SI 2003/1398 Sch.1 para.19, SI 2003/2155 Sch.2

2687. Police and Criminal Evidence Act 1984 (Tape-recording of Interviews) (No.1) Order 1991

applied: SI 2003/705

revoked: SI 2003/705 Art.4

2724. Customs Controls on Importation of Goods Regulations 1991

Reg.3, applied: SI 2003/3113 Sch.1

Reg.4, applied: SI 2003/3113 Sch.1

Reg.5, applied: SI 2003/3113 Sch.1

2740. Social Security (Attendance Allowance) Regulations 1991

Reg.7, amended: SI 2002/208 Reg.2, SI 2002/1406 Reg.2, SI 2003/2259 Reg.2

Reg.7, revoked (in part): SI 2003/2259 Reg.2

Reg.8, amended: SI 2002/3019 Reg.25, SI 2003/2259 Reg.2

Reg.8, revoked (in part): SI 2003/2259 Reg.2

2741. Social Security (Claims and Payments) Amendment Regulations 1991

revoked (in part): SI 2003/492 Sch.3 Part 1

2742. Disability Living Allowance and Disability Working Allowance (Consequential Provisions) Regulations 1991

Reg.1, amended: SI 2003/492 Sch.3 Part 1

Reg.15, revoked (in part): SI 2003/492 Sch.3 Part 1

2749. Simple Pressure Vessels (Safety) Regulations 1991

Sch.5 para.3, amended: SI 2003/1400 Sch.5

Sch.5 para.3, applied: SI 2003/1400 Sch.3, Sch.4

Sch.5 para.3, revoked (in part): SI 2003/1400 Sch.5

2773. Waltham Forest Housing Action Trust (Area and Constitution) Order 1991

revoked: SI 2002/86 Art.7

2794. Town and Country Planning (Development Plan) Regulations 1991

Reg.16, see *Test Valley BC v Hampshire CC* [2002] P.L.C.R. 2 (QBD (Admin Ct)), Jack Beatson, Q.C.

NO.

1991–cont.

2804. Town and Country Planning (Enforcement Notices and Appeals) Regulations 1991

applied: SI 2003/395 Reg.12

revoked (in part): SI 2003/394 Reg.11

2812. Peak Rail Light Railway Order 1991

Art.6, amended: SI 2003/2155 Sch.1 para.18

2839. Environmental Protection (Duty of Care) Regulations 1991

referred to: SSI 2003/533 Reg.2

Reg.2, amended: SI 2002/1559 Reg.19, SSI 2003/235 Sch.6 para.2

Reg.4, amended: SI 2003/63 Reg.3, SI 2003/1720 Reg.2, SSI 2003/533 Reg.3

2873. Criminal Justice Act 1988 (Designated Countries and Territories) Order 1991

Sch.1, amended: SI 2002/256 Sch.1, SI 2002/2844 Sch.1, SI 2004/1981 Art.2

2887. Disability Working Allowance (General) Regulations 1991

Part VII, applied: SI 2002/1334 Reg.2

Reg.2, amended: SI 2002/2469 Sch.8, SI 2003/44 Reg.3

Reg.6, see *Taylor v Inland Revenue Commissioners* [2004] EWCA Civ 174, [2004] S.T.C. 683 (CA), Peter Gibson, L.J.

Reg.6, amended: SI 2003/44 Reg.4

Reg.21, amended: SI 2003/44 Reg.5

Reg.42, amended: SI 2002/1333 Reg.3, Reg.4

Reg.47, amended: SI 2002/1333 Reg.3, Reg.4

Reg.51, amended: SI 2002/1333 Reg.5

Reg.51A, amended: SI 2002/14 Reg.3, SI 2002/525 Reg.3, SI 2002/1696 Reg.11, SI 2003/44 Reg.6

Reg.52, amended: SI 2002/829 Art.4

Sch.3 para.14, amended: SI 2002/525 Reg.5

Sch.3 para.24, amended: SI 2002/2469 Sch.5

Sch.3 para.25, amended: SI 2002/14 Reg.4

Sch.3 para.27A, added: SI 2003/44 Reg.7

Sch.3 para.50, amended: SI 2002/525 Reg.6

Sch.3 para.51, amended: SI 2002/525 Reg.6

Sch.3 para.52, amended: SI 2002/525 Reg.6, Reg.7

Sch.3 para.55, amended: SI 2003/762 Reg.11, SI 2004/1748 Sch.2 para.2

Sch.4 para.18, amended: SI 2002/14 Reg.5

Sch.5, amended: SI 2002/1333 Reg.6

Sch.5, substituted: SI 2002/829 Sch.2

2890. Social Security (Disability Living Allowance) Regulations 1991

Reg.4, amended: SI 2002/668 Art.12, SI 2003/526 Art.13, SI 2004/552 Art.13

Reg.9, amended: SI 2002/208 Reg.3, SI 2002/1406 Reg.3, SI 2003/2259 Reg.3

Reg.9, revoked (in part): SI 2003/2259 Reg.3

Reg.10, amended: SI 2002/208 Reg.3, SI 2002/3019 Reg.28, SI 2003/2259 Reg.3

NO.

1991–cont.

2890. Social Security (Disability Living Allowance) Regulations 1991–*cont.*

Reg.10, revoked (in part): SI 2003/2259 Reg.3

Reg.12, amended: SI 2002/648 Reg.2

2926. Rochdale Healthcare National Health Service Trust (Establishment) Order 1991

revoked (in part): SI 2002/308 Art.8

1992

14. Income Tax (Deposit-takers) (Non-residents) Regulations 1992

Reg.8, referred to: SI 2003/3297 Reg.16

31. Environmental Protection (Controls on Injurious Substances) Regulations 1992

Reg.5, amended: SI 2003/3274 Reg.9

34. Insolvency Fees (Amendment) Order 1992

revoked: SI 2004/593 Sch.1

89. Revenue Support Grant (Specified Bodies) Regulations 1992

Reg.3, amended: SI 2003/5 Reg.2

113. Cholsey and Wallingford Light Railway (Extension and Amendment) Order 1992

Art.6, amended: SI 2003/2155 Sch.1 para.18

129. Firemen's Pension Scheme Order 1992

Sch.2, added: SI 2004/1912 Sch.1 para.1, Sch.1 para.2, Sch.1 para.4, Sch.1 para.9, Sch.1 para.10, Sch.1 para.13, Sch.1 para.14, Sch.1 para.15, Sch.1 para.16, Sch.1 para.17, Sch.1 para.18, Sch.1 para.20, Sch.1 para.25, Sch.1 para.30, Sch.1 para.34, Sch.1 para.37, Sch.1 para.39, Sch.1 para.41, Sch.1 para.42, SSI 2004/385 Sch.1 para.1, Sch.1 para.2, Sch.1 para.4, Sch.1 para.9, Sch.1 para.10, Sch.1 para.13, Sch.1 para.14, Sch.1 para.15, Sch.1 para.16, Sch.1 para.17, Sch.1 para.18, Sch.1 para.20, Sch.1 para.25, Sch.1 para.30, Sch.1 para.34, Sch.1 para.37, Sch.1 para.39, Sch.1 para.41, Sch.1 para.42

Sch.2, amended: SI 2004/1912 Sch.1 para.3, Sch.1 para.6, Sch.1 para.8, Sch.1 para.9, Sch.1 para.11, Sch.1 para.12, Sch.1 para.13, Sch.1 para.15, Sch.1 para.18, Sch.1 para.19, Sch.1 para.21, Sch.1 para.22, Sch.1 para.24, Sch.1 para.26, Sch.1 para.27, Sch.1 para.28, Sch.1 para.29, Sch.1 para.31, Sch.1 para.33, Sch.1 para.34, Sch.1 para.36, Sch.1 para.37, Sch.1 para.38, Sch.1 para.40, Sch.1 para.42, Sch.1 para.43, SSI 2004/385 Sch.1 para.3, Sch.1 para.6, Sch.1 para.8, Sch.1 para.9, Sch.1 para.11, Sch.1 para.12, Sch.1 para.13, Sch.1 para.15, Sch.1 para.18, Sch.1 para.19, Sch.1 para.21, Sch.1 para.22, Sch.1 para.24, Sch.1 para.26, Sch.1 para.27, Sch.1 para.28, Sch.1 para.29, Sch.1 para.31, Sch.1 para.33, Sch.1 para.34, Sch.1 para.36, Sch.1 para.37,

NO.

1992–cont.

129. Firemen's Pension Scheme Order 1992–*cont.*

Sch.2, amended:–*cont.*
Sch.1 para.38, Sch.1 para.39, Sch.1 para.40, Sch.1 para.42, Sch.1 para.43

Sch.2, applied: SSI 2004/385 Art.1

Sch.2, referred to: SSI 2004/385 Art.2

Sch.2, revoked (in part): SI 2004/1912 Sch.1 para.6, Sch.1 para.9, Sch.1 para.22, Sch.1 para.23, SSI 2004/385 Sch.1 para.6, Sch.1 para.9, Sch.1 para.22, Sch.1 para.23

Sch.2, substituted: SI 2004/1912 Sch.1 para.5, Sch.1 para.7, Sch.1 para.13, Sch.1 para.15, Sch.1 para.32, Sch.1 para.35, Sch.1 para.39, SSI 2004/385 Sch.1 para.5, Sch.1 para.7, Sch.1 para.13, Sch.1 para.15, Sch.1 para.32, Sch.1 para.35

187. Fire Services (Appointments and Promotion) (Amendment) Regulations 1992

revoked: SI 2004/481 Sch.2

223. Town and Country Planning (General Permitted Development) (Scotland) Order 1992

applied: SSI 2002/410 Art.58, SSI 2004/219 Reg.5, Reg.8

Art.2, amended: SSI 2004/332 Sch.6 para.1, Sch.6 para.2

Art.3, disapplied: SSI 2004/219 Reg.5

Art.3, varied: 2004 asp 10 s.33

Art.4, applied: SSI 2004/219 Reg.5

Sch.1, applied: SSI 2004/219 Reg.1, Reg.13

Sch.1, referred to: SSI 2004/219 Reg.5

Sch.1 Part 6 para.18, applied: SSI 2004/219 Reg.5, Sch.1 para.14

Sch.1 Part 6 para.18A, added: SSI 2003/341 Reg.3

Sch.1 Part 11 para.29, varied: 2004 asp 10 s.33

Sch.1 Part 13 para.40, amended: SI 2003/2155 Sch.1 para.31

Sch.1 Part 20 para.67, amended: SI 2003/2155 Sch.1 para.31, Sch.2

224. Town and Country Planning (General Development Procedure) (Scotland) Order 1992

referred to: SSI 2003/1 Art.7

Art.2, amended: SSI 2004/332 Sch.7 para.1, Sch.7 para.2

Art.2A, added: SSI 2004/332 Sch.7 para.3

Art.3, amended: SI 2003/2155 Sch.1 para.32

Art.9, see *Macpherson v Edinburgh City Council* 2003 S.L.T. 1112 (OH), Lord Carloway

Art.12, amended: SSI 2003/1 Art.7

Art.14, amended: SSI 2003/1 Art.7

Art.15, amended: SSI 2003/1 Art.7

Art.23, amended: SSI 2004/332 Sch.7 para.4

Sch.5 para.7, added: SSI 2004/332 Sch.7 para.5

NO.

1992–cont.

231. Electricity (Northern Ireland) Order 1992

applied: 2002 c.40 Sch.15, SI 2003/419 Art.17, Art.18, Art.22, Art.38, Art.63

disapplied: SI 2003/419 Sch.2 para.5

referred to: 2003 c.21 Sch.17 para.120

Part II, applied: 2002 c.1 (NI) s.6, SI 2003/419 Art.2, Art.12, Art.63, SR 2003/77, SR 2003/143 Sch.1

Art.2, amended: SI 2003/419 Sch.5

Art.2, referred to: SI 2003/419 Art.2

Art.3, amended: SI 2003/419 Sch.3 para.1, Sch.5

Art.3, applied: SI 2003/419 Sch.4 para.7

Art.3, referred to: SI 2003/419 Art.2

Art.4, revoked: SI 2003/419 Sch.5

Art.5, revoked: SI 2003/419 Sch.5

Art.6, revoked: SI 2003/419 Sch.5

Art.7, applied: SI 2003/419 Art.9

Art.7, revoked: SI 2003/419 Sch.5

Art.8, amended: SI 2003/419 Art.28

Art.8, applied: SI 2003/419 Art.39, Art.60

Art.10, amended: SI 2003/419 Art.28, Sch.3 para.2

Art.10, applied: SI 2003/419 Art.20, Art.29, Sch.4 para.7, Sch.4 para.8

Art.10A, added: SI 2003/419 Art.28

Art.11, amended: SI 2003/419 Art.33, Sch.3 para.3

Art.11, applied: SI 2003/419 Art.62

Art.11A, amended: SI 2003/419 Sch.3 para.4, Sch.5

Art.12, amended: SI 2003/419 Sch.3 para.5

Art.13, amended: SI 2003/419 Sch.3 para.6, Sch.5

Art.15, amended: SI 2003/419 Sch.3 para.7

Art.15, applied: SI 2003/1397 Art.8

Art.15B, enabled: SI 2003/1371

Art.15B, referred to: SI 2003/1371

Art.16, amended: SI 2003/419 Sch.3 para.8

Art.17, amended: SI 2003/419 Art.36

Art.17A, added: SI 2003/419 Art.36

Art.18, substituted: 2002 c.40 Sch.9 para.9

Art.18, varied: SI 2003/1592 Sch.4 para.11

Art.18A, revoked: SI 2003/419 Sch.5

Art.19, applied: SI 2003/419 Art.12

Art.26, applied: SI 2003/419 Art.62

Art.28, applied: SI 2003/419 Sch.4 para.12

Art.28, revoked: SI 2003/419 Sch.5

Art.29, applied: SI 2003/419 Sch.4 para.12

Art.29, revoked: SI 2003/419 Sch.5

Art.30, revoked: SI 2003/419 Sch.5

Art.31, amended: SI 2003/419 Sch.3 para.9, Sch.5

Art.31, applied: SI 2003/419 Art.63, Sch.4 para.12

Art.32, amended: SI 2003/419 Sch.3 para.10

Art.33, amended: SI 2003/419 Sch.3 para.11

Art.35, amended: SI 2003/419 Sch.3 para.12

Art.35, applied: SI 2003/419 Art.57

NO.

NO.

1992–cont.

231. Electricity (Northern Ireland) Order 1992–*cont.*

Art.35, referred to: SI 2002/914 Art.8, SI 2003/419 Art.57, SSI 2002/163 Art.8, SSI 2004/170 Art.8

Art.35, revoked: SI 2003/419 Art.57, Sch.5

Art.36, revoked: SI 2003/419 Art.58, Sch.5

Art.38, amended: SI 2003/419 Sch.3 para.13

Art.39, applied: SI 2003/419 Art.13

Art.39, enabled: SR 2002/364

Art.40, applied: SI 2003/419 Art.13

Art.42, amended: SI 2003/419 Sch.3 para.14

Art.42, applied: SI 2003/419 Art.41, Art.45, Art.51

Art.45B, amended: SI 2003/419 Sch.3 para.15

Art.46, amended: 2002 c.40 Sch.9 para.20

Art.46, applied: SI 2003/419 Art.13

Art.46, revoked (in part): 2002 c.40 Sch.9 para.20

Art.48, applied: SI 2003/419 Sch.4 para.5

Art.48, revoked: SI 2003/419 Sch.5

Art.49, applied: SI 2003/419 Sch.4 para.5

Art.49, revoked: SI 2003/419 Sch.5

Art.50, amended: SI 2003/419 Sch.3 para.16

Art.50, applied: SI 2003/419 Art.6

Art.50, revoked (in part): SI 2003/419 Sch.5

Art.51, revoked: SI 2003/419 Sch.5

Art.52, amended: SI 2003/419 Sch.3 para.17

Art.52, applied: SI 2003/419 Art.62

Art.53, revoked: SI 2003/419 Sch.5

Art.54, revoked: SI 2003/419 Sch.5

Art.55, revoked: SI 2003/419 Sch.5

Art.56, revoked: SI 2003/419 Sch.5

Art.57, revoked: SI 2003/419 Sch.5

Art.58, applied: SI 2003/419 Art.13

Art.59, applied: SI 2003/419 Art.13, Art.63

Art.60, applied: SI 2003/419 Art.13

Art.61, amended: 2003 c.21 Sch.17 para.121, SI 2003/1400 Sch.6

Art.61, revoked: SI 2003/419 Sch.5

Art.62, amended: SI 2003/419 Sch.3 para.18

Art.63, amended: SI 2003/419 Sch.3 para.19

Art.64, varied: SI 2003/419 Art.66

Art.66, amended: SI 2003/419 Sch.3 para.20

Art.73, amended: SI 2002/3150 Sch.3 para.8

Sch.1, revoked: SI 2003/419 Sch.5

Sch.2, revoked: SI 2003/419 Sch.5

Sch.3, added: SI 2003/419 Art.64

Sch.4, amended: 2003 c.21 Sch.17 para.122, Sch.19

Sch.8, enabled: SR 2002/364

Sch.12, revoked: SI 2003/1398 Sch.1 para.20

235. Tourism (Northern Ireland) Order 1992

Art.11, amended: 2002 c.1 (NI) s.3, (NI) Sch.4

Art.11, applied: 2002 c.1 (NI) s.3

1992–cont.

247. Social Security (Miscellaneous Provisions) Amendment Regulations 1992

Reg.1, revoked (in part): SI 2003/492 Sch.3 Part 1

Reg.9, revoked (in part): SI 2003/492 Sch.3 Part 1

Reg.10, revoked (in part): SI 2003/492 Sch.3 Part 1

Reg.11, revoked (in part): SI 2003/492 Sch.3 Part 1

Reg.12, revoked (in part): SI 2003/492 Sch.3 Part 1

Reg.13, revoked (in part): SI 2003/492 Sch.3 Part 1

Reg.14, revoked (in part): SI 2003/492 Sch.3 Part 1

Reg.15, revoked (in part): SI 2003/492 Sch.3 Part 1

Reg.16, revoked (in part): SI 2003/492 Sch.3 Part 1

Reg.17, revoked (in part): SI 2003/492 Sch.3 Part 1

249. Act of Sederunt (Amendment of Ordinary Cause, Summary Cause and Small Claim Rules) 1992

r.3, revoked: SSI 2002/132 Sch.2

r.4, revoked: SSI 2002/133 Sch.2

280. Teachers Superannuation (Scotland) Regulations 1992

referred to: SSI 2004/89 Reg.2

Reg.1, amended: SSI 2002/288 Reg.3

Reg.1, substituted: SSI 2003/423 Sch.1, SSI 2004/89 Reg.5

Reg.1A, added: SSI 2002/288 Reg.13

Reg.2, amended: SSI 2003/423 Reg.3

Reg.2, amended: SSI 2003/423 Reg.4

Reg.2, revoked: SSI 2004/89 Reg.6

Reg.2, substituted: SSI 2003/423 Sch.1

Reg.3, revoked: SSI 2004/89 Reg.7

Reg.3, substituted: SSI 2003/423 Sch.1

Reg.4, revoked (in part): SSI 2004/89 Reg.8

Reg.4, substituted: SSI 2003/423 Sch.1

Reg.4A, amended: SSI 2003/423 Reg.9

Reg.5, amended: SSI 2002/288 Reg.4

Reg.5, substituted: SSI 2003/423 Sch.1

Reg.6, amended: SSI 2002/288 Reg.5

Reg.6, substituted: SSI 2003/423 Sch.1

Reg.7, amended: SSI 2002/288 Reg.6

Reg.7, substituted: SSI 2003/423 Sch.1

Reg.8, substituted: SSI 2003/423 Sch.1

Reg.9, amended: SSI 2002/288 Reg.7

Reg.9, amended: SSI 2002/288 Reg.12

Reg.9, substituted: SSI 2003/423 Sch.1

Reg.9A, substituted: SSI 2003/423 Sch.1

Reg.9B, substituted: SSI 2003/423 Sch.1

Reg.10, substituted: SSI 2003/423 Sch.1

Reg.11, amended: SSI 2003/423 Reg.5, SSI 2004/89 Reg.3

Reg.13, amended: SSI 2003/423 Reg.6, SSI 2004/89 Reg.4

Reg.15, amended: SSI 2002/288 Reg.8

NO.

1992–cont.

280. Teachers Superannuation (Scotland) Regulations 1992–*cont.*

Reg.16, amended: SSI 2002/288 Reg.9

Reg.16A, amended: SSI 2002/288 Reg.10

Reg.29, amended: SSI 2002/288 Reg.11, SSI 2003/423 Reg.7

Sch.1, amended: SSI 2002/288 Reg.14, SSI 2003/423 Reg.10

Sch.4 Part I para.2, amended: SSI 2003/423 Reg.11, SSI 2004/89 Reg.9

Sch.12, revoked: SSI 2004/89 Reg.10

Sch.12, substituted: SSI 2003/423 Reg.12

Sch.12 Part 1 para.1, revoked: SSI 2004/89 Reg.10

Sch.12 Part 1 para.1, substituted: SSI 2003/423 Reg.12

Sch.12 Part 1 para.2, revoked: SSI 2004/89 Reg.10

Sch.12 Part 1 para.2, substituted: SSI 2003/423 Reg.12

Sch.12 Part 1 para.3, revoked: SSI 2004/89 Reg.10

Sch.12 Part 1 para.3, substituted: SSI 2003/423 Reg.12

284. Port of Tilbury Transfer Scheme 1991 Confirmation Order 1992

referred to: SI 2003/527 Reg.42, SSI 2004/257 Reg.42

314. Common Agricultural Policy (Protection of Community Arrangements) Regulations 1992

Reg.3, applied: SI 2002/897 Reg.30, SR 2002/88 Reg.30

Reg.3, referred to: SSI 2002/110 Reg.29

315. Misuse of Drugs (Licence Fees) (Amendment) Regulations 1992

revoked: SI 2003/611 Sch.1

434. National Health Service (Service Committees and Tribunal) (Scotland) Regulations 1992

applied: 2002 asp 11 Sch.4 para.13, SSI 2004/163 Art.77, Art.78, Art.79

Reg.1, amended: SI 2002/3135 Sch.1 para.29

Reg.3, applied: SSI 2004/163 Art.33, Art.77

Reg.4, applied: SSI 2004/163 Art.78

Reg.5, referred to: SSI 2004/163 Art.77

Reg.7, applied: SSI 2004/163 Art.79, Art.80, Art.81

Reg.7, disapplied: SSI 2004/163 Art.80

Reg.8, applied: SSI 2004/163 Art.79, Art.81

Reg.9, applied: SSI 2004/163 Art.79, Art.81

Reg.9, referred to: SSI 2004/163 Art.81

Reg.10, applied: SSI 2004/163 Art.79, Art.81

Reg.16, applied: SSI 2004/163 Art.82

Reg.17, applied: SSI 2004/163 Art.82

Reg.18, applied: SSI 2004/163 Art.83

Reg.19, applied: SSI 2004/163 Art.84

Reg.21, revoked: SSI 2004/38 Sch.3

Reg.22, revoked: SSI 2004/38 Sch.3

Reg.23, revoked: SSI 2004/38 Sch.3

Reg.24, applied: SSI 2004/38 Reg.34

NO.

1992–cont.

434. National Health Service (Service Committees and Tribunal) (Scotland) Regulations 1992–*cont.*

Reg.24, revoked: SSI 2004/38 Sch.3

Reg.25, revoked: SSI 2004/38 Sch.3

Reg.25A, applied: SSI 2004/38 Reg.34

Reg.25A, revoked: SSI 2004/38 Sch.3

Reg.26, revoked: SSI 2004/38 Sch.3

Reg.27, revoked: SSI 2004/38 Sch.3

Reg.28, revoked: SSI 2004/38 Sch.3

Reg.29, revoked: SSI 2004/38 Sch.3

Reg.30, revoked: SSI 2004/38 Sch.3

Reg.31, revoked: SSI 2004/38 Sch.3

Reg.32, revoked: SSI 2004/38 Sch.3

Reg.33, revoked: SSI 2004/38 Sch.3

Reg.34, revoked: SSI 2004/38 Sch.3

Reg.35, revoked: SSI 2004/38 Sch.3

Reg.36, revoked: SSI 2004/38 Sch.3

Reg.37, revoked: SSI 2004/38 Sch.3

Reg.37A, revoked: SSI 2004/38 Sch.3

Reg.38, revoked: SSI 2004/38 Sch.3

Reg.39, revoked: SSI 2004/38 Sch.3

Reg.40, revoked: SSI 2004/38 Sch.3

Reg.41, revoked: SSI 2004/38 Sch.3

Reg.42, revoked: SSI 2004/38 Sch.3

Reg.43, revoked: SSI 2004/38 Sch.3

Reg.43B, revoked: SSI 2004/38 Sch.3

Reg.44, amended: SSI 2004/38 Sch.3

Reg.45, amended: SSI 2004/38 Sch.3

Reg.46, revoked (in part): SSI 2004/38 Sch.3

Reg.48, revoked (in part): SSI 2004/38 Sch.3

Sch.4, revoked: SSI 2004/38 Sch.3

458. National Health Service (Dental Charges) (Scotland) Amendment Regulations 1992

revoked: SSI 2003/158 Sch.4

462. Environmental Protection (Waste Recycling Payments) Regulations 1992

revoked (in part): SI 2004/639 Reg.4

Sch.1, substituted: SI 2002/531 Reg.2, SI 2003/596 Reg.2

471. Vehicle Inspectorate Trading Fund (Variation) Order 1992

referred to: SI 2003/942

478. Town and Country Planning (Special Enforcement Notices) (Scotland) Regulations 1992

revoked (in part): SI 2003/492 Sch.3 Part 1

483. Home Energy Efficiency Grants Regulations 1992

see *Keeping Newcastle Warm Ltd v Customs and Excise Commissioners (C353/00)* [2002] All E.R. (EC) 769 (ECJ), Judge Macken (President)

532. School Teachers Pay and Conditions Act 1991 (Commencement No 2 and Transitional Provision) Order 1992

revoked: 2002 c.32 Sch.22 Part 1

NO.

1992–cont.

548. Council Tax (Discount Disregards) Order 1992

Art.4, amended: SI 2003/673 Art.4

Art.6, substituted: SI 2003/3121 Art.4

Sch.1 Part III para.7, amended: SI 2004/1771 Sch.1 para.46

Sch.1 Part IV para.8, revoked (in part): SI 2003/673 Art.4

549. Chargeable Dwellings Order 1992

Art.2, see*John Grooms (Registered Charity) v Bond (Listing Officer)* [2003] R.V.R. 218 (Valuation Tribunal)

549. Council Tax (Chargeable Dwellings) Order 1992

Art.2, see *R. (on the application of Coleman (Listing Officer)) v Rotsztein* [2003] EWHC 1057, [2003] R.A. 152 (QBD (Admin Ct)), Sullivan, J.; see *Royal National Institute for the Blind v Williams (Listing Officer)* [2003] R.V.R. 215 (Valuation Tribunal), Judge not specified

Art.2, amended: SI 2003/3121 Art.2

Art.3, amended: SI 2003/3121 Art.2

Art.3, referred to: SI 2003/2613 Reg.1

Art.3A, added: SI 2003/3121 Art.2

Art.4, referred to: SI 2003/2613 Reg.1

551. Council Tax (Liability for Owners) Regulations 1992

Reg.2, amended: SI 2003/3125 Reg.2, SI 2004/2920 Reg.2

554. Council Tax (Reductions for Disabilities) Regulations 1992

applied: SI 2003/2613 Sch.1 para.17

referred to: SI 2003/2613 Sch.1 para.9

Reg.3, see *Sandwell MBC v Perks* [2003] EWHC 1749, [2003] R.V.R. 317 (QBD (Admin Ct)), Silber, J.

558. Council Tax (Exempt Dwellings) Order 1992

Art.3, amended: SI 2003/3121 Art.3

Art.3 Class G, see *Watson v Rhondda Cynon Taff CBC* [2001] EWHC Admin 913, [2002] R.V.R. 132 (QBD (Admin Ct)), Gibbs, J.

580. Nursing and Midwifery Student Allowances (Scotland) Regulations 1992

applied: SI 2002/195 Reg.4, Reg.28, SI 2002/3200 Reg.4, Reg.27, SR 2002/224 Reg.4, Reg.29

Reg.2, amended: SSI 2004/469 Reg.2

Reg.3, revoked (in part): SSI 2003/401 Reg.2

Reg.3, substituted: SSI 2002/423 Reg.4

Reg.4, amended: SSI 2002/423 Reg.5

Reg.5, amended: SSI 2002/423 Reg.6, Reg.7

Sch.1 para.1, added: SSI 2002/423 Reg.8

Sch.1 para.2, added: SSI 2002/423 Reg.8

Sch.1 para.2, amended: SSI 2004/469 Reg.2

Sch.1 para.3, added: SSI 2002/423 Reg.8

Sch.1 para.3, amended: SSI 2004/469 Reg.2

Sch.1 para.4, added: SSI 2002/423 Reg.8

Sch.1 para.4, amended: SSI 2004/469 Reg.2

NO.

1992–cont.

580. Nursing and Midwifery Student Allowances (Scotland) Regulations 1992–*cont.*

Sch.1 para.5, added: SSI 2002/423 Reg.8

Sch.1 para.6, added: SSI 2002/423 Reg.8

Sch.1 para.7, added: SSI 2002/423 Reg.8

Sch.1 para.7, amended: SSI 2004/469 Reg.2

Sch.1 para.8, added: SSI 2002/423 Reg.8

Sch.2 para.1, added: SSI 2002/423 Reg.8

Sch.2 para.2, added: SSI 2002/423 Reg.8

Sch.2 para.2, amended: SSI 2004/469 Reg.2

587. Education (London Residuary Body) (Property Transfer) Order 1992

Art.4, amended: SI 2002/2003 Art.2

Art.4, revoked (in part): SI 2002/2760 Art.2

605. Medicines Act 1968 (Application to Radiopharmaceutical-associated Products) Regulations 1992

Sch.1, amended: SI 2004/1031 Sch.10 para.9

612. Local Authorities (Calculation of Council Tax Base) Regulations 1992

Reg.1, amended: SI 2003/3012 Reg.2

Reg.5A, amended: SI 2003/3012 Reg.4

Reg.5AA, added: SI 2003/3012 Reg.3

Reg.6, amended: SI 2003/3012 Reg.5, SI 2003/3181 Reg.2

Reg.7, amended: SI 2003/3012 Reg.6

Reg.8, amended: SI 2003/3012 Reg.7

Reg.9, amended: SI 2003/3012 Reg.8

613. Council Tax (Administration and Enforcement) Regulations 1992

referred to: SI 2002/808 Art.2, SI 2003/768 Reg.2, SI 2003/2604 Art.2, SI 2004/927 Reg.2

Part V, applied: SI 2003/2613 Reg.4

Reg.1, amended: SI 2003/2604 Art.3, SI 2004/785 Reg.3, SI 2004/927 Reg.3

Reg.2, amended: SI 2003/2604 Art.4

Reg.4, amended: SI 2002/808 Art.38

Reg.14, substituted: SI 2004/785 Reg.4, SI 2004/927 Reg.4

Reg.18, see *Regentford Ltd v Thanet DC* [2004] EWHC 246, [2004] R.A. 113 (QBD (Admin Ct)), Lightman, J.

Reg.18, disapplied: SI 2003/2613 Reg.3

Reg.19, see *Regentford Ltd v Thanet DC* [2004] EWHC 246, [2004] R.A. 113 (QBD (Admin Ct)), Lightman, J.

Reg.32, amended: SI 2003/522 Reg.4, SI 2003/768 Reg.3, SI 2004/785 Reg.5, SI 2004/927 Reg.5

Reg.33, see *Regentford Ltd v Thanet DC* [2004] EWHC 246, [2004] R.A. 113 (QBD (Admin Ct)), Lightman, J.

Reg.34, see *R. v Lewes and Crowborough Magistrates Court Ex p. Mackelden* [2002] R.V.R. 363 (QBD), Collins, J.; see *Regentford Ltd v Thanet DC* [2004] EWHC 246, [2004] R.A. 113 (QBD (Admin Ct)), Lightman, J.

NO.

NO.

1992–cont.

613. Council Tax (Administration and Enforcement) Regulations 1992–*cont.*

Reg.35, amended: SI 2003/1715 Reg.3, SI 2003/2211 Reg.3

Reg.36A, added: SI 2004/785 Reg.5, SI 2004/927 Reg.5

Reg.37, amended: SI 2004/785 Reg.6, SI 2004/927 Reg.6

Reg.45, see *Nwankwo v Hendon Magistrates Court* [2003] EWHC 1659, [2004] R.V.R. 12 (QBD (Admin Ct)), Moses, J.

Reg.47, see *R. v Cannock Magistrates Court Ex p. Swaffer* [2003] R.V.R. 114 (QBD), Collins, J.

Reg.48, amended: SI 2003/1715 Reg.3, SI 2003/2211 Reg.3

Reg.50, amended: SI 2004/785 Reg.7, SI 2004/927 Reg.7

Sch.2, revoked (in part): SI 2003/1715 Reg.3, SI 2003/2211 Reg.3

Sch.5 para.1, amended: SI 2003/2211 Reg.4

Sch.5 para.1, substituted: SI 2004/1013 Reg.3

Sch.5 para.2, amended: SI 2003/2211 Reg.4, SI 2004/1013 Reg.3

618. Local Authorities (Members Interests) Regulations 1992

revoked (in part): SSI 2003/199 Sch.1

Reg.2, applied: SI 2002/975 Reg.2

635. National Health Service (General Medical Services) Regulations 1992

applied: SI 2002/553 Art.9, SI 2002/2469 Sch.12 para.5, SI 2003/2644 Reg.11, SI 2004/865 Art.9, Art.36, Art.41, SI 2004/1016 Art.9, SI 2004/1020 Sch.1 para.9

referred to: SI 2002/2802 Reg.4, SI 2003/784 Reg.1, SI 2003/1084 Reg.1, SI 2004/433 Art.42, SI 2004/477 Art.42, SI 2004/865 Art.60, Art.61, SI 2004/1016 Art.33

revoked (in part): SI 2004/865 Sch.2, SI 2004/1016 Sch.2

varied: SI 2004/585 Sch.1 para.9, SI 2004/865 Art.62, SI 2004/1016 Art.36, Art.38

see *Essex Strategic HA (formerly North Essex HA) v David-John* [2004] I.C.R. 112 (EAT), Judge DM Levy Q.C.

Reg.2, amended: SI 2002/554 Reg.2, SI 2002/881 Sch.1 para.9, SI 2002/1896 Reg.2, SI 2002/2469 Sch.5, Sch.7, SI 2002/2861 Reg.31, SI 2002/3135 Sch.1 para.30, SI 2003/699 Reg.3, SI 2003/1084 Reg.11, SI 2003/2624 Reg.3, SI 2003/2644 Reg.39

Reg.2, applied: SI 2003/2644 Reg.10

Reg.2, referred to: SI 2002/1882 Reg.10

Reg.2, revoked (in part): SI 2002/916 Reg.2, SI 2004/865 Sch.2

Reg.3, amended: SI 2002/1896 Reg.2

Reg.3, revoked (in part): SI 2004/865 Sch.2

Reg.4, amended: SI 2002/554 Reg.3, SI 2002/916 Reg.3, SI 2002/1896 Reg.2, SI 2002/2469 Sch.5, SI 2003/1084 Reg.12

1992–cont.

635. National Health Service (General Medical Services) Regulations 1992–*cont.*

Reg.4, applied: SI 2004/433 Art.3, Art.5, SI 2004/477 Art.3, Art.5

Reg.4, revoked (in part): SI 2004/865 Sch.2

Reg.5A, amended: SI 2002/554 Reg.4, SI 2002/916 Reg.4, SI 2002/2469 Sch.5

Reg.5A, revoked (in part): SI 2002/554 Reg.4, SI 2002/916 Reg.4

Reg.6, amended: SI 2002/554 Reg.5, SI 2002/916 Reg.5, SI 2002/1896 Reg.2, Reg.3, SI 2002/2469 Sch.5, Sch.7, SI 2003/2644 Reg.40

Reg.6, revoked (in part): SI 2004/865 Sch.2

Reg.7, amended: SI 2002/1896 Reg.2, Reg.4, SI 2002/2469 Sch.7, SI 2002/3135 Sch.1 para.30, SI 2003/2644 Reg.41

Reg.7, applied: SI 2003/2644 Reg.4, SI 2004/585 Reg.23, SI 2004/1020 Reg.23

Reg.7, revoked (in part): SI 2002/1896 Reg.4, SI 2004/865 Sch.2

Reg.7A, added: SI 2002/1896 Reg.5

Reg.7A, revoked (in part): SI 2004/865 Sch.2

Reg.7B, added: SI 2002/1896 Reg.5

Reg.7B, amended: SI 2002/2469 Sch.7, SI 2002/2802 Reg.5, SI 2003/2644 Reg.42

Reg.7B, revoked (in part): SI 2004/865 Sch.2

Reg.7C, added: SI 2002/1896 Reg.5

Reg.7C, amended: SI 2002/2469 Sch.7

Reg.7C, revoked (in part): SI 2004/865 Sch.2

Reg.7D, added: SI 2002/1896 Reg.5

Reg.7D, amended: SI 2002/2469 Sch.7, SI 2002/2802 Reg.5, SI 2003/2644 Reg.43

Reg.7D, revoked (in part): SI 2004/865 Sch.2

Reg.7E, added: SI 2002/1896 Reg.5

Reg.7E, amended: SI 2002/554 Sch.1 para.3, SI 2002/2469 Sch.7, SI 2003/2644 Reg.44

Reg.7E, revoked (in part): SI 2004/865 Sch.2

Reg.7F, added: SI 2002/1896 Reg.5

Reg.7F, amended: SI 2002/2469 Sch.7

Reg.7F, revoked (in part): SI 2004/865 Sch.2

Reg.7G, added: SI 2002/1896 Reg.5

Reg.7G, amended: SI 2002/2469 Sch.7, SI 2003/2644 Reg.46

Reg.7G, revoked (in part): SI 2004/865 Sch.2

Reg.7H, added: SI 2002/1896 Reg.5

Reg.7H, revoked (in part): SI 2004/865 Sch.2

Reg.8, amended: SI 2002/1896 Reg.2, SI 2002/2469 Sch.5, Sch.7

Reg.8, referred to: SI 2002/2469 Sch.7

Reg.8, revoked (in part): SI 2004/865 Sch.2

Reg.9, amended: SI 2002/1896 Reg.2, SI 2002/2469 Sch.7

Reg.9, revoked (in part): SI 2004/865 Sch.2

NO.

NO.

1992–cont.

635. National Health Service (General Medical Services) Regulations 1992–cont.

Reg.10, revoked (in part): SI 2002/554 Reg.6, SI 2002/916 Reg.6

Reg.11, revoked (in part): SI 2002/554 Reg.6, SI 2002/916 Reg.6

Reg.12, amended: SI 2002/2469 Sch.5

Reg.12, revoked (in part): SI 2004/865 Sch.2

Reg.12, substituted: SI 2002/554 Reg.7, SI 2002/916 Reg.7

Reg.13, amended: SI 2002/554 Reg.8, SI 2002/916 Reg.8, SI 2002/2469 Sch.5

Reg.13, revoked (in part): SI 2002/554 Reg.8, SI 2002/916 Reg.8, SI 2004/865 Sch.2

Reg.14, revoked (in part): SI 2002/554 Reg.9, SI 2002/916 Reg.9

Reg.15, amended: SI 2002/2469 Sch.5

Reg.15, revoked (in part): SI 2004/865 Sch.2

Reg.15, substituted: SI 2002/554 Reg.10, SI 2002/916 Reg.10

Reg.16, amended: SI 2002/2469 Sch.5

Reg.16, substituted: SI 2002/554 Reg.11, SI 2002/916 Reg.11

Reg.17, amended: SI 2002/554 Reg.12, SI 2002/916 Reg.12, SI 2002/2469 Sch.1 para.54, Sch.5

Reg.17, revoked (in part): SI 2004/865 Sch.2

Reg.18, amended: SI 2002/554 Reg.13, SI 2002/916 Reg.13, SI 2002/2469 Sch.5

Reg.18A, amended: SI 2002/554 Reg.14, SI 2002/916 Reg.14, SI 2002/2469 Sch.1 para.54, Sch.5

Reg.18A, applied: SI 2004/433 Art.3, Art.5, SI 2004/477 Art.3, Art.5, SI 2004/865 Art.38, Art.39, SI 2004/1016 Art.35

Reg.18B, amended: SI 2002/554 Reg.15, SI 2002/916 Reg.15, SI 2002/2469 Sch.5

Reg.18B, applied: SI 2004/433 Art.3, Art.5, SI 2004/477 Art.3, Art.5, SI 2004/865 Art.38, Art.39, SI 2004/1016 Art.35

Reg.18C, amended: SI 2002/554 Reg.16, SI 2002/916 Reg.16, SI 2002/2469 Sch.5

Reg.18C, applied: SI 2004/433 Art.8, Art.9, Art.10, SI 2004/477 Art.8, Art.9, Art.10

Reg.18D, amended: SI 2002/554 Reg.17, SI 2002/916 Reg.17, SI 2002/2469 Sch.5

Reg.18D, applied: SI 2004/433 Art.17, SI 2004/477 Art.17

Reg.18E, amended: SI 2002/554 Reg.18, SI 2002/916 Reg.18, SI 2002/1896 Reg.6, SI 2002/2469 Sch.5, SI 2002/3135 Sch.1 para.30, SI 2003/2644 Reg.47

Reg.18E, referred to: SI 2004/865 Art.60, Art.61

Reg.18E, revoked (in part): SI 2002/1896 Reg.6, SI 2003/1250 Sch.10 para.1, SI 2004/865 Sch.2

Reg.18EE, added: SI 2002/1896 Reg.7

Reg.18EE, amended: SI 2002/2469 Sch.7, SI 2002/2802 Reg.5, SI 2003/2644 Reg.48

1992–cont.

635. National Health Service (General Medical Services) Regulations 1992–cont.

Reg.18EE, revoked (in part): SI 2004/865 Sch.2

Reg.18EF, added: SI 2002/1896 Reg.7

Reg.18EF, amended: SI 2002/2469 Sch.7, SI 2003/2644 Reg.49

Reg.18EF, revoked (in part): SI 2004/865 Sch.2

Reg.18F, amended: SI 2002/554 Reg.19, SI 2002/916 Reg.19, SI 2002/1896 Reg.8, SI 2002/2469 Sch.1 para.54, Sch.5, Sch.7

Reg.18F, applied: SI 2004/433 Art.5, Art.8, SI 2004/477 Art.5, Art.8, SI 2004/865 Art.38, SI 2004/1016 Art.35

Reg.18F, revoked (in part): SI 2002/1896 Reg.8, SI 2004/865 Sch.2

Reg.18G, amended: SI 2002/554 Reg.20, SI 2002/916 Reg.20, SI 2002/1896 Reg.9, SI 2002/2469 Sch.5

Reg.18G, applied: SI 2004/433 Art.9, SI 2004/477 Art.9, SI 2004/865 Art.39

Reg.18G, referred to: SI 2004/477 Art.9

Reg.18G, revoked (in part): SI 2002/554 Reg.20, SI 2002/916 Reg.20, SI 2004/865 Sch.2

Reg.18G, varied: SI 2004/433 Art.9, SI 2004/865 Art.39, SI 2004/1016 Art.36

Reg.18GG, added: SI 2002/1896 Reg.10

Reg.18GG, amended: SI 2002/2469 Sch.7

Reg.18GG, applied: SI 2004/433 Art.9, SI 2004/477 Art.9, SI 2004/865 Art.39

Reg.18GG, referred to: SI 2004/477 Art.9

Reg.18GG, varied: SI 2004/433 Art.9, SI 2004/865 Art.39, SI 2004/1016 Art.36

Reg.18H, revoked (in part): SI 2002/554 Reg.21, SI 2002/916 Reg.21

Reg.18I, amended: SI 2002/1896 Reg.11

Reg.18I, revoked (in part): SI 2002/554 Reg.21, SI 2002/916 Reg.21

Reg.18J, amended: SI 2002/1896 Reg.12, SI 2002/2469 Sch.5, Sch.7

Reg.18J, referred to: SI 2002/2469 Sch.5

Reg.18J, revoked (in part): SI 2004/865 Sch.2

Reg.18J, substituted: SI 2002/554 Reg.22, SI 2002/916 Reg.22

Reg.18K, amended: SI 2002/554 Reg.23, SI 2002/916 Reg.23, SI 2002/2469 Sch.5

Reg.18K, revoked (in part): SI 2002/916 Reg.23, SI 2004/865 Sch.2

Reg.18L, amended: SI 2002/2469 Sch.5

Reg.18L, revoked (in part): SI 2004/865 Sch.2

Reg.18L, substituted: SI 2002/554 Reg.24, SI 2002/916 Reg.24

Reg.18M, added: SI 2002/1896 Reg.13

Reg.18M, amended: SI 2002/2469 Sch.7, SI 2003/2644 Reg.50

NO.

1992–cont.

635. National Health Service (General Medical Services) Regulations 1992–cont.

Reg.18M, revoked (in part): SI 2004/865 Sch.2

Reg.19, amended: SI 2002/1896 Reg.2, SI 2002/2469 Sch.5, Sch.7

Reg.19, applied: SI 2004/433 Art.3, Art.28, SI 2004/477 Art.3, Art.28, SI 2004/865 Art.7, Art.9, SI 2004/1016 Art.7, Art.9

Reg.19, referred to: SI 2002/2469 Sch.7

Reg.22, amended: SI 2002/1896 Reg.2, SI 2002/2469 Sch.7

Reg.22, revoked (in part): SI 2004/865 Sch.2

Reg.23, amended: SI 2002/1896 Reg.2, SI 2002/2469 Sch.7

Reg.23, applied: SI 2004/865 Art.5, Art.8, SI 2004/1016 Art.5, Art.8

Reg.23, revoked (in part): SI 2004/865 Sch.2

Reg.24, amended: SI 2002/1896 Reg.2, SI 2002/2469 Sch.7

Reg.24, revoked (in part): SI 2004/865 Sch.2

Reg.25, amended: SI 2002/1896 Reg.2, Reg.14, SI 2002/2469 Sch.1 para.54, Sch.5, Sch.7, SI 2003/1250 Sch.10 para.1

Reg.25, applied: SI 2004/433 Art.3, Art.13, Art.15, Art.30, SI 2004/477 Art.3, Art.13, Art.15, Art.30, SI 2004/865 Art.31, SI 2004/1016 Art.28

Reg.25, referred to: SI 2002/2469 Sch.7

Reg.25, revoked (in part): SI 2004/865 Sch.2

Reg.27, amended: SI 2002/1896 Reg.2, SI 2002/2469 Sch.7

Reg.27, revoked (in part): SI 2004/865 Sch.2

Reg.28, amended: SI 2002/1896 Reg.2, SI 2002/2469 Sch.5, Sch.7

Reg.28, applied: SI 2004/433 Art.24, SI 2004/477 Art.24

Reg.28, revoked (in part): SI 2004/865 Sch.2

Reg.29, applied: SI 2004/433 Art.24, SI 2004/477 Art.24

Reg.30, amended: SI 2002/1896 Reg.2, SI 2002/2469 Sch.7

Reg.30, revoked (in part): SI 2004/865 Sch.2

Reg.31, amended: SI 2002/1896 Reg.2, SI 2002/2469 Sch.7

Reg.31, applied: SI 2004/433 Art.24, SI 2004/477 Art.24

Reg.31, revoked (in part): SI 2004/865 Sch.2

Reg.32, amended: SI 2002/1896 Reg.2, SI 2002/2469 Sch.7

Reg.32, revoked (in part): SI 2004/865 Sch.2

Reg.33, amended: SI 2002/1896 Reg.2, SI 2002/2469 Sch.7

Reg.33, revoked (in part): SI 2004/865 Sch.2

Reg.33A, added: SI 2003/1084 Reg.13

Reg.33A, amended: SI 2002/1896 Reg.2, SI 2002/2469 Sch.7

Reg.33A, applied: SI 2004/865 Art.18

Reg.33A, referred to: SI 2004/865 Art.18

NO.

1992–cont.

635. National Health Service (General Medical Services) Regulations 1992–cont.

Reg.33A, revoked (in part): SI 2004/865 Sch.2

Reg.34, amended: SI 2002/1896 Reg.2, SI 2002/2469 Sch.7

Reg.34, applied: SI 2004/291 Sch.2 para.4, Sch.2 para.5, SI 2004/478 Sch.2 para.4, Sch.2 para.5, SI 2004/865 Art.60

Reg.34, revoked (in part): SI 2004/865 Sch.2

Reg.34A, amended: SI 2002/2469 Sch.7, SI 2002/2802 Reg.5

Reg.34A, revoked (in part): SI 2004/865 Sch.2

Reg.34A, substituted: SI 2002/1896 Reg.15

Reg.34B, amended: SI 2002/2469 Sch.5

Reg.35, amended: SI 2002/1896 Reg.2, SI 2002/2469 Sch.7, SI 2003/2644 Reg.51

Reg.35, applied: SI 2004/865 Art.41, SI 2004/1016 Art.38

Reg.35, revoked (in part): SI 2004/865 Sch.2

Reg.36, amended: SI 2002/1896 Reg.2, SI 2002/2469 Sch.7, SI 2002/2861 Reg.31

Reg.36, applied: SI 2004/865 Art.37

Reg.36, revoked (in part): SI 2004/865 Sch.2

Reg.36, varied: SI 2004/865 Art.37, SI 2004/1016 Art.34

Reg.37, amended: SI 2002/554 Reg.25, SI 2002/916 Reg.25, SI 2002/1896 Reg.2, SI 2002/2469 Sch.7

Reg.37, revoked (in part): SI 2004/865 Sch.2

Reg.38, amended: SI 2002/1896 Reg.2, SI 2002/2469 Sch.7

Reg.39, amended: SI 2002/1896 Reg.2, SI 2002/2469 Sch.7

Reg.40, amended: SI 2002/554 Reg.26, SI 2002/916 Reg.26, SI 2002/1896 Reg.2

Sch.2, applied: SI 2004/865 Art.16, SI 2004/1016 Art.16

Sch.2 para.1, amended: SI 2002/551 Reg.3, SI 2002/1896 Reg.2, SI 2002/2469 Sch.7, SI 2002/2861 Reg.31, SI 2002/3189 Reg.3, SI 2003/699 Reg.3, SI 2003/1084 Reg.14, SI 2003/2624 Reg.3

Sch.2 para.1, revoked (in part): SI 2004/865 Sch.2

Sch.2 para.1A, amended: SI 2002/2469 Sch.7

Sch.2 para.1A, revoked (in part): SI 2004/865 Sch.2

Sch.2 para.4, amended: SI 2002/1896 Reg.2, SI 2002/2469 Sch.7

Sch.2 para.4, applied: SI 2004/865 Art.13

Sch.2 para.4, revoked (in part): SI 2004/865 Sch.2

Sch.2 para.4, varied: SI 2004/1016 Art.13

Sch.2 para.5, amended: SI 2002/1896 Reg.2, SI 2002/2469 Sch.7

Sch.2 para.5, revoked (in part): SI 2004/865 Sch.2

1992–cont.

635. National Health Service (General Medical Services) Regulations 1992–cont.

Sch.2 para.6, amended: SI 2002/1896 Reg.2, SI 2002/2469 Sch.5, Sch.7

Sch.2 para.6, applied: SI 2004/865 Art.4, SI 2004/1016 Art.4

Sch.2 para.6, revoked (in part): SI 2004/865 Sch.2

Sch.2 para.7, applied: SI 2004/865 Art.11, SI 2004/1016 Art.11

Sch.2 para.9, amended: SI 2002/1896 Reg.2, SI 2002/2469 Sch.7

Sch.2 para.9, applied: SI 2004/865 Art.6, Art.11, Art.12, SI 2004/1016 Art.6, Art.11, Art.12

Sch.2 para.9, revoked (in part): SI 2004/865 Sch.2

Sch.2 para.9A, amended: SI 2002/1896 Reg.2, SI 2002/2469 Sch.7

Sch.2 para.9A, applied: SI 2004/865 Art.7, SI 2004/1016 Art.7, Art.12

Sch.2 para.9A, revoked (in part): SI 2004/865 Sch.2

Sch.2 para.10, amended: SI 2002/1896 Reg.2, SI 2002/2469 Sch.7

Sch.2 para.10, applied: SI 2004/865 Art.11, Art.12, SI 2004/1016 Art.11, Art.12

Sch.2 para.10, revoked (in part): SI 2004/865 Sch.2

Sch.2 para.11, amended: SI 2002/1896 Reg.2, SI 2002/2469 Sch.7

Sch.2 para.11, revoked (in part): SI 2004/865 Sch.2

Sch.2 para.12, amended: SI 2002/1896 Reg.2, SI 2002/2469 Sch.7

Sch.2 para.12, revoked (in part): SI 2004/865 Sch.2

Sch.2 para.13, amended: SI 2002/1896 Reg.2, SI 2002/2469 Sch.7

Sch.2 para.13, revoked (in part): SI 2004/865 Sch.2

Sch.2 para.14, amended: SI 2002/1896 Reg.2, SI 2002/2469 Sch.7

Sch.2 para.14, applied: SI 2004/865 Art.14, SI 2004/1016 Art.14

Sch.2 para.14, revoked (in part): SI 2004/865 Sch.2

Sch.2 para.16, applied: SI 2004/865 Art.33, SI 2004/1016 Art.30

Sch.2 para.17, amended: SI 2002/1896 Reg.2, SI 2002/2469 Sch.7

Sch.2 para.17, revoked (in part): SI 2004/865 Sch.2

Sch.2 para.18, amended: SI 2002/1896 Reg.2, SI 2002/2469 Sch.7

Sch.2 para.18, applied: SI 2004/291 Reg.30, Reg.31, SI 2004/433 Art.19, Art.20, SI 2004/477 Art.19, Art.20, SI 2004/478 Reg.30, Reg.31

Sch.2 para.18, revoked (in part): SI 2004/865 Sch.2

1992–cont.

635. National Health Service (General Medical Services) Regulations 1992–cont.

Sch.2 para.18A, amended: SI 2002/1896 Reg.16, SI 2002/2469 Sch.5, Sch.7, SI 2002/2548 Reg.12, SI 2002/3135 Sch.1 para.30, SI 2003/26 Reg.7

Sch.2 para.18A, applied: SI 2004/865 Art.74, Art.76, Art.79, Art.81, Art.84, Art.86, SI 2004/1016 Art.58, Art.59, Art.60, Art.61, Art.63, Art.64

Sch.2 para.18A, referred to: SI 2002/2469 Sch.5, SI 2004/865 Art.76, Art.79, Art.86, SI 2004/1016 Art.59, Art.60, Art.64

Sch.2 para.18A, revoked (in part): SI 2003/26 Reg.7, SI 2004/865 Sch.2

Sch.2 para.18A, varied: SI 2004/478 Sch.7 para.1, SI 2004/1016 Art.59, Art.60

Sch.2 para.18B, amended: SI 2002/2469 Sch.5, SI 2002/2548 Reg.13

Sch.2 para.18B, applied: SI 2004/865 Art.76, Art.81, Art.84, SI 2004/1016 Art.59, Art.61, Art.63

Sch.2 para.18B, revoked (in part): SI 2004/865 Sch.2

Sch.2 para.18B, varied: SI 2004/478 Sch.7 para.1

Sch.2 para.18C, amended: SI 2002/2469 Sch.5

Sch.2 para.18C, applied: SI 2004/865 Art.76, Art.86, SI 2004/1016 Art.59, Art.64

Sch.2 para.18C, varied: SI 2004/478 Sch.7 para.1

Sch.2 para.19, amended: SI 2002/1896 Reg.2, SI 2002/2469 Sch.7, SI 2003/1084 Reg.14

Sch.2 para.19, revoked (in part): SI 2004/865 Sch.2

Sch.2 para.20, amended: SI 2002/1896 Reg.2, SI 2002/2469 Sch.7, SI 2002/2548 Reg.13

Sch.2 para.20, revoked (in part): SI 2002/2548 Reg.13, SI 2004/865 Sch.2

Sch.2 para.21, amended: SI 2002/1896 Reg.2, SI 2002/2469 Sch.7

Sch.2 para.21, applied: SI 2004/865 Art.29, SI 2004/1016 Art.26

Sch.2 para.21, revoked (in part): SI 2004/865 Sch.2

Sch.2 para.21A, added: SI 2003/26 Reg.7

Sch.2 para.21A, amended: SI 2003/1250 Sch.10 para.1

Sch.2 para.21A, applied: SI 2004/865 Art.28, Art.29

Sch.2 para.21A, revoked (in part): SI 2004/865 Sch.2

Sch.2 para.22, amended: SI 2002/1896 Reg.16, SI 2002/2469 Sch.5, SI 2003/1250 Sch.10 para.1

Sch.2 para.22, revoked (in part): SI 2002/2548 Reg.13

1992–cont.

635. National Health Service (General Medical Services) Regulations 1992– *cont.*

Sch.2 para.22A, amended: SI 2003/1250 Sch.10 para.1

Sch.2 para.22A, revoked (in part): SI 2003/1250 Sch.10 para.1

Sch.2 para.23, amended: SI 2002/1896 Reg.2, Reg.16, SI 2002/2469 Sch.7

Sch.2 para.23, revoked (in part): SI 2004/865 Sch.2

Sch.2 para.23A, added: SI 2002/1896 Reg.16

Sch.2 para.23A, amended: SI 2002/554 Reg.31, Sch.1 para.8, SI 2002/2469 Sch.7, SI 2002/2802 Reg.5, SI 2003/2644 Reg.52

Sch.2 para.23A, revoked (in part): SI 2003/2644 Reg.52, SI 2004/865 Sch.2

Sch.2 para.24, amended: SI 2002/554 Reg.27, SI 2002/916 Reg.27, SI 2002/1896 Reg.2, SI 2002/2469 Sch.7

Sch.2 para.24, revoked (in part): SI 2004/865 Sch.2

Sch.2 para.27, amended: SI 2002/1896 Reg.2, SI 2002/2469 Sch.7

Sch.2 para.27, applied: SI 2004/865 Art.20, SI 2004/1016 Art.19

Sch.2 para.27, revoked (in part): SI 2004/865 Sch.2

Sch.2 para.28, amended: SI 2002/1896 Reg.2, SI 2002/2469 Sch.7

Sch.2 para.28, revoked (in part): SI 2004/865 Sch.2

Sch.2 para.28A, amended: SI 2002/2469 Sch.5, SI 2003/699 Reg.3, SI 2003/2624 Reg.3

Sch.2 para.28A, applied: SI 2004/865 Art.17, SI 2004/1016 Art.17

Sch.2 para.28A, revoked (in part): SI 2004/865 Sch.2

Sch.2 para.28B, added: SI 2003/699 Reg.3, SI 2003/2624 Reg.3

Sch.2 para.28B, revoked (in part): SI 2004/865 Sch.2

Sch.2 para.29, amended: SI 2002/554 Reg.27, SI 2002/916 Reg.27, SI 2002/1896 Reg.2, SI 2002/2469 Sch.7

Sch.2 para.29, applied: SI 2004/433 Art.26, SI 2004/477 Art.26, SI 2004/865 Art.21, SI 2004/1016 Art.20

Sch.2 para.29, referred to: SI 2004/865 Art.21

Sch.2 para.29, revoked (in part): SI 2004/865 Sch.2

Sch.2 para.29, varied: SI 2004/865 Art.21, Art.22, SI 2004/1016 Art.20, Art.21

Sch.2 para.29A, amended: SI 2002/554 Reg.27, SI 2002/916 Reg.27, SI 2002/1896 Reg.2, SI 2002/2469 Sch.7

1992–cont.

635. National Health Service (General Medical Services) Regulations 1992– *cont.*

Sch.2 para.29A, applied: SI 2004/433 Art.26, SI 2004/477 Art.26, SI 2004/865 Art.21, Art.22, SI 2004/1016 Art.20

Sch.2 para.29A, referred to: SI 2004/865 Art.22

Sch.2 para.29A, revoked (in part): SI 2004/865 Sch.2

Sch.2 para.29A, varied: SI 2004/865 Art.21, Art.22, SI 2004/1016 Art.20, Art.21

Sch.2 para.30, amended: SI 2002/1896 Reg.2, SI 2002/2469 Sch.7

Sch.2 para.30, revoked (in part): SI 2004/865 Sch.2

Sch.2 para.31, amended: SI 2002/1896 Reg.2, SI 2002/2469 Sch.7

Sch.2 para.31, applied: SI 2004/865 Art.15, SI 2004/1016 Art.15

Sch.2 para.31, revoked (in part): SI 2004/865 Sch.2

Sch.2 para.32, amended: SI 2002/554 Reg.27, SI 2002/916 Reg.27, SI 2002/1896 Reg.2, SI 2002/2469 Sch.5, Sch.7

Sch.2 para.32, revoked (in part): SI 2004/865 Sch.2

Sch.2 para.33, amended: SI 2002/554 Reg.27, SI 2002/916 Reg.27, SI 2002/1896 Reg.2, SI 2002/2469 Sch.7

Sch.2 para.33, revoked (in part): SI 2004/865 Sch.2

Sch.2 para.34, amended: SI 2002/554 Reg.27, SI 2002/916 Reg.27, SI 2002/1896 Reg.2, SI 2002/2469 Sch.5, Sch.7

Sch.2 para.34, revoked (in part): SI 2004/865 Sch.2

Sch.2 para.35, amended: SI 2002/1896 Reg.2, SI 2002/2469 Sch.7

Sch.2 para.36, amended: SI 2002/1896 Reg.2, SI 2002/2469 Sch.5

Sch.2 para.36, applied: SI 2004/865 Art.19, SI 2004/1016 Art.18

Sch.2 para.36, revoked (in part): SI 2004/865 Sch.2

Sch.2 para.36, varied: SI 2004/865 Art.37

Sch.2 para.36A, added: SI 2002/1896 Reg.16

Sch.2 para.36A, amended: SI 2002/2469 Sch.7, SI 2002/2802 Reg.5, SI 2003/2644 Reg.52

Sch.2 para.36A, revoked (in part): SI 2004/865 Sch.2

Sch.2 para.36A, substituted: SI 2003/2644 Reg.52

Sch.2 para.36B, added: SI 2002/1896 Reg.16

Sch.2 para.36B, amended: SI 2002/2469 Sch.7

Sch.2 para.36B, revoked (in part): SI 2004/865 Sch.2

1992–cont.

635. National Health Service (General Medical Services) Regulations 1992–cont.

Sch.2 para.36C, added: SI 2003/2644 Reg.52

Sch.2 para.36C, applied: SI 2004/865 Art.27

Sch.2 para.36C, revoked (in part): SI 2004/865 Sch.2

Sch.2 para.38, amended: SI 2002/1896 Reg.2, SI 2002/2469 Sch.7

Sch.2 para.38, applied: SI 2004/865 Art.35

Sch.2 para.38, revoked (in part): SI 2004/865 Sch.2

Sch.2 para.39, amended: SI 2002/1896 Reg.2, SI 2002/2469 Sch.7

Sch.2 para.39, revoked (in part): SI 2004/865 Sch.2

Sch.2 para.39, varied: SI 2004/865 Art.35, SI 2004/1016 Art.32

Sch.2 para.40, amended: SI 2003/1084 Reg.14

Sch.2 para.41, amended: SI 2002/1896 Reg.2, SI 2002/2469 Sch.7

Sch.2 para.42, amended: SI 2003/1084 Reg.14

Sch.2 para.42, revoked (in part): SI 2004/865 Sch.2

Sch.2 para.43, amended: SI 2002/1896 Reg.2, SI 2002/2469 Sch.7, SI 2002/3189 Reg.3, SI 2003/139 Reg.2, SI 2003/1084 Reg.14

Sch.2 para.43, revoked (in part): SI 2004/865 Sch.2

Sch.2 para.43A, added: SI 2003/1084 Reg.14

Sch.2 para.43A, revoked (in part): SI 2004/865 Sch.2

Sch.2 para.44, amended: SI 2002/551 Reg.3, SI 2002/2861 Reg.31, SI 2002/3189 Reg.3, SI 2003/1084 Reg.14

Sch.2 para.44, revoked (in part): SI 2004/865 Sch.2

Sch.2 para.45, amended: SI 2002/2861 Reg.31

Sch.2 para.45, revoked (in part): SI 2004/865 Sch.2

Sch.2 para.46, amended: SI 2003/1084 Reg.14

Sch.2 para.46, revoked (in part): SI 2004/865 Sch.2

Sch.2 para.47, amended: SI 2002/1896 Reg.2, SI 2002/2469 Sch.7

Sch.2 para.47, applied: SI 2004/865 Art.30, SI 2004/1016 Art.27

Sch.2 para.47, revoked (in part): SI 2004/865 Sch.2

Sch.2 para.47A, amended: SI 2003/784 Reg.2

Sch.2 para.47A, applied: SI 2004/865 Art.23, Art.24, Art.36, SI 2004/1016 Art.23, Art.33

1992–cont.

635. National Health Service (General Medical Services) Regulations 1992–cont.

Sch.2 para.47A, revoked (in part): SI 2004/865 Sch.2

Sch.2 para.47A, varied: SI 2004/865 Art.23, SI 2004/1016 Art.22

Sch.2 para.47B, amended: SI 2002/2469 Sch.5

Sch.2 para.48, applied: SI 2004/865 Art.25, SI 2004/1016 Art.24

Sch.2 para.49, amended: SI 2002/1896 Reg.2, SI 2002/2469 Sch.7, SI 2003/1084 Reg.14

Sch.2 para.49, applied: SI 2004/865 Art.26, SI 2004/1016 Art.25

Sch.2 para.49, revoked (in part): SI 2004/865 Sch.2

Sch.2 para.50, amended: SI 2002/1896 Reg.2, SI 2002/2469 Sch.7

Sch.2 para.50, applied: SI 2004/865 Art.36, SI 2004/1016 Art.33

Sch.2 para.50, revoked (in part): SI 2004/865 Sch.2

Sch.2 para.50A, added: SI 2002/1896 Reg.16

Sch.2 para.50A, amended: SI 2002/2469 Sch.7

Sch.2 para.50B, added: SI 2002/554 Reg.31, SI 2002/1896 Reg.16

Sch.2 para.50B, amended: SI 2002/2469 Sch.7

Sch.2 para.51, amended: SI 2002/1896 Reg.2, SI 2002/2469 Sch.7, SI 2003/2863 Reg.2

Sch.2 para.51, revoked (in part): SI 2004/865 Sch.2

Sch.3 Part I, revoked (in part): SI 2004/865 Sch.2

Sch.3 Part I, amended: SI 2002/916 Reg.28

Sch.3 Part I, revoked (in part): SI 2004/865 Sch.2

Sch.3 Part I, substituted: SI 2002/554 Reg.28

Sch.3 Part I para.1, amended: SI 2002/916 Reg.28

Sch.3 Part I para.1, substituted: SI 2002/554 Reg.28

Sch.3 Part I para.1, amended: SI 2002/916 Reg.28, SI 2002/2469 Sch.1 para.54, Sch.5

Sch.3 Part I para.1, substituted: SI 2002/554 Reg.28

Sch.3 Part I para.2, amended: SI 2002/916 Reg.28

Sch.3 Part I para.2, substituted: SI 2002/554 Reg.28

Sch.3 Part I para.2, amended: SI 2002/916 Reg.28

Sch.3 Part I para.2, substituted: SI 2002/554 Reg.28

NO.

NO.

1992–cont.

1992–cont.

635. National Health Service (General Medical Services) Regulations 1992– cont.

Sch.3 Part I para.3, amended: SI 2002/916 Reg.28

Sch.3 Part I para.3, substituted: SI 2002/554 Reg.28

Sch.3 Part I para.3, amended: SI 2002/916 Reg.28, SI 2002/2469 Sch.5

Sch.3 Part I para.3, substituted: SI 2002/554 Reg.28

Sch.3 Part I para.4, amended: SI 2002/916 Reg.28

Sch.3 Part I para.4, substituted: SI 2002/554 Reg.28

Sch.3 Part I para.4, amended: SI 2002/916 Reg.28, SI 2002/2469 Sch.5

Sch.3 Part I para.4, substituted: SI 2002/554 Reg.28

Sch.3 Part I para.5, amended: SI 2002/916 Reg.28

Sch.3 Part I para.5, substituted: SI 2002/554 Reg.28

Sch.3 Part I para.5, amended: SI 2002/916 Reg.28, SI 2002/2469 Sch.5

Sch.3 Part I para.5, substituted: SI 2002/554 Reg.28

Sch.3 Part I para.6, amended: SI 2002/916 Reg.28

Sch.3 Part I para.6, substituted: SI 2002/554 Reg.28

Sch.3 Part I para.6, amended: SI 2002/916 Reg.28, SI 2002/2469 Sch.5

Sch.3 Part I para.6, substituted: SI 2002/554 Reg.28

Sch.3 Part I para.7, amended: SI 2002/916 Reg.28

Sch.3 Part I para.7, substituted: SI 2002/554 Reg.28

Sch.3 Part I para.7, amended: SI 2002/916 Reg.28

Sch.3 Part I para.7, substituted: SI 2002/554 Reg.28

Sch.3 Part I para.8, amended: SI 2002/916 Reg.28

Sch.3 Part I para.8, substituted: SI 2002/554 Reg.28

Sch.3 Part I para.8, amended: SI 2002/916 Reg.28, SI 2002/1896 Reg.17, SI 2002/2469 Sch.5

Sch.3 Part I para.8, substituted: SI 2002/554 Reg.28

Sch.3 Part I para.9, amended: SI 2002/916 Reg.28

Sch.3 Part I para.9, substituted: SI 2002/554 Reg.28

Sch.3 Part I para.9, amended: SI 2002/916 Reg.28

Sch.3 Part I para.9, revoked (in part): SI 2002/554 Reg.28, SI 2002/916 Reg.28

635. National Health Service (General Medical Services) Regulations 1992– cont.

Sch.3 Part I para.9, substituted: SI 2002/554 Reg.28

Sch.3 Part I para.10, amended: SI 2002/916 Reg.28

Sch.3 Part I para.10, substituted: SI 2002/554 Reg.28

Sch.3 Part I para.10, amended: SI 2002/916 Reg.28

Sch.3 Part I para.10, revoked (in part): SI 2002/554 Reg.28, SI 2002/916 Reg.28

Sch.3 Part I para.10, substituted: SI 2002/554 Reg.28

Sch.3 Part I para.11, amended: SI 2002/916 Reg.28

Sch.3 Part I para.11, substituted: SI 2002/554 Reg.28

Sch.3 Part I para.11, amended: SI 2002/916 Reg.28, SI 2002/2469 Sch.5

Sch.3 Part I para.11, substituted: SI 2002/554 Reg.28

Sch.3 Part I para.12, amended: SI 2002/916 Reg.28

Sch.3 Part I para.12, substituted: SI 2002/554 Reg.28

Sch.3 Part I para.12, amended: SI 2002/916 Reg.28

Sch.3 Part I para.12, substituted: SI 2002/554 Reg.28

Sch.3 Part I para.13, amended: SI 2002/916 Reg.28

Sch.3 Part I para.13, substituted: SI 2002/554 Reg.28

Sch.3 Part I para.13, amended: SI 2002/554 Reg.28, SI 2002/916 Reg.28, SI 2002/2469 Sch.5

Sch.3 Part I para.13, substituted: SI 2002/554 Reg.28, SI 2002/916 Reg.28

Sch.3 Part I para.14, amended: SI 2002/916 Reg.28

Sch.3 Part I para.14, substituted: SI 2002/554 Reg.28

Sch.3 Part I para.15, amended: SI 2002/916 Reg.28

Sch.3 Part I para.15, substituted: SI 2002/554 Reg.28

Sch.3 Part I para.16, amended: SI 2002/916 Reg.28

Sch.3 Part I para.16, substituted: SI 2002/554 Reg.28

Sch.3 Part I para.17, amended: SI 2002/916 Reg.28

Sch.3 Part I para.17, substituted: SI 2002/554 Reg.28

Sch.3 Part I para.18, amended: SI 2002/916 Reg.28

Sch.3 Part I para.18, substituted: SI 2002/554 Reg.28

1992–cont.

635. National Health Service (General Medical Services) Regulations 1992– cont.

Sch.3 Part I para.19, amended: SI 2002/916 Reg.28

Sch.3 Part I para.19, substituted: SI 2002/554 Reg.28

Sch.3 Part I para.20, amended: SI 2002/916 Reg.28

Sch.3 Part I para.20, substituted: SI 2002/554 Reg.28

Sch.3 Part II para.1, revoked (in part): SI 2002/554 Reg.28, SI 2002/916 Reg.28

Sch.3 Part II para.2, revoked (in part): SI 2002/554 Reg.28, SI 2002/916 Reg.28

Sch.3 Part II para.3, revoked (in part): SI 2002/554 Reg.28, SI 2002/916 Reg.28

Sch.3 Part II para.4, revoked (in part): SI 2002/554 Reg.28, SI 2002/916 Reg.28

Sch.3 Part II para.5, revoked (in part): SI 2002/554 Reg.28, SI 2002/916 Reg.28

Sch.3 Part II para.6, revoked (in part): SI 2002/554 Reg.28, SI 2002/916 Reg.28

Sch.3 Part II para.7, revoked (in part): SI 2002/554 Reg.28, SI 2002/916 Reg.28

Sch.3 Part II para.8, revoked (in part): SI 2002/554 Reg.28, SI 2002/916 Reg.28

Sch.3 Part II para.9, revoked (in part): SI 2002/554 Reg.28, SI 2002/916 Reg.28

Sch.3 Part II para.10, revoked (in part): SI 2002/554 Reg.28, SI 2002/916 Reg.28

Sch.3 Part II para.11, revoked (in part): SI 2002/554 Reg.28, SI 2002/916 Reg.28

Sch.3 Part II para.12, revoked (in part): SI 2002/554 Reg.28, SI 2002/916 Reg.28

Sch.3 Part II para.13, revoked (in part): SI 2002/554 Reg.28, SI 2002/916 Reg.28

Sch.3 Part II para.14, revoked (in part): SI 2002/554 Reg.28, SI 2002/916 Reg.28

Sch.3 Part II para.15, revoked (in part): SI 2002/554 Reg.28, SI 2002/916 Reg.28

Sch.3 Part II para.16, revoked (in part): SI 2002/554 Reg.28, SI 2002/916 Reg.28

Sch.3 Part II para.17, revoked (in part): SI 2002/554 Reg.28, SI 2002/916 Reg.28

Sch.3 Part II para.18, revoked (in part): SI 2002/554 Reg.28, SI 2002/916 Reg.28

Sch.3 Part II para.19, revoked (in part): SI 2002/554 Reg.28, SI 2002/916 Reg.28

Sch.3 Part II para.20, revoked (in part): SI 2002/554 Reg.28, SI 2002/916 Reg.28

Sch.3 Part II para.21, revoked (in part): SI 2002/554 Reg.28, SI 2002/916 Reg.28

Sch.3 Part II para.22, revoked (in part): SI 2002/554 Reg.28, SI 2002/916 Reg.28

Sch.3 Part II para.23, revoked (in part): SI 2002/554 Reg.28, SI 2002/916 Reg.28

Sch.3 Part II para.24, revoked (in part): SI 2002/554 Reg.28, SI 2002/916 Reg.28

Sch.3 Part III, referred to: SI 2004/865 Art.60, Art.61

1992–cont.

635. National Health Service (General Medical Services) Regulations 1992– cont.

Sch.3 Part III para.5, substituted: SI 2003/1250 Sch.10 para.1

Sch.3 Part III para.6, amended: SI 2002/3135 Sch.1 para.30

Sch.3 Part III para.6A, amended: SI 2002/2469 Sch.7, SI 2003/2644 Reg.53

Sch.3 Part III para.6A, revoked (in part): SI 2004/865 Sch.2

Sch.3 Part III para.6A, substituted: SI 2002/1896 Reg.18

Sch.3 Part III para.13, amended: SI 2002/2469 Sch.5

Sch.3 Part III para.14, amended: SI 2002/2469 Sch.5

Sch.3 Part III para.15, amended: SI 2002/1896 Reg.18

Sch.3 Part III para.17, amended: SI 2002/2469 Sch.5

Sch.3 Part III para.18, amended: SI 2002/1896 Reg.18

Sch.3 Part III para.18, revoked (in part): SI 2004/865 Sch.2

Sch.3 Part III para.19, amended: SI 2002/2469 Sch.7

Sch.3 Part III para.19, revoked (in part): SI 2004/865 Sch.2

Sch.3 Part III para.19, substituted: SI 2002/1896 Reg.18

Sch.3 Part III para.19A, added: SI 2002/1896 Reg.18

Sch.3 Part III para.19A, amended: SI 2002/2469 Sch.7

Sch.3 Part III para.24, amended: SI 2002/2469 Sch.5

Sch.3 Part III para.25, amended: SI 2002/2469 Sch.7

Sch.3 Part III para.25, revoked (in part): SI 2004/865 Sch.2

Sch.3 Part III para.25, substituted: SI 2002/1896 Reg.18

Sch.3 Part III para.26, added: SI 2002/1896 Reg.18

Sch.3 Part III para.26, amended: SI 2002/2469 Sch.7

Sch.3 Part VII para.1, amended: SI 2002/1896 Reg.2

Sch.3 Part VII para.2, amended: SI 2002/1896 Reg.2

Sch.3 Part VII para.3, amended: SI 2002/1896 Reg.2

Sch.3 Part VII para.4, amended: SI 2002/1896 Reg.2

Sch.3 Part VII para.5, amended: SI 2002/1896 Reg.2

Sch.4 para.1, amended: SI 2002/1896 Reg.2, SI 2002/2469 Sch.7

Sch.4 para.1, revoked (in part): SI 2004/865 Sch.2

NO.

NO.

1992–cont.

635. National Health Service (General Medical Services) Regulations 1992–cont.

Sch.5 Part I para.3, amended: SI 2002/1896 Reg.2, SI 2002/2469 Sch.7

Sch.5 Part I para.3, revoked (in part): SI 2004/865 Sch.2

Sch.5 Part I para.5, amended: SI 2002/1896 Reg.2, SI 2002/2469 Sch.7

Sch.5 Part I para.5, revoked (in part): SI 2004/865 Sch.2

Sch.6A, added: SI 2003/1084 Reg.15

Sch.6A, revoked (in part): SI 2004/865 Sch.2

Sch.6B Part I, added: SI 2003/1084 Reg.15

Sch.6B Part I, revoked (in part): SI 2004/865 Sch.2

Sch.6B Part II, added: SI 2003/1084 Reg.15

Sch.6B Part II, revoked (in part): SI 2004/865 Sch.2

Sch.7, substituted: SI 2002/916 Reg.29

Sch.7A para.1, amended: SI 2002/2469 Sch.5

Sch.7A para.3, amended: SI 2002/2469 Sch.5

Sch.7A para.4, amended: SI 2002/2469 Sch.5

Sch.8 Part I para.8, amended: SI 2002/2469 Sch.5

Sch.8 Part I para.8, substituted: SI 2002/554 Reg.30, SI 2002/916 Reg.30

Sch.8 Part IV, amended: SI 2002/554 Reg.30, SI 2002/916 Reg.30

Sch.10, amended: SI 2002/1768 Reg.2, SI 2003/26 Reg.7, SI 2003/143 Reg.2

Sch.10, referred to: SI 2004/865 Art.62

Sch.10, revoked (in part): SI 2004/865 Sch.2

Sch.11, added: SI 2003/1005 Reg.2

Sch.11, amended: SI 2002/3189 Reg.3, SI 2003/26 Reg.7, SI 2003/143 Reg.3, SI 2003/699 Reg.3

Sch.11, referred to: SI 2004/865 Art.62

Sch.11, revoked (in part): SI 2004/865 Sch.2

Sch.12 para.5, amended: SI 2002/1896 Reg.2, SI 2002/2469 Sch.7

Sch.12 para.5, revoked (in part): SI 2004/865 Sch.2

Sch.12 para.10A, added: SI 2003/1084 Reg.16

Sch.12 para.10A, revoked (in part): SI 2004/865 Sch.2

Sch.12 para.20, substituted: SI 2003/1250 Sch.10 para.1

Sch.13 para.1, amended: SI 2002/1896 Reg.2, SI 2002/2469 Sch.7

Sch.13 para.1, revoked (in part): SI 2004/865 Sch.2

Sch.13 para.2A, added: SI 2003/1084 Reg.17

Sch.13 para.2A, revoked (in part): SI 2004/865 Sch.2

1992–cont.

635. National Health Service (General Medical Services) Regulations 1992–cont.

Sch.13 para.3, referred to: SI 2004/865 Art.36, SI 2004/1016 Art.33

655. Dental Practice Board Regulations 1992

Reg.8, amended: SI 2002/2469 Sch.1 para.55

661. National Health Service (General Dental Services) Regulations 1992

applied: SI 2002/553 Art.9, SI 2002/2469 Sch.12 para.5

referred to: SI 2002/2802 Reg.6

Reg.2, amended: SI 2002/1881 Reg.2, SI 2002/2469 Sch.5, Sch.7, SI 2002/2802 Reg.7, SI 2003/1976 Reg.3, SI 2004/865 Sch.1 para.9, SI 2004/1016 Sch.1 para.9

Reg.2, revoked (in part): SI 2004/1016 Sch.1 para.9

Reg.3, amended: SI 2002/2469 Sch.5

Reg.4, amended: SI 2002/1881 Reg.3, SI 2002/2469 Sch.1 para.56, Sch.5, SI 2004/696 Art.3

Reg.4, referred to: SI 2002/2469 Sch.5

Reg.4, revoked (in part): SI 2002/2469 Sch.1 para.56

Reg.5, amended: SI 2002/558 Reg.3, SI 2002/1881 Reg.4, SI 2002/2469 Sch.5, Sch.7, SI 2002/2802 Reg.7

Reg.5A, amended: SI 2002/2469 Sch.5

Reg.5C, amended: SI 2002/2469 Sch.5

Reg.5D, amended: SI 2002/2469 Sch.5

Reg.5E, amended: SI 2002/2469 Sch.5

Reg.5ZA, added: SI 2002/1881 Reg.5

Reg.5ZA, amended: SI 2002/558 Reg.4, SI 2002/2469 Sch.7, SI 2002/2802 Reg.7

Reg.5ZB, added: SI 2002/1881 Reg.5

Reg.5ZB, amended: SI 2002/558 Reg.5, SI 2002/2469 Sch.7, SI 2002/2802 Reg.7

Reg.5ZC, added: SI 2002/1881 Reg.5

Reg.5ZC, amended: SI 2002/2469 Sch.7

Reg.5ZD, added: SI 2002/1881 Reg.5

Reg.5ZD, amended: SI 2002/558 Reg.6, SI 2002/2469 Sch.7

Reg.6, amended: SI 2002/2469 Sch.5

Reg.7, amended: SI 2002/2469 Sch.5

Reg.8, amended: SI 2002/1881 Reg.6, SI 2002/2469 Sch.5

Reg.8, revoked (in part): SI 2002/1881 Reg.6

Reg.8A, added: SI 2002/1881 Reg.7

Reg.8B, added: SI 2002/1881 Reg.7

Reg.8B, amended: SI 2002/558 Reg.7, SI 2002/2469 Sch.7, SI 2002/2802 Reg.7

Reg.8C, added: SI 2002/1881 Reg.7

Reg.8C, amended: SI 2002/2469 Sch.7

Reg.8D, added: SI 2002/1881 Reg.7

Reg.8D, amended: SI 2002/558 Reg.8, SI 2002/2469 Sch.7, SI 2002/2802 Reg.7

Reg.8E, added: SI 2002/1881 Reg.7

NO.

1992–cont.

661. National Health Service (General Dental Services) Regulations 1992– *cont.*

Reg.8E, amended: SI 2002/558 Reg.9, SI 2002/2469 Sch.7

Reg.8F, added: SI 2002/1881 Reg.7

Reg.8F, amended: SI 2002/2469 Sch.7

Reg.8G, added: SI 2002/1881 Reg.7

Reg.8G, amended: SI 2002/2469 Sch.7

Reg.8G, revoked (in part): SI 2002/558 Reg.10

Reg.8H, added: SI 2002/1881 Reg.7

Reg.8H, amended: SI 2002/2802 Reg.7

Reg.8H, revoked (in part): SI 2002/2802 Reg.7

Reg.8H, substituted: SI 2002/2802 Reg.7

Reg.9, amended: SI 2002/2469 Sch.5, SI 2003/138 Reg.2, SI 2003/250 Reg.22

Reg.9, revoked (in part): SI 2003/138 Reg.2, SI 2003/250 Reg.22

Reg.10, amended: SI 2002/1881 Reg.8, SI 2002/2469 Sch.5, Sch.7, SI 2002/2802 Reg.7

Reg.10, revoked (in part): SI 2002/1881 Reg.8

Reg.11, amended: SI 2002/2469 Sch.5

Reg.12, amended: SI 2002/2469 Sch.5

Reg.13, amended: SI 2002/1881 Reg.9, SI 2002/2469 Sch.5

Reg.14, amended: SI 2002/2469 Sch.5

Reg.15, amended: SI 2002/2469 Sch.5

Reg.16, amended: SI 2002/2469 Sch.5

Reg.19, amended: SI 2003/1702 Reg.2

Reg.20, amended: SI 2002/2469 Sch.5

Reg.21, amended: SI 2002/2469 Sch.5

Reg.22, amended: SI 2002/2469 Sch.5

Reg.24, amended: SI 2002/1881 Reg.10, SI 2002/2469 Sch.5, Sch.7

Reg.25, amended: SI 2002/2469 Sch.5

Reg.26, amended: SI 2002/2469 Sch.5

Reg.27, amended: SI 2002/2469 Sch.5

Reg.28A, amended: SI 2002/1881 Reg.11

Reg.28A, revoked (in part): SI 2002/1881 Reg.11

Reg.28B, added: SI 2002/1881 Reg.11

Reg.28B, amended: SI 2002/1881 Reg.11, SI 2002/2469 Sch.7

Reg.28C, amended: SI 2002/1881 Reg.11

Reg.29, amended: SI 2002/2469 Sch.5

Reg.30, amended: SI 2002/2469 Sch.5

Reg.30A, amended: SI 2002/2469 Sch.5

Reg.31, amended: SI 2002/2469 Sch.5

Reg.32, amended: SI 2002/2469 Sch.5

Sch.1 Part I para.2, amended: SI 2002/1881 Reg.12, SI 2002/2469 Sch.7, SI 2003/2863 Reg.3

Sch.1 Part II para.4, amended: SI 2002/2469 Sch.5

Sch.1 Part II para.5, amended: SI 2002/2469 Sch.5

Sch.1 Part II para.8, amended: SI 2002/1881 Reg.12, SI 2002/2469 Sch.7

NO.

1992–cont.

661. National Health Service (General Dental Services) Regulations 1992– *cont.*

Sch.1 Part II para.9, amended: SI 2002/1881 Reg.12, SI 2002/2469 Sch.5, Sch.7

Sch.1 Part II para.11, amended: SI 2002/2469 Sch.5

Sch.1 Part II para.11A, amended: SI 2002/2469 Sch.5

Sch.1 Part II para.13, amended: SI 2002/2469 Sch.5

Sch.1 Part II para.15, amended: SI 2002/2469 Sch.5

Sch.1 Part III para.17, substituted: SI 2003/138 Reg.3

Sch.1 Part IV para.25, amended: SI 2002/2469 Sch.5

Sch.1 Part IV para.26, amended: SI 2002/2469 Sch.5

Sch.1 Part IV para.27, amended: SI 2002/2469 Sch.5

Sch.1 Part IV para.27B, amended: SI 2002/2469 Sch.5

Sch.1 Part IV para.31, amended: SI 2002/2469 Sch.5

Sch.1 Part IV para.31A, amended: SI 2003/782 Reg.2

Sch.1 Part IV para.31B, amended: SI 2002/2469 Sch.5

Sch.1 Part IV para.31D, amended: SI 2002/2469 Sch.5

Sch.1 Part IV para.31G, amended: SI 2002/2469 Sch.5

Sch.1 Part IV para.31H, added: SI 2002/1881 Reg.12

Sch.1 Part IV para.31H, amended: SI 2002/2469 Sch.7, SI 2002/2802 Reg.7, SI 2003/250 Reg.22

Sch.1 Part IV para.31J, added: SI 2002/1881 Reg.12

Sch.1 Part IV para.31J, amended: SI 2002/2469 Sch.7

Sch.1 Part V para.32, amended: SI 2002/2469 Sch.5

Sch.1 Part V para.33, amended: SI 2002/2469 Sch.5

Sch.1 Part V para.35, amended: SI 2002/1881 Reg.12, SI 2002/2469 Sch.5, SI 2003/250 Reg.22

Sch.1 Part VI para.39, amended: SI 2002/2469 Sch.5

Sch.1 Part VI para.41, amended: SI 2002/2469 Sch.5

Sch.1 Part VI para.42, amended: SI 2002/2469 Sch.5

Sch.1 Part VI para.43, amended: SI 2002/2469 Sch.5

Sch.1 Part VI para.44, amended: SI 2002/2469 Sch.5

Sch.2 Part I para.5B, added: SI 2002/1881 Reg.13

NO.

1992–cont.

661. National Health Service (General Dental Services) Regulations 1992–cont.

Sch.2 Part I para.5B, amended: SI 2002/2469 Sch.7, SI 2003/250 Reg.22

Sch.2 Part I para.8, amended: SI 2002/2469 Sch.5

Sch.2 Part I para.8, substituted: SI 2002/1881 Reg.13

Sch.2 Part I para.9, amended: SI 2002/2469 Sch.5

Sch.2 Part I para.11, substituted: SI 2002/1881 Reg.13

Sch.2 Part I para.14, amended: SI 2002/2469 Sch.5

Sch.2 Part I para.14, substituted: SI 2002/1881 Reg.13

Sch.2 Part I para.17, added: SI 2002/1881 Reg.13

Sch.2 Part I para.17, amended: SI 2002/2469 Sch.7

Sch.4 Part II para.1, amended: SI 2002/918 Reg.2, SI 2003/1702 Reg.2, SI 2003/1976 Reg.5

Sch.4 Part II para.2, amended: SI 2002/918 Reg.2, SI 2003/1702 Reg.2, SI 2003/1976 Reg.5

Sch.6 para.2, amended: SI 2002/2469 Sch.5

662. National Health Service (Pharmaceutical Services) Regulations 1992

applied: SI 2002/553 Art.9, SI 2002/2469 Sch.12 para.5, SI 2004/478 Sch.6 para.47

referred to: SI 2002/2861 Reg.2, SI 2003/1084 Reg.1

Reg.2, amended: SI 2002/2469 Sch.1 para.57, Sch.5, Sch.10, SI 2002/2861 Reg.3, Reg.15, SI 2002/3135 Sch.1 para.31, SI 2002/3189 Reg.2, SI 2003/699 Reg.2, SI 2003/1084 Reg.2, SI 2003/2624 Reg.2, SI 2003/3236 Reg.2, SI 2004/696 Sch.1 para.11, SI 2004/922 Reg.2, Sch.1, SI 2004/1018 Reg.2, SI 2004/1021 Reg.2, Sch.1, SI 2004/1771 Sch.1 para.45

Reg.2, revoked (in part): SI 2002/3189 Reg.2

Reg.2A, amended: SI 2002/2861 Reg.4

Reg.2A, revoked (in part): SI 2004/922 Sch.1

Reg.3, amended: SI 2002/2469 Sch.10, SI 2002/2861 Reg.15

Reg.4, see *Young v Evans-Jones* [2001] EWCA Civ 732, [2002] 1 P. & C.R. 14 (CA), Robert Walker, L.J.

Reg.4, amended: SI 2002/2469 Sch.10, SI 2002/2861 Reg.5, Reg.15, SI 2003/1084 Reg.3, SI 2004/1018 Reg.3

Reg.5, amended: SI 2002/888 Reg.10, SI 2002/2469 Sch.10, SI 2002/2861 Reg.6, Reg.15, SI 2004/922 Reg.4

Reg.6, amended: SI 2002/2469 Sch.10, SI 2002/2861 Reg.7, Reg.15, SI 2004/922 Reg.5, SI 2004/1021 Reg.3

Reg.6A, added: SI 2002/888 Reg.10

NO.

1992–cont.

662. National Health Service (Pharmaceutical Services) Regulations 1992–cont.

Reg.6A, amended: SI 2002/2469 Sch.7

Reg.7, amended: SI 2002/2469 Sch.10, SI 2002/2861 Reg.8, Reg.15, SI 2004/922 Reg.6

Reg.8, amended: SI 2002/2469 Sch.10, SI 2002/2861 Reg.9, Reg.15

Reg.8A, added: SI 2002/2016 Reg.5

Reg.8A, amended: SI 2002/2469 Sch.7, Sch.10

Reg.8A, applied: SI 2002/2016 Reg.4

Reg.9, amended: SI 2002/2469 Sch.10, SI 2002/2861 Reg.10, Reg.15, SI 2004/922 Reg.7, SI 2004/1021 Reg.4

Reg.9, referred to: SI 2004/291 Sch.6 para.47, SI 2004/627 Sch.5 para.46

Reg.10, amended: SI 2002/2469 Sch.10, SI 2002/2861 Reg.15

Reg.11, amended: SI 2002/2469 Sch.10, SI 2002/2861 Reg.11, SI 2004/922 Reg.8

Reg.12, amended: SI 2002/2016 Reg.5, SI 2002/2469 Sch.7, Sch.10, SI 2002/2861 Reg.12, Reg.15, SI 2003/1084 Reg.4, SI 2003/3236 Reg.3, SI 2004/922 Reg.9, SI 2004/1021 Reg.5

Reg.12, applied: SI 2004/291 Sch.6 para.47, Sch.6 para.48, SI 2004/478 Sch.6 para.47, Sch.6 para.48, SI 2004/627 Sch.5 para.46, Sch.5 para.47

Reg.12, revoked (in part): SI 2004/922 Reg.9, Sch.1

Reg.12, varied: SI 2004/291 Sch.6 para.48, SI 2004/478 Sch.6 para.48, SI 2004/627 Sch.5 para.47

Reg.13, amended: SI 2002/2469 Sch.10, SI 2002/2861 Reg.13, Reg.15, SI 2003/3236 Reg.4, SI 2004/922 Reg.10, SI 2004/1021 Reg.6

Reg.13, applied: SI 2004/291 Sch.6 para.47, Sch.6 para.48, SI 2004/478 Sch.6 para.47, Sch.6 para.48, SI 2004/627 Sch.5 para.46, Sch.5 para.47

Reg.13, revoked (in part): SI 2004/922 Reg.10, Sch.1

Reg.13, varied: SI 2004/291 Sch.6 para.48, SI 2004/478 Sch.6 para.48, SI 2004/627 Sch.5 para.47

Reg.14, amended: SI 2002/2469 Sch.10, SI 2002/2861 Reg.15

Reg.15, amended: SI 2002/888 Reg.10, SI 2002/2469 Sch.10

Reg.16A, amended: SI 2002/2469 Sch.10, SI 2003/1084 Reg.5

Reg.16B, added: SI 2003/1084 Reg.6, SI 2004/1018 Reg.4

Reg.16B, amended: SI 2004/922 Reg.11

Reg.17, amended: SI 2002/2016 Reg.5, SI 2002/2469 Sch.7, Sch.10, SI 2002/2861 Reg.15

NO.

NO.

1992–cont.

662. **National Health Service (Pharmaceutical Services) Regulations 1992–** *cont.*

Reg.18, amended: SI 2002/551 Reg.2, SI 2002/2469 Sch.10, SI 2002/2861 Reg.15, SI 2002/3189 Reg.2, SI 2003/1084 Reg.7, SI 2004/1018 Reg.5

Reg.18A, amended: SI 2002/2469 Sch.5

Reg.18B, amended: SI 2002/2469 Sch.5, SI 2003/1084 Reg.8, SI 2003/3236 Reg.5

Reg.19, see *Beynon v Customs and Excise Commissioners* [2002] EWHC 518, [2002] S.T.C. 699 (Ch D), Lawrence Collins, J.

Reg.19, amended: SI 2002/551 Reg.2, SI 2002/3189 Reg.2

Reg.19, revoked (in part): SI 2004/922 Sch.1

Reg.20, see *Beynon v Customs and Excise Commissioners* [2002] EWCA Civ 1870, [2003] S.T.C. 169 (CA), Aldous, L.J.; see *Beynon v Customs and Excise Commissioners* [2002] EWHC 518, [2002] S.T.C. 699 (Ch D), Lawrence Collins, J.; see *Beynon v Customs and Excise Commissioners* [2004] UKHL 53, [2004] 4 All E.R. 1091 (HL), Lord Nicholls of Birkenhead

Reg.20, amended: SI 2002/2469 Sch.5, Sch.10, SI 2002/2861 Reg.15

Reg.20, applied: SI 2004/291 Sch.5 para.1, SI 2004/478 Sch.5 para.1, Sch.6 para.47, SI 2004/627 Sch.3, Sch.5 para.39, Sch.5 para.46, SI 2004/922 Reg.24

Reg.20, substituted: SI 2004/922 Reg.13, SI 2004/1021 Reg.7

Reg.21, amended: SI 2002/2469 Sch.10, SI 2002/2861 Reg.15, SI 2004/922 Reg.14

Reg.21, applied: SI 2004/291 Sch.6 para.48, SI 2004/478 Sch.6 para.48

Reg.21A, revoked (in part): SI 2004/922 Sch.1

Reg.21B, amended: SI 2002/2469 Sch.5

Reg.21B, substituted: SI 2004/922 Reg.16, SI 2004/1021 Reg.8

Reg.21C, amended: SI 2002/2469 Sch.5, SI 2004/1021 Reg.9

Reg.21C, substituted: SI 2004/922 Reg.17

Reg.22, amended: SI 2002/2469 Sch.10, SI 2002/2861 Reg.15

Reg.24, amended: SI 2002/2469 Sch.10, SI 2004/922 Reg.18, Sch.1

Sch.2 Part I para.1, amended: SI 2004/922 Reg.19, Sch.1, SI 2004/1021 Reg.10

Sch.2 Part I para.1, substituted: SI 2003/1084 Reg.9, SI 2004/1018 Reg.6

Sch.2 Part I para.2, amended: SI 2002/2469 Sch.10, SI 2003/2863 Reg.5

Sch.2 Part II para.2A, amended: SI 2002/2469 Sch.5

Sch.2 Part II para.3, amended: SI 2002/3189 Reg.2, SI 2003/139 Reg.3, SI 2003/699 Reg.2, SI 2003/1084 Reg.9, SI 2003/

1992–cont.

662. **National Health Service (Pharmaceutical Services) Regulations 1992–** *cont.*

Sch.2 Part II para.3, amended:–*cont.* 2624 Reg.2, SI 2004/922 Reg.20, SI 2004/1018 Reg.6, SI 2004/1021 Reg.11

Sch.2 Part II para.3A, added: SI 2003/1084 Reg.9, SI 2004/1018 Reg.6

Sch.2 Part II para.3A, amended: SI 2004/922 Reg.20, SI 2004/1021 Reg.12

Sch.2 Part II para.4, amended: SI 2002/2469 Sch.5, Sch.10, SI 2002/2861 Reg.14, Reg.15

Sch.2 Part II para.5, amended: SI 2002/2469 Sch.5, SI 2003/1084 Reg.9, SI 2004/1018 Reg.6

Sch.2 Part II para.6, amended: SI 2002/2469 Sch.10

Sch.2 Part II para.7, amended: SI 2003/699 Reg.2, SI 2003/2624 Reg.2, SI 2004/922 Reg.20, SI 2004/1021 Reg.13

Sch.2 Part II para.8, amended: SI 2002/2469 Sch.5, Sch.10, SI 2003/1084 Reg.9, SI 2004/1018 Reg.6

Sch.2 Part II para.10, amended: SI 2002/2469 Sch.10

Sch.2 Part II para.10A, amended: SI 2003/783 Reg.2

Sch.2 Part II para.10B, amended: SI 2002/2469 Sch.5

Sch.2 Part III para.11, amended: SI 2002/2469 Sch.10, SI 2002/2861 Reg.15, SI 2002/3189 Reg.2

Sch.2 Part III para.11, substituted: SI 2004/922 Reg.21, SI 2004/1021 Reg.14

Sch.2 Part III para.11A, amended: SI 2002/3189 Reg.2, SI 2003/699 Reg.2, SI 2003/2624 Reg.2, SI 2004/922 Reg.21, SI 2004/1021 Reg.15

Sch.2 Part III para.11B, amended: SI 2002/551 Reg.2, SI 2002/2469 Sch.5, SI 2002/3189 Reg.2, SI 2003/699 Reg.2, SI 2003/1084 Reg.9, SI 2003/2624 Reg.2, SI 2004/922 Reg.21, SI 2004/1018 Reg.6

Sch.2 Part III para.11B, varied: SI 2004/291 Sch.6 para.50, SI 2004/478 Sch.6 para.49, SI 2004/627 Sch.5 para.50

Sch.2 Part III para.12, amended: SI 2002/551 Reg.2, SI 2002/2469 Sch.10, SI 2002/2861 Reg.15, SI 2002/3189 Reg.2

Sch.2 Part III para.13, amended: SI 2002/2469 Sch.10, SI 2004/1021 Reg.16

Sch.2 Part III para.13, revoked (in part): SI 2004/922 Sch.1

Sch.2 Part III para.13, substituted: SI 2004/922 Reg.21

Sch.2 Part III para.14, amended: SI 2002/2469 Sch.5

Sch.2 Part III para.14, substituted: SI 2004/922 Reg.21, SI 2004/1021 Reg.17

Sch.2 Part III para.15, amended: SI 2002/2469 Sch.5

NO.

1992–cont.

662. National Health Service (Pharmaceutical Services) Regulations 1992– *cont.*

Sch.2 Part III para.15, revoked (in part): SI 2004/922 Sch.1

Sch.3A, added: SI 2003/1084 Reg.10

Sch.3A, substituted: SI 2004/922 Reg.22

Sch.3 Part I, amended: SI 2002/2016 Reg.5, SI 2002/2469 Sch.10

Sch.3 Part II, amended: SI 2002/2469 Sch.10

664. National Health Service (Service Committees and Tribunal) Regulations 1992

applied: SI 2002/553 Art.9, SI 2002/2469 Sch.12 para.5, Sch.12 para.8, Sch.12 para.10, Sch.12 para.11, Sch.12 para.14, Sch.12 para.15, Sch.12 para.16, Sch.12 para.17, Sch.12 para.18, Sch.12 para.25, SI 2004/865 Art.95, Art.97, Art.98, SI 2004/1016 Art.71

varied: SI 2004/865 Art.95, Art.96

Reg.2, amended: SI 2002/2469 Sch.1 para.58, Sch.5, SI 2004/865 Sch.1 para.10

Reg.2, applied: SI 2002/2469 Sch.12 para.29

Reg.2, referred to: SI 2004/865 Art.95

Reg.2, revoked (in part): SI 2004/865 Sch.1 para.10, SI 2004/1016 Sch.1 para.10

Reg.2, varied: SI 2004/865 Art.95, Art.96, SI 2004/1016 Art.71, Art.72

Reg.3, amended: SI 2002/2469 Sch.5

Reg.3, applied: SI 2002/553 Art.9, SI 2002/2469 Sch.12 para.9, Sch.12 para.13

Reg.3, referred to: SI 2004/865 Art.95

Reg.3, revoked (in part): SI 2004/865 Sch.1 para.10, SI 2004/1016 Sch.1 para.10

Reg.3, varied: SI 2004/865 Art.95, Art.96, SI 2004/1016 Art.71, Art.72

Reg.4, amended: SI 2002/2469 Sch.5, SI 2004/865 Sch.1 para.10

Reg.4, applied: SI 2002/2469 Sch.12 para.7, Sch.12 para.11, SI 2004/865 Art.95, Art.96, SI 2004/1016 Art.71, Art.72

Reg.4, referred to: SI 2004/865 Art.95, SI 2004/1016 Art.71

Reg.4, revoked (in part): SI 2004/865 Sch.1 para.10, SI 2004/1016 Sch.1 para.10

Reg.4, varied: SI 2004/865 Art.95, Art.96, SI 2004/1016 Art.71, Art.72

Reg.5, amended: SI 2002/2469 Sch.5

Reg.5, applied: SI 2002/553 Art.9, SI 2002/2469 Sch.12 para.12

Reg.5, referred to: SI 2004/865 Art.95

Reg.5, revoked (in part): SI 2004/865 Sch.1 para.10, SI 2004/1016 Sch.1 para.10

Reg.5, varied: SI 2004/865 Art.95, Art.96, SI 2004/1016 Art.71, Art.72

Reg.6, amended: SI 2002/2469 Sch.5, SI 2004/865 Sch.1 para.10, SI 2004/1016 Sch.1 para.10

NO.

1992–cont.

664. National Health Service (Service Committees and Tribunal) Regulations 1992–*cont.*

Reg.6, referred to: SI 2002/2469 Sch.12 para.7, SI 2004/865 Art.95, SI 2004/1016 Art.71

Reg.6, varied: SI 2004/865 Art.95, Art.96, SI 2004/1016 Art.71, Art.72

Reg.7, amended: SI 2002/2469 Sch.5

Reg.7, referred to: SI 2004/865 Art.95

Reg.7, varied: SI 2004/865 Art.95, Art.96, SI 2004/1016 Art.71, Art.72

Reg.8, amended: SI 2002/2469 Sch.5, SI 2004/865 Sch.1 para.10, SI 2004/1016 Sch.1 para.10

Reg.8, applied: SI 2002/2469 Sch.12 para.14, Sch.12 para.15, SI 2004/865 Art.97, Art.98, Art.99, SI 2004/1016 Art.73, Art.74, Art.75

Reg.8, disapplied: SI 2004/865 Art.98, SI 2004/1016 Art.74

Reg.8, referred to: SI 2004/865 Art.95, Art.98, SI 2004/1016 Art.74

Reg.8, revoked (in part): SI 2004/865 Sch.1 para.10, SI 2004/1016 Sch.1 para.10

Reg.8, varied: SI 2004/865 Art.95, Art.96, SI 2004/1016 Art.71, Art.72

Reg.9, amended: SI 2002/2469 Sch.5, SI 2004/865 Sch.1 para.10, SI 2004/1016 Sch.1 para.10

Reg.9, applied: SI 2002/2469 Sch.12 para.16, SI 2004/865 Art.97, Art.99, SI 2004/1016 Art.73, Art.75

Reg.9, referred to: SI 2002/2469 Sch.12 para.16, SI 2004/865 Art.99, SI 2004/1016 Art.75

Reg.9, revoked (in part): SI 2004/1016 Sch.1 para.10

Reg.9, varied: SI 2004/865 Art.99, SI 2004/1016 Art.75

Reg.10, amended: SI 2002/2469 Sch.1 para.58, Sch.5, SI 2004/865 Sch.1 para.10

Reg.10, applied: SI 2004/865 Art.97, Art.99, SI 2004/1016 Art.73

Reg.10, referred to: SI 2004/865 Art.99, SI 2004/1016 Art.75

Reg.10, revoked (in part): SI 2004/865 Sch.1 para.10, SI 2004/1016 Sch.1 para.10

Reg.10, varied: SI 2004/865 Art.99, SI 2004/1016 Art.75

Reg.11, amended: SI 2002/2469 Sch.5, SI 2004/865 Sch.1 para.10, SI 2004/1016 Sch.1 para.10

Reg.11, applied: SI 2002/2469 Sch.12 para.17, Sch.12 para.18, Sch.12 para.19, SI 2004/865 Art.97, Art.99, SI 2004/1016 Art.73, Art.75

Reg.11, revoked (in part): SI 2004/865 Sch.1 para.10, SI 2004/1016 Sch.1 para.10

Reg.11, varied: SI 2004/865 Art.99, Art.101, Art.102, SI 2004/1016 Art.75, Art.77, Art.78

1992–cont.

664. National Health Service (Service Committees and Tribunal) Regulations 1992–*cont.*

Reg.12, amended: SI 2002/2469 Sch.5

Reg.12, applied: SI 2002/2469 Sch.12 para.17

Reg.13, amended: SI 2002/2469 Sch.5

Reg.15, amended: SI 2002/2469 Sch.1 para.58, Sch.10, SI 2003/1937 Sch.1 para.3

Reg.15, applied: SI 2002/553 Art.9, SI 2002/2469 Sch.12 para.20, Sch.12 para.22, Sch.12 para.23, Sch.12 para.24, SI 2004/865 Art.100, SI 2004/1016 Art.76

Reg.15, referred to: SI 2004/865 Art.100

Reg.15, revoked (in part): SI 2004/865 Sch.1 para.10, SI 2004/1016 Sch.1 para.10

Reg.15, varied: SI 2004/865 Art.100

Reg.16, amended: SI 2002/2469 Sch.5

Reg.16, applied: SI 2002/553 Art.9, SI 2004/865 Art.101, SI 2004/1016 Art.77

Reg.16, referred to: SI 2004/865 Art.101, SI 2004/1016 Art.77

Reg.16, revoked (in part): SI 2004/865 Sch.1 para.10, SI 2004/1016 Sch.1 para.10

Reg.16, varied: SI 2004/865 Art.101, Art.102, SI 2004/1016 Art.77

Reg.17, amended: SI 2002/2469 Sch.5

Reg.17, applied: SI 2004/865 Art.102, SI 2004/1016 Art.78

Reg.17, referred to: SI 2004/865 Art.102, SI 2004/1016 Art.78

Reg.17, revoked (in part): SI 2004/865 Sch.1 para.10, SI 2004/1016 Sch.1 para.10

Reg.17, varied: SI 2004/865 Art.102, SI 2004/1016 Art.78

Reg.18, amended: SI 2002/2469 Sch.10, SI 2003/1937 Sch.1 para.3

Reg.18, applied: SI 2002/2469 Sch.12 para.26, SI 2004/865 Art.103, SI 2004/1016 Art.79

Reg.18, referred to: SI 2004/865 Art.103

Reg.18, revoked (in part): SI 2004/865 Sch.1 para.10, SI 2004/1016 Sch.1 para.10

Reg.18, varied: SI 2004/865 Art.103, SI 2004/1016 Art.79

Reg.20, revoked (in part): SI 2004/865 Sch.1 para.10, SI 2004/1016 Sch.1 para.10

Reg.21, amended: SI 2002/2469 Sch.10

Reg.24, amended: SI 2002/2469 Sch.5, Sch.10, SI 2003/1937 Sch.1 para.3

Reg.24A, amended: SI 2002/2469 Sch.10

Reg.26, amended: SI 2002/2469 Sch.10

Reg.29, amended: SI 2002/2469 Sch.10

Reg.31B, amended: SI 2002/2469 Sch.5

Reg.32, amended: SI 2002/2469 Sch.10, SI 2003/1937 Sch.1 para.3, SI 2004/865 Sch.1 para.10, SI 2004/1016 Sch.1 para.10

Reg.33, amended: SI 2002/2469 Sch.10, SI 2003/1937 Sch.1 para.3

Reg.35, amended: SI 2002/2469 Sch.10

1992–cont.

664. National Health Service (Service Committees and Tribunal) Regulations 1992–*cont.*

Reg.37, amended: SI 2002/2469 Sch.5, SI 2004/865 Sch.1 para.10, SI 2004/1016 Sch.1 para.10

Sch.2, referred to: SI 2004/865 Art.95

Sch.2 para.1, varied: SI 2004/865 Art.95, Art.96, SI 2004/1016 Art.71, Art.72

Sch.2 Part I para.1, amended: SI 2002/2469 Sch.5

Sch.2 Part I para.1, varied: SI 2004/865 Art.95, Art.96, SI 2004/1016 Art.71, Art.72

Sch.2 Part I para.2, amended: SI 2002/2469 Sch.5, SI 2004/865 Sch.1 para.10

Sch.2 Part I para.2, revoked (in part): SI 2004/865 Sch.1 para.10, SI 2004/1016 Sch.1 para.10

Sch.2 Part I para.2, varied: SI 2004/865 Art.95, Art.96, SI 2004/1016 Art.71, Art.72

Sch.2 Part I para.3, varied: SI 2004/865 Art.95, Art.96, SI 2004/1016 Art.71, Art.72

Sch.2 Part I para.4, amended: SI 2002/2469 Sch.5

Sch.2 Part I para.4, varied: SI 2004/865 Art.95, Art.96, SI 2004/1016 Art.71, Art.72

Sch.2 Part I para.5, varied: SI 2004/865 Art.95, Art.96, SI 2004/1016 Art.71, Art.72

Sch.2 Part I para.6, amended: SI 2002/2469 Sch.5

Sch.2 Part I para.6, varied: SI 2004/865 Art.95, Art.96, SI 2004/1016 Art.71, Art.72

Sch.2 Part I para.7, varied: SI 2004/865 Art.95, Art.96, SI 2004/1016 Art.71, Art.72

Sch.2 Part I para.8, amended: SI 2002/2469 Sch.5, SI 2004/1771 Sch.1 para.44

Sch.2 Part I para.8, revoked (in part): SI 2004/865 Sch.1 para.10, SI 2004/1016 Sch.1 para.10

Sch.2 Part I para.8, varied: SI 2004/865 Art.95, Art.96, SI 2004/1016 Art.71, Art.72

Sch.2 para.2, varied: SI 2004/865 Art.95, Art.96, SI 2004/1016 Art.71, Art.72

Sch.2 para.3, varied: SI 2004/865 Art.95, Art.96, SI 2004/1016 Art.71, Art.72

Sch.2 para.4, varied: SI 2004/865 Art.95, Art.96, SI 2004/1016 Art.71, Art.72

Sch.2 para.5, varied: SI 2004/865 Art.95, Art.96, SI 2004/1016 Art.71, Art.72

Sch.2 para.6, varied: SI 2004/865 Art.95, Art.96, SI 2004/1016 Art.71, Art.72

Sch.2 para.7, varied: SI 2004/865 Art.95, Art.96, SI 2004/1016 Art.71, Art.72

Sch.2 para.8, varied: SI 2004/865 Art.95, Art.96, SI 2004/1016 Art.71, Art.72

Sch.2 para.9, varied: SI 2004/865 Art.95, Art.96, SI 2004/1016 Art.71, Art.72

Sch.2 para.10, varied: SI 2004/865 Art.95, Art.96, SI 2004/1016 Art.71, Art.72

Sch.2 para.11, varied: SI 2004/865 Art.95, Art.96, SI 2004/1016 Art.71, Art.72

1992–cont.

664. National Health Service (Service Committees and Tribunal) Regulations 1992–*cont.*

Sch.4, referred to: SI 2004/865 Art.95

Sch.4 para.1, amended: SI 2002/2469 Sch.5

Sch.4 para.1, varied: SI 2004/865 Art.95, Art.96, SI 2004/1016 Art.71, Art.72

Sch.4 para.2, amended: SI 2002/2469 Sch.5

Sch.4 para.2, revoked (in part): SI 2004/865 Sch.1 para.10, SI 2004/1016 Sch.1 para.10

Sch.4 para.2, varied: SI 2004/865 Art.95, Art.96, SI 2004/1016 Art.71, Art.72

Sch.4 para.3, amended: SI 2002/2469 Sch.5

Sch.4 para.3, varied: SI 2004/865 Art.95, Art.96, SI 2004/1016 Art.71, Art.72

Sch.4 para.4, amended: SI 2002/2469 Sch.5

Sch.4 para.4, varied: SI 2004/865 Art.95, Art.96, SI 2004/1016 Art.71, Art.72

Sch.4 para.5, amended: SI 2002/2469 Sch.5

Sch.4 para.5, varied: SI 2004/865 Art.95, Art.96, SI 2004/1016 Art.71, Art.72

Sch.4 para.6, amended: SI 2002/2469 Sch.5

Sch.4 para.6, varied: SI 2004/865 Art.95, Art.96, SI 2004/1016 Art.71, Art.72

Sch.4 para.7, amended: SI 2002/2469 Sch.5

Sch.4 para.7, varied: SI 2004/865 Art.95, Art.96, SI 2004/1016 Art.71, Art.72

Sch.4 para.8, varied: SI 2004/865 Art.95, Art.96, SI 2004/1016 Art.71, Art.72

Sch.4 para.9, amended: SI 2002/2469 Sch.5

Sch.4 para.9, revoked (in part): SI 2004/865 Sch.1 para.10, SI 2004/1016 Sch.1 para.10

Sch.4 para.9, varied: SI 2004/865 Art.95, Art.96, SI 2004/1016 Art.71, Art.72

Sch.4 para.10, varied: SI 2004/865 Art.95, Art.96, SI 2004/1016 Art.71, Art.72

Sch.5 Part I para.1, revoked (in part): SI 2004/865 Sch.1 para.10, SI 2004/1016 Sch.1 para.10

Sch.5 Part I para.1, varied: SI 2004/865 Art.99, Art.101, Art.102, SI 2004/1016 Art.75, Art.77, Art.78

Sch.5 Part I para.2, varied: SI 2004/865 Art.99, Art.101, Art.102, SI 2004/1016 Art.75, Art.77, Art.78

Sch.5 Part II para.3, revoked (in part): SI 2004/865 Sch.1 para.10, SI 2004/1016 Sch.1 para.10

Sch.5 Part II para.3, varied: SI 2004/865 Art.99, Art.101, Art.102, SI 2004/1016 Art.75, Art.77, Art.78

Sch.5 Part II para.4, revoked (in part): SI 2004/865 Sch.1 para.10, SI 2004/1016 Sch.1 para.10

Sch.5 Part II para.4, varied: SI 2004/865 Art.99, Art.101, Art.102, SI 2004/1016 Art.75, Art.77, Art.78

Sch.5 Part II para.5, revoked (in part): SI 2004/865 Sch.1 para.10, SI 2004/1016 Sch.1 para.10

1992–cont.

664. National Health Service (Service Committees and Tribunal) Regulations 1992–*cont.*

Sch.5 Part II para.5, varied: SI 2004/865 Art.99, Art.101, Art.102, SI 2004/1016 Art.75, Art.77, Art.78

Sch.5 Part II para.6, revoked (in part): SI 2004/865 Sch.1 para.10, SI 2004/1016 Sch.1 para.10

Sch.5 Part II para.6, varied: SI 2004/865 Art.99, Art.101, Art.102, SI 2004/1016 Art.75, Art.77, Art.78

Sch.5 Part II para.7, revoked (in part): SI 2004/865 Sch.1 para.10, SI 2004/1016 Sch.1 para.10

Sch.5 Part II para.7, varied: SI 2004/865 Art.99, Art.101, Art.102, SI 2004/1016 Art.75, Art.77, Art.78

Sch.5 Part II para.8, revoked (in part): SI 2004/865 Sch.1 para.10, SI 2004/1016 Sch.1 para.10

Sch.5 Part II para.8, varied: SI 2004/865 Art.99, Art.101, Art.102, SI 2004/1016 Art.75, Art.77, Art.78

Sch.5 Part II para.9, revoked (in part): SI 2004/865 Sch.1 para.10, SI 2004/1016 Sch.1 para.10

Sch.5 Part II para.9, varied: SI 2004/865 Art.99, Art.101, Art.102, SI 2004/1016 Art.75, Art.77, Art.78

Sch.5 Part III para.10, varied: SI 2004/865 Art.99, Art.101, Art.102, SI 2004/1016 Art.75, Art.77, Art.78

Sch.5 Part III para.11, varied: SI 2004/865 Art.99, Art.101, Art.102, SI 2004/1016 Art.75, Art.77, Art.78

Sch.5 Part III para.12, varied: SI 2004/865 Art.99, Art.101, Art.102, SI 2004/1016 Art.75, Art.77, Art.78

Sch.5 Part III para.13, varied: SI 2004/865 Art.99, Art.101, Art.102, SI 2004/1016 Art.75, Art.77, Art.78

Sch.5 Part III para.14, varied: SI 2004/865 Art.99, Art.101, Art.102, SI 2004/1016 Art.75, Art.77, Art.78

Sch.5 Part III para.15, varied: SI 2004/865 Art.99, Art.101, Art.102, SI 2004/1016 Art.75, Art.77, Art.78

Sch.5 Part III para.16, varied: SI 2004/865 Art.99, Art.101, Art.102, SI 2004/1016 Art.75, Art.77, Art.78

Sch.7, applied: SI 2004/865 Art.103

Sch.7 para.1, amended: SI 2002/2469 Sch.10

Sch.7 para.1, revoked (in part): SI 2004/865 Sch.1 para.10, SI 2004/1016 Sch.1 para.10

Sch.7 para.1, varied: SI 2004/865 Art.103, SI 2004/1016 Art.79

Sch.7 para.2, amended: SI 2002/2469 Sch.1 para.58, Sch.10

Sch.7 para.2, revoked (in part): SI 2004/865 Sch.1 para.10, SI 2004/1016 Sch.1 para.10

NO.

NO.

1992–cont.

1992–cont.

664. National Health Service (Service Committees and Tribunal) Regulations 1992–*cont.*

Sch.7 para.2, varied: SI 2004/865 Art.103, SI 2004/1016 Art.79

Sch.8 Part I, added: SI 2002/2469 Sch.1 para.58

Sch.8 Part I, amended: SI 2002/2469 Sch.1 para.58

Sch.8 Part II, amended: SI 2002/2469 Sch.1 para.58

Sch.9 para.2, amended: SI 2002/2469 Sch.10

Sch.9 para.5, amended: SI 2002/2469 Sch.10, SI 2003/1937 Sch.1 para.3

Sch.9 para.7, amended: SI 2002/2469 Sch.10, SI 2003/1937 Sch.1 para.3

666. Town and Country Planning (Control of Advertisements) Regulations 1992

applied: SI 2004/870 Reg.19, SI 2004/1962 Art.12

varied: SI 2003/284 Art.138

Reg.2, amended: SI 2003/2155 Sch.1 para.33, Sch.2

Reg.4, see *JC Decaux Ltd v Secretary of State for the Environment, Transport and the Regions* [2003] EWHC 407, [2003] J.P.L. 1567 (QBD (Admin Ct)), Sullivan, J.

Sch.2 Class D, see *Kensington and Chelsea RLBC v Harvey Nichols & Co Ltd* [2001] EWCA Civ 702, [2002] 1 P. & C.R. 29 (CA), Dyson, L.J.

Sch.3 Part 1 Class 8, see *R. (on the application of Cal Brown Ltd (t/a CB Advertising Ltd)) v Hounslow LBC* [2001] EWHC Admin 864, [2002] 2 P. & C.R. 22 (QBD (Admin Ct)), Goldring, J.

Sch.3 Part I Class 13, see *R. (on the application of Maiden Outdoor Advertising Ltd) v Lambeth LBC* [2003] EWHC 1224, [2004] J.P.L. 820 (QBD (Admin Ct)), Collins, J.

Sch.3 Part I Class 14, see *R. (on the application of Maiden Outdoor Advertising Ltd) v Lambeth LBC* [2003] EWHC 1224, [2004] J.P.L. 820 (QBD (Admin Ct)), Collins, J.

Sch.3 Class 8, see *Brent LBC v Maiden Outdoor Advertising Ltd* [2002] EWHC 1240, [2003] J.P.L. 192 (QBD (Admin Ct)), Sullivan, J.

712. Telecommunication Meters (Approval Fees) (British Approvals Board for Telecommunications) Order 1992

revoked: SI 2003/2155 Sch.2

747. Motor Vehicles (Competitions and Trials) (Scotland) Amendment Regulations 1992

revoked: SSI 2002/14 Reg.3

754. National Health Service (Travelling Expenses and Remission of Charges) (Scotland) Amendment Regulations 1992

revoked: SSI 2003/376 Sch.3 para.6

807. Industrial Relations (Northern Ireland) Order 1992

enabled: SR 2002/345, SR 2002/346, SR 2002/347

Part II, referred to: SR 2002/120 Sch.1

Art.2, referred to: SR 2002/120 Sch.1

Art.4, revoked (in part): SI 2003/2904 Sch.1

Art.84A, amended: SI 2002/2836 Sch.2 para.3

Art.84A, applied: SR 2002/120, SR 2002/120 Sch.1

Art.84A, enabled: SR 2002/120

Art.90, amended: SI 2003/2902 Sch.5 para.1

Art.90, applied: SR 2002/346 Art.2, SR 2002/347 Art.2

Art.90, enabled: SR 2002/346, SR 2002/347

Art.95, amended: SI 2003/2902 Sch.5 para.1

Art.95, applied: SR 2002/345 Art.2

Art.95, enabled: SR 2002/345

Sch.4 para.15, substituted: SI 2003/418 Sch.1 para.9

Sch.4 para.16, amended: SI 2003/418 Sch.3

810. Local Government (Miscellaneous Provisions) (Northern Ireland) Order 1992

Art.28, revoked: SI 2002/3149 Sch.1

Art.48, revoked: SI 2002/3149 Sch.1

Art.49, revoked: SI 2002/3149 Sch.1

814. Education (School Teachers Pay and Conditions) Order 1992

revoked: 2002 c.32 Sch.22 Part 1

905. Farm Woodland Premium Scheme 1992

applied: SSI 2004/381 Reg.4

Art.9, amended: SSI 2003/209 Sch.3 para.1

Art.14, applied: SSI 2004/381 Reg.4

Sch.1, substituted: SSI 2003/209 Sch.3 para.1

976. Libya (United Nations Sanctions) (Dependent Territories) Order 1992

Art.11, amended: 2002 c.8 s.2

977. Libya (United Nations Sanctions) (Channel Islands) Order 1992

Art.11, amended: 2002 c.8 s.2

988. School Teachers Pay and Conditions Act 1991 (Commencement No 3) Order 1992

revoked: 2002 c.32 Sch.22 Part 1

1026. Social Security (Claims and Payments) Amendment Regulations 1992

Reg.2, amended: SI 2003/492 Sch.3 Part 1

NO.

1992–cont.

1026. Social Security (Claims and Payments) Amendment Regulations 1992–*cont.*

Reg.3, revoked (in part): SI 2003/492 Sch.3 Part 1

Reg.4, revoked (in part): SI 2003/492 Sch.3 Part 1

Reg.5, revoked (in part): SI 2003/492 Sch.3 Part 1

Reg.6, revoked (in part): SI 2003/492 Sch.3 Part 1

Sch.1, revoked (in part): SI 2003/492 Sch.3 Part 1

1049. Teignmouth Harbour Revision Order 1992

referred to: SI 2003/2574 Art.1

revoked: SI 2003/2574 Sch.3

1104. National Health Service (Travelling Expenses and Remission of Charges) Amendment Regulations 1992

revoked: SI 2003/2382 Sch.2

1197. European Parliamentary (United Kingdom Representatives) Pensions (Amendment) Order 1992

applied: SI 2003/2922 Art.2

1267. Brechin and Bridge of Dun Light Railway Order 1992

Art.8, amended: SI 2003/2155 Sch.1 para.18

1276. Royal Cornwall Hospitals and West Cornwall Hospital National Health Service Trust (Change of Name) Order 1992

revoked: 2003 c.43 s.7

1293. Merchant Shipping (Ministry of Defence Commercially Managed Ships) Order 1992

Art.11, substituted: 2002 asp 17 Sch.3 para.32

1294. Merchant Shipping (Ministry of Defence Yachts) Order 1992

Art.11, amended: 2002 asp 17 Sch.3 para.33

1300. Extradition (British Antarctic Territory) (Commonwealth Countries, Colonies and Republic of Ireland) Order 1992

revoked: SI 2002/1823 Sch.5

1301. Official Secrets Act 1989 (Hong Kong) Order 1992

Sch.2, amended: 2002 c.8 s.2

1302. Serbia and Montenegro (United Nations Sanctions) Order 1992

Art.6, amended: 2002 c.8 s.2

Art.11, amended: 2002 c.8 s.2

1303. Serbia and Montenegro (United Nations Sanctions) (Dependent Territories) Order 1992

Art.6, amended: 2002 c.8 s.2

Art.11, amended: 2002 c.8 s.2

1308. Serbia and Montenegro (United Nations Sanctions) (Channel Islands) Order 1992

Art.6, amended: 2002 c.8 s.2

NO.

1992–cont.

1308. Serbia and Montenegro (United Nations Sanctions) (Channel Islands) Order 1992–*cont.*

Art.11, amended: 2002 c.8 s.2

1315. Transfer of Functions (Financial Services) Order 1992

Art.9, revoked (in part): SI 2002/2840 Sch.3

1327. Devon Ambulance Service National Health Service Trust (Establishment) Amendment Order 1992

revoked: 2003 c.43 s.7

1329. Council Tax (Valuation of Dwellings) (Scotland) Regulations 1992

Reg.2, see *Grampian Valuation Joint Board Assessor v Adron* 2003 S.C. 245 (1 Div), Lord Cullen L.P., Lord Kirkwood, Lord Marnoch; see *Lanarkshire Valuation Joint Board Assessor v Brownlie* 2003 S.C. 249 (1 Div), Lord Cullen L.P., Lord Kirkwood, Lord Marnoch

1331. Council Tax (Liability of Owners) (Scotland) Regulations 1992

Sch.1 para.1, see *Scottish Water v Clydecare Ltd* 2003 S.C. 330 (Ex Div), Lord Osborne, Lord Macfadyen, Lord Sutherland

Sch.1 para.3, substituted: SSI 2003/137 Reg.2

1332. Council Tax (Administration and Enforcement) (Scotland) Regulations 1992

Reg.1, amended: SSI 2002/166 Art.8

Reg.17, amended: SSI 2002/166 Art.8

Reg.20, varied: SSI 2002/33 Art.10

Reg.21, varied: SSI 2002/33 Art.10

Reg.22, varied: SSI 2002/33 Art.10

Reg.23, varied: SSI 2002/33 Art.10

Reg.24, varied: SSI 2002/33 Art.10

Reg.25, varied: SSI 2002/33 Art.10

Reg.27, varied: SSI 2002/33 Art.10

Reg.28, amended: SSI 2002/166 Art.8

Reg.28A, amended: SSI 2002/166 Art.8

Reg.30, amended: SSI 2002/166 Art.8

Sch.1 Part I para.1, varied: SSI 2002/33 Art.10

Sch.1 Part I para.2, varied: SSI 2002/33 Art.10

Sch.1 Part I para.3, varied: SSI 2002/33 Art.10

Sch.1 Part I para.4, varied: SSI 2002/33 Art.10

Sch.1 Part II para.5, varied: SSI 2002/33 Art.10

Sch.1 Part II para.6, varied: SSI 2002/33 Art.10

1408. Council Tax (Discounts) (Scotland) Order 1992

revoked: SSI 2003/176 Sch.4

1432. Police (Scotland) Amendment Regulations 1992

revoked: SSI 2004/257 Sch.4

1526. Special Constables (Amendment) Regulations 1992

revoked: SI 2002/3180 Reg.3

NO.

1992–cont.

1587. Advice and Assistance (Financial Conditions) (Scotland) Regulations 1992

Reg.3, revoked: SSI 2002/329 Reg.4

1672. Road Works (Sharing of Costs of Works) (Scotland) Regulations 1992

applied: SSI 2003/416 Reg.4, SSI 2003/509 Reg.10

revoked: SSI 2003/509 Reg.10

Reg.2, referred to: SSI 2003/416 Reg.4

1674. Road Works (Reinstatement) (Scotland) Regulations 1992

Reg.2, amended: SSI 2003/417 Reg.2, SSI 2003/512 Reg.2

Reg.3, amended: SSI 2003/417 Reg.2

Reg.4, amended: SSI 2003/417 Reg.2

Reg.7, amended: SSI 2003/417 Reg.2

Reg.8, amended: SSI 2003/417 Reg.2

1675. Road Works (Qualifications of Supervisors and Operatives) (Scotland) Regulations 1992

referred to: SI 2002/2934 Sch.1 Part 3

1676. Road Works (Inspection Fees) (Scotland) Regulations 1992

revoked: SSI 2003/415 Reg.4

Reg.3, amended: SSI 2002/13 Reg.2

1687. Street Works (Qualifications of Supervisors and Operatives) Regulations 1992

referred to: SI 2002/2934 Sch.1 Part 3

1688. Street Works (Inspection Fees) Regulations 1992

revoked (in part): SI 2002/2092 Reg.4

Reg.3, amended: SI 2002/3181 Reg.2, SI 2004/1809 Reg.2

1689. Street Works (Reinstatement) Regulations 1992

Reg.3, amended: SI 2002/1487 Reg.2

Reg.7, amended: SI 2002/1487 Reg.2

Reg.8, amended: SI 2002/1487 Reg.2

1690. Street Works (Sharing of Costs of Works) Regulations 1992

see *Thames Water Utilities Ltd v London Underground Ltd* [2004] EWCA Civ 615, (2004) 148 S.J.L.B. 633 (CA), Brooke, L.J.

Reg.2, see *British Telecommunications Plc v Gwynedd Council* [2004] EWCA Civ 942, [2004] 4 All E.R. 975 (CA), Auld, L.J.

Reg.3, see *British Telecommunications Plc v Gwynedd Council* [2004] EWCA Civ 942, [2004] 4 All E.R. 975 (CA), Auld, L.J.

1703. Housing (Right to Buy) (Prescribed Persons) Order 1992

Sch.1, amended: SI 2003/1615 Sch.1 para.46, SI 2004/696 Sch.1 para.12

1711. European Communities (Designation) (No.2) Order 1992

revoked (in part): SI 2003/2901 Sch.4

1718. Anatomy (Northern Ireland) Order 1992

revoked: 2004 c.30 Sch.7 Part 2

NO.

1992–cont.

1720. Competition and Service (Electricity) (Northern Ireland) Order 1992

Sch.1, revoked: SI 2003/419 Sch.5

1723. Firearms (Amendment) (Northern Ireland) Order 1992

revoked: SI 2004/702 Sch.8

1725. Housing (Northern Ireland) Order 1992

referred to: SI 2003/412 Art.1

Part III, applied: SI 2003/412 Art.120

Part III, referred to: SI 2003/412 Art.120

Part III, revoked: SI 2003/412 Sch.5

Art.6A, added: SI 2003/412 Art.139

Art.8, amended: SI 2003/412 Art.140

Art.13, amended: SI 2003/412 Art.141

Art.39, referred to: SI 2003/412 Art.120

Art.47, enabled: SR 2003/234, SR 2003/282

Art.50, disapplied: SI 2003/412 Art.120

Art.50, referred to: SI 2003/412 Art.120

Art.51, disapplied: SI 2003/412 Art.120

Art.51, referred to: SI 2003/412 Art.120

Art.54, applied: SI 2003/412 Art.120

Art.73, amended: SI 2003/412 Sch.4 para.11

Art.73, referred to: SI 2003/412 Art.120

Art.73, revoked (in part): SI 2003/412 Sch.4 para.11, Sch.5

Art.74, amended: SI 2003/412 Art.142

Art.74, applied: SI 2003/412 Art.142

Art.75, amended: SI 2003/412 Art.143

Art.75A, added: SI 2003/412 Sch.3

Art.75B, added: SI 2003/412 Sch.3

Art.75C, added: SI 2003/412 Sch.3

Art.75D, added: SI 2003/412 Sch.3

Art.75E, added: SI 2003/412 Sch.3

Art.75F, added: SI 2003/412 Sch.3

Art.75G, added: SI 2003/412 Sch.3

Art.75H, added: SI 2003/412 Sch.3

Art.75I, added: SI 2003/412 Sch.3

Art.75J, added: SI 2003/412 Sch.3

Art.75K, added: SI 2003/412 Sch.3

Art.75L, added: SI 2003/412 Sch.3

Art.75M, added: SI 2003/412 Sch.3

Art.75N, added: SI 2003/412 Sch.3

Art.80, applied: SI 2003/412 Art.43, Art.48, Art.58, Art.59, Art.60, Art.120

Art.85, applied: SI 2003/412 Art.81

Art.103, amended: SI 2003/412 Sch.4 para.12

Art.104, amended: SI 2003/412 Art.145, Sch.5

Sch.3, amended: SI 2003/412 Art.142

Sch.6, revoked (in part): SI 2003/412 Sch.5

1727. Vienna Document 1992 (Privileges and Immunities) Order 1992

revoked: SI 2003/2621 Art.4

1730. Crown Office (Forms and Proclamations Rules) Order 1992

Sch.1 Part I, amended: SI 2002/3131 Art.2

NO.

1992–cont.

1736. Merchant Shipping (Categorisation of Registries of Overseas Territories) Order 1992
revoked: SI 2003/1248 Art.1

1812. Child Support (Information, Evidence and Disclosure) Regulations 1992
Reg.2, amended: SI 2002/1204 Reg.4, SI 2003/3206 Reg.2
Reg.3, amended: SI 2003/3206 Reg.2
Reg.8, amended: SI 2004/2415 Reg.3
Reg.11, amended: SI 2004/1823 Art.16

1813. Child Support (Maintenance Assessment Procedure) Regulations 1992
applied: SI 2003/192 Art.8
Reg.1, amended: SI 2002/1703 Sch.2 para.3, SI 2003/2779 Reg.3
Reg.8D, amended: SI 2003/2779 Reg.3
Reg.17, amended: SI 2004/2415 Reg.4
Reg.20, amended: SI 2003/1050 Reg.5
Reg.23, amended: SI 2003/1050 Reg.5
Reg.27, see *C-V v Secretary of State for Work and Pensions* [2002] EWCA Civ 1854, [2003] 1 F.L.R. 829 (CA), Potter, L.J.
Reg.30, varied: SI 2003/192 Art.8
Reg.30A, amended: SI 2003/2779 Reg.3
Reg.35A, amended: SI 2003/328 Reg.5
Reg.40, amended: SI 2003/2779 Reg.3
Reg.40, revoked (in part): SI 2003/2779 Reg.3
Reg.40ZA, amended: SI 2003/2779 Reg.3
Reg.40ZA, revoked (in part): SI 2003/2779 Reg.3

1814. Council Tax Benefit (General) Regulations 1992
see *Arnott v Melton BC* [2002] EWCA Civ 1800, [2003] R.V.R. 166 (CA), Simon Brown, L.J.
applied: SI 2003/325 Reg.12, Reg.21, SI 2003/1338 Reg.2
referred to: SI 2003/325 Reg.1, Reg.12, SI 2003/770 Reg.2, SI 2003/2613 Sch.1 para.9, SI 2004/552 Art.21, Art.22
Reg.2, amended: SI 2002/490 Reg.5, SI 2002/841 Reg.4, SI 2002/1397 Sch.1 para.21, SI 2002/2402 Sch.3 para.1, SI 2002/2689 Reg.5, SI 2003/48 Reg.2, SI 2003/325 Reg.13, SI 2003/1338 Reg.8, SI 2003/2279 Reg.5, SI 2004/14 Reg.2, SI 2004/154 Reg.2, SI 2004/319 Reg.2, SI 2004/565 Reg.4, SI 2004/963 Reg.2, SI 2004/1141 Reg.2, SI 2004/2303 Reg.3, SI 2004/2327 Reg.3
Reg.4, amended: SI 2002/2689 Reg.5, SI 2003/325 Reg.13A, Reg.27, SI 2003/2275 Reg.4, SI 2004/2327 Reg.3
Reg.4, revoked (in part): SI 2004/2327 Reg.3
Reg.4A, amended: SI 2003/325 Reg.14, SI 2004/1232 Reg.2
Reg.4D, revoked: 2004 c.19 s.12
Reg.5, amended: SI 2002/2402 Sch.3 para.2
Reg.6, amended: SI 2002/2402 Sch.3 para.3

NO.

1992–cont.

1814. Council Tax Benefit (General) Regulations 1992–*cont.*
Reg.8, amended: SI 2003/325 Reg.15, SI 2003/1195 Reg.5, SI 2004/2327 Reg.3
Reg.8, applied: SI 2003/526 Art.21, SI 2004/552 Art.21, Art.22
Reg.8, substituted: SI 2003/325 Reg.15
Reg.9, amended: SI 2004/2327 Reg.3
Reg.9, applied: SI 2003/526 Art.21, SI 2004/552 Art.21
Reg.9, substituted: SI 2003/325 Reg.15
Reg.10, amended: SI 2002/668 Art.20, SI 2003/526 Art.21, SI 2003/1195 Reg.5, SI 2004/552 Art.21
Reg.10, substituted: SI 2003/325 Reg.15
Reg.11, amended: SI 2003/325 Reg.16, SI 2004/2327 Reg.3
Reg.11, revoked (in part): SI 2004/2327 Reg.3
Reg.13, amended: SI 2003/455 Sch.3 para.1, SI 2004/14 Reg.6, SI 2004/552 Art.21
Reg.13, substituted: SI 2003/325 Reg.17
Reg.13A, amended: SI 2002/499 Reg.2, SI 2002/2689 Reg.5, SI 2003/455 Sch.3 para.2, SI 2004/14 Reg.7
Reg.13A, applied: SI 2002/2005 Reg.13
Reg.13A, substituted: SI 2003/325 Reg.17
Reg.14, amended: SI 2004/14 Reg.8
Reg.14, substituted: SI 2003/325 Reg.17
Reg.15, amended: SI 2003/325 Reg.17, SI 2004/14 Reg.9, SI 2004/2327 Reg.3
Reg.15, revoked (in part): SI 2003/325 Reg.17, SI 2004/2327 Reg.3
Reg.15, substituted: SI 2003/325 Reg.17
Reg.16, amended: SI 2004/14 Reg.10
Reg.16, substituted: SI 2003/325 Reg.17
Reg.17, amended: SI 2003/325 Reg.17, SI 2004/565 Reg.10, SI 2004/2327 Reg.3
Reg.17, substituted: SI 2003/325 Reg.17
Reg.18, amended: SI 2002/2402 Sch.3 para.4, SI 2004/552 Art.22
Reg.18, substituted: SI 2003/325 Reg.17
Reg.19, amended: SI 2003/325 Reg.17
Reg.19, substituted: SI 2003/325 Reg.17
Reg.19, amended: SI 2002/2689 Reg.5, SI 2003/325 Reg.17
Reg.19, substituted: SI 2003/325 Reg.17
Reg.20, amended: SI 2003/325 Reg.17
Reg.20, substituted: SI 2003/325 Reg.17
Reg.20, amended: SI 2002/2689 Reg.5
Reg.20, substituted: SI 2003/325 Reg.17
Reg.21, substituted: SI 2003/325 Reg.17
Reg.22, amended: SI 2003/325 Reg.17
Reg.22, substituted: SI 2003/325 Reg.17
Reg.23, amended: SI 2003/325 Reg.17
Reg.23, substituted: SI 2003/325 Reg.17
Reg.24, substituted: SI 2003/325 Reg.17
Reg.24, amended: SI 2002/841 Reg.4, SI 2002/2402 Sch.3 para.5, SI 2004/565 Reg.10, SI 2004/2327 Reg.3
Reg.24, substituted: SI 2003/325 Reg.17

1992–cont.

1814. Council Tax Benefit (General) Regulations 1992–*cont.*

Reg.25, substituted: SI 2003/325 Reg.17

Reg.25, amended: SI 2002/2442 Reg.2

Reg.25, substituted: SI 2003/325 Reg.17

Reg.26, substituted: SI 2003/325 Reg.17

Reg.26, amended: SI 2002/2402 Sch.3 para.6

Reg.26, substituted: SI 2003/325 Reg.17

Reg.27, amended: SI 2003/325 Reg.17

Reg.27, substituted: SI 2003/325 Reg.17

Reg.27, revoked: SI 2004/2327 Reg.3

Reg.27, substituted: SI 2003/325 Reg.17

Reg.28, amended: SI 2003/325 Reg.17

Reg.28, substituted: SI 2003/325 Reg.17

Reg.29, substituted: SI 2003/325 Reg.17

Reg.30, substituted: SI 2003/325 Reg.17

Reg.31, amended: SI 2002/2402 Sch.3 para.7

Reg.31, substituted: SI 2003/325 Reg.17

Reg.32, substituted: SI 2003/325 Reg.17

Reg.33, substituted: SI 2003/325 Reg.17

Reg.34, amended: SI 2002/2402 Sch.3 para.8, SI 2004/2308 Reg.3, SI 2004/2327 Reg.3

Reg.34, substituted: SI 2003/325 Reg.17

Reg.35, revoked (in part): SI 2003/455 Sch.3 para.3

Reg.35, substituted: SI 2003/325 Reg.17

Reg.36, substituted: SI 2003/325 Reg.17

Reg.37, substituted: SI 2003/325 Reg.17

Reg.38, amended: SI 2002/1589 Reg.2, SI 2004/1708 Reg.4

Reg.40, amended: SI 2002/1763 Reg.2

Reg.42, amended: SI 2002/1589 Reg.3, Reg.4, SI 2002/2207 Reg.2, SI 2003/1701 Reg.2, Reg.3, SI 2003/1914 Reg.2, SI 2004/1708 Reg.2, Reg.3

Reg.42, revoked (in part): SI 2004/1708 Reg.3

Reg.47, amended: SI 2002/1589 Reg.3, Reg.5, SI 2003/1701 Reg.2, SI 2003/1914 Reg.2, SI 2004/1708 Reg.2

Reg.51, amended: SI 2004/319 Reg.5, SI 2004/2303 Reg.3

Reg.51, revoked (in part): SI 2004/154 Reg.2

Reg.52, amended: SI 2002/668 Art.20, SI 2003/325 Reg.19, SI 2003/526 Art.21, SI 2003/1195 Reg.5, SI 2003/2275 Reg.4, SI 2004/552 Art.21, SI 2004/2327 Reg.3

Reg.52, applied: SI 2003/526 Art.21, SI 2004/552 Art.21

Reg.52, revoked (in part): SI 2004/2327 Reg.3

Reg.52, substituted: SI 2003/325 Reg.19

Reg.53A, amended: SI 2003/1338 Reg.12, SI 2003/1589 Reg.4

Reg.53A, applied: SI 2004/14 Reg.28

Reg.53A, revoked (in part): SI 2003/1589 Reg.4

Reg.53A, substituted: SI 2004/14 Reg.11

1992–cont.

1814. Council Tax Benefit (General) Regulations 1992–*cont.*

Reg.53A, varied: SI 2004/14 Reg.28

Reg.53B, added: SI 2003/325 Reg.20

Reg.53B, amended: SI 2003/325 Reg.20, SI 2003/1338 Reg.3

Reg.53ZB, added: SI 2004/319 Reg.3

Reg.56, amended: SI 2003/1338 Reg.14, SI 2004/14 Reg.15, SI 2004/2303 Reg.3

Reg.56A, added: SI 2004/14 Reg.12

Reg.56B, added: SI 2004/319 Reg.4

Reg.57, revoked: SI 2004/14 Reg.13

Reg.57, varied: SI 2003/1338 Reg.5

Reg.58, revoked: SI 2004/14 Reg.13

Reg.59, amended: SI 2003/308 Reg.3, SI 2003/325 Reg.22, SI 2003/1338 Reg.13, SI 2004/2327 Reg.3

Reg.59B, added: SI 2003/325 Reg.22

Reg.59B, amended: SI 2003/325 Reg.22, SI 2004/290 Reg.4, SI 2004/2327 Reg.3

Reg.62, amended: SI 2002/1703 Sch.2 para.4, SI 2003/48 Reg.3, SI 2003/325 Reg.23, SI 2003/1589 Reg.4, SI 2003/1632 Reg.4

Reg.62, disapplied: SI 2003/1338 Reg.4

Reg.62, revoked (in part): SI 2003/1338 Reg.14, SI 2004/14 Reg.15

Reg.62BA, added: SI 2004/2303 Reg.3

Reg.63, amended: SI 2004/2308 Reg.3

Reg.65, amended: SI 2003/325 Reg.24, SI 2003/1338 Reg.19, SI 2004/14 Reg.25

Reg.66, amended: SI 2003/1589 Reg.4, SI 2004/14 Reg.17

Reg.66, revoked (in part): SI 2003/1338 Reg.15, SI 2003/1589 Reg.4, SI 2004/14 Reg.17

Reg.84, amended: SI 2002/1397 Sch.1 para.21

Reg.90, revoked (in part): SI 2003/1338 Reg.16, SI 2004/14 Reg.18

Reg.91, amended: SI 2003/325 Reg.26

Reg.92, amended: SI 2002/1397 Sch.1 para.21

Reg.93, revoked (in part): SI 2003/455 Sch.3 para.4

Reg.95, amended: SI 2004/14 Reg.19

Reg.95, revoked (in part): SI 2003/1589 Reg.4, SI 2004/14 Reg.19

Reg.96, added: SI 2004/574 Reg.2

Sch.A1 para.1, revoked: 2004 c.19 s.12

Sch.A1 para.2, revoked: 2004 c.19 s.12

Sch.A1 para.2A, revoked: 2004 c.19 s.12

Sch.A1 para.3, revoked: 2004 c.19 s.12

Sch.A1 para.4, revoked: 2004 c.19 s.12

Sch.A1 para.5, revoked: 2004 c.19 s.12

Sch.A1 para.6, revoked: 2004 c.19 s.12

Sch.A1 para.7, revoked: 2004 c.19 s.12

Sch.A1 para.8, revoked: 2004 c.19 s.12

Sch.A1 para.9, revoked: 2004 c.19 s.12

Sch.A1 para.10, revoked: 2004 c.19 s.12

1992–cont.

1814. Council Tax Benefit (General) Regula-tions 1992–*cont.*

Sch.1 Part I para.1, substituted: SI 2002/668 Sch.8, SI 2003/526 Sch.8, SI 2004/552 Sch.10

Sch.1 Part I para.2, amended: SI 2002/2019 Reg.2

Sch.1 Part I para.2, substituted: SI 2002/668 Sch.8, SI 2003/526 Sch.8, SI 2004/552 Sch.10

Sch.1 Part II para.3, amended: SI 2002/668 Art.20, SI 2002/2402 Sch.3 para.9, SI 2003/526 Art.21, SI 2004/552 Art.21

Sch.1 Part II para.3, applied: SI 2003/526 Art.21, SI 2004/552 Art.21

Sch.1 Part III para.4, amended: SI 2002/2497 Sch.2 para.1

Sch.1 Part III para.5, amended: SI 2002/2497 Sch.2 para.1

Sch.1 Part III para.6, amended: SI 2002/2497 Sch.2 para.1

Sch.1 Part III para.7, amended: SI 2002/2497 Sch.2 para.1

Sch.1 Part III para.8, amended: SI 2002/2497 Sch.2 para.1

Sch.1 Part III para.8A, amended: SI 2002/2497 Sch.2 para.1

Sch.1 Part III para.8A, revoked (in part): SI 2004/14 Reg.21

Sch.1 Part III para.9, amended: SI 2002/2497 Sch.2 para.1

Sch.1 Part III para.10, amended: SI 2002/2497 Sch.2 para.1

Sch.1 Part III para.11, amended: SI 2002/2497 Sch.2 para.1

Sch.1 Part III para.11, applied: SI 2002/2005 Reg.9, Reg.13

Sch.1 Part III para.12, amended: SI 2002/2497 Sch.2 para.1

Sch.1 Part III para.12, applied: SI 2002/2005 Reg.9

Sch.1 Part III para.13, amended: SI 2002/2497 Sch.2 para.1, SI 2003/455 Sch.3 para.5

Sch.1 Part III para.13, applied: SI 2002/2005 Reg.9

Sch.1 Part III para.14, amended: SI 2002/490 Reg.2, SI 2002/2497 Sch.2 para.1

Sch.1 Part III para.14A, amended: SI 2002/2497 Sch.2 para.1, SI 2003/1195 Reg.5

Sch.1 Part III para.14A, applied: SI 2003/526 Art.21, SI 2004/552 Art.21

Sch.1 Part III para.15, amended: SI 2002/2497 Sch.2 para.1, SI 2003/1731 Reg.3

Sch.1 Part III para.15, applied: SI 2003/526 Art.21, SI 2004/552 Art.21

Sch.1 Part III para.15, revoked (in part): SI 2004/2327 Reg.3

Sch.1 Part III para.16, amended: SI 2002/2020 Reg.2, SI 2002/2497 Sch.2 para.1, SI 2003/2279 Reg.5

Sch.1 Part III para.16, revoked (in part): SI 2003/2279 Reg.5

1992–cont.

1814. Council Tax Benefit (General) Regula-tions 1992–*cont.*

Sch.1 Part III para.17, amended: SI 2002/2497 Sch.2 para.1

Sch.1 Part III para.18, amended: SI 2002/2497 Sch.2 para.1

Sch.1 Part III para.19, amended: SI 2002/2497 Sch.2 para.1

Sch.1 Part IV, amended: SI 2002/668 Sch.9, SI 2002/2497 Sch.2 para.1

Sch.1 Part IV, substituted: SI 2003/526 Sch.9, SI 2004/552 Sch.11

Sch.1A Part I para.1, added: SI 2003/325 Reg.15

Sch.1A Part I para.1, amended: SI 2004/2327 Reg.3

Sch.1A Part I para.1, substituted: SI 2004/552 Sch.12

Sch.1A Part I para.2, added: SI 2003/325 Reg.15

Sch.1A Part I para.2, substituted: SI 2004/552 Sch.12

Sch.1A Part II para.3, added: SI 2003/325 Reg.15

Sch.1A Part II para.3, amended: SI 2004/552 Art.22

Sch.1A Part III para.4, added: SI 2003/325 Reg.15

Sch.1A Part III para.5, added: SI 2003/325 Reg.15

Sch.1A Part III para.6, added: SI 2003/325 Reg.15

Sch.1A Part III para.6, amended: SI 2003/325 Reg.15

Sch.1A Part III para.7, added: SI 2003/325 Reg.15

Sch.1A Part III para.8, added: SI 2003/325 Reg.15

Sch.1A Part III para.8, amended: SI 2003/325 Reg.15

Sch.1A Part III para.9, added: SI 2003/325 Reg.15

Sch.1A Part III para.10, added: SI 2003/325 Reg.15

Sch.1A Part III para.11, added: SI 2003/325 Reg.15

Sch.1A Part IV, added: SI 2003/325 Reg.15

Sch.1A Part IV, substituted: SI 2004/552 Sch.13

Sch.2 para.1, amended: SI 2002/668 Art.20, SI 2003/325 Reg.27, SI 2003/526 Art.21, SI 2004/154 Reg.2, SI 2004/552 Art.21

Sch.2 para.1, revoked (in part): SI 2004/154 Reg.2

Sch.3 para.1, amended: SI 2002/2497 Sch.2 para.1

Sch.3 para.2, amended: SI 2002/2497 Sch.2 para.1

Sch.3 para.3, amended: SI 2002/2497 Sch.2 para.1

1992–*cont.*

1814. Council Tax Benefit (General) Regulations 1992–*cont.*

Sch.3 para.4, amended: SI 2002/2497 Sch.2 para.1

Sch.3 para.4A, amended: SI 2002/2497 Sch.2 para.1

Sch.3 para.4B, amended: SI 2002/2497 Sch.2 para.1

Sch.3 para.5, amended: SI 2002/2497 Sch.2 para.1

Sch.3 para.6, amended: SI 2002/2497 Sch.2 para.1

Sch.3 para.7, amended: SI 2002/2497 Sch.2 para.1

Sch.3 para.8, amended: SI 2002/2497 Sch.2 para.1

Sch.3 para.9, amended: SI 2002/2497 Sch.2 para.1

Sch.3 para.10, amended: SI 2002/2497 Sch.2 para.1

Sch.3 para.11, amended: SI 2002/2497 Sch.2 para.1

Sch.3 para.12, amended: SI 2002/2497 Sch.2 para.1

Sch.3 para.13, amended: SI 2002/2497 Sch.2 para.1, SI 2004/2327 Reg.3

Sch.3 para.14, amended: SI 2002/2497 Sch.2 para.1

Sch.3 para.14, revoked: SI 2004/2327 Reg.3

Sch.3 para.15, amended: SI 2002/2497 Sch.2 para.1

Sch.3 para.16, amended: SI 2002/2402 Sch.3 para.10, SI 2002/2497 Sch.2 para.1, SI 2003/2634 Reg.2, SI 2004/552 Art.21

Sch.3 para.16, revoked (in part): SI 2003/2634 Reg.2

Sch.3 para.16, substituted: SI 2002/2402 Sch.3 para.10

Sch.3A para.1, added: SI 2003/325 Sch.2 Part I

Sch.3A para.2, added: SI 2003/325 Sch.2 Part I

Sch.3A para.3, added: SI 2003/325 Sch.2 Part I

Sch.3A para.3, amended: SI 2003/325 Sch.2 Part I

Sch.3A para.4, added: SI 2003/325 Sch.2 Part I

Sch.3A para.4, amended: SI 2003/325 Sch.2 Part I

Sch.3A para.4, varied: SI 2003/325 Sch.2 para.2

Sch.3A para.5, added: SI 2003/325 Sch.2 Part I

Sch.3A para.5, amended: SI 2003/325 Sch.2 Part I

Sch.3A para.6, added: SI 2003/325 Sch.2 Part I

Sch.3A para.7, added: SI 2003/325 Sch.2 Part I

1992–*cont.*

1814. Council Tax Benefit (General) Regulations 1992–*cont.*

Sch.3A para.8, added: SI 2003/325 Sch.2 Part I

Sch.3A para.8, varied: SI 2003/325 Sch.2 para.2

Sch.3A para.9, added: SI 2003/325 Sch.2 Part I

Sch.3A para.9, amended: SI 2003/325 Sch.2 Part I, SI 2004/552 Art.22

Sch.3A para.9, revoked (in part): SI 2003/325 Sch.2 Part I

Sch.3A para.9, varied: SI 2003/325 Sch.2 para.2

Sch.3A para.10, added: SI 2003/325 Sch.2 Part I

Sch.4 para.4B, added: SI 2003/511 Reg.5

Sch.4 para.10, substituted: SI 2004/1708 Reg.4

Sch.4 para.10A, added: SI 2002/2380 Reg.5

Sch.4 para.11, substituted: SI 2004/565 Reg.4

Sch.4 para.13, amended: SI 2002/2442 Reg.3, SI 2004/2308 Reg.2

Sch.4 para.14, amended: SI 2002/841 Reg.4

Sch.4 para.20, amended: SI 2002/668 Art.20, SI 2003/526 Art.21, SI 2004/552 Art.21

Sch.4 para.24, amended: SI 2003/2279 Reg.5, SI 2004/2308 Reg.4, SI 2004/2327 Reg.3

Sch.4 para.25, amended: SI 2004/1141 Reg.4

Sch.4 para.27, amended: SI 2004/1141 Reg.4

Sch.4 para.35, amended: SI 2004/2308 Reg.3

Sch.4 para.48, amended: SI 2004/565 Reg.4

Sch.4 para.52, amended: SI 2002/841 Reg.4

Sch.4 para.53, amended: SI 2002/841 Reg.4

Sch.4 para.54, amended: SI 2002/841 Reg.4

Sch.4 para.56, revoked: SI 2002/2402 Sch.3 para.11

Sch.4 para.57, amended: SI 2002/2402 Sch.3 para.11, SI 2003/2634 Reg.2, SI 2004/552 Art.21

Sch.4 para.60, revoked: 2004 c.19 s.12

Sch.4 para.61, revoked: 2004 c.19 s.12

Sch.4 para.62, amended: SI 2003/762 Reg.11, SI 2004/1748 Sch.2 para.2

Sch.4 para.63, revoked: SI 2004/565 Reg.4

Sch.4 para.64, revoked: SI 2004/565 Reg.4

Sch.4 para.64A, added: SI 2002/2314 Reg.5

Sch.4 para.64A, revoked: SI 2004/565 Reg.4

Sch.4 para.65, revoked: SI 2004/565 Reg.4

Sch.4 para.67, revoked: SI 2004/565 Reg.4

Sch.4 para.74, added: SI 2003/511 Reg.5

Sch.4 para.74, amended: SI 2003/2279 Reg.5

Sch.4 para.75, added: SI 2003/2279 Reg.5

Sch.4 para.75, revoked: SI 2004/565 Reg.4

Sch.4 para.76, added: SI 2003/2439 Reg.15

NO.

NO.

1992–cont.

1814. Council Tax Benefit (General) Regulations 1992–*cont.*

Sch.4 para.76, revoked: SI 2004/565 Reg.4

Sch.4A para.1, added: SI 2003/325 Sch.2 Part II

Sch.4A para.2, added: SI 2003/325 Sch.2 Part II

Sch.4A para.3, added: SI 2003/325 Sch.2 Part II

Sch.4A para.4, added: SI 2003/325 Sch.2 Part II

Sch.4A para.5, added: SI 2003/325 Sch.2 Part II

Sch.4A para.6, added: SI 2003/325 Sch.2 Part II

Sch.4A para.6, amended: SI 2003/325 Sch.2 Part II

Sch.4A para.7, added: SI 2003/325 Sch.2 Part II

Sch.4A para.8, added: SI 2003/325 Sch.2 Part II

Sch.4A para.9, added: SI 2003/325 Sch.2 Part II

Sch.4A para.10, added: SI 2003/325 Sch.2 Part II

Sch.4A para.11, added: SI 2003/325 Sch.2 Part II

Sch.4A para.12, added: SI 2003/325 Sch.2 Part II

Sch.4A para.13, added: SI 2003/325 Sch.2 Part II

Sch.4A para.14, added: SI 2003/325 Sch.2 Part II

Sch.4A para.15, added: SI 2003/325 Sch.2 Part II

Sch.4A para.16, added: SI 2003/325 Sch.2 Part II

Sch.4A para.17, added: SI 2003/325 Sch.2 Part II

Sch.4A para.18, added: SI 2003/325 Sch.2 Part II

Sch.4A para.19, added: SI 2003/325 Sch.2 Part II

Sch.4A para.20, added: SI 2003/325 Sch.2 Part II

Sch.4A para.21, added: SI 2003/325 Sch.2 Part II

Sch.4A para.21, amended: SI 2003/325 Sch.2 Part II, SI 2004/552 Art.22

Sch.4A para.22, added: SI 2003/325 Sch.2 Part II

Sch.4A para.23, added: SI 2003/325 Sch.2 Part II

Sch.4A para.23, varied: SI 2003/325 Sch.2 para.2

Sch.5A, applied: SI 2004/14 Reg.28

Sch.5 para.8, amended: SI 2002/2380 Reg.5, SI 2002/2402 Sch.3 para.12

Sch.5 para.8, applied: SI 2002/1792 Sch.5 para.20A

1992–cont.

1814. Council Tax Benefit (General) Regulations 1992–*cont.*

Sch.5 para.8, revoked (in part): SI 2004/14 Reg.22

Sch.5 para.18, amended: SI 2004/1141 Reg.3

Sch.5 para.21, amended: SI 2004/2327 Reg.3

Sch.5 para.23, amended: SI 2004/1141 Reg.3

Sch.5 para.33, substituted: SI 2004/565 Reg.4

Sch.5 para.34, revoked: SI 2003/2279 Reg.5

Sch.5 para.42, amended: SI 2004/565 Reg.4

Sch.5 para.46, amended: SI 2003/2279 Reg.5

Sch.5 para.47, amended: SI 2003/2279 Reg.5

Sch.5 para.49, revoked: SI 2003/1589 Reg.9

Sch.5 para.50, revoked: 2004 c.19 s.12

Sch.5 para.51, revoked: 2004 c.19 s.12

Sch.5 para.53, revoked: SI 2004/565 Reg.4

Sch.5 para.53A, added: SI 2002/2314 Reg.5

Sch.5 para.53A, revoked: SI 2004/565 Reg.4

Sch.5 para.54, revoked: SI 2004/565 Reg.4

Sch.5 para.56, revoked: SI 2004/565 Reg.4

Sch.5 para.60, substituted: SI 2004/1708 Reg.4

Sch.5 para.65, revoked: SI 2004/565 Reg.4

Sch.5 para.68, added: SI 2003/511 Reg.5

Sch.5 para.68, amended: SI 2003/2279 Reg.5

Sch.5 para.69, added: SI 2003/2279 Reg.5

Sch.5 para.70, added: SI 2003/2279 Reg.5

Sch.5 para.71, added: SI 2003/2279 Reg.5

Sch.5 para.71, revoked: SI 2004/565 Reg.4

Sch.5 para.72, added: SI 2003/2439 Reg.15

Sch.5 para.72, revoked: SI 2004/565 Reg.4

Sch.5A Part I para.1, revoked: SI 2004/14 Reg.23

Sch.5A Part I para.1A, added: SI 2004/14 Reg.23

Sch.5A Part I para.2, amended: SI 2004/14 Reg.23

Sch.5A Part I para.2, revoked (in part): SI 2004/14 Reg.23

Sch.5A Part I para.3, amended: SI 2004/14 Reg.23

Sch.5A Part II para.4, amended: SI 2004/14 Reg.23

Sch.5A Part II para.6, amended: SI 2004/14 Reg.23

Sch.5A Part III para.7, amended: SI 2004/14 Reg.23

Sch.5A Part IV para.8, amended: SI 2003/1589 Reg.4, SI 2004/14 Reg.23, SI 2004/781 Reg.4

Sch.5A Part IV para.8, revoked (in part): SI 2004/14 Reg.23

Sch.5B para.1, added: SI 2004/319 Sch.2

Sch.5B para.2, added: SI 2004/319 Sch.2

Sch.5B para.3, added: SI 2004/319 Sch.2

1992–cont.

1814. Council Tax Benefit (General) Regulations 1992–*cont.*

Sch.5B para.4, added: SI 2004/319 Sch.2

Sch.5B para.5, added: SI 2004/319 Sch.2

Sch.5B para.6, added: SI 2004/319 Sch.2

Sch.5B para.7, added: SI 2004/319 Sch.2

Sch.5ZA Part I para.1, added: SI 2003/325 Sch.2 Part III

Sch.5ZA Part I para.2, added: SI 2003/325 Sch.2 Part III

Sch.5ZA Part I para.3, added: SI 2003/325 Sch.2 Part III

Sch.5ZA Part I para.4, added: SI 2003/325 Sch.2 Part III

Sch.5ZA Part I para.4, amended: SI 2004/2327 Reg.3

Sch.5ZA Part I para.5, added: SI 2003/325 Sch.2 Part III

Sch.5ZA Part I para.6, added: SI 2003/325 Sch.2 Part III

Sch.5ZA Part I para.6, revoked (in part): SI 2003/325 Sch.2 Part III

Sch.5ZA Part I para.7, added: SI 2003/325 Sch.2 Part III

Sch.5ZA Part I para.8, added: SI 2003/325 Sch.2 Part III

Sch.5ZA Part I para.9, added: SI 2003/325 Sch.2 Part III

Sch.5ZA Part I para.10, added: SI 2003/325 Sch.2 Part III

Sch.5ZA Part I para.10, varied: SI 2003/325 Sch.2 para.2

Sch.5ZA Part I para.11, added: SI 2003/325 Sch.2 Part III

Sch.5ZA Part I para.12, added: SI 2003/325 Sch.2 Part III

Sch.5ZA Part I para.13, added: SI 2003/325 Sch.2 Part III

Sch.5ZA Part I para.14, added: SI 2003/325 Sch.2 Part III

Sch.5ZA Part I para.14, amended: SI 2003/325 Sch.2 Part III

Sch.5ZA Part I para.15, added: SI 2003/325 Sch.2 Part III

Sch.5ZA Part I para.16, added: SI 2003/325 Sch.2 Part III

Sch.5ZA Part I para.16, amended: SI 2004/1141 Reg.3

Sch.5ZA Part I para.17, added: SI 2003/325 Sch.2 Part III

Sch.5ZA Part I para.17, amended: SI 2003/325 Sch.2 Part III

Sch.5ZA Part I para.18, added: SI 2003/325 Sch.2 Part III

Sch.5ZA Part I para.19, added: SI 2003/325 Sch.2 Part III

Sch.5ZA Part I para.20, added: SI 2003/325 Sch.2 Part III

Sch.5ZA Part I para.21, added: SI 2003/325 Sch.2 Part III

1992–cont.

1814. Council Tax Benefit (General) Regulations 1992–*cont.*

Sch.5ZA Part I para.21, amended: SI 2003/325 Sch.2 Part III

Sch.5ZA Part I para.21, revoked (in part): SI 2003/325 Sch.2 Part III

Sch.5ZA Part I para.21, varied: SI 2003/325 Sch.2 para.2

Sch.5ZA Part I para.21A, added: SI 2003/325 Sch.2 Part III

Sch.5ZA Part I para.21A, applied: SI 2002/1792 Sch.5 para.20A

Sch.5ZA Part I para.22, added: SI 2003/325 Sch.2 Part III

Sch.5ZA Part I para.23, added: SI 2003/325 Sch.2 Part III

Sch.5ZA Part I para.24, added: SI 2003/325 Sch.2 Part III

Sch.5ZA Part I para.25, added: SI 2003/325 Sch.2 Part III

Sch.5ZA Part I para.25A, added: SI 2003/325 Sch.2 Part III

Sch.5ZA Part II para.26, added: SI 2003/325 Sch.2 Part III

Sch.5ZA Part II para.27, added: SI 2003/325 Sch.2 Part III

Sch.5ZA Part II para.28, added: SI 2003/325 Sch.2 Part III

Sch.5ZA Part II para.29, added: SI 2003/325 Sch.2 Part III

Sch.5ZA Part II para.29, revoked (in part): SI 2003/325 Sch.2 Part III

Sch.5ZA Part II para.30, added: SI 2003/325 Sch.2 Part III

Sch.6 Part II para.9, amended: SI 2003/325 Reg.25

Sch.6 Part II para.9, revoked (in part): SI 2003/1338 Reg.18, SI 2004/14 Reg.24

Sch.6 Part II para.9, substituted: SI 2003/325 Reg.25

Sch.6 Part VI para.13, revoked (in part): SI 2004/14 Reg.24

Sch.6 Part VII para.16, amended: SI 2004/14 Reg.24

1815. Child Support (Maintenance Assessments and Special Cases) Regulations 1992

Reg.1, see *M v Secretary of State for Work and Pensions* [2004] EWCA Civ 1343, [2004] 3 F.C.R. 507 (CA (Civ Div)), Kennedy, L.J.

Reg.1, amended: SI 2002/2469 Sch.8, SI 2003/328 Reg.6, SI 2003/2779 Reg.4

Reg.9, amended: SI 2002/1204 Reg.5, SI 2003/328 Reg.6, SI 2003/2779 Reg.4

Reg.10A, amended: SI 2003/328 Reg.6

Reg.10A, substituted: SI 2003/328 Reg.6

Reg.10B, added: SI 2003/2779 Reg.4

Reg.11, amended: SI 2003/328 Reg.6, SI 2003/2779 Reg.4

Sch.1 Part I para.1, amended: SI 2004/2415 Reg.5

NO.

1815. Child Support (Maintenance Assessments and Special Cases) Regulations 1992–*cont.*

Sch.1 Part I para.2, amended: SI 2003/328 Reg.6

Sch.1 Part I para.5, amended: SI 2003/328 Reg.6

Sch.1 Part II para.7, revoked (in part): SI 2003/328 Reg.6

Sch.1 Part III para.9A, amended: SI 2003/2779 Reg.4

Sch.1 Part III para.12, amended: SI 2003/328 Reg.6

Sch.1 Part III para.14B, added: SI 2003/328 Reg.6

Sch.1 Part III para.16, amended: SI 2003/328 Reg.6

Sch.1 Part IV para.22, amended: SI 2003/2779 Reg.4

Sch.2 para.15, amended: SI 2003/2779 Reg.4

Sch.2 para.18, amended: SI 2003/2779 Reg.4

Sch.2 para.22, amended: SI 2003/328 Reg.6

Sch.2 para.30, amended: SI 2002/2469 Sch.6

Sch.2 para.36A, added: SI 2004/2415 Reg.5

Sch.2 para.48C, amended: SI 2003/762 Reg.11, SI 2004/1748 Sch.2 para.2

Sch.2 para.48D, added: SI 2003/328 Reg.6

Sch.2 para.48E, added: SI 2003/328 Reg.6

Sch.2 para.48E, substituted: SI 2003/2779 Reg.4

Sch.2 para.48F, added: SI 2003/2779 Reg.4

Sch.3B para.1, amended: SI 2004/2415 Reg.5

Sch.3B para.7, amended: SI 2004/2415 Reg.5

Sch.3B para.8, amended: SI 2004/2415 Reg.5

Sch.3B para.14, amended: SI 2004/2415 Reg.5

Sch.3B para.20, amended: SI 2004/2415 Reg.5

Sch.4, amended: SI 2003/328 Reg.6

Sch.4, revoked (in part): SI 2003/328 Reg.6

1816. Child Support (Arrears, Interest and Adjustment of Maintenance Assessments) Regulations 1992

Reg.1, amended: SI 2002/3019 Reg.26

Reg.10A, amended: SI 2002/3019 Reg.26

Reg.10B, amended: SI 2002/3019 Reg.26

1822. Aylesbury Vale Community Healthcare National Health Service Trust (Establishment) Amendment Order 1992

revoked: 2003 c.43 s.7

1847. Crown Court (Amendment) Rules 1992

revoked: SI 2002/1688 r.11

NO.

1878. Act of Sederunt (Fees of Witnesses and Shorthand Writers in the Sheriff Court) 1992

Sch.1 para.1, amended: SSI 2004/152 Art.3

Sch.1 para.1, substituted: SSI 2002/280 Sch.1

Sch.1 para.2, substituted: SSI 2002/280 Sch.1

Sch.1 para.3, substituted: SSI 2002/280 Sch.1

Sch.1 para.4, substituted: SSI 2002/280 Sch.1

Sch.1 para.5, substituted: SSI 2002/280 Sch.1

Sch.1 para.6, substituted: SSI 2002/280 Sch.1

Sch.1 para.7, substituted: SSI 2002/280 Sch.1

Sch.1 para.8, substituted: SSI 2002/280 Sch.1

Sch.1 para.9, substituted: SSI 2002/280 Sch.1

Sch.1 para.10, substituted: SSI 2002/280 Sch.1

Sch.1 para.11, substituted: SSI 2002/280 Sch.1

Sch.1 para.12, substituted: SSI 2002/280 Sch.1

Sch.2 para.1, amended: SSI 2002/280 Art.2, SSI 2003/246 Art.2, SSI 2004/149 Art.2

Sch.2 para.4, amended: SSI 2002/280 Art.2, SSI 2003/246 Art.2, SSI 2004/149 Art.2

Sch.2 para.5, amended: SSI 2002/280 Art.2, SSI 2003/246 Art.2, SSI 2004/149 Art.2

1903. Town and Country Planning (Enforcement) (Inquiries Procedure) Rules 1992

applied: SI 2002/2685 r.3, r.25, SI 2003/1269 r.3, SI 2003/1270 r.3, r.25

revoked (in part): SI 2002/2686 r.26, SI 2003/1269 r.26

varied: SI 2002/2686 r.3

1904. Town and Country Planning (Enforcement Notices and Appeals) (Amendment) Regulations 1992

revoked (in part): SI 2003/394 Reg.11

1919. Environmentally Sensitive Areas (Loch Lomond) Designation Order 1992

Art.4, applied: SSI 2004/381 Reg.4

Art.4A, applied: SSI 2004/381 Reg.4

Art.5, applied: SSI 2004/381 Reg.4

Art.5A, applied: SSI 2004/381 Reg.4

Art.5D, applied: SSI 2004/381 Reg.4

1920. Environmentally Sensitive Areas (Breadalbane) Designation Order 1992

Art.4, applied: SSI 2004/381 Reg.4

Art.4A, applied: SSI 2004/381 Reg.4

Art.5, applied: SSI 2004/381 Reg.4

Art.5A, applied: SSI 2004/381 Reg.4

NO.

NO.

1992–cont.

1920. Environmentally Sensitive Areas (Breadalbane) Designation Order 1992–*cont.*

Art.5D, applied: SSI 2004/381 Reg.4

1957. Education (Government of Further Education Corporations) (Former Sixth Form Colleges) Regulations 1992

revoked (in part): SI 2002/1094 Sch.1 Part 2

1963. Education (Government of Further Education Corporations) (Former Further Education Colleges) Regulations 1992

revoked (in part): SI 2002/1094 Sch.1 Part 2

1971. Flavourings in Food Regulations 1992

Reg.11, revoked (in part): SI 2002/890 Sch.1, SI 2002/1886 Sch.1, SSI 2002/267 Sch.1

1974. Salmon (Definition of Methods of Net Fishing and Construction of Nets) (Scotland) Regulations 1992

applied: SSI 2002/138 Sch.2 para.2, SSI 2003/615 Sch.2 para.2

1975. Western Isles Islands Council (Ardveenish) Harbour Revision Order 1992

Art.3, revoked (in part): SSI 2002/410 Sch.2 Part II

Art.5, revoked: SSI 2002/410 Sch.2 Part II

Art.6, revoked: SSI 2002/410 Sch.2 Part II

Art.7, revoked: SSI 2002/410 Sch.2 Part II

Art.8, revoked: SSI 2002/410 Sch.2 Part II

Art.10, revoked: SSI 2002/410 Sch.2 Part II

Sch.1, revoked: SSI 2002/410 Sch.2 Part II

Sch.2, revoked: SSI 2002/410 Sch.2 Part II

1976. Western Isles Islands Council (Breasclete) Harbour Revision Order 1992

Art.3, revoked: SSI 2002/410 Sch.2 Part II

Art.4, revoked: SSI 2002/410 Sch.2 Part II

Art.5, revoked: SSI 2002/410 Sch.2 Part II

Art.6, revoked: SSI 2002/410 Sch.2 Part II

Art.7, revoked: SSI 2002/410 Sch.2 Part II

Art.8, revoked: SSI 2002/410 Sch.2 Part II

Art.10, revoked: SSI 2002/410 Sch.2 Part II

Sch.1, revoked: SSI 2002/410 Sch.2 Part II

Sch.2, revoked: SSI 2002/410 Sch.2 Part II

1978. Food Additives Labelling Regulations 1992

applied: SI 2004/554 Reg.3

referred to: SI 2003/1008 Reg.3

varied: SI 2002/329 Reg.9, SI 2003/945 Reg.3, SI 2003/3295 Reg.3

Sch.1 Part II, referred to: SI 2002/330 Reg.3

Sch.1 Part II, varied: SI 2002/379 Reg.5, SI 2003/1182 Reg.3, SI 2003/1713 Reg.3

1989. Child Support (Collection and Enforcement) Regulations 1992

Reg.8, amended: SI 2003/328 Reg.2

2014. East Hertfordshire Health National Health Service Trust (Change of Name) Order 1992

revoked: 2003 c.43 s.7

1992–cont.

2038. Town and Country Planning (Inquiries Procedure) Rules 1992

applied: SI 2002/1223 r.26, SI 2003/1266 r.23, SI 2003/1267 r.3

referred to: SI 2003/1266 r.23

revoked (in part): SI 2003/1266 r.23

see *R. (on the application of Elmbridge BC) v Secretary of State for the Environment, Transport and the Regions* [2002] Env. L.R.1 (QBD (Admin Ct)), Richards, J.

r.21, revoked (in part): SI 2003/1266 r.23

2039. Town and Country Planning Appeals (Determination by Inspectors) (Inquiries Procedure) Rules 1992

revoked (in part): SI 2003/1267 r.24

2069. Magistrates Courts (Attendance Centre) Rules 1992

r.1, amended: SI 2003/1236 r.55

r.2, revoked: SI 2003/1236 r.56

Sch.1, revoked: SI 2003/1236 r.57

2070. Magistrates Courts (Notice of Transfer) (Children's Evidence) Rules 1992

r.2, substituted: SI 2003/1236 r.60

r.6, amended: SI 2003/1236 r.61

r.6, revoked (in part): SI 2003/1236 r.61

r.7, revoked: SI 2003/1236 r.62

Sch.1, revoked: SI 2003/1236 r.63

2071. Magistrates Courts (Children and Young Persons) Rules 1992

Part I r.2., amended: SI 2003/1236 r.65

Part II r.4., amended: SI 2003/1236 r.66

Part II r.11., amended: SI 2003/1236 r.67

Part IV r.23., revoked: SI 2002/1687 r.10

Part IV r.24., revoked: SI 2002/1687 r.10

Part V r.25., amended: SI 2003/1236 r.68

Part V r.27., amended: SI 2003/1236 r.69

Part V r.29., revoked (in part): SI 2003/1236 r.70

Sch.2, amended: SI 2002/2469 Sch.1 para.59, SI 2003/1236 r.71

2086. Town and Country Planning (Enforcement of Control) (No.2) (Scotland) Regulations 1992

Reg.2, amended: SSI 2004/332 Sch.8 para.1

Reg.2A, added: SSI 2004/332 Sch.8 para.2

Reg.2B, added: SSI 2004/332 Sch.8 para.2

Reg.2C, added: SSI 2004/332 Sch.8 para.2

2111. Organic Products Regulations 1992

revoked (in part): SI 2002/3159 Sch.4, SI 2004/1604 Sch.3

2153. Education (Hilderstone College, Kent) Regulations 1992

revoked: SI 2002/1094 Sch.1 Part 1

2182. Fines (Deductions from Income Support) Regulations 1992

applied: SI 2004/176 Reg.5

Reg.1, amended: SI 2002/1397 Sch.1 para.22, SI 2002/3019 Reg.32, SI 2003/1360 Reg.2

Reg.1, varied: SI 2004/176 Reg.5

Reg.2, amended: SI 2002/3019 Reg.32

NO.

1992–cont.

2182. Fines (Deductions from Income Support) Regulations 1992–*cont.*
Reg.2, varied: SI 2004/176 Reg.5
Reg.2A, added: SI 2004/2889 Reg.2
Reg.3, amended: SI 2003/1360 Reg.2
Reg.3, varied: SI 2004/176 Reg.5
Reg.4, amended: SI 2002/3019 Reg.32, SI 2004/2889 Reg.2
Reg.4, varied: SI 2004/176 Reg.5
Reg.7, amended: SI 2002/3019 Reg.32
Reg.7, varied: SI 2004/176 Reg.5
Reg.8, varied: SI 2004/176 Reg.5
Sch.3, amended: SI 2002/3019 Reg.32
Sch.3, revoked (in part): SI 2003/1360 Reg.2

2357. Merchant Shipping (Passenger Ships of Classes IV, V, VI, &amp VI(A) Bridge Visibility) Regulations 1992
revoked: SI 2002/1473 Sch.1 para.2

2365. Fire Services (Appointments and Promotion) (Amendment) (No.2) Regulations 1992
revoked: SI 2004/481 Sch.2

2372. Electromagnetic Compatibility Regulations 1992
referred to: SI 2004/693 Sch.1
Reg.97, revoked: SI 2004/693 Sch.2

2412. National Health Service (General Medical Services) Amendment Regulations 1992
revoked (in part): SI 2004/865 Sch.2, SI 2004/1016 Sch.2

2461. East Cheshire National Health Service Trust (Establishment) Order 1992
revoked: 2003 c.43 s.7

2462. Cheshire Community Healthcare National Health Service Trust (Establishment) Order 1992
revoked: SI 2002/1496 Art.2, 2003 c.43 s.7

2463. Countess of Chester Hospital National Health Service Trust (Establishment) Order 1992
revoked: 2003 c.43 s.7

2464. Warrington Community Health Care National Health Service Trust (Establishment) Order 1992
revoked: 2003 c.43 s.7

2465. Southport and Formby Community Health Services National Health Service Trust (Establishment) Order 1992
revoked: 2003 c.43 s.7

2466. Halton General Hospital National Health Service Trust (Establishment) Order 1992
revoked: 2003 c.43 s.7

2467. Wigan and Leigh Health Services National Health Service Trust (Establishment) Order 1992
revoked: 2003 c.43 s.7

NO.

1992–cont.

2468. West Lancashire National Health Service Trust (Establishment) Order 1992
revoked: 2003 c.43 s.7

2469. Calderstones National Health Service Trust (Establishment) Order 1992
revoked: 2003 c.43 s.7

2470. Chorley and South Ribble National Health Service Trust (Establishment) Order 1992
revoked: SI 2002/2025 Art.6, 2003 c.43 s.7

2471. West Lindsey National Health Service Trust (Establishment) Order 1992
revoked: 2003 c.43 s.7

2472. Leicester General Hospital National Health Service Trust (Establishment) Order 1992
revoked: 2003 c.43 s.7

2473. Southern Derbyshire Mental Health National Health Service Trust (Establishment) Order 1992
revoked: 2003 c.43 s.7
Art.1, amended: SI 2002/1296 Art.2
Art.2, amended: SI 2002/1296 Art.2
Art.3, amended: SI 2002/1296 Art.2

2474. Chesterfield and North Derbyshire Royal Hospital National Health Service Trust (Establishment) Order 1992
revoked: 2003 c.43 s.7

2475. Nottinghamshire Ambulance Service National Health Service Trust (Establishment) Order 1992
revoked: 2003 c.43 s.7

2476. Derby City General Hospital National Health Service Trust (Establishment) Order 1992
revoked: 2003 c.43 s.7

2477. Central Nottinghamshire Healthcare National Health Service Trust (Establishment) Order 1992
revoked: 2003 c.43 s.7

2478. Queen's Medical Centre, Nottingham, University Hospital National Health Service Trust (Establishment) Order 1992
applied: SI 2003/3059 Sch.1
revoked: 2003 c.43 s.7

2479. Rotherham General Hospital's National Health Service Trust (Establishment) Order 1992
revoked: 2003 c.43 s.7

2480. Barnsley District General Hospital National Health Service Trust (Establishment) Order 1992
revoked: 2003 c.43 s.7

NO.

1992–cont.

2481. Community Health Services, Southern Derbyshire National Health Service Trust (Establishment) Order 1992

revoked: 2003 c.43 s.7

2482. Rotherham Priority Health Services National Health Service Trust (Establishment) Order 1992

revoked: SI 2002/1293 Art.2, 2003 c.43 s.7

2483. Leicester Royal Infirmary National Health Service Trust (Establishment) Order 1992

revoked: 2003 c.43 s.7

2484. Fosse Health, Leicestershire Community National Health Service Trust (Establishment) Order 1992

revoked: 2003 c.43 s.7

2485. South Lincolnshire Community and Mental Health Services National Health Service Trust (Establishment) Order 1992

revoked: 2003 c.43 s.7

2486. Glenfield Hospital National Health Service Trust (Establishment) Order 1992

revoked: 2003 c.43 s.7

2487. Huddersfield Health Care Services National Health Service Trust (Establishment) Order 1992

revoked: 2003 c.43 s.7

2488. Humberside Ambulance Service National Health Service Trust (Establishment) Order 1992

revoked: 2003 c.43 s.7

2489. North Yorkshire Ambulance Service National Health Service Trust (Establishment) Order 1992

revoked: 2003 c.43 s.7

2490. Pinderfields Hospitals National Health Service Trust (Establishment) Order 1992

revoked: 2003 c.43 s.7

2491. Pontefract Hospitals National Health Service Trust (Establishment) Order 1992

revoked: 2003 c.43 s.7

2492. Scunthorpe Community Health Care National Health Service Trust (Establishment) Order 1992

revoked: 2003 c.43 s.7

2493. West Yorkshire Metropolitan Ambulance Service National Health Service Trust (Establishment) Order 1992

applied: SI 2003/3059 Sch.1, Sch.2

referred to: SI 2004/569 Sch.1

revoked: 2003 c.43 s.7

2494. Scunthorpe and Goole Hospitals National Health Service Trust (Establishment) Order 1992

revoked: 2003 c.43 s.7

NO.

1992–cont.

2495. Wakefield and Pontefract Community Health National Health Service Trust (Establishment) Order 1992

revoked: SI 2002/1313 Art.6, 2003 c.43 s.7

2496. Grimsby Health National Health Service Trust (Establishment) Order 1992

revoked: 2003 c.43 s.7

2497. Leeds Community and Mental Health Services Teaching National Health Service Trust (Establishment) Order 1992

revoked: 2003 c.43 s.7

Art.1, amended: SI 2002/1615 Art.2

Art.2, amended: SI 2002/1615 Art.2

2498. Calderdale Healthcare National Health Service Trust (Establishment) Order 1992

revoked: 2003 c.43 s.7

2499. Royal Hull Hospitals National Health Service Trust (Establishment) Order 1992

revoked: 2003 c.43 s.7

2500. East Yorkshire Hospitals National Health Service Trust (Establishment) Order 1992

revoked: 2003 c.43 s.7

2501. North Hampshire, Loddon Community National Health Service Trust (Establishment) Order 1992

revoked: 2003 c.43 s.7

2502. Isle of Wight Community Healthcare National Health Service Trust (Establishment) Order 1992

revoked: 2003 c.43 s.7

2503. Wiltshire Ambulance Service National Health Service Trust (Establishment) Order 1992

revoked: 2003 c.43 s.7

2504. Hampshire Ambulance Service National Health Service Trust (Establishment) Order 1992

applied: SI 2003/3059 Sch.2

referred to: SI 2004/569 Sch.1

revoked: 2003 c.43 s.7

2505. Andover District Community Health Care National Health Service Trust (Establishment) Order 1992

revoked: 2003 c.43 s.7

2506. Portsmouth Hospitals National Health Service Trust (Establishment) Order 1992

applied: SI 2003/3059 Sch.1

revoked: 2003 c.43 s.7

Art.3, substituted: SI 2004/75 Art.2

2507. St Mary's Hospital National Health Service Trust (Establishment) Order 1992

revoked: 2003 c.43 s.7

1992–cont.

2508. Dorset Ambulance National Health Service Trust (Establishment) Order 1992
revoked: 2003 c.43 s.7

2509. Southampton University Hospitals National Health Service Trust (Establishment) Order 1992
revoked: 2003 c.43 s.7

2510. Whittington Hospital National Health Service Trust (Establishment) Order 1992
revoked: 2003 c.43 s.7

2511. Enfield Community Care National Health Service Trust (Establishment) Order 1992
revoked: 2003 c.43 s.7

2512. Havering Hospitals National Health Service Trust (Establishment) Order 1992
revoked: 2003 c.43 s.7

2513. Thameside Community Health Care National Health Service Trust (Establishment) Order 1992
revoked: 2003 c.43 s.7

2514. Mid Essex Community Health National Health Service Trust (Establishment) Order 1992
revoked: 2003 c.43 s.7

2515. BHB Community Health Care National Health Service Trust (Establishment) Order 1992
revoked: 2003 c.43 s.7

2516. Chase Farm Hospitals National Health Service Trust (Establishment) Order 1992
revoked: 2003 c.43 s.7

2517. Redbridge Health Care National Health Service Trust (Establishment) Order 1992
revoked: 2003 c.43 s.7

2518. Royal London Homoeopathic Hospital National Health Service Trust (Establishment) Order 1992
revoked: 2003 c.43 s.7

2519. Camden and Islington Community Health Services National Health Service Trust (Establishment) Order 1992
revoked: SI 2002/1323 Sch.1, 2003 c.43 s.7

2520. Worthing Priority Care National Health Service Trust (Establishment) Order 1992
revoked: SI 2002/1362 Art.6, 2003 c.43 s.7

2521. Crawley Horsham National Health Service Trust (Establishment) Order 1992
revoked: 2003 c.43 s.7

1992–cont.

2522. East Surrey Hospital and Community Healthcare National Health Service Trust (Establishment) Order 1992
revoked: 2003 c.43 s.7

2523. Richmond, Twickenham and Roehampton Healthcare National Health Service Trust (Establishment) Order 1992
revoked: 2003 c.43 s.7

2524. Merton and Sutton Community National Health Service Trust (Establishment) Order 1992
revoked: 2003 c.43 s.7

2525. Severn National Health Service Trust (Establishment) Order 1992
revoked: 2003 c.43 s.7

2526. Royal Devon and Exeter Healthcare National Health Service Trust (Establishment) Order 1992
revoked: 2003 c.43 s.7

2527. Gloucestershire Royal National Health Service Trust (Establishment) Order 1992
revoked: 2003 c.43 s.7

2528. Thanet Health Care National Health Service Trust (Establishment) Order 1992
revoked: 2003 c.43 s.7

2529. Canterbury and Thanet Community Healthcare National Health Service Trust (Establishment) Order 1992
revoked: 2003 c.43 s.7
Art.1, amended: SI 2003/1496 Art.2
Art.2, amended: SI 2003/1496 Art.2

2530. Queen Mary's Sidcup National Health Service Trust (Establishment) Order 1992
revoked: 2003 c.43 s.7

2531. Mid Kent Healthcare National Health Service Trust (Establishment) Order 1992
revoked: 2003 c.43 s.7

2532. Kent and Canterbury Hospitals National Health Service Trust (Establishment) Order 1992
revoked: 2003 c.43 s.7

2533. Greenwich Healthcare National Health Service Trust (Establishment) Order 1992
revoked: 2003 c.43 s.7

2534. Eastbourne and County Healthcare National Health Service Trust (Establishment) Order 1992
revoked: 2003 c.43 s.7
Art.1, amended: SI 2002/1495 Art.2, SI 2002/2397 Art.2
Art.2, amended: SI 2002/1495 Art.2, SI 2002/2397 Art.2

NO.

1992–cont.

2535. Bromley Hospitals National Health Service Trust (Establishment) Order 1992
revoked: 2003 c.43 s.7

2536. Brighton Health Care National Health Service Trust (Establishment) Order 1992
revoked: 2003 c.43 s.7
Art.1, amended: SI 2003/866 Art.2
Art.2, amended: SI 2003/866 Art.2
Art.3, amended: SI 2004/2894 Art.2
Art.4, substituted: SI 2004/2894 Art.3

2537. Northwick Park Hospital National Health Service Trust (Establishment) Order 1992
revoked: 2003 c.43 s.7

2538. Bedfordshire and Hertfordshire Ambulance and Paramedic Service National Health Service Trust (Establishment) Order 1992
referred to: SI 2004/569 Sch.1
revoked: 2003 c.43 s.7

2539. West London Healthcare National Health Service Trust (Establishment) Order 1992
revoked: 2003 c.43 s.7

2540. Hounslow and Spelthorne Community and Mental Health National Health Service Trust (Establishment) Order 1992
revoked: SI 2002/1323 Sch.1, 2003 c.43 s.7

2541. Riverside Mental Health National Health Service Trust (Establishment) Order 1992
revoked: 2003 c.43 s.7

2542. Northumberland Mental Health National Health Service Trust (Establishment) Order 1992
revoked: 2003 c.43 s.7

2543. South Tyneside Health Care National Health Service Trust (Establishment) Order 1992
revoked: 2003 c.43 s.7

2544. South Cumbria Community and Mental Health National Health Service Trust (Establishment) Order 1992
revoked: 2003 c.43 s.7

2545. Durham County Ambulance Service National Health Service Trust (Establishment) Order 1992
revoked: 2003 c.43 s.7

2546. Cumbria Ambulance Service National Health Service Trust (Establishment) Order 1992
revoked: 2003 c.43 s.7

2547. South West Durham Mental Health National Health Service Trust (Establishment) Order 1992
revoked: 2003 c.43 s.7

1992–cont.

2548. Westmorland Hospitals National Health Service Trust (Establishment) Order 1992
revoked: 2003 c.43 s.7

2549. West Cumbria Health Care National Health Service Trust (Establishment) Order 1992
revoked: 2003 c.43 s.7

2550. Gateshead Hospitals National Health Service Trust (Establishment) Order 1992
revoked: 2003 c.43 s.7

2551. South Tees Community and Mental Health National Health Service Trust (Establishment) Order 1992
revoked: 2003 c.43 s.7

2552. North Warwickshire National Health Service Trust (Establishment) Order 1992
revoked: SI 2002/2616 Art.2, 2003 c.43 s.7

2553. Walsall Community Health National Health Service Trust (Establishment) Order 1992
revoked: SI 2002/2616 Art.2, 2003 c.43 s.7

2554. Princess Royal Hospital National Health Service Trust (Establishment) Order 1992
revoked: 2003 c.43 s.7, SI 2003/2346 Art.6

2555. South Worcestershire Community National Health Service Trust (Establishment) Order 1992
revoked: 2003 c.43 s.7

2556. South Warwickshire General Hospitals National Health Service Trust (Establishment) Order 1992
revoked: 2003 c.43 s.7

2557. Shropshire's Mental Health National Health Service Trust (Establishment) Order 1992
revoked: 2003 c.43 s.7

2558. Mid-Staffordshire General Hospitals National Health Service Trust (Establishment) Order 1992
referred to: SI 2004/569 Sch.1
revoked: 2003 c.43 s.7

2559. North Staffordshire Hospital Centre National Health Service Trust (Establishment) Order 1992
revoked: 2003 c.43 s.7
Art.1, amended: SI 2003/792 Art.2
Art.2, amended: SI 2003/792 Art.2

2560. Kidderminster Health Care National Health Service Trust (Establishment) Order 1992
revoked: 2003 c.43 s.7

2561. Wolverley National Health Service Trust (Establishment) Order 1992
revoked: 2003 c.43 s.7

NO.

2562. Good Hope Hospital National Health Service Trust (Establishment) Order 1992

revoked: 2003 c.43 s.7

2563. Burton Hospitals National Health Service Trust (Establishment) Order 1992

revoked: 2003 c.43 s.7

2564. North East Worcestershire Community Health Care National Health Service Trust (Establishment) Order 1992

revoked: 2003 c.43 s.7

2565. West Suffolk Hospitals National Health Service Trust (Establishment) Order 1992

revoked: 2003 c.43 s.7

2566. Ipswich Hospital National Health Service Trust (Establishment) Order 1992

revoked: 2003 c.43 s.7

2567. Addenbrooke's National Health Service Trust (Establishment) Order 1992

revoked: 2003 c.43 s.7

2568. Papworth Hospital National Health Service Trust (Establishment) Order 1992

revoked: 2003 c.43 s.7

2569. James Paget Hospital National Health Service Trust (Establishment) Order 1992

revoked: 2003 c.43 s.7

2570. North West Anglia Health Care National Health Service Trust (Establishment) Order 1992

revoked: SI 2002/647 Art.8, 2003 c.43 s.7

2571. Lifespan Health Care Cambridge National Health Service Trust (Establishment) Order 1992

revoked: SI 2002/647 Art.8, 2003 c.43 s.7

2572. Peterborough Hospitals National Health Service Trust (Establishment) Order 1992

revoked: 2003 c.43 s.7

2573. Mid Anglia Community Health National Health Service Trust (Establishment) Order 1992

revoked: 2003 c.43 s.7

2574. Oxfordshire Learning Disability National Health Service Trust (Establishment) Order 1992

applied: SI 2003/3059 Sch.1

revoked: 2003 c.43 s.7

2575. South Buckinghamshire National Health Service Trust (Establishment) Order 1992

revoked: SI 2002/2419 Art.8, 2003 c.43 s.7

Art.3, amended: SI 2002/1490 Art.2

NO.

2576. Horton General Hospital National Health Service Trust (Establishment) Order 1992

revoked: 2003 c.43 s.7

2577. Two Shires Ambulance National Health Service Trust (Establishment) Order 1992

referred to: SI 2004/569 Sch.1

revoked: 2003 c.43 s.7

2578. Royal Berkshire Ambulance National Health Service Trust (Establishment) Order 1992

revoked: 2003 c.43 s.7

2579. Royal Berkshire and Battle Hospitals National Health Service Trust (Establishment) Order 1992

applied: SI 2003/3059 Sch.1, Sch.2

revoked: 2003 c.43 s.7

2580. Radcliffe Infirmary National Health Service Trust (Establishment) Order 1992

revoked: 2003 c.43 s.7

2581. West Berkshire Priority Care Service National Health Service Trust (Establishment) Order 1992

revoked: 2003 c.43 s.7

2582. East Berkshire Community Health National Health Service Trust (Establishment) Order 1992

revoked: SI 2002/1323 Sch.1, 2003 c.43 s.7

2583. East Suffolk Local Health Services National Health Service Trust (Establishment) Order 1992

revoked: 2003 c.43 s.7

2584. Southampton Community Health Services National Health Service Trust (Establishment) Order 1992

revoked: SI 2002/1323 Sch.1, 2003 c.43 s.7

2585. West Middlesex University Hospital National Health Service Trust (Establishment) Order 1992

revoked: 2003 c.43 s.7

2586. Mancunian Community Health National Health Service Trust (Establishment) Order 1992

revoked: 2003 c.43 s.7

2587. Bedford and Shires Health and Care National Health Service Trust (Establishment) Order 1992

revoked: 2003 c.43 s.7

2588. Avalon, Somerest, National Health Service Trust (Establishment) Order 1992

revoked: 2003 c.43 s.7

2595. Social Security (Miscellaneous Provisions) Amendment (No.2) Regulations 1992

Reg.1, amended: SI 2003/492 Sch.3 Part 1

Reg.2, revoked (in part): SI 2003/492 Sch.3 Part 1

NO.

NO.

1992–cont.

2595. Social Security (Miscellaneous Provisions) Amendment (No.2) Regulations 1992–cont.

Reg.3, revoked (in part): SI 2003/492 Sch.3 Part 1

Reg.4, revoked (in part): SI 2003/492 Sch.3 Part 1

Reg.5, revoked (in part): SI 2003/492 Sch.3 Part 1

Reg.6, revoked (in part): SI 2003/492 Sch.3 Part 1

Reg.7, revoked (in part): SI 2003/492 Sch.3 Part 1

Reg.8, revoked (in part): SI 2003/492 Sch.3 Part 1

2596. Food (Forces Exemptions) (Revocations) Regulations 1992

Sch.1 Part I, amended: SI 2003/1563 Reg.10, SI 2003/1564 Reg.10, SI 2003/1596 Reg.10, SI 2003/1659 Reg.11, SI 2003/2243 Reg.10, SI 2003/3037 Reg.11, SI 2003/3041 Reg.10, SI 2003/3044 Reg.10, SI 2003/3047 Reg.10, SI 2003/3053 Reg.10, SI 2003/3120 Reg.10, SI 2004/553 Reg.10

Sch.1 Part II, amended: SSI 2003/291 Reg.12, SSI 2003/293 Reg.11, SSI 2003/311 Reg.11, SSI 2003/527 Reg.11, SSI 2003/569 Reg.12, SSI 2004/6 Reg.11, SSI 2004/133 Reg.11

2645. Child Support (Maintenance Arrangements and Jurisdiction) Regulations 1992

Reg.3, varied: SI 2003/192 Art.8

Reg.7A, amended: SI 2002/2469 Sch.1 para.60, SI 2004/696 Sch.1 para.13

2668. Merchant Shipping (Prevention and Control of Pollution) (Bermuda) Order 1992

revoked: SI 2002/3147 Art.2

2677. Sheep Annual Premium Regulations 1992

Reg.5, amended: SI 2003/151 Reg.3

Reg.8, added: SI 2003/151 Reg.3

Reg.8A, revoked (in part): SI 2003/151 Reg.3

2730. Gwent Community Health National Health Service Trust (Establishment) Order 1992

revoked: 2003 c.43 s.7

2731. Wrexham Maelor Hospital National Health Service Trust (Establishment) Order 1992

revoked: 2003 c.43 s.7

2732. Glan Clwyd District General Hospital National Health Service Trust (Establishment) Order 1992

revoked: 2003 c.43 s.7

2733. Glan Hafren National Health Service Trust (Establishment) Order 1992

revoked: 2003 c.43 s.7

1992–cont.

2734. Llanelli Dinefwr National Health Service Trust (Establishment) Order 1992

revoked: 2003 c.43 s.7

2735. Ceredigion and Mid Wales National Health Service Trust (Establishment) Order 1992

revoked: 2003 c.43 s.7

2736. Swansea National Health Service Trust (Establishment) Order 1992

revoked: 2003 c.43 s.7

2737. Llandough Hospital National Health Service Trust (Establishment) Order 1992

revoked: 2003 c.43 s.7

2738. Bridgend and District National Health Service Trust (Establishment) Order 1992

revoked: 2003 c.43 s.7

2739. Gofal Cymuned Clwydian Community Care National Health Service Trust (Establishment) Order 1992

revoked: 2003 c.43 s.7

2740. South and East Wales Ambulance National Health Service Trust (Establishment) Order 1992

revoked: 2003 c.43 s.7

2741. Powys Health Care National Health Service Trust (Establishment) Order 1992

revoked: 2003 c.43 s.7, SI 2003/817 Art.2

2742. Carmarthen and District National Health Service Trust (Establishment) Order 1992

revoked: 2003 c.43 s.7

2783. Cigarettes (Maximum Tar Yield) (Safety) Regulations 1992

revoked: SI 2002/3041 Reg.16

2790. Statistics of Trade (Customs and Excise) Regulations 1992

Reg.3, amended: SI 2002/2498 Reg.3, SI 2003/2155 Sch.1 para.34, SI 2003/3131 Reg.3

Reg.3, revoked (in part): SI 2002/2498 Reg.3

Reg.4, amended: SI 2002/2498 Reg.3, SI 2003/3131 Reg.3

2792. Health and Safety (Display Screen Equipment) Regulations 1992

Reg.3, substituted: SI 2002/2174 Reg.3

Reg.5, amended: SI 2002/2174 Reg.3

Reg.6, amended: SI 2002/2174 Reg.3

2793. Manual Handling Operations Regulations 1992

see *Delaney v McGregor Construction (Highlands) Ltd* 2003 Rep. L.R. 56 (OH), Lady Paton

Reg.2, see *McIntosh v Edinburgh City Council* 2003 S.L.T. 827 (OH), Lord McEwan

Reg.3, see *Taylor v Glasgow City Council* 2002 S.C. 364 (Ex Div), Lord Carloway, Lord Marnoch, Lord Reed

NO.

NO.

1992–cont.

2793. Manual Handling Operations Regulations 1992–*cont.*

Reg.4, amended: SI 2002/2174 Reg.4

Reg.4, see *Davidson v Lothian and Borders Fire Board* 2003 S.L.T. 939 (Ex Div), Lord Marnoch, Lord Hamilton, Lord Macfadyen; see *Higgins v DHL International (UK) Ltd* 2003 S.L.T. 1301 (OH), Lady Paton; see *Kerr v North Ayrshire Council* 2002 Rep. L.R. 35 (OH), Lady Smith; see *King v Sussex Ambulance NHS Trust* [2002] EWCA Civ 953, [2002] I.C.R. 1413 (CA), Hale, L.J.; see *McDougall v Spiers* 2002 Rep. L.R. 80 (OH), Lady Paton; see *McDougall v Spiers* 2003 S.C. 491 (1 Div), Lady Cosgrove, Lord Carloway, Lord Cullen L.P.; see *McIntosh v Edinburgh City Council* 2003 S.L.T. 827 (OH), Lord McEwan; see *O'Neill v DSG Retail Ltd* [2002] EWCA Civ 1139, [2003] I.C.R. 222 (CA), Nelson, J.; see *Purdie v Glasgow City Council* 2002 Rep. L.R. 26 (OH), Lord Hamilton; see *R. (on the application of A) v East Sussex CC (No.2)* [2003] EWHC 167, (2003) 6 C.C.L. Rep. 194 (QBD (Admin Ct)), Munby, J.; see *Taylor v Glasgow City Council* 2002 S.C. 364 (Ex Div), Lord Carloway, Lord Marnoch, Lord Reed

2803. Police and Criminal Evidence Act 1984 (Tape-recording of Interviews) (No.2) Order 1992

applied: SI 2003/705

revoked: SI 2003/705 Art.4

2817. Transport and Works (Inquiries Procedure) Rules 1992

applied: SI 2004/2018 r.25

revoked: SI 2004/2018 r.25

2834. Property Misdescriptions (Specified Matters) Order 1992

Art.2, see *George Wimpey UK Ltd v Brown* 2003 S.L.T. 659 (HCJ), Lord Macfadyen, Lord Carloway, Temporary Judge Gordon Q.C.

2875. Telecommunications (Single Emergency Call Number) Regulations 1992

revoked: 2003 c.21 Sch.19

2876. Companies (Fees) (Amendment) Regulations 1992

revoked: SI 2004/2621 Sch.3

2885. Offshore Installations (Safety Case) Regulations 1992

applied: SI 2002/655 Reg.19, Reg.20, SI 2003/547 Reg.19, Sch.16, SI 2004/456 Reg.18

Reg.2, applied: SI 2002/655 Reg.22, SI 2003/547 Reg.22, SI 2004/456 Reg.21

Reg.2, varied: SI 2002/2175 Reg.3

Reg.4, applied: SI 2003/547 Sch.16, SI 2004/456 Sch.15

1992–cont.

2885. Offshore Installations (Safety Case) Regulations 1992–*cont.*

Reg.17, applied: SI 2003/547 Sch.16, SI 2004/456 Sch.15

2902. Transport and Works (Applications and Objections Procedure) Rules 1992

applied: SI 2002/366, SI 2002/412, SI 2002/1064, SI 2002/1065, SI 2002/1066, SI 2002/1997, SI 2002/1998, SI 2003/1075, SI 2003/3364

2903. Levying Bodies (General) Regulations 1992

Reg.8, disapplied: SI 2003/3072 Reg.4

2932. Provision and Use of Work Equipment Regulations 1992

Reg.2, see *Hammond v Commissioner of Police of the Metropolis* [2004] EWCA Civ 830, [2004] I.C.R. 1467 (CA), Brooke, L.J.

Reg.4, see *Hammond v Commissioner of Police of the Metropolis* [2004] EWCA Civ 830, [2004] I.C.R. 1467 (CA), Brooke, L.J.

Reg.5, see *Horton v Taplin Contracts Ltd* [2002] EWCA Civ 1604, [2003] B.L.R. 74 (CA), Bodey, J.; see *Wallis v Balfour Beatty Rail Maintenance Ltd* [2003] EWCA Civ 72, (2003) 147 S.J.L.B. 357 (CA), Morland, J.; see *Yorkshire Traction Co Ltd v Searby* [2003] EWCA Civ 1856, (2004) 148 S.J.L.B. 61 (CA), Chadwick, L.J.

Reg.6, see *Hammond v Commissioner of Police of the Metropolis* [2004] EWCA Civ 830, [2004] I.C.R. 1467 (CA), Brooke, L.J.; see *Hislop v Lynx Express Parcels* 2003 S.L.T. 785 (2 Div), Lord Gill L.J.C., Lord Osborne, Lord Weir

Reg.20, see *Horton v Taplin Contracts Ltd* [2002] EWCA Civ 1604, [2003] B.L.R. 74 (CA), Bodey, J.

2955. Council Tax (Dwellings and Part Residential Subjects) (Scotland) Regulations 1992

Reg.2, amended: SSI 2002/102 Reg.3

Reg.6, see *Scottish Water v Clydecare Ltd* 2003 S.C. 330 (Ex Div), Lord Osborne, Lord Macfadyen, Lord Sutherland

Reg.6, amended: SSI 2002/102 Reg.4

Sch.1 para.4, see *Scottish Water v Clydecare Ltd* 2003 S.C. 330 (Ex Div), Lord Osborne, Lord Macfadyen, Lord Sutherland

Sch.1 para.4, amended: SSI 2002/102 Reg.5

2961. Electricity Supply (Amendment) Regulations 1992

revoked: SI 2002/2665 Sch.5

2966. Personal Protective Equipment at Work Regulations 1992

referred to: SI 2003/2002 Reg.12

NO.

1992–cont.

2966. Personal Protective Equipment at Work Regulations 1992–*cont.*

Reg.4, see *Fytche v Wincanton Logistics Plc* [2004] UKHL 31, [2004] 4 All E.R. 221 (HL), Lord Nicholls of Birkenhead; see *Lane Group Plc v Farmiloe* [2004] P.I.Q.R. P22 (EAT), Judge Peter Clark

Reg.4, amended: SI 2002/2174 Reg.5

Reg.6, amended: SI 2002/2174 Reg.5

Reg.7, see *Fytche v Wincanton Logistics Plc* [2003] EWCA Civ 874, [2003] I.C.R. 1582 (CA), Waller, L.J.; see *Fytche v Wincanton Logistics Plc* [2004] UKHL 31, [2004] 4 All E.R. 221 (HL), Lord Nicholls of Birkenhead

Reg.9, amended: SI 2002/2174 Reg.5

2977. National Assistance (Assessment of Resources) Regulations 1992

applied: SI 2003/931 Reg.6, SI 2003/969 Reg.2, SSI 2002/266 Reg.2

see *Crookdake v Drury* [2003] EWHC 1938, (2004) 76 B.M.L.R. 99 (QBD), Owen, J.; see *R v Liverpool HA* [2002] Lloyd's Rep. Med. 23 (QBD), Munby, J.; see *R. (on the application of Beeson) v Dorset CC* [2001] EWHC Admin 986, [2002] H.R.L.R. 15 (QBD (Admin Ct)), Richards, J.

Reg.2, amended: SI 2003/627 Reg.2, SI 2003/897 Reg.3, SI 2003/2343 Reg.2, SI 2003/2530 Reg.2, SI 2004/2328 Reg.2, SI 2004/2879 Reg.2, SSI 2003/156 Reg.2, SSI 2003/425 Reg.2, SSI 2003/577 Reg.2

Reg.15, see *B (A Child) v Todd* [2002] P.I.Q.R. P11 (QBD), Stanley Burnton, J.

Reg.16, amended: SI 2002/2531 Reg.2, SI 2003/897 Reg.4, SSI 2003/577 Reg.3

Reg.16, see *B (A Child) v Todd* [2002] P.I.Q.R. P11 (QBD), Stanley Burnton, J.

Reg.16A, added: SI 2003/931 Reg.5

Reg.17, see *B (A Child) v Todd* [2002] P.I.Q.R. P11 (QBD), Stanley Burnton, J.

Reg.20, amended: SI 2002/410 Reg.2, SI 2002/814 Reg.2, SI 2003/627 Reg.3, SI 2003/897 Reg.2, SI 2004/760 Reg.3, SI 2004/1023 Reg.2, SSI 2004/103 Reg.2

Reg.20, referred to: SSI 2002/264 Art.2

Reg.22, see *B (A Child) v Todd* [2002] P.I.Q.R. P11 (QBD), Stanley Burnton, J.

Reg.25, see *R. (on the application of Beeson) v Dorset CC* [2002] EWCA Civ 1812, [2003] H.R.L.R. 11 (CA), Laws, L.J.

Reg.28, amended: SI 2002/814 Reg.2, SI 2003/627 Reg.4, SI 2003/897 Reg.2, SI 2003/931 Reg.5, SI 2004/760 Reg.4, SI 2004/1023 Reg.2, SSI 2004/103 Reg.3

Reg.28, referred to: SSI 2002/264 Art.2, SSI 2002/265 Reg.3, SSI 2002/266 Reg.2

Sch.2, applied: SI 2003/931 Reg.4, SSI 2002/265 Reg.3

Sch.2 para.3, amended: SI 2003/627 Reg.5, SI 2003/897 Reg.5, SSI 2003/156 Reg.3

NO.

1992–cont.

2977. National Assistance (Assessment of Resources) Regulations 1992–*cont.*

Sch.3, applied: SI 2003/931 Reg.4, SSI 2002/265 Reg.3

Sch.3 Part I para.10, amended: SI 2002/2531 Reg.3, SI 2003/897 Reg.6, SSI 2003/577 Reg.4

Sch.3 Part I para.10, substituted: SSI 2003/577 Reg.4

Sch.3 Part I para.17, amended: SI 2003/2343 Reg.3, SI 2003/2530 Reg.3

Sch.3 Part I para.28D, added: SI 2003/627 Reg.6, SI 2003/897 Reg.7, SSI 2003/156 Reg.4

Sch.3 Part I para.28E, added: SI 2003/627 Reg.6, SI 2003/897 Reg.7, SSI 2003/156 Reg.4

Sch.3 Part I para.28F, added: SI 2003/627 Reg.6, SI 2003/897 Reg.7, SSI 2003/156 Reg.4

Sch.3 Part I para.28G, added: SI 2003/627 Reg.6, SI 2003/897 Reg.7, SSI 2003/425 Reg.3

Sch.3 Part I para.28G, amended: SSI 2004/103 Reg.4

Sch.3 Part I para.28H, added: SI 2003/897 Reg.7, SI 2003/2343 Reg.3, SI 2003/2530 Reg.3, SSI 2003/425 Reg.3

Sch.3 Part I para.28H, amended: SI 2004/760 Reg.5, SI 2004/1023 Reg.3

Sch.3 Part I para.28I, added: SI 2003/2343 Reg.3, SI 2003/2530 Reg.3, SSI 2003/577 Reg.4

Sch.3 Part I para.28J, added: SI 2004/2328 Reg.3, SI 2004/2879 Reg.3, SSI 2004/389 Reg.2

Sch.3 Part II para.30, amended: SI 2002/2531 Reg.3, SI 2003/897 Reg.6, SSI 2003/577 Reg.4

Sch.4, applied: SI 2003/931 Reg.4, SSI 2002/265 Reg.3, SSI 2002/266 Reg.3

Sch.4 para.1A, applied: SI 2003/931 Reg.4, SSI 2002/265 Reg.2

Sch.4 para.1A, varied: SI 2003/969 Reg.2, SSI 2002/264 Art.2

Sch.4 para.2A, added: SI 2003/627 Reg.7, SI 2003/897 Reg.8, SSI 2003/156 Reg.5

Sch.4 para.6, amended: SI 2002/2531 Reg.4, SI 2003/897 Reg.8

Sch.4 para.6, substituted: SSI 2003/69 Reg.2

Sch.4 para.6A, added: SI 2003/627 Reg.7, SI 2003/897 Reg.8, SSI 2003/156 Reg.5

Sch.4 para.10, see *B (A Child) v Todd* [2002] P.I.Q.R. P11 (QBD), Stanley Burnton, J.

Sch.4 para.19, see *B (A Child) v Todd* [2002] P.I.Q.R. P11 (QBD), Stanley Burnton, J.

Sch.4 para.22, added: SI 2003/627 Reg.7, SI 2003/897 Reg.8, SSI 2003/156 Reg.5

Sch.4 para.23, added: SI 2003/627 Reg.7, SI 2003/897 Reg.8, SSI 2003/577 Reg.5

NO.

2977. National Assistance (Assessment of Resources) Regulations 1992–*cont.*

Sch.4 para.24, added: SI 2003/897 Reg.8, SI 2003/2343 Reg.4, SI 2003/2530 Reg.4, SSI 2004/389 Reg.3

Sch.4 para.25, added: SI 2004/2328 Reg.4, SI 2004/2879 Reg.4, SSI 2004/389 Reg.3

Sch.4 para.26, added: SI 2004/2328 Reg.4, SI 2004/2879 Reg.4

2984. New Roads and Street Works Act 1991 (Commencement No.5 and Transitional Provisions and Savings) Order 1992

Part II Art.10, see *Road Management Services (A13) Plc v London Power Networks Plc* [2003] B.L.R. 303 (QBD (T&CC)), Forbes, J.

2992. Licensing of Air Carriers Regulations 1992

applied: SI 2003/1400 Sch.4

Reg.2, amended: SI 2004/1256 Reg.3

Reg.18, amended: SI 2004/1256 Reg.3

2993. Access for Community Air Carriers to Intra-Community Air Routes Regulations 1992

Reg.2, amended: SI 2004/1256 Reg.4

Reg.4A, added: SI 2004/1256 Reg.4

Reg.5, amended: SI 2004/1256 Reg.4

Reg.6A, added: SI 2004/1256 Reg.4

2994. Air Fares Regulations 1992

Reg.2, amended: SI 2004/1256 Reg.5

3004. Workplace (Health, Safety and Welfare) Regulations 1992

see *Croft v Royal Mail Group Plc* [2002] I.R.L.R. 851 (EAT), Lindsay, J. (President); see *Gallagher v Kleinwort Benson (Trustees) Ltd* 2003 S.C.L.R. 384 (OH), Lord Reed; see *Purdie v Glasgow City Council* 2002 Rep. L.R. 26 (OH), Lord Hamilton

Reg.2, amended: SI 2002/2174 Reg.6

Reg.4, see *Mathieson v Aberdeenshire Council* 2003 S.L.T. (Sh Ct) 91 (Sh Ct (Grampian, Highland and Islands)), Sheriff GK Buchanan

Reg.4A, added: SI 2002/2174 Reg.6

Reg.5, amended: SI 2002/2174 Reg.6

Reg.5, see *Butler v Grampian University Hospitals NHS Trust* 2002 S.L.T. 985 (OH), Lord Macfadyen

Reg.6, revoked (in part): SI 2002/2174 Reg.6, SI 2002/2776 Sch.7 Part 2

Reg.7, amended: SI 2002/2174 Reg.6

Reg.8, see *Miller v Perth and Kinross Council* 2002 Rep. L.R. 22 (OH), Lord Hamilton

Reg.10, see *Butler v Grampian University Hospitals NHS Trust* 2002 S.L.T. 985 (OH), Lord Macfadyen

Reg.11, see *Butler v Grampian University Hospitals NHS Trust* 2002 S.L.T. 985 (OH), Lord Macfadyen

NO.

3004. Workplace (Health, Safety and Welfare) Regulations 1992–*cont.*

Reg.12, see *Anderson v Newham College of Further Education* [2002] EWCA Civ 505, [2003] I.C.R. 212 (CA), Sedley, L.J.; see *Harper v Staffordshire CC* [2003] EWHC 283, (2003) 147 S.J.L.B. 176 (QBD), Judge Wilkie Q.C.; see *Layden v Aldi GmbH & Co KG* 2002 S.L.T. (Sh Ct) 71 (Sh Ct (South Strathclyde, Dumfries and Galloway)), KA Ross; see *McGhee v Strathclyde Fire Brigade* 2002 S.L.T. 680 (OH), Lord Hamilton; see *Nisbet v Chief Constable of Strathclyde* 2003 S.C. 324 (Ex Div), Lord Osborne, Lord Dawson, Lord Weir; see *Simmons v British Steel Plc* 2002 S.L.T. 711 (OH), Lord Hardie

Reg.13, see *Mathieson v Aberdeenshire Council* 2003 S.L.T. (Sh Ct) 91 (Sh Ct (Grampian, Highland and Islands)), Sheriff GK Buchanan

Reg.17, see *Wallis v Balfour Beatty Rail Maintenance Ltd* [2003] EWCA Civ 72, (2003) 147 S.J.L.B. 357 (CA), Morland, J.

Reg.24, amended: SI 2002/2174 Reg.6

Reg.25, amended: SI 2002/2174 Reg.6

Reg.25A, added: SI 2002/2174 Reg.6

3006. Companies (Forms) (Amendment) Regulations 1992

Sch.2, applied: SI 2002/691 Reg.3

3045. Horses (Zootechnical Standards) Regulations 1992

Reg.3, applied: SI 2004/1397 Reg.3

3046. National Health Service (Superannuation, Premature Retirement and Injury Benefits) (Scotland) Amendment Regulations 1992

Reg.14, revoked: SSI 2003/344 Sch.2

Reg.15, revoked: SSI 2003/344 Sch.2

Reg.16, revoked: SSI 2003/344 Sch.2

3067. Asbestos (Prohibitions) Regulations 1992

applied: SI 2002/221 Sch.5 para.15, SI 2004/1964 Sch.6 para.14

disapplied: SI 2002/221 Sch.5 para.15

Reg.2, amended: SI 2003/1889 Reg.2

Reg.3, amended: SI 2003/1889 Reg.3

3068. Control of Asbestos at Work (Amendment) Regulations 1992

revoked: SI 2002/2675 Reg.27

3069. School Teachers Remuneration, Professional Duties and Working Time Order 1992

revoked: 2002 c.32 Sch.22 Part 1

3070. School Teachers Pay and Conditions Act 1991 (Commencement No.4) Order 1992

revoked: 2002 c.32 Sch.22 Part 1

3073. Supply of Machinery (Safety) Regulations 1992

referred to: SI 2004/693 Sch.1

NO.

1992–cont.

3073. Supply of Machinery (Safety) Regulations 1992–*cont.*

Reg.29, see *R. (on the application of Junttan Oy) v Bristol Magistrates Court* [2003] UKHL 55, [2004] 2 All E.R. 555 (HL), Lord Hobhouse of Woodborough

Sch.6 para.3, amended: SI 2004/693 Sch.2

Sch.6 para.3, revoked (in part): SI 2004/693 Sch.2

3078. Forest Reproductive Material (Amendment) Regulations 1992

revoked: SI 2002/3026 Reg.35

3082. Non-Domestic Rating Contributions (England) Regulations 1992

Sch.1, referred to: SI 2002/3021 Reg.2, SI 2003/3130 Reg.2

Sch.1 Part 1 para.1, amended: SI 2002/3021 Reg.3, SI 2003/3130 Reg.3

Sch.1 Part 1 para.3, amended: SI 2003/3130 Reg.3

Sch.1 Part 1 para.4, amended: SI 2002/3021 Reg.3, SI 2003/3130 Reg.3

Sch.1 Part II, substituted: SI 2002/3021 Reg.3, SI 2003/3130 Reg.3

Sch.2, referred to: SI 2002/3021 Reg.2, SI 2003/3130 Reg.2

Sch.2 Part 1 para.2, amended: SI 2002/3021 Reg.4, SI 2003/3130 Reg.4

Sch.2 Part 1 para.3, amended: SI 2003/3130 Reg.4

Sch.2 Part 1 para.4, amended: SI 2003/3130 Reg.4

Sch.2 Part 1 para.8, amended: SI 2002/3021 Reg.4, SI 2003/3130 Reg.4

3121. Value Added Tax (Place of Supply of Services) Order 1992

referred to: SI 2003/862 Art.2

Art.16A, added: SI 2003/862 Art.3

Art.17, amended: SI 2003/862 Art.4, Art.5

Art.18, amended: SI 2003/862 Art.5

3122. Value Added Tax (Cars) Order 1992

Art.2, amended: SI 2004/3084 Art.2

Art.2, revoked (in part): SI 2004/3084 Art.2

Art.4, see *General Motors Acceptance Corp (UK) Plc v Customs and Excise Commissioners* [2004] EWHC 192, [2004] S.T.C. 577 (Ch D), Field, J.

Art.8, see *Ball v Customs and Excise Commissioners* [2002] S.T.I. 1527 (V&DTr), CP Bishopp (Chairman)

Art.8, amended: SI 2002/1502 Art.2

Art.8, revoked (in part): SI 2002/1502 Art.2

3135. Excise Goods (Holding, Movement, Warehousing and REDS) Regulations 1992

referred to: SI 2004/1003 Reg.7

Reg.2, amended: SI 2002/501 Reg.28, SI 2002/2692 Reg.2

Reg.2, varied: SI 2003/2758 Sch.1 para.1, Sch.1 para.2, SI 2004/2064 Reg.6

NO.

1992–cont.

3135. Excise Goods (Holding, Movement, Warehousing and REDS) Regulations 1992–*cont.*

Reg.4, see *Greenalls Management Ltd v Customs and Excise Commissioners* [2002] EWHC 1691, [2002] 1 W.L.R. 3333 (Ch D), Jacob, J.; see *Greenalls Management Ltd v Customs and Excise Commissioners* [2003] EWCA Civ 896, [2003] 1 W.L.R. 2609 (CA), Schiemann, L.J.

Reg.4, amended: SI 2002/2692 Reg.2, SI 2004/1003 Reg.8

Reg.4, varied: SI 2003/2758 Sch.1 para.3

Reg.5, see *Greenalls Management Ltd v Customs and Excise Commissioners* [2003] EWCA Civ 896, [2003] 1 W.L.R. 2609 (CA), Schiemann, L.J.

Reg.5, amended: SI 2002/501 Reg.28, SI 2002/2692 Reg.2

Reg.5, revoked (in part): SI 2002/501 Reg.28

Reg.7, revoked (in part): SI 2002/501 Reg.28

Reg.10, amended: SI 2002/501 Reg.28

Reg.10, varied: SI 2004/2064 Reg.6

Reg.11, amended: SI 2002/501 Reg.28

Reg.11, revoked (in part): SI 2002/501 Reg.28

Reg.15, revoked (in part): SI 2002/501 Reg.28

3139. Personal Protective Equipment (EC Directive) Regulations 1992

revoked: SI 2002/1144 Sch.11 para.1

3146. Active Implantable Medical Devices Regulations 1992

revoked: SI 2002/618 Reg.66

Sch.2 para.10, amended: SI 2002/236 Reg.6

3147. Social Security Benefits (Amendments Consequential Upon the Introduction of Community Care) Regulations 1992

Sch.1 para.8, revoked (in part): SI 2003/492 Sch.3 Part 1

3152. Excise Duties (Deferred Payment) Regulations 1992

referred to: SI 2004/2065 Reg.19

Reg.2, amended: SI 2004/2065 Reg.5

Reg.3, amended: SI 2004/2065 Reg.5

Reg.5, amended: SI 2004/2065 Reg.5

Reg.5, applied: SI 2004/2065 Reg.19

Reg.6, amended: SI 2004/2065 Reg.5

Reg.6, applied: SI 2004/2065 Reg.23, Reg.24

Reg.11, amended: SI 2004/2065 Reg.5

3155. Excise Duties (Personal Reliefs) Order 1992

revoked: SI 2002/2691 Art.2

see *Gascoyne v Customs and Excise Commissioners* [2003] EWHC 257, [2003] Ch. 292 (Ch D), Neuberger, J.; see *Lindsay v Customs and Excise Commissioners* [2002] EWCA Civ 267, [2002] 1 W.L.R. 1766 (CA), Lord Phillips

NO.

1992–cont.

3155. Excise Duties (Personal Reliefs) Order 1992–*cont.*

see–*cont.*

of Worth Matravers, M.R.; see *R. (on the application of Hoverspeed Ltd) v Customs and Excise Commissioners* [2002] EWHC 1630, [2002] 3 W.L.R. 1219 (QBD (Admin Ct)), Brooke, L.J.

Art.2, see *Customs and Excise Commissioners v Newbury* [2003] EWHC 702, [2003] 1 W.L.R. 2131 (QBD (Admin Ct)), Hale, L.J.

3159. Specified Diseases (Notification and Slaughter) Order 1992

Art.2, amended: SI 2003/130 Art.18, SI 2003/326 Art.19, SSI 2003/91 Art.18

Art.4, revoked (in part): SSI 2003/353 Art.13

3170. Police (Scotland) Amendment (No.2) Regulations 1992

revoked: SSI 2004/257 Sch.4

3177. Ashford Hospitals National Health Service Trust (Change of Name) Order 1992

revoked: 2003 c.43 s.7

3182. Residential Accommodation (Determination of District Health Authority) Regulations 1992

Reg.2, amended: SI 2002/2469 Sch.5, Sch.11

3193. Customs and Excise Duties (Personal Reliefs for Goods Permanently Imported) Order 1992

varied: SI 2004/1002 Art.6

3204. Registered Homes (Northern Ireland) Order 1992

applied: SI 2004/1267 Sch.2 para.4, SR 2003/138 r.2, SR 2003/172 Reg.3

revoked: SI 2003/431 Sch.5

Part V, applied: SR 2003/138 r.14

Part V, referred to: SI 2003/417 Art.50

Art.10, applied: SR 2003/138 r.4, r.10

Art.16, applied: SI 2004/1267 Sch.2 para.4

Art.23, applied: SR 2003/138 r.4, r.10

Art.29, applied: SI 2003/417 Art.38

Art.30, amended: 2002 c.26 Sch.3 para.27

Art.30, applied: SI 2003/417 Art.50

Art.30, referred to: SI 2003/417 Art.50

Art.31, amended: 2002 c.26 Sch.3 para.28

Art.31, applied: SI 2003/417 Art.50

Art.32, amended: SI 2002/253 Sch.5 para.11

Art.33, applied: SI 2003/417 Art.50

Art.33, enabled: SR 2003/138

Art.34, applied: SI 2003/417 Art.50

Sch.1, applied: SI 2003/431 Sch.3 para.3

3222. Value Added Tax (Input Tax) Order 1992

Art.7, see *Crown & Cushion Hotel (Chipping Norton) Ltd v Customs and Excise Commissioners (Application for Permission to Appeal)* [2004] EWCA Civ 516, [2004] S.T.C. 1212 (CA), Waller, L.J.;

NO.

1992–cont.

3222. Value Added Tax (Input Tax) Order 1992–*cont.*

Art.7–*cont.*

see *Crown & Cushion Hotel (Chipping Norton) Ltd v Customs and Excise Commissioners* [2003] EWHC 1639, [2003] S.T.C. 1090 (Ch D), Lawrence Collins, J.; see *Customs and Excise Commissioners v Upton (t/a Fagomatic)* [2002] EWCA Civ 520, [2002] S.T.C. 640 (CA), Peter Gibson, L.J.; see *Customs and Excise Commissioners, Appellants* 2003 S.L.T. 1373 (Ex Div), Lord Marnoch, Lord Osborne, Lord Wheatley; see *Paterson v Customs and Excise Commissioners* [2002] S.T.I. 127 (V&DTr), T Gordon Coutts Q.C. (Chairman); see *Skellett (t/a Vidcom Computer Services) v Customs and Excise Commissioners* [2004] S.T.C. 201 (Ex Div), Lord Marnoch, Lord Osborne, Lord Wheatley

3230. Transport and Works (Descriptions of Works Interfering with Navigation) Order 1992

Art.2, enabled: SI 2003/2829

3232. Mallaig Harbour Revision Order 1992

Art.6, applied: SSI 2004/485 Art.8

Art.11, applied: SSI 2004/485 Art.8

3238. Non-Domestic Rating Contributions (Wales) Regulations 1992

Sch.2 Part I para.2, amended: SI 2002/3054 Reg.2, SI 2003/3211 Reg.2

Sch.4, substituted: SI 2002/3054 Sch.1, SI 2003/3211 Sch.1

3240. Environmental Information Regulations 1992

applied: SI 2003/3241 Reg.17

Reg.3, applied: SI 2003/750 Sch.5 para.12, SI 2003/751 Sch.6 para.12, SI 2004/1468 Sch.6 para.12

Reg.4, applied: SI 2002/2127 Reg.8, SI 2003/164 Reg.6, SSI 2002/6 Reg.8

3247. Disposal of Records (Scotland) Regulations 1992

Reg.4, amended: SSI 2003/522 Reg.2

3280. Genetically Modified Organisms (Deliberate Release) Regulations 1992

applied: SI 2002/2443 Reg.13, Reg.17, SI 2002/3188 Reg.14, Reg.18, SSI 2002/541 Reg.13, Reg.17

revoked (in part): SI 2002/2443 Sch.5, SI 2002/3188 Sch.5, SSI 2002/541 Sch.7

Reg.1, revoked: SSI 2002/541 Sch.7

Reg.2, revoked: SSI 2002/541 Sch.7

Reg.3, revoked: SSI 2002/541 Sch.7

Reg.4, revoked: SSI 2002/541 Sch.7

Reg.5, revoked: SSI 2002/541 Sch.7

Reg.6, revoked: SSI 2002/541 Sch.7

Reg.7, revoked: SSI 2002/541 Sch.7

Reg.8, revoked: SSI 2002/541 Sch.7

Reg.10, revoked: SSI 2002/541 Sch.7

NO.

1992–cont.

3280. Genetically Modified Organisms (Deliberate Release) Regulations 1992–*cont.*

Reg.11, revoked: SSI 2002/541 Sch.7

Reg.12, revoked: SSI 2002/541 Sch.7

Reg.14, referred to: SI 2002/800 Sch.1

Reg.14, revoked: SSI 2002/541 Sch.7

Reg.15, revoked: SSI 2002/541 Sch.7

Reg.16, applied: SI 2002/2443 Reg.17, SI 2002/3188 Reg.18, SSI 2002/541 Reg.17

Reg.16, referred to: SI 2002/800 Sch.1

Reg.16, revoked: SSI 2002/541 Sch.7

Reg.17, revoked: SSI 2002/541 Sch.7

Reg.18, revoked: SSI 2002/541 Sch.7

3287. Stamp Duty Reserve Tax (Amendment) Regulations 1992

varied: 2002 c.23 Sch.34 para.7, Sch.35 para.8

3288. Package Holidays and Package Tours Regulations 1992

see *Norfolk v My Travel Group Plc* [2004] 1 Lloyd's Rep. 106 (CC (Plymouth)), Judge Overend

3288. Package Travel, Package Holidays and Package Tours Regulations 1992

applied: SI 2003/1376 Sch.1, SI 2003/1400 Sch.3, Sch.4

referred to: SI 2003/1374 Sch.1

Reg.15, see *Lee v Airtours Holidays Ltd* [2004] 1 Lloyd's Rep. 683 (CC (Central London)), Judge Hallgarten Q.C.

Sch.2 para.2, revoked: SI 2003/1376 Art.3

Sch.3 para.7, revoked: SI 2003/1400 Sch.5

3289. Origin of Goods (Petroleum Products) (Amendment) Regulations 1992

revoked: SI 2002/2266 Reg.2

3301. Shellfish and Specified Fish (Third Country Imports) Order 1992

applied: SI 2004/853 Sch.6

3321. Yorkhill National Health Service Trust (Establishment) Order 1992

revoked: SSI 2004/107 Sch.2

1993

9. Rail Crossing Extinguishment and Diversion Orders Regulations 1993

Sch.1, amended: SI 2003/2155 Sch.1 para.35

22. Local Government Finance (Miscellaneous Provisions) (England) Order 1993

Art.3, applied: SI 2003/2613 Sch.1 para.8

27. Mayday Healthcare National Health Service Trust (Establishment) Order 1993

referred to: SI 2004/569 Sch.1

revoked: 2003 c.43 s.7

NO.

1993–cont.

28. Warrington Hospital National Health Service Trust (Establishment) Order 1993

revoked: 2003 c.43 s.7

29. West Midlands Ambulance Service National Health Service Trust (Establishment) Order 1993

referred to: SI 2004/569 Sch.1

revoked: 2003 c.43 s.7

Art.4, amended: SI 2003/2344 Art.2

34. North West London Mental Health National Health Service Trust (Establishment) Order 1993

revoked: 2003 c.43 s.7

69. Merchant Shipping (Navigational Equipment) Regulations 1993

revoked: SI 2002/1473 Sch.1 para.2

74. Copyright (Recording for Archives of Designated Class of Broadcasts and Cable Programmes) (Designated Bodies) Order 1993

referred to: SI 2003/2500 Sch.1 Part 1

Art.2, amended: SI 2003/2498 Sch.2

Art.3, amended: SI 2003/2498 Sch.2

80. A435 Trunk Road (Alcester to Gorcott Hill) De-Trunking Order 1993

revoked: SI 2004/2675 Art.2

81. A435 Trunk Road (Studley Bypass and Slip Roads) Order 1993

revoked: SI 2004/2679 Art.2

122. East Birmingham Hospital National Health Service Trust (Change of Name) Order 1993

revoked: 2003 c.43 s.7

123. Teddington Memorial Hospital National Health Service Trust (Establishment) Order 1993

revoked: 2003 c.43 s.7

152. Genetically Modified Organisms (Deliberate Release) Regulations 1993

referred to: SI 2002/2443 Sch.5, SI 2002/3188 Sch.5

revoked (in part): SI 2002/2443 Sch.5, SI 2002/3188 Sch.5, SSI 2002/541 Sch.7

155. North Mersey Community National Health Service Trust (Establishment) Amendment Order 1993

revoked: 2003 c.43 s.7

156. Shropshire's Mental Health National Health Service Trust (Establishment) Amendment Order 1993

revoked: 2003 c.43 s.7

157. Thameside Community Health Care National Health Service Trust (Change of Name) Order 1993

revoked: 2003 c.43 s.7

NO.

NO.

1993–cont.

1993–cont.

494. Council Tax (Deductions from Income Support) Regulations 1993–*cont.*

Reg.2, amended: SI 2002/3019 Reg.33

Reg.3, amended: SI 2002/3019 Reg.33

Reg.4, amended: SI 2002/3019 Reg.33

Reg.5, amended: SI 2002/3019 Reg.33

Reg.8, amended: SI 2002/3019 Reg.33

495. Deductions from Income Support (Miscellaneous Amendments) Regulations 1993

Reg.1, amended: SI 2003/492 Sch.3 Part 1

Reg.2, revoked (in part): SI 2003/492 Sch.3 Part 1

517. Common Agricultural Policy (Wine) Regulations 1993

applied: SSI 2002/325 Reg.7

523. National Health Service (Dental Services) (Miscellaneous Amendments) (Scotland) Regulations 1993

Reg.4, revoked: SSI 2003/158 Sch.4

539. Misuse of Drugs (Licence Fees) (Amendment) Regulations 1993

revoked: SI 2003/611 Sch.1

540. National Health Service (General Medical Services) Amendment Regulations 1993

revoked (in part): SI 2004/865 Sch.2, SI 2004/1016 Sch.2

543. Education (Teachers) Regulations 1993

applied: SI 2004/1729 Sch.2 para.14

varied: SI 2004/1744 Sch.1 para.2

Reg.10, see *Dorling v Sheffield City Council* [2002] E.L.R. 367 (Ch D), Patten, J.

Reg.14, applied: SI 2003/1662 Sch.1 para.1

Reg.15, applied: SI 2003/1662 Sch.1 para.2

Sch.2 Part I para.2, applied: SI 2003/1663 Sch.2 para.3

Sch.2 Part I para.3, applied: SI 2003/1662 Sch.2 para.11, SI 2004/1729 Sch.2 para.11

Sch.2 Part II, applied: SI 2003/1709 Art.5

Sch.3 para.3, applied: SI 2003/1662 Sch.1 para.4

577. Scottish Council for Postgraduate Medical and Dental Education Order 1993

revoked: SSI 2002/103 Art.7

Art.5, applied: SSI 2002/105

Sch.1 Part I, applied: SSI 2002/105

584. Child Support (Northern Ireland Reciprocal Arrangements) Regulations 1993

Reg.2, amended: SI 2002/771 Reg.2

Reg.2, revoked (in part): SI 2002/771 Reg.2

Sch.1A, referred to: SI 2002/771 Reg.3

Sch.1B, added: SI 2002/771 Sch.1

Sch.2, amended: SI 2002/771 Reg.4

Sch.3, added: SI 2002/771 Sch.2

586. National Blood Authority Regulations 1993

Reg.6, amended: SI 2004/696 Sch.1 para.14

592. Social Security (Northern Ireland) Order 1993

Art.4, applied: SI 2002/830, SI 2003/963, SI 2003/963 Art.5

Art.4, enabled: SI 2003/963, SI 2004/889

593. Reciprocal Enforcement of Maintenance Orders (Hague Convention Countries) Order 1993

Sch.1, amended: SI 2002/2838 Art.2

596. Veterinary Surgeons Qualifications (EEC Recognition) (Amendment) Order 1993

revoked: SI 2003/2919 Art.13

608. National Health Service (Travelling Expenses and Remission of Charges) Amendment Regulations 1993

revoked: SI 2003/2382 Sch.2

642. National Health Service (Travelling Expenses and Remission of Charges) (Scotland) Amendment Regulations 1993

revoked: SSI 2003/376 Sch.3 para.7

650. Social Security (Payments on account, Overpayments and Recovery) Amendment Regulations 1993

revoked (in part): SI 2003/492 Sch.3 Part 1

679. County of Wiltshire (Electoral Arrangements) Order 1993

revoked: SI 2004/2821 Art.5

693. Guy's and St Thomas National Health Service Trust (Establishment) Order 1993

revoked: 2003 c.43 s.7

694. Lewisham Hospital National Health Service Trust (Establishment) Order 1993

revoked: 2003 c.43 s.7

695. St Thomas Hospital National Health Service Trust Dissolution Order 1993

revoked: 2003 c.43 s.7

696. Guy's and Lewisham National Health Service Trust Dissolution Order 1993

revoked: 2003 c.43 s.7

697. Barts National Health Service Trust Dissolution Order 1993

revoked: 2003 c.43 s.7

698. King's Healthcare National Health Service Trust (Establishment) Amendment Order 1993

revoked: 2003 c.43 s.7

713. North Staffordshire Hospital Centre National Health Service Trust (Change of Name) Order 1993

revoked: 2003 c.43 s.7

743. Income Tax (Sub-contractors in the Construction Industry) Regulations 1993

referred to: SI 2003/536 Reg.2

Reg.2, amended: SI 2003/536 Reg.3, SI 2004/1075 Reg.3

Reg.7A, amended: SI 2002/2225 Reg.3

NO.

1993–cont.

743. Income Tax (Sub-contractors in the Construction Industry) Regulations 1993–*cont.*

Reg.7B, amended: SI 2002/2225 Reg.4

Reg.7C, amended: SI 2002/2225 Reg.5

Reg.8, applied: SI 2003/2682 Reg.70

Reg.8, substituted: SI 2004/1075 Reg.4

Reg.9, amended: SI 2003/536 Reg.4, SI 2004/1075 Reg.5

Reg.10, amended: SI 2003/536 Reg.5

Reg.12, amended: SI 2004/1075 Reg.6

Reg.13, amended: SI 2004/1075 Reg.6

Reg.14, amended: SI 2003/536 Reg.6

Reg.16, amended: SI 2004/1075 Reg.7

Reg.23A, amended: SI 2002/1397 Sch.1 para.24

Reg.24, amended: SI 2002/2225 Reg.6

Reg.25, amended: SI 2002/2225 Reg.7

Reg.41A, added: SI 2003/536 Reg.7

Reg.44B, added: SI 2003/536 Reg.8

Reg.44B, applied: SI 2003/2682 Reg.203

Reg.47, added: SI 2004/1075 Reg.8

Reg.48, added: SI 2004/1075 Reg.8

Reg.49, added: SI 2004/1075 Reg.8

Reg.50, added: SI 2004/1075 Reg.8

Reg.51, added: SI 2004/1075 Reg.8

Reg.52, added: SI 2004/1075 Reg.8

Reg.53, added: SI 2004/1075 Reg.8

Reg.53i, added: SI 2004/1075 Reg.8

744. Income Tax (Employments) Regulation 1993

Reg.49, see *Venables v Hornby (Inspector of Taxes)* [2002] EWCA Civ 1277, [2002] S.T.C. 1248 (CA), Chadwick, L.J.

744. Income Tax (Employments) Regulations 1993

applied: SI 2002/2820 Reg.4, SI 2003/2495 Reg.1, Reg.6, SI 2003/2682 Sch.1 para.10, SR 2002/379 Reg.4

referred to: 2003 c.1 s.710

revoked: SI 2003/2682 Sch.2

Reg.2, amended: SI 2002/680 Reg.4

Reg.2, applied: SI 2003/2682 Sch.1 para.16

Reg.2, revoked (in part): SI 2002/680 Reg.4

Reg.2A, added: SI 2002/680 Reg.5

Reg.2B, added: SI 2002/680 Reg.5

Reg.2C, added: SI 2002/680 Reg.5

Reg.2D, added: SI 2002/680 Reg.5

Reg.2D, amended: SI 2003/2494 Reg.3

Reg.2E, added: SI 2002/680 Reg.5

Reg.3, amended: SI 2003/2494 Reg.4

Reg.3, applied: SI 2003/2495 Reg.2

Reg.6, amended: SI 2002/680 Reg.6

Reg.7, see *Blackburn (Inspector of Taxes) v Keeling* [2003] EWCA Civ 1221, [2003] S.T.C. 1162 (CA), Carnwath, L.J.

Reg.13, amended: SI 2002/680 Reg.7

Reg.20, amended: SI 2002/680 Reg.8

Reg.20, applied: SI 2002/2172 Reg.3

Reg.23, applied: SI 2003/2495 Reg.1

1993–cont.

744. Income Tax (Employments) Regulations 1993–*cont.*

Reg.36, amended: SI 2002/1397 Sch.1 para.25

Reg.38, referred to: SI 2002/2172 Reg.6

Reg.39, referred to: SI 2002/2172 Reg.6

Reg.40, amended: SI 2003/2494 Reg.5

Reg.41, amended: SI 2003/536 Reg.9, SI 2003/2494 Reg.6

Reg.42, applied: SI 2003/2682 Sch.1 para.24

Reg.42A, added: SI 2003/2494 Reg.7

Reg.42B, added: SI 2003/2494 Reg.7

Reg.43, applied: SI 2003/2495 Reg.3, Reg.4

Reg.43, referred to: SI 2002/2172 Reg.6

Reg.46, applied: SI 2003/2682 Sch.1 para.17

Reg.46, referred to: SI 2003/2682 Sch.1 para.16, Sch.1 para.17

Reg.46AA, applied: SI 2003/2682 Sch.1 para.16

Reg.46ZC, added: SI 2003/2494 Reg.8

Reg.46ZD, added: SI 2003/2494 Reg.8

Reg.46ZE, added: SI 2003/2494 Reg.8

Reg.46ZF, added: SI 2003/2494 Reg.8

Reg.46ZG, added: SI 2003/2494 Reg.8

Reg.46ZH, added: SI 2003/2494 Reg.8

Reg.47, amended: SI 2003/2494 Reg.9

Reg.48, amended: SI 2003/2494 Reg.10

Reg.49, applied: SI 2003/2682 Sch.1 para.24

Reg.51, amended: SI 2003/2494 Reg.11

Reg.94, amended: SI 2002/1397 Sch.1 para.25

Reg.101, varied: SI 2003/2682 Sch.1 para.24

Reg.102, referred to: SI 2003/2495 Reg.4

Reg.106, applied: SI 2003/2682 Sch.1 para.26

Reg.107, applied: SI 2003/2682 Sch.1 para.26

Reg.108, applied: SI 2003/2682 Sch.1 para.26

751. Medicines Control Agency Trading Fund Order 1993

revoked: SI 2003/1076 Art.6

809. Devon Ambulance Service National Health Service Trust Dissolution Order 1993

revoked: 2003 c.43 s.7

810. Cornwall Community Healthcare National Health Service Trust Dissolution Order 1993

revoked: 2003 c.43 s.7

811. Walsgrave Hospitals National Health Service Trust (Establishment) Order 1993

revoked: 2003 c.43 s.7

812. Walsgrave Hospital National Health Service Trust Dissolution Order 1993

revoked: 2003 c.43 s.7

813. Cornwall Healthcare National Health Service Trust (Establishment) Order 1993

revoked: 2003 c.43 s.7

NO.

1993–cont.

813. Cornwall Healthcare National Health Service Trust (Establishment) Order 1993–*cont.*

Art.1, amended: SI 2002/1234 Art.2

Art.2, amended: SI 2002/1234 Art.2

814. Westcountry Ambulance Service National Health Service Trust (Establishment) Order 1993

referred to: SI 2004/569 Sch.1

revoked: 2003 c.43 s.7

822. Hinchingbrooke Health Care National Health Service Trust Dissolution Order 1993

revoked: 2003 c.43 s.7

823. Hinchingbrooke Health Care National Health Service Trust (Establishment) Order 1993

revoked: 2003 c.43 s.7

846. Social Security (Miscellaneous Provisions) Amendment Regulations 1993

Reg.4, revoked (in part): SI 2003/492 Sch.3 Part 1

848. Local Government (Direct Service Organisations) (Competition) Regulations 1993

revoked (in part): 2003 asp 1 s.60

893. Nurses, Midwives and Health Visitors (Professional Conduct) Rules 1993 Approval Order 1993

applied: SI 2004/1762 Art.2, Art.3, Art.4, Art.6, Art.9, Art.11

varied: SI 2004/1762 Art.1

Sch.1, amended: SI 2002/708 Sch.1, SSI 2002/142 Sch.1

Sch.1, applied: SI 2004/1762 Art.6, Art.7, Art.9, Art.10, Art.11

Sch.1, disapplied: SI 2004/1762 Art.6

Sch.1, referred to: SI 2004/1762 Art.8, Art.9, Art.10, Art.11

Sch.1, substituted: SI 2002/708 Sch.1, SSI 2002/59 Sch.1, SSI 2002/142 Sch.1

Sch.1, varied: SI 2004/1762 Art.4, Art.12

919. Act of Sederunt (Child Support Act 1991) (Amendment of Ordinary Cause and Summary Cause Rules) 1993

r.4, revoked: SSI 2002/132 Sch.2

938. Land Registry Trading Fund Order 1993

referred to: SI 2003/2094

Art.2, amended: SI 2003/2094 Art.2

Sch.1 para.1, substituted: SI 2003/2094 Sch.1

Sch.1 para.2, substituted: SI 2003/2094 Sch.1

Sch.1 para.3, substituted: SI 2003/2094 Sch.1

Sch.1 para.4, substituted: SI 2003/2094 Sch.1

Sch.1 para.5, substituted: SI 2003/2094 Sch.1

NO.

1993–cont.

938. Land Registry Trading Fund Order 1993–*cont.*

Sch.1 para.6, substituted: SI 2003/2094 Sch.1

961. Child Support Appeals (Jurisdiction of Courts) Order 1993

revoked (in part): SI 2002/1915 Art.2, SSI 2003/96 Art.6

994. National Health Service (Appointment of Consultants) (Scotland) Regulations 1993

applied: SSI 2002/103 Sch.1 Part III, SSI 2002/305 Sch.1 Part III, SSI 2002/534 Sch.1 Part III

996. Environmentally Sensitive Areas (Central Southern Uplands) Designation Order 1993

Art.4, applied: SSI 2004/381 Reg.4

Art.4A, applied: SSI 2004/381 Reg.4

Art.5, applied: SSI 2004/381 Reg.4

Art.5A, applied: SSI 2004/381 Reg.4

Art.5D, applied: SSI 2004/381 Reg.4

997. Environmentally Sensitive Areas (Western Southern Uplands) Designation Order 1993

Art.4, applied: SSI 2004/381 Reg.4

Art.4A, applied: SSI 2004/381 Reg.4

Art.5, applied: SSI 2004/381 Reg.4

Art.5A, applied: SSI 2004/381 Reg.4

Art.5D, applied: SSI 2004/381 Reg.4

1067. Airports Slot Allocation Regulations 1993

Reg.2, amended: SI 2004/1256 Reg.6

1069. Cornwall and Isles of Scilly Mental Handicap National Health Service Trust (Change of Name) Order 1993

revoked: 2003 c.43 s.7

1083. Peak Light Railway Order 1993

Art.6, amended: SI 2003/2155 Sch.1 para.18

1113. Social Security (Claims and Payments) Amendment (No.2) Regulations 1993

revoked (in part): SI 2003/492 Sch.3 Part 1

1155. Control of Pollution (Registers) (Scotland) Regulations 1993

Reg.2, amended: SSI 2003/168 Reg.9

Reg.7A, added: SSI 2003/168 Reg.9

1188. Serbia and Montenegro (United Nations Sanctions) Order 1993

Art.13, amended: 2002 c.8 s.2

1195. Serbia and Montenegro (United Nations Sanctions) (Dependent Territories) Order 1993

Art.12, amended: 2002 c.8 s.2

Art.13, amended: 2002 c.8 s.2

1213. Merchant Shipping (Local Passenger Vessels) (Masters Licences and Hours, Manning and Training) Regulations 1993

referred to: SI 2002/2934 Sch.1 Part 3

Reg.3, amended: SI 2002/2125 Sch.2 para.2

1993–cont.

1213. Merchant Shipping (Local Passenger Vessels) (Masters Licences and Hours, Manning and Training) Regulations 1993–*cont.*

Reg.11, revoked (in part): SI 2003/3049 Sch.2 para.1

1228. Beer Regulations 1993

Reg.4, amended: SI 2002/2692 Reg.3

Reg.13, amended: SI 2002/501 Reg.29, SI 2002/1265 Reg.2

Reg.15, amended: SI 2002/2692 Reg.3, SI 2004/1003 Reg.9

Reg.15, varied: SI 2003/2758 Sch.1 para.3

Reg.22, amended: SI 2002/1265 Reg.2

Reg.23, amended: SI 2002/1265 Reg.2

Sch.1, amended: SI 2002/1265 Reg.2

Sch.3, amended: SI 2002/1265 Reg.2

1244. Iraq (United Nations) (Sequestration of Assets) Order 1993

revoked: SI 2003/1519 Art.2

1245. Iraq (United Nations) (Sequestration of Assets) (Dependent Territories) Order 1993

revoked: SI 2003/1516 Art.2

Art.20, amended: SI 2003/2096 Sch.1 para.52

1250. Access to Health Records (Northern Ireland) Order 1993

Art.2, amended: SI 2004/311 Sch.1 para.15, Sch.2

Art.3, amended: SI 2004/311 Sch.1 para.15

Art.9, amended: SI 2004/311 Sch.1 para.15, Sch.2

Art.9, revoked (in part): SI 2004/311 Sch.1 para.15, Sch.2

1253. Serbia and Montenegro (United Nations Sanctions) (Channel Islands) Order 1993

Art.13, amended: 2002 c.8 s.2

1254. Serbia and Montenegro (United Nations Sanctions) (Isle of Man) Order 1993

Art.13, amended: 2002 c.8 s.2

1282. Treatment of Spruce Bark Order 1993

Sch.1, substituted: SI 2002/296 Sch.1

1283. Plant Health (Forestry) (Great Britain) Order 1993

varied: SI 2002/1478 Art.5, Art.6

Art.2, amended: SI 2002/295 Art.2, SI 2002/927 Art.2

Art.3, applied: SI 2002/1478 Sch.1

Art.12, applied: SI 2002/2589 Art.8

Art.12, referred to: SI 2002/1478 Art.4, SI 2002/2589 Art.8

Art.12, varied: SI 2002/1478 Art.4

Art.13, applied: SI 2002/2589 Art.8

Art.13, varied: SI 2002/1478 Art.4

Art.14, applied: SI 2002/2589 Art.7

Art.15, applied: SI 2002/2589 Art.7

Art.16, applied: SI 2002/2589 Art.7

1993–cont.

1283. Plant Health (Forestry) (Great Britain) Order 1993–*cont.*

Art.17, applied: SI 2002/2589 Art.7

Art.18, applied: SI 2002/2589 Art.7

Art.24, applied: SI 2002/2589 Art.11

Art.24, referred to: SI 2002/1478 Art.5, Art.6

Art.27, applied: SI 2002/2589 Art.11

Art.27, referred to: SI 2002/1478 Art.6

Art.28, amended: SI 2002/295 Art.2

Art.28A, applied: SI 2002/1478 Art.5, SI 2002/2589 Art.10

Art.28A, varied: SI 2002/1478 Art.5

Art.31, referred to: SI 2002/1478 Art.5, Art.6

Sch.2 Part A, applied: SI 2002/1478 Sch.1

Sch.3, applied: SI 2002/1478 Sch.1

Sch.4 Part A, applied: SI 2002/1478 Sch.1

Sch.4 Part A, referred to: SI 2002/2589 Sch.1

Sch.5 Part B, amended: SI 2002/295 Art.2, SI 2002/927 Art.2

Sch.6, substituted: SI 2002/295 Sch.1

Sch.7, revoked: SI 2002/295 Art.2

Sch.8, applied: SI 2002/2589 Art.7

1311. Seed Potatoes (Fees) (Scotland) Regulations 1993

revoked: SSI 2004/250 Reg.5

1317. Integrated Administration and Control System Regulations 1993

applied: SI 2002/646 Reg.3, SSI 2002/139 Sch.5 para.1, SSI 2003/129 Reg.1, Sch.7 para.1, SSI 2004/70 Reg.1, Sch.8 para.1, SSI 2004/381 Reg.3

Reg.2, amended: SI 2004/189 Reg.3

Reg.2A, amended: SI 2004/189 Reg.4

Reg.2C, amended: SI 2004/189 Reg.5

Reg.2F, added: SI 2004/189 Reg.6

Reg.9, amended: SI 2004/189 Reg.7

1320. Plant Health (Great Britain) Order 1993

applied: SI 2002/1299 Art.6, SI 2002/1350 Art.6, SI 2002/2573 Art.8, Art.12, Art.13, SI 2002/2762 Art.9, Art.12, SI 2004/1165 Reg.5, SI 2004/1452 Art.4, SI 2004/2697 Art.4, SSI 2002/223 Art.6, SSI 2002/483 Art.8, Art.13, SSI 2004/111 Reg.5, SSI 2004/255 Art.4, SSI 2004/488 Art.7

Art.2, amended: SI 2002/1067 Art.2, SI 2002/1805 Art.2, SI 2003/1157 Art.2, SI 2003/1851 Art.2, SI 2004/2365 Art.2, SSI 2002/164 Art.3, SSI 2003/224 Art.2, SSI 2004/440 Art.2

Art.3, amended: SI 2004/2365 Art.2, SSI 2004/440 Art.2

Art.3, applied: SI 2004/1165 Reg.3, SI 2004/2245 Reg.3

Art.9, amended: SI 2004/2365 Art.2, SSI 2004/440 Art.2

Art.11, amended: SI 2004/2365 Art.2, SSI 2004/440 Art.2

Art.11, varied: SI 2002/2573 Art.9, SI 2002/2762 Art.9, SI 2004/2590 Art.8, SSI 2002/483 Art.9, SSI 2004/488 Art.8

NO.

NO.

1993–cont.

1320. Plant Health (Great Britain) Order 1993–*cont.*

Art.12, applied: SI 2002/2573 Art.10, SI 2002/2762 Art.10, SI 2004/2590 Art.9, SSI 2002/483 Art.10, SSI 2004/488 Art.9

Art.12, varied: SI 2002/2573 Art.10, SI 2002/2762 Art.10, SI 2004/2590 Art.9, SSI 2002/483 Art.10, SSI 2004/488 Art.9

Art.13, applied: SI 2002/2573 Art.10, SI 2002/2762 Art.10, SI 2004/2590 Art.9, SSI 2002/483 Art.10, SSI 2004/488 Art.9

Art.14, applied: SI 2002/2573 Art.9, SI 2004/2590 Art.8, SSI 2002/483 Art.9, SSI 2004/488 Art.8

Art.14, varied: SI 2002/2573 Art.9, SI 2002/2762 Art.9, SI 2004/2590 Art.8, SSI 2002/483 Art.9, SSI 2004/488 Art.8

Art.15, applied: SI 2002/2573 Art.8, SI 2002/2762 Art.8, SI 2004/2590 Art.7, SSI 2002/483 Art.8, SSI 2004/488 Art.7

Art.16, applied: SI 2002/2573 Art.8, SI 2002/2762 Art.8, SI 2004/2590 Art.7, SSI 2002/483 Art.8, SSI 2004/488 Art.7

Art.17, applied: SI 2002/2573 Art.9, SI 2002/2762 Art.9, SI 2004/2590 Art.8, SSI 2002/483 Art.9, SSI 2004/488 Art.8

Art.22, applied: SI 2004/1165 Reg.5, SI 2004/1452 Art.4, SI 2004/2245 Reg.5, SI 2004/2697 Art.4, SSI 2004/111 Reg.2, Reg.5, SSI 2004/255 Art.4

Art.22, varied: SI 2004/2697 Art.4

Art.24, applied: SI 2004/1165 Reg.5, SI 2004/1452 Art.4, SI 2004/2245 Reg.5, SI 2004/2697 Art.4, SSI 2004/111 Reg.5, SSI 2004/255 Art.4

Art.24, varied: SI 2004/2590 Art.14, SSI 2004/488 Art.14

Art.25, applied: SI 2002/1299 Art.6, SI 2002/1350 Art.6, SI 2002/2573 Art.13, SI 2002/2762 Art.13, SI 2004/1165 Reg.5, Reg.6, SI 2004/1452 Art.4, SI 2004/2245 Reg.5, Reg.6, SI 2004/2697 Art.4, SSI 2002/223 Art.6, SSI 2002/483 Art.13, SSI 2004/111 Reg.5, Reg.6, SSI 2004/255 Art.4

Art.25, varied: SI 2004/2697 Art.4

Art.26, applied: SI 2004/1165 Reg.5, SI 2004/1452 Art.4, SI 2004/2245 Reg.5, SI 2004/2697 Art.4, SSI 2004/111 Reg.5, SSI 2004/255 Art.4

Art.26, varied: SI 2004/2590 Art.14, SSI 2004/488 Art.14

Art.27, applied: SI 2004/1165 Reg.5, SI 2004/1452 Art.4, SI 2004/2245 Reg.5, SI 2004/2697 Art.4, SSI 2004/111 Reg.5, SSI 2004/255 Art.4

Art.27, varied: SI 2004/2590 Art.14, SSI 2004/488 Art.14

Art.28, applied: SI 2002/2573 Art.13, SI 2002/2762 Art.13, SI 2004/1165 Reg.5, SI 2004/1452 Art.4, SI 2004/2245 Reg.5, SI 2004/2590 Art.13, SI 2004/

1993–cont.

1320. Plant Health (Great Britain) Order 1993–*cont.*

Art.28, applied:–*cont.*

2697 Art.4, SSI 2002/483 Art.13, SSI 2004/111 Reg.5, SSI 2004/255 Art.4, SSI 2004/488 Art.13

Art.28, varied: SSI 2004/488 Art.14

Art.30A, applied: SI 2002/2573 Art.12, SI 2002/2762 Art.12, SI 2004/2590 Art.11, SSI 2004/488 Art.11

Art.30A, varied: SI 2002/2573 Art.12, SI 2004/2590 Art.11, SSI 2002/483 Art.12, SSI 2004/488 Art.11

Art.32, applied: SI 2004/1165 Reg.5, SI 2004/1452 Art.4, SI 2004/2245 Reg.5, SI 2004/2697 Art.4, SSI 2004/111 Reg.5, SSI 2004/255 Art.4

Art.33, applied: SI 2004/1165 Reg.5, SI 2004/1452 Art.4, SI 2004/2245 Reg.5, SI 2004/2697 Art.4, SSI 2004/111 Reg.5, SSI 2004/255 Art.4

Sch.1 Part A, amended: SI 2003/1157 Art.2, SI 2003/1851 Art.2, SSI 2003/224 Art.2

Sch.1 Part A, substituted: SI 2003/1851 Art.2

Sch.1 Part B, amended: SI 2002/1067 Art.2, SI 2002/1805 Art.2, SI 2003/1157 Art.2, SI 2003/1851 Art.2, SI 2004/2365 Art.2, SSI 2002/164 Art.4, SSI 2003/224 Art.2, SSI 2004/440 Art.2

Sch.2 Part A, amended: SI 2003/1157 Art.2, SI 2003/1851 Art.2, SI 2004/2365 Art.2, SSI 2003/224 Art.2, SSI 2004/440 Art.2

Sch.2 Part B, amended: SI 2002/1067 Art.2, SI 2002/1805 Art.2, SI 2003/1157 Art.2, SI 2003/1851 Art.2, SI 2004/2365 Art.2, SSI 2002/164 Art.5, SSI 2003/224 Art.2, SSI 2004/440 Art.2

Sch.3 Part A, amended: SI 2004/2365 Art.2, SSI 2004/440 Art.2

Sch.3 Part B, amended: SI 2002/1067 Art.2, SI 2002/1805 Art.2, SI 2003/1157 Art.2, SI 2003/1851 Art.2, SI 2004/2365 Art.2, SSI 2002/164 Art.6, SSI 2003/224 Art.2, SSI 2004/440 Art.2

Sch.4 Part A, amended: SI 2003/1157 Art.2, SI 2003/1851 Art.2, SI 2004/2365 Art.2, SSI 2003/224 Art.2, SSI 2004/440 Art.2

Sch.4 Part A, applied: SI 2004/2245 Reg.3

Sch.4 Part A, disapplied: SI 2004/1165 Reg.3, SSI 2004/111 Reg.3

Sch.4 Part A, substituted: SSI 2003/224 Art.2

Sch.4 Part B, added: SI 2003/1851 Art.2

Sch.4 Part B, amended: SI 2003/1157 Art.2, SI 2004/2365 Art.2, SSI 2003/224 Art.2, SSI 2004/440 Art.2

Sch.4 Part B, revoked: SI 2003/1851 Art.2

Sch.4 Part B, substituted: SI 2003/1851 Art.2

Sch.5 Part A para.1, amended: SI 2004/2365 Art.2, SSI 2004/440 Art.2

NO.

NO.

1993–cont.

1320. Plant Health (Great Britain) Order 1993–*cont.*

Sch.5 Part A para.1, amended: SI 2003/1157 Art.2, SI 2003/1851 Art.2, SI 2004/2365 Art.2, SSI 2003/224 Art.2, SSI 2004/440 Art.2

Sch.5 Part A para.2, amended: SI 2003/1157 Art.2, SI 2003/1851 Art.2, SSI 2003/224 Art.2

Sch.5 Part B para.1, amended: SI 2003/1157 Art.2, SI 2003/1851 Art.2, SI 2004/2365 Art.2, SSI 2003/224 Art.2, SSI 2004/440 Art.2

Sch.5 Part B para.1, substituted: SI 2003/1157 Art.2, SI 2003/1851 Art.2, SSI 2003/224 Art.2

Sch.5 Part B para.2, substituted: SI 2003/1157 Art.2, SI 2003/1851 Art.2, SI 2004/2365 Art.2, SSI 2003/224 Art.2, SSI 2004/440 Art.2

Sch.5 Part B para.2, substituted: SI 2003/1157 Art.2, SI 2003/1851 Art.2, SSI 2003/224 Art.2

Sch.5 Part B para.3, amended: SI 2003/1157 Art.2, SI 2003/1851 Art.2, SSI 2003/224 Art.2

Sch.5 Part B para.3, substituted: SI 2004/2365 Art.2, SSI 2004/440 Art.2

Sch.5 Part B para.4, substituted: SI 2004/2365 Art.2, SSI 2004/440 Art.2

Sch.5 Part B para.6a, added: SI 2004/2365 Art.2, SSI 2004/440 Art.2

Sch.5 Part B para.7, amended: SI 2004/2365 Art.2, SSI 2004/440 Art.2

Sch.5 Part B para.8, amended: SI 2003/1157 Art.2, SI 2003/1851 Art.2, SI 2004/2365 Art.2, SSI 2003/224 Art.2, SSI 2004/440 Art.2

Sch.5A Part A para.1, added: SI 2004/2365 Art.2, SSI 2004/440 Art.2

Sch.5A Part A para.2, added: SI 2004/2365 Art.2, SSI 2004/440 Art.2

Sch.5A Part B para.1, added: SI 2004/2365 Art.2, SSI 2004/440 Art.2

Sch.5A Part B para.2, added: SI 2004/2365 Art.2, SSI 2004/440 Art.2

Sch.5A Part B para.3, added: SI 2004/2365 Art.2, SSI 2004/440 Art.2

Sch.5A Part B para.4, added: SI 2004/2365 Art.2, SSI 2004/440 Art.2

Sch.5A Part B para.5, added: SI 2004/2365 Art.2, SSI 2004/440 Art.2

Sch.5A Part B para.6, added: SI 2004/2365 Art.2, SSI 2004/440 Art.2

Sch.5A Part B para.7, added: SI 2004/2365 Art.2, SSI 2004/440 Art.2

Sch.8, amended: SI 2003/1157 Art.2, SI 2003/1851 Art.2, SI 2004/2365 Art.2, SSI 2003/224 Art.2, SSI 2004/440 Art.2

1353. Customs and Excise (Transit) Regulations 1993

Sch.1, applied: SI 2003/3113 Sch.1

1993–cont.

1507. Value Added Tax (Supply of Services) Order 1993

Art.3, amended: SI 2003/1055 Art.3

Art.3A, added: SI 2003/1055 Art.4

Art.3B, added: SI 2003/1055 Art.4

1520. Egg Products Regulations 1993

Sch.10 para.1, amended: SI 2004/2145 Reg.3, SI 2004/2731 Reg.3, SSI 2004/395 Reg.3

1543. First Community National Health Service Trust (Change of Name) Order 1993

revoked: 2003 c.43 s.7

1544. Mental Health Foundation of Mid Staffordshire National Health Service Trust (Change of Name) Order 1993

revoked: 2003 c.43 s.7

1571. European Communities (Designation) (No.2) Order 1993

varied: SI 2002/1819 Sch.3

1575. Iraq (United Nations) (Sequestration of Assets) (Isle of Man) Order 1993

revoked: SI 2003/1522 Art.2

1576. Family Law (Northern Ireland) Order 1993

Art.3, revoked: SI 2003/413 Sch.1

Art.12, enabled: SR 2002/137, SR 2003/75

Art.12, revoked (in part): SI 2003/435 Sch.5

Sch.2, amended: 2002 c.26 s.17, Sch.5 para.25

Sch.4, revoked: SI 2003/435 Sch.5

1578. Fire Services (Amendment) (Northern Ireland) Order 1993

Art.3, revoked: SI 2003/418 Sch.3

1607. Swanage Light Railway (Extension) Order 1993

Art.8, amended: SI 2003/2155 Sch.1 para.18

1622. Air Navigation (General) Regulations 1993

Reg.9, amended: SI 2002/733 Reg.3

Reg.10, amended: SI 2002/733 Reg.3

Reg.11, amended: SI 2002/733 Reg.3

Reg.17A, added: SI 2003/3286 Reg.3

Reg.18, amended: SI 2003/1365 Reg.3

Sch.1, amended: SI 2002/733 Reg.3

1636. Tower Hamlets Housing Action Trust (Area and Constitution) Order 1993

revoked: SI 2004/586 Art.7

1651. Tunbridge Wells and Eridge Light Railway Order 1993

Art.6, amended: SI 2003/2155 Sch.1 para.18

1678. Immigration (Transit Visa) Order 1993

revoked: SI 2003/1185 Sch.2

Art.2, amended: SI 2002/825 Art.2

Sch.1, amended: SI 2002/2758 Art.4

1760. Road Vehicles (Registration and Licensing) (Amendment) Regulations 1993

revoked: SI 2002/2742 Sch.1 Part I

NO.

1993–cont.

1780. Local Government Finance Act 1992 (Recovery of Community Charge) Saving Order 1993
Art.2, applied: 2002 c.16 Sch.2 para.27, Sch.2 para.29

1787. United Nations Arms Embargoes (Liberia, Somalia and the Former Yugoslavia) Order 1993
Art.2, amended: SI 2002/2628 Art.1
Art.3, amended: 2002 c.8 s.2
Art.7, amended: 2002 c.8 s.2
Art.8, amended: SI 2002/2628 Art.1
Sch.1 para.4, amended: SI 2002/2628 Art.1

1795. Hong Kong (British Nationality) (Amendment) Order 1993
amended: 2002 c.8 s.2
Art.2, amended: 2002 c.8 s.2
Art.3, amended: 2002 c.8 s.2
Sch.1, amended: 2002 c.8 s.2

1796. Immigration (Guernsey) Order 1993
Art.4, varied: SI 2003/2900 Art.3

1797. Immigration (Jersey) Order 1993
Art.4, varied: SI 2003/1252 Art.3
Sch.1 Part I para.18, varied: SI 2003/1252 Art.3

1798. Iraq (United Nations) (Sequestration of Assets) (Guernsey) Order 1993
revoked: SI 2003/1521 Art.2

1799. Iraq (United Nations) (Sequestration of Assets) (Jersey) Order 1993
revoked: SI 2003/1521 Art.2

1811. Cardiothoracic Centre-Liverpool National Health Service Trust (Establishment) Amendment Order 1993
revoked: 2003 c.43 s.7

1813. Channel Tunnel (International Arrangements) Order 1993
applied: SI 2002/2817 Reg.5
Sch.3 Part II para.3, amended: SI 2003/2799 Art.2
Sch.3 Part II para.4, revoked: SI 2003/2799 Art.2
Sch.3 Part II para.5, amended: SI 2003/2799 Art.2
Sch.3 Part II para.6, amended: SI 2003/2799 Art.2
Sch.4 para.5, disapplied: SI 2002/1241 Sch.1 para.22

1887. Norway Lobsters (Prohibition of Method of Fishing) Order 1993
revoked (in part): SI 2003/1855 Art.5

1898. Poultry Breeding Flocks and Hatcheries Order 1993
applied: SSI 2002/529 Art.3, Sch.1
Sch.2, applied: SSI 2002/529 Sch.1
Sch.2 Part I para.3, applied: SSI 2002/529 Sch.1

1909. Trade Union Ballots and Elections (Independent Scrutineer Qualifications) Order 1993
Art.7, substituted: SI 2002/2267 Art.2

NO.

1993–cont.

1932. Teddington Memorial Hospital National Health Service Trust (Establishment) Amendment Order 1993
revoked: 2003 c.43 s.7

1933. Money Laundering Regulations 1993
applied: SI 2003/3297 Reg.9
revoked: SI 2003/3075 Reg.1
Reg.2, referred to: SI 2003/3075 Reg.10
Reg.5, applied: SI 2003/171 Art.2, SI 2003/3075 Reg.10
Reg.13, amended: SI 2002/1555 Art.35, SI 2003/2096 Sch.1 para.53

1947. Tobacco Products Labelling (Safety) Amendment Regulations 1993
revoked: SI 2002/3041 Reg.16

1956. Act of Sederunt (Sheriff Court Ordinary Cause Rules 1993
r.16.2, see *Newman Shopfitters Ltd v MJ Gleeson Group Plc* 2003 S.L.T. (Sh Ct) 83 (Sh Pr), ID Macphail Q.C., Sheriff Principal; see *Samson v Fielding* 2003 S.L.T. (Sh Ct) 48 (Sh Pr), ID Macphail Q.C., Sheriff Principal

1956. Act of Sederunt (Sheriff Court Ordinary Cause Rules) 1993
r.2.1, see *Canmore Housing Association Ltd v Scott* 2003 S.L.T. (Sh Ct) 68 (Sh Pr), ID Macphail Q.C., Sheriff Principal; see *Drever v Drever* 2003 S.L.T. (Sh Ct) 8 (Sh Pr), Sir SST Young Q.C., Sheriff Principal; see *Graham Builders Merchants Ltd v Mann Engineering Ltd* 2003 S.C. 479 (1 Div), Lord Cullen L.P., Lord Abernethy, Lord MacLean
r.3., revoked: SSI 2002/132 Sch.2
r.3.3, see *Fab Tek Engineering Ltd v Carillion Construction Ltd* 2002 S.L.T. (Sh Ct) 113 (Sh Ct (Tayside, Central and Fife)), JS Forbes
r.3.5, see *Fab Tek Engineering Ltd v Carillion Construction Ltd* 2002 S.L.T. (Sh Ct) 113 (Sh Ct (Tayside, Central and Fife)), JS Forbes
r.4., revoked: SSI 2002/133 Sch.2
r.4.1, see *K and F, Applicants* 2002 S.L.T. (Sh Ct) 38 (Sh Pr), CGB Nicholson Q.C., Sheriff Principal
r.5.1, see *Fab Tek Engineering Ltd v Carillion Construction Ltd* 2002 S.L.T. (Sh Ct) 113 (Sh Ct (Tayside, Central and Fife)), JS Forbes
r.8.1, see *GMAC-RFA Ltd v Murray* 2003 Hous. L.R. 50 (Sh Pr), Sheriff Principal EF Bowen Q.C.
r.24.1, see *Trad Hire & Sales Ltd v Campbell* 2003 S.L.T. (Sh Ct) 41 (Sh Pr), BA Kerr Q.C., Sheriff Principal
r.33.7, see *Shields v Shields* 2002 S.C. 246 (Ex Div), Lord Marnoch, Lady Cosgrove, Lord Dawson
Sch.1, added: SSI 2004/197 r.2

NO.

1993–cont.

1956. Act of Sederunt (Sheriff Court Ordinary Cause Rules) 1993–*cont.*

Sch.1, amended: SSI 2002/560 Sch.3 para.4, SSI 2004/197 r.2

Sch.1, applied: SI 2002/1792 Sch.5 para.16

Sch.1, revoked: SSI 2004/197 r.2

Sch.1, substituted: SSI 2004/197 r.2

1957. Double Taxation Relief (Taxes on Income) (General) (Manufactured Overseas Dividends) Regulations 1993

revoked: SI 2003/2581 Reg.2

1976. Education (London Oratory School) (Exemption from Pay and Conditions Orders) Order 1993

revoked: 2002 c.32 Sch.22 Part 1

1998. Poultry Breeding Flocks, Hatcheries and Processed Animal Protein (Fees) Order 1993

revoked (in part): SI 2002/2875 Art.4, SSI 2002/529 Art.4

2004. Income Tax (Manufactured Overseas Dividends) Regulations 1993

Reg.2, amended: SI 2003/2582 Reg.3

Reg.3, amended: SI 2003/2582 Reg.4

Reg.3, revoked (in part): SI 2003/2582 Reg.4

Reg.4, amended: SI 2003/2582 Reg.5

Reg.4, referred to: SI 2003/3143 Reg.4

Reg.4, revoked (in part): SI 2004/2310 Sch.1 para.73

Reg.5, amended: SI 2003/2582 Reg.6, SI 2004/2310 Sch.1 para.73

Reg.5, referred to: SI 2003/3143 Reg.4

Reg.6, amended: SI 2003/2582 Reg.7, SI 2003/3143 Reg.5

Reg.7, amended: SI 2003/2582 Reg.8, SI 2003/3143 Reg.5

Reg.7, referred to: SI 2003/3143 Reg.4

Reg.7, revoked (in part): SI 2003/2582 Reg.8

Reg.8, amended: SI 2003/2582 Reg.9

Reg.9A, amended: SI 2003/2582 Reg.10

Reg.10, amended: SI 2003/2582 Reg.11

Reg.10, referred to: SI 2003/3143 Reg.4

Reg.14, amended: SI 2003/2582 Reg.12, SI 2003/3143 Reg.5

Reg.15, referred to: SI 2003/3143 Reg.4

2005. Cereal Seeds Regulations 1993

applied: SI 2002/3173 Reg.32

revoked (in part): SI 2002/3173 Reg.32

Reg.3, amended: SI 2003/56 Reg.2, SSI 2002/520 Reg.2, SSI 2002/564 Reg.3

Reg.8, amended: SI 2003/56 Reg.2, SSI 2002/520 Reg.2, SSI 2002/564 Reg.3

Reg.8, substituted: SSI 2002/520 Reg.2

Reg.9, amended: SI 2003/56 Reg.2, SSI 2002/520 Reg.2, SSI 2002/564 Reg.3

Reg.9, substituted: SSI 2002/520 Reg.2

Reg.9A, added: SSI 2002/520 Reg.2

Reg.9B, added: SI 2003/56 Reg.2, SSI 2002/520 Reg.2, SSI 2002/564 Reg.3

NO.

1993–cont.

2005. Cereal Seeds Regulations 1993–*cont.*

Reg.9C, added: SI 2003/56 Reg.2, SSI 2002/564 Reg.3

Sch.5 Part I para.8A, added: SI 2003/56 Reg.2, SSI 2002/520 Reg.2, SSI 2002/564 Reg.3

2006. Beet Seeds Regulations 1993

applied: SI 2002/3171 Reg.29

revoked (in part): SI 2002/3171 Reg.29

2007. Oil and Fibre Plant Seeds Regulations 1993

applied: SI 2004/2881 Reg.32, SSI 2004/317 Reg.22

revoked (in part): SI 2002/3174 Reg.32, SI 2004/2881 Reg.32, SSI 2004/317 Sch.8

Reg.3, amended: SI 2003/2529 Reg.3, SSI 2003/304 Reg.3

Reg.5, amended: SI 2003/2529 Reg.3, SSI 2003/304 Reg.3

Reg.5, applied: SSI 2004/317 Sch.2 para.4

Reg.8, amended: SI 2003/2529 Reg.3, SSI 2003/304 Reg.3

Reg.9, amended: SI 2003/2529 Reg.3, SSI 2003/304 Reg.3

Sch.4 Part I para.3A, added: SI 2003/2529 Reg.3, SSI 2003/304 Reg.3

Sch.4 Part I para.5A, added: SI 2003/2529 Reg.3, SSI 2003/304 Reg.3

Sch.4 Part I para.7, amended: SI 2003/2529 Reg.3, SSI 2003/304 Reg.3

Sch.4 Part I para.8, amended: SI 2003/2529 Reg.3, SSI 2003/304 Reg.3

Sch.4 Part II para.4, added: SI 2003/2529 Reg.3, SSI 2003/304 Reg.3

Sch.6 Part I, added: SI 2003/2529 Reg.3

Sch.6 Part I, amended: SSI 2003/304 Reg.3

2008. Vegetable Seeds Regulations 1993

revoked (in part): SI 2002/3175 Reg.32

2009. Fodder Plant Seeds Regulations 1993

referred to: SSI 2004/317 Reg.7

revoked (in part): SI 2002/3172 Reg.32

Reg.3, amended: SI 2003/56 Reg.3, SSI 2002/520 Reg.3, SSI 2002/564 Reg.4

Reg.8, amended: SI 2003/56 Reg.3, SSI 2002/520 Reg.3, SSI 2002/564 Reg.4

Reg.8, substituted: SSI 2002/520 Reg.3

Reg.9, amended: SI 2003/56 Reg.3, SSI 2002/520 Reg.3, SSI 2002/564 Reg.4

Reg.9, substituted: SSI 2002/520 Reg.3

Reg.9A, added: SSI 2002/520 Reg.3

Reg.9B, added: SI 2003/56 Reg.3, SSI 2002/520 Reg.3, SSI 2002/564 Reg.4

Reg.9C, added: SI 2003/56 Reg.3, SSI 2002/564 Reg.4

Sch.1, amended: SSI 2004/380 Reg.4

Sch.4 Part II para.6, amended: SSI 2004/380 Reg.5

Sch.5 Part I para.8A, added: SI 2003/56 Reg.3, SSI 2002/520 Reg.3, SSI 2002/564 Reg.4

NO.

1993–cont.

2009. Fodder Plant Seeds Regulations 1993–cont.

Sch.6 Part I, amended: SSI 2004/380 Reg.6
Sch.6 Part III, amended: SSI 2004/380 Reg.6

2049. National Health Service (Travelling Expenses and Remission of Charges) (Scotland) Amendment (No.2) Regulations 1993

revoked: SSI 2003/376 Sch.3 para.8

2072. Enforcement of Road Traffic Debts (Certificated Bailiffs) Regulations 1993

Sch.1 para.1, amended: SI 2003/1857 Reg.2
Sch.1 para.2, amended: SI 2003/1857 Reg.2
Sch.1 para.3, amended: SI 2003/1857 Reg.2
Sch.1 para.4, amended: SI 2003/1857 Reg.2
Sch.1 para.5, amended: SI 2003/1857 Reg.2
Sch.1 para.6, amended: SI 2003/1857 Reg.2
Sch.1 para.7, amended: SI 2003/1857 Reg.2
Sch.1 para.8, amended: SI 2003/1857 Reg.2

2073. Enforcement of Road Traffic Debts Order 1993

applied: SI 2004/3121 Sch.1
varied: SI 2003/300 Reg.22
Art.2, referred to: SI 2002/1808 Reg.22, SI 2003/300 Reg.22
Art.3, referred to: SI 2002/1808 Reg.22
Art.3, varied: SI 2003/300 Reg.22

2113. Social Security (Claims and Payments) Amendment (No.3) Regulations 1993

Reg.3, revoked (in part): SI 2003/492 Sch.3 Part 1

2153. Manchester, Liverpool Road (Castlefield Properties Limited) Light Railway Order 1993

Art.6, amended: SI 2003/2155 Sch.1 para.18

2154. East Kent Light Railway Order 1993

Art.2, amended: SI 2003/2155 Sch.1 para.19
Art.6, amended: SI 2003/2155 Sch.1 para.18

2166. Controlled Drugs (Substances Useful for Manufacture) (Intra-Community Trade) Regulations 1993

Sch.1 Part 2, amended: SI 2004/850 Reg.2
Sch.2, amended: SI 2004/850 Reg.2

2210. Dental Vocational Training Authority Regulations 1993

Reg.5, amended: SI 2004/696 Art.3, SI 2004/865 Sch.1 para.11, SI 2004/1016 Sch.1 para.11

2276. Income Tax (Employments) (Amendment) Regulations 1993

revoked: SI 2003/2682 Sch.2

2345. Environmentally Sensitive Areas (Cairngorms Straths) Designation Order 1993

Art.4, applied: SSI 2004/381 Reg.4
Art.4A, applied: SSI 2004/381 Reg.4
Art.5, applied: SSI 2004/381 Reg.4
Art.5A, applied: SSI 2004/381 Reg.4
Art.5D, applied: SSI 2004/381 Reg.4

NO.

1993–cont.

2355. Angola (United Nations Sanctions) Order 1993

revoked: SI 2003/1868 Sch.2
Art.5, amended: 2002 c.8 s.2
Art.6, amended: 2002 c.8 s.2

2356. Angola (United Nations Sanctions) (Dependent Territories) Order 1993

revoked: SI 2003/1868 Sch.2
Art.5, amended: 2002 c.8 s.2
Art.6, amended: 2002 c.8 s.2

2357. Angola (United Nations Sanctions) (Channel Islands) Order 1993

revoked: SI 2003/1868 Sch.2
Art.5, amended: 2002 c.8 s.2
Art.6, amended: 2002 c.8 s.2

2358. Angola (United Nations Sanctions) (Isle of Man) Order 1993

revoked: SI 2003/1868 Sch.2
Art.5, amended: 2002 c.8 s.2
Art.6, amended: 2002 c.8 s.2

2360. Clinical Thermometers (EEC Requirements) Regulations 1993

applied: SI 2003/1076 Sch.1 para.1

2407. Leasehold Reform (Collective Enfranchisement and Lease Renewal) Regulations 1993

Sch.1 para.2, revoked (in part): SI 2003/1990 Reg.3, SI 2004/670 Reg.3
Sch.2 para.4, amended: SI 2003/1990 Reg.3, SI 2004/670 Reg.3

2408. Rent Assessment Committee (England and Wales) (Leasehold Valuation Tribunal) Regulations 1993

revoked (in part): SI 2003/2099 Reg.25, SI 2004/681 Reg.25

2421. National Health Service (General Medical Services) Amendment (No.2) Regulations 1993

revoked (in part): SI 2004/865 Sch.2, SI 2004/1016 Sch.2

2529. Fodder Plant Seeds (Amendment) Regulations 1993

revoked (in part): SI 2002/3172 Reg.32

2538. Medicines (Applications for Grant of Product Licences-Products for Human Use) Regulations 1993

Reg.1, amended: SI 2002/236 Reg.7, SI 2003/2321 Reg.4
Reg.4, amended: SI 2002/236 Reg.7
Reg.4, revoked (in part): SI 2002/236 Reg.7
Sch.1 para.9, amended: SI 2002/236 Reg.7
Sch.1 para.10, amended: SI 2002/236 Reg.7
Sch.1 para.11, amended: SI 2002/236 Reg.7
Sch.1 para.17, amended: SI 2002/236 Reg.7, SI 2003/2321 Reg.4
Sch.1 para.18, amended: SI 2002/236 Reg.7, SI 2003/2321 Reg.4
Sch.1 para.21, amended: SI 2002/236 Reg.7
Sch.1 para.22, amended: SI 2002/236 Reg.7
Sch.2 para.1, amended: SI 2002/236 Reg.7

1993–cont.

2541. Birmingham Women's Health Care National Health Service Trust (Establishment) Order 1993
revoked: 2003 c.43 s.7

2542. Northern Birmingham Community Health National Health Service Trust (Establishment) Order 1993
revoked: 2003 c.43 s.7

2543. South Birmingham Community Health National Health Service Trust (Establishment) Order 1993
revoked: 2003 c.43 s.7

2544. Churchill John Radcliffe National Health Service Trust (Establishment) Order 1993
applied: SI 2003/3059 Sch.1, Sch.2
revoked: 2003 c.43 s.7

2545. City Hospital National Health Service Trust (Establishment) Order 1993
revoked: SI 2002/1364 Art.6, 2003 c.43 s.7

2546. Derbyshire Ambulance Service National Health Service Trust (Establishment) Order 1993
revoked: 2003 c.43 s.7

2547. Derbyshire Royal Infirmary National Health Service Trust (Establishment) Order 1993
revoked: 2003 c.43 s.7

2548. Dewsbury Health Care National Health Service Trust (Establishment) Order 1993
revoked: SI 2002/1341 Art.6, 2003 c.43 s.7

2549. East Wiltshire Health Care National Health Service Trust (Establishment) Order 1993
revoked: 2003 c.43 s.7

2550. East Yorkshire Community Healthcare National Health Service Trust (Establishment) Order 1993
revoked: 2003 c.43 s.7

2551. George Eliot Hospital National Health Service Trust (Establishment) Order 1993
applied: SI 2003/3059 Sch.1
revoked: 2003 c.43 s.7

2552. Hereford Hospitals National Health Service Trust (Establishment) Order 1993
revoked: 2003 c.43 s.7

2553. Hereford and Worcester Ambulance Service National Health Service Trust (Establishment) Order 1993
revoked: 2003 c.43 s.7

2554. Hull and Holderness Community Health National Health Service Trust (Establishment) Order 1993
revoked: 2003 c.43 s.7

1993–cont.

2555. Kent Ambulance National Health Service Trust (Establishment) Order 1993
revoked: 2003 c.43 s.7

2556. Kettering General Hospital National Health Service Trust (Establishment) Order 1993
revoked: 2003 c.43 s.7

2557. King's Mill Centre for Health Care Services National Health Service Trust (Establishment) Order 1993
revoked: 2003 c.43 s.7

2558. Leicestershire Ambulance and Paramedic Service National Health Service Trust (Establishment) Order 1993
revoked: 2003 c.43 s.7

2559. Leicestershire Mental Health Service National Health Service Trust (Establishment) Order 1993
revoked: 2003 c.43 s.7

2560. Lincoln Hospitals National Health Service Trust (Establishment) Order 1993
revoked: 2003 c.43 s.7

2561. Northampton General Hospital National Health Service Trust (Establishment) Order 1993
revoked: 2003 c.43 s.7

2562. Norwich Community Health Partnership National Health Service Trust (Establishment) Order 1993
revoked: 2003 c.43 s.7

2563. Nottingham Healthcare National Health Service Trust (Establishment) Order 1993
revoked: 2003 c.43 s.7

2564. Oxfordshire Ambulance National Health Service Trust (Establishment) Order 1993
revoked: 2003 c.43 s.7

2565. Oxfordshire Community Health National Health Service Trust (Establishment) Order 1993
revoked: 2003 c.43 s.7

2566. Oxfordshire Mental Healthcare National Health Service Trust (Establishment) Order 1993
applied: SI 2003/3059 Sch.1
revoked: 2003 c.43 s.7

2567. Pilgrim Health National Health Service Trust (Establishment) Order 1993
revoked: 2003 c.43 s.7

2568. Plymouth Hospitals National Health Service Trust (Establishment) Order 1993
referred to: SI 2004/569 Sch.2
revoked: 2003 c.43 s.7

NO.

1993–cont.

2569. Portsmouth Health Care National Health Service Trust (Establishment) Order 1993
revoked: SI 2002/1323 Sch.1, 2003 c.43 s.7

2570. Riverside Community Health Care National Health Service Trust (Establishment) Order 1993
revoked: SI 2002/1323 Sch.1, 2003 c.43 s.7

2571. Robert Jones and Agnes Hunt Orthopaedic and District Hospital National Health Service Trust (Establishment) Order 1993
revoked: 2003 c.43 s.7
Art.4, amended: SI 2003/2149 Art.2

2572. Rockingham Forest National Health Service Trust (Establishment) Order 1993
revoked: 2003 c.43 s.7

2573. Royal Shrewsbury Hospitals National Health Service Trust (Establishment) Order 1993
revoked: 2003 c.43 s.7, SI 2003/2346 Art.6

2574. Royal Wolverhampton Hospitals National Health Service Trust (Establishment) Order 1993
revoked: 2003 c.43 s.7

2575. Salisbury Health Care National Health Service Trust (Establishment) Order 1993
revoked: 2003 c.43 s.7

2576. Solihull Healthcare National Health Service Trust (Establishment) Order 1993
revoked: 2003 c.43 s.7

2577. Stoke Mandeville Hospital National Health Service Trust (Establishment) Order 1993
revoked: SI 2002/2419 Art.8, 2003 c.43 s.7

2578. Wandsworth Community Health National Health Service Trust (Establishment) Order 1993
revoked: 2003 c.43 s.7

2579. Warwickshire Ambulance Service National Health Service Trust-(Establishment) Order 1993
revoked: 2003 c.43 s.7
Art.1, amended: SI 2004/864 Art.2
Art.2, amended: SI 2004/864 Art.2
Art.3, amended: SI 2004/2896 Art.2
Art.4, amended: SI 2004/2896 Art.3

2580. South Warwickshire Mental Health National Health Service Trust (Establishment) Order 1993
revoked: 2003 c.43 s.7

2581. Winchester and Eastleigh Healthcare National Health Service Trust (Establishment) Order 1993
revoked: 2003 c.43 s.7

1993–cont.

2582. Worcester Royal Infirmary National Health Service Trust (Establishment) Order 1993
revoked: 2003 c.43 s.7

2589. Chichester Priority Care Services National Health Service Trust (Establishment) Order 1993
revoked: SI 2002/1362 Art.6, 2003 c.43 s.7

2590. Mental Health Services of Salford National Health Service Trust (Establishment) Order 1993
revoked: 2003 c.43 s.7, SI 2003/759 Art.6

2591. Hartlepool Community Care National Health Service Trust (Establishment) Order 1993
revoked: 2003 c.43 s.7

2592. Blackburn, Hyndburn and Ribble Valley Health Care National Health Service Trust (Establishment) Order 1993
revoked: SI 2002/2073 Art.8, 2003 c.43 s.7

2593. Northumberland Community Health National Health Service Trust (Establishment) Order 1993
revoked: 2003 c.43 s.7

2594. North Manchester Healthcare National Health Service Trust (Establishment) Order 1993
revoked: SI 2002/308 Art.8, 2003 c.43 s.7

2595. Community Healthcare Bolton National Health Service Trust (Establishment) Order 1993
revoked: SI 2002/1492 Art.2, 2003 c.43 s.7

2596. CommuniCare National Health Service Trust (Establishment) Order 1993
revoked (in part): SI 2002/1500 Art.2, 2003 c.43 s.7

2597. Blackpool, Wyre and Fylde Community Health Services National Health Service Trust (Establishment) Order 1993
revoked: SI 2002/1243 Art.6, 2003 c.43 s.7

2598. Blackpool Victoria Hospital National Health Service Trust (Establishment) Order 1993
revoked: SI 2002/1243 Art.6, 2003 c.43 s.7

2599. Bury Health Care National Health Service Trust (Establishment) Order 1993
revoked: SI 2002/308 Art.8, 2003 c.43 s.7

2600. Greater Manchester Ambulance Service National Health Service Trust (Establishment) Order 1993
referred to: SI 2004/569 Sch.1
revoked: 2003 c.43 s.7

2601. Lancashire Ambulance Service National Health Service Trust (Establishment) Order 1993
referred to: SI 2004/569 Sch.1
revoked: 2003 c.43 s.7

NO.

2602. Tameside and Glossop Acute Services National Health Service Trust (Establishment) Order 1993
revoked: 2003 c.43 s.7

2603. Darlington Memorial Hospital National Health Service Trust (Establishment) Order 1993
revoked: 2003 c.43 s.7

2604. Bolton Hospitals National Health Service Trust (Establishment) Order 1993
revoked: 2003 c.43 s.7

2605. Priority Healthcare Wearside National Health Service Trust (Establishment) Order 1993
revoked: SI 2002/1324 Art.6, 2003 c.43 s.7

2606. Community Health Care Service (North Derbyshire) National Health Service Trust (Establishment) Order 1993
revoked: SI 2002/1296 Art.4, 2003 c.43 s.7

2607. Wirral Community Healthcare National Health Service Trust (Establishment) Order 1993
revoked: 2003 c.43 s.7

2608. North Lakeland Healthcare National Health Service Trust (Establishment) Order 1993
revoked: 2003 c.43 s.7

2609. North Downs Community Health National Health Service Trust (Establishment) Order 1993
revoked: 2003 c.43 s.7

2610. South Durham Health Care National Health Service Trust (Establishment) Order 1993
revoked: 2003 c.43 s.7

2611. Salford Community Health Care National Health Service Trust (Establishment) Order 1993
revoked: 2003 c.43 s.7

2612. Community Health Care North Durham National Health Service Trust (Establishment) Order 1993
revoked: 2003 c.43 s.7

2613. Kingston and District Community National Health Service Trust (Establishment) Order 1993
revoked: 2003 c.43 s.7

2614. North Durham Acute Hospitals National Health Service Trust (Establishment) Order 1993
revoked: 2003 c.43 s.7

2615. Northampton Community Healthcare National Health Service Trust (Establishment) Order 1993
revoked: 2003 c.43 s.7

2616. Bishop Auckland Hospitals National Health Service Trust (Establishment) Order 1993
revoked: 2003 c.43 s.7

NO.

2617. Carlisle Hospitals National Health Service Trust (Establishment) Order 1993
revoked: 2003 c.43 s.7

2618. Cheviot and Wansbeck National Health Service Trust (Establishment) Order 1993
revoked: 2003 c.43 s.7

2619. City Hospitals Sunderland National Health Service Trust (Establishment) Order 1993
revoked: 2003 c.43 s.7

2620. West Cheshire National Health Service Trust (Establishment) Order 1993
revoked: 2003 c.43 s.7

2621. South Kent Community Healthcare National Health Service Trust (Establishment) Order 1993
revoked: 2003 c.43 s.7

2622. Stockport Acute Services National Health Service Trust (Establishment) Order 1993
revoked: 2003 c.43 s.7

2623. Guild Community Healthcare National Health Service Trust (Establishment) Order 1993
revoked: 2003 c.43 s.7

2624. North Tyneside Health Care National Health Service Trust (Establishment) Order 1993
revoked: 2003 c.43 s.7

2625. Preston Acute Hospitals National Health Service Trust (Establishment) Order 1993
revoked: SI 2002/2025 Art.6, 2003 c.43 s.7

2626. Tameside and Glossop Community and Priority Services National Health Service Trust (Establishment) Order 1993
revoked: 2003 c.43 s.7

2627. Hartlepool and Peterlee Hospitals National Health Service Trust (Establishment) Order 1993
revoked: 2003 c.43 s.7

2628. Stockport Healthcare National Health Service Trust (Establishment) Order 1993
revoked: 2003 c.43 s.7

2629. New Possibilities National Health Service Trust (Establishment) Order 1993
revoked: 2003 c.43 s.7, SI 2003/868 Art.2

2630. Shropshire's Community Health Service National Health Service Trust (Establishment) Order 1993
revoked: 2003 c.43 s.7

2633. South East London Mental Health National Health Service Trust (Establishment) Order 1993
revoked: 2003 c.43 s.7

NO.

1993–cont.

2634. Haringey Health Care National Health Service Trust (Establishment) Order 1993
revoked: 2003 c.43 s.7

2635. North Staffordshire Combined Healthcare National Health Service Trust (Establishment) Order 1993
revoked: 2003 c.43 s.7

2636. Lincoln District Healthcare National Health Service Trust (Establishment) Order 1993
revoked: 2003 c.43 s.7

2637. Swindon and Marlborough National Health Service Trust (Establishment) Order 1993
revoked: 2003 c.43 s.7

2638. Louth and District Healthcare National Health Service Trust (Establishment) Order 1993
revoked: 2003 c.43 s.7

2639. North Kent Healthcare National Health Service Trust (Establishment) Order 1993
revoked: 2003 c.43 s.7

2640. Medway National Health Service Trust (Establishment) Order 1993
revoked: 2003 c.43 s.7

2641. Queen Victoria Hospital National Health Service Trust (Establishment) Order 1993
revoked: 2003 c.43 s.7

2642. Dartford and Gravesham National Health Service Trust (Establishment) Order 1993
applied: SI 2003/3059 Sch.1
revoked: 2003 c.43 s.7

2643. Worthing and Southlands Hospitals National Health Service Trust (Establishment) Order 1993
revoked: 2003 c.43 s.7

2657. Norfolk Mental Health Care National Health Service Trust (Establishment) Order 1993
revoked: 2003 c.43 s.7
Art.1, amended: SI 2004/1626 Art.2
Art.2, amended: SI 2004/1626 Art.2
Art.3, amended: SI 2004/1626 Art.3

2665. Agriculture (Northern Ireland) Order 1993
Art.17, enabled: SR 2002/151
Art.30, enabled: SR 2002/151

2687. Employment Tribunals (Constitution and Procedure) Regulations 1993
r.11, see *Zietsman (t/a Berkshire Orthodontics) v Stubbington* [2002] I.C.R. 249 (EAT), Judge Peter Clark
r.20, see *Zietsman (t/a Berkshire Orthodontics) v Stubbington* [2002] I.C.R. 249 (EAT), Judge Peter Clark

NO.

1993–cont.

2687. Employment Tribunals (Constitution and Rules of Procedure) Regulations 1993
r.10, see *Scotford v Smithkline Beecham* [2002] I.C.R. 264 (EAT), Recorder Langstaff Q.C.
r.13, see *Andreou v Lord Chancellor's Department* [2002] EWCA Civ 1192, [2002] I.R.L.R. 728 (CA), Peter Gibson, L.J.
r.20, see *Scotford v Smithkline Beecham* [2002] I.C.R. 264 (EAT), Recorder Langstaff Q.C.
Reg.8, applied: SI 2002/655 Reg.22
Reg.12, see *Gee v Shell UK Ltd* [2002] EWCA Civ 1479, [2003] I.R.L.R. 82 (CA), Scott Baker, L.J.
Sch.1 para.9, see *Roberts v Skelmersdale College* [2003] EWCA Civ 954, [2003] I.C.R. 1127 (CA), Mummery, L.J.
Sch.1 r.12, see *Kovacs v Queen Mary & Westfield College* [2002] EWCA Civ 352, [2002] I.C.R. 919 (CA), Simon Brown, L.J.
Sch.4, applied: SI 2002/655 Reg.22

2688. Employment Tribunals (Constitution and Rules of Procedure) (Scotland) Regulations 1993
Reg.8, applied: SI 2002/655 Reg.22
Sch.4, applied: SI 2002/655 Reg.22

2732. Teachers (Education, Training and Recommendation for Registration) (Scotland) Regulations 1993
Reg.3, revoked (in part): SSI 2004/390 Reg.3
Reg.6, revoked (in part): SSI 2004/390 Reg.3

2755. Copyright (Certification of Licensing Scheme for Educational Recording of Broadcasts) (Open University Educational Enterprises Limited) Order 1993
revoked: SI 2003/187 Art.4
Sch.1, applied: SI 2003/187 Art.5
Sch.1, disapplied: SI 2003/187 Sch.1
Sch.1, referred to: SI 2003/187

2767. Environmentally Sensitive Areas (Central Borders) Designation Order 1993
Art.4, applied: SSI 2004/381 Reg.4
Art.4A, applied: SSI 2004/381 Reg.4
Art.5, applied: SSI 2004/381 Reg.4
Art.5A, applied: SSI 2004/381 Reg.4
Art.5D, applied: SSI 2004/381 Reg.4

2768. Environmentally Sensitive Areas (Stewartry) Designation Order 1993
Art.4, applied: SSI 2004/381 Reg.4
Art.4A, applied: SSI 2004/381 Reg.4
Art.5, applied: SSI 2004/381 Reg.4
Art.5A, applied: SSI 2004/381 Reg.4
Art.5D, applied: SSI 2004/381 Reg.4

NO.

1993–cont.

2807. Libya (United Nations Sanctions) Order 1993
Art.14, amended: 2002 c.8 s.2

2808. Libya (United Nations Sanctions) (Dependent Territories) Order 1993
Art.14, amended: 2002 c.8 s.2

2810. Education and Libraries (Northern Ireland) Order 1993
Part II, revoked: SI 2003/424 Art.16, Sch.3 Part I
Art.20, applied: SI 2003/424 Art.14
Art.29, referred to: SI 2003/424 Art.1
Art.29, revoked: SI 2003/424 Sch.3 Part I
Art.30, applied: SI 2003/1994 Sch.3 para.1
Sch.1, revoked: SI 2003/424 Art.16, Sch.3 Part I
Sch.4, amended: SI 2003/424 Sch.3 Part I

2811. Libya (United Nations Sanctions) (Channel Islands) Order 1993
Art.14, amended: 2002 c.8 s.2

2812. Libya (United Nations Sanctions) (Isle of Man) Order 1993
Art.14, amended: 2002 c.8 s.2

2815. Central Manchester National Health Service Trust (Change of Name) Order 1993
revoked: 2003 c.43 s.7

2816. Cleveland Ambulance National Health Service Trust (Establishment) Amendment Order 1993
revoked: 2003 c.43 s.7

2834. Mid Glamorgan Ambulance National Health Service Trust (Establishment) Order 1993
revoked: 2003 c.43 s.7

2835. Derwen National Health Service Trust (Establishment) Order 1993
revoked: 2003 c.43 s.7

2836. North Wales Ambulance National Health Service Trust (Establishment) Order 1993
revoked: 2003 c.43 s.7

2837. Rhondda Health Care National Health Service Trust (Establishment) Order 1993
revoked: 2003 c.43 s.7

2838. Velindre National Health Service Trust (Establishment) Order 1993
revoked: 2003 c.43 s.7
Art.3, amended: SI 2002/442 Art.2, SI 2002/2199 Art.2
Art.4, amended: SI 2002/442 Art.3, SI 2002/2199 Art.3

2839. Gwynedd Community Health National Health Service Trust (Establishment) Order 1993
revoked: 2003 c.43 s.7

2840. Nevill Hall and District National Health Service Trust (Establishment) Order 1993
revoked: 2003 c.43 s.7

NO.

1993–cont.

2841. Gwynedd Hospitals National Health Service Trust (Establishment) Order 1993
revoked: 2003 c.43 s.7

2848. East Anglian Ambulance National Health Service Trust (Establishment) Order 1993
revoked: 2003 c.43 s.7

2849. Norfolk Ambulance National Health Service Trust Dissolution Order 1993
revoked: 2003 c.43 s.7

2854. Employment Appeal Tribunal Rules 1993
added: SI 2004/2526 r.9
see *De Haney v Brent MIND* [2003] EWCA Civ 1637, [2004] I.C.R. 348 (CA), Carnwath, L.J.; see *Miriki v General Council of the Bar* [2001] EWCA Civ 1973, [2002] I.C.R. 505 (CA), Peter Gibson, L.J.
r.2, amended: SI 2004/2526 r.2
r.2, revoked (in part): SI 2004/2526 r.2
r.2A, added: SI 2004/2526 r.3
r.3, amended: SI 2004/2526 r.4
r.3, see *Chelminski v Gdynia America Shipping Lines (London) Ltd* [2004] EWCA Civ 871, [2004] 3 All E.R. 666 (CA), Pill, L.J.; see *Fenton v Newham Community Health Services NHS Trust* [2002] Emp. L.R. 1124 (EAT), Wall, J.; see *Sian v Abbey National Plc* [2004] I.C.R. 55 (EAT), Burton, J.
r.4, amended: SI 2004/2526 r.5
r.5, amended: SI 2004/2526 r.6
r.6, amended: SI 2004/2526 r.7
r.7, amended: SI 2004/2526 r.8
r.16B, amended: SI 2004/2526 r.10
r.16C, amended: SI 2004/2526 r.10
r.17, amended: SI 2004/2526 r.11, r.12
r.19, amended: SI 2004/2526 r.12
r.20, substituted: SI 2004/2526 r.13
r.22, amended: SI 2004/2526 r.14
r.23, amended: SI 2004/2526 r.15
r.26, amended: SI 2004/2526 r.17
r.30A, amended: SI 2004/2526 r.16
r.31, amended: SI 2004/2526 r.18
r.31A, amended: SI 2004/2526 r.16
r.33, amended: SI 2004/2526 r.19
r.34, substituted: SI 2004/2526 r.20
r.34A, added: SI 2004/2526 r.21
r.34B, added: SI 2004/2526 r.21
r.34C, added: SI 2004/2526 r.21
r.34D, added: SI 2004/2526 r.21
r.35, see *aPeters v Sat Katar Co Ltd (In Liquidation)* [2003] EWCA Civ 943, [2003] I.C.R. 1574 (CA), Peter Gibson, L.J.
r.36, amended: SI 2004/2526 r.22
r.37, amended: SI 2004/2526 r.23
Sch.1, amended: SI 2004/2526 r.24, r.25

NO.

1993–cont.

2856. Mid Essex Community and Mental Health National Health Service Trust (Establishment) Order 1993
revoked: 2003 c.43 s.7

2896. Community Health Sheffield National Health Service Trust (Establishment) Order 1993
revoked: 2003 c.43 s.7
Art.1, amended: SI 2003/760 Art.2
Art.2, amended: SI 2003/760 Art.2
Art.2, substituted: SI 2003/760 Art.4
Art.3, amended: SI 2004/2397 Art.2
Art.4, amended: SI 2003/760 Art.5, SI 2004/2397 Art.3

2908. Western Isles Islands Council (Brevig) Harbour Empowerment Order 1993
revoked: SSI 2002/410 Sch.2 Part II
Art.1, referred to: SSI 2002/410 Sch.2 Part II
Art.2, referred to: SSI 2002/410 Sch.2 Part II
Art.21, referred to: SSI 2002/410 Sch.2 Part II

2934. Dumfries and Galloway Acute and Maternity Hospitals National Health Service Trust (Establishment) Order 1993
revoked: SSI 2003/189 Sch.2

2946. Fire Services (Appointments and Promotion) (Amendment) Regulations 1993
revoked: SI 2004/481 Sch.2

3045. Land Registration (Leasehold Reform) Rules 1993
r.2, amended: 2003 c.14 Sch.20 para.3

3050. Notification of New Substances Regulations 1993
applied: SI 2002/655 Reg.18, SI 2003/547 Reg.18, Sch.15, SI 2004/456 Reg.17
Reg.2, amended: SI 2004/994 Reg.5
Reg.4, applied: SI 2004/456 Sch.14
Reg.5, applied: SI 2004/456 Sch.14
Reg.6, applied: SI 2004/456 Sch.14
Reg.11, applied: SI 2003/547 Sch.15, SI 2004/456 Sch.14
Reg.13, applied: SI 2003/547 Sch.15, SI 2004/456 Sch.14
Reg.23, applied: SI 2004/456 Sch.14
Sch.2 Part A, amended: SI 2002/2176 Reg.3, SI 2004/568 Sch.13 para.7
Sch.3, substituted: SI 2002/2176 Reg.3

3053. Commercial Agents (Council Directive) Regulations 1993
see *Bell Electric Ltd v Aweco Appliance Systems GmbH & Co KG* [2002] EWHC 872, [2002] C.L.C. 1246 (QBD), Elias, J.
Reg.2, see *Light v Ty Europe Ltd* [2003] EWCA Civ 1238, [2004] 1 Lloyd's Rep. 693 (CA), Tuckey, L.J.; see *Light v Ty Europe Ltd* [2003] EWHC 174, [2003] 1 All E.R. (Comm) 568 (QBD (Merc Ct)), Judge McGonigal; see *Mercantile International Group Plc v Chuan Soon*

NO.

1993–cont.

3053. Commercial Agents (Council Directive) Regulations 1993–*cont.*
Reg.2–*cont.*
Huat Industrial Group Ltd [2002] EWCA Civ 288, [2002] 1 All E.R. (Comm) 788 (CA), Rix, L.J.
Reg.8, see *Tigana Ltd v Decoro Ltd* [2003] EWHC 23, [2003] E.C.C. 23 (QBD), Davis, J.
Reg.17, see *Cooper v Pure Fishing (UK) Ltd (formerly Outdoor Technology Group (UK) Ltd)* [2004] EWCA Civ 375, [2004] 2 Lloyd's Rep. 518 (CA), Peter Gibson, L.J.; see *Frape v Emreco International Ltd* 2002 S.L.T. 371 (OH), Lord McEwan; see *Hardie Polymers Ltd v Polymerland Ltd* 2002 S.C.L.R. 64 (OH), Lord Macfadyen; see *Light v Ty Europe Ltd* [2003] EWCA Civ 1238, [2004] 1 Lloyd's Rep. 693 (CA), Tuckey, L.J.; see *Light v Ty Europe Ltd* [2003] EWHC 174, [2003] 1 All E.R. (Comm) 568 (QBD (Merc Ct)), Judge McGonigal; see *Tigana Ltd v Decoro Ltd* [2003] EWHC 23, [2003] E.C.C. 23 (QBD), Davis, J.
Reg.18, see *Cooper v Pure Fishing (UK) Ltd (formerly Outdoor Technology Group (UK) Ltd)* [2004] EWCA Civ 375, [2004] 2 Lloyd's Rep. 518 (CA), Peter Gibson, L.J.

3069. Children (Homes, Arrangements for Placement, Reviews and Representations) (Miscellaneous Amendments) Regulations 1993
Reg.2, revoked (in part): SI 2002/327 Reg.43

3074. Personal Protective Equipment (EC Directive) (Amendment) Regulations 1993
revoked: SI 2002/1144 Sch.11 para.1

3080. Act of Sederunt (Fees of Solicitors in the Sheriff Court) (Amendment and Further Provisions) 1993
Sch.1 Part 1, amended: SSI 2002/274 Sch.1, SSI 2003/162 Sch.1, SSI 2004/152 Sch.1
Sch.1 Part 1, added: SSI 2002/568 Sch.1, SSI 2004/152 Art.2
Sch.1 Part 1, amended: SSI 2002/235 Sch.1, SSI 2002/274 Sch.1, SSI 2002/568 Art.2, SSI 2003/162 Sch.1, SSI 2004/152 Art.2, Sch.1
Sch.1 Part 1, substituted: SSI 2004/152 Art.2
Sch.1 Part 1 para.1, amended: SSI 2002/274 Sch.1, SSI 2003/162 Sch.1, SSI 2004/152 Sch.1
Sch.1 Part 1 para.2, amended: SSI 2002/274 Sch.1, SSI 2003/162 Sch.1, SSI 2004/152 Sch.1
Sch.1 Part 1 para.3, amended: SSI 2002/274 Sch.1, SSI 2003/162 Sch.1, SSI 2004/152 Sch.1
Sch.1 para.14, amended: SSI 2002/235 Art.2, SSI 2002/568 Art.2

NO.

3080. Act of Sederunt (Fees of Solicitors in the Sheriff Court) (Amendment and Further Provisions) 1993–*cont.*

Sch.1 Reg.14, see *Allan v Jenkins* 2003 S.L.T. (Sh Ct) 111 (Sh Pr), Sheriff Principal EF Bowen Q.C.

3081. Police (Scotland) Amendment Regulations 1993

revoked: SSI 2004/257 Sch.4

3100. Credit Unions (Authorised Investments) Order 1993

revoked: SI 2002/1501 Art.3

3128. Act of Sederunt (Summary Suspension) 1993

Art.2, see *Ward v DRM Driver Training Centre (Glasgow)* 2002 S.L.T. (Sh Ct) 108 (Sh Pr), EF Bowen Q.C., Sheriff Principal

3136. Environmentally Sensitive Areas (Argyll Islands) Designation Order 1993

Art.4, applied: SSI 2004/381 Reg.4
Art.4A, applied: SSI 2004/381 Reg.4
Art.5, applied: SSI 2004/381 Reg.4
Art.5A, applied: SSI 2004/381 Reg.4
Art.5D, applied: SSI 2004/381 Reg.4

3138. Merchant Shipping (Registration of Ships) Regulations 1993

Reg.7, amended: 2002 c.8 s.2
Reg.31, applied: SI 2003/1535 Art.6, SI 2004/398 Art.6
Reg.89, amended: 2002 c.8 s.2

3140. Mid Essex Community Health National Health Service Trust Dissolution Order 1993

revoked: 2003 c.43 s.7

3141. New Possibilities National Health Service Trust Dissolution Order 1993

revoked: 2003 c.43 s.7

3149. Environmentally Sensitive Areas (Machair of the Uists and Benbecula, Barra and Vatersay) Designation Order 1993

Art.4, applied: SSI 2004/381 Reg.4
Art.4A, applied: SSI 2004/381 Reg.4
Art.5, applied: SSI 2004/381 Reg.4
Art.5A, applied: SSI 2004/381 Reg.4
Art.5D, applied: SSI 2004/381 Reg.4

3150. Environmentally Sensitive Areas (Shetland Islands) Designation Order 1993

Art.4, applied: SSI 2004/381 Reg.4
Art.4A, applied: SSI 2004/381 Reg.4
Art.5, applied: SSI 2004/381 Reg.4
Art.5A, applied: SSI 2004/381 Reg.4
Art.5D, applied: SSI 2004/381 Reg.4

3160. Roads (Northern Ireland) Order 1993

Art.2, amended: 2003 c.21 Sch.19
Art.8, see *Madden v Department of the Environment for Northern Ireland* [2003] N.I. 123 (CA (NI)), Carswell, L.C.J.
Art.12, amended: 2003 c.21 Sch.17 para.128

NO.

3160. Roads (Northern Ireland) Order 1993–*cont.*

Art.14, applied: SR 2003/112, SR 2003/149
Art.14, enabled: SR 2003/112, SR 2003/149
Art.15, applied: SR 2003/112, SR 2003/149
Art.15, enabled: SR 2003/112, SR 2003/149
Art.16, enabled: SR 2003/112, SR 2003/149
Art.68, applied: SR 2003/112, SR 2003/149
Art.68, enabled: SR 2003/112, SR 2003/149
Art.70, amended: 2003 c.21 Sch.17 para.128
Art.72, amended: 2003 c.21 Sch.17 para.128
Art.73, amended: 2003 c.21 Sch.17 para.128
Art.78, amended: 2003 c.21 Sch.17 para.128
Art.79, amended: 2003 c.21 Sch.17 para.128
Art.82, amended: 2003 c.21 Sch.17 para.128
Art.83, amended: 2003 c.21 Sch.17 para.128
Sch.1, applied: SR 2003/112 Art.6
Sch.1, referred to: SR 2003/149 Art.6
Sch.8, applied: SR 2003/112, SR 2003/149
Sch.9, amended: 2003 c.21 Sch.17 para.128

3167. Redundancy Payments (National Health Service) (Modification) Order 1993

Sch.1 para.1, substituted: SI 2002/2469 Sch.1 para.61
Sch.1 para.1A, substituted: SI 2002/2469 Sch.1 para.61
Sch.1 para.2ZA, added: SI 2004/696 Sch.1 para.15

3187. Advice and Assistance (Financial Limit) (Scotland) Regulations 1993

Reg.3, substituted: SSI 2004/308 Reg.2

3212. Lottery Duty Regulations 1993

Part IV regA.9, added: SI 2002/2355 Reg.4
Part IV regA.9, amended: SI 2002/2355 Reg.3
Reg.9, amended: SI 2002/2355 Reg.3, Reg.5
Reg.9, revoked (in part): SI 2002/2355 Reg.5

3228. Public Services Contracts Regulations 1993

applied: SI 2004/669 Art.2
referred to: SI 2003/1986 Art.3
see *Jobsin Co UK Plc (t/a Internet Recruitment Solutions) v Department of Health* [2001] EWCA Civ 1241, [2002] 1 C.M.L.R. 44 (CA), Dyson, L.J.
Reg.2, amended: SI 2003/46 Reg.4
Reg.7, applied: SI 2002/2114 Reg.8, SI 2003/2909 Reg.9
Reg.9, amended: SI 2003/46 Reg.4
Reg.11, amended: SI 2003/46 Reg.4
Reg.12, amended: SI 2003/46 Reg.4
Reg.13, amended: SI 2003/46 Reg.4
Reg.22, amended: SI 2003/46 Reg.4
Reg.23, amended: SI 2003/46 Reg.4
Reg.23, see *Luck (t/a G Luck Arboricultural & Horticultural) v Tower Hamlets LBC* [2003] EWCA Civ 52, [2003] 2 C.M.L.R. 12 (CA), Rix, L.J.
Reg.24, amended: SI 2003/46 Reg.4

NO.

1993–cont.

3228. Public Services Contracts Regulations 1993–*cont.*

Reg.32, see *Luck (t/a G Luck Arboricultural & Horticultural) v Tower Hamlets LBC* [2003] EWCA Civ 52, [2003] 2 C.M.L.R. 12 (CA), Rix, L.J.

Sch.2 Part A para.1, revoked: SI 2003/46 Reg.4

Sch.2 Part A para.2, revoked: SI 2003/46 Reg.4

Sch.2 Part A para.3, revoked: SI 2003/46 Reg.4

Sch.2 Part A para.4, revoked: SI 2003/46 Reg.4

Sch.2 Part A para.5, revoked: SI 2003/46 Reg.4

Sch.2 Part A para.6, revoked: SI 2003/46 Reg.4

Sch.2 Part B para.1, revoked: SI 2003/46 Reg.4

Sch.2 Part B para.2, revoked: SI 2003/46 Reg.4

Sch.2 Part B para.3, revoked: SI 2003/46 Reg.4

Sch.2 Part B para.4, revoked: SI 2003/46 Reg.4

Sch.2 Part B para.5, revoked: SI 2003/46 Reg.4

Sch.2 Part B para.6, revoked: SI 2003/46 Reg.4

Sch.2 Part B para.7, revoked: SI 2003/46 Reg.4

Sch.2 Part B para.8, revoked: SI 2003/46 Reg.4

Sch.2 Part B para.9, revoked: SI 2003/46 Reg.4

Sch.2 Part B para.10, revoked: SI 2003/46 Reg.4

Sch.2 Part B para.11, revoked: SI 2003/46 Reg.4

Sch.2 Part B para.12, revoked: SI 2003/46 Reg.4

Sch.2 Part B para.13, revoked: SI 2003/46 Reg.4

Sch.2 Part B para.14, revoked: SI 2003/46 Reg.4

Sch.2 Part B para.15, revoked: SI 2003/46 Reg.4

Sch.2 Part B para.16, revoked: SI 2003/46 Reg.4

Sch.2 Part B para.17, revoked: SI 2003/46 Reg.4

Sch.2 Part B para.18, revoked: SI 2003/46 Reg.4

Sch.2 Part B para.19, revoked: SI 2003/46 Reg.4

Sch.2 Part B para.20, revoked: SI 2003/46 Reg.4

Sch.2 Part E para.1, revoked: SI 2003/46 Reg.4

NO.

1993–cont.

3228. Public Services Contracts Regulations 1993–*cont.*

Sch.2 Part E para.2, revoked: SI 2003/46 Reg.4

Sch.2 Part E para.3, revoked: SI 2003/46 Reg.4

Sch.2 Part E para.4, revoked: SI 2003/46 Reg.4

Sch.2 Part E para.5, revoked: SI 2003/46 Reg.4

Sch.2 Part E para.6, revoked: SI 2003/46 Reg.4

Sch.2 Part E para.7, revoked: SI 2003/46 Reg.4

Sch.2 Part E para.8, revoked: SI 2003/46 Reg.4

Sch.2 Part E para.9, revoked: SI 2003/46 Reg.4

Sch.2 Part E para.10, revoked: SI 2003/46 Reg.4

Sch.2 Part E para.11, revoked: SI 2003/46 Reg.4

Sch.2 Part E para.12, revoked: SI 2003/46 Reg.4

Sch.2 Part E para.13, revoked: SI 2003/46 Reg.4

Sch.2 Part E para.14, revoked: SI 2003/46 Reg.4

Sch.2 Part F para.1, revoked: SI 2003/46 Reg.4

Sch.2 Part F para.2, revoked: SI 2003/46 Reg.4

Sch.2 Part F para.3, revoked: SI 2003/46 Reg.4

Sch.2 Part F para.4, revoked: SI 2003/46 Reg.4

Sch.2 Part F para.5, revoked: SI 2003/46 Reg.4

Sch.2 Part F para.6, revoked: SI 2003/46 Reg.4

Sch.2 Part F para.7, revoked: SI 2003/46 Reg.4

Sch.2 Part F para.8, revoked: SI 2003/46 Reg.4

Sch.2 Part F para.9, revoked: SI 2003/46 Reg.4

Sch.2 Part F para.10, revoked: SI 2003/46 Reg.4

Sch.2 Part F para.11, revoked: SI 2003/46 Reg.4

Sch.2 Part F para.12, revoked: SI 2003/46 Reg.4

Sch.2 Part F para.13, revoked: SI 2003/46 Reg.4

Sch.2 Part F para.14, revoked: SI 2003/46 Reg.4

Sch.2 Part G para.1, revoked: SI 2003/46 Reg.4

Sch.2 Part G para.2, revoked: SI 2003/46 Reg.4

NO.

1993–cont.

3228. Public Services Contracts Regulations 1993—*cont.*

Sch.2 Part G para.3, revoked: SI 2003/46 Reg.4

Sch.2 Part G para.4, revoked: SI 2003/46 Reg.4

Sch.2 Part G para.5, revoked: SI 2003/46 Reg.4

Sch.2 Part G para.6, revoked: SI 2003/46 Reg.4

Sch.2 Part G para.7, revoked: SI 2003/46 Reg.4

Sch.2 Part G para.8, revoked: SI 2003/46 Reg.4

Sch.2 Part G para.9, revoked: SI 2003/46 Reg.4

Sch.2 Part C para.1, revoked: SI 2003/46 Reg.4

Sch.2 Part C para.2, revoked: SI 2003/46 Reg.4

Sch.2 Part C para.3, revoked: SI 2003/46 Reg.4

Sch.2 Part C para.4, revoked: SI 2003/46 Reg.4

Sch.2 Part C para.5, revoked: SI 2003/46 Reg.4

Sch.2 Part C para.6, revoked: SI 2003/46 Reg.4

Sch.2 Part C para.7, revoked: SI 2003/46 Reg.4

Sch.2 Part C para.8, revoked: SI 2003/46 Reg.4

Sch.2 Part C para.9, revoked: SI 2003/46 Reg.4

Sch.2 Part C para.10, revoked: SI 2003/46 Reg.4

Sch.2 Part C para.11, revoked: SI 2003/46 Reg.4

Sch.2 Part C para.12, revoked: SI 2003/46 Reg.4

Sch.2 Part C para.13, revoked: SI 2003/46 Reg.4

Sch.2 Part C para.14, revoked: SI 2003/46 Reg.4

Sch.2 Part C para.15, revoked: SI 2003/46 Reg.4

Sch.2 Part C para.16, revoked: SI 2003/46 Reg.4

Sch.2 Part C para.17, revoked: SI 2003/46 Reg.4

Sch.2 Part C para.18, revoked: SI 2003/46 Reg.4

Sch.2 Part D para.1, revoked: SI 2003/46 Reg.4

Sch.2 Part D para.2, revoked: SI 2003/46 Reg.4

Sch.2 Part D para.3, revoked: SI 2003/46 Reg.4

Sch.2 Part D para.4, revoked: SI 2003/46 Reg.4

NO.

1993–cont.

3228. Public Services Contracts Regulations 1993—*cont.*

Sch.2 Part D para.5, revoked: SI 2003/46 Reg.4

Sch.2 Part D para.6, revoked: SI 2003/46 Reg.4

Sch.2 Part D para.7, revoked: SI 2003/46 Reg.4

Sch.2 Part D para.8, revoked: SI 2003/46 Reg.4

Sch.2 Part D para.9, revoked: SI 2003/46 Reg.4

Sch.2 Part D para.10, revoked: SI 2003/46 Reg.4

Sch.2 Part D para.11, revoked: SI 2003/46 Reg.4

Sch.2 Part D para.12, revoked: SI 2003/46 Reg.4

Sch.2 Part D para.13, revoked: SI 2003/46 Reg.4

Sch.2 Part D para.14, revoked: SI 2003/46 Reg.4

Sch.2 Part D para.15, revoked: SI 2003/46 Reg.4

Sch.2 Part D para.16, revoked: SI 2003/46 Reg.4

Sch.2 Part D para.17, revoked: SI 2003/46 Reg.4

Sch.3, amended: SSI 2003/242 Art.2

3252. Parliamentary Pensions (Additional Voluntary Contributions Scheme) Regulations 1993

Reg.7, amended: SI 2004/2417 Reg.3

Reg.9, amended: SI 2004/2417 Reg.4

3253. Parliamentary Pensions (Consolidation and Amendment) Regulations 1993

Reg.1, amended: SI 2002/1807 Reg.2

Reg.1, amended: SI 2002/1807 Reg.5, SI 2004/2416 Reg.7

Reg.1, amended: SI 2002/1807 Reg.7

Reg.1, amended: SI 2004/2416 Reg.8

Reg.1, amended: SI 2004/2416 Reg.9

Reg.2, amended: SI 2004/2416 Reg.2

Reg.2, amended: SI 2002/1807 Reg.2, SI 2002/1887 Reg.2, SI 2004/2416 Reg.4

Reg.2, amended: SI 2002/1807 Reg.3

Reg.2, amended: SI 2004/2416 Reg.10

Reg.3, amended: SI 2004/2416 Reg.3

Reg.3, substituted: SI 2004/2416 Reg.5

Reg.3, amended: SI 2002/1807 Reg.6

Reg.3, amended: SI 2004/2416 Reg.11

Reg.4, amended: SI 2002/1807 Reg.3

Reg.7, substituted: SI 2004/2416 Reg.6

Reg.8, amended: SI 2002/1807 Reg.4

Sch.1 para.6, amended: SI 2004/2416 Reg.12

Sch.5, added: SI 2002/1807 Reg.6

Sch.5 para.1A, added: SI 2002/1807 Reg.6

Sch.5 para.7, amended: SI 2002/1887 Reg.3

NO.

1993–cont.

3276. Land Registration (Official Searches) Rules 1993
applied: SI 2003/1953 Art.28

1994

Conservation (Natural Habitats) Regulations 1994
see *R. (on the application of Friends of the Earth) v Environment Agency* [2003] EWHC 3193, [2004] Env. L.R. 31 (QBD (Admin Ct)), Sullivan, J.

84. Chappel and Wakes Colne Light Railway Order 1994
Art.7, amended: SI 2003/2155 Sch.1 para.18

105. Medicines (Homoeopathic Medicinal Products for Human Use) Regulations 1994
Reg.1, amended: SI 2002/236 Reg.9, SI 2003/2321 Reg.5
Reg.1, applied: SI 2002/3170 Art.3
Reg.2, amended: SI 2002/236 Reg.9
Reg.5, amended: SI 2002/236 Reg.9
Reg.6, revoked (in part): SI 2002/542 Reg.2
Reg.9, revoked (in part): SI 2002/542 Reg.2
Reg.14, amended: SI 2002/542 Reg.2, SI 2003/625 Reg.2, SI 2004/666 Reg.2
Reg.15, amended: SI 2002/542 Reg.2, SI 2003/625 Reg.2, SI 2004/666 Reg.2
Sch.2 para.3, amended: SI 2002/542 Reg.2, SI 2003/625 Reg.2, SI 2004/666 Reg.2
Sch.4, amended: SI 2004/1031 Sch.10 para.10

157. Railways and Other Transport Systems (Approval of Works, Plant and Equipment) Regulations 1994
applied: SI 2002/366 Art.9, SI 2002/1064 Art.26, SI 2002/1166 Reg.16, SSI 2003/359 Art.3
Reg.4, see *Thames Trains Ltd v Health and Safety Executive* [2003] EWCA Civ 720, (2003) 147 S.J.L.B. 661 (CA), Waller, L.J.
Reg.4, amended: SI 2002/1166 Reg.36, SI 2004/129 Reg.31

161. South Manchester University Hospitals National Health Service Trust (Establishment) Order 1994
applied: SI 2003/3059 Sch.1
revoked: 2003 c.43 s.7

162. Dudley Priority Health National Health Service Trust (Establishment) Order 1994
revoked: SI 2002/2616 Art.2, 2003 c.43 s.7

163. Kent and Sussex Weald National Health Service Trust (Establishment) Order 1994
revoked: 2003 c.43 s.7

164. Salford Hospitals National Health Service Trust (Establishment) Order 1994
applied: SI 2003/3059 Sch.1
revoked: 2003 c.43 s.7

NO.

1994–cont.

165. Mid-Sussex National Health Service Trust (Establishment) Order 1994
revoked: SI 2002/1363 Art.6, 2003 c.43 s.7

166. Royal West Sussex National Health Service Trust (Establishment) Order 1994
revoked: 2003 c.43 s.7

167. Dorset Community National Health Service Trust (Establishment) Order 1994
revoked: 2003 c.43 s.7

168. Dudley Group of Hospitals National Health Service Trust (Establishment) Order 1994
applied: SI 2003/3059 Sch.1
revoked: 2003 c.43 s.7

169. Alexandra Health Care National Health Service Trust (Establishment) Order 1994
revoked: 2003 c.43 s.7

170. Coventry Healthcare National Health Service Trust (Establishment) Order 1994
revoked: SI 2002/2616 Art.2, 2003 c.43 s.7

171. South Birmingham Mental Health National Health Service Trust (Establishment) Order 1994
revoked: 2003 c.43 s.7, SI 2003/617 Art.6

172. Sandwell Healthcare National Health Service Trust (Establishment) Order 1994
revoked: SI 2002/1364 Art.6, 2003 c.43 s.7

173. Northern Birmingham Mental Health National Health Service Trust (Establishment) Order 1994
revoked: 2003 c.43 s.7, SI 2003/617 Art.6

174. Weald of Kent Community National Health Service Trust (Establishment) Order 1994
revoked: 2003 c.43 s.7

175. South Kent Hospitals National Health Service Trust (Establishment) Order 1994
revoked: 2003 c.43 s.7

176. Norfolk and Norwich Health Care National Health Service Trust (Establishment) Order 1994
revoked: 2003 c.43 s.7
Art.4, amended: SI 2003/791 Art.2

177. St Albans and Hemel Hempstead National Health Service Trust (Establishment) Order 1994
revoked: 2003 c.43 s.7

178. North Hampshire Hospitals National Health Service Trust (Establishment) Order 1994
revoked: 2003 c.43 s.7

179. Furness Hospitals National Health Service Trust (Establishment) Order 1994
revoked: 2003 c.43 s.7

NO.

1994–cont.

180. Trafford Healthcare National Health Service Trust (Establishment) Order 1994
revoked: 2003 c.43 s.7

181. East Surrey Learning Disability and Mental Health Service National Health Service Trust (Establishment) Order 1994
revoked: 2003 c.43 s.7

182. Surrey Ambulance National Health Service Trust (Establishment) Order 1994
revoked: 2003 c.43 s.7

183. Bexley Community Health National Health Service Trust (Establishment) Order 1994
revoked: 2003 c.43 s.7

184. Healthlands Mental Health National Health Service Trust (Establishment) Order 1994
revoked: 2003 c.43 s.7

185. Mancunian Community Health National Health Service Trust (Establishment) Order 1994
revoked: 2003 c.43 s.7

187. Insider Dealing (Securities and Regulated Markets) Order 1994
Art.9, amended: SI 2002/1874 Art.2
Art.10, amended: SI 2002/1874 Art.2
Sch.1, amended: SI 2002/1874 Art.2

188. Traded Securities (Disclosure) Regulations 1994
Sch.1 para.2, varied: SI 2003/1633 Sch.2 para.8

194. Community Health Care North Durham National Health Service Trust (Establishment) Amendment Order 1994
revoked: 2003 c.43 s.7

195. Northwick Park Hospital National Health Service Trust (Change of Name) Order 1994
revoked: 2003 c.43 s.7

196. Gateshead Healthcare National Health Service Trust (Establishment) Order 1994
revoked: 2003 c.43 s.7

197. Premier Health National Health Service Trust (Establishment) Order 1994
revoked: 2003 c.43 s.7

198. Northgate and Prudhoe National Health Service Trust (Establishment) Order 1994
revoked: 2003 c.43 s.7

199. Environmental Protection (Non-Refillable Refrigerant Containers) Regulations 1994
revoked: SI 2002/528 Reg.14

NO.

1994–cont.

229. Civil Legal Aid (General) (Amendment) Regulations 1994
Reg.107B, see *Brawley v Marczynski (No.2)* [2002] EWCA Civ 1453, [2003] 1 W.L.R. 813 (CA), Longmore, L.J.

307. Royal Hospital of St Bartholomew, the Royal London Hospital and London Chest Hospital National Health Service Trust (Establishment) Order 1994
revoked: 2003 c.43 s.7
Art.4, amended: SI 2003/1499 Art.2

308. Newham Healthcare National Health Service Trust (Establishment) Order 1994
revoked: 2003 c.43 s.7
Art.1, amended: SI 2004/1625 Art.2
Art.2, amended: SI 2004/1625 Art.2
Art.3, amended: SI 2004/1625 Art.3

309. Tavistock and Portman National Health Service Trust (Establishment) Order 1994
revoked: 2003 c.43 s.7

316. East Glamorgan National Health Service Trust (Establishment) Order 1994
revoked: 2003 c.43 s.7

317. Morriston Hospital National Health Service Trust (Establishment) Order 1994
revoked: 2003 c.43 s.7

323. Education (School Financial Statements) (Prescribed Particulars etc.) Regulations 1994
applied: SI 2002/536 Reg.3

326. Inshore Fishing (Prohibition of Fishing and Fishing Methods) (Scotland) Amendment Order 1994
revoked: SSI 2004/276 Sch.4

342. European Parliamentary Elections (Changes to the Franchise and Qualification of Representatives) Regulations 1994
Reg.3, consolidated: 2002 c.24, s.10
Reg.3, revoked: 2002 c.24 Sch.4
Reg.4, amended: SI 2004/1374 Reg.4
Reg.6, revoked: SI 2004/1267 Sch.7
Reg.16, revoked: SI 2004/1267 Sch.7

371. Docklands Light Railway (Penalty Fares and Provision of Police Services) Order 1994
Art.9, revoked: SI 2003/1615 Sch.1 para.47

391. Act of Sederunt (Fees of Messengers-at-Arms) 1994
applied: SSI 2002/566 Art.3
revoked: SSI 2002/566 Sch.2
Sch.1 para.15, amended: SSI 2002/513 Sch.1

392. Act of Sederunt (Fees of Sheriff Officers) 1994
applied: SSI 2002/567 Art.3
revoked: SSI 2002/567 Sch.2

1994–cont.

392. Act of Sederunt (Fees of Sheriff Officers) 1994–*cont.*
Sch.1 Part 1, amended: SSI 2002/515 Sch.1

400. Great Ormond Street Hospital for Children National Health Service Trust (Establishment) Order 1994
revoked: 2003 c.43 s.7

401. Royal Marsden National Health Service Trust (Establishment) Order 1994
revoked: 2003 c.43 s.7

402. Royal Brompton Hospital National Health Service Trust (Establishment) Order 1994
revoked: 2003 c.43 s.7

403. Moorfields Eye Hospital National Health Service Trust (Establishment) Order 1994
revoked: 2003 c.43 s.7

404. Bethlem and Maudsley National Health Service Trust (Establishment) Order 1994
revoked: 2003 c.43 s.7

426. Airports (Northern Ireland) Order 1994
Part IV, applied: 2002 c.40 Sch.15, SI 2003/419 Art.63
Art.12, amended: 2003 c.21 Sch.17 para.131
Art.12, revoked (in part): 2003 c.21 Sch.19
Art.18, applied: SR 2002/396 Art.2
Art.18, enabled: SR 2002/396
Art.19, applied: 2002 c.26 Sch.4 para.1
Art.35B, enabled: SI 2003/1371
Art.35B, referred to: SI 2003/1371
Art.45, amended: 2002 c.40 Sch.9 para.11
Art.45, revoked (in part): 2002 c.40 Sch.9 para.11
Art.45, varied: SI 2003/1592 Sch.4 para.13
Art.57, amended: SI 2002/3150 Sch.3 para.9
Sch.6, amended: 2002 c.40 Sch.9 para.12
Sch.9, revoked: SI 2003/419 Sch.5

429. Health and Personal Social Services (Northern Ireland) Order 1994
Art.3, enabled: SR 2003/200

440. Ozone Monitoring and Information Regulations 1994
revoked (in part): SI 2003/1848 Reg.11, SI 2003/2121 Sch.10, SR 2003/240 Reg.13, SSI 2003/428 Reg.16

482. Churchill John Radcliffe National Health Service Trust (Change of Name) Order 1994
revoked: 2003 c.43 s.7

522. Environmental Protection (Waste Recycling Payments) (Amendment) Regulations 1994
revoked (in part): SI 2004/639 Reg.4

533. Electricity Supply (Amendment) Regulations 1994
revoked: SI 2002/2665 Sch.5

1994–cont.

535. Misuse of Drugs (Licence Fees) (Amendment) Regulations 1994
revoked: SI 2003/611 Sch.1

570. Channel Tunnel (Security) Order 1994
Part II, applied: 2003 c.42 Sch.5 para.60, Sch.5 para.100, Sch.5 para.168, 2003 c.44 Sch.15 para.56, Sch.17 para.52
Art.2, amended: 2002 c.8 s.2
Art.4, applied: 2003 c.44 Sch.4 para.37, SI 2004/1500 Sch.2 para.29, SI 2004/1910 Sch.1
Art.5, applied: 2003 c.44 Sch.4 para.38, SI 2004/1500 Sch.2 para.30, SI 2004/1910 Sch.1
Art.6, applied: SI 2004/1910 Sch.1
Art.7, applied: SI 2004/1910 Sch.1
Art.8, applied: SI 2004/1910 Sch.1

573. Railways (London Regional Transport) (Exemptions) Order 1994
amended: SI 2003/1615 Sch.1 para.48
Art.2, amended: SI 2003/1615 Sch.1 para.48
Art.2, revoked (in part): SI 2003/1615 Sch.1 para.48
Art.3, amended: SI 2003/1615 Sch.1 para.48
Art.4, amended: SI 2003/1615 Sch.1 para.48
Art.5, amended: SI 2003/1615 Sch.1 para.48
Art.6, amended: SI 2003/1615 Sch.1 para.48

574. Railways (Heathrow Express) (Exemptions) Order 1994
Art.5, amended: SI 2002/2703 Art.2

581. Education (Middle Schools) (Amendment) Regulations 1994
applied: SI 2002/1983 Reg.7

602. Microbiological Research Authority Regulations 1994
revoked: SI 2003/505 Art.8

603. Microbiological Research Authority (Establishment and Constitution) Order 1994
revoked: SI 2003/505 Art.8

604. Enrolment of Deeds (Change of Name) Regulations 1994
Reg.2, amended: 2002 c.8 s.2

606. Railways (Class and Miscellaneous Exemptions) Order 1994
Art.3, applied: SI 2004/1072 Art.10
Art.5, applied: SI 2004/1072 Art.10
Art.6, applied: SI 2004/1072 Art.10
Art.7, disapplied: SI 2004/1072 Art.11

607. Railways (Alternative Closure Procedure) Order 1994
Sch.1, amended: SI 2003/1615 Sch.1 para.49

626. Council Tax (Discounts) (Scotland) Amendment Order 1994
revoked: SSI 2003/176 Sch.4

632. Secure Tenants (Compensation for Improvements) (Scotland) Regulations 1994
applied: SSI 2002/321 Art.4

NO.

1994–cont.

633. National Health Service (General Medical Services) Amendment Regulations 1994
revoked (in part): SI 2004/865 Sch.2, SI 2004/1016 Sch.2

636. National Health Service (Dental Charges) (Scotland) Amendment Regulations 1994
revoked: SSI 2003/158 Sch.4

651. Education (Special Educational Needs) (Approval of Independent Schools) Regulations 1994
referred to: SI 2002/808 Art.2
Reg.2, amended: SI 2002/2072 Reg.2
Reg.2A, added: SI 2002/2072 Reg.3

674. Common Agricultural Policy (Wine) Regulations 1994
applied: SSI 2002/325 Reg.7

691. Bowes Extension Light Railway Order 1994
Art.6, amended: SI 2003/2155 Sch.1 para.18

694. Hydrocarbon Oil (Amendment) (No.2) Regulations 1994
revoked: SI 2002/1773 Reg.20

704. Social Security Pensions (Home Responsibilities) Regulations 1994
Reg.1, amended: SI 2003/1767 Reg.2
Reg.2, amended: SI 2003/1767 Reg.2

745. Mid Essex Community Health National Health Service Trust Dissolution Order 1994
revoked: 2003 c.43 s.7

775. Income Tax (Employments) (Amendment) Regulations 1994
revoked: SI 2003/2682 Sch.2

777. Income Tax (Car Benefits) (Replacement Accessories) Regulations 1994
revoked: 2003 c.1 Sch.8 Part 2

778. Income Tax (Replacement Cars) Regulations 1994
revoked: 2003 c.1 Sch.8 Part 2

782. European Parliamentary Elections (Northern Ireland) (Amendment) Regulations 1994
revoked: SI 2004/1267 Sch.7

797. North Kent Healthcare National Health Service Trust (Establishment) Amendment Order 1994
revoked: 2003 c.43 s.7

798. South Birmingham Community Health National Health Service Trust (Change of Name) Order 1994
revoked: 2003 c.43 s.7

827. Gateshead Community Health National Health Service Trust Dissolution Order 1994
revoked: 2003 c.43 s.7

828. Mancunian Community Health National Health Service Trust Dissolution Order 1994
revoked: 2003 c.43 s.7

1994–cont.

829. Northgate National Health Service Trust Dissolution Order 1994
revoked: 2003 c.43 s.7

830. Royal London Hospital and Associated Community Services National Health Service Trust Dissolution Order 1994
revoked: 2003 c.43 s.7

831. West Dorset Mental Health National Health Service Trust Dissolution Order 1994
revoked: 2003 c.43 s.7

832. Premier Health National Health Service Trust Dissolution Order 1994
revoked: 2003 c.43 s.7

833. West Dorset Community Health National Health Service Trust Dissolution Order 1994
revoked: 2003 c.43 s.7

848. Harrow and Hillingdon Healthcare National Health Service Trust (Establishment) Order 1994
revoked: SI 2002/1323 Sch.1, 2003 c.43 s.7

849. Royal Victoria Infirmary and Associated Hospitals National Health Service Trust (Establishment) Order 1994
revoked: 2003 c.43 s.7

850. University College London Hospitals National Health Service Trust (Establishment) Order 1994
revoked: 2003 c.43 s.7

851. Newcastle City Health National Health Service Trust (Establishment) Order 1994
revoked: 2003 c.43 s.7

852. Mount Vernon and Watford Hospitals National Health Service Trust (Establishment) Order 1994
revoked: 2003 c.43 s.7

853. Hammersmith Hospitals National Health Service Trust (Establishment) Order 1994
revoked: 2003 c.43 s.7

854. West Herts Community Health National Health Service Trust (Establishment) Order 1994
revoked: 2003 c.43 s.7

855. Chelsea and Westminster Healthcare National Health Service Trust (Establishment) Order 1994
revoked: 2003 c.43 s.7

856. South East London Mental Health National Health Service Trust (Change of Name and Miscellaneous Amendments) Order 1994
revoked: 2003 c.43 s.7

858. Harrow Community Health Services National Health Service Trust Dissolution Order 1994
revoked: 2003 c.43 s.7

NO.

1994–cont.

859. Royal Victoria Infirmary and Associated Hospitals National Health Service Trust Dissolution Order 1994
revoked: 2003 c.43 s.7

860. Mount Vernon Hospital National Health Service Trust Dissolution Order 1994
revoked: 2003 c.43 s.7

861. Newcastle Mental Health National Health Service Trust Dissolution Order 1994
revoked: 2003 c.43 s.7

862. Dacorum and St Albans Community National Health Service Trust Dissolution Order 1994
revoked: 2003 c.43 s.7

863. Hillingdon Community Health National Health Service Trust Dissolution Order 1994
revoked: 2003 c.43 s.7

867. Local Government Changes for England Regulations 1994
Reg.27, applied: SI 2002/187 Art.1

955. Travellers Allowances Order 1994
varied: SI 2004/1002 Art.6

1047. Education (Special Educational Needs) Regulations 1994
revoked (in part): SI 2002/152 Reg.25
Reg.6, applied: SI 2002/152 Reg.26
Reg.7, applied: SI 2002/152 Reg.26
Reg.8, applied: SI 2002/152 Reg.26
Reg.9, applied: SI 2002/152 Reg.26
Reg.10, applied: SI 2002/152 Reg.26
Reg.11, applied: SI 2002/152 Reg.26
Reg.13, applied: SI 2002/152 Reg.26
Reg.14, applied: SI 2002/152 Reg.26
Reg.15, applied: SI 2002/152 Reg.26
Reg.16, applied: SI 2002/152 Reg.26
Reg.17, applied: SI 2002/152 Reg.26

1056. Waste Management Licensing Regulations 1994
applied: SI 2002/1689 Reg.3
referred to: SI 2003/595 Reg.2, SSI 2003/171 Reg.3
Reg.1, amended: SI 2003/595 Reg.3, SI 2003/780 Reg.3, Reg.4, SSI 2003/171 Reg.4, SSI 2003/593 Reg.7
Reg.3, amended: SI 2002/1559 Sch.5 para.2, SSI 2003/235 Sch.6 para.4
Reg.4, see *R. (on the application of Thornby Farms Ltd) v Daventry DC* [2002] EWCA Civ 31, [2003] Q.B. 503 (CA), Pill, L.J.
Reg.4, added: SI 2003/780 Reg.6
Reg.4, substituted: SI 2003/595 Reg.4, SI 2003/780 Reg.5, SSI 2003/171 Reg.5
Reg.5, amended: SI 2003/595 Reg.5, SI 2003/780 Reg.7
Reg.10, amended: SI 2002/1559 Sch.5 para.2, SI 2004/70 Reg.3, SSI 2003/235 Sch.6 para.4

NO.

1994–cont.

1056. Waste Management Licensing Regulations 1994–*cont.*
Reg.12, amended: SI 2002/1087 Reg.2, SI 2004/70 Reg.4, SSI 2004/275 Reg.4
Reg.16, amended: SI 2002/2980 Reg.6, SSI 2003/170 Reg.15, SSI 2004/275 Reg.5
Reg.17, amended: SSI 2003/171 Reg.6, SSI 2004/275 Reg.6
Reg.17, applied: SI 2003/2635 Reg.45
Reg.17, referred to: SSI 2003/593 Reg.4
Reg.18, amended: SI 2003/2635 Reg.48, SSI 2003/171 Reg.7, SSI 2003/593 Reg.7, SSI 2004/275 Reg.7
Reg.18, applied: SI 2003/2635 Reg.45
Reg.18, revoked (in part): SSI 2003/171 Reg.7
Reg.18A, added: SSI 2003/171 Reg.8
Reg.18A, amended: SSI 2004/275 Reg.8
Sch.1A para.1, added: SI 2003/595 Sch.1, SI 2003/780 Sch.1, SSI 2003/171 Reg.9
Sch.1A para.1, amended: SSI 2004/275 Reg.9
Sch.1A para.2, added: SI 2003/595 Sch.1, SI 2003/780 Sch.1, SSI 2003/171 Reg.9
Sch.1A para.2, amended: SSI 2004/275 Reg.9
Sch.3, applied: SI 2003/2635 Reg.45
Sch.3, referred to: SSI 2003/593 Reg.4
Sch.3 para.3, revoked (in part): SI 2002/2980 Reg.6
Sch.3 para.7, amended: SSI 2004/275 Reg.10
Sch.3 para.7, substituted: SSI 2003/171 Reg.10
Sch.3 para.8, substituted: SSI 2004/275 Reg.11
Sch.3 para.9, amended: SSI 2004/275 Reg.12
Sch.3 para.9, substituted: SSI 2003/171 Reg.10
Sch.3 para.10, substituted: SSI 2004/275 Reg.13
Sch.3 para.12, substituted: SSI 2004/275 Reg.14
Sch.3 para.12A, added: SSI 2004/275 Reg.14
Sch.3 para.13, see *Environment Agency v R Newcomb & Sons Ltd* [2002] EWHC 2095, [2003] Env. L.R. 12 (QBD (Admin Ct)), Newman, J.
Sch.3 para.18, applied: SSI 2003/593 Reg.4
Sch.3 para.19, see *Environment Agency v R Newcomb & Sons Ltd* [2002] EWHC 2095, [2003] Env. L.R. 12 (QBD (Admin Ct)), Newman, J.
Sch.3 para.19, amended: SSI 2004/275 Reg.15
Sch.3 para.19, substituted: SSI 2003/171 Reg.10
Sch.3 para.25, applied: SSI 2003/235 Reg.4
Sch.3 para.25, referred to: SI 2002/1559 Reg.4

NO.

1994–cont.

1056. Waste Management Licensing Regulations 1994–cont.

Sch.3 para.29, amended: SI 2002/2980 Reg.6, SSI 2003/170 Reg.15

Sch.3 para.30, amended: SSI 2004/275 Reg.16

Sch.3 para.41, amended: SI 2003/2635 Reg.48, SSI 2003/593 Reg.7

Sch.3 para.45, amended: SI 2003/2635 Reg.48, SSI 2003/593 Reg.7, SSI 2004/275 Reg.17

Sch.3 para.45, applied: SI 2003/2635 Reg.47

Sch.3 para.45, referred to: SSI 2003/593 Reg.6

Sch.3 para.45, varied: SI 2003/2635 Reg.45, SSI 2003/593 Reg.4

Sch.3 para.46, added: SSI 2004/275 Reg.18

Sch.3A Part I, added: SSI 2003/171 Reg.11

Sch.3A Part I, amended: SSI 2004/275 Reg.19

Sch.3A Part II para.1, added: SSI 2003/171 Reg.11

Sch.3A Part II para.1, amended: SSI 2004/275 Reg.19

Sch.3A Part II para.2, added: SSI 2003/171 Reg.11

Sch.3A Part II para.3, added: SSI 2003/171 Reg.11

Sch.4 Part I para.4, see *R. (on the application of Blewett) v Derbyshire CC* [2003] EWHC 2775, [2004] Env. L.R. 29 (QBD (Admin Ct)), Sullivan, J.

Sch.4 Part I para.13, amended: SSI 2003/171 Reg.12, SSI 2004/275 Reg.20

Sch.4 Part III, substituted: SSI 2004/275 Reg.21

Sch.4 Part III para.1, substituted: SSI 2004/275 Reg.21

Sch.4 Part III para.2, substituted: SSI 2004/275 Reg.21

Sch.4 Part III para.3, substituted: SSI 2004/275 Reg.21

Sch.4 Part III para.4, substituted: SSI 2004/275 Reg.21

Sch.4 Part III para.5, substituted: SSI 2004/275 Reg.21

Sch.4 Part III para.6, substituted: SSI 2004/275 Reg.21

Sch.4 Part III para.7, substituted: SSI 2004/275 Reg.21

Sch.4 Part III para.8, substituted: SSI 2004/275 Reg.21

Sch.4 Part III para.9, substituted: SSI 2004/275 Reg.21

Sch.4 Part III para.10, substituted: SSI 2004/275 Reg.21

Sch.4 Part III para.11, substituted: SSI 2004/275 Reg.21

Sch.4 Part III para.12, substituted: SSI 2004/275 Reg.21

NO.

1994–cont.

1056. Waste Management Licensing Regulations 1994–cont.

Sch.4 Part III para.13, substituted: SSI 2004/275 Reg.21

Sch.4 Part III para.14, substituted: SSI 2004/275 Reg.21

Sch.4 Part III para.15, substituted: SSI 2004/275 Reg.21

Sch.4 Part IV, substituted: SSI 2004/275 Reg.22

Sch.4 Part IV para.1, substituted: SSI 2004/275 Reg.22

Sch.4 Part IV para.2, substituted: SSI 2004/275 Reg.22

Sch.4 Part IV para.3, substituted: SSI 2004/275 Reg.22

Sch.4 Part IV para.4, substituted: SSI 2004/275 Reg.22

Sch.4 Part IV para.5, substituted: SSI 2004/275 Reg.22

Sch.4 Part IV para.6, substituted: SSI 2004/275 Reg.22

Sch.4 Part IV para.7, substituted: SSI 2004/275 Reg.22

Sch.4 Part IV para.8, substituted: SSI 2004/275 Reg.22

Sch.4 Part IV para.9, substituted: SSI 2004/275 Reg.22

Sch.4 Part IV para.10, substituted: SSI 2004/275 Reg.22

Sch.4 Part IV para.11, substituted: SSI 2004/275 Reg.22

Sch.4 Part IV para.12, substituted: SSI 2004/275 Reg.22

Sch.4 Part IV para.13, substituted: SSI 2004/275 Reg.22

1065. European Convention on Cinematographic Co-production Order 1994

Sch.1, amended: SI 2002/1398 Art.3, SI 2002/2635 Art.3, SI 2003/828 Art.3, SI 2003/2630 Art.3, SI 2004/724 Art.2, SI 2004/2031 Art.2, Art.3

1089. European Parliamentary Elections Act 1993 (Commencement) Order 1994

revoked: 2002 c.24 Sch.4

1191. Export of Goods (Control) Order 1994

applied: SI 2003/335 Sch.1, SSI 2003/93 Sch.1

Appendix 1., revoked: SI 2002/2059 Art.2

Sch.1 Part I, revoked: SI 2002/2059 Art.2

Sch.1 Part I para.1, revoked: SI 2002/2059 Art.2

Sch.1 Part I para.1, added: SI 2003/1938 Sch.1 para.1

Sch.1 Part I para.1, revoked: SI 2002/2059 Art.2, SI 2003/1938 Sch.2

Sch.1 Part I para.1, revoked: SI 2002/2059 Art.2

NO.

NO.

1994–cont.

1191. Export of Goods (Control) Order 1994–*cont.*

Sch.1 Part I para.2, revoked: SI 2002/2059 Art.2

Sch.1 Part I para.2, added: SI 2003/1938 Sch.1 para.1

Sch.1 Part I para.2, revoked: SI 2002/2059 Art.2, SI 2003/1938 Sch.2

Sch.1 Part I para.3, added: SI 2003/1938 Sch.1 para.1

Sch.1 Part I para.3, revoked: SI 2002/2059 Art.2, SI 2003/1938 Sch.2

Sch.1 Part II para.1, revoked: SI 2002/2059 Art.2

Sch.1 Part II para.2, revoked: SI 2002/2059 Art.2

Sch.1 Part III, revoked: SI 2002/2059 Art.2

Sch.1 Part III, added: SI 2002/2059 Art.2, SI 2003/1938 Sch.1 para.2

Sch.1 Part III, amended: SI 2002/2059 Art.2, Sch.1

Sch.1 Part III, revoked: SI 2002/2059 Art.2, SI 2003/1938 Sch.2

Sch.1 Part III, revoked: SI 2002/2059 Art.2

Sch.1 Part III para.1, added: SI 2003/1938 Sch.1 para.2

Sch.1 Part III para.1, revoked: SI 2002/2059 Art.2, SI 2003/1938 Sch.2

Sch.1 Part III para.1, revoked: SI 2002/2059 Art.2

Sch.1 Part III para.1A, revoked: SI 2002/2059 Art.2

Sch.1 Part III para.1B, revoked: SI 2002/2059 Art.2

Sch.1 Part III para.1C, revoked: SI 2002/2059 Art.2

Sch.1 Part III para.1D, revoked: SI 2002/2059 Art.2

Sch.1 Part III para.1E, revoked: SI 2002/2059 Art.2

Sch.1 Part III para.2, added: SI 2003/1938 Sch.1 para.2

Sch.1 Part III para.2, revoked: SI 2002/2059 Art.2, SI 2003/1938 Sch.2

Sch.1 Part III para.2, revoked: SI 2002/2059 Art.2

Sch.1 Part III para.2A, revoked: SI 2002/2059 Art.2

Sch.1 Part III para.2B, revoked: SI 2002/2059 Art.2

Sch.1 Part III para.2C, revoked: SI 2002/2059 Art.2

Sch.1 Part III para.2D, revoked: SI 2002/2059 Art.2

Sch.1 Part III para.2E, revoked: SI 2002/2059 Art.2

Sch.1 Part III para.3A, revoked: SI 2002/2059 Art.2

Sch.1 Part III para.3B, revoked: SI 2002/2059 Art.2

1994–cont.

1191. Export of Goods (Control) Order 1994–*cont.*

Sch.1 Part III para.3C, revoked: SI 2002/2059 Art.2

Sch.1 Part III para.3D, revoked: SI 2002/2059 Art.2

Sch.1 Part III para.3E, revoked: SI 2002/2059 Art.2

Sch.1 Part III para.4A, revoked: SI 2002/2059 Art.2

Sch.1 Part III para.4B, revoked: SI 2002/2059 Art.2

Sch.1 Part III para.4C, revoked: SI 2002/2059 Art.2

Sch.1 Part III para.4D, revoked: SI 2002/2059 Art.2

Sch.1 Part III para.4E, revoked: SI 2002/2059 Art.2

Sch.1 Part III para.5A1, revoked: SI 2002/2059 Art.2

Sch.1 Part III para.5A2, revoked: SI 2002/2059 Art.2

Sch.1 Part III para.5B1, revoked: SI 2002/2059 Art.2

Sch.1 Part III para.5B2, revoked: SI 2002/2059 Art.2

Sch.1 Part III para.5C1, revoked: SI 2002/2059 Art.2

Sch.1 Part III para.5C2, revoked: SI 2002/2059 Art.2

Sch.1 Part III para.5D1, revoked: SI 2002/2059 Art.2

Sch.1 Part III para.5D2, revoked: SI 2002/2059 Art.2

Sch.1 Part III para.5E1, revoked: SI 2002/2059 Art.2

Sch.1 Part III para.5E2, revoked: SI 2002/2059 Art.2

Sch.1 Part III para.6A, revoked: SI 2002/2059 Art.2

Sch.1 Part III para.6B, revoked: SI 2002/2059 Art.2

Sch.1 Part III para.6C, revoked: SI 2002/2059 Art.2

Sch.1 Part III para.6D, revoked: SI 2002/2059 Art.2

Sch.1 Part III para.6E, revoked: SI 2002/2059 Art.2

Sch.1 Part III para.7A, revoked: SI 2002/2059 Art.2

Sch.1 Part III para.7B, revoked: SI 2002/2059 Art.2

Sch.1 Part III para.7C, revoked: SI 2002/2059 Art.2

Sch.1 Part III para.7D, revoked: SI 2002/2059 Art.2

Sch.1 Part III para.7E, revoked: SI 2002/2059 Art.2

Sch.1 Part III para.8A, revoked: SI 2002/2059 Art.2

NO.

NO.

1994–cont.

1191. Export of Goods (Control) Order 1994–*cont.*

Sch.1 Part III para.8B, revoked: SI 2002/2059 Art.2

Sch.1 Part III para.8C, revoked: SI 2002/2059 Art.2

Sch.1 Part III para.8D, revoked: SI 2002/2059 Art.2

Sch.1 Part III para.8E, revoked: SI 2002/2059 Art.2

Sch.1 Part III para.9A, revoked: SI 2002/2059 Art.2

Sch.1 Part III para.9B, revoked: SI 2002/2059 Art.2

Sch.1 Part III para.9C, revoked: SI 2002/2059 Art.2

Sch.1 Part III para.9D, revoked: SI 2002/2059 Art.2

Sch.1 Part III para.9E, revoked: SI 2002/2059 Art.2

Sch.3, amended: SI 2002/2059 Art.2, SI 2003/1938 Sch.2

1210. Isle of Wight (Structural Change) Order 1994

varied: SI 2004/222 Art.2

1212. Income Tax (Employments) (Notional Payments) Regulations 1994

revoked: SI 2003/2682 Sch.2

Reg.2, amended: 2003 c.1 Sch.8 Part 2

Reg.2, revoked (in part): 2003 c.1 Sch.8 Part 2

Reg.3, revoked: 2003 c.1 Sch.8 Part 2

Reg.3A, revoked: 2003 c.1 Sch.8 Part 2

Reg.3B, revoked: 2003 c.1 Sch.8 Part 2

Reg.4, revoked: 2003 c.1 Sch.8 Part 2

Reg.5, revoked: 2003 c.1 Sch.8 Part 2

Reg.6, revoked: 2003 c.1 Sch.8 Part 2

Reg.7, revoked: 2003 c.1 Sch.8 Part 2

Reg.8, revoked: 2003 c.1 Sch.8 Part 2

Reg.8A, revoked: 2003 c.1 Sch.8 Part 2

1227. Service Subsidy Agreements (Tendering) (Amendment) Regulations 1994

revoked (in part): SI 2002/2090 Sch.2

1268. Surrey Ambulance National Health Service Trust (Change of Name) Order 1994

revoked: 2003 c.43 s.7

1269. Salford Hospitals National Health Service Trust (Change of Name) Order 1994

revoked: 2003 c.43 s.7

1291. Habitat (Water Fringe) Regulations 1994

applied: SI 2003/2261 Sch.3 Part I

1293. Habitat (Salt-Marsh) Regulations 1994

applied: SI 2003/2261 Sch.3 Part I

1303. Education (Lay Members of Appeal Committees) Regulations 1994

applied: SI 2002/2899 Reg.4, SI 2002/3178 Sch.1 para.4, SI 2003/3227 Sch.1 para.4

1994–cont.

1303. Education (Lay Members of Appeal Committees) Regulations 1994–*cont.*

revoked (in part): SI 2002/3178 Reg.9, SI 2003/3227 Reg.11

1323. Haiti (United Nations Sanctions) Order 1994

Art.8, amended: 2002 c.8 s.2

Art.11, amended: 2002 c.8 s.2

1324. Haiti (United Nations Sanctions) (Dependent Territories) Order 1994

Art.8, amended: 2002 c.8 s.2

Art.11, amended: 2002 c.8 s.2

1325. Haiti (United Nations Sanctions) (Channel Islands) Order 1994

Art.8, amended: 2002 c.8 s.2

Art.11, amended: 2002 c.8 s.2

1326. Haiti (United Nations Sanctions) (Isle of Man) Order 1994

Art.8, amended: 2002 c.8 s.2

Art.11, amended: 2002 c.8 s.2

1364. Road Vehicles (Registration and Licensing) (Amendment) Regulations 1994

revoked: SI 2002/2742 Sch.1 Part I

1402. Medicines (Child Safety) Amendment Regulations 1994

revoked: SI 2003/2317 Reg.7

1405. Channel Tunnel (Miscellaneous Provisions) Order 1994

applied: SI 2002/2817 Reg.5

Art.2, amended: SI 2004/2589 Art.3

Art.3, amended: SI 2004/2589 Art.3

Sch.1, amended: SI 2004/2589 Art.3

Sch.2 Part III, added: SI 2004/2589 Art.3

1423. Oil and Fibre Plant Seeds (Amendment) Regulations 1994

revoked (in part): SI 2002/3174 Reg.32, SI 2004/2881 Reg.32, SSI 2004/317 Sch.8

1435. Cleveland Tertiary College (Government) Regulations 1994

revoked: SI 2002/1094 Sch.1 Part 1

1443. Act of Sederunt (Rules of the Court of Session 1994

para.38.4, see *M v Chief Constable of Strathclyde* 2003 S.L.T. 1007 (OH), Lord McCluskey

1443. Act of Sederunt (Rules of the Court of Session 1994) 1994

see *King v Global Marine (UK) Ltd* 2003 S.C. 269 (2 Div), Lord Gill L.J.C., Lord Caplan, Lord Johnston

Appendix 1., added: SSI 2002/514 Sch.1, SSI 2003/223 Sch.1

Appendix 1., amended: SSI 2002/570 Sch.1, SSI 2003/537 r.2, SSI 2004/52 r.2, Sch.1 Part 1, Sch.1 Part 2, SSI 2004/291 Sch.1, SSI 2004/331 r.2, Sch.1 Part 1, Sch.1 Part 2

r.42.1, see *Finlayson v British Steel Plc* 2003 S.L.T. 903 (OH), Lord Mackay of Drumadoon

NO.

1994–cont.

1443. Act of Sederunt (Rules of the Court of Session 1994) 1994–*cont.*

Sch.2 r.2.1, see *VP Packaging Ltd v ADF Partnership* 2002 S.L.T. 1224 (OH), Lord Wheatley

Sch.2 Part 2 para.7.7, applied: SSI 2002/494 Reg.41

Sch.2 Part 2 para.10.1, amended: SSI 2004/52 r.2

Sch.2 Part 3, added: SSI 2004/52 r.2

Sch.2 Part 3 para.13.6, substituted: SSI 2003/537 r.2

Sch.2 Part 3 para.13.8, substituted: SSI 2003/537 r.2

Sch.2 Part 3 para.13.9, substituted: SSI 2003/537 r.2

Sch.2 Part 3 para.13.10, amended: SSI 2003/537 r.2

Sch.2 Part 3 para.13.11, amended: SSI 2003/537 r.2

Sch.2 Part 3 para.16.2A, added: SSI 2004/52 r.2

Sch.2 Part 3 para.16.6, amended: SSI 2004/52 r.2

Sch.2 Part 3 para.16.8, amended: SSI 2004/52 r.2

Sch.2 Part 3 para.16.15, amended: SSI 2002/560 Sch.3 para.5

Sch.2 Part 3 para.22.4, substituted: SSI 2004/331 r.2

Sch.2 Part 3 para.25.2, substituted: SSI 2003/537 r.2

Sch.2 Part 3 para.26.3, substituted: SSI 2003/537 r.2

Sch.2 Part 3 para.26.6, amended: SSI 2004/52 r.2

Sch.2 Part 3 para.26.6, revoked (in part): SSI 2004/52 r.2

Sch.2 Part 3 para.33.5, amended: SSI 2004/331 r.2

Sch.2 Part 3 para.39.1, amended: SSI 2004/331 r.2

Sch.2 Part 3 para.40.7A, amended: SSI 2004/331 r.2

Sch.2 Part 3 para.40.21, substituted: SSI 2004/52 r.2

Sch.2 Part 3 para.41.3A, added: SSI 2004/331 r.2

Sch.2 Part 3 para.41.4, amended: SSI 2004/52 r.2, SSI 2004/331 r.2

Sch.2 Part 3 para.41.20, amended: SSI 2004/331 r.2

Sch.2 Part 3 para.41.25, amended: SSI 2004/52 r.2

Sch.2 Part 3 para.41.43A, added: SSI 2003/222 r.2

Sch.2 Part 3 para.41.43A, amended: SSI 2004/331 r.2

Sch.2 Part 3 para.41.43B, added: SSI 2003/222 r.2

1994–cont.

1443. Act of Sederunt (Rules of the Court of Session 1994) 1994–*cont.*

Sch.2 Part 3 para.41.43B, amended: SSI 2004/331 r.2

Sch.2 Part 3 para.41.46, added: SSI 2003/223 r.2

Sch.2 Part 3 para.41.46A, added: SSI 2003/223 r.2, SSI 2004/331 r.2

Sch.2 Part 3 para.41.47, added: SSI 2003/223 r.2

Sch.2 Part 3 para.41.47, amended: SSI 2004/331 r.2

Sch.2 Part 3 para.41.47, revoked (in part): SSI 2004/331 r.2

Sch.2 Part 3 para.41.48, added: SSI 2003/223 r.2

Sch.2 Part 3 para.41.49, added: SSI 2003/223 r.2

Sch.2 Part 3 para.41.49, substituted: SSI 2004/331 r.2

Sch.2 Part 3 para.41.50, added: SSI 2003/223 r.2

Sch.2 Part 3 para.41.50, revoked: SSI 2004/331 r.2

Sch.2 Part 3 para.41.51, added: SSI 2003/223 r.2

Sch.2 Part 3 para.41.52, added: SSI 2003/223 r.2

Sch.2 Part 3 para.41.54, added: SSI 2003/223 r.2

Sch.2 Part 3 para.41.55, added: SSI 2004/331 r.2

Sch.2 Part 3 para.41.56, added: SSI 2004/331 r.2

Sch.2 Part 3 para.41.57, added: SSI 2004/331 r.2

Sch.2 Part 3 para.41.58, added: SSI 2004/331 r.2

Sch.2 Part 3 para.42.16, added: SSI 2003/194 Sch.2, SSI 2004/151 r.2

Sch.2 Part 3 para.42.16, amended: SSI 2002/301 Sch.1, SSI 2003/194 r.2, Sch.1, SSI 2003/247 r.2, SSI 2004/150 r.2, SSI 2004/151 r.2

Sch.2 Part 3 para.42.16, revoked (in part): SSI 2003/194 r.2, r.2

Sch.2 Part 3 para.42.16, substituted: SSI 2004/151 Sch.1

Sch.2 Part 4, substituted: SSI 2002/570 r.2

Sch.2 Part 4 para.43.1, amended: SSI 2004/291 r.2

Sch.2 Part 4 para.43.11, amended: SSI 2004/331 r.2

Sch.2 Part 4 para.43.15, applied: SI 2002/1792 Reg.21

Sch.2 Part 4 para.49.89, amended: SSI 2004/52 r.2

Sch.2 Part 4 para.58.8A, amended: SSI 2004/52 r.2

Sch.2 Part 4 para.59.1, amended: SSI 2003/537 r.2, SSI 2004/331 r.2

NO.

NO.

1994–cont.

1443. Act of Sederunt (Rules of the Court of Session 1994) 1994–*cont.*

Sch.2 Part 5, added: SSI 2002/514 Art.2

Sch.2 Part 5, added: SSI 2004/331 r.2

Sch.2 Part 5 para.62.26, substituted: SSI 2004/52 r.2

Sch.2 Part 5 para.62.27, substituted: SSI 2004/52 r.2

Sch.2 Part 5 para.62.28, substituted: SSI 2004/52 r.2

Sch.2 Part 5 para.62.29, substituted: SSI 2004/52 r.2

Sch.2 Part 5 para.62.30, substituted: SSI 2004/52 r.2

Sch.2 Part 5 para.62.31, substituted: SSI 2004/52 r.2

Sch.2 Part 5 para.62.32, substituted: SSI 2004/52 r.2

Sch.2 Part 5 para.62.33, substituted: SSI 2004/52 r.2

Sch.2 Part 5 para.62.34, substituted: SSI 2004/52 r.2

Sch.2 Part 5 para.62.35, substituted: SSI 2004/52 r.2

Sch.2 Part 5 para.62.36, substituted: SSI 2004/52 r.2

Sch.2 Part 5 para.62.37, substituted: SSI 2004/52 r.2

Sch.2 Part 5 para.62.38, substituted: SSI 2004/52 r.2

Sch.2 Part 5 para.62.39, substituted: SSI 2004/52 r.2

Sch.2 Part 5 para.62.40, substituted: SSI 2004/52 r.2

Sch.2 Part 5 para.62.41, substituted: SSI 2004/52 r.2

Sch.2 Part 5 para.62.42, substituted: SSI 2004/52 r.2

Sch.2 Part 5 para.64.2, amended: SSI 2004/52 r.2

Sch.2 Part 5 para.64.6, amended: SSI 2004/52 r.2

Sch.2 Part 5 para.64.9, amended: SSI 2004/52 r.2

Sch.2 Part 5 para.67.33, substituted: SSI 2004/52 r.2

Sch.2 Part 5 para.67.34, substituted: SSI 2004/52 r.2

Sch.2 Part 5 para.67.35, substituted: SSI 2004/52 r.2

Sch.2 Part 5 para.67.36, substituted: SSI 2004/52 r.2

Sch.2 Part 5 para.67.37, substituted: SSI 2004/52 r.2

Sch.2 Part 5 para.67.38, substituted: SSI 2004/52 r.2

Sch.2 Part 5 para.67.39, substituted: SSI 2004/52 r.2

Sch.2 Part 5 para.67.40, substituted: SSI 2004/52 r.2

1994–cont.

1443. Act of Sederunt (Rules of the Court of Session 1994) 1994–*cont.*

Sch.2 Part 5 para.67.41, substituted: SSI 2004/52 r.2

Sch.2 Part 5 para.74.1, amended: SSI 2003/385 r.2

Sch.2 Part 5 para.74.4, amended: SSI 2003/385 r.2

Sch.2 Part 5 para.74.5, amended: SSI 2003/385 r.2

Sch.2 Part 5 para.74.9, amended: SSI 2003/385 r.2

Sch.2 Part 5 para.74.10, amended: SSI 2003/385 r.2

Sch.2 Part 5 para.74.11, amended: SSI 2003/385 r.2

Sch.2 Part 5 para.74.12, amended: SSI 2003/385 r.2

Sch.2 Part 5 para.74.13, amended: SSI 2003/385 r.2

Sch.2 Part 5 para.74.13, substituted: SSI 2003/385 r.2

Sch.2 Part 5 para.74.14, amended: SSI 2003/385 r.2

Sch.2 Part 5 para.74.14, substituted: SSI 2003/385 r.2

Sch.2 Part 5 para.74.15, amended: SSI 2003/385 r.2

Sch.2 Part 5 para.74.15, substituted: SSI 2003/385 r.2

Sch.2 Part 5 para.74.17, amended: SSI 2003/385 r.2

Sch.2 Part 5 para.74.24, amended: SSI 2003/385 r.2

Sch.2 Part 5 para.74.25, amended: SSI 2003/385 r.2

Sch.2 Part 5 para.74.30A, added: SSI 2003/385 r.2

Sch.2 Part 5 para.76A.1, added: SSI 2003/222 r.2

Sch.2 Part 5 para.76A.1, substituted: SSI 2004/331 r.2

Sch.2 Part 5 para.76A.2, added: SSI 2003/222 r.2

Sch.2 Part 5 para.76A.2, substituted: SSI 2004/331 r.2

Sch.2 Part 5 para.76A.3, added: SSI 2003/222 r.2

Sch.2 Part 5 para.76A.3, substituted: SSI 2004/331 r.2

Sch.2 Part 5 para.76A.4, added: SSI 2003/222 r.2

Sch.2 Part 5 para.76A.4, substituted: SSI 2004/331 r.2

Sch.2 Part 5 para.76A.5, added: SSI 2003/222 r.2

Sch.2 Part 5 para.76A.5, substituted: SSI 2004/331 r.2

Sch.2 Part 5 para.76A.6, added: SSI 2003/222 r.2

NO.

1994–cont.

1443. Act of Sederunt (Rules of the Court of Session 1994) 1994–*cont.*

Sch.2 Part 5 para.76A.6, substituted: SSI 2004/331 r.2

Sch.2 Part 5 para.76A.7, added: SSI 2003/222 r.2

Sch.2 Part 5 para.76A.7, substituted: SSI 2004/331 r.2

Sch.2 Part 5 para.76A.8, added: SSI 2003/222 r.2

Sch.2 Part 5 para.76A.8, substituted: SSI 2004/331 r.2

Sch.2 Part 5 para.76A.9, added: SSI 2003/222 r.2

Sch.2 Part 5 para.76A.9, substituted: SSI 2004/331 r.2

Sch.2 Part 5 para.76A.10, added: SSI 2003/222 r.2

Sch.2 Part 5 para.76A.10, substituted: SSI 2004/331 r.2

Sch.2 Part 5 para.76A.11, added: SSI 2003/222 r.2

Sch.2 Part 5 para.76A.11, substituted: SSI 2004/331 r.2

Sch.2 Part 5 para.76A.12, added: SSI 2003/222 r.2

Sch.2 Part 5 para.76A.12, substituted: SSI 2004/331 r.2

Sch.2 r.13.6, see *Karl Construction Ltd v Palisade Properties Plc* 2002 S.C. 270 (OH), Lord Drummond Young

Sch.2 r.14.3, see *Institute of Chartered Accountants of Scotland, Petitioners* 2002 S.L.T. 921 (OH), Lord Menzies

Sch.2 r.14.8, see *Van Overwaele v Hacking & Paterson* 2002 S.C. 62 (Ex Div), Lord Coulsfield, Lord Johnston, Lord Prosser

Sch.2 r.24.4, see *Magee v Glasgow City Council* 2003 S.L.T. 777 (OH), Temporary Judge JG Reid Q.C.

Sch.2 r.29.1, see *Beattie v Royal Bank of Scotland Plc* 2003 S.L.T. 564 (OH), Lord Reed; see *VP Packaging Ltd v ADF Partnership* 2002 S.L.T. 1224 (OH), Lord Wheatley

Sch.2 r.37.1, see *Benson v Scottish Lion Engineering Ltd* 2002 S.C. 228 (2 Div), Lord Gill L.J.C., Lord MacLean, Lady Paton; see *Benson v Scottish Lion Engineering Ltd* 2002 S.C.L.R. 162 (OH), Lord Kingarth

Sch.2 r.40.12, see *Drever v Drever* 2003 S.L.T. (Sh Ct) 8 (Sh Pr), Sir SST Young Q.C., Sheriff Principal

Sch.2 r.42.4, see *Magee v Glasgow City Council* 2003 S.L.T. 777 (OH), Temporary Judge JG Reid Q.C.

Sch.2 r.42.10, see *McNair's Executrix v Wrights Insulation Co Ltd* 2003 S.L.T. 1311 (OH), Lord Carloway

Sch.2 r.42.13, see *Earl v Kvaerner Energy Ltd* 2002 S.L.T. 1167 (OH), Lord Eassie

NO.

1994–cont.

1443. Act of Sederunt (Rules of the Court of Session 1994) 1994–*cont.*

Sch.2 r.42.14, see *Magee v Glasgow City Council* 2003 S.L.T. 777 (OH), Temporary Judge JG Reid Q.C.

Sch.2 r.43.1, see *Tudhope v Finlay Park (t/a Park Hutchison Solicitors)* 2003 S.L.T. 1305 (OH), Lady Paton

Sch.2 r.43.2, see *Higgins v DHL International (UK) Ltd* 2003 S.L.T. 1301 (OH), Lady Paton

Sch.2 r.43.6, see *Higgins v DHL International (UK) Ltd* 2003 S.L.T. 1301 (OH), Lady Paton

Sch.2 r.53.8, see *Vaughan Engineering Ltd v Hinkins & Frewin Ltd* 2003 S.L.T. 428 (OH), Lord Clarke

Sch.2 r.58, see *Davidson v Scottish Ministers (No.1)* 2002 S.C. 205 (Ex Div), Lord Marnoch, Lord Hardie, Lord Weir

Sch.2 r.58.3, see *Davidson v Scottish Ministers (No.1)* 2002 S.C. 205 (Ex Div), Lord Marnoch, Lord Hardie, Lord Weir; see *Vaughan Engineering Ltd v Hinkins & Frewin Ltd* 2003 S.L.T. 428 (OH), Lord Clarke

1443. Act of Sederunt (Rules of the Court of Session) 1994

r.42.14, see *S v S* 2003 S.C.L.R. 261 (Ex Div), Lord Macfadyen, Lord Cameron of Lochbroom, Lord Kirkwood

1443. Act of Sederunt (Rules of the Court of Session) 1994

Sch.2 r.30.2, see *Hay v Institute of Chartered Accountants in Scotland* 2003 S.L.T. 612 (OH), Lady Paton

1447. Diseases of Fish (Control) Regulations 1994

Reg.2, substituted: SI 2002/284 Sch.1 para.1

Reg.3, substituted: SI 2002/284 Sch.1 para.1

Reg.4, substituted: SI 2002/284 Sch.1 para.1

Reg.5, substituted: SI 2002/284 Sch.1 para.1

Reg.6, substituted: SI 2002/284 Sch.1 para.1

Reg.7, substituted: SI 2002/284 Sch.1 para.1

Reg.8, substituted: SI 2002/284 Sch.1 para.1

Reg.11, amended: SI 2002/284 Sch.1 para.4

Reg.12, substituted: SI 2002/284 Sch.1 para.5

Reg.13, amended: SI 2002/284 Sch.1 para.6

Reg.15, amended: SI 2002/284 Sch.1 para.7

Sch.1 para.1, revoked (in part): SI 2002/284 Sch.1 para.8

Sch.1 para.2, revoked (in part): SI 2002/284 Sch.1 para.8

1511. Children's Homes Amendment Regulations 1994

revoked (in part): SI 2002/327 Reg.43

1519. Traffic Signs Regulations and General Directions 1994

applied: SI 2002/1066 Sch.12 para.8, SI 2004/757 Sch.14 para.8

1994–cont.

1519. Traffic Signs Regulations and General Directions 1994–*cont.*

Reg.1, revoked: SI 2002/3113 Reg.2
Reg.2, revoked: SI 2002/3113 Reg.2
Reg.3, revoked: SI 2002/3113 Reg.2
Reg.4, revoked: SI 2002/3113 Reg.2
Reg.5, revoked: SI 2002/3113 Reg.2
Reg.6, revoked: SI 2002/3113 Reg.2
Reg.7, revoked: SI 2002/3113 Reg.2
Reg.8, revoked: SI 2002/3113 Reg.2
Reg.9, revoked: SI 2002/3113 Reg.2
Reg.10, revoked: SI 2002/3113 Reg.2
Reg.11, revoked: SI 2002/3113 Reg.2
Reg.12, revoked: SI 2002/3113 Reg.2
Reg.13, revoked: SI 2002/3113 Reg.2
Reg.14, revoked: SI 2002/3113 Reg.2
Reg.14A, revoked: SI 2002/3113 Reg.2
Reg.15, revoked: SI 2002/3113 Reg.2
Reg.16, revoked: SI 2002/3113 Reg.2
Reg.17, revoked: SI 2002/3113 Reg.2
Reg.18, revoked: SI 2002/3113 Reg.2
Reg.19, revoked (in part): SI 2002/3020 Reg.1, SI 2002/3113 Reg.2, SSI 2002/549 Reg.1
Reg.20, revoked: SI 2002/3113 Reg.2
Reg.21, revoked: SI 2002/3113 Reg.2
Reg.22, revoked: SI 2002/3113 Reg.2
Reg.23, revoked: SI 2002/3113 Reg.2
Reg.24, revoked: SI 2002/3113 Reg.2
Reg.25, revoked: SI 2002/3113 Reg.2
Reg.26, revoked: SI 2002/3113 Reg.2
Reg.27, revoked: SI 2002/3113 Reg.2
Reg.28, revoked: SI 2002/3113 Reg.2
Reg.29, revoked: SI 2002/3113 Reg.2
Reg.30, revoked: SI 2002/3113 Reg.2
Reg.31, revoked: SI 2002/3113 Reg.2
Reg.32, revoked: SI 2002/3113 Reg.2
Reg.33, revoked: SI 2002/3113 Reg.2
Reg.34, revoked: SI 2002/3113 Reg.2
Reg.35, revoked: SI 2002/3113 Reg.2
Reg.36, revoked: SI 2002/3113 Reg.2
Reg.37, revoked: SI 2002/3113 Reg.2
Reg.38, revoked: SI 2002/3113 Reg.2
Reg.39, revoked (in part): SI 2002/3020 Reg.1, SI 2002/3113 Reg.2, SSI 2002/549 Reg.1
Reg.40, revoked: SI 2002/3113 Reg.2
Reg.41, revoked: SI 2002/3113 Reg.2
Reg.42, revoked: SI 2002/3113 Reg.2
Reg.43, revoked: SI 2002/3113 Reg.2
Reg.44, revoked: SI 2002/3113 Reg.2
Reg.45, revoked: SI 2002/3113 Reg.2
Reg.46, revoked: SI 2002/3113 Reg.2
Reg.50, applied: SI 2002/3113 Reg.58
Sch.2, revoked (in part): SI 2002/3020 Reg.1, SSI 2002/549 Reg.1

1534. West Lindsey National Health Service Trust (Establishment) Amendment Order 1994

revoked: 2003 c.43 s.7

1994–cont.

1555. Ashford Hospitals National Health Service Trust (Establishment) Amendment Order 1994

revoked: 2003 c.43 s.7

1623. Employment Tribunals Extension of Jurisdiction (England and Wales) Order 1994

applied: 2002 c.22 Sch.3, Sch.5
Art.3, see *Johnston v Miller Bros & FP Butler Ltd* [2002] I.C.R. 744 (EAT), Recorder Langstaff Q.C.; see *Sweeney v Peninsula Business Services Ltd* [2004] I.R.L.R. 49 (EAT), Rimer, J.
Art.4, applied: SI 2004/1861 Sch.1 para.7
Art.7, amended: SI 2004/752 Reg.17

1624. Employment Tribunals Extension of Jurisdiction (Scotland) Order 1994

applied: 2002 c.22 Sch.3, Sch.5
Art.4, applied: SI 2004/1861 Sch.1 para.7
Art.7, amended: SI 2004/752 Reg.17

1647. Lancaster Port Commission Harbour Revision Order 1994

Art.3, revoked: SI 2003/2724 Sch.3

1662. European Parliamentary (United Kingdom Representatives) Pensions (Consolidation and Amendment) Order 1994

applied: SI 2003/2922 Art.2
amended: SI 2003/2922 Art.2
Art.3, amended: SI 2003/2922 Art.2
Art.5, amended: SI 2003/1416 Art.2
Art.7, amended: SI 2003/1416 Art.3
Art.10, amended: SI 2003/1416 Art.4
Art.14, amended: SI 2003/1416 Art.5
Art.16, amended: SI 2003/1416 Art.6
Sch.5 para.1, substituted: SI 2003/1416 Art.5
Sch.5 para.1A, added: SI 2003/1416 Art.5
Sch.5 para.1A, substituted: SI 2003/1416 Art.5
Sch.5 para.2, substituted: SI 2003/1416 Art.5
Sch.5 para.3, substituted: SI 2003/1416 Art.5
Sch.5 para.4, substituted: SI 2003/1416 Art.5
Sch.5 para.5, substituted: SI 2003/1416 Art.5
Sch.5 para.6, substituted: SI 2003/1416 Art.5
Sch.5 para.7, added: SI 2003/1416 Art.5
Sch.5 para.7, substituted: SI 2003/1416 Art.5
Sch.5 para.8, added: SI 2003/1416 Art.5
Sch.5 para.8, substituted: SI 2003/1416 Art.5

1663. European Parliament (Pay and Pensions) Act 1979 (Section 3 (Amendment)) Order 1994

applied: SI 2003/2922 Art.2

1701. Organic Aid (Scotland) Regulations 1994

applied: SI 2003/2261 Sch.3 Part I, SSI 2004/143 Reg.3, Reg.11, Reg.15, Sch.8, SSI 2004/381 Reg.4
Reg.8, amended: SSI 2004/143 Reg.26
Reg.12, applied: SSI 2004/381 Reg.4

NO.

1994–cont.

1721. Organic Farming (Aid) Regulations 1994
applied: SI 2003/1235 Reg.8
Reg.2, amended: SI 2002/3159 Reg.15

1729. Nitrate Sensitive Areas Regulations 1994
applied: SI 2003/2261 Sch.3 Part I
Sch.6 para.1, amended: SI 2002/744 Reg.3
Sch.6 para.3, amended: SI 2002/744 Reg.3
Sch.6 para.4, amended: SI 2002/744 Reg.3
Sch.6 para.6, amended: SI 2002/744 Reg.3
Sch.6 para.6B, amended: SI 2002/744 Reg.3

1761. Wirral Tramway Light Railway Order 1994
Art.2, amended: SI 2003/2155 Sch.2
Art.20, amended: SI 2003/2155 Sch.1 para.18
Art.20, revoked (in part): SI 2003/2155 Sch.2

1774. Insurance Premium Tax Regulations 1994
Reg.11, amended: SI 2003/2096 Sch.1 para.54
Reg.43, amended: 2002 asp 17 Sch.3 para.34

1809. Non Domestic Rating (Alteration of Lists and Appeals) (Amendment) Regulations 1994
see *National Car Parks Ltd v Baird (Valuation Officer)* [2004] EWCA Civ 967, [2004] R.A. 245 (CA), Sir Andrew Morritt V.C.

1811. Special Commissioners (Jurisdiction and Procedure) Regulations 1994
applied: SI 2002/2172 Reg.14
referred to: SI 2002/2976 Reg.1, SI 2003/968 Reg.2
Reg.2, amended: SI 2002/2976 Reg.3, SI 2003/968 Reg.3
Reg.3, see *Arkwright (Williams Personal Representative) v Inland Revenue Commissioners* [2004] S.T.C. (S.C.D.) 89 (Sp Comm), Nuala Brice
Reg.7, amended: SI 2002/2976 Reg.4
Reg.7A, added: SI 2002/2976 Reg.5
Reg.8, amended: SI 2003/968 Reg.4
Reg.10, amended: SI 2003/968 Reg.5
Reg.12A, added: SI 2003/968 Reg.6
Reg.14, amended: SI 2003/968 Reg.7
Reg.15, amended: SI 2003/968 Reg.8
Reg.15, substituted: SI 2002/2976 Reg.6
Reg.15, see *Businessman v Inspector of Taxes* [2003] S.T.C. (S.C.D.) 403 (Sp Comm), John F Avery Jones
Reg.21, see *Lavery v Macleod (Inspector of Taxes) (No.2)* [2003] S.T.C. (S.C.D.) 413 (Sp Comm), AN Brice; see *Robertson v Inland Revenue Commissioners (No.2)* [2002] S.T.C. (S.C.D.) 242 (Sp Comm), J Gordon Reid Q.C.
Reg.23, see *Arkwright (Williams Personal Representative) v Inland Revenue Commissioners* [2004] S.T.C. (S.C.D.) 89 (Sp Comm), Nuala Brice

NO.

1994–cont.

1812. General Commissioners (Jurisdiction and Procedure) Regulations 1994
applied: SI 2002/2172 Reg.8, Reg.14
referred to: SI 2002/2976 Reg.1
Reg.2, amended: SI 2002/2976 Reg.8
Reg.6A, added: SI 2002/2976 Reg.9
Reg.10, see *R. (on the application of Werner) v Inland Revenue Commissioners* [2002] EWCA Civ 979, [2002] S.T.C. 1213 (CA), Hart, J.; see *Slater Ltd v Beacontree General Commissioners (No.1)* [2002] S.T.C. 246 (Ch D), Lightman, J.
Reg.13, substituted: SI 2002/2976 Reg.10
Reg.16, see *McCullough (Inspector of Taxes) v Ahluwalia* [2004] EWCA Civ 889, [2004] S.T.C. 1295 (CA), Waller, L.J.
Reg.22, see *New World Medical Ltd v Cormack (Inspector of Taxes)* [2002] EWHC 1787, [2002] S.T.C. 1245 (Ch D), Blackburne, J.

1818. Education (National Curriculum) (Modern Foreign Languages) (Amendment) Order 1994
revoked (in part): SI 2004/260 Art.2

1842. Protection of Wrecks (Designation No 1) Order 1994
revoked: SI 2004/2395 Sch.2 para.6

1882. Statutory Maternity Pay (Compensation of Employers) and Miscellaneous Amendment Regulations 1994
Reg.1, amended: SI 2003/672 Reg.2
Reg.1, revoked (in part): SI 2003/672 Reg.2
Reg.2, amended: SI 2002/225 Reg.2, SI 2004/698 Reg.2
Reg.3, amended: SI 2002/225 Reg.2, SI 2003/672 Reg.3
Reg.4, applied: SI 2003/2682 Reg.203
Reg.4, substituted: SI 2003/672 Reg.4
Reg.5, applied: SI 2003/2682 Reg.203
Reg.5, substituted: SI 2003/672 Reg.4
Reg.6, applied: SI 2003/2682 Reg.203
Reg.6, substituted: SI 2003/672 Reg.4
Reg.7, amended: SI 2003/672 Reg.5
Reg.7A, added: SI 2003/672 Reg.6

1886. Gas Safety (Installation and Use) Regulations 1994
Reg.35, see *MacKenzie v Aberdeen City Council* 2002 Hous. L.R. 88 (Sh Ct (Grampian, Highland and Islands)), DJ Cusine

1890. European Molecular Biology Laboratory (Immunities and Privileges) Order 1994
Art.14, amended: 2002 c.8 s.2

1896. Litter (Northern Ireland) Order 1994
Art.7, applied: SR 2002/248 Reg.9
Art.12, applied: SR 2002/248 Reg.9
Art.13, applied: SR 2002/248 Reg.9
Art.17, applied: SR 2002/248 Reg.9
Art.17, enabled: SR 2002/248

NO.

1994–cont.

1897. Rates (Amendment) (Northern Ireland) Order 1994
Art.5, revoked (in part): SI 2004/703 Sch.4

1898. Social Security (Incapacity for Work) (Northern Ireland) Order 1994
Art.4, revoked (in part): 2002 c.21 Sch.6
Art.6, enabled: SR 2002/86
Art.12, revoked: 2002 c.21 Sch.6
Sch.1, revoked: 2002 c.21 Sch.6

1911. Road Vehicles (Registration and Licensing) (Amendment) (No.2) Regulations 1994
revoked: SI 2002/2742 Sch.1 Part I

1931. Prisons and Young Offenders Institutions (Scotland) Rules 1994
Part 1 r.3, amended: SSI 2002/107 r.2
Part 2 r.13, amended: SSI 2002/107 r.3
Part 2A, applied: SSI 2002/107 r.12
Part 2A r.14A, substituted: SSI 2002/107 r.4
Part 2A r.14B, substituted: SSI 2002/107 r.4
Part 2A r.14C, substituted: SSI 2002/107 r.4
Part 2A r.14D, substituted: SSI 2002/107 r.4
Part 2A r.14E, substituted: SSI 2002/107 r.4
Part 2A r.14F, substituted: SSI 2002/107 r.4
Part 6 r.42, amended: SSI 2002/107 r.5
Part 7 r.62B, amended: SSI 2003/242 Art.3
Part 9 r.91, amended: SSI 2002/107 r.6
Part 9 r.91, referred to: SSI 2002/107 r.12
Part 9 r.92, revoked (in part): SSI 2002/107 r.7
Part 14 r.120, substituted: SSI 2002/107 r.8
Part 14 r.120A, substituted: SSI 2002/107 r.8
Part 14 r.121, substituted: SSI 2002/107 r.8
Part 14 r.122, substituted: SSI 2002/107 r.8
Part 14 r.123, substituted: SSI 2002/107 r.8
Part 14 r.123A, substituted: SSI 2002/107 r.8
Part 14 r.124, substituted: SSI 2002/107 r.8
Part 14 r.125, substituted: SSI 2002/107 r.8
Part 14 r.126, substituted: SSI 2002/107 r.8
Part 16 r.133, amended: SSI 2002/107 r.9
Part 16 r.134, amended: SSI 2002/107 r.10
r.54, see *Dudley (Fiona Jacqueline) v HM Advocate* 2003 J.C. 53 (HCJ), Lord Cameron of Lochbroom, Lord Gill L.J.C., Lord Kirkwood
Sch.4, amended: SSI 2002/107 r.11

1932. Medicines (Advertising) Regulations 1994
referred to: SI 2003/1374 Sch.1
Reg.2, amended: SI 2002/236 Reg.10, SI 2003/2321 Reg.6
Reg.6, amended: SI 2004/1480 Reg.2
Reg.6, revoked (in part): SI 2004/1480 Reg.2
Reg.23, applied: SI 2003/1376 Sch.1
Sch.1, substituted: SI 2004/1480 Reg.2

1933. Medicines (Monitoring of Advertising) Regulations 1994
applied: SI 2004/1975 Art.7, Art.8, Art.11
Reg.2, amended: SI 2002/236 Reg.11, SI 2003/3093 Art.2
Reg.4, amended: SI 2003/3093 Art.3

NO.

1994–cont.

1933. Medicines (Monitoring of Advertising) Regulations 1994*–cont.*
Reg.5, amended: SI 2003/3093 Art.4
Reg.9, substituted: SI 2003/3093 Art.5
Reg.10, revoked: SI 2003/3093 Art.6
Reg.11, amended: SI 2003/3093 Art.7
Reg.11, revoked (in part): SI 2003/3093 Art.7

1994/1931. Prisons and Young Offenders Institutions (Scotland) Rules 1994
r.88, see *Tolmie v Scottish Ministers* 2003 S.C. 265 (2 Div), Lord Gill L.J.C., Lord Caplan, Lord MacLean

2005. Railway Pensions (Transfer and Miscellaneous Provisions) Order 1994
Sch.1 Part II para.8, varied: SI 2003/1633 Sch.2 para.8

2023. Police Authorities (Selection Panel) Regulations 1994
Reg.4, amended: SI 2002/1282 Reg.3
Reg.6, amended: SI 2002/1282 Reg.4

2095. Police (Scotland) Amendment Regulations 1994
revoked: SSI 2004/257 Sch.4

2145. Compulsory Purchase of Land Regulations 1994
revoked (in part): SI 2004/2595 Reg.5, SI 2004/2732 Reg.5

2155. Pig Carcase (Grading) Regulations 1994
Reg.2, amended: SI 2003/2949 Reg.2, SI 2004/106 Reg.2, SI 2004/1505 Reg.2, SSI 2003/565 Reg.2, SSI 2004/279 Reg.2
Reg.6, amended: SI 2004/1505 Reg.2

2217. Companies (Fees) (Amendment) Regulations 1994
revoked: SI 2004/2621 Sch.3

2231. Police (Scotland) Amendment (No.2) Regulations 1994
revoked: SSI 2004/257 Sch.4

2249. Marketing of Gas Oil (Sulphur Content) Regulations 1994
revoked: SR 2002/28 Reg.6

2286. Organic Products (Amendment) Regulations 1994
revoked (in part): SI 2002/3159 Sch.4, SI 2004/1604 Sch.3

2318. Income Tax (Authorised Unit Trusts) (Interest Distributions) Regulations 1994
revoked: SI 2003/1830 Reg.11

2319. Social Security (Claims and Payments) Amendment Regulations 1994
revoked (in part): SI 2003/492 Sch.3 Part 1

2326. Personal Protective Equipment (EC Directive) (Amendment) Regulations 1994
revoked: SI 2002/1144 Sch.11 para.1

NO.

1994–cont.

2328. General Product Safety Regulations 1994

applied: SI 2003/1400 Sch.3, Sch.4

2421. Insolvent Partnerships Order 1994

applied: SI 2002/2708 Art.11, SI 2003/2093 Art.3, SI 2004/2443 Sch.4 para.14

referred to: SI 2002/1308 Art.1

varied: SI 2002/1308 Art.2

Art.4, amended: SI 2002/2708 Art.4

Art.7, amended: SI 2002/1308 Art.3

Art.8, amended: SI 2002/1308 Art.4

Art.19, amended: SI 2002/2708 Art.5

Sch.1, substituted: SI 2002/2708 Sch.1

Sch.1 Part I, substituted: SI 2002/2708 Sch.1

Sch.1 Part II, substituted: SI 2002/2708 Sch.1

Sch.2 para.2, added: SI 2002/2708 Art.7

Sch.2 para.2, amended: SI 2002/1555 Art.36

Sch.2 para.4, added: SI 2002/2708 Art.7

Sch.2 para.5, added: SI 2002/2708 Art.7

Sch.3, see *Lancefield v Lancefield* [2002] B.P.I.R. 1108 (Ch D), Neuberger, J.

Sch.3 Part I para.3, added: SI 2002/1308 Art.5, SI 2002/2708 Art.8

Sch.3 Part I para.4, applied: SI 2003/2553 Reg.16

Sch.3 Part I para.5, applied: SI 2003/2553 Reg.16

Sch.3 Part II para.6, added: SI 2002/1308 Art.5

Sch.4 Part I para.3, added: SI 2002/1308 Art.5

Sch.4 Part I para.3, substituted: SI 2002/2708 Art.9

Sch.4 Part II para.5, added: SI 2002/1308 Art.5

Sch.4 Part II para.6, amended: SI 2002/2708 Art.9

Sch.4 Part II para.8, added: SI 2002/1308 Art.5

Sch.5 para.1, added: SI 2002/1308 Art.5

Sch.5 para.2, added: SI 2002/1308 Art.5

Sch.6 para.1, added: SI 2002/1308 Art.5

Sch.6 para.4, added: SI 2002/1308 Art.5

Sch.9, amended: SI 2002/1308 Sch.1, SI 2002/2708 Art.10, Sch.2

2464. Merchant Shipping (Gas Carriers) Regulations 1994

Reg.1, amended: SI 2004/929 Reg.2

Reg.1A, added: SI 2004/929 Reg.3

Reg.3, substituted: SI 2004/929 Reg.4

Reg.4, substituted: SI 2004/929 Reg.5

Reg.5, substituted: SI 2004/929 Reg.5

Reg.6, substituted: SI 2004/929 Reg.5

Reg.10, amended: SI 2004/929 Reg.6

Reg.10, revoked (in part): SI 2004/929 Reg.6

Reg.11, substituted: SI 2004/929 Reg.7

2488. Roads (Traffic Calming) (Scotland) Regulations 1994

applied: SI 2002/3113 Reg.16

Reg.7, amended: SSI 2002/419 Reg.2

NO.

1994–cont.

2507. Insolvency Regulations 1994

referred to: SI 2003/3363 Sch.1 para.1, SI 2004/584 r.3

Reg.5, amended: SI 2004/472 Sch.1 para.1

Reg.7, applied: SI 2003/3363 Sch.1 para.2

Reg.8, applied: SI 2003/3363 Sch.1 para.2

Reg.9, amended: SI 2004/472 Sch.1 para.2

Reg.9, varied: SI 2003/1633 Sch.2 para.2, SI 2004/472 Sch.1 para.2

Reg.14, applied: SI 2003/3363 Sch.1 para.1

Reg.22, applied: SI 2003/3363 Sch.1 para.2

Reg.23, applied: SI 2003/3363 Sch.1 para.2

Reg.23A, amended: SI 2004/472 Sch.1 para.3

Reg.23A, varied: SI 2003/1633 Sch.2 para.2, SI 2004/472 Sch.1 para.3

Reg.28, applied: SI 2003/3363 Sch.1 para.1

Reg.32, applied: SI 2003/3363 Sch.1 para.2

Reg.33, revoked: SI 2004/472 Sch.1 para.4

Reg.34, revoked: SI 2004/472 Sch.1 para.4

Reg.35, amended: SI 2004/472 Sch.1 para.5

Reg.36, revoked: SI 2004/472 Sch.1 para.4

Sch.2, amended: SI 2004/472 Sch.1 para.6, Sch.1 para.7

2522. Chesterfield and North Derbyshire Royal Hospital National Health Service Trust (Establishment) Amendment Order 1994

revoked: 2003 c.43 s.7

2524. Salmon (Fish Passes and Screens) (Scotland) Regulations 1994

applied: SSI 2002/138 Sch.2 para.3, SSI 2003/615 Sch.2 para.3

2541. Insolvency Fees (Amendment) Order 1994

revoked: SI 2004/593 Sch.1

2563. Coal Mining Subsidence (Subsidence Adviser) Regulations 1994

revoked: SI 2004/2241 Reg.2

2576. British Coal Staff Superannuation Scheme (Modification) Regulations 1994

Sch.1, varied: SI 2003/1633 Sch.2 para.8

2577. Mineworkers Pension Scheme (Modification) Regulations 1994

Sch.1, varied: SI 2003/1633 Sch.2 para.8

2583. Trade Mark Rules 1994

r.31, see *CERNIVET Trade Mark* [2002] R.P.C. 30 (Appointed Person), Geoffrey Hobbs Q.C.

2591. Scottish Milk Marketing Board (Residual Functions) Regulations 1994

Reg.4, applied: SSI 2003/534

2616. Solicitors (Non-Contentious Business) Remuneration Order 1994

applied: SI 2002/1892 Sch.1 Part TABLEe, SI 2002/1893 para.1, para.4, SI 2003/1933 Sch.1 Part II, Sch.1 Part V, SI 2003/1936 para.1, para.4, SI 2004/1888 Sch.1 Part TABLEe

NO.

NO.

1994–cont.

2620. National Health Service (General Medical Services) Amendment (No.2) Regulations 1994

revoked (in part): SI 2004/865 Sch.2, SI 2004/1016 Sch.2

Reg.2, revoked (in part): SI 2004/865 Sch.2

2627. Spongiform Encephalopathy (Miscellaneous Amendments) Order 1994

Art.2, revoked (in part): SSI 2003/353 Art.13

2673. Former Yugoslavia (United Nations Sanctions) Order 1994

Art.8, amended: 2002 c.8 s.2

2674. Former Yugoslavia (United Nations Sanctions) (Dependent Territories) Order 1994

Art.8, amended: 2002 c.8 s.2

2675. Former Yugoslavia (United Nations Sanctions) (Channel Islands) Order 1994

Art.8, amended: 2002 c.8 s.2

2676. Former Yugoslavia (United Nations Sanctions) (Isle of Man) Order 1994

Art.8, amended: 2002 c.8 s.2

2690. East Birmingham Hospital National Health Service Trust (Establishment) Amendment Order 1994

revoked: 2003 c.43 s.7

2710. Habitats (Scotland) Regulations 1994

applied: SI 2003/2261 Sch.3 Part I, SSI 2004/381 Reg.4

Reg.12, applied: SSI 2004/381 Reg.4

2716. Conservation (Natural Habitats &c.) Regulations 1994

Reg.48, see *R. (on the application of Medway Council) v Secretary of State for Transport, Local Government and the Regions* [2002] EWHC 2516, [2003] J.P.L. 583 (QBD (Admin Ct)), Maurice Kay, J.

Reg.49, see *R. (on the application of Medway Council) v Secretary of State for Transport, Local Government and the Regions* [2002] EWHC 2516, [2003] J.P.L. 583 (QBD (Admin Ct)), Maurice Kay, J.

2716. Conservation (Natural Habitats, c.) Regulations 1994

applied: SSI 2003/129 Sch.2 para.11

referred to: SI 2002/2127 Reg.13, 2003 asp 2 Sch.2 para.14, SSI 2004/70 Sch.2 para.11

Reg.2, amended: SSI 2004/475 Reg.4

Reg.3, amended: 2003 asp 2 Sch.2 para.15, SSI 2004/475 Reg.5

Reg.10, amended: SSI 2004/475 Reg.6

Reg.10, applied: 2002 asp 3 s.54

Reg.11, amended: SSI 2004/475 Reg.7

Reg.17, revoked (in part): SSI 2004/475 Reg.8

Reg.18, applied: SSI 2004/475 Reg.20

Reg.18, substituted: SSI 2004/475 Reg.9

Reg.19, substituted: SSI 2004/475 Reg.9

Reg.20, substituted: SSI 2004/475 Reg.9

1994–cont.

2716. Conservation (Natural Habitats, c.) Regulations 1994–*cont.*

Reg.21, substituted: SSI 2004/475 Reg.9

Reg.22, applied: SSI 2004/475 Reg.21

Reg.22, substituted: SSI 2004/475 Reg.9

Reg.23, revoked (in part): SSI 2004/475 Reg.22

Reg.24, revoked (in part): SSI 2004/475 Reg.22

Reg.25, revoked (in part): SSI 2004/475 Reg.22

Reg.26, revoked (in part): SSI 2004/475 Reg.22

Reg.27, revoked (in part): SSI 2004/475 Reg.22

Reg.29, amended: SI 2003/2155 Sch.1 para.36

Reg.32, revoked (in part): SSI 2004/475 Reg.22

Reg.39, amended: SSI 2004/475 Reg.10

Reg.39, applied: SI 2002/2127 Reg.13, SSI 2002/6 Reg.13

Reg.40, amended: SSI 2004/475 Reg.11

Reg.41, amended: SSI 2004/475 Reg.12

Reg.41, applied: SI 2002/2127 Reg.13, SSI 2002/6 Reg.13

Reg.43, amended: SSI 2004/475 Reg.13

Reg.43, applied: SI 2002/2127 Reg.13, SSI 2002/6 Reg.13

Reg.44, amended: SSI 2004/475 Reg.14

Reg.44, applied: SI 2002/2127 Reg.13, SSI 2002/6 Reg.13

Reg.46, amended: SSI 2004/475 Reg.15

Reg.47, amended: SSI 2004/475 Reg.16

Reg.53A, added: SSI 2004/475 Reg.16

Reg.60, disapplied: SI 2002/2618 Art.17, SI 2004/2190 Art.18

Reg.69A, added: 2003 asp 2 Sch.2 para.16

Reg.87, revoked (in part): SSI 2004/475 Reg.22

Reg.88, revoked (in part): SSI 2004/475 Reg.22

Reg.89, revoked (in part): SSI 2004/475 Reg.22

Reg.90, revoked (in part): SSI 2004/475 Reg.22

Reg.91, revoked (in part): SSI 2004/475 Reg.22

Reg.92, revoked (in part): SSI 2004/475 Reg.22

Reg.93, revoked (in part): SSI 2004/475 Reg.22

Reg.98, revoked (in part): SSI 2004/475 Reg.22

Reg.99, revoked (in part): SSI 2004/475 Reg.22

Reg.101, amended: SSI 2004/475 Reg.17

Reg.101A, added: SSI 2004/475 Reg.18

Reg.102, amended: SSI 2004/475 Reg.19

Sch.1 para.1, revoked (in part): SSI 2004/475 Reg.22

NO.

NO.

1994–cont.

2716. Conservation (Natural Habitats, c.) Regulations 1994–*cont.*

Sch.1 para.2, revoked (in part): SSI 2004/475 Reg.22

Sch.1 para.3, revoked (in part): SSI 2004/475 Reg.22

Sch.1 para.4, revoked (in part): SSI 2004/475 Reg.22

Sch.1 para.5, revoked (in part): SSI 2004/475 Reg.22

Sch.1 para.6, applied: SSI 2004/475 Reg.21

Sch.1 para.6, revoked (in part): SSI 2004/475 Reg.22

Sch.1 para.7, revoked (in part): SSI 2004/475 Reg.22

Sch.1 para.8, revoked (in part): SSI 2004/475 Reg.22

2716. Conservation (Natural Habitats, &c) Regulations 1994

Reg.44, see *R. (on the application of PPG11 Ltd) v Dorset CC* [2003] EWHC 1311, [2004] Env. L.R. 5 (QBD (Admin Ct)), Mackay, J.

2716. Conservation (Natural Habitats, &c.) Regulations 1994

Reg.39, see *R. (on the application of Newsum) v Welsh Assembly* [2004] EWHC 50, [2004] Env. L.R. 39 (QBD (Admin Ct)), Pitchford, J.

Reg.40, see *R. (on the application of Newsum) v Welsh Assembly* [2004] EWHC 50, [2004] Env. L.R. 39 (QBD (Admin Ct)), Pitchford, J.

Reg.44, see *Moggridge v National Assembly for Wales* [2003] EWHC 2188, [2004] Env. L.R.18 (QBD (Admin Ct)), Pitchford, J.; see *R. (on the application of Brown) v Secretary of State for Transport* [2003] EWHC 819, [2004] Env. L.R. 2 (QBD (Admin Ct)), Collins, J.; see *R. (on the application of Newsum) v Welsh Assembly* [2004] EWHC 50, [2004] Env. L.R. 39 (QBD (Admin Ct)), Pitchford, J.

2759. Milk Marketing Board (Residuary Functions) Regulations 1994

Reg.4, referred to: SI 2002/128(a)

2784. Liverpool Obstetric and Gynaecology Services National Health Service Trust (Change of Name) Order 1994

revoked: 2003 c.43 s.7

2795. Criminal Justice (Northern Ireland) Order 1994

Art.11, applied: 2002 c.29 s.82, s.148, s.163, s.230

Art.14, amended: 2002 c.26 Sch.11 para.6

Art.14, applied: 2002 c.29 s.163, s.164, s.165, s.169, s.170, s.171, s.172, s.182, s.183, s.308

Art.14, disapplied: 2002 c.29 s.163

Art.16, amended: 2002 c.29 Sch.11 para.26

Art.18, revoked (in part): SI 2003/1247 Sch.2

2809. Ports (Northern Ireland) Order 1994

Art.23A, added: SI 2003/2867 Sch.1 para.34

1994–cont.

2841. Urban Waste Water Treatment (England and Wales) Regulations 1994

Reg.3, amended: SI 2003/1788 Reg.4

Reg.3, applied: SI 2003/1788 Reg.2, Reg.3

Reg.3, revoked (in part): SI 2003/1788 Reg.4

Reg.12, revoked (in part): SI 2003/1788 Reg.4

2842. Urban Waste Water Treatment (Scotland) Regulations 1994

Reg.3, amended: SSI 2003/273 Reg.4

Reg.3, applied: SSI 2003/273 Reg.2

Reg.3, revoked (in part): SSI 2003/273 Reg.4

Reg.12, revoked (in part): SSI 2003/273 Reg.4

2844. Dangerous Substances and Preparations (Safety) (Consolidation) Regulations 1994

Reg.1, amended: SI 2004/1031 Sch.10 para.11

Reg.1, revoked (in part): SI 2004/1031 Sch.10 para.11

Reg.3A, revoked (in part): SI 2002/1770 Reg.2

Reg.6D, referred to: SI 2002/1689 Reg.8, SR 2002/301 Reg.8

Sch.2, amended: SI 2002/2479 Sch.1 Part 1, Sch.1 Part 2, Sch.1 Part 3, SI 2002/3010 Sch.1 Part I, Sch.1 Part II, Sch.1 Part III, SI 2004/1417 Reg.2, Sch.1 Part 1, Sch.1 Part 2, Sch.2

Sch.2, referred to: SI 2002/1689 Reg.8, SR 2002/301 Reg.8

2853. Beef Carcase (Classification) (Amendment) Regulations 1994

revoked (in part): SI 2004/1317 Reg.16, SSI 2004/280 Reg.17

2867. Units of Measurement Regulations 1994

see *Thoburn v Sunderland City Council* [2002] EWHC 195, [2003] Q.B. 151 (QBD (Admin Ct)), Laws, L.J.

2889. Alternative Names in Welsh Order 1994

Sch.1, amended: SI 2002/881 Sch.1 para.10

2899. Gaming Clubs (Bankers Games) Regulations 1994

Reg.4, revoked (in part): SI 2002/1130 Reg.2

Reg.7, amended: SI 2002/1130 Reg.2

Reg.8, amended: SI 2002/1130 Reg.2

Reg.11, added: SI 2002/1130 Reg.2

Reg.12, added: SI 2002/1130 Reg.2

Reg.13, added: SI 2002/1130 Reg.2

Reg.13, amended: SI 2002/1407 Reg.2

Sch.1 para.8, amended: SI 2002/1130 Reg.2

Sch.1 para.9, added: SI 2002/1130 Reg.2

Sch.3, added: SI 2002/1130 Reg.2

Sch.4 para.1, added: SI 2002/1130 Reg.2

Sch.4 para.2, added: SI 2002/1130 Reg.2

Sch.4 para.3, added: SI 2002/1130 Reg.2

Sch.4 para.4, added: SI 2002/1130 Reg.2

Sch.4 para.5, added: SI 2002/1130 Reg.2

Sch.4 para.6, added: SI 2002/1130 Reg.2

NO.

NO.

1994–cont.

1994–cont.

2899. Gaming Clubs (Bankers Games) Regulations 1994–*cont.*

Sch.4 para.7, added: SI 2002/1130 Reg.2

Sch.4 para.8, added: SI 2002/1130 Reg.2

Sch.4 para.9, added: SI 2002/1130 Reg.2

Sch.4 para.10, added: SI 2002/1130 Reg.2

Sch.4 para.11, added: SI 2002/1130 Reg.2

Sch.4 para.12, added: SI 2002/1130 Reg.2

Sch.4 para.13, added: SI 2002/1130 Reg.2

Sch.4 para.14, added: SI 2002/1130 Reg.2

2943. Social Security (Claims and Payments) Amendment (No.2) Regulations 1994

revoked (in part): SI 2003/492 Sch.3 Part 1

2944. Social Security (Claims and Payments) Amendment (No.3) Regulations 1994

revoked (in part): SI 2003/492 Sch.3 Part 1

2945. Social Security (Incapacity Benefit Increases for Dependants) Regulations 1994

Reg.3, substituted: SI 2003/937 Reg.2

Reg.6, revoked: SI 2003/937 Reg.2

Reg.7, revoked: SI 2003/937 Reg.2

Reg.8, revoked: SI 2003/937 Reg.2

Reg.9, amended: SI 2003/937 Reg.2

Reg.9, revoked (in part): SI 2003/937 Reg.2

2946. Social Security (Incapacity Benefit) Regulations 1994

Reg.2A, revoked (in part): SI 2003/937 Reg.2

Reg.2B, amended: SI 2002/2497 Sch.2 para.1, SI 2003/455 Sch.4 para.4

Reg.7A, added: SI 2002/2690 Reg.10

Reg.7B, added: SI 2002/2690 Reg.10

Reg.7C, added: SI 2003/1068 Reg.2

Reg.8, amended: SI 2002/2311 Reg.3, SI 2003/2262 Reg.3, SI 2004/2301 Reg.3

Reg.10, amended: SI 2002/668 Art.14, SI 2003/526 Art.15, SI 2004/552 Art.14

Reg.18, amended: SI 2002/2311 Reg.3

Reg.18, revoked (in part): SI 2002/2311 Reg.3

Reg.19, amended: SI 2002/491 Reg.4

2973. Industry-Wide Coal Staff Superannuation Scheme Regulations 1994

Part 1, varied: SI 2003/1633 Sch.2 para.8

Part 1 para.1, varied: SI 2003/1633 Sch.2 para.8

Part 1 para.10, varied: SI 2003/1633 Sch.2 para.8

Part 1 para.11, varied: SI 2003/1633 Sch.2 para.8

Part 1 para.12, varied: SI 2003/1633 Sch.2 para.8

Part 1 para.13, varied: SI 2003/1633 Sch.2 para.8

Part 1 para.14, varied: SI 2003/1633 Sch.2 para.8

Part 1 para.15, varied: SI 2003/1633 Sch.2 para.8

2973. Industry-Wide Coal Staff Superannuation Scheme Regulations 1994–*cont.*

Part 1 para.16, varied: SI 2003/1633 Sch.2 para.8

Part 1 para.17, varied: SI 2003/1633 Sch.2 para.8

Part 1 para.18, varied: SI 2003/1633 Sch.2 para.8

Part 1 para.19, varied: SI 2003/1633 Sch.2 para.8

Part 1 para.1a, varied: SI 2003/1633 Sch.2 para.8

Part 1 para.2, varied: SI 2003/1633 Sch.2 para.8

Part 1 para.20, varied: SI 2003/1633 Sch.2 para.8

Part 1 para.21, varied: SI 2003/1633 Sch.2 para.8

Part 1 para.2a, varied: SI 2003/1633 Sch.2 para.8

Part 1 para.3, varied: SI 2003/1633 Sch.2 para.8

Part 1 para.3a, varied: SI 2003/1633 Sch.2 para.8

Part 1 para.4, varied: SI 2003/1633 Sch.2 para.8

Part 1 para.4a, varied: SI 2003/1633 Sch.2 para.8

Part 1 para.5, varied: SI 2003/1633 Sch.2 para.8

Part 1 para.6, varied: SI 2003/1633 Sch.2 para.8

Part 1 para.7, varied: SI 2003/1633 Sch.2 para.8

Part 1 para.8, varied: SI 2003/1633 Sch.2 para.8

Part 1 para.9, varied: SI 2003/1633 Sch.2 para.8

Part 2, varied: SI 2003/1633 Sch.2 para.8

Appendix 1., varied: SI 2003/1633 Sch.2 para.8

Appendix 10., varied: SI 2003/1633 Sch.2 para.8

Appendix 11., varied: SI 2003/1633 Sch.2 para.8

Appendix 12., varied: SI 2003/1633 Sch.2 para.8

Appendix 13., varied: SI 2003/1633 Sch.2 para.8

Appendix 14., varied: SI 2003/1633 Sch.2 para.8

Appendix 15., varied: SI 2003/1633 Sch.2 para.8

Appendix 16., varied: SI 2003/1633 Sch.2 para.8

Appendix 17., varied: SI 2003/1633 Sch.2 para.8

Appendix 18., varied: SI 2003/1633 Sch.2 para.8

NO.

1994–cont.

2973. Industry-Wide Coal Staff Superannuation Scheme Regulations 1994– *cont.*

Appendix 19 para.1., varied: SI 2003/1633 Sch.2 para.8

Appendix 19 para.10., varied: SI 2003/1633 Sch.2 para.8

Appendix 19 para.11., varied: SI 2003/1633 Sch.2 para.8

Appendix 19 para.12., varied: SI 2003/1633 Sch.2 para.8

Appendix 19 para.13., varied: SI 2003/1633 Sch.2 para.8

Appendix 19 para.14., varied: SI 2003/1633 Sch.2 para.8

Appendix 19 para.15., varied: SI 2003/1633 Sch.2 para.8

Appendix 19 para.16., varied: SI 2003/1633 Sch.2 para.8

Appendix 19 para.2., varied: SI 2003/1633 Sch.2 para.8

Appendix 19 para.3., varied: SI 2003/1633 Sch.2 para.8

Appendix 19 para.4., varied: SI 2003/1633 Sch.2 para.8

Appendix 19 para.5., varied: SI 2003/1633 Sch.2 para.8

Appendix 19 para.6., varied: SI 2003/1633 Sch.2 para.8

Appendix 19 para.7., varied: SI 2003/1633 Sch.2 para.8

Appendix 19 para.8., varied: SI 2003/1633 Sch.2 para.8

Appendix 19 para.9., varied: SI 2003/1633 Sch.2 para.8

Appendix 2., varied: SI 2003/1633 Sch.2 para.8

Appendix 20., varied: SI 2003/1633 Sch.2 para.8

Appendix 3., varied: SI 2003/1633 Sch.2 para.8

Appendix 4., varied: SI 2003/1633 Sch.2 para.8

Appendix 5., varied: SI 2003/1633 Sch.2 para.8

Appendix 6., varied: SI 2003/1633 Sch.2 para.8

Appendix 7., varied: SI 2003/1633 Sch.2 para.8

Appendix 8., varied: SI 2003/1633 Sch.2 para.8

Appendix 9., varied: SI 2003/1633 Sch.2 para.8

Sch.1 Part 1 para.1, varied: SI 2003/1633 Sch.2 para.8

Sch.1 Part 1 para.2, varied: SI 2003/1633 Sch.2 para.8

Sch.1 Part 1 para.3, varied: SI 2003/1633 Sch.2 para.8

Sch.1 Part 1 para.4, varied: SI 2003/1633 Sch.2 para.8

NO.

1994–cont.

2973. Industry-Wide Coal Staff Superannuation Scheme Regulations 1994– *cont.*

Sch.1 Part 1 para.5, varied: SI 2003/1633 Sch.2 para.8

Sch.1 Part 1 para.6, varied: SI 2003/1633 Sch.2 para.8

Sch.1 Part 1 para.7, varied: SI 2003/1633 Sch.2 para.8

Sch.1 Part 1 para.8, varied: SI 2003/1633 Sch.2 para.8

Sch.1 Part 1 para.9, varied: SI 2003/1633 Sch.2 para.8

Sch.1 Part 1 para.10, varied: SI 2003/1633 Sch.2 para.8

Sch.1 Part 1 para.11, varied: SI 2003/1633 Sch.2 para.8

Sch.1 Part 1 para.12, varied: SI 2003/1633 Sch.2 para.8

Sch.1 Part 1 para.13, varied: SI 2003/1633 Sch.2 para.8

Sch.1 Part 1 para.14, varied: SI 2003/1633 Sch.2 para.8

Sch.1 Part 1 para.15, varied: SI 2003/1633 Sch.2 para.8

Sch.1 Part 1 para.16, varied: SI 2003/1633 Sch.2 para.8

Sch.1 Part 1 para.17, varied: SI 2003/1633 Sch.2 para.8

Sch.1 Part 1 para.18, varied: SI 2003/1633 Sch.2 para.8

Sch.1 Part 1 para.19, varied: SI 2003/1633 Sch.2 para.8

Sch.1 Part 1 para.20, varied: SI 2003/1633 Sch.2 para.8

Sch.1 Part 1 para.21, varied: SI 2003/1633 Sch.2 para.8

Sch.1 Part 1 para.22, varied: SI 2003/1633 Sch.2 para.8

Sch.1 Part 1 para.23, varied: SI 2003/1633 Sch.2 para.8

Sch.1 Part 1 para.24, varied: SI 2003/1633 Sch.2 para.8

Sch.1 Part 1 para.25, varied: SI 2003/1633 Sch.2 para.8

Sch.1 Part 1 para.26, varied: SI 2003/1633 Sch.2 para.8

Sch.1 Part 1 para.27, varied: SI 2003/1633 Sch.2 para.8

Sch.1 Part 1 para.28, varied: SI 2003/1633 Sch.2 para.8

Sch.1 Part 1 para.29, varied: SI 2003/1633 Sch.2 para.8

Sch.1 Part 1 para.30, varied: SI 2003/1633 Sch.2 para.8

Sch.1 Part 1 para.31, varied: SI 2003/1633 Sch.2 para.8

Sch.1 Part 1 para.32, varied: SI 2003/1633 Sch.2 para.8

Sch.1 Part 1 para.33, varied: SI 2003/1633 Sch.2 para.8

1994–cont.

2973. Industry-Wide Coal Staff Superannuation Scheme Regulations 1994– *cont.*

Sch.1 Part 1 para.34, varied: SI 2003/1633 Sch.2 para.8

Sch.1 Part 1 para.35, varied: SI 2003/1633 Sch.2 para.8

Sch.1 Part 1 para.36, varied: SI 2003/1633 Sch.2 para.8

Sch.1 Part 1 para.37, varied: SI 2003/1633 Sch.2 para.8

Sch.1 Part 1 para.38, varied: SI 2003/1633 Sch.2 para.8

Sch.1 Part 1 para.39, varied: SI 2003/1633 Sch.2 para.8

Sch.1 Part 1 para.40, varied: SI 2003/1633 Sch.2 para.8

Sch.1 Part 1 para.41, varied: SI 2003/1633 Sch.2 para.8

Sch.1 Part 1 para.42, varied: SI 2003/1633 Sch.2 para.8

Sch.1 Part 1 para.43, varied: SI 2003/1633 Sch.2 para.8

Sch.1 Part 1 para.44, varied: SI 2003/1633 Sch.2 para.8

Sch.1 Part 1 para.45, varied: SI 2003/1633 Sch.2 para.8

Sch.1 Part 1 para.46, varied: SI 2003/1633 Sch.2 para.8

Sch.1 Part 1 para.47, varied: SI 2003/1633 Sch.2 para.8

Sch.1 Part 1 para.48, varied: SI 2003/1633 Sch.2 para.8

Sch.1 Part 1 para.49, varied: SI 2003/1633 Sch.2 para.8

Sch.1 Part 1 para.50, varied: SI 2003/1633 Sch.2 para.8

Sch.1 Part 1 para.51, varied: SI 2003/1633 Sch.2 para.8

Sch.1 Part 2 para.1, varied: SI 2003/1633 Sch.2 para.8

Sch.1 Part 2 para.2, varied: SI 2003/1633 Sch.2 para.8

Sch.1 Part 2 para.3, varied: SI 2003/1633 Sch.2 para.8

Sch.1 Part 2 para.4, varied: SI 2003/1633 Sch.2 para.8

Sch.1 Part 2 para.5, varied: SI 2003/1633 Sch.2 para.8

Sch.1 Part 2 para.6, varied: SI 2003/1633 Sch.2 para.8

Sch.1 Part 2 para.7, varied: SI 2003/1633 Sch.2 para.8

Sch.1 Part 2 para.8, varied: SI 2003/1633 Sch.2 para.8

Sch.1 Part 2 para.9, varied: SI 2003/1633 Sch.2 para.8

Sch.1 Part 2 para.10, varied: SI 2003/1633 Sch.2 para.8

Sch.1 Part 2 para.11, varied: SI 2003/1633 Sch.2 para.8

1994–cont.

2973. Industry-Wide Coal Staff Superannuation Scheme Regulations 1994– *cont.*

Sch.1 Part 2 para.12, varied: SI 2003/1633 Sch.2 para.8

Sch.1 Part 2 para.13, varied: SI 2003/1633 Sch.2 para.8

Sch.1 Part 2 para.14, varied: SI 2003/1633 Sch.2 para.8

Sch.1 Part 2 para.15, varied: SI 2003/1633 Sch.2 para.8

Sch.1 Part 2 para.16, varied: SI 2003/1633 Sch.2 para.8

Sch.1 Part 2 para.17, varied: SI 2003/1633 Sch.2 para.8

Sch.1 Part 2 para.18, varied: SI 2003/1633 Sch.2 para.8

Sch.1 Part 2 para.19, varied: SI 2003/1633 Sch.2 para.8

Sch.1 Part 2 para.20, varied: SI 2003/1633 Sch.2 para.8

Sch.1 Part 2 para.21, varied: SI 2003/1633 Sch.2 para.8

Sch.1 Part 2 para.22, varied: SI 2003/1633 Sch.2 para.8

Sch.1 Part 2 para.23, varied: SI 2003/1633 Sch.2 para.8

Sch.1 Part 2 para.24, varied: SI 2003/1633 Sch.2 para.8

Sch.1 Part 2 para.25, varied: SI 2003/1633 Sch.2 para.8

Sch.1 Part 2 para.26, varied: SI 2003/1633 Sch.2 para.8

Sch.1 Part 2 para.27, varied: SI 2003/1633 Sch.2 para.8

Sch.1 Part 2 para.28, varied: SI 2003/1633 Sch.2 para.8

Sch.1 Part 2 para.29, varied: SI 2003/1633 Sch.2 para.8

Sch.1 Part 2 para.30, varied: SI 2003/1633 Sch.2 para.8

Sch.1 Part 2 para.31, varied: SI 2003/1633 Sch.2 para.8

Sch.1 Part 2 para.32, varied: SI 2003/1633 Sch.2 para.8

Sch.1 Part 2 para.33, varied: SI 2003/1633 Sch.2 para.8

Sch.1 Part 2 para.34, varied: SI 2003/1633 Sch.2 para.8

Sch.1 Part 2 para.35, varied: SI 2003/1633 Sch.2 para.8

Sch.1 Part 2 para.36, varied: SI 2003/1633 Sch.2 para.8

Sch.1 Part 2 para.37, varied: SI 2003/1633 Sch.2 para.8

Sch.1 Part 2 para.38, varied: SI 2003/1633 Sch.2 para.8

Sch.1 Part 2 para.39, varied: SI 2003/1633 Sch.2 para.8

Sch.1 Part 2 para.40, varied: SI 2003/1633 Sch.2 para.8

1994–cont.

2973. Industry-Wide Coal Staff Superannuation Scheme Regulations 1994– *cont.*

Sch.1 Part 2 para.41, varied: SI 2003/1633 Sch.2 para.8

Sch.1 Part 2 para.42, varied: SI 2003/1633 Sch.2 para.8

Sch.1 Part 2 para.43, varied: SI 2003/1633 Sch.2 para.8

Sch.1 Part 2 para.44, varied: SI 2003/1633 Sch.2 para.8

Sch.1 Part 2 para.45, varied: SI 2003/1633 Sch.2 para.8

Sch.1 Part 2 para.46, varied: SI 2003/1633 Sch.2 para.8

Sch.1 Part 2 para.47, varied: SI 2003/1633 Sch.2 para.8

Sch.1 Part 2 para.48, varied: SI 2003/1633 Sch.2 para.8

Sch.1 Part 2 para.49, varied: SI 2003/1633 Sch.2 para.8

Sch.1 Part 2 para.50, varied: SI 2003/1633 Sch.2 para.8

Sch.1 Part 2 para.51, varied: SI 2003/1633 Sch.2 para.8

Sch.1 Part 2 para.52, varied: SI 2003/1633 Sch.2 para.8

Sch.1 Part 2 para.53, varied: SI 2003/1633 Sch.2 para.8

Sch.1 Part 2 para.54, varied: SI 2003/1633 Sch.2 para.8

Sch.1 Part 2 para.55, varied: SI 2003/1633 Sch.2 para.8

Sch.1 Part 2 para.56, varied: SI 2003/1633 Sch.2 para.8

Sch.1 Part 2 para.57, varied: SI 2003/1633 Sch.2 para.8

Sch.1 Part 2 para.58, varied: SI 2003/1633 Sch.2 para.8

Sch.1 Part 2 para.59, varied: SI 2003/1633 Sch.2 para.8

Sch.1 Part 2 para.60, varied: SI 2003/1633 Sch.2 para.8

Sch.1 Part 2 para.61, varied: SI 2003/1633 Sch.2 para.8

Sch.1 Part 2 para.62, varied: SI 2003/1633 Sch.2 para.8

Sch.1 Part 2 para.63, varied: SI 2003/1633 Sch.2 para.8

Sch.1 Part 2 para.64, varied: SI 2003/1633 Sch.2 para.8

Sch.1 Part 2 para.65, varied: SI 2003/1633 Sch.2 para.8

Sch.1 Part 2 para.66, varied: SI 2003/1633 Sch.2 para.8

Sch.1 Part 2 para.67, varied: SI 2003/1633 Sch.2 para.8

Sch.1 Part 2 para.68, varied: SI 2003/1633 Sch.2 para.8

1994–cont.

2987. Medicines (Restrictions on the Administration of Veterinary Medicinal Products) Regulations 1994

Reg.2, amended: SI 2002/236 Reg.12

2998. Borders General Hospital National Health Service Trust (Establishment) Order 1994

revoked: SSI 2003/189 Sch.2

3017. Medical Devices Regulations 1994

revoked: SI 2002/618 Reg.66

Reg.2, amended: SI 2002/236 Reg.13

Reg.3, amended: SI 2002/236 Reg.13

3021. Electricity Supply (Amendment) (No.2) Regulations 1994

revoked: SI 2002/2665 Sch.5

3024. Charitable Institutions (Fund-Raising) Regulations 1994

Reg.7, see *Supporting Link Alliance Ltd, Re* [2004] EWHC 523, [2004] 1 W.L.R. 1549 (Ch D), Sir Andrew Morritt V.C.

3046. Court of Protection Rules 1994

r.21, see *R (Execution of Statutory Will), Re* [2003] W.T.L.R. 1051 (Ch D), Ferris, J.

3076. Energy Information (Refrigerators and Freezers) Regulations 1994

applied: SI 2004/1468 Reg.13

revoked: SI 2004/1468 Reg.17

Sch.6 Part III para.15, revoked (in part): SI 2003/1398 Sch.1 para.23

3082. Meat Products (Hygiene) Regulations 1994

applied: SI 2002/843 Reg.56, Reg.101, SI 2002/1387 Reg.4, SI 2003/2756 Reg.48, SI 2004/2640 Reg.4, SSI 2003/411 Reg.49

referred to: SI 2002/1227 Reg.4, SI 2002/1416 Reg.101, SI 2003/1482 Reg.49, SI 2003/3177 Reg.4, SI 2004/1214 Reg.4, SI 2004/1430 Reg.4, SI 2004/1740 Reg.4, SSI 2002/255 Reg.99, SSI 2002/445 Reg.4

Reg.10, amended: SSI 2002/35 Reg.3

Reg.10, revoked (in part): SSI 2002/35 Reg.3

Sch.2 Part VI para.3A, substituted: SI 2002/118 Reg.2, SI 2002/129 Reg.2, SSI 2002/35 Reg.3

Sch.2 Part VI para.3B, substituted: SI 2002/118 Reg.2, SI 2002/129 Reg.2

3093. Treatment of Spruce Bark (Amendment) Order 1994

revoked: SI 2002/296 Art.3

3099. Habitat (Broadleaved Woodland) (Wales) Regulations 1994

applied: SI 2003/2261 Sch.3 Part I

3100. Habitat (Water Fringe) (Wales) Regulations 1994

applied: SI 2003/2261 Sch.3 Part I

3101. Habitat (Coastal Belt) (Wales) Regulations 1994

applied: SI 2003/2261 Sch.3 Part I

NO.

NO.

1994–cont.

3102. Habitat (Species-Rich Grassland) (Wales) Regulations 1994
applied: SI 2003/2261 Sch.3 Part I

3117. Motor Vehicle Tyres (Safety) Regulations 1994
Reg.2, amended: SI 2003/1316 Reg.3
Reg.4, substituted: SI 2003/1316 Reg.4
Reg.5, substituted: SI 2003/1316 Reg.4
Reg.6, substituted: SI 2003/1316 Reg.4
Reg.7, amended: SI 2003/2762 Reg.2
Reg.7, substituted: SI 2003/1316 Reg.4
Reg.9, amended: SI 2003/1316 Reg.5
Reg.10, amended: SI 2003/1316 Reg.5
Reg.12, amended: SI 2003/1316 Reg.5
Sch.1 para.1, amended: SI 2003/1316 Reg.6

3118. Church Representation Rules (Amendment) Resolution 1994
referred to: SI 2004/1889

3123. Non-Domestic Rating (Railways, Telecommunications and Canals) Regulations 1994
Reg.4, amended: SI 2003/2155 Sch.1 para.37

3130. Vocational Training for General Medical Practice (European Requirements) Regulations 1994
applied: SI 2003/2644 Reg.4, SI 2004/865 Art.110, Art.117, SI 2004/1016 Art.86, SSI 2004/163 Art.97
revoked: SI 2003/1250 Sch.10 Part 2
varied: SI 2004/1947 Reg.10
Reg.2, amended: SI 2003/3148 Reg.14
Reg.3A, added: SI 2003/3148 Reg.14
Reg.5, applied: SI 2003/2644 Reg.6, SI 2004/585 Reg.23, SI 2004/865 Art.110, SI 2004/1016 Art.86, SI 2004/1020 Reg.23, SSI 2004/114 Sch.1 para.3, SSI 2004/163 Art.97
Reg.5, disapplied: SI 2004/865 Art.110, SI 2004/1016 Art.86, SSI 2004/163 Art.97
Reg.5, varied: SI 2004/865 Art.117, SI 2004/1016 Art.93, SSI 2004/163 Art.100

3140. Construction (Design and Management) Regulations 1994
Reg.10, see *McCook v Lobo* [2002] EWCA Civ 1760, [2003] I.C.R. 89 (CA), Judge, L.J.

3141. Diseases of Poultry Order 1994
revoked (in part): SI 2003/1078 Art.18, SI 2003/1079 Art.17, SSI 2003/354 Art.19

3142. Marketing Authorisations for Veterinary Medicinal Products Regulations 1994
applied: SI 2004/2750 Reg.13
Reg.1, amended: SI 2002/269 Reg.3, Reg.4
Reg.1, revoked (in part): SI 2002/269 Reg.5
Reg.2, amended: SI 2002/269 Reg.6
Reg.3, see *Department for the Environment, Food and Rural Affairs v Atkinson* [2002] EWHC 2028, [2002] 3 C.M.L.R. 38 (QBD (Admin Ct)), Brooke, L.J.
Reg.3, amended: SI 2002/269 Reg.7

1994–cont.

3142. Marketing Authorisations for Veterinary Medicinal Products Regulations 1994–*cont.*
Reg.4, substituted: SI 2002/269 Reg.8
Reg.5, applied: SI 2004/2750 Sch.6 para.4
Reg.5, substituted: SI 2002/269 Reg.9
Reg.6, amended: SI 2002/269 Reg.10
Reg.6, applied: SI 2004/2750 Reg.6
Reg.7, substituted: SI 2002/269 Reg.11
Reg.8, substituted: SI 2002/269 Reg.11
Reg.9, referred to: SI 2004/2750 Reg.13
Reg.10, amended: SI 2002/269 Reg.12
Reg.11, substituted: SI 2002/269 Reg.13
Reg.12, amended: SI 2002/269 Reg.14
Reg.13, amended: SI 2002/269 Reg.15
Reg.15, revoked: SI 2002/269 Reg.16
Reg.16, see *Department for the Environment, Food and Rural Affairs v Atkinson* [2002] EWHC 2028, [2002] 3 C.M.L.R. 38 (QBD (Admin Ct)), Brooke, L.J.
Sch.1 para.1, substituted: SI 2002/269 Sch.1
Sch.1 para.2, substituted: SI 2002/269 Sch.1
Sch.1 para.3, substituted: SI 2002/269 Sch.1
Sch.2 para.1, substituted: SI 2002/269 Sch.1
Sch.2 para.2, substituted: SI 2002/269 Sch.1

3144. Medicines for Human Use (Marketing Authorisations Etc.) Regulations 1994
applied: SI 2003/1076 Art.1
Reg.1, amended: SI 2002/236 Reg.8, SI 2003/2321 Reg.7, SI 2004/1031 Sch.10 para.12
Reg.1, applied: SI 2002/3170 Art.3
Reg.4, amended: SI 2002/236 Reg.8
Reg.5, amended: SI 2002/236 Reg.8
Reg.5, revoked (in part): SI 2002/542 Reg.3
Reg.5A, added: SI 2002/542 Reg.3
Reg.6, revoked (in part): SI 2002/542 Reg.3
Reg.6A, added: SI 2003/2321 Reg.7
Reg.8, amended: SI 2002/236 Reg.8
Reg.8, revoked: SI 2002/542 Reg.3
Reg.9, revoked (in part): SI 2004/2990 Reg.7
Sch.1 para.2, amended: SI 2002/236 Reg.8, SI 2004/1031 Sch.10 para.12
Sch.1 para.3, amended: SI 2004/865 Sch.1 para.12, SI 2004/1016 Sch.1 para.12
Sch.2 para.3, amended: SI 2002/236 Reg.8
Sch.2 para.4, amended: SI 2002/236 Reg.8
Sch.3 para.3A, added: SI 2003/2321 Reg.7
Sch.3 para.6, amended: SI 2002/236 Reg.8, SI 2003/2321 Reg.7
Sch.3 para.7, amended: SI 2002/236 Reg.8
Sch.3 para.8, amended: SI 2002/236 Reg.8
Sch.3 para.9, amended: SI 2002/236 Reg.8
Sch.3 para.10, amended: SI 2002/236 Reg.8
Sch.3 para.11, amended: SI 2002/236 Reg.8
Sch.3 para.12, amended: SI 2002/236 Reg.8
Sch.5, applied: SI 2004/1031 Reg.46
Sch.5 para.2, amended: SI 2002/236 Reg.8
Sch.5 para.5, amended: SI 2003/1618 Reg.2

NO.

1994–cont.

3144. Medicines for Human Use (Marketing Authorisations Etc.) Regulations 1994–cont.

Sch.5 para.6, amended: SI 2002/542 Reg.3

Sch.5A para.3, added: SI 2003/1618 Reg.3

Sch.7 para.2, revoked: SI 2003/2317 Reg.7

3159. Unfair Terms in Consumer Contracts Regulations 1994

Reg.3, see *Bankers Insurance Co Ltd v South* [2003] EWHC 380, [2004] Lloyd's Rep. I.R. 1 (QBD), Buckley, J.; see *Director General of Fair Trading v First National Bank Plc* [2001] UKHL 52, [2002] 1 A.C. 481 (HL), Lord Bingham of Cornhill

Reg.4, see *Bankers Insurance Co Ltd v South* [2003] EWHC 380, [2004] Lloyd's Rep. I.R. 1 (QBD), Buckley, J.; see *Director General of Fair Trading v First National Bank Plc* [2001] UKHL 52, [2002] 1 A.C. 481 (HL), Lord Bingham of Cornhill

Reg.5, see *Bankers Insurance Co Ltd v South* [2003] EWHC 380, [2004] Lloyd's Rep. I.R. 1 (QBD), Buckley, J.

3162. Gloucester Harbour Revision Order 1994

Art.3, applied: SI 2002/3268 Art.4

Art.3, revoked: SI 2002/3268 Sch.3

Art.5, revoked: SI 2002/3268 Sch.3

Sch.1, revoked: SI 2002/3268 Sch.3

3173. Bournewood Community and Mental Health National Health Service Trust (Establishment) Order 1994

revoked: 2003 c.43 s.7

Art.1, amended: SI 2002/1338 Art.2

Art.2, amended: SI 2002/1338 Art.2

3174. Manchester Children's Hospitals National Health Service Trust (Establishment) Order 1994

revoked: 2003 c.43 s.7

3175. Grantham and District Hospital National Health Service Trust (Establishment) Order 1994

revoked: 2003 c.43 s.7

3176. Sussex Ambulance Service National Health Service Trust (Establishment) Order 1994

revoked: 2003 c.43 s.7

3177. Black Country Mental Health National Health Service Trust (Establishment) Order 1994

revoked: 2003 c.43 s.7

Art.1, amended: SI 2003/844 Art.2

Art.2, amended: SI 2003/844 Art.2

Art.2, substituted: SI 2003/844 Art.4

3178. Pathfinder National Health Service Trust (Establishment) Order 1994

revoked: 2003 c.43 s.7

NO.

1994–cont.

3179. Princess Alexandra Hospital National Health Service Trust (Establishment) Order 1994

applied: SI 2003/3059 Sch.1

revoked: 2003 c.43 s.7

3180. Essex and Herts Community National Health Service Trust (Establishment) Order 1994

revoked: 2003 c.43 s.7

3181. Homerton Hospital National Health Service Trust (Establishment) Order 1994

revoked: 2003 c.43 s.7

3182. Birmingham Children's Hospital National Health Service Trust (Establishment) Order 1994

revoked: 2003 c.43 s.7

3183. St James's and Seacroft University Hospitals National Health Service Trust (Establishment) Order 1994

revoked: 2003 c.43 s.7

3184. Royal Liverpool and Broadgreen University Hospitals National Health Service Trust (Establishment) Order 1994

revoked: 2003 c.43 s.7

3185. Fosse Health, Leicestershire Community National Health Service Trust (Establishment) Order 1994

revoked: 2003 c.43 s.7

3186. United Leeds Teaching Hospitals National Health Service Trust (Establishment) Order 1994

revoked: 2003 c.43 s.7

3187. Air Navigation (Dangerous Goods) Regulations 1994

applied: SI 2002/1689 Reg.7, SR 2002/301 Reg.7

revoked: SI 2002/2786 Sch.1

Reg.4, see *R. v Tropical Express Ltd* [2001] EWCA Crim 1182, [2002] 1 Cr. App. R. (S.) 27 (CA (Crim Div)), Kay, L.J.

Reg.6, see *R. v Tropical Express Ltd* [2001] EWCA Crim 1182, [2002] 1 Cr. App. R. (S.) 27 (CA (Crim Div)), Kay, L.J.

3196. Social Security (Claims and Payments) Amendment (No.4) Regulations 1994

revoked (in part): SI 2003/492 Sch.3 Part 1

3197. Wolverhampton Health Care National Health Service Trust (Establishment) Order 1994

revoked: 2003 c.43 s.7, SI 2003/868 Art.2

3204. Firearms (Amendment) (Northern Ireland) Order 1994

revoked: SI 2004/702 Sch.8

3226. Exchange Gains and Losses (Transitional Provisions) Regulations 1994

Reg.1, amended: SI 2002/1969 Reg.3

Reg.2, amended: SI 2002/1969 Reg.4

NO.

3226. Exchange Gains and Losses (Transitional Provisions) Regulations 1994– *cont.*

Reg.3, see *Finance Ltd v Inspector of Taxes* [2003] S.T.C. (S.C.D.) 344 (Sp Comm), AN Brice (Chairman)

Reg.3, revoked: SI 2002/1969 Reg.5

Reg.4, revoked: SI 2002/1969 Reg.5

Reg.5, revoked: SI 2002/1969 Reg.5

Reg.6, revoked: SI 2002/1969 Reg.5

Reg.7, amended: SI 2002/1969 Reg.6

Reg.8, amended: SI 2002/1969 Reg.7

Reg.13, amended: SI 2002/1969 Reg.8

Reg.13, revoked (in part): SI 2002/1969 Reg.8

Reg.14, substituted: SI 2002/1969 Reg.9

Reg.15, revoked: SI 2002/1969 Reg.10

Reg.16, revoked: SI 2002/1969 Reg.10

Reg.17, revoked: SI 2002/1969 Reg.11

Reg.18, revoked: SI 2002/1969 Reg.11

Reg.19, revoked: SI 2002/1969 Reg.11

Reg.20, revoked: SI 2002/1969 Reg.11

Reg.21, revoked: SI 2002/1969 Reg.11

Reg.22, revoked: SI 2002/1969 Reg.11

3227. Exchange Gains and Losses (Alternative Method of Calculation of Gain or Loss) Regulations 1994

referred to: SI 2002/1969 Reg.12

Reg.2, revoked: SI 2002/1969 Reg.13

Reg.3, revoked: SI 2002/1969 Reg.13

Reg.7, amended: SI 2002/1969 Reg.14

Reg.7, applied: SI 2002/1970 Reg.3

Reg.7, revoked (in part): SI 2002/1969 Reg.14

Reg.8, applied: SI 2002/1970 Reg.3, Reg.7

Reg.8, revoked: SI 2002/1969 Reg.15

Reg.9, applied: SI 2002/1970 Reg.3

Reg.9, referred to: SI 2002/1970 Reg.3

Reg.9, revoked: SI 2002/1969 Reg.15

Reg.10, applied: SI 2002/1970 Reg.7

Reg.11, amended: SI 2002/1969 Reg.16

Reg.12, revoked: SI 2002/1969 Reg.17

3231. Exchange Gains and Losses (Insurance Companies) Regulations 1994

referred to: SI 2002/1969 Reg.18

Reg.1, amended: SI 2002/1969 Reg.19

Reg.2, revoked: SI 2002/1969 Reg.20

Reg.3, revoked: SI 2002/1969 Reg.20

Reg.4, revoked: SI 2002/1969 Reg.20

Reg.5, revoked: SI 2002/1969 Reg.20

Reg.5A, revoked: SI 2002/1969 Reg.20

Reg.7, amended: SI 2002/1969 Reg.21

Reg.7A, added: SI 2002/1969 Reg.22

Reg.7B, added: SI 2002/1969 Reg.22

Reg.8, amended: SI 2002/1969 Reg.23

Reg.8A, revoked: SI 2002/1969 Reg.24

Reg.9, amended: SI 2002/1969 Reg.25

Reg.11, amended: SI 2002/1969 Reg.26

Reg.12, amended: SI 2002/1969 Reg.27

NO.

3246. Control of Substances Hazardous to Health Regulations 1994

Reg.7, see *Dugmore v Swansea NHS Trust* [2002] EWCA Civ 1689, [2003] 1 All E.R. 333 (CA), Hale, L.J.

3247. Chemicals (Hazard Information and Packaging for Supply) Regulations 1994

applied: SI 2002/1689 Reg.16

revoked: SI 2002/1689 Sch.7

3251. Education (Inter-authority Recoupment) Regulations 1994

Reg.3, varied: SI 2003/2959 Reg.9

3259. Electricity (Non-Fossil Fuel Sources) (England and Wales) Order 1994

Sch.1, referred to: SSI 2004/170 Art.8

3260. Electrical Equipment (Safety) Regulations 1994

referred to: SI 2003/750 Sch.5 para.12, SI 2003/751 Sch.6 para.12

3264. Compulsory Purchase by Ministers (Inquiries Procedure) Rules 1994

referred to: SI 2004/2730 Sch.1

3267. Act of Sederunt (Fees of Sheriff Officers) (No.2) 1994

revoked: SSI 2002/567 Sch.2

3268. Act of Sederunt (Fees of Messengers-at-Arms) (No.2) 1994

revoked: SSI 2002/566 Sch.2

3272. Public Service Vehicles (Traffic Regulation Conditions) (Amendment) Regulations 1994

disapplied: SI 2004/2682 Reg.2

3275. Electricity (Non-Fossil Fuel Sources) (Scotland) Order 1994

Sch.1, referred to: SSI 2004/170 Art.8

3279. Non-Domestic Rating (Chargeable Amounts) Regulations 1994

Reg.36, amended: SI 2004/1297 Reg.2

3282. Electricity Supply Industry (Rateable Values) Order 1994

see *R. (on the application of Edison First Power Ltd) v Secretary of State for the Environment, Transport and the Regions* [2003] UKHL 20, [2003] 4 All E.R. 209 (HL), Lord Hoffmann

3296. Road Vehicles (Registration and Licensing) (Amendment) (No.3) Regulations 1994

revoked: SI 2002/2742 Sch.1 Part I

1995

art.6(1. Town and Country Planning (General Development Procedure) Order 1995

see *R. (on the application of Pridmore) v Salisbury DC* [2004] EWHC 2511, [2004] 47 E.G.C.S.165 (QBD (Admin)), Newman, J.

NO.

1995–cont.

11. Pigs (Records, Identification and Movement) Order 1995

applied: SSI 2002/34 Art.4, Art.11

restored: SI 2002/2303 Art.14

revoked (in part): SI 2002/2154 Art.14, SI 2002/2303 Art.14, SI 2003/2632 Art.28, SI 2004/996 Art.28

substituted: SI 2002/2154 Art.14

Art.5, amended: SI 2002/241 Art.2, SI 2002/281 Art.2, SSI 2002/34 Art.11

Art.7, amended: SI 2002/241 Art.2, SI 2002/281 Art.2

Art.8, amended: SSI 2002/540 Art.2

Art.8, applied: SI 2002/242 Art.3, SI 2002/280 Art.3, SI 2002/2152 Art.3

Art.8, referred to: SI 2002/242 Art.3, SI 2002/280 Art.3, SI 2002/2152 Art.3, SI 2002/2304 Art.3

Art.8, substituted: SI 2002/241 Art.2, SI 2002/281 Art.2

Art.9, substituted: SI 2002/241 Art.2, SI 2002/281 Art.2

Art.10, revoked (in part): SSI 2002/540 Art.2

Art.11, amended: SI 2002/241 Art.2, SI 2002/281 Art.2, SSI 2002/34 Art.11

Art.12, amended: SSI 2002/540 Art.2

Art.12, applied: SI 2002/280 Art.3, SI 2002/2152 Art.3, SI 2002/2304 Art.3

Art.12, referred to: SI 2002/242 Art.3

Art.13, substituted: SI 2002/241 Art.2, SI 2002/281 Art.2

Art.14, revoked (in part): SI 2002/241 Art.2, SI 2002/281 Art.2

Art.15, amended: SSI 2002/34 Art.11, SSI 2002/540 Art.2

Art.16, amended: SSI 2002/540 Art.2

Art.20, added: SI 2002/241 Art.2, SI 2002/281 Art.2

Sch.2, amended: SSI 2002/34 Sch.3, SSI 2002/540 Art.2

Sch.2, substituted: SI 2002/241 Sch.1, SI 2002/281 Sch.1, SSI 2002/221 Sch.1

Sch.3, amended: SSI 2002/34 Sch.3

Sch.3, substituted: SI 2002/241 Sch.1, SI 2002/281 Sch.1, SSI 2002/221 Sch.1

Sch.4, amended: SSI 2002/34 Sch.3

Sch.4, substituted: SI 2002/241 Sch.1, SI 2002/281 Sch.1, SSI 2002/221 Sch.1

Sch.5, amended: SSI 2002/34 Sch.3

Sch.5, revoked (in part): SSI 2002/540 Art.2

Sch.6, amended: SSI 2002/34 Sch.3, SSI 2002/540 Art.2

Sch.6, substituted: SI 2002/241 Sch.1, SI 2002/281 Sch.1, SSI 2002/221 Sch.1

Sch.7, added: SSI 2002/540 Art.2

Sch.7, amended: SSI 2002/34 Sch.3, SSI 2002/540 Art.2

Sch.7, substituted: SI 2002/241 Sch.1, SI 2002/281 Sch.1, SSI 2002/221 Sch.1

1995–cont.

44. District of Bromsgrove (Electoral Arrangements) Order 1995

revoked: SI 2003/158 Art.12

77. Infant Formula and Follow-on Formula Regulations 1995

Reg.1, amended: SI 2003/3208 Reg.3, SI 2004/313 Reg.3, SSI 2004/7 Reg.3

Reg.2, amended: SI 2003/3208 Reg.4, SI 2004/313 Reg.4, SSI 2004/7 Reg.4

Reg.3, amended: SI 2003/3208 Reg.4, SI 2004/313 Reg.4, SSI 2004/7 Reg.4

Reg.5, amended: SI 2003/3208 Reg.5, SI 2004/313 Reg.5, SSI 2004/7 Reg.5

Reg.6, amended: SI 2003/3208 Reg.5, SI 2004/313 Reg.5, SSI 2004/7 Reg.5

Reg.8, amended: SI 2003/3208 Reg.6, SI 2004/313 Reg.6, SSI 2004/7 Reg.6

Reg.9, amended: SI 2003/3208 Reg.6, SI 2004/313 Reg.6, SSI 2004/7 Reg.6

Reg.12A, added: SI 2003/3208 Reg.7, SI 2004/313 Reg.7, SSI 2004/7 Reg.7

Reg.22, amended: SI 2003/3208 Reg.8, SI 2004/313 Reg.8

Reg.22, revoked (in part): SSI 2004/7 Reg.8

Reg.23, substituted: SI 2003/3208 Reg.9, SI 2004/313 Reg.9, SSI 2004/7 Reg.9

Sch.7A, added: SI 2003/3208 Sch.1, SI 2004/313 Sch.1, SSI 2004/7 Sch.1

Sch.7B, added: SI 2003/3208 Sch.1, SI 2004/313 Sch.1, SSI 2004/7 Sch.1

80. National Health Service (General Medical Services) Amendment Regulations 1995

revoked (in part): SI 2004/865 Sch.2, SI 2004/1016 Sch.2

88. Princess Royal Hospital National Health Service Trust (Establishment) Amendment Order 1995

revoked: 2003 c.43 s.7

91. Royal Hull Hospitals National Health Service Trust (Establishment) Amendment Order 1995

revoked: 2003 c.43 s.7

92. Cumbria Ambulance Service National Health Service Trust (Establishment) Amendment Order 1995

revoked: 2003 c.43 s.7

99. Teddington Memorial Hospital National Health Service Trust (Establishment) Amendment Order 1995

revoked: 2003 c.43 s.7

117. North Hampshire Hospitals National Health Service Trust (Establishment) Amendment Order 1995

revoked: 2003 c.43 s.7

121. Council Tax and Non-Domestic Rating (Demand Notices) (England) Amendment Regulations 1995

Reg.3, revoked (in part): SI 2002/180 Sch.1

NO.

1995–cont.

137. **Police (Scotland) Amendment Regulations 1995**
revoked: SSI 2004/257 Sch.4

141. **West Wales Ambulance National Health Service Trust (Establishment) Order 1995**
revoked: 2003 c.43 s.7

142. **Cardiff Community Healthcare National Health Service Trust (Establishment) Order 1995**
revoked: 2003 c.43 s.7

143. **University Dental Hospital National Health Service Trust (Establishment) Order 1995**
revoked: 2003 c.43 s.7

164. **Valuation Timetable (Scotland) Order 1995**
see *Magell Ltd v Dumfries and Galloway Regional Assessor* [2004] R.A. 188 (LVAC), Lord Gill L.J.C., Lord Clarke, Lord Nimmo Smith

187. **Cleveland (Structural Change) Order 1995**
varied: SI 2004/222 Art.2

201. **Public Supply Contracts Regulations 1995**
applied: SI 2004/669 Art.2
referred to: SI 2003/1986 Art.3
Reg.2, amended: SI 2003/46 Reg.5
Reg.7, applied: SI 2002/2114 Reg.8, SI 2003/2909 Reg.9
Reg.9, amended: SI 2003/46 Reg.5
Reg.11, amended: SI 2003/46 Reg.5
Reg.12, amended: SI 2003/46 Reg.5
Reg.13, amended: SI 2003/46 Reg.5
Reg.22, amended: SI 2003/46 Reg.5
Reg.23, amended: SI 2003/46 Reg.5
Sch.1, amended: SI 2002/881 Sch.1 para.11, SSI 2003/242 Art.4
Sch.3 Part A para.1, revoked: SI 2003/46 Reg.5
Sch.3 Part A para.2, revoked: SI 2003/46 Reg.5
Sch.3 Part A para.3, revoked: SI 2003/46 Reg.5
Sch.3 Part A para.4, revoked: SI 2003/46 Reg.5
Sch.3 Part A para.5, revoked: SI 2003/46 Reg.5
Sch.3 Part A para.6, revoked: SI 2003/46 Reg.5
Sch.3 Part B para.1, revoked: SI 2003/46 Reg.5
Sch.3 Part B para.2, revoked: SI 2003/46 Reg.5
Sch.3 Part B para.3, revoked: SI 2003/46 Reg.5
Sch.3 Part B para.4, revoked: SI 2003/46 Reg.5
Sch.3 Part B para.5, revoked: SI 2003/46 Reg.5

NO.

1995–cont.

201. **Public Supply Contracts Regulations 1995**–*cont.*
Sch.3 Part B para.6, revoked: SI 2003/46 Reg.5
Sch.3 Part B para.7, revoked: SI 2003/46 Reg.5
Sch.3 Part B para.8, revoked: SI 2003/46 Reg.5
Sch.3 Part B para.9, revoked: SI 2003/46 Reg.5
Sch.3 Part B para.10, revoked: SI 2003/46 Reg.5
Sch.3 Part B para.11, revoked: SI 2003/46 Reg.5
Sch.3 Part B para.12, revoked: SI 2003/46 Reg.5
Sch.3 Part B para.13, revoked: SI 2003/46 Reg.5
Sch.3 Part B para.14, revoked: SI 2003/46 Reg.5
Sch.3 Part B para.15, revoked: SI 2003/46 Reg.5
Sch.3 Part B para.16, revoked: SI 2003/46 Reg.5
Sch.3 Part B para.17, revoked: SI 2003/46 Reg.5
Sch.3 Part B para.18, revoked: SI 2003/46 Reg.5
Sch.3 Part E para.1, revoked: SI 2003/46 Reg.5
Sch.3 Part E para.2, revoked: SI 2003/46 Reg.5
Sch.3 Part E para.3, revoked: SI 2003/46 Reg.5
Sch.3 Part E para.4, revoked: SI 2003/46 Reg.5
Sch.3 Part E para.5, revoked: SI 2003/46 Reg.5
Sch.3 Part E para.6, revoked: SI 2003/46 Reg.5
Sch.3 Part E para.7, revoked: SI 2003/46 Reg.5
Sch.3 Part E para.8, revoked: SI 2003/46 Reg.5
Sch.3 Part E para.9, revoked: SI 2003/46 Reg.5
Sch.3 Part E para.10, revoked: SI 2003/46 Reg.5
Sch.3 Part E para.11, revoked: SI 2003/46 Reg.5
Sch.3 Part E para.12, revoked: SI 2003/46 Reg.5
Sch.3 Part E para.13, revoked: SI 2003/46 Reg.5
Sch.3 Part C para.1, revoked: SI 2003/46 Reg.5
Sch.3 Part C para.2, revoked: SI 2003/46 Reg.5
Sch.3 Part C para.3, revoked: SI 2003/46 Reg.5

1995–cont.

201. Public Supply Contracts Regulations 1995–*cont.*

Sch.3 Part C para.4, revoked: SI 2003/46 Reg.5

Sch.3 Part C para.5, revoked: SI 2003/46 Reg.5

Sch.3 Part C para.6, revoked: SI 2003/46 Reg.5

Sch.3 Part C para.7, revoked: SI 2003/46 Reg.5

Sch.3 Part C para.8, revoked: SI 2003/46 Reg.5

Sch.3 Part C para.9, revoked: SI 2003/46 Reg.5

Sch.3 Part C para.10, revoked: SI 2003/46 Reg.5

Sch.3 Part C para.11, revoked: SI 2003/46 Reg.5

Sch.3 Part C para.12, revoked: SI 2003/46 Reg.5

Sch.3 Part C para.13, revoked: SI 2003/46 Reg.5

Sch.3 Part C para.14, revoked: SI 2003/46 Reg.5

Sch.3 Part C para.15, revoked: SI 2003/46 Reg.5

Sch.3 Part C para.16, revoked: SI 2003/46 Reg.5

Sch.3 Part D para.1, revoked: SI 2003/46 Reg.5

Sch.3 Part D para.2, revoked: SI 2003/46 Reg.5

Sch.3 Part D para.3, revoked: SI 2003/46 Reg.5

Sch.3 Part D para.4, revoked: SI 2003/46 Reg.5

Sch.3 Part D para.5, revoked: SI 2003/46 Reg.5

Sch.3 Part D para.6, revoked: SI 2003/46 Reg.5

Sch.3 Part D para.7, revoked: SI 2003/46 Reg.5

Sch.3 Part D para.8, revoked: SI 2003/46 Reg.5

Sch.3 Part D para.9, revoked: SI 2003/46 Reg.5

Sch.3 Part D para.10, revoked: SI 2003/46 Reg.5

Sch.3 Part D para.11, revoked: SI 2003/46 Reg.5

Sch.3 Part D para.12, revoked: SI 2003/46 Reg.5

Sch.3 Part D para.13, revoked: SI 2003/46 Reg.5

Sch.3 Part D para.14, revoked: SI 2003/46 Reg.5

204. Toy (Safety) Regulations 1995

Reg.4, see *Brighton and Hove City Council v Woolworths Plc* [2002] EWHC 2565, (2003) 167 J.P. 21 (QBD (Admin Ct)), Field, J.

1995–cont.

204. Toy (Safety) Regulations 1995–*cont.*

Reg.13, see *Brighton and Hove City Council v Woolworths Plc* [2002] EWHC 2565, (2003) 167 J.P. 21 (QBD (Admin Ct)), Field, J.

204. Toys (Safety) Regulations 1995

Sch.2 Part 1 para.6, amended: SI 2004/1769 Reg.20

208. Education (School Financial Statements) (Prescribed Particulars etc.) Regulations 1995

applied: SI 2002/536 Reg.3

215. Police Regulations 1995

revoked: SI 2003/527 Sch.4 Part 1

Reg.4, amended: SI 2002/1758 Reg.2

Reg.12, amended: SI 2002/3162 Reg.2

Reg.13A, amended: SI 2002/2529 Reg.2

Reg.13A, applied: SI 2002/2529 Reg.4

Reg.13B, amended: SI 2002/3162 Reg.3

Reg.14, amended: SI 2002/1758 Reg.3

Reg.16, see *Surrey Police Authority v Beckett* [2001] EWCA Civ 1253, [2002] I.C.R. 257 (CA), Simon Brown, L.J.

Reg.20A, added: SI 2002/1758 Reg.4

Reg.39, amended: SI 2002/1758 Reg.5

Reg.42A, added: SI 2002/1758 Reg.6

Reg.45, amended: 2002 c.8 s.1

Sch.13 para.1, amended: SI 2002/1758 Reg.7

216. Income Tax (Employments) (Amendment) Regulations 1995

revoked: SI 2003/2682 Sch.2

236. Fruit Juices and Fruit Nectars (England, Wales and Scotland) (Amendment) Regulations 1995

revoked (in part): SI 2003/1564 Reg.10, SI 2003/3041 Reg.10, SSI 2003/293 Reg.11

266. World Trade Organisation (Immunities and Privileges) Order 1995

Art.13, amended: 2002 c.8 s.2

Art.14, amended: 2002 c.8 s.2

289. Isle of Wight (Staff Transfer) Order 1995

varied: SI 2004/222 Art.2

300. National Health Service Pension Scheme Regulations 1995

applied: SI 2002/561 Reg.3, SI 2002/1311 Reg.5

referred to: SI 2003/631 Reg.2

Part r Reg.3, see *Roy v National Health Pensions Agency* [2002] EWHC 3107, [2003] O.P.L.R. 151 (Ch D), Patten, J.

Part U Reg.1, see *Roy v National Health Pensions Agency* [2002] EWHC 3107, [2003] O.P.L.R. 151 (Ch D), Patten, J.

Part M, applied: SI 2002/1311 Reg.6

Reg.1, amended: SI 2003/2322 Reg.2

Reg.1, applied: SI 2002/1311 Reg.7

Reg.1, amended: SI 2003/631 Sch.1 para.2, SI 2004/665 Reg.3

Reg.1, amended: SI 2002/561 Sch.1 para.3, Sch.1 para.4

NO.

NO.

1995–cont.

300. National Health Service Pension Scheme Regulations 1995–*cont.*

Reg.1, amended: SI 2002/561 Sch.1 para.7, Sch.1 para.8

Reg.1, amended: SI 2003/2322 Reg.2

Reg.1, amended: SI 2002/2469 Sch.5, Sch.11

Reg.1A, added: SI 2004/665 Reg.3

Reg.2, amended: SI 2002/561 Sch.1 para.1, SI 2002/2469 Sch.1 para.62, SI 2003/631 Reg.3, SI 2004/696 Art.3, Sch.1 para.16

Reg.2, amended: SI 2004/665 Reg.3, SI 2004/696 Art.3

Reg.2, applied: SI 2002/1311 Reg.10

Reg.2, amended: SI 2003/631 Sch.1 para.1, SI 2004/665 Reg.3

Reg.2, amended: SI 2002/561 Sch.1 para.5

Reg.3, amended: SI 2002/561 Sch.1 para.2

Reg.3, amended: SI 2004/696 Art.3

Reg.3, applied: SI 2002/1311 Reg.3, Reg.5, Reg.6, Reg.9

Reg.3, applied: SI 2002/1311 Reg.6

Reg.3, disapplied: SI 2002/1311 Reg.5, Reg.6

Reg.3, amended: SI 2003/631 Sch.1 para.5

Reg.4, amended: SI 2004/696 Art.3

Reg.4, amended: SI 2003/2322 Reg.2

Reg.4, substituted: SI 2002/561 Sch.1 para.9

Reg.4, applied: SI 2002/1311 Reg.5

Reg.5, amended: SI 2003/2322 Reg.2

Reg.5, applied: SI 2002/1311 Reg.9

Reg.6, applied: SI 2002/1311 Reg.4, Reg.6, Reg.9

Reg.6, substituted: SI 2002/561 Sch.1 para.6

Reg.6, amended: SI 2003/631 Sch.1 para.4

Reg.11, amended: SI 2004/696 Art.3

Reg.11, applied: SI 2002/561 Reg.3

s.art S Reg.2, amended: SI 2003/631 Sch.1 para.3

s.art S Reg.2, applied: SI 2002/1311 Reg.11

Sch.2 para.1, amended: SI 2002/561 Sch.1 para.10, SI 2002/2469 Sch.1 para.62, Sch.5, SI 2003/631 Reg.4

Sch.2 para.1, applied: SI 2002/561 Reg.3

Sch.2 para.2, amended: SI 2002/561 Sch.1 para.10, SI 2002/2469 Sch.5, SI 2003/631 Reg.3, Reg.4

Sch.2 para.2A, added: SI 2002/561 Sch.1 para.10

Sch.2 para.3, amended: SI 2002/561 Sch.1 para.10, SI 2002/2469 Sch.5, SI 2003/631 Reg.4

Sch.2 para.4, amended: SI 2002/2469 Sch.5

Sch.2 para.5, amended: SI 2002/2469 Sch.1 para.62, Sch.5

Sch.2 para.6, amended: SI 2002/561 Sch.1 para.10, SI 2003/631 Reg.4

Sch.2 para.8, amended: SI 2002/2469 Sch.6

Sch.2 para.9, amended: SI 2002/561 Sch.1 para.10, SI 2003/631 Reg.3, SI 2003/2322 Reg.2, SI 2004/665 Reg.3

Sch.2 para.9A, added: SI 2002/561 Sch.1 para.10

1995–cont.

300. National Health Service Pension Scheme Regulations 1995–*cont.*

Sch.2 para.10, amended: SI 2002/561 Sch.1 para.10, SI 2002/2469 Sch.6

Sch.2 para.11A, added: SI 2003/2322 Reg.2

Sch.2 para.19, amended: SI 2002/561 Sch.1 para.10

304. Genetically Modified Organisms (Deliberate Release) Regulations 1995

referred to: SI 2002/2443 Sch.5, SI 2002/3188 Sch.5

revoked (in part): SI 2002/2443 Sch.5, SI 2002/3188 Sch.5, SSI 2002/541 Sch.7

309. Medicines (Advisory Board on the Registration of Homoeopathic Products) Order 1995

Art.2, amended: SI 2002/236 Reg.14

310. Social Security (Incapacity Benefit) (Transitional) Regulations 1995

Reg.5, referred to: SI 2002/491 Reg.6

Reg.7, applied: SI 2002/491 Reg.6

Reg.7, revoked: SI 2002/491 Reg.5

Reg.7, varied: SI 2002/491 Reg.6

Reg.18, amended: SI 2002/668 Art.15, SI 2003/526 Art.16, SI 2004/552 Art.15

311. Social Security (Incapacity for Work) (General) Regulations 1995

Reg.10, applied: SI 2003/2439 Reg.8, SI 2004/959 Reg.4, Reg.8

Reg.10A, amended: SI 2002/491 Reg.2

Reg.17, amended: SI 2002/491 Reg.3, SI 2002/2311 Reg.4, SI 2003/2262 Reg.4, SI 2004/2301 Reg.4

Reg.17, referred to: SI 2002/491 Reg.6

Reg.17, varied: SI 2002/491 Reg.6

Reg.27, see *Howker v Secretary of State for Work and Pensions* [2002] EWCA Civ 1623, [2003] I.C.R. 405 (CA), Peter Gibson, L.J.

356. Milk Development Council Order 1995

Art.2, amended: SI 2004/964 Art.3

Art.8, substituted: SI 2004/964 Art.4

365. National Health Service Superannuation Scheme (Scotland) Regulations 1995

applied: SSI 2003/344 Reg.4, Reg.6, Reg.8, Reg.10, Reg.11, Reg.14

Part M, applied: SSI 2003/344 Reg.6

Reg.1, amended: SSI 2003/55 Reg.4

Reg.1, amended: SSI 2003/517 Reg.3

Reg.1, applied: SSI 2003/344 Reg.7

Reg.1, amended: SSI 2003/55 Reg.6, Reg.7, Reg.8

Reg.1, amended: SSI 2003/55 Reg.11

Reg.1, amended: SSI 2003/517 Reg.6

Reg.1, amended: SSI 2003/55 Reg.13

Reg.2, amended: SSI 2003/55 Reg.3

Reg.2, applied: SSI 2003/344 Reg.10

Reg.2, referred to: SSI 2003/344 Reg.10

NO.

NO.

1995–cont.

365. National Health Service Superannuation Scheme (Scotland) Regulations 1995–*cont.*

Reg.2, amended: SSI 2003/270 Reg.3

Reg.2, amended: SSI 2003/517 Reg.5

Reg.2, amended: SSI 2003/55 Reg.6, Reg.9

Reg.3, amended: SSI 2003/55 Reg.5

Reg.3, applied: SSI 2003/344 Reg.3, Reg.6, Reg.9

Reg.3, amended: SSI 2003/55 Reg.6

Reg.3, applied: SSI 2003/344 Reg.6

Reg.3, disapplied: SSI 2003/344 Reg.5

Reg.3, varied: SSI 2003/344 Reg.6

Reg.3, amended: SSI 2003/270 Reg.6

Reg.4, substituted: SSI 2003/55 Reg.12

Reg.4, applied: SSI 2003/344 Reg.5

Reg.5, amended: SSI 2003/517 Reg.4

Reg.5, applied: SSI 2003/344 Reg.9

Reg.5, amended: SSI 2003/55 Reg.6

Reg.6, amended: SSI 2003/270 Reg.4

Reg.6, substituted: SSI 2003/55 Reg.10

Reg.7, applied: SSI 2003/344 Reg.4, Reg.6, Reg.9

s.art S Reg.2, amended: SSI 2003/270 Reg.5

s.art S Reg.2, applied: SSI 2003/344 Reg.11

Sch.1 Part I para.1, amended: SSI 2003/55 Reg.15, SSI 2003/270 Reg.8

Sch.1 Part I para.2, amended: SSI 2003/55 Reg.16, SSI 2003/270 Reg.9

Sch.1 Part I para.2A, added: SSI 2003/55 Reg.16

Sch.1 Part I para.2B, added: SSI 2003/55 Reg.16

Sch.1 Part II para.3, amended: SSI 2003/55 Reg.17, SSI 2003/270 Reg.10

Sch.1 Part II para.6, amended: SSI 2003/55 Reg.18, SSI 2003/270 Reg.11

Sch.1 Part III para.9, amended: SSI 2003/55 Reg.19, SSI 2003/517 Reg.7

Sch.1 Part III para.9A, added: SSI 2003/55 Reg.19

Sch.1 Part III para.9B, added: SSI 2003/517 Reg.8

Sch.1 Part IV para.10, amended: SSI 2003/55 Reg.20

Sch.1 Part VII para.18, amended: SSI 2003/55 Reg.21

402. Local Government Changes for England (Property Transfer and Transitional Payments) Regulations 1995

Reg.16, see *Durham CC v Darlington BC* [2003] EWHC 2598, [2004] B.L.G.R. 311 (QBD (Admin Ct)), Stanley Burnton, J.

Reg.18, see *Durham CC v Darlington BC* [2003] EWHC 2598, [2004] B.L.G.R. 311 (QBD (Admin Ct)), Stanley Burnton, J.

414. National Health Service (Pharmaceutical Services) (Scotland) Regulations 1995

referred to: SSI 2002/111 Reg.2

1995–cont.

414. National Health Service (Pharmaceutical Services) (Scotland) Regulations 1995–*cont.*

Reg.2, amended: SI 2002/3135 Sch.1 para.32, SI 2004/1771 Sch.1 para.43, SI 2004/1860 Art.3, SSI 2002/111 Reg.2, SSI 2003/296 Reg.2, SSI 2004/212 Sch.1 para.4

Reg.2, revoked (in part): SSI 2003/296 Reg.2

Reg.3, revoked (in part): SSI 2002/111 Reg.2

Reg.5, applied: SSI 2004/386 Reg.3

Reg.5, see *Lloyds Pharmacy Ltd v National Appeal Panel for Entry to the Pharmaceutical Lists* 2003 S.L.T. 830 (OH), Lady Smith; see *Sainsbury's Supermarkets Ltd v National Appeal Panel for Entry to the Pharmaceutical Lists* 2003 S.L.T. 688 (OH), Lord Carloway

Reg.9, amended: SSI 2002/111 Reg.2

Reg.11, revoked (in part): SSI 2004/212 Sch.1 para.4

Sch.1 para.1, revoked (in part): SSI 2002/111 Reg.2, SSI 2003/296 Reg.3

Sch.1 para.3, amended: SSI 2002/111 Reg.2, SSI 2003/296 Reg.3, SSI 2004/212 Sch.1 para.4

Sch.1 para.3, revoked (in part): SSI 2004/212 Sch.1 para.4

Sch.1 para.11, revoked (in part): SSI 2002/111 Reg.2

Sch.4 Part I para.6, amended: SSI 2003/296 Reg.4

Sch.4 Part II para.14, amended: SSI 2003/296 Reg.5

416. National Health Service (General Medical Services) (Scotland) Regulations 1995

applied: SSI 2003/64 Sch.1 para.3, Sch.1 para.11, SSI 2004/142 Art.42, SSI 2004/163 Art.9, Art.31

referred to: SSI 2002/111 Reg.3

revoked: SSI 2004/114 Sch.2

varied: SSI 2004/163 Art.51, Art.52, Art.53

Reg.2, amended: SSI 2002/111 Reg.3, SSI 2003/443 Reg.2

Reg.2, revoked (in part): SSI 2003/443 Reg.2

Reg.4, amended: SSI 2004/41 Reg.2

Reg.4, applied: SSI 2004/142 Art.3, Art.4

Reg.5, amended: SSI 2004/41 Reg.2

Reg.7A, amended: SI 2002/3135 Sch.1 para.33

Reg.11, applied: SSI 2004/142 Art.9, Art.17

Reg.11, referred to: SSI 2004/142 Art.8

Reg.11, varied: SSI 2004/142 Art.9

Reg.14, applied: SSI 2004/142 Art.8

Reg.17, applied: SSI 2004/142 Art.9

Reg.17, varied: SSI 2004/142 Art.9

Reg.24, applied: SSI 2004/142 Art.3, Art.4, Art.13, Art.15, Art.30, SSI 2004/163 Art.26

Reg.25, applied: SSI 2004/163 Art.5, Art.8

NO.

416. National Health Service (General Medical Services) (Scotland) Regulations 1995–*cont.*

Reg.27, amended: SSI 2003/443 Reg.4

Reg.27, applied: SSI 2004/142 Art.28, SSI 2004/163 Art.7, Art.9

Reg.27, revoked (in part): SSI 2003/443 Reg.4

Reg.29, applied: SSI 2004/142 Art.24

Reg.30, applied: SSI 2004/142 Art.24

Reg.31, applied: SSI 2004/142 Art.24

Reg.34, applied: SSI 2003/64 Sch.1 para.6, Sch.1 para.7, Sch.1 para.8, Sch.1 para.11

Reg.34, disapplied: SSI 2003/64 Sch.1 para.6

Reg.35, amended: SSI 2002/111 Reg.3

Reg.35, applied: SSI 2003/64 Reg.13, Sch.1 para.2, SSI 2004/115 Sch.1 para.4, Sch.1 para.5, SSI 2004/116 Sch.3 para.4, Sch.3 para.5

Reg.35, referred to: SSI 2003/64 Reg.13A, Sch.1 para.11

Reg.35, varied: SSI 2004/163 Art.51

Reg.36, applied: SSI 2004/163 Art.33

Reg.36, referred to: SSI 2004/163 Art.33

Sch.1, applied: SSI 2004/163 Art.16

Sch.1 para.1, amended: SSI 2002/111 Reg.3, SSI 2003/443 Reg.3

Sch.1 para.4, applied: SSI 2004/163 Art.13

Sch.1 para.6, applied: SSI 2004/163 Art.4

Sch.1 para.7, applied: SSI 2004/163 Art.11

Sch.1 para.9, applied: SSI 2004/163 Art.6, Art.7

Sch.1 para.9A, applied: SSI 2004/163 Art.11, Art.12

Sch.1 para.10, applied: SSI 2004/163 Art.30

Sch.1 para.10, varied: SSI 2004/163 Art.30

Sch.1 para.12, referred to: SSI 2004/163 Art.25

Sch.1 para.12A, applied: SSI 2004/163 Art.21, Art.22, Art.31

Sch.1 para.12A, varied: SSI 2004/163 Art.21

Sch.1 para.13, applied: SSI 2003/64 Sch.1 para.5

Sch.1 para.13, referred to: SSI 2003/64 Sch.1 para.5

Sch.1 para.14, applied: SSI 2004/163 Art.14

Sch.1 para.16, applied: SSI 2004/163 Art.28

Sch.1 para.17, applied: SSI 2004/115 Reg.30, Reg.31, SSI 2004/142 Art.19, Art.20

Sch.1 para.17A, amended: SI 2002/3135 Sch.1 para.33, SSI 2004/41 Reg.2

Sch.1 para.17A, applied: SSI 2004/163 Art.64, Art.65, Art.66, Art.67, Art.69, Art.70

Sch.1 para.17A, referred to: SSI 2004/163 Art.65, Art.66

Sch.1 para.17B, applied: SSI 2004/163 Art.65, Art.67, Art.69

Sch.1 para.17C, applied: SSI 2004/163 Art.65, Art.70

NO.

416. National Health Service (General Medical Services) (Scotland) Regulations 1995–*cont.*

Sch.1 para.18, amended: SSI 2003/64 Reg.15, SSI 2004/41 Reg.2

Sch.1 para.19, amended: SSI 2003/64 Reg.15, SSI 2004/41 Reg.2

Sch.1 para.19, applied: SSI 2004/163 Art.24

Sch.1 para.20A, amended: SSI 2004/41 Reg.2

Sch.1 para.20B, added: SSI 2003/443 Reg.5

Sch.1 para.23, applied: SSI 2004/163 Art.15, Art.19

Sch.1 para.24, applied: SSI 2003/64 Sch.1 para.5, SSI 2004/142 Art.26, SSI 2004/163 Art.20

Sch.1 para.24, referred to: SSI 2004/163 Art.20

Sch.1 para.24, varied: SSI 2004/163 Art.20

Sch.1 para.27, applied: SSI 2004/142 Art.26

Sch.1 para.29, amended: SSI 2002/111 Reg.3

Sch.1 para.29, applied: SSI 2004/163 Art.17

Sch.1 para.29A, amended: SSI 2003/443 Reg.3

Sch.1 para.29B, amended: SSI 2003/443 Reg.3

Sch.1 para.29C, added: SSI 2003/443 Reg.3

Sch.1 para.30, amended: SSI 2002/111 Reg.3

Sch.1 para.32, applied: SSI 2004/163 Art.18

Sch.1 para.34, applied: SSI 2004/163 Art.23

Sch.1 para.35, applied: SSI 2004/163 Art.31

Sch.9, applied: SSI 2003/64 Sch.1 para.5

Sch.9, referred to: SSI 2003/64 Sch.1 para.5

Sch.10, amended: SSI 2002/438 Reg.2, SSI 2003/11 Reg.2

Sch.11, amended: SSI 2002/111 Reg.3, SSI 2003/11 Reg.3, SSI 2003/310 Reg.2

Sch.11, applied: SSI 2003/64 Sch.1 para.10

Sch.11, referred to: SSI 2003/64 Sch.1 para.6, Sch.1 para.10

418. Town and Country (General Permitted Development) Order 1995

Sch.2 Part 24, see *Wandsworth LBC v Secretary of State for Transport, Local Government and the Regions* [2003] EWHC 622, [2004] 1 P. & C.R. 32 (QBD (Admin Ct)), Sullivan, J.

418. Town and Country Planning (General Permitted Development) Order 1995

applied: 2002 c.i s.40, 2003 c.iii s.16

referred to: SI 2003/956 Art.13

see *R. (on the application of Cal Brown Ltd (t/a CB Advertising Ltd)) v Hounslow LBC* [2001] EWHC Admin 864, [2002] 2 P. & C.R. 22 (QBD (Admin Ct)), Goldring, J.; see *Taylor & Sons (Farms) v Secretary of State for the Environment, Transport and the Regions* [2001] EWCA Civ 1254, [2002] P.L.C.R. 11 (CA), Schiemann, L.J.

Art.1, amended: SI 2003/956 Sch.6 para.1, Sch.6 para.2

NO.

418. Town and Country Planning (General Permitted Development) Order 1995– *cont.*

Art.3, amended: SI 2003/956 Sch.6 para.3

Art.3, applied: SI 2002/2618 Art.17

Art.3, referred to: SI 2004/2190 Art.18

Art.3, see *Hill v Secretary of State for Transport, Local Government and the Regions* [2003] EWHC 279, [2004] 1 P. & C.R. 5 (QBD (Admin Ct)), Collins, J.

Art.14, see *R. (on the application of Hartley Property Trust Ltd) v Secretary of State for the Environment, Transport and the Regions* [2001] EWHC Admin 935, [2002] P.L.C.R. 21 (QBD (Admin Ct)), Gibbs, J.

Sch.2 Part 1 Class B, see *R. (on the application of Watts) v Secretary of State for the Environment, Transport and the Regions* [2002] EWHC 993, [2002] J.P.L. 1473 (QBD (Admin Ct)), Ouseley, J.

Sch.2 Part 2 Class A, see *Lowe v First Secretary of State* [2003] EWHC 537, [2003] 2 P. & C.R. 24 (QBD (Admin Ct)), Sir Richard Tucker

Sch.2 Part 4 Class B, see *Ramsey v Secretary of State for the Environment, Transport and the Regions* [2002] EWCA Civ 118, Times, March 4, 2002 (CA), Keene, L.J.

Sch.2 Part 4 Class E, see *Crockett v Secretary of State for Transport, Local Government and the Regions* [2002] EWHC 2272, (2002) 99(43) L.S.G. 37 (QBD (Admin Ct)), Maurice Kay, J.

Sch.2 Part 11, applied: SI 2002/2618 Art.17

Sch.2 Part 11, referred to: SI 2004/2190 Art.18

Sch.2 Part 17, amended: SI 2003/2155 Sch.1 para.38

Sch.2 Part 24 paraA, amended: SI 2003/2155 Sch.1 para.38, SI 2004/945 Art.3

Sch.2 Part 24 paraA, substituted: SI 2002/1878 Sch.1

Sch.2 Part 24 paraA.1, amended: SI 2003/2155 Sch.1 para.38, SI 2004/945 Art.3

Sch.2 Part 24 paraA.1, substituted: SI 2002/1878 Sch.1

Sch.2 Part 24 paraA.2, amended: SI 2003/2155 Sch.1 para.38, SI 2004/945 Art.3

Sch.2 Part 24 paraA.2, substituted: SI 2002/1878 Sch.1

Sch.2 Part 24 paraA.3, amended: SI 2003/2155 Sch.1 para.38, SI 2004/945 Art.3

Sch.2 Part 24 paraA.3, substituted: SI 2002/1878 Sch.1

Sch.2 Part 24 paraA.4, amended: SI 2003/2155 Sch.1 para.38, Sch.2, SI 2004/945 Art.3

Sch.2 Part 24 paraA.4, substituted: SI 2002/1878 Sch.1

NO.

419. Town and Country Planning (General Development Procedure) Order 1995

referred to: SI 2003/956 Art.11

Art.1, see *R. (on the application of Murray) v Hampshire CC (No.1)* [2002] EWHC 1401, [2003] J.P.L. 224 (QBD (Admin Ct)), Burton, J.

Art.1, amended: SI 2003/956 Sch.1 para.1, Sch.1 para.2, SI 2003/2047 Art.2, SI 2004/1434 Art.2

Art.4, amended: SI 2003/956 Sch.1 para.3

Art.5A, added: SI 2002/1877 Art.3

Art.6, amended: SI 2003/956 Sch.1 para.4

Art.8, amended: SI 2004/1231 Art.4

Art.8, see *R. (on the application of Gavin) v Haringey LBC* [2003] EWHC 2591, [2004] 2 P. & C.R. 13 (QBD (Admin Ct)), Richards, J.

Art.10, amended: SI 2003/2047 Art.3, Art.4

Art.22, amended: SI 2003/2047 Art.5, SI 2004/1434 Art.3

Art.23, amended: SI 2003/956 Sch.1 para.5, SI 2003/2047 Art.6, SI 2004/1434 Art.4

Art.25, amended: SI 2003/956 Sch.1 para.6, SI 2003/2047 Art.7, SI 2004/1434 Art.5

Art.27A, added: SI 2003/956 Sch.1 para.7

Sch.1 Part 2, amended: SI 2003/2047 Art.8

Sch.2 Part 1, amended: SI 2003/956 Sch.1 para.8

Sch.3, amended: SI 2003/956 Sch.1 para.9

447. Income Tax (Employments) (Amendment No 2) Regulations 1995

revoked: SI 2003/2682 Sch.2

449. Medical Devices (Consultation Requirements) (Fees) Regulations 1995

Reg.1, amended: SI 2002/236 Reg.15

Reg.3, amended: SI 2002/542 Reg.4, SI 2003/625 Reg.3, SI 2004/666 Reg.3

450. Police and Criminal Evidence Act 1984 (Codes of Practice) (No.3) Order 1995

revoked: SI 2003/703 Art.4

477. Broadgreen Hospital National Health Service Trust Dissolution Order 1995

revoked: 2003 c.43 s.7

478. Fosse Health, Leicestershire Community National Health Service Trust Dissolution Order 1995

revoked: 2003 c.43 s.7

479. Royal Liverpool University Hospital National Health Service Trust Dissolution Order 1995

revoked: 2003 c.43 s.7

480. St James's University Hospital National Health Service Trust Dissolution Order 1995

revoked: 2003 c.43 s.7

1995–cont.

481. Weybourne Community National Health Service Trust Dissolution Order 1995

revoked: 2003 c.43 s.7

490. Antarctic Regulations 1995

Sch.1, added: SI 2002/2054 Sch.1 Part A

Sch.1, amended: SI 2002/2054 Reg.2, SI 2003/323 Reg.2, Sch.1, SI 2004/2782 Sch.1

Sch.1, substituted: SI 2002/2054 Sch.1 Part B

Sch.2, substituted: SI 2004/2782 Sch.2

Sch.2 para.1, substituted: SI 2004/2782 Sch.2

Sch.2 para.2, substituted: SI 2004/2782 Sch.2

Sch.2 para.3, substituted: SI 2004/2782 Sch.2

Sch.2 para.4, substituted: SI 2004/2782 Sch.2

Sch.2 para.5, substituted: SI 2004/2782 Sch.2

Sch.2 para.6, substituted: SI 2004/2782 Sch.2

Sch.2 para.7, substituted: SI 2004/2782 Sch.2

Sch.2 para.8, substituted: SI 2004/2782 Sch.2

Sch.2 para.9, substituted: SI 2004/2782 Sch.2

Sch.2 para.10, substituted: SI 2004/2782 Sch.2

Sch.2 para.11, substituted: SI 2004/2782 Sch.2

Sch.2 para.12, substituted: SI 2004/2782 Sch.2

Sch.2 para.13, substituted: SI 2004/2782 Sch.2

Sch.2 para.14, substituted: SI 2004/2782 Sch.2

Sch.2 para.15, substituted: SI 2004/2782 Sch.2

Sch.2 para.16, substituted: SI 2004/2782 Sch.2

Sch.2 para.17, substituted: SI 2004/2782 Sch.2

Sch.2 para.18, substituted: SI 2004/2782 Sch.2

Sch.2 para.19, substituted: SI 2004/2782 Sch.2

Sch.2 para.20, substituted: SI 2004/2782 Sch.2

Sch.2 para.21, substituted: SI 2004/2782 Sch.2

Sch.2 para.22, substituted: SI 2004/2782 Sch.2

Sch.2 para.23, substituted: SI 2004/2782 Sch.2

Sch.2 para.24, substituted: SI 2004/2782 Sch.2

Sch.2 para.25, substituted: SI 2004/2782 Sch.2

1995–cont.

490. Antarctic Regulations 1995–cont.

Sch.2 para.26, substituted: SI 2004/2782 Sch.2

Sch.2 para.27, substituted: SI 2004/2782 Sch.2

Sch.2 para.28, substituted: SI 2004/2782 Sch.2

Sch.2 para.29, substituted: SI 2004/2782 Sch.2

Sch.2 para.30, substituted: SI 2004/2782 Sch.2

Sch.2 para.31, substituted: SI 2004/2782 Sch.2

Sch.2 para.32, substituted: SI 2004/2782 Sch.2

Sch.2 para.33, substituted: SI 2004/2782 Sch.2

Sch.2 para.34, substituted: SI 2004/2782 Sch.2

Sch.2 para.35, substituted: SI 2004/2782 Sch.2

Sch.2 para.36, substituted: SI 2004/2782 Sch.2

Sch.2 para.37, substituted: SI 2004/2782 Sch.2

Sch.2 para.38, substituted: SI 2004/2782 Sch.2

Sch.2 para.39, substituted: SI 2004/2782 Sch.2

Sch.2 para.40, substituted: SI 2004/2782 Sch.2

Sch.2 para.41, substituted: SI 2004/2782 Sch.2

Sch.2 para.42, substituted: SI 2004/2782 Sch.2

Sch.2 para.43, substituted: SI 2004/2782 Sch.2

Sch.2 para.44, substituted: SI 2004/2782 Sch.2

Sch.2 para.45, substituted: SI 2004/2782 Sch.2

Sch.2 para.46, substituted: SI 2004/2782 Sch.2

Sch.2 para.47, substituted: SI 2004/2782 Sch.2

Sch.2 para.48, substituted: SI 2004/2782 Sch.2

Sch.2 para.49, substituted: SI 2004/2782 Sch.2

Sch.2 para.50, substituted: SI 2004/2782 Sch.2

Sch.2 para.51, substituted: SI 2004/2782 Sch.2

Sch.2 para.52, substituted: SI 2004/2782 Sch.2

Sch.2 para.53, substituted: SI 2004/2782 Sch.2

Sch.2 para.54, substituted: SI 2004/2782 Sch.2

Sch.2 para.55, substituted: SI 2004/2782 Sch.2

NO.

NO.

1995–cont.

1995–cont.

490. Antarctic Regulations 1995–*cont.*

Sch.2 para.56, substituted: SI 2004/2782 Sch.2

Sch.2 para.57, substituted: SI 2004/2782 Sch.2

Sch.2 para.58, substituted: SI 2004/2782 Sch.2

Sch.2 para.59, substituted: SI 2004/2782 Sch.2

Sch.2 para.60, substituted: SI 2004/2782 Sch.2

Sch.2 para.61, substituted: SI 2004/2782 Sch.2

Sch.2 para.62, substituted: SI 2004/2782 Sch.2

Sch.2 para.63, substituted: SI 2004/2782 Sch.2

Sch.2 para.64, substituted: SI 2004/2782 Sch.2

Sch.2 para.65, substituted: SI 2004/2782 Sch.2

Sch.2 para.66, substituted: SI 2004/2782 Sch.2

Sch.2 para.67, substituted: SI 2004/2782 Sch.2

Sch.2 para.68, substituted: SI 2004/2782 Sch.2

Sch.2 para.69, substituted: SI 2004/2782 Sch.2

Sch.2 para.70, substituted: SI 2004/2782 Sch.2

Sch.2 para.71, substituted: SI 2004/2782 Sch.2

Sch.2 para.72, substituted: SI 2004/2782 Sch.2

Sch.2 para.73, substituted: SI 2004/2782 Sch.2

Sch.2 para.74, substituted: SI 2004/2782 Sch.2

Sch.2 para.75, added: SI 2002/2054 Sch.2

Sch.2 para.75, substituted: SI 2004/2782 Sch.2

Sch.2 para.76, added: SI 2002/2054 Sch.2

Sch.2 para.76, substituted: SI 2004/2782 Sch.2

493. Avon (Structural Change) Order 1995

varied: SI 2004/222 Art.2

506. Misuse of Drugs (Licence Fees) (Amendment) Regulations 1995

revoked: SI 2003/611 Sch.1

510. Marriages (Approved Premises) Regulations 1995

Reg.7, amended: SI 2003/1961 Reg.2

516. Income-related Benefits Schemes (Miscellaneous Amendments) Regulations 1995

Reg.28, applied: SI 2002/1792 Sch.1 para.6

519. Barking Barrage Order 1995

Art.3, amended: SI 2003/2155 Sch.1 para.22

Sch.5, amended: SI 2003/2155 Sch.1 para.17, Sch.2

539. Fresh Meat (Hygiene and Inspection) Regulations 1995

applied: 2002 asp 11 Sch.3 para.4, SI 2002/ 76 Reg.6, SI 2002/843 Reg.46, Reg.56, Reg.82, Reg.91, Reg.101, SI 2002/1227 Reg.4, SI 2002/1387 Reg.4, SI 2002/ 1416 Reg.46, Reg.101, SI 2003/409 Sch.1 Part I, SI 2003/1482 Reg.49, SI 2003/ 2756 Reg.48, SI 2003/3177 Reg.4, SI 2004/1214 Reg.4, SI 2004/1430 Reg.4, SI 2004/1740 Reg.4, SI 2004/2640 Reg.4, SSI 2002/234 Reg.3, SSI 2002/ 255 Reg.43, Reg.81, Reg.88, Reg.89, Reg.99, SSI 2002/445 Reg.4, SSI 2003/ 411 Reg.49

Reg.4, applied: SSI 2002/234 Reg.3

Reg.8, applied: SI 2002/843 Reg.77, SI 2002/1416 Reg.77, SI 2004/853 Reg.12

Sch.12 para.9, amended: SI 2002/8 Reg.30

Sch.12 para.9, substituted: SI 2002/118 Reg.3, SI 2002/129 Reg.3, SSI 2002/35 Reg.4

Sch.17A para.1, added: SI 2002/889 Reg.3, SI 2002/1476 Reg.3, SSI 2002/234 Sch.1

Sch.17A para.2, added: SI 2002/889 Reg.3, SI 2002/1476 Reg.3, SSI 2002/234 Sch.1

Sch.17A para.3, added: SI 2002/889 Reg.3, SI 2002/1476 Reg.3, SSI 2002/234 Sch.1

Sch.17A para.4, added: SI 2002/889 Reg.3, SI 2002/1476 Reg.3, SSI 2002/234 Sch.1

Sch.17A para.5, added: SI 2002/889 Reg.3, SI 2002/1476 Reg.3, SSI 2002/234 Sch.1

Sch.17A para.6, added: SI 2002/889 Reg.3, SI 2002/1476 Reg.3, SSI 2002/234 Sch.1

Sch.17A para.7, added: SI 2002/889 Reg.3, SI 2002/1476 Reg.3, SSI 2002/234 Sch.1

Sch.17B para.1, added: SI 2002/889 Reg.3, SI 2002/1476 Reg.3, SSI 2002/234 Sch.1

Sch.17B para.2, added: SI 2002/889 Reg.3, SI 2002/1476 Reg.3, SSI 2002/234 Sch.1

Sch.17B para.3, added: SI 2002/889 Reg.3, SI 2002/1476 Reg.3, SSI 2002/234 Sch.1

Sch.17B para.4, added: SI 2002/889 Reg.3, SI 2002/1476 Reg.3, SSI 2002/234 Sch.1

Sch.17B para.5, added: SI 2002/889 Reg.3, SI 2002/1476 Reg.3, SSI 2002/234 Sch.1

Sch.17B para.6, added: SI 2002/889 Reg.3, SI 2002/1476 Reg.3, SSI 2002/234 Sch.1

Sch.17B para.7, added: SI 2002/889 Reg.3, SI 2002/1476 Reg.3, SSI 2002/234 Sch.1

Sch.17C para.1, added: SI 2002/889 Reg.3, SI 2002/1476 Reg.3, SSI 2002/234 Sch.1

Sch.17C para.2, added: SI 2002/889 Reg.3, SI 2002/1476 Reg.3, SSI 2002/234 Sch.1

Sch.17C para.3, added: SI 2002/889 Reg.3, SI 2002/1476 Reg.3, SSI 2002/234 Sch.1

Sch.17C para.4, added: SI 2002/889 Reg.3, SI 2002/1476 Reg.3, SSI 2002/234 Sch.1

Sch.17C para.5, added: SI 2002/889 Reg.3, SI 2002/1476 Reg.3, SSI 2002/234 Sch.1

Sch.17C para.6, added: SI 2002/889 Reg.3, SI 2002/1476 Reg.3, SSI 2002/234 Sch.1

NO.

539. Fresh Meat (Hygiene and Inspection) Regulations 1995–*cont.*

Sch.17C para.7, added: SI 2002/889 Reg.3, SI 2002/1476 Reg.3, SSI 2002/234 Sch.1

540. Poultry Meat, Farmed Game Bird Meat and Rabbit Meat (Hygiene and Inspection) Regulations 1995

applied: 2002 asp 11 Sch.3 para.4, SI 2002/843 Reg.56, Reg.101, SI 2002/1227 Reg.4, SI 2002/1387 Reg.4, SI 2002/1416 Reg.101, SI 2003/409 Sch.1 Part I, SI 2003/1482 Reg.49, SI 2003/2756 Reg.48, SI 2003/3177 Reg.4, SI 2004/1214 Reg.4, SI 2004/1430 Reg.4, SI 2004/1740 Reg.4, SI 2004/2640 Reg.4, SSI 2002/234 Reg.3, SSI 2002/255 Reg.99, SSI 2002/445 Reg.4, SSI 2003/411 Reg.49

Reg.2, amended: SSI 2002/87 Reg.2

Reg.4, applied: SSI 2002/234 Reg.3

Reg.8, amended: SI 2002/889 Reg.4, SI 2002/1476 Reg.4, SSI 2002/234 Reg.5

Reg.8, applied: SI 2004/853 Reg.12

Reg.13, amended: SI 2002/47 Reg.2

Reg.18, amended: SI 2002/47 Reg.2, SSI 2002/87 Reg.2

Reg.18, substituted: SSI 2002/234 Reg.5

Sch.5 Part I para.5, substituted: SI 2002/47 Reg.2, SSI 2002/87 Reg.2

Sch.8 para.11, amended: SI 2002/47 Reg.2, SSI 2002/87 Reg.2

Sch.14 para.1, amended: SI 2002/47 Reg.2, SSI 2002/87 Reg.2

547. Police (Amendment) Regulations 1995

revoked: SI 2003/527 Sch.4 Part 1

553. Local Authorities (Members Allowance) (Amendment) Regulations 1995

revoked (in part): SI 2003/1021 Reg.33

572. Valuation Appeal Committee (Procedure in Appeals under the Valuation Acts) (Scotland) Regulations 1995

Reg.3, applied: SSI 2003/452 r.11

Reg.4, applied: SSI 2003/452 r.11

574. State Hospitals Board for Scotland Order 1995

Sch.1 Part II, amended: SSI 2003/242 Art.5

Sch.1 Part III, amended: SI 2003/1590 Sch.1 para.22

596. Police (Scotland) Amendment (No.2) Regulations 1995

revoked: SSI 2004/257 Sch.4

599. Council Tax (Discounts) (Scotland) Amendment Order 1995

revoked: SSI 2003/176 Sch.4

600. Humberside (Structural Change) Order 1995

varied: SI 2004/222 Art.2

NO.

610. North Yorkshire (District of York) (Structural and Boundary Changes) Order 1995

varied: SI 2004/222 Art.2

614. Animal By-Products (Identification) Regulations 1995

referred to: SI 2003/2754 Reg.2

Reg.2, amended: SI 2002/3231 Reg.2, SI 2003/1484 Reg.3, SI 2003/1849 Reg.2, SI 2003/2754 Reg.3, SSI 2003/53 Reg.2, SSI 2003/411 Sch.5 para.1

Reg.3, amended: SI 2002/3231 Reg.2, SI 2003/1849 Reg.2, SSI 2003/53 Reg.2

Reg.4, amended: SI 2002/3231 Reg.2, SI 2003/1849 Reg.2, SSI 2003/53 Reg.2, SSI 2003/411 Sch.5 para.1

Reg.4, substituted: SI 2002/1472 Reg.2, SI 2002/1619 Reg.2, SSI 2002/283 Reg.2

Reg.5, amended: SI 2002/3231 Reg.2, SI 2003/1484 Reg.4, SI 2003/1849 Reg.2, SI 2003/2754 Reg.4, SSI 2003/53 Reg.2, SSI 2003/411 Sch.5 para.1

Reg.6, amended: SI 2002/3231 Reg.2, SI 2003/1484 Reg.5, SI 2003/1849 Reg.2, SI 2003/2754 Reg.5, SSI 2003/53 Reg.2, SSI 2003/411 Sch.5 para.1

Reg.6, revoked (in part): SI 2002/3231 Reg.2, SI 2003/1849 Reg.2, SSI 2003/53 Reg.2

Reg.6, substituted: SI 2002/1472 Reg.2, SI 2002/1619 Reg.2, SSI 2002/283 Reg.2

Reg.7, amended: SI 2002/3231 Reg.2, SI 2003/1484 Reg.6, SI 2003/1849 Reg.2, SI 2003/2754 Reg.6, SSI 2003/53 Reg.2, SSI 2003/411 Sch.5 para.1

Reg.8, amended: SI 2002/3231 Reg.2, SI 2003/1849 Reg.2, SSI 2003/53 Reg.2

Reg.8, substituted: SI 2002/1472 Reg.2, SI 2002/1619 Reg.2, SSI 2002/283 Reg.2

Reg.9, amended: SI 2002/3231 Reg.2, SI 2003/1484 Reg.7, SI 2003/1849 Reg.2, SI 2003/2754 Reg.7, SSI 2003/53 Reg.2, SSI 2003/411 Sch.5 para.1

Reg.9, substituted: SI 2002/1472 Reg.2, SI 2002/1619 Reg.2, SSI 2002/283 Reg.2

Reg.10, amended: SI 2002/3231 Reg.2, SI 2003/1484 Reg.8, SI 2003/1849 Reg.2, SI 2003/2754 Reg.8, SSI 2003/53 Reg.2, SSI 2003/411 Sch.5 para.1

Reg.10, substituted: SI 2002/1472 Reg.2, SI 2002/1619 Reg.2, SSI 2002/283 Reg.2

615. Common Agricultural Policy (Wine) Regulations 1995

applied: SSI 2002/325 Reg.7

621. Family Health Services Appeal Authority (Establishment and Constitution) Order 1995

Art.3, amended: SI 2002/2469 Sch.1 para.63

622. Family Health Services Appeal Authority Regulations 1995

Reg.1, amended: SI 2002/2469 Sch.1 para.64, SI 2004/696 Art.3

NO.

622. Family Health Services Appeal Authority Regulations 1995–*cont.*

Reg.7, amended: SI 2002/2469 Sch.1 para.64, SI 2004/21 Reg.2, SI 2004/696 Art.3, Sch.1 para.17, SI 2004/1771 Sch.1 para.42

Reg.12, amended: SI 2002/2469 Sch.1 para.64

642. National Health Service (Travelling Expenses and Remission of Charges) Amendment Regulations 1995

revoked: SI 2003/2382 Sch.2

700. National Health Service (Travelling Expenses and Remission of Charges) (Scotland) Amendment Regulations 1995

revoked: SSI 2003/376 Sch.3 para.9

703. National Health Service (Dental Charges) (Scotland) Amendment Regulations 1995

revoked: SSI 2003/158 Sch.4

731. Welfare of Animals (Slaughter or Killing) Regulations 1995

Reg.3A, substituted: SSI 2002/255 Sch.8 Part I

Sch.1 para.9, amended: SI 2003/3272 Reg.2, SSI 2004/13 Reg.2

Sch.4 para.6, amended: SI 2003/3272 Reg.2, SSI 2004/13 Reg.2

Sch.6 para.2, revoked (in part): SI 2003/3272 Reg.2

Sch.7 Part III para.7, amended: SSI 2002/238 Reg.2

Sch.7 Part III para.8, amended: SSI 2002/238 Reg.2

Sch.7 Part III para.10, amended: SSI 2002/238 Reg.2

Sch.9 para.2, amended: SI 2003/3272 Reg.2, SSI 2004/13 Reg.2

734. Companies (Welsh Language Forms and Documents) (Amendment) Regulations 1995

Sch.1, applied: SI 2003/62 Reg.3

735. Measuring Equipment (Capacity Measures and Testing Equipment) Regulations 1995

Reg.13, amended: SI 2003/214 Sch.1 para.6

736. Companies (Forms) (Amendment) Regulations 1995

Sch.2, applied: SI 2002/691 Reg.3

738. Offshore Installations and Pipeline Works (Management and Administration) Regulations 1995

Reg.2, amended: SI 2002/2175 Reg.2

Reg.3, amended: SI 2002/2175 Reg.2

739. European Parliamentary (United Kingdom Representatives) Pensions (Additional Voluntary Contributions Scheme) (No.2) Order 1995

applied: SI 2003/2922 Art.2

amended: SI 2003/2922 Art.2

NO.

739. European Parliamentary (United Kingdom Representatives) Pensions (Additional Voluntary Contributions Scheme) (No.2) Order 1995–*cont.*

Art.3, amended: SI 2003/2922 Art.2

Art.7, amended: SI 2004/2418 Art.3

Art.9, amended: SI 2003/2922 Art.2, SI 2004/2418 Art.4

Art.13, amended: SI 2003/2922 Art.2

740. Stornaway Harbour Revision Order 1995

revoked: SSI 2003/435 Sch.3

743. Offshore Installations (Prevention of Fire and Explosion, and Emergency Response) Regulations 1995

Reg.2, varied: SI 2002/2175 Reg.3

755. Children (Northern Ireland) Order 1995

applied: 2002 c.11 (NI), SI 2003/431 Art.9, Art.15, SI 2003/435 Sch.2 para.2, SI 2003/439 Sch.1 para.3, SR 2002/79 Reg.5, 2004 c.6 s.3

Part IV, applied: SI 2003/493 Reg.18

Part VI, applied: 2002 c.21 Sch.5 para.10A

Part IX, amended: SI 2003/431 Sch.4

Part XI, applied: SI 2002/635 Reg.2, SI 2002/896 Sch.1 para.8, SI 2003/417 Art.31

Art.2, amended: 2002 c.11 (NI) s.7, 2002 c.21 Sch.6, SI 2003/431 Sch.4, Sch.5

Art.2, applied: SI 2002/2006 Reg.19

Art.3, see *L1 (Care Proceedings: Criminal Trial), Re* [2004] N.I. 136 (Fam Div (NI)), Gillen, J.

Art.6, applied: SR 2003/255 Art.5

Art.15, applied: SR 2002/224 Reg.16, Sch.3 para.1, SR 2002/265 Sch.7 para.1

Art.17A, added: 2002 c.6 (NI) s.4

Art.18, amended: 2002 c.11 (NI) s.7, 2002 c.21 Sch.3 para.52

Art.18A, added: 2002 c.6 (NI) s.5

Art.18A, applied: 2002 c.6 (NI) s.1

Art.18B, added: 2002 c.6 (NI) s.6

Art.18C, added: 2002 c.6 (NI) s.9

Art.18C, amended: 2002 c.21 Sch.3 para.53, Sch.6

Art.18C, applied: SI 2003/417 Art.16

Art.18D, added: 2002 c.6 (NI) s.7

Art.24, amended: 2002 c.21 Sch.3 para.54

Art.25, amended: 2002 c.11 (NI) s.2

Art.27, amended: SI 2003/431 Sch.4

Art.27, applied: SI 2003/431 Art.23, Art.40, SI 2003/493 Reg.16, SR 2002/224 Reg.16, Sch.3 para.1, SR 2002/265 Sch.7 para.1

Art.34A, added: 2002 c.11 (NI) s.1

Art.34A, applied: 2002 c.11 (NI) s.6

Art.34B, added: 2002 c.11 (NI) s.2

Art.34B, applied: 2002 c.11 (NI) s.6

Art.34C, added: 2002 c.11 (NI) s.2

Art.34D, added: 2002 c.11 (NI) s.2

Art.34D, applied: SI 2003/439 Art.3

NO.

1995–cont.

755. Children (Northern Ireland) Order 1995–*cont.*

Art.34E, added: 2002 c.11 (NI) s.3

Art.34E, applied: SI 2003/439 Art.3

Art.34F, added: 2002 c.11 (NI) s.3

Art.35, amended: 2002 c.11 (NI) s.2, SI 2003/431 Sch.4

Art.35, applied: SI 2003/439 Art.3, SR 2002/224 Reg.16, Sch.3 para.1, SR 2002/265 Sch.7 para.1

Art.35, substituted: 2002 c.11 (NI) s.4

Art.35A, added: 2002 c.11 (NI) s.4

Art.35A, applied: SI 2003/439 Art.3

Art.35B, added: 2002 c.11 (NI) s.4

Art.35B, applied: SI 2003/439 Art.3

Art.35C, added: 2002 c.11 (NI) s.4

Art.35D, added: 2002 c.11 (NI) s.5

Art.36, applied: SR 2002/224 Reg.16, Sch.3 para.1, SR 2002/265 Sch.7 para.1

Art.36, revoked: 2002 c.11 (NI) s.7

Art.37, amended: SI 2003/431 Sch.4

Art.37, revoked: 2002 c.11 (NI) s.7

Art.39, amended: 2002 c.21 Sch.3 para.55

Art.44, amended: SI 2003/435 Sch.4 para.11

Art.46, amended: 2002 c.11 (NI) s.7

Art.50, see *J (Freeing for Adoption: Adoption Agencies: Procedural Requirements), Re* [2004] N.I. 10 (Fam Div (NI)), Gillen, J.; see *L1 (Care Proceedings: Criminal Trial), Re* [2004] N.I. 136 (Fam Div (NI)), Gillen, J.

Art.50, applied: SI 2002/635 Reg.2, SI 2002/896 Sch.1 para.1, Sch.1 para.2

Art.63, applied: SI 2002/896 Sch.1 para.74

Art.68, applied: SI 2002/635 Sch.1 para.3, SI 2002/896 Sch.1 para.74

Art.69, applied: SI 2002/635 Sch.1 para.3, SI 2002/896 Sch.1 para.74

Art.70, amended: 2002 c.26 Sch.12 para.51, SI 2003/431 Sch.4

Art.73, revoked (in part): SI 2003/431 Sch.5

Art.74, amended: SI 2003/431 Sch.4

Art.74, revoked (in part): SI 2003/431 Sch.5

Art.75, amended: SI 2003/431 Sch.4

Art.75, applied: SI 2003/431 Art.40

Art.77, amended: SI 2003/431 Sch.4

Art.78, amended: SI 2003/431 Sch.4

Art.78A, added: SI 2003/431 Sch.4

Art.79, applied: SI 2002/635 Sch.1 para.3, SI 2002/896 Sch.1 para.78

Art.79, revoked: SI 2003/431 Sch.5

Art.80, applied: SI 2002/635 Reg.2, SI 2002/896 Sch.1 para.5

Art.80, revoked: SI 2003/431 Sch.5

Art.81, applied: SI 2002/635 Sch.1 para.3, SI 2002/896 Sch.1 para.78

Art.81, revoked: SI 2003/431 Sch.5

Art.82, applied: SI 2002/635 Reg.2, SI 2002/896 Sch.1 para.5

Art.82, revoked: SI 2003/431 Sch.5

Art.83, revoked: SI 2003/431 Sch.5

Art.84, revoked: SI 2003/431 Sch.5

NO.

1995–cont.

755. Children (Northern Ireland) Order 1995–*cont.*

Art.85, revoked: SI 2003/431 Sch.5

Art.86, revoked: SI 2003/431 Sch.5

Art.87, revoked: SI 2003/431 Sch.5

Art.88, revoked: SI 2003/431 Sch.5

Art.89, revoked (in part): SI 2003/431 Sch.5

Art.90, amended: SI 2003/431 Sch.4

Art.90, revoked (in part): SI 2003/431 Sch.5

Art.91, amended: SI 2003/431 Sch.4

Art.91, revoked (in part): SI 2003/431 Sch.5

Art.92, amended: SI 2003/431 Sch.4

Art.93, amended: SI 2003/431 Sch.4

Art.94, amended: SI 2003/431 Sch.4

Art.94A, added: SI 2003/431 Sch.4

Art.95, applied: SI 2002/635 Sch.1 para.3, SI 2002/896 Sch.1 para.78

Art.95, revoked: SI 2003/431 Sch.5

Art.96, applied: SI 2002/635 Reg.2, SI 2002/896 Sch.1 para.5

Art.96, revoked: SI 2003/431 Sch.5

Art.97, applied: SI 2002/635 Sch.1 para.3, SI 2002/896 Sch.1 para.78

Art.97, revoked: SI 2003/431 Sch.5

Art.98, applied: SI 2002/635 Reg.2, SI 2002/896 Sch.1 para.5

Art.98, revoked: SI 2003/431 Sch.5

Art.99, revoked: SI 2003/431 Sch.5

Art.100, revoked: SI 2003/431 Sch.5

Art.101, revoked: SI 2003/431 Sch.5

Art.102, revoked: SI 2003/431 Sch.5

Art.103, revoked: SI 2003/431 Sch.5

Art.104, revoked: SI 2003/431 Sch.5

Art.105, amended: SI 2003/431 Sch.4

Art.105, revoked (in part): SI 2003/431 Sch.5

Art.106, amended: SI 2003/431 Sch.4

Art.107, amended: SI 2003/431 Sch.4

Art.107, revoked (in part): SI 2003/431 Sch.4, Sch.5

Art.110, applied: SI 2002/635 Reg.2, SI 2002/896 Sch.1 para.6

Art.117, applied: SI 2002/635 Sch.1 para.3, SI 2002/896 Sch.1 para.77

Art.118, applied: SI 2003/439 Sch.1 para.4

Art.132, applied: SI 2002/635 Sch.1 para.3, SI 2002/896 Sch.1 para.76

Art.149, amended: SI 2003/431 Sch.4

Art.152, amended: SI 2003/431 Sch.5

Art.153, amended: SI 2003/431 Sch.4

Art.155, referred to: 2003 c.1 s.721

Art.164, enabled: SR 2002/119, SR 2002/350

Art.165, amended: 2002 c.26 s.11

Art.166, see *B and N (Children) (Allocation of Proceedings), Re* [2002] N.I. 197 (Fam Div (NI)), Gillen, J.

Art.171, see *L1 (Care Proceedings: Criminal Trial), Re* [2004] N.I. 136 (Fam Div (NI)), Gillen, J.

Art.172, revoked: SI 2003/435 Sch.5

NO.

1995–cont.

755. Children (Northern Ireland) Order 1995–cont.

Art.176, amended: SI 2003/431 Sch.4

Art.176, applied: SI 2003/424 Art.17

Art.183, amended: 2002 c.21 Sch.3 para.56

Sch.1, applied: SI 2003/412 Art.15, Art.16, Art.85, SR 2002/224 Reg.16, Sch.3 para.1, SR 2002/265 Sch.7 para.1

Sch.2, amended: 2002 c.11 (NI) s.7

Sch.4, amended: 2002 c.26 Sch.12 para.52

Sch.5, amended: SI 2003/431 Sch.4

Sch.7, enabled: SR 2002/119, SR 2002/350

Sch.9, revoked: SI 2003/412 Sch.5, SI 2003/413 Sch.1, SI 2003/431 Sch.5, SI 2003/435 Sch.5

757. Children's Evidence (Northern Ireland) Order 1995

Art.4, amended: SI 2003/435 Sch.4 para.12

Sch.1, amended: SI 2003/435 Sch.4 para.12

Sch.2, revoked: SI 2003/435 Sch.5, SI 2004/1501 Sch.2

769. Glan-y-Mor National Health Service Trust (Establishment) Order 1995

revoked: 2003 c.43 s.7

770. University Hospital of Wales Healthcare National Health Service Trust (Establishment) Order 1995

revoked: 2003 c.43 s.7

792. Homewood National Health Service Trust Dissolution Order 1995

revoked: 2003 c.43 s.7

798. Local Government Changes for England (Capital Finance) Regulations 1995

revoked: SI 2004/2044 Art.3

801. United Leeds Teaching Hospitals National Health Service Trust Dissolution Order 1995

revoked: 2003 c.43 s.7

829. Social Security (Incapacity Benefit) (Consequential and Transitional Amendments and Savings) Regulations 1995

Reg.1, amended: SI 2003/492 Sch.3 Part 1

Reg.21, revoked (in part): SI 2003/492 Sch.3 Part 1

842. Newham Community Health Services National Health Service Trust (Establishment) Order 1995

revoked: 2003 c.43 s.7

843. City and Hackney Community Services National Health Service Trust (Establishment) Order 1995

revoked: 2003 c.43 s.7

844. University Hospital Birmingham National Health Service Trust (Establishment) Order 1995

revoked: 2003 c.43 s.7

NO.

1995–cont.

845. Royal Orthopaedic Hospital National Health Service Trust (Establishment) Order 1995

revoked: 2003 c.43 s.7

846. Wolverley National Health Service Trust Dissolution Order 1995

revoked: 2003 c.43 s.7

847. Tower Hamlets Healthcare National Health Service Trust (Establishment) Order 1995

revoked: 2003 c.43 s.7

848. Surrey Heartlands National Health Service Trust (Establishment) Order 1995

revoked: 2003 c.43 s.7

849. Local Authorities (Companies) Order 1995

Part V, referred to: SI 2004/533 Art.9

Art.8, referred to: SI 2004/533 Art.9

Art.8, revoked: SI 2004/533 Art.9

Art.12, revoked: SI 2004/533 Art.9

Art.13, applied: SI 2004/533 Art.9

Art.13, revoked: SI 2004/533 Art.9

Art.14, amended: SI 2002/2118 Art.2, SI 2002/2298 Art.2

Art.14, referred to: SI 2004/533 Art.9

Art.14, revoked: SI 2004/533 Art.9

Art.15, amended: SI 2002/2118 Art.2

Art.15, applied: SI 2002/2298 Art.3

Art.15, referred to: SI 2004/533 Art.9

Art.15, revoked: SI 2004/533 Art.9

Art.15, substituted: SI 2002/2298 Art.2

Art.15, varied: SI 2002/2298 Art.3

Art.16, amended: SI 2002/2118 Art.2

Art.16, applied: SI 2002/2298 Art.3

Art.16, referred to: SI 2002/2298 Art.3

Art.16, revoked: SI 2004/533 Art.9

Art.17, revoked: SI 2004/533 Art.9

Art.18, revoked: SI 2004/533 Art.9

853. Income Tax (Employments) (Incapacity Benefit) Regulations 1995

revoked: SI 2003/2682 Sch.2

866. National Health Service (Injury Benefits) Regulations 1995

referred to: SI 2004/865 Art.114

varied: SI 2004/865 Art.114

Reg.2, amended: SI 2002/2469 Sch.1 para.65, Sch.2, Sch.5, SI 2003/631 Reg.3, SI 2004/696 Sch.1 para.18, SI 2004/865 Sch.1 para.13, SI 2004/1016 Sch.1 para.13

Reg.2, revoked (in part): SI 2004/1016 Sch.1 para.13

Reg.3, amended: SI 2002/2469 Sch.5, SI 2004/665 Reg.2

Reg.3, revoked (in part): SI 2004/865 Sch.1 para.13, SI 2004/1016 Sch.1 para.13

Reg.4, amended: SI 2004/665 Reg.2

Reg.4A, amended: SI 2002/2469 Sch.5, SI 2004/865 Sch.1 para.13, SI 2004/1016 Sch.1 para.13

NO.

1995–cont.

866. National Health Service (Injury Benefits) Regulations 1995–*cont.*

Reg.18A, added: SI 2004/665 Reg.2

Reg.21A, added: SI 2004/665 Reg.2

887. Plant Protection Products Regulations 1995

applied: SI 2002/1689 Reg.3, Reg.9, SI 2003/660 Reg.2, Sch.1, SSI 2003/129 Sch.2 para.8, SSI 2004/70 Sch.2 para.8

revoked (in part): SI 2003/3241 Sch.5, SSI 2003/579 Sch.5

Reg.2, amended: SI 2002/526 Reg.2, SI 2002/1460 Reg.2, SI 2002/2874 Reg.2

Reg.4, applied: SI 2003/660 Reg.2, Sch.1

Reg.5, applied: SI 2002/1460 Reg.3, SI 2003/660 Sch.1

Reg.7, amended: SI 2002/2874 Reg.2, SSI 2002/537 Reg.2

Reg.7, applied: SI 2002/1460 Reg.3, SI 2003/660 Sch.1

Reg.7, varied: SI 2002/526 Reg.3

Reg.8, applied: SI 2003/660 Sch.1

Reg.9, applied: SI 2003/660 Sch.1

Reg.10, applied: SI 2003/660 Reg.2, Sch.1

Reg.13, applied: SI 2002/1460 Reg.3, SI 2003/660 Reg.2, Sch.1

Reg.27, revoked (in part): SI 2002/2874 Reg.2, SSI 2002/537 Reg.2

Sch.AA1, added: SI 2002/2874 Sch.1

Sch.AA1, substituted: SI 2003/1787 Sch.1

Sch.A1, added: SI 2002/2874 Sch.1, SSI 2002/537 Sch.1

Sch.1 para.2, amended: SI 2002/2874 Reg.2, SSI 2002/537 Reg.2

Sch.2 para.1, amended: SI 2002/2874 Reg.2, SSI 2002/537 Reg.2

Sch.2 para.4, referred to: SI 2002/1689 Reg.8

Sch.4, amended: SSI 2002/117 Reg.2, SSI 2002/279 Reg.2, SSI 2002/537 Reg.2

891. Heather Moorland (Livestock Extensification) (Scotland) Regulations 1995

applied: SSI 2004/381 Reg.4

Reg.13, applied: SSI 2004/381 Reg.4

910. Prisons (Scotland) Act 1989 (Release of Prisoners etc.) Order 1995

revoked: 2003 asp 7 s.27

911. Prisoners and Criminal Proceedings (Scotland) Act 1993 (Release of Prisoners etc.) Order 1995

revoked: 2003 asp 7 s.28

912. Local Authorities Etc (Allowances) (Scotland) Regulations 1995

Reg.20, amended: SSI 2002/15 Reg.3, SSI 2004/146 Reg.3

Reg.21, amended: SSI 2002/15 Reg.4, SSI 2004/146 Reg.4

Sch.2, amended: SSI 2002/15 Reg.5, SSI 2004/146 Reg.5

NO.

1995–cont.

918. Llandough Hospital National Health Service Trust (Change of Name) Order 1995

revoked: 2003 c.43 s.7

964. Stornoway (Ferry Terminal) Harbour Revision Order 1995

referred to: SSI 2003/435 Art.1

968. East Surrey Hospital and Community Healthcare National Health Service Trust (Change of Name) Order 1995

revoked: 2003 c.43 s.7

971. Justices of the Peace (Size and Chairmanship of Bench) Rules 1995

applied: SI 2002/193 r.21

revoked: SI 2002/193 r.20

r.10., varied: SI 2002/193 r.21

r.12., varied: SI 2002/193 r.21

r.13., varied: SI 2002/193 r.21

r.14., varied: SI 2002/193 r.21

r.15., varied: SI 2002/193 r.21

r.16., varied: SI 2002/193 r.21

r.17., varied: SI 2002/193 r.21

993. Hyde Park and The Regent's Park (Vehicle Parking) Regulations 1995

Reg.6, substituted: SI 2004/1307 Reg.3

Reg.7, amended: SI 2004/1307 Reg.3

996. Robert Jones and Agnes Hunt Orthopaedic and District Hospital National Health Service Trust (Establishment) Amendment Order 1995

revoked: 2003 c.43 s.7

1014. Measuring Equipment (Liquid Fuel and Lubricants) Regulations 1995

Reg.6, substituted: SI 2003/2110 Reg.3

Reg.6A, added: SI 2003/2110 Reg.4

Reg.7, amended: SI 2003/2110 Reg.5

Reg.10A, amended: SI 2003/2110 Reg.6

Reg.17, amended: SI 2003/2110 Reg.7

Reg.17A, added: SI 2003/2110 Reg.8

Reg.18, amended: SI 2003/214 Sch.1 para.7, SI 2003/2110 Reg.9

Reg.19, amended: SI 2003/2110 Reg.10

Reg.26, revoked: SI 2003/2110 Reg.11

1019. Local Government Pension Scheme Regulations 1995

Part C Reg.2, see *Newham LBC v Skingle* [2002] EWHC 1013, [2002] 3 All E.R. 287 (Ch D), Jacob, J.

Reg.C2, see *Newham LBC v Skingle* [2003] EWCA Civ 280, [2003] 2 All E.R. 761 (CA), Jonathan Parker, L.J.

1030. Antarctic Act 1994 (Overseas Territories) Order 1995

Sch.1 Part IV para.31, amended: 2002 c.8 s.2

1032. United Nations Arms Embargoes (Dependent Territories) Order 1995

varied: SI 2004/2036 Art.2

Art.2, amended: SI 2002/2631 Art.1

Art.3, amended: 2002 c.8 s.2

Art.8, amended: 2002 c.8 s.2

Art.9, amended: SI 2002/2631 Art.1

NO.

1995–cont.

1032. United Nations Arms Embargoes (Dependent Territories) Order 1995– *cont.*

Sch.3 para.4, amended: SI 2002/2631 Art.1

1036. Parliamentary Constituencies (Wales) Order 1995

applied: SI 2004/1204 Art.1

1045. Child Support and Income Support (Amendment) Regulations 1995

see *C-V v Secretary of State for Work and Pensions* [2002] EWCA Civ 1854, [2003] 1 F.L.R. 829 (CA), Potter, L.J.

1046. Excise Goods (Drawback) Regulations 1995

referred to: SI 2004/1003 Reg.7

1054. Civil Aviation (Air Travel Organisers Licensing) Regulations 1995

Reg.1, amended: SI 2003/1741 Reg.2

Reg.3, amended: SI 2003/1741 Reg.2

1086. Dairy Products (Hygiene) Regulations 1995

Part V, referred to: SI 2003/1596 Sch.1

Reg.22, applied: SI 2002/1387 Reg.15, SI 2004/2640 Reg.15

Reg.22, referred to: SI 2002/1227 Reg.15, SI 2003/3177 Reg.15, SI 2004/1214 Reg.15, SI 2004/1430 Reg.15, SI 2004/1740 Reg.15, SSI 2002/445 Reg.15

Reg.22, substituted: SI 2002/1227 Sch.8 para.1, SI 2002/1387 Sch.8 para.1

1116. Medicines (Products for Human Use-Fees) Regulations 1995

applied: SI 2004/1031 Reg.17, Reg.38

Reg.2, amended: SI 2002/236 Reg.16, SI 2002/542 Reg.5, SI 2003/625 Reg.4, SI 2003/2321 Reg.8, SI 2004/666 Reg.4, SI 2004/1157 Reg.2

Reg.3A, added: SI 2003/625 Reg.4

Reg.3A, amended: SI 2004/666 Reg.5

Reg.3B, added: SI 2003/625 Reg.4

Reg.3B, amended: SI 2003/2321 Reg.9, SI 2004/666 Sch.1

Reg.3BA, added: SI 2003/625 Reg.4, SI 2004/666 Reg.5

Reg.3BB, added: SI 2003/625 Reg.4, SI 2004/666 Reg.5

Reg.3BC, added: SI 2003/625 Reg.4, SI 2004/666 Reg.5

Reg.3BD, added: SI 2003/625 Reg.4, SI 2004/666 Reg.5

Reg.3C, added: SI 2003/625 Reg.4

Reg.4, amended: SI 2004/666 Reg.6, SI 2004/1157 Reg.3

Reg.5, amended: SI 2004/666 Reg.7, SI 2004/1157 Reg.3

Reg.6, amended: SI 2002/542 Sch.1, SI 2003/625 Sch.1, SI 2004/666 Sch.1

Reg.6A, amended: SI 2002/236 Reg.16

Reg.6B, amended: SI 2002/236 Reg.16

Reg.6C, amended: SI 2002/236 Reg.16

NO.

1995–cont.

1116. Medicines (Products for Human Use-Fees) Regulations 1995–*cont.*

Reg.7, amended: SI 2004/666 Reg.8, SI 2004/1157 Reg.4

Reg.7A, added: SI 2004/1157 Reg.4

Reg.8, amended: SI 2004/666 Reg.9, SI 2004/1157 Reg.4

Reg.9, amended: SI 2004/1157 Reg.4

Reg.9A, added: SI 2003/625 Reg.4

Reg.9B, added: SI 2003/625 Reg.4

Reg.9C, added: SI 2003/625 Reg.4

Reg.10, amended: SI 2002/542 Sch.1, SI 2003/625 Sch.1, SI 2004/666 Sch.1

Reg.10, revoked: SI 2004/1157 Reg.5

Reg.11, amended: SI 2002/542 Sch.1, SI 2003/625 Sch.1, SI 2004/666 Sch.1

Reg.12, amended: SI 2004/1157 Reg.5

Reg.12A, added: SI 2002/542 Reg.5

Reg.12B, added: SI 2002/542 Reg.5

Reg.13, amended: SI 2004/666 Reg.10, SI 2004/1157 Reg.6

Reg.13A, added: SI 2004/1157 Reg.6

Reg.14, amended: SI 2004/1157 Reg.7

Reg.14A, added: SI 2004/1157 Reg.7

Reg.16, amended: SI 2003/625 Reg.4

Reg.18A, added: SI 2004/666 Reg.11

Reg.18B, added: SI 2004/666 Reg.11

Reg.18C, added: SI 2004/666 Reg.11

Reg.19, amended: SI 2004/1157 Reg.8

Reg.20, amended: SI 2004/1157 Reg.8

Sch.1 Part I para.1, amended: SI 2002/236 Reg.16, SI 2002/542 Reg.5, SI 2004/666 Reg.12, SI 2004/1157 Reg.9

Sch.1 Part II, substituted: SI 2004/1157 Reg.9

Sch.1 Part II para.1, amended: SI 2002/236 Reg.16, SI 2002/542 Reg.5, Sch.1, SI 2003/625 Sch.1, SI 2003/2321 Reg.10, SI 2004/666 Sch.1

Sch.1 Part II para.1A, added: SI 2002/542 Reg.5

Sch.1 Part II para.1A, amended: SI 2003/625 Sch.1, SI 2004/666 Sch.1

Sch.1 Part II para.4, amended: SI 2002/542 Reg.5, SI 2003/625 Sch.1, SI 2004/666 Sch.1

Sch.1 Part II para.5, amended: SI 2002/542 Sch.1, SI 2003/625 Sch.1, SI 2004/666 Sch.1, SI 2004/1157 Reg.9

Sch.1 Part II para.6, amended: SI 2002/542 Sch.1, SI 2003/625 Sch.1, SI 2004/666 Sch.1

Sch.1 Part II para.7, amended: SI 2002/542 Sch.1, SI 2003/625 Sch.1, SI 2004/666 Sch.1

Sch.1 Part IIA para.2, amended: SI 2002/236 Reg.16, SI 2002/542 Sch.1, SI 2003/625 Sch.1, SI 2004/666 Sch.1

Sch.1 Part III, substituted: SI 2004/1157 Reg.9

Sch.1 Part III para.1, amended: SI 2002/236 Reg.16, SI 2002/542 Reg.5, SI 2003/2321 Reg.11

1995–cont.

1116. Medicines (Products for Human Use-Fees) Regulations 1995–*cont.*

Sch.1 Part III para.2, amended: SI 2002/542 Reg.5, Sch.1, SI 2003/625 Sch.1, SI 2003/2321 Reg.11, SI 2004/666 Sch.1

Sch.1 Part III para.3, amended: SI 2002/542 Sch.1, SI 2003/625 Sch.1, SI 2003/2321 Reg.11, SI 2004/666 Sch.1

Sch.1 Part III para.4, amended: SI 2002/236 Reg.16, SI 2003/2321 Reg.11

Sch.1 Part III para.5, amended: SI 2002/236 Reg.16, SI 2003/2321 Reg.11

Sch.1 Part III para.5A, added: SI 2002/542 Reg.5

Sch.1 Part III para.5A, amended: SI 2003/625 Sch.1, SI 2004/666 Sch.1

Sch.1 Part III para.6, amended: SI 2002/542 Reg.5, Sch.1, SI 2003/625 Sch.1, SI 2004/666 Sch.1

Sch.1 Part III para.7, amended: SI 2002/542 Sch.1, SI 2003/625 Sch.1, SI 2004/666 Sch.1, SI 2004/1157 Reg.9

Sch.1 Part III para.8, amended: SI 2002/542 Sch.1, SI 2003/625 Sch.1, SI 2004/666 Sch.1, SI 2004/1157 Reg.9

Sch.1 Part III para.9, amended: SI 2002/542 Sch.1, SI 2003/625 Sch.1, SI 2004/666 Sch.1

Sch.1 Part IIIA para.1, added: SI 2003/625 Reg.4

Sch.1 Part IIIA para.2, added: SI 2003/625 Reg.4

Sch.1 Part IIIA para.2, amended: SI 2004/666 Sch.1

Sch.1 Part IIIA para.3, added: SI 2003/625 Reg.4

Sch.1 Part III para.10, amended: SI 2002/542 Sch.1, SI 2003/625 Sch.1, SI 2004/666 Sch.1

Sch.1 Part III para.11, amended: SI 2002/542 Sch.1, SI 2003/625 Sch.1, SI 2004/666 Sch.1

Sch.1 Part III para.12, amended: SI 2002/542 Sch.1, SI 2003/625 Sch.1

Sch.1 Part III para.12, revoked: SI 2004/1157 Reg.9

Sch.1 Part III para.13, amended: SI 2002/542 Reg.5

Sch.1 Part III para.14, amended: SI 2003/2321 Reg.11

Sch.1 Part III para.15, added: SI 2002/542 Reg.5

Sch.1 Part III para.15, amended: SI 2003/625 Sch.1, SI 2004/666 Sch.1

Sch.1 Part IV para.1, added: SI 2002/542 Reg.5

Sch.1 Part IV para.1, amended: SI 2003/625 Sch.1, SI 2004/666 Sch.1

Sch.1 Part IV para.2, added: SI 2002/542 Reg.5

Sch.1 Part IV para.2, amended: SI 2003/625 Sch.1, SI 2004/666 Sch.1

1995–cont.

1116. Medicines (Products for Human Use-Fees) Regulations 1995–*cont.*

Sch.2 para.1, amended: SI 2003/625 Reg.4, SI 2004/666 Reg.13

Sch.2 para.2, amended: SI 2002/542 Sch.1, SI 2003/625 Reg.4, Sch.1, SI 2004/666 Sch.1

Sch.2 para.3, amended: SI 2003/625 Reg.4

Sch.2 para.4, amended: SI 2003/625 Reg.4

Sch.2 para.4A, added: SI 2004/666 Reg.13

Sch.2 para.5, amended: SI 2002/542 Sch.1, SI 2003/625 Reg.4, Sch.1, SI 2004/666 Sch.1

Sch.2 para.5A, added: SI 2003/625 Reg.4

Sch.2 para.5A, amended: SI 2004/666 Sch.1

Sch.2 para.7, added: SI 2004/1157 Reg.10

Sch.2 para.8, added: SI 2004/1157 Reg.10

Sch.3 Part I para.1, amended: SI 2002/236 Reg.16, SI 2003/2321 Reg.12

Sch.3 Part III, amended: SI 2004/1157 Reg.11

Sch.3 Part III, added: SI 2004/1157 Reg.11

Sch.3 Part III para.1, amended: SI 2002/542 Sch.1, SI 2003/625 Sch.1, SI 2004/666 Sch.1

Sch.3 Part III para.2, amended: SI 2002/542 Sch.1, SI 2003/625 Sch.1, SI 2004/666 Sch.1

Sch.3 Part III para.3, amended: SI 2002/542 Sch.1, SI 2003/625 Sch.1, SI 2004/666 Sch.1

Sch.3 Part III para.7, amended: SI 2002/542 Sch.1, SI 2003/625 Sch.1, SI 2004/666 Sch.1

Sch.3 Part III para.8, amended: SI 2002/542 Sch.1, SI 2003/625 Sch.1, SI 2004/666 Sch.1

Sch.3 Part IV para.1, amended: SI 2002/236 Reg.16

Sch.4 para.4A, amended: SI 2002/236 Reg.16

Sch.4 para.5, amended: SI 2004/1157 Reg.12

Sch.4 para.6, amended: SI 2004/1157 Reg.12

Sch.5 para.1A, added: SI 2003/2321 Reg.13

Sch.5 para.1A, amended: SI 2004/666 Reg.14

Sch.5 para.2, amended: SI 2003/2321 Reg.13

Sch.5 para.2, substituted: SI 2003/625 Reg.4

Sch.5 para.2B, added: SI 2002/542 Reg.5

Sch.5 para.3, amended: SI 2004/1157 Reg.13

Sch.5 para.4, amended: SI 2004/1157 Reg.13

Sch.5 para.4A, amended: SI 2004/1157 Reg.13

Sch.5 para.5, amended: SI 2004/1157 Reg.13

Sch.5 para.5A, added: SI 2003/625 Reg.4

Sch.5 para.6, amended: SI 2002/236 Reg.16

Sch.5 para.8, added: SI 2004/1157 Reg.13

1203. Customs Traders (Accounts and Records) Regulations 1995

Reg.3, applied: SI 2003/3113 Sch.1

NO.

1995–cont.

1203. Customs Traders (Accounts and Records) Regulations 1995–*cont.*

Reg.4, applied: SI 2003/3113 Sch.1

Reg.5, applied: SI 2003/3113 Sch.1

Reg.9, applied: SI 2003/3113 Sch.1

1210. Merchant Shipping (Survey and Certification) Regulations 1995

Reg.1, amended: SI 2002/1473 Sch.2 para.4, SI 2003/771 Reg.3, SI 2004/1107 Reg.3, SI 2004/2883 Reg.3

Reg.2, amended: SI 2004/302 Reg.12

1211. Life Assurance (Apportionment of Receipts of Participating Funds) (Applicable Percentage) (Amendment) Order 1995

revoked: SI 2003/1860 Art.3

1223. Income Tax (Employments) (Amendment No 3) Regulations 1995

revoked: SI 2003/2682 Sch.2

1235. Bexley Community Health National Health Service Trust (Change of Name) Order 1995

revoked: 2003 c.43 s.7

1236. Foxfield Light Railway Order 1995

Art.7, amended: SI 2003/2155 Sch.1 para.18

1268. Value Added Tax (Special Provisions) Order 1995

Art.2, amended: SI 2002/1280 Art.3, SI 2004/3085 Art.2

Art.2, revoked (in part): SI 2004/3085 Art.2

Art.5, amended: SI 2004/779 Art.3, Art.4

Art.5, applied: SI 2002/1502 Art.1, SI 2002/1503 Art.1

Art.11, revoked: SI 2002/1280 Art.4

Art.12, amended: SI 2002/1503 Art.2

Art.12, revoked (in part): SI 2002/1503 Art.2

1284. Income Tax (Employments) (Amendment No 4) Regulations 1995

revoked: SI 2003/2682 Sch.2

1300. Northampton and Lamport Light Railway Order 1995

Art.5, amended: SI 2003/2155 Sch.1 para.18

1311. Durham County Ambulance Service National Health Service Trust (Establishment) Amendment Order 1995

revoked: 2003 c.43 s.7

1336. Local Government (Direct Service Organisations) (Competition) (Amendment) Regulations 1995

revoked (in part): 2003 asp 1 s.60

1342. Middlesbrough College (Government) Regulations 1995

revoked: SI 2002/1094 Sch.1 Part 1

1344. Teesside Tertiary College (Government) Regulationsv 1995

revoked: SI 2002/1094 Sch.1 Part 1

1372. Dairy Products (Hygiene) (Scotland) Regulations 1995

Part V, referred to: SSI 2003/311 Sch.1

Reg.2, amended: SSI 2002/445 Sch.8 para.1

1995–cont.

1372. Dairy Products (Hygiene) (Scotland) Regulations 1995–*cont.*

Reg.22, substituted: SSI 2002/445 Sch.8 para.1

1397. Vehicle Excise Duty (Designation of Small Islands) Order 1995

Sch.1, amended: SI 2002/1072 Art.2

1423. Companies (Fees) (Amendment) Regulations 1995

revoked: SI 2004/2621 Sch.3

1444. Trade Marks (EC Measures Relating to Counterfeit Goods) Regulations 1995

revoked: SI 2004/1473 Sch.1

1459. Inheritance Tax (Delivery of Accounts) (Scotland) Regulations 1995

revoked: SI 2002/1733 Sch.1

1461. Inheritance Tax (Delivery of Accounts) Regulations 1995

revoked: SI 2002/1733 Sch.1

1469. Calderdale Healthcare National Health Service Trust (Establishment) Amendment Order 1995

revoked: 2003 c.43 s.7

1470. Road Vehicles (Registration and Licensing) (Amendment) Regulations 1995

revoked: SI 2002/2742 Sch.1 Part I

1482. Cereal Seeds (Amendment) Regulations 1995

revoked (in part): SI 2002/3173 Reg.32

1537. Public Offers of Securities Regulations 1995

Reg.2, amended: SI 2002/765 Reg.5

Reg.2, varied: SI 2003/1633 Sch.2 para.8

Reg.3, varied: SI 2003/1633 Sch.2 para.8, Sch.2 para.10

Reg.7, amended: SI 2004/355 Art.6

Reg.7, varied: SI 2003/1633 Sch.2 para.8

Sch.4 Part I para.1, amended: SI 2004/355 Art.7

1551. Double Taxation Relief (Manufactured Overseas Dividends) (Amendment) Regulations 1995

revoked: SI 2003/2581 Reg.2

1555. Betting and Gaming Duties (Payment) Regulations 1995

revoked: SI 2003/2503 Reg.3

1569. Ridge Danyers College (Government) Regulations 1995

revoked: SI 2002/1094 Sch.1 Part 1

1613. Social Security (Income Support and Claims and Payments) Amendment Regulations 1995

referred to: SSI 2003/376 Sch.1 para.2, Sch.1 para.4

Reg.3, revoked (in part): SI 2003/492 Sch.3 Part 1

Sch.2 para.1, revoked (in part): SI 2003/492 Sch.3 Part 1

NO.

NO.

1995–cont.

1613. Social Security (Income Support and Claims and Payments) Amendment Regulations 1995–*cont.*

Sch.2 para.2, revoked (in part): SI 2003/492 Sch.3 Part 1

Sch.2 para.3, revoked (in part): SI 2003/492 Sch.3 Part 1

Sch.2 para.4, revoked (in part): SI 2003/492 Sch.3 Part 1

Sch.2 para.5, revoked (in part): SI 2003/492 Sch.3 Part 1

Sch.2 para.6, revoked (in part): SI 2003/492 Sch.3 Part 1

Sch.2 para.7, revoked (in part): SI 2003/492 Sch.3 Part 1

Sch.2 para.8, revoked (in part): SI 2003/492 Sch.3 Part 1

Sch.2 para.9, revoked (in part): SI 2003/492 Sch.3 Part 1

1622. Armagh Observatory and Planetarium (Northern Ireland) Order 1995

Art.8, substituted: SI 2003/418 Sch.1 para.6

1623. Arts Council (Northern Ireland) Order 1995

Art.4, applied: SR 2003/253 Art.3

Art.8, revoked (in part): SI 2003/418 Sch.3

1644. Housing Benefit (General) Amendment Regulations 1995

Reg.10, amended: SI 2003/363 Reg.4, SI 2003/1338 Reg.22, SI 2003/2399 Reg.15, SI 2004/14 Reg.30

1671. Active Implantable Medical Devices (Amendment and Transitional Provisions) Regulations 1995

revoked: SI 2002/618 Reg.66

1709. Royal Orthopaedic Hospital National Health Service Trust (Establishment) Amendment Order 1995

revoked: 2003 c.43 s.7

1717. EMPLOYMENT TRIBUNALS (ENFORCEMENT OF ORDERS UNDER THE CIVIL JURISDICTION AND JUDGMENTS ACT 1982) (SCOTLAND) REGULATIONS 1995

revoked: SI 2002/2972 Reg.1

1730. Insurance Companies (Taxation of Reinsurance Business) Regulations 1995

referred to: SI 2003/2573 Reg.2

referred to: SI 2004/2257 Reg.2

Reg.2, amended: SI 2003/2573 Reg.3

Reg.3, amended: SI 2004/2189 Reg.3, SI 2004/2257 Reg.3, SI 2004/2310 Sch.1 para.74

Reg.4, amended: SI 2003/2573 Reg.4, SI 2004/2189 Reg.4, SI 2004/2257 Reg.4

Reg.4, applied: SI 2004/2257 Reg.1

Reg.4, referred to: SI 2004/2189 Reg.1

Reg.5, amended: SI 2003/1828 Reg.3, SI 2003/2573 Reg.5, SI 2004/2189 Reg.4, SI 2004/2257 Reg.4

1995–cont.

1730. Insurance Companies (Taxation of Reinsurance Business) Regulations 1995–*cont.*

Reg.5, applied: SI 2004/2257 Reg.1

Reg.5, varied: SI 2004/2257 Reg.1

Reg.6, amended: SI 2003/2573 Reg.6, SI 2004/2310 Sch.1 para.74

Reg.7, amended: SI 2003/2573 Reg.7, SI 2003/2642 Reg.2

Reg.7A, added: SI 2003/2573 Reg.8

Reg.9, amended: SI 2003/2573 Reg.9, SI 2004/2189 Reg.5, SI 2004/2257 Reg.5

Reg.9, revoked (in part): SI 2004/2189 Reg.5, SI 2004/2257 Reg.5

Reg.10, substituted: SI 2002/1409 Art.4

Reg.11, amended: SI 2003/1828 Reg.4, SI 2003/2573 Reg.10

Reg.11, revoked (in part): SI 2003/2573 Reg.10

Reg.11A, added: SI 2003/2573 Reg.11

Reg.13, added: SI 2003/1828 Reg.5

Reg.13, amended: SI 2003/2573 Reg.12

Reg.13, revoked (in part): SI 2003/2573 Reg.12

1739. Education Authority Bursaries (Scotland) Regulations 1995

Reg.2, amended: SSI 2004/469 Reg.3

Sch.1 para.2, amended: SSI 2004/469 Reg.3

Sch.1 para.2A, amended: SSI 2004/469 Reg.3

Sch.1 para.2B, amended: SSI 2004/469 Reg.3

Sch.1 para.4, amended: SSI 2004/469 Reg.3

Sch.2 para.2, amended: SSI 2004/469 Reg.3

1747. Cleveland (Further Provision) Order 1995

varied: SI 2004/222 Art.2

1748. Local Government Changes for England (Miscellaneous Provision) Regulations 1995

Reg.4, revoked: SI 2004/2044 Art.3

1763. Food Safety (General Food Hygiene) Regulations 1995

see *Wei Hai Restaurant Ltd v Kingston upon Hull City Council* [2001] EWHC Admin 490, (2002) 166 J.P. 185 (QBD (Admin Ct)), Forbes, J.

Reg.2, amended: SI 2003/666 Reg.22, SI 2003/3042 Reg.22, SI 2004/656 Reg.15, SI 2004/1509 Reg.15, SI 2004/1727 Reg.2, SSI 2004/394 Reg.2

Reg.2, see *Greene King Plc v Harlow DC* [2003] EWHC 2852, [2004] 1 W.L.R. 2338 (QBD (Admin Ct)), Goldring, J.

Sch.1 Part I, referred to: SSI 2003/299 Reg.5, SSI 2003/568 Reg.5

Sch.1 Part II, referred to: SSI 2003/299 Reg.5, SSI 2003/568 Reg.5

Sch.1 Part V, referred to: SSI 2003/299 Reg.5, SSI 2003/568 Reg.5

NO.

1995–cont.

1763. Food Safety (General Food Hygiene) Regulations 1995–*cont.*

Sch.1 Part VI, referred to: SSI 2003/299 Reg.5, SSI 2003/568 Reg.5

Sch.1 Part VII, referred to: SSI 2003/299 Reg.5, SSI 2003/568 Reg.5

Sch.1 Part VIII, referred to: SSI 2003/299 Reg.5, SSI 2003/568 Reg.5

Sch.1 Part IX, referred to: SSI 2003/299 Reg.5, SSI 2003/568 Reg.5

Sch.1 Part X, referred to: SSI 2003/299 Reg.5, SSI 2003/568 Reg.5

1769. Buckinghamshire (Borough of Milton Keynes) (Structural Change) Order 1995

varied: SI 2004/222 Art.2

1770. East Sussex (Boroughs of Brighton and Hove) (Structural Change) Order 1995

varied: SI 2004/222 Art.2

1771. Dorset (Boroughs of Poole and Bournemouth) (Structural Change) Order 1995

varied: SI 2004/222 Art.2

1772. Durham (Borough of Darlington) (Structural Change) Order 1995

varied: SI 2004/222 Art.2

1773. Derbyshire (City of Derby) (Structural Change) Order 1995

varied: SI 2004/222 Art.2

1774. Wiltshire (Borough of Thamesdown) (Structural Change) Order 1995

varied: SI 2004/222 Art.2

1775. Hampshire (Cities of Portsmouth and Southampton) (Structural Change) Order 1995

varied: SI 2004/222 Art.2

1776. Bedfordshire (Borough of Luton) (Structural Change) Order 1995

varied: SI 2004/222 Art.2

1779. Staffordshire (City of Stoke-on-Trent) (Structural and Boundary Changes) Order 1995

varied: SI 2004/222 Art.2

1801. Social Security (Adjudication) Regulations 1995

Reg.10, see *Anderson v Secretary of State for Work and Pensions* 2002 S.L.T. 68 (OH), Lord Eassie

1803. Merchant Shipping (Ships Doctors) Regulations 1995

Reg.2, amended: SI 2002/3135 Sch.1 para.35

1879. Aberdeen and Grampian Tourist Board Scheme Order 1995

revoked: SSI 2004/397 Sch.2

1880. Angus and City of Dundee Tourist Board Scheme Order 1995

revoked: SSI 2004/397 Sch.2

NO.

1995–cont.

1881. Argyll, the Isles, Loch Lomond, Stirling and Trossachs Tourist Board Scheme Order 1995

revoked: SSI 2004/397 Sch.2

1882. Ayrshire and Arran Tourist Board Scheme Order 1995

revoked: SSI 2004/396 Sch.2

1883. Dumfries and Galloway Tourist Board Scheme Order 1995

revoked: SSI 2004/396 Sch.2

1884. Edinburgh and Lothians Tourist Board Scheme Order 1995

revoked: SSI 2004/396 Sch.2

1885. Greater Glasgow and Clyde Valley Tourist Board Scheme Order 1995

revoked: SSI 2004/396 Sch.2

1886. Highlands of Scotland Tourist Board Scheme Order 1995

revoked: SSI 2004/397 Sch.2

1887. Kingdom of Fife Tourist Board Scheme Order 1995

revoked: SSI 2004/397 Sch.2

1888. Orkney Tourist Board Scheme Order 1995

revoked: SSI 2004/397 Sch.2

1889. Perthshire Tourist Board Scheme Order 1995

revoked: SSI 2004/397 Sch.2

1890. Scottish Borders Tourist Board Scheme Order 1995

revoked: SSI 2004/396 Sch.2

1891. Shetland Tourist Board Scheme Order 1995

revoked: SSI 2004/397 Sch.2

1892. Western Isles Tourist Board Scheme Order 1995

revoked: SSI 2004/397 Sch.2

1947. Satellite Communications Services Regulations 1995

revoked: SI 2003/2155 Sch.2

1948. Local Government Elections (Changes to the Franchise and Qualification of Members) Regulations 1995

Reg.4, consolidated: 2002 c.24 Sch.1 para.4

1967. Drug Trafficking Act 1994 (Enforcement of Northern Ireland Confiscation Orders) Order 1995

revoked: 2002 c.29 Sch.12

1970. Air Navigation (No.2) Order 1995

referred to: SI 2002/1078 Art.2

Art.55, see *R. v Tagg (Heather Susan)* [2001] EWCA Crim 1230, [2002] 1 Cr. App. R. 2 (CA (Crim Div)), Rose, L.J.

Art.57, see *R. v Tagg (Heather Susan)* [2001] EWCA Crim 1230, [2002] 1 Cr. App. R. 2 (CA (Crim Div)), Rose, L.J.

1979. Venture Capital Trust Regulations 1995

Reg.8, applied: SI 2004/2199 Reg.3

NO.

1995–cont.

1980. Trade Union and Labour Relations (Northern Ireland) Order 1995

applied: 2002 c.22 s.46, SI 2003/2902 Sch.2, Sch.3, Sch.4

Art.15, enabled: SR 2003/331

Art.40, amended: SR 2002/24 Sch.1, SR 2003/241 Sch.1

Art.144, amended: SI 2004/311 Sch.1 para.16, Sch.2

2007. Western Isles Islands Council (Various Harbours Jurisdiction and Byelaws) Harbour Revision Order 1995

revoked: SSI 2002/410 Sch.2 Part II

2015. Children (Short-term Placements) (Miscellaneous Amendments) Regulations 1995

Reg.2, revoked (in part): SI 2002/57 Reg.51, SI 2003/237 Reg.53

2020. Police (Amendment No 2) Regulations 1995

revoked: SI 2003/527 Sch.4 Part 1

2038. Borehole Sites and Operations Regulations 1995

Reg.2, applied: SI 2002/2776 Reg.3

2049. Financial Markets and Insolvency (Money Market) Regulations 1995

applied: 2002 c.29 s.282

2051. Stamp Duty Reserve Tax (Tradepoint) Regulations 1995

Reg.2, amended: SI 2003/2078 Reg.3

Reg.4, amended: SI 2003/2078 Reg.4

Reg.5, amended: SI 2003/2078 Reg.5

2061. Returning Officers (Parliamentary Constituencies) (England) Order 1995

referred to: SI 2002/1057 Art.2

Art.4B, added: SI 2002/1057 Art.14

Sch.2, amended: SI 2002/1057 Art.14

2065. Education (Further Education Institutions Information) (England) Regulations 1995

revoked: SI 2003/51 Reg.2

2089. Education (Pupil Registration) Regulations 1995

applied: SI 2003/1910 Sch.1 para.3, SI 2003/ 3234 Sch.1 para.3, Sch.1 para.6, SI 2004/ 1026 Sch.1 para.7, Sch.2 para.5

see *R. (on the application of M) v B LBC* [2002] EWHC 2483, [2003] E.L.R. 144 (QBD (Admin Ct)), Jack Beatson, Q.C.

Reg.9, amended: SI 2002/3178 Reg.8, SI 2003/3227 Reg.9

2092. Companies (Summary Financial Statement) Regulations 1995

Reg.2, amended: SI 2002/1780 Reg.2

Reg.7, amended: SI 2002/1780 Reg.3

Sch.1 para.1, amended: SI 2002/1780 Reg.4

Sch.1 para.2A, added: SI 2002/1780 Reg.5

Sch.1 para.3, revoked (in part): SI 2002/1780 Reg.5

NO.

1995–cont.

2092. Companies (Summary Financial Statement) Regulations 1995–*cont.*

Sch.2 para.1, varied: SI 2003/1633 Sch.2 para.2

Sch.2 para.2, varied: SI 2003/1633 Sch.2 para.2

Sch.2 para.2A, added: SI 2002/1780 Reg.6

Sch.2 para.2A, varied: SI 2003/1633 Sch.2 para.2

Sch.2 para.3, revoked (in part): SI 2002/1780 Reg.6

Sch.2 para.3, varied: SI 2003/1633 Sch.2 para.2

Sch.2 para.4, varied: SI 2003/1633 Sch.2 para.2

Sch.2 para.5, varied: SI 2003/1633 Sch.2 para.2

Sch.2 para.6, varied: SI 2003/1633 Sch.2 para.2

Sch.2 para.7, varied: SI 2003/1633 Sch.2 para.2

Sch.3 para.3A, added: SI 2002/1780 Reg.7

Sch.3 para.4, revoked (in part): SI 2002/1780 Reg.7

2093. Patents Rules 1995

applied: SI 2002/247 Reg.16, Reg.22, SI 2002/3052 Sch.1 para.2

referred to: SI 2002/247 Reg.22, SI 2003/ 513 r.2

varied: SI 2002/247 Reg.22

see *Entertainment UK Ltd's Patent* [2002] R.P.C. 11 (PO), P Hayward

r.2, amended: SI 2004/2358 Sch.2 para.2

r.3, revoked (in part): SI 2004/2177 Art.5

r.4, amended: SI 2003/513 r.3, SI 2004/2177 Art.4

r.4A, added: SI 2003/513 r.4

r.6, substituted: SI 2004/2358 r.3

r.7, referred to: SI 2002/247 Reg.22

r.9, substituted: SI 2004/3205 Art.4

r.13, substituted: SI 2004/3205 Art.5

r.15, amended: SI 2004/2358 r.4

r.15, revoked (in part): SI 2004/2358 r.4

r.16, amended: SI 2003/513 r.5, SI 2004/ 2358 r.5

r.18, amended: SI 2003/513 r.6

r.19, applied: SI 2002/3052 Sch.1 para.2

r.20, amended: SI 2003/513 r.7

r.22A, added: SI 2004/2358 r.6

r.23, substituted: SI 2004/2358 r.7

r.24, amended: SI 2004/2358 Sch.2 para.3

r.25, amended: SI 2002/529 r.3

r.25, substituted: SI 2004/2358 r.8

r.26, substituted: SI 2004/2358 r.8

r.28, substituted: SI 2004/2358 r.9

r.28A, substituted: SI 2004/2358 r.9

r.29, substituted: SI 2004/2358 r.9

r.31, amended: SI 2003/513 r.8

r.32, amended: SI 2004/2358 Sch.2 para.4

r.33, amended: SI 2002/529 r.4, SI 2004/ 2358 Sch.2 para.3

NO.

1995–cont.

2093. Patents Rules 1995–*cont.*
r.34, amended: SI 2004/2358 Sch.2 para.3
r.36, applied: SI 2002/3052 Sch.1 para.2
r.36A, added: SI 2004/2358 r.10
r.37, applied: SI 2002/3052 Sch.1 para.2, Sch.2 para.2
r.40, amended: SI 2003/513 r.9, SI 2004/2358 Sch.2 para.5
r.45, amended: SI 2004/2358 r.11
r.46, amended: SI 2004/2358 r.12
r.47, amended: SI 2004/2358 r.13
r.57, substituted: SI 2004/3205 Art.6
r.58, substituted: SI 2004/3205 Art.7
r.72, amended: SI 2004/3205 Art.8
r.73, amended: SI 2004/3205 Art.8
r.78, amended: SI 2003/513 r.10
r.81, amended: SI 2004/2358 Sch.2 para.6
r.82, amended: SI 2004/2358 Sch.2 para.7
r.85, amended: SI 2002/529 r.5, SI 2004/2358 Sch.2 para.8, Sch.2 para.9
r.85, revoked (in part): SI 2004/2358 Sch.2 para.8
r.91, amended: SI 2004/2358 Sch.2 para.10
r.92, see *Haberman v Comptroller General of Patents* [2003] EWHC 430, [2004] R.P.C. 21 (Pat Ct), Peter Prescott Q.C.
r.98, revoked: SI 2004/2177 Art.5
r.99, revoked: SI 2004/2177 Art.5
r.102, amended: SI 2004/2358 Sch.2 para.3
r.107, amended: SI 2004/2358 Sch.2 para.11
r.110, substituted: SI 2004/2358 r.14
r.110, varied: SI 2004/2358 r.20
r.110, see *Abbott Laboratories SPC Application* [2004] R.P.C. 20 (PO), RJ Walker
r.110A, added: SI 2004/2358 r.15
r.112A, added: SI 2004/2358 r.16
r.113, amended: SI 2004/2358 Sch.2 para.12
r.113, revoked (in part): SI 2004/2358 Sch.2 para.12
r.113A, added: SI 2004/2358 r.17
r.115, substituted: SI 2004/2177 Art.4
Sch.1, amended: SI 2003/513 Sch.1
Sch.1, revoked: SI 2004/2177 Art.5
Sch.4 para.1, amended: SI 2003/513 r.12
Sch.4 para.3, amended: SI 2003/513 r.12
Sch.4 para.4, amended: SI 2003/513 r.12
Sch.4 para.5, revoked: SI 2004/2358 Sch.2 para.13
Sch.4A Part 1, added: SI 2004/2358 Sch.1
Sch.4A Part 2, added: SI 2004/2358 Sch.1
Sch.4A Part 3, added: SI 2004/2358 Sch.1
Sch.4A Part 4, added: SI 2004/2358 Sch.1

2109. Fire Services (Appointments and Promotion) (Amendment) Regulations 1995
revoked: SI 2004/481 Sch.2

2131. Police (Scotland) Amendment (No.3) Regulations 1995
revoked: SSI 2004/257 Sch.4

NO.

1995–cont.

2142. Oswestry Light Railway Order 1995
Art.8, amended: SI 2003/2155 Sch.1 para.18

2143. Great Central (Nottingham) Railway Order 1995
Art.10, amended: SI 2003/2155 Sch.1 para.18

2148. Wild Game Meat (Hygiene and Inspection) Regulations 1995
applied: 2002 asp 11 Sch.3 para.4, SI 2002/843 Reg.56, Reg.101, SI 2002/1227 Reg.4, SI 2002/1387 Reg.4, SI 2002/1416 Reg.101, SI 2003/409 Sch.1 Part I, SI 2003/1482 Reg.49, SI 2003/2756 Reg.48, SI 2003/3177 Reg.4, SI 2004/1214 Reg.4, SI 2004/1430 Reg.4, SI 2004/1740 Reg.4, SI 2004/2640 Reg.4, SSI 2002/255 Reg.99, SSI 2002/445 Reg.4, SSI 2003/411 Reg.49

2211. Aberdeen and Grampian Tourist Board Scheme Amendment Order 1995
revoked: SSI 2004/397 Sch.2

2212. Angus and City of Dundee Tourist Board Scheme Amendment Order 1995
revoked: SSI 2004/397 Sch.2

2213. Argyll, the Isles, Loch Lomond, Stirling and Trossachs Tourist Board Scheme Amendment Order 1995
revoked: SSI 2004/397 Sch.2

2214. Scottish Borders Tourist Board Scheme Amendment Order 1995
revoked: SSI 2004/396 Sch.2

2232. Ayrshire and Arran Tourist Board Scheme Amendment Order 1995
revoked: SSI 2004/396 Sch.2

2233. Dumfries and Galloway Tourist Board Scheme Amendment Order 1995
revoked: SSI 2004/396 Sch.2

2234. Edinburgh and Lothians Tourist Board Scheme Amendment Order 1995
revoked: SSI 2004/396 Sch.2

2235. Greater Glasgow and Clyde Valley Tourist Board Scheme Amendment Order 1995
revoked: SSI 2004/396 Sch.2

2236. Highlands of Scotland Tourist Board Scheme Amendment Order 1995
revoked: SSI 2004/397 Sch.2

2237. Kingdom of Fife Tourist Board Scheme Amendment Order 1995
revoked: SSI 2004/397 Sch.2

2238. Orkney Tourist Board Scheme Amendment Order 1995
revoked: SSI 2004/397 Sch.2

2239. Perthshire Tourist Board Scheme Amendment Order 1995
revoked: SSI 2004/397 Sch.2

2240. Shetland Tourist Board Scheme Amendment Order 1995
revoked: SSI 2004/397 Sch.2

NO.

1995–cont.

2241. Western Isles Tourist Board Scheme Amendment Order 1995
revoked: SSI 2004/397 Sch.2

2287. Income Support (General) Amendment and Transitional Regulations 1995
referred to: SSI 2003/376 Sch.1 para.2, Sch.1 para.4
Reg.3, applied: SI 2002/1792 Sch.1 para.6

2303. Income-related Benefits Schemes and Social Security (Claims and Payments) (Miscellaneous Amendments) Regulations 1995
Reg.1, amended: SI 2003/492 Sch.3 Part 1
Reg.10, revoked (in part): SI 2003/492 Sch.3 Part 1

2352. National Health Service (Travelling Expenses and Remission of Charges) Amendment No 2 Regulations 1995
revoked: SI 2003/2382 Sch.2

2379. East Surrey Learning Disability and Mental Health Service National Health Service Trust (Change of Name) Order 1995
revoked: 2003 c.43 s.7

2487. Medical Devices Fees Regulations 1995
revoked: SI 2002/618 Reg.66

2489. Footwear (Indication of Composition) Labelling Regulations 1995
applied: SI 2003/1400 Sch.3, Sch.4

2498. Merchant Shipping (Reporting Requirements for Ships Carrying Dangerous or Polluting Goods) Regulations 1995
Reg.2, amended: 2002 c.8 s.2, SI 2004/2110 Sch.1 para.1
Reg.2, revoked (in part): SI 2004/2110 Sch.1 para.1
Reg.3, amended: SI 2004/2110 Sch.1 para.2
Reg.4, amended: SI 2004/2110 Sch.1 para.3
Reg.4, revoked (in part): SI 2004/2110 Sch.1 para.3
Reg.5, substituted: SI 2004/2110 Sch.1 para.4
Reg.6, revoked: SI 2004/2110 Sch.1 para.5
Reg.7, revoked: SI 2004/2110 Sch.1 para.5
Reg.8, revoked: SI 2004/2110 Sch.1 para.5
Reg.9, amended: SI 2004/2110 Sch.1 para.6
Reg.11, amended: SI 2004/2110 Sch.1 para.7
Reg.12, revoked: SI 2004/2110 Sch.1 para.8
Reg.13, revoked: SI 2004/2110 Sch.1 para.8
Reg.14, revoked: SI 2004/2110 Sch.1 para.8
Reg.15, amended: SI 2004/2110 Sch.1 para.9
Reg.15, revoked (in part): SI 2004/2110 Sch.1 para.9
Reg.18, amended: SI 2004/2110 Sch.1 para.10
Reg.19, amended: SI 2004/2110 Sch.1 para.11
Reg.19, revoked (in part): SI 2004/2110 Sch.1 para.11

NO.

1995–cont.

2501. Low Moor Tramway Light Railway Order 1995
Art.7, amended: SI 2003/2155 Sch.1 para.18

2507. Motorways Traffic (Scotland) Regulations 1995
Sch.1 para.3, added: SSI 2004/53 Reg.3

2518. Value Added Tax Regulations 1995
referred to: SI 2002/2918 Reg.2, SI 2002/3027 Reg.2, SI 2003/532 Reg.2, SI 2003/3220 Reg.2, SI 2004/767 Reg.3
see *Musashi Autoparts Europe Ltd (formerly TAP Manufacturing Ltd) v Customs and Excise Commissioners* [2003] EWHC 343, [2003] S.T.C. 449 (Ch D), Lightman, J.
Part III, added: SI 2003/3220 Reg.3
Part VIIA, added: SI 2003/3220 Reg.19
Part XIV Reg.101, see *Southampton Leisure Holdings Plc v Customs and Excise Commissioners* [2002] V. & D.R. 235 (V&DTr (London)), Nuala Brice (Chairman)
Reg.2, amended: SI 2004/1082 Reg.3
Reg.5, amended: SI 2004/1675 Reg.2
Reg.6, amended: SI 2004/1675 Reg.3
Reg.9, amended: SI 2003/2096 Sch.1 para.56
Reg.10, amended: SI 2003/2096 Sch.1 para.57
Reg.13, amended: SI 2003/3220 Reg.4
Reg.13A, added: SI 2003/3220 Reg.5
Reg.13B, added: SI 2003/3220 Reg.6
Reg.14, amended: SI 2003/3220 Reg.7, Reg.8, Reg.9
Reg.14, revoked (in part): SI 2003/3220 Reg.7
Reg.15, amended: SI 2003/1485 Reg.3
Reg.16, amended: SI 2003/3220 Reg.10
Reg.24, amended: SI 2003/1485 Reg.4, SI 2003/2096 Sch.1 para.58
Reg.24, see *General Motors Acceptance Corp (UK) Plc v Customs and Excise Commissioners* [2004] EWHC 192, [2004] S.T.C. 577 (Ch D), Field, J.
Reg.25, amended: SI 2004/1675 Reg.4
Reg.25, applied: SI 2004/1929 Reg.2
Reg.25, see *Hindle (t/a DJ Baker Bar) v Customs and Excise Commissioners* [2003] EWHC 1665, [2004] S.T.C. 412 (Ch D), Neuberger, J.
Reg.29, amended: SI 2003/1114 Reg.3
Reg.29., see *Local Authorities Mutual Investment Trust v Customs and Excise Commissioners* [2003] EWHC 2766, [2004] S.T.C. 246 (Ch D), Lawrence Collins, J.
Reg.31, amended: SI 2003/3220 Reg.11
Reg.35, see *R. (on the application of Cardiff City Council) v Customs and Excise Commissioners* [2002] EWHC 2085, [2002] S.T.C. 1318 (QBD (Admin Ct)), Stanley Burnton, J.; see *R. (on the*

1995–cont.

2518. Value Added Tax Regulations 1995– cont.

Reg.35–cont.

application of Cardiff City Council) v Customs and Excise Commissioners [2003] EWCA Civ 1456, [2004] S.T.C. 356 (CA), Schiemann, L.J.

Reg.38, see *General Motors Acceptance Corp (UK) Plc v Customs and Excise Commissioners* [2004] EWHC 192, [2004] S.T.C. 577 (Ch D), Field, J.

Reg.40, amended: SI 2004/1675 Reg.5

Reg.40, see *Hindle (t/a DJ Baker Bar) v Customs and Excise Commissioners* [2003] EWHC 1665, [2004] S.T.C. 412 (Ch D), Neuberger, J.

Reg.49, amended: SI 2002/1142 Reg.3

Reg.50, amended: SI 2002/1142 Reg.4

Reg.50, revoked (in part): SI 2002/1142 Reg.4

Reg.51, amended: SI 2002/1142 Reg.5

Reg.52, amended: SI 2002/1142 Reg.6, SI 2003/1069 Reg.3, SI 2004/767 Reg.4

Reg.53, amended: SI 2003/1069 Reg.4, SI 2004/767 Reg.5

Reg.54, amended: SI 2004/767 Reg.5

Reg.55A, added: SI 2002/1142 Reg.7

Reg.55A, amended: SI 2003/1069 Reg.5, SI 2003/3220 Reg.18

Reg.55B, added: SI 2002/1142 Reg.7

Reg.55B, amended: SI 2003/3220 Reg.17

Reg.55C, added: SI 2002/1142 Reg.7

Reg.55D, added: SI 2002/1142 Reg.7

Reg.55D, amended: SI 2003/1069 Reg.5, SI 2003/3220 Reg.18

Reg.55E, added: SI 2002/1142 Reg.7

Reg.55F, added: SI 2002/1142 Reg.7

Reg.55G, added: SI 2002/1142 Reg.7

Reg.55H, added: SI 2002/1142 Reg.7

Reg.55H, amended: SI 2003/1069 Reg.5

Reg.55H, substituted: SI 2003/3220 Reg.19

Reg.55J, added: SI 2002/1142 Reg.7

Reg.55J, substituted: SI 2003/3220 Reg.19

Reg.55JA, added: SI 2002/1142 Reg.7, SI 2003/1069 Reg.5

Reg.55JA, substituted: SI 2003/3220 Reg.19

Reg.55JB, added: SI 2002/1142 Reg.7

Reg.55K, added: SI 2002/1142 Reg.7

Reg.55K, amended: SI 2003/1069 Reg.6, SI 2003/3220 Reg.20, SI 2004/767 Reg.6

Reg.55K, referred to: SI 2004/767 Reg.2

Reg.55K, revoked (in part): SI 2003/3220 Reg.18

Reg.55L, added: SI 2002/1142 Reg.7

Reg.55L, amended: SI 2003/1069 Reg.7

Reg.55M, added: SI 2002/1142 Reg.7

Reg.55M, amended: SI 2003/1069 Reg.7

Reg.55N, added: SI 2002/1142 Reg.7

Reg.55N, amended: SI 2003/3220 Reg.18

Reg.55P, added: SI 2002/1142 Reg.7

1995–cont.

2518. Value Added Tax Regulations 1995– cont.

Reg.55Q, added: SI 2002/1142 Reg.7

Reg.55R, added: SI 2002/1142 Reg.7

Reg.55T, added: SI 2002/1142 Reg.7

Reg.55U, added: SI 2002/1142 Reg.7

Reg.55V, added: SI 2002/1142 Reg.7

Reg.57A, added: SI 2002/1142 Reg.8

Reg.58, amended: SI 2004/767 Reg.7

Reg.60, amended: SI 2004/767 Reg.8

Reg.61, substituted: SI 2004/767 Reg.9

Reg.64A, added: SI 2004/767 Reg.10

Reg.66, amended: SI 2002/1142 Reg.9

Reg.69A, added: SI 2002/1142 Reg.9

Reg.71, substituted: SI 2002/1142 Reg.9

Reg.83, amended: SI 2003/3220 Reg.12

Reg.84, amended: SI 2002/2918 Reg.3, Reg.4, SI 2003/1069 Reg.8, Reg.9, SI 2003/3220 Reg.13

Reg.85, applied: SI 2004/1933 Sch.2 para.4

Reg.85, see *Royal & Sun Alliance Insurance Group Plc v Customs and Excise Commissioners* [2003] UKHL 29, [2003] 1 W.L.R. 1387 (HL), Lord Woolf

Reg.86, applied: SI 2004/1933 Sch.2 para.4

Reg.87, amended: SI 2003/3220 Reg.14

Reg.88, amended: SI 2003/3220 Reg.15

Reg.89, amended: SI 2003/3220 Reg.16

Reg.90, applied: SI 2004/1933 Sch.2 para.4

Reg.90A, applied: SI 2004/1933 Sch.2 para.4

Reg.90B, applied: SI 2004/1933 Sch.2 para.4

Reg.91, applied: SI 2004/1933 Sch.2 para.4

Reg.93, applied: SI 2004/1933 Sch.2 para.4

Reg.94B, added: SI 2003/2318 Reg.3

Reg.95, amended: SI 2003/2318 Reg.4

Reg.99, amended: SI 2002/1074 Reg.3

Reg.101, see *Customs and Excise Commissioners v Southern Primary Housing Association Ltd* [2003] S.T.I. 310 (V&DTr), John F Avery Jones (Chairman); see *Dial-a-Phone Ltd v Customs and Excise Commissioners* [2004] EWCA Civ 603, [2004] S.T.C. 987 (CA), Waller, L.J.; see *JDL Ltd v Customs and Excise Commissioners* [2002] S.T.C. 1 (Ch D), Lawrence Collins, J.

Reg.102A, added: SI 2003/3220 Reg.21

Reg.102B, added: SI 2003/3220 Reg.21

Reg.102C, added: SI 2003/3220 Reg.21

Reg.106, substituted: SI 2002/1074 Reg.4

Reg.106A, added: SI 2002/1074 Reg.5

Reg.107, amended: SI 2002/1074 Reg.6

Reg.107A, added: SI 2002/1074 Reg.7

Reg.107B, added: SI 2002/1074 Reg.7

Reg.107C, added: SI 2002/1074 Reg.7

Reg.107D, added: SI 2002/1074 Reg.7

Reg.107E, added: SI 2002/1074 Reg.7

NO.

1995–cont.

2518. Value Added Tax Regulations 1995– cont.

Reg.109, see *Royal & Sun Alliance Insurance Group Plc v Customs and Excise Commissioners* [2003] UKHL 29, [2003] 1 W.L.R.1387 (HL), LordWoolf

Reg.115, see *Centralan Property Ltd v Customs and Excise Commissioners* [2003] EWHC 44, [2003] S.T.C. 290 (Ch D), Sir Andrew Morritt V.C.

Reg.117, amended: SI 2003/1485 Reg.5, SI 2004/1082 Reg.4

Reg.117, revoked (in part): SI 2003/1485 Reg.5

Reg.120, amended: SI 2003/2318 Reg.5

Reg.121A, added: SI 2003/2318 Reg.6

Reg.121B, added: SI 2003/2318 Reg.6

Reg.121C, added: SI 2003/2318 Reg.6

Reg.129, revoked (in part): SI 2003/1485 Reg.6

Reg.130, revoked: SI 2003/1485 Reg.6

Reg.131, revoked (in part): SI 2003/1485 Reg.6

Reg.138, amended: SI 2004/1082 Reg.5

Reg.139, amended: SI 2004/1082 Reg.6

Reg.166A, amended: SI 2002/3027 Reg.3

Reg.170, amended: SI 2002/3027 Reg.4

Reg.170A, added: SI 2002/3027 Reg.5

Reg.171, amended: SI 2002/3027 Reg.6, SI 2003/3220 Reg.22, Reg.23

Reg.172F, added: SI 2002/3027 Reg.8

Reg.172G, added: SI 2002/3027 Reg.8

Reg.172H, added: SI 2002/3027 Reg.8

Reg.172I, added: SI 2002/3027 Reg.8

Reg.172I, amended: SI 2003/532 Reg.3

Reg.172I, revoked (in part): SI 2003/532 Reg.4

Reg.172J, added: SI 2002/3027 Reg.8

Reg.172ZC, added: SI 2002/3027 Reg.7

Reg.207, amended: SI 2003/2096 Sch.1 para.59

s.art VIIA Reg.55S, added: SI 2002/1142 Reg.7

Sch.1, amended: SI 2004/1675 Sch.1

2561. Local Authorities (Calculation of Council Tax Base) (Wales) Regulations 1995

Reg.1, amended: SI 2004/3094 Reg.2

Reg.5A, added: SI 2004/3094 Reg.3

Reg.6, amended: SI 2004/3094 Reg.4

Reg.7, amended: SI 2004/3094 Reg.5

Reg.8, amended: SI 2004/3094 Reg.6

Reg.9, amended: SI 2004/3094 Reg.7

2562. Local Authorities (Precepts) (Wales) Regulations 1995

Reg.5, varied: SI 2002/1129 Art.5

Sch.1 Part II para.8, varied: SI 2002/1129 Art.5

2607. Measuring Instruments (EC Requirements) (Electrical Energy Meters) Regulations 1995

Reg.2, amended: SI 2002/3082 Sch.1 para.1

NO.

1995–cont.

2607. Measuring Instruments (EC Requirements) (Electrical Energy Meters) Regulations 1995– *cont.*

Reg.5, amended: SI 2002/3082 Sch.1 para.2

Reg.5A, added: SI 2002/3082 Sch.1 para.3

Reg.10, substituted: SI 2002/3082 Sch.1 para.4

Sch.1 para.6, added: SI 2002/3082 Sch.1 para.5

2632. North Eastern Combined Fire Services Area Administration Scheme Order 1995

Sch.1 para.4, amended: SSI 2002/141 Art.2

Sch.1 para.5, amended: SSI 2002/141 Art.2

Sch.1 para.6, amended: SSI 2002/141 Art.2

Sch.1 para.11, amended: SSI 2002/141 Art.2

2633. Northern Combined Fire Services Area Administration Scheme Order 1995

Sch.1 para.4, amended: SSI 2002/141 Art.2

Sch.1 para.5, amended: SSI 2002/141 Art.2

Sch.1 para.6, amended: SSI 2002/141 Art.2

Sch.1 para.11, amended: SSI 2002/141 Art.2

2634. South Eastern Combined Fire Services Area Administration Scheme Order 1995

Sch.1 para.4, amended: SSI 2002/141 Art.2

Sch.1 para.5, amended: SSI 2002/141 Art.2

Sch.1 para.6, amended: SSI 2002/141 Art.2

Sch.1 para.11, amended: SSI 2002/141 Art.2

2635. Central Combined Fire Services Area Administration Scheme Order 1995

Sch.1 para.4, amended: SSI 2002/141 Art.2

Sch.1 para.5, amended: SSI 2002/141 Art.2

Sch.1 para.6, amended: SSI 2002/141 Art.2

Sch.1 para.11, amended: SSI 2002/141 Art.2

2636. Mid and South Western Combined Fire Services Area Administration Scheme Order 1995

Sch.1 para.4, amended: SSI 2002/141 Art.2

Sch.1 para.5, amended: SSI 2002/141 Art.2

Sch.1 para.6, amended: SSI 2002/141 Art.2

Sch.1 para.11, amended: SSI 2002/141 Art.2

2637. Mid Eastern Combined Fire Services Area Administration Scheme Order 1995

Sch.1 para.4, amended: SSI 2002/141 Art.2

Sch.1 para.5, amended: SSI 2002/141 Art.2

Sch.1 para.6, amended: SSI 2002/141 Art.2

Sch.1 para.11, amended: SSI 2002/141 Art.2

2638. Central Scotland Combined Police Area Amalgamation Scheme Order 1995

referred to: SSI 2002/458(a)

Sch.1, referred to: SSI 2002/140

Sch.1 para.5, amended: SSI 2002/140 Sch.1

Sch.1 para.6, amended: SSI 2002/140 Sch.1

Sch.1 para.7, amended: SSI 2002/140 Sch.1

Sch.1 para.12, amended: SSI 2002/140 Sch.1

1995–cont.

2639. Grampian Combined Police Area Amalgamation Scheme Order 1995
referred to: SSI 2002/458(b)
Sch.1, referred to: SSI 2002/140
Sch.1 para.5, amended: SSI 2002/140 Sch.2
Sch.1 para.6, amended: SSI 2002/140 Sch.2
Sch.1 para.7, amended: SSI 2002/140 Sch.2
Sch.1 para.12, amended: SSI 2002/140 Sch.2

2640. Lothian and Borders Combined Police Area Amalgamation Scheme Order 1995
referred to: SSI 2002/458(c)
Sch.1, referred to: SSI 2002/140
Sch.1 para.5, amended: SSI 2002/140 Sch.3
Sch.1 para.6, amended: SSI 2002/140 Sch.3
Sch.1 para.7, amended: SSI 2002/140 Sch.3
Sch.1 para.12, amended: SSI 2002/140 Sch.3

2641. Northern Combined Police Area Amalgamation Scheme Order 1995
referred to: SSI 2002/458(d)
Sch.1, referred to: SSI 2002/140
Sch.1 para.5, amended: SSI 2002/140 Sch.4
Sch.1 para.6, amended: SSI 2002/140 Sch.4
Sch.1 para.7, amended: SSI 2002/140 Sch.4
Sch.1 para.12, amended: SSI 2002/140 Sch.4

2642. Strathclyde Combined Police Area Amalgamation Scheme Order 1995
referred to: SSI 2002/458(e)
Sch.1, referred to: SSI 2002/140
Sch.1 para.5, amended: SSI 2002/140 Sch.5
Sch.1 para.6, amended: SSI 2002/140 Sch.5
Sch.1 para.7, amended: SSI 2002/140 Sch.5
Sch.1 para.12, amended: SSI 2002/140 Sch.5

2643. Tayside Combined Police Area Amalgamation Scheme Order 1995
referred to: SSI 2002/458(f)
Sch.1, referred to: SSI 2002/140
Sch.1 para.5, amended: SSI 2002/140 Sch.6
Sch.1 para.6, amended: SSI 2002/140 Sch.6
Sch.1 para.7, amended: SSI 2002/140 Sch.6
Sch.1 para.12, amended: SSI 2002/140 Sch.6

2644. Statutory Nuisance (Appeals) Regulations 1995
Reg.2, see *East Devon DC v Farr* [2002] EWHC 115, [2002] Env. L.R. 31 (QBD (Admin Ct)), Elias, J.

2645. Blyth Harbour Act 1986 (Amendment) Order 1995
revoked: SI 2004/148 Sch.3

2653. Marketing of Fruit Plant Material Regulations 1995
Sch.1, referred to: SSI 2004/471 Reg.2
Sch.1, substituted: SI 2004/2603 Reg.2, SSI 2004/471 Sch.1

2697. Kent Ambulance National Health Service Trust (Establishment) Amendment Order 1995
revoked: 2003 c.43 s.7

1995–cont.

2700. Air Navigation (Hong Kong) Order 1995
Art.98, amended: 2002 c.8 s.2

2702. Child Support (Northern Ireland) Order 1995
Art.4, enabled: SR 2002/323, SR 2003/191
Art.19, enabled: SR 2002/323, SR 2003/191

2705. Jobseekers (Northern Ireland) Order 1995
applied: 2002 c.11 (NI) s.6, SR 2002/56 Reg.4
Part II, applied: SI 2003/492 Reg.19
Art.2, applied: SR 2002/378 Reg.35
Art.3, applied: SI 2003/493 Reg.10, SR 2002/79 Reg.11, SR 2003/28 Reg.9
Art.3, enabled: SR 2002/332
Art.3, referred to: SR 2002/79 Reg.5, Reg.12, Reg.13
Art.4, referred to: SR 2002/79 Reg.4
Art.5, applied: SR 2002/79 Reg.5, Reg.10
Art.5A, applied: SR 2002/79 Reg.11, Reg.16
Art.6, applied: 2002 c.5 (NI) s.3, SR 2002/79 Reg.4
Art.6, enabled: SR 2002/128, SR 2002/132, SR 2002/267, SR 2002/322, SR 2003/154, SR 2003/195, SR 2003/261, SR 2003/267
Art.7, enabled: SR 2002/80
Art.8, enabled: SR 2002/243, SR 2002/388
Art.10, enabled: SR 2002/388
Art.14, enabled: SR 2002/128, SR 2002/132, SR 2002/203, SR 2002/222, SR 2002/270, SR 2002/275, SR 2002/295, SR 2002/299, SR 2002/363, SR 2003/1, SR 2003/154, SR 2003/195, SR 2003/351
Art.15, enabled: SR 2002/132, SR 2003/195
Art.16, applied: SI 2003/2682 Reg.64
Art.18, applied: SR 2002/79 Reg.10, Reg.11
Art.18, referred to: SR 2002/79 Reg.5
Art.21, applied: SR 2002/79 Reg.5
Art.21, enabled: SR 2002/275
Art.22A, applied: SR 2002/79 Reg.11
Art.23, enabled: SR 2002/132, SR 2002/363
Art.28, enabled: SR 2002/80, SR 2002/323, SR 2003/191
Art.31, revoked (in part): 2002 c.21 Sch.6
Art.36, enabled: SR 2002/80, SR 2002/128, SR 2002/203, SR 2002/275, SR 2002/295, SR 2002/322, SR 2002/332, SR 2002/363, SR 2002/388, SR 2003/1, SR 2003/154, SR 2003/195, SR 2003/261, SR 2003/267
Art.39, enabled: SR 2002/323
Sch.1, enabled: SR 2002/132, SR 2002/275, SR 2002/363, SR 2003/1
Sch.1, revoked: SI 2003/435 Sch.5
Sch.2, revoked (in part): 2002 c.14 (NI) Sch.3, 2002 c.21 Sch.6

NO.

1995–cont.

2709. Reciprocal Enforcement of Maintenance Orders (United States of America) Order 1995
Sch.1, amended: SI 2003/776 Art.2

2716. Other Fuel Substitutes (Rates of Excise Duty etc) Order 1995
applied: SI 2004/2063 Art.5
referred to: SI 2002/3042 Art.2
Art.2, amended: SI 2004/2062 Art.3
Art.2, revoked (in part): SI 2004/2062 Art.3
Art.3, amended: SI 2002/3042 Art.3, SI 2004/2062 Art.4
Art.4, amended: SI 2002/3042 Art.3, Art.4, SI 2004/2062 Art.4, Art.5
Art.5, amended: SI 2002/3042 Art.3, Art.5, SI 2004/2062 Art.4, Art.6
Art.6, revoked: SI 2002/3042 Art.6

2717. Other Fuel Substitutes (Payment of Excise Duty etc) Regulations 1995
applied: SI 2004/2065 Reg.8
revoked: SI 2004/2065 Reg.4
Reg.2, amended: SI 2002/1928 Reg.9
Reg.6, referred to: SI 2004/2065 Reg.14
Sch.2, referred to: SI 2002/1928 Reg.6
Sch.2, revoked: SI 2002/1928 Reg.9
Sch.3 para.12, added: SI 2002/1928 Reg.9

2769. Traffic Signs General (Amendment) Directions 1995
revoked: SI 2002/3113 Reg.2

2797. Gwent Community Health National Health Service Trust (Establishment) Amendment Order 1995
revoked: 2003 c.43 s.7

2800. National Health Service Litigation Authority (Establishment and Constitution) Order 1995
Art.4, amended: SI 2002/2621 Art.2

2801. National Health Service Litigation Authority Regulations 1995
Reg.1, amended: SI 2002/2469 Sch.1 para.66, SI 2002/2861 Reg.32, SI 2004/696 Art.3, Sch.1 para.19
Reg.7, amended: SI 2004/696 Art.3, Sch.1 para.19

2808. Medicines (Exemption from Licences) (Clinical Trials) Order 1995
revoked: SI 2004/1031 Sch.11
Art.3, applied: SI 2004/1031 Sch.12 para.4
Art.4, amended: SI 2002/2469 Sch.1 para.67
Art.4, referred to: SI 2004/1031 Sch.12 para.4

2809. Medicines (Exemption from Licences and Certificates) (Clinical Trials) Order 1995
revoked: SI 2004/1031 Sch.11

2815. Lottery Duty (Instant Chances) Regulations 1995
Reg.5, amended: SI 2002/2354 Reg.3

2869. Goods Vehicles (Licensing of Operators) Regulations 1995
Reg.31, amended: SI 2003/2096 Sch.1 para.60

NO.

1995–cont.

2894. Local Government Changes For England (Designation of Authorities) Order 1995
varied: SI 2004/222 Art.2

2895. Local Government Changes for England (Payments to Designated Authorities) (Minimum Revenue Provision) Regulations 1995
revoked: SI 2004/2044 Art.4
varied: SI 2004/2044 Art.4

2909. Public Service Vehicles (Operators Licences) (Fees) Regulations 1995
Reg.3, amended: SI 2002/2535 Reg.2
Sch.1, amended: SI 2004/1876 Reg.2
Sch.1, substituted: SI 2002/2535 Sch.1

2927. Social Security (Income Support, Claims and Payments and Adjudication) Amendment Regulations 1995
Reg.1, revoked (in part): SI 2003/492 Sch.3 Part 1
Reg.3, revoked (in part): SI 2003/492 Sch.3 Part 1

2971. Western Isles Islands Council (Leverburgh) Harbour Revision Order 1995
revoked: SSI 2002/410 Sch.2 Part II
Art.1, referred to: SSI 2002/410 Sch.2 Part II
Art.2, referred to: SSI 2002/410 Sch.2 Part II
Art.20, referred to: SSI 2002/410 Sch.2 Part II
Art.27, referred to: SSI 2002/410 Sch.2 Part II
Art.28, referred to: SSI 2002/410 Sch.2 Part II

2993. Police (Amendment) (Northern Ireland) Order 1995
Art.7, revoked (in part): SI 2004/1500 Sch.3

2994. Road Traffic (Northern Ireland) Order 1995
Art.9, see *Attorney General for Northern Ireland's Reference (Nos.2, 6, 7 and 8 of 2003), Re* [2004] N.I. 50 (CA (Crim Div) (NI)), Lord Carswell L.C.J.
Art.9, applied: 2003 c.32 Sch.3 para.3, 2003 c.44 Sch.17 para.53
Art.10, applied: 2003 c.32 Sch.3 para.3
Art.12, applied: 2003 c.32 Sch.3 para.3
Art.14, see *Attorney General for Northern Ireland's Reference (Nos.2, 6, 7 and 8 of 2003), Re* [2004] N.I. 50 (CA (Crim Div) (NI)), Lord Carswell L.C.J.
Art.14, applied: 2003 c.32 Sch.3 para.3, 2003 c.44 Sch.17 para.54
Art.15, see *Russell (Superintendent of the Royal Ulster Constabulary) v Devine* [2003] UKHL 24, [2003] 1 W.L.R. 1187 (HL (NI)), Lord Bingham of Cornhill
Art.15, applied: 2003 c.32 Sch.3 para.3
Art.16, applied: 2003 c.32 Sch.3 para.3
Art.17, applied: 2003 c.32 Sch.3 para.3
Art.18, see *Russell (Superintendent of the Royal Ulster Constabulary) v Devine* [2003] UKHL 24, [2003] 1 W.L.R. 1187 (HL (NI)), Lord Bingham of Cornhill
Art.18, applied: 2003 c.32 Sch.3 para.3

1995–cont.

2994. Road Traffic (Northern Ireland) Order 1995–*cont.*

Art.25, amended: 2002 c.21 Sch.3 para.57

Art.55, enabled: SR 2002/8, SR 2002/197, SR 2002/256, SR 2002/294, SR 2002/375, SR 2003/19, SR 2003/38, SR 2003/39, SR 2003/145

Art.60, applied: SR 2003/303 Reg.6

Art.61, applied: SR 2003/303 Reg.3, Reg.4, Reg.16

Art.61, enabled: SR 2002/47, SR 2003/101, SR 2003/303

Art.62, enabled: SR 2002/47, SR 2003/101, SR 2003/303

Art.63, applied: SR 2003/303 Reg.20

Art.63, disapplied: SR 2003/303 Reg.6

Art.63, enabled: SR 2003/303

Art.65, enabled: SR 2002/48, SR 2003/102

Art.67, enabled: SR 2002/48, SR 2003/102

Art.72, enabled: SR 2003/303

Art.72, referred to: SI 2003/2994 Art.2

Art.74, applied: SR 2002/116 Reg.7

Art.75, applied: SR 2003/8 Reg.2, SR 2003/303 Reg.22, Sch.1

Art.75, enabled: SR 2003/101, SR 2003/303

Art.76, applied: SR 2003/8 Reg.2

Art.81, applied: SR 2003/303 Reg.22, Sch.1

Art.81, enabled: SR 2003/101, SR 2003/303

Art.83, applied: SI 2003/1593 Sch.1 Part II

Art.84, applied: SI 2003/1593 Sch.1 Part II

Art.110, enabled: SR 2002/8, SR 2002/47, SR 2002/48, SR 2002/197, SR 2002/256, SR 2002/294, SR 2002/375, SR 2003/19, SR 2003/38, SR 2003/39, SR 2003/101, SR 2003/102, SR 2003/145, SR 2003/303

3000. Goods Vehicles (Licensing of Operators) (Fees) Regulations 1995

referred to: SI 2004/1878 Reg.3

Sch.1 Part I, amended: SI 2002/2778 Reg.2, SI 2004/1878 Reg.2

Sch.1 Part II, amended: SI 2002/2778 Reg.2, SI 2004/1878 Reg.2

Sch.1 Part II, applied: SI 2004/1878 Reg.3

3001. Police (Scotland) Amendment (No.4) Regulations 1995

revoked: SSI 2004/257 Sch.4

3026. Strathclyde Passenger Transport Authority (Constitution, Membership and Transitional and Consequential Provisions) Order 1995

Art.12, amended: SSI 2003/128 Art.2

3052. Motor Vehicles (Authorisation of Special Types) (Amendment) Order 1995

revoked: SI 2003/1998 Art.2

3055. Social Security (Claims and Payments) Amendment Regulations 1995

revoked (in part): SI 2003/492 Sch.3 Part 1

1995–cont.

3056. Valuation Tribunals (Wales) Regulations 1995

Reg.4, revoked (in part): SI 2004/1312 Reg.3

Reg.7, revoked (in part): SI 2004/1312 Reg.3

3093. National Health Service (General Medical Services) Amendment (No.2) Regulations 1995

revoked (in part): SI 2004/865 Sch.2, SI 2004/1016 Sch.2

3094. Act of Sederunt (Fees of Messengers-at-Arms) 1995

revoked: SSI 2002/566 Sch.2

3095. Act of Sederunt (Fees of Sheriff Officers) 1995

revoked: SSI 2002/567 Sch.2

3103. Retirement Benefits Schemes (Information Powers) Regulations 1995

Reg.2, amended: SI 2002/3006 Reg.3, SI 2003/2155 Sch.1 para.23

Reg.2, substituted: SI 2002/3006 Reg.3

Reg.5, amended: SI 2002/3006 Reg.4

Reg.6, amended: SI 2002/3006 Reg.5

Reg.7, amended: SI 2002/3006 Reg.6

Reg.8, amended: SI 2002/3006 Reg.7

Reg.10, amended: SI 2002/3006 Reg.8

Reg.11, amended: SI 2002/3006 Reg.9

Reg.11A, added: SI 2002/3006 Reg.10

Reg.11B, added: SI 2002/3006 Reg.10

Reg.11C, added: SI 2002/3006 Reg.10

Reg.12, amended: SI 2002/3006 Reg.11

Reg.14, amended: SI 2002/3006 Reg.12

Reg.15, amended: SI 2002/3006 Reg.13

3105. Local Government (Changes for the Registration Service in Avon, Cleveland, Humberside and North Yorkshire) Order 1995

varied: SI 2004/222 Art.2

3107. Traffic Signs (Amendment) Regulations and General Directions 1995

Reg.1, revoked: SI 2002/3113 Reg.2

Reg.2, revoked: SI 2002/3113 Reg.2

Reg.3, revoked: SI 2002/3113 Reg.2

Sch.1, revoked: SI 2002/3113 Reg.2

3113. Special Educational Needs Tribunal Regulations 1995

Reg.36, see *O v Harrow LBC* [2001] EWCA Civ 2046, [2002] 1 W.L.R. 928 (CA), Simon Brown, L.J.

3123. Sweeteners in Food Regulations 1995

referred to: SI 2002/379 Reg.5, SI 2003/1182 Reg.3

Reg.2, amended: SI 2002/330 Reg.2, SI 2003/1182 Reg.2, SI 2003/1713 Reg.2, SSI 2003/274 Reg.3

Reg.3, amended: SI 2003/1182 Reg.2, SI 2003/1713 Reg.2, SSI 2003/274 Reg.4, Reg.5

Reg.5, amended: SSI 2003/274 Reg.6

Reg.5A, amended: SSI 2003/274 Reg.7

1995–cont.

3123. Sweeteners in Food Regulations 1995–*cont.*

Reg.10, amended: SSI 2004/6 Reg.11, SSI 2004/133 Reg.11

Sch.1, amended: SI 2002/330 Sch.1, SI 2002/379 Sch.1, SSI 2002/61 Sch.1

3124. Colours in Food Regulations 1995

Reg.12, amended: SSI 2004/133 Reg.11

Reg.12, revoked (in part): SI 2003/1563 Reg.10, SI 2003/3047 Reg.10, SSI 2003/527 Reg.11, SSI 2004/6 Reg.11

Sch.2, amended: SI 2003/3037 Reg.11

Sch.2 para.1, amended: SI 2003/3037 Reg.11

Sch.2 para.2, amended: SI 2003/3037 Reg.11

Sch.2 para.3, amended: SI 2003/3037 Reg.11

Sch.2 para.4, amended: SI 2003/3037 Reg.11

Sch.2 para.5, amended: SI 2003/3037 Reg.11

Sch.2 para.6, amended: SI 2003/1596 Reg.10, SI 2003/3037 Reg.11, SI 2003/3053 Reg.10, SSI 2003/311 Reg.11

Sch.2 para.7, amended: SI 2003/3037 Reg.11

Sch.2 para.8, amended: SI 2003/3037 Reg.11

Sch.2 para.9, amended: SI 2003/3037 Reg.11

Sch.2 para.10, amended: SI 2003/3037 Reg.11

Sch.2 para.11, amended: SI 2003/3037 Reg.11

Sch.2 para.12, amended: SI 2003/3037 Reg.11

Sch.2 para.13, amended: SI 2003/3037 Reg.11

Sch.2 para.14, amended: SI 2003/3037 Reg.11

Sch.2 para.15, amended: SI 2003/3037 Reg.11

Sch.2 para.16, amended: SI 2003/3037 Reg.11

Sch.2 para.17, amended: SI 2003/1564 Reg.10, SI 2003/3037 Reg.11, SI 2003/3041 Reg.10, SSI 2003/293 Reg.11

Sch.2 para.18, amended: SI 2003/3037 Reg.11

Sch.2 para.19, amended: SI 2003/3037 Reg.11

Sch.2 para.20, amended: SI 2003/3037 Reg.11

Sch.2 para.21, amended: SI 2003/1659 Reg.11, SI 2003/3037 Reg.11, SSI 2003/291 Reg.12

Sch.2 para.22, amended: SI 2003/3037 Reg.11

Sch.2 para.23, amended: SI 2003/3037 Reg.11

1995–cont.

3124. Colours in Food Regulations 1995–*cont.*

Sch.2 para.24, amended: SI 2003/3037 Reg.11

Sch.2 para.25, amended: SI 2003/3037 Reg.11

Sch.2 para.26, amended: SI 2003/3037 Reg.11

Sch.2 para.27, amended: SI 2003/3037 Reg.11

Sch.2 para.28, amended: SI 2003/3037 Reg.11

Sch.2 para.29, amended: SI 2003/3037 Reg.11

Sch.2 para.30, amended: SI 2003/3037 Reg.11

Sch.2 para.31, amended: SI 2003/3037 Reg.11

Sch.2 para.32, amended: SI 2003/3037 Reg.11

Sch.2 para.33, amended: SI 2003/3037 Reg.11

Sch.3, amended: SSI 2004/133 Reg.11

Sch.6, amended: SI 2002/890 Sch.1, SI 2002/1886 Sch.1, SSI 2002/267 Sch.1

3127. Avon Fire Services (Combination Scheme) Order 1995

Sch.1 Part II para.6, amended: 2003 c.26 Sch.8 Part 2

Sch.1 Part III para.20, revoked (in part): 2003 c.26 Sch.8 Part 2

Sch.1 Part IV para.21, revoked: 2003 c.26 Sch.8 Part 2

3128. Merchant Shipping (Port State Control) Regulations 1995

referred to: SI 2003/1636 Reg.2

Part I, substituted: SI 2003/1636 Reg.5

Reg.2, amended: SI 2003/1636 Reg.3, Reg.4

Reg.6, amended: SI 2003/1636 Reg.6

Reg.7, substituted: SI 2003/1636 Reg.7

Reg.7A, added: SI 2003/1636 Reg.8

Reg.7B, added: SI 2003/1636 Reg.8

Reg.8, substituted: SI 2003/1636 Reg.9

Reg.9, amended: SI 2003/1636 Reg.10

Reg.10, amended: SI 2003/1636 Reg.11

Reg.11, amended: SI 2003/1636 Reg.12

Reg.12, amended: SI 2003/1636 Reg.13

Reg.14, amended: SI 2003/1636 Reg.6

Reg.16, amended: SI 2003/1636 Reg.14

Reg.18, amended: SI 2003/1636 Reg.15

3131. Cleveland Fire Services (Combination Scheme) Order 1995

Sch.1 Part II para.6, amended: 2003 c.26 Sch.8 Part 2

Sch.1 Part III para.20, revoked (in part): 2003 c.26 Sch.8 Part 2

Sch.1 Part IV para.21, revoked: 2003 c.26 Sch.8 Part 2

NO.

1995–cont.

3132. Humberside Fire Services (Combination Scheme) Order 1995

Sch.1 Part II para.6, amended: 2003 c.26 Sch.8 Part 2

Sch.1 Part III para.20, revoked (in part): 2003 c.26 Sch.8 Part 2

Sch.1 Part IV para.21, revoked: 2003 c.26 Sch.8 Part 2

3133. North Yorkshire Fire Services (Combination Scheme) Order 1995

Sch.1 Part II para.6, amended: 2003 c.26 Sch.8 Part 2

Sch.1 Part III para.20, revoked (in part): 2003 c.26 Sch.8 Part 2

Sch.1 Part IV para.21, revoked: 2003 c.26 Sch.8 Part 2

3163. Reporting of Injuries, Diseases and Dangerous Occurrences Regulations 1995

Reg.2, amended: SI 2004/568 Sch.13 para.8

Sch.2 Part I para.6, amended: SI 2004/568 Sch.13 para.8

Sch.2 Part I para.17A, substituted: SI 2004/568 Sch.13 para.8

Sch.2 Part IV para.59, amended: SI 2004/568 Sch.13 para.8

3187. Miscellaneous Food Additives Regulations 1995

referred to: SI 2003/945 Reg.3, SI 2003/1008 Reg.3, SI 2004/554 Reg.3, SSI 2004/413 Reg.2

Reg.2, amended: SI 2002/329 Reg.3, SI 2003/945 Reg.2, SI 2003/1008 Reg.2, SI 2004/2601 Reg.3, SSI 2003/132 Reg.2, SSI 2004/413 Reg.3

Reg.2, referred to: SI 2002/330 Reg.3

Reg.2, varied: SI 2003/1182 Reg.3, SI 2003/1713 Reg.3

Reg.10, amended: SSI 2003/291 Reg.12, SSI 2003/293 Reg.11, SSI 2003/311 Reg.11, SSI 2003/527 Reg.11, SSI 2004/133 Reg.11

Reg.10, revoked (in part): SI 2003/1563 Reg.10, SI 2003/1596 Reg.10, SI 2003/3047 Reg.10, SI 2003/3053 Reg.10, SSI 2004/6 Reg.11

Reg.11, amended: SI 2002/329 Reg.4, SI 2004/2601 Reg.4, SSI 2004/413 Reg.4

Sch.2 Part A, amended: SI 2003/3120 Reg.10, SI 2004/553 Reg.10, SSI 2004/133 Reg.11

Sch.2 Part B, amended: SI 2003/1563 Reg.10, SI 2003/3047 Reg.10, SI 2003/3120 Reg.10, SI 2004/553 Reg.10, SSI 2003/527 Reg.11, SSI 2004/133 Reg.11

Sch.2 Part C, amended: SI 2003/3120 Reg.10, SI 2004/553 Reg.10, SSI 2004/133 Reg.11

Sch.2 Part D, amended: SI 2003/3120 Reg.10, SI 2004/553 Reg.10, SSI 2004/133 Reg.11

NO.

1995–cont.

3187. Miscellaneous Food Additives Regulations 1995–cont.

Sch.3, amended: SI 2003/1659 Reg.11, SI 2003/3037 Reg.11, SI 2003/3120 Reg.10, SI 2003/3295 Reg.2, SI 2004/553 Reg.10, SI 2004/554 Reg.2, SSI 2003/291 Reg.12, SSI 2003/599 Reg.2, SSI 2004/133 Reg.11

Sch.3, substituted: SI 2002/329 Reg.6

Sch.4, amended: SI 2002/329 Reg.7

Sch.6, amended: SI 2003/2243 Reg.10, SI 2003/3044 Reg.10, SSI 2003/527 Reg.11, SSI 2003/569 Reg.12

Sch.7, amended: SI 2003/1564 Reg.10, SI 2003/1596 Reg.10, SI 2003/1659 Reg.11, SI 2003/3037 Reg.11, SI 2003/3041 Reg.10, SI 2003/3053 Reg.10, SI 2003/3120 Reg.10, SI 2004/553 Reg.10, SSI 2003/291 Reg.12, SSI 2003/293 Reg.11, SSI 2003/311 Reg.11, SSI 2004/133 Reg.11

Sch.7, substituted: SI 2003/1564 Reg.10

Sch.9, amended: SI 2003/1563 Reg.10, SI 2003/1564 Reg.10, SI 2003/1596 Reg.10, SI 2003/1659 Reg.11, SI 2003/2243 Reg.10, SI 2003/3037 Reg.11, SI 2003/3041 Reg.10, SI 2003/3044 Reg.10, SI 2003/3047 Reg.10, SI 2003/3053 Reg.10, SSI 2003/291 Reg.12, SSI 2003/293 Reg.11, SSI 2003/311 Reg.11, SSI 2003/527 Reg.11, SSI 2004/6 Reg.11

3199. National Health Service (General Medical Services) (Scotland) Amendment Regulations 1995

revoked: SSI 2004/114 Sch.2

3201. National Health Service (Service Committees and Tribunal) (Scotland) Amendment Regulations 1995

revoked: SSI 2004/38 Sch.3

3204. City of Sunderland College (Government) Regulations 1995

revoked: SI 2002/1094 Sch.1 Part 1

3205. Minced Meat and Meat Preparations (Hygiene) Regulations 1995

applied: SI 2002/8 Reg.6, SI 2002/843 Reg.56, Reg.101, SI 2002/1387 Reg.4, SI 2003/2756 Reg.48, SI 2004/2640 Reg.4, SSI 2003/411 Reg.49

referred to: SI 2002/1227 Reg.4, SI 2002/1416 Reg.101, SI 2003/1482 Reg.49, SI 2003/3177 Reg.4, SI 2004/1214 Reg.4, SI 2004/1430 Reg.4, SI 2004/1740 Reg.4, SSI 2002/255 Reg.99, SSI 2002/445 Reg.4

Reg.7, amended: SSI 2002/35 Reg.5

Reg.8, amended: SSI 2002/35 Reg.5

3208. European Specialist Medical Qualifications Order 1995

applied: SI 2003/1250 Sch.8 para.9, Sch.8 para.13, SI 2004/1947 Reg.4

revoked: SI 2003/1250 Sch.10 Part 2

varied: SI 2003/1250 Sch.8 para.20, SI 2004/1947 Reg.9

1995–cont.

3208. European Specialist Medical Qualifications Order 1995–*cont.*

Part V Art.12, see *R. (on the application of Hollingworth) v Specialist Training Authority of the Medical Royal Colleges* [2003] EWCA Civ 452, (2003) 74 B.M.L.R. 24 (CA), Keene, L.J.

Art.2, amended: SI 2003/3148 Reg.10

Art.3, amended: SI 2003/3148 Reg.10

Art.3, applied: SI 2003/1250 Sch.8 para.13

Art.3, referred to: SI 2003/1250 Sch.8 para.11

Art.6, applied: SI 2003/1250 Sch.8 para.11

Art.7, amended: SI 2002/849 Reg.2

Art.7, applied: SI 2003/1250 Sch.8 para.10

Art.8, amended: SI 2002/849 Reg.2

Art.8, applied: SI 2003/1250 Sch.8 para.9

Art.8, referred to: SI 2003/1250 Sch.8 para.9

Art.8A, added: SI 2003/3148 Reg.10

Art.8A, applied: SI 2003/1250 Sch.8 para.12

Art.8A, referred to: SI 2003/1250 Sch.8 para.9

Art.9, see *Lambiris v Specialist Training Authority of the Medical Royal Colleges* [2003] EWCA Civ 609, [2003] 2 C.M.L.R. 38 (CA), Buxton, L.J.

Art.9, amended: SI 2003/3148 Reg.10

Art.9, applied: SI 2003/1250 Sch.8 para.9, Sch.8 para.12

Art.10, amended: SI 2003/3148 Reg.10

Art.13, applied: SI 2003/1250 Sch.8 para.9, Sch.8 para.11, Sch.8 para.12, Sch.8 para.14

Art.14, applied: SI 2003/1250 Sch.8 para.12, Sch.8 para.15, Sch.8 para.16, Sch.8 para.17

Sch.2 Part II, amended: SI 2002/849 Reg.2

Sch.4, substituted: SI 2003/3148 Sch.4 Part II

Sch.6 para.2, applied: SI 2003/1250 Sch.8 para.16

3210. Street Works (Northern Ireland) Order 1995

applied: SR 2002/10 Reg.5

Art.3, enabled: SR 2002/10

Art.13, applied: SR 2002/10 Reg.3

Art.13, enabled: SR 2002/10, SR 2003/236

Art.14, applied: SR 2002/10 Reg.3, Reg.4, Reg.6, Sch.1 para.2, Sch.1 para.6, SR 2003/236 Sch.1

Art.14, enabled: SR 2002/10

Art.15, applied: SR 2002/10 Reg.3, Reg.4, Reg.7, SR 2003/236 Sch.1

Art.15, enabled: SR 2002/10

Art.16, applied: SR 2002/10 Reg.8

Art.17, applied: SR 2002/10 Reg.3, Reg.4, SR 2003/236 Sch.1

Art.17, enabled: SR 2002/10

Art.18, applied: SR 2002/10 Reg.3, Reg.9

Art.18, enabled: SR 2002/10

Art.21, applied: SR 2002/10 Reg.11, Sch.1 para.9

Art.21, disapplied: SR 2002/10 Reg.10

Art.22, enabled: SR 2002/10

1995–cont.

3210. Street Works (Northern Ireland) Order 1995–*cont.*

Art.23, applied: SR 2002/10 Reg.12, Sch.1 para.9

Art.23, enabled: SR 2002/10

Art.24, applied: SR 2002/10 Reg.13, Sch.1 para.9

Art.24, enabled: SR 2002/10

Art.30, applied: SR 2002/10 Reg.3, SR 2003/236 Sch.1

Art.40, applied: SR 2002/10 Reg.3, Reg.10

Art.45, applied: SR 2002/10 Reg.3

Art.54, applied: SR 2002/10 Reg.5

Art.54, enabled: SR 2002/10

Sch.2, amended: 2003 c.21 Sch.17 para.135, Sch.19

Sch.2, applied: SR 2002/10 Reg.3, SR 2003/236 Sch.1

Sch.3, referred to: SI 2003/412 Sch.4 para.1

3213. Pensions (Northern Ireland) Order 1995

referred to: SR 2002/74 Reg.1

Art.4, amended: SI 2002/3150 Sch.3 para.10

Art.10, applied: SR 2002/74 Reg.6, Reg.12

Art.10, enabled: SR 2002/74

Art.17, enabled: SR 2002/279

Art.19, enabled: SR 2002/279, SR 2003/256

Art.21, enabled: SR 2002/279, SR 2003/256

Art.22, applied: SR 2002/74 Reg.5

Art.22, referred to: SR 2002/74 Reg.2

Art.23, applied: SR 2002/74 Reg.2, Reg.9

Art.23, enabled: SR 2002/74

Art.26A, applied: SR 2002/74 Reg.6

Art.26A, disapplied: SR 2002/74 Reg.5

Art.26A, referred to: SR 2002/74 Reg.2, Reg.4

Art.26A, varied: SR 2002/74 Reg.2

Art.26B, applied: SR 2002/74 Reg.3, Reg.6

Art.26B, disapplied: SR 2002/74 Reg.5

Art.26B, enabled: SR 2002/74

Art.26B, referred to: SR 2002/74 Reg.3, Reg.4

Art.26B, varied: SR 2002/74 Reg.3

Art.26C, disapplied: SR 2002/74 Reg.4

Art.26C, enabled: SR 2002/74

Art.29, amended: SI 2002/3150 Sch.3 para.11

Art.35, enabled: SR 2003/256

Art.40, applied: SR 2002/352 Sch.6 para.35

Art.40, enabled: SR 2002/109, SR 2003/256

Art.47, applied: SR 2002/74 Reg.7, Reg.9

Art.47, enabled: SR 2003/256

Art.49, applied: SR 2002/352 Reg.81

Art.49, enabled: SR 2003/256

Art.49A, applied: SR 2002/74 Reg.7, Reg.12

Art.49A, disapplied: SR 2002/74 Reg.12

Art.49A, enabled: SR 2002/74

Art.49A, referred to: SR 2002/74 Reg.12

Art.56, enabled: SR 2002/64, SR 2003/256

NO.

1995–cont.

3213. Pensions (Northern Ireland) Order 1995–cont.

Art.57, enabled: SR 2002/64

Art.58, enabled: SR 2002/64

Art.59, enabled: SR 2002/64

Art.60, amended: SR 2002/64 Reg.5

Art.60, enabled: SR 2003/256

Art.61, enabled: SR 2002/64

Art.67, enabled: SR 2002/109

Art.71A, applied: SR 2002/74 Reg.7

Art.71A, enabled: SR 2002/74

Art.72A, applied: SR 2002/74 Reg.8, Reg.9, Reg.10, Reg.13

Art.72A, enabled: SR 2002/74

Art.72B, applied: SR 2002/74 Reg.13

Art.72B, enabled: SR 2002/74

Art.73, applied: SR 2002/74 Reg.11

Art.73, enabled: SR 2002/64

Art.74, applied: SR 2002/74 Reg.11

Art.75, applied: 2004 c.12 s.199

Art.75, enabled: SR 2002/64

Art.81, enabled: SR 2003/256

Art.89, disapplied: 2002 c.29 s.273

Art.89, enabled: SR 2002/109

Art.90, enabled: SR 2002/109

Art.106, amended: SI 2002/3150 Sch.3 para.12

Art.115, enabled: SR 2002/74, SR 2003/256

Art.116, enabled: SR 2003/256

Art.121, disapplied: SR 2002/74 Reg.11

Art.121, enabled: SR 2002/74

Art.122, enabled: SR 2002/64, SR 2003/256

Art.124, revoked: 2002 c.21 Sch.6

Art.133, referred to: SR 2002/109 Sch.1

Art.139, referred to: SR 2002/109 Sch.1

Art.140, referred to: SR 2002/109 Sch.1

Art.143, referred to: SR 2002/109 Sch.1

Art.164, applied: SR 2002/352 Reg.6, Reg.111, Reg.126

Art.164, referred to: SR 2002/352 Reg.126, Sch.5 para.1

Art.166, enabled: SR 2002/64, SR 2002/74, SR 2002/109, SR 2002/279

Sch.3, referred to: SR 2002/109 Sch.1

Sch.5, referred to: SR 2002/109 Sch.1

3225. Lloyd's Underwriters (Gilt-edged Securities) (Periodic Accounting for Tax on Interest) Regulations 1995

Reg.9, amended: 2002 asp 17 Sch.3 para.35

3237. Insurance Companies (Overseas Life Assurance Business) (Compliance) Regulations 1995

Reg.2, amended: SI 2004/2200 Reg.12

3243. Church Representation Rules (Amendment) Resolution 1995

referred to: SI 2004/1889

3264. Local Government Changes (Rent Act Registration Areas) Order 1995

varied: SI 2004/222 Art.2

NO.

1995–cont.

3267. Food (Miscellaneous Revocations and Amendments) Regulations 1995

Reg.3, amended: SSI 2003/291 Reg.12

Sch.1, amended: SI 2002/890 Sch.1, SI 2002/1886 Sch.1, SSI 2002/267 Sch.1, SSI 2003/293 Reg.11

3297. Duration of Copyright and Rights in Performances Regulations 1995

Reg.15, applied: SI 2003/2498 Reg.39

Reg.23, see *Sweeney v Macmillan Publishers Ltd* [2002] R.P.C. 35 (Ch D), Lloyd, J.

Reg.24, see *Sweeney v Macmillan Publishers Ltd* [2002] R.P.C. 35 (Ch D), Lloyd, J.

3299. Electrical Contracting (London Exhibition Halls) Order 1995

applied: SI 2004/2181 Sch.2

3321. Education (Mandatory Awards) Regulations 1995

referred to: SI 2002/3200 Sch.3 para.4

1996

30. Social Security (Persons From Abroad) Miscellaneous Amendments Regulations 1996

Reg.1, amended: SI 2003/492 Sch.3 Part 1

Reg.10, revoked (in part): SI 2003/492 Sch.3 Part 1

Reg.12, applied: SI 2003/653 Reg.5

75. Merchant Shipping (Distress Signals and Prevention of Collisions) Regulations 1996

Reg.1, amended: SI 2004/302 Sch.1 para.16

90. London Ambulance Service National Health Service Trust (Establishment) Order 1996

revoked: 2003 c.43 s.7

Art.3, amended: SI 2004/2394 Art.2

Art.4, amended: SI 2004/2394 Art.3

146. Health Authorities (Wales) Establishment Order 1996

revoked: SI 2003/813 Art.9

177. National Health Service (General Dental Services) (Scotland) Regulations 1996

applied: SSI 2004/292 Reg.2, Reg.8

Reg.2, amended: SSI 2003/131 Reg.2, SSI 2004/292 Reg.7

Reg.2, applied: SSI 2004/292 Reg.8

Reg.4, amended: SSI 2004/37 Reg.2

Reg.4, applied: SSI 2004/386 Reg.3

Reg.5, amended: SSI 2004/292 Reg.7

Reg.5, applied: SSI 2004/292 Reg.2

Reg.5A, amended: SSI 2002/192 Reg.2

Reg.6, applied: SSI 2004/292 Reg.8

Reg.6, revoked: SSI 2004/292 Reg.7

Reg.7, revoked: SSI 2004/292 Reg.7

Reg.8, applied: SSI 2004/292 Reg.8

Reg.8, revoked: SSI 2004/292 Reg.7

Reg.12, amended: SSI 2003/131 Reg.2

Reg.13, amended: SSI 2004/37 Reg.2

NO.

NO.

1996–cont.

177. National Health Service (General Dental Services) (Scotland) Regulations 1996–*cont.*

Reg.22, amended: SSI 2002/99 Reg.2, SSI 2002/268 Reg.2, SSI 2003/131 Reg.2, SSI 2003/422 Reg.2

Reg.23, amended: SSI 2003/131 Reg.2

Reg.36, substituted: SSI 2004/292 Reg.7

Sch.1 Part II para.7, referred to: SSI 2003/158 Reg.3

Sch.1 Part II para.13, referred to: SSI 2003/158 Reg.3

Sch.1 Part III para.17, referred to: SSI 2003/158 Reg.3

Sch.1 Part III para.17, substituted: SSI 2002/99 Reg.2

Sch.1 Part IV para.31E, added: SSI 2002/99 Reg.2

Sch.1 Part V para.35, amended: SSI 2004/37 Reg.2

Sch.4 Part II para.1, amended: SSI 2002/192 Reg.2, SSI 2003/422 Reg.2

Sch.4 Part II para.2, amended: SSI 2002/192 Reg.2, SSI 2003/422 Reg.2

Sch.7, revoked: SSI 2004/292 Reg.7

178. Contracting Out (Administration of the Teachers Superannuation Scheme) Order 1996

revoked: SI 2003/1668 Art.4

180. Charities (Exception from Registration) Regulations 1996

Reg.4, amended: SI 2002/1598 Reg.2

190. Copyright (Certification of Licensing Scheme for Educational Recording of Broadcasts) (Open University Educational Enterprises Limited) (Amendment) Order 1996

revoked: SI 2003/187 Art.4

192. Equipment and Protective Systems Intended for Use in Potentially Explosive Atmospheres Regulations 1996

referred to: SI 2002/2776 Sch.3 para.1

207. Jobseeker's Allowance Regulations 1996

referred to: SI 2002/3072 Reg.2, SI 2004/552 Art.24

see *Collins v Secretary of State for Work and Pensions (C138/02)* [2004] 3 W.L.R. 1236 (ECJ), Judge Skouris (President)

Reg.1, amended: SI 2002/841 Reg.3, SI 2002/1411 Reg.2, SI 2002/1589 Reg.2, SI 2002/1763 Reg.2, SI 2002/2314 Reg.2, SI 2002/2402 Sch.2 para.1, SI 2002/2689 Reg.3, SI 2003/1121 Sch.2 para.1, SI 2003/1195 Reg.6, SI 2003/2279 Reg.3, SI 2004/565 Reg.5, SI 2004/963 Reg.2, SI 2004/1141 Reg.2, SI 2004/1708 Reg.6

Reg.1, see *Walter v Secretary of State for Social Security* [2001] EWCA Civ 1913, [2002] 1 C.M.L.R. 27 (CA), Keene, L.J.

Reg.2A, revoked (in part): SI 2003/455 Sch.2 para.1

1996–cont.

207. Jobseeker's Allowance Regulations 1996–*cont.*

Reg.3A, amended: SI 2002/1701 Reg.2

Reg.3D, referred to: SI 2002/1703 Reg.8

Reg.3E, amended: SI 2002/1701 Reg.2, SI 2002/2689 Reg.3

Reg.4, see *Walter v Secretary of State for Social Security* [2001] EWCA Civ 1913, [2002] 1 C.M.L.R. 27 (CA), Keene, L.J.

Reg.5, amended: SI 2002/3072 Reg.3

Reg.12, substituted: SI 2002/3072 Reg.4

Reg.14, amended: SI 2004/1869 Reg.3

Reg.15, amended: SI 2002/3072 Reg.5

Reg.15, see *Walter v Secretary of State for Social Security* [2001] EWCA Civ 1913, [2002] 1 C.M.L.R. 27 (CA), Keene, L.J.

Reg.17, applied: SI 2003/2682 Reg.169

Reg.18, amended: SI 2004/1008 Reg.2

Reg.19, amended: SI 2004/1869 Reg.3

Reg.23, applied: SI 2004/867 Reg.3, SI 2004/869 Reg.3

Reg.23A, applied: SI 2004/867 Reg.3, SI 2004/869 Reg.3

Reg.30, amended: SI 2002/3072 Reg.6

Reg.34, amended: SI 2002/1397 Sch.1 para.26

Reg.46, amended: SI 2003/511 Reg.3

Reg.47, amended: SI 2002/490 Reg.7

Reg.48, amended: SI 2002/2314 Reg.2, SI 2003/511 Reg.3

Reg.50, amended: SI 2004/1869 Reg.3

Reg.51, amended: SI 2003/511 Reg.3

Reg.52, amended: SI 2002/2689 Reg.3

Reg.53, amended: SI 2004/963 Reg.4

Reg.55, amended: SI 2004/1869 Reg.3

Reg.55A, added: SI 2004/1869 Reg.3

Reg.72, amended: SI 2004/1008 Reg.2

Reg.75, amended: SI 2002/2314 Reg.2, SI 2003/2438 Reg.6, SI 2004/959 Reg.23

Reg.75, applied: SSI 2003/176 Art.8

Reg.75, referred to: SI 2002/1792 Sch.2 para.5, SI 2002/2005 Reg.4, SI 2003/673 Art.3, SI 2004/934 Reg.7, SI 2004/959 Reg.21

Reg.75, revoked (in part): SI 2002/2314 Reg.2

Reg.75, varied: SI 2004/868 Reg.3, SI 2004/869 Reg.3, SI 2004/934 Reg.7

Reg.76, amended: SI 2002/2402 Sch.2 para.2

Reg.77, amended: SI 2002/2402 Sch.2 para.3

Reg.79, amended: SI 2002/668 Art.21, SI 2003/526 Art.22, SI 2004/552 Art.23

Reg.83, amended: SI 2003/455 Sch.2 para.2

Reg.83, applied: SI 2003/455 Reg.8, SI 2003/526 Art.23, SI 2004/552 Art.24, SSI 2003/176 Art.4

Reg.83, revoked (in part): SI 2003/455 Sch.2 para.2, SI 2003/1121 Sch.2 para.2

Reg.84, amended: SI 2003/455 Sch.2 para.3

NO.

1996–cont.

207. Jobseeker's Allowance Regulations 1996–cont.

Reg.84, applied: SI 2003/455 Reg.8, SI 2003/526 Art.23, SI 2004/552 Art.24, SSI 2003/176 Art.4

Reg.84, revoked (in part): SI 2003/455 Sch.2 para.3, SI 2003/1121 Sch.2 para.3

Reg.85, amended: SI 2003/455 Sch.2 para.4, SI 2004/1232 Reg.4

Reg.85, applied: SI 2003/526 Art.23, SI 2003/654 Reg.7, SI 2004/552 Art.24

Reg.85, revoked (in part): SI 2003/1121 Sch.2 para.4

Reg.86A, applied: SSI 2003/176 Art.4

Reg.86A, revoked (in part): SI 2003/1121 Sch.2 para.5

Reg.86B, amended: SI 2003/455 Sch.2 para.5

Reg.86B, applied: SSI 2003/176 Art.4

Reg.86B, revoked (in part): SI 2003/1121 Sch.2 para.6

Reg.86C, amended: SI 2004/565 Reg.6

Reg.86C, revoked (in part): SI 2004/565 Reg.6

Reg.87, applied: SI 2002/1792 Sch.1 para.6

Reg.88, amended: SI 2003/455 Sch.2 para.6

Reg.89, amended: SI 2003/455 Sch.2 para.7

Reg.96, amended: SI 2002/2402 Sch.2 para.4, SI 2003/1731 Reg.4

Reg.96, applied: SI 2003/455 Reg.8

Reg.98, amended: SI 2002/2689 Reg.3

Reg.103, amended: SI 2003/455 Sch.2 para.8

Reg.104, amended: SI 2002/2442 Reg.2, SI 2004/1141 Reg.5

Reg.104, revoked (in part): SI 2003/455 Sch.2 para.9

Reg.105, amended: SI 2002/841 Reg.3, SI 2003/455 Sch.2 para.10

Reg.105, revoked (in part): SI 2003/455 Sch.2 para.10

Reg.106, revoked: SI 2003/455 Sch.2 para.11

Reg.109, revoked: SI 2003/455 Sch.2 para.11

Reg.110, revoked (in part): SI 2003/455 Sch.2 para.12

Reg.113, amended: SI 2002/841 Reg.3, SI 2003/455 Sch.2 para.13, SI 2004/2308 Reg.3

Reg.117, revoked (in part): SI 2003/455 Sch.2 para.14

Reg.121, amended: SI 2003/455 Sch.2 para.15, SI 2003/511 Reg.3

Reg.121, revoked (in part): SI 2003/455 Sch.2 para.15

Reg.130, amended: SI 2002/1589 Reg.2, SI 2004/1708 Reg.6

Reg.131, amended: SI 2002/1589 Reg.3, Reg.4, SI 2002/2207 Reg.2, SI 2003/455 Sch.2 para.16, SI 2003/1701 Reg.2, Reg.3, SI 2003/1914 Reg.2, SI 2004/1708 Reg.2, Reg.3

1996–cont.

207. Jobseeker's Allowance Regulations 1996–cont.

Reg.131, revoked (in part): SI 2004/1708 Reg.3

Reg.136, amended: SI 2002/1589 Reg.3, Reg.5, SI 2003/1701 Reg.2, SI 2003/1914 Reg.2, SI 2004/1708 Reg.2

Reg.136A, amended: SI 2003/455 Sch.2 para.17

Reg.138, amended: SI 2003/455 Sch.2 para.17

Reg.140, amended: SI 2003/455 Sch.2 para.18

Reg.145, referred to: SI 2003/526 Sch.15, SI 2004/552 Sch.19

Reg.146G, referred to: SI 2003/526 Sch.15, SI 2004/552 Sch.19

Reg.148, amended: SI 2003/455 Sch.2 para.19

Reg.148, applied: SI 2003/526 Art.23, SI 2004/552 Art.24

Reg.148, referred to: SI 2003/526 Sch.15, SI 2004/552 Sch.19

Reg.148, revoked (in part): SI 2003/455 Sch.2 para.19, SI 2003/1121 Sch.2 para.7

Reg.148A, referred to: SI 2003/526 Sch.15, SI 2004/552 Sch.19

Reg.148A, revoked (in part): SI 2003/1121 Sch.2 para.8

Reg.150, amended: SI 2003/511 Reg.3

Reg.153, amended: SI 2003/511 Reg.3

Reg.156, applied: SI 2003/2682 Reg.169

Reg.172, amended: SI 2002/668 Art.23, SI 2003/526 Art.24, SI 2004/552 Art.25

Sch.A1 para.1, amended: SI 2003/511 Reg.3

Sch.A1 para.2, amended: SI 2003/511 Reg.3

Sch.A1 para.3, amended: SI 2003/511 Reg.3

Sch.A1 para.4, amended: SI 2003/511 Reg.3

Sch.A1 para.5, amended: SI 2003/511 Reg.3

Sch.A1 para.6, amended: SI 2003/511 Reg.3

Sch.A1 para.7, amended: SI 2003/511 Reg.3

Sch.A1 para.8, amended: SI 2003/511 Reg.3

Sch.A1 para.9, amended: SI 2003/511 Reg.3

Sch.A1 para.10, amended: SI 2003/511 Reg.3

Sch.A1 para.11, amended: SI 2003/511 Reg.3

Sch.A1 para.12, amended: SI 2003/511 Reg.3

Sch.A1 para.13, amended: SI 2003/511 Reg.3

Sch.A1 para.14, amended: SI 2003/511 Reg.3

Sch.A1 para.15, amended: SI 2003/511 Reg.3

Sch.A1 para.16, amended: SI 2003/511 Reg.3

Sch.A1 para.17, amended: SI 2003/511 Reg.3

Sch.1 Part I para.1, amended: SI 2002/668 Sch.10

Sch.1 Part I para.1, substituted: SI 2003/526 Sch.10, SI 2004/552 Sch.14

Sch.1 Part I para.2, amended: SI 2002/668 Sch.10, SI 2002/2019 Reg.2

Sch.1 Part I para.2, applied: SI 2002/1792 Sch.1 para.6

Sch.1 Part I para.2, revoked: SI 2003/455 Sch.2 para.20

NO.

NO.

1996–cont.

207. Jobseeker's Allowance Regulations 1996–*cont.*

Sch.1 Part I para.2, substituted: SI 2003/526 Sch.10, SI 2004/552 Sch.14

Sch.1 Part I para.3, amended: SI 2002/668 Sch.10

Sch.1 Part I para.3, applied: SI 2002/1792 Sch.1 para.6

Sch.1 Part I para.3, revoked: SI 2003/1121 Sch.2 para.9

Sch.1 Part I para.3, substituted: SI 2003/526 Sch.10, SI 2004/552 Sch.14

Sch.1 Part II para.4, amended: SI 2002/668 Art.22, SI 2003/526 Art.23, SI 2004/552 Art.24

Sch.1 Part II para.4, applied: SI 2002/1792 Sch.1 para.6, SI 2003/526 Art.23

Sch.1 Part II para.4, revoked: SI 2003/455 Sch.2 para.20

Sch.1 Part III para.5, amended: SI 2003/511 Reg.3

Sch.1 Part III para.6, amended: SI 2003/511 Reg.3

Sch.1 Part III para.7, amended: SI 2003/511 Reg.3

Sch.1 Part III para.7, revoked (in part): SI 2003/455 Sch.2 para.20

Sch.1 Part III para.8, amended: SI 2003/511 Reg.3

Sch.1 Part III para.9, amended: SI 2003/511 Reg.3

Sch.1 Part III para.9A, amended: SI 2003/511 Reg.3

Sch.1 Part III para.10, amended: SI 2003/511 Reg.3

Sch.1 Part III para.11, amended: SI 2003/511 Reg.3

Sch.1 Part III para.12, amended: SI 2003/511 Reg.3

Sch.1 Part III para.12, applied: SI 2002/2005 Reg.9

Sch.1 Part III para.13, amended: SI 2003/511 Reg.3

Sch.1 Part III para.13, applied: SI 2002/2005 Reg.9

Sch.1 Part III para.14, amended: SI 2003/455 Sch.2 para.20, SI 2003/511 Reg.3

Sch.1 Part III para.14, applied: SI 2002/2005 Reg.9, SSI 2003/176 Art.4

Sch.1 Part III para.15, amended: SI 2002/490 Reg.2, SI 2003/511 Reg.3

Sch.1 Part III para.15A, amended: SI 2003/455 Sch.2 para.20, SI 2003/511 Reg.3, SI 2003/1195 Reg.6

Sch.1 Part III para.15A, applied: SI 2002/1792 Sch.1 para.6, SI 2003/526 Art.23, SI 2004/552 Art.24

Sch.1 Part III para.15A, revoked (in part): SI 2003/455 Sch.2 para.20

Sch.1 Part III para.16, amended: SI 2003/511 Reg.3

1996–cont.

207. Jobseeker's Allowance Regulations 1996–*cont.*

Sch.1 Part III para.16, applied: SI 2002/1792 Sch.1 para.6, SI 2003/526 Art.23, SI 2004/552 Art.24

Sch.1 Part III para.16, revoked: SI 2003/455 Sch.2 para.20

Sch.1 Part III para.17, amended: SI 2002/2020 Reg.3, SI 2003/511 Reg.3, SI 2003/2279 Reg.3

Sch.1 Part III para.17, revoked (in part): SI 2003/2279 Reg.3

Sch.1 Part III para.18, amended: SI 2003/511 Reg.3

Sch.1 Part III para.19, amended: SI 2003/511 Reg.3

Sch.1 Part IV, amended: SI 2002/668 Sch.11, SI 2003/455 Sch.2 para.20, SI 2003/511 Reg.3

Sch.1 Part IV, substituted: SI 2003/526 Sch.11, SI 2004/552 Sch.15

Sch.1 Part IVA para.20A, amended: SI 2003/511 Reg.3

Sch.1 Part IVA para.20B, amended: SI 2003/511 Reg.3

Sch.1 Part IVA para.20C, amended: SI 2003/511 Reg.3

Sch.1 Part IVA para.20D, amended: SI 2003/511 Reg.3

Sch.1 Part IVA para.20E, amended: SI 2003/511 Reg.3

Sch.1 Part IVA para.20F, amended: SI 2003/511 Reg.3

Sch.1 Part IVA para.20G, amended: SI 2003/511 Reg.3

Sch.1 Part IVA para.20H, amended: SI 2003/455 Sch.2 para.20, SI 2003/511 Reg.3

Sch.1 Part IVA para.20H, applied: SSI 2003/176 Art.4

Sch.1 Part IVA para.20I, amended: SI 2002/490 Reg.2, SI 2003/511 Reg.3

Sch.1 Part IVA para.20IA, amended: SI 2003/511 Reg.3, SI 2003/1195 Reg.6

Sch.1 Part IVA para.20J, amended: SI 2002/2020 Reg.3, SI 2002/2380 Reg.3, SI 2003/511 Reg.3, SI 2003/2279 Reg.3

Sch.1 Part IVA para.20J, revoked (in part): SI 2003/2279 Reg.3

Sch.1 Part IVA para.20K, amended: SI 2003/511 Reg.3

Sch.1 Part IVA para.20L, amended: SI 2003/511 Reg.3

Sch.1 Part IVB para.20M, amended: SI 2002/668 Sch.12, SI 2003/511 Reg.3

Sch.1 Part IVB para.20M, substituted: SI 2003/526 Sch.12, SI 2004/552 Sch.16

Sch.2, applied: SI 2002/1792 Sch.2 para.7

Sch.2 para.1, amended: SI 2004/2825 Reg.2

Sch.2 para.3, amended: SI 2004/2327 Reg.6

Sch.2 para.5, referred to: SI 2003/526 Sch.15, SI 2004/552 Sch.19

1996–cont.

207. Jobseeker's Allowance Regulations 1996–*cont.*

Sch.2 para.6, amended: SI 2002/3019 Reg.30

Sch.2 para.6, referred to: SI 2003/526 Sch.15, SI 2004/552 Sch.19

Sch.2 para.7, referred to: SI 2003/526 Sch.15, SI 2004/552 Sch.19

Sch.2 para.9, amended: SI 2004/2825 Reg.2

Sch.2 para.9, referred to: SI 2003/526 Sch.15, SI 2004/552 Sch.19

Sch.2 para.10, referred to: SI 2003/526 Sch.15, SI 2004/552 Sch.19

Sch.2 para.11, amended: SI 2004/2825 Reg.2

Sch.2 para.11, referred to: SI 2003/526 Sch.15, SI 2004/552 Sch.19

Sch.2 para.13, amended: SI 2002/841 Reg.6, SI 2002/3019 Reg.30

Sch.2 para.14, applied: SI 2002/1792 Sch.2 para.7

Sch.2 para.15, applied: SI 2002/1792 Sch.2 para.7

Sch.2 para.17, amended: SI 2002/668 Art.22, SI 2002/3019 Reg.30, SI 2003/526 Art.23, SI 2003/1195 Reg.6, SI 2004/552 Art.24, SI 2004/2327 Reg.6

Sch.2 para.17, applied: SI 2003/526 Art.23, SI 2004/552 Art.24

Sch.2 para.18, applied: SI 2002/1792 Sch.1 para.6

Sch.3, revoked: SI 2003/1121 Sch.2 para.10

Sch.5, amended: SI 2002/668 Sch.13 Part I, SI 2003/455 Sch.2 para.21, SI 2003/1121 Sch.2 para.11, SI 2003/1195 Reg.6

Sch.5, applied: SI 2003/526 Sch.13 Part II

Sch.5, referred to: SI 2002/1792 Sch.1 para.6, SI 2004/552 Sch.17 Part II, Sch.18 Part II

Sch.5, substituted: SI 2003/526 Sch.13 Part I, SI 2004/552 Sch.17 Part I

Sch.5A, amended: SI 2002/668 Sch.14, SI 2003/1121 Sch.2 para.12, SI 2004/552 Sch.18 Part I

Sch.5A, revoked: SI 2004/565 Reg.6

Sch.5A, substituted: SI 2003/526 Sch.14

Sch.6 para.1, amended: SI 2003/511 Reg.3

Sch.6 para.2, amended: SI 2003/511 Reg.3

Sch.6 para.3, amended: SI 2003/511 Reg.3

Sch.6 para.4, amended: SI 2003/511 Reg.3

Sch.6 para.5, amended: SI 2003/511 Reg.3

Sch.6 para.6, amended: SI 2003/511 Reg.3

Sch.6 para.7, amended: SI 2003/511 Reg.3

Sch.6 para.8, amended: SI 2003/511 Reg.3

Sch.6 para.9, amended: SI 2003/511 Reg.3

Sch.6 para.10, amended: SI 2003/511 Reg.3

Sch.6 para.11, amended: SI 2003/511 Reg.3

Sch.6 para.12, amended: SI 2003/511 Reg.3

Sch.6 para.13, amended: SI 2003/511 Reg.3

Sch.6 para.14, amended: SI 2003/511 Reg.3

Sch.6 para.15, amended: SI 2003/511 Reg.3

Sch.6 para.16, amended: SI 2003/511 Reg.3

1996–cont.

207. Jobseeker's Allowance Regulations 1996–*cont.*

Sch.6 para.17, amended: SI 2003/455 Sch.2 para.22, SI 2003/511 Reg.3

Sch.6 para.18, amended: SI 2003/511 Reg.3

Sch.6 para.18, revoked: SI 2003/455 Sch.2 para.22

Sch.6 para.19, amended: SI 2003/511 Reg.3

Sch.6 para.20, amended: SI 2003/511 Reg.3

Sch.6 para.21, amended: SI 2003/511 Reg.3

Sch.6A para.1, amended: SI 2003/511 Reg.3

Sch.6A para.2, amended: SI 2003/511 Reg.3

Sch.6A para.3, amended: SI 2003/511 Reg.3

Sch.6A para.4, amended: SI 2003/511 Reg.3

Sch.6A para.5, amended: SI 2003/511 Reg.3

Sch.6A para.6, amended: SI 2003/511 Reg.3

Sch.6A para.7, amended: SI 2003/511 Reg.3

Sch.7 para.4, amended: SI 2002/2689 Reg.3

Sch.7 para.5, amended: SI 2002/2689 Reg.3

Sch.7 para.6A, added: SI 2002/2402 Sch.2 para.5, SI 2003/455 Sch.2 para.23

Sch.7 para.6B, added: SI 2003/455 Sch.2 para.23

Sch.7 para.12, substituted: SI 2004/1708 Reg.6

Sch.7 para.12A, added: SI 2002/2380 Reg.3

Sch.7 para.14, substituted: SI 2004/565 Reg.5

Sch.7 para.15, amended: SI 2002/2442 Reg.3, SI 2004/2308 Reg.2

Sch.7 para.17, amended: SI 2002/841 Reg.3

Sch.7 para.20, amended: SI 2002/668 Art.22, SI 2003/526 Art.23, SI 2004/552 Art.24

Sch.7 para.26, amended: SI 2003/455 Sch.2 para.23, SI 2003/2279 Reg.3, SI 2004/2308 Reg.4

Sch.7 para.26, revoked (in part): SI 2003/455 Sch.2 para.23

Sch.7 para.26A, added: SI 2003/455 Sch.2 para.23

Sch.7 para.27, amended: SI 2004/1141 Reg.4

Sch.7 para.29, amended: SI 2004/1141 Reg.4

Sch.7 para.41, amended: SI 2004/2308 Reg.3

Sch.7 para.50, amended: SI 2004/565 Reg.5

Sch.7 para.53, amended: SI 2002/841 Reg.3

Sch.7 para.54, amended: SI 2002/841 Reg.3

Sch.7 para.55, amended: SI 2002/841 Reg.3

Sch.7 para.56, amended: SI 2003/762 Reg.11, SI 2004/1748 Sch.2 para.2

Sch.7 para.57, revoked: SI 2004/565 Reg.5

Sch.7 para.58, revoked: SI 2004/565 Reg.5

Sch.7 para.60, revoked: SI 2004/565 Reg.5

Sch.7 para.60A, added: SI 2002/2314 Reg.2

Sch.7 para.60A, revoked: SI 2004/565 Reg.5

Sch.7 para.61, revoked: SI 2004/565 Reg.5

Sch.7 para.63, revoked: SI 2004/565 Reg.5

Sch.7 para.70, substituted: SI 2004/98 Reg.3

Sch.7 para.72, added: SI 2003/511 Reg.3

1996–cont.

207. Jobseeker's Allowance Regulations 1996–*cont.*

Sch.7 para.72, amended: SI 2003/2279 Reg.3

Sch.7 para.73, added: SI 2003/2279 Reg.3

Sch.7 para.73, revoked: SI 2004/565 Reg.5

Sch.7 para.74, added: SI 2003/2439 Reg.16

Sch.7 para.74, revoked: SI 2004/565 Reg.5

Sch.8 para.1, see *Secretary of State for Work and Pensions v Miah* [2003] EWCA Civ 1111, [2003] 4 All E.R. 702 (CA), Ward, L.J.

Sch.8 para.5, amended: SI 2003/511 Reg.3

Sch.8 para.12, amended: SI 2002/2380 Reg.3, SI 2003/455 Sch.2 para.24

Sch.8 para.12, applied: SI 2002/1792 Sch.5 para.20A

Sch.8 para.22, amended: SI 2004/1141 Reg.3

Sch.8 para.25, amended: SI 2003/455 Sch.2 para.24

Sch.8 para.27, amended: SI 2004/1141 Reg.3

Sch.8 para.32, substituted: SI 2004/565 Reg.5

Sch.8 para.40, amended: SI 2004/565 Reg.5

Sch.8 para.42, amended: SI 2003/2279 Reg.3

Sch.8 para.43, amended: SI 2003/2279 Reg.3

Sch.8 para.45, revoked: SI 2004/565 Reg.5

Sch.8 para.45A, added: SI 2002/2314 Reg.2

Sch.8 para.45A, revoked: SI 2004/565 Reg.5

Sch.8 para.46, revoked: SI 2004/565 Reg.5

Sch.8 para.48, revoked: SI 2004/565 Reg.5

Sch.8 para.52, substituted: SI 2004/1708 Reg.6

Sch.8 para.59, added: SI 2003/511 Reg.3

Sch.8 para.59, amended: SI 2003/2279 Reg.3

Sch.8 para.60, added: SI 2003/2279 Reg.3

Sch.8 para.61, added: SI 2003/2279 Reg.3

Sch.8 para.61A, added: SI 2003/2279 Reg.3, SI 2004/2308 Reg.4

Sch.8 para.62, added: SI 2003/2279 Reg.3

Sch.8 para.62, revoked: SI 2004/565 Reg.5

Sch.8 para.63, added: SI 2003/2439 Reg.16

Sch.8 para.63, revoked: SI 2004/565 Reg.5

221. Police (Promotion) (Scotland) Regulations 1996

applied: SSI 2004/257 Reg.9

Reg.1, amended: SSI 2004/257 Reg.49

251. National Health Service (Clinical Negligence Scheme) Regulations 1996

Reg.1, amended: SI 2002/1073 Reg.2, SI 2002/2469 Sch.1 para.68

Reg.3, amended: SI 2002/1073 Reg.3, SI 2002/2469 Sch.1 para.68, SI 2004/696 Sch.1 para.20

Reg.4, substituted: SI 2002/1073 Reg.4

1996–cont.

255. Bridgend and District National Health Service Trust (Dissolution) Order 1996

revoked: 2003 c.43 s.7

256. Glan Hafren National Health Service Trust (Dissolution) Order 1996

revoked: 2003 c.43 s.7

257. Bridgend and District National Health Service Trust (Establishment) Order 1996

revoked: 2003 c.43 s.7

258. Glan Hafren National Health Service Trust (Establishment) Order 1996

revoked: 2003 c.43 s.7

259. North Glamorgan National Health Service Trust (Establishment) Order 1996

revoked: 2003 c.43 s.7

263. Charter Trustees Regulations 1996

Reg.14, revoked: SI 2004/533 Art.7

266. European Communities (Designation) Order 1996

Sch.1, amended: SI 2002/2840 Sch.3

274. Education (Northern Ireland) Order 1996

applied: SR 2002/224 Reg.17, SR 2002/265 Sch.6 para.14

Art.22, amended: 2002 c.26 Sch.3 para.37

Art.22, revoked (in part): 2002 c.26 Sch.13

Art.32, revoked: SI 2003/424 Sch.3 Part I

275. Gas (Northern Ireland) Order 1996

applied: 2002 c.40 Sch.15, SI 2003/419 Art.17, Art.18, Art.22, Art.38, Art.63

disapplied: SI 2003/419 Sch.2 para.5

referred to: SR 2002/291 Reg.3, Reg.12, 2003 c.21 Sch.17 para.140

Part II, applied: 2002 c.1 (NI) s.6, SI 2003/419 Art.2, Art.14, Art.31, Art.32, Art.63, Art.66, Sch.4 para.15, SR 2002/291 Reg.11, SR 2003/143 Sch.1

Art.2, amended: SI 2003/419 Sch.5

Art.2, referred to: SI 2003/419 Art.2

Art.3, amended: SR 2002/291 Reg.4

Art.3, referred to: SI 2003/419 Art.2

Art.4, revoked: SI 2003/419 Sch.5

Art.5, applied: SR 2002/291 Reg.11

Art.5, revoked: SI 2003/419 Sch.5

Art.6, amended: SI 2003/419 Art.30

Art.6, applied: SI 2003/419 Art.40

Art.8, amended: SI 2003/419 Art.30, Sch.3 para.21, Sch.5

Art.8, applied: SI 2003/419 Art.20, Art.31, Art.32, Sch.4 para.9, Sch.4 para.15, SR 2002/291 Reg.10

Art.8A, added: SI 2003/419 Art.30

Art.9, amended: SI 2003/419 Sch.3 para.22, SR 2002/291 Reg.5

Art.9, applied: SR 2002/291 Reg.10

Art.9A, added: SR 2002/291 Reg.6

Art.9A, applied: SR 2002/291 Reg.10

1996–cont.

275. Gas (Northern Ireland) Order 1996– *cont.*

Art.10, amended: SI 2003/419 Art.34, Sch.3 para.23

Art.10, applied: SI 2003/419 Art.62

Art.10A, added: SR 2002/291 Reg.7

Art.10A, amended: SI 2003/419 Sch.3 para.24, Sch.5

Art.10A, applied: SR 2002/291 Reg.10

Art.11, amended: SI 2003/419 Art.32, Art.35, Sch.3 para.25

Art.11, applied: SI 2003/419 Art.32

Art.12, amended: SI 2003/419 Sch.3 para.26

Art.14, amended: SI 2003/419 Sch.3 para.27

Art.14, applied: SR 2002/291 Reg.10

Art.15, amended: SI 2003/419 Sch.3 para.28

Art.15B, enabled: SI 2003/1371

Art.15B, referred to: SI 2003/1371

Art.16, amended: SI 2003/419 Sch.3 para.29

Art.17, amended: SI 2003/419 Art.37, Sch.3 para.30

Art.17A, added: SI 2003/419 Art.37

Art.18, amended: 2002 c.40 Sch.9 para.13, SI 2003/419 Sch.3 para.31

Art.18, revoked (in part): 2002 c.40 Sch.9 para.13

Art.18, varied: SI 2003/1592 Sch.4 para.14

Art.18A, added: SR 2002/291 Reg.8

Art.18A, applied: SR 2002/291 Reg.10

Art.18A, revoked: SI 2003/419 Sch.5

Art.19, revoked: SI 2003/419 Sch.5

Art.20, applied: SI 2003/419 Sch.4 para.12

Art.20, revoked: SI 2003/419 Sch.5

Art.21, revoked: SI 2003/419 Sch.5

Art.23, amended: 2002 c.40 Sch.9 para.22

Art.23, applied: SI 2003/419 Art.15

Art.23, revoked (in part): 2002 c.40 Sch.9 para.22

Art.25, applied: SI 2003/419 Sch.4 para.6

Art.25, revoked: SI 2003/419 Sch.5

Art.26, applied: SI 2003/419 Sch.4 para.6

Art.26, revoked: SI 2003/419 Sch.5

Art.27, amended: SI 2003/419 Sch.3 para.32

Art.27, applied: SI 2003/419 Art.6

Art.27, revoked (in part): SI 2003/419 Sch.5

Art.28, revoked: SI 2003/419 Sch.5

Art.29, amended: SI 2003/419 Sch.3 para.33

Art.29, applied: SI 2003/419 Art.62

Art.30, amended: SI 2003/419 Sch.3 para.34, Sch.5

Art.30, applied: SI 2003/419 Art.63, Sch.4 para.12

Art.30, revoked (in part): SI 2003/419 Sch.5

Art.31, revoked: SI 2003/419 Sch.5

Art.32, revoked: SI 2003/419 Sch.5

Art.33, revoked: SI 2003/419 Sch.5

Art.34, revoked (in part): SI 2003/419 Sch.5

Art.36, amended: SI 2003/419 Sch.3 para.35

Art.38A, added: SR 2002/291 Reg.9

Art.40, applied: SI 2003/419 Art.15

1996–cont.

275. Gas (Northern Ireland) Order 1996– *cont.*

Art.44, amended: 2003 c.21 Sch.17 para.141, SI 2003/1400 Sch.6

Art.44, revoked: SI 2003/419 Sch.5

Art.45, amended: SI 2003/419 Sch.3 para.36

Art.45, applied: SI 2003/419 Art.63

Art.46, amended: SI 2003/419 Sch.3 para.37

Art.48, amended: SI 2003/419 Sch.3 para.38

Sch.1, revoked: SI 2003/419 Sch.5

Sch.3, amended: 2003 c.21 Sch.17 para.142, Sch.19

Sch.4, added: SI 2003/419 Art.64

Sch.5, substituted: SI 2003/419 Sch.3 para.39

Sch.6, revoked: SI 2003/419 Sch.5

279. Extradition (Designated Commonwealth Countries) Order 1991 (Amendment) Order 1996

revoked: SI 2003/1870 Art.3

280. Merchant Shipping (Categorisation of Registries of Overseas Territories) (Gibraltar) Order 1996

revoked: SI 2003/1248 Art.1

282. Merchant Shipping (Prevention of Pollution) (Law of the Sea Convention) Order 1996

enabled: SI 2004/303

Art.2, enabled: SI 2004/303, SI 2004/930

293. Fossil Fuel Levy (Scotland) Regulations 1996

Sch.3 Part II para.3, amended: SSI 2002/94 Reg.2

294. Mental Health (After-care under Supervision) Regulations 1996

Reg.2, amended: SI 2002/2469 Sch.5

Sch.2, amended: SI 2002/2469 Sch.5

300. Children (Allocation of Proceedings) Order (Northern Ireland) 1996

Art.10, see *B and N (Children) (Allocation of Proceedings), Re* [2002] N.I. 197 (Fam Div (NI)), Gillen, J.

325. Water Services Charges (Billing and Collection) (Scotland) Order 1996

revoked: 2002 asp 3 Sch.7 para.23

326. Domestic Sewerage Charges (Reduction) (Scotland) Regulations 1996

revoked: 2002 asp 3 Sch.7 para.23

341. Health and Safety (Safety Signs and Signals) Regulations 1996

referred to: SI 2002/2676 Sch.2, SI 2002/2677 Sch.7, SI 2002/2776 Sch.5

Reg.2, amended: SI 2004/568 Sch.13 para.9

345. Deregulation (Fair Trading Act 1973) (Amendment) (Merger Reference Time Limits) Order 1996

revoked: 2002 c.40 Sch.26

377. Bath and North East Somerset District Council (Staff Transfer) Order 1996

varied: SI 2004/222 Art.2

NO.

1996–cont.

378. **East Riding of Yorkshire District Council (Staff Transfer) Order 1996**
varied: SI 2004/222 Art.2

384. **North Lincolnshire District Council (Staff Transfer) Order 1996**
varied: SI 2004/222 Art.2

386. **North East Lincolnshire District Council (Staff Transfer) Order 1996**
varied: SI 2004/222 Art.2

387. **South Gloucestershire District Council (Staff Transfer) Order 1996**
varied: SI 2004/222 Art.2

388. **North Yorkshire (District of York) (Staff Transfer) Order 1996**
varied: SI 2004/222 Art.2

397. **Humberside (Staff Transfer) Order 1996**
varied: SI 2004/222 Art.2

398. **Cleveland (Staff Transfer) Order 1996**
varied: SI 2004/222 Art.2

400. **Avon (Staff Transfer) Order 1996**
varied: SI 2004/222 Art.2

401. **University College London Hospitals National Health Service Trust (Establishment) Order 1996**
revoked: 2003 c.43 s.7

408. **North Lincolnshire &amp East Riding of Yorkshire District Councils (Staff Transfer) Order 1996**
varied: SI 2004/222 Art.2

410. **National Health Service (Travelling Expenses and Remission of Charges) Amendment Regulations 1996**
revoked: SI 2003/2382 Sch.2

425. **Social Security (Industrial Injuries and Diseases) (Miscellaneous Amendments) Regulations 1996**
Reg.3, revoked (in part): SI 2003/492 Sch.3 Part 1

429. **National Health Service (Travelling Expenses and Remission of Charges) (Scotland) Amendment Regulations 1996**
revoked: SSI 2003/376 Sch.3 para.10

439. **Gas (Calculation of Thermal Energy) Regulations 1996**
Reg.14, amended: SI 2002/3130 Reg.2

444. **British Nationality (Fees) Regulations 1996**
revoked: SI 2003/3157 Reg.2
Reg.2, amended: 2002 c.8 s.2

446. **Local Government Changes for England (Miscellaneous Provision) Order 1996**
varied: SI 2004/222 Art.2

469. **Local Authorities (Members Allowances) (Amendment) Regulations 1996**
revoked (in part): SI 2003/1021 Reg.33

NO.

1996–cont.

472. **National Health Service (Dental Charges) (Scotland) Amendment Regulations 1996**
revoked: SSI 2003/158 Sch.4

481. **Child Support (Maintenance Assessments and Special Cases) and Social Security (Claims and Payments) Amendment Regulations 1996**
Reg.1, amended: SI 2003/492 Sch.3 Part 1
Reg.5, revoked (in part): SI 2003/492 Sch.3 Part 1
Reg.6, revoked (in part): SI 2003/492 Sch.3 Part 1

489. **Ashworth, Broadmoor and Rampton Hospital Authorities (Functions and Membership) Regulations 1996**
revoked: SI 2002/559 Art.2

494. **Cardiff (St Mellons Community) Order 1996**
varied: SI 2004/218 Art.2

506. **Environmental Protection (Controls on Substances that Deplete the Ozone Layer) Regulations 1996**
revoked: SI 2002/528 Reg.14

507. **Leicestershire (City of Leicester and District of Rutland) (Structural Change) Order 1996**
varied: SI 2004/222 Art.2

513. **Act of Adjournal (Criminal Procedure Rules) 1996**
see *Higson v Clark* 2003 S.L.T. 253 (HCJ), Lord Marnoch, Lady Cosgrove, Lord Hamilton
r.40.5, see *HM Advocate v Bain (David)* 2002 S.L.T. 340 (HCJ Appeal), Lord Reed
Sch.2 Appendix, amended: SSI 2002/137 r.2, SSI 2002/387 Sch.1, SSI 2002/454 r.2, Sch.1, Sch.2, Sch.3, SSI 2002/517 Sch.1, SSI 2003/387 Sch.1, SSI 2003/468 r.2, Sch.1, Sch.2, Sch.3, SSI 2004/195 r.2, Sch.1, Sch.2, SSI 2004/206 Sch.1, Sch.2, SSI 2004/346 r.2, Sch.1, SSI 2004/434 r.2, Sch.1 Part 1, Sch.1 Part 2, Sch.1 Part 3, SSI 2004/481 r.2, Sch.1 Part 1, Sch.1 Part 2
Sch.2 Appendix, referred to: SSI 2003/387 Art.3
Sch.2 Part I para.2a, amended: SSI 2003/468 r.2
Sch.2 Part I para.2b, amended: SSI 2004/434 r.2
Sch.2 Part I para.2b, revoked (in part): SSI 2003/468 r.2
Sch.2 Part I para.2ba, added: SSI 2004/434 r.2
Sch.2 Part I para.2d, amended: SSI 2004/434 r.2
Sch.2 Part I para.2e, amended: SSI 2003/468 r.2
Sch.2 Part I para.3, amended: SSI 2003/468 r.2
Sch.2 Part III, added: SSI 2004/434 r.2

1996–cont.

513. Act of Adjournal (Criminal Procedure Rules) 1996–cont.

Sch.2 Part III para.8a, amended: SSI 2002/454 r.2, SSI 2003/468 r.2

Sch.2 Part III para.8Aa, amended: SSI 2004/481 r.2

Sch.2 Part III para.9a, substituted: SSI 2003/468 r.2

Sch.2 Part III para.9ca, added: SSI 2002/454 r.2

Sch.2 Part III para.9cb, added: SSI 2002/454 r.2

Sch.2 Part III para.9d, amended: SSI 2002/454 r.2

Sch.2 Part III para.9e, amended: SSI 2002/454 r.2

Sch.2 Part III para.9g, amended: SSI 2002/454 r.2

Sch.2 Part III para.9ja, added: SSI 2002/454 r.2

Sch.2 Part III para.9jb, added: SSI 2002/454 r.2

Sch.2 Part III para.9jc, added: SSI 2002/454 r.2

Sch.2 Part III para.13A, amended: SSI 2004/481 r.2

Sch.2 Part III para.15, amended: SSI 2003/387 Art.3

Sch.2 Part III para.15a, amended: SSI 2002/387 Art.3

Sch.2 Part III para.15a, revoked (in part): SSI 2002/387 Art.3

Sch.2 Part III para.15da, added: SSI 2002/387 Art.3

Sch.2 Part III para.15o, added: SSI 2002/387 Art.3

Sch.2 Part III para.15p, added: SSI 2003/387 Art.3

Sch.2 Part IV, added: SSI 2003/468 r.2

Sch.2 Part IV para.16, amended: SSI 2002/454 r.2, SSI 2003/468 r.2

Sch.2 Part IV para.19B, amended: SSI 2004/346 r.2

Sch.2 Part IV para.19I, amended: SSI 2004/346 r.2

Sch.2 Part IV para.19n, amended: SSI 2003/387 Art.3

Sch.2 Part IV para.19s, added: SSI 2003/387 Art.3

Sch.2 Part IV para.19s, substituted: SSI 2003/468 r.2

Sch.2 Part V para.20b, substituted: SSI 2003/468 r.2

Sch.2 Part V para.20ba, substituted: SSI 2004/206 r.2

Sch.2 Part V para.20j, amended: SSI 2003/468 r.2

Sch.2 Part V para.20k, substituted: SSI 2003/468 r.2

Sch.2 Part V para.20lb, substituted: SSI 2003/468 r.2

1996–cont.

513. Act of Adjournal (Criminal Procedure Rules) 1996–cont.

Sch.2 Part V para.20t, added: SSI 2004/481 r.2

Sch.2 Part VI, added: SSI 2004/195 r.2

Sch.2 Part VI para.21d, added: SSI 2002/454 r.2

Sch.2 Part VI para.23, revoked (in part): SSI 2004/195 r.2

Sch.2 Part VII, revoked: SSI 2004/346 r.2

Sch.2 Part VII, substituted: SSI 2004/346 r.2

Sch.2 Part VII, substituted: SSI 2004/195 r.2

Sch.2 Part VII, added: SSI 2003/120 r.2

Sch.2 Part VII, added: SSI 2003/468 r.2

Sch.2 Part VII, added: SSI 2004/206 r.2

Sch.2 Part VII, added: SSI 2004/481 r.2

Sch.2 Part VII para.31, applied: SSI 2003/179 Reg.6

Sch.2 Part VII para.33b, amended: SSI 2002/454 r.2

Sch.2 Part VII para.33e, added: SSI 2002/454 r.2

Sch.2 Part VII para.34, amended: SSI 2002/517 r.2

Sch.2 Part VII para.34e, added: SSI 2002/517 r.2

Sch.2 Part VII para.37AA.9, amended: SSI 2003/468 r.2

Sch.2 Part VII para.42, amended: SSI 2002/137 r.2

Sch.2 Part VII para.42b, amended: SSI 2002/137 r.2

Sch.2 Part VII para.42c, amended: SSI 2002/137 r.2

Sch.2 Part VII para.43a, revoked (in part): SSI 2002/136 r.2

519. Lands Tribunal for Scotland (Amendment) (Fees) Rules 1996

Sch.1, amended: SSI 2003/452 Sch.3

Sch.1, referred to: SSI 2003/452 r.29

539. Royal Liverpool Children's Hospital and Community Services National Health Service Trust (Change of Name) Order 1996

revoked: 2003 c.43 s.7

551. Gas Safety (Management) Regulations 1996

applied: SI 2003/547 Reg.21, Sch.18, SI 2004/456 Reg.20, Sch.17

Reg.11, applied: SI 2003/547 Sch.18, SI 2004/456 Sch.17

590. Accounts and Audit Regulations 1996

revoked (in part): SI 2003/533 Reg.3

596. Misuse of Drugs (Licence Fees) (Amendment) Regulations 1996

revoked: SI 2003/611 Sch.1

597. Social Security (Contributions) (Re-rating and National Insurance Fund Payments) Order 1996

Art.5, revoked (in part): 2002 c.19 Sch.2

1996–cont.

600. Energy Information (Washing Machines) Regulations 1996
Sch.5 Part III para.15, revoked (in part): SI 2003/1398 Sch.1 para.26

601. Energy Information (Tumble Driers) Regulations 1996
Sch.5 Part III para.15, revoked (in part): SI 2003/1398 Sch.1 para.27

604. Public Airport Companies (Capital Finance) Order 1996
referred to: SI 2004/533 Art.10
revoked (in part): 2003 c.26 Sch.8 Part 1
Sch.1, amended: SI 2003/1035 Art.2

615. Education (Areas to which Pupils and Students Belong) Regulations 1996
Reg.8, referred to: SI 2002/1330 Reg.8, SI 2003/1994 Reg.8

623. National Health Service Contracts (Dispute Resolution) Regulations 1996
applied: SI 2004/865 Art.69
Reg.1A, added: SI 2004/865 Sch.1 para.14, SI 2004/1016 Sch.1 para.14

624. Health Authorities (England) Establishment Order 1996
revoked: SI 2002/553 Sch.3

640. Community Health Councils Regulations 1996
applied: SI 2003/2660 Art.2
revoked (in part): SI 2004/905 Reg.31
Reg.1, amended: SI 2002/2469 Sch.1 para.69
Reg.3, amended: SI 2002/2106 Reg.2
Reg.7, amended: SI 2002/2469 Sch.1 para.69
Reg.13, amended: SI 2002/2469 Sch.2
Reg.14, amended: SI 2002/2469 Sch.2
Reg.16, amended: SI 2002/2469 Sch.1 para.69, Sch.9
Reg.17, amended: SI 2002/2469 Sch.1 para.69
Reg.18, amended: SI 2002/2469 Sch.1 para.69, Sch.2, Sch.9
Reg.19, amended: SI 2002/2469 Sch.1 para.69, Sch.2
Reg.22, revoked: SI 2002/2106 Reg.2
Sch.1 para.6, substituted: SI 2002/2106 Reg.2

654. National Health Service (Functions of Health Authorities in London) Regulations 1996
revoked: SI 2002/2375 Sch.4

656. Avon (Coroners) Order 1996
varied: SI 2004/222 Art.2

657. Cleveland (Coroners) Order 1996
varied: SI 2004/222 Art.2

658. Humberside (Coroners) Order 1996
varied: SI 2004/222 Art.2

659. York and North Yorkshire (Coroners) Order 1996
varied: SI 2004/222 Art.2

1996–cont.

665. Nuclear Generating Stations (Security) Regulations 1996
applied: SI 2003/403 Reg.12
revoked: SI 2003/403 Reg.1

669. National Health Service (Functions of Health Authorities) (Complaints) Regulations 1996
Reg.1, amended: SI 2004/865 Sch.1 para.15, SI 2004/1016 Sch.1 para.15
Reg.2, amended: SI 2002/2469 Sch.5

672. Social Security (Claims and Payments Etc.) Amendment Regulations 1996
Reg.2, revoked (in part): SI 2003/492 Sch.3 Part 1
Reg.4, revoked (in part): SI 2003/492 Sch.3 Part 1

686. National Health Service (Existing Liabilities Scheme) Regulations 1996
Reg.3, amended: SI 2002/2469 Sch.1 para.70, SI 2004/696 Sch.1 para.21

696. Common Agricultural Policy (Wine) Regulations 1996
applied: SSI 2002/325 Reg.7
revoked (in part): SSI 2002/325 Reg.19

699. Police (Amendment) Regulations 1996
revoked: SI 2003/527 Sch.4 Part 1

701. National Health Service (Appointment of Consultants) Regulations 1996
Reg.2, amended: SI 2002/2469 Sch.1 para.71, SI 2004/696 Sch.1 para.22
Reg.4, amended: SI 2003/1250 Sch.10 para.3
Reg.5, amended: SI 2004/696 Art.3
Reg.5, revoked (in part): SI 2002/2469 Sch.1 para.71
Sch.1 para.2, amended: SI 2002/2469 Sch.1 para.71

702. National Health Service (General Medical Services) Amendment Regulations 1996
revoked (in part): SI 2004/865 Sch.2, SI 2004/1016 Sch.2

707. Health Authorities (Membership and Procedure) Regulations 1996
Reg.1, amended: SI 2002/556 Reg.2, SI 2002/2469 Sch.9, SI 2004/696 Art.3, Sch.1 para.23, SI 2004/865 Sch.1 para.16
Reg.1, revoked (in part): SI 2004/1016 Sch.1 para.16
Reg.2, amended: SI 2004/1771 Sch.1 para.41
Reg.2, substituted: SI 2002/556 Reg.3
Reg.8, amended: SI 2002/556 Reg.4
Reg.10, amended: SI 2004/696 Art.3, Sch.1 para.23, SI 2004/865 Sch.1 para.16, SI 2004/1016 Sch.1 para.16
Reg.14, amended: SI 2004/865 Sch.1 para.16, SI 2004/1016 Sch.1 para.16

NO.

1996–cont.

707. Health Authorities (Membership and Procedure) Regulations 1996–cont.

Reg.16, amended: SI 2004/865 Sch.1 para.16, SI 2004/1016 Sch.1 para.16

Sch.1, revoked (in part): SI 2002/556 Reg.6

Sch.2, amended: SI 2004/17 Reg.2

Sch.5 para.10, revoked: SI 2003/506 Sch.2

708. National Health Service (Functions of Health Authorities and Administration Arrangements) Regulations 1996

Sch.1, amended: SI 2002/920 Art.4

714. Trade Marks (International Registration) Order 1996

Art.2, amended: SI 2002/692 Art.3

Art.3, amended: SI 2004/948 Art.3

Art.4, amended: SI 2002/692 Art.4

Art.6, amended: SI 2002/692 Art.5

Art.6, applied: SI 2002/692 Art.12

Art.9, amended: SI 2002/692 Art.6

Art.9, applied: SI 2002/692 Art.13

Art.9A, added: SI 2004/948 Art.4

Art.10, amended: SI 2002/692 Art.7

Art.10, applied: SI 2002/692 Art.13, SI 2004/948 Art.8

Art.10, substituted: SI 2004/948 Art.5

Art.10C, referred to: SI 2004/948 Art.8

Art.11, amended: SI 2004/948 Art.6

Art.11, applied: SI 2002/692 Art.13

Art.11, substituted: SI 2002/692 Art.8

Art.12, amended: SI 2002/692 Art.9

Art.12A, added: SI 2002/692 Art.10

Art.13, amended: SI 2004/948 Art.7

Art.22, amended: 2002 c.8 s.2

Art.24, amended: SI 2002/692 Art.11

725. Business Tenancies (Northern Ireland) Order 1996

applied: 2003 c.14 Sch.17A para.9

Art.23, varied: SR 2003/73 Sch.1

Art.26, see *Fujitsu Telecommunications Europe Ltd v Brunswick (9 Lanyon Place) Ltd* BT/90/2002 (Lands Tr (NI)), Michael R Curry FRICS

729. Trade Marks Act 1994 (Isle of Man) Order 1996

Sch.1 para.1A, added: SI 2004/1497 Sch.1 para.1

Sch.1 para.1B, added: SI 2004/1497 Sch.1 para.1

Sch.1 para.1C, added: SI 2004/1497 Sch.1 para.1

Sch.1 para.4A, added: SI 2004/1497 Sch.1 para.2

Sch.1 para.4B, added: SI 2004/1497 Sch.1 para.2

Sch.1 para.10, amended: SI 2004/1497 Sch.1 para.3

Sch.1 para.11A, added: SI 2002/3148 Art.2

NO.

1996–cont.

736. Richmond Adult and Community College (Government) Regulations 1996

revoked: SI 2002/1094 Sch.1 Part 1

741. Housing (Valuation Bands for Improvement and Repairs Grants) (Scotland) Order 1996

revoked: SSI 2003/314 Art.3

744. Water and Sewerage Authorities (Rate of Return) (Scotland) Order 1996

revoked: 2002 asp 3 Sch.7 para.23

772. Adventure Activities Licensing Regulations 1996

revoked: SI 2004/1309 Reg.20

Sch.1, applied: SI 2004/1309 Reg.19

787. Humberside (Coroners) (Amendment) Order 1996

varied: SI 2004/222 Art.2

804. Income Tax (Employments) (Amendment) Regulations 1996

revoked: SI 2003/2682 Sch.2

825. Pipelines Safety Regulations 1996

Reg.13A, added: SI 2003/2563 Reg.2

842. National Health Service (General Medical Services) (Scotland) Amendment Regulations 1996

revoked: SSI 2004/114 Sch.2

871. Royal Free Hampstead National Health Service Trust (Amendment) Order 1996

revoked: 2003 c.43 s.7

872. Lincoln Hospitals National Health Service Trust (Change of Name) Order 1996

revoked: 2003 c.43 s.7

873. Hartlepool and East Durham National Health Service Trust (Establishment) Order 1996

revoked: 2003 c.43 s.7

874. Worcestershire Community Healthcare National Health Service Trust (Establishment) Order 1996

revoked: 2003 c.43 s.7

875. South Durham National Health Service Trust (Establishment) Order 1996

revoked: 2003 c.43 s.7

876. South West Durham Mental Health National Health Service Trust Dissolution Order 1996

revoked: 2003 c.43 s.7

877. Louth and District Healthcare National Health Service Trust Dissolution Order 1996

revoked: 2003 c.43 s.7

879. Hartlepool and Peterlee Hospitals National Health Service Trust Dissolution Order 1996

revoked: 2003 c.43 s.7

NO.

1996–cont.

880. South Durham Health Care National Health Service Trust Dissolution Order 1996
revoked: 2003 c.43 s.7

881. University College London Hospitals National Health Service Trust Dissolution Order 1996
revoked: 2003 c.43 s.7

882. Birmingham Heartlands Hospital National Health Service Trust Dissolution Order 1996
revoked: 2003 c.43 s.7

883. Birmingham Heartlands and Solihull (Teaching) National Health Service Trust (Establishment) Order 1996
revoked: 2003 c.43 s.7

884. South Worcestershire Community National Health Service Trust Dissolution Order 1996
revoked: 2003 c.43 s.7

885. North East Worcestershire Community Health Care National Health Service Trust Dissolution Order 1996
revoked: 2003 c.43 s.7

886. Royal National Throat, Nose and Ear Hospital National Health Service Trust Dissolution Order 1996
revoked: 2003 c.43 s.7

887. Hartlepool Community Care National Health Service Trust Dissolution Order 1996
revoked: 2003 c.43 s.7

888. Protection of Water Against Agricultural Nitrate Pollution (England and Wales) Regulations 1996
Reg.2, amended: SI 2002/2297 Sch.1 para.1
Reg.3, amended: SI 2002/2297 Sch.1 para.2, Sch.1 para.3, SI 2002/2614 Reg.9
Reg.3, applied: SI 2002/2614 Reg.9
Reg.3A, added: SI 2002/2297 Sch.1 para.4
Reg.3B, added: SI 2002/2297 Sch.1 para.4
Reg.3C, added: SI 2002/2297 Sch.1 para.4
Reg.3D, added: SI 2002/2297 Sch.1 para.4
Reg.4, applied: SI 2002/2614 Reg.9
Reg.6, amended: SI 2002/2297 Sch.1 para.5, Sch.1 para.6
Reg.6, applied: SI 2002/2614 Reg.9
Reg.7, amended: SI 2002/2614 Reg.9
Sch.1, amended: SI 2002/2297 Sch.1 para.7
Sch.1A, added: SI 2002/2297 Sch.1 para.8
Sch.1B, added: SI 2002/2297 Sch.1 para.8
Sch.2 para.1, amended: SI 2002/2297 Sch.1 para.9
Sch.2 para.2, amended: SI 2002/2297 Sch.1 para.9

897. Returning Officers (Parliamentary Constituencies) (Wales) Order 1996
Sch.1, substituted: SI 2004/1204 Art.2

NO.

1996–cont.

913. Offshore Installations and Wells (Design and Construction, etc.) Regulations 1996
Reg.2, varied: SI 2002/2175 Reg.3

972. Special Waste Regulations 1996
applied: SI 2002/1689 Reg.3
Reg.1, amended: SSI 2004/112 Reg.2
Reg.2, substituted: SSI 2004/112 Reg.2
Reg.2A, added: SSI 2004/112 Reg.2
Reg.2B, added: SSI 2004/112 Reg.2
Reg.3, amended: SSI 2004/112 Reg.2
Reg.4A, added: SSI 2004/112 Reg.2
Reg.5, amended: SSI 2004/112 Reg.2
Reg.15, amended: SSI 2004/112 Reg.2
Reg.15A, added: SSI 2004/112 Reg.2
Reg.17A, added: SSI 2004/112 Reg.2
Reg.19A, added: SSI 2004/112 Reg.2
Sch.1 Part I, amended: SSI 2004/112 Sch.1
Sch.2 Part I, amended: SSI 2004/112 Reg.2

980. Income Tax (Employments) (Amendment No 2) Regulations 1996
revoked: SI 2003/2682 Sch.2

982. Walton Centre for Neurology and Neurosurgery National Health Service Trust (Establishment) Amendment Order 1996
revoked: 2003 c.43 s.7

983. South Manchester University Hospitals National Health Service Trust (Establishment) Amendment Order 1996
revoked: 2003 c.43 s.7

984. North Durham Acute Hospitals National Health Service Trust (Establishment) Amendment Order 1996
revoked: 2003 c.43 s.7

985. West Middlesex University Hospital National Health Service Trust (Establishment) Amendment Order 1996
revoked: 2003 c.43 s.7

986. Gloucestershire Royal National Health Service Trust (Establishment) Amendment Order 1996
revoked: 2003 c.43 s.7

987. Swindon and Marlborough National Health Service Trust (Establishment) Amendment Order 1996
revoked: 2003 c.43 s.7

988. Hull and Holderness Community Health National Health Service Trust (Establishment) Amendment Order 1996
revoked: 2003 c.43 s.7

989. Bishop Auckland Hospitals National Health Service Trust (Establishment) Amendment Order 1996
revoked: 2003 c.43 s.7

990. Hereford Hospitals National Health Service Trust (Establishment) Amendment Order 1996
revoked: 2003 c.43 s.7

1996–cont.

991. Rochdale Healthcare National Health Service Trust (Establishment) Amendment Order 1996
revoked: 2003 c.43 s.7

992. Wellhouse National Health Service Trust (Establishment) Amendment Order 1996
revoked: 2003 c.43 s.7

993. Essex Rivers Healthcare National Health Service Trust (Establishment) Amendment Order 1996
revoked: 2003 c.43 s.7

994. Dartford and Gravesham National Health Service Trust (Establishment) Amendment Order 1996
revoked: 2003 c.43 s.7

996. St James's and Seacroft University Hospitals National Health Service Trust (Establishment) Amendment Order 1996
revoked: 2003 c.43 s.7

997. Thameside Community Health Care National Health Service Trust (Establishment) Amendment Order 1996
revoked: 2003 c.43 s.7

998. South Buckinghamshire National Health Service Trust (Establishment) Amendment Order 1996
revoked: 2003 c.43 s.7

999. South Devon Health Care National Health Service Trust (Establishment) Amendment Order 1996
revoked: 2003 c.43 s.7

1000. Bexley Community Health National Health Service Trust (Establishment) Amendment Order 1996
revoked: 2003 c.43 s.7

1001. Norfolk and Norwich Health Care National Health Service Trust (Establishment) Amendment Order 1996
revoked: 2003 c.43 s.7

1002. East Yorkshire Community Health-care National Health Service Trust (Establishment) Amendment Order 1996
revoked: 2003 c.43 s.7

1012. Civil Legal Aid (Financial Conditions) (Scotland) Regulations 1996
Reg.4, revoked: SSI 2002/330 Reg.5

1021. Lands Tribunal (Fees) Rules 1996
r.6, added: SI 2002/770 r.2
r.6, referred to: SI 2002/770 r.3
r.7, added: SI 2002/770 r.2

1022. Lands Tribunal Rules 1996
applied: SI 2002/221 Sch.2 para.10, Sch.4 para.12, SI 2002/1711 Reg.10, SI 2004/248 Reg.10
Part IIA r.5A, amended: SI 2003/2945 r.4
Part IIA r.5A, substituted: SI 2003/2945 r.3
Part IIA r.5B, amended: SI 2003/2945 r.6
Part IIA r.5B, substituted: SI 2003/2945 r.3

1996–cont.

1022. Lands Tribunal Rules 1996–cont.
Part IIA r.5C, amended: SI 2003/2945 r.6
Part IIA r.5C, substituted: SI 2003/2945 r.3
Part IIA r.5D, amended: SI 2003/2945 r.6
Part IIA r.5D, substituted: SI 2003/2945 r.3
Part IIA r.5E, amended: SI 2003/2945 r.6
Part IIA r.5E, substituted: SI 2003/2945 r.3
Part IIA r.5F, amended: SI 2003/2945 r.5
Part IIA r.5F, substituted: SI 2003/2945 r.3
Part IIA r.5G, amended: SI 2003/2945 r.6
Part IIA r.5G, substituted: SI 2003/2945 r.3
Part IIA r.5H, amended: SI 2003/2945 r.6
Part IIA r.5H, substituted: SI 2003/2945 r.3
Part III r.6, amended: SI 2003/2945 r.6
Part VIII r.28, amended: SI 2003/2945 r.7
Part VIII r.52, amended: SI 2003/2945 r.8
r.16, see *Girls Day School Trust (1872)'s Application, Re* [2002] 2 E.G.L.R. 89 (Lands Tr), PH Clarke FRICS
r.28, see *Henriques v Stephens (Valuation Officer)* [2003] R.V.R. 266 (Lands Tr), PR Francis FRICS
r.32, see *Aslam v South Bedfordshire DC (Rate of Interest)* [2001] EWCA Civ 515, [2002] R.V.R. 16 (CA), Chadwick, L.J.; see *Goldstein v Conley* [2001] EWCA Civ 637, [2002] 1 W.L.R. 281 (CA), Clarke, L.J.

1023. Employment Protection (Continuity of Employment of National Health Service Employees) (Modification) Order 1996
Art.1, amended: SI 2002/2469 Sch.1 para.72, SI 2004/696 Sch.1 para.24

1092. Chemicals (Hazard Information and Packaging for Supply) (Amendment) Regulations 1996
revoked: SI 2002/1689 Sch.7

1141. Juries (Northern Ireland) Order 1996
Sch.2, amended: 2002 c.26 Sch.4 para.38, Sch.12 para.53, Sch.13

1172. Occupational Pension Schemes (Contracting-out) Regulations 1996
Reg.3, amended: SI 2002/681 Reg.2
Reg.3, revoked (in part): SI 2002/681 Reg.2
Reg.6, revoked (in part): SI 2002/681 Reg.2
Reg.9, amended: SI 2002/681 Reg.2
Reg.16, amended: SI 2002/681 Reg.2
Reg.18, amended: SI 2002/681 Reg.2
Reg.19, substituted: SI 2002/681 Reg.2
Reg.20, substituted: SI 2002/681 Reg.2
Reg.20A, added: SI 2002/681 Reg.2
Reg.23, amended: SI 2002/681 Reg.2
Reg.31, amended: SI 2002/681 Reg.2
Reg.51, amended: SI 2002/681 Reg.2
Reg.52, amended: SI 2002/681 Reg.2
Reg.60, amended: SI 2002/681 Reg.2
Reg.61, amended: SI 2002/681 Reg.2
Reg.62, amended: SI 2002/681 Reg.2
Reg.63, amended: SI 2002/681 Reg.2
Reg.72, amended: SI 2002/681 Reg.2

1996–cont.

1211. Deregulation (Salmon Fisheries (Scotland) Act 1868) Order 1996
revoked: 2003 asp 15 Sch.4 Part 2

1215. Local Authorities (Members Interests) (Amendment) Regulations 1996
revoked (in part): SSI 2003/199 Sch.1

1216. Occupational Pension Schemes (Member-nominated Trustees and Directors) Regulations 1996
Reg.9, amended: SI 2002/2327 Reg.3
Reg.15, amended: SI 2002/2327 Reg.4
Reg.20, amended: SI 2002/2327 Reg.5
Sch.3 para.3, amended: SI 2002/2327 Reg.6

1251. Hydrocarbon Oil (Designated Markers) Regulations 1996
Reg.2, amended: SI 2002/1773 Reg.19

1267. Churnet Valley Light Railway Order 1996
Art.7, amended: SI 2003/2155 Sch.1 para.18

1295. International Oil Pollution Compensation Fund 1992 (Immunities and Privileges) Order 1996
Art.13, amended: 2002 c.8 s.2
Art.14, amended: 2002 c.8 s.2
Art.15, amended: 2002 c.8 s.2

1297. Commissioner for Complaints (Northern Ireland) Order 1996
applied: SR 2002/66 Reg.11
Art.4, enabled: SR 2002/320
Sch.2, amended: 2002 c.1 (NI) Sch.1 para.19, (NI) Sch.4, 2002 c.9 (NI) Sch.1 para.17, 2003 c.6 Sch.1 para.14, SI 2003/410 Art.5, Sch.1 para.21, SI 2003/412 Art.146, SI 2003/431 Sch.4, SI 2003/439 Sch.2 para.14

1298. Ombudsman (Northern Ireland) Order 1996
Art.5, enabled: SR 2002/320
Sch.2, amended: SI 2003/419 Sch.1 para.13, Sch.5

1299. Proceeds of Crime (Northern Ireland) Order 1996
applied: 2002 c.29 s.8, s.94, s.118, s.158
Part II, revoked: 2002 c.29 Sch.11 para.31, Sch.12
Part III, revoked: 2002 c.29 Sch.11 para.31, Sch.12
Art.2, amended: 2002 c.29 Sch.11 para.31, Sch.12
Art.2, revoked (in part): 2002 c.29 Sch.11 para.31, Sch.12
Art.3, revoked: 2002 c.29 Sch.11 para.31
Art.32, applied: 2002 c.29 s.41, s.49, s.51, s.53, s.79, s.120, s.125, s.128, s.145, s.190, s.197, s.199, s.201, s.227
Art.48, applied: SI 2003/120 Art.5
Art.48, referred to: SI 2003/120 Art.5
Art.49, amended: 2002 c.29 Sch.11 para.31, Sch.12
Art.49, applied: SI 2003/120 Art.6, SI 2003/335 Sch.1, SSI 2003/93 Sch.1

1996–cont.

1299. Proceeds of Crime (Northern Ireland) Order 1996–*cont.*
Art.49, revoked (in part): 2002 c.29 Sch.11 para.31, Sch.12
Art.50, amended: 2002 c.29 Sch.11 para.31
Art.50, applied: SI 2003/120 Art.6, SI 2003/335 Sch.1, SSI 2003/93 Sch.1
Art.51, amended: 2002 c.29 Sch.11 para.31
Art.51, applied: SI 2003/120 Art.6, SI 2003/335 Sch.1, SSI 2003/93 Sch.1
Art.52, amended: 2002 c.29 Sch.11 para.31
Art.52, applied: SI 2003/120 Art.6
Art.52, revoked (in part): 2002 c.29 Sch.11 para.31, Sch.12
Art.53, applied: SI 2003/120 Art.5
Art.54, amended: 2002 c.29 Sch.11 para.31, Sch.12
Art.54, applied: SI 2003/120 Art.6
Art.54, revoked (in part): 2002 c.29 Sch.11 para.31, Sch.12
Art.54A, added: 2002 c.29 Sch.11 para.31
Art.55, amended: 2002 c.29 Sch.11 para.31, Sch.12
Art.55, applied: SI 2003/120 Art.6
Art.55, revoked (in part): 2002 c.29 Sch.11 para.31, Sch.12
Art.56, amended: 2002 c.29 Sch.11 para.31, Sch.12
Art.56, applied: SI 2003/120 Art.6
Art.56, revoked (in part): 2002 c.29 Sch.11 para.31, Sch.12
Sch.2, amended: 2002 c.29 Sch.11 para.31, Sch.12
Sch.2, applied: SI 2003/120 Art.6, SI 2003/335 Sch.1, SSI 2003/93 Sch.1
Sch.2, enabled: SR 2003/141
Sch.2, revoked: 2002 c.29 Sch.11 para.31, Sch.12
Sch.3, revoked: 2002 c.29 Sch.12

1312. Income Tax (Employments) (Amendment No 3) Regulations 1996
revoked: SI 2003/2682 Sch.2

1313. National Health Service (Appointment of Consultants) (Wales) Regulations 1996
Reg.4, amended: SI 2003/1250 Sch.10 para.4

1320. Road Traffic Offenders (Northern Ireland) Order 1996
Art.2, amended: SI 2003/2903 Sch.1 para.12
Art.7, amended: SI 2003/2903 Sch.1 para.13
Art.28, amended: SI 2003/2903 Sch.1 para.14
Art.36, applied: 2003 c.32 s.55
Art.47, applied: 2003 c.32 s.55
Art.84, referred to: SI 2002/3153 Sch.2 para.5
Art.92A, applied: 2003 c.32 s.55
Sch.1, amended: SI 2003/2903 Sch.1 para.15, Sch.2
Sch.1, referred to: 2003 c.32 Sch.3 para.7

NO.

1996–cont.

1333. Disability Discrimination (Sub-leases and Sub-tenancies) Regulations 1996
revoked: SI 2004/153 Reg.3

1345. Social Security and Child Support (Jobseeker's Allowance) (Consequential Amendments) Regulations 1996
Reg.2, revoked: SI 2003/493 Sch.2 Part 1
Reg.23, revoked (in part): SI 2003/492 Sch.3 Part 1

1346. National Health Service (Travelling Expenses and Remission of Charges) Amendment (No.2) Regulations 1996
revoked: SI 2003/2382 Sch.2

1350. Radioactive Material (Road Transport) (Great Britain) Regulations 1996
referred to: SI 2002/2776 Sch.5
revoked: SI 2002/1093 Reg.8

1353. Recreational Craft Regulations 1996
referred to: SI 2004/693 Sch.1
revoked: SI 2004/1464 Reg.1
Sch.15, amended: SI 2004/693 Sch.2

1392. Aerodromes (Designation) (Facilities for Consultation) Order 1996
Sch.1, amended: SI 2002/2421 Art.2

1393. Rules of the Air Regulations 1996
Sch.1, amended: SI 2003/64 Reg.2

1419. Cromarty Firth Port Authority Harbour Revision Order 1996
applied: SSI 2003/491 Art.1
Art.3, revoked (in part): SSI 2003/491 Sch.3
Art.6, revoked: SSI 2003/491 Sch.3

1434. Welfare Food Regulations 1996
applied: SI 2003/731 Reg.3
see *R. (on the application of T) v Secretary of State for Health* [2002] EWHC 1887, (2003) 6 C.C.L. Rep. 277 (QBD (Admin Ct)), Sir Edwin Jowitt
Reg.2, amended: SI 2003/702 Reg.2, SI 2003/1864 Reg.2, SI 2004/696 Art.3
Reg.3, amended: SI 2003/702 Reg.3, SI 2003/1864 Reg.3, SI 2004/723 Reg.2, Reg.3
Reg.4, amended: SI 2003/702 Reg.4, SI 2003/1864 Reg.4, SI 2004/723 Reg.2
Reg.5, amended: SI 2003/702 Reg.5, SI 2003/1864 Reg.5, SI 2004/723 Reg.2, Reg.4
Reg.6, amended: SI 2003/702 Reg.6, SI 2003/1864 Reg.6, SI 2004/723 Reg.2
Reg.7, amended: SI 2002/550 Reg.2, SI 2003/702 Reg.7, SI 2004/723 Reg.2
Reg.8, amended: SI 2003/702 Reg.8, SI 2003/1864 Reg.7
Reg.12, amended: SI 2003/702 Reg.9
Reg.13, amended: SI 2003/702 Reg.10
Reg.15, amended: SI 2003/702 Reg.11
Sch.1, amended: SI 2003/702 Reg.12
Sch.2A para.1, added: SI 2004/723 Reg.5
Sch.2A para.2, added: SI 2004/723 Reg.5

NO.

1996–cont.

1434. Welfare Food Regulations 1996–*cont.*
Sch.2A para.3, added: SI 2004/723 Reg.5
Sch.4 Part I para.2, amended: SI 2004/723 Reg.2
Sch.6, amended: SI 2003/702 Reg.13, SI 2004/2311 Reg.2

1436. Social Security (Disability Living Allowance and Claims and Payments) Amendment Regulations 1996
Reg.3, revoked (in part): SI 2003/492 Sch.3 Part 1

1444. Companies (Fees) (Amendment) Regulations 1996
revoked: SI 2004/2621 Sch.3

1451. Oil and Fibre Plant Seeds (Amendment) Regulations 1996
revoked (in part): SI 2002/3174 Reg.32, SI 2004/2881 Reg.32, SSI 2004/317 Sch.8

1452. Vegetable Seeds (Amendment) Regulations 1996
revoked (in part): SI 2002/3175 Reg.32

1453. Fodder Plant Seeds (Amendment) Regulations 1996
revoked (in part): SI 2002/3172 Reg.32

1455. Disability Discrimination (Meaning of Disability) Regulations 1996
see *Murray v Newham Citizens Advice Bureau Ltd* [2003] I.C.R. 643 (EAT), Judge Serota Q.C.

1455. Meaning of Disability Regulations 1996
Reg.3, see *Power v Panasonic UK Ltd* [2003] I.R.L.R. 151 (EAT), Recorder Slade Q.C.

1456. Disability Discrimination (Employment) Regulations 1996
revoked: SI 2004/153 Reg.3

1460. Social Security (Claims and Payments) (Jobseeker's Allowance Consequential Amendments) Regulations 1996
revoked (in part): SI 2003/492 Sch.3 Part 1

1461. Protected Rights (Transfer Payment) Regulations 1996
Reg.4A, added: SI 2002/681 Reg.3
Reg.5, amended: SI 2002/681 Reg.3

1469. Financial Markets and Insolvency Regulations 1996
applied: 2002 c.29 s.282
Reg.6, amended: SI 2003/2096 Sch.1 para.62, SI 2004/2312 Art.3
Reg.7, amended: SI 2003/2096 Sch.1 para.63
Reg.8, amended: SI 2003/2096 Sch.1 para.64

1470. Inheritance Tax (Delivery of Accounts) Regulations 1996
revoked: SI 2002/1733 Sch.1

1472. Inheritance Tax (Delivery of Accounts) (Scotland) Regulations 1996
revoked: SI 2002/1733 Sch.1

NO.

1996–cont.

1475. Inshore Fishing (Prohibition of Fishing and Fishing Methods) (Scotland) Amendment Order 1996
revoked: SSI 2004/276 Sch.4

1493. European Parliamentary (United Kingdom Representatives) Pensions (Amendment) Order 1996
applied: SI 2003/2922 Art.2
amended: SI 2003/2922 Art.2

1499. Food Labelling Regulations 1996
applied: SI 2003/1659 Reg.7, SI 2003/2075 Reg.4, Reg.5, SI 2003/3037 Reg.6, Reg.7, SI 2003/3120 Reg.5, SI 2004/553 Reg.5, Reg.6, SI 2004/554 Reg.3, SI 2004/1396 Reg.4, Reg.5, SSI 2003/291 Reg.7, SSI 2004/6 Reg.4, Reg.8

disapplied: SI 2003/1387 Reg.6

referred to: SI 2003/474 Reg.2, SI 2003/1008 Reg.3, SI 2003/1659 Reg.6, SI 2003/1719 Reg.6, SI 2003/2647 Reg.2, SI 2004/249 Reg.2, SSI 2003/278 Reg.6, SSI 2003/291 Reg.6, SSI 2004/133 Reg.5

varied: SI 2002/329 Reg.9, SI 2003/945 Reg.3, SI 2003/3295 Reg.3

Part II, applied: SI 2003/1564 Reg.5, SI 2003/3207 Reg.8, SI 2004/314 Reg.8, SSI 2004/8 Reg.8

Part II, referred to: SI 2003/1563 Reg.5, SI 2003/1596 Reg.5, SI 2003/1659 Reg.6, SI 2003/2243 Reg.4, SI 2003/3037 Reg.6, SI 2003/3041 Reg.5, SI 2003/3044 Reg.4, SI 2003/3047 Reg.5, SI 2003/3053 Reg.5, SI 2003/3120 Reg.5, SI 2004/553 Reg.5, SSI 2003/291 Reg.6, SSI 2003/293 Reg.5, SSI 2003/311 Reg.5, SSI 2003/527 Reg.5, SSI 2003/569 Reg.5, SSI 2004/133 Reg.5

Reg.2, amended: SI 2003/2075 Reg.9, SI 2003/2647 Reg.3, SI 2004/249 Reg.3, SI 2004/1396 Reg.9, SI 2004/1512 Reg.3, SI 2004/2145 Reg.4, SI 2004/2558 Reg.3, SI 2004/2731 Reg.4, SI 2004/2824 Reg.3, SI 2004/3022 Reg.3, SSI 2003/578 Reg.3, SSI 2004/6 Reg.10, SSI 2004/269 Reg.3, SSI 2004/395 Reg.4, SSI 2004/472 Reg.3

Reg.3, amended: SI 2003/2647 Reg.4, SI 2004/249 Reg.4, SI 2004/2824 Reg.4, SI 2004/3022 Reg.4, SSI 2003/578 Reg.4, SSI 2004/472 Reg.4

Reg.4, revoked (in part): SI 2003/1563 Reg.10, SI 2003/1596 Reg.10, SI 2003/1659 Reg.11, SI 2003/2243 Reg.10, SI 2003/3037 Reg.11, SI 2003/3044 Reg.10, SI 2003/3047 Reg.10, SI 2003/3053 Reg.10

Reg.5, applied: SI 2003/1387 Reg.7, SI 2003/1719 Reg.7, SSI 2003/278 Reg.7

Reg.6, applied: SI 2003/461 Reg.4, SI 2003/1635 Reg.4, SSI 2003/145 Reg.4, SSI 2004/6 Reg.5

NO.

1996–cont.

1499. Food Labelling Regulations 1996– *cont.*
Reg.7, applied: SI 2003/461 Reg.4, SI 2003/1635 Reg.4

Reg.8, applied: SI 2003/461 Reg.4, SI 2003/1635 Reg.4

Reg.13, amended: SI 2004/2824 Reg.5, SI 2004/3022 Reg.5, SSI 2004/472 Reg.5

Reg.14, amended: SI 2003/474 Reg.3, SI 2003/832 Reg.3, SI 2003/2647 Reg.5, SI 2004/249 Reg.5, SI 2004/2824 Reg.6, SI 2004/3022 Reg.6, SSI 2002/524 Reg.3, SSI 2003/578 Reg.5, SSI 2004/472 Reg.6

Reg.15, amended: SI 2004/2824 Reg.7, SI 2004/3022 Reg.7, SSI 2004/472 Reg.7

Reg.17, amended: SI 2004/2824 Reg.8, SI 2004/3022 Reg.8, SSI 2004/472 Reg.8

Reg.18, amended: SI 2004/2824 Reg.9, SI 2004/3022 Reg.9, SSI 2004/472 Reg.9

Reg.19, amended: SI 2003/2647 Reg.4, SI 2004/249 Reg.4, SSI 2003/578 Reg.4

Reg.23, amended: SI 2003/2075 Reg.9, SI 2004/1396 Reg.9, SI 2004/2824 Reg.10, SI 2004/3022 Reg.10, SSI 2004/6 Reg.10, SSI 2004/472 Reg.10

Reg.27, amended: SI 2004/2824 Reg.11, SI 2004/3022 Reg.11, SSI 2004/472 Reg.11

Reg.34, referred to: SI 2002/330 Reg.3

Reg.34, varied: SI 2002/379 Reg.5, SI 2003/1182 Reg.3, SI 2003/1713 Reg.3

Reg.34A, added: SI 2003/2647 Reg.6, SI 2004/249 Reg.6, SSI 2003/578 Reg.6

Reg.34B, added: SI 2004/2824 Reg.12, SI 2004/3022 Reg.12, SSI 2004/472 Reg.12

Reg.35, applied: SI 2003/3037 Reg.7, SSI 2003/569 Reg.7

Reg.35, varied: SI 2003/1563 Reg.6, SI 2003/1564 Reg.6, SI 2003/1596 Reg.6, SI 2003/1659 Reg.7, SI 2003/2243 Reg.6, SI 2003/3041 Reg.6, SI 2003/3044 Reg.6, SI 2003/3047 Reg.6, SI 2003/3053 Reg.6, SI 2003/3120 Reg.6, SI 2004/553 Reg.6, SSI 2003/291 Reg.7, SSI 2003/293 Reg.6, SSI 2003/311 Reg.6, SSI 2003/527 Reg.6, SSI 2004/133 Reg.6

Reg.36, applied: SI 2003/3037 Reg.7, SSI 2003/569 Reg.7

Reg.36, varied: SI 2003/1563 Reg.6, SI 2003/1564 Reg.6, SI 2003/1596 Reg.6, SI 2003/1659 Reg.7, SI 2003/2243 Reg.6, SI 2003/3044 Reg.6, SI 2003/3047 Reg.6, SI 2003/3053 Reg.6, SI 2003/3120 Reg.6, SI 2004/553 Reg.6, SSI 2003/291 Reg.7, SSI 2003/293 Reg.6, SSI 2003/311 Reg.6, SSI 2003/527 Reg.6, SSI 2004/133 Reg.6

Reg.38, applied: SSI 2003/569 Reg.7

Reg.38, varied: SI 2003/1563 Reg.6, SI 2003/1564 Reg.6, SI 2003/1596 Reg.6, SI 2003/1659 Reg.7, SI 2003/2243 Reg.6, SI 2003/3041 Reg.6, SI 2003/

NO.

1996–cont.

1499. Food Labelling Regulations 1996– cont.

Reg.38, varied:–*cont.*
3044 Reg.6, SI 2003/3047 Reg.6, SI 2003/3053 Reg.6, SI 2003/3120 Reg.6, SI 2004/553 Reg.6, SSI 2003/291 Reg.7, SSI 2003/293 Reg.6, SSI 2003/311 Reg.6, SSI 2003/527 Reg.6, SSI 2004/133 Reg.6

Reg.47, amended: SI 2003/2647 Reg.4, SI 2004/249 Reg.4, SSI 2003/578 Reg.4

Reg.49, amended: SI 2003/1659 Reg.11, SI 2003/3037 Reg.11, SSI 2003/291 Reg.12, SSI 2003/311 Reg.11, SSI 2004/6 Reg.11, SSI 2004/133 Reg.11

Reg.49, revoked (in part): SI 2003/1563 Reg.10, SI 2003/1596 Reg.10, SI 2003/3047 Reg.10, SI 2003/3053 Reg.10, SSI 2003/527 Reg.11

Reg.50, amended: SI 2003/474 Reg.4, SI 2003/832 Reg.4, SI 2003/2647 Reg.7, SI 2004/249 Reg.7, SI 2004/2824 Reg.13, SI 2004/3022 Reg.13, SSI 2002/524 Reg.4, SSI 2003/578 Reg.7, SSI 2004/472 Reg.13

Sch.AA1 para.1, added: SI 2004/2824 Sch.1, SI 2004/3022 Sch.1, SSI 2004/472 Sch.1

Sch.AA1 para.2, added: SI 2004/2824 Sch.1, SI 2004/3022 Sch.1, SSI 2004/472 Sch.1

Sch.AA1 para.3, added: SI 2004/2824 Sch.1, SI 2004/3022 Sch.1, SSI 2004/472 Sch.1

Sch.AA1 para.4, added: SI 2004/2824 Sch.1, SI 2004/3022 Sch.1, SSI 2004/472 Sch.1

Sch.AA1 para.5, added: SI 2004/2824 Sch.1, SI 2004/3022 Sch.1, SSI 2004/472 Sch.1

Sch.AA1 para.6, added: SI 2004/2824 Sch.1, SI 2004/3022 Sch.1, SSI 2004/472 Sch.1

Sch.AA1 para.7, added: SI 2004/2824 Sch.1, SI 2004/3022 Sch.1, SSI 2004/472 Sch.1

Sch.AA1 para.8, added: SI 2004/2824 Sch.1, SI 2004/3022 Sch.1, SSI 2004/472 Sch.1

Sch.AA1 para.9, added: SI 2004/2824 Sch.1, SI 2004/3022 Sch.1, SSI 2004/472 Sch.1

Sch.AA1 para.10, added: SI 2004/2824 Sch.1, SI 2004/3022 Sch.1, SSI 2004/472 Sch.1

Sch.AA1 para.11, added: SI 2004/2824 Sch.1, SI 2004/3022 Sch.1, SSI 2004/472 Sch.1

Sch.AA1 para.12, added: SI 2004/2824 Sch.1, SI 2004/3022 Sch.1, SSI 2004/472 Sch.1

Sch.1 para.1, revoked (in part): SI 2003/461 Reg.11, SI 2003/1635 Reg.11, SSI 2003/145 Reg.11

Sch.3, substituted: SI 2003/474 Reg.5, SI 2003/832 Reg.5, SSI 2002/524 Reg.5

Sch.3 Part I, amended: SI 2003/474 Reg.5, SI 2003/832 Reg.5, SI 2003/1563 Reg.10, SI 2003/3047 Reg.10, SI 2004/2824 Reg.15, SI 2004/3022 Reg.15, SSI 2002/524 Reg.5, SSI 2003/527 Sch.2, SSI 2004/472 Reg.15

Sch.3 Part I, substituted: SI 2003/474 Reg.5, SI 2003/832 Reg.5, SSI 2002/524 Reg.5

NO.

1996–cont.

1499. Food Labelling Regulations 1996– cont.

Sch.3 Part II, added: SI 2003/474 Reg.5, SI 2003/832 Reg.5, SSI 2002/524 Reg.5

Sch.3 Part II, substituted: SI 2003/474 Reg.5, SI 2003/832 Reg.5, SSI 2002/524 Reg.5

Sch.4A para.1, added: SI 2003/2075 Sch.4, SI 2004/1396 Sch.4, SSI 2004/6 Sch.4

Sch.4A para.2, added: SI 2003/2075 Sch.4, SI 2004/1396 Sch.4, SSI 2004/6 Sch.4

Sch.4A para.3, added: SI 2003/2075 Sch.4, SI 2004/1396 Sch.4, SSI 2004/6 Sch.4

Sch.4A para.4, added: SI 2003/2075 Sch.4, SI 2004/1396 Sch.4, SSI 2004/6 Sch.4

Sch.7, referred to: SI 2003/3120 Reg.5, SI 2004/553 Reg.5, SSI 2004/133 Reg.5

Sch.7 Part I para.5, amended: SI 2004/1512 Reg.4, SI 2004/2558 Reg.4, SSI 2004/269 Reg.4

Sch.8 Part I, referred to: SI 2002/330 Reg.3

Sch.8 Part I, varied: SI 2002/379 Reg.5, SI 2003/1182 Reg.3, SI 2003/1713 Reg.3

Sch.9, amended: SI 2003/1659 Reg.11, SI 2003/2243 Reg.10, SI 2003/3037 Reg.11, SI 2003/3044 Reg.10, SI 2003/3120 Reg.10, SI 2004/553 Reg.10, SSI 2003/291 Reg.12, SSI 2003/293 Reg.11, SSI 2003/569 Reg.12, SSI 2004/6 Reg.11

1500. Hill Livestock (Compensatory Allowances) Regulations 1996
applied: SSI 2003/129 Reg.4, SSI 2004/70 Reg.4

1503. National Health Service (Wheelchair Charges) Regulations 1996
Reg.1, amended: SI 2004/696 Art.3
Reg.2, amended: SI 2004/696 Art.3

1504. National Health Service (General Medical Services, Pharmaceutical Services and Charges for Drugs and Appliances) (Scotland) Amendment Regulations 1996
Reg.2, revoked: SSI 2004/114 Sch.2

1507. Ancient Monuments (Class Consents) (Scotland) Order 1996
applied: SSI 2003/129 Sch.2 para.12
referred to: SSI 2004/70 Sch.2 para.12

1513. Health and Safety (Consultation with Employees) Regulations 1996
applied: SI 2002/377 Sch.1 para.36, SI 2002/3199 Sch.2 para.20, SI 2003/3118 Sch.2 para.20, SI 2003/3170 Sch.3 para.20

1527. Landfill Tax Regulations 1996
referred to: SI 2003/605 Reg.2
Reg.2, amended: SI 2004/769 Reg.2
Reg.9, amended: SI 2003/2096 Sch.1 para.66
Reg.31, amended: SI 2003/605 Reg.3, SI 2004/769 Reg.3
Reg.31, revoked (in part): SI 2003/605 Reg.3
Reg.33, amended: SI 2003/2313 Reg.3, SR 2003/46 Sch.11 para.6

1996–cont.

1527. Landfill Tax Regulations 1996–cont.
Reg.33, revoked (in part): SI 2003/605 Reg.4
Reg.33A, amended: SI 2002/1 Reg.3
Reg.34, applied: SI 2003/1325 Art.6
Reg.38, amended: SI 2002/1 Reg.4
Reg.38, revoked (in part): SI 2002/1 Reg.4
Reg.39, amended: SI 2002/1 Reg.5
Reg.47, amended: SI 2003/2096 Sch.1 para.67
Reg.49, amended: 2002 asp 17 Sch.3 para.36

1536. Occupational Pension Schemes (Minimum Funding Requirement and Actuarial Valuations) Regulations 1996
Reg.2, amended: SI 2002/380 Reg.2, SI 2004/3031 Reg.2
Reg.2, varied: SI 2003/1633 Sch.2 para.8
Reg.7, see *Pitmans Trustees Ltd v Telecommunications Group Plc* [2004] EWHC 181, [2004] Pens. L.R. 213 (Ch D), Sir Andrew Morritt V.C.
Reg.7, amended: SI 2002/380 Reg.2
Reg.12, amended: SI 2002/380 Reg.2
Reg.16, amended: SI 2002/380 Reg.2
Reg.17, amended: SI 2002/380 Reg.2
Reg.17, applied: SI 2002/380 Reg.2
Reg.18, amended: SI 2002/380 Reg.2
Reg.20, amended: SI 2002/380 Reg.2
Reg.20, revoked (in part): SI 2002/380 Reg.2
Reg.21, amended: SI 2002/380 Reg.2
Sch.1 Part I para.6, substituted: SI 2004/3031 Reg.3
Sch.2 Part I para.1, amended: SI 2002/380 Reg.2
Sch.2 Part I para.2, amended: SI 2002/380 Reg.2
Sch.2 Part I para.5, substituted: SI 2002/380 Reg.2
Sch.2 Part I para.6, substituted: SI 2002/380 Reg.2
Sch.2 Part II, amended: SI 2002/380 Reg.2
Sch.3 Part I para.5, substituted: SI 2002/380 Reg.2
Sch.4 para.1, amended: SI 2002/380 Reg.2

1537. Personal and Occupational Pension Schemes (Protected Rights) Regulations 1996
Reg.4, amended: SI 2002/681 Reg.4
Reg.5, substituted: SI 2002/681 Reg.4
Reg.7, amended: SI 2002/681 Reg.4
Reg.9, amended: SI 2002/681 Reg.4
Reg.12, amended: SI 2002/681 Reg.4
Reg.12, revoked (in part): SI 2002/681 Reg.4
Reg.13, amended: SI 2002/681 Reg.4
Reg.13, revoked (in part): SI 2002/681 Reg.4

1592. Construction (Health, Safety and Welfare) Regulations 1996
see *Delaney v McGregor Construction (Highlands) Ltd* 2003 Rep. L.R. 56 (OH), Lady Paton

1996–cont.

1592. Construction (Health, Safety and Welfare) Regulations 1996–cont.
Reg.4, see *McCook v Lobo* [2002] EWCA Civ 1760, [2003] I.C.R. 89 (CA), Judge, L.J.
Reg.5, see *Horton v Taplin Contracts Ltd* [2002] EWCA Civ 1604, [2003] B.L.R. 74 (CA), Bodey, J.; see *McCook v Lobo* [2002] EWCA Civ 1760, [2003] I.C.R. 89 (CA), Judge, L.J.
Reg.6, see *McCook v Lobo* [2002] EWCA Civ 1760, [2003] I.C.R. 89 (CA), Judge, L.J.

1619. Stansted Airport Aircraft Movement Limit (Amendment) Order 1996
revoked: SI 2004/1946 Art.2

1630. General Medical Council (Constitution) Amendment Order 1996
revoked: SI 2002/3136 Art.9

1632. Deregulation and Contracting Out (Northern Ireland) Order 1996
Part II, applied: SI 2004/1109 Art.4
Art.12, amended: SI 2002/3150 Sch.3 para.13
Art.13, applied: SI 2004/1109 Art.4
Art.14, applied: SI 2004/1109 Art.4
Art.15, applied: SI 2004/1109 Art.4
Art.16, applied: SI 2004/1109 Art.4
Art.17, amended: 2002 c.10 (NI) s.7
Sch.3, amended: SI 2002/3150 Sch.3 para.14
Sch.5, revoked: SI 2004/1109 Sch.1

1642. Police (Conduct) (Scotland) Regulations 1996
applied: SSI 2004/257 Reg.15, Reg.37, Sch.2 para.1, Sch.2 para.2, Sch.2 para.4
referred to: SSI 2004/257 Reg.24
Reg.6, see *McAdam v Wood* 2002 S.L.T. 23 (OH), Lord Wheatley
Reg.7, see *McAdam v Wood* 2002 S.L.T. 23 (OH), Lord Wheatley
Reg.22, amended: SSI 2004/257 Reg.48
Reg.22, revoked (in part): SSI 2004/257 Reg.48
Sch.1 para.8, amended: SSI 2004/257 Reg.48

1643. Police (Efficiency) (Scotland) Regulations 1996
applied: SSI 2004/257 Reg.15

1647. Adventure Activities (Enforcing Authority and Licensing Amendment) Regulations 1996
revoked: SI 2004/1359 Reg.3

1655. Occupational Pension Schemes (Disclosure of Information) Regulations 1996
Reg.1, amended: SI 2002/1383 Reg.3
Reg.5, amended: SI 2002/459 Reg.2, SI 2002/1383 Reg.3
Sch.2 para.6ZA, added: SI 2002/1383 Reg.3

1656. Work in Compressed Air Regulations 1996
applied: SI 2003/547 Sch.6, SI 2004/456 Sch.5

NO.

1996–cont.

1656. Work in Compressed Air Regulations 1996–*cont.*
Reg.8, applied: SI 2002/325 Reg.3
Reg.12, applied: SI 2002/325 Reg.3

1680. Local Government (Discretionary Payments) Regulations 1996
referred to: SI 2004/928 Reg.5
see *Nicholls v Greenwich LBC* [2003] EWCA Civ 416, [2003] I.C.R. 1020 (CA), Mummery, L.J.
Reg.33, amended: SI 2003/1022 Reg.9
Reg.39, amended: SI 2003/1022 Reg.9

1684. Runnymede and Spelthorne (Borough Boundaries) Order 1996
varied: SI 2004/222 Art.2

1685. Police (Promotion) Regulations 1996
Reg.2, amended: SI 2002/767 Reg.2, SI 2003/2595 Reg.2
Reg.3, amended: SI 2002/767 Reg.3, SI 2003/2595 Reg.3
Reg.5, amended: SI 2003/2595 Reg.4
Reg.6, amended: SI 2003/2595 Reg.5
Reg.7, amended: SI 2003/2595 Reg.6
Reg.7, substituted: SI 2002/767 Reg.4
Sch.1 para.4, amended: SI 2003/2595 Reg.7
Sch.1 para.5, amended: SI 2003/2595 Reg.7
Sch.2 para.1, amended: SI 2003/2595 Reg.8
Sch.2 para.2, amended: SI 2003/2595 Reg.8

1749. Merchant Shipping (Mandatory Ship Reporting) Regulations 1996
revoked: SI 2002/1473 Sch.1 para.2

1765. City of Bristol College (Government) Regulations 1996
revoked: SI 2002/1094 Sch.1 Part 1

1768. Cornwall and Isles of Scilly Learning Disabilities National Health Service Trust (Change of Name) Order 1996
revoked: 2003 c.43 s.7

1769. West Lambeth Community Care National Health Service Trust (Change of Name) Order 1996
revoked: 2003 c.43 s.7

1784. Plant Health Fees (Scotland) Regulations 1996
Reg.4A, added: SSI 2004/249 Reg.2
Sch.3, added: SSI 2004/249 Sch.1

1803. Child Benefit, Child Support and Social Security (Miscellaneous Amendments) Regulations 1996
Reg.1, amended: SI 2003/492 Sch.3 Part 1
Reg.3, revoked: SI 2003/493 Sch.2 Part 1
Reg.4, revoked: SI 2003/493 Sch.2 Part 1
Reg.18, revoked (in part): SI 2003/492 Sch.3 Part 1
Reg.19, revoked (in part): SI 2003/492 Sch.3 Part 1
Reg.20, revoked (in part): SI 2003/492 Sch.3 Part 1
Reg.21, revoked (in part): SI 2003/492 Sch.3 Part 1

NO.

1996–cont.

1815. Merchant Shipping (Navigational Warnings) Regulations 1996
revoked: SI 2002/1473 Sch.1 para.2

1829. South Tynedale Railway (Light Railway) Order 1996
Art.7, amended: SI 2003/2155 Sch.1 para.18

1836. Disability Discrimination (Services and Premises) Regulations 1996
Reg.9, revoked: SI 2002/1980 Reg.4

1847. Occupational Pension Schemes (Transfer Values) Regulations 1996
Reg.1, amended: SI 2003/1727 Reg.2
Reg.8, amended: SI 2003/1727 Reg.2

1863. Cheshire (Boroughs of Halton and Warrington) (Structural Change) Order 1996
varied: SI 2004/222 Art.2

1865. Devon (City of Plymouth and Borough of Torbay) (Structural Change) Order 1996
varied: SI 2004/222 Art.2

1866. Shropshire (District of The Wrekin) (Structural Change) Order 1996
varied: SI 2004/222 Art.2

1867. Hereford and Worcester (Structural, Boundary and Electoral Changes) Order 1996
varied: SI 2004/222 Art.2
Art.6, revoked: SI 2002/3224 Art.9
Art.7, revoked: SI 2002/187 Art.11
Sch.3, revoked: SI 2002/187 Art.11

1868. Lancashire (Boroughs of Blackburn and Blackpool) (Structural Change) Order 1996
varied: SI 2004/222 Art.2

1875. Essex (Boroughs of Colchester, Southend-on-Sea and Thurrock and District of Tendring) (Structural, Boundary and Electoral Changes) Order 1996
varied: SI 2004/222 Art.2

1876. Kent (Borough of Gillingham and City of Rochester upon Medway) (Structural Change) Order 1996
varied: SI 2004/222 Art.2

1877. Nottinghamshire (City of Nottingham) (Structural Change) Order 1996
varied: SI 2004/222 Art.2

1878. Cambridgeshire (City of Peterborough) (Structural, Boundary and Electoral Changes) Order 1996
varied: SI 2004/222 Art.2

1879. Berkshire (Structural Change) Order 1996
varied: SI 2004/222 Art.2
Art.9, revoked (in part): SI 2002/2243 Art.10

1883. Local Authorities (Contracting Out of Investment Functions) Order 1996
Art.2, amended: SI 2004/2044 Art.5
Art.4, amended: SI 2004/2044 Art.5
Art.4, revoked (in part): SI 2004/2044 Art.5

NO.

1996–cont.

1898. Welsh Language Schemes (Public Bodies) Order 1996
Sch.1, amended: SI 2004/1771 Sch.1 para.40

1905. Deregulation (Building) (Initial Notices and Final Certificates) Order 1996
Art.3, revoked (in part): 2004 c.22 Sch.1

1908. Community Trade Mark Regulations 1996
Reg.2, amended: SI 2004/949 Reg.3, SI 2004/2332 Reg.8
Reg.3, amended: SI 2004/949 Reg.5, SI 2004/2332 Reg.9
Reg.4, substituted: SI 2004/2332 Reg.10
Reg.6, amended: SI 2004/2332 Reg.11
Reg.7, amended: SI 2004/2332 Reg.12
Reg.8A, added: SI 2004/2332 Reg.13
Reg.9, substituted: SI 2004/2332 Reg.15
Reg.10, substituted: SI 2004/2332 Reg.14
Reg.11, amended: SI 2004/949 Reg.4

1909. Insolvent Companies (Reports on Conduct of Directors) Rules 1996
r.3, amended: SI 2003/2096 Sch.1 para.69
r.4, amended: SI 2003/2096 Sch.1 para.70

1919. Employment Rights (Northern Ireland) Order 1996
applied: 2002 c.1 (NI) Sch.2 para.3, (NI) Sch.2 para.5, 2002 c.9 (NI) Sch.1 para.21, 2002 c.22 s.46, SI 2003/417 Art.2, SI 2003/435 Sch.3 para.10, SI 2003/457 Art.3, SR 2002/120 Sch.1, SR 2003/61 Reg.4
referred to: 2002 c.21 s.64, SR 2002/377 Reg.2, Reg.30
Part I, applied: SR 2002/298 Reg.8, SR 2002/352 Reg.13, SR 2002/377 Reg.2, SR 2003/174 Reg.3
Part I, referred to: SR 2002/120 Sch.1
Part I, applied: SI 2003/2902 Art.27, Art.28, SR 2002/377 Reg.31, SR 2003/173 Reg.15
Part I, referred to: SR 2002/120 Sch.1
Part I, varied: SR 2003/61 Reg.5
Part V, applied: SR 2002/352 Reg.17
Part VA, applied: SR 2002/120 Sch.1
Part VA, referred to: SI 2003/2902 Sch.1 para.15
Part IX, added: SI 2002/2836 Art.3
Part IX, applied: SR 2002/298 Reg.6
Part IX, added: SI 2002/2836 Art.4
Part IXA, added: SI 2002/2836 Art.15
Part XI, applied: SR 2002/120 Sch.1, SR 2002/377 Reg.28, Reg.29, SR 2003/61 Reg.5, SR 2003/173 Reg.16
Part XI, referred to: SR 2002/120
Part XI, referred to: SR 2003/173 Reg.16
Part XII, applied: SR 2002/120 Sch.1, SR 2003/61 Reg.4, Reg.5, Reg.12, 2004 c.17 Sch.2 para.3
Part XII, disapplied: SI 2003/435 Sch.3 para.10
Part XIII, applied: SR 2002/120 Sch.1

NO.

1996–cont.

1919. Employment Rights (Northern Ireland) Order 1996–*cont.*
Art.2, amended: SI 2002/2836 Sch.2 para.4, SR 2002/298 Sch.2 para.2
Art.20, amended: SI 2002/2836 Sch.2 para.4
Art.21, amended: SI 2002/2836 Sch.2 para.4
Art.22, amended: SI 2003/2902 Sch.5 para.2
Art.23, amended: SI 2002/2836 Sch.2 para.4, SI 2003/2902 Sch.5 para.2, SR 2002/24 Sch.1, SR 2003/241 Sch.1
Art.23, applied: SR 2003/173 Reg.15
Art.23, referred to: SI 2003/2902 Art.27, Art.28
Art.33, applied: SI 2003/2902 Art.27, Art.28
Art.35, amended: SI 2003/2902 Art.24
Art.35, revoked (in part): SI 2003/2902 Art.25
Art.36, applied: SI 2003/2902 Art.27, Art.28
Art.39A, added: SI 2003/2902 Art.26
Art.39B, added: SI 2003/2902 Art.26
Art.55, applied: SI 2003/2902 Sch.2, Sch.3, Sch.4
Art.59, amended: SI 2002/2836 Sch.2 para.4
Art.61, revoked (in part): SR 2002/298 Sch.2 para.2
Art.63, amended: SR 2002/24 Sch.1, SR 2003/241 Sch.1
Art.67K, amended: SI 2004/311 Sch.1 para.17
Art.67KA, added: 2003 c.6 s.26
Art.68A, amended: SI 2003/3049 Sch.2 para.4
Art.68A, substituted: SI 2004/1713 Sch.2 para.3
Art.70C, amended: SI 2002/2836 Sch.2 para.4
Art.70C, applied: SR 2002/377 Reg.28
Art.70C, enabled: SR 2002/355, SR 2002/377, SR 2003/222
Art.70D, added: 2002 c.21 Sch.1 para.2, SI 2002/2836 Art.15
Art.70D, substituted: SI 2003/2902 Sch.5 para.2
Art.71, amended: 2002 c.21 Sch.1 para.2, SI 2002/2836 Sch.2 para.4, SI 2003/2902 Sch.5 para.2
Art.71, applied: SI 2003/2902 Sch.2, Sch.3, Sch.4, SR 2003/173 Reg.16
Art.72, amended: 2002 c.21 Sch.1 para.2
Art.74, applied: SI 2003/2902 Sch.2, Sch.3, Sch.4
Art.92, applied: SR 2003/173 Reg.14
Art.92, referred to: SR 2003/173 Reg.14
Art.92A, added: SI 2003/2902 Art.31
Art.93, amended: SI 2003/2902 Art.31
Art.93, applied: SR 2003/173 Reg.14
Art.94, amended: SI 2003/2902 Art.31
Art.95, amended: SI 2003/2902 Art.31
Art.95, applied: SR 2003/173 Reg.14

1996–cont.

1919. Employment Rights (Northern Ireland) Order 1996–*cont.*

Art.97, revoked (in part): SR 2002/298 Sch.2 para.2

Art.103, amended: SI 2002/2836 Art.14

Art.103, enabled: SR 2002/355

Art.105, amended: SI 2002/2836 Art.14

Art.105, enabled: SR 2002/355

Art.106, amended: SI 2002/2836 Art.14

Art.106, enabled: SR 2002/355

Art.107, enabled: SR 2002/355

Art.107A, applied: SR 2002/377 Reg.19

Art.107A, enabled: SR 2002/377, SR 2003/222

Art.107B, enabled: SR 2002/377, SR 2003/222

Art.107C, enabled: SR 2002/377, SR 2003/222

Art.107D, enabled: SR 2002/377, SR 2003/222

Art.108, enabled: SR 2002/110, SR 2002/135, SR 2002/355

Art.110, amended: SI 2002/2836 Sch.2 para.4

Art.112A, enabled: SR 2002/377

Art.112B, enabled: SR 2002/377, SR 2003/220, SR 2003/222

Art.112B, referred to: SR 2003/220 Reg.2

Art.112B, varied: SR 2003/220 Sch.1

Art.112C, applied: SR 2002/377 Reg.12

Art.112C, enabled: SR 2002/377, SR 2003/222

Art.112C, referred to: SR 2002/377 Reg.12

Art.112D, enabled: SR 2002/377, SR 2003/222

Art.112E, enabled: SR 2002/377, SR 2003/222

Art.112F, enabled: SR 2003/174

Art.112G, enabled: SR 2003/173

Art.112G, referred to: SR 2003/173 Reg.5

Art.112H, applied: SR 2003/174 Reg.6, Reg.7

Art.112H, enabled: SR 2003/174

Art.112I, applied: SR 2003/174 Reg.7

Art.112I, enabled: SR 2003/174

Art.118, referred to: SR 2002/120 Sch.1

Art.118, revoked (in part): SR 2002/298 Sch.2 para.2

Art.120, amended: SI 2002/2836 Sch.2 para.4

Art.121, amended: SI 2002/2836 Sch.2 para.4

Art.124, amended: SI 2002/2836 Sch.2 para.4, SR 2002/298 Sch.2 para.2

Art.124, applied: SR 2002/298 Reg.5

Art.127, amended: SR 2002/298 Sch.2 para.2

Art.129, amended: SR 2002/298 Sch.2 para.2

Art.129, applied: SR 2002/377 Reg.3

Art.129, referred to: SI 2003/2902 Art.27, Art.28

1996–cont.

1919. Employment Rights (Northern Ireland) Order 1996–*cont.*

Art.130, amended: SI 2003/2902 Sch.5 para.2

Art.130A, added: SI 2003/2902 Art.23

Art.131, amended: SI 2002/2836 Sch.2 para.4

Art.131, applied: SR 2002/377 Reg.29

Art.131, enabled: SR 2002/355, SR 2002/377, SR 2003/222

Art.132, referred to: SR 2002/120 Sch.1

Art.132A, substituted: SI 2003/3049 Sch.2 para.4, SI 2004/1713 Sch.2 para.3

Art.135, amended: SI 2003/3049 Sch.2 para.4, SI 2004/1713 Sch.2 para.3

Art.135B, substituted: 2002 c.21 Sch.1 para.4

Art.135C, added: SI 2002/2836 Art.15

Art.137, amended: 2002 c.21 Sch.1 para.4, SR 2002/298 Sch.2 para.2

Art.137, referred to: SR 2002/120 Sch.1

Art.138, amended: SI 2002/2836 Sch.2 para.4

Art.140, amended: 2002 c.21 Sch.1 para.4, SI 2003/2902 Sch.5 para.2, SR 2002/298 Sch.2 para.2

Art.140, disapplied: SR 2003/173 Reg.16

Art.141, amended: SR 2002/298 Sch.2 para.2

Art.141, disapplied: SR 2003/173 Reg.16

Art.142, amended: SI 2003/2902 Art.32

Art.142, applied: SR 2002/120 Sch.1, SR 2002/378 Reg.34

Art.145, applied: SI 2003/2902 Sch.2, Sch.3, Sch.4, SR 2002/378 Reg.34

Art.146, amended: SI 2003/2902 Art.23, Sch.5 para.2

Art.151, amended: SI 2003/2902 Art.23, Sch.5 para.2, SR 2002/120 Art.5

Art.151, applied: SR 2002/120 Art.5

Art.152, amended: SI 2003/2902 Sch.5 para.2

Art.154, amended: SI 2003/2902 Art.23, SR 2002/24 Sch.1, SR 2003/241 Sch.1

Art.154, applied: SR 2002/120 Sch.1

Art.157, amended: SI 2003/2902 Art.23, Sch.5 para.2

Art.158, amended: SR 2002/24 Sch.1, SR 2003/241 Sch.1

Art.158, referred to: SR 2002/120 Sch.1

Art.158A, added: SI 2003/2902 Art.29

Art.161, disapplied: SR 2002/120 Sch.1

Art.162A, revoked: SI 2003/2902 Sch.5 para.2

Art.163, applied: SR 2003/173 Reg.16

Art.163, referred to: SR 2003/173 Reg.16

Art.164, applied: SR 2003/173 Reg.16

Art.165, applied: SR 2003/173 Reg.16

Art.166, applied: SR 2003/173 Reg.16

Art.167, applied: SR 2003/173 Reg.16

Art.171, amended: SR 2002/298 Sch.2 para.2

NO.

NO.

1996–cont.

1919. Employment Rights (Northern Ireland) Order 1996–*cont.*

Art.173, applied: SR 2002/120 Sch.1

Art.174, applied: SR 2002/120 Sch.1

Art.176, applied: SR 2002/120 Sch.1

Art.180, amended: SR 2002/298 Sch.2 para.2

Art.180, applied: SR 2002/298 Sch.2 para.5

Art.198, applied: SI 2003/2902 Sch.2, Sch.3, Sch.4

Art.229, applied: SR 2002/120 Art.6

Art.231, amended: SR 2002/24 Sch.1, SR 2003/241 Sch.1

Art.236, amended: SI 2002/2836 Sch.2 para.4

Art.237, amended: 2002 c.21 Sch.1 para.2

Art.237, revoked (in part): 2002 c.21 Sch.6

Art.240, applied: SR 2002/298 Sch.2 para.5, SR 2003/61 Reg.5

Art.240, revoked: SR 2002/298 Sch.2 para.2

Art.242, amended: SI 2002/2836 Sch.2 para.4

Art.242, revoked (in part): SR 2002/298 Sch.2 para.2

Art.243, amended: 2003 c.6 s.26, Sch.4

Art.245, amended: SR 2002/298 Sch.2 para.2

Art.245, applied: SR 2002/298 Reg.10

Art.245, revoked (in part): SR 2002/298 Sch.2 para.2

Art.251, amended: SI 2002/2836 Sch.2 para.4, SI 2003/2902 Sch.5 para.2

1921. Industrial Tribunals (Northern Ireland) Order 1996

Art.9, amended: SI 2003/2902 Art.3, Art.4, Art.5

Art.9, applied: SI 2003/2902 Art.19

Art.9A, added: SI 2003/2902 Art.6

Art.11, amended: SI 2003/2902 Art.7

Art.13, amended: SI 2003/1247 Sch.1 para.18, Sch.2

Art.15, amended: SI 2003/2902 Art.8

Art.15A, added: SI 2003/2902 Art.8

Art.20, amended: SI 2002/2836 Sch.2 para.5, SI 2003/2902 Art.3, SI 2003/3049 Sch.2 para.5, SI 2004/1713 Sch.2 para.4, SR 2002/298 Sch.2 para.3

Art.20, applied: SR 2002/120 Sch.1, SR 2002/378 Reg.34

Art.21, amended: SI 2003/2902 Sch.5 para.3

Art.21, revoked (in part): SI 2003/2902 Art.3

Art.21, substituted: SI 2003/2902 Art.3

Art.22, disapplied: SI 2003/435 Sch.3 para.11

Art.69, amended: SI 2003/2902 Art.33

1923. Personal Social Services (Direct Payments) (Northern Ireland) Order 1996

revoked: 2002 c.6 (NI) Sch.1

1996–cont.

1996. Disability Discrimination (Guidance and Code of Practice) (Appointed Day) Order 1996

Art.3, referred to: SI 2004/2300 Art.2

2009. Local Government Changes for England (Sheriffs) Order 1996

varied: SI 2004/222 Art.2

2034. Grimsby Health National Health Service Trust (Change of Name) Order 1996

revoked: 2003 c.43 s.7

2070. Asylum Appeals (Procedure) Rules 1996

r.2, see *R. v Special Adjudicator Ex p. Bashir* [2002] Imm. A.R.1 (QBD), Harrison, J.

2075. Health and Safety at Work etc Act 1974 (Application to Environmentally Hazardous Substances) Regulations 1996

revoked: SI 2002/282 Reg.4

2083. Education (National Curriculum) (Exceptions) Regulations 1996

revoked (in part): SI 2002/2048 Reg.11

2089. Carriage of Dangerous Goods by Rail Regulations 1996

referred to: SI 2002/2676 Sch.2, SI 2002/2677 Sch.7, SI 2002/2776 Sch.5

Reg.1, revoked: SI 2004/568 Sch.14

Reg.2, amended: SI 2003/1431 Reg.3

Reg.2, revoked: SI 2004/568 Sch.14

Reg.5, revoked: SI 2004/568 Sch.14

Reg.6, revoked: SI 2004/568 Sch.14

Reg.7, revoked: SI 2004/568 Sch.14

Reg.8, revoked: SI 2004/568 Sch.14

Reg.9, amended: SI 2003/1431 Reg.3

Reg.9, revoked: SI 2004/568 Sch.14

Reg.10, revoked: SI 2004/568 Sch.14

Reg.11, revoked: SI 2004/568 Sch.14

Reg.12, revoked: SI 2004/568 Sch.14

Reg.13, revoked: SI 2004/568 Sch.14

Reg.14, revoked: SI 2004/568 Sch.14

Reg.15, revoked: SI 2004/568 Sch.14

Reg.16, revoked: SI 2004/568 Sch.14

Reg.17, revoked: SI 2004/568 Sch.14

Reg.18, revoked: SI 2004/568 Sch.14

Reg.19, revoked: SI 2004/568 Sch.14

Reg.20, revoked: SI 2004/568 Sch.14

Reg.21, revoked: SI 2004/568 Sch.14

Reg.22, revoked: SI 2004/568 Sch.14

Reg.23, revoked: SI 2004/568 Sch.14

Reg.24, revoked: SI 2004/568 Sch.14

Reg.25, revoked: SI 2004/568 Sch.14

Reg.26, revoked: SI 2004/568 Sch.14

Reg.27, revoked: SI 2004/568 Sch.14

Reg.28, revoked: SI 2004/568 Sch.14

Reg.29, revoked: SI 2004/568 Sch.14

Reg.29A, revoked: SI 2004/568 Sch.14

Reg.30, revoked: SI 2004/568 Sch.14

Reg.31, revoked: SI 2004/568 Sch.14

Reg.32, revoked: SI 2004/568 Sch.14

NO.

NO.

1996–cont.

2089. Carriage of Dangerous Goods by Rail Regulations 1996–cont.

Reg.33, revoked: SI 2004/568 Sch.14

Reg.34, revoked: SI 2004/568 Sch.14

Sch.1 para.1, amended: SI 2003/1431 Reg.3

Sch.1 para.1, revoked: SI 2004/568 Sch.14

Sch.1 para.2, amended: SI 2003/1431 Reg.3

Sch.1 para.2, revoked: SI 2004/568 Sch.14

Sch.1 para.3, amended: SI 2003/1431 Reg.3

Sch.1 para.3, revoked: SI 2004/568 Sch.14

Sch.2 para.1, revoked: SI 2004/568 Sch.14

Sch.2 para.2, revoked: SI 2004/568 Sch.14

Sch.2 para.3, revoked: SI 2004/568 Sch.14

Sch.2 para.4, revoked: SI 2004/568 Sch.14

Sch.2 para.5, revoked: SI 2004/568 Sch.14

Sch.2 para.6, revoked: SI 2004/568 Sch.14

Sch.2 para.7, revoked: SI 2004/568 Sch.14

Sch.2 para.8, revoked: SI 2004/568 Sch.14

Sch.3 para.1, revoked: SI 2004/568 Sch.14

Sch.3 para.2, revoked: SI 2004/568 Sch.14

Sch.3 para.3, revoked: SI 2004/568 Sch.14

Sch.3 para.4, revoked: SI 2004/568 Sch.14

Sch.3 para.5, revoked: SI 2004/568 Sch.14

Sch.3 para.6, revoked: SI 2004/568 Sch.14

Sch.3 para.7, revoked: SI 2004/568 Sch.14

Sch.3 para.8, revoked: SI 2004/568 Sch.14

Sch.3 para.9, revoked: SI 2004/568 Sch.14

Sch.3 para.10, revoked: SI 2004/568 Sch.14

Sch.3 para.11, revoked: SI 2004/568 Sch.14

Sch.3 para.12, revoked: SI 2004/568 Sch.14

Sch.3A para.1, revoked: SI 2004/568 Sch.14

Sch.3A para.2, revoked: SI 2004/568 Sch.14

Sch.4 para.1, revoked: SI 2004/568 Sch.14

Sch.4 para.2, revoked: SI 2004/568 Sch.14

Sch.4 para.3, revoked: SI 2004/568 Sch.14

Sch.4 para.4, revoked: SI 2004/568 Sch.14

Sch.4 para.5, revoked: SI 2004/568 Sch.14

Sch.4 para.6, revoked: SI 2004/568 Sch.14

Sch.5 para.1, revoked: SI 2004/568 Sch.14

Sch.5 para.2, revoked: SI 2004/568 Sch.14

Sch.5 para.3, revoked: SI 2004/568 Sch.14

Sch.5 para.4, revoked: SI 2004/568 Sch.14

Sch.5 para.5, revoked: SI 2004/568 Sch.14

Sch.5 para.5A, revoked: SI 2004/568 Sch.14

Sch.5 para.6, revoked: SI 2004/568 Sch.14

Sch.5 para.7, revoked: SI 2004/568 Sch.14

Sch.5 para.8, revoked: SI 2004/568 Sch.14

Sch.5 para.9, revoked: SI 2004/568 Sch.14

Sch.6 para.1, revoked: SI 2004/568 Sch.14

Sch.6 para.2, revoked: SI 2004/568 Sch.14

Sch.6 para.3, revoked: SI 2004/568 Sch.14

Sch.6 para.4, revoked: SI 2004/568 Sch.14

Sch.7 Part I para.1, revoked: SI 2004/568 Sch.14

Sch.7 Part I para.2, revoked: SI 2004/568 Sch.14

Sch.7 Part I para.3, revoked: SI 2004/568 Sch.14

Sch.7 Part I para.4, revoked: SI 2004/568 Sch.14

1996–cont.

2089. Carriage of Dangerous Goods by Rail Regulations 1996–cont.

Sch.7 Part I para.5, revoked: SI 2004/568 Sch.14

Sch.7 Part I para.6, revoked: SI 2004/568 Sch.14

Sch.7 Part I para.7, revoked: SI 2004/568 Sch.14

Sch.7 Part I para.8, revoked: SI 2004/568 Sch.14

Sch.7 Part I para.9, revoked: SI 2004/568 Sch.14

Sch.7 Part I para.10, revoked: SI 2004/568 Sch.14

Sch.7 Part II para.11, revoked: SI 2004/568 Sch.14

Sch.7 Part II para.12, revoked: SI 2004/568 Sch.14

Sch.7 Part II para.13, revoked: SI 2004/568 Sch.14

Sch.7 Part II para.14, revoked: SI 2004/568 Sch.14

Sch.7 Part II para.15, revoked: SI 2004/568 Sch.14

Sch.8, revoked: SI 2004/568 Sch.14

Sch.9, revoked: SI 2004/568 Sch.14

2090. Packaging, Labelling and Carriage of Radioactive Material by Rail Regulations 1996

referred to: SI 2002/2776 Sch.5

revoked: SI 2002/2099 Sch.2

2092. Carriage of Dangerous Goods (Classification, Packaging and Labelling) and Use of Transportable Pressure Receptacles Regulations 1996

applied: SI 2002/1689 Reg.7, SI 2002/2675 Reg.23, Sch.2 para.1

referred to: SI 2002/2676 Sch.2, SI 2002/2677 Sch.7, SI 2002/2776 Sch.5

revoked: SI 2004/568 Sch.14

Reg.3, amended: SI 2003/1431 Reg.4

Reg.9, applied: SI 2002/1689 Reg.8, Reg.9

Reg.9, substituted: SI 2002/1689 Reg.18

Reg.10, applied: SI 2002/1689 Reg.8, Reg.9

Reg.10, substituted: SI 2002/1689 Reg.18

Reg.11, amended: SI 2002/1689 Reg.18

Reg.22, revoked (in part): SI 2002/2776 Sch.7 Part 2

Sch.8 para.1, amended: SI 2003/1431 Reg.4

Sch.8 para.2, amended: SI 2003/1431 Reg.4

Sch.8 para.3, amended: SI 2003/1431 Reg.4

Sch.8 para.4, amended: SI 2003/1431 Reg.4

Sch.8 para.5, amended: SI 2003/1431 Reg.4

Sch.8 para.6, amended: SI 2003/1431 Reg.4

Sch.8 para.7, amended: SI 2003/1431 Reg.4

Sch.8 para.8, amended: SI 2003/1431 Reg.4

Sch.8 para.9, amended: SI 2003/1431 Reg.4

Sch.8 para.10, amended: SI 2003/1431 Reg.4

NO.

1996–cont.

2093. Carriage of Explosives by Road Regulations 1996

referred to: SI 2002/2676 Sch.2, SI 2002/2677 Sch.7, SI 2002/2776 Sch.5

revoked: SI 2004/568 Sch.14

2094. Carriage of Dangerous Goods by Road (Driver Training) Regulations 1996

revoked: SI 2004/568 Sch.14

Reg.4, applied: SI 2002/655 Reg.13, SI 2003/547 Reg.13, Reg.14, SI 2004/456 Reg.12, Reg.13, SI 2004/568 Reg.33

Reg.4, referred to: SI 2002/655 Reg.14

2095. Carriage of Dangerous Goods by Road Regulations 1996

applied: SI 2002/2675 Reg.23

referred to: SI 2002/2676 Sch.2, SI 2002/2677 Sch.7, SI 2002/2776 Sch.5

Reg.1, revoked: SI 2004/568 Sch.14

Reg.2, revoked: SI 2004/568 Sch.14

Reg.3, revoked: SI 2004/568 Sch.14

Reg.4, revoked: SI 2004/568 Sch.14

Reg.7, revoked: SI 2004/568 Sch.14

Reg.8, revoked: SI 2004/568 Sch.14

Reg.9, revoked: SI 2004/568 Sch.14

Reg.10, revoked: SI 2004/568 Sch.14

Reg.11, amended: SI 2003/1431 Reg.5

Reg.11, revoked: SI 2004/568 Sch.14

Reg.12, revoked: SI 2004/568 Sch.14

Reg.13, revoked: SI 2004/568 Sch.14

Reg.14, revoked: SI 2004/568 Sch.14

Reg.15, revoked: SI 2004/568 Sch.14

Reg.16, revoked: SI 2004/568 Sch.14

Reg.17, revoked: SI 2004/568 Sch.14

Reg.18, revoked: SI 2004/568 Sch.14

Reg.19, revoked: SI 2004/568 Sch.14

Reg.20, substituted: SI 2002/2776 Sch.6 para.10

Reg.21, revoked: SI 2004/568 Sch.14

Reg.22, revoked: SI 2004/568 Sch.14

Reg.23, revoked: SI 2004/568 Sch.14

Reg.24, revoked: SI 2004/568 Sch.14

Reg.25, revoked: SI 2004/568 Sch.14

Reg.25A, revoked: SI 2004/568 Sch.14

Reg.26, revoked: SI 2004/568 Sch.14

Reg.27, revoked: SI 2004/568 Sch.14

Reg.28, revoked: SI 2004/568 Sch.14

Reg.29, revoked: SI 2004/568 Sch.14

Sch.1, revoked: SI 2004/568 Sch.14

Sch.2 para.1, revoked: SI 2004/568 Sch.14

Sch.2 para.2, revoked: SI 2004/568 Sch.14

Sch.2 para.3, revoked: SI 2004/568 Sch.14

Sch.2 para.3A, revoked: SI 2004/568 Sch.14

Sch.2 para.4, revoked: SI 2004/568 Sch.14

Sch.2 para.5, revoked: SI 2004/568 Sch.14

Sch.2 para.6, revoked: SI 2004/568 Sch.14

Sch.2 para.7, revoked: SI 2004/568 Sch.14

Sch.2 para.8, revoked: SI 2004/568 Sch.14

Sch.2 para.9, revoked: SI 2004/568 Sch.14

Sch.2 para.10, revoked: SI 2004/568 Sch.14

NO.

1996–cont.

2095. Carriage of Dangerous Goods by Road Regulations 1996–*cont.*

Sch.2 para.11, revoked: SI 2004/568 Sch.14

Sch.3 para.1, amended: SI 2003/1431 Reg.5

Sch.3 para.1, revoked: SI 2004/568 Sch.14

Sch.3 para.2, amended: SI 2003/1431 Reg.5

Sch.3 para.2, revoked: SI 2004/568 Sch.14

Sch.3 para.3, amended: SI 2003/1431 Reg.5

Sch.3 para.3, revoked: SI 2004/568 Sch.14

Sch.3 para.4, amended: SI 2003/1431 Reg.5

Sch.3 para.4, revoked: SI 2004/568 Sch.14

Sch.3 para.5, amended: SI 2003/1431 Reg.5

Sch.3 para.5, revoked: SI 2004/568 Sch.14

Sch.4 para.1, revoked: SI 2004/568 Sch.14

Sch.4 Part I para.1, revoked: SI 2004/568 Sch.14

Sch.4 Part I para.2, revoked: SI 2004/568 Sch.14

Sch.4 Part I para.3, revoked: SI 2004/568 Sch.14

Sch.4 Part I para.4, revoked: SI 2004/568 Sch.14

Sch.4 Part I para.5, revoked: SI 2004/568 Sch.14

Sch.4 Part I para.6, revoked: SI 2004/568 Sch.14

Sch.4 Part I para.7, revoked: SI 2004/568 Sch.14

Sch.4 Part I para.7A, revoked: SI 2004/568 Sch.14

Sch.4 Part I para.8, revoked: SI 2004/568 Sch.14

Sch.4 Part I para.9, revoked: SI 2004/568 Sch.14

Sch.4 Part I para.10, revoked: SI 2004/568 Sch.14

Sch.4 Part I para.11, revoked: SI 2004/568 Sch.14

Sch.4 Part I para.12, revoked: SI 2004/568 Sch.14

Sch.4 para.2, revoked: SI 2004/568 Sch.14

Sch.4 Part II para.13, revoked: SI 2004/568 Sch.14

Sch.4 Part II para.14, revoked: SI 2004/568 Sch.14

Sch.4 Part II para.15, revoked: SI 2004/568 Sch.14

Sch.4 Part II para.16, revoked: SI 2004/568 Sch.14

Sch.4 Part II para.17, revoked: SI 2004/568 Sch.14

Sch.4 para.3, revoked: SI 2004/568 Sch.14

Sch.4 para.4, revoked: SI 2004/568 Sch.14

Sch.4 para.5, revoked: SI 2004/568 Sch.14

Sch.4 para.6, revoked: SI 2004/568 Sch.14

Sch.4 para.7, revoked: SI 2004/568 Sch.14

Sch.4 para.8, revoked: SI 2004/568 Sch.14

Sch.4 para.9, revoked: SI 2004/568 Sch.14

Sch.4 para.10, revoked: SI 2004/568 Sch.14

Sch.5 para.1, revoked: SI 2004/568 Sch.14

Sch.5 para.2, revoked: SI 2004/568 Sch.14

1996–cont.

2095. Carriage of Dangerous Goods by Road Regulations 1996–cont.

Sch.5 para.3, revoked: SI 2004/568 Sch.14
Sch.5 para.4, revoked: SI 2004/568 Sch.14
Sch.5 para.5, revoked: SI 2004/568 Sch.14
Sch.5 para.6, revoked: SI 2004/568 Sch.14
Sch.5 para.7, revoked: SI 2004/568 Sch.14
Sch.5 para.8, revoked: SI 2004/568 Sch.14
Sch.5 para.9, revoked: SI 2004/568 Sch.14
Sch.5 para.10, revoked: SI 2004/568 Sch.14
Sch.5 para.11, revoked: SI 2004/568 Sch.14
Sch.5 para.12, revoked: SI 2004/568 Sch.14
Sch.5 para.13, revoked: SI 2004/568 Sch.14
Sch.5 para.14, revoked: SI 2004/568 Sch.14
Sch.5 para.15, revoked: SI 2004/568 Sch.14
Sch.5 para.16, revoked: SI 2004/568 Sch.14
Sch.5 para.17, revoked: SI 2004/568 Sch.14
Sch.5 para.17A, revoked: SI 2004/568 Sch.14
Sch.5 para.18, revoked: SI 2004/568 Sch.14
Sch.5 para.19, revoked: SI 2004/568 Sch.14
Sch.6 para.1, revoked: SI 2004/568 Sch.14
Sch.6 para.2, revoked: SI 2004/568 Sch.14
Sch.6 para.3, revoked: SI 2004/568 Sch.14
Sch.6 para.4, revoked: SI 2004/568 Sch.14
Sch.6 para.5, revoked: SI 2004/568 Sch.14
Sch.6 para.6, revoked: SI 2004/568 Sch.14
Sch.6 para.7, revoked: SI 2004/568 Sch.14
Sch.6 para.8, revoked: SI 2004/568 Sch.14
Sch.6 para.9, revoked: SI 2004/568 Sch.14
Sch.6 para.10, revoked: SI 2004/568 Sch.14
Sch.6 para.11, revoked: SI 2004/568 Sch.14
Sch.6 para.12, revoked: SI 2004/568 Sch.14
Sch.6 para.13, revoked: SI 2004/568 Sch.14
Sch.6 para.14, revoked: SI 2004/568 Sch.14
Sch.6 para.15, revoked: SI 2004/568 Sch.14
Sch.6 para.16, revoked: SI 2004/568 Sch.14
Sch.6 para.17, revoked: SI 2004/568 Sch.14
Sch.6 para.18, revoked: SI 2004/568 Sch.14
Sch.6 para.19, revoked: SI 2004/568 Sch.14
Sch.6 para.20, revoked: SI 2004/568 Sch.14
Sch.7 para.1, revoked: SI 2004/568 Sch.14
Sch.7 Part I para.1, revoked: SI 2004/568 Sch.14
Sch.7 Part I para.2, revoked: SI 2004/568 Sch.14
Sch.7 Part I para.3, revoked: SI 2004/568 Sch.14
Sch.7 Part I para.4, revoked: SI 2004/568 Sch.14
Sch.7 Part I para.5, revoked: SI 2004/568 Sch.14
Sch.7 Part I para.6, revoked: SI 2004/568 Sch.14
Sch.7 Part I para.7, revoked: SI 2004/568 Sch.14
Sch.7 Part I para.8, revoked: SI 2004/568 Sch.14
Sch.7 Part I para.9, revoked: SI 2004/568 Sch.14

1996–cont.

2095. Carriage of Dangerous Goods by Road Regulations 1996–cont.

Sch.7 Part I para.10, revoked: SI 2004/568 Sch.14
Sch.7 Part I para.12, revoked: SI 2004/568 Sch.14
Sch.7 Part I para.13, revoked: SI 2004/568 Sch.14
Sch.7 para.2, revoked: SI 2004/568 Sch.14
Sch.7 Part II para.14, revoked: SI 2004/568 Sch.14
Sch.7 Part II para.15, revoked: SI 2004/568 Sch.14
Sch.7 para.3, revoked: SI 2004/568 Sch.14
Sch.7 para.4, revoked: SI 2004/568 Sch.14
Sch.7 para.5, revoked: SI 2004/568 Sch.14
Sch.7 para.6, revoked: SI 2004/568 Sch.14
Sch.7 para.7, revoked: SI 2004/568 Sch.14
Sch.7 para.8, revoked: SI 2004/568 Sch.14
Sch.7 para.9, revoked: SI 2004/568 Sch.14
Sch.7 para.10, revoked: SI 2004/568 Sch.14
Sch.7 para.12, revoked: SI 2004/568 Sch.14
Sch.7 para.13, revoked: SI 2004/568 Sch.14
Sch.8 para.1, revoked: SI 2004/568 Sch.14
Sch.8 para.2, revoked: SI 2004/568 Sch.14
Sch.8 para.3, revoked: SI 2004/568 Sch.14
Sch.8 para.4, revoked: SI 2004/568 Sch.14
Sch.8 para.5, revoked: SI 2004/568 Sch.14
Sch.8 para.6, revoked: SI 2004/568 Sch.14
Sch.9 para.1, revoked: SI 2004/568 Sch.14
Sch.9 para.2, revoked: SI 2004/568 Sch.14
Sch.9 para.3, revoked: SI 2004/568 Sch.14
Sch.9 para.4, revoked: SI 2004/568 Sch.14
Sch.9A para.1, revoked: SI 2004/568 Sch.14
Sch.9A para.2, revoked: SI 2004/568 Sch.14
Sch.9A para.3, revoked: SI 2004/568 Sch.14
Sch.9A para.4, revoked: SI 2004/568 Sch.14
Sch.9A para.5, revoked: SI 2004/568 Sch.14
Sch.9A para.6, revoked: SI 2004/568 Sch.14
Sch.9A para.7, revoked: SI 2004/568 Sch.14
Sch.9A para.8, revoked: SI 2004/568 Sch.14
Sch.9A para.9, revoked: SI 2004/568 Sch.14
Sch.9A para.10, revoked: SI 2004/568 Sch.14
Sch.10 Part I para.1, revoked: SI 2004/568 Sch.14
Sch.10 Part I para.2, revoked: SI 2004/568 Sch.14
Sch.10 Part I para.3, revoked: SI 2004/568 Sch.14
Sch.10 Part I para.4, revoked: SI 2004/568 Sch.14
Sch.10 Part I para.5, revoked: SI 2004/568 Sch.14
Sch.10 Part I para.6, revoked: SI 2004/568 Sch.14
Sch.10 Part I para.7, revoked: SI 2004/568 Sch.14
Sch.10 Part I para.8, revoked: SI 2004/568 Sch.14

1996–cont.

2095. Carriage of Dangerous Goods by Road Regulations 1996–*cont.*

Sch.10 Part I para.9, revoked: SI 2004/568 Sch.14

Sch.10 Part I para.10, revoked: SI 2004/568 Sch.14

Sch.10 Part I para.11, amended: SI 2003/1431 Reg.5

Sch.10 Part I para.11, revoked: SI 2004/568 Sch.14

Sch.10 Part I para.12, revoked: SI 2004/568 Sch.14

Sch.10 Part I para.13, revoked: SI 2004/568 Sch.14

Sch.10 Part I para.14, revoked: SI 2004/568 Sch.14

Sch.10 Part I para.15, revoked: SI 2004/568 Sch.14

Sch.10 Part I para.16, revoked: SI 2004/568 Sch.14

Sch.10 Part I para.17, revoked: SI 2004/568 Sch.14

Sch.10 Part I para.18, revoked: SI 2004/568 Sch.14

Sch.10 Part I para.19, revoked: SI 2004/568 Sch.14

Sch.10 Part I para.20, revoked: SI 2004/568 Sch.14

Sch.10 Part I para.21, revoked: SI 2004/568 Sch.14

Sch.10 Part I para.22, revoked: SI 2004/568 Sch.14

Sch.10 Part I para.23, revoked: SI 2004/568 Sch.14

Sch.10 Part I para.24, revoked: SI 2004/568 Sch.14

Sch.10 Part I para.25, revoked: SI 2004/568 Sch.14

Sch.10 Part II, revoked: SI 2004/568 Sch.14

Sch.11 para.1, revoked: SI 2004/568 Sch.14

Sch.11 para.2, revoked: SI 2004/568 Sch.14

Sch.11 para.3, revoked: SI 2004/568 Sch.14

Sch.11 para.4, revoked: SI 2004/568 Sch.14

Sch.11 para.5, revoked: SI 2004/568 Sch.14

Sch.11 para.6, revoked: SI 2004/568 Sch.14

Sch.11 para.7, revoked: SI 2004/568 Sch.14

Sch.11 para.8, revoked: SI 2004/568 Sch.14

Sch.11 para.9, revoked: SI 2004/568 Sch.14

Sch.11 para.10, revoked: SI 2004/568 Sch.14

Sch.11 para.11, revoked: SI 2004/568 Sch.14

Sch.11 para.12, revoked: SI 2004/568 Sch.14

Sch.11 para.13, revoked: SI 2004/568 Sch.14

Sch.11 para.14, revoked: SI 2004/568 Sch.14

Sch.11 para.15, revoked: SI 2004/568 Sch.14

Sch.11 para.16, revoked: SI 2004/568 Sch.14

Sch.11 para.17, revoked: SI 2004/568 Sch.14

Sch.11 para.18, revoked: SI 2004/568 Sch.14

Sch.12 Part I para.1, revoked: SI 2002/2776 Sch.7 Part 2, SI 2004/568 Sch.14

Sch.12 Part I para.2, revoked: SI 2002/2776 Sch.7 Part 2, SI 2004/568 Sch.14

1996–cont.

2095. Carriage of Dangerous Goods by Road Regulations 1996–*cont.*

Sch.12 Part I para.3, revoked: SI 2002/2776 Sch.7 Part 2, SI 2004/568 Sch.14

Sch.12 Part I para.4, revoked: SI 2002/2776 Sch.7 Part 2, SI 2004/568 Sch.14

Sch.12 Part I para.5, revoked: SI 2002/2776 Sch.7 Part 2, SI 2004/568 Sch.14

Sch.12 Part I para.6, revoked: SI 2002/2776 Sch.7 Part 2, SI 2004/568 Sch.14

Sch.12 Part I para.7, revoked: SI 2002/2776 Sch.7 Part 2, SI 2004/568 Sch.14

Sch.12 Part I para.8, revoked: SI 2002/2776 Sch.7 Part 2, SI 2004/568 Sch.14

Sch.12 Part II para.9, revoked: SI 2002/2776 Sch.7 Part 2, SI 2004/568 Sch.14

Sch.12 Part II para.10, revoked: SI 2002/2776 Sch.7 Part 2, SI 2004/568 Sch.14

Sch.12 Part II para.11, revoked: SI 2002/2776 Sch.7 Part 2, SI 2004/568 Sch.14

Sch.12 Part II para.12, revoked: SI 2002/2776 Sch.7 Part 2, SI 2004/568 Sch.14

Sch.12 Part II para.13, revoked: SI 2002/2776 Sch.7 Part 2, SI 2004/568 Sch.14

Sch.12 Part II para.14, revoked: SI 2002/2776 Sch.7 Part 2, SI 2004/568 Sch.14

Sch.12 Part II para.15, revoked: SI 2002/2776 Sch.7 Part 2, SI 2004/568 Sch.14

Sch.12 Part II para.16, revoked: SI 2002/2776 Sch.7 Part 2, SI 2004/568 Sch.14

Sch.12 Part II para.17, revoked: SI 2002/2776 Sch.7 Part 2, SI 2004/568 Sch.14

Sch.12 Part II para.18, revoked: SI 2002/2776 Sch.7 Part 2, SI 2004/568 Sch.14

Sch.12 Part III para.19, revoked: SI 2002/2776 Sch.7 Part 2, SI 2004/568 Sch.14

Sch.12 Part III para.20, revoked: SI 2002/2776 Sch.7 Part 2, SI 2004/568 Sch.14

Sch.12 Part III para.21, revoked: SI 2002/2776 Sch.7 Part 2, SI 2004/568 Sch.14

Sch.12 Part III para.22, revoked: SI 2002/2776 Sch.7 Part 2, SI 2004/568 Sch.14

Sch.12 Part III para.23, revoked: SI 2002/2776 Sch.7 Part 2, SI 2004/568 Sch.14

Sch.12 Part III para.24, revoked: SI 2002/2776 Sch.7 Part 2, SI 2004/568 Sch.14

Sch.12 Part III para.25, revoked: SI 2002/2776 Sch.7 Part 2, SI 2004/568 Sch.14

Sch.12 Part III para.26, revoked: SI 2002/2776 Sch.7 Part 2, SI 2004/568 Sch.14

Sch.12 Part IV, revoked: SI 2002/2776 Sch.7 Part 2, SI 2004/568 Sch.14

Sch.12 Part V, revoked: SI 2002/2776 Sch.7 Part 2, SI 2004/568 Sch.14

Sch.12 Part VI, revoked: SI 2002/2776 Sch.7 Part 2, SI 2004/568 Sch.14

2096. Fire Services (Appointments and Promotion) (Amendment) Regulations 1996

revoked: SI 2004/481 Sch.2

NO.

1996–cont.

2097. Fresh Meat (Beef Controls) (No.2) Regulations 1996
Sch.1, applied: SI 2002/843 Reg.33
Sch.1, referred to: SI 2002/1416 Reg.33, SSI 2002/255 Reg.33

2125. General Medical Council (Constitution of Fitness to Practise Committees) Rules Order of Council 1996
revoked: SI 2003/1344 Art.2
Sch.1, substituted: SI 2002/2572 Sch.1 para.7
Sch.1, varied: SI 2003/1344 Sch.1

2128. Merchant Shipping (Prevention of Pollution) (Limits) Regulations 1996
Sch.1, applied: SI 2004/2668 Art.1

2154. Merchant Shipping (Prevention of Oil Pollution) Regulations 1996
amended: SI 2004/303 Reg.2
Reg.1, amended: SI 2004/303 Reg.2
Reg.1A, added: SI 2004/303 Reg.3
Reg.4, substituted: SI 2004/303 Reg.4
Reg.5, substituted: SI 2004/303 Reg.4
Reg.6, substituted: SI 2004/303 Reg.4
Reg.7, substituted: SI 2004/303 Reg.4
Reg.8, substituted: SI 2004/303 Reg.4
Reg.31, substituted: SI 2004/303 Reg.5
Reg.33, amended: SI 2004/303 Reg.6, SI 2004/2110 Reg.22
Reg.35, amended: SI 2004/303 Reg.7

2186. Goods Vehicles (Licensing of Operators) (Temporary Use in Great Britain) Regulations 1996
Reg.4, amended: SI 2004/462 Reg.2
Reg.5, amended: SI 2004/462 Reg.2
Reg.6, amended: SI 2004/462 Reg.2
Reg.7, amended: SI 2004/462 Reg.2
Reg.13, substituted: SI 2004/462 Reg.2
Reg.25, substituted: SI 2004/462 Reg.2
Reg.30A, added: SI 2004/462 Reg.2
Reg.30B, added: SI 2004/462 Reg.2
Reg.30C, added: SI 2004/462 Reg.2
Reg.30D, added: SI 2004/462 Reg.2
Reg.30E, added: SI 2004/462 Reg.2
Reg.31, amended: SI 2004/462 Reg.2
Sch.2 para.31, added: SI 2004/462 Reg.2
Sch.2 para.32, added: SI 2004/462 Reg.2

2194. Animal Test Certificates Regulations 1996
revoked: SI 2003/3309 Reg.2

2288. South and East Wales Ambulance National Health Service Trust (Establishment) (Amendment) Order 1996
revoked: 2003 c.43 s.7

2306. Social Security (Claims and Payments and Adjudication) Amendment Regulations 1996
Reg.1, amended: SI 2003/492 Sch.3 Part 1
Reg.2, revoked (in part): SI 2003/492 Sch.3 Part 1
Reg.3, revoked (in part): SI 2003/492 Sch.3 Part 1

NO.

1996–cont.

2306. Social Security (Claims and Payments and Adjudication) Amendment Regulations 1996–*cont.*
Reg.4, revoked (in part): SI 2003/492 Sch.3 Part 1
Reg.5, revoked (in part): SI 2003/492 Sch.3 Part 1
Reg.6, revoked (in part): SI 2003/492 Sch.3 Part 1
Reg.7, revoked (in part): SI 2003/492 Sch.3 Part 1

2344. Social Security (Jobseeker's Allowance Consequential Amendments) (Deductions) Regulations 1996
Reg.25, revoked (in part): SI 2003/492 Sch.3 Part 1

2362. National Health Service (Travelling Expenses and Remission of Charges) Amendment (No.3) Regulations 1996
revoked: SI 2003/2382 Sch.2

2374. European Communities (Recognition of Professional Qualifications) (Second General System) Regulations 1996
applied: SI 2002/253 Art.9, SI 2002/254 Art.12
referred to: SI 2002/254 Art.9
revoked: SI 2002/2934 Reg.27
Sch.2 Part I, amended: SI 2002/880 Sch.1 para.7, SI 2002/881 Sch.1 para.12

2381. Income Tax (Employments) (Amendment No 4) Regulations 1996
revoked: SI 2003/2682 Sch.2

2391. National Health Service (Travelling Expenses and Remission of Charges) (Scotland) Amendment (No.2) Regulations 1996
revoked: SSI 2003/376 Sch.3 para.11

2403. Cornwall (Coroners Districts) (Amendment) Order 1996
revoked: SI 2003/3224 Art.4

2431. Income Support and Social Security (Claims and Payments) (Miscellaneous Amendments) Regulations 1996
Reg.7, revoked (in part): SI 2003/492 Sch.3 Part 1

2444. Civil Legal Aid (Scotland) Regulations 1996
revoked: SSI 2002/494 Sch.1
Reg.14A, amended: SSI 2002/88 Reg.2, SSI 2002/254 Reg.2

2447. Advice and Assistance (Scotland) (Consolidation and Amendment) Regulations 1996
referred to: SSI 2003/163 Reg.3, SSI 2003/421 Reg.3
Reg.2, amended: SSI 2003/421 Reg.4
Reg.6, amended: SSI 2003/421 Reg.5
Reg.7, amended: SSI 2003/163 Reg.4, SSI 2003/421 Reg.6

NO.

NO.

1996–cont.

2447. Advice and Assistance (Scotland) (Consolidation and Amendment) Regulations 1996–*cont.*

Reg.8, substituted: SSI 2004/492 Reg.3

Reg.10, substituted: SSI 2004/492 Reg.4

Reg.15A, added: SSI 2004/492 Reg.5

Reg.16, amended: SSI 2002/495 Reg.2, SSI 2003/163 Reg.5, SSI 2004/49 Reg.4

Reg.21, amended: SSI 2004/492 Reg.6

Sch.2 para.5, amended: SSI 2003/163 Reg.6, SSI 2003/421 Reg.7

Sch.3 Part I para.1, substituted: SSI 2004/262 Sch.1

Sch.3 Part I para.2, substituted: SSI 2004/262 Sch.1

Sch.3 Part I para.3, substituted: SSI 2004/262 Sch.1

Sch.3 Part II para.1, substituted: SSI 2004/262 Sch.1

Sch.3 Part II para.1.D, substituted: SSI 2004/262 Sch.1

Sch.3 Part II para.2, substituted: SSI 2004/262 Sch.1

Sch.3 Part II para.3, substituted: SSI 2004/262 Sch.1

2475. Personal and Occupational Pension Schemes (Pensions Ombudsman) Regulations 1996

Reg.1, see *R. (on the application of Britannic Asset Management Ltd) v Pensions Ombudsman* [2002] EWHC 441, [2002] O.P.L.R. 175 (QBD (Admin Ct)), Lightman, J.

Reg.2, see *R. (on the application of Britannic Asset Management Ltd) v Pensions Ombudsman* [2002] EWCA Civ 1405, [2002] 4 All E.R. 860 (CA), Chadwick, L.J.; see *R. (on the application of Britannic Asset Management Ltd) v Pensions Ombudsman* [2002] EWHC 441, [2002] O.P.L.R. 175 (QBD (Admin Ct)), Lightman, J.

Reg.4, amended: SI 2002/1555 Art.37

2489. Local Authorities Traffic Orders (Procedure) (England and Wales) Regulations 1996

Reg.6, amended: SI 2004/696 Art.3, Sch.1 para.25

Reg.7, see *R. (on the application of LPC Group Plc) v Leicester City Council* [2002] EWHC 2485, [2003] R.T.R. 11 (QBD (Admin Ct)), Sir Christopher Bellamy, Q.C.

2503. Chemical Weapons (Notification) Regulations 1996

Reg.3, amended: SI 2004/2406 Reg.2

Reg.4, amended: SI 2004/2406 Reg.2

Reg.5, amended: SI 2004/2406 Reg.2

2507. Act of Sederunt (Sheriff Court Bankruptcy Rules) 1996

Sch.1 Part 1, amended: SSI 2002/560 Sch.3 para.6

1996–cont.

2517. Occupational Pension Schemes (Modification of Schemes) Regulations 1996

Reg.6, amended: SI 2002/681 Reg.5

2519. Social Security (Jobseeker's Allowance and Payments on Account) (Miscellaneous Amendments) Regulations 1996

Reg.3, revoked (in part): SI 2003/492 Sch.3 Part 1

2547. Local Government Changes (Rent Act Registration Areas) Order 1996

varied: SI 2004/222 Art.2

2554. Income Tax (Employments) (Amendment No 5) Regulations 1996

revoked: SI 2003/2682 Sch.2

2555. Criminal Legal Aid (Scotland) Regulations 1996

Reg.5, amended: SSI 2003/249 Reg.3, SSI 2004/282 Reg.2

Reg.18, amended: SSI 2002/441 Reg.2

2567. Jobseeker's Allowance (Transitional Provisions) Regulations 1996

Reg.3, amended: SI 2002/2497 Sch.2 para.3

2570. Social Security (Back to Work Bonus) (No.2) Regulations 1996

revoked: SI 2003/1589 Reg.8

Reg.1, varied: SI 2003/1589 Reg.10

Reg.3, amended: SI 2002/490 Reg.6

Reg.4, amended: SI 2002/2497 Sch.2 para.1

Reg.8, amended: SI 2002/1397 Sch.1 para.27

Reg.17, amended: SI 2002/3197 Reg.7

Reg.17, varied: SI 2003/1589 Reg.10

Reg.22, amended: SI 2002/1397 Sch.1 para.27

Reg.23, amended: SI 2002/1397 Sch.1 para.27

2588. Central Nottinghamshire Healthcare National Health Service Trust (Establishment) Amendment Order 1996

revoked: 2003 c.43 s.7

2602. Essex Ambulance Service National Health Service Trust (Establishment) Amendment Order 1996

revoked: 2003 c.43 s.7

2628. Specified Diseases (Notification) Order 1996

Sch.1 Part I, amended: SI 2003/130 Art.18, SI 2003/326 Art.19, SSI 2003/91 Art.18

2631. Income Tax (Employments) (Amendment No 6) Regulations 1996

revoked: SI 2003/2682 Sch.2

2654. Double Taxation Relief (Manufactured Overseas Dividends) (Amendment) Regulations 1996

revoked: SI 2003/2581 Reg.2

2660. Duffield and Wirksworth Light Railway Order 1996

Art.5, amended: SI 2003/2155 Sch.1 para.18

NO.

1996–cont.

2671. Asylum (Designated Countries of Destination and Designated Safe Third Countries) Order 1996

see *R. (on the application of Javed) v Secretary of State for the Home Department* [2001] EWCA Civ 789, [2002] Q.B. 129 (CA), Lord Phillips of Worth Matravers, M.R.

2709. Act of Sederunt (Proceedings in the Sheriff Court under the Debtors (Scotland) Act 1987) (Amendment) 1996

revoked: SSI 2002/560 Sch.4

2714. Greater Manchester (Light Rapid Transit System) (Eccles Extension) Order 1996

Art.2, amended: SI 2003/2155 Sch.2

Art.5, amended: SI 2003/2155 Sch.1 para.18

Art.11, amended: SI 2003/2155 Sch.1 para.18

Art.20, applied: SI 2002/1327 Art.28

Art.35, applied: SI 2002/1327 Art.28

Art.36, applied: SI 2002/1327 Art.28

Art.37, applied: SI 2002/1327 Art.28

Art.38, applied: SI 2002/1327 Art.28

Art.40, applied: SI 2002/1327 Art.28

Art.41, applied: SI 2002/1327 Art.28

Art.42, applied: SI 2002/1327 Art.28

Art.43, applied: SI 2002/1327 Art.28

Art.44, applied: SI 2002/1327 Art.28

Art.45, applied: SI 2002/1327 Art.28

Art.46, applied: SI 2002/1327 Art.28

Art.47, applied: SI 2002/1327 Art.28

Art.51, applied: SI 2002/1327 Art.28

Sch.9 para.1, amended: SI 2003/2155 Sch.1 para.17, Sch.2

Sch.9 para.2, amended: SI 2003/2155 Sch.1 para.17, Sch.2

2744. Social Security (Invalid Care Allowance) Amendment Regulations 1996

Reg.3, amended: SI 2002/2497 Sch.2 para.1

2745. Social Security Benefit (Computation of Earnings) Regulations 1996

Reg.2, amended: SI 2002/2469 Sch.8, SI 2002/2823 Reg.2

Reg.7, amended: SI 2002/2823 Reg.2

Reg.7, applied: SI 2003/526 Art.6, SI 2004/552 Art.6

Reg.9, amended: SI 2002/2823 Reg.2

Reg.10, amended: SI 2002/2823 Reg.2

Reg.11, varied: SI 2002/1792 Reg.17B

Reg.12, amended: SI 2002/2469 Sch.6

Reg.12, varied: SI 2002/1792 Reg.17B, SI 2002/3197 Reg.3

Reg.13, amended: SI 2002/2823 Reg.2

Reg.13, varied: SI 2002/1792 Reg.17B

Reg.14, varied: SI 2002/1792 Reg.17B

Sch.1 para.7, amended: SI 2002/2469 Sch.6

Sch.2 para.2, amended: SI 2002/842 Reg.2

Sch.3 para.1, amended: SI 2002/2823 Reg.2

Sch.3 para.2, amended: SI 2002/2823 Reg.2

NO.

1996–cont.

2758. Multiplex Licence (Broadcasting of Programmes in Gaelic) Order 1996

varied: 2003 c.21 Sch.18 para.29

2763. Dog Fouling (Fixed Penalties) Order 1996

Art.3, revoked (in part): SI 2002/425 Art.3, SI 2004/909 Art.3

2766. Isle of Wight Community Healthcare National Health Service Trust Dissolution Order 1996

revoked: 2003 c.43 s.7

2767. St Mary's Hospital National Health Service Trust Dissolution Order 1996

revoked: 2003 c.43 s.7

2768. Isle of Wight Healthcare National Health Service Trust (Establishment) Order 1996

revoked: 2003 c.43 s.7

2793. Disability Discrimination (Questions and Replies) Order 1996

revoked: SI 2004/1168 Art.2

2798. Civil Aviation (Investigation of Air Accidents and Incidents) Regulations 1996

Reg.8, amended: SI 2004/1256 Reg.7

Reg.9, amended: SI 2004/1256 Reg.7

Reg.13, amended: SI 2004/1256 Reg.7

2800. Vehicle Registration (Sale of Information) Regulations 1996

revoked: SI 2002/2742 Sch.1 Part I

2803. Employment Tribunals (Interest on Awards in Discrimination Cases) Regulations 1996

applied: SI 2003/1660 Reg.30, SI 2003/1661 Reg.30

Reg.1, amended: SI 2003/1660 Sch.5 para.3, SI 2003/1661 Sch.5 para.3

2826. Local Government Changes for England (Capital Finance) (Amendment) Regulations 1996

revoked: SI 2004/2044 Art.3

2839. Approval of Codes of Management Practice (Residential Property) Order 1996

varied: SI 2004/1802 Art.3

2855. Act of Sederunt (Fees of Messengers-at-Arms) 1996

revoked: SSI 2002/566 Sch.2

2858. Act of Sederunt (Fees of Sheriff Officers) 1996

revoked: SSI 2002/567 Sch.2

2860. Royal Surrey County and St Luke's Hospitals National Health Service Trust (Change of Name) Order 1996

revoked: 2003 c.43 s.7

2867. Bodmin and Wenford Light Railway Order 1996

Art.8, amended: SI 2003/2155 Sch.1 para.18

1996–cont.

2880. Drug Trafficking Act 1994 (Designated Countries and Territories) Order 1996

Sch.1, amended: SI 2002/257 Sch.1, SI 2002/2846 Sch.1

2887. Home Repair Assistance Regulations 1996

revoked: SI 2002/1860 Sch.6

2888. Disabled Facilities Grants and Home Repair Assistance (Maximum Amounts) Order 1996

Art.2, amended: SI 2002/837 Art.2

2890. Housing Renewal Grants Regulations 1996

referred to: SI 2002/2798 Reg.2

Reg.2, amended: SI 2002/2469 Sch.8, SI 2002/2798 Reg.3, SI 2003/2504 Reg.4, SI 2004/253 Reg.4

Reg.5, amended: SI 2003/2504 Reg.5, SI 2004/253 Reg.5

Reg.5, revoked (in part): SI 2003/2504 Reg.5, SI 2004/253 Reg.5

Reg.7, amended: SI 2003/2504 Reg.6, SI 2004/253 Reg.6

Reg.9, amended: SI 2002/2798 Reg.4

Reg.10, amended: SI 2002/530 Reg.5, SI 2002/2798 Reg.5, SI 2003/2504 Reg.7, SI 2004/253 Reg.7

Reg.12, amended: SI 2002/2798 Reg.6, SI 2003/2504 Reg.8, SI 2004/253 Reg.8

Reg.13, amended: SI 2003/2504 Reg.9, SI 2004/253 Reg.9

Reg.14, amended: SI 2002/530 Reg.7, SI 2002/2798 Reg.7

Reg.18, amended: SI 2002/2798 Reg.8, SI 2003/2504 Reg.10, SI 2004/253 Reg.10

Reg.19, amended: SI 2002/530 Reg.9, SI 2002/2798 Reg.9, SI 2003/2504 Reg.11, SI 2004/253 Reg.11

Reg.24, amended: SI 2003/2504 Reg.12, SI 2004/253 Reg.12

Reg.26, amended: SI 2002/2469 Sch.6

Reg.30, amended: SI 2003/2504 Reg.13, SI 2004/253 Reg.13

Reg.30, substituted: SI 2004/253 Reg.13

Reg.31, amended: SI 2002/2798 Reg.10, SI 2003/2504 Reg.14, SI 2004/253 Reg.14

Reg.31, revoked (in part): SI 2003/2504 Reg.14, SI 2004/253 Reg.14

Reg.31, substituted: SI 2004/253 Reg.14

Reg.38, amended: SI 2002/530 Reg.11, SI 2002/2798 Reg.11

Reg.40, amended: SI 2003/2504 Reg.15, SI 2004/253 Reg.15

Reg.40, substituted: SI 2004/253 Reg.15

Reg.41, amended: SI 2002/2798 Reg.12

Reg.43, amended: SI 2002/2798 Reg.13, SI 2003/2504 Reg.16, SI 2004/253 Reg.16

Reg.43, substituted: SI 2004/253 Reg.16

Reg.46, amended: SI 2002/2798 Reg.14

1996–cont.

2890. Housing Renewal Grants Regulations 1996–*cont.*

Sch.1 Part I para.1, amended: SI 2002/2798 Reg.15, SI 2003/2504 Reg.17, SI 2004/253 Reg.17

Sch.1 Part I para.1, substituted: SI 2004/253 Reg.17

Sch.1 Part I para.2, amended: SI 2002/2798 Reg.15, SI 2003/2504 Reg.17, SI 2004/253 Reg.17

Sch.1 Part I para.2, substituted: SI 2004/253 Reg.17

Sch.1 Part II para.3, amended: SI 2002/530 Reg.15, SI 2002/2798 Reg.15, SI 2003/2504 Reg.17, SI 2004/253 Reg.17

Sch.1 Part II para.3, substituted: SI 2004/253 Reg.17

Sch.1 Part III para.10A, added: SI 2002/530 Reg.15, SI 2002/2798 Reg.15

Sch.1 Part III para.12, amended: SI 2002/530 Reg.15, SI 2002/2798 Reg.15, SI 2003/2504 Reg.17, SI 2004/253 Reg.17

Sch.1 Part III para.13, amended: SI 2003/2504 Reg.17, SI 2004/253 Reg.17

Sch.1 Part III para.13, substituted: SI 2004/253 Reg.17

Sch.1 Part III para.14, amended: SI 2002/530 Reg.15, SI 2002/2798 Reg.15

Sch.1 Part III para.15, amended: SI 2003/2504 Reg.17, SI 2004/253 Reg.17

Sch.1 Part III para.18, amended: SI 2004/253 Reg.17

Sch.1 Part IV, amended: SI 2002/2798 Reg.15

Sch.1 Part IV, substituted: SI 2004/253 Reg.17

Sch.2 para.5, amended: SI 2003/2504 Reg.18, SI 2004/253 Reg.18

Sch.2 para.12, substituted: SI 2003/2504 Reg.18, SI 2004/253 Reg.18

Sch.2 para.18, substituted: SI 2003/2504 Reg.18, SI 2004/253 Reg.18

Sch.3 para.2, amended: SI 2002/530 Reg.16, SI 2002/2798 Reg.16

Sch.3 para.4, substituted: SI 2003/2504 Reg.19, SI 2004/253 Reg.19

Sch.3 para.6, amended: SI 2003/2504 Reg.19, SI 2004/253 Reg.19

Sch.3 para.11, amended: SI 2002/530 Reg.16, SI 2002/2798 Reg.16

Sch.3 para.13, amended: SI 2003/2504 Reg.19, SI 2004/253 Reg.19

Sch.3 para.13, substituted: SI 2004/253 Reg.19

Sch.3 para.13A, added: SI 2002/530 Reg.16, SI 2002/2798 Reg.16

Sch.3 para.24, amended: SI 2002/530 Reg.16, SI 2002/2798 Reg.16

Sch.3 para.31, amended: SI 2002/530 Reg.16, SI 2002/2798 Reg.16

Sch.3 para.51, amended: SI 2003/2504 Reg.19, SI 2004/253 Reg.19

NO.

1996–cont.

2890. Housing Renewal Grants Regulations 1996–*cont.*

Sch.3 para.52, amended: SI 2003/2504 Reg.19, SI 2004/253 Reg.19

Sch.3 para.53, amended: SI 2003/2504 Reg.19, SI 2004/253 Reg.19

Sch.3 para.53, substituted: SI 2004/253 Reg.19

Sch.3 para.54, substituted: SI 2003/2504 Reg.19, SI 2004/253 Reg.19

Sch.3 para.55, revoked (in part): SI 2003/2504 Reg.19, SI 2004/253 Reg.19

Sch.3 para.59, amended: SI 2003/762 Reg.11, SI 2004/1748 Sch.2 para.2

Sch.3 para.61, substituted: SI 2002/530 Reg.16, SI 2002/2798 Reg.16

Sch.3 para.70, added: SI 2002/530 Reg.16, SI 2002/2798 Reg.16

Sch.3 para.71, added: SI 2003/2504 Reg.19, SI 2004/253 Reg.19

Sch.4 para.6, substituted: SI 2003/2504 Reg.20, SI 2004/253 Reg.20

Sch.4 para.9, amended: SI 2002/530 Reg.17, SI 2002/2798 Reg.17, SI 2003/2504 Reg.20, SI 2004/253 Reg.20

Sch.4 para.9, substituted: SI 2004/253 Reg.20

Sch.4 para.52, substituted: SI 2002/530 Reg.17, SI 2002/2798 Reg.17

Sch.4 para.64, added: SI 2002/530 Reg.17, SI 2002/2798 Reg.17

Sch.4 para.65, added: SI 2002/530 Reg.17, SI 2002/2798 Reg.17

2891. Housing Renewal Grants (Prescribed Form and Particulars) Regulations 1996

Reg.2, substituted: SI 2003/2707 Reg.3, SI 2004/254 Reg.3

Sch.1, added: SI 2002/667 Sch.1 para.3, Sch.1 para.7, Sch.1 para.8, SI 2004/254 Sch.1 para.17, Sch.1 para.25, Sch.1 para.31, Sch.1 para.32

Sch.1, amended: SI 2002/667 Sch.1 para.1, Sch.1 para.2, Sch.1 para.4, Sch.1 para.5, Sch.1 para.6, Sch.1 para.9, Sch.1 para.10, SI 2002/1397 Sch.1 para.28, SI 2002/2799 Sch.1 para.1, Sch.1 para.2, Sch.1 para.3, Sch.1 para.4, Sch.1 para.5, Sch.1 para.6, Sch.1 para.7, Sch.1 para.8, Sch.1 para.9, Sch.1 para.10, SI 2003/2707 Sch.1, SI 2004/254 Sch.1 para.1, Sch.1 para.2, Sch.1 para.3, Sch.1 para.4, Sch.1 para.6, Sch.1 para.7, Sch.1 para.8, Sch.1 para.9, Sch.1 para.10, Sch.1 para.11, Sch.1 para.12, Sch.1 para.13, Sch.1 para.14, Sch.1 para.15, Sch.1 para.16, Sch.1 para.19, Sch.1 para.20, Sch.1 para.21, Sch.1 para.22, Sch.1 para.23, Sch.1 para.24, Sch.1 para.26, Sch.1 para.27, Sch.1 para.28, Sch.1 para.29, Sch.1 para.30, Sch.1 para.33, Sch.1 para.34

NO.

1996–cont.

2891. Housing Renewal Grants (Prescribed Form and Particulars) Regulations 1996–*cont.*

Sch.1, revoked: SI 2004/254 Sch.1 para.5, Sch.1 para.18

2907. Child Support Departure Direction and Consequential Amendments Regulations 1996

Reg.1, amended: SI 2002/1703 Sch.2 para.5

Reg.9, amended: SI 2003/328 Reg.4, SI 2003/2779 Reg.2

Reg.12, amended: SI 2003/328 Reg.4, SI 2003/2779 Reg.2

Reg.23, amended: SI 2002/1204 Reg.3

Reg.32A, see *R. (on the application of Denson) v Child Support Agency* [2002] EWHC 154, [2002] 1 F.L.R. 938 (QBD (Admin Ct)), Munby, J.

Reg.32B, see *R. (on the application of Denson) v Child Support Agency* [2002] EWHC 154, [2002] 1 F.L.R. 938 (QBD (Admin Ct)), Munby, J.

2908. Merchant Shipping (Ship Inspection and Survey Organisations) Regulations 1996

Reg.2, amended: SI 2004/1266 Reg.3

2911. Utilities Contracts Regulations 1996

Reg.2, amended: SI 2003/46 Reg.6

Reg.14, amended: SI 2003/46 Reg.6

Reg.15, amended: SI 2003/46 Reg.6

Reg.17, amended: SI 2003/46 Reg.6

Reg.18, amended: SI 2003/46 Reg.6

Reg.23, amended: SI 2003/46 Reg.6

Reg.31, amended: SI 2003/46 Reg.6

Sch.1, amended: SI 2003/1615 Sch.1 para.50, SSI 2003/331 Sch.1 para.9

Sch.5 Part A para.1, revoked: SI 2003/46 Reg.6

Sch.5 Part A para.2, revoked: SI 2003/46 Reg.6

Sch.5 Part A para.3, revoked: SI 2003/46 Reg.6

Sch.5 Part A para.4, revoked: SI 2003/46 Reg.6

Sch.5 Part A para.5, revoked: SI 2003/46 Reg.6

Sch.5 Part A para.6, revoked: SI 2003/46 Reg.6

Sch.5 Part A para.7, revoked: SI 2003/46 Reg.6

Sch.5 Part A para.8, revoked: SI 2003/46 Reg.6

Sch.5 Part A para.9, revoked: SI 2003/46 Reg.6

Sch.5 Part A para.10, revoked: SI 2003/46 Reg.6

Sch.5 Part A para.11, revoked: SI 2003/46 Reg.6

Sch.5 Part A para.12, revoked: SI 2003/46 Reg.6

1996–cont.

2911. Utilities Contracts Regulations 1996– cont.

Sch.5 Part B para.1, revoked: SI 2003/46 Reg.6

Sch.5 Part B para.2, revoked: SI 2003/46 Reg.6

Sch.5 Part B para.3, revoked: SI 2003/46 Reg.6

Sch.5 Part B para.4, revoked: SI 2003/46 Reg.6

Sch.5 Part B para.5, revoked: SI 2003/46 Reg.6

Sch.5 Part B para.6, revoked: SI 2003/46 Reg.6

Sch.5 Part B para.7, revoked: SI 2003/46 Reg.6

Sch.5 Part B para.8, revoked: SI 2003/46 Reg.6

Sch.5 Part B para.9, revoked: SI 2003/46 Reg.6

Sch.5 Part B para.10, revoked: SI 2003/46 Reg.6

Sch.5 Part B para.11, revoked: SI 2003/46 Reg.6

Sch.5 Part B para.12, revoked: SI 2003/46 Reg.6

Sch.5 Part B para.13, revoked: SI 2003/46 Reg.6

Sch.5 Part B para.14, revoked: SI 2003/46 Reg.6

Sch.5 Part B para.15, revoked: SI 2003/46 Reg.6

Sch.5 Part B para.16, revoked: SI 2003/46 Reg.6

Sch.5 Part B para.17, revoked: SI 2003/46 Reg.6

Sch.5 Part B para.18, revoked: SI 2003/46 Reg.6

Sch.5 Part B para.19, revoked: SI 2003/46 Reg.6

Sch.5 Part B para.20, revoked: SI 2003/46 Reg.6

Sch.5 Part E para.1, revoked: SI 2003/46 Reg.6

Sch.5 Part E para.2, revoked: SI 2003/46 Reg.6

Sch.5 Part E para.3, revoked: SI 2003/46 Reg.6

Sch.5 Part E para.4, revoked: SI 2003/46 Reg.6

Sch.5 Part E para.5, revoked: SI 2003/46 Reg.6

Sch.5 Part E para.6, revoked: SI 2003/46 Reg.6

Sch.5 Part E para.7, revoked: SI 2003/46 Reg.6

Sch.5 Part F para.1, revoked: SI 2003/46 Reg.6

Sch.5 Part F para.2, revoked: SI 2003/46 Reg.6

1996–cont.

2911. Utilities Contracts Regulations 1996– cont.

Sch.5 Part F para.3, revoked: SI 2003/46 Reg.6

Sch.5 Part F para.4, revoked: SI 2003/46 Reg.6

Sch.5 Part F para.5, revoked: SI 2003/46 Reg.6

Sch.5 Part F para.6, revoked: SI 2003/46 Reg.6

Sch.5 Part F para.7, revoked: SI 2003/46 Reg.6

Sch.5 Part F para.8, revoked: SI 2003/46 Reg.6

Sch.5 Part F para.9, revoked: SI 2003/46 Reg.6

Sch.5 Part F para.10, revoked: SI 2003/46 Reg.6

Sch.5 Part F para.11, revoked: SI 2003/46 Reg.6

Sch.5 Part F para.12, revoked: SI 2003/46 Reg.6

Sch.5 Part F para.13, revoked: SI 2003/46 Reg.6

Sch.5 Part F para.14, revoked: SI 2003/46 Reg.6

Sch.5 Part F para.15, revoked: SI 2003/46 Reg.6

Sch.5 Part F para.16, revoked: SI 2003/46 Reg.6

Sch.5 Part F para.17, revoked: SI 2003/46 Reg.6

Sch.5 Part F para.18, revoked: SI 2003/46 Reg.6

Sch.5 Part F para.19, revoked: SI 2003/46 Reg.6

Sch.5 Part F para.20, revoked: SI 2003/46 Reg.6

Sch.5 Part F para.21, revoked: SI 2003/46 Reg.6

Sch.5 Part G para.1, revoked: SI 2003/46 Reg.6

Sch.5 Part G para.2, revoked: SI 2003/46 Reg.6

Sch.5 Part G para.3, revoked: SI 2003/46 Reg.6

Sch.5 Part G para.4, revoked: SI 2003/46 Reg.6

Sch.5 Part G para.5, revoked: SI 2003/46 Reg.6

Sch.5 Part G para.6, revoked: SI 2003/46 Reg.6

Sch.5 Part G para.7, revoked: SI 2003/46 Reg.6

Sch.5 Part G para.8, revoked: SI 2003/46 Reg.6

Sch.5 Part G para.9, revoked: SI 2003/46 Reg.6

Sch.5 Part G para.10, revoked: SI 2003/46 Reg.6

1996–cont.

2911. Utilities Contracts Regulations 1996– cont.

Sch.5 Part G para.11, revoked: SI 2003/46 Reg.6

Sch.5 Part G para.12, revoked: SI 2003/46 Reg.6

Sch.5 Part G para.13, revoked: SI 2003/46 Reg.6

Sch.5 Part G para.14, revoked: SI 2003/46 Reg.6

Sch.5 Part H para.1, revoked: SI 2003/46 Reg.6

Sch.5 Part H para.2, revoked: SI 2003/46 Reg.6

Sch.5 Part H para.3, revoked: SI 2003/46 Reg.6

Sch.5 Part H para.4, revoked: SI 2003/46 Reg.6

Sch.5 Part H para.5, revoked: SI 2003/46 Reg.6

Sch.5 Part H para.6, revoked: SI 2003/46 Reg.6

Sch.5 Part H para.7, revoked: SI 2003/46 Reg.6

Sch.5 Part H para.8, revoked: SI 2003/46 Reg.6

Sch.5 Part H para.9, revoked: SI 2003/46 Reg.6

Sch.5 Part C para.1, revoked: SI 2003/46 Reg.6

Sch.5 Part C para.2, revoked: SI 2003/46 Reg.6

Sch.5 Part C para.3, revoked: SI 2003/46 Reg.6

Sch.5 Part C para.4, revoked: SI 2003/46 Reg.6

Sch.5 Part C para.5, revoked: SI 2003/46 Reg.6

Sch.5 Part C para.6, revoked: SI 2003/46 Reg.6

Sch.5 Part C para.7, revoked: SI 2003/46 Reg.6

Sch.5 Part C para.8, revoked: SI 2003/46 Reg.6

Sch.5 Part C para.9, revoked: SI 2003/46 Reg.6

Sch.5 Part C para.10, revoked: SI 2003/46 Reg.6

Sch.5 Part C para.11, revoked: SI 2003/46 Reg.6

Sch.5 Part C para.12, revoked: SI 2003/46 Reg.6

Sch.5 Part C para.13, revoked: SI 2003/46 Reg.6

Sch.5 Part C para.14, revoked: SI 2003/46 Reg.6

Sch.5 Part C para.15, revoked: SI 2003/46 Reg.6

Sch.5 Part C para.16, revoked: SI 2003/46 Reg.6

1996–cont.

2911. Utilities Contracts Regulations 1996– cont.

Sch.5 Part C para.17, revoked: SI 2003/46 Reg.6

Sch.5 Part C para.18, revoked: SI 2003/46 Reg.6

Sch.5 Part D para.1, revoked: SI 2003/46 Reg.6

Sch.5 Part D para.2, revoked: SI 2003/46 Reg.6

Sch.5 Part D para.3, revoked: SI 2003/46 Reg.6

Sch.5 Part D para.4, revoked: SI 2003/46 Reg.6

Sch.5 Part D para.5, revoked: SI 2003/46 Reg.6

Sch.5 Part D para.6, revoked: SI 2003/46 Reg.6

Sch.5 Part D para.7, revoked: SI 2003/46 Reg.6

Sch.5 Part D para.8, revoked: SI 2003/46 Reg.6

Sch.5 Part D para.9, revoked: SI 2003/46 Reg.6

Sch.5 Part D para.10, revoked: SI 2003/46 Reg.6

Sch.5 Part D para.11, revoked: SI 2003/46 Reg.6

Sch.5 Part D para.12, revoked: SI 2003/46 Reg.6

Sch.5 Part D para.13, revoked: SI 2003/46 Reg.6

Sch.5 Part D para.14, revoked: SI 2003/46 Reg.6

Sch.5 Part D para.15, revoked: SI 2003/46 Reg.6

Sch.5 Part D para.16, revoked: SI 2003/46 Reg.6

Sch.5 Part D para.17, revoked: SI 2003/46 Reg.6

Sch.5 Part D para.18, revoked: SI 2003/46 Reg.6

Sch.5 Part D para.19, revoked: SI 2003/46 Reg.6

2912. Leicestershire Fire Services (Combination Scheme) Order 1996

Sch.1 Part II para.6, amended: 2003 c.26 Sch.8 Part 2

Sch.1 Part III para.20, revoked (in part): 2003 c.26 Sch.8 Part 2

Sch.1 Part IV para.21, revoked: 2003 c.26 Sch.8 Part 2

2914. Denbighshire and Wrexham (Areas) Order 1996

varied: SI 2004/218 Art.2

2915. Bridgend and The Vale of Glamorgan (Areas) Order 1996

varied: SI 2004/218 Art.2

NO.

1996–cont.

2916. Wiltshire Fire Services (Combination Scheme) Order 1996

Sch.1 Part II para.6, amended: 2003 c.26 Sch.8 Part 2

Sch.1 Part III para.20, revoked (in part): 2003 c.26 Sch.8 Part 2

Sch.1 Part IV para.21, revoked: 2003 c.26 Sch.8 Part 2

2917. Staffordshire Fire Services (Combination Scheme) Order 1996

Sch.1 Part II para.6, amended: 2003 c.26 Sch.8 Part 2

Sch.1 Part III para.20, revoked (in part): 2003 c.26 Sch.8 Part 2

Sch.1 Part IV para.21, revoked: 2003 c.26 Sch.8 Part 2

2918. Bedfordshire Fire Services (Combination Scheme) Order 1996

Sch.1 Part II para.6, amended: 2003 c.26 Sch.8 Part 2

Sch.1 Part III para.20, revoked (in part): 2003 c.26 Sch.8 Part 2

Sch.1 Part IV para.21, revoked: 2003 c.26 Sch.8 Part 2

2919. Derbyshire Fire Services (Combination Scheme) Order 1996

Sch.1 Part II para.6, amended: 2003 c.26 Sch.8 Part 2

Sch.1 Part III para.20, revoked (in part): 2003 c.26 Sch.8 Part 2

Sch.1 Part IV para.21, revoked: 2003 c.26 Sch.8 Part 2

2920. Dorset Fire Services (Combination Scheme) Order 1996

Sch.1 Part II para.6, amended: 2003 c.26 Sch.8 Part 2

Sch.1 Part III para.20, revoked (in part): 2003 c.26 Sch.8 Part 2

Sch.1 Part IV para.21, revoked: 2003 c.26 Sch.8 Part 2

2921. Durham Fire Services (Combination Scheme) Order 1996

Sch.1 Part II para.6, amended: 2003 c.26 Sch.8 Part 2

Sch.1 Part III para.20, revoked (in part): 2003 c.26 Sch.8 Part 2

Sch.1 Part IV para.21, revoked: 2003 c.26 Sch.8 Part 2

2922. East Sussex Fire Services (Combination Scheme) Order 1996

Sch.1 Part II para.6, amended: 2003 c.26 Sch.8 Part 2

Sch.1 Part III para.20, revoked (in part): 2003 c.26 Sch.8 Part 2

Sch.1 Part IV para.21, revoked: 2003 c.26 Sch.8 Part 2

2923. Hampshire Fire Services (Combination Scheme) Order 1996

Sch.1 Part II para.6, amended: 2003 c.26 Sch.8 Part 2

NO.

1996–cont.

2923. Hampshire Fire Services (Combination Scheme) Order 1996–cont.

Sch.1 Part III para.20, revoked (in part): 2003 c.26 Sch.8 Part 2

Sch.1 Part IV para.21, revoked: 2003 c.26 Sch.8 Part 2

2924. Buckinghamshire Fire Services (Combination Scheme) Order 1996

Sch.1 Part II para.6, amended: 2003 c.26 Sch.8 Part 2

Sch.1 Part III para.20, revoked (in part): 2003 c.26 Sch.8 Part 2

Sch.1 Part IV para.21, revoked: 2003 c.26 Sch.8 Part 2

2925. Cosmetic Products (Safety) Regulations 1996

applied: SI 2002/1689 Reg.3, SR 2002/301 Reg.3

revoked: SI 2003/835 Sch.1

Reg.2, referred to: SI 2002/2677

Reg.8, amended: SI 2002/3135 Sch.1 para.36

Sch.1, applied: SI 2003/835 Reg.2

Sch.2 Part I, applied: SI 2003/835 Reg.2

2967. Copyright and Related Rights Regulations 1996

referred to: SI 2003/2500 Sch.1 Part 1

Reg.16, amended: SI 2003/2498 Sch.1 para.27

2969. Income Tax (Employments) (Notional Payments) (Amendment) Regulations 1996

revoked: 2003 c.1 Sch.8 Part 2

2988. Social Security (Claims and Payments) Amendment (No.2) Regulations 1996

revoked (in part): SI 2003/492 Sch.3 Part 1

2991. Insurance Companies (Reserves) (Tax) Regulations 1996

Reg.2, amended: SI 2004/3260 Reg.2

Reg.7, amended: SI 2002/1409 Art.5

Reg.8, amended: SI 2002/1409 Art.5

3010. Merchant Shipping (Dangerous or Noxious Liquid Substances in Bulk) Regulations 1996

Reg.2, amended: SI 2004/930 Reg.2

Reg.3A, added: SI 2004/930 Reg.3

Reg.6, amended: SI 2004/930 Reg.4

Reg.8A, added: SI 2004/930 Reg.5

Reg.9, substituted: SI 2004/930 Reg.6

Reg.10, substituted: SI 2004/930 Reg.6

Reg.11, substituted: SI 2004/930 Reg.6

Reg.15, amended: SI 2004/930 Reg.7

3012. Mid Essex Community and Mental Health National Health Service Trust (Establishment) Amendment Order 1996

revoked: 2003 c.43 s.7

NO.

1996–cont.

3039. Personal Protective Equipment (EC Directive) (Amendment) Regulations 1996

revoked: SI 2002/1144 Sch.11 para.1

3040. Bridlington Harbour Revision Order 1996

Art.15, revoked: SI 2004/1426 Sch.3

3047. Surface Waters (Abstraction for Drinking Water) (Classification) (Scotland) Regulations 1996

Reg.1, amended: SSI 2003/331 Sch.1 para.10

Reg.9, amended: SSI 2003/331 Sch.1 para.10

Reg.10, amended: SSI 2003/331 Sch.1 para.10

Reg.11, amended: SSI 2003/331 Sch.1 para.10

Reg.14, amended: SSI 2003/331 Sch.1 para.10

3055. Litter (Fixed Penalty) Order 1996

revoked (in part): SI 2002/424 Art.3, SI 2004/909 Art.3, SSI 2003/268 Art.3

3100. Air Navigation (Dangerous Goods) (Amendment) Regulations 1996

revoked: SI 2002/2786 Sch.1

3102. European Nursing and Midwifery Qualifications Designation Order 1996

Art.2, amended: SI 2003/3148 Reg.5

Art.6, amended: SI 2003/3148 Reg.5

Sch.1, amended: SI 2003/3148 Reg.5

Sch.2 Part I, substituted: SI 2003/3148 Sch.1

Sch.2 Part I para.1, substituted: SI 2003/3148 Sch.1

Sch.2 Part I para.2, substituted: SI 2003/3148 Sch.1

Sch.2 Part I para.3, substituted: SI 2003/3148 Sch.1

Sch.2 Part I para.4, substituted: SI 2003/3148 Sch.1

Sch.2 Part I para.5, substituted: SI 2003/3148 Sch.1

Sch.2 Part I para.6, substituted: SI 2003/3148 Sch.1

Sch.2 Part I para.7, substituted: SI 2003/3148 Sch.1

Sch.2 Part I para.8, substituted: SI 2003/3148 Sch.1

Sch.2 Part I para.9, substituted: SI 2003/3148 Sch.1

Sch.2 Part I para.10, substituted: SI 2003/3148 Sch.1

Sch.2 Part I para.11, substituted: SI 2003/3148 Sch.1

Sch.2 Part I para.12, substituted: SI 2003/3148 Sch.1

Sch.2 Part I para.13, substituted: SI 2003/3148 Sch.1

Sch.2 Part I para.14, substituted: SI 2003/3148 Sch.1

Sch.2 Part I para.15, substituted: SI 2003/3148 Sch.1

NO.

1996–cont.

3102. European Nursing and Midwifery Qualifications Designation Order 1996–*cont.*

Sch.2 Part I para.16, substituted: SI 2003/3148 Sch.1

Sch.2 Part I para.17, substituted: SI 2003/3148 Sch.1

Sch.2 Part II, substituted: SI 2003/3148 Sch.1

Sch.2 Part II para.18, substituted: SI 2003/3148 Sch.1

Sch.2 Part II para.19, substituted: SI 2003/3148 Sch.1

Sch.2 Part II para.20, substituted: SI 2003/3148 Sch.1

Sch.2 Part II para.21, substituted: SI 2003/3148 Sch.1

Sch.2 Part II para.22, substituted: SI 2003/3148 Sch.1

Sch.2 Part II para.23, substituted: SI 2003/3148 Sch.1

Sch.2 Part II para.24, substituted: SI 2003/3148 Sch.1

Sch.2 Part II para.25, substituted: SI 2003/3148 Sch.1

Sch.2 Part II para.26, substituted: SI 2003/3148 Sch.1

Sch.2 Part II para.27, substituted: SI 2003/3148 Sch.1

Sch.2 Part II para.28, substituted: SI 2003/3148 Sch.1

Sch.2 Part II para.29, substituted: SI 2003/3148 Sch.1

Sch.2 Part II para.30, substituted: SI 2003/3148 Sch.1

Sch.2 Part II para.31, substituted: SI 2003/3148 Sch.1

Sch.2 Part II para.32, substituted: SI 2003/3148 Sch.1

Sch.2 Part II para.33, substituted: SI 2003/3148 Sch.1

Sch.2 Part II para.34, substituted: SI 2003/3148 Sch.1

3118. Local Government (Changes for the Registration Service in Bedfordshire, Buckinghamshire, Derbyshire, Dorset, Durham, East Sussex, Hampshire, Leicestershire, Staffordshire and Wiltshire) Order 1996

varied: SI 2004/222 Art.2

3119. Housing Renewal Grants and Home Repair Assistance (Amendment) Regulations 1996

revoked: SI 2002/1860 Sch.6

3124. Products of Animal Origin (Import and Export) Regulations 1996

applied: SI 2002/2 Reg.12, SI 2002/8 Reg.12, SI 2002/130 Reg.12, SI 2003/1736 Reg.4, SI 2003/3003 Reg.6, SI 2003/3229 Reg.4, SSI 2003/299 Reg.4, SSI 2003/568 Reg.4

NO.

3124. Products of Animal Origin (Import and Export) Regulations 1996–*cont.*

referred to: SI 2002/47, SI 2002/1476, SSI 2002/234

Reg.2, disapplied: SI 2002/1227 Sch.7, SI 2002/1387 Sch.7, SI 2003/3177 Reg.67, SI 2004/1430 Reg.67, SSI 2002/445 Sch.7

Reg.3, disapplied: SI 2002/1227 Sch.7, SI 2002/1387 Sch.7, SI 2003/3177 Reg.67, SI 2004/1430 Reg.67, SSI 2002/445 Sch.7

Reg.4, disapplied: SI 2002/1227 Sch.7, SI 2002/1387 Sch.7, SI 2003/3177 Reg.67, SI 2004/1430 Reg.67, SSI 2002/445 Sch.7

Reg.5, disapplied: SI 2002/1227 Sch.7, SI 2002/1387 Sch.7, SI 2003/3177 Reg.67, SI 2004/1430 Reg.67, SSI 2002/445 Sch.7

Reg.6, applied: SI 2003/1736 Reg.10, SI 2003/3003 Reg.12, SI 2003/3229 Reg.10, SSI 2003/299 Reg.10, SSI 2003/568 Reg.10

Reg.6, disapplied: SI 2002/1227 Sch.7, SI 2002/1387 Sch.7, SI 2003/3177 Reg.67, SI 2004/1430 Reg.67, SSI 2002/445 Sch.7

Reg.7, disapplied: SI 2002/1227 Sch.7, SI 2002/1387 Sch.7, SI 2003/3177 Reg.67, SI 2004/1430 Reg.67, SSI 2002/445 Sch.7

Reg.8, disapplied: SI 2002/1227 Sch.7, SI 2002/1387 Sch.7, SI 2003/3177 Reg.67, SI 2004/1430 Reg.67, SSI 2002/445 Sch.7

Reg.19, disapplied: SI 2002/1227 Sch.7, SI 2002/1387 Sch.7, SSI 2002/445 Sch.7

Reg.19, revoked (in part): SI 2003/3177 Sch.6, SI 2004/1430 Sch.6

Reg.20, disapplied: SI 2002/1227 Sch.7, SI 2002/1387 Sch.7, SSI 2002/445 Sch.7

Reg.20, revoked (in part): SI 2003/3177 Sch.6, SI 2004/1430 Sch.6

Reg.21, see *R. v Matudi (Misawki Kurawku)* [2003] EWCA Crim 697, [2003] E.H.L.R. 13 (CA (Crim Div)), Scott Baker, L.J.

Reg.21, disapplied: SI 2002/1227 Sch.7, SI 2002/1387 Sch.7, SSI 2002/445 Sch.7

Reg.21, revoked (in part): SI 2003/3177 Sch.6, SI 2004/1430 Sch.6

Reg.22, disapplied: SI 2002/1227 Sch.7, SI 2002/1387 Sch.7, SSI 2002/445 Sch.7

Reg.22, revoked (in part): SI 2003/3177 Sch.6, SI 2004/1430 Sch.6

Reg.23, disapplied: SI 2002/1227 Sch.7, SI 2002/1387 Sch.7, SSI 2002/445 Sch.7

Reg.23, revoked (in part): SI 2003/3177 Sch.6, SI 2004/1430 Sch.6

Reg.24, disapplied: SI 2002/1227 Sch.7, SI 2002/1387 Sch.7, SSI 2002/445 Sch.7

NO.

3124. Products of Animal Origin (Import and Export) Regulations 1996–*cont.*

Reg.24, revoked (in part): SI 2003/3177 Sch.6, SI 2004/1430 Sch.6

Reg.25, see *Southampton Port HA v Seahawk Marine Foods Ltd* [2002] EWCA Civ 54, [2002] E.H.L.R. 15 (CA), Buxton, L.J.

Reg.25, disapplied: SI 2002/1227 Sch.7, SI 2002/1387 Sch.7, SSI 2002/445 Sch.7

Reg.25, revoked (in part): SI 2003/3177 Sch.6, SI 2004/1430 Sch.6

Reg.26, disapplied: SI 2002/1227 Sch.7, SI 2002/1387 Sch.7, SSI 2002/445 Sch.7

Reg.26, revoked (in part): SI 2003/3177 Sch.6, SI 2004/1430 Sch.6

Reg.27, disapplied: SI 2002/1227 Sch.7, SI 2002/1387 Sch.7, SSI 2002/445 Sch.7

Reg.27, revoked (in part): SI 2003/3177 Sch.6, SI 2004/1430 Sch.6

Reg.28, disapplied: SI 2002/1227 Sch.7, SI 2002/1387 Sch.7, SI 2003/3177 Reg.67, SI 2004/1430 Reg.67, SSI 2002/445 Sch.7

Reg.29, disapplied: SI 2002/1227 Sch.7, SI 2002/1387 Sch.7, SI 2003/3177 Reg.67, SI 2004/1430 Reg.67, SSI 2002/445 Sch.7

Reg.30, disapplied: SI 2002/1227 Sch.7, SI 2002/1387 Sch.7, SI 2003/3177 Reg.67, SI 2004/1430 Reg.67, SSI 2002/445 Sch.7

Reg.30A, disapplied: SI 2002/1227 Sch.7, SI 2002/1387 Sch.7, SI 2003/3177 Reg.67, SI 2004/1430 Reg.67, SSI 2002/445 Sch.7

Reg.31, disapplied: SI 2002/1227 Sch.7, SI 2002/1387 Sch.7, SI 2003/3177 Reg.67, SI 2004/1430 Reg.67, SSI 2002/445 Sch.7

Reg.32, disapplied: SI 2002/1227 Sch.7, SI 2002/1387 Sch.7, SI 2003/3177 Reg.67, SI 2004/1430 Reg.67, SSI 2002/445 Sch.7

Reg.33, disapplied: SI 2002/1227 Sch.7, SI 2002/1387 Sch.7, SI 2003/3177 Reg.67, SI 2004/1430 Reg.67, SSI 2002/445 Sch.7

Reg.34, disapplied: SI 2002/1227 Sch.7, SI 2002/1387 Sch.7, SI 2003/3177 Reg.67, SI 2004/1430 Reg.67, SSI 2002/445 Sch.7

Reg.35, disapplied: SI 2002/1227 Sch.7, SI 2002/1387 Sch.7, SI 2003/3177 Reg.67, SI 2004/1430 Reg.67, SSI 2002/445 Sch.7

Reg.36, disapplied: SI 2002/1227 Sch.7, SI 2002/1387 Sch.7, SI 2003/3177 Reg.67, SI 2004/1430 Reg.67, SSI 2002/445 Sch.7

Reg.37, see *R. v Matudi (Misawki Kurawku)* [2003] EWCA Crim 697, [2003] E.H.L.R. 13 (CA (Crim Div)), Scott Baker, L.J.

NO.

NO.

1996–cont.

3124. Products of Animal Origin (Import and Export) Regulations 1996–*cont.*

Reg.37, disapplied: SI 2002/1227 Sch.7, SI 2002/1387 Sch.7, SI 2003/3177 Reg.67, SI 2004/1430 Reg.67, SSI 2002/445 Sch.7

Reg.38, disapplied: SI 2002/1227 Sch.7, SI 2002/1387 Sch.7, SI 2003/3177 Reg.67, SI 2004/1430 Reg.67, SSI 2002/445 Sch.7

Reg.39, disapplied: SI 2002/1227 Sch.7, SI 2002/1387 Sch.7, SI 2003/3177 Reg.67, SI 2004/1430 Reg.67, SSI 2002/445 Sch.7

Reg.40, disapplied: SI 2002/1227 Sch.7, SI 2002/1387 Sch.7, SI 2003/3177 Reg.67, SI 2004/1430 Reg.67, SSI 2002/445 Sch.7

Sch.2 para.6, amended: SI 2002/889 Reg.5, SI 2002/1476 Reg.5, SSI 2002/234 Reg.6

Sch.2 para.7, amended: SI 2002/47 Reg.3, SI 2002/889 Reg.5, SI 2002/1476 Reg.5, SSI 2002/87 Reg.3, SSI 2002/234 Reg.6

Sch.3 para.9, amended: SI 2003/1736 Reg.3, SI 2003/3003 Reg.4, Reg.5, SI 2003/3229 Reg.3, SSI 2003/299 Reg.3, SSI 2003/405 Reg.3, SSI 2003/466 Reg.3, SSI 2003/568 Reg.3

Sch.3 para.12, amended: SI 2003/1736 Reg.3, SI 2003/3003 Reg.4, Reg.5, SI 2003/3229 Reg.3, SSI 2003/299 Reg.3, SSI 2003/405 Reg.3, SSI 2003/466 Reg.3, SSI 2003/568 Reg.3

Sch.4, disapplied: SI 2002/1387 Sch.7, SI 2003/3177 Reg.67, SI 2004/1430 Reg.67, SSI 2002/445 Sch.7

Sch.5 Part I, disapplied: SI 2002/1227 Sch.7, SI 2002/1387 Sch.7, SI 2003/3177 Reg.67, SI 2004/1430 Reg.67, SSI 2002/445 Sch.7

3125. Fresh Meat (Import Conditions) Regulations 1996

revoked (in part): SI 2003/3177 Sch.6, SI 2004/1430 Sch.6

Reg.1, amended: SI 2002/1227 Sch.8 para.2, SI 2002/1387 Sch.8 para.2, SSI 2002/445 Sch.8 para.2

Reg.14, disapplied: SI 2002/1227 Sch.7, SI 2002/1387 Sch.7, SSI 2002/445 Sch.7

Sch.1 para.3, revoked (in part): SI 2003/3177 Sch.6

Sch.1 para.4, revoked (in part): SI 2003/3177 Sch.6

Sch.1 para.8, revoked (in part): SI 2003/3177 Sch.6

Sch.1 para.9, revoked (in part): SI 2003/3177 Sch.6

Sch.1 para.10, revoked (in part): SI 2003/3177 Sch.6

Sch.1 para.12, revoked (in part): SI 2003/3177 Sch.6

1996–cont.

3125. Fresh Meat (Import Conditions) Regulations 1996–*cont.*

Sch.1 para.13, revoked (in part): SI 2003/3177 Sch.6

Sch.1 para.15, revoked (in part): SI 2003/3177 Sch.6

Sch.1 para.16, revoked (in part): SI 2003/3177 Sch.6

Sch.1 para.17, revoked (in part): SI 2003/3177 Sch.6

Sch.1 para.18, revoked (in part): SI 2003/3177 Sch.6

Sch.1 para.19, revoked (in part): SI 2003/3177 Sch.6

Sch.1 para.21, revoked (in part): SI 2003/3177 Sch.6

Sch.1 para.22, revoked (in part): SI 2003/3177 Sch.6

Sch.1 para.23, revoked (in part): SI 2003/3177 Sch.6

Sch.1 para.24, revoked (in part): SI 2003/3177 Sch.6

Sch.1 para.25, revoked (in part): SI 2003/3177 Sch.6

Sch.1 para.27, revoked (in part): SI 2003/3177 Sch.6

Sch.1 para.28, revoked (in part): SI 2003/3177 Sch.6

Sch.1 para.31, revoked (in part): SI 2003/3177 Sch.6

Sch.1 para.33, revoked (in part): SI 2003/3177 Sch.6

Sch.1 para.34, revoked (in part): SI 2003/3177 Sch.6

Sch.1 para.36, revoked (in part): SI 2003/3177 Sch.6

Sch.2 Part I para.11, revoked (in part): SI 2003/3177 Sch.6

Sch.2 Part I para.14, revoked (in part): SI 2003/3177 Sch.6

Sch.2 Part I para.16, revoked (in part): SI 2003/3177 Sch.6

Sch.2 Part I para.18, revoked (in part): SI 2003/3177 Sch.6

Sch.2 Part I para.29, revoked (in part): SI 2003/3177 Sch.6

3126. Occupational Pension Schemes (Winding Up) Regulations 1996

applied: SI 2002/459 Reg.12

referred to: SI 2004/1140 Reg.1

Reg.3, amended: SI 2004/1140 Reg.3

Reg.3, revoked (in part): SI 2004/1140 Reg.2

Reg.4, amended: SI 2002/380 Reg.3, SI 2004/403 Reg.2

Reg.4A, added: SI 2002/380 Reg.3

Reg.4A, amended: SI 2004/403 Reg.2

Reg.4B, added: SI 2004/403 Reg.2

Reg.13, amended: SI 2002/380 Reg.3

3127. Occupational Pension Schemes (Investment) Regulations 1996

Reg.2, amended: SI 2002/681 Reg.6

NO.

NO.

1996–cont.

3127. Occupational Pension Schemes (Investment) Regulations 1996–*cont.*

Reg.5, varied: SI 2003/1633 Sch.2 para.8

Reg.8, varied: SI 2003/1633 Sch.2 para.8

3128. Occupational Pension Schemes (Deficiency on Winding Up etc.) Regulations 1996

Reg.3, amended: SI 2002/380 Reg.4, SI 2004/403 Reg.3

Reg.3A, added: SI 2002/380 Reg.4

Reg.3A, amended: SI 2004/403 Reg.3

Reg.3B, added: SI 2004/403 Reg.3

3140. Films (Exhibition Periods) Order 1996

applied: SI 2004/2181 Sch.2

3142. Arable Area Payments Regulations 1996

Reg.2, amended: SI 2002/3159 Reg.15

3147. Employment Protection (Continuity of Employment) Regulations 1996

Reg.2, amended: SI 2004/752 Reg.17

3151. Advanced Television Services Regulations 1996

revoked: SI 2003/1901 Reg.2

Reg.1, referred to: SI 2003/1901 Reg.2

Reg.1, varied: SI 2003/1901 Reg.2

Reg.3, referred to: SI 2003/1901 Reg.2

Reg.3, varied: SI 2003/1901 Reg.2

Reg.6, applied: SI 2003/1901 Reg.2

Reg.6, referred to: SI 2003/1901 Reg.2

Reg.6, varied: SI 2003/1901 Reg.2

Reg.8, referred to: SI 2003/1901 Reg.2

Reg.8, varied: SI 2003/1901 Reg.2

Reg.9, applied: SI 2003/1901 Reg.2

Reg.9, referred to: SI 2003/1901 Reg.2

Reg.9, varied: SI 2003/1901 Reg.2

Reg.14, referred to: SI 2003/1901 Reg.2

Reg.14, varied: SI 2003/1901 Reg.2

Reg.15, referred to: SI 2003/1901 Reg.2

Reg.15, varied: SI 2003/1901 Reg.2

Reg.16, referred to: SI 2003/1901 Reg.2

Reg.16, varied: SI 2003/1901 Reg.2

Reg.17, referred to: SI 2003/1901 Reg.2

Reg.17, varied: SI 2003/1901 Reg.2

Sch.2, referred to: SI 2003/1901 Reg.2

Sch.2 para.1, varied: SI 2003/1901 Reg.2

Sch.2 para.2, varied: SI 2003/1901 Reg.2

Sch.2 para.3, varied: SI 2003/1901 Reg.2

Sch.2 para.4, varied: SI 2003/1901 Reg.2

Sch.2 para.5, varied: SI 2003/1901 Reg.2

Sch.2 para.6, varied: SI 2003/1901 Reg.2

Sch.2 para.7, varied: SI 2003/1901 Reg.2

Sch.2 para.8, varied: SI 2003/1901 Reg.2

Sch.2 para.9, varied: SI 2003/1901 Reg.2

Sch.2 para.10, varied: SI 2003/1901 Reg.2

Sch.2 para.11, varied: SI 2003/1901 Reg.2

Sch.2 para.12, varied: SI 2003/1901 Reg.2

Sch.2 para.13, varied: SI 2003/1901 Reg.2

1996–cont.

3153. United Nations Arms Embargoes (Somalia, Liberia and Rwanda) (Isle of Man) Order 1996

Art.2, amended: SI 2002/2630 Art.1

Art.3, amended: 2002 c.8 s.2

Art.7, amended: 2002 c.8 s.2

Art.8, amended: SI 2002/2630 Art.1

Sch.1 para.4, amended: SI 2002/2630 Art.1

3154. United Nations Arms Embargoes (Somalia, Liberia and Rwanda) (Channel Islands) Order 1996

Art.2, amended: SI 2002/2629 Art.1

Art.3, amended: 2002 c.8 s.2, SI 2002/2629 Art.1

Art.5, amended: SI 2002/2629 Art.1

Art.7, amended: 2002 c.8 s.2, SI 2002/2629 Art.1

Art.8, amended: SI 2002/2629 Art.1

Art.11, amended: SI 2002/2629 Art.1

Sch.1 para.4, amended: SI 2002/2629 Art.1

3158. Licensing (Northern Ireland) Order 1996

applied: SI 2004/1267 Reg.99

3160. Criminal Justice (Northern Ireland) Order 1996

Art.2, amended: 2002 c.26 Sch.12 para.55, SI 2003/1247 Sch.1 para.19, SI 2004/702 Sch.7 para.13

Art.2, applied: SI 2003/495 Reg.7

Art.3, see *Attorney General of Northern Ireland's Reference (No.2 of 2002), Re* [2003] N.I. 21 (CA (NI)), Carswell, L.C.J.

Art.4, amended: SI 2004/702 Sch.7 para.14

Art.5, amended: 2002 c.26 Sch.11 para.8

Art.6, amended: 2002 c.26 Sch.11 para.9

Art.7, amended: 2002 c.26 Sch.11 para.10

Art.9, amended: 2002 c.26 Sch.11 para.11, Sch.12 para.56

Art.10, amended: SI 2004/702 Sch.7 para.15

Art.13, amended: SI 2004/702 Sch.7 para.16

Art.15, amended: SI 2004/702 Sch.7 para.17

Art.18, amended: 2002 c.26 Sch.12 para.57, Sch.12 para.59

Art.19, amended: 2002 c.26 Sch.12 para.58, SI 2004/702 Sch.7 para.18

Art.20, amended: SI 2004/702 Sch.7 para.19

Art.21, amended: 2002 c.26 Sch.11 para.12

Art.21A, added: SI 2003/1247 Art.32

Art.24, see *Attorney General for Northern Ireland's Reference (No.11 of 2003), Re* [2004] N.I. 144 (CA (Crim Div) (NI)), Lord Carswell L.C.J.

Art.24, amended: SI 2004/702 Sch.7 para.20

Art.26, see *Attorney General for Northern Ireland's Reference (No.1 of 2003), Re* [2004] N.I. 30 (CA (Crim Div) (NI)), Lord Carswell L.C.J.

Art.29, amended: 2002 c.26 Sch.11 para.13

Art.31, amended: 2002 c.26 Sch.11 para.14

Art.34, amended: 2002 c.26 Sch.11 para.15

NO.

1996–cont.

3160. Criminal Justice (Northern Ireland) Order 1996–cont.

Art.34, revoked: SI 2003/1247 Art.32, Sch.2

Art.35, revoked: SI 2003/1247 Sch.2

Art.44, revoked: SI 2004/1501 Sch.2

Art.57, amended: SI 2003/1247 Art.32

Sch.2, amended: 2002 c.26 Sch.12 para.59

3162. Rates (Amendment) (Northern Ireland) Order 1996

Art.8, revoked: SI 2004/703 Sch.4

3170. Judicial Committee (Fees) Order 1996

revoked: SI 2003/1879 Art.3

3183. Bovine Spongiform Encephalopathy (No.2) Order 1996

applied: SI 2002/843 Reg.104, Sch.9 para.1, Sch.9 para.2, Sch.9 para.3, Sch.9 para.4, SI 2002/1416 Reg.104, SSI 2002/255 Reg.102, Sch.9 para.1, Sch.9 para.2, Sch.9 para.3, Sch.9 para.4

revoked (in part): SI 2002/843 Sch.9 Part I, SI 2002/1416 Sch.9 Part I, SSI 2002/255 Sch.9 Part I

varied: SI 2002/1416 Sch.9 para.1, Sch.9 para.2, Sch.9 para.3

Art.9, applied: SI 2002/843 Sch.9 para.5, SSI 2002/255 Sch.9 para.5

Art.9, varied: SI 2002/1416 Sch.9 para.5

Art.12, applied: SI 2002/843 Sch.9 para.6, SSI 2002/255 Sch.9 para.6

Art.12, varied: SI 2002/1416 Sch.9 para.6

Art.13, applied: SI 2002/843 Sch.9 para.7, SSI 2002/255 Sch.9 para.7

Art.13, varied: SI 2002/1416 Sch.9 para.7

Art.14, applied: SI 2002/843 Sch.9 para.7, SSI 2002/255 Sch.9 para.7

Art.14, varied: SI 2002/1416 Sch.9 para.7

Art.16, applied: SI 2002/843 Sch.9 para.8, Sch.9 para.9, SSI 2002/255 Sch.9 para.8, Sch.9 para.9

Art.16, varied: SI 2002/1416 Sch.9 para.8, Sch.9 para.9

Art.17, applied: SSI 2002/255 Sch.9 para.10

Sch.1 Part 1, varied: SI 2002/1416 Sch.9 para.4

3184. Bovine Spongiform Encephalopathy Compensation Order 1996

applied: SSI 2002/255 Reg.102, Sch.9 para.11

revoked (in part): SI 2002/843 Sch.9 Part I, SI 2002/1416 Sch.9 Part I, SSI 2002/255 Sch.9 Part I

3188. Merchant Shipping (High-Speed Craft) Regulations 1996

referred to: SI 2002/1473 Reg.4, SI 2003/2950 Reg.3

revoked: SI 2004/302 Reg.12

3195. Social Security (Child Maintenance Bonus) Regulations 1996

Reg.1, amended: SI 2002/1397 Sch.1 para.29

Reg.4, amended: SI 2002/2497 Sch.2 para.1

NO.

1996–cont.

3195. Social Security (Child Maintenance Bonus) Regulations 1996–cont.

Reg.8, amended: SI 2002/3197 Reg.7

Reg.16, revoked (in part): SI 2003/492 Sch.3 Part 1

3197. Advanced Television Services (Amendment) Regulations 1996

revoked: SI 2003/1901 Reg.2

3205. Local Authorities (Contracting out of Allocation of Housing and Homelessness Functions) Order 1996

Art.3, see *Adan v Newham LBC* [2001] EWCA Civ 1916, [2002] 1 WL.R. 2120 (CA), Brooke, L.J.

3207. Social Security (Incapacity for Work and Miscellaneous Amendments) Regulations 1996

Reg.2, see *Howker v Secretary of State for Work and Pensions* [2002] EWCA Civ 1623, [2003] I.C.R. 405 (CA), Peter Gibson, L.J.

3215. High Court and County Courts (Allocation of Arbitration Proceedings) Order 1996

Art.5, amended: SI 2002/439 Art.11

3225. Immigration (Restrictions on Employment) Order 1996

revoked: SI 2004/755 Art.5

Sch.1 Part II para.13, amended: 2002 c.8 s.2

3232. Police (Scotland) Amendment Regulations 1996

revoked: SSI 2004/257 Sch.4

3243. Merchant Shipping (Fees) Regulations 1996

Reg.2, amended: SI 2004/1977 Reg.3

Sch.1 Part I para.1, amended: SI 2003/788 Reg.2, SI 2004/302 Sch.1 para.15, SI 2004/1977 Reg.4

Sch.1 Part I para.2, amended: SI 2003/788 Reg.2, SI 2004/1977 Reg.4

Sch.1 Part I para.3, amended: SI 2003/788 Reg.2

Sch.1 Part II, amended: SI 2004/1977 Reg.4

Sch.1 Part III, amended: SI 2004/1977 Reg.4

Sch.1 Part III, substituted: SI 2004/1977 Reg.4

Sch.1 Part IV, substituted: SI 2004/1977 Reg.4

Sch.1 Part V, amended: SI 2004/1977 Reg.4

Sch.1 Part VI, amended: SI 2004/1977 Reg.4

Sch.1 Part VII, substituted: SI 2003/788 Reg.2

Sch.1 Part VIII, amended: SI 2003/788 Reg.2

Sch.1 Part XII para.2, amended: SI 2003/788 Reg.2, SI 2004/1977 Reg.4

Sch.1 Part XIII, substituted: SI 2004/1977 Reg.4

Sch.1 Part XIII para.1, substituted: SI 2004/1977 Reg.4

Sch.1 Part XIII para.2, substituted: SI 2004/1977 Reg.4

1996–cont.

3243. Merchant Shipping (Fees) Regulations 1996–*cont.*
Sch.1 Part XIV, added: SI 2004/1977 Reg.4

3255. Secure Accommodation (Scotland) Regulations 1996
applied: SSI 2002/162 Art.8
referred to: SSI 2002/63 r.3
Reg.3, varied: SSI 2002/162 Art.5

3261. Children's Hearings (Scotland) Rules 1996
applied: SSI 2002/63 r.4

3262. Arrangements to Look After Children (Scotland) Regulations 1996
referred to: SI 2003/493 Reg.16

3263. Fostering of Children (Scotland) Regulations 1996
applied: SI 2002/2005 Reg.14, SI 2003/493 Reg.36
referred to: SI 2003/493 Reg.16
Reg.7, referred to: 2003 c.14 Sch.36 para.4
Reg.14, applied: SSI 2003/231 Sch.3 para.6
Reg.14, referred to: 2003 c.14 Sch.36 para.4
Reg.16, referred to: 2003 c.14 Sch.36 para.4

3265. Markets, Sales and Lairs (Amendment) Order 1996
revoked (in part): SI 2003/1723 Art.11, SI 2003/1967 Art.11

3266. Adoption Agencies (Scotland) Regulations 1996
Reg.8, amended: SI 2002/3135 Sch.1 para.37
Reg.8, referred to: SSI 2003/19 Reg.22
Reg.9, amended: SI 2002/3135 Sch.1 para.37
Reg.9, varied: SSI 2003/19 Sch.4
Reg.10, varied: SSI 2003/19 Sch.4
Reg.11, applied: SSI 2003/19 Reg.22
Reg.11, varied: SSI 2003/19 Sch.4
Reg.12, applied: SI 2002/2788 Reg.2, SI 2002/2820 Reg.11, SI 2002/2822 Reg.2, SR 2002/377 Reg.2, SR 2002/378 Reg.2, SR 2002/379 Reg.11, SR 2002/382 Reg.1
Reg.12, varied: SSI 2003/19 Sch.4
Reg.19, applied: SR 2002/377 Reg.15
Reg.19, varied: SSI 2003/19 Sch.4
Reg.21, varied: SSI 2003/19 Sch.4
Reg.23, varied: SSI 2003/19 Sch.4
Reg.24, amended: SSI 2003/242 Art.6
Sch.2 Part 1 para.17, amended: SI 2002/3135 Sch.1 para.37
Sch.2 Part II para.15, amended: SI 2002/3135 Sch.1 para.37
Sch.2 Part IV para.25, amended: SI 2002/3135 Sch.1 para.37

3272. Firearms (Amendment) Act 1988 (Firearms Consultative Committee) Order 1996
revoked: SI 2002/127 Art.3

13946. Act of Adjournal (Criminal Procedure Rules) 1996
r.40.3, see *Stevens (Andrew) v HM Advocate* 2002 S.L.T. 1249 (HCJ), Lady Paton

1997

2. Bedfordshire and Hertfordshire Ambulance and Paramedic Service National Health Service Trust (Establishment) Amendment Order 1997
revoked: 2003 c.43 s.7

7. Plant Protection Products (Amendment) Regulations 1997
revoked (in part): SI 2003/3241 Sch.5, SSI 2003/579 Sch.5
Reg.3, revoked (in part): SSI 2002/117 Reg.4

10. Town and Country Planning (Fees for Applications and Deemed Applications) (Scotland) Regulations 1997
revoked: SSI 2004/219 Reg.15
Reg.1, referred to: SSI 2002/122 Reg.1
Reg.12, amended: SSI 2002/122 Reg.2
Reg.13, amended: SSI 2002/122 Reg.2
Reg.14, amended: SSI 2002/122 Reg.2
Sch.1 Part II para.4, amended: SSI 2002/122 Reg.3
Sch.1 Part II para.5, amended: SSI 2002/122 Reg.3
Sch.1 Part II para.6, amended: SSI 2002/122 Reg.3
Sch.1 Part II para.7, amended: SSI 2002/122 Reg.3
Sch.1 Part III, substituted: SSI 2002/122 Sch.1
Sch.1 Part III para.14, amended: SSI 2002/122 Reg.3

15. Police and Criminal Evidence Act 1984 (Application to the Armed Forces) Order 1997
applied: SI 2003/2273 Art.17

37. Town and Country Planning (Fees for Applications and Deemed Applications) (Amendment) Regulations 1997
Reg.2, revoked (in part): SI 2002/768 Reg.3
Reg.3, revoked (in part): SI 2002/768 Reg.3

57. Electronic Lodgement of Tax Returns Order 1997
disapplied: SI 2003/282 Reg.2

93. Education (Fees and Awards) (Scotland) Regulations 1997
Reg.2, amended: SSI 2004/469 Reg.4
Sch.1 para.2, amended: SSI 2004/469 Reg.4
Sch.1 para.5, amended: SSI 2004/469 Reg.4
Sch.1 para.6, amended: SSI 2004/469 Reg.4
Sch.2 para.2, amended: SSI 2004/469 Reg.4
Sch.2 para.4, amended: SSI 2004/469 Reg.4
Sch.3 para.3, amended: SSI 2004/469 Reg.4
Sch.3 para.5, amended: SSI 2004/469 Reg.4

102. Yorkshire Dales Light Railway Order 1997
Art.9, amended: SI 2003/2155 Sch.1 para.18

150. Diseases of Poultry (Amendment) Order 1997
revoked (in part): SI 2003/1078 Art.18, SI 2003/1079 Art.17, SSI 2003/354 Art.19

1997–cont.

157. City of Gloucester (Electoral Changes) Order 1997
varied: SI 2004/222 Art.2

166. Organic Products (Amendment) Regulations 1997
revoked (in part): SI 2002/3159 Sch.4, SI 2004/1604 Sch.3

169. Courts-Martial (Army) Rules 1997
Part III r.16, amended: SI 2002/230 r.2
Part III r.17, amended: SI 2002/230 r.2
Part V r.37, amended: SI 2002/230 r.2
Part V r.38, amended: SI 2002/230 r.2
Part V r.40, amended: SI 2002/230 r.2
Part V r.41, amended: SI 2002/230 r.2
Sch.2, amended: SI 2002/230 r.2

170. Courts-Martial (Royal Navy) Rules 1997
Part I r.2, amended: SI 2004/66 Art.3
Part II r.8, amended: SI 2004/66 Art.3
Part II r.9, amended: SI 2004/66 Art.3
Part III r.14, amended: SI 2002/231 r.2
Part III r.15, amended: SI 2002/231 r.2
Part V r.28, amended: SI 2002/231 r.2
Part V r.31, amended: SI 2002/231 r.2
Part V r.33, amended: SI 2002/231 r.2
Sch.2, amended: SI 2002/231 r.2

171. Courts-Martial (Royal Air Force) Rules 1997
Part III r.16, amended: SI 2002/229 r.2
Part III r.17, amended: SI 2002/229 r.2
Part V r.37, amended: SI 2002/229 r.2
Part V r.38, amended: SI 2002/229 r.2
Part V r.40, amended: SI 2002/229 r.2
Part V r.41, amended: SI 2002/229 r.2
Sch.2, amended: SI 2002/229 r.2

179. Forest of Dean (Parishes and Electoral Changes) Order 1997
varied: SI 2004/222 Art.2

194. Assured Tenancies and Agricultural Occupancies (Forms) Regulations 1997
Reg.3, amended: SI 2002/337 Reg.3, SI 2003/260 Reg.2, SI 2003/307 Reg.2
Sch.1, added: SI 2003/307 Sch.1
Sch.1, amended: SI 2002/337 Reg.4, Sch.1, SI 2003/260 Reg.2, Sch.1
Sch.1, referred to: SI 2003/260 Reg.3
Sch.1, revoked (in part): SI 2003/307 Reg.3

214. Income Tax (Employments) (Amendment) Regulations 1997
revoked: SI 2003/2682 Sch.2

248. Electricity (Non-Fossil Fuel Sources) (England and Wales) Order 1997
Sch.1, referred to: SSI 2004/170 Art.8

264. London Underground (East London Line Extension) Order 1997
see *Bishopsgate Space Management Ltd v London Underground Ltd* [2004] 2 E.G.L.R. 175 (Lands Tr), George Bartlett Q.C. (President)

1997–cont.

264. London Underground (East London Line Extension) Order 1997–*cont.*
Sch.9 para.1, amended: SI 2003/2155 Sch.1 para.17, Sch.2
Sch.9 para.2, amended: SI 2003/2155 Sch.1 para.17

265. Life Assurance and Other Policies (Keeping of Information and Duties of Insurers) Regulations 1997
Reg.2, amended: SI 2002/444 Reg.3

266. Potato Industry Development Council Order 1997
Art.2, amended: SI 2002/3062 Art.3
Art.6, amended: SI 2002/3062 Art.4
Art.8, amended: SI 2002/3062 Art.5
Art.9, amended: SI 2002/3062 Art.6
Art.9, revoked (in part): SI 2002/3062 Art.6

274. Construction Contracts (Northern Ireland) Order 1997
Art.4, amended: 2003 c.21 Sch.17 para.143

276. Road Traffic Regulation (Northern Ireland) Order 1997
Art.4, amended: SI 2002/3153 Sch.5 para.7
Art.5, applied: SR 2002/10 Reg.13
Art.28, enabled: SR 2002/143, SR 2003/214
Art.43, applied: 2003 c.32 Sch.3 para.2
Reg.15, applied: SR 2003/303 Reg.6

278. Territorial Sea Act 1987 (Jersey) Order 1997
Sch.1 para.2, amended: SI 2002/250 Art.2
Sch.1 para.2, varied: SI 2002/250 Art.2

284. Wireless Telegraphy (Channel Islands) (Amendment) Order 1997
Art.2, varied: SI 2004/307 Art.3, SI 2004/308 Art.3

288. Education (Chief Inspector of Schools in Wales) Order 1997
revoked: SI 2002/260 Art.3

290. Wireless Telegraphy (Television Licence Fees) Regulations 1997
referred to: SI 2003/663 Reg.2, SI 2004/692 Reg.7
revoked: SI 2004/692 Sch.6
Reg.3, varied: SI 2003/3142 Art.10
Reg.4, amended: SI 2003/663 Reg.7
Sch.2 Part I, amended: SI 2002/641 Reg.3, SI 2003/663 Reg.3, Reg.8
Sch.2 Part II para.1, amended: SI 2003/663 Reg.9
Sch.2 Part II para.2, amended: SI 2003/663 Reg.9
Sch.2 Part II para.3, amended: SI 2003/663 Reg.9
Sch.2 Part II para.4, amended: SI 2003/663 Reg.9
Sch.2 Part II para.5, amended: SI 2003/663 Reg.9
Sch.2 Part II para.6, amended: SI 2003/663 Reg.9
Sch.2 Part II para.7, amended: SI 2003/663 Reg.9

NO.

290. Wireless Telegraphy (Television Licence Fees) Regulations 1997–*cont.*

Sch.2 Part II para.8, amended: SI 2003/663 Reg.9

Sch.2 Part II para.8, substituted: SI 2003/663 Reg.9

Sch.2 Part II para.8, amended: SI 2003/663 Reg.9

Sch.2 Part II para.9, amended: SI 2003/663 Reg.9

Sch.2 Part II para.10, added: SI 2003/663 Reg.9

Sch.2 Part II para.10, amended: SI 2003/663 Reg.9

Sch.2 Part III para.1, amended: SI 2002/641 Reg.3, SI 2003/663 Reg.4

Sch.3, amended: SI 2002/641 Reg.4, SI 2003/663 Reg.5

Sch.4, amended: SI 2002/641 Reg.5, SI 2003/663 Reg.6

291. Act of Sederunt (Child Care and Maintenance Rules 1997

see *Edinburgh City Council v W* 2002 Fam. L.R. 67 (Sh Pr), CGB Nicholson Q.C., Sheriff Principal; see *K and F, Applicants* 2002 S.L.T. (Sh Ct) 38 (Sh Pr), CGB Nicholson Q.C., Sheriff Principal; see *S v N* 2002 S.L.T. 589 (Ex Div), Lord Emslie, Lord Cameron of Lochbroom, Lord Reed

291. Act of Sederunt (Child Care and Maintenance Rules) 1997

Part 2, added: SSI 2003/44 r.6

Part 2 r.2.25, amended: SSI 2003/44 r.4

Part 2 r.2.26, amended: SSI 2003/44 r.5

Part 5 r.5.43, amended: SSI 2002/560 Sch.3 para.7

Sch.1, amended: SSI 2003/44 Sch.1

302. Civil Jurisdiction and Judgments Act 1982 (Interim Relief) Order 1997

see *Lewis v Eliades* [2002] EWHC 335, [2002] C.P. Rep. 28 (QBD), McCombe, J.

307. Reserve Forces (Call-out and Recall) (Exemptions Etc.) Regulations 1997

Reg.2, amended: SI 2002/3135 Sch.1 para.38

319. Local Authorities (Capital Finance) Regulations 1997

applied: SI 2002/377 Sch.1 para.19

revoked: 2003 c.26 Sch.8 Part 1

Reg.2, varied: SI 2003/1633 Sch.2 para.4

Reg.12A, referred to: SI 2003/533 Reg.7

Reg.12B, added: SI 2003/515 Reg.2, SI 2003/915 Reg.2

Reg.12B, amended: SI 2004/459 Reg.2

Reg.16, amended: SI 2003/515 Reg.2

Reg.16, applied: SI 2002/377 Sch.2 para.14, SI 2002/432 Reg.8, SI 2003/507 Reg.19, SI 2004/1576 Reg.16

NO.

319. Local Authorities (Capital Finance) Regulations 1997–*cont.*

Reg.16, referred to: SI 2002/3199 Reg.1, SI 2003/453 Sch.1 para.14, SI 2003/3118 Reg.2, SI 2003/3247 Sch.1 para.14, SI 2004/2506 Sch.1 para.16

Reg.81, amended: SI 2003/43 Reg.2

Reg.104B, added: SI 2003/43 Reg.2

Reg.104B, applied: SI 2003/3146 Reg.16

Reg.112, amended: SI 2002/2299 Reg.2

Reg.123, amended: SI 2002/2299 Reg.2

Reg.130, amended: SI 2002/2299 Reg.2

Reg.136, amended: SI 2002/2299 Reg.2

Reg.136, applied: SI 2003/3146 Reg.28, SI 2003/3239 Reg.22

Reg.154, amended: SI 2002/2469 Sch.8

Reg.158, amended: SI 2002/2469 Sch.6

320. Hovercraft (Fees) Regulations 1997

Reg.5, amended: SI 2004/1976 Reg.2

Reg.9, amended: SI 2004/1976 Reg.2

322. Registration of Homoeopathic Veterinary Medicinal Products Regulations 1997

Reg.2, applied: SI 2004/2750 Reg.12

330. Countryside Premium Scheme (Scotland) Regulations 1997

applied: SSI 2004/381 Reg.4

Reg.12, applied: SSI 2004/381 Reg.4

Sch.2, amended: SSI 2004/113 Reg.2

348. Merchant Shipping (Training and Certification) Regulations 1997

referred to: SI 2002/2934 Sch.1 Part 3

Reg.2, amended: SI 2004/302 Sch.1 para.14

362. Water Services Charges (Billing and Collection) (Scotland) Order 1997

revoked: 2002 asp 3 Sch.7 para.23

363. Domestic Sewerage Charges (Reduction) (Scotland) Regulations 1997

revoked: 2002 asp 3 Sch.7 para.23

394. Council Tax and Non-Domestic Rating (Demand Notices) (England) (Amendment) Regulations 1997

Reg.6, revoked: SI 2002/180 Sch.1

401. Road Vehicles (Registration and Licensing) (Amendment) Regulations 1997

revoked: SI 2002/2742 Sch.1 Part I

417. Weald of Kent Community National Health Service Trust Dissolution Order 1997

revoked: 2003 c.43 s.7

418. Maidstone Priority Care National Health Service Trust Dissolution Order 1997

revoked: 2003 c.43 s.7

419. Invicta Community Care National Health Service Trust (Establishment) Order 1997

revoked: SI 2002/1337 Art.6, 2003 c.43 s.7

NO.

1997-cont.

456. Wiltshire County Council (Borough of Thamesdown) (Staff Transfer) Order 1997
varied: SI 2004/222 Art.2

458. Dorset County Council (Boroughs of Poole and Bournemouth) (Staff Transfer) Order 1997
varied: SI 2004/222 Art.2

459. Derbyshire County Council (City of Derby) (Staff Transfer) Order 1997
varied: SI 2004/222 Art.2

460. Durham County Council (Borough of Darlington) (Staff Transfer) Order 1997
varied: SI 2004/222 Art.2

461. East Sussex County Council (Boroughs of Brighton and Hove) (Staff Transfer) Order 1997
varied: SI 2004/222 Art.2

468. Hampshire County Council (Cities of Portsmouth and Southampton) (Staff Transfer) Order 1997
varied: SI 2004/222 Art.2

469. Staffordshire County Council (City of Stoke-on-Trent) (Staff Transfer) Order 1997
varied: SI 2004/222 Art.2

470. Personal Pension Schemes (Appropriate Schemes) Regulations 1997
Reg.6A, added: SI 2002/681 Reg.8

473. Friendly Societies (Modification of the Corporation Tax Acts) Regulations 1997
added: SI 2004/2310 Sch.1 para.75
added: SI 2003/23 Reg.10
Reg.2, amended: SI 2004/822 Reg.3
Reg.2A, added: SI 2004/822 Reg.4
Reg.3, revoked: SI 2004/822 Reg.5
Reg.4, revoked: SI 2004/822 Reg.5
Reg.4A, amended: SI 2003/23 Reg.3
Reg.6, amended: SI 2003/23 Reg.4, SI 2004/822 Reg.6
Reg.7A, added: SI 2004/822 Reg.7
Reg.9, amended: SI 2003/23 Reg.5, SI 2004/822 Reg.8
Reg.13, amended: SI 2003/23 Reg.6, SI 2004/822 Reg.9
Reg.13, revoked (in part): SI 2004/822 Reg.9
Reg.14, substituted: SI 2004/822 Reg.10
Reg.15, revoked: SI 2004/822 Reg.11
Reg.19, amended: SI 2004/822 Reg.12
Reg.19A, amended: SI 2004/822 Reg.13
Reg.20, amended: SI 2004/822 Reg.14
Reg.20A, amended: SI 2004/822 Reg.15
Reg.21A, revoked (in part): SI 2004/822 Reg.16
Reg.21B, amended: SI 2003/23 Reg.7
Reg.21B, revoked: SI 2004/822 Reg.17
Reg.22, amended: SI 2004/822 Reg.18
Reg.23, revoked: SI 2004/822 Reg.19
Reg.25, revoked: SI 2004/822 Reg.20

NO.

1997-cont.

473. Friendly Societies (Modification of the Corporation Tax Acts) Regulations 1997-*cont.*
Reg.27, revoked: SI 2004/822 Reg.21
Reg.28, amended: SI 2004/822 Reg.22
Reg.30, revoked: SI 2004/822 Reg.23
Reg.30B, amended: SI 2004/822 Reg.24
Reg.30C, amended: SI 2004/822 Reg.25
Reg.30D, amended: SI 2004/822 Reg.26
Reg.32, substituted: SI 2004/822 Reg.27
Reg.32A, added: SI 2004/822 Reg.28
Reg.33, amended: SI 2004/822 Reg.29
Reg.34, revoked: SI 2004/822 Reg.30
Reg.35, revoked: SI 2004/822 Reg.30
Reg.36, amended: SI 2003/23 Reg.8, SI 2004/822 Reg.31
Reg.37, amended: SI 2004/822 Reg.32
Reg.39A, added: SI 2004/822 Reg.33
Reg.40, revoked: SI 2004/822 Reg.34
Reg.40A, added: SI 2004/822 Reg.35
Reg.43A, added: SI 2004/822 Reg.36
Reg.44, revoked: SI 2004/822 Reg.37
Reg.44A, added: SI 2004/822 Reg.38
Reg.45, amended: SI 2004/822 Reg.39
Reg.45, revoked (in part): SI 2004/822 Reg.39
Reg.47, revoked: SI 2004/822 Reg.40
Reg.49, revoked: SI 2004/822 Reg.40
Reg.50, revoked: SI 2004/822 Reg.40
Reg.50A, added: SI 2003/23 Reg.9
Reg.50A, revoked: SI 2004/822 Reg.40
Reg.50B, added: SI 2003/23 Reg.9
Reg.50B, revoked: SI 2004/822 Reg.40
Reg.51, revoked: SI 2004/822 Reg.40
Reg.52, revoked: SI 2004/822 Reg.40
Reg.53A, substituted: SI 2002/1409 Art.6
Reg.53D, revoked: SI 2004/822 Reg.40
Reg.53E, revoked: SI 2004/822 Reg.40
Reg.53F, revoked: SI 2004/822 Reg.40
Reg.53G, revoked: SI 2004/822 Reg.40
Reg.53J, revoked: SI 2004/822 Reg.40

476. Leicestershire County Council (City of Leicester and District of Rutland) (Staff Transfer) Order 1997
varied: SI 2004/222 Art.2

478. Bedfordshire County Council (Borough of Luton) (Staff Transfer) Order 1997
varied: SI 2004/222 Art.2

479. Buckinghamshire County Council (Borough of Milton Keynes) (Staff Transfer) Order 1997
varied: SI 2004/222 Art.2

488. East Sussex (Coroners) Order 1997
varied: SI 2004/222 Art.2

489. Hampshire (Coroners) Order 1997
varied: SI 2004/222 Art.2

490. Leicestershire (Coroners) Order 1997
varied: SI 2004/222 Art.2

1997–cont.

492. Staffordshire (Coroners) Order 1997
varied: SI 2004/222 Art.2

493. Wiltshire (Coroners) Order 1997
varied: SI 2004/222 Art.2

494. Bedfordshire (Coroners) Order 1997
varied: SI 2004/222 Art.2

495. Buckinghamshire (Coroners) Order 1997
varied: SI 2004/222 Art.2

496. Derbyshire (Coroners) Order 1997
varied: SI 2004/222 Art.2

497. Dorset (Coroners) Order 1997
varied: SI 2004/222 Art.2

498. Durham (Coroners) Order 1997
varied: SI 2004/222 Art.2

529. Merchant Shipping (Minimum Standards of Safety Communications) Regulations 1997
Reg.2, amended: SI 2004/1266 Reg.4

542. Common Agricultural Policy (Wine) (Amendment) Regulations 1997
revoked (in part): SSI 2002/325 Reg.19

562. Merchant Shipping (Light Dues) Regulations 1997
Sch.2 Part II para.1, amended: SI 2002/504 Reg.2
Sch.2 Part II para.3, amended: SI 2002/504 Reg.2, SI 2004/610 Reg.2

573. Education (Individual Pupils Achievements) (Information) (Wales) Regulations 1997
revoked: SI 2004/1026 Sch.5
Reg.2, amended: SI 2002/46 Reg.2
Reg.3, amended: SI 2002/46 Reg.2
Reg.7, amended: SI 2002/46 Reg.2
Sch.1 Part 1 para.1, amended: SI 2002/46 Reg.2
Sch.2 para.1, amended: SI 2002/46 Reg.2
Sch.2 para.1, revoked (in part): SI 2002/46 Reg.2
Sch.3 para.1, amended: SI 2002/46 Reg.2
Sch.3 para.1, revoked (in part): SI 2002/46 Reg.2

581. Pontefract Hospitals National Health Service Trust Dissolution Order 1997
revoked: 2003 c.43 s.7

582. Pinderfields and Pontefract Hospitals National Health Service Trust (Establishment) Order 1997
revoked: SI 2002/1341 Art.6, 2003 c.43 s.7

583. Pinderfields Hospitals National Health Service Trust Dissolution Order 1997
revoked: 2003 c.43 s.7

585. National Health Service (Dental Charges) (Scotland) Amendment Regulations 1997
revoked: SSI 2003/158 Sch.4

586. Council Tax (Discounts) (Scotland) Amendment Order 1997
revoked: SSI 2003/176 Sch.4

1997–cont.

616. Seeds (Miscellaneous Amendments) Regulations 1997
revoked (in part): SI 2002/3173 Reg.32
Reg.2, revoked (in part): SSI 2004/317 Sch.8
Reg.4, amended: SSI 2004/317 Sch.8

619. Housing (Right to Acquire) Regulations 1997
Reg.2, applied: SI 2002/1091 Art.2

640. Leasehold Reform (Notices) Regulations 1997
Sch.1, amended: SI 2002/1715 Sch.1, SI 2002/3187 Sch.1, SI 2002/3209 Sch.1, SI 2003/991 Reg.2

647. Merchant Shipping (Ro-Ro Passenger Ship Survivability) Regulations 1997
revoked: SI 2004/2884 Reg.11
Reg.2, amended: SI 2004/302 Sch.1 para.13

648. Producer Responsibility Obligations (Packaging Waste) Regulations 1997
referred to: SSI 2003/613 Reg.3
see *R. (on the application of Valpak Ltd) v Environment Agency* [2002] EWHC 1510, [2002] Env. L.R. 36 (QBD (Admin Ct)), Moses, J.
Reg.2, amended: SI 2003/3238 Sch.1 para.1, SI 2003/3294 Reg.4, SSI 2003/613 Reg.4
Reg.3, amended: SI 2003/3238 Sch.1 para.2, SI 2003/3294 Reg.5, SSI 2003/613 Reg.5
Reg.3, revoked (in part): SI 2003/3238 Sch.1 para.2, SI 2003/3294 Reg.5
Reg.4, revoked (in part): SI 2003/3238 Sch.1 para.2, SI 2003/3294 Reg.5, SSI 2003/613 Reg.5
Reg.5, amended: SI 2003/3238 Sch.1 para.3, SI 2003/3294 Reg.6, SSI 2003/613 Reg.6
Reg.6, amended: SI 2003/3238 Sch.1 para.3, SI 2003/3294 Reg.6, SSI 2003/613 Reg.6
Reg.6, revoked (in part): SI 2003/3238 Sch.1 para.3, SI 2003/3294 Reg.6, SSI 2003/613 Reg.6
Reg.7, substituted: SI 2003/3238 Sch.1 para.3, SI 2003/3294 Reg.6, SSI 2003/613 Reg.6
Reg.8, revoked (in part): SI 2003/3238 Sch.1 para.3, SI 2003/3294 Reg.6, SSI 2003/613 Reg.6
Reg.9, amended: SI 2003/3238 Sch.1 para.3, SI 2003/3294 Reg.6, SSI 2003/613 Reg.6
Reg.11, amended: SI 2003/3238 Sch.1 para.3, SI 2003/3294 Reg.6, SSI 2003/613 Reg.6
Reg.11, revoked (in part): SI 2003/3238 Sch.1 para.3, SI 2003/3294 Reg.6, SSI 2003/613 Reg.6
Reg.12, amended: SI 2003/3238 Sch.1 para.3, SI 2003/3294 Reg.6, SSI 2003/613 Reg.6
Reg.12, revoked (in part): SI 2003/3238 Sch.1 para.3, SI 2003/3294 Reg.6, SSI 2003/613 Reg.6

1997–cont.

648. Producer Responsibility Obligations (Packaging Waste) Regulations 1997–
cont.

Reg.13, amended: SI 2003/3238 Sch.1 para.3, SI 2003/3294 Reg.6, SSI 2003/613 Reg.6

Reg.13, revoked (in part): SI 2003/3238 Sch.1 para.3, SI 2003/3294 Reg.6, SSI 2003/613 Reg.6

Reg.14, revoked (in part): SI 2003/3238 Sch.1 para.3, SI 2003/3294 Reg.6, SSI 2003/613 Reg.6

Reg.15, amended: SI 2003/3238 Sch.1 para.3, SI 2003/3294 Reg.6, SSI 2003/613 Reg.6

Reg.17, amended: SI 2003/3238 Sch.1 para.3, SI 2003/3294 Reg.6, SSI 2003/613 Reg.6

Reg.17, revoked (in part): SI 2003/3238 Sch.1 para.3, SI 2003/3294 Reg.6, SSI 2003/613 Reg.6

Reg.17A, added: SI 2003/3238 Sch.1 para.3, SI 2003/3294 Reg.6, SSI 2003/613 Reg.6

Reg.18, amended: SI 2003/3294 Reg.7

Reg.18, substituted: SI 2003/3238 Sch.1 para.4, SI 2003/3294 Reg.7, SSI 2003/613 Reg.7

Reg.19, amended: SI 2003/3238 Sch.1 para.4, SI 2003/3294 Reg.7, SSI 2003/613 Reg.7

Reg.19, substituted: SI 2003/3238 Sch.1 para.4

Reg.20, amended: SI 2003/3294 Reg.7

Reg.20, substituted: SI 2003/3238 Sch.1 para.4

Reg.21, amended: SI 2003/3238 Sch.1 para.4, SI 2003/3294 Reg.7, SSI 2003/613 Reg.7

Reg.21, substituted: SI 2003/3238 Sch.1 para.4

Reg.21A, added: SI 2003/3238 Sch.1 para.5, SI 2003/3294 Reg.8, SSI 2003/613 Reg.8

Reg.21B, added: SI 2003/3238 Sch.1 para.5, SI 2003/3294 Reg.8, SSI 2003/613 Reg.8

Reg.21C, amended: SI 2003/3294 Reg.7

Reg.21C, substituted: SI 2003/3238 Sch.1 para.4

Reg.21C, added: SI 2003/3238 Sch.1 para.5, SI 2003/3294 Reg.8, SSI 2003/613 Reg.8

Reg.21D, added: SI 2003/3238 Sch.1 para.5, SI 2003/3294 Reg.8, SSI 2003/613 Reg.8

Reg.22, amended: SI 2003/3238 Sch.1 para.6, SI 2003/3294 Reg.9, SSI 2003/613 Reg.9

Reg.24, amended: SI 2003/3238 Sch.1 para.6, SI 2003/3294 Reg.9, SSI 2003/613 Reg.9

Reg.24, revoked (in part): SI 2003/3238 Sch.1 para.6, SI 2003/3294 Reg.9, SSI 2003/613 Reg.9

1997–cont.

648. Producer Responsibility Obligations (Packaging Waste) Regulations 1997–
cont.

Reg.25, amended: SI 2003/3238 Sch.1 para.7, SI 2003/3294 Reg.10, SSI 2003/613 Reg.10

Reg.25A, amended: SI 2003/3238 Sch.1 para.7, SI 2003/3294 Reg.10, SSI 2003/613 Reg.10

Reg.26, amended: SI 2003/3238 Sch.1 para.7, SI 2003/3294 Reg.10, SSI 2003/613 Reg.10

Reg.27, amended: SI 2003/3238 Sch.1 para.7, SI 2003/3294 Reg.10, SSI 2003/613 Reg.10

Reg.28, amended: SI 2003/3238 Sch.1 para.7, SI 2003/3294 Reg.10, SSI 2003/613 Reg.10

Reg.28, revoked (in part): SI 2003/3238 Sch.1 para.7, SI 2003/3294 Reg.10, SSI 2003/613 Reg.10

Reg.34, amended: SI 2003/3238 Sch.1 para.8, SI 2003/3294 Reg.11, SSI 2003/613 Reg.11

Sch.1 para.3, amended: SI 2003/3238 Sch.1 para.9, SI 2003/3294 Reg.12, SSI 2003/613 Reg.12

Sch.1 para.4, amended: SI 2003/3238 Sch.1 para.9, SI 2003/3294 Reg.12, SSI 2003/613 Reg.12

Sch.1 para.4, revoked (in part): SI 2003/3238 Sch.1 para.9, SI 2003/3294 Reg.12

Sch.2 para.2, amended: SI 2003/3238 Sch.1 para.10, SI 2003/3294 Reg.13, SSI 2003/613 Reg.13

Sch.2 para.4, amended: SI 2002/732 Reg.2, SI 2002/813 Reg.2, SSI 2002/147 Reg.2

Sch.2 para.4, substituted: SI 2003/3238 Sch.1 para.10, SI 2003/3294 Reg.13, SSI 2003/613 Reg.13

Sch.2 para.5, amended: SI 2002/732 Reg.2, SI 2002/813 Reg.2, SSI 2002/147 Reg.2

Sch.2 para.5, substituted: SI 2003/3238 Sch.1 para.10, SI 2003/3294 Reg.13, SSI 2003/613 Reg.13

Sch.2 para.6, revoked (in part): SI 2003/3238 Sch.1 para.10, SI 2003/3294 Reg.13, SSI 2003/613 Reg.13

Sch.2A para.1, added: SI 2003/3238 Sch.1 para.11, SI 2003/3294 Reg.14, SSI 2003/613 Reg.14

Sch.2A para.2, added: SI 2003/3238 Sch.1 para.11, SI 2003/3294 Reg.14, SSI 2003/613 Reg.14

Sch.3 Part I para.1, amended: SI 2003/3238 Sch.1 para.12, SI 2003/3294 Reg.15, SSI 2003/613 Reg.15

Sch.3 Part II para.2, amended: SI 2003/3238 Sch.1 para.12, SI 2003/3294 Reg.15, SSI 2003/613 Reg.15

NO.

NO.

1997–cont.

648. Producer Responsibility Obligations (Packaging Waste) Regulations 1997– cont.

Sch.3 Part III para.3, amended: SI 2003/3238 Sch.1 para.12, SI 2003/3294 Reg.15, SSI 2003/613 Reg.15

Sch.3 Part III para.3, revoked (in part): SI 2003/3238 Sch.1 para.12, SI 2003/3294 Reg.15, SSI 2003/613 Reg.15

Sch.3 Part IV para.4, amended: SI 2003/3238 Sch.1 para.12, SI 2003/3294 Reg.15, SSI 2003/613 Reg.15

Sch.3 Part IV para.4, revoked (in part): SI 2003/3238 Sch.1 para.12, SI 2003/3294 Reg.15, SSI 2003/613 Reg.15

Sch.3 Part IV para.5, amended: SI 2003/3238 Sch.1 para.12, SI 2003/3294 Reg.15, SSI 2003/613 Reg.15

Sch.3 Part IV para.5, revoked (in part): SI 2003/3238 Sch.1 para.12, SI 2003/3294 Reg.15, SSI 2003/613 Reg.15

Sch.3 Part V para.6, amended: SI 2003/3238 Sch.1 para.12, SI 2003/3294 Reg.15, SSI 2003/613 Reg.15

Sch.3 Part V para.6, revoked (in part): SI 2003/3238 Sch.1 para.12, SI 2003/3294 Reg.15, SSI 2003/613 Reg.15

Sch.3 Part V para.7, amended: SI 2003/3238 Sch.1 para.12, SI 2003/3294 Reg.15, SSI 2003/613 Reg.15

Sch.3 Part V para.7, revoked (in part): SI 2003/3238 Sch.1 para.12, SI 2003/3294 Reg.15, SSI 2003/613 Reg.15

Sch.3 Part V para.8, amended: SI 2003/3238 Sch.1 para.12, SI 2003/3294 Reg.15, SSI 2003/613 Reg.15

Sch.3 Part V para.8, revoked (in part): SI 2003/3238 Sch.1 para.12, SI 2003/3294 Reg.15, SSI 2003/613 Reg.15

Sch.4 Part IV para.10, amended: SI 2003/3238 Sch.1 para.13, SI 2003/3294 Reg.16, SSI 2003/613 Reg.16

Sch.4 Part IV para.11, amended: SI 2003/3238 Sch.1 para.13, SI 2003/3294 Reg.16, SSI 2003/613 Reg.16

Sch.4 Part IV para.11, revoked (in part): SI 2003/3238 Sch.1 para.13, SI 2003/3294 Reg.16, SSI 2003/613 Reg.16

Sch.4 Part IV para.12, amended: SI 2003/3238 Sch.1 para.13, SI 2003/3294 Reg.16, SSI 2003/613 Reg.16

Sch.5 para.1, amended: SI 2003/3238 Sch.1 para.14, SI 2003/3294 Reg.17, SSI 2003/613 Reg.17

Sch.5 para.2, amended: SI 2003/3238 Sch.1 para.14, SI 2003/3294 Reg.17, SSI 2003/613 Reg.17

Sch.6, amended: SI 2003/3238 Sch.1 para.15, SI 2003/3294 Reg.18, SSI 2003/613 Reg.18

1997–cont.

648. Producer Responsibility Obligations (Packaging Waste) Regulations 1997– cont.

Sch.7 para.1, substituted: SI 2003/3238 Sch.1 para.16, SI 2003/3294 Reg.19, SSI 2003/613 Reg.19

Sch.7 para.2, substituted: SI 2003/3238 Sch.1 para.16, SI 2003/3294 Reg.19, SSI 2003/613 Reg.19

Sch.7 para.3, substituted: SI 2003/3238 Sch.1 para.16, SI 2003/3294 Reg.19, SSI 2003/613 Reg.19

Sch.9 Part II para.16, amended: SI 2003/3238 Sch.1 para.17, SI 2003/3294 Reg.20, SSI 2003/613 Reg.20

Sch.9 Part III para.21, amended: SI 2003/2096 Sch.1 para.71

Sch.10, revoked (in part): SI 2003/3238 Sch.1 para.18, SI 2003/3294 Reg.21, SSI 2003/613 Reg.21

654. Good Laboratory Practice Regulations 1997

referred to: SI 2002/2776 Sch.5

656. Council Tax (Chargeable Dwellings, Exempt Dwellings and Discount Disregards) Amendment Order 1997

Art.3, amended: 2002 c.8 s.2

657. Council Tax (Additional Provisions for Discount Disregards) Amendment Regulations 1997

Reg.2, amended: 2002 c.8 s.2

665. Occupational Pension Schemes (Pensions Compensation Provisions) Regulations 1997

Reg.3A, revoked: SI 2004/3350 Art.3

Reg.5, amended: SI 2004/3350 Art.3

Reg.5, revoked (in part): SI 2004/3350 Art.3

Reg.6, revoked (in part): SI 2004/3350 Art.3

Reg.7, revoked: SI 2004/3350 Art.3

Reg.10, revoked: SI 2004/3350 Art.3

668. Vehicle Inspectorate Trading Fund (Appropriation of Additional Assets) Order 1997

referred to: SI 2003/942

679. Local Government Changes for England (Education) (Miscellaneous Provisions) Order 1997

varied: SI 2004/222 Art.2

685. Leasehold Reform and Housing (Excluded Tenancies) (Designated Rural Areas) (Wales) Order 1997

Art.3, applied: SI 2003/54 Art.5

Art.3, varied: SI 2003/54 Art.5

687. Sheriff Court Fees Order 1997

Art.7, substituted: SSI 2002/269 Art.2

Art.9, amended: SSI 2003/97 Art.2

Sch.1, amended: SSI 2003/97 Art.2

Sch.1, substituted: SSI 2002/269 Sch.1

688. Court of Session etc Fees Order 1997

Art.5, substituted: SSI 2002/270 Art.2

NO.

1997–cont.

688. Court of Session etc Fees Order 1997–*cont.*
Sch.1, substituted: SSI 2002/270 Sch.1

693. Community Care (Direct Payments) (Scotland) Regulations 1997
revoked: SSI 2003/243 Sch.1

694. Medical Devices Fees (Amendment) Regulations 1997
revoked: SI 2002/618 Reg.66

717. Registration of Births, Deaths and Marriages (Fees) (Scotland) Order 1997
revoked: SSI 2002/389 Art.3

727. Civil Legal Aid (Scotland) Amendment Regulations 1997
revoked: SSI 2002/494 Sch.1

728. Council Tax (Exempt Dwellings) (Scotland) Order 1997
Art.2, amended: SSI 2002/101 Art.2
Art.3, see *Scottish Water v Clydecare Ltd* 2003 S.C. 330 (Ex Div), Lord Osborne, Lord Macfadyen, Lord Sutherland
Sch.1, see *Scottish Water v Clydecare Ltd* 2003 S.C. 330 (Ex Div), Lord Osborne, Lord Macfadyen, Lord Sutherland
Sch.1 para.8, amended: SSI 2002/101 Art.2

730. National Health Service (General Medical Services) Amendment Regulations 1997
revoked (in part): SI 2004/865 Sch.2, SI 2004/1016 Sch.2

733. Dairy Produce Quotas Regulations 1997
applied: SI 2002/794 Art.3
revoked (in part): SI 2002/457 Sch.4, SI 2002/897 Sch.4, SR 2002/88 Sch.4, SSI 2002/110 Reg.34
Reg.11, applied: SR 2002/88 Reg.35
Reg.11, disapplied: SI 2002/457 Reg.35
Reg.30, applied: SI 2002/457 Reg.35, SR 2002/88 Reg.35
Reg.30A, applied: SI 2002/457 Reg.35
Reg.31, applied: SI 2002/457 Reg.35, SR 2002/88 Reg.35

734. Community Care (Direct Payments) Regulations 1997
revoked (in part): SI 2003/762 Reg.12, SI 2004/1748 Reg.13

735. Offshore Installations (Safety Zones) Order 1997
Sch.1, amended: SI 2002/2467 Art.3, SI 2003/2743 Art.3

748. National Health Service (Travelling Expenses and Remission of Charges) Amendment Regulations 1997
revoked: SI 2003/2382 Sch.2

750. Town and Country Planning Appeals (Determination by Appointed Person) (Inquiries Procedure) (Scotland) Rules 1997
r.3, amended: SSI 2004/332 Sch.9 para.1

NO.

1997–cont.

750. Town and Country Planning Appeals (Determination by Appointed Person) (Inquiries Procedure) (Scotland) Rules 1997–*cont.*
r.3A, added: SSI 2004/332 Sch.9 para.2
r.12, amended: SSI 2004/332 Sch.9 para.4
r.14, amended: SSI 2004/332 Sch.9 para.3
r.22, amended: SSI 2004/332 Sch.9 para.5
r.24, substituted: SSI 2004/332 Sch.9 para.6
r.24A, added: SSI 2004/332 Sch.9 para.7

775. Borough of Thurrock (Electoral Changes) Order 1997
varied: SI 2004/222 Art.2
Art.1, revoked: SI 2002/2234 Art.7
Art.2, revoked: SI 2002/2234 Art.7
Art.3, revoked (in part): SI 2002/1670 Art.5, SI 2002/2234 Art.7
Sch.1, revoked: SI 2002/2234 Art.7
Sch.2, revoked: SI 2002/2234 Art.7

776. District of the Medway Towns (Parishes and Electoral Changes) Order 1997
varied: SI 2004/222 Art.2
Art.1, revoked: SI 2002/2235 Art.8
Art.3, revoked: SI 2002/2235 Art.8
Sch.1, revoked: SI 2002/2235 Art.8

777. City of Peterborough (Parishes and Electoral Changes) Order 1997
revoked: SI 2003/161 Art.12
varied: SI 2004/222 Art.2
Art.1, revoked: SI 2003/161 Art.12
Art.3, revoked: SI 2003/161 Art.12
Art.4, revoked (in part): SI 2002/2876 Art.5, SI 2003/161 Art.12
Art.5, revoked: SI 2003/161 Art.12
Art.6, revoked: SI 2003/161 Art.12
Art.7, revoked: SI 2003/161 Art.12
Art.8, amended: SI 2002/2876 Art.5
Art.8, revoked (in part): SI 2002/2876 Art.5, SI 2003/161 Art.12
Sch.1, revoked: SI 2003/161 Art.12
Sch.2, revoked: SI 2003/161 Art.12
Sch.3, revoked: SI 2003/161 Art.12
Sch.4, revoked: SI 2003/161 Art.12
Sch.5, revoked: SI 2003/161 Art.12

779. Borough of Halton (Electoral Changes) Order 1997
varied: SI 2004/222 Art.2
Art.1, revoked: SI 2002/2242 Art.7
Art.2, revoked: SI 2002/2242 Art.7
Art.3, revoked (in part): SI 2002/1670 Art.5, SI 2002/2242 Art.7
Art.4, revoked (in part): SI 2002/2242 Art.7
Sch.1, revoked: SI 2002/2242 Art.7
Sch.2, revoked: SI 2002/2242 Art.7

780. District of The Wrekin (Parishes and Electoral Changes) Order 1997
varied: SI 2004/222 Art.2
Art.1, revoked: SI 2002/2373 Art.21
Art.3, revoked: SI 2002/2373 Art.21

NO.

1997–cont.

780. District of The Wrekin (Parishes and Electoral Changes) Order 1997–cont.
Art.5, revoked: SI 2002/2373 Art.21
Art.6, revoked: SI 2002/2373 Art.21
Art.7, revoked: SI 2002/2373 Art.21
Art.8, revoked: SI 2002/2373 Art.21
Art.9, revoked: SI 2002/2373 Art.21
Art.10, revoked: SI 2002/2373 Art.21
Sch.1, revoked: SI 2002/2373 Art.21

781. Borough of Warrington (Parishes and Electoral Changes) Order 1997. 1997
varied: SI 2004/222 Art.2
Art.1, revoked: SI 2002/2237 Art.10
Art.3, revoked: SI 2002/2237 Art.10
Art.4, revoked (in part): SI 2002/1670 Art.5
Art.7, revoked: SI 2002/2237 Art.10
Art.8, revoked: SI 2002/2237 Art.10
Sch.1, revoked: SI 2002/2237 Art.10
Sch.2, revoked: SI 2002/2237 Art.10

782. Borough of Blackburn (Parishes and Electoral Changes) Order 1997
varied: SI 2004/222 Art.2
Art.3, revoked: SI 2002/3223 Art.7
Art.4, revoked (in part): SI 2002/2876 Art.5
Art.5, amended: SI 2002/2876 Art.5
Art.5, revoked (in part): SI 2002/2876 Art.5

783. Borough of Blackpool (Electoral Changes) Order 1997
varied: SI 2004/222 Art.2
Art.1, revoked: SI 2002/2240 Art.6
Art.2, revoked: SI 2002/2240 Art.6
Sch.1, revoked: SI 2002/2240 Art.6

785. Occupational Pension Schemes (Assignment, Forfeiture, Bankruptcy etc.) Regulations 1997
Reg.2, amended: SI 2002/681 Reg.9

790. Home Energy Efficiency Scheme Regulations 1997
applied: SSI 2002/312 Reg.5
referred to: SSI 2004/188 Reg.2
Reg.2, amended: SSI 2003/529 Reg.2
Reg.3A, amended: SSI 2004/188 Reg.3
Reg.4, amended: SSI 2003/284 Reg.2, SSI 2003/529 Reg.2, SSI 2004/188 Reg.4
Reg.15, amended: SSI 2004/188 Reg.5
Reg.17, amended: SSI 2004/188 Reg.6
Reg.19, amended: SSI 2004/188 Reg.7

792. Social Security (Social Fund and Claims and Payments) (Miscellaneous Amendments) Regulations 1997
Reg.8, revoked (in part): SI 2003/492 Sch.3 Part 1

793. Social Security (Miscellaneous Amendments) (No.2) Regulations 1997
Reg.1, revoked (in part): SI 2003/492 Sch.3 Part 1
Reg.2, revoked (in part): SI 2003/492 Sch.3 Part 1

NO.

1997–cont.

793. Social Security (Miscellaneous Amendments) (No.2) Regulations 1997–cont.
Reg.3, revoked (in part): SI 2003/492 Sch.3 Part 1
Reg.4, revoked (in part): SI 2003/492 Sch.3 Part 1
Reg.5, revoked (in part): SI 2003/492 Sch.3 Part 1
Reg.6, revoked (in part): SI 2003/492 Sch.3 Part 1
Reg.7, revoked (in part): SI 2003/492 Sch.3 Part 1

796. Town and Country Planning (Inquiries Procedure) (Scotland) Rules 1997
r.3, amended: SSI 2004/332 Sch.10 para.1
r.3A, added: SSI 2004/332 Sch.10 para.2
r.12, amended: SSI 2004/332 Sch.10 para.3
r.13, amended: SSI 2004/332 Sch.10 para.4
r.15, amended: SSI 2004/332 Sch.10 para.5
r.22, amended: SSI 2004/332 Sch.10 para.6
r.24, substituted: SSI 2004/332 Sch.10 para.7
r.24A, added: SSI 2004/332 Sch.10 para.8

799. Electricity (Non-Fossil Fuel Sources) (Scotland) Order 1997
Sch.1, referred to: SSI 2004/170 Art.8

817. Banking Act 1987 (Exempt Transactions) Regulations 1997
Sch.2, amended: SI 2003/1615 Sch.1 para.51

818. National Health Service (Optical Charges and Payments) Regulations 1997
Reg.1, amended: SI 2002/35 Reg.2, SI 2002/186 Reg.2, SI 2002/1326 Reg.2, SI 2002/2469 Sch.5, SI 2003/657 Reg.2, SI 2003/955 Reg.2, SI 2003/2381 Reg.2, SI 2004/642 Reg.2, Reg.3, SI 2004/696 Art.3, SI 2004/1014 Reg.2, SI 2004/1138 Reg.2, SI 2004/1659 Reg.2
Reg.2, amended: SI 2004/696 Art.3
Reg.8, amended: SI 2002/547 Reg.2, SI 2003/657 Reg.3, SI 2003/955 Reg.3, SI 2003/2381 Reg.2, SI 2004/642 Reg.2, Reg.3, SI 2004/696 Art.3, SI 2004/936 Reg.3, SI 2004/1014 Reg.3, SI 2004/1042 Reg.3
Reg.8, applied: SI 2004/1042 Reg.5
Reg.8, revoked (in part): SI 2003/657 Reg.3, SI 2003/955 Reg.3
Reg.9, amended: SI 2002/2469 Sch.5, SI 2003/301 Reg.2
Reg.10, amended: SI 2004/696 Art.3
Reg.11, amended: SI 2002/2469 Sch.6, SI 2004/696 Art.3
Reg.12, amended: SI 2003/301 Reg.3
Reg.12, applied: SI 2004/1014 Reg.6
Reg.12A, added: SI 2003/657 Reg.4, SI 2003/955 Reg.4
Reg.13, amended: SI 2003/301 Reg.4
Reg.17, applied: SI 2004/1014 Reg.6

NO.

1997-cont.

818. National Health Service (Optical Charges and Payments) Regulations 1997-*cont.*

Reg.19, amended: SI 2002/547 Reg.3, SI 2002/917 Reg.3, SI 2003/657 Reg.5, SI 2003/955 Reg.5, SI 2004/642 Reg.3, SI 2004/1014 Reg.4

Sch.1, amended: SI 2002/547 Reg.4, SI 2002/917 Reg.4, SI 2003/657 Reg.6, SI 2003/955 Reg.6, SI 2004/642 Reg.4, SI 2004/696 Art.3, SI 2004/1014 Reg.5

Sch.2 para.1, amended: SI 2002/547 Reg.4, SI 2003/657 Reg.6, SI 2003/955 Reg.6, SI 2004/642 Reg.4, SI 2004/696 Art.3, SI 2004/1014 Reg.5

Sch.2 para.2, amended: SI 2002/547 Reg.4, SI 2003/657 Reg.6, SI 2003/955 Reg.6, SI 2004/642 Reg.4, SI 2004/1014 Reg.5

Sch.3, substituted: SI 2002/547 Sch.1, SI 2002/917 Sch.1, SI 2003/657 Sch.1, SI 2003/955 Sch.1, SI 2004/642 Sch.1, SI 2004/1014 Sch.1

822. Channel Tunnel Rail Link (Fees for Requests for Planning Approval) Regulations 1997

Sch.2, amended: SI 2003/2155 Sch.1 para.25
Sch.4, amended: SI 2003/2155 Sch.1 para.25

827. Social Security and Child Support (Miscellaneous Amendments) Regulations 1997

Reg.7, revoked (in part): SI 2003/492 Sch.3 Part 1

829. Farm Woodland Premium Scheme 1997

applied: SSI 2004/381 Reg.4
Art.7A, added: SSI 2003/209 Sch.3 para.2
Art.9, amended: SSI 2003/209 Sch.3 para.2
Art.14, applied: SSI 2004/381 Reg.4
Sch.1, substituted: SSI 2003/209 Sch.3 para.2

830. Loch Ewe, Isle of Ewe, Wester Ross, Scallops Several Fishery Order 1997

Art.1, amended: SSI 2002/185 Art.2
Art.2, amended: SSI 2002/185 Art.2
Art.2A, added: SSI 2002/185 Art.2
Art.2B, added: SSI 2002/185 Art.2
Art.3, amended: SSI 2002/185 Art.2
Art.5, amended: SSI 2002/185 Art.2
Art.5, revoked (in part): SSI 2002/185 Art.2
Sch.1, substituted: SSI 2002/185 Sch.1

831. Lifts Regulations 1997

applied: SI 2004/129 Reg.3
referred to: SI 2004/693 Sch.1
Sch.15 para.2, amended: SI 2004/693 Sch.2
Sch.15 para.2, revoked (in part): SI 2004/693 Sch.2

832. West Cheshire National Health Service Trust Dissolution Order 1997

revoked: 2003 c.43 s.7

NO.

1997-cont.

833. Wirral and West Cheshire Community National Health Service Trust (Establishment) Order 1997

revoked: SI 2002/1244 Art.8, 2003 c.43 s.7

834. Wirral Community Healthcare National Health Service Trust Dissolution Order 1997

revoked: 2003 c.43 s.7

835. Calderdale Healthcare National Health Service Trust (Establishment) Amendment Order 1997

revoked: 2003 c.43 s.7

836. Worcester Royal Infirmary National Health Service Trust (Establishment) Amendment Order 1997

revoked: 2003 c.43 s.7

837. Carlisle Hospitals National Health Service Trust (Establishment) Amendment Order 1997

revoked: 2003 c.43 s.7

852. Housing Benefit and Council Tax Benefit (General) Amendment Regulations 1997

Reg.4, amended: SI 2003/1338 Reg.23, SI 2004/14 Reg.31

857. Welfare Food (Amendment) Regulations 1997

revoked: SI 2002/550 Reg.3

866. Education (Northern Ireland) Order 1997

Art.15, amended: SI 2003/424 Art.20, Sch.3 Part I
Art.25, amended: SI 2003/424 Art.28

869. Race Relations (Northern Ireland) Order 1997

referred to: SR 2002/120 Sch.1
Art.11, amended: SR 2003/318 Art.2
Art.52, applied: SI 2003/2902 Sch.2, Sch.3, Sch.4
Art.64, amended: SI 2003/435 Sch.4 para.13
Art.69, enabled: SR 2003/318
Sch.2 para.4, revoked: 2003 c.21 Sch.19
Sch.2 para.9, revoked: 2003 c.21 Sch.19

875. Derwen National Health Service Trust (Dissolution) Order 1997

revoked: 2003 c.43 s.7

876. Pembrokeshire and Derwen National Health Service Trust (Establishment) Order 1997

revoked: 2003 c.43 s.7

877. Pembrokeshire National Health Service Trust (Dissolution) Order 1997

revoked: 2003 c.43 s.7

933. Queen Elizabeth II Conference Centre Trading Fund Order 1997

referred to: SI 2002/1951
Art.2, amended: SI 2002/1951 Art.2
Sch.1, substituted: SI 2002/1951 Sch.1

NO.

NO.

1997–cont.

943. National Health Service (General Medical Services) (Scotland) Amendment Regulations 1997
revoked: SSI 2004/114 Sch.2

959. Fire Services (Appointments and Promotion) (Amendment) Regulations 1997
revoked: SI 2004/481 Sch.2

969. European Parliamentary Elections (Northern Ireland) (Amendment) Regulations 1997
revoked: SI 2004/1267 Sch.7

980. National Health Service (Indicative Amounts) Regulations 1997
Reg.2, amended: SI 2002/2469 Sch.7
Reg.3, amended: SI 2002/2469 Sch.5, SI 2004/865 Sch.1 para.17
Reg.3, substituted: SI 2004/1016 Sch.1 para.17

981. National Health Service (General Medical Services) Amendment (No.2) Regulations 1997
revoked (in part): SI 2004/865 Sch.2, SI 2004/1016 Sch.2

1002. Kingston and District Community National Health Service Trust (Establishment) Amendment Order 1997
revoked: 2003 c.43 s.7

1012. National Health Service (Travelling Expenses and Remission of Charges) (Scotland) Amendment Regulations 1997
revoked: SSI 2003/376 Sch.3 para.12

1055. Magistrates Courts (Criminal Procedure and Investigations Act 1996) (Tainted Acquittals) Rules 1997
r.1, amended: SI 2003/1236 r.73
r.3, revoked: SI 2003/1236 r.74
r.4, amended: SI 2003/1236 r.75
r.6, amended: SI 2003/1236 r.76
r.7, amended: SI 2003/1236 r.77
Sch.1, revoked: SI 2003/1236 r.78

1081. Timeshare Regulations 1997
Reg.8, revoked (in part): SI 2003/1922 Reg.3
Reg.13, revoked (in part): SI 2003/1398 Sch.1 para.28

1093. Dairy Produce Quotas (Amendment) (Time Limits) Regulations 1997
revoked (in part): SI 2002/457 Sch.4, SI 2002/897 Sch.4, SR 2002/88 Sch.4, SSI 2002/110 Reg.34

1154. Open-ended Investment Companies (Tax) Regulations 1997
applied: SI 2003/3297 Reg.16
Reg.5, revoked (in part): SI 2002/1973 Reg.3
Reg.7, amended: SI 2002/1973 Reg.4
Reg.9, amended: SI 2002/1973 Reg.5
Reg.10, revoked (in part): SI 2004/2310 Sch.1 para.76
Reg.11, revoked: SI 2002/1973 Reg.6
Reg.17, revoked: SI 2002/1973 Reg.6

1997–cont.

1154. Open-ended Investment Companies (Tax) Regulations 1997–*cont.*
Reg.18, revoked: SI 2002/1973 Reg.6
Reg.19, revoked (in part): SI 2002/1973 Reg.7
Reg.21, revoked: SI 2002/1973 Reg.8
Reg.25, amended: SI 2004/2310 Sch.1 para.76
Reg.28, referred to: SI 2003/3297 Reg.16
Reg.28, substituted: SI 2003/1831 Reg.2

1160. Hedgerows Regulations 1997
Reg.2, amended: SI 2003/2155 Sch.1 para.39
Reg.5, see *Conwy CBC v Lloyd* [2003] EWHC 264, (2003) 167 J.P. 223 (QBD (Admin Ct)), Maurice Kay, J.
Reg.6, see *Conwy CBC v Lloyd* [2003] EWHC 264, (2003) 167 J.P. 223 (QBD (Admin Ct)), Maurice Kay, J.

1177. Health Services (Primary Care) (Northern Ireland) Order 1997
Part II, applied: SI 2004/311 Art.7
Art.3, applied: SI 2003/1250 Art.10, Sch.8 para.22
Art.4, amended: SI 2003/1250 Sch.9 para.7
Art.12, revoked: SI 2003/1250 Sch.9 para.7
Art.23, revoked: SI 2004/311 Sch.2
Art.25, revoked: SI 2004/311 Sch.2

1179. Property (Northern Ireland) Order 1997
Art.1, enabled: SR 2002/252
Art.35, enabled: SR 2002/229
Art.35A, enabled: SR 2002/229

1180. Protection from Harassment (Northern Ireland) Order 1997
applied: SI 2003/1593 Sch.1 Part II
Art.6, applied: 2003 c.44 Sch.17 para.55

1182. Social Security Administration (Fraud) (Northern Ireland) Order 1997
referred to: 2002 c.22 s.55
Art.6, amended: SI 2003/418 Sch.2 para.5
Art.7, amended: SI 2003/418 Sch.2 para.5
Art.7, revoked (in part): SI 2003/418 Sch.3
Sch.1, revoked: 2002 c.22 Sch.8 Part 2

1186. South Lincolnshire Community and Mental Health Services National Health Service Trust (Establishment) Amendment Order 1997
revoked: 2003 c.43 s.7

1213. District of Herefordshire (Electoral Changes) Order 1997
revoked: SI 2002/187 Art.11

1220. Offshore Installations (Safety Zones) (No.2) Order 1997
Sch.1, amended: SI 2003/2743 Art.3

1225. Glan Hafren National Health Service Trust (Establishment) Amendment Order 1997
revoked: 2003 c.43 s.7

NO.

1997–cont.

1266. Greater Manchester (Light Rapid Transit System) (Airport Extension) Order 1997
referred to: SI 2002/1327 Sch.1
Art.2, amended: SI 2003/2155 Sch.2
Art.6, amended: SI 2003/2155 Sch.1 para.18
Art.12, amended: SI 2003/2155 Sch.1 para.18
Sch.10 para.1, amended: SI 2003/2155 Sch.1 para.17, Sch.2
Sch.10 para.2, amended: SI 2003/2155 Sch.1 para.17, Sch.2

1291. European Parliamentary (United Kingdom Representatives) Pensions (Amendment) Order 1997
applied: SI 2003/2922 Art.2

1320. Merchant Shipping (Safe Manning, Hours of Work and Watchkeeping) Regulations 1997
Reg.2, amended: SI 2002/2125 Sch.2 para.3
Reg.6, revoked: SI 2002/2125 Sch.2 para.3
Reg.7, revoked: SI 2002/2125 Sch.2 para.3
Reg.8, revoked: SI 2002/2125 Sch.2 para.3
Reg.9, revoked: SI 2002/2125 Sch.2 para.3
Reg.10, revoked: SI 2002/2125 Sch.2 para.3
Reg.17, amended: SI 2002/2125 Sch.2 para.3
Reg.17, revoked (in part): SI 2002/2125 Sch.2 para.3

1325. Leicestershire Ambulance and Paramedic Service National Health Service Trust (Establishment) Amendment Order 1997
revoked: 2003 c.43 s.7

1328. British Nationality (Fees) (Amendment) Regulations 1997
revoked: SI 2003/3157 Reg.2

1331. Surface Waters (Fishlife) (Classification) Regulations 1997
Reg.4, amended: SI 2003/1053 Reg.2

1335. Novel Foods and Novel Food Ingredients Regulations 1997
Reg.2, amended: SI 2004/2335 Reg.9, SSI 2004/432 Reg.8
Sch.1, amended: SI 2004/2335 Reg.9, SSI 2004/432 Reg.8

1341. Merchant Shipping (Mandatory Ships Routeing) Regulations 1997
revoked: SI 2002/1473 Sch.1 para.2

1372. Control of trade in Endangered Species Regulations 1997
see *R. v Humphrey (Raymond Leslie)* [2003] EWCA Crim 1915, [2004] 1 Cr. App. R. (S.) 39 (CA (Crim Div)), Gray, J.

1376. Horizon National Health Service Trust (Establishment) Amendment Order 1997
revoked: 2003 c.43 s.7

1400. West Yorkshire Metropolitan Ambulance Service National Health Service Trust (Establishment) Amendment Order 1997
revoked: 2003 c.43 s.7

NO.

1997–cont.

1413. Miscellaneous Food Additives (Amendment) Regulations 1997
applied: SI 2004/554 Reg.3
referred to: SI 2003/945 Reg.3, SI 2003/1008 Reg.3
varied: SI 2002/329 Reg.9
Reg.12, amended: SSI 2003/293 Reg.11

1431. Distress for Customs and Excise Duties and Other Indirect Taxes Regulations 1997
Reg.2, amended: SI 2002/761 Reg.39

1460. Chemicals (Hazard Information and Packaging for Supply) (Amendment) Regulations 1997
revoked: SI 2002/1689 Sch.7

1473. National Health Service (General Medical Services) (Scotland) Amendment (No.2) Regulations 1997
revoked: SSI 2004/114 Sch.2

1480. Welfare of Animals (Transport) Order 1997
Art.12, applied: SI 2004/853 Reg.7
Sch.9, applied: SI 2004/853 Reg.7

1482. Leicestershire Ambulance and Paramedic Service National Health Service Trust (Establishment) Amendment (No.2) Order 1997
revoked: 2003 c.43 s.7

1483. Horizon National Health Service Trust (Establishment) Amendment (No.2) Order 1997
revoked: 2003 c.43 s.7

1499. Contaminants in Food Regulations 1997
revoked (in part): SI 2002/890 Sch.1, SI 2002/1886 Sch.1, SSI 2002/267 Sch.1

1509. Merchant Shipping (Cargo Ship Construction) Regulations 1997
Reg.4, amended: SI 2004/302 Sch.1 para.12
Reg.7, amended: SI 2004/2151 Reg.3

1529. General Medical Council (Professional Performance) Rules Order of Council 1997
applied: SI 2003/1340 Art.4
Part I r.2, amended: SI 2002/2572 Sch.1 para.5, SI 2003/1343 Sch.1
Part I r.2, varied: SI 2003/1340 Art.4
Part II r.3, amended: SI 2002/2572 Sch.1 para.5
Part II r.3, applied: SI 2003/1344 Sch.1
Part II r.3, varied: SI 2003/1340 Art.4
Part II r.5, amended: SI 2002/2572 Sch.1 para.5
Part II r.5, applied: SI 2003/1344 Sch.1
Part II r.5, revoked (in part): SI 2002/2572 Sch.1 para.5
Part II r.6, amended: SI 2002/2572 Sch.1 para.5
Part II r.6, applied: SI 2003/1344 Sch.1
Part III r.7, substituted: SI 2003/1343 Sch.1

NO.

NO.

1997–cont.

1529. General Medical Council (Professional Performance) Rules Order of Council 1997–*cont.*

Part III r.8, amended: SI 2002/2572 Sch.1 para.5

Part III r.12, amended: SI 2002/2572 Sch.1 para.5

Part III r.13, amended: SI 2002/2572 Sch.1 para.5

Part V r.26, amended: SI 2002/2572 Sch.1 para.5

Part VIA r.30A, amended: SI 2003/1343 Sch.1

Part VIA r.30C, amended: SI 2003/1343 Sch.1

Part VIA r.30D, amended: SI 2003/1343 Sch.1

Part VIA r.30E, amended: SI 2002/2572 Sch.1 para.5

Part VIA r.30F, added: SI 2003/1343 Sch.1

Part VII r.31, amended: SI 2002/2572 Sch.1 para.5

Part VII r.32, amended: SI 2002/2572 Sch.1 para.5

Part VII r.33, revoked (in part): SI 2002/2572 Sch.1 para.5

Part VII r.34, revoked: SI 2002/2572 Sch.1 para.5

r.25, see *Sadler v General Medical Council* [2003] UKPC 59, [2003] 1 W.L.R. 2259 (PC (UK)), Lord Walker of Gestingthorpe

Sch.1 para.9, amended: SI 2002/2572 Sch.1 para.5

Sch.1 para.10, amended: SI 2002/2572 Sch.1 para.5

Sch.1 para.12, substituted: SI 2002/2572 Sch.1 para.5

Sch.3 Part I para.2A, amended: SI 2002/2572 Sch.1 para.5

Sch.3 Part III para.10, amended: SI 2002/2572 Sch.1 para.5

Sch.3 Part IV para.12, amended: SI 2002/2572 Sch.1 para.5

1612. Local Government Pension Scheme Regulations 1997

applied: SI 2003/2437 Reg.3, SI 2003/2963 Reg.3, Reg.5

referred to: SI 2003/1022 Reg.2, SI 2003/3004 Reg.2, SI 2004/928 Reg.5

Part V, added: SI 2003/1022 Reg.5

Reg.4, amended: SI 2004/573 Reg.3

Reg.5, amended: SI 2002/206 Reg.3

Reg.5, substituted: SI 2003/3004 Reg.3

Reg.5A, substituted: SI 2003/3004 Reg.3

Reg.5B, substituted: SI 2003/3004 Reg.3

Reg.6, amended: SI 2002/819 Reg.3, SI 2003/3004 Reg.4, SI 2004/573 Reg.4

Reg.6, disapplied: SI 2002/819 Reg.4

Reg.9, amended: SI 2003/2249 Sch.1, SI 2004/573 Reg.5

Reg.13, amended: SI 2002/206 Reg.4

1997–cont.

1612. Local Government Pension Scheme Regulations 1997–*cont.*

Reg.13, revoked (in part): SI 2004/573 Reg.6

Reg.17, amended: SI 2003/2249 Sch.1

Reg.18, amended: SI 2003/2249 Sch.1

Reg.19, amended: SI 2004/573 Reg.7

Reg.20, revoked (in part): SI 2004/573 Reg.8

Reg.21, amended: SI 2003/2249 Sch.1

Reg.21, revoked (in part): SI 2004/573 Reg.9

Reg.27, amended: SI 2004/573 Reg.10

Reg.27, revoked (in part): SI 2004/573 Reg.10

Reg.28, amended: SI 2002/206 Reg.5, SI 2004/573 Reg.11

Reg.28, revoked (in part): SI 2004/573 Reg.11

Reg.29, substituted: SI 2004/573 Reg.12

Reg.30, revoked: SI 2004/573 Reg.12

Reg.32, amended: SI 2003/1022 Reg.3, SI 2003/3004 Reg.5, SI 2004/573 Reg.13

Reg.32, referred to: SI 2002/819 Reg.4

Reg.32A, amended: SI 2004/573 Reg.14

Reg.36, amended: SI 2004/573 Reg.15

Reg.39, revoked: SI 2002/206 Reg.6

Reg.41, amended: SI 2004/573 Reg.16

Reg.48, revoked: SI 2004/573 Reg.17

Reg.52, amended: SI 2004/573 Reg.18

Reg.52, revoked (in part): SI 2004/573 Reg.18

Reg.53, revoked: SI 2004/573 Reg.18

Reg.55, amended: SI 2003/2249 Sch.1

Reg.66, revoked (in part): SI 2004/573 Reg.19

Reg.76A, added: SI 2004/573 Reg.20

Reg.77, amended: SI 2004/573 Reg.21

Reg.78, amended: SI 2003/3004 Reg.6

Reg.79, amended: SI 2003/2249 Sch.1

Reg.80, amended: SI 2004/573 Reg.22

Reg.80, revoked (in part): SI 2004/573 Reg.22

Reg.82, amended: SI 2004/573 Reg.23

Reg.83, amended: SI 2004/573 Reg.24

Reg.87, amended: SI 2004/573 Reg.25

Reg.87, revoked (in part): SI 2004/573 Reg.25

Reg.88, revoked (in part): SI 2004/573 Reg.26

Reg.93, amended: SI 2002/206 Reg.7

Reg.98, amended: SI 2004/573 Reg.27

Reg.99, substituted: SI 2004/573 Reg.28

Reg.100, amended: SI 2004/573 Reg.29

Reg.101, amended: SI 2004/573 Reg.30

Reg.102, amended: SI 2004/573 Reg.31

Reg.103, amended: SI 2004/573 Reg.32

Reg.106A, added: SI 2004/573 Reg.33

Reg.116, applied: SI 2002/819 Reg.4

Reg.121, amended: SI 2002/206 Reg.8

Reg.121, revoked (in part): SI 2002/206 Reg.8

Reg.123, amended: SI 2002/206 Reg.9

1997–cont.

1612. Local Government Pension Scheme Regulations 1997–cont.

Reg.125, disapplied: SI 2002/819 Reg.4

Reg.126, revoked: SI 2004/573 Reg.34

Reg.131, amended: SI 2003/1022 Reg.4

Reg.133, revoked (in part): SI 2004/573 Reg.35

Reg.143, revoked: SI 2004/573 Reg.36

Sch.1, amended: SI 2003/1022 Reg.6, SI 2003/2249 Sch.1, SI 2003/3004 Reg.7, SI 2004/928 Reg.3

Sch.2, amended: SI 2002/206 Reg.10, SI 2004/573 Reg.37

Sch.2A, referred to: SI 2003/3004 Reg.8

Sch.2A, substituted: SI 2003/3004 Sch.1

Sch.2A para.1, substituted: SI 2003/3004 Sch.1

Sch.2A para.2, substituted: SI 2003/3004 Sch.1

Sch.2A para.3, substituted: SI 2003/3004 Sch.1

Sch.2A para.4, substituted: SI 2003/3004 Sch.1

Sch.2A para.5, substituted: SI 2003/3004 Sch.1

Sch.2A para.6, substituted: SI 2003/3004 Sch.1

Sch.2A para.7, substituted: SI 2003/3004 Sch.1

Sch.2A para.8, substituted: SI 2003/3004 Sch.1

Sch.2A para.9, substituted: SI 2003/3004 Sch.1

Sch.2A para.10, substituted: SI 2003/3004 Sch.1

Sch.2A para.11, substituted: SI 2003/3004 Sch.1

Sch.2A para.12, substituted: SI 2003/3004 Sch.1

Sch.3, added: SI 2003/1022 Reg.7

Sch.3, amended: SI 2002/206 Reg.11, SI 2003/1022 Reg.7

Sch.3 para.1, amended: SI 2003/1022 Reg.7

Sch.4, amended: SI 2004/573 Reg.38

Sch.4 para.1, amended: SI 2003/3004 Reg.9

Sch.4 para.8, amended: SI 2004/573 Reg.38

Sch.4 para.8, revoked (in part): SI 2004/573 Reg.38

Sch.5 Part II, added: SI 2004/573 Reg.39

Sch.5 Part II, amended: SI 2002/206 Reg.12, SI 2004/573 Reg.39

Sch.6 Part I para.5, amended: SI 2004/573 Reg.40

Sch.6 Part I para.5, revoked (in part): SI 2004/573 Reg.40

Sch.6 Part II para.6, amended: SI 2004/573 Reg.40

Sch.8 Part I para.1, added: SI 2003/1022 Sch.1

Sch.8 Part I para.2, added: SI 2003/1022 Sch.1

1997–cont.

1612. Local Government Pension Scheme Regulations 1997–cont.

Sch.8 Part I para.3, added: SI 2003/1022 Sch.1

Sch.8 Part II para.4, added: SI 2003/1022 Sch.1

Sch.8 Part II para.4, amended: SI 2003/2249 Reg.3, SI 2004/928 Reg.4

Sch.8 Part III para.5, added: SI 2003/1022 Sch.1

Sch.8 Part III para.6, added: SI 2003/1022 Sch.1

Sch.8 Part III para.7, added: SI 2003/1022 Sch.1

Sch.8 Part III para.8, added: SI 2003/1022 Sch.1

Sch.8 Part III para.9, added: SI 2003/1022 Sch.1

Sch.8 Part III para.10, added: SI 2003/1022 Sch.1

Sch.8 Part III para.10, amended: SI 2004/573 Reg.41

Sch.8 Part III para.11, added: SI 2003/1022 Sch.1

Sch.8 Part III para.12, added: SI 2003/1022 Sch.1

Sch.8 Part III para.13, added: SI 2003/1022 Sch.1

Sch.8 Part III para.14, added: SI 2003/1022 Sch.1

Sch.8 Part III para.15, added: SI 2003/1022 Sch.1

Sch.8 Part III para.16, added: SI 2003/1022 Sch.1

Sch.8 Part III para.17, added: SI 2003/1022 Sch.1

Sch.8 Part III para.18, added: SI 2003/1022 Sch.1

Sch.8 Part III para.19, added: SI 2003/1022 Sch.1

Sch.8 Part III para.20, added: SI 2003/1022 Sch.1

Sch.8 Part IV para.21, added: SI 2003/1022 Sch.1

Sch.8 Part IV para.21, amended: SI 2004/573 Reg.41

Sch.8 Part IV para.22, added: SI 2003/1022 Sch.1

Sch.8 Part IV para.23, added: SI 2003/1022 Sch.1

Sch.8 Part V para.24, added: SI 2003/1022 Sch.1

Sch.8 Part V para.25, added: SI 2003/1022 Sch.1

1624. Energy Information (Combined Washer-driers) Regulations 1997

Sch.5 Part III para.15, revoked (in part): SI 2003/1398 Sch.1 para.29

1639. Royal Parks and Other Open Spaces Regulations 1997

Reg.3, amended: SI 2004/1308 Reg.2

NO.

1997–cont.

1639. Royal Parks and Other Open Spaces Regulations 1997–*cont.*

Reg.4, see *Phillips v DPP* [2002] EWHC 2093, [2003] R.T.R. 8 (QBD (Admin Ct)), McCombe, J.

Reg.4, amended: SI 2004/1308 Reg.2

Sch.1 para.13, revoked: SI 2004/1308 Reg.2

Sch.1 para.19, revoked: SI 2004/1308 Reg.2

Sch.2 Part I, see *Phillips v DPP* [2002] EWHC 2093, [2003] R.T.R. 8 (QBD (Admin Ct)), McCombe, J.

Sch.2 Part II para.1, substituted: SI 2004/1308 Reg.2

1688. Golden Valley Railway Order 1997

Art.10, amended: SI 2003/2155 Sch.1 para.18

1713. Confined Spaces Regulations 1997

referred to: SI 2003/2002 Reg.12

1723. Nurses, Midwives and Health Visitors (Supervisors of Midwives) Amendment Rules Approval Order 1997

varied: SI 2004/1762 Art.1

1724. James Paget Hospital National Health Service Trust (Change of Name) Order 1997

revoked: 2003 c.43 s.7

1729. Animals and Animal Products (Examination for Residues and Maximum Residue Limits) Regulations 1997

Reg.6, amended: SI 2004/147 Reg.2

Reg.9, applied: SI 2004/853 Reg.13

Sch.1, applied: SI 2004/853 Reg.13

1740. Supply of Beer (Tied Estate) (Amendment) Order 1997

revoked: SI 2002/3204 Art.2

1755. Broadcasting Act 1996 (British Broadcasting Corporation-Transmission Network) (Guernsey) Order 1997

Art.2, amended: SI 2003/3192 Art.4

Sch.1 para.1, revoked: SI 2003/3192 Art.4

1756. Broadcasting Act 1996 (British Broadcasting Corporation-Transmission Network) (Isle of Man) Order 1997

Art.2, amended: SI 2003/3193 Art.4

Sch.1 para.1, revoked: SI 2003/3193 Art.4

1757. Broadcasting Act 1996 (British Broadcasting Corporation-Transmission Network) (Jersey) Order 1997

Art.2, amended: SI 2003/3203 Art.4

Sch.1 para.1, revoked: SI 2003/3203 Art.4

1766. Extradition (Safety of Maritime Navigation) Order 1997

Sch.2 Part I, amended: SI 2003/1244 Art.2

Sch.2 Part II, amended: SI 2003/1244 Art.2

Sch.3 Part IA, amended: SI 2003/1244 Art.3

Sch.3 Part IB, amended: SI 2003/1244 Art.4

1769. Extradition (Torture) Order 1997

Sch.2, amended: SI 2003/1251 Art.2

Sch.3 Part I, amended: SI 2003/1251 Art.3

NO.

1997–cont.

1772. Further Education (Northern Ireland) Order 1997

applied: SI 2002/1663 Reg.3, SI 2003/424 Art.11, SI 2003/439 Sch.1 para.7, SR 2002/352 Reg.4

referred to: SR 2003/61 Sch.3

Art.5, applied: SI 2003/1994 Sch.3 para.1

Art.14, amended: SI 2003/424 Sch.2 para.7, SR 2003/110 Art.2

Art.14, enabled: SR 2003/110

Art.15, amended: SR 2003/110 Art.3

Art.21, amended: SI 2003/424 Art.37

Sch.4, amended: SI 2003/424 Sch.3 Part I

1773. Merchant Shipping (Salvage Convention) (Jersey) Order 1997

revoked: SI 2004/1284 Sch.1

1830. Prescription Only Medicines (Human Use) Order 1997

applied: SI 2002/254 Sch.2 para.24

Art.1, amended: SI 2002/549 Art.2, SI 2002/2469 Sch.4, SI 2003/696 Art.2, SI 2003/1590 Sch.1 para.21, SI 2003/2915 Art.2, SI 2004/696 Art.3, SI 2004/1031 Sch.10 para.13, SI 2004/1189 Art.2, SI 2004/1771 Sch.1 para.39, SI 2004/2693 Art.2

Art.2, amended: SI 2002/549 Art.3, SI 2003/696 Art.3

Art.3, amended: SI 2003/696 Art.4

Art.3, substituted: SI 2002/549 Art.4

Art.3A, added: SI 2002/549 Art.5

Art.3A, amended: SI 2003/696 Art.5

Art.3B, added: SI 2003/696 Art.6

Art.3B, amended: SI 2004/1031 Sch.10 para.13

Art.3B, referred to: SI 2004/291 Sch.6 para.43, SI 2004/627 Sch.5 para.42, SSI 2004/115 Sch.5 para.41, SSI 2004/116 Sch.1 para.13

Art.3C, added: SI 2003/696 Art.6

Art.4, revoked: SI 2002/549 Art.11

Art.5A, added: SI 2003/696 Art.7

Art.6, revoked: SI 2002/549 Art.11

Art.7, amended: SI 2004/2693 Art.3

Art.7A, added: SI 2004/2693 Art.4

Art.8, amended: SI 2002/549 Art.6, SI 2003/696 Art.8

Art.10, substituted: SI 2003/696 Art.9

Art.12, substituted: SI 2004/2 Art.2

Art.12A, amended: SI 2002/2469 Sch.1 para.73, SI 2004/696 Art.3

Art.12B, amended: SI 2002/2469 Sch.5, SI 2004/865 Sch.1 para.18, SI 2004/1016 Sch.1 para.18, SI 2004/2261 Sch.1 para.2, SSI 2004/212 Sch.1 para.5

Art.12C, amended: SI 2002/2469 Sch.1 para.73, SI 2003/696 Art.10

Art.12D, added: SI 2003/696 Art.11

Art.12E, added: SI 2003/696 Art.11

Art.13A, added: SI 2002/549 Art.7

Art.13A, amended: SI 2003/696 Art.12

NO.

1997–cont.

1830. Prescription Only Medicines (Human Use) Order 1997–*cont.*

Art.15, amended: SI 2002/549 Art.8, SI 2003/696 Art.13

Sch.3, amended: SI 2003/696 Art.14

Sch.3A, added: SI 2002/549 Art.9

Sch.3A, amended: SI 2003/696 Art.15, SI 2003/2915 Art.3, SI 2004/2 Art.3, SI 2004/1189 Art.3, SI 2004/2693 Art.5

Sch.3B, added: SI 2003/696 Art.16

Sch.5 Part I, amended: SI 2003/1590 Sch.1 para.21

Sch.5 Part I, applied: SI 2003/1571 Art.6

Sch.5 Part III, amended: SI 2003/1590 Sch.1 para.21, SI 2004/2 Art.4, SI 2004/1189 Art.4, SI 2004/2693 Art.6

Sch.5 Part III, applied: SI 2003/1571 Art.6

Sch.7 Part II, amended: SI 2002/2469 Sch.1 para.73, SI 2004/696 Art.3

Sch.7 Part IIA, added: SI 2003/696 Art.17

Sch.7 Part III, amended: SI 2002/549 Art.10, SI 2003/1590 Sch.1 para.21, SI 2004/1189 Art.5, SI 2004/1771 Sch.1 para.39

1840. Fire Precautions (Workplace) Regulations 1997

Part II, applied: SI 2003/1910 Sch.1 para.3, SI 2003/1934 Sch.1 para.3, SI 2003/3230 Sch.1 para.3, SI 2003/3234 Sch.1 para.3

Reg.9, amended: SI 2002/2776 Sch.6 para.8, SI 2003/2457 Reg.8, Reg.9, Reg.10, Reg.11

Reg.9A, added: SI 2003/2457 Reg.12

Reg.17, amended: SI 2003/2457 Reg.13

1841. Council Tax Benefit (General) Amendment Regulations 1997

revoked: SI 2004/154 Reg.3

1844. West Mercia (Police Area and Authority) Order 1997

varied: SI 2004/222 Art.2

1845. Cheshire (Police Area and Authority) Order 1997

varied: SI 2004/222 Art.2

1846. Cambridgeshire (Police Area and Authority) Order 1997

varied: SI 2004/222 Art.2

1847. Essex (Police Area and Authority) Order 1997

varied: SI 2004/222 Art.2

1848. Thames Valley (Police Authority) Order 1997

varied: SI 2004/222 Art.2

1849. Devon and Cornwall (Police Area and Authority) Order 1997

varied: SI 2004/222 Art.2

1850. Nottinghamshire (Police Area and Authority) Order 1997

varied: SI 2004/222 Art.2

1852. Leasehold Valuation Tribunals (Fees) Order 1997

revoked (in part): SI 2003/2270 Art.2, SI 2004/680 Art.2

NO.

1997–cont.

1853. Leasehold Valuation Tribunals (Service Charges, Insurance or Appointment of Managers Applications) Order 1997

revoked (in part): SI 2003/2269 Art.2, SI 2004/677 Art.2

1855. Lancashire (Police Area and Authority) Order 1997

varied: SI 2004/222 Art.2

1856. Broadcasting (Technical Services) Order 1997

Art.2, amended: SI 2003/2155 Sch.1 para.40

1857. Kent (Police Area and Authority) Order 1997

varied: SI 2004/222 Art.2

1861. General Medical Council (Legal Assessors) (Amendment) Rules 1997

revoked: SI 2004/2625 r.6

1886. Telecommunications (Voice Telephony) Regulations 1997

revoked: 2003 c.21 Sch.19

1900. Genetically Modified Organisms (Deliberate Release and Risk Assessment-Amendment) Regulations 1997

referred to: SI 2002/2443 Sch.5, SI 2002/3188 Sch.5

Reg.2, revoked (in part): SI 2002/2443 Sch.5, SI 2002/3188 Sch.5, SSI 2002/541 Sch.7

1908. Police (Property) Regulations 1997

applied: SI 2002/1372 Reg.5

Reg.3, amended: SI 2002/2313 Reg.2

Reg.5, amended: SI 2002/2313 Reg.3

Reg.6, amended: SI 2002/2313 Reg.4

Reg.7, amended: SI 2002/2313 Reg.5

Reg.8, amended: SI 2002/2313 Reg.4

1931. Education (National Curriculum) (Assessment Arrangements for the Core Subjects) (Key Stage 1) (England) (Amendment) Order 1997

revoked: 2002 c.32 Sch.22 Part 3

1941. Energy Efficiency (Refrigerators and Freezers) Regulations 1997

Sch.3 Part III para.15, revoked (in part): SI 2003/1398 Sch.1 para.30

1950. Humber Bridge (Revision of Tolls and Vehicle Classification) Order 1997

see *R. (on the application of Confederation of Passenger Transport UK) v Humber Bridge Board* [2002] EWHC 2261, [2002] N.P.C. 136 (QBD (Admin Ct)), Newman, J.

1953. Cromarty Firth Port Authority Harbour Revision Order 1997

applied: SSI 2003/491 Art.1

1963. National Board for Nursing, Midwifery and Health Visiting for England (Constitution and Administration) Amendment Order 1997

varied: SI 2004/1762 Art.1

NO.

1997–cont.

1966. Education (School Inspection) Regulations 1997

Reg.8, applied: SI 2003/1921 Reg.5

1968. Education (Assisted Places) Regulations 1997

Reg.10, amended: SI 2002/1879 Reg.2, SI 2002/1979 Reg.2, SI 2003/1705 Reg.2, SI 2003/1854 Reg.2, SI 2004/1812 Reg.2, SI 2004/1965 Reg.2

Sch.2 para.1, amended: SI 2002/1879 Reg.2, SI 2002/1979 Reg.2, SI 2003/1705 Reg.2, SI 2003/1854 Reg.2, SI 2004/1812 Reg.2, SI 2004/1965 Reg.2

Sch.2 para.2, amended: SI 2002/1879 Reg.2, SI 2002/1979 Reg.2, SI 2003/1705 Reg.2, SI 2003/1854 Reg.2, SI 2004/1812 Reg.2, SI 2004/1965 Reg.2

1969. Education (Assisted Places) (Incidental Expenses) Regulations 1997

Reg.2, amended: SI 2002/1880 Reg.2, SI 2003/1707 Reg.2, SI 2003/1779 Reg.2, SI 2004/1807 Reg.2, SI 2004/1970 Reg.2

Reg.2, substituted: SI 2002/1984 Reg.2

Reg.4, amended: SI 2002/1880 Reg.2, SI 2003/1707 Reg.2, SI 2003/1779 Reg.2, SI 2004/1807 Reg.2, SI 2004/1970 Reg.2

Reg.9, amended: SI 2003/1707 Reg.2, SI 2003/1779 Reg.2

1972. Education (Fees and Awards) Regulations 1997

Reg.2, amended: SI 2003/3280 Reg.2

Reg.5, applied: SI 2003/3280 Reg.1

Reg.6, applied: SI 2003/3280 Reg.1

Reg.6A, applied: SI 2003/3280 Reg.1

Reg.6B, applied: SI 2003/3280 Reg.1

Reg.7, applied: SI 2003/3280 Reg.1

Reg.8, amended: SI 2003/3280 Reg.2

Sch.1 para.6, amended: SI 2003/3280 Reg.2

Sch.1 para.8, amended: SI 2003/3280 Reg.2

Sch.1 para.9, amended: SI 2003/3280 Reg.2

1984. Rent Officers (Housing Benefit Functions) Order 1997

Art.2, amended: SI 2003/2398 Art.2, SI 2004/2101 Art.2

Art.3, amended: SI 2003/2398 Art.2

Art.4B, added: SI 2003/2398 Art.2

Art.4C, added: SI 2003/2398 Art.2

Art.4D, added: SI 2003/2398 Art.2

Art.4E, added: SI 2003/2398 Art.2

Art.5, amended: SI 2003/2398 Art.2

Art.6, amended: SI 2003/2398 Art.2

Art.7A, substituted: SI 2003/2398 Art.2

Sch.1 Part I para.4, see *R. (on the application of Cumpsty) v Rent Service* [2002] EWHC 2526, Times, December 5, 2002 (QBD (Admin Ct)), Pitchford, J.

Sch.1 Part I para.4, revoked (in part): SI 2003/478 Art.2

Sch.1 Part 1 para.4, see *R. (on the application of Dinsdale) v Rent Service* [2001] EWCA Civ 1559, [2002] H.L.R. 32 (CA), Sedley, L.J.

NO.

1997–cont.

1984. Rent Officers (Housing Benefit Functions) Order 1997–*cont.*

Sch.1 Part I para.5, amended: SI 2003/2398 Art.2

Sch.1 Part II para.7, revoked (in part): SI 2003/478 Art.2

Sch.1 Part IV para.11, revoked (in part): SI 2003/478 Art.2

Sch.3A Part I para.1, added: SI 2003/2398 Sch.2

Sch.3A Part I para.2, added: SI 2003/2398 Sch.2

Sch.3A Part I para.3, added: SI 2003/2398 Sch.2

Sch.3A Part I para.4, added: SI 2003/2398 Sch.2

Sch.3A Part II, added: SI 2003/2398 Sch.2

1987. Anglian Harbours National Health Service Trust Dissolution Order 1997

revoked: 2003 c.43 s.7

1992. Local Government Changes for England (Lord-Lieutenants and Sheriffs) Order 1997

varied: SI 2004/222 Art.2

1995. Rent Officers (Housing Benefit Functions) (Scotland) Order 1997

Art.2, amended: SI 2003/2398 Art.3, SI 2004/2101 Art.2

Art.3, amended: SI 2003/2398 Art.3

Art.4B, added: SI 2003/2398 Art.3

Art.4C, added: SI 2003/2398 Art.3

Art.4D, added: SI 2003/2398 Art.3

Art.4E, added: SI 2003/2398 Art.3

Art.5, amended: SI 2003/2398 Art.3

Art.6, amended: SI 2003/2398 Art.3

Art.7A, substituted: SI 2003/2398 Art.3

Sch.1 Part I para.4, revoked (in part): SI 2003/478 Art.3

Sch.1 Part I para.5, amended: SI 2003/2398 Art.3

Sch.1 Part II para.7, revoked (in part): SI 2003/478 Art.3

Sch.1 Part IV para.11, revoked (in part): SI 2003/478 Art.3

Sch.3A Part I para.1, added: SI 2003/2398 Sch.2

Sch.3A Part I para.2, added: SI 2003/2398 Sch.2

Sch.3A Part I para.3, added: SI 2003/2398 Sch.2

Sch.3A Part I para.4, added: SI 2003/2398 Sch.2

Sch.3A Part II, added: SI 2003/2398 Sch.2

2009. Education (National Curriculum) (Assessment Arrangements for English, Welsh, Mathematics and Science) (Key Stage 2) (Wales) Order 1997

revoked: 2002 c.32 Sch.22 Part 3, SI 2004/2915 Art.2

Art.4, applied: SI 2002/438 Sch.1 para.1

NO.

1997–cont.

2009. Education (National Curriculum) (Assessment Arrangements for English, Welsh, Mathematics and Science) (Key Stage 2) (Wales) Order 1997–*cont.*

Art.5, applied: SI 2002/438 Sch.1 para.1
Art.6, applied: SI 2002/438 Sch.1 para.1
Art.7, applied: SI 2002/438 Sch.1 para.1
Art.8, applied: SI 2002/438 Sch.1 para.1
Art.9, applied: SI 2002/438 Sch.1 para.1

2010. Education (National Curriculum) (Key Stage 3 Assessment Arrangements) (Wales) Order 1997

revoked: 2002 c.32 Sch.22 Part 3
Art.4, applied: SI 2002/438 Sch.1 para.1
Art.5, applied: SI 2002/438 Sch.1 para.1
Art.6, applied: SI 2002/438 Sch.1 para.1
Art.7, applied: SI 2002/438 Sch.1 para.1
Art.8, applied: SI 2002/438 Sch.1 para.1
Art.9, applied: SI 2002/438 Sch.1 para.1
Art.10, applied: SI 2002/438 Sch.1 para.1
Art.11, applied: SI 2002/438 Sch.1 para.1
Art.12, applied: SI 2002/438 Sch.1 para.1

2011. Education (National Curriculum) (Assessment Arrangements for English, Welsh, Mathematics and Science) (Key Stage 1) (Wales) Order 1997

revoked: 2002 c.32 Sch.22 Part 3, SI 2002/45 Art.2

2042. Processed Cereal-based Foods and Baby Foods for Infants and Young Children Regulations 1997

revoked (in part): SI 2003/3207 Reg.13, SI 2004/314 Reg.13, SSI 2004/8 Reg.14

2046. Allocation of Housing and Homelessness (Amendment) (No.2) Regulations 1997

revoked: 2002 c.7 s.14

2169. Local Government Changes for England (Direct Labour Organisations) (East Riding of Yorkshire District Council) Order 1997

varied: SI 2004/222 Art.2

2173. Education (Further Education Institutions Information) (England) (Amendment) Regulations 1997

revoked: SI 2003/51 Reg.2

2176. Education (National Curriculum) (Assessment Arrangements for Key Stages 1, 2 and 3) (England) (Amendment) Order 1997

revoked: 2002 c.32 Sch.22 Part 3

2196. Gaming Duty Regulations 1997

Reg.5, amended: SI 2002/2310 Reg.4, SI 2003/2247 Reg.4, SI 2004/2243 Reg.4

2205. Social Security (Recovery of Benefits) Regulations 1997

see *Bruce v Genesis Fast Food Ltd* [2003] EWHC 788, [2004] P.I.Q.R. P9 (QBD), McKinnon, J.

NO.

1997–cont.

2205. Social Security (Recovery of Benefits) Regulations 1997–*cont.*

Reg.2, amended: SI 2004/1141 Reg.7

2238. Food (Pistachios from Iran) (Emergency Control) Order 1997

revoked (in part): SI 2003/1119 Reg.7, SI 2003/1956 Reg.7, SI 2003/2288 Reg.7, SSI 2003/414 Reg.7

2289. National Health Service (Proposals for Pilot Schemes) and (Miscellaneous Amendments) Regulations 1997

applied: SI 2002/553 Art.9, SI 2002/2469 Sch.12 para.5
Reg.1, amended: SI 2002/2469 Sch.1 para.74
Reg.2, revoked (in part): SI 2004/865 Sch.1 para.19, SI 2004/1016 Sch.1 para.19, SSI 2004/212 Sch.1 para.6
Reg.3, revoked (in part): SI 2004/865 Sch.1 para.19, SI 2004/1016 Sch.1 para.19, SSI 2004/212 Sch.1 para.6

2290. Social Security (Claims and Payments and Adjudication) Amendment No 2 Regulations 1997

Reg.1, amended: SI 2003/492 Sch.3 Part 1
Reg.5, revoked (in part): SI 2003/492 Sch.3 Part 1
Reg.6, revoked (in part): SI 2003/492 Sch.3 Part 1

2294. Fireworks (Safety) Regulations 1997

applied: SI 2003/3085 Reg.5, SI 2004/1836 Reg.6
referred to: SI 2003/1376 Sch.1, SI 2004/1836 Reg.9
Reg.6, applied: SI 2003/1376 Sch.1, SI 2003/1593 Sch.1 Part I

2305. Social Security (Miscellaneous Amendments) (No.4) Regulations 1997

Reg.5, revoked (in part): SI 2003/492 Sch.3 Part 1

2308. Children (Protection from Offenders) (Miscellaneous Amendments) Regulations 1997

Reg.3, revoked (in part): SI 2002/57 Reg.51, SI 2003/237 Reg.53
Reg.4, revoked (in part): SI 2002/327 Reg.43

2365. Bovine Spongiform Encephalopathy Compensation (Amendment) Order 1997

revoked (in part): SSI 2002/255 Sch.9 Part I

2367. Merchant Shipping (Dangerous Goods and Marine Pollutants) Regulations 1997

applied: SI 2002/1689 Reg.7, SR 2002/301 Reg.7
referred to: SI 2002/1689 Reg.8A
amended: SI 2004/2110 Sch.2 para.1
Reg.2, amended: 2002 c.8 s.2, SI 2004/2110 Sch.2 para.1, Sch.2 para.2
Reg.9, amended: SI 2004/2110 Sch.2 para.3

NO.

1997–cont.

2367. Merchant Shipping (Dangerous Goods and Marine Pollutants) Regulations 1997–*cont.*

Reg.10, amended: SI 2004/2110 Sch.2 para.4, Sch.2 para.5

Reg.21, amended: SI 2004/2110 Sch.2 para.6, Sch.2 para.7

2387. Bovine Spongiform Encephalopathy (No.2) (Amendment) Order 1997

revoked (in part): SSI 2002/255 Sch.9 Part I

2389. Airports (Groundhandling) Regulations 1997

Reg.19, amended: SI 2004/1256 Reg.8

2393. National Health Service (Travelling Expenses and Remission of Charges) Amendment (No.2) Regulations 1997

revoked: SI 2003/2382 Sch.2

2400. Zebra, Pelican and Puffin Pedestrian Crossings Regulations and General Directions 1997

Reg.18, applied: 2004 c.18 Sch.7 para.3, Sch.7 para.4

Reg.20, applied: 2004 c.18 Sch.7 para.3, Sch.7 para.4

Reg.22, amended: SI 2003/2155 Sch.1 para.41

2430. Stamp Duty Reserve Tax (Amendment) Regulations 1997

varied: 2002 c.23 Sch.34 para.7, Sch.35 para.8

2439. Vehicle Excise Duty (Immobilisation, Removal and Disposal of Vehicles) Regulations 1997

Reg.10, amended: SI 2002/745 Reg.2

2455. National Health Service (Travelling Expenses and Remission of Charges) (Scotland) Amendment (No.2) Regulations 1997

revoked: SSI 2003/376 Sch.3 para.13

2456. Local Government Changes for England (Direct Labour Organisations) (County of Leicestershire and District of Rutland) Order 1997

varied: SI 2004/222 Art.2

2468. National Health Service (General Medical Services) Amendment (No.3) Regulations 1997

revoked (in part): SI 2004/865 Sch.2, SI 2004/1016 Sch.2

2471. Surface Waters (Fishlife) (Classification) (Scotland) Regulations 1997

Reg.4, amended: SSI 2003/85 Reg.2

Reg.5A, added: SSI 2003/85 Reg.2

2499. Plant Protection Products (Amendment) (No.2) Regulations 1997

revoked (in part): SI 2003/3241 Sch.5, SSI 2003/579 Sch.5

NO.

1997–cont.

2518. Greater Manchester Ambulance Service National Health Service Trust (Establishment) Amendment Order 1997

revoked: 2003 c.43 s.7

2537. Imported Food Regulations 1997

Sch.1 para.21, added: SI 2002/1227 Sch.8 para.3, SI 2002/1387 Sch.8 para.3, SSI 2002/445 Sch.8 para.3

2544. Coroners Records (Fees for Copies) Rules 1997

revoked: SI 2002/2401 r.4

2570. Angola (United Nations Prohibition of Flights) (Dependent Territories) Order 1997

revoked: SI 2003/1868 Sch.2

2571. Angola (United Nations Prohibition of Flights) Order 1997

revoked: SI 2003/1868 Sch.2

2572. Angola (United Nations Sanctions) Order 1997

revoked: SI 2003/1868 Sch.2

Art.5, amended: 2002 c.8 s.2

Art.10, amended: 2002 c.8 s.2

2573. Angola (United Nations Sanctions) (Dependent Territories) Order 1997

revoked: SI 2003/1868 Sch.2

Art.5, amended: 2002 c.8 s.2

Art.10, amended: 2002 c.8 s.2

2581. Merchant Shipping (Oil Pollution) (Bermuda) Order 1997

revoked: SI 2002/3147 Art.2

2594. Angola (United Nations Sanctions) (Channel Islands) Order 1997

revoked: SI 2003/1868 Sch.2

Art.5, amended: 2002 c.8 s.2

Art.9, amended: 2002 c.8 s.2

Art.10, amended: 2002 c.8 s.2

2595. Angola (United Nations Sanctions) (Isle of Man) Order 1997

revoked: SI 2003/1868 Sch.2

Art.5, amended: 2002 c.8 s.2

Art.9, amended: 2002 c.8 s.2

Art.10, amended: 2002 c.8 s.2

2605. Nevill Hall and District National Health Service Trust (Establishment) Amendment Order 1997

revoked: 2003 c.43 s.7

2666. Air Navigation (Dangerous Goods) (Second Amendment) Regulations 1997

revoked: SI 2002/2786 Sch.1

2676. Social Security (National Insurance Number Information Exemption) Regulations 1997

Reg.7, revoked: SI 2003/495 Sch.1 Part 1

2679. Education (Teachers) (Amendment) (No.2) Regulations 1997

referred to: SI 2003/1663 Sch.1 para.2, SI 2003/1709 Art.5, SI 2004/1744 Sch.1 para.2

1997–cont.

2690. Mersey Regional Ambulance Service National Health Service Trust (Establishment) Amendment Order 1997
revoked: 2003 c.43 s.7

2695. Berkshire Fire Services (Combination Scheme) Order 1997
Sch.1 Part II para.6, amended: 2003 c.26 Sch.8 Part 2
Sch.1 Part III para.20, revoked (in part): 2003 c.26 Sch.8 Part 2
Sch.1 Part IV para.21, revoked: 2003 c.26 Sch.8 Part 2

2696. Cambridgeshire Fire Services (Combination Scheme) Order 1997
Sch.1 Part II para.6, amended: 2003 c.26 Sch.8 Part 2
Sch.1 Part III para.20, revoked (in part): 2003 c.26 Sch.8 Part 2
Sch.1 Part IV para.21, revoked: 2003 c.26 Sch.8 Part 2

2697. Cheshire Fire Services (Combination Scheme) Order 1997
Sch.1 Part II para.6, amended: 2003 c.26 Sch.8 Part 2
Sch.1 Part III para.20, revoked (in part): 2003 c.26 Sch.8 Part 2
Sch.1 Part IV para.21, revoked: 2003 c.26 Sch.8 Part 2

2698. Devon Fire Services (Combination Scheme) Order 1997
Sch.1 Part II para.6, amended: 2003 c.26 Sch.8 Part 2
Sch.1 Part III para.20, revoked (in part): 2003 c.26 Sch.8 Part 2
Sch.1 Part IV para.21, revoked: 2003 c.26 Sch.8 Part 2

2699. Essex Fire Services (Combination Scheme) Order 1997
Sch.1 Part II para.6, amended: 2003 c.26 Sch.8 Part 2
Sch.1 Part III para.20, revoked (in part): 2003 c.26 Sch.8 Part 2
Sch.1 Part IV para.21, revoked: 2003 c.26 Sch.8 Part 2

2700. Hereford and Worcester Fire Services (Combination Scheme) Order 1997
Sch.1 Part II para.6, amended: 2003 c.26 Sch.8 Part 2
Sch.1 Part III para.20, revoked (in part): 2003 c.26 Sch.8 Part 2
Sch.1 Part IV para.21, revoked: 2003 c.26 Sch.8 Part 2

2701. Kent Fire Services (Combination Scheme) Order 1997
Sch.1 Part II para.6, amended: 2003 c.26 Sch.8 Part 2
Sch.1 Part III para.20, revoked (in part): 2003 c.26 Sch.8 Part 2
Sch.1 Part IV para.21, revoked: 2003 c.26 Sch.8 Part 2

1997–cont.

2702. Shropshire Fire Services (Combination Scheme) Order 1997
Sch.1 Part II para.6, amended: 2003 c.26 Sch.8 Part 2
Sch.1 Part III para.20, revoked (in part): 2003 c.26 Sch.8 Part 2
Sch.1 Part IV para.21, revoked: 2003 c.26 Sch.8 Part 2

2709. Education (Individual Pupils Achievements) (Information) (Wales) (Amendment) Regulations 1997
revoked: SI 2004/1026 Sch.5

2744. Value Added Tax (Drugs, Medicines and Aids for the Handicapped) Order 1997
see *BUPA Hospitals Ltd v Customs and Excise Commissioners* [2002] 3 C.M.L.R. 40 (V&DTr), Stephen Oliver Q.C. (Chairman)

2760. Lancashire Fire Services (Combination Scheme) Order 1997
Sch.1 Part II para.6, amended: 2003 c.26 Sch.8 Part 2
Sch.1 Part III para.20, revoked (in part): 2003 c.26 Sch.8 Part 2
Sch.1 Part IV para.21, revoked: 2003 c.26 Sch.8 Part 2

2761. Nottinghamshire Fire Services (Combination Scheme) Order 1997
Sch.1 Part II para.6, amended: 2003 c.26 Sch.8 Part 2
Sch.1 Part III para.20, revoked (in part): 2003 c.26 Sch.8 Part 2
Sch.1 Part IV para.21, revoked: 2003 c.26 Sch.8 Part 2

2764. Relocation Grants Regulations 1997
revoked: SI 2002/1860 Sch.6

2767. South Yorkshire Metropolitan Ambulance and Paramedic Service National Health Service Trust (Establishment) Amendment Order 1997
revoked: 2003 c.43 s.7

2776. Diving at Work Regulations 1997
applied: SI 2002/1587 Reg.3, Reg.15
Reg.6, applied: SI 2002/325 Reg.3

2777. Industrial Pollution Control (Northern Ireland) Order 1997
applied: SI 2002/3153 Sch.1 para.20, SR 2002/28 Sch.1 para.1
revoked: SI 2002/3153 Sch.6 Part I
Art.3, enabled: SR 2003/96
Art.6, amended: SR 2003/46 Sch.11 para.11
Art.7, amended: SI 2002/3153 Sch.5 para.8
Art.8, applied: SR 2002/28 Sch.1 para.2, Sch.1 para.8
Art.10, applied: SR 2003/210 Reg.3, Reg.4
Art.11, applied: SR 2003/210 Reg.3, Reg.4
Art.17, referred to: SI 2002/3153 Sch.1 para.14

1997–cont.

2778. Waste and Contaminated Land (Northern Ireland) Order 1997

Part II, applied: SI 2002/3153 Art.6, Sch.1 para.20, SR 2002/248 Reg.3, Reg.6, Reg.7, Reg.8

Part II, referred to: SR 2002/271 Reg.2

Part II, varied: SR 2002/248 Reg.9

Art.1, enabled: SR 2002/185, SR 2003/489

Art.2, amended: 2003 c.21 Sch.17 para.144

Art.2, enabled: SR 2002/248, SR 2002/271

Art.4, applied: SR 2002/248 Reg.4

Art.4, disapplied: SR 2002/248 Reg.10

Art.4, enabled: SR 2002/248

Art.4, referred to: SR 2002/271 Reg.2

Art.5, amended: SR 2003/46 Sch.11 para.12

Art.5, applied: SI 2002/3153 Art.6

Art.5, enabled: SR 2002/271

Art.6, referred to: SR 2002/271 Reg.2

Art.19, applied: SI 2002/3153 Art.7

Art.20, applied: SR 2002/248 Reg.5, Reg.9

Art.20, enabled: SR 2002/248

Art.32, applied: SR 2003/97

Art.32, enabled: SR 2003/97

Art.38, referred to: SR 2002/271 Reg.2

Art.39, referred to: SR 2002/271 Reg.2

Art.47, amended: SI 2002/3153 Art.5

Art.47, applied: SI 2002/3153 Art.6, SR 2002/248 Reg.10

Art.47, referred to: SI 2002/3153 Art.6

Sch.5, referred to: SI 2003/412 Sch.4 para.1

Sch.5, revoked: 2002 c.4 (NI) s.5, SI 2002/3153 Sch.6 Part I

2788. Staffordshire Ambulance Service National Health Service Trust (Establishment) Amendment Order 1997

revoked: 2003 c.43 s.7

2789. Horse Passports Order 1997

revoked (in part): SI 2003/2780 Reg.25

Art.4, applied: SI 2003/2780 Reg.3

2817. National Health Service (Vocational Training for General Medical Practice) Regulations 1997

applied: SI 2002/1882 Reg.4, SI 2003/1250 Sch.8 para.5, Sch.8 para.6, SI 2003/2644 Reg.4, SI 2004/865 Art.110, Art.118, SI 2004/1016 Art.86, SI 2004/1947 Reg.4

revoked: SI 2003/1250 Sch.10 Part 2

varied: SI 2004/1947 Reg.8

Reg.2, amended: SI 2003/3148 Reg.13

Reg.2, varied: SI 2004/865 Art.118, SI 2004/1016 Art.94

Reg.4, amended: SI 2002/2469 Sch.1 para.75, Sch.5

Reg.4, varied: SI 2004/865 Art.118, SI 2004/1016 Art.94

Reg.5, amended: SI 2003/3148 Reg.13

Reg.5, applied: SI 2003/1250 Art.10, Art.11, Sch.8 para.22, SI 2004/865 Art.110, SI 2004/1016 Art.86

Reg.5, referred to: SI 2003/1250 Sch.8 para.22

1997–cont.

2817. National Health Service (Vocational Training for General Medical Practice) Regulations 1997–cont.

Reg.5, varied: SI 2004/865 Art.118, SI 2004/1016 Art.94

Reg.6, amended: SI 2003/3148 Reg.13

Reg.6, applied: SI 2003/1250 Sch.8 para.2, SI 2003/2644 Reg.4

Reg.6, referred to: SI 2004/585 Reg.23, SI 2004/1020 Reg.23

Reg.7, applied: SI 2003/1250 Sch.8 para.3, Sch.8 para.4

Reg.7, referred to: SI 2003/1250 Sch.8 para.4

Reg.8, applied: SI 2003/1250 Sch.8 para.2

Reg.9, applied: SI 2003/2644 Reg.4, SI 2004/1020 Reg.23

Reg.10, applied: SI 2003/2644 Reg.4, SI 2004/585 Reg.23, SI 2004/1020 Reg.23

Reg.11, applied: SI 2003/2644 Reg.4, SI 2004/585 Reg.23, SI 2004/1020 Reg.23

Reg.12, amended: SI 2003/3148 Reg.13

Reg.12, applied: SI 2003/1250 Art.8, SI 2004/1020 Reg.23

Reg.12A, applied: SI 2003/1250 Sch.8 para.6

Reg.12A, referred to: SI 2003/1250 Sch.8 para.5

Reg.13, applied: SI 2003/1250 Sch.8 para.6

Reg.13, referred to: SI 2003/1250 Sch.8 para.6

Reg.14, amended: SI 2002/2469 Sch.1 para.75, SI 2004/696 Art.3

2824. Act of Sederunt (Fees of Sheriff Officers) 1997

revoked: SSI 2002/567 Sch.2

2825. Act of Sederunt (Fees of Messengers-at-Arms) 1997

revoked: SSI 2002/566 Sch.2

2827. Non-Domestic Rating (Rural Areas and Rateable Value Limits) (Scotland) Order 1997

Art.3, amended: SSI 2003/141 Art.2

Sch.1, amended: SSI 2004/91 Art.3, Art.4

2844. Sheep Annual Premium and Suckler Cow Premium Quotas Regulations 1997

applied: SI 2003/2261 Reg.17

revoked: SI 2003/2261 Reg.18

2847. Relocation Grants (Form of Application) Regulations 1997

revoked: SI 2002/1860 Sch.6

Sch.1, added: SI 2002/666 Sch.1 para.3, Sch.1 para.7, Sch.1 para.8

Sch.1, amended: SI 2002/666 Sch.1 para.1, Sch.1 para.2, Sch.1 para.4, Sch.1 para.5, Sch.1 para.6, Sch.1 para.9, Sch.1 para.10, SI 2002/1397 Sch.1 para.30, SI 2002/2800 Sch.1 para.1, Sch.1 para.2, Sch.1 para.3, Sch.1 para.4, Sch.1 para.5, Sch.1 para.6, Sch.1 para.7, Sch.1 para.8, Sch.1 para.9, Sch.1 para.10, SI 2003/762 Reg.11, SI 2004/1748 Sch.2 para.2

NO.

1997–cont.

2886. Merchant Shipping (Master's Discretion) Regulations 1997

revoked: SI 2002/1473 Sch.1 para.2

2893. Charges for Inspections and Controls Regulations 1997

Sch.1, amended: SI 2004/1697 Reg.2, SI 2004/1871 Reg.2

2914. Cosmetic Products (Safety) (Amendment) Regulations 1997

revoked: SI 2003/835 Sch.1

2918. Education (Particulars of Independent Schools) Regulations 1997

revoked (in part): 2002 c.32 Sch.22 Part 3, SI 2003/1934 Reg.12, SI 2003/3230 Reg.10

2928. European Specialist Medical Qualifications Amendment Regulations 1997

revoked: SI 2003/1250 Sch.10 Part 2

2929. National Health Service (Pilot Schemes-Health Service Bodies) Regulations 1997

applied: SI 2004/865 Art.68, SSI 2004/163 Art.58

Reg.1, amended: SI 2002/2469 Sch.1 para.76, SI 2004/865 Sch.1 para.20, SI 2004/1016 Sch.1 para.20, SSI 2004/212 Sch.1 para.7

Reg.2, revoked (in part): SI 2002/2469 Sch.1 para.76

Reg.3, amended: SI 2002/2469 Sch.1 para.76

Reg.3, applied: SI 2004/865 Art.68, SSI 2004/163 Art.58

2931. Telecommunications (Interconnection) Regulations 1997

revoked: 2003 c.21 Sch.19

Reg.6, see *British Telecommunications Plc v Director General of Telecommunications (Permission to Intervene)* [2003] CAT 20, [2004] Comp. A.R. 187 (Competition Appeal Tribunal), Sir Christopher Bellamy (President); see *British Telecommunications Plc v Office of Communications (formerly Director General of Telecommunications)* [2004] CAT 8 (CAT), Sir Christopher Bellamy (President)

2932. Telecommunications (Open Network Provision and Leased Lines) Regulations 1997

revoked: 2003 c.21 Sch.19

2938. Southend Health Care Services National Health Service Trust (Change of Name) Order 1997

revoked: 2003 c.43 s.7

2964. Specified Risk Material Order 1997

applied: SI 2002/843 Reg.104, SI 2002/1416 Reg.104, SSI 2002/255 Reg.102

revoked (in part): SI 2003/3177 Sch.6, SI 2004/1430 Sch.6

Art.2, revoked (in part): SI 2004/1430 Sch.6

NO.

1997–cont.

2964. Specified Risk Material Order 1997–cont.

Art.3, amended: SI 2002/843 Sch.8 para.1, SI 2002/1416 Sch.8 para.1, SSI 2002/255 Sch.8 para.1

Art.4, amended: SI 2002/843 Sch.8 para.2, SI 2002/1416 Sch.8 para.2, SSI 2002/255 Sch.8 para.2

Art.4, revoked (in part): SI 2004/1430 Sch.6

Art.5, revoked (in part): SI 2002/843 Sch.9 Part I, SI 2002/1416 Sch.9 Part I, SSI 2002/255 Sch.9 Part I

Art.6, amended: SI 2002/843 Sch.8 para.3, SI 2002/1416 Sch.8 para.3, SSI 2002/255 Sch.8 para.3

Art.6, revoked (in part): SI 2004/1430 Sch.6

Art.7, revoked (in part): SI 2002/843 Sch.9 Part I, SI 2002/1416 Sch.9 Part I, SSI 2002/255 Sch.9 Part I

Art.8, applied: SI 2002/843 Sch.9 para.1, SSI 2002/255 Sch.9 para.1

Art.8, revoked (in part): SI 2002/843 Sch.9 Part I, SI 2002/1416 Sch.9 Part I, SSI 2002/255 Sch.9 Part I

Art.8, varied: SI 2002/1416 Sch.9 para.1

Art.9, revoked (in part): SI 2002/843 Sch.9 Part I, SI 2002/1416 Sch.9 Part I, SSI 2002/255 Sch.9 Part I

Art.10, applied: SI 2002/843 Sch.9 para.2, SSI 2002/255 Sch.9 para.2

Art.10, revoked (in part): SI 2002/843 Sch.9 Part I, SI 2002/1416 Sch.9 Part I, SSI 2002/255 Sch.9 Part I

Art.10, varied: SI 2002/1416 Sch.9 para.2

Art.11, revoked (in part): SI 2002/843 Sch.9 Part I, SI 2002/1416 Sch.9 Part I, SSI 2002/255 Sch.9 Part I

Art.12, applied: SI 2002/843 Sch.9 para.3, SSI 2002/255 Sch.9 para.3

Art.12, revoked (in part): SI 2002/843 Sch.9 Part I, SI 2002/1416 Sch.9 Part I, SSI 2002/255 Sch.9 Part I

Art.12, varied: SI 2002/1416 Sch.9 para.3

Art.13, revoked (in part): SI 2002/843 Sch.9 Part I, SI 2002/1416 Sch.9 Part I, SSI 2002/255 Sch.9 Part I

Art.14, revoked (in part): SI 2002/843 Sch.9 Part I, SI 2002/1416 Sch.9 Part I, SSI 2002/255 Sch.9 Part I

Sch.2, amended: SI 2002/843 Sch.8 para.4, SI 2002/1416 Sch.8 para.4, SSI 2002/255 Sch.8 para.4

2965. Specified Risk Material Regulations 1997

applied: SI 2002/843 Reg.104, SI 2002/1416 Reg.104, SSI 2002/255 Reg.102

revoked (in part): SSI 2002/255 Sch.9 Part I

Reg.3, amended: SI 2002/843 Sch.8 para.1, SI 2002/1416 Sch.8 para.1

Reg.4, amended: SI 2002/843 Sch.8 para.2, SI 2002/1416 Sch.8 para.2

1997-cont.

2965. Specified Risk Material Regulations 1997-cont.

Reg.5, revoked (in part): SI 2002/843 Sch.9 Part I, SI 2002/1416 Sch.9 Part I

Reg.6, applied: SI 2002/843 Sch.9 para.1, Sch.9 para.2, SSI 2002/255 Sch.9 para.1, Sch.9 para.2

Reg.6, revoked (in part): SI 2002/843 Sch.9 Part I, SI 2002/1416 Sch.9 Part I

Reg.6, varied: SI 2002/1416 Sch.9 para.1, Sch.9 para.2

Reg.7, revoked (in part): SI 2002/843 Sch.9 Part I, SI 2002/1416 Sch.9 Part I

Reg.8, revoked (in part): SI 2002/843 Sch.9 Part I, SI 2002/1416 Sch.9 Part I

Reg.9, revoked (in part): SI 2002/843 Sch.9 Part I, SI 2002/1416 Sch.9 Part I

Reg.10, revoked (in part): SI 2002/843 Sch.9 Part I, SI 2002/1416 Sch.9 Part I

Reg.11, revoked (in part): SI 2002/843 Sch.9 Part I, SI 2002/1416 Sch.9 Part I

Reg.13, revoked (in part): SI 2002/843 Sch.9 Part I, SI 2002/1416 Sch.9 Part I

Reg.14, revoked (in part): SI 2002/843 Sch.9 Part I, SI 2002/1416 Sch.9 Part I

Reg.15, applied: SI 2002/843 Sch.9 para.3, SSI 2002/255 Sch.9 para.3

Reg.15, revoked (in part): SI 2002/843 Sch.9 Part I, SI 2002/1416 Sch.9 Part I

Reg.15, varied: SI 2002/1416 Sch.9 para.3

Reg.15A, applied: SI 2002/843 Sch.9 para.4, SSI 2002/255 Sch.9 para.4

Reg.15A, revoked (in part): SI 2002/843 Sch.9 Part I, SI 2002/1416 Sch.9 Part I

Reg.15A, varied: SI 2002/1416 Sch.9 para.4

Reg.16, applied: SI 2002/843 Sch.9 para.5, SSI 2002/255 Sch.9 para.5

Reg.16, revoked (in part): SI 2002/843 Sch.9 Part I, SI 2002/1416 Sch.9 Part I

Reg.16, varied: SI 2002/1416 Sch.9 para.5

Reg.16A, applied: SI 2002/843 Reg.33, Reg.47, SI 2002/1416 Reg.33, Reg.47

Reg.17, revoked (in part): SI 2002/843 Sch.9 Part I, SI 2002/1416 Sch.9 Part I

Reg.18, applied: SI 2002/843 Sch.9 para.6, SSI 2002/255 Sch.9 para.6

Reg.18, revoked (in part): SI 2002/843 Sch.9 Part I, SI 2002/1416 Sch.9 Part I

Reg.18, varied: SI 2002/1416 Sch.9 para.6

Reg.19, revoked (in part): SI 2002/843 Sch.9 Part I, SI 2002/1416 Sch.9 Part I

Reg.20, revoked (in part): SI 2002/843 Sch.9 Part I, SI 2002/1416 Sch.9 Part I

Reg.21, revoked (in part): SI 2002/843 Sch.9 Part I, SI 2002/1416 Sch.9 Part I

Reg.22, revoked (in part): SI 2002/843 Sch.9 Part I, SI 2002/1416 Sch.9 Part I

Reg.23, revoked (in part): SI 2002/843 Sch.9 Part I, SI 2002/1416 Sch.9 Part I

Reg.24, revoked (in part): SI 2002/843 Sch.9 Part I, SI 2002/1416 Sch.9 Part I

1997-cont.

2965. Specified Risk Material Regulations 1997-cont.

Reg.25, revoked (in part): SI 2002/843 Sch.9 Part I, SI 2002/1416 Sch.9 Part I

Reg.26, applied: SSI 2002/255 Sch.9 para.7

Reg.26, revoked (in part): SI 2002/843 Sch.9 Part I, SI 2002/1416 Sch.9 Part I

Reg.27, revoked (in part): SI 2002/843 Sch.9 Part I, SI 2002/1416 Sch.9 Part I

Reg.28, applied: SI 2002/843 Sch.9 para.7, SSI 2002/255 Sch.9 para.8

Reg.28, revoked (in part): SI 2002/843 Sch.9 Part I, SI 2002/1416 Sch.9 Part I

Reg.28, varied: SI 2002/1416 Sch.9 para.7

2975. OSPAR Commission (Immunities and Privileges) Order 1997

Art.13, amended: 2002 c.8 s.2

2983. Civil Evidence (Northern Ireland) Order 1997

Sch.1, revoked: SI 2004/1501 Sch.2

3001. Teachers Pensions Regulations 1997

applied: SI 2003/453 Reg.15, SI 2003/3247 Reg.16, SI 2004/587 Reg.33

referred to: SI 2004/587 Reg.2

see *Healey v Bridgend CBC* [2002] EWCA Civ 1996, [2004] I.C.R. 561 (CA), Ward, L.J.

Reg.C1, see *Secretary of State for Education and Skills v Bailey* [2003] EWHC 1873, [2004] I.C.R. 181 (Ch D), Pumfrey, J.

Reg.1, amended: SI 2004/587 Reg.8

Reg.1, amended: SI 2004/587 Reg.12

Reg.1, substituted: SI 2004/587 Reg.26

Reg.1A, added: SI 2004/587 Reg.4

Reg.2, amended: SI 2004/587 Reg.9

Reg.2, amended: SI 2004/587 Reg.23

Reg.2, amended: SI 2002/3058 Reg.3, SI 2004/587 Reg.27

Reg.3, amended: SI 2004/587 Reg.3

Reg.3, amended: SI 2004/587 Reg.5

Reg.3, amended: SI 2004/587 Reg.28

Reg.3A, amended: SI 2003/2096 Sch.1 para.72, SI 2004/587 Reg.6

Reg.4, amended: SI 2004/587 Reg.7

Reg.4, amended: SI 2004/587 Reg.13

Reg.4, applied: SI 2003/3139 Reg.6, SI 2004/2733 Reg.6

Reg.4, amended: SI 2004/587 Reg.24

Reg.4, amended: SI 2002/3058 Reg.4

Reg.4A, added: SI 2004/587 Reg.25

Reg.5, amended: SI 2002/3058 Reg.5

Reg.7, amended: SI 2002/3058 Reg.6

Reg.9, amended: SI 2004/587 Reg.10

Reg.10, amended: SI 2004/587 Reg.11

Reg.19, amended: SI 2004/587 Reg.14

Reg.19A, added: SI 2004/587 Reg.15

Reg.20, amended: SI 2004/587 Reg.16

Reg.25, amended: SI 2004/587 Reg.17

Reg.26, amended: SI 2004/587 Reg.18

Reg.28, amended: SI 2004/587 Reg.19

Reg.31, amended: SI 2004/587 Reg.20

NO.

1997–cont.

3001. Teachers Pensions Regulations 1997– cont.

Reg.33, amended: SI 2004/587 Reg.21

Reg.34, amended: SI 2004/587 Reg.22

Sch.1, amended: SI 2004/587 Reg.29

Sch.2 Part I para.2, amended: SI 2004/587 Reg.30

Sch.2 Part I para.5, amended: SI 2002/3058 Reg.7, SI 2004/587 Reg.30

Sch.2 Part II para.24, amended: SI 2004/587 Reg.30

Sch.2 Part II para.26, substituted: SI 2004/587 Reg.30

Sch.10 Part VI para.35, amended: SI 2004/587 Reg.31

Sch.10 PartVI para.35A, added: SI 2004/587 Reg.31

Sch.10 Part VI para.37, amended: SI 2004/587 Reg.31

Sch.13 Part I, revoked: SI 2004/587 Reg.32

Sch.15 Part II para.9, amended: SI 2002/3058 Reg.8

3002. Mink Keeping Order 1997

applied: SI 2002/221 Art.3, Sch.5 para.14, SI 2004/1964 Art.3, Sch.6 para.13

3008. Long Residential Tenancies (Principal Forms) Regulations 1997

Sch.1, amended: SI 2002/2227 Reg.2, SI 2003/233 Reg.2

3018. Merchant Shipping (Port Waste Reception Facilities) Regulations 1997

revoked: SI 2003/1809 Reg.1

Reg.10, applied: SI 2003/1809 Reg.7

Reg.11, applied: SI 2003/1809 Reg.7

3025. Road Vehicles (Statutory Off-Road Notification) Regulations 1997

revoked: SI 2002/2742 Sch.1 Part I

3032. Copyright and Rights in Databases Regulations 1997

see *British Horseracing Board Ltd v William Hill Organisation Ltd* [2001] EWCA Civ 1268, [2002] E.C.C. 24 (CA), Peter Gibson, L.J.

Reg.2, amended: SI 2003/2501 Reg.3

Reg.12, amended: SI 2003/2501 Reg.4

Reg.18, amended: SI 2003/2501 Reg.5

Reg.20A, added: 2003 c.28 s.8

Reg.26, substituted: SI 2003/2501 Reg.6

Reg.27, amended: SI 2003/2501 Reg.7

Reg.28, substituted: SI 2003/2501 Reg.8

Reg.29, amended: SI 2003/2501 Reg.9

Reg.30, substituted: SI 2003/2501 Reg.10

Sch.2 para.15, amended: SI 2003/1398 Sch.1 para.31

3034. Social Security (Claims and Payments) Amendment Regulations 1997

revoked (in part): SI 2003/492 Sch.3 Part 1

NO.

1997–cont.

3046. Food (Pistachios from Iran) (Emergency Control) (Amendment) Order 1997

revoked (in part): SI 2003/1956 Reg.7, SI 2003/2288 Reg.7

3049. Homeless Persons (Priority Need) (Scotland) Order 1997

revoked: 2003 asp 10 s.1

3058. Road Traffic (Vehicle Emissions) (Fixed Penalty) Regulations 1997

revoked (in part): SI 2002/1808 Reg.25, SI 2003/300 Reg.25, SSI 2003/212 Reg.24

Reg.5, applied: SSI 2003/212 Reg.24

Reg.6, applied: SSI 2003/212 Reg.24

Reg.7, applied: SSI 2003/212 Reg.24

Reg.8, applied: SSI 2003/212 Reg.24

Reg.9, applied: SSI 2003/212 Reg.24

Reg.10, applied: SSI 2003/212 Reg.24

Reg.11, applied: SSI 2003/212 Reg.24

Reg.12, applied: SSI 2003/212 Reg.24

3061. Town and Country Planning (Use Classes) (Scotland) Order 1997

Sch.1, referred to: SSI 2004/219 Reg.6

3062. Specified Risk Material (Amendment) Regulations 1997

revoked (in part): SSI 2002/255 Sch.9 Part I

3067. Local Government (Changes for the Registration Service in Berkshire, Cambridgeshire, Cheshire, Devon, Essex, Hereford and Worcester, Kent, Lancashire, Nottinghamshire and Shropshire) Order 1997

varied: SI 2004/222 Art.2

3070. Advice and Assistance (Assistance by Way of Representation) (Scotland) Regulations 1997

revoked: SSI 2003/179 Sch.1

Reg.3, amended: SSI 2002/37 Reg.3

Reg.8A, amended: SSI 2002/37 Reg.4

1998

4. National Health Service (General Medical Services) (Scotland) Amendment Regulations 1998

revoked: SSI 2004/114 Sch.2

5. National Health Service (Vocational Training for General Medical Practice) (Scotland) Regulations 1998

applied: SI 2003/1250 Sch.8 para.5, Sch.8 para.6, SI 2004/1947 Reg.4, SSI 2003/64 Sch.2 para.1, SSI 2004/163 Art.97

revoked: SI 2003/1250 Sch.10 Part 2

varied: SI 2004/1947 Reg.7

Reg.2, amended: SI 2002/3135 Sch.1 para.39, SI 2003/3148 Reg.11

Reg.2, referred to: SSI 2004/163 Art.97

Reg.2, varied: SSI 2004/163 Art.101

Reg.4, varied: SSI 2004/163 Art.101

Reg.5, amended: SI 2003/3148 Reg.11

NO.

1998–cont.

5. National Health Service (Vocational Training for General Medical Practice) (Scotland) Regulations 1998– *cont.*

Reg.5, applied: SI 2003/1250 Art.10, Art.11, Sch.8 para.22, SSI 2004/163 Art.97

Reg.5, referred to: SI 2003/1250 Sch.8 para.22

Reg.5, varied: SSI 2004/163 Art.101

Reg.6, amended: SI 2003/3148 Reg.11

Reg.6, applied: SI 2003/1250 Sch.8 para.2

Reg.6, referred to: SI 2004/585 Reg.23

Reg.7, applied: SI 2003/1250 Sch.8 para.3

Reg.8, applied: SI 2003/1250 Sch.8 para.2

Reg.9, applied: SSI 2004/114 Sch.1 para.4

Reg.10, applied: SI 2004/585 Reg.23, SSI 2004/114 Sch.1 para.3, Sch.1 para.4

Reg.11, applied: SI 2004/585 Reg.23, SSI 2004/114 Sch.1 para.3, Sch.1 para.4

Reg.12, amended: SI 2003/3148 Reg.11

Reg.12, applied: SI 2003/1250 Art.8

Reg.12A, applied: SI 2003/1250 Sch.8 para.6

Reg.12A, referred to: SI 2003/1250 Sch.8 para.5

Reg.13, applied: SI 2003/1250 Sch.8 para.6

Reg.13, referred to: SI 2003/1250 Sch.8 para.6

9. Criminal Justice (Children) (Northern Ireland) Order 1998

Art.6, applied: SI 2003/435 Sch.2 para.2

Art.8, referred to: SI 2003/1247 Art.15

Sch.1, amended: SI 2003/1247 Sch.1 para.22

Sch.5, revoked (in part): SI 2003/435 Sch.5, SI 2003/1247 Sch.2

12. Beef Carcase (Classification) (Amendment) Regulations 1998

revoked (in part): SI 2004/1317 Reg.16, SSI 2004/280 Reg.17

47. Council Tax and Non-Domestic Rating (Demand Notices) (England) (Amendment) (Rural Rate Relief) Regulations 1998

Reg.2, revoked (in part): SI 2002/180 Sch.1

54. Local Government Changes (Rent Act Registration Areas) Order 1998

varied: SI 2004/222 Art.2

55. Immigration (Transit Visa) (Amendment) Order 1998

revoked: SI 2003/1185 Sch.2

93. Rating Lists (Valuation Date) Order 1998

revoked (in part): SI 2002/3186 Art.3, SI 2003/329 Art.3

105. Council Tax (Prescribed Classes of Dwellings) (Wales) Regulations 1998

Reg.2, amended: SI 2004/452 Reg.3

Reg.3, amended: SI 2004/3094 Reg.8

Reg.3, substituted: SI 2004/452 Reg.3

Reg.5A, added: SI 2004/452 Reg.3

NO.

1998–cont.

119. Local Government Finance (New Parishes) Regulations 1998

varied: SI 2004/222 Art.2

124. Birmingham Northern Relief Road Toll Order 1998

applied: SI 2003/2186 Reg.3

193. Frenchay Healthcare National Health Service Trust (Establishment) Amendment Order 1998

revoked: 2003 c.43 s.7

201. Potatoes Originating in Egypt Regulations 1998

revoked (in part): SI 2004/1165 Reg.8, SI 2004/2245 Reg.8

Reg.5, substituted: SI 2002/120 Reg.2

Reg.5A, amended: SI 2002/120 Reg.2

Sch.1, amended: SI 2002/120 Reg.2, SI 2002/2902 Reg.2, SI 2002/3226 Reg.2

211. Education (Student Loans) Regulations 1998

referred to: SSI 2003/285 Reg.2

Reg.3, amended: SI 2002/1329 Reg.3, SSI 2002/282 Reg.3

Reg.6, amended: SI 2003/1647 Reg.2, SI 2004/1030 Reg.4, SSI 2002/282 Reg.4, SSI 2003/285 Reg.3, SSI 2004/256 Reg.2

Reg.6, substituted: SI 2002/1433 Reg.3

261. Museums and Galleries (Northern Ireland) Order 1998

Art.10, revoked (in part): SI 2003/418 Sch.3

276. Children (Protection at Work) Regulations 1998

see *Ashby v Addison (t/a Brayton News)* [2003] I.C.R. 667 (EAT), Judge Burke Q.C.

321. Chichester Priority Care Services National Health Service Trust (Establishment) Amendment Order 1998

revoked: 2003 c.43 s.7

322. Leeds Community and Mental Health Services Teaching National Health Service Trust (Establishment) Amendment Order 1998

revoked: 2003 c.43 s.7

323. Northallerton Health Services National Health Service Trust (Establishment) Amendment Order 1998

revoked: 2003 c.43 s.7

341. Council Tax (Discounts) (Scotland) Amendment Order 1998

revoked: SSI 2003/176 Sch.4

355. Devon (Coroners) Order 1998

varied: SI 2004/222 Art.2

356. Cheshire (Coroners) Order 1998

varied: SI 2004/222 Art.2

357. Essex (Coroners) Order 1998

varied: SI 2004/222 Art.2

358. Kent (Coroners) Order 1998

varied: SI 2004/222 Art.2

359. Hereford and Worcester (Coroners) Order 1998

varied: SI 2004/222 Art.2

NO.

360. Lancashire (Coroners) Order 1998
referred to: SI 2002/2257 Art.3
varied: SI 2004/222 Art.2

361. Nottinghamshire (Coroners) Order 1998
varied: SI 2004/222 Art.2

362. Peterborough (Coroners) Order 1998
varied: SI 2004/222 Art.2

363. Shropshire (Coroners) Order 1998
varied: SI 2004/222 Art.2

366. Local Government Pension Scheme (Scotland) Regulations 1998
Reg.5, amended: SSI 2002/311 Reg.2
Sch.2 para.3, substituted: SSI 2002/311 Reg.2
Sch.5 Part II, amended: SSI 2002/311 Reg.2

442. Essex County Council (Boroughs of Southend-on-Sea and Thurrock) (Staff Transfer) Order 1998
varied: SI 2004/222 Art.2

443. Cambridgeshire County Council (City of Peterborough) (Staff Transfer) Order 1998
varied: SI 2004/222 Art.2

444. Hereford and Worcester (Staff Transfer) Order 1998
varied: SI 2004/222 Art.2

445. Lancashire County Council (Boroughs of Blackburn with Darwen and Blackpool) (Staff Transfer) Order 1998
varied: SI 2004/222 Art.2

446. Cheshire County Council (Boroughs of Halton and Warrington) (Staff Transfer) Order 1998
varied: SI 2004/222 Art.2

447. Nottinghamshire County Council (City of Nottingham) (Staff Transfer) Order 1998
varied: SI 2004/222 Art.2

448. Shropshire County Council (District of The Wrekin) (Staff Transfer) Order 1998
varied: SI 2004/222 Art.2

449. Kent County Council (Borough of Gillingham and City of Rochester upon Medway) (Staff Transfer) Order 1998
varied: SI 2004/222 Art.2

450. Berkshire County Council (Staff Transfer) Order 1998
varied: SI 2004/222 Art.2

451. Devon County Council (City of Plymouth and Borough of Torbay) (Staff Transfer) Order 1998
varied: SI 2004/222 Art.2

453. Common Agricultural Policy (Wine) (Amendment) Regulations 1998
revoked (in part): SSI 2002/325 Reg.19

NO.

462. Town and Country Planning (General Permitted Development) (Amendment) Order 1998
Art.3, revoked (in part): SI 2002/1878 Art.4

463. Specified Animal Pathogens Order 1998
applied: SI 2003/2329 Art.3, SI 2003/2456 Art.3, SSI 2003/426 Art.3, SSI 2003/586 Art.3
Art.4, applied: SI 2003/130 Art.4, SI 2003/326 Art.4, SI 2003/2913 Art.3
Art.4, disapplied: SSI 2003/91 Art.4

466. Berkshire (Coroners) Order 1998
varied: SI 2004/222 Art.2

472. Secure Training Centre Rules 1998
r.2, amended: SI 2003/3005 r.2
r.3, amended: SI 2003/3005 r.2
r.10, amended: SI 2003/3005 r.2
r.27, amended: SI 2003/3005 r.2
r.30, amended: SI 2003/3005 r.2
r.42, amended: SI 2003/3005 r.2
r.45A, amended: SI 2003/3005 r.2

493. Police (Amendment) Regulations 1998
revoked: SI 2003/527 Sch.4 Part 1

494. Health and Safety (Enforcing Authority) Regulations 1998
applied: SI 2004/1359 Reg.2
varied: SI 2004/1359 Reg.2
Reg.3, disapplied: SI 2002/1689 Reg.14, SI 2004/568 Reg.58
Sch.2 para.4A, added: SI 2002/2675 Reg.27

496. Area Tourist Boards Amending Scheme (Scotland) Order 1998
revoked: SSI 2004/396 Sch.2

500. Shropshire's Community and Mental Health Services National Health Service Trust (Establishment) Order 1998
revoked: SI 2002/2616 Art.2, 2003 c.43 s.7

501. Surrey Hampshire Borders National Health Service Trust (Establishment) Order 1998
revoked: 2003 c.43 s.7

502. Dissolution of the North Downs Community Health National Health Service Trust and the Heathlands Mental Health National Health Service Trust Order 1998
revoked: 2003 c.43 s.7

504. Building Societies (Accounts and Related Provisions) Regulations 1998
Sch.2 Part I, varied: SI 2003/1633 Sch.2 para.2, Sch.2 para.6
Sch.2 Part II, varied: SI 2003/1633 Sch.2 para.2, Sch.2 para.6
Sch.2 Part III para.1, varied: SI 2003/1633 Sch.2 para.2
Sch.2 Part III para.2, varied: SI 2003/1633 Sch.2 para.2

NO.

NO.

1998–cont.

504. Building Societies (Accounts and Related Provisions) Regulations 1998–*cont.*

Sch.2 Part III para.3, varied: SI 2003/1633 Sch.2 para.2, Sch.2 para.3, Sch.2 para.12

Sch.2 Part III para.4, varied: SI 2003/1633 Sch.2 para.2

Sch.2 Part III para.5, varied: SI 2003/1633 Sch.2 para.2

Sch.2 Part III para.6, varied: SI 2003/1633 Sch.2 para.2

Sch.2 Part III para.7, varied: SI 2003/1633 Sch.2 para.2

Sch.2 Part III para.8, varied: SI 2003/1633 Sch.2 para.2

Sch.2 Part III para.9, varied: SI 2003/1633 Sch.2 para.2, Sch.2 para.12

Sch.2 Part III para.10, varied: SI 2003/1633 Sch.2 para.2

Sch.2 Part III para.11, varied: SI 2003/1633 Sch.2 para.2

Sch.2 Part III para.12, varied: SI 2003/1633 Sch.2 para.2

Sch.2 Part III para.13, varied: SI 2003/1633 Sch.2 para.2

Sch.2 Part III para.14, varied: SI 2003/1633 Sch.2 para.2

Sch.2 Part III para.15, varied: SI 2003/1633 Sch.2 para.2

Sch.2 Part III para.16, varied: SI 2003/1633 Sch.2 para.2

Sch.2 Part III para.17, varied: SI 2003/1633 Sch.2 para.2

Sch.2 Part III para.18, varied: SI 2003/1633 Sch.2 para.2

515. Shropshire's Community Health Service National Health Service Trust (Dissolution) Order 1998

revoked: 2003 c.43 s.7

516. Dissolution of the South Warwickshire Health Care National Health Service Trust and the South Warwickshire Mental Health National Health Service Trust Order 1998

revoked: 2003 c.43 s.7

517. South Warwickshire Combined Care National Health Service Trust (Establishment) Order 1998

revoked: SI 2002/2616 Art.2, 2003 c.43 s.7

518. Shropshire's Mental Health National Health Service Trust (Dissolution) Order 1998

revoked: 2003 c.43 s.7

543. Control of Lead at Work Regulations 1998

applied: SI 2002/655 Reg.3, Reg.8

revoked: SI 2002/2676 Reg.15

545. Environmental Protection (Controls on Hexachloroethane) Regulations 1998

revoked: SI 2003/602 Reg.6

1998–cont.

558. Wireless Telegraphy (Television Licence Fees) (Amendment) Regulations 1998

revoked: SI 2004/692 Sch.6

562. Income-related Benefits (Subsidy to Authorities) Order 1998

Art.1, amended: SI 2002/3116 Art.2

Art.2, amended: SI 2004/646 Sch.1 para.1

Art.4, amended: SI 2003/3179 Art.2, SI 2004/646 Sch.1 para.2

Art.6, amended: SI 2004/646 Sch.1 para.3

Art.11, amended: SI 2003/3179 Art.3, SI 2004/646 Sch.1 para.4

Art.13, amended: SI 2002/1859 Art.2, SI 2003/3179 Art.4, SI 2004/646 Sch.1 para.5

Art.13, revoked (in part): SI 2003/3179 Art.4

Art.14, amended: SI 2002/3116 Art.3, SI 2003/3179 Art.5

Art.17, amended: SI 2003/3179 Art.6

Art.17, revoked (in part): SI 2003/3179 Art.6

Art.18, amended: SI 2002/1397 Sch.1 para.31, SI 2002/3116 Art.4, SI 2003/3179 Art.7

Art.18, revoked (in part): SI 2003/3179 Art.7

Art.19, amended: SI 2003/3179 Art.8

Art.20A, added: SI 2004/646 Sch.1 para.6

Sch.1, amended: SI 2002/1859 Art.6, SI 2003/3179 Art.10

Sch.1, referred to: SI 2003/3179 Art.9

Sch.1, substituted: SI 2002/1859 Sch.1, SI 2003/3179 Sch.1

Sch.4 Part II para.6, see *R. (on the application of Isle of Anglesey CC) v Secretary of State for Work and Pensions* [2003] EWHC 2518, [2004] B.L.G.R. 614 (QBD (Admin Ct)), Lindsay, J.

Sch.4 Part V, referred to: SI 2003/3179 Art.11

Sch.4 Part V para.18, amended: SI 2002/1859 Sch.2

Sch.4 Part V para.18, substituted: SI 2003/3179 Sch.2

Sch.4A Part I para.1, added: SI 2004/646 Sch.1 para.7

Sch.4A Part II para.2, added: SI 2004/646 Sch.1 para.7

Sch.4A Part II para.3, added: SI 2004/646 Sch.1 para.7

Sch.4A Part III, added: SI 2004/646 Sch.1 para.7

Sch.4A Part IV para.4, added: SI 2004/646 Sch.1 para.7

Sch.4A Part IV para.5, added: SI 2004/646 Sch.1 para.7

Sch.4A Part V, added: SI 2004/646 Sch.1 para.7

Sch.5 para.1, amended: SI 2002/1859 Art.5, SI 2002/3116 Art.2, SI 2003/3179 Art.12

572. Road Vehicles Registration Fee Regulations 1998

revoked: SI 2002/2742 Sch.1 Part I

NO.

1998–cont.

577. Police Pensions (Amendment) Regulations 1998

Reg.5, revoked (in part): SI 2003/527 Sch.4 Part 1

582. Charter Trustees (Hereford) Order 1998

varied: SI 2004/222 Art.2

610. National Health Service (Dental Charges) (Scotland) Amendment Regulations 1998

revoked: SSI 2003/158 Sch.4

614. Local Government Changes for England (Education) (Miscellaneous Provisions) Order 1998

varied: SI 2004/222 Art.2

631. National Health Service (Primary Care) Act 1997 (Commencement No 4) Order 1998

Art.3, revoked (in part): SI 2004/287 Art.4

632. National Health Service (Functions of Health Authorities) (Prescribing Incentive Schemes) Regulations 1998

revoked (in part): SI 2004/865 Sch.2, SI 2004/1016 Sch.2

Reg.1, amended: SI 2002/2469 Sch.5

Reg.1, revoked (in part): SI 2004/865 Sch.2

Reg.2, amended: SI 2002/2469 Sch.5

Reg.2, revoked (in part): SI 2004/865 Sch.2

634. Water Services Charges (Billing and Collection) (Scotland) Order 1998

revoked: 2002 asp 3 Sch.7 para.23

635. Domestic Sewerage Charges (Reduction) (Scotland) Regulations 1998

revoked: 2002 asp 3 Sch.7 para.23

637. National Crime Squad (Discipline) (Senior Police Members) Regulations 1998

revoked: SI 2003/2596 Reg.2

638. National Crime Squad (Complaints) Regulations 1998

revoked: SI 2004/643 Reg.29

Reg.3, revoked: SI 2003/2602 Reg.10

Reg.4, revoked: SI 2003/2602 Reg.10

Reg.5, revoked: SI 2003/2602 Reg.10

Reg.6, revoked: SI 2003/2602 Reg.10

Reg.7, revoked: SI 2003/2602 Reg.10

Reg.8, revoked: SI 2003/2602 Reg.10

Reg.9, revoked: SI 2003/2602 Reg.10

Reg.10, revoked: SI 2003/2602 Reg.10

Reg.11, revoked: SI 2003/2602 Reg.10

Reg.12, revoked: SI 2003/2602 Reg.10

Reg.19, applied: SI 2004/671 Art.4

639. National Crime Squad (Senior Police Members) (Appeals) Order 1998

applied: SI 2003/2598 Art.2

revoked: SI 2003/2598 Art.2

641. NCIS (Complaints) Regulations 1998

revoked: SI 2004/643 Reg.29

NO.

1998–cont.

642. National Health Service (Optical Charges and Payments) (Scotland) Regulations 1998

Reg.1, amended: SSI 2002/17 Reg.2, SSI 2002/224 Reg.2, SSI 2003/218 Reg.3, SSI 2003/431 Reg.2, SSI 2004/97 Reg.2, SSI 2004/168 Reg.2

Reg.2, amended: SSI 2004/168 Reg.2

Reg.8, amended: SSI 2002/86 Reg.2, SSI 2003/218 Reg.3, SSI 2003/431 Reg.2, SSI 2004/97 Reg.2, SSI 2004/168 Reg.2

Reg.8, revoked (in part): SSI 2003/218 Reg.3

Reg.10, amended: SSI 2004/168 Reg.2

Reg.11, amended: SSI 2004/168 Reg.2

Reg.12, applied: SSI 2004/97 Reg.3

Reg.12A, added: SSI 2003/218 Reg.3

Reg.17, applied: SSI 2004/97 Reg.3

Reg.19, amended: SSI 2002/86 Reg.2, SSI 2003/218 Reg.3, SSI 2004/97 Reg.2

Sch.1, amended: SSI 2002/86 Reg.2, SSI 2003/218 Reg.3, SSI 2004/97 Reg.2, SSI 2004/168 Reg.2

Sch.2, substituted: SSI 2002/86 Sch.1, SSI 2003/218 Sch.1, SSI 2004/97 Sch.1

Sch.3 para.1, amended: SSI 2002/86 Reg.2, SSI 2003/218 Reg.3, SSI 2004/97 Reg.2, SSI 2004/168 Reg.2

Sch.3 para.2, amended: SSI 2002/86 Reg.2, SSI 2003/218 Reg.3, SSI 2004/97 Reg.2

643. Births, Deaths, Marriages and Divorces (Fees) (Scotland) Regulations 1998

Reg.2, amended: SSI 2002/390 Reg.3, SSI 2003/89 Reg.2

Sch.1 Part I, amended: SSI 2002/390 Reg.4

Sch.2 Part I, amended: SSI 2002/390 Reg.5

Sch.2 Part II, amended: SSI 2002/390 Reg.6

Sch.3, amended: SSI 2002/390 Reg.7

644. Local Education Authority (Behaviour Support Plans) Regulations 1998

Reg.3, amended: SI 2002/2469 Sch.1 para.77

Reg.5, disapplied: SI 2003/3082 Reg.2

646. National Health Service (Pilot Schemes Miscellaneous Provisions and Consequential Amendments) Regulations 1998

referred to: SI 2004/865 Art.60

varied: SSI 2004/163 Art.51

Reg.3, amended: SI 2002/2469 Sch.2

Reg.3, applied: SI 2002/2375 Reg.4

Reg.3, revoked (in part): SI 2004/865 Sch.2, SI 2004/1016 Sch.2, SSI 2004/212 Sch.2

Reg.4, amended: SI 2002/2469 Sch.1 para.78

Reg.4, revoked (in part): SI 2004/865 Sch.2, SI 2004/1016 Sch.2, SSI 2004/212 Sch.2

Reg.5, revoked (in part): SI 2003/1250 Sch.10 para.5, SI 2004/865 Sch.2, SI 2004/1016 Sch.2, SSI 2004/212 Sch.2

NO.

1998-cont.

648. Construction Contracts (England and Wales) Exclusion Order 1998

Art.3A, added: SI 2004/696 Sch.1 para.26

649. Scheme for Construction Contracts (England and Wales) Regulations 1998

see *David McLean Housing Contractors Ltd v Swansea Housing Association Ltd* [2002] B.L.R. 125 (QBD (T&CC)), Judge Humphrey Lloyd Q.C.; see *Pegram Shopfitters Ltd v Tally Weijl (UK) Ltd* [2003] EWCA Civ 1750, [2004] 1 W.L.R. 2082 (CA), May, L.J.; see *Pegram Shopfitters Ltd v Tally Weijl (UK) Ltd* [2003] EWHC 984, [2003] 1 W.L.R. 2990 (QBD (T&CC)), Judge Thornton Q.C.; see *Thomas-Fredric's (Construction) Ltd v Wilson* [2003] EWCA Civ 1494, [2004] B.L.R. 23 (CA), Simon Brown, L.J.

Sch.1 Part I para.2, see *Ide Contracting Ltd v RG Carter Cambridge Ltd* [2004] B.L.R.172 (QBD (T&CC)), Judge Havery Q.C.

Sch.1 Part I para.3, see *Ide Contracting Ltd v RG Carter Cambridge Ltd* [2004] B.L.R.172 (QBD (T&CC)), Judge Havery Q.C.

Sch.1 Part I para.6, see *Ide Contracting Ltd v RG Carter Cambridge Ltd* [2004] B.L.R.172 (QBD (T&CC)), Judge Havery Q.C.

Sch.1 Part I para.19, see *Simons Construction Ltd v Aardvark Developments Ltd* [2003] EWHC 2474, [2004] B.L.R. 117 (QBD (T&CC)), Judge Richard Seymour Q.C.

651. Surrey and Sussex Healthcare National Health Service Trust (Establishment) Order 1998

revoked: 2003 c.43 s.7

652. Dissolution of the Surrey Heartlands National Health Service Trust and the East Surrey Priority Care National Health Service Trust Order 1998

revoked: 2003 c.43 s.7

653. Surrey Oaklands National Health Service Trust (Establishment) Order 1998

referred to: SI 2004/569 Sch.1

revoked: 2003 c.43 s.7

657. National Health Service (Service Committees and Tribunal) (Scotland) Amendment Regulations 1998

revoked: SSI 2004/38 Sch.3

659. National Health Service (Choice of Medical Practitioner) (Scotland) Regulations 1998

revoked: SSI 2004/163 Art.102

varied: SSI 2004/163 Art.51, Art.52

Reg.1, amended: SI 2002/3135 Sch.1 para.41

Reg.1, varied: SSI 2004/163 Art.54

Reg.2, applied: SSI 2004/163 Art.3, Art.14

Reg.2, varied: SSI 2004/163 Art.54

Reg.3, applied: SSI 2004/163 Art.3, Art.14

NO.

1998-cont.

659. National Health Service (Choice of Medical Practitioner) (Scotland) Regulations 1998-*cont.*

Reg.4, applied: SSI 2004/142 Art.28, Art.30, Art.31, Art.32, SSI 2004/163 Art.14, Art.60, Art.61

Reg.5, applied: SSI 2004/163 Art.51, Art.55

Reg.5, varied: SSI 2004/163 Art.54

Reg.6, applied: SSI 2004/163 Art.61

Reg.7, applied: SSI 2004/163 Art.10

Reg.7, varied: SSI 2004/163 Art.54

660. National Health Service (General Medical Services) (Scotland) Amendment (No.2) Regulations 1998

revoked: SSI 2004/114 Sch.2

665. National Health Service (Pilot Schemes Part II Practitioners) Regulations 1998

revoked (in part): SI 2004/865 Sch.2, SI 2004/1016 Sch.2, SSI 2004/212 Sch.2

Reg.1, amended: SI 2002/2469 Sch.1 para.79

668. National Health Service (Choice of Medical Practitioner) Regulations 1998

referred to: SI 2004/865 Art.60, Art.61

revoked (in part): SI 2004/865 Sch.2

varied: SI 2004/1016 Art.55

Reg.1, amended: SI 2002/2469 Sch.5

Reg.1, revoked (in part): SI 2004/865 Sch.2

Reg.1, varied: SI 2004/865 Art.63

Reg.2, applied: SI 2004/865 Art.3, Art.14, SI 2004/1016 Art.3, Art.14

Reg.2, varied: SI 2004/865 Art.63

Reg.3, amended: SI 2002/2469 Sch.5

Reg.3, applied: SI 2004/865 Art.3, Art.14, SI 2004/1016 Art.3, Art.14

Reg.4, amended: SI 2002/2469 Sch.5

Reg.4, applied: SI 2004/433 Art.28, Art.29, Art.30, Art.31, Art.32, SI 2004/477 Art.28, Art.29, Art.30, Art.31, Art.32, SI 2004/865 Art.14, Art.70, Art.71, SI 2004/1016 Art.14, Art.54

Reg.4, referred to: SI 2004/865 Art.60

Reg.4, revoked (in part): SI 2004/865 Sch.2

Reg.5, amended: SI 2002/2469 Sch.5

Reg.5, applied: SI 2004/865 Art.64

Reg.5, referred to: SI 2004/865 Art.60

Reg.5, revoked (in part): SI 2004/865 Sch.2

Reg.5, varied: SI 2004/865 Art.63

Reg.6, referred to: SI 2004/865 Art.71

Reg.6, varied: SI 2004/1016 Art.55

Reg.7, applied: SI 2004/865 Art.10, SI 2004/1016 Art.10

Reg.7, varied: SI 2004/865 Art.63

Reg.8, amended: SI 2002/2469 Sch.5

669. National Health Service (Vocational Training for General Medical Practice) Amendment Regulations 1998

revoked: SI 2003/1250 Sch.10 Part 2

NO.

1998–cont.

670. North Wales Ambulance National Health Service Trust (Dissolution) Order 1998
revoked: 2003 c.43 s.7

671. Mid Glamorgan Ambulance National Health Service Trust (Dissolution) Order 1998
revoked: 2003 c.43 s.7

677. West Wales Ambulance National Health Service Trust (Dissolution) Order 1998
revoked: 2003 c.43 s.7

678. Welsh Ambulance Services National Health Service Trust (Establishment) Order 1998
revoked: 2003 c.43 s.7

679. South and East Wales Ambulance National Health Service Trust (Dissolution) Order 1998
revoked: 2003 c.43 s.7

682. National Health Service (General Medical Services) Amendment Regulations 1998
revoked (in part): SI 2004/865 Sch.2, SI 2004/1016 Sch.2

684. River Ewe Salmon Fishery District (Baits and Lures) Regulations 1998
revoked: SSI 2003/614 Reg.2

685. Broadcasting Digital Terrestrial Sound (Technical Service) Order 1998
Art.2, amended: SI 2003/2155 Sch.1 para.42

687. Scheme for Construction Contracts (Scotland) Regulations 1998
Sch.1 Part II, see *Karl Construction (Scotland) Ltd v Sweeney Civil Engineering (Scotland) Ltd* 2002 S.C.L.R. 766 (Ex Div), Lord Marnoch, Lord Clarke, Lord Dawson
Sch.1 para.23, see *Peterhead Harbours Trustees v Lilley Construction Ltd* 2003 S.L.T. 731 (OH), Lord Mackay of Drumadoon

691. Welfare Food (Amendment) Regulations 1998
revoked: SI 2002/550 Reg.3

692. Dissolution of the Crawley Horsham National Health Service Trust and the East Surrey Healthcare National Health Service Trust Order 1998
revoked: 2003 c.43 s.7

725. Civil Legal Aid (Scotland) Amendment Regulations 1998
revoked: SSI 2002/494 Sch.1

754. Northwick Park and St Mark's National Health Service Trust (Establishment) Amendment Order 1998
revoked: 2003 c.43 s.7

770. Llandough Hospital and Community National Health Service Trust (Establishment) Amendment Order 1998
revoked: 2003 c.43 s.7

NO.

1998–cont.

783. Dissolution of the Royal Brompton Hospital National Health Service Trust and the Harefield Hospital National Health Service Trust Order 1998
revoked: 2003 c.43 s.7

784. Royal Brompton and Harefield National Health Service Trust (Establishment) Order 1998
revoked: 2003 c.43 s.7

799. Education (Grant-maintained and Grant-maintained Special Schools) (Finance) Regulations 1998
applied: SI 2002/377 Reg.26
Reg.5, applied: SI 2002/377 Sch.3 para.4, SI 2003/453 Sch.2 para.4
Reg.9, applied: SI 2003/453 Reg.25, SI 2003/3247 Reg.25

800. Dissolution of the Ashford Hospital National Health Service Trust and the St Peter's Hospital National Health Service Trust Order 1998
revoked: 2003 c.43 s.7

801. Ashford and St Peter's Hospitals National Health Service Trust (Establishment) Order 1998
revoked: 2003 c.43 s.7

805. Thames Gateway National Health Service Trust (Establishment) Order 1998
revoked: SI 2002/1337 Art.6, 2003 c.43 s.7

806. Horton General Hospital National Health Service Trust (Dissolution) Order 1998
revoked: 2003 c.43 s.7

807. Dissolution of the North Kent Healthcare National Health Service Trust and the Thameslink Healthcare Services National Health Service Trust Order 1998
revoked: 2003 c.43 s.7

810. Relocation Grants (Form of Application) (Amendment) Regulations 1998
revoked: SI 2002/1860 Sch.6

811. European Primary and Specialist Dental Qualifications Regulations 1998
Reg.2, amended: SI 2003/3148 Reg.7, SI 2004/1947 Reg.12
Reg.4, amended: SI 2003/3148 Reg.7
Reg.6, revoked (in part): SI 2004/1947 Reg.12
Reg.9, amended: SI 2003/3148 Reg.7
Reg.10, amended: SI 2003/3148 Reg.7, SI 2004/1947 Reg.12
Reg.13, substituted: SI 2003/3148 Reg.7
Reg.16, amended: SI 2003/3148 Reg.7
Sch.1 Part I, amended: SI 2004/1947 Reg.12
Sch.1 Part I, substituted: SI 2003/3148 Sch.2 Part II
Sch.1 Part II, amended: SI 2004/1947 Reg.12

NO.

1998–cont.

811. European Primary and Specialist Dental Qualifications Regulations 1998–*cont.*

Sch.1 Part II, substituted: SI 2003/3148 Sch.2 Part II

Sch.2, amended: SI 2003/3148 Reg.7

812. Walsgrave Hospitals National Health Service Trust (Establishment) Amendment Order 1998

revoked: 2003 c.43 s.7

813. Rugby National Health Service Trust (Dissolution) Order 1998

revoked: 2003 c.43 s.7

814. North Warwickshire National Health Service Trust (Establishment) Amendment Order 1998

revoked: 2003 c.43 s.7

815. Lancaster Priority Services National Health Service Trust (Dissolution) Order 1998

revoked: 2003 c.43 s.7

816. Morecambe Bay Hospitals National Health Service Trust (Establishment) Order 1998

revoked: 2003 c.43 s.7

817. Lancaster Acute Hospitals National Health Service Trust (Dissolution) Order 1998

revoked: 2003 c.43 s.7

818. Westmorland Hospitals National Health Service Trust (Dissolution) Order 1998

revoked: 2003 c.43 s.7

819. South Cumbria Community and Mental Health National Health Service Trust (Dissolution) Order 1998

revoked: 2003 c.43 s.7

820. Furness Hospitals National Health Service Trust (Dissolution) Order 1998

revoked: 2003 c.43 s.7

821. Bay Community National Health Service Trust (Establishment) Order 1998

revoked: 2003 c.43 s.7

822. Community Health Care North Durham National Health Service Trust (Dissolution) Order 1998

revoked: 2003 c.43 s.7

823. Bishop Auckland Hospitals National Health Service Trust (Dissolution) Order 1998. 1998

revoked: 2003 c.43 s.7

824. Gateshead Hospitals National Health Service Trust (Dissolution) Order 1998

revoked: 2003 c.43 s.7

NO.

1998–cont.

825. Cheviot and Wansbeck, North Tyneside Health Care, and Northumberland Community Health National Health Service Trusts (Dissolution) Order 1998

revoked: 2003 c.43 s.7

826. Gateshead Healthcare National Health Service Trust (Dissolution) Order 1998

revoked: 2003 c.43 s.7

827. Newcastle upon Tyne Hospitals National Health Service Trust (Establishment) Order 1998

revoked: 2003 c.43 s.7

828. South Durham National Health Service Trust (Dissolution) Order 1998

revoked: 2003 c.43 s.7

829. Durham County Priority Services National Health Service Trust (Establishment) Order 1998

revoked: 2003 c.43 s.7

830. North Durham Acute Hospitals National Health Service Trust (Dissolution) Order 1998

revoked: 2003 c.43 s.7

831. Freeman Group of Hospitals and the Royal Victoria Infirmary and Associated Hospitals National Health Service Trusts (Dissolution) Order 1998

revoked: 2003 c.43 s.7

832. South Durham Health Care National Health Service Trust (Establishment) Order 1998

revoked: SI 2002/2420 Art.6, 2003 c.43 s.7

833. Darlington Memorial Hospital National Health Service Trust (Dissolution) Order 1998

revoked: 2003 c.43 s.7

834. Gateshead Health National Health Service Trust (Establishment) Order 1998

revoked: 2003 c.43 s.7

835. North Durham Health Care National Health Service Trust (Establishment) Order 1998

revoked: SI 2002/2420 Art.6, 2003 c.43 s.7

836. Northumbria Health Care National Health Service Trust (Establishment) Order 1998

revoked: 2003 c.43 s.7

837. Leeds Teaching Hospitals National Health Service Trust (Establishment) Order 1998

applied: SI 2003/3059 Sch.1

revoked: 2003 c.43 s.7

Art.4, amended: SI 2004/487 Art.2

NO.

1998–cont.

838. United Leeds Teaching Hospitals National Health Service Trust (Dissolution) Order 1998
revoked: 2003 c.43 s.7

839. St James and Seacroft University Hospitals National Health Service Trust (Dissolution) Order 1998
revoked: 2003 c.43 s.7

845. Canterbury and Thanet Community Healthcare National Health Service Trust (Establishment) Amendment Order 1998
revoked: 2003 c.43 s.7

846. South Kent Community Healthcare National Health Service Trust (Dissolution) Order 1998
revoked: 2003 c.43 s.7

848. Southern Derbyshire Acute Hospitals National Health Service Trust (Establishment) Order 1998
revoked: 2003 c.43 s.7

849. Derbyshire Royal Infirmary National Health Service Trust (Dissolution) Order 1998
revoked: 2003 c.43 s.7

850. Derby City General Hospital National Health Service Trust (Dissolution) Order 1998
revoked: 2003 c.43 s.7

871. Cattle Identification Regulations 1998
applied: SI 2002/2152 Art.3, Sch.1 para.15, SI 2002/2304 Art.3, SSI 2002/34 Art.4
Reg.2, amended: SSI 2002/1 Reg.3
Reg.3, applied: SI 2002/242 Art.3, SI 2002/280 Art.3, SI 2002/2152 Art.3, SI 2002/2304 Art.3
Reg.26, amended: SSI 2002/255 Sch.8 Part III

880. Education (Publication of Local Education Authority Inspection Reports) Regulations 1998
Reg.4, amended: SI 2002/2469 Sch.1 para.80

911. Council Tax Benefit (General) Amendment Regulations 1998
revoked: SI 2004/154 Reg.3

948. Local Authorities (Transport Charges) Regulations 1998
Reg.2, amended: SI 2003/1615 Sch.1 para.52
Sch.1, substituted: SI 2003/1615 Sch.1 para.52

954. Fertilisers (Mammalian Meat and Bone Meal) Regulations 1998
referred to: SI 2002/843 Reg.13, SI 2002/1416 Reg.13
revoked (in part): SI 2002/843 Sch.9 Part I, SI 2002/1416 Sch.9 Part I, SSI 2002/255 Sch.9 Part I

NO.

1998–cont.

955. Fertilisers (Mammalian Meat and Bone Meal) (Conditions of Manufacture) Regulations 1998
applied: SI 2002/843 Reg.104, SI 2002/1416 Reg.104, SSI 2002/255 Reg.102
revoked (in part): SI 2002/843 Sch.9 Part I, SI 2002/1416 Sch.9 Part I, SSI 2002/255 Sch.9 Part I
Reg.9, applied: SI 2002/843 Sch.9 para.1, Sch.9 para.2, SI 2002/1416 Sch.9 para.2, SSI 2002/255 Sch.9 para.1, Sch.9 para.2
Reg.9, varied: SI 2002/1416 Sch.9 para.1

957. Lifespan Health Care Cambridge National Health Service Trust (Establishment) Amendment Order 1998
revoked: 2003 c.43 s.7

972. Advice and Assistance (Assistance by Way of Representation) (Scotland) Amendment Regulations 1998
revoked: SSI 2003/179 Sch.1

994. Food Safety (Fishery Products and Live Shellfish) (Hygiene) Regulations 1998
applied: SI 2004/12 Art.3
Sch.3 Part 7 para.2, amended: SI 2004/2145 Reg.5, SI 2004/2731 Reg.5, SSI 2004/395 Reg.5

995. Road Vehicles Registration Fee (Amendment) Regulations 1998
revoked: SI 2002/2742 Sch.1 Part I

1011. Merchant Shipping (Fire Protection Small Ships) Regulations 1998
applied: SI 2003/2950 Reg.3
Reg.1, amended: SI 2003/2951 Reg.12, SI 2004/302 Sch.1 para.11

1012. Merchant Shipping (Fire Protection Large Ships) Regulations 1998
Reg.1, amended: SI 2003/2950 Reg.4, SI 2003/2951 Reg.2, Reg.3, Reg.4, SI 2004/302 Sch.1 para.10
Reg.7, amended: SI 2003/2951 Reg.5
Reg.12A, added: SI 2003/2951 Reg.7
Reg.24, amended: SI 2003/2951 Reg.6
Reg.25A, added: SI 2003/2951 Reg.7
Reg.28, amended: SI 2003/2951 Reg.7
Reg.30A, added: SI 2003/2951 Reg.8
Reg.32A, added: SI 2003/2951 Reg.9
Reg.34A, added: SI 2003/2951 Reg.7
Reg.35, amended: SI 2003/2951 Reg.7
Reg.36, amended: SI 2003/2951 Reg.7
Reg.48A, added: SI 2003/2951 Reg.10
Reg.50A, added: SI 2003/2951 Reg.11
Reg.50B, added: SI 2003/2951 Reg.11
Reg.50C, added: SI 2003/2951 Reg.11

1014. Immigration (Transit Visa) (Amendment No 2) Order 1998
revoked: SI 2003/1185 Sch.2

1021. Plants Breeders Rights (Fees) Regulations 1998
applied: SI 2002/247 Reg.25
Sch.1 Part I, substituted: SI 2002/1677 Sch.1

NO.

NO.

1998–cont.

1021. Plants Breeders Rights (Fees) Regulations 1998–*cont.*

Sch.1 Part II, substituted: SI 2002/1677 Sch.1

Sch.1 Part III, substituted: SI 2002/1677 Sch.1

Sch.1 Part IV, substituted: SI 2002/1677 Sch.1

1027. Plant Breeders Rights Regulations 1998

applied: SI 2002/247 Reg.11, Reg.12, Reg.16, Reg.19, Reg.23

varied: SI 2002/247 Reg.23

Reg.10, disapplied: SI 2002/247 Reg.23

1029. Road Works (Inspection Fees) (Scotland) Amendment Regulations 1998

revoked: SSI 2002/13 Reg.3

1046. Medicated Feedingstuffs Regulations 1998

Reg.2, amended: SI 2002/697 Reg.2, SR 2002/161 Reg.2

Reg.3, amended: SI 2003/752 Reg.2

Reg.4, amended: SI 2002/697 Reg.2, SR 2002/161 Reg.2

Reg.5, amended: SI 2003/752 Reg.2

Reg.6, revoked: SI 2002/697 Reg.2, SR 2002/161 Reg.2

Reg.7, amended: SI 2002/697 Reg.2

Reg.7, revoked (in part): SR 2002/161 Reg.2

Reg.10, amended: SI 2003/752 Reg.2

Reg.11, amended: SI 2002/697 Reg.2

Reg.11, revoked (in part): SR 2002/161 Reg.2

Reg.12, amended: SI 2003/752 Reg.2

Reg.13, revoked: SI 2002/697 Reg.2, SR 2002/161 Reg.2

Reg.14, amended: SI 2002/697 Reg.2

Reg.14, revoked (in part): SR 2002/161 Reg.2

Reg.35, amended: SI 2002/697 Reg.2, SI 2003/752 Reg.2, SI 2004/1036 Reg.3, SR 2002/161 Reg.2

Reg.35, revoked (in part): SI 2003/752 Reg.2

Sch.1, substituted: SI 2002/697 Sch.1, SI 2003/752 Sch.1, SI 2004/1036 Sch.2, SR 2002/161 Sch.1

Sch.1 Part I, substituted: SI 2003/752 Sch.1, SI 2004/1036 Sch.2

Sch.1 Part II, substituted: SI 2003/752 Sch.1, SI 2004/1036 Sch.2

1058. Carriage by Air Acts (Application of Provisions) (Fourth Amendment) Order 1998

revoked: SI 2004/1899 Sch.4

1064. Federal Republic of Yugoslavia (United Nations Sanctions) (Dependent Territories) Order 1998

Art.5, amended: 2002 c.8 s.2

Art.6, amended: 2002 c.8 s.2

1065. Federal Republic of Yugoslavia (United Nations Sanctions) Order 1998

Art.5, amended: 2002 c.8 s.2

Art.6, amended: 2002 c.8 s.2

1998–cont.

1071. Family Homes and Domestic Violence (Northern Ireland) Order 1998

applied: SI 2003/435 Sch.2 para.2

Sch.2 Part II, applied: SI 2003/412 Art.14, Art.15, Art.16

Sch.3, revoked: SI 2003/435 Sch.5

1072. Federal Republic of Yugoslavia (United Nations Sanctions) (Channel Islands) Order 1998

Art.5, amended: 2002 c.8 s.2

Art.6, amended: 2002 c.8 s.2

1073. Federal Republic of Yugoslavia (United Nations Sanctions) (Isle of Man) Order 1998

Art.5, amended: 2002 c.8 s.2

Art.6, amended: 2002 c.8 s.2

1074. Road Traffic (New Drivers) (Northern Ireland) Order 1998

Art.2, amended: SI 2003/2903 Sch.1 para.17

Art.4, amended: SI 2003/2903 Sch.1 para.18

Art.5, amended: SI 2003/2903 Sch.1 para.19

Art.6, amended: SI 2003/2903 Sch.1 para.20

Art.7, amended: SI 2003/2903 Sch.1 para.21

Art.9, amended: SI 2003/2903 Sch.1 para.22

Sch.1 Part I para.1, amended: SI 2003/2903 Sch.1 para.24

Sch.1 Part I para.2, amended: SI 2003/2903 Sch.1 para.25

Sch.1 Part III para.5, amended: SI 2003/2903 Sch.1 para.26

Sch.1 Part III para.6, amended: SI 2003/2903 Sch.1 para.27

Sch.1 Part IV para.8, amended: SI 2003/2903 Sch.1 para.28

Sch.1 Part IV para.9, amended: SI 2003/2903 Sch.1 para.29

Sch.1 Part V para.10, amended: SI 2003/2903 Sch.1 para.30

Sch.1 Part V para.11, amended: SI 2003/2903 Sch.1 para.31

1103. Nurses, Midwives and Health Visitors (Professional Conduct) (Amendment) Rules 1998 Approval Order 1998

varied: SI 2004/1762 Art.1

1113. Housing Renewal Grants (Prescribed Form and Particulars) (Welsh Form and Particulars) Regulations 1998

Sch.1, amended: SI 2002/2799 Sch.1 para.1, Sch.1 para.2, Sch.1 para.3, Sch.1 para.4, Sch.1 para.5, Sch.1 para.6, Sch.1 para.7, Sch.1 para.8, Sch.1 para.9, Sch.1 para.10

1130. Cash Ratio Deposits (Eligible Liabilities) Order 1998

Art.2, amended: SI 2004/1862 Reg.14

Art.2, varied: SI 2003/1633 Sch.2 para.5

Sch.1 para.2, varied: SI 2003/1633 Sch.2 para.5

Sch.1 para.9, varied: SI 2003/1633 Sch.2 para.5

NO.

NO.

1998–cont.

1130. Cash Ratio Deposits (Eligible Liabilities) Order 1998–*cont.*
Sch.1 para.11, varied: SI 2003/1633 Sch.2 para.5

1165. Packaging (Essential Requirements) Regulations 1998
revoked: SI 2003/1941 Reg.1

1170. Coventry Healthcare National Health Service Trust (Establishment) Amendment Order 1998
revoked: 2003 c.43 s.7

1171. Bromley Hospitals National Health Service Trust (Establishment) Amendment Order 1998
revoked: 2003 c.43 s.7

1172. Rotherham Priority Health Services National Health Service Trust (Establishment) Amendment Order 1998
revoked: 2003 c.43 s.7

1174. Social Security (Miscellaneous Amendments) (No.4) Regulations 1998
Reg.8, revoked (in part): SI 2003/492 Sch.3 Part 1

1177. Measuring Instruments (EEC Requirements) (Fees) Regulations 1998
referred to: SI 2004/1300 Reg.2
revoked: SI 2004/1300 Reg.2
Sch.2 para.1, amended: SI 2002/511 Reg.2, SI 2003/551 Reg.2
Sch.3 para.1, amended: SI 2002/511 Reg.2, SI 2003/551 Reg.2
Sch.5 para.1, amended: SI 2002/511 Reg.2, SI 2003/551 Reg.2
Sch.6 para.1, amended: SI 2002/511 Reg.2, SI 2003/551 Reg.2

1187. Black Country Mental Health National Health Service Trust (Establishment) Amendment Order 1998
revoked: 2003 c.43 s.7

1190. Local Land Charges (Amendment) Rules 1998
revoked: SI 2003/2502 r.3

1202. Action Programme for Nitrate Vulnerable Zones (England and Wales) Regulations 1998
applied: SI 2002/2614 Reg.11
Reg.2, amended: SI 2003/1852 Reg.2
Reg.8, amended: SI 2002/2614 Reg.11, SI 2003/1852 Reg.2
Reg.8, substituted: SI 2002/2614 Reg.11
Sch.1 para.9, amended: SI 2003/1852 Reg.2
Sch.1 para.9, varied: SI 2002/2614 Reg.11
Sch.1 para.15, substituted: SI 2002/2614 Reg.11, SI 2003/1852 Reg.2

1203. Consumer Credit Licensing (Appeals) Regulations 1998
Reg.23, amended: SI 2003/1400 Sch.5
Reg.23, revoked (in part): SI 2003/1400 Sch.5

1998–cont.

1213. Cumbria Ambulance Service National Health Service Trust (Establishment) Amendment Order 1998
revoked: 2003 c.43 s.7

1227. Oxford Radcliffe Hospital National Health Service Trust (Change of Name) Order 1998
revoked: 2003 c.43 s.7

1228. Seed Potatoes (Fees) Regulations 1998
revoked (in part): SI 2004/1316 Reg.4

1240. Broadcasting (Local Delivery Services) Order 1998
Sch.1 Part I, amended: SI 2003/2155 Sch.2
Sch.1 Part II para.5, amended: SI 2003/2155 Sch.1 para.43

1258. Merchant Shipping (Convention on Limitation of Liability for Maritime Claims) (Amendment) Order 1998
Art.7, revoked (in part): SI 2004/1273 Art.3
Sch.1, amended: SI 2004/1273 Art.3

1265. Employment Rights (Dispute Resolution) (Northern Ireland) Order 1998
Art.8, referred to: SR 2002/120 Sch.1

1269. Cash Ratio Deposits (Value Bands and Ratios) Order 1998
revoked: SI 2004/1270 Art.2

1271. Restriction on Agreements and Conduct (Specified Domestic Electrical Goods) Order 1998
applied: SI 2004/2181 Sch.2

1280. Enfield Community Care National Health Service Trust (Establishment) Amendment Order 1998
revoked: 2003 c.43 s.7

1285. Oxfordshire Mental Healthcare National Health Service Trust (Establishment) Amendment Order 1998
revoked: 2003 c.43 s.7

1328. General Osteopathic Council (Registration) Rules Order of Council 1998
Sch.1, amended: SI 2003/3148 Reg.15
Sch.1, revoked: SI 2004/1947 Reg.14
Sch.1, substituted: SI 2004/1947 Reg.14

1332. Bolton Sixth Form College (Government) Regulations 1998
revoked: SI 2002/1094 Sch.1 Part 1

1338. General Optical Council (Disciplinary Committee (Constitution) Rules) Order of Council 1998
Sch.1, amended: SI 2004/259 Sch.1
Sch.1, substituted: SI 2004/259 Sch.1

1340. Railways Regulations 1998
applied: SI 2003/1400 Sch.4
Reg.30, amended: 2002 c.8 s.2

1341. Queen Mary's Sidcup National Health Service Trust (Establishment) Amendment Order 1998
revoked: 2003 c.43 s.7

1998–cont.

1376. Plastic Materials and Articles in Contact with Food Regulations 1998
referred to: SI 2003/302 Reg.2, SSI 2003/9 Reg.2

Reg.1A, added: SI 2002/2364 Reg.3, SI 2002/2834 Reg.3, SSI 2002/498 Reg.3

Reg.2, amended: SI 2002/2364 Reg.4, SI 2002/2834 Reg.4, SSI 2002/498 Reg.4

Reg.3, amended: SI 2002/2364 Reg.5, SI 2002/2834 Reg.5, SSI 2002/498 Reg.5

Reg.4, substituted: SI 2002/2364 Reg.6

Reg.4A, added: SI 2002/2364 Reg.7, SI 2002/2834 Reg.7, SSI 2002/498 Reg.7

Reg.5, amended: SI 2002/2364 Reg.8, SI 2002/2834 Reg.8, SSI 2002/498 Reg.8

Reg.6, amended: SI 2002/2364 Reg.9, SI 2002/2834 Reg.9, SSI 2002/498 Reg.9

Reg.6, substituted: SI 2002/2834 Reg.9

Reg.7A, substituted: SI 2002/2364 Reg.10, SI 2002/2834 Reg.10, SSI 2002/498 Reg.10

Reg.8A, added: SI 2002/2364 Reg.11, SI 2002/2834 Reg.11, SSI 2002/498 Reg.11

Reg.8B, added: SI 2002/2364 Reg.11, SI 2002/2834 Reg.11, SSI 2002/498 Reg.11

Reg.10, amended: SI 2002/2364 Reg.12, SI 2002/2834 Reg.12, SI 2002/3008 Reg.3, SI 2003/302 Reg.3, SSI 2002/498 Reg.12, SSI 2003/9 Reg.3

Reg.10, substituted: SI 2002/2834 Reg.12

Reg.11, amended: SI 2002/2364 Reg.13, SI 2002/2834 Reg.13, SSI 2002/498 Reg.13

Reg.12, amended: SI 2002/2364 Reg.14, SI 2002/2834 Reg.14, SSI 2002/498 Reg.14

Sch.1 Part I, amended: SI 2002/2364 Sch.1 Part I, Sch.1 Part II, Sch.1 Part III, SI 2002/2834 Sch.1 Part I, Sch.1 Part II, Sch.1 Part III, SI 2002/3008 Reg.4, Sch.1 Part I, Sch.1 Part II, Sch.1 Part III, Sch.1 Part IV, SI 2003/302 Reg.4, Sch.1 Part I, Sch.1 Part II, Sch.1 Part III, Sch.1 Part IV, SSI 2002/498 Sch.1 Part I, Sch.1 Part II, Sch.1 Part III, SSI 2003/9 Reg.4, Sch.1 Part I, Sch.1 Part II, Sch.1 Part III, Sch.1 Part IV

Sch.1 Part I, referred to: SI 2003/302 Reg.4

Sch.1 Part I, substituted: SI 2002/2364 Sch.1 Part IV, SI 2002/2834 Sch.1 Part IV, SSI 2002/498 Sch.1 Part IV

Sch.1 Part I, varied: SI 2002/2364 Sch.1

Sch.1 Part II para.4, amended: SI 2002/3008 Reg.4, SI 2003/302 Reg.4, SSI 2003/9 Reg.4

Sch.1 Part II para.4, substituted: SI 2002/2364 Reg.15, SI 2002/2834 Reg.15, SSI 2002/498 Reg.15

Sch.2B, added: SSI 2002/498 Reg.17

Sch.2B, amended: SI 2002/2364 Sch.3, SI 2002/2834 Sch.3, SI 2002/3008 Sch.3, SI 2003/302 Sch.3, SSI 2002/498 Sch.3, SSI 2003/9 Sch.3

1998–cont.

1376. Plastic Materials and Articles in Contact with Food Regulations 1998—cont.

Sch.2 Part I, amended: SI 2002/2364 Reg.16, Sch.2 Part I, Sch.2 Part II, Sch.2 Part III, SI 2002/2834 Reg.16, Sch.2 Part I, Sch.2 Part II, Sch.2 Part III, SI 2002/3008 Reg.5, Sch.2 Part I, Sch.2 Part II, SI 2003/302 Reg.5, Sch.2 Part I, Sch.2 Part II, SSI 2002/498 Reg.16, Sch.2 Part I, Sch.2 Part II, Sch.2 Part III, SSI 2003/9 Reg.5, Sch.2 Part I, Sch.2 Part II

Sch.2 Part I, referred to: SI 2003/302 Reg.5

Sch.2 Part II, added: SI 2002/2364 Sch.2 Part IV, SI 2002/2834 Sch.2 Part IV, SSI 2002/498 Sch.2 Part IV

Sch.2 Part II, amended: SI 2002/2364 Reg.16, SI 2002/3008 Sch.2 Part III, Sch.2 Part IV, SI 2003/302 Sch.2 Part III, Sch.2 Part IV, SSI 2003/9 Sch.2 Part III, Sch.2 Part IV

Sch.2 Part II, referred to: SI 2003/302 Reg.5

Sch.2 Part II para.1, added: SI 2002/2364 Sch.2 Part IV, SI 2002/2834 Sch.2 Part IV

Sch.2 Part II para.1, amended: SI 2002/2364 Reg.16

Sch.2 Part II para.2, added: SI 2002/2364 Sch.2 Part IV, SI 2002/2834 Sch.2 Part IV

Sch.2 Part II para.2, amended: SI 2002/2364 Reg.16

Sch.2 Part II para.3, added: SI 2002/2364 Sch.2 Part IV, SI 2002/2834 Sch.2 Part IV

Sch.2 Part II para.3, amended: SI 2002/2364 Reg.16

Sch.2 Part II para.4, added: SI 2002/2364 Sch.2 Part IV, SI 2002/2834 Sch.2 Part IV

Sch.2 Part II para.4, amended: SI 2002/2364 Reg.16

Sch.2 Part II para.5, added: SI 2002/2364 Sch.2 Part IV, SI 2002/2834 Sch.2 Part IV

Sch.2 Part II para.5, amended: SI 2002/2364 Reg.16

Sch.2 Part III para.1, amended: SI 2002/2364 Reg.16, SI 2002/2834 Reg.16, SSI 2002/498 Reg.16

Sch.2 Part III para.2, amended: SI 2002/2364 Reg.16, SI 2002/2834 Reg.16, SSI 2002/498 Reg.16

Sch.2 Part III para.3, amended: SI 2002/2364 Reg.16, SI 2002/2834 Reg.16, SSI 2002/498 Reg.16

Sch.2 Part III para.4, amended: SI 2002/2364 Reg.16, SI 2002/2834 Reg.16, SI 2002/3008 Reg.5, SI 2003/302 Reg.5, SSI 2002/498 Reg.16, SSI 2003/9 Reg.5

Sch.2 Part III para.4, substituted: SI 2002/2364 Reg.16, SI 2002/2834 Reg.16, SI 2002/3008 Reg.5, SSI 2002/498 Reg.16

Sch.2 Part III para.5, added: SI 2002/2364 Reg.16, SI 2002/2834 Reg.16, SSI 2002/498 Reg.16

NO.

1376. Plastic Materials and Articles in Contact with Food Regulations 1998—*cont.*

Sch.3 para.4, amended: SI 2002/2364 Reg.18, SI 2002/2834 Reg.18, SSI 2002/498 Reg.18

Sch.3 para.8, amended: SI 2002/2364 Reg.18, SI 2002/2834 Reg.18, SSI 2002/498 Reg.18

1381. Social Security (Claims and Payments) Amendment Regulations 1998

revoked (in part): SI 2003/492 Sch.3 Part 1

1398. Food Labelling (Amendment) Regulations 1998

Reg.18, amended: SSI 2004/6 Reg.11, SSI 2004/133 Reg.11

1417. Greenwich Healthcare National Health Service Trust (Establishment) Amendment Order 1998

revoked: 2003 c.43 s.7

1419. Merchant Shipping (Navigation Bridge Visibility) Regulations 1998

revoked: SI 2002/1473 Sch.1 para.2

1424. National Health Service (Service Committees and Tribunal) (Scotland) Amendment (No.2) Regulations 1998

Reg.3, revoked: SSI 2004/38 Sch.3

Reg.4, revoked: SSI 2004/38 Sch.3

1430. Inheritance Tax (Delivery of Accounts) (Scotland) Regulations 1998

revoked: SI 2002/1733 Sch.1

1431. Inheritance Tax (Delivery of Accounts) Regulations 1998

revoked: SI 2002/1733 Sch.1

1446. National Savings Stock Register (Closure of Register to Gilts) Order 1998

Art.16, amended: SI 2004/1662 Sch.1 para.27

Art.18, amended: SI 2004/1662 Sch.1 para.27

Art.19, amended: SI 2004/1662 Sch.1 para.27

Art.20, amended: SI 2004/1662 Sch.1 para.27

Art.25, substituted: SI 2004/1662 Sch.1 para.27

Art.29, amended: SI 2004/1662 Sch.1 para.27

1448. Road Humps (Scotland) Regulations 1998

applied: SI 2002/3113 Reg.16, Reg.34

Reg.7, amended: SSI 2002/419 Reg.3

1451. National Health Service Superannuation Scheme (Scotland) (Additional Voluntary Contributions) Regulations 1998

Reg.2, amended: SSI 2004/62 Reg.3

Reg.2, revoked (in part): SSI 2004/62 Reg.3

NO.

1451. National Health Service Superannuation Scheme (Scotland) (Additional Voluntary Contributions) Regulations 1998—*cont.*

Reg.3, amended: SSI 2004/62 Reg.4

Reg.4, amended: SSI 2004/62 Reg.5

Reg.6, amended: SSI 2004/62 Reg.6

Reg.8, amended: SSI 2004/62 Reg.7

Reg.10, substituted: SSI 2004/62 Reg.8

Reg.11, amended: SSI 2004/62 Reg.9

Reg.12, amended: SSI 2004/62 Reg.10

Reg.14, amended: SSI 2004/62 Reg.11

Reg.15, amended: SSI 2004/62 Reg.12

Reg.16, amended: SSI 2004/62 Reg.13

Sch.1 Part I para.1, substituted: SSI 2004/62 Reg.14

Sch.1 Part I para.2, substituted: SSI 2004/62 Reg.14

Sch.1 Part I para.3, substituted: SSI 2004/62 Reg.14

Sch.1 Part I para.4, substituted: SSI 2004/62 Reg.14

Sch.1 Part I para.5, substituted: SSI 2004/62 Reg.14

Sch.1 Part I para.6, substituted: SSI 2004/62 Reg.14

Sch.1 Part I para.7, substituted: SSI 2004/62 Reg.14

Sch.1 Part I para.8, substituted: SSI 2004/62 Reg.14

Sch.1 Part I para.9, substituted: SSI 2004/62 Reg.14

Sch.1 Part I para.10, substituted: SSI 2004/62 Reg.14

Sch.1 Part II para.7, substituted: SSI 2004/62 Reg.14

Sch.1 Part II para.8, substituted: SSI 2004/62 Reg.14

Sch.1 Part II para.9, substituted: SSI 2004/62 Reg.14

Sch.1 Part II para.10, substituted: SSI 2004/62 Reg.14

Sch.1 Part II para.11, substituted: SSI 2004/62 Reg.14

Sch.1 Part II para.12, substituted: SSI 2004/62 Reg.14

Sch.1 Part II para.13, substituted: SSI 2004/62 Reg.14

Sch.1 Part II para.14, substituted: SSI 2004/62 Reg.14

Sch.1 Part II para.15, substituted: SSI 2004/62 Reg.14

Sch.1 Part II para.16, substituted: SSI 2004/62 Reg.14

Sch.1 Part II para.17, substituted: SSI 2004/62 Reg.14

Sch.1 Part III para.14, substituted: SSI 2004/62 Reg.14

Sch.1 Part III para.18, substituted: SSI 2004/62 Reg.14

NO.

NO.

1998–cont.

1451. National Health Service Superannuation Scheme (Scotland) (Additional Voluntary Contributions) Regulations 1998–*cont.*

Sch.1 Part IV para.15, substituted: SSI 2004/62 Reg.14

Sch.1 Part IV para.19, substituted: SSI 2004/62 Reg.14

1460. Mental Health Review Tribunals (Regions) Order 1998

revoked (in part): SI 2003/2251 Art.4

1461. Air Passenger Duty and Other Indirect Taxes (Interest Rate) Regulations 1998

referred to: SI 2003/230 Reg.2

Reg.4, amended: SI 2003/230 Reg.3

Reg.5, amended: SI 2003/230 Reg.4

1493. New Northern Ireland Assembly Elections (Returning Officer's Charges) Order 1998

Sch.1 Part A para.1, amended: SI 2003/3029 Art.2

Sch.1 Part A para.2, amended: SI 2003/3029 Art.2

Sch.1 Part A para.3, amended: SI 2003/3029 Art.2

Sch.1 Part A para.4, amended: SI 2003/3029 Art.2

Sch.1 Part A para.5, added: SI 2003/3029 Art.2

Sch.1 Part B para.1, amended: SI 2003/3029 Art.2

Sch.1 Part B para.7, amended: SI 2003/3029 Art.2

Sch.1 Part B para.10, revoked: SI 2003/3029 Art.2

1500. Merchant Shipping (Control of Pollution) (SOLAS) Order 1998

enabled: SI 2004/302

1504. Criminal Justice (Children) (Northern Ireland) Order 1998

applied: SI 2003/439 Sch.1 para.13, SR 2003/137 Art.3

Part IIIA, added: 2002 c.26 s.58

Art.2, amended: 2002 c.26 Sch.11 para.17, Sch.12 para.67

Art.3A, added: 2002 c.26 s.57

Art.3B, added: 2002 c.26 s.57

Art.3C, added: 2002 c.26 s.57

Art.4, revoked: 2002 c.26 Sch.13

Art.8, amended: 2002 c.26 Sch.12 para.68

Art.10A, added: 2002 c.26 s.58

Art.10A, varied: 2002 c.26 s.89

Art.10B, added: 2002 c.26 s.58

Art.10B, varied: 2002 c.26 s.89

Art.10C, added: 2002 c.26 s.58

Art.10D, added: 2002 c.26 s.58

Art.12, applied: SI 2003/1247 Art.6

Art.13, amended: 2002 c.26 Sch.12 para.69

Art.13, applied: SI 2003/1247 Art.6

Art.22, applied: SI 2004/1988 Art.8

1998–cont.

1504. Criminal Justice (Children) (Northern Ireland) Order 1998–*cont.*

Art.30, amended: 2002 c.26 Sch.11 para.18, Sch.12 para.70

Art.33A, added: 2002 c.26 s.59

Art.33A, varied: 2002 c.26 s.89

Art.33B, added: 2002 c.26 s.59

Art.33C, added: 2002 c.26 s.59

Art.33D, added: 2002 c.26 s.59

Art.33E, added: 2002 c.26 s.59

Art.35, applied: 2002 c.29 s.185

Art.36A, added: 2002 c.26 s.54

Art.36A, varied: 2002 c.26 s.89

Art.36B, added: 2002 c.26 s.54

Art.36C, added: 2002 c.26 s.54

Art.36D, added: 2002 c.26 s.54

Art.36E, added: 2002 c.26 s.55

Art.36E, varied: 2002 c.26 s.89

Art.36F, added: 2002 c.26 s.55

Art.36G, added: 2002 c.26 s.55

Art.36H, added: 2002 c.26 s.55

Art.36I, added: 2002 c.26 s.55

Art.36J, added: 2002 c.26 s.60

Art.36K, added: 2002 c.26 s.60

Art.36L, added: 2002 c.26 s.60

Art.37, amended: 2002 c.26 Sch.12 para.71

Art.39, amended: 2002 c.26 s.64, Sch.12 para.72

Art.41, amended: 2002 c.26 Sch.12 para.73

Art.44, amended: 2002 c.26 Sch.12 para.74

Art.44A, added: 2002 c.26 s.56

Art.44B, added: 2002 c.26 s.56

Art.44C, added: 2002 c.26 s.56

Art.44D, added: 2002 c.26 s.56

Art.44D, applied: 2002 c.26 s.89

Art.44E, added: 2002 c.26 s.56

Art.44F, added: 2002 c.26 s.56

Art.44F, applied: 2002 c.26 s.89

Art.44G, added: 2002 c.26 s.56

Art.45, amended: 2002 c.26 s.65, Sch.11 para.19

Art.45, applied: 2002 c.26 s.70, SI 2004/702 Art.63

Art.46, applied: SI 2004/702 Art.63

Art.53, amended: 2002 c.26 Sch.11 para.20

Art.54, amended: 2002 c.26 Sch.11 para.21

Art.54, revoked (in part): 2002 c.26 Sch.11 para.21, Sch.13

Art.55, revoked: 2002 c.26 Sch.13

Art.56, amended: 2002 c.26 Sch.12 para.75

Art.56, enabled: SR 2003/137

Art.56, revoked: 2004 c.4 s.9, Sch.4

Art.57, revoked (in part): 2004 c.4 s.9, Sch.4

Sch.1A, added: 2002 c.26 Sch.10

Sch.5, revoked (in part): 2002 c.26 Sch.13, Sch.13, 2003 c.44 Sch.37 Part 7

NO.

NO.

1998–cont.

1506. Social Security (Northern Ireland) Order 1998

applied: SR 2002/108 Reg.2, SR 2003/18 Reg.19, SR 2003/28 Reg.12, SR 2003/156 Reg.2, 2004 c.6 s.24

Part II, applied: 2002 c.21 s.50, s.63, 2002 c.26 Sch.1, Sch.6, 2004 c.6 s.2, SI 2004/1987 Art.7

Part II, referred to: 2002 c.14 (NI) Sch.1 para.4

Part II, varied: 2002 c.21 Sch.4 para.19

Art.2, enabled: SI 2002/527, SI 2002/1378, SI 2003/492, SI 2003/916, SR 2003/18

Art.4, amended: 2002 c.14 (NI) Sch.1 para.5, (NI) Sch.3

Art.6, amended: 2002 c.26 Sch.3 para.24

Art.7, amended: 2002 c.26 Sch.3 para.25

Art.7, revoked (in part): 2002 c.26 Sch.13

Art.8, applied: SR 2002/403 Reg.19

Art.8, enabled: SR 2002/403

Art.9, amended: 2002 c.14 (NI) Sch.1 para.6

Art.9, applied: 2002 c.14 (NI) s.6, SI 2004/960 Reg.2, SI 2004/1987 Art.7

Art.9, revoked (in part): 2002 c.21 Sch.6

Art.10, applied: 2002 c.14 (NI) s.6, (NI) s.7, SI 2003/492 Reg.12, Reg.23, Reg.36, Reg.38, SI 2003/493 Reg.38, SR 2002/14 Reg.3, SR 2003/191 Reg.36

Art.10, enabled: SI 2002/527, SI 2002/1378, SI 2003/492, SI 2003/916, SR 2002/14, SR 2002/67, SR 2002/80, SR 2003/224

Art.11, applied: 2002 c.14 (NI) s.6, (NI) s.7, (NI) s.8, SI 2003/492 Reg.23, Reg.36, Reg.38, SI 2003/493 Reg.38, SR 2003/28 Reg.17, SR 2003/191 Reg.34

Art.11, enabled: SI 2002/527, SI 2003/916, SR 2002/67, SR 2002/80, SR 2003/191, SR 2003/224

Art.12, amended: 2002 c.14 (NI) Sch.1 para.7

Art.12, enabled: SR 2002/132

Art.13, applied: SR 2002/403 Reg.3, Reg.27

Art.13, enabled: SI 2002/1378, SI 2003/916, SI 2004/3377, SR 2002/403

Art.13, varied: SI 2002/2926 Reg.4

Art.14, applied: SR 2002/403 Reg.27

Art.14, varied: SI 2002/2926 Reg.5

Art.15, applied: SR 2002/403 Reg.27, SR 2003/18 Reg.15, Reg.23

Art.15, enabled: SI 2002/1378, SR 2002/403

Art.15, varied: SI 2002/2926 Reg.6, Reg.7

Art.16, enabled: SI 2002/1378, SI 2003/916, SR 2002/403

Art.16, varied: SI 2002/2926 Reg.9

Art.17, varied: SI 2002/2926 Reg.10

Art.18, enabled: SR 2003/191

Art.21, enabled: SI 2003/916

Art.22, amended: 2002 c.14 (NI) Sch.1 para.8

Art.22, enabled: SI 2003/916

Art.23, enabled: SI 2003/916

Art.25, enabled: SI 2003/916

Art.26, enabled: SI 2003/916

Art.27, amended: 2002 c.14 (NI) Sch.1 para.9

1998–cont.

1506. Social Security (Northern Ireland) Order 1998–*cont.*

Art.28, amended: 2002 c.14 (NI) Sch.1 para.10, (NI) Sch.3

Art.28, enabled: SI 2002/1378, SR 2002/403

Art.28, varied: SI 2002/2926 Reg.11

Art.39, varied: SI 2002/2926 Reg.12

Art.59, revoked: 2004 c.3 Sch.2 Part 2

Art.68, applied: 2002 c.21 s.49

Art.74, amended: 2002 c.21 Sch.4 para.17

Art.74, enabled: SI 2002/1378, SI 2003/916, SR 2002/79, SR 2002/80, SR 2002/403, SR 2003/18, SR 2003/154, SR 2003/191, SR 2003/312

Art.75, amended: 2002 c.21 Sch.4 para.18

Art.75, enabled: SI 2004/3377

Sch.1, enabled: SR 2002/403

Sch.1, revoked (in part): 2002 c.26 Sch.13

Sch.2, amended: 2002 c.10 (NI) Sch.1 para.10, 2002 c.14 (NI) Sch.1 para.11, (NI) Sch.3

Sch.2, enabled: SI 2002/1378, SR 2002/79, SR 2003/312

Sch.2, substituted: SR 2002/321 Art.2

Sch.3, added: 2002 c.14 (NI) Sch.1 para.12

Sch.4, enabled: SI 2002/1378, SI 2003/916, SR 2002/403, SR 2003/18

Sch.4, varied: SI 2002/2926 Reg.9

Sch.6, revoked: 2002 c.10 (NI) Sch.2

1510. Wireless Telegraphy (Isle of Man) Order 1998

Art.2, revoked (in part): SI 2003/3198 Art.3

1511. Wireless Telegraphy (Guernsey) Order 1998

Art.2, revoked (in part): SI 2003/3195 Art.3

1512. Wireless Telegraphy (Jersey) Order 1998

Art.2, revoked (in part): SI 2003/3197 Art.3

1530. Export of Goods (Federal Republic of Yugoslavia) (Control) Order 1998

revoked: SI 2002/315 Art.2

1531. Federal Republic of Yugoslavia (Supply and Sale of Equipment) (Penalties and Licences) Regulations 1998

revoked: SI 2002/316 Reg.2

1532. Education (School Performance Targets) (England) Regulations 1998

referred to: SI 2003/1970 Reg.2

revoked: SI 2004/2858 Sch.2

Reg.2, amended: SI 2002/2105 Reg.4

Reg.3, amended: SI 2002/840 Reg.3

Reg.3A, amended: SI 2002/2105 Reg.5

Reg.4, amended: SI 2003/1970 Reg.3

Reg.4, revoked (in part): SI 2003/1970 Reg.3

Reg.5, amended: SI 2003/1970 Reg.4

Reg.6, amended: SI 2002/840 Reg.4, SI 2002/2105 Reg.6, SI 2003/1970 Reg.5

Reg.6, disapplied: SI 2004/2683 Art.2, SI 2004/2810 Art.2

1998–cont.

1532. Education (School Performance Targets) (England) Regulations 1998–cont.
Reg.6, revoked (in part): SI 2003/1970 Reg.5
Sch.2, disapplied: SI 2004/2683 Art.2, SI 2004/2810 Art.2

1539. Road Traffic (Permitted Parking Area and Special Parking Area) (City of Edinburgh) Designation Order 1998
Sch.2 para.1, amended: SSI 2002/188 Art.2

1543. Bradford Community Health National Health Service Trust (Establishment) Amendment Order 1998
revoked: 2003 c.43 s.7

1561. Merchant Shipping (International Safety Management (ISM) Code) Regulations 1998
Reg.3, amended: SI 2004/302 Sch.1 para.9

1565. Meters (Approval of Pattern or Construction and Manner of Installation) Regulations 1998
Reg.2, amended: SI 2002/3129 Sch.1 para.1
Reg.4, amended: SI 2002/3129 Sch.1 para.2
Reg.5, amended: SI 2002/3129 Sch.1 para.3
Reg.10, amended: SI 2002/3129 Sch.1 para.4

1566. Meters (Certification) Regulations 1998
Reg.2, amended: SI 2002/3129 Sch.1 para.5
Reg.3, substituted: SI 2002/3129 Sch.1 para.6
Reg.4, substituted: SI 2002/3129 Sch.1 para.7
Reg.5, substituted: SI 2002/3129 Sch.1 para.8
Reg.6, amended: SI 2002/3129 Sch.1 para.9
Reg.11, substituted: SI 2002/3129 Sch.1 para.10

1576. Special Health Authorities (Amendment) Regulations 1998
Reg.4, revoked: SI 2003/506 Sch.2

1580. Telecommunications (Open Network Provision) (Voice Telephony) Regulations 1998
revoked: 2003 c.21 Sch.19

1594. National Health Service (Scotland) (Injury Benefits) Regulations 1998
Reg.2, amended: SSI 2004/212 Sch.1 para.8
Reg.3, revoked (in part): SSI 2004/212 Sch.1 para.8
Reg.4A, revoked (in part): SSI 2004/212 Sch.1 para.8

1609. Merchant Shipping (Small Workboats and Pilot Boats) Regulations 1998
Reg.5, applied: SI 2004/302 Reg.3

1645. Sheep and Goats Spongiform Encephalopathy Order 1998
applied: SI 2002/843 Reg.104, Sch.9 para.2, SI 2002/1416 Reg.104, SSI 2002/255 Reg.102, Sch.9 para.2, Sch.9 para.6

1998–cont.

1645. Sheep and Goats Spongiform Encephalopathy Order 1998–cont.
revoked (in part): SI 2002/843 Sch.9 Part I, SI 2002/1416 Sch.9 Part I, SSI 2002/255 Sch.9 Part I
varied: SI 2002/1416 Sch.9 para.2
Art.4, applied: SI 2002/843 Sch.9 para.1, SSI 2002/255 Sch.9 para.1
Art.4, varied: SI 2002/1416 Sch.9 para.1
Art.5, applied: SI 2002/843 Sch.9 para.1, SSI 2002/255 Sch.9 para.1
Art.5, varied: SI 2002/1416 Sch.9 para.1
Art.6, applied: SI 2002/843 Sch.9 para.3, SSI 2002/255 Sch.9 para.3
Art.6, varied: SI 2002/1416 Sch.9 para.3
Art.7, applied: SI 2002/843 Sch.9 para.4, SSI 2002/255 Sch.9 para.4
Art.7, varied: SI 2002/1416 Sch.9 para.4

1646. Sheep and Goats Spongiform Encephalopathy Regulations 1998
applied: SI 2002/843 Reg.104, Sch.9 para.5, SSI 2002/255 Reg.102, Sch.9 para.5
revoked (in part): SI 2002/843 Sch.9 Part I, SI 2002/1416 Sch.9 Part I, SSI 2002/255 Sch.9 Part I
varied: SI 2002/1416 Sch.9 para.5

1647. Sheep and Goats Spongiform Encephalopathy (Compensation) Order 1998. 1998
applied: SSI 2002/255 Reg.102
revoked (in part): SI 2002/843 Sch.9 Part I, SI 2002/1416 Sch.9 Part I, SSI 2002/255 Sch.9 Part I

1664. Medical Act 1983 (Approved Medical Practices and Conditions of Residence) and National Health Service (General Medical Services) (Amendment) Regulations 1998
Reg.2, amended: SI 2003/1250 Sch.10 para.2, SI 2004/865 Sch.1 para.21, SI 2004/1016 Sch.1 para.21
Reg.3, amended: SI 2004/696 Art.3, SI 2004/865 Sch.1 para.21, SI 2004/1016 Sch.1 para.21
Reg.4, revoked (in part): SI 2004/865 Sch.2, SI 2004/1016 Sch.2

1667. Medical Act 1983 (Approved Medical Practices and Conditions of Residence) and National Health Service (General Medical Services) (Scotland) Amendment Regulations 1998
Reg.4, revoked: SSI 2004/114 Sch.2

1691. Merchant Shipping (Distress Messages) Regulations 1998
Reg.3, revoked: SI 2002/1473 Sch.1 para.5
Reg.4, revoked: SI 2002/1473 Sch.1 para.5
Reg.5, revoked: SI 2002/1473 Sch.1 para.5
Reg.6, revoked: SI 2002/1473 Sch.1 para.5
Reg.7, revoked: SI 2002/1473 Sch.1 para.5
Reg.8, revoked: SI 2002/1473 Sch.1 para.5

NO.

1998—cont.

1692. Merchant Shipping (Co-operation with Search and Rescue Services) Regulations 1998
revoked: SI 2002/1473 Sch.1 para.2

1708. M4 Motorway (Hillingdon and Hounslow) (Speed Limits) Regulations 1998
revoked: SI 2002/1651 Reg.3

1713. Faculty Jurisdiction (Appeals) Rules 1998
Part II r.4, applied: SI 2002/1892 Sch.1 Part TABLEa, SI 2003/1933 Sch.1 Part II, SI 2004/1888 Sch.1 Part TABLEa
Part II r.5, applied: SI 2002/1892 Sch.1 Part TABLEa, SI 2003/1933 Sch.1 Part II, SI 2004/1888 Sch.1 Part TABLEa
Part II r.6, applied: SI 2002/1892 Sch.1 Part TABLEa, SI 2003/1933 Sch.1 Part II, SI 2004/1888 Sch.1 Part TABLEa
Part IV r.17, applied: SI 2002/1892 Sch.1 Part TABLEa, SI 2003/1933 Sch.1 Part II, SI 2004/1888 Sch.1 Part TABLEa
Part V r.19, applied: SI 2002/1892 Sch.1 Part TABLEa, SI 2003/1933 Sch.1 Part II, SI 2004/1888 Sch.1 Part TABLEa

1715. National Institutions of The Church of England (Transfer of Functions) Order 1998
applied: SI 2002/1894, SI 2003/1932

1727. Cosmetic Products (Safety) (Amendment) Regulations 1998
revoked: SI 2003/835 Sch.1

1733. East Berkshire Community Health National Health Service Trust (Establishment) Amendment Order 1998
revoked: 2003 c.43 s.7

1749. Government Stock (Amendment) Regulations 1998
Reg.4, amended: SI 2002/2521 Sch.2 Part II

1751. Air Carrier Liability Order 1998
revoked: SI 2004/1418 Reg.6

1752. Angola (United Nations Sanctions) Order 1998
revoked: SI 2003/1868 Sch.2
Art.6, amended: 2002 c.8 s.2
Art.8, amended: 2002 c.8 s.2

1753. Angola (United Nations Sanctions) (Dependent Territories) Order 1998
revoked: SI 2003/1868 Sch.2
Art.6, amended: 2002 c.8 s.2
Art.9, amended: 2002 c.8 s.2

1756. Angola (United Nations Sanctions) (Channel Islands) Order 1998
revoked: SI 2003/1868 Sch.2
Art.6, amended: 2002 c.8 s.2
Art.9, amended: 2002 c.8 s.2

1757. Angola (United Nations Sanctions) (Isle of Man) Order 1998
revoked: SI 2003/1868 Sch.2
Art.6, amended: 2002 c.8 s.2
Art.8, amended: 2002 c.8 s.2

NO.

1998—cont.

1759. Education (Northern Ireland) Order 1998
Part VII, applied: SI 2003/424 Art.4
Art.3, amended: SI 2003/424 Art.19
Art.3, referred to: SI 2003/424 Art.19
Art.4, amended: SI 2003/424 Sch.2 para.8
Art.5, amended: SI 2003/424 Sch.2 para.9
Art.11, amended: SI 2003/424 Art.27
Art.23, amended: SI 2003/424 Art.21
Art.35, amended: SI 2003/424 Art.35
Art.36, amended: SI 2003/424 Art.35
Art.44, revoked: SI 2003/424 Sch.1 para.7, Sch.3 Part II
Art.45, revoked: SI 2003/424 Sch.1 para.7, Sch.3 Part II
Art.46, revoked: SI 2003/424 Sch.1 para.7, Sch.3 Part II
Art.47, revoked: SI 2003/424 Sch.1 para.7, Sch.3 Part II
Art.48, revoked: SI 2003/424 Sch.1 para.7, Sch.3 Part II
Art.49, revoked: SI 2003/424 Sch.1 para.7, Sch.3 Part II
Art.50, revoked: SI 2003/424 Sch.1 para.7, Sch.3 Part II
Art.51, revoked: SI 2003/424 Sch.1 para.7, Sch.3 Part II
Art.52, revoked: SI 2003/424 Sch.1 para.7, Sch.3 Part II
Art.53, revoked: SI 2003/424 Sch.1 para.7, Sch.3 Part II
Art.54, revoked: SI 2003/424 Sch.1 para.7, Sch.3 Part II
Art.55, amended: SI 2003/424 Sch.1 para.8
Art.59, amended: SI 2003/424 Sch.1 para.9
Art.61, amended: SI 2003/424 Sch.1 para.10
Art.61, applied: SI 2003/424 Art.4
Art.63, amended: SI 2003/424 Sch.1 para.11
Art.63, applied: SI 2003/424 Art.4
Art.65, revoked: SI 2003/424 Sch.1 para.12, Sch.3 Part II
Art.66, revoked: SI 2003/424 Sch.1 para.12, Sch.3 Part II
Art.67, amended: SI 2003/424 Sch.1 para.13
Art.67A, added: SI 2003/424 Sch.1 para.14
Art.72, amended: SI 2003/424 Sch.1 para.15
Art.83, amended: SI 2003/424 Art.34
Art.83, revoked (in part): SI 2003/424 Sch.3 Part I
Art.86, applied: SI 2003/424 Art.36
Sch.1 para.12, revoked (in part): SI 2003/418 Sch.3
Sch.3 para.13, revoked (in part): SI 2003/418 Sch.3

1760. Education (Student Support) (Northern Ireland) Order 1998
applied: SI 2002/2086 Reg.3, Reg.7, SR 2002/224 Reg.22
Art.2, applied: SR 2002/224 Reg.10

NO.

1998–cont.

1760. Education (Student Support) (Northern Ireland) Order 1998–*cont.*

Art.3, applied: SI 2002/2820 Reg.4, SR 2002/224 Reg.5, Reg.40, SR 2002/379 Reg.4

Art.3, enabled: SR 2002/111, SR 2002/224, SR 2002/272, SR 2003/121, SR 2003/166, SR 2003/339

Art.4, applied: SR 2002/224 Reg.22, Reg.33

Art.4, referred to: SR 2002/224 Reg.6

Art.8, enabled: SR 2002/111, SR 2002/224, SR 2003/121, SR 2003/166, SR 2003/339

Art.9, referred to: SR 2002/265 Reg.5

Sch.1, referred to: SR 2002/265 Reg.5

1762. Producer Responsibility Obligations (Northern Ireland) Order 1998

Art.3, applied: SR 2002/239

Art.3, enabled: SR 2002/239

Art.3, referred to: SR 2002/239

Art.4, enabled: SR 2002/239

1763. Public Interest Disclosure (Northern Ireland) Order 1998

Art.16, revoked: 2003 c.6 s.26, Sch.4

1778. Patents (Fees) Rules 1998

applied: SI 2002/247 Reg.24

Sch.1 Part A, amended: SI 2004/2358 Sch.3 para.2, Sch.3 para.3, Sch.3 para.4, Sch.3 para.5, Sch.3 para.6, Sch.3 para.7

1796. Cattle Database Regulations 1998

Reg.7, amended: SI 2002/94 Reg.2, SI 2002/304 Reg.2, SSI 2002/22 Reg.2

1799. Hertfordshire (Coroners Districts) (Amendment) Order 1998

referred to: SI 2002/3084 Art.2

revoked: SI 2002/3084 Art.4

1802. Restriction of Liberty Order (Scotland) Regulations 1998

Reg.2, amended: SSI 2002/119 Reg.2

Sch.1, substituted: SSI 2002/119 Reg.3

Sch.1 para.1, substituted: SSI 2002/119 Reg.3

Sch.1 para.2, substituted: SSI 2002/119 Reg.3

Sch.1 para.3, substituted: SSI 2002/119 Reg.3

Sch.2 para.1, referred to: SSI 2002/119 Reg.5

Sch.2 para.1, revoked: SSI 2002/119 Reg.4

Sch.2 para.2, amended: SSI 2002/119 Reg.4

Sch.2 para.2, referred to: SSI 2002/119 Reg.5

Sch.2 para.2, revoked (in part): SSI 2002/119 Reg.4

Sch.2 para.3, referred to: SSI 2002/119 Reg.5

Sch.2 para.3, revoked: SSI 2002/119 Reg.4

Sch.2 para.4, referred to: SSI 2002/119 Reg.5

Sch.2 para.4, revoked: SSI 2002/119 Reg.4

1811. Social Security (Guardian's Allowances) Amendment Regulations 1998

revoked: SI 2003/495 Sch.1 Part 1

1831. Local Government Pension Scheme (Management and Investment of Funds) Regulations 1998

Reg.9A, amended: SI 2002/1852 Reg.2

NO.

1998–cont.

1831. Local Government Pension Scheme (Management and Investment of Funds) Regulations 1998–*cont.*

Reg.11, amended: SI 2003/2719 Reg.3

Reg.11A, added: SI 2003/2719 Reg.3

Sch.1 Part I, substituted: SI 2003/2719 Sch.1

Sch.1 Part I para.1, substituted: SI 2003/2719 Sch.1

Sch.1 Part I para.2, substituted: SI 2003/2719 Sch.1

Sch.1 Part I para.3, substituted: SI 2003/2719 Sch.1

Sch.1 Part I para.4, substituted: SI 2003/2719 Sch.1

Sch.1 Part I para.5, substituted: SI 2003/2719 Sch.1

Sch.1 Part I para.6, substituted: SI 2003/2719 Sch.1

Sch.1 Part I para.7, substituted: SI 2003/2719 Sch.1

Sch.1 Part I para.8, substituted: SI 2003/2719 Sch.1

Sch.1 Part I para.9, substituted: SI 2003/2719 Sch.1

Sch.1 Part I para.9A, substituted: SI 2003/2719 Sch.1

Sch.1 Part I para.9B, substituted: SI 2003/2719 Sch.1

Sch.1 Part I para.10, substituted: SI 2003/2719 Sch.1

Sch.1 Part I para.11, substituted: SI 2003/2719 Sch.1

Sch.1 Part III, amended: SI 2003/2066 Reg.13

1833. Working Time Regulations 1998

disapplied: SI 2002/2055 Reg.3

referred to: SI 2002/2125 Reg.3, SI 2003/1684 Reg.2, SI 2003/2002 Reg.12

see *Maconnachie v Leisure Leagues UK Ltd* [2002] I.R.L.R. 600 (EAT), Judge A Wilkie Q.C.; see *Marshalls Clay Products Ltd v Caulfield* [2004] EWCA Civ 422, [2004] 2 C.M.L.R. 45 (CA), Judge, L.J.

see *Rich v Forbuoys Ltd* [2002] Emp. L.R. 1041 (EAT), Judge Peter Clark

see *Rich v Forbuoys Ltd* [2002] Emp. L.R. 1041 (EAT), Judge Peter Clark

Reg.2, amended: SI 2002/3128 Reg.3, SI 2003/1684 Reg.3

Reg.2, see *Ashby v Addison (t/a Brayton News)* [2003] I.C.R. 667 (EAT), Judge Burke Q.C.; see *Burton v Higham (t/a Ace Appointments)* [2003] I.R.L.R. 257 (EAT), Judge McMullen Q.C.; see *Byrne Bros (Formwork) Ltd v Baird* [2002] I.C.R. 667 (EAT), Recorder Underhill Q.C.; see *Redrow Homes (Yorkshire) Ltd v Wright* [2004] EWCA Civ 469, [2004] 3 All E.R. 98 (CA), Pill, L.J.

Reg.3, added: SI 2002/3128 Reg.4

Reg.3, amended: SI 2002/3128 Reg.4

Reg.4, amended: SI 2002/3128 Reg.5

NO.

NO.

1998–cont.

1833. Working Time Regulations 1998–*cont.*
Reg.5A, added: SI 2002/3128 Reg.6
Reg.6, revoked (in part): SI 2002/3128 Reg.7
Reg.6A, added: SI 2002/3128 Reg.8
Reg.7, amended: SI 2002/3128 Reg.9
Reg.9, amended: SI 2002/3128 Reg.10
Reg.10, amended: SI 2002/3128 Reg.11
Reg.10, see *Prison Service v Bewley* [2004] I.C.R. 422 (EAT), Judge Peter Clark
Reg.11, amended: SI 2002/3128 Reg.12
Reg.12, amended: SI 2002/3128 Reg.13
Reg.13, see *Canada Life Ltd v Gray* [2004] I.C.R. 673 (EAT), Judge Peter Clark; see *List Design Group Ltd v Douglas* [2002] I.C.R. 686 (EAT), Bell, J.; see *MPB Structures Ltd v Munro* [2002] I.R.L.R. 601 (EAT), Lord Johnston; see *Toulson v South Tyneside MBC* [2003] 1 C.M.L.R. 28 (EAT), Recorder Burke Q.C.; see *Voteforce Associates Ltd v Quinn* [2002] I.C.R. 1 (EAT), Judge Peter Clark
Reg.14, see *Canada Life Ltd v Gray* [2004] I.C.R. 673 (EAT), Judge Peter Clark
Reg.16, see *Bamsey v Albon Engineering & Manufacturing Plc* [2003] I.C.R. 1224 (EAT), Judge Ansell; see *Bamsey v Albon Engineering & Manufacturing Plc* [2004] EWCA Civ 359, [2004] 2 C.M.L.R. 59 (CA), Auld, L.J.; see *Blackburn v Gridquest Ltd (t/a Select Employment)* [2002] EWCA Civ 1037, [2002] I.C.R. 1206 (CA), Pill, L.J.; see *Blackburn v Gridquest Ltd (t/a Select Employment)* [2002] I.C.R. 682 (EAT), Judge Peter Clark; see *Marshalls Clay Products Ltd v Caulfield* [2004] I.C.R. 436 (EAT), Burton, J.; see *MPB Structures Ltd v Munro* 2003 S.C. 485 (1 Div), Lord Cullen L.P., Lord Carloway, Lady Cosgrove; see *Voteforce Associates Ltd v Quinn* [2002] I.C.R. 1 (EAT), Judge Peter Clark
Reg.18, amended: SI 2003/3049 Sch.2 para.6, SI 2004/1713 Sch.2 para.5
Reg.18, substituted: SI 2003/1684 Reg.4
Reg.19, amended: SI 2002/3128 Reg.14
Reg.21, amended: SI 2003/1684 Reg.5
Reg.23, see *Prison Service v Bewley* [2004] I.C.R. 422 (EAT), Judge Peter Clark
Reg.24A, added: SI 2003/1684 Reg.6
Reg.25, amended: SI 2002/3128 Reg.15
Reg.25A, added: SI 2003/1684 Reg.7
Reg.25B, added: SI 2003/1684 Reg.8
Reg.26, amended: SI 2002/3128 Reg.16
Reg.26, revoked: SI 2003/1684 Reg.9
Reg.27, amended: SI 2002/3128 Reg.18
Reg.27A, added: SI 2002/3128 Reg.17
Reg.28, amended: SI 2002/3128 Reg.19
Reg.28, substituted: SI 2003/1684 Reg.10
Reg.29, substituted: SI 2003/1684 Reg.10
Reg.30, amended: SI 2002/3128 Reg.20, SI 2003/1684 Reg.11, SI 2004/752 Reg.17

1998–cont.

1833. Working Time Regulations 1998–*cont.*
Reg.30, applied: 2002 c.22 Sch.3, Sch.4, Sch.5
Reg.35, amended: SI 2004/2516 Reg.2
Reg.35, see *MPB Structures Ltd v Munro* [2002] I.R.L.R. 601 (EAT), Lord Johnston; see *MPB Structures Ltd v Munro* 2003 S.C. 485 (1 Div), Lord Cullen L.P., Lord Carloway, Lady Cosgrove
s.230, see *Inland Revenue Commissioners v Post Office Ltd* [2003] I.C.R. 546 (EAT), Burton, J.
Sch.1, referred to: SI 2004/753 Sch.1 para.147
Sch.3 para.1, added: SI 2003/1684 Reg.12
Sch.3 para.2, added: SI 2003/1684 Reg.12
Sch.3 para.3, added: SI 2003/1684 Reg.12
Sch.3 para.4, added: SI 2003/1684 Reg.12
Sch.3 para.5, added: SI 2003/1684 Reg.12
Sch.3 para.6, added: SI 2003/1684 Reg.12
Sch.3 para.7, added: SI 2003/1684 Reg.12
Sch.3 para.8, added: SI 2003/1684 Reg.12

1866. Education (School Inspection) (Wales) Regulations 1998
Reg.7, amended: SI 2004/784 Reg.2
Reg.8, amended: SI 2004/784 Reg.2
Reg.13, amended: SI 2004/784 Reg.2

1867. Education (School Performance Information) (Wales) Regulations 1998
revoked: SI 2004/1025 Sch.4

1870. Individual Savings Account Regulations 1998
referred to: SI 2004/1863 Sch.1 para.7
Reg.2, amended: SI 2003/2066 Reg.13, SI 2003/2747 Reg.3, SI 2004/1677 Reg.3, SI 2004/2996 Reg.3, Reg.4
Reg.4, amended: SI 2002/1974 Reg.3, SI 2004/2996 Reg.5
Reg.4, revoked (in part): SI 2004/2996 Reg.5
Reg.4A, added: SI 2002/3158 Reg.3
Reg.4B, added: SI 2002/3158 Reg.4
Reg.4C, added: SI 2004/2996 Reg.6
Reg.6, amended: SI 2003/2747 Reg.4
Reg.7, amended: SI 2002/1409 Art.7, SI 2003/2747 Reg.5, Reg.6, SI 2004/2996 Reg.7, Reg.8, Reg.9, Reg.10, Reg.11
Reg.8, amended: SI 2003/2747 Reg.7, SI 2004/2996 Reg.12
Reg.9, amended: SI 2004/2996 Reg.13
Reg.12, amended: SI 2002/3158 Reg.5, SI 2003/2155 Sch.1 para.24
Reg.12, revoked (in part): SI 2002/1974 Reg.4
Reg.13, revoked (in part): SI 2002/1974 Reg.5, SI 2002/3158 Reg.6
Reg.14, amended: SI 2004/2996 Reg.14
Reg.14, revoked (in part): SI 2004/2996 Reg.14
Reg.20, amended: SI 2003/2096 Sch.1 para.73
Reg.22, amended: SI 2004/2996 Reg.15

1998-cont.

1870. Individual Savings Account Regulations 1998–*cont.*

Reg.23, amended: SI 2004/2996 Reg.16

Reg.25, amended: SI 2004/2996 Reg.17

Reg.31, amended: SI 2002/3158 Reg.7, SI 2003/2747 Reg.8, SI 2004/2996 Reg.18

Reg.31, revoked (in part): SI 2004/2996 Reg.19

Reg.35, amended: SI 2002/453 Reg.4, SI 2004/2996 Reg.20, Reg.21

Reg.36, amended: SI 2002/453 Reg.5, SI 2004/2996 Reg.22

Reg.36, revoked (in part): SI 2002/453 Reg.5

Reg.36, varied: SI 2002/3158 Reg.8

1871. Individual Savings Account (Insurance Companies) Regulations 1998

Reg.13, revoked (in part): SI 2004/2680 Reg.22

Reg.15, revoked: SI 2004/2680 Reg.22

Reg.16, revoked: SI 2004/2680 Reg.22

1878. School Standards and Framework Act 1998 (Education Action Zones) (Modification) Regulations 1998

revoked (in part): SI 2003/2694 Sch.1 Part 1

1881. Special Immigration Appeals Commission (Procedure) Rules 1998

applied: SI 2003/1034 r.56

revoked: SI 2003/1034 r.55

1885. Education (National Curriculum) (Attainment Targets and Programmes of Study in Geography) (Wales) Order 1998

revoked: 2002 c.32 Sch.22 Part 3

1886. Education (National Curriculum) (Attainment Targets and Programmes of Study in Art) (Wales) Order 1998

revoked: 2002 c.32 Sch.22 Part 3

1888. Education (National Curriculum) (Attainment Targets and Programmes of Study in History) (Wales) Order 1998

revoked: 2002 c.32 Sch.22 Part 3

1889. Education (National Curriculum) (Attainment Targets and Programmes of Study in Music) (Wales) Order 1998

revoked: 2002 c.32 Sch.22 Part 3

1890. Education (National Curriculum) (Attainment Targets and Programmes of Study in Technology) (Wales) Order 1998

revoked: 2002 c.32 Sch.22 Part 3

1891. Income Tax (Employments) (Notional Payments) (Amendment) Regulations 1998

revoked: SI 2003/2682 Sch.2

Reg.4, revoked: 2003 c.1 Sch.8 Part 2

Reg.5, revoked: 2003 c.1 Sch.8 Part 2

Reg.6, revoked: 2003 c.1 Sch.8 Part 2

1998-cont.

1908. Dartford-Thurrock Crossing Regulations 1998

Reg.1, amended: SI 2003/496 Reg.2

Reg.3, amended: SI 2003/496 Reg.2

Reg.4, amended: SI 2003/496 Reg.2

Reg.5, amended: SI 2003/496 Reg.2, SI 2004/1441 Reg.2

Reg.8, amended: SI 2003/496 Reg.2

1936. Greater Manchester (Light Rapid Transit System) (Ashton-under-Lyne Extension) Order 1998

Art.2, amended: SI 2003/2155 Sch.2

Art.5, amended: SI 2003/2155 Sch.1 para.18

Art.12, amended: SI 2003/2155 Sch.1 para.18

Sch.10 para.1, amended: SI 2003/2155 Sch.1 para.17, Sch.2

1937. Local Authorities (Capital Finance) (Amendment No 3) Regulations 1998

Reg.12, revoked (in part): SI 2004/2044 Art.4

1938. Scottish Legal Aid Board (Employment of Solicitors to Provide Criminal Legal Assistance) Regulations 1998

Reg.3, revoked (in part): SSI 2003/511 Reg.3

1943. Education (Infant Class Sizes) (Wales) Regulations 1998

Reg.2, amended: SI 2003/2959 Reg.10

Reg.3, amended: SI 2003/2959 Reg.10

1947. Education (Infant Class Sizes) (Transitional Provisions) Regulations 1998

revoked (in part): SI 2003/2694 Sch.1 Part 2

1948. Education Act 1996 (Infant Class Sizes) (Modification) Regulations 1998

revoked (in part): SI 2003/2694 Sch.1 Part 2

1964. Education Action Forum (Proceedings) Regulations 1998

Reg.6, substituted: SI 2002/2301 Reg.2

1968. School Standards and Framework Act 1998 (Infant Class Sizes) (Modification) Regulations 1998

revoked (in part): SI 2003/2694 Sch.1 Part 2

1976. Education (National Curriculum) (Key Stage 3 Assessment Arrangements) (Wales) (Amendment) Order 1998

revoked: 2002 c.32 Sch.22 Part 3

1977. Education (National Curriculum) (Assessment Arrangements for English, Welsh, Mathematics and Science) (Key Stage 2) (Wales) (Amendment) Order 1998

revoked: 2002 c.32 Sch.22 Part 3, SI 2004/2915 Art.2

1986. Education (National Curriculum) (Attainment Targets and Programmes of Study in Technology) (England) Order 1998

revoked: 2002 c.32 Sch.22 Part 3

NO.

1998–cont.

1987. Education (National Curriculum) (Attainment Targets and Programmes of Study in Physical Education) (England) Order 1998

revoked: 2002 c.32 Sch.22 Part 3

1988. Education (National Curriculum) (Attainment Targets and Programmes of Study in History) (England) Order 1998

revoked: 2002 c.32 Sch.22 Part 3

1989. Education (National Curriculum) (Attainment Targets and Programmes of Study in Geography) (England) Order 1998

revoked: 2002 c.32 Sch.22 Part 3

1990. Education (National Curriculum) (Attainment Targets and Programmes of Study in Art) (England) Order 1998

revoked: 2002 c.32 Sch.22 Part 3

1991. Education (National Curriculum) (Attainment Targets and Programmes of Study in Music) (England) Order 1998

revoked: 2002 c.32 Sch.22 Part 3

1992. Harrow and Hillingdon Healthcare National Health Service Trust (Establishment) Amendment Order 1998

revoked: 2003 c.43 s.7

1998. National Health Service (Primary Care) Act 1997 (Commencement No 5) Order 1998

Art.3, revoked (in part): SI 2004/287 Art.4

2003. Education (Student Support) Regulations 1998

applied: SI 2002/3200 Reg.3

2021. Education (National Curriculum) (Exceptions at Key Stage 4) Regulations 1998

revoked: 2002 c.32 Sch.22 Part 3

2033. Cardiff Community Healthcare National Health Service Trust (Establishment) Amendment Order 1998

revoked: 2003 c.43 s.7

2034. East Glamorgan National Health Service Trust (Establishment) Amendment Order 1998

revoked: 2003 c.43 s.7

2051. Motor Vehicles (EC Type Approval) Regulations 1998

Reg.3, amended: SI 2002/1835 Reg.2, SI 2004/2186 Reg.3

Sch.1, amended: SI 2002/1835 Reg.3, SI 2002/2743 Reg.2, SI 2003/1019 Reg.2, SI 2003/2428 Reg.2, SI 2004/73 Reg.2, SI 2004/2186 Reg.4, Reg.5

2070. Merchant Shipping (Radio Installations) Regulations 1998

Reg.3, amended: SI 2004/302 Sch.1 para.8

NO.

1998–cont.

2115. School Standards and Framework Act 1998 (School Teachers Pay and Conditions) (Transitional Provisions) Regulations 1998

revoked (in part): SI 2003/2694 Sch.1 Part 2

2116. Mid Essex Hospital Services National Health Service Trust (Establishment) Amendment Order 1998

revoked: 2003 c.43 s.7

2153. Gaming (Bingo) Act (Variation of Monetary Limit) Order 1998

revoked: SI 2002/1909 Art.3

2159. District of Purbeck (Electoral Changes) Order 1998

varied: SI 2004/222 Art.2

2197. Service Subsidy Agreements (Tendering) (Amendment) Regulations 1998

revoked (in part): SI 2002/2090 Sch.2

2220. Education (Further Education Institutions Information) (England) (Amendment) Regulations 1998

revoked: SI 2003/51 Reg.2

2223. Dental Practice Boards (Personal Dental Services) Regulations 1998

Reg.2, amended: SI 2002/2469 Sch.1 para.81, Sch.5

Reg.5, amended: SI 2002/2469 Sch.5

2224. National Health Service (Pilot Schemes for Personal Dental Services Miscellaneous Provisions and Consequential Amendments) Regulations 1998

Reg.2, amended: SI 2002/2469 Sch.6

2230. School Standards and Framework Act 1998 (Admissions) (Modifications) Regulations 1998

revoked (in part): SI 2003/2694 Sch.1 Part 2

2231. Social Security (Welfare to Work) Regulations 1998

Reg.9, revoked: SI 2004/154 Reg.3

2248. School Standards and Framework Act 1998 (Intervention in Schools Causing Concern) (Modification) Regulations 1998

revoked (in part): SI 2003/2694 Sch.1 Part 2

2249. Motor Vehicles (Authorisation of Special Types) (Amendment) Order 1998

revoked: SI 2003/1998 Art.2

2251. High Court of Justiciary (Proceedings in the Netherlands) (United Nations) Order 1998

Art.3, see *HM Advocate v Al-Megrahi (No.5)* 2002 J.C. 38 (HCJ Appeal), Lord Kirkwood, Lord Carloway, Lord Hamilton, Lord Nimmo Smith, Lord Wheatley

2258. National Health Service (Dental Charges) (Scotland) Amendment (No.2) Regulations 1998

revoked: SSI 2003/158 Sch.4

NO.

1998–cont.

2306. Provision and Use of Work Equipment Regulations 1998
applied: SI 2002/2776 Reg.5
referred to: SI 2003/2002 Reg.12
see *Delaney v McGregor Construction (Highlands) Ltd* 2003 Rep. L.R. 56 (OH), Lady Paton
Reg.10, amended: SI 2002/2174 Reg.7
Reg.11, amended: SI 2002/2174 Reg.7
Reg.11, see *R. v Colthrop Board Mills Ltd* [2002] EWCA Crim 520, [2002] 2 Cr. App. R. (S.) 80 (CA (Crim Div)), Gibbs, J.
Reg.18, amended: SI 2002/2174 Reg.7
Reg.35, amended: SI 2002/2174 Reg.7
Sch.1, amended: SI 2004/129 Reg.32

2307. Lifting Operations and Lifting Equipment Regulations 1998
referred to: SI 2003/2002 Reg.12
see *Delaney v McGregor Construction (Highlands) Ltd* 2003 Rep. L.R. 56 (OH), Lady Paton
Reg.2, amended: SI 2002/2174 Reg.8
Reg.3, amended: SI 2002/2174 Reg.8

2310. Stockport Healthcare National Health Service Trust (Establishment) Amendment Order 1998
revoked: 2003 c.43 s.7

2313. Compulsory Purchase by Public Authorities (Inquiries Procedure) (Scotland) Rules 1998
r.3, amended: SSI 2003/503 Sch.1 para.18

2314. Sports Grounds and Sporting Events (Designation) (Scotland) Order 1998
revoked: SSI 2004/356 Sch.3
Sch.1 Part I, amended: SSI 2002/382 Art.2

2333. Borough of Boston (Electoral Changes) Order 1998
varied: SI 2004/222 Art.2

2334. City of Lincoln (Electoral Changes) Order 1998
varied: SI 2004/222 Art.2

2335. District of East Lindsey (Electoral Changes) Order 1998
varied: SI 2004/222 Art.2

2336. District of South Holland (Electoral Changes) Order 1998
varied: SI 2004/222 Art.2

2337. District of South Kesteven (Electoral Changes) Order 1998
varied: SI 2004/222 Art.2

2338. District of North Kesteven (Parishes and Electoral Changes) Order 1998
varied: SI 2004/222 Art.2

2342. District of Wansbeck (Electoral Changes) Order 1998
varied: SI 2004/222 Art.2

2343. District of Tynedale (Electoral Changes) Order 1998
varied: SI 2004/222 Art.2

NO.

1998–cont.

2344. Borough of Castle Morpeth (Electoral Changes) Order 1998
varied: SI 2004/222 Art.2

2345. Borough of Blyth Valley (Electoral Changes) Order 1998
varied: SI 2004/222 Art.2

2346. Borough of Berwick-upon-Tweed (Electoral Changes) Order 1998
varied: SI 2004/222 Art.2

2347. District of Alnwick (Electoral Changes) Order 1998
varied: SI 2004/222 Art.2

2353. Electricity (Non-Fossil Fuel Sources) (England and Wales) Order 1998
Sch.1, referred to: SSI 2004/170 Art.8

2366. District of West Lindsey (Electoral Changes) Order 1998
varied: SI 2004/222 Art.2

2367. Horse Passports (Amendment) Order 1998
revoked (in part): SI 2003/2780 Reg.25

2405. Specified Risk Material (Amendment) Regulations 1998
revoked (in part): SSI 2002/255 Sch.9 Part I

2409. Prohibition of Keeping or Release of Live Fish (Specified Species) Order 1998
Art.2, amended: SI 2003/25 Art.2, SI 2003/416 Art.2
Sch.1, referred to: SI 2003/416 Art.2
Sch.1, substituted: SI 2003/25 Art.2, SI 2003/416 Sch.1

2411. Merchant Shipping and Fishing Vessels (Health and Safety at Work) (Employment of Young Persons) Regulations 1998
Reg.2, amended: SI 2002/2125 Sch.2 para.4
Reg.6, amended: SI 2002/2125 Sch.2 para.4
Reg.6, referred to: SI 2002/2125 Reg.5
Reg.6, revoked (in part): SI 2002/2125 Sch.2 para.4
Reg.8, amended: SI 2002/3135 Sch.1 para.40

2417. National Health Service (Travelling Expenses and Remission of Charges) Amendment Regulations 1998
revoked: SI 2003/2382 Sch.2

2428. Medicines (Products for Animal Use-Fees) Regulations 1998
revoked: SI 2004/2750 Reg.18
Reg.2, amended: SI 2003/2957 Reg.2, Sch.1
Reg.3, substituted: SI 2003/2957 Reg.2
Reg.12, amended: SI 2002/2569 Sch.1, SI 2003/2957 Reg.2
Reg.13, amended: SI 2002/2569 Sch.1, SI 2003/2957 Reg.2
Reg.14, amended: SI 2003/2957 Reg.2
Reg.15, amended: SI 2003/2957 Reg.2
Reg.16, amended: SI 2003/2957 Reg.2
Reg.17, amended: SI 2003/2957 Reg.2
Reg.19, amended: SI 2003/2957 Reg.2

NO.

1998–cont.

2428. Medicines (Products for Animal Use-Fees) Regulations 1998–cont.

Sch.1 Part I, amended: SI 2003/2957 Sch.2

Sch.1 Part I, substituted: SI 2003/2957 Sch.2

Sch.1 Part II para.1, amended: SI 2002/2569 Sch.1, SI 2003/2957 Reg.3, Sch.4

Sch.1 Part II para.2, amended: SI 2002/2569 Sch.1, SI 2003/2957 Reg.3, Sch.4

Sch.1 Part II para.3, amended: SI 2002/2569 Sch.1, SI 2003/2957 Reg.3, Sch.4

Sch.1 Part II para.4, amended: SI 2003/2957 Reg.3

Sch.1 Part II para.5, amended: SI 2003/2957 Reg.3

Sch.1 Part II para.6, amended: SI 2002/2569 Sch.1, SI 2003/2957 Reg.3, Sch.4

Sch.1 Part II para.7, amended: SI 2002/2569 Sch.1, SI 2003/2957 Reg.3, Sch.4

Sch.1 Part II para.8, amended: SI 2002/2569 Sch.1, SI 2003/2957 Reg.3

Sch.1 Part II para.9, amended: SI 2002/2569 Sch.1, SI 2003/2957 Reg.3, Sch.4

Sch.1 Part II para.10, added: SI 2003/2957 Reg.3

Sch.1 Part II para.10, amended: SI 2003/2957 Reg.3

Sch.1 Part III para.4, amended: SI 2002/2569 Sch.1, SI 2003/2957 Sch.4

Sch.1 Part III para.5, amended: SI 2002/2569 Sch.1, SI 2003/2957 Sch.4

Sch.1 Part IV para.1, amended: SI 2002/2569 Sch.1, SI 2003/2957 Sch.4

Sch.1 Part IV para.2, amended: SI 2002/2569 Sch.1, SI 2003/2957 Sch.4

Sch.1 Part IV para.3, amended: SI 2002/2569 Sch.1, SI 2003/2957 Sch.3

Sch.1 Part IV para.4, substituted: SI 2003/2957 Reg.3

Sch.1 Part IV para.5, amended: SI 2002/2569 Sch.1, SI 2003/2957 Sch.4

Sch.1 Part IV para.6, amended: SI 2002/2569 Sch.1, SI 2003/2957 Sch.4

Sch.1 Part IV para.7, amended: SI 2002/2569 Sch.1, SI 2003/2957 Sch.4

Sch.1 Part V para.1, amended: SI 2002/2569 Sch.1, SI 2003/2957 Sch.4

Sch.1 Part V para.2, amended: SI 2002/2569 Sch.1, SI 2003/2957 Sch.4

Sch.1 Part V para.3, amended: SI 2002/2569 Sch.1, SI 2003/2957 Sch.4

Sch.1 Part V para.4, substituted: SI 2003/2957 Reg.3

Sch.2 para.2, amended: SI 2002/2569 Sch.1, SI 2003/2957 Sch.4

Sch.2 para.3, amended: SI 2002/2569 Sch.1, SI 2003/2957 Sch.4

Sch.3 Part II para.1, amended: SI 2002/2569 Reg.2, SI 2003/2957 Reg.3

Sch.3 Part II para.2, amended: SI 2002/2569 Reg.2

Sch.3 Part III, amended: SI 2002/2569 Reg.2

NO.

1998–cont.

2428. Medicines (Products for Animal Use-Fees) Regulations 1998–cont.

Sch.5 Part I, amended: SI 2003/2957 Reg.3

Sch.5 Part II para.1, amended: SI 2002/2569 Sch.1, SI 2003/2957 Sch.4

Sch.5 Part II para.2, amended: SI 2002/2569 Sch.1, SI 2003/2957 Reg.3, Sch.4

Sch.6 para.1, amended: SI 2002/2569 Sch.1, SI 2003/2957 Sch.4

Sch.6 para.2, amended: SI 2002/2569 Sch.1, SI 2003/2957 Sch.4

Sch.6 para.2A, added: SI 2003/2957 Reg.3

Sch.7 para.4, amended: SI 2003/2957 Reg.3

2431. Specified Risk Material (Coming into Force Date) (Amendment) Regulations 1998

revoked (in part): SSI 2002/255 Sch.9 Part I

2451. Gas Safety (Installation and Use) Regulations 1998

applied: SI 2002/2776 Reg.3

Reg.3, referred to: SI 2002/440 Sch.1

2452. Crime and Disorder Strategies (Prescribed Descriptions) Order 1998

revoked (in part): SI 2004/118 Art.4

2456. Rail Vehicle Accessibility Regulations 1998

applied: SI 2002/285 Art.4

referred to: SI 2002/656 Art.2, Art.4, SI 2002/657 Art.2, Art.4, SI 2002/1694 Art.4, SI 2002/1699 Art.2, SI 2003/1562 Art.2, SI 2003/1687 Art.2, SI 2004/955 Art.2, SI 2004/1410 Art.2, SI 2004/2180 Art.2

Reg.4, disapplied: SI 2002/285 Art.4, SI 2002/656 Art.4, SI 2002/657 Art.4, SI 2002/1694 Art.4, SI 2002/2873 Art.4, SI 2003/1436 Art.3

Reg.4, referred to: SI 2002/656 Art.6, SI 2002/1188 Art.4, SI 2003/1687 Art.3, SI 2003/2408 Art.3

Reg.5, applied: SI 2002/656 Art.5

Reg.5, disapplied: SI 2002/656 Art.4

Reg.5, referred to: SI 2002/656 Art.5, Art.6

Reg.6, disapplied: SI 2002/656 Art.4, SI 2002/1694 Art.4, SI 2002/1699 Art.3, Art.6, Art.7, SI 2002/2873 Art.4, SI 2003/1436 Art.3

Reg.6, referred to: SI 2002/656 Art.6, SI 2002/1699 Art.9, SI 2004/1205 Art.3

Reg.7, applied: SI 2004/954 Art.3

Reg.7, disapplied: SI 2002/1694 Art.4, SI 2003/1436 Art.3, SI 2004/955 Art.3, Art.4

Reg.7, referred to: SI 2004/954 Art.4, SI 2004/955 Art.6

Reg.8, applied: SI 2004/1410 Art.3

Reg.8, disapplied: SI 2002/285 Art.4, SI 2002/1694 Art.4, SI 2003/1436 Art.3, SI 2003/1704 Art.4

Reg.8, referred to: SI 2003/1687 Art.3, Art.4, SI 2004/1205 Art.3, SI 2004/1410 Art.5

1998–cont.

2456. Rail Vehicle Accessibility Regulations 1998–*cont.*

Reg.10, referred to: SI 2002/1188 Art.4, SI 2004/1205 Art.3

Reg.11, disapplied: SI 2002/656 Art.4, SI 2002/1694 Art.4, SI 2002/2873 Art.4, SI 2003/1436 Art.3

Reg.11, referred to: SI 2002/656 Art.6, SI 2002/1188 Art.4, SI 2003/1687 Art.3, Art.5, SI 2003/2408 Art.3, SI 2004/1205 Art.3

Reg.12, applied: SI 2004/954 Art.3

Reg.12, disapplied: SI 2002/1694 Art.4, SI 2002/1699 Art.4, Art.6, SI 2003/1436 Art.3

Reg.12, referred to: SI 2002/1188 Art.4, SI 2002/1699 Art.9, SI 2003/1687 Art.3, SI 2004/954 Art.4

Reg.13, disapplied: SI 2002/285 Art.4, SI 2002/656 Art.4, SI 2002/657 Art.4, SI 2002/1617 Art.3, SI 2002/1694 Art.4, SI 2002/2873 Art.4, SI 2003/1436 Art.3

Reg.13, referred to: SI 2002/656 Art.6, SI 2002/1188 Art.4, SI 2003/1687 Art.3, Art.6, Art.9, SI 2003/2408 Art.3, SI 2004/1205 Art.3

Reg.14, applied: SI 2004/954 Art.3, SI 2004/1410 Art.3

Reg.14, disapplied: SI 2003/1562 Art.3, SI 2003/1704 Art.3

Reg.14, referred to: SI 2003/1562 Art.4, SI 2003/1704 Art.5, Art.9, SI 2004/954 Art.3, Art.4, SI 2004/1410 Art.5, SI 2004/2180 Art.3

Reg.15, disapplied: SI 2003/1436 Art.3

Reg.15, referred to: SI 2003/1687 Art.3

Reg.16, disapplied: SI 2002/285 Art.4, SI 2002/1694 Art.4, SI 2002/2873 Art.4

Reg.16, referred to: SI 2002/1188 Art.4, SI 2002/2873 Art.5, SI 2003/2408 Art.3, SI 2004/1302 Art.3, Art.5

Reg.18, disapplied: SI 2002/1699 Art.5, Art.7, SI 2002/2873 Art.4

Reg.18, referred to: SI 2002/1699 Art.9

Reg.19, disapplied: SI 2002/285 Art.4, SI 2002/1694 Art.4, SI 2002/2873 Art.4, SI 2003/1704 Art.3

Reg.19, referred to: SI 2002/1188 Art.4

Reg.20, applied: SI 2003/1562 Art.3, SI 2003/1704 Art.3, Art.5, SI 2004/954 Art.3, SI 2004/955 Art.5, SI 2004/1410 Art.3, SI 2004/2180 Art.3

Reg.20, disapplied: SI 2002/656 Art.4, SI 2003/1704 Art.3, SI 2004/955 Art.3, Art.4

Reg.20, referred to: SI 2002/656 Art.6, SI 2004/955 Art.6

Reg.23, applied: SI 2002/2873 Art.6

Reg.23, disapplied: SI 2002/2873 Art.4

Reg.23, referred to: SI 2002/1188 Art.4, SI 2002/2873 Art.6, SI 2004/1205 Art.3, Art.4

1998–cont.

2461. Borough of Taunton Deane (Electoral Changes) Order 1998

varied: SI 2004/222 Art.2

2462. District of South Somerset (Electoral Changes) Order 1998

varied: SI 2004/222 Art.2

2463. District of West Somerset (Electoral Changes) Order 1998

varied: SI 2004/222 Art.2

2464. District of Mendip (Electoral Changes) Order 1998

varied: SI 2004/222 Art.2

2465. District of Sedgemoor (Electoral Changes) Order 1998

varied: SI 2004/222 Art.2

2478. Leeds Community and Mental Health Services Teaching National Health Service Trust (Establishment) Amendment (No.2) Order 1998

revoked: 2003 c.43 s.7

2482. Late Payment of Commercial Debts (Interest) (Legal Aid Exceptions) Order 1998

revoked (in part): SI 2002/1674 Reg.4, SSI 2002/335 Reg.2

2484. Income Tax (Employments) (Amendment) Regulations 1998

revoked: SI 2003/2682 Sch.2

2485. East Yorkshire Hospitals National Health Service Trust (Establishment) Amendment Order 1998

revoked: 2003 c.43 s.7

2486. Bromley Hospitals National Health Service Trust (Establishment) Amendment (No.2) Order 1998

revoked: 2003 c.43 s.7

2487. District of South Hams (Electoral Changes) Order 1998

varied: SI 2004/222 Art.2

2506. Borough of Corby (Electoral Changes) Order 1998

varied: SI 2004/222 Art.2

2507. District of Daventry (Electoral Changes) Order 1998

varied: SI 2004/222 Art.2

2508. Borough of Kettering (Electoral Changes) Order 1998

varied: SI 2004/222 Art.2

2509. District of South Northamptonshire (Electoral Changes) Order 1998

varied: SI 2004/222 Art.2

2510. Borough of Wellingborough (Electoral Changes) Order 1998

varied: SI 2004/222 Art.2

2511. Borough of Northampton (Electoral Changes) Order 1998

varied: SI 2004/222 Art.2

2512. District of East Northamptonshire (Electoral Changes) Order 1998

varied: SI 2004/222 Art.2

1998–cont.

2513. Crime and Disorder Strategies (Prescribed Descriptions) (Amendment) Order 1998

revoked (in part): SI 2004/118 Art.4

2514. Merchant Shipping (Passenger Ship Construction Ships of Classes I, II and II(A)) Regulations 1998

Reg.2, amended: SI 2004/302 Sch.1 para.7

Reg.3, amended: SI 2004/302 Sch.1 para.7

Reg.44, amended: SI 2004/2884 Reg.11

Reg.75, amended: SI 2002/1650 Reg.2

Reg.91, amended: SI 2002/1650 Reg.2

2515. Merchant Shipping (Passenger Ship Construction Ships of Classes III to VI(A)) Regulations 1998

Reg.2, amended: SI 2004/302 Sch.1 para.6

Reg.3, amended: SI 2004/302 Sch.1 para.6

Reg.51, amended: SI 2002/1650 Reg.3

Reg.60, amended: SI 2002/1650 Reg.3

Reg.62, amended: SI 2002/1650 Reg.3

Reg.73, amended: SI 2002/1650 Reg.3

2526. Education (School Information) (England) Regulations 1998

revoked: SI 2002/2897 Reg.2

Reg.3, amended: SI 2002/1172 Reg.3

Reg.9, amended: SI 2002/1172 Reg.4

Reg.11, amended: SI 2002/1172 Reg.5

Sch.2 para.6, amended: SI 2002/1172 Reg.6

Sch.2 para.9, amended: SI 2002/1172 Reg.7

Sch.2 para.10, amended: SI 2002/1172 Reg.7

Sch.2 para.11, amended: SI 2002/1172 Reg.7

Sch.2 para.12, amended: SI 2002/1172 Reg.8

Sch.2 para.13, substituted: SI 2002/1172 Reg.9

Sch.3 para.2, amended: SI 2002/1172 Reg.10

2535. Religious Character of Schools (Designation Procedure) Regulations 1998

applied: SI 2004/764

referred to: SI 2003/800, SI 2003/2749, SI 2003/3259, SI 2003/3262, SI 2004/150, SI 2004/1160, SI 2004/1169, SI 2004/1513, SI 2004/1725, SI 2004/1734, SI 2004/1971, SI 2004/2474, SI 2004/2476, SI 2004/2477, SI 2004/2478, SI 2004/2564, SI 2004/2565, SI 2004/2698, SI 2004/2892

Reg.3, applied: SI 2003/1377 Reg.16

Reg.9, amended: SI 2003/1558 Reg.58

2536. Air Navigation (Dangerous Goods) (Third Amendment) Regulations 1998

revoked: SI 2002/2786 Sch.1

2547. District of Eden (Electoral Changes) Order 1998

varied: SI 2004/222 Art.2

2548. District of South Lakeland (Electoral Changes) Order 1998

varied: SI 2004/222 Art.2

2549. City of Carlisle (Electoral Changes) Order 1998

varied: SI 2004/222 Art.2

1998–cont.

2551. Borough of Broxbourne (Electoral Changes) Order 1998

varied: SI 2004/222 Art.2

2552. Borough of Dacorum (Electoral Changes) Order 1998

varied: SI 2004/222 Art.2

2553. District of East Hertfordshire (Electoral Changes) Order 1998

varied: SI 2004/222 Art.2

2554. Borough of Hertsmere (Electoral Changes) Order 1998

varied: SI 2004/222 Art.2

2555. District of North Hertfordshire (Electoral Changes) Order 1998

varied: SI 2004/222 Art.2

2556. District of Three Rivers (Parishes and Electoral Changes) Order 1998

varied: SI 2004/222 Art.2

2557. Borough of Stevenage (Electoral Changes) Order 1998

varied: SI 2004/222 Art.2

2558. City of St Albans (Electoral Changes) Order 1998

varied: SI 2004/222 Art.2

2559. Borough of Watford (Electoral Changes) Order 1998

varied: SI 2004/222 Art.2

2560. District of Welwyn Hatfield (Electoral Changes) Order 1998

varied: SI 2004/222 Art.2

2569. Borough of Allerdale (Electoral Changes) Order 1998

varied: SI 2004/222 Art.2

2570. Borough of Copeland (Electoral Changes) Order 1998

varied: SI 2004/222 Art.2

2571. Borough of Barrow-in-Furness (Electoral Changes) Order 1998

varied: SI 2004/222 Art.2

2573. Employers Liability (Compulsory Insurance) Regulations 1998

Sch.2 para.6, substituted: SI 2003/1615 Sch.1 para.53

Sch.2 para.15, added: SI 2004/2882 Reg.2

2576. Education (National Curriculum) (Attainment Targets and Programmes of Study in Welsh) (Amendment) Order 1998

revoked (in part): 2002 c.32 Sch.22 Part 3

2623. Nurses, Midwives and Health Visitors (Miscellaneous Amendments) Order 1998

varied: SI 2004/1762 Art.1

2647. Merchant Shipping (Carriage of Nautical Publications) Regulations 1998

revoked: SI 2002/1473 Sch.1 para.2

2649. Nurses, Midwives and Health Visitors (Midwives Amendment) Rules Approval Order 1998

varied: SI 2004/1762 Art.1

1998–cont.

2667. Dudley Priority Health National Health Service Trust (Establishment) Amendment Order 1998
revoked: 2003 c.43 s.7

2668. Act of Sederunt (Fees of Messengers-at-Arms) 1998
revoked: SSI 2002/566 Sch.2

2669. Act of Sederunt (Fees of Sheriff Officers) 1998
revoked: SSI 2002/567 Sch.2

2670. School Standards and Framework Act 1998 (Modification) Regulations 1998
Reg.2, revoked (in part): SI 2003/2694 Sch.1 Part 2
Reg.3, revoked (in part): SI 2003/2694 Sch.1 Part 2
Reg.4, revoked (in part): SI 2003/2694 Sch.1 Part 2
Reg.7, revoked (in part): SI 2003/2694 Sch.1 Part 2
Reg.8, revoked (in part): SI 2003/2694 Sch.1 Part 2
Reg.9, revoked (in part): SI 2003/2694 Sch.1 Part 2

2682. Magistrates Courts (Sex Offender and Anti-social Behaviour Orders) Rules 1998
revoked: SI 2002/2782 r.3
r.6, applied: SI 2002/2784 r.3
r.7, applied: SI 2002/2784 r.3
Sch.5, applied: SI 2002/2784 r.3
Sch.6, applied: SI 2002/2784 r.3

2699. City of Bristol (Electoral Changes) Order 1998
varied: SI 2004/222 Art.2

2700. District of Bath and North East Somerset (Electoral Changes) Order 1998
varied: SI 2004/222 Art.2

2701. District of South Gloucestershire (Electoral Changes) Order 1998
varied: SI 2004/222 Art.2

2702. District of North Somerset (Electoral Changes) Order 1998
varied: SI 2004/222 Art.2

2705. Education (Individual Pupils Achievements) (Information) (Wales) (Amendment) Regulations 1998
revoked: SI 2004/1026 Sch.5

2708. Protection of Wrecks (Designation No 2) Order 1998
revoked: SI 2004/2395 Sch.2 para.7

2709. Borders Primary Care National Health Service Trust (Establishment) Order 1998
revoked: SSI 2003/189 Sch.2

2710. Tayside Primary Care National Health Service Trust (Establishment) Order 1998
revoked: SSI 2004/107 Sch.2

1998–cont.

2711. Lothian Primary Care National Health Service Trust (Establishment) Order 1998
revoked: SSI 2004/107 Sch.2

2712. Fife Primary Care National Health Service Trust (Establishment) Order 1998
revoked: SSI 2003/448 Sch.2

2713. Forth Valley Primary Care National Health Service Trust (Establishment) Order 1998
revoked: SSI 2004/107 Sch.2

2714. Dumfries and Galloway Primary Care National Health Service Trust (Establishment) Order 1998
revoked: SSI 2003/189 Sch.2

2715. Ayrshire and Arran Primary Care National Health Service Trust (Establishment) Order 1998
revoked: SSI 2004/107 Sch.2

2716. Argyll and Clyde Acute Hospitals National Health Service Trust (Establishment) Order 1998
revoked: SSI 2003/325 Sch.2

2717. Lothian University Hospitals National Health Service Trust (Establishment) Order 1998
revoked: SSI 2003/597 Sch.1

2718. Grampian University Hospitals National Health Service Trust (Establishment) Order 1998
revoked: SSI 2004/107 Sch.2

2719. Greater Glasgow Primary Care National Health Service Trust (Establishment) Order 1998
revoked: SSI 2004/107 Sch.2

2720. Grampian Primary Care National Health Service Trust (Establishment) Order 1998
revoked: SSI 2004/107 Sch.2

2721. Highland Primary Care National Health Service Trust (Establishment) Order 1998
revoked: SSI 2004/107 Sch.2

2722. Highland Acute Hospitals National Health Service Trust (Establishment) Order 1998
revoked: SSI 2004/107 Sch.2

2723. Fife Acute Hospitals National Health Service Trust (Establishment) Order 1998
revoked: SSI 2003/448 Sch.2

2724. Lanarkshire Acute Hospitals National Health Service Trust (Establishment) Order 1998
revoked: SSI 2004/107 Sch.2

2725. Forth Valley Acute Hospitals National Health Service Trust (Establishment) Order 1998
revoked: SSI 2004/107 Sch.2

NO.

1998–cont.

2728. Tayside University Hospitals National Health Service Trust (Establishment) Order 1998

revoked: SSI 2004/107 Sch.2

2729. North Glasgow University Hospitals National Health Service Trust (Establishment) Order 1998

revoked: SSI 2004/107 Sch.2

2730. South Glasgow University Hospitals National Health Service Trust (Establishment) Order 1998

revoked: SSI 2004/107 Sch.2

2731. West Lothian Healthcare National Health Service Trust (Establishment) Order 1998

revoked: SSI 2004/107 Sch.2

2732. Lanarkshire Primary Care National Health Service Trust (Establishment) Order 1998

revoked: SSI 2004/107 Sch.2

Art.3, amended: SSI 2003/259 Art.2

2733. Renfrewshire and Inverclyde Primary Care National Health Service Trust (Establishment) Order 1998

revoked: SSI 2003/325 Sch.2

2734. Lomond and Argyll Primary Care National Health Service Trust (Establishment) Order 1998

revoked: SSI 2003/325 Sch.2

2735. Ayrshire and Arran Acute Hospitals National Health Service Trust (Establishment) Order 1998

revoked: SSI 2004/107 Sch.2

2746. Groundwater Regulations 1998

applied: SSI 2003/129 Sch.2 para.3

referred to: SSI 2004/70 Sch.2 para.3

2763. Education (School Government) (Transition to New Framework) Regulations 1998

revoked (in part): SI 2003/348 Reg.2

2765. Late Payment of Commercial Debts (Rate of Interest) (No.2) Order 1998

revoked (in part): SI 2002/1675 Art.2, SSI 2002/336 Art.2

2771. Merchant Shipping (Vessels in Commercial Use for Sport or Pleasure) Regulations 1998

referred to: SI 2003/2950 Reg.3

Reg.4, referred to: SI 2004/302 Reg.3

Reg.5, referred to: SI 2004/302 Reg.3

Sch.1, amended: SI 2002/1473 Sch.1 para.6, Sch.2 para.5

Sch.2, amended: SI 2002/1473 Sch.1 para.6, Sch.2 para.5

2772. National Health Service (Travelling Expenses and Remission of Charges) (Scotland) Amendment Regulations 1998

revoked: SSI 2003/376 Sch.3 para.14

NO.

1998–cont.

2795. Health and Safety at Work (Amendment) (Northern Ireland) Order 1998

Sch.1 para.20, revoked (in part): SI 2003/418 Sch.3

2796. Local Government (Amendment) (Northern Ireland) Order 1998

revoked: SI 2003/412 Sch.5

2834. School Standards and Framework Act 1998 (Home-School Agreements) (Modification) Regulations 1998

revoked (in part): SI 2003/2694 Sch.1 Part 2

2837. London Ambulance Service National Health Service Trust (Establishment) Amendment Order 1998

revoked: 2003 c.43 s.7

2838. National Health Service (General Medical Services) Amendment (No.2) Regulations 1998

revoked (in part): SI 2004/865 Sch.2, SI 2004/1016 Sch.2

2839. Criminal Justice (Northern Ireland) Order 1998

Art.5, amended: SI 2003/1247 Art.33

2841. Hereford and Worcester Ambulance Service National Health Service Trust (Establishment) Amendment Order 1998

revoked: 2003 c.43 s.7

2843. Borough of Congleton (Electoral Changes) Order 1998

varied: SI 2004/222 Art.2

2844. Borough of Ellesmere Port &amp Neston (Electoral Changes) Order 1998

varied: SI 2004/222 Art.2

2845. Borough of Crewe and Nantwich (Electoral Changes) Order 1998

varied: SI 2004/222 Art.2

2846. Borough of Vale Royal (Electoral Changes) Order 1998

varied: SI 2004/222 Art.2

2847. Borough of Macclesfield (Electoral Changes) Order 1998

varied: SI 2004/222 Art.2

2866. City of Chester (Electoral Changes) Order 1998

varied: SI 2004/222 Art.2

2880. Charges for Inspections and Controls (Amendment) Regulations 1998

Reg.6, revoked (in part): SI 2002/457 Sch.4, SI 2002/897 Sch.4, SR 2002/88 Sch.4

2884. Motor Vehicles (Authorisation of Special Types) (Amendment) (No.2) Order 1998

revoked: SI 2003/1998 Art.2

2885. Carriage of Dangerous Goods (Amendment) Regulations 1998

revoked: SI 2004/568 Sch.14

NO.

1998–cont.

2888. Local Government Pension Scheme (Management and Investment of Funds) (Scotland) Regulations 1998
referred to: SSI 2003/138 Reg.2
Reg.9A, amended: SSI 2003/138 Reg.3
Reg.9A, applied: SSI 2003/138 Reg.5
Reg.9A, referred to: SSI 2003/138 Reg.5
Reg.11, amended: SSI 2004/134 Reg.3
Reg.11A, added: SSI 2004/134 Reg.3
Sch.1 Part I, substituted: SSI 2004/134 Sch.1 Part I
Sch.1 Part I para.1, substituted: SSI 2004/134 Sch.1 Part I
Sch.1 Part I para.2, substituted: SSI 2004/134 Sch.1 Part I
Sch.1 Part I para.3, substituted: SSI 2004/134 Sch.1 Part I
Sch.1 Part I para.4, substituted: SSI 2004/134 Sch.1 Part I
Sch.1 Part I para.5, substituted: SSI 2004/134 Sch.1 Part I
Sch.1 Part I para.6, substituted: SSI 2004/134 Sch.1 Part I
Sch.1 Part I para.7, substituted: SSI 2004/134 Sch.1 Part I
Sch.1 Part I para.8, substituted: SSI 2004/134 Sch.1 Part I
Sch.1 Part I para.9, substituted: SSI 2004/134 Sch.1 Part I
Sch.1 Part I para.9B, substituted: SSI 2004/134 Sch.1 Part I
Sch.1 Part I para.10, amended: SSI 2003/138 Reg.4
Sch.1 Part I para.10, substituted: SSI 2004/134 Sch.1 Part I
Sch.1 Part I para.11, substituted: SSI 2004/134 Sch.1 Part I
Sch.1 Part III para.15, amended: SSI 2003/138 Reg.4

2911. General Teaching Council for Wales Order 1998
Art.3, amended: SI 2002/2940 Art.2

2920. Life Assurance (Apportionment of Receipts of Participating Funds) (Applicable Percentage) (Amendment) Order 1998
revoked: SI 2003/1860 Art.3

2923. Chichester Priority Care Services National Health Service Trust (Change of Name) Order 1998
revoked: 2003 c.43 s.7

2927. Action Programme for Nitrate Vulnerable Zones (Scotland) Regulations 1998
revoked (in part): SSI 2003/51 Reg.9
Sch.1 para.15, revoked: SSI 2003/51 Reg.9

2947. Queen's Medical Centre, Nottingham, University Hospital National Health Service Trust (Establishment) Amendment Order 1998
revoked: 2003 c.43 s.7

NO.

1998–cont.

2948. Herefordshire Community Health National Health Service Trust (Establishment) Amendment Order 1998
revoked: 2003 c.43 s.7

2949. Warwickshire Ambulance Service National Health Service Trust (Establishment) Amendment Order 1998
revoked: 2003 c.43 s.7

2950. South Tees Acute Hospitals National Health Service Trust (Establishment) Amendment Order 1998
revoked: 2003 c.43 s.7

2963. Non-Domestic Rating (Rural Settlements) (Wales) Order 1998
Art.3, revoked: SI 2002/331 Art.5

2964. Riverside Mental Health, the North West London Mental Health and the West London Healthcare National Health Service Trusts (Dissolution) Order 1998
revoked: 2003 c.43 s.7

2965. Ealing, Hammersmith and Fulham Mental Health National Health Service Trust (Establishment) Order 1998
revoked: 2003 c.43 s.7

2966. Brent, Kensington &amp Chelsea and Westminster Mental Health National Health Service Trust (Establishment) Order 1998
revoked: 2003 c.43 s.7
Art.1, amended: SI 2002/1361 Art.2
Art.2, amended: SI 2002/1361 Art.2
Art.4, amended: SI 2002/1361 Art.3

2971. Electricity Supply (Amendment) Regulations 1998
revoked: SI 2002/2665 Sch.5

2972. North Staffordshire Combined Healthcare National Health Service Trust (Establishment) Amendment Order 1998
revoked: 2003 c.43 s.7

2997. Housing (Right to Buy) (Limits on Discount) Order 1998
referred to: SI 2003/498 Art.2
Art.3, amended: SI 2003/498 Art.3
Art.3A, added: SI 2003/498 Art.3
Sch.1, substituted: SI 2003/498 Art.3
Sch.2, added: SI 2003/498 Art.3

2998. Home Repair Assistance (Extension) Regulations 1998
revoked: SI 2002/1860 Sch.6

3039. Social Security (Claims and Payments) Amendment (No.2) Regulations 1998
revoked (in part): SI 2003/492 Sch.3 Part 1

NO.

NO.

1998–cont.

3068. Leicestershire Mental Health Service and the Fosse Health, Leicestershire Community National Health Service Trusts (Dissolution) Order 1998

revoked: 2003 c.43 s.7

3069. Leicestershire and Rutland Healthcare National Health Service Trust (Establishment) Order 1998

revoked: 2003 c.43 s.7

Art.3, substituted: SI 2002/1437 Art.3

3070. BSE Offspring Slaughter Regulations 1998

revoked (in part): SI 2002/843 Sch.9 Part I, SI 2002/1416 Sch.9 Part I, SSI 2002/255 Sch.9 Part I

3071. Bovine Spongiform Encephalopathy (No.2) (Amendment) Order 1998

revoked (in part): SSI 2002/255 Sch.9 Part I

3081. Controlled Foreign Companies (Excluded Countries) Regulations 1998

Reg.7, amended: SI 2002/1963 Reg.2

Reg.7, revoked (in part): SI 2002/1963 Reg.2

Sch.2 Part II, amended: SI 2002/2406 Reg.2

3082. Walsgrave Hospitals National Health Service Trust (Establishment) Amendment Order 1998

revoked: 2003 c.43 s.7

3088. Companies (Fees) (Amendment) Regulations 1998

revoked: SI 2004/2621 Sch.3

3090. M4 Motorway (London Borough of Hounslow) (Bus Lane) Order 1998

Art.2, amended: SI 2002/1672 Art.2

Art.3, amended: SI 2002/1672 Art.2

3094. Vehicle Excise Duty (Reduced Pollution) Regulations 1998

revoked: SI 2002/2742 Sch.1 Part I

Reg.14, amended: SI 2003/1814 Reg.2

3097. Education (Government of New Schools on Transition to New Framework) Regulations 1998

revoked (in part): SI 2003/1558 Reg.2

3098. Southampton Community Health Services National Health Service Trust (Establishment) Amendment Order 1998

revoked: 2003 c.43 s.7

3106. Chemicals (Hazard Information and Packaging for Supply) (Amendment) Regulations 1998

revoked: SI 2002/1689 Sch.7

3111. Road Vehicles (Authorised Weight) Regulations 1998

applied: SI 2003/1998 Art.40, Art.46, Art.50, Art.51, Art.52, Art.53, Sch.1 para.16, Sch.1 para.21, Sch.1 para.22, Sch.1 para.29, Sch.1 para.35, Sch.2 para.2, Sch.3 para.21, Sch.3 para.24, Sch.4 para.17, Sch.10 para.12, Sch.11 para.7, Sch.11 para.8

1998–cont.

3111. Road Vehicles (Authorised Weight) Regulations 1998–*cont.*

disapplied: SI 2003/1998 Sch.10 para.12

referred to: SI 2003/1998 Art.29, Art.35, Art.42, Art.49

varied: SI 2003/1998 Sch.1 para.28, Sch.11 para.7

Sch.1, applied: SI 2003/1998 Sch.1 para.28, Sch.10 para.9

Sch.1 para.1, varied: SI 2003/1998 Sch.10 para.9

Sch.1 para.2, varied: SI 2003/1998 Sch.10 para.9

Sch.3, applied: SI 2003/1998 Sch.1 para.29, Sch.10 para.10

Sch.3 para.1, varied: SI 2003/1998 Sch.1 para.29, Sch.10 para.10

Sch.3 para.2, varied: SI 2003/1998 Sch.1 para.29, Sch.10 para.10

Sch.3 para.3, varied: SI 2003/1998 Sch.1 para.29, Sch.10 para.10

Sch.3 para.4, varied: SI 2003/1998 Sch.1 para.29, Sch.10 para.10

3129. Building (Local Authority Charges) Regulations 1998

Reg.5, amended: SI 2004/533 Art.12

3130. School Standards and Framework Act 1998 (Admissions) (Modifications No 2) Regulations 1998

revoked (in part): SI 2003/2694 Sch.1 Part 2

3132. Civil Procedure Rules 1998

see *A (A Child) v Ministry of Defence* [2003] EWHC 849, [2003] P.I.Q.R. P33 (QBD), Bell, J.; see *Legal & General Assurance Society Ltd v CCA Stationery Ltd* [2003] EWHC 1491, [2003] Pens. L.R. 261 (Ch D), Etherton, J.; see *London & Argyll Developments Ltd v Mount Cook Land Ltd (No.1)* [2002] 50 E.G.C.S. 111 (Ch D), Peter Leaver Q.C.

applied: SI 2002/1985 Reg.24, SI 2003/1372 r.65, SI 2004/400 Reg.13, SI 2004/1861 Sch.1 para.41, Sch.4 para.10

referred to: SI 2002/3219 r.2, SI 2004/3129 r.2

see *Ahmed v Kennedy* [2002] EWCA Civ 1793, [2003] 1 W.L.R. 1820 (CA), Simon Brown, L.J.; see *Attorney General v Ebert* [2001] EWHC Admin 695, [2002] 2 All E.R. 789 (QBD (Admin Ct)), Brooke, L.J.; see *Cairnstores Ltd v Aktiebolaget Hassle* [2002] F.S.R. 35 (Pat Ct), Pumfrey, J.; see *CIL International Ltd v Vitrashop Ltd* [2002] F.S.R. 4 (Pat Ct), Pumfrey, J.; see *Cordle v Cordle* [2001] EWCA Civ 1791, [2002] 1 W.L.R. 1441 (CA), Thorpe, L.J.; see *Dendron GmbH v University of California (Parallel Proceedings: Use of Evidence)* [2004] EWHC 589, [2004] I.L.Pr. 35 (Pat Ct), Laddie, J.; see *Designers Guild Ltd v Russell Williams (Textiles) Ltd (t/a Washington DC) (Costs) (No.1)* [2003] 1

1998–cont.

3132. Civil Procedure Rules 1998–*cont.*

see–*cont.*

Costs L.R. 128 (HL), Judge not specified; see *Dunnett v Railtrack Plc* [2002] EWCA Civ 303, [2002] 1 W.L.R. 2434 (CA), Brooke, L.J.; see *English v Emery Reimbold & Strick Ltd* [2002] EWCA Civ 605, [2002] 1 W.L.R. 2409 (CA), Lord Phillips of Worth Matravers, M.R.; see *Halsey v Milton Keynes General NHS Trust* [2004] EWCA Civ 576, [2004] 1 W.L.R. 3002 (CA), Ward, L.J.; see *Highberry Ltd v Colt Telecom Group Plc (No.1)* [2002] EWHC 2503, [2003] 1 B.C.L.C. 290 (Ch D (Companies Court)), Lawrence Collins, J.; see *Hollins v Russell* [2003] EWCA Civ 718, [2003] 1 W.L.R. 2487 (CA), Brooke, L.J.; see *John v PricewaterhouseCoopers (formerly Price Waterhouse) (Costs)* [2002] 1 W.L.R. 953 (Ch D), Ferris, J.; see *Markem Corp v Zipher Ltd (No.2)* [2004] R.P.C. 11 (Pat Ct), Judge Fysh Q.C.; see *Montali v Goldman Sachs Services Ltd* [2002] I.C.R. 1251 (EAT), Judge Peter Clark; see *Paul Thomas Construction Ltd v Hyland* (2002) 18 Const. L.J. 345 (QBD (T&CC)), Judge Wilcox; see *Phoenix Finance Ltd v Federation International de l'Automobile (Costs)* [2002] EWHC 1242, [2003] C.P. Rep. 1 (Ch D), Sir Andrew Morritt V.C.; see *R. (on the application of Cowl) v Plymouth City Council* [2001] EWCA Civ 1935, [2002] 1 W.L.R. 803 (CA), Lord Woolf of Barnes, L.C.J.; see *Rouse v Freeman* Times, January 8, 2002 (QBD), Gross, J.; see *Sayers v SmithKline Beecham Plc* [2001] EWCA Civ 2017, [2002] 1 W.L.R. 2274 (CA), Longmore, L.J.; see *Scriven, Re* [2004] EWCA Civ 683, [2004] B.P.I.R. 972 (CA), Clarke, L.J.; see *Southward v Banham* [2002] B.P.I.R. 1253 (Ch D), Judge Weeks Q.C.; see *Van Aken v Camden LBC* [2002] EWCA Civ 1724, [2003] 1 W.L.R. 684 (CA), Jonathan Parker, L.J.; see *Various Ledward Claimants v Kent and Medway HA* [2003] EWHC 2551, [2004] 1 Costs L.R. 101 (QBD), Hallett, J.

see *Darrell v Miller* [2003] EWHC 2811, [2004] B.P.I.R. 470 (Ch D), Lewison, J.

Part 1, see *Norwich Union Linked Life Assurance Ltd v Mercantile Credit Co Ltd* [2003] EWHC 3064, [2004] 4 E.G.C.S. 109 (Ch D), David Richards, J

Part 1 r.1, see *Boyd & Hutchinson (A Firm) v Foenander* [2003] EWCA Civ 1516, [2004] B.P.I.R. 20 (CA), Chadwick, L.J.; see *Maresca v Motor Insurance Repair Research Centre* [2004] 4 All E.R. 254 (EAT), Rimer, J.; see *O'Brien v Chief Constable of South Wales* [2003] EWCA Civ 1085, [2004] C.P. Rep. 5 (CA), Brooke, L.J.

1998–cont.

3132. Civil Procedure Rules 1998–*cont.*

Part 1 r.1.1, see *ES v Chesterfield and North Derbyshire Royal Hospital NHS Trust* [2003] EWCA Civ 1284, [2004] C.P. Rep. 9 (CA), Brooke, L.J.; see *Hampshire Waste Services Ltd v Intending Trespassers upon Chineham Incinerator Site* [2003] EWHC 1738, [2004] Env. L.R. 9 (Ch D), Sir Andrew Morritt V.C.

Part 1 r.1.3, see *Reed Executive Plc v Reed Business Information Ltd (Costs: Alternative Dispute Resolution)* [2004] EWCA Civ 887, [2004] 1 W.L.R. 3026 (CA), Auld, L.J.; see *Tasyurdu v Immigration Appeal Tribunal* [2003] EWCA Civ 447, [2003] C.P. Rep. 61 (CA), Lord Phillips of Worth Matravers, M.R.

Part 1 r.31.12, see *Arsenal Football Club Plc v Elite Sports Distribution Ltd* [2002] EWHC 3057, [2003] F.S.R. 26 (Ch D), Geoffrey Vos Q.C.

Part 1 r.31.16, see *Arsenal Football Club Plc v Elite Sports Distribution Ltd* [2002] EWHC 3057, [2003] F.S.R. 26 (Ch D), Geoffrey Vos Q.C.

Part I Sch.1 r.31.22, see *Smithkline Beecham Plc v Apotex Europe Ltd* [2003] EWHC 127, (2003) 26(5) I.P.D. 26031 (Pat Ct), Laddie, J.

Part II, see *Siboti K/S v BP France SA* [2003] EWHC 1278, [2003] 2 Lloyd's Rep. 364 (QBD (Comm Ct)), Gross, J.

Part 2 r.2.1, amended: SI 2003/1242 r.3

Part 2 r.2.1, see *Contract Facilities Ltd v Rees Estate (Application to Strike Out)* [2003] EWCA Civ 1105, (2003) 147 S.J.L.B. 933 (CA), Waller, L.J.

Part 2 r.2.3, amended: SI 2004/2072 r.3

Part 2 r.2.8, see *Crichton v Wellingborough BC* [2002] EWHC 2988, [2004] Env. L.R. 11 (QBD (Admin Ct)), Gibbs, J.; see *Di Placito v Slater* [2003] EWHC 1233, [2003] W.T.L.R. 805 (Ch D), Launcelot Henderson Q.C.

Part 3, see *Reality Group Ltd v Chance* [2002] F.S.R. 13 (Ch D), Patten, J.; see *Totty v Snowden* [2001] EWCA Civ 1415, [2002] 1 W.L.R. 1384 (CA), Kay, L.J.

Part 3 r.3, see *B v H Bauer Publishing Ltd* [2002] E.M.L.R. 8 (QBD), Eady, J.; see *Independents Advantage Insurance Co v Personal Representatives of Cook (Deceased)* [2002] EWHC 2681, [2003] Lloyd's Rep. P.N. 109 (Ch D), Lloyd, J.; see *Maresca v Motor Insurance Repair Research Centre* [2004] 4 All E.R. 254 (EAT), Rimer, J.

Part 3 r.3.1, see *A v National Blood Authority (No. 2)* [2002] Lloyd's Rep. Med. 487 (QBD), Burton, J.; see *AB v Leeds Teaching Hospitals NHS Trust* [2003] EWHC 1034, [2003] 3 Costs L.R. 405 (QBD), Gage, J.; see *Ambrose v Kaye*

NO.

NO.

1998–cont.

3132. Civil Procedure Rules 1998–cont.

Part 3 r.3.1–cont.

[2002] EWCA Civ 91, [2002] C.P. Rep. 33 (CA), Chadwick, L.J.; see *CIBC MellonTrust Co v Mora Hotel Corp NV* [2002] EWCA Civ 1688, [2003] 1 All E.R. 564 (CA), Peter Gibson, L.J.; see *Citibank NA v Rafidian Bank* [2003] EWHC 1950, [2003] 2 All E.R. (Comm.) 1054 (QBD), Tugendhat, J.; see *Contract Facilities Ltd v Rees Estate (Application to Strike Out)* [2003] EWCA Civ 1105, (2003) 147 S.J.L.B. 933 (CA), Waller, L.J.; see *Luckies v Simons* [2002] EWHC 2504, [2003] 2 P. & C.R. 30 (Ch D), Judge Rich Q.C.; see *Nur Saed v Ealing Hospital NHS Trust* [2002] Lloyd's Rep. Med. 121 (QBD), Mackay, J.; see *Olatawura v Abiloye* [2002] EWCA Civ 998, [2003] 1 W.L.R. 275 (CA), Simon Brown, L.J.; see *R. (on the application of G) v Ealing LBC (No.2)* [2002] EWHC 250, Times, March 18, 2002 (QBD (Admin Ct)), Munby, J.; see *Reckitt Benkiser (UK) Ltd v Home Pairfum Ltd* [2004] EWHC 302, [2004] F.S.R. 37 (Ch D), Laddie, J.; see *Robert v Momentum Services Ltd* [2003] EWCA Civ 299, [2003] 1 W.L.R. 1577 (CA), Dyson, L.J.; see *Tarajan Overseas Ltd v Kaye* [2001] EWCA Civ 1859, Times, January 22, 2002 (CA), Tuckey, L.J.

Part 3 r.3.1.2, see *Kalmneft JSC v Glencore International AG* [2002] 1 All E.R. 76 (QBD (Comm Ct)), Colman, J.

Part 3 r.3.3, amended: SI 2004/2072 r.4

Part 3 r.3.3, see *Bhamjee v Forsdick* [2003] EWCA Civ 1113, [2004] 1 W.L.R. 88 (CA), Lord Phillips of Worth Matravers, M.R.; see *Orford v Rasmi Electronics Ltd* [2002] EWCA Civ 1672, [2003] C.P.L.R. 213 (CA), Bodey, J.

Part 3 r.3.4, amended: SI 2004/2072 r.5

Part 3 r.3.4, see *Atlasview Ltd v Brightview Ltd* [2004] EWHC 1056, [2004] 2 B.C.L.C. 191 (Ch D (Companies Ct)), Jonathan Crow; see *Bhamjee v Forsdick* [2003] EWCA Civ 1113, [2004] 1 W.L.R. 88 (CA), Lord Phillips of Worth Matravers, M.R.; see *Bowthorpe Holdings Ltd v Hills* [2002] EWHC 2331, [2003] 1 B.C.L.C. 226 (Ch D), Sir Andrew Morritt V.C.; see *Independents Advantage Insurance Co v Personal Representatives of Cook (Deceased)* [2003] EWCA Civ 1103, [2004] P.N.L.R. 3 (CA), Chadwick, L.J.; see *Kaberry v Freethcartwright (A Firm) (formerly Freeth Cartwright Hunt Dickens) (No.1)* [2003] B.P.I.R. 606 (QBD), Douglas Brown, J.; see *Meherali v Hampshire CC* [2002] EWHC 2655, [2003] E.L.R. 338 (QBD), Judge Zucker Q.C.; see *Popek v National Westminster Bank Plc* [2002] EWCA Civ 42, [2002] C.P.L.R. 370 (CA), Dyson, L.J.; see

1998–cont.

3132. Civil Procedure Rules 1998–cont.

Part 3 r.3.4–cont.

Reckitt Benkiser (UK) Ltd v Home Pairfum Ltd [2004] EWHC 302, [2004] F.S.R. 37 (Ch D), Laddie, J.; see *Robert v Momentum Services Ltd* [2003] EWCA Civ 299, [2003] 1 W.L.R. 1577 (CA), Dyson, L.J.; see *Taylor v Anderson* [2002] EWCA Civ 1680, [2003] R.T.R. 21 (CA), Chadwick, L.J.; see *Temseel Holdings Ltd v Beaumonts Chartered Accountants* [2002] EWHC 2642, [2003] P.N.L.R. 27 (QBD (Comm Ct)), Tomlinson, J.; see *Thames Trains Ltd v Health and Safety Executive* [2002] EWHC 1415, [2003] P.I.Q.R. P14 (QBD), Morland, J.

Part 3 r.3.4.2, see *Man Nutzfahrzeuge AG v Ernst & Young* [2003] EWHC 2245, [2004] P.N.L.R. 19 (QBD (Comm Ct)), Cooke, J.

Part 3 r.3.7, amended: SI 2002/2058 r.3, SI 2003/1242 r.4

Part 3 r.3.9, see *Audergon v La Baguette Ltd* [2002] EWCA Civ 10, [2002] C.P. Rep. 27 (CA), Jonathan Parker, L.J.; see *Citibank NA v Rafidian Bank* [2003] EWHC 1950, [2003] 2 All E.R. (Comm.) 1054 (QBD), Tugendhat, J.; see *Flaxman-Binns v Lincolnshire CC* [2004] EWCA Civ 424, [2004] 1 W.L.R. 2232 (CA), Lord Phillips of Worth Matravers, M.R.; see *Grupo Torras SA v Al-Sabah (Costs)* [2003] EWHC 262, [2003] 2 Costs L.R. 294 (QBD), Treacy, J.; see *Hansom v E Rex Makin & Co* [2003] EWCA Civ 1801, (2004) 148 S.J.L.B. 57 (CA), Mance, L.J.; see *Meredith v Colleys Valuation Services Ltd* [2001] EWCA Civ 1456, [2002] C.P. Rep. 10 (CA), Peter Gibson, L.J.; see *Parnall v Hurst* [2003] W.T.L.R. 997 (Ch D), Peter Langan Q.C.; see *Price v Price (t/a Poppyland Headware)* [2003] EWCA Civ 888, [2003] 3 All E.R. 911 (CA), Brooke, L.J.; see *RC Residuals Ltd (formerly Regent Chemicals Ltd) v Linton Fuel Oils Ltd* [2002] EWCA Civ 911, [2002] 1 W.L.R. 2782 (CA), Kay, L.J.; see *Robert v Momentum Services Ltd* [2003] EWCA Civ 299, [2003] 1 W.L.R. 1577 (CA), Dyson, L.J.; see *Sayers v Clarke Walker (Permission to Appeal: Extension of Time Limits)* [2002] EWCA Civ 645, [2002] 1 W.L.R. 3095 (CA), Brooke, L.J.; see *Southern & District Finance Plc v Turner* [2003] EWCA Civ 1574, (2003) 147 S.J.L.B. 1362 (CA), Brooke, L.J.; see *Witt v Dunton* [2004] EWHC 110, [2004] B.P.I.R. 853 (Ch D), Lewison, J.; see *Woodhouse v Consignia Plc* [2002] EWCA Civ 275, [2002] 1 W.L.R. 2558 (CA), Brooke, L.J.

Part 3 r.3.9.1, see *Smith v Bromley LBC* [2002] C.P. Rep. 32 (Ch D), Garland, J.

1998–cont.

3132. Civil Procedure Rules 1998–*cont.*

Part 3 r.3.10, see *Ahmed v Kennedy* [2002] EWHC 2061, [2002] EWHC 2060, [2002] 4 All E.R. 764 (QBD), Hooper, J.; see *Bloomsbury Publishing Group Plc v News Group Newspapers Ltd (Continuation of Injunction)* [2003] EWHC 1205, [2003] 1 W.L.R. 1633 (Ch D), Sir Andrew Morritt V.C.; see *Fawdry & Co v Murfitt* [2002] EWCA Civ 643, [2003] Q.B. 104 (CA), Hale, L.J.; see *Lloyds Bank Plc v Ellicott* [2002] EWCA Civ 1333, [2003] B.P.I.R. 632 (CA), Ward, L.J.; see *Maridive & Oil Services SAE v CNA Insurance Co (Europe) Ltd* [2002] EWCA Civ 369, [2002] 1 All E.R. (Comm) 653 (CA), Mance, L.J.; see *Shiblaq v Sadikoglu (Application to Set Aside) (No.2)* [2004] EWHC 1890, [2004] 2 All E.R. (Comm) 596 (QBD (Comm)), Colman, J.; see *Southern & District Finance Plc v Turner* [2003] EWCA Civ 1574, (2003) 147 S.J.L.B. 1362 (CA), Brooke, L.J.

Part 3 r.3.11, added: SI 2004/2072 r.6

Part 3 r.3.20, see *Hampshire Waste Services Ltd v Intending Trespassers upon Chineham Incinerator Site* [2003] EWHC 1738, [2004] Env. L.R. 9 (Ch D), Sir Andrew Morritt V.C.

Part 5 r.5.4, substituted: SI 2004/2072 r.7

Part 5 r.5.4, see *Law Debenture Trust Corp (Channel Islands) Ltd v Lexington Insurance Co (Application for Disclosure)* [2003] EWHC 2297, (2003) 153 N.L.J. 1551 (QBD (Comm Ct)), Colman, J.; see *X Charity Trusts, Re* [2003] EWHC 1462, [2003] 1 W.L.R. 2751 (Ch D), Sir Andrew Morritt V.C.

Part 5 r.5.4A, added: SI 2004/1306 r.3

Part 5 r.5.5, added: SI 2002/2058 r.4

Part 6, added: SI 2002/2058 Sch.1

Part 6, see *Charles v NTL Group Ltd* [2002] EWCA Civ 2004, [2003] C.P. Rep. 44 (CA), Kay, L.J.

Part 6 r.6.2, see *Cranfield v Bridgegrove Ltd* [2003] EWCA Civ 656, [2003] 1 W.L.R. 2441 (CA), Dyson, L.J.; see *Phillips v Symes (Stay of Proceedings)* [2002] 1 W.L.R. 853 (Ch D), Hart, J.

Part 6 r.6.5, see *Nanglegan v Royal Free Hampstead NHS Trust* [2001] EWCA Civ 127, [2002] 1 W.L.R. 1043 (CA), Thorpe, L.J.

Part 6 r.6.7, see *Anderton v Clwyd CC* [2002] EWCA Civ 933, [2002] 1 W.L.R. 3174 (CA), Mummery, L.J.; see *Consignia Plc v Sealy* [2002] EWCA Civ 878, [2002] 3 All E.R. 801 (CA), Hart, J.; see *Godwin v Swindon BC* [2001] EWCA Civ 1478, [2002] 1 W.L.R. 997 (CA), May, L.J.

1998–cont.

3132. Civil Procedure Rules 1998–*cont.*

Part 6 r.6.8, see *Knauf UK GmbH v British Gypsum Ltd (No.1)* [2001] EWCA Civ 1570, [2002] 1 W.L.R. 907 (CA), Henry, L.J.; see *Nanglegan v Royal Free Hampstead NHS Trust* [2001] EWCA Civ 127, [2002] 1 W.L.R. 1043 (CA), Thorpe, L.J.

Part 6 r.6.9, see *Anderton v Clwyd CC* [2002] EWCA Civ 933, [2002] 1 W.L.R. 3174 (CA), Mummery, L.J.; see *Cranfield v Bridgegrove Ltd* [2003] EWCA Civ 656, [2003] 1 W.L.R. 2441 (CA), Dyson, L.J.; see *Wilkey v BBC* [2002] EWCA Civ 1561, [2003] 1 W.L.R. 1 (CA), Simon Brown, L.J.

Part 6 r.6.10, amended: SI 2004/1306 r.4

Part 6 r.6.17, see *Anderton v Clwyd CC* [2002] EWCA Civ 933, [2002] 1 W.L.R. 3174 (CA), Mummery, L.J.

Part 6 r.6.18, amended: SI 2002/2058 r.5

Part 6 r.6.19, amended: SI 2002/2058 r.5

Part 6 r.6.19, see *Swithenbank Foods Ltd v Bowers* [2002] EWHC 2257, [2002] 2 All E.R. (Comm) 974 (QBD (Merc Ct)), Judge McGonigal

Part 6 r.6.20, amended: SI 2004/2072 r.8

Part 6 r.6.20, see *Apple Corps Ltd v Apple Computer Inc* [2004] EWHC 768, [2004] I.L.Pr. 34 (Ch D), Mann, J.; see *Booth v Phillips* [2004] EWHC 1437, [2004] 1 W.L.R. 3292 (QBD (Comm Ct)), Nigel Teare Q.C.; see *Burrows v Jamaica Private Power Co Ltd* [2002] 1 All E.R. (Comm) 374 (QBD (Comm Ct)), Moore-Bick, J.; see *Credit Agricole Indosuez v Unicof Ltd* [2003] EWHC 2676, [2004] 1 Lloyd's Rep. 196 (QBD (Comm Ct)), Cooke, J.; see *Konamaneni v Rolls Royce Industrial Power (India) Ltd* [2002] 1 W.L.R. 1269 (Ch D), Lawrence Collins, J.; see *Morin v Bonhams & Brooks Ltd* [2003] EWHC 467, [2003] 2 All E.R. (Comm) 36 (QBD (Comm Ct)), Jonathan Hirst, Q.C.; see *MRG (Japan) Ltd v Engelhard Metals Japan Ltd* [2003] EWHC 3418, [2004] 1 Lloyd's Rep. 731 (QBD (Comm Ct)), Toulson, J.; see *Navigation Maritime Bulgare v Rustal Trading Ltd (The Ivan Zagubanski)* [2002] 1 Lloyd s Rep. 106 (QBD (Comm Ct)), Aikens, J.

Part 6 r.6.21, see *Swiss Reinsurance Co Ltd v United India Insurance Co* [2003] EWHC 741, [2004] I.L.Pr. 4 (QBD (Comm Ct)), Gross, J.

Part 6 r.6.24, see *Arros Invest Ltd v Nishanov* [2004] EWHC 576, [2004] I.L.Pr. 22 (Ch D), Lawrence Collins, J.; see *Shiblaq v Sadikoglu (Application to Set Aside) (No.2)* [2004] EWHC 1890, [2004] 2 All E.R. (Comm) 596 (QBD (Comm)), Colman, J.

1998–cont.

3132. Civil Procedure Rules 1998–*cont.*

Part 7, see *Cable & Wireless Plc v IBM United Kingdom Ltd* [2002] EWHC 2059, [2002] 2 All E.R. (Comm) 1041 (QBD (Comm Ct)), Colman, J.; see *Scribes West Ltd v Anstalt (No.2)* [2004] EWCA Civ 965, [2004] 4 All E.R. 653 (CA), Brooke, L.J.

Part 7 r.7.5, see *Anderton v Clwyd CC* [2002] EWCA Civ 933, [2002] 1 W.L.R. 3174 (CA), Mummery, L.J.; see *Arros Invest Ltd v Nishanov* [2004] EWHC 576, [2004] I.L.Pr. 22 (Ch D), Lawrence Collins, J.; see *Nagusina Naviera v Allied Maritime Inc* [2002] C.L.C. 385 (QBD (Comm Ct)), Andrew Smith, J.; see *Nagusina Naviera v Allied Maritime Inc* [2002] EWCA Civ 1147, [2003] 2 C.L.C. 1 (CA), Mance, L.J.

Part 7 r.7.6, see *Anderton v Clwyd CC* [2002] EWCA Civ 933, [2002] 1 W.L.R. 3174 (CA), Mummery, L.J.; see *Cranfield v Bridgegrove Ltd* [2003] EWCA Civ 656, [2003] 1 W.L.R. 2441 (CA), Dyson, L.J.; see *Hashtroodi v Hancock* [2004] EWCA Civ 652, [2004] 1 W.L.R. 3206 (CA), Thorpe, L.J.; see *Nagusina Naviera v Allied Maritime Inc* [2002] C.L.C. 385 (QBD (Comm Ct)), Andrew Smith, J.; see *Nanglegan v Royal Free Hampstead NHS Trust* [2001] EWCA Civ 127, [2002] 1 W.L.R. 1043 (CA), Thorpe, L.J.; see *Totty v Snowden* [2001] EWCA Civ 1415, [2002] 1 W.L.R. 1384 (CA), Kay, L.J.

Part 7 r.7.12, added: SI 2003/3361 r.3

Part 8, see *Associated Newspapers Ltd v Impac Ltd* [2002] F.S.R. 18 (QBD), Master Turner; see *Comsite Projects Ltd v Andritz AG* [2003] EWHC 958, (2004) 20 Const. L.J. 24 (QBD (T&CC)), Judge Kirkham; see *Scribes West Ltd v Anstalt (No.2)* [2004] EWCA Civ 965, [2004] 4 All E.R. 653 (CA), Brooke, L.J.

Part 8 r.8, see *CI v NS* [2004] EWHC 659, [2004] W.T.L.R. 1113 (Fam Div), Baron, J

Part 8 r.8.1, see *Cable & Wireless Plc v IBM United Kingdom Ltd* [2002] EWHC 2059, [2002] 2 All E.R. (Comm) 1041 (QBD (Comm Ct)), Colman, J.

Part 8 r.8.2A, see *Owens Corning Fiberglas (UK) Pension Plan Ltd, Re* [2002] Pens. L.R. 323 (Ch D), Neuberger, J.

Part 8 r.8.3, see *Hormel Foods Corp v Antilles Landscape Investment* [2003] EWHC 1912, (2004) 27(1) I.P.D. 27005 (Ch D), Lindsay, J.

Part 8 r.8.5, see *Parnall v Hurst* [2003] W.T.L.R. 997 (Ch D), Peter Langan Q.C.

Part 8 r.8.6, see *Parnall v Hurst* [2003] W.T.L.R. 997 (Ch D), Peter Langan Q.C.

Part 11, see *Midland Resources Ltd v Gonvarri Industrial SA* [2002] I.L.Pr. 8 (QBD (Comm Ct)), Judge Chambers Q.C.

1998–cont.

3132. Civil Procedure Rules 1998–*cont.*

Part 11 r.11, see *Ennstone Building Products Ltd v Stanger Ltd (No.1)* [2002] B.L.R. 82 (QBD (T&CC)), Judge Kirkham; see *Owusu v Jackson* [2002] EWCA Civ 877, [2003] 1 C.L.C. 246 (CA), Brooke, L.J.; see *SSQ Europe SA v Johann & Backes OHG* [2002] 1 Lloyd's Rep. 465 (QBD (Merc Ct)), Judge Havelock-Allan Q.C.

Part 13 r.13.3, see *ED&F Man Liquid Products Ltd v Patel* [2003] EWCA Civ 472, [2003] C.P. Rep. 51 (CA), Peter Gibson, L.J.

Part 13 r.13.5, revoked: SI 2004/1306 r.21

Part 15 r.15.4, see *SSQ Europe SA v Johann & Backes OHG* [2002] 1 Lloyd's Rep. 465 (QBD (Merc Ct)), Judge Havelock-Allan Q.C.

Part 16, see *Maridive & Oil Services SAE v CNA Insurance Co (Europe) Ltd* [2002] EWCA Civ 369, [2002] 1 All E.R. (Comm) 653 (CA), Mance, L.J.

Part 16 r.16.3, see *Khiaban v Beard* [2003] EWCA Civ 358, [2003] 1 W.L.R. 1626 (CA), Dyson, L.J.

Part 17 r.17, see *Hoechst UK Ltd v Inland Revenue Commissioners* [2003] EWHC 1002, [2004] S.T.C. 1486 (Ch D), Park, J.; see *Pounds v Eckford Rands (A firm)* [2003] Lloyd's Rep. P.N. 195 (QBD), Judge Peter Clark

Part 17 r.17.4, see *Goode v Martin* [2001] EWCA Civ 1899, [2002] 1 W.L.R. 1828 (CA), Brooke, L.J.; see *Hemmingway v Smith Roddam (A Firm)* [2003] EWCA Civ 1342, (2003) 147 S.J.L.B. 1089 (CA), Clarke, L.J.; see *Kuwait Airways Corp v Iraqi Airways Corp (No.9) (Statement of Claim)* [2002] EWCA Civ 515, [2002] C.P. Rep. 47 (CA), Longmore, L.J.; see *Smith v Henniker-Major & Co* [2002] B.C.C. 544 (Ch D), Rimer, J.

Part 17 r.22.1, see *Clarke v Marlborough Fine Art (London) Ltd (Amendments)* [2002] 1 W.L.R. 1731 (Ch D), Patten, J.

Part 19 r.19.2, see *Kooltrade Ltd v XTS Ltd (Joinder of Action)* [2002] F.S.R. 49 (Pat Ct), Pumfrey, J.

Part 19 r.19.3, see *Parsons v George* [2004] EWCA Civ 912, [2004] 1 W.L.R. 3264 (CA), Sir Andrew Morritt V.C.

Part 19 r.19.4A, see *R. (on the application of Morris) v Westminster City Council (No.1)* [2003] EWHC 2266, [2004] H.L.R. 18 (QBD (Admin Ct)), Keith, J.

Part 19 r.19.5, see *Horne-Roberts v Smithkline Beecham Plc* [2001] EWCA Civ 2006, [2002] 1 W.L.R. 1662 (CA), Keene, L.J.; see *Parsons v George* [2004] EWCA Civ 912, [2004] 1 W.L.R. 3264 (CA), Sir Andrew Morritt V.C.

Part 19 r.19.7, see *Murphy v McGlynn* [2002] W.T.L.R. 231 (Ch D), Lloyd, J.

NO.

1998–cont.

3132. Civil Procedure Rules 1998–*cont.*

Part 19 r.19.7A, added: SI 2002/2058 r.6

Part 19 r.19.8, see *Berti v Steele Raymond (A Firm)* [2001] EWCA Civ 2079, [2002] B.P.I.R. 683 (CA), Robert Walker, L.J.; see *Piggott v Aulton (Deceased)* [2003] EWCA Civ 24, [2003] C.P. Rep. 35 (CA), Arden, L.J.

Part 19 r.19.8A, substituted: SI 2002/2058 r.6

Part 19 r.19.9, see *Konamaneni v Rolls Royce Industrial Power (India) Ltd* [2002] 1 W.L.R. 1269 (Ch D), Lawrence Collins, J.

Part 20, see *Lloyds Bank Plc v Ellicott* [2002] EWCA Civ 1333, [2003] B.P.I.R. 632 (CA), Ward, L.J.; see *Prettys v Carter* [2002] P.N.L.R. 11 (QBD), Judge Playford Q.C.; see *Societe Internationale de Telecommunications Aeronautiques SC v Wyatt Co (UK) Ltd (Costs)* [2002] EWHC 2401, (2003) 147 S.J.L.B. 27 (Ch D), Park, J.

Part 20 r.20.7, amended: SI 2003/2113 r.3

Part 20 r.20.8, amended: SI 2003/2113 r.4

Part 21, see *Masterman-Lister v Jewell* [2002] EWCA Civ 1889, [2003] 1 W.L.R. 1511 (CA), Kennedy, L.J.

Part 21 r.21.1, amended: SI 2003/3361 r.4

Part 21 r.21.4, see *R. (on the application of Hussain) v Birmingham CC* [2002] EWHC 949, [2002] C.P. Rep. 54 (QBD (Admin Ct)), Forbes, J.

Part 21 r.21.10, see *Drinkall v Whitwood* [2003] EWCA Civ 1547, [2004] 1 W.L.R. 462 (CA), Simon Brown, L.J.

Part 22 r.22, see *Binks v Securicor Omega Express Ltd* [2003] EWCA Civ 993, [2003] 1 W.L.R. 2557 (CA), Maurice Kay, J.

Part 23, see *McKay v Rogers* [2002] EWHC 2825, [2004] B.P.I.R. 1272 (Ch D), Hart, J.; see *Phillipps v Associated Newspapers Ltd* [2004] EWHC 190, [2004] 1 W.L.R. 2106 (QBD), Eady, J.

Part 23 r.23.12, added: SI 2004/2072 r.9

Part 24, see *Chiemgauer Membran und Zeltbau GmbH (formerly Koch Hightex GmbH) v New Millennium Experience Co Ltd (formerly Millennium Central Ltd) (No.2)* [2002] B.P.I.R. 42 (Ch D), Geoffrey Vos Q.C.; see *Evans v First Secretary of State* [2003] EWCA Civ 1523, [2004] Env. L.R. 17 (CA), Simon Brown, L.J.; see *Kellar v BBR Graphic Engineers (Yorks) Ltd* [2002] B.P.I.R. 544 (Ch D), Roger Kaye Q.C.; see *Lewis v Eliades* [2003] EWHC 368, [2003] 1 All E.R. (Comm) 850 (QBD), Nelson, J.; see *Olatawura v Abiloye* [2002] EWCA Civ 998, [2003] 1 W.L.R. 275 (CA), Simon Brown, L.J.; see *Rhondda Cynon Taff CBC v Watkins* [2003] EWCA Civ 129, [2003] 1 W.L.R. 1864 (CA), Schiemann, L.J.; see *Trafigura Beheer BV v Golden Stavraetos*

NO.

1998–cont.

3132. Civil Procedure Rules 1998–*cont.*

Part 24–*cont.*

Maritime Inc (The Sonia) [2002] EWHC 1154, [2002] 2 All E.R. (Comm) 984 (QBD (Comm Ct)), Morison, J.

Part 24 r.24, see *Anglo Eastern Trust Ltd v Kermanshahchi* [2002] EWCA Civ 198, [2002] C.P. Rep. 36 (CA), Park, J.; see *Independents Advantage Insurance Co v Personal Representatives of Cook (Deceased)* [2002] EWHC 2681, [2003] Lloyd's Rep. P.N. 109 (Ch D), Lloyd, J.; see *Independents Advantage Insurance Co v Personal Representatives of Cook (Deceased)* [2003] EWCA Civ 1103, [2004] P.N.L.R. 3 (CA), Chadwick, L.J.; see *Kaberry v Freethcartwright (A Firm) (formerly Freeth Cartwright Hunt Dickens) (No.1)* [2003] B.P.I.R. 606 (QBD), Douglas Brown, J.; see *Spencer v Sillitoe* [2002] EWCA Civ 1579, [2003] E.M.L.R. 10 (CA), Buxton, L.J.

Part 24 r.24, see *Manx Electricity Authority v JP Morgan Chase Bank* [2003] B.L.R. 477 (CA), Rix, L.J.

Part 24 r.24.1, see *Petrotrade Inc v Texaco Ltd* [2002] 1 W.L.R. 947 (Note) (CA), Clarke, L.J.

Part 24 r.24.2, see *Arthur JS Hall & Co v Simons* [2002] 1 A.C. 615 (HL), Lord Hoffmann; see *Bavarian Lager Co Ltd v Secretary of State for Trade and Industry* [2002] U.K.C.L.R. 160 (QBD), Tomlinson, J.; see *Bernhard Schulte GmbH & Co KG v Nile Holdings Ltd* [2004] EWHC 977, [2004] 2 Lloyd's Rep. 352 (QBD (Comm Ct)), Cooke, J.; see *Bowthorpe Holdings Ltd v Hills* [2002] EWHC 2331, [2003] 1 B.C.L.C. 226 (Ch D), Sir Andrew Morritt V.C.; see *ED&F Man Liquid Products Ltd v Patel* [2003] EWCA Civ 472, [2003] C.P. Rep. 51 (CA), Peter Gibson, L.J.; see *Entertainment UK Ltd's Patent* [2002] R.P.C. 11 (PO), P Hayward; see *Equitable Life Assurance Society v Bowley* [2003] EWHC 2263, [2003] B.C.C. 829 (QBD (Comm Ct)), Langley, J.; see *HIH Casualty & General Insurance Ltd v Axa Corporate Solutions (formerly Axa Reassurance SA)* [2002] Lloyd's Rep. I.R. 325 (QBD), Jules Sher Q.C.; see *Man Nutzfahrzeuge AG v Ernst & Young* [2003] EWHC 2245, [2004] P.N.L.R. 19 (QBD (Comm Ct)), Cooke, J.; see *Meherali v Hampshire CC* [2002] EWHC 2655, [2003] E.L.R. 338 (QBD), Judge Zucker Q.C.; see *Taylor v Midland Bank Trust Co Ltd (No.2)* [2002] W.T.L.R. 95 (CA), Rattee, J.; see *Temseel Holdings Ltd v Beaumonts Chartered Accountants* [2002] EWHC 2642, [2003] P.N.L.R. 27 (QBD (Comm Ct)), Tomlinson, J.; see *Wallis v Valentine* [2002] EWCA Civ 1034,

NO.

1998–cont.

3132. Civil Procedure Rules 1998–*cont.*

Part 24 r.24.2–*cont.*

[2003] E.M.L.R. 8 (CA), Sir Murray Stuart-Smith

Part 24 r.24.4, see *Orford v Rasmi Electronics Ltd* [2002] EWCA Civ 1672, [2003] C.P.L.R. 213 (CA), Bodey, J.

Part 25, see *Olatawura v Abiloye* [2002] EWCA Civ 998, [2003] 1 W.L.R. 275 (CA), Simon Brown, L.J.

Part 25 PD 25 para.8.5, see *Elvee Ltd v Taylor* [2001] EWCA Civ 1943, [2002] F.S.R. 48 (CA), Chadwick, L.J.

Part 25 r.25, see *Myers v Design Inc (International) Ltd* [2003] EWHC 103, [2003] 1 W.L.R. 1642 (Ch D), Lightman, J.

Part 25 r.25.1, amended: SI 2002/2058 r.7

Part 25 r.25.1, see *Capital One Developments Ltd v Customs and Excise Commissioners* [2002] EWHC 197, [2002] S.T.C. 479 (Ch D), Neuberger, J.; see *NHS Trust v T (Adult Patient: Refusal of Medical Treatment)* [2004] EWHC 1279, [2004] 3 F.C.R. 297 (Fam Div), Charles, J.; see *Parker v CS Structured Credit Fund Ltd* [2003] EWHC 391, [2003] 1 W.L.R. 1680 (Ch D), Gabriel Moss Q.C.

Part 25 r.25.1.3, see *Somerset-Leeke v Kay Trustees (Security for Costs)* [2003] EWHC 1243, [2004] 3 All E.R. 406 (Ch D), Jacob, J.

Part 25 r.25.13, amended: SI 2002/3219 r.3

Part 25 r.25.13, revoked (in part): SI 2002/3219 r.3

Part 25 r.25.13, see *De Beer v Kanaar & Co (No.1)* [2001] EWCA Civ 1318, [2003] 1 W.L.R. 38 (CA), Jonathan Parker, L.J.; see *Naghshineh v Chaffe* [2003] EWHC 2107, [2003] N.P.C. 146 (Ch D), Jonathan Crow; see *Quicksons (South & West) Ltd v Katz (No.1)* [2003] EWHC 1981, [2003] 4 All E.R. 864 (Ch D (Companies Ct)), Evans-Lombe, J.; see *Thistle Hotels Ltd (formerly Thistle Hotels Plc) v Gamma Four Ltd* [2004] EWHC 322, [2004] 2 B.C.L.C. 174 (Ch D), Sonia Proudman Q.C.

Part 25 r.25.15, see *Bell Electric Ltd v Aweco Appliance Systems GmbH & Co KG (Application to Stay Appeal)* [2002] EWCA Civ 1501, [2003] 1 All E.R. 344 (CA), Potter, L.J.; see *Nasser v United Bank of Kuwait (Security for Costs)* [2001] EWCA Civ 556, [2002] 1 W.L.R. 1868 (CA), Mance, L.J.

Part 26 r.26.10, see *Maguire v Molin* [2002] EWCA Civ 1083, [2003] 1 W.L.R. 644 (CA), Dyson, L.J.

Part 27, see *Avinue Ltd v Sunrule Ltd* [2003] EWCA Civ 1942, [2004] 1 W.L.R. 634 (CA), Arden, L.J.

NO.

1998–cont.

3132. Civil Procedure Rules 1998–*cont.*

Part 27 r.27.14, see *Voice & Script International Ltd v Alghafar* [2003] EWCA Civ 736, [2003] C.P. Rep. 53 (CA), Judge, L.J.

Part 28 r.28.4, amended: SI 2002/2058 r.8

Part 28 r.28.5, substituted: SI 2002/2058 r.9

Part 28 r.28.6, amended: SI 2002/2058 r.8

Part 29 r.29.2, amended: SI 2002/2058 r.8

Part 29 r.29.5, amended: SI 2002/2058 r.8

Part 29 r.29.6, substituted: SI 2002/2058 r.10

Part 29 r.29.7, amended: SI 2002/2058 r.11

Part 29 r.29.8, amended: SI 2002/2058 r.8

Part 30 r.30.1, amended: SI 2003/2113 r.5

Part 30 r.30.1, substituted: SI 2003/2113 r.5

Part 30 r.30.8, restored: SI 2003/3361 r.5

Part 30 r.30.8, substituted: SI 2004/1306 r.5

Part 31 r.31.1, varied: SI 2003/421 r.40

Part 31 r.31.2, varied: SI 2003/421 r.40

Part 31 r.31.2, see *SmithKline Beecham Plc v Generics (UK) Ltd* [2003] EWCA Civ 1109, [2004] 1 W.L.R. 1479 (CA), Aldous, L.J.

Part 31 r.31.3, varied: SI 2003/421 r.40

Part 31 r.31.3, see *Bennett v Compass Group UK & Ireland Ltd* [2002] EWCA Civ 642, [2002] C.P. Rep. 58 (CA), Clarke, L.J.

Part 31 r.31.4, varied: SI 2003/421 r.40

Part 31 r.31.5, varied: SI 2003/421 r.40

Part 31 r.31.6, varied: SI 2003/421 r.40

Part 31 r.31.6, see *Bennett v Compass Group UK & Ireland Ltd* [2002] EWCA Civ 642, [2002] C.P. Rep. 58 (CA), Clarke, L.J.

Part 31 r.31.7, varied: SI 2003/421 r.40

Part 31 r.31.8, varied: SI 2003/421 r.40

Part 31 r.31.8, see *Bennett v Compass Group UK & Ireland Ltd* [2002] EWCA Civ 642, [2002] C.P. Rep. 58 (CA), Clarke, L.J.

Part 31 r.31.9, varied: SI 2003/421 r.40

Part 31 r.31.10, varied: SI 2003/421 r.40

Part 31 r.31.11, varied: SI 2003/421 r.40

Part 31 r.31.12, varied: SI 2003/421 r.40

Part 31 r.31.12, see *Bennett v Compass Group UK & Ireland Ltd* [2002] EWCA Civ 642, [2002] C.P. Rep. 58 (CA), Clarke, L.J.; see *Rigg v Associated Newspapers Ltd* [2003] EWHC 710, [2004] E.M.L.R. 4 (QBD), Gray, J.

Part 31 r.31.13, varied: SI 2003/421 r.40

Part 31 r.31.14, varied: SI 2003/421 r.40

Part 31 r.31.14, see *Bennett v Compass Group UK & Ireland Ltd* [2002] EWCA Civ 642, [2002] C.P. Rep. 58 (CA), Clarke, L.J.; see *Lucas v Barking, Havering and Redbridge Hospitals NHS Trust* [2003] EWCA Civ 1102, [2004] 1 W.L.R. 220 (CA), Waller, L.J.; see *Rigg v Associated Newspapers Ltd* [2003] EWHC 710, [2004] E.M.L.R. 4 (QBD), Gray, J.

Part 31 r.31.15, varied: SI 2003/421 r.40

Part 31 r.31.16, varied: SI 2003/421 r.40

NO.

1998–cont.

3132. Civil Procedure Rules 1998–*cont.*

Part 31 r.31.16, see *Black v Sumitomo Corp* [2001] EWCA Civ 1819, [2002] 1 W.L.R. 1562 (CA), Rix, L.J.; see *Medisys Plc v Arthur Andersen (A Firm)* [2002] Lloyd's Rep. P.N. 323 (QBD), Cooke, J.; see *Rose v Lynx Express Ltd* [2003] EWHC 2937, [2004] 1 B.C.L.C. 397 (Ch D), John Powell, Q.C.

Part 31 r.31.17, varied: SI 2003/421 r.40

Part 31 r.31.17, see *Frankson v Secretary of State for the Home Department* [2003] EWCA Civ 655, [2003] 1 W.L.R. 1952 (CA), Scott Baker, L.J.; see *Skyward Builders Plc, Re* [2002] EWHC 1788, [2002] 2 B.C.L.C. 750 (Ch D), Blackburne, J.

Part 31 r.31.18, varied: SI 2003/421 r.40

Part 31 r.31.19, varied: SI 2003/421 r.40

Part 31 r.31.20, varied: SI 2003/421 r.40

Part 31 r.31.20, see *Al-Fayed v Commissioner of Police of the Metropolis* [2002] EWCA Civ 780, Times, June 17, 2002 (CA), Clarke, L.J.

Part 31 r.31.21, varied: SI 2003/421 r.40

Part 31 r.31.22, varied: SI 2003/421 r.40

Part 31 r.31.22, see *Knight v Department of Social Security* [2002] I.R.L.R. 249 (EAT), Maurice Kay, J.; see *Law Debenture Trust Corp (Channel Islands) Ltd v Lexington Insurance Co (Application for Disclosure)* [2003] EWHC 2297, (2003) 153 N.L.J. 1551 (QBD (Comm Ct)), Colman, J.; see *Lilly ICOS Ltd v Pfizer Ltd (No.2)* [2002] EWCA Civ 2, [2002] 1 W.L.R. 2253 (CA), Buxton, L.J.; see *Marlwood Commercial Inc v Kozeny* [2004] EWCA Civ 798, [2004] 3 All E.R. 648 (CA), Peter Gibson, L.J.; see *SmithKline Beecham Plc v Generics (UK) Ltd* [2003] EWCA Civ 1109, [2004] 1 W.L.R. 1479 (CA), Aldous, L.J.

Part 31 r.31.23, varied: SI 2003/421 r.40

Part 31.r.31.17, see *SmithKline Beecham Plc v Generics (UK) Ltd* [2003] EWCA Civ 1109, [2004] 1 W.L.R. 1479 (CA), Aldous, L.J.

Part 32, see *Clarke v Marlborough Fine Art (London) Ltd (Amendments)* [2002] 1 W.L.R. 1731 (Ch D), Patten, J.

Part 32 r.32.1, see *Jones v Warwick University* [2003] EWCA Civ 151, [2003] 1 W.L.R. 954 (CA), Lord Woolf of Barnes, L.C.J.; see *O'Brien v Chief Constable of South Wales* [2003] EWCA Civ 1085, [2004] C.P. Rep. 5 (CA), Brooke, L.J.; see *R. (on the application of G) v Ealing LBC (No.2)* [2002] EWHC 250, Times, March 18, 2002 (QBD (Admin Ct)), Munby, J.

Part 32 r.32.5, see *Douglas v Hello! Ltd (No.5)* [2003] EWCA Civ 332, [2003] C.P. Rep. 42 (CA), Lord Woolf of Barnes, L.C.J.

NO.

1998–cont.

3132. Civil Procedure Rules 1998–*cont.*

Part 33 r.33.2, see *Sunley v Gowland White (Surveyors & Estate Agents) Ltd* [2003] EWCA Civ 240, [2004] P.N.L.R. 15 (CA), Clarke, L.J.

Part 33 r.33.4, see *Douglas v Hello! Ltd (No.5)* [2003] EWCA Civ 332, [2003] C.P. Rep. 42 (CA), Lord Woolf of Barnes, L.C.J.; see *Tsavliris Russ (Worldwide Salvage & Towage) Ltd v RL Baron Shipping Co SA (The Green Opal)* [2003] 1 Lloyd's Rep. 523 (QBD (Adm Ct)), Tomlinson, J.

Part 34, substituted: SI 2002/2058 r.12

Part 34, added: SI 2002/2058 Sch.2

Part 34, added: SI 2003/2113 r.9

Part 34, see *Individual Homes Ltd v Macbream Investments Ltd* Times, November 14, 2002 (Ch D), AG Steinfeld Q.C.

Part 34 r.34.1, amended: SI 2002/2058 r.12

Part 34 r.34.1, substituted: SI 2002/2058 r.12

Part 34 r.34.1, amended: SI 2002/2058 r.12

Part 34 r.34.2, amended: SI 2002/2058 r.12

Part 34 r.34.2, substituted: SI 2002/2058 r.12

Part 34 r.34.2, amended: SI 2002/2058 r.12

Part 34 r.34.3, amended: SI 2002/2058 r.12

Part 34 r.34.3, substituted: SI 2002/2058 r.12

Part 34 r.34.3, amended: SI 2002/2058 r.12

Part 34 r.34.4, amended: SI 2002/2058 r.12

Part 34 r.34.4, substituted: SI 2002/2058 r.12

Part 34 r.34.4, amended: SI 2002/2058 r.12

Part 34 r.34.4, see *R. (on the application of Brooks) v Parole Board* [2004] EWCA Civ 80, (2004) 148 S.J.L.B. 233 (CA), Kennedy, L.J.

Part 34 r.34.5, amended: SI 2002/2058 r.12

Part 34 r.34.5, substituted: SI 2002/2058 r.12

Part 34 r.34.5, amended: SI 2002/2058 r.12

Part 34 r.34.6, amended: SI 2002/2058 r.12

Part 34 r.34.6, substituted: SI 2002/2058 r.12

Part 34 r.34.6, amended: SI 2002/2058 r.12

Part 34 r.34.7, amended: SI 2002/2058 r.12

Part 34 r.34.7, substituted: SI 2002/2058 r.12

Part 34 r.34.7, amended: SI 2002/2058 r.12

Part 34 r.34.8, amended: SI 2002/2058 r.12

Part 34 r.34.8, substituted: SI 2002/2058 r.12

Part 34 r.34.8, amended: SI 2002/2058 r.12

Part 34 r.34.9, amended: SI 2002/2058 r.12

Part 34 r.34.9, substituted: SI 2002/2058 r.12

Part 34 r.34.9, amended: SI 2002/2058 r.12

Part 34 r.34.10, amended: SI 2002/2058 r.12

Part 34 r.34.10, substituted: SI 2002/2058 r.12

Part 34 r.34.10, amended: SI 2002/2058 r.12

Part 34 r.34.11, amended: SI 2002/2058 r.12

Part 34 r.34.11, substituted: SI 2002/2058 r.12

Part 34 r.34.11, amended: SI 2002/2058 r.12

Part 34 r.34.12, amended: SI 2002/2058 r.12

Part 34 r.34.12, substituted: SI 2002/2058 r.12

1998–cont.

3132. Civil Procedure Rules 1998–*cont.*

Part 34 r.34.12, amended: SI 2002/2058 r.12

Part 34 r.34.13, amended: SI 2002/2058 r.12

Part 34 r.34.13, substituted: SI 2002/2058 r.12

Part 34 r.34.13, amended: SI 2002/2058 r.12, SI 2003/2113 r.7

Part 34 r.34.13A, added: SI 2003/3361 r.6

Part 34 r.34.13A, amended: SI 2002/2058 r.12

Part 34 r.34.14, amended: SI 2002/2058 r.12

Part 34 r.34.14, substituted: SI 2002/2058 r.12

Part 34 r.34.14, amended: SI 2002/2058 r.12

Part 34 r.34.15, amended: SI 2002/2058 r.12

Part 34 r.34.15, substituted: SI 2002/2058 r.12

Part 34 r.34.15, amended: SI 2002/2058 r.12

Part 34 r.34.16, amended: SI 2002/2058 r.12, SI 2004/1306 r.6

Part 34 r.34.16, substituted: SI 2003/2113 r.8

Part 34 r.34.17, amended: SI 2002/2058 r.12

Part 34 r.34.18, amended: SI 2002/2058 r.12

Part 34 r.34.19, amended: SI 2002/2058 r.12

Part 34 r.34.20, amended: SI 2002/2058 r.12

Part 34 r.34.21, amended: SI 2002/2058 r.12

Part 34 r.34.22, amended: SI 2002/2058 r.12

Part 34 r.34.23, amended: SI 2002/2058 r.12, SI 2003/3361 r.7, SI 2004/1306 r.7

Part 34 r.34.24, amended: SI 2002/2058 r.12

Part 35, see *Practice Guide (Fam Div: Instructing a Single Joint Expert)* [2003] 1 FLR 573 (Fam Div), District Judge Gerald Angel (Chairman)

Part 35 r.35.1, see *ES v Chesterfield and North Derbyshire Royal Hospital NHS Trust* [2003] EWCA Civ 1284, [2004] C.P. Rep. 9 (CA), Brooke, L.J.

Part 35 r.35.3, see *Pearce v Ove Arup Partnership Ltd (Copying)* (2002) 25(2) I.P.D. 25011 (Ch D), Jacob, J.

Part 35 r.35.7, see *Layland v Fairview New Homes Plc* [2002] EWHC 1350, [2003] C.P.L.R. 19 (Ch D), Neuberger, J.; see *Peet v Mid Kent Area Healthcare NHS Trust* [2001] EWCA Civ 1703, [2002] 1 W.L.R. 210 (CA), Lord Woolf of Barnes, L.C.J.

Part 35 r.35.10, see *Lucas v Barking, Havering and Redbridge Hospitals NHS Trust* [2003] EWCA Civ 1102, [2004] 1 W.L.R. 220 (CA), Waller, L.J.; see *Wade v Varney* [2003] EWCA Civ 1279, [2003] W.T.L.R. 1535 (CA), Tuckey, L.J.

Part 36, see *Higgs v Camden and Islington HA* [2003] EWHC 15, [2003] 2 Costs L.R. 211 (QBD), Fulford, J.; see *Kastor Navigation Co Ltd v AGF MAT (The Kastor Too)* [2004] EWCA Civ 277, [2004] 2 Lloyd's Rep. 119 (CA), Tuckey, L.J.; see *Kiam v MGN Ltd (Costs)* [2002] EWCA Civ 66, [2002] 1 W.L.R. 2810 (CA), Simon Brown, L.J.; see *Mamidoil-Jetoil Greek*

1998–cont.

3132. Civil Procedure Rules 1998–*cont.*

Part 36–*cont.*

Petroleum Co SA v Okta Crude Oil Refinery AD (Costs) [2002] EWHC 2462, [2003] 1 Lloyd's Rep. 42 (QBD (Comm Ct)), Aikens, J.; see *Padgham v Rochelle (Costs)* [2002] EWHC 2747, [2003] W.T.L.R. 71 (Ch D), L Henderson Q.C.

Part 36 r.36, see *Garratt v Saxby* [2004] EWCA Civ 341, [2004] 1 W.L.R. 2152 (CA), Ward, L.J.; see *Neave v Neave (Costs)* [2003] EWCA Civ 325, (2003) 100(14) L.S.G. 27 (CA), Chadwick, L.J.; see *Phillipps v Associated Newspapers Ltd* [2004] EWHC 190, [2004] 1 W.L.R. 2106 (QBD), Eady, J.

Part 36 r.36.1, see *Charles v NTL Group Ltd* [2002] EWCA Civ 2004, [2003] C.P. Rep. 44 (CA), Kay, L.J.; see *Mitchells v James (Costs)* [2002] EWCA Civ 997, [2004] 1 W.L.R. 158 (CA), Peter Gibson, L.J.; see *Neave v Neave (Costs)* [2003] EWCA Civ 325, (2003) 100(14) L.S.G. 27 (CA), Chadwick, L.J.

Part 36 r.36.2A, added: SI 2004/3129 r.4

Part 36 r.36.3, amended: SI 2004/3129 r.3

Part 36 r.36.4, amended: SI 2004/3129 r.5

Part 36 r.36.6, amended: SI 2002/3219 r.4

Part 36 r.36.6, revoked (in part): SI 2002/3219 r.4

Part 36 r.36.6, see *Flynn v Scougall* [2004] EWCA Civ 873, [2004] 1 W.L.R. 3069 (CA (Civ Div)), Brooke, L.J.

Part 36 r.36.10, amended: SI 2004/3129 r.6

Part 36 r.36.10, see *Huck v Robson* [2002] EWCA Civ 398, [2003] 1 W.L.R. 1340 (CA), Jonathan Parker, L.J.

Part 36 r.36.11, see *Flynn v Scougall* [2004] EWCA Civ 873, [2004] 1 W.L.R. 3069 (CA (Civ Div)), Brooke, L.J.

Part 36 r.36.13, see *Dyson Appliances Ltd v Hoover Ltd (Costs)* [2002] EWHC 2229, [2003] F.S.R. 21 (Pat Ct), Jacob, J.; see *GKN Westland Helicopters Ltd v Korean Air Lines Co Ltd* [2003] EWHC 1120, [2003] 2 All E.R. (Comm.) 578 (QBD (Comm Ct)), Morison, J.

Part 36 r.36.14, see *Mitchells v James (Costs)* [2002] EWCA Civ 997, [2004] 1 W.L.R. 158 (CA), Peter Gibson, L.J.; see *Neave v Neave (Costs)* [2003] EWCA Civ 325, (2003) 100(14) L.S.G. 27 (CA), Chadwick, L.J.

Part 36 r.36.20, amended: SI 2004/3129 r.7

Part 36 r.36.20, see *Excelsior Commercial & Industrial Holdings Ltd v Salisbury Hamer Aspden & Johnson (Costs)* [2002] EWCA Civ 879, [2002] C.P. Rep. 67 (CA), Lord Woolf of Barnes, L.C.J.; see *Huck v Robson* [2002] EWCA Civ 398, [2003] 1 W.L.R. 1340 (CA), Jonathan Parker, L.J.; see *Irvine v Talksport Ltd (Damages)*

NO.

1998–cont.

3132. Civil Procedure Rules 1998–*cont.*

Part 36 r.36.20–*cont.*

[2002] EWHC 539, [2003] E.M.L.R. 6 (Ch D), Laddie, J.; see *Peninsular Business Services Ltd v Citation Plc (No.2)* [2004] F.S.R 18 (Ch D), Judge Maddocks; see *Uttley v Uttley* [2002] P.I.Q.R. P12 (QBD), Hallett, J.

Part 36 r.36.21, amended: SI 2004/3129 r.8

Part 36 r.36.21, see *Ali Reza-Delta Transport Co Ltd v United Arab Shipping Co SAG (Costs)* [2003] EWCA Civ 811, [2004] 1 W.L.R. 168 (CA), Peter Gibson, L.J.; see *Dyson Appliances Ltd v Hoover Ltd (Costs)* [2002] EWHC 2229, [2003] F.S.R. 21 (Pat Ct), Jacob, J.; see *East West Corp v DKBS 1912 (Costs)* [2002] EWHC 253, [2002] 2 Lloyd's Rep. 222 (QBD (Comm Ct)), Thomas, J.; see *East West Corp v DKBS 1912 (Costs)* [2003] EWCA Civ 174, [2003] 1 Lloyd's Rep. 265 (CA), Brooke, L.J.; see *Excelsior Commercial & Industrial Holdings Ltd v Salisbury Hamer Aspden & Johnson (Costs)* [2002] EWCA Civ 879, [2002] C.P. Rep. 67 (CA), Lord Woolf of Barnes, L.C.J.; see *Harper v Staffordshire CC* [2003] EWHC 283, (2003) 147 S.J.L.B. 176 (QBD), Judge Wilkie Q.C.; see *Huck v Robson* [2002] EWCA Civ 398, [2003] 1 W.L.R. 1340 (CA), Jonathan Parker, L.J.; see *KR v Bryn Alyn Community (Holdings) Ltd (In Liquidation) (Permission to Amend)* [2003] EWCA Civ 383, [2003] C.P. Rep. 49 (CA), Waller, L.J.; see *Mitchells v James (Costs)* [2002] EWCA Civ 997, [2004] 1 W.L.R. 158 (CA), Peter Gibson, L.J.; see *Neave v Neave (Costs)* [2003] EWCA Civ 325, (2003) 100(14) L.S.G. 27 (CA), Chadwick, L.J.; see *Padgham v Rochelle (Costs)* [2002] EWHC 2747, [2003] W.T.L.R. 71 (Ch D), L Henderson Q.C.; see *Petrotrade Inc v Texaco Ltd* [2002] 1 W.L.R. 947 (Note) (CA), Clarke, L.J.; see *Reid Minty (A Firm) v Taylor* [2001] EWCA Civ 1723, [2002] 1 W.L.R. 2800 (CA), May, L.J.; see *Seashore Marine SA v Phoenix Assurance Plc (The Vergina) (No.3)* [2002] 1 Lloyd's Rep. 238 (QBD (Comm Ct)), Aikens, J.

Part 36 r.36.23, amended: SI 2004/3129 r.9

Part 36 r.36.23, see *Williams v Devon CC* [2003] EWCA Civ 365, [2003] P.I.Q.R. Q4 (CA), Latham, L.J.

Part 37 r.37.1, amended: SI 2002/3219 r.5

Part 39 r.39.3, see *Brazil v Brazil* [2002] EWCA Civ 1135, [2003] C.P. Rep. 7 (CA), Mummery, L.J.; see *Hackney LBC v Driscoll* [2003] EWCA Civ 1037, [2003] 1 W.L.R. 2602 (CA), Brooke, L.J.; see *Thakerar v Northwich Park Hospital NHS Trust* [2002] EWCA Civ 617, [2002] C.P. Rep. 50 (CA), Sedley, L.J.

NO.

1998–cont.

3132. Civil Procedure Rules 1998–*cont.*

Part 39 r.39.6#, see *Tracto Teknik GmbH v LKL International Pty Ltd* [2003] EWHC 1563, [2003] 2 B.C.L.C. 519 (Pat Ct), Pumfrey, J.; see *Watson v Bluemoor Properties Ltd* [2002] EWCA Civ 1875, [2003] C.P. Rep. 33 (CA), Sullivan, J.

Part 40 r.40.2, see *Giambrone v JMC Holidays Ltd (formerly t/a Sunworld Holidays Ltd)* [2002] EWHC 495, [2002] C.P.L.R. 440 (QBD), Nelson, J.

Part 40 r.40.4, amended: SI 2002/2058 r.13

Part 40 r.40.20, see *Financial Services Authority (FSA) v Rourke (t/a JE Rourke & Co)* [2002] C.P. Rep. 14 (Ch D), Neuberger, J.

Part 41 r.41.1, amended: SI 2004/3129 r.10, r.11

Part 41 r.41.1, substituted: SI 2004/3129 Sch.1 Part II

Part 41 r.41.1, amended: SI 2004/3129 r.10

Part 41 r.41.1, substituted: SI 2004/3129 Sch.1 Part II

Part 41 r.41.2, amended: SI 2004/3129 r.10

Part 41 r.41.2, substituted: SI 2004/3129 Sch.1 Part II

Part 41 r.41.2, amended: SI 2004/3129 r.10

Part 41 r.41.2, substituted: SI 2004/3129 Sch.1 Part II

Part 41 r.41.3, amended: SI 2004/3129 r.10

Part 41 r.41.3, substituted: SI 2004/3129 Sch.1 Part II

Part 41 r.41.3, amended: SI 2004/3129 r.10

Part 41 r.41.3, substituted: SI 2004/3129 Sch.1 Part II

Part 41 r.41.4, amended: SI 2004/3129 r.10

Part 41 r.41.4, substituted: SI 2004/3129 Sch.1 Part II

Part 41 r.41.5, amended: SI 2004/3129 r.10

Part 41 r.41.5, substituted: SI 2004/3129 Sch.1 Part II

Part 41 r.41.6, amended: SI 2004/3129 r.10

Part 41 r.41.6, substituted: SI 2004/3129 Sch.1 Part II

Part 41 r.41.7, amended: SI 2004/3129 r.10

Part 41 r.41.7, substituted: SI 2004/3129 Sch.1 Part II

Part 41 r.41.8, amended: SI 2004/3129 r.10

Part 41 r.41.8, substituted: SI 2004/3129 Sch.1 Part II

Part 41 r.41.9, amended: SI 2004/3129 r.10

Part 41 r.41.9, substituted: SI 2004/3129 Sch.1 Part II

Part 41 r.41.10, amended: SI 2004/3129 r.10

Part 41 r.41.10, substituted: SI 2004/3129 Sch.1 Part II

Part 42 r.42.2, amended: SI 2004/1306 r.8

Part 43, see *R. v Mashhour (Costs)* [2003] 2 Costs L.R. 318 (Supreme Court Costs Office), Master GN Pollard

NO.

1998–cont.

3132. Civil Procedure Rules 1998–*cont.*

Part 43 PD 43 para.6.4, see *Leigh v Michelin Tyre Plc* [2003] EWCA Civ 1766, [2004] 1 W.L.R. 846 (CA), Dyson, L.J.

Part 43 PD 43 para.6.6, see *Leigh v Michelin Tyre Plc* [2003] EWCA Civ 1766, [2004] 1 W.L.R. 846 (CA), Dyson, L.J.

Part 43 r.43.2, amended: SI 2003/1242 r.5, SI 2003/1329 r.3, SI 2003/2113 r.10

Part 43 r.43.2, see *Papera Traders Co Ltd v Hyundai Merchant Marine Co Ltd (The Eurasian Dream) (No.2)* [2002] EWHC 2130, [2002] 2 All E.R. (Comm) 1083 (QBD (Comm Ct)), Cresswell, J.

Part 44, see *Derbyshire, The* [2003] 1 All E.R. (Comm) 784 (QBD (Adm Ct)), Colman, J.; see *Giambrone v JMC Holidays Ltd (formerly t/a Sunworld Holidays Ltd) (Costs)* [2002] EWHC 2932, [2003] 1 All E.R. 982 (QBD), Morland, J.; see *Inline Logistics Ltd v UCI Logistics Ltd (Costs: Recovery of Insurance Premium)* [2002] EWHC 519, [2002] 2 Costs L.R. 304 (Ch D), Ferris, J.; see *Kiam v MGN Ltd (Costs)* [2002] EWCA Civ 66, [2002] 1 W.L.R. 2810 (CA), Simon Brown, L.J.; see *Q v Q (Costs: Summary Assessment)* [2002] 2 F.L.R. 668 (Fam Div), Wilson, J.; see *Reid Minty (A Firm) v Taylor* [2001] EWCA Civ 1723, [2002] 1 W.L.R. 2800 (CA), May, L.J.; see *South Coast Shipping Co Ltd v Havant BC* [2002] 3 All E.R. 779 (Ch D), Pumfrey, J.

Part 44 r.44, see *Hadjimilitis v Tsavliris (Costs)* [2003] 1 F.L.R. 81 (Fam Div), Alison Ball Q.C.; see *Lynch v Paul Davidson Taylor (A Firm)* [2004] EWHC 89, [2004] 1 W.L.R. 1753 (QBD), Hughes, J.

Part 44 r.44.3, see *Aaron v Shelton* [2004] EWHC 1162, [2004] 3 All E.R. 561 (QBD), Jack, J.; see *Ali Reza-Delta Transport Co Ltd v United Arab Shipping Co SAG (Costs)* [2003] EWCA Civ 811, [2004] 1 W.L.R. 168 (CA), Peter Gibson, L.J.; see *Budgen v Andrew Gardner Partnership* [2002] EWCA Civ 1125, [2003] C.P. Rep. 8 (CA), Simon Brown, L.J.; see *C v C (Costs: Ancillary Relief)* [2003] EWHC 2321, [2004] 1 F.L.R. 291 (Fam Div), Charles, J.; see *Charles v NTL Group Ltd* [2002] EWCA Civ 2004, [2003] C.P. Rep. 44 (CA), Kay, L.J.; see *Douglas v Hello! Ltd (No.9)* [2004] EWHC 63, [2004] 2 Costs L.R. 304 (Ch D), Lindsay, J.; see *Good (Deceased) (Costs), Re* [2002] EWHC 640, [2002] W.T.L.R. 1305 (Ch D), Rimer, J.; see *Norris v Norris* [2003] EWCA Civ 1084, [2003] 1 W.L.R. 2960 (CA), Dame Elizabeth Butler-Sloss (President); see *Peninsular Business Services Ltd v Citation Plc (No.2)* [2004] F.S.R 18 (Ch D), Judge Maddocks; see *Powell v Herefordshire HA* [2002] EWCA Civ 1786, [2003] 3 All E.R.

NO.

1998–cont.

3132. Civil Procedure Rules 1998–*cont.*

Part 44 r.44.3–*cont.*

253 (CA), Kay, L.J.; see *Purfleet Farms Ltd v Secretary of State for Transport, Local Government and the Regions* [2002] EWCA Civ 1430, [2003] 1 P. & C.R. 20 (CA), Potter, L.J.; see *Reed Executive Plc v Reed Business Information Ltd (Costs: Alternative Dispute Resolution)* [2004] EWCA Civ 887, [2004] 1 W.L.R. 3026 (CA), Auld, L.J.; see *SCT Finance Ltd v Bolton* [2002] EWCA Civ 56, [2003] 3 All E.R. 434 (CA), Wilson, J.; see *Societe Internationale de Telecommunications Aeronautiques SC v Wyatt Co (UK) Ltd (Costs)* [2002] EWHC 2401, (2003) 147 S.J.L.B. 27 (Ch D), Park, J.; see *Spice Girls Ltd v Aprilia World Service BV* [2002] EWCA Civ 15, [2002] E.M.L.R. 27 (CA), Sir Andrew Morritt V.C.; see *Summit Property Ltd v Pitmans (Costs)* [2001] EWCA Civ 2020, [2002] C.P.L.R. 97 (CA), Longmore, L.J.

Part 44 r.44.3.8, see *Dyson Appliances Ltd v Hoover Ltd (Costs: Interim Payment)* [2003] EWHC 624, [2004] 1 W.L.R. 1264 (Pat Ct), Laddie, J.

Part 44 r.44.3B, see *Grupo Torras SA v Al-Sabah (Costs)* [2003] EWHC 262, [2003] 2 Costs L.R. 294 (QBD), Treacy, J.

Part 44 r.44.4, see *SCT Finance Ltd v Bolton* [2002] EWCA Civ 56, [2003] 3 All E.R. 434 (CA), Wilson, J.; see *Shaina Investment Corp v Standard Bank London Ltd (Indemnity Costs)* [2002] C.P.L.R. 14 (Ch D), M Kallipetis Q.C.; see *Sharratt v London Central Bus Co Ltd (No.2)* [2004] EWCA Civ 575, [2004] 3 All E.R. 325 (CA), Kennedy, L.J.

Part 44 r.44.5, see *Aaron v Shelton* [2004] EWHC 1162, [2004] 3 All E.R. 561 (QBD), Jack, J.; see *Higgs v Camden and Islington HA* [2003] EWHC 15, [2003] 2 Costs L.R. 211 (QBD), Fulford, J.; see *Leigh v Michelin Tyre Plc* [2003] EWCA Civ 1766, [2004] 1 W.L.R. 846 (CA), Dyson, L.J.; see *Lownds v Home Office* [2002] EWCA Civ 365, [2002] 1 W.L.R. 2450 (CA), Lord Woolf of Barnes, L.C.J.; see *Ortwein v Rugby Mansions Ltd* [2003] EWHC 2077, [2004] 1 Costs L.R. 26 (Ch D), Lloyd, J.; see *Young v JR Smart (Builders) Ltd (Costs)* [2004] EWHC 103, [2004] 2 Costs L.R. 298 (QBD), Henriques, J.

Part 44 r.44.12A, amended: SI 2002/2058 r.14, SI 2003/2113 r.11

Part 44 r.44.12A, see *Crosbie v Munroe* [2003] EWCA Civ 350, [2003] 1 W.L.R. 2033 (CA), Brooke, L.J.

Part 44 r.44.15, amended: SI 2002/2058 r.15

Part 44 r.44.15, see *Inline Logistics Ltd v UCI Logistics Ltd (Costs: Recovery of Insurance Premium)* [2002] EWHC 519, [2002] 2 Costs L.R. 304 (Ch D), Ferris, J.

NO.

1998–cont.

3132. Civil Procedure Rules 1998–*cont.*

Part 44 r.44.16, amended: SI 2002/2058 r.16

Part 45, added: SI 2003/2113 r.12

Part 45, disapplied: SI 2003/2113 r.18

Part 45, added: SI 2004/1306 Sch.1 Part II

Part 45, added: SI 2004/2072 Sch.1 Part II

Part 45 r.45.1, substituted: SI 2003/2113 r.12

Part 45 r.45.1, amended: SI 2003/2113 r.12

Part 45 r.45.1, substituted: SI 2003/2113 r.12

Part 45 r.45.2, substituted: SI 2003/2113 r.12

Part 45 r.45.3, substituted: SI 2003/2113 r.12

Part 45 r.45.4, substituted: SI 2003/2113 r.12

Part 45 r.45.5, substituted: SI 2003/2113 r.12

Part 45 r.45.6, substituted: SI 2003/2113 r.12

Part 45 r.45.7, substituted: SI 2003/2113 r.12

Part 45 r.45.8, substituted: SI 2003/2113 r.12

Part 45 r.45.9, substituted: SI 2003/2113 r.12

Part 45 r.45.9, see *Sharratt v London Central Bus Co Ltd (No.2)* [2004] EWCA Civ 575, [2004] 3 All E.R. 325 (CA), Kennedy, L.J.

Part 45 r.45.10, amended: SI 2003/3361 r.8, SI 2004/2072 r.11

Part 45 r.45.10, substituted: SI 2003/2113 r.12

Part 45 r.45.11, amended: SI 2003/3361 r.9

Part 45 r.45.11, substituted: SI 2003/2113 r.12

Part 45 r.45.12, substituted: SI 2003/2113 r.12

Part 45 r.45.13, substituted: SI 2003/2113 r.12

Part 45 r.45.14, substituted: SI 2003/2113 r.12

Part 45 r.45.15, substituted: SI 2003/2113 r.12

Part 45 r.45.16, substituted: SI 2003/2113 r.12

Part 45 r.45.17, substituted: SI 2003/2113 r.12

Part 45 r.45.18, substituted: SI 2003/2113 r.12

Part 45 r.45.19, substituted: SI 2003/2113 r.12

Part 45 r.45.20, substituted: SI 2003/2113 r.12

Part 45 r.45.21, substituted: SI 2003/2113 r.12

Part 45 r.45.22, substituted: SI 2003/2113 r.12

Part 47, see *Grupo Torras SA v Al-Sabah (Costs)* [2003] EWHC 262, [2003] 2 Costs L.R. 294 (QBD), Treacy, J.

Part 47 r.47, see *Wills v Crown Estate Commissioners* [2003] EWHC 1718, [2003] 4 Costs L.R. 581 (Ch D), Peter Smith, J.

Part 47 r.47.6, applied: SI 2002/2058 r.34

Part 47 r.47.14, amended: SI 2002/2058 r.17

Part 47 r.47.19, amended: SI 2002/2058 r.18

Part 47 r.47.19, see *Crosbie v Munroe* [2003] EWCA Civ 350, [2003] 1 W.L.R. 2033 (CA), Brooke, L.J.

Part 48, see *Joseph v Boyd & Hutchinson* [2003] EWHC 413, [2003] 3 Costs L.R. 358 (Ch D), Patten, J.

Part 48 PD 48 para 52.5, see *Hatton v Kendrick* [2002] EWCA Civ 1783, [2003] C.P. Rep. 32 (CA), Scott Baker, L.J.

Part 48 r.48, see *Lynch v Paul Davidson Taylor (A Firm)* [2004] EWHC 89, [2004] 1 W.L.R. 1753 (QBD), Hughes, J.

NO.

1998–cont.

3132. Civil Procedure Rules 1998–*cont.*

Part 48 r.48.1, see *Individual Homes Ltd v Macbream Investments Ltd* Times, November 14, 2002 (Ch D), AG Steinfeld Q.C.; see *Totalise Plc v Motley Fool Ltd* [2001] EWCA Civ 1897, [2002] 1 W.L.R. 1233 (CA), Aldous, L.J.

Part 48 r.48.2, see *Individual Homes Ltd v Macbream Investments Ltd* Times, November 14, 2002 (Ch D), AG Steinfeld Q.C.

Part 48 r.48.6, amended: SI 2002/2058 r.19

Part 48 r.48.6, applied: SI 2002/2058 r.34

Part 48 r.48.6, see *Ahmed v Powell* [2003] P.N.L.R. 22 (Sup Ct Costs Office), Chief Master Hurst; see *Hatton v Kendrick* [2002] EWCA Civ 1783, [2003] C.P. Rep. 32 (CA), Scott Baker, L.J.; see *Joseph v Boyd & Hutchinson* [2003] EWHC 413, [2003] 3 Costs L.R. 358 (Ch D), Patten, J.; see *R. (on the application of Wulfsohn) v Legal Services Commission* [2002] EWCA Civ 250, [2002] C.P. Rep. 34 (CA), Schiemann, L.J.; see *United Building & Plumbing Contractors v Kajla* [2002] EWCA Civ 628, [2002] C.P. Rep. 53 (CA), Tuckey, L.J.

Part 48 r.48.7, amended: SI 2002/2058 r.20

Part 49, see *Dardana Ltd v Yukos Oil Co (No.2)* [2002] 2 Lloyd's Rep. 261 (QBD (Comm Ct)), Judge Chambers Q.C.; see *Fawdry & Co v Murfitt* [2002] EWCA Civ 643, [2003] Q.B. 104 (CA), Hale, L.J.; see *Nagusina Naviera v Allied Maritime Inc* [2002] C.L.C. 385 (QBD (Comm Ct)), Andrew Smith, J.; see *Nagusina Naviera v Allied Maritime Inc* [2002] EWCA Civ 1147, [2003] 2 C.L.C. 1 (CA), Mance, L.J.; see *Navigation Maritime Bulgare v Rustal Trading Ltd (The Ivan Zagubanski)* [2002] 1 Lloyd s Rep. 106 (QBD (Comm Ct)), Aikens, J.

Part 49 r.49, revoked (in part): SI 2002/3219 r.6

Part 51, see *Joseph v Boyd & Hutchinson* [2003] EWHC 413, [2003] 3 Costs L.R. 358 (Ch D), Patten, J.; see *Taylor v Anderson* [2002] EWCA Civ 1680, [2003] R.T.R. 21 (CA), Chadwick, L.J.; see *Woodhouse v Consignia Plc* [2002] EWCA Civ 275, [2002] 1 W.L.R. 2558 (CA), Brooke, L.J.

Part 51 PD para.19, see *Overseas & Commercial Developments Ltd v Cox* [2002] EWCA Civ 635, [2002] B.P.I.R. 1150 (CA), Dyson, L.J.

Part 51 r.51, see *Hansom v E Rex Makin & Co* [2003] EWCA Civ 1801, (2004) 148 S.J.L.B. 57 (CA), Mance, L.J.

Part 51 r.51 para.19, see *Flaxman-Binns v Lincolnshire CC* [2004] EWCA Civ 424, [2004] 1 W.L.R. 2232 (CA), Lord Phillips of Worth Matravers, M.R.

NO.

1998-cont.

3132. Civil Procedure Rules 1998-*cont.*

Part 52, added: SI 2003/2113 r.14

Part 52, see *Colley v Council for Licensed Conveyancers (Right of Appeal)* [2001] EWCA Civ 1137, [2002] 1 W.L.R. 160 (CA), Sir Andrew Morritt V.C.; see *Gurney v Spence (Inspector of Taxes)* [2002] S.T.C. 758 (Ch D), Jacob, J.; see *Hansen v Great Future International Ltd* [2003] EWCA Civ 1646, [2004] C.P. Rep. 14 (CA), Waller, L.J.; see *Joop v Canadelle Ltd Partnership of Canada* [2002] R.P.C. 45 (Ch D), Pumfrey, J.; see *Lucas v Millman* [2002] EWHC 2470, [2003] 1 W.L.R. 271 (QBD (Admin Ct)), Kennedy, L.J.; see *Morris v Wiltshire (Costs)* [2002] 1 Costs. L.R. 167 (QBD), Roderick Evans, J.; see *Practice Direction (PO: 1/2003 (Revised))* [2003] R.P.C. 46 (PO), Not specified

Part 52 PD 52, see *Harvey Shopfitters Ltd v ADI Ltd* [2003] EWCA Civ 1757, [2004] 2 All E.R. 982 (CA), Dame Elizabeth Butler-Sloss (President); see *Medina Housing Association Ltd v Connolly* [2002] EWCA Civ 1263, [2003] C.P. Rep. 4 (CA), Peter Gibson, L.J.

Part 52 r.52, see *Contract Facilities Ltd v Rees Estate (Application to Strike Out)* [2003] EWCA Civ 1105, (2003) 147 S.J.L.B. 933 (CA), Waller, L.J.

Part 52 r.52 para.4, see *Aujla v Sanghera* [2004] EWCA Civ 121, (2004) 148 S.J.L.B. 147 (CA), Thorpe, L.J.

Part 52 r.52.1, see *Slot v Isaac* [2002] EWCA Civ 481, [2002] C.P. Rep. 57 (CA), Brooke, L.J.

Part 52 r.52.3, see *Foenander v Bond Lewis & Co* [2001] EWCA Civ 759, [2002] 1 W.L.R. 525 (CA), Brooke, L.J.; see *James v Baily Gibson & Co* [2002] EWCA Civ 1690, (2002) 99(46) L.S.G. 33 (CA), May, L.J.; see *Plymouth City Council v Hoskin* [2002] EWCA Civ 684, [2002] C.P. Rep. 55 (CA), Pill, L.J.; see *Sengupta v Holmes* [2002] EWCA Civ 1104, Times, August 19, 2002 (CA), Laws, L.J.; see *Sierra Leone v Davenport (No.2)* [2002] EWCA Civ 230, [2002] C.P.L.R. 236 (CA), Jonathan Parker, L.J.; see *Slot v Isaac* [2002] EWCA Civ 481, [2002] C.P. Rep. 57 (CA), Brooke, L.J.; see *Societe Internationale de Telecommunications Aeronautiques SC v Wyatt Co (UK) Ltd (Costs)* [2002] EWHC 2401, (2003) 147 S.J.L.B. 27 (Ch D), Park, J.; see *Wilkinson v Lord Chancellor's Department* [2003] EWCA Civ 95, [2003] 1 W.L.R. 1254 (CA), Hale, L.J.

Part 52 r.52.4, see *Barnet LBC v Hurst* [2002] EWCA Civ 1009, [2003] 1 W.L.R. 722 (CA), Brooke, L.J.; see *Kirin-Amgen Inc v Transkaryotic Therapies Inc (No.2)* [2002] R.P.C. 2 (Pat Ct), Neuberger, J.; see *Sayers v Clarke Walker (Permission to*

NO.

1998-cont.

3132. Civil Procedure Rules 1998-*cont.*

Part 52 r.52.4-*cont.*

Appeal: Extension of Time Limits) [2002] EWCA Civ 645, [2002] 1 W.L.R. 3095 (CA), Brooke, L.J.

Part 52 r.52.7, see *Aoun v Bahri (No.1)* [2002] EWCA Civ 1141, [2003] C.P. Rep. 6 (CA), Brooke, L.J.

Part 52 r.52.9, see *Barings Plc (In Liquidation) v Coopers & Lybrand (No.6) (Application to Set Aside Permission to Appeal)* [2002] EWCA Civ 1155, [2003] C.P. Rep. 2 (CA), Jonathan Parker, L.J.; see *Bell Electric Ltd v Aweco Appliance Systems GmbH & Co KG (Application to Stay Appeal)* [2002] EWCA Civ 1501, [2003] 1 All E.R. 344 (CA), Potter, L.J.; see *Carr v Bower Cotton (A Firm) (Application to Strike Out)* [2002] EWCA Civ 789, [2002] C.P. Rep. 60 (CA), Chadwick, L.J.; see *Hammond Suddards Solicitors v Agrichem International Holdings Ltd (Stay of Proceedings)* [2001] EWCA Civ 1915, [2002] C.P. Rep. 21 (CA), Clarke, L.J.; see *Komercni Banka AS v Stone & Rolls Ltd* [2003] EWCA Civ 311, [2003] C.P. Rep. 58 (CA), Potter, L.J.; see *Mamidoil-Jetoil Greek Petroleum Co SA v Okta Crude Oil Refinery AD (No.4)* [2003] EWCA Civ 617, [2003] 2 Lloyd's Rep 645 (CA), Clarke, L.J.

Part 52 r.52.10, amended: SI 2004/2072 r.13

Part 52 r.52.10, see *Kiam v MGN Ltd* [2002] EWCA Civ 43, [2003] Q.B. 281 (CA), Simon Brown, L.J.; see *Southampton City Council v G* [2002] EWHC 1516, [2002] E.L.R. 698 (QBD (Admin)), Sullivan, J.

Part 52 r.52.11, see *Assicurazioni Generali SpA v Arab Insurance Group (BSC)* [2002] EWCA Civ 1642, [2003] 1 W.L.R. 577 (CA), Clarke, L.J.; see *Audergon v La Baguette Ltd* [2002] EWCA Civ 10, [2002] C.P. Rep. 27 (CA), Jonathan Parker, L.J.; see *Bhopal v Sphere Drake Insurance Plc* [2002] Lloyd's Rep. I.R. 413 (CA), Wilson, J.; see *El du Pont de Nemours & Co v ST Dupont (Appeals: Procedure)* Times, November 7, 2002 (Ch D), Neuberger, J.; see *Evans v Tiger Investments Ltd* [2002] EWCA Civ 161, [2002] 2 B.C.L.C. 185 (CA), Potter, L.J.; see *Frewen v Secretary of State for Trade and Industry* [2002] EWHC 2688, [2003] 2 B.C.L.C. 305 (Ch D), Park, J.; see *King v Telegraph Group Ltd* [2004] EWCA Civ 613, [2004] 3 Costs L.R. 449 (CA), Brooke, L.J.; see *Ministere de l'Agriculture de la Foret v Bernard Matthews Plc* [2002] EWHC 190, [2002] E.T.M.R. 90 (Ch D), Lawrence Collins, J.

Part 52 r.52.11.3, see *Hayes v Transco Plc* [2003] EWCA Civ 1261, (2003) 147 S.J.L.B. 1089 (CA), Clarke, L.J.

Part 52 r.52.12, amended: SI 2003/3361 r.10

NO.

1998–cont.

3132. Civil Procedure Rules 1998–*cont.*

Part 52 r.52.12, see *Garratt v Saxby* [2004] EWCA Civ 341, [2004] 1 W.L.R. 2152 (CA), Ward, L.J.

Part 52 r.52.13, see *Barnet LBC v Hurst* [2002] EWCA Civ 1009, [2003] 1 W.L.R. 722 (CA), Brooke, L.J.; see *Hatton v Kendrick* [2002] EWCA Civ 1783, [2003] C.P. Rep. 32 (CA), Scott Baker, L.J.; see *Sawden v Sawden* [2004] EWCA Civ 339, [2004] 1 F.C.R. 776 (CA), Ward, L.J.

Part 52 r.52.16, amended: SI 2003/3361 r.11

Part 52 r.52.16, see *Hansen v Great Future International Ltd* [2003] EWCA Civ 1646, [2004] C.P. Rep. 14 (CA), Waller, L.J.

Part 53, see *Downtex v Flatley* [2003] EWCA Civ 1282, (2003) 147 S.J.L.B. 1152 (CA), Chadwick, L.J.; see *Phillipps v Associated Newspapers Ltd* [2004] EWHC 190, [2004] 1 W.L.R. 2106 (QBD), Eady, J.

Part 54, added: SI 2003/364 Sch.1 Part 2

Part 54, see *Practice Statement (Admin Ct: Administration of Justice)* [2002] 1 W.L.R. 810 (QBD (Admin Ct)), Scott Baker, J.; see *R. (on the application of G) v Ealing LBC (No.2)* [2002] EWHC 250, Times, March 18, 2002 (QBD (Admin Ct)), Munby, J.; see *R. (on the application of Heather) v Leonard Cheshire Foundation* [2002] EWCA Civ 366, [2002] 2 All E.R. 936 (CA), Lord Woolf of Barnes, L.C.J.

Part 54 PD 54 para.8.5, see *R. (on the application of Payne) v Caerphilly CBC (Costs)* [2004] EWCA Civ 433, (2004) 148 S.J.L.B. 384 (CA), Dyson, L.J.

Part 54 PD 54 para.8.6, see *R. (on the application of Payne) v Caerphilly CBC (Costs)* [2004] EWCA Civ 433, (2004) 148 S.J.L.B. 384 (CA), Dyson, L.J.

Part 54 r.54.1, amended: SI 2003/364 r.3

Part 54 r.54.1, substituted: SI 2003/364 Sch.1 Part 1

Part 54 r.54.1, amended: SI 2003/364 r.3, r.5

Part 54 r.54.1, revoked (in part): SI 2003/3361 r.12

Part 54 r.54.1, substituted: SI 2003/364 Sch.1 Part 1

Part 54 r.54.1, see *R. (on the application of A) v Partnerships in Care Ltd* [2002] EWHC 529, [2002] 1 W.L.R. 2610 (QBD (Admin Ct)), Keith, J.

Part 54 r.54.2, amended: SI 2003/364 r.3

Part 54 r.54.2, substituted: SI 2003/364 Sch.1 Part 1

Part 54 r.54.2, amended: SI 2003/364 r.3, r.5

Part 54 r.54.2, substituted: SI 2003/364 Sch.1 Part 1

Part 54 r.54.3, amended: SI 2003/364 r.3

Part 54 r.54.3, substituted: SI 2003/364 Sch.1 Part 1

Part 54 r.54.3, amended: SI 2003/364 r.3, r.5, SI 2003/3361 r.13

NO.

1998–cont.

3132. Civil Procedure Rules 1998–*cont.*

Part 54 r.54.3, substituted: SI 2003/364 Sch.1 Part 1

Part 54 r.54.4, amended: SI 2003/364 r.3

Part 54 r.54.4, substituted: SI 2003/364 Sch.1 Part 1

Part 54 r.54.4, amended: SI 2003/364 r.3, r.5

Part 54 r.54.4, substituted: SI 2003/364 Sch.1 Part 1

Part 54 r.54.5, amended: SI 2003/364 r.3

Part 54 r.54.5, substituted: SI 2003/364 Sch.1 Part 1

Part 54 r.54.5, amended: SI 2003/364 r.3

Part 54 r.54.5, substituted: SI 2003/364 Sch.1 Part 1

Part 54 r.54.6, amended: SI 2003/364 r.3

Part 54 r.54.6, substituted: SI 2003/364 Sch.1 Part 1

Part 54 r.54.6, amended: SI 2003/364 r.3

Part 54 r.54.6, substituted: SI 2003/364 Sch.1 Part 1

Part 54 r.54.7, amended: SI 2003/364 r.3

Part 54 r.54.7, substituted: SI 2003/364 Sch.1 Part 1

Part 54 r.54.7, amended: SI 2003/364 r.3

Part 54 r.54.7, substituted: SI 2003/364 Sch.1 Part 1

Part 54 r.54.8, amended: SI 2003/364 r.3

Part 54 r.54.8, substituted: SI 2003/364 Sch.1 Part 1

Part 54 r.54.8, amended: SI 2003/364 r.3

Part 54 r.54.8, substituted: SI 2003/364 Sch.1 Part 1

Part 54 r.54.8, see *R. (on the application of Mount Cook Land Ltd) v Westminster City Council* [2003] EWCA Civ 1346, [2004] C.P. Rep. 12 (CA), Auld, L.J.

Part 54 r.54.9, amended: SI 2003/364 r.3

Part 54 r.54.9, substituted: SI 2003/364 Sch.1 Part 1

Part 54 r.54.9, amended: SI 2003/364 r.3

Part 54 r.54.9, substituted: SI 2003/364 Sch.1 Part 1

Part 54 r.54.10, amended: SI 2003/364 r.3

Part 54 r.54.10, substituted: SI 2003/364 Sch.1 Part 1

Part 54 r.54.10, amended: SI 2003/364 r.3

Part 54 r.54.10, substituted: SI 2003/364 Sch.1 Part 1

Part 54 r.54.11, amended: SI 2003/364 r.3

Part 54 r.54.11, substituted: SI 2003/364 Sch.1 Part 1

Part 54 r.54.11, amended: SI 2003/364 r.3

Part 54 r.54.11, substituted: SI 2003/364 Sch.1 Part 1

Part 54 r.54.12, amended: SI 2003/364 r.3

Part 54 r.54.12, substituted: SI 2003/364 Sch.1 Part 1

Part 54 r.54.12, amended: SI 2003/364 r.3

Part 54 r.54.12, substituted: SI 2003/364 Sch.1 Part 1

1998–cont.

3132. Civil Procedure Rules 1998–*cont.*

Part 54 r.54.13, amended: SI 2003/364 r.3

Part 54 r.54.13, substituted: SI 2003/364 Sch.1 Part 1

Part 54 r.54.13, amended: SI 2003/364 r.3

Part 54 r.54.13, substituted: SI 2003/364 Sch.1 Part 1

Part 54 r.54.14, amended: SI 2003/364 r.3

Part 54 r.54.14, substituted: SI 2003/364 Sch.1 Part 1

Part 54 r.54.14, amended: SI 2003/364 r.3

Part 54 r.54.14, substituted: SI 2003/364 Sch.1 Part 1

Part 54 r.54.15, amended: SI 2003/364 r.3

Part 54 r.54.15, substituted: SI 2003/364 Sch.1 Part 1

Part 54 r.54.15, amended: SI 2003/364 r.3

Part 54 r.54.15, substituted: SI 2003/364 Sch.1 Part 1

Part 54 r.54.15, see *R. (on the application of Opoku) v Southwark College Principal* [2002] EWHC 2092, [2003] 1 W.L.R. 234 (QBD (Admin Ct)), Lightman, J.

Part 54 r.54.16, amended: SI 2002/2058 r.21, SI 2003/364 r.3

Part 54 r.54.16, substituted: SI 2003/364 Sch.1 Part 1

Part 54 r.54.16, amended: SI 2003/364 r.3, r.5

Part 54 r.54.16, substituted: SI 2003/364 Sch.1 Part 1

Part 54 r.54.17, amended: SI 2003/364 r.3

Part 54 r.54.17, substituted: SI 2003/364 Sch.1 Part 1

Part 54 r.54.17, amended: SI 2003/364 r.3

Part 54 r.54.17, substituted: SI 2003/364 Sch.1 Part 1

Part 54 r.54.18, amended: SI 2003/364 r.3

Part 54 r.54.18, substituted: SI 2003/364 Sch.1 Part 1

Part 54 r.54.18, amended: SI 2003/364 r.3

Part 54 r.54.18, substituted: SI 2003/364 Sch.1 Part 1

Part 54 r.54.19, amended: SI 2003/364 r.3

Part 54 r.54.19, substituted: SI 2003/364 Sch.1 Part 1

Part 54 r.54.19, amended: SI 2003/364 r.3

Part 54 r.54.19, substituted: SI 2003/364 Sch.1 Part 1

Part 54 r.54.20, amended: SI 2003/364 r.3

Part 54 r.54.20, substituted: SI 2003/364 Sch.1 Part 1

Part 54 r.54.20, amended: SI 2003/364 r.3, r.5

Part 54 r.54.20, substituted: SI 2003/364 Sch.1 Part 1

Part 54 r.54.21, amended: SI 2003/364 r.3

Part 54 r.54.21, substituted: SI 2003/364 Sch.1 Part 1

Part 54 r.54.22, amended: SI 2003/364 r.3, SI 2003/1329 r.4

1998–cont.

3132. Civil Procedure Rules 1998–*cont.*

Part 54 r.54.22, revoked (in part): SI 2003/1329 r.4

Part 54 r.54.22, substituted: SI 2003/364 Sch.1 Part 1

Part 54 r.54.23, amended: SI 2003/364 r.3

Part 54 r.54.23, substituted: SI 2003/364 Sch.1 Part 1

Part 54 r.54.24, amended: SI 2003/364 r.3

Part 54 r.54.24, substituted: SI 2003/364 Sch.1 Part 1

Part 54 r.54.25, amended: SI 2003/364 r.3

Part 54 r.54.25, substituted: SI 2003/364 Sch.1 Part 1

Part 54 r.54.26, amended: SI 2003/364 r.3

Part 54 r.54.26, substituted: SI 2003/364 Sch.1 Part 1

Part 54 r.54.27, amended: SI 2003/364 r.3

Part 54 r.54.27, substituted: SI 2003/364 Sch.1 Part 1

Part 55, added: SI 2002/2058 Sch.3

Part 55 r.55.1, amended: SI 2004/1306 r.10

Part 55 r.55.1, see *Drury v Secretary of State for the Environment, Food and Rural Affairs* [2004] EWCA Civ 200, [2004] 1 W.L.R. 1906 (CA), Ward, L.J.

Part 55 r.55.2, amended: SI 2002/2058 r.22, SI 2004/1306 r.11

Part 55 r.55.3, see *Scribes West Ltd v Anstalt (No.2)* [2004] EWCA Civ 965, [2004] 4 All E.R. 653 (CA), Brooke, L.J.

Part 55 r.55.9, amended: SI 2004/1306 r.12

Part 55 r.55.11, amended: SI 2004/1306 r.13

Part 55 r.55.12, amended: SI 2004/1306 r.14

Part 55 r.55.12, substituted: SI 2004/1306 r.14

Part 56 r.56.2, amended: SI 2004/1306 r.15

Part 56 r.56.2, revoked (in part): SI 2004/1306 r.15

Part 56 r.56.3, substituted: SI 2004/1306 r.16

Part 56 r.56.4, amended: SI 2002/3219 r.7

Part 56 r.56.6, see *Foenander v Bond Lewis & Co* [2001] EWCA Civ 759, [2002] 1 W.L.R. 525 (CA), Brooke, L.J.

Part 57, added: SI 2002/2058 Sch.4

Part 57 r.57.1, amended: SI 2002/2058 r.23

Part 57 r.57.2, amended: SI 2002/2058 r.23, SI 2003/2113 r.15

Part 57 r.57.3, amended: SI 2002/2058 r.23

Part 57 r.57.4, amended: SI 2002/2058 r.23

Part 57 r.57.5, amended: SI 2002/2058 r.23

Part 57 r.57.6, amended: SI 2002/2058 r.23

Part 57 r.57.7, amended: SI 2002/2058 r.23

Part 57 r.57.8, amended: SI 2002/2058 r.23

Part 57 r.57.9, amended: SI 2002/2058 r.23, SI 2003/3361 r.14

Part 57 r.57.10, amended: SI 2002/2058 r.23

Part 57 r.57.11, amended: SI 2002/2058 r.23

Part 57 r.57.12, amended: SI 2002/2058 r.23

Part 57 r.57.13, amended: SI 2002/2058 r.23

Part 57 r.57.14, amended: SI 2002/2058 r.23

1998–cont.

3132. Civil Procedure Rules 1998–*cont.*

Part 57 r.57.15, amended: SI 2002/2058 r.23

Part 57 r.57.16, amended: SI 2002/2058 r.23, SI 2004/1306 r.17

Part 58, see *Practice Statement (QBD: Admiralty and Commercial Courts: Procedure)* Times, April 2, 2002 (QBD), Moore-Bick, J.

Part 61, see *Practice Statement (QBD: Admiralty and Commercial Courts: Procedure)* Times, April 2, 2002 (QBD), Moore-Bick, J.

Part 61 r.61.11, see *ICL Shipping Ltd v Chin Tai Steel Enterprise Co Ltd (The ICL Vikraman)* [2003] EWHC 2320, [2004] 1 W.L.R. 2254 (QBD (Comm Ct)), Colman, J.

Part 62, see *Nagusina Naviera v Allied Maritime Inc* [2002] C.L.C. 385 (QBD (Comm Ct)), Andrew Smith, J.; see *Practice Statement (QBD: Admiralty and Commercial Courts: Procedure)* Times, April 2, 2002 (QBD), Moore-Bick, J.

Part 62 r.62.10, see *Department of Economic Policy and Development of the City of Moscow v Bankers Trust Co* [2003] EWHC 1377, [2003] 1 W.L.R. 2885 (QBD (Comm Ct)), Cooke, J.; see *Department of Economic Policy and Development of the City of Moscow v Bankers Trust Co* [2004] EWCA Civ 314, [2004] 3 W.L.R. 533 (CA), Sir Andrew Morritt V.C.

Part 62 r.62.20, amended: SI 2002/2058 r.24

Part 62 r.62.21, amended: SI 2002/2058 r.25

Part 63 r.63.1, added: SI 2002/3219 Sch.1

Part 63 r.63.2, added: SI 2002/3219 Sch.1

Part 63 r.63.3, added: SI 2002/3219 Sch.1

Part 63 r.63.4, added: SI 2002/3219 Sch.1

Part 63 r.63.5, added: SI 2002/3219 Sch.1

Part 63 r.63.6, added: SI 2002/3219 Sch.1

Part 63 r.63.7, added: SI 2002/3219 Sch.1

Part 63 r.63.7, amended: SI 2003/3361 r.15

Part 63 r.63.8, added: SI 2002/3219 Sch.1

Part 63 r.63.9, added: SI 2002/3219 Sch.1

Part 63 r.63.9, amended: SI 2003/3361 r.16

Part 63 r.63.10, added: SI 2002/3219 Sch.1

Part 63 r.63.11, added: SI 2002/3219 Sch.1

Part 63 r.63.12, added: SI 2002/3219 Sch.1

Part 63 r.63.13, added: SI 2002/3219 Sch.1

Part 63 r.63.14, added: SI 2002/3219 Sch.1

Part 63 r.63.15, added: SI 2002/3219 Sch.1

Part 63 r.63.16, added: SI 2002/3219 Sch.1

Part 63 r.63.16, substituted: SI 2003/3361 r.17

Part 63 r.63.17, added: SI 2002/3219 Sch.1

Part 64 r.64.1, added: SI 2002/2058 Sch.5

Part 64 r.64.1, see *CI v NS* [2004] EWHC 659, [2004] W.T.L.R. 1113 (Fam Div), Baron, J

Part 64 r.64.2, added: SI 2002/2058 Sch.5

Part 64 r.64.3, added: SI 2002/2058 Sch.5

Part 64 r.64.4, added: SI 2002/2058 Sch.5

Part 64 r.64.5, added: SI 2002/2058 Sch.5

1998–cont.

3132. Civil Procedure Rules 1998–*cont.*

Part 64 r.64.6, added: SI 2002/2058 Sch.5

Part 65 r.65.1, added: SI 2004/1306 Sch.2

Part 65 r.65.2, added: SI 2004/1306 Sch.2

Part 65 r.65.3, added: SI 2004/1306 Sch.2

Part 65 r.65.3, amended: SI 2004/2072 r.14

Part 65 r.65.4, added: SI 2004/1306 Sch.2

Part 65 r.65.5, added: SI 2004/1306 Sch.2

Part 65 r.65.6, added: SI 2004/1306 Sch.2

Part 65 r.65.7, added: SI 2004/1306 Sch.2

Part 65 r.65.8, added: SI 2004/1306 Sch.2

Part 65 r.65.9, added: SI 2004/1306 Sch.2

Part 65 r.65.10, added: SI 2004/1306 Sch.2

Part 65 r.65.11, added: SI 2004/1306 Sch.2

Part 65 r.65.12, added: SI 2004/1306 Sch.2

Part 65 r.65.13, added: SI 2004/1306 Sch.2

Part 65 r.65.14, added: SI 2004/1306 Sch.2

Part 65 r.65.15, added: SI 2004/1306 Sch.2

Part 65 r.65.16, added: SI 2004/1306 Sch.2

Part 65 r.65.17, added: SI 2004/1306 Sch.2

Part 65 r.65.18, added: SI 2004/1306 Sch.2

Part 65 r.65.19, added: SI 2004/1306 Sch.2

Part 65 r.65.20, added: SI 2004/1306 Sch.2

Part 65 r.65.21, added: SI 2004/1306 Sch.2

Part 65 r.65.22, added: SI 2004/1306 Sch.2

Part 65 r.65.23, added: SI 2004/1306 Sch.2

Part 65 r.65.24, added: SI 2004/1306 Sch.2

Part 65 r.65.25, added: SI 2004/1306 Sch.2

Part 65 r.65.26, added: SI 2004/1306 Sch.2

Part 65 r.65.27, added: SI 2004/1306 Sch.2

Part 65 r.65.28, added: SI 2004/1306 Sch.2

Part 65 r.65.29, added: SI 2004/1306 Sch.2

Part 65 r.65.30, added: SI 2004/1306 Sch.2

Part 68 r.68.1, added: SI 2002/2058 Sch.6

Part 68 r.68.2, added: SI 2002/2058 Sch.6

Part 68 r.68.3, added: SI 2002/2058 Sch.6

Part 68 r.68.4, added: SI 2002/2058 Sch.6

Part 69 r.69.1, added: SI 2002/2058 Sch.7

Part 69 r.69.2, added: SI 2002/2058 Sch.7

Part 69 r.69.3, added: SI 2002/2058 Sch.7

Part 69 r.69.4, added: SI 2002/2058 Sch.7

Part 69 r.69.5, added: SI 2002/2058 Sch.7

Part 69 r.69.6, added: SI 2002/2058 Sch.7

Part 69 r.69.7, added: SI 2002/2058 Sch.7

Part 69 r.69.8, added: SI 2002/2058 Sch.7

Part 69 r.69.9, added: SI 2002/2058 Sch.7

Part 69 r.69.10, added: SI 2002/2058 Sch.7

Part 69 r.69.10, amended: SI 2004/1306 r.19

Part 69 r.69.10, substituted: SI 2004/1306 r.19

Part 69 r.69.11, added: SI 2002/2058 Sch.7

Part 70 r.70.1, amended: SI 2002/2058 r.27

Part 70 r.70.5, amended: SI 2002/2058 r.28, SI 2003/2113 r.16

Part 74 r.74.1, added: SI 2002/2058 Sch.8

Part 74 r.74.2, added: SI 2002/2058 Sch.8

Part 74 r.74.3, added: SI 2002/2058 Sch.8

Part 74 r.74.4, added: SI 2002/2058 Sch.8

Part 74 r.74.5, added: SI 2002/2058 Sch.8

Part 74 r.74.6, added: SI 2002/2058 Sch.8

1998–cont.

3132. Civil Procedure Rules 1998–*cont.*

Part 74 r.74.7, added: SI 2002/2058 Sch.8
Part 74 r.74.8, added: SI 2002/2058 Sch.8
Part 74 r.74.8, see *Citibank NA v Rafidian Bank* [2003] EWHC 1950, [2003] 2 All E.R. (Comm.) 1054 (QBD), Tugendhat, J.
Part 74 r.74.9, added: SI 2002/2058 Sch.8
Part 74 r.74.10, added: SI 2002/2058 Sch.8
Part 74 r.74.11, added: SI 2002/2058 Sch.8
Part 74 r.74.12, added: SI 2002/2058 Sch.8
Part 74 r.74.13, added: SI 2002/2058 Sch.8
Part 74 r.74.14, added: SI 2002/2058 Sch.8
Part 74 r.74.15, added: SI 2002/2058 Sch.8
Part 74 r.74.16, added: SI 2002/2058 Sch.8
Part 74 r.74.17, added: SI 2002/2058 Sch.8
Part 74 r.74.18, added: SI 2002/2058 Sch.8
Part 74 r.74.19, added: SI 2002/2058 Sch.8
Part 74 r.74.19, amended: SI 2003/3361 r.18
Part 74 r.74.20, added: SI 2002/2058 Sch.8
Part 74 r.74.21, added: SI 2002/2058 Sch.8
Part 74 r.74.22, added: SI 2002/2058 Sch.8
Part 74 r.74.23, added: SI 2002/2058 Sch.8
Part 74 r.74.24, added: SI 2002/2058 Sch.8
Part 74 r.74.25, added: SI 2002/2058 Sch.8
Part 74 r.74.26, added: SI 2002/2058 Sch.8
Part 75 r.75.1, added: SI 2002/2058 Sch.9
Part 75 r.75.2, added: SI 2002/2058 Sch.9
Part 75 r.75.3, added: SI 2002/2058 Sch.9
Part 75 r.75.4, added: SI 2002/2058 Sch.9
Part 75 r.75.5, added: SI 2002/2058 Sch.9
Part 75 r.75.6, added: SI 2002/2058 Sch.9
Part 75 r.75.7, added: SI 2002/2058 Sch.9
Part 75 r.75.8, added: SI 2002/2058 Sch.9
Part 75 r.75.9, added: SI 2002/2058 Sch.9
Part 75 r.75.10, added: SI 2002/2058 Sch.9
Part 75 r.75.11, added: SI 2002/2058 Sch.9
r.1.1, see *Dicker v Scammell* [2003] EWHC 1601, [2003] N.P.C. 90 (QBD), McCombe, J.
r.44.4, see *Habib Bank Ltd v Ahmed (Permission to Appeal)* [2004] EWCA Civ 805, [2004] B.P.I.R. 864 (CA), Auld, L.J.
Sch.1 Ord.11 r.1, see *ABCI (formerly Arab Business Consortium International Finance & Investment Co) v Banque Franco-Tunisienne (Costs)* [2003] EWCA Civ 205, [2003] 2 Lloyd's Rep 146 (CA), Mance, L.J.
Sch.1 Part 15 para.6A, revoked: SI 2002/2058 Sch.10
Sch.1 Part 15 para.7, revoked: SI 2002/2058 Sch.10
Sch.1 Part 15 para.9, revoked: SI 2002/2058 Sch.10
Sch.1 Part 15 para.11, revoked: SI 2002/2058 Sch.10
Sch.1 Part 15 para.12, revoked: SI 2002/2058 Sch.10
Sch.1 Part 15 para.12A, revoked: SI 2002/2058 Sch.10

1998–cont.

3132. Civil Procedure Rules 1998–*cont.*

Sch.1 Part 15 para.13, revoked: SI 2002/2058 Sch.10
Sch.1 Part 15 para.13A, revoked: SI 2002/2058 Sch.10
Sch.1 Part 15 para.14, revoked: SI 2002/2058 Sch.10
Sch.1 Part 15 para.15, revoked: SI 2002/2058 Sch.10
Sch.1 Part 15 para.16, revoked: SI 2002/2058 Sch.10
Sch.1 Part 15 para.17, revoked: SI 2002/2058 Sch.10
Sch.1 Part 17 para.1, amended: SI 2003/3361 r.19
Sch.1 Part 30 paraA.1, revoked: SI 2002/2058 Sch.10
Sch.1 Part 30 para.1, revoked: SI 2002/2058 Sch.10
Sch.1 Part 30 para.2, revoked: SI 2002/2058 Sch.10
Sch.1 Part 30 para.3, revoked: SI 2002/2058 Sch.10
Sch.1 Part 30 para.4, revoked: SI 2002/2058 Sch.10
Sch.1 Part 30 para.5, revoked: SI 2002/2058 Sch.10
Sch.1 Part 30 para.6, revoked: SI 2002/2058 Sch.10
Sch.1 Part 30 para.7, revoked: SI 2002/2058 Sch.10
Sch.1 Part 30 para.8, revoked: SI 2002/2058 Sch.10
Sch.1 Part 44 para.1, revoked: SI 2002/2058 Sch.10
Sch.1 Part 44 para.2, revoked: SI 2002/2058 Sch.10
Sch.1 Part 44 para.3, revoked: SI 2002/2058 Sch.10
Sch.1 Part 44 para.4, revoked: SI 2002/2058 Sch.10
Sch.1 Part 44 para.5, revoked: SI 2002/2058 Sch.10
Sch.1 Part 44 para.6, revoked: SI 2002/2058 Sch.10
Sch.1 Part 44 para.7, revoked: SI 2002/2058 Sch.10
Sch.1 Part 44 para.8, revoked: SI 2002/2058 Sch.10
Sch.1 Part 44 para.9, revoked: SI 2002/2058 Sch.10
Sch.1 Part 44 para.10, revoked: SI 2002/2058 Sch.10
Sch.1 Part 44 para.11, revoked: SI 2002/2058 Sch.10
Sch.1 Part 44 para.12, revoked: SI 2002/2058 Sch.10
Sch.1 Part 45 para.1A, added: SI 2003/3361 r.20
Sch.1 Part 45 para.2, amended: SI 2003/3361 r.21

1998–cont.

3132. Civil Procedure Rules 1998–*cont.*

Sch.1 Part 45 para.8, amended: SI 2003/
3361 r.22

Sch.1 Ord.46 r.2, see *Patel v Singh* [2002]
EWCA Civ 1938, [2003] C.P.L.R. 149
(CA), Peter Gibson, L.J.

Sch.1 Part 46 para.8, amended: SI 2003/
3361 r.23

Sch.1 Part 46 para.9, amended: SI 2003/
3361 r.24

Sch.1 Part 47 para.2, revoked: SI 2003/3361
r.25

Sch.1 Part 47 para.4, amended: SI 2003/3361
r.26

Sch.1 Part 47 para.5, amended: SI 2003/3361
r.27

Sch.1 Part 47 para.6, amended: SI 2003/3361
r.28

Sch.1 Part 51 paraA.1, revoked: SI 2002/2058
Sch.10

Sch.1 Part 51 para.1, revoked: SI 2002/2058
Sch.10

Sch.1 Part 51 para.2, revoked: SI 2002/2058
Sch.10

Sch.1 Part 51 para.3, revoked: SI 2002/2058
Sch.10

Sch.1 Part 52 para.1, amended: SI 2002/2058
r.30

Sch.1 Part 52 para.7A, added: SI 2003/3361
r.29

Sch.1 Part 69 para.1, revoked: SI 2002/2058
Sch.10

Sch.1 Part 69 para.2, revoked: SI 2002/2058
Sch.10

Sch.1 Part 69 para.3, revoked: SI 2002/2058
Sch.10

Sch.1 Part 69 para.4, revoked: SI 2002/2058
Sch.10

Sch.1 Part 70 para.1, revoked: SI 2002/2058
Sch.10

Sch.1 Part 70 para.2, revoked: SI 2002/2058
Sch.10

Sch.1 Part 70 para.3, revoked: SI 2002/2058
Sch.10

Sch.1 Part 70 para.4, revoked: SI 2002/2058
Sch.10

Sch.1 Part 70 para.5, revoked: SI 2002/2058
Sch.10

Sch.1 Part 70 para.6, revoked: SI 2002/2058
Sch.10

Sch.1 Part 71 para.1, revoked: SI 2002/2058
Sch.10

Sch.1 Part 71 para.2, revoked: SI 2002/2058
Sch.10

Sch.1 Part 71 para.3, revoked: SI 2002/2058
Sch.10

Sch.1 Part 71 para.4, revoked: SI 2002/2058
Sch.10

Sch.1 Part 71 para.5, revoked: SI 2002/2058
Sch.10

1998–cont.

3132. Civil Procedure Rules 1998–*cont.*

Sch.1 Part 71 para.6, revoked: SI 2002/2058
Sch.10

Sch.1 Part 71 para.7, revoked: SI 2002/2058
Sch.10

Sch.1 Part 71 para.9, revoked: SI 2002/2058
Sch.10

Sch.1 Part 71 para.10, revoked: SI 2002/2058
Sch.10

Sch.1 Part 71 para.11, revoked: SI 2002/2058
Sch.10

Sch.1 Part 71 para.12, revoked: SI 2002/2058
Sch.10

Sch.1 Part 71 para.13, revoked: SI 2002/2058
Sch.10

Sch.1 Part 71 para.15, revoked: SI 2002/2058
Sch.10

Sch.1 Part 71 para.16, revoked: SI 2002/2058
Sch.10

Sch.1 Part 71 para.17, revoked: SI 2002/2058
Sch.10

Sch.1 Part 71 para.18, revoked: SI 2002/2058
Sch.10

Sch.1 Part 71 para.19, revoked: SI 2002/2058
Sch.10

Sch.1 Part 71 para.20, revoked: SI 2002/2058
Sch.10

Sch.1 Part 71 para.21, revoked: SI 2002/2058
Sch.10

Sch.1 Part 71 para.22, revoked: SI 2002/2058
Sch.10

Sch.1 Part 71 para.23, revoked: SI 2002/2058
Sch.10

Sch.1 Part 71 para.24, revoked: SI 2002/2058
Sch.10

Sch.1 Part 71 para.25, revoked: SI 2002/2058
Sch.10

Sch.1 Part 71 para.26, revoked: SI 2002/2058
Sch.10

Sch.1 Part 71 para.27, revoked: SI 2002/2058
Sch.10

Sch.1 Part 71 para.28, revoked: SI 2002/2058
Sch.10

Sch.1 Part 71 para.29, revoked: SI 2002/2058
Sch.10

Sch.1 Part 71 para.30, revoked: SI 2002/2058
Sch.10

Sch.1 Part 71 para.31, revoked: SI 2002/2058
Sch.10

Sch.1 Part 71 para.32, revoked: SI 2002/2058
Sch.10

Sch.1 Part 71 para.33, revoked: SI 2002/2058
Sch.10

Sch.1 Part 71 para.34, revoked: SI 2002/2058
Sch.10

Sch.1 Part 71 para.35, revoked: SI 2002/2058
Sch.10

Sch.1 Part 71 para.36, revoked: SI 2002/2058
Sch.10

Sch.1 Part 71 para.37, revoked: SI 2002/2058
Sch.10

1998–cont.

3132. Civil Procedure Rules 1998–*cont.*

Sch.1 Part 71 para.38, revoked: SI 2002/2058 Sch.10

Sch.1 Part 71 para.39, revoked: SI 2002/2058 Sch.10

Sch.1 Part 71 para.39A, revoked: SI 2002/2058 Sch.10

Sch.1 Part 71 para.40, revoked: SI 2002/2058 Sch.10

Sch.1 Part 71 para.41, revoked: SI 2002/2058 Sch.10

Sch.1 Part 71 para.42, revoked: SI 2002/2058 Sch.10

Sch.1 Part 71 para.43, revoked: SI 2002/2058 Sch.10

Sch.1 Part 71 para.44, revoked: SI 2002/2058 Sch.10

Sch.1 Part 71 para.45, revoked: SI 2002/2058 Sch.10

Sch.1 Part 71 para.46, revoked: SI 2002/2058 Sch.10

Sch.1 Part 71 para.47, revoked: SI 2002/2058 Sch.10

Sch.1 Part 71 para.48, revoked: SI 2002/2058 Sch.10

Sch.1 Part 71 para.49, revoked: SI 2002/2058 Sch.10

Sch.1 Part 71 para.50, revoked: SI 2002/2058 Sch.10

Sch.1 Part 71 para.51, revoked: SI 2002/2058 Sch.10

Sch.1 Part 71 para.52, revoked: SI 2002/2058 Sch.10

Sch.1 Part 71 para.53, revoked: SI 2002/2058 Sch.10

Sch.1 Part 71 para.54, revoked: SI 2002/2058 Sch.10

Sch.1 Part 71 para.55, revoked: SI 2002/2058 Sch.10

Sch.1 Part 71 para.56, revoked: SI 2002/2058 Sch.10

Sch.1 Part 71 para.57, revoked: SI 2002/2058 Sch.10

Sch.1 Part 77 para.15, amended: SI 2002/2058 r.31

Sch.1 Part 77 para.16, amended: SI 2002/2058 r.31

Sch.1 Part 79 para.9, amended: SI 2003/3361 r.30

Sch.1 RSC Ord.85, see *Pennington v Waine (No.2)* [2003] W.T.L.R. 1011 (Ch D), Judge Hegarty Q.C.

Sch.1 Part 85 para.1, revoked: SI 2002/2058 Sch.10

Sch.1 Part 85 para.2, revoked: SI 2002/2058 Sch.10

Sch.1 Part 85 para.3, revoked: SI 2002/2058 Sch.10

Sch.1 Part 85 para.5, revoked: SI 2002/2058 Sch.10

1998–cont.

3132. Civil Procedure Rules 1998–*cont.*

Sch.1 Part 85 para.6, revoked: SI 2002/2058 Sch.10

Sch.1 Part 87 para.1, revoked: SI 2002/2058 Sch.10

Sch.1 Part 87 para.2, revoked: SI 2002/2058 Sch.10

Sch.1 Part 87 para.3, revoked: SI 2002/2058 Sch.10

Sch.1 Part 87 para.4, revoked: SI 2002/2058 Sch.10

Sch.1 Part 87 para.5, revoked: SI 2002/2058 Sch.10

Sch.1 Part 87 para.6, revoked: SI 2002/2058 Sch.10

Sch.1 Part 91 para.1, revoked: SI 2003/2113 r.19

Sch.1 Part 91 para.2, revoked: SI 2003/2113 r.19

Sch.1 Part 91 para.3, revoked: SI 2003/2113 r.19

Sch.1 Part 91 para.4, revoked: SI 2003/2113 r.19

Sch.1 Part 91 para.5, revoked: SI 2003/2113 r.19

Sch.1 Part 91 para.5A, revoked: SI 2003/2113 r.19

Sch.1 Part 91 para.6, revoked: SI 2003/2113 r.19

Sch.1 Part 92 para.1, revoked: SI 2002/2058 Sch.10

Sch.1 Part 92 para.2, revoked: SI 2002/2058 Sch.10

Sch.1 Part 92 para.3A, revoked: SI 2002/2058 Sch.10

Sch.1 Part 92 para.4, revoked: SI 2002/2058 Sch.10

Sch.1 Part 92 para.5, revoked: SI 2002/2058 Sch.10

Sch.1 Part 93 para.6, revoked: SI 2002/2058 Sch.10

Sch.1 Part 93 para.21, revoked: SI 2002/2058 Sch.10

Sch.1 Part 93 para.22, amended: SI 2003/3361 r.31

Sch.1 Part 94 para.16, revoked: SI 2004/1306 r.21

Sch.1 Part 98 para.1, revoked: SI 2004/1306 r.21

Sch.1 Part 98 para.2, revoked: SI 2004/1306 r.21

Sch.1 Part 98 para.3, revoked: SI 2004/1306 r.21

Sch.1 Part 98 para.4, revoked: SI 2004/1306 r.21

Sch.1 Part 99 paraA.1, revoked: SI 2002/2058 Sch.10

Sch.1 Part 99 para.1, revoked: SI 2002/2058 Sch.10

Sch.1 Part 99 para.2, revoked: SI 2002/2058 Sch.10

NO.

NO.

1998–cont.

3132. Civil Procedure Rules 1998–*cont.*

Sch.1 Part 99 para.3, revoked: SI 2002/2058 Sch.10

Sch.1 RSC Ord.99 r.3, see *Parnall v Hurst* [2003] W.T.L.R. 997 (Ch D), Peter Langan Q.C.

Sch.1 Part 99 para.4, revoked: SI 2002/2058 Sch.10

Sch.1 Part 99 para.5, revoked: SI 2002/2058 Sch.10

Sch.1 Part 99 para.6, revoked: SI 2002/2058 Sch.10

Sch.1 Part 99 para.7, revoked: SI 2002/2058 Sch.10

Sch.1 Part 99 para.8, revoked: SI 2002/2058 Sch.10

Sch.1 Part 99 para.9, revoked: SI 2002/2058 Sch.10

Sch.1 Part 99 para.10, revoked: SI 2002/2058 Sch.10

Sch.1 RSC Ord.106 r.12, see *Lucas v Millman* [2002] EWHC 2470, [2003] 1 W.L.R. 271 (QBD (Admin Ct)), Kennedy, L.J.

Sch.1 RSC Ord.106 r.13, see *Lucas v Millman* [2002] EWHC 2470, [2003] 1 W.L.R. 271 (QBD (Admin Ct)), Kennedy, L.J.

Sch.1 RSC Ord.106 r.15, see *Lucas v Millman* [2002] EWHC 2470, [2003] 1 W.L.R. 271 (QBD (Admin Ct)), Kennedy, L.J.

Sch.1 Part 108 para.1, revoked: SI 2002/2058 Sch.10

Sch.1 Part 108 para.2, revoked: SI 2002/2058 Sch.10

Sch.1 Part 108 para.3, revoked: SI 2002/2058 Sch.10

Sch.1 Part 108 para.4, revoked: SI 2002/2058 Sch.10

Sch.1 Part 108 para.5, revoked: SI 2002/2058 Sch.10

Sch.1 Part 108 para.6, revoked: SI 2002/2058 Sch.10

Sch.1 Part 114 para.1, revoked: SI 2002/2058 Sch.10

Sch.1 Part 114 para.2, revoked: SI 2002/2058 Sch.10

Sch.1 Part 114 para.3, revoked: SI 2002/2058 Sch.10

Sch.1 Part 114 para.4, revoked: SI 2002/2058 Sch.10

Sch.1 Part 114 para.5, revoked: SI 2002/2058 Sch.10

Sch.1 Part 114 para.6, revoked: SI 2002/2058 Sch.10

Sch.1 Part 115, added: SI 2003/2113 r.17

Sch.1 Part 115 para.8, amended: SI 2002/2058 r.32

Sch.2 Part 4 para.3, revoked: SI 2003/2113 r.19

Sch.2 Part 5 para.12, revoked: SI 2002/2058 Sch.10

1998–cont.

3132. Civil Procedure Rules 1998–*cont.*

Sch.2 Part 5 para.13, revoked: SI 2002/2058 Sch.10

Sch.2 Part 5 para.14, revoked: SI 2002/2058 Sch.10

Sch.2 Part 6 para.6, revoked: SI 2003/1242 r.7

Sch.2 Part 16 para.7, amended: SI 2003/3361 r.32

Sch.2 Part 19 para.15, revoked: SI 2002/2058 Sch.10

Sch.2 Part 24 para.8, revoked: SI 2002/2058 Sch.10

Sch.2 Part 24 para.9, revoked: SI 2002/2058 Sch.10

Sch.2 Part 24 para.10, revoked: SI 2002/2058 Sch.10

Sch.2 Part 24 para.11, revoked: SI 2002/2058 Sch.10

Sch.2 Part 24 para.12, revoked: SI 2002/2058 Sch.10

Sch.2 Part 24 para.13, revoked: SI 2002/2058 Sch.10

Sch.2 Part 24 para.14, revoked: SI 2002/2058 Sch.10

Sch.2 Part 24 para.15, revoked: SI 2002/2058 Sch.10

Sch.2 Part 29 para.1, amended: SI 2003/3361 r.33

Sch.2 Part 29 r.1, see *Benson v Richards* [2002] EWCA Civ 1402, Independent, October 17, 2002 (CA), Sir Andrew Morritt V.C.

Sch.2 Part 29 r.1.7, see *Bell v Tuohy* [2002] EWCA Civ 423, [2002] 1 W.L.R. 2703 (CA), Neuberger, J.

Sch.2 Part 35 para.1, revoked: SI 2002/2058 Sch.10

Sch.2 Part 35 para.2, revoked: SI 2002/2058 Sch.10

Sch.2 Part 35 para.3, revoked: SI 2002/2058 Sch.10

Sch.2 Part 35 para.3A, revoked: SI 2002/2058 Sch.10

Sch.2 Part 35 para.4, revoked: SI 2002/2058 Sch.10

Sch.2 Part 35 para.5, revoked: SI 2002/2058 Sch.10

Sch.2 Part 35 para.6, revoked: SI 2002/2058 Sch.10

Sch.2 Part 37 para.1, revoked: SI 2002/2058 Sch.10

Sch.2 Part 37 para.6, revoked: SI 2002/2058 Sch.10

Sch.2 Part 37 para.8, revoked: SI 2002/2058 Sch.10

Sch.2 Part 42 para.13, amended: SI 2002/2058 r.33

Sch.2 Part 42 para.13, revoked (in part): SI 2002/2058 r.33

NO.

1998–cont.

3132. Civil Procedure Rules 1998–*cont.*

Sch.2 Part 42 para.14, amended: SI 2002/2058 r.33

Sch.2 Part 48B para.1, revoked: SI 2002/2058 r.35

Sch.2 Part 48B para.1A, revoked: SI 2002/2058 r.35

Sch.2 Part 48B para.2, revoked: SI 2002/2058 r.35

Sch.2 Part 48B para.3, revoked: SI 2002/2058 r.35

Sch.2 Part 48B para.4, revoked: SI 2002/2058 r.35

Sch.2 Part 48B para.5, revoked: SI 2002/2058 r.35

Sch.2 Part 48D para.1, revoked: SI 2003/2113 r.19

Sch.2 Part 48D para.2, revoked: SI 2003/2113 r.19

Sch.2 Part 48D para.3, revoked: SI 2003/2113 r.19

Sch.2 Part 48D para.4, revoked: SI 2003/2113 r.19

Sch.2 Part 48D para.5, revoked: SI 2003/2113 r.19

Sch.2 Part 49 para.4A, revoked: SI 2003/2113 r.19

Sch.2 Part 49 para.5, revoked: SI 2003/2113 r.19

Sch.2 Part 49 para.6B, revoked: SI 2004/1306 r.21

Sch.2 Part 49 para.17, amended: SI 2003/3361 r.34, SI 2004/2072 r.15

Sch.2 Part 49 para.18B, revoked: SI 2003/2113 r.19

Sch.2 Part 49 para.20, revoked: SI 2002/2058 Sch.10

3134. County Borough of Bridgend (Electoral Arrangements) Order 1998

varied: SI 2004/218 Art.2

3135. County Borough of Caerphilly (Electoral Arrangements) Order 1998

varied: SI 2004/218 Art.2

3136. County of Carmarthenshire (Electoral Arrangements) Order 1998

varied: SI 2004/218 Art.2

3137. County Borough of Conwy (Electoral Arrangements) Order 1998

varied: SI 2004/218 Art.2

3138. County Borough of Rhondda Cynon Taff (Electoral Arrangements) Order 1998

varied: SI 2004/218 Art.2

3139. County of Denbighshire (Electoral Arrangements) Order 1998

varied: SI 2004/218 Art.2

3140. County of Flintshire (Electoral Arrangements) Order 1998

varied: SI 2004/218 Art.2

NO.

1998–cont.

3142. County Borough of Wrexham (Electoral Arrangements) Order 1998

varied: SI 2004/218 Art.2

3143. County of Powys (Electoral Arrangements) Order 1998

varied: SI 2004/218 Art.2

3162. Fair Employment and Treatment (Northern Ireland) Order 1998

referred to: SR 2002/120 Sch.1

Art.38, amended: SI 2003/2902 Sch.5 para.4

Art.38, applied: SI 2003/2902 Art.18, Art.20, Art.22, Art.28

Art.46, amended: SI 2003/2902 Sch.5 para.4

Art.50, applied: SR 2002/367

Art.50, enabled: SR 2002/367

Art.51, applied: SR 2002/367

Art.51, enabled: SR 2002/367

Art.52, applied: SR 2002/367

Art.53, applied: SR 2002/367

Art.54, applied: SR 2002/367

Art.55, applied: SR 2002/367

Art.56, applied: SR 2002/367

Art.57, applied: SR 2002/367

Art.58, applied: SR 2002/367

Art.59, applied: SR 2002/367

Art.60, applied: SR 2002/367

Art.61, applied: SR 2002/367

Art.62, applied: SR 2002/367

Art.63, applied: SR 2002/367

Art.64, applied: SR 2002/367

Art.65, applied: SR 2002/367

Art.81, amended: SI 2003/2902 Sch.5 para.4

Art.82, amended: 2002 c.26 Sch.3 para.29

Art.82, applied: 2002 c.26 Sch.1, Sch.6

Art.82, revoked (in part): 2002 c.26 Sch.13

Art.84, amended: SI 2003/2902 Art.9, Art.10, Art.11

Art.84, revoked (in part): SI 2003/2902 Art.9, Art.13, Art.14

Art.84A, added: SI 2003/2902 Art.12

Art.84B, added: SI 2003/2902 Art.13

Art.85A, added: SI 2003/2902 Art.14

Art.85B, added: SI 2003/2902 Art.14

Art.88, amended: SI 2003/2902 Art.11

Art.88, applied: SR 2002/120 Sch.1

3164. Rates (Amendment) (Northern Ireland) Order 1998

Sch.2 para.9, revoked: SI 2004/703 Sch.4

3167. Potatoes Originating in Egypt (Amendment) Regulations 1998

revoked (in part): SI 2004/1165 Reg.8, SI 2004/2245 Reg.8

3172. School Standards and Framework Act 1998 (Proposals under section 211 of the Education Act 1996) (Transitional Provisions) Regulations 1998

revoked: SI 2003/2694 Sch.1 Part 1

NO.

1998–cont.

3175. Corporation Tax (Instalment Payments) Regulations 1998
varied: 2002 c.23 s.93
Reg.3, amended: 2002 c.23 s.92

3177. European Single Currency (Taxes) Regulations 1998
Reg.2, amended: SI 2002/1971 Reg.3
Reg.6, amended: SI 2004/2310 Sch.1 para.77
Reg.6, revoked (in part): SI 2004/2310 Sch.1 para.77
Reg.7, revoked: SI 2002/1971 Reg.4
Reg.8, revoked: SI 2002/1971 Reg.4
Reg.9, revoked: SI 2002/1971 Reg.4
Reg.10, revoked: SI 2002/1971 Reg.4
Reg.11, revoked: SI 2002/1971 Reg.4

3186. Building Societies (Business Names) Regulations 1998
Sch.1, amended: SI 2002/881 Sch.1 para.13, SI 2002/1397 Sch.1 para.32

3192. Homerton Hospital National Health Service Trust (Establishment) Amendment Order 1998
revoked: 2003 c.43 s.7

3217. School Standards and Framework Act 1998 (Modification) (No.2) Regulations 1998
revoked (in part): SI 2003/2694 Sch.1 Part 2

3219. Local Authorities Etc (Allowances) (Scotland) Amendment Regulations 1998
revoked: SSI 2002/15 Reg.6

3235. Control of Asbestos at Work (Amendment) Regulations 1998
revoked: SI 2002/2675 Reg.27

3237. Teaching and Higher Education Act 1998 (Commencement No 4 and Transitional Provisions) Order 1998
Art.3, applied: SI 2002/1330 Reg.7, SI 2003/1994 Reg.7
Art.4, applied: SI 2002/1330 Reg.7, SI 2003/1994 Reg.7

3256. Act of Sederunt (Fees of Messengers-at-Arms) (Amendment) 1998
revoked: SSI 2002/566 Sch.2

3257. Housing Benefit (General) Amendment (No.2) Regulations 1998
Reg.3, see *Campbell v South Northamptonshire DC* [2004] EWCA Civ 409, [2004] 3 All E.R. 387 (CA), Peter Gibson, L.J.
Reg.7, see *R. (on the application of Tucker) v Secretary of State for Social Security* [2001] EWCA Civ 1646, [2002] H.L.R. 27 (CA), Waller L.J.

3261. City and County of Swansea (Electoral Arrangements) (No.2) Order 1998
varied: SI 2004/218 Art.2

NO.

1998–cont.

3269. Tyne and Wear Passenger Transport (Sunderland) Order 1998
Sch.10 para.1, amended: SI 2003/2155 Sch.1 para.17, Sch.2
Sch.10 para.2, amended: SI 2003/2155 Sch.1 para.17
Sch.10 para.3, amended: SI 2003/2155 Sch.1 para.18
Sch.10 para.3, revoked (in part): SI 2003/2155 Sch.2
Sch.10 para.4, amended: SI 2003/2155 Sch.1 para.18

3270. Local Government Finance (New Parishes) (Amendment) Regulations 1998
varied: SI 2004/222 Art.2

3271. City and County of Cardiff (Electoral Arrangements) Order 1998
varied: SI 2004/218 Art.2

3314. North West Wales National Health Service Trust (Establishment) Order 1998
revoked: 2003 c.43 s.7

3315. Swansea (1999) National Health Service Trust (Establishment) Order 1998
revoked: 2003 c.43 s.7

3316. Carmarthenshire National Health Service Trust (Establishment) Order 1998
revoked: 2003 c.43 s.7

3317. Conwy and Denbighshire National Health Service Trust (Establishment) Order 1998
revoked: 2003 c.43 s.7

3318. Pontypridd and Rhondda National Health Service Trust (Establishment) Order 1998
revoked: 2003 c.43 s.7

3319. Bro Morgannwg National Health Service Trust (Establishment) Order 1998
revoked: 2003 c.43 s.7

3320. North East Wales National Health Service Trust (Establishment) Order 1998
revoked: 2003 c.43 s.7

3321. Gwent Healthcare National Health Service Trust (Establishment) Order 1998
revoked: 2003 c.43 s.7

1999

Reg.13. Working Time (Amendment) Regulations 1999
see *Brown v Kigass Aero Components Ltd* [2002] I.C.R. 697 (EAT), Lindsay, J.

Reg.14. Working Time (Amendment) Regulations 1999
see *Brown v Kigass Aero Components Ltd* [2002] I.C.R. 697 (EAT), Lindsay, J.

NO.

1999–cont.

Reg.2. Working Time (Amendment) Regulations 1999

see *Brown v Kigass Aero Components Ltd* [2002] I.C.R. 697 (EAT), Lindsay, J.

1. School Standards and Framework Act 1998 (School Playing Fields) (Modification) (England) Regulations 1999

revoked: SI 2003/2694 Sch.1 Part 1

2. Education (School Premises) Regulations 1999

applied: SI 2003/1910 Sch.1 para.5, SI 2003/3234 Sch.1 para.5

6. Rent Acts (Maximum Fair Rent) Order 1999

see *Spath Holme Ltd v North Western Rent Assessment Committee* [2001] EWHC Admin 541, [2003] H.L.R. 13 (QBD (Admin Ct)), Collins, J.

11. Medway National Health Service Trust (Establishment) Amendment Order 1999

revoked: 2003 c.43 s.7

17. Merchant Shipping (Pilot Transfer Arrangements) Regulations 1999

revoked: SI 2002/1473 Sch.1 para.2

40. Health and Safety at Work etc Act 1974 (Application to Environmentally Hazardous Substances) (Amendment) Regulations 1999

revoked: SI 2002/282 Reg.4

58. Warrington Hospital National Health Service Trust (Establishment) Amendment Order 1999

revoked: 2003 c.43 s.7

60. Durham County Priority Services National Health Service Trust (Change of Name) Order 1999

revoked: 2003 c.43 s.7

62. Sandwell Healthcare National Health Service Trust (Establishment) Amendment Order 1999

revoked: 2003 c.43 s.7

67. European Communities (Recognition of Professional Qualifications) (Second General System) (Amendment) Regulations 1999

revoked: SI 2002/2934 Reg.27

68. Housing Renewal Grants (Common Parts) Order 1999

revoked: SI 2002/1860 Sch.6

70. Income Tax (Employments) (Amendment) Regulations 1999

revoked: SI 2003/2682 Sch.2

101. Financing of Maintained Schools Regulations 1999

applied: SI 2002/377 Reg.24, Reg.25, Reg.32, SI 2003/3247 Reg.23, Reg.24, SI 2004/2506 Reg.3, Reg.6

referred to: SI 2002/122 Sch.2

revoked (in part): SI 2004/2506 Reg.3

Part IV, referred to: SI 2004/2506 Reg.3

NO.

1999–cont.

101. Financing of Maintained Schools Regulations 1999–*cont.*

Reg.2, revoked: SI 2003/3118 Reg.3

Reg.3, amended: SI 2002/136 Reg.2

Reg.3, revoked (in part): SI 2002/136 Reg.2, SI 2003/3118 Reg.3

Reg.5, revoked: SI 2003/3118 Reg.3

Reg.7, amended: SI 2002/136 Reg.2

Reg.11, applied: SI 2002/122 Reg.2

Reg.18, applied: SI 2002/377 Reg.25, SI 2003/453 Reg.24, SI 2003/3247 Reg.24

Reg.19, amended: SI 2002/136 Reg.2

Reg.19, applied: SI 2003/873 Reg.5

Reg.20, amended: SI 2002/136 Reg.2

Reg.22, amended: SI 2002/136 Reg.2

Reg.22, referred to: SI 2002/122 Sch.2

Reg.23A, added: SI 2002/136 Reg.2

Reg.25, revoked (in part): SI 2004/2507 Reg.3

Reg.26, revoked (in part): SI 2004/2507 Reg.3

Reg.27, revoked (in part): SI 2004/2507 Reg.3

Reg.28, revoked (in part): SI 2004/2507 Reg.3

Sch.2, revoked: SI 2003/3118 Reg.3

Sch.2 para.1, amended: SI 2002/136 Reg.2

Sch.2 para.1, referred to: SI 2002/1187 Reg.21

Sch.2 para.1, revoked: SI 2003/3118 Reg.3

Sch.2 para.2, referred to: SI 2002/1187 Reg.21

Sch.2 para.2, revoked: SI 2003/3118 Reg.3

Sch.2 para.2A, added: SI 2002/136 Reg.2

Sch.2 para.2A, revoked: SI 2003/3118 Reg.3

Sch.2 para.3, referred to: SI 2002/1187 Reg.21

Sch.2 para.3, revoked: SI 2003/3118 Reg.3

Sch.2 para.4, referred to: SI 2002/1187 Reg.21

Sch.2 para.4, revoked: SI 2003/3118 Reg.3

Sch.2 para.5, referred to: SI 2002/1187 Reg.21

Sch.2 para.5, revoked: SI 2003/3118 Reg.3

Sch.2 para.6, referred to: SI 2002/1187 Reg.21

Sch.2 para.6, revoked: SI 2003/3118 Reg.3

Sch.2 para.7, referred to: SI 2002/1187 Reg.21

Sch.2 para.7, revoked: SI 2003/3118 Reg.3

Sch.2 para.8, referred to: SI 2002/1187 Reg.21

Sch.2 para.8, revoked: SI 2003/3118 Reg.3

Sch.2 para.9, referred to: SI 2002/1187 Reg.21

Sch.2 para.9, revoked: SI 2003/3118 Reg.3

Sch.2 para.10, referred to: SI 2002/1187 Reg.21

Sch.2 para.10, revoked: SI 2003/3118 Reg.3

Sch.2 para.11, referred to: SI 2002/1187 Reg.21

NO.

NO.

1999–cont.

1999–cont.

101. Financing of Maintained Schools Regulations 1999–*cont.*

Sch.2 para.11, revoked: SI 2003/3118 Reg.3

Sch.2 para.12, referred to: SI 2002/1187 Reg.21

Sch.2 para.12, revoked: SI 2003/3118 Reg.3

Sch.2 para.13, referred to: SI 2002/1187 Reg.21

Sch.2 para.13, revoked: SI 2003/3118 Reg.3

Sch.2 para.14, amended: SI 2002/136 Reg.2

Sch.2 para.14, referred to: SI 2002/1187 Reg.21

Sch.2 para.14, revoked: SI 2003/3118 Reg.3

Sch.2 para.15, referred to: SI 2002/1187 Reg.21

Sch.2 para.15, revoked: SI 2003/3118 Reg.3

Sch.2 para.16, revoked: SI 2003/3118 Reg.3

Sch.2 para.17, revoked: SI 2003/3118 Reg.3

Sch.2 para.18, revoked: SI 2003/3118 Reg.3

Sch.2 para.19, revoked: SI 2003/3118 Reg.3

Sch.2 para.19, substituted: SI 2002/136 Reg.2

Sch.2 para.20, referred to: SI 2002/1187 Reg.21

Sch.2 para.20, revoked: SI 2003/3118 Reg.3

Sch.2 para.21, referred to: SI 2002/1187 Reg.21

Sch.2 para.21, revoked: SI 2003/3118 Reg.3

Sch.2 para.22, referred to: SI 2002/1187 Reg.21

Sch.2 para.22, revoked: SI 2003/3118 Reg.3

Sch.2 para.23, referred to: SI 2002/1187 Reg.21

Sch.2 para.23, revoked: SI 2003/3118 Reg.3

Sch.2 para.24, revoked: SI 2003/3118 Reg.3

Sch.2 para.25, revoked: SI 2003/3118 Reg.3

Sch.2 para.26, revoked: SI 2003/3118 Reg.3

Sch.2 para.27, revoked: SI 2003/3118 Reg.3

Sch.2 para.28, amended: SI 2002/136 Reg.2

Sch.2 para.28, revoked: SI 2003/3118 Reg.3

Sch.2 para.29, revoked: SI 2003/3118 Reg.3

Sch.2 para.30, revoked: SI 2003/3118 Reg.3

Sch.2 para.31, revoked: SI 2003/3118 Reg.3

Sch.2 para.32, revoked: SI 2003/3118 Reg.3

Sch.2 para.33, revoked: SI 2003/3118 Reg.3

Sch.2 para.33, substituted: SI 2002/136 Reg.2

Sch.2 para.34, revoked: SI 2003/3118 Reg.3

Sch.2 para.34, substituted: SI 2002/136 Reg.2

Sch.2 para.35, revoked: SI 2003/3118 Reg.3

Sch.2 para.36, revoked: SI 2003/3118 Reg.3

Sch.2 para.37, revoked: SI 2003/3118 Reg.3

Sch.2 para.38, revoked: SI 2003/3118 Reg.3

Sch.2 para.39, revoked: SI 2003/3118 Reg.3

Sch.2 para.40, revoked: SI 2003/3118 Reg.3

Sch.2 para.40A, amended: SI 2003/538 Reg.2

Sch.2 para.40A, revoked: SI 2003/3118 Reg.3

101. Financing of Maintained Schools Regulations 1999–*cont.*

Sch.2 para.41, revoked: SI 2003/3118 Reg.3

Sch.2 para.42, revoked: SI 2003/3118 Reg.3

Sch.2 para.43, revoked: SI 2003/3118 Reg.3

Sch.2 para.44, revoked: SI 2003/3118 Reg.3

Sch.2 para.45, revoked: SI 2003/3118 Reg.3

Sch.3, amended: SI 2002/136 Reg.2

Sch.3 para.29A, added: SI 2002/136 Reg.2

Sch.4, applied: SI 2002/377 Sch.3 para.2, Sch.3 para.3, Sch.3 para.4, SI 2003/453 Sch.2 para.2, Sch.2 para.3

Sch.4 para.4, applied: SI 2003/453 Sch.2 para.2

Sch.4 para.7, applied: SI 2003/453 Sch.2 para.4

Sch.5, referred to: SI 2004/2506 Reg.3

125. Education (Objections to Admission Arrangements) Regulations 1999

Reg.1, amended: SI 2002/2901 Reg.2

Reg.2, applied: SI 2003/1041 Reg.7

Reg.2, substituted: SI 2002/2901 Reg.2

Reg.4, substituted: SI 2002/2901 Reg.2

Reg.5, amended: SI 2002/2901 Reg.2

Reg.8, amended: SI 2002/2901 Reg.2

Reg.10, amended: SI 2002/2901 Reg.2

126. Education (Determination of Admission Arrangements) Regulations 1999

Reg.2, amended: SI 2002/2896 Reg.2

Reg.3, substituted: SI 2002/2896 Reg.2

Reg.5, amended: SI 2002/2896 Reg.2

Reg.5A, added: SI 2002/2896 Reg.2

Reg.6, amended: SI 2002/2896 Reg.2

Reg.8, amended: SI 2002/2896 Reg.2

Reg.9, substituted: SI 2002/2896 Reg.2

Reg.10, amended: SI 2002/2896 Reg.2

129. School Standards and Framework Act 1998 (School Attendance Targets) (Modification) Regulations 1999

revoked (in part): SI 2003/2694 Sch.1 Part 2

135. Caradon (Parishes) Order 1999

revoked: SI 2002/2602 Art.10

Art.2, referred to: SI 2002/2602 Art.10

157. Miscellaneous Products of Animal Origin (Import Conditions) Regulations 1999

revoked (in part): SI 2003/3177 Sch.6, SI 2004/1430 Sch.6

Reg.4, disapplied: SI 2002/1387 Sch.7, SSI 2002/445 Sch.7

160. Petroleum (Current Model Clauses) Order 1999

disapplied: SI 2004/352 Reg.3

167. M4 Motorway (Hillingdon and Hounslow) (Speed Limits) (Amendment) Regulations 1999

revoked: SI 2002/1651 Reg.3

NO.

1999–cont.

197. Chemicals (Hazard Information and Packaging for Supply) (Amendment) Regulations 1999
revoked: SI 2002/1689 Sch.7

199. Mid-Sussex National Health Service Trust (Establishment) Amendment Order 1999
revoked: 2003 c.43 s.7

214. Advice and Assistance (Assistance by Way of Representation) (Scotland) Amendment Regulations 1999
revoked: SSI 2003/179 Sch.1

220. National Institute for Clinical Excellence (Establishment and Constitution) Order 1999
Art.4, amended: SI 2002/1760 Art.2

229. Local Education Authority (Post-Compulsory Education Awards) Regulations 1999
revoked (in part): SI 2002/1856 Reg.2
Reg.4, applied: SI 2002/1856 Reg.2, Reg.5

251. Education (School Information) (England) (Amendment) Regulations 1999
revoked: SI 2002/2897 Reg.2

257. Transport of Dangerous Goods (Safety Advisers) Regulations 1999
revoked: SI 2004/568 Sch.14
Reg.4, disapplied: SI 2002/1227 Sch.7
Reg.7, applied: SI 2002/655 Reg.15, SI 2003/547 Reg.15, SI 2004/456 Reg.14, SI 2004/568 Reg.32
Sch.1 para.2, amended: SI 2002/2099 Reg.31

260. National Institute for Clinical Excellence Regulations 1999
Reg.1, amended: SI 2004/696 Art.3
Reg.4, amended: SI 2002/1759 Reg.2
Reg.4, revoked (in part): SI 2002/1759 Reg.2
Reg.5, amended: SI 2004/696 Art.3, Sch.1 para.27
Reg.9, amended: SI 2002/1759 Reg.3

268. European Economic Interest Grouping (Fees) Regulations 1999
revoked: SI 2004/2643 Sch.1
Reg.2, amended: SI 2002/2928 Reg.4
Sch.1, amended: SI 2002/401 Reg.2, SI 2002/2928 Reg.3

269. Police (Retention and Disposal of Items seized under section 60 of the Criminal Justice and Public Order Act 1994) Regulations 1999
revoked (in part): SI 2002/1372 Reg.3

275. Processed Cereal-based Foods and Baby Foods for Infants and Young Children (Amendment) Regulations 1999
revoked (in part): SI 2003/3207 Reg.13, SI 2004/314 Reg.13, SSI 2004/8 Reg.14

NO.

1999–cont.

278. European Communities (Immunities and Privileges of the North-East Atlantic Fisheries Commission) Order 1999
Art.12, amended: 2002 c.8 s.2
Art.13, amended: 2002 c.8 s.2

280. Federal Republic of Yugoslavia (United Nations Sanctions) (Amendment) Order 1999
Art.4, amended: 2002 c.8 s.2

281. Federal Republic of Yugoslavia (United Nations Sanctions) (Dependent Territories) (Amendment) Order 1999
Art.4, amended: 2002 c.8 s.2

283. Departments (Northern Ireland) Order 1999
Art.8, enabled: SR 2003/163
Sch.2, amended: 2002 c.1 (NI) Sch.4

284. Federal Republic of Yugoslavia (United Nations Sanctions) (Channel Islands) (Amendment) Order 1999
Art.4, amended: 2002 c.8 s.2

285. Federal Republic of Yugoslavia (United Nations Sanctions) (Isle of Man) (Amendment) Order 1999
Art.4, amended: 2002 c.8 s.2

291. Police and Criminal Evidence Act 1984 (Codes of Practice No 5) Order 1999
revoked: SI 2003/703 Art.4

292. Housing (Right to Buy) (Limits on Discount) (Wales) Order 1999
Art.3, amended: SI 2003/803 Art.3

293. Town and Country Planning (Environmental Impact Assessment) (England and Wales) Regulations 1999
applied: SI 2002/2127 Reg.3
see *R. (on the application of Blewett) v Derbyshire CC* [2003] EWHC 2775, [2004] Env. L.R. 29 (QBD (Admin Ct)), Sullivan, J.; see *R. (on the application of Fernback) v Harrow LBC* [2001] EWHC Admin 278, [2002] Env. L.R. 10 (QBD (Admin Ct)), Richards, J.; see *R. (on the application of Gavin) v Haringey LBC* [2003] EWHC 2591, [2004] 2 P. & C.R. 13 (QBD (Admin Ct)), Richards, J.; see *R. (on the application of Goodman) v Lewisham LBC* [2002] EWHC 1769, [2003] Env. L.R. 16 (QBD (Admin Ct)), Sir Richard Tucker; see *R. (on the application of Malster) v Ipswich BC* [2001] EWHC Admin 711, [2002] P.L.C.R. 14 (QBD (Admin Ct)), Sullivan, J.; see *R. (on the application of Payne) v Caerphilly CBC* [2003] EWCA Civ 71, [2003] Env. L.R. 31 (CA), Dyson, L.J.; see *R. (on the application of Portland Port Ltd) v Weymouth and Portland BC* [2001] EWHC Admin 1171, [2002] 2 P. & C.R. 29 (QBD (Admin Ct)), Harrison, J.

1999–cont.

293. Town and Country Planning (Environmental Impact Assessment) (England and Wales) Regulations 1999–*cont.*

Reg.2, see *R. (on the application of PPG11 Ltd) v Dorset CC* [2003] EWHC 1311, [2004] Env. L.R. 5 (QBD (Admin Ct)), Mackay, J.

Reg.3, see *Evans v First Secretary of State* [2003] EWHC 411, [2003] P.& C.R. 29 (QBD (Admin Ct)), Lightman, J.; see *R. (on the application of PPG11 Ltd) v Dorset CC* [2003] EWHC 1311, [2004] Env. L.R. 5 (QBD (Admin Ct)), Mackay, J.; see *R. (on the application of Richardson) v North Yorkshire CC* [2003] EWCA Civ 1860, [2004] 1 W.L.R. 1920 (CA), Simon Brown, L.J.; see *R. (on the application of Richardson) v North Yorkshire CC* [2003] EWHC 764, [2004] Env. L.R. 13 (QBD (Admin Ct)), Richards, J.

Reg.4, see *Evans v First Secretary of State* [2003] EWHC 411, [2003] P.& C.R. 29 (QBD (Admin Ct)), Lightman, J.; see *R. (on the application of Orchard) v Secretary of State for the Home Department* [2003] EWCA Civ 37, [2004] Env. L.R. 12 (CA), Scott Baker, L.J.

Reg.6, see *Younger Homes (Northern) Ltd v First Secretary of State* [2003] EWHC 3058, [2004] J.P.L. 950 (QBD (Admin Ct)), Ouseley, J.

Reg.7, see *R. (on the application of Lebus) v South Cambridgeshire DC* [2002] EWHC 2009, [2003] Env. L.R. 17 (QBD (Admin Ct)), Sullivan, J.

Reg.8, see *Younger Homes (Northern) Ltd v First Secretary of State* [2003] EWHC 3058, [2004] J.P.L. 950 (QBD (Admin Ct)), Ouseley, J.

Reg.21, see *R. (on the application of Richardson) v North Yorkshire CC* [2003] EWCA Civ 1860, [2004] 1 W.L.R. 1920 (CA), Simon Brown, L.J.; see *R. (on the application of Richardson) v North Yorkshire CC* [2003] EWHC 764, [2004] Env. L.R. 13 (QBD (Admin Ct)), Richards, J.

Sch.2, see *R. (on the application of Goodman) v Lewisham LBC* [2003] EWCA Civ 140, [2003] Env. L.R. 28 (CA), Buxton, L.J.; see *R. (on the application of Orchard) v Secretary of State for the Home Department* [2003] EWCA Civ 37, [2004] Env. L.R. 12 (CA), Scott Baker, L.J.

Sch.3, see *Evans v First Secretary of State* [2003] EWCA Civ 1523, [2004] Env. L.R. 17 (CA), Simon Brown, L.J.

293. Town and Country Planning (Environmental Impact Assessment)(England and Wales) Regulations 1999

Sch.2 para.10, see *R. (on the application of Prokopp) v London Underground Ltd* [2003] EWHC 960, [2003] 19 E.G.C.S. 119 (QBD (Admin Ct)), Collins, J.

1999–cont.

303. Carriage of Dangerous Goods (Amendment) Regulations 1999

revoked: SI 2004/568 Sch.14

Reg.6, revoked: SI 2002/2099 Sch.2

Sch.5 para.1, revoked: SI 2002/2099 Sch.2

Sch.5 para.2, revoked: SI 2002/2099 Sch.2

Sch.5 para.3, revoked: SI 2002/2099 Sch.2

Sch.5 para.4, revoked: SI 2002/2099 Sch.2

Sch.5 para.5, revoked: SI 2002/2099 Sch.2

Sch.5 para.6, revoked: SI 2002/2099 Sch.2

Sch.5 para.7, revoked: SI 2002/2099 Sch.2

Sch.5 para.8, revoked: SI 2002/2099 Sch.2

Sch.5 para.9, revoked: SI 2002/2099 Sch.2

Sch.5 para.10, revoked: SI 2002/2099 Sch.2

Sch.5 para.11, revoked: SI 2002/2099 Sch.2

Sch.5 para.12, revoked: SI 2002/2099 Sch.2

Sch.5 para.13, revoked: SI 2002/2099 Sch.2

Sch.5 para.14, revoked: SI 2002/2099 Sch.2

Sch.5 para.15, revoked: SI 2002/2099 Sch.2

Sch.5 para.16, revoked: SI 2002/2099 Sch.2

326. National Health Service (General Medical Services) Amendment Regulations 1999

revoked (in part): SI 2004/865 Sch.2

336. Merchant Shipping (Carriage of Cargoes) Regulations 1999

referred to: SI 2003/2002 Reg.12

358. Corporation Tax (Treatment of Unrelieved Surplus Advance Corporation Tax) Regulations 1999

Reg.22, amended: SI 2003/1861 Reg.2

360. Offshore Petroleum Production and Pipe-lines (Assessment of Environmental Effects) Regulations 1999

Reg.6, applied: SI 2002/1355 Reg.7

362. Education (Transition to New Framework) (New Schools, Groups and Miscellaneous) Regulations 1999

Reg.1, revoked (in part): SI 2003/2694 Sch.1 Part 2

Reg.4, revoked (in part): SI 2003/2694 Sch.1 Part 2

Reg.5, revoked (in part): SI 2003/2694 Sch.1 Part 2

Reg.6, revoked (in part): SI 2003/2694 Sch.1 Part 2

Reg.7, revoked (in part): SI 2003/2694 Sch.1 Part 2

Reg.8, revoked (in part): SI 2003/2694 Sch.1 Part 2

Reg.9, revoked (in part): SI 2003/2694 Sch.1 Part 2

Reg.10, revoked (in part): SI 2003/2694 Sch.1 Part 2

Reg.11, revoked (in part): SI 2003/2694 Sch.1 Part 2

Reg.12, revoked (in part): SI 2003/2694 Sch.1 Part 2

Reg.13, revoked (in part): SI 2003/2694 Sch.1 Part 2

NO.

1999–cont.

362. Education (Transition to New Framework) (New Schools, Groups and Miscellaneous) Regulations 1999– *cont.*

Reg.14, revoked (in part): SI 2003/2694 Sch.1 Part 2

Reg.15, revoked (in part): SI 2003/2694 Sch.1 Part 2

Reg.16, revoked (in part): SI 2003/2694 Sch.1 Part 2

Reg.17, revoked (in part): SI 2003/2694 Sch.1 Part 2

Reg.18, revoked (in part): SI 2003/2694 Sch.1 Part 2

Reg.19, revoked (in part): SI 2003/2694 Sch.1 Part 2

Reg.20, revoked (in part): SI 2003/2694 Sch.1 Part 2

Reg.21, revoked (in part): SI 2003/2694 Sch.1 Part 2

Reg.22, revoked (in part): SI 2003/2694 Sch.1 Part 2

Reg.23, revoked (in part): SI 2003/2694 Sch.1 Part 2

Reg.24, revoked (in part): SI 2003/2694 Sch.1 Part 2

Reg.25, revoked (in part): SI 2003/2694 Sch.1 Part 2

Reg.26, revoked (in part): SI 2003/2694 Sch.1 Part 2

Reg.27, revoked (in part): SI 2003/2694 Sch.1 Part 2

Reg.28, revoked (in part): SI 2003/2694 Sch.1 Part 2

Reg.29, revoked (in part): SI 2003/2694 Sch.1 Part 2

Reg.30, revoked (in part): SI 2003/2694 Sch.1 Part 2

Reg.31, revoked (in part): SI 2003/2694 Sch.1 Part 2

Reg.32, revoked (in part): SI 2003/2694 Sch.1 Part 2

Reg.33, revoked (in part): SI 2003/2694 Sch.1 Part 2

Reg.34, revoked (in part): SI 2003/2694 Sch.1 Part 2

Reg.35, revoked (in part): SI 2003/2694 Sch.1 Part 2

Reg.36, revoked (in part): SI 2003/2694 Sch.1 Part 2

Reg.37, revoked (in part): SI 2003/2694 Sch.1 Part 2

Reg.38, revoked (in part): SI 2003/2694 Sch.1 Part 2

Reg.39, revoked (in part): SI 2003/2694 Sch.1 Part 2

Reg.40, revoked (in part): SI 2003/2694 Sch.1 Part 2

Reg.41, revoked (in part): SI 2003/2694 Sch.1 Part 2

NO.

1999–cont.

362. Education (Transition to New Framework) (New Schools, Groups and Miscellaneous) Regulations 1999– *cont.*

Reg.42, revoked (in part): SI 2003/2694 Sch.1 Part 2

Reg.43, revoked (in part): SI 2003/2694 Sch.1 Part 2

Reg.44, revoked (in part): SI 2003/2694 Sch.1 Part 2

Reg.45, revoked (in part): SI 2003/2694 Sch.1 Part 2

Reg.46, revoked (in part): SI 2003/2694 Sch.1 Part 2

Reg.47, revoked (in part): SI 2003/2694 Sch.1 Part 2

Reg.48, revoked (in part): SI 2003/2694 Sch.1 Part 2

Reg.49, revoked (in part): SI 2003/2694 Sch.1 Part 2

Reg.50, revoked (in part): SI 2003/2694 Sch.1 Part 2

Reg.51, revoked (in part): SI 2003/2694 Sch.1 Part 2

Reg.52, revoked (in part): SI 2003/2694 Sch.1 Part 2

Reg.53, revoked (in part): SI 2003/2694 Sch.1 Part 2

Reg.57, revoked (in part): SI 2003/2694 Sch.1 Part 2

Reg.58, revoked (in part): SI 2003/2694 Sch.1 Part 2

Reg.59, revoked (in part): SI 2003/2694 Sch.1 Part 2

Reg.60, revoked (in part): SI 2003/2694 Sch.1 Part 2

Reg.61, revoked (in part): SI 2003/2694 Sch.1 Part 2

370. Birmingham Children's Hospital National Health Service Trust (Establishment) Amendment Order 1999

revoked: 2003 c.43 s.7

391. Channel Tunnel Rail Link (Nomination) Order 1999

Art.3, amended: SI 2003/2306 Art.2, SI 2003/2834 Art.3

Art.4, amended: SI 2003/2834 Art.4

Art.5, added: SI 2003/2834 Art.5

394. Local Elections (Principal Areas) (Amendment) Rules 1999

see *R. (on the application of De Beer) v Balabanoff* [2002] EWHC 670, Times, April 25, 2002 (QBD (Admin Ct)), Scott Baker, J.

398. Education (School Organisation Committees) (Initial Financial Arrangements) (England) Regulations 1999

revoked: SI 2003/2694 Sch.1 Part 1

NO.

1999–cont.

421. Local Authorities (Goods and Services) (Public Bodies) (No.1) Order 1999
revoked: 2003 c.43 s.7

423. Lifecare National Health Service Trust (Dissolution) Order 1999
revoked: 2003 c.43 s.7

437. Control of Substances Hazardous to Health Regulations 1999
applied: SI 2002/655 Reg.3
revoked: SI 2002/2677 Reg.18

439. Electricity (Non-Fossil Fuel Sources) (Scotland) Order 1999
Sch.1, referred to: SSI 2004/170 Art.8

449. National Assembly for Wales (Disqualification) Order 1999
referred to: SI 2003/437
revoked: SI 2003/437 Art.3

450. National Assembly for Wales (Representation of the People) Order 1999
applied: SI 2002/3053 Sch.1 para.10, Sch.1 para.11
revoked: SI 2003/284 Art.1
Appendix 1., amended: SI 2002/834 Art.23
Appendix 2., amended: SI 2002/834 Art.24
Appendix 3., amended: SI 2002/834 Art.26
Art.2, amended: SI 2002/834 Art.4, Art.14
Art.4, amended: SI 2002/834 Art.5
Art.7, amended: SI 2002/834 Art.6
Art.8, amended: SI 2002/834 Art.7
Art.8, revoked (in part): SI 2002/834 Art.7
Art.9, amended: SI 2002/834 Art.8
Art.11, amended: SI 2002/834 Art.9
Art.12, amended: SI 2002/834 Art.10
Art.12, revoked (in part): SI 2002/834 Art.10
Art.14, applied: SI 2002/3053 Sch.1 para.1, Sch.1 para.3, Sch.1 para.4, Sch.1 para.5
Art.17, applied: SI 2002/3053 Sch.1 para.8
Art.20, applied: SI 2002/3053 Art.3
Art.20, enabled: SI 2002/3053
Art.23, amended: SI 2002/834 Art.11
Art.23, revoked (in part): SI 2002/834 Art.11
Art.25, amended: SI 2002/834 Art.12
Art.31, amended: SI 2002/834 Art.13
Art.34, amended: SI 2002/834 Art.14
Art.36, revoked: SI 2002/834 Art.15
Art.37, substituted: SI 2002/834 Art.16
Art.39, revoked: SI 2002/834 Art.16
Art.40, revoked: SI 2002/834 Art.16
Art.43, revoked: SI 2002/834 Art.16
Art.44, revoked: SI 2002/834 Art.16
Art.45, revoked: SI 2002/834 Art.16
Art.46, amended: SI 2002/834 Art.16
Art.47, revoked: SI 2002/834 Art.16
Art.48, revoked: SI 2002/834 Art.16
Art.49, revoked: SI 2002/834 Art.16
Art.50, substituted: SI 2002/834 Art.16
Art.51, amended: SI 2002/834 Art.16
Art.51, revoked (in part): SI 2002/834 Art.16
Art.51, varied: SI 2002/834 Art.16

NO.

1999–cont.

450. National Assembly for Wales (Representation of the People) Order 1999–cont.
Art.52, revoked (in part): SI 2002/834 Art.16
Art.52, varied: SI 2002/834 Art.16
Art.55, revoked: SI 2002/834 Art.16
Art.57, revoked: SI 2002/834 Art.16
Art.58, amended: SI 2002/834 Art.16
Art.59, amended: SI 2002/834 Art.16
Art.60, amended: SI 2002/834 Art.14
Art.61, revoked (in part): SI 2002/834 Art.16
Art.61, varied: SI 2002/834 Art.16
Art.62, varied: SI 2002/834 Art.16
Art.62A, added: SI 2002/834 Art.17
Art.65, revoked: SI 2002/834 Art.16
Art.66, amended: SI 2002/834 Art.21
Art.69, amended: SI 2002/834 Art.18
Art.73, revoked: SI 2002/834 Art.18
Art.74, revoked: SI 2002/834 Art.18
Art.75, revoked: SI 2002/834 Art.18
Art.76, revoked: SI 2002/834 Art.18
Art.77, revoked: SI 2002/834 Art.18
Art.78, revoked (in part): SI 2002/834 Art.18
Art.80, revoked: SI 2002/834 Art.18
Art.90, amended: SI 2002/834 Art.19
Art.93, amended: SI 2002/834 Art.14
Art.94, revoked (in part): SI 2002/834 Art.20
Art.98, amended: SI 2002/834 Art.14
Art.99, substituted: SI 2002/834 Art.20
Art.110, revoked: SI 2002/834 Art.20
Art.111, revoked: SI 2002/834 Art.20
Art.112, revoked: SI 2002/834 Art.20
Art.113, revoked: SI 2002/834 Art.20
Art.114, revoked: SI 2002/834 Art.20
Art.115, revoked: SI 2002/834 Art.20
Art.119, revoked (in part): SI 2002/834 Art.20
Art.121, revoked (in part): SI 2002/834 Art.20
Art.122, amended: SI 2002/834 Art.20
Art.123, amended: SI 2002/834 Art.20
Art.124, amended: SI 2002/834 Art.20
Art.131, revoked (in part): SI 2002/834 Art.20
Art.138, revoked (in part): SI 2002/834 Art.20
Art.139, amended: SI 2002/834 Art.20
Art.143A, added: SI 2002/834 Art.20
Art.147, amended: SI 2002/834 Art.14
Art.148, amended: SI 2002/834 Art.20
Sch.1 para.1, amended: SI 2002/834 Art.22
Sch.1 para.1, revoked: SI 2002/834 Art.22
Sch.1 para.2, amended: SI 2002/834 Art.22
Sch.1 para.3, amended: SI 2002/834 Art.22
Sch.1 para.3, substituted: SI 2002/834 Art.22
Sch.1 para.4, amended: SI 2002/834 Art.22
Sch.1 para.4, substituted: SI 2002/834 Art.22
Sch.1 para.5, amended: SI 2002/834 Art.22

NO.

1999–cont.

450. National Assembly for Wales (Representation of the People) Order 1999– cont.

Sch.1 para.5, revoked: SI 2002/834 Art.22

Sch.1 para.6, amended: SI 2002/834 Art.22

Sch.1 para.6, revoked: SI 2002/834 Art.22

Sch.1 para.7, amended: SI 2002/834 Art.22

Sch.2 para.1, amended: SI 2002/834 Art.23

Sch.2 para.1, revoked (in part): SI 2002/834 Art.23

Sch.2 para.2, amended: SI 2002/834 Art.23

Sch.2 para.2, revoked: SI 2002/834 Art.23

Sch.2 para.3, amended: SI 2002/834 Art.23, SI 2002/881 Sch.1 para.14

Sch.2 para.4, amended: SI 2002/834 Art.23

Sch.2 para.5, amended: SI 2002/834 Art.23

Sch.2 para.5, substituted: SI 2002/834 Art.23

Sch.2 para.6, amended: SI 2002/834 Art.23

Sch.2 para.7, amended: SI 2002/834 Art.23

Sch.2 para.7, revoked: SI 2002/834 Art.23

Sch.2 para.8, amended: SI 2002/834 Art.23

Sch.2 para.8, revoked (in part): SI 2002/834 Art.23

Sch.2 para.9, amended: SI 2002/834 Art.23

Sch.2 para.10, amended: SI 2002/834 Art.23

Sch.2 para.11, amended: SI 2002/834 Art.23

Sch.2 para.12, amended: SI 2002/834 Art.23

Sch.2 para.13, amended: SI 2002/834 Art.23

Sch.2 para.14, amended: SI 2002/834 Art.23

Sch.2 para.15, amended: SI 2002/834 Art.23

Sch.2 para.16, amended: SI 2002/834 Art.23

Sch.2 para.17, amended: SI 2002/834 Art.23

Sch.3 para.1, amended: SI 2002/834 Art.24

Sch.3 para.2, amended: SI 2002/834 Art.24

Sch.3 para.3, amended: SI 2002/834 Art.24

Sch.3 para.4, amended: SI 2002/834 Art.24

Sch.3 para.4A, added: SI 2002/834 Art.24

Sch.3 para.4A, amended: SI 2002/834 Art.24

Sch.3 para.5, amended: SI 2002/834 Art.24

Sch.3 para.6, amended: SI 2002/834 Art.24

Sch.3 para.7, amended: SI 2002/834 Art.24

Sch.3 para.7, substituted: SI 2002/834 Art.24

Sch.3 para.8, amended: SI 2002/834 Art.24

Sch.3 para.9, amended: SI 2002/834 Art.24

Sch.3 para.10, amended: SI 2002/834 Art.24

Sch.3 para.11, amended: SI 2002/834 Art.24

Sch.3 para.11, substituted: SI 2002/834 Art.24

Sch.3 para.12, amended: SI 2002/834 Art.24

Sch.3 para.12, revoked: SI 2002/834 Art.24

Sch.3 para.13, amended: SI 2002/834 Art.24

Sch.3 para.13, substituted: SI 2002/834 Art.24

Sch.3 para.14, amended: SI 2002/834 Art.24

Sch.3 para.14A, added: SI 2002/834 Art.24

Sch.3 para.14A, amended: SI 2002/834 Art.24

NO.

1999–cont.

450. National Assembly for Wales (Representation of the People) Order 1999– cont.

Sch.3 para.15, amended: SI 2002/834 Art.24

Sch.3 para.15, revoked: SI 2002/834 Art.24

Sch.3 para.16, amended: SI 2002/834 Art.24

Sch.3 para.16, substituted: SI 2002/834 Art.24

Sch.3 para.17, amended: SI 2002/834 Art.24

Sch.3 para.17, substituted: SI 2002/834 Art.24

Sch.3 para.18, amended: SI 2002/834 Art.24

Sch.3 para.18, substituted: SI 2002/834 Art.24

Sch.3 para.19, amended: SI 2002/834 Art.24

Sch.3 para.19, substituted: SI 2002/834 Art.24

Sch.3 para.20, amended: SI 2002/834 Art.24

Sch.3 para.20, substituted: SI 2002/834 Art.24

Sch.3 para.21, amended: SI 2002/834 Art.24

Sch.3 para.21, substituted: SI 2002/834 Art.24

Sch.3 para.22, amended: SI 2002/834 Art.24

Sch.3 para.22, substituted: SI 2002/834 Art.24

Sch.3 para.23, amended: SI 2002/834 Art.24

Sch.3 para.23, substituted: SI 2002/834 Art.24

Sch.3 para.24, amended: SI 2002/834 Art.24

Sch.3 para.24, substituted: SI 2002/834 Art.24

Sch.3 para.25, amended: SI 2002/834 Art.24

Sch.3 para.25, substituted: SI 2002/834 Art.24

Sch.3 para.26, amended: SI 2002/834 Art.24

Sch.3 para.26, substituted: SI 2002/834 Art.24

Sch.3 para.27, amended: SI 2002/834 Art.24

Sch.3 para.27, substituted: SI 2002/834 Art.24

Sch.4 Part I para.1, amended: SI 2002/834 Art.25

Sch.4 Part I para.2, amended: SI 2002/834 Art.25

Sch.4 Part I para.3, amended: SI 2002/834 Art.25

Sch.4 Part II para.4, amended: SI 2002/834 Art.25

Sch.4 Part II para.5, amended: SI 2002/834 Art.25

Sch.4 Part II para.6, amended: SI 2002/834 Art.25

1999–cont.

450. **National Assembly for Wales (Representation of the People) Order 1999–**
cont.

Sch.4 Part II para.7, amended: SI 2002/834
Art.25

Sch.4 Part II para.8, amended: SI 2002/834
Art.25

Sch.4 Part II para.9, amended: SI 2002/834
Art.25

Sch.4 Part II para.10, amended: SI 2002/834
Art.25

Sch.4 Part II para.11, amended: SI 2002/834
Art.25

Sch.4 Part II para.12, amended: SI 2002/834
Art.25

Sch.4 Part II para.13, amended: SI 2002/834
Art.25

Sch.4 Part II para.14, amended: SI 2002/834
Art.25

Sch.4 Part II para.15, amended: SI 2002/834
Art.25

Sch.4 Part II para.16, amended: SI 2002/834
Art.25

Sch.4 Part II para.17, amended: SI 2002/834
Art.25

Sch.4 Part II para.18, amended: SI 2002/834
Art.25

Sch.4 Part II para.19, amended: SI 2002/834
Art.25

Sch.4 Part II para.20, amended: SI 2002/834
Art.25

Sch.4 Part II para.21, amended: SI 2002/834
Art.25

Sch.4 Part II para.22, amended: SI 2002/834
Art.25

Sch.4 Part III para.23, amended: SI 2002/834
Art.25

Sch.4 Part III para.24, amended: SI 2002/834
Art.25

Sch.4 Part III para.25, amended: SI 2002/834
Art.25

Sch.4 Part III para.26, amended: SI 2002/834
Art.25

Sch.4 Part III para.27, amended: SI 2002/834
Art.25

Sch.4 Part III para.28, amended: SI 2002/834
Art.25

Sch.4 Part III para.29, amended: SI 2002/834
Art.25

Sch.4 Part III para.30, amended: SI 2002/834
Art.25

Sch.4 Part III para.31, amended: SI 2002/834
Art.25

Sch.4 Part III para.32, amended: SI 2002/834
Art.25

Sch.4 Part III para.33, amended: SI 2002/834
Art.25

Sch.4 Part III para.34, amended: SI 2002/834
Art.25

Sch.4 Part III para.35, amended: SI 2002/834
Art.25

1999–cont.

450. **National Assembly for Wales (Representation of the People) Order 1999–**
cont.

Sch.4 Part III para.36, amended: SI 2002/834
Art.25

Sch.4 Part III para.37, amended: SI 2002/834
Art.25

Sch.4 Part III para.38, amended: SI 2002/834
Art.25

Sch.4 Part III para.39, amended: SI 2002/834
Art.25

Sch.4 Part III para.40, amended: SI 2002/834
Art.25

Sch.4 Part III para.41, amended: SI 2002/834
Art.25

Sch.4 Part III para.42, amended: SI 2002/834
Art.25

Sch.4 Part III para.43, amended: SI 2002/834
Art.25

Sch.4 Part IV para.44, amended: SI 2002/
834 Art.25

Sch.4 Part IV para.45, amended: SI 2002/
834 Art.25

Sch.4 Part IV para.46, amended: SI 2002/
834 Art.25

Sch.4 Part IV para.47, amended: SI 2002/834
Art.25

Sch.4 Part IV para.48, amended: SI 2002/
834 Art.25

Sch.4 Part IV para.49, amended: SI 2002/
834 Art.25

Sch.4 Part IV para.50, amended: SI 2002/
834 Art.25

Sch.4 Part IV para.51, amended: SI 2002/834
Art.25

Sch.4 Part IV para.52, amended: SI 2002/
834 Art.25

Sch.4 Part IV para.53, amended: SI 2002/
834 Art.25

Sch.4 Part IV para.54, amended: SI 2002/
834 Art.25

Sch.4 Part IV para.55, amended: SI 2002/
834 Art.25

Sch.4 Part IV para.56, amended: SI 2002/
834 Art.25

Sch.4 Part IV para.57, amended: SI 2002/834
Art.25

Sch.4 Part IV para.58, amended: SI 2002/
834 Art.25

Sch.4 Part IV para.59, amended: SI 2002/
834 Art.25

Sch.4 Part IV para.60, amended: SI 2002/
834 Art.25

Sch.4 Part IV para.61, amended: SI 2002/834
Art.25

Sch.4 Part IV para.62, amended: SI 2002/
834 Art.25

Sch.4 Part IV para.63, amended: SI 2002/
834 Art.25

Sch.4 Part IV para.64, amended: SI 2002/
834 Art.25

NO.

1999–cont.

450. National Assembly for Wales (Representation of the People) Order 1999– cont.

Sch.5 Part I para.1, amended: SI 2002/834 Art.26

Sch.5 Part I para.2, amended: SI 2002/834 Art.26

Sch.5 Part II para.3, amended: SI 2002/834 Art.26

Sch.5 Part II para.4, amended: SI 2002/834 Art.26

Sch.5 Part II para.5, amended: SI 2002/834 Art.26

Sch.5 Part II para.6, amended: SI 2002/834 Art.26

Sch.5 Part II para.7, amended: SI 2002/834 Art.26

Sch.5 Part II para.8, amended: SI 2002/834 Art.26

Sch.5 Part II para.9, amended: SI 2002/834 Art.26

Sch.5 Part II para.10, amended: SI 2002/834 Art.26

Sch.5 Part II para.11, amended: SI 2002/834 Art.26

Sch.5 Part II para.12, amended: SI 2002/834 Art.26

Sch.5 Part II para.13, amended: SI 2002/834 Art.26

Sch.5 Part II para.14, amended: SI 2002/834 Art.26

Sch.5 Part II para.15, amended: SI 2002/834 Art.26

Sch.5 Part II para.16, amended: SI 2002/834 Art.26

Sch.5 Part II para.17, amended: SI 2002/834 Art.26

Sch.5 Part II para.18, amended: SI 2002/834 Art.26

Sch.5 Part II para.19, amended: SI 2002/834 Art.26

Sch.5 Part II para.20, amended: SI 2002/834 Art.26

Sch.5 Part II para.21, amended: SI 2002/834 Art.26

Sch.5 Part III para.22, amended: SI 2002/834 Art.26

Sch.5 Part III para.23, amended: SI 2002/834 Art.26

Sch.5 Part III para.24, amended: SI 2002/834 Art.26

Sch.5 Part III para.25, amended: SI 2002/834 Art.26

Sch.5 Part III para.26, amended: SI 2002/834 Art.26

Sch.5 Part III para.27, amended: SI 2002/834 Art.26

Sch.5 Part III para.28, amended: SI 2002/834 Art.26

Sch.5 Part III para.29, amended: SI 2002/834 Art.26

NO.

1999–cont.

450. National Assembly for Wales (Representation of the People) Order 1999– cont.

Sch.5 Part III para.30, amended: SI 2002/834 Art.26

Sch.5 Part III para.31, amended: SI 2002/834 Art.26

Sch.5 Part III para.32, amended: SI 2002/834 Art.26

Sch.5 Part III para.33, amended: SI 2002/834 Art.26

Sch.5 Part III para.34, amended: SI 2002/834 Art.26

Sch.5 Part III para.35, amended: SI 2002/834 Art.26

Sch.5 Part III para.36, amended: SI 2002/834 Art.26

Sch.5 Part III para.37, amended: SI 2002/834 Art.26

Sch.5 Part III para.38, amended: SI 2002/834 Art.26

Sch.5 Part III para.39, amended: SI 2002/834 Art.26

Sch.5 Part III para.40, amended: SI 2002/834 Art.26

Sch.5 Part III para.41, amended: SI 2002/834 Art.26

Sch.5 Part III para.42, amended: SI 2002/834 Art.26

Sch.5 Part III para.43, amended: SI 2002/834 Art.26

Sch.5 Part III para.44, amended: SI 2002/834 Art.26

Sch.5 Part III para.45, amended: SI 2002/834 Art.26

Sch.5 Part III para.46, amended: SI 2002/834 Art.26

Sch.5 Part III para.47, amended: SI 2002/834 Art.26

Sch.5 Part III para.48, amended: SI 2002/834 Art.26

Sch.5 Part III para.49, amended: SI 2002/834 Art.26

Sch.5 Part III para.50, amended: SI 2002/834 Art.26

Sch.5 Part III para.51, amended: SI 2002/834 Art.26

Sch.5 Part III para.51, applied: SI 2002/3053 Sch.1 para.5

Sch.5 Part III para.52, amended: SI 2002/834 Art.26

Sch.5 Part III para.52, applied: SI 2002/3053 Sch.1 para.5

Sch.5 Part III para.53, amended: SI 2002/834 Art.26

Sch.5 Part III para.54, amended: SI 2002/834 Art.26

Sch.5 Part III para.55, amended: SI 2002/834 Art.26

Sch.5 Part III para.56, amended: SI 2002/834 Art.26

1999–cont.

450. National Assembly for Wales (Representation of the People) Order 1999–cont.

Sch.5 Part IV para.57, amended: SI 2002/834 Art.26

Sch.5 Part IV para.58, amended: SI 2002/834 Art.26

Sch.5 Part IV para.59, amended: SI 2002/834 Art.26

Sch.5 Part IV para.60, amended: SI 2002/834 Art.26

Sch.5 Part V para.61, amended: SI 2002/834 Art.26

Sch.5 Part V para.62, amended: SI 2002/834 Art.26

Sch.5 Part V para.63, amended: SI 2002/834 Art.26

Sch.5 Part V para.64, amended: SI 2002/834 Art.26

Sch.5 Part VI para.65, amended: SI 2002/834 Art.26

Sch.5 Part VII para.66, amended: SI 2002/834 Art.26

Sch.5 Part VII para.67, amended: SI 2002/834 Art.26

Sch.5 Part VII para.68, amended: SI 2002/834 Art.26

Sch.5 Part VII para.69, amended: SI 2002/834 Art.26

Sch.5 Part VII para.70, amended: SI 2002/834 Art.26

Sch.6, revoked: SI 2002/834 Art.27

451. Education (Budget Statements) (Wales) Regulations 1999

revoked: SI 2002/122 Reg.3

482. Common Agricultural Policy (Wine) (Amendment) Regulations 1999

revoked (in part): SSI 2002/325 Reg.19

483. Crime and Disorder Strategies (Prescribed Descriptions) (Amendment) Order 1999

revoked (in part): SI 2004/118 Art.4

491. Criminal Legal Aid (Fixed Payments) (Scotland) Regulations 1999

see *Vickers v Buchanan* 2002 S.L.T. 686 (HCJ Appeal), Lord Coulsfield, Lord MacLean, Lord Sutherland

Reg.2, amended: SSI 2002/442 Reg.2, SSI 2004/51 Reg.3

Reg.4, amended: SSI 2004/263 Reg.3

Reg.4A, added: SSI 2002/247 Reg.3

Sch.1 Part 1, amended: SSI 2002/247 Reg.4, SSI 2003/249 Reg.4

Sch.1 Part 1, substituted: SSI 2004/51 Sch.1, SSI 2004/126 Sch.1, SSI 2004/263 Sch.1

492. Scottish Local Elections Amendment (No.2) Rules 1999

revoked: SSI 2002/457 Sch.1

1999–cont.

495. Education (Amount to Follow Permanently Excluded Pupil) Regulations 1999

Reg.1, amended: SI 2003/3227 Reg.10, SI 2004/402 Reg.2, Reg.3

Reg.2, amended: SI 2002/408 Reg.2, SI 2003/3227 Reg.10, SI 2004/402 Reg.3

Reg.4, amended: SI 2003/3227 Reg.10, SI 2004/402 Reg.2

498. Insurance Companies (Capital Redemption Business) (Modification of the Corporation Tax Acts) Regulations 1999

Reg.4, revoked: SI 2004/2310 Sch.1 para.78

499. Education (School Organisation Plans) (Wales) Regulations 1999

revoked: SI 2003/1732 Reg.2

506. Competition Act 1998 (Competition Commission) Transitional, Consequential and Supplemental Provisions Order 1999

Art.22, revoked: 2002 c.40 Sch.26

Art.41, revoked: 2004 c.27 Sch.8

539. Specified Risk Material (Inspection Charges) Regulations 1999

revoked (in part): SSI 2002/255 Sch.9 Part I

545. Local Government (Parishes and Parish Councils) Regulations 1999

varied: SI 2004/222 Art.2

551. Common Investment (Amendment) Scheme 1999

revoked: SI 2004/266 Art.7

584. National Minimum Wage Regulations 1999

referred to: SI 2004/1930 Reg.7

Reg.3, see *Walton v Independent Living Organisation Ltd* [2002] I.C.R. 1406 (EAT), Holland, J.; see *Walton v Independent Living Organisation Ltd* [2003] EWCA Civ 199, [2003] I.C.R. 688 (CA), Aldous, L.J.

Reg.6, see *Walton v Independent Living Organisation Ltd* [2002] I.C.R. 1406 (EAT), Holland, J.; see *Walton v Independent Living Organisation Ltd* [2003] EWCA Civ 199, [2003] I.C.R. 688 (CA), Aldous, L.J.

Reg.11, amended: SI 2002/1999 Reg.2, SI 2003/1923 Reg.2, SI 2004/1930 Reg.2

Reg.12, amended: SI 2004/1930 Reg.3

Reg.12, revoked (in part): SI 2004/1930 Reg.3

Reg.13, amended: SI 2002/1999 Reg.3, SI 2003/1923 Reg.3, SI 2004/1930 Reg.4

Reg.14A, added: SI 2002/1999 Reg.4

Reg.15, see *British Nursing Association v Inland Revenue (National Minimum Wage Compliance Team)* [2002] EWCA Civ 494, [2003] I.C.R. 19 (CA), Buxton, L.J.

Reg.24, substituted: SI 2004/1161 Reg.2

Reg.25, substituted: SI 2004/1161 Reg.2

NO.

1999–cont.

584. National Minimum Wage Regulations 1999–cont.

Reg.26, amended: SI 2004/1161 Reg.3

Reg.26, substituted: SI 2004/1161 Reg.2

Reg.28, see *Walton v Independent Living Organisation Ltd* [2002] I.C.R. 1406 (EAT), Holland, J.; see *Walton v Independent Living Organisation Ltd* [2003] EWCA Civ 199, [2003] I.C.R. 688 (CA), Aldous, L.J.

Reg.36, amended: SI 2003/1923 Reg.4, SI 2004/1930 Reg.5

Reg.36A, added: SI 2003/1923 Reg.5

Reg.38, amended: SI 2004/1930 Reg.6

590. Organic Farming Regulations 1999

applied: SI 2003/1235 Reg.8

610. Education (Transfer of Functions Concerning School Lunches) (Wales) Order 1999

Art.2, amended: SI 2003/1717 Reg.4

Art.2, revoked (in part): SI 2003/1717 Reg.4

Art.4, amended: SI 2003/1717 Reg.4

Art.5, substituted: SI 2003/1717 Reg.4

611. Housing (Right to Buy) (Cost Floor) (Scotland) Order 1999

applied: SSI 2002/317 Art.3

614. Local Authorities Traffic Orders (Procedure) (Scotland) Regulations 1999

Reg.21, substituted: SSI 2002/31 Reg.3

616. Health Authorities (England) Establishment Order 1996 Amendment and the Cambridgeshire and Norfolk Health Authorities (Establishment etc.) Order 1999

revoked: SI 2002/553 Sch.3

625. North Bristol National Health Service Trust (Establishment) Order 1999

revoked: 2003 c.43 s.7

626. Frenchay Healthcare and the Southmead Health Services National Health Service Trusts (Dissolution) Order 1999

revoked: 2003 c.43 s.7

630. Swindon and Marlborough National Health Service Trust (Establishment) Amendment Order 1999

revoked: 2003 c.43 s.7

631. Mancunian Community Health National Health Service Trust (Establishment) Amendment Order 1999

revoked: 2003 c.43 s.7

632. St Helens and Knowsley Hospital Services National Health Service Trust (Establishment) Amendment Order 1999

revoked: 2003 c.43 s.7

633. Cornwall Healthcare National Health Service Trust (Establishment) Amendment Order 1999

revoked: 2003 c.43 s.7

NO.

1999–cont.

634. Trecare National Health Service Trust (Dissolution) Order 1999

revoked: 2003 c.43 s.7

636. Lincoln District Healthcare National Health Service Trust (Establishment) Amendment Order 1999

revoked: 2003 c.43 s.7

640. North Staffordshire Combined Healthcare National Health Service Trust (Establishment) Amendment Order 1999

revoked: 2003 c.43 s.7

641. National Health Service Estate Management and Health Building Agency Trading Fund Order 1999

Sch.1, amended: SI 2004/696 Sch.1 para.28

646. Animal By-Products Order 1999

applied: SI 2002/1387 Reg.24, Reg.39, SI 2002/2875 Art.3, SI 2003/255 Art.6, SI 2003/1470 Art.6, SI 2003/1968 Art.7, SSI 2002/445 Reg.21, Reg.24, Reg.29, Reg.39, SSI 2002/529 Art.3, Sch.1, SSI 2003/411 Reg.2

disapplied: SI 2003/482 Art.6

revoked (in part): SI 2003/1482 Reg.51, SI 2003/2756 Reg.51, SSI 2003/411 Sch.6

Art.3, amended: SSI 2002/255 Sch.8 para.1

Art.5, see *R. (on the application of Feakins) v Secretary of State for the Environment, Food and Rural Affairs* [2002] EWHC 2574, [2003] Env. L.R. 20 (QBD (Admin Ct)), Goldring, J.; see *R. (on the application of Langton) v Department for the Environment, Food and Rural Affairs* [2001] EWHC Admin 1047, [2002] Env. L.R. 20 (QBD (Admin Ct)), Nigel Pleming Q.C.; see *R. (on the application of Langton) v Derbyshire CC* [2001] EWHC Admin 564, [2002] E.H.L.R. 6 (QBD (Admin Ct)), Elias, J.

Art.5, applied: SI 2002/1387 Reg.22

Art.5, referred to: SI 2002/1387 Reg.29, SSI 2002/445 Reg.22, Reg.29

Art.7, amended: SSI 2002/255 Sch.8 para.2

Art.8, amended: SSI 2002/255 Sch.8 para.3

Art.35, revoked (in part): SSI 2002/255 Sch.9 Part I

Sch.6 Part II para.1, revoked (in part): SSI 2002/255 Sch.9 Part I

658. Appropriation (Northern Ireland) Order 1999

revoked: 2002 c.7 (NI) Sch.3

659. Energy Efficiency (Northern Ireland) Order 1999

varied: 2002 c.1 (NI) s.5

Art.3, amended: 2002 c.1 (NI) Sch.3 para.16, (NI) Sch.3 para.17

Art.3, applied: 2002 c.1 (NI) s.2

Art.4, varied: SR 2003/163 Art.4

Art.7, amended: 2002 c.1 (NI) Sch.3 para.18

NO.

1999–cont.

660. Strategic Planning (Northern Ireland) Order 1999
Art.5, disapplied: SI 2003/430 Art.29

662. Water (Northern Ireland) Order 1999
applied: SI 2003/419 Art.63
Art.5, applied: SR 2002/331 Reg.26
Art.5, enabled: SR 2003/194
Art.10, amended: SI 2002/3153 Sch.5 para.6
Art.10, revoked (in part): SI 2002/3153 Sch.6 Part I
Art.16, referred to: SR 2003/7 Reg.3
Art.17, applied: SR 2003/7 Reg.3
Art.17, enabled: SR 2003/7
Art.17, referred to: SR 2003/7 Reg.3
Art.18, applied: SR 2003/7 Reg.4
Art.18, enabled: SR 2003/7
Art.19, referred to: SR 2003/7 Reg.3
Art.30, amended: SI 2002/3153 Sch.5 para.6, Sch.6 Part I
Art.30, enabled: SR 2003/7
Sch.7, amended: SI 2002/3153 Sch.6 Part I
Sch.7, revoked: SI 2003/419 Sch.5

663. Northern Ireland (Modification of Enactments-No 1) Order 1999
Sch.1 para.1, revoked: SI 2003/413 Sch.1
Sch.1 para.2, revoked: SI 2003/413 Sch.1
Sch.1 para.5, revoked: SI 2003/413 Sch.1
Sch.1 para.10, revoked: SI 2003/413 Sch.1
Sch.1 para.11, revoked: SI 2003/413 Sch.1

665. Judicial Committee (Devolution Issues) Rules Order 1999
Sch.1 Part V para.5.11, amended: SI 2003/1880 Art.2
Sch.1 Part V para.5.27, amended: SI 2003/1880 Art.2
Sch.1 Part V para.5.33, amended: SI 2003/1880 Art.2
Sch.1 Part V para.5.41, amended: SI 2003/1880 Art.2
Sch.1 Part V para.5.43, amended: SI 2003/1880 Art.2
Sch.1 Part V para.5.61, amended: SI 2003/1880 Art.2, Sch.1

670. Diplomatic Privileges (British Nationals) Order 1999
amended: 2002 c.8 s.2

671. Social Security Contributions (Transfer of Functions, etc.) (Northern Ireland) Order 1999
referred to: 2002 c.22 s.55
Art.7, amended: SI 2002/2836 Art.10
Art.7, applied: SR 2002/378 Reg.42
Art.7, enabled: SI 2002/2366, SR 2002/379, SR 2003/276
Art.8, enabled: SI 2002/3120
Art.10, amended: SI 2002/2836 Art.10
Art.10, enabled: SI 2002/3120
Art.12, enabled: SI 2002/2976, SI 2002/3120
Art.13, amended: SI 2002/2836 Art.10

NO.

1999–cont.

671. Social Security Contributions (Transfer of Functions, etc.) (Northern Ireland) Order 1999–*cont.*
Art.23, amended: SI 2002/2836 Sch.2 para.7
Art.23, enabled: SI 2002/2366, SI 2002/3120, SR 2002/379, SR 2003/276
Sch.1 para.15, revoked: 2002 c.22 Sch.8 Part 2
Sch.1 para.32, revoked: SI 2002/2836 Art.17
Sch.1 para.38, referred to: SR 2002/109 Sch.1
Sch.1 para.40, referred to: SR 2002/109 Sch.1
Sch.1 para.48, referred to: SR 2002/109 Sch.1
Sch.3 para.45, revoked (in part): 2004 c.3 Sch.2 Part 2
Sch.4 para.1, revoked: 2004 c.3 Sch.2 Part 2
Sch.4 para.3, revoked: 2004 c.3 Sch.2 Part 2
Sch.4 para.8, revoked: 2004 c.3 Sch.2 Part 2

672. National Assembly for Wales (Transfer of Functions) Order 1999
applied: SI 2002/652, SI 2002/2118, SI 2003/2676, SI 2003/2963, SI 2004/675
referred to: SI 2003/3233, 2004 c.5 s.118
Art.5, applied: SI 2002/1985, SI 2002/2787
Art.6, applied: SI 2002/676 Art.2
Sch.1, amended: 2002 c.38 s.145, SI 2002/2626 Sch.2 para.23, 2003 c.26 Sch.8 Part 2, 2003 c.37 s.100, Sch.9 Part 3, 2003 c.43 Sch.14 Part 2, Sch.14 Part 4
Sch.1, referred to: 2002 c.7 s.17, 2003 c.38 s.55, s.56, 2003 c.40 s.2, SI 2003/940 Art.3, 2004 c.17 s.11, 2004 c.21 s.62
Sch.1, revoked: 2003 c.37 Sch.9 Part 3
Sch.1, varied: 2002 c.15 s.177, 2002 c.17 s.40, 2002 c.38 s.145, SI 2002/1860 Sch.5 para.8, 2003 c.43 s.197, 2003 c.4 s.6, 2003 c.37 s.100, 2003 c.38 s.17, s.42, SI 2003/992 Reg.2, 2004 c.18 s.96, 2004 c.23 s.67, 2004 c.31 s.44, 2004 c.34 s.267
Sch.2, amended: 2003 c.28 Sch.1, 2003 c.37 s.100, 2003 c.43 Sch.14 Part 2
Sch.2, applied: SI 2002/1998
Sch.3, applied: SI 2002/676 Art.2

680. Scottish Parliament (Disqualification) Order 1999
revoked: SI 2003/409 Art.4
Sch.1 Part I, amended: 2002 c.8 s.1, SI 2002/881 Sch.1 para.15

681. Magistrates Courts (Hearsay Evidence in Civil Proceedings) Rules 1999
see *R. (on the application of McCann) v Manchester Crown Court* [2002] UKHL 39, [2003] 1 A.C. 787 (HL), Lord Steyn

686. Scottish Ambulance Service Board Order 1999
Sch.1 Part II, amended: SSI 2003/242 Art.7
Sch.1 Part III, amended: SI 2003/1590 Sch.1 para.20

687. Supreme Court Fees Order 1999
revoked: SI 2004/3121 Sch.2

NO.

1999–cont.

687. Supreme Court Fees Order 1999– *cont.*

Art.5, amended: SI 2003/717 Art.2, SI 2004/2100 Art.2

Art.5, revoked (in part): SI 2003/717 Art.2

Sch.1, amended: SI 2002/222 Art.3, Art.4, Art.5, SI 2003/646 Art.3, Art.5, Art.6, Art.7, Art.8, Art.9, Art.10, Art.11, Art.12, Art.13, Art.14, Art.15, Art.16, Art.17, Art.18, Art.19, Art.20, Art.21, Art.22, Art.23, Art.24, Art.25

Sch.1, referred to: SI 2003/646 Art.2

Sch.1, substituted: SI 2003/646 Art.4

688. Non-Contentious Probate Fees Order 1999

varied: SI 2003/1239 Art.3

Sch.1, referred to: SI 2003/1239 Art.3

Sch.1, substituted: SI 2003/1239 Art.2

689. County Court Fees Order 1999

revoked: SI 2004/3121 Sch.2

Art.5, amended: SI 2003/718 Art.2, SI 2004/2098 Art.2

Art.5, revoked (in part): SI 2003/718 Art.2

Sch.1, amended: SI 2002/223 Art.3, Art.4, Art.5, Art.6, SI 2003/648 Art.3, Art.4, Art.5, Art.6, Art.7, Art.8, Art.9, Art.10, Art.11, Art.12, Art.13, Art.14, Art.15, Art.16, Art.17, Art.18, Art.19, Art.20, Art.21, Art.22, Art.23, Art.24, Art.25, Art.26, Art.27, Art.28, Art.29, Art.30, Art.31

Sch.1, referred to: SI 2003/648 Art.2

690. Family Proceedings Fees Order 1999

revoked: SI 2004/3114 Sch.2

Art.4, amended: SI 2003/719 Art.2, SI 2004/2103 Art.2

Art.4, revoked (in part): SI 2003/719 Art.2

Sch.1, amended: SI 2003/645 Art.3, Art.4, Art.5, Art.6, Art.7, Art.8, Art.9, Art.10, Art.11, Art.12, Art.13, Art.14, Art.15, Art.16, Art.17, Art.18, Art.19, Art.20

Sch.1, referred to: SI 2003/645 Art.2

692. Crown Office Fees Order 1999

revoked: SI 2003/92 Art.3

694. National Health Service Information Authority Regulations 1999

Reg.1, amended: SI 2004/696 Art.3

Reg.3, amended: SI 2004/696 Art.3, Sch.1 para.29

695. National Health Service Information Authority (Establishment and Constitution) Order 1999

referred to: SI 2004/1119 Sch.1

700. Education (School Organisation Committees) (England) Regulations 1999

applied: SI 2003/507 Reg.6, Reg.24, SI 2003/1200 Reg.14

Reg.2, amended: SI 2004/3052 Reg.6

Reg.4, amended: SI 2004/3052 Reg.7

Reg.6, amended: SI 2004/3052 Reg.8

Reg.11, amended: SI 2004/3052 Reg.9

NO.

1999–cont.

700. Education (School Organisation Committees) (England) Regulations 1999–*cont.*

Sch.1 para.1, substituted: SI 2004/3052 Reg.10

Sch.1 para.2, substituted: SI 2004/3052 Reg.10

Sch.1 para.3, amended: SI 2004/3052 Reg.10

Sch.1 para.4, revoked: SI 2004/3052 Reg.10

701. Education (School Organisation Plans) (England) Regulations 1999

Reg.3, amended: SI 2003/1201 Reg.3

Reg.4, amended: SI 2003/1201 Reg.4

Reg.6, substituted: SI 2003/1201 Reg.5

Reg.7, substituted: SI 2003/1201 Reg.5

Reg.8, amended: SI 2003/1201 Reg.6

Reg.12, amended: SI 2003/1201 Reg.7, Reg.8

702. Education (References to Adjudicator) Regulations 1999

Reg.2, amended: SI 2004/3052 Reg.12

Reg.3, added: SI 2004/3052 Reg.13

703. Education (Governors Allowances) Regulations 1999

revoked (in part): SI 2003/523 Reg.3

705. Staffing of Grant-maintained and Grant-maintained Special Schools (Transitional Provisions) Regulations 1999

revoked (in part): SI 2003/2694 Sch.1 Part 2

707. East Durham and Houghall Community College (Government) Regulations 1999

revoked: SI 2002/1094 Sch.1 Part 1

709. Leicester College (Government) Regulations 1999

revoked: SI 2002/1094 Sch.1 Part 1

713. Road Vehicles (Statutory Off-Road Notification) (Amendment) Regulations 1999

revoked: SI 2002/2742 Sch.1 Part I

717. European Parliamentary Elections Act 1999 (Commencement) Order 1999

revoked: 2002 c.24 Sch.4

724. National Health Service (Dental Services) (Miscellaneous Amendments) (Scotland) Regulations 1999

Reg.15, revoked: SSI 2003/158 Sch.4

Reg.16, revoked: SSI 2003/158 Sch.4

Reg.17, revoked: SSI 2003/158 Sch.4

726. Clinical Standards Board for Scotland Order 1999

revoked: SSI 2002/534 Art.7

Art.5, applied: SSI 2002/535

Sch.1 Part I, applied: SSI 2002/535

728. Prison Rules 1999

see *R. (on the application of Carroll) v Secretary of State for the Home Department* [2001] EWCA Civ 1224, [2002] 1 W.L.R. 545 (CA), Lord Woolf of Barnes, L.C.J.

NO.

1999–cont.

728. Prison Rules 1999–*cont.*

Part I r.2, amended: SI 2002/2116 Sch.1 para.1, SI 2003/3301 r.3

Part I r.2, see *R. (on the application of Van Hoogstraten) v Governor of Belmarsh Prison* [2002] EWHC 1965, [2003] 1 W.L.R. 263 (QBD (Admin Ct)), Jackson, J.

Part II r.20, amended: SI 2002/3135 Sch.1 para.42

Part II r.35, amended: SI 2003/3301 r.4

Part II r.43, amended: SI 2003/3301 r.5

Part II r.53, amended: SI 2002/2116 Sch.1 para.2

Part II r.53A, added: SI 2002/2116 Sch.1 para.3

Part II r.54, amended: SI 2002/2116 Sch.1 para.4

Part II r.55, amended: SI 2002/2116 Sch.1 para.5

Part II r.55, revoked (in part): SI 2002/2116 Sch.1 para.5

Part II r.55A, added: SI 2002/2116 Sch.1 para.6

Part II r.57, amended: SI 2002/2116 Sch.1 para.7

Part II r.59, amended: SI 2002/2116 Sch.1 para.8

Part II r.59A, added: SI 2002/2116 Sch.1 para.9

Part II r.60, amended: SI 2002/2116 Sch.1 para.10

Part VI r.82, amended: SI 2002/2116 Sch.1 para.11

r.4, see *R. (on the application of B) v Wakefield Prison Governor* [2001] EWHC Admin 917, [2002] 1 F.C.R. 445 (QBD (Admin Ct)), Harrison, J.

r.12, see *CF v Secretary of State for the Home Department* [2004] EWHC 111, [2004] 2 F.L.R. 517 (Fam Div), Munby, J.

r.39, see *Watkins v Secretary of State for the Home Department* [2004] EWCA Civ 966, [2004] 4 All E.R. 1158 (CA), Brooke, L.J.

r.43, see *Duggan v Full Sutton Prison Governor* [2003] EWHC 361, [2003] 2 All E.R. 678 (Ch D), Hart, J.; see *Duggan v Full Sutton Prison Governor* [2004] EWCA Civ 78, [2004] 1 W.L.R. 1010 (CA), Peter Gibson, L.J.

730. Police (Conduct) Regulations 1999

revoked: SI 2004/645 Reg.2

Reg.4, amended: SI 2003/2599 Reg.2

Reg.15A, added: SI 2003/2599 Reg.3

Reg.16, amended: SI 2003/2599 Reg.4

Reg.17, amended: SI 2003/2599 Reg.5

Reg.18, amended: SI 2003/2599 Reg.6

Reg.30, amended: SI 2003/2599 Reg.7

Reg.31, applied: SI 2003/527 Reg.15

Reg.37, amended: SI 2003/2599 Reg.8

NO.

1999–cont.

730. Police (Conduct) Regulations 1999–*cont.*

Sch.2 Part II para.2, amended: SI 2003/2599 Reg.9

Sch.2 Part II para.3, amended: SI 2003/2599 Reg.9

731. Police (Conduct) (Senior Officers) Regulations 1999

applied: SI 2003/527 Sch.2 para.1, SI 2003/2596 Reg.2

disapplied: SI 2003/2596 Reg.2

revoked: SI 2004/645 Reg.2

Reg.4, amended: SI 2003/2596 Reg.3

Reg.24, amended: SI 2003/2596 Reg.4

732. Police (Efficiency) Regulations 1999

referred to: SI 2003/528 Reg.2

Reg.3, amended: SI 2003/528 Reg.3, SI 2003/2600 Reg.2

Reg.4, amended: SI 2003/2600 Reg.3

Reg.4, substituted: SI 2003/528 Reg.4

Reg.5, amended: SI 2003/528 Reg.5

Reg.6, amended: SI 2003/528 Reg.6

Reg.7, amended: SI 2003/528 Reg.7

Reg.8, amended: SI 2003/528 Reg.8

Reg.9, amended: SI 2003/528 Reg.9

Reg.10, amended: SI 2003/528 Reg.10, SI 2003/2600 Reg.4

Reg.11, amended: SI 2003/528 Reg.11

Reg.12, amended: SI 2003/528 Reg.12

Reg.13, amended: SI 2003/528 Reg.13

Reg.14, amended: SI 2003/2600 Reg.5

Reg.15, amended: SI 2003/528 Reg.14

Reg.16, amended: SI 2003/528 Reg.15

Reg.17, amended: SI 2003/528 Reg.16

Reg.17, applied: SI 2003/527 Reg.15

Reg.18A, added: SI 2003/528 Reg.17

Reg.22, amended: SI 2003/2600 Reg.6

Reg.23, revoked: SI 2003/527 Sch.4 Part 1

741. Misuse of Drugs (Licence Fees) (Amendment) Regulations 1999

revoked: SI 2003/611 Sch.1

743. Control of Major Accident Hazards Regulations 1999

Reg.2, amended: SI 2002/2469 Sch.1 para.82

749. National Health Service (General Medical Services) (Scotland) Amendment Regulations 1999

revoked: SSI 2004/114 Sch.2

751. Inshore Fishing (Prohibition of Fishing and Fishing Methods) (Scotland) Amendment Order 1999

revoked: SSI 2004/276 Sch.4

765. Wireless Telegraphy (Television Licence Fees) (Amendment) Regulations 1999

revoked: SI 2004/692 Sch.6

NO.

1999–cont.

766. National Board for Nursing, Midwifery and Health Visiting for England (Constitution and Administration) Amendment Order 1999
varied: SI 2004/1762 Art.1

767. National Health Service (Charges for Drugs and Appliances and Travelling Expenses and Remission of Charges) Amendment Regulations 1999
revoked: SI 2003/2382 Sch.2

785. Road Traffic (NHS Charges) Regulations 1999
Reg.4, amended: SI 2002/2995 Reg.2, SI 2004/560 Reg.2

Reg.4, substituted: SI 2002/237 Reg.2

Reg.4A, amended: SSI 2002/528 Reg.2

Reg.4B, amended: SSI 2004/76 Reg.2

Reg.4C, added: SSI 2004/76 Reg.2

Reg.6, amended: SSI 2002/56 Reg.2, SSI 2002/528 Reg.2, SSI 2004/76 Reg.2

Reg.13, amended: SSI 2002/528 Reg.2, SSI 2004/76 Reg.2

787. Scottish Parliament (Elections etc.) Order 1999
revoked: SI 2002/2779 Art.2

Sch.3 para.3, amended: SI 2002/881 Sch.1 para.16

790. Mulberry National Health Service Trust (Dissolution) Order 1999
revoked: 2003 c.43 s.7

791. Derbyshire Ambulance Service, the Leicestershire Ambulance and Paramedic Service and the Nottinghamshire Ambulance Service National Health Service Trusts (Dissolution) Order 1999
revoked: 2003 c.43 s.7

792. South Lincolnshire Community and Mental Health Services National Health Service Trust (Establishment) Amendment Order 1999
revoked: 2003 c.43 s.7

793. Merton and Sutton Community, the Richmond, Twickenham and Roehampton Healthcare and the Wandsworth Community Health National Health Service Trusts (Dissolution) Order 1999
revoked: 2003 c.43 s.7

794. South West London Community National Health Service Trust (Establishment) Order 1999
applied: SI 2003/3059 Sch.1

revoked: SI 2002/1323 Sch.1, 2003 c.43 s.7

795. Teddington Memorial Hospital National Health Service Trust (Establishment) Amendment Order 1999
revoked: 2003 c.43 s.7

NO.

1999–cont.

796. Northumbria Ambulance Service and the Durham County Ambulance Service National Health Service Trust (Dissolution) Order 1999
revoked: 2003 c.43 s.7

797. North East Ambulance Service National Health Service Trust (Establishment) Order 1999
referred to: SI 2004/569 Sch.1

revoked: 2003 c.43 s.7

798. Tees, East and North Yorkshire Ambulance Service National Health Service Trust (Establishment) Order 1999
referred to: SI 2004/569 Sch.1

revoked: 2003 c.43 s.7

799. Cleveland Ambulance, the Humberside Ambulance Service and the North Yorkshire Ambulance Service National Health Service Trusts (Dissolution) Order 1999
revoked: 2003 c.43 s.7

800. Hartlepool and East Durham, the North Tees Health and the South Tees Community and Mental Health National Health Service Trusts (Dissolution) Order 1999
revoked: 2003 c.43 s.7

801. North Tees and Hartlepool National Health Service Trust (Establishment) Order 1999
revoked: 2003 c.43 s.7

818. Police Appeals Tribunals Rules 1999
disapplied: SI 2003/2598 Art.2

r.5, amended: SI 2003/2597 r.2

821. National Crime Squad (Secretary of State's Objectives) Order 1999
revoked: SI 2002/779 Art.2

822. NCIS (Secretary of State's Objectives) Order 1999
revoked: SI 2002/778 Art.2

824. Income Tax (Employments) (Amendment No 2) Regulations 1999
revoked: SI 2003/2682 Sch.2

826. Velindre National Health Service Trust (Establishment) Amendment Order 1999
revoked: 2003 c.43 s.7

833. Education (Recognised Bodies) Order 1999
revoked (in part): SI 2002/1661 Art.3

834. Education (Listed Bodies) Order 1999
revoked (in part): SI 2002/1667 Art.3

847. Tees and North East Yorkshire National Health Service Trust (Establishment) Order 1999
revoked: 2003 c.43 s.7

848. Epsom and St Helier National Health Service Trust (Establishment) Order 1999
revoked: 2003 c.43 s.7

1999–cont.

848. Epsom and St Helier National Health Service Trust (Establishment) Order 1999–cont.

Art.1, amended: SI 2003/1500 Art.2

Art.2, amended: SI 2003/1500 Art.2

849. Epsom Health Care and the St Helier National Health Service Trusts (Dissolution) Order 1999

revoked: 2003 c.43 s.7

850. Allington, the East Suffolk Local Health Services and the Mid Anglia Community Health National Health Service Trusts (Dissolution) Order 1999

revoked: 2003 c.43 s.7

851. Local Health Partnerships National Health Service Trust (Establishment) Order 1999

revoked: 2003 c.43 s.7

Art.1, amended: SI 2004/1624 Art.2

Art.2, amended: SI 2004/1624 Art.2

Art.3, amended: SI 2004/1624 Art.3

855. Public Trustee (Fees) Order 1999

applied: SI 2003/690 Art.11, SI 2004/799 Art.8

Part VII, applied: SI 2003/690 Art.11

Art.7, amended: SI 2002/2232 Art.2, SI 2003/690 Art.2

Art.11, amended: SI 2003/690 Art.3, SI 2004/799 Art.2

Art.17, amended: SI 2002/2232 Art.3, SI 2003/690 Art.4, SI 2004/799 Art.3

Art.18, amended: SI 2003/690 Art.5

Art.19, amended: SI 2003/690 Art.6, SI 2004/799 Art.4

Art.20, amended: SI 2003/690 Art.7, SI 2004/799 Art.5

Art.24, amended: SI 2003/690 Art.8, SI 2004/799 Art.6

Art.29, amended: SI 2003/690 Art.9

Art.30, amended: SI 2003/690 Art.10, SI 2004/799 Art.7

873. National Health Service (Liabilities to Third Parties Scheme) Regulations 1999

Reg.1, amended: SI 2002/2469 Sch.1 para.83

Reg.3, amended: SI 2002/2469 Sch.1 para.83, SI 2004/696 Sch.1 para.30

874. National Health Service (Property Expenses Scheme) Regulations 1999

Reg.1, amended: SI 2002/2469 Sch.1 para.84

Reg.3, amended: SI 2002/2469 Sch.1 para.84, SI 2004/696 Sch.1 para.31

881. Overseas Insurers (Tax Representatives) Regulations 1999

Reg.2, amended: SI 2002/443 Reg.4

Reg.10, amended: SI 2002/443 Reg.5

Reg.12, referred to: SI 2002/443 Reg.10

Sch.1 Part I para.1, amended: SI 2002/443 Reg.6

1999–cont.

881. Overseas Insurers (Tax Representatives) Regulations 1999–cont.

Sch.1 Part II para.4, amended: SI 2002/443 Reg.7

Sch.1 Part III para.8, substituted: SI 2002/443 Reg.8

Sch.1 Part III para.10, amended: SI 2002/443 Reg.9

882. Bovine Spongiform Encephalopathy (Feeding Stuffs and Surveillance) Regulations 1999

applied: SI 2002/843 Reg.104, Sch.9 Part VII, SI 2002/1416 Reg.104, SSI 2002/255 Reg.102, Sch.9 Part VII

revoked (in part): SI 2002/843 Sch.9 Part I, SI 2002/1416 Sch.9 Part I, SSI 2002/255 Sch.9 Part I

varied: SI 2002/1416 Sch.9 Part VII

884. Southampton University Hospitals National Health Service Trust (Establishment) Amendment Order 1999

revoked: 2003 c.43 s.7

885. Cornwall Healthcare National Health Service Trust (Establishment) Amendment (No.2) Order 1999

revoked: 2003 c.43 s.7

886. Weston Park Hospital National Health Service Trust (Dissolution) Order 1999

revoked: 2003 c.43 s.7

887. Central Sheffield University Hospitals National Health Service Trust (Establishment) Amendment Order 1999

revoked: 2003 c.43 s.7

888. North Sefton &amp West Lancashire Community National Health Service Trust (Establishment) Order 1999

revoked: 2003 c.43 s.7

889. Southport and Formby, the Southport and Formby Community Health Services and the West Lancashire National Health Service Trusts (Dissolution) Order 1999

revoked: 2003 c.43 s.7

890. Southport &amp Ormskirk Hospital National Health Service Trust (Establishment) Order 1999

revoked: 2003 c.43 s.7

891. Bath Mental Health Care National Health Service Trust (Establishment) Amendment Order 1999

revoked: 2003 c.43 s.7

892. Barnet and Chase Farm Hospitals National Health Service Trust (Establishment) Order 1999

revoked: 2003 c.43 s.7

893. Chase Farm Hospitals and the Wellhouse National Health Service Trusts (Dissolution) Order 1999

revoked: 2003 c.43 s.7

NO.

1999–cont.

894. Bedford and Shires Health and Care and the South Bedfordshire Community Health Care National Health Service Trusts (Dissolution) Order 1999
revoked: 2003 c.43 s.7

895. Bedfordshire and Luton Community National Health Service Trust (Establishment) Order 1999
revoked: 2003 c.43 s.7

896. East Kent Hospitals National Health Service Trust (Establishment) Order 1999
applied: SI 2003/3059 Sch.1, Sch.2
revoked: 2003 c.43 s.7

897. Kent and Canterbury Hospitals, the South Kent Hospitals and the Thanet Health Care National Health Service Trusts (Dissolution) Order 1999
revoked: 2003 c.43 s.7

898. Community Health South London National Health Service Trust (Establishment) Order 1999
revoked: SI 2002/1323 Sch.1, 2003 c.43 s.7

899. South London and Maudsley National Health Service Trust (Establishment) Order 1999
revoked: 2003 c.43 s.7

900. Bethlem and Maudsley, the Lambeth Healthcare, the Lewisham and Guy's Mental Health and the Optimum Health Services National Health Service Trusts (Dissolution) Order 1999
revoked: 2003 c.43 s.7

903. Education (Individual Pupil Information) (Prescribed Persons) Regulations 1999
Reg.1, amended: SI 2004/1377 Reg.3
Reg.2, amended: SI 2004/1377 Reg.4
Reg.3, amended: SI 2004/1377 Reg.5

908. Parkside National Health Service Trust (Establishment) Amendment Order 1999
revoked: 2003 c.43 s.7

909. Royal London Homoeopathic National Health Service Trust (Dissolution) Order 1999
revoked: 2003 c.43 s.7

910. East Midlands Ambulance Service National Health Service Trust (Establishment) Order 1999
revoked: 2003 c.43 s.7

913. North West London Hospitals National Health Service Trust (Establishment) Order 1999
revoked: 2003 c.43 s.7

914. Central Middlesex Hospital and the Northwick Park and St Mark's National Health Service Trusts (Dissolution) Order 1999
revoked: 2003 c.43 s.7

NO.

1999–cont.

921. Bovine Spongiform Encephalopathy (No.2) (Amendment) Order 1999
revoked (in part): SSI 2002/255 Sch.9 Part I

929. Act of Sederunt (Summary Applications, Statutory Applications and Appeals etc Rules) 1999
r.2.6, see *Ward v DRM Driver Training Centre (Glasgow)* 2002 S.L.T. (Sh Ct) 108 (Sh Pr), EF Bowen Q.C., Sheriff Principal
Part 2 r.2.4, amended: SSI 2004/197 r.3
Part 2 r.2.6, amended: SSI 2004/197 r.3
Part 2 r.2.7, amended: SSI 2002/7 r.3, SSI 2002/130 r.2, SSI 2004/197 r.3
Part 2 r.2.11, amended: SSI 2003/26 r.3
Part 2 r.2.12, amended: SSI 2003/26 r.3, SSI 2004/197 r.3
Part 2 r.2.12, revoked (in part): SSI 2004/197 r.3
Part 2 r.2.22A, added: SSI 2002/7 r.3
Part 3, revoked: SSI 2002/563 r.2
Part 3, added: SSI 2002/129 r.2
Part 3, added: SSI 2002/130 r.2
Part 3, added: SSI 2002/563 r.2
Part 3, added: SSI 2003/27 r.2
Part 3, added: SSI 2003/261 r.2
Part 3, added: SSI 2003/319 Art.2
Part 3, referred to: SSI 2004/455 r.2
Part 3, revoked: SSI 2004/455 r.2
Part 3, added: SSI 2003/346 r.2
Part 3, added: SSI 2003/556 r.2
Part 3, added: SSI 2004/222 r.2
Part 3, added: SSI 2004/334 r.2
Part 3, added: SSI 2004/455 r.2
Part 3, referred to: SSI 2004/455 r.1
Part 3 r.3.8.4, amended: SSI 2003/26 r.3
Part 3 r.3.15.2, amended: SSI 2004/197 r.3
Part 3 r.3.16.1, amended: SSI 2002/146 r.2
Part 3 r.3.16.3, substituted: SSI 2004/197 r.3
Part 3 r.3.16.4, amended: SSI 2002/146 r.2
Part 3 r.3.16.6, amended: SSI 2002/146 r.2
Part 3 r.3.16.8, amended: SSI 2002/146 r.2
Part 3 r.3.16.10, added: SSI 2002/146 r.2
Part 3 r.3.16.11, added: SSI 2002/146 r.2
Part 3 r.3.16.12, added: SSI 2002/146 r.2
Part 3 r.3.16.13, added: SSI 2002/146 r.2
Part 3 r.3.19.1, substituted: SSI 2003/98 r.2
Part 3 r.3.19.6, added: SSI 2003/98 r.2
Part 3 r.3.19.7, added: SSI 2003/98 r.2
Part 3 r.3.19.8, added: SSI 2003/98 r.2
Part 3 r.3.19.9, added: SSI 2003/98 r.2
Part 3 r.3.19.10, added: SSI 2003/98 r.2
Part 3 r.3.19.11, added: SSI 2003/98 r.2
Part 3 r.3.19.12, added: SSI 2003/98 r.2
Part 3 r.3.19.13, added: SSI 2003/98 r.2
Part 3 r.3.19.14, added: SSI 2003/98 r.2
Part 3 r.3.19.15, added: SSI 2003/98 r.2
Part 3 r.3.19.16, added: SSI 2003/98 r.2
Part 3 r.3.19.17, added: SSI 2003/98 r.2
Part 3 r.3.19.18, added: SSI 2003/98 r.2
Part 3 r.3.19.19, added: SSI 2003/98 r.2

NO.

NO.

1999–cont.

929. **Act of Sederunt (Summary Applica-tions, Statutory Applications and Appeals etc Rules) 1999**–*cont.*
Part 3 r.3.19.20, added: SSI 2003/98 r.2
Part 3 r.3.19.21, added: SSI 2003/98 r.2
Part 3 r.3.19.22, added: SSI 2003/98 r.2
Part 3 r.3.19.23, added: SSI 2003/98 r.2
Part 3 r.3.19.24, added: SSI 2003/98 r.2
Part 3 r.3.27.5, referred to: SSI 2004/455 r.1
Part 3 r.3.27.12, referred to: SSI 2004/455 r.1
Part 3 r.3.27.13, referred to: SSI 2004/455 r.1
Part 3 r.3.27.14, referred to: SSI 2004/455 r.1
Part 3 r.3.27.15, referred to: SSI 2004/455 r.1
Part 3 r.3.27.16, referred to: SSI 2004/455 r.1
Part 3 r.3.27.17, referred to: SSI 2004/455 r.1
Part 3 r.3.27.18, referred to: SSI 2004/455 r.1
r.3.7.2, see *McAuley v Wigtown Divisional Licensing Board* [2002] 23 S.L.L.P. 25 (Sh Ct), JR Smith
Sch.1, amended: SSI 2002/7 Sch.2, SSI 2002/130 Sch.1, SSI 2004/455 Sch.1
Sch.1, referred to: SSI 2004/455 r.2

930. **Wireless Telegraphy (Exemption) Regulations 1999**
revoked: SI 2003/74 Sch.1
Reg.4, amended: SI 2002/1590 Reg.2

942. **National Assembly for Wales (Return-ing Officers Charges) Order 1999**
revoked: SI 2002/3053 Art.4

948. **European Parliamentary Elections (Returning Officers) Order 1999**
revoked: SI 2003/3362 Art.2

982. **Sweeteners in Food (Amendment) Regulations 1999**
Reg.3, amended: SSI 2004/6 Reg.11

991. **Social Security and Child Support (Decisions and Appeals) Regulations 1999**
applied: SI 2003/1050 Reg.6
referred to: SI 2002/1379 Reg.1
revoked (in part): SI 2003/916 Reg.34
Reg.1, amended: SI 2002/1379 Reg.2, SI 2002/1703 Sch.2 para.6, SI 2002/3019 Reg.16, SI 2003/916 Reg.36, SI 2003/1050 Reg.3, SI 2003/1886 Reg.15, SI 2004/959 Reg.24
Reg.1, referred to: SI 2002/1792 Sch.5 para.20A
Reg.3, amended: SI 2002/428 Reg.4, SI 2002/490 Reg.8, SI 2002/1379 Reg.3, SI 2002/1703 Sch.2 para.6, SI 2003/1050 Reg.3, SI 2003/1886 Reg.15
Reg.3, revoked: SI 2003/916 Reg.34
Reg.3A, amended: SI 2002/1204 Reg.2
Reg.3A, revoked: SI 2003/916 Reg.34
Reg.4, revoked: SI 2003/916 Reg.34
Reg.5, revoked: SI 2003/916 Reg.34
Reg.5, substituted: SI 2004/2283 Reg.3
Reg.5A, amended: SI 2003/129 Reg.2
Reg.5A, revoked: SI 2003/916 Reg.34

1999–cont.

991. **Social Security and Child Support (Decisions and Appeals) Regulations 1999**–*cont.*
Reg.6, amended: SI 2002/428 Reg.4, SI 2002/490 Reg.8, SI 2002/3019 Reg.17, SI 2003/1050 Reg.3, SI 2003/1886 Reg.15, SI 2003/2274 Reg.5, SI 2004/959 Reg.24
Reg.6, revoked: SI 2003/916 Reg.34
Reg.6A, amended: SI 2003/1050 Reg.3
Reg.6A, revoked: SI 2003/916 Reg.34
Reg.6B, amended: SI 2002/1204 Reg.2, SI 2004/2415 Reg.2
Reg.6B, revoked: SI 2003/916 Reg.34
Reg.7, amended: SI 2002/428 Reg.4, SI 2002/490 Reg.8, SI 2002/3019 Reg.18, SI 2002/3197 Reg.6, SI 2003/1050 Reg.3, SI 2003/1886 Reg.15, SI 2003/2274 Reg.5, SI 2004/647 Reg.2, SI 2004/959 Reg.24, SI 2004/2327 Reg.4
Reg.7, referred to: SI 2004/647 Reg.4
Reg.7, revoked: SI 2003/916 Reg.34
Reg.7A, revoked: SI 2003/916 Reg.34
Reg.7B, amended: SI 2002/1204 Reg.2, SI 2003/328 Reg.3, SI 2003/1050 Reg.3
Reg.7B, revoked (in part): SI 2002/1204 Reg.2, SI 2003/916 Reg.34
Reg.7C, revoked: SI 2003/916 Reg.34
Reg.8, revoked: SI 2003/916 Reg.34
Reg.9, revoked: SI 2003/916 Reg.34
Reg.9A, added: SI 2002/1379 Reg.4
Reg.9A, revoked: SI 2003/916 Reg.34
Reg.10, revoked: SI 2003/916 Reg.34
Reg.11, revoked: SI 2003/916 Reg.34
Reg.11A, amended: SI 2002/1379 Reg.5
Reg.11A, revoked: SI 2003/916 Reg.34
Reg.12, revoked: SI 2003/916 Reg.34
Reg.12A, revoked: SI 2003/916 Reg.34
Reg.13, amended: SI 2002/3019 Reg.19
Reg.13, revoked: SI 2003/916 Reg.34
Reg.14, amended: SI 2002/3019 Reg.20
Reg.14, revoked: SI 2003/916 Reg.34
Reg.14A, added: SI 2002/1379 Reg.6
Reg.14A, revoked: SI 2003/916 Reg.34
Reg.15, revoked: SI 2003/916 Reg.34
Reg.15A, revoked: SI 2003/916 Reg.34
Reg.15B, revoked: SI 2003/916 Reg.34
Reg.15C, revoked: SI 2003/916 Reg.34
Reg.15D, revoked: SI 2003/916 Reg.34
Reg.16, revoked: SI 2003/916 Reg.34
Reg.17, revoked: SI 2003/916 Reg.34
Reg.18, revoked: SI 2003/916 Reg.34
Reg.19, revoked: SI 2003/916 Reg.34
Reg.20, revoked: SI 2003/916 Reg.34
Reg.21, revoked: SI 2003/916 Reg.34
Reg.22, revoked: SI 2003/916 Reg.34
Reg.23, revoked: SI 2003/916 Reg.34
Reg.24, revoked: SI 2003/916 Reg.34
Reg.25, amended: SI 2002/1379 Reg.7
Reg.25, revoked: SI 2003/916 Reg.34

NO.

1999–cont.

991. Social Security and Child Support (Decisions and Appeals) Regulations 1999–cont.

Reg.26, revoked: SI 2003/916 Reg.34

Reg.27, revoked: SI 2003/916 Reg.34

Reg.28, revoked: SI 2003/916 Reg.34

Reg.29, amended: SI 2002/1379 Reg.8

Reg.29, revoked: SI 2003/916 Reg.34

Reg.30, revoked: SI 2003/916 Reg.34

Reg.30A, revoked: SI 2003/916 Reg.34

Reg.31, amended: SI 2002/1204 Reg.2, SI 2002/1379 Reg.9

Reg.31, revoked: SI 2003/916 Reg.34

Reg.31, varied: SI 2002/1915 Art.5, SSI 2003/96 Art.5

Reg.32, amended: SI 2002/1379 Reg.10

Reg.32, revoked: SI 2003/916 Reg.34

Reg.32, varied: SI 2002/1915 Art.5, SSI 2003/96 Art.5

Reg.33, amended: SI 2002/1379 Reg.11

Reg.33, revoked: SI 2003/916 Reg.34

Reg.34, revoked: SI 2003/916 Reg.34

Reg.38A, amended: SI 2002/1379 Reg.12

Reg.47, substituted: SI 2002/1379 Reg.13

Reg.49, amended: SI 2002/1379 Reg.14

Reg.51, revoked (in part): SI 2002/1379 Reg.15

Reg.53, amended: SI 2002/1379 Reg.16

Reg.53, applied: SI 2003/916 Reg.21

Reg.54, amended: SI 2002/1379 Reg.17

Reg.57, amended: SI 2002/1379 Reg.18

Reg.57A, substituted: SI 2002/1379 Reg.19

Reg.58, amended: SI 2002/1379 Reg.20

Reg.58, revoked (in part): SI 2002/1379 Reg.20

Sch.2, added: SI 2002/1379 Reg.21

Sch.2 para.1, revoked: SI 2003/916 Reg.34

Sch.2 para.2, revoked: SI 2003/916 Reg.34

Sch.2 para.3, revoked: SI 2003/916 Reg.34

Sch.2 para.4, revoked: SI 2003/916 Reg.34

Sch.2 para.5, amended: SI 2003/1581 Reg.2

Sch.2 para.5, revoked: SI 2003/916 Reg.34

Sch.2 para.5, substituted: SI 2002/1379 Reg.21

Sch.2 para.6, revoked: SI 2003/916 Reg.34

Sch.2 para.7, revoked: SI 2003/916 Reg.34

Sch.2 para.8, revoked: SI 2003/916 Reg.34

Sch.2 para.9, revoked: SI 2003/916 Reg.34

Sch.2 para.10, revoked: SI 2003/916 Reg.34

Sch.2 para.11, revoked: SI 2003/916 Reg.34

Sch.2 para.12, revoked: SI 2003/916 Reg.34

Sch.2 para.13, revoked: SI 2003/916 Reg.34

Sch.2 para.13A, added: SI 2002/3019 Reg.21

Sch.2 para.13A, revoked: SI 2003/916 Reg.34

Sch.2 para.14, revoked: SI 2003/916 Reg.34

Sch.2 para.15, revoked: SI 2003/916 Reg.34

Sch.2 para.16, revoked: SI 2003/916 Reg.34

Sch.2 para.17, revoked: SI 2003/916 Reg.34

NO.

1999–cont.

991. Social Security and Child Support (Decisions and Appeals) Regulations 1999–cont.

Sch.2 para.18, revoked: SI 2003/916 Reg.34

Sch.2 para.19, revoked: SI 2003/916 Reg.34

Sch.2 para.19A, revoked: SI 2003/916 Reg.34

Sch.2 para.20, revoked: SI 2003/916 Reg.34

Sch.2 para.21, revoked: SI 2003/916 Reg.34

Sch.2 para.22, revoked: SI 2003/916 Reg.34

Sch.2 para.23, revoked: SI 2003/916 Reg.34

Sch.2 para.24, revoked: SI 2003/916 Reg.34

Sch.2 para.25, revoked: SI 2003/916 Reg.34

Sch.2 para.26, revoked: SI 2003/916 Reg.34

Sch.2 para.27, revoked: SI 2003/916 Reg.34

Sch.3 para.4, amended: SI 2002/1379 Reg.22

Sch.3A para.1, applied: SI 2002/105 Reg.1, SI 2002/338 Reg.1, SI 2003/2693 Reg.1, SI 2004/440 Reg.1, SI 2004/1520 Reg.1, SI 2004/2174 Reg.1

Sch.3A para.3, amended: SI 2002/398 Reg.3

Sch.3A para.4, amended: SI 2003/1731 Reg.5

Sch.3A para.8, amended: SI 2002/398 Reg.3

Sch.3B para.1, added: SI 2002/3019 Reg.22

Sch.3B para.2, added: SI 2002/3019 Reg.22

Sch.3B para.3, added: SI 2002/3019 Reg.22

Sch.3B para.4, added: SI 2002/3019 Reg.22

Sch.3B para.5, added: SI 2002/3019 Reg.22

Sch.3B para.5, substituted: SI 2003/2274 Reg.5

Sch.3B para.6, added: SI 2002/3019 Reg.22

1001. Education (Student Loans) (Scotland) Regulations 1999

applied: SSI 2003/461 Reg.27

1006. Anti-Pollution Works Regulations 1999

see *Eastern Counties Leather Plc v Eastern Counties Leather Group Ltd* [2002] EWHC 494, [2002] Env. L.R. 34 (Ch D), Blackburne, J.

1012. Family Proceedings (Miscellaneous Amendments) Rules 1999

r.4, revoked (in part): SI 2003/184 r.20

1024. Health Authorities (England) Establishment Order 1996 Amendment and the Cambridgeshire and Norfolk Health Authorities (Establishment etc.) (Amendment) Order 1999

revoked: SI 2002/553 Sch.3

1025. Highways (Road Humps) Regulations 1999

applied: SI 2002/3113 Reg.16, Reg.34

1026. Highways (Traffic Calming) Regulations 1999

applied: SI 2002/3113 Reg.16

referred to: SI 2002/1327 Art.7

1027. Social Security Contributions (Decisions and Appeals) Regulations 1999

Reg.3, amended: SI 2002/3120 Reg.3

NO.

1999–cont.

1027. Social Security Contributions (Decisions and Appeals) Regulations 1999– *cont.*

Reg.4, amended: SI 2002/3120 Reg.3
Reg.8, amended: SI 2002/3120 Reg.3
Reg.11, amended: SI 2002/3120 Reg.3
Reg.12, amended: SI 2002/3120 Reg.3

1029. Personal Portfolio Bonds (Tax) Regulations 1999

Reg.2, applied: SI 2004/1450 Reg.12
Reg.6, amended: SI 2002/455 Reg.2

1042. Scotland Act 1998 (Consequential Modifications) (No.1) Order 1999

Sch.1 Part II para.14, revoked: SI 2003/435 Sch.5

1052. South Downs Health National Health Service Trust (Establishment) Amendment Order 1999

revoked: 2003 c.43 s.7

1053. Non-Road Mobile Machinery (Emission of Gaseous and Particulate Pollutants) Regulations 1999

referred to: SI 2004/693 Sch.1
Appendix 1 para.1., revoked: SI 2002/1649 Reg.3
Appendix 2 para.1., revoked: SI 2002/1649 Reg.3
Appendix 2 para.2., revoked: SI 2002/1649 Reg.3
Appendix 3 para.1., revoked: SI 2002/1649 Reg.3
Reg.2, amended: SI 2002/1649 Reg.2, Reg.3, SI 2004/2034 Reg.3
Reg.3, amended: SI 2004/2034 Reg.4
Reg.3, revoked (in part): SI 2004/2034 Reg.4
Reg.4, amended: SI 2004/2034 Reg.5
Reg.5, amended: SI 2004/2034 Reg.6
Reg.6, amended: SI 2002/1649 Reg.3
Reg.6, substituted: SI 2004/2034 Reg.7
Reg.7, substituted: SI 2004/2034 Reg.8
Reg.7A, added: SI 2004/2034 Reg.9
Reg.8, amended: SI 2002/1649 Reg.3
Reg.9, amended: SI 2002/1649 Reg.3, SI 2004/2034 Reg.10
Reg.11, amended: SI 2002/1649 Reg.3
Reg.13, amended: SI 2002/1649 Reg.3
Reg.15, substituted: SI 2004/2034 Reg.11
Reg.15A, added: SI 2004/2034 Reg.12
Reg.15B, added: SI 2004/2034 Reg.12
Reg.16, amended: SI 2004/693 Sch.2, SI 2004/2034 Reg.13
Reg.16, revoked (in part): SI 2004/693 Sch.2
Sch.1 para.1, revoked: SI 2002/1649 Reg.3
Sch.1 para.2, revoked: SI 2002/1649 Reg.3
Sch.1 para.3, revoked: SI 2002/1649 Reg.3
Sch.1 para.4, revoked: SI 2002/1649 Reg.3
Sch.1 para.5, revoked: SI 2002/1649 Reg.3
Sch.1 para.6, revoked: SI 2002/1649 Reg.3
Sch.1 para.7, revoked: SI 2002/1649 Reg.3
Sch.2, revoked: SI 2002/1649 Reg.3
Sch.3 para.1, revoked: SI 2002/1649 Reg.3

NO.

1999–cont.

1053. Non-Road Mobile Machinery (Emission of Gaseous and Particulate Pollutants) Regulations 1999–*cont.*

Sch.3 para.2, revoked: SI 2002/1649 Reg.3
Sch.3 para.3, revoked: SI 2002/1649 Reg.3
Sch.4, revoked: SI 2002/1649 Reg.3
Sch.5, revoked: SI 2002/1649 Reg.3
Sch.6, revoked: SI 2002/1649 Reg.3
Sch.7 para.1, revoked: SI 2002/1649 Reg.3
Sch.7 para.2, revoked: SI 2002/1649 Reg.3
Sch.7 para.3, revoked: SI 2002/1649 Reg.3

1057. National Health Service (General Medical Services) (Scotland) Amendment (No.2) Regulations 1999

revoked: SSI 2004/114 Sch.2

1064. School Standards and Framework Act 1998 (Admissions and Standard Numbers) (Modification) Regulations 1999

revoked (in part): SI 2003/2694 Sch.1 Part 2

1066. Education (Information as to Provision of Education) (England) Regulations 1999

Reg.4, substituted: SI 2003/190 Reg.3
Sch.2 Part I para.1, revoked: SI 2003/190 Reg.3
Sch.2 Part I para.2, revoked: SI 2003/190 Reg.3
Sch.2 Part II para.3, revoked: SI 2003/190 Reg.3
Sch.2 Part II para.4, revoked: SI 2003/190 Reg.3
Sch.2 Part II para.5, revoked: SI 2003/190 Reg.3
Sch.2 Part II para.6, revoked: SI 2003/190 Reg.3
Sch.2 Part II para.7, revoked: SI 2003/190 Reg.3

1069. Highland Primary Care National Health Service Trust (Establishment) Amendment Order 1999

revoked: SSI 2004/107 Sch.2

1071. Lothian University Hospitals National Health Service Trust (Establishment) Amendment Order 1999

revoked: SSI 2003/597 Sch.1

1074. Police (Conduct)(Senior Officers)(Scotland) Regulations 1999

applied: SSI 2004/257 Reg.37, Sch.2 para.1, Sch.2 para.2, Sch.2 para.4
referred to: SSI 2004/257 Reg.24
Reg.3, amended: SSI 2004/257 Reg.47
Sch.1 para.8, amended: SSI 2004/257 Reg.47

1080. Education (Lower Primary Class Sizes) (Scotland) Regulations 1999

applied: SSI 2003/75 Reg.3

1094. Scottish Parliamentary Elections (Returning Officers Charges) Order 1999

revoked: SI 2003/122 Art.2

NO.

1999–cont.

1096. Scotland Act 1998 (Transitory and Transitional Provisions) (Statutory Instruments) Order 1999

Art.3, applied: SSI 2003/522

Art.12, applied: SSI 2003/522

1099. Education (Nursery Education and Early Years Development) (Wales) Regulations 1999

revoked: SI 2003/893 Reg.2

1102. Sex Discrimination (Gender Reassignment) Regulations 1999

Reg.4, see *Chief Constable of West Yorkshire v A* [2002] I.C.R. 552 (EAT), Lindsay, J. (President)

1103. Bovines and Bovine Products (Trade) Regulations 1999

Reg.2, amended: SI 2002/2325 Reg.2, SI 2002/2357 Reg.2, SSI 2002/449 Reg.2

Reg.2, revoked (in part): SI 2002/2325 Reg.2

Reg.3, amended: SI 2002/2325 Reg.2, SI 2002/2357 Reg.2, SSI 2002/449 Reg.2

Reg.5A, added: SI 2002/2325 Reg.2, SI 2002/2357 Reg.2, SSI 2002/449 Reg.2

Reg.10, amended: SI 2002/2325 Reg.2, SI 2002/2357 Reg.2, SSI 2002/449 Reg.2

Reg.11, amended: SSI 2002/449 Reg.2

Reg.12, amended: SI 2002/2325 Reg.2, SI 2002/2357 Reg.2, SSI 2002/449 Reg.2

Reg.12, revoked (in part): SI 2002/2325 Reg.2, SI 2002/2357 Reg.2, SSI 2002/449 Reg.2

Reg.13, amended: SI 2002/2325 Reg.2, SI 2002/2357 Reg.2, SSI 2002/449 Reg.2

Reg.13, revoked (in part): SI 2002/2325 Reg.2, SI 2002/2357 Reg.2, SSI 2002/449 Reg.2

Reg.17, amended: SI 2002/2325 Reg.2, SI 2002/2357 Reg.2, SSI 2002/449 Reg.2

Sch.1, substituted: SI 2002/2325 Reg.2, SI 2002/2357 Reg.2, SSI 2002/449 Sch.1

Sch.2, amended: SI 2002/1174 Reg.2

Sch.2, substituted: SI 2002/2325 Reg.2, SI 2002/2357 Reg.2, SSI 2002/449 Sch.1

Sch.3, substituted: SI 2002/2325 Reg.2, SI 2002/2357 Reg.2, SSI 2002/449 Sch.1

Sch.6 para.1, amended: SI 2002/2325 Reg.2, SI 2002/2357 Reg.2, SSI 2002/449 Reg.2

1111. District Salmon Fishery Boards Order 1999

revoked: 2003 asp 15 Sch.4 Part 2

1115. Argyll and Clyde Acute Hospitals National Health Service Trust (Establishment) Amendment Order 1999

revoked: SSI 2003/325 Sch.2

1118. Cardiff and District Community National Health Service Trust (Establishment) Order 1999

revoked: 2003 c.43 s.7

NO.

1999–cont.

1119. University Hospital of Wales and Llandough Hospital National Health Service Trust (Establishment) Order 1999

revoked: 2003 c.43 s.7

1120. National Health Service Trusts (Wales) (Dissolution) Order 1999

revoked: 2003 c.43 s.7

1125. International Mobile Satellite Organisation (Immunities and Privileges) Order 1999

Art.15, amended: 2002 c.8 s.2

Art.16, amended: 2002 c.8 s.2

1131. Students Allowances (Scotland) Regulations 1999

Reg.2, amended: SSI 2004/469 Reg.5

Sch.1 para.2, amended: SSI 2004/469 Reg.5

Sch.1 para.3, amended: SSI 2004/469 Reg.5

Sch.1 para.4, amended: SSI 2004/469 Reg.5

Sch.1 para.7, amended: SSI 2004/469 Reg.5

Sch.2 para.2, amended: SSI 2004/469 Reg.5

1136. Miscellaneous Food Additives (Amendment) Regulations 1999

applied: SI 2004/554 Reg.3

referred to: SI 2003/945 Reg.3, SI 2003/1008 Reg.3

varied: SI 2002/329 Reg.9

Reg.14, amended: SI 2003/1563 Reg.10, SI 2003/1596 Reg.10, SI 2003/1659 Reg.11, SI 2003/3037 Reg.11, SI 2003/3047 Reg.10, SI 2003/3053 Reg.10, SSI 2003/291 Reg.12, SSI 2003/293 Reg.11, SSI 2003/311 Reg.11, SSI 2003/527 Reg.11, SSI 2004/6 Reg.11, SSI 2004/133 Reg.11

1148. Water Supply (Water Fittings) Regulations 1999

Reg.5, referred to: SI 2004/701 Reg.2

1167. Southend Community Care Services National Health Service Trust (Establishment) Amendment Order 1999

revoked: 2003 c.43 s.7

1168. St George's Healthcare National Health Service Trust (Establishment) Amendment Order 1999

revoked: 2003 c.43 s.7

1169. South Birmingham Mental Health National Health Service Trust (Establishment) Amendment Order 1999

revoked: 2003 c.43 s.7

1170. Lerwick Harbour Revision Order 1999

applied: SSI 2003/211 Art.10

Art.4, revoked: SSI 2003/211 Sch.1

Art.5, revoked: SSI 2003/211 Sch.1

Art.6, revoked: SSI 2003/211 Sch.1

Art.7, revoked: SSI 2003/211 Sch.1

Art.8, revoked: SSI 2003/211 Sch.1

Art.9, revoked: SSI 2003/211 Sch.1

Art.15, amended: SSI 2003/211 Art.18

Art.16, amended: SSI 2003/211 Art.18

Art.17, amended: SSI 2003/211 Art.18

NO.

NO.

1999–cont.

1999–cont.

1170. Lerwick Harbour Revision Order 1999–*cont.*
Art.18, revoked: SSI 2003/211 Sch.1

1176. Land in Care Scheme (Tir Gofal) (Wales) Regulations 1999
Reg.2, amended: SI 2003/529 Reg.2
Reg.9, amended: SI 2003/529 Reg.6
Sch.2, revoked: SI 2003/529 Reg.3
Sch.2, substituted: SI 2003/529 Reg.3
Sch.3, revoked: SI 2003/529 Reg.4
Sch.3, substituted: SI 2003/529 Reg.4
Sch.4, added: SI 2003/529 Reg.5
Sch.4, amended: SI 2003/529 Reg.5
Sch.4, revoked: SI 2003/529 Reg.5
Sch.4, substituted: SI 2003/529 Reg.5

1214. European Parliamentary Elections Regulations 1999
revoked: SI 2004/293 Reg.126
Sch.2, varied: SI 2002/185 Sch.3 Part I
Sch.3 Part I para.6, varied: SI 2002/185 Sch.3 Part I
Sch.3 Part I para.22, varied: SI 2002/185 Sch.3 Part I
Sch.3 Part I para.24, varied: SI 2002/185 Sch.3 Part I

1218. Luton and Dunstable Hospital National Health Service Trust (Establishment) Amendment Order 1999
revoked: 2003 c.43 s.7

1236. Education (National Curriculum) (Key Stage 1 Assessment Arrangements) (England) Order 1999
revoked: SI 2003/1037 Art.2

1266. National Crime Squad (Complaints) (Amendment) Regulations 1999
revoked: SI 2004/643 Reg.29

1268. European Parliamentary Elections (Northern Ireland) (Amendment) Regulations 1999
revoked: SI 2004/1267 Sch.7

1273. NCIS (Complaints) (Amendment) Regulations 1999
revoked: SI 2004/643 Reg.29

1278. Warehousekeepers and Owners of Warehoused Goods Regulations 1999
Reg.2, amended: SI 2004/2064 Reg.7
Reg.3, applied: SI 2004/2065 Reg.6
Reg.11, amended: SI 2002/501 Reg.30, SI 2004/2064 Reg.7

1286. Education (Adjudicators Inquiry Procedure etc.) Regulations 1999
Reg.15, referred to: SI 2003/507 Reg.23

1287. Education (Head Teachers) Regulations 1999
revoked (in part): SI 2003/2045 Reg.5

1289. Pembrokeshire (Llangwm and Hook Community) Order 1999
varied: SI 2004/218 Art.2

1306. Wirral Tramway Order 1999
Art.25, amended: SI 2003/2155 Sch.1 para.18, Sch.2

1319. Scotland Act 1998 (Cross-Border Public Authorities) (Specification) Order 1999
referred to: SI 2002/2636
Sch.1, amended: SI 2003/1250 Sch.10 para.6

1321. Swansea (1999) National Health Service Trust (Change of Name) Order 1999
revoked: 2003 c.43 s.7

1326. Social Security (Hospital In-Patients, Attendance Allowance and Disability Living Allowance) (Amendment) Regulations 1999
applied: SI 2002/881 Sch.1 para.9

1328. Harrow College (Government) Regulations 1999
revoked: SI 2002/1094 Sch.1 Part 1

1329. Education (Nursery Education and Early Years Development) (England) Regulations 1999
Reg.1, amended: SI 2002/2466 Reg.3, SI 2003/2939 Reg.2
Reg.2, amended: SI 2003/2939 Reg.2
Reg.3, amended: SI 2002/2466 Reg.4
Reg.3, revoked: SI 2003/2939 Reg.2
Reg.4, amended: SI 2002/2466 Reg.5
Reg.4, revoked: SI 2003/2939 Reg.2
Sch.1, revoked: SI 2003/2939 Reg.2
Sch.1 para.1, revoked: SI 2003/2939 Reg.2
Sch.1 para.2, revoked: SI 2003/2939 Reg.2
Sch.1 para.3, revoked: SI 2003/2939 Reg.2
Sch.1 para.4, revoked: SI 2003/2939 Reg.2
Sch.1 para.5, revoked: SI 2003/2939 Reg.2
Sch.1 para.6, revoked: SI 2003/2939 Reg.2

1351. Scotland Act 1998 (Transitory and Transitional Provisions) (Complaints of Maladministration) Order 1999
referred to: 2002 asp 11 Sch.7 para.1
Art.3, applied: SSI 2002/467 Art.3
Art.4, applied: 2002 asp 11 Sch.7 para.1

1352. Election Petition (Amendment) Rules 1999
see *Ahmed v Kennedy* [2002] EWHC 2061, [2002] EWHC 2060, [2002] 4 All E.R. 764 (QBD), Hooper, J.

1373. European Specialist Medical Qualifications Amendment Regulations 1999
revoked: SI 2003/1250 Sch.10 Part 2

1377. European Parliamentary Elections (Local Returning Officers Charges) Order 1999
revoked: SI 2004/1299 Art.3

1378. European Parliamentary Elections (Returning Officers Charges) Order 1999
revoked: SI 2004/1298 Art.3

NO.

1999–cont.

1379. Scotland Act 1998 (Transitory and Transitional Provisions) (Publication and Interpretation etc of Acts of the Scottish Parliament) Order 1999
referred to: SSI 2002/166 Art.2
Sch.1 para.4, applied: SSI 2002/199 Reg.12, 2003 asp 5 s.19, 2004 asp 10 s.31
Sch.1 para.13, applied: SSI 2002/118 Art.3
Sch.1 para.13, referred to: SSI 2002/168 Art.3
Sch.2, amended: SI 2002/881 Sch.1 para.17, SI 2002/3135 Sch.1 para.43, SI 2004/1771 Sch.1 para.38

1384. Pathfinder National Health Service Trust (Change of Name) Order 1999
revoked: 2003 c.43 s.7

1385. Education (Al-Furqan Primary School, Tyseley) (Exemption from Pay and Conditions) Order 1999
revoked: 2002 c.32 Sch.22 Part 1

1392. Walsgrave Hospitals National Health Service Trust (Establishment) Amendment Order 1999
revoked: 2003 c.43 s.7

1402. European Parliamentary Elections (Welsh Forms) (Amendment) Order 1999
revoked: SI 2004/1373 Art.3

1414. Radcliffe Infirmary National Health Service Trust (Dissolution) Order 1999
revoked: 2003 c.43 s.7

1437. Northern Ireland (Location of Victims Remains) Act 1999 (Immunities and Privileges) Order 1999
Art.7, amended: 2002 c.8 s.2
Art.8, amended: 2002 c.8 s.2

1439. Education Development Plans (Wales) Regulations 1999
revoked: SI 2002/1187 Reg.2

1441. Education (Inspection of Nursery Education) (Wales) Regulations 1999
Reg.4, amended: SI 2004/1743 Reg.6

1452. Aeroplane Noise Regulations 1999
Reg.3, amended: SI 2004/1256 Reg.9
Reg.4, amended: SI 2004/1256 Reg.9
Reg.5, amended: SI 2004/1256 Reg.9
Reg.6, amended: SI 2004/1256 Reg.9
Reg.7, amended: SI 2004/1256 Reg.9
Reg.8, amended: SI 2004/1256 Reg.9
Reg.9, amended: SI 2004/1256 Reg.9
Reg.10, amended: SI 2004/1256 Reg.9
Reg.11, amended: SI 2004/1256 Reg.9
Reg.12, amended: SI 2004/1256 Reg.9
Reg.13, amended: SI 2004/1256 Reg.9
Reg.14, amended: SI 2004/1256 Reg.9
Reg.18, amended: SI 2004/1256 Reg.9
Reg.18, applied: SI 2002/798 Art.14, Art.15
Reg.19, amended: SI 2004/1256 Reg.9
Reg.27, amended: SI 2004/1256 Reg.9
Reg.30, amended: SI 2004/1256 Reg.9

NO.

1999–cont.

1468. Horserace Betting Levy (Bookmakers Committee) Regulations 1999
revoked: SI 2003/1909 Reg.8

1470. Education (School Performance Information) (Wales) (Amendment) Regulations 1999
revoked: SI 2004/1025 Sch.4

1497. Education (Individual Pupils Achievements) (Information) (Wales) (Amendment) Regulations 1999
revoked: SI 2004/1026 Sch.5

1510. Social Security Act 1998 (Commencement No 7 and Consequential and Transitional Provisions) Order 1999
Art.4, revoked (in part): SI 2003/492 Sch.3 Part 1

1513. Olive Oil (Designations of Origin) Regulations 1999
applied: SI 2003/2577 Reg.17
revoked: SI 2003/2577 Reg.17

1517. Energy Information (Lamps) Regulations 1999
Sch.4 Part III para.12, revoked (in part): SI 2003/1398 Sch.1 para.33

1540. Natural Mineral Water, Spring Water and Bottled Drinking Water Regulations 1999
referred to: SI 2003/3042 Reg.2
Reg.2, amended: SI 2003/666 Reg.3, SI 2003/3042 Reg.3, SI 2004/656 Reg.3, SI 2004/1509 Reg.3, SSI 2003/139 Reg.3, SSI 2004/132 Reg.3
Reg.3, amended: SI 2003/666 Reg.4, SI 2003/3042 Reg.4, SSI 2003/139 Reg.4
Reg.4, amended: SI 2003/666 Reg.5, SI 2003/3042 Reg.5, SSI 2003/139 Reg.5
Reg.5, amended: SI 2003/666 Reg.6, SI 2003/3042 Reg.6, SSI 2003/139 Reg.6
Reg.7, amended: SI 2004/656 Reg.4, SI 2004/1509 Reg.4, SSI 2004/132 Reg.4
Reg.7A, added: SI 2004/656 Reg.5, SI 2004/1509 Reg.5, SSI 2004/132 Reg.5
Reg.9A, added: SI 2004/656 Reg.6, SI 2004/1509 Reg.6, SSI 2004/132 Reg.6
Reg.10, amended: SI 2003/666 Reg.7, SI 2003/3042 Reg.7, SI 2004/656 Reg.7, Reg.8, SI 2004/1509 Reg.7, Reg.8, SSI 2003/139 Reg.7, SSI 2004/132 Reg.7, Reg.8
Reg.11, amended: SI 2004/656 Reg.9, SI 2004/1509 Reg.9, SSI 2004/132 Reg.9
Reg.11, substituted: SI 2003/666 Reg.8, SI 2003/3042 Reg.8, SSI 2003/139 Reg.8
Reg.11A, added: SI 2004/656 Reg.10, SI 2004/1509 Reg.10, SSI 2004/132 Reg.10
Reg.12, amended: SI 2003/666 Reg.9, SI 2003/3042 Reg.9
Reg.12, substituted: SSI 2003/139 Reg.9
Reg.13, amended: SI 2003/666 Reg.10, SI 2003/3042 Reg.10, SSI 2003/139 Reg.10

NO.

1999–cont.

1540. Natural Mineral Water, Spring Water and Bottled Drinking Water Regulations 1999–*cont.*

Reg.13, revoked (in part): SSI 2003/139 Reg.10

Reg.16, substituted: SI 2003/666 Reg.11, SI 2003/3042 Reg.11, SSI 2003/139 Reg.11

Reg.17, amended: SI 2003/666 Reg.12, SI 2004/656 Reg.11, SI 2004/1509 Reg.11, SSI 2003/139 Reg.12, SSI 2004/132 Reg.11

Reg.17, substituted: SI 2003/3042 Reg.12

Reg.18, amended: SI 2003/666 Reg.13, SI 2003/3042 Reg.13, SI 2004/656 Reg.12, SI 2004/1509 Reg.12, SSI 2003/139 Reg.13, SSI 2004/132 Reg.12

Reg.18, substituted: SI 2003/3042 Reg.13

Reg.19, amended: SI 2003/666 Reg.14, SI 2003/3042 Reg.14, SSI 2003/139 Reg.14

Sch.1 Part I para.2, amended: SI 2003/666 Reg.15, SI 2003/3042 Reg.15, SI 2004/656 Reg.13, SI 2004/1509 Reg.13, SSI 2003/139 Reg.15, SSI 2004/132 Reg.13

Sch.1 Part I para.2, referred to: SI 2003/666 Reg.15, SI 2003/3042 Reg.15

Sch.1 Part II para.2, amended: SI 2003/666 Reg.15, SI 2003/3042 Reg.15, SI 2004/656 Reg.13, SI 2004/1509 Reg.13, SSI 2003/139 Reg.15, SSI 2004/132 Reg.13

Sch.1 Part II para.2, referred to: SI 2003/666 Reg.15, SI 2003/3042 Reg.15

Sch.2, amended: SI 2003/666 Reg.16, SI 2003/3042 Reg.16, SSI 2003/139 Reg.16

Sch.3 Part I para.1, amended: SI 2003/666 Reg.17, SI 2003/3042 Reg.17, SSI 2004/132 Reg.14

Sch.3 Part I para.1, substituted: SSI 2003/139 Sch.1

Sch.3 Part I para.2, substituted: SSI 2003/139 Sch.1

Sch.3 Part II, amended: SI 2003/3042 Reg.18, Reg.19, Reg.20, Reg.21

Sch.3 Part II, substituted: SI 2003/666 Reg.18, Reg.19, Reg.20, Reg.21, SSI 2003/139 Sch.1

Sch.5 para.1, added: SI 2004/656 Sch.1, SI 2004/1509 Sch.1, SSI 2004/132 Sch.1

Sch.5 para.2, added: SI 2004/656 Sch.1, SI 2004/1509 Sch.1, SSI 2004/132 Sch.1

Sch.5 para.3, added: SI 2004/656 Sch.1, SI 2004/1509 Sch.1, SSI 2004/132 Sch.1

Sch.5 para.4, added: SI 2004/656 Sch.1, SI 2004/1509 Sch.1, SSI 2004/132 Sch.1

Sch.5 para.5, added: SI 2004/656 Sch.1, SI 2004/1509 Sch.1, SSI 2004/132 Sch.1

Sch.5 para.6, added: SI 2004/656 Sch.1, SI 2004/1509 Sch.1, SSI 2004/132 Sch.1

Sch.5 para.7, added: SI 2004/656 Sch.1, SI 2004/1509 Sch.1, SSI 2004/132 Sch.1

Sch.5 para.8, added: SI 2004/656 Sch.1, SI 2004/1509 Sch.1, SSI 2004/132 Sch.1

NO.

1999–cont.

1540. Natural Mineral Water, Spring Water and Bottled Drinking Water Regulations 1999–*cont.*

Sch.6, added: SI 2004/656 Sch.1, SI 2004/1509 Sch.1, SSI 2004/132 Sch.1

Sch.7, added: SI 2004/656 Sch.1, SI 2004/1509 Sch.1, SSI 2004/132 Sch.1

1541. Relocation Grants (Form of Application) (Amendment) Regulations 1999

revoked: SI 2002/1860 Sch.6

1549. Public Interest Disclosure (Prescribed Persons) Order 1999

Sch.1, amended: SI 2002/1555 Art.38, SI 2004/664 Sch.1 para.1

Sch.1, substituted: SI 2003/1993 Sch.1

Sch.1, varied: SI 2004/664 Art.11, Art.12, Art.13, Art.14

1552. Cosmetic Products (Safety) (Amendment) Regulations 1999

revoked: SI 2003/835 Sch.1

1555. Railtrack (Luton Parkway Station Land Acquisition) Order 1999

Sch.2 para.3, amended: SI 2003/2155 Sch.1 para.17

Sch.2 para.6, amended: SI 2003/2155 Sch.2

1565. Excise Goods (Sales on Board Ships and Aircraft) Regulations 1999

referred to: SI 2004/1003 Reg.7

Part VII, applied: SI 2002/501 Reg.8, Reg.11, Reg.15

1601. Goods Infringing Intellectual Property Rights (Customs) Regulations 1999

revoked: SI 2004/1473 Sch.1

Reg.6, revoked: SI 2003/2316 Reg.2

1603. Contaminants in Food (Amendment) Regulations 1999

revoked (in part): SSI 2002/267 Sch.1

1617. Excise Duties (Personal Reliefs) (Amendment) Order 1999

revoked: SI 2002/2691 Art.2

see *R. (on the application of Hoverspeed Ltd) v Customs and Excise Commissioners* [2002] EWHC 1630, [2002] 3 W.L.R. 1219 (QBD (Admin Ct)), Brooke, L.J.

1618. Goods Infringing Intellectual Property Rights (Consequential Provisions) Regulations 1999

revoked: SI 2004/1473 Sch.1

1619. General Teaching Council for Wales (Constitution) Regulations 1999

Sch.1 Part 1, substituted: SI 2003/389 Reg.2

Sch.1 Part 2, substituted: SI 2003/389 Reg.2

1620. National Health Service (General Medical Services) (Scotland) Amendment (No.3) Regulations 1999

revoked: SSI 2004/114 Sch.2

1627. National Health Service (General Medical Services) Amendment (No.2) Regulations 1999

revoked (in part): SI 2004/865 Sch.2

NO.

NO.

1999–cont.

1644. Merchant Shipping (Additional Safety Measures for Bulk Carriers) Regulations 1999

Reg.4, amended: SI 2004/2151 Reg.2

Reg.5, amended: SI 2004/2151 Reg.2

Reg.9, amended: SI 2004/2151 Reg.2

Reg.12, amended: SI 2004/2151 Reg.2

Reg.12A, added: SI 2004/2151 Sch.1

Reg.12B, added: SI 2004/2151 Sch.1

Reg.12C, added: SI 2004/2151 Sch.1

Reg.12D, added: SI 2004/2151 Sch.1

Reg.12E, added: SI 2004/2151 Sch.1

Reg.15, amended: SI 2004/2151 Reg.2

1661. Town and Country Planning (General Permitted Development) (Amendment) Order 1999

Art.3, revoked (in part): SI 2002/1878 Art.4

1663. Feeding Stuffs (Sampling and Analysis) Regulations 1999

referred to: SI 2003/1296 Reg.2, SI 2003/1677 Reg.2, SI 2003/1850 Reg.13, SI 2003/2912 Reg.4, SI 2003/3119 Reg.4

Reg.1, amended: SI 2003/1296 Reg.3, SI 2003/1677 Reg.3, SSI 2003/277 Reg.3

Reg.3, substituted: SI 2003/1296 Reg.4, SI 2003/1677 Reg.4, SSI 2003/277 Reg.4

Reg.3, varied: SI 2004/2334 Reg.7, SSI 2004/433 Reg.7

Reg.4, varied: SI 2004/2334 Reg.7, SSI 2004/433 Reg.7

Reg.5, varied: SI 2004/2334 Reg.7, SSI 2004/433 Reg.7

Reg.6, amended: SI 2003/1296 Reg.5, SI 2003/1677 Reg.5, SI 2004/2146 Reg.2, SI 2004/2734 Reg.2, SSI 2003/277 Reg.5, SSI 2004/414 Reg.2

Reg.6, referred to: SSI 2004/433 Reg.6

Reg.6, substituted: SSI 2003/277 Reg.5

Reg.6, varied: SI 2004/2334 Reg.7, SSI 2004/433 Reg.7

Reg.6A, added: SI 2003/1296 Reg.6, SI 2003/1677 Reg.6, SSI 2003/277 Reg.6

Reg.7, varied: SI 2004/2334 Reg.7, SSI 2004/433 Reg.7

Reg.8, varied: SI 2004/2334 Reg.7, SSI 2004/433 Reg.7

Sch.1 Part I, varied: SI 2004/2334 Reg.7, SSI 2004/433 Reg.7

Sch.1 Part II, referred to: SSI 2004/433 Reg.6

Sch.1 Part II para.1, varied: SI 2004/2334 Reg.7, SSI 2004/433 Reg.7

Sch.1 Part II para.2, varied: SI 2004/2334 Reg.7, SSI 2004/433 Reg.7

Sch.1 Part II para.3, varied: SI 2004/2334 Reg.7, SSI 2004/433 Reg.7

Sch.1 Part II para.4, varied: SI 2004/2334 Reg.7, SSI 2004/433 Reg.7

Sch.1 Part II para.5, amended: SI 2002/892 Reg.13, SI 2002/1797 Reg.11

Sch.1 Part II para.5, varied: SI 2004/2334 Reg.7, SSI 2004/433 Reg.7

1999–cont.

1663. Feeding Stuffs (Sampling and Analysis) Regulations 1999–*cont.*

Sch.1 Part II para.6, varied: SI 2004/2334 Reg.7, SSI 2004/433 Reg.7

Sch.1 Part II para.7, varied: SI 2004/2334 Reg.7, SSI 2004/433 Reg.7

Sch.1 Part II para.8, varied: SI 2004/2334 Reg.7, SSI 2004/433 Reg.7

Sch.1 Part II para.9, varied: SI 2004/2334 Reg.7, SSI 2004/433 Reg.7

Sch.1 Part II para.10, varied: SI 2004/2334 Reg.7, SSI 2004/433 Reg.7

Sch.1 Part III para.1, varied: SI 2004/2334 Reg.7, SSI 2004/433 Reg.7

Sch.1 Part III para.2, varied: SI 2004/2334 Reg.7, SSI 2004/433 Reg.7

Sch.1 Part III para.3, varied: SI 2004/2334 Reg.7, SSI 2004/433 Reg.7

Sch.1 Part III para.4, varied: SI 2004/2334 Reg.7, SSI 2004/433 Reg.7

Sch.2 Part I para.3, amended: SI 2002/892 Reg.13, SI 2002/1797 Reg.11, SI 2003/1503 Reg.14, SI 2003/1850 Reg.14, SI 2003/2912 Reg.5, SI 2003/3119 Reg.5, SI 2004/1301 Reg.5, SI 2004/1749 Reg.5, SI 2004/2688 Reg.4, SSI 2002/285 Reg.12

Sch.2 Part II, amended: SI 2003/1296 Reg.7, SI 2003/1677 Reg.7, SSI 2003/277 Reg.7

Sch.3 Part I, varied: SI 2004/2334 Reg.7, SSI 2004/433 Reg.7

Sch.3 Part II, amended: SI 2002/1797 Reg.11, SI 2003/1503 Reg.15, SI 2003/1850 Reg.15, SI 2003/2912 Reg.6, SI 2003/3119 Reg.6, SI 2004/1301 Reg.6, SI 2004/1749 Reg.6, SI 2004/2688 Reg.4, SSI 2002/285 Reg.12

Sch.3 Part II, substituted: SI 2002/892 Reg.13

Sch.3 Part II, varied: SI 2004/2334 Reg.7, SSI 2004/433 Reg.7

1671. Education (School Organisation Proposals) (Wales) Regulations 1999

referred to: SI 2004/908 Reg.3

Reg.2, amended: SI 2004/908 Reg.4

Reg.3A, added: SI 2004/908 Reg.5

Sch.1, applied: SI 2002/432 Sch.2 para.1, SI 2004/1576 Reg.2

Sch.1 Part I para.1, amended: SI 2004/908 Reg.6

Sch.2 Part 1 para.6, amended: SI 2004/908 Reg.7

Sch.2A para.1, added: SI 2004/908 Sch.1

Sch.2A para.2, added: SI 2004/908 Sch.1

Sch.2A para.3, added: SI 2004/908 Sch.1

Sch.2A para.4, added: SI 2004/908 Sch.1

Sch.2A para.5, added: SI 2004/908 Sch.1

Sch.3 Part II para.5, substituted: SI 2004/908 Reg.9

Sch.4 Part I para.1, amended: SI 2004/908 Reg.10

NO.

1999–cont.

1671. Education (School Organisation Proposals) (Wales) Regulations 1999–
cont.

Sch.4 Part II para.4, amended: SI 2004/908 Reg.10

Sch.4 Part III para.6, amended: SI 2004/908 Reg.10

Sch.4 Part III para.6, revoked (in part): SI 2004/908 Reg.10

Sch.4 Part III para.7, revoked (in part): SI 2004/908 Reg.10

Sch.4 Part III para.13, amended: SI 2004/908 Reg.10

Sch.4 Part III para.18A, added: SI 2004/908 Reg.10

Sch.4 Part IV para.29, amended: SI 2004/908 Reg.10

1676. Energy Information (Dishwashers) Regulations 1999

Sch.5 Part III para.12, revoked (in part): SI 2003/1398 Sch.1 para.34

1723. Traffic Signs General (Amendment) Directions 1999

revoked: SI 2002/3113 Reg.2

1726. General Teaching Council for England (Constitution) Regulations 1999

Reg.2, amended: SI 2004/1935 Reg.2

Reg.2, revoked (in part): SI 2004/1935 Reg.2

Reg.4, amended: SI 2004/1935 Reg.2

Reg.5, amended: SI 2004/1935 Reg.2

Reg.5, revoked (in part): SI 2004/1935 Reg.2

Reg.6, amended: SI 2004/1935 Reg.2

Reg.8, amended: SI 2004/1935 Reg.2

Reg.10, amended: SI 2004/1935 Reg.2

Reg.10, revoked (in part): SI 2004/1935 Reg.2

1736. Visiting Forces and International Headquarters (Application of Law) Order 1999

Art.8, applied: SR 2003/303 Reg.6

1737. Carriage by Air Acts (Application of Provisions) (Fifth Amendment) Order 1999

revoked: SI 2004/1899 Sch.4

1742. Appropriation (No.2) (Northern Ireland) Order 1999

revoked: 2002 c.7 (NI) Sch.3

1747. Scotland Act 1998 (Cross-Border Public Authorities) (Adaptation of Functions etc.) Order 1999

Art.3, amended: SI 2002/2636 Art.2

Sch.16 Part I para.1, amended: SI 2002/2636 Art.3

Sch.16 Part II para.2, amended: SI 2002/2636 Art.3

Sch.16 Part II para.4, added: SI 2002/2636 Art.3

Sch.16 Part II para.5, added: SI 2002/2636 Art.3

Sch.16 Part III para.6, added: SI 2002/2636 Art.3

NO.

1999–cont.

1747. Scotland Act 1998 (Cross-Border Public Authorities) (Adaptation of Functions etc.) Order 1999–*cont.*

Sch.16 Part IV para.7, added: SI 2002/2636 Art.3

1751. Copyright (Application to Other Countries) Order 1999

Sch.1, amended: SI 2003/774 Art.2

Sch.2, amended: SI 2003/774 Art.3

Sch.3, amended: SI 2003/774 Art.4

Sch.3, revoked: SI 2003/774 Art.4

Sch.5 para.2, revoked: SI 2003/774 Art.5

1752. Performances (Reciprocal Protection) (Convention Countries) Order 1999

revoked: SI 2003/773 Art.4

1768. Mount Vernon and Watford Hospitals National Health Service Trust (Establishment) Amendment Order 1999

revoked: 2003 c.43 s.7

1769. Hillingdon Hospital National Health Service Trust (Establishment) Amendment Order 1999

revoked: 2003 c.43 s.7

1770. Wiltshire and Swindon Health Care National Health Service Trust (Establishment) Order 1999

revoked: SI 2002/1335 Art.2, 2003 c.43 s.7

1771. Wiltshire Health Care and the East Wiltshire Health Care National Health Service Trusts (Dissolution) Order 1999

revoked: 2003 c.43 s.7

1773. Newham Community Health Services National Health Service Trust (Establishment) Amendment Order 1999

revoked: 2003 c.43 s.7

1774. Wireless Telegraphy (Licence Charges) Regulations 1999

revoked: SI 2002/1700 Sch.1

1775. Federal Republic of Yugoslavia (Supply and Sale of Equipment) (Penalties and Licences) (Amendment) Regulations 1999

revoked: SI 2002/316 Reg.2

1779. Education (Transfer of Functions Concerning School Lunches) (Wales) (No.2) Order 1999

Art.2, amended: SI 2003/1717 Reg.5

Art.2, revoked (in part): SI 2003/1717 Reg.5

Art.4, amended: SI 2003/1717 Reg.5

1781. Education (Individual Pupil Information) (Prescribed Persons) (Wales) Regulations 1999

revoked: SI 2004/549 Reg.1

1783. Environmental Impact Assessment (Land Drainage Improvement Works) Regulations 1999

applied: SI 2002/2127 Reg.3, SI 2003/164 Reg.3

NO.

NO.

1999–cont.

1811. Education (School Performance and Unauthorised Absence Targets) (Wales) Regulations 1999
applied: SI 2002/1187 Reg.19
Reg.3, amended: SI 2004/2914 Reg.2
Reg.4, amended: SI 2004/2914 Reg.2
Reg.9, amended: SI 2004/2914 Reg.2

1812. Education (School Information) (Wales) Regulations 1999
Reg.3, amended: SI 2002/1400 Reg.2, SI 2004/1736 Reg.2
Reg.10, amended: SI 2004/1736 Reg.2
Reg.12, amended: SI 2004/1736 Reg.2
Sch.1 Part II para.21, amended: SI 2004/1736 Reg.2
Sch.3 para.16, amended: SI 2004/2914 Reg.3
Sch.3 para.16, revoked: SI 2004/1736 Reg.2
Sch.3 para.18, amended: SI 2002/1400 Reg.2
Sch.3 para.18, revoked (in part): SI 2002/1400 Reg.2
Sch.3 para.19, revoked (in part): SI 2004/2914 Reg.3
Sch.4 Part I para.1, added: SI 2004/1736 Reg.2
Sch.4 Part I para.2, added: SI 2004/1736 Reg.2
Sch.4 Part I para.3, added: SI 2004/1736 Reg.2
Sch.4 Part I para.4, added: SI 2004/1736 Reg.2
Sch.4 Part I para.5, added: SI 2004/1736 Reg.2
Sch.4 Part II para.6, added: SI 2004/1736 Reg.2
Sch.4 Part II para.7, added: SI 2004/1736 Reg.2
Sch.4 Part II para.8, added: SI 2004/1736 Reg.2
Sch.4 Part II para.9, added: SI 2004/1736 Reg.2
Sch.4 Part II para.10, added: SI 2004/1736 Reg.2
Sch.4 Part II para.11, added: SI 2004/1736 Reg.2
Sch.4 Part II para.12, added: SI 2004/1736 Reg.2
Sch.4 Part II para.13, added: SI 2004/1736 Reg.2
Sch.4 Part II para.14, added: SI 2004/1736 Reg.2
Sch.4 Part II para.15, added: SI 2004/1736 Reg.2
Sch.4 Part II para.16, added: SI 2004/1736 Reg.2
Sch.4 Part III para.17, added: SI 2004/1736 Reg.2
Sch.4 Part III para.18, added: SI 2004/1736 Reg.2

1999–cont.

1812. Education (School Information) (Wales) Regulations 1999–*cont.*
Sch.4 Part IV para.19, added: SI 2004/1736 Reg.2

1814. Designation of Schools Having a Religious Character (Wales) Order 1999
Sch.1 Part I, amended: SI 2004/1734 Art.4
Sch.1 Part II, amended: SI 2004/1734 Art.4

1815. Education (National Curriculum) (Temporary Exceptions for Individual Pupils) (Wales) Regulations 1999
revoked: 2002 c.32 Sch.22 Part 3

1820. Scotland Act 1998 (Consequential Modifications) (No.2) Order 1999
Sch.2 Part I para.29, revoked: 2003 asp 8 Sch.6 para.24
Sch.2 Part I para.74, revoked: 2003 asp 13 Sch.5 Part 2
Sch.2 Part I para.90, revoked: SI 2002/794 Sch.2

1823. Royal Hospital of St Bartholomew, the Royal London Hospital and London Chest Hospital National Health Service Trust (Change of Name) Order 1999
revoked: 2003 c.43 s.7

1825. Leicestershire and Rutland Healthcare National Health Service Trust (Establishment) Amendment Order 1999
revoked: 2003 c.43 s.7

1856. General Chiropractic Council (Registration) Rules Order of Council 1999
applied: SI 2002/2704 Sch.1 para.8
Sch.1, amended: SI 2003/3148 Reg.18
Sch.1, applied: SI 2002/2704 Sch.1 para.11, Sch.1 para.12
Sch.1, disapplied: SI 2002/2704 Sch.1 para.8, Sch.1 para.10
Sch.1, referred to: SI 2002/2704 Sch.1 para.3, Sch.1 para.10
Sch.1, revoked: SI 2004/1947 Reg.17
Sch.1, substituted: SI 2003/3148 Reg.18, SI 2004/1947 Reg.17
Sch.1, varied: SI 2004/1877 Sch.1

1857. General Chiropractic Council (Registration During Transitional Period) Rules Order of Council 1999
Sch.1, amended: SI 2003/3148 Reg.17
Sch.1, applied: SI 2002/2704 Sch.1 para.6
Sch.1, revoked: SI 2004/1947 Reg.16
Sch.1, substituted: SI 2003/3148 Reg.17, SI 2004/1947 Reg.16

1858. East Kent Hospitals National Health Service Trust (Establishment) Amendment Order 1999
revoked: 2003 c.43 s.7

1861. Beet Seeds (Amendment) Regulations 1999
revoked (in part): SI 2002/3171 Reg.29

NO.

NO.

1999–cont.

1999–cont.

1862. **Oil and Fibre Plant Seeds (Amendment) Regulations 1999**
revoked (in part): SI 2002/3174 Reg.32, SI 2004/2881 Reg.32, SSI 2004/317 Sch.8

1863. **Vegetable Seeds (Amendment) Regulations 1999**
revoked (in part): SI 2002/3175 Reg.32

1864. **Fodder Plant Seeds (Amendment) Regulations 1999**
revoked (in part): SI 2002/3172 Reg.32

1868. **Education (Exclusion from School) (Prescribed Periods) Regulations 1999**
revoked (in part): SI 2002/3178 Reg.9, SI 2003/3227 Reg.11

1871. **Feedingstuffs (Zootechnical Products) Regulations 1999**
Reg.2, amended: SI 2002/696 Reg.3, SI 2003/545 Reg.2, Reg.3, SI 2004/1036 Reg.2, SR 2002/162 Reg.3
Reg.2, applied: SI 2003/752 Reg.3
Reg.10, amended: SI 2003/545 Reg.3
Reg.11, amended: SI 2003/545 Reg.3
Reg.12, amended: SI 2003/545 Reg.3
Reg.13, amended: SI 2003/545 Reg.3
Reg.14, amended: SI 2003/545 Reg.3
Reg.15, amended: SI 2003/545 Reg.3
Reg.17, amended: SI 2003/545 Reg.3
Reg.75, amended: SI 2003/545 Reg.3
Reg.75, substituted: SI 2002/696 Reg.4, SR 2002/162 Reg.4
Sch.1 para.4, added: SI 2003/545 Reg.2
Sch.3 Part I, substituted: SI 2002/696 Sch.1, SR 2002/162 Sch.1
Sch.3 Part II, substituted: SI 2002/696 Sch.1, SI 2003/545 Sch.1, SI 2004/1036 Sch.1, SR 2002/162 Sch.1
Sch.3 Part III, substituted: SI 2002/696 Sch.1, SI 2003/545 Sch.1, SI 2004/1036 Sch.1, SR 2002/162 Sch.1

1872. **Feeding Stuffs (Establishments and Intermediaries) Regulations 1999**
referred to: SI 2003/1296 Reg.14, SI 2003/1677 Reg.14
Reg.2, amended: SI 2003/989 Reg.8, SI 2003/1026 Reg.15, SR 2003/219 r.7, SSI 2003/101 Reg.6
Reg.98, amended: SI 2002/892 Reg.14, SI 2002/1797 Reg.12, SI 2003/1296 Reg.15, SI 2003/1677 Reg.15, SR 2002/263 Reg.12, SSI 2003/277 Reg.17
Reg.99, amended: SI 2002/892 Reg.14, SI 2002/1797 Reg.12, SI 2003/1296 Reg.16, SI 2003/1677 Reg.16, SR 2002/263 Reg.12, SSI 2003/277 Reg.18
Reg.106, amended: SI 2002/892 Reg.14, SI 2002/1797 Reg.12, SI 2003/1296 Reg.17, SI 2003/1677 Reg.17, SR 2002/263 Reg.12, SR 2003/287 Reg.14, SSI 2003/277 Reg.19

1875. **Tayside Primary Care National Health Service Trust (Establishment) Amendment Order 1999**
revoked: SSI 2004/107 Sch.2

1876. **Cross-Border Credit Transfers Regulations 1999**
Reg.2, amended: SI 2002/765 Reg.6
Reg.12, amended: SI 2003/3075 Sch.2 para.3
Sch.1, amended: SI 2003/2066 Reg.13

1892. **Town and Country Planning (Trees) Regulations 1999**
see *Robinson v East Riding of Yorkshire Council* [2002] EWCA Civ 1660, [2003] J.P.L. 894 (CA), Scott Baker, L.J.
Reg.10, applied: SI 2002/412 Art.14, SI 2002/1066 Art.17, SI 2002/1327 Art.14
Reg.10, disapplied: SI 2004/757 Art.20
Reg.11, revoked (in part): SI 2003/390 Reg.13
Reg.12, revoked (in part): SI 2003/390 Reg.13
Reg.13, revoked (in part): SI 2003/390 Reg.13
Reg.14, revoked (in part): SI 2003/390 Reg.13
Reg.15, revoked (in part): SI 2003/390 Reg.13
Reg.16, revoked (in part): SI 2003/390 Reg.13
Sch.1, applied: SI 2002/1327 Art.14
Sch.1, referred to: SI 2002/412 Art.14, SI 2002/1066 Art.17, SI 2004/757 Art.20

1922. **Merchant Shipping (Liability of Shipowners and Others) (Rate of Interest) Order 1999**
Art.3, amended: SI 2003/3136 Art.2, SI 2004/931 Art.3

1925. **Collective Redundancies and Transfer of Undertakings (Protection of Employment) (Amendment) Regulations 1999**
see *Ashford School v Nixon* [2002] Emp. L.R. 556 (EAT), Wall, J.

1949. **Education (Parent Governor Representatives) Regulations 1999**
Reg.10, see *R. (on the application of Transport and General Workers Union) v Walsall MBC* [2001] EWHC Admin 452, [2002] E.L.R. 329 (QBD (Admin Ct)), Harrison, J.

1957. **Merchant Shipping (Marine Equipment) Regulations 1999**
applied: SI 2004/302 Reg.6
Reg.2, amended: SI 2004/1266 Reg.5
Reg.4, amended: SI 2004/302 Sch.1 para.5

1958. **Social Security Act 1998 (Commencement No 8, and Savings and Consequential and Transitional Provisions) Order 1999**
Art.4, revoked (in part): SI 2003/492 Sch.3 Part 1, SI 2003/495 Sch.1 Part 1
Sch.2, revoked (in part): SI 2003/495 Sch.1 Part 1

NO.

1999–cont.

1958. Social Security Act 1998 (Commencement No 8, and Savings and Consequential and Transitional Provisions) Order 1999–*cont.*

Sch.3 para.1, revoked: SI 2003/493 Sch.2 Part 1

Sch.3 para.2, revoked: SI 2003/493 Sch.2 Part 1

Sch.9 para.1, revoked: SI 2003/492 Sch.3 Part 1

Sch.9 para.2, revoked: SI 2003/492 Sch.3 Part 1

Sch.9 para.3, revoked: SI 2003/492 Sch.3 Part 1

Sch.9 para.4, revoked: SI 2003/492 Sch.3 Part 1

Sch.9 para.5, revoked: SI 2003/492 Sch.3 Part 1

Sch.10 para.1, revoked: SI 2003/492 Sch.3 Part 1

Sch.10 para.2, revoked: SI 2003/492 Sch.3 Part 1

Sch.10 para.3, revoked: SI 2003/492 Sch.3 Part 1

Sch.10 para.4, revoked: SI 2003/492 Sch.3 Part 1

Sch.10 para.5, revoked: SI 2003/492 Sch.3 Part 1

1992. Disability Discrimination Code of Practice (Goods, Facilities, Services and Premises) Order 1999

referred to: SI 2002/721 Art.2

2001. Pressure Equipment Regulations 1999

applied: SI 2004/568 Reg.5, Reg.38, Reg.39, Reg.40, Reg.41

referred to: SI 2004/568 Reg.40, SI 2004/693 Sch.1

Reg.2, amended: SI 2002/1267 Reg.2

Reg.26, amended: SI 2002/1267 Reg.2

Sch.8 para.2, amended: SI 2002/1267 Reg.2, SI 2004/693 Sch.2

Sch.8 para.2, revoked (in part): SI 2004/693 Sch.2

2020. Education (Grants in respect of Voluntary Aided Schools) Regulations 1999

Reg.2, amended: SI 2002/1720 Reg.2

Reg.3, amended: SI 2002/1720 Reg.2, SI 2003/507 Reg.29, SI 2004/1576 Reg.20

2024. Quarries Regulations 1999

Reg.2, amended: SI 2002/2174 Reg.9

Reg.3, applied: SI 2002/2776 Reg.3

Reg.33, amended: SI 2002/2174 Reg.9

Reg.45, amended: SI 2002/2174 Reg.9

Sch.5 Part II, revoked: SI 2002/2099 Sch.2

2032. INTELSAT (Immunities and Privileges) (Amendment) Order 1999

amended: 2002 c.8 s.2

Art.2, amended: 2002 c.8 s.2

NO.

1999–cont.

2034. International Organisations (Immunities and Privileges) Miscellaneous Provisions Order 1999

Sch.1, amended: SI 2002/1826 Sch.1

2083. Unfair Terms in Consumer Contract Regulations 1999

Reg.5, see *Picardi (t/a Picardi Architects) v Cuniberti* [2002] EWHC 2923, [2003] B.L.R. 487 (QBD (T&CC)), Judge Toulmin Q.C.

Sch.2, see *Picardi (t/a Picardi Architects) v Cuniberti* [2002] EWHC 2923, [2003] B.L.R. 487 (QBD (T&CC)), Judge Toulmin Q.C.

2083. Unfair Terms in Consumer Contracts Regulations 1999

applied: SI 2003/1400 Sch.4

referred to: SI 2003/1374 Sch.1

see *R. (on the application of Khatun) v Newham LBC* [2003] EWHC 2326, [2004] Eu. L.R. 116 (QBD (Admin Ct)), Newman, J.; see *Westminster Building Co Ltd v Beckingham* [2004] EWHC 138, [2004] B.L.R. 163 (QBD (T&CC)), Judge Thornton Q.C.

Reg.3, amended: SI 2004/2095 Reg.24

Reg.3, see *Standard Bank London Ltd v Apostolakis (No.1)* [2002] C.L.C. 933 (QBD (Comm Ct)), Longmore, J.

Reg.5, amended: SI 2004/2095 Reg.24

Reg.5, see *Bairstow Eves London Central Ltd v Smith* [2004] EWHC 263, [2004] 2 E.G.L.R. 25 (QBD), Gross, J.; see *Bryen & Langley Ltd v Boston* [2004] EWHC 2450, [2004] N.P.C. 165 (QBD (TCC)), Judge Richard Seymour Q.C.; see *Lovell Projects Ltd v Legg* [2003] B.L.R. 452 (QBD (T&CC)), Judge Moseley Q.C.

Reg.6, see *Bairstow Eves London Central Ltd v Smith* [2004] EWHC 263, [2004] 2 E.G.L.R. 25 (QBD), Gross, J.

Sch.1 Part I para.1, amended: SI 2003/3182 Art.2

Sch.1 Part I para.2, amended: SI 2003/3182 Art.2

Sch.1 Part I para.3, amended: SI 2003/3182 Art.2

Sch.1 Part I para.4, amended: SI 2003/3182 Art.2

Sch.1 Part I para.5, amended: SI 2003/3182 Art.2

Sch.1 Part I para.6, amended: SI 2003/3182 Art.2

Sch.1 Part I para.7, amended: SI 2003/3182 Art.2

Sch.1 Part I para.8, amended: SI 2003/3182 Art.2

Sch.1 Part I para.9, amended: SI 2003/3182 Art.2

Sch.1 Part I para.10, amended: SI 2003/3182 Art.2

NO.

NO.

1999–cont.

2085. Redbridge Health Care National Health Service Trust (Establishment) Amendment Order 1999
revoked: 2003 c.43 s.7

2093. Telecommunications (Data Protection and Privacy) Regulations 1999
applied: SI 2003/1904 Sch.1 para.2, Sch.1 para.3
revoked: SI 2003/2426 Reg.3
Part IV, applied: SI 2003/2426 Sch.2 para.2
Part V, referred to: SI 2003/1374 Sch.1
Reg.22, applied: SI 2003/2426 Sch.2 para.3
Reg.23, applied: SI 2003/2426 Sch.2 para.3, Sch.2 para.4
Reg.24, applied: SI 2003/2426 Sch.2 para.3
Reg.25, applied: SI 2003/2426 Sch.2 para.3, Sch.2 para.4
Reg.28, revoked (in part): SI 2003/2155 Sch.2
Reg.30, amended: SI 2003/2155 Sch.1 para.44
Reg.30, referred to: SI 2003/2155 Sch.1 para.45
Reg.30, revoked (in part): SI 2003/2155 Sch.2

2101. European Parliamentary (United Kingdom Representatives) Pensions (Additional Voluntary Contributions Scheme) (Amendment) Order 1999
applied: SI 2003/2922 Art.2

2104. Education (Annual Parents Meetings) (England) Regulations 1999
revoked: SI 2003/1921 Reg.2

2112. Church Representation Rules (Amendment) Resolution 1999
referred to: SI 2004/1889

2120. Stansted Airport Aircraft Movement Limit (Amendment) Order 1999
revoked: SI 2004/1946 Art.2

2129. Welsh Highland Railway Order 1999
Art.21, amended: SI 2003/2155 Sch.1 para.18, Sch.2
Sch.3 para.3, substituted: SI 2003/2155 Sch.1 para.17
Sch.3 para.6, amended: SI 2003/2155 Sch.2

2134. New Forest (Confirmation of the Byelaws of the Verderers of the New Forest) Order 1999
revoked: SI 2003/3298 Art.3

2138. Appointment of Queen's Counsel Fees Order 1999
revoked: SI 2002/2037 Art.3

2149. Motor Vehicles (Type Approval and Approval Marks) (Fees) Regulations 1999
Reg.3, amended: SI 2003/2258 Reg.2, SI 2004/2106 Reg.3
Reg.4, amended: SI 2003/2258 Reg.2, SI 2004/2106 Reg.4
Reg.9, amended: SI 2003/2258 Reg.2, SI 2004/2106 Reg.4

1999–cont.

2149. Motor Vehicles (Type Approval and Approval Marks) (Fees) Regulations 1999–*cont.*
Reg.10, amended: SI 2003/2258 Reg.2, SI 2004/2106 Reg.4
Reg.11, amended: SI 2003/2258 Reg.2, SI 2004/2106 Reg.4
Reg.13, amended: SI 2003/2258 Reg.2, SI 2004/2106 Reg.4
Sch.1 Part I, substituted: SI 2003/2258 Reg.2, SI 2004/2106 Sch.1
Sch.1 Part II, substituted: SI 2003/2258 Reg.2, SI 2004/2106 Sch.1
Sch.1 Part III, substituted: SI 2003/2258 Reg.2, SI 2004/2106 Sch.1
Sch.2, substituted: SI 2003/2258 Reg.2, SI 2004/2106 Sch.1
Sch.3, substituted: SI 2003/2258 Reg.2, SI 2004/2106 Sch.1
Sch.4 Part I, substituted: SI 2003/2258 Reg.2, SI 2004/2106 Sch.1
Sch.4 Part II, substituted: SI 2003/2258 Reg.2, SI 2004/2106 Sch.1
Sch.4 Part III, substituted: SI 2003/2258 Reg.2, SI 2004/2106 Sch.1
Sch.5 Part I, amended: SI 2004/2106 Reg.6
Sch.5 Part I, substituted: SI 2003/2258 Reg.2
Sch.5 Part II, amended: SI 2004/2106 Reg.7
Sch.5 Part II, substituted: SI 2003/2258 Reg.2
Sch.5 Part III, amended: SI 2004/2106 Reg.8
Sch.5 Part III, substituted: SI 2003/2258 Reg.2

2155. Income Tax (Employments) (Amendment No 3) Regulations 1999
revoked: SI 2003/2682 Sch.2

2157. Education (Governors Annual Reports) (England) Regulations 1999
Reg.3A, added: SI 2002/2214 Reg.2
Sch.1 para.1, substituted: SI 2002/1171 Sch.1
Sch.1 para.2, substituted: SI 2002/1171 Sch.1
Sch.1 para.3, substituted: SI 2002/1171 Sch.1
Sch.1 para.4, substituted: SI 2002/1171 Sch.1
Sch.1 para.5, substituted: SI 2002/1171 Sch.1
Sch.1 para.6, substituted: SI 2002/1171 Sch.1
Sch.1 para.7, substituted: SI 2002/1171 Sch.1
Sch.1 para.8, applied: SI 2004/1076 Reg.5
Sch.1 para.8, disapplied: SI 2004/1076 Reg.5
Sch.1 para.8, substituted: SI 2002/1171 Sch.1
Sch.1 para.8, varied: SI 2004/1076 Reg.5
Sch.1 para.9, substituted: SI 2002/1171 Sch.1
Sch.1 para.10, substituted: SI 2002/1171 Sch.1
Sch.1 para.11, substituted: SI 2002/1171 Sch.1
Sch.1 para.12, substituted: SI 2002/1171 Sch.1
Sch.1 para.13, substituted: SI 2002/1171 Sch.1
Sch.1 para.14, substituted: SI 2002/1171 Sch.1

2160. Education (School Teachers Pay and Conditions) (No.2) Order 1999
Art.3, referred to: 2002 c.32 s.147

NO.

1999–cont.

2163. Education (School Government) (England) Regulations 1999
revoked (in part): SI 2003/348 Reg.2
Reg.1, amended: SI 2003/348 Reg.2
Reg.1, revoked (in part): SI 2003/348 Reg.2, Reg.2
Reg.2, amended: SI 2003/348 Reg.2
Reg.2, revoked (in part): SI 2003/348 Reg.2, Reg.2
Reg.3, amended: SI 2003/348 Reg.2
Reg.3, revoked (in part): SI 2003/348 Reg.2, Reg.2
Reg.4, amended: SI 2003/348 Reg.2
Reg.4, revoked (in part): SI 2003/348 Reg.2, Reg.2
Reg.5, amended: SI 2003/348 Reg.2
Reg.5, revoked (in part): SI 2003/348 Reg.2, Reg.2
Reg.6, revoked (in part): SI 2003/348 Reg.2, Reg.2
Reg.7, revoked: SI 2003/348 Reg.2
Reg.8, revoked: SI 2003/348 Reg.2
Reg.9, revoked (in part): SI 2003/348 Reg.2, Reg.2
Reg.10, revoked (in part): SI 2003/348 Reg.2, Reg.2
Reg.11, revoked (in part): SI 2003/348 Reg.2, Reg.2
Reg.12, revoked (in part): SI 2003/348 Reg.2, Reg.2
Reg.13, revoked: SI 2003/348 Reg.2
Reg.14, revoked: SI 2003/348 Reg.2
Reg.15, amended: SI 2003/348 Reg.2
Reg.15, revoked (in part): SI 2003/348 Reg.2, Reg.2
Reg.16, amended: SI 2003/348 Reg.2
Reg.16, revoked (in part): SI 2003/348 Reg.2, Reg.2
Reg.17, revoked (in part): SI 2003/348 Reg.2, Reg.2
Reg.18, amended: SI 2003/348 Reg.2
Reg.18, revoked (in part): SI 2003/348 Reg.2, Reg.2
Reg.19, revoked (in part): SI 2003/348 Reg.2, Reg.2
Reg.20, revoked (in part): SI 2003/348 Reg.2, Reg.2
Reg.21, amended: SI 2003/1377 Reg.2
Reg.21, revoked (in part): SI 2003/1377 Reg.2, SI 2003/1558 Reg.3
Reg.22, revoked: SI 2003/1377 Reg.2
Reg.23, revoked: SI 2003/1377 Reg.2
Reg.24, revoked: SI 2003/1377 Reg.2
Reg.25, revoked: SI 2003/1377 Reg.2
Reg.26, revoked: SI 2003/1558 Reg.3
Reg.27, revoked: SI 2003/1558 Reg.3
Reg.28, amended: SI 2003/1377 Reg.2
Reg.28, revoked: SI 2003/1377 Reg.2
Reg.29, amended: SI 2003/1377 Reg.2
Reg.29, revoked: SI 2003/1377 Reg.2
Reg.30, amended: SI 2003/1377 Reg.2

NO.

1999–cont.

2163. Education (School Government) (England) Regulations 1999–*cont.*
Reg.30, revoked: SI 2003/1377 Reg.2
Reg.31, revoked: SI 2003/1558 Reg.3
Reg.32, revoked (in part): SI 2003/1377 Reg.2, SI 2003/1558 Reg.3
Reg.33, revoked: SI 2003/1377 Reg.2
Reg.34, amended: SI 2003/1377 Reg.2
Reg.34, revoked (in part): SI 2003/1377 Reg.2, SI 2003/1558 Reg.3
Reg.35, revoked: SI 2003/1377 Reg.2
Reg.36, revoked: SI 2003/1377 Reg.2
Reg.37, revoked: SI 2003/1377 Reg.2
Reg.38, revoked: SI 2003/1377 Reg.2
Reg.39, revoked: SI 2003/1377 Reg.2
Reg.40, revoked (in part): SI 2002/2113 Reg.6, SI 2003/1377 Reg.2
Reg.41, revoked: SI 2003/1377 Reg.2
Reg.42, amended: SI 2002/3178 Reg.8, SI 2003/1377 Reg.2
Reg.42, revoked: SI 2003/1377 Reg.2
Reg.43, revoked: SI 2003/1377 Reg.2
Reg.44, revoked: SI 2003/1377 Reg.2
Reg.45, amended: SI 2003/1377 Reg.2
Reg.45, revoked: SI 2003/1377 Reg.2
Reg.46, revoked: SI 2003/1377 Reg.2
Reg.47, revoked: SI 2003/1377 Reg.2
Reg.48, amended: SI 2002/3178 Reg.8
Reg.48, revoked: SI 2003/1377 Reg.2
Reg.49, revoked: SI 2003/1377 Reg.2
Reg.50, revoked: SI 2003/1377 Reg.2
Reg.51, revoked: SI 2003/1377 Reg.2
Reg.52, revoked: SI 2003/1377 Reg.2
Reg.53, revoked: SI 2003/1377 Reg.2
Reg.54, revoked: SI 2003/1377 Reg.2
Reg.55, revoked: SI 2003/1377 Reg.2
Reg.56, revoked (in part): SI 2003/1377 Reg.2, Reg.2
Reg.57, amended: SI 2003/1377 Reg.2
Reg.57, revoked: SI 2003/1377 Reg.2
Reg.58, revoked: SI 2003/348 Reg.2
Sch.1 para.1, revoked: SI 2003/348 Reg.2
Sch.1 para.2, revoked: SI 2003/348 Reg.2
Sch.1 para.3, revoked: SI 2003/348 Reg.2
Sch.1 para.4, revoked: SI 2003/348 Reg.2
Sch.2 para.1, revoked: SI 2003/348 Reg.2
Sch.2 para.2, revoked: SI 2003/348 Reg.2
Sch.2 para.3, revoked: SI 2003/348 Reg.2
Sch.2 para.4, revoked: SI 2003/348 Reg.2
Sch.2 para.5, revoked: SI 2003/348 Reg.2
Sch.2 para.6, revoked: SI 2003/348 Reg.2
Sch.3 para.1, revoked: SI 2003/348 Reg.2
Sch.3 para.2, revoked: SI 2003/348 Reg.2
Sch.3 para.3, revoked: SI 2003/348 Reg.2
Sch.3 para.4, revoked: SI 2003/348 Reg.2
Sch.3 para.5, revoked: SI 2003/348 Reg.2
Sch.3 para.6, revoked: SI 2003/348 Reg.2
Sch.3 para.7, revoked: SI 2003/348 Reg.2
Sch.3 para.8, revoked: SI 2003/348 Reg.2
Sch.4 para.1, revoked: SI 2003/348 Reg.2

NO.

NO.

1999–cont.

2163. Education (School Government) (England) Regulations 1999–*cont.*
Sch.4 para.2, revoked: SI 2003/348 Reg.2
Sch.4 para.3, revoked: SI 2003/348 Reg.2
Sch.4 para.4, revoked: SI 2003/348 Reg.2
Sch.4 para.5, revoked: SI 2003/348 Reg.2
Sch.4 para.6, revoked: SI 2003/348 Reg.2
Sch.4 para.7, revoked: SI 2003/348 Reg.2
Sch.4 para.8, revoked: SI 2003/348 Reg.2
Sch.4 para.9, revoked: SI 2003/348 Reg.2
Sch.5 para.1, revoked: SI 2003/348 Reg.2
Sch.5 para.2, revoked: SI 2003/348 Reg.2
Sch.5 para.3, revoked: SI 2003/348 Reg.2
Sch.5 para.4, revoked: SI 2003/348 Reg.2
Sch.5 para.5, revoked: SI 2003/348 Reg.2
Sch.5 para.6, revoked: SI 2003/348 Reg.2
Sch.5 para.7, revoked: SI 2003/348 Reg.2
Sch.5 para.8, revoked: SI 2003/348 Reg.2
Sch.5 para.9, revoked: SI 2003/348 Reg.2
Sch.5 para.10, revoked: SI 2003/348 Reg.2
Sch.5 para.11, revoked: SI 2003/348 Reg.2
Sch.5 para.12, revoked (in part): SI 2003/348 Reg.2
Sch.5 para.13, revoked (in part): SI 2003/348 Reg.2
Sch.5 para.14, revoked (in part): SI 2003/348 Reg.2
Sch.5 para.15, revoked (in part): SI 2003/348 Reg.2
Sch.5 para.16, revoked (in part): SI 2003/348 Reg.2

2164. Education (Transfer of Functions Concerning School Lunches etc.) (England) (No.2) Order 1999
Art.2, amended: SI 2003/689 Reg.2
Art.2, revoked (in part): SI 2003/689 Reg.2
Art.3, amended: SI 2003/689 Reg.2
Art.4, amended: SI 2003/689 Reg.2

2166. Education (Teachers Qualifications and Health Standards) (England) Regulations 1999
referred to: SI 2003/107 Reg.2, SI 2003/1663 Sch.1 para.2
revoked (in part): SI 2003/1662 Sch.1 Part 1, SI 2003/3139 Reg.4
see *R. (on the application of Verner) v Derby City Council* [2003] EWHC 2708, [2004] I.C.R. 535 (QBD (Admin Ct)), Lindsay, J.
Part III, applied: SI 2003/1963 Reg.3
Reg.7, see *Dorling v Sheffield City Council* [2002] E.L.R. 367 (Ch D), Patten, J.; see *R. (on the application of Dorling) v Sheffield City Council* [2002] EWHC 2505, [2003] I.C.R. 424 (QBD (Admin Ct)), Goldring, J.
Reg.11, applied: SI 2003/1662 Sch.1 para.1
Reg.12, applied: SI 2003/1662 Sch.1 para.2
Reg.13, applied: SI 2003/1662 Sch.1 para.3
Reg.15, applied: SI 2003/1662 Sch.1 para.4
Sch.1 Part II para.6, revoked: SI 2003/1663 Sch.1 Part 1

1999–cont.

2166. Education (Teachers Qualifications and Health Standards) (England) Regulations 1999–*cont.*
Sch.1 Part II para.7, revoked: SI 2003/1663 Sch.1 Part 1
Sch.2 Part 1 para.1, revoked: SI 2003/1663 Sch.1 Part 1
Sch.2 Part 1 para.2, applied: SI 2003/1663 Sch.2 para.3
Sch.2 Part 1 para.2, revoked: SI 2003/1663 Sch.1 Part 1
Sch.2 Part 1 para.3, applied: SI 2003/1662 Sch.2 para.11
Sch.2 Part 1 para.3, revoked: SI 2003/1663 Sch.1 Part 1
Sch.2 Part 1 para.4, applied: SI 2003/1663 Sch.2 para.5
Sch.2 Part 1 para.4, revoked: SI 2003/1663 Sch.1 Part 1
Sch.2 Part 1 para.4A, applied: SI 2003/1663 Sch.2 para.6
Sch.2 Part 1 para.4A, revoked: SI 2003/1663 Sch.1 Part 1
Sch.2 Part II, applied: SI 2003/1662 Sch.2 para.9
Sch.2 Part II para.5, amended: SI 2002/1434 Reg.3
Sch.2 Part II para.5, applied: SI 2003/1663 Sch.1 para.3, Sch.2 para.7, SI 2003/1709 Art.6
Sch.2 Part II para.5, revoked: SI 2003/1663 Sch.1 Part 1
Sch.2 Part II para.6, applied: SI 2003/1663 Sch.1 para.3, Sch.2 para.7, SI 2003/1709 Art.6
Sch.2 Part II para.6, revoked: SI 2003/1663 Sch.1 Part 1
Sch.2 Part II para.7, applied: SI 2003/1663 Sch.1 para.3, Sch.2 para.7, SI 2003/1709 Art.6
Sch.2 Part II para.7, revoked: SI 2003/1663 Sch.1 Part 1
Sch.2 Part II para.8, applied: SI 2003/1663 Sch.1 para.3, Sch.2 para.7, SI 2003/1709 Art.6
Sch.2 Part II para.8, revoked: SI 2003/1663 Sch.1 Part 1
Sch.2 Part II para.9, applied: SI 2003/1662 Sch.1 para.6, SI 2003/1663 Sch.1 para.3, Sch.2 para.7, SI 2003/1709 Art.6
Sch.2 Part II para.9, revoked: SI 2003/1663 Sch.1 Part 1
Sch.2 Part II para.10, applied: SI 2003/1663 Sch.1 para.3, Sch.2 para.7, SI 2003/1709 Art.6
Sch.2 Part II para.10, revoked: SI 2003/1663 Sch.1 Part 1
Sch.2 Part II para.11, applied: SI 2003/1663 Sch.1 para.3, Sch.2 para.7, SI 2003/1709 Art.6
Sch.2 Part II para.11, revoked: SI 2003/1663 Sch.1 Part 1

NO.

1999–cont.

2166. Education (Teachers Qualifications and Health Standards) (England) Regulations 1999–cont.

Sch.2 Part III, applied: SI 2003/1662 Sch.2 para.9

Sch.2 Part III para.12, amended: SI 2002/1434 Reg.3

Sch.2 Part III para.12, applied: SI 2003/1663 Sch.1 para.4, Sch.2 para.8, SI 2003/1709 Art.6

Sch.2 Part III para.12, revoked: SI 2003/1663 Sch.1 Part 1

Sch.2 Part III para.13, applied: SI 2003/1663 Sch.1 para.4, Sch.2 para.8, SI 2003/1709 Art.6

Sch.2 Part III para.13, revoked: SI 2003/1663 Sch.1 Part 1

Sch.2 Part III para.14, applied: SI 2003/1663 Sch.1 para.4, Sch.2 para.8, SI 2003/1709 Art.6

Sch.2 Part III para.14, revoked: SI 2003/1663 Sch.1 Part 1

Sch.2 Part III para.15, applied: SI 2003/1663 Sch.1 para.4, Sch.2 para.8, SI 2003/1709 Art.6

Sch.2 Part III para.15, revoked: SI 2003/1663 Sch.1 Part 1

Sch.2 Part III para.16, applied: SI 2003/1663 Sch.1 para.4, Sch.2 para.8, SI 2003/1709 Art.6

Sch.2 Part III para.16, revoked: SI 2003/1663 Sch.1 Part 1

Sch.2 Part III para.17, applied: SI 2003/1663 Sch.1 para.4, Sch.2 para.8, SI 2003/1709 Art.6

Sch.2 Part III para.17, revoked: SI 2003/1663 Sch.1 Part 1

Sch.2 Part III para.18, applied: SI 2003/1663 Sch.1 para.4, Sch.2 para.8, SI 2003/1709 Art.6

Sch.2 Part III para.18, revoked: SI 2003/1663 Sch.1 Part 1

Sch.2 Part IV para.19, added: SI 2002/1434 Reg.4

Sch.2 Part IV para.19, applied: SI 2003/1662 Sch.1 para.5

Sch.2 Part IV para.19, revoked: SI 2003/1663 Sch.1 Part 1

Sch.3 para.1, applied: SI 2002/2086 Reg.5, SI 2003/1662 Sch.2 para.2, SI 2003/1663 Sch.2 para.6, SI 2003/1709 Art.7, SI 2003/1917 Reg.5

Sch.3 Part I para.6, amended: SI 2003/107 Reg.3

Sch.3 Part I para.7, amended: SI 2002/1434 Reg.5

Sch.3 Part I para.7A, added: SI 2002/1434 Reg.6

Sch.3 para.2, applied: SI 2003/1662 Sch.1 para.4

Sch.3 para.2, referred to: SI 2003/1663 Sch.2 para.6, SI 2003/1709 Art.7

NO.

1999–cont.

2166. Education (Teachers Qualifications and Health Standards) (England) Regulations 1999–cont.

Sch.3 para.3, referred to: SI 2002/2086 Reg.5

Sch.3 para.4, referred to: SI 2002/2086 Reg.5

Sch.3 para.5, referred to: SI 2002/2086 Reg.5

Sch.3 para.6, referred to: SI 2002/2086 Reg.5

Sch.3 para.7, referred to: SI 2003/1663 Sch.2 para.6, SI 2003/1709 Art.7

Sch.3 para.7A, referred to: SI 2003/1663 Sch.2 para.6, SI 2003/1709 Art.7

Sch.3 para.9, referred to: SI 2003/1663 Sch.2 para.6, SI 2003/1709 Art.7

2170. Environmental Protection (Restriction on Use of Lead Shot) (England) Regulations 1999

referred to: SI 2002/2102

Sch.1, amended: SI 2003/2512 Reg.2

Sch.1, substituted: SI 2002/2102 Sch.1

Sch.2, amended: SI 2002/2102 Reg.2

2176. Salford Royal Hospitals National Health Service Trust (Establishment) Amendment Order 1999

revoked: 2003 c.43 s.7

2187. Education (National Curriculum) (Key Stage 1 Assessment Arrangements) (England) (Amendment) Order 1999

revoked: SI 2003/1037 Art.2

2188. Education (National Curriculum) (Key Stage 2 Assessment Arrangements) (England) Order 1999

revoked: SI 2003/1038 Art.2

2189. Education (National Curriculum) (Key Stage 3 Assessment Arrangements) (England) Order 1999

revoked: SI 2003/1039 Art.2

2196. Cereal Seeds (Amendment) (England) Regulations 1999

revoked: SI 2002/3173 Reg.32

2205. Merchant Shipping and Fishing Vessels (Personal Protective Equipment) Regulations 1999

referred to: SI 2003/2002 Reg.12

2206. Offshore Installations (Safety Zones) (No.3) Order 1999

Sch.1, amended: SI 2003/2743 Art.3

2208. Dartford-Thurrock Crossing (Amendment) Regulations 1999

revoked: SI 2003/496 Reg.3

2212. Education (Maintained Special Schools) (England) Regulations 1999

Reg.2, amended: SI 2002/2469 Sch.8

Reg.7, amended: SI 2002/2469 Sch.1 para.85

1999–cont.

2213. Education (School Organisation Proposals) (England) Regulations 1999

referred to: SI 2003/1229 Reg.2

Reg.2, amended: SI 2003/1229 Reg.3

Reg.2, applied: SI 2003/1229 Reg.18

Reg.3, substituted: SI 2003/1229 Reg.4

Reg.4, amended: SI 2003/1229 Reg.5

Reg.5, amended: SI 2003/1229 Reg.6

Reg.7, amended: SI 2003/1229 Reg.7

Reg.9, amended: SI 2004/3052 Reg.3

Reg.9, substituted: SI 2003/1229 Reg.8

Reg.10, amended: SI 2003/1229 Reg.9

Reg.10A, added: SI 2003/1229 Reg.10

Reg.10B, added: SI 2003/1229 Reg.10

Reg.10C, added: SI 2003/1229 Reg.10

Reg.12, amended: SI 2003/1229 Reg.11

Reg.14, amended: SI 2003/1229 Reg.12

Sch.1 para.1, substituted: SI 2003/1229 Reg.13

Sch.1 Part I para.1, applied: SI 2003/1229 Reg.18

Sch.1 Part I para.1, substituted: SI 2003/1229 Reg.13

Sch.1 Part I para.2, amended: SI 2003/1229 Reg.13

Sch.1 Part I para.2, substituted: SI 2003/1229 Reg.13

Sch.1 Part I para.3, substituted: SI 2003/1229 Reg.13

Sch.1 Part I para.3A, added: SI 2003/1229 Reg.13

Sch.1 Part I para.3A, amended: SI 2004/3052 Reg.4

Sch.1 Part I para.3A, substituted: SI 2003/1229 Reg.13

Sch.1 Part I para.4, substituted: SI 2003/1229 Reg.13

Sch.1 Part I para.5, substituted: SI 2003/1229 Reg.13

Sch.1 Part I para.6, substituted: SI 2003/1229 Reg.13

Sch.1 Part I para.7, substituted: SI 2003/1229 Reg.13

Sch.1 Part I para.8, substituted: SI 2003/1229 Reg.13

Sch.1 Part I para.9, substituted: SI 2003/1229 Reg.13

Sch.1 Part I para.10, substituted: SI 2003/1229 Reg.13

Sch.1 para.2, substituted: SI 2003/1229 Reg.13

Sch.1 Part II para.11, added: SI 2003/1229 Reg.13

Sch.1 Part II para.11, substituted: SI 2003/1229 Reg.13

Sch.1 Part II para.12, added: SI 2003/1229 Reg.13

Sch.1 Part II para.12, substituted: SI 2003/1229 Reg.13

1999–cont.

2213. Education (School Organisation Proposals) (England) Regulations 1999–*cont.*

Sch.1 Part II para.13, added: SI 2003/1229 Reg.13

Sch.1 Part II para.13, substituted: SI 2003/1229 Reg.13

Sch.1 para.3, substituted: SI 2003/1229 Reg.13

Sch.1 para.4, substituted: SI 2003/1229 Reg.13

Sch.1 para.5, substituted: SI 2003/1229 Reg.13

Sch.1 para.6, substituted: SI 2003/1229 Reg.13

Sch.1 para.7, substituted: SI 2003/1229 Reg.13

Sch.1 para.8, substituted: SI 2003/1229 Reg.13

Sch.1 para.9, substituted: SI 2003/1229 Reg.13

Sch.1 para.10, substituted: SI 2003/1229 Reg.13

Sch.2 Part II para.5, substituted: SI 2003/1229 Reg.14

Sch.2 Part II para.7A, added: SI 2003/1229 Reg.14

Sch.2 Part II para.9A, added: SI 2003/1229 Reg.14

Sch.2 Part II para.10, substituted: SI 2003/1229 Reg.14

Sch.2 Part II para.12, amended: SI 2003/1229 Reg.14

Sch.2 Part III para.16, substituted: SI 2003/1229 Reg.14

Sch.3 Part I para.1, amended: SI 2003/1229 Reg.15

Sch.3 Part II para.4, amended: SI 2003/1229 Reg.15

Sch.3 Part II para.5, amended: SI 2003/1229 Reg.15

Sch.3 Part III para.9A, added: SI 2003/1229 Reg.15

Sch.3 Part III para.9B, added: SI 2003/1229 Reg.15

Sch.3 Part III para.9C, added: SI 2003/1229 Reg.15

Sch.3 Part III para.13, amended: SI 2003/1229 Reg.15

Sch.3 Part III para.18A, amended: SI 2003/1229 Reg.15

Sch.3 Part III para.18B, added: SI 2003/1229 Reg.15

Sch.3 Part IV para.24, amended: SI 2003/1229 Reg.15

Sch.3 Part IV para.25, amended: SI 2003/1229 Reg.15

Sch.3 Part V para.36, amended: SI 2003/1229 Reg.15

Sch.4, amended: SI 2003/1229 Reg.16

1999–cont.

2213. Education (School Organisation Proposals) (England) Regulations 1999–*cont.*

Sch.5 Part I para.3, amended: SI 2003/1229 Reg.17

2214. Education (National Curriculum) (Modern Foreign Languages) (Amendment) Order 1999

revoked: 2002 c.32 Sch.22 Part 3

2228. Environmental Impact Assessment (Forestry) (England and Wales) Regulations 1999

Reg.3, referred to: SI 2002/2127 Reg.3

2242. Education (School Government) (Wales) Regulations 1999

Reg.42, amended: SI 2003/3227 Reg.9
Reg.48, amended: SI 2003/3227 Reg.9

2244. Railway Safety Regulations 1999

Reg.6, applied: SI 2003/547 Sch.17, SI 2004/456 Sch.16

2256. Education (Modification of Enactments Relating to Employment) Order 1999

revoked (in part): SI 2003/1964 Art.1
see *Murphy v Slough BC* [2004] I.C.R. 1163 (EAT), Silber, J.
Art.2, see *Green v Victoria Road Primary School Governing Body* [2003] I.C.R. 713 (EAT), Judge Ansell
Art.3, see *Green v Victoria Road Primary School Governing Body* [2003] I.C.R. 713 (EAT), Judge Ansell; see *Green v Victoria Road Primary School Governing Body* [2004] EWCA Civ 11, [2004] 2 All E.R. 763 (CA), Pill, L.J.
Art.6, see *Green v Victoria Road Primary School Governing Body* [2004] EWCA Civ 11, [2004] 2 All E.R. 763 (CA), Pill, L.J.

2257. Education (Non-Maintained Special Schools) (England) Regulations 1999

Sch.1 Part III para.21, amended: SI 2002/1982 Reg.3

2258. Education (School Meals Staff) (England) Regulations 1999

revoked: SI 2003/1963 Reg.2

2262. Education (New Schools) (England) Regulations 1999

Part I, applied: SI 2003/1558 Reg.2
Part II, applied: SI 2003/1558 Reg.2
Part III, applied: SI 2003/1558 Reg.2
Part IV, applied: SI 2003/1558 Reg.2
Part VI, referred to: SI 2003/1558 Reg.2
Reg.1, revoked: SI 2003/1558 Reg.2
Reg.2, revoked: SI 2003/1558 Reg.2
Reg.3, revoked: SI 2003/1558 Reg.2
Reg.4, revoked: SI 2003/1558 Reg.2
Reg.5, revoked: SI 2003/1558 Reg.2
Reg.6, revoked: SI 2003/1558 Reg.2
Reg.7, revoked: SI 2003/1558 Reg.2
Reg.8, revoked: SI 2003/1558 Reg.2
Reg.9, revoked: SI 2003/1558 Reg.2

1999–cont.

2262. Education (New Schools) (England) Regulations 1999–*cont.*

Reg.10, revoked: SI 2003/1558 Reg.2
Reg.11, revoked: SI 2003/1558 Reg.2
Reg.12, revoked: SI 2003/1558 Reg.2
Reg.13, revoked: SI 2003/1558 Reg.2
Reg.14, revoked: SI 2003/1558 Reg.2
Reg.15, revoked: SI 2003/1558 Reg.2
Reg.16, revoked: SI 2003/1558 Reg.2
Reg.17, revoked: SI 2003/1558 Reg.2
Reg.18, revoked: SI 2003/1558 Reg.2
Reg.19, revoked: SI 2003/1558 Reg.2
Reg.20, revoked: SI 2003/1558 Reg.2
Reg.21, revoked: SI 2003/1558 Reg.2
Reg.22, revoked: SI 2003/1558 Reg.2
Reg.23, revoked: SI 2003/1558 Reg.2
Reg.24, revoked: SI 2003/1558 Reg.2
Reg.25, revoked: SI 2003/1558 Reg.2
Reg.26, revoked: SI 2003/1558 Reg.2
Reg.27, revoked: SI 2003/1558 Reg.2
Reg.28, revoked: SI 2003/1558 Reg.2
Reg.29, revoked: SI 2003/1558 Reg.2
Reg.30, revoked: SI 2003/1558 Reg.2
Reg.31, amended: SI 2002/2113 Reg.8, SI 2003/348 Reg.2
Reg.31, revoked (in part): SI 2002/2113 Reg.8, SI 2003/1558 Reg.2
Reg.32, revoked: SI 2003/1558 Reg.2
Reg.33, revoked: SI 2003/1558 Reg.2
Reg.34, revoked: SI 2003/1558 Reg.2
Reg.35, revoked: SI 2003/1558 Reg.2
Reg.36, revoked: SI 2003/1558 Reg.2
Reg.37, revoked: SI 2003/1558 Reg.2
Reg.38, revoked: SI 2003/1558 Reg.2
Reg.39, revoked: SI 2003/1558 Reg.2
Reg.40, revoked: SI 2003/1558 Reg.2
Reg.41, revoked: SI 2003/1558 Reg.2
Reg.42, revoked: SI 2003/1558 Reg.2
Reg.43, revoked: SI 2003/1558 Reg.2
Reg.44, revoked: SI 2003/1558 Reg.2
Reg.45, revoked: SI 2003/1963 Reg.2
Reg.46, revoked: SI 2003/1963 Reg.2
Reg.47, revoked: SI 2003/1963 Reg.2
Reg.48, revoked: SI 2003/1963 Reg.2
Reg.49, revoked: SI 2003/1963 Reg.2
Reg.50, revoked: SI 2003/1963 Reg.2
Reg.51, revoked: SI 2003/1963 Reg.2
Reg.52, revoked: SI 2003/1963 Reg.2
Reg.53, revoked: SI 2003/1558 Reg.2
Reg.54, revoked: SI 2003/1558 Reg.2
Reg.55, revoked: SI 2003/1558 Reg.2
Reg.56, revoked: SI 2003/1558 Reg.2
Reg.57, revoked: SI 2003/1558 Reg.2
Reg.58, revoked: SI 2003/1558 Reg.2
Reg.59, revoked: SI 2003/1558 Reg.2
Reg.60, revoked: SI 2003/1558 Reg.2
Reg.61, revoked: SI 2003/1558 Reg.2
Reg.62, revoked: SI 2003/1558 Reg.2

NO.

1999–cont.

2263. Education (Student Support) (Dance and Drama) Regulations 1999

Reg.4, applied: SI 2002/3200 Reg.11, SR 2002/224 Reg.11

Reg.4, referred to: SI 2002/195 Reg.11

2265. Education (Student Fees) (Exceptions) (England) Regulations 1999

applied: SI 2002/1330 Sch.1, SI 2003/1994 Sch.1

2267. Education (Transition to New Framework) (Miscellaneous Provisions) Regulations 1999

Reg.4, revoked (in part): SI 2003/2694 Sch.1 Part 2

Reg.5, revoked (in part): SI 2003/2694 Sch.1 Part 2

Reg.6, revoked: SI 2004/2858 Sch.2

Reg.8, revoked (in part): SI 2003/2694 Sch.1 Part 2

Reg.10, revoked (in part): SI 2003/2694 Sch.1 Part 2

2277. Redundancy Payments (Continuity of Employment in Local Government, etc.) (Modification) Order 1999

Sch.1 para.1, substituted: SI 2004/1682 Art.2

Sch.1 para.1A, added: SI 2004/1682 Art.2

Sch.1 para.1B, added: SI 2004/1682 Art.2

Sch.1 para.2, revoked: SI 2004/1682 Art.2

Sch.1 para.4A, added: SI 2004/1682 Art.2

Sch.1 para.4A, substituted: SI 2002/532 Art.2

Sch.1 para.4A, added: SI 2004/1682 Art.2

Sch.1 para.4AA, substituted: SI 2002/532 Art.2

Sch.1 para.4ZA, added: SI 2004/1682 Art.2

Sch.1 para.4ZB, added: SI 2004/1682 Art.2

Sch.1 para.4ZC, added: SI 2004/1682 Art.2

Sch.1 para.5A, added: SI 2002/532 Art.2

Sch.1 para.6, substituted: SI 2004/1682 Art.2

Sch.1 para.6A, substituted: SI 2004/1682 Art.2

Sch.1 para.6AA, added: SI 2002/532 Art.2

Sch.1 para.7AA, added: SI 2002/532 Art.2

Sch.1 para.8, amended: SI 2004/1682 Art.2

Sch.1 para.8AA, added: SI 2002/532 Art.2

Sch.1 para.8B, added: SI 2004/1682 Art.2

Sch.1 para.9A, substituted: SI 2002/532 Art.2

Sch.1 para.9AA, substituted: SI 2002/532 Art.2

Sch.1 para.9ZA, added: SI 2004/1682 Art.2

Sch.1 para.11A, added: SI 2004/1682 Art.2

Sch.1 para.13A, added: SI 2004/1682 Art.2

Sch.1 para.13B, added: SI 2004/1682 Art.2

Sch.1 para.15A, added: SI 2004/1682 Art.2

Sch.1 para.17A, added: SI 2002/532 Art.2

Sch.1 para.17A, varied: SI 2004/664 Art.11, Art.12, Art.13, Art.14

Sch.1 para.17B, added: SI 2004/664 Sch.1 para.2

NO.

1999–cont.

2277. Redundancy Payments (Continuity of Employment in Local Government, etc.) (Modification) Order 1999–*cont.*

Sch.1 para.17C, added: SI 2004/664 Sch.1 para.2

Sch.1 para.19A, added: SI 2004/1682 Art.2

Sch.1 para.19B, added: SI 2004/1682 Art.2

Sch.1 para.19C, added: SI 2004/1682 Art.2

Sch.1 para.19D, added: SI 2004/1682 Art.2

Sch.1 para.21A, added: SI 2004/1682 Art.2

Sch.1 para.21B, added: SI 2004/1682 Art.2

Sch.1 para.22, substituted: SI 2004/1682 Art.2

Sch.1 para.22A, added: SI 2004/1682 Art.2

Sch.1 para.24A, added: SI 2004/1682 Art.2

Sch.1 para.24B, added: SI 2004/1682 Art.2

Sch.1 para.24C, added: SI 2004/1682 Art.2

Sch.1 para.24D, added: SI 2004/1682 Art.2

Sch.1 para.26, added: SI 2004/1682 Art.2

Sch.1 para.32, added: SI 2004/1682 Art.2

Sch.1 para.33, added: SI 2004/1682 Art.2

Sch.1 para.37A, added: SI 2004/1682 Art.2

Sch.1 para.38A, added: SI 2002/532 Art.2

Sch.1 para.41A, added: SI 2004/1682 Art.2

Sch.1 para.45, added: SI 2002/532 Art.2

Sch.1 para.46, added: SI 2002/532 Art.2

Sch.1 para.47, added: SI 2002/532 Art.2

Sch.1 para.48, added: SI 2004/1682 Art.2

Sch.1 para.49, added: SI 2004/1682 Art.2

Sch.1 para.50, added: SI 2004/1682 Art.2

Sch.1 para.51, added: SI 2004/1682 Art.2

Sch.1 para.52, added: SI 2004/1682 Art.2

Sch.1 para.53, added: SI 2004/1682 Art.2

Sch.1 para.54, added: SI 2004/1682 Art.2

Sch.1 para.55, added: SI 2004/1682 Art.2

Sch.1 para.56, added: SI 2004/1682 Art.2

Sch.1 para.57, added: SI 2004/1682 Art.2

Sch.1 para.58, added: SI 2004/1682 Art.2

Sch.1 para.59, added: SI 2004/1682 Art.2

Sch.1 para.60, added: SI 2004/1682 Art.2

Sch.2 Part II para.4A, added: SI 2004/1682 Art.2

Sch.2 Part II para.19, amended: SI 2002/1397 Sch.1 para.33

2307. Wigan and Leigh Health Services National Health Service Trust (Establishment) Amendment Order 1999

revoked: 2003 c.43 s.7

2308. Blackburn, Hyndburn and Ribble Valley Health Care National Health Service Trust (Establishment) Amendment Order 1999

revoked: 2003 c.43 s.7

2315. Relocation Grants (Form of Application) (Welsh Form of Application) Regulations 1999

revoked: SI 2002/1860 Sch.6

Sch.1, amended: SI 2002/2800 Sch.1 para.1, Sch.1 para.2, Sch.1 para.3, Sch.1 para.4, Sch.1 para.5, Sch.1 para.6, Sch.1 para.7, Sch.1 para.8, Sch.1 para.9, Sch.1 para.10

NO.

1999–cont.

2325. Feeding Stuffs (Enforcement) Regulations 1999

referred to: SI 2003/1296 Reg.8, SI 2003/1677 Reg.8, SI 2003/1850 Reg.16, SI 2003/2912 Reg.7, SI 2003/3119 Reg.7

Reg.2, amended: SI 2002/892 Reg.15, SI 2002/1797 Reg.13, SI 2003/1026 Reg.8, SR 2002/263 Reg.13, SSI 2002/285 Reg.13

Reg.3, amended: SI 2003/1026 Reg.9

Reg.4, amended: SI 2003/1026 Reg.10

Reg.6, amended: SI 2003/1026 Reg.11

Reg.6A, added: SI 2003/1026 Reg.12

Reg.6AA, added: SI 2003/1026 Reg.12, SI 2003/2264 Reg.2

Reg.6B, added: SI 2003/1026 Reg.12

Reg.7, amended: SI 2002/1797 Reg.13, SI 2003/989 Reg.7, SI 2003/1026 Reg.13, SI 2003/1296 Reg.9, SI 2003/1503 Reg.17, SI 2003/1677 Reg.9, SI 2003/1850 Reg.17, SI 2003/2912 Reg.8, SI 2003/3119 Reg.8, SI 2004/1301 Reg.8, SI 2004/1749 Reg.8, SI 2004/2688 Reg.5, SR 2003/287 Reg.9

Reg.7, substituted: SSI 2003/277 Reg.9

Reg.8, amended: SI 2002/892 Reg.15, SI 2002/1797 Reg.13, SR 2002/263 Reg.13

Reg.8, substituted: SI 2003/1296 Reg.10, SI 2003/1677 Reg.10, SR 2003/287 Reg.10, SSI 2003/277 Reg.10

Reg.9, amended: SI 2002/892 Reg.15, SI 2002/1797 Reg.13, SI 2003/989 Reg.7, SI 2003/1026 Reg.13, SI 2003/1503 Reg.19, SI 2003/1850 Reg.19, SI 2003/2912 Reg.10, SI 2003/3119 Reg.10, SI 2004/1301 Reg.10, SI 2004/1749 Reg.10, SI 2004/2688 Reg.5

Reg.9, applied: SI 2003/1026 Reg.13

Reg.9, substituted: SSI 2003/277 Reg.11

Reg.10, added: SR 2003/287 Reg.11

Reg.10, amended: SI 2002/892 Reg.15, SI 2002/1797 Reg.13, SI 2003/989 Reg.7, SI 2003/1026 Reg.13, SI 2003/1296 Reg.11, SI 2003/1677 Reg.11, SI 2003/1850 Reg.20, SI 2003/2912 Reg.11, SI 2003/3119 Reg.11, SI 2004/1301 Reg.11, SI 2004/2688 Reg.5, SR 2003/287 Reg.11, SSI 2003/277 Reg.12

Reg.10, applied: SI 2003/1026 Reg.13

Reg.10, substituted: SI 2003/1503 Reg.20, SI 2003/1677 Reg.11, SI 2004/1749 Reg.11, SR 2003/287 Reg.11, SSI 2002/285 Reg.13, SSI 2003/277 Reg.12

Reg.11, amended: SI 2003/1503 Reg.18, SI 2003/1850 Reg.18, SI 2003/2912 Reg.9, SI 2003/3119 Reg.9, SI 2004/1301 Reg.9, SI 2004/1749 Reg.9, SI 2004/2688 Reg.5

Reg.11, substituted: SI 2003/1296 Reg.12, SI 2003/1677 Reg.12, SR 2003/287 Reg.12, SSI 2003/277 Reg.13

NO.

1999–cont.

2325. Feeding Stuffs (Enforcement) Regulations 1999–*cont.*

Reg.11A, amended: SI 2003/1503 Reg.18, SI 2003/1850 Reg.18, SI 2003/2912 Reg.9, SI 2003/3119 Reg.9, SI 2004/1301 Reg.9, SI 2004/1749 Reg.9, SI 2004/2688 Reg.5

Reg.11A, substituted: SI 2003/1296 Reg.12, SI 2003/1677 Reg.12, SR 2003/287 Reg.12, SSI 2003/277 Reg.13

Reg.11B, amended: SI 2003/1503 Reg.18, SI 2003/1850 Reg.18, SI 2003/2912 Reg.9, SI 2003/3119 Reg.9, SI 2004/1301 Reg.9, SI 2004/1749 Reg.9, SI 2004/2688 Reg.5

Reg.12, amended: SI 2003/1026 Reg.14, SI 2003/1296 Reg.13, SI 2003/1677 Reg.13, SR 2003/287 Reg.13

Reg.12, revoked (in part): SSI 2003/277 Reg.14

Reg.13, amended: SR 2003/287 Reg.13

Reg.13, revoked (in part): SSI 2003/277 Reg.15

2336. Railtrack (Leeds Bridges) Order 1999

Sch.6 para.1, amended: SI 2003/2155 Sch.1 para.17, Sch.2

2337. Primary Care Trusts (Consultation on Establishment, Dissolution and Transfer of Staff) Regulations 1999

applied: SI 2002/553 Art.9, SI 2002/2469 Sch.12 para.5

Reg.1, amended: SI 2002/880 Sch.1 para.8, SI 2002/2469 Sch.3, SI 2004/865 Sch.1 para.22, SI 2004/1771 Sch.1 para.37

Reg.2, amended: SI 2002/2469 Sch.3, SI 2004/696 Art.3, SI 2004/865 Sch.1 para.22

Reg.3, amended: SI 2002/2469 Sch.3, SI 2004/696 Art.3, SI 2004/865 Sch.1 para.22

Reg.4, amended: SI 2002/2469 Sch.3

Reg.5, amended: SI 2002/2469 Sch.3

Reg.6, amended: SI 2002/2469 Sch.3

2356. Companies (Forms) (Amendment) Regulations 1999

Sch.1, applied: SI 2002/691 Reg.3

2357. Companies (Welsh Language Forms) (Amendment) Regulations 1999

Sch.1, applied: SI 2003/62 Reg.3

2358. Social Security (Claims and Payments) Amendment Regulations 1999

revoked (in part): SI 2003/492 Sch.3 Part 1

2372. University College London Hospitals National Health Service Trust (Establishment) Amendment Order 1999

revoked: 2003 c.43 s.7

2382. Keith and Dufftown Light Railway Order 1999

Art.6, amended: SI 2003/2155 Sch.1 para.18

1999–cont.

2383. Stamp Duty Reserve Tax (UK Depositary Interests in Foreign Securities) Regulations 1999
varied: 2002 c.23 Sch.34 para.7, Sch.35 para.8

2393. Isle of Wight (Electoral Changes) Order 1999
varied: SI 2004/222 Art.2

2395. Magistrates Courts Committees (Constitution) Regulations 1999
Reg.8, amended: SI 2003/2252 Reg.2
Reg.8, revoked (in part): SI 2003/2252 Reg.2

2396. Justices of the Peace (Size and Chairmanship of Bench) (Amendment) Rules 1999
revoked: SI 2002/193 r.20

2422. Social Security Act 1998 (Commencement No 9, and Savings and Consequential and Transitional Provisions) Order 1999
revoked (in part): SI 2003/492 Sch.3 Part 1
Art.3, revoked (in part): SI 2003/492 Sch.3 Part 1
Sch.7 para.1, revoked (in part): SI 2003/492 Sch.3 Part 1
Sch.7 para.2, revoked (in part): SI 2003/492 Sch.3 Part 1
Sch.7 para.3, revoked (in part): SI 2003/492 Sch.3 Part 1
Sch.7 para.4, revoked (in part): SI 2003/492 Sch.3 Part 1
Sch.7 para.5, revoked (in part): SI 2003/492 Sch.3 Part 1
Sch.7 para.6, revoked (in part): SI 2003/492 Sch.3 Part 1
Sch.8 para.1, revoked (in part): SI 2003/492 Sch.3 Part 1
Sch.8 para.2, revoked (in part): SI 2003/492 Sch.3 Part 1
Sch.8 para.3, revoked (in part): SI 2003/492 Sch.3 Part 1
Sch.8 para.4, revoked (in part): SI 2003/492 Sch.3 Part 1
Sch.8 para.5, revoked (in part): SI 2003/492 Sch.3 Part 1

2450. Telecommunications (Licence Modification) (Standard Schedules) Regulations 1999
revoked: 2003 c.21 Sch.19
Sch.1 Part 2 para.31.2, amended: SI 2003/1398 Sch.1 para.35

2451. Telecommunications (Licence Modification) (Fixed Voice Telephony and International Facilities Operator Licences) Regulations 1999
revoked: 2003 c.21 Sch.19

2452. Telecommunications (Licence Modification) (Mobile Public Telecommunication Operators) Regulations 1999
referred to: SI 2003/1397 Art.11
revoked: 2003 c.21 Sch.19

1999–cont.

2453. Telecommunications (Licence Modification) (British Telecommunications plc) Regulations 1999
referred to: SI 2003/1397 Art.11
revoked: 2003 c.21 Sch.19

2454. Telecommunications (Licence Modification) (Cable and Local Delivery Operator Licences) Regulations 1999
revoked: 2003 c.21 Sch.19

2455. Telecommunications (Licence Modification) (Kingston Communications (Hull) PLC) Regulations 1999
referred to: SI 2003/1397 Art.11
revoked: 2003 c.21 Sch.19

2465. Borough of Elmbridge (Electoral Changes) Order 1999
varied: SI 2004/222 Art.2

2467. District of East Devon (Electoral Changes) Order 1999
varied: SI 2004/222 Art.2

2468. City of Exeter (Electoral Changes) Order 1999
varied: SI 2004/222 Art.2

2469. District of North Devon (Electoral Changes) Order 1999
varied: SI 2004/222 Art.2

2470. District of Mid Devon (Electoral Changes) Order 1999
varied: SI 2004/222 Art.2

2471. District of Teignbridge (Electoral Changes) Order 1999
varied: SI 2004/222 Art.2

2472. District of Torridge (Electoral Changes) Order 1999
varied: SI 2004/222 Art.2

2473. Borough of West Devon (Electoral Changes) Order 1999
varied: SI 2004/222 Art.2
Sch.1, amended: SI 2004/2678 Art.2

2474. Borough of Epsom and Ewell (Electoral Changes) Order 1999
varied: SI 2004/222 Art.2

2475. Borough of Guildford (Electoral Changes) Order 1999
varied: SI 2004/222 Art.2

2476. District of Mole Valley (Electoral Changes) Order 1999
varied: SI 2004/222 Art.2

2477. Borough of Reigate and Banstead (Electoral Changes) Order 1999
varied: SI 2004/222 Art.2

2478. Borough of Runnymede (Electoral Changes) Order 1999
varied: SI 2004/222 Art.2

2479. Borough of Spelthorne (Electoral Changes) Order 1999
varied: SI 2004/222 Art.2

2480. District of Tandridge (Electoral Changes) Order 1999
varied: SI 2004/222 Art.2

NO.

1999–cont.

2481. Borough of Surrey Heath (Electoral Changes) Order 1999

varied: SI 2004/222 Art.2

2482. Borough of Waverley (Electoral Changes) Order 1999

varied: SI 2004/222 Art.2

2483. Borough of Woking (Electoral Changes) Order 1999

varied: SI 2004/222 Art.2

2503. District of Chester-le-Street (Electoral Changes) Order 1999

varied: SI 2004/222 Art.2

2506. Education (Special Educational Needs) (Information) (England) Regulations 1999

Reg.2, amended: SI 2002/2469 Sch.8

Reg.3, applied: SI 2002/2897 Sch.3 para.6

Reg.4, amended: SI 2002/2469 Sch.7

2507. National Health Service (Travelling Expenses and Remission of Charges) Amendment Regulations 1999

revoked: SI 2003/2382 Sch.2

2512. Medicines (Products for Animal Use-Fees) (Amendment) Regulations 1999

revoked: SI 2004/2750 Reg.18

2536. Stamp Duty Reserve Tax (Amendment) Regulations 1999

varied: 2002 c.23 Sch.34 para.7, Sch.35 para.8

2537. Stamp Duty (Collection and Recovery of Penalties) Regulations 1999

Sch.1 Part II, amended: 2002 asp 17 Sch.3 para.37

Sch.1 Part II, substituted: 2002 asp 17 Sch.3 para.37

2539. Stamp Duty (Exempt Instruments) (Amendment) Regulations 1999

Reg.4, amended: 2003 c.14 Sch.20 para.3

2541. Health Act 1999 (Fund-holding Practices) (Transfer of Assets, Savings, Rights and Liabilities and Transitional Provisions) Order 1999

Art.8, amended: SI 2002/2469 Sch.5

Art.16, amended: SI 2002/2469 Sch.1 para.86

2546. Competition Act 1998 (Application for Designation of Professional Rules) Regulations 1999

revoked: 2002 c.40 Sch.26

2548. County Court Fees (Amendment) Order 1999

revoked: SI 2004/3121 Sch.2

2549. Family Proceedings Fees (Amendment) Order 1999

revoked: SI 2004/3114 Sch.2

2556. Social Security (Miscellaneous Amendments) (No.2) Regulations 1999

Reg.7, revoked (in part): SI 2003/492 Sch.3 Part 1

NO.

1999–cont.

2561. Welfare Food (Amendment) Regulations 1999

revoked: SI 2002/550 Reg.3

2566. Social Security and Child Support (Tax Credits) Consequential Amendments Regulations 1999

Reg.4, revoked (in part): SI 2003/492 Sch.3 Part 1

2567. Merchant Shipping (Accident Reporting and Investigation) Regulations 1999

Reg.6, amended: SI 2004/1266 Reg.6

2569. Supreme Court Fees (Amendment) Order 1999

revoked: SI 2004/3121 Sch.2

2578. Education (Further Education Institutions Information) (England) (Amendment) Regulations 1999

revoked: SI 2003/51 Reg.2

2579. City of Durham (Electoral Changes) Order 1999

varied: SI 2004/222 Art.2

2580. District of Derwentside (Electoral Changes) Order 1999

varied: SI 2004/222 Art.2

2581. District of Easington (Electoral Changes) Order 1999

varied: SI 2004/222 Art.2

2582. Borough of Sedgefield (Electoral Changes) Order 1999

varied: SI 2004/222 Art.2

2583. District of Teesdale (Electoral Changes) Order 1999

varied: SI 2004/222 Art.2

2584. District of Wear Valley (Electoral Changes) Order 1999

varied: SI 2004/222 Art.2

2625. Relocation Grants (Form of Application) (Amendment) (England) Regulations 1999

revoked: SI 2002/1860 Sch.6

2638. Disability Discrimination Code of Practice (Trade Organisations) Order 1999

referred to: SI 2004/2300 Art.2

2655. Scunthorpe Community Health Care National Health Service Trust (Dissolution) Order 1999

revoked: 2003 c.43 s.7

2656. Doncaster Healthcare National Health Service Trust Change of Name and (Establishment) Amendment Order 1999

revoked: 2003 c.43 s.7

2666. New School (Admissions) (England) Regulations 1999

revoked: SI 2003/1041 Reg.2

1999–cont.

2674. East Yorkshire Hospitals and the Royal Hull Hospitals National Health Service Trusts (Dissolution) Order 1999
revoked: 2003 c.43 s.7

2675. Hull and East Yorkshire Hospitals National Health Service Trust (Establishment) Order 1999
revoked: 2003 c.43 s.7

2687. East Yorkshire Community Healthcare and the Hull and Holderness Community Health National Health Service Trusts (Dissolution) Order 1999
revoked: 2003 c.43 s.7

2688. Hull and East Riding Community Health National Health Service Trust (Establishment) Order 1999
revoked: 2003 c.43 s.7

2690. Borough of Amber Valley (Electoral Changes) Order 1999
varied: SI 2004/222 Art.2

2691. District of Bolsover (Electoral Changes) Order 1999
varied: SI 2004/222 Art.2

2692. Borough of Chesterfield (Electoral Changes) Order 1999
varied: SI 2004/222 Art.2

2693. District of Derbyshire Dales (Electoral Changes) Order 1999
varied: SI 2004/222 Art.2

2694. Borough of Erewash (Electoral Changes) Order 1999
varied: SI 2004/222 Art.2

2695. Borough of High Peak (Electoral Changes) Order 1999
varied: SI 2004/222 Art.2

2696. District of North East Derbyshire (Electoral Changes) Order 1999
varied: SI 2004/222 Art.2

2697. District of South Derbyshire (Electoral Changes) Order 1999
varied: SI 2004/222 Art.2

2721. Merchant Shipping (Life-Saving Appliances For Ships Other Than Ships Of Classes III To VI(A)) Regulations 1999
Reg.7, amended: SI 2004/2259 Reg.2
Reg.8, amended: SI 2004/2259 Reg.2
Reg.38, revoked: SI 2002/1473 Sch.1 para.7
Reg.42, amended: SI 2004/2259 Reg.2
Reg.43, amended: SI 2004/2259 Reg.2
Reg.63, amended: SI 2004/2259 Reg.2
Reg.64, amended: SI 2004/2259 Reg.2

2722. Merchant Shipping (Musters, Training and Decision Support Systems) Regulations 1999
applied: SI 2002/2125 Reg.5
Reg.3, amended: SI 2004/302 Sch.1 para.4

1999–cont.

2725. Consumer Credit (Content of Quotations) and Consumer Credit (Advertisements) (Amendment) Regulations 1999
Reg.7, revoked: SI 2004/1484 Reg.11

2733. Changing of School Session Times (England) Regulations 1999
applied: SI 2004/108 Art.2
disapplied: SI 2002/3063 Art.2, SI 2003/1671 Art.2, SI 2004/1712 Art.2, SI 2004/2685 Art.2

2734. Housing Benefit (General) Amendment (No.3) Regulations 1999
Reg.13, amended: SI 2003/363 Reg.5

2743. Prosecution of Offences (Youth Courts Time Limits) Regulations 1999
referred to: SI 2003/917 Reg.2
revoked: SI 2003/917 Reg.2

2766. Home Repair Assistance (Extension) (England) Regulations 1999
revoked: SI 2002/1860 Sch.6

2768. Children (Protection from Offenders) (Amendment) Regulations 1999
Reg.2, revoked (in part): SI 2002/57 Reg.51

2782. Borough of Sefton (Electoral Changes) Order 1999
revoked (in part): SI 2003/1977 Art.11
varied: SI 2004/222 Art.2

2784. Justices Clerks Rules 1999
Sch.1 para.39, amended: SI 2002/3220 Art.2

2788. European Communities (Designation) (No.3) Order 1999
varied: SI 2002/1819 Sch.3

2789. Criminal Evidence (Northern Ireland) Order 1999
Art.1, enabled: SR 2003/323, SR 2003/476
Art.2, amended: 2002 c.26 Sch.13
Art.3, amended: SI 2003/1247 Sch.1 para.24
Art.3, revoked (in part): SI 2003/1247 Sch.1 para.24, Sch.2
Art.7, applied: SI 2004/1501 Art.20
Art.23, amended: SI 2003/1247 Sch.1 para.25
Art.26, amended: SI 2003/1247 Art.34
Art.26, applied: SI 2004/1501 Art.11
Art.28, applied: SI 2004/1501 Art.17
Sch.1 para.1, amended: SI 2004/1501 Sch.2
Sch.1 para.1, revoked (in part): SI 2004/1501 Sch.2

2790. Employment Relations (Northern Ireland) Order 1999
Art.1, enabled: SR 2002/214, SR 2002/317, SR 2003/332
Art.12, applied: SI 2003/2902 Sch.1 para.14
Art.15, applied: SI 2003/2902 Sch.1 para.14
Art.20, revoked (in part): 2002 c.21 Sch.6
Art.21, enabled: SR 2002/286
Art.24, amended: SI 2002/2836 Sch.2 para.6, SI 2003/2902 Sch.5 para.5
Art.33, enabled: SR 2002/24, SR 2003/241

NO.

1999–cont.

2790. Employment Relations (Northern Ireland) Order 1999–cont.

Art.39, enabled: SR 2002/24, SR 2002/214, SR 2002/317, SR 2003/241, SR 2003/332

Sch.4 Part III para.13, revoked (in part): 2002 c.21 Sch.6

2795. Health Act 1999 (Supplementary and Consequential Provisions) Order 1999

Art.3, revoked: SI 2004/664 Art.8

Art.4, revoked: SI 2004/664 Art.8

Art.5, revoked: SI 2004/664 Art.8

2801. Commission for Health Improvement (Membership and Procedure) Regulations 1999

Reg.1, amended: SI 2002/880 Sch.1 para.9, SI 2002/2469 Sch.2, SI 2004/1771 Sch.1 para.36

Reg.5, amended: SI 2002/880 Sch.1 para.10, SI 2002/881 Sch.1 para.18, SI 2002/2469 Sch.2

2802. Education (School Meals Staff) (Wales) Regulations 1999

Reg.1, amended: SI 2003/1717 Reg.6

2817. Education (Teachers Qualifications and Health Standards) (Wales) Regulations 1999

applied: SI 2004/1729 Sch.2 para.14

referred to: SI 2002/2938 Reg.2, SI 2004/1744 Sch.1 para.2

Reg.3, amended: SI 2002/2938 Reg.3, SI 2003/140 Reg.2

Reg.4, amended: SI 2002/1663 Reg.5

Reg.5, revoked: SI 2004/2733 Reg.4

Reg.6, revoked: SI 2004/2733 Reg.4

Reg.7, revoked: SI 2004/2733 Reg.4

Reg.8, revoked: SI 2004/1729 Sch.1 Part 1

Reg.9, revoked: SI 2004/1729 Sch.1 Part 1

Reg.10, revoked: SI 2004/1729 Sch.1 Part 1

Reg.11, amended: SI 2004/1729 Reg.9

Reg.11, applied: SI 2004/1729 Reg.5

Reg.12, amended: SI 2004/1729 Reg.9

Reg.12, applied: SI 2004/1729 Reg.5

Reg.13, amended: SI 2004/1729 Reg.9

Reg.13, applied: SI 2004/1729 Reg.5

Reg.14, applied: SI 2004/1729 Reg.5

Sch.1 Part I, revoked: SI 2004/1729 Sch.1 Part 1

Sch.1 Part II para.4, revoked: SI 2004/1744 Sch.1 Part 1

Sch.1 Part II para.5, revoked: SI 2004/1729 Sch.1 Part 1

Sch.1 Part II para.6, revoked: SI 2004/1744 Sch.1 Part 1

Sch.1 Part II para.7, revoked: SI 2004/1744 Sch.1 Part 1

Sch.2 Part 1 para.1, revoked: SI 2004/1744 Sch.1 Part 1

Sch.2 Part 1 para.2, revoked: SI 2004/1744 Sch.1 Part 1

NO.

1999–cont.

2817. Education (Teachers Qualifications and Health Standards) (Wales) Regulations 1999–cont.

Sch.2 Part 1 para.3, applied: SI 2004/1729 Sch.2 para.11

Sch.2 Part 1 para.3, revoked: SI 2004/1744 Sch.1 Part 1

Sch.2 Part 1 para.4, applied: SI 2004/1744 Sch.2 para.4

Sch.2 Part 1 para.4, revoked: SI 2004/1744 Sch.1 Part 1

Sch.2 Part II, applied: SI 2002/1663 Reg.3, SI 2004/1729 Sch.2 para.9

Sch.2 Part II para.5, applied: SI 2003/1709 Art.6, SI 2004/1744 Sch.2 para.5

Sch.2 Part II para.5, revoked: SI 2004/1744 Sch.1 Part 1

Sch.2 Part II para.5, varied: SI 2004/1744 Sch.1 para.3

Sch.2 Part II para.6, applied: SI 2003/1709 Art.6, SI 2004/1744 Sch.2 para.5

Sch.2 Part II para.6, revoked: SI 2004/1744 Sch.1 Part 1

Sch.2 Part II para.6, varied: SI 2004/1744 Sch.1 para.3

Sch.2 Part II para.7, applied: SI 2003/1709 Art.6, SI 2004/1744 Sch.2 para.5

Sch.2 Part II para.7, revoked: SI 2004/1744 Sch.1 Part 1

Sch.2 Part II para.7, varied: SI 2004/1744 Sch.1 para.3

Sch.2 Part II para.8, applied: SI 2003/1709 Art.6, SI 2004/1744 Sch.2 para.5

Sch.2 Part II para.8, revoked: SI 2004/1744 Sch.1 Part 1

Sch.2 Part II para.8, varied: SI 2004/1744 Sch.1 para.3

Sch.2 Part II para.9, applied: SI 2003/1709 Art.6, SI 2004/1744 Sch.2 para.5

Sch.2 Part II para.9, revoked: SI 2004/1744 Sch.1 Part 1

Sch.2 Part II para.9, varied: SI 2004/1744 Sch.1 para.3

Sch.2 Part II para.10, applied: SI 2003/1709 Art.6, SI 2004/1744 Sch.2 para.5

Sch.2 Part II para.10, revoked: SI 2004/1744 Sch.1 Part 1

Sch.2 Part II para.10, varied: SI 2004/1744 Sch.1 para.3

Sch.2 Part II para.11, applied: SI 2003/1709 Art.6, SI 2004/1744 Sch.2 para.5

Sch.2 Part II para.11, revoked: SI 2004/1744 Sch.1 Part 1

Sch.2 Part II para.11, varied: SI 2004/1744 Sch.1 para.3

Sch.2 Part III, applied: SI 2002/1663 Reg.3, SI 2004/1729 Sch.2 para.9

Sch.2 Part III para.12, applied: SI 2003/1709 Art.6, SI 2004/1744 Sch.2 para.6

Sch.2 Part III para.12, revoked: SI 2004/1744 Sch.1 Part 1

1999–cont.

2817. Education (Teachers Qualifications and Health Standards) (Wales) Regulations 1999–*cont.*

Sch.2 Part III para.12, varied: SI 2004/1744 Sch.1 para.4

Sch.2 Part III para.13, applied: SI 2003/1709 Art.6, SI 2004/1744 Sch.2 para.6

Sch.2 Part III para.13, revoked: SI 2004/1744 Sch.1 Part 1

Sch.2 Part III para.13, varied: SI 2004/1744 Sch.1 para.4

Sch.2 Part III para.14, applied: SI 2003/1709 Art.6, SI 2004/1744 Sch.2 para.6

Sch.2 Part III para.14, revoked: SI 2004/1744 Sch.1 Part 1

Sch.2 Part III para.14, varied: SI 2004/1744 Sch.1 para.4

Sch.2 Part III para.15, applied: SI 2003/1709 Art.6, SI 2004/1744 Sch.2 para.6

Sch.2 Part III para.15, revoked: SI 2004/1744 Sch.1 Part 1

Sch.2 Part III para.15, varied: SI 2004/1744 Sch.1 para.4

Sch.2 Part III para.16, applied: SI 2003/1709 Art.6, SI 2004/1744 Sch.2 para.6

Sch.2 Part III para.16, revoked: SI 2004/1744 Sch.1 Part 1

Sch.2 Part III para.16, varied: SI 2004/1744 Sch.1 para.4

Sch.2 Part III para.17, applied: SI 2003/1709 Art.6, SI 2004/1744 Sch.2 para.6

Sch.2 Part III para.17, revoked: SI 2004/1744 Sch.1 Part 1

Sch.2 Part III para.17, varied: SI 2004/1744 Sch.1 para.4

Sch.2 Part III para.18, applied: SI 2003/1709 Art.6, SI 2004/1744 Sch.2 para.6

Sch.2 Part III para.18, revoked: SI 2004/1744 Sch.1 Part 1

Sch.2 Part III para.18, varied: SI 2004/1744 Sch.1 para.4

Sch.3, referred to: SI 2004/1729 Sch.1 para.2

Sch.3 para.1, applied: SI 2002/2086 Reg.5

Sch.3 para.1, revoked: SI 2004/1729 Sch.1 Part 1

Sch.3 Part I para.1, added: SI 2002/2938 Reg.4

Sch.3 Part I para.1, amended: SI 2002/2938 Reg.5, SI 2003/140 Reg.2, SI 2003/2458 Reg.2

Sch.3 Part I para.1, applied: SI 2004/1729 Sch.1 para.2, Sch.2 para.2

Sch.3 Part I para.1, revoked: SI 2004/1729 Sch.1 Part 1

Sch.3 Part I para.2, added: SI 2002/2938 Reg.4

Sch.3 Part I para.2, amended: SI 2003/2458 Reg.2

Sch.3 Part I para.2, applied: SI 2004/1729 Sch.1 para.1

1999–cont.

2817. Education (Teachers Qualifications and Health Standards) (Wales) Regulations 1999–*cont.*

Sch.3 Part I para.2, revoked: SI 2004/1729 Sch.1 Part 1

Sch.3 Part I para.2A, added: SI 2002/2938 Reg.4, SI 2003/2458 Reg.2

Sch.3 Part I para.2A, applied: SI 2004/1729 Sch.1 para.2

Sch.3 Part I para.2A, revoked: SI 2004/1729 Sch.1 Part 1

Sch.3 Part I para.3, added: SI 2002/2938 Reg.4

Sch.3 Part I para.3, applied: SI 2004/1729 Sch.1 para.1

Sch.3 Part I para.3, revoked: SI 2004/1729 Sch.1 Part 1

Sch.3 Part I para.4, added: SI 2002/2938 Reg.4

Sch.3 Part I para.4, revoked: SI 2004/1729 Sch.1 Part 1

Sch.3 Part I para.5, added: SI 2002/2938 Reg.4

Sch.3 Part I para.5, revoked: SI 2004/1729 Sch.1 Part 1

Sch.3 Part I para.6, added: SI 2002/2938 Reg.4

Sch.3 Part I para.6, revoked: SI 2004/1729 Sch.1 Part 1

Sch.3 Part I para.7, added: SI 2002/2938 Reg.4

Sch.3 Part I para.7, revoked: SI 2004/1729 Sch.1 Part 1

Sch.3 Part I para.8, added: SI 2002/2938 Reg.4

Sch.3 Part I para.8, revoked: SI 2004/1729 Sch.1 Part 1

Sch.3 Part I para.9, added: SI 2002/2938 Reg.4

Sch.3 Part I para.9, revoked: SI 2004/1729 Sch.1 Part 1

Sch.3 Part I para.10, added: SI 2002/2938 Reg.4, Reg.5

Sch.3 Part I para.10, applied: SI 2003/543 Sch.1 para.17

Sch.3 Part I para.10, revoked: SI 2004/1729 Sch.1 Part 1

Sch.3 Part I para.11, added: SI 2002/2938 Reg.4, Reg.5

Sch.3 Part I para.11, applied: SI 2003/543 Sch.1 para.18

Sch.3 Part I para.11, revoked: SI 2004/1729 Sch.1 Part 1

Sch.3 para.2, revoked: SI 2004/1729 Sch.1 Part 1

Sch.3 Part II para.12, added: SI 2002/2938 Reg.6

Sch.3 Part II para.12, revoked: SI 2004/1729 Sch.1 Part 1

Sch.3 Part II para.13, added: SI 2002/2938 Reg.6

NO.

1999–cont.

2817. Education (Teachers Qualifications and Health Standards) (Wales) Regulations 1999—*cont.*

Sch.3 Part II para.13, revoked: SI 2004/1729 Sch.1 Part 1

Sch.3 Part II para.14, added: SI 2002/2938 Reg.6

Sch.3 Part II para.14, revoked: SI 2004/1729 Sch.1 Part 1

Sch.3 Part II para.15, added: SI 2002/2938 Reg.6

Sch.3 Part II para.15, revoked: SI 2004/1729 Sch.1 Part 1

Sch.3 Part II para.16, added: SI 2002/2938 Reg.6

Sch.3 Part II para.16, revoked: SI 2004/1729 Sch.1 Part 1

Sch.3 Part II para.17, added: SI 2002/2938 Reg.6

Sch.3 Part II para.17, revoked: SI 2004/1729 Sch.1 Part 1

Sch.3 Part II para.18, added: SI 2002/2938 Reg.6

Sch.3 Part II para.18, revoked: SI 2004/1729 Sch.1 Part 1

Sch.3 Part II para.19, added: SI 2002/2938 Reg.6

Sch.3 Part II para.19, revoked: SI 2004/1729 Sch.1 Part 1

Sch.3 para.3, referred to: SI 2002/2086 Reg.5

Sch.3 para.3, revoked: SI 2004/1729 Sch.1 Part 1

Sch.3 para.4, referred to: SI 2002/2086 Reg.5

Sch.3 para.4, revoked: SI 2004/1729 Sch.1 Part 1

Sch.3 para.5, referred to: SI 2002/2086 Reg.5

Sch.3 para.5, revoked: SI 2004/1729 Sch.1 Part 1

Sch.3 para.6, referred to: SI 2002/2086 Reg.5

Sch.3 para.6, revoked: SI 2004/1729 Sch.1 Part 1

Sch.3 para.7, applied: SI 2003/543 Sch.1 para.20

Sch.3 para.7, revoked: SI 2004/1729 Sch.1 Part 1

Sch.3 para.8, revoked: SI 2004/1729 Sch.1 Part 1

Sch.3 para.9, revoked: SI 2004/1729 Sch.1 Part 1

2842. Major Precepting Authorities (Excessive Budget Requirements-Payments) (England) Regulations 1999

revoked: 2003 c.26 Sch.8 Part 1

NO.

1999–cont.

2860. Social Security Act 1998 (Commencement No 11, and Savings and Consequential and Transitional Provisions) Order 1999

revoked (in part): SI 2003/492 Sch.3 Part 1

Art.3, revoked (in part): SI 2003/492 Sch.3 Part 1

Sch.3 para.1, revoked (in part): SI 2003/492 Sch.3 Part 1

Sch.3 para.2, revoked (in part): SI 2003/492 Sch.3 Part 1

Sch.3 para.3, revoked (in part): SI 2003/492 Sch.3 Part 1

Sch.3 para.4, revoked (in part): SI 2003/492 Sch.3 Part 1

Sch.3 para.5, revoked (in part): SI 2003/492 Sch.3 Part 1

Sch.3 para.6, revoked (in part): SI 2003/492 Sch.3 Part 1

Sch.3 para.7, revoked (in part): SI 2003/492 Sch.3 Part 1

Sch.3 para.8, revoked (in part): SI 2003/492 Sch.3 Part 1

Sch.3 para.9, revoked (in part): SI 2003/492 Sch.3 Part 1

Sch.3 para.10, revoked (in part): SI 2003/492 Sch.3 Part 1

Sch.3 para.11, revoked (in part): SI 2003/492 Sch.3 Part 1

Sch.3 para.12, revoked (in part): SI 2003/492 Sch.3 Part 1

Sch.3 para.13, revoked (in part): SI 2003/492 Sch.3 Part 1

Sch.4 para.1, revoked (in part): SI 2003/492 Sch.3 Part 1

Sch.4 para.2, revoked (in part): SI 2003/492 Sch.3 Part 1

Sch.4 para.3, revoked (in part): SI 2003/492 Sch.3 Part 1

Sch.4 para.4, revoked (in part): SI 2003/492 Sch.3 Part 1

Sch.4 para.5, revoked (in part): SI 2003/492 Sch.3 Part 1

Sch.4 para.6, revoked (in part): SI 2003/492 Sch.3 Part 1

2864. Motor Vehicles (Driving Licences) Regulations 1999

referred to: SI 2002/2641 Reg.2, SI 2003/636 Reg.2

Reg.8, amended: SI 2002/2641 Reg.3

Reg.9, amended: SI 2003/166 Reg.2, SI 2004/696 Sch.1 para.32

Reg.12, amended: SI 2003/636 Reg.3

Reg.16, amended: SI 2003/222 Reg.3

Reg.16, referred to: SI 2003/222 Reg.2

Reg.23, amended: SI 2003/2003 Reg.2

Reg.24, amended: SI 2003/2003 Reg.3

Reg.24, revoked (in part): SI 2003/2003 Reg.3

Reg.30, amended: SI 2002/2641 Reg.4, SI 2003/2003 Reg.4

1999–cont.

2864. Motor Vehicles (Driving Licences) Regulations 1999–*cont.*

Reg.35, amended: SI 2003/2003 Reg.3

Reg.37, amended: SI 2003/2003 Reg.5

Reg.38, applied: SI 2003/636 Reg.6

Reg.40, amended: SI 2002/2641 Reg.5

Reg.40, applied: SI 2003/636 Reg.6

Reg.42, amended: SI 2003/166 Reg.3

Reg.47, amended: SI 2002/2641 Reg.6, SI 2003/2003 Reg.6

Reg.47, applied: SI 2003/636 Reg.6

Reg.48, amended: SI 2002/2641 Reg.7, SI 2003/2003 Reg.3

Reg.51, amended: SI 2003/166 Reg.4

Reg.54, amended: SI 2004/1519 Reg.2

Reg.54, substituted: SI 2003/636 Reg.4

Reg.72, amended: SI 2003/166 Reg.5

Reg.73, amended: SI 2003/166 Reg.6

Reg.73, revoked (in part): SI 2003/166 Reg.6

Reg.80, see *Momoh v Gallacher* 2003 S.L.T. 1155 (HCJ), Lord Hamilton, Lord Clarke, Lord Marnoch

Reg.80, amended: SI 2003/166 Reg.7

Sch.2, referred to: SI 2002/2379 Art.2, SI 2004/301 Art.2

Sch.3 Part 1, substituted: SI 2004/265 Sch.1

Sch.3 Part 2, substituted: SI 2004/265 Sch.1

Sch.5, amended: SI 2002/2641 Sch.1

Sch.5, referred to: SI 2002/2641 Reg.8

Sch.6 para.2, applied: SI 2002/975 Reg.2

Sch.7 Part 1, substituted: SI 2003/636 Sch.1 Part 1

Sch.7 Part 1 paraA, substituted: SI 2003/636 Sch.1 Part 1

Sch.7 Part 1 paraB, substituted: SI 2003/636 Sch.1 Part 1

Sch.7 Part 1 paraC, substituted: SI 2003/636 Sch.1 Part 1

Sch.7 Part 1 paraD, substituted: SI 2003/636 Sch.1 Part 1

Sch.7 Part 1 paraE, substituted: SI 2003/636 Sch.1 Part 1

Sch.7 Part 1 paraF, substituted: SI 2003/636 Sch.1 Part 1

Sch.7 Part 1, substituted: SI 2003/636 Sch.1 Part 1

Sch.7 Part 2, substituted: SI 2003/636 Sch.1 Part 2

Sch.7 Part 2 paraA, substituted: SI 2003/636 Sch.1 Part 2

Sch.7 Part 2 paraB, substituted: SI 2003/636 Sch.1 Part 2

Sch.7 Part 2 paraC, substituted: SI 2003/636 Sch.1 Part 2

Sch.7 Part 2 paraD, substituted: SI 2003/636 Sch.1 Part 2

Sch.7 Part 2 paraE, substituted: SI 2003/636 Sch.1 Part 2

Sch.7 Part 2 paraF, substituted: SI 2003/636 Sch.1 Part 2

1999–cont.

2864. Motor Vehicles (Driving Licences) Regulations 1999–*cont.*

Sch.7 Part 2, substituted: SI 2003/636 Sch.1 Part 2

Sch.7 Part 3, substituted: SI 2003/636 Sch.2 Part 1

Sch.7 Part 3 paraA, substituted: SI 2003/636 Sch.2 Part 1

Sch.7 Part 3 paraB, substituted: SI 2003/636 Sch.2 Part 1

Sch.7 Part 3 paraC, substituted: SI 2003/636 Sch.2 Part 1

Sch.7 Part 3 paraD, substituted: SI 2003/636 Sch.2 Part 1

Sch.7 Part 3 paraE, substituted: SI 2003/636 Sch.2 Part 1

Sch.7 Part 3 paraF, substituted: SI 2003/636 Sch.2 Part 1

Sch.7 Part 3, substituted: SI 2003/636 Sch.2 Part 1

Sch.7 Part 3 paraH, substituted: SI 2003/636 Sch.2 Part 1

Sch.7 Part 4, substituted: SI 2003/636 Sch.2 Part 2

Sch.7 Part 4 paraA, substituted: SI 2003/636 Sch.2 Part 2

Sch.7 Part 4 paraB, substituted: SI 2003/636 Sch.2 Part 2

Sch.7 Part 4 paraC, substituted: SI 2003/636 Sch.2 Part 2

Sch.7 Part 4 paraD, substituted: SI 2003/636 Sch.2 Part 2

Sch.7 Part 4 paraE, substituted: SI 2003/636 Sch.2 Part 2

Sch.7 Part 4 paraF, substituted: SI 2003/636 Sch.2 Part 2

Sch.7 Part 4, substituted: SI 2003/636 Sch.2 Part 2

Sch.7 Part 4 paraH, substituted: SI 2003/636 Sch.2 Part 2

Sch.8 Part 1, amended: SI 2003/3313 Reg.2

Sch.8 Part 1, substituted: SI 2003/2003 Sch.1

Sch.8 Part 1 paraA, amended: SI 2003/3313 Reg.2

Sch.8 Part 1 paraA, substituted: SI 2003/166 Reg.8, SI 2003/2003 Sch.1

Sch.8 Part 1 paraB, amended: SI 2003/3313 Reg.2

Sch.8 Part 1 paraB, substituted: SI 2003/2003 Sch.1

Sch.8 Part 1 paraC, amended: SI 2003/3313 Reg.2

Sch.8 Part 1 paraC, substituted: SI 2003/2003 Sch.1

Sch.8 Part 1 paraD, amended: SI 2003/3313 Reg.2

Sch.8 Part 1 paraD, substituted: SI 2003/2003 Sch.1

Sch.8 Part 1 paraE, amended: SI 2003/3313 Reg.2

NO.

NO.

1999–cont.

1999–cont.

2864. Motor Vehicles (Driving Licences) Regulations 1999–*cont.*

Sch.8 Part 1 paraE, substituted: SI 2003/2003 Sch.1

Sch.8 Part 1 paraF, amended: SI 2003/3313 Reg.2

Sch.8 Part 1 paraF, substituted: SI 2003/2003 Sch.1

Sch.8 Part 2, amended: SI 2003/3313 Reg.2

Sch.8 Part 2, substituted: SI 2003/2003 Sch.1

Sch.8 Part 2 paraA, amended: SI 2003/3313 Reg.2

Sch.8 Part 2 paraA, substituted: SI 2003/166 Reg.8, SI 2003/2003 Sch.1

Sch.8 Part 2 paraB, amended: SI 2003/3313 Reg.2

Sch.8 Part 2 paraB, substituted: SI 2003/2003 Sch.1

Sch.8 Part 2 paraC, amended: SI 2003/3313 Reg.2

Sch.8 Part 2 paraC, substituted: SI 2003/2003 Sch.1

Sch.8 Part 2 paraD, amended: SI 2003/3313 Reg.2

Sch.8 Part 2 paraD, substituted: SI 2003/2003 Sch.1

Sch.8 Part 2 paraE, amended: SI 2003/3313 Reg.2

Sch.8 Part 2 paraE, substituted: SI 2003/2003 Sch.1

Sch.8 Part 2 paraF, amended: SI 2003/3313 Reg.2

Sch.8 Part 2 paraF, substituted: SI 2003/2003 Sch.1

Sch.8 Part 2, amended: SI 2003/3313 Reg.2

Sch.8 Part 2, substituted: SI 2003/2003 Sch.1

Sch.8 Part 3, amended: SI 2003/3313 Reg.2

Sch.8 Part 3, substituted: SI 2003/2003 Sch.1

Sch.8 Part 3 paraA, amended: SI 2003/3313 Reg.2

Sch.8 Part 3 paraA, substituted: SI 2003/2003 Sch.1

Sch.8 Part 3 paraB, amended: SI 2003/3313 Reg.2

Sch.8 Part 3 paraB, substituted: SI 2003/2003 Sch.1

Sch.8 Part 3 paraC, amended: SI 2003/3313 Reg.2

Sch.8 Part 3 paraC, substituted: SI 2003/2003 Sch.1

Sch.8 Part 3 paraD, amended: SI 2003/3313 Reg.2

Sch.8 Part 3 paraD, substituted: SI 2003/2003 Sch.1

Sch.8 Part 3 paraE, amended: SI 2003/3313 Reg.2

Sch.8 Part 3 paraE, substituted: SI 2003/2003 Sch.1

2864. Motor Vehicles (Driving Licences) Regulations 1999–*cont.*

Sch.8 Part 3 paraF, amended: SI 2003/3313 Reg.2

Sch.8 Part 3 paraF, substituted: SI 2003/2003 Sch.1

Sch.8 Part 3, amended: SI 2003/3313 Reg.2

Sch.8 Part 3, substituted: SI 2003/2003 Sch.1

Sch.8 Part 4, amended: SI 2003/3313 Reg.2

Sch.8 Part 4, substituted: SI 2003/2003 Sch.1

Sch.8 Part 4 paraA, amended: SI 2003/3313 Reg.2

Sch.8 Part 4 paraA, substituted: SI 2003/2003 Sch.1

Sch.8 Part 4 paraB, amended: SI 2003/3313 Reg.2

Sch.8 Part 4 paraB, substituted: SI 2003/2003 Sch.1

Sch.8 Part 4 paraC, amended: SI 2003/3313 Reg.2

Sch.8 Part 4 paraC, substituted: SI 2003/2003 Sch.1

Sch.8 Part 4 paraD, amended: SI 2003/3313 Reg.2

Sch.8 Part 4 paraD, substituted: SI 2003/2003 Sch.1

Sch.8 Part 4 paraE, amended: SI 2003/3313 Reg.2

Sch.8 Part 4 paraE, substituted: SI 2003/2003 Sch.1

Sch.8 Part 4 paraF, amended: SI 2003/3313 Reg.2

Sch.8 Part 4 paraF, substituted: SI 2003/2003 Sch.1

Sch.8 Part 4, amended: SI 2003/3313 Reg.2

Sch.8 Part 4, substituted: SI 2003/2003 Sch.1

Sch.8 Part 5 paraA, amended: SI 2003/3313 Reg.2

Sch.8 Part 5 paraA, substituted: SI 2003/2003 Sch.1, SI 2003/3313 Sch.1

Sch.8 Part 5 paraB, amended: SI 2003/3313 Reg.2

Sch.8 Part 5 paraB, substituted: SI 2003/2003 Sch.1, SI 2003/3313 Sch.1

Sch.8 Part 5 paraC, amended: SI 2003/3313 Reg.2

Sch.8 Part 5 paraC, substituted: SI 2003/2003 Sch.1, SI 2003/3313 Sch.1

Sch.8 Part 5 paraD, amended: SI 2003/3313 Reg.2

Sch.8 Part 5 paraD, substituted: SI 2003/2003 Sch.1, SI 2003/3313 Sch.1

Sch.8 Part 5 para.1, amended: SI 2003/3313 Reg.2

Sch.8 Part 5 para.1, substituted: SI 2003/166 Reg.8, SI 2003/2003 Sch.1, SI 2003/3313 Sch.1

NO.

NO.

1999–cont.

2864. Motor Vehicles (Driving Licences) Regulations 1999–cont.

Sch.8 Part 5 para.2, amended: SI 2003/3313 Reg.2

Sch.8 Part 5 para.2, substituted: SI 2003/2003 Sch.1, SI 2003/3313 Sch.1

Sch.8 Part 5 para.3, amended: SI 2003/3313 Reg.2

Sch.8 Part 5 para.3, substituted: SI 2003/2003 Sch.1, SI 2003/3313 Sch.1

Sch.8 Part 5 para.4, amended: SI 2003/3313 Reg.2

Sch.8 Part 5 para.4, substituted: SI 2003/2003 Sch.1, SI 2003/3313 Sch.1

Sch.8 Part 5 para.5, amended: SI 2003/3313 Reg.2

Sch.8 Part 5 para.5, substituted: SI 2003/2003 Sch.1, SI 2003/3313 Sch.1

Sch.8 Part 5 para.6, amended: SI 2003/3313 Reg.2

Sch.8 Part 5 para.6, substituted: SI 2003/2003 Sch.1, SI 2003/3313 Sch.1

Sch.8 Part 6 para.1, amended: SI 2003/3313 Reg.2

Sch.8 Part 6 para.1, substituted: SI 2003/2003 Sch.1

Sch.8 Part 6 para.2, amended: SI 2003/3313 Reg.2

Sch.8 Part 6 para.2, substituted: SI 2003/2003 Sch.1

Sch.8 Part 6 para.3, amended: SI 2003/3313 Reg.2

Sch.8 Part 6 para.3, substituted: SI 2003/2003 Sch.1

Sch.8 Part 7 para.1, amended: SI 2003/3313 Reg.2

Sch.8 Part 7 para.1, substituted: SI 2003/2003 Sch.1

Sch.8 Part 7 para.2, amended: SI 2003/3313 Reg.2

Sch.8 Part 7 para.2, substituted: SI 2003/2003 Sch.1

Sch.8 Part 7 para.3, amended: SI 2003/3313 Reg.2

Sch.8 Part 7 para.3, substituted: SI 2003/2003 Sch.1

Sch.12 paraA, substituted: SI 2003/166 Reg.9

2879. Education (Islamia Primary School, Brent) (Exemption from Pay and Conditions) Order 1999

revoked: 2002 c.32 Sch.22 Part 1

2888. Education (School Teacher Appraisal) (Wales) Regulations 1999

applied: SI 2002/1394 Reg.19, Reg.33

revoked: SI 2002/1394 Reg.2

2920. Motor Cycles Etc (EC Type Approval) Regulations 1999

Reg.3, amended: SI 2003/1099 Reg.2, SI 2004/1948 Reg.2

Reg.4, amended: SI 2003/1099 Reg.2

1999–cont.

2920. Motor Cycles Etc (EC Type Approval) Regulations 1999–cont.

Reg.10A, added: SI 2003/1099 Reg.2

Reg.18A, added: SI 2003/1099 Reg.2

Reg.26, amended: SI 2003/1099 Reg.2

Sch.1, amended: SI 2003/1099 Reg.2, SI 2004/1948 Reg.3, SI 2004/2539 Reg.2

Sch.1A para.1, added: SI 2003/1099 Sch.1

Sch.1A para.2, added: SI 2003/1099 Sch.1

Sch.2 para.4, revoked (in part): SI 2003/1099 Reg.2

2921. University Hospitals of Leicester National Health Service Trust (Establishment) Order 1999

revoked: 2003 c.43 s.7

Art.4, amended: SI 2003/2150 Art.2

2922. District of Kennet (Electoral Changes) Order 1999

varied: SI 2004/222 Art.2

2923. District of North Wiltshire (Electoral Changes) Order 1999

varied: SI 2004/222 Art.2

2924. District of Salisbury (Electoral Changes) Order 1999

varied: SI 2004/222 Art.2

2926. District of West Wiltshire (Electoral Changes) Order 1999

varied: SI 2004/222 Art.2

2927. Borough of Swindon (Electoral Changes) Order 1999

varied: SI 2004/222 Art.2

2934. Wireless Telegraphy (Cordless Telephone Apparatus) (Restriction and Marking) Order 1999

Art.3, amended: SI 2003/2155 Sch.1 para.46

Art.3, revoked (in part): SI 2003/2155 Sch.2

2955. Northern Birmingham Mental Health National Health Service Trust (Establishment) Amendment Order 1999

revoked: 2003 c.43 s.7

2978. Road Vehicles (Brake Linings Safety) Regulations 1999

Reg.2, amended: SI 2003/3314 Reg.3

Reg.5, substituted: SI 2003/3314 Reg.4

2979. Financial Markets and Insolvency (Settlement Finality) Regulations 1999

applied: 2002 c.29 s.282

Reg.2, amended: SI 2002/765 Reg.7, SI 2002/1555 Art.39

Reg.6, amended: SI 2002/1555 Art.39

Reg.7, amended: SI 2002/1555 Art.39

Reg.10, amended: SI 2002/1555 Art.39

Reg.14, amended: SI 2003/2096 Sch.1 para.75

Reg.19, amended: SI 2003/2096 Sch.1 para.76

1999–cont.

2981. River Thames (Hungerford Foot-bridges) Order 1999

see *Ocean Leisure Ltd v Westminster City Council* [2004] EWCA Civ 970, [2004] B.L.R. 393 (CA), Potter, L.J.

Art.2, amended: SI 2003/1615 Sch.1 para.54

Sch.10 Part III para.24, amended: SI 2003/2155 Sch.2

Sch.10 Part III para.25, amended: SI 2003/2155 Sch.1 para.18

Sch.10 Part III para.27, amended: SI 2003/2155 Sch.1 para.18

Sch.10 Part IV para.28, amended: SI 2003/1615 Sch.1 para.54

Sch.10 Part IV para.29, amended: SI 2003/1615 Sch.1 para.54

Sch.10 Part IV para.30, amended: SI 2003/1615 Sch.1 para.54

Sch.10 Part V para.40, amended: SI 2003/1615 Sch.1 para.54

Sch.10 Part V para.41, amended: SI 2003/1615 Sch.1 para.54

Sch.10 Part V para.42, amended: SI 2003/1615 Sch.1 para.54

Sch.10 Part V para.43, amended: SI 2003/1615 Sch.1 para.54

Sch.10 Part V para.44, amended: SI 2003/1615 Sch.1 para.54

Sch.10 Part V para.45, amended: SI 2003/1615 Sch.1 para.54

Sch.10 Part V para.47, amended: SI 2003/1615 Sch.1 para.54

Sch.10 Part V para.48, amended: SI 2003/1615 Sch.1 para.54

Sch.10 Part V para.49, amended: SI 2003/1615 Sch.1 para.54

Sch.10 Part V para.50, amended: SI 2003/1615 Sch.1 para.54

Sch.10 Part V para.51, amended: SI 2003/1615 Sch.1 para.54

Sch.11 para.1, amended: SI 2003/2155 Sch.1 para.17, Sch.2

Sch.11 para.2, amended: SI 2003/2155 Sch.1 para.17

2998. Fishing Vessels (EC Directive on Harmonised Safety Regime) Regulations 1999

Reg.2, amended: SI 2003/1112 Reg.5

Reg.4, amended: SI 2003/1112 Reg.6

Reg.6, substituted: SI 2003/1112 Reg.7

Reg.8, amended: SI 2003/1112 Reg.8

Reg.9, amended: SI 2003/1112 Reg.9

Reg.10, amended: SI 2003/1112 Reg.10

Reg.15, amended: SI 2003/1112 Reg.11

Reg.17, amended: SI 2003/1112 Reg.12

Sch.3i Part I para.1, amended: SI 2003/1112 Reg.13

Sch.3i Part I para.2, amended: SI 2003/1112 Reg.13

Sch.3i Part I para.3, amended: SI 2003/1112 Reg.13

1999–cont.

2998. Fishing Vessels (EC Directive on Harmonised Safety Regime) Regulations 1999–*cont.*

Sch.3i Part I para.4, amended: SI 2003/1112 Reg.13

Sch.3i Part I para.5, amended: SI 2003/1112 Reg.13, Reg.14

Sch.3i Part I para.6, amended: SI 2003/1112 Reg.13

Sch.3i Part I para.7, amended: SI 2003/1112 Reg.13

Sch.3i Part I para.8, amended: SI 2003/1112 Reg.13

Sch.3i Part I para.9, amended: SI 2003/1112 Reg.13

Sch.3i Part I para.10, amended: SI 2003/1112 Reg.13

Sch.3i Part I para.11, amended: SI 2003/1112 Reg.13

Sch.3i Part I para.12, amended: SI 2003/1112 Reg.13

Sch.3i Part I para.13, amended: SI 2003/1112 Reg.13

Sch.3i Part I para.14, amended: SI 2003/1112 Reg.13

Sch.3i Part I para.15, amended: SI 2003/1112 Reg.13

Sch.3i Part I para.16, amended: SI 2003/1112 Reg.13

Sch.3i Part I para.17, amended: SI 2003/1112 Reg.13

Sch.3i Part I para.18, amended: SI 2003/1112 Reg.13

Sch.3i Part I para.19, amended: SI 2003/1112 Reg.13

Sch.3i Part I para.20, amended: SI 2003/1112 Reg.13

Sch.3i Part I para.21, amended: SI 2003/1112 Reg.13

Sch.3i Part I para.22, amended: SI 2003/1112 Reg.13

Sch.3i Part I para.23, amended: SI 2003/1112 Reg.13

Sch.3i Part I para.24, amended: SI 2003/1112 Reg.13

Sch.3i Part I para.25, amended: SI 2003/1112 Reg.13

Sch.3i Part I para.25, substituted: SI 2003/1112 Reg.15

Sch.3i Part I para.26, amended: SI 2003/1112 Reg.13

Sch.3i Part I para.27, amended: SI 2003/1112 Reg.13

Sch.3i Part I para.28, amended: SI 2003/1112 Reg.13

Sch.3i Part I para.29, amended: SI 2003/1112 Reg.13

Sch.3i Part I para.30, amended: SI 2003/1112 Reg.13, Reg.16

Sch.3i Part I para.31, amended: SI 2003/1112 Reg.13

1999–cont.

2998. Fishing Vessels (EC Directive on Harmonised Safety Regime) Regulations 1999–*cont.*

Sch.3i Part I para.32, amended: SI 2003/1112 Reg.13

Sch.3i Part I para.33, amended: SI 2003/1112 Reg.13

Sch.3i Part I para.34, amended: SI 2003/1112 Reg.13

Sch.3i Part I para.35, amended: SI 2003/1112 Reg.13

Sch.3i Part I para.36, amended: SI 2003/1112 Reg.13

Sch.3i Part I para.37, amended: SI 2003/1112 Reg.13

Sch.3i Part I para.38, amended: SI 2003/1112 Reg.13

Sch.3i Part I para.39, amended: SI 2003/1112 Reg.13

Sch.3i Part I para.40, amended: SI 2003/1112 Reg.13

Sch.3i Part I para.41, amended: SI 2003/1112 Reg.13, Reg.17

Sch.3i Part I para.42, amended: SI 2003/1112 Reg.13

Sch.3i Part II para.1, amended: SI 2003/1112 Reg.13

Sch.3i Part II para.2, amended: SI 2003/1112 Reg.13

Sch.3i Part II para.3, amended: SI 2003/1112 Reg.13

Sch.4 Part I para.1, added: SI 2003/1112 Sch.1

Sch.4 Part I para.2, added: SI 2003/1112 Sch.1

Sch.4 Part I para.3, added: SI 2003/1112 Sch.1

Sch.4 Part I para.4, added: SI 2003/1112 Sch.1

Sch.4 Part I para.5, added: SI 2003/1112 Sch.1

Sch.4 Part I para.6, added: SI 2003/1112 Sch.1

Sch.4 Part I para.7, added: SI 2003/1112 Sch.1

Sch.4 Part I para.8, added: SI 2003/1112 Sch.1

Sch.4 Part I para.9, added: SI 2003/1112 Sch.1

Sch.4 Part I para.10, added: SI 2003/1112 Sch.1

Sch.4 Part I para.11, added: SI 2003/1112 Sch.1

Sch.4 Part I para.12, added: SI 2003/1112 Sch.1

Sch.4 Part I para.13, added: SI 2003/1112 Sch.1

Sch.4 Part I para.14, added: SI 2003/1112 Sch.1

Sch.4 Part I para.15, added: SI 2003/1112 Sch.1

1999–cont.

2998. Fishing Vessels (EC Directive on Harmonised Safety Regime) Regulations 1999–*cont.*

Sch.4 Part I para.16, added: SI 2003/1112 Sch.1

Sch.4 Part I para.17, added: SI 2003/1112 Sch.1

Sch.4 Part I para.18, added: SI 2003/1112 Sch.1

Sch.4 Part I para.19, added: SI 2003/1112 Sch.1

Sch.4 Part I para.20, added: SI 2003/1112 Sch.1

Sch.4 Part I para.21, added: SI 2003/1112 Sch.1

Sch.4 Part I para.22, added: SI 2003/1112 Sch.1

Sch.4 Part I para.23, added: SI 2003/1112 Sch.1

Sch.4 Part I para.24, added: SI 2003/1112 Sch.1

Sch.4 Part I para.25, added: SI 2003/1112 Sch.1

Sch.4 Part I para.26, added: SI 2003/1112 Sch.1

Sch.4 Part I para.27, added: SI 2003/1112 Sch.1

Sch.4 Part I para.28, added: SI 2003/1112 Sch.1

Sch.4 Part I para.29, added: SI 2003/1112 Sch.1

Sch.4 Part I para.30, added: SI 2003/1112 Sch.1

Sch.4 Part I para.31, added: SI 2003/1112 Sch.1

Sch.4 Part I para.32, added: SI 2003/1112 Sch.1

Sch.4 Part I para.33, added: SI 2003/1112 Sch.1

Sch.4 Part I para.34, added: SI 2003/1112 Sch.1

Sch.4 Part I para.35, added: SI 2003/1112 Sch.1

Sch.4 Part I para.36, added: SI 2003/1112 Sch.1

Sch.4 Part I para.37, added: SI 2003/1112 Sch.1

Sch.4 Part I para.38, added: SI 2003/1112 Sch.1

Sch.4 Part I para.39, added: SI 2003/1112 Sch.1

Sch.4 Part I para.40, added: SI 2003/1112 Sch.1

Sch.4 Part I para.41, added: SI 2003/1112 Sch.1

Sch.4 Part I para.42, added: SI 2003/1112 Sch.1

Sch.4 Part I para.43, added: SI 2003/1112 Sch.1

Sch.4 Part I para.44, added: SI 2003/1112 Sch.1

NO.

NO.

1999–cont.

2998. Fishing Vessels (EC Directive on Harmonised Safety Regime) Regulations 1999–cont.

Sch.4 Part I para.45, added: SI 2003/1112 Sch.1

Sch.4 Part I para.46, added: SI 2003/1112 Sch.1

Sch.4 Part I para.47, added: SI 2003/1112 Sch.1

Sch.4 Part I para.48, added: SI 2003/1112 Sch.1

Sch.4 Part I para.49, added: SI 2003/1112 Sch.1

Sch.4 Part I para.50, added: SI 2003/1112 Sch.1

Sch.4 Part I para.51, added: SI 2003/1112 Sch.1

Sch.4 Part I para.52, added: SI 2003/1112 Sch.1

Sch.4 Part I para.53, added: SI 2003/1112 Sch.1

Sch.4 Part I para.54, added: SI 2003/1112 Sch.1

Sch.4 Part I para.55, added: SI 2003/1112 Sch.1

Sch.4 Part I para.56, added: SI 2003/1112 Sch.1

Sch.4 Part I para.57, added: SI 2003/1112 Sch.1

Sch.4 Part I para.58, added: SI 2003/1112 Sch.1

Sch.4 Part I para.59, added: SI 2003/1112 Sch.1

Sch.4 Part I para.60, added: SI 2003/1112 Sch.1

Sch.4 Part I para.61, added: SI 2003/1112 Sch.1

Sch.4 Part I para.62, added: SI 2003/1112 Sch.1

Sch.4 Part I para.63, added: SI 2003/1112 Sch.1

Sch.4 Part I para.64, added: SI 2003/1112 Sch.1

Sch.4 Part I para.65, added: SI 2003/1112 Sch.1

Sch.4 Part I para.66, added: SI 2003/1112 Sch.1

Sch.4 Part I para.67, added: SI 2003/1112 Sch.1

Sch.4 Part I para.68, added: SI 2003/1112 Sch.1

Sch.4 Part I para.69, added: SI 2003/1112 Sch.1

Sch.4 Part II para.1, added: SI 2003/1112 Sch.1

Sch.4 Part II para.2, added: SI 2003/1112 Sch.1

Sch.4 Part II para.3, added: SI 2003/1112 Sch.1

1999–cont.

3010. Justices of the Peace (Commission Areas) Order 1999

Art.2, amended: SI 2003/640 Art.3

Art.2, referred to: SI 2003/2818 Art.12

Sch.1 Part I, amended: SI 2002/1440 Art.3

Sch.1 Part II, amended: SI 2003/641 Art.3

3036. Glenfield Hospital, the Leicester General Hospital and the Leicester Royal Infirmary National Health Service Trusts (Dissolution) Order 1999

revoked: 2003 c.43 s.7

3042. Price Marking Order 1999

revoked: SI 2004/102 Art.2

3050. Avalon, Somerset, National Health Service Trust (Change of Name) Order 1999

revoked: 2003 c.43 s.7

3056. Asylum Support (Interim Provisions) Regulations 1999

see *Anufrijeva v Southwark LBC* [2002] EWHC 3163, (2003) 6 C.C.L. Rep. 25 (QBD), Newman, J.

Reg.2, amended: SI 2002/471 Reg.3, Reg.4, SI 2004/566 Reg.2

Reg.5, revoked (in part): SI 2002/471 Reg.5

3084. Home Repair Assistance (Extension) (Wales) Regulations 1999

revoked: SI 2002/1860 Sch.6

3088. Water Appointment (Competition Commission) Regulations 1999

Reg.3, amended: SI 2003/1398 Sch.1 para.36

Reg.7, substituted: SI 2003/1398 Sch.1 para.36

Reg.8, substituted: SI 2003/1398 Sch.1 para.36

Reg.10A, added: SI 2003/1398 Sch.1 para.36

Reg.11, amended: SI 2003/1398 Sch.1 para.36

3099. Greater London Magistrates Courts Authority (Constitution) Regulations 1999

Reg.15, amended: SI 2003/385 Reg.2

Sch.4 para.4, amended: SI 2004/76 Reg.2

3106. Good Laboratory Practice Regulations 1999

referred to: SI 2002/2676 Sch.2, SI 2002/2677 Sch.7, SI 2002/2776 Sch.5, SR 2003/34 Sch.7, SR 2003/35 Sch.2

Reg.2, amended: SI 2004/994 Reg.2

Reg.5, amended: SI 2004/994 Reg.2

Reg.9, amended: SI 2004/994 Reg.2

Sch.1 Part I para.1, amended: SI 2004/994 Reg.2

Sch.1 Part I para.2, amended: SI 2004/994 Reg.2

Sch.1 Part I para.3, amended: SI 2004/994 Reg.2

Sch.1 Part I para.4, amended: SI 2004/994 Reg.2

1999–cont.

3106. Good Laboratory Practice Regulations 1999–*cont.*

Sch.1 Part II para.1, amended: SI 2004/994 Reg.2

Sch.1 Part II para.2, amended: SI 2004/994 Reg.2

Sch.1 Part III para.1, amended: SI 2004/994 Reg.2

Sch.1 Part III para.2, amended: SI 2004/994 Reg.2

Sch.1 Part III para.3, amended: SI 2004/994 Reg.2

Sch.1 Part III para.4, amended: SI 2004/994 Reg.2

Sch.1 Part III para.5, amended: SI 2004/994 Reg.2

Sch.1 Part IV para.1, amended: SI 2004/994 Reg.2

Sch.1 Part IV para.2, amended: SI 2004/994 Reg.2

Sch.1 Part IV para.3, amended: SI 2004/994 Reg.2

Sch.1 Part IV para.4, amended: SI 2004/994 Reg.2

Sch.1 Part V para.1, amended: SI 2004/994 Reg.2

Sch.1 Part V para.2, amended: SI 2004/994 Reg.2

Sch.1 Part VI para.1, amended: SI 2004/994 Reg.2

Sch.1 Part VI para.2, amended: SI 2004/994 Reg.2

Sch.1 Part VII para.1, amended: SI 2004/994 Reg.2

Sch.1 Part VII para.2, amended: SI 2004/994 Reg.2

Sch.1 Part VII para.3, amended: SI 2004/994 Reg.2

Sch.1 Part VII para.4, amended: SI 2004/994 Reg.2

Sch.1 Part VIII para.1, amended: SI 2004/994 Reg.2

Sch.1 Part VIII para.2, amended: SI 2004/994 Reg.2

Sch.1 Part VIII para.3, amended: SI 2004/994 Reg.2

Sch.1 Part IX para.1, amended: SI 2004/994 Reg.2

Sch.1 Part IX para.2, amended: SI 2004/994 Reg.2

Sch.1 Part X para.1, amended: SI 2004/994 Reg.2

Sch.1 Part X para.2, amended: SI 2004/994 Reg.2

Sch.1 Part X para.3, amended: SI 2004/994 Reg.2

Sch.1 Part X para.4, amended: SI 2004/994 Reg.2

Sch.2 Part I para.1, amended: SI 2004/994 Reg.2

1999–cont.

3106. Good Laboratory Practice Regulations 1999–*cont.*

Sch.2 Part I para.2, amended: SI 2004/994 Reg.2

Sch.2 Part I para.3, amended: SI 2004/994 Reg.2

Sch.2 Part I para.4, amended: SI 2004/994 Reg.2

Sch.2 Part I para.5, amended: SI 2004/994 Reg.2

Sch.2 Part I para.6, amended: SI 2004/994 Reg.2

Sch.2 Part I para.7, amended: SI 2004/994 Reg.2

Sch.2 Part I para.8, amended: SI 2004/994 Reg.2

Sch.2 Part I para.9, amended: SI 2004/994 Reg.2

Sch.2 Part I para.10, amended: SI 2004/994 Reg.2

Sch.2 Part I para.11, amended: SI 2004/994 Reg.2

Sch.2 Part I para.12, amended: SI 2004/994 Reg.2

Sch.2 Part I para.13, amended: SI 2004/994 Reg.2

Sch.2 Part II para.1, amended: SI 2004/994 Reg.2

Sch.2 Part II para.2, amended: SI 2004/994 Reg.2

Sch.2 Part II para.3, amended: SI 2004/994 Reg.2

Sch.2 Part II para.4, amended: SI 2004/994 Reg.2

3107. Motor Fuel (Composition and Content) Regulations 1999

referred to: SI 2003/3078 Reg.2

Reg.2, amended: SI 2003/3078 Reg.3

Reg.2, referred to: SI 2002/1689 Reg.8, SR 2002/301 Reg.8

Reg.3, amended: SI 2003/3078 Reg.4

Reg.4, amended: SI 2003/3078 Reg.5

Reg.5, amended: SI 2003/3078 Reg.5

Reg.5A, added: SI 2003/3078 Reg.6

Reg.6, amended: SI 2003/3078 Reg.7

Reg.7, amended: SI 2003/3078 Reg.8

Sch.1 para.5, amended: SI 2003/3078 Reg.9

3108. Social Security (Claims and Information) Regulations 1999

Reg.4, amended: SI 2002/2497 Sch.2 para.1

Reg.5, revoked (in part): SI 2003/492 Sch.3 Part 1

Reg.17, amended: SI 2002/2497 Sch.2 para.1

Sch.3 para.2, revoked (in part): SI 2003/492 Sch.3 Part 1

3110. Tax Credit (New Category of Child Care Provider) Regulations 1999

Reg.4, applied: SI 2002/2005 Reg.14

NO.

NO.

1999–cont.

3121. Value Added Tax (Input Tax) (Specified Supplies) Order 1999

see *WHA Ltd v Customs and Excise Commissioners* [2003] EWHC 305, [2003] S.T.C. 648 (Ch D), Lloyd, J.

Art.3, see *Water Hall Group Plc v Customs and Excise Commissioners* [2003] V. & D.R. 257 (V&DTr), Peter H Lawson (Chairman)

3132. Consular Fees (No.2) Order 1999

Art.2, amended: SI 2003/1871 Art.2

Art.2, revoked (in part): SI 2002/2634 Art.2

Sch.1 Part II, amended: SI 2002/1627 Art.2, SI 2002/2634 Art.2, SI 2003/1871 Art.2, SI 2003/2920 Art.2

Sch.1 Part II, substituted: SI 2003/1871 Art.2

3135. Afghanistan (United Nations Sanctions) (Isle of Man) Order 1999

Art.4, amended: 2002 c.8 s.2

3147. Welfare Reform and Pensions (Northern Ireland) Order 1999

referred to: SR 2002/63 Art.1, SR 2002/126 Art.1

Part IV, applied: 2002 c.29 s.275

Art.1, enabled: SR 2002/25, SR 2002/63, SR 2002/126, SR 2003/204

Art.3, enabled: SR 2002/268, SR 2002/410, SR 2003/256

Art.5, enabled: SR 2003/256

Art.12, applied: SR 2002/127 Reg.2, Reg.3, Reg.5, Reg.6

Art.12, enabled: SR 2002/127

Art.12, referred to: SR 2002/127 Reg.3

Art.13, applied: SR 2002/127 Reg.3

Art.13, enabled: SR 2002/127

Art.14, referred to: SR 2002/109 Sch.1

Art.26, applied: 2002 c.29 s.275, 2004 c.12 s.220, Sch.36 para.18

Art.27, referred to: SR 2002/352 Reg.137

Art.31, referred to: SR 2002/352 Reg.137

Art.40, amended: 2002 c.26 s.21, Sch.13

Art.50, revoked (in part): 2002 c.10 (NI) Sch.2

Art.69, amended: 2002 c.10 (NI) Sch.1 para.11

Art.69, enabled: SR 2002/323

Art.73, enabled: SR 2002/127, SR 2002/268, SR 2002/323

Art.75, enabled: SR 2002/86

Sch.2 para.4, referred to: SR 2002/109 Sch.1

Sch.5 para.1, applied: SR 2002/352 Reg.133

Sch.5 para.6, enabled: SR 2003/256

Sch.5 para.10, enabled: SR 2003/256

Sch.8 Part I para.10, revoked: 2002 c.21 Sch.6

Sch.8 Part I para.13, revoked: 2002 c.21 Sch.6

Sch.9 Part I para.46, referred to: SR 2002/109 Sch.1

Sch.9 Part I para.47, referred to: SR 2002/109 Sch.1

1999–cont.

3154. European Specialist Medical Qualifications Amendment (No.2) Regulations 1999

revoked: SI 2003/1250 Sch.10 Part 2

3164. Croydon Community National Health Service Trust (Change of Name) Order 1999

revoked: 2003 c.43 s.7

3165. Chemicals (Hazard Information and Packaging for Supply) (Amendment) (No.2) Regulations 1999

revoked: SI 2002/1689 Sch.7

3178. Social Security Act 1998 (Commencement No 12 and Consequential and Transitional Provisions) Order 1999

Art.3, revoked (in part): SI 2003/492 Sch.3 Part 1

Sch.6 para.1, revoked (in part): SI 2003/492 Sch.3 Part 1

Sch.6 para.2, revoked (in part): SI 2003/492 Sch.3 Part 1

Sch.6 para.3, revoked (in part): SI 2003/492 Sch.3 Part 1

Sch.6 para.4, revoked (in part): SI 2003/492 Sch.3 Part 1

Sch.6 para.5, revoked (in part): SI 2003/492 Sch.3 Part 1

Sch.6 para.6, revoked (in part): SI 2003/492 Sch.3 Part 1

Sch.6 para.7, revoked (in part): SI 2003/492 Sch.3 Part 1

Sch.6 para.8, revoked (in part): SI 2003/492 Sch.3 Part 1

Sch.6 para.9, revoked (in part): SI 2003/492 Sch.3 Part 1

Sch.6 para.10, revoked (in part): SI 2003/492 Sch.3 Part 1

Sch.6 para.11, revoked (in part): SI 2003/492 Sch.3 Part 1

Sch.6 para.12, revoked (in part): SI 2003/492 Sch.3 Part 1

Sch.6 para.13, revoked (in part): SI 2003/492 Sch.3 Part 1

Sch.6 para.14, revoked (in part): SI 2003/492 Sch.3 Part 1

Sch.6 para.15, revoked (in part): SI 2003/492 Sch.3 Part 1

Sch.6 para.16, revoked (in part): SI 2003/492 Sch.3 Part 1

Sch.6 para.17, revoked (in part): SI 2003/492 Sch.3 Part 1

Sch.9 para.1, revoked (in part): SI 2003/492 Sch.3 Part 1

Sch.9 para.2, revoked (in part): SI 2003/492 Sch.3 Part 1

Sch.9 para.3, revoked (in part): SI 2003/492 Sch.3 Part 1

Sch.9 para.4, revoked (in part): SI 2003/492 Sch.3 Part 1

NO.

NO.

1999–cont.

3178. Social Security Act 1998 (Commencement No 12 and Consequential and Transitional Provisions) Order 1999–*cont.*

Sch.9 para.5, revoked (in part): SI 2003/492 Sch.3 Part 1

Sch.9 para.6, revoked (in part): SI 2003/492 Sch.3 Part 1

Sch.9 para.7, revoked (in part): SI 2003/492 Sch.3 Part 1

Sch.9 para.8, revoked (in part): SI 2003/492 Sch.3 Part 1

Sch.9 para.9, revoked (in part): SI 2003/492 Sch.3 Part 1

Sch.9 para.10, revoked (in part): SI 2003/492 Sch.3 Part 1

3179. National Health Service (Choice of Medical Practitioner) Amendment Regulations 1999

revoked: SI 2004/865 Sch.2, SI 2004/1016 Sch.2

3181. Education (School Day and School Year) (England) Regulations 1999

Reg.3, varied: SI 2004/1191 Art.3

3205. Betting and Gaming Duties Act 1981 (Bingo Prize Limit) Order 1999

revoked: SI 2004/155 Art.3

3210. Merchant Shipping (Radio) (Fishing Vessels) Regulations 1999

Reg.3, amended: SI 2002/2201 Sch.1 para.54

Reg.21, amended: SI 2002/2201 Sch.1 para.55

Reg.22, amended: SI 2002/2201 Sch.1 para.55

Reg.23, amended: SI 2002/2201 Sch.1 para.55

Reg.24, amended: SI 2002/2201 Sch.1 para.55

Reg.25, amended: SI 2002/2201 Sch.1 para.55

Reg.26, amended: SI 2002/2201 Sch.1 para.55

3232. Ionising Radiations Regulations 1999

applied: SI 2002/655 Reg.3, Reg.9, SI 2003/547 Reg.3, Reg.9, Sch.6, SI 2004/456 Reg.8, Sch.5

Part II, applied: SI 2002/1093 Reg.24

Part V, applied: SI 2002/1093 Reg.67

Reg.6, applied: SI 2002/655 Sch.8

Reg.20, applied: SI 2002/1093 Reg.67

Reg.21, applied: SI 2002/1093 Reg.67

Reg.22, applied: SI 2002/1093 Reg.67

Reg.23, applied: SI 2002/1093 Reg.67

Reg.24, applied: SI 2002/1093 Reg.67

Reg.25, applied: SI 2002/1093 Reg.67

Reg.26, applied: SI 2002/1093 Reg.67

Reg.35, applied: SI 2003/547 Sch.8

Sch.1 para.1, applied: SI 2002/655 Reg.9, Sch.8, SI 2003/547 Reg.9, Sch.8, SI 2004/456 Reg.8

Sch.4, referred to: SI 2002/1093 Reg.68

1999–cont.

3232. Ionising Radiations Regulations 1999–*cont.*

Sch.4 Part I para.1, applied: SI 2002/1093 Reg.67

Sch.4 Part I para.2, applied: SI 2002/1093 Reg.67

Sch.4 Part I para.6, applied: SI 2002/1093 Reg.67

Sch.4 Part I para.7, applied: SI 2002/1093 Reg.67

Sch.4 Part I para.8, applied: SI 2002/1093 Reg.67

Sch.9 para.7, revoked: SI 2002/2099 Sch.2

3242. Management of Health and Safety at Work Regulations 1999

referred to: SI 2002/2675 Reg.14, SI 2002/2676 Reg.12, SI 2002/2677 Reg.13

Reg.2, substituted: SI 2003/2457 Reg.3

Reg.3, applied: SI 2003/1910 Sch.1 para.3, SI 2003/1934 Sch.1 para.3, SI 2003/3230 Sch.1 para.3, SI 2003/3234 Sch.1 para.3

Reg.3, substituted: SI 2003/2457 Reg.4

Reg.16, see *Hardman v Mallon (t/a Orchard Lodge Nursing Home)* [2002] 2 C.M.L.R. 59 (EAT), J McMullen Q.C.

Reg.19, revoked (in part): SI 2003/2457 Reg.5

Reg.21, applied: SI 2002/2675 Reg.28, SI 2002/2677 Reg.21

Reg.22, substituted: SI 2003/2457 Reg.6

3243. Wireless Telegraphy (Licence Charges) (Amendment) Regulations 1999

revoked: SI 2002/1700 Sch.1

3244. Environmental Protection (Controls on Injurious Substances) Regulations 1999

revoked (in part): SI 2003/721 Reg.2, SI 2003/1511 Reg.2

3251. Local Government (Best Value) Performance Plans and reviews order 1999

Art.3, revoked: SI 2003/662 Art.2

Art.4, amended: SI 2002/305 Art.4

Art.4, revoked: SI 2003/662 Art.2

Art.5, revoked: SI 2002/305 Art.5

Art.6, amended: SI 2003/662 Art.2

3264. Stamp Duty Reserve Tax (Amendment No 2) Regulations 1999

varied: 2002 c.23 Sch.34 para.7, Sch.35 para.8

3280. Town and Country Planning (Development Plan) (England) Regulations 1999

applied: SI 2004/2205 Reg.3, Reg.4, Reg.5

Reg.2, amended: SI 2004/2205 Sch.1 para.1

Reg.24, applied: SI 2004/2205 Sch.1 para.2

Reg.24, referred to: SI 2004/2205 Sch.1 para.2

Reg.24, revoked: SI 2004/2205 Sch.1 para.2

Reg.24A, added: SI 2004/2205 Sch.1 para.3

1999–cont.

3280. Town and Country Planning (Development Plan) (England) Regulations 1999–cont.

Reg.25, revoked: SI 2004/2205 Sch.1 para.4

Reg.26, amended: SI 2004/2205 Sch.1 para.5

Reg.27, revoked: SI 2004/2205 Sch.1 para.6

Reg.28, applied: SI 2004/2205 Sch.1 para.6, Sch.1 para.7

Reg.29, revoked: SI 2004/2205 Sch.1 para.7

Reg.30, substituted: SI 2004/2205 Sch.1 para.8

Reg.31, amended: SI 2004/2205 Sch.1 para.9

Reg.33, amended: SI 2004/2205 Sch.1 para.10

Reg.35, amended: SI 2004/2205 Sch.1 para.11

Reg.46, added: SI 2004/2205 Sch.1 para.12

Sch.1, amended: SI 2004/2205 Sch.1 para.13, Sch.1 para.14

3311. Registration of Births, Deaths and Marriages (Fees) Order 1999

revoked: SI 2002/3076 Art.3

3312. Maternity and Parental Leave etc Regulations 1999

applied: SI 2003/543 Reg.18, Sch.1 para.4

Reg.2, amended: SI 2002/2789 Reg.4

Reg.4, amended: SI 2002/2789 Reg.5

Reg.5, amended: SI 2002/2789 Reg.6

Reg.6, amended: SI 2002/2789 Reg.7

Reg.7, amended: SI 2002/2789 Reg.8

Reg.7, referred to: SI 2003/543 Reg.9

Reg.9, substituted: SI 2002/2789 Reg.9

Reg.11, amended: SI 2002/2789 Reg.10

Reg.12, revoked: SI 2002/2789 Reg.11

Reg.18, substituted: SI 2002/2789 Reg.12

Reg.18A, substituted: SI 2002/2789 Reg.12

Reg.19, see *South Central Trains Ltd v Rodway* [2004] I.R.L.R. 777 (EAT), Judge Birtles

Reg.19, amended: SI 2002/2789 Reg.13

Reg.20, amended: SI 2002/2789 Reg.14

Sch.2 para.7, see *South Central Trains Ltd v Rodway* [2004] I.R.L.R. 777 (EAT), Judge Birtles

3323. Transnational Information and Consultation of Employees Regulations 1999

Reg.3, amended: SI 2004/1079 Sch.1 para.4

Reg.32, applied: 2002 c.22 Sch.3, Sch.4, Sch.5, SI 2003/2902 Sch.2, Sch.3, Sch.4

Reg.41, amended: SI 2004/2518 Reg.2

Reg.46A, added: SI 2004/2326 Reg.53

3339. Travel Documents (Fees) Regulations 1999

Reg.3, amended: SI 2002/2155 Reg.3, Reg.4, SI 2004/579 Reg.2

3379. Non-Domestic Rating (Chargeable Amounts) (England) Regulations 1999

Reg.10, amended: SI 2004/1297 Reg.4

1999–cont.

3379. Non-Domestic Rating (Chargeable Amounts) (England) Regulations 1999–cont.

Reg.13, amended: SI 2004/1297 Reg.5

Reg.27A, amended: SI 2004/1297 Reg.6

Reg.37, amended: SI 2004/1297 Reg.7

Sch.2 para.3, amended: SI 2004/1297 Reg.8

Sch.2 para.4, amended: SI 2004/1297 Reg.8

Sch.2 para.5, amended: SI 2004/1297 Reg.8

Sch.2 para.6, amended: SI 2004/1297 Reg.8

Sch.2 para.9, amended: SI 2004/1297 Reg.8

3381. Peterlee Education Action Zone Order 1999

varied: SI 2002/3086 Art.3

3382. Easington and Seaham Education Action Zone Order 1999

varied: SI 2002/3087 Art.3

3383. Dingle Granby Toxteth Education Action Zone Order 1999

varied: SI 2002/3088 Art.3

3384. Community Learning Partnership Barrow-in-Furness Education Action Zone Order 1999

varied: SI 2002/3093 Art.3

3385. Sunderland Building Our Future Education Action Zone Order 1999

varied: SI 2002/3089 Art.3

3386. Learning Together East Cleveland Education Action Zone Order 1999

varied: SI 2002/3090 Art.3

3387. Wolverhampton Education Action Zone Order 1999

varied: SI 2002/3091 Art.3

3388. North Gillingham Education Action Zone Order 1999

varied: SI 2002/3092 Art.3

3389. Rainbow Education Action Zone in Stoke on Trent Order 1999

varied: SI 2002/3097 Art.3

3390. Leigh Park Education Action Zone Order 1999

varied: SI 2002/3094 Art.3

3391. Ashington Education Action Zone Order 1999

varied: SI 2002/3095 Art.3

3392. Breaking the Cycle Bridgwater Education Action Zone Order 1999

varied: SI 2002/3096 Art.3

3393. Bolton Education Action Zone Order 1999

varied: SI 2002/3098 Art.3

3394. Coventry Millennium Education Action Zone Order 1999

varied: SI 2002/3099 Art.3

3395. Downham and Bellingham Education Action Zone Order 1999

varied: SI 2002/3100 Art.3

3396. Epicentre LEAP Ellesmere Port Cheshire Education Action Zone Order 1999

varied: SI 2002/3101 Art.3

1999–cont.

3397. Clacton and Harwich Education Action Zone Order 1999
varied: SI 2002/3102 Art.3

3398. Challenge for Corby Education Action Zone Order 1999
varied: SI 2002/3103 Art.3

3399. Action for Learning Partnership, Bedford Education Action Zone Order 1999
varied: SI 2002/3104 Art.3

3400. Withernsea and Southern Holderness Rural Achievement Education Zone Order 1999
varied: SI 2002/3105 Art.3

3406. Wakefield Community Learning Partnership Education Action Zone Order 1999
varied: SI 2002/3109 Art.3

3407. South Bradford Community Learning Partnership Education Action Zone Order 1999
varied: SI 2002/3107 Art.3

3408. Speke Garston Excellent Education Action Zone Order 1999
varied: SI 2002/3106 Art.3

3412. Gloucester Education Achievement Zone Order 1999
varied: SI 2002/3108 Art.3

3414. Camborne, Pool and Redruth Success Zone Education Action Zone Order 1999
varied: SI 2002/3085 Art.3

3424. Police (Secretary of State's Objectives) (No.3) Order 1999
revoked: SI 2002/695 Art.2

3432. Health Development Agency Regulations 1999
Reg.1, amended: SI 2004/696 Art.3
Reg.3, amended: SI 2002/2469 Sch.3, SI 2004/20 Reg.2, SI 2004/696 Art.3

3441. Water Industry (Charges) (Vulnerable Groups) Regulations 1999
Reg.2, amended: SI 2003/552 Reg.2

3443. Pet Travel Scheme (Pilot Arrangements) (England) Order 1999
disapplied: SI 2004/853 Sch.6
revoked: SI 2004/2363 Sch.2
Art.2A, amended: SI 2002/2850 Art.2
Art.6, amended: SI 2002/2850 Art.2
Art.6A, amended: SI 2002/2850 Art.2
Art.7, amended: SI 2002/2850 Art.2
Art.7A, substituted: SI 2002/2850 Art.2
Art.8, applied: SI 2004/2363 Reg.21
Sch.2 Part I, amended: SI 2002/2850 Art.2
Sch.4 Part 1, added: SI 2002/2850 Art.2
Sch.4 Part 1, amended: SI 2002/2850 Art.2
Sch.6 para.1, amended: SI 2002/1011 Art.2
Sch.6 para.1, substituted: SI 2002/2850 Art.2
Sch.6 para.2, substituted: SI 2002/2850 Art.2

1999–cont.

3443. Pet Travel Scheme (Pilot Arrangements) (England) Order 1999–cont.
Sch.6 para.3, substituted: SI 2002/2850 Art.2
Sch.6 para.4, substituted: SI 2002/2850 Art.2
Sch.6 para.5, substituted: SI 2002/2850 Art.2, SI 2004/828 Art.2
Sch.6 para.6, substituted: SI 2002/2850 Art.2, SI 2004/828 Art.2
Sch.6 para.7, substituted: SI 2002/2850 Art.2, SI 2004/828 Art.2
Sch.6 para.8, substituted: SI 2002/2850 Art.2, SI 2004/828 Art.2

3448. Telecommunications (Interconnection) (Carrier Pre-selection) Regulations 1999
revoked: 2003 c.21 Sch.19

3449. Telecommunications (Interconnection) (Number Portability, etc.) Regulations 1999
revoked: 2003 c.21 Sch.19

3450. National Health Service Trusts (Wales) (Dissolution No 2) Order 1999
revoked: 2003 c.43 s.7

3451. Cardiff and Vale National Health Service Trust Establishment Order 1999
revoked: 2003 c.43 s.7

3453. Central Rating List (Wales) Regulations 1999
Reg.1, amended: SI 2003/3225 Reg.2
Sch.1 Part 2, amended: SI 2003/3225 Reg.2

3466. Northern Birmingham Community Health and the Southern Birmingham Community Health National Health Service Trusts (Dissolution) Order 1999
revoked: 2003 c.43 s.7

3467. Birmingham Specialist Community Health National Health Service Trust (Establishment) Order 1999
revoked: SI 2002/2616 Art.2, 2003 c.43 s.7

3471. Alexandra Health Care, the Kidderminster Health Care, the Worcestershire Community Healthcare and the Worcester Royal Infirmary National Health Service Trusts (Dissolution) Order 1999
revoked: 2003 c.43 s.7

3472. Worcestershire Community and Mental Health National Health Service Trust (Establishment) Order 1999
revoked: 2003 c.43 s.7
Art.1, amended: SI 2002/1360 Art.2
Art.2, amended: SI 2002/1360 Art.2
Art.3, substituted: SI 2002/1360 Art.3

NO.

1999–cont.

3473. Worcestershire Acute Hospitals National Health Service Trust (Establishment) Order 1999

applied: SI 2003/3059 Sch.1

revoked: 2003 c.43 s.7

3483. Pesticides (Maximum Residue Levels in Crops, Food and Feeding Stuffs) (England and Wales) Regulations 1999

Reg.2, amended: SI 2002/1767 Reg.2, SI 2002/2723 Reg.2, SI 2003/661 Reg.2, SI 2003/2591 Reg.2, SI 2004/676 Reg.2, SI 2004/1393 Reg.2, SI 2004/2559 Reg.2

Reg.4, revoked (in part): SI 2003/661 Reg.2

Reg.6, amended: SI 2002/2723 Reg.2

Sch.1, amended: SI 2002/1767 Reg.2, SI 2002/2723 Reg.2, SI 2003/661 Reg.2, SI 2003/2591 Reg.2, SI 2004/676 Reg.2, SI 2004/1393 Reg.2, SI 2004/2559 Reg.2

Sch.2 Part 1, amended: SI 2002/1767 Reg.2, SI 2002/2723 Reg.2, SI 2003/661 Reg.2, SI 2003/2591 Reg.2, SI 2004/2559 Reg.2

Sch.2 Part 1, varied: SI 2004/676 Reg.2

Sch.2 Part 2, amended: SI 2002/1767 Reg.2, Sch.1, SI 2002/2723 Sch.1, SI 2003/661 Sch.1, SI 2003/2591 Reg.2, Sch.1, SI 2004/1393 Reg.2, Sch.1, SI 2004/2559 Reg.2, Sch.1

Sch.2 Part 2, referred to: SI 2004/676 Reg.2

Sch.2 Part 2, substituted: SI 2004/2559 Reg.2

Sch.2 Part 2, varied: SI 2004/676 Reg.2, Sch.1

3491. Family Proceedings (Amendment No.2) Rules 1999

r.2.69, see *Norris v Norris* [2003] EWCA Civ 1084, [2003] 1 W.L.R. 2960 (CA), Dame Elizabeth Butler-Sloss (President)

2000

Reg.12(5. Community Legal Service (Costs) Regulations 2000

see *Hill v Bailey* [2003] EWHC 2835, [2004] 1 All E.R. 1210 (Ch D), Lightman, J.

Reg.3(2. Welfare of Farmed Animals (England) Regulations 2000

see *R. (on the application of Compassion in World Farming Ltd) v Secretary of State for the Environment, Food and Rural Affairs* [2003] EWHC 2850, [2004] Eu. L.R. 382 (QBD (Admin Ct)), Newman, J.

11. Community Care (Direct Payments) Amendment Regulations 2000

revoked: SI 2003/762 Reg.12

22. Potatoes Originating in Egypt (Amendment) (England) Regulations 2000

revoked: SI 2004/1165 Reg.8

NO.

2000–cont.

51. Sea Fishing (Enforcement of Community Control Measures) Order 2000

Art.2, amended: SI 2003/229 Art.7, SI 2003/1535 Art.7, SI 2004/38 Art.3, SI 2004/398 Art.23, SR 2003/59 Art.7

Art.3, amended: SI 2004/398 Art.23

Sch.1, amended: SI 2003/229 Art.7, SI 2004/398 Art.23, SR 2003/59 Art.7

89. Primary Care Trusts (Membership, Procedure and Administration Arrangements) Regulations 2000

Reg.1, amended: SI 2002/881 Sch.1 para.19, SI 2002/2469 Sch.2, SI 2002/2861 Reg.33, SI 2003/1616 Reg.2, SI 2004/664 Sch.1 para.3, SI 2004/696 Art.3, Sch.1 para.33, SI 2004/865 Sch.1 para.23, SI 2004/1771 Sch.1 para.35

Reg.2, amended: SI 2002/557 Reg.2

Reg.2, applied: SI 2002/64 Art.4, SI 2002/65 Art.4, SI 2002/66 Art.4, SI 2002/67 Art.4, SI 2002/68 Art.4, SI 2002/69 Art.4, SI 2002/70 Art.4, SI 2002/71 Art.4, SI 2002/137 Art.4, SI 2002/138 Art.4, SI 2002/139 Art.4, SI 2002/140 Art.4, SI 2002/141 Art.4, SI 2002/142 Art.4, SI 2002/143 Art.4, SI 2002/144 Art.4, SI 2002/145 Art.4, SI 2002/146 Art.4, SI 2002/147 Art.4, SI 2002/148 Art.4, SI 2002/149 Art.4, SI 2002/150 Art.4, SI 2002/166 Art.4, SI 2002/356 Art.4, SI 2002/357 Art.4, SI 2002/358 Art.4, SI 2002/617 Art.4, SI 2002/634 Art.4, SI 2002/722 Art.4, SI 2002/723 Art.4, SI 2002/724 Art.4, SI 2002/725 Art.4, SI 2002/726 Art.4, SI 2002/727 Art.4, SI 2002/728 Art.4, SI 2002/894 Art.4, SI 2002/938 Art.4, SI 2002/939 Art.4, SI 2002/940 Art.4, SI 2002/941 Art.4, SI 2002/942 Art.4, SI 2002/943 Art.4, SI 2002/944 Art.4, SI 2002/945 Art.4, SI 2002/946 Art.4, SI 2002/947 Art.4, SI 2002/951 Art.4, SI 2002/957 Art.4, SI 2002/959 Art.4, SI 2002/997 Art.4

Reg.3, amended: SI 2002/557 Reg.3

Reg.4, amended: SI 2002/557 Reg.4

Reg.5, amended: SI 2002/880 Sch.1 para.11, SI 2002/881 Sch.1 para.20, SI 2002/2469 Sch.1 para.87, SI 2002/2861 Reg.33, SI 2003/1616 Reg.3, SI 2004/664 Sch.1 para.3, SI 2004/696 Art.3, Sch.1 para.33, SI 2004/865 Sch.1 para.23, SI 2004/1771 Sch.1 para.35

Reg.5, revoked (in part): SI 2002/557 Reg.5, SI 2003/1616 Reg.3

Reg.6, amended: SI 2003/1616 Reg.4

Reg.9, amended: SI 2003/1616 Reg.5

Reg.10, amended: SI 2003/1616 Reg.6

Reg.11, amended: SI 2003/1616 Reg.7

Reg.12, revoked: SI 2002/2375 Sch.4

Sch.1, amended: SI 2002/38 Reg.3, SI 2004/18 Reg.2

NO.

2000–cont.

123. Health Service Medicines (Control of Prices of Branded Medicines) Regulations 2000
Reg.2, amended: SI 2002/236 Reg.17
Reg.5, amended: SI 2004/865 Sch.1 para.24, SI 2004/1016 Sch.1 para.22

128. Pressure Systems Safety Regulations 2000
Reg.2, amended: SI 2004/568 Sch.13 para.10
Sch.1 Part I para.9, substituted: SI 2004/568 Sch.13 para.10
Sch.1 Part I para.13, substituted: SI 2004/568 Sch.13 para.10
Sch.1 Part II para.3, amended: SI 2004/568 Sch.13 para.10

136. Trade Marks Rules 2000
r.5, revoked (in part): SI 2004/947 r.3
r.8, amended: SI 2004/947 r.4
r.8A, added: SI 2004/947 r.5
r.11, amended: SI 2004/947 r.6
r.13, substituted: SI 2004/947 r.7
r.13C, disapplied: SI 2004/948 Art.8
r.14, amended: SI 2004/947 r.8
r.18, amended: SI 2004/947 r.9
r.21, amended: SI 2004/947 r.10
r.23, amended: SI 2004/947 r.11
r.25, amended: SI 2004/947 r.12
r.31, see *CB Richard Ellis Inc v Groupement Carte Bleue* [2002] R.P.C. 31 (TMR), A Knight
r.31, substituted: SI 2004/947 r.13
r.31A, substituted: SI 2004/947 r.13
r.31B, substituted: SI 2004/947 r.13
r.32, see *FIRETRACE Trade Mark* [2002] R.P.C. 15 (TMR), Mike Knight
r.32, substituted: SI 2004/947 r.13
r.32A, substituted: SI 2004/947 r.13
r.32B, substituted: SI 2004/947 r.13
r.33, see *FIRETRACE Trade Mark* [2002] R.P.C. 15 (TMR), Mike Knight
r.33, substituted: SI 2004/947 r.13
r.34, amended: SI 2004/947 r.14
r.35, amended: SI 2004/947 r.15
r.47, amended: SI 2004/947 r.16
r.54, see *Joop v Canadelle Ltd Partnership of Canada* [2002] R.P.C. 45 (Ch D), Pumfrey, J.; see *Nettec Solutions Ltd's Trade Mark Application* [2003] R.P.C. 17 (Appointed Person), Ruth Annand
r.55, see *Joop v Canadelle Ltd Partnership of Canada* [2002] R.P.C. 45 (Ch D), Pumfrey, J.
r.63, amended: SI 2004/947 r.17
r.65, substituted: SI 2004/947 r.18
r.68, see *FIRETRACE Trade Mark* [2002] R.P.C. 15 (TMR), Mike Knight
r.68, amended: SI 2004/947 r.19

155. Public Order (Prescribed Forms) Regulations (Northern Ireland) 2000
revoked: SI 2004/416 Reg.3

NO.

2000–cont.

157. Telecommunications (Data Protection and Privacy) (Amendment) Regulations 2000
revoked: SI 2003/2426 Reg.3

168. Immigration and Asylum Act 1999 (Commencement No.2 and Transitional Provisions) Order 2000
see *R. v Hobbs (Stephen Paul)* [2002] EWCA Crim 387, [2002] 2 Cr. App. R. 22 (CA (Crim Div)), Pill, L.J.

177. Firearms (Amendment) Act 1988(Firearms Consultative Committee) Order 2000
revoked: SI 2002/127 Art.3

181. Sea Fishing (Enforcement of Community Satellite Monitoring Measures) Order 2000
Art.4, amended: SI 2002/794 Sch.1 para.46

189. Data Protection Tribunal (Enforcement Appeals) Rules 2000
r.2, amended: SI 2002/2722 r.3
r.3, amended: SI 2002/2722 r.4
r.5, amended: SI 2002/2722 r.5
r.6, amended: SI 2002/2722 r.4
r.7, amended: SI 2002/2722 r.5
r.12, amended: SI 2002/2722 r.5, r.6
r.14, amended: SI 2002/2722 r.5
r.16, amended: SI 2002/2722 r.5
r.18, amended: SI 2002/2722 r.4, r.5
r.20, amended: SI 2002/2722 r.5
r.22, amended: SI 2002/2722 r.5

209. Hillingdon Primary Care Trust (Establishment) Order 2000
referred to: SI 2004/569 Sch.1
Art.1, amended: SI 2002/1405 Sch.1
Art.4, revoked: SI 2002/1405 Sch.1

210. South Manchester Primary Care Trust (Establishment) Order 2000
Art.1, amended: SI 2002/1405 Sch.1
Art.4, revoked: SI 2002/1405 Sch.1

211. Daventry and South Northamptonshire Primary Care Trust (Establishment) Order 2000
Art.1, amended: SI 2002/1405 Sch.1
Art.4, revoked: SI 2002/1405 Sch.1
Art.8, revoked: SI 2003/1740 Sch.1
Sch.1, amended: SI 2004/543 Sch.1

214. Major Precepting Authorities (Excessive Budget Requirements Payments) (England) Regulations 2000
revoked: 2003 c.26 Sch.8 Part 1

218. Central Derby Primary Care Trust (Establishment) Order 2000
Art.1, amended: SI 2002/1405 Sch.1
Art.4, revoked: SI 2002/1405 Sch.1
Art.8, revoked: SI 2003/1740 Sch.1
Sch.1, amended: SI 2002/1116 Art.2

219. North East Lincolnshire Primary Care Trust (Establishment) Order 2000
Art.1, amended: SI 2002/1405 Sch.1
Art.4, revoked: SI 2002/1405 Sch.1

NO.

2000–cont.

219. North East Lincolnshire Primary Care Trust (Establishment) Order 2000–
cont.
Art.8, revoked: SI 2003/1740 Sch.1
Sch.1, amended: SI 2004/543 Sch.1

220. National Health Service (General Medical Services) Amendment Regulations 2000
revoked: SI 2004/865 Sch.2

223. Newark and Sherwood Primary Care Trust (Establishment) Order 2000
Art.1, amended: SI 2002/1405 Sch.1
Art.4, revoked: SI 2002/1405 Sch.1
Art.8, revoked: SI 2003/1740 Sch.1

226. Mansfield District Primary Care Trust (Establishment) Order 2000
Art.1, amended: SI 2002/1405 Sch.1
Art.4, revoked: SI 2002/1405 Sch.1
Art.8, revoked: SI 2003/1740 Sch.1

227. Sea Fish (Specified Sea Areas) (Regulation of Nets and Other Fishing Gear) (Scotland) Order 2000
Art.4, see *Urquhart v Sinclair* 2003 S.L.T. 824 (HCJ), Lord Cullen L.J.G., Lord Caplan, Lord Marnoch

237. Maidstone and Tunbridge Wells National Health Service Trust (Establishment) Order 2000
revoked: 2003 c.43 s.7

238. Kent and Sussex Weald and the Mid Kent Healthcare National Health Service Trusts (Dissolution) Order 2000
revoked: 2003 c.43 s.7

251. Judicial Committee (Osteopaths Rules) Order 2000
revoked: 2002 c.17 Sch.9 Part 2

254. Nelson and West Merton Primary Care Trust (Establishment) Order 2000
Art.1, amended: SI 2002/1009 Art.2, SI 2002/1405 Sch.1
Art.2, amended: SI 2002/1009 Art.2
Art.4, revoked: SI 2002/1405 Sch.1
Art.8, revoked: SI 2002/1009 Art.3
Sch.1, substituted: SI 2002/1009 Art.3

255. Poole Bay Primary Care Trust (Establishment) Order 2000
revoked: SI 2002/1325 Sch.1

256. Poole Central and North Primary Care Trust (Establishment) Order 2000
revoked: SI 2002/1325 Sch.1

257. Southampton East Healthcare Primary Care Trust (Establishment) Order 2000
Art.1, amended: SI 2002/1405 Sch.1
Art.4, revoked: SI 2002/1405 Sch.1
Art.8, revoked: SI 2003/1740 Sch.1
Sch.1, substituted: SI 2002/729 Art.2

NO.

2000–cont.

260. Competition Act 1998 (Concurrency) Regulations 2000
revoked: SI 2004/1077 Reg.10

261. Competition Commission Appeal Tribunal Rules 2000
revoked: SI 2003/1372 r.70

varied: 2002 c.40 Sch.24 para.12, SI 2003/767 Art.2, SI 2003/1372 r.69

see *Freeserve.com Plc v Director General of Telecommunications (Application for Time Extension)* [2002] CAT 9, [2003] Comp. A.R. 57 (Competition Commission Appeal Tribunal), Sir Christopher Bellamy (President)

r.6, see *Hasbro UK Ltd v Director General of Fair Trading (Application for Time Extension)* [2003] CAT 1, [2003] Comp. A.R. 47 (Competition Commission Appeal Tribunal), Sir Christopher Bellamy (President)

r.10, see *Hasbro UK Ltd v Director General of Fair Trading (Withdrawal of Appeal: Costs)* [2003] Comp. A.R. 59 (Competition Commission Appeal Tribunal), Sir Christopher Bellamy (President)

r.16, see *Aberdeen Journals Ltd v Director General of Fair Trading (Preliminary Hearing: Jurisdiction)* [2002] Comp. A.R. 1 (Competition Commission Appeal Tribunal), Sir Christopher Bellamy Q.C. (President); see *BetterCare Group Ltd v Director General of Fair Trading (Preliminary Hearing: Jurisdiction)* [2002] Comp. A.R. 9 (CCAT), Sir Christopher Bellamy Q.C. (President)

r.26, see *Aberdeen Journals Ltd v Office of Fair Trading (Costs)* [2003] CAT 21, [2004] Comp. A.R. 189 (Competition Appeal Tribunal), Sir Christopher Bellamy (President); see *Aquavitae (UK) Ltd v Director General of Water Services (Costs)* [2003] CAT 23, [2004] Comp. A.R. 203 (Competition Appeal Tribunal), Sir Christopher Bellamy (President)

r.27, see *Aberdeen Journals Ltd v Director General of Fair Trading (Penalty: Calculation of Interest)* [2003] CAT 13, [2004] Comp. A.R. 69 (Competition Commission Appeal Tribunal), Sir Christopher Bellamy (President)

r.32, see *Genzyme Ltd v Office of Fair Trading (Disclosure of Confidential Information)* [2003] CAT 7, [2003] Comp. A.R. 288 (Competition Appeal Tribunal), Sir Christopher Bellamy (President)

262. Competition Act 1998 (Small Agreements and Conduct of Minor Significance) Regulations 2000
Sch.1 para.1, amended: SI 2002/765 Reg.8

2000–cont.

263. Competition Act 1998 (Notification of Excluded Agreements and Appealable Decisions) Regulations 2000

revoked: SI 2004/1078 Reg.3

264. Humber Bridge (Revision of Tolls and Vehicle Classification) Order 2000

see *R. (on the application of Confederation of Passenger Transport UK) v Humber Bridge Board* [2002] EWHC 2261, [2002] N.P.C. 136 (QBD (Admin Ct)), Newman, J.

265. Immigration (Regularisation Period for Overstayers) Regulations 2000

applied: SI 2003/754 Sch.2 para.2, Sch.2 para.3, Sch.2 para.6

283. North Peterborough Primary Care Trust (Establishment) Order 2000

Art.1, amended: SI 2002/1405 Sch.1
Art.4, revoked: SI 2002/1405 Sch.1
Art.8, revoked: SI 2003/1740 Sch.1
Sch.1, amended: SI 2004/543 Sch.1

284. South Peterborough Primary Care Trust (Establishment) Order 2000

Art.1, amended: SI 2002/1405 Sch.1
Art.4, revoked: SI 2002/1405 Sch.1
Art.8, revoked: SI 2003/1740 Sch.1
Sch.1, amended: SI 2004/543 Sch.1

285. Tendring Primary Care Trust (Establishment) Order 2000

Art.1, amended: SI 2002/1405 Sch.1
Art.4, revoked: SI 2002/1405 Sch.1
Art.8, revoked: SI 2003/1740 Sch.1
Sch.1, amended: SI 2004/543 Sch.1

286. Fenland Primary Care Trust (Establishment) Order 2000

Art.1, amended: SI 2002/1121 Art.2, SI 2002/1405 Sch.1
Art.2, amended: SI 2002/1121 Art.2
Art.4, revoked: SI 2002/1405 Sch.1
Art.8, revoked: SI 2003/1740 Sch.1
Sch.1, substituted: SI 2002/1121 Art.3

287. Epping Forest Primary Care Trust (Establishment) Order 2000

applied: SI 2003/3059 Sch.1
Art.1, amended: SI 2002/1405 Sch.1
Art.4, revoked: SI 2002/1405 Sch.1
Art.8, revoked: SI 2003/1740 Sch.1
Sch.1, amended: SI 2004/543 Sch.1

293. Competition Act 1998 (Director's rules) Order 2000

revoked: SI 2004/2751 Art.3

r.14, see *Argos Ltd v Office of Fair Trading (Case Management: New Material)* [2003] CAT 24, [2004] Comp. A.R. 212 (Competition Appeal Tribunal), Sir Christopher Bellamy (President); see *Claymore Dairies Ltd v Office of Fair Trading (Stay of Proceedings)* [2003] CAT 18, [2004] Comp. A.R. 177 (Competition Appeal Tribunal), Sir Christopher Bellamy (President); see *Freeserve.com Plc v Director General of Telecommunications (Application for*

2000–cont.

293. Competition Act 1998 (Director's rules) Order 2000–*cont.*

r.14–*cont.*
Further Time Extension) [2003] CAT 22, [2004] Comp. A.R. 199 (Competition Appeal Tribunal), Sir Christopher Bellamy (President); see *Pernod-Ricard SA v Office of Fair Trading (Admissibility: Initial Consideration)* [2003] CAT 19, [2004] Comp. A.R. 181 (Competition Appeal Tribunal), Sir Christopher Bellamy (President)

Sch.1 para.26, amended: SI 2003/1398 Sch.1 para.38

Sch.1 para.26, revoked (in part): SI 2003/1398 Sch.1 para.38

Sch.1 para.28, revoked: SI 2003/1398 Sch.1 para.38

Sch.1 para.30, amended: SI 2003/1398 Sch.1 para.38

294. Education (Exclusion from School) (Prescribed Periods) (Amendment) (England) Regulations 2000

revoked: SI 2002/3178 Reg.9

297. Education (Pupil Information) (England) Regulations 2000

Reg.2, amended: SI 2002/1680 Reg.3
Reg.10, amended: SI 2003/1006 Reg.3
Reg.10, substituted: SI 2002/1680 Reg.4
Sch.1 Part 1 para.1, amended: SI 2003/1006 Reg.4
Sch.1 Part 1 para.1, varied: SI 2004/1076 Reg.6
Sch.1 Part 1 para.2, amended: SI 2003/1006 Reg.4
Sch.1 Part 1 para.3, amended: SI 2003/1006 Reg.4
Sch.1 Part 2 para.5, amended: SI 2002/1680 Reg.5
Sch.2 para.1, revoked (in part): SI 2003/1006 Reg.5
Sch.2 para.1, varied: SI 2004/1076 Reg.6
Sch.2 para.3, amended: SI 2003/1006 Reg.5
Sch.3 para.1, amended: SI 2003/1006 Reg.6
Sch.3 para.1, varied: SI 2004/1076 Reg.6
Sch.3 para.3, amended: SI 2003/1006 Reg.6
Sch.5 Part 1 para.1, added: SI 2002/1680 Sch.1
Sch.5 Part 1 para.1, amended: SI 2003/1006 Reg.7
Sch.5 Part 1 para.1, varied: SI 2004/1076 Reg.6
Sch.5 Part 2 para.2, added: SI 2002/1680 Sch.1
Sch.5 Part 2 para.2, amended: SI 2003/1006 Reg.7
Sch.5 Part 2 para.2, varied: SI 2004/1076 Reg.6
Sch.5 Part 3 para.3, added: SI 2002/1680 Sch.1
Sch.5 Part 3 para.3, amended: SI 2003/1006 Reg.7

NO.

2000–cont.

297. Education (Pupil Information) (England) Regulations 2000–*cont.*

Sch.5 Part 3 para.3, varied: SI 2004/1076 Reg.6

Sch.5 Part 4 para.4, added: SI 2002/1680 Sch.1

Sch.5 Part 4 para.4, amended: SI 2003/1006 Reg.7

Sch.5 Part 4 para.4, varied: SI 2004/1076 Reg.6

Sch.5 Part 5 para.5, added: SI 2002/1680 Sch.1

Sch.5 Part 5 para.5, amended: SI 2003/1006 Reg.7

Sch.5 Part 5 para.5, varied: SI 2004/1076 Reg.6

299. Water Undertakers (Rateable Values) (Wales) Order 2000

Art.2, amended: SI 2003/944 Art.2

Art.5, amended: SI 2003/944 Art.2

Art.7, amended: SI 2003/944 Art.2

300. Crime and Disorder Strategies (Prescribed Descriptions) (Amendment) Order 2000

revoked (in part): SI 2004/118 Art.4

307. Southend on Sea Primary Care Trust (Establishment) Order 2000

Art.1, amended: SI 2002/1405 Sch.1

Art.4, revoked: SI 2002/1405 Sch.1

Sch.1, amended: SI 2004/543 Sch.1

308. Greater London Authority (Elections and Acceptance of Office) Order 2000

revoked: SI 2002/1044 Art.3

309. Competition Act 1998 (Determination of Turnover for Penalties) Order 2000

Art.2, amended: SI 2004/1259 Art.2

Art.3, substituted: SI 2004/1259 Art.2

Sch.1 para.1, amended: SI 2004/1259 Art.2

Sch.1 para.3, amended: SI 2004/1259 Art.2

Sch.1 para.5, amended: SI 2004/1259 Art.2

Sch.1 para.6, amended: SI 2004/1259 Art.2

310. Competition Act 1998 (Land and Vertical Agreements Exclusion) Order 2000

revoked: SI 2004/1260 Art.2

see *Vendo Plc v Adams* [2002] N.I. 95 (Ch D (NI)), Girvan, J.

311. Competition Act 1998 (Transitional, Consequential and Supplemental Provisions) Order 2000

Art.9, revoked (in part): 2002 c.40 Sch.26, SI 2003/1398 Sch.1 para.39, SI 2003/3180 Sch.1 para.8

Art.31, revoked: SI 2003/1398 Sch.1 para.39

312. London Borough of Bexley (Electoral Changes) Order 2000

varied: SI 2004/222 Art.2

313. London Borough of Havering (Electoral Changes) Order 2000

varied: SI 2004/222 Art.2

NO.

2000–cont.

314. London Borough of Richmond upon Thames (Electoral Changes) Order 2000

varied: SI 2004/222 Art.2

315. London Borough of Wandsworth (Electoral Changes) Order 2000

varied: SI 2004/222 Art.2

316. London Borough of Harrow (Electoral Changes) Order 2000

varied: SI 2004/222 Art.2

317. London Borough of Hounslow (Electoral Changes) Order 2000

varied: SI 2004/222 Art.2

318. London Borough of Merton (Electoral Changes) Order 2000

varied: SI 2004/222 Art.2

319. London Borough of Lambeth (Electoral Changes) Order 2000

varied: SI 2004/222 Art.2

333. London Borough of Barnet (Electoral Changes) Order 2000

varied: SI 2004/222 Art.2

334. London Borough of Ealing (Electoral Changes) Order 2000

varied: SI 2004/222 Art.2

335. London Borough of Redbridge (Electoral Changes) Order 2000

varied: SI 2004/222 Art.2

336. London Borough of Waltham Forest (Electoral Changes) Order 2000

varied: SI 2004/222 Art.2

339. Local Government Best Value (Exemption) (England) Order 2000

revoked: SI 2003/3343 Art.3

350. Potatoes Originating in Egypt (Amendment) (Wales) Regulations 2000

revoked: SI 2004/2245 Reg.8

352. BG plc (Rateable Value) (Wales) Order 2000

Art.3, amended: SI 2003/944 Art.3

369. Competition Act 1998 (Determination of Turnover for Penalties) Order 2000

Sch.1, amended: SI 2002/765 Reg.9

375. Food (Peanuts from Egypt) (Emergency Control) (England and Wales) Order 2000

revoked (in part): SI 2003/2074 Reg.7, SI 2003/2910 Reg.7

388. Weighing Equipment (Automatic Gravimetric Filling Instruments) Regulations 2000

Reg.8, amended: SI 2003/214 Sch.1 para.8

406. South Essex Mental Health and Community Care National Health Service Trust (Establishment) Order 2000

revoked: 2003 c.43 s.7

Art.1, amended: SI 2002/1498 Art.2

Art.2, amended: SI 2002/1498 Art.2

Art.3, amended: SI 2004/2897 Art.2

NO.

2000–cont.

406. South Essex Mental Health and Community Care National Health Service Trust (Establishment) Order 2000–*cont.*

Art.4, amended: SI 2004/2897 Art.3

407. Southend Community Care Services and the Thameside Community Healthcare National Health Service Trusts (Dissolution) Order 2000

revoked: 2003 c.43 s.7

410. United Lincolnshire Hospitals National Health Service Trust (Establishment) Order 2000

revoked: 2003 c.43 s.7

411. Grantham and District Hospital, the Lincoln and Louth and the Pilgrim Health National Health Service Trusts (Dissolution) Order 2000

revoked: 2003 c.43 s.7

415. Data Protection (Subject Access Modification) (Social Work) Order 2000

Sch.1 para.1, amended: SI 2002/2469 Sch.1 para.88, SI 2002/3220 Art.3, SI 2004/696 Sch.1 para.34

426. Channel Tunnel (Alcoholic Liquor and Tobacco Products) Order 2000

revoked: SI 2003/2758 Art.6

Art.2, revoked: SI 2002/2693 Art.3

Art.3, substituted: SI 2002/2693 Art.4

Art.4, amended: SI 2002/2693 Art.5

Art.5, amended: SI 2002/2693 Art.5, Art.6

Art.5A, added: SI 2002/2693 Art.7

Art.6, revoked (in part): SI 2002/2693 Art.8

Sch.1 para.1, substituted: SI 2002/2693 Art.9

Sch.1 para.2, substituted: SI 2002/2693 Art.9

Sch.1 para.3, substituted: SI 2002/2693 Art.9

Sch.1 para.4, substituted: SI 2002/2693 Art.9

Sch.1 para.5, substituted: SI 2002/2693 Art.9

Sch.1 para.6, substituted: SI 2002/2693 Art.9

Sch.1 para.7, substituted: SI 2002/2693 Art.9

Sch.1 para.8, substituted: SI 2002/2693 Art.9

Sch.1 para.9, substituted: SI 2002/2693 Art.9

Sch.2 para.1, amended: SI 2002/2693 Art.10

Sch.2 para.2, amended: SI 2002/2693 Art.11

427. Greater London Authority Elections (No.2) Rules 2000

r.4., varied: SI 2002/185 Sch.3 Part I

r.5., substituted: SI 2004/227 r.2

r.7., revoked: SI 2004/227 r.3

r.8., substituted: SI 2004/227 r.2

r.8., varied: SI 2002/185 Sch.3 Part I

r.9, added: SI 2004/227 r.2

Sch.1 Part IV para.20, substituted: SI 2004/227 Sch.1 para.1

NO.

2000–cont.

427. Greater London Authority Elections (No.2) Rules 2000–*cont.*

Sch.1 Part IV para.23A, added: SI 2004/227 Sch.1 para.2

Sch.1 Part IV para.24, amended: SI 2004/227 Sch.1 para.3

Sch.1 Part IV para.24A, added: SI 2004/227 Sch.1 para.4

Sch.1 Part IV para.26, amended: SI 2004/227 Sch.1 para.5

Sch.1 Part IV para.27, amended: SI 2004/227 Sch.1 para.6

Sch.1 Part IV para.34, substituted: SI 2004/227 Sch.1 para.7

Sch.1 Part IV para.38, amended: SI 2004/227 Sch.1 para.8

Sch.1 Part IV para.39, amended: SI 2004/227 Sch.1 para.9

Sch.1 Part IV para.40, amended: SI 2004/227 Sch.1 para.10

Sch.1 Part IV para.41, amended: SI 2004/227 Sch.1 para.11

Sch.1 Part VI para.48, amended: SI 2004/227 Sch.1 para.12

Sch.1 Part VI para.49, amended: SI 2004/227 Sch.1 para.13

Sch.1 Part VI para.50, amended: SI 2004/227 Sch.1 para.14

Sch.2 Part IV para.20, substituted: SI 2004/227 Sch.2 para.1

Sch.2 Part IV para.24A, added: SI 2004/227 Sch.2 para.2

Sch.2 Part IV para.25, amended: SI 2004/227 Sch.2 para.3

Sch.2 Part IV para.25A, added: SI 2004/227 Sch.2 para.4

Sch.2 Part IV para.26, amended: SI 2004/227 Sch.2 para.5

Sch.2 Part IV para.27, amended: SI 2004/227 Sch.2 para.6

Sch.2 Part IV para.28, amended: SI 2004/227 Sch.2 para.7

Sch.2 Part IV para.35, substituted: SI 2004/227 Sch.2 para.8

Sch.2 Part IV para.39, amended: SI 2004/227 Sch.2 para.9

Sch.2 Part IV para.40, amended: SI 2004/227 Sch.2 para.10

Sch.2 Part IV para.41, amended: SI 2004/227 Sch.2 para.11

Sch.2 Part IV para.42, amended: SI 2004/227 Sch.2 para.12

Sch.2 Part IV para.44, amended: SI 2004/227 Sch.2 para.13

Sch.2 Part VI para.51, amended: SI 2004/227 Sch.2 para.14

Sch.2 Part VI para.52, amended: SI 2004/227 Sch.2 para.15

Sch.2 Part VI para.53, amended: SI 2004/227 Sch.2 para.16

NO.

NO.

2000–cont.

427. Greater London Authority Elections (No.2) Rules 2000–*cont.*

Sch.2 PartVIII para.59, revoked: SI 2004/227 Sch.2 para.17

Sch.3 Part IV para.20, substituted: SI 2004/227 Sch.3 para.1

Sch.3 Part IV para.24A, added: SI 2004/227 Sch.3 para.2

Sch.3 Part IV para.25, amended: SI 2004/227 Sch.3 para.3

Sch.3 Part IV para.25A, added: SI 2004/227 Sch.3 para.4

Sch.3 Part IV para.26, amended: SI 2004/227 Sch.3 para.5

Sch.3 Part IV para.27, amended: SI 2004/227 Sch.3 para.6

Sch.3 Part IV para.28, amended: SI 2004/227 Sch.3 para.7

Sch.3 Part IV para.35, substituted: SI 2004/227 Sch.3 para.8

Sch.3 Part IV para.39, amended: SI 2004/227 Sch.3 para.9

Sch.3 Part IV para.40, amended: SI 2004/227 Sch.3 para.10

Sch.3 Part IV para.41, amended: SI 2004/227 Sch.3 para.11

Sch.3 Part IV para.42, amended: SI 2004/227 Sch.3 para.12

Sch.3 Part IV para.44, amended: SI 2004/227 Sch.3 para.13

Sch.3 Part IV para.46, amended: SI 2004/227 Sch.3 para.14

Sch.3 Part VII para.53, amended: SI 2004/227 Sch.3 para.15

Sch.3 Part VII para.54, amended: SI 2004/227 Sch.3 para.16

Sch.3 Part VII para.55, amended: SI 2004/227 Sch.3 para.17

Sch.5, amended: SI 2004/227 Sch.4 para.1, Sch.4 para.2, Sch.4 para.3, Sch.4 para.4, Sch.4 para.5, Sch.4 para.6, Sch.4 para.7, Sch.4 para.8, Sch.4 para.9

Sch.7 Part I para.1, revoked: SI 2004/227 r.3

Sch.7 Part I para.2, revoked: SI 2004/227 r.3

Sch.7 Part I para.3, revoked: SI 2004/227 r.3

Sch.7 Part II para.1, revoked: SI 2004/227 r.3

Sch.7 Part II para.2, revoked: SI 2004/227 r.3

Sch.7 Part II para.3, revoked: SI 2004/227 r.3

Sch.7 Part II para.4, revoked: SI 2004/227 r.3

Sch.7 Part II para.5, revoked: SI 2004/227 r.3

Sch.8, substituted: SI 2004/227 Sch.5

Sch.8 para.1, substituted: SI 2004/227 Sch.5

Sch.8 para.2, substituted: SI 2004/227 Sch.5

Sch.8 para.2, varied: SI 2002/185 Sch.3 Part I

Sch.12 para.1, added: SI 2004/227 Sch.6

Sch.12 para.2, added: SI 2004/227 Sch.6

Sch.12 para.3, added: SI 2004/227 Sch.6

Sch.12 para.4, added: SI 2004/227 Sch.6

Sch.12 para.5, added: SI 2004/227 Sch.6

2000–cont.

427. Greater London Authority Elections (No.2) Rules 2000–*cont.*

Sch.12 para.6, added: SI 2004/227 Sch.6

Sch.12 para.7, added: SI 2004/227 Sch.6

Sch.12 para.8, added: SI 2004/227 Sch.6

Sch.12 para.9, added: SI 2004/227 Sch.6

Sch.12 para.10, added: SI 2004/227 Sch.6

428. Knowsley Industrial Park (Rail Terminal) Order 2000

Art.2, amended: SI 2003/2155 Sch.2

Sch.4 para.1, amended: SI 2003/2155 Sch.1 para.17, Sch.2

441. Community Legal Service (Costs) Regulations 2000

referred to: SI 2003/649 Reg.2

Reg.2, amended: SI 2003/649 Reg.3

Reg.4, applied: SI 2003/421 r.47

Reg.7, amended: SI 2003/649 Reg.4

Reg.10, amended: SI 2003/649 Reg.5

476. Croydon Tramlink (Penalty Fares) Order 2000

revoked: SI 2003/1614 Art.3

478. Financing of Maintained Schools (England) Regulations 2000

applied: SI 2002/377 Reg.24, Reg.25, Reg.32, SI 2003/3247 Reg.23, Reg.24, Reg.28

revoked: SI 2002/377 Reg.2

Reg.18, applied: SI 2002/377 Reg.25, SI 2003/453 Reg.24, SI 2003/3247 Reg.24

479. Community Health Councils Amendment (Wales) Regulations 2000

revoked: SI 2004/905 Reg.31

480. Animals (Scientific Procedures) Act 1986 (Fees) Order 2000

Art.2, amended: SI 2002/473 Art.2

Art.3, amended: SI 2002/473 Art.2

516. Community Legal Service (Financial) Regulations 2000

referred to: SI 2002/709 Reg.2, SI 2003/650 Reg.2, SI 2004/2899 Reg.4

Part II, added: SI 2003/2838 Reg.3

Part II, added: SI 2004/2899 Reg.2

Reg.2, amended: SI 2003/650 Reg.3

Reg.3, amended: SI 2002/709 Reg.4

Reg.4, amended: SI 2002/709 Reg.5, SI 2003/650 Reg.4

Reg.5, amended: SI 2002/709 Reg.6, SI 2003/650 Reg.5

Reg.5A, amended: SI 2002/709 Reg.7, SI 2002/1766 Reg.4, SI 2003/650 Reg.6

Reg.5B, amended: SI 2003/650 Reg.7

Reg.5B, revoked (in part): SI 2003/650 Reg.7

Reg.19, amended: SI 2002/709 Reg.8, SI 2002/1766 Reg.5, SI 2003/762 Reg.11, SI 2004/1748 Sch.2 para.1, SI 2004/2899 Reg.3

Reg.33, amended: SI 2003/762 Reg.11, SI 2004/1748 Sch.2 para.1

Reg.35, amended: SI 2002/709 Reg.9

2000–cont.

516. Community Legal Service (Financial) Regulations 2000–cont.
Reg.38, amended: SI 2002/709 Reg.10, SI 2003/650 Reg.8, Reg.9, SI 2003/2838 Reg.4
Reg.43, amended: SI 2003/650 Reg.10

522. East London and The City Mental Health National Health Service Trust (Establishment) Order 2000
revoked: 2003 c.43 s.7

534. Council Tax and Non-Domestic Rating (Demand Notices) (England) (Amendment) (No.2) Regulations 2000
revoked: SI 2002/180 Sch.1

535. East and North Hertfordshire National Health Service Trust (Establishment) Order 2000
revoked: 2003 c.43 s.7

536. East Hertfordshire and the North Hertfordshire National Health Service Trusts (Dissolution) Order 2000
revoked: 2003 c.43 s.7

541. Asylum Support Appeals (Procedure) Rules 2000
r.3, amended: SI 2003/1735 r.3
r.4, amended: SI 2003/1735 r.4
r.6, amended: SI 2003/1735 r.5, r.6
r.13, amended: SI 2003/1735 r.7
Sch.1, amended: SI 2003/1735 Sch.1

555. Railtrack plc (Rateable Value) (Wales) Order 2000
Art.2, amended: SI 2003/944 Art.4
Art.5, amended: SI 2003/944 Art.4

595. National Health Service Trusts and Primary Care Trusts (Pharmaceutical Services Remuneration Special Arrangement) Order 2000
revoked: SI 2002/2469 Reg.19

601. National Health Service (General Medical Services) Amendment (No.2) Regulations 2000
revoked: SI 2004/865 Sch.2

605. National Health Service (Pension Scheme and Compensation for Premature Retirement) Amendment Regulations 2000
Reg.1, amended: SI 2002/1311 Sch.2
Reg.16, revoked: SI 2002/1311 Sch.2

617. NHS Bodies and Local Authorities Partnership Arrangements Regulations 2000
Reg.2, amended: SI 2002/2469 Sch.7, SI 2003/629 Reg.2
Reg.3, amended: SI 2003/629 Reg.3, SI 2004/696 Sch.1 para.35
Reg.3, revoked (in part): SI 2002/2469 Sch.1 para.89
Reg.4, amended: SI 2002/2469 Sch.7, SI 2003/629 Reg.4

2000–cont.

617. NHS Bodies and Local Authorities Partnership Arrangements Regulations 2000–cont.
Reg.6, amended: SI 2003/629 Reg.5
Reg.7, amended: SI 2002/2469 Sch.7
Reg.8, amended: SI 2003/629 Reg.6
Reg.9, amended: SI 2002/2469 Sch.7, SI 2003/629 Reg.7

618. National Health Service (Payments by Local Authorities to NHS Bodies) (Prescribed Functions) Regulations 2000
Reg.2, amended: SI 2004/865 Sch.1 para.25

619. National Health Service Pension Scheme (Additional Voluntary Contributions) Regulations 2000
Reg.2, amended: SI 2002/610 Reg.3
Reg.6, amended: SI 2002/610 Reg.4
Reg.10, substituted: SI 2002/610 Reg.5
Sch.1 Part II para.13, amended: SI 2002/610 Reg.6

620. National Health Service (Charges for Drugs and Appliances) Regulations 2000
applied: SI 2003/2382 Reg.4
referred to: SI 2003/1084 Reg.1
Reg.2, amended: SI 2002/548 Reg.2, SI 2002/2352 Reg.2, SI 2003/699 Reg.4, SI 2003/1084 Reg.18, SI 2004/663 Reg.3, SI 2004/696 Art.3, SI 2004/865 Sch.1 para.26, SI 2004/1771 Sch.1 para.34
Reg.2, revoked (in part): SI 2002/548 Reg.2
Reg.3, amended: SI 2002/548 Reg.3, SI 2002/2352 Reg.3, SI 2003/585 Reg.2, SI 2003/1084 Reg.19, SI 2004/663 Reg.2, SI 2004/865 Sch.1 para.26
Reg.3, referred to: SI 2003/2382 Reg.5
Reg.4, amended: SI 2002/548 Reg.4, SI 2002/1386 Reg.2, SI 2002/2352 Reg.4, SI 2003/585 Reg.2, SI 2004/663 Reg.2, SI 2004/865 Sch.1 para.26
Reg.5, amended: SI 2002/548 Reg.5, SI 2002/2352 Reg.5, SI 2003/585 Reg.2, SI 2004/663 Reg.2, SI 2004/696 Art.3
Reg.6, amended: SI 2002/548 Reg.6, SI 2002/2352 Reg.6, SI 2003/585 Reg.2, SI 2003/699 Reg.4, SI 2004/663 Reg.2, SI 2004/696 Art.3, SI 2004/865 Sch.1 para.26
Reg.6A, amended: SI 2002/548 Reg.7, SI 2003/585 Reg.2, SI 2004/663 Reg.2
Reg.7, amended: SI 2002/2352 Reg.7, SI 2004/696 Art.3
Reg.7A, added: SI 2004/663 Reg.3
Reg.8, amended: SI 2002/2352 Reg.8
Reg.9, amended: SI 2002/548 Reg.8, SI 2002/2352 Reg.9, SI 2003/585 Reg.2, SI 2004/663 Reg.2
Reg.10, amended: SI 2002/2352 Reg.10, SI 2004/696 Art.3
Reg.11, amended: SI 2002/2352 Reg.11, SI 2004/696 Art.3

NO.

2000–cont.

620. National Health Service (Charges for Drugs and Appliances) Regulations 2000–*cont.*

Sch.1, amended: SI 2002/548 Reg.9, SI 2003/585 Reg.2, SI 2004/663 Reg.2

Sch.1, referred to: SI 2003/2382 Reg.6

621. National Health Service (Travelling Expenses and Remission of Charges) Amendment Regulations 2000

revoked: SI 2003/2382 Sch.2

622. Local Authorities (Members Allowances) (Amendment) (England) Regulations 2000

revoked: SI 2003/1021 Reg.33

623. Local Authorities (Members Allowances) (Amendment) (England) (No.2) Regulations 2000

revoked: SI 2003/1021 Reg.33

627. Community Legal Service (Funding) Order 2000

referred to: SI 2003/651 Art.2, SI 2003/851 Art.2

Art.5, amended: SI 2003/651 Art.3, Art.4, Art.5, SI 2003/851 Art.3, SI 2004/597 Art.3, SI 2004/2900 Art.2, Art.3, Art.4

Art.6, amended: SI 2003/651 Art.6

Art.7, amended: SI 2004/2900 Art.5

Sch.1 Part V, amended: SI 2004/2900 Art.6

630. Wireless Telegraphy (Television Licence Fees) (Amendment) Regulations 2000

revoked: SI 2004/692 Sch.6

636. Social Security (Immigration and Asylum) Consequential Amendments Regulations 2000

Reg.1, amended: SI 2003/492 Sch.3 Part 1

Reg.2, amended: SI 2002/2497 Sch.2 para.1, SI 2003/2274 Reg.6

Reg.5, revoked (in part): SI 2003/492 Sch.3 Part 1

Reg.12, amended: SI 2002/2497 Sch.2 para.1

Reg.12, applied: SI 2003/653 Reg.5

Reg.12, revoked (in part): 2004 c.19 s.12

Sch.1 Part II para.1, amended: SI 2002/2497 Sch.2 para.1

Sch.1 Part II para.2, amended: SI 2002/2497 Sch.2 para.1

Sch.1 Part II para.3, amended: SI 2002/2497 Sch.2 para.1

Sch.1 Part II para.4, amended: SI 2002/2497 Sch.2 para.1

639. County Court Fees (Amendment) Order 2000

revoked: SI 2004/3121 Sch.2

640. Family Proceedings Fees (Amendment) Order 2000

revoked: SI 2004/3114 Sch.2

641. Supreme Court Fees (Amendment) Order 2000

revoked: SI 2004/3121 Sch.2

NO.

2000–cont.

645. Excise Goods (Export Shops) Regulations 2000

referred to: SI 2004/1003 Reg.7

656. Food Standards Act 1999 (Transitional and Consequential Provisions and Savings) (England and Wales) Regulations 2000

referred to: SI 2004/2146

Reg.14, applied: SI 2002/892, SI 2003/1296, SI 2003/1503, SI 2003/1850, SI 2003/2912, SI 2003/3119, SI 2004/1301, SI 2004/2688

661. National Health Service (Functions of Health Authorities) (Prescribing Incentive Schemes) Amendment Regulations 2000

revoked: SI 2004/865 Sch.2

662. Commission for Health Improvement (Functions) Regulations 2000

revoked (in part): SI 2003/1587 Reg.23

Reg.1, amended: SI 2002/2469 Sch.1 para.90, SI 2002/2861 Reg.34

Reg.2, amended: SI 2002/2469 Sch.1 para.90

Reg.2, applied: SI 2003/993 Reg.4, Reg.10, Reg.19, Reg.21

Reg.2, revoked (in part): SI 2002/2469 Sch.1 para.90

Reg.8, amended: SI 2002/2469 Sch.3

Reg.9, amended: SI 2002/2469 Sch.3

Reg.12, amended: SI 2002/2469 Sch.1 para.90, Sch.3

Reg.13, amended: SI 2002/2469 Sch.3

Reg.14, amended: SI 2002/2469 Sch.1 para.90

Reg.15, amended: SI 2002/2469 Sch.1 para.90

Reg.16, amended: SI 2002/2469 Sch.3

685. Carriers Liability (Clandestine Entrants and Sale of Transporters) Regulations 2000

revoked: SI 2002/2817 Reg.15

687. Scotland Act 1998 (Designation of Receipts) Order 2000

revoked: SI 2004/953 Art.3

688. Social Security (Maternity Allowance) (Earnings) Regulations 2000

Reg.2, amended: SI 2002/2690 Reg.16

Reg.3, amended: SI 2002/2690 Reg.17

Reg.4, amended: SI 2002/2690 Reg.18

Reg.4, revoked (in part): SI 2002/2690 Reg.18

Reg.5, substituted: SI 2002/2690 Reg.19, SI 2003/659 Reg.2

Reg.6, amended: SI 2002/2690 Reg.20, SI 2003/659 Reg.3

692. Conditional Fee Agreements Regulations 2000

see *Benaim UK Ltd v Davies Middleton & Davies Ltd* [2004] EWHC 737, (2004) 154 N.L.J. 617 (QBD (T&CC)), Judge

2000–cont.

692. Conditional Fee Agreements Regulations 2000–cont.

see–cont.

Rich Q.C.; see *Hollins v Russell* [2003] EWCA Civ 718, [2003] 1 W.L.R. 2487 (CA), Brooke, L.J.; see *Thornley v Lang* [2003] EWCA Civ 1484, [2004] 1 W.L.R. 378 (CA), Lord Phillips of Worth Matravers, M.R.

Reg.1, see *Sharratt v London Central Bus Co Ltd (No.1)* [2003] 1 All E.R. 353 (Supreme Court Costs Office), Chief Master Hurst

Reg.2, see *Myler v Williams* [2003] EWHC 1587, [2003] 4 Costs L.R. 566 (QBD), Crane, J.

Reg.3A, added: SI 2003/1240 Reg.2

Reg.3A, amended: SI 2003/3344 Reg.2

Reg.4, see *Sharratt v London Central Bus Co Ltd (No.1)* [2003] 1 All E.R. 353 (Supreme Court Costs Office), Chief Master Hurst

Reg.6, amended: SI 2003/1240 Reg.2

695. Primary Care Trusts (Functions) (England) Regulations 2000

revoked: SI 2002/2375 Sch.4

Reg.2, amended: SI 2002/555 Reg.2

Reg.3, amended: SI 2002/555 Reg.3

Reg.3, revoked (in part): SI 2002/555 Reg.3

Reg.4, revoked (in part): SI 2002/555 Reg.4

Sch.3, amended: SI 2002/555 Reg.5

Sch.4, amended: SI 2002/555 Reg.6

696. Health Authorities (Membership and Procedure) Amendment Regulations 2000

Reg.1, amended: SI 2003/506 Sch.2

Sch.1 para.5, revoked: SI 2003/506 Sch.2

698. Dairy Produce Quotas (Amendment) (England) Regulations 2000

revoked: SI 2002/457 Sch.4

701. Homeless (England) Regulations 2000

Reg.3 Class E, see *Kaya v Haringey LBC* [2001] EWCA Civ 677, [2002] H.L.R. 1 (CA), Buxton, L.J.

701. Homelessness (England) Regulations 2000

Reg.4, substituted: SI 2004/1235 Reg.3

702. Allocation of Housing (England) Regulations 2000

revoked: SI 2002/3264 Reg.6

704. Asylum Support Regulations 2000

see *R. (on the application of T) v Secretary of State for Health* [2002] EWHC 1887, (2003) 6 C.C.L. Rep. 277 (QBD (Admin Ct)), Sir Edwin Jowitt

Reg.3, amended: SI 2002/3110 Reg.2

Reg.6, see *R. (on the application of Mani) v Lambeth LBC* [2002] EWHC 735, (2002) 5 C.C.L. Rep. 486 (QBD (Admin Ct)), Wilson, J.; see *R. (on the application of Westminster City Council) v National Asylum Support Service* [2002] UKHL 38,

2000–cont.

704. Asylum Support Regulations 2000–cont.

Reg.6–cont.

[2002] 1 W.L.R. 2956 (HL), Lord Hoffmann

Reg.10, amended: SI 2002/472 Reg.4, SI 2002/2619 Reg.2, SI 2003/755 Reg.2, SI 2004/763 Reg.2, SI 2004/1313 Reg.2

Reg.10, revoked (in part): SI 2002/472 Reg.4

Reg.10A, added: SI 2003/241 Reg.2

Reg.10A, amended: SI 2004/1313 Reg.3

Reg.11, amended: SI 2002/472 Reg.4

Reg.11, revoked: SI 2004/1313 Reg.4

Reg.13, see *R. (on the application of Hetoja) v Secretary of State for the Home Department* [2002] EWHC 2146, Times, November 11, 2002 (QBD (Admin Ct)), Lightman, J.

Reg.23, see *R. (on the application of Mani) v Lambeth LBC* [2002] EWHC 735, (2002) 5 C.C.L. Rep. 486 (QBD (Admin Ct)), Wilson, J.

Sch.1, amended: SI 2002/3110 Sch.1 para.2, Sch.1 para.3, Sch.1 para.4, Sch.1 para.5, Sch.1 para.6, Sch.1 para.7, Sch.1 para.8, SI 2004/1313 Reg.5

Sch.1, referred to: SI 2002/3110 Sch.1 para.1

718. Revenue Support Grant (Specified Bodies) (Wales) Regulations 2000

Reg.3, amended: SI 2003/706 Reg.2

Reg.3, revoked (in part): SI 2003/706 Reg.2

720. Relocation Grants (Form of Application) (Amendment) (England) Regulations 2000

revoked: SI 2002/1860 Sch.6

721. Employment Zones Regulations 2000

applied: SI 2002/2005 Reg.4, SI 2003/2438 Reg.2, SI 2004/934 Reg.3

revoked: SI 2003/2438 Reg.8

727. Social Security Contributions (Intermediaries) Regulations 2000

referred to: SI 2003/2079 Reg.3

see *R. (on the application of Professional Contractors Group Ltd) v Inland Revenue Commissioners* [2001] EWCA Civ 1945, [2002] S.T.C. 165 (CA), Robert Walker, L.J.

Reg.2, amended: SI 2002/703 Reg.3, SI 2002/705 Reg.3, SI 2003/2079 Reg.4, SI 2004/770 Reg.35

Reg.3, amended: SI 2004/770 Reg.35

Reg.4, amended: SI 2004/770 Reg.35

Reg.5, amended: SI 2004/770 Reg.35

Reg.6, amended: SI 2003/2079 Reg.5

Reg.6, see *FS Consulting Ltd v McCaul (Inspector of Taxes)* [2002] S.T.C. (S.C.D.) 138 (Sp Comm), Nuala Brice; see *Synaptek Ltd v Young (Inspector of Taxes)* [2003] EWHC 645, [2003] S.T.C. 543 (Ch D), Hart, J.; see *Tilbury Consulting Ltd v Gittins (Inspector of Taxes) (No.2)* [2004] S.T.C. (S.C.D.) 72 (Sp Comm), Stephen Oliver Q.C.; see *Usetech Ltd v Young*

NO.

NO.

2000–cont.

727. Social Security Contributions (Inter-mediaries) Regulations 2000–*cont.*

Reg.6–*cont.*

(Inspector of Taxes) [2004] EWHC 2248, [2004] S.T.C.1671 (Ch D), Park, J.

Reg.7, amended: SI 2002/703 Reg.4, Reg.5, SI 2002/705 Reg.4, Reg.5, SI 2003/2079 Reg.6, SI 2004/770 Reg.35

Reg.7, applied: SI 2003/2079 Reg.7

Reg.7, varied: SI 2003/2079 Reg.7

Reg.8, amended: SI 2002/703 Reg.6, SI 2002/705 Reg.6

Reg.8, varied: SI 2003/2079 Reg.7

728. Social Security Contributions (Inter-mediaries) (Northern Ireland) Regula-tions 2000

referred to: SI 2003/2080 Reg.3

Reg.2, amended: SI 2003/2080 Reg.4, SI 2004/770 Reg.35

Reg.3, amended: SI 2004/770 Reg.35

Reg.4, amended: SI 2004/770 Reg.35

Reg.5, amended: SI 2004/770 Reg.35

Reg.6, amended: SI 2003/2080 Reg.5

Reg.7, amended: SI 2003/2080 Reg.6, SI 2004/770 Reg.35

Reg.7, varied: SI 2003/2080 Reg.7

Reg.8, varied: SI 2003/2080 Reg.7

729. Social Fund Winter Fuel Payment Regulations 2000

applied: 2004 c.10 s.3

referred to: 2004 c.10 s.3

Reg.1, amended: SI 2003/1121 Reg.5, SI 2004/2154 Reg.2

Reg.2, amended: SI 2002/2660 Reg.3, SI 2003/2192 Reg.2, SI 2004/2154 Reg.2

Reg.2, substituted: SI 2003/1737 Reg.2

Reg.3, amended: SI 2004/2154 Reg.2

Reg.4, amended: SI 2004/2154 Reg.2

730. Radio Equipment and Telecommuni-cations Terminal Equipment Regula-tions 2000

referred to: SI 2004/693 Sch.1

varied: SI 2003/3144 Reg.2

Reg.1, amended: SI 2003/1903 Reg.2

Reg.2, amended: SI 2003/1903 Reg.2, SI 2003/3144 Reg.2

Reg.2, referred to: SI 2003/1903 Reg.3

Reg.3, amended: SI 2003/1903 Reg.2

Reg.3, applied: SI 2003/1903 Reg.3

Reg.5, amended: SI 2003/1903 Reg.2

Reg.6, amended: SI 2003/1903 Reg.2

Reg.7, substituted: SI 2003/1903 Reg.2

Reg.10, amended: SI 2003/1903 Reg.2

Reg.12, amended: SI 2003/3144 Reg.2

Reg.13, amended: SI 2003/3144 Reg.2

Reg.13, substituted: SI 2003/1903 Reg.2

Reg.14, amended: SI 2003/1903 Reg.2

Reg.17, revoked: SI 2003/1903 Reg.2

Reg.18, amended: SI 2003/1903 Reg.2, SI 2003/3144 Reg.2

Reg.18A, added: SI 2003/3144 Reg.2

2000–cont.

730. Radio Equipment and Telecommuni-cations Terminal Equipment Regula-tions 2000–*cont.*

Reg.19, amended: SI 2003/1903 Reg.2

Reg.21, amended: SI 2003/3144 Reg.2

Reg.22, amended: SI 2003/3144 Reg.2

Sch.8 Part I, revoked: SI 2003/1903 Reg.2

Sch.8 Part II, revoked: SI 2003/1903 Reg.2

Sch.8 Part III, revoked: SI 2003/1903 Reg.2

Sch.8 Part III para.1, revoked: SI 2003/1903 Reg.2

Sch.8 Part III para.2, revoked: SI 2003/1903 Reg.2

Sch.8 Part III para.3, revoked: SI 2003/1903 Reg.2

Sch.9 para.1, amended: SI 2003/1903 Reg.2, SI 2004/693 Sch.2

Sch.9 para.1, revoked (in part): SI 2004/693 Sch.2

Sch.9 para.1, substituted: SI 2003/3144 Reg.2

Sch.9 Part I para.1, substituted: SI 2003/3144 Reg.2

Sch.9 Part I para.2, substituted: SI 2003/3144 Reg.2

Sch.9 Part I para.3, substituted: SI 2003/3144 Reg.2

Sch.9 Part I para.4, substituted: SI 2003/3144 Reg.2

Sch.9 para.2, substituted: SI 2003/3144 Reg.2

Sch.9 Part II para.5, substituted: SI 2003/3144 Reg.2

Sch.9 Part II para.6, substituted: SI 2003/3144 Reg.2

Sch.9 Part II para.7, substituted: SI 2003/3144 Reg.2

Sch.9 Part II para.8, substituted: SI 2003/3144 Reg.2

Sch.9 Part II para.9, substituted: SI 2003/3144 Reg.2

Sch.9 Part II para.10, substituted: SI 2003/3144 Reg.2

Sch.9 Part II para.11, substituted: SI 2003/3144 Reg.2

Sch.9 Part II para.12, substituted: SI 2003/3144 Reg.2

Sch.9 Part II para.13, substituted: SI 2003/3144 Reg.2

Sch.9 Part II para.14, substituted: SI 2003/3144 Reg.2

Sch.9 Part II para.15, substituted: SI 2003/3144 Reg.2

Sch.9 Part II para.16, substituted: SI 2003/3144 Reg.2

Sch.9 Part II para.17, substituted: SI 2003/3144 Reg.2

Sch.9 Part II para.18, substituted: SI 2003/3144 Reg.2

Sch.9 Part II para.19, substituted: SI 2003/3144 Reg.2

2000–cont.

730. Radio Equipment and Telecommunications Terminal Equipment Regulations 2000–cont.

Sch.9 Part II para.20, substituted: SI 2003/3144 Reg.2

Sch.9 Part II para.21, substituted: SI 2003/3144 Reg.2

Sch.9 Part II para.22, substituted: SI 2003/3144 Reg.2

Sch.9 para.3, substituted: SI 2003/3144 Reg.2

Sch.9 para.4, substituted: SI 2003/3144 Reg.2

732. West Hertfordshire Hospitals National Health Service Trust (Establishment) Order 2000

revoked: 2003 c.43 s.7

733. Mount Vernon and Watford Hospitals and the St Albans and Hemel Hempstead National Health Service Trust (Dissolution) Order 2000

revoked: 2003 c.43 s.7

742. Appropriation (Northern Ireland) Order 2000

revoked: SI 2003/1885 Sch.4

750. Occupational Pension Schemes (Contracting-out) (Payment and Recovery of Remaining Balances) Regulations 2000

Reg.3, amended: SI 2002/681 Reg.10

755. Social Security (Contributions) (Re-rating and National Insurance Funds Payments) Order 2000

Art.4, revoked (in part): 2002 c.19 Sch.2

768. Genetically Modified and Novel Foods (Labelling) (England) Regulations 2000

Reg.2, amended: SI 2003/2647 Reg.8

Reg.3, amended: SI 2003/2647 Reg.8

Reg.9, amended: SI 2003/2647 Reg.8

780. London Borough of Barking and Dagenham (Electoral Changes) Order 2000

varied: SI 2004/222 Art.2

781. London Borough of Croydon (Electoral Changes) Order 2000

varied: SI 2004/222 Art.2

782. London Borough of Hackney (Electoral Changes) Order 2000

varied: SI 2004/222 Art.2

783. London Borough of Haringey (Electoral Changes) Order 2000

varied: SI 2004/222 Art.2

784. London Borough of Islington (Electoral Changes) Order 2000

varied: SI 2004/222 Art.2

785. Royal Borough of Kensington and Chelsea (Electoral Changes) Order 2000

varied: SI 2004/222 Art.2

2000–cont.

786. London Borough of Southwark (Electoral Changes) Order 2000

varied: SI 2004/222 Art.2

787. London Borough of Tower Hamlets (Electoral Changes) Order 2000

varied: SI 2004/222 Art.2

788. City of Westminster (Electrol Changes) Order 2000

varied: SI 2004/222 Art.2

797. Commission for Health Improvement (Functions) Amendment Regulations 2000

revoked: SI 2003/1587 Reg.23

798. National Assistance (Sums for Personal Requirements) Regulations 2000

revoked: SI 2004/2335 Reg.8

824. Community Legal Service (Cost Protection) Regulations 2000

Reg.3, see *Hinde v Harbourne* [2003] EWHC 3109, [2004] 2 Costs L.R. 289 (Ch D), Neuberger, J.

837. National Health Service (Travelling Expenses and Remission of Charges) Amendment (No.2) Regulations 2000

revoked: SI 2003/2382 Sch.2

841. Stockport Acute Services and the Stockport Healthcare National Health Service Trusts (Dissolution) Order 2000

revoked: 2003 c.43 s.7

842. Stockport National Health Service Trust (Establishment) Order 2000

applied: SI 2003/3059 Sch.1

revoked: 2003 c.43 s.7

845. Medical Food (England) Regulations 2000

Reg.2, amended: SI 2004/2145 Reg.6

846. Phoenix National Health Service Trust (Dissolution) Order 2000

revoked: 2003 c.43 s.7

847. Andover District Community Health Care National Health Service Trust (Dissolution) Order 2000

revoked: 2003 c.43 s.7

864. Derby North East Education Action Zone Order 2000

varied: SI 2003/556 Art.3

865. Bristol Education Action Zone Order 2000

varied: SI 2003/561 Art.3

867. Great Yarmouth Achievement Education Action Zone Order 2000

varied: SI 2003/555 Art.3

897. Social Security (Work-focused Interviews) Regulations 2000

applied: SI 2002/1703 Reg.16

Reg.2, amended: SI 2002/1703 Sch.1

Reg.2, revoked (in part): SI 2002/1703 Sch.1

Reg.3, revoked: SI 2002/1703 Sch.1

Reg.4, revoked: SI 2002/1703 Sch.1

Reg.5, revoked: SI 2002/1703 Sch.1

NO.

2000–cont.

897. Social Security (Work-focused Interviews) Regulations 2000–*cont.*

Reg.6, revoked: SI 2002/1703 Sch.1

Reg.7, revoked: SI 2002/1703 Sch.1

Reg.8, revoked: SI 2002/1703 Sch.1

Reg.9, revoked: SI 2002/1703 Sch.1

Reg.10, revoked: SI 2002/1703 Sch.1

Reg.11, revoked: SI 2002/1703 Sch.1

Reg.12, revoked: SI 2002/1703 Sch.1

Reg.13, revoked: SI 2002/1703 Sch.1

Reg.14, revoked: SI 2002/1703 Sch.1

Reg.15, revoked: SI 2002/1703 Sch.1

Reg.16, revoked (in part): SI 2002/1703 Sch.1

Sch.1, revoked: SI 2002/1703 Sch.1

Sch.1A, revoked: SI 2002/1703 Sch.1

Sch.2 para.1, revoked: SI 2002/1703 Sch.1

Sch.2 para.2, revoked: SI 2002/1703 Sch.1

Sch.2 para.3, revoked: SI 2002/1703 Sch.1

Sch.2 para.4, revoked: SI 2002/1703 Sch.1

Sch.2 para.5, revoked: SI 2002/1703 Sch.1

Sch.2 para.6, revoked: SI 2002/1703 Sch.1

Sch.3 para.1, revoked: SI 2002/1703 Sch.1

Sch.3 para.2, revoked: SI 2002/1703 Sch.1

Sch.3 para.3, revoked: SI 2002/1703 Sch.1

Sch.3 para.4, revoked: SI 2002/1703 Sch.1

Sch.3 para.5, revoked: SI 2002/1703 Sch.1

Sch.3 para.6, revoked: SI 2002/1703 Sch.1

Sch.6 para.2, revoked (in part): SI 2002/1703 Sch.1

Sch.6 para.3, revoked (in part): SI 2002/1703 Sch.1

911. Financing of Maintained Schools (Amendment) (Wales) Regulations 2000

revoked: SI 2004/2506 Reg.3

928. Air Quality (England) Regulations 2000

Sch.1, added: SI 2002/3043 Reg.2

Sch.1, amended: SI 2002/3043 Reg.2

Sch.1 para.3, substituted: SI 2002/3043 Reg.2

Sch.1 para.4, amended: SI 2002/3043 Reg.2

Sch.1 para.5, amended: SI 2002/3043 Reg.2

929. Education (School Teachers Pay and Conditions) (No.2) Order 2000

revoked: 2002 c.32 Sch.22 Part 1

932. Weighing Equipment (Non-automatic Weighing Machines) Regulations 2000

applied: SI 2003/2454 Reg.5, SI 2003/2761 Reg.4

Reg.3, amended: SI 2003/2761 Reg.17

Reg.3, applied: SI 2003/2761 Reg.4

Reg.36, amended: SI 2003/214 Sch.1 para.9

934. Greenwich Park (Vehicle Parking) Regulations 2000

Reg.5, substituted: SI 2004/1307 Reg.2

Reg.6, amended: SI 2004/1307 Reg.2

NO.

2000–cont.

937. Supreme Court Fees (Amendment No 2) Order 2000

revoked: SI 2004/3121 Sch.2

939. County Fees (Amendment No 2) Order 2000

revoked: SI 2004/3121 Sch.2

944. Education (Student Loans) (Repayment) Regulations 2000

Reg.2, amended: SI 2002/2087 Reg.2

Reg.9, amended: SI 2004/2752 Reg.4

Reg.10, amended: SI 2004/2752 Reg.5

Reg.11, amended: SI 2002/2087 Reg.3

Reg.13, amended: SI 2002/2087 Reg.4, SI 2004/2752 Reg.7

Reg.13A, added: SI 2004/2752 Reg.6

Reg.13B, added: SI 2004/2752 Reg.6

Reg.13C, added: SI 2004/2752 Reg.6

Reg.13D, added: SI 2004/2752 Reg.6

Reg.13E, added: SI 2004/2752 Reg.6

Reg.15, amended: SI 2002/2087 Reg.5, SI 2004/2752 Reg.7, Reg.8

Reg.29, amended: SI 2004/2752 Reg.7

Reg.34, applied: SI 2002/680 Reg.2

Reg.35, amended: SI 2002/2087 Reg.6

Reg.36, amended: SI 2002/2859 Reg.3

Reg.36, referred to: SI 2002/2859 Reg.2

Reg.43, amended: SI 2002/2087 Reg.7

Reg.56, amended: SI 2004/2752 Reg.7

945. Income Tax (Electronic Communications) Regulations 2000

revoked: SI 2003/282 Reg.11

961. Oxford Radcliffe Hospitals National Health Service Trust (Establishment) Amendment Order 2000

revoked: 2003 c.43 s.7

966. Inheritance Tax (Delivery of Accounts) (Scotland) Regulations 2000

revoked: SI 2002/1733 Sch.1

967. Inheritance Tax (Delivery of Accounts) Regulations 2000

revoked: SI 2002/1733 Sch.1

972. Dairy Produce Quotas (Amendment) (Wales) Regulations 2000

revoked: SI 2002/897 Sch.4

993. Blackpool, Wyre and Fylde Community Health Services National Health Service Trust (Establishment) Amendment Order 2000

revoked: 2003 c.43 s.7

1012. Wireless Telegraphy (Exemption) (Amendment) Regulations 2000

revoked: SI 2003/74 Sch.1

1015. Commission for Health Improvement (Functions) (Wales) Regulations 2000

revoked: SI 2003/993 Reg.22

NO.

2000–cont.

1038. General Osteopathic Council (Application for Registration and Fees) Rules Order of Council 2000
Sch.1, amended: SI 2003/3148 Reg.16, SI 2004/1947 Reg.15

1048. Pensions on Divorce etc (Provision of Information) Regulations 2000
Reg.3, applied: SI 2002/427 Reg.7
Reg.3, varied: SI 2002/836 Reg.7, SI 2003/291 Reg.2
Reg.4, amended: SI 2003/1727 Reg.3

1052. Pension Sharing (Valuation) Regulations 2000
Reg.1, amended: SI 2003/1727 Reg.4
Reg.5, amended: SI 2003/1727 Reg.4

1053. Pension Sharing (Implementation and Discharge of Liability) Regulations 2000
Reg.1, amended: SI 2003/1727 Reg.5
Reg.16, amended: SI 2003/1727 Reg.5

1054. Pension Sharing (Pension Credit Benefit) Regulations 2000
applied: SI 2002/427 Reg.9, Reg.18
Reg.1, amended: SI 2003/1727 Reg.6
Reg.24, applied: SI 2002/427 Reg.9, Reg.18, SI 2003/291 Reg.3
Reg.24, varied: SI 2002/836 Reg.9, Reg.18
Reg.27, amended: SI 2003/1727 Reg.6

1059. Ionising Radiation (Medical Exposure) Regulations 2000
Reg.2, amended: SI 2004/1031 Sch.10 para.14
Reg.6, applied: SI 2004/1769 Reg.21

1071. Access to Justice Act 1999 (Destination of Appeals) Order 2000
Art.1, see *Jones v T Mobile (UK) Ltd* [2003] EWCA Civ 1162, [2004] C.P. Rep. 10 (CA), Kennedy, L.J.; see *Persaud v Dulovic* [2002] EWHC 889, [2002] C.P. Rep. 56 (QBD), Silber, J.
Art.4, see *Persaud v Dulovic* [2002] EWHC 889, [2002] C.P. Rep. 56 (QBD), Silber, J.; see *Scribes West Ltd v Anstalt (No.2)* [2004] EWCA Civ 965, [2004] 4 All E.R. 653 (CA), Brooke, L.J.
Art.4, amended: SI 2002/439 Art.12, SI 2003/490 Art.2

1075. Sea Fishing (Enforcement of Community Control Measures) (Wales) Order 2000
Art.2, amended: SI 2003/559 Art.2
Sch.1, amended: SI 2003/559 Art.2

1076. Bro Morgannwg National Health Service Trust (Establishment) Amendment Order 2000
revoked: 2003 c.43 s.7

1078. Sea Fishing (Enforcement of Community Satellite Monitoring Measures) (Wales) Order 2000
Art.2, amended: SI 2002/677 Reg.3
Art.3, amended: SI 2002/677 Reg.4

NO.

2000–cont.

1078. Sea Fishing (Enforcement of Community Satellite Monitoring Measures) (Wales) Order 2000–*cont.*
Art.4, referred to: SI 2002/677 Reg.1
Art.4, revoked (in part): SI 2002/677 Reg.5
Art.5, amended: SI 2002/677 Reg.6
Art.6, amended: SI 2002/677 Reg.7
Art.7, amended: SI 2002/677 Reg.8

1080. Allocation of Housing (Wales) Regulations 2000
revoked: SI 2003/239 Reg.6

1081. Sea Fishing (Enforcement of Community Conservation Measures) Order 2000
Art.2, amended: SI 2002/426 Art.3
Art.4, amended: SI 2002/426 Art.4
Art.9, amended: SI 2002/794 Sch.1 para.47
Art.13, amended: SI 2002/426 Art.5
Sch.1, amended: SI 2002/426 Art.6

1082. Social Security (National Insurance Number Information Exemption) Regulations 2000
Reg.2, revoked: SI 2003/493 Sch.2 Part 1
Reg.3, revoked: SI 2003/495 Sch.1 Part 1

1085. Retirement Benefits Schemes (Sharing of Pensions on Divorce or Annulment) Regulations 2000
Reg.5, applied: SR 2002/352 Reg.21

1090. Financing of Maintained Schools (England) (No.2) Regulations 2000
applied: SI 2002/377 Reg.24, Reg.25, SI 2003/3247 Reg.23, Reg.24
referred to: SI 2003/453 Reg.23, Reg.24

1098. Education (National Curriculum) (Attainment Targets and Programmes of Study in Physical Education) (Wales) Order 2000
revoked: 2002 c.32 Sch.22 Part 3

1099. Education (National Curriculum) (Attainment Targets and Programmes of Study in Science) (Wales) Order 2000
revoked: 2002 c.32 Sch.22 Part 3

1100. Education (National Curriculum) (Attainment Targets and Programmes of Study in Mathematics) (Wales) Order 2000
revoked: 2002 c.32 Sch.22 Part 3

1101. Education (National Curriculum) (Attainment Targets and Programmes of Study in Welsh) Order 2000
revoked: 2002 c.32 Sch.22 Part 3

1105. Organisation for Joint Armament Cooperation (Immunities and Privileges) Order 2000
Art.14, amended: 2002 c.8 s.2
Art.15, substituted: 2002 c.8 s.2
Art.16, amended: 2002 c.8 s.2

1110. Equality (Disability, etc.) (Northern Ireland) Order 2000
Art.10, amended: SI 2003/435 Sch.4 para.16

NO.

2000–cont.

1119. European Communities (Lawyer's Practice) Regulations 2000
Reg.1, amended: SI 2004/1628 Reg.2
Reg.2, amended: SI 2004/1628 Reg.3
Reg.12, amended: SI 2004/1628 Reg.4
Reg.13, amended: SI 2004/1628 Reg.5
Reg.14, applied: SI 2003/435 Art.2
Reg.21, applied: SI 2004/1628 Reg.2
Reg.22, applied: SI 2004/1628 Reg.2
Sch.3 Part 1, amended: SI 2003/435 Sch.4 para.17, SI 2004/1628 Reg.6
Sch.4 para.7, amended: SI 2004/1628 Reg.7
Sch.4 para.24, substituted: SI 2004/1628 Reg.7

1121. Education (Student Support) Regulations 2000
Sch.1 para.8, see *R. (on the application of Ayiwe) v Hackney LBC* [2001] EWHC Admin 806, [2002] E.L.R. 343 (QBD (Admin Ct)), Newman, J.

1139. National Police Records (Recordable Offences) Regulations 2000
Sch.1 para.5, substituted: SI 2003/2823 Reg.2
Sch.1 para.26, revoked: SI 2003/2823 Reg.2
Sch.1 para.27, substituted: SI 2003/2823 Reg.2
Sch.1 para.51, revoked: SI 2003/2823 Reg.2
Sch.1 para.53, added: SI 2003/2823 Reg.2
Sch.1 para.54, added: SI 2003/2823 Reg.2

1140. Education (National Curriculum) (Exceptions at Key Stage 4) (England) Regulations 2000
revoked: SI 2003/252 Reg.2
Reg.3, amended: SI 2002/2048 Reg.3
Reg.4, revoked (in part): SI 2002/2048 Reg.4
Reg.5, amended: SI 2002/2048 Reg.5
Reg.7, amended: SI 2002/2048 Reg.6
Reg.8, amended: SI 2002/2048 Reg.7
Reg.8, revoked (in part): SI 2002/2048 Reg.7
Reg.9, substituted: SI 2002/2048 Reg.8
Reg.10, revoked: SI 2002/2048 Reg.9
Reg.11, revoked: SI 2002/2048 Reg.9
Reg.12, amended: SI 2002/2048 Reg.10
Reg.13, revoked: SI 2002/2048 Reg.9

1146. Foundation Subject (Amendment) (England) Order 2000
revoked: 2002 c.32 Sch.22 Part 3

1152. Income Tax (Employments) (Amendment) Regulations 2000
revoked: SI 2003/2682 Sch.2

1153. Education (National Curriculum) (Attainment Targets and Programmes of Study in Art) (Wales) Order 2000
revoked: 2002 c.32 Sch.22 Part 3

1154. Education (National Curriculum) (Attainment Targets and Programmes of Study in English) (Wales) Order 2000
revoked: 2002 c.32 Sch.22 Part 3

NO.

2000–cont.

1155. Education (National Curriculum) (Attainment Targets and Programmes of Study in Geography) (Wales) Order 2000
revoked: 2002 c.32 Sch.22 Part 3

1156. Education (National Curriculum) (Attainment Targets and Programmes of Study in History) (Wales) Order 2000
revoked: 2002 c.32 Sch.22 Part 3

1157. Education (National Curriculum) (Attainment Targets and Programmes of Study in Modern Foreign Languages) (Wales) Order 2000
revoked: 2002 c.32 Sch.22 Part 3

1158. Education (National Curriculum) (Attainment Targets and Programmes of Study in Music) (Wales) Order 2000
revoked: 2002 c.32 Sch.22 Part 3

1159. Education (National Curriculum) (Attainment Targets and Programmes of Study in Technology) (Wales) Order 2000
revoked: 2002 c.32 Sch.22 Part 3

1161. Immigration (Leave to Enter and Remain) Order 2000
applied: SI 2003/2818 Art.11
referred to: SI 2004/475 Art.2
Art.1, amended: SI 2004/475 Art.3
Art.1, varied: SI 2003/2818 Sch.2 para.4
Art.3, amended: SI 2004/475 Art.4
Art.4, varied: SI 2003/2818 Sch.2 para.4
Art.6, varied: SI 2003/2818 Sch.2 para.4

1167. Blackburn with Darwen Primary Care Trust (Establishment) Order 2000
Art.1, amended: SI 2002/1405 Sch.1
Art.4, revoked: SI 2002/1405 Sch.1
Art.8, revoked: SI 2003/1740 Sch.1

1168. Trafford South Primary Care Trust (Establishment) Order 2000
Art.1, amended: SI 2002/1405 Sch.1
Art.4, revoked: SI 2002/1405 Sch.1
Art.8, revoked: SI 2003/1740 Sch.1

1212. Gaming Act (Variation of Fees) Order 2000
Sch.1, amended: SI 2002/637 Art.3, SI 2002/642 Art.3

1213. Gaming Act (Variation of Monetary Limits) Order 2000
Art.3, revoked: SI 2002/1904 Art.4

1236. London Borough of Lewisham (Electoral Changes) Order 2000
varied: SI 2004/222 Art.2

1240. East Riding Health Authority (Change of Name) Order 2000
revoked: SI 2002/553 Sch.3

1241. County Durham Health Authority (Change of Name) Order 2000
revoked: SI 2002/553 Sch.3

NO.

2000–cont.

1242. Education (National Curriculum) (Key Stage 1 Assessment Arrangements) (England) (Amendment) Order 2000
revoked: SI 2003/1037 Art.2

1271. Local Government (Best Value) (Reviews and Performance Plans) (Wales) Order 2000
revoked: SI 2002/886 Art.5

1280. Home Energy Efficiency Scheme (England) Regulations 2000
Reg.4, amended: SI 2002/115 Reg.3, SI 2003/1017 Reg.2, SI 2003/2263 Reg.2, SI 2004/2430 Reg.2
Reg.5, amended: SI 2002/115 Reg.4
Reg.6, amended: SI 2002/115 Reg.5, SI 2003/1017 Reg.2, SI 2003/2263 Reg.2

1298. Pet Travel Scheme (Pilot Arrangements) (England) (Amendment) Order 2000
revoked: SI 2004/2363 Sch.2

1306. Recognition and Derecognition Ballots (Qualified Persons) Order 2000
Art.4, substituted: SI 2002/2268 Art.2

1315. In Vitro Diagnostic Medical Devices Regulations 2000
revoked: SI 2002/618 Reg.66

1317. Civil Procedure (Amendment No.3) Rules 2000
r.39, see *Inline Logistics Ltd v UCI Logistics Ltd (Costs: Recovery of Insurance Premium)* [2002] EWHC 519, [2002] 2 Costs L.R. 304 (Ch D), Ferris, J.

1323. Education (School Day and School Year) (Wales) Regulations 2000
Reg.3, amended: SI 2002/107 Reg.3
Reg.4, amended: SI 2002/1556 Reg.2
Reg.5, added: SI 2002/107 Reg.4

1341. Pitcairn Court of Appeal Order 2000
Art.3, amended: SI 2004/2669 Art.2
Art.3A, added: SI 2004/2669 Art.3
Art.3B, added: SI 2004/2669 Art.3
Sch.1 para.1, revoked: SI 2002/249 Art.2
Sch.1 para.2, revoked: SI 2002/249 Art.2
Sch.1 para.3, revoked: SI 2002/249 Art.2
Sch.1 para.5, revoked: SI 2002/249 Art.2

1343. Virgin Islands (Constitution) (Amendment) Order 2000
Art.2, amended: 2002 c.8 s.2

1346. Air Navigation (Jersey) Order 2000
Sch.1 para.57A, added: SI 2002/1078 Art.2

1347. Flags (Northern Ireland) Order 2000
Art.3, amended: 2002 c.26 s.67

1362. Mid-Sussex National Health Service Trust (Establishment) Amendment Order 2000
revoked: 2003 c.43 s.7

1366. Social Security (Claims and Payments) Amendment Regulations 2000
revoked (in part): SI 2003/492 Sch.3 Part 1

NO.

2000–cont.

1381. Immigration (Transit Visa) (Amendment) Order 2000
revoked: SI 2003/1185 Sch.2

1384. Hertsmere Primary Care Trust (Establishment) Order 2000
Art.1, amended: SI 2002/1405 Sch.1
Art.4, revoked: SI 2002/1405 Sch.1
Art.8, revoked: SI 2003/1740 Sch.1
Sch.1, amended: SI 2004/543 Sch.1

1403. Stakeholder Pension Schemes Regulations 2000
Reg.1, amended: SI 2002/1383 Reg.4, SI 2002/1555 Art.40, SI 2002/2098 Reg.2
Reg.1, varied: SI 2003/1633 Sch.2 para.8
Reg.11, amended: SI 2002/2098 Reg.3
Reg.12, amended: SI 2002/1480 Reg.2
Reg.12, substituted: SI 2002/2098 Reg.4
Reg.15, amended: SI 2002/1555 Art.40, SI 2002/2098 Reg.5
Reg.18, amended: SI 2002/1383 Reg.4

1408. Burma (Sale, Supply and Export of Goods) (Penalties) Regulations 2000
revoked: SI 2004/1315 Sch.1
Reg.2, amended: SI 2003/2742 Reg.2

1410. Local Government (Early Termination of Employment) (Discretionary Compensation) (England and Wales) Regulations 2000
see *R. (on the application of Foster) v Eastbourne BC* [2004] EWCA Civ 36, [2004] I.C.R. 1149 (CA), Lord Brown of Eaton-under-Heywood

1410. Local Government (Early Termination of Employment) (Discretionary Compensation)(England and Wales) Regulations 2000
referred to: SI 2004/928 Reg.5
Reg.6, amended: SI 2002/769 Reg.3
Reg.6, applied: SI 2002/769 Reg.11
Reg.7, amended: SI 2002/769 Reg.4
Reg.17, amended: SI 2002/769 Reg.5
Reg.19, amended: SI 2002/769 Reg.6
Reg.21, amended: SI 2002/769 Reg.7
Reg.24, amended: SI 2002/769 Reg.8
Sch.1 para.1, amended: SI 2002/769 Reg.9, SI 2003/1022 Reg.9
Sch.4 para.1, amended: SI 2002/769 Reg.10
Sch.4 para.2, amended: SI 2002/769 Reg.10
Sch.4 para.3, amended: SI 2002/769 Reg.10
Sch.5 para.1, amended: SI 2002/769 Reg.10
Sch.5 para.2, amended: SI 2002/769 Reg.10
Sch.5 para.3, amended: SI 2002/769 Reg.10
Sch.5 para.4, amended: SI 2002/769 Reg.10
Sch.5 para.5, amended: SI 2002/769 Reg.10
Sch.5 para.6, amended: SI 2002/769 Reg.10

1411. National Minimum Wage (Increase in Development Rate for Young Workers) Regulations 2000
revoked: SI 2002/1999 Sch.1

NO.

2000–cont.

1413. Barking, Havering and Redbridge Hospitals National Health Service Trust (Establishment) Order 2000
applied: SI 2003/3059 Sch.1, Sch.2
revoked: 2003 c.43 s.7

1414. Whipps Cross Hospital National Health Service Trust (Establishment) Order 2000
revoked: 2003 c.43 s.7

1415. North East London Mental Health National Health Service Trust (Establishment) Order 2000
revoked: 2003 c.43 s.7

1416. BHB Community Health Care, the Forest Healthcare, the Havering Hospitals and the Redbridge Health Care National Health Service Trusts (Dissolution) Order 2000
revoked: 2003 c.43 s.7

1417. District of Bridgnorth (Electoral Changes) Order 2000
varied: SI 2004/222 Art.2

1418. Borough of Oswestry (Electoral Changes) Order 2000
varied: SI 2004/222 Art.2

1419. District of North Shropshire (Electoral Changes) Order 2000
varied: SI 2004/222 Art.2

1420. District of South Shropshire (Electoral Changes) Order 2000
varied: SI 2004/222 Art.2

1472. Burma (Freezing of Funds) Regulations 2000
Reg.1, amended: SI 2003/1810 Reg.2

1474. Metropolitan Police (Capital Finance) Order 2000
revoked: SI 2004/533 Art.13

1483. Social Security (Benefits for Widows and Widowers) (Consequential Amendments) Regulations 2000
Reg.9, revoked (in part): SI 2003/492 Sch.3 Part 1
Reg.10, revoked (in part): SI 2003/492 Sch.3 Part 1

1487. Borough of Southend-on-Sea (Electoral Changes) Order 2000
varied: SI 2004/222 Art.2

1492. Housing Grants (Additional Purposes) (England) Order 2000
revoked: SI 2002/1860 Sch.6

1504. London Regional Transport (Transitional Modifications) Order 2000
revoked: SI 2003/1615 Sch.1 para.55

1510. Processed Cereal-based Foods and Baby Foods for Infants and Young Children (Amendment) (England) Regulations 2000
revoked: SI 2003/3207 Reg.13

NO.

2000–cont.

1549. Greater London Authority Act 1999 (Consequential Amendments) (Police) Order 2000
Art.4, revoked: SI 2003/527 Sch.4 Part 1
Art.11, revoked: SI 2004/645 Reg.2
Art.12, revoked: SI 2004/645 Reg.2

1551. Part-time Workers (Prevention of Less Favourable Treatment) Regulations 2000
Reg.2, see *Matthews v Kent and Medway Towns Fire Authority* [2004] EWCA Civ 844, [2004] 3 All E.R. 620 (CA), Jonathan Parker, L.J.; see *Matthews v Kent and Medway Towns Fire Authority* [2004] I.C.R. 257 (EAT), Judge Birtles
Reg.2, amended: SI 2002/2035 Reg.2
Reg.5, see *Matthews v Kent and Medway Towns Fire Authority* [2004] I.C.R. 257 (EAT), Judge Birtles
Reg.8, amended: SI 2002/2035 Reg.2
Reg.8, revoked (in part): SI 2002/2035 Reg.2

1553. Greater London Authority Act 1999 (Consequential Amendments of Subordinate Legislation) (Fire etc Authority) Order 2000
Sch.1 para.4, revoked: SI 2003/1021 Reg.33

1556. Eritrea and Ethiopia (United Nations Sanctions) Order 2000
Art.5, amended: 2002 c.8 s.2
Art.7, amended: 2002 c.8 s.2

1557. Eritrea and Ethiopia (United Nations Sanctions) (Overseas Territories) Order 2000
Art.5, amended: 2002 c.8 s.2
Art.7, amended: 2002 c.8 s.2

1558. Eritrea and Ethiopia (United Nations Sanctions) (Isle of Man) Order 2000
Art.5, amended: 2002 c.8 s.2
Art.7, amended: 2002 c.8 s.2

1559. Eritrea and Ethiopia (United Nations Sanctions) (Channel Islands) Order 2000
Art.5, amended: 2002 c.8 s.2
Art.7, amended: 2002 c.8 s.2

1562. Air Navigation Order 2000
applied: SI 2002/2786 Reg.3, Reg.5, SI 2003/1902 Sch.8 para.5, Sch.8 para.7, Sch.8 para.8, Sch.8 para.9
referred to: SI 2002/798 Art.3, SI 2003/777 Art.2, SI 2004/705 Art.2
Art.4, amended: SI 2003/2905 Art.11
Art.8, amended: SI 2003/777 Art.3
Art.9A, added: SI 2003/777 Art.3
Art.9B, added: SI 2003/777 Art.3
Art.20, amended: SI 2002/264 Art.3
Art.21, applied: SI 2003/1902 Sch.8 para.2
Art.22, amended: SI 2002/1628 Art.3
Art.24A, added: SI 2002/1628 Art.3
Art.27, amended: SI 2004/1256 Reg.10
Art.34A, added: SI 2003/2905 Art.3
Art.34A, amended: SI 2004/705 Art.3

2000–cont.

1562. Air Navigation Order 2000–*cont.*
Art.36, enabled: SI 2002/733
Art.37, amended: SI 2002/264 Art.4
Art.40, amended: SI 2002/264 Art.5
Art.45, amended: SI 2002/264 Art.3
Art.47, enabled: SI 2003/1365
Art.54A, added: SI 2003/777 Art.4
Art.60, enabled: SI 2002/2786, SI 2004/3214
Art.62, amended: SI 2002/264 Art.6
Art.62, revoked (in part): SI 2002/264 Art.6
Art.72, applied: SI 2004/756 Reg.10
Art.84, amended: SI 2003/2905 Art.11
Art.84, enabled: SI 2003/64
Art.87A, added: SI 2002/264 Art.7
Art.88A, added: SI 2003/2905 Art.4
Art.92, substituted: SI 2003/2905 Art.4
Art.93, substituted: SI 2003/2905 Art.4
Art.94, substituted: SI 2003/2905 Art.4
Art.94A, amended: SI 2004/705 Art.4, Art.5
Art.101, amended: SI 2003/2905 Art.6
Art.102, amended: SI 2003/2905 Art.6
Art.104, amended: SI 2003/2905 Art.11
Art.109A, added: SI 2002/264 Art.8
Art.111, amended: SI 2002/264 Art.9
Art.113, amended: SI 2004/1256 Reg.10
Art.117, applied: SI 2002/2786 Reg.19
Art.117A, added: SI 2003/2905 Art.7
Art.117A, enabled: SI 2003/3286
Art.118, amended: SI 2003/2905 Art.8
Art.119, amended: SI 2003/2905 Art.6
Art.122, amended: SI 2003/2905 Art.9
Art.126, amended: SI 2003/2905 Art.11
Art.129, amended: SI 2002/264 Art.3, Art.7, Art.10, SI 2002/1628 Art.3, SI 2003/777 Art.4, SI 2003/2905 Art.5, Art.11
Art.129, enabled: SI 2002/2786
Art.134, substituted: SI 2004/77 Reg.3
Sch.3 Part A, amended: SI 2002/264 Art.11
Sch.3 Part A, referred to: SI 2002/798 Art.4, Art.12
Sch.4 para.4, amended: SI 2003/2905 Art.10
Sch.4 para.5, amended: SI 2002/264 Art.3, SI 2003/2905 Art.10
Sch.5 para.2, amended: SI 2003/777 Art.5
Sch.5 para.3, amended: SI 2003/777 Art.5
Sch.5 para.4, amended: SI 2003/777 Art.5
Sch.8 Part A, added: SI 2002/1628 Art.3
Sch.8 Part A, amended: SI 2002/264 Art.9, SI 2003/777 Art.6
Sch.8 Part B para.1, amended: SI 2002/1628 Art.3
Sch.8 Part C, added: SI 2002/1628 Art.3
Sch.9 Part A para.1, amended: SI 2004/705 Art.6
Sch.9 Part A para.1, substituted: SI 2003/2905 Art.5
Sch.9 Part A para.2, substituted: SI 2003/2905 Art.5

2000–cont.

1562. Air Navigation Order 2000–*cont.*
Sch.9 Part B para.1, amended: SI 2004/705 Art.7
Sch.9 Part B para.1, substituted: SI 2003/2905 Art.5
Sch.9 Part B para.2, substituted: SI 2003/2905 Art.5
Sch.9 Part B para.3, amended: SI 2004/705 Art.8
Sch.9 Part B para.3, substituted: SI 2003/2905 Art.5
Sch.9 para.1, substituted: SI 2003/2905 Art.5
Sch.9 para.2, amended: SI 2002/264 Art.12
Sch.9 para.2, substituted: SI 2003/2905 Art.5
Sch.10 Part A, amended: SI 2002/264 Art.13
Sch.12 Part A, amended: SI 2003/2905 Art.3, Art.5
Sch.12 Part B, amended: SI 2003/2905 Art.9
Sch.12 Part C, added: SI 2003/2905 Art.9

1595. Education (National Curriculum) (Attainment Targets and Programmes of Study in Modern Foreign Languages) (England) Order 2000
revoked: SI 2004/256 Art.2, SI 2004/1793 Art.2

1596. Social Security and Child Support (Miscellaneous Amendments) Regulations 2000
Reg.1, amended: SI 2003/492 Sch.3 Part 1
Reg.3, revoked (in part): SI 2003/492 Sch.3 Part 1

1597. Education (National Curriculum) (Attainment Targets and Programmes of Study in Music) (England) Order 2000
revoked: 2002 c.32 Sch.22 Part 3

1598. Education (National Curriculum) (Attainment Targets and Programmes of Study in Mathematics) (England) Order 2000
revoked: 2002 c.32 Sch.22 Part 3

1599. Education (National Curriculum) (Attainment Targets and Programmes of Study in Design and Technology) (England) Order 2000
revoked: SI 2004/261 Art.2, SI 2004/1794 Art.2

1600. Education (National Curriculum) (Attainment Targets and Programmes of Study in Science) (England) Order 2000
revoked: 2002 c.32 Sch.22 Part 3, SI 2004/1217 Art.2, SI 2004/1800 Art.2

1601. Education (National Curriculum) (Attainment Targets and Programmes of Study in Information and Communication Technology) (England) Order 2000
revoked: 2002 c.32 Sch.22 Part 3

NO.

2000–cont.

1602. Education (National Curriculum) (Attainment Targets and Programmes of Study in Art and Design) (England) Order 2000

revoked: 2002 c.32 Sch.22 Part 3

1603. Education (National Curriculum) (Attainment Target and Programmes of Study in Citizenship) (England) Order 2000

revoked: 2002 c.32 Sch.22 Part 3

1604. Education (National Curriculum) (Attainment Targets and Programmes of Study in English) (England) Order 2000

revoked: 2002 c.32 Sch.22 Part 3

1605. Education (National Curriculum) (Attainment Targets and Programmes of Study in Geography) (England) Order 2000

revoked: 2002 c.32 Sch.22 Part 3

1606. Education (National Curriculum) (Attainment Targets and Programmes of Study in History) (England) Order 2000

revoked: 2002 c.32 Sch.22 Part 3

1607. Education (National Curriculum) (Attainment Targets and Programmes of Study in Physical Education) (England) Order 2000

revoked: 2002 c.32 Sch.22 Part 3

1618. Transport of Animals (Cleansing and Disinfection) (England) (No.2) Order 2000

referred to: SI 2002/242 Art.8, SI 2002/2152 Art.6

revoked: SI 2003/255 Art.9

Sch.1, applied: SI 2002/2152 Sch.1 para.13

1619. Veterinary Surgeons and Veterinary Practitioners (Registration) Regulations Order of Council 2000

revoked: SI 2003/3342 Sch.1

1624. Town and Country Planning (Inquiries Procedure) (England) Rules 2000

applied: SI 2002/1223 r.3, r.26

referred to: SI 2003/956 Art.12

r.2, amended: SI 2003/956 Sch.2 para.1, Sch.2 para.2

r.2, substituted: SI 2003/956 Sch.2 para.1

r.6, amended: SI 2003/956 Sch.2 para.3

r.10, amended: SI 2003/956 Sch.2 para.4

r.13, amended: SI 2003/956 Sch.2 para.5

r.14, amended: SI 2003/956 Sch.2 para.6

r.18, amended: SI 2003/956 Sch.2 para.7

r.22, substituted: SI 2003/956 Sch.2 para.8

r.22A, added: SI 2003/956 Sch.2 para.9

1625. Town and Country Planning Appeals (Determination by Inspectors) (Inquiries Procedure) (England) Rules 2000

referred to: SI 2003/956 Art.12

NO.

2000–cont.

1625. Town and Country Planning Appeals (Determination by Inspectors) (Inquiries Procedure) (England) Rules 2000–*cont.*

r.2, amended: SI 2003/956 Sch.3 para.1, Sch.3 para.2

r.2, substituted: SI 2003/956 Sch.3 para.1

r.6, amended: SI 2003/956 Sch.3 para.3

r.10, amended: SI 2003/956 Sch.3 para.4

r.14, amended: SI 2003/956 Sch.3 para.5

r.15, see *Edward Ware New Homes Ltd v Secretary of State for Transport, Local Government and the Regions* [2003] EWCA Civ 566, [2004] 1 P. & C.R. 6 (CA), Kennedy, L.J.

r.15, amended: SI 2003/956 Sch.3 para.6

r.18, see *Edward Ware New Homes Ltd v Secretary of State for Transport, Local Government and the Regions* [2003] EWCA Civ 566, [2004] 1 P. & C.R. 6 (CA), Kennedy, L.J.

r.19, amended: SI 2003/956 Sch.3 para.7

r.23, substituted: SI 2003/956 Sch.3 para.8

r.23A, added: SI 2003/956 Sch.3 para.9

1626. Town and Country Planning (Hearings Procedure) (England) Rules 2000

referred to: SI 2003/956 Art.12

see *Jory v Secretary of State for Transport, Local Government and the Regions* [2002] EWHC 2724, Times, December 3, 2002 (QBD (Admin Ct)), Sullivan, J.

r.2, amended: SI 2003/956 Sch.4 para.1, Sch.4 para.2

r.2, substituted: SI 2003/956 Sch.4 para.1

r.6, amended: SI 2003/956 Sch.4 para.3

r.7, amended: SI 2003/956 Sch.4 para.4

r.15, amended: SI 2003/956 Sch.4 para.5

r.16, amended: SI 2003/956 Sch.4 para.6

r.19, substituted: SI 2003/956 Sch.4 para.7

r.19A, added: SI 2003/956 Sch.4 para.8

1628. Town and Country Planning (Appeals) (Written Representations Procedure) (England) Regulations 2000

referred to: SI 2003/956 Art.14

Reg.2, amended: SI 2003/956 Sch.7 para.1, Sch.7 para.2

Reg.2, substituted: SI 2003/956 Sch.7 para.1

Reg.3, amended: SI 2003/956 Sch.7 para.3

Reg.7, amended: SI 2003/956 Sch.7 para.4

Reg.11A, added: SI 2003/956 Sch.7 para.5

1641. Pet Travel Scheme (Pilot Arrangements) (England) (Amendment) (No.3) Order 2000

revoked: SI 2004/2363 Sch.2

1645. National Health Service (General Medical Services) Amendment (No.3) Regulations 2000

revoked: SI 2004/865 Sch.2

NO.

2000–cont.

1669. East London and The City Mental Health National Health Service Trust (Establishment) Amendment Order 2000
revoked: 2003 c.43 s.7

1673. Animals and Animal Products (Import and Export) (England and Wales) Regulations 2000
revoked (in part): SI 2004/853 Reg.35
Reg.12, applied: SI 2002/242 Art.3, SI 2002/280 Art.3, SI 2002/2152 Art.3, SI 2002/2304 Art.3, SI 2003/254 Sch.1 para.7, SI 2003/483 Sch.1 para.7, SI 2003/1279 Sch.1 para.7, SI 2003/1414 Sch.1 para.7, SI 2003/1729 Sch.1 para.7, SI 2003/1966 Sch.1 para.7
Reg.13, referred to: SI 2002/2 Reg.20, SI 2002/8 Reg.20, SI 2002/76 Reg.20, SI 2002/119 Reg.14, SI 2002/130 Reg.19
Sch.3 Part 1 para.9, amended: SI 2002/430 Reg.2, SI 2002/467 Reg.2, SI 2002/956 Reg.2, SI 2002/1039 Reg.2
Sch.3 Part 1 para.16, added: SI 2002/430 Reg.2, SI 2002/467 Reg.2
Sch.3 Part 1 para.16, amended: SI 2002/956 Reg.2, SI 2002/1039 Reg.2

1674. Railways (Interoperability) (Notified Bodies) Regulations 2000
revoked: SI 2002/1166 Reg.37

1675. Borough of North Warwickshire (Electoral Changes) Order 2000
varied: SI 2004/222 Art.2

1676. Borough of Rugby (Electoral Changes) Order 2000
varied: SI 2004/222 Art.2

1677. District of Warwick (Electoral Changes) Order 2000
varied: SI 2004/222 Art.2

1678. Wireless Telegraphy (Licence Charges) (Amendment) Regulations 2000
revoked: SI 2002/1700 Sch.1

1679. Cosmetic Products (Safety) (Amendment) Regulations 2000
revoked: SI 2003/835 Sch.1

1707. National Health Service (General Medical Services) Amendment (Wales) Regulations 2000
revoked: SI 2004/1016 Sch.2

1708. National Health Service (Choice of Medical Practitioner) Amendment (Wales) Regulations 2000
revoked: SI 2004/1016 Sch.2

1710. Relocation Grants (Forms of Application) (Amendment) (Wales) Regulations 2000
revoked: SI 2002/1860 Sch.6

1711. Telecommunications (Licence Modification) (Satellite Operator Licences) Regulations 2000
revoked: 2003 c.21 Sch.19

NO.

2000–cont.

1712. Telecommunications (Licence Modification) (Regional Public Access Mobile Radio Operator Licences) Regulations 2000
revoked: 2003 c.21 Sch.19

1713. Telecommunications (Licence Modifications) (Amendment) Regulations 2000
revoked: 2003 c.21 Sch.19

1714. Telecommunications (Licence Modification) (Mobile Data Operator Licences) Regulations 2000
revoked: 2003 c.21 Sch.19

1715. Telecommunications (Licence Modification) (Paging Operator Licences) Regulations 2000
revoked: 2003 c.21 Sch.19

1717. Education (Outturn Statements) (Wales) Regulations 2000
revoked: SI 2003/873 Reg.3

1718. West Norfolk Primary Care Trust (Establishment) Order 2000
Art.1, amended: SI 2002/1405 Sch.1
Art.4, revoked: SI 2002/1405 Sch.1
Art.8, revoked: SI 2003/1740 Sch.1
Sch.1, amended: SI 2004/543 Sch.1

1725. Borough of Shrewsbury and Atcham (Electoral Changes) Order 2000
varied: SI 2004/222 Art.2

1748. Herefordshire Primary Care Trust (Establishment) Order 2000
Art.1, amended: SI 2002/1405 Sch.1
Art.4, revoked: SI 2002/1405 Sch.1

1749. Herefordshire Community Health National Health Service Trust (Dissolution) Order 2000
revoked: 2003 c.43 s.7

1763. Health Service Medicines (Control of Prices of Specified Generic Medicines) Regulations 2000
Reg.2, amended: SI 2002/236 Reg.17, SI 2002/2861 Reg.35

1764. London Borough of Bromley (Electoral Changes) Order 2000
varied: SI 2004/222 Art.2

1765. London Borough of Camden (Electoral Changes) Order 2000
varied: SI 2004/222 Art.2

1766. London Borough of Hillingdon (Electoral Changes) Order 2000
varied: SI 2004/222 Art.2

1767. Royal Borough of Kingston upon Thames (Electoral Changes) Order 2000
varied: SI 2004/222 Art.2

1768. London Borough of Newham (Electoral Changes) Order 2000
varied: SI 2004/222 Art.2

1789. Oil and Fibre Plant Seeds (Amendment) (England) Regulations 2000
revoked: SI 2002/3174 Reg.32

NO.

2000–cont.

1790. Vegetable Seeds (Amendment) (England) Regulations 2000
revoked: SI 2002/3175 Reg.32

1791. Beet Seeds (Amendment) (England) Regulations 2000
revoked: SI 2002/3171 Reg.29

1792. Fodder Plant Seeds (Amendment) (England) Regulations 2000
revoked: SI 2002/3172 Reg.32

1793. Cereal Seeds (Amendment) (England) Regulations 2000
revoked: SI 2002/3173 Reg.32

1797. Consumer Credit (Advertisements and Content of Quotations) (Amendment) Regulations 2000
Reg.2, revoked: SI 2004/1484 Reg.11

1803. Medical Act 1983 (Amendment) Order 2000
Art.3, revoked: SI 2002/3135 Sch.1 para.44
Art.4, revoked: SI 2002/3135 Sch.1 para.44
Art.5, revoked: SI 2002/3135 Sch.1 para.44
Art.6, revoked: SI 2002/3135 Sch.1 para.44
Art.7, revoked: SI 2002/3135 Sch.1 para.44
Art.8, revoked: SI 2002/3135 Sch.1 para.44
Art.9, revoked: SI 2002/3135 Sch.1 para.44
Art.10, revoked: SI 2002/3135 Sch.1 para.44
Art.11, revoked: SI 2002/3135 Sch.1 para.44
Art.12, revoked: SI 2002/3135 Sch.1 para.44
Art.13, revoked: SI 2002/3135 Sch.1 para.44
Art.14, revoked: SI 2002/3135 Sch.1 para.44
Art.15, revoked (in part): SI 2002/3135 Sch.1 para.44
Art.16, revoked: SI 2002/3135 Sch.1 para.44
Art.18, applied: SI 2004/2608
Art.18, enabled: SI 2004/2608

1815. International Seabed Authority (Immunities and Privileges) Order 2000
Art.16, amended: 2002 c.8 s.2
Art.17, amended: 2002 c.8 s.2
Art.19, amended: 2002 c.8 s.2

1817. European Court of Human Rights (Immunities and Privileges) Order 2000
Art.4, amended: 2002 c.8 s.2

1818. Angola (United Nations Sanctions) (Amendment) Order 2000
revoked: SI 2003/1868 Sch.2

1819. Angola (United Nations Sanctions) (Overseas Territories) (Amendment) Order 2000
revoked: SI 2003/1868 Sch.2

1836. Angola (United Nations Sanctions) (Isle of Man) (Amendment) Order 2000
revoked: SI 2003/1868 Sch.2

1837. Angola (United Nations Sanctions) (Channel Islands) (Amendment) Order 2000
revoked: SI 2003/1868 Sch.2

NO.

2000–cont.

1844. London Borough of Hammersmith and Fulham (Electoral Changes) Order 2000
varied: SI 2004/222 Art.2

1845. London Borough of Enfield (Electoral Changes) Order 2000
varied: SI 2004/222 Art.2

1846. London Borough of Brent (Electoral Changes) Order 2000
varied: SI 2004/222 Art.2

1847. London Borough of Sutton (Electoral Changes) Order 2000
varied: SI 2004/222 Art.2

1849. Special Immigration Appeals Commission (Procedure) (Amendment) Rules 2000
revoked: SI 2003/1034 r.55

1866. Medical Food (Wales) Regulations 2000
Reg.2, amended: SI 2004/2731 Reg.6

1868. Community Care (Direct Payments) Amendment (Wales) Regulations 2000
revoked: SI 2004/1748 Reg.13

1870. Welfare of Farmed Animals (England) Regulations 2000
Reg.2, amended: SI 2002/1646 Reg.2, SI 2003/299 Reg.3
Reg.4, revoked: SI 2002/1646 Reg.2
Reg.5, substituted: SI 2002/1646 Reg.2
Reg.5A, added: SI 2002/1646 Reg.2
Reg.8A, added: SI 2003/299 Reg.3
Reg.12, amended: SI 2002/1646 Reg.2
Sch.1 para.2, amended: SI 2002/1646 Reg.2
Sch.1 para.7, amended: SI 2002/1646 Reg.2
Sch.2 para.1, revoked: SI 2002/1646 Reg.2
Sch.2 para.2, revoked: SI 2002/1646 Reg.2
Sch.2 para.3, revoked: SI 2002/1646 Reg.2
Sch.2 para.4, revoked: SI 2002/1646 Reg.2
Sch.2 para.5, revoked: SI 2002/1646 Reg.2
Sch.2 para.6, revoked: SI 2002/1646 Reg.2
Sch.2 para.7, revoked: SI 2002/1646 Reg.2
Sch.2 para.8, revoked: SI 2002/1646 Reg.2
Sch.2 para.9, revoked: SI 2002/1646 Reg.2
Sch.2 para.10, revoked: SI 2002/1646 Reg.2
Sch.3, substituted: SI 2002/1646 Reg.2
Sch.3A para.1, added: SI 2002/1646 Sch.1
Sch.3A para.2, added: SI 2002/1646 Sch.1
Sch.3A para.3, added: SI 2002/1646 Sch.1
Sch.3A para.4, added: SI 2002/1646 Sch.1
Sch.3A para.5, added: SI 2002/1646 Sch.1
Sch.3A para.6, added: SI 2002/1646 Sch.1
Sch.3A para.7, added: SI 2002/1646 Sch.1
Sch.3B para.1, added: SI 2002/1646 Sch.1
Sch.3B para.2, added: SI 2002/1646 Sch.1
Sch.3B para.3, added: SI 2002/1646 Sch.1
Sch.3C para.1, added: SI 2002/1646 Sch.1
Sch.3C para.2, added: SI 2002/1646 Sch.1
Sch.3C para.3, added: SI 2002/1646 Sch.1
Sch.3C para.4, added: SI 2002/1646 Sch.1

2000–cont.

1870. Welfare of Farmed Animals (England) Regulations 2000–*cont.*

Sch.3C para.5, added: SI 2002/1646 Sch.1
Sch.3C para.6, added: SI 2002/1646 Sch.1
Sch.3D para.1, added: SI 2002/1646 Sch.1
Sch.3D para.2, added: SI 2002/1646 Sch.1
Sch.3D para.3, added: SI 2002/1646 Sch.1
Sch.3D para.4, added: SI 2002/1646 Sch.1
Sch.3D para.5, added: SI 2002/1646 Sch.1
Sch.3D para.6, added: SI 2002/1646 Sch.1
Sch.3D para.7, added: SI 2002/1646 Sch.1
Sch.3D para.8, added: SI 2002/1646 Sch.1
Sch.3D para.9, added: SI 2002/1646 Sch.1
Sch.6 Part I para.1, substituted: SI 2003/299 Reg.3
Sch.6 Part II para.2, substituted: SI 2003/299 Reg.3
Sch.6 Part II para.3, substituted: SI 2003/299 Reg.3
Sch.6 Part II para.4, substituted: SI 2003/299 Reg.3
Sch.6 Part II para.5, substituted: SI 2003/299 Reg.3
Sch.6 Part II para.6, substituted: SI 2003/299 Reg.3
Sch.6 Part II para.7, substituted: SI 2003/299 Reg.3
Sch.6 Part II para.8, substituted: SI 2003/299 Reg.3
Sch.6 Part II para.9, substituted: SI 2003/299 Reg.3
Sch.6 Part II para.10, substituted: SI 2003/299 Reg.3
Sch.6 Part II para.11, substituted: SI 2003/299 Reg.3
Sch.6 Part II para.12, substituted: SI 2003/299 Reg.3
Sch.6 Part II para.13, substituted: SI 2003/299 Reg.3
Sch.6 Part II para.13, referred to: SI 2003/299 Reg.2
Sch.6 Part II para.13, substituted: SI 2003/299 Reg.3
Sch.6 Part II para.14, substituted: SI 2003/299 Reg.3
Sch.6 Part II para.15, substituted: SI 2003/299 Reg.3
Sch.6 Part II para.16, substituted: SI 2003/299 Reg.3
Sch.6 Part II para.17, substituted: SI 2003/299 Reg.3
Sch.6 Part II para.18, substituted: SI 2003/299 Reg.3
Sch.6 Part II para.19, substituted: SI 2003/299 Reg.3
Sch.6 Part II para.20, substituted: SI 2003/299 Reg.3
Sch.6 Part II para.21, substituted: SI 2003/299 Reg.3
Sch.6 Part II para.22, substituted: SI 2003/299 Reg.3

2000–cont.

1870. Welfare of Farmed Animals (England) Regulations 2000–*cont.*

Sch.6 Part II para.23, substituted: SI 2003/299 Reg.3
Sch.6 Part II para.24, substituted: SI 2003/299 Reg.3
Sch.6 Part II para.25, substituted: SI 2003/299 Reg.3
Sch.6 Part II para.26, substituted: SI 2003/299 Reg.3
Sch.6 Part III para.17, substituted: SI 2003/299 Reg.3
Sch.6 Part III para.18, substituted: SI 2003/299 Reg.3
Sch.6 Part III para.19, substituted: SI 2003/299 Reg.3
Sch.6 Part III para.27, substituted: SI 2003/299 Reg.3
Sch.6 Part III para.28, substituted: SI 2003/299 Reg.3
Sch.6 Part III para.29, substituted: SI 2003/299 Reg.3
Sch.6 Part IV para.20, substituted: SI 2003/299 Reg.3
Sch.6 Part IV para.21, substituted: SI 2003/299 Reg.3
Sch.6 Part IV para.22, substituted: SI 2003/299 Reg.3
Sch.6 Part IV para.23, substituted: SI 2003/299 Reg.3
Sch.6 Part IV para.24, substituted: SI 2003/299 Reg.3
Sch.6 Part IV para.30, substituted: SI 2003/299 Reg.3
Sch.6 Part IV para.31, substituted: SI 2003/299 Reg.3
Sch.6 Part IV para.32, substituted: SI 2003/299 Reg.3
Sch.6 Part IV para.33, substituted: SI 2003/299 Reg.3
Sch.6 Part IV para.34, substituted: SI 2003/299 Reg.3
Sch.6 Part IV para.35, substituted: SI 2003/299 Reg.3
Sch.6 Part IV para.36, substituted: SI 2003/299 Reg.3
Sch.6 Part IV para.37, substituted: SI 2003/299 Reg.3
Sch.6 Part IV para.38, substituted: SI 2003/299 Reg.3
Sch.6 Part IV para.39, substituted: SI 2003/299 Reg.3
Sch.6 Part IV para.40, substituted: SI 2003/299 Reg.3
Sch.6 Part IV para.41, substituted: SI 2003/299 Reg.3
Sch.6 Part IV para.42, substituted: SI 2003/299 Reg.3
Sch.6 Part V para.25, substituted: SI 2003/299 Reg.3

NO.

2000–cont.

1870. Welfare of Farmed Animals (England) Regulations 2000–*cont.*

Sch.6 Part V para.26, substituted: SI 2003/299 Reg.3

Sch.6 Part V para.27, substituted: SI 2003/299 Reg.3

Sch.6 Part V para.28, substituted: SI 2003/299 Reg.3

Sch.6 Part V para.29, referred to: SI 2003/299 Reg.2

Sch.6 Part V para.29, substituted: SI 2003/299 Reg.3

Sch.6 Part V para.43, substituted: SI 2003/299 Reg.3

Sch.6 Part V para.44, substituted: SI 2003/299 Reg.3

Sch.6 Part V para.45, substituted: SI 2003/299 Reg.3

Sch.6 Part V para.46, substituted: SI 2003/299 Reg.3

Sch.6 Part V para.47, substituted: SI 2003/299 Reg.3

Sch.6 Part VI para.30, substituted: SI 2003/299 Reg.3

Sch.6 Part VI para.31, substituted: SI 2003/299 Reg.3

Sch.6 Part VI para.37, referred to: SI 2003/299 Reg.2

Sch.6 Part VI para.37, substituted: SI 2003/299 Reg.3

Sch.6 Part VI para.38, referred to: SI 2003/299 Reg.2

Sch.6 Part VI para.38, substituted: SI 2003/299 Reg.3

Sch.6 Part VI para.39, referred to: SI 2003/299 Reg.2

Sch.6 Part VI para.39, substituted: SI 2003/299 Reg.3

Sch.6 Part VI para.48, substituted: SI 2003/299 Reg.3

Sch.6 Part VI para.49, substituted: SI 2003/299 Reg.3

Sch.6 Part VI para.50, substituted: SI 2003/299 Reg.3

Sch.6 Part VI para.51, substituted: SI 2003/299 Reg.3

Sch.6 Part VI para.52, substituted: SI 2003/299 Reg.3

1881. General Medical Council (Legal Assessors) (Amendment) Rules 2000

revoked: SI 2004/2625 r.6

1882. Foundation Subject (Amendment) (Wales) Order 2000

revoked: 2002 c.32 Sch.22 Part 3

1887. National Health Service (General Medical Services) Amendment (No.3) (Wales) Regulations 2000

revoked: SI 2004/1016 Sch.2

NO.

2000–cont.

1925. Genetically Modified and Novel Foods (Labelling) (Wales) Regulations 2000

Reg.2, amended: SI 2004/249 Reg.8

Reg.3, amended: SI 2004/249 Reg.8

Reg.9, amended: SI 2004/249 Reg.8

1926. Social Security (Work-focused Interviews for Lone Parents) and Miscellaneous Amendments Regulations 2000

Reg.1, amended: SI 2002/670 Reg.2, SI 2003/400 Reg.2, SI 2004/565 Reg.7

Reg.2, amended: SI 2002/670 Reg.2, SI 2004/959 Reg.25

Reg.4, amended: SI 2002/670 Reg.2, SI 2002/1703 Sch.2 para.7, SI 2004/959 Reg.25, SI 2004/2244 Reg.10

Reg.4, revoked (in part): SI 2003/400 Reg.2

Reg.7, amended: SI 2004/959 Reg.25

Reg.10, amended: SI 2003/492 Sch.3 Part 1

Sch.2 para.1, revoked (in part): SI 2003/492 Sch.3 Part 1

1940. Air Quality (Wales) Regulations 2000

Sch.1 Part I, amended: SI 2002/3182 Reg.2

Sch.1 Part II para.2, substituted: SI 2002/3182 Reg.2

Sch.1 Part II para.3, amended: SI 2002/3182 Reg.2

Sch.1 Part II para.4, amended: SI 2002/3182 Reg.2

1942. Airedale Primary Care Trust (Establishment) Order 2000

Art.1, amended: SI 2002/1405 Sch.1

Art.4, revoked: SI 2002/1405 Sch.1

1943. Bradford South and West Primary Care Trust (Establishment) Order 2000

Art.1, amended: SI 2002/1405 Sch.1

Art.4, revoked: SI 2002/1405 Sch.1

1944. North Bradford Primary Care Trust (Establishment) Order 2000

Art.1, amended: SI 2002/1405 Sch.1

Art.4, revoked: SI 2002/1405 Sch.1

1945. Bradford City Primary Care Trust (Establishment) Order 2000

Art.1, amended: SI 2002/1405 Sch.1, SI 2004/1630 Art.2

Art.2, amended: SI 2004/1630 Art.2

Art.4, revoked: SI 2002/1405 Sch.1

1961. Doncaster Central Primary Care Trust (Establishment) Order 2000

Art.1, amended: SI 2002/1405 Sch.1

Art.4, revoked: SI 2002/1405 Sch.1

Sch.1, amended: SI 2004/543 Sch.1

1962. Bexley Primary Care Trust (Establishment) Order 2000

Art.1, amended: SI 2002/1405 Sch.1, SI 2003/2168 Art.2

Art.2, added: SI 2003/2168 Art.4

Art.2, amended: SI 2003/2168 Art.2

NO.

2000–cont.

1962. Bexley Primary Care Trust (Establishment) Order 2000–cont.
Art.4, revoked: SI 2002/1405 Sch.1

1964. North Manchester Primary Care Trust (Establishment) Order 2000
Art.1, amended: SI 2002/1405 Sch.1
Art.4, revoked: SI 2002/1405 Sch.1

1965. Central Manchester Primary Care Trust (Establishment) Order 2000
Art.1, amended: SI 2002/1405 Sch.1
Art.4, revoked: SI 2002/1405 Sch.1

1970. Public Service Vehicles Accessibility Regulations 2000
Reg.4, amended: SI 2002/2981 Reg.2
Reg.7, amended: SI 2003/1818 Reg.2, SI 2004/1881 Reg.2
Reg.18, amended: SI 2003/1818 Reg.2
Sch.1 Part I para.5, amended: SI 2002/2981 Reg.2

1973. Pollution Prevention and Control (England and Wales) Regulations 2000
amended: SI 2004/107 Reg.8
applied: SI 2002/843 Reg.64, Reg.68, SI 2002/1416 Reg.64, Reg.68, SI 2004/107 Reg.3, Reg.6, SSI 2002/255 Reg.63, Reg.67
referred to: SI 2002/2980 Reg.2, SI 2004/434 Reg.2
see *R. (on the application of Furness) v Environment Agency* [2001] EWHC Admin 1058, [2002] Env. L.R. 26 (QBD (Admin Ct)), Turner, J.
Reg.2, amended: SI 2002/1559 Sch.5 para.1, SI 2002/2688 Reg.3, SI 2002/2980 Reg.5, SI 2003/3296 Reg.2, SI 2004/107 Reg.8
Reg.4, amended: SI 2002/1559 Sch.5 para.1, SI 2003/3296 Reg.2
Reg.4, applied: SI 2002/1559 Reg.8, Reg.11
Reg.5, amended: SI 2002/1559 Sch.5 para.1
Reg.6, amended: SI 2002/1559 Sch.5 para.1
Reg.8, amended: SI 2004/107 Reg.8
Reg.9, applied: SI 2004/434 Reg.3
Reg.10, amended: SI 2002/1559 Sch.5 para.1, SI 2004/107 Reg.8
Reg.10, applied: SI 2002/1559 Sch.4 para.1, SI 2002/2980 Reg.3, SI 2004/107 Reg.3, Reg.5, Reg.7
Reg.11, disapplied: SI 2002/1559 Reg.6
Reg.12, amended: SI 2002/1559 Sch.5 para.1, SI 2003/3311 Sch.5 para.1
Reg.12, disapplied: SI 2002/1559 Reg.6
Reg.12A, added: SI 2004/107 Reg.8
Reg.14, amended: SI 2004/107 Reg.8
Reg.17, amended: SI 2002/1559 Sch.5 para.1, SI 2004/107 Reg.8
Reg.17, applied: SI 2002/1559 Sch.4 para.1, SI 2002/2688 Reg.4, Reg.5, SI 2002/2980 Reg.3, SI 2004/107 Reg.3, Reg.4
Reg.17, varied: SI 2004/107 Reg.4

NO.

2000–cont.

1973. Pollution Prevention and Control (England and Wales) Regulations 2000–cont.
Reg.19, amended: SI 2002/2980 Reg.5
Reg.19, disapplied: SI 2002/1559 Reg.15
Reg.20, amended: SI 2002/2980 Reg.5
Reg.21, disapplied: SI 2002/1559 Reg.15
Reg.24, applied: SI 2002/2980 Reg.3, SI 2004/107 Reg.3, Reg.6
Reg.27, amended: SI 2002/1559 Sch.5 para.1
Reg.28, amended: SI 2002/1559 Sch.5 para.1
Reg.28, applied: SI 2004/107 Reg.6
Reg.32, amended: SI 2002/1559 Sch.5 para.1
Reg.36, amended: SI 2002/1559 Sch.5 para.1
Reg.37, amended: SI 2002/1559 Sch.5 para.1
Sch.1 Part 1, amended: SI 2003/1699 Reg.2
Sch.1 Part 1, applied: SI 2004/107 Reg.4, Reg.5
Sch.1 Part 1, referred to: SI 2002/2980 Reg.3
Sch.1 Part 1, amended: SI 2003/1699 Reg.2
Sch.1 Part 1, applied: SI 2004/107 Reg.4, Reg.5
Sch.1 Part 1, added: SI 2004/107 Sch.1
Sch.1 Part 1, amended: SI 2002/1559 Reg.6, SI 2002/2980 Reg.5
Sch.1 Part 1, applied: SI 2002/1559 Reg.8, SI 2004/107 Reg.4, Reg.5
Sch.1 Part 1, referred to: SI 2002/1559 Reg.6, Sch.4 para.1, Sch.4 para.2, Sch.4 para.4
Sch.1 Part 1, substituted: SI 2002/2980 Reg.5
Sch.1 Part 1 para.1, applied: SI 2004/107 Reg.4, Reg.5
Sch.1 Part 1 para.2, applied: SI 2004/107 Reg.4, Reg.5
Sch.1 Part 2 para.2, amended: SI 2004/107 Reg.8
Sch.1 Part 2 para.3, amended: SI 2004/107 Reg.8
Sch.1 Part 2 para.4, amended: SI 2004/107 Reg.8
Sch.1 Part 2 para.5, amended: SI 2004/107 Reg.8
Sch.1 Part 2 para.6, amended: SI 2004/107 Reg.8
Sch.1 Part 2 para.7, amended: SI 2004/107 Reg.8
Sch.1 Part 2 para.7A, added: SI 2004/107 Reg.8
Sch.1 Part 2 para.9, amended: SI 2004/107 Reg.8
Sch.1 Part 2 para.10, amended: SI 2004/107 Reg.8
Sch.1 Part 3 para.17, amended: SI 2002/2980 Reg.5
Sch.1 Part 3 para.18, revoked: SI 2002/2980 Reg.5

2000–cont.

1973. Pollution Prevention and Control (England and Wales) Regulations 2000–cont.

Sch.1 Part 3 para.21, substituted: SI 2004/107 Reg.8

Sch.3 Part 1 para.1, amended: SI 2002/1559 Sch.4 para.4

Sch.3 Part 1 para.1, varied: SI 2002/2980 Reg.4

Sch.3 Part 1 para.2, amended: SI 2002/275 Reg.2, SI 2002/1559 Sch.5 para.1, SI 2002/1702 Reg.2, SI 2002/2980 Reg.5, SI 2003/1699 Reg.2, SI 2003/3296 Reg.2, SI 2004/1375 Reg.9

Sch.3 Part 1 para.4, varied: SI 2002/2980 Reg.4

Sch.3 Part 1 para.5, amended: SI 2004/107 Reg.8

Sch.3 Part 1 para.6, amended: SI 2002/2980 Reg.5

Sch.3 Part 1 para.6, varied: SI 2002/2980 Reg.4

Sch.3 Part 2 para.9, applied: SI 2004/434 Reg.3

Sch.3 Part 2 para.9, disapplied: SI 2004/434 Reg.3

Sch.3 Part 2 para.9, referred to: SI 2004/434 Reg.3

Sch.3 Part 2 para.10, amended: SI 2002/275 Reg.2

Sch.3 Part 2 para.10, referred to: SI 2004/434 Reg.3

Sch.3 Part 3 para.12, added: SI 2004/107 Sch.2

Sch.3 Part 3 para.12, varied: SI 2004/107 Reg.4

Sch.3 Part 3 para.13, added: SI 2004/107 Sch.2

Sch.3 Part 3 para.13, varied: SI 2004/107 Reg.4

Sch.3 Part 3 para.14, added: SI 2004/107 Sch.2

Sch.3 Part 3 para.14, varied: SI 2004/107 Reg.4

Sch.3 Part 3 para.15, added: SI 2004/107 Sch.2

Sch.3 Part 3 para.15, varied: SI 2004/107 Reg.4

Sch.3 Part 3 para.16, added: SI 2004/107 Sch.2

Sch.3 Part 3 para.16, varied: SI 2004/107 Reg.4

Sch.3 Part 3 para.17, added: SI 2004/107 Sch.2

Sch.3 Part 3 para.17, varied: SI 2004/107 Reg.4

Sch.3 Part 4 para.18, added: SI 2004/107 Sch.2

Sch.3 Part 4 para.18, applied: SI 2004/107 Reg.4, Reg.5

Sch.3 Part 4 para.19, added: SI 2004/107 Sch.2

2000–cont.

1973. Pollution Prevention and Control (England and Wales) Regulations 2000–cont.

Sch.4 Part 1 para.1, amended: SI 2002/2980 Reg.5, SI 2004/107 Reg.8

Sch.4 Part 1 para.1A, added: SI 2002/1559 Sch.5 para.1

Sch.4 Part 1 para.1B, added: SI 2002/2980 Reg.5

Sch.4 Part 1 para.1B, referred to: SI 2002/2980 Reg.3

Sch.4 Part 1 para.1C, added: SI 2004/107 Reg.8

Sch.4 Part 1 para.1C, referred to: SI 2004/107 Reg.3

Sch.4 Part 1 para.3A, added: SI 2004/107 Reg.8

Sch.4 Part 1 para.5, disapplied: SI 2002/1559 Reg.6

Sch.4 Part 1 para.8, substituted: SI 2004/107 Reg.8

Sch.4 Part 2 para.9, amended: SI 2002/2469 Sch.5, Sch.8, SI 2003/3296 Reg.2

Sch.4 Part 2 para.10, substituted: SI 2004/107 Reg.8

Sch.7 Part 1 para.1, amended: SI 2002/2980 Reg.5

Sch.7 Part 1 para.1, varied: SI 2004/107 Reg.4

Sch.7 Part 1 para.2, varied: SI 2004/107 Reg.4

Sch.7 Part 1 para.2A, added: SI 2004/107 Reg.8

Sch.7 Part 1 para.2A, varied: SI 2004/107 Reg.4

Sch.7 Part 1 para.3, varied: SI 2004/107 Reg.4

Sch.7 Part 2 para.4, amended: SI 2004/107 Reg.8

Sch.7 Part 2 para.4, disapplied: SI 2002/1559 Reg.6

Sch.7 Part 2 para.4, varied: SI 2004/107 Reg.4

Sch.7 Part 2 para.5, varied: SI 2004/107 Reg.4

Sch.7 Part 2 para.6, varied: SI 2004/107 Reg.4

Sch.7 Part 2 para.7, varied: SI 2004/107 Reg.4

Sch.7 Part 2 para.8, varied: SI 2004/107 Reg.4

Sch.7 Part 2 para.9, varied: SI 2004/107 Reg.4

Sch.7 Part 2 para.10, varied: SI 2004/107 Reg.4

Sch.7 Part 2 para.11, varied: SI 2004/107 Reg.4

Sch.7 Part 2 para.12, varied: SI 2004/107 Reg.4

Sch.7 Part 3 para.13, varied: SI 2004/107 Reg.4

Sch.7 Part 3 para.14, varied: SI 2004/107 Reg.4

NO.

2000–cont.

1973. Pollution Prevention and Control (England and Wales) Regulations 2000–*cont.*

Sch.7 Part 3 para.15, varied: SI 2004/107 Reg.4

Sch.7 Part 3 para.16, varied: SI 2004/107 Reg.4

Sch.8 para.2, amended: SI 2004/1375 Reg.9

Sch.9 para.1, amended: SI 2002/1559 Sch.5 para.1, SI 2002/2980 Reg.5

1974. Education (Outturn Statements) (England) Regulations 2000

applied: SI 2002/536 Reg.3

1977. London Borough of Greenwich (Electoral Changes) Order 2000

varied: SI 2004/222 Art.2

1979. General Teaching Council for Wales (Functions) Regulations 2000

Reg.2, amended: SI 2004/1741 Reg.2

Reg.3A, added: SI 2004/1741 Reg.2

Reg.4, substituted: SI 2004/1741 Reg.2

Reg.16, amended: SI 2004/1741 Reg.2

Reg.17, amended: SI 2004/1741 Reg.2

Reg.18, added: SI 2004/1741 Reg.2

Reg.19, added: SI 2004/1741 Reg.2

Sch.1 para.16, amended: SI 2004/1741 Reg.2

Sch.1 para.19, amended: SI 2004/1741 Reg.2

Sch.1 para.21, substituted: SI 2004/1741 Reg.2

Sch.2 para.1, amended: SI 2004/1741 Reg.2

Sch.2 para.2, amended: SI 2004/1741 Reg.2

Sch.2 para.3, amended: SI 2004/1741 Reg.2

Sch.2 para.4, amended: SI 2004/1741 Reg.2

Sch.2 para.5, amended: SI 2004/1741 Reg.2

Sch.2 para.6, amended: SI 2004/1741 Reg.2

Sch.2 para.7, amended: SI 2004/1741 Reg.2

Sch.2 para.8, amended: SI 2004/1741 Reg.2

Sch.2 para.9, amended: SI 2004/1741 Reg.2

Sch.2 para.10, amended: SI 2004/1741 Reg.2

Sch.2 para.11, amended: SI 2004/1741 Reg.2

Sch.2 para.12, amended: SI 2004/1741 Reg.2

Sch.2 para.12, substituted: SI 2004/1741 Reg.2

Sch.2 para.13, amended: SI 2004/1741 Reg.2

Sch.2 para.13A, amended: SI 2004/1741 Reg.2

Sch.2 para.13B, amended: SI 2004/1741 Reg.2

Sch.2 para.14, amended: SI 2004/1741 Reg.2

1980. Education (National Curriculum) (Modern Foreign Languages) (Wales) Order 2000

revoked: 2002 c.32 Sch.22 Part 3

1982. Social Security (Joint Claims Consequential Amendments) Regulations 2000

Reg.2, revoked (in part): SI 2003/492 Sch.3 Part 1

NO.

2000–cont.

1989. National Minimum Wage Regulations 1999 (Amendment) Regulations 2000

Reg.3, revoked: SI 2002/1999 Sch.1

Reg.10, amended: SI 2002/1999 Sch.1

1992. National Health Service (General Medical Services) Amendment (No.2) (Wales) Regulations 2000

revoked: SI 2004/1016 Sch.2

2013. Police (Amendment) Regulations 2000

revoked: SI 2003/527 Sch.4 Part 1

2014. North Stoke Primary Care Trust (Establishment) Order 2000

Art.1, amended: SI 2002/1405 Sch.1

Art.4, revoked: SI 2002/1405 Sch.1

Sch.1, amended: SI 2002/1113 Art.2, SI 2002/1392 Art.2

2015. Milton Keynes Primary Care Trust (Establishment) Order 2000

applied: SI 2003/3059 Sch.1

Art.1, amended: SI 2002/1405 Sch.1

Art.4, revoked: SI 2002/1405 Sch.1

Sch.1, amended: SI 2004/543 Sch.1

2027. Sheep and Goats Identification (England) Order 2000

applied: SI 2002/240 Art.9, Art.13, SI 2002/2153 Art.9, Art.10, Art.13

revoked: SI 2002/240 Art.18

Art.3, applied: SI 2002/240 Art.3

Art.8, applied: SI 2002/240 Art.4, Art.5, Art.7, Art.8, Art.9, Art.12, SI 2002/2153 Art.4, Art.5, Art.7, Art.8, Art.9, Art.12, SI 2002/2302 Art.7

Art.15, applied: SI 2002/240 Art.7, SI 2002/2153 Art.7, Art.8, SI 2002/2302 Art.7

2033. General Medical Council (Voluntary Erasure and Restoration) Regulations Order of Council 2000

revoked: SI 2003/1341 Art.2

Sch.1, applied: SI 2003/1341 Sch.1

Sch.1, revoked: SI 2003/1342 Art.2

2042. Sunderland West Primary Care Trust (Establishment) Order 2000

revoked: SI 2002/1325 Sch.1

2043. Dartford, Gravesham and Swanley Primary Care Trust (Establishment) Order 2000

applied: SI 2003/3059 Sch.1

Art.1, amended: SI 2002/1405 Sch.1

Art.4, revoked: SI 2002/1405 Sch.1

Sch.1, amended: SI 2004/543 Sch.1

2044. Birmingham Specialist Community Health National Health Service Trust (Establishment) Amendment Order 2000

revoked: 2003 c.43 s.7

2047. Faculty Jurisdiction Rules 2000

referred to: SI 2002/1892 Sch.1 Part TABLE, SI 2003/1933 Sch.1 Part I

Part II r.3, referred to: SI 2003/1933 Sch.1 Part I, SI 2004/1888 Sch.1 Part TABLE

NO.

2000–cont.

2047. Faculty Jurisdiction Rules 2000–cont.
Part II r.5, referred to: SI 2004/1888 Sch.1 Part TABLE
Part II r.6, applied: SI 2003/1933 Sch.1 Part I
Part II r.6, referred to: SI 2004/1888 Sch.1 Part TABLE
Part III r.7, applied: SI 2003/1933 Sch.1 Part I
Part III r.9, applied: SI 2003/1933 Sch.1 Part I
Part III r.9, referred to: SI 2004/1888 Sch.1 Part TABLE
Part IV r.18, applied: SI 2003/1933 Sch.1 Part I
Part IV r.18, referred to: SI 2004/1888 Sch.1 Part TABLE
Part IV r.25, applied: SI 2003/1933 Sch.1 Part I
Part IV r.25, referred to: SI 2004/1888 Sch.1 Part TABLE

2048. Faculty Jurisdiction (Care of Places of Worship) Rules 2000
applied: SI 2004/1888 Sch.1 Part TABLE
referred to: SI 2002/1892 Sch.1 Part TABLE, SI 2003/1933 Sch.1 Part I

2051. General Medical Council (Fitness to Practise Committees) Rules Order of Council 2000
Sch.1, revoked: SI 2003/1344 Sch.1

2052. General Medical Council (Constitution of Interim Orders Committee) Rules Order of Council 2000
revoked: SI 2003/1344 Art.2
Sch.1, substituted: SI 2002/2572 Sch.1 para.8
Sch.1, varied: SI 2003/1344 Sch.1

2053. General Medical Council (Interim Orders Committee) (Procedure) Rules Order of Council 2000
Sch.1, added: SI 2002/2572 Sch.1 para.6
Sch.1, substituted: SI 2002/2572 Sch.1 para.6

2054. General Medical Council (Interim Orders Committee) (Transitional Provisions) Rules Order of Council 2000
revoked: SI 2004/2608 Sch.1

2058. Borough of Nuneaton and Bedworth (Electoral Changes) Order 2000
varied: SI 2004/222 Art.2
Art.3, revoked: SI 2002/1962 Art.6
Sch.2, revoked: SI 2002/1962 Art.6

2059. District of Stratford on Avon (Electoral Changes) Order 2000
varied: SI 2004/222 Art.2

2074. Donations to Charity by Individuals (Appropriate Declarations) Regulations 2000
Reg.2, amended: SI 2003/2155 Sch.1 para.23

2081. Research and Development (Prescribed Activities) Regulations 2000
revoked: SI 2004/712 Reg.3

2088. Supply of New Cars Order 2000
applied: SI 2004/2181 Sch.2

NO.

2000–cont.

2110. Foreign Package Holidays (Tour Operators and Travel Agents) Order 2000
applied: SI 2004/2181 Sch.2

2119. Evaluation of Active Substances for Pesticides (Fees) Regulations 2000
Reg.3, added: SI 2004/694 Reg.2
Reg.4, added: SI 2004/694 Reg.2

2122. Education (School Government) (Terms of Reference) (England) Regulations 2000
Reg.6, applied: SI 2003/1377 Reg.16

2126. Football Spectators (Prescription) Order 2000
revoked: SI 2004/2409 Art.2

2129. Tonnage Tax (Training Requirement) Regulations 2000
referred to: SI 2003/2320 Reg.1
Reg.4, amended: SI 2003/2320 Reg.3
Reg.4, applied: SI 2003/2320 Reg.2
Reg.5, applied: SI 2003/2320 Reg.2
Reg.15, amended: SI 2002/2265 Reg.3, SI 2003/2320 Reg.4, SI 2004/2255 Reg.3
Reg.21, amended: SI 2002/2265 Reg.3, SI 2003/2320 Reg.5, SI 2004/2255 Reg.3

2151. Dartford-Thurrock Crossing (Amendment) Regulations 2000
revoked: SI 2003/496 Reg.3

2154. Torbay Primary Care Trust (Establishment) Order 2000
Art.1, amended: SI 2002/1405 Sch.1
Art.4, revoked: SI 2002/1405 Sch.1
Art.8, revoked: SI 2002/1118 Art.2

2155. Bournemouth Primary Care Trust (Establishment) Order 2000
Art.1, amended: SI 2002/1405 Sch.1, SI 2003/2664 Art.2
Art.2, amended: SI 2003/2664 Art.2
Art.4, revoked: SI 2002/1405 Sch.1

2156. South Hams and West Devon Primary Care Trust (Establishment) Order 2000
Art.1, amended: SI 2002/1405 Sch.1
Art.4, revoked: SI 2002/1405 Sch.1
Sch.1, amended: SI 2004/543 Sch.1

2157. North Dorset Primary Care Trust (Establishment) Order 2000
Art.1, amended: SI 2002/1405 Sch.1
Art.4, revoked: SI 2002/1405 Sch.1
Sch.1, amended: SI 2004/543 Sch.1

2158. Carrick Primary Care Trust (Establishment) Order 2000
revoked: SI 2002/1325 Sch.1

2173. Wiltshire College (Government) Regulations 2000
revoked: SI 2002/1094 Sch.1 Part 1

2174. Teacher Training Agency (Additional Functions) (No.2) Order 2000
Art.2, amended: SI 2002/2513 Art.2, SI 2003/2038 Art.4
Art.2, revoked (in part): SI 2003/2038 Art.4

NO.

2000–cont.

2174. Teacher Training Agency (Additional Functions) (No.2) Order 2000–*cont.*

Art.4, amended: SI 2003/537 Reg.2, SI 2003/2038 Art.5

2190. Transport and Works (Applications and Objections Procedure) (England and Wales) Rules 2000

applied: SI 2002/1327, SI 2002/1943, SI 2002/2398, SI 2003/2829, SI 2003/2830, SI 2003/2831, SI 2003/2907, SI 2004/389, SI 2004/757, SI 2004/933, SI 2004/1817

r.4, amended: SI 2003/1615 Sch.1 para.56, SI 2003/2155 Sch.1 para.17, Sch.2

Sch.7 Part I, amended: SI 2002/1965 r.3

Sch.7 Part II para.1, amended: SI 2002/1965 r.4

2195. Education (Change of Category of Maintained Schools) (England) Regulations 2000

Reg.2, amended: SI 2003/2136 Reg.3

Reg.11, amended: SI 2003/2136 Reg.4

Reg.12, substituted: SI 2003/2136 Reg.5

Reg.13, substituted: SI 2003/2136 Reg.6

Reg.14, amended: SI 2003/2136 Reg.7

Reg.16, amended: SI 2003/2136 Reg.8

Reg.16A, added: SI 2003/2136 Reg.9

Sch.1, amended: SI 2003/2136 Reg.10

Sch.2, substituted: SI 2003/2136 Sch.1

Sch.4 Part I, substituted: SI 2003/2136 Sch.2

Sch.4 para.1, substituted: SI 2003/2136 Sch.2

Sch.4 Part II, substituted: SI 2003/2136 Sch.2

Sch.4 Part III, substituted: SI 2003/2136 Sch.2

Sch.4 Part IV, substituted: SI 2003/2136 Sch.2

Sch.4 Part V, substituted: SI 2003/2136 Sch.2

Sch.4 Part VI para.1, substituted: SI 2003/2136 Sch.2

Sch.5, revoked: SI 2003/2136 Reg.13

2197. Education (Student Support) (European Institutions) Regulations 2000

Sch.1 para.8, see *R. (on the application of Haracoglou) v Department for Education and Skills* [2001] EWHC Admin 678, [2002] E.L.R. 177 (QBD (Admin Ct)), Hooper, J.

2212. Land Registration (Conduct of Business) Regulations 2000

Reg.2, varied: SI 2003/1953 Art.6

Reg.3, varied: SI 2003/1953 Art.6

Reg.5, varied: SI 2003/1953 Art.6

Reg.6, varied: SI 2003/1953 Art.6

2213. Land Registration (Hearings Procedure) Rules 2000

applied: SI 2003/1953 Art.6

NO.

2000–cont.

2243. Immigration (Removal Directions) Regulations 2000

Reg.4, see *R. (on the application of Pharis) v Secretary of State for the Home Department* [2004] EWCA Civ 654, [2004] 1 W.L.R. 2590 (CA), Brooke, L.J.

2244. Immigration and Asylum Appeals (One-Stop Procedure) Regulations 2000

Reg.4, amended: SI 2002/2731 Reg.2

Sch.1 Part II, amended: SI 2002/2731 Reg.3

2246. Immigration and Asylum Appeals (Notices) Regulations 2000

revoked: 2002 c.41 Sch.9

2250. Medicines (Products for Animal Use-Fees) (Amendment) Regulations 2000

revoked: SI 2004/2750 Reg.18

2265. General Chiropractic Council (Appeals Against Decisions of the Registrar) Rules Order 2000

referred to: SI 2004/1877 Sch.1

2266. Animals and Animal Products (Import and Export) (England and Wales) (Amendment) Regulations 2000

revoked (in part): SI 2004/853 Reg.35

2310. County Court Fees (Amendment No 4) Order 2000

revoked: SI 2004/3121 Sch.2

2324. School Teachers Remuneration Order 2000

revoked: 2002 c.32 Sch.22 Part 1

2326. Immigration (European Economic Area) Regulations 2000

applied: 2002 c.41 s.11, SI 2003/2818 Art.11, 2004 c.6 s.2, SI 2004/1219 Reg.2, Reg.4, Reg.6

revoked: 2002 c.41 Sch.9

varied: SI 2002/1241 Sch.1 para.7, Sch.1 para.11, Sch.1 para.14

Reg.2, amended: SI 2003/549 Reg.2, SI 2004/1219 Reg.3, SI 2004/1236 Reg.2

Reg.2, varied: SI 2002/1241 Sch.1 para.1, SI 2003/2818 Sch.2 para.5

Reg.3, amended: SI 2004/1236 Reg.2

Reg.3, varied: SI 2002/1241 Sch.1 para.2

Reg.5, applied: SI 2002/1792 Reg.2, SI 2004/1219 Reg.5

Reg.5, disapplied: SI 2004/1219 Reg.5

Reg.5, varied: SI 2004/1219 Reg.5

Reg.6, amended: SI 2003/549 Reg.2, SI 2003/3188 Reg.2

Reg.6, applied: SI 2002/1241 Reg.2, SI 2004/1219 Reg.6

Reg.7, varied: SI 2002/1241 Sch.1 para.3

Reg.9, amended: SI 2003/549 Reg.2

Reg.9, varied: SI 2002/1241 Sch.1 para.4

Reg.10, disapplied: SI 2004/1219 Reg.5

Reg.10, varied: SI 2002/1241 Sch.1 para.5

NO.

2000–cont.

2326. Immigration (European Economic Area) Regulations 2000–cont.

Reg.12, see *R. (on the application of Kimani) v Lambeth LBC* [2003] EWCA Civ 1150, [2004] 1 W.L.R. 272 (CA), Lord Phillips of Worth Matravers, M.R.

Reg.12, varied: SI 2002/1241 Sch.1 para.6, SI 2003/2818 Sch.2 para.5

Reg.14, varied: SI 2002/1241 Sch.1 para.8

Reg.15, disapplied: SI 2004/1219 Reg.5

Reg.15, varied: SI 2002/1241 Sch.1 para.9

Reg.16, varied: SI 2002/1241 Sch.1 para.10

Reg.17, varied: SI 2002/1241 Sch.1 para.12

Reg.18, varied: SI 2002/1241 Sch.1 para.13

Reg.20, amended: SI 2003/549 Reg.2

Reg.21, applied: SI 2004/1219 Reg.6

Reg.21, varied: SI 2002/1241 Sch.1 para.15, SI 2003/2818 Sch.2 para.5

Reg.22, varied: SI 2002/1241 Sch.1 para.16

Reg.24, varied: SI 2002/1241 Sch.1 para.17

Reg.25, revoked (in part): SI 2003/549 Reg.2

Reg.25, varied: SI 2002/1241 Sch.1 para.18

Reg.26, varied: SI 2002/1241 Sch.1 para.19

Reg.26A, added: SI 2003/549 Reg.2

Reg.27, substituted: SI 2003/549 Reg.2

Reg.28, substituted: SI 2003/549 Reg.2

Reg.29, applied: SI 2004/1219 Reg.6

Reg.29, substituted: SI 2003/549 Reg.2

Reg.30, substituted: SI 2003/549 Reg.2

Reg.30, varied: SI 2002/1241 Sch.1 para.20

Reg.31, substituted: SI 2003/549 Reg.2

Reg.32, substituted: SI 2003/549 Reg.2

Reg.33, substituted: SI 2003/549 Reg.2

Reg.33, added: SI 2003/549 Reg.2

Reg.33, amended: SI 2003/3188 Reg.2, SI 2004/1236 Reg.2

Reg.34, substituted: SI 2003/549 Reg.2

Reg.35, substituted: SI 2003/549 Reg.2

Reg.35, varied: SI 2002/1241 Sch.1 para.21

Reg.36, substituted: SI 2003/549 Reg.2

Reg.36, varied: SI 2002/1241 Sch.1 para.21

Sch.2, substituted: SI 2003/549 Reg.2, SI 2003/3188 Reg.2

Sch.2 para.1, substituted: SI 2003/549 Reg.2, SI 2003/3188 Reg.2

Sch.2 para.2, substituted: SI 2003/549 Reg.2, SI 2003/3188 Reg.2

Sch.2 para.3, substituted: SI 2003/549 Reg.2, SI 2003/3188 Reg.2

2329. Football (Offences) (Designation of Football Matches) Order 2000

revoked: SI 2004/2410 Art.2

2330. Education (Grants for Disabled Post-graduate Students) Regulations 2000

Reg.2, amended: SI 2003/3280 Reg.3, SI 2004/1658 Reg.5

Reg.2, applied: SI 2002/2104 Reg.4, SI 2003/1588 Reg.4

Reg.2, referred to: SI 2004/1658 Reg.4

2000–cont.

2330. Education (Grants for Disabled Post-graduate Students) Regulations 2000–cont.

Reg.2, revoked (in part): SI 2004/1658 Reg.5

Reg.3, amended: SI 2003/1588 Reg.5, SI 2004/1658 Reg.6

Reg.9, amended: SI 2002/2104 Reg.3, SI 2003/1588 Reg.6, SI 2004/1658 Reg.7

Sch.1 para.4, amended: SI 2003/3280 Reg.3

Sch.1 para.6, amended: SI 2003/3280 Reg.3

Sch.1 para.7, amended: SI 2003/3280 Reg.3

2333. Immigration and Asylum Appeals (Procedure) Rules 2000

revoked: SI 2003/652 r.60

see *Daqlawi v Secretary of State for the Home Department* 2003 S.L.T. 755 (OH), Lord Menzies

Part I r.4, applied: SI 2003/652 r.61

r.16, see *R. (on the application of Maqsood) v Special Adjudicator* [2001] EWHC Admin 1003, [2002] Imm. A.R. 268 (QBD (Admin Ct)), Stanley Burnton, J.

r.18, see *R. (on the application of Tataw) v Immigration Appeal Tribunal* [2003] EWCA Civ 925, [2003] I.N.L.R. 585 (CA), May, L.J.

r.30, see *R. (on the application of Rahmani) v Secretary of State for the Home Department* [2002] Imm. A.R. 627 (QBD (Admin Ct)), Sir Richard Tucker

r.33, see *Benkaddouri v Secretary of State for the Home Department* [2003] EWCA Civ 1250, [2004] I.N.L.R. 1 (CA), Sedley, L.J.

r.41, see *R. (on the application of Maqsood) v Special Adjudicator* [2001] EWHC Admin 1003, [2002] Imm. A.R. 268 (QBD (Admin Ct)), Stanley Burnton, J.

2334. Consumer Protection (Distance Selling) Regulations 2000

applied: SI 2003/1400 Sch.4

referred to: SI 2003/1374 Sch.1

Reg.3, amended: SI 2004/2095 Reg.25

Reg.5, amended: SI 2004/2095 Reg.25

Reg.6, amended: SI 2004/2095 Reg.25

Reg.15, applied: SI 2004/2095 Reg.11

Reg.24, applied: SI 2003/1376 Sch.1

Sch.2 para.1, revoked: SI 2004/2095 Reg.25

Sch.2 para.2, revoked: SI 2004/2095 Reg.25

Sch.2 para.3, revoked: SI 2004/2095 Reg.25

Sch.2 para.4, revoked: SI 2004/2095 Reg.25

2335. Sheep and Goats Identification (Wales) Regulations 2000

applied: SI 2002/274 Reg.9, Reg.10, Reg.13, SI 2002/1357 Art.9, Art.10, Art.13, SI 2002/2302 Art.9, Art.10

revoked: SI 2002/274 Reg.18

Reg.3, applied: SI 2002/274 Reg.3

Reg.7, applied: SI 2002/274 Reg.4, Reg.5, Reg.7, Reg.8, Reg.9, SI 2002/1357 Art.4, Art.5, Art.7, Art.8, Art.9, Art.12, SI 2002/2302 Art.4, Art.5, Art.7, Art.8, Art.9, Art.12

NO.

2335. Sheep and Goats Identification (Wales) Regulations 2000–*cont.*
Reg.14, applied: SI 2002/274 Reg.7, SI 2002/1357 Art.7, SI 2002/2302 Art.7

2336. Social Security (Payments on account, Overpayments and Recovery) Amendment Regulations 2000
revoked (in part): SI 2003/492 Sch.3 Part 1

2338. Birmingham North East Primary Care Trust (Establishment) Order 2000
revoked: SI 2002/1325 Sch.1

2339. Greater Yardley Primary Care Trust (Establishment) Order 2000
revoked: SI 2002/1325 Sch.1

2367. Naval Custody Rules 2000
Part I r.2., amended: SI 2004/66 Art.4
Part III r.16., amended: SI 2004/66 Art.4
Part IV r.18., amended: SI 2004/66 Art.4

2370. Summary Appeal Court (Navy) Rules 2000
Part I r.2, amended: SI 2004/66 Art.5
Part II r.10, amended: SI 2004/1949 r.3
Part II r.12, amended: SI 2004/66 Art.5
Part II r.15, amended: SI 2004/66 Art.5
Part III r.22, amended: SI 2004/66 Art.5
Part IV r.23, amended: SI 2004/1949 r.4
Part IV r.24, amended: SI 2004/1949 r.5
Part IV r.25, amended: SI 2004/1949 r.6
Part IX r.60, amended: SI 2004/1949 r.7

2371. Summary Appeal Court (Army) Rules 2000
Part II r.10, amended: SI 2004/1950 r.3
Part IV r.23, amended: SI 2004/1950 r.4
Part IV r.24, amended: SI 2004/1950 r.5
Part IV r.25, amended: SI 2004/1950 r.6
Part IX r.60, amended: SI 2004/1950 r.7

2372. Summary Appeal Court (Air Force) Rules 2000
Part I r.2., amended: SI 2004/1951 r.3
Part II r.10., amended: SI 2004/1951 r.4
Part IV r.23., amended: SI 2004/1951 r.5
Part IV r.24., amended: SI 2004/1951 r.6
Part IV r.25., amended: SI 2004/1951 r.7
Part IX r.60., amended: SI 2004/1951 r.8

2376. Administration of Oaths (Summary Appeal Court) (Navy) Order 2000
Art.2, amended: SI 2004/66 Art.6, SI 2004/1937 Art.7

2377. Administration of Oaths (Summary Appeal Court) (Army) Order 2000
Art.2, amended: SI 2004/1937 Art.7

2378. Administration of Oaths (Summary Appeal Court) (Air Force) Order 2000
Art.2, amended: SI 2004/1937 Art.7

2381. Chemicals (Hazard Information and Packaging for Supply) (Amendment) Regulations 2000
revoked: SI 2002/1689 Sch.7

NO.

2383. National Health Service (General Medical Services) Amendment (No.4) Regulations 2000
revoked: SI 2004/865 Sch.2

2387. West Suffolk Hospitals National Health Service Trust (Establishment) Amendment Order 2000
revoked: 2003 c.43 s.7

2389. King's Healthcare National Health Service Trust (Change of Name) Order 2000
revoked: 2003 c.43 s.7

2392. Morecambe Bay Primary Care Trust (Establishment) Order 2000
Art.1, amended: SI 2002/1405 Sch.1
Art.4, revoked: SI 2002/1405 Sch.1

2394. Swine Fever (Movement Restriction Areas) Order 2000
revoked: SI 2003/2329 Art.19

2408. Gaming Duty (Amendment) Regulations 2000
revoked: SI 2002/2310 Reg.3

2409. Wireless Telegraphy (Interception and Disclosure of Messages) (Designation) Regulations 2000
revoked: SI 2003/3104 Reg.2

2410. Telecommunications (Services for Disabled Persons) Regulations 2000
revoked: 2003 c.21 Sch.19

2413. Companies (Welsh Language Forms) (Amendment) Regulations 2000
Sch.1, applied: SI 2003/62 Reg.3

2417. Regulation of Investigatory Powers (Prescription of Offices, Ranks and Positions) Order 2000
revoked: SI 2003/3171 Art.11
Sch.1 Part I, amended: SI 2002/794 Sch.1 para.48, SI 2002/1298 Art.2, SI 2002/1555 Art.41

2418. Regulation of Investigatory Powers (Authorisations Extending to Scotland) Order 2000
Sch.1, amended: SI 2002/1555 Art.42

2419. Education (Restriction of Employment) Regulations 2000
revoked: SI 2003/1184 Reg.3
Reg.2, varied: SI 2003/1184 Reg.3
Reg.5, see *R. (on the application of Dorling) v Sheffield City Council* [2002] EWHC 2505, [2003] I.C.R. 424 (QBD (Admin Ct)), Goldring, J.
Reg.5, applied: SI 2002/816 Reg.4, Sch.4 para.1
Reg.5, varied: SI 2003/1184 Reg.3
Reg.13, applied: SI 2002/816 Reg.4, Sch.4 para.1

NO.

2000–cont.

2444. Immigration and Asylum Act 1999 (Commencement No.6, Transitional and Consequential Provisions) Order 2000

see *R. (on the application of Kariharan) v Secretary of State for the Home Department* [2001] EWHC Admin 1004, [2002] Imm. A.R. 281 (QBD (Admin Ct)), Stanley Burnton, J.

Art.3, see *Pardeepan v Secretary of State for the Home Department* [2002] Imm. A.R. 249 (IAT), Collins, J.

Sch.2 para.1, see *Pardeepan v Secretary of State for the Home Department* [2002] Imm. A.R. 249 (IAT), Collins, J.

2446. Immigration Appeals (Family Visitor) (No.2) Regulations 2000

revoked: 2002 c.41 Sch.9

Reg.2, amended: SI 2002/1147 Reg.3

Reg.3, applied: SI 2002/1147 Reg.3

Reg.3, revoked: SI 2002/1147 Reg.3

Reg.4, applied: SI 2002/1147 Reg.3

Reg.4, revoked: SI 2002/1147 Reg.3

2481. Feeding Stuffs Regulations 2000

Reg.2, amended: SI 2002/892 Reg.3, SI 2003/1026 Reg.3, SI 2003/1503 Reg.3

Reg.7, amended: SI 2002/892 Reg.4, SI 2003/1026 Reg.4, SI 2003/1503 Reg.4, SI 2003/2912 Reg.3, SI 2004/1301 Reg.3, SI 2004/2688 Reg.3

Reg.11, amended: SI 2002/892 Reg.5

Reg.14, amended: SI 2003/1026 Reg.5, SI 2004/2688 Reg.2

Reg.14, substituted: SI 2003/1503 Reg.5

Reg.15, substituted: SI 2004/2688 Reg.2

Reg.19, amended: SI 2002/892 Reg.6

Reg.19A, added: SI 2003/1503 Reg.6

Reg.25, amended: SI 2002/892 Reg.4, Reg.7, SI 2003/1026 Reg.4, SI 2003/1503 Reg.7, Reg.8, SI 2003/2912 Reg.3, SI 2004/1301 Reg.3, SI 2004/2688 Reg.3

Reg.27, revoked (in part): SI 2002/892 Reg.8

Sch.3 Part 1, amended: SI 2003/2912 Reg.2, SI 2004/1301 Reg.2, SI 2004/2688 Reg.2

Sch.3 Part 1, substituted: SI 2002/892 Sch.1, SI 2003/1026 Reg.6, Sch.1, SI 2003/1503 Sch.1, SI 2003/2912 Sch.1

Sch.4 Part I para.14, revoked (in part): SI 2003/1503 Reg.10

Sch.4 Part I para.15, amended: SI 2003/1503 Reg.10

Sch.4 Part I para.19, substituted: SI 2003/1503 Reg.10

Sch.7 Part I, amended: SI 2002/892 Sch.2, SI 2003/1503 Reg.11, SI 2004/1301 Sch.1, SI 2004/2688 Sch.1

Sch.7 Part I, referred to: SI 2004/2688 Reg.2

Sch.7 Part II, amended: SI 2002/892 Sch.2

Sch.7 Part II, revoked: SI 2003/1503 Reg.11

Sch.8, amended: SI 2002/892 Reg.11, SI 2004/1301 Sch.2

NO.

2000–cont.

2481. Feeding Stuffs Regulations 2000– cont.

Sch.9 Part A, amended: SI 2002/892 Sch.3

Sch.10 Part II, revoked: SI 2003/1503 Reg.12

2485. County of Cumbria (Electoral Changes) Order 2000

varied: SI 2004/222 Art.2

2486. County of Cheshire (Electoral Changes) Order 2000

varied: SI 2004/222 Art.2

2487. County of Hertfordshire (Electoral Changes) Order 2000

varied: SI 2004/222 Art.2

2488. County of Lincolnshire (Electoral Changes) Order 2000

varied: SI 2004/222 Art.2

2489. County of Northamptonshire (Electoral Changes) Order 2000

varied: SI 2004/222 Art.2

2490. County of Northumberland (Electoral Changes) Order 2000

varied: SI 2004/222 Art.2

2491. County of Somerset (Electoral Changes) Order 2000

varied: SI 2004/222 Art.2

2524. Animals and Animal Products (Import and Export) (England and Wales) (Amendment) (No.1) Regulations 2000

revoked (in part): SI 2004/853 Reg.35

2531. Building Regulations 2000

applied: SI 2002/2871 Reg.3, Reg.4, SI 2003/2692 Reg.3

referred to: SI 2002/2871 Reg.3, Reg.4

varied: SI 2004/1808 Reg.3

Reg.2, amended: SI 2002/2871 Reg.2, SI 2003/2692 Reg.2, SI 2004/1465 Reg.2, SI 2004/1808 Reg.2

Reg.3, amended: SI 2003/2692 Reg.2, SI 2004/1808 Reg.2

Reg.5, amended: SI 2002/2871 Reg.2, SI 2003/2692 Reg.2

Reg.6, amended: SI 2002/2871 Reg.2, SI 2003/2692 Reg.2, SI 2004/1465 Reg.2, SI 2004/1808 Reg.2

Reg.8, amended: SI 2004/1808 Reg.2

Reg.8, substituted: SI 2002/2871 Reg.2

Reg.9, amended: SI 2004/1808 Reg.2

Reg.12, amended: SI 2002/440 Reg.2, SI 2004/1808 Reg.2

Reg.12, applied: SI 2002/2871 Reg.3, Reg.4, SI 2003/2692 Reg.3, SI 2004/1808 Reg.3

Reg.14, see *Manchester City Council v Railtrack Plc* [2002] EWHC 2719, [2003] E.H.L.R. 8 (QBD (Admin Ct)), Silber, J.

Reg.15, amended: SI 2002/440 Reg.2

Reg.15, applied: SI 2002/2871 Reg.3, Reg.4, SI 2003/2692 Reg.3, SI 2004/1808 Reg.3

Reg.16A, added: SI 2002/440 Reg.2

Reg.16A, disapplied: SI 2002/440 Reg.3

Reg.16A, substituted: SI 2004/1808 Reg.2

NO.

2000–cont.

2531. Building Regulations 2000–cont.
Reg.20, amended: SI 2002/440 Reg.2, SI 2002/2871 Reg.2
Reg.20A, added: SI 2002/2871 Reg.2
Reg.20A, amended: SI 2004/1465 Reg.2
Sch.1, amended: SI 2003/2692 Reg.2, Sch.1, SI 2004/1465 Reg.2
Sch.1, referred to: SI 2003/2692 Reg.2
Sch.1, substituted: SI 2002/2871 Sch.1, Sch.2, SI 2004/1465 Sch.1
Sch.2A, added: SI 2002/440 Sch.1
Sch.2A, amended: SI 2003/2692 Reg.2, SI 2004/1808 Reg.2, Sch.1 Part 1
Sch.2A, applied: SI 2003/2692 Reg.3
Sch.2A, referred to: SI 2004/1808 Reg.3
Sch.2B para.1, added: SI 2004/1808 Sch.1 Part 2
Sch.2B para.2, added: SI 2004/1808 Sch.1 Part 2
Sch.2B para.3, added: SI 2004/1808 Sch.1 Part 2

2532. Building (Approved Inspectors etc.) Regulations 2000
applied: SI 2002/2872 Reg.3, Reg.4
referred to: SI 2002/2872 Reg.4
Reg.11, amended: SI 2002/2872 Reg.2
Reg.12A, added: SI 2002/2872 Reg.2
Reg.12A, amended: SI 2004/1466 Reg.2
Reg.31, amended: SI 2002/2872 Reg.2

2547. North Hampshire Primary Care Trust (Establishment) Order 2000
Art.1, amended: SI 2002/1405 Sch.1
Art.4, revoked: SI 2002/1405 Sch.1

2554. Nurses, Midwives and Health Visitors (Training) Amendment Rules Approval Order 2000
varied: SI 2004/1762 Art.1

2560. Teacher Training Incentive (Wales) Regulations 2000
Reg.2, amended: SI 2003/140 Reg.3

2562. West London Mental Health National Health Service Trust (Establishment) Order 2000
revoked: 2003 c.43 s.7

2585. Great Central Railway (East Leake Branch, etc.) Order 2000
Art.10, amended: SI 2003/2155 Sch.1 para.18

2599. District of Craven (Electoral Changes) Order 2000
referred to: SI 2002/1032
varied: SI 2004/222 Art.2

2600. District of Hambleton (Electoral Changes) Order 2000
varied: SI 2004/222 Art.2

2601. Borough of Harrogate (Electoral Changes) Order 2000
varied: SI 2004/222 Art.2

2602. District of Richmondshire (Electoral Changes) Order 2000
varied: SI 2004/222 Art.2

NO.

2000–cont.

2603. District of Ryedale (Electoral Changes) Order 2000
varied: SI 2004/222 Art.2

2604. Borough of Scarborough (Electoral Changes) Order 2000
varied: SI 2004/222 Art.2

2605. District of Selby (Electoral Changes) Order 2000
varied: SI 2004/222 Art.2

2606. Isle of Wight (Electoral Changes) Order 2000
varied: SI 2004/222 Art.2

2619. Protection of Children Act Tribunal Regulations 2000
revoked: SI 2002/816 Reg.36

2620. Dual-Use Items (Export Control) Regulations 2000
applied: SI 2003/335 Sch.1, SSI 2003/93 Sch.1
revoked: SI 2003/2764 Sch.6
Reg.2, amended: SI 2002/50 Reg.2
Sch.1A, added: SI 2002/50 Reg.3
Sch.1A, amended: SI 2002/2033 Reg.3, SI 2003/504 Reg.2
Sch.2 para.4, amended: SI 2002/50 Reg.4, SI 2002/2033 Reg.2

2662. Milton Keynes Community Health National Health Service Trust (Dissolution) Order 2000
revoked: 2003 c.43 s.7

2663. Aylesbury Vale Community Healthcare National Health Service Trust (Establishment) Amendment Order 2000
revoked: 2003 c.43 s.7

2687. Merchant Shipping (Passenger Ships on Domestic Voyages) Regulations 2000
applied: SI 2003/2950 Reg.3
Reg.2, amended: SI 2003/771 Reg.2, SI 2004/1107 Reg.2, SI 2004/2883 Reg.2
Reg.3, amended: SI 2004/2883 Reg.2
Reg.4, amended: SI 2004/302 Sch.1 para.3
Reg.4, referred to: SI 2004/302 Reg.3
Reg.5, amended: SI 2002/1473 Sch.2 para.6
Reg.5, revoked (in part): SI 2002/1473 Sch.1 para.8
Reg.6, amended: SI 2003/771 Reg.2, SI 2004/2883 Reg.2
Reg.7A, added: SI 2004/2883 Reg.2
Reg.7B, added: SI 2004/2883 Reg.2
Reg.7C, added: SI 2004/2883 Reg.2
Reg.9, amended: SI 2004/2883 Reg.2

2688. Railways (Safety Case) Regulations 2000
applied: SI 2003/547 Reg.20, Sch.17, SI 2003/1400 Sch.4, SI 2004/456 Reg.19
referred to: SI 2003/579 Reg.2
Reg.2, amended: SI 2003/579 Reg.3
Reg.2, applied: SI 2002/655 Reg.22, SI 2003/547 Reg.22

NO.

2000–cont.

2688. Railways (Safety Case) Regulations 2000–*cont.*
Reg.3, revoked: SI 2003/579 Reg.4
Reg.4, revoked (in part): SI 2003/579 Reg.5
Reg.5, amended: SI 2003/579 Reg.6
Reg.5, revoked (in part): SI 2003/579 Reg.6
Reg.7, amended: SI 2003/579 Reg.7
Reg.7, revoked (in part): SI 2003/579 Reg.7
Reg.9, applied: SI 2003/579 Reg.10
Reg.9, disapplied: SI 2003/579 Reg.10
Reg.9, substituted: SI 2003/579 Reg.8
Reg.11, amended: SI 2003/579 Reg.9
Reg.11, applied: SI 2003/547 Sch.17
Sch.3, revoked: SI 2002/2099 Sch.2

2689. Lowestoft Primary Care Trust (Establishment) Order 2000
Art.1, amended: SI 2002/1405 Sch.1
Art.4, revoked: SI 2002/1405 Sch.1
Sch.1, amended: SI 2004/543 Sch.1

2691. Pension Sharing (Consequential and Miscellaneous Amendments) Regulations 2000
Reg.3, revoked (in part): SI 2004/1140 Reg.2

2699. Telecommunications (Lawful Business Practice) (Interception of Communications) Regulations 2000
Reg.3, amended: SI 2003/2426 Reg.34

2704. Education (Teachers Qualifications and Health Standards) (England) (Amendment) Regulations 2000
revoked: SI 2003/1662 Sch.1 Part 1

2724. Immigration (Designation of Travel Bans) Order 2000
Sch.1, referred to: SI 2003/3285 Art.2
Sch.1 Part 1, amended: SI 2002/192 Art.2, SI 2002/3018 Art.3
Sch.1 Part 1, substituted: SI 2003/3285 Sch.1
Sch.1 Part 2, amended: SI 2002/795 Art.2, SI 2002/3018 Art.3, SI 2003/236 Art.2
Sch.1 Part 2, substituted: SI 2003/3285 Sch.1

2726. Specified Risk Material (Amendment) (England) Order 2000
revoked: SI 2003/3177 Sch.6

2727. Electricity from Non-Fossil Fuel Sources Saving Arrangements Order 2000
Art.7, amended: SI 2003/2096 Sch.1 para.77

2735. Immigration Services Commissioner (Registration Fee) Order 2000
revoked: SI 2002/2011 Art.4

2739. Immigration Services Tribunal Rules 2000
referred to: SI 2002/1716 r.1
r.20, amended: SI 2002/1716 r.2
r.21, amended: SI 2002/1716 r.3
r.21, substituted: SI 2002/1716 r.3

2741. East Gloucestershire National Health Service Trust (Establishment) Amendment Order 2000
revoked: 2003 c.43 s.7

NO.

2000–cont.

2742. Income Tax (Sub-contractors in the Construction Industry and Employments) (Amendment) Regulations 2000
Reg.3, revoked: SI 2003/2682 Sch.2

2765. Cosmetic Products (Safety) (Amendment) (No.2) Regulations 2000
revoked: SI 2003/835 Sch.1

2792. Fixed Penalty Order 2000
Sch.1, amended: SI 2003/1254 Sch.1

2811. Specified Risk Material (Amendment) (Wales) Order 2000
revoked: SI 2004/1430 Sch.6

2812. European Communities (Designation) (No.3) Order 2000
varied: SI 2002/248 Sch.3
Art.2, applied: SI 2002/3183, SI 2003/1848

2820. Harlow Primary Care Trust (Establishment) Order 2000
applied: SI 2003/3059 Sch.1
Art.1, amended: SI 2002/1405 Sch.1
Art.4, revoked: SI 2002/1405 Sch.1
Sch.1, amended: SI 2004/543 Sch.1

2822. Judicial Committee (Chiropractors Rules) Order 2000
revoked: 2002 c.17 Sch.9 Part 2

2831. Genetically Modified Organisms (Contained Use) Regulations 2000
applied: SI 2002/655 Reg.17, SI 2002/2677 Sch.3 para.5, SI 2003/547 Reg.17, SI 2004/456 Sch.16
referred to: SI 2002/2443 Sch.5, SI 2002/3188 Sch.5
Reg.9, applied: SI 2004/456 Sch.13
Reg.10, applied: SI 2004/456 Sch.13
Reg.11, applied: SI 2004/456 Sch.13
Reg.12, applied: SI 2004/456 Sch.13
Reg.14, applied: SI 2002/655 Reg.17, SI 2003/547 Reg.17, SI 2004/456 Reg.16
Reg.15, applied: SI 2002/655 Reg.17, SI 2003/547 Reg.17, SI 2004/456 Reg.16, Sch.13
Reg.16, applied: SI 2002/2443 Reg.12, SI 2002/3188 Reg.13, SSI 2002/541 Reg.12
Reg.17, applied: SI 2004/456 Sch.16
Reg.18, applied: SI 2004/456 Sch.13
Reg.22, amended: SI 2002/63 Reg.3
Reg.23, amended: SI 2002/63 Reg.4
Reg.23A, added: SI 2002/63 Reg.5
Reg.24, amended: SI 2002/63 Reg.6
Reg.24A, added: SI 2002/63 Reg.7
Reg.31, revoked (in part): SI 2002/2443 Sch.5, SI 2002/3188 Sch.5, SSI 2002/541 Sch.7
Sch.10 para.4, applied: SI 2004/456 Sch.13
Sch.10 para.5, applied: SI 2004/456 Sch.13

2853. Local Authorities (Functions and Responsibilities) (England) Regulations 2000
Reg.4, amended: SI 2004/1158 Reg.2

NO.

2000–cont.

2853. Local Authorities (Functions and Responsibilities) (England) Regulations 2000–*cont.*

Sch.1, amended: SI 2002/1916 Reg.6, SI 2004/2748 Sch.1 para.1, Sch.1 para.2

Sch.1, substituted: SI 2004/2211 Sch.1

Sch.2 para.4, substituted: SI 2004/2748 Sch.1 Part 2

Sch.2 para.5, substituted: SI 2004/2748 Sch.1 Part 2

Sch.2 para.6, substituted: SI 2004/2748 Sch.1 Part 2

2870. National Health Service (Travelling Expenses and Remission of Charges) Amendment (No.3) Regulations 2000

revoked: SI 2003/2382 Sch.2

2872. Education (Foundation Body) (England) Regulations 2000

Reg.7, applied: SI 2003/507 Reg.19

Reg.22, applied: SI 2003/507 Reg.19

2885. Northern Lincolnshire and Goole Hospitals National Health Service Trust (Establishment) Order 2000

revoked: 2003 c.43 s.7

2886. Walsgrave Hospitals National Health Service Trust Change of Name and (Establishment) Amendment Order 2000

revoked: 2003 c.43 s.7

2891. Child Benefit (General) Amendment Regulations 2000

applied: 2004 c.6 s.2

revoked: SI 2003/493 Sch.2 Part 1

2900. Animals and Animal Products (Import and Export) (England and Wales) (Amendment) (No.2) Regulations 2000

revoked (in part): SI 2004/853 Reg.35

2906. Education (Restriction of Employment) (Wales) Regulations 2000

Reg.4, revoked: SI 2003/542 Reg.2

2908. Nottinghamshire Healthcare National Health Service Trust (Establishment) Order 2000

revoked: 2003 c.43 s.7

2909. Sheffield Teaching Hospitals National Health Service Trust (Establishment) Order 2000

applied: SI 2003/3059 Sch.1

revoked: 2003 c.43 s.7

2911. Farm Waste Grant (Nitrate Vulnerable Zones) (England) (No.2) Scheme 2000

revoked: SI 2003/562 Art.7

Art.2, amended: SI 2002/2614 Reg.10

2956. Utilities Act 2000 (Supply of Information) Regulations 2000

Reg.5, amended: SI 2003/1398 Sch.1 para.40

NO.

2000–cont.

2961. National Clinical Assessment Authority (Establishment and Constitution) Order 2000

referred to: SI 2004/1119 Sch.1

Art.4, amended: SI 2004/2147 Art.2

2962. National Clinical Assessment Authority Regulations 2000

Reg.1, amended: SI 2004/696 Art.3

Reg.3, amended: SI 2004/696 Art.3

2963. Potatoes Originating in Egypt (Amendment) (No.2) (England) Regulations 2000

revoked: SI 2004/1165 Reg.8

2976. Cattle (Identification of Older Animals) Regulations 2000

Reg.7, amended: SI 2002/95 Reg.2

2977. Dairy Produce Quotas (Amendment) (England) (No.2) Regulations 2000

revoked: SI 2002/457 Sch.4

2982. Isle of Wight Primary Care Trust (Establishment) Order 2000

Art.1, amended: SI 2002/1405 Sch.1

Art.4, revoked: SI 2002/1405 Sch.1

2988. Collective Conditional Fee Agreements Regulations 2000

see *Gliddon v Lloyd Maunder Ltd* (2003) 153 N.L.J. 318 (Supreme Court Costs Office), Master O'Hare; see *Thornley v Lang* [2003] EWCA Civ 1484, [2004] 1 W.L.R. 378 (CA), Lord Phillips of Worth Matravers, M.R.

Reg.4, amended: SI 2003/1240 Reg.3, SI 2003/3344 Reg.3

Reg.5, amended: SI 2003/1240 Reg.3, SI 2003/3344 Reg.3

2993. National Health Service Bodies and Local Authorities Partnership Arrangements (Wales) Regulations 2000

Reg.2, amended: SI 2004/1390 Reg.2

Reg.3, amended: SI 2004/1390 Reg.2

Reg.4, amended: SI 2004/1390 Reg.2

Reg.7, amended: SI 2004/1390 Reg.2

Reg.9, amended: SI 2004/1390 Reg.2

Reg.10, amended: SI 2004/1390 Reg.2

2998. Telecommunications (Licence Modifications) (Amendment No 2) Regulations 2000

revoked: 2003 c.21 Sch.19

3026. Education (Exclusion from School) (Prescribed Periods) (Amendment) (Wales) Regulations 2000

revoked: SI 2003/3227 Reg.11

3027. School Government (Terms of Reference) (Wales) Regulations 2000

Reg.2, amended: SI 2002/1396 Reg.2

Reg.10, added: SI 2002/1396 Reg.2

NO.

2000–cont.

3040. Medical Act 1983 (Approved Medical Practices and Conditions of Residence) and National Health Service (General Medical Services) (Amendment) Regulations 2000

Reg.3, revoked (in part): SI 2004/865 Sch.2, SI 2004/1016 Sch.2

3044. England Rural Development Programme (Enforcement) Regulations 2000

Sch.1 Part II, amended: SI 2002/271 Reg.11, SI 2003/289 Reg.11, SI 2003/1235 Reg.11, SI 2004/145 Reg.10

3047. Beef Labelling (Enforcement) (England) Regulations 2000

Reg.5, amended: SI 2002/2315 Reg.2

Reg.13A, added: SI 2002/2315 Reg.2

3048. Countryside Stewardship Regulations 2000

Sch.1 Part I, amended: SI 2004/114 Reg.2

Sch.1 Part II, substituted: SI 2004/114 Sch.1

Sch.1 Part III, substituted: SI 2004/114 Sch.2

3049. Environmentally Sensitive Areas (Stage I) Designation Order 2000

Sch.1 Part 3, amended: SI 2004/115 Art.2

Sch.2 Part 3, amended: SI 2004/115 Art.2

Sch.3 Part 3, amended: SI 2004/115 Art.2

Sch.4 Part 3, amended: SI 2004/115 Art.2

Sch.5 Part 3, amended: SI 2004/115 Art.2

3050. Environmentally Sensitive Areas (Stage II) Designation Order 2000

Sch.1 Part 3, amended: SI 2004/115 Art.3

Sch.2 Part 3, amended: SI 2004/115 Art.3

Sch.3 Part 3, amended: SI 2004/115 Art.3

Sch.4 Part 3, amended: SI 2004/115 Art.3

Sch.5 Part 3, amended: SI 2004/115 Art.3

3051. Environmentally Sensitive Areas (Stage III) Designation Order 2000

Sch.1 Part 3, amended: SI 2004/115 Art.4

Sch.2 Part 3, amended: SI 2004/115 Art.4

Sch.3 Part 3, amended: SI 2004/115 Art.4

Sch.4 Part 3, amended: SI 2004/115 Art.4

Sch.5 Part 3, amended: SI 2004/115 Art.4

Sch.6 Part 3, amended: SI 2004/115 Art.4

3052. Environmentally Sensitive Areas (Stage IV) Designation Order 2000

Sch.1 Part 3, amended: SI 2004/115 Art.5

Sch.2 Part 3, amended: SI 2004/115 Art.5

Sch.3 Part 3, amended: SI 2004/115 Art.5

Sch.4 Part 3, amended: SI 2004/115 Art.5

Sch.5 Part 3, amended: SI 2004/115 Art.5

Sch.6 Part 3, amended: SI 2004/115 Art.5

3053. Asylum Support (Amendment) Regulations 2000

revoked: SI 2002/2619 Reg.3

3089. Town and Country Planning (Costs of Inquiries etc.) (Standard Daily Amount) (England) Regulations 2000

varied: SI 2002/452 Reg.3

NO.

2000–cont.

3120. Social Security (Incapacity Benefit) Miscellaneous Amendments Regulations 2000

Reg.3, revoked (in part): SI 2003/492 Sch.3 Part 1

Reg.5, revoked (in part): SI 2003/492 Sch.3 Part 1

3122. Teachers (Compulsory Registration) (Wales) Regulations 2000

revoked: SI 2004/1744 Sch.1 Part 1

3123. Dairy Produce Quotas (Amendment) (Wales) (No.2) Regulations 2000

revoked: SI 2002/897 Sch.4

3124. Doncaster Royal Infirmary and Montagu Hospital and the Bassetlaw Hospital and Community Services National Health Service Trusts (Dissolution) Order 2000

revoked: 2003 c.43 s.7

3125. Doncaster and Bassetlaw Hospitals National Health Service Trust (Establishment) Order 2000

revoked: 2003 c.43 s.7

3127. Common Agricultural Policy Support Schemes (Modulation) Regulations 2000

Reg.2, amended: SI 2004/2330 Reg.2

Reg.3, amended: SI 2004/2330 Reg.2

Reg.4, amended: SI 2004/2330 Reg.2

3128. Animals and Animal Products (Import and Export) (England and Wales) (Amendment) (No.3) Regulations 2000

revoked (in part): SI 2004/853 Reg.35

3165. Registration of Births, Deaths and Marriages (Fees) (Amendment) Order 2000

revoked: SI 2002/3076 Art.3

3173. Child Support (Variations) (Modification of Statutory Provisions) Regulations 2000

Reg.8, amended: SI 2002/1204 Reg.10

3174. Child Support (Temporary Compensation Payment Scheme) Regulations 2000

Reg.3, amended: SI 2002/1854 Reg.3

3176. Social Security (Child Maintenance Premium and Miscellaneous Amendments) Regulations 2000

Reg.1, substituted: SI 2004/98 Reg.4

Reg.2, revoked (in part): SI 2004/98 Reg.4

Reg.4, substituted: SI 2003/231 Reg.2

3183. Registered Parties (Non-constituent and Non-affiliated Organisations) Order 2000

varied: SI 2004/366 Art.5

Sch.1 Part I, amended: SI 2002/414 Art.2

3184. Water Supply (Water Quality) Regulations 2000

Reg.2, amended: SI 2002/2469 Reg.7, Reg.11, Sch.1 para.91

NO.

2000–cont.

3184. Water Supply (Water Quality) Regulations 2000–*cont.*

Reg.20, amended: SI 2002/2469 Sch.1 para.91

Reg.24, amended: SI 2002/2469 Sch.1 para.91

Reg.31, applied: SR 2002/331 Reg.30

Reg.35, amended: SI 2002/2469 Sch.1 para.91

3185. Child Support (Decisions and Appeals) (Amendment) Regulations 2000

Reg.14, amended: SI 2003/347 Reg.2

Reg.15, amended: SI 2003/347 Reg.2

3186. Child Support (Transitional Provisions) Regulations 2000

Reg.2, amended: SI 2003/328 Reg.9, SI 2003/2779 Reg.7, SI 2004/2415 Reg.8

Reg.3, amended: SI 2003/328 Reg.9, SI 2004/2415 Reg.8

Reg.4, amended: SI 2002/1204 Reg.8

Reg.4A, added: SI 2004/2415 Reg.8

Reg.5A, added: SI 2004/2415 Reg.8

Reg.7, amended: SI 2003/2779 Reg.7

Reg.9, amended: SI 2002/1204 Reg.8, SI 2004/2415 Reg.8

Reg.9A, added: SI 2004/2415 Reg.8

Reg.9B, added: SI 2004/2415 Reg.8

Reg.10, amended: SI 2002/1204 Reg.8, SI 2003/328 Reg.9

Reg.11, amended: SI 2003/328 Reg.9

Reg.12, amended: SI 2002/1204 Reg.8

Reg.13, amended: SI 2002/1204 Reg.8

Reg.13, substituted: SI 2002/1204 Reg.8

Reg.14, amended: SI 2002/1204 Reg.8

Reg.15, amended: SI 2002/1204 Reg.8, SI 2003/328 Reg.9

Reg.16, amended: SI 2003/328 Reg.9, SI 2003/347 Reg.3, SI 2004/2415 Reg.8

Reg.17, amended: SI 2002/1204 Reg.8, SI 2003/2779 Reg.7

Reg.21, amended: SI 2002/1204 Reg.8

Reg.22, amended: SI 2002/1204 Reg.8, SI 2003/328 Reg.9

Reg.23, amended: SI 2002/1204 Reg.8

Reg.23A, added: SI 2002/1204 Reg.8

Reg.24, amended: SI 2002/1204 Reg.8, SI 2003/328 Reg.9, SI 2003/2779 Reg.7

Reg.25, amended: SI 2003/328 Reg.9, SI 2003/2779 Reg.7

Reg.27, amended: SI 2002/1204 Reg.8, SI 2003/328 Reg.9, SI 2003/2779 Reg.7, SI 2004/2415 Reg.8

Reg.28, amended: SI 2002/1204 Reg.8, SI 2003/328 Reg.9

Reg.33, amended: SI 2003/328 Reg.9

3216. Merchant Shipping (Carriage of Packaged Irradiated Nuclear Fuel etc.) (INF Code) Regulations 2000

Reg.2, amended: 2002 c.8 s.2

NO.

2000–cont.

3226. Transport Tribunal Rules 2000

Part I r.3, amended: SI 2002/643 r.5

Part IIA r.10A, added: SI 2002/643 r.4, r.6

Part IIA r.10B, added: SI 2002/643 r.4, r.6

Part IIA r.10C, added: SI 2002/643 r.4, r.6

Part IIA r.10D, added: SI 2002/643 r.4, r.6

Part IIA r.10E, added: SI 2002/643 r.4, r.6

Part IVA r.18A, added: SI 2002/643 r.4, r.7

Part IVA r.18B, added: SI 2002/643 r.4, r.7

Part IVA r.18C, added: SI 2002/643 r.4, r.7

Part IVA r.18D, added: SI 2002/643 r.4, r.7

Part IVA r.18E, added: SI 2002/643 r.4, r.7

Part V r.20, substituted: SI 2002/643 r.8

Part V r.26, amended: SI 2002/643 r.9

Part V r.28, amended: SI 2002/643 r.10

Part V r.35, amended: SI 2002/643 r.11

r.14, see *Coakley v Secretary of State for Transport (Locus of Commissioner to Appear)* 2003 S.C. 455 (Court of Session (Inner House, Extra Division)), Lord Kirkwood, Lady Cosgrove, Lord Marnoch

3236. Non-automatic Weighing Instruments Regulations 2000

applied: SI 2003/2454 Reg.5, SI 2003/2761 Reg.3, SR 2002/309 Reg.5

Reg.3, applied: SR 2002/309 Reg.5

Reg.9, applied: SI 2004/1300 Reg.6

Reg.10, applied: SI 2004/1300 Reg.7

Reg.12, applied: SI 2004/1300 Reg.8

Reg.23, applied: SI 2003/2761 Reg.16

Reg.24, applied: SI 2003/2761 Reg.16

3241. Iraq (United Nations Sanctions) Order 2000

applied: SI 2003/1519 Art.3, SI 2004/1498

referred to: SI 2003/1347, SI 2004/1660 Reg.4

Art.1, amended: 2002 c.8 s.2, SI 2004/1498 Art.5, SI 2004/1660 Reg.3, SI 2004/1779 Reg.4

Art.1, referred to: SI 2003/1347

Art.1, revoked (in part): SI 2003/1347 Art.2

Art.2, amended: SI 2003/1519 Sch.1 para.1, SI 2004/1498 Art.5, SI 2004/1660 Reg.3

Art.3, amended: SI 2004/1498 Art.5

Art.3, substituted: SI 2003/1519 Sch.1 para.2

Art.3A, added: SI 2004/1498 Art.5

Art.4, revoked: SI 2004/1498 Art.5

Art.4, substituted: SI 2003/1519 Sch.1 para.3

Art.4A, added: SI 2004/1498 Art.5

Art.4A, amended: SI 2004/1660 Reg.3

Art.5, amended: SI 2003/1519 Sch.1 para.4, SI 2004/1498 Art.5

Art.5, varied: SI 2004/1498 Art.6

Art.5A, added: SI 2003/1519 Sch.1 para.5

Art.5A, amended: SI 2004/1498 Art.5, SI 2004/1660 Reg.3

Art.5A, disapplied: SI 2004/1660 Reg.4

Art.5A, varied: SI 2004/1498 Art.6

Art.6, amended: SI 2003/1519 Sch.1 para.6, SI 2004/1498 Art.5

NO.

2000–cont.

3241. Iraq (United Nations Sanctions) Order 2000–*cont.*

Art.8, amended: SI 2003/1519 Sch.1 para.7, SI 2004/1498 Art.5

Art.9, varied: SI 2004/1498 Art.6

Art.10, varied: SI 2004/1498 Art.6

Art.11, amended: SI 2003/1519 Sch.1 para.8, SI 2004/1498 Art.5

Art.11, varied: SI 2004/1498 Art.6

Art.12, varied: SI 2004/1498 Art.6

3242. Iraq (United Nations Sanctions) (Overseas Territories) Order 2000

applied: SI 2003/1516 Art.3

referred to: SI 2003/1347

Art.1, amended: 2002 c.8 s.2

Art.1, referred to: SI 2003/1347

Art.1, revoked (in part): SI 2003/1347 Art.2

Art.2, amended: SI 2003/1516 Sch.3 para.1, SI 2004/2671 Sch.1 para.1

Art.3, amended: SI 2004/2671 Sch.1 para.2

Art.3, substituted: SI 2003/1516 Sch.3 para.2

Art.3A, added: SI 2004/2671 Sch.1 para.3

Art.4, revoked: SI 2004/2671 Sch.1 para.4

Art.4, substituted: SI 2003/1516 Sch.3 para.3

Art.4A, added: SI 2004/2671 Sch.1 para.4

Art.5, amended: SI 2003/1516 Sch.3 para.4, SI 2004/2671 Sch.1 para.5

Art.5A, added: SI 2003/1516 Sch.3 para.5

Art.5A, amended: SI 2004/2671 Sch.1 para.6

Art.6, amended: SI 2003/1516 Sch.3 para.6, SI 2004/2671 Sch.1 para.6a

Art.8, amended: SI 2003/1516 Sch.3 para.7, SI 2004/2671 Sch.1 para.7

Art.11, amended: SI 2003/1516 Sch.3 para.8, SI 2004/2671 Sch.1 para.8

3244. Iraq (United Nations Sanctions) (Channel Islands) Order 2000

applied: SI 2003/1521 Art.3

referred to: SI 2003/1347, SI 2004/1978, SI 2004/1978 Art.6

Art.1, amended: 2002 c.8 s.2

Art.1, referred to: SI 2003/1347

Art.1, revoked (in part): SI 2003/1347 Art.2

Art.2, amended: SI 2003/1521 Sch.1 para.1, SI 2004/1978 Sch.1 para.1

Art.2, substituted: SI 2003/1521 Sch.1 para.1

Art.3, amended: SI 2004/1978 Sch.1 para.2, Sch.1 para.3

Art.3, substituted: SI 2003/1521 Sch.1 para.2

Art.3A, added: SI 2004/1978 Sch.1 para.4

Art.4, applied: SI 2004/1978 Art.6

Art.4, referred to: SI 2004/1978 Art.6

Art.4, revoked: SI 2004/1978 Sch.1 para.5

Art.4, substituted: SI 2003/1521 Sch.1 para.3

Art.4A, added: SI 2004/1978 Sch.1 para.6

Art.5, amended: SI 2003/1521 Sch.1 para.4, SI 2004/1978 Sch.1 para.7

Art.5, applied: SI 2004/1978 Art.6

Art.5A, added: SI 2003/1521 Sch.1 para.5

NO.

2000–cont.

3244. Iraq (United Nations Sanctions) (Channel Islands) Order 2000–*cont.*

Art.5A, amended: SI 2004/1978 Sch.1 para.8

Art.5A, applied: SI 2004/1978 Art.6

Art.6, amended: SI 2003/1521 Sch.1 para.6, SI 2004/1978 Sch.1 para.9

Art.8, amended: SI 2003/1521 Sch.1 para.7, SI 2004/1978 Sch.1 para.10

Art.9, applied: SI 2004/1978 Art.6

Art.10, applied: SI 2004/1978 Art.6

Art.11, amended: SI 2003/1521 Sch.1 para.8, SI 2004/1978 Sch.1 para.11

Art.11, applied: SI 2004/1978 Art.6

Art.12, applied: SI 2004/1978 Art.6

3245. Iraq (United Nations Sanctions) (Isle of Man) Order 2000

applied: SI 2003/1522 Art.3

referred to: SI 2003/1347, SI 2004/1982, SI 2004/1982 Art.5

Art.1, amended: 2002 c.8 s.2

Art.1, referred to: SI 2003/1347

Art.1, revoked (in part): SI 2003/1347 Art.2

Art.2, amended: SI 2003/1522 Sch.1 para.1, SI 2004/1982 Sch.1 para.1

Art.3, amended: SI 2004/1982 Sch.1 para.2, Sch.1 para.3

Art.3, substituted: SI 2003/1522 Sch.1 para.2

Art.3A, added: SI 2004/1982 Sch.1 para.4

Art.4, revoked: SI 2004/1982 Sch.1 para.5

Art.4, substituted: SI 2003/1522 Sch.1 para.3

Art.4A, added: SI 2004/1982 Sch.1 para.6

Art.5, amended: SI 2003/1522 Sch.1 para.4, SI 2004/1982 Sch.1 para.7

Art.5A, added: SI 2003/1522 Sch.1 para.5

Art.5A, amended: SI 2004/1982 Sch.1 para.8

Art.6, amended: SI 2003/1522 Sch.1 para.6, SI 2004/1982 Sch.1 para.9

Art.8, amended: SI 2003/1522 Sch.1 para.7, SI 2004/1982 Sch.1 para.10

Art.11, amended: SI 2003/1522 Sch.1 para.8, SI 2004/1982 Sch.1 para.11

3253. Scotland Act 1998 (Transfer of Functions to the Scottish Ministers etc.) (No.2) Order 2000

Art.2, disapplied: SI 2003/2617 Art.2

Art.3, referred to: SI 2003/2617 Art.3

Sch.1, disapplied: SI 2003/2617 Art.2

Sch.1 para.2, referred to: SI 2003/2617 Sch.1 para.1

Sch.1 para.2, revoked (in part): SI 2003/2617 Art.4

Sch.1 para.3, referred to: SI 2003/2617 Sch.1 para.2

Sch.1 para.3, revoked (in part): SI 2003/2617 Art.4

Sch.2, referred to: SI 2003/2617 Art.3

3255. Social Security (Australia) Order 2000

Art.2, applied: 2004 c.35 s.299

NO.

NO.

2000–cont.

3272. Local Authorities (Executive Arrangements) (Access to Information) (England) Regulations 2000
Reg.1, amended: SI 2002/716 Reg.3
Reg.2, amended: SI 2002/716 Reg.4
Reg.7, amended: SI 2002/716 Reg.5
Reg.9, amended: SI 2002/716 Reg.14
Reg.10, amended: SI 2002/716 Reg.14
Reg.11, amended: SI 2002/716 Reg.14
Reg.13, amended: SI 2002/716 Reg.6
Reg.14, amended: SI 2002/716 Reg.7
Reg.15, amended: SI 2002/716 Reg.8, Reg.14
Reg.16, amended: SI 2002/716 Reg.9
Reg.18, amended: SI 2002/716 Reg.10
Reg.21, amended: SI 2002/716 Reg.11
Reg.22, amended: SI 2002/716 Reg.12
Reg.23, amended: SI 2002/716 Reg.13

3274. Vehicle Excise Duty (Reduced Pollution) (Amendment) Regulations 2000
revoked: SI 2002/2742 Sch.1 Part I

3278. Magistrates Courts Warrants (Specification of Provisions) Order 2000
Art.2, amended: SI 2004/1835 Art.2

3285. District of Bassetlaw (Electoral Changes) Order 2000
varied: SI 2004/222 Art.2

3294. Common Agricultural Policy Support Schemes (Modulation) (Wales) Regulations 2000
Reg.2, amended: SI 2004/2662 Reg.2
Reg.3, amended: SI 2004/2662 Reg.2

3295. District of Ashfield (Electoral Changes) Order 2000
varied: SI 2004/222 Art.2

3296. Borough of Broxtowe (Electoral Changes) Order 2000
varied: SI 2004/222 Art.2

3297. Borough of Gedling (Electoral Changes) Order 2000
varied: SI 2004/222 Art.2

3298. District of Mansfield (Electoral Changes) Order 2000
varied: SI 2004/222 Art.2

3299. District of Newark and Sherwood (Electoral Changes) Order 2000
varied: SI 2004/222 Art.2

3300. City of Nottingham (Electoral Changes) Order 2000
varied: SI 2004/222 Art.2

3301. Borough of Rushcliffe (Electoral Changes) Order 2000
varied: SI 2004/222 Art.2

3304. Dual-Use Items (Export Control) (Amendment) Regulations 2000
revoked: SI 2003/2764 Sch.6

2000–cont.

3305. Crime and Disorder Act 1998 (Service of Prosecution Evidence) Regulations 2000
Reg.2, see *Fehily v Governor of Wandsworth Prison* [2002] EWHC 1295, [2003] 1 Cr. App. R. 10 (QBD (Admin Ct)), Rose, L.J.
Reg.3, see *Fehily v Governor of Wandsworth Prison* [2002] EWHC 1295, [2003] 1 Cr. App. R. 10 (QBD (Admin Ct)), Rose, L.J.

3314. Street Works (Sharing of Costs of Works) (England) Regulations 2000
applied: SI 2002/1327 Sch.5 para.2, SI 2002/2091 Reg.4
Reg.2, referred to: SI 2002/2091 Reg.4

3315. Exchange Gains and Losses (Miscellaneous Modifications) Regulations 2000
referred to: SI 2002/1969 Reg.28
Reg.2, revoked: SI 2002/1969 Reg.29
Reg.3, revoked: SI 2002/1969 Reg.29
Reg.4, revoked: SI 2002/1969 Reg.29
Reg.5, revoked: SI 2002/1969 Reg.29
Reg.11, revoked: SI 2002/1969 Reg.30

3323. Coffee Extracts and Chicory Extracts (England) Regulations 2000
referred to: SI 2003/1008 Reg.3
Reg.5, amended: SI 2003/1563 Reg.10

3325. Companies (Fees) (Amendment) Regulations 2000
revoked: SI 2004/2621 Sch.3

3326. East Manchester Education Action Zone (Variation) Order 2000
revoked: 2002 c.32 Sch.15 para.2

3327. Education (Recognised Bodies) (England) Order 2000
revoked: SI 2003/1865 Art.3

3332. Education (Listed Bodies) (England) Order 2000
revoked: SI 2002/1377 Art.3

3337. Newham Education Action Zone (Variation) Order 2000
revoked: 2002 c.32 Sch.15 para.2

3339. Cattle (Identification of Older Animals) (Wales) Regulations 2000
Reg.7, amended: SI 2002/273 Reg.2

3357. Whole of Government Accounts (Designation of Bodies) Order 2000
Sch.1, amended: SI 2002/454 Sch.1

3363. Borough of Rugby (Electoral Changes) (No.2) Order 2000
varied: SI 2004/222 Art.2

3364. District of South Shropshire (Electoral Changes) (Amendment) Order 2000
varied: SI 2004/222 Art.2

3365. Borough of Taunton Deane (Electoral Changes) (Amendment) Order 2000
varied: SI 2004/222 Art.2

3366. Borough of Waverley (Electoral Changes) (Amendment) Order 2000
varied: SI 2004/222 Art.2

NO.

2000–cont.

3371. Young Offender Institution Rules 2000

Part I r.2, amended: SI 2002/2117 Sch.1 para.1

Part II r.27, amended: SI 2002/3135 Sch.1 para.45

Part II r.38, applied: SI 2002/152 Reg.24

Part II r.58, amended: SI 2002/2117 Sch.1 para.2

Part II r.58A, added: SI 2002/2117 Sch.1 para.3

Part II r.59, amended: SI 2002/2117 Sch.1 para.4

Part II r.60, amended: SI 2002/2117 Sch.1 para.5

Part II r.60, revoked (in part): SI 2002/2117 Sch.1 para.5

Part II r.60A, added: SI 2002/2117 Sch.1 para.6

Part II r.63, amended: SI 2002/2117 Sch.1 para.7

Part II r.65, amended: SI 2002/2117 Sch.1 para.8

Part II r.65, revoked (in part): SI 2002/2117 Sch.1 para.8

Part VI r.86, amended: SI 2002/2117 Sch.1 para.9

3384. Individual Learning Accounts (Wales) Regulations 2000

revoked: SI 2003/918 Reg.2

3402. Mink Keeping (England) Order 2000

applied: SI 2002/221 Sch.5 para.14, SI 2004/1964 Sch.6 para.13

3412. European Economic Interest Grouping (Fees) (Amendment) Regulations 2000

revoked: SI 2004/2643 Sch.1

2001

6. Pet Travel Scheme (Pilot Arrangements) (England) (Amendment) Order 2001

revoked: SI 2004/2363 Sch.2

9. Fishing Vessels (Code of Practice for the Safety of Small Fishing Vessels) Regulations 2001

referred to: SI 2002/2201 Reg.4

Reg.2, amended: SI 2002/2201 Sch.1 para.57

Reg.3, amended: SI 2002/2201 Sch.1 para.58

Reg.6, amended: SI 2002/2201 Sch.1 para.59

16. Norfolk and Norwich Health Care National Health Service Trust Change of Name and (Establishment) Amendment Order 2001

revoked: 2003 c.43 s.7

18. Social Security (Claims and Payments) Amendment Regulations 2001

revoked (in part): SI 2003/492 Sch.3 Part 1

21. Employment Rights (Increase of Limits) Order 2001

revoked: SI 2002/10 Art.2

NO.

2001–cont.

25. Motor Vehicles (Approval) Regulations 2001

Reg.3, amended: SI 2004/623 Reg.3

Reg.5, amended: SI 2004/623 Reg.4

Reg.6, amended: SI 2004/623 Reg.5

Reg.11, amended: SI 2004/623 Reg.6

Sch.2 para.1, revoked (in part): SI 2004/623 Reg.7

Sch.2 para.2, amended: SI 2004/623 Reg.7

Sch.2 para.6, revoked: SI 2004/623 Reg.7

Sch.3, amended: SI 2004/623 Sch.1

Sch.4, amended: SI 2004/623 Sch.2

Sch.5, amended: SI 2004/623 Sch.3

Sch.6 Part II, amended: SI 2004/623 Reg.11

Sch.6 Part III, amended: SI 2004/623 Reg.11

44. South Staffordshire Healthcare National Health Service Trust (Establishment) Order 2001

revoked: 2003 c.43 s.7

51. First Community Health, the Foundation and the Premier Health National Health Service Trusts (Dissolution) Order 2001

revoked: 2003 c.43 s.7

52. Immigration Appeals (Family Visitor) (Amendment) Regulations 2001

revoked: 2002 c.41 Sch.9

60. Miscellaneous Food Additives (Amendment) (England) Regulations 2001

referred to: SI 2003/1008 Reg.3

65. Whipps Cross Hospital National Health Service Trust (Establishment) Amendment Order 2001

revoked: 2003 c.43 s.7

66. Wyre Forest Primary Care Trust (Establishment) Order 2001

Art.1, amended: SI 2002/1405 Sch.1

Art.4, revoked: SI 2002/1405 Sch.1

67. Burntwood, Lichfield and Tamworth Primary Care Trust (Establishment) Order 2001

Art.1, amended: SI 2002/1405 Sch.1

Art.4, revoked: SI 2002/1405 Sch.1

Sch.1, amended: SI 2002/1114 Art.2

82. Registration of Political Parties (Prohibited Words and Expressions) Order 2001

varied: SI 2004/366 Art.5

83. Registration of Political Parties (Fees) Order 2001

varied: SI 2004/366 Art.5

96. North East Lincolnshire and the Scunthorpe and Goole Hospitals National Health Service Trusts (Dissolution) Order 2001

revoked: 2003 c.43 s.7

NO.

97. Central Sheffield University Hospitals and the Northern General Hospital National Health Service Trusts (Dissolution) Order 2001
revoked: 2003 c.43 s.7

117. Personal Pension Schemes (Restriction on Discretion to Approve) (Permitted Investments) Regulations 2001
Reg.2, amended: SI 2003/2066 Reg.13

128. Chesterfield Primary Care Trust (Establishment) Order 2001
Art.1, amended: SI 2002/1405 Sch.1
Art.4, revoked: SI 2002/1405 Sch.1

129. Gedling Primary Care Trust (Establishment) Order 2001
Art.1, amended: SI 2002/1405 Sch.1
Art.4, revoked: SI 2002/1405 Sch.1

130. Amber Valley Primary Care Trust (Establishment) Order 2001
Art.1, amended: SI 2002/1405 Sch.1
Art.4, revoked: SI 2002/1405 Sch.1

131. North Sheffield Primary Care Trust (Establishment) Order 2001
Art.1, amended: SI 2002/1405 Sch.1
Art.4, revoked: SI 2002/1405 Sch.1
Sch., amended: SI 2004/543 Sch.1
Sch., substituted: SI 2004/1413 Sch.1

132. North Lincolnshire Primary Care Trust (Establishment) Order 2001
Art.1, amended: SI 2002/1405 Sch.1
Art.4, revoked: SI 2002/1405 Sch.1
Sch., amended: SI 2004/543 Sch.1

133. North Eastern Derbyshire Primary Care Trust (Establishment) Order 2001
Art.1, amended: SI 2002/1405 Sch.1
Art.4, revoked: SI 2002/1405 Sch.1

134. Melton, Rutland and Harborough Primary Care Trust (Establishment) Order 2001
Art.1, amended: SI 2002/1405 Sch.1
Art.4, revoked: SI 2002/1405 Sch.1

136. Leicester City West Primary Care Trust (Establishment) Order 2001
Art.1, amended: SI 2002/1405 Sch.1
Art.4, revoked: SI 2002/1405 Sch.1

137. Doncaster East Primary Care Trust (Establishment) Order 2001
Art.1, amended: SI 2002/1405 Sch.1
Art.4, revoked: SI 2002/1405 Sch.1

138. Doncaster West Primary Care Trust (Establishment) Order 2001
Art.1, amended: SI 2002/1405 Sch.1
Art.4, revoked: SI 2002/1405 Sch.1

139. Care Standards Act 2000 (Commencement No.2 and Transitional Provisions) (Wales) Order 2001
Art.3, applied: SI 2002/920 Art.3, Sch.1 para.7, Sch.1 para.8, Sch.1 para.9

NO.

140. Children's Homes Amendment (Wales) Regulations 2001
revoked: SI 2002/327 Reg.43

152. Merchant Shipping (Mandatory Surveys for Ro-Ro Ferry and High Speed Passenger Craft) Regulations 2001
referred to: SI 2004/2884 Reg.7
Reg.2, amended: SI 2004/1266 Reg.7

154. United Lincolnshire Hospitals National Health Service Trust (Establishment) Amendment Order 2001
revoked: 2003 c.43 s.7

155. Child Support (Maintenance Calculations and Special Cases) Regulations 2001
Reg.1, amended: SI 2002/3019 Reg.27, SI 2003/328 Reg.8, SI 2003/2779 Reg.6
Reg.4, amended: SI 2002/2497 Sch.2 para.1, SI 2002/3019 Reg.27, SI 2003/2779 Reg.6
Reg.5, amended: SI 2002/3019 Reg.27, SI 2003/1195 Reg.7, SI 2003/2779 Reg.6
Reg.5, revoked (in part): SI 2004/2415 Reg.7
Reg.8, amended: SI 2003/328 Reg.8
Reg.11, amended: SI 2003/2779 Reg.6
Reg.15, amended: SI 2003/347 Reg.2
Sch.Part II para.4, amended: SI 2004/2415 Reg.7
Sch.Part II para.6, amended: SI 2003/328 Reg.8
Sch.Part II para.6, revoked (in part): SI 2003/328 Reg.8
Sch.Part III para.8, amended: SI 2002/1204 Reg.7
Sch.Part III para.9, revoked (in part): SI 2003/328 Reg.8
Sch.Part IV para.11, amended: SI 2003/328 Reg.8
Sch.Part IV para.11, revoked (in part): SI 2003/328 Reg.8
Sch.Part IV para.13, revoked (in part): SI 2003/328 Reg.8
Sch.Part IV para.13, substituted: SI 2002/1204 Reg.7
Sch.Part IV para.13A, added: SI 2003/328 Reg.8
Sch.Part VI para.17, added: SI 2004/2415 Reg.7

156. Child Support (Variations) Regulations 2001
Reg.1, amended: SI 2004/2415 Reg.9
Reg.7, amended: SI 2002/1204 Reg.9, SI 2003/328 Reg.10, SI 2004/2415 Reg.9
Reg.9, amended: SI 2002/1204 Reg.9
Reg.16, amended: SI 2002/1204 Reg.9
Reg.18, amended: SI 2002/1204 Reg.9
Reg.19, amended: SI 2002/1204 Reg.9
Reg.20, amended: SI 2002/1204 Reg.9
Reg.27, amended: SI 2004/2415 Reg.9
Reg.28, amended: SI 2003/2779 Reg.8

NO.

2001–cont.

156. Child Support (Variations) Regulations 2001–cont.
Reg.33, amended: SI 2003/347 Reg.2

157. Child Support (Maintenance Calculation Procedure) Regulations 2001
Reg.1, amended: SI 2002/1204 Reg.6
Reg.5, amended: SI 2003/328 Reg.7
Reg.8, amended: SI 2003/2779 Reg.5
Reg.9A, added: SI 2002/1204 Reg.6
Reg.10, amended: SI 2003/328 Reg.7
Reg.14, amended: SI 2003/2779 Reg.5
Reg.14, revoked (in part): SI 2003/2779 Reg.5
Reg.15, amended: SI 2003/2779 Reg.5
Reg.15, revoked (in part): SI 2003/2779 Reg.5
Reg.25, amended: SI 2003/328 Reg.7
Reg.26, amended: SI 2002/1204 Reg.6
Reg.27, amended: SI 2002/1204 Reg.6
Reg.28, amended: SI 2002/1204 Reg.6
Reg.29, amended: SI 2002/1204 Reg.6, SI 2003/328 Reg.7, SI 2004/2415 Reg.6
Reg.30, amended: SI 2003/328 Reg.7, SI 2003/347 Reg.2
Reg.31, amended: SI 2002/1204 Reg.6, SI 2003/328 Reg.7, SI 2004/2415 Reg.6
Sch.3 para.1, added: SI 2003/328 Sch.1
Sch.3 para.2, added: SI 2003/328 Sch.1
Sch.3 para.3, added: SI 2003/328 Sch.1
Sch.3 para.4, added: SI 2003/328 Sch.1
Sch.3 para.5, added: SI 2003/328 Sch.1

158. Child Support (Consequential Amendments and Transitional Provisions) Regulations 2001
Reg.2, amended: SI 2003/495 Sch.1 Part 1
Reg.5, revoked: SI 2003/495 Sch.1 Part 1
Reg.10, amended: SI 2003/347 Reg.2

161. Child Support (Information, Evidence and Disclosure and Maintenance Arrangements and Jurisdiction) (Amendment) Regulations 2001
Reg.10, amended: SI 2003/347 Reg.2

162. Child Support (Collection and Enforcement and Miscellaneous Amendments) Regulations 2001
Reg.6, amended: SI 2003/347 Reg.2

163. South Stoke Primary Care Trust (Establishment) Order 2001
Art.1, amended: SI 2002/1405 Sch.1
Art.4, revoked: SI 2002/1405 Sch.1
Sch., amended: SI 2002/1112 Art.2, SI 2002/1393 Art.2

174. Greater Derby Primary Care Trust (Establishment) Order 2001
Art.1, amended: SI 2002/1405 Sch.1
Art.4, revoked: SI 2002/1405 Sch.1

175. Eastern Leicester Primary Care Trust (Establishment) Order 2001
Art.1, amended: SI 2002/1405 Sch.1
Art.4, revoked: SI 2002/1405 Sch.1

NO.

2001–cont.

176. Ashfield Primary Care Trust (Establishment) Order 2001
Art.1, amended: SI 2002/1405 Sch.1
Art.4, revoked: SI 2002/1405 Sch.1

177. Rushcliffe Primary Care Trust (Establishment) Order 2001
Art.1, amended: SI 2002/1405 Sch.1
Art.4, revoked: SI 2002/1405 Sch.1

181. Nottingham City Primary Care Trust (Establishment) Order 2001
referred to: SI 2004/569 Sch.1
Art.1, amended: SI 2002/1405 Sch.1
Art.4, revoked: SI 2002/1405 Sch.1

182. Sheffield West Primary Care Trust (Establishment) Order 2001
Art.1, amended: SI 2002/1405 Sch.1
Art.4, revoked: SI 2002/1405 Sch.1
Sch., substituted: SI 2004/1413 Sch.1

183. Sheffield South West Primary Care Trust (Establishment) Order 2001
Art.1, amended: SI 2002/1405 Sch.1
Art.4, revoked: SI 2002/1405 Sch.1
Sch., substituted: SI 2004/1413 Sch.1

184. South East Sheffield Primary Care Trust (Establishment) Order 2001
Art.1, amended: SI 2002/1405 Sch.1
Art.4, revoked: SI 2002/1405 Sch.1
Sch., substituted: SI 2004/1413 Sch.1

185. Erewash Primary Care Trust (Establishment) Order 2001
Art.1, amended: SI 2002/1405 Sch.1
Art.4, revoked: SI 2002/1405 Sch.1

186. Bassetlaw Primary Care Trust (Establishment) Order 2001
Art.1, amended: SI 2002/1405 Sch.1
Art.4, revoked: SI 2002/1405 Sch.1

187. Broxtowe &amp Hucknall Primary Care Trust (Establishment) Order 2001
Art.1, amended: SI 2002/1405 Sch.1
Art.4, revoked: SI 2002/1405 Sch.1
Sch., amended: SI 2004/543 Sch.1

192. Terrorism Act 2000 (Crown Servants and Regulators) Regulations 2001
Reg.2, amended: SI 2003/3075 Sch.2 para.4
Reg.3, amended: SI 2003/3075 Sch.2 para.4
Reg.4, amended: SI 2002/1555 Art.43
Reg.4, revoked (in part): SI 2002/1555 Art.43

200. European Communities (Recognition of Professional Qualifications) (Second General System) (Amendment) Regulations 2001
revoked: SI 2002/2934 Reg.27

207. Social Security Benefits Up-rating (No.2) Order 2001
revoked: SI 2002/668 Art.24

211. Solihull Primary Care Trust (Establishment) Order 2001
Art.1, amended: SI 2002/1405 Sch.1
Art.4, revoked: SI 2002/1405 Sch.1
Sch., amended: SI 2004/543 Sch.1

NO.

NO.

2001–cont.

212. **Solihull Healthcare National Health Service Trust (Dissolution) Order 2001**
revoked: 2003 c.43 s.7

213. **Newcastle, North Tyneside and North-umberland Mental Health National Health Service Trust (Establishment) Order 2001**
revoked: 2003 c.43 s.7

214. **Newcastle City Health and the North-umberland Mental Health National Health Service Trusts (Dissolution) Order 2001**
revoked: 2003 c.43 s.7

219. **Major Precepting Authorities (Excessive Budget Requirements-Payments) (England) Regulations 2001**
revoked: 2003 c.26 Sch.8 Part 1

220. **Lincoln District Healthcare and the South Lincolnshire Healthcare National Health Service Trusts (Dissolution) Order 2001**
revoked: 2003 c.43 s.7

221. **Lincolnshire Healthcare National Health Service Trust (Establishment) Order 2001**
revoked: 2003 c.43 s.7
Art.1, amended: SI 2002/891 Art.2
Art.2, amended: SI 2002/891 Art.2

238. **Detention Centre Rules 2001**
Part II r.33, amended: SI 2002/3135 Sch.1 para.47

248. **Bromley Primary Care Trust (Establishment) Order 2001**
Art.1, amended: SI 2002/1405 Sch.1
Art.4, revoked: SI 2002/1405 Sch.1

249. **Tower Hamlets Primary Care Trust (Establishment) Order 2001**
Art.1, amended: SI 2002/1405 Sch.1
Art.4, revoked: SI 2002/1405 Sch.1

260. **Charities (Exception from Registration) (Amendment) Regulations 2001**
revoked: SI 2002/1598 Reg.3

268. **Vale of Aylesbury Primary Care Trust (Establishment) Order 2001**
applied: SI 2003/3059 Sch.1
Art.1, amended: SI 2002/1405 Sch.1
Art.4, revoked: SI 2002/1405 Sch.1
Sch., amended: SI 2004/543 Sch.1

269. **Hertfordshire Partnership National Health Service Trust (Establishment) Order 2001**
revoked: 2003 c.43 s.7

271. **Avon and Western Wiltshire Mental Health Care National Health Service Trust (Change of Name) Order 2001**
revoked: 2003 c.43 s.7

2001–cont.

272. **City and Hackney Primary Care Trust (Establishment) Order 2001**
Art.1, amended: SI 2002/1405 Sch.1, SI 2003/2663 Art.2
Art.2, amended: SI 2003/2663 Art.2
Art.4, revoked: SI 2002/1405 Sch.1

273. **Lincolnshire South West Primary Care Trust (Establishment) Order 2001**
Art.1, amended: SI 2002/1235 Art.2, SI 2002/1405 Sch.1
Art.2, amended: SI 2002/1235 Art.2
Art.4, revoked: SI 2002/1405 Sch.1
Sch., amended: SI 2004/543 Sch.1

274. **West Lincolnshire Primary Care Trust (Establishment) Order 2001**
Art.1, amended: SI 2002/1405 Sch.1
Art.4, revoked: SI 2002/1405 Sch.1
Sch., amended: SI 2004/543 Sch.1, SI 2004/2248 Sch.1

278. **Teddington, Twickenham and Hamptons Primary Care Trust (Establishment) Order 2001**
Art.1, amended: SI 2002/1008 Art.2, SI 2002/1405 Sch.1
Art.2, amended: SI 2002/1008 Art.2
Art.4, amended: SI 2002/1008 Art.3
Art.4, revoked: SI 2002/1405 Sch.1
Sch.1, amended: SI 2004/543 Sch.1
Sch.1, substituted: SI 2002/1008 Art.3

279. **Kingston Primary Care Trust (Establishment) Order 2001**
Art.1, amended: SI 2002/1405 Sch.1
Art.4, revoked: SI 2002/1405 Sch.1

282. **Hastings and St Leonards Primary Care Trust (Establishment) Order 2001**
Art.1, amended: SI 2002/1405 Sch.1
Art.4, revoked: SI 2002/1405 Sch.1

283. **Bexhill and Rother Primary Care Trust (Establishment) Order 2001**
Art.1, amended: SI 2002/1405 Sch.1
Art.4, revoked: SI 2002/1405 Sch.1
Sch., amended: SI 2004/543 Sch.1

284. **South West Kent Primary Care Trust (Establishment) Order 2001**
Art.1, amended: SI 2002/1405 Sch.1
Art.4, revoked: SI 2002/1405 Sch.1

285. **Maidstone and Malling Primary Care Trust (Establishment) Order 2001**
Art.1, amended: SI 2002/1123 Art.2, SI 2002/1405 Sch.1
Art.2, amended: SI 2002/1123 Art.2
Art.4, revoked: SI 2002/1405 Sch.1
Sch., substituted: SI 2002/1123 Art.3

286. **Northamptonshire Healthcare National Health Service Trust (Establishment) Order 2001**
revoked: 2003 c.43 s.7

2001–cont.

311. Carriers Liability (Clandestine Entrants and Sale of Transporters) (Amendment) Regulations 2001
revoked: SI 2002/2817 Reg.15

318. Merger Report (Interbrew SA and Bass PLC) (Interim Provision) Order 2001
revoked: SI 2002/108 Art.2

322. South West Dorset Primary Care Trust (Establishment) Order 2001
Art.1, amended: SI 2002/1405 Sch.1
Art.4, revoked: SI 2002/1405 Sch.1
Sch.1, amended: SI 2004/543 Sch.1

323. Berkshire Healthcare National Health Service Trust (Establishment) Order 2001
revoked: 2003 c.43 s.7

324. North Essex Mental Health Partnership National Health Service Trust (Establishment) Order 2001
applied: SI 2003/3059 Sch.1
revoked: 2003 c.43 s.7

325. Exeter Primary Care Trust (Establishment) Order 2001
Art.1, amended: SI 2002/1405 Sch.1
Art.4, revoked: SI 2002/1405 Sch.1

326. East Berkshire National Health Service Trust for People with Learning Disabilities and the West Berkshire Priority Care Service National Health Service Trust (Dissolution) Order 2001
revoked: 2003 c.43 s.7

328. Barnet Primary Care Trust (Establishment) Order 2001
Art.1, amended: SI 2002/1405 Sch.1
Art.4, revoked: SI 2002/1405 Sch.1

329. Haringey Primary Care Trust (Establishment) Order 2001
Art.1, amended: SI 2002/1405 Sch.1, SI 2003/1501 Art.2
Art.2, amended: SI 2003/1501 Art.2
Art.4, revoked: SI 2002/1405 Sch.1

331. East Hampshire Primary Care Trust (Establishment) Order 2001
applied: SI 2003/3059 Sch.1
Art.1, amended: SI 2002/1405 Sch.1
Art.4, revoked: SI 2002/1405 Sch.1
Sch.1, amended: SI 2004/543 Sch.1

332. Mid-Sussex Primary Care Trust (Establishment) Order 2001
Art.1, amended: SI 2002/1405 Sch.1
Art.4, revoked: SI 2002/1405 Sch.1
Sch.1, amended: SI 2004/543 Sch.1

333. Buckinghamshire Mental Health National Health Service Trust (Establishment) Order 2001
applied: SI 2003/3059 Sch.1
revoked: 2003 c.43 s.7

2001–cont.

334. Aylesbury Vale Community Healthcare National Health Service Trust (Dissolution) Order 2001
revoked: 2003 c.43 s.7

335. South Wiltshire Primary Care Trust (Establishment) Order 2001
Art.1, amended: SI 2002/1405 Sch.1
Art.4, revoked: SI 2002/1405 Sch.1
Sch.1, amended: SI 2004/543 Sch.1

341. Representation of the People (England and Wales) Regulations 2001
applied: SI 2003/1557 Reg.7, SI 2004/293 Sch.2 para.14
see *R. (on the application of Robertson) v Wakefield MDC* [2001] EWHC Admin 915, [2002] Q.B. 1052 (QBD (Admin Ct)), Maurice Kay, J.
Part II, applied: SI 2004/870 Reg.10
Part III, applied: SI 2004/870 Reg.10
Part V, applied: SI 2004/870 Reg.10
Part V, referred to: SI 2004/294 Reg.5
Part V, applied: SI 2004/294 Reg.5, SI 2004/870 Reg.10
Reg.1, applied: SI 2004/870 Reg.10
Reg.2, applied: SI 2004/870 Reg.10
Reg.3, amended: SI 2002/1871 Reg.5
Reg.3, applied: SI 2004/870 Reg.10
Reg.3, varied: SI 2003/1557 Sch.2 para.1, SI 2004/870 Sch.3, SI 2004/1962 Sch.2 Part 3
Reg.4, applied: SI 2004/870 Reg.10
Reg.4, varied: SI 2004/870 Sch.3, SI 2004/1962 Sch.2 Part 3
Reg.5, applied: SI 2004/870 Reg.10
Reg.5, varied: SI 2004/870 Sch.3, SI 2004/1962 Sch.2 Part 3
Reg.6, applied: SI 2004/870 Reg.10
Reg.6, varied: SI 2004/870 Sch.3, SI 2004/1962 Sch.2 Part 3
Reg.7, applied: SI 2004/870 Reg.10
Reg.7, substituted: SI 2002/1871 Reg.6
Reg.7, varied: SI 2004/870 Sch.3, SI 2004/1962 Sch.2 Part 3
Reg.8, applied: SI 2004/870 Reg.10
Reg.8, varied: SI 2004/870 Sch.3, SI 2004/1962 Sch.2 Part 3
Reg.9, applied: SI 2004/870 Reg.10
Reg.10, amended: SI 2002/1871 Reg.7
Reg.10, applied: SI 2004/870 Reg.10
Reg.10, revoked (in part): SI 2002/1871 Reg.7
Reg.11, applied: SI 2004/870 Reg.10
Reg.11, varied: SI 2004/870 Sch.3
Reg.12, applied: SI 2004/870 Reg.10
Reg.13, applied: SI 2004/870 Reg.10
Reg.15, applied: SI 2004/1962 Sch.1
Reg.24, varied: SI 2003/1557 Sch.2 para.1
Reg.26, amended: SI 2002/1871 Reg.8, SI 2003/1899 Reg.4, SI 2004/1848 Reg.4
Reg.26, varied: SI 2003/1557 Sch.2 para.1
Reg.33, varied: SI 2003/1557 Sch.2 para.1

2001–cont.

341. Representation of the People (England and Wales) Regulations 2001–*cont.*

Reg.36, amended: SI 2002/1871 Reg.9

Reg.42, varied: SI 2003/1557 Sch.2 para.1

Reg.43, amended: SI 2002/1871 Reg.10

Reg.45, amended: SI 2002/1871 Reg.11

Reg.46, revoked: SI 2002/1871 Reg.3

Reg.47, revoked: SI 2002/1871 Reg.3

Reg.48, revoked: SI 2002/1871 Reg.3

Reg.48, varied: SI 2003/284 Sch.1 para.2

Reg.49, revoked: SI 2002/1871 Reg.3

Reg.50, applied: SI 2004/870 Reg.10

Reg.50, varied: SI 2004/870 Sch.3, Sch.4, SI 2004/1962 Sch.2 Part 3

Reg.51, applied: SI 2004/870 Reg.10

Reg.51, varied: SI 2004/870 Sch.3, Sch.4, SI 2004/1962 Sch.2 Part 3

Reg.52, applied: SI 2004/870 Reg.10

Reg.52, varied: SI 2004/870 Sch.3, SI 2004/1962 Sch.2 Part 3

Reg.53, amended: SI 2002/881 Sch.1 para.21, SI 2004/1771 Sch.1 para.32

Reg.53, applied: SI 2004/870 Reg.10

Reg.53, varied: SI 2004/1962 Sch.2 Part 3

Reg.54, applied: SI 2004/870 Reg.10

Reg.54, varied: SI 2004/1962 Sch.2 Part 3

Reg.55, varied: SI 2004/870 Sch.3, SI 2004/1962 Sch.2 Part 3

Reg.56, applied: SI 2004/870 Reg.10

Reg.56, varied: SI 2004/870 Sch.3, SI 2004/1962 Sch.2 Part 3

Reg.57, applied: SI 2004/870 Reg.10

Reg.57, varied: SI 2004/870 Sch.3, SI 2004/1962 Sch.2 Part 3

Reg.58, applied: SI 2004/870 Reg.10

Reg.58, varied: SI 2004/870 Sch.3, SI 2004/1962 Sch.2 Part 3

Reg.59, applied: SI 2004/870 Reg.10

Reg.59, varied: SI 2004/870 Sch.3, SI 2004/1962 Sch.2 Part 3

Reg.60, applied: SI 2004/870 Reg.10

Reg.60, varied: SI 2004/1962 Sch.2 Part 3

Reg.61, applied: SI 2004/870 Reg.10

Reg.61, varied: SI 2004/870 Sch.3, SI 2004/1962 Sch.2 Part 3

Reg.62, varied: SI 2004/870 Sch.3

Reg.63, applied: SI 2004/870 Reg.10

Reg.64, varied: SI 2004/870 Sch.3

Reg.65, applied: SI 2002/185 Sch.3 para.41, SI 2004/294 Reg.5

Reg.65, referred to: SI 2004/294 Reg.5

Reg.65, varied: SI 2004/294 Reg.7

Reg.66, varied: SI 2004/870 Sch.3

Reg.67, varied: SI 2004/870 Sch.3

Reg.68, varied: SI 2004/870 Sch.3

Reg.70, varied: SI 2004/870 Sch.3

Reg.71, varied: SI 2003/1557 Sch.2 para.1, SI 2004/870 Sch.3

Reg.72, amended: SI 2002/1871 Reg.12

2001–cont.

341. Representation of the People (England and Wales) Regulations 2001–*cont.*

Reg.72, varied: SI 2004/870 Sch.3, Sch.4

Reg.73, varied: SI 2004/870 Sch.3

Reg.74, varied: SI 2004/870 Sch.3

Reg.75, varied: SI 2004/870 Sch.3

Reg.76, varied: SI 2004/870 Sch.3

Reg.76, see *Knight v Nicholls* [2004] EWCA Civ 68, [2004] 1 W.L.R. 1653 (CA), Tuckey, L.J.

Reg.77, amended: SI 2002/1871 Reg.13

Reg.77, varied: SI 2004/870 Sch.3

Reg.78, varied: SI 2004/870 Sch.3

Reg.79, varied: SI 2004/870 Sch.3

Reg.80, applied: SI 2004/870 Reg.10

Reg.80, varied: SI 2004/870 Sch.3

Reg.81, applied: SI 2004/870 Reg.10

Reg.81, varied: SI 2004/870 Sch.3

Reg.82, applied: SI 2004/870 Reg.10

Reg.82, varied: SI 2004/870 Sch.3

Reg.83, applied: SI 2004/870 Reg.10

Reg.83, varied: SI 2004/870 Sch.3

Reg.84, applied: SI 2004/870 Reg.10

Reg.84, varied: SI 2004/870 Sch.3

Reg.85, amended: SI 2002/1871 Reg.14

Reg.85, applied: SI 2004/870 Reg.10

Reg.85, varied: SI 2004/870 Sch.3

Reg.86, applied: SI 2004/870 Reg.10

Reg.86, varied: SI 2004/870 Sch.3

Reg.87, applied: SI 2004/870 Reg.10

Reg.87, varied: SI 2004/870 Sch.3

Reg.88, applied: SI 2004/870 Reg.10

Reg.88, varied: SI 2004/870 Sch.3

Reg.89, applied: SI 2004/870 Reg.10

Reg.89, varied: SI 2004/870 Sch.3

Reg.90, applied: SI 2004/870 Reg.10

Reg.91, applied: SI 2004/870 Reg.10

Reg.91, varied: SI 2004/870 Sch.3

Reg.92, added: SI 2002/1871 Reg.15

Reg.92, applied: SI 2004/870 Reg.10

Reg.92, varied: SI 2004/1962 Sch.2 Part 3

Reg.93, added: SI 2002/1871 Reg.15

Reg.93, applied: SI 2004/870 Reg.10

Reg.93, varied: SI 2004/1962 Sch.2 Part 3

Reg.94, added: SI 2002/1871 Reg.15

Reg.94, applied: SI 2004/870 Reg.10

Reg.95, added: SI 2002/1871 Reg.15

Reg.95, applied: SI 2004/870 Reg.10

Reg.96, added: SI 2002/1871 Reg.15

Reg.96, applied: SI 2004/870 Reg.10

Reg.97, added: SI 2002/1871 Reg.15

Reg.97, applied: SI 2004/870 Reg.10

Reg.98, added: SI 2002/1871 Reg.15

Reg.98, applied: SI 2004/870 Reg.10

Reg.98, varied: SI 2004/1962 Sch.2 Part 3

Reg.99, added: SI 2002/1871 Reg.15

Reg.99, applied: SI 2004/870 Reg.10

Reg.100, added: SI 2002/1871 Reg.15

Reg.100, applied: SI 2004/870 Reg.10

NO.

2001-cont.

341. Representation of the People (England and Wales) Regulations 2001-cont.

Reg.100, varied: SI 2004/1962 Art.8

Reg.101, added: SI 2002/1871 Reg.15

Reg.101, applied: SI 2004/870 Reg.10

Reg.102, added: SI 2002/1871 Reg.15

Reg.102, applied: SI 2004/870 Reg.10

Reg.103, added: SI 2002/1871 Reg.15

Reg.103, applied: SI 2004/870 Reg.10

Reg.104, added: SI 2002/1871 Reg.15

Reg.104, applied: SI 2004/870 Reg.10

Reg.105, added: SI 2002/1871 Reg.15

Reg.105, applied: SI 2004/870 Reg.10

Reg.106, added: SI 2002/1871 Reg.15

Reg.106, applied: SI 2004/870 Reg.10

Reg.106, varied: SI 2004/1962 Sch.2 Part 3

Reg.107, added: SI 2002/1871 Reg.15

Reg.107, applied: SI 2004/870 Reg.10

Reg.108, added: SI 2002/1871 Reg.15

Reg.108, applied: SI 2004/870 Reg.10

Reg.109, added: SI 2002/1871 Reg.15

Reg.109, applied: SI 2004/870 Reg.10

Reg.110, added: SI 2002/1871 Reg.15

Reg.110, applied: SI 2004/870 Reg.10

Reg.111, added: SI 2002/1871 Reg.15

Reg.111, applied: SI 2004/870 Reg.10

Reg.112, added: SI 2002/1871 Reg.15

Reg.112, applied: SI 2004/870 Reg.10

Reg.113, added: SI 2002/1871 Reg.15

Reg.113, applied: SI 2004/870 Reg.10

Reg.114, added: SI 2002/1871 Reg.15

Reg.114, amended: SI 2003/3075 Sch.2 para.5

Reg.114, applied: SI 2004/870 Reg.10

Reg.114, see *R. (on the application of Robertson) v Secretary of State* [2003] EWHC 1760, [2003] A.C.D. 78 (QBD (Admin Ct)), Maurice Kay, J.

Reg.115, added: SI 2002/1871 Reg.15

Reg.115, applied: SI 2004/870 Reg.10

Reg.115, varied: SI 2004/1962 Sch.2 Part 3

Sch.3, amended: SI 2004/294 Sch.3 para.2, Sch.3 para.3

Sch.3, varied: SI 2002/185 Sch.3 Part I, SI 2004/870 Sch.3

343. Feeding Stuffs (Wales) Regulations 2001

referred to: SI 2003/989 Reg.2, SI 2003/1850 Reg.2

Reg.2, amended: SI 2003/989 Reg.3, SI 2003/1850 Reg.3

Reg.7, amended: SI 2002/1797 Reg.3, SI 2003/989 Reg.4, SI 2003/1850 Reg.4, SI 2003/3119 Reg.3, SI 2004/1749 Reg.3

Reg.12, amended: SI 2003/989 Reg.5

Reg.12, substituted: SI 2003/1850 Reg.5

Reg.17, amended: SI 2002/1797 Reg.4

Reg.17A, added: SI 2003/1850 Reg.6

NO.

2001-cont.

343. Feeding Stuffs (Wales) Regulations 2001-cont.

Reg.24, amended: SI 2002/1797 Reg.3, Reg.5, SI 2003/989 Reg.4, SI 2003/1850 Reg.7, Reg.8, SI 2003/3119 Reg.3, SI 2004/1749 Reg.3

Reg.25, revoked (in part): SI 2002/1797 Reg.6

Sch.3 Part II, referred to: SI 2003/3119 Reg.2

Sch.3 Part II, substituted: SI 2003/3119 Sch.1

Sch.3 Part V, amended: SI 2004/1749 Reg.2

Sch.3 Part VII, substituted: SI 2003/989 Reg.6

Sch.3 Part IX, added: SI 2003/3119 Reg.2

Sch.3 Part IX, amended: SI 2003/3119 Reg.2, SI 2004/1749 Reg.2

Sch.3 Part IX, substituted: SI 2002/1797 Sch.1, SI 2003/989 Sch.1, SI 2003/1850 Sch.1

Sch.4 Part I para.14, revoked (in part): SI 2003/1850 Reg.10

Sch.4 Part I para.15, amended: SI 2003/1850 Reg.10

Sch.4 Part I para.19, substituted: SI 2003/1850 Reg.10

Sch.7 Part I, amended: SI 2002/1797 Sch.2, SI 2003/1850 Reg.11, SI 2004/1749 Sch.1

Sch.7 Part II, amended: SI 2002/1797 Sch.2

Sch.7 Part II, revoked: SI 2003/1850 Reg.11

Sch.8, amended: SI 2002/1797 Reg.9, SI 2004/1749 Sch.2

Sch.9 Part A, amended: SI 2002/1797 Sch.3

Sch.10 Part II, revoked: SI 2003/1850 Reg.12

344. Chingford, Wanstead and Woodford Primary Care Trust (Establishment) Order 2001

revoked: SI 2003/1066 Art.2

Art.1, amended: SI 2002/1405 Sch.1

Art.4, revoked: SI 2002/1405 Sch.1

345. North Cheshire Hospitals National Health Service Trust (Establishment) Order 2001

applied: SI 2003/3059 Sch.1

revoked: 2003 c.43 s.7

346. Slough Primary Care Trust (Establishment) Order 2001

Art.1, amended: SI 2002/1405 Sch.1

Art.4, revoked: SI 2002/1405 Sch.1

Sch.1, amended: SI 2004/543 Sch.1

347. Wokingham Primary Care Trust (Establishment) Order 2001

Art.1, amended: SI 2002/1405 Sch.1

Art.4, revoked: SI 2002/1405 Sch.1

348. Barking and Dagenham Primary Care Trust (Establishment) Order 2001

Art.1, amended: SI 2002/1405 Sch.1

Art.4, substituted: SI 2002/1405 Sch.1

349. Walthamstow, Leyton and Leytonstone Primary Care Trust (Establishment) Order 2001

revoked: SI 2003/1066 Art.2

NO.

2001–cont.

349. Walthamstow, Leyton and Leytonstone Primary Care Trust (Establishment) Order 2001–cont.
Art.1, amended: SI 2002/1405 Sch.1
Art.4, revoked: SI 2002/1405 Sch.1

350. Newham Primary Care Trust (Establishment) Order 2001
referred to: SI 2004/569 Sch.1
Art.1, amended: SI 2002/1405 Sch.1
Art.4, revoked: SI 2002/1405 Sch.1

351. Reading Primary Care Trust (Establishment) Order 2001
Art.1, amended: SI 2002/1405 Sch.1
Art.4, revoked: SI 2002/1405 Sch.1

352. Redbridge Primary Care Trust (Establishment) Order 2001
revoked: SI 2003/1066 Art.2
Art.1, amended: SI 2002/1405 Sch.1
Art.4, revoked: SI 2002/1405 Sch.1

364. Watford and Three Rivers Primary Care Trust (Establishment) Order 2001
Art.1, amended: SI 2002/1405 Sch.1
Art.4, revoked: SI 2002/1405 Sch.1
Sch.1, amended: SI 2004/543 Sch.1

365. Welwyn Hatfield Primary Care Trust (Establishment) Order 2001
Art.1, amended: SI 2002/1405 Sch.1
Art.4, revoked: SI 2002/1405 Sch.1
Sch.1, amended: SI 2004/543 Sch.1

369. Luton Primary Care Trust (Establishment) Order 2001
Art.1, amended: SI 2002/1405 Sch.1
Art.4, revoked: SI 2002/1405 Sch.1

370. Uttlesford Primary Care Trust (Establishment) Order 2001
Art.1, amended: SI 2002/1405 Sch.1
Art.4, revoked: SI 2002/1405 Sch.1
Sch.1, amended: SI 2004/543 Sch.1

371. South East Hertfordshire Primary Care Trust (Establishment) Order 2001
Art.1, amended: SI 2002/1405 Sch.1
Art.4, revoked: SI 2002/1405 Sch.1
Sch.1, amended: SI 2004/543 Sch.1

381. Bedford Primary Care Trust (Establishment) Order 2001
Art.1, amended: SI 2002/1405 Sch.1
Art.4, revoked: SI 2002/1405 Sch.1

382. Dacorum Primary Care Trust (Establishment) Order 2001
Art.1, amended: SI 2002/1405 Sch.1
Art.4, revoked: SI 2002/1405 Sch.1
Sch.1, amended: SI 2004/543 Sch.1

383. Great Yarmouth Primary Care Trust (Establishment) Order 2001
Art.1, amended: SI 2002/1405 Sch.1
Art.4, revoked: SI 2002/1405 Sch.1
Sch.1, amended: SI 2004/543 Sch.1

NO.

2001–cont.

385. Norwich Primary Care Trust (Establishment) Order 2001
Art.1, amended: SI 2002/1405 Sch.1
Art.4, revoked: SI 2002/1405 Sch.1

386. St Albans and Harpenden Primary Care Trust (Establishment) Order 2001
Art.1, amended: SI 2002/1405 Sch.1
Art.4, revoked: SI 2002/1405 Sch.1
Sch.1, amended: SI 2004/543 Sch.1

387. Thurrock Primary Care Trust (Establishment) Order 2001
Art.1, amended: SI 2002/1405 Sch.1
Art.4, revoked: SI 2002/1405 Sch.1
Sch.1, amended: SI 2004/543 Sch.1

388. Basildon Primary Care Trust (Establishment) Order 2001
Art.1, amended: SI 2002/1405 Sch.1
Art.4, revoked: SI 2002/1405 Sch.1

389. Bedfordshire Heartlands Primary Care Trust (Establishment) Order 2001
Art.1, amended: SI 2002/1405 Sch.1
Art.4, revoked: SI 2002/1405 Sch.1
Sch.1, amended: SI 2004/543 Sch.1

390. Royston, Buntingford and Bishop's Stortford Primary Care Trust (Establishment) Order 2001
applied: SI 2003/3059 Sch.1
Art.1, amended: SI 2002/1405 Sch.1
Art.4, revoked: SI 2002/1405 Sch.1
Sch.1, amended: SI 2004/543 Sch.1

392. Afghanistan (United Nations Sanctions) (Overseas Territories) Order 2001
revoked: SI 2002/112 Art.1

393. Afghanistan (United Nations Sanctions) (Channel Islands) Order 2001
revoked: SI 2002/258 Art.1
Art.2, amended: SI 2003/1521 Art.3

394. Afghanistan (United Nations Sanctions) (Isle of Man) Order 2001
revoked: SI 2002/259 Art.1

396. Afghanistan (United Nations Sanctions) Order 2001
revoked: SI 2002/111 Art.1

400. Representation of the People (Northern Ireland) Regulations 2001
applied: SI 2003/1557 Reg.7
Reg.3, amended: SI 2002/1873 Reg.5
Reg.3, varied: SI 2003/1557 Sch.2 para.4
Reg.10, amended: SI 2002/1873 Reg.7
Reg.10, revoked (in part): SI 2002/1873 Reg.7
Reg.12A, added: SI 2002/1873 Reg.8
Reg.24, varied: SI 2003/1557 Sch.2 para.4
Reg.26, amended: SI 2002/1873 Reg.10, SI 2003/1942 Reg.4
Reg.26, varied: SI 2003/1557 Sch.2 para.4
Reg.33, varied: SI 2003/1557 Sch.2 para.4
Reg.42, varied: SI 2003/1557 Sch.2 para.4

NO.

2001–cont.

400. Representation of the People (Northern Ireland) Regulations 2001–*cont.*
Reg.53, amended: SI 2002/881 Sch.1 para.22
Reg.107, amended: SI 2003/3075 Sch.2 para.6
Reg.107, revoked (in part): SI 2003/3075 Sch.2 para.6

402. Terrorism Act 2000 (Code of Practice on Video Recording of Interviews) (Northern Ireland) Order 2001
revoked: SI 2003/1100 Art.3

424. Organic Farming Scheme (Wales) Regulations 2001
applied: SI 2003/2261 Sch.3 Part I
referred to: SI 2004/105 Reg.2
Reg.1, amended: SI 2004/105 Reg.3
Reg.2, amended: SI 2002/3159 Reg.15, SI 2004/105 Reg.4
Reg.5A, added: SI 2004/105 Reg.5
Reg.5B, added: SI 2004/105 Reg.5
Reg.5C, added: SI 2004/105 Reg.5
Reg.6, amended: SI 2004/105 Reg.6
Reg.7, amended: SI 2004/105 Reg.7
Reg.10, amended: SI 2004/105 Reg.8
Reg.12, amended: SI 2004/105 Reg.9
Reg.16, amended: SI 2004/105 Reg.10
Sch.1 Part I, amended: SI 2004/105 Reg.11
Sch.1 Part IA, added: SI 2004/105 Reg.11
Sch.2 para.1, amended: SI 2004/105 Reg.12
Sch.2 para.2, amended: SI 2004/105 Reg.12
Sch.2 para.3, amended: SI 2004/105 Reg.12
Sch.2 para.4, amended: SI 2004/105 Reg.12
Sch.2 para.5, amended: SI 2004/105 Reg.12
Sch.2 para.6, amended: SI 2004/105 Reg.12
Sch.2 para.7, amended: SI 2004/105 Reg.12
Sch.2 para.8, amended: SI 2004/105 Reg.12
Sch.2 para.9, amended: SI 2004/105 Reg.12
Sch.2 para.10, amended: SI 2004/105 Reg.12
Sch.2 para.10, substituted: SI 2004/105 Reg.12

430. Organic Products Regulations 2001
revoked: SI 2004/1604 Sch.3

432. Organic Farming (England Rural Development Programme) Regulations 2001
applied: SI 2003/1235 Reg.8, Reg.12
revoked: SI 2003/1235 Reg.12
Reg.7, disapplied: SI 2003/1235 Reg.12

436. Stockport Primary Care Trust (Establishment) Order 2001
Art.1, amended: SI 2002/1405 Sch.1
Art.4, revoked: SI 2002/1405 Sch.1

437. Bootle and Litherland Primary Care Trust (Establishment) Order 2001
Art.1, amended: SI 2002/1133 Art.2, SI 2002/1405 Sch.1
Art.2, amended: SI 2002/1133 Art.2
Art.4, revoked: SI 2002/1405 Sch.1
Sch.1, substituted: SI 2002/1133 Art.3

NO.

2001–cont.

438. Heywood and Middleton Primary Care Trust (Establishment) Order 2001
Art.1, amended: SI 2002/1405 Sch.1
Art.4, revoked: SI 2002/1405 Sch.1

439. Bebington and West Wirral Primary Care Trust (Establishment) Order 2001
Art.1, amended: SI 2002/1405 Sch.1
Art.4, revoked: SI 2002/1405 Sch.1

440. Trafford North Primary Care Trust (Establishment) Order 2001
Art.1, amended: SI 2002/1405 Sch.1
Art.4, revoked: SI 2002/1405 Sch.1

441. Carers (Services) and Direct Payments (Amendment) (England) Regulations 2001
Reg.3, revoked: SI 2003/762 Reg.12
Reg.4, revoked: SI 2003/762 Reg.12

442. Disabled Children (Direct Payments) (England) Regulations 2001
revoked: SI 2003/762 Reg.12

446. Political Parties, Elections and Referendums Act 2000 (Disapplication of Part IV for Northern Ireland Parties, etc.) Order 2001
varied: SI 2004/366 Art.5

465. Plymouth Primary Care Trust (Establishment) Order 2001
Art.1, amended: SI 2002/1405 Sch.1, SI 2003/2944 Art.2
Art.2, amended: SI 2003/2944 Art.2
Art.4, revoked: SI 2002/1405 Sch.1

466. Mid Devon Primary Care Trust (Establishment) Order 2001
Art.1, amended: SI 2002/1405 Sch.1
Art.4, revoked: SI 2002/1405 Sch.1
Sch.1, amended: SI 2004/543 Sch.1

467. Teignbridge Primary Care Trust (Establishment) Order 2001
Art.1, amended: SI 2002/1405 Sch.1
Art.4, revoked: SI 2002/1405 Sch.1
Art.8, revoked: SI 2002/1118 Art.2
Sch.1, amended: SI 2004/543 Sch.1

468. East Devon Primary Care Trust (Establishment) Order 2001
Art.1, amended: SI 2002/1405 Sch.1
Art.4, revoked: SI 2002/1405 Sch.1
Sch.1, amended: SI 2004/543 Sch.1

469. Mendip Primary Care Trust (Establishment) Order 2001
Art.1, amended: SI 2002/1405 Sch.1
Art.4, revoked: SI 2002/1405 Sch.1
Sch.1, amended: SI 2004/543 Sch.1

470. West Wiltshire Primary Care Trust (Establishment) Order 2001
Art.1, amended: SI 2002/1405 Sch.1
Art.4, revoked: SI 2002/1405 Sch.1
Sch.1, amended: SI 2004/543 Sch.1

2001–cont.

471. Somerset Coast Primary Care Trust (Establishment) Order 2001
Art.1, amended: SI 2002/1405 Sch.1
Art.4, revoked: SI 2002/1405 Sch.1
Sch.1, amended: SI 2004/543 Sch.1

472. North Devon Primary Care Trust (Establishment) Order 2001
Art.1, amended: SI 2002/1405 Sch.1
Art.4, revoked: SI 2002/1405 Sch.1
Sch.1, amended: SI 2004/543 Sch.1

473. Bath and North East Somerset Primary Care Trust (Establishment) Order 2001
Art.1, amended: SI 2002/1405 Sch.1
Art.4, revoked: SI 2002/1405 Sch.1
Sch.1, amended: SI 2004/543 Sch.1

474. South and East Dorset Primary Care Trust (Establishment) Order 2001
Art.1, amended: SI 2002/1405 Sch.1
Art.4, revoked: SI 2002/1405 Sch.1

475. Financing of Maintained Schools (England) Regulations 2001
applied: SI 2002/377 Reg.2, Reg.11, Reg.14, Reg.32, SI 2002/536 Reg.3, SI 2003/3247 Reg.23, Reg.24, Reg.28
revoked: SI 2003/453 Reg.2
Reg.11, applied: SI 2002/377 Reg.18, Reg.19
Reg.20, applied: SI 2002/377 Reg.18, Reg.19, SI 2003/453 Reg.24, SI 2003/3247 Reg.24

478. Parent Governor Representatives (England) Regulations 2001
Reg.2, amended: SI 2003/2045 Reg.7

488. Social Security (Miscellaneous Amendments) Regulations 2001
Reg.11, revoked: SI 2003/492 Sch.3 Part 1

489. North East Oxfordshire Primary Care Trust (Establishment) Order 2001
Art.1, amended: SI 2002/1405 Sch.1
Art.4, revoked: SI 2002/1405 Sch.1

490. Oxford City Primary Care Trust (Establishment) Order 2001
Art.1, amended: SI 2002/1405 Sch.1
Art.4, revoked: SI 2002/1405 Sch.1
Sch.1, amended: SI 2004/543 Sch.1

491. Cherwell Vale Primary Care Trust (Establishment) Order 2001
applied: SI 2003/3059 Sch.1
Art.1, amended: SI 2002/1405 Sch.1
Art.4, revoked: SI 2002/1405 Sch.1
Sch.1, amended: SI 2004/543 Sch.1

495. Financing of Maintained Schools (Amendment) (Wales) Regulations 2001
revoked: SI 2004/2506 Reg.3

496. Tir Mynydd (Wales) Regulations 2001
applied: SI 2003/4 Sch.1
Reg.2, amended: SI 2002/1806 Reg.3
Reg.2A, added: SI 2002/1806 Reg.4
Reg.2A, referred to: SI 2003/4 Sch.1
Reg.3, substituted: SI 2002/1806 Reg.5

2001–cont.

496. Tir Mynydd (Wales) Regulations 2001–*cont.*
Reg.3A, added: SI 2002/1806 Reg.6
Reg.4, amended: SI 2002/1806 Reg.7
Reg.6, amended: SI 2002/1806 Reg.8
Reg.7, amended: SI 2002/1806 Reg.9
Reg.8, amended: SI 2002/1806 Reg.10
Reg.9, revoked (in part): SI 2002/1806 Reg.11
Reg.10, amended: SI 2002/1806 Reg.12
Reg.11, revoked: SI 2002/1806 Reg.13
Reg.12, amended: SI 2002/1806 Reg.14
Reg.13, amended: SI 2002/1806 Reg.15
Reg.14, amended: SI 2002/1806 Reg.16
Reg.15, revoked: SI 2002/1806 Reg.17
Sch.1 Part A para.1, substituted: SI 2002/1806 Reg.18
Sch.1 Part A para.2, substituted: SI 2002/1806 Reg.18
Sch.1 Part A para.3, substituted: SI 2002/1806 Reg.18
Sch.1 Part C para.4, substituted: SI 2002/1806 Reg.18

497. Representation of the People (Scotland) Regulations 2001
applied: SI 2003/1557 Reg.7, SI 2004/293 Sch.2 para.14
Part V, applied: SI 2002/2779 Sch.5 para.2
Reg.3, amended: SI 2002/1872 Reg.5
Reg.3, varied: SI 2003/1557 Sch.2 para.2
Reg.7, substituted: SI 2002/1872 Reg.6
Reg.24, varied: SI 2003/1557 Sch.2 para.2
Reg.26, amended: SI 2002/1872 Reg.7, SI 2003/1892 Reg.4, SI 2004/1960 Reg.4
Reg.26, varied: SI 2003/1557 Sch.2 para.2
Reg.33, varied: SI 2003/1557 Sch.2 para.2
Reg.36, amended: SI 2002/1872 Reg.8
Reg.42, varied: SI 2003/1557 Sch.2 para.2
Reg.43, amended: SI 2002/1872 Reg.9
Reg.45, amended: SI 2002/1872 Reg.10
Reg.46, revoked: SI 2002/1872 Reg.3
Reg.47, revoked: SI 2002/1872 Reg.3
Reg.48, revoked: SI 2002/1872 Reg.3
Reg.49, revoked: SI 2002/1872 Reg.3
Reg.53, amended: SI 2002/881 Sch.1 para.23, SI 2004/1771 Sch.1 para.30
Reg.71, amended: SI 2002/1872 Reg.11
Reg.71, varied: SI 2003/1557 Sch.2 para.2
Reg.72, amended: SI 2002/1872 Reg.12
Reg.85, amended: SI 2002/1872 Reg.13
Reg.92, added: SI 2002/1872 Reg.14
Reg.93, added: SI 2002/1872 Reg.14
Reg.93, referred to: SI 2002/2779 Sch.1 para.3
Reg.94, added: SI 2002/1872 Reg.14
Reg.95, added: SI 2002/1872 Reg.14
Reg.96, added: SI 2002/1872 Reg.14
Reg.97, added: SI 2002/1872 Reg.14
Reg.98, added: SI 2002/1872 Reg.14
Reg.99, added: SI 2002/1872 Reg.14

2001–cont.

497. Representation of the People (Scotland) Regulations 2001–cont.

Reg.100, added: SI 2002/1872 Reg.14

Reg.101, added: SI 2002/1872 Reg.14

Reg.102, added: SI 2002/1872 Reg.14

Reg.103, added: SI 2002/1872 Reg.14

Reg.104, added: SI 2002/1872 Reg.14

Reg.105, added: SI 2002/1872 Reg.14

Reg.106, added: SI 2002/1872 Reg.14

Reg.107, added: SI 2002/1872 Reg.14

Reg.108, added: SI 2002/1872 Reg.14

Reg.109, added: SI 2002/1872 Reg.14

Reg.110, added: SI 2002/1872 Reg.14

Reg.111, added: SI 2002/1872 Reg.14

Reg.112, added: SI 2002/1872 Reg.14

Reg.113, added: SI 2002/1872 Reg.14

Reg.113, amended: SI 2003/3075 Sch.2 para.7

Reg.114, added: SI 2002/1872 Reg.14

Reg.115, added: SI 2002/1872 Reg.14

500. North Tees Primary Care Trust (Establishment) Order 2001

Art.1, amended: SI 2002/1405 Sch.1

Art.4, revoked: SI 2002/1405 Sch.1

501. Yorkshire Wolds and Coast Primary Care Trust (Establishment) Order 2001

Art.1, amended: SI 2002/1405 Sch.1

Art.4, revoked: SI 2002/1405 Sch.1

502. Eastern Hull Primary Care Trust (Establishment) Order 2001

Art.1, amended: SI 2002/1405 Sch.1

Art.4, revoked: SI 2002/1405 Sch.1

503. Pollution Prevention and Control (England and Wales) (Amendment) Regulations 2001

Reg.2, revoked (in part): SI 2002/275 Reg.3

504. Wakefield West Primary Care Trust (Establishment) Order 2001

Art.1, amended: SI 2002/1405 Sch.1

Art.4, revoked: SI 2002/1405 Sch.1

505. North Tyneside Primary Care Trust (Establishment) Order 2001

Art.1, amended: SI 2002/1405 Sch.1

Art.4, revoked: SI 2002/1405 Sch.1

506. Eastern Wakefield Primary Care Trust (Establishment) Order 2001

Art.1, amended: SI 2002/1405 Sch.1

Art.4, revoked: SI 2002/1405 Sch.1

507. Carlisle and District Primary Care Trust (Establishment) Order 2001

Art.1, amended: SI 2002/1405 Sch.1

Art.4, revoked: SI 2002/1405 Sch.1

Sch.1, amended: SI 2004/543 Sch.1

508. Selby and York Primary Care Trust (Establishment) Order 2001

Art.1, amended: SI 2002/1405 Sch.1

Art.4, revoked: SI 2002/1405 Sch.1

Sch.1, amended: SI 2004/543 Sch.1

2001–cont.

509. West Hull Primary Care Trust (Establishment) Order 2001

Art.1, amended: SI 2002/1405 Sch.1

Art.4, revoked: SI 2002/1405 Sch.1

511. East Yorkshire Primary Care Trust (Establishment) Order 2001

Art.1, amended: SI 2002/1405 Sch.1

Art.4, revoked: SI 2002/1405 Sch.1

Sch.1, amended: SI 2004/543 Sch.1

512. West Cumbria Primary Care Trust (Establishment) Order 2001

Art.1, amended: SI 2002/1405 Sch.1

Art.4, revoked: SI 2002/1405 Sch.1

513. Newcastle Primary Care Trust (Establishment) Order 2001

Art.1, amended: SI 2002/1405 Sch.1

Art.4, revoked: SI 2002/1405 Sch.1

514. Eden Valley Primary Care Trust (Establishment) Order 2001

Art.1, amended: SI 2002/1405 Sch.1

Art.4, revoked: SI 2002/1405 Sch.1

515. Hartlepool Primary Care Trust (Establishment) Order 2001

Art.1, amended: SI 2002/1405 Sch.1

Art.4, revoked: SI 2002/1405 Sch.1

518. Social Security Amendment (Joint Claims) Regulations 2001

Reg.5, revoked (in part): SI 2003/492 Sch.3 Part 1

519. Salford Primary Care Trust (Establishment) Order 2001

Art.1, amended: SI 2002/1405 Sch.1

Art.4, revoked: SI 2002/1405 Sch.1

520. Southport and Formby Primary Care Trust (Establishment) Order 2001

Art.1, amended: SI 2002/1405 Sch.1

Art.4, revoked: SI 2002/1405 Sch.1

521. Chorley and South Ribble Primary Care Trust (Establishment) Order 2001

Art.1, amended: SI 2002/1405 Sch.1

Art.4, revoked: SI 2002/1405 Sch.1

Sch.1, amended: SI 2004/543 Sch.1

522. West Lancashire Primary Care Trust (Establishment) Order 2001

Art.1, amended: SI 2002/1405 Sch.1

Art.4, revoked: SI 2002/1405 Sch.1

523. South East Oxfordshire Primary Care Trust (Establishment) Order 2001

applied: SI 2003/3059 Sch.1

Art.1, amended: SI 2002/1405 Sch.1

Art.4, revoked: SI 2002/1405 Sch.1

Sch.1, amended: SI 2004/543 Sch.1

524. Newbury and Community Primary Care Trust (Establishment) Order 2001

Art.1, amended: SI 2002/1405 Sch.1

Art.4, revoked: SI 2002/1405 Sch.1

525. South West Oxfordshire Primary Care Trust (Establishment) Order 2001

applied: SI 2003/3059 Sch.1

2001–cont.

525. South West Oxfordshire Primary Care Trust (Establishment) Order 2001– *cont.*
Art.1, amended: SI 2002/1405 Sch.1
Art.4, revoked: SI 2002/1405 Sch.1
Sch.1, amended: SI 2004/543 Sch.1

526. Enfield Primary Care Trust (Establishment) Order 2001
Art.1, amended: SI 2002/1405 Sch.1
Art.4, revoked: SI 2002/1405 Sch.1

527. Havering Primary Care Trust (Establishment) Order 2001
Art.1, amended: SI 2002/1405 Sch.1
Art.4, revoked: SI 2002/1405 Sch.1

528. Greenwich Primary Care Trust (Establishment) Order 2001
Art.1, amended: SI 2002/1405 Sch.1, SI 2004/1643 Art.2
Art.2, amended: SI 2004/1643 Art.2
Art.4, revoked: SI 2002/1405 Sch.1

536. Nurses, Midwives and Health Visitors (Professional Conduct) (Amendment) Rules 2001 Approval Order 2001
varied: SI 2004/1762 Art.1

539. Colchester Primary Care Trust (Establishment) Order 2001
Art.1, amended: SI 2002/1405 Sch.1
Art.4, revoked: SI 2002/1405 Sch.1
Sch.1, amended: SI 2004/543 Sch.1

543. Huntingdonshire Primary Care Trust (Establishment) Order 2001
Art.1, amended: SI 2002/1405 Sch.1
Art.4, revoked: SI 2002/1405 Sch.1
Sch.1, amended: SI 2004/543 Sch.1

544. Financial Services and Markets Act 2000 (Regulated Activities) Order 2001
Part II, added: SI 2003/1476 Art.7
Part II, added: SI 2004/2737 Art.3
Part II, substituted: SI 2002/1776 Art.3
Art.2, amended: SI 2002/1777 Art.2
Art.3, amended: SI 2002/682 Art.2, SI 2003/1475 Art.3, SI 2003/1476 Art.3
Art.4, amended: SI 2002/682 Art.11, SI 2003/1476 Art.3
Art.5, amended: SI 2002/682 Art.3
Art.6, amended: SI 2002/1310 Art.4
Art.9, amended: SI 2002/682 Art.12
Art.9, applied: SI 2003/1633 Sch.2 para.7
Art.9A, added: SI 2002/682 Art.3
Art.9AA, added: SI 2002/1776 Art.3
Art.9B, added: SI 2002/682 Art.4
Art.9B, disapplied: SI 2002/682 Art.9
Art.9B, referred to: SI 2002/682 Art.9
Art.9C, added: SI 2002/682 Art.4
Art.9C, applied: SI 2004/2095 Reg.17
Art.9D, added: SI 2002/682 Art.4
Art.9E, added: SI 2002/682 Art.4
Art.9F, added: SI 2002/682 Art.4

2001–cont.

544. Financial Services and Markets Act 2000 (Regulated Activities) Order 2001–*cont.*
Art.9G, added: SI 2002/682 Art.4
Art.9G, applied: SI 2002/682 Art.1, Art.10
Art.9H, added: SI 2002/682 Art.4
Art.9H, applied: SI 2002/682 Art.1, Art.10
Art.9I, added: SI 2002/682 Art.4
Art.9J, added: SI 2002/682 Art.4
Art.9K, added: SI 2002/682 Art.4
Art.10, disapplied: SI 2004/2095 Reg.17
Art.12, applied: SI 2004/2095 Reg.17
Art.12A, added: SI 2002/1776 Art.3
Art.14, referred to: SI 2004/1450 Reg.14
Art.17, varied: SI 2003/1633 Sch.2 para.8, Sch.2 para.9
Art.18A, added: SI 2003/2822 Art.3
Art.20, amended: SI 2002/1776 Art.3
Art.21, amended: SI 2003/1476 Art.4
Art.21, referred to: SI 2004/1450 Reg.14
Art.22, amended: SI 2003/1476 Art.4
Art.22, applied: SI 2004/2615 Sch.1 para.11
Art.24, amended: SI 2002/1776 Art.3, SI 2003/1476 Art.4
Art.25, amended: SI 2003/1476 Art.5
Art.25, referred to: SI 2004/1450 Reg.14
Art.25A, added: SI 2003/1475 Art.4
Art.25A, referred to: SI 2004/2615 Art.2
Art.26, amended: SI 2003/1475 Art.5
Art.27, amended: SI 2003/1475 Art.6
Art.28, amended: SI 2003/1476 Art.5
Art.28A, added: SI 2003/1475 Art.7
Art.29, amended: SI 2003/1475 Art.8, SI 2003/1476 Art.5
Art.29, applied: SI 2004/2615 Sch.1 para.11
Art.29A, added: SI 2003/1475 Art.9
Art.30, amended: SI 2003/1476 Art.5
Art.31, varied: SI 2003/1633 Sch.2 para.8, Sch.2 para.9
Art.33, amended: SI 2003/1475 Art.10, SI 2003/1476 Art.5
Art.33A, added: SI 2003/1475 Art.11
Art.35, amended: SI 2003/1476 Art.5
Art.36, amended: SI 2002/1776 Art.3, SI 2003/1476 Art.5
Art.36, substituted: SI 2003/1475 Art.12
Art.37, referred to: SI 2004/1450 Reg.14
Art.39, amended: SI 2002/1776 Art.3, SI 2003/1476 Art.6
Art.40, referred to: SI 2004/1450 Reg.14
Art.44, amended: SI 2002/1776 Art.3, SI 2003/1476 Art.8
Art.45, amended: SI 2002/682 Art.13
Art.45, referred to: SI 2004/1450 Reg.14
Art.46, amended: SI 2002/682 Art.13
Art.49, amended: SI 2002/682 Art.13
Art.50, amended: SI 2002/1776 Art.3
Art.51, referred to: SI 2004/1450 Reg.14
Art.51A, added: SI 2002/1776 Art.3
Art.52A, added: SI 2002/1776 Art.3

NO.

NO.

2001–cont.

544. Financial Services and Markets Act 2000 (Regulated Activities) Order 2001–cont.

Art.52B, applied: SI 2004/2738 Reg.3

Art.52B, enabled: SI 2004/2738

Art.52B, referred to: SI 2004/2737 Art.4

Art.53, amended: SI 2003/1476 Art.9

Art.53, referred to: SI 2004/1450 Reg.14, SI 2004/2737 Art.4

Art.53A, added: SI 2003/1475 Art.13

Art.53A, referred to: SI 2004/2615 Art.2

Art.54, amended: SI 2003/1475 Art.14, SI 2003/1476 Art.9

Art.54A, added: SI 2003/1475 Art.15

Art.55, amended: SI 2002/1776 Art.3, SI 2003/1476 Art.9

Art.55, substituted: SI 2003/1475 Art.16

Art.58A, added: SI 2002/1776 Art.3

Art.60A, added: SI 2002/1776 Art.3

Art.61, applied: SI 2004/1484 Reg.10

Art.63A, added: SI 2002/1776 Art.3

Art.63A, substituted: SI 2003/1475 Art.17

Art.64, amended: SI 2002/682 Art.5

Art.64, referred to: SI 2004/1450 Reg.14, SI 2004/2615 Art.2

Art.65, substituted: SI 2002/1776 Art.3

Art.66, amended: SI 2003/1475 Art.18, SI 2003/1476 Art.10

Art.67, amended: SI 2003/1475 Art.19, SI 2003/1476 Art.10

Art.68, amended: SI 2003/1476 Art.10

Art.69, amended: SI 2002/682 Art.13, SI 2003/1476 Art.10

Art.70, amended: SI 2003/1476 Art.10

Art.72, amended: SI 2003/1475 Art.20, SI 2003/1476 Art.10

Art.72, applied: SI 2004/2615 Sch.1 para.12

Art.72A, added: SI 2002/1776 Art.2

Art.72B, added: SI 2003/1476 Art.11

Art.72B, applied: SI 2004/2095 Reg.11

Art.72C, added: SI 2003/1476 Art.11

Art.72D, added: SI 2003/1476 Art.11

Art.74A, added: SI 2002/682 Art.6

Art.77, varied: SI 2003/1633 Sch.2 para.8

Art.78, varied: SI 2003/1633 Sch.2 para.8

Art.92, added: SI 2003/1476 Art.13

Art.93, added: SI 2003/1476 Art.13

Art.94, added: SI 2003/1476 Art.13

Art.95, added: SI 2003/1476 Art.13

Art.96, added: SI 2003/1476 Art.13

Art.97, added: SI 2004/1610 Art.3

Sch.1 Part II paraI, applied: SI 2004/1450 Reg.12

Sch.1 Part II paraIII, applied: SI 2004/1450 Reg.12

Sch.4 Part I, added: SI 2003/1476 Art.12

Sch.4 Part II, added: SI 2003/1476 Art.12

Sch.4 Part III, added: SI 2003/1476 Art.12

2001–cont.

561. Road Vehicles (Display of Registration Marks) Regulations 2001

Reg.2, referred to: SI 2002/2742 Reg.42

Reg.5, applied: SI 2002/2742 Reg.42

Reg.6, applied: SI 2002/2742 Reg.42

Reg.11, amended: SI 2002/2687 Reg.3

Reg.12, amended: SI 2002/2687 Reg.4

Reg.14, amended: SI 2002/2687 Reg.5

Reg.14A, added: SI 2002/2687 Reg.5

570. Education (Outturn Statements) (England) Regulations 2001

revoked: SI 2002/536 Reg.3

574. Mid-Hampshire Primary Care Trust (Establishment) Order 2001

Art.1, amended: SI 2002/1405 Sch.1

Art.4, revoked: SI 2002/1405 Sch.1

Sch.1, amended: SI 2004/543 Sch.1

575. North Hertfordshire and Stevenage Primary Care Trust (Establishment) Order 2001

Art.1, amended: SI 2002/1405 Sch.1

Art.4, revoked: SI 2002/1405 Sch.1

Sch.1, amended: SI 2004/543 Sch.1

600. Special Educational Needs Tribunal Regulations 2001

Reg.2, amended: SI 2002/2787 Reg.3

Reg.2, revoked (in part): SI 2002/2787 Reg.3

Reg.3, revoked: SI 2002/2787 Reg.4

Reg.4, revoked: SI 2002/2787 Reg.4

Reg.5, revoked: SI 2002/2787 Reg.4

Reg.6, revoked: SI 2002/2787 Reg.4

Reg.7, amended: SI 2002/2787 Reg.5

Reg.7, applied: SI 2002/1985 Reg.27

Reg.9, amended: SI 2002/2787 Reg.6

Reg.10, amended: SI 2002/2787 Reg.7

Reg.12, amended: SI 2002/2787 Reg.8

Reg.13, amended: SI 2002/2787 Reg.9

Reg.15, amended: SI 2002/2787 Reg.10

Reg.16, amended: SI 2002/2787 Reg.11

Reg.17, amended: SI 2002/2787 Reg.12

Reg.18, amended: SI 2002/2787 Reg.13

Reg.19, amended: SI 2002/2787 Reg.14

Reg.20, amended: SI 2002/2787 Reg.15

Reg.21, amended: SI 2002/2787 Reg.16

Reg.26, amended: SI 2002/2787 Reg.17

Reg.28, amended: SI 2002/2787 Reg.18

Reg.30, amended: SI 2002/2787 Reg.19

Reg.30, revoked (in part): SI 2002/2787 Reg.19

Reg.32, applied: SI 2002/1985 Reg.5

Reg.34, amended: SI 2002/2787 Reg.20

Reg.35, see *E v X LBC* [2002] EWHC 915, [2002] E.L.R. 453 (QBD (Admin Ct)), Stanley Burnton, J.

Reg.36, see *M v Worcestershire CC* [2002] EWHC 1292, [2003] E.L.R. 31 (QBD (Admin Ct)), Lawrence Collins, J.

Reg.46, amended: SI 2002/2787 Reg.21

NO.

NO.

2001–cont.

600. Special Educational Needs Tribunal Regulations 2001–*cont.*
Reg.48, see *Southampton City Council v G* [2002] EWHC 1516, [2002] E.L.R. 698 (QBD (Admin Ct)), Sullivan, J.
Reg.48, amended: SI 2002/2787 Reg.22

601. New Forest Primary Care Trust (Establishment) Order 2001
Art.1, amended: SI 2002/1405 Sch.1
Art.4, amended: SI 2002/1405 Sch.1
Sch.1, amended: SI 2004/543 Sch.1

607. Homeless Persons (Priority Need) (Wales) Order 2001
Art.3, amended: SI 2004/696 Art.3

643. Pig Industry Restructuring Grant (Wales) Scheme 2001
Art.2, amended: SI 2003/2726 Art.2

649. Sea Fish (Specified Sea Areas) (Regulation of Nets and Other Fishing Gear) Order 2001
referred to: SI 2003/1560 Art.2
Art.2, amended: SI 2003/1560 Art.3
Art.3, amended: SI 2003/1560 Art.4, Art.5
Art.6, revoked (in part): SI 2003/1560 Art.6

650. Prohibition of Fishing with Multiple Trawls Order 2001
revoked: SI 2003/1559 Art.5

651. Disabled Facilities Grants and Home Repair Assistance (Maximum Amounts) (Amendment) (England) Order 2001
revoked: SI 2002/1860 Sch.6

655. Carlisle Hospitals, the North Lakeland Healthcare and the West Cumbria Health Care National Health Service Trusts (Dissolution) Order 2001
revoked: 2003 c.43 s.7

656. North Cumbria Acute Hospitals National Health Service Trust (Establishment) Order 2001
revoked: 2003 c.43 s.7

657. South Gloucestershire Primary Care Trust (Establishment) Order 2001
Art.1, amended: SI 2002/1405 Sch.1
Art.4, revoked: SI 2002/1405 Sch.1
Sch.1, amended: SI 2004/543 Sch.1

661. Environmental Protection (Waste Recycling Payments) (Amendment) (England) Regulations 2001
revoked: SI 2002/531 Reg.3

686. Common Agricultural Policy (Wine) (England and Northern Ireland) Regulations 2001
Reg.2, amended: SI 2003/114 Reg.2, SI 2004/1046 Reg.2
Reg.5, amended: SI 2003/114 Reg.2
Reg.6, amended: SI 2003/114 Reg.2
Reg.6, substituted: SI 2004/1046 Reg.2
Reg.6A, added: SI 2003/114 Reg.2
Reg.6B, added: SI 2003/114 Reg.2
Reg.8, amended: SI 2003/114 Reg.2

2001–cont.

686. Common Agricultural Policy (Wine) (England and Northern Ireland) Regulations 2001–*cont.*
Reg.13, revoked: SI 2003/114 Reg.2
Reg.14, amended: SI 2003/114 Reg.2
Reg.16, amended: SI 2003/114 Reg.2, SI 2004/1046 Reg.2
Reg.19, amended: SI 2004/1046 Reg.2
Sch.1, substituted: SI 2003/114 Sch.1, SI 2004/1046 Sch.1
Sch.2 Part I, amended: SI 2003/114 Reg.2
Sch.2 Part III, amended: SI 2004/1046 Sch.2
Sch.2 Part IV, amended: SI 2003/114 Reg.2
Sch.2 Part V, amended: SI 2003/114 Reg.2
Sch.3, revoked: SI 2003/114 Reg.2, SI 2004/1046 Reg.2
Sch.4, revoked: SI 2003/114 Reg.2
Sch.5 para.2, amended: SI 2003/114 Reg.2
Sch.5 para.4, amended: SI 2003/114 Reg.2
Sch.6, added: SI 2004/1046 Sch.3
Sch.7 para.1, added: SI 2004/1046 Sch.3
Sch.7 para.2, added: SI 2004/1046 Sch.3

701. M11 London-Cambridge Motorway (Redbridge-Stump Cross Section) Scheme 1970 (Revocation) Scheme 2001
revoked: SI 2004/445 Art.2

706. National Health Service (General Medical Services) Amendment Regulations 2001
revoked: SI 2004/865 Sch.2

707. National Health Service (Dental Charges) Amendment Regulations 2001
revoked: SI 2002/544 Reg.3

713. National Treatment Agency (Establishment and Constitution) Order 2001
Art.4, amended: SI 2003/1827 Art.2

715. National Treatment Agency Regulations 2001
Reg.1, amended: SI 2004/696 Art.3
Reg.3, amended: SI 2004/696 Art.3, Sch.1 para.36

716. Calderdale Healthcare and the Huddersfield Health Care Services National Health Service Trusts (Dissolution) Order 2001
revoked: 2003 c.43 s.7

717. Calderdale and Huddersfield National Health Service Trust (Establishment) Order 2001
revoked: 2003 c.43 s.7

718. Wrightington, Wigan and Leigh National Health Service Trust (Establishment) Order 2001
revoked: 2003 c.43 s.7

NO.

719. **Wigan and Leigh Health Services and the Wrightington Hospital National Health Service Trusts (Dissolution) Order 2001**
revoked: 2003 c.43 s.7

724. **Local Government (Best Value) Performance Indicators and Performance Standards Order 2001**
revoked: SI 2002/523 Art.18

725. **Gaming Act (Variation of Fees) (England and Wales) Order 2001**
Sch.1, revoked: SI 2002/637 Art.3

726. **Gaming Act (Variation of Fees) (England and Wales and Scotland) Order 2001**
Sch.1, amended: SI 2002/642 Art.3

727. **Gaming (Bingo) Act (Fees) (Amendment) Order 2001**
revoked: SI 2002/640 Art.3

728. **Lotteries (Gaming Board Fees) Order 2001**
revoked: SI 2002/639 Art.9

730. **Wireless Telegraphy (Exemption) (Amendment) Regulations 2001**
revoked: SI 2003/74 Sch.1

740. **Health Authorities (Establishment and Abolition) (England) Order 2001**
revoked: SI 2002/553 Sch.3

742. **National Health Service (Travelling Expenses and Remission of Charges) Amendment Regulations 2001**
revoked: SI 2003/2382 Sch.2

743. **Retained Organs Commission (Establishment and Constitution) Order 2001**
referred to: SI 2004/1119 Sch.1

747. **National Health Service (Functions of Health Authorities and Administration Arrangements) (England) Regulations 2001**
revoked: SI 2002/2375 Sch.4
Reg.5, amended: SI 2002/881 Sch.1 para.24
Reg.6, amended: SI 2002/881 Sch.1 para.24

748. **Retained Organs Commission Regulations 2001**
Reg.3, revoked (in part): SI 2002/34 Reg.2

756. **Government Resources and Accounts Act 2000 (Investment by Devolved Administrations) (Public-Private Partnership Business) Order 2001**
varied: SI 2003/1633 Sch.2 para.8

757. **Gaming Act (Variation of Monetary Limits) Order 2001**
Art.2, revoked: SI 2002/1904 Art.4

758. **Welfare Food (Amendment) Regulations 2001**
revoked: SI 2002/550 Reg.3

NO.

759. **Value Added Tax (Electronic Communications) (Incentives) Regulations 2001**
revoked: SI 2004/1675 Reg.1

761. **Insolvency Fees (Amendment) Order 2001**
revoked: SI 2004/593 Sch.1

769. **Social Security (Crediting and Treatment of Contributions, and National Insurance Numbers) Regulations 2001**
Reg.4, amended: SI 2004/1361 Reg.2
Reg.5, amended: SI 2002/2366 Reg.19
Reg.6, amended: SI 2002/2366 Reg.19
Reg.6A, added: SI 2004/1361 Reg.2
Reg.9, applied: SI 2002/2014 Reg.5

771. **Oxfordshire Community Health National Health Service Trust (Dissolution) Order 2001**
revoked: 2003 c.43 s.7

772. **Wireless Telegraphy (Television Licence Fees) (Amendment) Regulations 2001**
revoked: SI 2004/692 Sch.6

780. **Relocation Grants (Form of Application) (Amendment) (England) Regulations 2001**
revoked: SI 2002/1860 Sch.6

784. **Portsmouth City Primary Care Trust (Establishment) Order 2001**
Art.1, amended: SI 2002/1405 Sch.1, SI 2003/2662 Art.2
Art.2, amended: SI 2003/2662 Art.2
Art.4, revoked: SI 2002/1405 Sch.1

788. **Street Works (Inspection Fees) (Amendment) (England) Regulations 2001**
revoked: SI 2002/2092 Reg.4

790. **County of Cumbria (Electoral Changes) (Amendment) Order 2001**
varied: SI 2004/222 Art.2

794. **National Health Service Appointments Commission Regulations 2001**
Reg.1, amended: SI 2004/696 Art.3
Reg.3, amended: SI 2002/2469 Sch.3, SI 2004/696 Art.3, Sch.1 para.37

798. **School Organisation Proposals by the Learning and Skills Council for England Regulations 2001**
revoked: SI 2003/507 Reg.30
Reg.2, amended: SI 2002/2469 Sch.8
Reg.6, amended: SI 2002/2469 Sch.7

811. **Credit Unions (Increase in Limits on Deposits by persons too young to be members and of Periods for the Repayment of Loans) Order 2001**
revoked: SI 2002/1501 Art.3

824. **Court of Protection Rules 2001**
Part III r.9, amended: SI 2002/833 r.3
Part IV r.24, amended: SI 2002/833 r.4
Part V r.29, amended: SI 2002/833 r.5

2001–cont.

824. Court of Protection Rules 2001–*cont.*
Part VII r.43, amended: SI 2002/833 r.6
Part VIII r.46, amended: SI 2002/833 r.7
Part XIII r.65, amended: SI 2004/1291 r.3
Part XIII r.65, revoked (in part): SI 2004/1291 r.3
Part XIII r.66, amended: SI 2004/1291 r.4
Part XV r.73, amended: SI 2004/1662 Sch.1 para.28
Part XVII r.76, amended: SI 2002/833 r.8, SI 2004/1291 r.5
Part XVII r.77, amended: SI 2002/833 r.9
Part XVII r.77A, added: SI 2002/833 r.10
Part XVII r.77A, applied: SI 2004/1291 r.11
Part XVII r.78, amended: SI 2002/833 r.11, SI 2004/1291 r.6
Part XVII r.78, revoked (in part): SI 2004/1291 r.6
Part XVII r.78A, added: SI 2004/1291 r.7
Part XVII r.79, amended: SI 2002/833 r.12
Part XVII r.79, applied: SI 2004/1291 r.11
Part XVII r.80A, added: SI 2004/1291 r.8
Part XVII r.80A, applied: SI 2004/1291 r.11
Part XVII r.81, revoked: SI 2002/833 r.13
Part XVIII r.84, amended: SI 2004/1291 r.9
Part XVIII r.86, amended: SI 2002/833 r.14
Appendix 1., added: SI 2002/833 r.15
Appendix 1., amended: SI 2002/833 r.15, SI 2003/1733 r.2, SI 2004/1291 r.10
Appendix 1., referred to: SI 2004/1291 r.11
Appendix 1., revoked: SI 2002/833 r.15
Appendix 1., substituted: SI 2002/833 r.15

825. Court of Protection (Enduring Powers of Attorney) Rules 2001
Part I r.3., amended: SI 2002/1944 r.2
Part II r.7., amended: SI 2002/832 r.3
Part IV r.23., amended: SI 2002/832 r.4
Part V r.25., amended: SI 2002/832 r.5
Part VA r.25A., added: SI 2002/832 r.6
Part VI r.26., amended: SI 2002/832 r.7
Part VI r.26A., added: SI 2002/832 r.8
Sch.1, amended: SI 2002/1944 Sch.1
Sch.2, amended: SI 2002/832 r.9

826. Education Standards Fund (England) Regulations 2001
revoked: SI 2002/510 Sch.2

827. Education (School Performance Targets) (England) (Amendment) Regulations 2001
revoked: SI 2004/2858 Sch.2

832. Education (Pupil Records) (Wales) Regulations 2001
revoked: SI 2004/1026 Sch.5

838. Climate Change Levy (General) Regulations 2001
Reg.2, amended: SI 2003/604 Reg.3
Reg.5, amended: SI 2003/604 Reg.4
Reg.6A, added: SI 2002/1152 Reg.2
Reg.6A, amended: SI 2003/604 Reg.5
Reg.6B, added: SI 2002/1152 Reg.2

2001–cont.

838. Climate Change Levy (General) Regulations 2001–*cont.*
Reg.6C, added: SI 2002/1152 Reg.2
Reg.6D, added: SI 2002/1152 Reg.2
Reg.6D, amended: SI 2003/604 Reg.6
Reg.6E, added: SI 2002/1152 Reg.2
Reg.6E, amended: SI 2003/604 Reg.6, Reg.7
Reg.6F, added: SI 2002/1152 Reg.2
Reg.6G, added: SI 2002/1152 Reg.2
Reg.8, amended: SI 2003/604 Reg.4, Reg.8
Reg.12, amended: SI 2003/604 Reg.4
Reg.27, amended: SI 2003/604 Reg.4
Reg.33, amended: SI 2003/604 Reg.4
Reg.34, amended: SI 2003/604 Reg.4
Reg.35, amended: SI 2003/604 Reg.4
Reg.36, amended: SI 2003/604 Reg.4
Reg.38, amended: SI 2003/604 Reg.4
Reg.39, amended: SI 2003/604 Reg.4
Reg.43, amended: SI 2003/604 Reg.4
Reg.46, revoked (in part): SI 2003/604 Reg.10
Reg.46, substituted: SI 2003/604 Reg.9
Reg.47, amended: SI 2003/604 Reg.11, Reg.12, Reg.13, SI 2003/2633 Reg.2
Reg.47, revoked (in part): SI 2003/604 Reg.14
Reg.48, amended: SI 2003/604 Reg.15, Reg.16, Reg.18
Reg.49, amended: SI 2003/604 Reg.17, Reg.18
Reg.51A, added: SI 2003/604 Reg.19
Reg.51B, added: SI 2003/604 Reg.19
Reg.51C, added: SI 2003/604 Reg.19
Reg.51D, added: SI 2003/604 Reg.19
Reg.51E, added: SI 2003/604 Reg.19
Reg.51F, added: SI 2003/604 Reg.19
Reg.51G, added: SI 2003/604 Reg.19
Reg.51H, added: SI 2003/604 Reg.19
Reg.51I, added: SI 2003/604 Reg.19
Reg.51J, added: SI 2003/604 Reg.19
Reg.51K, added: SI 2003/604 Reg.19
Reg.51L, added: SI 2003/604 Reg.19
Reg.51M, added: SI 2003/604 Reg.19
Reg.59, amended: SI 2003/604 Reg.4
Reg.60, amended: SI 2003/604 Reg.4, Reg.20
Sch.para.1, amended: SI 2003/604 Reg.21
Sch.para.2, amended: SI 2003/604 Reg.21
Sch.para.3, amended: SI 2003/604 Reg.21
Sch.para.4, amended: SI 2003/604 Reg.21
Sch.para.5, amended: SI 2003/604 Reg.21
Sch.para.6, amended: SI 2003/604 Reg.21
Sch.para.7, amended: SI 2003/604 Reg.21
Sch.para.8, amended: SI 2003/604 Reg.21
Sch.para.9, amended: SI 2003/604 Reg.21
Sch.para.10, amended: SI 2003/604 Reg.21
Sch.para.11, amended: SI 2003/604 Reg.21
Sch.para.12, amended: SI 2003/604 Reg.21
Sch.para.13, amended: SI 2003/604 Reg.21

NO.

2001–cont.

838. Climate Change Levy (General) Regulations 2001–*cont.*
Sch.para.14, amended: SI 2003/604 Reg.21
Sch.para.15, amended: SI 2003/604 Reg.21
Sch.2 para.1, added: SI 2003/604 Reg.22
Sch.2 para.2, added: SI 2003/604 Reg.22
Sch.2 para.3, added: SI 2003/604 Reg.22
Sch.2 para.4, added: SI 2003/604 Reg.22
Sch.2 para.5, added: SI 2003/604 Reg.22
Sch.2 para.6, added: SI 2003/604 Reg.22
Sch.2 para.7, added: SI 2003/604 Reg.22
Sch.2 para.8, added: SI 2003/604 Reg.22
Sch.2 para.9, added: SI 2003/604 Reg.22
Sch.2 para.10, added: SI 2003/604 Reg.22
Sch.2 para.11, added: SI 2003/604 Reg.22
Sch.2 para.12, added: SI 2003/604 Reg.22
Sch.2 para.13, added: SI 2003/604 Reg.22

847. Rail Vehicle Accessibility (Gatwick Express Class 460 Vehicles) Exemption Order 2001
Art.5, amended: SI 2004/2150 Art.2

848. Rail Vehicle Accessibility (South West Trains Class 458 Vehicles) Exemption Order 2001
revoked: SI 2002/656 Art.8

853. Transport Act 2000 (Civil Aviation Authority Pension Scheme) Order 2001
Sch.1, amended: SI 2002/1555 Art.44

855. Criminal Defence Service (Funding) Order 2001
varied: SI 2004/2045 Art.2
Art.2, amended: SI 2002/714 Art.4, SI 2004/2045 Art.3
Art.3, amended: SI 2002/714 Art.5, SI 2003/642 Art.2
Art.9, amended: SI 2004/2045 Art.4
Art.9A, added: SI 2004/2045 Art.5
Sch.1 para.20, amended: SI 2002/714 Art.6
Sch.2 Part 2 para.1, amended: SI 2004/2045 Art.6
Sch.4 Part 1 para.2, amended: SI 2004/2045 Art.7
Sch.4 Part 1 para.4, amended: SI 2004/2045 Art.7
Sch.4 Part 2 para.7, amended: SI 2004/2045 Art.8
Sch.4 Part 2 para.8, amended: SI 2004/2045 Sch.1, Sch.2
Sch.4 Part 4 para.17A, added: SI 2004/2045 Art.9
Sch.4 Part 4 para.19, amended: SI 2004/2045 Art.9
Sch.4 Part 4 para.22, amended: SI 2004/2045 Art.9
Sch.4 para.5, see *R. v Knight (Costs)* [2003] 3 Costs L.R. 496 (Supreme Court Costs Office), Costs Judge Rogers
Sch.4 Part 5 para.26, amended: SI 2004/2045 Art.10
Sch.5, amended: SI 2004/2045 Sch.3

NO.

2001–cont.

856. Criminal Defence Service (Recovery of Defence Costs Orders) Regulations 2001
Reg.3, amended: SI 2004/1195 Reg.2
Reg.4, amended: SI 2004/1195 Reg.2
Reg.9, amended: SI 2002/713 Reg.3, SI 2003/643 Reg.2
Reg.11, amended: SI 2004/1195 Reg.3
Reg.13, amended: SI 2004/1195 Reg.4
Reg.17, amended: SI 2004/1195 Reg.5

865. Immigration (European Economic Area) (Amendment) Regulations 2001
revoked: 2002 c.41 Sch.9

868. Immigration and Asylum Appeals (Notices) (Amendment) Regulations 2001
revoked: 2002 c.41 Sch.9

880. Biocidal Products Regulations 2001
applied: SI 2002/1689 Reg.16, SI 2003/2913 Art.12, SI 2003/3273 Art.12, SSI 2003/586 Art.12
Reg.2, amended: SI 2003/429 Reg.3
Reg.39A, added: SI 2003/429 Reg.3
Sch.12A para.1, added: SI 2003/429 Sch.1
Sch.12A para.2, added: SI 2003/429 Sch.1
Sch.12A para.3, added: SI 2003/429 Sch.1
Sch.12A para.4, added: SI 2003/429 Sch.1
Sch.12A para.5, added: SI 2003/429 Sch.1
Sch.12A para.6, added: SI 2003/429 Sch.1
Sch.12A para.7, added: SI 2003/429 Sch.1
Sch.12A para.8, added: SI 2003/429 Sch.1
Sch.12A para.9, added: SI 2003/429 Sch.1
Sch.12A para.10, added: SI 2003/429 Sch.1
Sch.12A para.11, added: SI 2003/429 Sch.1
Sch.12A para.12, added: SI 2003/429 Sch.1
Sch.12A para.13, added: SI 2003/429 Sch.1
Sch.12A para.14, added: SI 2003/429 Sch.1
Sch.12A para.15, added: SI 2003/429 Sch.1
Sch.12A para.16, added: SI 2003/429 Sch.1
Sch.12A para.17, added: SI 2003/429 Sch.1
Sch.12A para.18, added: SI 2003/429 Sch.1
Sch.12A para.19, added: SI 2003/429 Sch.1

888. North Cumbria Mental Health and Learning Disabilities National Health Service Trust (Establishment) Order 2001
revoked: 2003 c.43 s.7

889. Education (National Curriculum) (Key Stage 3 Assessment Arrangements) (Wales) (Amendment) Order 2001
revoked: 2002 c.32 Sch.22 Part 3

890. Education (Individual Pupils Achievements) (Information) (Wales) (Amendment) Regulations 2001
revoked: SI 2004/1026 Sch.5

891. Education (Education Standards Grants) (Wales) Regulations 2001
revoked: SI 2002/438 Reg.12

NO.

2001–cont.

907. Financing of Maintained Schools (England) (Amendment) Regulations 2001
applied: SI 2002/377 Reg.2

910. Social Security Benefits Up-rating Regulations 2001
revoked: SI 2002/684 Reg.5, SI 2004/583 Reg.5

918. Air Navigation (Dangerous Goods) (Amendment) Regulations 2001
revoked: SI 2002/2786 Sch.1

928. Billericay, Brentwood and Wickford Primary Care Trust (Establishment) Order 2001
Art.1, amended: SI 2002/1405 Sch.1
Art.4, revoked: SI 2002/1405 Sch.1
Sch., amended: SI 2004/543 Sch.1

929. Maldon and South Chelmsford Primary Care Trust (Establishment) Order 2001
Art.1, amended: SI 2002/1405 Sch.1
Art.4, revoked: SI 2002/1405 Sch.1
Sch., amended: SI 2004/543 Sch.1

930. North Hampshire, Loddon Community National Health Service Trust (Dissolution) Order 2001
revoked: 2003 c.43 s.7

931. Newcastle upon Tyne Hospitals National Health Service Trust (Establishment) Amendment Order 2001
revoked: 2003 c.43 s.7

932. City and Hackney Community Services, the Newham Community Health Services and the Tower Hamlets Healthcare National Health Service Trusts (Dissolution) Order 2001
revoked: 2003 c.43 s.7

946. Liberia (United Nations Sanctions) (Overseas Territories) Order 2001
Art.1, amended: 2002 c.8 s.2
Art.6, amended: 2002 c.8 s.2

947. Liberia (United Nations Sanctions) Order 2001
Art.1, amended: 2002 c.8 s.2
Art.6, amended: 2002 c.8 s.2

948. Liberia (United Nations Sanctions) (Isle of Man) Order 2001
Art.1, amended: 2002 c.8 s.2
Art.6, amended: 2002 c.8 s.2

949. Liberia (United Nations Sanctions) (Channel Islands) Order 2001
Art.1, amended: 2002 c.8 s.2
Art.2, amended: SI 2003/1521 Art.3
Art.6, amended: 2002 c.8 s.2

951. Education (Student Support) Regulations 2001
revoked: SI 2002/195 Reg.3
Part IX, applied: SI 2002/195 Reg.3

NO.

2001–cont.

951. Education (Student Support) Regulations 2001–*cont.*
Reg.5, see *R. (on the application of Theophilus) v Lewisham LBC* [2002] EWHC 1371, [2002] 3 All E.R. 851 (QBD (Admin Ct)), Silber, J.
Reg.16, amended: SI 2002/174 Reg.3
Reg.30, amended: SI 2002/174 Reg.4

958. Maximum Number of Judges (Northern Ireland) Order 2001
revoked: SI 2004/1985 Art.2

962. European Convention on Extradition Order 2001
applied: SI 2002/419 Reg.2
Art.2, amended: SI 2003/1873 Art.2
Sch.3 Part I, amended: SI 2002/1829 Art.2, SI 2003/408 Art.2, SI 2003/1873 Art.2
Sch.4 Part 2A, added: SI 2002/1829 Sch.1
Sch.4 Part 3A, added: SI 2003/408 Sch.1
Sch.4 Part 9, amended: SI 2003/408 Art.2
Sch.4 Part 12A, added: SI 2002/1829 Sch.2
Sch.4 Part 32A, added: SI 2003/408 Sch.2
Sch.4 Part 33A, added: SI 2003/1873 Art.2
Sch.5 Part I, amended: SI 2003/408 Art.2

964. Stamp Duty and Stamp Duty Reserve Tax (Definition of Unit Trust Scheme and Open-ended Investment Company) Regulations 2001
varied: 2002 c.23 Sch.34 para.7, Sch.35 para.8

965. Social Security Contributions and Benefits (Northern Ireland) Act 1992 (Modification of Section 10(7)) Regulations 2001
revoked: SI 2004/770 Sch.1

966. Social Security Contributions and Benefits Act 1992 (Modification of Section 10(7)) Regulations 2001
revoked: SI 2004/770 Sch.1

967. Companies (Disqualification Orders) Regulations 2001
Reg.9, amended: SI 2004/1940 Reg.3
Sch.1, amended: SI 2002/1834 Sch.1

969. Limited Liability Partnerships (Fees) (No.2) Regulations 2001
applied: SI 2004/2620 Sch.3
revoked: SI 2004/2620 Reg.3
Sch., amended: SI 2002/2895 Reg.3
Sch., applied: SI 2004/2620 Reg.3

972. Birmingham (Kitts Green and Shard End) Education Action Zone (Variation) Order 2001
revoked: 2002 c.32 Sch.15 para.2

973. Bristol Education Action Zone (Variation) Order 2001
revoked: 2002 c.32 Sch.15 para.2

2001–cont.

1002. Housing Benefit and Council Tax Benefit (Decisions and Appeals) Regulations 2001

Reg.1, amended: SI 2002/1379 Reg.23, SI 2002/1703 Sch.2 para.8, SI 2003/2275 Reg.5

Reg.1, revoked (in part): SI 2002/1703 Sch.2 para.8

Reg.4, amended: SI 2002/490 Reg.9, SI 2002/1379 Reg.24, SI 2002/1703 Sch.2 para.8, SI 2003/2275 Reg.5, SI 2003/2399 Reg.16

Reg.5, amended: SI 2002/1703 Sch.2 para.8

Reg.7, amended: SI 2002/490 Reg.9, SI 2002/1703 Sch.2 para.8, SI 2003/1050 Reg.4, SI 2003/1338 Reg.24, SI 2003/2275 Reg.5, SI 2003/2399 Reg.16, SI 2004/14 Reg.34

Reg.7, revoked (in part): SI 2002/1703 Sch.2 para.8

Reg.8, amended: SI 2002/490 Reg.9, SI 2003/325 Reg.28, SI 2003/1050 Reg.4, SI 2003/1338 Reg.24, SI 2003/2275 Reg.5, SI 2003/2399 Reg.16, SI 2004/14 Reg.34

Reg.10A, added: SI 2002/1379 Reg.25

Reg.18, amended: SI 2002/1379 Reg.26

Reg.19, amended: SI 2002/1379 Reg.27

Reg.20, amended: SI 2002/1703 Sch.2 para.8

Reg.23, amended: SI 2002/1379 Reg.28

Sch.para.6, added: SI 2003/1581 Reg.3

1004. Social Security (Contributions) Regulations 2001

applied: SI 2002/2820 Reg.4, SR 2002/379 Reg.4

referred to: SI 2002/2924 Reg.2, SI 2003/193 Reg.2, SI 2003/1059 Reg.2, SI 2003/2085 Reg.3, SI 2003/2682 Reg.69, SI 2004/770 Reg.2

Reg.1, amended: SI 2002/307 Reg.3, SI 2003/193 Reg.3, SI 2003/2085 Reg.4, SI 2003/2155 Sch.1 para.23, SI 2004/770 Reg.3, Sch.1, SI 2004/2096 Reg.3

Reg.3, amended: SI 2002/2366 Reg.4

Reg.3, revoked (in part): SI 2002/2366 Reg.4

Reg.9, amended: SI 2003/193 Reg.4

Reg.10, amended: SI 2002/238 Reg.3, SI 2003/193 Reg.5, SI 2004/220 Reg.3

Reg.11, amended: SI 2002/238 Reg.4, SI 2004/220 Reg.4

Reg.14, applied: SI 2002/2822 Reg.38, SR 2002/378 Reg.38

Reg.15, applied: SI 2002/2822 Reg.38, SR 2002/378 Reg.38

Reg.21, substituted: SI 2003/193 Reg.6

Reg.22, amended: SI 2002/307 Reg.4, SI 2003/2085 Reg.5

Reg.22A, added: SI 2002/307 Reg.5

Reg.22A, amended: SI 2004/770 Reg.4

Reg.25, applied: SI 2002/2822 Reg.39

2001–cont.

1004. Social Security (Contributions) Regulations 2001–*cont.*

Reg.27, amended: SI 2004/770 Reg.5

Reg.30, substituted: SI 2002/2366 Reg.5

Reg.31, substituted: SI 2002/2366 Reg.6

Reg.32, revoked: SI 2004/770 Sch.1

Reg.33, revoked: SI 2004/770 Sch.1

Reg.34, revoked: SI 2004/770 Sch.1

Reg.35, revoked: SI 2004/770 Sch.1

Reg.36, amended: SI 2004/770 Reg.7

Reg.37, revoked: SI 2004/770 Sch.1

Reg.40, amended: SI 2003/2085 Reg.6, SI 2004/770 Reg.9

Reg.40, revoked (in part): SI 2003/2085 Reg.6

Reg.42, amended: SI 2004/770 Reg.10

Reg.43, amended: SI 2002/2924 Reg.3

Reg.47, amended: SI 2003/2958 Reg.3

Reg.48, amended: SI 2004/1362 Reg.3

Reg.49, amended: SI 2003/193 Reg.7

Reg.50, substituted: SI 2002/2366 Reg.7

Reg.50A, added: SI 2004/1362 Reg.4

Reg.51, amended: SI 2004/770 Reg.11

Reg.52, substituted: SI 2002/2366 Reg.8, SI 2004/770 Reg.12

Reg.54, amended: SI 2002/2366 Reg.9

Reg.55, amended: SI 2002/2366 Reg.10, SI 2004/770 Reg.13

Reg.57, amended: SI 2004/770 Reg.14

Reg.60, amended: SI 2002/2366 Reg.11

Reg.61, substituted: SI 2002/2366 Reg.12

Reg.65, amended: SI 2002/2366 Reg.13

Reg.65A, added: SI 2004/1362 Reg.5

Reg.67, amended: SI 2004/770 Reg.15

Reg.69, amended: SI 2004/2096 Reg.4

Reg.70, amended: SI 2002/2929 Reg.3

Reg.71, amended: SI 2004/770 Reg.16

Reg.72, amended: SI 2004/770 Reg.17, Sch.1

Reg.73, amended: SI 2004/770 Reg.18, Sch.1

Reg.76, amended: SI 2004/770 Reg.19

Reg.80, amended: SI 2004/770 Reg.20

Reg.80, revoked (in part): SI 2004/770 Sch.1

Reg.80A, revoked: SI 2004/770 Sch.1

Reg.84, substituted: SI 2003/193 Reg.8

Reg.85, revoked: SI 2003/193 Reg.9

Reg.86, amended: SI 2004/770 Reg.22, Sch.1

Reg.90, amended: SI 2003/193 Reg.10

Reg.90A, added: SI 2004/770 Reg.23

Reg.90B, added: SI 2004/770 Reg.23

Reg.90C, added: SI 2004/770 Reg.23

Reg.90D, added: SI 2004/770 Reg.23

Reg.90E, added: SI 2004/770 Reg.23

Reg.90F, added: SI 2004/770 Reg.23

Reg.90G, added: SI 2004/770 Reg.23

Reg.90H, added: SI 2004/770 Reg.23

Reg.90I, added: SI 2004/770 Reg.23

Reg.90J, added: SI 2004/770 Reg.23

2001–cont.

1004. Social Security (Contributions) Regulations 2001–*cont.*

Reg.90K, added: SI 2004/770 Reg.23
Reg.90L, added: SI 2004/770 Reg.23
Reg.90M, added: SI 2004/770 Reg.23
Reg.90N, added: SI 2004/770 Reg.23
Reg.90O, added: SI 2004/770 Reg.23
Reg.90P, added: SI 2004/770 Reg.23
Reg.90Q, added: SI 2004/770 Reg.23
Reg.90R, added: SI 2004/770 Reg.23
Reg.94, amended: SI 2003/193 Reg.11
Reg.94A, added: SI 2003/2958 Reg.4
Reg.95, amended: SI 2003/193 Reg.12
Reg.99, amended: SI 2003/193 Reg.13
Reg.100, substituted: SI 2003/193 Reg.14
Reg.101, amended: SI 2002/2366 Reg.14
Reg.102, amended: SI 2002/2366 Reg.15
Reg.103, amended: SI 2003/193 Reg.15, SI 2004/770 Reg.24
Reg.110, amended: SI 2002/2366 Reg.16
Reg.111, applied: SI 2003/495 Reg.9
Reg.114, applied: SI 2003/495 Reg.9
Reg.115, applied: SI 2003/495 Reg.9
Reg.120, amended: SI 2003/964 Reg.4
Reg.123, applied: SI 2002/2822 Reg.39
Reg.125, amended: SI 2004/944 Reg.2
Reg.127, amended: SI 2003/964 Reg.5
Reg.128, amended: SI 2003/964 Reg.9
Reg.131, substituted: SI 2003/964 Reg.6
Reg.133, amended: SI 2003/964 Reg.7
Reg.134, amended: SI 2003/964 Reg.8
Reg.136, amended: SI 2003/964 Reg.9
Reg.139, amended: SI 2003/964 Reg.10
Reg.140, applied: SI 2003/495 Reg.9
Reg.143, amended: SI 2004/770 Reg.25
Reg.145, applied: SR 2002/378 Reg.32
Reg.145, referred to: SI 2002/2822 Reg.32
Reg.146, applied: SI 2002/2821 Reg.4, SR 2002/382 Reg.4
Reg.149, amended: SI 2002/2366 Reg.17
Reg.155A, added: SI 2002/2366 Reg.18
Reg.155A, amended: SI 2004/770 Reg.26
Reg.156, amended: SI 2003/964 Reg.11
Sch.2 para.5, amended: SI 2003/2085 Reg.7
Sch.2 para.7, substituted: SI 2003/2085 Reg.7, SI 2004/2096 Reg.5
Sch.2 para.8, revoked: SI 2003/2085 Reg.7
Sch.2 para.9, revoked: SI 2003/2085 Reg.7
Sch.2 para.10, amended: SI 2003/1059 Reg.3
Sch.2 para.10, revoked: SI 2003/2085 Reg.7
Sch.2 para.11, amended: SI 2003/1059 Reg.3
Sch.2 para.11, substituted: SI 2003/2085 Reg.7
Sch.2 para.11A, added: SI 2003/1059 Reg.3
Sch.2 para.11A, amended: SI 2003/2085 Reg.7
Sch.2 para.12, revoked: SI 2003/2085 Reg.7
Sch.2 para.13, amended: SI 2004/770 Reg.27

2001–cont.

1004. Social Security (Contributions) Regulations 2001–*cont.*

Sch.3, applied: SI 2002/2822 Reg.39
Sch.3, referred to: SI 2003/2085 Reg.8
Sch.3 Part I para.1, amended: SI 2003/2085 Reg.9
Sch.3 Part II para.2, amended: SI 2004/770 Reg.28
Sch.3 Part III para.1, substituted: SI 2003/2085 Reg.10
Sch.3 Part III para.2, substituted: SI 2003/2085 Reg.10
Sch.3 Part IV para.1, substituted: SI 2003/2085 Reg.11
Sch.3 Part IV para.2, revoked: SI 2003/2085 Reg.11
Sch.3 Part IV para.3, revoked: SI 2003/2085 Reg.11
Sch.3 Part IV para.4, revoked: SI 2003/2085 Reg.11
Sch.3 Part IV para.5, revoked: SI 2003/2085 Reg.11
Sch.3 Part IV para.7, revoked: SI 2003/2085 Reg.11
Sch.3 Part IV para.8, revoked: SI 2003/2085 Reg.11
Sch.3 Part IV para.11, amended: SI 2003/2085 Reg.11
Sch.3 Part V, applied: SI 2002/1792 Reg.17A
Sch.3 Part V para.1, amended: SI 2002/307 Reg.6, SI 2004/770 Reg.28
Sch.3 Part V para.1, varied: SI 2003/1633 Sch.2 para.8
Sch.3 Part V para.2, amended: SI 2004/770 Reg.28
Sch.3 Part V para.2, varied: SI 2003/1633 Sch.2 para.8
Sch.3 Part V para.3, substituted: SI 2004/770 Reg.28
Sch.3 Part V para.3, varied: SI 2003/1633 Sch.2 para.8
Sch.3 Part V para.4, substituted: SI 2004/770 Reg.28
Sch.3 Part V para.4, varied: SI 2003/1633 Sch.2 para.8
Sch.3 Part V para.5, substituted: SI 2003/2958 Reg.5
Sch.3 Part V para.5, varied: SI 2003/1633 Sch.2 para.8
Sch.3 Part V para.5A, substituted: SI 2003/2958 Reg.5
Sch.3 Part V para.5A, varied: SI 2003/1633 Sch.2 para.8
Sch.3 Part V para.5B, substituted: SI 2003/2958 Reg.5
Sch.3 Part V para.5B, varied: SI 2003/1633 Sch.2 para.8
Sch.3 Part V para.6, substituted: SI 2003/2958 Reg.5
Sch.3 Part V para.6, varied: SI 2003/1633 Sch.2 para.8

2001–cont.

1004. Social Security (Contributions) Regulations 2001–cont.

Sch.3 Part V para.6A, varied: SI 2003/1633 Sch.2 para.8

Sch.3 Part V para.7, amended: SI 2004/770 Reg.28

Sch.3 Part V para.7, varied: SI 2003/1633 Sch.2 para.8

Sch.3 Part V para.8, varied: SI 2003/1633 Sch.2 para.8

Sch.3 Part VI para.2, substituted: SI 2004/770 Reg.28

Sch.3 Part VI para.3, amended: SI 2004/770 Reg.28

Sch.3 Part VII para.1, amended: SI 2003/2340 Reg.2

Sch.3 Part VII para.2, amended: SI 2004/770 Reg.28

Sch.3 Part VII para.3, amended: SI 2004/770 Reg.28

Sch.3 Part VII para.8, added: SI 2003/2340 Reg.2

Sch.3 Part VII para.9, added: SI 2003/2340 Reg.2

Sch.3 Part VII para.9, substituted: SI 2003/2958 Reg.5

Sch.3 Part VII para.10, added: SI 2004/770 Reg.28

Sch.3 Part VII para.11, added: SI 2004/770 Reg.28

Sch.3 Part VIII para.2, amended: SI 2004/770 Reg.28

Sch.3 Part VIII para.3, amended: SI 2004/770 Reg.28

Sch.3 Part VIII para.4, added: SI 2004/770 Reg.28

Sch.3 Part VIII para.4A, added: SI 2004/770 Reg.28

Sch.3 Part VIII para.4B, added: SI 2004/770 Reg.28

Sch.3 Part VIII para.4C, added: SI 2004/770 Reg.28

Sch.3 Part VIII para.4D, added: SI 2004/770 Reg.28

Sch.3 Part VIII para.5, added: SI 2004/770 Reg.28

Sch.3 Part VIII para.7, amended: SI 2004/770 Reg.28

Sch.3 Part VIII para.7A, added: SI 2002/307 Reg.7

Sch.3 Part VIII para.7B, added: SI 2002/307 Reg.7

Sch.3 Part VIII para.7B, amended: SI 2004/770 Reg.28

Sch.3 Part VIII para.7C, added: SI 2002/307 Reg.7

Sch.3 Part VIII para.7C, amended: SI 2004/770 Reg.28

Sch.3 Part VIII para.7D, added: SI 2002/307 Reg.7

2001–cont.

1004. Social Security (Contributions) Regulations 2001–cont.

Sch.3 Part VIII para.7D, substituted: SI 2004/770 Reg.28

Sch.3 Part VIII para.8, amended: SI 2004/770 Reg.28

Sch.3 Part VIII para.9, substituted: SI 2002/307 Reg.7

Sch.3 Part VIII para.10, amended: SI 2004/770 Reg.28

Sch.3 Part VIII para.11, amended: SI 2004/770 Reg.28

Sch.3 Part VIII para.12, amended: SI 2004/770 Reg.28

Sch.3 Part VIII para.15, added: SI 2004/770 Reg.28

Sch.3 Part IX para.1, substituted: SI 2003/2085 Reg.12

Sch.3 Part IX para.2, revoked: SI 2003/2085 Reg.12

Sch.3 Part IX para.2, substituted: SI 2003/2085 Reg.12

Sch.3 Part IX para.3, substituted: SI 2003/2085 Reg.12

Sch.3 Part IX para.3A, revoked: SI 2003/2085 Reg.12

Sch.3 Part IX para.3A, substituted: SI 2003/2085 Reg.12

Sch.3 Part IX para.4, revoked: SI 2003/2085 Reg.12

Sch.3 Part IX para.4, substituted: SI 2003/2085 Reg.12

Sch.3 Part IX para.5, substituted: SI 2003/2085 Reg.12

Sch.3 Part IX para.6, amended: SI 2003/2085 Reg.12

Sch.3 Part IX para.6, substituted: SI 2003/2085 Reg.12

Sch.3 Part IX para.7, substituted: SI 2003/2085 Reg.12

Sch.3 Part IX para.7A, substituted: SI 2003/2085 Reg.12

Sch.3 Part IX para.8, revoked: SI 2003/2085 Reg.12

Sch.3 Part IX para.8, substituted: SI 2003/2085 Reg.12

Sch.3 Part IX para.9, substituted: SI 2003/2085 Reg.12

Sch.3 Part IX para.10, revoked: SI 2003/2085 Reg.12

Sch.3 Part IX para.10, substituted: SI 2003/2085 Reg.12

Sch.3 Part IX para.11, revoked: SI 2003/2085 Reg.12

Sch.3 Part IX para.11, substituted: SI 2003/2085 Reg.12

Sch.3 Part IX para.12, revoked: SI 2003/2085 Reg.12

Sch.3 Part IX para.12, substituted: SI 2003/2085 Reg.12

NO.

2001–cont.

1004. Social Security (Contributions) Regulations 2001–*cont.*

Sch.3 Part IX para.13, revoked: SI 2003/2085 Reg.12

Sch.3 Part IX para.13, substituted: SI 2003/2085 Reg.12

Sch.3 Part IX para.14, revoked: SI 2003/2085 Reg.12

Sch.3 Part IX para.14, substituted: SI 2003/2085 Reg.12

Sch.3 Part IX para.15, revoked: SI 2003/2085 Reg.12

Sch.3 Part IX para.15, substituted: SI 2003/2085 Reg.12

Sch.3 Part IX para.16, amended: SI 2003/1059 Reg.4

Sch.3 Part IX para.16, substituted: SI 2003/2085 Reg.12

Sch.3 Part IX para.16A, substituted: SI 2003/2085 Reg.12

Sch.3 Part IX para.17, added: SI 2003/1059 Reg.4

Sch.3 Part IX para.17, amended: SI 2003/2085 Reg.12

Sch.3 Part IX para.17, substituted: SI 2003/2085 Reg.12

Sch.3 Part X para.1, amended: SI 2002/2924 Reg.4, SI 2003/2085 Reg.13

Sch.3 Part X para.3, amended: SI 2004/2096 Reg.6

Sch.3 Part X para.4, amended: SI 2004/770 Reg.28

Sch.3 Part X para.5, amended: SI 2004/173 Reg.2

Sch.3 Part X para.8, substituted: SI 2004/770 Reg.28

Sch.3 Part X para.10, substituted: SI 2004/770 Reg.28

Sch.3 Part X para.11, amended: SI 2004/770 Reg.28

Sch.3 Part X para.14, substituted: SI 2004/770 Reg.28

Sch.3 Part X para.16, added: SI 2002/2924 Reg.4

Sch.3 Part X para.17, added: SI 2003/2085 Reg.13

Sch.4 Part I para.1, amended: SI 2002/2929 Reg.4, SI 2004/770 Reg.29, Reg.30

Sch.4 Part I para.2, amended: SI 2004/770 Reg.29

Sch.4 Part I para.2, substituted: SI 2004/770 Reg.30

Sch.4 Part I para.3, amended: SI 2004/770 Reg.29, Reg.30

Sch.4 Part I para.4, amended: SI 2002/2929 Reg.5, SI 2004/770 Reg.29

Sch.4 Part I para.4A, added: SI 2002/2929 Reg.6

Sch.4 Part I para.4A, amended: SI 2004/770 Reg.29, Reg.30

NO.

2001–cont.

1004. Social Security (Contributions) Regulations 2001–*cont.*

Sch.4 Part I para.5, amended: SI 2004/770 Reg.29

Sch.4 Part I para.5, substituted: SI 2004/770 Reg.30

Sch.4 Part II para.6, amended: SI 2004/770 Reg.29, Reg.31, SI 2004/2096 Reg.7

Sch.4 Part II para.7, amended: SI 2002/2929 Reg.7, SI 2003/193 Reg.16, SI 2003/1337 Reg.2, SI 2003/2085 Reg.14, SI 2004/770 Reg.29, Reg.31, SI 2004/2246 Reg.2

Sch.4 Part II para.7, revoked (in part): SI 2003/193 Reg.16, SI 2004/770 Sch.1

Sch.4 Part II para.8, amended: SI 2004/770 Reg.29

Sch.4 Part II para.8, substituted: SI 2004/2096 Reg.7

Sch.4 Part II para.9, amended: SI 2003/193 Reg.16, SI 2003/1337 Reg.3, SI 2004/770 Reg.29, Reg.31

Sch.4 Part III para.10, amended: SI 2004/770 Reg.29, Reg.32

Sch.4 Part III para.11, amended: SI 2003/193 Reg.16, SI 2004/770 Reg.29, Reg.32

Sch.4 Part III para.11, revoked (in part): SI 2004/770 Reg.32

Sch.4 Part III para.12, amended: SI 2004/770 Reg.29, Reg.32

Sch.4 Part III para.13, amended: SI 2004/770 Reg.29, Reg.32

Sch.4 Part III para.14, amended: SI 2004/770 Reg.29, Reg.32

Sch.4 Part III para.15, amended: SI 2004/770 Reg.29, Reg.32

Sch.4 Part III para.16, amended: SI 2004/770 Reg.29, Reg.32

Sch.4 Part III para.17, amended: SI 2004/770 Reg.29, Reg.32

Sch.4 Part III para.17A, added: SI 2004/770 Reg.32

Sch.4 Part III para.17A, amended: SI 2004/770 Reg.29

Sch.4 Part III para.18, amended: SI 2004/770 Reg.29

Sch.4 Part III para.19, amended: SI 2004/770 Reg.29, Reg.32

Sch.4 Part III para.20, amended: SI 2004/770 Reg.29

Sch.4 Part III para.21, amended: SI 2004/770 Reg.29, SI 2004/2096 Reg.7

Sch.4 Part III para.22, amended: SI 2003/193 Reg.16, SI 2004/770 Reg.29, Reg.32

Sch.4 Part III para.22, revoked (in part): SI 2003/193 Reg.16

Sch.4 Part III para.23, amended: SI 2003/2085 Reg.14, SI 2004/770 Reg.29, Reg.32, SI 2004/2096 Reg.7

Sch.4 Part III para.24, amended: SI 2004/770 Reg.29, Reg.32

Sch.4 Part III para.25, amended: SI 2004/770 Reg.29, Reg.32

NO.

2001-cont.

1004. Social Security (Contributions) Regulations 2001-*cont.*

Sch.4 Part III para.26, amended: SI 2003/193 Reg.16, SI 2004/770 Reg.29, Reg.32

Sch.4 Part III para.27, amended: SI 2004/770 Reg.29, Reg.32

Sch.4 Part III para.28, amended: SI 2004/770 Reg.29, Reg.32

Sch.4 Part III para.29, amended: SI 2004/770 Reg.29, Reg.32

Sch.4 Part IV para.30, amended: SI 2004/770 Reg.29

Sch.4 Part IV para.31, amended: SI 2004/770 Reg.29, Reg.33

Sch.5 para.1, amended: SI 2004/2096 Reg.8

Sch.5 para.2, amended: SI 2004/2096 Reg.8

Sch.5 para.3, amended: SI 2004/2096 Reg.8

Sch.6 Part 1, applied: SI 2002/1792 Sch.6 para.2, SR 2003/28 Sch.6 para.2

1005. National Assistance (Sums for Personal Requirements) (England) Regulations 2001

revoked: SI 2002/411 Reg.3

1016. Borough of Rushmoor (Electoral Changes) Order 2001

varied: SI 2004/222 Art.2

1017. District of East Hampshire (Electoral Changes) Order 2001

varied: SI 2004/222 Art.2

1018. Borough of Test Valley (Electoral Changes) Order 2001

varied: SI 2004/222 Art.2

1019. Borough of Basingstoke and Deane (Electoral Changes) Order 2001

varied: SI 2004/222 Art.2

1020. Borough of Fareham (Electoral Changes) Order 2001

varied: SI 2004/222 Art.2

Art.3, revoked: SI 2002/1962 Art.6

Sch.2, revoked: SI 2002/1962 Art.6

1021. Borough of Eastleigh (Parishes and Electoral Changes) Order 2001

varied: SI 2004/222 Art.2

1022. Borough of Gosport (Electoral Changes) Order 2001

varied: SI 2004/222 Art.2

Art.3, revoked: SI 2002/1962 Art.6

Sch.2, revoked: SI 2002/1962 Art.6

1023. District of Hart (Parishes and Electoral Changes) Order 2001

varied: SI 2004/222 Art.2

1024. City of Southampton (Electoral Changes) Order 2001

varied: SI 2004/222 Art.2

1025. Borough of Havant (Electoral Changes) Order 2001

varied: SI 2004/222 Art.2

1026. District of New Forest (Parishes and Electoral Changes) Order 2001

varied: SI 2004/222 Art.2

NO.

2001-cont.

1027. City of Portsmouth (Electoral Changes) Order 2001

varied: SI 2004/222 Art.2

1028. City of Winchester (Electoral Changes) Order 2001

varied: SI 2004/222 Art.2

1032. Pensions Appeal Tribunals (Late Appeals) Regulations 2001

Reg.2, amended: 2004 c.32 s.7

1042. National Care Standards Commission (Membership and Procedure) Regulations 2001

revoked: SI 2004/664 Art.7

varied: SI 2004/664 Art.11, Art.12, Art.13, Art.14

Reg.1, amended: SI 2003/1590 Sch.1 para.16

Reg.1, varied: SI 2004/664 Art.11, Art.12, Art.13, Art.14

Reg.5, amended: SI 2002/880 Sch.1 para.12, SI 2002/881 Sch.1 para.25

1060. Financial Services and Markets Act 2000 (Promotion of Collective Investment Schemes) (Exemptions) Order 2001

Art.2, amended: SI 2002/1310 Art.3

Art.3, amended: SI 2002/2157 Art.8

Art.5A, added: SI 2002/2157 Art.8

Art.8, amended: SI 2002/2157 Art.9

Art.10A, added: SI 2002/2157 Art.10

Art.10A, amended: SI 2003/2067 Art.2

Art.22, amended: SI 2002/1310 Art.3

Art.29, added: SI 2003/2067 Art.2

Art.30, added: SI 2003/2067 Art.2

1066. National Assistance (Assessment of Resources) (Amendment) (No.2) (England) Regulations 2001

Reg.3, revoked: SI 2002/410 Reg.4

Reg.4, revoked: SI 2002/410 Reg.4

1077. Community Legal Service (Funding) (Counsel in Family Proceedings) Order 2001

Art.2, amended: SI 2003/2590 Art.3

Art.2, revoked (in part): SI 2003/2590 Art.3

Art.8, amended: SI 2003/2590 Art.4

Art.10A, added: SI 2003/2590 Art.5

Art.11, amended: SI 2003/2590 Art.6

Art.13, amended: SI 2003/2590 Art.7

Art.16, amended: SI 2003/2590 Art.8

Sch.1 para.1, amended: SI 2003/2590 Art.9

Sch.1 para.2, amended: SI 2003/2590 Art.9

Sch.1 para.3, amended: SI 2003/2590 Art.9

Sch.1 para.4, amended: SI 2003/2590 Art.9

Sch.2 para.2, amended: SI 2003/2590 Art.10

1081. Income Tax (Electronic Communications) (Miscellaneous Amendments) Regulations 2001

Reg.1, amended: SI 2003/282 Reg.11, SI 2003/2682 Sch.2

Reg.2, revoked: SI 2003/282 Reg.11

Reg.3, revoked: SI 2003/282 Reg.11

Reg.4, revoked: SI 2003/282 Reg.11

NO.

2001–cont.

1081. Income Tax (Electronic Communications) (Miscellaneous Amendments) Regulations 2001–*cont.*

Reg.5, revoked: SI 2003/282 Reg.11
Reg.6, revoked: SI 2003/282 Reg.11
Reg.7, revoked: SI 2003/2682 Sch.2
Reg.8, revoked: SI 2003/2682 Sch.2
Reg.9, revoked: SI 2003/2682 Sch.2
Reg.10, revoked: SI 2003/2682 Sch.2
Reg.11, revoked: SI 2003/2682 Sch.2
Reg.12, revoked: SI 2003/2682 Sch.2
Reg.13, revoked: SI 2003/2682 Sch.2
Reg.14, revoked: SI 2003/2682 Sch.2
Reg.15, revoked: SI 2003/2682 Sch.2
Reg.16, revoked: SI 2003/2682 Sch.2
Reg.17, revoked: SI 2003/2682 Sch.2
Reg.18, revoked: SI 2003/2682 Sch.2
Reg.19, revoked: SI 2003/2682 Sch.2
Reg.20, revoked: SI 2003/2682 Sch.2
Reg.21, revoked: SI 2003/2682 Sch.2

1090. Limited Liability Partnerships Regulations 2001

referred to: SI 2003/61 Reg.1
Reg.3, referred to: SI 2002/690 Reg.1
Reg.4, applied: SI 2002/503, SI 2004/2620
Reg.4, referred to: SI 2002/690 Reg.1, SI 2002/2895
Reg.5, applied: SI 2003/2093 Art.3
Sch.1, amended: SI 2004/355 Art.8
Sch.2, applied: SI 2002/503, SI 2004/2620
Sch.2, referred to: SI 2002/2895
Sch.2 Part I, amended: SI 2004/355 Art.9
Sch.3, amended: SI 2004/355 Art.10

1091. Offshore Combustion Installations (Prevention and Control of Pollution) Regulations 2001

Reg.4, amended: SI 2003/3311 Sch.5 para.3

1110. School Governors Annual Reports (Wales) Regulations 2001

Reg.2, amended: SI 2004/1735 Reg.2
Reg.3, amended: SI 2004/1735 Reg.2
Reg.6, amended: SI 2004/1735 Reg.2
Sch.1 para.1, substituted: SI 2004/1735 Reg.2
Sch.1 para.2, substituted: SI 2004/1735 Reg.2
Sch.1 para.3, substituted: SI 2004/1735 Reg.2
Sch.1 para.4, substituted: SI 2004/1735 Reg.2
Sch.1 para.5, substituted: SI 2004/1735 Reg.2
Sch.1 para.6, amended: SI 2002/1401 Reg.2
Sch.1 para.6, revoked (in part): SI 2002/1401 Reg.2
Sch.1 para.6, substituted: SI 2004/1735 Reg.2
Sch.1 para.7, revoked: SI 2004/1735 Reg.2
Sch.1 para.7, substituted: SI 2004/1735 Reg.2

NO.

2001–cont.

1110. School Governors Annual Reports (Wales) Regulations 2001–*cont.*

Sch.1 para.8, substituted: SI 2002/1401 Reg.2, SI 2004/1735 Reg.2
Sch.1 para.9, substituted: SI 2004/1735 Reg.2
Sch.1 para.10, substituted: SI 2004/1735 Reg.2
Sch.1 para.11, substituted: SI 2004/1735 Reg.2
Sch.1 para.12, substituted: SI 2004/1735 Reg.2
Sch.1 para.13, substituted: SI 2004/1735 Reg.2
Sch.1 para.14, substituted: SI 2004/1735 Reg.2
Sch.2 Part 1 para.1, added: SI 2004/1735 Reg.2
Sch.2 Part 1 para.2, added: SI 2004/1735 Reg.2
Sch.2 Part 1 para.3, added: SI 2004/1735 Reg.2
Sch.2 Part 1 para.4, added: SI 2004/1735 Reg.2
Sch.2 Part 1 para.5, added: SI 2004/1735 Reg.2
Sch.2 Part 2 para.6, added: SI 2004/1735 Reg.2
Sch.2 Part 2 para.7, added: SI 2004/1735 Reg.2
Sch.2 Part 2 para.8, added: SI 2004/1735 Reg.2
Sch.2 Part 2 para.9, added: SI 2004/1735 Reg.2
Sch.2 Part 2 para.10, added: SI 2004/1735 Reg.2
Sch.2 Part 2 para.11, added: SI 2004/1735 Reg.2
Sch.2 Part 2 para.12, added: SI 2004/1735 Reg.2
Sch.2 Part 2 para.13, added: SI 2004/1735 Reg.2
Sch.2 Part 2 para.14, added: SI 2004/1735 Reg.2
Sch.2 Part 2 para.15, added: SI 2004/1735 Reg.2
Sch.2 Part 2 para.16, added: SI 2004/1735 Reg.2
Sch.2 Part 3 para.17, added: SI 2004/1735 Reg.2
Sch.2 Part 3 para.18, added: SI 2004/1735 Reg.2
Sch.2 Part 4 para.19, added: SI 2004/1735 Reg.2

1123. Income Tax (Car Benefits) (Reduction of Value of Appropriate Percentage) Regulations 2001

Reg.8, revoked: 2003 c.1 Sch.8 Part 2

2001–cont.

1131. General Optical Council (Registration and Enrolment (Amendment) Rules) Order of Council 2001
revoked: SI 2002/775 Sch.1

1135. Postal Services Act 2000 (Determination of Turnover for Penalties) Order 2001
Art.2, amended: SI 2002/125 Art.2

1138. Climate Change Levy (Use as Fuel) Regulations 2001
Sch.para.34A, added: SI 2003/665 Reg.2
Sch.para.34B, added: SI 2003/665 Reg.2
Sch.para.34C, added: SI 2003/665 Reg.2
Sch.para.34D, added: SI 2003/665 Reg.2
Sch.para.44, added: SI 2003/665 Reg.2
Sch.para.45, added: SI 2003/665 Reg.2
Sch.para.46, added: SI 2003/665 Reg.2

1140. Climate Change Levy (Combined Heat and Power Stations) Prescribed Conditions and Efficiency Percentages Regulations 2001
Reg.5, revoked (in part): SI 2003/861 Reg.2

1149. Postal Services Act 2000 (Consequential Modifications No 1) Order 2001
Sch.1 Part 1 para.18, revoked: SI 2003/2908 Sch.2
Sch.1 Part 1 para.38, revoked: SI 2003/2908 Sch.2
Sch.1 Part 1 para.60, revoked: 2003 asp 13 Sch.5 Part 2

1154. Tir Mynydd (Cross-border Holdings) (Wales) Regulations 2001
Reg.2, revoked (in part): SI 2002/1806 Reg.20
Reg.4, amended: SI 2002/1806 Reg.21

1163. Double Taxation Relief (Surrender of Relievable Tax Within a Group) Regulations 2001
Reg.4, amended: SI 2003/1829 Reg.2

1167. Discretionary Financial Assistance Regulations 2001
Reg.3, amended: SI 2002/490 Reg.10

1168. Criminal Defence Service (Representation Order Appeals) Regulations 2001
Reg.3, amended: SI 2002/1620 Reg.3
Reg.5, amended: SI 2002/1620 Reg.4

1169. Criminal Defence Service (Choice in Very High Cost Cases) Regulations 2001
referred to: SI 2004/598 Reg.1
Reg.2, amended: SI 2004/598 Reg.2
Reg.3, amended: SI 2004/598 Reg.3

1170. Employment Tribunals (Constitution and Rules of Procedure) (Scotland) Regulations 2001
applied: SI 2002/302 Art.9, SI 2002/303 Art.9, SI 2003/285 Art.9, SI 2003/286 Art.9, SI 2004/368 Art.9, SI 2004/369 Art.9

2001–cont.

1170. Employment Tribunals (Constitution and Rules of Procedure) (Scotland) Regulations 2001–cont.
revoked: SI 2004/1861 Reg.1
Reg.11, applied: SI 2004/456 Reg.21
Reg.11, disapplied: SI 2003/547 Reg.22
Sch.1 para.16, amended: SI 2003/1673 Reg.31
Sch.5, applied: SI 2004/456 Reg.21
Sch.5, disapplied: SI 2003/547 Reg.22

1171. Employment Tribunal (Constitution and Rules of Procedure) Regulations 2001
Sch.1 r.14, see *Kopel v Safeway Stores Plc* [2003] I.R.L.R. 753 (EAT), Mitting, J.

1171. Employment Tribunals (Constitution and Rules of Procedure) Regulations 2001
applied: SI 2002/302 Art.9, SI 2002/303 Art.9, SI 2003/285 Art.9, SI 2003/286 Art.9, SI 2004/369 Art.9
revoked: SI 2004/1861 Reg.1
see *Montali v Goldman Sachs Services Ltd* [2002] I.C.R. 1251 (EAT), Judge Peter Clark
r.10, see *XXX v YYY* [2004] I.R.L.R. 137 (EAT), Mitting, J.
Reg.10, see *Maresca v Motor Insurance Repair Research Centre* [2004] 4 All E.R. 254 (EAT), Rimer, J.
Reg.11, applied: SI 2004/456 Reg.21
Reg.11, disapplied: SI 2003/547 Reg.22
Reg.11, see *Jackson v Ghost Ltd* [2003] I.R.L.R. 824 (EAT), Judge Peter Clark
Sch.1 para.3, see *Bartholomew v Southwark LBC* [2004] I.C.R. 358 (EAT), Burton, J.
Sch.1 para.4, see *Maresca v Motor Insurance Repair Research Centre* [2004] 4 All E.R. 254 (EAT), Rimer, J.
Sch.1 para.7, see *HM Prison Service v Dolby* [2003] I.R.L.R. 694 (EAT), Recorder Bowers Q.C.
Sch.1 r.10, see *Williams v Ferrosan Ltd* [2004] I.R.L.R. 607 (EAT), Hooper, J.
Sch.1 para.13, see *Bartholomew v Southwark LBC* [2004] I.C.R. 358 (EAT), Burton, J.
Sch.1 r.13, see *Williams v Ferrosan Ltd* [2004] I.R.L.R. 607 (EAT), Hooper, J.
Sch.1 para.14, see *McPherson v BNP Paribas SA (London Branch)* [2004] EWCA Civ 569, [2004] 3 All E.R. 266 (CA), Thorpe, L.J.
Sch.1 r.14, see *Health Development Agency v Parish* [2004] I.R.L.R. 550 (EAT), Judge Richardson; see *Kovacs v Queen Mary & Westfield College* [2002] EWCA Civ 352, [2002] I.C.R. 919 (CA), Simon Brown, L.J.
Sch.1 para.15, see *HM Prison Service v Dolby* [2003] I.R.L.R. 694 (EAT), Recorder Bowers Q.C.; see *X v Stevens (Commissioner of Police of the*

NO.

2001–cont.

1171. Employment Tribunals (Constitution and Rules of Procedure) Regulations 2001–*cont.*
Sch.1 para.15–*cont.*
Metropolis) [2003] I.C.R.1031 (EAT), Burton, J.
Sch.1 r.15, see *Bolch v Chipman* [2004] I.R.L.R. 140 (EAT), Burton, J.
Sch.1 para.16, amended: SI 2003/1673 Reg.31
Sch.1 para.16, see *X v Stevens (Commissioner of Police of the Metropolis)* [2003] I.C.R. 1031 (EAT), Burton, J.
Sch.5, applied: SI 2004/456 Reg.21
Sch.5, disapplied: SI 2003/547 Reg.22

1175. West of Cornwall Primary Care Trust (Establishment) Order 2001
Art.1, amended: SI 2002/1405 Sch.1
Art.4, revoked: SI 2002/1405 Sch.1

1177. Financial Services and Markets Act 2000 (Carrying on Regulated Activities by Way of Business) Order 2001
Art.1, amended: SI 2003/1476 Art.18
Art.3, amended: SI 2003/1476 Art.18
Art.3A, added: SI 2003/1475 Art.25

1178. National Health Service (General Medical Services) Amendment (No.2) Regulations 2001
revoked: SI 2004/865 Sch.2

1179. Land Registration Fees Order 2001
revoked: SI 2003/165 Art.1

1184. European Parliamentary Elections (Franchise of Relevant Citizens of the Union) Regulations 2001
applied: 2002 c.24 s.8, SI 2003/1557 Reg.6
Reg.1, varied: SI 2003/1557 Sch.1 para.1
Reg.2, consolidated: 2002 c.24 Sch.1 para.4
Reg.4, varied: SI 2003/1557 Sch.1 para.2
Reg.5, applied: 2002 c.24 Sch.1 para.4
Reg.5, varied: SI 2003/1557 Sch.1 para.3
Reg.6, varied: SI 2003/1557 Sch.1 para.4
Reg.8, amended: SI 2003/1557 Reg.5
Reg.8, applied: SI 2004/293 Sch.4 para.20
Reg.8, varied: SI 2003/1557 Sch.1 para.5
Reg.9, varied: SI 2003/1557 Sch.1 para.6
Reg.10, varied: SI 2003/1557 Sch.1 para.7
Reg.11, consolidated: 2002 c.24 s.8
Reg.11, revoked (in part): 2002 c.24 Sch.4
Sch., varied: SI 2003/1557 Sch.1 para.8

1185. ACAS Arbitration Scheme (England and Wales) Order 2001
revoked: SI 2004/753 Art.3

1193. Care Standards Act 2000 (Commencement No 4) (England) Order 2001
varied: SI 2004/664 Art.11, Art.12, Art.13, Art.14
Art.2, varied: SI 2004/664 Art.11, Art.12, Art.13, Art.14

NO.

2001–cont.

1197. King's Mill Centre for Health Care Services National Health Service Trust Change of Name and (Establishment) Amendment Order 2001
revoked: 2003 c.43 s.7

1198. West Hampshire National Health Service Trust (Establishment) Order 2001
revoked: 2003 c.43 s.7
Art.1, amended: SI 2004/766 Art.2
Art.2, amended: SI 2004/766 Art.2
Art.3, amended: SI 2004/766 Art.4

1201. Financial Services and Markets Act 2000 (Exemption) Order 2001
Art.2, amended: SI 2003/1675 Art.2
Art.5, amended: SI 2003/1675 Art.2
Sch.Part I para.15A, added: SI 2003/47 Art.2
Sch.Part II para.21, substituted: SI 2002/1310 Art.4
Sch.Part III para.27, substituted: SI 2003/1675 Art.2
Sch.Part IV para.47, substituted: SI 2003/1675 Art.2
Sch.Part IV para.48, substituted: SI 2003/1675 Art.2

1208. Weighing Equipment (Beltweighers) Regulations 2001
Reg.14, amended: SI 2003/214 Sch.1 para.10

1209. Further Education Teachers Qualifications (England) Regulations 2001
Reg.2, amended: SI 2003/2039 Reg.4
Reg.3, amended: SI 2003/2039 Reg.4
Reg.5, revoked: SI 2003/2039 Reg.4

1214. General Teaching Council for England (Additional Functions) Order 2001
revoked: SI 2003/1662 Sch.1 Part 1, SI 2003/2039 Reg.3

1217. Financial Services and Markets Act 2000 (Appointed Representatives) Regulations 2001
Reg.1, amended: SI 2003/1475 Art.23, SI 2003/1476 Art.14, SI 2004/453 Reg.2
Reg.2, amended: SI 2003/1475 Art.23, SI 2003/1476 Art.14, SI 2004/453 Reg.3, SI 2004/2737 Art.5
Reg.3, amended: SI 2003/1475 Art.23, SI 2003/1476 Art.14

1221. Nottingham Community Health National Health Service Trust (Dissolution) Order 2001
revoked: 2003 c.43 s.7

1223. Nottingham Healthcare and the Central Nottinghamshire Healthcare National Health Service Trusts (Dissolution) Order 2001
revoked: 2003 c.43 s.7

1224. South Buckinghamshire National Health Service Trust (Establishment) Amendment Order 2001
revoked: 2003 c.43 s.7

2001–cont.

1227. Financial Services and Markets Act 2000 (Professions) (Non-Exempt Activities) Order 2001

Art.1, amended: SI 2002/1777 Art.3

Art.2, amended: SI 2003/1476 Art.16

Art.4, amended: SI 2002/682 Art.7, SI 2004/2737 Art.5

Art.4A, added: SI 2003/1476 Art.16

Art.5, amended: SI 2003/1476 Art.16

Art.5A, added: SI 2003/1476 Art.16

Art.6, amended: SI 2003/1476 Art.16

Art.6A, substituted: SI 2003/1475 Art.24

Art.6B, substituted: SI 2003/1475 Art.24

Art.8, amended: SI 2002/682 Art.7

1228. Open-Ended Investment Companies Regulations 2001

applied: SI 2003/1400 Sch.4

Reg.2, amended: SI 2003/2066 Reg.13

Reg.14, applied: SSI 2003/231 Sch.2 para.1

Reg.15, amended: SI 2003/2066 Reg.8

Reg.17, amended: SI 2003/2066 Reg.13

Reg.21, applied: SSI 2003/231 Sch.2 para.1

Reg.25, applied: SSI 2003/231 Sch.2 para.1

Reg.30, applied: SI 2002/912 Sch.1, SI 2002/915 Sch.1

1230. North and East Devon Partnership National Health Service Trust (Establishment) Order 2001

revoked: 2003 c.43 s.7

Art.1, amended: SI 2002/731 Art.2

Art.2, amended: SI 2002/731 Art.2

Art.3, substituted: SI 2002/731 Art.3

1242. Foot-and-Mouth Disease (Ascertainment of Value) (No.4) Order 2001

Art.2, see *R. (on the application of J&PM Dockeray (A Firm)) v Secretary of State for the Environment, Food and Rural Affairs* [2002] EWHC 420, [2002] H.R.L.R. 27 (QBD (Admin Ct)), Collins, J.

1244. Plymouth Community Services National Health Service Trust (Dissolution) Order 2001

revoked: 2003 c.43 s.7

1245. Exeter and District Community Health Service National Health Service Trust (Dissolution) Order 2001

revoked: 2003 c.43 s.7

1247. Dorset Community National Health Service Trust (Dissolution) Order 2001

revoked: 2003 c.43 s.7

1248. Bath and West Community National Health Service Trust (Dissolution) Order 2001

revoked: 2003 c.43 s.7

2001–cont.

1249. Essex and Herts Community, the Mid Essex Community and Mental Health, and the North East Essex Mental Health National Health Service Trusts (Dissolution) Order 2001

revoked: 2003 c.43 s.7

1250. Norwich Community Health Partnership National Health Service Trust (Dissolution) Order 2001

revoked: 2003 c.43 s.7

1251. Adoption of Children from Overseas Regulations 2001

revoked: SI 2003/1173 Reg.7

1258. Camden and Islington Mental Health National Health Service Trust (Establishment) Order 2001

revoked: 2003 c.43 s.7

Art.2, amended: SI 2002/1494 Art.2

Art.4, amended: SI 2002/1494 Art.3

1266. Teachers (Compulsory Registration) (England) Regulations 2001

revoked: SI 2003/1663 Sch.1 Part 1

1268. General Teaching Council for England (Disciplinary Functions) Regulations 2001

Reg.2, amended: SI 2003/1186 Reg.3

Reg.9, amended: SI 2003/1186 Reg.4

Reg.13A, added: SI 2003/1186 Reg.5

Reg.18, amended: SI 2003/1186 Reg.6

Reg.20, amended: SI 2003/1186 Reg.7

Reg.29, substituted: SI 2003/1186 Reg.8

Sch.para.1, substituted: SI 2003/1186 Reg.9

Sch.para.2, substituted: SI 2003/1186 Reg.9

Sch.para.3, substituted: SI 2003/1186 Reg.9

Sch.para.4, substituted: SI 2003/1186 Reg.9

Sch.para.5, substituted: SI 2003/1186 Reg.9

Sch.para.6, substituted: SI 2003/1186 Reg.9

Sch.para.7, substituted: SI 2003/1186 Reg.9

Sch.para.8, substituted: SI 2003/1186 Reg.9

Sch.Part 1 para.1, substituted: SI 2003/1186 Reg.9

Sch.Part 1 para.2, substituted: SI 2003/1186 Reg.9

Sch.Part 1 para.3, substituted: SI 2003/1186 Reg.9

Sch.Part 1 para.4, substituted: SI 2003/1186 Reg.9

Sch.Part 1 para.5, substituted: SI 2003/1186 Reg.9

Sch.Part 1 para.6, substituted: SI 2003/1186 Reg.9

Sch.Part 1 para.7, substituted: SI 2003/1186 Reg.9

Sch.Part 2 para.8, substituted: SI 2003/1186 Reg.9

Sch.Part 2 para.9, substituted: SI 2003/1186 Reg.9

Sch.Part 2 para.10, substituted: SI 2003/1186 Reg.9

Sch.Part 2 para.11, substituted: SI 2003/1186 Reg.9

2001-cont.

1268. General Teaching Council for England (Disciplinary Functions) Regulations 2001–*cont.*

Sch. Part 2 para.12, substituted: SI 2003/1186 Reg.9

Sch. Part 2 para.13, substituted: SI 2003/1186 Reg.9

Sch. Part 2 para.14, substituted: SI 2003/1186 Reg.9

1269. Education (Restriction of Employment) (Amendment) Regulations 2001

revoked: SI 2003/1184 Reg.3

1272. Adoption of Children from Overseas (Wales) Regulations 2001

Reg.2, amended: SI 2003/1634 Reg.2

Reg.3, amended: SI 2003/1634 Reg.2

1275. Disabled Facilities Grants and Home Repair Assistance (Maximum Amounts) (Amendment) (Wales) Order 2001

revoked: SI 2002/1860 Sch.6

1280. Local Authorities (Members Allowances) (England) Regulations 2001

revoked: SI 2003/1021 Reg.33

1286. Education (National Curriculum) (Assessment Arrangements) (England) (Amendment) Order 2001

revoked (in part): SI 2003/1037 Art.2, SI 2003/1038 Art.2, SI 2003/1039 Art.2

1288. Horizon and the West Herts Community Health National Health Service Trusts (Dissolution) Order 2001

revoked: 2003 c.43 s.7

1289. Mancunian Community Health National Health Service Trust (Dissolution) Order 2001

revoked: 2003 c.43 s.7

1290. Bay Community National Health Service Trust (Dissolution) Order 2001

revoked: 2003 c.43 s.7

1291. Northampton Community Healthcare and the Rockingham Forest National Health Service Trusts (Dissolution) Order 2001

revoked: 2003 c.43 s.7

1295. Bridgend Valleys Railway Order 2001

Art.9, amended: SI 2003/2155 Sch.1 para.18

1298. Local Authorities (Conduct of Referendums) (England) Regulations 2001

Reg.2, amended: SI 2004/226 Reg.2

Reg.2, applied: SI 2004/293 Sch.2 para.26, Sch.3 para.2, SI 2004/294 Reg.2

Reg.10, amended: SI 2002/521 Reg.2

Reg.14, varied: SI 2002/185 Sch.3 Part I

Reg.15, amended: SI 2004/226 Reg.2

Reg.15, revoked (in part): SI 2004/226 Reg.2

Reg.15, varied: SI 2002/185 Sch.3 Part I

Reg.16, amended: SI 2004/226 Reg.2

Reg.16, revoked (in part): SI 2004/226 Reg.2

2001-cont.

1298. Local Authorities (Conduct of Referendums) (England) Regulations 2001–*cont.*

Reg.16, varied: SI 2002/185 Sch.3 Part I

Reg.17, amended: SI 2004/226 Reg.2

Sch.3, amended: SI 2002/521 Reg.2

Sch.5 Part I para.1, substituted: SI 2004/226 Sch.1

Sch.5 Part I para.2, substituted: SI 2004/226 Sch.1

Sch.5 Part II, substituted: SI 2004/226 Sch.1

Sch.5 Part III, substituted: SI 2004/226 Sch.1

Sch.5 Part IV, substituted: SI 2004/226 Sch.1

Sch.5 Part V, substituted: SI 2004/226 Sch.1

Sch.5 Part V, varied: SI 2002/185 Sch.3 Part I

1303. Restriction on Pithing (Wales) Regulations 2001

Reg.2, revoked (in part): SI 2002/1416 Sch.9 Part I

1313. Ravensbourne Priority Health National Health Service Trust (Dissolution) Order 2001

revoked: 2003 c.43 s.7

1329. Electoral Commission (Limit on Public Awareness Expenditure) Order 2001

revoked: SI 2002/505 Art.3

1330. Barnet, Enfield and Haringey Mental Health National Health Service Trust (Establishment) Order 2001

revoked: 2003 c.43 s.7

1331. Barnet Community Healthcare, the Enfield Community Care and the Haringey Health Care National Health Service Trusts (Dissolution) Order 2001

revoked: 2003 c.43 s.7

1335. Financial Services and Markets Act 2000 (Financial Promotion) Order 2001

Art.1, amended: SI 2002/1777 Art.4

Art.2, amended: SI 2002/1310 Art.2

Art.6, amended: SI 2002/2157 Art.3

Art.8A, added: SI 2002/2157 Art.3

Art.12, amended: SI 2002/2157 Art.4

Art.18, amended: SI 2002/2157 Art.5

Art.18A, added: SI 2002/2157 Art.5

Art.20, amended: SI 2002/1310 Art.2

Art.20B, added: SI 2002/2157 Art.6

Art.20B, amended: SI 2003/2067 Art.3

Art.28B, added: SI 2003/1676 Art.3

Art.29, amended: SI 2003/1676 Art.4

Art.30, amended: SI 2003/1676 Art.4

Art.41, varied: SI 2003/1633 Sch.2 para.15

Art.42, varied: SI 2003/1633 Sch.2 para.15

Art.46, amended: SI 2003/1676 Art.4

Art.49, amended: SI 2002/1310 Art.2

Sch.1 Part I para.1, varied: SI 2003/1633 Sch.2 para.8

Sch.1 Part I para.2, varied: SI 2003/1633 Sch.2 para.8

2001-cont.

1335. Financial Services and Markets Act 2000 (Financial Promotion) Order 2001-*cont.*

Sch.1 Part I para.3, varied: SI 2003/1633 Sch.2 para.8

Sch.1 Part I para.4, varied: SI 2003/1633 Sch.2 para.8

Sch.1 Part I para.5, varied: SI 2003/1633 Sch.2 para.8

Sch.1 Part I para.6, varied: SI 2003/1633 Sch.2 para.8

Sch.1 Part I para.7, varied: SI 2003/1633 Sch.2 para.8

Sch.1 Part I para.8, varied: SI 2003/1633 Sch.2 para.8

Sch.1 Part I para.9, varied: SI 2003/1633 Sch.2 para.8

Sch.1 Part I para.10, varied: SI 2003/1633 Sch.2 para.8

Sch.1 Part I para.10A, added: SI 2003/1676 Art.5

Sch.1 Part I para.10A, varied: SI 2003/1633 Sch.2 para.8

Sch.1 Part I para.10B, added: SI 2003/1676 Art.5

Sch.1 Part I para.10B, varied: SI 2003/1633 Sch.2 para.8

Sch.1 Part I para.11, amended: SI 2003/1676 Art.5

Sch.1 Part I para.11, varied: SI 2003/1633 Sch.2 para.8

Sch.1 Part II para.12, varied: SI 2003/1633 Sch.2 para.8

Sch.1 Part II para.13, varied: SI 2003/1633 Sch.2 para.8

Sch.1 Part II para.14, varied: SI 2003/1633 Sch.2 para.8

Sch.1 Part II para.15, applied: SI 2003/1633 Sch.2 para.15

Sch.1 Part II para.15, varied: SI 2003/1633 Sch.2 para.8

Sch.1 Part II para.16, varied: SI 2003/1633 Sch.2 para.8

Sch.1 Part II para.17, varied: SI 2003/1633 Sch.2 para.8

Sch.1 Part II para.18, varied: SI 2003/1633 Sch.2 para.8

Sch.1 Part II para.19, varied: SI 2003/1633 Sch.2 para.8

Sch.1 Part II para.20, varied: SI 2003/1633 Sch.2 para.8

Sch.1 Part II para.21, varied: SI 2003/1633 Sch.2 para.8

Sch.1 Part II para.22, varied: SI 2003/1633 Sch.2 para.8

Sch.1 Part II para.23, varied: SI 2003/1633 Sch.2 para.8

Sch.1 Part II para.24, varied: SI 2003/1633 Sch.2 para.8

Sch.1 Part II para.25, varied: SI 2003/1633 Sch.2 para.8

2001-cont.

1335. Financial Services and Markets Act 2000 (Financial Promotion) Order 2001-*cont.*

Sch.1 Part II para.26, varied: SI 2003/1633 Sch.2 para.8

Sch.1 Part II para.27, varied: SI 2003/1633 Sch.2 para.8

Sch.1 Part II para.28, varied: SI 2003/1633 Sch.2 para.8

Sch.1 Part II para.29, varied: SI 2003/1633 Sch.2 para.8

Sch.3 Part II, amended: SI 2002/1310 Art.2

Sch.3 Part III, amended: SI 2002/1310 Art.2

Sch.4 Part II para.22, amended: SI 2002/1310 Art.2

Sch.4 Part II para.28, amended: SI 2002/1310 Art.2

Sch.4 Part II para.31, amended: SI 2002/1310 Art.2

Sch.4 Part III para.45, amended: SI 2002/1310 Art.2

Sch.4 Part III para.47, amended: SI 2002/1310 Art.2

1337. Local Government (Best Value Performance Indicators) (Wales) Order 2001

revoked: SI 2002/757 Art.2

1338. The South Wales Sea Fisheries District (Variation) Order 2001

see *R. (on the application of South Wales Sea Fisheries Committee) v National Assembly for Wales* [2001] EWHC Admin 1162, [2002] R.V.R. 134 (QBD (Admin Ct)), Richards, J.

1344. Dual-Use Items (Export Control) (Amendment) Regulations 2001

revoked: SI 2003/2764 Sch.6

1347. Leeds Supertram (Extension) Order 2001

Sch.9 para.1, amended: SI 2003/2155 Sch.1 para.17, Sch.2

Sch.9 para.2, amended: SI 2003/2155 Sch.1 para.17, Sch.1 para.18

Sch.9 para.3, amended: SI 2003/2155 Sch.1 para.17

Sch.9 para.3, revoked (in part): SI 2003/2155 Sch.2

1358. National Health Service (Charges for Drugs and Appliances) (Wales) Regulations 2001

Reg.2, amended: SI 2003/2624 Reg.4, SI 2004/1016 Sch.1 para.24, SI 2004/1018 Reg.7, SI 2004/1605 Reg.2, SI 2004/1771 Sch.1 para.29

Reg.2, revoked (in part): SI 2004/1771 Sch.1 para.29

Reg.3, amended: SI 2004/1016 Sch.1 para.24, SI 2004/1018 Reg.8, SI 2004/1605 Sch.1

Reg.4, amended: SI 2004/1016 Sch.1 para.24, SI 2004/1605 Sch.1

Reg.5, amended: SI 2004/1605 Sch.1

NO.

NO.

2001–cont.

1358. National Health Service (Charges for Drugs and Appliances) (Wales) Regulations 2001–cont.

Reg.6, amended: SI 2003/2624 Reg.4, SI 2004/1016 Sch.1 para.24, SI 2004/1605 Sch.1

Reg.7, amended: SI 2004/1605 Sch.1

Reg.8, amended: SI 2004/1605 Reg.4

Reg.10, amended: SI 2004/1605 Sch.1

1389. Partnerships (Unrestricted Size) No 16 Regulations 2001

Reg.2, amended: SI 2002/1555 Art.45

Reg.2, revoked (in part): SI 2002/1555 Art.45

Reg.3, added: SI 2002/1555 Art.45

1391. Education (Teachers Qualifications and Health Standards) (England) (Amendment) Regulations 2001

revoked: SI 2003/1663 Sch.1 Part 1

1395. Social Security (Breach of Community Order) Regulations 2001

Reg.3, amended: SI 2002/490 Reg.11

1399. Scottish Parliament (Elections etc.) (Amendment) Order 2001

revoked: SI 2002/2779 Art.2

1403. Immigration and Asylum Act 1999 (Part V Exemption Educational Institutions and Health Sector Bodies) Order 2001

Sch.3 para.1, amended: SI 2002/2469 Sch.1 para.92, SI 2004/696 Sch.1 para.38

1408. National Assistance (Sums for Personal Requirements) (Wales) Regulations 2001

revoked: SI 2002/815 Reg.3

1420. Financial Services and Markets Act 2000 (Service of Notices) Regulations 2001

varied: SI 2002/1775 Reg.15, SI 2004/1862 Reg.6

1422. Stop Now Orders (E.C Directive) Regulations 2001

revoked: 2002 c.40 Sch.26

Reg.2, amended: SI 2002/2013 Reg.16

Sch.1 para.6, substituted: SI 2002/236 Reg.18

Sch.1 para.11, added: SI 2002/2013 Reg.16

1424. General Teaching Council for Wales (Disciplinary Functions) Regulations 2001

Reg.2, amended: SI 2003/503 Reg.3

Reg.8, amended: SI 2003/503 Reg.4

Reg.9, amended: SI 2003/503 Reg.5

Reg.18, amended: SI 2003/503 Reg.6

Reg.21A, added: SI 2003/503 Reg.7

Reg.28, revoked: SI 2003/542 Reg.2

1426. Transportable Pressure Vessels Regulations 2001

revoked: SI 2004/568 Sch.14

Sch.3, amended: SI 2003/1431 Reg.6

2001–cont.

1435. Greenwich Healthcare National Health Service Trust Change of Name and (Establishment) Amendment Order 2001

revoked: 2003 c.43 s.7

1437. Criminal Defence Service (General) (No.2) Regulations 2001

referred to: SI 2003/644 Reg.2

Part IV, added: SI 2004/1196 Reg.4

Reg.2, amended: SI 2002/712 Reg.4, SI 2003/644 Reg.3, SI 2004/2046 Reg.2

Reg.3, amended: SI 2002/712 Reg.5, SI 2002/2785 Reg.2, SI 2004/1196 Reg.2

Reg.4, amended: SI 2002/712 Reg.6

Reg.4A, added: SI 2004/1196 Reg.3

Reg.5, amended: SI 2002/712 Reg.7, SI 2002/2785 Reg.2, SI 2003/644 Reg.4, Reg.5, SI 2003/2378 Reg.2

Reg.6, amended: SI 2002/712 Reg.8

Reg.7, amended: SI 2002/712 Reg.9

Reg.10, amended: SI 2002/712 Reg.10

Reg.13, amended: SI 2002/712 Reg.11

Reg.14, amended: SI 2002/712 Reg.12

Reg.17, amended: SI 2002/712 Reg.13

Reg.22, amended: SI 2004/1196 Reg.5

Sch.1 para.8, amended: SI 2003/762 Reg.11, SI 2004/1748 Sch.2 para.1

Sch.2, substituted: SI 2002/712 Reg.14

Reg.14, see *R. v Conroy (Costs)* [2004] 1 Costs L.R. 182 (Crown Ct (Bristol)), Judge Crowther Q.C.

Reg.22, see *R. v Conroy (Costs)* [2004] 1 Costs L.R. 182 (Crown Ct (Bristol)), Judge Crowther Q.C.

1440. Coffee Extracts and Chicory Extracts (Wales) Regulations 2001

applied: SI 2004/554 Reg.3

referred to: SI 2003/945 Reg.3

varied: SI 2002/329 Reg.9

Reg.5, amended: SI 2003/3047 Reg.10

1442. District of Cannock Chase (Electoral Changes) Order 2001

varied: SI 2004/222 Art.2

1443. Borough of East Staffordshire (Electoral Changes) Order 2001

varied: SI 2004/222 Art.2

1444. District of Lichfield (Electoral Changes) Order 2001

varied: SI 2004/222 Art.2

1445. Borough of Newcastle-under-Lyme (Electoral Changes) Order 2001

varied: SI 2004/222 Art.2

1446. District of South Staffordshire (Electoral Changes) Order 2001

varied: SI 2004/222 Art.2

1447. Borough of Stafford (Electoral Changes) Order 2001

varied: SI 2004/222 Art.2

1448. District of Staffordshire Moorlands (Electoral Changes) Order 2001

varied: SI 2004/222 Art.2

NO.

2001–cont.

1448. District of Staffordshire Moorlands (Electoral Changes) Order 2001–*cont.*
Sch.1, amended: SI 2004/2677 Art.2

1449. City of Stoke-on-Trent (Electoral Changes) Order 2001
varied: SI 2004/222 Art.2

1450. Borough of Tamworth (Electoral Changes) Order 2001
varied: SI 2004/222 Art.2

1452. Civil Aviation Act 1982 (Overseas Territories) Order 2001
applied: SI 2003/433, SI 2004/2038

1453. European Convention on Extradition (Fiscal Offences) Order 2001
Art.1, amended: SI 2002/1830 Art.2
Sch.3, amended: SI 2002/1830 Art.2, SI 2003/436 Art.2, SI 2003/1878 Art.2
Sch.4, added: SI 2002/1830 Art.2, SI 2003/436 Art.2

1501. Housing (Right to Acquire) (Discount) Order 2001
revoked: SI 2002/1091 Art.3

1537. South Tees Acute Hospitals National Health Service Trust Change of Name and (Establishment) Amendment Order 2001
revoked: 2003 c.43 s.7

1543. National Health Service (Payments by Local Authorities to Health Authorities) (Prescribed Functions) (Wales) Regulations 2001
Reg.2, amended: SI 2004/1016 Sch.1 para.23

1606. Southern Derbyshire Mental Health National Health Service Trust Change of Name and (Establishment) Amendment Order 2001
revoked: 2003 c.43 s.7

1612. Community Health Services, Southern Derbyshire National Health Service Trust (Dissolution) Order 2001
revoked: 2003 c.43 s.7

1625. North Mersey Community National Health Service Trust (Establishment) Amendment Order 2001
revoked: 2003 c.43 s.7

1631. Sea Fishing (Enforcement of Community Quota and Third Country Fishing Measures) Order 2001
revoked: SI 2002/272 Art.13

1644. BSE Monitoring (England) Regulations 2001
applied: SI 2002/843 Reg.104, Sch.9 para.1, Sch.9 para.2
revoked: SI 2002/843 Sch.9 Part I
Reg.3, applied: SI 2002/843 Sch.9 para.3

1663. Teddington Memorial Hospital and Community National Health Service Trust (Dissolution) Order 2001
revoked: 2003 c.43 s.7

NO.

2001–cont.

1664. Kingston and District Community National Health Service Trust (Dissolution) Order 2001
revoked: 2003 c.43 s.7

1665. Halton General Hospital and the Warrington Hospital National Health Service Trusts (Dissolution) Order 2001
revoked: 2003 c.43 s.7

1666. Salford Community Health Care National Health Service Trust (Dissolution) Order 2001
revoked: 2003 c.43 s.7

1669. Medicines (Products for Animal Use-Fees) (Amendment) Regulations 2001
revoked: SI 2004/2750 Reg.18

1678. National Health Service (Functions of Health Authorities) (General Dental Services Incentive Schemes) Regulations 2001
Reg.1, amended: SI 2002/2469 Sch.7
Reg.2, amended: SI 2002/2469 Sch.1 para.93, Sch.7

1691. Processed Cereal-based Foods and Baby Foods for Infants and Young Children (Amendment) (Wales) Regulations 2001
revoked: SI 2004/314 Reg.13

1700. Representation of the People (England and Wales) (Amendment) Regulations 2001
Reg.4, revoked: SI 2002/1871 Reg.3

1704. Animal By-Products (Amendment) (England) Order 2001
revoked: SI 2003/1482 Reg.51

1708. Sex Offenders (Notification Requirements) (Prescribed Police Stations) Regulations 2001
revoked: SI 2004/875 Reg.3

1712. Tobacco Products Regulations 2001
Reg.3, amended: SI 2002/2692 Reg.4, SI 2003/1523 Reg.2
Reg.12, amended: SI 2002/2692 Reg.4, SI 2004/1003 Reg.10
Reg.12, revoked (in part): SI 2003/1523 Reg.2
Reg.12, varied: SI 2003/2758 Sch.1 para.3
Reg.23, amended: SI 2002/2692 Reg.4

1730. Education (Student Support) Regulations 2001 (Amendment) Regulations 2001
revoked: SI 2002/195 Reg.3

1734. Education (Mandatory Awards) Regulations 2001
applied: SI 2002/1330 Reg.6
revoked: SI 2002/1330 Sch.6
Sch.2 Part III para.14, amended: SI 2002/173 Reg.3, SI 2002/232 Reg.4

NO.

2001-cont.

1735. Animal By-Products (Amendment) (Wales) Order 2001
revoked: SI 2003/2756 Reg.51

1742. National Patient Safety Agency Regulations 2001
Reg.1, amended: SI 2004/696 Art.3
Reg.3, amended: SI 2004/696 Art.3, Sch.1 para.39

1743. National Patient Safety Agency (Establishment and Constitution) Order 2001
Art.4, amended: SI 2003/1077 Art.2

1744. General Social Care Council (Appointments and Procedure) Regulations 2001
Reg.4, amended: SI 2003/1590 Sch.1 para.15, SI 2004/1771 Sch.1 para.28

1748. Scottish Parliament (Elections etc.) (Amendment) (No.2) Order 2001
revoked: SI 2002/2779 Art.2

1749. Representation of the People (Scotland) (Amendment) Regulations 2001
Reg.4, revoked: SI 2002/1872 Reg.3

1750. Scottish Parliament (Elections etc.) (Amendment) (No.3) Order 2001
revoked: SI 2002/2779 Art.2

1757. General Insurance Reserves (Tax) Regulations 2001
Reg.2, amended: SI 2003/2862 Reg.4
Reg.3, amended: SI 2003/2862 Reg.5
Reg.3, revoked (in part): SI 2003/2862 Reg.5
Reg.4, amended: SI 2003/2862 Reg.6
Reg.5, substituted: SI 2003/2862 Reg.7
Reg.6, amended: SI 2003/2096 Sch.1 para.78, SI 2003/2862 Reg.8
Reg.7, amended: SI 2003/2862 Reg.9
Reg.7, revoked (in part): SI 2003/2862 Reg.9
Reg.8, amended: SI 2003/2862 Reg.10
Reg.10, added: SI 2003/2862 Reg.11

1783. Financial Services and Markets Act 2000 (Compensation Scheme Electing Participants) Regulations 2001
Reg.1, amended: SI 2003/1476 Art.15, SI 2003/2066 Reg.7
Reg.2, amended: SI 2003/1476 Art.15, SI 2003/2066 Reg.7
Reg.3, amended: SI 2003/1476 Art.15, SI 2003/2066 Reg.7
Reg.4, amended: SI 2003/1476 Art.15, SI 2003/2066 Reg.7

1787. Miscellaneous Food Additives (Amendment) (Wales) Regulations 2001
applied: SI 2004/554 Reg.3
referred to: SI 2003/945 Reg.3
varied: SI 2002/329 Reg.9
Reg.6, revoked (in part): SI 2002/329 Reg.9

NO.

2001-cont.

1788. National Health Service (General Medical Services) Amendment (No.2) (Wales) Regulations 2001
revoked: SI 2004/1016 Sch.2

1817. Social Security Contributions (Share Options) Regulations 2001
Reg.4, amended: SI 2003/2155 Sch.1 para.24

1819. Financial Services and Markets Act 2000 (Regulations Relating to Money Laundering) Regulations 2001
revoked: SI 2003/3075 Reg.1

1828. Day Care and Child Minding (National Standards) (England) Regulations 2001
revoked: SI 2003/1996 Reg.2

1829. Child Minding and Day Care (Applications for Registration) (England) Regulations 2001
Reg.2, amended: SI 2003/1995 Reg.3
Reg.3, amended: SI 2003/1995 Reg.4
Sch.1 para.1, substituted: SI 2003/1995 Reg.5
Sch.1 para.4, revoked: SI 2003/1995 Reg.6
Sch.1 para.12, revoked: SI 2003/1995 Reg.6
Sch.1 para.13, revoked: SI 2003/1995 Reg.6
Sch.1 para.14, revoked: SI 2003/1995 Reg.6
Sch.1 para.15, amended: SI 2003/1995 Reg.7
Sch.1 para.16, amended: SI 2003/1995 Reg.8
Sch.1 para.17, revoked: SI 2003/1995 Reg.6

1833. National Health Service (General Medical Services) Amendment (Wales) Regulations 2001
revoked: SI 2004/1016 Sch.2

1846. Sex Offenders (Notice Requirements) (Foreign Travel) Regulations 2001
varied: SI 2004/1220 Reg.3

1866. Financial Investigations (Northern Ireland) Order 2001
Art.1, enabled: SR 2003/140
Art.3, revoked (in part): 2002 c.29 Sch.12
Art.4, revoked (in part): 2002 c.29 Sch.12

1867. Liberia (United Nations Sanctions) (Overseas Territories) (No.2) Order 2001
Art.1, amended: SI 2003/1876 Art.2
Art.3A, added: SI 2003/1876 Art.2
Art.4, amended: SI 2003/1876 Art.2
Art.6, amended: SI 2003/1876 Art.2
Sch.2 para.1, amended: SI 2003/1876 Art.2

1887. Central Manchester and Manchester Children's University Hospitals National Health Service Trust (Establishment) Order 2001
revoked: 2003 c.43 s.7

1888. Mersey Care National Health Service Trust (Establishment) Order 2001
revoked: 2003 c.43 s.7

NO.

2001–cont.

1889. North Sefton &amp West Lancashire Community National Health Service Trust (Establishment) Amendment Order 2001
revoked: 2003 c.43 s.7

1895. Central Manchester Healthcare and the Manchester Children's Hospitals National Health Service Trusts (Dissolution) Order 2001
revoked: 2003 c.43 s.7

1910. Rotherham Priority Health Services National Health Service Trust (Establishment) Amendment Order 2001
revoked: 2003 c.43 s.7

1915. Winchester and Eastleigh Healthcare National Health Service Trust (Establishment) Amendment Order 2001
revoked: 2003 c.43 s.7

1916. Southampton Community Health Services National Health Service Trust (Establishment) Amendment Order 2001
revoked: 2003 c.43 s.7

1975. Ealing, Hammersmith and Fulham Mental Health National Health Service Trust (Dissolution) Order 2001
revoked: 2003 c.43 s.7

2070. Housing Grants (Additional Purposes) (Wales) Order 2001
revoked: SI 2002/1860 Sch.6

2072. Relocation Grants (Forms of Application) (Amendment) (Wales) Regulations 2001
revoked: SI 2002/1860 Sch.6

2127. Health and Safety at Work etc Act 1974 (Application outside Great Britain) Order 2001
applied: SI 2002/1689 Reg.17, SI 2002/2675 Reg.26, SI 2002/2676 Reg.14, SI 2002/2677 Reg.17, SI 2002/2776 Reg.12

2128. Air Navigation (Overseas Territories) Order 2001
Art.4, amended: SI 2004/2038 Art.3
Art.8, amended: SI 2004/2038 Art.4
Art.9A, added: SI 2004/2038 Art.4
Art.9B, added: SI 2004/2038 Art.4
Art.20, amended: SI 2004/2038 Art.5
Art.34A, added: SI 2004/2038 Art.6
Art.37, amended: SI 2004/2038 Art.7
Art.40, amended: SI 2004/2038 Art.8
Art.45, amended: SI 2004/2038 Art.5
Art.62, amended: SI 2004/2038 Art.9
Art.62, revoked (in part): SI 2004/2038 Art.9
Art.78A, added: SI 2004/2038 Art.10
Art.84, amended: SI 2004/2038 Art.11
Art.88, substituted: SI 2004/2038 Art.12
Art.88A, added: SI 2004/2038 Art.13
Art.101, amended: SI 2004/2038 Art.14
Art.102, amended: SI 2004/2038 Art.14
Art.103, amended: SI 2004/2038 Art.14

NO.

2001–cont.

2128. Air Navigation (Overseas Territories) Order 2001–cont.
Art.104, amended: SI 2004/2038 Art.14
Art.104, substituted: SI 2004/2038 Art.15
Art.105, amended: SI 2004/2038 Art.14
Art.105, substituted: SI 2004/2038 Art.15
Art.106, amended: SI 2004/2038 Art.14
Art.107, amended: SI 2004/2038 Art.14
Art.108, amended: SI 2004/2038 Art.14
Art.109, amended: SI 2004/2038 Art.14
Art.109A, added: SI 2004/2038 Art.16
Art.109A, amended: SI 2004/2038 Art.14
Art.110, amended: SI 2004/2038 Art.14
Art.111, amended: SI 2004/2038 Art.14
Art.112, amended: SI 2004/2038 Art.14
Art.117A, added: SI 2004/2038 Art.17
Art.118, amended: SI 2004/2038 Art.18
Art.119, amended: SI 2004/2038 Art.19
Art.125, amended: SI 2004/2038 Art.20
Art.130, amended: SI 2003/433 Art.2, SI 2004/2038 Art.5, Art.21
Art.136, added: SI 2003/433 Art.2
Art.137, added: SI 2003/433 Art.2
Sch.2 Part B para.1, amended: SI 2004/2038 Art.22
Sch.3 Part A, amended: SI 2004/2038 Art.23
Sch.4 para.4, amended: SI 2004/2038 Art.24
Sch.4 para.5, amended: SI 2004/2038 Art.5, Art.24
Sch.5 para.2, amended: SI 2004/2038 Art.25
Sch.5 para.3, substituted: SI 2004/2038 Art.25
Sch.5 para.4, amended: SI 2004/2038 Art.25
Sch.9 para.2, amended: SI 2004/2038 Art.26
Sch.12 Part A, amended: SI 2004/2038 Art.27
Sch.13 Part VI para.31, amended: SI 2004/2038 Art.28
Sch.14 Part ANNEX, amended: SI 2004/2038 Art.29
Sch.14 para.7, amended: SI 2004/2038 Art.29
Sch.14 para.8, amended: SI 2004/2038 Art.29
Sch.14 para.9, amended: SI 2004/2038 Art.29
Sch.14 para.18A, added: SI 2004/2038 Art.29
Sch.14 para.19, amended: SI 2004/2038 Art.29
Sch.15 para.1, substituted: SI 2004/2038 Art.30
Sch.15 Part I para.1, substituted: SI 2004/2038 Art.30
Sch.15 para.2, substituted: SI 2004/2038 Art.30

NO.

2001–cont.

2128. Air Navigation (Overseas Territories) Order 2001–*cont.*

Sch.15 Part II para.2, substituted: SI 2004/2038 Art.30

Sch.15 Part II para.3, substituted: SI 2004/2038 Art.30

Sch.15 para.3, substituted: SI 2004/2038 Art.30

Sch.15 Part III para.4, substituted: SI 2004/2038 Art.30

Sch.15 Part III para.5, substituted: SI 2004/2038 Art.30

Sch.15 Part III para.6, substituted: SI 2004/2038 Art.30

Sch.15 Part III para.7, substituted: SI 2004/2038 Art.30

Sch.15 Part III para.8, substituted: SI 2004/2038 Art.30

Sch.15 para.4, substituted: SI 2004/2038 Art.30

Sch.15 Part IV para.9, substituted: SI 2004/2038 Art.30

Sch.15 para.5, substituted: SI 2004/2038 Art.30

Sch.15 Part V para.10, substituted: SI 2004/2038 Art.30

Sch.15 para.6, substituted: SI 2004/2038 Art.30

Sch.15 Part VI para.11, substituted: SI 2004/2038 Art.30

Sch.15 para.7, substituted: SI 2004/2038 Art.30

Sch.15 Part VII para.12, substituted: SI 2004/2038 Art.30

Sch.15 Part VII para.13, substituted: SI 2004/2038 Art.30

Sch.15 para.8, substituted: SI 2004/2038 Art.30

Sch.15 Part VIII para.14, substituted: SI 2004/2038 Art.30

Sch.15 Part VIII para.15, substituted: SI 2004/2038 Art.30

Sch.15 Part VIII para.16, substituted: SI 2004/2038 Art.30

Sch.15 Part VIII para.17, substituted: SI 2004/2038 Art.30

Sch.15 Part VIII para.18, substituted: SI 2004/2038 Art.30

Sch.15 Part VIII para.19, substituted: SI 2004/2038 Art.30

Sch.15 para.9, substituted: SI 2004/2038 Art.30

Sch.15 para.10, substituted: SI 2004/2038 Art.30

Sch.15 para.11, substituted: SI 2004/2038 Art.30

Sch.19 Part A, added: SI 2004/2038 Art.31

Sch.19 Part B, added: SI 2004/2038 Art.31

Sch.19 Part C, added: SI 2004/2038 Art.31

NO.

2001–cont.

2186. Carers (Services) and Direct Payments (Amendment) (Wales) Regulations 2001

Reg.3, revoked: SI 2004/1748 Reg.13

Reg.4, revoked: SI 2004/1748 Reg.13

2187. Social Security (Contributions) (Amendment No 4) Regulations 2001

Reg.3, revoked (in part): SI 2004/770 Sch.1

2188. Financial Services and Markets Act 2000 (Disclosure of Confidential Information) Regulations 2001

applied: SI 2003/1102 Reg.16, Reg.50, SI 2004/353 Reg.16, Reg.50, SI 2004/1045 Reg.18, Reg.38

varied: SI 2003/1102 Reg.50

Reg.2, amended: SI 2003/693 Reg.3, SI 2003/1473 Reg.10, SI 2003/2066 Reg.12, SI 2004/1862 Reg.11

Reg.4, amended: SI 2003/1092 Reg.3, SI 2003/2174 Reg.4

Reg.4, revoked (in part): SI 2003/1092 Reg.3

Reg.8, amended: SI 2003/2066 Reg.12

Reg.9, amended: SI 2003/693 Reg.3, SI 2003/2066 Reg.12

Reg.10, amended: SI 2003/2066 Reg.12

Reg.11, revoked (in part): SI 2003/2066 Reg.12

Reg.12B, added: SI 2002/1775 Reg.16

Reg.12BI, added: SI 2003/1092 Reg.3

Reg.12BI, revoked: SI 2003/1092 Reg.3

Reg.12C, added: SI 2003/2174 Reg.4

Reg.15, amended: SI 2003/2066 Reg.12

Sch.1 Part 1, amended: SI 2003/1092 Reg.3, SI 2003/2174 Reg.4, SI 2003/2817 Reg.2

Sch.2, amended: SI 2003/1092 Reg.3, SI 2003/2174 Reg.4

2189. Children (Leaving Care) (Wales) Regulations 2001

Reg.2, amended: SI 2002/2935 Reg.12

Reg.3, revoked (in part): SI 2002/1855 Reg.2

Reg.4, amended: SI 2002/1855 Reg.2, SI 2004/1732 Reg.2

2192. Disabled Children (Direct Payments) (Wales) Regulations 2001

revoked: SI 2004/1748 Reg.13

2193. Common Agricultural Policy (Wine) (Wales) Regulations 2001

Reg.2, amended: SI 2003/1776 Reg.3, SI 2004/2599 Reg.2

Reg.5, amended: SI 2003/1776 Reg.3

Reg.6, amended: SI 2003/1776 Reg.3

Reg.6, substituted: SI 2004/2599 Reg.2

Reg.6A, added: SI 2003/1776 Reg.3

Reg.6B, added: SI 2003/1776 Reg.3

Reg.8, amended: SI 2003/1776 Reg.3

Reg.13, revoked: SI 2003/1776 Reg.3

Reg.14, amended: SI 2003/1776 Reg.3

Reg.16, amended: SI 2003/1776 Reg.3, SI 2004/2599 Reg.2

Reg.19, amended: SI 2004/2599 Reg.2

NO.

2001–cont.

2193. Common Agricultural Policy (Wine) (Wales) Regulations 2001–*cont.*

Sch.1, substituted: SI 2003/1776 Sch.1, SI 2004/2599 Sch.1

Sch.2 Part I, amended: SI 2003/1776 Reg.3

Sch.2 Part III, amended: SI 2004/2599 Sch.2

Sch.2 Part IV, amended: SI 2003/1776 Reg.3

Sch.2 Part V, amended: SI 2003/1776 Reg.3

Sch.3, amended: SI 2003/1776 Reg.3

Sch.3, revoked: SI 2004/2599 Reg.2

Sch.4, revoked: SI 2003/1776 Reg.3

Sch.5 para.2, amended: SI 2003/1776 Reg.3

Sch.5 para.4, amended: SI 2003/1776 Reg.3

Sch.6, added: SI 2004/2599 Sch.3

Sch.7 Part 1 para.1, added: SI 2004/2599 Sch.3

Sch.7 Part 2 para.2, added: SI 2004/2599 Sch.3

2218. Special Educational Needs (Provision of Information by Local Education Authorities) (England) Regulations 2001

Reg.1, amended: SI 2002/2469 Sch.1 para.94, Sch.8

Reg.3, amended: SI 2002/2469 Sch.7

2254. Police and Criminal Evidence Act 1984 (Codes of Practice) (Modification) Order 2001

revoked: SI 2002/1150 Art.4

2256. Financial Services and Markets Act 2000 (Rights of Action) Regulations 2001

Reg.3, amended: SI 2002/1775 Reg.18

Reg.6, amended: SI 2002/2706 Reg.3

Reg.7, referred to: SI 2002/1775 Reg.6

Reg.7, varied: SI 2002/1775 Reg.6

2265. Wireless Telegraphy (Licence Charges) (Amendment) Regulations 2001

revoked: SI 2002/1700 Sch.1

2284. Local Authorities (Alternative Arrangements) (Wales) Regulations 2001

Reg.4, amended: SI 2002/810 Reg.2, Reg.3

Reg.4, applied: SI 2002/2880 Reg.2

Reg.5, amended: SI 2002/810 Reg.4

Sch.1, amended: SI 2002/810 Reg.5, SI 2003/2676 Reg.7

Sch.3, amended: SI 2003/155 Reg.2

2285. Road User Charging (Charges and Penalty Charges) (London) Regulations 2001

Reg.2, amended: SI 2003/109 Reg.3

Reg.4, amended: SI 2003/109 Reg.4

Reg.6, amended: SI 2003/109 Reg.5

Reg.11, amended: SI 2003/109 Reg.6

2287. Local Authorities (Executive Arrangements) (Discharge of Functions) (Wales) Regulations 2001

revoked: SI 2002/802 Reg.13

NO.

2001–cont.

2289. Conduct of Members (Model Code of Conduct) (Wales) Order 2001

Art.4, added: SI 2004/1510 Art.3

Sch.1 Part III para.15, amended: SI 2004/163 Art.3

2290. Local Authorities (Executive Arrangements) (Decisions, Documents and Meetings) (Wales) Regulations 2001

varied: SI 2002/802 Reg.11

Reg.5, amended: SI 2002/1385 Reg.2

2291. Local Authorities Executive Arrangements (Functions and Responsibilities) (Wales) Regulations 2001

Sch.1, added: SI 2002/783 Reg.2

Sch.1, amended: SI 2002/783 Reg.2, SI 2003/2676 Reg.6

Sch.3, amended: SI 2003/153 Reg.2

2292. Local Authorities (Referendums) (Petitions and Directions) (Wales) Regulations 2001

Reg.3, amended: SI 2003/398 Reg.3

Reg.3, revoked (in part): SI 2003/398 Reg.3

Reg.3A, added: SI 2003/398 Reg.3

Reg.4, substituted: SI 2003/398 Reg.3

Reg.5, substituted: SI 2003/398 Reg.3

Reg.9, amended: SI 2003/398 Reg.3

Reg.14, amended: SI 2003/398 Reg.3

Reg.16, amended: SI 2003/398 Reg.3

Reg.17, applied: SI 2004/870 Reg.4, Reg.17

Reg.19, applied: SI 2004/870 Reg.4, Reg.17

Reg.20, applied: SI 2004/870 Reg.17

Reg.23, applied: SI 2004/870 Reg.14

Reg.24, applied: SI 2004/870 Reg.14

2294. Sweeteners in Food (Amendment) (England) Regulations 2001

referred to: SI 2003/1008 Reg.3

Reg.4, revoked (in part): SI 2002/379 Reg.5

2295. Child Support, Pensions and Social Security Act 2000 (Commencement No 9) Order 2001

Art.2, revoked (in part): SI 2002/437 Art.2

2301. Damages (Personal Injury) Order 2001

see *Cooke v United Bristol Healthcare NHS Trust* [2003] EWCA Civ 1370, [2004] 1 W.L.R. 251 (CA), Laws, L.J.; see *Page v Plymouth Hospitals NHS Trust* [2004] EWHC 1154, [2004] 3 All E.R. 367 (QBD), Davis, J.

2313. Road User Charging (Enforcement and Adjudication) (London) Regulations 2001

Reg.2, amended: SI 2003/108 Reg.3

Reg.8, amended: SI 2003/108 Reg.4

Reg.10, amended: SI 2003/108 Reg.5

Reg.11, amended: SI 2003/108 Reg.6

Reg.12, amended: SI 2003/108 Reg.7

Reg.13, amended: SI 2003/108 Reg.8

Reg.16, amended: SI 2003/108 Reg.9

Reg.17, amended: SI 2003/108 Reg.10

NO.

2001–cont.

2313. Road User Charging (Enforcement and Adjudication) (London) Regulations 2001–*cont.*

Reg.20, amended: SI 2003/108 Reg.11

Reg.21, amended: SI 2003/108 Reg.12

2315. Air Quality Limit Values Regulations 2001

applied: SI 2003/2121 Sch.6

revoked: SI 2003/2121 Sch.10

Reg.2, amended: SI 2002/3117 Reg.2

Reg.2A, added: SI 2002/3117 Reg.2

Reg.7, amended: SI 2002/3117 Reg.2

Reg.11, amended: SI 2002/3117 Reg.2

Reg.13, amended: SI 2002/3117 Reg.2

Sch.1 Part V, added: SI 2002/3117 Reg.2

Sch.1 Part VI, added: SI 2002/3117 Reg.2

Sch.2 Part I, amended: SI 2002/3117 Reg.2

Sch.2 Part II, amended: SI 2002/3117 Reg.2

Sch.3, amended: SI 2002/3117 Reg.2

Sch.3 Part I, amended: SI 2002/3117 Reg.2

Sch.3 Part II, amended: SI 2002/3117 Reg.2

Sch.3 Part III, amended: SI 2002/3117 Reg.2

Sch.4 Part I, amended: SI 2002/3117 Reg.2

Sch.5 Part I, amended: SI 2002/3117 Reg.2

Sch.6 Part I, amended: SI 2002/3117 Reg.2

Sch.6 Part II, amended: SI 2002/3117 Reg.2

Sch.6 Part IIIA, amended: SI 2002/3117 Reg.2

Sch.6 Part IIIB, amended: SI 2002/3117 Reg.2

Sch.6 Part IV, amended: SI 2002/3117 Reg.2

Sch.6 Part V, added: SI 2002/3117 Reg.2

Sch.6 Part V, amended: SI 2002/3117 Reg.2

Sch.6 Part VI, added: SI 2002/3117 Reg.2

Sch.6 Part VI, amended: SI 2002/3117 Reg.2

2340. Discretionary Housing Payments (Grants) Order 2001

Art.1, amended: SI 2004/2329 Art.2

Art.3, amended: SI 2004/2329 Art.2

Art.4, substituted: SI 2004/2329 Art.2

Art.6, substituted: SI 2004/2329 Art.2

Art.6A, added: SI 2004/2329 Art.2

2355. Education (Student Support) (Amendment) (No.2) Regulations 2001

revoked: SI 2002/195 Reg.3

2356. Potatoes Originating in Egypt (Amendment) (Wales) Regulations 2001

revoked: SI 2004/2245 Reg.8

2360. BSE Monitoring (Wales) Regulations 2001

applied: SI 2002/1416 Reg.104

revoked: SI 2002/1416 Sch.9 Part I

varied: SI 2002/1416 Sch.9 para.1, Sch.9 para.2

Reg.3, varied: SI 2002/1416 Sch.9 para.3

2376. Processed Animal Protein (England) Regulations 2001

applied: SI 2002/843 Reg.104, Sch.9 para.7, Sch.9 para.8

NO.

2001–cont.

2376. Processed Animal Protein (England) Regulations 2001–*cont.*

Reg.4, revoked: SI 2002/843 Sch.9 Part I

Reg.5, applied: SI 2002/843 Sch.9 para.1

Reg.5, revoked: SI 2002/843 Sch.9 Part I

Reg.6, applied: SI 2002/843 Sch.9 para.2

Reg.6, revoked: SI 2002/843 Sch.9 Part I

Reg.7, applied: SI 2002/843 Sch.9 para.3

Reg.7, revoked: SI 2002/843 Sch.9 Part I

Reg.8, revoked: SI 2002/843 Sch.9 Part I

Reg.9, revoked: SI 2002/843 Sch.9 Part I

Reg.12, revoked: SI 2002/843 Sch.9 Part I

Reg.13, applied: SI 2002/843 Sch.9 para.4

Reg.13, revoked: SI 2002/843 Sch.9 Part I

Reg.14, applied: SI 2002/843 Sch.9 para.5

Reg.14, revoked: SI 2002/843 Sch.9 Part I

Reg.15, applied: SI 2002/843 Sch.9 para.6

Reg.15, revoked: SI 2002/843 Sch.9 Part I

Reg.16, revoked: SI 2002/843 Sch.9 Part I

Sch.1 para.1, revoked: SI 2002/843 Sch.9 Part I

Sch.1 para.2, revoked: SI 2002/843 Sch.9 Part I

Sch.1 para.3, revoked: SI 2002/843 Sch.9 Part I

Sch.1 para.4, revoked: SI 2002/843 Sch.9 Part I

Sch.1 para.5, revoked: SI 2002/843 Sch.9 Part I

Sch.2 para.1, revoked: SI 2002/843 Sch.9 Part I

Sch.2 para.2, revoked: SI 2002/843 Sch.9 Part I

Sch.2 para.3, revoked: SI 2002/843 Sch.9 Part I

Sch.3 para.1, revoked: SI 2002/843 Sch.9 Part I

Sch.3 para.2, revoked: SI 2002/843 Sch.9 Part I

2377. Immigration (Designation of Travel Bans) (Amendment) Order 2001

revoked: SI 2003/3285 Sch.2

2379. International Criminal Court Act 2001 (Enforcement of Fines, Forfeiture and Reparation Orders) Regulations 2001

Reg.4, amended: SI 2002/822 Reg.2

Reg.5, amended: SI 2002/822 Reg.2

2383. Financial Services and Markets Act 2000 (Collective Investment Schemes Constituted in Other EEA States) Regulations 2001

Reg.2, amended: SI 2003/2066 Reg.11

Reg.3, amended: SI 2003/2066 Reg.11

Reg.4, amended: SI 2003/2066 Reg.11

2385. Relocation Grants (Form of Application) (Amendment No 2) (England) Regulations 2001

revoked: SI 2002/1860 Sch.6

NO.

2001–cont.

2407. North Middlesex Hospital National Health Service Trust (Change of Name) Order 2001
revoked: 2003 c.43 s.7

2429. Borough of Ribble Valley (Electoral Changes) Order 2001
varied: SI 2004/222 Art.2

2430. Borough of Rossendale (Electoral Changes) Order 2001
varied: SI 2004/222 Art.2

2431. Borough of South Ribble (Electoral Changes) Order 2001
varied: SI 2004/222 Art.2
Art.7, amended: SI 2002/1031 Art.2

2432. District of West Lancashire (Electoral Changes) Order 2001
varied: SI 2004/222 Art.2

2433. Borough of Wyre (Electoral Changes) Order 2001
varied: SI 2004/222 Art.2

2434. District of Uttlesford (Electoral Changes) Order 2001
varied: SI 2004/222 Art.2

2435. District of Tendring (Electoral Changes) Order 2001
varied: SI 2004/222 Art.2

2436. District of Maldon (Electoral Changes) Order 2001
varied: SI 2004/222 Art.2

2437. District of Harlow (Electoral Changes) Order 2001
varied: SI 2004/222 Art.2

2438. Borough of Colchester (Electoral Changes) Order 2001
varied: SI 2004/222 Art.2

2439. Borough of Chelmsford (Electoral Changes) Order 2001
varied: SI 2004/222 Art.2

2440. Borough of Castle Point (Electoral Changes) Order 2001
varied: SI 2004/222 Art.2

2441. Borough of Brentwood (Electoral Changes) Order 2001
varied: SI 2004/222 Art.2

2442. District of Braintree (Electoral Changes) Order 2001
varied: SI 2004/222 Art.2

2443. District of Basildon (Electoral Changes) Order 2001
varied: SI 2004/222 Art.2

2444. District of Epping Forest (Electoral Changes) Order 2001
varied: SI 2004/222 Art.2
Sch.2, amended: SI 2002/2982 Art.2

2469. Borough of Hyndburn (Electoral Changes) Order 2001
varied: SI 2004/222 Art.2

2470. City of Lancaster (Electoral Changes) Order 2001
varied: SI 2004/222 Art.2

NO.

2001–cont.

2471. Borough of Pendle (Electoral Changes) Order 2001
varied: SI 2004/222 Art.2

2472. Borough of Preston (Electoral Changes) Order 2001
varied: SI 2004/222 Art.2

2473. Borough of Burnley (Electoral Changes) Order 2001
varied: SI 2004/222 Art.2
Art.3, amended: SI 2002/2992 Art.2

2475. Borough of Fylde (Electoral Changes) Order 2001
varied: SI 2004/222 Art.2

2477. Plant Protection Products (Fees) Regulations 2001
revoked: SI 2003/660 Reg.4
Sch.1, added: SI 2002/2733 Reg.2
Sch.1, amended: SI 2002/2733 Reg.2

2480. Police and Criminal Evidence Act 1984 (Tape-recording of Interviews) (Amendment) Order 2001
revoked: SI 2003/705 Art.4

2495. Telecommunications (Licence Modifications) (Amendment) Regulations 2001
revoked: 2003 c.21 Sch.19

2501. Inspection of Education and Training (Wales) Regulations 2001
Reg.2, substituted: SI 2004/783 Reg.2
Reg.3, amended: SI 2004/783 Reg.2
Reg.4, amended: SI 2004/783 Reg.2

2505. International Criminal Court Act 2001 (Elements of Crimes) Regulations 2001
revoked (in part): SI 2004/1080 Reg.3

2506. National Lottery (Licence Fees) Order 2001
Art.3, amended: SI 2002/3124 Art.2, SI 2003/2771 Art.2

2509. Financial Services and Markets Act 2000 (Consultation with Competent Authorities) Regulations 2001
Reg.2, amended: SI 2003/2066 Reg.6, SI 2004/1862 Reg.13
Reg.3, amended: SI 2003/2066 Reg.6, SI 2004/1862 Reg.13
Reg.4, amended: SI 2003/2066 Reg.6, SI 2004/1862 Reg.13
Reg.5, amended: SI 2003/2066 Reg.6, SI 2004/1862 Reg.13
Reg.6, amended: SI 2003/2066 Reg.6
Reg.6, substituted: SI 2004/1862 Reg.13
Reg.7, added: SI 2004/1862 Reg.13

2511. Financial Services and Markets Act 2000 (EEA Passport Rights) Regulations 2001
Reg.1, amended: SI 2002/765 Reg.10, SI 2003/1473 Reg.8, SI 2003/2066 Reg.2
Reg.2, amended: SI 2002/765 Reg.10, SI 2003/2066 Reg.3, SI 2004/1862 Reg.14

NO.

2001—cont.

2511. Financial Services and Markets Act 2000 (EEA Passport Rights) Regulations 2001—*cont.*

Reg.3, amended: SI 2003/1473 Reg.8, SI 2003/2066 Reg.3, SI 2004/1862 Reg.14

Reg.4, amended: SI 2003/2066 Reg.3

Reg.5, amended: SI 2003/2066 Reg.3

Reg.10, amended: SI 2003/1473 Reg.8

Reg.11, amended: SI 2003/2066 Reg.4

Reg.12, amended: SI 2003/2066 Reg.4

2513. Police (Northern Ireland) Order 2001

Art.4, revoked: SI 2004/702 Sch.8

2537. Agricultural Subsidies (Appeals) (Wales) Regulations 2001

Reg.5, revoked (in part): SI 2003/411 Reg.2

Reg.8, amended: SI 2003/411 Reg.2

Reg.8, revoked (in part): SI 2003/411 Reg.2

Reg.11, amended: SI 2003/411 Reg.2

2541. Capital Allowances (Energy-saving Plant and Machinery) Order 2001

Art.2, amended: SI 2002/1818 Art.3, SI 2003/1744 Art.3, SI 2004/2093 Art.2

Art.3, amended: SI 2002/1818 Art.4, SI 2003/1744 Art.4, SI 2004/2093 Art.2

Art.4, amended: SI 2003/1744 Art.5

Art.5, amended: SI 2002/1818 Art.5

2550. Welsh Language Schemes (Public Bodies) Order 2001

Sch.1, amended: SI 2004/664 Art.4

2556. Education (Chief Inspector of Schools in England) Order 2001

revoked: SI 2002/252 Art.3

2557. Afghanistan (United Nations Sanctions) (Amendment) Order 2001

revoked: SI 2002/111 Art.1

2558. Afghanistan (United Nations Sanctions) (Overseas Territories) (Amendment) Order 2001

revoked: SI 2002/112 Art.1

2561. Central Council for Education and Training in Social Work (Transfer Scheme) Order 2001

Art.7, revoked: SI 2002/797 Art.4

2562. Afghanistan (United Nations Sanctions) (Channel Islands) (Amendment) Order 2001

revoked: SI 2002/258 Art.1

2564. Life Sentences (Northern Ireland) Order 2001

Art.3, see *Hinton's Application for Judicial Review, Re* [2003] N.I. 139 (QBD (NI)), Kerr, J.

Art.5, applied: SR 2003/293 Art.2

Art.6, see *Hinton's Application for Judicial Review, Re* [2003] N.I. 139 (QBD (NI)), Kerr, J.

Art.8, see *Hinton's Application for Judicial Review, Re* [2003] N.I. 139 (QBD (NI)), Kerr, J.

Art.10, applied: SR 2003/293 Art.2

NO.

2001—cont.

2564. Life Sentences (Northern Ireland) Order 2001—*cont.*

Art.11, see *King's Application for Judicial Review, Re* [2003] N.I. 43 (CA (NI)), Nicholson, L.J.

Art.11, applied: SR 2003/293 Art.2

Sch.2 para.6, amended: 2002 c.26 Sch.7 para.18

2566. Afghanistan (United Nations Sanctions) (Isle of Man) (Amendment) Order 2001

revoked: SI 2002/259 Art.1

2568. Secretaries of State for Transport, Local Government and the Regions and for Environment, Food and Rural Affairs Order 2001

Art.15, revoked: SI 2002/2626 Art.17

2579. Bermuda Constitution (Amendment) Order 2001

Art.2, revoked: SI 2003/456 Art.2

2581. Foreign Package Holidays (Tour Operators and Travel Agents) Order 2001

applied: SI 2004/2181 Sch.2

2599. Northern Ireland Assembly (Elections) Order 2001

Appendix 1 para.1., varied: 2003 c.3 s.1

Art.3, applied: 2003 c.12 s.2, SI 2003/3029

Sch.1, added: SI 2002/1964 Art.2

Sch.1, amended: SI 2003/2752 Art.2, SI 2003/2989 Art.2

Sch.1, applied: 2003 c.12 s.2, SI 2003/3029

Sch.1, substituted: SI 2002/1964 Art.2

Sch.1, varied: 2003 c.12 s.1

Sch.2, amended: SI 2002/1964 Art.3

2613. Education (Mandatory Awards) (Amendment) Regulations 2001

revoked: SI 2002/1330 Sch.6

2622. Education (Teacher Training Bursaries) (England) Regulations 2001

revoked: SI 2002/508 Reg.5

2624. District of Rochford (Electoral Changes) Order 2001

varied: SI 2004/222 Art.2

2626. Health and Safety (Fees) Regulations 2001

revoked: SI 2002/655 Reg.26

2631. Primary Care Trusts (Membership, Procedure and Administration Arrangements) Amendment (England) Regulations 2001

revoked: SI 2002/38 Reg.2

2634. Financial Services and Markets Act 2000 (Insolvency) (Definition of Insurer) Order 2001

Art.2, amended: SI 2002/1242 Art.2

NO.

2001-cont.

2636. Financial Services and Markets Act 2000 (Transitional Provisions) (Authorised Persons etc.) Order 2001
Art.67, varied: SI 2003/1181 Art.4

2646. Football (Disorder) (Duration of Powers) Order 2001
revoked: 2002 c.12 s.1

2650. Specified Risk Material (Amendment) (England) Order 2001
revoked: SI 2003/3177 Sch.6

2662. Transport of Animals (Cleansing and Disinfection) (Wales) Order 2001
referred to: SI 2002/280 Art.8, SI 2002/2304 Art.5, Art.6
revoked: SI 2003/482 Art.9
Sch.1, applied: SI 2002/2304 Sch.1 para.13

2665. Legal Officers (Annual Fees) Order 2001
revoked: SI 2002/1893 Art.3
Sch.1, amended: SI 2002/1893 Sch.1 Part TABLE, Sch.1 Part TABLEa

2666. Parochial Fees Order 2001
revoked: SI 2002/1894 Art.4

2671. Ecclesiastical Judges, Legal Officers and Others (Fees) Order 2001
revoked: SI 2002/1892 Art.2
Sch.1, referred to: SI 2002/1892 Art.1
Sch.1 Part II, referred to: SI 2002/1892 Art.1

2679. Sweeteners in Food (Amendment) (Wales) Regulations 2001
applied: SI 2004/554 Reg.3
Reg.4, revoked (in part): SI 2002/330 Reg.3

2682. Welfare of Farmed Animals (Wales) Regulations 2001
Reg.2, amended: SI 2002/1898 Reg.2
Reg.4, revoked: SI 2002/1898 Reg.2
Reg.5, substituted: SI 2002/1898 Reg.2
Reg.5A, added: SI 2002/1898 Reg.2
Reg.8A, added: SI 2003/1726 Reg.3
Reg.12, amended: SI 2002/1898 Reg.2
Sch.1 para.2, amended: SI 2002/1898 Reg.2
Sch.1 para.7, amended: SI 2002/1898 Reg.2
Sch.2 para.1, revoked: SI 2002/1898 Reg.2
Sch.2 para.2, revoked: SI 2002/1898 Reg.2
Sch.2 para.3, revoked: SI 2002/1898 Reg.2
Sch.2 para.4, revoked: SI 2002/1898 Reg.2
Sch.2 para.5, revoked: SI 2002/1898 Reg.2
Sch.2 para.6, revoked: SI 2002/1898 Reg.2
Sch.2 para.7, revoked: SI 2002/1898 Reg.2
Sch.2 para.8, revoked: SI 2002/1898 Reg.2
Sch.2 para.9, revoked: SI 2002/1898 Reg.2
Sch.2 para.10, revoked: SI 2002/1898 Reg.2
Sch.3, substituted: SI 2002/1898 Reg.2
Sch.3A para.1, added: SI 2002/1898 Sch.1
Sch.3A para.2, added: SI 2002/1898 Sch.1
Sch.3A para.3, added: SI 2002/1898 Sch.1
Sch.3A para.4, added: SI 2002/1898 Sch.1
Sch.3A para.5, added: SI 2002/1898 Sch.1
Sch.3A para.6, added: SI 2002/1898 Sch.1
Sch.3A para.7, added: SI 2002/1898 Sch.1

NO.

2001-cont.

2682. Welfare of Farmed Animals (Wales) Regulations 2001–*cont.*
Sch.3B para.1, added: SI 2002/1898 Sch.1
Sch.3B para.2, added: SI 2002/1898 Sch.1
Sch.3B para.3, added: SI 2002/1898 Sch.1
Sch.3C para.1, added: SI 2002/1898 Sch.1
Sch.3C para.2, added: SI 2002/1898 Sch.1
Sch.3C para.3, added: SI 2002/1898 Sch.1
Sch.3C para.4, added: SI 2002/1898 Sch.1
Sch.3C para.5, added: SI 2002/1898 Sch.1
Sch.3C para.6, added: SI 2002/1898 Sch.1
Sch.3C para.7, added: SI 2002/1898 Sch.1
Sch.3D para.1, added: SI 2002/1898 Sch.1
Sch.3D para.2, added: SI 2002/1898 Sch.1
Sch.3D para.3, added: SI 2002/1898 Sch.1
Sch.3D para.4, added: SI 2002/1898 Sch.1
Sch.3D para.5, added: SI 2002/1898 Sch.1
Sch.3D para.6, added: SI 2002/1898 Sch.1
Sch.3D para.7, added: SI 2002/1898 Sch.1
Sch.3D para.8, added: SI 2002/1898 Sch.1
Sch.3D para.9, added: SI 2002/1898 Sch.1
Sch.6 Part I para.1, substituted: SI 2003/1726 Reg.3
Sch.6 Part II para.2, substituted: SI 2003/1726 Reg.3
Sch.6 Part II para.3, substituted: SI 2003/1726 Reg.3
Sch.6 Part II para.4, substituted: SI 2003/1726 Reg.3
Sch.6 Part II para.5, substituted: SI 2003/1726 Reg.3
Sch.6 Part II para.6, substituted: SI 2003/1726 Reg.3
Sch.6 Part II para.7, substituted: SI 2003/1726 Reg.3
Sch.6 Part II para.8, substituted: SI 2003/1726 Reg.3
Sch.6 Part II para.9, substituted: SI 2003/1726 Reg.3
Sch.6 Part II para.10, substituted: SI 2003/1726 Reg.3
Sch.6 Part II para.11, substituted: SI 2003/1726 Reg.3
Sch.6 Part II para.12, substituted: SI 2003/1726 Reg.3
Sch.6 Part II para.13, substituted: SI 2003/1726 Reg.3
Sch.6 Part II para.14, substituted: SI 2003/1726 Reg.3
Sch.6 Part II para.15, substituted: SI 2003/1726 Reg.3
Sch.6 Part II para.16, substituted: SI 2003/1726 Reg.3
Sch.6 Part II para.17, substituted: SI 2003/1726 Reg.3
Sch.6 Part II para.18, substituted: SI 2003/1726 Reg.3
Sch.6 Part II para.19, substituted: SI 2003/1726 Reg.3
Sch.6 Part II para.20, substituted: SI 2003/1726 Reg.3

NO.

2001–cont.

2682. Welfare of Farmed Animals (Wales) Regulations 2001–cont.

Sch.6 Part II para.21, substituted: SI 2003/1726 Reg.3

Sch.6 Part II para.22, substituted: SI 2003/1726 Reg.3

Sch.6 Part II para.23, substituted: SI 2003/1726 Reg.3

Sch.6 Part II para.24, substituted: SI 2003/1726 Reg.3

Sch.6 Part II para.25, substituted: SI 2003/1726 Reg.3

Sch.6 Part II para.26, substituted: SI 2003/1726 Reg.3

Sch.6 Part III para.17, substituted: SI 2003/1726 Reg.3

Sch.6 Part III para.18, substituted: SI 2003/1726 Reg.3

Sch.6 Part III para.19, substituted: SI 2003/1726 Reg.3

Sch.6 Part III para.27, substituted: SI 2003/1726 Reg.3

Sch.6 Part III para.28, substituted: SI 2003/1726 Reg.3

Sch.6 Part III para.29, substituted: SI 2003/1726 Reg.3

Sch.6 Part IV para.20, substituted: SI 2003/1726 Reg.3

Sch.6 Part IV para.21, substituted: SI 2003/1726 Reg.3

Sch.6 Part IV para.22, substituted: SI 2003/1726 Reg.3

Sch.6 Part IV para.23, substituted: SI 2003/1726 Reg.3

Sch.6 Part IV para.24, substituted: SI 2003/1726 Reg.3

Sch.6 Part IV para.30, substituted: SI 2003/1726 Reg.3

Sch.6 Part IV para.31, substituted: SI 2003/1726 Reg.3

Sch.6 Part IV para.32, substituted: SI 2003/1726 Reg.3

Sch.6 Part IV para.33, substituted: SI 2003/1726 Reg.3

Sch.6 Part IV para.34, substituted: SI 2003/1726 Reg.3

Sch.6 Part IV para.35, substituted: SI 2003/1726 Reg.3

Sch.6 Part IV para.36, substituted: SI 2003/1726 Reg.3

Sch.6 Part IV para.37, substituted: SI 2003/1726 Reg.3

Sch.6 Part IV para.38, substituted: SI 2003/1726 Reg.3

Sch.6 Part IV para.39, substituted: SI 2003/1726 Reg.3

Sch.6 Part IV para.40, substituted: SI 2003/1726 Reg.3

Sch.6 Part IV para.41, substituted: SI 2003/1726 Reg.3

NO.

2001–cont.

2682. Welfare of Farmed Animals (Wales) Regulations 2001–cont.

Sch.6 Part IV para.42, substituted: SI 2003/1726 Reg.3

Sch.6 Part V para.25, substituted: SI 2003/1726 Reg.3

Sch.6 Part V para.26, substituted: SI 2003/1726 Reg.3

Sch.6 Part V para.27, substituted: SI 2003/1726 Reg.3

Sch.6 Part V para.28, substituted: SI 2003/1726 Reg.3

Sch.6 Part V para.29, substituted: SI 2003/1726 Reg.3

Sch.6 Part V para.43, substituted: SI 2003/1726 Reg.3

Sch.6 Part V para.44, substituted: SI 2003/1726 Reg.3

Sch.6 Part V para.45, substituted: SI 2003/1726 Reg.3

Sch.6 Part V para.46, substituted: SI 2003/1726 Reg.3

Sch.6 Part V para.47, substituted: SI 2003/1726 Reg.3

Sch.6 Part VI para.30, substituted: SI 2003/1726 Reg.3

Sch.6 Part VI para.31, substituted: SI 2003/1726 Reg.3

Sch.6 Part VI para.37, substituted: SI 2003/1726 Reg.3

Sch.6 Part VI para.39, substituted: SI 2003/1726 Reg.3

Sch.6 Part VI para.48, substituted: SI 2003/1726 Reg.3

Sch.6 Part VI para.49, substituted: SI 2003/1726 Reg.3

Sch.6 Part VI para.50, substituted: SI 2003/1726 Reg.3

Sch.6 Part VI para.51, substituted: SI 2003/1726 Reg.3

Sch.6 Part VI para.52, substituted: SI 2003/1726 Reg.3

2683. Air Quality Limit Values (Wales) Regulations 2001

revoked: SI 2002/3183 Reg.13

2720. Representation of the People (Form of Canvass) (England and Wales) Regulations 2001

revoked: SI 2002/1871 Reg.3

2734. Foot-and-Mouth Disease (Ascertainment of Value) (No.5) Order 2001

Art.2, see *R. (on the application of J&PM Dockeray (A Firm)) v Secretary of State for the Environment, Food and Rural Affairs* [2002] EWHC 420, [2002] H.R.L.R. 27 (QBD (Admin Ct)), Collins, J.

2743. Education (Grants) (Music, Ballet and Choir Schools) (England) Regulations 2001

Reg.5, amended: SI 2002/2004 Reg.2

Reg.11, amended: SI 2002/2004 Reg.3

NO.

2001–cont.

2743. Education (Grants) (Music, Ballet and Choir Schools) (England) Regulations 2001–*cont.*

Sch.1 Part II para.8, amended: SI 2002/2004 Reg.4

Sch.1 Part III para.14, amended: SI 2002/2004 Reg.4

Sch.1 Part III para.15, amended: SI 2002/2004 Reg.4

Sch.1 Part IV para.18, amended: SI 2002/2004 Reg.4

Sch.1 Part V para.20, amended: SI 2002/2004 Reg.4

Sch.2 para.1, amended: SI 2002/2004 Reg.5

Sch.2 para.3, amended: SI 2002/2004 Reg.5

Sch.2 para.5, amended: SI 2002/2004 Reg.5

2747. Teacher Training Agency (Additional Functions) (England) (No.2) Order 2001

revoked: SI 2002/507 Art.3

2748. Transport (Scotland) Act 2001 (Conditions attached to PSV Operator's Licence and Competition Test for Exercise of Bus Functions) Order 2001

applied: SI 2003/1400 Sch.4

2750. Education Maintenance Allowance (Pilot Areas) Regulations 2001

referred to: SI 2003/553 Reg.3

revoked: SI 2004/1006 Reg.2

Reg.2, amended: SI 2002/1841 Reg.3, Reg.4, SI 2003/553 Reg.4

Reg.5, amended: SI 2003/553 Reg.5

Reg.6, amended: SI 2002/1841 Reg.5, SI 2003/553 Reg.6

Reg.8, amended: SI 2003/553 Reg.7

Sch.1, substituted: SI 2003/553 Sch.1

Sch.1 Part I, substituted: SI 2003/553 Sch.1

Sch.1 Part II, substituted: SI 2003/553 Sch.1

2751. Agricultural Holdings (Units of Production) (England) Order 2001

revoked: SI 2002/1925 Art.3

2763. National Minimum Wage Regulations 1999 (Amendment) (No.2) Regulations 2001

Reg.2, revoked: SI 2002/1999 Sch.1

Reg.3, revoked: SI 2002/1999 Sch.1

Reg.4, revoked: SI 2003/1923 Sch.1

Reg.6, amended: SI 2002/1999 Sch.1

2780. Processed Animal Protein (Wales) Regulations 2001

applied: SI 2002/1416 Reg.104, Sch.9 para.7, Sch.9 para.8

Reg.2, amended: SI 2002/1416 Sch.8 para.1

Reg.3, amended: SI 2002/1416 Sch.8 para.2

Reg.3, revoked (in part): SI 2002/1416 Sch.8 para.2

Reg.4, revoked: SI 2002/1416 Sch.9 Part I

Reg.5, revoked: SI 2002/1416 Sch.9 Part I

Reg.5, varied: SI 2002/1416 Sch.9 para.1

Reg.6, revoked: SI 2002/1416 Sch.9 Part I

NO.

2001–cont.

2780. Processed Animal Protein (Wales) Regulations 2001–*cont.*

Reg.6, varied: SI 2002/1416 Sch.9 para.2

Reg.7, revoked: SI 2002/1416 Sch.9 Part I

Reg.7, varied: SI 2002/1416 Sch.9 para.3

Reg.8, revoked: SI 2002/1416 Sch.9 Part I

Reg.9, revoked: SI 2002/1416 Sch.9 Part I

Reg.10, amended: SI 2002/1416 Sch.8 para.3

Reg.11, amended: SI 2002/1416 Sch.8 para.4

Reg.12, revoked: SI 2002/1416 Sch.9 Part I

Reg.13, revoked: SI 2002/1416 Sch.9 Part I

Reg.13, varied: SI 2002/1416 Sch.9 para.4

Reg.14, revoked: SI 2002/1416 Sch.9 Part I

Reg.14, varied: SI 2002/1416 Sch.9 para.5

Reg.15, revoked: SI 2002/1416 Sch.9 Part I

Reg.15, varied: SI 2002/1416 Sch.9 para.6

Reg.16, revoked: SI 2002/1416 Sch.9 Part I

Sch.1 para.1, revoked: SI 2002/1416 Sch.9 Part I

Sch.1 para.2, revoked: SI 2002/1416 Sch.9 Part I

Sch.1 para.3, revoked: SI 2002/1416 Sch.9 Part I

Sch.1 para.4, revoked: SI 2002/1416 Sch.9 Part I

Sch.1 para.5, revoked: SI 2002/1416 Sch.9 Part I

Sch.2 para.1, revoked: SI 2002/1416 Sch.9 Part I

Sch.2 para.2, revoked: SI 2002/1416 Sch.9 Part I

Sch.2 para.3, revoked: SI 2002/1416 Sch.9 Part I

Sch.3 para.1, revoked: SI 2002/1416 Sch.9 Part I

Sch.3 para.2, revoked: SI 2002/1416 Sch.9 Part I

2781. Local Authorities (Members Allowances) (Amendment) (Wales) Regulations 2001

revoked (in part): SI 2003/895 Reg.15

2793. Road User Charging And Workplace Parking Levy (Classes Of Motor Vehicles) (England) Regulations 2001

applied: SI 2002/1040 Sch.2

2800. Education (Mandatory Awards) (Amendment) (No.2) Regulations 2001

revoked: SI 2002/1330 Sch.6

2812. Relevant Authorities (Standards Committee) Regulations 2001

Reg.7, amended: SI 2003/1483 Reg.3, SI 2004/2617 Reg.2

2817. Representation of the People (Form of Canvass) (Scotland) Regulations 2001

revoked: SI 2002/1872 Reg.3

2857. Education (Grants etc.) (Dance and Drama) (England) Regulations 2001

Reg.3, amended: SI 2002/2064 Reg.3

Reg.7, amended: SI 2002/2064 Reg.4

NO.

NO.

2001–cont.

2857. Education (Grants etc.) (Dance and Drama) (England) Regulations 2001– *cont.*

Sch.1 Part I para.1, amended: SI 2002/2064 Reg.5

Sch.1 Part I para.2, amended: SI 2002/2064 Reg.5

Sch.1 Part II para.6, amended: SI 2002/2064 Reg.5

Sch.1 Part II para.8, amended: SI 2002/2064 Reg.5

Sch.1 Part II para.10, amended: SI 2002/2064 Reg.5

Sch.2 Part 1, substituted: SI 2002/2064 Reg.6

Sch.2 Part 2, substituted: SI 2002/2064 Reg.6

2866. Local Government Pension Scheme (Her Majesty's Chief Inspector of Schools in England) (Transfers) Regulations 2001

Reg.3, amended: SI 2002/819 Reg.2

2870. Railtrack (Shortlands Junction) Order 2001

Sch.4 para.3, amended: SI 2003/2155 Sch.1 para.17

Sch.4 para.6, amended: SI 2003/2155 Sch.2

Sch.5 Part II para.1, amended: SI 2003/2155 Sch.1 para.18

Sch.5 Part II para.1, revoked (in part): SI 2003/2155 Sch.2

Sch.5 Part II para.2, amended: SI 2003/2155 Sch.1 para.18

2874. Children (Leaving Care) (England) Regulations 2001

Reg.4, amended: SI 2002/546 Reg.9

2879. Value Added Tax (Refund of Tax to Museums and Galleries) Order 2001

Sch.1, amended: SI 2004/1709 Art.3, Art.4, Art.5, Art.6

2890. National Health Service (General Medical Services) (Electronic Communications) Order 2001

revoked: SI 2004/865 Sch.2

2896. Education (Teachers Qualifications and Health Standards) (England) (Amendment No 2) Regulations 2001

revoked: SI 2003/1663 Sch.1 Part 1

2897. Education (Induction Arrangements for School Teachers) (Consolidation) (England) Regulations 2001

applied: SI 2002/509 Reg.4, SI 2003/1663 Sch.3 para.1

referred to: SI 2003/106 Reg.2, SI 2003/2148 Reg.2

Reg.3, amended: SI 2003/2148 Reg.3

Reg.6, amended: SI 2003/2148 Reg.4

Reg.8, amended: SI 2003/2148 Reg.5

Reg.10, amended: SI 2003/2148 Reg.6

Reg.11, amended: SI 2003/2148 Reg.7

Reg.16, amended: SI 2003/2148 Reg.8

2001–cont.

2897. Education (Induction Arrangements for School Teachers) (Consolidation) (England) Regulations 2001–*cont.*

Reg.17, amended: SI 2003/2148 Reg.9

Reg.18, amended: SI 2003/2148 Reg.10

Reg.18, applied: SI 2003/1663 Sch.3 para.1

Reg.20, substituted: SI 2003/2148 Reg.11

Sch.2 para.4A, added: SI 2003/2148 Reg.12

Sch.2 para.4B, added: SI 2003/2148 Reg.12

Sch.2 para.5, substituted: SI 2003/2148 Reg.12

Sch.2 para.9, amended: SI 2003/106 Reg.3

Sch.2 para.16, amended: SI 2003/2148 Reg.12

Sch.2 para.18, amended: SI 2003/2148 Reg.12

Sch.2 para.19, added: SI 2002/2063 Reg.3

2916. EC Competition Law (Articles 84 and 85) Enforcement Regulations 2001

applied: SI 2003/1400 Sch.3, Sch.4

Reg.2, amended: SI 2003/767 Art.3

Reg.4, amended: SI 2002/42 Reg.3

Reg.20, amended: SI 2002/42 Reg.4

Reg.25, amended: SI 2002/42 Reg.5

Reg.25, revoked (in part): SI 2003/1398 Sch.1 para.41

Reg.26, substituted: SI 2003/1398 Sch.1 para.41

Reg.27, amended: SI 2003/767 Art.3

Reg.29, revoked: SI 2003/1400 Sch.5

Reg.32, amended: SI 2003/1398 Sch.1 para.41

Reg.33, amended: SI 2003/1400 Sch.5

Reg.35, revoked (in part): 2002 c.40 Sch.26

Sch.1, amended: SI 2002/42 Reg.6, SI 2003/1398 Sch.1 para.41

Sch.1, revoked: SI 2003/1398 Sch.1 para.41

Sch.2 para.1, amended: SI 2003/767 Art.3

Sch.2 para.5, amended: SI 2003/767 Art.3

2917. Limited Liability Partnerships (Welsh Language Forms) Regulations 2001

Sch.1, applied: SI 2003/61 Reg.3

2944. Education (School Performance Targets) (England) (Amendment) (No.2) Regulations 2001

revoked: SI 2004/2858 Sch.2

2962. Education (School Teachers Pay and Conditions) (No.5) Order 2001

revoked: 2002 c.32 Sch.22 Part 1

2963. Local Elections (Declaration of Acceptance of Office) (Amendment) (Wales) Order 2001

revoked: SI 2004/1508 Art.4

2967. Financial Services and Markets Act 2000 (Transitional Provisions, Repeals and Savings) (Financial Services Compensation Scheme) Order 2001

Art.3, amended: SI 2004/952 Art.2

Sch.1 Part 1, amended: SI 2003/2134 Art.9

NO.

2001–cont.

2968. Financial Services and Markets Act 2000 (Treatment of Assets of Insurers on Winding Up) Regulations 2001
revoked: SI 2003/1102 Reg.51

2973. Dartford-Thurrock Crossing (Amendment) Regulations 2001
revoked: SI 2003/496 Reg.3

2975. Radiation (Emergency Preparedness and Public Information) Regulations 2001
Reg.2, amended: SI 2002/2099 Sch.4 para.3, SI 2002/2469 Sch.1 para.95, SI 2004/568 Sch.13 para.11
Reg.3, amended: SI 2002/2099 Sch.4 para.4, SI 2004/568 Sch.13 para.11
Reg.14, applied: SI 2003/547 Reg.9, Sch.8, SI 2004/456 Reg.8
Reg.18, amended: SI 2002/2099 Sch.4 para.5
Reg.19, amended: SI 2002/2099 Sch.4 para.6
Reg.22, revoked: SI 2002/2099 Sch.4 para.7
Sch.2 Part I, substituted: SI 2002/2099 Sch.4 para.8
Sch.2 Part II para.2, amended: SI 2002/2099 Sch.4 para.9
Sch.4 Part I, substituted: SI 2002/2099 Sch.4 para.10

2982. Agricultural Holdings (Units of Production) (Wales) Order 2001
revoked: SI 2003/4 Art.3

2983. Agricultural Holdings (Units of Production) (Wales) (No.2) Order 2001
revoked: SI 2003/4 Art.3

2992. Foster Placement (Children) and Adoption Agencies Amendment (England) Regulations 2001
Reg.2, revoked: SI 2002/57 Reg.51

3021. Gaming Duty (Amendment) Regulations 2001
revoked: SI 2003/2247 Reg.3

3022. Excise Duty Points (Duty Suspended Movements of Excise Goods) Regulations 2001
referred to: SI 2004/1003 Reg.7
Reg.2, varied: SI 2003/2758 Sch.1 para.4, Sch.1 para.5
Reg.2A, varied: SI 2003/2758 Sch.1 para.6
Reg.7, see *Customs and Excise Commissioners v Arena Corp Ltd (In Provisional Liquidation)* [2004] EWCA Civ 371, [2004] B.P.I.R. 415 (CA), Carnwath, L.J.; see *Customs and Excise Commissioners v Jack Baars Wholesale* [2004] EWHC 18, [2004] B.P.I.R. 543 (Ch D (Companies Ct)), Lindsay, J.

3064. Agricultural Holdings (Units of Production) (Wales)(No.3) Order 2001
revoked: SI 2003/4 Art.3

2001–cont.

3065. National Health Service (Travelling Expenses and Remission of Charges) Amendment (No.2) Regulations 2001
revoked: SI 2003/2382 Sch.2

3071. Education (Fast Track Bursaries and Grants) (England) Regulations 2001
Reg.2, amended: SI 2003/2039 Reg.5
Reg.5, amended: SI 2003/2039 Reg.5

3074. Children (Leaving Care) Social Security Benefits Regulations 2001
Reg.2, amended: SI 2004/565 Reg.12

3088. General Betting Duty Regulations 2001
Reg.3, amended: SI 2003/2631 Reg.3
Reg.7, revoked: SI 2003/2631 Reg.3
Reg.9, applied: SI 2003/2631 Reg.4
Reg.9, revoked: SI 2003/2631 Reg.3
Reg.10, amended: SI 2003/2631 Reg.3, SI 2004/768 Reg.2
Reg.10, applied: SI 2003/2631 Reg.4
Reg.10, referred to: SI 2003/2631 Reg.4
Reg.10, revoked (in part): SI 2003/2631 Reg.3
Reg.11, amended: SI 2003/2631 Reg.3, SI 2004/768 Reg.2

3142. Energy Information and Energy Efficiency (Miscellaneous Amendments) Regulations 2001
varied: SI 2004/1468 Reg.17

3203. Southampton Community Health Services National Health Service Trust (Establishment) Amendment (No.2) Order 2001
revoked: 2003 c.43 s.7

3209. Merchant Shipping (Domestic Passenger Ships) (Safety Management Code) Regulations 2001
Reg.3, amended: SI 2004/302 Sch.1 para.2

3210. Social Security (Jobcentre Plus Interviews) Regulations 2001
applied: SI 2002/1703 Reg.16
Reg.2, revoked (in part): SI 2002/1703 Sch.1
Reg.3, revoked: SI 2002/1703 Sch.1
Reg.4, revoked: SI 2002/1703 Sch.1
Reg.5, revoked: SI 2002/1703 Sch.1
Reg.6, revoked: SI 2002/1703 Sch.1
Reg.7, revoked: SI 2002/1703 Sch.1
Reg.8, revoked: SI 2002/1703 Sch.1
Reg.9, revoked: SI 2002/1703 Sch.1
Reg.10, revoked: SI 2002/1703 Sch.1
Reg.11, revoked: SI 2002/1703 Sch.1
Reg.12, revoked: SI 2002/1703 Sch.1
Reg.13, revoked: SI 2002/1703 Sch.1
Reg.14, revoked: SI 2002/1703 Sch.1
Reg.15, amended: SI 2002/1703 Sch.1, SI 2003/492 Sch.3 Part 1
Sch.1, revoked: SI 2002/1703 Sch.1
Sch.2 para.1, revoked (in part): SI 2003/492 Sch.3 Part 1
Sch.2 para.2, revoked: SI 2002/1703 Sch.1

NO.

2001–cont.

3231. Northern Ireland Act 2000 (Restoration of Devolved Government) (No.2) Order 2001
revoked: SI 2002/2574 Art.2

3243. Education (School Teachers Pay and Conditions) (No.6) Order 2001
revoked: SI 2002/2223 Art.1

3244. Accounts and Audit (Amendment) (England) Regulations 2001
revoked: SI 2003/533 Reg.3

3245. Bracknell Forest Primary Care Trust (Establishment) Order 2001
Art.1, amended: SI 2002/1405 Sch.1
Art.4, revoked: SI 2002/1405 Sch.1

3246. Windsor, Ascot and Maidenhead Primary Care Trust (Establishment) Order 2001
Art.1, amended: SI 2002/1405 Sch.1
Art.4, revoked: SI 2002/1405 Sch.1
Sch.1, amended: SI 2004/543 Sch.1

3252. Social Security (Notification of Change of Circumstances) Regulations 2001
Reg.5, amended: SI 2002/1789 Art.8, SI 2003/2800 Art.3, SI 2003/3209 Reg.3
Reg.5, revoked (in part): SI 2003/492 Sch.3 Part 1

3253. Disability Discrimination (Providers of Services) (Adjustment of Premises) Regulations 2001
Reg.1, amended: SI 2004/1429 Reg.2
Reg.1, substituted: SI 2004/1429 Reg.2
Sch.1 para.2, amended: SI 2004/1429 Reg.2

3256. Working Time (Amendment) Regulations 2001
see *Toulson v South Tyneside MBC* [2003] 1 C.M.L.R. 28 (EAT), Recorder Burke Q.C.

3258. Southern Norfolk Primary Care Trust (Establishment) Order 2001
Art.1, amended: SI 2002/1405 Sch.1
Art.4, revoked: SI 2002/1405 Sch.1
Sch.1, amended: SI 2004/543 Sch.1

3265. Electricity (Standards of Performance) Regulations 2001
Reg.3, amended: SI 2002/476 Reg.2, SI 2002/742 Reg.3
Reg.5A, added: SI 2002/742 Reg.4
Reg.9, revoked: SI 2002/476 Reg.3, SI 2002/742 Reg.5
Reg.10, revoked: SI 2002/476 Reg.3, SI 2002/742 Reg.5
Reg.11, revoked: SI 2002/476 Reg.3, SI 2002/742 Reg.5
Reg.12, revoked: SI 2002/476 Reg.3, SI 2002/742 Reg.5
Reg.13A, added: SI 2002/476 Reg.4, SI 2002/742 Reg.6
Reg.13B, added: SI 2002/476 Reg.4, SI 2002/742 Reg.6
Reg.14, amended: SI 2002/476 Reg.5, SI 2002/742 Reg.7

NO.

2001–cont.

3265. Electricity (Standards of Performance) Regulations 2001–*cont.*
Reg.16, amended: SI 2002/476 Reg.6, SI 2002/742 Reg.8
Reg.16, revoked (in part): SI 2002/476 Reg.6, SI 2002/742 Reg.8
Reg.17, amended: SI 2002/476 Reg.7, SI 2002/742 Reg.9
Reg.18, amended: SI 2002/476 Reg.8, SI 2002/742 Reg.10
Reg.19, amended: SI 2002/476 Reg.9, SI 2002/742 Reg.11
Sch.1 Part I, amended: SI 2002/476 Reg.10, SI 2002/742 Reg.12

3267. Gas (Connection Charges) Regulations 2001
Reg.3, amended: SI 2002/1488 Reg.2

3269. Electricity from Non-Fossil Fuel Sources (Scotland) Saving Arrangements Order 2001
Art.2, amended: SSI 2002/93 Art.2
Art.4A, added: SSI 2002/93 Art.2

3293. Police (Amendment) Regulations 2001
revoked: SI 2003/527 Sch.4 Part 1

3295. Chiltern and South Bucks Primary Care Trust (Establishment) Order 2001
applied: SI 2003/3059 Sch.1
Art.1, amended: SI 2002/1405 Sch.1
Art.4, revoked: SI 2002/1405 Sch.1

3296. Wycombe Primary Care Trust (Establishment) Order 2001
applied: SI 2003/3059 Sch.1
Art.1, amended: SI 2002/1405 Sch.1
Art.4, revoked: SI 2002/1405 Sch.1

3297. Rushmoor and Hart Primary Care Trust (Establishment) Order 2001
varied: SI 2002/730 Art.2, SI 2002/1115 Art.2
Art.1, amended: SI 2002/730 Art.2, SI 2002/1115 Art.2, SI 2002/1405 Sch.1
Art.2, amended: SI 2002/730 Art.2, SI 2002/1115 Art.2
Art.4, revoked: SI 2002/1405 Sch.1

3316. Energy Efficiency (Ballasts for Fluorescent Lighting) Regulations 2001
Sch.3 Part III para.12, revoked (in part): SI 2003/1398 Sch.1 para.42

3335. Building (Amendment) Regulations 2001
Reg.3, referred to: SI 2002/440 Reg.4

3347. Local Authorities (Goods and Services) (Public Bodies) (England) (No.4) Order 2001
Art.3, amended: SI 2003/2155 Sch.1 para.25

3352. Railway Administration Order Rules 2001
Part 2 r.2.8, amended: SI 2002/1555 Art.46

NO.

2001–cont.

3353. Gas (Applications for Licences and Extensions and Restrictions of Licences) Regulations 2001
revoked: SI 2004/2542 Reg.2
Reg.8, substituted: SI 2003/847 Reg.2
Sch.1, added: SI 2003/847 Reg.3
Sch.2 para.1, revoked: SI 2003/847 Reg.4
Sch.2 para.2, revoked: SI 2003/847 Reg.4
Sch.2 para.3, revoked: SI 2003/847 Reg.4
Sch.2 para.4, revoked: SI 2003/847 Reg.4
Sch.2 para.5, revoked: SI 2003/847 Reg.4
Sch.2 para.6, revoked: SI 2003/847 Reg.4
Sch.2 para.7, revoked: SI 2003/847 Reg.4
Sch.2 para.8, revoked: SI 2003/847 Reg.4
Sch.2 para.9, revoked: SI 2003/847 Reg.4
Sch.3 Part I, revoked: SI 2003/847 Reg.5
Sch.3 Part I para.3, added: SI 2003/847 Reg.5
Sch.3 Part I para.3, revoked: SI 2003/847 Reg.5
Sch.3 Part I para.6, amended: SI 2003/847 Reg.5
Sch.3 Part I para.6, revoked (in part): SI 2003/847 Reg.5
Sch.3 Part II para.2, revoked: SI 2003/847 Reg.5
Sch.3 Part II para.3, revoked: SI 2003/847 Reg.5
Sch.3 Part II para.4, revoked: SI 2003/847 Reg.5
Sch.3 Part II para.5, revoked: SI 2003/847 Reg.5
Sch.3 Part III para.2, added: SI 2003/847 Reg.5
Sch.3 Part III para.2, revoked: SI 2003/847 Reg.5
Sch.3 Part III para.3, revoked: SI 2003/847 Reg.5
Sch.3 Part III para.4, revoked: SI 2003/847 Reg.5
Sch.3 Part III para.5, revoked: SI 2003/847 Reg.5
Sch.3 Part III para.6, amended: SI 2003/847 Reg.5
Sch.3 Part III para.6, revoked (in part): SI 2003/847 Reg.5
Sch.4, substituted: SI 2003/847 Reg.6

3354. Electricity (Applications for Licences and Extensions and Restrictions of Licences) Regulations 2001
revoked: SI 2004/2541 Reg.2
Reg.8, substituted: SI 2003/848 Reg.2
Sch.1, added: SI 2003/848 Reg.3
Sch.2 para.1, revoked: SI 2003/848 Reg.4
Sch.2 para.2, revoked: SI 2003/848 Reg.4
Sch.2 para.3, revoked: SI 2003/848 Reg.4
Sch.2 para.4, revoked: SI 2003/848 Reg.4
Sch.2 para.5, revoked: SI 2003/848 Reg.4
Sch.2 para.6, revoked: SI 2003/848 Reg.4
Sch.2 para.7, revoked: SI 2003/848 Reg.4
Sch.2 para.8, revoked: SI 2003/848 Reg.4

NO.

2001–cont.

3354. Electricity (Applications for Licences and Extensions and Restrictions of Licences) Regulations 2001–*cont.*
Sch.3 Part I para.2, revoked: SI 2003/848 Reg.5
Sch.3 Part II para.2, revoked: SI 2003/848 Reg.5
Sch.3 Part II para.3, revoked: SI 2003/848 Reg.5
Sch.3 Part II para.4, revoked: SI 2003/848 Reg.5
Sch.3 Part II para.5, revoked: SI 2003/848 Reg.5
Sch.3 Part II para.6, revoked: SI 2003/848 Reg.5
Sch.3 Part III para.3, added: SI 2003/848 Reg.5
Sch.3 Part III para.3, revoked: SI 2003/848 Reg.5
Sch.3 Part III para.4, revoked: SI 2003/848 Reg.5
Sch.3 Part III para.5, revoked: SI 2003/848 Reg.5
Sch.3 Part III para.6, revoked: SI 2003/848 Reg.5
Sch.3 Part III para.7, revoked: SI 2003/848 Reg.5
Sch.3 Part III para.8, revoked: SI 2003/848 Reg.5
Sch.3 Part III para.9, revoked (in part): SI 2003/848 Reg.5
Sch.3 Part IV, revoked: SI 2003/848 Reg.5
Sch.3 Part IV para.2, revoked: SI 2003/848 Reg.5
Sch.3 Part IV para.2, added: SI 2003/848 Reg.5
Sch.3 Part IV para.3, revoked: SI 2003/848 Reg.5
Sch.3 Part IV para.3, added: SI 2003/848 Reg.5
Sch.3 Part IV para.6, revoked (in part): SI 2003/848 Reg.5
Sch.4, substituted: SI 2003/848 Reg.6

3357. Borough of Darlington (Electoral Changes) Order 2001
varied: SI 2004/222 Art.2

3358. District of East Riding (Electoral Changes) Order 2001
varied: SI 2004/222 Art.2
Sch.1, amended: SI 2002/1033 Art.2

3359. Borough of North Lincolnshire (Electoral Changes) Order 2001
varied: SI 2004/222 Art.2

3360. City of Kingston upon Hull (Electoral Changes) Order 2001
varied: SI 2004/222 Art.2

3361. Borough of North East Lincolnshire (Electoral Changes) Order 2001
varied: SI 2004/222 Art.2

2001-cont.

3362. City of York (Electoral Changes) Order 2001
varied: SI 2004/222 Art.2

3363. Terrorism (United Nations Measures) (Channel Islands) Order 2001
Art.1, amended: 2002 c.8 s.2
Art.2, amended: SI 2002/258 Art.1
Art.6, amended: SI 2002/258 Art.1
Art.12, amended: SI 2002/258 Art.1

3364. Terrorism (United Nations Measures) (Isle of Man) Order 2001
Art.1, amended: 2002 c.8 s.2
Art.2, amended: SI 2002/259 Art.1, SI 2002/1555 Art.47

3365. Terrorism (United Nations Measures) Order 2001
Art.1, amended: 2002 c.8 s.2
Art.2, amended: SI 2002/111 Art.1, SI 2003/1297 Reg.2, SI 2003/2209 Reg.2, SI 2003/2430 Reg.3, SI 2004/2309 Reg.3
Art.4, amended: SI 2003/1297 Reg.3

3366. Terrorism (United Nations Measures) (Overseas Territories) Order 2001
Art.1, amended: 2002 c.8 s.2
Art.2, amended: SI 2002/112 Art.1

3386. National Health Service (General Medical Services) Amendment (No.3) Regulations 2001
revoked: SI 2004/865 Sch.2

3435. Education (School Teachers Pay and Conditions) (No.7) Order 2001
revoked: SI 2002/2223 Art.1

3442. Colours in Food (Amendment) (England) Regulations 2001
referred to: SI 2003/1008 Reg.3

3443. Children (Protection from Offenders) (Amendment) (Wales) Regulations 2001
Reg.2, revoked (in part): SI 2003/237 Reg.53

3446. Education (School Performance Information) (England) Regulations 2001
referred to: SI 2004/2141 Reg.3
Reg.2, amended: SI 2002/2017 Reg.3, SI 2003/537 Reg.4, SI 2003/2135 Reg.3
Reg.7A, added: SI 2002/2017 Reg.4
Reg.10, amended: SI 2002/2017 Reg.5
Reg.14, amended: SI 2002/2017 Reg.6
Reg.16, amended: SI 2002/2017 Reg.7
Reg.16, revoked (in part): SI 2002/2017 Reg.7, SI 2003/2135 Reg.4
Sch.1 para.1, amended: SI 2003/2135 Reg.5
Sch.1 para.1, varied: SI 2004/1076 Reg.7
Sch.2 para.2, amended: SI 2003/2135 Reg.6, SI 2004/2141 Reg.4
Sch.2A para.1, added: SI 2002/2017 Sch.1
Sch.2A para.2, added: SI 2002/2017 Sch.1
Sch.3 Part I para.2, amended: SI 2002/2017 Reg.9, SI 2004/2141 Reg.5
Sch.3 Part I para.3, substituted: SI 2004/2141 Reg.5

2001-cont.

3446. Education (School Performance Information) (England) Regulations 2001-*cont.*
Sch.3 Part I para.4, amended: SI 2004/2141 Reg.5
Sch.3 Part I para.4, revoked (in part): SI 2004/2141 Reg.5
Sch.3 Part I para.5, substituted: SI 2004/2141 Reg.5
Sch.3 Part II para.6, amended: SI 2002/2017 Reg.9
Sch.3 Part II para.7, amended: SI 2003/2135 Reg.7
Sch.3 Part II para.8, revoked: SI 2002/2017 Reg.9
Sch.3 Part II para.10, amended: SI 2003/2135 Reg.7
Sch.5 para.1, amended: SI 2002/2017 Reg.10
Sch.5 para.2, amended: SI 2002/2017 Reg.10
Sch.5 para.3, amended: SI 2002/2017 Reg.10
Sch.5 para.4, amended: SI 2002/2017 Reg.10
Sch.5 para.5, amended: SI 2002/2017 Reg.10
Sch.5 para.5, substituted: SI 2003/2135 Reg.8
Sch.5 para.5A, added: SI 2003/2135 Reg.8
Sch.5 para.5A, amended: SI 2002/2017 Reg.10
Sch.5 para.6, amended: SI 2002/2017 Reg.10
Sch.5 para.7, amended: SI 2002/2017 Reg.10
Sch.5 para.8, amended: SI 2002/2017 Reg.10
Sch.5 para.9, amended: SI 2002/2017 Reg.10
Sch.5 para.10, amended: SI 2002/2017 Reg.10
Sch.5 para.10, substituted: SI 2003/2135 Reg.8
Sch.5 para.11, added: SI 2002/2017 Reg.10
Sch.5 para.11, amended: SI 2002/2017 Reg.10
Sch.5 para.11, substituted: SI 2003/2135 Reg.8
Sch.5 para.11A, added: SI 2002/2017 Reg.10, SI 2003/2135 Reg.8
Sch.5 para.11A, amended: SI 2002/2017 Reg.10
Sch.5 para.12, added: SI 2002/2017 Reg.10
Sch.5 para.12, amended: SI 2002/2017 Reg.10
Sch.6 para.5, substituted: SI 2003/2135 Reg.9
Sch.6 para.5A, added: SI 2003/2135 Reg.9
Sch.7 Part II para.2, amended: SI 2002/2017 Reg.11
Sch.8, amended: SI 2002/2017 Sch.2
Sch.8, revoked: SI 2003/2135 Reg.4

NO.

3446. Education (School Performance Information) (England) Regulations 2001–*cont.*

Sch.9, referred to: SI 2002/3179 Reg.9

Sch.9 para.4, substituted: SI 2002/2017 Reg.13

Sch.9 para.6, amended: SI 2002/3178 Reg.8

Sch.10, referred to: SI 2002/3179 Reg.9

3455. Education (Special Educational Needs) (England) (Consolidation) Regulations 2001

see *E v X LBC* [2002] EWHC 915, [2002] E.L.R. 453 (QBD (Admin Ct)), Stanley Burnton, J.

Reg.2, amended: SI 2002/2469 Sch.1 para.96, Sch.7, Sch.8

Reg.6, amended: SI 2002/2469 Sch.7

Reg.7, amended: SI 2002/2469 Sch.7

Reg.9, amended: SI 2002/2469 Sch.7, SI 2002/3135 Sch.1 para.49

Reg.12, amended: SI 2002/2469 Sch.7

Reg.18, amended: SI 2002/2469 Sch.7, SI 2003/537 Reg.3

Sch.2, amended: SI 2002/2469 Sch.7

3458. Race Relations Act 1976 (Statutory Duties) Order 2001

Art.4, applied: SI 2002/377 Sch.1 para.27, SI 2002/3199 Sch.1 para.21, SI 2003/3118 Sch.1 para.19, SI 2003/3170 Sch.1 para.21

Sch.1, amended: SI 2002/2469 Sch.1 para.97, SI 2003/3006 Art.5, SI 2004/664 Sch.1 para.6

Sch.3, amended: SI 2003/3006 Art.5

3462. Public Record Office (Fees) (No.2) Regulations 2001

revoked: SI 2003/871 Reg.3

3463. Burnley, Pendle and Rossendale Primary Care Trust (Establishment) Order 2001

Art.1, amended: SI 2002/1405 Sch.1

Art.4, revoked: SI 2002/1405 Sch.1

Sch.1, amended: SI 2004/543 Sch.1

3464. Fylde Primary Care Trust (Establishment) Order 2001

Art.1, amended: SI 2002/1405 Sch.1

Art.4, revoked: SI 2002/1405 Sch.1

3482. City of Derby (Electoral Changes) Order 2001

varied: SI 2004/222 Art.2

3487. Wyre Primary Care Trust (Establishment) Order 2001

Art.1, amended: SI 2002/1405 Sch.1

Art.4, revoked: SI 2002/1405 Sch.1

Sch.1, amended: SI 2004/543 Sch.1

3488. Ashton, Leigh and Wigan Primary Care Trust (Establishment) Order 2001

Art.1, amended: SI 2002/1405 Sch.1

Art.4, revoked: SI 2002/1405 Sch.1

Sch.1, amended: SI 2004/543 Sch.1

NO.

3489. Hyndburn and Ribble Valley Primary Care Trust (Establishment) Order 2001

Art.1, amended: SI 2002/1405 Sch.1

Art.4, revoked: SI 2002/1405 Sch.1

Sch.1, amended: SI 2004/543 Sch.1

3490. Central Liverpool Primary Care Trust (Establishment) Order 2001

applied: SI 2003/3059 Sch.1

Art.1, amended: SI 2002/1405 Sch.1

Art.4, revoked: SI 2002/1405 Sch.1

3491. Preston Primary Care Trust (Establishment) Order 2001

Art.1, amended: SI 2002/1405 Sch.1

Art.4, revoked: SI 2002/1405 Sch.1

3492. South Liverpool Primary Care Trust (Establishment) Order 2001

Art.1, amended: SI 2002/1405 Sch.1

Art.4, revoked: SI 2002/1405 Sch.1

3493. North Liverpool Primary Care Trust (Establishment) Order 2001

Art.1, amended: SI 2002/1405 Sch.1

Art.4, revoked: SI 2002/1405 Sch.1

3495. European Communities (Designation) (No.3) Order 2001

Sch.3, amended: SI 2003/2901 Sch.4

3510. Seeds (National Lists of Varieties) Regulations 2001

Reg.2, amended: SI 2004/2949 Reg.2

Reg.3, amended: SI 2004/2949 Reg.2

Reg.4, applied: SI 2002/3171 Reg.18, SI 2002/3172 Reg.20, SI 2002/3173 Reg.20, SI 2002/3174 Reg.19, SI 2002/3175 Reg.19, SI 2004/2881 Reg.19, SSI 2004/317 Reg.8

Reg.5, amended: SI 2004/2949 Reg.2

Reg.6, amended: SI 2004/2949 Reg.2

Reg.9, amended: SI 2004/2949 Reg.2

Reg.12, amended: SI 2004/2949 Reg.2

Reg.14, amended: SI 2004/2949 Reg.2

Reg.15, amended: SI 2004/2949 Reg.2

Reg.25, revoked (in part): SSI 2004/317 Sch.8

Sch.1 Part I, referred to: SSI 2004/317 Reg.6

Sch.1 Part I para.1, amended: SI 2004/2949 Reg.2

Sch.1 Part II para.2, amended: SI 2004/2949 Reg.2

3523. Passenger Car (Fuel Consumption and CO2 Emissions Information) Regulations 2001

Reg.4, amended: SI 2004/1661 Reg.3

Reg.8, amended: SI 2004/1661 Reg.4

Sch.3 para.1, substituted: SI 2004/1661 Reg.5

Sch.3 para.2, substituted: SI 2004/1661 Reg.5

3540. Local Government Elections (Wales) Order 2001

varied: SI 2004/222 Art.2

2001–cont.

3544. Financial Services and Markets Act 2000 (Regulated Activities) (Amendment) Order 2001
Art.1, amended: SI 2002/1777 Art.5

3546. Specified Risk Material (Amendment) (Wales) (No.2) Regulations 2001
Reg.3, revoked: SI 2004/1430 Sch.6

3555. Borough of Swale (Electoral Changes) Order 2001
varied: SI 2004/222 Art.2

3556. District of Thanet (Electoral Changes) Order 2001
varied: SI 2004/222 Art.2

3557. District of Sevenoaks (Electoral Changes) Order 2001
varied: SI 2004/222 Art.2

3558. District of Shepway (Electoral Changes) Order 2001
varied: SI 2004/222 Art.2

3559. Borough of Tunbridge Wells (Electoral Changes) Order 2001
varied: SI 2004/222 Art.2

3560. Borough of Dartford (Electoral Changes) Order 2001
varied: SI 2004/222 Art.2

3563. Borough of Ashford (Electoral Changes) Order 2001
varied: SI 2004/222 Art.2

3564. City of Canterbury (Electoral Changes) Order 2001
varied: SI 2004/222 Art.2

3574. Potatoes Originating in Egypt (Amendment) (England) Regulations 2001
revoked: SI 2004/1165 Reg.8

3575. Local Authorities (Model Code of Conduct) (England) Order 2001
see *R. (on the application of Richardson) v North Yorkshire CC* [2003] EWCA Civ 1860, [2004] 1 W.L.R. 1920 (CA), Simon Brown, L.J.; see *R. (on the application of Richardson) v North Yorkshire CC* [2003] EWHC 764, [2004] Env. L.R. 13 (QBD (Admin Ct)), Richards, J.
Art.4, amended: SI 2002/1719 Art.2
Art.4, revoked (in part): SI 2002/1044 Art.4
Sch.1 para.12, see *R. (on the application of Richardson) v North Yorkshire CC* [2003] EWCA Civ 1860, [2004] 1 W.L.R. 1920 (CA), Simon Brown, L.J.

3576. Parish Councils (Model Code of Conduct) Order 2001
Art.3, amended: SI 2002/1719 Art.3

3577. National Park and Broads Authorities (Model Code of Conduct) (England) Order 2001
Art.3, amended: SI 2002/1719 Art.4

3578. Police Authorities (Model Code of Conduct) Order 2001
Art.3, amended: SI 2002/1719 Art.5

2001–cont.

3586. Borough of Maidstone (Electoral Changes) Order 2001
varied: SI 2004/222 Art.2

3587. Borough of Gravesham (Electoral Changes) Order 2001
varied: SI 2004/222 Art.2

3588. District of Dover (Electoral Changes) Order 2001
varied: SI 2004/222 Art.2

3606. Goods Vehicles (Authorisation of International Journeys) (Fees) Regulations 2001
Reg.3, amended: SI 2004/1883 Reg.2

3609. Leeds West Primary Care Trust (Establishment) Order 2001
Art.1, amended: SI 2002/1405 Sch.1
Art.4, revoked: SI 2002/1405 Sch.1

3610. Leeds North East Primary Care Trust (Establishment) Order 2001
Art.1, amended: SI 2002/1405 Sch.1
Art.4, revoked: SI 2002/1405 Sch.1

3615. Tonbridge and Malling (Electoral Changes) Order 2001
varied: SI 2004/222 Art.2

3620. East Leeds Primary Care Trust (Establishment) Order 2001
Art.1, amended: SI 2002/1405 Sch.1
Art.4, revoked: SI 2002/1405 Sch.1

3621. Homerton Hospital National Health Service Trust (Change of Name) Order 2001
revoked: 2003 c.43 s.7

3622. South Leeds Primary Care Trust (Establishment) Order 2001
applied: SI 2003/3059 Sch.1
Art.1, amended: SI 2002/1405 Sch.1
Art.4, revoked: SI 2002/1405 Sch.1

3627. South Hampshire Rapid Transit Order 2001
Art.2, amended: SI 2003/2155 Sch.2
Sch.11 para.1, amended: SI 2003/2155 Sch.1 para.17, Sch.2
Sch.11 para.3, amended: SI 2003/2155 Sch.1 para.18, Sch.2

3629. Financial Services and Markets Act 2000 (Consequential Amendments) (Taxes) Order 2001
Art.107, revoked: 2003 c.1 Sch.8 Part 2

3635. Insurers (Winding Up) Rules 2001
referred to: SI 2003/1102 Reg.52
r.5, substituted: SI 2003/1102 Reg.53
r.11, amended: SI 2003/1102 Reg.54
r.20, amended: SI 2003/1102 Reg.55
r.22, amended: SI 2003/1102 Reg.56
r.24, amended: SI 2003/1102 Reg.57, SI 2004/353 Reg.51
r.26, amended: SI 2003/1102 Reg.58

3641. Money Laundering Regulations 2001
applied: SI 2003/3297 Reg.9
revoked: SI 2003/3075 Reg.1

NO.

2001-cont.

3644. Human Rights Act 1998 (Designated Derogation) Order 2001
see *A v Secretary of State for the Home Department* [2002] EWCA Civ 1502, [2004] Q.B. 335 (CA), Lord Woolf of Barnes, L.C.J.; see *A v Secretary of State for the Home Department* [2002] H.R.L.R. 45 (Sp Imm App Comm), Collins, J. (Chairman)

3645. Financial Services and Markets Act 2000 (Misleading Statements and Practices) Order 2001
Art.1, amended: SI 2002/1777 Art.6
Art.2, amended: SI 2003/1474 Art.2, SI 2003/1476 Art.17
Art.3, amended: SI 2003/1474 Art.2, SI 2003/1476 Art.17

3647. Financial Services and Markets Act 2000 (Consequential Amendments and Savings) (Industrial Assurance) Order 2001
applied: SI 2002/1555 Art.2
Sch.1 Part III para.31, amended: SI 2002/1555 Art.48
Sch.1 Part III para.34, substituted: SI 2002/1555 Art.48
Sch.1 Part III para.36A, added: SI 2002/1555 Art.48

3649. Financial Services and Markets Act 2000 (Consequential Amendments and Repeals) Order 2001
Art.152, referred to: SR 2002/109 Sch.1
Art.285, revoked: SI 2003/1400 Sch.5
Art.518, revoked: SI 2004/2044 Art.4

3650. Financial Services and Markets Act 2000 (Miscellaneous Provisions) Order 2001
Art.1, amended: SI 2002/1777 Art.7

3659. High Peak and Dales Primary Care Trust (Establishment) Order 2001
Art.1, amended: SI 2002/1405 Sch.1
Art.4, revoked: SI 2002/1405 Sch.1

3660. Leeds North West Primary Care Trust (Establishment) Order 2001
Art.1, amended: SI 2002/1405 Sch.1
Art.4, revoked: SI 2002/1405 Sch.1

3661. Blackpool Primary Care Trust (Establishment) Order 2001
Art.1, amended: SI 2002/1405 Sch.1
Art.4, revoked: SI 2002/1405 Sch.1

3662. Bolton Primary Care Trust (Establishment) Order 2001
Art.1, amended: SI 2002/1405 Sch.1
Art.4, revoked: SI 2002/1405 Sch.1

3669. Oil and Fibre Plant Seeds (Amendment) (Wales) Regulations 2001
revoked: SI 2004/2881 Reg.32

3682. London Underground (East London Line Extension) (No.2) Order 2001
Art.28, amended: SI 2003/1615 Sch.1 para.57

NO.

2001-cont.

3682. London Underground (East London Line Extension) (No.2) Order 2001– *cont.*
Sch.9 para.1, amended: SI 2003/2155 Sch.1 para.17, Sch.2

3709. Farm Waste Grant (Nitrate Vulnerable Zones) (Wales) Scheme 2001
revoked: SI 2004/1606 Art.7

3721. Income Support (General) (Standard Interest Rate Amendment) (No.3) Regulations 2001
revoked: SI 2002/105 Reg.3

3733. Pennine Care National Health Service Trust (Establishment) and the Tameside and Glossop Community and Priority Services National Health Service Trust (Dissolution) Order 2001
revoked: 2003 c.43 s.7

3737. Education (Teachers Qualifications and Health Standards) (England) (Amendment) (No.3) Regulations 2001
revoked: SI 2003/1662 Sch.1 Part 1

3738. Health and Social Care Act 2001 (Commencement No 6) (England) Order 2001
Sch.2, referred to: SI 2002/2469 Reg.16

3740. National Health Service (General Medical Services Supplementary List) Regulations 2001
applied: SI 2003/2644 Reg.11
revoked: SI 2004/585 Sch.2
varied: SI 2002/2469 Sch.12 para.3, SI 2004/585 Sch.1 para.9
Reg.2, amended: SI 2002/1920 Reg.9, SI 2002/2469 Sch.5, Sch.7, SI 2003/2644 Reg.23
Reg.2, revoked (in part): SI 2002/1920 Reg.9
Reg.3, amended: SI 2002/2469 Sch.7, SI 2003/2644 Reg.24
Reg.4, amended: SI 2002/2469 Sch.7, SI 2002/3135 Sch.1 para.50, SI 2003/1250 Sch.10 para.7, SI 2003/2644 Reg.25
Reg.5, amended: SI 2002/2469 Sch.7
Reg.5, substituted: SI 2003/2644 Reg.26
Reg.6, amended: SI 2002/848 Reg.2, SI 2002/2469 Sch.7, SI 2002/3135 Sch.1 para.50, SI 2003/1250 Sch.10 para.7, SI 2003/2644 Reg.27
Reg.7, amended: SI 2002/2469 Sch.7, SI 2003/2644 Reg.28
Reg.8, amended: SI 2002/2469 Sch.7, SI 2003/2644 Reg.29
Reg.9, amended: SI 2002/2469 Sch.7, SI 2003/2644 Reg.30
Reg.10, amended: SI 2002/2469 Sch.7, SI 2002/3135 Sch.1 para.50, SI 2003/2644 Reg.31
Reg.10, applied: SI 2003/2644 Reg.4, SI 2004/585 Reg.23

NO.

2001–cont.

3740. National Health Service (General Medical Services Supplementary List) Regulations 2001–*cont.*

Reg.11, amended: SI 2002/2469 Sch.7, SI 2003/2644 Reg.32

Reg.12, amended: SI 2002/2469 Sch.7

Reg.13, amended: SI 2002/2469 Sch.7, SI 2003/2644 Reg.33

Reg.14, amended: SI 2002/2469 Sch.7, SI 2003/2644 Reg.34

Reg.15, amended: SI 2002/2469 Sch.7

Reg.16, amended: SI 2002/2469 Sch.7, SI 2003/2644 Reg.35

Reg.17, amended: SI 2002/2469 Sch.7, SI 2003/2644 Reg.36

Reg.18, amended: SI 2002/2469 Sch.7

Reg.19, amended: SI 2002/2469 Sch.7

Reg.21, added: SI 2003/2644 Reg.37

3742. National Health Service (General Medical Services) Amendment (No.4) Regulations 2001

revoked: SI 2004/865 Sch.2

3743. Family Health Services Appeal Authority (Primary Care Act) Regulations 2001

applied: SI 2002/2469 Sch.12 para.31, Sch.12 para.32

revoked: SI 2004/865 Sch.2

Reg.2, amended: SI 2002/2469 Sch.7

Reg.4, amended: SI 2002/2469 Sch.7

Reg.7, amended: SI 2002/2469 Sch.7

Reg.8, amended: SI 2002/2469 Sch.7

Reg.10, amended: SI 2002/2469 Sch.7

Reg.13, amended: SI 2002/2469 Sch.7

Reg.13, applied: SI 2002/2469 Sch.12 para.33

Reg.14, amended: SI 2002/2469 Sch.7

Reg.16, amended: SI 2002/2469 Sch.7

Reg.17, amended: SI 2002/2469 Sch.7

3744. Abolition of the NHS Tribunal (Consequential Provisions) Regulations 2001

Reg.2, amended: SI 2002/2469 Sch.1 para.98

Reg.3, amended: SI 2002/2469 Sch.1 para.98

Reg.4, applied: SI 2002/2469 Sch.12 para.39, Sch.12 para.40

Reg.5, applied: SI 2002/2469 Sch.12 para.41

Reg.6, amended: SI 2002/2469 Sch.1 para.98, Sch.7

Reg.6, applied: SI 2002/2469 Sch.12 para.42, Sch.12 para.43, Sch.12 para.44, SI 2002/3038 Reg.5, SI 2002/3040 Reg.3, SI 2003/506 Reg.3, SI 2003/2123 Reg.4, SI 2003/2773 Reg.3, SI 2003/3060 Reg.3, SI 2003/3279 Reg.4, SI 2004/570 Reg.3, SI 2004/668 Reg.3

3745. Smoke Control Areas (Authorised Fuels) (England) Regulations 2001

Sch.1 para.3, amended: SI 2002/3046 Reg.2

NO.

2001–cont.

3745. Smoke Control Areas (Authorised Fuels) (England) Regulations 2001–*cont.*

Sch.1 para.11A, added: SI 2002/3046 Reg.2

Sch.1 para.11B, added: SI 2002/3046 Reg.2

Sch.1 para.15, amended: SI 2002/3046 Reg.2

Sch.1 para.28, amended: SI 2002/3046 Reg.2

Sch.1 para.29, amended: SI 2002/3046 Reg.2

Sch.1 para.31, amended: SI 2002/3046 Reg.2

3746. Variation of Stamp Duties Regulations 2001

referred to: 2002 c.23 s.110

revoked: SI 2003/1056 Reg.8

3747. Stamp Duty (Disadvantaged Areas) Regulations 2001

amended: 2003 c.14 Sch.20 para.3

3748. Finance Act 2001, Section 92(8), (Specified Day) Order 2001

amended: 2003 c.14 Sch.20 para.3

3750. Family Health Services Appeal Authority (Procedure) Rules 2001

applied: SI 2002/1095 Art.4, SI 2002/2469 Sch.12 para.53

referred to: SI 2002/2469 Sch.12 para.54, Sch.12 para.61, Sch.12 para.73, Sch.12 para.76

Part I r.1, amended: SI 2002/1921 r.2

Part I r.2, amended: SI 2002/1921 r.2, SI 2002/2469 Sch.1 para.99, Sch.5, SI 2004/865 Sch.1 para.27, SI 2004/1016 Sch.1 para.25

Part I r.2, revoked (in part): SI 2004/1016 Sch.1 para.25

Part II r.5, amended: SI 2002/2469 Sch.5

Part II r.5, referred to: SI 2002/2469 Sch.12 para.51, SI 2004/585 Sch.1 para.14, SI 2004/1020 Sch.1 para.14

Part II r.6, amended: SI 2002/2469 Sch.5

Part II r.6, applied: SI 2002/2469 Sch.12 para.52, SI 2004/585 Sch.1 para.15, SI 2004/1020 Sch.1 para.15

Part II r.8, applied: SI 2002/2469 Sch.12 para.57

Part II r.12, amended: SI 2002/2469 Sch.5

Part II r.13, amended: SI 2002/2469 Sch.5

Part II r.13, applied: SI 2002/2469 Sch.12 para.56, Sch.12 para.57

Part II r.14, amended: SI 2002/2469 Sch.5

Part III, applied: SI 2002/2469 Sch.12 para.60, SI 2004/585 Sch.1 para.16, SI 2004/1020 Sch.1 para.16

Part III r.15, amended: SI 2002/2469 Sch.5, SI 2004/865 Sch.1 para.27, SI 2004/1016 Sch.1 para.25

Part III r.19, applied: SI 2002/2469 Sch.12 para.65

Part III r.25, applied: SI 2002/2469 Sch.12 para.64

NO.

2001–cont.

3750. Family Health Services Appeal Authority (Procedure) Rules 2001– *cont.*

Part III r.26, applied: SI 2002/2469 Sch.12 para.65

Part IV r.29, amended: SI 2002/2469 Sch.5

Part IV r.32, applied: SI 2002/2469 Sch.12 para.69, SI 2004/585 Sch.1 para.17, SI 2004/1020 Sch.1 para.17

Part IV r.33, applied: SI 2002/2469 Sch.12 para.69, SI 2004/585 Sch.1 para.17, SI 2004/1020 Sch.1 para.17

Part IV r.36, amended: SI 2002/2469 Sch.5

Part IV r.37, applied: SI 2002/2469 Sch.12 para.69, SI 2004/585 Sch.1 para.17, SI 2004/1020 Sch.1 para.17

Part IV r.38, amended: SI 2002/2469 Sch.5

Part IV r.41, amended: SI 2002/2469 Sch.5

Part IV r.42, amended: SI 2002/2469 Sch.5

Part IV r.42, applied: SI 2002/2469 Sch.12 para.70, SI 2004/585 Sch.1 para.18, SI 2004/1020 Sch.1 para.18

Part IV r.43, applied: SI 2002/2469 Sch.12 para.70, Sch.12 para.71, SI 2004/585 Sch.1 para.18, SI 2004/1020 Sch.1 para.18

Part IV r.44, applied: SI 2002/2469 Sch.12 para.69, Sch.12 para.75, SI 2004/585 Sch.1 para.17, SI 2004/1020 Sch.1 para.17

Part IV r.45, applied: SI 2002/2469 Sch.12 para.69, SI 2004/585 Sch.1 para.17, SI 2004/1020 Sch.1 para.17

Part V r.46, amended: SI 2002/2469 Sch.5, SI 2004/865 Sch.1 para.27, SI 2004/1016 Sch.1 para.25

Part V r.46, applied: SI 2002/2469 Sch.12 para.77, SI 2004/585 Sch.1 para.19, SI 2004/1020 Sch.1 para.19

3751. Medicines (Products for Animal Use-Fees)(Amendment No 2) Regulations 2001

revoked: SI 2004/2750 Reg.18

3755. Uncertificated Securities Regulations 2001

applied: SI 2004/1611 Reg.11, Reg.15, Reg.25

referred to: SI 2003/1633 Reg.2

Reg.3, amended: SI 2003/1633 Reg.3, Reg.4, SI 2004/1662 Sch.1 para.29, SI 2004/2044 Art.6

Reg.3, revoked (in part): SI 2004/2044 Art.6

Reg.19, amended: SI 2003/1633 Reg.5

Reg.21, amended: SI 2003/1633 Reg.6, Reg.8, SI 2004/1662 Sch.1 para.29, SI 2004/2044 Art.6

Reg.21, applied: SI 2004/1611 Reg.4

Reg.21, revoked (in part): SI 2004/2044 Art.6

Reg.22, amended: SI 2003/1633 Reg.6, Reg.9

Reg.24, amended: SI 2003/1633 Reg.6, Reg.10

Reg.27, amended: SI 2003/1633 Reg.11

NO.

2001–cont.

3755. Uncertificated Securities Regulations 2001–*cont.*

Reg.38, amended: SI 2004/1662 Sch.1 para.29

Reg.48, amended: SI 2004/1662 Sch.1 para.29

Sch.1 para.12, amended: SI 2003/1633 Reg.12

Sch.1 para.25, amended: SI 2003/1633 Reg.12

Sch.2, added: SI 2003/1398 Sch.1 para.43

Sch.2 para.3, amended: SI 2003/1398 Sch.1 para.43, SI 2003/3180 Sch.1 para.9

Sch.2 para.4, amended: SI 2003/1398 Sch.1 para.43

Sch.2 para.4, revoked (in part): SI 2003/1398 Sch.1 para.43

Sch.2 para.5, revoked: SI 2003/1398 Sch.1 para.43

Sch.4, amended: SI 2003/1633 Reg.6

Sch.4 para.12, amended: SI 2003/1633 Reg.6, Reg.7, Reg.8, SI 2004/1662 Sch.1 para.29

Sch.4 para.13, amended: SI 2003/1633 Reg.6, Reg.7, SI 2004/1662 Sch.1 para.29

Sch.4 para.16, amended: SI 2003/1633 Reg.13

Sch.4 para.19, amended: SI 2003/1633 Reg.8, SI 2004/1662 Sch.1 para.29

Sch.4 para.19, revoked (in part): SI 2004/2044 Art.6

3762. Smoke Control Areas (Authorised Fuels) (Wales) Regulations 2001

Sch.1 para.3, amended: SI 2002/3160 Reg.2

Sch.1 para.5, amended: SI 2002/3160 Reg.2

Sch.1 para.10A, added: SI 2002/3160 Reg.2

Sch.1 para.10B, added: SI 2002/3160 Reg.2

Sch.1 para.14, amended: SI 2002/3160 Reg.2

Sch.1 para.27, amended: SI 2002/3160 Reg.2

Sch.1 para.28, amended: SI 2002/3160 Reg.2

Sch.1 para.30, amended: SI 2002/3160 Reg.2

3767. Social Security Amendment (Residential Care and Nursing Homes) Regulations 2001

Sch.1 Part I para.12, amended: SI 2002/398 Reg.4

Sch.1 Part I para.14, amended: SI 2002/398 Reg.4

Sch.1 Part I para.17, amended: SI 2002/398 Reg.4

Sch.1 Part II para.15, amended: SI 2002/398 Reg.4

Sch.1 Part II para.16, amended: SI 2002/398 Reg.4

Sch.1 Part II para.18, amended: SI 2002/398 Reg.4

Sch.1 Part II para.20, amended: SI 2002/398 Reg.4

2001–cont.

3775. Miscellaneous Food Additives (Amendment) (England) (No.2) Regulations 2001
referred to: SI 2003/1008 Reg.3
Reg.9, amended: SI 2003/1563 Reg.10, SI 2003/1596 Reg.10, SI 2003/1659 Reg.11
Reg.9, revoked (in part): SI 2003/1008 Reg.3

3787. Primary Care Trusts (Membership, Procedure and Administration Arrangements) Amendment (No.2) (England) Regulations 2001
Reg.1, amended: SI 2002/557 Reg.6

3788. Care Trusts (Applications and Consultation) Regulations 2001
Reg.3, amended: SI 2002/2469 Sch.3
Reg.6, amended: SI 2002/2469 Sch.3

3798. Health Service Medicines (Information on the Prices of Specified Generic Medicines) Regulations 2001
Reg.2, amended: SI 2002/236 Reg.19, SI 2002/2861 Reg.36

3799. Enterprise Management Incentives (Gross Asset Requirement) Order 2001
revoked: 2003 c.1 Sch.8 Part 2

3811. South Wales Sea Fisheries Committee (Levies) Regulations 2001
revoked: SI 2003/3072 Reg.5

3814. Plant Protection Products (Amendment) (No.3) Regulations 2001
revoked: SI 2002/526 Reg.4

3815. Education Development Plans (England) Regulations 2001
Reg.2, amended: SI 2002/423 Reg.2
Reg.5, varied: SI 2002/423 Reg.4
Reg.11, varied: SI 2002/423 Reg.5
Reg.13, varied: SI 2002/423 Reg.6
Reg.15, varied: SI 2002/423 Reg.5
Reg.16, varied: SI 2002/423 Reg.5
Reg.18, varied: SI 2002/423 Reg.7

3821. Staffordshire Moorlands Primary Care Trust (Establishment) Order 2001
Art.1, amended: SI 2002/1405 Sch.1
Art.4, revoked: SI 2002/1405 Sch.1

3823. Dudley South Primary Care Trust (Establishment) Order 2001
Art.1, amended: SI 2002/1405 Sch.1
Art.4, revoked: SI 2002/1405 Sch.1

3825. Dudley Beacon and Castle Primary Care Trust (Establishment) Order 2001
Art.1, amended: SI 2002/1405 Sch.1
Art.4, revoked: SI 2002/1405 Sch.1

3829. Newcastle-under-Lyme Primary Care Trust (Establishment) Order 2001
Art.1, amended: SI 2002/1405 Sch.1
Art.4, revoked: SI 2002/1405 Sch.1
Sch.1, amended: SI 2004/543 Sch.1

2001–cont.

3835. Ealing Primary Care Trust (Establishment) Order 2001
Art.1, amended: SI 2002/1405 Sch.1
Art.4, revoked: SI 2002/1405 Sch.1

3850. Hounslow Primary Care Trust (Establishment) Order 2001
Art.1, amended: SI 2002/1405 Sch.1
Art.4, revoked: SI 2002/1405 Sch.1

3851. Hammersmith and Fulham Primary Care Trust (Establishment) Order 2001
Art.1, amended: SI 2002/1405 Sch.1
Art.4, revoked: SI 2002/1405 Sch.1

3852. Care Standards Act 2000 (Commencement No 9 (England) and Transitional and Savings Provisions) Order 2001
applied: SI 2002/3210 Art.4
varied: SI 2004/664 Art.11, Art.12, Art.13, Art.14
Art.2, applied: SI 2002/57 Reg.50
Art.3, amended: SI 2002/1790 Art.2, SI 2002/2001 Art.2, SI 2002/3210 Art.2
Sch.1 para.1, amended: SI 2002/3210 Art.2
Sch.1 para.2, amended: SI 2002/1790 Art.2, SI 2002/2001 Art.2, SI 2002/3210 Art.2
Sch.1 para.3, applied: SI 2002/3210 Art.4
Sch.1 para.3, revoked (in part): SI 2002/2001 Art.2
Sch.1 para.5, amended: SI 2002/2001 Art.2
Sch.1 para.5, varied: SI 2002/2001 Art.3
Sch.1 para.6, amended: SI 2002/1493 Art.5, SI 2002/1790 Art.2
Sch.1 para.6, revoked: SI 2002/2001 Art.2
Sch.1 para.10, amended: SI 2002/1493 Art.5, SI 2002/1790 Art.2, SI 2002/2001 Art.2, SI 2002/3210 Art.2
Sch.1 para.10, revoked (in part): SI 2002/2001 Art.2
Sch.1 para.13, amended: SI 2002/1790 Art.2, SI 2002/2001 Art.2, SI 2002/3210 Art.2
Sch.1 para.14, amended: SI 2002/1790 Art.2, SI 2002/2001 Art.2, SI 2002/3210 Art.2
Sch.1 para.15, amended: SI 2002/1493 Art.5, SI 2002/1790 Art.2, SI 2002/2001 Art.2, SI 2002/3210 Art.2
Sch.1 para.15, applied: SI 2002/57 Reg.50

3853. Fur Farming (Compensation Scheme) (England) Order 2001
applied: SI 2002/221 Art.13
revoked: SI 2002/221 Art.14

3872. Veterinary Surgeons and Veterinary Practitioners (Registration) (Amendment) Regulations Order of Council 2001
revoked: SI 2003/219 Art.3
Sch.1, amended: SI 2003/219 Sch.1

3880. District of Forest of Dean (Electoral Changes) Order 2001
varied: SI 2004/222 Art.2
Art.1, amended: SI 2002/1035 Art.2

NO.

2001–cont.

3881. Borough of Tewkesbury (Electoral Changes) Order 2001
varied: SI 2004/222 Art.2

3882. Borough of Cheltenham (Electoral Changes) Order 2001
varied: SI 2004/222 Art.2
Art.3, revoked: SI 2002/1962 Art.6
Sch.2, revoked: SI 2002/1962 Art.6

3883. District of Stroud (Parishes and Electoral Changes) Order 2001
varied: SI 2004/222 Art.2

3884. City of Gloucester (Electoral Changes) Order 2001
varied: SI 2004/222 Art.2

3885. District of Cotswold (Electoral Changes) Order 2001
varied: SI 2004/222 Art.2

3886. Severn Bridges Tolls Order 2001
revoked: SI 2002/3004 Art.3

3887. Statistics of Trade (Customs and Excise) (Amendment) Regulations 2001
revoked: SI 2002/2498 Reg.4

3888. Criminal Justice and Police Act 2001 (Consequential Amendments) (Police Ranks) Regulations 2001
Reg.3, revoked: SI 2003/527 Sch.4 Part 1
Reg.5, revoked: SI 2004/645 Reg.2
Reg.6, revoked: SI 2004/645 Reg.2

3889. District of Waveney (Electoral Changes) Order 2001
varied: SI 2004/222 Art.2
Art.6, amended: SI 2002/2983 Art.2

3890. Borough of Ipswich (Electoral Changes) Order 2001
varied: SI 2004/222 Art.2

3891. District of Mid Suffolk (Electoral Changes) Order 2001
varied: SI 2004/222 Art.2

3892. District of Suffolk Coastal (Electoral Changes) Order 2001
varied: SI 2004/222 Art.2

3893. District of Forest Heath (Electoral Changes) Order 2001
varied: SI 2004/222 Art.2

3894. District of Babergh (Electoral Changes) Order 2001
varied: SI 2004/222 Art.2
Sch.1, amended: SI 2002/1036 Art.2

3895. Borough of St Edmundsbury (Electoral Changes) Order 2001
varied: SI 2004/222 Art.2

3898. Plant Protection Products (Payments) Regulations 2001
Reg.3, revoked: SI 2003/660 Reg.4

3909. Colours in Food (Amendment)(-Wales) Regulations 2001
applied: SI 2004/554 Reg.3

3917. Scotland Act 1998 (Agency Arrangements) (Specification) Order 2001
revoked: SI 2002/800 Art.3

NO.

2001–cont.

3919. European Communities (Designation) (No.4) Order 2001
Art.2, amended: SI 2002/248 Art.5

3921. Organisation for the Prohibition of Chemical Weapons (Immunities and Privileges) Order 2001
Art.13, amended: 2002 c.8 s.2
Art.14, amended: 2002 c.8 s.2

3923. Child Abduction and Custody (Parties to Conventions) (Amendment) Order 2001
revoked: SI 2003/1518 Art.2

3925. Double Taxation Relief (Taxes on Income) (Lithuania) Order 2001
Sch.1, applied: SI 2002/2847 Sch.1
Sch.1, substituted: SI 2002/2847 Sch.1

3926. Dentists Act 1984 (Amendment) Order 2001
Part II, applied: SI 2002/1625 Art.4
Part II, referred to: SI 2002/2463 Sch.1 para.6
Art.8, applied: 2002 c.17 s.31
Art.10, applied: 2002 c.17 s.31
Art.10, revoked (in part): 2002 c.17 s.31

3929. Civil Jurisdiction and Judgments Order 2001
Sch.2 Part II para.4, see *McGowan v Summit at Lloyds* 2002 S.C. 638 (Ex Div), Lord Reed, Lady Cosgrove, Lord Marnoch

3937. Regulatory Reform (Special Occasions Licensing) Order 2001
Art.3, amended: SI 2002/3205 Art.2
Art.4, amended: SI 2002/1062 Art.2, SI 2002/3205 Art.2
Art.5, amended: SI 2002/1062 Art.2
Art.6, amended: SI 2002/1062 Art.2
Art.6, revoked (in part): SI 2002/1062 Art.2
Art.8, amended: SI 2002/1062 Art.2, SI 2002/3205 Art.2
Sch.1 para.1, added: SI 2002/1062 Art.2
Sch.1 para.2, added: SI 2002/1062 Art.2
Sch.1 para.3, added: SI 2002/1062 Art.2
Sch.1 para.4, added: SI 2002/1062 Art.2

3952. Rail Vehicle Accessibility (Croydon Tramlink Class CR4000 Vehicles) Exemption Order 2001
Art.9, amended: SI 2002/3001 Art.2

3955. Rail Vehicle Accessibility (C2C Class 357/0 Vehicles) Exemption Order 2001
Art.5, amended: SI 2002/3002 Art.2

3959. Northern Ireland (Date of Next Assembly Poll) Order 2001
revoked: 2003 c.3 s.1

3964. Medicines (Pharmacies) (Applications for Registration and Fees) Amendment Regulations 2001
revoked: SI 2002/3024 Reg.3

3965. Care Homes Regulations 2001
applied: SI 2004/2071 Reg.41, Sch.10 para.3, Sch.10 para.4
referred to: SI 2004/2071 Sch.6 para.1

NO.

2001–cont.

3965. Care Homes Regulations 2001–*cont.*
varied: SI 2004/664 Art.11, Art.12, Art.13, Art.14

Reg.2, amended: SI 2003/1590 Sch.1 para.14, SI 2004/664 Art.3, SI 2004/865 Sch.1 para.28, SI 2004/1770 Reg.2

Reg.3, amended: SI 2003/1845 Reg.2, SI 2004/696 Sch.1 para.40, SI 2004/2071 Sch.6 para.2

Reg.3, referred to: SI 2004/692 Sch.4 para.5

Reg.5, amended: SI 2003/1703 Reg.2

Reg.5A, added: SI 2003/1703 Reg.2

Reg.7, amended: SI 2002/865 Reg.2

Reg.7, revoked (in part): SI 2002/865 Reg.2

Reg.9, amended: SI 2002/865 Reg.2

Reg.9, revoked (in part): SI 2002/865 Reg.2

Reg.18, amended: SI 2004/1770 Reg.2

Reg.19, amended: SI 2002/865 Reg.2, SI 2003/534 Reg.2, SI 2004/1770 Reg.2

Reg.19, revoked (in part): SI 2002/865 Reg.2, SI 2003/534 Reg.2

Reg.23, amended: SI 2002/865 Reg.3

Reg.33, substituted: SI 2004/1770 Reg.2

Reg.36, amended: SI 2003/1703 Reg.2

Reg.43, amended: SI 2002/865 Reg.3, SI 2003/1703 Reg.2

Reg.45, amended: SI 2003/1845 Reg.3

Reg.45, revoked: SI 2004/2071 Sch.6 para.3

Reg.46, amended: SI 2003/1845 Reg.4

Reg.46, revoked (in part): SI 2003/1845 Reg.4, SI 2004/2071 Sch.6 para.3

Reg.47, added: SI 2003/1845 Reg.5

Reg.47, revoked: SI 2004/2071 Sch.6 para.3

Sch.2, amended: SI 2002/865 Reg.2

Sch.2, revoked: SI 2002/865 Reg.2

Sch.2, substituted: SI 2004/1770 Sch.1

Sch.2 para.1, substituted: SI 2004/1770 Sch.1

Sch.2 para.2, substituted: SI 2004/1770 Sch.1

Sch.2 para.3, substituted: SI 2004/1770 Sch.1

Sch.2 para.4, substituted: SI 2004/1770 Sch.1

Sch.2 para.5, substituted: SI 2004/1770 Sch.1

Sch.2 para.6, substituted: SI 2004/1770 Sch.1

Sch.2 para.7, substituted: SI 2004/1770 Sch.1

Sch.2 para.8, substituted: SI 2004/1770 Sch.1

Sch.2 para.9, substituted: SI 2004/1770 Sch.1

Sch.4, amended: SI 2002/865 Reg.3, SI 2004/1770 Reg.2

Sch.6, revoked: SI 2004/1770 Reg.2

3966. Environmental Impact Assessment (Uncultivated Land and Semi-natural Areas) (England) Regulations 2001
Reg.12, applied: SI 2002/2127 Reg.12

NO.

2001–cont.

3967. Children's Homes Regulations 2001
varied: SI 2004/664 Art.11, Art.12, Art.13, Art.14

Reg.2, amended: SI 2002/2469 Sch.8, SI 2004/664 Art.3, SI 2004/865 Sch.1 para.29, SI 2004/1016 Sch.1 para.27

Reg.4, varied: SI 2004/664 Art.11, Art.12, Art.13, Art.14

Reg.6, amended: SI 2002/865 Reg.4

Reg.6, revoked (in part): SI 2002/865 Reg.4

Reg.8, amended: SI 2002/865 Reg.4

Reg.8, revoked (in part): SI 2002/865 Reg.4

Reg.17, amended: SI 2002/865 Reg.5

Reg.21, amended: SI 2004/865 Sch.1 para.29, SI 2004/1016 Sch.1 para.27

Reg.21, revoked (in part): SI 2004/865 Sch.1 para.29, SI 2004/1016 Sch.1 para.27

Reg.26, amended: SI 2002/865 Reg.4

Reg.26, revoked (in part): SI 2002/865 Reg.4

Reg.41, amended: SI 2002/865 Reg.5

Sch.2, amended: SI 2002/865 Reg.4

Sch.2, revoked: SI 2002/865 Reg.4

Sch.5, amended: SI 2002/2469 Sch.7

3968. Private and Voluntary Health Care (England) Regulations 2001
varied: SI 2004/664 Art.11, Art.12, Art.13, Art.14

Reg.2, amended: SI 2004/664 Sch.1 para.4, SI 2004/865 Sch.1 para.30, SI 2004/1771 Sch.1 para.25

Reg.3, amended: SI 2004/865 Sch.1 para.30

Reg.4, amended: SI 2004/865 Sch.1 para.30

Reg.10, amended: SI 2002/865 Reg.10

Reg.10, revoked (in part): SI 2002/865 Reg.10

Reg.12, amended: SI 2002/865 Reg.10

Reg.12, revoked (in part): SI 2002/865 Reg.10

Reg.19, amended: SI 2002/865 Reg.10

Reg.19, revoked (in part): SI 2002/865 Reg.10

Reg.24, amended: SI 2004/1031 Sch.10 para.15

Reg.51, amended: SI 2002/865 Reg.11

Sch.2, amended: SI 2002/865 Reg.10

3969. National Care Standards Commission (Registration) Regulations 2001
applied: SI 2004/2071 Reg.42

referred to: SI 2004/2071 Sch.7 para.1

varied: SI 2004/664 Art.11, Art.12, Art.13, Art.14

Reg.1, varied: SI 2004/664 Art.11, Art.12, Art.13, Art.14

Reg.2, amended: SI 2002/2469 Sch.8, SI 2003/369 Reg.2, SI 2004/664 Sch.1 para.5, SI 2004/1771 Sch.1 para.26, SI 2004/2071 Sch.7 para.2

Reg.3, amended: SI 2002/865 Reg.8, SI 2003/1845 Reg.6

Reg.3, revoked (in part): SI 2002/865 Reg.8

NO.

2001–cont.

3969. National Care Standards Commission (Registration) Regulations 2001– *cont.*

Reg.8, amended: SI 2002/865 Reg.9, SI 2003/369 Reg.2, SI 2004/2071 Sch.7 para.3

Reg.9, amended: SI 2003/369 Reg.2, SI 2004/2071 Sch.7 para.4

Reg.11, amended: SI 2002/865 Reg.9

Reg.11, revoked (in part): SI 2002/865 Reg.9

Reg.15, amended: SI 2002/2469 Sch.7

Sch.1 Part I para.1, revoked (in part): SI 2002/865 Reg.9

Sch.1 Part I para.2, amended: SI 2002/865 Reg.9

Sch.1 Part I para.4, amended: SI 2003/1845 Reg.6, SI 2004/2071 Sch.7 para.5

Sch.1 Part III para.17, amended: SI 2002/865 Reg.9

Sch.2 para.4, amended: SI 2002/865 Reg.8

Sch.2 para.8, amended: SI 2004/696 Art.3

Sch.2 para.10, amended: SI 2002/865 Reg.8, SI 2003/369 Reg.2, SI 2003/2323 Reg.4

Sch.2 para.10, revoked (in part): SI 2003/2323 Reg.4

Sch.3 Part I para.8, revoked: SI 2002/865 Reg.8

Sch.3 Part II para.3, substituted: SI 2002/865 Reg.8

Sch.3 Part II para.11, revoked: SI 2002/865 Reg.8

Sch.3 Part II para.12, amended: SI 2002/865 Reg.8

Sch.3 Part II para.13, amended: SI 2002/865 Reg.8

Sch.7 Part II para.6, amended: SI 2004/2071 Sch.7 para.6

Sch.7 Part II para.9, amended: SI 2004/2071 Sch.7 para.6

Sch.7 Part II para.10, added: SI 2003/369 Reg.2

3980. National Care Standards Commission (Fees and Frequency of Inspections) Regulations 2001

revoked: SI 2003/753 Reg.7

Reg.1, varied: SI 2004/664 Art.11, Art.12, Art.13, Art.14

Reg.2, amended: SI 2002/1505 Reg.2, SI 2002/2070 Reg.2, SI 2002/3211 Reg.2

Reg.3, amended: SI 2002/1505 Reg.2, SI 2002/2070 Reg.2, SI 2002/3211 Reg.2

Reg.5, amended: SI 2002/1505 Reg.2, SI 2002/2070 Reg.2, SI 2002/3211 Reg.2

Reg.6, amended: SI 2002/1505 Reg.2, SI 2002/2070 Reg.2, SI 2002/3211 Reg.2

3981. Goods Vehicles (Enforcement Powers) Regulations 2001

Reg.15, applied: SI 2003/336 Sch.1 Part 2

Reg.17, applied: SI 2003/336 Sch.1 Part 2

Reg.18, applied: SI 2003/336 Sch.1 Part 2

NO.

2001–cont.

3993. General Teaching Council for England (Deduction of Fees) Regulations 2001

Reg.3, amended: SI 2003/2039 Reg.6

Reg.6, amended: SI 2003/2039 Reg.6

Reg.6, substituted: SI 2003/985 Reg.3

Sch.1 para.7, added: SI 2003/985 Reg.4

3994. Education Standards Fund (England) (Amendment) Regulations 2001

revoked: SI 2002/510 Sch.2

3998. Misuse of Drugs Regulations 2001

Reg.2, amended: SI 2003/2429 Reg.2, SI 2004/1771 Sch.1 para.24

Reg.6, amended: SI 2003/2429 Reg.2, SI 2004/1771 Sch.1 para.24

Reg.6A, added: SI 2003/1653 Reg.2

Reg.7, amended: SI 2003/2429 Reg.2

Reg.8, amended: SI 2003/2429 Reg.2

Reg.9, amended: SI 2003/2429 Reg.2

Reg.10, amended: SI 2003/2429 Reg.2

Reg.11, amended: SI 2004/1771 Sch.1 para.24

Reg.14, applied: SI 2004/627 Sch.5 para.38

Reg.15, applied: SI 2004/627 Sch.5 para.38

Reg.16, applied: SI 2004/627 Sch.5 para.38

Reg.17, applied: SI 2004/627 Sch.5 para.38

Reg.18, amended: SI 2004/1031 Sch.10 para.16

Reg.18, applied: SI 2004/627 Sch.5 para.38

Reg.19, applied: SI 2004/627 Sch.5 para.38

Reg.20, applied: SI 2004/627 Sch.5 para.38

Reg.21, applied: SI 2004/627 Sch.5 para.38

Reg.23, applied: SI 2004/627 Sch.5 para.38

Reg.26, applied: SI 2004/627 Sch.5 para.38

Reg.27, applied: SI 2004/627 Sch.5 para.38

Sch.2, referred to: SI 2004/291 Sch.6 para.39, SI 2004/478 Sch.6 para.39, SI 2004/627 Sch.5 para.38

Sch.2 para.1, amended: SI 2003/1432 Reg.2

Sch.3, referred to: SI 2004/478 Sch.6 para.39

Sch.4, referred to: SI 2004/291 Sch.6 para.39, Sch.6 para.42, SI 2004/478 Sch.6 para.39, Sch.6 para.42, SI 2004/627 Sch.5 para.38, Sch.5 para.41, SSI 2004/115 Sch.5 para.39, SSI 2004/116 Sch.1 para.11

Sch.4 Part I para.1, amended: SI 2003/1432 Reg.2

Sch.4 Part II para.1, amended: SI 2003/1432 Reg.2

Sch.5, applied: SI 2004/478 Sch.6 para.39

Sch.5, referred to: SI 2004/291 Sch.6 para.39, Sch.6 para.42, SI 2004/478 Sch.6 para.39, Sch.6 para.42, SI 2004/627 Sch.5 para.38, Sch.5 para.41, SSI 2003/64 Sch.1 para.9, SSI 2004/115 Sch.5 para.39, SSI 2004/116 Sch.1 para.11

Sch.8 para.1, added: SI 2003/2429 Sch.1

Sch.8 para.1, revoked (in part): SI 2004/1771 Sch.1 para.24

4001. Countryside Access (Draft Maps) (Wales) Regulations 2001

Reg.3, applied: SI 2002/1796 Reg.3

NO.

2001–cont.

4001. Countryside Access (Draft Maps) (Wales) Regulations 2001–*cont.*
Reg.7, applied: SI 2002/1796 Reg.3
Sch.1, amended: SI 2002/1796 Reg.12

4003. Environmental Protection (Restriction on Use of Lead Shot) (Wales) Regulations 2001
revoked: SI 2002/1730 Reg.6

4008. Relocation Grants (Forms of Application) (Amendment No 2) (Wales) Regulations 2001
revoked: SI 2002/1860 Sch.6

4011. Electricity and Gas (Energy Efficiency Obligations) Order 2001
Art.6, amended: SI 2003/1180 Art.2
Art.10, amended: SI 2003/1180 Art.2
Art.12, amended: SI 2003/1180 Art.2
Sch.2 para.2, amended: SI 2003/1180 Art.2
Sch.2 para.3, added: SI 2003/1180 Art.2

4013. Magistrates Courts (Detention and Forfeiture of Terrorist Cash) (No.2) Rules 2001
r.4, amended: SI 2003/1236 r.80
r.4, revoked (in part): SI 2003/1236 r.80
r.5, amended: SI 2003/1236 r.81
r.5, revoked (in part): SI 2003/1236 r.81
r.6, amended: SI 2003/1236 r.82
r.7, amended: SI 2003/1236 r.83
Sch.1, amended: SI 2003/1236 r.84

4014. Immigration and Asylum Appeals (Procedure) (Amendment) Rules 2001
revoked: 2002 c.41 Sch.9

4020. Education (Information About Individual Pupils) (England) Regulations 2001
referred to: SI 2002/3112 Reg.2
Reg.2, amended: SI 2002/3112 Reg.3
Reg.4, amended: SI 2002/3112 Reg.4
Sch.1 Part I, substituted: SI 2002/3112 Sch.1
Sch.1 Part I para.1, substituted: SI 2002/3112 Sch.1
Sch.1 Part I para.2, substituted: SI 2002/3112 Sch.1
Sch.1 Part I para.3, substituted: SI 2002/3112 Sch.1
Sch.1 Part I para.4, substituted: SI 2002/3112 Sch.1
Sch.1 Part I para.5, substituted: SI 2002/3112 Sch.1
Sch.1 Part I para.6, amended: SI 2003/689 Reg.3
Sch.1 Part I para.6, substituted: SI 2002/3112 Sch.1
Sch.1 Part I para.7, amended: SI 2003/3277 Reg.4
Sch.1 Part I para.7, substituted: SI 2002/3112 Sch.1
Sch.1 Part I para.8, substituted: SI 2002/3112 Sch.1

NO.

2001–cont.

4020. Education (Information About Individual Pupils) (England) Regulations 2001–*cont.*
Sch.1 Part I para.9, substituted: SI 2002/3112 Sch.1
Sch.1 Part I para.10, substituted: SI 2002/3112 Sch.1
Sch.1 Part I para.11, substituted: SI 2002/3112 Sch.1
Sch.1 Part I para.12, substituted: SI 2002/3112 Sch.1
Sch.1 Part I para.13, substituted: SI 2002/3112 Sch.1
Sch.1 Part I para.14, substituted: SI 2002/3112 Sch.1
Sch.1 Part I para.15, substituted: SI 2002/3112 Sch.1
Sch.1 Part II, substituted: SI 2002/3112 Sch.1
Sch.1 Part II para.1, substituted: SI 2002/3112 Sch.1
Sch.1 Part II para.2, substituted: SI 2002/3112 Sch.1
Sch.1 Part II para.3, substituted: SI 2002/3112 Sch.1
Sch.1 Part II para.4, substituted: SI 2002/3112 Sch.1

4022. Social Security (Loss of Benefit) Regulations 2001
Reg.2, amended: SI 2002/486 Reg.2, SI 2002/1792 Reg.25
Reg.3A, added: SI 2002/1792 Reg.25

4027. Aggregates Levy (Registration and Miscellaneous Provisions) Regulations 2001
referred to: SI 2003/465 Reg.2
Reg.3, revoked (in part): SI 2002/1929 Reg.3
Reg.3, substituted: SI 2003/465 Reg.3

4030. Road Traffic (NHS Charges) Amendment Regulations 2001
revoked: SI 2002/237 Reg.4

4040. Insurers (Winding Up) (Scotland) Rules 2001
referred to: SI 2003/1102 Reg.52
r.5, substituted: SI 2003/1102 Reg.53
r.11, amended: SI 2003/1102 Reg.54
r.19, amended: SI 2003/1102 Reg.55
r.21, amended: SI 2003/1102 Reg.56
r.23, amended: SI 2003/1102 Reg.57, SI 2004/353 Reg.51
r.24, amended: SI 2003/1102 Reg.58

4043. National Health Service (Travelling Expenses and Remission of Charges) Amendment (No.3) Regulations 2001
revoked: SI 2003/2382 Sch.2

4046. Import and Export Restrictions (Foot-And-Mouth Disease) (No.14) Regulations 2001
revoked: SI 2002/2 Reg.29

NO.

2001—cont.

4047. Import and Export Restrictions (Foot-and-Mouth Disease) (Wales) (No.14) Regulations 2001
revoked: SI 2002/8 Reg.29

4049. Welfare Reform and Pensions Act 1999 (Commencement No 12) Order 2001
Art.2, revoked (in part): SI 2002/153 Art.3

4050. Transport Act 2000 (Consequential Amendments) Order 2001
Sch.1 Part II para.7, revoked: 2004 c.22 Sch.1

4052. District of Lewes (Electoral Changes) Order 2001
varied: SI 2004/222 Art.2

4053. District of Wealden (Electoral Changes) Order 2001
varied: SI 2004/222 Art.2

4054. District of Rother (Electoral Changes) Order 2001
varied: SI 2004/222 Art.2

4055. City of Brighton and Hove (Electoral Changes) Order 2001
varied: SI 2004/222 Art.2

4056. Borough of Hastings (Electoral Changes) Order 2001
varied: SI 2004/222 Art.2
Art.3, revoked: SI 2002/1962 Art.6
Sch.2, revoked: SI 2002/1962 Art.6

4057. Borough of Eastbourne (Electoral Changes) Order 2001
varied: SI 2004/222 Art.2

4062. Borough of Milton Keynes (Electoral Changes) Order 2001
varied: SI 2004/222 Art.2
Art.1, amended: SI 2002/1034 Art.2

4063. City of Oxford (Electoral Changes) Order 2001
varied: SI 2004/222 Art.2
Art.3, revoked: SI 2002/1962 Art.6
Sch.2, revoked: SI 2002/1962 Art.6

4064. District of Vale of White Horse (Electoral Changes) Order 2001
varied: SI 2004/222 Art.2

4065. District of Cherwell (Electoral Changes) Order 2001
varied: SI 2004/222 Art.2

4066. Borough of Bedford (Electoral Changes) Order 2001
varied: SI 2004/222 Art.2

4067. District of Mid Bedfordshire (Electoral Changes) Order 2001
varied: SI 2004/222 Art.2

4068. District of South Bedfordshire (Electoral Changes) Order 2001
varied: SI 2004/222 Art.2

NO.

2001—cont.

4118. Lancashire Care National Health Service Trust (Establishment) and the Guild Community Healthcare National Health Service Trust and the North Sefton and the West Lancashire Community National Health Service Trust (Dissolution) Order 2001
applied: SI 2003/3059 Sch.1
revoked: 2003 c.43 s.7

4119. Gloucestershire Hospitals and the Gloucestershire Partnership National Health Service Trusts (Establishment) and the East Gloucestershire National Health Service Trust, the Gloucestershire Royal National Health Service Trust and the Severn Nation 2001
revoked: 2003 c.43 s.7

4120. 5 Boroughs Partnership National Health Service Trust (Establishment) and the Warrington Community Health Care National Health Service Trust (Dissolution) Order 2001
revoked: 2003 c.43 s.7
Art.3, amended: SI 2004/2893 Art.2
Art.4, amended: SI 2004/2893 Art.3

4122. Castle Point and Rochford Primary Care Trust (Establishment) Order 2001
Art.1, amended: SI 2002/1405 Sch.1
Art.4, revoked: SI 2002/1405 Sch.1

4125. Ipswich Primary Care Trust (Establishment) Order 2001
Art.1, amended: SI 2002/1405 Sch.1
Art.4, revoked: SI 2002/1405 Sch.1
Sch.1, amended: SI 2004/543 Sch.1

4126. Central Suffolk Primary Care Trust (Establishment) Order 2001
Art.1, amended: SI 2002/1405 Sch.1
Art.4, revoked: SI 2002/1405 Sch.1
Sch.1, amended: SI 2004/543 Sch.1

4127. Suffolk West Primary Care Trust (Establishment) Order 2001
Art.1, amended: SI 2002/1405 Sch.1
Art.4, revoked: SI 2002/1405 Sch.1

4128. Cambridge City Primary Care Trust (Establishment) Order 2001
Art.1, amended: SI 2002/1405 Sch.1
Art.4, revoked: SI 2002/1405 Sch.1

4129. Broadland Primary Care Trust (Establishment) Order 2001
Art.1, amended: SI 2002/1405 Sch.1
Art.4, revoked: SI 2002/1405 Sch.1

4130. Chelmsford Primary Care Trust (Establishment) Order 2001
Art.1, amended: SI 2002/1405 Sch.1
Art.4, revoked: SI 2002/1405 Sch.1
Sch.1, amended: SI 2004/543 Sch.1

NO.

2001—cont.

4131. North Norfolk Primary Care Trust (Establishment) Order 2001
Art.1, amended: SI 2002/1405 Sch.1
Art.4, revoked: SI 2002/1405 Sch.1
Sch.1, amended: SI 2004/543 Sch.1

4132. Hinckley and Bosworth Primary Care Trust (Establishment) Order 2001
Art.1, amended: SI 2002/1405 Sch.1
Art.4, revoked: SI 2002/1405 Sch.1
Sch.1, amended: SI 2004/543 Sch.1

4133. Barnsley Primary Care Trust (Establishment) Order 2001
Art.1, amended: SI 2002/1405 Sch.1
Art.4, revoked: SI 2002/1405 Sch.1

4134. South Leicestershire Primary Care Trust (Establishment) Order 2001
Art.1, amended: SI 2002/1405 Sch.1
Art.4, revoked: SI 2002/1405 Sch.1

4135. East Lincolnshire Primary Care Trust (Establishment) Order 2001
Art.1, amended: SI 2002/1405 Sch.1
Art.4, revoked: SI 2002/1405 Sch.1

4136. Charnwood and North West Leicestershire Primary Care Trust (Establishment) Order 2001
Art.1, amended: SI 2002/1405 Sch.1
Art.4, revoked: SI 2002/1405 Sch.1
Sch.1, amended: SI 2004/543 Sch.1

4137. Derbyshire Dales and South Derbyshire Primary Care Trust (Establishment) Order 2001
Art.1, amended: SI 2002/1405 Sch.1
Art.4, revoked: SI 2002/1405 Sch.1

4138. Rotherham Primary Care Trust (Establishment) Order 2001
Art.1, amended: SI 2002/1405 Sch.1
Art.4, revoked: SI 2002/1405 Sch.1

4139. Bristol South and West Primary Care Trust (Establishment) Order 2001
Art.1, amended: SI 2002/1405 Sch.1
Art.4, revoked: SI 2002/1405 Sch.1
Sch.1, amended: SI 2004/543 Sch.1

4140. Taunton Deane Primary Care Trust (Establishment) Order 2001
Art.1, amended: SI 2002/1405 Sch.1
Art.4, revoked: SI 2002/1405 Sch.1

4141. West Gloucestershire Primary Care Trust (Establishment) Order 2001
Art.1, amended: SI 2002/1405 Sch.1
Art.4, revoked: SI 2002/1405 Sch.1

4142. Central Cornwall Primary Care Trust (Establishment) Order 2001
Art.1, amended: SI 2002/1405 Sch.1
Art.4, revoked: SI 2002/1405 Sch.1

4143. North and East Cornwall Primary Care Trust (Establishment) Order 2001
Art.1, amended: SI 2002/1405 Sch.1
Art.4, revoked: SI 2002/1405 Sch.1
Sch.1, amended: SI 2004/543 Sch.1

NO.

2001—cont.

4144. Cheltenham and Tewkesbury Primary Care Trust (Establishment) Order 2001
Art.1, amended: SI 2002/1405 Sch.1
Art.4, revoked: SI 2002/1405 Sch.1

4145. Cotswold and Vale Primary Care Trust (Establishment) Order 2001
Art.1, amended: SI 2002/1405 Sch.1
Art.4, revoked: SI 2002/1405 Sch.1

4146. Bristol North Primary Care Trust (Establishment) Order 2001
Art.1, amended: SI 2002/1405 Sch.1
Art.4, revoked: SI 2002/1405 Sch.1

4147. South Somerset Primary Care Trust (Establishment) Order 2001
Art.1, amended: SI 2002/1405 Sch.1
Art.4, revoked: SI 2002/1405 Sch.1

4148. Suffolk Coastal Primary Care Trust (Establishment) Order 2001
Art.1, amended: SI 2002/1405 Sch.1
Art.4, revoked: SI 2002/1405 Sch.1
Sch.1, amended: SI 2004/543 Sch.1

4150. Care Standards Act 2000 (Commencement No 10 (England) and Transitional, Savings and Amendment Provisions) Order 2001
varied: SI 2004/664 Art.11, Art.12, Art.13, Art.14
Art.3, amended: SI 2002/1493 Art.6, SI 2002/1790 Art.3, SI 2002/2001 Art.4, SI 2002/3210 Art.3

2002

Act of Sederunt (Summary Cause Rules) 2002
see *Reid v First Glasgow Ltd* 2003 Rep. L.R. 66 (Sh Pr), EF Bowen Q.C., Sheriff Principal

2. Import and Export Restrictions (Foot-And-Mouth Disease) Regulations 2002
revoked: SI 2002/76 Reg.29

8. Import and Export Restrictions (Foot-and-Mouth Disease) (Wales) Regulations 2002
revoked: SI 2002/130 Reg.28
Sch.2, substituted: SI 2002/85 Sch.1

10. Employment Rights (Increase of Limits) Order 2002
revoked: SI 2002/2927 Art.2

38. Primary Care Trusts (Membership, Procedure and Administration Arrangements) Amendment (No.3) (England) Regulations 2002
Reg.1, amended: SI 2002/557 Reg.7

45. Education (National Curriculum) (Assessment Arrangements for English, Welsh, Mathematics and Science) (Key Stage 1) (Wales) Order 2002
revoked: 2002 c.32 Sch.22 Part 3
Art.4, applied: SI 2002/438 Sch.1 para.1

NO.

2002–cont.

45. Education (National Curriculum) (Assessment Arrangements for English, Welsh, Mathematics and Science) (Key Stage 1) (Wales) Order 2002–*cont.*

Art.5, applied: SI 2002/438 Sch.1 para.1

Art.6, applied: SI 2002/438 Sch.1 para.1

Art.7, applied: SI 2002/438 Sch.1 para.1

Art.8, applied: SI 2002/438 Sch.1 para.1

46. Education (Individual Pupils Achievements) (Information) (Wales) (Amendment) Regulations 2002

revoked: SI 2004/1026 Sch.5

48. District of West Oxfordshire (Electoral Changes) Order 2002

varied: SI 2004/222 Art.2

49. District of South Oxfordshire (Electoral Changes) Order 2002

varied: SI 2004/222 Art.2

50. Dual-Use Items (Export Control) (Amendment) Regulations 2002

revoked: SI 2003/2764 Sch.6

57. Fostering Services Regulations 2002

applied: SI 1991/1507 Reg.4, SI 2002/2005 Reg.14

varied: SI 2004/664 Art.11, Art.12, Art.13, Art.14

Reg.2, amended: SI 2002/865 Reg.7, SI 2002/2469 Sch.8, SI 2004/664 Art.3, SI 2004/865 Sch.1 para.31

Reg.3, varied: SI 2004/664 Art.11, Art.12, Art.13, Art.14

Reg.5, amended: SI 2002/865 Reg.6

Reg.5, revoked (in part): SI 2002/865 Reg.6

Reg.7, amended: SI 2002/865 Reg.6

Reg.7, revoked (in part): SI 2002/865 Reg.6

Reg.20, amended: SI 2002/865 Reg.6

Reg.20, revoked (in part): SI 2002/865 Reg.6

Reg.27, amended: SI 2002/865 Reg.7

Reg.38, referred to: SI 1991/1507 Reg.4

Reg.39, revoked (in part): SI 2002/865 Reg.7

Reg.44, amended: SI 2002/865 Reg.7

Reg.48, amended: SI 2002/865 Reg.7

Reg.50, amended: SI 2002/865 Reg.7

Sch.1 para.7, revoked: SI 2002/865 Reg.6

Sch.5 para.7, applied: SI 1991/1507 Reg.4

Sch.5 para.8, applied: SI 1991/1507 Reg.4

Sch.5 para.9, applied: SI 1991/1507 Reg.4

Sch.5 para.10, applied: SI 1991/1507 Reg.4

Sch.5 para.11, applied: SI 1991/1507 Reg.4

Sch.5 para.12, applied: SI 1991/1507 Reg.4

Sch.5 para.13, applied: SI 1991/1507 Reg.4

Sch.5 para.14, applied: SI 1991/1507 Reg.4

Sch.5 para.15, applied: SI 1991/1507 Reg.4

Sch.6 para.4, applied: SI 1991/1507 Reg.4

Sch.6 para.5, applied: SI 1991/1507 Reg.4

Sch.6 para.6, applied: SI 1991/1507 Reg.4

Sch.6 para.7, applied: SI 1991/1507 Reg.4

Sch.6 para.8, applied: SI 1991/1507 Reg.4

Sch.8, amended: SI 2002/2469 Sch.7

NO.

2002–cont.

64. Oldham Primary Care Trust (Establishment) Order 2002

Art.1, amended: SI 2002/1405 Sch.1

Art.4, revoked: SI 2002/1405 Sch.1

65. Warrington Primary Care Trust (Establishment) Order 2002

Art.1, amended: SI 2002/1405 Sch.1

Art.4, revoked: SI 2002/1405 Sch.1

66. Halton Primary Care Trust (Establishment) Order 2002

Art.1, amended: SI 2002/1405 Sch.1

Art.4, revoked: SI 2002/1405 Sch.1

67. Knowsley Primary Care Trust (Establishment) Order 2002

Art.1, amended: SI 2002/1405 Sch.1

Art.4, revoked: SI 2002/1405 Sch.1

68. Rochdale Primary Care Trust (Establishment) Order 2002

Art.1, amended: SI 2002/1405 Sch.1

Art.4, revoked: SI 2002/1405 Sch.1

69. Bury Primary Care Trust (Establishment) Order 2002

Art.1, amended: SI 2002/1405 Sch.1

Art.4, revoked: SI 2002/1405 Sch.1

70. St Helens Primary Care Trust (Establishment) Order 2002

Art.1, amended: SI 2002/1405 Sch.1

Art.4, revoked: SI 2002/1405 Sch.1

71. South Cambridgeshire Primary Care Trust (Establishment) Order 2002

Art.1, amended: SI 2002/1405 Sch.1

Art.4, revoked: SI 2002/1405 Sch.1

Sch.1, amended: SI 2004/543 Sch.1

76. Import and Export Restrictions (Foot-And-Mouth Disease) (No.2) Regulations 2002

revoked: SI 2002/119 Reg.23

79. Social Fund Maternity and Funeral Expenses (General) Amendment Regulations 2002

Reg.3, amended: SI 2002/470 Reg.2

82. Nurses, Midwives and Health Visitors (Professional Conduct) (Amendment) Rules 2002 Approval Order 2002

revoked: 1999 c.8 Sch.5

varied: SI 2004/1762 Art.1

85. Import and Export Restrictions (Foot-and-Mouth Disease) (Wales) (Amendment) Regulations 2002

revoked: SI 2002/130 Reg.28

93. Electricity (Connection Charges) Regulations 2002

Reg.2, amended: SI 2002/3232 Reg.3

Reg.3, amended: SI 2002/3232 Reg.3

Reg.6, amended: SI 2002/3232 Reg.3

Reg.7, amended: SI 2002/3232 Reg.3

Reg.8A, added: SI 2002/3232 Reg.3

NO.

2002–cont.

102. Council Tax (Dwellings and Part Residential Subjects) (Scotland) Amendment Regulations 2002

see *Scottish Water v Clydecare Ltd* 2003 S.C. 330 (Ex Div), Lord Osborne, Lord Macfadyen, Lord Sutherland

105. Income Support (General) (Standard Interest Rate Amendment) Regulations 2002

revoked: SI 2002/338 Reg.3

111. Al-Qa'ida and Taliban (United Nations Measures) Order 2002

Art.1, amended: 2002 c.8 s.2, SI 2002/251 Art.2

Art.3, amended: 2002 c.8 s.2

Art.5, amended: 2002 c.8 s.2

Art.6, amended: 2002 c.8 s.2

112. Al-Qa'ida and Taliban (United Nations Measures) (Overseas Territories) Order 2002

varied: SI 2004/2036 Art.2

Art.1, amended: 2002 c.8 s.2, SI 2002/266 Art.2

Art.2, amended: SI 2002/266 Art.3, Art.4

Art.2, revoked (in part): SI 2002/266 Art.3

Art.6, amended: 2002 c.8 s.2

Art.8, varied: SI 2004/2036 Art.2

Art.13, amended: SI 2002/266 Art.5

Art.15, amended: SI 2002/266 Art.6

Art.16, amended: SI 2002/266 Art.6

Sch.3 para.2, amended: SI 2002/266 Art.7

119. Import and Export Restrictions (Foot-And-Mouth Disease)(No.3) Regulations 2002

revoked: SI 2002/468 Reg.2

120. Potatoes Originating in Egypt (Amendment) (Wales) Regulations 2002

revoked: SI 2004/2245 Reg.8

123. Street Works (Charges for Occupation of the Highway) (England) (Middlesbrough Borough Council) Order 2002

revoked: SI 2004/2175 Art.2

124. Street Works (Charges for Occupation of the Highway) (England) (London Borough of Camden) Order 2002

revoked: SI 2004/2175 Art.2

130. Import and Export Restrictions (Foot-and-Mouth Disease) (Wales) (No.2) Regulations 2002

revoked: SI 2002/431 Reg.2

136. Financing of Maintained Schools (Amendment) (Wales) Regulations 2002

revoked: SI 2004/2506 Reg.3

137. Scarborough, Whitby and Ryedale Primary Care Trust (Establishment) Order 2002

Art.1, amended: SI 2002/1405 Sch.1

NO.

2002–cont.

137. Scarborough, Whitby and Ryedale Primary Care Trust (Establishment) Order 2002–*cont.*

Art.4, revoked: SI 2002/1405 Sch.1

138. Middlesbrough Primary Care Trust (Establishment) Order 2002

Art.1, amended: SI 2002/1405 Sch.1

Art.4, revoked: SI 2002/1405 Sch.1

Sch.1, amended: SI 2004/543 Sch.1

139. Sunderland Teaching Primary Care Trust (Establishment) Order 2002

Art.1, amended: SI 2002/1405 Sch.1

Art.4, revoked: SI 2002/1405 Sch.1

140. Langbaurgh Primary Care Trust (Establishment) Order 2002

Art.1, amended: SI 2002/1405 Sch.1

Art.4, revoked: SI 2002/1405 Sch.1

Sch.1, amended: SI 2004/543 Sch.1

141. Sedgefield Primary Care Trust (Establishment) Order 2002

Art.1, amended: SI 2002/1405 Sch.1

Art.4, revoked: SI 2002/1405 Sch.1

142. Easington Primary Care Trust (Establishment) Order 2002

Art.1, amended: SI 2002/1405 Sch.1

Art.4, revoked: SI 2002/1405 Sch.1

143. North Kirklees Primary Care Trust (Establishment) Order 2002

Art.1, amended: SI 2002/1405 Sch.1

Art.4, revoked: SI 2002/1405 Sch.1

144. Calderdale Primary Care Trust (Establishment) Order 2002

Art.1, amended: SI 2002/1405 Sch.1

Art.4, revoked: SI 2002/1405 Sch.1

Sch.1, amended: SI 2004/543 Sch.1

145. Derwentside Primary Care Trust (Establishment) Order 2002

Art.1, amended: SI 2002/1405 Sch.1

Art.4, revoked: SI 2002/1405 Sch.1

146. Gateshead Primary Care Trust (Establishment) Order 2002

Art.1, amended: SI 2002/1405 Sch.1

Art.4, revoked: SI 2002/1405 Sch.1

147. Durham Dales Primary Care Trust (Establishment) Order 2002

Art.1, amended: SI 2002/1405 Sch.1

Art.4, revoked: SI 2002/1405 Sch.1

148. Durham and Chester-le-Street Primary Care Trust (Establishment) Order 2002

Art.1, amended: SI 2002/1405 Sch.1

Art.4, revoked: SI 2002/1405 Sch.1

149. Craven, Harrogate and Rural District Primary Care Trust (Establishment) Order 2002

Art.1, amended: SI 2002/1405 Sch.1

Art.4, revoked: SI 2002/1405 Sch.1

150. Darlington Primary Care Trust (Establishment) Order 2002

Art.1, amended: SI 2002/1405 Sch.1

Art.4, revoked: SI 2002/1405 Sch.1

NO.

2002–cont.

152. Education (Special Education Needs) (Wales) Regulations 2002

Reg.9, amended: SI 2002/3135 Sch.1 para.51

Reg.18, amended: SI 2003/1717 Reg.7

166. South Tyneside Primary Care Trust (Establishment) Order 2002

Art.1, amended: SI 2002/1405 Sch.1

Art.4, revoked: SI 2002/1405 Sch.1

173. Education (Mandatory Awards) Regulations 2001 (Amendment) (No.3) Regulations 2002

revoked: SI 2002/232 Reg.2

183. Food and Animal Feedingstuffs (Products of Animal Origin from China) (Control) (England) Regulations 2002

revoked: SI 2002/1614 Reg.6

185. Local Authorities (Mayoral Elections) (England and Wales) Regulations 2002

Appendix 999., substituted: SI 2004/225 Sch.1

Reg.2, amended: SI 2004/225 Reg.2

Reg.3, amended: SI 2004/225 Reg.2

Reg.5, substituted: SI 2004/225 Reg.2

Sch.1, amended: SI 2004/225 Reg.2

Sch.2, amended: SI 2004/225 Reg.2

Sch.3, referred to: SI 2004/225 Reg.2

Sch.3 Part I, substituted: SI 2004/225 Sch.1

Sch.3 Part I para.1, substituted: SI 2004/225 Sch.1

Sch.3 Part I para.2, substituted: SI 2004/225 Sch.1

Sch.3 Part II, substituted: SI 2004/225 Sch.1

Sch.3 Part II para.3, substituted: SI 2004/225 Sch.1

Sch.3 Part II para.4, substituted: SI 2004/225 Sch.1

Sch.3 Part III para.5, substituted: SI 2004/225 Sch.1

Sch.3 Part III para.6, substituted: SI 2004/225 Sch.1

Sch.3 Part III para.7, substituted: SI 2004/225 Sch.1

Sch.3 Part III para.8, substituted: SI 2004/225 Sch.1

Sch.3 Part III para.9, substituted: SI 2004/225 Sch.1

Sch.3 Part III para.10, substituted: SI 2004/225 Sch.1

Sch.3 Part III para.11, substituted: SI 2004/225 Sch.1

Sch.3 Part III para.12, substituted: SI 2004/225 Sch.1

Sch.3 Part III para.13, substituted: SI 2004/225 Sch.1

Sch.3 Part III para.14, substituted: SI 2004/225 Sch.1

Sch.3 Part IV para.15, substituted: SI 2004/225 Sch.1

NO.

2002–cont.

185. Local Authorities (Mayoral Elections) (England and Wales) Regulations 2002–*cont.*

Sch.3 Part IV para.16, substituted: SI 2004/225 Sch.1

Sch.3 Part IV para.17, substituted: SI 2004/225 Sch.1

Sch.3 Part IV para.18, substituted: SI 2004/225 Sch.1

Sch.3 Part IV para.19, substituted: SI 2004/225 Sch.1

Sch.3 Part IV para.20, substituted: SI 2004/225 Sch.1

Sch.3 Part IV para.21, substituted: SI 2004/225 Sch.1

Sch.3 Part IV para.22, substituted: SI 2004/225 Sch.1

Sch.3 Part IV para.23, substituted: SI 2004/225 Sch.1

Sch.3 Part IV para.24, substituted: SI 2004/225 Sch.1

Sch.3 Part IV para.25, substituted: SI 2004/225 Sch.1

Sch.3 Part IV para.26, substituted: SI 2004/225 Sch.1

Sch.3 Part IV para.27, substituted: SI 2004/225 Sch.1

Sch.3 Part IV para.28, substituted: SI 2004/225 Sch.1

Sch.3 Part IV para.29, substituted: SI 2004/225 Sch.1

Sch.3 Part IV para.30, substituted: SI 2004/225 Sch.1

Sch.3 Part IV para.31, substituted: SI 2004/225 Sch.1

Sch.3 Part IV para.32, substituted: SI 2004/225 Sch.1

Sch.3 Part IV para.33, substituted: SI 2004/225 Sch.1

Sch.3 Part IV para.34, substituted: SI 2004/225 Sch.1

Sch.3 Part IV para.35, substituted: SI 2004/225 Sch.1

Sch.3 Part IV para.36, substituted: SI 2004/225 Sch.1

Sch.3 Part IV para.37, substituted: SI 2004/225 Sch.1

Sch.3 Part IV para.38, substituted: SI 2004/225 Sch.1

Sch.3 Part IV para.39, substituted: SI 2004/225 Sch.1

Sch.3 Part IV para.40, substituted: SI 2004/225 Sch.1

Sch.3 Part IV para.41, substituted: SI 2004/225 Sch.1

Sch.3 Part IV para.42, substituted: SI 2004/225 Sch.1

Sch.3 Part IV para.43, substituted: SI 2004/225 Sch.1

Sch.3 Part IV para.44, substituted: SI 2004/225 Sch.1

NO.

2002–cont.

185. Local Authorities (Mayoral Elections) (England and Wales) Regulations 2002–*cont.*

Sch.3 Part IV para.45, substituted: SI 2004/ 225 Sch.1

Sch.3 Part V para.46, substituted: SI 2004/ 225 Sch.1

Sch.3 Part V para.47, substituted: SI 2004/ 225 Sch.1

Sch.3 Part VI para.48, substituted: SI 2004/ 225 Sch.1

Sch.3 Part VI para.49, substituted: SI 2004/ 225 Sch.1

Sch.3 Part VII para.50, substituted: SI 2004/ 225 Sch.1

Sch.3 Part VII para.51, substituted: SI 2004/ 225 Sch.1

Sch.3 Part VII para.52, substituted: SI 2004/ 225 Sch.1

Sch.3 Part VII para.53, substituted: SI 2004/ 225 Sch.1

Sch.3 Part VIII para.54, substituted: SI 2004/ 225 Sch.1

187. County of Herefordshire District Council (Electoral Changes) Order 2002

varied: SI 2004/222 Art.2

192. Immigration (Designation of Travel Bans) (Amendment) Order 2002

revoked: SI 2003/3285 Sch.2

193. Justices of the Peace (Size and Chairmanship of Bench) Rules 2002

r.2, amended: SI 2004/1514 r.2

r.6, amended: SI 2004/1514 r.3

r.7, substituted: SI 2004/1514 r.4

r.8, substituted: SI 2004/1514 r.4

r.10, revoked (in part): SI 2004/1514 r.5

r.11, substituted: SI 2004/1514 r.6

195. Education (Student Support) Regulations 2002

revoked: SI 2002/3200 Reg.3

see *R. (on the application of Douglas) v North Tyneside MBC* [2003] EWCA Civ 1847, [2004] 1 W.L.R. 2363 (CA), Thorpe, L.J.

Reg.2, amended: SI 2002/1318 Reg.3

Reg.12, amended: SI 2002/1318 Reg.4, SI 2002/2088 Reg.3

Reg.13, amended: SI 2002/1318 Reg.4

Reg.15, amended: SI 2002/1318 Reg.5, SI 2002/3059 Reg.3

Reg.15, applied: SI 1987/1967 Reg.62, SI 1992/1814 Reg.42, SI 1996/207 Reg.131

Reg.17, amended: SI 2002/3059 Reg.4

Reg.18, amended: SI 2002/1318 Reg.6

Reg.20, amended: SI 2002/1318 Reg.7, SI 2002/2088 Reg.4

Reg.24, amended: SI 2002/1318 Reg.8

Reg.30, amended: SI 2002/1318 Reg.9

Sch.3 Part I para.1, amended: SI 2002/3059 Reg.5

NO.

2002–cont.

195. Education (Student Support) Regulations 2002–*cont.*

Sch.3 Part II para.2, amended: SI 2002/1318 Reg.10

202. Animal Gatherings (Interim Measures) (England) Order 2002

revoked: SI 2003/253 Art.11

Art.1, amended: SI 2002/2152 Art.13, SI 2003/31 Art.2

Art.2, amended: SI 2002/1328 Art.3, SI 2002/1765 Art.2

Sch.1 para.1, amended: SI 2002/1765 Art.2

Sch.1 para.2, amended: SI 2002/1765 Art.2

Sch.1 para.2, substituted: SI 2002/1328 Art.4

Sch.1 para.4, amended: SI 2002/1765 Art.2

Sch.1 para.6, amended: SI 2002/1328 Art.5

203. Food and Animal Feedingstuffs (Products of Animal Origin from China) (Control) (Wales) Regulations 2002

revoked: SI 2002/1798 Reg.6

205. Income Tax (Exemption of Minor Benefits) Regulations 2002

Reg.2, amended: SI 2003/1434 Reg.2

Reg.3, amended: SI 2003/1434 Reg.3

Reg.3, revoked (in part): SI 2003/1434 Reg.3

Reg.4, amended: SI 2003/1434 Reg.4

Reg.5, added: SI 2004/3087 Reg.2

Reg.6, added: SI 2004/3087 Reg.2

221. Fur Farming (Compensation Scheme) (England) Order 2002

applied: SI 2004/1964 Art.10

revoked: SI 2004/1964 Art.11

Art.6, applied: SI 2004/1964 Art.10

232. Education (Mandatory Awards) Regulations 2001 (Amendment) (No.4) Regulations 2002

revoked: SI 2002/1330 Sch.6

233. Police Act 1997 (Criminal Records) Regulations 2002

Reg.4, amended: SI 2004/367 Reg.2

Reg.4, substituted: SI 2003/1418 Reg.2

Reg.4A, amended: SI 2004/367 Reg.2

Reg.6, amended: SI 2003/520 Reg.2

Reg.7, substituted: SI 2003/520 Reg.3

Reg.8, amended: SI 2003/520 Reg.4

Reg.8, substituted: SI 2004/1759 Reg.2

Reg.12, amended: SI 2004/367 Reg.3

Sch.2, revoked: SI 2003/137 Reg.3

Sch.3, referred to: SI 2004/367 Reg.4

Sch.3, substituted: SI 2004/367 Sch.1, SI 2004/2592 Sch.1

236. Medicines (Codification Amendments Etc.) Regulations 2002

Reg.6, revoked: SI 2002/618 Reg.66

Reg.13, revoked: SI 2002/618 Reg.66

240. Sheep and Goats Identification and Movement (Interim Measures) (England) Order 2002

revoked: SI 2002/2153 Art.19

2002–cont.

240. Sheep and Goats Identification and Movement (Interim Measures) (England) Order 2002–*cont.*

Art.2, amended: SI 2002/764 Art.3, SI 2002/1349 Art.3

Art.4, amended: SI 2002/764 Art.4, SI 2002/1349 Art.4

Art.5, amended: SI 2002/764 Art.5, SI 2002/1349 Art.5

Art.6, amended: SI 2002/764 Art.6

Art.9, amended: SI 2002/764 Art.7, SI 2002/1349 Art.6

Art.12, amended: SI 2002/764 Art.8, SI 2002/1349 Art.7

Art.16A, added: SI 2002/1349 Art.8

Sch.1, added: SI 2002/1349 Sch.1

241. Pigs (Records, Identification and Movement) (Interim Measures) (England) Order 2002

revoked: SI 2002/2154 Art.14

242. Disease Control (Interim Measures) (England) Order 2002

revoked: SI 2002/2152 Art.12

Art.2, amended: SI 2002/907 Art.2, SI 2002/1348 Art.2, SI 2002/1764 Art.2

Art.3, amended: SI 2002/907 Art.2, SI 2002/1348 Art.2, SI 2002/1764 Art.2

Art.3, applied: SI 2002/240 Art.2, Art.4, Art.5

Art.3, revoked (in part): SI 2002/1764 Art.2

Art.5, amended: SI 2002/1348 Art.2

Art.5, revoked: SI 2002/1764 Art.2

Art.6, amended: SI 2002/1348 Art.2

Art.6, revoked: SI 2002/1764 Art.2

Art.7, amended: SI 2002/1348 Art.2

Art.8, amended: SI 2002/1348 Art.2

Art.14, revoked: SI 2002/1764 Art.2

253. Nursing and Midwifery Order (2001) 2002

applied: SI 2000/89 Reg.5, SI 2001/1042 Reg.5, 2002 c.17 s.29, SI 2002/2375 Reg.11, SI 2002/2376 Reg.4, SI 2004/905 Reg.9, SI 2004/1762 Art.7, Art.14

Part V, applied: SI 2004/1762 Art.6, Art.7, SI 2004/1763 Art.2, SI 2004/1767 Sch.1

Part VI, applied: SI 2004/1767 Sch.1

Art.3, varied: SI 2002/1125 Art.2

Art.5, applied: SI 1987/235 Sch.1 para.4, 1989 c.41 s.48, s.102, SI 1990/1718 Art.5, SI 1990/2024 Reg.4, 1996 c.18 s.55, SI 2001/341 Reg.53, SI 2001/497 Reg.53, SI 2004/905 Reg.9, SI 2004/1767 Sch.1, SR 2002/386 Reg.2, Reg.4, SSI 2003/176 Art.7

Art.5, enabled: SI 2004/1767

Art.6, applied: SI 2004/1767 Sch.1

Art.6, enabled: SI 2004/1765

Art.6, referred to: SI 2004/1765 Art.6

Art.7, applied: SI 2004/1654 Sch.1

Art.7, enabled: SI 2004/1654, SI 2004/1767

Art.9, applied: SI 2004/1767 Sch.1

2002–cont.

253. Nursing and Midwifery Order (2001) 2002–*cont.*

Art.9, enabled: SI 2004/1767

Art.10, applied: SI 2004/1767 Sch.1

Art.10, enabled: SI 2004/1767

Art.12, enabled: SI 2004/1767

Art.13, applied: SI 2004/1654 Sch.1, SI 2004/1767 Sch.1

Art.13, enabled: SI 2004/1767

Art.13, referred to: SI 2004/1767 Sch.1

Art.14, applied: SI 2004/1767 Sch.1

Art.14, enabled: SI 2004/1766

Art.15, applied: 1989 c.41 s.45, SI 2004/1764 Sch.1

Art.15, enabled: SI 2004/1767

Art.18, applied: SI 2002/2375 Reg.9

Art.19, applied: SI 2004/1762 Art.9, Art.11, SI 2004/1767 Sch.1

Art.19, enabled: SI 2004/1767

Art.21, applied: SI 2004/1761 Sch.1

Art.22, applied: SI 2004/1761 Sch.1, SI 2004/1763 Art.2, SI 2004/1767 Sch.1

Art.22, enabled: SI 2004/1761

Art.22, referred to: SI 2004/1761 Sch.1

Art.26, applied: SI 2004/1761 Sch.1

Art.26, enabled: SI 2004/1761

Art.27, varied: SI 2002/1125 Art.2

Art.29, applied: SI 2004/1761 Sch.1, SI 2004/1762 Art.6, Art.7, Art.9, Art.10, Art.11

Art.30, applied: SI 2004/1761 Sch.1, SI 2004/1762 Art.9, Art.10, Art.11

Art.30, enabled: SI 2004/1761

Art.30, referred to: SI 2004/1762 Art.10

Art.31, applied: SI 2004/1761 Sch.1, SI 2004/1763 Art.2

Art.32, applied: SI 2004/1761 Sch.1, SI 2004/1767 Sch.1

Art.32, enabled: SI 2004/1761

Art.32, referred to: SI 2004/1761 Sch.1

Art.33, applied: SI 2004/1761 Sch.1, SI 2004/1762 Art.8, Art.9, SI 2004/1767 Sch.1

Art.33, disapplied: SI 2004/1762 Art.8

Art.33, enabled: SI 2004/1654, SI 2004/1761

Art.37, applied: SI 2004/1763 Art.2, SI 2004/1767 Sch.1

Art.37, enabled: SI 2004/1767

Art.37, referred to: SI 2004/1767 Sch.1

Art.38, applied: SI 2004/1761 Sch.1, SI 2004/1762 Art.6, Art.7, SI 2004/1767 Sch.1

Art.38, referred to: SI 2004/1762 Art.6, Art.7

Art.38, varied: SI 2004/1762 Art.6, Art.7

Art.41, applied: SI 2004/1764 Sch.1

Art.42, applied: SI 2001/3998 Reg.11, SI 2002/2375 Reg.9, SI 2004/551 Art.3, SI 2004/1764 Sch.1

Art.42, enabled: SI 2004/1764

Art.43, applied: SI 2002/2375 Reg.9, SI 2004/551 Art.3, SI 2004/1764 Sch.1

Art.43, enabled: SI 2004/1764

Art.44, applied: SI 2000/1139 Sch.1 para.27

NO.

NO.

2002–cont.

2002–cont.

253. Nursing and Midwifery Order (2001) 2002–*cont.*

Art.46, enabled: SI 2004/1763

Art.47, applied: SI 2003/1738 Sch.1, SI 2004/1654, SI 2004/1654 Sch.1, SI 2004/1761 Sch.1, SI 2004/1764 Sch.1, SI 2004/1767, SI 2004/1767 Sch.1

Art.47, enabled: SI 2003/1738, SI 2004/1654, SI 2004/1761, SI 2004/1762, SI 2004/1764, SI 2004/1767

Art.47, referred to: SI 2004/1764

Art.47, varied: SI 2002/1125 Art.2

Art.48, applied: SI 2004/1654, SI 2004/1761 Sch.1, SI 2004/1767

Art.48, referred to: SI 2004/1764

Art.54, enabled: SI 2002/923, SI 2002/1125, SI 2004/1762

Sch.1 Part I para.8, varied: SI 2002/1125 Art.2

Sch.1 Part I para.10, applied: SI 2004/293 Sch.2 para.16

Sch.1 Part I para.15A, added: 2003 c.43 Sch.12 para.7

Sch.1 Part II para.17, applied: SI 2003/1738 Sch.1

Sch.1 Part II para.17, enabled: SI 2003/1738

Sch.2, applied: 2002 c.9 (NI) Sch.1 para.20, (NI) Sch.1 para.21, SI 2003/3148 Reg.3

Sch.2 para.10, applied: SI 1987/235 Sch.1 para.4, SI 1990/1718 Art.5, SI 1990/2024 Reg.4, SI 1995/414 Reg.2, SI 1995/416 Reg.2, SI 1999/450 Sch.2 para.3, SI 1999/787 Sch.3 para.3, SSI 2001/430 Reg.2

Sch.2 para.17, applied: SI 2004/1762 Art.13

Sch.2 para.18, amended: SI 2002/2469 Sch.1 para.100

Sch.2 para.18, applied: SI 2002/2375 Reg.9

Sch.2 para.18, referred to: SI 2002/2375 Sch.3

Sch.2 para.20, enabled: SI 2002/923

Sch.2 para.21, enabled: SI 2002/923

Sch.2 para.23, enabled: SI 2002/923

Sch.2 para.25, enabled: SI 2002/923

Sch.4, amended: SI 2002/2469 Sch.1 para.100, SI 2003/3148 Reg.4, SI 2004/1947 Reg.2

Sch.4, applied: SI 2004/1764 Sch.1

Sch.4, enabled: SI 2004/1764

Sch.5 para.3, revoked: SI 2003/1398 Sch.1 para.44

Sch.5 para.7, referred to: SI 2004/1771 Art.1

254. Health Professions Order 2002

applied: SI 1964/939 Reg.2, 1968 c.67 s.58, SI 1974/494 Reg.2, SI 1975/1023 Sch.1 para.10, 1984 c.39 s.3, SI 1990/2639 Sch.1 Part III, 1994 c.23 Sch.9 Part II, SI 1995/574 Sch.1 Part III, SI 1999/686 Sch.1 Part III, SI 2001/1042 Reg.5, SI 2002/2376 Reg.4, SI 2003/2461 Art.2, SI 2003/2462 Art.2, SSI 2001/137, SSI 2002/103 Sch.1 Part III, SSI 2002/190

254. Health Professions Order 2002–*cont.*

applied: SI 1964/939 Reg.2–*cont.*

Reg.3, SSI 2002/305 Sch.1 Part III, SSI 2002/534 Sch.1 Part III, SSI 2003/231 Sch.4 para.10

referred to: 1999 c.8 s.60

Part V, applied: SI 2003/1572 Sch.1, SI 2003/1578 Art.2, SI 2003/1700 Art.2, Art.3, Art.4, Art.5

Art.3, applied: SSI 2001/424 Art.2

Art.3, varied: SI 2002/1124 Art.2

Art.5, applied: SI 1964/939 Reg.2, 1972 c.58 s.32, SI 1974/494 Reg.2, 1977 c.49 s.41, 1978 c.29 s.27, SI 1978/41 Reg.5, SI 2003/1572 Sch.1, SI 2003/1700 Art.10

Art.5, enabled: SI 2003/1572

Art.6, applied: SI 2003/1571, SI 2003/1572 Sch.1, SI 2003/1576 Sch.1

Art.6, enabled: SI 2003/1571, SI 2004/2522

Art.6, referred to: SI 2003/1571 Art.5

Art.7, applied: SI 2003/1572 Sch.1, SI 2004/2524 Sch.1

Art.7, enabled: SI 2003/1572, SI 2004/2524

Art.9, applied: SI 2003/1572 Sch.1

Art.9, enabled: SI 2003/1572

Art.9, referred to: SI 2003/1579 Sch.1

Art.10, amended: SI 2004/2033 Art.10

Art.10, applied: SI 2003/1572 Sch.1

Art.10, enabled: SI 2003/1572

Art.11, applied: SI 2003/1572 Sch.1

Art.11, enabled: SI 2003/1572

Art.12, applied: SI 2003/1572 Sch.1

Art.12, enabled: SI 2003/1572

Art.13, amended: SI 2004/2033 Art.3

Art.13, applied: SI 2003/1572 Sch.1

Art.19, applied: SI 2003/1209 Sch.1

Art.21, applied: SI 2003/1209 Sch.1, SI 2003/1575 Sch.1, SI 2003/1576 Sch.1

Art.21, varied: SI 2003/1700 Art.8, Art.9

Art.22, applied: SI 2003/1572 Sch.1, SI 2003/1576 Sch.1, SI 2003/1578 Art.2

Art.22, enabled: SI 2003/1574, SI 2003/1575, SI 2003/1576

Art.22, referred to: SI 2003/1700 Art.2

Art.22, varied: SI 2003/1700 Art.8, Art.9

Art.23, applied: SI 2003/1573 Sch.1

Art.23, enabled: SI 2003/1573

Art.23, varied: SI 2003/1700 Art.8, Art.9

Art.24, enabled: SI 2003/1573

Art.24, varied: SI 2003/1700 Art.8, Art.9

Art.25, varied: SI 2003/1700 Art.8, Art.9

Art.26, applied: SI 2003/1574 Sch.1

Art.26, enabled: SI 2003/1574

Art.26, referred to: SI 2003/1574 Sch.1

Art.26, varied: SI 2003/1700 Art.8, Art.9

Art.27, varied: SI 2002/1124 Art.2, SI 2003/1700 Art.8, Art.9

Art.28, varied: SI 2003/1700 Art.8, Art.9

NO.

2002–cont.

254. Health Professions Order 2002–*cont.*

Art.29, applied: SI 2003/1575 Sch.1, SI 2003/1576 Sch.1, SI 2003/1700 Art.8, Art.9

Art.29, varied: SI 2003/1700 Art.8, Art.9

Art.30, applied: SI 2003/1575 Sch.1, SI 2003/1576 Sch.1

Art.30, enabled: SI 2003/1575, SI 2003/1576

Art.30, varied: SI 2003/1700 Art.8, Art.9

Art.31, varied: SI 2003/1700 Art.8, Art.9

Art.32, applied: SI 2003/1573 Sch.1, SI 2003/1574 Sch.1, SI 2003/1575 Sch.1, SI 2003/1576 Sch.1, SI 2003/1579 Sch.1

Art.32, enabled: SI 2003/1573, SI 2003/1575, SI 2003/1576

Art.32, varied: SI 2003/1700 Art.8, Art.9

Art.33, applied: SI 2003/1575 Sch.1, SI 2003/1576 Sch.1, SI 2003/1700 Art.10, SI 2004/2524 Sch.1

Art.33, enabled: SI 2003/1572, SI 2003/1575, SI 2003/1576, SI 2004/2524

Art.33, varied: SI 2003/1700 Art.8, Art.9

Art.34, enabled: SI 2003/1577

Art.34, varied: SI 2003/1700 Art.8, Art.9

Art.35, enabled: SI 2003/1577

Art.35, varied: SI 2003/1700 Art.8, Art.9

Art.36, enabled: SI 2003/1577

Art.36, varied: SI 2003/1700 Art.8, Art.9

Art.37, amended: SI 2004/2033 Art.10

Art.37, applied: SI 2003/1572 Sch.1, SI 2003/1578 Art.2, SI 2003/1579 Sch.1

Art.37, enabled: SI 2003/1579

Art.37, referred to: SI 2003/1579 Sch.1

Art.38, amended: SI 2004/2033 Art.10

Art.38, applied: SI 2003/1572 Sch.1, SI 2003/1700 Art.2, Art.3, Art.4, Art.5, Art.6

Art.38, disapplied: SI 2003/1700 Art.8, Art.9

Art.38, varied: SI 2003/1700 Art.8, Art.9

Art.40, enabled: SI 2003/1578

Art.41, applied: SI 2003/1209, SI 2003/1209 Sch.1, SI 2003/1572, SI 2003/1572 Sch.1, SI 2003/1573, SI 2003/1573 Sch.1, SI 2003/1574, SI 2003/1575 Sch.1, SI 2003/1576 Sch.1, SI 2003/1577, SI 2003/1577 Sch.1, SI 2003/1579, SI 2003/1579 Sch.1, SI 2004/2524, SI 2004/2524 Sch.1

Art.41, enabled: SI 2003/1572, SI 2003/1573, SI 2003/1574, SI 2003/1575, SI 2003/1576, SI 2003/1579, SI 2004/2524, SI 2004/3318

Art.41, varied: SI 2002/1124 Art.2

Art.42, applied: SI 2003/1209, SI 2003/1572, SI 2003/1573, SI 2003/1577, SI 2003/1579, SI 2004/2524

Art.47, amended: SI 2004/2033 Art.10

Art.48, enabled: SI 2002/922, SI 2002/1124, SI 2003/1700, SI 2004/2525

Sch.1 Part I para.1, amended: SI 2004/2033 Art.3

NO.

2002–cont.

254. Health Professions Order 2002–*cont.*

Sch.1 Part I para.2, enabled: SI 2004/3318

Sch.1 Part I para.3, amended: SI 2004/2033 Art.3

Sch.1 Part I para.9, varied: SI 2002/1124 Art.2

Sch.1 Part I para.16A, added: 2003 c.43 Sch.12 para.8

Sch.1 Part II para.17, varied: SI 2002/1124 Art.2

Sch.1 Part II para.18, applied: SI 2003/1209 Sch.1

Sch.1 Part II para.18, enabled: SI 2003/1209, SI 2003/1574, SI 2003/1575, SI 2003/1576

Sch.2 para.1, amended: SI 2004/2033 Art.3

Sch.2 para.3, amended: SI 2004/2033 Art.3

Sch.2 para.17, applied: SI 2003/1700 Art.2, Art.7, Art.10, Art.12

Sch.2 para.20, amended: SI 2004/2033 Art.3

Sch.2 para.20, enabled: SI 2002/922

Sch.2 para.25, added: SI 2004/2033 Art.3

Sch.2 para.25, applied: SI 2004/2033 Art.2

Sch.2 para.25, disapplied: SI 2004/2033 Art.2

Sch.2 para.26, added: SI 2004/2033 Art.3

Sch.2 para.27, added: SI 2004/2033 Art.3

Sch.3 para.1, amended: SI 2003/3148 Reg.20, SI 2004/1947 Reg.19, SI 2004/2033 Art.3, Art.10

258. Al-Qa'ida and Taliban (United Nations Measures) (Channel Islands) Order 2002

Art.1, amended: 2002 c.8 s.2

259. Al-Qa'ida and Taliban (United Nations Measures) (Isle of Man) Order 2002

Art.1, amended: 2002 c.8 s.2

271. Hill Farm Allowance Regulations 2002

applied: SI 2002/1925 Sch.1

referred to: SI 2000/3044 Sch.1 Part II

Reg.7, referred to: SI 2002/1925 Sch.1

272. Sea Fishing (Enforcement of Community Quota and Third Country Fishing Measures) Order 2002

revoked: SI 2003/772 Art.13

274. Sheep and Goats Identification and Movement (Interim Measures) (Wales) Regulations 2002

revoked: SI 2002/1354 Reg.2

Reg.2, amended: SI 2002/811 Art.3

Reg.3, applied: SI 2002/1357 Art.3

Reg.4, amended: SI 2002/811 Art.4

Reg.5, amended: SI 2002/811 Art.5

Reg.6, amended: SI 2002/811 Art.6

Reg.9, amended: SI 2002/811 Art.7

Reg.12, amended: SI 2002/811 Art.8

278. School Budget Shares (Prescribed Purposes) (England) Regulations 2002

applied: SI 2002/377 Sch.2 para.28

NO.

2002–cont.

280. Disease Control (Interim Measures) (Wales) Order 2002
revoked: SI 2002/2304 Art.12
Art.2, amended: SI 2002/1038 Art.2, SI 2002/1356 Art.2, SI 2002/2061 Art.2
Art.3, amended: SI 2002/1038 Art.2, SI 2002/1356 Art.2, SI 2002/2061 Art.2
Art.3, applied: SI 1995/11 Art.13, SI 2002/1357 Art.4, Art.5, Art.12
Art.3, revoked (in part): SI 2002/2061 Art.2
Art.5, amended: SI 2002/1356 Art.2
Art.5, revoked: SI 2002/2061 Art.2
Art.6, amended: SI 2002/1356 Art.2
Art.6, revoked: SI 2002/2061 Art.2
Art.7, amended: SI 2002/1356 Art.2
Art.8, amended: SI 2002/1356 Art.2
Art.14, revoked: SI 2002/2061 Art.2

281. Pigs (Records, Identification and Movement) (Interim Measures) (Wales) Order 2002
revoked: SI 2002/2303 Art.14
Art.8, applied: SI 2003/1414 Sch.1 para.10, Sch.2 para.3
Art.8, referred to: SI 2003/1414 Sch.2 para.2

282. Health and Safety at Work etc Act 1974 (Application to Environmentally Hazardous Substances) Regulations 2002
Reg.2, amended: SI 2004/463 Reg.2

283. Animal Gatherings (Interim Measures) (Wales) Order 2002
revoked: SI 2002/2304 Art.1
varied: SI 2003/481 Art.11
Art.1, amended: SI 2002/2304 Art.13, SI 2003/169 Art.2
Art.2, amended: SI 2002/1358 Art.3, SI 2002/2060 Art.2
Sch.1 para.1, amended: SI 2002/2060 Art.2
Sch.1 para.2, amended: SI 2002/2060 Art.2
Sch.1 para.2, substituted: SI 2002/1358 Art.4
Sch.1 para.4, amended: SI 2002/2060 Art.2
Sch.1 para.6, amended: SI 2002/1358 Art.5

307. Social Security (Contributions) (Amendment No 2) Regulations 2002
Reg.3, revoked: SI 2004/770 Sch.1

308. Manchester Healthcare National Health Service Trust (Dissolution) Order 2002
see *R. v Pennine Acute Hospitals NHS Trust (formerly Rochdale Healthcare NHS Trust)* [2003] EWCA Crim 3436, [2004] 1 All E.R. 1324 (CA (Crim Div)), Tuckey, L.J.

308. Pennine Acute Hospitals National Health Service Trust (Establishment) and the Bury Health Care National Health Service Trust, the Rochdale Healthcare National Health Service Trust, the Oldham National Health Service Trust and the North Manchester 2002
applied: SI 2003/3059 Sch.1

NO.

2002–cont.

308. Pennine Acute Hospitals National Health Service Trust (Establishment) and the Bury Health Care National Health Service Trust, the Rochdale Healthcare–*cont.*
revoked: 2003 c.43 s.7

317. Companies (Fees) (Amendment) Regulations 2002
revoked: SI 2004/2621 Sch.3

324. Care Homes (Wales) Regulations 2002
Reg.2, amended: SI 2002/2935 Reg.2, SI 2004/1016 Sch.1 para.26, Sch.1 para.28, SI 2004/1314 Reg.2
Reg.3, amended: SI 2004/1756 Reg.37
Reg.3, referred to: SI 2004/692 Sch.4 para.5
Reg.5, amended: SI 2003/1004 Reg.2
Reg.5A, added: SI 2003/1004 Reg.2
Reg.7, amended: SI 2002/2622 Reg.2
Reg.9, amended: SI 2002/2622 Reg.2
Reg.19, amended: SI 2002/2622 Reg.2
Reg.39, amended: SI 2003/1004 Reg.2
Sch.2 para.2, amended: SI 2002/2622 Reg.2, SI 2004/2414 Reg.2
Sch.2 para.7, substituted: SI 2002/2622 Reg.2
Sch.2 para.8, added: SI 2004/2414 Reg.2

325. Private and Voluntary Health Care (Wales) Regulations 2002
Reg.2, amended: SI 2004/1771 Sch.1 para.23
Reg.9, amended: SI 2002/2622 Reg.4
Reg.11, amended: SI 2002/2622 Reg.4
Reg.18, amended: SI 2002/2622 Reg.4
Sch.2 para.2, amended: SI 2002/2622 Reg.4, SI 2004/2414 Reg.4
Sch.2 para.8, substituted: SI 2002/2622 Reg.4
Sch.2 para.9, added: SI 2004/2414 Reg.4

326. General Teaching Council for Wales (Fees) Regulations 2002
Reg.3, amended: SI 2004/1745 Reg.3
Reg.4, amended: SI 2004/1745 Reg.3

327. Children's Homes (Wales) Regulations 2002
Part III, referred to: SI 1991/1507 Reg.4
Part IV, referred to: SI 1991/1507 Reg.4
Part V, referred to: SI 1991/1507 Reg.4
Reg.6, amended: SI 2002/2622 Reg.3
Reg.8, amended: SI 2002/2622 Reg.3
Reg.12, varied: SI 2002/324 Reg.33
Reg.15, varied: SI 2002/324 Reg.33
Reg.16, varied: SI 2002/324 Reg.33
Reg.17, varied: SI 2002/324 Reg.33
Reg.18, varied: SI 2002/324 Reg.33
Reg.23, varied: SI 2002/324 Reg.33
Reg.26, amended: SI 2002/2622 Reg.3
Reg.29, applied: SI 2002/324 Reg.33
Reg.29, varied: SI 2002/324 Reg.33
Sch.2 para.2, amended: SI 2002/2622 Reg.3, SI 2004/2414 Reg.3

2002–cont.

327. Children's Homes (Wales) Regulations 2002–*cont.*

Sch.2 para.7, substituted: SI 2002/2622 Reg.3

Sch.2 para.8, added: SI 2004/2414 Reg.3

Sch.5, applied: SI 2002/324 Sch.6 para.10

Sch.5, varied: SI 2002/324 Reg.33

329. Miscellaneous Food Additives (Amendment) (Wales) Regulations 2002

applied: SI 2004/554 Reg.3

referred to: SI 2003/945 Reg.3

Reg.3, referred to: SI 1995/3187 Reg.11

Reg.8, referred to: SI 1995/3187 Reg.11

Reg.9, amended: SI 2003/3037 Reg.11, SI 2003/3047 Reg.10, SI 2003/3053 Reg.10

Reg.9, revoked (in part): SI 2003/945 Reg.3

330. Sweeteners in Food (Amendment) (Wales) Regulations 2002

applied: SI 2004/554 Reg.3

Reg.3, revoked (in part): SI 2003/1713 Reg.3

334. Food (Star Anise from Third Countries) (Emergency Control) (England) Order 2002

revoked: SI 2003/2338 Art.2

Art.3, amended: SI 2002/602 Art.3

Art.5, amended: SI 2002/602 Art.4

337. Assured Tenancies and Agricultural Occupancies (Forms) (Amendment) (England) Regulations 2002

revoked: SI 2003/260 Reg.3

338. Income Support (General) (Standard Interest Rate Amendment) (No.2) Regulations 2002

revoked: SI 2003/2693 Reg.3

355. Social Security (Claims and Payments) Amendment Regulations 2002

revoked (in part): SI 2003/492 Sch.3 Part 1

356. South Huddersfield Primary Care Trust (Establishment) Order 2002

Art.1, amended: SI 2002/1405 Sch.1

Art.4, revoked: SI 2002/1405 Sch.1

357. Hambleton and Richmondshire Primary Care Trust (Establishment) Order 2002

Art.1, amended: SI 2002/1405 Sch.1

Art.4, revoked: SI 2002/1405 Sch.1

358. Huddersfield Central Primary Care Trust (Establishment) Order 2002

Art.1, amended: SI 2002/1405 Sch.1

Art.4, revoked: SI 2002/1405 Sch.1

377. Financing of Maintained Schools (England) Regulations 2002

applied: SI 2003/3247 Reg.23, Reg.24, Reg.28

revoked: SI 2003/3247 Reg.2

Part IV, applied: SI 2003/453 Reg.7

Reg.8, applied: SI 2002/535 Sch.3, SI 2003/453 Reg.18

Reg.11, applied: SI 2002/535 Sch.3

2002–cont.

377. Financing of Maintained Schools (England) Regulations 2002–*cont.*

Reg.14, applied: SI 2002/535 Sch.3

Reg.17, amended: SI 2002/2763 Reg.2, SI 2002/2868 Reg.3

Reg.17, applied: SI 2002/535 Sch.3

Reg.17A, added: SI 2002/2763 Reg.2, SI 2002/2868 Reg.3

Reg.18, applied: SI 2002/535 Sch.3, SI 2003/3247 Reg.24

Reg.19, applied: SI 2002/535 Sch.3

Reg.21, applied: SI 2002/535 Sch.2, Sch.3, SI 2003/453 Reg.17, Reg.18, Reg.20, SI 2003/3247 Reg.24

Reg.22, applied: SI 2002/535 Sch.3, SI 2003/453 Reg.20

Reg.23, applied: SI 2002/535 Sch.3

Reg.24, applied: SI 2002/535 Sch.3

Reg.25, applied: SI 2002/535 Sch.3

Reg.26, applied: SI 2002/535 Sch.3

Reg.27, applied: SI 2002/535 Sch.3

Reg.32, applied: SI 2003/453 Reg.20

Sch.1 para.1, applied: SI 2002/535 Sch.1

Sch.1 para.2, applied: SI 2002/535 Sch.1

Sch.1 para.3, applied: SI 2002/535 Sch.1

Sch.1 para.4, applied: SI 2002/535 Sch.1

Sch.1 para.5, applied: SI 2002/535 Sch.1

Sch.1 para.6, applied: SI 2002/535 Sch.1

Sch.1 para.7, applied: SI 2002/535 Sch.1

Sch.1 para.8, applied: SI 2002/535 Sch.1

Sch.1 para.9, applied: SI 2002/535 Sch.1

Sch.1 para.10, applied: SI 2002/535 Sch.1

Sch.1 para.11, applied: SI 2002/535 Sch.1

Sch.1 para.12, applied: SI 2002/535 Sch.1

Sch.1 para.13, applied: SI 2002/535 Sch.1

Sch.1 para.14, applied: SI 2002/535 Sch.1

Sch.1 para.15, applied: SI 2002/535 Sch.1

Sch.1 para.16, amended: SI 2002/2469 Sch.1 para.101

Sch.1 para.16, applied: SI 2002/535 Sch.1

Sch.1 para.17, applied: SI 2002/535 Sch.1

Sch.1 para.19, applied: SI 2002/535 Sch.1

Sch.1 para.20, applied: SI 2002/535 Sch.1

Sch.1 para.21, applied: SI 2002/535 Sch.1

Sch.1 para.22, applied: SI 2002/535 Sch.1

Sch.1 para.23, applied: SI 2002/535 Sch.1

Sch.1 para.24, applied: SI 2002/535 Sch.1

Sch.1 para.25, applied: SI 2002/535 Sch.1

Sch.1 para.26, applied: SI 2002/535 Sch.1

Sch.1 para.27, applied: SI 2002/535 Sch.1

Sch.1 para.28, applied: SI 2002/535 Sch.1

Sch.1 para.29, applied: SI 2002/535 Sch.1

Sch.1 para.30, applied: SI 2002/535 Sch.1

Sch.1 para.31, applied: SI 2002/535 Sch.1

Sch.1 para.32, applied: SI 2002/535 Sch.2

Sch.1 para.33, applied: SI 2002/535 Sch.1

Sch.1 para.34, applied: SI 2002/535 Sch.1

Sch.1 para.35, applied: SI 2002/535 Sch.1

Sch.1 para.38, applied: SI 2002/535 Sch.1

Sch.1 para.39, applied: SI 2002/535 Sch.1

NO.

2002–cont.

377. Financing of Maintained Schools (England) Regulations 2002–*cont.*
Sch.1 para.40, applied: SI 2002/535 Sch.1
Sch.1 para.41, applied: SI 2002/535 Sch.1
Sch.1 para.42, applied: SI 2002/535 Sch.1
Sch.1 para.43, applied: SI 2002/535 Sch.1
Sch.1 para.44, applied: SI 2002/535 Sch.1
Sch.1 para.45, applied: SI 2002/535 Sch.1
Sch.2, applied: SI 2002/535 Sch.3
Sch.4 para.28, added: SI 2002/2062 Reg.2

378. School Budget Shares (Prescribed Purposes) (England) Regulations 2002
referred to: SI 2003/453 Sch.1 para.28, SI 2003/3247 Sch.1 para.28
Reg.2, revoked: SI 2004/444 Reg.2
Reg.3, amended: SI 2004/444 Reg.2
Reg.4, revoked: SI 2004/444 Reg.2

379. Sweeteners in Food (Amendment) (England) Regulations 2002
referred to: SI 2003/1008 Reg.3
Reg.5, revoked (in part): SI 2003/1182 Reg.3

398. Social Security Amendment (Residential Care and Nursing Homes) Regulations 2002
Reg.2, revoked (in part): SI 2003/492 Sch.3 Part 1

401. European Economic Interest Grouping (Fees) (Amendment) Regulations 2002
revoked: SI 2004/2643 Sch.1

402. Food (Star Anise from Third Countries) (Emergency Control) (Wales) Order 2002
revoked: SI 2003/2661 Art.2

410. National Assistance (Assessment of Resources) (Amendment) (England) Regulations 2002
revoked: SI 2003/627 Reg.8

411. National Assistance (Sums for Personal Requirements) (England) Regulations 2002
revoked: SI 2003/628 Reg.3

412. Chester Guided Busway Order 2002
Sch.5 para.3, amended: SI 2003/2155 Sch.1 para.17
Sch.5 para.6, amended: SI 2003/2155 Sch.2

414. Registered Parties (Non-constituent and Non-affiliated Organisations) (Amendment) Order 2002
varied: SI 2004/366 Art.5

427. Occupational and Personal Pension Schemes (Bankruptcy) Regulations 2002
referred to: SI 2002/836 Reg.1
revoked: SI 2002/836 Reg.20

428. Social Security (Claims and Payments and Miscellaneous Amendments) Regulations 2002
Reg.1, revoked (in part): SI 2003/492 Sch.3 Part 1

NO.

2002–cont.

428. Social Security (Claims and Payments and Miscellaneous Amendments) Regulations 2002–*cont.*
Reg.2, revoked: SI 2003/492 Sch.3 Part 1
Reg.3, revoked: SI 2003/492 Sch.3 Part 1

432. School Organisation Proposals by the National Council for Education and Training for Wales Regulations 2002
revoked: SI 2004/1576 Reg.21

435. Education (QCA Levy) Regulations 2002
Reg.5, amended: SI 2002/1331 Reg.2

442. Velindre National Health Service Trust (Establishment) Amendment Order 2002
revoked: 2003 c.43 s.7

454. Whole of Government Accounts (Designation of Bodies) Order 2002
Sch.2, varied: SI 2004/664 Art.11, Art.12, Art.13, Art.14

457. Dairy Produce Quotas Regulations 2002
Reg.3, amended: SI 2004/312 Reg.5, Sch.1, Sch.2
Reg.4, substituted: SI 2004/312 Reg.6
Reg.5, amended: SI 2004/312 Sch.1
Reg.7, amended: SI 2004/312 Sch.1
Reg.8, amended: SI 2004/312 Sch.1, Sch.2
Reg.12, substituted: SI 2004/312 Reg.7
Reg.14, amended: SI 2004/312 Sch.1
Reg.15, amended: SI 2004/312 Sch.1
Reg.17, amended: SI 2004/312 Sch.1, Sch.2
Reg.18, amended: SI 2004/312 Sch.2
Reg.19, amended: SI 2004/312 Sch.1
Reg.21, amended: SI 2004/312 Sch.1, Sch.2
Reg.23, amended: SI 2004/312 Reg.8, Sch.2
Reg.25, amended: SI 2004/312 Sch.2
Reg.26, amended: SI 2004/312 Reg.9
Reg.28, amended: SI 2004/312 Sch.1
Reg.31, amended: SI 2004/312 Reg.10, Reg.11, Sch.2
Reg.33, substituted: SI 2004/312 Reg.12
Sch.1 para.1, amended: SI 2004/312 Reg.13
Sch.1 para.12, amended: SI 2004/312 Reg.13
Sch.2 para.9, amended: SI 2004/312 Sch.1
Sch.2 para.17, amended: SI 2004/312 Sch.1
Sch.2 para.19, amended: SI 2004/312 Sch.1
Sch.3 para.1, amended: SI 2004/312 Sch.2

458. Dairy Produce Quotas (General Provisions) Regulations 2002
Reg.7, applied: 1992 c.53 Sch.1 Part I, Sch.1 Part II

467. Animals and Animal Products (Import and Export) (England and Wales) (Amendment) (England) Regulations 2002
revoked: SI 2004/853 Reg.35

NO.

2002–cont.

475. Gas (Standards of Performance) Regulations 2002
Reg.2, amended: SI 2002/741 Reg.2, Reg.6
Reg.4A, added: SI 2002/741 Reg.3
Reg.4B, added: SI 2002/741 Reg.3
Reg.4C, added: SI 2002/741 Reg.3
Reg.5, substituted: SI 2002/741 Reg.4
Reg.5, amended: SI 2002/741 Reg.5, Reg.6
Reg.6, substituted: SI 2002/741 Reg.4
Reg.6, amended: SI 2002/741 Reg.6
Reg.7, substituted: SI 2002/741 Reg.4
Reg.7, amended: SI 2002/741 Reg.6, Reg.7
Reg.8, substituted: SI 2002/741 Reg.4
Reg.8, amended: SI 2002/741 Reg.6, Reg.8
Reg.9, substituted: SI 2002/741 Reg.4
Reg.10, substituted: SI 2002/741 Reg.4
Reg.10, amended: SI 2002/741 Reg.9
Reg.11, amended: SI 2002/741 Reg.10
Sch.1 Part 1, amended: SI 2002/741 Reg.11

476. Electricity (Standards of Performance) (Amendment) Regulations 2002
revoked: SI 2002/742 Reg.2

492. Social Security (Guardian's Allowances) Amendment Regulations 2002
revoked: SI 2003/495 Sch.1 Part 1

498. Non-Domestic Rating (Alteration of Lists and Appeals)(Amendment)(England) Regulations 2002
Reg.6, revoked: SI 2003/2000 Reg.3

501. Excise Goods (Accompanying Documents) Regulations 2002
applied: SI 1993/1228 Reg.13
referred to: SI 1992/3135 Reg.11, SI 2004/1003 Reg.7
Part II, applied: SI 1988/809 Reg.17
Reg.2, varied: SI 2003/2758 Sch.1 para.7, Sch.1 para.8, Sch.1 para.9
Reg.15, varied: SI 2003/2758 Sch.1 para.10
Reg.17, varied: SI 2003/2758 Sch.1 para.10
Reg.21, varied: SI 2003/2758 Sch.1 para.11, Sch.1 para.12

505. Electoral Commission (Limit on Public Awareness Expenditure) Order 2002
varied: SI 2004/366 Art.5

508. Education (Teacher Training Bursaries) (England) Regulations 2002
applied: SI 2002/507 Art.2
Reg.2, amended: SI 2003/3094 Reg.3
Reg.3, amended: SI 2003/3094 Reg.4

509. Education (Bursaries for School Teacher Training) (England) Regulations 2002
revoked: SI 2002/3005 Reg.2
Reg.2, amended: SI 2002/756 Reg.2, SI 2002/1137 Reg.3
Reg.4, amended: SI 2002/1137 Reg.3
Reg.4, revoked (in part): SI 2002/1137 Reg.3
Reg.7, amended: SI 2002/756 Reg.2

NO.

2002–cont.

510. Education Standards Fund (England) Regulations 2002
Reg.2, amended: SI 2002/1738 Reg.3
Reg.5, amended: SI 2002/1738 Reg.4
Sch.1 para.2, amended: SI 2002/1738 Reg.5
Sch.1 para.6, amended: SI 2002/1738 Reg.5

523. Local Government (Best Value) Performance Indicators and Performance Standards Order 2002
revoked: SI 2003/530 Art.19

526. Plant Protection Products (Amendment) Regulations 2002
revoked: SI 2002/1460 Reg.4

528. Environmental Protection (Controls on Ozone-Depleting Substances) Regulations 2002
referred to: SI 2002/800 Sch.1

531. Environmental Protection (Waste Recycling Payments) (Amendment) (England) Regulations 2002
revoked: SI 2003/596 Reg.3

532. Redundancy Payments (Continuity of Employment in Local Government, etc.) (Modification) (Amendment) Order 2002
varied: SI 2004/664 Art.11, Art.12, Art.13, Art.14
Art.2, varied: SI 2004/664 Art.11, Art.12, Art.13, Art.14

536. Education (Outturn Statements) (England) Regulations 2002
revoked: SI 2003/1153 Reg.3

543. National Health Service (England) (Pilot Schemes Miscellaneous Provisions and Consequential Amendments) Amendment Regulations 2002
revoked: SI 2003/1250 Sch.10 Part 2, SI 2004/865 Sch.2

544. National Health Service (Dental Charges) Amendment Regulations 2002
revoked: SI 2003/586 Reg.3

545. National Health Service (Functions of Health Authorities) (England) (Support of Provision of Services and Appraisal) Regulations 2002
revoked: SI 2004/865 Sch.2
Reg.1, amended: SI 2002/2469 Sch.7, SI 2003/1937 Sch.1 para.5
Reg.2, amended: SI 2003/1937 Sch.1 para.5
Reg.2, applied: SI 2002/2375 Reg.4

550. Welfare Food (Amendment) Regulations 2002
revoked: SI 2004/723 Reg.6

551. National Health Service (Pharmaceutical Services) and (General Medical Services) (No.2) Amendment Regulations 2002
Reg.3, revoked: SI 2004/865 Sch.2

2002–cont.

552. National Care Standards Commission (Inspection of Schools and Colleges) Regulations 2002

varied: SI 2004/664 Art.11, Art.12, Art.13, Art.14

Reg.1, varied: SI 2004/664 Art.11, Art.12, Art.13, Art.14

Reg.2, varied: SI 2004/664 Art.11, Art.12, Art.13, Art.14

553. Health Authorities (Establishment and Abolition) (England) Order 2002

Art.7, applied: SI 1992/635 Reg.18L

Sch.1, amended: SI 2002/2469 Reg.3, SI 2004/37 Art.2

554. National Health Service (General Medical Services) Amendment Regulations 2002

revoked: SI 2004/865 Sch.2

564. Rochdale Healthcare National Health Service Trust (Transfer of Trust Property) Order 2002

see *R. v Pennine Acute Hospitals NHS Trust (formerly Rochdale Healthcare NHS Trust)* [2003] EWCA Crim 3436, [2004] 1 All E.R. 1324 (CA (Crim Div)), Tuckey, L.J.

570. Act of Sederunt (Rules of the Court of Session Amendment No.2) (Personal Injuries Actions) 2002

see *Tudhope v Finlay Park (t/a Park Hutchison Solicitors)* 2003 S.L.T. 1305 (OH), Lady Paton

580. National Health Service (Travelling Expenses and Remission of Charges) Amendment Regulations 2002

revoked: SI 2003/2382 Sch.2

603. National Care Standards Commission (Director of Private and Voluntary Health Care) Regulations 2002

revoked: SI 2004/664 Art.6

varied: SI 2004/664 Art.11, Art.12, Art.13, Art.14

Reg.1, varied: SI 2004/664 Art.11, Art.12, Art.13, Art.14

Reg.3, varied: SI 2004/664 Art.11, Art.12, Art.13, Art.14

615. Police and Criminal Evidence Act 1984 (Codes of Practice) (Temporary Modifications to Code D) Order 2002

revoked: SI 2003/704 Art.4

616. South Birmingham Primary Care Trust (Establishment) Order 2002

Art.1, amended: SI 2002/1405 Sch.1

Art.4, revoked: SI 2002/1405 Sch.1

617. Central Cheshire Primary Care Trust (Establishment) Order 2002

Art.1, amended: SI 2002/1405 Sch.1

Art.4, revoked: SI 2002/1405 Sch.1

Sch.1, amended: SI 2004/543 Sch.1

2002–cont.

618. Medical Devices Regulations 2002

applied: SI 2002/1689 Reg.3, SI 2003/1076 Art.1, Sch.1 para.1, SR 2002/301 Reg.3

Reg.2, amended: SI 2003/1697 Reg.2

Reg.4, amended: SI 2003/1697 Reg.3

Reg.5, amended: SI 2003/1697 Reg.4

Reg.7, amended: SI 2003/1697 Reg.5

Reg.13, amended: SI 2003/1697 Reg.6

Reg.17, amended: SI 2003/1697 Reg.7

Reg.18, amended: SI 2003/1697 Reg.8

Reg.19A, added: SI 2003/1697 Reg.9

Reg.20, amended: SI 2003/1697 Reg.10

Reg.32, amended: SI 2003/1697 Reg.11

Reg.44A, added: SI 2003/1697 Reg.12

Reg.45, amended: SI 2003/1697 Reg.13

Reg.47, amended: SI 2003/1697 Reg.14

Reg.52, amended: SI 2003/1697 Reg.15

Reg.54, amended: SI 2003/1697 Reg.16

Reg.59, amended: SI 2003/1697 Reg.17

Reg.61, amended: SI 2003/1400 Sch.5

634. North Warwickshire Primary Care Trust (Establishment) Order 2002

Art.1, amended: SI 2002/1405 Sch.1

Art.4, revoked: SI 2002/1405 Sch.1

635. Disqualification from Caring for Children (England) Regulations 2002

varied: SI 2004/664 Art.11, Art.12, Art.13, Art.14

637. Gaming Act (Variation of Fees) (England and Wales) Order 2002

referred to: SI 2003/508 Art.2

revoked: SI 2003/508 Art.3

Sch.1, referred to: SI 2003/508 Art.2

638. Awards For All (England) Joint Scheme (Authorisation) Order 2002

revoked: SI 2003/664 Art.3

639. Lotteries (Gaming Board Fees) Order 2002

revoked: SI 2004/532 Art.9

641. Wireless Telegraphy (Television Licence Fees) (Amendment) Regulations 2002

revoked: SI 2004/692 Sch.6

642. Gaming Act (Variation of Fees) (England and Wales and Scotland) Order 2002

referred to: SI 2003/509 Art.2

Sch.1, amended: SI 2003/509 Art.3

Sch.1, referred to: SI 2003/509 Art.2

647. Cambridgeshire and Peterborough Mental Health Partnership National Health Service Trust (Establishment) and the Lifespan Health Care Cambridge National Health Service Trust and the North West Anglia Health Care National Health Service Trust (Diss 2002

referred to: SI 2004/569 Sch.1

revoked: 2003 c.43 s.7

Art.2, amended: SI 2002/1690 Art.2

Art.4, amended: SI 2003/2427 Art.2

NO.

2002–cont.

651. Blaenau Gwent and Caerphilly (Trede-gar and Rhymney) Order 2002
varied: SI 2004/218 Art.2

652. Neath Port Talbot and Swansea (Trebanos and Clydach) Order 2002
varied: SI 2004/218 Art.2

654. Rhondda Cynon Taff and Vale of Glamorgan (Llanharry, Pont-y-clun, Penllyn, Welsh St Donats and Pendoylan) Order 2002
varied: SI 2004/218 Art.2

655. Health and Safety (Fees) Regulations 2002
revoked: SI 2003/547 Reg.26

656. Rail Vehicle Accessibility (South West Trains Class 458 Vehicles) Exemption Order 2002
Art.2, substituted: SI 2002/1762 Art.2
Art.5, substituted: SI 2002/1762 Art.2
Art.6, amended: SI 2002/1762 Art.2, SI 2004/2149 Art.2
Art.7, substituted: SI 2004/2149 Art.2

658. Transport Act 2000 (Commencement No 8 and Transitional Provisions) Order 2002
Sch.1 Part 2, amended: SI 2002/846 Art.2

666. Relocation Grants (Form of Applica-tion) (Amendment) (England) Regula-tions 2002
revoked: SI 2002/1860 Sch.6

668. Social Security Benefits Up-rating Order 2002
revoked: SI 2003/526 Art.26

680. Income Tax (Employments and Elec-tronic Communications) (Miscella-neous Provisions) Regulations 2002
Reg.3, revoked: SI 2003/2682 Sch.2
Reg.4, revoked: SI 2003/2682 Sch.2
Reg.5, revoked: SI 2003/2682 Sch.2
Reg.6, revoked: SI 2003/2682 Sch.2
Reg.7, revoked: SI 2003/2682 Sch.2
Reg.8, revoked: SI 2003/2682 Sch.2

684. Social Security Benefits Up-rating Regulations 2002
revoked: SI 2003/601 Reg.5, SI 2004/583 Reg.5
Reg.2, revoked: SI 2003/601 Reg.5
Reg.3, revoked: SI 2003/601 Reg.5
Reg.4, revoked: SI 2003/601 Reg.5

689. Companies (Disqualification Orders) (Amendment) Regulations 2002
revoked: SI 2002/1834 Reg.3

694. Police Authorities (Best Value) Performance Indicators Order 2002
revoked: SI 2003/519 Art.3

695. Police (Secretary of State's Objec-tives) Order 2002
revoked: SI 2003/830 Art.2

2002–cont.

704. Financial Services and Markets Act 2000 (Permission and Applications) (Credit Unions etc.) Order 2002
Art.2, amended: SI 2002/1501 Art.17
Art.3, applied: SI 2002/1501 Art.5, Art.6

708. Nurses, Midwives and Health Visitors (Professional Conduct) (Amendment No 2) Rules 2002 Approval Order 2002
revoked: 1999 c.8 Sch.5
varied: SI 2004/1762 Art.1

719. ABRO Trading Fund Order 2002
referred to: SI 2003/105 Art.1
Art.4, amended: SI 2003/105 Art.2

722. Swindon Primary Care Trust (Estab-lishment) Order 2002
Art.1, amended: SI 2002/1405 Sch.1
Art.4, revoked: SI 2002/1405 Sch.1

723. Kennet and North Wiltshire Primary Care Trust (Establishment) Order 2002
Art.1, amended: SI 2002/1405 Sch.1
Art.4, revoked: SI 2002/1405 Sch.1
Sch.1, amended: SI 2004/543 Sch.1

724. Ellesmere Port and Neston Primary Care Trust (Establishment) Order 2002
Art.1, amended: SI 2002/1405 Sch.1
Art.4, revoked: SI 2002/1405 Sch.1

725. Cheshire West Primary Care Trust (Establishment) Order 2002
Art.1, amended: SI 2002/1405 Sch.1
Art.4, revoked: SI 2002/1405 Sch.1
Sch.1, amended: SI 2004/543 Sch.1

726. Eastern Cheshire Primary Care Trust (Establishment) Order 2002
Art.1, amended: SI 2002/1405 Sch.1
Art.4, revoked: SI 2002/1405 Sch.1

727. Poole Primary Care Trust (Establish-ment) Order 2002
Art.1, amended: SI 2002/1405 Sch.1
Art.4, revoked: SI 2002/1405 Sch.1

728. Birkenhead and Wallasey Primary Care Trust (Establishment) Order 2002
Art.1, amended: SI 2002/1405 Sch.1
Art.4, revoked: SI 2002/1405 Sch.1

730. Rushmoor and Hart Primary Care Trust (Change of Name) Order 2002
revoked: SI 2002/1115 Art.3

731. North and East Devon Partnership National Health Service Trust Change of Name and (Establishment) Amendment Order 2002
revoked: 2003 c.43 s.7

756. Education (Bursaries for School Teacher Training) (England) (Amend-ment) Regulations 2002
revoked: SI 2002/3005 Reg.2

2002–cont.

761. Aggregates Levy (General) Regulations 2002

Part III, applied: SI 2002/1927 Reg.3, Reg.4, SI 2004/1959 Reg.3, Reg.9

Reg.15, applied: SI 2002/1927 Reg.5, SI 2004/1959 Reg.10

Reg.16, applied: SI 2002/1927 Reg.5, SI 2004/1959 Reg.10

Sch.1, amended: SI 2003/466 Reg.3

Sch.1, referred to: SI 2003/466 Reg.2

762. Value Added Tax (Health and Welfare) Order 2002

see *Kingscrest Associates Ltd (t/a Kingscrest Residential Care Homes) v Customs and Excise Commissioners* [2003] B.V.C. 2592 (V&DTr), Adrian Shipwright (Chairman)

773. Food (Figs, Hazelnuts and Pistachios from Turkey) (Emergency Control) (England) Regulations 2002

applied: SI 2002/821 Reg.3

revoked: SI 2002/2351 Reg.7

774. Food (Peanuts from China) (Emergency Control) (England) Regulations 2002

revoked: SI 2002/2350 Reg.7

775. General Optical Council (Registration and Enrolment (Amendment) Rules) Order of Council 2002

referred to: SI 2003/1080

revoked: SI 2003/1080 Art.2

782. Asylum Support (Repeal) Order 2002

revoked: 2002 c.41 s.61

786. Humber Bridge (Revision of Tolls) Order 2002

see *R. (on the application of Confederation of Passenger Transport UK) v Humber Bridge Board* [2002] EWHC 2261, [2002] N.P.C. 136 (QBD (Admin Ct)), Newman, J.

787. Hemp (Third Country Imports) Regulations 2002

Reg.11, amended: SI 2002/1924 Reg.2

Reg.15, amended: SI 2002/1924 Reg.2

788. Reciprocal Enforcement of Maintenance Orders (Designation of Reciprocating Countries) Order 2002

applied: SI 2002/789

referred to: SI 2002/789 Art.1

794. Ministry of Agriculture, Fisheries and Food (Dissolution) Order 2002

Art.2, applied: SI 2002/892, SI 2003/1296, SI 2003/1503, SI 2003/1850, SI 2003/2912, SI 2003/3119, SI 2004/1301, SI 2004/2688

Art.2, referred to: SI 2004/2146

Art.6, applied: SI 2002/892, SI 2003/1296, SI 2003/1503, SI 2003/1850, SI 2003/2912, SI 2003/3119, SI 2004/1301

Art.6, referred to: SI 2004/2146

2002–cont.

795. Immigration (Designation of Travel Bans) (Amendment No 2) Order 2002

revoked: SI 2003/3285 Sch.2

796. Criminal Injuries Compensation (Northern Ireland) Order 2002

Art.1, enabled: SR 2002/148, SR 2002/205

Art.3, enabled: SR 2002/204

Art.7, applied: 1967 c.13 Sch.4

Art.12, revoked (in part): 2002 c.21 Sch.6

800. Scotland Act 1998 (Agency Arrangements) (Specification) (No.2) Order 2002

Sch.1, amended: SSI 2002/541 Sch.6

802. Local Authorities (Executive Arrangements) (Discharge of Functions) (Wales) Regulations 2002

Reg.12, amended: SI 2002/2941 Reg.2, SI 2003/147 Reg.3

811. Sheep and Goats Identification and Movement (Interim Measures) (Wales) (Amendment) Order 2002

revoked: SI 2002/1354 Reg.2

812. Child Minding and Day Care (Wales) Regulations 2002

Reg.4, amended: SI 2002/2171 Reg.2, SI 2002/2622 Reg.6, SI 2003/2708 Reg.2

Reg.4, revoked (in part): SI 2002/2622 Reg.6

Reg.4A, added: SI 2003/2708 Reg.2

Reg.4B, added: SI 2003/2708 Reg.2

Reg.5, amended: SI 2003/2708 Reg.2

Reg.6, amended: SI 2003/2708 Reg.2

Reg.16, amended: SI 2002/2171 Reg.2, SI 2002/2622 Reg.6

Reg.16, revoked (in part): SI 2002/2622 Reg.6

Sch.2 para.2, amended: SI 2002/2622 Reg.6, SI 2004/2414 Reg.7

Sch.2 para.7, substituted: SI 2002/2622 Reg.6

Sch.2 para.8, added: SI 2004/2414 Reg.7

814. National Assistance (Assessment of Resources) (Amendment) (Wales) Regulations 2002

revoked: SI 2003/897 Reg.9

815. National Assistance (Sums for Personal Requirements) (Wales) Regulations 2002

revoked: SI 2003/892 Reg.3

816. Protection of Children and Vulnerable Adults and Care Standards Tribunal Regulations 2002

applied: SI 2003/463 Art.15, Art.20, SI 2004/2071 Sch.10 para.5

Reg.1, amended: SI 2003/626 Reg.2, SI 2003/1060 Reg.2, SI 2003/2043 Reg.2, SI 2004/664 Sch.1 para.7, SI 2004/2073 Reg.2

Reg.1, varied: SI 2004/664 Art.11, Art.12, Art.13, Art.14

2002–cont.

816. Protection of Children and Vulnerable Adults and Care Standards Tribunal Regulations 2002–*cont.*

Reg.3, amended: SI 2003/1060 Reg.3, SI 2004/696 Art.3

Reg.4, amended: SI 2003/626 Reg.3, SI 2003/1060 Reg.4, SI 2003/2043 Reg.3

Reg.4A, added: SI 2004/2073 Reg.3

Reg.6, amended: SI 2003/626 Reg.4, SI 2003/1060 Reg.5, SI 2003/2043 Reg.4, SI 2004/2073 Reg.4

Reg.6A, added: SI 2003/626 Reg.5

Reg.6A, amended: SI 2003/2043 Reg.5

Reg.7, amended: SI 2003/626 Reg.6, SI 2003/2043 Reg.6, SI 2004/2073 Reg.5

Reg.8, amended: SI 2003/626 Reg.7

Reg.9, amended: SI 2003/2043 Reg.7

Reg.10, amended: SI 2004/2073 Reg.6

Reg.16, amended: SI 2003/626 Reg.8

Reg.23, amended: SI 2003/2043 Reg.8

Reg.25, amended: SI 2003/2043 Reg.9

Reg.26, amended: SI 2003/2043 Reg.10

Reg.33, amended: SI 2004/2073 Reg.7

Reg.35, amended: SI 2003/626 Reg.9, SI 2003/1060 Reg.6, SI 2003/2043 Reg.11, SI 2004/2073 Reg.8

Sch.1 para.1, amended: SI 2004/2073 Reg.9

Sch.1 para.4, revoked: SI 2004/2073 Reg.9

Sch.2 para.1, amended: SI 2004/2073 Reg.10

Sch.2 para.1, varied: SI 2003/463 Art.15

Sch.2 para.2, varied: SI 2003/463 Art.15

Sch.2 para.3, amended: SI 2004/2073 Reg.10

Sch.2 para.3, varied: SI 2003/463 Art.15

Sch.2 para.4, revoked: SI 2004/2073 Reg.10

Sch.2 para.4, varied: SI 2003/463 Art.15

Sch.2 para.5, amended: SI 2003/1060 Reg.7

Sch.2 para.5, varied: SI 2003/463 Art.15

Sch.2 para.6, varied: SI 2003/463 Art.15

Sch.3 para.4, revoked: SI 2004/2073 Reg.11

Sch.4 para.5, revoked: SI 2004/2073 Reg.12

Sch.4 para.8, amended: SI 2003/1060 Reg.7

Sch.5 para.5, revoked: SI 2004/2073 Reg.13

Sch.5 para.8, amended: SI 2003/1060 Reg.7

Sch.6 para.1, added: SI 2003/626 Sch.1

Sch.6 para.2, added: SI 2003/626 Sch.1

Sch.6 para.3, added: SI 2003/626 Sch.1

Sch.6 para.4, added: SI 2003/626 Sch.1

Sch.6 para.4, revoked: SI 2004/2073 Reg.14

Sch.6 para.5, added: SI 2003/626 Sch.1

Sch.6 para.6, added: SI 2003/626 Sch.1

Sch.7 para.1, added: SI 2003/626 Sch.1

Sch.7 para.2, added: SI 2003/626 Sch.1

Sch.7 para.3, added: SI 2003/626 Sch.1

Sch.7 para.4, added: SI 2003/626 Sch.1

Sch.7 para.5, added: SI 2003/626 Sch.1

Sch.7 para.5, revoked: SI 2004/2073 Reg.15

Sch.8 para.1, added: SI 2003/1060 Sch.1

Sch.8 para.2, added: SI 2003/1060 Sch.1

Sch.8 para.3, added: SI 2003/1060 Sch.1

2002–cont.

816. Protection of Children and Vulnerable Adults and Care Standards Tribunal Regulations 2002–*cont.*

Sch.8 para.4, added: SI 2003/1060 Sch.1

Sch.8 para.4, revoked: SI 2004/2073 Reg.16

Sch.8 para.5, added: SI 2003/1060 Sch.1

Sch.8 para.6, added: SI 2003/1060 Sch.1

Sch.9 para.1, added: SI 2003/2043 Sch.1

Sch.9 para.2, added: SI 2003/2043 Sch.1

Sch.9 para.3, added: SI 2003/2043 Sch.1

Sch.9 para.4, added: SI 2003/2043 Sch.1

Sch.9 para.4, revoked: SI 2004/2073 Reg.17

Sch.9 para.5, added: SI 2003/2043 Sch.1

Sch.9 para.6, added: SI 2003/2043 Sch.1

Sch.9 para.7, added: SI 2003/2043 Sch.1

820. Food (Peanuts from China) (Emergency Control) (Wales) Regulations 2002

revoked: SI 2002/2295 Reg.7

Reg.3, amended: SI 2002/1728 Reg.3

821. Food (Figs, Hazelnuts and Pistachios from Turkey) (Emergency Control) (Wales) Regulations 2002

revoked: SI 2002/2296 Reg.7

Reg.3, amended: SI 2002/1726 Reg.3

826. Zimbabwe (Freezing of Funds, other Financial Assets or Economic Resources) Regulations 2002

Reg.1, amended: SI 2002/2530 Reg.2

830. Social Security (Contributions) (Rerating and National Insurance Funds Payments) Order 2002

Art.2, revoked: 2002 c.19 Sch.2

Art.5, amended: 2002 c.19 Sch.2

Art.5, revoked (in part): 2002 c.19 Sch.2

834. National Assembly for Wales (Representation of the People) (Amendment) Order 2002

revoked: SI 2003/284 Art.1

838. Education (School Teachers Pay and Conditions) Order 2002

revoked: SI 2002/2223 Art.1

840. Education (School Performance Targets) (England) (Amendment) Regulations 2002

revoked: SI 2004/2858 Sch.2

843. TSE (England) Regulations 2002

referred to: SI 2003/1482 Reg.51, Sch.4 para.1

Reg.3, amended: SI 2002/1253 Reg.2

Reg.9, amended: SI 2002/1253 Reg.2

Reg.13, amended: SI 2003/1482 Sch.4 para.3

Reg.28, amended: SI 2002/2860 Reg.2

Reg.29A, added: SI 2002/2860 Reg.2

Reg.29B, added: SI 2002/2860 Reg.2

Reg.29C, added: SI 2002/2860 Reg.2

Reg.29D, added: SI 2002/2860 Reg.2

Reg.29E, added: SI 2002/2860 Reg.2

Reg.29F, added: SI 2002/2860 Reg.2

2002–cont.

843. TSE (England) Regulations 2002–*cont.*
Reg.33, revoked (in part): SI 2003/1482 Sch.4 para.2
Reg.34, revoked (in part): SI 2003/1482 Sch.4 para.2
Reg.34A, added: SI 2003/1482 Sch.4 para.4
Reg.36, applied: SI 1997/2964 Art.6
Reg.40, substituted: SI 2003/1482 Sch.4 para.5
Reg.52, revoked: SI 2003/1482 Sch.4 para.2
Reg.54, revoked: SI 2003/1482 Sch.4 para.2
Reg.56, revoked (in part): SI 2003/1482 Sch.4 para.2
Reg.63, revoked: SI 2003/1482 Sch.4 para.2
Reg.64, revoked: SI 2003/1482 Sch.4 para.2
Reg.65, revoked: SI 2003/1482 Sch.4 para.2
Reg.66, revoked: SI 2003/1482 Sch.4 para.2
Reg.67, revoked: SI 2003/1482 Sch.4 para.2
Reg.68, revoked: SI 2003/1482 Sch.4 para.2
Reg.69, revoked (in part): SI 2003/1482 Sch.4 para.2
Reg.71, revoked (in part): SI 2002/1253 Reg.2
Reg.86A, added: SI 2004/1518 Reg.3
Reg.99, amended: SI 2002/1253 Reg.2
Sch.5, substituted: SI 2003/1482 Sch.4 para.6
Sch.6 Part I para.1, revoked: SI 2003/1482 Sch.4 para.2
Sch.6 Part I para.2, revoked: SI 2003/1482 Sch.4 para.2
Sch.6 Part I para.3, revoked: SI 2003/1482 Sch.4 para.2
Sch.6 Part I para.4, revoked: SI 2003/1482 Sch.4 para.2
Sch.6 Part I para.5, revoked: SI 2003/1482 Sch.4 para.2
Sch.6 Part I para.6, revoked: SI 2003/1482 Sch.4 para.2
Sch.6 Part I para.7, revoked: SI 2003/1482 Sch.4 para.2
Sch.6 Part I para.8, revoked: SI 2003/1482 Sch.4 para.2
Sch.6 Part II para.1, revoked: SI 2003/1482 Sch.4 para.2
Sch.6 Part II para.2, revoked: SI 2003/1482 Sch.4 para.2
Sch.6 Part II para.3, revoked: SI 2003/1482 Sch.4 para.2
Sch.6 Part II para.4, revoked: SI 2003/1482 Sch.4 para.2
Sch.6 Part II para.5, revoked: SI 2003/1482 Sch.4 para.2
Sch.6 Part II para.6, revoked: SI 2003/1482 Sch.4 para.2
Sch.6 Part II para.7, revoked: SI 2003/1482 Sch.4 para.2
Sch.6A Part I para.1, added: SI 2004/1518 Reg.4
Sch.6A Part I para.2, added: SI 2004/1518 Reg.4

2002–cont.

843. TSE (England) Regulations 2002–*cont.*
Sch.6A Part I para.3, added: SI 2004/1518 Reg.4
Sch.6A Part I para.4, added: SI 2004/1518 Reg.4
Sch.6A Part I para.5, added: SI 2004/1518 Reg.4
Sch.6A Part I para.6, added: SI 2004/1518 Reg.4
Sch.6A Part I para.7, added: SI 2004/1518 Reg.4
Sch.6A Part I para.8, added: SI 2004/1518 Reg.4
Sch.6A Part II para.9, added: SI 2004/1518 Reg.4
Sch.6A Part II para.10, added: SI 2004/1518 Reg.4
Sch.6A Part II para.11, added: SI 2004/1518 Reg.4
Sch.6A Part II para.12, added: SI 2004/1518 Reg.4
Sch.6A Part II para.13, added: SI 2004/1518 Reg.4
Sch.6A Part II para.14, added: SI 2004/1518 Reg.4
Sch.6A Part III para.15, added: SI 2004/1518 Reg.4
Sch.6A Part III para.16, added: SI 2004/1518 Reg.4
Sch.6A Part IV para.17, added: SI 2004/1518 Reg.4

848. National Health Service (General Medical Services Supplementary List) (Amendment) Regulations 2002
revoked: SI 2003/1250 Sch.10 Part 2

849. European Specialist Medical Qualifications Amendment Regulations 2002
revoked: SI 2003/1250 Sch.10 Part 2

865. Care Standards Act 2000 (Establishments and Agencies) (Miscellaneous Amendments) Regulations 2002
varied: SI 2004/664 Art.11, Art.12, Art.13, Art.14
Reg.8, varied: SI 2004/664 Art.11, Art.12, Art.13, Art.14
Reg.9, varied: SI 2004/664 Art.11, Art.12, Art.13, Art.14

868. Zimbabwe (Sale, Supply, Export and Shipment of Equipment) (Penalties and Licences) Regulations 2002
revoked: SI 2004/559 Sch.1

881. Nursing and Midwifery Order 2001 (Consequential Amendments) Order 2002
Sch.1 para.9, revoked (in part): SI 2004/865 Sch.2, SI 2004/1016 Sch.2

886. Local Government (Whole Authority Analyses and Improvement Plans) (Wales) Order 2002
Art.3, amended: SI 2004/1575 Art.2

2002–cont.

886. Local Government (Whole Authority Analyses and Improvement Plans) (Wales) Order 2002–*cont.*

Art.3A, added: SI 2004/1575 Art.2

888. National Health Service (Local Pharmaceutical Services and Pharmaceutical Services) Regulations 2002

Reg.1, amended: SI 2002/2469 Sch.7

Reg.2, amended: SI 2002/2469 Sch.7

Reg.3, amended: SI 2002/2469 Sch.7

Reg.4, amended: SI 2002/2469 Sch.7

Reg.4, applied: SI 1992/662 Reg.8A

Reg.5, amended: SI 2002/2469 Sch.7

Reg.6, amended: SI 2002/2469 Sch.7

Reg.7, amended: SI 2002/2469 Sch.7

Reg.7A, added: SI 2002/2861 Reg.37

Reg.7A, amended: SI 2002/2469 Sch.7

Reg.8, amended: SI 2002/2469 Sch.7

Reg.9, amended: SI 2002/2469 Sch.7

890. Contaminants in Food (England) Regulations 2002

revoked: SI 2003/1478 Reg.12

Reg.2, amended: SI 2002/1923 Reg.2

891. Lincolnshire Healthcare National Health Service Trust (Change of Name) Order 2002

revoked: 2003 c.43 s.7

892. Feeding Stuffs (Amendment) Regulations 2002

referred to: SI 1999/1663 Sch.2 para.3, SI 1999/1872 Reg.98, Reg.106, SI 1999/2325 Reg.11A, Reg.11, Reg.11B, Reg.7, Reg.8, SI 2000/2481 Reg.2

894. Walsall Primary Care Trust (Establishment) Order 2002

applied: SI 2003/3059 Sch.1

Art.1, amended: SI 2002/1405 Sch.1, SI 2003/1983 Art.2

Art.2, amended: SI 2003/1983 Art.2

Art.4, revoked: SI 2002/1405 Sch.1

896. Disqualification from Caring for Children (Wales) Regulations 2002

revoked: SI 2004/2695 Reg.2

897. Dairy Produce Quotas (Wales) Regulations 2002

Reg.3, amended: SI 2004/911 Reg.5, Sch.1, Sch.2

Reg.4, substituted: SI 2004/911 Reg.6

Reg.5, amended: SI 2004/911 Sch.1

Reg.7, amended: SI 2004/911 Sch.1

Reg.8, amended: SI 2004/911 Sch.1, Sch.2

Reg.12, substituted: SI 2004/911 Reg.7

Reg.14, amended: SI 2004/911 Sch.1

Reg.15, amended: SI 2004/911 Sch.1

Reg.17, amended: SI 2004/911 Sch.1, Sch.2

Reg.19, amended: SI 2004/911 Sch.1

Reg.21, amended: SI 2004/911 Sch.1, Sch.2

Reg.23, amended: SI 2004/911 Reg.8, Sch.2

Reg.26, amended: SI 2004/911 Reg.9

Reg.28, amended: SI 2004/911 Sch.1

2002–cont.

897. Dairy Produce Quotas (Wales) Regulations 2002–*cont.*

Reg.31, amended: SI 2004/911 Reg.10, Reg.11, Sch.2

Reg.33, substituted: SI 2004/911 Reg.12

Sch.1 para.1, amended: SI 2004/911 Reg.13

Sch.1 para.12, amended: SI 2004/911 Reg.13

Sch.2 para.9, amended: SI 2004/911 Sch.1

Sch.2 para.17, amended: SI 2004/911 Sch.1

Sch.2 para.19, amended: SI 2004/911 Sch.1

912. Companies (Particulars of Usual Residential Address) (Confidentiality Orders) Regulations 2002

applied: SI 2002/915 Reg.10

913. Limited Liability Partnerships (No.2) Regulations 2002

referred to: SI 2003/61 Reg.1

Reg.3, referred to: SI 2002/690 Reg.1

914. Renewables Obligation Order 2002

Art.2, amended: SI 2004/924 Art.2

Art.3, amended: SI 2004/924 Art.2

Art.4, amended: SI 2004/924 Art.2

Art.4, referred to: SI 2003/2562 Sch.2 para.2

Art.5, amended: SI 2004/924 Art.2

Art.8, amended: SI 2004/924 Art.2

Art.8, revoked (in part): SI 2004/924 Art.2

Art.9, amended: SI 2004/924 Art.2

Art.10, amended: SI 2004/924 Art.2

Art.12, amended: SI 2004/924 Art.2

Sch.2 para.6, amended: SI 2004/924 Art.2

915. Limited Liability Partnerships (Particulars of Usual Residential Address) (Confidentiality Orders) Regulations 2002

applied: 1985 c.6 s.288A, 2000 c.12 s.2, s.9, SI 2002/502 Reg.3, SI 2002/503 Reg.3

Reg.13, applied: SI 2002/502 Reg.3, SI 2002/503 Reg.3

916. National Health Service (General Medical Services) (Amendment) (Wales) Regulations 2002

revoked: SI 2004/1016 Sch.2

919. Registration of Social Care and Independent Health Care (Wales) Regulations 2002

Reg.2, amended: SI 2003/237 Reg.50, SI 2003/710 Reg.19, SI 2003/2527 Reg.29, SI 2003/2709 Reg.2, SI 2004/219 Reg.33, SI 2004/1756 Reg.34

Reg.4, amended: SI 2002/2622 Reg.5, SI 2003/237 Reg.50

Reg.4, revoked (in part): SI 2002/2622 Reg.5

Reg.6, amended: SI 2003/237 Reg.50

Reg.8, amended: SI 2002/2622 Reg.5, SI 2003/237 Reg.50

Reg.8, revoked (in part): SI 2002/2622 Reg.5

Reg.9, amended: SI 2003/237 Reg.50, SI 2004/219 Reg.33

Reg.10, amended: SI 2003/237 Reg.50

Reg.12, amended: SI 2003/237 Reg.50

Reg.13, amended: SI 2003/237 Reg.50

NO.

2002–cont.

919. Registration of Social Care and Independent Health Care (Wales) Regulations 2002–*cont.*

Reg.14, amended: SI 2003/237 Reg.50

Reg.15, amended: SI 2003/237 Reg.50

Reg.17, substituted: SI 2003/2709 Reg.2

Reg.18, amended: SI 2003/2709 Reg.2

Sch.1 Part I para.1, amended: SI 2003/237 Reg.50, SI 2004/219 Reg.33

Sch.1 Part I para.1, revoked (in part): SI 2002/2622 Reg.5

Sch.1 Part I para.2, amended: SI 2003/237 Reg.50

Sch.1 Part I para.3, amended: SI 2002/2935 Reg.3, SI 2003/237 Reg.50

Sch.1 Part II para.4, amended: SI 2003/237 Reg.50

Sch.1 Part II para.5, amended: SI 2003/237 Reg.50

Sch.1 Part II para.6, amended: SI 2003/237 Reg.50

Sch.1 Part II para.7, amended: SI 2003/237 Reg.50

Sch.1 Part II para.8, amended: SI 2003/237 Reg.50

Sch.1 Part II para.9, amended: SI 2003/237 Reg.50

Sch.1 Part II para.10, amended: SI 2003/237 Reg.50

Sch.1 Part II para.11, amended: SI 2003/237 Reg.50

Sch.1 Part II para.12, amended: SI 2003/237 Reg.50

Sch.1 Part II para.13, amended: SI 2003/237 Reg.50

Sch.1 Part II para.14, amended: SI 2003/237 Reg.50

Sch.1 Part II para.15, amended: SI 2003/237 Reg.50

Sch.1 Part III para.16, amended: SI 2003/237 Reg.50

Sch.2 para.1, amended: SI 2003/237 Reg.50

Sch.2 para.2, amended: SI 2003/237 Reg.50

Sch.2 para.3, amended: SI 2003/237 Reg.50

Sch.2 para.4, amended: SI 2002/2622 Reg.5, SI 2003/237 Reg.50

Sch.2 para.5, amended: SI 2003/237 Reg.50

Sch.2 para.6, amended: SI 2003/237 Reg.50

Sch.2 para.7, amended: SI 2003/237 Reg.50

Sch.2 para.8, amended: SI 2003/237 Reg.50

Sch.2 para.9, amended: SI 2003/237 Reg.50

Sch.2 para.9A, added: SI 2002/2622 Reg.5

Sch.2 para.9A, amended: SI 2003/237 Reg.50

Sch.2 para.10, amended: SI 2002/2622 Reg.5, SI 2003/237 Reg.50

Sch.3 Part I para.1, amended: SI 2003/237 Reg.50

Sch.3 Part I para.2, amended: SI 2003/237 Reg.50

NO.

2002–cont.

919. Registration of Social Care and Independent Health Care (Wales) Regulations 2002–*cont.*

Sch.3 Part I para.3, amended: SI 2003/237 Reg.50

Sch.3 Part I para.4, amended: SI 2003/237 Reg.50

Sch.3 Part I para.5, amended: SI 2003/237 Reg.50

Sch.3 Part I para.6, amended: SI 2003/237 Reg.50

Sch.3 Part I para.7, amended: SI 2003/237 Reg.50

Sch.3 Part I para.8, amended: SI 2003/237 Reg.50

Sch.3 Part I para.8, revoked: SI 2002/2622 Reg.5

Sch.3 Part II para.9, amended: SI 2003/237 Reg.50

Sch.3 Part II para.10, amended: SI 2003/237 Reg.50

Sch.3 Part II para.11, amended: SI 2003/237 Reg.50

Sch.3 Part II para.12, amended: SI 2002/2622 Reg.5, SI 2003/237 Reg.50

Sch.3 Part II para.13, amended: SI 2002/2622 Reg.5, SI 2003/237 Reg.50

Sch.3 Part II para.13A, added: SI 2002/2622 Reg.5

Sch.3 Part II para.13A, amended: SI 2003/237 Reg.50

Sch.7 Part I para.1, revoked (in part): SI 2002/2622 Reg.5

Sch.7 Part I para.3, revoked: SI 2003/2709 Reg.2

Sch.8 para.1, substituted: SI 2003/2709 Reg.2

Sch.8 para.2, substituted: SI 2003/2709 Reg.2

Sch.8 para.3, substituted: SI 2003/2709 Reg.2

Sch.8 para.4, amended: SI 2002/2622 Reg.5

Sch.8 para.4, substituted: SI 2003/2709 Reg.2

Sch.8 para.5, substituted: SI 2003/2709 Reg.2

Sch.8 para.6, substituted: SI 2003/2709 Reg.2

Sch.8 para.7, substituted: SI 2003/2709 Reg.2

Sch.8 para.8, substituted: SI 2003/2709 Reg.2

Sch.8 para.9, substituted: SI 2003/2709 Reg.2

Sch.8 para.9A, added: SI 2002/2171 Reg.2

Sch.8 para.9A, substituted: SI 2002/2622 Reg.5, SI 2003/2709 Reg.2

Sch.8 para.10, amended: SI 2002/2171 Reg.2

Sch.8 para.10, revoked (in part): SI 2002/2622 Reg.5

NO.

2002–cont.

919. Registration of Social Care and Independent Health Care (Wales) Regulations 2002–*cont.*
Sch.8 para.10, substituted: SI 2003/2709 Reg.2

920. Care Standards Act 2000 (Commencement No.8 (Wales) and Transitional, Savings and Consequential Provisions) Order 2002
Art.2, applied: SI 2003/237 Reg.52
Sch.1 para.6, applied: SI 2002/921 Reg.3
Sch.2 para.3, applied: SI 2002/921 Reg.3

921. Registration of Social Care and Independent Healthcare (Fees) (Wales) Regulations 2002
Reg.2, amended: SI 2002/3161 Reg.6, SI 2003/237 Reg.51, SI 2003/710 Reg.20, SI 2003/781 Reg.33, SI 2003/2527 Reg.28, SI 2004/219 Reg.34, SI 2004/1756 Reg.35
Reg.3, amended: SI 2003/237 Reg.51, SI 2003/710 Reg.20, SI 2004/219 Reg.34, SI 2004/1756 Reg.35
Reg.4, amended: SI 2003/237 Reg.51, SI 2003/710 Reg.20
Reg.7, amended: SI 2002/2935 Reg.4
Reg.10, added: SI 2002/3161 Reg.6
Reg.11, added: SI 2003/781 Reg.33
Reg.12, added: SI 2003/237 Reg.51
Reg.12A, added: SI 2003/710 Reg.20
Reg.13, added: SI 2003/710 Reg.20
Reg.13i, added: SI 2003/710 Reg.20, SI 2003/2527 Reg.28
Reg.15, added: SI 2004/219 Reg.34
Reg.16, added: SI 2004/1756 Reg.35

928. Contracting Out (Local Education Authority Functions) (England) Order 2002
Sch.2, amended: SI 2003/2704 Art.3
Sch.3, amended: SI 2003/2704 Art.4

931. Food (Jelly Confectionery) (Emergency Control) (England) Regulations 2002
Reg.2, amended: SI 2004/1151 Reg.2
Reg.3, amended: SI 2004/1151 Reg.2
Reg.5, amended: SI 2004/1151 Reg.2

938. Rowley Regis and Tipton Primary Care Trust (Establishment) Order 2002
Art.1, amended: SI 2002/1405 Sch.1
Art.4, revoked: SI 2002/1405 Sch.1
Sch.1, amended: SI 2004/543 Sch.1

939. Eastern Birmingham Primary Care Trust (Establishment) Order 2002
Art.1, amended: SI 2002/1405 Sch.1
Art.4, revoked: SI 2002/1405 Sch.1

940. Coventry Primary Care Trust (Establishment) Order 2002
Art.1, amended: SI 2002/1405 Sch.1, SI 2003/2766 Art.2
Art.2, amended: SI 2003/2766 Art.2

NO.

2002–cont.

940. Coventry Primary Care Trust (Establishment) Order 2002–*cont.*
Art.4, revoked: SI 2002/1405 Sch.1
Sch.1, amended: SI 2004/543 Sch.1

941. Shropshire County Primary Care Trust (Establishment) Order 2002
Art.1, amended: SI 2002/1405 Sch.1
Art.4, revoked: SI 2002/1405 Sch.1
Sch.1, amended: SI 2004/543 Sch.1

942. South Warwickshire Primary Care Trust (Establishment) Order 2002
Art.1, amended: SI 2002/1405 Sch.1
Art.4, revoked: SI 2002/1405 Sch.1
Sch.1, amended: SI 2004/543 Sch.1

943. Telford and Wrekin Primary Care Trust (Establishment) Order 2002
Art.1, amended: SI 2002/1405 Sch.1
Art.4, revoked: SI 2002/1405 Sch.1

944. Rugby Primary Care Trust (Establishment) Order 2002
Art.1, amended: SI 2002/1405 Sch.1
Art.4, revoked: SI 2002/1405 Sch.1

945. Redditch and Bromsgrove Primary Care Trust (Establishment) Order 2002
Art.1, amended: SI 2002/1405 Sch.1
Art.4, revoked: SI 2002/1405 Sch.1
Sch.1, amended: SI 2004/543 Sch.1

946. Cannock Chase Primary Care Trust (Establishment) Order 2002
Art.1, amended: SI 2002/1405 Sch.1
Art.4, revoked: SI 2002/1405 Sch.1

947. South Worcestershire Primary Care Trust (Establishment) Order 2002
Art.1, amended: SI 2002/1405 Sch.1
Art.4, revoked: SI 2002/1405 Sch.1
Sch.1, amended: SI 2004/543 Sch.1

949. Oldbury and Smethwick Primary Care Trust (Establishment) Order 2002
Art.1, amended: SI 2002/1405 Sch.1
Art.4, revoked: SI 2002/1405 Sch.1

951. East Staffordshire Primary Care Trust (Establishment) Order 2002
Art.1, amended: SI 2002/1405 Sch.1
Art.4, revoked: SI 2002/1405 Sch.1

956. Animals and Animal Products (Import and Export) (England and Wales) (Amendment) (England) (No.2) Regulations 2002
revoked: SI 2004/853 Reg.35

957. Wednesbury and West Bromwich Primary Care Trust (Establishment) Order 2002
Art.1, amended: SI 2002/1405 Sch.1
Art.4, revoked: SI 2002/1405 Sch.1
Sch.1, amended: SI 2004/543 Sch.1

958. Heart of Birmingham Teaching Primary Care Trust (Establishment) Order 2002
Art.1, amended: SI 2002/1405 Sch.1

NO.

2002–cont.

958. Heart of Birmingham Teaching Primary Care Trust (Establishment) Order 2002–*cont.*

Art.4, revoked: SI 2002/1405 Sch.1

959. North Birmingham Primary Care Trust (Establishment) Order 2002

Art.1, amended: SI 2002/1405 Sch.1

Art.4, revoked: SI 2002/1405 Sch.1

960. Medway Primary Care Trust (Establishment) Order 2002

Sch.1, amended: SI 2004/543 Sch.1

980. Northampton Primary Care Trust (Establishment) Order 2002

Art.1, amended: SI 2002/1405 Sch.1

Art.4, revoked: SI 2002/1405 Sch.1

Sch.1, amended: SI 2004/543 Sch.1

982. East Elmbridge and Mid Surrey Primary Care Trust (Establishment) Order 2002

Sch.1, amended: SI 2004/543 Sch.1

983. Canterbury and Coastal Primary Care Trust (Establishment) Order 2002

Sch.1, amended: SI 2004/543 Sch.1

985. Horsham and Chanctonbury Primary Care Trust (Establishment) Order 2002

Sch.1, amended: SI 2004/543 Sch.1, SI 2004/2248 Sch.1

986. Guildford and Waverley Primary Care Trust (Establishment) Order 2002

Sch.1, amended: SI 2004/543 Sch.1

987. Western Sussex Primary Care Trust (Establishment) Order 2002

Sch.1, amended: SI 2004/2248 Sch.1

988. East Surrey Primary Care Trust (Establishment) Order 2002

Sch.1, amended: SI 2004/543 Sch.1

990. East Kent Coastal Primary Care Trust (Establishment) Order 2002

Sch.1, amended: SI 2004/543 Sch.1

991. Brighton and Hove City Primary Care Trust (Establishment) Order 2002

Sch.1, amended: SI 2004/543 Sch.1

992. Ashford Primary Care Trust (Establishment) Order 2002

Sch.1, amended: SI 2004/543 Sch.1

995. Woking Area Primary Care Trust (Establishment) Order 2002

Art.1, amended: SI 2004/904 Art.2

Art.2, amended: SI 2004/904 Art.2

997. Northamptonshire Heartlands Primary Care Trust (Establishment) Order 2002

Art.1, amended: SI 2002/1405 Sch.1

Art.4, revoked: SI 2002/1405 Sch.1

Sch.1, amended: SI 2004/543 Sch.1

1003. Southwark Primary Care Trust (Establishment) Order 2002

referred to: SI 2004/569 Sch.1

NO.

2002–cont.

1004. Kensington and Chelsea Primary Care Trust (Establishment) Order 2002

referred to: SI 2004/569 Sch.1

1005. Brent Primary Care Trust (Establishment) Order 2002

Art.1, amended: SI 2003/2649 Art.2

Art.2, amended: SI 2003/2649 Art.2

1011. Pet Travel Scheme (Pilot Arrangements) (England) (Amendment) Order 2002

revoked: SI 2004/2363 Sch.2

1015. Bus Service Operators Grant (England) Regulations 2002

referred to: SI 2004/9 Reg.2

Reg.2, amended: SI 2003/1036 Reg.3, SI 2004/9 Reg.3

Reg.3, amended: SI 2003/1036 Reg.4, SI 2004/9 Reg.4

1031. Borough of South Ribble (Electoral Changes) (Amendment) Order 2002

varied: SI 2004/222 Art.2

1032. District of Craven (Ribble Banks Parish Council) (Electoral Changes) Order 2002

varied: SI 2004/222 Art.2

1033. District of East Riding (Electoral Changes) (Amendment) Order 2002

varied: SI 2004/222 Art.2

1034. Borough of Milton Keynes (Electoral Changes) (Amendment) Order 2002

varied: SI 2004/222 Art.2

1035. District of Forest of Dean (Electoral Changes) (Amendment) Order 2002

varied: SI 2004/222 Art.2

1036. District of Babergh (Electoral Changes) (Amendment) Order 2002

varied: SI 2004/222 Art.2

1064. Heathrow Express Railway Extension Order 2002

Sch.3 para.1, amended: SI 2003/2155 Sch.1 para.17, Sch.2

1065. Piccadilly Line (Heathrow T5 Extension) Order 2002

Sch.6 para.3, amended: SI 2003/2155 Sch.1 para.17

Sch.6 para.6, amended: SI 2003/2155 Sch.2

1066. Docklands Light Railway (Silvertown and London City Airport Extension) Order 2002

Art.2, amended: SI 2003/2155 Sch.2

Sch.10 para.1, amended: SI 2003/2155 Sch.1 para.17, Sch.2

Sch.10 para.2, amended: SI 2003/2155 Sch.1 para.18, Sch.2

1069. Police and Criminal Evidence Act 1984 (Visual Recording of Interviews) (Certain Police Areas) Order 2002

revoked: SI 2003/2463 Art.2

2002–cont.

1077. Overseas Territories (Zimbabwe) (Restrictive Measures) Order 2002
varied: SI 2004/2036 Art.2
Art.2, amended: SI 2004/1111 Art.2, Art.3
Art.4, substituted: SI 2004/1111 Art.4
Art.5, amended: SI 2004/1111 Art.5
Art.6, amended: SI 2004/1111 Art.6
Art.19, amended: SI 2004/1111 Art.7
Sch.2 para.1, amended: SI 2004/1111 Art.8
Sch.3, substituted: SI 2004/1111 Art.9
Sch.3 para.1, substituted: SI 2004/1111 Art.9
Sch.3 para.2, substituted: SI 2004/1111 Art.9
Sch.3 para.3, substituted: SI 2004/1111 Art.9
Sch.3 para.4, substituted: SI 2004/1111 Art.9
Sch.3 para.5, substituted: SI 2004/1111 Art.9
Sch.3 para.6, substituted: SI 2004/1111 Art.9
Sch.3 para.7, substituted: SI 2004/1111 Art.9
Sch.3 para.8, substituted: SI 2004/1111 Art.9
Sch.3 para.9, substituted: SI 2004/1111 Art.9
Sch.3 para.10, substituted: SI 2004/1111 Art.9
Sch.3 para.11, substituted: SI 2004/1111 Art.9
Sch.3 para.12, substituted: SI 2004/1111 Art.9
Sch.3 para.13, substituted: SI 2004/1111 Art.9
Sch.3 para.14, substituted: SI 2004/1111 Art.9
Sch.3 para.15, substituted: SI 2004/1111 Art.9
Sch.3 para.16, substituted: SI 2004/1111 Art.9
Sch.3 para.17, substituted: SI 2004/1111 Art.9
Sch.3 para.18, substituted: SI 2004/1111 Art.9
Sch.3 para.19, substituted: SI 2004/1111 Art.9
Sch.3 para.20, substituted: SI 2004/1111 Art.9
Sch.3 para.21, substituted: SI 2004/1111 Art.9
Sch.3 para.22, substituted: SI 2004/1111 Art.9
Sch.3 para.23, substituted: SI 2004/1111 Art.9
Sch.3 para.24, substituted: SI 2004/1111 Art.9
Sch.3 para.25, substituted: SI 2004/1111 Art.9
Sch.3 para.26, substituted: SI 2004/1111 Art.9
Sch.3 para.27, substituted: SI 2004/1111 Art.9
Sch.3 para.28, substituted: SI 2004/1111 Art.9
Sch.3 para.29, substituted: SI 2004/1111 Art.9
Sch.3 para.30, substituted: SI 2004/1111 Art.9
Sch.3 para.31, substituted: SI 2004/1111 Art.9
Sch.3 para.32, substituted: SI 2004/1111 Art.9
Sch.4, amended: SI 2002/2627 Art.2, Art.3
Sch.4, substituted: SI 2004/1111 Art.10

1090. Food (Jelly Confectionery) (Emergency Control) (Wales) Regulations 2002
Reg.2, amended: SI 2004/1262 Reg.2

2002–cont.

1090. Food (Jelly Confectionery) (Emergency Control) (Wales) Regulations 2002–cont.
Reg.3, amended: SI 2004/1262 Reg.2
Reg.5, amended: SI 2004/1262 Reg.2

1093. Radioactive Material (Road Transport) Regulations 2002
applied: SI 1987/37 Reg.25
referred to: SI 2002/2676 Sch.2, SI 2002/2677 Sch.7, SI 2002/2776 Sch.5
Reg.2, amended: SI 2003/1867 Reg.2
Reg.5, amended: SI 2003/1867 Reg.2
Reg.41, amended: SI 2003/1867 Reg.2
Reg.49, revoked (in part): SI 2003/1867 Reg.2
Reg.66, amended: SI 2003/1867 Reg.2
Reg.69, amended: SI 2003/1867 Reg.2
Sch.1, amended: SI 2003/1867 Reg.2
Sch.7 para.4, amended: SI 2003/1867 Reg.2
Sch.8 Part XIII para.3, amended: SI 2003/1867 Reg.2

1095. Health and Social Care Act 2001 (Commencement No 8) Order 2002
Art.2, amended: SI 2002/1170 Art.2
Art.4, added: SI 2002/1170 Art.3

1096. Football Spectators (World Cup Control Period) Order 2002
revoked: SI 2002/1143 Art.2

1119. Eastleigh and Test Valley South Primary Care Trust (Establishment) Order 2002
Sch.1, amended: SI 2004/543 Sch.1

1129. Bridgend (Cynffig, Cornelly and Pyle Communities) (Electoral Changes) Order 2002
varied: SI 2004/218 Art.2
Art.2, amended: SI 2002/1432 Art.2
Art.4, amended: SI 2002/1432 Art.2

1137. Education (Bursaries for School Teacher Training) (England) (Amendment) (No.2) Regulations 2002
revoked: SI 2002/3005 Reg.2

1144. Personal Protective Equipment Regulations 2002
applied: SI 2002/2675 Reg.10, SI 2002/2676 Reg.6, SI 2002/2677 Reg.7, SR 2003/33 Reg.10
referred to: SI 2004/693 Sch.1, SR 2003/34 Reg.7, SR 2003/35 Reg.6
Sch.10 para.1, amended: SI 2004/693 Sch.2
Sch.10 para.1, revoked (in part): SI 2004/693 Sch.2

1147. Immigration Appeals (Family Visitor) Regulations 2002
revoked: 2002 c.41 Sch.9

1150. Police and Criminal Evidence Act 1984 (Codes of Practice) (Modifications to Code C and Code D) (Certain Police Areas) Order 2002
revoked: SI 2003/704 Art.4
Art.3, amended: SI 2002/1863 Art.2

2002–cont.

1166. Railways (Interoperability) (High-Speed) Regulations 2002

Reg.11, applied: SI 1994/157 Reg.4

Reg.12, applied: SI 1994/157 Reg.4

Reg.13, applied: SI 1994/157 Reg.4

Reg.14, applied: SI 1994/157 Reg.4

Reg.15, applied: SI 1994/157 Reg.4

Reg.16, applied: SI 1994/157 Reg.4

Reg.17, applied: SI 1994/157 Reg.4

1169. Nurses, Midwives and Health Visitors (Amendment) Rules Approval Order 2002

revoked: 1999 c.8 Sch.5

varied: SI 2004/1762 Art.1

1172. Education (School Information) (England) (Amendment) Regulations 2002

revoked: SI 2002/2897 Reg.2

1227. Products of Animal Origin (Third Country Imports) (England) Regulations 2002

revoked: SI 2003/3177 Sch.6

Reg.2, amended: SI 2003/812 Reg.3

Reg.3, substituted: SI 2002/3206 Reg.2

Reg.3A, substituted: SI 2002/3206 Reg.2

Reg.4, amended: SI 2003/812 Reg.4

Reg.12A, added: SI 2003/812 Reg.5

Reg.13, amended: SI 2003/812 Reg.6

Reg.16, substituted: SI 2003/812 Reg.7

Reg.28, amended: SI 2003/812 Reg.8

Reg.45, amended: SI 2002/3206 Reg.2

Reg.53, amended: SI 2002/3206 Reg.2

Reg.63, amended: SI 2002/3206 Reg.2

Sch.2 Part I, amended: SI 2002/2151 Reg.2, SI 2002/2570 Reg.2

Sch.2 Part I, substituted: SI 2002/3206 Sch.1

Sch.2 Part I para.1, substituted: SI 2002/3206 Sch.1

Sch.2 Part I para.2, substituted: SI 2002/3206 Sch.1

Sch.2 Part I para.3, substituted: SI 2002/3206 Sch.1

Sch.2 Part I para.4, substituted: SI 2002/3206 Sch.1

Sch.2 Part II, substituted: SI 2002/3206 Sch.1

Sch.2 Part II para.1, substituted: SI 2002/3206 Sch.1

Sch.2 Part II para.2, substituted: SI 2002/3206 Sch.1

Sch.2 Part II para.3, substituted: SI 2002/3206 Sch.1

Sch.2 Part II para.4, substituted: SI 2002/3206 Sch.1

Sch.2 Part II para.5, substituted: SI 2002/3206 Sch.1

Sch.2 Part II para.6, substituted: SI 2002/3206 Sch.1

Sch.2 Part II para.7, substituted: SI 2002/3206 Sch.1

2002–cont.

1227. Products of Animal Origin (Third Country Imports) (England) Regulations 2002–*cont.*

Sch.2 Part II para.8, substituted: SI 2002/3206 Sch.1

Sch.2 Part II para.9, substituted: SI 2002/3206 Sch.1

Sch.2 Part II para.10, substituted: SI 2002/3206 Sch.1

Sch.2 Part II para.11, substituted: SI 2002/3206 Sch.1

Sch.2 Part II para.12, substituted: SI 2002/3206 Sch.1

Sch.2 Part II para.13, substituted: SI 2002/3206 Sch.1

Sch.2 Part II para.14, substituted: SI 2002/3206 Sch.1

Sch.2 Part II para.15, substituted: SI 2002/3206 Sch.1

Sch.2 Part II para.16, substituted: SI 2002/3206 Sch.1

Sch.2 Part II para.17, substituted: SI 2002/3206 Sch.1

Sch.2 Part II para.18, substituted: SI 2002/3206 Sch.1

Sch.2 Part II para.19, substituted: SI 2002/3206 Sch.1

Sch.2 Part II para.20, substituted: SI 2002/3206 Sch.1

Sch.2 Part II para.21, substituted: SI 2002/3206 Sch.1

Sch.2 Part II para.22, substituted: SI 2002/3206 Sch.1

Sch.2 Part II para.23, substituted: SI 2002/3206 Sch.1

Sch.2 Part II para.24, substituted: SI 2002/3206 Sch.1

Sch.2 Part II para.25, substituted: SI 2002/3206 Sch.1

Sch.2 Part II para.26, substituted: SI 2002/3206 Sch.1

Sch.2 Part II para.27, substituted: SI 2002/3206 Sch.1

Sch.2 Part II para.28, substituted: SI 2002/3206 Sch.1

Sch.2 Part II para.29, substituted: SI 2002/3206 Sch.1

Sch.2 Part II para.30, substituted: SI 2002/3206 Sch.1

Sch.2 Part II para.31, substituted: SI 2002/3206 Sch.1

Sch.2 Part II para.32, substituted: SI 2002/3206 Sch.1

Sch.2 Part II para.33, substituted: SI 2002/3206 Sch.1

Sch.2 Part III para.1, substituted: SI 2002/3206 Sch.1

Sch.2 Part III para.2, substituted: SI 2002/3206 Sch.1

Sch.2 Part III para.3, substituted: SI 2002/3206 Sch.1

2002–cont.

1227. Products of Animal Origin (Third Country Imports) (England) Regulations 2002–*cont.*

Sch.2 Part III para.4, substituted: SI 2002/3206 Sch.1

Sch.2 Part III para.5, substituted: SI 2002/3206 Sch.1

Sch.2 Part III para.6, substituted: SI 2002/3206 Sch.1

Sch.2 Part III para.7, substituted: SI 2002/3206 Sch.1

Sch.2 Part III para.8, substituted: SI 2002/3206 Sch.1

Sch.2 Part III para.9, substituted: SI 2002/3206 Sch.1

Sch.2 Part III para.10, substituted: SI 2002/3206 Sch.1

Sch.2 Part IV, substituted: SI 2002/3206 Sch.1

Sch.2 Part IV para.1, substituted: SI 2002/3206 Sch.1

Sch.2 Part IV para.2, substituted: SI 2002/3206 Sch.1

Sch.2 Part IV para.3, substituted: SI 2002/3206 Sch.1

Sch.2 Part V, substituted: SI 2002/2639 Reg.2, SI 2002/3206 Sch.1

Sch.2 Part V, added: SI 2002/2639 Reg.2

Sch.2 Part V, substituted: SI 2002/2639 Reg.2, SI 2002/3206 Sch.1

Sch.2 Part V para.1, substituted: SI 2002/2639 Reg.2, SI 2002/3206 Sch.1

Sch.2 Part V para.2, substituted: SI 2002/2639 Reg.2, SI 2002/3206 Sch.1

Sch.2 Part VI para.1, substituted: SI 2002/3206 Sch.1

Sch.2 Part VI para.2, substituted: SI 2002/3206 Sch.1

Sch.2 Part VII, substituted: SI 2002/3206 Sch.1

Sch.2 Part VII para.1, substituted: SI 2002/3206 Sch.1

Sch.2 Part VII para.2, substituted: SI 2002/3206 Sch.1

Sch.2 Part VIII, substituted: SI 2002/3206 Sch.1

Sch.2 Part VIII para.1, substituted: SI 2002/3206 Sch.1

Sch.2 Part VIII para.2, substituted: SI 2002/3206 Sch.1

Sch.2 Part VIII para.3, substituted: SI 2002/3206 Sch.1

Sch.2 Part VIII para.4, substituted: SI 2002/3206 Sch.1

Sch.2 Part VIII para.5, substituted: SI 2002/3206 Sch.1

Sch.2 Part VIII para.6, substituted: SI 2002/3206 Sch.1

Sch.2 Part VIII para.7, substituted: SI 2002/3206 Sch.1

2002–cont.

1227. Products of Animal Origin (Third Country Imports) (England) Regulations 2002–*cont.*

Sch.2 Part VIII para.8, substituted: SI 2002/3206 Sch.1

Sch.2 Part VIII para.9, substituted: SI 2002/3206 Sch.1

Sch.2 Part VIII para.10, substituted: SI 2002/3206 Sch.1

Sch.2 Part VIII para.11, substituted: SI 2002/3206 Sch.1

Sch.2 Part VIII para.12, substituted: SI 2002/3206 Sch.1

Sch.2 Part VIII para.13, substituted: SI 2002/3206 Sch.1

Sch.2 Part VIII para.14, substituted: SI 2002/3206 Sch.1

Sch.2 Part VIII para.15, substituted: SI 2002/3206 Sch.1

Sch.2 Part VIII para.16, substituted: SI 2002/3206 Sch.1

Sch.2 Part IX, substituted: SI 2002/3206 Sch.1

Sch.2 Part IX para.1, substituted: SI 2002/3206 Sch.1

Sch.2 Part IX para.2, substituted: SI 2002/3206 Sch.1

Sch.2 Part IX para.2, amended: SI 2002/2570 Reg.2

Sch.2 Part IX para.2, substituted: SI 2002/3206 Sch.1

Sch.2 Part IX para.3, substituted: SI 2002/3206 Sch.1

Sch.2 Part IX para.4, substituted: SI 2002/3206 Sch.1

Sch.2 Part IX para.5, substituted: SI 2002/3206 Sch.1

Sch.2 Part IX para.5, revoked: SI 2002/2570 Reg.2

Sch.2 Part IX para.5, substituted: SI 2002/3206 Sch.1

Sch.2 Part IX para.6, substituted: SI 2002/3206 Sch.1

Sch.2 Part IX para.7, substituted: SI 2002/3206 Sch.1

Sch.2 Part IX para.7, revoked: SI 2002/2570 Reg.2

Sch.2 Part IX para.7, substituted: SI 2002/3206 Sch.1

Sch.2 Part IX para.8, substituted: SI 2002/3206 Sch.1

Sch.2 Part IX para.9, substituted: SI 2002/3206 Sch.1

Sch.2 Part IX para.10, substituted: SI 2002/3206 Sch.1

Sch.2 Part IX para.11, substituted: SI 2002/3206 Sch.1

Sch.2 Part IX para.12, substituted: SI 2002/3206 Sch.1

Sch.2 Part IX para.13, substituted: SI 2002/3206 Sch.1

2002–cont.

1227. Products of Animal Origin (Third Country Imports) (England) Regulations 2002–*cont.*

Sch.2 Part IX para.14, substituted: SI 2002/3206 Sch.1

Sch.2 Part IX para.15, substituted: SI 2002/3206 Sch.1

Sch.2 Part IX para.16, substituted: SI 2002/3206 Sch.1

Sch.2 Part IX para.17, substituted: SI 2002/3206 Sch.1

Sch.2 Part IX para.18, substituted: SI 2002/3206 Sch.1

Sch.2 Part IX para.19, substituted: SI 2002/3206 Sch.1

Sch.2 Part IX para.20, substituted: SI 2002/3206 Sch.1

Sch.2 Part IX para.21, substituted: SI 2002/3206 Sch.1

Sch.2 Part IX para.22, substituted: SI 2002/3206 Sch.1

Sch.2 Part IX para.23, substituted: SI 2002/3206 Sch.1

Sch.2 Part IX para.24, substituted: SI 2002/3206 Sch.1

Sch.2 Part IX para.25, substituted: SI 2002/3206 Sch.1

Sch.2 Part IX para.26, substituted: SI 2002/3206 Sch.1

Sch.2 Part IX para.27, substituted: SI 2002/3206 Sch.1

Sch.2 Part IX para.28, substituted: SI 2002/3206 Sch.1

Sch.2 Part IX para.29, substituted: SI 2002/3206 Sch.1

Sch.2 Part IX para.30, substituted: SI 2002/3206 Sch.1

Sch.2 Part IX para.31, substituted: SI 2002/3206 Sch.1

Sch.2 Part IX para.32, substituted: SI 2002/3206 Sch.1

Sch.2 Part IX para.33, substituted: SI 2002/3206 Sch.1

Sch.2 Part IX para.34, substituted: SI 2002/3206 Sch.1

Sch.2 Part IX para.35, substituted: SI 2002/3206 Sch.1

Sch.2 Part IX para.36, substituted: SI 2002/3206 Sch.1

Sch.2 Part IX para.37, substituted: SI 2002/3206 Sch.1

Sch.2 Part IX para.38, substituted: SI 2002/3206 Sch.1

Sch.2 Part IX para.39, substituted: SI 2002/3206 Sch.1

Sch.2 Part IX para.40, substituted: SI 2002/3206 Sch.1

Sch.2 Part IX para.41, substituted: SI 2002/3206 Sch.1

Sch.2 Part IX para.42, substituted: SI 2002/3206 Sch.1

2002–cont.

1227. Products of Animal Origin (Third Country Imports) (England) Regulations 2002–*cont.*

Sch.2 Part IX para.43, substituted: SI 2002/3206 Sch.1

Sch.2 Part IX para.44, substituted: SI 2002/3206 Sch.1

Sch.2 Part IX para.45, substituted: SI 2002/3206 Sch.1

Sch.2 Part IX para.46, substituted: SI 2002/3206 Sch.1

Sch.2 Part IX para.47, substituted: SI 2002/3206 Sch.1

Sch.2 Part IX para.48, substituted: SI 2002/3206 Sch.1

Sch.2 Part IX para.49, substituted: SI 2002/3206 Sch.1

Sch.2 Part IX para.50, substituted: SI 2002/3206 Sch.1

Sch.2 Part IX para.51, substituted: SI 2002/3206 Sch.1

Sch.2 Part IX para.52, substituted: SI 2002/3206 Sch.1

Sch.2 Part IX para.53, substituted: SI 2002/3206 Sch.1

Sch.2 Part IX para.54, substituted: SI 2002/3206 Sch.1

Sch.2 Part IX para.55, substituted: SI 2002/3206 Sch.1

Sch.2 Part IX para.56, substituted: SI 2002/3206 Sch.1

Sch.2 Part IX para.57, substituted: SI 2002/3206 Sch.1

Sch.2 Part IX para.58, substituted: SI 2002/3206 Sch.1

Sch.2 Part IX para.59, substituted: SI 2002/3206 Sch.1

Sch.2 Part IX para.60, substituted: SI 2002/3206 Sch.1

Sch.2 Part IX para.61, substituted: SI 2002/3206 Sch.1

Sch.2 Part IX para.62, substituted: SI 2002/3206 Sch.1

Sch.6 Part I, amended: SI 2003/812 Reg.9

1234. Cornwall Healthcare National Health Service Trust Change of Name and (Establishment) Amendment Order 2002

revoked: 2003 c.43 s.7

1242. Financial Services and Markets Act 2000 (Administration Orders Relating to Insurers) Order 2002

applied: SI 2003/2093 Art.3

Art.1, amended: SI 2003/2134 Art.3

Art.3, amended: SI 2003/2134 Art.4, SI 2004/353 Reg.52

Art.4, amended: SI 2003/2134 Art.5

Art.5, substituted: SI 2003/2134 Art.6

Sch.1 para.1, substituted: SI 2003/2134 Art.7

Sch.1 para.2, substituted: SI 2003/2134 Art.7

Sch.1 para.3, substituted: SI 2003/2134 Art.7

NO.

2002–cont.

1242. Financial Services and Markets Act 2000 (Administration Orders Relating to Insurers) Order 2002–*cont.*
Sch.1 para.4, substituted: SI 2003/2134 Art.7
Sch.1 para.5, substituted: SI 2003/2134 Art.7
Sch.1 para.6, substituted: SI 2003/2134 Art.7
Sch.1 para.8, amended: SI 2003/2134 Art.7

1243. Blackpool, Fylde and Wyre Hospitals National Health Service Trust (Establishment) and the Blackpool, Wyre and Fylde Community Health Services National Health Service Trust and the Blackpool Victoria Hospital National Health Service Trust (Dissolu 2002
revoked: 2003 c.43 s.7

1244. Cheshire and Wirral Partnership National Health Service Trust (Establishment) and the Wirral and West Cheshire Community National Health Service Trust (Dissolution) Order 2002
revoked: 2003 c.43 s.7
Art.4, amended: SI 2004/469 Art.2

1250. National Care Standards Commission (Children's Rights Director) Regulations 2002
revoked: SI 2004/615 Reg.4
varied: SI 2004/664 Art.11, Art.12, Art.13, Art.14
Reg.1, varied: SI 2004/664 Art.11, Art.12, Art.13, Art.14
Reg.3, varied: SI 2004/664 Art.11, Art.12, Art.13, Art.14

1251. Manchester Mental Health and Social Care Trust (Establishment) Order 2002
revoked: 2003 c.43 s.7

1266. Police and Criminal Evidence Act 1984 (Codes of Practice) (Visual Recording of Interviews) Order 2002
revoked: SI 2004/1887 Art.4

1293. Rotherham Priority Health Services National Health Service Trust (Dissolution) Order 2002
revoked: 2003 c.43 s.7

1294. Barnsley Community and Priority Services National Health Service Trust (Dissolution) Order 2002
revoked: 2003 c.43 s.7

1295. Doncaster Healthcare National Health Service Trust (Establishment) Amendment Order 2002
revoked: 2003 c.43 s.7

1296. Southern Derbyshire Mental Health National Health Service Trust Change of Name and (Establishment) Amendment Order and the Community Health Care Service (North Derbyshire) National Health Service Trust (Dissolution) Order 2002
revoked: 2003 c.43 s.7

NO.

2002–cont.

1297. Sheffield Children's Hospital National Health Service Trust Change of Name and (Establishment) Amendment Order 2002
revoked: 2003 c.43 s.7

1299. Plant Health (Phytophthora ramorum) (England) Order 2002
revoked: SI 2002/2573 Art.15
Art.2, referred to: SI 2002/2573 Art.15
Art.3, applied: SI 2002/2573 Art.15

1311. National Health Service (Compensation for Premature Retirement) Regulations 2002
Reg.2, amended: SI 2002/2469 Sch.9, SI 2003/631 Reg.3, SI 2004/696 Sch.1 para.41
Reg.4, applied: SI 1995/300 Reg.2
Reg.8, applied: SI 1995/300 Reg.2
Reg.9, applied: SI 1995/300 Reg.2

1313. South West Yorkshire Mental Health National Health Service Trust (Establishment) and the Wakefield and Pontefract Community National Health Service Trust (Dissolution) Order 2002
applied: SI 2003/3059 Sch.1
revoked: 2003 c.43 s.7

1318. Education (Student Support) (Amendment) Regulations 2002
revoked: SI 2002/3200 Reg.3

1322. Bradford District Care Trust (Establishment) and the Bradford Community Health National Health Service Trust (Dissolution) Order 2002
revoked: 2003 c.43 s.7

1323. National Health Service Trusts (Dissolution) Order 2002
revoked: 2003 c.43 s.7

1327. Greater Manchester (Light Rapid Transit System) (Trafford Depot) Order 2002
Art.2, amended: SI 2003/2155 Sch.2
Sch.5 para.1, amended: SI 2003/2155 Sch.1 para.17, Sch.2
Sch.5 para.2, amended: SI 2003/2155 Sch.1 para.17, Sch.2

1328. Animal Gatherings (Interim Measures) (England) (Amendment) Order 2002
revoked: SI 2003/253 Art.11

1329. Education (Student Loans) (Amendment) (England and Wales) Regulations 2002
referred to: SI 2002/1433 Reg.1

1330. Education (Mandatory Awards) Regulations 2002
applied: SI 2003/1994 Reg.6
revoked: SI 2003/1994 Sch.6
Sch.2 Part III para.12, amended: SI 2002/3060 Reg.3

2002–cont.

1330. Education (Mandatory Awards) Regulations 2002–*cont.*

Sch.2 Part III para.15, amended: SI 2002/3060 Reg.3

Sch.3 Part I para.1, amended: SI 2002/3060 Reg.4

Sch.3 Part II para.2, amended: SI 2002/2089 Reg.3, SI 2002/3060 Reg.4

Sch.5 para.1, amended: SI 2002/2089 Reg.4

1335. Wiltshire and Swindon Health Care National Health Service Trust (Dissolution) Order 2002

revoked: 2003 c.43 s.7

1337. West Kent National Health Service and Social Care Trust (Establishment) and the Thames Gateway National Health Service Trust and Invicta Community Care National Health Service Trust (Dissolution) Order 2002

revoked: 2003 c.43 s.7

1338. Bournewood Community and Mental Health National Health Service Trust Change of Name Order 2002

revoked: 2003 c.43 s.7

1341. Mid Yorkshire Hospitals National Health Service Trust (Establishment) and the Pinderfields and Pontefract Hospitals National Health Service Trust and the Dewsbury Health Care National Health Service Trust (Dissolution) Order 2002

applied: SI 2003/3059 Sch.1

revoked: 2003 c.43 s.7

1342. Northallerton Health Services National Health Service Trust (Dissolution) Order 2002

revoked: 2003 c.43 s.7

1349. Sheep and Goat Identification and Movement (Interim Measures) (England) (Amendment) (No.2) Order 2002

applied: SI 2002/2304 Sch.1 para.15

1350. Plant Health (Phytophthora ramorum) (Wales) Order 2002

revoked: SI 2002/2762 Art.15

1355. Offshore Chemicals Regulations 2002

applied: SI 1985/1699 Sch.1 para.15A

Reg.3, applied: SI 1985/1699 Sch.1 para.15A

1357. Sheep and Goats Identification and Movement (Interim Measures) (Wales) Order 2002

applied: SI 2002/2302 Art.13

revoked: SI 2002/2302 Art.19

Art.7, applied: SI 2002/2302 Art.7

Art.8, applied: SI 2002/2302 Art.8

Art.9, applied: SI 2002/2302 Art.9

2002–cont.

1358. Animal Gatherings (Interim Measures) (Wales) (Amendment) Order 2002

revoked: SI 2003/481 Art.11

1360. Worcestershire Community and Mental Health National Health Service Trust Change of Name and (Establishment) Amendment Order 2002

revoked: 2003 c.43 s.7

1361. Brent, Kensington, Chelsea and Westminster Mental Health National Health Service Trust Change of Name and (Establishment) Amendment Order 2002

revoked: 2003 c.43 s.7

1362. West Sussex Health and Social Care National Health Service Trust (Establishment) and the Worthing Priority National Health Service Trust and Sussex Weald and Downs National Health Service Trust (Dissolution) Order 2002

revoked: 2003 c.43 s.7

1363. Brighton and Sussex University Hospitals National Health Service Trust (Establishment) and the Mid Sussex National Health Service Trust (Dissolution) Order 2002

revoked: 2003 c.43 s.7, SI 2003/868 Art.2

1364. Sandwell and West Birmingham Hospitals National Health Service Trust (Establishment) and the City Hospital National Health Service Trust and Sandwell Healthcare National Health Service Trust (Dissolution) Order 2002

revoked: 2003 c.43 s.7

Art.3, amended: SI 2003/2345 Art.2

Art.4, substituted: SI 2003/2345 Art.3

1377. Education (Listed Bodies) (England) Order 2002

revoked: SI 2004/2753 Art.1

1384. East Lancashire (Heywood Extension) Light Railway Order 2002

Art.7, amended: SI 2003/2155 Sch.1 para.18

1387. Products of Animal Origin (Third Country Imports) (Wales) Regulations 2002

referred to: SI 2003/976 Reg.2

revoked: SI 2004/1430 Sch.6

Reg.2, amended: SI 2003/976 Reg.3

Reg.3, substituted: SI 2002/3230 Reg.2

Reg.4, amended: SI 2003/976 Reg.4

Reg.12A, added: SI 2003/976 Reg.5

Reg.13, amended: SI 2003/976 Reg.6

Reg.16, substituted: SI 2003/976 Reg.7

Reg.28, amended: SI 2003/976 Reg.8

Reg.53, amended: SI 2002/3230 Reg.2

Reg.63, amended: SI 2002/3230 Reg.2

Sch.2 Part I, substituted: SI 2002/3230 Sch.1

NO.

NO.

2002–cont.

1387. Products of Animal Origin (Third Country Imports) (Wales) Regulations 2002–*cont.*

Sch.2 Part I para.1, substituted: SI 2002/3230 Sch.1

Sch.2 Part I para.2, substituted: SI 2002/3230 Sch.1

Sch.2 Part I para.3, substituted: SI 2002/3230 Sch.1

Sch.2 Part I para.4, substituted: SI 2002/3230 Sch.1

Sch.2 Part I para.5, substituted: SI 2002/3230 Sch.1

Sch.2 Part I para.6, substituted: SI 2002/3230 Sch.1

Sch.2 Part I para.7, substituted: SI 2002/3230 Sch.1

Sch.2 Part I para.8, substituted: SI 2002/3230 Sch.1

Sch.2 Part I para.9, substituted: SI 2002/3230 Sch.1

Sch.2 Part II, substituted: SI 2002/3230 Sch.1

Sch.2 Part II para.1, substituted: SI 2002/3230 Sch.1

Sch.2 Part II para.2, substituted: SI 2002/3230 Sch.1

Sch.2 Part II para.3, substituted: SI 2002/3230 Sch.1

Sch.2 Part II para.4, substituted: SI 2002/3230 Sch.1

Sch.2 Part II para.5, substituted: SI 2002/3230 Sch.1

Sch.2 Part II para.6, substituted: SI 2002/3230 Sch.1

Sch.2 Part II para.7, substituted: SI 2002/3230 Sch.1

Sch.2 Part II para.8, substituted: SI 2002/3230 Sch.1

Sch.2 Part II para.9, substituted: SI 2002/3230 Sch.1

Sch.2 Part II para.10, substituted: SI 2002/3230 Sch.1

Sch.2 Part II para.11, substituted: SI 2002/3230 Sch.1

Sch.2 Part II para.12, substituted: SI 2002/3230 Sch.1

Sch.2 Part II para.13, substituted: SI 2002/3230 Sch.1

Sch.2 Part II para.13i, substituted: SI 2002/3230 Sch.1

Sch.2 Part II para.14, substituted: SI 2002/3230 Sch.1

Sch.2 Part II para.14i, substituted: SI 2002/3230 Sch.1

Sch.2 Part II para.15, substituted: SI 2002/3230 Sch.1

Sch.2 Part II para.15i, substituted: SI 2002/3230 Sch.1

Sch.2 Part II para.16, substituted: SI 2002/3230 Sch.1

2002–cont.

1387. Products of Animal Origin (Third Country Imports) (Wales) Regulations 2002–*cont.*

Sch.2 Part II para.16i, substituted: SI 2002/3230 Sch.1

Sch.2 Part II para.17, substituted: SI 2002/3230 Sch.1

Sch.2 Part II para.17i, substituted: SI 2002/3230 Sch.1

Sch.2 Part II para.18, substituted: SI 2002/3230 Sch.1

Sch.2 Part II para.18i, substituted: SI 2002/3230 Sch.1

Sch.2 Part II para.19, substituted: SI 2002/3230 Sch.1

Sch.2 Part II para.19i, substituted: SI 2002/3230 Sch.1

Sch.2 Part II para.20, substituted: SI 2002/3230 Sch.1

Sch.2 Part II para.20i, substituted: SI 2002/3230 Sch.1

Sch.2 Part II para.21, substituted: SI 2002/3230 Sch.1

Sch.2 Part II para.21i, substituted: SI 2002/3230 Sch.1

Sch.2 Part II para.22, substituted: SI 2002/3230 Sch.1

Sch.2 Part II para.22i, substituted: SI 2002/3230 Sch.1

Sch.2 Part II para.23, substituted: SI 2002/3230 Sch.1

Sch.2 Part II para.23i, substituted: SI 2002/3230 Sch.1

Sch.2 Part II para.24, substituted: SI 2002/3230 Sch.1

Sch.2 Part II para.24i, substituted: SI 2002/3230 Sch.1

Sch.2 Part II para.25, substituted: SI 2002/3230 Sch.1

Sch.2 Part II para.25i, substituted: SI 2002/3230 Sch.1

Sch.2 Part II para.26, substituted: SI 2002/3230 Sch.1

Sch.2 Part II para.26i, substituted: SI 2002/3230 Sch.1

Sch.2 Part II para.27, substituted: SI 2002/3230 Sch.1

Sch.2 Part II para.27i, substituted: SI 2002/3230 Sch.1

Sch.2 Part II para.28, substituted: SI 2002/3230 Sch.1

Sch.2 Part II para.28i, substituted: SI 2002/3230 Sch.1

Sch.2 Part II para.29, substituted: SI 2002/3230 Sch.1

Sch.2 Part II para.29i, substituted: SI 2002/3230 Sch.1

Sch.2 Part II para.30, substituted: SI 2002/3230 Sch.1

Sch.2 Part II para.30i, substituted: SI 2002/3230 Sch.1

NO.

NO.

2002–cont.

2002–cont.

1387. Products of Animal Origin (Third Country Imports) (Wales) Regulations 2002–*cont.*

Sch.2 Part II para.31, substituted: SI 2002/ 3230 Sch.1

Sch.2 Part II para.31i, substituted: SI 2002/ 3230 Sch.1

Sch.2 Part II para.32, substituted: SI 2002/ 3230 Sch.1

Sch.2 Part II para.32i, substituted: SI 2002/ 3230 Sch.1

Sch.2 Part II para.33, substituted: SI 2002/ 3230 Sch.1

Sch.2 Part II para.33i, substituted: SI 2002/ 3230 Sch.1

Sch.2 Part II para.34, substituted: SI 2002/ 3230 Sch.1

Sch.2 Part II para.35, substituted: SI 2002/ 3230 Sch.1

Sch.2 Part II para.36, substituted: SI 2002/ 3230 Sch.1

Sch.2 Part II para.37, substituted: SI 2002/ 3230 Sch.1

Sch.2 Part II para.38, substituted: SI 2002/ 3230 Sch.1

Sch.2 Part II para.39, substituted: SI 2002/ 3230 Sch.1

Sch.2 Part II para.40, substituted: SI 2002/ 3230 Sch.1

Sch.2 Part II para.41, substituted: SI 2002/ 3230 Sch.1

Sch.2 Part II para.42, substituted: SI 2002/ 3230 Sch.1

Sch.2 Part II para.43, substituted: SI 2002/ 3230 Sch.1

Sch.2 Part II para.44, substituted: SI 2002/ 3230 Sch.1

Sch.2 Part II para.45, substituted: SI 2002/ 3230 Sch.1

Sch.2 Part II para.46, substituted: SI 2002/ 3230 Sch.1

Sch.2 Part II para.47, substituted: SI 2002/ 3230 Sch.1

Sch.2 Part II para.48, substituted: SI 2002/ 3230 Sch.1

Sch.2 Part II para.49, substituted: SI 2002/ 3230 Sch.1

Sch.2 Part II para.50, substituted: SI 2002/ 3230 Sch.1

Sch.2 Part II para.51, substituted: SI 2002/ 3230 Sch.1

Sch.2 Part II para.52, substituted: SI 2002/ 3230 Sch.1

Sch.2 Part II para.53, substituted: SI 2002/ 3230 Sch.1

Sch.2 Part II para.54, substituted: SI 2002/ 3230 Sch.1

Sch.2 Part II para.55, substituted: SI 2002/ 3230 Sch.1

Sch.2 Part II para.56, substituted: SI 2002/ 3230 Sch.1

1387. Products of Animal Origin (Third Country Imports) (Wales) Regulations 2002–*cont.*

Sch.2 Part II para.57, substituted: SI 2002/ 3230 Sch.1

Sch.2 Part II para.58, substituted: SI 2002/ 3230 Sch.1

Sch.2 Part II para.59, substituted: SI 2002/ 3230 Sch.1

Sch.2 Part II para.60, substituted: SI 2002/ 3230 Sch.1

Sch.2 Part II para.61, substituted: SI 2002/ 3230 Sch.1

Sch.2 Part II para.62, substituted: SI 2002/ 3230 Sch.1

Sch.2 Part II para.63, substituted: SI 2002/ 3230 Sch.1

Sch.2 Part II para.64, substituted: SI 2002/ 3230 Sch.1

Sch.2 Part II para.65, substituted: SI 2002/ 3230 Sch.1

Sch.2 Part II para.66, substituted: SI 2002/ 3230 Sch.1

Sch.2 Part II para.67, substituted: SI 2002/ 3230 Sch.1

Sch.2 Part II para.68, substituted: SI 2002/ 3230 Sch.1

Sch.2 Part II para.69, substituted: SI 2002/ 3230 Sch.1

Sch.2 Part III para.1, substituted: SI 2002/ 3230 Sch.1

Sch.2 Part III para.2, substituted: SI 2002/ 3230 Sch.1

Sch.2 Part III para.3, substituted: SI 2002/ 3230 Sch.1

Sch.2 Part III para.4, substituted: SI 2002/ 3230 Sch.1

Sch.2 Part III para.5, substituted: SI 2002/ 3230 Sch.1

Sch.2 Part III para.6, substituted: SI 2002/ 3230 Sch.1

Sch.2 Part III para.7, substituted: SI 2002/ 3230 Sch.1

Sch.2 Part III para.8, substituted: SI 2002/ 3230 Sch.1

Sch.2 Part III para.9, substituted: SI 2002/ 3230 Sch.1

Sch.2 Part III para.10, substituted: SI 2002/ 3230 Sch.1

Sch.2 Part III para.70, substituted: SI 2002/ 3230 Sch.1

Sch.2 Part III para.71, substituted: SI 2002/ 3230 Sch.1

Sch.2 Part III para.72, substituted: SI 2002/ 3230 Sch.1

Sch.2 Part III para.73, substituted: SI 2002/ 3230 Sch.1

Sch.2 Part III para.74, substituted: SI 2002/ 3230 Sch.1

Sch.2 Part III para.75, substituted: SI 2002/ 3230 Sch.1

2002–cont.

1387. Products of Animal Origin (Third Country Imports) (Wales) Regulations 2002–cont.

Sch.2 Part III para.76, substituted: SI 2002/3230 Sch.1

Sch.2 Part III para.77, substituted: SI 2002/3230 Sch.1

Sch.2 Part III para.78, substituted: SI 2002/3230 Sch.1

Sch.2 Part III para.79, substituted: SI 2002/3230 Sch.1

Sch.2 Part III para.80, substituted: SI 2002/3230 Sch.1

Sch.2 Part III para.81, substituted: SI 2002/3230 Sch.1

Sch.2 Part III para.82, substituted: SI 2002/3230 Sch.1

Sch.2 Part III para.83, substituted: SI 2002/3230 Sch.1

Sch.2 Part III para.84, substituted: SI 2002/3230 Sch.1

Sch.2 Part III para.85, substituted: SI 2002/3230 Sch.1

Sch.2 Part III para.86, substituted: SI 2002/3230 Sch.1

Sch.2 Part IV, substituted: SI 2002/3230 Sch.1

Sch.2 Part IV para.1, substituted: SI 2002/3230 Sch.1

Sch.2 Part IV para.2, substituted: SI 2002/3230 Sch.1

Sch.2 Part IV para.3, substituted: SI 2002/3230 Sch.1

Sch.2 Part IV para.87, substituted: SI 2002/3230 Sch.1

Sch.2 Part IV para.88, substituted: SI 2002/3230 Sch.1

Sch.2 Part IV para.89, substituted: SI 2002/3230 Sch.1

Sch.2 Part IV para.90, substituted: SI 2002/3230 Sch.1

Sch.2 Part IV para.91, substituted: SI 2002/3230 Sch.1

Sch.2 Part V, amended: SI 2002/3011 Reg.2

Sch.2 Part V, substituted: SI 2002/3230 Sch.1

Sch.2 Part V, added: SI 2002/3011 Reg.2

Sch.2 Part V, amended: SI 2002/3011 Reg.2

Sch.2 Part V, substituted: SI 2002/3230 Sch.1

Sch.2 Part V para.1, amended: SI 2002/3011 Reg.2

Sch.2 Part V para.1, substituted: SI 2002/3230 Sch.1

Sch.2 Part V para.1, amended: SI 2002/3011 Reg.2

Sch.2 Part V para.1, substituted: SI 2002/3230 Sch.1

Sch.2 Part V para.1, amended: SI 2002/3011 Reg.2

2002–cont.

1387. Products of Animal Origin (Third Country Imports) (Wales) Regulations 2002–cont.

Sch.2 Part V para.1, substituted: SI 2002/3230 Sch.1

Sch.2 Part V para.2, amended: SI 2002/3011 Reg.2

Sch.2 Part V para.2, substituted: SI 2002/3230 Sch.1

Sch.2 Part V para.2, amended: SI 2002/3011 Reg.2

Sch.2 Part V para.2, substituted: SI 2002/3230 Sch.1

Sch.2 Part V para.2, amended: SI 2002/3011 Reg.2

Sch.2 Part V para.2, substituted: SI 2002/3230 Sch.1

Sch.2 Part V para.92, amended: SI 2002/3011 Reg.2

Sch.2 Part V para.92, substituted: SI 2002/3230 Sch.1

Sch.2 Part V para.93, amended: SI 2002/3011 Reg.2

Sch.2 Part V para.93, substituted: SI 2002/3230 Sch.1

Sch.2 Part V para.94, amended: SI 2002/3011 Reg.2

Sch.2 Part V para.94, substituted: SI 2002/3230 Sch.1

Sch.2 Part V para.95, amended: SI 2002/3011 Reg.2

Sch.2 Part V para.95, substituted: SI 2002/3230 Sch.1

Sch.2 Part VI para.1, substituted: SI 2002/3230 Sch.1

Sch.2 Part VI para.2, substituted: SI 2002/3230 Sch.1

Sch.2 Part VI para.96, substituted: SI 2002/3230 Sch.1

Sch.2 Part VI para.97, substituted: SI 2002/3230 Sch.1

Sch.2 Part VI para.98, substituted: SI 2002/3230 Sch.1

Sch.2 Part VI para.99, substituted: SI 2002/3230 Sch.1

Sch.2 Part VII, substituted: SI 2002/3230 Sch.1

Sch.2 Part VII para.1, substituted: SI 2002/3230 Sch.1

Sch.2 Part VII para.2, substituted: SI 2002/3230 Sch.1

Sch.2 Part VII para.100, substituted: SI 2002/3230 Sch.1

Sch.2 Part VII para.101, substituted: SI 2002/3230 Sch.1

Sch.2 Part VIII, substituted: SI 2002/3230 Sch.1

Sch.2 Part VIII para.1, substituted: SI 2002/3230 Sch.1

Sch.2 Part VIII para.2, substituted: SI 2002/3230 Sch.1

2002–cont.

1387. Products of Animal Origin (Third Country Imports) (Wales) Regulations 2002–*cont.*

Sch.2 Part VIII para.3, substituted: SI 2002/3230 Sch.1

Sch.2 Part VIII para.4, substituted: SI 2002/3230 Sch.1

Sch.2 Part VIII para.5, substituted: SI 2002/3230 Sch.1

Sch.2 Part VIII para.6, substituted: SI 2002/3230 Sch.1

Sch.2 Part VIII para.7, substituted: SI 2002/3230 Sch.1

Sch.2 Part VIII para.8, substituted: SI 2002/3230 Sch.1

Sch.2 Part VIII para.9, substituted: SI 2002/3230 Sch.1

Sch.2 Part VIII para.10, substituted: SI 2002/3230 Sch.1

Sch.2 Part VIII para.11, substituted: SI 2002/3230 Sch.1

Sch.2 Part VIII para.12, substituted: SI 2002/3230 Sch.1

Sch.2 Part VIII para.13, substituted: SI 2002/3230 Sch.1

Sch.2 Part VIII para.14, substituted: SI 2002/3230 Sch.1

Sch.2 Part VIII para.15, substituted: SI 2002/3230 Sch.1

Sch.2 Part VIII para.16, substituted: SI 2002/3230 Sch.1

Sch.2 Part VIII para.102, substituted: SI 2002/3230 Sch.1

Sch.2 Part VIII para.103, substituted: SI 2002/3230 Sch.1

Sch.2 Part VIII para.104, substituted: SI 2002/3230 Sch.1

Sch.2 Part VIII para.105, substituted: SI 2002/3230 Sch.1

Sch.2 Part VIII para.106, substituted: SI 2002/3230 Sch.1

Sch.2 Part VIII para.107, substituted: SI 2002/3230 Sch.1

Sch.2 Part VIII para.108, substituted: SI 2002/3230 Sch.1

Sch.2 Part VIII para.109, substituted: SI 2002/3230 Sch.1

Sch.2 Part VIII para.110, substituted: SI 2002/3230 Sch.1

Sch.2 Part VIII para.111, substituted: SI 2002/3230 Sch.1

Sch.2 Part VIII para.112, substituted: SI 2002/3230 Sch.1

Sch.2 Part VIII para.113, substituted: SI 2002/3230 Sch.1

Sch.2 Part VIII para.114, substituted: SI 2002/3230 Sch.1

Sch.2 Part VIII para.115, substituted: SI 2002/3230 Sch.1

Sch.2 Part VIII para.116, substituted: SI 2002/3230 Sch.1

2002–cont.

1387. Products of Animal Origin (Third Country Imports) (Wales) Regulations 2002–*cont.*

Sch.2 Part VIII para.117, substituted: SI 2002/3230 Sch.1

Sch.2 Part VIII para.118, substituted: SI 2002/3230 Sch.1

Sch.2 Part VIII para.119, substituted: SI 2002/3230 Sch.1

Sch.2 Part VIII para.120, substituted: SI 2002/3230 Sch.1

Sch.2 Part VIII para.121, substituted: SI 2002/3230 Sch.1

Sch.2 Part VIII para.122, substituted: SI 2002/3230 Sch.1

Sch.2 Part VIII para.123, substituted: SI 2002/3230 Sch.1

Sch.2 Part VIII para.124, substituted: SI 2002/3230 Sch.1

Sch.2 Part IX, substituted: SI 2002/3230 Sch.1

Sch.2 Part IX para.1, substituted: SI 2002/3230 Sch.1

Sch.2 Part IX para.2, substituted: SI 2002/3230 Sch.1

Sch.2 Part IX para.3, substituted: SI 2002/3230 Sch.1

Sch.2 Part IX para.4, substituted: SI 2002/3230 Sch.1

Sch.2 Part IX para.5, substituted: SI 2002/3230 Sch.1

Sch.2 Part IX para.6, substituted: SI 2002/3230 Sch.1

Sch.2 Part IX para.7, substituted: SI 2002/3230 Sch.1

Sch.2 Part IX para.8, substituted: SI 2002/3230 Sch.1

Sch.2 Part IX para.9, substituted: SI 2002/3230 Sch.1

Sch.2 Part IX para.10, substituted: SI 2002/3230 Sch.1

Sch.2 Part IX para.11, substituted: SI 2002/3230 Sch.1

Sch.2 Part IX para.12, substituted: SI 2002/3230 Sch.1

Sch.2 Part IX para.13, substituted: SI 2002/3230 Sch.1

Sch.2 Part IX para.14, substituted: SI 2002/3230 Sch.1

Sch.2 Part IX para.15, substituted: SI 2002/3230 Sch.1

Sch.2 Part IX para.16, substituted: SI 2002/3230 Sch.1

Sch.2 Part IX para.17, substituted: SI 2002/3230 Sch.1

Sch.2 Part IX para.18, substituted: SI 2002/3230 Sch.1

Sch.2 Part IX para.19, substituted: SI 2002/3230 Sch.1

Sch.2 Part IX para.20, substituted: SI 2002/3230 Sch.1

2002–cont.

1387. Products of Animal Origin (Third Country Imports) (Wales) Regulations 2002–*cont.*

Sch.2 Part IX para.21, substituted: SI 2002/ 3230 Sch.1

Sch.2 Part IX para.22, substituted: SI 2002/ 3230 Sch.1

Sch.2 Part IX para.23, substituted: SI 2002/ 3230 Sch.1

Sch.2 Part IX para.24, substituted: SI 2002/ 3230 Sch.1

Sch.2 Part IX para.25, substituted: SI 2002/ 3230 Sch.1

Sch.2 Part IX para.26, substituted: SI 2002/ 3230 Sch.1

Sch.2 Part IX para.27, substituted: SI 2002/ 3230 Sch.1

Sch.2 Part IX para.28, substituted: SI 2002/ 3230 Sch.1

Sch.2 Part IX para.29, substituted: SI 2002/ 3230 Sch.1

Sch.2 Part IX para.30, substituted: SI 2002/ 3230 Sch.1

Sch.2 Part IX para.31, substituted: SI 2002/ 3230 Sch.1

Sch.2 Part IX para.32, substituted: SI 2002/ 3230 Sch.1

Sch.2 Part IX para.33, substituted: SI 2002/ 3230 Sch.1

Sch.2 Part IX para.34, substituted: SI 2002/ 3230 Sch.1

Sch.2 Part IX para.35, substituted: SI 2002/ 3230 Sch.1

Sch.2 Part IX para.36, substituted: SI 2002/ 3230 Sch.1

Sch.2 Part IX para.37, substituted: SI 2002/ 3230 Sch.1

Sch.2 Part IX para.38, substituted: SI 2002/ 3230 Sch.1

Sch.2 Part IX para.39, substituted: SI 2002/ 3230 Sch.1

Sch.2 Part IX para.40, substituted: SI 2002/ 3230 Sch.1

Sch.2 Part IX para.41, substituted: SI 2002/ 3230 Sch.1

Sch.2 Part IX para.42, substituted: SI 2002/ 3230 Sch.1

Sch.2 Part IX para.43, substituted: SI 2002/ 3230 Sch.1

Sch.2 Part IX para.44, substituted: SI 2002/ 3230 Sch.1

Sch.2 Part IX para.45, substituted: SI 2002/ 3230 Sch.1

Sch.2 Part IX para.46, substituted: SI 2002/ 3230 Sch.1

Sch.2 Part IX para.47, substituted: SI 2002/ 3230 Sch.1

Sch.2 Part IX para.48, substituted: SI 2002/ 3230 Sch.1

Sch.2 Part IX para.49, substituted: SI 2002/ 3230 Sch.1

2002–cont.

1387. Products of Animal Origin (Third Country Imports) (Wales) Regulations 2002–*cont.*

Sch.2 Part IX para.50, substituted: SI 2002/ 3230 Sch.1

Sch.2 Part IX para.51, substituted: SI 2002/ 3230 Sch.1

Sch.2 Part IX para.52, substituted: SI 2002/ 3230 Sch.1

Sch.2 Part IX para.53, substituted: SI 2002/ 3230 Sch.1

Sch.2 Part IX para.54, substituted: SI 2002/ 3230 Sch.1

Sch.2 Part IX para.55, substituted: SI 2002/ 3230 Sch.1

Sch.2 Part IX para.56, substituted: SI 2002/ 3230 Sch.1

Sch.2 Part IX para.57, substituted: SI 2002/ 3230 Sch.1

Sch.2 Part IX para.58, substituted: SI 2002/ 3230 Sch.1

Sch.2 Part IX para.59, substituted: SI 2002/ 3230 Sch.1

Sch.2 Part IX para.60, substituted: SI 2002/ 3230 Sch.1

Sch.2 Part IX para.61, substituted: SI 2002/ 3230 Sch.1

Sch.2 Part IX para.62, substituted: SI 2002/ 3230 Sch.1

Sch.2 Part IX para.125, substituted: SI 2002/ 3230 Sch.1

Sch.2 Part IX para.126, substituted: SI 2002/ 3230 Sch.1

Sch.2 Part IX para.127, substituted: SI 2002/ 3230 Sch.1

Sch.2 Part IX para.128, substituted: SI 2002/ 3230 Sch.1

Sch.2 Part IX para.129, substituted: SI 2002/ 3230 Sch.1

Sch.2 Part IX para.130, substituted: SI 2002/ 3230 Sch.1

Sch.2 Part IX para.131, substituted: SI 2002/ 3230 Sch.1

Sch.2 Part IX para.132, substituted: SI 2002/ 3230 Sch.1

Sch.2 Part IX para.133, substituted: SI 2002/ 3230 Sch.1

Sch.2 Part IX para.134, substituted: SI 2002/ 3230 Sch.1

Sch.2 Part IX para.135, substituted: SI 2002/ 3230 Sch.1

Sch.2 Part IX para.136, substituted: SI 2002/ 3230 Sch.1

Sch.2 Part IX para.137, substituted: SI 2002/ 3230 Sch.1

Sch.2 Part IX para.138, substituted: SI 2002/ 3230 Sch.1

Sch.2 Part IX para.139, substituted: SI 2002/ 3230 Sch.1

Sch.2 Part IX para.140, substituted: SI 2002/ 3230 Sch.1

2002–cont.

1387. Products of Animal Origin (Third Country Imports) (Wales) Regulations 2002–*cont.*

Sch.2 Part IX para.141, substituted: SI 2002/ 3230 Sch.1

Sch.2 Part IX para.142, substituted: SI 2002/ 3230 Sch.1

Sch.2 Part IX para.143, substituted: SI 2002/ 3230 Sch.1

Sch.2 Part IX para.144, substituted: SI 2002/ 3230 Sch.1

Sch.2 Part IX para.145, substituted: SI 2002/ 3230 Sch.1

Sch.2 Part IX para.146, substituted: SI 2002/ 3230 Sch.1

Sch.2 Part IX para.147, substituted: SI 2002/ 3230 Sch.1

Sch.2 Part IX para.148, substituted: SI 2002/ 3230 Sch.1

Sch.2 Part IX para.149, substituted: SI 2002/ 3230 Sch.1

Sch.2 Part IX para.150, substituted: SI 2002/ 3230 Sch.1

Sch.2 Part IX para.151, substituted: SI 2002/ 3230 Sch.1

Sch.2 Part IX para.152, substituted: SI 2002/ 3230 Sch.1

Sch.2 Part IX para.153, substituted: SI 2002/ 3230 Sch.1

Sch.2 Part IX para.154, substituted: SI 2002/ 3230 Sch.1

Sch.2 Part IX para.155, substituted: SI 2002/ 3230 Sch.1

Sch.2 Part IX para.156, substituted: SI 2002/ 3230 Sch.1

Sch.2 Part IX para.157, substituted: SI 2002/ 3230 Sch.1

Sch.2 Part IX para.158, substituted: SI 2002/ 3230 Sch.1

Sch.2 Part IX para.159, substituted: SI 2002/ 3230 Sch.1

Sch.2 Part IX para.160, substituted: SI 2002/ 3230 Sch.1

Sch.2 Part IX para.161, substituted: SI 2002/ 3230 Sch.1

Sch.2 Part IX para.162, substituted: SI 2002/ 3230 Sch.1

Sch.2 Part IX para.163, substituted: SI 2002/ 3230 Sch.1

Sch.2 Part IX para.164, substituted: SI 2002/ 3230 Sch.1

Sch.2 Part IX para.165, substituted: SI 2002/ 3230 Sch.1

Sch.2 Part IX para.166, substituted: SI 2002/ 3230 Sch.1

Sch.2 Part IX para.167, substituted: SI 2002/ 3230 Sch.1

Sch.2 Part IX para.168, substituted: SI 2002/ 3230 Sch.1

Sch.2 Part IX para.169, substituted: SI 2002/ 3230 Sch.1

2002–cont.

1387. Products of Animal Origin (Third Country Imports) (Wales) Regulations 2002–*cont.*

Sch.2 Part IX para.170, substituted: SI 2002/ 3230 Sch.1

Sch.2 Part IX para.171, substituted: SI 2002/ 3230 Sch.1

Sch.2 Part IX para.172, substituted: SI 2002/ 3230 Sch.1

Sch.2 Part IX para.173, substituted: SI 2002/ 3230 Sch.1

Sch.2 Part IX para.174, substituted: SI 2002/ 3230 Sch.1

Sch.2 Part IX para.175, substituted: SI 2002/ 3230 Sch.1

Sch.2 Part IX para.176, substituted: SI 2002/ 3230 Sch.1

Sch.2 Part IX para.177, substituted: SI 2002/ 3230 Sch.1

Sch.2 Part IX para.178, substituted: SI 2002/ 3230 Sch.1

Sch.2 Part IX para.179, substituted: SI 2002/ 3230 Sch.1

Sch.2 Part IX para.180, substituted: SI 2002/ 3230 Sch.1

Sch.2 Part IX para.181, substituted: SI 2002/ 3230 Sch.1

Sch.2 Part IX para.182, substituted: SI 2002/ 3230 Sch.1

Sch.2 Part IX para.183, substituted: SI 2002/ 3230 Sch.1

Sch.2 Part IX para.184, substituted: SI 2002/ 3230 Sch.1

Sch.2 Part IX para.185, substituted: SI 2002/ 3230 Sch.1

Sch.2 Part IX para.186, substituted: SI 2002/ 3230 Sch.1

Sch.2 Part IX para.187, substituted: SI 2002/ 3230 Sch.1

Sch.2 Part IX para.188, substituted: SI 2002/ 3230 Sch.1

Sch.2 Part IX para.189, substituted: SI 2002/ 3230 Sch.1

Sch.2 Part IX para.190, substituted: SI 2002/ 3230 Sch.1

Sch.2 Part IX para.191, substituted: SI 2002/ 3230 Sch.1

Sch.2 Part IX para.192, substituted: SI 2002/ 3230 Sch.1

Sch.2 Part IX para.193, substituted: SI 2002/ 3230 Sch.1

Sch.2 Part IX para.194, substituted: SI 2002/ 3230 Sch.1

Sch.2 Part IX para.195, substituted: SI 2002/ 3230 Sch.1

Sch.2 Part IX para.196, substituted: SI 2002/ 3230 Sch.1

Sch.2 Part IX para.197, substituted: SI 2002/ 3230 Sch.1

Sch.2 Part IX para.198, substituted: SI 2002/ 3230 Sch.1

NO.

NO.

2002–cont.

1387. Products of Animal Origin (Third Country Imports) (Wales) Regulations 2002–*cont.*

Sch.2 Part IX para.199, substituted: SI 2002/3230 Sch.1

Sch.2 Part IX para.200, substituted: SI 2002/3230 Sch.1

Sch.2 Part IX para.201, substituted: SI 2002/3230 Sch.1

Sch.2 Part IX para.202, substituted: SI 2002/3230 Sch.1

Sch.2 Part IX para.203, substituted: SI 2002/3230 Sch.1

Sch.2 Part IX para.204, substituted: SI 2002/3230 Sch.1

Sch.2 Part IX para.205, substituted: SI 2002/3230 Sch.1

Sch.2 Part IX para.206, substituted: SI 2002/3230 Sch.1

Sch.2 Part IX para.207, substituted: SI 2002/3230 Sch.1

Sch.2 Part IX para.208, substituted: SI 2002/3230 Sch.1

Sch.2 Part IX para.209, substituted: SI 2002/3230 Sch.1

Sch.2 Part IX para.210, substituted: SI 2002/3230 Sch.1

Sch.2 Part IX para.211, substituted: SI 2002/3230 Sch.1

Sch.2 Part IX para.212, substituted: SI 2002/3230 Sch.1

Sch.2 Part IX para.213, substituted: SI 2002/3230 Sch.1

Sch.2 Part IX para.214, substituted: SI 2002/3230 Sch.1

Sch.2 Part IX para.215, substituted: SI 2002/3230 Sch.1

Sch.2 Part IX para.216, substituted: SI 2002/3230 Sch.1

Sch.2 Part IX para.217, substituted: SI 2002/3230 Sch.1

Sch.2 Part IX para.218, substituted: SI 2002/3230 Sch.1

Sch.2 Part IX para.219, substituted: SI 2002/3230 Sch.1

Sch.2 Part IX para.220, substituted: SI 2002/3230 Sch.1

Sch.2 Part IX para.221, substituted: SI 2002/3230 Sch.1

Sch.2 Part IX para.222, substituted: SI 2002/3230 Sch.1

Sch.6 Part I, amended: SI 2003/976 Reg.9

1416. TSE (Wales) Regulations 2002

Reg.13, amended: SI 2003/2756 Sch.4 para.3

Reg.33, revoked (in part): SI 2003/2756 Sch.4 para.2

Reg.34, revoked (in part): SI 2003/2756 Sch.4 para.2

Reg.34A, added: SI 2003/2756 Sch.4 para.4

Reg.36, applied: SI 1997/2964 Art.6

2002–cont.

1416. TSE (Wales) Regulations 2002–*cont.*

Reg.40, substituted: SI 2003/2756 Sch.4 para.5

Reg.52, revoked: SI 2003/2756 Sch.4 para.2

Reg.54, revoked: SI 2003/2756 Sch.4 para.2

Reg.56, revoked (in part): SI 2003/2756 Sch.4 para.2

Reg.63, revoked: SI 2003/2756 Sch.4 para.2

Reg.64, revoked: SI 2003/2756 Sch.4 para.2

Reg.65, revoked: SI 2003/2756 Sch.4 para.2

Reg.66, revoked: SI 2003/2756 Sch.4 para.2

Reg.67, revoked: SI 2003/2756 Sch.4 para.2

Reg.68, revoked: SI 2003/2756 Sch.4 para.2

Reg.69, revoked (in part): SI 2003/2756 Sch.4 para.2

Reg.86A, added: SI 2004/2735 Reg.3

Sch.5, substituted: SI 2003/2756 Sch.4 para.6

Sch.6 Part 1 para.1, revoked: SI 2003/2756 Sch.4 para.2

Sch.6 Part 1 para.2, revoked: SI 2003/2756 Sch.4 para.2

Sch.6 Part 1 para.3, revoked: SI 2003/2756 Sch.4 para.2

Sch.6 Part 1 para.4, revoked: SI 2003/2756 Sch.4 para.2

Sch.6 Part 1 para.5, revoked: SI 2003/2756 Sch.4 para.2

Sch.6 Part 1 para.6, revoked: SI 2003/2756 Sch.4 para.2

Sch.6 Part 1 para.7, revoked: SI 2003/2756 Sch.4 para.2

Sch.6 Part 1 para.8, revoked: SI 2003/2756 Sch.4 para.2

Sch.6 Part II para.1, revoked: SI 2003/2756 Sch.4 para.2

Sch.6 Part II para.2, revoked: SI 2003/2756 Sch.4 para.2

Sch.6 Part II para.3, revoked: SI 2003/2756 Sch.4 para.2

Sch.6 Part II para.4, revoked: SI 2003/2756 Sch.4 para.2

Sch.6 Part II para.5, revoked: SI 2003/2756 Sch.4 para.2

Sch.6 Part II para.6, revoked: SI 2003/2756 Sch.4 para.2

Sch.6 Part II para.7, revoked: SI 2003/2756 Sch.4 para.2

Sch.6A Part I para.1, added: SI 2004/2735 Reg.4

Sch.6A Part I para.2, added: SI 2004/2735 Reg.4

Sch.6A Part I para.3, added: SI 2004/2735 Reg.4

Sch.6A Part I para.4, added: SI 2004/2735 Reg.4

Sch.6A Part I para.5, added: SI 2004/2735 Reg.4

Sch.6A Part I para.6, added: SI 2004/2735 Reg.4

NO.

2002–cont.

1416. TSE (Wales) Regulations 2002–*cont.*

Sch.6A Part I para.7, added: SI 2004/2735 Reg.4

Sch.6A Part I para.8, added: SI 2004/2735 Reg.4

Sch.6A Part II para.9, added: SI 2004/2735 Reg.4

Sch.6A Part II para.10, added: SI 2004/2735 Reg.4

Sch.6A Part II para.11, added: SI 2004/2735 Reg.4

Sch.6A Part II para.12, added: SI 2004/2735 Reg.4

Sch.6A Part II para.13, added: SI 2004/2735 Reg.4

Sch.6A Part II para.14, added: SI 2004/2735 Reg.4

Sch.6A Part III para.15, added: SI 2004/2735 Reg.4

Sch.6A Part III para.16, added: SI 2004/2735 Reg.4

Sch.6A Part IV para.17, added: SI 2004/2735 Reg.4

1417. Tax Credit (New Category of Child Care Provider) Regulations 2002

Reg.4, applied: SI 1987/1973 Reg.46A, SI 2002/2005 Reg.14

1434. Education (Teachers Qualifications and Health Standards) (England) (Amendment) Regulations 2002

revoked: SI 2003/1662 Sch.1 Part 1

1437. Leicestershire and Rutland Healthcare National Health Service Trust Change of Name and (Establishment) Amendment Order 2002

revoked: 2003 c.43 s.7

1438. Health Service (Control of Patient Information) Regulations 2002

Reg.1, amended: SI 2004/1031 Sch.10 para.17

1460. Plant Protection Products (Amendment) (No.2) Regulations 2002

revoked: SI 2002/2874 Reg.3

1473. Merchant Shipping (Safety of Navigation) Regulations 2002

disapplied: SI 2000/2687 Reg.5

referred to: SI 1998/2771 Sch.1, Sch.2, SI 2004/2110 Sch.3 para.1

Reg.2, amended: SI 2004/2110 Sch.3 para.2

Reg.4, amended: SI 2004/302 Sch.1 para.1, SI 2004/2110 Sch.3 para.3, Sch.3 para.4, Sch.3 para.5, Sch.3 para.6, Sch.3 para.7

Reg.5, applied: SI 1981/569 Sch.1 Part I, SI 1981/570 Sch.1

1478. Plant Health (Forestry) (Phytophthora ramorum) (Great Britain) Order 2002

revoked: SI 2002/2589 Art.13

NO.

2002–cont.

1489. St Helens and Knowsley Community Health National Health Service Trust (Dissolution) Order 2002

revoked: 2003 c.43 s.7

1490. South Buckinghamshire National Health Service Trust (Establishment) Amendment Order 2002

revoked: 2003 c.43 s.7

1491. South Tees Acute Hospitals National Health Service Trust (Establishment) Amendment Order 2002

revoked: 2003 c.43 s.7

1492. Community Healthcare Bolton National Health Service Trust (Dissolution) Order 2002

revoked: 2003 c.43 s.7

1493. Care Standards Act 2000 (Commencement No 14 (England) and Transitional, Savings and Amendment Provisions) Order 2002

Art.4, applied: SI 2001/4150 Art.3

1494. Camden and Islington Mental Health National Health Service Trust (Establishment) Amendment Order 2002

revoked: 2003 c.43 s.7

1495. Eastbourne and County National Health Service Trust Change of Name and (Establishment) Amendment Order 2002

revoked: SI 2002/2397 Art.3, 2003 c.43 s.7

1496. Cheshire Community Healthcare National Health Service Trust (Dissolution) Order 2002

revoked: 2003 c.43 s.7

1497. North Mersey Community National Health Service Trust (Dissolution) Order 2002

revoked: 2003 c.43 s.7

1498. South Essex Mental Health and Community Care National Health Service Trust Change of Name and (Establishment) Amendment Order 2002

revoked: 2003 c.43 s.7

1499. Chester and Halton Community National Health Service Trust (Dissolution) Order 2002

revoked: 2003 c.43 s.7

1500. CommuniCare National Health Service Trust (Dissolution) Order 2002

revoked: 2003 c.43 s.7

1505. National Care Standards Commission (Fees and Frequency of Inspections) (Amendment) Regulations 2002

varied: SI 2004/664 Art.11, Art.12, Art.13, Art.14

Reg.1, varied: SI 2004/664 Art.11, Art.12, Art.13, Art.14

Reg.2, varied: SI 2004/664 Art.11, Art.12, Art.13, Art.14

2002–cont.

1555. Financial Services and Markets Act 2000 (Consequential Amendments) Order 2002

Art.58, revoked: SI 2004/355 Art.11

1559. Landfill (England and Wales) Regulations 2002

Reg.2, amended: SI 2004/1375 Reg.4

Reg.3, see *Blackland Park Exploration Ltd v Environment Agency* [2003] EWCA Civ 1795, [2004] Env. L.R. 33 (CA), Scott Baker, L.J.; see *Blackland Park Exploration Ltd v Environment Agency* [2003] EWHC 691, [2003] Env. L.R. 33 (Ch D), Blackburne, J.

Reg.4, amended: SI 2004/1375 Reg.4

Reg.8, applied: SI 2000/1973 Reg.10, Reg.12, Reg.17, Reg.27

Reg.8, referred to: SI 2000/1973 Reg.17

Reg.9, see *Blackland Park Exploration Ltd v Environment Agency* [2003] EWCA Civ 1795, [2004] Env. L.R. 33 (CA), Scott Baker, L.J.

Reg.10, amended: SI 2004/1375 Reg.5

Reg.10, revoked (in part): SI 2004/1375 Reg.5

Reg.12, amended: SI 2004/1375 Reg.5

Reg.15, applied: SI 1994/1056 Reg.10, SI 2000/1973 Reg.27, Sch.9 para.1

Reg.16, applied: SI 2000/1973 Reg.27, Reg.32

Reg.17, see *Blackland Park Exploration Ltd v Environment Agency* [2003] EWCA Civ 1795, [2004] Env. L.R. 33 (CA), Scott Baker, L.J.

Reg.17, applied: SI 1994/1056 Reg.3, Reg.10, SI 2000/1973 Reg.5, Sch.9 para.1

Sch.1 para.1, substituted: SI 2004/1375 Sch.1 para.1

Sch.1 Part I para.1, substituted: SI 2004/1375 Sch.1 para.1

Sch.1 Part I para.2, substituted: SI 2004/1375 Sch.1 para.1

Sch.1 Part I para.3, substituted: SI 2004/1375 Sch.1 para.1

Sch.1 para.2, substituted: SI 2004/1375 Sch.1 para.1

Sch.1 Part II para.4, substituted: SI 2004/1375 Sch.1 para.1

Sch.1 Part II para.5, substituted: SI 2004/1375 Sch.1 para.1

Sch.1 Part II para.6, substituted: SI 2004/1375 Sch.1 para.1

Sch.1 Part II para.7, substituted: SI 2004/1375 Sch.1 para.1

Sch.1 para.3, substituted: SI 2004/1375 Sch.1 para.1

Sch.1 Part III para.8, substituted: SI 2004/1375 Sch.1 para.1

Sch.1 Part III para.9, substituted: SI 2004/1375 Sch.1 para.1

Sch.1 Part III para.10, substituted: SI 2004/1375 Sch.1 para.1

2002–cont.

1559. Landfill (England and Wales) Regulations 2002–*cont.*

Sch.1 Part III para.11, substituted: SI 2004/1375 Sch.1 para.1

Sch.1 Part III para.12, substituted: SI 2004/1375 Sch.1 para.1

Sch.1 Part III para.13, substituted: SI 2004/1375 Sch.1 para.1

Sch.1 Part III para.14, substituted: SI 2004/1375 Sch.1 para.1

Sch.1 Part III para.15, substituted: SI 2004/1375 Sch.1 para.1

Sch.1 Part III para.16, substituted: SI 2004/1375 Sch.1 para.1

Sch.1 Part III para.17, substituted: SI 2004/1375 Sch.1 para.1

Sch.1 Part III para.18, substituted: SI 2004/1375 Sch.1 para.1

Sch.1 para.4, substituted: SI 2004/1375 Sch.1 para.1

Sch.1 Part IV para.19, substituted: SI 2004/1375 Sch.1 para.1

Sch.1 Part IV para.20, substituted: SI 2004/1375 Sch.1 para.1

Sch.3 para.4, amended: SI 2004/1375 Reg.7

Sch.4 para.1, amended: SI 2004/1375 Reg.8

Sch.4 para.1, applied: SI 1994/1056 Reg.10, SI 2000/1973 Reg.27, Sch.9 para.1

Sch.4 para.3, amended: SI 2004/1375 Reg.8

1563. Seeds (Fees) (Amendment) (England) Regulations 2002

Sch.1, amended: SI 2002/3171 Reg.29, SI 2002/3172 Reg.32, SI 2002/3173 Reg.32, SI 2002/3174 Reg.32, SI 2002/3175 Reg.32

1588. Lincolnshire (Coroners Districts) Order 2002

revoked: SI 2003/2753 Art.4

1590. Wireless Telegraphy (Exemption) (Amendment) Regulations 2002

revoked: SI 2003/74 Sch.1

1592. Regulatory Reform (Vaccine Damage Payments Act 1979) Order 2002

Art.4, applied: 1979 c.17 s.7B

Sch.1, applied: 1979 c.17 s.7B

1594. A46 Trunk Road (Ashchurch Station Bridge) Order 2002

Art.2, referred to: SI 2002/1595 Art.2

1597. European Communities (Recognition of Qualifications and Experience) (Third General System) Regulations 2002

Sch.1 para.3, substituted: SI 2002/2036 Reg.2

1614. Food and Animal Feedingstuffs (Products of Animal Origin from China) (Emergency Control) (England) Regulations 2002

revoked: SI 2002/2151 Reg.3

2002–cont.

1615. Leeds Community and Mental Health Services Teaching National Health Service Trust (Change of Name) Order 2002
revoked: 2003 c.43 s.7

1625. General Dental Council (Constitution) Order 2002
Art.1, amended: SI 2002/3134 Art.2
Art.3, substituted: SI 2004/2627 Art.2
Art.3A, added: SI 2002/3134 Art.2
Art.3B, added: SI 2002/3134 Art.2
Art.3B, amended: SI 2004/2627 Art.2
Art.3C, added: SI 2002/3134 Art.2
Art.4, substituted: SI 2002/3134 Art.2

1661. Education (Recognised Bodies) (Wales) Order 2002
revoked: SI 2003/3124 Art.3

1663. Further Education Teachers Qualifications (Wales) Regulations 2002
applied: SI 1999/2817 Reg.4
Reg.2, amended: SI 2004/1745 Reg.2
Reg.3, amended: SI 2003/1717 Reg.8, SI 2004/1745 Reg.2

1664. Street Works (Charges for Occupation of the Highway) (England) (Transport for London) Order 2002
revoked: SI 2004/2175 Art.2

1670. Boroughs of Halton, Thurrock and Warrington (Changes to Years of Elections) Order 2002
varied: SI 2004/222 Art.2

1677. Plant Breeders Rights (Fees) (Amendment) Regulations 2002
referred to: SI 1998/1021 Sch.1 Part I, Sch.1 Part II, Sch.1 Part III, Sch.1 Part IV

1687. Magistrates Courts (Special Measures Directions) Rules 2002
r.1, amended: SI 2004/184 r.2
r.2, amended: SI 2004/184 r.2
r.4, amended: SI 2004/184 r.2
r.7, amended: SI 2004/184 r.2
r.8, amended: SI 2004/184 r.2
r.9A, added: SI 2004/184 r.2
Sch.1, amended: SI 2004/184 r.2

1688. Crown Court (Special Measures Directions and Directions Prohibiting Cross-examination) Rules 2002
Part I r.1, amended: SI 2004/185 r.2
Part II r.2, amended: SI 2004/185 r.2
Part II r.4, amended: SI 2004/185 r.2
Part II r.7, amended: SI 2004/185 r.2
Part II r.8, amended: SI 2004/185 r.2
Part II r.9A, added: SI 2004/185 r.2
Sch.1, amended: SI 2004/185 r.2

1689. Chemicals (Hazard Information and Packaging for Supply) Regulations 2002
applied: SI 1993/3050 Sch.2 Part A, SI 2002/2675 Sch.2 para.1
referred to: SI 2002/2676 Sch.2, SI 2002/2677 Sch.7, SI 2002/2776 Sch.5

2002–cont.

1689. Chemicals (Hazard Information and Packaging for Supply) Regulations 2002–*cont.*
Reg.8A, added: SI 2004/568 Sch.11 para.2

1690. Cambridgeshire and Peterborough Mental Health Partnership National Health Service Trust (Establishment) and the Lifespan Health Care Cambridge National Health Service Trust and the North West Anglia Health Care National Health Service Trust (Diss 2002
revoked: 2003 c.43 s.7

1700. Wireless Telegraphy (Licence Charges) Regulations 2002
Reg.3, amended: SI 2003/2155 Sch.1 para.47
Reg.4, amended: SI 2003/2983 Reg.3
Reg.4, varied: SI 2003/2984 Reg.3
Reg.5, amended: SI 2003/2983 Reg.3
Reg.5, varied: SI 2003/2984 Reg.3
Sch.2, amended: SI 2003/2983 Reg.3
Sch.2, varied: SI 2003/2984 Reg.3

1703. Social Security (Jobcentre Plus Interviews) Regulations 2002
Reg.2, amended: SI 2002/2497 Sch.2 para.1, SI 2004/959 Reg.26
Reg.4, amended: SI 2002/2497 Sch.2 para.1, SI 2004/959 Reg.26
Reg.8, amended: SI 2003/2439 Reg.17
Reg.12, amended: SI 2002/2497 Sch.2 para.1
Reg.16, amended: SI 2004/959 Reg.26
Sch.2 para.1, revoked (in part): SI 2003/492 Sch.3 Part 1

1710. Access to the Countryside (Provisional and Conclusive Maps) (England) Regulations 2002
Reg.2, amended: SI 2003/32 Reg.2
Reg.2, applied: SI 2003/1591 Reg.6
Reg.8, amended: SI 2003/32 Reg.2
Reg.8, applied: SI 2003/1591 Reg.8
Reg.9, applied: SI 2003/1591 Reg.9
Reg.10, applied: SI 2003/1591 Reg.9
Reg.11, applied: SI 2003/1591 Reg.9
Reg.12, applied: SI 2003/1591 Reg.9
Reg.15, amended: SI 2003/32 Reg.2
Reg.16, varied: SI 2003/1591 Reg.10
Reg.22, substituted: SI 2003/32 Reg.2
Reg.27, applied: SI 2003/1591 Reg.7
Reg.38, applied: SI 2003/1591 Reg.7
Reg.39, applied: SI 2003/1591 Reg.7
Reg.47, amended: SI 2003/32 Reg.2
Reg.54, applied: SI 2003/1591 Reg.7
Reg.55, applied: SI 2003/1591 Reg.7

1714. North Derbyshire Tertiary College (Dissolution) Order 2002
applied: SI 2002/2996

1715. Leasehold Reform (Notices) (Amendment) (England) Regulations 2002
Sch.1, referred to: SI 2004/1005 Sch.2

NO.

2002–cont.

1727. Tax Credits Act 2002 (Commencement No 1) Order 2002

Art.3, substituted: SI 2002/2158 Art.2

1733. Inheritance Tax (Delivery of Accounts) (Excepted Estates) Regulations 2002

revoked: SI 2004/2543 Reg.11

Reg.3, amended: SI 2003/1658 Reg.2

1758. Police (Amendment) Regulations 2002

revoked: SI 2003/527 Sch.4 Part 1

1761. Protection of Military Remains Act 1986 (Designation of Vessels and Controlled Sites) Order 2002

Art.3, amended: SI 2003/405 Art.2

1765. Animal Gatherings (Interim Measures) (England) (Amendment) (No.2) Order 2002

revoked: SI 2003/253 Art.11

1768. National Health Service (General Medical Services) Amendment (No.3) Regulations 2002

revoked: SI 2004/865 Sch.2

1773. Hydrocarbon Oil (Marking) Regulations 2002

varied: 1972 c.68 s.2

1775. Electronic Commerce Directive (Financial Services and Markets) Regulations 2002

Reg.10, applied: SI 2001/2188 Reg.12B

Reg.19, added: SI 2002/2015 Reg.2

1781. District of Wycombe (Electoral Changes) Order 2002

varied: SI 2004/222 Art.2

1783. Borough of Bournemouth (Electoral Changes) Order 2002

varied: SI 2004/222 Art.2

1784. District of Chiltern (Electoral Changes) Order 2002

varied: SI 2004/222 Art.2

1785. District of South Bucks (Electoral Changes) Order 2002

varied: SI 2004/222 Art.2

1786. Borough of Torbay (Electoral Changes) Order 2002

varied: SI 2004/222 Art.2

1787. Borough of Luton (Electoral Changes) Order 2002

varied: SI 2004/222 Art.2

1788. District of Aylesbury Vale (Electoral Changes) Order 2002

varied: SI 2004/222 Art.2

1789. Social Security (Electronic Communications) (Child Benefit) Order 2002

revoked (in part): SI 2003/492 Sch.2 para.1, SI 2003/2800 Art.4

Art.7, revoked: SI 2003/495 Sch.1 Part 1

1792. State Pension Credit Regulations 2002

referred to: SI 2004/552 Art.26

NO.

2002–cont.

1792. State Pension Credit Regulations 2002–*cont.*

Part III, applied: SI 1987/1968 Sch.9 para.4, SI 1988/664 Reg.7

Reg.1, amended: SI 2002/3019 Reg.23, SI 2002/3197 Sch.1 para.1, SI 2003/2274 Reg.2, SI 2004/1141 Reg.2, SI 2004/2327 Reg.7

Reg.1, applied: SI 1987/1971 Reg.43, SI 1992/1814 Reg.35, SI 2001/4022 Reg.3A

Reg.2, amended: SI 2003/2274 Reg.2, SI 2004/1232 Reg.5

Reg.3, amended: SI 2003/2274 Reg.2

Reg.4, substituted: SI 2002/3019 Reg.23

Reg.5, amended: SI 2002/3019 Reg.23, SI 2002/3197 Sch.1 para.2, SI 2003/2274 Reg.2

Reg.5, revoked (in part): SI 2003/2274 Reg.2

Reg.6, amended: SI 2002/3197 Reg.4, SI 2004/552 Art.26

Reg.6, applied: SI 1987/1968 Sch.9A para.10, SI 1999/991 Reg.13, SI 2003/526 Art.25

Reg.6, referred to: SI 2002/3019 Reg.36, SI 2003/526 Sch.16, SI 2004/552 Sch.20

Reg.7, amended: SI 2002/3019 Reg.23, SI 2002/3197 Reg.4, SI 2004/552 Art.26

Reg.7, applied: SI 2003/526 Art.25, SI 2004/552 Art.26

Reg.7, referred to: SI 2003/526 Sch.16, SI 2004/552 Sch.20

Reg.10, amended: SI 2002/3019 Reg.23, SI 2003/2274 Reg.2, SI 2004/647 Reg.3

Reg.10, applied: SI 1999/991 Reg.6, Reg.7, SI 2002/3019 Reg.37

Reg.13, applied: SI 1987/1971 Reg.2

Reg.13A, added: SI 2002/3019 Reg.23

Reg.13A, applied: SI 1987/1968 Sch.9 para.4

Reg.13B, added: SI 2002/3019 Reg.23

Reg.13B, amended: SI 2002/3197 Sch.1 para.3

Reg.15, amended: SI 2002/3019 Reg.23, SI 2003/2274 Reg.2, SI 2004/2327 Reg.7

Reg.15, applied: SI 1987/1968 Sch.9 para.4

Reg.15, referred to: SI 1987/1968 Sch.9 para.4

Reg.16, added: SI 2002/3197 Sch.1 para.4

Reg.16, amended: SI 2002/3197 Sch.1 para.4, SI 2004/2327 Reg.7

Reg.17, amended: SI 2002/3019 Reg.23, SI 2002/3197 Sch.1 para.5

Reg.17, revoked (in part): SI 2002/3197 Sch.1 para.5

Reg.17A, added: SI 2002/3019 Reg.23

Reg.17A, amended: SI 2002/3197 Reg.3

Reg.17B, added: SI 2002/3019 Reg.23

Reg.17B, amended: SI 2002/3197 Reg.3

Reg.17ZA, added: SI 2004/647 Reg.3

Reg.21, amended: SI 2002/3019 Reg.23, SI 2002/3197 Sch.1 para.6, SI 2004/647 Reg.3

Reg.21, applied: SI 1992/1814 Reg.35

2002–cont.

1792. State Pension Credit Regulations 2002–*cont.*

Reg.21, referred to: SI 1987/1971 Reg.43

Reg.22, amended: SI 2002/3197 Sch.1 para.7

Reg.24A, added: SI 2002/3019 Reg.23

Sch.1 Part I para.1, amended: SI 2002/3197 Sch.1 para.8, SI 2003/2274 Reg.2

Sch.1 Part I para.1, applied: SI 1999/991 Reg.13

Sch.1 Part I para.2, amended: SI 2002/3197 Sch.1 para.8

Sch.1 Part II para.4, amended: SI 2002/3197 Sch.1 para.8, SI 2003/2274 Reg.2

Sch.1 Part III para.6, amended: SI 2002/3197 Sch.1 para.8

Sch.1 Part III para.6, applied: SI 1999/991 Reg.14

Sch.2, applied: SI 1987/1968 Sch.9 para.5, Sch.9 para.6, Sch.9 para.7, Sch.9 para.8, Sch.9A para.2, Sch.9A para.3, SI 1987/1971 Sch.4A para.12, SI 1992/1814 Sch.4A para.12, SI 1999/991 Reg.7, Reg.13

Sch.2 para.1, amended: SI 2002/3197 Sch.1 para.9, SI 2004/2825 Reg.2

Sch.2 para.1, applied: SI 1987/1968 Sch.9A para.3

Sch.2 para.1, revoked (in part): SI 2002/3197 Sch.1 para.9

Sch.2 para.2, amended: SI 2002/3197 Sch.1 para.9, SI 2003/2274 Reg.2

Sch.2 para.4, amended: SI 2004/2327 Reg.7

Sch.2 para.5, amended: SI 2002/3019 Reg.23, SI 2002/3197 Sch.1 para.9

Sch.2 para.5, applied: SI 1987/1968 Sch.9 para.3, Sch.9A para.3

Sch.2 para.6, referred to: SI 2003/526 Sch.16, SI 2004/552 Sch.20

Sch.2 para.7, amended: SI 2002/3019 Reg.23, SI 2002/3197 Sch.1 para.9, SI 2004/2825 Reg.2

Sch.2 para.7, applied: SI 1987/1968 Sch.9A para.3, SI 1999/991 Reg.7

Sch.2 para.7, referred to: SI 2003/526 Sch.16

Sch.2 para.8, referred to: SI 2003/526 Sch.16, SI 2004/552 Sch.20

Sch.2 para.9, amended: SI 2002/3197 Sch.1 para.9, SI 2004/2825 Reg.2

Sch.2 para.9, applied: SI 1987/1968 Sch.9A para.11

Sch.2 para.9, referred to: SI 1987/1968 Sch.9A para.4, SI 2003/526 Sch.16, SI 2004/552 Sch.20

Sch.2 para.11, applied: SI 1999/991 Reg.7

Sch.2 para.12, applied: SI 1999/991 Reg.7

Sch.2 para.13, amended: SI 2002/3019 Reg.23

Sch.2 para.14, amended: SI 2002/3197 Sch.1 para.9, SI 2003/1195 Reg.8, SI 2003/2274 Reg.2, SI 2004/552 Art.26, SI 2004/2327 Reg.7

2002–cont.

1792. State Pension Credit Regulations 2002–*cont.*

Sch.2 para.14, applied: SI 1987/1968 Sch.9 para.3, Sch.9A para.3, SI 2003/526 Art.25, SI 2004/552 Art.26

Sch.3 para.1, amended: SI 2002/3019 Reg.23, SI 2002/3197 Reg.4, Sch.1 para.10, SI 2003/2274 Reg.2, SI 2004/552 Art.26

Sch.3 para.1, applied: SI 2003/526 Art.25

Sch.3 para.2, amended: SI 2002/3019 Reg.23, SI 2002/3197 Sch.1 para.10, SI 2003/1195 Reg.8

Sch.3 para.2, applied: SI 2001/155 Reg.5

Sch.3 para.2, revoked (in part): SI 2003/1195 Reg.8

Sch.3 para.2, varied: SI 2002/3019 Reg.36

Sch.4 para.1, amended: SI 2003/2274 Reg.2

Sch.4 para.1, applied: SI 1988/664 Reg.16

Sch.4 para.4, amended: SI 2003/2274 Reg.2

Sch.4 para.5, amended: SI 2003/2274 Reg.2

Sch.4 para.6, amended: SI 2003/2274 Reg.2

Sch.4 para.7A, added: SI 2002/3197 Sch.1 para.11

Sch.4 para.11, amended: SI 2002/3019 Reg.23, SI 2002/3197 Sch.1 para.11

Sch.4 para.11, revoked (in part): SI 2002/3019 Reg.23

Sch.4 para.13, amended: SI 2002/3197 Sch.1 para.11

Sch.4 para.14, amended: SI 2002/3197 Sch.1 para.11

Sch.4 para.17, added: SI 2003/2274 Reg.2

Sch.4 para.18, added: SI 2003/2274 Reg.2

Sch.5 Part I para.1A, added: SI 2003/2274 Reg.2

Sch.5 Part I para.4, amended: SI 2004/2327 Reg.7

Sch.5 Part I para.9A, added: SI 2002/3019 Reg.23

Sch.5 Part I para.9A, amended: SI 2003/2274 Reg.2

Sch.5 Part I para.12, amended: SI 2002/3197 Sch.1 para.12

Sch.5 Part I para.13, amended: SI 2003/2274 Reg.2

Sch.5 Part I para.15, amended: SI 2002/3197 Sch.1 para.12, SI 2004/1141 Reg.3

Sch.5 Part I para.16, substituted: SI 2002/3019 Reg.23

Sch.5 Part I para.20, amended: SI 2002/3019 Reg.23, SI 2002/3197 Sch.1 para.12, SI 2003/2274 Reg.2

Sch.5 Part I para.20, revoked (in part): SI 2003/2274 Reg.2

Sch.5 Part I para.20A, added: SI 2002/3197 Sch.1 para.12

Sch.5 Part I para.20A, applied: SI 1987/1971 Sch.5ZA para.21A, SI 1992/1814 Sch.5ZA para.21A

NO.

2002–cont.

1792. State Pension Credit Regulations 2002–*cont.*

Sch.5 Part I para.20A, substituted: SI 2003/2274 Reg.2

Sch.5 Part II para.24, amended: SI 2002/3019 Reg.23

Sch.5 Part II para.25, amended: SI 2002/3019 Reg.23

Sch.5 Part II para.26, amended: SI 2002/3019 Reg.23

Sch.5 Part II para.27, amended: SI 2002/3019 Reg.23

Sch.5 Part II para.27, revoked: SI 2003/2274 Reg.2

Sch.5 Part II para.28, amended: SI 2002/3019 Reg.23

Sch.6, applied: SI 1988/664 Reg.16

Sch.6 para.2, amended: SI 2002/3197 Sch.1 para.13

Sch.6 para.2A, added: SI 2002/3197 Sch.1 para.13

Sch.6 para.2B, added: SI 2003/2274 Reg.2

Sch.6 para.4, amended: SI 2002/3197 Sch.1 para.13

Sch.6 para.4, revoked (in part): SI 2002/3197 Sch.1 para.13

Sch.6 para.4A, added: SI 2002/3197 Sch.1 para.13

Sch.6 para.6, amended: SI 2002/3197 Sch.1 para.13

Sch.6 para.7, added: SI 2002/3197 Sch.1 para.13

1794. Countryside Access (Appeals Procedures) (Wales) Regulations 2002

Reg.2, amended: SI 2003/142 Sch.2 para.1

Reg.4, substituted: SI 2003/142 Sch.2 para.2

Reg.5, amended: SI 2003/142 Sch.2 para.3

Reg.6, amended: SI 2003/142 Sch.2 para.4, Sch.2 para.5, Sch.2 para.6, Sch.2 para.7

Reg.12, amended: SI 2003/142 Sch.2 para.8, Sch.2 para.9

Reg.22, amended: SI 2003/142 Sch.2 para.10, Sch.2 para.11

Reg.36, amended: SI 2003/142 Sch.2 para.12

Reg.36, substituted: SI 2003/142 Sch.2 para.13

1797. Feeding Stuffs (Amendment) (Wales) Regulations 2002

referred to: SI 1999/1663 Sch.2 para.3, SI 1999/1872 Reg.98, Reg.99, Reg.106, SI 1999/2325 Reg.11, Reg.11A, Reg.11B, Reg.7, Reg.8

1804. National Health Service (General Medical Services) (Amendment) (No.3) (Wales) Regulations 2002

revoked: SI 2004/1016 Sch.2

NO.

2002–cont.

1817. Food for Particular Nutritional Uses (Addition of Substances for Specific Nutritional Purposes) (England) Regulations 2002

Reg.2, amended: SI 2004/649 Reg.3

Reg.3, amended: SI 2004/649 Reg.4

Sch.1, amended: SI 2004/649 Reg.5

Sch.2, substituted: SI 2004/649 Sch.1

Sch.3, added: SI 2004/649 Sch.2

1823. Extradition (Overseas Territories) Order 2002

varied: SI 2004/2036 Art.2

Art.2, applied: SI 2002/1825 Art.2

Sch.2 Part I para.1, amended: SI 2002/1825 Sch.1 para.1

Sch.2 Part I para.2, amended: SI 2002/1825 Sch.1 para.2

Sch.2 Part II para.6, amended: SI 2002/1825 Sch.1 para.3

Sch.2 Part III para.7, amended: SI 2002/1825 Sch.1 para.4

Sch.2 Part III para.9, amended: SI 2002/1825 Sch.1 para.5

Sch.2 Part III para.10, amended: SI 2002/1825 Sch.1 para.6

Sch.2 Part III para.12, amended: SI 2002/1825 Sch.1 para.7

Sch.2 Part IV para.19, varied: SI 2002/1825 Sch.1 para.8

Sch.2 Part IV para.20, amended: SI 2002/1825 Sch.1 para.9

Sch.2 Part V para.21, amended: SI 2002/1825 Sch.1 para.10

Sch.2 Part VI para.27A, added: SI 2002/1825 Sch.1 para.11

Sch.2 Part VI para.28, amended: SI 2002/1825 Sch.1 para.12

Sch.2 Part VI para.35, amended: SI 2002/1825 Sch.1 para.13

1836. Local Access Forums (England) Regulations 2002

Reg.8A, added: SI 2003/2713 Reg.18

1837. Penalties for Disorderly Behaviour (Amount of Penalty) Order 2002

Art.2, amended: SI 2004/2468 Art.2

Sch.1 Part I, amended: SI 2003/2155 Sch.1 para.48, SI 2004/316 Art.2, SI 2004/2468 Sch.1 Part I

Sch.1 Part I, substituted: SI 2004/2468 Sch.1

Sch.1 Part II, amended: SI 2004/316 Art.2

Sch.1 Part II, substituted: SI 2004/2468 Sch.1

1841. Education Maintenance Allowance (Pilot Areas) (Amendment) Regulations 2002

revoked: SI 2004/1006 Reg.2

1856. Local Education Authority (Post-Compulsory Education Awards)(-Wales) Regulations 2002

applied: SI 2002/1857 Sch.1

NO.

2002–cont.

1857. Education (Assembly Learning Grant Scheme) (Wales) Regulations 2002
Sch.1, applied: SI1987/1967 Reg.62, SI1992/1814 Reg.42, SI 1996/207 Reg.131, SI 1996/2890 Reg.43

1860. Regulatory Reform (Housing Assistance) (England and Wales) Order 2002
Art.3, applied: 1985 c.70 s.20A, 1988 c.9 s.25, 2004 c.34 s.3

1863. Police and Criminal Evidence Act 1984 (Codes of Practice) (Modifications to Code C and Code D) (Certain Police Areas) (Amendment) Order 2002
revoked: SI 2003/704 Art.4

1870. Seeds (Fees) (Amendment) (Wales) (No.2) Regulations 2002
Sch.1, revoked: SI 2004/2881 Reg.32

1871. Representation of the People (England and Wales) (Amendment) Regulations 2002
Reg.4, revoked: SI 2003/1899 Reg.2
Reg.15, see *R. (on the application of Robertson) v Secretary of State* [2003] EWHC 1760, [2003] A.C.D. 78 (QBD (Admin Ct)), Maurice Kay, J.
Sch.1 Part I, revoked: SI 2003/1899 Reg.2
Sch.1 Part II, referred to: SI 2001/341 Reg.26
Sch.1 Part II, revoked: SI 2003/1899 Reg.2

1872. Representation of the People (Scotland) (Amendment) Regulations 2002
Reg.4, revoked: SI 2003/1892 Reg.2
Sch.1 Part I, revoked: SI 2003/1892 Reg.2
Sch.1 Part II, referred to: SI 2001/497 Reg.26
Sch.1 Part II, revoked: SI 2003/1892 Reg.2

1873. Representation of the People (Northern Ireland) (Amendment) Regulations 2002
Reg.4, revoked: SI 2003/1942 Reg.2
Sch.2 Part I, revoked: SI 2003/1942 Reg.2
Sch.2 Part II, revoked: SI 2003/1942 Reg.2

1882. National Health Service (General Medical Services Supplementary List) (Wales) Regulations 2002
applied: SI 2004/1020 Sch.1 para.9
referred to: SI 2002/2802 Reg.2
revoked: SI 2004/1020 Sch.2
Reg.4, amended: SI 2002/3135 Sch.1 para.52, SI 2003/1250 Sch.10 para.8
Reg.6, amended: SI 2002/2802 Reg.3, SI 2002/3135 Sch.1 para.52, SI 2003/1250 Sch.10 para.8
Reg.9, amended: SI 2002/2802 Reg.3
Reg.10, amended: SI 2002/3135 Sch.1 para.52
Reg.10, applied: SI 2004/1020 Reg.23
Reg.11, amended: SI 2002/2802 Reg.3
Reg.15, amended: SI 2002/2802 Reg.3

NO.

2002–cont.

1886. Contaminants in Food (Wales) Regulations 2002
revoked: SI 2003/1721 Reg.12

1889. Companies (Disclosure of Information) (Designated Authorities) (No.2) Order 2002
Art.3, applied: 1989 c.40 s.87

1892. Ecclesiastical Judges, Legal Officers and Others (Fees) Order 2002
revoked: SI 2003/1933 Art.2
Sch.1, referred to: SI 2003/1933 Art.1

1893. Legal Officers (Annual Fees) Order 2002
revoked: SI 2003/1936 Art.3

1894. Parochial Fees Order 2002
revoked: SI 2003/1932 Art.4

1895. Local Authorities (Allowances for Members of County and County Borough Councils and National Park Authorities) (Wales) Regulations 2002
applied: SI 2004/2555 Reg.6, Reg.14

1896. National Health Service (General Medical Services) (Amendment) (Wales) (No.2) Regulations 2002
revoked: SI 2004/1016 Sch.2

1911. Wireless Telegraphy (Public Fixed Wireless Access Licences) Regulations 2002
referred to: SI 2003/397
Sch.1 Part I, amended: SI 2003/397 Reg.2

1913. Superannuation (Admission to Schedule 1 to the Superannuation Act 1972) Order 2002
Art.4, amended: SI 2003/1073 Art.4

1919. Health and Social Care Act 2001 (Commencement No 3) (Wales) Order 2002
Art.2, applied: SI 2002/1920 Reg.6

1920. Abolition of the NHS Tribunal (Consequential Provisions) Regulations 2002
Reg.6, applied: SI 2002/1881 Reg.14, SI 2003/3190 Reg.4, SI 2003/3279 Reg.4, SI 2004/570 Reg.3, SI 2004/668 Reg.3
Reg.8, revoked: SI 2004/865 Sch.2

1923. Contaminants in Food (England) (Amendment) Regulations 2002
revoked: SI 2003/1478 Reg.12

1925. Agricultural Holdings (Units of Production) (England) Order 2002
revoked: SI 2003/2151 Art.3

1927. Aggregates Levy (Northern Ireland Tax Credit) Regulations 2002
revoked: SI 2004/1959 Reg.12

1928. Biodiesel and Bioblend Regulations 2002
applied: SI 2004/2065 Reg.8
revoked: SI 2004/2065 Reg.4
Reg.7, referred to: SI 2004/2065 Reg.14

NO.

2002–cont.

1950. Social Security (Claims and Payments) Amendment (No.2) Regulations 2002
revoked (in part): SI 2003/492 Sch.3 Part 1

1962. Local Authorities (Scheme for Elections of Specified Councils) (England) Order 2002
varied: SI 2004/222 Art.2

1969. Exchange Gains and Losses (Transitional Provisions and Savings) Regulations 2002
applied: SI 2002/1970 Reg.3

1970. Exchange Gains and Losses (Bringing into Account Gains or Losses) Regulations 2002
Reg.2, amended: SI 2004/3259 Reg.3
Reg.3, amended: SI 2004/3259 Reg.4
Reg.6, amended: SI 2004/3259 Reg.5
Reg.6, revoked (in part): SI 2004/3259 Reg.5
Reg.7, amended: SI 2004/3259 Reg.6
Reg.9, amended: SI 2004/3259 Reg.7
Reg.11, amended: SI 2004/3259 Reg.8
Reg.13, amended: SI 2004/3259 Reg.9
Reg.14, added: SI 2004/3259 Reg.10

1985. Special Educational Needs and Disability Tribunal (General Provisions and Disability Claims Procedure) Regulations 2002
Reg.27, applied: SI 2001/600 Reg.7, Reg.21

1998. Wye Navigation Order 2002
Art.2, amended: SI 2003/2155 Sch.1 para.19

1999. National Minimum Wage Regulations 1999 (Amendment) Regulations 2002
Reg.2, revoked: SI 2003/1923 Sch.1
Reg.3, revoked: SI 2003/1923 Sch.1

2001. Care Standards Act 2000 (Commencement and Transitional Provisions) (Amendment) (England) Order 2002
varied: SI 2004/664 Art.11, Art.12, Art.13, Art.14

2002. Education Act 2002 (Commencement No 1) Order 2002
Art.4, amended: SI 2002/2018 Art.4

2005. Working Tax Credit (Entitlement and Maximum Rate) Regulations 2002
applied: SI 2003/653 Reg.3
referred to: SI 1996/2890 Sch.3 para.54, SI 2003/701 Reg.2, SI 2003/742 Reg.26
Reg.2, amended: SI 2003/701 Reg.3, SI 2003/2815 Reg.13
Reg.2, varied: SI 2003/742 Reg.27
Reg.3, varied: SI 2003/742 Reg.28
Reg.4, amended: SI 2003/701 Reg.4, SI 2004/762 Reg.5
Reg.4, applied: SI 2002/2014 Reg.10
Reg.4, varied: SI 1996/2890 Sch.2 para.18, SI 2003/742 Reg.29
Reg.5, amended: SI 2004/762 Reg.6
Reg.5, substituted: SI 2003/701 Reg.5
Reg.5A, added: SI 2004/762 Reg.7

NO.

2002–cont.

2005. Working Tax Credit (Entitlement and Maximum Rate) Regulations 2002–cont.
Reg.6, substituted: SI 2003/701 Reg.6
Reg.7A, added: SI 2003/701 Reg.7
Reg.7B, added: SI 2003/701 Reg.7
Reg.7C, added: SI 2003/701 Reg.7
Reg.9, amended: SI 2003/2815 Reg.14
Reg.9, applied: SI 2002/2014 Reg.8, Reg.26, SI 2002/3196 Reg.9, SR 2002/403 Reg.9
Reg.9, referred to: SI 2002/2014 Reg.8, Reg.26
Reg.9, substituted: SI 2003/701 Reg.8
Reg.9B, amended: SI 2004/762 Reg.8
Reg.10, amended: SI 2003/701 Reg.9
Reg.10, varied: SI 2003/742 Reg.30
Reg.11, substituted: SI 2003/701 Reg.10
Reg.11, varied: SI 2003/742 Reg.31
Reg.12, amended: SI 2003/701 Reg.11
Reg.13, amended: SI 2003/701 Reg.12
Reg.13, applied: SI 2002/3196 Reg.9, SR 2002/403 Reg.9
Reg.13, revoked (in part): SI 2004/762 Reg.9
Reg.13, varied: SI 2003/742 Reg.32
Reg.14, amended: SI 2003/701 Reg.13, SI 2003/2815 Reg.15, SI 2004/762 Reg.10, SI 2004/1276 Reg.2, SI 2004/2663 Reg.3
Reg.14, applied: SI 2002/2014 Reg.26, Reg.31, SI 2002/3196 Reg.9, SI 2003/463 Art.4, SR 2002/403 Reg.9
Reg.14, revoked (in part): SI 2003/701 Reg.13, SI 2004/762 Reg.10
Reg.14, varied: SI 2003/742 Reg.33
Reg.15, amended: SI 2003/701 Reg.14
Reg.15, applied: SI 2002/2008 Reg.7, SI 2002/2014 Reg.22, Reg.27
Reg.16, amended: SI 2003/701 Reg.15
Reg.16, applied: SI 2002/2008 Reg.7, SI 2002/2014 Reg.21, Reg.22, Reg.27
Reg.16, revoked (in part): SI 2003/701 Reg.15
Reg.17, applied: SI 2002/2014 Reg.26, SI 2002/3196 Reg.9, SR 2002/403 Reg.9
Reg.18, amended: SI 2003/2815 Reg.16, SI 2004/762 Reg.11
Reg.18, applied: SI 1987/1971 Sch.3 para.16, Sch.3A para.9, SI 1992/1814 Sch.3 para.16
Reg.20, amended: SI 2003/701 Reg.16
Reg.20, applied: SI 1975/556 Reg.7B, SI 1987/1967 Sch.2 para.12, SI 1987/1971 Sch.3 para.16, Sch.3A para.9, SI 1992/1814 Sch.4A para.21, Sch.3A para.9, SI 1996/207 Sch.1 para.14, SI 1996/2890 Sch.1 para.12, Sch.2 para.18, SI 2002/2008 Reg.7
Reg.20, referred to: SI 1987/481 Reg.5, Reg.6, Reg.7, SI 1987/1971 Reg.23, Sch.3 para.16, Sch.4 para.58, SI 1992/1814 Reg.15, Sch.1 para.13, Sch.3 para.16, Sch.4 para.57, SI 1994/2946 Reg.2B
Reg.20, varied: SI 2003/742 Reg.34
Sch.2, amended: SI 2004/941 Sch.1

NO.

2002–cont.

2005. Working Tax Credit (Entitlement and Maximum Rate) Regulations 2002– *cont.*

Sch.2, applied: SI 1992/1814 Sch.3A para.5, Sch.4A para.21, SI 2002/1792 Sch.6 para.4, SR 2003/28 Sch.6 para.4

Sch.2, referred to: SI 1987/1971 Sch.4 para.58, SI 1992/1814 Sch.4 para.57

2006. Tax Credits (Definition and Calculation of Income) Regulations 2002

referred to: SI 2003/742 Reg.35

Reg.2, amended: SI 2003/732 Reg.4, SI 2003/2815 Reg.3, SI 2004/762 Reg.13

Reg.2, varied: SI 2003/742 Reg.36

Reg.3, amended: SI 2003/732 Reg.5, SI 2003/2815 Reg.4

Reg.3, varied: SI 2003/742 Reg.37

Reg.4, amended: SI 2003/732 Reg.6, SI 2003/2815 Reg.5, SI 2004/762 Reg.14, SI 2004/2663 Reg.2

Reg.4, varied: SI 2003/742 Reg.38

Reg.5, amended: SI 2003/732 Reg.7

Reg.7, amended: SI 2003/732 Reg.8, SI 2003/2815 Reg.6

Reg.7, revoked (in part): SI 2003/732 Reg.8

Reg.8, substituted: SI 2003/2815 Reg.7

Reg.10, amended: SI 2003/732 Reg.9, SI 2003/2815 Reg.8

Reg.11, amended: SI 2003/2815 Reg.9

Reg.12, amended: SI 2003/732 Reg.10, SI 2003/2815 Reg.10

Reg.16, amended: SI 2004/762 Reg.15

Reg.19, amended: SI 2003/732 Reg.11, SI 2003/762 Reg.11, SI 2003/2815 Reg.11, SI 2004/762 Reg.16, SI 2004/1748 Sch.2 para.3

Reg.19, applied: SI 2002/2005 Reg.4

2007. Child Tax Credit Regulations 2002

applied: SI 2003/653 Reg.3

referred to: SI 2003/738 Reg.2, SI 2003/742 Reg.22

Reg.2, amended: SI 2003/738 Reg.3, SI 2003/2815 Reg.17

Reg.2, revoked (in part): SI 2003/738 Reg.3

Reg.2, varied: SI 2003/742 Reg.23

Reg.3, amended: SI 2004/762 Reg.2

Reg.3, applied: SI 2002/2005 Reg.2, Reg.14, SI 2002/2006 Reg.2, SI 2002/2173 Reg.3, SI 2003/654 Reg.2, SI 2003/2170 Art.2

Reg.3, varied: SI 2003/742 Reg.24

Reg.5, amended: SI 2003/738 Reg.4, Reg.5, Reg.6

Reg.6, applied: SI 2002/2005 Reg.19

Reg.7, amended: SI 2004/941 Reg.2

Reg.7, applied: SI 1988/1724 Reg.1A

Reg.7, varied: SI 2003/742 Reg.25

Reg.8, applied: SI 2002/2014 Reg.26A

Reg.8, referred to: SI 2002/3196 Reg.9, SR 2002/403 Reg.9

NO.

2002–cont.

2008. Tax Credits (Income Thresholds and Determination of Rates) Regulations 2002

Reg.3, amended: SI 2004/941 Reg.4

Reg.3, applied: SI 2002/2173 Reg.12A

Reg.4, amended: SI 2003/2815 Reg.18

2011. Immigration Services Commissioner (Registration Fee) Order 2002

revoked: SI 2004/802 Art.7

2013. Electronic Commerce (EC Directive) Regulations 2002

applied: SI 2003/2500 Reg.2, SI 2004/1818 Reg.8

varied: SI 2003/115 Reg.2, SI 2004/1178 Reg.2

Reg.3, amended: SI 2004/1178 Reg.3

Reg.3, disapplied: SI 2003/115 Reg.2, SI 2003/2500 Reg.2, SI 2004/1178 Reg.2, SI 2004/1818 Reg.8

Reg.6, applied: 1988 c.48 s.97A, s.191JA

Reg.6, referred to: SI 2003/1374 Sch.1

Reg.7, referred to: SI 2003/1374 Sch.1

Reg.8, referred to: SI 2003/1374 Sch.1

Reg.9, referred to: SI 2003/1374 Sch.1

Reg.11, referred to: SI 2003/1374 Sch.1

2014. Tax Credits (Claims and Notifications) Regulations 2002

applied: SI 2002/3036 Reg.3, Reg.4, Reg.5

referred to: SI 2003/723 Reg.2, SI 2003/742 Reg.39, SI 2003/3240 Reg.2

Reg.2, amended: SI 2003/723 Reg.3

Reg.2, varied: SI 2003/742 Reg.40

Reg.3, amended: SI 2003/723 Reg.3

Reg.4, amended: SI 2003/723 Reg.3

Reg.5, amended: SI 2003/723 Reg.3

Reg.6, amended: SI 2003/723 Reg.3

Reg.7, amended: SI 2003/723 Reg.3

Reg.7, disapplied: SI 2003/653 Reg.3

Reg.7, referred to: SI 2003/962 Art.5

Reg.8, amended: SI 2003/2815 Reg.20, SI 2003/3240 Reg.3

Reg.8, disapplied: SI 2003/653 Reg.3

Reg.11, amended: SI 2003/723 Reg.3, SI 2004/762 Reg.3

Reg.11, applied: SI 2003/654 Reg.3

Reg.11, varied: SI 2003/742 Reg.41

Reg.12, applied: SI 2003/654 Reg.3

Reg.13, varied: SI 2003/742 Reg.42

Reg.15, varied: SI 2003/742 Reg.43

Reg.16, varied: SI 2003/742 Reg.44

Reg.18, applied: SI 2002/3237 Reg.27, SR 2003/18 Reg.27

Reg.19, amended: SI 2003/723 Reg.3

Reg.20, applied: SI 2002/2005 Reg.9A

Reg.21, amended: SI 2003/723 Reg.4, SI 2004/1241 Reg.3

Reg.22, amended: SI 2003/723 Reg.3

Reg.22, referred to: SI 2002/2007 Reg.5

Reg.23, varied: SI 2003/742 Reg.45

NO.

2002–cont.

2014. Tax Credits (Claims and Notifications) Regulations 2002–*cont.*

Reg.24, amended: SI 2003/723 Reg.3, SI 2004/762 Reg.3

Reg.25, amended: SI 2003/723 Reg.3

Reg.26, amended: SI 2003/2815 Reg.21, SI 2003/3240 Reg.4

Reg.26A, added: SI 2004/762 Reg.3

Reg.27, amended: SI 2003/723 Reg.5

Reg.29A, added: SI 2004/1241 Reg.4

Reg.30, varied: SI 2003/742 Reg.46

Reg.31, varied: SI 2003/742 Reg.47

Reg.33, amended: SI 2003/2815 Reg.22

Reg.33, substituted: SI 2004/762 Reg.3

Reg.34, amended: SI 2003/742 Reg.47A

Reg.34, substituted: SI 2004/762 Reg.3

2016. National Health Service (Local Pharmaceutical Services and Pharmaceutical Services) (No.2) Regulations 2002

Reg.1, amended: SI 2002/2469 Sch.7

Reg.2, amended: SI 2002/2469 Sch.7

Reg.3, amended: SI 2002/2469 Sch.7

Reg.4, amended: SI 2002/2469 Sch.7

2022. Bus Service Operators Grant (Wales) Regulations 2002

Reg.2, amended: SI 2003/943 Reg.3, SI 2004/1827 Reg.3

Reg.3, amended: SI 2003/943 Reg.4, SI 2004/1827 Reg.4

2025. Lancashire Teaching Hospitals National Health Service Trust (Establishment) and the Chorley and South Ribble National Health Service Trust and Preston Acute Hospitals National Health Service Trust (Dissolution) Order 2002

revoked: 2003 c.43 s.7

2033. Dual-Use Items (Export Control) (Amendment) (No.2) Regulations 2002

revoked: SI 2003/2764 Sch.6

2034. Fixed-term Employees (Prevention of Less Favourable Treatment) Regulations 2002

applied: 1996 c.17 s.21, 1996 c.18 s.203

see *Allen v National Australia Group Europe Ltd* [2004] I.R.L.R. 847 (EAT (SC)), Judge McMullen Q.C.

Reg.3, applied: 1996 c.17 s.18

Reg.6, applied: 1996 c.17 s.18, 1996 c.18 s.105, s.108, s.109

Reg.9, applied: 1996 c.17 s.18

2048. Education (National Curriculum) (Exceptions at Key Stage 4) (England) (Amendment) Regulations 2002

revoked: SI 2003/252 Reg.2

NO.

2002–cont.

2051. Homelessness (Priority Need for Accommodation) (England) Order 2002

see *R. (on the application of Berhe) v Hillingdon LBC* [2003] EWHC 2075, [2004] 1 F.L.R. 439 (QBD (Admin Ct)), Sullivan, J.

2055. Merchant Shipping (Medical Examination) Regulations 2002

Reg.3, amended: SI 2003/3049 Sch.2 para.8, SI 2004/1713 Sch.2 para.7

2060. Animal Gatherings (Interim Measures) (Wales) (Amendment) (No.2) Order 2002

revoked: SI 2003/481 Art.11

2070. National Care Standards Commission (Fees and Frequency of Inspections) Amendment (No.2) Regulations 2002

varied: SI 2004/664 Art.11, Art.12, Art.13, Art.14

Reg.1, varied: SI 2004/664 Art.11, Art.12, Art.13, Art.14

Reg.2, varied: SI 2004/664 Art.11, Art.12, Art.13, Art.14

2073. East Lancashire Hospitals National Health Service Trust (Establishment) and the Blackburn, Hyndburn and Ribble Valley Health Care National Health Service Trust and Burnley Health Care National Health Service Trust (Dissolution) Order 2002

applied: SI 2003/3059 Sch.1

revoked: 2003 c.43 s.7

2086. Education (Teacher Student Loans) (Repayment etc.) Regulations 2002

Reg.3, applied: SI 2000/944 Reg.11

Reg.11, applied: SI 1987/1967 Sch.9 para.11A, SI 1992/1814 Sch.4 para.10A, SI 1996/207 Sch.7 para.12A

2088. Education (Student Support)(Amendment)(No.2) Regulations 2002

revoked: SI 2002/3200 Reg.3

2089. Education (Mandatory Awards) (Amendment) Regulations 2002

revoked: SI 2003/1994 Sch.6

2090. Service Subsidy Agreements (Tendering) (England) Regulations 2002

Reg.2, amended: SI 2004/609 Reg.3

Reg.3, amended: SI 2004/609 Reg.4

Reg.3A, added: SI 2004/609 Reg.5

2092. Street Works (Inspection Fees) (England) Regulations 2002

referred to: SI 2004/572 Reg.2

Reg.3, amended: SI 2004/572 Reg.3

2099. Packaging, Labelling and Carriage of Radioactive Material by Rail Regulations 2002

referred to: SI 2002/2676 Sch.2, SI 2002/2677 Sch.7

NO.

NO.

2002–cont.

2002–cont.

2099. Packaging, Labelling and Carriage of Radioactive Material by Rail Regulations 2002–*cont.*
revoked: SI 2004/568 Sch.14
Reg.4, referred to: SI 2001/2975 Reg.3

2103. School Teachers Remuneration Order 2002
revoked: 2002 c.32 Sch.22 Part 1

2105. Education (School Performance Targets) (England) (Amendment) (No.2) Regulations 2002
revoked: SI 2004/2858 Sch.2

2113. Education Act 2002 (Transitional Provisions etc.) (England) Regulations 2002
Reg.3, revoked (in part): SI 2002/2316 Reg.5

2114. Schools Forums (England) Regulations 2002
Reg.1, amended: SI 2004/447 Reg.2
Reg.4, amended: SI 2004/447 Reg.2
Reg.6, amended: SI 2004/447 Reg.2

2125. Merchant Shipping (Hours of Work) Regulations 2002
referred to: SI 1993/1213 Reg.3
Reg.2, amended: SI 2004/1469 Reg.2
Reg.3, amended: SI 2003/3049 Sch.2 para.9, SI 2004/1469 Reg.2, SI 2004/1713 Sch.2 para.8
Reg.3, revoked (in part): SI 2004/1469 Reg.2
Reg.15, amended: SI 2004/1469 Reg.2

2151. Products of Animal Origin (Third Country Imports) (England) (Amendment) Regulations 2002
revoked: SI 2002/3206 Reg.3

2152. Disease Control (Interim Measures) (England) (No.2) Order 2002
revoked: SI 2003/254 Art.16
Art.1, amended: SI 2003/30 Art.2
Art.2, amended: SI 2002/2300 Art.2
Art.3, amended: SI 2002/2300 Art.2, SI 2003/30 Art.2
Art.3, applied: SI 2002/2153 Art.4, Art.5, Art.12, SI 2002/2154 Art.11
Art.3, referred to: SI 2002/2154 Art.8
Art.5, revoked: SI 2002/2300 Art.2
Art.6, amended: SI 2002/2300 Art.2
Art.8, substituted: SI 2003/30 Art.2

2153. Sheep and Goats Identification and Movement (Interim Measures) (England) (No.2) Order 2002
applied: SI 2003/1729 Sch.1 para.12, Sch.2 para.6, Sch.2 para.7, Sch.2 para.8
Art.1, amended: SI 2003/29 Art.3, SI 2003/502 Art.2, SI 2003/1728 Art.2
Art.2, amended: SI 2003/29 Art.4
Art.2A, added: SI 2003/29 Art.5
Art.4, amended: SI 2003/29 Art.6, SI 2003/502 Art.2
Art.5, amended: SI 2003/29 Art.7, SI 2003/502 Art.2
Art.6, amended: SI 2003/29 Art.8

2153. Sheep and Goats Identification and Movement (Interim Measures) (England) (No.2) Order 2002–*cont.*
Art.6, applied: SI 2003/1279 Art.4, SI 2003/1729 Art.9
Art.7, amended: SI 2003/29 Art.9
Art.9, amended: SI 2003/29 Art.10
Art.12, amended: SI 2003/29 Art.11, SI 2003/502 Art.2
Art.13, amended: SI 2003/29 Art.12

2154. Pigs (Records, Identification and Movement) (Interim Measures) (England) (No.2) Order 2002
applied: SI 2003/1729 Art.12
revoked: SI 2003/2632 Art.28
Art.1, amended: SI 2003/28 Art.2
Art.8, applied: SI 2003/254 Sch.1 para.10, Sch.2 para.3, SI 2003/1279 Sch.1 para.10, Sch.2 para.3, SI 2003/1729 Sch.1 para.10, Sch.2 para.4
Art.8, referred to: SI 2003/254 Sch.2 para.2, SI 2003/1279 Sch.2 para.2, SI 2003/1729 Sch.2 para.3
Art.10, applied: SI 2003/254 Art.3, SI 2003/1279 Art.3

2171. Child Minding and Day Care (Wales) (Amendment) Regulations 2002
revoked: SI 2002/2622 Reg.7

2172. Working Tax Credit (Payment by Employers) Regulations 2002
applied: SI 2002/2173 Reg.8, Reg.9
referred to: SI 2003/962 Art.5
Reg.2, amended: SI 2003/715 Reg.4, SI 2004/762 Reg.17
Reg.3, amended: SI 2003/715 Reg.5, SI 2004/762 Reg.17
Reg.4, amended: SI 2003/715 Reg.6
Reg.5, amended: SI 2003/715 Reg.6
Reg.6, amended: SI 2003/715 Reg.6, Reg.7, SI 2004/762 Reg.17
Reg.6, applied: SI 1993/744 Reg.42A, SI 2003/2495 Reg.1, SI 2003/2682 Reg.191
Reg.7, amended: SI 2003/715 Reg.6
Reg.7, applied: SI 1993/743 Reg.9, Reg.52, SI 1993/744 Reg.42B, Reg.41, SI 2001/1004 Reg.90K, Sch.4 para.11, SI 2003/2682 Reg.203
Reg.8, amended: SI 2003/715 Reg.6, SI 2004/762 Reg.17
Reg.12, amended: SI 2003/715 Reg.8
Reg.13, amended: SI 2003/715 Reg.9

2173. Tax Credits (Payments by the Board) Regulations 2002
referred to: SI 2003/723 Reg.6, SI 2003/742 Reg.48, SI 2003/962 Art.5
Reg.1, amended: SI 2003/723 Reg.7
Reg.2, varied: SI 2003/742 Reg.49
Reg.3, amended: SI 2003/723 Reg.8, SI 2004/1241 Reg.5
Reg.3, varied: SI 2003/742 Reg.50
Reg.8, amended: SI 2003/723 Reg.9

2002–cont.

2173. Tax Credits (Payments by the Board) Regulations 2002–*cont.*
Reg.10, substituted: SI 2003/723 Reg.10
Reg.12A, added: SI 2004/762 Reg.18
Reg.13, amended: SI 2003/723 Reg.11
Reg.14, amended: SI 2003/723 Reg.12

2183. Road Traffic (Permitted Parking Area and Special Parking Area) (County of Essex) (Borough of Brentwood) Order 2002
Art.3, amended: SI 2002/2440 Art.2

2199. Velindre National Health Service Trust (Establishment) Amendment (No.2) Order 2002
revoked: 2003 c.43 s.7

2201. Fishing Vessels (Safety of 15-24 Metre Vessels) Regulations 2002
applied: SI 1975/330 r.1B

2216. Disability Discrimination Codes of Practice (Education) (Appointed Day) Order 2002
see *McAuley Catholic High School v CC* [2003] EWHC 3045, [2004] 2 All E.R. 436 (QBD (Admin Ct)), Silber, J.

2223. Education (School Teachers Pay and Conditions) (No.2) Order 2002
referred to: SI 2003/1708 Reg.3
revoked: SI 2003/2169 Art.1

2233. Witham, Braintree and Halstead Care Trust (Establishment) Order 2002
Sch.1, amended: SI 2004/543 Sch.1

2234. Borough of Thurrock (Electoral Changes) Order 2002
varied: SI 2004/222 Art.2
Art.4, amended: SI 2003/1091 Art.2

2235. Borough of Medway (Electoral Changes) Order 2002
varied: SI 2004/222 Art.2

2236. City of Plymouth (Electoral Changes) Order 2002
varied: SI 2004/222 Art.2

2237. Borough of Warrington (Electoral Changes) Order 2002
varied: SI 2004/222 Art.2
Art.4, amended: SI 2003/1089 Art.2

2238. District of East Dorset (Electoral Changes) Order 2002
varied: SI 2004/222 Art.2

2239. District of North Dorset (Electoral Changes) Order 2002
varied: SI 2004/222 Art.2

2240. Borough of Blackpool (Electoral Changes) Order 2002
varied: SI 2004/222 Art.2

2241. Borough of Christchurch (Electoral Changes) Order 2002
varied: SI 2004/222 Art.2

2242. Borough of Halton (Electoral Changes) Order 2002
varied: SI 2004/222 Art.2

2002–cont.

2243. District of West Berkshire (Electoral Changes) Order 2002
varied: SI 2004/222 Art.2

2258. Town and Country Planning (Fees for Applications and Deemed Applications) (Amendment No.2) (Wales) Regulations 2002
revoked: SI 2004/2736 Reg.3

2295. Food (Peanuts from China) (Emergency Control) (Wales) (No.2) Regulations 2002
Reg.2, amended: SI 2003/2299 Reg.2

2296. Food (Figs, Hazelnuts and Pistachios from Turkey) (Emergency Control) (Wales) (No.2) Regulations 2002
Reg.2, amended: SI 2003/2292 Reg.2
Reg.4, amended: SI 2003/2292 Reg.2

2300. Disease Control (Interim Measures) (England) (No.2) (Amendment) Order 2002
revoked: SI 2003/254 Art.16

2302. Sheep and Goats Identification and Movement (Interim Measures) (Wales) (No.2) Order 2002
Art.1, amended: SI 2003/167 Art.3, SI 2003/946 Art.3, SI 2003/1966 Art.24
Art.2, amended: SI 2003/167 Art.4
Art.2A, added: SI 2003/167 Art.5
Art.4, amended: SI 2003/167 Art.6
Art.5, amended: SI 2003/167 Art.7
Art.6, amended: SI 2003/167 Art.8
Art.6, applied: SI 2003/1414 Art.4, SI 2003/1966 Art.9
Art.7, amended: SI 2003/167 Art.9, SI 2003/946 Art.4
Art.9, amended: SI 2003/167 Art.10
Art.12, amended: SI 2003/167 Art.11
Art.13, amended: SI 2003/167 Art.12

2303. Pigs (Records, Identification and Movement) (Interim Measures) (Wales) (No.2) Order 2002
revoked: SI 2004/996 Art.28
Art.1, amended: SI 2003/170 Art.2, SI 2003/2763 Art.2
Art.3, amended: SI 2003/170 Art.2
Art.8, applied: SI 2003/483 Sch.1 para.10, SI 2003/1966 Sch.1 para.10, Sch.2 para.4
Art.8, disapplied: SI 2003/483 Sch.2 para.3
Art.8, referred to: SI 2003/483 Sch.2 para.2, SI 2003/1966 Sch.2 para.3
Art.10, applied: SI 2003/483 Art.3, SI 2003/1414 Art.3, SI 2003/1966 Art.12

2304. Disease Control (Interim Measures) (Wales) (No.2) Order 2002
revoked: SI 2003/483 Art.16
Art.1, amended: SI 2003/168 Art.2
Art.2, amended: SI 2002/2480 Art.2
Art.3, amended: SI 2002/2480 Art.2, SI 2003/168 Art.2
Art.3, applied: SI 2002/2302 Art.4, Art.5, Art.12, SI 2002/2303 Art.11

2002–cont.

2304. Disease Control (Interim Measures) (Wales) (No.2) Order 2002–*cont.*
Art.3, referred to: SI 2002/2303 Art.8
Art.4, amended: SI 2002/2480 Art.2
Art.5, revoked: SI 2002/2480 Art.2
Art.6, amended: SI 2002/2480 Art.2
Art.8, substituted: SI 2003/168 Art.2
Art.8A, substituted: SI 2003/168 Art.2
Art.8B, substituted: SI 2003/168 Art.2
Art.8C, substituted: SI 2003/168 Art.2
Art.9, amended: SI 2002/2480 Art.2

2310. Gaming Duty (Amendment) Regulations 2002
revoked: SI 2004/2243 Reg.3

2326. Police and Criminal Evidence Act 1984 (Department of Trade and Industry Investigations) Order 2002
referred to: SI 1999/1747 Sch.16 para.2

2350. Food (Peanuts from China) (Emergency Control) (England) (No.2) Regulations 2002
Reg.2, amended: SI 2003/1958 Reg.2, SI 2004/1265 Reg.2
Reg.4, amended: SI 2003/1958 Reg.2

2351. Food (Figs, Hazelnuts and Pistachios from Turkey) (Emergency Control) (England) (No.2) Regulations 2002
Reg.2, amended: SI 2003/1957 Reg.2, SI 2004/1265 Reg.3
Reg.4, amended: SI 2003/1957 Reg.2

2353. National Health Service (Miscellaneous Dental Charges Amendments) Regulations 2002
Reg.2, revoked: SI 2003/2382 Sch.2
Reg.3, revoked: SI 2003/2382 Sch.2
Reg.4, revoked: SI 2003/2382 Sch.2
Reg.5, revoked: SI 2003/2382 Sch.2
Reg.6, revoked: SI 2003/2382 Sch.2

2364. Plastic Materials and Articles in Contact with Food (Amendment) (England) Regulations 2002
applied: SI 1990/2463 Sch.1

2368. Borough of Weymouth and Portland (Electoral Changes) Order 2002
varied: SI 2004/222 Art.2
Art.6, amended: SI 2003/1090 Art.2

2369. City of Cambridge (Electoral Changes) Order 2002
varied: SI 2004/222 Art.2

2370. District of West Dorset (Electoral Changes) Order 2002
varied: SI 2004/222 Art.2

2371. Borough of Bracknell Forest (Electoral Changes) Order 2002
varied: SI 2004/222 Art.2

2372. Royal Borough of Windsor and Maidenhead (Electoral Changes) Order 2002
varied: SI 2004/222 Art.2

2002–cont.

2373. Borough of Telford and Wrekin (Electoral Changes) Order 2002
varied: SI 2004/222 Art.2

2374. District of South Cambridgeshire (Electoral Changes) Order 2002
varied: SI 2004/222 Art.2
Art.6, amended: SI 2003/711 Art.2

2375. National Health Service (Functions of Strategic Health Authorities and Primary Care Trusts and Administration Arrangements) (England) Regulations 2002
Reg.2, amended: SI 2003/1497 Reg.2, SI 2004/865 Sch.1 para.32, SI 2004/1031 Sch.10 para.18
Reg.3, amended: SI 2003/1497 Reg.3, SI 2004/865 Sch.1 para.32
Reg.4, amended: SI 2002/2548 Reg.16
Reg.4, revoked (in part): SI 2004/865 Sch.1 para.32
Reg.6, revoked (in part): SI 2004/865 Sch.1 para.32
Reg.9, amended: SI 2003/1497 Reg.4, SI 2004/865 Sch.1 para.32
Reg.9, revoked (in part): SI 2003/1497 Reg.4
Reg.10, amended: SI 2003/1497 Reg.5, SI 2004/865 Sch.1 para.32
Reg.10, revoked (in part): SI 2004/865 Sch.1 para.32
Reg.11, amended: SI 2003/1497 Reg.6, SI 2004/865 Sch.1 para.32
Sch.3, amended: SI 2004/865 Sch.1 para.32

2380. Social Security (Miscellaneous Amendments) (No.2) Regulations 2002
applied: SI 1992/2977 Sch.4 para.6

2382. Road Vehicles (Registration and Licensing) (Amendment) Regulations 2002
revoked: SI 2002/2742 Sch.1 Part I

2397. Eastbourne and County National Health Service Trust Change of Name and (Establishment) Amendment Order (No.2) 2002
revoked: 2003 c.43 s.7

2398. Strand Road, Preston Railway Order 2002
Art.5, amended: SI 2003/2155 Sch.1 para.18

2402. Income-related Benefits and Jobseeker's Allowance (Working Tax Credit and Child Tax Credit) (Amendment) Regulations 2002
Sch.1 para.5, revoked: SI 2003/455 Sch.4 para.5
Sch.2 para.5, revoked: SI 2003/455 Sch.4 para.5
Sch.3 para.5, revoked: SI 2003/455 Sch.4 para.6
Sch.3 para.10, amended: SI 2003/770 Reg.2
Sch.3 para.11, amended: SI 2003/770 Reg.2

NO.

2002–cont.

2402. Income-related Benefits and Jobseeker's Allowance (Working Tax Credit and Child Tax Credit) (Amendment) Regulations 2002–*cont.*

Sch.4 para.5, revoked: SI 2003/455 Sch.4 para.6

Sch.4 para.10, amended: SI 2003/770 Reg.2

Sch.4 para.11, amended: SI 2003/770 Reg.2

2419. Buckinghamshire Hospitals National Health Service Trust (Establishment) and the South Buckinghamshire National Health Service Trust and Stoke Mandeville Hospital National Health Service Trust (Dissolution) Order 2002

applied: SI 2003/3059 Sch.1

revoked: 2003 c.43 s.7

2420. County Durham and Darlington Acute Hospitals National Health Service Trust (Establishment) and the North Durham Health Care National Health Service Trust and South Durham Health Care National Health Service Trust (Dissolution) Order 2002

revoked: 2003 c.43 s.7

2439. Education Act 2002 (Commencement No 2 and Savings and Transitional Provisions) Order 2002

Sch.1 Part 2 para.4, substituted: SI 2003/606 Art.2, SI 2003/2992 Art.3

2441. Social Security (Claims and Payments and Miscellaneous Amendments) (No.2) Regulations 2002

revoked (in part): SI 2003/492 Sch.3 Part 1

Reg.2, revoked (in part): SI 2003/492 Sch.3 Part 1

Reg.3, revoked (in part): SI 2003/492 Sch.3 Part 1

Reg.5, revoked (in part): SI 2003/492 Sch.3 Part 1

Reg.9, revoked (in part): SI 2003/492 Sch.3 Part 1

Reg.10, revoked (in part): SI 2003/492 Sch.3 Part 1

2443. Genetically Modified Organisms (Deliberate Release) Regulations 2002

referred to: SI 2002/3188 Reg.4, Reg.30

Reg.2, amended: SI 2004/2411 Reg.2

Reg.3, referred to: SI 2002/3188 Reg.4

Reg.4, referred to: SI 2002/3188 Reg.5

Reg.15, amended: SI 2004/2411 Reg.2

Reg.17A, added: SI 2004/2411 Reg.2

Reg.19, referred to: SI 2002/3188 Reg.20

Reg.21, amended: SI 2004/2411 Reg.2

Reg.29, referred to: SI 2002/3188 Reg.30

Reg.30, referred to: SI 2002/3188 Reg.31

Reg.33, referred to: SI 2002/3188 Reg.34

Reg.38, referred to: SI 2002/3188 Reg.40

NO.

2002–cont.

2466. Education (Nursery Education and Early Years Development) (England) (Amendment) Regulations 2002

revoked: SI 2003/2939 Reg.3

2467. Offshore Installations (Safety Zones) (No.2) Order 2002

Sch.1, amended: SI 2003/845 Art.3

2469. National Health Service Reform and Health Care Professions Act 2002 (Supplementary, Consequential etc Provisions) Regulations 2002

Sch.1 Part 2 para.54, revoked (in part): SI 2004/865 Sch.2, SI 2004/1016 Sch.2

Sch.1 Part 2 para.67, revoked: SI 2004/1031 Sch.11

Sch.1 Part 2 para.78, revoked (in part): SI 2004/865 Sch.2, SSI 2004/212 Sch.2

Sch.1 Part 2 para.79, revoked (in part): SI 2004/865 Sch.2, SSI 2004/212 Sch.2

Sch.2, amended: SI 2004/865 Sch.2

Sch.2, varied: SI 2004/664 Art.11, Art.12, Art.13, Art.14

Sch.5, amended: SI 2004/865 Sch.2, SI 2004/1016 Sch.2

Sch.7, amended: SI 2004/865 Sch.2, SI 2004/1016 Sch.2

Sch.7, varied: SI 2004/664 Art.11, Art.12, Art.13, Art.14

Sch.8, varied: SI 2004/664 Art.11, Art.12, Art.13, Art.14

2479. Dangerous Substances and Preparations (Safety) (Consolidation) (Amendment No 2) Regulations 2002

revoked: SI 2002/3010 Reg.2

2480. Disease Control (Interim Measures) (Wales) (No.2) (Amendment) Order 2002

revoked: SI 2003/483 Art.16

2513. Teacher Training Agency (Additional Functions) (No.2) (Amendment) Order 2002

revoked: SI 2003/2038 Art.2

2525. Nitrate Vulnerable Zones (Additional Designations) (England) Regulations 2002

revoked: SI 2002/2614 Reg.12

2527. Police and Criminal Evidence Act 1984 (Visual Recording of Interviews) (Certain Police Areas) (No.2) Order 2002

revoked: SI 2003/2463 Art.2

2529. Police (Amendment) (No.2) Regulations 2002

revoked: SI 2003/527 Sch.4 Part 1

2548. National Health Service (Out of Hours Medical Services) and National Health Service (General Medical Services) Amendment Regulations 2002

applied: SI 2004/865 Art.90

referred to: SI 2004/865 Art.90

NO.

2002–cont.

2548. National Health Service (Out of Hours Medical Services) and National Health Service (General Medical Services) Amendment Regulations 2002–*cont.*

revoked: SI 2004/865 Sch.2

Reg.1, referred to: SI 2004/627 Sch.6 para.1

Reg.1, varied: SI 2004/291 Sch.7 para.1, SI 2004/627 Sch.6 para.1, SI 2004/865 Art.90

Reg.2, referred to: SI 2004/627 Sch.6 para.1

Reg.2, varied: SI 2004/291 Sch.7 para.1, SI 2004/627 Sch.6 para.1, SI 2004/865 Art.90

Reg.3, referred to: SI 2004/627 Sch.6 para.1

Reg.3, varied: SI 2004/291 Sch.7 para.1, SI 2004/627 Sch.6 para.1, SI 2004/865 Art.90

Reg.4, applied: SI 2004/865 Art.90

Reg.4, referred to: SI 2004/627 Sch.6 para.1

Reg.4, varied: SI 2004/291 Sch.7 para.1, SI 2004/627 Sch.6 para.1, SI 2004/865 Art.90

Reg.5, amended: SI 2003/26 Reg.8

Reg.5, applied: SI 1992/635 Sch.2 para.18A, SI 2003/26 Reg.4, SI 2004/291 Sch.7 para.2, SI 2004/627 Sch.6 para.2, SI 2004/865 Art.90

Reg.5, referred to: SI 2004/627 Sch.6 para.1

Reg.5, varied: SI 2004/291 Sch.7 para.1, SI 2004/627 Sch.6 para.1, SI 2004/865 Art.90

Reg.6, referred to: SI 2004/627 Sch.6 para.1

Reg.6, varied: SI 2004/291 Sch.7 para.1, SI 2004/627 Sch.6 para.1, SI 2004/865 Art.90

Reg.7, applied: SI 2004/865 Art.90

Reg.7, referred to: SI 2004/627 Sch.6 para.1

Reg.7, varied: SI 2004/291 Sch.7 para.1, SI 2004/627 Sch.6 para.1, SI 2004/865 Art.90

Reg.8, applied: SI 1992/635 Sch.2 para.18A, SI 2003/26 Reg.3, SI 2004/291 Sch.7 para.6, SI 2004/627 Sch.6 para.5, Sch.6 para.6, SI 2004/865 Art.76, Art.77

Reg.8, referred to: SI 2004/627 Sch.6 para.1

Reg.8, varied: SI 2004/291 Sch.7 para.1, SI 2004/627 Sch.6 para.1, SI 2004/865 Art.90

Reg.9, applied: SI 1992/635 Sch.2 para.18A, SI 2003/26 Reg.3, SI 2004/291 Sch.7 para.5, SI 2004/627 Sch.6 para.4, Sch.6 para.6, SI 2004/865 Art.78

Reg.9, referred to: SI 2004/627 Sch.6 para.1

Reg.9, varied: SI 2004/291 Sch.7 para.1, SI 2004/627 Sch.6 para.1, SI 2004/865 Art.90

Reg.10, amended: SI 2003/26 Reg.8

Reg.10, applied: SI 2004/865 Art.90

Reg.10, referred to: SI 2004/627 Sch.6 para.1

NO.

2002–cont.

2548. National Health Service (Out of Hours Medical Services) and National Health Service (General Medical Services) Amendment Regulations 2002–*cont.*

Reg.10, varied: SI 2004/291 Sch.7 para.1, SI 2004/627 Sch.6 para.1, SI 2004/865 Art.90

Reg.11, amended: SI 2003/26 Reg.8

Reg.11, applied: SI 2004/291 Sch.7 para.5, Sch.7 para.6, Sch.7 para.7, SI 2004/627 Sch.6 para.4, Sch.6 para.5, Sch.6 para.6

Reg.11, referred to: SI 2004/627 Sch.6 para.1

Reg.11, varied: SI 2004/291 Sch.7 para.1, SI 2004/627 Sch.6 para.1, SI 2004/865 Art.90

Sch.1 para.7, varied: SI 2004/865 Art.90

2550. Education (Pupil Referral Units) (Appeals Against Permanent Exclusion) (England) Regulations 2002

applied: SI 2002/2952 Sch.1 para.4

revoked: SI 2002/3179 Reg.10

2569. Medicines (Products for Animal Use-Fees) (Amendment) Regulations 2002

revoked: SI 2004/2750 Reg.18

2570. Products of Animal Origin (Third Country Imports) (England) (Amendment) (No.2) Regulations 2002

revoked: SI 2002/3206 Reg.3

2572. General Medical Council (Fitness to Practise Committees) (Amendment) Rules Order of Council 2002

Sch.1 para.7, revoked: SI 2003/1344 Sch.1

Sch.1 para.8, revoked: SI 2003/1344 Sch.1

2573. Plant Health (Phytophthora ramorum) (England) (No.2) Order 2002

revoked: SI 2004/2590 Art.16

2593. District of Penwith (Electoral Changes) Order 2002

varied: SI 2004/222 Art.2

2594. District of Carrick (Electoral Changes) Order 2002

varied: SI 2004/222 Art.2

2595. District of Fenland (Electoral Changes) Order 2002

varied: SI 2004/222 Art.2

2596. District of East Cambridgeshire (Electoral Changes) Order 2002

varied: SI 2004/222 Art.2

2597. District of Harborough (Electoral Changes) Order 2002

varied: SI 2004/222 Art.2

2598. District of North West Leicestershire (Electoral Changes) Order 2002

varied: SI 2004/222 Art.2

2599. Borough of Melton (Electoral Changes) Order 2002

varied: SI 2004/222 Art.2

NO.

2002–cont.

2600. Borough of Slough (Electoral Changes) Order 2002
varied: SI 2004/222 Art.2

2601. Borough of Restormel (Electoral Changes) Order 2002
varied: SI 2004/222 Art.2

2602. District of Caradon (Electoral Changes) Order 2002
varied: SI 2004/222 Art.2

2603. District of North Cornwall (Electoral Changes) Order 2002
varied: SI 2004/222 Art.2

2604. District of Kerrier (Electoral Changes) Order 2002
varied: SI 2004/222 Art.2

2616. National Health Service Trusts (Miscellaneous Dissolutions) Order 2002
revoked: 2003 c.43 s.7

2617. Basildon and Thurrock General Hospitals National Health Service Trust (Change of Name) Order 2002
revoked: 2003 c.43 s.7

2619. Asylum Support (Amendment) (No.2) Regulations 2002
revoked: SI 2003/755 Reg.3

2623. Freedom of Information (Additional Public Authorities) Order 2002
Sch.1, varied: SI 2004/664 Art.11, Art.12, Art.13, Art.14

2639. Products of Animal Origin (Third Country Imports) (England) (Amendment) (No.3) Regulations 2002
revoked: SI 2002/3206 Reg.3

2660. Social Security (Claims and Payments and Miscellaneous Amendments) (No.3) Regulations 2002
Reg.2, revoked (in part): SI 2003/492 Sch.3 Part 1

2665. Electricity Safety, Quality and Continuity Regulations 2002
Sch.3 Part IV para.4, amended: SI 2003/2155 Sch.1 para.49
Sch.3 Part IV para.4, varied: SI 2004/1822 Sch.1 para.20

2675. Control of Asbestos at Work Regulations 2002
applied: SI 2002/2677 Reg.5, SI 2003/547 Reg.3, Reg.7, Sch.6, SI 2004/456 Reg.6, Sch.5
Reg.23, amended: SI 2004/568 Sch.13 para.12
Reg.23, revoked (in part): SI 2004/568 Sch.13 para.12
Sch.2 para.1, amended: SI 2004/568 Sch.13 para.12

2676. Control of Lead at Work Regulations 2002
applied: SI 2002/2677 Reg.5, SI 2003/547 Reg.3, Reg.8, SI 2004/456 Reg.7

NO.

2002–cont.

2676. Control of Lead at Work Regulations 2002–*cont.*
Sch.2, substituted: SI 2004/568 Sch.13 para.13

2677. Control of Substances Hazardous to Health Regulations 2002
applied: SI 2003/547 Reg.3, Sch.6, SI 2004/456 Sch.5
Reg.2, amended: SI 2003/978 Reg.2
Reg.7, amended: SI 2003/978 Reg.2
Reg.13, amended: SI 2003/978 Reg.2
Sch.1, amended: SI 2003/978 Reg.2
Sch.7, substituted: SI 2004/568 Sch.13 para.14

2682. Town and Country Planning (Enforcement Notices and Appeals) (England) Regulations 2002
referred to: SI 2003/956 Art.16
Reg.3, amended: SI 2003/956 Sch.9 para.1
Reg.4, referred to: SI 2002/2683 Reg.5
Reg.5, amended: SI 2003/956 Sch.9 para.2
Reg.6, applied: SI 2002/2683 Reg.7
Reg.9, applied: SI 2002/2683 Reg.7
Reg.10A, added: SI 2003/956 Sch.9 para.3

2683. Town and Country Planning (Enforcement) (Written Representations Procedure) (England) Regulations 2002
referred to: SI 2003/956 Art.16
Reg.2, amended: SI 2003/956 Sch.13 para.1, Sch.13 para.2
Reg.2, substituted: SI 2003/956 Sch.13 para.1
Reg.3, amended: SI 2003/956 Sch.13 para.3
Reg.7, amended: SI 2003/956 Sch.13 para.4
Reg.10A, added: SI 2003/956 Sch.13 para.5

2684. Town and Country Planning (Enforcement) (Hearings Procedure) (England) Rules 2002
referred to: SI 2003/956 Art.16
r.2, amended: SI 2003/956 Sch.12 para.1, Sch.12 para.2
r.4, applied: SI 2002/2682 Reg.9
r.5, amended: SI 2003/956 Sch.12 para.3
r.6, amended: SI 2003/956 Sch.12 para.4
r.15, amended: SI 2003/956 Sch.12 para.5
r.16, amended: SI 2003/956 Sch.12 para.6
r.19, substituted: SI 2003/956 Sch.12 para.7
r.20, added: SI 2003/956 Sch.12 para.8

2685. Town and Country Planning (Enforcement) (Determination by Inspectors) (Inquiries Procedure) (England) Rules 2002
referred to: SI 2003/956 Art.16
varied: SI 2002/2684 r.3, SI 2002/2686 r.3
r.2, amended: SI 2003/956 Sch.11 para.1, Sch.11 para.2
r.2, substituted: SI 2003/956 Sch.11 para.1
r.4, applied: SI 2002/2682 Reg.9
r.6, amended: SI 2003/956 Sch.11 para.3
r.9, amended: SI 2003/956 Sch.11 para.4

2002–cont.

2685. Town and Country Planning (Enforcement) (Determination by Inspectors) (Inquiries Procedure) (England) Rules 2002–*cont.*

r.15, amended: SI 2003/956 Sch.11 para.5
r.16, amended: SI 2003/956 Sch.11 para.6
r.20, amended: SI 2003/956 Sch.11 para.7
r.24, substituted: SI 2003/956 Sch.11 para.8
r.24A, added: SI 2003/956 Sch.11 para.9

2686. Town and Country Planning (Enforcement) (Inquiries Procedure) (England) Rules 2002

applied: SI 2002/2685 r.3, r.25
referred to: SI 2003/956 Art.16
varied: SI 2002/2684 r.3
r.2, amended: SI 2003/956 Sch.10 para.1, Sch.10 para.2
r.4, applied: SI 2002/2682 Reg.9
r.8, amended: SI 2003/956 Sch.10 para.3
r.11, amended: SI 2003/956 Sch.10 para.4
r.16, amended: SI 2003/956 Sch.10 para.5
r.17, amended: SI 2003/956 Sch.10 para.6
r.21, amended: SI 2003/956 Sch.10 para.7
r.25, substituted: SI 2003/956 Sch.10 para.8
r.25A, added: SI 2003/956 Sch.10 para.9

2690. Social Security, Statutory Maternity Pay and Statutory Sick Pay (Miscellaneous Amendments) Regulations 2002

Reg.3, referred to: SI 2003/526 Art.1

2693. Channel Tunnel (Alcoholic Liquor and Tobacco Products) (Amendment) Order 2002

revoked: SI 2003/2758 Art.6

2704. General Chiropractic Council (Registration of Chiropractors with Foreign Qualifications) Rules Order of Council 2002

Sch.1 Part III para.9, amended: SI 2003/3148 Reg.19, SI 2004/1947 Reg.18
Sch.1 Part III para.10, amended: SI 2004/1947 Reg.18
Sch.1 Part III para.11, amended: SI 2004/1947 Reg.18
Sch.1 Part III para.12, amended: SI 2004/1947 Reg.18

2710. Insolvency Practitioners (Amendment) Regulations 2002

Reg.2, amended: SI 2002/2748 Reg.2
Reg.2, revoked (in part): SI 2002/2748 Reg.2

2733. Plant Protection Products (Fees) (Amendment) Regulations 2002

revoked: SI 2003/660 Reg.4

2742. Road Vehicles (Registration and Licensing) Regulations 2002

applied: SI 1981/1694 Reg.13
Reg.3, amended: SI 2004/1773 Reg.3
Reg.9A, added: SI 2002/2981 Reg.2
Reg.9A, amended: SI 2003/3073 Reg.2
Reg.10, amended: SI 2003/3110 Reg.2
Reg.10A, added: SI 2003/3073 Reg.3

2002–cont.

2742. Road Vehicles (Registration and Licensing) Regulations 2002–*cont.*

Reg.13, amended: SI 2004/238 Reg.3, SI 2004/1773 Reg.4
Reg.14, amended: SI 2004/238 Reg.4, SI 2004/1773 Reg.5
Reg.15, amended: SI 2003/3073 Reg.4
Reg.16, amended: SI 2004/238 Reg.5, SI 2004/1773 Reg.6
Reg.17, amended: SI 2003/2635 Reg.34
Reg.17A, added: SI 2003/2635 Reg.34
Reg.18, amended: SI 2003/3073 Reg.5, SI 2004/238 Reg.6, SI 2004/1773 Reg.7
Reg.20, referred to: SI 2001/2285 Reg.6
Reg.21, amended: SI 2003/2154 Reg.3, SI 2004/238 Reg.7, SI 2004/1773 Reg.8
Reg.21, applied: SI 2001/2285 Reg.6
Reg.21, referred to: SI 2001/2285 Reg.6
Reg.21, revoked: SI 2003/3073 Reg.8
Reg.22, amended: SI 2003/2154 Reg.3, SI 2003/3073 Reg.5, Reg.8, SI 2004/238 Reg.8, SI 2004/1773 Reg.9
Reg.22, applied: SI 2001/2285 Reg.6
Reg.23, amended: SI 2003/3073 Reg.5, Reg.8
Reg.23, applied: SI 2001/2285 Reg.6
Reg.24, amended: SI 2003/2154 Reg.3, SI 2003/3073 Reg.5, Reg.8, SI 2004/238 Reg.9, SI 2004/1773 Reg.10
Reg.24, applied: SI 2001/2285 Reg.6
Reg.25, amended: SI 2003/3073 Reg.5, SI 2004/238 Reg.10, SI 2004/1773 Reg.11
Reg.25, applied: SI 2001/2285 Reg.6
Reg.25, revoked: SI 2003/3073 Reg.8
Reg.26A, added: SI 2003/3073 Reg.6
Reg.26A, revoked (in part): SI 2003/3073 Reg.8
Reg.27, amended: SI 2003/2154 Reg.4
Reg.27A, added: SI 2003/3073 Reg.7
Reg.30, amended: SI 2004/238 Reg.11
Reg.33, amended: SI 2003/2154 Reg.5
Reg.47, amended: SI 2003/2154 Reg.6
Sch.2 para.13, amended: SI 2003/2335 Reg.3, SI 2004/1872 Reg.2
Sch.3 para.7, amended: SI 2004/2099 Reg.2
Sch.5 para.3, substituted: SI 2003/2154 Sch.1
Sch.5 para.4, substituted: SI 2003/2154 Sch.1
Sch.8, amended: SI 2003/2635 Reg.34

2758. Immigration (Transit Visa) (Amendment No 2) Order 2002

revoked: SI 2003/1185 Sch.2

2759. National Health Service Act 1977 and National Health Service and Community Care Act 1990 (Amendment) Regulations 2002

Reg.2, amended: SI 2002/2932 Reg.2

NO.

2002–cont.

2763. **Financing of Maintained Schools (England) (Amendment No 2) Regulations 2002**
revoked: SI 2002/2868 Reg.2

2776. **Dangerous Substances and Explosive Atmospheres Regulations 2002**
applied: 1928 c.32 s.18, SI 1982/630 Reg.8
referred to: SI 1979/427 Reg.2, SI 2003/2002 Reg.12
Sch.5, substituted: SI 2004/568 Sch.13 para.15

2779. **Scottish Parliament (Elections etc.) Order 2002**
applied: SI 2003/122 Art.4, Sch.1 para.4, SI 2003/1557 Reg.7
Art.3, varied: SI 2003/1557 Sch.2 para.5
Art.16, applied: SI 2003/122 Art.4, Sch.1 para.1
Art.19, applied: SI 2003/122, SI 2003/122 Art.3, Art.4
Art.22, varied: SI 2003/1557 Sch.2 para.5
Sch.3 para.2, amended: SI 2004/1771 Sch.1 para.22
Sch.4 para.7, varied: SI 2003/1557 Sch.2 para.5

2782. **Magistrates Courts (Sex Offender Orders) Rules 2002**
revoked: SI 2004/1054 r.3
r.5, amended: SI 2003/1236 r.86
r.5, revoked (in part): SI 2003/1236 r.86
Sch.2, revoked: SI 2003/1236 r.87
Sch.3, revoked: SI 2003/1236 r.87
Sch.4, revoked: SI 2003/1236 r.87

2784. **Magistrates Courts (Anti-Social Behaviour Orders) Rules 2002**
r.4, amended: SI 2003/1236 r.89
r.4, revoked (in part): SI 2003/1236 r.89
r.5, see *R. (on the application of M) v Secretary of State for Constitutional Affairs* [2004] EWCA Civ 312, [2004] 1 W.L.R. 2298 (CA), Lord Phillips of Worth Matravers, M.R.
Sch.2, revoked: SI 2003/1236 r.90
Sch.3, revoked: SI 2003/1236 r.90
Sch.4, revoked: SI 2003/1236 r.90
Sch.6, revoked: SI 2003/1236 r.90

2786. **Air Navigation (Dangerous Goods) Regulations 2002**
referred to: SI 2002/1689 Reg.8A

2788. **Paternity and Adoption Leave Regulations 2002**
applied: SI 2003/543 Reg.18, Sch.1 para.4, SI 2003/921 Reg.3
referred to: SI 2004/923 Reg.2
Reg.2, varied: SI 2003/921 Reg.4
Reg.3, varied: SI 2003/921 Reg.5
Reg.4, referred to: SI 2002/2822 Reg.4
Reg.4, varied: SI 2003/921 Reg.6
Reg.5, varied: SI 2003/921 Reg.6
Reg.6, varied: SI 2003/921 Reg.6
Reg.7, varied: SI 2003/921 Reg.6

NO.

2002–cont.

2788. **Paternity and Adoption Leave Regulations 2002**–*cont.*
Reg.8, varied: SI 2003/921 Reg.7
Reg.9, varied: SI 2003/921 Reg.7
Reg.10, varied: SI 2003/921 Reg.7
Reg.11, varied: SI 2003/921 Reg.8
Reg.15, varied: SI 2003/921 Reg.9
Reg.16, varied: SI 2003/921 Reg.9
Reg.17, revoked (in part): SI 2004/923 Reg.3
Reg.17, varied: SI 2003/921 Reg.9
Reg.18, varied: SI 2003/921 Reg.10
Reg.20, varied: SI 2003/921 Reg.11
Reg.22, varied: SI 2003/921 Reg.12
Reg.27, amended: SI 2004/923 Reg.4

2800. **Relocation Grants (Forms of Application) (Amendment) (Wales) Regulations 2002**
revoked: SI 2002/1860 Sch.6

2802. **National Health Service (General Medical Services Supplementary List) (Wales) (Amendment), the National Health Service (General Medical Services) (Amendment) (Wales) (No.3), the National Health Service (General Dental Services) (Amendment) (Wale 2002**
Reg.4, revoked: SI 2004/1016 Sch.2
Reg.5, revoked: SI 2004/1016 Sch.2

2812. **Freedom of Information Act 2000 (Commencement No 2) Order 2002**
Sch.2 Part I, varied: SI 2004/664 Art.11, Art.12, Art.13, Art.14

2816. **Carriers Liability (Clandestine Entrants) (Level of Penalty Code of Practice) Order 2002**
revoked: 1999 c.33 s.32A

2817. **Carriers Liability Regulations 2002**
Reg.5, amended: SI 2004/244 Reg.2

2818. **Statutory Paternity Pay and Statutory Adoption Pay (Weekly Rates) Regulations 2002**
Reg.2, amended: SI 2004/552 Art.11
Reg.2, applied: SI 2003/526 Art.11, SI 2004/552 Art.11
Reg.2, substituted: SI 2004/925 Reg.2
Reg.3, amended: SI 2004/552 Art.11
Reg.3, applied: SI 2003/526 Art.11

2819. **Statutory Paternity Pay and Statutory Adoption Pay (National Health Service Employees) Regulations 2002**
Reg.1, amended: SI 2004/696 Sch.1 para.42

2820. **Statutory Paternity Pay and Statutory Adoption Pay (Administration) Regulations 2002**
applied: SI 2003/1192 Reg.3
Reg.2, varied: SI 2003/1192 Reg.3
Reg.3, applied: SI 1993/743 Reg.52, SI 1993/744 Reg.42B, SI 2001/1004 Reg.90K, SI 2003/2682 Reg.203
Reg.4, applied: SI 2003/2682 Reg.203

NO.

2002–cont.

2820. Statutory Paternity Pay and Statutory Adoption Pay (Administration) Regulations 2002–*cont.*
Reg.5, applied: SI 1993/743 Reg.52, SI 1993/744 Reg.42B, SI 2001/1004 Reg.90K, Sch.4 para.22, SI 2003/2682 Reg.203
Reg.11, varied: SI 2003/1192 Reg.3

2821. Statutory Paternity Pay and Statutory Adoption Pay (Persons Abroad and Mariners) Regulations 2002
applied: SI 2003/1193 Reg.3
Reg.1, varied: SI 2003/1193 Reg.3
Reg.5, varied: SI 2003/1193 Reg.3
Reg.6, varied: SI 2003/1193 Reg.3

2822. Statutory Paternity Pay and Statutory Adoption Pay (General) Regulations 2002
applied: SI 2003/500 Reg.3
Reg.11, amended: SI 2004/488 Reg.2
Reg.17, applied: SI 2003/500 Reg.4
Reg.17, referred to: SI 2003/500 Reg.3
Reg.17, varied: SI 2003/1194 Reg.3
Reg.18, applied: SI 2003/500 Reg.4
Reg.18, referred to: SI 2003/500 Reg.3
Reg.18, varied: SI 2003/1194 Reg.3
Reg.19, applied: SI 2003/500 Reg.4
Reg.19, referred to: SI 2003/500 Reg.3
Reg.19, varied: SI 2003/1194 Reg.3
Reg.26, applied: SI 2003/500 Reg.4
Reg.26, referred to: SI 2003/500 Reg.3
Reg.26, varied: SI 2003/1194 Reg.3
Reg.27, applied: SI 2003/500 Reg.4
Reg.27, referred to: SI 2003/500 Reg.3
Reg.27, varied: SI 2003/1194 Reg.3
Reg.28, applied: SI 2003/500 Reg.4
Reg.28, referred to: SI 2003/500 Reg.3
Reg.28, varied: SI 2003/1194 Reg.3
Reg.31, applied: SI 2003/500 Reg.4
Reg.31, referred to: SI 2003/500 Reg.3
Reg.31, varied: SI 2003/1194 Reg.3
Reg.32, applied: SI 2002/2821 Reg.2, Reg.3, SI 2003/500 Reg.4
Reg.32, referred to: SI 2003/500 Reg.3
Reg.32, varied: SI 2003/1194 Reg.3
Reg.33, applied: SI 2003/500 Reg.4
Reg.33, referred to: SI 2003/500 Reg.3
Reg.33, varied: SI 2003/1194 Reg.3
Reg.34, applied: SI 2003/500 Reg.4
Reg.34, referred to: SI 2003/500 Reg.3
Reg.34, varied: SI 2003/1194 Reg.3
Reg.35, applied: SI 2003/500 Reg.4
Reg.35, referred to: SI 2003/500 Reg.3
Reg.35, varied: SI 2003/1194 Reg.3
Reg.36, applied: SI 2003/500 Reg.4
Reg.36, referred to: SI 2003/500 Reg.3
Reg.36, varied: SI 2003/1194 Reg.3
Reg.37, applied: SI 2003/500 Reg.4
Reg.37, referred to: SI 2003/500 Reg.3
Reg.37, varied: SI 2003/1194 Reg.3
Reg.38, applied: SI 2003/500 Reg.4

NO.

2002–cont.

2822. Statutory Paternity Pay and Statutory Adoption Pay (General) Regulations 2002–*cont.*
Reg.38, referred to: SI 2003/500 Reg.3
Reg.38, varied: SI 2003/1194 Reg.3
Reg.39, applied: SI 2002/2818 Reg.2, Reg.3, SI 2003/500 Reg.4
Reg.39, referred to: SI 2003/500 Reg.3
Reg.39, varied: SI 2003/1194 Reg.3
Reg.40, applied: SI 2002/2818 Reg.2, Reg.3, SI 2003/500 Reg.4
Reg.40, referred to: SI 2003/500 Reg.3
Reg.40, varied: SI 2003/500 Reg.3, SI 2003/1194 Reg.3
Reg.41, applied: SI 2003/500 Reg.4
Reg.41, referred to: SI 2003/500 Reg.3
Reg.41, varied: SI 2003/1194 Reg.3
Reg.42, applied: SI 2003/500 Reg.4
Reg.42, referred to: SI 2003/500 Reg.3
Reg.42, varied: SI 2003/1194 Reg.3
Reg.43, amended: SI 2003/2096 Sch.1 para.79
Reg.43, applied: SI 2003/500 Reg.4
Reg.43, referred to: SI 2003/500 Reg.3
Reg.43, varied: SI 2003/1194 Reg.3
Reg.44, applied: SI 2003/500 Reg.4
Reg.44, referred to: SI 2003/500 Reg.3
Reg.44, varied: SI 2003/1194 Reg.3
Reg.45, applied: SI 2003/500 Reg.4
Reg.45, referred to: SI 2003/500 Reg.3
Reg.45, varied: SI 2003/1194 Reg.3
Reg.46, applied: SI 2003/500 Reg.4
Reg.46, referred to: SI 2003/500 Reg.3
Reg.46, varied: SI 2003/1194 Reg.3
Reg.47, applied: SI 2003/500 Reg.4
Reg.47, referred to: SI 2003/500 Reg.3
Reg.47, varied: SI 2003/1194 Reg.3

2834. Plastic Materials and Articles in Contact with Food (Amendment) (Wales) Regulations 2002
referred to: SI 1990/2463 Sch.1
Reg.5, referred to: SI 1998/1376 Reg.10
Reg.6, referred to: SI 1998/1376 Reg.10
Reg.8, referred to: SI 1998/1376 Reg.10
Reg.10, referred to: SI 1998/1376 Reg.10
Reg.12, referred to: SI 1998/1376 Reg.10
Reg.15, referred to: SI 1998/1376 Reg.10
Reg.16, referred to: SI 1998/1376 Reg.10
Reg.17, referred to: SI 1998/1376 Reg.10

2836. Employment (Northern Ireland) Order 2002
applied: SR 2002/380
referred to: SR 2002/363
Art.1, enabled: SR 2002/356
Art.3, applied: SR 2002/359
Art.4, applied: SR 2002/359
Art.5, applied: SR 2002/359, SR 2002/378, SR 2002/381, SR 2002/382, SR 2003/223
Art.5, enabled: SR 2003/221, SR 2003/277

NO.

2002–cont.

2836. Employment (Northern Ireland) Order 2002–cont.

Art.6, applied: SR 2002/359, SR 2002/378, SR 2002/381, SR 2002/382, SR 2003/223

Art.6, enabled: SR 2003/221, SR 2003/277

Art.8, applied: SR 2002/379 Reg.3, Reg.7

Art.8, enabled: SR 2002/379, SR 2003/276

Art.9, enabled: SR 2002/379, SR 2003/276

Art.11, enabled: SR 2002/379, SR 2003/276

Art.16, enabled: SR 2002/379, SR 2003/276

Art.17, applied: SR 2002/378, SR 2003/223

Sch.1 para.1, amended: SI 2003/2902 Sch.5 para.6

Sch.2 para.2, applied: SR 2002/378, SR 2003/223

2850. Pet Travel Scheme (Pilot Arrangements) (England) (Amendment) (No.2) Order 2002

revoked: SI 2004/2363 Sch.2

2861. National Health Service (Local Pharmaceutical Services Etc.) Regulations 2002

Reg.31, revoked: SI 2004/865 Sch.2

2865. Tobacco Advertising and Promotion Act 2002 (Commencement) Order 2002

Art.2, amended: SI 2003/258 Art.2

Art.3, added: SI 2003/258 Art.2

2868. Financing of Maintained Schools (England) (Amendment No 3) Regulations 2002

applied: SI 2003/453 Reg.15

revoked: SI 2003/453 Reg.2

2871. Building (Amendment) (No.2) Regulations 2002

Reg.1, amended: SI 2003/3133 Reg.2

Reg.4, amended: SI 2003/3133 Reg.2

2872. Building (Approved Inspectors etc.) (Amendment) Regulations 2002

Reg.1, amended: SI 2003/3133 Reg.2

Reg.4, amended: SI 2003/3133 Reg.2

2874. Plant Protection Products (Amendment) (No.3) Regulations 2002

revoked: SI 2003/3241 Sch.5

2876. Borough of Blackburn with Darwen and the City of Peterborough (Changes to Years of Elections) Order 2002

varied: SI 2004/222 Art.2

2882. District of Blaby (Electoral Changes) Order 2002

varied: SI 2004/222 Art.2

2883. District of Chichester (Electoral Changes) Order 2002

varied: SI 2004/222 Art.2

2884. Borough of Worthing (Electoral Changes) Order 2002

varied: SI 2004/222 Art.2

NO.

2002–cont.

2885. District of Arun (Electoral Changes) Order 2002

varied: SI 2004/222 Art.2

2886. Borough of Charnwood (Electoral Changes) Order 2002

varied: SI 2004/222 Art.2

2887. Borough of Poole (Electoral Changes) Order 2002

varied: SI 2004/222 Art.2

2888. Borough of Hinckley and Bosworth (Electoral Changes) Order 2002

varied: SI 2004/222 Art.2

2889. Borough of Oadby and Wigston (Electoral Changes) Order 2002

varied: SI 2004/222 Art.2

2890. District of Horsham (Electoral Changes) Order 2002

varied: SI 2004/222 Art.2

2891. District of Mid Sussex (Electoral Changes) Order 2002

varied: SI 2004/222 Art.2

2892. Borough of Reading (Electoral Changes) Order 2002

varied: SI 2004/222 Art.2

2894. Companies (Fees) (Amendment No 2) Regulations 2002

revoked: SI 2004/2621 Sch.3

2895. Limited Liability Partnerships (Fees) (Amendment) Regulations 2002

revoked: SI 2004/2620 Reg.3

2897. Education (School Information) (England) Regulations 2002

Part 4, disapplied: SI 2003/1041 Sch.1 para.9

Sch.3 para.9, varied: SI 2004/1076 Reg.8

2898. Education (Variation of Admission Arrangements) (England) Regulations 2002

applied: SI 1999/2213 Reg.9

2902. Potatoes Originating in Egypt (Amendment) (England) Regulations 2002

revoked (in part): SI 2004/1165 Reg.8

2903. Education (Co-ordination of Admission Arrangements) (Primary Schools) (England) Regulations 2002

Reg.3, amended: SI 2003/2751 Reg.2, SI 2004/1515 Reg.3

Reg.4, amended: SI 2003/2751 Reg.2

Reg.4, revoked (in part): SI 2003/2751 Reg.2

Reg.5, amended: SI 2004/1515 Reg.4

Reg.6, amended: SI 2003/2751 Reg.2, SI 2004/1515 Reg.5

Reg.9, added: SI 2003/2751 Reg.2

Sch.1 para.4, revoked: SI 2004/1515 Reg.6

2904. Education (Co-ordination of Admission Arrangements) (Secondary Schools) (England) Regulations 2002

Reg.3, amended: SI 2004/1516 Reg.3

Reg.5, amended: SI 2004/1516 Reg.4

Reg.6, amended: SI 2004/1516 Reg.5

Sch.1 para.1, amended: SI 2004/1516 Reg.6

NO.

NO.

2002–cont.

2002–cont.

2904. Education (Co-ordination of Admission Arrangements) (Secondary Schools) (England) Regulations 2002–*cont.*

Sch.1 para.4A, added: SI 2004/1516 Reg.7

Sch.1 para.6, revoked: SI 2004/1516 Reg.8

2926. Tax Credits (Appeals) Regulations 2002

referred to: SI 2002/3237, SR 2003/18, SR 2003/18 Reg.15, Reg.19, Reg.23

Reg.7, revoked (in part): SI 2004/372 Reg.2

2927. Employment Rights (Increase of Limits) (No.2) Order 2002

revoked: SI 2003/3038 Art.2

2928. European Economic Interest Grouping (Fees) (Amendment No.2) Regulations 2002

revoked: SI 2004/2643 Sch.1

2929. Social Security (Contributions)(Amendment No 5) Regulations 2002

Reg.4, revoked: SI 2004/770 Sch.1

2933. Release of Short-Term Prisoners on Licence (Amendment of Requisite Period) Order 2002

revoked: SI 2003/1602 Art.2

2934. European Communities (Recognition of Professional Qualifications) (Second General System) Regulations 2002

applied: SI 1994/1056 Reg.4

referred to: SI 1994/1056 Reg.4

Sch.2 Part 1, amended: SI 2004/1771 Sch.1 para.21, SI 2004/2033 Art.4

2938. Education (Teachers Qualifications and Health Standards) (Wales) (Amendment) Regulations 2002

revoked: SI 2004/1729 Sch.1 Part 1

2939. Food for Particular Nutritional Uses (Addition of Substances for Specific Nutritional Purposes) (Wales) Regulations 2002

referred to: SI 2004/1012 Reg.2

Reg.2, amended: SI 2004/1012 Reg.3

Reg.3, amended: SI 2004/1012 Reg.4

Sch.1, amended: SI 2004/1012 Reg.5

Sch.2, substituted: SI 2004/1012 Sch.1

Sch.3, added: SI 2004/1012 Sch.2

2941. Local Authorities (Executive Arrangements) (Discharge of Functions) (Amendment) (Wales) Regulations 2002

revoked: SI 2003/147 Reg.2

2952. Education Act 2002 (Commencement No.3 and Savings and Transitional Provisions) Order 2002

Sch.1 para.4, applied: SI 2002/3178 Reg.9, SI 2002/3179 Reg.10

2954. City of Plymouth (Scheme for Elections) Order 2002

varied: SI 2004/222 Art.2

2977. Vehicles Crime (Registration of Registration Plate Suppliers) (England and Wales) Regulations 2002

Reg.7, amended: SI 2003/228 Reg.2

2978. School Companies Regulations 2002

Reg.8, amended: SI 2003/2049 Reg.3

2982. District of Epping Forest (Electoral Changes) (Amendment) Order 2002

varied: SI 2004/222 Art.2

2983. District of Waveney (Electoral Changes) (Amendment) Order 2002

varied: SI 2004/222 Art.2

2984. District of Huntingdonshire (Electoral Changes) Order 2002

varied: SI 2004/222 Art.2

2985. District of Wyre Forest (Electoral Changes) Order 2002

varied: SI 2004/222 Art.2

2986. Borough of Redditch (Electoral Changes) Order 2002

varied: SI 2004/222 Art.2

2987. District of Wychavon (Electoral Changes) Order 2002

varied: SI 2004/222 Art.2

2988. City of Leicester (Electoral Changes) Order 2002

varied: SI 2004/222 Art.2

2989. District of Wokingham (Electoral Changes) Order 2002

varied: SI 2004/222 Art.2

2990. Borough of Crawley (Electoral Changes) Order 2002

varied: SI 2004/222 Art.2

2991. District of Adur (Electoral Changes) Order 2002

varied: SI 2004/222 Art.2

Art.4, amended: SI 2003/984 Art.4

Sch.2, revoked: SI 2003/984 Art.4

2992. Borough of Burnley (Electoral Changes) (Amendment) Order 2002

varied: SI 2004/222 Art.2

2998. Magistrates Courts (Detention and Forfeiture of Cash) Rules 2002

r.4, amended: SI 2003/1236 r.92

r.4, revoked (in part): SI 2003/1236 r.92

r.5, amended: SI 2003/1236 r.93

r.5, revoked (in part): SI 2003/1236 r.93

r.6, revoked (in part): SI 2003/1236 r.94

r.7, amended: SI 2003/1236 r.95

r.12, added: SI 2003/638 r.2

Sch.1, amended: SI 2003/1236 r.96

3004. Severn Bridges Tolls Order 2002

revoked: SI 2003/3276 Art.3

3007. Commission for Patient and Public Involvement in Health (Functions) Regulations 2002

Reg.1A, added: SI 2003/2044 Reg.2

Reg.2, amended: SI 2003/2044 Reg.3

Reg.3, amended: SI 2004/664 Art.4, Art.5

Reg.3, varied: SI 2004/664 Art.11, Art.12, Art.13, Art.14

NO.

2002–cont.

3007. Commission for Patient and Public Involvement in Health (Functions) Regulations 2002–*cont.*

Reg.4, amended: SI 2003/497 Reg.2, SI 2004/664 Art.4, Art.5

Reg.4, varied: SI 2004/664 Art.11, Art.12, Art.13, Art.14

Reg.5, amended: SI 2003/497 Reg.3, SI 2004/664 Art.4, Art.5

Reg.5, varied: SI 2004/664 Art.11, Art.12, Art.13, Art.14

Reg.8, amended: SI 2003/497 Reg.4, SI 2004/696 Sch.1 para.43

Reg.9, amended: SI 2003/497 Reg.5, SI 2004/540 Reg.3

3008. Plastic Materials and Articles in Contact with Food (Amendment) (England) (No.2) Regulations 2002

referred to: SI 1998/1376 Reg.10

Reg.4, referred to: SI 1998/1376 Reg.10

Reg.6, referred to: SI 1998/1376 Reg.10

3016. Proceeds of Crime Act 2002 (Recovery of Cash in Summary Proceedings Minimum Amount) Order 2002

revoked: SI 2004/420 Art.3

3018. Immigration (Designation of Travel Bans) (Amendment No 3) Order 2002

revoked: SI 2003/3285 Sch.2

3019. State Pension Credit (Consequential, Transitional and Miscellaneous Provisions) Regulations 2002

Reg.29, referred to: SI 2003/2379 Reg.1

Reg.32, revoked (in part): SI 2003/1360 Reg.3

Reg.36, amended: SI 2002/3197 Reg.7, SI 2003/2274 Reg.3

Reg.36, revoked (in part): SI 2003/1195 Reg.9

Reg.38, applied: SI 2004/647 Reg.4

3024. Medicines (Pharmacies) (Applications for Registration and Fees) Amendment Regulations 2002

revoked: SI 2003/3141 Reg.3

3038. Commission for Patient and Public Involvement in Health (Membership and Procedure) Regulations 2002

Reg.1, amended: SI 2004/696 Art.3, Sch.1 para.44, SI 2004/865 Sch.1 para.33

Reg.5, amended: SI 2004/540 Reg.5, SI 2004/664 Sch.1 para.8, SI 2004/696 Art.3, Sch.1 para.44, SI 2004/865 Sch.1 para.33

Reg.5, varied: SI 2004/664 Art.11, Art.12, Art.13, Art.14

Sch.2 Part 1 para.1, amended: SI 2004/865 Sch.1 para.33

3039. Counter Fraud and Security Management Service (Establishment and Constitution) Order 2002

applied: 2004 c.35 Sch.3, Sch.8

NO.

2002–cont.

3040. Counter Fraud and Security Management Service Regulations 2002

Reg.1, amended: SI 2004/696 Art.3, Sch.1 para.45, SI 2004/865 Sch.1 para.34, SI 2004/1016 Sch.1 para.30

Reg.3, amended: SI 2004/696 Art.3, Sch.1 para.45, SI 2004/865 Sch.1 para.34, SI 2004/1016 Sch.1 para.30

3041. Tobacco Products (Manufacture, Presentation and Sale) (Safety) Regulations 2002

applied: SI 2003/1593 Sch.1 Part I

referred to: SI 2003/1376 Sch.1

Reg.7, applied: SI 2004/765 Reg.5, SSI 2004/144 Reg.5

3045. Sale and Supply of Goods to Consumers Regulations 2002

Reg.15, referred to: SI 2003/1374 Sch.1

3048. Local Authority (Overview and Scrutiny Committees Health Scrutiny Functions) Regulations 2002

Reg.1, amended: SI 2004/696 Art.3, Sch.1 para.46, SI 2004/1427 Reg.2

Reg.4, amended: SI 2004/696 Sch.1 para.46

Reg.4A, added: SI 2004/696 Sch.1 para.46

3053. National Assembly for Wales (Returning Officers Charges) Order 2002

Art.3, amended: SI 2003/3117 Art.2

Sch.1 Part II para.6A, added: SI 2003/3117 Art.2

3059. Education (Student Support) (Amendment) (No.3) Regulations 2002

revoked: SI 2003/1065 Reg.3

3060. Education (Mandatory Awards) (Amendment) (No.2) Regulations 2002

revoked: SI 2003/1994 Sch.6

3075. Police and Criminal Evidence Act 1984 (Codes of Practice) (Statutory Powers of Stop and Search) Order 2002

revoked: SI 2004/1887 Art.4

3078. Withholding and Withdrawal of Support (Travel Assistance and Temporary Accommodation) Regulations 2002

see *R. (on the application of M) v Islington LBC* [2003] EWHC 1388, [2003] 2 F.L.R. 903 (QBD (Admin Ct)), Wilson, J.

Reg.2, see *R. (on the application of Kimani) v Lambeth LBC* [2003] EWCA Civ 1150, [2004] 1 W.L.R. 272 (CA), Lord Phillips of Worth Matravers, M.R.

Reg.3, see *R. (on the application of Grant) v Lambeth LBC* [2004] EWHC 1524, [2004] 3 F.C.R. 494 (QBD (Admin Ct)), Mitting, J.

NO.

2002–cont.

3080. Zoo Licensing Act 1981 (Amendment) (England and Wales) Regulations 2002
referred to: SI 2003/992 Reg.2, Reg.4
Reg.3, applied: SI 2003/992 Reg.2
Reg.4, applied: SI 2003/992 Reg.2
Reg.5, applied: SI 2003/992 Reg.2
Reg.6, applied: SI 2003/992 Reg.2
Reg.7, applied: SI 2003/992 Reg.2
Reg.8, applied: SI 2003/992 Reg.2
Reg.9, applied: SI 2003/992 Reg.2
Reg.10, applied: SI 2003/992 Reg.2
Reg.11, applied: SI 2003/992 Reg.2
Reg.12, applied: SI 2003/992 Reg.2
Reg.13, applied: SI 2003/992 Reg.2
Reg.14, applied: SI 2003/992 Reg.2
Reg.15, applied: SI 2003/992 Reg.2
Reg.16, applied: SI 2003/992 Reg.2
Reg.17, applied: SI 2003/992 Reg.2
Reg.18, applied: SI 2003/992 Reg.2
Reg.19, applied: SI 2003/992 Reg.2
Reg.20, applied: SI 2003/992 Reg.2
Reg.21, applied: SI 2003/992 Reg.2
Reg.22, applied: SI 2003/992 Reg.2
Reg.23, applied: SI 2003/992 Reg.2
Reg.24, applied: SI 2003/992 Reg.2
Reg.25, applied: SI 2003/992 Reg.2
Reg.26, applied: SI 2003/992 Reg.2

3083. Judicial Pensions and Retirement Act 1993 (Certain Qualifying Judicial Offices) (Amendment) Order 2002
revoked: SI 2003/2775 Art.3

3084. Hertfordshire (Coroners Districts) Order 2002
revoked: SI 2004/2192 Art.4

3113. Traffic Signs Regulations and General Directions 2002
applied: 2003 c.iii Sch.3 para.1
referred to: 2003 c.iii s.4, Sch.3 para.3, 2004 c.18 Sch.7 para.9
referred to: SI 2003/393 Reg.2
Reg.5, amended: SI 2003/2155 Sch.1 para.50
Reg.10, referred to: 2004 c.18 Sch.7 para.3, Sch.7 para.4
Reg.26, amended: SI 2003/2155 Sch.1 para.50
Reg.27, amended: SI 2003/2155 Sch.1 para.50
Reg.29, referred to: 2004 c.18 Sch.7 para.3, Sch.7 para.4
Reg.42, amended: SI 2004/1275 Reg.2
Reg.58, amended: SI 2003/393 Reg.3
Reg.004, referred to: SI 1981/1694 Reg.8B, Reg.8E, Reg.8F

3117. Air Quality Limit Values (Amendment) Regulations 2002
revoked: SI 2003/2121 Sch.10

NO.

2002–cont.

3133. Proceeds of Crime Act 2002 (Enforcement in different parts of the United Kingdom) Order 2002
Art.6, applied: SI 2003/421 r.30, r.31, r.32
Art.11, applied: SI 1994/1443 Sch.2 para.76A.12

3135. Medical Act 1983 (Amendment) Order 2002
applied: SI 2004/2610 Art.1
referred to: SI 2004/1731 Art.1, SI 2004/2608 Sch.1
Art.4, referred to: SI 2003/1340 Art.2, Art.3, Art.4
Art.13, applied: SI 2004/477 Art.3, SI 2004/585 Reg.26, SI 2004/2610 Art.3
Art.13, referred to: SI 2004/433 Art.3, SI 2004/585 Reg.24, Reg.26, SI 2004/1020 Reg.24, Reg.26, SI 2004/1731 Art.2, SSI 2004/142 Art.3, Art.4
Art.14, applied: SI 2004/477 Art.3
Art.14, referred to: SI 2004/433 Art.3, SI 2004/585 Reg.24, Reg.26, SI 2004/1020 Reg.24, Reg.26, SI 2004/1731 Art.2, SSI 2004/142 Art.3, Art.4
Art.16, enabled: SI 2003/1340, SI 2004/1731, SI 2004/2610
Sch.1 Part I para.1, revoked: SI 2003/1250 Art.30
Sch.1 Part I para.10, referred to: SI 2003/1250 Sch.8 para.23
Sch.1 Part II para.30, revoked (in part): SI 2004/865 Sch.2, SI 2004/1016 Sch.2
Sch.1 Part II para.33, revoked: SSI 2004/212 Sch.2
Sch.2, referred to: SI 2003/1340 Art.2, Art.3, Art.4
Sch.2 para.37, applied: SI 2004/2610 Art.4

3149. Local Government (Miscellaneous Provisions) (Northern Ireland) Order 2002
Art.4, applied: SR 2003/58
Art.4, enabled: SR 2003/58

3150. Company Directors Disqualification (Northern Ireland) Order 2002
applied: 2002 c.40 Sch.15
Art.1, enabled: SR 2003/345
Art.10, applied: SR 2003/358 r.1, r.4, 2004 c.35 s.201
Art.11, applied: SR 2003/358 r.1, r.4, 2004 c.35 s.201
Art.17, varied: SR 2003/346 Art.5
Art.19, varied: SR 2003/346 Art.5
Art.21, disapplied: SR 2003/346 Art.4
Art.24, enabled: SR 2003/358
Art.26, disapplied: SR 2003/346 Art.4
Art.26, enabled: SR 2003/346
Sch.4, disapplied: SR 2003/346 Art.4

3152. Insolvency (Northern Ireland) Order 2002
Art.1, enabled: SR 2003/545

2002–cont.

3153. Environment (Northern Ireland) Order 2002

Art.1, enabled: SR 2003/49, SR 2003/113

Art.4, applied: SR 2003/46

Art.4, enabled: SR 2003/46

Sch.1 Part I para.20, applied: SR 2003/209 Reg.2

Sch.1 Part I para.20, enabled: SR 2003/209

3154. Housing Support Services (Northern Ireland) Order 2002

Art.1, enabled: SR 2003/171

Art.3, applied: SR 2003/172 Reg.3

Art.3, enabled: SR 2003/172

Art.4, applied: SI 2002/2006 Reg.19, SR 2003/28 Sch.5 para.20, SR 2003/172 Reg.2

Art.4, enabled: SR 2003/172

Art.5, applied: SR 2003/172

3157. Kava-kava in Food (Wales) Regulations 2002

revoked: SI 2003/2755 Reg.2

3159. Organic Products (Wales) Regulations 2002

revoked: SI 2004/1604 Sch.3

Reg.3, applied: SI 1996/3142 Reg.2

3162. Police (Amendment) (No.3) Regulations 2002

revoked: SI 2003/527 Sch.4 Part 1

3169. Kava-kava in Food (England) Regulations 2002

Reg.2, amended: SI 2004/455 Reg.2

Reg.3, amended: SI 2004/455 Reg.2

3171. Beet Seed (England) Regulations 2002

Reg.2, amended: SI 2004/2385 Reg.2

Reg.8, amended: SI 2004/2385 Reg.2

Reg.10, amended: SI 2004/2385 Reg.2

Reg.11, amended: SI 2004/2385 Reg.2

Reg.17, amended: SI 2004/2385 Reg.2

Reg.18, amended: SI 2004/2385 Reg.2

Reg.21, amended: SI 2004/2385 Reg.2

Reg.23, amended: SI 2004/2385 Reg.2

Sch.1 Part II para.11, amended: SI 2004/2385 Reg.2

Sch.1 Part II para.17, amended: SI 2004/2385 Reg.2

Sch.1 Part III para.23, revoked (in part): SI 2004/2385 Reg.2

Sch.1 Part III para.25, amended: SI 2004/2385 Reg.2

Sch.1 Part III para.26, amended: SI 2004/2385 Reg.2

Sch.1 Part III para.27, revoked (in part): SI 2004/2385 Reg.2

Sch.1 Part IV para.34, amended: SI 2004/2385 Reg.2

Sch.3 para.3, amended: SI 2004/2385 Reg.2

Sch.10, amended: SI 2004/2385 Reg.2

2002–cont.

3172. Fodder Plant Seed (England) Regulations 2002

applied: SI 2002/3174 Reg.21, SI 2002/3175 Reg.21

referred to: SI 2002/3173 Reg.22

Reg.2, amended: SI 2004/2387 Reg.2

Reg.3, amended: SI 2004/2387 Reg.2

Reg.8, amended: SI 2004/2387 Reg.2

Reg.9, amended: SI 2004/2387 Reg.2

Reg.11, amended: SI 2004/2387 Reg.2

Reg.11, revoked (in part): SI 2004/2387 Reg.2

Reg.12, amended: SI 2004/2387 Reg.2

Reg.19, amended: SI 2004/2387 Reg.2

Reg.20, amended: SI 2004/2387 Reg.2

Reg.23, amended: SI 2004/2387 Reg.2

Reg.24, amended: SI 2004/2387 Reg.2

Reg.26, amended: SI 2004/2387 Reg.2

Reg.26, revoked (in part): SI 2004/2387 Reg.2

Sch.1 Part II para.11, amended: SI 2004/2387 Reg.2

Sch.1 Part II para.17, amended: SI 2004/2387 Reg.2

Sch.1 Part III para.25, amended: SI 2004/2387 Reg.2

Sch.1 Part III para.26, amended: SI 2004/2387 Reg.2

Sch.1 Part III para.33, amended: SI 2004/2387 Reg.2

Sch.1 Part III para.34, amended: SI 2004/2387 Reg.2

Sch.1 Part III para.39, amended: SI 2004/2387 Reg.2

Sch.1 Part III para.40A, added: SI 2004/2387 Reg.2

Sch.1 Part III para.41, substituted: SI 2004/2387 Reg.2

Sch.1 Part III para.42, amended: SI 2004/2387 Reg.2

Sch.1 Part III para.44, amended: SI 2004/2387 Reg.2

Sch.1 Part V para.57, amended: SI 2004/2387 Reg.2

Sch.1 Part V para.58, amended: SI 2004/2387 Reg.2

Sch.1 Part V para.59, added: SI 2004/2387 Reg.2

Sch.4 Part II para.5, amended: SI 2004/2387 Reg.2

Sch.4 Part II para.11, amended: SI 2004/2387 Reg.2

Sch.4 Part II para.12, amended: SI 2004/2387 Reg.2

Sch.4 Part II para.13, amended: SI 2004/2387 Reg.2

Sch.4 Part II para.14, amended: SI 2004/2387 Reg.2

Sch.5, amended: SI 2004/2387 Reg.2

Sch.6 para.18A, added: SI 2004/2387 Reg.2

2002–cont.

3172. Fodder Plant Seed (England) Regulations 2002–*cont.*

Sch.8 Part III para.5, amended: SI 2004/2387 Reg.2

Sch.8 Part IV para.9, amended: SI 2004/2387 Reg.2

Sch.8 Part IV para.10, amended: SI 2004/2387 Reg.2

Sch.8 Part IV para.11, amended: SI 2004/2387 Reg.2

Sch.8 Part IV para.12, amended: SI 2004/2387 Reg.2

Sch.8 Part IV para.13A, added: SI 2004/2387 Reg.2

Sch.8 Part VI para.25, amended: SI 2004/2387 Reg.2

Sch.8 Part VI para.28A, added: SI 2004/2387 Reg.2

Sch.10, amended: SI 2004/2387 Reg.2

3173. Cereal Seed (England) Regulations 2002

applied: SI 2002/3172 Reg.22

Reg.2, amended: SI 2004/2386 Reg.2

Reg.9, amended: SI 2004/2386 Reg.2

Reg.11, amended: SI 2004/2386 Reg.2

Reg.13, amended: SI 2004/2386 Reg.2

Reg.19, amended: SI 2004/2386 Reg.2

Reg.20, amended: SI 2004/2386 Reg.2

Reg.23, amended: SI 2004/2386 Reg.2

Reg.24, amended: SI 2004/2386 Reg.2

Reg.26, amended: SI 2004/2386 Reg.2

Sch.1 Part II para.16, amended: SI 2004/2386 Reg.2

Sch.1 Part II para.22, amended: SI 2004/2386 Reg.2

Sch.1 Part III para.30, amended: SI 2004/2386 Reg.2

Sch.1 Part III para.31, amended: SI 2004/2386 Reg.2

Sch.1 Part III para.38, amended: SI 2004/2386 Reg.2

Sch.1 Part III para.39, amended: SI 2004/2386 Reg.2

Sch.1 Part III para.44, amended: SI 2004/2386 Reg.2

Sch.1 Part III para.45A, added: SI 2004/2386 Reg.2

Sch.1 Part III para.46, substituted: SI 2004/2386 Reg.2

Sch.1 Part III para.47, amended: SI 2004/2386 Reg.2

Sch.1 Part III para.49, amended: SI 2004/2386 Reg.2

Sch.1 Part IV para.56, amended: SI 2004/2386 Reg.2

Sch.1 Part IV para.57, amended: SI 2004/2386 Reg.2

Sch.1 Part IV para.58, added: SI 2004/2386 Reg.2

Sch.4 Part II para.14, amended: SI 2004/2386 Reg.2

2002–cont.

3173. Cereal Seed (England) Regulations 2002–*cont.*

Sch.4 Part II para.15, amended: SI 2004/2386 Reg.2

Sch.5, amended: SI 2004/2386 Reg.2

Sch.6 para.18A, added: SI 2004/2386 Reg.2

Sch.10, amended: SI 2004/2386 Reg.2

3174. Oil and Fibre Plant Seed (England) Regulations 2002

applied: SI 2002/3172 Reg.22

Reg.2, amended: SI 2003/3101 Reg.2, SI 2004/2388 Reg.2

Reg.3, amended: SI 2003/3101 Reg.2

Reg.6, amended: SI 2003/3101 Reg.2

Reg.8, amended: SI 2003/3101 Reg.2

Reg.9, amended: SI 2004/2388 Reg.2

Reg.10, amended: SI 2003/3101 Reg.2, SI 2004/2388 Reg.2

Reg.11, amended: SI 2003/3101 Reg.2, SI 2004/2388 Reg.2

Reg.12, amended: SI 2004/2388 Reg.2

Reg.18, amended: SI 2004/2388 Reg.2

Reg.19, amended: SI 2004/2388 Reg.2

Reg.24, amended: SI 2004/2388 Reg.2

Reg.26, amended: SI 2003/3101 Reg.2, SI 2004/2388 Reg.2

Reg.26, revoked (in part): SI 2004/2388 Reg.2

Sch.1 Part I para.1, amended: SI 2003/3101 Reg.2

Sch.1 Part II para.13, amended: SI 2003/3101 Reg.2

Sch.1 Part II para.16, amended: SI 2004/2388 Reg.2

Sch.1 Part II para.22, amended: SI 2004/2388 Reg.2

Sch.1 Part III para.27, amended: SI 2003/3101 Reg.2

Sch.1 Part III para.30, amended: SI 2004/2388 Reg.2

Sch.1 Part III para.31, amended: SI 2004/2388 Reg.2

Sch.1 Part III para.35, amended: SI 2003/3101 Reg.2

Sch.1 Part III para.38, amended: SI 2004/2388 Reg.2

Sch.1 Part III para.39, amended: SI 2004/2388 Reg.2

Sch.1 Part III para.43, amended: SI 2003/3101 Reg.2

Sch.1 Part III para.43, substituted: SI 2004/2388 Reg.2

Sch.1 Part III para.44, amended: SI 2004/2388 Reg.2

Sch.1 Part III para.45A, added: SI 2004/2388 Reg.2

Sch.1 Part III para.46, substituted: SI 2004/2388 Reg.2

Sch.1 Part III para.47, amended: SI 2004/2388 Reg.2

2002–cont.

3174. Oil and Fibre Plant Seed (England) Regulations 2002–*cont.*

Sch.1 Part III para.47, revoked (in part): SI 2004/2388 Reg.2

Sch.1 Part III para.49, amended: SI 2004/2388 Reg.2

Sch.1 Part III para.52A, added: SI 2004/2388 Reg.2

Sch.1 Part III para.53, substituted: SI 2004/2388 Reg.2

Sch.1 Part III para.56, amended: SI 2004/2388 Reg.2

Sch.1 Part IV para.63, amended: SI 2004/2388 Reg.2

Sch.1 Part V para.64, amended: SI 2003/3101 Reg.2

Sch.1 Part V para.69, amended: SI 2004/2388 Reg.2

Sch.1 Part V para.70, amended: SI 2004/2388 Reg.2

Sch.1 Part V para.71, amended: SI 2004/2388 Reg.2

Sch.1 Part V para.72, added: SI 2004/2388 Reg.2

Sch.2 para.3A, added: SI 2003/3101 Reg.2

Sch.3 para.1, amended: SI 2003/3101 Reg.2

Sch.3 para.2, amended: SI 2003/3101 Reg.2, SI 2004/2388 Reg.2

Sch.3 para.5, amended: SI 2003/3101 Reg.2

Sch.3 para.6, amended: SI 2003/3101 Reg.2

Sch.3 para.7, amended: SI 2003/3101 Reg.2

Sch.3 para.7A, added: SI 2003/3101 Reg.2

Sch.3 para.9A, added: SI 2003/3101 Reg.2

Sch.3 para.10, amended: SI 2003/3101 Reg.2

Sch.3 para.12, amended: SI 2003/3101 Reg.2

Sch.4 Part I para.2, amended: SI 2003/3101 Reg.2

Sch.4 Part I para.3, amended: SI 2003/3101 Reg.2

Sch.4 Part II para.6, amended: SI 2003/3101 Reg.2

Sch.4 Part II para.7, amended: SI 2003/3101 Reg.2

Sch.4 Part II para.8, amended: SI 2003/3101 Reg.2

Sch.4 Part II para.9, amended: SI 2003/3101 Reg.2

Sch.4 Part III para.10, amended: SI 2003/3101 Reg.2

Sch.5, amended: SI 2003/3101 Reg.2, SI 2004/2388 Reg.2

Sch.6 para.18A, added: SI 2004/2388 Reg.2

Sch.6 para.21A, added: SI 2004/2388 Reg.2

Sch.7, amended: SI 2003/3101 Reg.2

Sch.8 Part IV para.8, amended: SI 2003/3101 Reg.2

Sch.8 Part VI para.24, amended: SI 2003/3101 Reg.2

Sch.10, added: SI 2004/2388 Reg.2

Sch.10, amended: SI 2003/3101 Reg.2, SI 2004/2388 Reg.2

2002–cont.

3175. Vegetable Seed (England) Regulations 2002

applied: SI 2002/3172 Reg.22

disapplied: SI 2002/3176 Reg.24, Sch.2 Part I, Sch.3 Part I

referred to: SI 2002/3176 Reg.32

Reg.2, amended: SI 2004/2389 Reg.2

Reg.12, amended: SI 2004/2389 Reg.2

Reg.18, amended: SI 2004/2389 Reg.2

Reg.19, amended: SI 2004/2389 Reg.2

Sch.1 Part III para.21, amended: SI 2004/2389 Reg.2

Sch.8 Part III para.5, revoked: SI 2004/2389 Reg.2

Sch.8 Part IV para.11, revoked: SI 2004/2389 Reg.2

Sch.8 Part IV para.16, revoked: SI 2004/2389 Reg.2

Sch.10, amended: SI 2004/2389 Reg.2

3176. Seed (Registration, Licensing and Enforcement) (England) Regulations 2002

Reg.2, amended: SI 2003/3101 Reg.3, SI 2004/2390 Reg.2

Sch.1 Part I para.2A, added: SI 2004/2390 Reg.2

Sch.1 Part I para.5, added: SI 2004/2390 Reg.2

Sch.1 Part II para.3A, added: SI 2004/2390 Reg.2

Sch.1 Part II para.4A, added: SI 2004/2390 Reg.2

Sch.1 Part II para.5, substituted: SI 2004/2390 Reg.2

Sch.5, applied: SI 2002/3171 Reg.20, Reg.24, SI 2002/3172 Reg.23, Reg.27, SI 2002/3173 Reg.23, SI 2002/3174 Reg.23, Reg.27, SI 2002/3175 Reg.22, Reg.27, SI 2004/2881 Reg.23, Reg.27

Sch.5 para.4, amended: SI 2004/2390 Reg.2

Sch.5 para.6, amended: SI 2004/2390 Reg.2

Sch.5 para.13, amended: SI 2003/3101 Reg.3

3178. Education (Pupil Exclusions and Appeals) (Maintained Schools) (England) Regulations 2002

varied: SI 2004/657 Art.3

see *R. (on the application of Begum (Shabina)) v Denbigh High School Governors* [2004] EWHC 1389, [2004] E.L.R. 374 (QBD (Admin Ct)), Bennett, J.

Reg.4, amended: SI 2004/402 Reg.8

Reg.4, applied: SI 1999/2163 Reg.42

Reg.5, applied: SI 1999/2163 Reg.42, Reg.48

Reg.6, applied: SI 1999/2163 Reg.42

Reg.7, applied: SI 1999/2163 Reg.42

Reg.7A, added: SI 2004/402 Reg.4

Reg.7B, added: SI 2004/402 Reg.9

Reg.8, revoked (in part): SI 2003/1377 Reg.2

Sch.1, applied: SI 2004/402 Reg.7

Sch.1 para.1, varied: SI 2002/3179 Sch.1 para.1, Sch.1 para.2, Sch.1 para.3

2002–cont.

3178. Education (Pupil Exclusions and Appeals) (Maintained Schools) (England) Regulations 2002–*cont.*
Sch.1 para.2, amended: SI 2004/402 Reg.6
Sch.1 para.2, applied: SI 2002/3179 Reg.8A, Reg.8
Sch.1 para.2, varied: SI 2002/3179 Sch.1 para.3, Sch.1 para.4, Sch.1 para.5
Sch.1 para.3, varied: SI 2002/3179 Sch.1 para.3
Sch.1 para.4, varied: SI 2002/3179 Sch.1 para.3
Sch.1 para.5, varied: SI 2002/3179 Sch.1 para.3
Sch.1 para.6, varied: SI 2002/3179 Sch.1 para.3
Sch.1 para.7, varied: SI 2002/3179 Sch.1 para.3
Sch.1 para.8, varied: SI 2002/3179 Sch.1 para.3
Sch.1 para.9, varied: SI 2002/3179 Sch.1 para.3
Sch.1 para.10, varied: SI 2002/3179 Sch.1 para.3, Sch.1 para.6
Sch.1 para.11, varied: SI 2002/3179 Sch.1 para.3
Sch.1 para.12, varied: SI 2002/3179 Sch.1 para.3
Sch.1 para.13, varied: SI 2002/3179 Sch.1 para.3
Sch.1 para.14, varied: SI 2002/3179 Sch.1 para.3, Sch.1 para.7
Sch.1 para.15, varied: SI 2002/3179 Sch.1 para.3
Sch.1 para.16, varied: SI 2002/3179 Sch.1 para.3

3179. Education (Pupil Exclusions and Appeals) (Pupil Referral Units) (England) Regulations 2002
Reg.5, amended: SI 2004/402 Reg.10
Reg.8A, added: SI 2004/402 Reg.5
Reg.9, amended: SI 2004/402 Reg.10

3183. Air Quality Limit Values (Wales) Regulations 2002
applied: SI 2003/1848 Sch.4
Reg.10, applied: SI 2003/1848 Reg.5
Sch.6 Part II, referred to: SI 2003/1848 Sch.4
Sch.7, referred to: SI 2003/1848 Reg.5

3189. National Health Service (Pharmaceutical Services) and (General Medical Services) (Amendment) (Wales) Regulations 2002
Reg.3, revoked: SI 2004/1016 Sch.2

3199. LEA Budget, Schools Budget and Individual Schools Budget (England) Regulations 2002
Reg.5, applied: SI 2003/3170 Sch.2 para.1
Sch.2 para.1, applied: SI 2003/3170 Sch.2 para.1
Sch.2 para.2, applied: SI 2003/3170 Sch.2 para.1

2002–cont.

3199. LEA Budget, Schools Budget and Individual Schools Budget (England) Regulations 2002–*cont.*
Sch.2 para.3, applied: SI 2003/3170 Sch.2 para.1
Sch.2 para.15, referred to: SI 2003/453 Reg.13
Sch.2 para.24, applied: SI 2003/3170 Sch.2 para.1, Sch.2 para.2, Sch.2 para.3
Sch.2 para.25, referred to: SI 2003/453 Reg.13
Sch.2 para.27, referred to: SI 2003/453 Reg.13
Sch.2 para.31, referred to: SI 2003/453 Reg.21

3200. Education (Student Support) (No.2) Regulations 2002
applied: SI 2003/1994 Sch.3 para.4
referred to: SI 2003/1065 Reg.2, SI 2004/161 Reg.3
Part VIII, referred to: SI 2004/161 Reg.18
Reg.2, amended: SI 2003/3280 Reg.4, SI 2004/161 Reg.4
Reg.3, revoked (in part): SI 2004/161 Reg.5
Reg.6, amended: SI 2004/161 Reg.6
Reg.10, amended: SI 2004/161 Reg.7
Reg.11, amended: SI 2004/161 Sch.3
Reg.12, amended: SI 2003/1065 Reg.4
Reg.13, amended: SI 2004/161 Sch.3
Reg.14, amended: SI 2004/161 Reg.8
Reg.15, amended: SI 2004/161 Reg.9, Sch.3
Reg.15, applied: SI 1987/1967 Reg.62, SI 1992/1814 Reg.42, SI 1996/207 Reg.131, SI 1996/2890 Reg.43
Reg.16, amended: SI 2003/1065 Reg.5, SI 2004/161 Sch.3
Reg.17, amended: SI 2004/161 Sch.3
Reg.17A, added: SI 2004/161 Reg.10
Reg.17A, amended: SI 2004/1602 Reg.5
Reg.19, amended: SI 2003/1065 Reg.6, SI 2004/161 Reg.11, Reg.12, Sch.3
Reg.19, revoked (in part): SI 2004/161 Reg.12
Reg.21, revoked: SI 2004/161 Reg.13
Reg.22, amended: SI 2004/161 Reg.14
Reg.23, amended: SI 2003/1065 Reg.7, SI 2004/161 Reg.11, Reg.15, Sch.3
Reg.24, amended: SI 2004/161 Reg.16
Reg.25, amended: SI 2004/161 Reg.17
Reg.26, amended: SI 2003/1065 Reg.8
Reg.26, revoked (in part): SI 2003/1065 Reg.8
Reg.27, amended: SI 2004/1602 Reg.6, SI 2004/2041 Reg.4
Reg.27, substituted: SI 2004/161 Sch.1
Reg.28, substituted: SI 2004/161 Sch.1
Reg.29, amended: SI 2003/1065 Reg.9
Reg.29, substituted: SI 2004/161 Sch.1
Reg.30, substituted: SI 2004/161 Sch.1
Reg.31, substituted: SI 2004/161 Sch.1
Reg.32, substituted: SI 2004/161 Sch.1
Reg.33, substituted: SI 2004/161 Sch.1

NO.

2002–cont.

3200. Education (Student Support) (No.2) Regulations 2002–cont.

Reg.34, substituted: SI 2004/161 Sch.1

Reg.35, substituted: SI 2004/161 Sch.1

Reg.36, substituted: SI 2004/161 Sch.1

Reg.37, substituted: SI 2004/161 Sch.1

Reg.38, amended: SI 2004/161 Reg.19

Reg.39, amended: SI 2004/2041 Reg.5

Sch.1 para.4, amended: SI 2003/3280 Reg.4

Sch.1 para.6, amended: SI 2003/3280 Reg.4

Sch.1 para.8, amended: SI 2003/3280 Reg.4

Sch.3, referred to: SI 2004/161 Reg.20

Sch.3 para.1, amended: SI 2004/2598 Reg.4

Sch.3 para.1, substituted: SI 2004/161 Sch.2

Sch.3 Part I para.1, substituted: SI 2004/161 Sch.2

Sch.3 para.2, substituted: SI 2004/161 Sch.2

Sch.3 Part II para.2, substituted: SI 2004/161 Sch.2

Sch.3 Part II para.3, substituted: SI 2004/161 Sch.2

Sch.3 Part II para.4, amended: SI 2003/1065 Reg.10

Sch.3 Part II para.4, substituted: SI 2004/161 Sch.2

Sch.3 Part II para.5, substituted: SI 2004/161 Sch.2

Sch.3 Part II para.6, amended: SI 2003/1065 Reg.11

Sch.3 Part II para.6, substituted: SI 2004/161 Sch.2

Sch.3 para.3, substituted: SI 2004/161 Sch.2

Sch.3 Part III para.7, substituted: SI 2004/161 Sch.2

Sch.3 Part III para.8, substituted: SI 2004/161 Sch.2

Sch.3 Part III para.9, substituted: SI 2004/161 Sch.2

Sch.3 para.4, amended: SI 2004/1602 Reg.7, SI 2004/2598 Reg.5

Sch.3 para.4, substituted: SI 2004/161 Sch.2

Sch.3 para.5, amended: SI 2004/2598 Reg.6

Sch.3 para.5, substituted: SI 2004/161 Sch.2

Sch.3 para.6, substituted: SI 2004/161 Sch.2

Sch.3 para.7, substituted: SI 2004/161 Sch.2

Sch.3 para.8, substituted: SI 2004/161 Sch.2

Sch.3 para.9, substituted: SI 2004/161 Sch.2

3206. Products of Animal Origin (Third Country Imports) (England) (Amendment) (No 4) Regulations 2002

revoked: SI 2003/3177 Sch.6

3207. Flexible Working (Procedural Requirements) Regulations 2002

applied: SI 2004/2333 Sch.1 para.18

referred to: SI 2003/694 Sch.1 para.13

Reg.14, applied: SI 2003/694 Sch.1 para.98, SI 2004/2333 Sch.1 para.119

NO.

2002–cont.

3210. Care Standards Act 2000 (Commencement and Transitional Provisions) (Amendment No 2) (England) Order 2002

Art.4, applied: SI 2001/3852 Sch.1 para.2, SI 2001/3980 Reg.5

3211. National Care Standards Commission (Fees and Frequency of Inspections) Amendment (No.3) Regulations 2002

varied: SI 2004/664 Art.11, Art.12, Art.13, Art.14

Reg.1, varied: SI 2004/664 Art.11, Art.12, Art.13, Art.14

Reg.2, varied: SI 2004/664 Art.11, Art.12, Art.13, Art.14

3212. Nurses Agencies Regulations 2002

varied: SI 2004/664 Art.11, Art.12, Art.13, Art.14

Reg.2, amended: SI 2004/664 Art.3, SI 2004/1770 Reg.4, SI 2004/1771 Sch.1 para.20

Reg.2, varied: SI 2004/664 Art.11, Art.12, Art.13, Art.14

Reg.3, substituted: SI 2004/1269 Reg.2

Reg.12, amended: SI 2003/2323 Reg.3, SI 2004/1770 Reg.4

Reg.12, applied: SI 2001/3965 Reg.19

Reg.14, amended: SI 2004/1770 Reg.4

Reg.16, amended: SI 2004/1770 Reg.4

Sch.3 para.13, added: SI 2003/2323 Reg.3

3213. Residential Family Centres Regulations 2002

varied: SI 2004/664 Art.11, Art.12, Art.13, Art.14

Reg.2, amended: SI 2004/664 Art.3, SI 2004/865 Sch.1 para.35

Reg.2, varied: SI 2004/664 Art.11, Art.12, Art.13, Art.14

Reg.4, varied: SI 2004/664 Art.11, Art.12, Art.13, Art.14

3214. Domiciliary Care Agencies Regulations 2002

applied: SI 2004/2071 Reg.44

varied: SI 2004/664 Art.11, Art.12, Art.13, Art.14

Reg.2, amended: SI 2004/664 Art.3, SI 2004/1770 Reg.3

Reg.2, varied: SI 2004/664 Art.11, Art.12, Art.13, Art.14

Reg.3, substituted: SI 2004/2071 Sch.9 para.1

Reg.12, amended: SI 2004/1770 Reg.3

Reg.12, substituted: SI 2003/2323 Reg.2

Reg.15, amended: SI 2004/1770 Reg.3

Reg.17, amended: SI 2004/1770 Reg.3

Sch.3 para.13, added: SI 2003/2323 Reg.2

Sch.4 para.5, added: SI 2004/1770 Reg.3

3218. District of South Norfolk (Electoral Changes) Order 2002

varied: SI 2004/222 Art.2

NO.

2002–cont.

3219. Civil Procedure (Amendment No.2) Rules 2002
see *Practice Direction (PO: 1/2003 (Revised))* [2003] R.P.C. 46 (PO), Not specified

3221. District of Breckland (Electoral Changes) Order 2002
varied: SI 2004/222 Art.2

3222. City of Norwich (Electoral Changes) Order 2002
varied: SI 2004/222 Art.2

3223. Borough of Blackburn with Darwen (Electoral Changes) Order 2002
varied: SI 2004/222 Art.2

3224. District of Malvern Hills (Electoral Changes) Order 2002
varied: SI 2004/222 Art.2

3225. City of Worcester (Electoral Changes) Order 2002
varied: SI 2004/222 Art.2

3227. Borough of King's Lynn and West Norfolk (Electoral Changes) Order 2002
varied: SI 2004/222 Art.2

3228. Borough of Great Yarmouth (Electoral Changes) Order 2002
varied: SI 2004/222 Art.2

3230. Products of Animal Origin (Third Country Imports) (Wales) (Amendment) (No.2) Regulations 2002
revoked: SI 2004/1430 Sch.6

3264. Allocation of Housing (England) Regulations 2002
Reg.5, substituted: SI 2004/1235 Reg.2

3270. Carmarthenshire and Pembrokeshire (Clynderwen, Cilymaenllwyd and Henllanfallteg) Order 2002
varied: SI 2004/218 Art.2

3271. Newport (Caerleon and Malpas) Order 2002
varied: SI 2004/218 Art.2

3272. Ceredigion and Pembrokeshire (St Dogmaels) Order 2002
varied: SI 2004/218 Art.2

3273. Cardiff and Vale of Glamorgan (Michaelston and Grangetown) Order 2002
varied: SI 2004/218 Art.2

3274. County of Gwynedd (Electoral Changes) Order 2002
varied: SI 2004/218 Art.2

3275. County of Monmouthshire (Electoral Changes) Order 2002
varied: SI 2004/218 Art.2

3276. County Borough of Newport (Electoral Changes) Order 2002
varied: SI 2004/218 Art.2

3277. County Borough of The Vale of Glamorgan (Electoral Changes) Order 2002
varied: SI 2004/218 Art.2

NO.

2002–cont.

3278. County of Ceredigion (Electoral Changes) Order 2002
varied: SI 2004/218 Art.2

3279. County Borough of Torfaen (Electoral Changes) Order 2002
varied: SI 2004/218 Art.2

2003

4. Agricultural Holdings (Units of Production) (Wales) Order 2003
revoked: SI 2004/1218 Art.3

21. Veterinary Surgeons and Veterinary Practitioners (Registration) (Amendment) Regulations Order of Council 2003
revoked: SI 2003/3342 Art.2, Sch.1

26. National Health Service (Out of Hours Provision of Personal Medical Services and Miscellaneous Amendments) (England) Regulations 2003
revoked: SI 2004/865 Sch.2
Reg.3, applied: SI 2004/865 Art.78
Reg.4, applied: SI 2004/865 Art.75, Art.77, Art.80, Art.83, Art.85, Art.89
Reg.4, varied: SI 2004/865 Art.77, Art.80
Reg.5, applied: SI 2004/865 Art.77, Art.83, Art.85
Reg.5, referred to: SI 2004/865 Art.89
Reg.6, applied: SI 2004/865 Art.77, Art.89
Reg.6, referred to: SI 2004/865 Art.89

28. Pigs (Records, Identification and Movement) (Interim Measures) (England) (No.2) (Amendment) Order 2003
revoked: SI 2003/2632 Art.28

30. Disease Control (Interim Measures) (England) (No.2) (Amendment) Order 2003
revoked: SI 2003/254 Art.16

31. Animal Gatherings (Interim Measures) (England) (Amendment) Order 2003
revoked: SI 2003/253 Art.11

33. Electronic Communications (Universal Service) Regulations 2003
Reg.4, amended: SI 2003/330 Reg.3
Reg.4, applied: 2003 c.21 Sch.18 para.7
Reg.4, varied: 2003 c.21 Sch.18 para.7
Reg.5, applied: 2003 c.21 Sch.18 para.7
Reg.5, varied: 2003 c.21 Sch.18 para.7
Reg.6, varied: 2003 c.21 Sch.18 para.7

54. Housing (Right to Acquire and Right to Buy) (Designated Rural Areas and Designated Regions) (Wales) Order 2003
referred to: SI 2003/1147 Art.2
Art.1, amended: SI 2003/1147 Art.3
Art.2, amended: SI 2003/1147 Art.4
Sch.1, amended: SI 2003/1147 Art.5

NO.

2003—cont.

74. Wireless Telegraphy (Exemption) Regulations 2003
Reg.3, revoked (in part): SI 2003/2155 Sch.2
Reg.4, amended: SI 2003/2155 Sch.1 para.51
Sch.3 Part I, amended: SI 2003/2155 Sch.1 para.51

77. Tobacco Advertising and Promotion (Sponsorship) Transitional Regulations 2003
Reg.3, amended: SI 2003/1415 Reg.2

82. Proceeds of Crime Act 2002 (Appeals under Part 2) Order 2003
applied: SI 2003/428 r.17
Art.6, applied: SI 2003/428 r.3, r.14
Art.7, applied: SI 2003/428 r.14, r.15
Art.8, applied: SI 2003/428 r.18
Art.8, referred to: SI 2003/428 r.19
Art.12, applied: SI 2003/428 r.22
Art.15, referred to: SI 2003/428 r.22

107. Education (Teachers Qualifications and Health Standards) (England) (Amendment) Regulations 2003
revoked: SI 2003/1662 Sch.1 Part 1

116. Police Act 1997 (Criminal Records) (Amendment) Regulations 2003
revoked: SI 2003/137 Reg.2

118. Intercountry Adoption (Hague Convention) Regulations 2003
Reg.2, amended: SI 2004/1868 Reg.2
Reg.9, applied: SI 2004/1868 Reg.1
Reg.10, amended: SI 2004/1868 Reg.2
Reg.10, applied: SI 2004/190 Reg.2, Reg.3
Reg.12, referred to: SI 1984/265 Sch.2 para.1
Reg.18, applied: SI 1984/265 r.47A
Reg.21, referred to: SI 1984/265 r.30.
Reg.22, applied: SI 2003/1255 Reg.5
Reg.32, referred to: SI 1984/265 r.30.

120. Proceeds of Crime Act 2002 (Commencement No 4, Transitional Provisions and Savings) Order 2003
Art.3, amended: SI 2003/333 Art.14
Art.5, amended: SI 2003/333 Art.14

139. National Health Service (General Medical Services) and (Pharmaceutical Services) (Amendment) (Wales) Regulations 2003
Reg.2, revoked: SI 2004/1016 Sch.2

140. Education (Teachers Qualifications and Health Standards) (Amendment) (Wales) Regulations 2003
revoked: SI 2004/1729 Sch.1 Part 1

142. Countryside Access (Exclusion or Restriction of Access) (Wales) Regulations 2003
applied: SI 2002/1794 Reg.6

143. National Health Service (General Medical Services) (Amendment) (Wales) Regulations 2003
revoked: SI 2004/1016 Sch.2

NO.

2003—cont.

149. Local Health Boards (Constitution, Membership and Procedures) (Wales) Regulations 2003
applied: SI 2004/905 Reg.9
Reg.2, amended: SI 2004/1016 Sch.1 para.36
Reg.3, amended: SI 2004/1771 Sch.1 para.19
Sch.2 Part II, amended: SI 2004/1771 Sch.1 para.19

157. District of Broadland (Electoral Changes) Order 2003
varied: SI 2004/222 Art.2

158. District of Bromsgrove (Electoral Changes) Order 2003
varied: SI 2004/222 Art.2

159. Borough of Middlesbrough (Electoral Changes) Order 2003
varied: SI 2004/222 Art.2

160. District of North Norfolk (Electoral Changes) Order 2003
varied: SI 2004/222 Art.2

161. City of Peterborough (Electoral Changes) Order 2003
varied: SI 2004/222 Art.2
Art.1, amended: SI 2004/721 Art.2
Art.4, amended: SI 2004/721 Art.2

162. Borough of Redcar and Cleveland (Electoral Changes) Order 2003
varied: SI 2004/222 Art.2

168. Disease Control (Interim Measures) (Wales) (No.2) (Amendment) Order 2003
revoked: SI 2003/483 Art.16

169. Animal Gatherings (Interim Measures) (Wales) (Amendment) Order 2003
revoked: SI 2003/481 Art.11

170. Pigs (Records, Identification and Movement) (Interim Measures) (Wales) (No.2) (Amendment) Order 2003
revoked: SI 2004/996 Art.28

171. Proceeds of Crime Act 2002 (Failure to Disclose Money Laundering Specified Training) Order 2003
Art.2, amended: SI 2003/3075 Sch.2 para.8

172. Proceeds of Crime Act 2002 (References to Financial Investigators) Order 2003
Sch.1, amended: SI 2004/8 Sch.1 para.2, Sch.1 para.3, Sch.1 para.4, Sch.1 para.5
Sch.1, referred to: SI 2004/8 Sch.1 para.1

174. Proceeds of Crime Act 2002 (Application of Police and Criminal Evidence Act 1984 and Police and Criminal Evidence (Northern Ireland) Order 1989) Order 2003
Art.3, applied: SI 2003/425 Art.6
Art.3, disapplied: SI 2003/425 Art.15, Art.25
Art.3, varied: SI 2003/425 Art.5
Art.4, disapplied: SI 2003/425 Art.5, Art.6
Art.4, varied: SI 2003/425 Art.15, Art.25
Art.5, disapplied: SI 2003/425 Art.5, Art.6

2003–cont.

325. Housing Benefit and Council Tax Benefit (State Pension Credit) Regulations 2003

applied: SI 2001/1002 para.6, SI 2004/552 Art.20

Reg.2, applied: SI 1987/1971 Reg.72B

Reg.2, varied: SI 1987/1971 Reg.68B

Reg.3, amended: SI 2003/2275 Reg.2

Reg.3A, added: SI 2003/2275 Reg.2

Reg.6, amended: SI 2003/2275 Reg.2

Reg.8, added: SI 2003/2634 Reg.4

Reg.8, amended: SI 2003/2275 Reg.2, SI 2003/2634 Reg.4, SI 2004/290 Reg.2

Reg.8, revoked (in part): SI 2003/2634 Reg.4

Reg.9, revoked (in part): SI 2004/14 Reg.32

Reg.11, revoked: SI 2003/2275 Reg.2

Reg.12, applied: SI 1992/1814 Reg.59B, Reg.62BA, SI 2004/552 Art.22

Reg.13A, added: SI 2003/2275 Reg.2

Reg.15, amended: SI 2003/2275 Reg.2

Reg.17, added: SI 2003/2634 Reg.4

Reg.17, amended: SI 2003/2275 Reg.2, SI 2003/2634 Reg.4, SI 2004/290 Reg.2

Reg.17, revoked (in part): SI 2003/2634 Reg.4

Reg.18, revoked (in part): SI 2004/14 Reg.32

Reg.19, revoked: SI 2003/2275 Reg.2

Reg.20, amended: SI 2003/2275 Reg.2

Reg.22, amended: SI 2003/2275 Reg.2

Reg.23, amended: SI 2003/2275 Reg.2

Reg.24, amended: SI 2003/2275 Reg.2

Reg.25, amended: SI 2003/2275 Reg.2

Reg.27, revoked (in part): SI 2003/2275 Reg.2

Reg.31, revoked: SI 2003/1195 Reg.10

Sch.2 Part I, added: SI 2003/2634 Reg.4

Sch.2 Part I, amended: SI 2003/2275 Reg.2, SI 2003/2634 Reg.4

Sch.2 Part I, revoked: SI 2003/2634 Reg.4

Sch.2 para.2, amended: SI 2003/2275 Reg.2

Sch.2 para.2, revoked (in part): SI 2003/2275 Reg.2

Sch.2 Part II, added: SI 2003/2275 Reg.2

Sch.2 Part II, amended: SI 2003/2275 Reg.2, SI 2003/2634 Reg.4

Sch.2 Part III, amended: SI 2003/2275 Reg.2, SI 2003/2279 Reg.6

330. Electronic Communications (Market Analysis) Regulations 2003

Reg.8, varied: 2003 c.21 Sch.18 para.10

Reg.11, varied: 2003 c.21 Sch.18 para.10

332. Child Minding and Day Care (Suspension of Registration) (England) Regulations 2003

applied: SI 2002/816 Reg.6A, Reg.6, Reg.7, Reg.8

varied: SI 2003/463 Art.19, Art.20

Reg.3, applied: SI 2003/463 Art.19

Reg.4, applied: SI 2003/463 Art.19

Reg.5, applied: SI 2003/463 Art.19

Reg.6, applied: SI 2003/463 Art.19

2003–cont.

332. Child Minding and Day Care (Suspension of Registration) (England) Regulations 2003–*cont.*

Reg.7, applied: SI 2003/463 Art.19

Reg.8, applied: SI 2002/816 Reg.4, Sch.7 para.1, SI 2003/463 Art.19, Art.20

333. Proceeds of Crime Act 2002 (Commencement No 5, Transitional Provisions, Savings and Amendment) Order 2003

Art.7, substituted: SI 2003/531 Art.3

Art.8, substituted: SI 2003/531 Art.4

348. School Governance (Constitution) (England) Regulations 2003

applied: SI 2000/2195 Reg.16A, Reg.11, Reg.13, Reg.14, SI 2003/1377 Reg.17

disapplied: SI 2004/530 Reg.3

Part 5, applied: SI 1999/2262 Reg.31, SI 2000/2195 Reg.12, SI 2003/1965 Reg.32, Reg.37, SI 2004/530 Reg.16, SI 2004/2042 Reg.37, Reg.42

Reg.3, amended: SI 2003/1916 Reg.2

Reg.4, amended: SI 2003/1916 Reg.2, SI 2004/450 Reg.2

Reg.5, applied: SI 2003/1558 Reg.55

Reg.7, applied: SI 2000/2195 Reg.16A

Reg.9, applied: SI 2003/1558 Reg.55

Reg.12, amended: SI 2003/1916 Reg.2

Reg.17, applied: SI 2003/1377 Reg.9, SI 2003/1965 Reg.24

Reg.18, applied: SI 2003/1965 Reg.24

Reg.20, applied: SI 2003/1962 Reg.6, SI 2003/1965 Reg.24

Reg.21, applied: SI 2003/1965 Reg.24

Reg.21, varied: SI 2003/1965 Sch.6 para.1, SI 2004/2042 Sch.7 para.1

Reg.22, applied: SI 2003/1377 Reg.9, SI 2003/1965 Reg.24

Reg.23, applied: SI 2003/1965 Reg.24

Reg.24, applied: SI 2003/1965 Reg.24

Reg.25, applied: SI 2003/1965 Reg.24

Reg.25, varied: SI 2003/1965 Sch.6 para.2, SI 2004/2042 Sch.7 para.2

Reg.26, applied: SI 2003/1965 Reg.24

Reg.27, applied: SI 2003/1965 Reg.24

Reg.27, varied: SI 2003/1965 Sch.6 para.3, SI 2004/2042 Sch.7 para.3

Reg.28, applied: SI 2003/1558 Reg.53, SI 2003/1965 Reg.24

Reg.29, applied: SI 2003/1558 Reg.53, SI 2003/1965 Reg.24

Reg.29, varied: SI 2000/2195 Sch.4 para.1, SI 2003/1965 Sch.6 para.4, SI 2004/2042 Sch.7 para.4

Reg.30, applied: SI 2003/1558 Reg.53, SI 2003/1965 Reg.24

Reg.30, varied: SI 2000/2195 Sch.4 para.1, SI 2003/1965 Sch.6 para.5, SI 2004/2042 Sch.7 para.5

Reg.31, applied: SI 2003/1965 Reg.24, Reg.32, SI 2004/2042 Reg.37

NO.

NO.

2003–cont.

348. School Governance (Constitution) (England) Regulations 2003–*cont.*

Reg.31, varied: SI 2000/2195 Sch.4 para.1, SI 2003/1965 Sch.6 para.6, SI 2004/2042 Sch.7 para.6

Reg.32, applied: SI 2003/1965 Reg.24

Reg.32, varied: SI 2003/1965 Sch.6 para.6, Sch.6 para.7, SI 2004/2042 Sch.7 para.7

Reg.33, varied: SI 2000/2195 Sch.4 para.1

Reg.34, substituted: SI 2003/1916 Reg.2

Sch.1 para.8, amended: SI 2004/450 Reg.2

Sch.2, applied: SI 2003/1558 Reg.55

Sch.3 para.2, amended: SI 2004/696 Art.3

Sch.4, applied: SI 2003/1558 Reg.55

Sch.5 para.2, applied: SI 2003/1558 Sch.3 para.2

Sch.6, applied: SI 1999/2163 Reg.15, SI 2003/1377 Reg.15, SI 2003/1965 Reg.19, Reg.24, SI 2004/2042 Reg.20

Sch.6 para.1, applied: SI 2003/1965 Reg.19, SI 2004/2042 Reg.20

Sch.6 para.1, varied: SI 2003/1965 Sch.6 para.8, SI 2004/2042 Sch.7 para.8

Sch.6 para.2, applied: SI 2003/1962 Reg.6

Sch.6 para.3, applied: SI 2003/1962 Reg.6

Sch.6 para.4, applied: SI 2003/1962 Reg.6

Sch.6 para.4, substituted: SI 2004/450 Reg.2

Sch.6 para.5, applied: SI 2003/1377 Reg.15, SI 2003/1962 Reg.6

Sch.6 para.5, varied: SI 2003/1965 Sch.6 para.8

Sch.6 para.6, applied: SI 2003/1962 Reg.6

Sch.6 para.7, applied: SI 2003/1962 Reg.6

Sch.6 para.8, applied: SI 2003/1962 Reg.6

Sch.6 para.9, applied: SI 2003/1962 Reg.6

Sch.6 para.10, applied: SI 2003/1377 Reg.9, SI 2003/1962 Reg.6

Sch.6 para.11, applied: SI 2003/1962 Reg.6

367. Voluntary Adoption Agencies and the Adoption Agencies (Miscellaneous Amendments) Regulations 2003

referred to: SI 2003/365 Sch.1 para.3

varied: SI 2004/664 Art.11, Art.12, Art.13, Art.14

Reg.1, amended: SI 2004/664 Art.3

Reg.1, varied: SI 2004/664 Art.11, Art.12, Art.13, Art.14

368. National Care Standards Commission (Fees and Frequency of Inspections) (Adoption Agencies) Regulations 2003

varied: SI 2004/664 Art.11, Art.12, Art.13, Art.14

Reg.1, varied: SI 2004/664 Art.11, Art.12, Art.13, Art.14

Reg.2, amended: SI 2004/664 Art.3

2003–cont.

369. National Care Standards Commission (Registration) (Amendment) Regulations 2003

varied: SI 2004/664 Art.11, Art.12, Art.13, Art.14

Reg.1, varied: SI 2004/664 Art.11, Art.12, Art.13, Art.14

Reg.2, varied: SI 2004/664 Art.11, Art.12, Art.13, Art.14

370. Local Authority Adoption Service (England) Regulations 2003

Reg.2, varied: SI 2004/664 Art.11, Art.12, Art.13, Art.14

Sch.2 para.6, varied: SI 2004/664 Art.11, Art.12, Art.13, Art.14

373. Consistent Financial Reporting (England) Regulations 2003

Sch.1, amended: SI 2004/393 Reg.2

394. Town and Country Planning (Enforcement Notices and Appeals) (Wales) Regulations 2003

Reg.3, referred to: SI 2003/395 Reg.5

Reg.5, applied: SI 2003/395 Reg.7

Reg.8, applied: SI 2003/395 Reg.7

410. Strategic Investment and Regeneration of Sites (Northern Ireland) Order 2003

applied: SR 2003/120

Part II, applied: SR 2003/120 Art.2

Art.5, enabled: SR 2003/120

412. Housing (Northern Ireland) Order 2003

Art.1, enabled: SR 2003/270, SR 2003/528

413. Marriage (Northern Ireland) Order 2003

applied: 2004 c.19 s.24

Art.1, enabled: SR 2003/466

Art.4, applied: 2004 c.19 s.23

Art.7, applied: 2004 c.19 s.23

417. Protection of Children and Vulnerable Adults (Northern Ireland) Order 2003

Part III, amended: SI 2003/431 Sch.5

Art.2, amended: SI 2003/431 Sch.4

Art.6, amended: SI 2003/431 Sch.4, Sch.5

Art.11, amended: SI 2003/431 Sch.4

Art.12, amended: SI 2003/431 Sch.4

Art.13, amended: SI 2003/431 Sch.4

Art.15, amended: SI 2003/431 Sch.4

Art.18, amended: SI 2003/431 Sch.4

Art.27, amended: SI 2003/431 Sch.4

Art.34, amended: SI 2003/431 Sch.4

Art.38, amended: SI 2003/431 Sch.4

Art.42, amended: SI 2003/431 Sch.4

Art.43, amended: SI 2003/431 Sch.4

Art.44, amended: SI 2003/431 Sch.4

Art.48, amended: SI 2003/431 Sch.4

Art.50, revoked: SI 2003/431 Sch.5

Sch.1 para.2, amended: 2004 c.19 s.5

418. Audit and Accountability (Northern Ireland) Order 2003

Art.3, disapplied: SR 2003/253 Art.3

NO.

2003–cont.

418. Audit and Accountability (Northern Ireland) Order 2003–*cont.*
Art.4, enabled: SR 2003/253

419. Energy (Northern Ireland) Order 2003
Art.1, enabled: SR 2003/203

420. Budget (Northern Ireland) Order 2003
Art.6, revoked: SI 2004/707 Art.3
Art.8, revoked: SI 2004/707 Art.4

426. Northern Ireland Arms Decommissioning Act 1997 (Amnesty Period) Order 2003
revoked: SI 2004/464 Art.3

430. Planning (Amendment) (Northern Ireland) Order 2003
Art.1, enabled: SR 2003/188, SR 2003/443

431. Health and Personal Social Services (Quality, Improvement and Regulation) (Northern Ireland) Order 2003
Art.1, enabled: SR 2003/239, SR 2003/348

432. European Communities (Designation) Order 2003
revoked: SI 2003/1246 Art.3

435. Access to Justice (Northern Ireland) Order 2003
applied: SI 2004/1500 Art.30
Art.1, enabled: SR 2003/344, SR 2003/439, SR 2003/440
Art.48, enabled: SR 2003/440
Sch.2 para.2, amended: 2004 c.19 Sch.2 para.25

437. National Assembly for Wales (Disqualification) Order 2003
referred to: SI 2003/284 Sch.5 para.9
Sch.1 Part 1, amended: SI 2004/664 Art.4

439. Commissioner for Children and Young People (Northern Ireland) Order 2003
Art.1, enabled: SR 2003/400
Sch.1 Part II para.13, amended: 2004 c.4 s.9, Sch.4

453. Financing of Maintained Schools (England) Regulations 2003
applied: SI 2003/3247 Reg.28
referred to: SI 2003/3247 Reg.6
Reg.8, applied: SI 2003/475 Reg.2, SI 2003/3170 Sch.3 para.32, SI 2003/3247 Reg.18, Reg.19
Reg.12, applied: SI 2003/3247 Sch.2 para.1
Reg.15, amended: SI 2003/3247 Reg.2
Reg.15, applied: SI 2003/3247 Sch.2 para.1
Reg.15, referred to: SI 2003/3247 Reg.2
Reg.16, amended: SI 2003/3247 Reg.2
Reg.16, referred to: SI 2003/3247 Reg.2
Reg.17, applied: SI 2003/3247 Sch.2 para.1
Reg.18, applied: SI 2003/3247 Sch.2 para.1
Reg.21, applied: SI 2003/3247 Reg.18, Reg.19
Reg.22, applied: SI 2003/3247 Sch.2 para.1
Reg.23, applied: SI 2003/3247 Sch.2 para.1
Reg.24, applied: SI 2003/3247 Sch.2 para.1

NO.

2003–cont.

453. Financing of Maintained Schools (England) Regulations 2003–*cont.*
Reg.25, applied: SI 2003/3247 Sch.2 para.1
Reg.28, applied: SI 2003/3247 Sch.2 para.1
Sch.1 para.8, applied: SI 2003/3247 Sch.2 para.1
Sch.1 para.29, applied: SI 2003/3247 Sch.2 para.1

455. Social Security (Working Tax Credit and Child Tax Credit) (Consequential Amendments) Regulations 2003
Reg.7, amended: SI 2003/1731 Reg.6, SI 2004/565 Reg.11
Reg.8, amended: SI 2003/1731 Reg.6, SI 2004/565 Reg.11
Sch.1 para.16, amended: SI 2003/1731 Reg.6
Sch.1 para.21, revoked (in part): SI 2003/1731 Reg.6
Sch.2 para.2, revoked (in part): SI 2003/1731 Reg.6
Sch.2 para.3, revoked (in part): SI 2003/1731 Reg.6
Sch.2 para.16, amended: SI 2003/1731 Reg.6
Sch.2 para.21, amended: SI 2003/1731 Reg.6
Sch.2 para.21, revoked (in part): SI 2003/1731 Reg.6
Sch.4 para.2, amended: SI 2003/1731 Reg.6

467. Customs (Presentation of Goods for Export) Regulations 2003
Reg.2, amended: SI 2003/2155 Sch.1 para.52

473. Local Health Boards (Transfer of Property, Rights and Liabilities) (Wales) Order 2003
applied: SI 2003/813 Art.8

474. Food Labelling (Amendment) (England) Regulations 2003
Reg.3, referred to: SI 1996/1499 Reg.50
Reg.5, referred to: SI 1996/1499 Reg.50

481. Animal Gatherings (Interim Measures) (Wales) Order 2003
revoked: SI 2003/1967 Art.11

482. Transport of Animals (Cleansing and Disinfection) (Wales) Order 2003
applied: SI 2003/483 Art.13
referred to: SI 2003/1414 Art.14
revoked: SI 2003/1470 Art.9

483. Disease Control (Interim Measures) (Wales) Order 2003
revoked: SI 2003/1414 Art.17

489. Whole of Government Accounts (Designation of Bodies) Order 2003
Sch.1, amended: SI 2004/664 Art.4, Art.5
Sch.1, varied: SI 2004/664 Art.11, Art.12, Art.13, Art.14

492. Child Benefit and Guardian's Allowance (Administration) Regulations 2003
applied: SI 2003/493 Reg.39, SI 2003/494 Reg.3, Reg.4, Reg.5
Part 5, applied: SI 2003/916 Sch.2 para.6

NO.

NO.

2003–cont.

492. Child Benefit and Guardian's Allowance (Administration) Regulations 2003–*cont.*

Reg.5, applied: SI 2003/916 Sch.2 para.6

Reg.6, amended: SI 2004/761 Reg.2

Reg.6, substituted: SI 2003/1945 Reg.3, SI 2003/2107 Reg.3

Reg.7, amended: SI 2004/1240 Reg.2

Reg.7, applied: SI 2003/916 Sch.2 para.6

Reg.10, applied: SI 2003/916 Sch.2 para.6

Reg.11, applied: SI 2003/916 Sch.2 para.6

Reg.18, applied: SI 2003/916 Sch.2 para.6

Reg.19, applied: SI 2003/916 Sch.2 para.6

Reg.23, applied: SI 2003/916 Sch.2 para.6

Reg.23, referred to: SI 2003/916 Reg.19

Reg.26, applied: SI 2003/916 Sch.2 para.6

Reg.28, applied: SI 2003/916 Sch.2 para.6

Reg.29, applied: SI 2003/916 Sch.2 para.6

Reg.30, applied: SI 2003/916 Sch.2 para.6

Reg.31, applied: SI 2003/916 Sch.2 para.6

Reg.32, applied: SI 2003/916 Sch.2 para.6

Reg.33, applied: SI 2003/916 Sch.2 para.6

Reg.34, applied: SI 2003/916 Sch.2 para.6

Reg.35, disapplied: SI 2003/916 Sch.2 para.6

Reg.37, disapplied: SI 2003/916 Sch.2 para.6

Reg.38, disapplied: SI 2003/916 Sch.2 para.6

Reg.39, disapplied: SI 2003/916 Sch.2 para.6

Reg.41, disapplied: SI 2003/916 Sch.2 para.6

Reg.42, disapplied: SI 2003/916 Sch.2 para.6

Sch.2, applied: SI 2003/493 Reg.39, SI 2003/495 Reg.10

Sch.2, referred to: SI 2003/916 Reg.4

Sch.2 Part 1 para.2, amended: SI 2003/2155 Sch.1 para.23

493. Child Benefit (General) Regulations 2003

Reg.1, amended: SI 2004/761 Reg.4

Reg.4, applied: SI 2003/916 Sch.2 para.7

Reg.9, amended: SI 2004/761 Reg.5

Reg.21, amended: SI 2004/1244 Reg.3

Reg.24, applied: SI 2003/916 Sch.2 para.7

Reg.25, amended: SI 2004/1244 Reg.4

Reg.28, applied: SI 2003/916 Sch.2 para.7

495. Guardian's Allowance (General) Regulations 2003

Reg.8, applied: SI 2003/916 Sch.2 para.8

Reg.10, applied: SI 2003/492 Reg.34

499. Social Security Contributions and Benefits Act 1992 (Application of Parts 12ZA and 12ZB to Adoptions from Overseas) Regulations 2003

applied: SI 2003/500 Reg.2, Reg.3

Sch.1, amended: SI 2004/488 Reg.3

Sch.2, amended: SI 2004/488 Reg.3

2003–cont.

500. Statutory Paternity Pay (Adoption) and Statutory Adoption Pay (Adoptions from Overseas) Regulations 2003

revoked: SI 2003/1194 Reg.19

505. Health Protection Agency (Yr Asiantaeth Diogelu Iechyd) (Establishment) Order 2003

applied: 2004 c.17 s.8

revoked: 2004 c.17 Sch.3 para.19

Art.3, applied: SI 2003/506 Reg.12

506. Health Protection Agency (Yr Asiantaeth Diogelu Iechyd) Regulations 2003

revoked: 2004 c.17 Sch.3 para.20

Reg.1, amended: SI 2004/664 Art.4, SI 2004/696 Art.3, Sch.1 para.47, SI 2004/865 Sch.1 para.36, SI 2004/1016 Sch.1 para.32

Reg.3, amended: SI 2004/696 Sch.1 para.47, SI 2004/865 Sch.1 para.36, SI 2004/1016 Sch.1 para.32

507. School Organisation Proposals by the Learning and Skills Council for England Regulations 2003

Reg.4, amended: SI 2004/696 Art.3

Reg.16, amended: SI 2004/696 Art.3

509. Gaming Act (Variation of Fees) (England and Wales and Scotland) Order 2003

applied: SI 2004/531 Art.2

Sch.1, amended: SI 2004/531 Art.3

519. Police Authorities (Best Value) Performance Indicators Order 2003

revoked: SI 2004/644 Art.4

Sch.3, amended: SI 2003/1265 Art.2

523. Education (Governors Allowances) (England) Regulations 2003

disapplied: SI 2004/530 Reg.3

526. Social Security Benefits Up-rating Order 2003

revoked: SI 2004/552 Art.27

527. Police Regulations 2003

applied: SI 1996/1685 Reg.2

Reg.3, amended: 2003 c.20 Sch.5 para.4, SI 2003/2594 Reg.2

Reg.4, amended: SI 2003/2594 Reg.3

Reg.5, amended: SI 2003/2594 Reg.4

Reg.8, amended: SI 2003/2594 Reg.5

Reg.21, amended: SI 2003/2594 Reg.6

Reg.29, applied: SI 1996/1685 Reg.2

530. Local Government (Best Value) Performance Indicators and Performance Standards Order 2003

referred to: SI 2004/589 Art.3

Art.2, substituted: SI 2004/644 Art.3

Art.3, amended: SI 2004/589 Art.4

Art.6, amended: SI 2004/589 Art.5

Art.7, amended: SI 2004/589 Art.6

Art.8, amended: SI 2004/589 Art.7

Art.9, substituted: SI 2004/589 Art.8

2003-cont.

530. Local Government (Best Value) Performance Indicators and Performance Standards Order 2003-*cont.*

Art.10, substituted: SI 2003/864 Art.2

Art.11, amended: SI 2004/589 Art.9

Art.12, substituted: SI 2004/589 Art.10

Art.13, substituted: SI 2004/589 Art.11

Art.15, substituted: SI 2004/589 Art.12

Art.16, amended: SI 2004/1176 Art.2

Sch.1, amended: SI 2004/589 Art.4

Sch.4, amended: SI 2004/589 Art.5

Sch.5, amended: SI 2004/589 Art.6

Sch.6, amended: SI 2004/589 Art.7

Sch.7, amended: SI 2004/589 Art.8

Sch.8A Part 1, added: SI 2003/864 Art.2

Sch.8A Part 2, added: SI 2003/864 Art.2

Sch.9, amended: SI 2004/589 Art.9

Sch.10, substituted: SI 2004/589 Art.10

Sch.11, substituted: SI 2004/589 Art.11

Sch.13, amended: SI 2004/589 Art.12

Sch.14, substituted: SI 2004/1176 Art.2

533. Accounts and Audit Regulations 2003

Reg.7, amended: SI 2004/556 Reg.2

536. Income Tax (Sub-contractors in the Construction Industry and Employments) (Amendment) Regulations 2003

Reg.1, amended: SI 2003/2682 Sch.2

Reg.9, revoked: SI 2003/2682 Sch.2

538. Financing of Maintained Schools (Amendment) (Wales) Regulations 2003

revoked: SI 2004/2506 Reg.3

541. Immigration Employment Document (Fees) Regulations 2003

Reg.3, amended: SI 2003/1277 Reg.2, SI 2004/1044 Reg.2, SI 2004/1485 Reg.2

Reg.4, amended: SI 2003/1277 Reg.2, SI 2003/2447 Reg.2, SI 2003/2626 Reg.2, SI 2004/1485 Reg.2

Reg.4A, added: SI 2003/1277 Reg.2

Reg.4B, added: SI 2003/1277 Reg.2

Reg.4B, revoked: SI 2004/1485 Reg.2

Reg.4C, added: SI 2003/2447 Reg.2

Reg.4D, added: SI 2003/2626 Reg.2

Reg.5, revoked (in part): SI 2003/2447 Reg.2, SI 2003/2626 Reg.2

Reg.5, substituted: SI 2004/1044 Reg.2

Reg.6, amended: SI 2004/1044 Reg.2

Sch.1, revoked: SI 2004/1044 Reg.2

542. Education (Supply of Information) (Wales) Regulations 2003

applied: SI 2003/3230 Reg.6

Reg.5, applied: SI 2001/1424 Reg.9

Reg.7, applied: SI 2001/1424 Reg.9

543. Education (Induction Arrangements for School Teachers) (Wales) Regulations 2003

applied: SI 2003/1663 Sch.3 para.1

2003-cont.

543. Education (Induction Arrangements for School Teachers) (Wales) Regulations 2003-*cont.*

Reg.2, amended: SI 2004/872 Reg.3, SI 2004/1745 Reg.4

Reg.6, amended: SI 2004/872 Reg.4, SI 2004/1745 Reg.4

Reg.8, amended: SI 2004/872 Reg.5

Reg.9, amended: SI 2004/872 Reg.6

Reg.16, applied: SI 2003/1663 Sch.3 para.1

Reg.18, amended: SI 2004/872 Reg.7

Reg.18, substituted: SI 2004/872 Reg.7

Sch.1 para.4, substituted: SI 2004/872 Reg.8

Sch.1 para.4A, added: SI 2004/872 Reg.8

Sch.1 para.4B, added: SI 2004/872 Reg.8

Sch.1 para.5, substituted: SI 2004/872 Reg.8

Sch.1 para.9, amended: SI 2004/872 Reg.8

Sch.1 para.17, substituted: SI 2004/1745 Reg.4

Sch.1 para.18, substituted: SI 2004/1745 Reg.4

Sch.1 para.20, added: SI 2004/872 Reg.8

Sch.1 para.20, amended: SI 2004/1745 Reg.4

546. Medicated Feedingstuffs (Amendment) Regulations 2003

revoked: SI 2003/752 Reg.3

547. Health and Safety (Fees) Regulations 2003

revoked: SI 2004/456 Reg.25

548. British Nationality (General) Regulations 2003

Reg.2, amended: SI 2003/3158 Reg.3

Reg.5A, added: SI 2004/1726 Reg.3

Reg.5A, amended: SI 2004/2109 Reg.2

Reg.6, substituted: SI 2003/3158 Reg.4

Sch.2 para.14, amended: SI 2004/1726 Reg.4

Sch.3 para.1, amended: SI 2003/3158 Reg.5

Sch.3 para.2, amended: SI 2003/3158 Reg.5

Sch.3 para.3, added: SI 2003/3158 Reg.5

Sch.3 para.3, amended: SI 2003/3158 Reg.5

553. Education Maintenance Allowance (Pilot Areas) (Amendment) Regulations 2003

revoked: SI 2004/1006 Reg.2

582. Motor Vehicles (Type Approval for Goods Vehicles) (Great Britain) (Amendment) Regulations 2003

applied: SI 1982/1271 Reg.2

586. National Health Service (Dental Charges) Amendment Regulations 2003

revoked: SI 2004/1091 Reg.4

595. Waste Management Licensing (Amendment) (England) Regulations 2003

referred to: SI 1994/1056 Reg.5

596. Environmental Protection (Waste Recycling Payments) (Amendment) (England) Regulations 2003

revoked: SI 2004/639 Reg.4

NO.

2003–cont.

601. Social Security Benefits Up-rating Regulations 2003
revoked: SI 2004/583 Reg.5

602. Environmental Protection (Controls on Hexachloroethane) Regulations 2003
revoked: SI 2003/3274 Reg.9

606. Education Act 2002 (Commencement No 2 and Savings and Transitional Provisions) (Amendment) Order 2003
revoked: SI 2003/2992 Art.2

617. Birmingham and Solihull Mental Health National Health Service Trust (Establishment) and the Northern Birmingham Mental Health National Health Service Trust and South Birmingham Mental Health National Health Service Trust (Dissolution) Order 2003
revoked: 2003 c.43 s.7

627. National Assistance (Assessment of Resources) (Amendment) (England) Regulations 2003
revoked: SI 2004/760 Reg.6

628. National Assistance (Sums for Personal Requirements) (England) Regulations 2003
Reg.2, amended: SI 2004/760 Reg.2

645. Family Proceedings Fees (Amendment) Order 2003
revoked: SI 2004/3114 Sch.2

646. Supreme Court Fees (Amendment) Order 2003
revoked: SI 2004/3121 Sch.2

648. County Court Fees (Amendment) Order 2003
revoked: SI 2004/3121 Sch.2

652. Immigration and Asylum Appeals (Procedure) Rules 2003
Part 2 r.5, applied: SI 2003/801 r.5
Part 2 r.6, applied: SI 2003/801 r.5, r.6
Part 2 r.8, applied: SI 2003/801 r.5, r.6
Part 2 r.9, referred to: SI 2003/801 r.6
Part 2 r.10, applied: SI 2003/801 r.5
Part 2 r.11, applied: SI 2003/801 r.5
Part 2 r.12, applied: SI 2003/801 r.5, r.8
Part 2 r.13, applied: SI 2003/801 r.23
Part 3 r.14, applied: SI 2003/801 r.10
Part 3 r.15, applied: SI 2003/801 r.10, r.11
Part 3 r.17, applied: SI 2003/801 r.10, r.11
Part 3 r.18, applied: SI 2003/801 r.10, r.14
Part 3 r.19, applied: SI 2003/801 r.10, r.12
Part 3 r.20, applied: SI 2003/801 r.10
Part 3 r.21, applied: SI 2003/801 r.10, r.11, r.12
Part 3 r.22, applied: SI 2003/801 r.10
Part 3 r.23, applied: SI 2003/801 r.10
Part 3 r.24, applied: SI 2003/801 r.10
Part 3 r.25, applied: SI 2003/801 r.10
Part 4 r.26, applied: SI 2003/801 r.16
Part 4 r.27, applied: SI 2003/801 r.16, r.17

NO.

2003–cont.

652. Immigration and Asylum Appeals (Procedure) Rules 2003–*cont.*
Part 4 r.29, applied: SI 2003/801 r.16, r.17
Part 4 r.30, applied: SI 2003/801 r.16
Part 6, applied: SI 2003/801 r.20
Part 6 r.39, applied: SI 2003/801 r.20
Part 6 r.40, disapplied: SI 2003/801 r.20
Part 6 r.45, applied: SI 2003/801 r.14
Part 6 r.45, disapplied: SI 2003/801 r.20
Part 6 r.53, applied: SI 2003/801 r.20
r.30, see *E v Secretary of State for the Home Department* [2004] EWCA Civ 49, [2004] Q.B. 1044 (CA), Lord Phillips of Worth Matravers, M.R.

653. Tax Credits (Immigration) Regulations 2003
referred to: SI 2003/742 Reg.53
Reg.2, varied: SI 2003/742 Reg.54
Reg.3, varied: SI 2003/742 Reg.55
Reg.4, varied: SI 2003/742 Reg.56

654. Tax Credits (Residence) Regulations 2003
referred to: SI 2003/742 Reg.51
Reg.2, varied: SI 2003/742 Reg.52
Reg.3, amended: SI 2004/1243 Reg.3

655. Private Hire Vehicles (London) (Transitional and Saving Provisions) Regulations 2003
Reg.5, amended: SI 2003/3028 Reg.3
Reg.6, amended: SI 2003/3028 Reg.4

660. Plant Protection Products (Fees) Regulations 2003
Reg.1, amended: SI 2004/1159 Reg.2
Reg.2, amended: SI 2004/1159 Reg.2
Reg.3A, added: SI 2004/1159 Reg.2
Sch.1, substituted: SI 2004/1159 Sch.1

663. Wireless Telegraphy (Television Licence Fees) (Amendment) Regulations 2003
revoked: SI 2004/692 Sch.6

664. Awards for All (England) Joint Scheme (Authorisation) Order 2003
revoked: SI 2004/691 Art.3

666. Natural Mineral Water, Spring Water and Bottled Drinking Water (Amendment) (England) Regulations 2003
Reg.17, disapplied: SI 1999/1540 Reg.11, Reg.12, Reg.16
Reg.18, disapplied: SI 1999/1540 Reg.11, Reg.12, Reg.16
Reg.19, disapplied: SI 1999/1540 Reg.11, Reg.12, Reg.16
Reg.20, disapplied: SI 1999/1540 Reg.11, Reg.12, Reg.16
Reg.21, disapplied: SI 1999/1540 Reg.11, Reg.12, Reg.16

671. National Health Service (Travelling Expenses and Remission of Charges) (Amendment) Regulations 2003
revoked: SI 2003/2382 Sch.2

2003–cont.

694. ACAS (Flexible Working) Arbitration Scheme (England and Wales) Order 2003

revoked: SI 2004/2333 Art.3

Sch.1, applied: SI 2004/2333 Art.6

699. National Health Service (Amendments Relating to Prescribing by Nurses and Pharmacists etc.) (England) Regulations 2003

Reg.3, revoked: SI 2004/865 Sch.2

702. Welfare Food (Amendment) Regulations 2003

revoked: SI 2004/723 Reg.6

703. Police and Criminal Evidence Act 1984 (Codes of Practice) (Codes B to E) (No.2) Order 2003

revoked: SI 2004/1887 Art.4

704. Police and Criminal Evidence Act 1984 (Codes of Practice) (Modifications to Codes C and D) (Certain Police Areas) Order 2003

revoked: SI 2004/1887 Art.4

Art.3, amended: SI 2004/78 Art.2

711. District of South Cambridgeshire (Electoral Changes) (Amendment) Order 2003

varied: SI 2004/222 Art.2

717. Supreme Court Fees (Amendment No 2) Order 2003

revoked: SI 2004/3121 Sch.2

718. County Court Fees (Amendment No 2) Order 2003

revoked: SI 2004/3121 Sch.2

719. Family Proceedings Fees (Amendment No 2) Order 2003

revoked: SI 2004/3114 Sch.2

721. Creosote (Prohibition on Use and Marketing) Regulations 2003

revoked: SI 2003/1511 Reg.2

731. Tax Credits (Provision of Information) (Functions Relating to Health) Regulations 2003

disapplied: SI 2003/1650 Reg.2

referred to: SI 2004/1895 Reg.2

742. Tax Credits (Polygamous Marriages) Regulations 2003

Reg.47A, added: SI 2004/762 Reg.19

753. National Care Standards Commission (Fees and Frequency of Inspections) Regulations 2003

revoked: SI 2004/662 Reg.7

varied: SI 2004/664 Art.11, Art.12, Art.13, Art.14

Reg.1, varied: SI 2004/664 Art.11, Art.12, Art.13, Art.14

Reg.2, varied: SI 2004/664 Art.11, Art.12, Art.13, Art.14

Reg.7, varied: SI 2004/664 Art.11, Art.12

2003–cont.

754. Nationality, Immigration and Asylum Act 2002 (Commencement No 4) Order 2003

Sch.1, amended: SI 2003/1339 Art.3, SI 2003/2993 Art.3

Sch.2 para.1, amended: SI 2003/1339 Art.4

Sch.2 para.2, amended: SI 2003/1040 Art.2

755. Asylum Support (Amendment) (No.2) Regulations 2003

revoked: SI 2004/763 Reg.3

757. Anglian Water Parks Byelaws (Extension) Order 2003

Art.2, varied: SI 2004/1106 Art.2

759. Bolton, Salford and Trafford Mental Health National Health Service Trust (Establishment) and the Mental Health Services of Salford National Health Service Trust (Dissolution) Order 2003

revoked: 2003 c.43 s.7

760. Community Health Sheffield National Health Service Trust (Change of Name) and (Establishment) Amendment Order 2003

revoked: 2003 c.43 s.7

762. Community Care, Services for Carers and Children's Services (Direct Payments) (England) Regulations 2003

Reg.2, applied: SI 2003/1216 Reg.4

769. Education (School Teachers Pay and Conditions) Order 2003

referred to: SI 2003/1708 Reg.3

revoked: SI 2003/2169 Art.1

772. Sea Fishing (Enforcement of Community Quota and Third Country Fishing Measures) (England) Order 2003

revoked: SI 2004/1237 Art.14

773. Performances (Reciprocal Protection) (Convention Countries and Isle of Man) Order 2003

referred to: SI 2003/2500 Sch.1 Part 2

774. Copyright (Application to Other Countries) (Amendment) Order 2003

referred to: SI 2003/2500 Sch.1 Part 2

778. Common Investment (Closure of High Yield Fund) Scheme 2003

revoked: SI 2004/266 Art.7

Art.2, amended: SI 2003/1027 Art.2

780. Waste Management Licensing (Amendment) (Wales) Regulations 2003

referred to: SI 1994/1056 Reg.5

781. Residential Family Centres (Wales) Regulations 2003

Reg.2, amended: SI 2004/1016 Sch.1 para.31

784. National Health Service (General Medical Services) (Amendment) (No.2) (Wales) Regulations 2003

revoked: SI 2004/1016 Sch.2

NO.

NO.

2003–cont.

2003–cont.

791. Norfolk and Norwich Health Care National Health Service Trust (Establishment) Amendment Order 2003
revoked: 2003 c.43 s.7

792. North Staffordshire Hospital National Health Service Trust (Change of Name) Order 2003
revoked: 2003 c.43 s.7

801. Immigration and Asylum Appeals (Fast Track Procedure) Rules 2003
Sch.1, amended: SI 2004/1891 r.2

812. Products of Animal Origin (Third Country Imports) (England) (Amendment) Regulations 2003
revoked: SI 2003/3177 Sch.6

813. Health Authorities (Transfer of Functions, Staff, Property, Rights and Liabilities and Abolition) (Wales) Order 2003
varied: SI 2003/818 Art.5
Art.2, amended: SI 2003/814 Art.2
Art.4A, added: SI 2003/814 Art.2

817. Powys Health Care National Health Service Trust (Dissolution) Order 2003
revoked: 2003 c.43 s.7

832. Food Labelling (Amendment) (Wales) Regulations 2003
Reg.3, referred to: SI 1996/1499 Reg.50
Reg.5, referred to: SI 1996/1499 Reg.50

834. Bradford Hospitals National Health Service Trust (Change of Name) and (Establishment) Amendment Order 2003
revoked: 2003 c.43 s.7

835. Cosmetic Products (Safety) Regulations 2003
referred to: SI 2004/2152 Reg.1, Sch.1 Part 1, Sch.6
revoked: SI 2004/2152 Reg.2
Reg.5, applied: SI 2004/2152 Reg.16
Reg.9, amended: SI 2004/994 Reg.4
Sch.3 Part I, referred to: SI 2004/2152 Sch.3
Sch.4 Part I, referred to: SI 2004/2152 Sch.4

844. Black Country Mental Health National Health Service Trust (Change of Name) and (Establishment) Amendment Order 2003
revoked: 2003 c.43 s.7

847. Gas (Applications for Licences and Extensions and Restrictions of Licences)(Amendment) Regulations 2003
revoked: SI 2004/2542 Reg.2

858. Electricity (Applications for Licences and Extensions and Restrictions of Licences) (Amendment) Regulations 2003
revoked: SI 2004/2541 Reg.2

866. Brighton Health Care National Health Service Trust (Change of Name) Order 2003
revoked: 2003 c.43 s.7

868. National Health Service Trusts (Dissolutions) Order 2003
revoked: 2003 c.43 s.7

871. Public Records Office (Fees) Regulations 2003
revoked: SI 2004/750 Reg.3

892. National Assistance (Sums for Personal Requirements) (Wales) Regulations 2003
revoked: SI 2004/1024 Reg.3

897. National Assistance (Assessment of Resources) (Amendment) (Wales) Regulations 2003
Reg.2, revoked: SI 2004/1023 Reg.4

907. Local Authorities (Charges for Specified Welfare Services) (England) Regulations 2003
applied: SI 1992/2977 Sch.3 para.28E

916. Child Benefit and Guardian's Allowance (Decisions and Appeals) Regulations 2003
Reg.18, applied: SI 2003/492 Reg.6
Reg.19, applied: SI 2003/492 Reg.6
Reg.20, applied: SI 2003/492 Reg.6

931. National Assistance (Residential Accommodation)(Additional Payments, Relevant Contributions and Assessment of Resources)(-Wales) Regulations 2003
Reg.4, disapplied: SI 1992/2977 Reg.16A
Reg.4, referred to: SI 1992/2977 Reg.16A, Reg.28

938. Tax Credits Act 2002 (Commencement No 3 and Transitional Provisions and Savings) Order 2003
Art.2, referred to: SR 2003/213 Reg.1

945. Miscellaneous Food Additives (Amendment) (Wales) Regulations 2003
applied: SI 2004/554 Reg.3
Reg.3, revoked (in part): SI 2004/554 Reg.3

962. Tax Credits Act 2002 (Commencement No 4, Transitional Provisions and Savings) Order 2003
Art.2, referred to: SR 2003/213 Reg.1
Sch.1, referred to: SR 2003/213 Reg.1

974. Preserved Counties (Amendment to Boundaries) (Wales) Order 2003
varied: SI 2004/218 Art.2

976. Products of Animal Origin (Third Country Imports) (Wales) (Amendment) Regulations 2003
revoked: SI 2004/1430 Sch.6

984. District of Adur (Scheme for Elections of Specified Council) Order 2003
varied: SI 2004/222 Art.2

2003–cont.

989. Feeding Stuffs (Amendment) (Wales) Regulations 2003

applied: SI 1999/2325 Reg.11, Reg.11A, Reg.11B

referred to: SI 1999/1663 Sch.2 para.3, SI 1999/2325 Reg.11, Reg.11A, Reg.11B, Reg.7

1005. National Health Service (General Medical Services) (Amendment) (No.3) (Wales) Regulations 2003

revoked: SI 2004/1016 Sch.2

1008. Miscellaneous Food Additives (Amendment) (England) Regulations 2003

Reg.3, revoked (in part): SI 2003/3295 Reg.3

1021. Local Authorities (Members Allowances) (England) Regulations 2003

referred to: SI 2003/1692 Reg.2

Part 2, applied: SI 2004/1777 Art.15

Part 2, referred to: SI 2004/1778 Art.15

Part 3, applied: SI 2004/1777 Art.15

Part 3, referred to: SI 2004/1778 Art.15

Reg.17, amended: SI 2003/1692 Reg.3

Reg.23, amended: SI 2003/1692 Reg.4

Reg.24, amended: SI 2004/2596 Reg.3

Reg.25, amended: SI 2003/1692 Reg.5, SI 2004/2596 Reg.4

Reg.26, amended: SI 2003/1692 Reg.6

Reg.26A, added: SI 2004/2596 Reg.6

Reg.28, amended: SI 2004/2596 Reg.5

Reg.34, amended: SI 2003/1692 Reg.7

1022. Local Government Pension Scheme and Discretionary Compensation (Local Authority Members in England) Regulations 2003

applied: SI 2004/928 Reg.5

1026. Feeding Stuffs (Amendment) Regulations 2003

applied: SI 1999/1663 Sch.2 para.3, SI 1999/2325 Reg.11, Reg.11A, Reg.11B

referred to: SI 1999/2325 Reg.11A, Reg.7, Reg.9, Reg.10, Reg.11

1027. Common Investment (Closure of High Yield Fund) (Amendment) Scheme 2003

revoked: SI 2004/266 Art.7

1037. Education (National Curriculum) (Key Stage 1 Assessment Arrangements) (England) Order 2003

revoked: SI 2004/2783 Art.2

1050. Social Security and Child Support (Miscellaneous Amendments) Regulations 2003

Reg.1, amended: SI 2003/1189 Reg.3

Reg.6, added: SI 2003/1189 Reg.4

Reg.6, revoked: SI 2003/1189 Reg.2

1052. Fee for Initial Assessment of Active Substances for Pesticides Regulations 2003

revoked: SI 2004/695 Reg.3

2003–cont.

1056. Stamp Duty (Disadvantaged Areas) (Application of Exemptions) Regulations 2003

Reg.2, amended: 2003 c.14 Sch.20 para.3

Reg.5, amended: 2003 c.14 Sch.20 para.3

1063. East Sussex Hospitals National Health Service Trust (Establishment) and the Eastbourne Hospitals National Health Service Trust and Hastings and Rother National Health Service Trust (Dissolution) Amendment Order 2003

revoked: 2003 c.43 s.7

1075. Network Rail (West Coast Main Line) Order 2003

Sch.12 para.1, amended: SI 2003/2155 Sch.1 para.17, Sch.2

Sch.12 para.2, amended: SI 2003/2155 Sch.1 para.17, Sch.2

Sch.13 Part II para.14, amended: SI 2003/2155 Sch.1 para.18

Sch.13 Part II para.14, revoked (in part): SI 2003/2155 Sch.2

Sch.13 Part II para.15, amended: SI 2003/2155 Sch.1 para.18

Sch.13 Part II para.16, amended: SI 2003/2155 Sch.1 para.18

Sch.13 Part II para.17, amended: SI 2003/2155 Sch.1 para.18

1076. Medicines and Healthcare Products Regulatory Agency Trading Fund Order 2003

Sch.1 para.1, amended: SI 2004/994 Reg.3

1080. General Optical Council (Registration and Enrolment (Amendment) Rules) Order of Council 2003

referred to: SI 2004/258

revoked: SI 2004/258 Art.2

1081. General Dental Council (Constitution of Committees) Order of Council 2003

Art.1, amended: SI 2004/67 Art.2

Art.2, amended: SI 2004/67 Art.2

Art.7, added: SI 2004/67 Art.2

1084. National Health Service (Pharmaceutical Services) (General Medical Services) and (Charges for Drugs and Appliances) Amendment Regulations 2003

Reg.11, revoked: SI 2004/865 Sch.2

Reg.12, revoked: SI 2004/865 Sch.2

Reg.13, revoked: SI 2004/865 Sch.2

Reg.14, revoked: SI 2004/865 Sch.2

Reg.15, revoked: SI 2004/865 Sch.2

Reg.16, revoked: SI 2004/865 Sch.2

Reg.17, revoked: SI 2004/865 Sch.2

1088. Borough of Hartlepool (Electoral Changes) Order 2003

varied: SI 2004/222 Art.2

NO.

2003–cont.

1089. Borough of Warrington (Electoral Changes) (Amendment) Order 2003
varied: SI 2004/222 Art.2

1090. Borough of Weymouth and Portland (Electoral Changes) (Amendment) Order 2003
varied: SI 2004/222 Art.2

1091. Borough of Thurrock (Electoral Changes) (Amendment) Order 2003
varied: SI 2004/222 Art.2

1092. Financial Services and Markets Act 2000 (Disclosure of Confidential Information) (Amendment) Regulations 2003
revoked: SI 2003/2174 Reg.3

1102. Insurers (Reorganisation and Winding Up) Regulations 2003
applied: SI 1986/1915 r.4.84
revoked: SI 2004/353 Reg.53
see *Pan Atlantic Insurance Co Ltd, Re* [2003] EWHC 1696, [2003] B.C.C. 847 (Ch D (Companies Ct)), Lloyd, J.
Part III, referred to: SI 2004/353 Reg.53
Part IV, referred to: SI 2004/353 Reg.53
Reg.28, applied: SI 2001/3635 r.24

1116. Companies (Acquisition of Own Shares)(Treasury Shares) Regulations 2003
Sch.1 para.12, revoked (in part): SI 2003/3031 Reg.3

1119. Food (Pistachios from Iran) (Emergency Control) (Wales) Regulations 2003
revoked: SI 2003/2288 Reg.7

1153. Education (Outturn Statements) (England) Regulations 2003
applied: SI 2004/1279 Reg.3
revoked: SI 2004/1279 Reg.3

1184. Education (Prohibition from Teaching or Working with Children) Regulations 2003
Reg.8, amended: SI 2004/1493 Reg.3
Sch.2 para.14A, added: SI 2004/1493 Reg.4
Sch.2 para.14AA, added: SI 2004/1493 Reg.4
Sch.2 para.14B, added: SI 2004/1493 Reg.4
Sch.2 para.14BB, added: SI 2004/1493 Reg.4
Sch.2 para.14C, added: SI 2004/1493 Reg.4
Sch.2 para.14D, added: SI 2004/1493 Reg.4
Sch.2 para.14E, added: SI 2004/1493 Reg.4
Sch.2 para.14F, added: SI 2004/1493 Reg.4
Sch.2 para.14G, added: SI 2004/1493 Reg.4
Sch.2 para.14H, added: SI 2004/1493 Reg.4
Sch.2 para.14I, added: SI 2004/1493 Reg.4
Sch.2 para.14J, added: SI 2004/1493 Reg.4
Sch.2 para.14K, added: SI 2004/1493 Reg.4
Sch.2 para.14L, added: SI 2004/1493 Reg.4
Sch.2 para.14M, added: SI 2004/1493 Reg.4
Sch.2 para.14N, added: SI 2004/1493 Reg.4
Sch.2 para.14O, added: SI 2004/1493 Reg.4

NO.

2003–cont.

1184. Education (Prohibition from Teaching or Working with Children) Regulations 2003–cont.
Sch.2 para.14P, added: SI 2004/1493 Reg.4
Sch.2 para.14Q, added: SI 2004/1493 Reg.4
Sch.2 para.14R, added: SI 2004/1493 Reg.4
Sch.2 para.14S, added: SI 2004/1493 Reg.4
Sch.2 para.14T, added: SI 2004/1493 Reg.4
Sch.2 para.14U, added: SI 2004/1493 Reg.4
Sch.2 para.14V, added: SI 2004/1493 Reg.4
Sch.2 para.14W, added: SI 2004/1493 Reg.4
Sch.2 para.14X, added: SI 2004/1493 Reg.4
Sch.2 para.14Y, added: SI 2004/1493 Reg.4
Sch.2 para.14Z, added: SI 2004/1493 Reg.4

1185. Immigration (Passenger Transit Visa) Order 2003
Art.2, amended: SI 2003/2628 Art.2
Art.3, amended: SI 2003/2628 Art.2
Art.3A, added: SI 2003/2628 Art.2
Art.3A, amended: SI 2004/1304 Art.2
Art.3A, revoked (in part): SI 2004/1304 Art.2
Sch.1, amended: SI 2004/1304 Art.2
Sch.1, substituted: SI 2003/1598 Sch.1, SI 2003/2628 Sch.1

1194. Statutory Paternity Pay (Adoption) and Statutory Adoption Pay (Adoptions from Overseas) (No.2) Regulation 2003
Reg.3, amended: SI 2004/488 Reg.4

1200. Education (Additional Secondary School Proposals) Regulations 2003
Reg.12, amended: SI 2003/1421 Reg.2

1235. Organic Farming (England Rural Development Programme) Regulations 2003
applied: SI 2003/2261 Sch.3 Part I
referred to: SI 2000/3044 Sch.1 Part II

1247. Criminal Justice (Northern Ireland) Order 2003
Part II, applied: 2004 c.4 Sch.2 para.4
Art.1, enabled: SR 2003/307, SR 2003/352
Art.4, amended: 2004 c.4 s.12
Art.5, amended: 2004 c.4 s.12
Art.6, amended: 2004 c.4 s.12
Art.6, applied: 2004 c.4 Sch.2 para.4
Art.12, amended: SI 2004/1500 Art.29
Art.16, applied: 1996 c.25 s.1
Art.19, applied: 1968 c.34 (NI) Sch.1, 1992 c.34 s.2, s.4, 1997 c.51 Sch.1 para.3, Sch.2 para.2, SI 1998/9 Sch.1 para.1, SI 1999/2789 Art.3
Art.20, applied: 1968 c.34 (NI) Sch.1, 1992 c.34 s.2, 1997 c.51 Sch.1 para.3, Sch.2 para.2, SI 1998/9 Sch.1 para.1, SI 1999/2789 Art.3, 2003 c.44 Sch.17 para.108
Art.21, applied: 1968 c.34 (NI) Sch.1, SI 1981/1675 Sch.2 para.23, 1992 c.34 s.2, 1996 c.29 Sch.1 para.2, 1997 c.51 Sch.1 para.3, Sch.2 para.2, SI 1998/9 Sch.1 para.1, SI 1999/2789 Art.3, 2003 c.44 Sch.17 para.109

NO.

2003–cont.

1247. Criminal Justice (Northern Ireland) Order 2003–*cont.*

Sch.1 para.3, revoked: 2004 c.4 Sch.4

1250. General and Specialist Medical Practice (Education, Training and Qualifications) Order 2003

Art.4, applied: SI 2004/1020 Reg.23, SSI 2004/114 Sch.1 para.4

Art.4, referred to: SI 2004/585 Reg.23, SI 2004/1020 Reg.23

Art.5, applied: SI 2004/1016 Art.86, SI 2004/1020 Reg.23, SSI 2004/114 Sch.1 para.4, SSI 2004/163 Art.97

Art.5, referred to: SI 2004/585 Reg.23, SI 2004/865 Art.110, SI 2004/1020 Reg.23

Art.8, amended: SI 2004/1947 Reg.5

Art.10, amended: SI 2004/865 Sch.1 para.37, SI 2004/1016 Sch.1 para.33, SI 2004/2261 Sch.1 para.3

Art.10, applied: SI 2004/585 Reg.23, SI 2004/1020 Reg.23, SSI 2004/114 Sch.1 para.4

Art.10, referred to: SI 2004/585 Reg.23, SI 2004/1020 Reg.23

Art.10, revoked (in part): SI 2004/1016 Sch.1 para.33, SI 2004/2261 Sch.1 para.3

Art.11, amended: SI 2004/865 Sch.1 para.37, SI 2004/1016 Sch.1 para.33, SI 2004/1947 Reg.5

Art.12, amended: SI 2004/865 Sch.1 para.37, SI 2004/1016 Sch.1 para.33

Art.15, amended: SI 2004/1947 Reg.5

Art.31, applied: SI 2004/865 Art.110, Art.117, Art.118, SI 2004/1016 Art.86, SSI 2004/163 Art.97, Art.100, Art.101

Sch.1, amended: SI 2004/865 Sch.1 para.37, SI 2004/1016 Sch.1 para.33, SI 2004/1947 Reg.5, SI 2004/2261 Sch.1 para.3

Sch.3 Part 1, added: SI 2004/1947 Reg.5

Sch.3 Part 1, amended: SI 2004/1947 Reg.5

Sch.6A, added: SI 2004/1947 Reg.5

Sch.7, amended: SI 2004/1947 Reg.5

Sch.8 Part 1, applied: SI 2004/1947 Reg.4

Sch.8 Part 1 para.5, amended: SI 2004/1947 Reg.5

Sch.8 Part 1 para.6, amended: SI 2004/1947 Reg.5

Sch.8 Part 1 para.9, amended: SI 2004/1947 Reg.5

Sch.8 Part 1 para.12, amended: SI 2004/1947 Reg.5

Sch.8 Part 2 para.22, amended: SI 2004/865 Sch.1 para.37, SI 2004/1016 Sch.1 para.33, SI 2004/2261 Sch.1 para.3

Sch.8 Part 2 para.22, revoked (in part): SI 2004/865 Sch.1 para.37, SI 2004/1016 Sch.1 para.33, SI 2004/2261 Sch.1 para.3

Sch.9 para.2, revoked (in part): SI 2004/865 Sch.1 para.37, SI 2004/1016 Sch.1 para.33

Sch.9 para.3, revoked (in part): SI 2004/2261 Sch.1 para.3

NO.

2003–cont.

1250. General and Specialist Medical Practice (Education, Training and Qualifications) Order 2003–*cont.*

Sch.9 para.6, revoked (in part): SI 2004/865 Sch.1 para.37, SI 2004/1016 Sch.1 para.33, SI 2004/2261 Sch.1 para.3

Sch.10 Part 1 para.1, revoked (in part): SI 2004/865 Sch.1 para.37, SI 2004/1016 Sch.1 para.33

Sch.10 Part 1 para.5, revoked (in part): SI 2004/1016 Sch.1 para.33

Sch.10 Part 1 para.5, substituted: SI 2004/865 Sch.1 para.37

Sch.10 Part 1 para.7, revoked (in part): SI 2004/865 Sch.1 para.37, SI 2004/1016 Sch.1 para.33

Sch.10 Part 2, applied: SI 2004/865 Art.110, Art.117, Art.118, SI 2004/1016 Art.86, SSI 2004/163 Art.97, Art.100, Art.101

1265. Police Authorities (Best Value) Performance Indicators (Amendment) Order 2003

revoked: SI 2004/644 Art.4

1266. Town and Country Planning (Inquiries Procedure) (Wales) Rules 2003

applied: SI 2003/1267 r.3, r.24, SI 2003/1269 r.3, SI 2003/1271 r.3

1267. Town and Country Planning Appeals (Determination by Inspectors) (Inquiries Procedure) (Wales) Rules 2003

applied: SI 2003/1266 r.3, SI 2003/1271 r.3

1269. Town and Country Planning (Enforcement) (Inquiries Procedure) (Wales) Rules 2003

applied: SI 2003/1268 r.3, SI 2003/1270 r.3, r.25

1270. Town and Country Planning (Enforcement) (Determination by Inspectors) (Inquiries Procedure) (Wales) Rules 2003

applied: SI 2003/1268 r.3

r.25, applied: SI 2003/1269 r.26

1276. York Health Services National Health Service Trust (Change of Name) and (Establishment) Amendment Order 2003

revoked: 2003 c.43 s.7

1279. Disease Control (Interim Measures) (England) (No.2) Order 2003

revoked: SI 2003/1729 Art.23

1286. Magistrates&apos Courts (Miscellaneous Amendments) Rules 2003

r.85, revoked: SI 2004/1054 r.3

r.87, revoked: SI 2004/1054 r.3

1296. Feeding Stuffs (Sampling and Analysis), the Feeding Stuffs (Enforcement) and the Feeding Stuffs (Establishments and Intermediaries) (Amendment) (England) Regulations 2003

applied: SI 1999/1663 Sch.2 para.3

2003–cont.

1296. Feeding Stuffs (Sampling and Analysis), the Feeding Stuffs (Enforcement) and the Feeding Stuffs (Establishments and Intermediaries) (Amendment) (England) Regulations 2003–cont.
referred to: SI 1999/1872 Reg.98, Reg.99, Reg.106

1297. Terrorism (United Nations Measures) Order 2001 (Amendment) Regulations 2003
Reg.2, revoked: SI 2003/2209 Reg.3

1327. Education (National Curriculum) (Foundation Stage Profile Assessment Arrangements) (England) Order 2003
Art.4, amended: SI 2004/622 Art.2

1336. Transport of Animals (Cleansing and Disinfection) (England) (No.2) Order 2003
revoked: SI 2003/1724 Art.11

1338. Housing Benefit and Council Tax Benefit (State Pension Credit) (Abolition of Benefit Periods) Amendment Regulations 2003
Reg.4, revoked: SI 2004/14 Reg.33
Reg.5, revoked: SI 2004/14 Reg.33
Reg.6, revoked: SI 2004/14 Reg.33
Reg.8, revoked: SI 2004/14 Reg.33
Reg.9, revoked: SI 2004/14 Reg.33
Reg.10, revoked: SI 2004/14 Reg.33
Reg.11, revoked: SI 2004/14 Reg.33
Reg.12, revoked: SI 2004/14 Reg.33
Reg.13, revoked (in part): SI 2004/14 Reg.33
Reg.14, revoked: SI 2004/14 Reg.33
Reg.15, revoked: SI 2004/14 Reg.33
Reg.16, revoked: SI 2004/14 Reg.33
Reg.17, revoked: SI 2004/14 Reg.33
Reg.18, revoked: SI 2004/14 Reg.33
Reg.19, revoked: SI 2004/14 Reg.33
Reg.20, revoked: SI 2004/14 Reg.33
Reg.21, revoked: SI 2004/14 Reg.33
Reg.22, revoked: SI 2004/14 Reg.33
Reg.23, revoked: SI 2004/14 Reg.33
Reg.24, revoked: SI 2004/14 Reg.33

1341. General Medical Council (Voluntary Erasure and Restoration following Voluntary Erasure) Regulations Order of Council 2003
revoked: SI 2004/2609 Art.2
Sch.1, applied: SI 1987/2174, SI 1988/2255 para.46A, para.46B, SI 1997/1529 r.30A, r.30D, r.30F, SI 2004/2609 Sch.1
Sch.1, disapplied: SI 2004/2609 Sch.1
Sch.1, referred to: SI 1987/2174, SI 1988/2255 para.46A

1342. General Medical Council (Restoration and Registration Fees Amendment) Regulations Order of Council 2003
referred to: SI 1987/2174

2003–cont.

1342. General Medical Council (Restoration and Registration Fees Amendment) Regulations Order of Council 2003–cont.
revoked: SI 2004/2612 Art.2
Sch.1, applied: SI 1987/2174, SI 1988/2255 para.46A, SI 1997/1529 r.30A, r.30D, SI 2004/2612 Sch.1
Sch.1, disapplied: SI 2004/2612 Sch.1
Sch.1, referred to: SI 1988/2255 para.46A
Sch.1, revoked: SI 2004/2612 Sch.1

1368. Enterprise Act 2002 (Super-complaints to Regulators) Order 2003
Sch.1, amended: SI 2003/3182 Art.4

1370. Enterprise Act 2002 (Merger Fees and Determination of Turnover) Order 2003
Art.10, amended: SI 2004/1079 Sch.1 para.5

1372. Competition Appeal Tribunal Rules 2003
Part I r.5, applied: SI 2004/2068 r.3
Part II r.8, applied: SI 2004/2068 r.3
Part II r.8, disapplied: SI 2004/2068 r.4
Part II r.12, amended: SI 2004/2068 Sch.1 para.1
Part II r.14, applied: SI 2004/2068 r.3
Part II r.16, amended: SI 2004/2068 Sch.1 para.2
Part II r.16, applied: SI 2004/2068 r.3
Part IV r.43, amended: SI 2004/2068 Sch.1 para.3
Part V r.55, amended: SI 2004/2068 Sch.1 para.4
Part V r.62, amended: SI 2004/2068 Sch.1 para.5
Part V r.63, amended: SI 2004/2068 Sch.1 para.6
r.16, see *British Telecommunications Plc v Director General of Telecommunications (Permission to Intervene)* [2003] CAT 20, [2004] Comp. A.R. 187 (Competition Appeal Tribunal), Sir Christopher Bellamy (President); see *Umbro Holdings Ltd v Office of Fair Trading (Permission to Intervene)* [2003] CAT 25, [2004] Comp. A.R. 214 (Competition Appeal Tribunal), Sir Christopher Bellamy (President)
r.19, see *Pernod-Ricard SA v Office of Fair Trading (Admissibility: Initial Consideration)* [2003] CAT 19, [2004] Comp. A.R. 181 (Competition Appeal Tribunal), Sir Christopher Bellamy (President)

1374. Enterprise Act 2002 (Part 8 Community Infringements Specified UK Laws) Order 2003
Sch.1, amended: SI 2004/2095 Reg.27

NO.

1376. Enterprise Act 2002 (Part 8 Notice to OFT of Intended Prosecution Specified Enactments, Revocation and Transitional Provision) Order 2003

Sch.1, amended: SI 2004/2095 Reg.28

1377. School Governance (Procedures) (England) Regulations 2003

applied: SI 2003/1965 Reg.25

disapplied: SI 2004/530 Reg.3

Reg.3, varied: SI 2003/1965 Sch.7 para.1, SI 2004/2042 Sch.8 para.1

Reg.5, varied: SI 2003/1965 Sch.7 para.2, Sch.7 para.3, SI 2004/2042 Sch.8 para.2, Sch.8 para.3

Reg.6, varied: SI 2003/1965 Sch.7 para.4, SI 2004/2042 Sch.8 para.3, Sch.8 para.6

Reg.8, varied: SI 2003/1965 Sch.7 para.5, Sch.7 para.6, SI 2004/2042 Sch.8 para.3, Sch.8 para.5, Sch.8 para.7

Reg.10, varied: SI 2003/1965 Sch.7 para.5, SI 2004/2042 Sch.8 para.4

Reg.11, applied: SI 2003/1965 Reg.30, SI 2004/2042 Reg.6, Reg.35

Reg.11, varied: SI 2003/1965 Sch.7 para.7, Sch.7 para.9, SI 2004/2042 Sch.8 para.6, Sch.8 para.7

Reg.12, amended: SI 2004/450 Reg.3

Reg.12, varied: SI 2003/1965 Sch.7 para.7, Sch.7 para.8, SI 2004/2042 Sch.8 para.6

Reg.13, varied: SI 2003/1965 Sch.7 para.3, Sch.7 para.7, SI 2004/2042 Sch.8 para.3, Sch.8 para.6

Reg.14, substituted: SI 2003/1916 Reg.3

Reg.14, varied: SI 2003/1965 Sch.7 para.8, Sch.7 para.9, SI 2004/2042 Sch.8 para.3, Sch.8 para.7

Reg.15, applied: SI 2003/1962 Reg.7

Reg.15, varied: SI 2003/1965 Sch.7 para.3, Sch.7 para.10, SI 2004/2042 Sch.8 para.3, Sch.8 para.8

Reg.16, amended: SI 2003/1963 Reg.8

Reg.16, applied: SI 2003/1962 Reg.3

Reg.16, varied: SI 2003/1962 Reg.4, SI 2003/1965 Sch.7 para.9, SI 2004/2042 Sch.8 para.7

Reg.17, applied: SI 2003/1962 Reg.3

Reg.17, varied: SI 2003/1962 Reg.4, SI 2003/1965 Sch.7 para.7, SI 2004/2042 Sch.8 para.6

Reg.18, applied: SI 2003/1962 Reg.3

Reg.18, varied: SI 2003/1962 Reg.4, SI 2003/1965 Sch.7 para.5, SI 2004/2042 Sch.8 para.7

Reg.19, varied: SI 2003/1965 Sch.7 para.11, SI 2004/2042 Sch.8 para.9

Reg.21, varied: SI 2003/1965 Sch.7 para.5, Sch.7 para.9, SI 2004/2042 Sch.8 para.4, Sch.8 para.7

Reg.23, varied: SI 2003/1965 Sch.7 para.5, SI 2004/2042 Sch.8 para.4

NO.

1377. School Governance (Procedures) (England) Regulations 2003–*cont.*

Reg.24, varied: SI 2003/1965 Sch.7 para.3, Sch.7 para.5, Sch.7 para.7, SI 2004/2042 Sch.8 para.3, Sch.8 para.6, Sch.8 para.7

Sch.1 para.1, substituted: SI 2003/1916 Reg.4

Sch.1 para.1, varied: SI 2003/1965 Sch.7 para.3, SI 2004/2042 Sch.8 para.3

Sch.1 para.2, substituted: SI 2003/1916 Reg.4

Sch.1 para.2, varied: SI 2004/2042 Sch.8 para.10

Sch.1 para.3, substituted: SI 2003/1916 Reg.4

Sch.1 para.3, varied: SI 2003/1965 Sch.7 para.3, Sch.7 para.5, SI 2004/2042 Sch.8 para.3, Sch.8 para.7

1397. Enterprise Act 2002 (Commencement No 3, Transitional and Transitory Provisions and Savings) Order 2003

Art.4, applied: SI 2003/3180 Art.3

Art.5, applied: SI 2004/2751 Sch.1 para.19

Art.5, referred to: SI 2003/1398 Art.3

1399. Enterprise Act 2002 (Part 8 Designated Enforcers Criteria for Designation, Designation of Public Bodies as Designated Enforcers and Transitional Provisions) Order 2003

Sch.1, amended: SI 2003/3182 Art.3

1414. Disease Control (Interim Measures) (Wales) (No.2) Order 2003

revoked: SI 2003/1966 Art.23

1416. European Parliament (United Kingdom Representatives) Pensions (Amendment) Order 2003

applied: SI 2003/2922 Art.2

1417. Land Registration Rules 2003

applied: SI 2003/1953 Art.5, Art.26

referred to: SI 2003/1953 Art.20

Part 1 r.3, disapplied: SI 2004/1830 r.3

Part 1 r.3, varied: SI 2004/1830 r.3

Part 3 r.16, referred to: SI 2004/1830 r.8

Part 5, applied: SI 2003/1953 Art.14

Part 5 r.41, varied: SI 2003/1953 Art.14

Part 5 r.51, varied: SI 2003/1953 Art.14

Part 6 r.54, applied: SI 2004/595 Sch.3 Part 1

Part 6 r.54, varied: SI 2004/1830 r.3

Part 8 r.92, disapplied: SI 2003/1953 Art.18

Part 12 r.126, disapplied: SI 2004/1830 r.3

Part 12 r.127, disapplied: SI 2004/1830 r.3

Part 13, applied: SI 2003/1953 Art.28

Part 13 r.132, applied: SI 2004/595 Sch.3 Part 2, Sch.3 Part 3

Part 13 r.133, applied: SI 2003/1953 Art.27

Part 13 r.135, applied: SI 2003/1953 Art.27

Part 13 r.136, varied: SI 2004/1830 r.3

Part 13 r.137, applied: SI 2004/595 Sch.3 Part 4

Part 13 r.137, varied: SI 2004/1830 r.3

Part 13 r.138, varied: SI 2004/1830 r.3

Part 13 r.140, applied: SI 2003/1953 Sch.1

NO.

2003–cont.

1417. Land Registration Rules 2003–cont.
Part13 r.144, applied: SI 2004/595 Sch.3 Part 2
Part 13 r.146, applied: SI 2003/1953 Art.21
Part 13 r.151, applied: SI 2003/1953 Art.28
Part 13 r.151, varied: SI 2003/1953 Art.28
Part 13 r.152, applied: SI 2003/1953 Art.28
Part 13 r.153, applied: SI 2003/1953 Art.28
Part 13 r.154, applied: SI 2003/1953 Art.28
Part 14 r.184, amended: SI 2003/2096 Sch.1 para.80
Part 15 r.198, applied: SI 2004/1830 r.10, r.11
Part 15 r.203, disapplied: SI 2003/1953 Art.24
Part 15 r.204, applied: SI 2004/595 Sch.3 Part 4
Part 15 r.204, disapplied: SI 2003/1953 Art.24
Part 15 r.208, applied: SI 2004/1830 r.3
Part 15 r.210, applied: SI 2004/1830 r.3
Part 15 r.211, applied: SI 2004/1830 r.3
Part 15 r.214, disapplied: SI 2004/1830 r.3
Part 15 r.216, applied: SI 2003/2114 r.6
Sch.1, applied: SI 2004/1830 r.3
Sch.1, referred to: SI 2003/1953 Art.12, Art.16
Sch.1, varied: SI 2004/1830 r.25, r.26
Sch.2, applied: SI 2003/2040 Art.2
Sch.4, applied: SI 2004/595 Sch.4
Sch.6 Part 3 paraA, varied: SI 2004/1830 r.3
Sch.6 Part 3 paraB, varied: SI 2004/1830 r.3
Sch.6 Part 3 paraC, varied: SI 2004/1830 r.3
Sch.6 Part 3 paraD, varied: SI 2004/1830 r.3
Sch.6 Part 3 paraE, varied: SI 2004/1830 r.3
Sch.6 Part 3 paraF, varied: SI 2004/1830 r.3
Sch.6 Part 3, varied: SI 2004/1830 r.3
Sch.6 Part 3 paraH, varied: SI 2004/1830 r.3
Sch.6 Part 3 paraI, varied: SI 2004/1830 r.3
Sch.6 Part 3 paraJ, varied: SI 2004/1830 r.3
Sch.6 Part 4 paraA, varied: SI 2004/1830 r.3
Sch.6 Part 4 paraB, varied: SI 2004/1830 r.3
Sch.6 Part 4 paraC, varied: SI 2004/1830 r.3
Sch.6 Part 4 paraD, varied: SI 2004/1830 r.3
Sch.6 Part 4 paraE, varied: SI 2004/1830 r.3
Sch.6 Part 4 paraF, varied: SI 2004/1830 r.3
Sch.6 Part 4, varied: SI 2004/1830 r.3
Sch.6 Part 4 paraH, varied: SI 2004/1830 r.3
Sch.6 Part 4 paraI, varied: SI 2004/1830 r.3
Sch.6 Part 4 paraJ, varied: SI 2004/1830 r.3

1431. Carriage of Dangerous Goods and Transportable Pressure Vessels (Amendment) Regulations 2003
revoked: SI 2004/568 Sch.14

1447. Land Registration Rules 2003
applied: SI 2003/2092 Art.1
r.118, applied: SI 2003/2092 Art.9, Sch.3 Part 1
r.132, applied: SI 2003/2092 Sch.3 Part 2
r.137, applied: SI 2003/2092 Sch.3 Part 4
r.140, applied: SI 2003/2092 Art.9
r.204, applied: SI 2003/2092 Sch.3 Part 4

NO.

2003–cont.

1447. Land Registration Rules 2003–cont.
Sch.4, applied: SI 2003/2092 Sch.3 Part 1
Sch.4, referred to: SI 2003/2092 Sch.4

1470. Transport of Animals (Cleansing and Disinfection) (Wales) (No.2) Order 2003
revoked: SI 2003/1968 Art.11

1471. Tobacco Products (Descriptions of Products) Order 2003
referred to: SI 2001/1712 Reg.3

1476. Financial Services and Markets Act 2000 (Regulated Activities) (Amendment) (No.2) Order 2003
Art.20, revoked (in part): SI 2004/1610 Art.2

1482. Animal By-Products Regulations 2003
applied: SI 2002/843 Reg.13, Reg.40, SI 2003/1724 Art.7
Reg.26, applied: SI 2003/3177 Reg.22, SI 2004/1214 Reg.22, SI 2004/2640 Reg.22
Reg.26, referred to: SI 2004/1214 Reg.22, SI 2004/1740 Reg.22

1483. Local Authorities (Code of Conduct) (Local Determination) Regulations 2003
Reg.2, amended: SI 2004/2617 Reg.4
Reg.4, amended: SI 2004/2617 Reg.5
Reg.5, substituted: SI 2004/2617 Reg.6
Reg.6, amended: SI 2004/2617 Reg.7
Reg.7, amended: SI 2004/2617 Reg.8

1496. Canterbury and Thanet Community Healthcare National Health Service Trust (Change of Name) Amendment Order 2003
revoked: 2003 c.43 s.7

1499. Royal Hospital of St Bartholomew, the Royal London Hospital and London Chest Hospital National Health Service Trust (Establishment) Amendment Order 2003
revoked: 2003 c.43 s.7

1500. Epsom and St Helier National Health Service Trust (Change of Name) Amendment Order 2003
revoked: 2003 c.43 s.7

1503. Feeding Stuffs, the Feeding Stuffs (Sampling and Analysis) and the Feeding Stuffs (Enforcement) (Amendment) (England) Regulations 2003
applied: SI 1999/2325 Reg.11, Reg.11A, Reg.11B
referred to: SI 1999/2325 Reg.7, SI 2000/2481 Reg.2
Reg.6, see *R. (on the application of ABNA Ltd) v Secretary of State for Health* [2003] EWHC 2420, [2004] 2 C.M.L.R. 39 (QBD (Admin Ct)), Davis, J.

NO.

2003–cont.

1503. Feeding Stuffs, the Feeding Stuffs (Sampling and Analysis) and the Feeding Stuffs (Enforcement) (Amendment) (England) Regulations 2003–*cont.*

Reg.10, see *R. (on the application of ABNA Ltd) v Secretary of State for Health* [2003] EWHC 2420, [2004] 2 C.M.L.R. 39 (QBD (Admin Ct)), Davis, J.

1511. Creosote (Prohibition on Use and Marketing) (No.2) Regulations 2003

Reg.8, added: SI 2003/2650 Reg.2

1516. Iraq (United Nations Sanctions) (Overseas Territories) Order 2003

applied: SI 2000/3242 Art.5A

varied: SI 2004/2036 Art.2

Art.4, amended: SI 2004/1983 Art.2

Art.6, substituted: SI 2004/2671 Art.2

Art.10a, added: SI 2004/1983 Art.3

Art.13, amended: SI 2004/2671 Art.3

Art.14, amended: SI 2004/2671 Art.4

1519. Iraq (United Nations Sanctions) Order 2003

applied: SI 2004/1498

referred to: SI 2000/3241 Art.5A

Sch.1 para.1, amended: SI 2004/1498 Art.4

Sch.1 para.1, revoked (in part): SI 2004/1498 Art.4

Sch.1 para.3, revoked: SI 2004/1498 Art.4

Sch.1 para.7, revoked (in part): SI 2004/1498 Art.4

1521. Iraq (United Nations Sanctions) (Channel Islands) Order 2003

referred to: SI 2000/3244 Art.5A, SI 2004/1978

Art.4, amended: SI 2004/1978 Sch.1 para.1

Art.10A, added: SI 2004/1978 Sch.1 para.2

Sch.1 para.1, amended: SI 2004/1978 Sch.1 para.3

Sch.1 para.1, revoked (in part): SI 2004/1978 Sch.1 para.3

Sch.1 para.3, revoked: SI 2004/1978 Sch.1 para.3

Sch.1 para.4, revoked: SI 2004/1978 Sch.1 para.3

Sch.1 para.7, revoked (in part): SI 2004/1978 Sch.1 para.3

1522. Iraq (United Nations Sanctions) (Isle of Man) Order 2003

referred to: SI 2000/3245 Art.5A, SI 2004/1982, SI 2004/1982 Art.4

Art.4, amended: SI 2004/1982 Sch.1 para.1

Art.10A, added: SI 2004/1982 Sch.1 para.2

Sch.1 para.1, revoked (in part): SI 2004/1982 Sch.1 para.3

Sch.1 para.3, revoked: SI 2004/1982 Sch.1 para.3

Sch.1 para.4, revoked: SI 2004/1982 Sch.1 para.3

Sch.1 para.7, revoked (in part): SI 2004/1982 Sch.1 para.3

NO.

2003–cont.

1535. Sea Fishing (Restriction on Days at Sea) (No.2) Order 2003

revoked (in part): SI 2004/398 Art.24

Art.2, amended: SI 2004/38 Art.2

Art.3, amended: SI 2004/38 Art.2

Art.4, amended: SI 2004/38 Art.2

1558. New Schools (General) (England) Regulations 2003

Part 1, applied: SI 2003/1965 Reg.11, SI 2004/2042 Reg.11

Part 2, applied: SI 2003/1965 Reg.11, SI 2004/2042 Reg.11

Part 3, applied: SI 1998/2535 Reg.9, SI 2003/1965 Reg.11, Reg.32, Reg.37, SI 2004/2042 Reg.11, Reg.37, Reg.42

Part 4, applied: SI 2003/1965 Reg.32, Reg.37, SI 2004/2042 Reg.37, Reg.42

Part 5, applied: SI 2003/1965 Reg.11, SI 2004/2042 Reg.11

Part 6, applied: SI 2003/1965 Reg.11, SI 2004/2042 Reg.11

Part 7, applied: SI 2003/1965 Reg.11, SI 2004/2042 Reg.11

Reg.10, amended: SI 2004/450 Reg.4

Reg.44, amended: SI 2004/450 Reg.4

Reg.45, amended: SI 2004/450 Reg.4

Reg.51, amended: SI 2004/450 Reg.4

Sch.1 para.2, amended: SI 2004/696 Art.3, Sch.1 para.48

Sch.2 para.4, substituted: SI 2004/450 Reg.4

1563. Specified Sugar Products (England) Regulations 2003

applied: SI 2000/3323 Reg.5

1571. Health Professions (Parts of and Entries in the Register) Order of Council 2003

Sch.1, amended: SI 2004/2033 Art.11, SI 2004/2522 Art.2

1572. Health Professions Council (Registration and Fees) Rules Order of Council 2003

Sch.1, added: SI 2004/2524 Sch.1

Sch.1, amended: SI 2004/2524 Sch.1

Sch.1, referred to: SI 2003/1571 Art.5

Sch.1, substituted: SI 2004/2524 Sch.1

1589. Social Security (Back to Work Bonus and Lone Parent Run-on) (Amendment and Revocation) Regulations 2003

Reg.3, revoked: SI 2004/14 Reg.35

Reg.4, revoked: SI 2004/14 Reg.35

Reg.7, revoked: SI 2004/14 Reg.35

Reg.10, amended: SI 2004/1655 Reg.2

1590. Health Professions Order 2001 (Consequential Amendments) Order 2003

Sch.1 Part 2 para.16, varied: SI 2004/664 Art.11, Art.12, Art.13, Art.14

2003–cont.

1592. Enterprise Act 2002 (Protection of Legitimate Interests) Order 2003
Art.1, amended: SI 2003/3180 Sch.1 para.10
Art.3, amended: SI 2003/3180 Sch.1 para.10
Art.4, amended: SI 2003/3180 Sch.1 para.10
Art.4A, added: SI 2003/3180 Sch.1 para.10
Art.5, amended: SI 2003/3180 Sch.1 para.10
Art.8, amended: SI 2003/3180 Sch.1 para.10
Art.14, amended: SI 2003/3180 Sch.1 para.10
Sch.2 para.5, applied: SI 1997/3032 Sch.2 para.15
Sch.2 para.10, applied: SI 1997/3032 Sch.2 para.15
Sch.2 para.11, applied: SI 1997/3032 Sch.2 para.15
Sch.3 para.1, amended: SI 2003/3180 Sch.1 para.10
Sch.3 para.2, amended: SI 2003/3180 Sch.1 para.10
Sch.4 para.15, amended: SI 2003/3180 Sch.1 para.10

1596. Condensed Milk and Dried Milk (England) Regulations 2003
Reg.8, amended: SI 2004/2145 Reg.7

1617. Strategic Health Authorities (Consultation on Changes) Regulations 2003
Reg.2, amended: SI 2004/696 Art.3

1633. Uncertificated Securities (Amendment) (Eligible Debt Securities) Regulations 2003
Reg.3, revoked (in part): SI 2004/2044 Art.7
Reg.8, revoked (in part): SI 2004/2044 Art.7
Reg.14, revoked (in part): SI 2004/2044 Art.7
Sch.1 Part 3 para.18, revoked (in part): SI 2004/2044 Art.7
Sch.1 Part 3 para.19, revoked (in part): SI 2004/2044 Art.7
Sch.1 Part 3 para.20, revoked (in part): SI 2004/2044 Art.7
Sch.1 Part 3 para.21, revoked (in part): SI 2004/2044 Art.7
Sch.1 Part 3 para.22, revoked (in part): SI 2004/2044 Art.7
Sch.1 Part 3 para.23, revoked (in part): SI 2004/2044 Art.7
Sch.1 Part 3 para.24, revoked (in part): SI 2004/2044 Art.7
Sch.1 Part 3 para.25, revoked (in part): SI 2004/2044 Art.7
Sch.1 Part 3 para.26, revoked (in part): SI 2004/2044 Art.7
Sch.1 Part 3 para.27, revoked (in part): SI 2004/2044 Art.7
Sch.1 Part 3 para.28, revoked (in part): SI 2004/2044 Art.7
Sch.1 Part 3 para.29, revoked (in part): SI 2004/2044 Art.7
Sch.1 Part 3 para.30, revoked (in part): SI 2004/2044 Art.7
Sch.1 Part 3 para.31, revoked (in part): SI 2004/2044 Art.7

2003–cont.

1633. Uncertificated Securities (Amendment) (Eligible Debt Securities) Regulations 2003–cont.
Sch.1 Part 3 para.32, revoked (in part): SI 2004/2044 Art.7
Sch.1 Part 3 para.33, revoked (in part): SI 2004/2044 Art.7
Sch.2 para.2, revoked (in part): SI 2004/2044 Art.7
Sch.2 para.4, revoked (in part): SI 2004/2044 Art.7
Sch.2 para.17, revoked (in part): SI 2004/2044 Art.7

1650. Tax Credits (Provision of Information) (Functions Relating to Health) (No.2) Regulations 2003
referred to: SI 2004/1895 Reg.2

1658. Inheritance Tax (Delivery of Accounts) (Excepted Estates) (Amendment) Regulations 2003
revoked: SI 2004/2543 Reg.11

1660. Employment Equality (Religion or Belief) Regulations 2003
applied: 1996 c.17 s.21, 1996 c.18 s.126, SI 2004/1861 Sch.1 para.22
Reg.2, amended: SI 2003/2828 Reg.3
Reg.9A, added: SI 2003/2828 Reg.3
Reg.20, amended: SI 2004/437 Reg.3
Reg.27, amended: SI 2003/2828 Reg.3
Reg.28, applied: 1996 c.17 s.18, 2002 c.22 Sch.3, Sch.4, Sch.5
Reg.30, amended: SI 2003/2828 Reg.3
Reg.31, applied: SI 1998/3132 Sch.2 para.17
Reg.33, amended: SI 2004/752 Reg.17
Reg.33, applied: SI 1998/3132 Sch.2 para.17
Reg.33, referred to: SI 2004/752 Reg.14
Reg.34, amended: SI 2004/752 Reg.17
Reg.39, amended: SI 2003/2037 Reg.6
Sch.1A para.1, added: SI 2003/2828 Reg.3
Sch.1A para.2, added: SI 2003/2828 Reg.3
Sch.1A para.3, added: SI 2003/2828 Reg.3
Sch.1A para.4, added: SI 2003/2828 Reg.3
Sch.1A para.5, added: SI 2003/2828 Reg.3
Sch.1A para.6, added: SI 2003/2828 Reg.3
Sch.1A para.7, added: SI 2003/2828 Reg.3
Sch.1B para.1, added: SI 2004/437 Reg.3
Sch.1B para.2, added: SI 2004/437 Reg.3
Sch.1B para.3, added: SI 2004/437 Reg.3
Sch.4 Part 1 para.1, applied: SI 1998/3132 Sch.2 para.17
Sch.4 Part 1 para.2, amended: SI 2004/2520 Reg.2

1661. Employment Equality (Sexual Orientation) Regulations 2003
applied: 1996 c.17 s.21, 1996 c.18 s.126, SI 2004/1861 Sch.1 para.22
Reg.2, amended: SI 2003/2827 Reg.3
Reg.7, see *R. (on the application of Amicus) v Secretary of State for Trade and Industry* [2004] EWHC 860, [2004] I.R.L.R. 430 (QBD (Admin Ct)), Richards, J.

NO.

2003–cont.

1661. Employment Equality (Sexual Orientation) Regulations 2003–*cont.*

Reg.9A, added: SI 2003/2827 Reg.3

Reg.20, see *R. (on the application of Amicus) v Secretary of State for Trade and Industry* [2004] EWHC 860, [2004] I.R.L.R. 430 (QBD (Admin Ct)), Richards, J.

Reg.25, see *R. (on the application of Amicus) v Secretary of State for Trade and Industry* [2004] EWHC 860, [2004] I.R.L.R. 430 (QBD (Admin Ct)), Richards, J.

Reg.27, amended: SI 2003/2827 Reg.3

Reg.28, applied: 1996 c.17 s.18, 2002 c.22 Sch.3, Sch.4, Sch.5

Reg.30, amended: SI 2003/2827 Reg.3

Reg.31, applied: SI 1998/3132 Sch.2 para.17

Reg.33, amended: SI 2004/752 Reg.17

Reg.33, applied: SI 1998/3132 Sch.2 para.17

Reg.33, referred to: SI 2004/752 Reg.14

Reg.34, amended: SI 2004/752 Reg.17

Sch.1A para.1, added: SI 2003/2827 Reg.3

Sch.1A para.2, added: SI 2003/2827 Reg.3

Sch.1A para.3, added: SI 2003/2827 Reg.3

Sch.1A para.4, added: SI 2003/2827 Reg.3

Sch.1A para.5, added: SI 2003/2827 Reg.3

Sch.1A para.6, added: SI 2003/2827 Reg.3

Sch.1A para.7, added: SI 2003/2827 Reg.3

Sch.4 Part 1 para.1, applied: SI 1998/3132 Sch.2 para.17

Sch.4 Part 1 para.2, amended: SI 2004/2519 Reg.2

1662. Education (School Teachers Qualifications) (England) Regulations 2003

applied: SI 2001/3071 Reg.5

referred to: SI 2003/1663 Sch.1 para.2

Reg.10, applied: SI 2003/1663 Sch.2 para.6

Sch.2 Part 1 para.7, referred to: SI 2003/1663 Sch.2 para.6

Sch.2 Part 1 para.9, referred to: SI 2003/1663 Sch.2 para.6, SI 2003/1709 Art.7

Sch.2 Part 1 para.10, applied: SI 2003/1709 Art.7

Sch.2 Part 1 para.10, referred to: SI 2003/1663 Sch.2 para.6, SI 2003/1709 Art.7

1663. Education (Specified Work and Registration) (England) Regulations 2003

Sch.2 para.4, applied: SI 2003/1662 Sch.2 para.11

1667. Education Act 2002 (Commencement No.6 and Transitional and Saving Provisions) Order 2003

Sch.1 para.1, revoked: SI 2004/571 Sch.1

1677. Feeding Stuffs (Sampling and Analysis), the Feeding Stuffs (Enforcement) and the Feeding Stuffs (Establishments and Intermediaries) (Amendment) (Wales) Regulations 2003

referred to: SI 1999/1872 Reg.98, Reg.99, Reg.106, SI 1999/2325 Reg.8

NO.

2003–cont.

1701. Social Security Amendment (Students and Income-related Benefits) Regulations 2003

Reg.2, revoked (in part): SI 2003/1914 Reg.3

1706. Home Loss Payments (England) Regulations 2003

revoked: SI 2004/1631 Reg.3

1708. Education (School Teachers Pay and Conditions) (Amendment) Regulations 2003

revoked: SI 2003/2169 Art.1

1711. Immigration (Leave to Remain) (Fees) Regulations 2003

Reg.3, amended: SI 2004/580 Reg.3

Reg.3A, added: SI 2004/580 Reg.4

Reg.5, amended: SI 2004/580 Reg.5

1712. Immigration (Leave to Remain) (Prescribed Forms and Procedures) Regulations 2003

referred to: SI 2004/581 Reg.2

Reg.3A, added: SI 2004/581 Reg.3

Reg.5A, added: SI 2004/2576 Reg.3

Reg.6, amended: SI 2004/581 Reg.4

Reg.6, revoked (in part): SI 2004/581 Reg.4

Reg.10, amended: SI 2004/581 Reg.5

Reg.11, amended: SI 2004/581 Reg.6

Reg.12, amended: SI 2004/581 Reg.7

Sch.1A, added: SI 2004/581 Sch.1

Sch.3A, added: SI 2004/2576 Sch.1

1713. Sweeteners in Food (Amendment) (Wales) Regulations 2003

applied: SI 2004/554 Reg.3

1722. Food (Brazil Nuts) (Emergency Control) (England) Regulations 2003

Reg.2, amended: SI 2004/1265 Reg.4

Reg.6, amended: SI 2003/2988 Reg.2

1723. Animal Gatherings (England) Order 2003

applied: SI 2003/1729 Sch.2 para.1

revoked: SI 2004/1202 Art.14

1729. Disease Control (England) Order 2003

applied: SI 2003/1723 Art.3, SI 2004/1202 Art.4

referred to: SI 2003/2632 Art.23

1736. Collagen and Gelatine (Intra-Community Trade) (England) Regulations 2003

revoked: SI 2003/3003 Reg.3

1745. Charitable Deductions (Approved Schemes) (Amendment) Regulations 2003

applied: SI 1986/2211 Reg.4A

1787. Plant Protection Products (Amendment) Regulations 2003

revoked: SI 2003/3241 Sch.5

1788. Urban Waste Water Treatment (England and Wales) (Amendment) Regulations 2003

Reg.2, applied: SI 1994/2841 Reg.3

NO.

NO.

2003–cont.

1809. Merchant Shipping and Fishing Vessels (Port Waste Reception Facilities) Regulations 2003

Reg.6, applied: SI 1996/3243 Sch.1 para.1

Reg.8, applied: SI 1996/3243 Sch.1 para.1

Reg.9, applied: SI 1996/3243 Sch.1 para.1

Reg.15, applied: SI 1996/3243 Sch.1 para.2

1814. Vehicle Excise Duty (Reduced Pollution) (Amendment) Regulations 2003

revoked: SI 2003/2335 Reg.2

1830. Income Tax (Authorised Unit Trusts) (Interest Distributions) Regulations 2003

applied: SI 2003/3297 Reg.16

Reg.2, varied: SI 1997/1154 Reg.28

Reg.5, varied: SI 1997/1154 Reg.28

Reg.6, varied: SI 1997/1154 Reg.28

Reg.7, varied: SI 1997/1154 Reg.28

Reg.8, varied: SI 1997/1154 Reg.28

Reg.9, referred to: SI 2003/3297 Reg.16

Reg.9, varied: SI 1997/1154 Reg.28

Reg.10, varied: SI 1997/1154 Reg.28

1845. Care Homes (Adult Placements) (Amendment) Regulations 2003

varied: SI 2004/664 Art.11, Art.12, Art.13, Art.14

Reg.1, varied: SI 2004/664 Art.11, Art.12, Art.13, Art.14

1846. Horticultural Produce (Community Grading Rules) (England and Wales) Regulations 2003

revoked: SI 2004/2604 Reg.2

1850. Feeding Stuffs, the Feeding Stuffs (Sampling and Analysis) and the Feeding Stuffs (Enforcement) (Amendment) (Wales) Regulations 2003

applied: SI 1999/2325 Reg.11, Reg.11A, Reg.11B

referred to: SI 1999/1663 Sch.2 para.3

1856. Home Loss Payments (Prescribed Amounts) (Wales) Regulations 2003

revoked: SI 2004/1758 Reg.3

1864. Welfare Food (Amendment No 2) Regulations 2003

revoked: SI 2004/723 Reg.6

1875. Immigration (Provision of Physical Data) Regulations 2003

referred to: SI 2004/474 Reg.2

Reg.2, amended: SI 2004/474 Reg.3

Reg.5, substituted: SI 2004/474 Reg.4

Sch.1, amended: SI 2004/474 Reg.5, SI 2004/1834 Reg.2

1885. Budget (No.2) (Northern Ireland) Order 2003

Art.4, revoked: SI 2004/707 Art.3

Art.5, revoked: SI 2004/707 Art.4

Art.6, revoked: SI 2004/707 Art.5

2003–cont.

1886. Social Security (Jobcentre Plus Interviews for Partners) Regulations 2003

applied: SI 1999/991 Reg.6, Reg.7

Reg.2, amended: SI 2004/959 Reg.27

Reg.2, applied: SI 1999/991 Reg.7

1892. Representation of the People (Form of Canvass) (Scotland) Regulations 2003

applied: SI 2001/497 Reg.26

revoked: SI 2004/1960 Reg.2

1899. Representation of the People (Form of Canvass) (England and Wales) Regulations 2003

revoked: SI 2004/1848 Reg.2

Sch.1 Part II, referred to: SI 2001/341 Reg.26

1900. Communications Act 2003 (Commencement No 1) Order 2003

Art.3, applied: SI 2003/1902, SI 2003/2983

Art.3, revoked (in part): SI 2003/3142 Art.1

1901. Advanced Television Services Regulations 2003

Reg.3, amended: SI 2003/2750 Reg.2

1904. Electronic Communications (Universal Service) Order 2003

Sch.1 para.2, amended: SI 2003/2426 Reg.35

Sch.1 para.3, amended: SI 2003/2426 Reg.35

1905. Export of Goods (Control) (Amendment) Order 2003

revoked: SI 2003/1938 Sch.2

1907. Greater London Authority Elections (Election Addresses) Order 2003

Art.7, applied: SI 2004/294 Reg.7

1910. Education (Independent School Standards) (England) Regulations 2003

Sch.1 para.3, applied: SI 2003/1934 Sch.1 para.3

Sch.1 para.7, applied: SI 2003/1934 Sch.1 para.3

1923. National Minimum Wage Regulations 1999 (Amendment) Regulations 2003

Reg.2, revoked: SI 2004/1930 Reg.8

Reg.3, revoked: SI 2004/1930 Reg.8

1932. Parochial Fees Order 2003

revoked: SI 2004/1890 Art.4

1933. Ecclesiastical Judges, Legal Officers and Others (Fees) Order 2003

applied: SI 2003/1936 para.4

Sch.1, referred to: SI 2004/1888 Art.1

Sch.1 Part I, referred to: SI 2004/1888 Art.1

1937. National Health Service Reform and Health Care Professions Act 2002 (Supplementary, Consequential etc Provisions) Regulations 2003

Sch.1 Part 2 para.5, revoked: SI 2004/865 Sch.2

NO.

2003–cont.

1940. Food (Hot Chilli and Hot Chilli Products) (Emergency Control) (England) Regulations 2003
Reg.2, amended: SI 2004/142 Reg.2
Reg.6, amended: SI 2004/142 Reg.2

1941. Packaging (Essential Requirements) Regulations 2003
referred to: SI 2004/693 Sch.1
Reg.2, amended: SI 2004/1188 Reg.2
Sch.2 para.1, amended: SI 2004/1188 Reg.2
Sch.3 para.1, amended: SI 2004/1188 Reg.2
Sch.4 para.2, amended: SI 2004/693 Sch.2
Sch.4 para.2, revoked (in part): SI 2004/693 Sch.2
Sch.5, added: SI 2004/1188 Reg.2

1945. Child Benefit and Guardian's Allowance (Administration) (Amendment) Regulations 2003
revoked: SI 2003/2106 Reg.2

1956. Food (Pistachios from Iran) (Emergency Control) (England) Regulations 2003
Reg.2, amended: SI 2004/1265 Reg.5

1959. Motor Cycles Etc (Single Vehicle Approval) Regulations 2003
Reg.5, applied: SI 2003/1960 Reg.3, Reg.4
Reg.8, applied: SI 2003/1960 Reg.6
Reg.11, applied: SI 2003/1960 Reg.8
Sch.2, applied: SI 2003/1960 Reg.4
Sch.2, referred to: SI 2003/1960 Reg.4

1962. School Governance (Collaboration) (England) Regulations 2003
disapplied: SI 2004/530 Reg.3

1963. School Staffing (England) Regulations 2003
applied: SI 2003/1962 Reg.3
disapplied: SI 2004/530 Reg.3
Part 1, applied: SI 2003/1965 Reg.26
Part 2, applied: SI 2003/1965 Reg.26
Part 4, applied: SI 2003/1965 Reg.26
Reg.3, varied: SI 2004/2042 Sch.9 para.1
Reg.4, varied: SI 2003/1965 Sch.8 para.2, SI 2004/2042 Sch.9 para.3
Reg.5, varied: SI 2003/1965 Sch.8 para.3, SI 2004/2042 Sch.9 para.2
Reg.6, varied: SI 2004/2042 Sch.9 para.3
Reg.7, varied: SI 2004/2042 Sch.9 para.3
Reg.10, varied: SI 2003/1965 Sch.8 para.1, SI 2004/2042 Sch.9 para.4
Reg.13, varied: SI 2003/1965 Sch.8 para.2
Reg.16, varied: SI 2003/1965 Sch.8 para.4, SI 2004/2042 Sch.9 para.5
Reg.17, varied: SI 2003/1965 Sch.8 para.5, SI 2004/2042 Sch.9 para.6
Reg.18, applied: SI 2003/1964 Art.3
Reg.18, varied: SI 2003/1965 Sch.8 para.6, SI 2004/2042 Sch.9 para.7, Sch.9 para.8
Reg.19, varied: SI 2004/2042 Sch.9 para.9
Reg.22, varied: SI 2004/2042 Sch.9 para.10
Reg.25, varied: SI 2004/2042 Sch.9 para.3
Reg.27, varied: SI 2004/2042 Sch.9 para.11

NO.

2003–cont.

1963. School Staffing (England) Regulations 2003*–cont.*
Reg.28, varied: SI 2003/1965 Sch.8 para.7, Sch.8 para.8, SI 2004/2042 Sch.9 para.12
Reg.29, varied: SI 2003/1965 Sch.8 para.7
Reg.30, varied: SI 2003/1965 Sch.8 para.7, Sch.8 para.9, SI 2004/2042 Sch.9 para.13
Reg.31, varied: SI 2003/1965 Sch.8 para.7, Sch.8 para.9, SI 2004/2042 Sch.9 para.13
Reg.33, varied: SI 2004/2042 Sch.9 para.14
Sch.1, applied: SI 2003/1965 Reg.26
Sch.1 para.2, amended: SI 2003/2725 Reg.2
Sch.1 para.2, varied: SI 2003/1965 Sch.8 para.5, Sch.8 para.7, SI 2004/2042 Sch.9 para.6

1964. Education (Modification of Enactments Relating to Employment) (England) Order 2003
Sch.1, amended: SI 2004/2325 Art.2

1965. Federation of Schools (Community Schools, Community Special Schools, Voluntary Controlled Schools and Maintained Nursery Schools) (England) Regulations 2003
disapplied: SI 2004/530 Reg.3
revoked: SI 2004/2042 Reg.2
Reg.13, amended: SI 2003/2133 Reg.2

1966. Disease Control (Wales) Order 2003
applied: SI 2003/1967 Art.3, SI 2004/1803 Art.4
referred to: SI 2004/996 Art.23

1967. Animal Gatherings (Wales) Order 2003
applied: SI 2003/1966 Sch.2 para.1
revoked: SI 2004/1803 Art.14

1968. Transport of Animals (Cleansing and Disinfection) (Wales) (No.3) Order 2003
applied: SI 2003/1966 Art.20

1970. Education (School Performance Targets) (Amendment) (England) Regulations 2003
revoked: SI 2004/2858 Sch.2

1977. Borough of Sefton (Electoral Changes) Order 2003
varied: SI 2004/222 Art.2

1979. Borough of St Helens (Electoral Changes) Order 2003
varied: SI 2004/222 Art.2

1980. Borough of Wirral (Electoral Changes) Order 2003
varied: SI 2004/222 Art.2

1987. Service Charges (Consultation Requirements) (England) Regulations 2003
Reg.4, amended: SI 2004/2665 Reg.2, SI 2004/2939 Reg.2

NO.

2003–cont.

1993. Public Interest Disclosure (Prescribed Persons) (Amendment) Order 2003

Sch.1, varied: SI 2004/664 Art.11, Art.12, Art.13, Art.14

1994. Education (Mandatory Awards) Regulations 2003

applied: SI 2002/3200 Sch.3 para.9

Reg.2, amended: SI 2004/1038 Reg.4

Reg.6, amended: SI 2004/1038 Reg.5

Reg.6, revoked (in part): SI 2004/1038 Reg.5

Reg.21, amended: SI 2004/1038 Sch.1

Sch.1, amended: SI 2004/1038 Reg.6, Sch.1

Sch.2 Part 1 para.2, amended: SI 2004/1038 Sch.1

Sch.2 Part 2 para.5, amended: SI 2004/1038 Sch.1

Sch.2 Part 2 para.7, amended: SI 2004/1038 Sch.1

Sch.2 Part 2 para.9, amended: SI 2004/1038 Sch.1

Sch.2 Part 3 para.12, amended: SI 2004/1038 Sch.1

Sch.2 Part 3 para.13, amended: SI 2004/1038 Sch.1, SI 2004/1792 Reg.2

Sch.2 Part 3 para.14, amended: SI 2004/1038 Sch.1

Sch.3 Part 1 para.1, amended: SI 2004/1038 Sch.1

Sch.3 Part 2 para.4, amended: SI 2004/1038 Sch.1

Sch.3 Part 2 para.6, amended: SI 2004/1038 Sch.1

Sch.3 Part 3 para.8, amended: SI 2004/1038 Sch.1

Sch.4 para.2, amended: SI 2004/1038 Sch.1

Sch.5 para.4, amended: SI 2004/1038 Sch.1

1999. Non-Domestic Rating (Alteration of Lists and Appeals) (Amendment) (England) Regulations 2003

applied: SI 1993/291 Reg.13

2000. Non-Domestic Rating (Transitional Period) (Amendment) (England) Regulations 2003

applied: SI 1990/608 Reg.18

2042. Mental Health (Correspondence of Patients, Patient Advocacy and Liaison Services) Regulations 2003

Reg.2, amended: SI 2004/696 Sch.1 para.49

2074. Food (Peanuts from Egypt) (Emergency Control) (England) Regulations 2003

Reg.2, amended: SI 2004/1265 Reg.6

2075. Meat Products (England) Regulations 2003

varied: SI 2003/3295 Reg.3

Sch.2, applied: SI 1996/1499 Sch.4A para.1

2076. Capital Allowances (Environmentally Beneficial Plant and Machinery) Order 2003

Art.2, amended: SI 2004/2094 Art.2

NO.

2003–cont.

2076. Capital Allowances (Environmentally Beneficial Plant and Machinery) Order 2003–cont.

Art.3, amended: SI 2004/2094 Art.2

2092. Land Registration Fee Order 2003

revoked: SI 2004/595 Art.15

2093. Enterprise Act 2002 (Commencement No 4 and Transitional Provisions and Savings) Order 2003

Sch.2, amended: SI 2003/3340 Art.2

2098. Leasehold Valuation Tribunals (Fees)(England) Regulations 2003

Reg.4, applied: SI 2003/2099 Reg.7

Reg.5, applied: SI 2003/2099 Reg.7

2099. Leasehold Valuation Tribunals (Procedure) (England) Regulations 2003

Reg.1, amended: SI 2004/3098 Reg.3

Reg.3, amended: SI 2004/3098 Reg.4

Reg.13, amended: SI 2004/3098 Reg.5

Reg.17, amended: SI 2004/3098 Reg.6

Sch.1 para.8, added: SI 2004/3098 Reg.7

Sch.2 para.1, amended: SI 2004/3098 Reg.8

Sch.2 para.6, amended: SI 2004/3098 Reg.8

Sch.2 para.7, added: SI 2004/3098 Reg.8

2104. Food Protection (Emergency Prohibitions) (Scallops) (England) Order 2003

referred to: SI 2003/2185

revoked: SI 2003/2185 Art.2

2121. Air Quality Limit Values Regulations 2003

Reg.2, amended: SI 2004/2888 Reg.4, Reg.5

Reg.9, amended: SI 2004/2888 Reg.5

Reg.11, amended: SI 2004/2888 Reg.4

Reg.16, revoked (in part): SI 2004/2888 Reg.4

Sch.2 Part II, amended: SI 2004/2888 Reg.5

2123. Patients Forums (Membership and Procedure) Regulations 2003

Reg.1, amended: SI 2004/696 Art.3, Sch.1 para.50, SI 2004/865 Sch.1 para.38

Reg.2, amended: SI 2004/540 Reg.4, SI 2004/696 Art.3

Reg.4, amended: SI 2004/696 Art.3, Sch.1 para.50, SI 2004/865 Sch.1 para.38

Reg.6, amended: SI 2004/540 Reg.4

2124. Patients Forums (Functions) Regulations 2003

Reg.2, amended: SI 2004/696 Art.3

Reg.3, amended: SI 2004/540 Reg.2, SI 2004/696 Art.3, Sch.1 para.51, SI 2004/865 Sch.1 para.39

Reg.3, applied: SI 1986/975 Sch.1 para.2, SI 1992/635 Sch.2 para.51, SI 1992/661 Sch.1 para.2, SI 1992/662 Sch.2 para.2, SI 2004/291 Sch.6 para.90, SI 2004/627 Sch.5 para.84

Reg.5, amended: SI 2004/696 Sch.1 para.51

Reg.6, amended: SI 2004/540 Reg.2

Reg.7, amended: SI 2004/696 Art.3

2003–cont.

2124. Patients Forums (Functions) Regulations 2003–*cont.*

Reg.8, amended: SI 2004/696 Art.3, Sch.1 para.51

2133. Federation of Schools (Community Schools, Community Special Schools, Voluntary Controlled Schools and Maintained Nursery Schools) (England) (Amendment) Regulations 2003

disapplied: SI 2004/530 Reg.3

revoked: SI 2004/2042 Reg.2

2149. Robert Jones and Agnes Hunt Orthopaedic and District Hospital National Health Service Trust (Establishment) Amendment Order 2003

revoked: 2003 c.43 s.7

2150. University Hospitals of Leicester National Health Service Trust (Establishment) Amendment Order 2003

revoked: 2003 c.43 s.7

2151. Agricultural Holdings (Units of Production) (England) Order 2003

revoked: SI 2004/1811 Art.3

2156. Borough of Knowsley (Electoral Changes) Order 2003

varied: SI 2004/222 Art.2

2169. Education (School Teachers Pay and Conditions) (No.2) Order 2003

revoked: SI 2004/2142 Art.2

2186. M6 Toll (Collection of Tolls) Regulations 2003

applied: SI 1982/1163 Reg.7

2208. Crime Prevention (Designated Areas) Order 2003

Art.2, amended: SI 2004/2674 Art.2

2209. Terrorism (United Nations Measures) Order 2001 (Amendment No 2) Regulations 2003

revoked: SI 2003/2430 Reg.2

2254. Food (Brazil Nuts) (Emergency Control) (Wales) Regulations 2003

Reg.6, amended: SI 2004/245 Reg.2

2261. Sheep Annual Premium and Suckler Cow Premium Quotas Regulations 2003

Reg.4, applied: SSI 2004/381 Reg.4

Reg.6, applied: SSI 2004/381 Reg.4

Reg.8, applied: SSI 2004/381 Reg.4

Reg.12, applied: SSI 2004/381 Reg.4

2275. Housing Benefit and Council Tax Benefit (State Pension Credit and Miscellaneous Amendments) Regulations 2003

Reg.5, amended: SI 2003/2526 Reg.2

2276. Delayed Discharges (Mental Health Care) (England) Order 2003

Art.2, applied: SI 2003/2277 Reg.3

2003–cont.

2288. Food (Pistachios from Iran) (Emergency Control) (Wales) (No.2) Regulations 2003

Reg.6, amended: SI 2004/245 Reg.3

Reg.7, amended: SI 2004/245 Reg.3

2314. Religious Character of Schools (Designation Procedure) (Independent Schools) (England) Regulations 2003

applied: SI 2004/72, SI 2004/354, SI 2004/1378, SI 2004/2089

referred to: SI 2003/3108, SI 2003/3284

2316. Goods Infringing Intellectual Property Rights (Customs) Regulations 2003

revoked: SI 2004/1473 Sch.1

2317. Medicines (Child Safety) Regulations 2003

Reg.1, amended: SI 2004/1771 Sch.1 para.15

2323. Care Standards Act 2000 (Domiciliary Care Agencies and Nurses Agencies) (Amendment) (England) Regulations 2003

varied: SI 2004/664 Art.11, Art.12, Art.13, Art.14

Reg.4, varied: SI 2004/664 Art.11, Art.12, Art.13, Art.14

2327. Kimberley Process (Fees) Regulations 2003

revoked: SI 2004/686 Reg.5

2344. West Midlands Ambulance Service National Health Service Trust (Establishment) Amendment Order 2003

revoked: 2003 c.43 s.7

2345. Sandwell and West Birmingham Hospitals National Health Service Trust (Establishment) Amendment Order 2003

revoked: 2003 c.43 s.7

2346. Shrewsbury and Telford Hospital National Health Service Trust (Establishment) and the Princess Royal Hospital National Health Service Trust and the Royal Shrewsbury Hospitals National Health Service Trust (Dissolution) Order 2003

revoked: 2003 c.43 s.7

Art.3, amended: SI 2004/2895 Art.2

Art.4, amended: SI 2004/2895 Art.3

2382. National Health Service (Travel Expenses and Remission of Charges) Regulations 2003

Reg.2, amended: SI 2004/663 Reg.5

Reg.3, amended: SI 2004/696 Art.3, SI 2004/865 Sch.1 para.40

Reg.3, applied: SI 1992/662 Sch.2 para.11B

Reg.4, referred to: SI 1992/662 Sch.2 para.11B

Reg.5, amended: SI 2004/663 Reg.5, SI 2004/936 Reg.2

Reg.5, applied: SI 1992/662 Sch.2 para.11B

2003–cont.

2382. National Health Service (Travel Expenses and Remission of Charges) Regulations 2003–*cont.*

Reg.12, amended: SI 2004/696 Art.3

Reg.14, amended: SI 2004/663 Reg.5

Sch.1, amended: SI 2004/663 Reg.6

2397. Police and Criminal Evidence Act 1984 (Remote Reviews of Detention) (Specified Police Stations) Regulations 2003

revoked: SI 2004/1503 Reg.2

2399. Housing Benefit (General) (Local Housing Allowance) Amendment Regulations 2003

Reg.14, revoked: SI 2004/14 Reg.36

Sch.1, referred to: SI 2004/781 Reg.5

2426. Privacy and Electronic Communications (EC Directive) Regulations 2003

applied: SI 2003/1904 Sch.1 para.2, Sch.1 para.3

Reg.26, amended: SI 2004/1039 Reg.2

2427. Cambridgeshire and Peterborough Mental Health Partnership National Health Service Trust (Establishment) and the Lifespan Health Care Cambridge National Health Service Trust and the North West Anglia Health Care National Health Service Trust (Diss 2003

revoked: 2003 c.43 s.7

2430. Terrorism (United Nations Measures) Order 2001 (Amendment No 3) Regulations 2003

revoked: SI 2004/2309 Reg.2

2434. Royal Cornwall Hospitals and West Cornwall Hospital National Health Service Trust (Establishment) Amendment Order 2003

revoked: 2003 c.43 s.7

2438. Employment Zones Regulations 2003

applied: SI 1996/207 Reg.75, SI 2004/934 Reg.3

Reg.1, amended: SI 2004/1043 Reg.2

Reg.2, amended: SI 2004/1043 Reg.2

Reg.7, added: SI 2004/1043 Reg.2

Reg.8, added: SI 2004/1043 Reg.2

2439. Social Security (Incapacity Benefit Work-focused Interviews) Regulations 2003

disapplied: SI 2002/1703 Reg.8

2453. Education (Information About Post-16 Individual Pupils) (Wales) Regulations 2003

revoked: SI 2003/3237 Reg.1

2454. Weighing Equipment (Automatic Rail-weighbridges) Regulations 2003

applied: SI 1963/1710 Reg.1

2003–cont.

2455. Food (Hot Chilli and Hot Chilli Products) (Emergency Control) (Wales) Regulations 2003

Reg.2, amended: SI 2004/392 Reg.2

Reg.6, amended: SI 2004/245 Reg.4

2458. Education (Teachers' Qualifications and Health Standards) (Amendment No 2) (Wales) Regulations 2003

revoked: SI 2004/1729 Sch.1 Part 1

2494. Income Tax (Employments) (Amendment) Regulations 2003

revoked: SI 2003/2682 Sch.2

2495. Income Tax (Incentive Payments for Voluntary Electronic Communication of PAYE Returns) Regulations 2003

applied: SI 1993/744 Reg.3, SI 2003/2682 Reg.99

2498. Copyright and Related Rights Regulations 2003

applied: SI 2003/2500 Reg.2

2505. City of Liverpool (Electoral Changes) Order 2003

varied: SI 2004/222 Art.2

2506. Borough of Stockton-on-Tees (Electoral Changes) Order 2003

varied: SI 2004/222 Art.2

2507. City of Coventry (Electoral Changes) Order 2003

varied: SI 2004/222 Art.2

2508. Borough of Solihull (Electoral Changes) Order 2003

varied: SI 2004/222 Art.2

2509. City of Wolverhampton (Electoral Changes) Order 2003

varied: SI 2004/222 Art.2

2510. Borough of Sandwell (Electoral Changes) Order 2003

varied: SI 2004/222 Art.2

2511. Borough of Walsall (Electoral Changes) Order 2003

varied: SI 2004/222 Art.2

2527. Nurses Agencies (Wales) Regulations 2003

Reg.2, amended: SI 2004/1771 Sch.1 para.14

Reg.12, amended: SI 2003/3054 Reg.2

Sch.2 para.2, amended: SI 2004/2414 Reg.5

Sch.2 para.10, added: SI 2004/2414 Reg.5

Sch.3 para.4, amended: SI 2004/2414 Reg.5

Sch.3 para.14, added: SI 2004/2414 Reg.5

2529. Oil and Fibre Plant Seeds (Amendment) (Wales) Regulations 2003

revoked: SI 2004/2881 Reg.32

2531. Disability Discrimination (Prescribed Periods for Accessibility Strategies and Plans for Schools) (Wales) Regulations 2003

applied: SI 2003/3234 Sch.1 para.5

NO.

2003–cont.

2573. Insurance Companies (Taxation of Reinsurance Business) (Amendment No 2) Regulations 2003

Reg.4, revoked (in part): SI 2004/2189 Reg.6, SI 2004/2257 Reg.6

Reg.5, revoked (in part): SI 2004/2189 Reg.6, SI 2004/2257 Reg.6

Reg.9, revoked (in part): SI 2004/2189 Reg.6, SI 2004/2257 Reg.6

2577. Olive Oil (Marketing Standards) Regulations 2003

Reg.2, amended: SI 2004/2661 Reg.2

Reg.4, amended: SI 2004/2661 Reg.2

Reg.6, amended: SI 2004/2661 Reg.2

Reg.8, amended: SI 2004/2661 Reg.2

2599. Police (Conduct) (Amendment) Regulations 2003

revoked: SI 2004/645 Reg.2

2601. National Crime Squad (Dispensation from Requirement to Investigate Complaints) Regulations 2003

revoked: SI 2004/643 Reg.29

Reg.4, applied: SI 2004/671 Art.4

2604. Council Tax and Non-Domestic Rating (Electronic Communications) (England) Order 2003

Art.1, amended: SI 2003/3052 Art.3

2613. Council Tax and Non-Domestic Rating (Demand Notices) (England) Regulations 2003

referred to: SI 2003/3081 Reg.2

Reg.1, amended: SI 2003/3081 Reg.3

Sch.1 para.8A, added: SI 2003/3081 Reg.4

Sch.1 para.9, amended: SI 2003/3081 Reg.4

Sch.1 para.10, substituted: SI 2003/3081 Reg.4

Sch.1 para.17, amended: SI 2003/3081 Reg.4

Sch.2 Part 1 para.6, amended: SI 2003/3081 Reg.5

Sch.2 Part 3 para.3, amended: SI 2003/3081 Reg.5

Sch.3 Part 3 para.4, amended: SI 2003/3081 Reg.6

2624. National Health Service (Amendments concerning Supplementary and Independent Nurse Prescribing) (Wales) Regulations 2003

Reg.3, revoked: SI 2004/1016 Sch.2

2627. Democratic Republic of the Congo (Restrictive Measures) (Overseas Territories) Order 2003

varied: SI 2004/2036 Art.2

2635. End-of-Life Vehicles Regulations 2003

Reg.18, applied: SSI 2003/593 Sch.1 para.2

Sch.5 Part 1 para.1, referred to: SI 1994/1056 Sch.3 para.41

Sch.5 Part 2 para.1, referred to: SI 1994/1056 Sch.3 para.41

NO.

2003–cont.

2644. National Health Service (Personal Medical Services) (Services List) and the (General Medical Services Supplementary List) and (General Medical Services) Amendment Regulations 2003

applied: SI 2001/3740 Reg.11

revoked: SI 2004/585 Sch.2

varied: SI 2004/585 Sch.1 para.9

Reg.6, referred to: SI 2004/865 Art.60, Art.61

Reg.10, applied: SI 2001/3740 Reg.4, SI 2004/585 Reg.23

Reg.21, applied: SI 1992/635 Sch.2 para.23A, SI 2001/3740 Reg.3

2647. Food (Provisions relating to Labelling) (England) Regulations 2003

Reg.5, referred to: SI 1996/1499 Reg.50

Reg.6, referred to: SI 1996/1499 Reg.50

Reg.8, revoked: SI 2004/2335 Reg.9

2682. Income Tax (Pay As You Earn) Regulations 2003

applied: SI 2001/1004 Reg.67, SI 2004/2502 Reg.2

Reg.35, applied: SI 2001/1004 Sch.4 para.6, Sch.4 para.26

Reg.66, applied: SI 2002/2172 Reg.6

Reg.67, applied: SI 2001/1004 Sch.4 para.9, SI 2002/2172 Reg.6

Reg.68, applied: SI 1993/743 Reg.49, SI 2001/1004 Reg.90H, Sch.4 para.11

Reg.72, amended: SI 2004/851 Reg.3

Reg.72A, added: SI 2004/851 Reg.4

Reg.72B, added: SI 2004/851 Reg.4

Reg.72C, added: SI 2004/851 Reg.4

Reg.72D, added: SI 2004/851 Reg.4

Reg.73, applied: SI 1993/743 Reg.53, SI 2001/1004 Reg.90N, SI 2004/1864 Reg.8

Reg.73, referred to: SI 2002/2172 Reg.6

Reg.81, amended: SI 2004/851 Reg.5

Reg.81A, added: SI 2004/851 Reg.6

Reg.98, applied: SI 2001/1004 Sch.4 para.2

Reg.99, applied: SI 2001/1004 Sch.4 para.2

Reg.199, applied: SI 1993/743 Reg.49, SI 2001/1004 Reg.90H

Reg.205, applied: SI 2001/1004 Reg.90N, Reg.90P

Reg.206, applied: SI 2001/1004 Reg.90N

2693. Income Support (General) (Standard Interest Rate Amendment) Regulations 2003

revoked: SI 2004/440 Reg.3

2713. Access to the Countryside (Exclusions and Restrictions) (England) Regulations 2003

Reg.9, referred to: SI 2002/1836 Reg.8A

Reg.15, referred to: SI 2002/1836 Reg.8A

Reg.16, referred to: SI 2002/1836 Reg.8A

2756. Animal By-Products (Wales) Regulations 2003

applied: SI 2002/1416 Reg.13, Reg.40

NO.

2003–cont.

2756. Animal By-Products (Wales) Regulations 2003–*cont.*
Reg.26, applied: SI 2004/1430 Reg.22
Reg.26, referred to: SI 2004/1430 Reg.22

2758. Channel Tunnel (Alcoholic Liquor and Tobacco Products) Order 2003
Art.2, amended: SI 2004/1004 Art.3
Sch.1, added: SI 2004/1004 Art.4

2760. Stamp Duty and Stamp Duty Land Tax (Variation of the Finance Act 2003) Regulations 2003
revoked: SI 2003/2816 Reg.3

2761. Weighing Equipment (Automatic Catchweighing Instruments) Regulations 2003
applied: SI 1963/1710 Reg.1
referred to: SI 2000/932 Reg.3

2763. Pigs (Records, Identification and Movement) (Interim Measures) (Wales) (No.2) (Amendment) (No.2) Order 2003
revoked: SI 2004/996 Art.28

2764. Export of Goods, Transfer of Technology and Provision of Technical Assistance (Control) Order 2003
Art.11, amended: SI 2004/2741 Art.2
Sch.1 Part I paraML.21, amended: SI 2004/1050 Art.2
Sch.1 Part II paraPL.8001, applied: SI 2003/2765 Sch.1 para.1
Sch.5, substituted: SI 2004/2561 Art.2

2767. Borough of Dudley (Electoral Changes) Order 2003
varied: SI 2004/222 Art.2

2769. City of Birmingham (Electoral Changes) Order 2003
varied: SI 2004/222 Art.2

2773. NHSU Regulations 2003
Reg.1, amended: SI 2004/696 Art.3, SI 2004/865 Sch.1 para.41
Reg.3, amended: SI 2004/696 Art.3, SI 2004/865 Sch.1 para.41

2780. Horse Passports (England) Regulations 2003
revoked: SI 2004/1397 Reg.26

2816. Stamp Duty and Stamp Duty Land Tax (Variation of the Finance Act 2003) (No.2) Regulations 2003
referred to: 2004 c.12 Sch.39 para.6, Sch.39 para.11, Sch.39 para.14
revoked: 2004 c.12 Sch.39 para.14

2818. Nationality, Immigration and Asylum Act 2002 (Juxtaposed Controls) Order 2003
Sch.1, referred to: SI 2002/2817 Reg.5

2824. National Health Service (Improved Access, Quality Information Preparation and Violent Patients Schemes) (England) Regulations 2003
revoked: SI 2004/865 Sch.2

NO.

2003–cont.

2862. General Insurance Reserves (Tax) (Amendment) Regulations 2003
Reg.8, applied: SI 2001/1757 Reg.10

2863. National Health Service (General Medical Services etc.) (Patients Forums) Amendment Regulations 2003
Reg.2, revoked: SI 2004/865 Sch.2

2910. Food (Peanuts from Egypt) (Emergency Control) (Wales) Regulations 2003
Reg.6, amended: SI 2004/245 Reg.4

2951. Merchant Shipping (Fire Protection) Regulations (Amendment) Regulations 2003
applied: SI 1998/1012 Reg.1

2957. Medicines (Products for Animal Use Fees) (Amendment) Regulations 2003
revoked: SI 2004/2750 Reg.18

2959. Education Act 2002 (Transitional Provisions and Consequential Amendments) (No.2) (Wales) Regulations 2003
Reg.7, applied: SI 2003/3227 Reg.11, SI 2003/3246 Reg.10

2994. Department for Transport (Driver Licensing and Vehicle Registration Fees) Order 2003
applied: SI 2004/265
enabled: SI 2003/3110

3011. Council Tax (Prescribed Classes of Dwellings) (England) Regulations 2003
referred to: SI 2003/2613 Sch.1 para.9
Reg.2, amended: SI 2004/926 Reg.2
Reg.6, amended: SI 2004/926 Reg.2
Sch.1 para.2A, added: SI 2004/926 Reg.2

3037. Cocoa and Chocolate Products (Wales) Regulations 2003
applied: SI 2004/554 Reg.3

3041. Fruit Juices and Fruit Nectars (Wales) Regulations 2003
applied: SI 2004/554 Reg.3

3042. Natural Mineral Water, Spring Water and Bottled Drinking Water (Amendment) (Wales) Regulations 2003
Reg.17, applied: SI 1999/1540 Reg.2
Reg.18, applied: SI 1999/1540 Reg.2
Reg.19, applied: SI 1999/1540 Reg.2
Reg.20, applied: SI 1999/1540 Reg.2
Reg.21, applied: SI 1999/1540 Reg.2

3044. Honey (Wales) Regulations 2003
applied: SI 2004/554 Reg.3

3047. Specified Sugar Products (Wales) Regulations 2003
applied: SI 2001/1440 Reg.5, SI 2004/554 Reg.3

NO.

2003–cont.

3049. Merchant Shipping (Working Time Inland Waterways) Regulations 2003
applied: 1996 c.17 s.21, SI 2002/2055 Reg.3, SI 2002/2125 Reg.3
disapplied: SI 1998/1833 Reg.18
referred to: 1996 c.18 s.45A, s.101A, s.104
Reg.18, applied: 1996 c.17 s.18

3053. Condensed Milk and Dried Milk (Wales) Regulations 2003
applied: SI 2004/554 Reg.3
Reg.8, amended: SI 2004/2731 Reg.7

3059. NHS Professionals Special Health Authority (Establishment and Constitution) Order 2003
Art.6, added: SI 2004/648 Art.2, SI 2004/951 Art.3
Art.7, added: SI 2004/648 Art.2, SI 2004/951 Art.3
Art.8, added: SI 2004/648 Art.2, SI 2004/951 Art.3
Sch.1, added: SI 2004/648 Sch.1, SI 2004/951 Sch.1
Sch.2, added: SI 2004/648 Sch.1, SI 2004/951 Sch.1

3060. NHS Professionals Special Health Authority Regulations 2003
Reg.1, amended: SI 2004/664 Art.4, SI 2004/696 Art.3, Sch.1 para.52, SI 2004/865 Sch.1 para.42
Reg.3, amended: SI 2004/696 Art.3, Sch.1 para.52

3075. Money Laundering Regulations 2003
applied: SI 2001/341 Reg.114
referred to: 1998 c.47 Sch.3 para.25
Reg.3, applied: SI 2003/171 Art.2
Reg.21, applied: 1994 c.23 s.83

3085. Fireworks Regulations 2003
revoked: SI 2004/1836 Reg.2

3087. City of Wakefield (Electoral Changes) Order 2003
varied: SI 2004/222 Art.2

3088. Borough of Calderdale (Electoral Changes) Order 2003
varied: SI 2004/222 Art.2

3089. City of Leeds (Electoral Changes) Order 2003
varied: SI 2004/222 Art.2

3090. Borough of Barnsley (Electoral Changes) Order 2003
varied: SI 2004/222 Art.2
Art.1, amended: SI 2004/128 Art.2
Art.2, amended: SI 2004/128 Art.2
Art.4, amended: SI 2004/128 Art.2
Art.7, amended: SI 2004/128 Art.2

3091. Borough of Kirklees (Electoral Changes) Order 2003
varied: SI 2004/222 Art.2

3096. Regulatory Reform (Business Tenancies) (England and Wales) Order 2003
applied: SI 2004/1005 Sch.2

NO.

2003–cont.

3096. Regulatory Reform (Business Tenancies) (England and Wales) Order 2003–*cont.*
Art.29, applied: SI 2004/1306 r.20
Sch.1, applied: 1954 c.56 s.38A
Sch.2 para.1, applied: 1954 c.56 s.38A
Sch.2 para.2, applied: 1954 c.56 s.38A
Sch.2 para.3, applied: 1954 c.56 s.38A
Sch.2 para.4, applied: 1954 c.56 s.38A
Sch.2 para.5, applied: 1954 c.56 s.38A
Sch.2 para.6, applied: 1954 c.56 s.38A
Sch.2 para.7, applied: 1954 c.56 s.38A
Sch.2 para.8, applied: 1954 c.56 s.38A
Sch.3, applied: 1954 c.56 s.38A

3102. Export (Penalty) Regulations 2003
Reg.6, referred to: SI 1986/590 r.8A
Reg.9, applied: SI 1986/590 r.20

3103. Extradition Act 2003 (Commencement and Savings) Order 2003
Art.3, substituted: SI 2003/3312 Art.2
Art.5, substituted: SI 2003/3258 Art.2

3112. Financial Collateral Arrangements Regulations 2003
revoked: SI 2003/3226 Reg.2

3118. LEA Budget, Schools Budget and Individual Schools Budget (Wales) Regulations 2003
Sch.1 para.9, amended: SI 2004/696 Art.3
Sch.2 para.30, referred to: SI 2004/2506 Reg.18

3132. Powys (Llanbadarn Fynydd, Llanbister and Abbey Cwmhir) Order 2003
varied: SI 2004/218 Art.2

3134. Denbighshire (Rhuddlan, Rhyl, Dyserth and Prestatyn) Order 2003
varied: SI 2004/218 Art.2

3135. Merchant Shipping (Liability of Shipowners and Others) (Rate of Interest) (Amendment) Order 2003
revoked: SI 2004/931 Art.3

3137. Cardiff (Llandaff North, Whitchurch, Llanishen, Lisvane, Ely and St Fagans Communities) Order 2003
varied: SI 2004/218 Art.2

3142. Office of Communications Act 2002 (Commencement No 3) and Communications Act 2003 (Commencement No 2) Order 2003
referred to: SI 2004/307 Art.1, SI 2004/308 Art.1
Art.4, amended: SI 2004/545 Art.2, SI 2004/697 Art.2
Art.4, revoked (in part): SI 2004/1492 Art.2
Sch.2, amended: SI 2004/545 Art.2, SI 2004/697 Art.2

3146. Local Authorities (Capital Finance and Accounting) (England) Regulations 2003
Reg.1, amended: SI 2004/534 Reg.2, SI 2004/3055 Reg.2

2003–cont.

3146. Local Authorities (Capital Finance and Accounting) (England) Regulations 2003–*cont.*

Reg.12, amended: SI 2004/534 Reg.3, SI 2004/3055 Reg.3

Reg.13, substituted: SI 2004/534 Reg.4

Reg.20A, added: SI 2004/3055 Reg.4

Reg.22, amended: SI 2004/3055 Reg.5

Reg.25, amended: SI 2004/534 Reg.5

Reg.28, amended: SI 2004/3055 Reg.6

Reg.33, amended: SI 2004/3055 Reg.7

3170. LEA Budget, Schools Budget and Individual Schools Budget (England) Regulations 2003

Sch.2 para.1, amended: SI 2004/659 Reg.2

Sch.2 para.1, varied: SI 2004/659 Sch.1, SI 2004/804 Reg.2

Sch.2 para.2, varied: SI 2004/657 Art.3

Sch.2 para.3, varied: SI 2004/592 Art.3

Sch.3 para.15, amended: SI 2004/659 Reg.2

Sch.3 para.15, referred to: SI 2003/3247 Reg.13

Sch.3 para.15, varied: SI 2004/592 Art.4

Sch.3 para.25, varied: SI 2004/657 Art.3

Sch.3 para.26, referred to: SI 2003/3247 Reg.13

Sch.3 para.28, referred to: SI 2003/3247 Reg.13

Sch.3 para.33, referred to: SI 2003/3247 Reg.20

3177. Products of Animal Origin (Third Country Imports) (England) Regulations 2003

revoked: SI 2004/1214 Reg.68

Reg.2, amended: SI 2004/82 Reg.2

Reg.62, substituted: SI 2004/390 Reg.3

Reg.65, amended: SI 2004/390 Reg.4

3190. Commission for Social Care Inspection (Membership) Regulations 2003

Reg.1, amended: SI 2004/696 Sch.1 para.53, SI 2004/865 Sch.1 para.43

Reg.4, amended: SI 2004/696 Art.3, Sch.1 para.53, SI 2004/865 Sch.1 para.43

3192. Broadcasting (Guernsey) Order 2003

Sch.2, revoked (in part): SI 2004/715 Art.2

3193. Broadcasting (Isle of Man) Order 2003

Sch.1 para.17, amended: SI 2004/309 Sch.1 Part 1

Sch.1 para.18, amended: SI 2004/309 Sch.1 Part 1

3195. Communications (Bailiwick of Guernsey) Order 2003

Art.1, amended: SI 2004/715 Sch.1 para.1

Art.6, amended: SI 2004/1116 Art.2

Sch.2 para.2, substituted: SI 2004/715 Sch.1 para.2

Sch.2 para.65, revoked: SI 2004/1116 Art.2

2003–cont.

3196. Wireless Telegraphy (Jersey) Order 2003

Sch.1 Part I para.5, amended: SI 2004/308 Sch.2 Part 1

3197. Communications (Jersey) Order 2003

Art.1, amended: SI 2004/716 Art.3

Art.6, amended: SI 2004/1114 Art.2

Sch.2 para.1, amended: SI 2004/308 Sch.2 Part 3

Sch.2 para.20, amended: SI 2004/308 Sch.2 Part 3

Sch.2 para.23, amended: SI 2004/308 Sch.2 Part 3

Sch.2 para.33, revoked: SI 2004/308 Sch.2 Part 3

Sch.2 para.58, amended: SI 2004/308 Sch.2 Part 3

Sch.2 para.62, revoked: SI 2004/1114 Art.2

Sch.2 para.69, amended: SI 2004/308 Sch.2 Part 3

Sch.2 para.76, amended: SI 2004/308 Sch.2 Part 3

Sch.2 para.82, amended: SI 2004/308 Sch.2 Part 3

Sch.2 para.86, amended: SI 2004/308 Sch.2 Part 3

Sch.2 para.94, amended: SI 2004/308 Sch.2 Part 3

Sch.2 para.106, substituted: SI 2004/308 Sch.2 Part 3

Sch.2 para.108, amended: SI 2004/308 Sch.2 Part 3

Sch.2 para.108, revoked (in part): SI 2004/308 Sch.2 Part 3

Sch.2 para.109, amended: SI 2004/308 Sch.2 Part 3

Sch.2 para.110, amended: SI 2004/308 Sch.2 Part 3

Sch.2 para.110, revoked (in part): SI 2004/308 Sch.2 Part 3

Sch.2 para.111, amended: SI 2004/308 Sch.2 Part 3

3198. Communications (Isle of Man) Order 2003

referred to: SI 2004/692

Art.1, amended: SI 2004/718 Art.2

Art.6, amended: SI 2004/1115 Art.2

Sch.2 para.17, amended: SI 2004/309 Sch.1 Part 2

Sch.2 para.46, amended: SI 2004/309 Sch.1 Part 2

Sch.2 para.54, amended: SI 2004/309 Sch.1 Part 2

Sch.2 para.71, amended: SI 2004/309 Sch.1 Part 2

3203. Broadcasting (Jersey) Order 2003

Sch.1 para.46, amended: SI 2004/308 Sch.2 Part 2

Sch.1 para.58, revoked: SI 2004/308 Sch.2 Part 2

2003–cont.

3203. Broadcasting (Jersey) Order 2003– *cont.*
Sch.2, revoked (in part): SI 2004/716 Art.2

3227. Education (Pupil Exclusions and Appeals) (Maintained Schools) (Wales) Regulations 2003
Reg.4, applied: SI 1999/2242 Reg.42
Reg.5, amended: SI 2004/1805 Reg.3
Reg.5, applied: SI 1999/2242 Reg.42
Reg.6, amended: SI 2004/1805 Reg.5
Reg.6, applied: SI 1999/2242 Reg.42, Reg.48
Reg.6, varied: SI 2004/1805 Reg.5
Reg.7, applied: SI 1999/2242 Reg.42
Reg.8, applied: SI 1999/2242 Reg.42
Reg.8A, added: SI 2004/1805 Reg.7
Sch.1 para.1, varied: SI 2003/3246 Reg.8, Sch.1 para.1, Sch.1 para.2, Sch.1 para.3
Sch.1 para.2, varied: SI 2003/3246 Reg.8, Sch.1 para.3, Sch.1 para.4
Sch.1 para.3, varied: SI 2003/3246 Reg.8
Sch.1 para.4, varied: SI 2003/3246 Reg.8, Sch.1 para.3
Sch.1 para.5, varied: SI 2003/3246 Reg.8, Sch.1 para.3
Sch.1 para.6, varied: SI 2003/3246 Reg.8, Sch.1 para.3
Sch.1 para.7, varied: SI 2003/3246 Reg.8
Sch.1 para.8, varied: SI 2003/3246 Reg.8
Sch.1 para.9, varied: SI 2003/3246 Reg.8
Sch.1 para.10, varied: SI 2003/3246 Reg.8, Sch.1 para.5
Sch.1 para.11, varied: SI 2003/3246 Reg.8
Sch.1 para.12, varied: SI 2003/3246 Reg.8
Sch.1 para.13, varied: SI 2003/3246 Reg.8
Sch.1 para.14, varied: SI 2003/3246 Reg.8, Sch.1 para.6
Sch.1 para.15, varied: SI 2003/3246 Reg.8
Sch.1 para.16, varied: SI 2003/3246 Reg.8

3234. Independent School Standards (Wales) Regulations 2003
Sch.1 para.3, applied: SI 2003/3230 Sch.1 para.3
Sch.1 para.7, applied: SI 2003/3230 Sch.1 para.3

3239. Local Authorities (Capital Finance and Accounting) (Wales) Regulations 2003
Reg.1, amended: SI 2004/1010 Reg.2
Reg.2, amended: SI 2004/1010 Reg.2
Reg.3, amended: SI 2004/1010 Reg.2
Reg.5A, added: SI 2004/1010 Reg.2
Reg.6, amended: SI 2004/1010 Reg.2
Reg.9, amended: SI 2004/1010 Reg.2
Reg.9A, added: SI 2004/1010 Reg.2
Reg.18, amended: SI 2004/1010 Reg.2
Reg.19, amended: SI 2004/1010 Reg.2
Reg.20, amended: SI 2004/1010 Reg.2
Reg.21, substituted: SI 2004/1010 Reg.2
Reg.22, amended: SI 2004/1010 Reg.2
Reg.24, amended: SI 2004/1010 Reg.2

2003–cont.

3239. Local Authorities (Capital Finance and Accounting) (Wales) Regulations 2003–*cont.*
Reg.25, substituted: SI 2004/1010 Reg.2

3241. Plant Protection Products Regulations 2003
applied: SI 2003/660 Reg.2
Reg.4, applied: SI 2003/660 Reg.2
Reg.5, applied: SI 2003/660 Sch.1
Reg.7, applied: SI 2003/660 Sch.1
Reg.8, applied: SI 2003/660 Sch.1
Reg.9, applied: SI 2003/660 Sch.1
Reg.10, applied: SI 2003/660 Reg.2, Sch.1
Reg.11, applied: SI 2003/660 Sch.1
Reg.13, applied: SI 2003/660 Reg.2, Sch.1
Reg.27, amended: SI 2004/1810 Reg.2
Reg.27, revoked (in part): SI 2004/1810 Reg.2
Sch.1, substituted: SI 2004/1810 Sch.1

3242. Water Environment (Water Framework Directive) (England and Wales) Regulations 2003
Reg.2, applied: SI 2003/3245 Reg.5
Reg.2, varied: SI 2003/3245 Reg.5
Reg.4, referred to: SI 2003/3245 Reg.5
Reg.5, applied: SI 2003/3245 Reg.5
Reg.6, applied: SI 2003/3245 Reg.5
Reg.7, applied: SI 2003/3245 Reg.5
Reg.8, applied: SI 2003/3245 Reg.5
Reg.9, applied: SI 2003/3245 Reg.5
Reg.10, applied: SI 2003/3245 Reg.5
Reg.11, applied: SI 2003/3245 Reg.5
Reg.12, applied: SI 2003/3245 Reg.5
Reg.12, varied: SI 2003/3245 Reg.5
Reg.13, applied: SI 2003/3245 Reg.5
Reg.13, varied: SI 2003/3245 Reg.5
Reg.14, applied: SI 2003/3245 Reg.5
Reg.14, varied: SI 2003/3245 Reg.5
Reg.15, applied: SI 2003/3245 Reg.5
Reg.16, applied: SI 2003/3245 Reg.5
Reg.17, applied: SI 2003/3245 Reg.5
Reg.18, applied: SI 2003/3245 Reg.5
Reg.19, applied: SI 2003/3245 Reg.5
Reg.20, applied: SI 2003/3245 Reg.5

3246. Education (Pupil Exclusions and Appeals) (Pupil Referral Units) (Wales) Regulations 2003
Reg.6, amended: SI 2004/1805 Reg.4
Reg.7, amended: SI 2004/1805 Reg.6
Reg.9A, added: SI 2004/1805 Reg.8

3247. Financing of Maintained Schools (England) (No.2) Regulations 2003
Reg.1, varied: SI 2004/657 Art.3
Reg.6, disapplied: SI 2004/592 Art.7
Reg.15, varied: SI 2004/592 Art.5
Reg.26, amended: SI 2004/659 Reg.3
Sch.2 para.1, varied: SI 2004/592 Art.6
Sch.2 para.3, substituted: SI 2004/659 Reg.3

NO.

2003–cont.

3279. Commission for Healthcare Audit and Inspection (Membership) Regulations 2003
Reg.1, amended: SI 2004/696 Sch.1 para.54, SI 2004/865 Sch.1 para.44, SI 2004/1016 Sch.1 para.34
Reg.4, amended: SI 2004/696 Art.3, Sch.1 para.54, SI 2004/865 Sch.1 para.44, SI 2004/1016 Sch.1 para.34

3299. Media Ownership (Local Radio and Appointed News Provider) Order 2003
Art.2A, added: SI 2004/1944 Art.5

3310. Controls on Certain Azo Dyes and Blue Colourant Regulations 2003
Reg.4, amended: SI 2004/2913 Reg.2
Sch.3, added: SI 2004/2913 Reg.2

3311. Greenhouse Gas Emissions Trading Scheme Regulations 2003
applied: SI 2000/1973 Reg.12, SI 2001/1091 Reg.4, SSI 2000/323 Reg.9

3333. Extradition Act 2003 (Designation of Part 1 Territories) Order 2003
Art.2, amended: SI 2004/1898 Art.2

3334. Extradition Act 2003 (Designation of Part 2 Territories) Order 2003
Art.2, amended: SI 2004/1898 Art.2
Art.3, amended: SI 2004/1898 Art.2

3362. European Parliamentary Elections (Returning Officers) Order 2003
revoked: SI 2004/1056 Art.2

3363. Insolvency Practitioners and Insolvency Services Account (Fees) Order 2003
Art.3, amended: SI 2004/476 Art.2

3596. Police (Conduct) (Senior Officers) (Amendment) Regulations 2003
revoked: SI 2004/645 Reg.2

2004

13. Road Traffic (Permitted Parking Area and Special Parking Area) (County of Bedfordshire) (Districts of Mid-Bedfordshire and South Bedfordshire) Order 2004
Art.3, amended: SI 2004/538 Art.2
Sch.1 para.7, amended: SI 2004/538 Art.2

14. Housing Benefit and Council Tax Benefit (Abolition of Benefit Periods) Amendment Regulations 2004
referred to: SI 2004/319 Reg.1

24. European Parliament (Representation) Act 2003 (Commencement No 3) Order 2004
referred to: SI 2004/320 Art.2

38. Sea Fishing (Restriction on Days at Sea) (No.2) (Amendment) Order 2004
revoked (in part): SI 2004/398 Art.24

NO.

2004–cont.

78. Police and Criminal Evidence Act 1984 (Codes of Practice) (Modifications to Codes C and D) (Certain Police Areas) (Amendment) Order 2004
revoked: SI 2004/1887 Art.4

82. Products of Animal Origin (Third Country Imports) (England) (Amendment) Regulations 2004
revoked: SI 2004/1214 Reg.68

107. Solvent Emissions (England and Wales) Regulations 2004
Reg.3, applied: SI 2000/1973 Sch.3 para.5

118. Crime and Disorder Strategies (Prescribed Descriptions) (England) Order 2004
Art.2, amended: SI 2004/696 Sch.1 para.55
Art.3, amended: SI 2004/865 Sch.1 para.45

120. City of Sheffield (Electoral Changes) Order 2004
varied: SI 2004/222 Art.2

121. Borough of Doncaster (Electoral Changes) Order 2004
varied: SI 2004/222 Art.2

122. City of Bradford (Electoral Changes) Order 2004
varied: SI 2004/222 Art.2

123. Borough of Rotherham (Electoral Changes) Order 2004
varied: SI 2004/222 Art.2

124. Borough of Oldham (Electoral Changes) Order 2004
varied: SI 2004/222 Art.2

125. Borough of Rochdale (Electoral Changes) Order 2004
varied: SI 2004/222 Art.2
Art.2, amended: SI 2004/1073 Art.2
Art.5, amended: SI 2004/1073 Art.2

126. City of Salford (Electoral Changes) Order 2004
varied: SI 2004/222 Art.2

127. Borough of Tameside (Electoral Changes) Order 2004
varied: SI 2004/222 Art.2

128. Borough of Barnsley (Electoral Changes) (Amendment) Order 2004
varied: SI 2004/222 Art.2

129. Cableway Installations Regulations 2004
applied: SI 1998/2306 Sch.1
Reg.2, amended: SI 2004/1230 Reg.2
Reg.4, applied: SI 1994/157 Reg.4
Reg.5, applied: SI 1994/157 Reg.4
Reg.6, applied: SI 1994/157 Reg.4
Reg.7, applied: SI 1994/157 Reg.4
Reg.8, applied: SI 1994/157 Reg.4
Reg.9, applied: SI 1994/157 Reg.4
Reg.10, applied: SI 1994/157 Reg.4
Reg.11, applied: SI 1994/157 Reg.4
Reg.12, applied: SI 1994/157 Reg.4
Reg.19, amended: SI 2004/1230 Reg.2
Reg.25, amended: SI 2004/1230 Reg.2

2004–cont.

145. Hill Farm Allowance Regulations 2004

referred to: SI 2000/3044 Sch.1 Part II

175. Collection of Fines (Pilot Schemes) Order 2004

applied: SI 2004/176 Reg.1, SI 2004/1407 Reg.1

Art.1, amended: SI 2004/1406 Art.2

Art.2, amended: SI 2004/1406 Art.3

Art.2, revoked (in part): SI 2004/1406 Art.4

Sch.1 Part I, applied: SI 2004/176 Reg.1, Reg.7

Sch.1 Part II, applied: SI 2004/176 Reg.1, Reg.7

176. Fines Collection Regulations 2004

Reg.4A, added: SI 2004/1407 Reg.2

181. Education (Penalty Notices) (England) Regulations 2004

Reg.20, amended: SI 2004/920 Reg.2

190. Independent Review of Determinations (Adoption) Regulations 2004

applied: SI 1983/1964 Reg.11A

Reg.1, amended: SI 2004/1868 Reg.3

Reg.2, amended: SI 2004/1868 Reg.3

Reg.3, amended: SI 2004/1868 Reg.3

Reg.12, amended: SI 2004/1081 Reg.3

215. General Medical Council (Suspension and Removal of Members from Office) Rules Order of Council 2004

Sch.1, amended: SI 2004/2608 Sch.1

218. Local Government (Ordinary Day of Election) (Wales) Order 2004

Art.2, enabled: SI 2002/1432

219. Domiciliary Care Agencies (Wales) Regulations 2004

Reg.3, amended: SI 2004/1756 Reg.38

Reg.4, varied: SSI 2004/219 Reg.10

Reg.5, varied: SSI 2004/219 Reg.10

Reg.6, varied: SSI 2004/219 Reg.10

Sch.2 para.3, amended: SI 2004/2414 Reg.6

Sch.2 para.11, added: SI 2004/2414 Reg.6

Sch.3 para.4, amended: SI 2004/2414 Reg.6

Sch.3 para.13, added: SI 2004/2414 Reg.6

244. Carriers&apos Liability (Amendment) Regulations 2004

referred to: SI 2004/250, SI 2004/251

249. Food (Provisions relating to Labelling) (Wales) Regulations 2004

Reg.5, referred to: SI 1996/1499 Reg.50

Reg.6, referred to: SI 1996/1499 Reg.50

256. Education (National Curriculum) (Attainment Targets and Programmes of Study in Modern Foreign Languages in respect of the Third Key Stage) (England) Order 2004

revoked: SI 2004/1793 Art.2

2004–cont.

261. Education (National Curriculum) (Attainment Targets and Programmes of Study in Design and Technology in respect of the First, Second and Third Key Stages) (England) Order 2004

revoked: SI 2004/1794 Art.2

288. Health and Social Care (Community Health and Standards) Act 2003 Commencement (No.2) Order 2004

Art.1, amended: SI 2004/866 Art.2

Art.2, amended: SI 2004/866 Art.2

Art.6, amended: SI 2004/866 Art.2, SI 2004/1009 Art.2

Art.7, amended: SI 2004/866 Art.2

Art.9, added: SI 2004/866 Art.2

291. National Health Service (General Medical Services Contracts) Regulations 2004

applied: SI 2004/627 Reg.19

Part 1, applied: SI 2002/2375 Reg.9

Reg.2, amended: SI 2004/2694 Reg.2

Reg.4, amended: SI 2004/2694 Reg.3

Reg.4, applied: SI 2004/2694 Reg.19

Reg.4, referred to: SI 2004/627 Reg.19

Reg.5, applied: SSI 2004/115 Reg.5

Reg.5, referred to: SI 2004/627 Reg.19

Reg.9, applied: SI 2004/433 Art.4, Art.6, Art.7, Art.10, Art.14, SI 2004/627 Reg.19

Reg.9, referred to: SI 2004/865 Art.42

Reg.15, applied: SI 2004/865 Art.47

Reg.17, applied: SI 2004/433 Art.17

Reg.18, applied: SI 2004/433 Art.26

Reg.24, applied: SI 2004/865 Art.52

Reg.24, referred to: SI 2004/865 Art.52

Reg.27, applied: SI 2004/865 Art.31

Reg.29, applied: SI 2004/433 Art.24

Reg.30, applied: SI 2004/433 Art.19, Art.20

Reg.30, varied: SI 2004/865 Art.93

Sch.1, referred to: SI 2004/865 Art.105

Sch.2 para.4, amended: SI 2004/2694 Reg.4

Sch.3, applied: SI 2002/2375 Sch.3

Sch.3, referred to: SI 2004/433 Art.24, SI 2004/627 Reg.19

Sch.3 para.4, applied: SI 2004/433 Art.20

Sch.3 para.4, referred to: SI 2004/865 Art.92

Sch.3 para.5, applied: SI 2004/433 Art.20

Sch.3 para.5, referred to: SI 2004/865 Art.92

Sch.3 para.6, referred to: SI 2004/433 Art.24, SI 2004/865 Art.92

Sch.6 Part 1 para.4, applied: SI 2004/865 Art.45

Sch.6 Part 1 para.4, referred to: SI 2004/865 Art.14, Art.45

Sch.6 Part 1 para.5, referred to: SI 2004/865 Art.32

Sch.6 Part 1 para.6, applied: SI 2004/865 Art.33

Sch.6 Part 1 para.6, referred to: SI 2004/865 Art.33

2004–cont.

291. National Health Service (General Medical Services Contracts) Regulations 2004–*cont.*

Sch.6 Part 1 para.7, amended: SI 2004/2694 Reg.5

Sch.6 Part 1 para.11, amended: SI 2004/2694 Reg.5

Sch.6 Part 1 para.11, referred to: SI 2004/865 Art.92

Sch.6 Part 1 para.13, referred to: SI 2004/865 Art.92

Sch.6 Part 2 para.14, applied: SI 2004/627 Reg.19

Sch.6 Part 2 para.15, referred to: SI 2004/433 Art.32, SI 2004/865 Art.3, Art.4

Sch.6 Part 2 para.16, applied: SI 1992/662 Reg.20, SI 2004/865 Art.46

Sch.6 Part 2 para.16, referred to: SI 2004/865 Art.10, Art.11, Art.46

Sch.6 Part 2 para.17, referred to: SI 2004/865 Art.10

Sch.6 Part 2 para.18, applied: SI 2004/865 Art.44

Sch.6 Part 2 para.19, applied: SI 2004/865 Art.48

Sch.6 Part 2 para.19, referred to: SI 2004/865 Art.5

Sch.6 Part 2 para.20, referred to: SI 2004/865 Art.6, Art.44

Sch.6 Part 2 para.23, applied: SI 2004/865 Art.48

Sch.6 Part 2 para.23, referred to: SI 2004/865 Art.8

Sch.6 Part 2 para.23, varied: SI 2004/865 Art.48

Sch.6 Part 2 para.24, applied: SI 2004/865 Art.48

Sch.6 Part 2 para.24, referred to: SI 2004/865 Art.8, Art.48

Sch.6 Part 2 para.24, varied: SI 2004/865 Art.8

Sch.6 Part 2 para.28, referred to: SI 2004/433 Art.24

Sch.6 Part 2 para.29, referred to: SI 2004/433 Art.32

Sch.6 Part 2 para.31, amended: SI 2004/2694 Reg.5

Sch.6 Part 2 para.31, applied: SI 2002/2375 Reg.10

Sch.6 Part 2 para.35, applied: SI 2002/2375 Reg.10

Sch.6 Part 3 para.39, applied: SI 1992/662 Reg.20, Sch.2 para.11

Sch.6 Part 3 para.40, referred to: SI 2004/865 Art.18

Sch.6 Part 3 para.42, applied: SI 1992/662 Sch.2 para.11

Sch.6 Part 3 para.43, amended: SI 2004/2694 Reg.5

Sch.6 Part 3 para.44, applied: SI 2000/620 Reg.3

2004–cont.

291. National Health Service (General Medical Services Contracts) Regulations 2004–*cont.*

Sch.6 Part 3 para.47, applied: SI 2004/865 Art.49

Sch.6 Part 3 para.47, referred to: SI 2004/865 Art.49

Sch.6 Part 3 para.48, amended: SI 2004/2694 Reg.5

Sch.6 Part 3 para.50, amended: SI 2004/2694 Reg.5

Sch.6 Part 3 para.51, applied: SI 2004/627 Sch.5 para.51

Sch.6 Part 4 para.53, amended: SI 2004/2694 Reg.5

Sch.6 Part 4 para.57, applied: SI 2004/865 Art.44

Sch.6 Part 4 para.57, referred to: SI 2004/865 Art.16

Sch.6 Part 4 para.58, applied: SI 2004/865 Art.44

Sch.6 Part 4 para.58, referred to: SI 2004/865 Art.16

Sch.6 Part 4 para.59, applied: SI 2004/865 Art.44

Sch.6 Part 4 para.59, referred to: SI 2004/865 Art.16

Sch.6 Part 4 para.60, applied: SI 2004/865 Art.44

Sch.6 Part 4 para.64, amended: SI 2004/2694 Reg.5

Sch.6 Part 4 para.64, referred to: SI 2004/865 Art.34

Sch.6 Part 4 para.65, referred to: SI 2004/865 Art.17

Sch.6 Part 4 para.66, referred to: SI 2004/865 Art.105

Sch.6 Part 4 para.68, amended: SI 2004/2694 Reg.5

Sch.6 Part 4 para.69, amended: SI 2004/906 Reg.4

Sch.6 Part 4 para.69, applied: SI 2004/865 Art.29, Art.44

Sch.6 Part 4 para.69, referred to: SI 2004/865 Art.29, Art.44, Art.50

Sch.6 Part 4 para.70, referred to: SI 2004/865 Art.91, Art.92

Sch.6 Part 4 para.70, varied: SI 2004/433 Art.21, Art.22

Sch.6 Part 4 para.71, referred to: SI 2004/865 Art.92

Sch.6 Part 4 para.72, amended: SI 2004/2694 Reg.5

Sch.6 Part 4 para.72, referred to: SI 2004/865 Art.92

Sch.6 Part 5 para.73, applied: SI 2004/865 Art.44

Sch.6 Part 5 para.73, referred to: SI 2004/865 Art.19

Sch.6 Part 5 para.77, amended: SI 2004/2694 Reg.5

2004–cont.

291. National Health Service (General Medical Services Contracts) Regulations 2004–*cont.*

Sch.6 Part 5 para.79, applied: SI 2004/865 Art.26

Sch.6 Part 5 para.80, referred to: SI 2004/865 Art.25

Sch.6 Part 5 para.81, amended: SI 2004/2694 Reg.5

Sch.6 Part 5 para.81, referred to: SI 2004/865 Art.53

Sch.6 Part 5 para.82, referred to: SI 2004/865 Art.15

Sch.6 Part 5 para.86, applied: SI 2004/865 Art.44

Sch.6 Part 5 para.87, referred to: SI 2004/865 Art.27

Sch.6 Part 5 para.89, referred to: SI 2004/865 Art.20

Sch.6 Part 6 para.92, applied: SI 1992/662 Sch.2 para.14, SI 2004/865 Art.24

Sch.6 Part 6 para.92, referred to: SI 2004/865 Art.51

Sch.6 Part 6 para.93, referred to: SI 2004/865 Art.51

Sch.6 Part 6 para.94, referred to: SI 2004/865 Art.51

Sch.6 Part 6 para.95, referred to: SI 2004/865 Art.51

Sch.6 Part 6 para.96, referred to: SI 2004/865 Art.51

Sch.6 Part 6 para.97, applied: SI 1986/975 Sch.1 para.8C, SI 1992/662 Sch.2 para.14

Sch.6 Part 6 para.98, referred to: SI 2004/865 Art.51

Sch.6 Part 6 para.98, substituted: SI 2004/2694 Reg.5

Sch.6 Part 7 para.101, amended: SI 2004/2694 Reg.5

Sch.6 Part 7 para.101, referred to: SI 2004/433 Art.33

Sch.6 Part 7 para.102, referred to: SI 2004/433 Art.33

Sch.6 Part 7 para.102, varied: SI 2004/433 Art.33

Sch.6 Part 8 para.104, referred to: SI 2004/433 Art.23

Sch.6 Part 8 para.111, applied: SI 2004/2694 Reg.19

Sch.6 Part 8 para.113, applied: SI 2004/865 Art.55

Sch.6 Part 8 para.113, referred to: SI 2004/433 Art.12, SI 2004/865 Art.55, SSI 2004/115 Sch.5 para.101

Sch.6 Part 8 para.113, varied: SI 2004/433 Art.34

Sch.6 Part 8 para.114A, added: SI 2004/906 Reg.4

Sch.6 Part 8 para.115, referred to: SI 2004/865 Art.28, Art.97, Art.98, Art.99, Art.101, Art.102

2004–cont.

291. National Health Service (General Medical Services Contracts) Regulations 2004–*cont.*

Sch.6 Part 9 para.122, amended: SI 2004/2694 Reg.5

Sch.6 Part 9 para.124, applied: SI 2004/585 Reg.23

Sch.7, referred to: SI 2004/433 Art.23, SI 2004/865 Art.92

Sch.7 para.1, varied: SI 2004/433 Art.21, Art.22

Sch.7 para.2, applied: SI 2004/865 Art.87, Art.88

Sch.7 para.2, referred to: SI 2004/865 Art.74, Art.76, Art.79, Art.81, Art.82, Art.84, Art.86, Art.88, Art.91

Sch.7 para.2, varied: SI 2004/865 Art.74

Sch.7 para.4, applied: SI 2004/865 Art.82, Art.87, Art.88

Sch.7 para.4, referred to: SI 2004/865 Art.81, Art.84, Art.88

Sch.7 para.5, referred to: SI 2004/865 Art.78

Sch.7 para.6, applied: SI 2004/865 Art.87, Art.88

Sch.7 para.6, referred to: SI 2004/865 Art.86, Art.88

Sch.7 para.6, varied: SI 2004/433 Art.21, Art.22

Sch.7 para.7, referred to: SI 2004/865 Art.78

Sch.10, referred to: SI 2004/865 Art.30

293. European Parliamentary Elections Regulations 2004

applied: SI 2004/1298 Sch.1 para.3, SI 2004/1299 Sch.1 para.4

Reg.2, varied: SI 2004/294 Reg.7

Reg.6, applied: SI 2004/294 Reg.7

Reg.6, disapplied: SI 2004/294 Reg.7

Reg.7, applied: SI 2004/294 Reg.7, SI 2004/1298 Sch.1 para.1

Reg.15, applied: SI 2004/1298 Art.4, SI 2004/1299 Art.4

Reg.15, enabled: SI 2004/1298, SI 2004/1299

Reg.32, referred to: SI 1979/521 r.18

Reg.52, varied: SI 2004/1373 Art.6

Reg.87, applied: SI 1979/521 r.18

Reg.89, applied: SI 1979/521 r.6

Reg.89, referred to: SI 1979/521 r.4

Reg.94, applied: SI 1979/521 r.5

Reg.94, referred to: SI 1979/521 r.7

Reg.96, applied: SI 1979/521 r.10

Reg.101, applied: SI 1979/521 r.11

Reg.120, enabled: SI 2004/1415

Reg.122, applied: SI 1979/521 r.20

Sch.1 Part 2 para.4, referred to: SI 2004/1373 Art.4

Sch.1 Part 3 para.21, referred to: SI 2004/1373 Art.4

Sch.1 Part 3 para.21, varied: SI 2004/1373 Art.6

2004–cont.

293. European Parliamentary Elections Regulations 2004–*cont.*

Sch.1 Part 3 para.29, varied: SI 2004/1373 Art.6

Sch.1 Part 3 para.30, varied: SI 2004/1373 Art.6

Sch.1 Part 3 para.33, varied: SI 2004/1373 Art.5

Sch.1 Part 3 para.36, varied: SI 2004/1373 Art.5

Sch.1 Part 3 para.40, varied: SI 2004/1373 Art.5

Sch.2 Part 1 para.6, varied: SI 2004/1373 Art.6

Sch.2 Part 2 para.16, amended: SI 2004/1771 Sch.1 para.12

Sch.2 Part 3 para.27, varied: SI 2004/294 Reg.7

Sch.2 Part 3 para.28, varied: SI 2004/1373 Art.6

Sch.2 Part 3 para.52, varied: SI 2004/1373 Art.6

Sch.3 Part 1 para.1, varied: SI 2004/294 Sch.1

Sch.3 Part 1 para.2, varied: SI 2004/294 Sch.1

Sch.3 Part 1 para.3, varied: SI 2004/294 Sch.1

Sch.3 Part 1 para.4, varied: SI 2004/294 Sch.1

Sch.3 Part 1 para.5, varied: SI 2004/294 Sch.1

Sch.3 Part 1 para.6, varied: SI 2004/294 Sch.1

Sch.3 Part 1 para.7, varied: SI 2004/294 Sch.1

Sch.3 Part 1 para.8, varied: SI 2004/294 Sch.1, SI 2004/1373 Art.6

Sch.3 Part 1 para.9, varied: SI 2004/294 Sch.1

Sch.3 Part 1 para.10, varied: SI 2004/294 Sch.1

Sch.3 Part 1 para.11, varied: SI 2004/294 Sch.1

Sch.3 Part 1 para.12, varied: SI 2004/294 Sch.1

Sch.3 Part 1 para.13, varied: SI 2004/294 Sch.1

Sch.3 Part 1 para.14, varied: SI 2004/294 Sch.1

Sch.3 Part 1 para.15, varied: SI 2004/294 Sch.1

Sch.3 Part 1 para.16, varied: SI 2004/294 Sch.1

Sch.3 Part 1 para.17, varied: SI 2004/294 Sch.1

Sch.3 Part 1 para.18, varied: SI 2004/294 Sch.1

Sch.3 Part 1 para.19, varied: SI 2004/294 Sch.1

Sch.3 Part 1 para.20, varied: SI 2004/294 Sch.1

Sch.3 Part 1 para.21, varied: SI 2004/294 Sch.1

2004–cont.

293. European Parliamentary Elections Regulations 2004–*cont.*

Sch.3 Part 1 para.22, varied: SI 2004/294 Sch.1

Sch.3 Part 1 para.23, varied: SI 2004/294 Sch.1

Sch.3 Part 1 para.24, varied: SI 2004/294 Sch.1

Sch.3 Part 1 para.25, varied: SI 2004/294 Sch.1

Sch.3 Part 1 para.26, varied: SI 2004/294 Sch.1

Sch.3 Part 1 para.27, varied: SI 2004/294 Sch.1, SI 2004/1373 Art.6

Sch.3 Part 1 para.28, varied: SI 2004/294 Sch.1, SI 2004/1373 Art.5

294. Representation of the People (Combination of Polls) (England and Wales) Regulations 2004

Reg.5, applied: SI 2002/185 Sch.3 para.26, Sch.3 para.38, Sch.3 para.39, Sch.3 para.40, Sch.3 para.41, Sch.3 para.51

Reg.5, referred to: SI 1986/2214 Sch.3, SI 1986/2215 Sch.3 para.20, SI 2000/427 Sch.8, Sch.9, Sch.10

302. Merchant Shipping (High Speed Craft) Regulations 2004

applied: SI 1972/674 Art.7A, SI 1995/1210 Reg.2, SI 1997/1509 Reg.4, SI 1998/1011 Reg.1, SI 1998/1012 Reg.1, SI 1998/1561 Reg.3, SI 1998/2070 Reg.3, SI 1998/2514 Reg.3, SI 1998/2515 Reg.3, SI 1999/1957 Reg.4, SI 2000/2687 Reg.4, SI 2002/1473 Reg.4

Reg.2, referred to: SI 2001/3209 Reg.3

Reg.7A, added: SI 2004/2883 Reg.4

305. Liberia (United Nations Sanctions) (Isle of Man) Order 2004

referred to: SI 2004/1120 Art.2

Art.1, amended: SI 2004/1120 Art.3

Art.2, amended: SI 2004/1120 Art.4, Art.5

Art.2, substituted: SI 2004/1120 Art.4

Art.6A, added: SI 2004/1120 Art.6

Art.6B, added: SI 2004/1120 Art.6

Art.6C, added: SI 2004/1120 Art.6

Art.6D, added: SI 2004/1120 Art.6

Art.16, amended: SI 2004/1120 Art.7, Art.8

306. Liberia (United Nations Sanctions) (Channel Islands) Order 2004

referred to: SI 2004/1113 Art.2

Art.1, amended: SI 2004/1113 Art.3

Art.2, amended: SI 2004/1113 Art.4, Art.5

Art.6A, added: SI 2004/1113 Art.6

Art.6B, added: SI 2004/1113 Art.6

Art.6C, added: SI 2004/1113 Art.6

Art.6D, added: SI 2004/1113 Art.6

Art.16, amended: SI 2004/1113 Art.7, Art.8

307. Communications (Bailiwick of Guernsey) Order 2004

referred to: SI 2004/692

2004–cont.

308. Broadcasting and Communications (Jersey) Order 2004
referred to: SI 2004/692

318. Trade in Controlled Goods (Embargoed Destinations) Order 2004
Art.8, amended: SI 2004/1049 Art.2
Sch.1, amended: SI 2004/2741 Art.3

347. Liberia (Restrictive Measures) (Overseas Territories) Order 2004
Art.1, amended: SI 2004/1112 Art.2
Art.2, amended: SI 2004/1112 Art.3, Art.4
Art.2, substituted: SI 2004/1112 Art.3
Art.8A, added: SI 2004/1112 Art.5
Art.8B, added: SI 2004/1112 Art.5
Art.8C, added: SI 2004/1112 Art.5
Art.8D, added: SI 2004/1112 Art.5
Art.17, amended: SI 2004/1112 Art.6, Art.7
Sch.2 para.1, amended: SI 2004/1112 Art.8
Sch.2 para.2, amended: SI 2004/1112 Art.9

349. Sudan (Restrictive Measures) (Overseas Territories) Order 2004
Art.2, amended: SI 2004/1980 Art.2
Art.5, amended: SI 2004/1980 Art.3

353. Insurers (Reorganisation and Winding Up) Regulations 2004
Reg.9, amended: SI 2004/546 Reg.2
Reg.14, amended: SI 2004/546 Reg.2
Reg.21, amended: SI 2004/546 Reg.2
Reg.28, applied: SI 2001/4040 r.23
Reg.29, applied: SI 2001/3635 r.24
Reg.33, amended: SI 2004/546 Reg.2
Reg.51, amended: SI 2004/546 Reg.2

356. Borough of Bolton (Electoral Changes) Order 2004
varied: SI 2004/222 Art.2

357. Borough of Bury (Electoral Changes) Order 2004
varied: SI 2004/222 Art.2

358. Borough of South Tyneside (Electoral Changes) Order 2004
varied: SI 2004/222 Art.2

359. City of Manchester (Electoral Changes) Order 2004
varied: SI 2004/222 Art.2

360. Borough of Stockport (Electoral Changes) Order 2004
varied: SI 2004/222 Art.2

361. Borough of Gateshead (Electoral Changes) Order 2004
varied: SI 2004/222 Art.2

362. City of Sunderland (Electoral Changes) Order 2004
varied: SI 2004/222 Art.2

363. City of Newcastle upon Tyne (Electoral Changes) Order 2004
varied: SI 2004/222 Art.2

364. Borough of North Tyneside (Electoral Changes) Order 2004
varied: SI 2004/222 Art.2

2004–cont.

365. Borough of Wigan (Electoral Changes) Order 2004
varied: SI 2004/222 Art.2

390. Products of Animal Origin (Third Country Imports) (England) (Amendment No 2) Regulations 2004
revoked: SI 2004/1214 Reg.68

400. High Court Enforcement Officers Regulations 2004
Reg.3, amended: SI 2004/673 Reg.3
Sch.1, amended: SI 2004/673 Reg.4

433. General Medical Services Transitional and Consequential Provisions Order 2004
Part 2, applied: SI 2004/865 Art.93
Art.1, amended: SI 2004/865 Sch.1 para.46
Art.3, amended: SI 2004/865 Sch.1 para.46
Art.3, applied: SI 2004/865 Art.2
Art.4, amended: SI 2004/865 Sch.1 para.46
Art.5, applied: SI 2004/865 Art.2
Art.12, amended: SI 2004/865 Sch.1 para.46
Art.13, amended: SI 2004/865 Sch.1 para.46
Art.13, applied: SI 1986/975 Sch.1 para.8C, SI 1992/662 Reg.2, SI 2000/620 Reg.2, SI 2004/865 Art.2
Art.15, applied: SI 2004/865 Art.74, Art.76, Art.79, Art.86
Art.22, amended: SI 2004/865 Sch.1 para.46
Art.24, applied: SI 2004/865 Art.92
Art.25, applied: SI 2004/865 Art.92

440. Income Support (General) (Standard Interest Rate Amendment) Regulations 2004
revoked: SI 2004/1520 Reg.3

450. School Governance (Constitution, Procedures and New Schools) (England) (Amendment) Regulations 2004
disapplied: SI 2004/530 Reg.3

454. Financial Services and Markets Act 2000 (Transitional Provisions) (Complaints Relating to General Insurance and Mortgages) Order 2004
Art.1, amended: SI 2004/1609 Art.2
Art.2, amended: SI 2004/1609 Art.3
Art.10, revoked: SI 2004/1609 Art.4
Art.11, amended: SI 2004/1609 Art.5
Art.12, added: SI 2004/1609 Art.6

456. Health and Safety (Fees) Regulations 2004
Reg.12, substituted: SI 2004/568 Sch.10 para.2
Reg.13, substituted: SI 2004/568 Sch.10 para.2
Reg.14, substituted: SI 2004/568 Sch.10 para.2
Sch.10, substituted: SI 2004/568 Sch.10 para.3
Sch.11, substituted: SI 2004/568 Sch.10 para.4

NO.

2004–cont.

456. Health and Safety (Fees) Regulations 2004–cont.
Sch.12, substituted: SI 2004/568 Sch.10 para.5

458. Cumbria (Coroners&apos Districts) Order 2004
revoked: SI 2004/535 Art.4

472. Insolvency (Amendment) Regulations 2004
disapplied: SI 2004/584 r.3

477. General Medical Services Transitional and Consequential Provisions (Wales) Order 2004
Part 2, applied: SI 2004/1016 Art.69
Art.1, amended: SI 2004/1016 Sch.1 para.35
Art.3, amended: SI 2004/1016 Sch.1 para.35
Art.3, applied: SI 2004/1016 Art.2
Art.4, amended: SI 2004/1016 Sch.1 para.35
Art.5, applied: SI 2004/1016 Art.2
Art.12, amended: SI 2004/1016 Sch.1 para.35
Art.13, amended: SI 2004/1016 Sch.1 para.35
Art.13, applied: SI 2004/1016 Art.2, Sch.1 para.4
Art.15, applied: SI 2004/1016 Art.58, Art.60, Art.64
Art.22, amended: SI 2004/1016 Sch.1 para.35
Art.24, applied: SI 2004/1016 Art.68
Art.25, applied: SI 2004/1016 Art.68

478. National Health Service (General Medical Services Contracts) (Wales) Regulations 2004
Reg.9, applied: SI 2004/477 Art.4, Art.6, Art.10, Art.14, SI 2004/1016 Art.39
Reg.9, referred to: SI 2004/1016 Art.39
Reg.15, referred to: SI 2004/1016 Art.44
Reg.17, applied: SI 2004/477 Art.17
Reg.18, applied: SI 2004/477 Art.26
Reg.24, applied: SI 1992/662 Sch.2 para.13
Reg.24, referred to: SI 2004/1016 Art.49
Reg.24, varied: SI 2004/1016 Art.49
Reg.27, applied: SI 2004/1016 Art.28
Reg.29, applied: SI 2004/477 Art.24, Art.27
Reg.30, applied: SI 2004/477 Art.19, Art.20, SI 2004/1016 Art.69
Sch.1, applied: SI 2004/1016 Art.81
Sch.3, applied: SI 2004/477 Art.24
Sch.3 para.4, applied: SI 2004/477 Art.20, SI 2004/1016 Art.68
Sch.3 para.5, applied: SI 2004/477 Art.20, SI 2004/1016 Art.68
Sch.3 para.6, applied: SI 2004/477 Art.24, SI 2004/1016 Art.68
Sch.5, applied: SI 1992/662 Sch.2 para.13
Sch.6 Part 1 para.4, applied: SI 2004/1016 Art.14, Art.42
Sch.6 Part 1 para.4, referred to: SI 2004/1016 Art.42
Sch.6 Part 1 para.4, varied: SI 2004/1016 Art.42

NO.

2004–cont.

478. National Health Service (General Medical Services Contracts) (Wales) Regulations 2004–cont.
Sch.6 Part 1 para.5, applied: SI 2004/1016 Art.29
Sch.6 Part 1 para.6, applied: SI 2004/1016 Art.30
Sch.6 Part 1 para.6, referred to: SI 2004/1016 Art.30
Sch.6 Part 1 para.11, applied: SI 2004/1016 Art.68
Sch.6 Part 1 para.13, applied: SI 2004/1016 Art.68
Sch.6 Part 2 para.15, applied: SI 2004/477 Art.32, SI 2004/1016 Art.3, Art.4
Sch.6 Part 2 para.16, applied: SI 2004/1016 Art.10
Sch.6 Part 2 para.16, referred to: SI 2004/1016 Art.43
Sch.6 Part 2 para.16, varied: SI 2004/1016 Art.11, Art.43
Sch.6 Part 2 para.17, applied: SI 2004/1016 Art.10
Sch.6 Part 2 para.18, applied: SI 2004/1016 Art.41
Sch.6 Part 2 para.19, applied: SI 2004/1016 Art.5
Sch.6 Part 2 para.19, referred to: SI 2004/1016 Art.45
Sch.6 Part 2 para.20, applied: SI 2004/1016 Art.6, Art.41
Sch.6 Part 2 para.23, varied: SI 2004/1016 Art.8, Art.45
Sch.6 Part 2 para.24, varied: SI 2004/1016 Art.8
Sch.6 Part 2 para.28, applied: SI 2004/477 Art.24
Sch.6 Part 2 para.29, applied: SI 2004/477 Art.32
Sch.6 Part 3 para.39, applied: SI 1992/662 Sch.2 para.7, Sch.2 para.11
Sch.6 Part 3 para.42, referred to: SI 1992/662 Sch.2 para.11
Sch.6 Part 3 para.44, applied: SI 2001/1358 Reg.3
Sch.6 Part 3 para.47, applied: SI 2004/1016 Art.46
Sch.6 Part 3 para.47, referred to: SI 2004/1016 Art.46
Sch.6 Part 4 para.56, applied: SI 2004/1016 Art.16
Sch.6 Part 4 para.56, referred to: SI 2004/1016 Art.41
Sch.6 Part 4 para.57, applied: SI 2004/1016 Art.16
Sch.6 Part 4 para.57, referred to: SI 2004/1016 Art.41
Sch.6 Part 4 para.58, applied: SI 2004/1016 Art.16
Sch.6 Part 4 para.58, referred to: SI 2004/1016 Art.41

2004–cont.

478. National Health Service (General Medical Services Contracts) (Wales) Regulations 2004–cont.

Sch.6 Part 4 para.59, referred to: SI 2004/1016 Art.41

Sch.6 Part 4 para.63, applied: SI 2004/1016 Art.31

Sch.6 Part 4 para.64, applied: SI 2004/1016 Art.17

Sch.6 Part 4 para.65, applied: SI 2004/1016 Art.81

Sch.6 Part 4 para.68, amended: SI 2004/1017 Reg.4

Sch.6 Part 4 para.68, applied: SI 2004/1016 Art.26, Art.41, Art.47

Sch.6 Part 4 para.68, referred to: SI 2004/1016 Art.41

Sch.6 Part 4 para.69, applied: SI 2004/1016 Art.67, Art.68

Sch.6 Part 4 para.69, varied: SI 2004/477 Art.21, Art.22

Sch.6 Part 4 para.70, applied: SI 2004/1016 Art.68

Sch.6 Part 4 para.71, applied: SI 2004/1016 Art.68

Sch.6 Part 5 para.72, applied: SI 2004/1016 Art.18

Sch.6 Part 5 para.72, referred to: SI 2004/1016 Art.41

Sch.6 Part 5 para.77, applied: SI 2004/1016 Art.25

Sch.6 Part 5 para.78, applied: SI 2004/1016 Art.24

Sch.6 Part 5 para.79, applied: SI 2004/1016 Art.50

Sch.6 Part 5 para.80, applied: SI 2004/1016 Art.15

Sch.6 Part 5 para.84, referred to: SI 2004/1016 Art.41

Sch.6 Part 5 para.87, applied: SI 2004/1016 Art.19

Sch.6 Part 6 para.90, applied: SI 2004/1016 Art.23, Art.48

Sch.6 Part 6 para.90, referred to: SI 2004/1016 Art.48

Sch.6 Part 6 para.91, applied: SI 2004/1016 Art.48

Sch.6 Part 6 para.92, applied: SI 1992/662 Sch.2 para.14, SI 2004/1016 Art.48

Sch.6 Part 6 para.93, applied: SI 2004/1016 Art.48

Sch.6 Part 6 para.94, applied: SI 2004/1016 Art.48

Sch.6 Part 6 para.95, applied: SI 1992/662 Sch.2 para.14

Sch.6 Part 6 para.95, referred to: SI 1986/975 Sch.1 para.8C

Sch.6 Part 6 para.96, applied: SI 2004/1016 Art.48

Sch.6 Part 7 para.98, referred to: SI 2004/477 Art.33

2004–cont.

478. National Health Service (General Medical Services Contracts) (Wales) Regulations 2004–cont.

Sch.6 Part 7 para.99, referred to: SI 2004/477 Art.33

Sch.6 Part 7 para.100, referred to: SI 2004/477 Art.33

Sch.6 Part 7 para.100, varied: SI 2004/477 Art.33

Sch.6 Part 8, added: SI 2004/1017 Reg.4

Sch.6 Part 8 para.102, referred to: SI 2004/477 Art.23

Sch.6 Part 8 para.111, applied: SI 2004/477 Art.12, SI 2004/1016 Art.52

Sch.6 Part 8 para.111, referred to: SI 2004/477 Art.34, SI 2004/1016 Art.52

Sch.6 Part 8 para.111, varied: SI 2004/477 Art.34

Sch.6 Part 8 para.113, applied: SI 2004/1016 Art.73, Art.74, Art.75, Art.77, Art.78

Sch.7, referred to: SI 2004/477 Art.23

Sch.7 para.1, varied: SI 2004/477 Art.21, Art.22

Sch.7 para.2, applied: SI 2004/1016 Art.58, Art.59, Art.60, Art.61, Art.62, Art.63, Art.64, Art.66, Art.67

Sch.7 para.2, referred to: SI 2004/1016 Art.65, Art.66

Sch.7 para.2, varied: SI 2004/1016 Art.60

Sch.7 para.4, applied: SI 2004/1016 Art.61, Art.63, Art.66

Sch.7 para.4, referred to: SI 2004/1016 Art.62, Art.65, Art.66

Sch.7 para.4, varied: SI 2004/1016 Art.62, Art.63, Art.64

Sch.7 para.5, varied: SI 2004/477 Art.21, Art.22

Sch.7 para.6, applied: SI 2004/1016 Art.66

Sch.10, applied: SI 2004/1016 Art.27

480. Health and Social Care (Community Health and Standards) Act 2003 (Commencement No 1) (Wales) Order 2004

Art.1, amended: SI 2004/1019 Art.2

Art.2, amended: SI 2004/1019 Art.2

Art.4, amended: SI 2004/1019 Art.2

Art.4, revoked (in part): SI 2004/1019 Art.2

Art.5, amended: SI 2004/1019 Art.2

Art.6, amended: SI 2004/1019 Art.2

545. Office of Communications Act 2002 (Commencement No 3) and Communications Act 2003 (Commencement No 2) (Amendment) Order 2004

applied: SI 2003/3195 Art.1, SI 2003/3197 Art.1, SI 2003/3198 Art.1

551. Health Professions Wales (Establishment, Membership, Constitution and Functions) Order 2004

applied: SI 2004/550 Art.3

NO.

2004–cont.

552. Social Security Benefits Up-rating Order 2004
applied: SI 2004/583 Reg.2, Reg.3

553. Jam and Similar Products (Wales) Regulations 2004
applied: SI 2004/554 Reg.3

568. Carriage of Dangerous Goods and Use of Transportable Pressure Equipment Regulations 2004
applied: 1928 c.32 s.18, SI 1987/37 Reg.25, SI 1991/1531 Reg.10, SI 1993/208 Reg.5, SI 1993/3050 Sch.2 Part A, SI 1995/3163 Sch.2 para.6, SI 2000/128 Sch.1 para.3, Sch.1 para.9, SI 2002/2675 Reg.23, Sch.2 para.1
referred to: SI 2002/1689 Reg.8A, SI 2002/2676 Sch.2, SI 2002/2776 Sch.5
Part 4, applied: SI 1978/1723 Reg.1A
Reg.2, referred to: SI 1987/37 Reg.25, SI 2001/2975 Reg.3
Reg.4, referred to: SI 2000/128 Sch.1 para.3, SI 2001/2975 Reg.3
Reg.20, applied: SI 2001/2975 Reg.3
Reg.21, applied: SI 2001/2975 Reg.3
Reg.24, applied: SI 2004/456 Reg.12
Reg.28, applied: SI 2001/2975 Reg.3
Reg.32, applied: SI 2004/456 Reg.12
Reg.33, applied: SI 2004/456 Reg.12

585. National Health Service (Performers Lists) Regulations 2004
applied: SI 2004/865 Art.101, Art.102
Reg.6, referred to: SI 2004/865 Art.60, Art.61
Reg.10, amended: SI 2004/2694 Reg.16
Reg.21, amended: SI 2004/2694 Reg.17
Sch.1 para.7, applied: SI 2004/865 Art.106

595. Land Registration Fee Order 2004
Art.1, amended: SI 2004/1833 Art.3
Art.5, amended: SI 2004/1833 Art.4
Art.6, amended: SI 2004/1833 Art.5
Art.9, amended: SI 2004/1833 Art.6
Sch.3 Part 1, amended: SI 2004/1833 Art.7
Sch.3 Part 2, amended: SI 2004/1833 Art.8

615. Commission for Social Care Inspection (Childrens Rights Director) Regulations 2004
Reg.2, varied: SI 2004/664 Art.11, Art.12, Art.13, Art.14
Reg.3, varied: SI 2004/664 Art.11, Art.12, Art.13, Art.14
Reg.4, varied: SI 2004/664 Art.11, Art.12, Art.13, Art.14

627. National Health Service (Personal Medical Services Agreements) Regulations 2004
applied: SI 2004/865 Art.59
Reg.2, amended: SI 2004/2694 Reg.6
Reg.3, amended: SI 2004/2694 Reg.7
Reg.4, revoked: SI 2004/2694 Reg.8
Reg.5, amended: SI 2004/2694 Reg.9
Reg.5, revoked (in part): SI 2004/2694 Reg.9

NO.

2004–cont.

627. National Health Service (Personal Medical Services Agreements) Regulations 2004–*cont.*
Reg.6, amended: SI 2004/2694 Reg.10
Reg.6, varied: SI 2004/865 Art.71
Reg.7, amended: SI 2004/2694 Reg.11
Reg.9, amended: SI 2004/2694 Reg.12
Reg.9, varied: SI 2004/865 Art.68
Reg.15, amended: SI 2004/2694 Reg.13
Reg.20, applied: SI 2004/865 Art.60
Sch.1, referred to: SI 2004/865 Art.105
Sch.4, applied: SI 2002/2375 Reg.9, Sch.3
Sch.4, referred to: SI 2004/865 Art.60
Sch.4 para.2, amended: SI 2004/2694 Reg.14
Sch.5 Part 1 para.5, amended: SI 2004/2694 Reg.15
Sch.5 Part 1 para.9, amended: SI 2004/2694 Reg.15
Sch.5 Part 2 para.15, applied: SI 1992/662 Reg.20
Sch.5 Part 2 para.19, applied: SI 2004/865 Art.64
Sch.5 Part 2 para.20, applied: SI 2004/865 Art.64
Sch.5 Part 2 para.30, amended: SI 2004/2694 Reg.15
Sch.5 Part 2 para.30, applied: SI 2002/2375 Reg.10
Sch.5 Part 2 para.34, applied: SI 2002/2375 Reg.10
Sch.5 Part 3 para.38, amended: SI 2004/2694 Reg.15
Sch.5 Part 3 para.47, amended: SI 2004/2694 Reg.15
Sch.5 Part 3 para.50, amended: SI 2004/2694 Reg.15
Sch.5 Part 4 para.53, amended: SI 2004/2694 Reg.15
Sch.5 Part 4 para.63, amended: SI 2004/2694 Reg.15
Sch.5 Part 4 para.66, referred to: SI 2004/865 Art.105
Sch.5 Part 4 para.69, amended: SI 2004/906 Reg.5
Sch.5 Part 5 para.73, amended: SI 2004/2694 Reg.15
Sch.5 Part 5 para.77, amended: SI 2004/2694 Reg.15
Sch.5 Part 5 para.80, amended: SI 2004/2694 Reg.15
Sch.5 Part 6 para.86, amended: SI 2004/2694 Reg.15
Sch.5 Part 6 para.86, applied: SI 1992/662 Sch.2 para.14
Sch.5 Part 6 para.91, applied: SI 1986/975 Sch.1 para.8C
Sch.5 Part 6 para.92, substituted: SI 2004/2694 Reg.15
Sch.5 Part 7 para.95, amended: SI 2004/2694 Reg.15

NO.

NO.

2004–cont.

627. National Health Service (Personal Medical Services Agreements) Regulations 2004–cont.

Sch.5 Part 8 para.98, amended: SI 2004/2694 Reg.15

Sch.5 Part 8 para.103, revoked: SI 2004/2694 Reg.15

Sch.5 Part 8 para.104, amended: SI 2004/2694 Reg.15

Sch.5 Part 8 para.105, referred to: SI 2004/865 Art.60, Art.67

Sch.5 Part 8 para.106A, added: SI 2004/906 Reg.5

Sch.5 Part 9 para.113, amended: SI 2004/2694 Reg.15

Sch.6, referred to: SI 2004/865 Art.60

Sch.6 para.1, applied: SI 2004/865 Art.60

Sch.6 para.2, referred to: SI 2004/865 Art.60, Art.75, Art.77, Art.80, Art.83, Art.85, Art.89

Sch.6 para.3, referred to: SI 2004/865 Art.60, Art.83, Art.85

Sch.6 para.4, referred to: SI 2004/865 Art.78

Sch.6 para.5, referred to: SI 2004/865 Art.60

Sch.6 para.6, referred to: SI 2004/865 Art.78

Sch.9, applied: SI 2004/865 Art.61

Sch.9, referred to: SI 2004/865 Art.61

629. National Health Service (General Medical Services Contracts) (Prescription of Drugs etc.) Regulations 2004

Sch.1, referred to: SI 2000/123 Reg.5, SI 2000/618 Reg.2, SI 2004/865 Art.62

Sch.2, applied: SI 1992/662 Sch.2 para.11

Sch.2, referred to: SI 1992/662 Sch.2 para.3, SI 2004/865 Art.62

648. NHS Professionals Special Health Authority (Establishment and Constitution) Amendment Order 2004

revoked: SI 2004/951 Art.2

652. Ministry of Defence Police Appeal Tribunals Regulations 2004

applied: SI 2004/653 Reg.28, Reg.35, SI 2004/654 Reg.9, Reg.14, Reg.20

656. Natural Mineral Water, Spring Water and Bottled Drinking Water (Amendment) (England) Regulations 2004

referred to: SI 1999/1540 Reg.18

658. Education (School Teachers&apos Pay and Conditions) Order 2004

referred to: SI 2002/2677 Sch.7

revoked: SI 2004/2142 Art.2

661. Commission for Healthcare Audit and Inspection (Fees and Frequency of Inspections) Regulations 2004

varied: SI 2004/664 Art.11, Art.12, Art.13

varied: SI 2004/664 Art.11, Art.12, Art.13, Art.14

2004–cont.

662. Commission for Social Care Inspection (Fees and Frequency of Inspections) Regulations 2004

applied: SI 2004/2071 Reg.43

referred to: SI 2004/2071 Sch.8 para.1

varied: SI 2004/664 Art.11, Art.12, Art.13, Art.14

Reg.2, amended: SI 2004/2071 Sch.8 para.2

Reg.2, varied: SI 2004/664 Art.11, Art.12, Art.13, Art.14

Reg.3, amended: SI 2004/2071 Sch.8 para.3

Reg.4, amended: SI 2004/2071 Sch.8 para.4

Reg.4, varied: SI 2004/664 Art.11, Art.12, Art.13, Art.14

Reg.5, amended: SI 2004/2071 Sch.8 para.5

Reg.6, amended: SI 2004/2071 Sch.8 para.6

Reg.7, varied: SI 2004/664 Art.11, Art.12, Art.13, Art.14

671. Independent Police Complaints Commission (Transitional Provisions) Order 2004

Art.2, amended: SI 2004/1092 Art.2

Art.4, amended: SI 2004/1092 Art.2

672. Independent Police Complaints Commission (Forces Maintained Otherwise than by Police Authorities) Order 2004

Art.3, amended: SI 2004/1573 Art.12

674. Recovery of Duties and Taxes Etc Due in Other Member States (Corresponding UK Claims, Procedure and Supplementary) Regulations 2004

referred to: SI 2004/800 Reg.2

Reg.8, revoked (in part): SI 2004/800 Reg.3

Sch.2 para.1, amended: SI 2004/800 Reg.4

683. Leasehold Valuation Tribunals (Fees) (Wales) Regulations 2004

Reg.4, applied: SI 2004/681 Reg.7

Reg.5, applied: SI 2004/681 Reg.7

696. Health and Social Care (Community Health and Standards) Act 2003 (Supplementary and Consequential Provision) (NHS Foundation Trusts) Order 2004

Sch.5, varied: SI 2004/664 Art.11, Art.12, Art.13, Art.14

702. Firearms (Northern Ireland) Order 2004

Art.2, referred to: SI 2004/1500 Sch.2 para.16

720. Borough of Trafford (Electoral Changes) Order 2004

varied: SI 2004/222 Art.2

721. City of Peterborough (Electoral Changes) (Amendment) Order 2004

varied: SI 2004/222 Art.2

752. Employment Act 2002 (Dispute Resolution) Regulations 2004

applied: SI 1996/3147 Reg.2

NO.

2004–cont.

752. Employment Act 2002 (Dispute Reso-
lution) Regulations 2004–*cont.*
Reg.15, applied: SI 1975/2048 Art.5, SI 1977/
842 Art.5, SI 1994/1623 Art.7, SI 1994/
1624 Art.7, SI 1998/1833 Reg.30, SI
2004/1168 Art.4
Reg.15, referred to: SI 2003/1660 Reg.34, SI
2003/1661 Reg.34

754. Compromise Agreements (Descrip-
tion of Person) Order 2004
Art.3, revoked: SI 2004/2515 Art.2

759. Health and Social Care (Community
Health and Standards) Act 2003
Commencement (No.3) Order 2004
varied: SI 2004/664 Art.11, Art.12, Art.13,
Art.14
Art.6, varied: SI 2004/664 Art.11, Art.12,
Art.13, Art.14

828. Pet Travel Scheme (Pilot Arrange-
ments) (England) (Amendment)
Order 2004
revoked: SI 2004/2363 Sch.2

853. Animals and Animal Products (Import
and Export) Regulations 2004
applied: SI 1974/2211 Art.4A
Reg.2, substituted: SI 2004/2363 Reg.19
Sch.3 Part I para.10, amended: SI 2004/2363
Reg.19

865. General Medical Services and Perso-
nal Medical Services Transitional and
Consequential Provisions Order 2004
Art.1, applied: SI 1986/975 Sch.1 para.8C, SI
1992/662 Reg.2, SI 2000/620 Reg.2
Art.34, revoked: SI 2004/2694 Reg.18
Art.53, applied: SI 2004/291 Sch.6 para.81
Sch.1 para.1, applied: SSI 2004/163 Art.94
Sch.1 para.5, applied: SSI 2004/163 Art.94

905. Community Health Councils Regula-
tions 2004
Reg.9, amended: SI 2004/1771 Sch.1 para.13
Reg.20, applied: SI 2004/478 Sch.6 para.88

915. Railway Safety Accreditation Scheme
Regulations 2004
Reg.2, amended: SI 2004/1573 Art.12
Reg.4, amended: SI 2004/1573 Art.12
Reg.5, amended: SI 2004/1573 Art.12
Reg.6, amended: SI 2004/1573 Art.12
Sch.1 para.1, amended: SI 2004/1573 Art.12
Sch.1 para.2, amended: SI 2004/1573 Art.12
Sch.1 para.2, revoked (in part): SI 2004/1573
Art.12
Sch.1 para.3, amended: SI 2004/1573 Art.12
Sch.1 para.4, amended: SI 2004/1573 Art.12
Sch.1 para.5, amended: SI 2004/1573 Art.12
Sch.1 para.6, amended: SI 2004/1573 Art.12
Sch.1 para.7, amended: SI 2004/1573 Art.12
Sch.1 para.8, amended: SI 2004/1573 Art.12
Sch.1 para.9, amended: SI 2004/1573 Art.12
Sch.1 para.10, amended: SI 2004/1573 Art.12
Sch.1 para.11, amended: SI 2004/1573 Art.12

NO.

2004–cont.

916. Private Security Industry Act 2001
(Modification of Local Enactments)
Order 2004
revoked: SI 2004/1268 Art.4

934. Employment Zones (Allocation to
Contractors) Pilot Regulations 2004
applied: SI 2003/2438 Reg.2

938. Freedom of Information (Additional
Public Authorities) Order 2004
Art.2, amended: SI 2004/1870 Art.2

957. Primary Medical Services (Scotland)
Act 2004 (Consequential Modifica-
tions) Order 2004
Sch.1 para.4, disapplied: SSI 2004/163
Art.98
Sch.1 para.7, disapplied: SSI 2004/163 Art.99

959. Social Security (Working Neighbour-
hoods) Regulations 2004
applied: SI 1996/207 Reg.75, SI 2000/1926
Reg.2, Reg.4, SI 2002/1703 Reg.2, Reg.4,
Reg.16
referred to: SI 2003/1886 Reg.2
Reg.2, applied: SI 2002/1703 Reg.2, Reg.4,
Reg.16, SI 2003/1886 Reg.2

1002. Customs and Excise Duties (Travel-
lers Allowances and Personal
Reliefs)(New Member States) Order
2004
varied: SI 2003/2758 Art.2

1003. Excise Duty Points (Etc.)(New
Member States) Regulations 2004
varied: SI 2003/2758 Art.2

1020. National Health Service (Performers
Lists) (Wales) Regulations 2004
applied: SI 2004/1016 Art.73, Art.74, Art.75,
Art.77, Art.78
Sch.1 para.7, applied: SI 2004/1016 Art.82

1022. National Health Service (General
Medical Services Contracts)
(Prescription of Drugs Etc.) (Wales)
Regulations 2004
Sch.1, referred to: SI 2001/1543 Reg.2
Sch.2, referred to: SI 1992/662 Sch.2 para.3,
Sch.2 para.11, SI 2001/1543 Reg.2

1025. Education (School Performance
Information) (Wales) Regulations
2004
Reg.2, amended: SI 2004/2914 Reg.4
Reg.11, amended: SI 2004/2914 Reg.4
Sch.3 Part 1 para.1, revoked (in part): SI 2004/
2914 Reg.4
Sch.3 Part 3 para.3, revoked: SI 2004/2914
Reg.4
Sch.3 Part 5 para.5, amended: SI 2004/2914
Reg.4

1026. Education (Pupil Information)
(Wales) Regulations 2004
Reg.7, amended: SI 2004/2914 Reg.5
Sch.3 para.2, amended: SI 2004/2914 Reg.5
Sch.3 para.2, revoked (in part): SI 2004/2914
Reg.5

NO.

2004–cont.

1026. Education (Pupil Information) (Wales) Regulations 2004–cont.
Sch.4 para.2, amended: SI 2004/2914 Reg.5

1031. Medicines for Human Use (Clinical Trials) Regulations 2004
applied: 1968 c.67 s.3, s.4, s.7, s.8, 1971 c.69 s.1, SI 1976/1726 Reg.1, SI 1978/40 Reg.3, SI 1989/684 Sch.1 para.9B, SI 1997/1830 Art.3B
Reg.15, applied: 2000 asp 4 s.51
Reg.18, applied: SI 1995/1116 Reg.14A
Reg.19, applied: SI 1995/1116 Reg.14A
Reg.20, applied: SI 1995/1116 Reg.14A
Reg.24, applied: SI 1995/1116 Reg.7A
Reg.27, applied: SI 1995/1116 Reg.2
Reg.31, applied: SI 1995/1116 Reg.2
Reg.44, applied: SI 1995/1116 Reg.7
Sch.3 Part 2 para.11, applied: SI 1995/1116 Reg.7A, Sch.1 para.7, Sch.5 para.8
Sch.5, applied: SI 1989/684 Sch.1 para.9B
Sch.8, applied: SI 1989/684 Sch.1 para.9B
Sch.12, applied: SI 1995/1116 Reg.14A

1034. Crime (International Co-operation) Act 2003 (Designation of Prosecuting Authorities) Order 2004
Art.2, amended: SI 2004/1747 Art.2

1073. Borough of Rochdale (Electoral Changes) (Amendment) Order 2004
varied: SI 2004/222 Art.2

1111. Overseas Territories (Zimbabwe) (Restrictive Measures) (Amendment) Order 2004
varied: 1887 c.54, 1945 c.7

1112. Liberia (Restrictive Measures) (Overseas Territories) (Amendment) Order 2004
varied: 1945 c.7

1159. Plant Protection Products (Fees) (Amendment) Regulations 2004
referred to: SI 2003/660 Reg.3A

1192. Courts Boards Areas Order 2004
Sch.1, substituted: SI 2004/1303 Sch.1

1214. Products of Animal Origin (Third Country Imports) (England) Regulations 2004
revoked: SI 2004/1740 Reg.68

1217. Education (National Curriculum) (Attainment Targets and Programmes of Study in Science in respect of the First, Second Third and Fourth Key Stages) (England) Order 2004
revoked: SI 2004/1800 Art.2

1219. Accession (Immigration and Worker Registration) Regulations 2004
Reg.2, amended: SI 2004/1236 Reg.3
Reg.5, applied: SI 2000/701 Reg.4, SI 2002/1792 Reg.2

1231. Town and Country Planning (London Borough of Camden) Special Development Order 2004
Art.4, added: SI 2004/2355 Art.3

NO.

2004–cont.

1231. Town and Country Planning (London Borough of Camden) Special Development Order 2004–cont.
Art.4, amended: SI 2004/2355 Art.3

1264. Liberia (Freezing of Funds and Economic Resources) Regulations 2004
Reg.1, amended: SI 2004/1710 Reg.2, SI 2004/2574 Reg.3

1267. European Parliamentary Elections (Northern Ireland) Regulations 2004
Reg.16, enabled: SI 2004/1405
Reg.76, amended: SI 2004/1374 Reg.3

1301. Feeding Stuffs, the Feeding Stuffs (Sampling and Analysis) and the Feeding Stuffs (Enforcement) (Amendment) (England) Regulations 2004
applied: SI 1999/1663 Sch.2 para.3, SI 1999/2325 Reg.11, Reg.11A, Reg.11B, Reg.7
referred to: SI 1999/2325 Reg.9

1309. Adventure Activities Licensing Regulations 2004
applied: SI 2004/1359 Reg.2

1317. Beef Carcase (Classification) (England) Regulations 2004
Reg.9, applied: 1967 c.22 Sch.1 para.10A

1396. Meat Products (Wales) Regulations 2004
applied: SI 1996/1499 Sch.4A para.1

1409. Offshore Installations (Safety Zones) (No.2) Order 2004
Sch.1, amended: SI 2004/1746 Art.3

1418. Air Carrier Liability Regulations 2004
Reg.4, amended: SI 2004/1974 Reg.3

1450. Child Trust Funds Regulations 2004
Reg.2, amended: SI 2004/2676 Reg.3
Reg.6, amended: SI 2004/2676 Reg.4
Reg.7, amended: SI 2004/2676 Reg.5
Reg.8, amended: SI 2004/2676 Reg.6
Reg.10, amended: SI 2004/2676 Reg.7
Reg.12, amended: SI 2004/2676 Reg.8
Reg.13, amended: SI 2004/2676 Reg.9
Reg.14, amended: SI 2004/2676 Reg.10
Reg.18, amended: SI 2004/2676 Reg.11
Reg.18A, added: SI 2004/2676 Reg.12
Reg.21, amended: SI 2004/2676 Reg.13
Reg.33, amended: SI 2004/2676 Reg.14
Sch.1 para.2, amended: SI 2004/2676 Reg.15
Sch.1 para.3, amended: SI 2004/2676 Reg.15

1478. National Health Service (General Medical Services Contracts) (Wales) Regulations 2004
Sch.6, applied: SI 2004/1020 Reg.23

1482. Consumer Credit (Agreements) (Amendment) Regulations 2004
Reg.4, amended: SI 2004/2619 Reg.2
Reg.5, amended: SI 2004/2619 Reg.2
Reg.9, amended: SI 2004/2619 Reg.2
Reg.10, amended: SI 2004/2619 Reg.2
Reg.11, amended: SI 2004/2619 Reg.2

NO.

NO.

2004-cont.

1483. Consumer Credit (Early Settlement) Regulations 2004
Reg.3, amended: SI 2004/2619 Reg.4

1484. Consumer Credit (Advertisements) Regulations 2004
Sch.2 para.1, amended: SI 2004/2619 Reg.3
Sch.2 para.2, amended: SI 2004/2619 Reg.3
Sch.2 para.3, amended: SI 2004/2619 Reg.3
Sch.2 para.4, amended: SI 2004/2619 Reg.3
Sch.2 para.5, amended: SI 2004/2619 Reg.3
Sch.2 para.6, amended: SI 2004/2619 Reg.3
Sch.2 para.7, amended: SI 2004/2619 Reg.3
Sch.2 para.7, substituted: SI 2004/2619 Reg.3
Sch.3 para.5, amended: SI 2004/2619 Reg.3

1487. Wildlife and Countryside Act 1981(England and Wales) (Amendment) Regulations 2004
referred to: SI 2004/1733 Reg.3

1498. Iraq (United Nations Sanctions)(Amendment) Order 2004
Art.6, applied: SI 2000/3241 Art.6, Art.8, SI 2000/3242 Art.6, Art.8

1509. Natural Mineral Water, Spring Water and Bottled Drinking Water (Amendment) (Wales) Regulations 2004
referred to: SI 1999/1540 Reg.18

1520. Income Support (General) (Standard Interest Rate Amendment) (No.2) Regulations 2004
revoked: SI 2004/2174 Reg.3

1611. Government Stock Regulations 2004
Reg.7, applied: SI 1998/1446 Art.25, SI 2004/1662 Sch.1 para.20
Reg.7, disapplied: SI 2001/3755 Sch.4 para.12
Reg.7, referred to: 1889 c.6 s.4, 1892 c.39 s.8, SI 1972/764 Reg.41, SI 1976/2012 Reg.14, Reg.41, Reg.42, SI 1984/779 Reg.17, SI 1991/1031 Reg.17, SI 1998/1446 Art.16
Reg.8, applied: SI 1998/1446 Art.25
Reg.8, disapplied: SI 2001/3755 Sch.4 para.12
Reg.9, disapplied: SI 2001/3755 Reg.38, Sch.4 para.12
Reg.12, disapplied: SI 2001/3755 Sch.4 para.12
Reg.13, disapplied: SI 2001/3755 Sch.4 para.12
Reg.14, disapplied: SI 2001/3755 Sch.4 para.12
Reg.16, disapplied: SI 2001/3755 Sch.4 para.12
Reg.17, disapplied: SI 2001/3755 Sch.4 para.12
Reg.18, disapplied: SI 2001/3755 Sch.4 para.12
Reg.19, disapplied: SI 2001/3755 Sch.4 para.12
Reg.20, disapplied: SI 2001/3755 Sch.4 para.12

2004-cont.

1611. Government Stock Regulations 2004-cont.
Reg.21, disapplied: SI 2001/3755 Sch.4 para.12
Reg.22, disapplied: SI 2001/3755 Sch.4 para.12
Reg.23, disapplied: SI 2001/3755 Sch.4 para.12
Reg.24, disapplied: SI 2001/3755 Sch.4 para.12
Reg.25, disapplied: SI 1998/1446 Art.16
Reg.28, disapplied: SI 2001/3755 Sch.4 para.12
Reg.30, disapplied: SI 2001/3755 Sch.4 para.12
Reg.31, disapplied: SI 2001/3755 Sch.4 para.12

1633. Environmental Assessment of Plans and Programmes Regulations 2004
Reg.14, applied: SSI 2004/258 Reg.19, Reg.20

1654. Nursing and Midwifery Council (Fees) Rules Order of Council 2004
Sch.1, applied: SI 2004/1767 Sch.1

1660. Iraq (United Nations Sanctions) Order 2000 (Amendment) Regulations 2004
referred to: SI 2000/3241 Art.5A
Reg.3, revoked (in part): SI 2004/1779 Reg.3

1697. Charges for Inspections and Controls (Amendment) Regulations 2004
revoked: SI 2004/1871 Reg.2

1705. Local Government (Best Value Authorities) (Power to Trade) (England) Order 2004
Art.1, amended: SI 2004/2307 Art.2
Art.2, amended: SI 2004/2307 Art.2
Art.4, added: SI 2004/2307 Art.2
Sch.1, added: SI 2004/2307 Sch.1
Sch.1, amended: SI 2004/2573 Art.2

1710. Liberia (Freezing of Funds and Economic Resources) (Amendment) Regulations 2004
revoked: SI 2004/2574 Reg.2

1729. Education (School Teachers Qualifications) (Wales) Regulations 2004
referred to: SI 2004/1744 Sch.1 para.2
Reg.5, applied: SI 1999/2817 Reg.11, Reg.12, Reg.13, SI 2003/543 Sch.1 para.17, Sch.1 para.18, Sch.1 para.20
Sch.2 Part 1 para.10, applied: SI 2003/543 Sch.1 para.20
Sch.2 Part 1 para.12, applied: SI 2003/543 Sch.1 para.17
Sch.2 Part 1 para.13, applied: SI 2003/543 Sch.1 para.18

1740. Products of Animal Origin (Third Country Imports) (England) (No.2) Regulations 2004
revoked: SI 2004/2640 Reg.68

NO.

2004-cont.

1744. Education (Specified Work and Registration) (Wales) Regulations 2004
Sch.2 para.3, applied: SI 2004/1729 Sch.2 para.11, Sch.2 para.13

1749. Feeding Stuffs, the Feeding Stuffs (Sampling and Analysis) and the Feeding Stuffs (Enforcement) (Amendment) (Wales) Regulations 2004
applied: SI 1999/1663 Sch.2 para.3
referred to: SI 1999/2325 Reg.11, Reg.11A, Reg.11B, Reg.7, Reg.9

1756. Adult Placement Schemes (Wales)-Regulations 2004
applied: SI 2002/324 Reg.3, SI 2004/219 Reg.3

1765. Nurses and Midwives (Parts of and Entries in the Register) Order of Council 2004
Sch.2, referred to: SI 2004/1762 Art.8, Art.9

1769. Justification of Practices Involving Ionising Radiation Regulations 2004
Reg.20, referred to: SI 1995/204 Sch.2 para.6

1848. Representation of the People (Form of Canvass) (England and Wales) Regulations 2004
Sch.1 Part II, referred to: SI 2001/341 Reg.26

1861. Employment Tribunals (Constitution and Rules of Procedure) Regulations 2004
Reg.1, amended: SI 2004/2351 Reg.2
Reg.2, amended: SI 2004/2351 Reg.2
Reg.3, amended: SI 2004/2351 Reg.2
Reg.15, amended: SI 2004/2351 Reg.2
Reg.16, amended: SI 2004/2351 Reg.2
Reg.20, amended: SI 2004/2351 Reg.2
Sch.1 para.8, amended: SI 2004/2351 Reg.2
Sch.1 para.9, amended: SI 2004/2351 Reg.2
Sch.1 para.30, amended: SI 2004/2351 Reg.2
Sch.1 para.48, amended: SI 2004/2351 Reg.2
Sch.4 para.3, amended: SI 2004/2351 Reg.2
Sch.5 para.3, amended: SI 2004/2351 Reg.2

1863. Tax Avoidance Schemes (Prescribed Descriptions of Arrangements) Regulations 2004
referred to: SI 2004/2429 Reg.2
Reg.1, amended: SI 2004/2429 Reg.3
Reg.2, amended: SI 2004/2429 Reg.4
Sch.1 Part 1, applied: SI 2004/1864 Reg.6
Sch.1 Part 1, referred to: SI 2004/1864 Reg.8
Sch.1 Part 1 para.1, amended: SI 2004/2429 Reg.5
Sch.1 Part 1 para.5A, added: SI 2004/2429 Reg.5
Sch.1 Part 2, applied: SI 2004/1864 Reg.1, Reg.6

1864. Tax Avoidance Schemes (Information) Regulations 2004
Reg.3, applied: SI 2004/1865 Reg.6
Reg.4, amended: SI 2004/2613 Reg.3
Reg.4, applied: SI 2004/2613 Reg.1

NO.

2004-cont.

1865. Tax Avoidance Schemes (Promoters and Prescribed Circumstances) Regulations 2004
Reg.6, added: SI 2004/2613 Reg.2
Reg.6, applied: SI 2004/1864 Reg.4

1899. Carriage by Air Acts (Application of Provisions) Order 2004
Art.2, amended: SI 2004/1974 Reg.2

1931. Value Added Tax (Groups eligibility) Order 2004
applied: SI 2004/1933 Sch.1

1944. Community Radio Order 2004
Art.2, applied: SI 2003/3299 Art.2A

1960. Representation of the People (Form of Canvass) (Scotland) Regulations 2004
applied: SI 2001/497 Reg.26

1972. Care Standards Act 2000 (Extension of the Application of Part 2 to Adult Placement Schemes) (England) Regulations 2004
applied: SI 2004/2071 Reg.40

1978. Iraq (United Nations Sanctions) (Channel Islands) (Amendment) Order 2004
Art.6, applied: SI 2000/3244 Art.6, Art.8

1982. Iraq (United Nations Sanctions) (Isle of Man) (Amendment) Order 2004
Art.6, applied: SI 2000/3245 Art.6, Art.8

2033. Health Professions (Operating Department Practitioners and Miscellaneous Amendments) Order 2004
Art.3, applied: SI 2004/2525 Art.2

2040. Food Protection (Emergency Prohibitions) (Scallops) (Irish Sea) Order 2004
referred to: SI 2004/2686
revoked: SI 2004/2686 Art.2
Art.4, substituted: SI 2004/2123 Art.2
Sch.1, substituted: SI 2004/2123 Art.2

2064. Excise Warehousing (Energy Products) Regulations 2004
Reg.2, applied: SI 2004/2065 Reg.7

2065. Biofuels and Other Fuel Substitutes (Payment of Excise Duties etc.) Regulations 2004
Reg.21, applied: SI 1992/3152 Reg.6, Reg.11

2071. Adult Placement Schemes (England) Regulations 2004
applied: SI 2001/3965 Reg.3
Reg.2, referred to: SI 2002/3214 Reg.3

2095. Financial Services (Distance Marketing) Regulations 2004
applied: 1974 c.39 s.84, SI 2003/1376 Sch.1

2098. County Court Fees (Amendment) Order 2004
revoked: SI 2004/3121 Sch.2

2100. Supreme Court Fees (Amendment) Order 2004
revoked: SI 2004/3121 Sch.2

NO.

2004–cont.

2110. Merchant Shipping (Vessel Traffic Monitoring and Reporting Requirements) Regulations 2004
applied: SI 1996/2154 Reg.33

2152. Cosmetic Products (Safety) Regulations 2004
Reg.5, amended: SI 2004/2988 Reg.2
Reg.12, amended: SI 2004/2988 Reg.2
Reg.13, amended: SI 2004/2988 Reg.2
Reg.16, amended: SI 2004/2988 Reg.2
Sch.2 para.38, added: SI 2004/2988 Reg.2
Sch.2 para.39, added: SI 2004/2988 Reg.2
Sch.2 para.40, added: SI 2004/2988 Reg.2
Sch.2 para.41, added: SI 2004/2988 Reg.2
Sch.3 Part 1, amended: SI 2004/2988 Reg.2
Sch.4 Part 1, amended: SI 2004/2988 Reg.2, Sch.1 Part 1, Sch.1 Part 2
Sch.4 Part 2, amended: SI 2004/2988 Reg.2
Sch.5 Part I, amended: SI 2004/2988 Reg.2
Sch.6, amended: SI 2004/2988 Reg.2
Sch.6 Part I, amended: SI 2004/2988 Reg.2, Sch.1 Part 3
Sch.7 Part 1, amended: SI 2004/2988 Reg.2
Sch.13, revoked: SI 2004/2988 Reg.2

2189. Insurance Companies (Taxation of Reinsurance Business)(Amendment) Regulations 2004
revoked: SI 2004/2257 Reg.6

2204. Town and Country Planning (Local Development) (England) Regulations 2004
referred to: SI 2004/2205 Reg.6
Reg.17, referred to: SI 2004/2205 Reg.6
Reg.18, referred to: SI 2004/2205 Reg.6
Reg.19, referred to: SI 2004/2205 Reg.6
Reg.28, applied: SI 2004/2205 Reg.6
Reg.28, referred to: SI 2004/2205 Reg.6

2244. Social Security (Quarterly Work-focused Interviews for Certain Lone Parents) Regulations 2004
applied: SI 2000/1926 Reg.4

2326. European Public Limited-Liability Company Regulations 2004
applied: 1996 c.17 s.21
Reg.29, referred to: SI 1999/3323 Reg.46A
Reg.33, applied: SI 1993/2854 r.16AA, r.20, r.26, r.31
Reg.33, referred to: SI 1993/2854 r.16AA
Reg.41, applied: 1996 c.17 s.18
Reg.42, applied: 1996 c.18 s.105, s.108, s.109
Reg.42, referred to: 1996 c.18 s.105
Reg.45, applied: 1996 c.17 s.18
Reg.46, applied: 1996 c.17 s.20

2004–cont.

2326. European Public Limited-Liability Company Regulations 2004–*cont.*
Reg.47, applied: SI 1993/2854 r.4, r.5, r.7

2357. Regulatory Reform (Patents) Order 2004
Art.20, applied: SI 2004/2358 r.20
Art.21, applied: SI 2004/2358 r.20
Art.22, applied: SI 2004/2358 r.20

2363. Non Commercial Movement of Pet Animals (England) Regulations 2004
applied: SI 1974/2211 Art.5A, Art.6
disapplied: SI 1974/2211 Art.4B

2601. Miscellaneous Food Additives (Amendment) (England) Regulations 2004
Reg.3, referred to: SI 1995/3187 Reg.11

2608. General Medical Council (Fitness to Practise) Rules Order of Council 2004
Sch.1, applied: SI 2004/2607 Sch.1, SI 2004/2609 Sch.1, SI 2004/2612 Sch.1
Sch.1, varied: SI 2004/2607 Sch.1

2660. Police Federation (Amendment) Regulations 2004
applied: SI 1969/1787 Reg.6

2665. Service Charges (Consultation Requirements) (Amendment) (England) Regulations 2004
revoked: SI 2004/2939 Reg.3

2688. Feeding Stuffs, the Feeding Stuffs (Sampling and Analysis) and the Feeding Stuffs (Enforcement) (Amendment) (England) (No.2) Regulations 2004
applied: SI 1999/2325 Reg.7
referred to: SI 1999/1663 Sch.2 para.3, SI 1999/2325 Reg.11A, Reg.11B, Reg.11

2824. Food Labelling (Amendment) (England) (No.2) Regulations 2004
Reg.3, applied: SI 1996/1499 Reg.50
Reg.5, applied: SI 1996/1499 Reg.50
Reg.6, applied: SI 1996/1499 Reg.50
Reg.7, applied: SI 1996/1499 Reg.50
Reg.8, applied: SI 1996/1499 Reg.50
Reg.9, applied: SI 1996/1499 Reg.50
Reg.12, applied: SI 1996/1499 Reg.50
Reg.15, applied: SI 1996/1499 Reg.50

2884. Merchant Shipping (Ro-Ro Passenger Ships) (Stability) Regulations 2004
applied: SI 1998/2514 Reg.44